D0437983

Matthew
Henry's
Commentary

Publishers' Note

For two hundred and fifty years *Matthew Henry's Commentary* has been the most widely used of all Bible Commentaries. The complete Commentary was originally published in five volumes, and is still available in an attractive modern setting in six handsome library volumes.

The need for a condensed version of this great work, which would retain all the best of the larger work in a form easier of access to the busy student, and unencumbered by material now of little help or quite out of date, has long been apparent.

Rev. Dr. Leslie F. Church, formerly President, and for many years Connexional Editor to the Methodist Church in Great Britain and Ireland (Epworth Press), was so greatly impressed with this need that, in the midst of an extremely busy period of his life, he consented to read, examine with care, and reduce the contents of the six volumes into one handy book. The masterly way with which this brilliant piece of editorial work has been done will be readily discerned by all who are familiar with the larger work, and will arouse the admiration of older students. It was a monumental undertaking, and it has given a new lease of life to one of the most useful books of reference ever produced for the Bible student.

The Publishers take this opportunity of expressing very sincere thanks to the Editor for his great achievement. They would like also to make acknowledgment of the help given to the Editor by the Rev. C. Lester Johnson, B.Sc., and to express their appreciation of the diligence and care of the Rev. F. S. Fitzsimmonds, B.A., B.D., M.Th., in the formidable task of reading the proofs.

C. H. Spurgeon is reported to have said that "every minister ought to read *Matthew Henry* entirely and carefully through once at least". That these ministers have been able to give the time to do much more than that and bring to their task the necessary thought, critical appreciation and editorial work, places all who will use this book greatly in their debt.

All the best in *Matthew Henry*—the expositions, commentary, the metaphors, analogies and illustrations of the complete work—has been retained here *in Matthew Henry's own words* in condensed form. This preserves for a new generation of Bible students all that is most valuable in the larger work, which has been the mainstay of preaching for more than two centuries.

ZONDERVAN CLASSIC REFERENCE SERIES

Matthew Henry's Commentary

IN ONE VOLUME

GENESIS TO REVELATION

Edited by

Rev. Leslie F. Church, Ph.D., F.R.Hist.S.

ZondervanPublishingHouse
Grand Rapids, Michigan

A Division of HarperCollinsPublishers

Matthew Henry's Commentary
Marshall, Morgan & Scott, Ltd., © 1960
Copyright © 1961 by The Zondervan Corporation

Requests for information should be addressed to:

🏭 ZondervanPublishingHouse
Grand Rapids, Michigan 49530

ISBN 0-310-26010-8

Printed in the United States of America

98 99 00 01 02 03 04 /❖ DC/ 60 59 58 57 56

Introduction

By WILBUR M. SMITH, D.D. *1675*

Almost without exception, I have always had an aversion to abbreviated editions of any great classic. The author of any notable work can only be accurately known, and his work properly understood, by one having the actual words the author wrote before him, and not some mangled re-phrased abbreviated edition. The book I am now about to refer to is, for me, one of those few exceptions. I am referring to a new edition of the superlative, abidingly valuable *Commentary on the Bible* by Matthew Henry which makes available all the best of Matthew Henry in one large volume (9½ x 6½ inches), of nearly 2,000 double column pages.

It is an abbreviated edition but it has two virtues which so many similar attempts of reducing famous classics do not begin to possess. First of all, *everything here is in Matthew Henry's own words,* that is, though some of his passages and even paragraphs have been omitted, what is here is the original Matthew Henry. Secondly, the condensation is not radical. I would judge that there are, in this one volume, nearly 3,000,000 words, and that is about all of Matthew Henry that any Bible student needs 250 years after this commentary was written. There was a time, when for many ministers, Matthew Henry was about the only commentary which they used or even had available, but today not only do we have hundreds of commentaries on various parts of the Scripture, but some of these *must* be consulted, especially for archeological and historical matters.

This task occupied the gifted editor, Dr. Leslie F. Church, for the last years of his very active life. In 1929 he was appointed to the faculty of Richmond College, a Methodist school in England, where he exercised a great deal of influence. In 1935 he was appointed Connexional Editor for the Methodist Church in Great Britain and Ireland (Epworth Press), with responsibility for its magazines, manuscripts, etc., a position he held for eighteen years. He was honored by the Presidential chair for the Methodist Conference in 1943. Retiring in 1953, he devoted time to various editorial pursuits, the last four years before his passing in January 1961 to the work on Matthew Henry, which is now being published by Marshall, Morgan, and Scott in London, and by the Zondervan Publishing House in Grand Rapids.

I have tried to test this work as far as eliminations are concerned in three places. I find that Psalm 89 is given 4,000 words in the original, and 3,500 in this abbreviated edition. To Deuteronomy 33, Matthew Henry gave 4,500 words and the condensed work 4,000. I find that it is concerning such a passage as Zechariah 6:9-15, that a greater difference is revealed. Matthew Henry gave these seven verses 2,200 words, whereas in the condensation we have about 1,000.

The book is most attractively bound. The type is clear and the paper is of commendable quality. Frankly, I wouldn't be a bit surprised if this new, somewhat abridged edition will soon be in far greater demand than the older six-volume edition. I think this is all that a twentieth-century Bible student needs of Matthew Henry.

May I on this occasion take the liberty of quoting some words which the learned commentator wrote in his diary on New Year's Day 1704, when he was only forty-two years of age. (He died at the age of fifty-two.)

"This New Year's Day I have in much Weakness, and compassed about with many Infirmities, upon my Knees made a fresh Surrender of myself, my whole self, all I am, all I have, all I can do, to God the Father, Son, and Holy Ghost, my Creator, Owner, Ruler and Benefactor; all my Affections to be ruled by the Divine Grace, and all my Affairs overruled by the Divine Providence, so as I may not come short of glorifying God in this World, and being glorified with him in a better World.

"Confirming and ratifying all former Resignations of myself to God, and lamenting all the Disagreeableness of my Heart and Life therewith, and depending upon the Merit of the Redeemer to make this and all my other Services acceptable, and the Grace of the Sanctifier to enable me to make good these engagements, I again bind my Soul with a Bond to the Lord, and commit myself entirely to him; particularly, as to the Events of this Year which I am now entering upon, not knowing the Things that may abide me in it.

"If this Year should be a Year of continued Health and Comfort, I commit myself to the Grace of God to be preserved from carnal Security, and to be enabled in a Day of Prosperity to serve God with joy.

"If my Opportunities as a Minister should be this Year continued, I commit my Studies, and Ministerial Labours at home and abroad, to the Blessing of God; having afresh consecrated them all to his Service and Honor, earnestly desiring Mercy of the Lord to be Faithful and Successful.

"If I should be this Year at any time tried with Doubts concerning my Duty, I commit myself to the Divine Conduct, with an unbyass'd Desire, praying to know what God will have me to do, with a fixed Resolution by His Grace to follow his Direction in the Integrity of my Heart.

"If I should this Year be afflicted in my Body, Family, Name or Estate, I commit my All to the Divine Dispose; the Will of the Lord be done; only begging that the Grace of God may go along with the Providence of God in all my Afflictions, to enable me both to bear them well and to use them well.

"If this Year I should be disturbed or molested in the Exercise of my Ministry, if I should be silenced, or otherways suffer for well-doing, I commit the keeping of my Soul to God as to a faithful Creator; depending upon him to guide me in my Call to suffer, and to make that clear, and to preserve me from perplexing Snares; depending upon him to support and comfort me under my Sufferings, and to bring Glory to himself out of them, and then welcome his whole Will."

I commend this edition wholeheartedly.

W. M. S.

Pasadena, Calif.

Foreword

The Commentary

The Commentary on the Bible by Matthew Henry is, in many senses, unique. It has continued to be useful for two and a half centuries, and, in spite of increasing knowledge, its profound insight into spiritual and eternal truth makes its essential teaching invaluable today.

It is a practical and devotional work written by a man who has been described as one of the greatest commentators of all time. It was not produced by a recluse, isolated in his study and concerned only with academic values, but is the outcome of personal and pastoral experience. In family worship in his father's home, and later in daily prayers with his own family, and in the homes of his neighbours, he not only studied the Scriptures but learned how best to apply them to the lives and needs of people young and old, rich and poor.

Matthew Henry described his work as "methodized and practical expositions . . . in plain and homely dress". Its purpose, he said, was "to promote knowledge of the Scriptures, in order to the reforming of men's hearts and lives". Realizing the chronological and textual problems involved, he was not dogmatic in his interpretations, but agreed with Augustine that the Word of God "had enough in it that is easy to nourish the meanest to life eternal" but enough, also, to demand the industry and humility of the greatest scholars.

He wrote with confidence and authority on the basic principles of conduct and belief, but with a modesty which commanded, and should still command, respect. "I have no sufficiency of my own," he said, "but by the grace of God I am what I am, and that grace will, I trust, be sufficient for me."

As he set himself to his tremendous task, whilst fulfilling a busy pastoral ministry, he besought his friends to pray that he "might be given understanding . . . and be found the faithful servant of the Lord Jesus, who am less than the least of all that call Him Master".

With a deep sense of vocation he began his work not as one who wanted to be remembered as a scholar—though he was familiar with the Classics and Patristics—but rather as a pastor anxious to guide his flock. That is why his work is valuable, not only historically as descriptive of the Puritan outlook, but as a challenging exposition of the mercy and justice of God, and as a reliable guide to the right conduct of all who try to do His will.

No wonder that George Whitefield read the Commentary through four times—read it literally on his knees—and spoke always of "the great Matthew Henry" to whom he owed so much. The direct influence of his writing on the religious leaders of the 18th century was felt indirectly by many of the great personalities of the period and they, in turn, have passed it down the years to us. The hymns of William Cowper, for example, were undoubtedly inspired by the spirit and even the phrasing of Matthew Henry. Without him we should never have had the poignant prayer "O for a closer walk with God", nor the sturdy comfort of "God moves in a mysterious way, His wonders to perform".

In reading Matthew Henry's comment on Leviticus viii. 35, one recognises words that Charles Wesley later used in his great hymn, "A charge to keep I have". This is part of Matthew Henry's actual command: "They attended to keep the charge of the Lord: we have every one of us a charge to keep, an eternal God to glorify, an immortal soul to provide for, needful duty to be done, our generation to serve; and it must be our daily care to keep this charge, for it is the charge of the Lord our Master."

Some of the terse epigrams and unforgettable phrases have become proverbial to the English-speaking people everywhere. But, what is more important, many of his interpretations of the Word of God have helped to create and strengthen the standards of morality by which the Christian may shape and direct his life.

Matthew Henry: The Commentator

In Broad Oak, a Welsh farmhouse at Iscoid, Flintshire, Matthew Henry was born, on October 18, 1662. His father, Philip Henry, a well-known clergyman, was one of two thousand who resigned or were ejected from their livings because they "dissented" to the conditions laid down in the Act of Uniformity, and were afterwards called "Dissenters". His mother was of an ancient and honourable family. She had a modest inheritance, so Philip Henry was able to live at Broad Oak and exercise a selfless ministry amongst the people of the district. Matthew was their second son—so frail at his birth that he was baptised when he was only a day old, lest he died within the week. As a boy he was physically weak, but mentally and, indeed, spiritually strong. (He is said to have read aloud a chapter of the Bible when he was only three years old!)

In Broad Oak, Philip Henry frequently boarded and trained a candidate for the ministry, who repaid him by acting as tutor to the children. One of these young students, a certain William Turner, gave Matthew his first love for Latin, and in the Commentary there are many apposite quotations from the Classics. Until he was eighteen, the education of Matthew was supervised by his father, a considerable scholar and a gifted teacher. Because of the increasing laxity at the Universities of Oxford and Cambridge, Matthew was sent, in 1680, to the Academy at Islington, London. (The "Dissenting Academies" which were established in 1662 and the following years maintained a high standard of academic education at a time when the ancient universities had betrayed their trust and forfeited the respect of serious-minded educationists, who desired intellectual freedom.) At Islington the famous Thomas Doolittle, M.A. (late of Pembroke College, Cambridge), was the Principal, and his Assistant Tutor was Thomas Vincent, M.A. (Christ Church, Oxford). Like other Academies it was forced, by persecution, to move from place to place on five occasions, but, in spite of such breaks in continuity, it was considered by many to be the foremost Presbyterian Academy. Of its Principal, Matthew Henry said, "He was very studious and diligent", but of its accommodation he described its rooms as "very straight and little". When the Academy was compelled to remove to Battersea, London, Matthew returned home, in 1682. At Broad Oak, though he was of considerable help to his father in pastoral work, he realised that there was not much likelihood of his getting a "call" to a settled pastorate. The village was remote, the restrictions on dissenting ministers were severe, and he had no desire to live in comparative idleness.

He decided to return to London to go to Gray's Inn and study Law. It was soon apparent that his remarkable memory and easy eloquence promised well for a distinguished future. But at this time he was greatly influenced by the preaching of Dr. Stillingfleet at St. Andrew's, Holborn, and by Dr. Tillotson at Lawrence Jewry. At this time, also, he gathered some of his friends in a small group which met for prayer and Bible study, just as, later, the Wesleys founded the Holy Club at Oxford.

Returning to Broad Oak, he began to preach as a candidate for the ministry. The people who heard him in Chester were so impressed that they asked him to become their pastor. After much self-examination, he decided to answer the "call". Certain London ministers ordained him, privately, on May 9th 1687, but in 1702 he obtained a document certifying the regularity of his Presbyterian ordination fifteen years earlier.

He held the pastorate in Chester from 1687 to 1712.

His first wife, Katherine Hardware, died of small-pox, as she gave birth to a child. Subsequently he married the grand-daughter of Peter Warburton, a judge of the Court of Common Pleas. Though three of their nine children died in infancy, this marriage was as happy as the first had been. No domestic tragedy could mar the beauty of his home life. It was moulded on the pattern of Broad Oak, where his father's house was often described as "a house of God and a gate of heaven". In Chester Matthew Henry conducted family prayers in his home at the beginning and the end of the day. In the morning he expounded the Old Testament, and in the evening the New Testament. Probably these expositions, amended as the result of questions and comments from his family and his neighbours, were the basis of his Commentary.

In public services he usually prayed for half an hour, preached for an hour, and joined in singing Psalms from a selection he himself had made. His sermons were expository, never political but always practical in their application to the problems of ordinary life. They frequently contained some reference to the condition of the people of the Reformed Churches, who were suffering severe persecution on the Continent.

On Saturday afternoons he held catechism classes for children, in preparation for their attendance at the Sacrament of the Lord's Supper, which, he stressed, was a fulfilment of their baptismal covenant.

Though he had strong personal convictions on the cardinal doctrines, he was not intolerant, and visited all who were in need, whatever might be the communion to which they belonged. He preached on six days a week to various congregations within a radius of thirty miles, but always contrived to be in his own pulpit at Chester on Sunday. His influence in the city grew rapidly, and a new meeting-house was built to accommodate the large congregations which now came to hear him.

After recovering from a serious illness in 1704, he began his *Notes on the New Testament*, and the entry in his diary concluded with a typical prayer: "The Lord help me to set about it with great humility."

Six years later, in 1710, an urgent "call" came to him from the congregation in Silver Street, Hackney, London. He was reluctant to leave Chester, but felt that his work on the Commentary would be helped by easier access to books and to Biblical scholars in London. "I look back with sorrow for leaving Chester," he said; "I look forward with fear; but unto Thee, O Lord, do I look up."

It was not surprising that his attempt to discharge the duties of a large pastorate and, at the same time, to write a detailed commentary on the whole Bible overtaxed his physical resources.

He was troubled by the poor quality of religious life in England, and this increased his weakness. In 1714, whilst paying a visit to his old friends in Chester, he died, from apoplexy, at Nantwich. He was only fifty-two, and it seemed a tragic ending; but as one of his relatives said: "I believe it was most agreeable to him to have so short a passage from his work to his reward." To have exercised so virile and continuous a ministry, to have been a pastor with such intimate insight into the problems of his people, and to have produced so monumental a work as his Commentary, was an astonishing achievement. For two and a half centuries innumerable people have been enlightened and inspired by his interpretation of the Scriptures. Its essentials have stood the test of time, as, in his own day, they stood the test of human experience. The explanation is, surely, that it had its origin in his fellowship with his Master and in his constant concern for the deepest needs of the people committed to his care.

The New Edition of the Commentary

Matthew Henry began his Commentary, November 1704. The first volume was published 1708 (folio). This first volume with four others appeared in uniform edition 1710 (folio). Before he died he completed volume 6 up to Acts and after his death, the Epistles and Revelation were prepared by thirteen nonconformist divines.

For many years a standard six-volume edition has been, and indeed remains, very popular. There has been, however, in recent years a persistent and increasing demand for a shorter version which, at a lower price, should be available to an even wider public.

In reducing the six volumes to one, certain principles have been strictly observed.

1. The work is still produced in Matthew Henry's words. Even archaisms have frequently been retained, since emphasis is strengthened by the very quaintness of their appeal. Abbreviation has not been accomplished by any kind of paraphrase.
2. Obvious anachronisms have been, in the light of present knowledge, omitted.
3. Factual errors in minor details of background material have also been corrected, but the corrections are such as Matthew Henry himself would have sanctioned, for the sake of accuracy. For example, references to the "seasons" do not correspond with natural conditions in the Middle East. The physical features and climate of Palestine and Syria make the times of harvest quite different from those in the Western world.
4. Many quaint phrases and aphorisms have been retained, since, although they are not used in modern speech, they reveal the personality of the commentator, and often express truth with point and piquancy.
5. Where, in certain places, imagination has dispensed with evidence, we have not included such unimportant passages; e.g. of Noah's drunkenness Matthew Henry comments, "We have reason to believe he was never drunk before nor since" (Gen. 9, 21).

This one-volume edition we hope will be justified by its usefulness in private devotions, in groups for Bible study, and in the public and private exposition of eternal Truth as revealed in Holy Scripture.

This is a valuable aid to the preacher and speaker. It is not a museum-piece, but a sincere and vivid interpretation. It may be that you will not agree with all its conclusions, but it cannot but help you to form your own with confidence.

L. F. C.

Contents

THE BOOKS OF THE OLD TESTAMENT

THE BOOKS OF THE NEW TESTAMENT

THE OLD TESTAMENT

GENESIS

We have now before us the holy Bible, or *book*, for so *bible* signifies. We call it *the book*, for it is incomparably the best book that ever was written, the book of books. We call it the holy book, because it was written by holy men, and indited by the Holy Ghost. The great things of God's law and gospel are here *written* for us, that they might be transmitted to distant places and ages more pure and entire than possibly they could be by report and tradition. This is the *light that shines in a dark place* (2 Pet. i. 19), and a dark place indeed the world would be without the Bible.

We have before us that part of the Bible which we call the *Old Testament*. This is called a *testament*, or *covenant* (Διαθήκη), because it was a settled declaration of the *will* of God concerning man in a federal way, and had its force from the designed death of the great testator, *the Lamb slain from the foundation of the world*, Rev. xiii. 8. It is called the *Old Testament*, with relation to the *New*, which does not cancel and supersede it, but crowns and perfects it, by the bringing in of that better hope which was typified and foretold in it.

We have before us that part of the Old Testament which we call the *Pentateuch*, or five books of Moses. In our Saviour's distribution of the books of the Old Testament into the *law*, the *prophets*, and the *psalms*, or *Hagiographa*, these are the *law*.

We have before us the first and longest of those five books, which we call *Genesis*, written, some think, when Moses was in Midian, for the instruction and comfort of his suffering brethren in Egypt: I rather think he wrote it in the wilderness, after he had been in the mount with God, where, probably, he received full and particular instructions for the writing of it. *Genesis* is a name borrowed from the Greek. It signifies the *original*, or *generation*: it is a history of originals—the creation of the world, the entrance of sin and death into it, the invention of arts, the rise of nations, and especially the planting of the church, and the state of it in its early days. It is also a history of the generations of Adam, Noah, Abraham, &c. The beginning of the New Testament is called *Genesis* too (Matt. i. 1), Βίβλος γενέσεως, the book of the *genesis*, or *generation*, of Jesus Christ. Blessed be God for that book which shows us our remedy, as this opens our wound. Lord, open our eyes, that we may see the wondrous things both of thy law and gospel!

CHAPTER 1

A plain and full account of the creation of the world in answer to that first enquiry "Where is God my Maker?" Concerning this the pagan philosophers wretchedly blundered, some asserting the world's eternity and self-existence, others ascribing it to a fortuitous concourse of atoms: thus "the world by wisdom knew not God", but took a great deal of pains to lose him. The holy scripture by revealed religion lays down, at first, this principle. That this world was, in the beginning of time, created by a Being of infinite wisdom and power, who was himself before all time and all worlds. The first verse of the Bible gives us a surer and better, a more satisfying and useful, knowledge of the origin of the universe, than all the volumes of the philosophers.

We have three things in this chapter:—I. A general idea given us of the work of creation, ver. 1, 2. II. A particular account of the several days' work, registered, as in a journal, distinctly and in order. The review and approbation of the whole work, ver. 31.

Verses 1–2

The work of creation in its epitome and in its embryo.

I. In its epitome, *v.* 1, where we find the first article of our creed, that *God the Father Almighty is the Maker of heaven and earth.*

1. Observe, in this verse, four things:—

(1) The effect produced—the whole frame and furniture of the universe. The world is a great house, consisting of upper and lower stories, the structure stately and magnificent, uniform and convenient, and every room well and wisely furnished. The heavens are not only beautified to our eye with glorious lamps which garnish its outside, of whose creation we here read, but they are within replenished with glorious beings, out of our sight. In the visible world it is easy to observe, [1] Great variety, several sorts of beings vastly differing in their nature and constitution from each other. [2] Great beauty. The azure sky and verdant earth are charming to the eye of the curious spectator. How transcendent then must the beauty of the Creator be! [3] Great exactness and accuracy. To those that, with the help of microscopes, narrowly look into the works of nature, they appear far more fine than any of the works of art. [4] Great power. It is not a lump of dead and inactive matter, the earth itself has a magnetic power. [5] Great order, a mutual dependence of beings, an exact harmony of motions, and an admirable chain and connection of causes. [6] Great mystery. There are phenomena in nature which cannot be solved. But from what we see of heaven and earth we may infer the eternal power and Godhead of the great Creator. Our duty as Christians is always to keep heaven in our eye and the earth under our feet.

(2) The author and cause of this great work— GOD. The Hebrew word is *Elohim*, which bespeaks, [1] The power of God the Creator. *El* signifies *the strong God*; and what less than almighty strength could bring all things out of nothing? [2] The plurality of persons in the Godhead, Father, Son, and Holy Ghost. This plural name of God, in Hebrew, which speaks of him as many though he is one, confirming our faith in the doctrine of the Trinity, which, though but darkly intimated in the Old Testament, is clearly revealed in the New. We are often told that the world was made by him, and nothing made without him, John i. 3, 10; Eph. iii. 9; Col. i. 16; Heb. i. 2.

(3) The manner in which this work was effected: *God created it*, that is, made it out of nothing. There was not any pre-existent matter out of which the world was produced. No artificer can work, unless he has something to work on. But by the almighty power of God it is not only possible that something should be made of nothing (the God of nature is not subject to the laws of nature), but in the creation it is impossible it should be otherwise, for nothing is more injurious to the honour of the Eternal Mind than the supposition of eternal matter.

(4) When this work was produced: *In the beginning*, that is, in the beginning of time, when that clock was first set a-going: time began with the production of those beings that are measured by time. Before the beginning of time there was none but that Infinite Being that inhabits eternity. But to us it is enough to say, *In the beginning was the Word*, John i. 1.

2. Let us learn hence, (1) That atheism is folly, and atheists are the greatest fools in nature; for they see there is a world that could not make itself, and yet they will not own there is a God that made it. (2) That God is sovereign Lord of all by an incontestable right. (3) That with God all things are possible, and therefore happy are the people that have him for their God, and whose help and hope stand in his name, Ps. cxxi. 2; cxxiv. 8. (4) That the God we serve is worthy of all blessing and praise, Neh. ix. 5, 6. If all is of him, all must be to him.

II. The work of creation in its embryo, *v.* 2, where we have an account of the first matter and the first mover.

1. A chaos was the first matter. It is here called the earth; it is also called *the deep*, both for its vastness and because the waters which were afterwards separated from the earth were now mixed with it. The Creator could have made his work perfect at first, but by this gradual proceeding he would show what is, ordinarily, the method of his providence and grace. Observe the description of this chaos. (1) There was nothing in it desirable to be seen, for it was *without form and void. Tohu* and *Bohu, confusion* and *emptiness*; so these words are rendered, Isa. xxxiv. 11. To those who have their hearts in heaven this lower world, in comparison with that upper, still appears to be nothing but confusion and emptiness. (2) If there had been anything desirable to be seen, yet there was no light to see it by; for *darkness*, thick darkness, *was upon the face of the deep.* This chaos represents the state of an unregenerate graceless soul: *there* is disorder, confusion, and every evil work; it is empty of all good, for it is without God; it is dark till almighty grace effects a blessed change.

2. The Spirit of God was the first mover: He *moved upon the face of the waters.* The Spirit of God begins to work, and, if he work, who or what shall hinder? God is said to make the world by his Spirit, Ps. xxxiii. 6; Job xxvi. 13; and by the same mighty worker the new creation is effected. He moved upon the face of the deep. God is not only the author of all being, but the fountain of life and spring of motion. Dead matter would be for ever dead if he did not quicken it. And this makes it credible to us that God should raise the dead.

Verses 3–5

We have here a further account of the first day's work, in which observe, 1. That the first of all visible beings which God created was light, that by it we might see his works and his glory in them, and might work our works while it is day. Light is the great beauty and blessing of the universe. In the new creation, the first thing wrought in the soul is *light*: the blessed Spirit captivates the will and affections by enlightening the understanding. Those that by sin were darkness by grace become light in the world. 2. That the light was made by the word of God's power. He said, *Let there be light*; he willed and appointed it, and it was done immediately. The word of God is quick and powerful. Christ is the Word, the essential eternal Word, and by him the light was produced, for *in him was light, and he is the true light, the light of the world*, John i. 9; ix. 5. The divine light which shines in sanctified souls is wrought by the power of God, giving the knowledge of the glory of God in the face of Christ, as, at first, *God commanded the light to shine out of darkness*, 2 Cor. iv. 6. 3. That the light which God willed, when it was produced, he approved of: *God saw the light that it was good.* If the light is good, how good is he that is the fountain of light, from whom we receive it. 4. That God *divided the light from the darkness.* Yet he divided time between them, the

day for light and the night for darkness, in a constant and regular succession to each other. Though the darkness was now scattered by the light, yet it takes its turn with the light, and has its place, because it has its use; for, as the light of the morning befriends the business of the day, so the shadows of the evening befriend the repose of the night, and draw the curtains about us, that we may sleep the better. 5. That God divided them from each other by distinguishing names: *He called the light day, and the darkness he called night.* He gave them names, as the Lord of both. Let us acknowledge God in the constant succession of day and night, and consecrate both to his honour, by working for him every day and resting in him every night. 6. That this was the first day's work, and a good day's work it was. *The evening and the morning were the first day.* This was not only the first day of the world, but the first day of the week. I observe it to the honour of that day, because the new world began on the first day of the week likewise, in the resurrection of Christ, as the light of the world, early in the morning. In him the dayspring from on high has visited the world.

Verses 6–8

We have here an account of the second day's work, the creation of the firmament, in which observe, 1. The command of God concerning it: *Let there be a firmament*, an *expansion*, so the Hebrew word signifies, like a sheet spread, or a curtain drawn out. This firmament is not a wall of partition, but a way of intercourse. See Job xxvi. 7; xxxvii. 18; Ps. civ. 3; Amos ix. 6. 2. The creation of it. Lest it should seem as if God had only commanded it to be done, and someone else had done it, he adds, *And God made the firmament.* What God requires of us he himself works in us, or it is not done. He that commands faith, holiness, and love, creates them by the power of his grace going along with his word. 3. The use and design of it—to *divide the waters from the waters*, that is, to distinguish between the waters that are wrapped up in the clouds and those that cover the sea. God has, in the firmament of his power, chambers, store-chambers, whence he *watereth the earth.* O what a great God is he who has thus provided for the comfort of all that serve him. 4. The naming of it: *He called the firmament heaven.* It is the visible heaven, the pavement of the holy city; above the firmament God is said to have his throne (Ezek. i. 26). We should be led by the contemplation of the heavens that are in our eye to consider *our Father who is in heaven.* The height of the heavens should remind us of God's supremacy and the infinite distance there is between us and him; the brightness of the heavens and their purity should remind us of his glory, and majesty, and perfect holiness; the vastness of the heavens, their encompassing of the earth, and the influence they have upon it, should remind us of his immensity and universal providence.

Verses 9–13

Hitherto the power of the Creator had been employed about the upper part of the visible world; the light of heaven was kindled, and the firmament of heaven fixed: but now he descends to this lower world, the earth, which was designed for the children of men, designed both for their habitation and for their maintenance; and here we have an account of the fitting of it for both, the building of their house and the spreading of their table.

I. How the earth was prepared to be a habitation for man, by the gathering of the waters together, and the making of the dry land to appear. 1. The waters which had covered the earth were ordered to retire, and to gather into one place. The waters thus collected he called *seas.* Waters and seas often, in scripture, signify troubles and afflictions, Ps. xlii. 7; lxix. 2, 14, 15. God's own people are not exempted from these in this world; but it is their comfort that they are only waters under the heaven (there are none in heaven), and that they are all in the place that God has appointed them and within the bounds that he has set for them. 2. The dry land was made to appear, and emerge out of the waters, and was called *earth*, and *given to the children of men*. The earth, it seems, was in being before; but it was of no use, because it was under water. Thus many of God's gifts are received in vain, because they are buried; make them to appear, and they become serviceable.

II. How the earth was furnished for the maintenance and support of man, *v.* 11, 12. Present provision was now made, by the immediate products of the upstart earth. It became fruitful, and brought forth grass for the cattle and herb for the service of man. Provision was likewise made for time to come, every one *having its seed in itself after its kind*, that, during the continuance of man upon the earth, food might be fetched out of the earth for his use and benefit. Observe here, 1. That not only the earth is the Lord's, but *the fulness thereof*, and he is the rightful owner and sovereign disposer, not only of it, but of all its furniture. The earth was *emptiness* (*v.* 2), but now, by a word's speaking, it has become full of God's riches. 2. That common providence is a continued creation, and in it *our Father worketh hitherto*. The earth still remains under the efficacy of this command, to bring forth grass, and herbs, and its annual products. They are standing instances of the unwearied power and unexhausted goodness of the world's great Maker and Master. 3. That though God, ordinarily, makes use of the agency of second causes, according to their nature, yet he neither needs them nor is tied to them. 4. That it is good to provide things necessary before we have occasions to use them: before the beasts and man were made, here were grass and herbs prepared for them. 5. That God must have the glory of all the benefit we receive from the products of the earth.

Verses 14–19

This is the history of the fourth day's work, the creating of the sun, moon, and stars, that garniture which is not only so much the beauty of the upper world, but so much the blessing of this lower. Of the creation of the lights of heaven we have an account,

I. In general, *v.* 14, 15, where we have, 1. The command given concerning them: *Let there be lights in the firmament of heaven.* God had said, *Let there be light* (*v.* 3), and there was light; but this was, as it were, a chaos of light, scattered and confused: now it was collected and modelled, and so rendered both more glorious and more serviceable. God is the God of order, and not of confusion; and, as he is light, so he is the Father and former of lights. 2. The use they were intended to be to this earth. (1) They must be for the distinction of times, of day and night, summer and winter, and thus, *under the sun*, there is *a season to every purpose*, Eccl. iii. 1. (2) They must be for the direction of actions. They are for signs of the change of weather, that the husbandman may order his affairs with discretion, foreseeing, by the face of the sky, when second causes have begun to work, whether it will be fair or foul, Matt. xvi. 2, 3. They do also *give light upon the earth*, that we may *walk* (John xi. 9), and *work* (John ix. 4), according as the duty of every day requires. The lights of heaven shine for us, for our pleasure and advantage. The lights of heaven are made to serve us, and they do it faithfully, and shine in their season, without fail: but we are set as lights in this world to serve God; and do we in like manner answer the end of our creation? We burn our Master's candles, but do not mind our Master's work.

II. In particular, *v.* 16–18.

1. Observe, The lights of heaven are the sun, moon, and stars; and all these are the work of God's hands. (1) The sun is the greatest light of all. Let us learn from Ps. xix. 1–6 how to give unto God the glory due unto his name, as the Maker of the sun. (2) The moon is a less light, and yet is here reckoned one of the greater lights. Those are most valuable that are most serviceable; and those are the greater lights, not that have the best gifts, but that humbly and faithfully do the most good with them. (3) *He made the stars also,* for the scriptures were written, not to gratify our curiosity and make us astronomers, but to lead us to God, and make us saints. Now these lights are deputy-governors, rulers under him. Here the less light, the moon, is said to rule *the night*; but in Ps. cxxxvi. 9 the stars are mentioned as sharers in that government: *The moon and stars to rule by night.* The best and most honourable way of ruling is by giving light and doing good: those command respect that live a useful life, and so shine as lights.

2. Learn from all this, (1) The sin and folly of that ancient idolatry, the worshipping of the sun, moon, and stars. But the account here given of them plainly shows that they are both God's creatures and man's servants; and therefore it is both a great affront to God and a great reproach to ourselves to make deities of them and give them divine honours. (2) The duty and wisdom of daily worshipping that God who made all these things, and to offer the solemn sacrifice of prayer and praise every morning and evening.

Verses 20–23

We do not read of the creation of any living creature till the fifth day, of which these verses give us an account. It was on the fifth day that the fish and fowl were created, and both out of the waters. Observe, 1. The making of the fish and fowl, at first, *v.* 20, 21. God commanded them to be produced. He said, *Let the waters bring forth abundantly.* This command he himself executed: *God created great whales, &c.* Insects, which perhaps are as various and as numerous as any species of animals, and their structure as curious, were part of this day's work. Mr. Boyle (I remember) says he admires the Creator's wisdom and power as much in an ant as in an elephant. The curious formation of the bodies of animals, their different sizes, shapes, and natures, with the admirable powers of the sensitive life with which they are endued, when duly considered, serve, not only to silence and shame the objections of atheists and infidels, but to raise high thoughts and high praises of God in pious and devout souls, Ps. civ. 25, &c. 2. The blessing of them, in order to their continuance. Life is a wasting thing. Its strength is not the strength of stones. It is a candle that will burn out, if it be not first blown out; and therefore the wise Creator not only made the individuals, but provided for the propagation of the several kinds: *God blessed them, saying, Be fruitful, and multiply,* *v.* 22.

Verses 24–25

We have here the first part of the sixth day's work, and this day were made the beasts of the earth, the cattle, and the creeping things that pertain to the earth. Here, as before, 1. *The Lord gave the word*; he said, *Let the earth bring forth.* 2. He also did the work; he made them all after their kind, not only of divers shapes, but of divers natures, manners, food, and fashions—some living upon grass and herbs, others upon flesh—some bold, and others timorous—

some for man's service, and not his sustenance, as the horse—others for his sustenance, and not his service, as the sheep—others for both, as the ox—and some for neither, as the wild beasts.

Verses 26–28

The second part of the sixth day's work, the creation of man.

I. That man was made last of all the creatures, that it might not be suspected that he had been, in any way, a helper to God in the creation of the world. Yet it was both an honour and a favour to him that he was made last: an honour, for the method of the creation was to advance from that which was less perfect to that which was more so; and a favour, for it was not fit he should be lodged in the palace designed for him till it was completely fitted up and furnished for his reception. Man, as soon as he was made, had the whole visible creation before him, both to contemplate and to take the comfort of.

II. That man's creation was a more signal and immediate act of divine wisdom and power than that of the other creatures. Hitherto, it had been said, "Let there be light," and "Let there be a firmament," and "Let the earth, or waters, bring forth" such a thing; but now the word of command is turned into a word of consultation, "*Let us make man*, for whose sake the rest of the creatures were made: this is a work we must take into our own hands." In the former he speaks as one having authority, in this as one having affection; as if he had said, "Having at last settled the preliminaries, let us now apply ourselves to the business, *Let us make man*." Man was to be a creature different from all that had been hitherto made. Flesh and spirit, heaven and earth, must be put together in him, and he must be allied to both worlds. And therefore God himself not only undertakes to make him, but is pleased so to express himself as if he called a council to consider of the making of him: *Let us make man*. The three persons of the Trinity, Father, Son, and Holy Ghost, consult about it and concur in it. Let him rule man who said, *Let us make man*.

III. That man was made in God's image and after his likeness, two words to express the same thing and making each other the more expressive; *image* and *likeness* denote the likest image. Still between God and man there is an infinite distance. Christ only is the *express* image of God's person, as the Son of his Father, having the same nature. It is only some of God's honour that is put upon man, who is God's image only as the shadow in the glass, or the king's impress upon the coin. God's image upon man consists in these three things:—1. In his nature and constitution, not those of his body (for God has not a body), but those of his soul. This honour indeed God has put upon the body of man, that the Word was made flesh, the Son of God was clothed with a body like ours and will shortly clothe ours with a glory like that of his. But it is the soul, the great soul, of man, that does especially bear God's image. The soul of man, considered in its three noble faculties, understanding, will, and active power, is perhaps the brightest, clearest looking-glass in nature, wherein to see God. 2. In his place and authority: *Let us make man in our image, and let him have dominion.* As he has the government of the inferior creatures, he is, as it were, God's representative, or viceroy, upon earth. Yet his government of himself by the freedom of his will has in it more of God's image than his government of the creatures. 3. In his purity and rectitude. God's image upon man consists in knowledge, righteousness, and true holiness, Eph. iv. 24; Col. iii. 10. Thus holy, thus happy, were our first parents, in having the image of God upon them.

IV. That man was made male and female, and blessed with the blessing of fruitfulness and increase. God said, *Let us make man*, and immediately it follows, *So God created man*; he performed what he resolved. With us saying and doing are two things, but they are not so with God. It would seem that of the rest of the creatures God made many couples; but of man *did not he make one?* Whence Christ gathers an argument against divorce, Matt. xix. 4, 5. Our first father, Adam, was confined to one wife; and, if he had put her away, there was no other for him to marry, which plainly intimated that the bond of marriage was not to be dissolved at pleasure. God made but one male and one female, that all the nations of men might know themselves to be made of one blood, descendants from one common stock, and might thereby be induced to love one another. He gave them, 1. A large inheritance: *Replenish the earth;* it is this that is bestowed upon the children of men. They were made *to dwell upon the face of all the earth*, Acts xvii. 26. This is the place in which God has set man to be a probationer for a better state. 2. A numerous lasting family, to enjoy this inheritance.

V. That God gave to man, when he had made him, a dominion over the inferior creatures, *over the fish of the sea and over the fowl of the air*. Though man provides for neither, he has power over both. God designed hereby to put an honour upon man. God's providence continues so much of it to the children of men as is necessary to the safety and support of their lives.

Verses 29–30

The third part of the sixth day's work, a gracious provision of food for all flesh, Ps. cxxxvi. 25.

I. Food provided for man, *v.* 29. Herbs and fruits must be his meat. See here, 1. That which should make us humble. As we were made out of the earth, so we are maintained out of it. There is meat that endures to everlasting life; the Lord evermore give us this. 2. That which should make us thankful. The Lord is for the body; from him we receive all the supports and comforts of this life. He gives us all things richly to enjoy, not only for necessity, but plenty, dainties, and varieties, for ornament and delight. 3. That which should make us temperate and content with our lot. If God gives us food for our lives, let us not, with murmuring Israel, ask food for our lusts, Ps. lxxviii. 18; see Dan. i. 15.

II. Food provided for the beasts, *v.* 30. *Doth God take care for oxen?* Yes, certainly, he provides food convenient for them, and not for oxen only, but even the young lions and the young ravens are the care of his providence. He is a great housekeeper, a very rich and bountiful one, that satisfies the desire of every living thing. He that feeds his birds will not starve his babes.

Verse 31

The approbation and conclusion of the whole work of creation.

I. The review God took of his work: He *saw that every thing that he had made.* So he does still; all the works of his hands are under his eye. Omniscience cannot be separated from omnipotence. But this was the Eternal Mind's solemn reflection upon the copies of its own wisdom and the products of its own power. God has hereby set us an example of reviewing our works. When we have finished a day's work, and are entering upon the rest of the night, we should commune with our own hearts about what we have been doing that day.

II. The complacency God took in his work. He did not pronounce it good till he had seen it so, to teach us not to answer a matter before we hear it. 1. It was good. Good, for it is all agreeable to the mind of the Creator, just as he would have it to be. Good, for it answers the end of its creation, and is fit for the purpose for which it was designed. Good, for it is serviceable to man, whom God had appointed lord of the visible creation. Good, for it is all for God's glory. 2. It was very good. Of each day's work (except the second) it was said that it was good, but now, it is very good. For, (1) Now man was made, who was the chief of the ways of God, who was designed to be the visible image of the Creator's glory and the mouth of the creation in his praises. (2) Now all was made; every part was good, but all together very good. The glory and goodness, the beauty and harmony, of God's works, both of providence and grace, as this of creation, will best appear when they are perfected. Therefore judge nothing before the time.

III. The time when this work was concluded: *The evening and the morning were the sixth day*; so that in six days God made the world. We are not to think but that God could have made the world in an instant. He that said, *Let there be light, and there was light*, could have said, "Let there be a world," and there would have been a world, *in a moment, in the twinkling of an eye*, as at the resurrection, 1 Cor. xv. 52. But he did it in his own way and in his own time. So much would the sabbath conduce to the keeping up of religion in the world that God had an eye to it in the timing of his creation.

CHAPTER 2

This chapter is an appendix to the history of the creation, more particularly explaining and enlarging upon that part of the history which relates immediately to man. We have in it, I. The institution and sanctification of the sabbath, ver. 1-3. II. A more particular account of man's creation, ver. 4-7. III. A description of the garden of Eden, and the placing of man in it under the obligations of a law and covenant, ver. 8-17. IV. The creation of the woman, her marriage to the man, and the institution of the ordinance of marriage, ver. 18, &c.

Verses 1-3

I. The settlement of the kingdom of nature, in God's resting from the work of creation, *v*. 1, 2. Here observe, 1. The creatures made both in heaven and earth are disciplined, and under command. Every one knows and keeps his place. 2. The heavens and the earth are finished pieces, and so are all the creatures in them. 3. After the end of the first six days God ceased from all works of creation. He has so ended his work. In miracles, he has controlled nature, but never changed its settled course. 4. The eternal God did not rest, as one weary, but as one well-pleased.

II. The commencement of the kingdom of grace, in the sanctification of the sabbath day, *v*. 3. Observe, 1. The solemn observance of one day in seven, as a day of holy rest and holy work, to God's honour, is the indispensable duty of all those to whom God has revealed his holy sabbaths. 2. Sabbaths are as ancient as the world; and I see no reason to doubt that the sabbath, being now instituted in innocency, was religiously observed by the people of God throughout the patriarchal age. 3. The sabbath of the Lord is truly honourable, and we have reason to honour it in obedience to him. 4. The sabbath day is a blessed day, for God blessed it, and that which he blesses is blessed indeed. God has promised, on that day, to meet us and bless us. 5. The sabbath day is a holy day, for God has sanctified it.

Verses 4-7

In these verses, I. Here is a name given to the Creator which we have not yet met with, and that

is *Jehovah*—the LORD, in capital letters, which are constantly used in our English translation to intimate that in the original it is *Jehovah*. All along, in the first chapter, he was called *Elohim—a God of power*; but now *Jehovah Elohim—a God of power and perfection*, a finishing God. *Jehovah* is that great and incommunicable name of God which denotes his having his being of himself, and his giving being to all things.

II. Further notice taken of the production of plants and herbs, because they were made and appointed to be food for man, *v*. 5, 6. Here observe, 1. The earth did not bring forth its fruits of itself, but purely by the almighty power of God. Thus grace in the soul, that plant of renown, grows not of itself in nature's soil, but is the work of God's own hands. 2. Rain also is the gift of God; it came not till *the Lord God caused it to rain*. 3. Though God, ordinarily, works by means, yet he is not tied to them. 4. Some way or other God will take care to water the plants that are of his own planting. Though as yet there was no rain, God made a mist equivalent to a shower, and with it *watered the whole face of the ground*. Divine grace descends like a mist, or silent dew, and waters the church without noise, Deut. xxxii. 2.

III. A more particular account of the creation of man, *v*. 7. Man is a little world, consisting of heaven and earth, soul and body. Now here we have an account of the origin of both.

1. The mean origin, and yet the curious structure, of the body of man. (1) The matter was despicable. He was made *of the dust of the ground*, a very unlikely thing to make a man of; but the same infinite power that made the world of nothing made man, its masterpiece, of next to nothing. He was not made of gold-dust, powder of pearl, or diamond dust, but common dust, dust of the ground. Our fabric is earthly, and the fashioning of it like that of an earthen vessel, Job x. 9. What have we then to be proud of? (2) Yet the Maker was great, and the make fine. Of the other creatures it is said that they were *created* and *made*; but of man that he was *formed*, which denotes a gradual process in the work with great accuracy and exactness. *The workmanship exceeded the materials*. Let us present our bodies to God as living sacrifices (Rom. xii. 1).

2. The high origin and the admirable serviceableness of the soul of man. (1) It takes its rise from the breath of heaven. It was not made of the earth, as the body was; it came immediately from God. Let the soul which God has breathed into us breathe after him. Into his hands let us commit our spirits, for from his hands we had them. (2) The soul is the man. The body would be worthless, useless, loathsome carcase, if the soul did not animate it. Since the extraction of the soul is so noble, and its nature and faculties are so excellent, let us not be of those fools that despise their own souls, by preferring their bodies before them, Prov. xv. 32. He that made the soul is alone able to new-make it.

Verses 8-15

Man consisting of body and soul, a body made out of the earth and a rational immortal soul the breath of heaven, we have, in these verses, the provision that was made for the happiness of both; he that made him took care to make him happy, if he could but have kept himself so and known when he was well off.

I. A description of the garden of Eden, which was intended for the mansion and demesne of this great lord, the palace of this prince. The inspired penman, in this history, writing for the Jews first, and calculating his narratives for the infant state of the church, describes things by their outward sensible appearances, and leaves us, by further discoveries of the divine light, to be led into the understanding of the mysteries couched under them. Therefore he does not so much insist upon the happiness of Adam's mind as upon that of his outward state.

1. The place appointed for Adam's residence was a garden; not an ivory house nor a palace overlaid with gold, but a garden, furnished and adorned by nature, not by art. The heaven was the roof of Adam's house, and never was any roof so curiously ceiled and painted. The earth was his floor, and never was any floor so richly inlaid. The shadow of the trees was his retirement; under them were his dining-rooms, his lodging-rooms, and never were any rooms so finely hung as these: Solomon's, in all their glory, were not arrayed like them. Nature is content with a little and that which is most natural, grace with less, but lust with nothing.

2. The contrivance and furniture of this garden were the immediate work of God's wisdom and power. The Lord God planted this garden. No delights can be agreeable nor satisfying to a soul but those that God himself has provided and appointed for it; no true paradise, but of God's planting.

3. The situation of this garden was extremely sweet. It was in *Eden*, which signifies *delight* and *pleasure*. The place is here particularly pointed out by such marks and bounds as were sufficient. Let it be our care to make sure of a place in the heavenly paradise, and then we need not perplex ourselves with a search after the place of the earthly paradise.

4. The trees with which this garden was planted. (1) It had all the best and choicest trees. God, as a tender Father, consulted not only Adam's profit, but his pleasure; for there is a pleasure consistent with innocency, nay, there is a true and transcendent pleasure in innocency. But, (2) It had two extra-ordinary trees peculiar to itself; on earth there were not their like. [1] There was *the tree of life in the midst of the garden*, which was chiefly intended to be a sign and seal to Adam, assuring him of the continuance of life and happiness, even to immortality and everlasting bliss, through the grace and favour of his Maker, upon condition of his perseverance in this state of innocency and obedience. Of this he might eat and live. Christ is now to us the tree of life (Rev. ii. 7; xxii. 2). [2] There was *the tree of the knowledge of good and evil*, so called, not because it had any virtue in it to beget or increase useful knowledge, but, *First*, Because there was an express positive revelation of the will of God concerning this tree, so that by it he might know moral good and evil. What is good? It is good not to eat of this tree. What is evil? It is evil to eat of this tree. The distinction between all other moral good and evil was written in the heart of man by nature; but this, which resulted from a positive law, was written upon this tree. *Secondly*, Because, in the event, it proved to give Adam an experimental knowledge of good by the loss of it and of evil by the sense of it. As the covenant of grace has in it, not only *Believe and be saved*, but also, *Believe not and be damned* (Mark xvi. 16), so the covenant of innocency had in it, not only "Do this and live," which was sealed and confirmed by the tree of life, but "Fail and die," which Adam was assured of by this other tree: "Touch it at your peril; " so that, in these two trees, God set before him *good and evil, the blessing and the curse*, Deut. xxx. 19. These two trees were as two sacraments.

5. The rivers with which this garden was watered, *v.* 10–14. These four rivers (or one river branched into four streams) contributed much both to the pleasantness and the fruitfulness of this garden. In the heavenly paradise there is a river infinitely sur-passing these; for it is a river of the water of life, not coming out of Eden, as this, but proceeding out of the throne of God and of the Lamb (Rev. xxii. 1), a river that *makes glad the city of our God*, Ps. xlvi. 4. Havilah had gold, and spices, and precious stones; but Eden had that which was infinitely better, the tree of life, and communion with God. So we may say of the Africans and Indians: "They have the gold, but we have the gospel. The gold of their land is good, but the riches of ours are infinitely better."

II. The placing of man in this paradise of delight, *v.* 15, where observe,

1. How God put him in possession of it. (1) Man was made *out* of paradise; for, after God had formed him, he put him into the garden: he was made of common clay, not of paradise-dust. He could not plead a tenant-right to the garden, for he was not born upon the premises, nor had anything but what he received. (2) The same God that was the author of his being was the author of his bliss. He that made us is alone able to make us happy. (3) It adds much to the comfort of any condition if we have plainly seen God going before us and putting us into it. If we have not forced providence, but taken the hints of direction it has given us, we may hope to find a paradise. See Ps. xlvii. 4.

2. How God appointed him to dress the garden and to keep it. Paradise itself was not a place of exemption from work. Note here, (1) We were none of us sent into the world to be idle. He that made us these souls and bodies has given us something to work with; he that gave us being has given us business, to serve him and our generation, and to work out our salvation. (2) Secular employments will very well consist with a state of innocency and a life of communion with God. (3) The husbandman's calling is an ancient and honourable calling; it was needful even in paradise. It was a calling giving man an opportunity of admiring the Creator. While his hands were about his trees, his heart might be with his God. (4) There is a true pleasure in the business which God calls us to, and employs us in.

III. The command which God gave to man in innocency, and the covenant he then took him into. Hitherto we have seen God as man's powerful Creator and his bountiful Benefactor; now he appears as his Ruler and Lawgiver.

Verses 16–17

Observe here, I. God's authority over man, as a creature that had reason and freedom of will. The Lord God commanded the man, who stood now as the father and representative of all mankind, to receive law, as he had lately received a nature. The brute-creatures have their respective instincts; but man was made capable of performing reasonable service, and therefore received, not only the command of a Creator, but the command of a Prince and Master.

II. The particular act of this authority, in pre-scribing to him what he should do.

1. A confirmation of his present happiness to him, in that grant, *Of every tree in the garden thou mayest freely eat*. This was not only an allowance of liberty to him, but it was, withal, an assurance of life to him, immortal life, upon his obedience. Thus, upon condition of perfect personal and perpetual obedi-ence, Adam was sure of paradise to himself and his heirs for ever.

2. A trial of his obedience, upon pain of the for-feiture of all his happiness: "Know, Adam, that thou art now upon thy good behaviour, thou art put into paradise upon trial; be observant, be obedient, and thou art made for ever; otherwise thou wilt be as miserable as now thou art happy." Here,

(1) Adam is threatened with death in case of disobedience. Observe, [1] Even Adam, in innocency, was awed with a threatening. [2] The penalty threatened is death. [3] This was threatened as the immediate consequence of sin.

(2) Adam is tried with a positive law, not to eat of the fruit *of the tree of knowledge.* [1] Because the reason of it is fetched purely from the will of the Law-maker. Adam had in his nature an aversion to that which was evil in itself, and therefore he is tried in a thing which was evil only because it was forbidden. [2] Because the restraint of it is laid upon the desires of the flesh and of the mind, which, in the corrupt nature of man, are the two great fountains of sin. This prohibition checked both his appetite towards sensitive delights and his ambition of curious knowledge, that his body might be ruled by his soul and his soul by his God.

Verses 18–20

I. An instance of the Creator's care of man and his fatherly concern for his comfort, *v.* 18. He lets him know, for his encouragement in his obedience, that he was a friend.

1. How God graciously pitied his solitude. He that made him knew both him and what was good for him, better than he did himself, and he said, "It is not good that he should continue thus alone." (1) It is not for his comfort; for man is a sociable creature. Perfect solitude would turn a paradise into a desert, and a palace into a dungeon. (2) It is not for the increase and continuance of his kind. God could have made a world of men at first, to replenish the earth. God saw fit to make up that number by a succession of generations, which, as God had formed man, must be from two, and those male and female; one will be ever one.

2. How God graciously resolved to provide society for him. The result of this reasoning concerning him was this kind resolution, *I will make a help-meet for him.* Note hence, (1) In our best state in this world we have need of one another's help. (2) It is God only who perfectly knows our wants, and is perfectly able to supply them all, Phil. iv. 19. In him alone our help is, and from him are all our helpers. (3) A suitable wife is a help-meet, and is from the Lord. (4) Family-society, if it is agreeable, is a redress sufficient for the grievance of solitude. He that has a good God, a good heart, and a good wife, to converse with, and yet complains he wants conversation, would not have been easy and content in paradise.

II. An instance of the creatures' subjection to man, and his dominion over them (*v.* 19, 20). Thus God gave man livery and seisin of the fair estate he had granted him, and put him in possession of his dominion over the creatures. God brought them to him, that he might name them, and so might give, 1. A proof of his knowledge, as a creature endued with the faculties both of reason and speech. And, 2. A proof of his power. It is an act of authority to impose names. God gave names to the day and night, to the firmament, to the earth, and to the sea; and he *calleth the stars by their names,* to show that he is the supreme Lord of these. But he gave Adam leave to name the beasts and fowls, as their subordinate lord; for, having made him in his own image, he thus put some of his honour upon him.

III. An instance of the creatures' insufficiency to be a happiness for man: *But* (among them all) *for Adam there was not found a help-meet for him.* Observe here, 1. The dignity and excellency of the human nature. 2. The vanity of this world and the things of it; put them all together, and they will not make a help-meet for man. They will not suit the

nature of his soul, nor supply its needs, nor satisfy its just desires, nor run parallel with its never-failing duration.

Verses 21–25

Here we have, I. The making of the woman, to be a help-meet for Adam. Observe, 1. That Adam was first formed, then Eve (1 Tim. ii. 13). If man is the head, she is the crown, a crown to her husband, the crown of the visible creation. The man was dust refined, but the woman was dust double-refined, one remove further from the earth. 2. That Adam slept while his wife was in making as one that had cast all his care on God, with a cheerful resignation of himself and all his affairs to his Maker's will and wisdom. Jehovah-jireh, let the Lord provide when and whom he pleases. 3. That *God caused a sleep to fall on Adam,* and made it a deep sleep. While he knows no sin, God will take care he shall feel no pain. 4. That the woman was *made of a rib out of the side of Adam*; not made out of his head to rule over him, nor out of his feet to be trampled upon by him, but out of his side to be equal with him, under his arm to be protected, and near his heart to be beloved.

II. The marriage of the woman to Adam. Marriage is honourable, but this surely was the most honourable marriage that ever was, in which God himself had all along an immediate hand. Marriages (they say) are made in heaven: we are sure this was, for the man, the woman, the match, were all God's own work; he, by his power, made them *both,* and now, by his ordinance, made them *one.* 1. God, as *her* Father, brought the woman to the man, as his second self, and a help-meet for him. That wife that is of God's making by special grace, and of God's bringing by special providence, is likely to prove a help-meet for a man. 2. From God, as *his* Father, Adam received her. God's gifts to us are to be received with a humble thankful acknowledgment of his wisdom in suiting them to us, and his favour in bestowing them on us. Further, in token of his acceptance of her, he gave her a name, not peculiar to her, but common to her sex: *She shall be called woman, Ishah,* a *she-man,* differing from man in sex only, not in nature.

III. The institution of the ordinance of marriage, and the settling of the law of it, *v.* 24. The sabbath and marriage were two ordinances instituted in innocency, the former for the preservation of the church, the latter for the preservation of the world of mankind. It appears (by Matt. xix. 4, 5) that it was God himself who said here, "A man must leave all his relations, to cleave to his wife." 1. See here how great the virtue of a divine ordinance is; the bonds of it are stronger even than those of nature. 2. See how necessary it is that children should take their parents' consent along with them in their marriage. 3. See what need there is both of prudence and prayer in the choice of this relation, which is so near and so lasting. 4. See how firm the bond of marriage is, not to be divided and weakened by having many wives (Mal. ii. 15) nor to be broken or cut off by divorce, for any cause but fornication, or voluntary desertion. 5. See how dear the affection ought to be between husband and wife, such as there is to our own bodies, Eph. v. 28.

IV. An evidence of the purity and innocency of that state wherein our first parents were created, *v.* 25. They were both naked. They needed no clothes for defence against cold nor heat. Nay, they needed none for decency; they were naked, and had no reason to be ashamed. *They knew not what shame was,* so the Chaldee reads it. Those that had no sin in their conscience might well have no shame in their faces, though they had no clothes to their backs.

CHAPTER 3

We have here an account of the sin and misery of our first parents, the wrath and curse of God against them, the peace of the creation disturbed, and its beauty stained and sullied, all bad, very bad. I. The innocent tempted, ver. 1–5. II. The tempted transgressing, ver. 6–8. III. The transgressors arraigned, ver. 9, 10. IV. Upon their arraignment, convicted, ver. 11–13. V. Upon their conviction, sentenced, ver. 14–19. VI. After sentence, reprieved, ver. 20, 21. VII. Notwithstanding their reprieve, execution in part done, ver. 22–24. And, were it not for the gracious intimations here given of redemption by the promised seed, they, and all their degenerate guilty race, would have been left to endless despair.

Verses 1–5

I. The tempter, and that was the devil, in the shape and likeness of a serpent.

1. It is certain it was the devil that beguiled Eve. The devil and Satan is the old serpent (Rev. xii. 9), a malignant spirit, by creation an angel of light and an immediate attendant upon God's throne, but by sin become an apostate from his first state and a rebel against God's crown and dignity. He knew he could not destroy man but by debauching him. The game therefore which Satan had to play was to draw our first parents to sin, and so to separate between them and their God. The whole race of mankind had here, as it were, but one neck, and at that Satan struck.

2. It was the devil in the likeness of a serpent. (1) Many a dangerous temptation comes to us in gay fine colours that are but skin-deep, and seems to come from above; for Satan can seem an angel of light. And, (2) Because it is a subtle creature. Many instances are given of the subtlety of the serpent. Observe, There is not anything by which the devil serves himself and his own interest more than by unsanctified subtlety.

II. The person tempted was the woman, now alone, and at a distance from her husband, but near the forbidden tree. It was the devil's subtlety. 1. To assault the weaker vessel with his temptations. 2. It was his policy to enter into discourse with her when she was alone. There are many temptations to which solitude gives great advantage; but the communion of saints contributes much to their strength and safety. 3. He took advantage by finding her near the forbidden tree, and probably gazing upon the fruit of it, only to satisfy her curiosity. Those that would not eat the forbidden fruit must not come near the forbidden tree. 4. Satan tempted Eve, that by her he might tempt Adam.

III. The temptation itself, and the artificial management of it. That which the devil aimed at was to persuade Eve to eat forbidden fruit; and to do this, he took the same method that he does still. He questioned whether it was a sin or no, *v.* 1. He denied that there was any danger in it, *v.* 4. He suggested much advantage by it, *v.* 5. And these are his common topics.

1. He questioned whether it was a sin or no to eat of this tree, and whether really the fruit of it was forbidden.

(1) *He said to the woman, Yea, hath God said, You shall not eat?* The first word intimated something said before, perhaps some discourse Eve had with herself, which Satan took hold of, and grafted this question upon. Observe here, [1] He does not discover his design at first, but puts a question which seemed innocent: "I hear a piece of news, pray is it true? Has God forbidden you to eat of this tree?" [2] He quotes the command fallaciously as if it were a prohibition, not only of that tree, but of all. [3] He seems to speak it tauntingly, upbraiding the woman with her shyness of meddling with that tree. [4] It is the subtlety of Satan to blemish the reputation of the divine law as uncertain or unreasonable, and so to draw people to sin.

(2) In answer to this question the woman gives him a plain and full account of the law they were under, *v.* 2, 3. Here observe, [1] It was her weakness to enter into discourse with the serpent. It is a dangerous thing to treat with a temptation, which ought at first to be rejected with disdain and abhorrence. The garrison that sounds a parley is not far from being surrendered. [2] It was her wisdom to take notice of the liberty God had granted them. "Yea," says she, "we may eat of the fruit of the trees, thanks to our Maker, we have plenty and variety enough allowed us." [3] It was an instance of her resolution that she adhered to the command, and faithfully repeated it, as of unquestionable certainty: "We must not eat, therefore we will not touch. It is forbidden in the highest degree, and the authority of the prohibition is sacred to us." [4] She seems a little to waver about the threatening, all she makes of that is, *Lest you die.*

2. He denies that there was any danger in it, insisting that, though it might be the transgressing of a precept, yet it would not be the incurring of a penalty: *You shall not surely die.* Either, (1) "It is not certain that you shall die," so some. Satan teaches men first to doubt and then to deny; he makes them sceptics first, and so by degrees makes them atheists. Or, (2) "It is certain you shall not die," so others. He avers his contradiction with the same phrase of assurance that God had used in ratifying the threatening. He concealed his own misery, that he might draw them into the like: thus he still deceives sinners into their own ruin. Hope of impunity is a great support to all iniquity.

3. He promises them advantage by it, *v.* 5. He could not have persuaded them to run the hazard of ruining themselves if he had not suggested to them a great probability of bettering themselves.

(1) He insinuates to them the great improvements they would make by eating of this fruit. And he suits the temptation to the pure state they were now in, intellectual delights and satisfactions. These were the baits with which he covered his hook. [1] "*Your eyes shall be opened;* you shall have much more of the power and pleasure of contemplation than now you have; you shall see further into things than now you do." [2] "*You shall be as gods*, as *Elohim*, mighty gods; not only omniscient, but omnipotent too." [3] "You shall know *good and evil*, that is, every thing that is desirable to be known." To support this part of the temptation, he abuses the name given to this tree: he perverts the sense of it, as if this tree would give them a speculative notional knowledge of the natures, kinds, and originals, of good and evil. And [4] All this presently: "*In the day you eat thereof* you will find a sudden and immediate change for the better." Now in all these insinuations he aims to beget in them, *First*, Discontent with their present state. *Secondly*, Ambition of preferment, as if they were fit to be gods.

(2) He insinuates to them that God had no good design upon them, in forbidding them this fruit, as if he durst not let them eat of that tree because then they would know their own strength, and would be able to cope with him. Now, [1] This was a great affront to God, and the highest indignity that could be done him, a reproach to his power, as if he feared his creatures, and much more a reproach to his goodness, as if he hated the work of his own hands and would not have those whom he has made to be made happy. [2] It was a most dangerous snare to our first parents, as it tended to alienate their affections from God.

Verses 6–8

Satan, at length, gains his point, and the stronghold is taken by his wiles.

I. We have here the inducements that moved them to transgress. 1. She saw no harm in this tree, more than in any of the rest. It seemed as good for food as any of them, and why should this be forbidden them rather than any of the rest? We are often betrayed into snares by an inordinate desire to have our senses gratified. It was the more coveted because it was prohibited. In us (that is, in our flesh, in our corrupt nature) there dwells a strange spirit of contradiction. *Nitimur in vetitum—We desire what is prohibited.* 2. She imagined more virtue in this tree than in any of the rest, that it was a tree not only not to be dreaded, but *to be desired to make one wise.* See here how the desire of unnecessary knowledge, under the mistaken notion of wisdom, proves hurtful and destructive to many. Our first parents, who knew so much, did not know this—that they knew enough.

II. The steps of the transgression, not steps upward, but downward. 1. She *saw.* She should have turned away her eyes from beholding vanity; but she enters into temptation, by looking with pleasure on the forbidden fruit. Observe, a great deal of sin comes in at the eyes. 2. She *took.* It was her own act and deed. The devil did not take it, and put it into her mouth, whether she would or no; but she herself took it. Satan may tempt, but he cannot force; may persuade us to cast ourselves down, but he cannot cast us down, Matt. iv. 6. 3. She *did eat.* Perhaps she did not intend, when she looked, to take, nor, when she took, to eat; but this was the result. Note, The way of sin is down-hill; a man cannot stop himself when he will. Suppress the first emotions of sin, and leave it off before it be meddled with. *Obsta principiis—Nip mischief in the bud.* 4. She *gave also to her husband with her.* She gave it to him, persuading him with the same arguments that the serpent had used with her, adding this to all the rest, that she herself had eaten of it, and found it so far from being deadly that it was extremely pleasant and grateful. As was the devil, so was Eve, no sooner a sinner than a tempter. 5. *He did eat,* overcome by his wife's importunity. In neglecting the tree of life of which he was allowed to eat, and eating of the tree of knowledge which was forbidden, he plainly showed a contempt of the favours God had bestowed on him, and a preference given to those God did not see fit for him. He would be both his own carver and his own master, would have what he pleased and do what he pleased: his sin was, in one word, *disobedience* (Rom. v. 19). The human nature being lodged entirely in our first parents, henceforward it could not but be transmitted from them under an attainder of guilt, a stain of dishonour, and an hereditary disease of sin and corruption. And can we say, then, that Adam's sin had but little harm in it?

III. The immediate consequences of the transgression.

1. Shame seized them unseen, *v.* 7.

(1) The strong convictions they fell under, in their own bosoms: *The eyes of them both were opened.* It is not meant of the eyes of the body, but the eyes of their consciences were opened, their hearts smote them for what they had done. Now, when it was too late, they saw the folly of eating forbidden fruit. They saw the happiness they had fallen from, and the misery they had fallen into. They saw a law in their members warring against the law of their minds. The text tells us that they saw *that they were naked,* that is, [1] That they were stripped, deprived of all the honours and joys of their paradise-state. They were disarmed; their defence had departed from them. [2] That they were shamed. They saw themselves laid open to the contempt and reproach of heaven, and earth, and their own consciences. Now see here, *First,* What a dishonour and disquietment sin is; it makes mischief wherever it is admitted. *Secondly,* What a deceiver Satan is. He told our first parents, when he tempted them, that their eyes should be opened; and so they were, but not as they understood it; they were opened to their shame and grief.

(2) The sorry shift they made to palliate these convictions, and to arm themselves against them: *They sewed,* or platted, *fig-leaves together*; and to cover, at least, part of their shame from one another, they *made themselves aprons.* See here what is commonly the folly of those that have sinned. [1] That they are more solicitous to save their credit before men than to obtain their pardon from God. [2] That the excuses men make, to cover and extenuate their sins, are vain and frivolous. Like the aprons of fig-leaves, they make the matter never the better, but the worse; the shame, thus hidden, becomes the more shameful.

2. Fear seized them immediately upon their eating the forbidden fruit, *v.* 8. Observe here, (1) What was the cause and occasion of their fear: They *heard the voice of the Lord God walking in the garden in the cool of the day.* It was the approach of the Judge that put them into a fright; and yet he came in such a manner as made it formidable only to guilty consciences. He came in the cool of the day, not in the night, when all fears are double fearful, nor in the heat of day, for he came not in the heat of his anger. They heard his voice, and probably it was a still small voice, like that in which he came to enquire after Elijah. (2) What was the effect and evidence of their fear: *They hid themselves from the presence of the Lord God*—a sad change! God had become a terror to them, and then no marvel that they had become a terror to themselves. Their own consciences accused them, and set their sin before them in its proper colours. Their fig-leaves failed them, and would do them no service. Knowing themselves guilty, they durst not stand a trial, but absconded, and fled from justice. See here, [1] The falsehood of the tempter. He promised them they should be safe, but now they cannot so much as think themselves so; he promised them they should be knowing, but they see themselves at a loss, and know not so much as where to hide themselves; he promised them they should be as gods, great, and bold, and daring, but they are as criminals discovered. [2] The folly of sinners, to think it either possible or desirable to hide themselves from God. [3] The fear that attends sin. All that amazing fear of God's appearances, the accusations of conscience, the approaches of trouble, the assaults of inferior creatures, and the arrests of death, which is common among men, is the effect of sin.

Verses 9–10

The arraignment of these deserters before the righteous Judge.

I. The startling question with which God pursued Adam and arrested him: *Where art thou?* Not, In what *place*? but, In what *condition*? "Is this all thou hast gotten by eating forbidden fruit? Note, 1. This enquiry after Adam may be looked upon as a gracious pursuit, in kindness to him, and in order to his recovery. Note, 2. If sinners will but consider where they are, they will not rest till they return to God.

II. The trembling answer which Adam gave to this question: *I heard thy voice in the garden, and I was afraid, v.* 10. He does not own his guilt, and yet in effect confesses it by owning his shame and fear.

Verses 11 13

The offenders found guilty by their own confession, and yet endeavouring to excuse and extenuate their fault.

I. How their confession was extorted from them. God put it to the man: *Who told thee that thou wast naked? v.* 11. "How camest thou to be sensible of thy nakedness as thy shame?" *Hast thou eaten of the forbidden tree?* Note, Though God knows all our sins, yet he will know them from us,'and requires from us an ingenuous confession of them; not that he may be informed, but that we may be humbled. The question put to the woman was, *What is this that thou hast done? v.* 13. Note, It concerns those who have eaten forbidden fruit themselves, and especially those who have enticed others to eat it likewise, seriously to consider what they have done. In eating forbidden fruit, we have offended a great and gracious God. In enticing others to eat of it, we do the devil's work, make ourselves guilty of other men's sins, and accessory to their ruin.

II. How their crime was extenuated by them in their confession. It was to no purpose to plead *not guilty*. Instead of aggravating the sin, and taking shame to themselves, they excuse the sin, and lay the shame and blame on others. 1. Adam lays all the blame upon his wife. Learn, hence, never to be brought to sin by that which will not bring us off in the judgment; let us therefore never act against our consciences, nor ever displease God, to please the best friend we have in the world. But this is not the worst of it. He not only lays the blame upon his wife, but expresses it so as tacitly to reflect on God himself. He insinuates that God was accessory to his sin: he gave him the woman, and she gave him the fruit. Note, There is a strange proneness in those that are tempted to say that they are tempted of God, as if our abusing God's gifts would excuse our violation of God's laws. 2. Eve lays all the blame upon the serpent: *The serpent beguiled me.* Sin is a brat that nobody is willing to own, a sign that it is a scandalous thing. Learn hence, (1) That Satan's temptations are all beguilings, his arguments are all fallacies, his allurements are all cheats. Sin deceives us, and, by deceiving, cheats us. It is by the *deceitfulness of sin* that the heart is hardened. See Rom. vii. 11; Heb. iii. 13. (2) Satan's subtlety will not justify us in sin: though he is the tempter, we are the sinners; and indeed it is our own lust that draws us aside and entices us, Jam. i. 14.

Verses 14–15

God immediately proceeds to pass sentence; and, in these verses, he begins (where the sin began) with the serpent, because he was already convicted of rebellion against God.

I. The sentence passed upon the tempter may be considered as lighting upon the serpent. The devil's instruments must share in the devil's punishments. Now, 1. The serpent is here laid under the curse of God: *Thou art cursed above all cattle.* Unsanctified subtlety often proves a great curse to a man; and the more crafty men are to do evil the more mischief they do. 2. He is here laid under man's reproach and enmity. (1) He is to be for ever looked upon as a vile and despicable creature. His crime was that he tempted Eve to eat that which she should not; his punishment was that he was necessitated to eat that which he would not: *Dust thou shalt eat.* (2) He is to be for ever looked upon as a venomous noxious creature, and a proper object of hatred and detestation. The serpent is hurtful to man, and often bruises his heel, because it can reach no higher; nay, notice is taken of his biting the horses' heels, *ch.* xlix. 17. But man is victorious over the serpent, and bruises his head, that is, gives him a mortal wound, aiming to destroy the whole generation of vipers. This sentence pronounced upon the serpent is much fortified by that promise of God to his people, *Thou shalt tread upon the lion and the adder* (Ps. xci. 13),

and that of Christ to his disciples, *They shall take up serpents* (Mark xvi. 18). Observe here, The serpent and the woman had just now been very familiar and friendly in discourse about the forbidden fruit, and a wonderful agreement there was between them; but here they are irreconcilably set at variance. Note, Sinful friendships justly end in mortal feuds: those that unite in wickedness will not unite long.

II. This sentence may be considered as levelled at the devil, who only made use of the serpent as his vehicle in this appearance, but was himself the principal agent.

1. A perpetual reproach is here fastened upon that great enemy both to God and man. Under the cover of the serpent, he is here sentenced to be, (1) Degraded and accursed of God. *How art thou fallen, O Lucifer!* He that would be above God, and would head a rebellion against him, is justly exposed here to contempt, and God will humble those that will not humble themselves. (2) Detested and abhorred of all mankind. He is here condemned to a state of war and irreconcilable enmity. (3) Destroyed and ruined at last by *the great Redeemer*, signified by the breaking of his head. His subtle politics shall all be baffled, his usurped power shall be entirely crushed.

2. A perpetual quarrel is here commenced between the kingdom of God and the kingdom of the devil among men. It is the fruit of this enmity, (1) That there is a continual conflict between grace and corruption in the hearts of God's people. (2) That there is likewise a continual struggle between the wicked and the godly in this world.

3. A gracious promise is here made of Christ, as the deliverer of fallen man from the power of Satan. It was said in the hearing of our first parents, who, doubtless, saw a door of hope opened to them. Here was the dawning of the gospel day. No sooner was the wound given than the remedy was provided and revealed. Notice is here given them of three things concerning Christ:—(1) His incarnation, that he should be *the seed of the woman*, the seed of *that* woman; therefore his genealogy (Luke iii) goes so high as to show him to be the son of Adam, but God does the woman the honour to call him rather her seed, because she it was whom the devil had beguiled, and on whom Adam had laid the blame; herein God magnifies his grace, in that,-though the woman was first in the transgression, yet she shall be saved *by* childbearing (as some read it), that is, by the promised seed who shall descend from her, 1 Tim. ii. 15. He was likewise to be the seed of a woman only, of a virgin. (2) His sufferings and death, pointed at in Satan's *bruising his heel*, that is, his human nature. Satan tempted Christ in the wilderness, to draw him into sin; and some think it was Satan that terrified Christ in his agony, to drive him to despair. It was the devil that put it into the heart of Judas to betray Christ, of Peter to deny him, of the chief priests to prosecute him, of the false witnesses to accuse him, and of Pilate to condemn him, aiming in all this, by destroying the Saviour, to ruin the salvation; but, on the contrary, it was by death that Christ *destroyed him that had the power of death*, Heb. ii. 14. Christ's heel was bruised when his feet were pierced and nailed to the cross, and Christ's sufferings are continued in the sufferings of the saints for his name. The devil tempts them, casts them into prison, persecutes and slays them, and so bruises the heel of Christ, who is afflicted in their afflictions. But, while the heel is bruised on earth, it is well that the head is safe in heaven. (3) His victory over Satan thereby. Satan had now trampled upon the woman, and insulted her; but the seed of the woman should be raised up in the fulness of time to *triumph over him*, Col. ii. 15. *He shall bruise his head* that is, he shall destroy all his politics and all his powers,

and give a total overthrow to his kingdom and interest. Christ baffled Satan's temptations; by his death, he gave a fatal blow to the devil's kingdom, a wound to the head of this beast, that can never be healed.

Verse 16

We have here the sentence passed upon the woman for her sin.

I. She is here put into a state of sorrow, one particular of which only is specified, that in bringing forth children; but it includes grief and fear. Note, Sin brought sorrow into the world; had we known no guilt, we should have known no grief. The sorrows are here said to be multiplied; *greatly multiplied.* No marvel that our sorrows are multiplied when our sins are: both are innumerable evils. The sorrows of child-bearing are multiplied; and if the children prove wicked and foolish, they are, more than ever, the heaviness of her that bore them.

II. *Wives, be in subjection to your own husbands;* but the entrance of sin has made that duty a punishment, which otherwise it would not have been. If Eve had not eaten forbidden fruit herself, and tempted her husband to eat it, she would never have complained of her subjection; therefore it ought never to be complained of, though harsh; but sin must be complained of, that made it so. Those wives who not only despise and disobey their husbands, but domineer over them, do not consider that they not only violate a divine law, but thwart a divine sentence.

III. Observe here how mercy is mixed with wrath in this sentence. The woman shall have sorrow, but it shall be in bringing forth children, and the sorrow shall be *forgotten for joy that a child is born,* John xvi. 21. The sentence was not a curse, to bring her to ruin, but a chastisement, to bring her to repentance.

Verses 17–19

The sentence passed upon Adam, which is prefaced with a recital of his crime.

I. God put marks of his displeasure on Adam in three instances:—

1. His habitation is, by this sentence, cursed: *Cursed is the ground for thy sake;* and the effect of that curse is, *Thorns and thistles shall it bring forth unto thee.* What good fruits it produces must be extorted from it by the ingenuity and industry of man. But observe a mixture of mercy in this sentence. (1) Adam himself is not cursed, as the serpent was (*v.* 14). God had blessings in store for him. (2) He is yet above ground. The earth does not open and swallow him up, notwithstanding its degeneracy from its primitive beauty and fruitfulness.

2. His employments and enjoyments are all embittered to him.

(1) His business shall henceforth become a toil to him, and he shall go on with it *in the sweat of his face,* v. 19. His business, before he sinned, was a constant pleasure to him; the garden was then dressed without any uneasy labour. If Adam had not sinned, he had not sweated. Labour is our duty, which we must faithfully perform.

(2) His food shall henceforth become (in comparison with what it had been) unpleasant to him. *In sorrow* (v. 17) and *in the sweat of his face* (v. 19) he must eat of it. All, even the happiest in this world, have some allays to their joy: troops of diseases, disasters, and deaths, in various shapes, entered the world with sin, and still ravage it. Yet, in this part of the sentence, there is also a mixture of mercy. He shall sweat, but his toil shall make his rest the more welcome when he returns to his earth, as to his bed; he shall grieve, but he shall not starve; he shall have sorrow, but in that sorrow he shall eat bread, which shall strengthen his heart under his sorrows.

3. His life also is but short. Considering how full of trouble his days are, it is in favour to him that they are few; yet death being dreadful to nature (yea, even though life be unpleasant) *that* concludes the sentence. "Thou shalt *return to the ground out of which thou wast taken*; thy body, that part of thee which was taken out of the ground, shall return to it again; for *dust thou art.*" "Thy body shall be forsaken by thy soul, and become itself a lump of dust; and then it shall be lodged in the grave, the proper place for it, and mingle itself with the dust of the earth," *our dust,* Ps. civ. 29. *Earth to earth, dust to dust.* Observe here, (1) That man is a mean frail creature, *little* as dust, the small dust of the balance —*light* as dust, altogether lighter than vanity—*weak* as dust, and of no consistency. (2) That he is a mortal dying creature. A great man is but a great mass of dust, and must return to his earth. (3) That sin brought death into the world. If Adam had not sinned, he would not have died, Rom. v. 12.

II. We must not go off from this sentence upon our first parents till we have considered two things:—

1. How fitly the sad consequences of sin upon the soul of Adam and his sinful race were represented. Though that misery only is mentioned which affected the body, yet that was a pattern of spiritual miseries, the curse that entered into the soul. (1) The pains of a woman in travail represent the terrors and pangs of a guilty conscience, awakened to a sense of sin. (2) The state of subjection to which the woman was reduced represents that loss of spiritual liberty and freedom of will which is the effect of sin. (3) The curse of barrenness which was brought upon the earth, and its produce of briars and thorns, are a fit representation of the barrenness of a corrupt and sinful soul in that which is good and its fruitfulness in evil. (4) The toil and sweat bespeak the difficulty which, through the infirmity of the flesh, man labours under, in the service of God and the work of religion.

2. How admirably the satisfaction our Lord Jesus made by his death and sufferings answered to the sentence here passed upon our first parents. (1) Did travailing pains come in with sin? We read of the *travail of Christ's soul* (Isa. liii. 11). (2) Did subjection come in with sin? Christ was made under the law, Gal. iv. 4. (3) Did the curse come in with sin? Christ was made a curse for us, died a cursed death, Gal. iii. 13. (4) Did thorns come in with sin? He was crowned with thorns for us. (5) Did sweat come in with sin? He for us did sweat as it were great drops of blood. (6) Did sorrow come in with sin? He was a man of sorrows, his soul was, in his agony, exceedingly sorrowful. (7) Did death come in with sin? He became obedient unto death. Thus is the plaster as wide as the wound. Blessed be God for Jesus Christ!

Verse 20

God having named the man, and called him *Adam,* which signifies *red earth,* Adam named the woman, *Eve,* that is, *life.* Adam bears the name of the dying body, Eve that of the living soul. The reason of the name is here given: *Because she was* (that is, was to be) *the mother of all living.* He had before called her *Ishah—woman,* as a wife; here he calls her *Evah—life,* as a mother. Now, 1. If this was done by divine direction, it was an instance of God's favour, and was a seal of the covenant, and an assurance to them that he had not reversed that blessing wherewith he had blessed them: *Be fruitful and multiply.* It was likewise a confirmation of the promise now made, that the seed of the woman, of this woman, should break the serpent's head. 2. If Adam did it of himself, it was an instance of his faith in the word of God. (1) The blessing of a reprieve, that he should spare such sinners to be the parents of all living. (2) The blessing of a Redeemer, the promised seed, to whom Adam had an eye, in calling his wife *Eve—life.*

Verse 21

We have here a further instance of God's care concerning our first parents, notwithstanding their sin. Though he corrects his disobedient children, yet he does not disinherit them, but, like a tender father, provides the herb of the field for their food and *coats of skins* for their clothing. God is to be acknowledged with thankfulness, not only in giving us food, but in giving us clothes also, *ch.* xxviii. 20. The wool and the flax are his, as well as *the corn and the wine,* Hos. ii. 9. Adam and Eve made for themselves aprons of fig-leaves, a covering too narrow for them to *wrap themselves in,* Isa. xxviii. 20. Such are all the rags of our own righteousness. But God made them coats of skins, large, and strong, and durable, and fit for them; such is the righteousness of Christ. Therefore *put on the Lord Jesus Christ.*

Verses 22–24

Sentence being passed upon the offenders, we have here execution, in part, done upon them immediately.

I. How they were justly disgraced and shamed before God and the holy angels, by the ironical upbraiding of them with the issue of their enterprise: "*Behold, the man has become as one of us, to know good and evil ! A goodly god he makes ! Does he not ?*" This was said to awaken and humble them, and to bring them to a sense of their sin and folly, and to repentance for it. God thus *fills their faces with shame, that they may seek his name,* Ps. lxxxiii. 16. He puts them to this confusion, in order to their conversion.

II. How they were justly discarded, and shut out of paradise.

1. The reason God gave why he shut man out of paradise; not only because he had put forth his hand, and taken of the tree of knowledge, which was his sin, but lest he should again put forth his hand, and take also of the tree of life and flatter himself with a conceit that thereby he should live for ever.

2. The method God took in expelling and excluding him from this garden of pleasure. He turned him out, and kept him out.

(1) He turned him out, from the garden to the common. This signified the exclusion of him, and all his guilty race, from that communion with God which was the bliss and glory of paradise. His acquaintance with God was lessened and lost, and that correspondence which had been settled between man and his Maker was interrupted and broken off. But whither did he send him when he turned him out of Eden ? He might justly have chased him out of the world (Job xviii. 18), but he only chased him out of the garden. But man was only sent to till the ground out of which he was taken. He was sent to a place of toil, not to a place of torment. He was sent to the ground, not to the grave—to the work-house, not to the dungeon, not to the prison-house—to hold the plough, not to drag the chain. His tilling the ground would be recompensed by his eating of its fruits; and his converse with the earth whence he was taken was improvable to good purposes, to keep him humble, and to remind him of his latter end. Observe, then, that though our first parents were excluded from the privileges of their state of innocency, yet they were not abandoned to despair, God's thoughts of love designing them for a second state of probation upon new terms.

(2) He kept him out, and forbade him all hopes of a re-entry; for he *placed at the east of the garden of Eden* a detachment of *cherubim,* God's hosts, armed with a dreadful and irresistible power, to keep

the way that led to the tree of life, so that he could neither steal nor force an entry. Now this intimated to Adam, [1] That God was displeased with him. [2] That the angels were at war with him; no peace with the heavenly hosts, while he was in rebellion against their Lord and ours. [3] That the way to the tree of life was shut up, namely, that way which, at first, he was put into, the way of spotless innocency. It was henceforward in vain for him and his to expect righteousness, life, and happiness, by virtue of the first covenant, for it was irreparably broken. We are all undone if we be judged by that covenant. God revealed this to Adam, not to drive him to despair, but to oblige and quicken him to look for life and happiness in the promised seed, by whom the flaming sword is removed. God and his angels are reconciled to us, and a new and living way into the holiest is consecrated and laid open for us.

CHAPTER 4

In this chapter we have both the world and the church in a family. As all mankind were represented in Adam, so that great distinction of mankind into saints and sinners was here represented in Cain and Abel, and an early instance is given of the enmity which was later put between the seed of the woman and the seed of the serpent. We have here, I. The birth, names, and callings, of Cain and Abel, ver. 1, 2. II. Their religion, and different success in it, ver. 3, 4 and part of ver. 5. III. Cain's anger at God, and the reproof of him for that anger, ver. 5–7. IV. Cain's murder of his brother, and the process against him for that murder. The murder committed, ver. 8. The proceedings against him. 1. His arraignment, ver. 9, former part. 2. His plea, ver. 9, latter part. 3. His conviction, ver. 10. 4. The sentence passed upon him, ver. 11, 12. 5. His complaint against the sentence, ver. 13, 14. 6. The ratification of the sentence, ver. 15. 7. The execution of the sentence, ver. 15, 16. V. The family and posterity of Cain, ver. 17–24. VI. The birth of another son and grandson of Adam, ver. 25, 26.

Verses 1–2

Adam and Eve had many sons and daughters, *ch.* v. 4. But Cain and Abel seem to have been the two eldest.

I. The names of their two sons. 1. *Cain* signifies *possession*; for Eve, when she bore him, said with joy, and thankfulness, and great expectation, *I have gotten a man from the* LORD. Observe, Children are God's gifts, and he must be acknowledged in the building up of our families. It doubles and sanctifies our comfort in them when we see them coming to us from the hand of God, who will not forsake the works and gifts of his own hand. 2. *Abel* signifies *vanity*. When she thought she had obtained the promised seed in Cain, she was so taken up with that possession that another son was as vanity to her.

II. The employments of Cain and Abel. 1. They both had a calling. God gave their father a calling, even in innocency, and he gave them one. Note, It is the will of God that we should every one of us have something to do in this world. Parents ought to bring up their children to business. "Give them a Bible and a calling (said good Mr. Dod), and God be with them." 2. Their employments were different, that they might trade and exchange with one another, as there was occasion. The members of the body politic have need one of another, and mutual love is helped by mutual commerce. 3. Their employments belonged to the husbandman's calling, their father's profession. 4. Abel, though the younger brother, yet entered first into his calling, and probably his example drew in Cain. 5. Abel chose that employment which most befriended contemplation and devotion, for to these a pastoral life has been looked upon as being peculiarly favourable.

Verses 3–5

Here we have, I. The devotions of Cain and Abel. *In the process of time* Cain and Abel brought to

Adam, as the priest of the family, each of them *an offering to the Lord*. God would thus try Adam's faith in the promise and his obedience to the remedial law; he would thus settle a correspondence again between heaven and earth, and give *shadows of good things to come*. Observe here, 1. That the religious worship of God is no novel invention, but an ancient institution. It is that which was *from the beginning* (1 John i. 1); it is the *good old way*, Jer. vi. 16. 2. That it is a good thing for children to be well taught when they are young, and trained up betimes in religious services, that when they come to be capable of acting for themselves they may, of their own accord, *bring an offering to God*. 3. That we should every one of us honour God with what we have, according as he has prospered us. 4. That hypocrites and evil doers may be found going as far as the best of God's people in the external services of religion. Cain brought an offering with Abel; nay, Cain's offering is mentioned first, as if he were the more forward of the two. The Pharisee and the publican went to the temple to pray, Luke xviii. 10.

II. The different success of their devotions. That which is to be aimed at in all acts of religion is God's acceptance: we speed well if we attain this, but in vain do we worship if we miss of it, 2 Cor. v. 9. God had *respect to Abel and to his offering*, and showed his acceptance of it, probably by fire from heaven; but to *Cain and his offering he had not respect*.

1. There was a difference in the characters of the persons offering. Cain was a wicked man and therefore his sacrifice was *a vain oblation*, Isa. i. 13. God had no respect to Cain himself, and therefore no respect to his offering. But Abel was a righteous man; he is called *righteous Abel* (Matt. xxiii. 35); his heart was upright and his life was pious. God had respect to him as a holy man, and therefore to his offering as a holy offering.

2. There was a difference in the offerings they brought. It is expressly said (Heb. xi. 4), Abel's was a *more excellent sacrifice* than Cain's: either, (1) In the nature of it, or, (2) In the qualities of the offering. Cain brought *of the fruit of the ground*, any thing that came next to hand, what he had not occasion for himself. But Abel was curious in the choice of his offering: not the lame, nor the lean, nor the refuse, but the *firstlings of the flock*—the best he had, *and the fat thereof*—the best of those best.

3. The great difference was this, that Abel offered in faith, and Cain did not. There was a difference in the principle upon which they went. Abel offered with an eye to God's will as his rule, and God's glory as his end, but Cain did what he did only for company's sake, or to save his credit, not in faith, and so it turned into sin to him. Abel was a penitent; Cain was unhumbled; his confidence was within himself.

III. Cain's displeasure at the difference God made between his sacrifice and Abel's. Cain was very wroth, which presently appeared in his very looks. This anger bespeaks, 1. His enmity to God. He should have been angry at himself for his own infidelity and hypocrisy, by which he had forfeited God's acceptance. Note, It is a certain sign of an unhumbled heart to quarrel with those rebukes which we have, by our own sin, brought upon ourselves. 2. His envy of his brother. He conceived a hatred of him as an enemy. Note, (1) It is common for those who have rendered themselves unworthy of God's favour to have indignation against those who are dignified by it. The Pharisees walked in this way of Cain, when they *neither entered into the kingdom of God themselves* nor *suffered those that were entering to go in*, Luke xi. 52. (2) Envy is a sin that commonly carries with it its own punishment, in the rottenness of the bones.

Verses 6–7

God is here reasoning with Cain, to convince him of the sin and folly of his anger and discontent, and to bring him into a good temper again, that further mischief might be prevented. Thus the father of the prodigal argued the case with the elder son (Luke xv. 28, &c.).

I. God puts Cain himself upon enquiring into the cause of his discontent: *Why is thy countenance fallen ?* Observe, 1. That God takes notice of all our sinful passions and discontents. 2. *"Why am I wroth?* Is there a real cause, a just cause, a proportionable cause for it ? Why am I so soon angry ?"

II. To reduce Cain to his right mind again, it is here made evident to him,

1. That he had no reason to be angry at God.

(1) God sets before Cain life and a blessing: either, [1] "If thou hadst done well, as thy brother did, thou shouldst have been accepted, as he was." Or, [2] "If now thou do well, if thou repent of thy sin, reform thy heart and life, and bring thy sacrifice in a better manner, thou shalt yet be accepted, thy sin shall be pardoned, thy comfort and honour restored, and all shall be well." See how early the gospel was preached, and the benefit of it here offered even to one of the chief of sinners.

(2) He sets before him death and a curse: "If now thou wilt not do well, if thou persist in this wrath, and, instead of humbling thyself before God, harden thyself against him, *sin lies at the door*," that is, [1] Further sin. "Now that anger is in thy heart, murder is at the door." Or, [2] The punishment of sin. So near akin are sin and punishment that the same word in Hebrew signifies both. If sin be harboured in the house, the curse waits at the door, like a bailiff, ready to arrest the sinner whenever he looks out. "If thou doest not well, *sin* (that is, *the sin-offering*), lies at the door, and thou mayest take the benefit of it." The same word signifies *sin* and *a sacrifice for sin*. Christ, the great sin-offering, is said to *stand at the door*, Rev. iii. 20. All this considered, Cain had no reason to be angry at God, but at himself only.

2. That he had no reason to be angry at his brother: "*Unto thee shall be his desire*, he shall continue his respect to thee as an elder brother, and thou, as the first-born, shalt rule over him as much as ever." God's acceptance of Abel's offering did not transfer the birth-right to him. God did not so intend it; Abel did not so interpret it; why then should he be so much exasperated ?

Verse 8

Abel's murder, which may be considered two ways:—

I. As Cain's sin; and a scarlet, crimson, sin it was, a sin of the first magnitude. See in it, 1. Adam's eating forbidden fruit seemed but a little sin, but it opened the door to the greatest. 2. A fruit of the enmity which is in the seed of the serpent against the seed of the woman. So early did he that was after the flesh *persecute him that was after the Spirit*. 3. See also what comes of *envy, hatred, malice, and all uncharitableness*; if they be indulged and cherished in the soul, they are in danger of involving men in the horrid guilt of murder itself. Many were the aggravations of Cain's sin. (1) It was his own brother that he murdered, his younger brother, whom he ought to have protected. (2) He was a good brother, one who had never done him any wrong. (3) God himself had told him what would come of it, yet he persisted in his barbarous design. (4) He covered it with a show of friendship and kindness. According to the Septuagint Cain said to Abel, *Let us go into the field*. The Chaldee paraphrase adds that Cain maintained that there was no judgment to come, no future state, and that when Abel spoke in defence of the truth Cain took that occasion to fall upon him. However, (5) That which the scripture tells us was the reason why he slew him was a sufficient aggravation of the murder; it was *because his own works were evil and his brother's righteous*. Nay, (6) In killing his brother, he directly struck at God himself; he hated Abel because God loved him.

II. As Abel's suffering. Death reigned ever since Adam sinned, but we read not of any taken captive by him till now; and now, 1. The first that dies is a saint, one that was accepted and beloved of God. The first that went to the grave went to heaven. Nay, 2. The first that dies is a martyr, and dies for his religion. Abel's death has not only no curse in it, but it has a crown in it.

Verses 9–12

The trial and condemnation of the first murderer.

I. The arraignment of Cain: *The Lord said unto Cain, Where is Abel thy brother?* He asks him, that he may draw from him a confession of his crime, for those who would be justified before God must accuse themselves, and the penitent will do so.

II. Cain's plea: he pleads *not guilty*, and adds rebellion to his sin. For, 1. He endeavours to cover a deliberate murder with a deliberate lie: *I know not*. Thus, in Cain, the devil was both a murderer and a liar from the beginning. Those are strangely blind that think it possible to conceal their sins from a God that sees all, and those are strangely hard that think it desirable to conceal them from a God who pardons those only that confess. 2. He impudently charges his Judge with folly and injustice, in putting this question to him: *Am I my brother's keeper?* He should have humbled himself, and have said, *Am I not my brother's murderer?* Some think he reflects on God and his providence, as if he had said, "Art not thou his keeper? If he be missing, on thee be the blame, and not on me, who never undertook to keep him." Note, Those who are unconcerned in the affairs of their brethren, and take no care, when they have opportunity, to prevent their hurt in their bodies, goods, or good name, especially in their souls, do, in effect, speak Cain's language. See Lev. xix. 17; Phil. ii. 4.

III. The conviction of Cain, *v.* 10. "The evidence against thee is clear and incontestable: *The voice of thy brother's blood cries*." He speaks as if the blood itself were both witness and prosecutor, before God's own knowledge testified against him. Observe here, 1. Murder is a crying sin, none more so. The patient sufferers cried for pardon (*Father, forgive them*), but their blood cries for vengeance. 2. The blood is said to cry from the ground, the earth, which is said *to open her mouth to receive his brother's blood from his hand, v.* 11. 3. In the original the word is plural, thy brother's *bloods*, not only his blood, but the blood of all those that might have descended from him. How well is it for us that the blood of Christ speaks better things than that of Abel! Heb. xii. 24. Abel's blood cried for vengeance, Christ's blood cries for pardon.

IV. The sentence passed upon Cain: *And now art thou cursed from the earth, v.* 11.

1. He is cursed. The curse for Adam's disobedience terminated on the ground: *Cursed is the ground for thy sake;* but that for Cain's rebellion fell immediately upon himself: *Thou art cursed*. We have all deserved this curse, and it is only in Christ that believers are saved from it and inherit the blessing, Gal. iii. 10, 13.

2. He is cursed from the earth. Cain found his punishment where he chose his portion and set his heart. Two things we expect from the earth, and by this curse both are denied to Cain and taken from

him: *sustenance* and *settlement*. (1) Sustenance out of the earth is here withheld from him. It is a curse upon him in his enjoyments, and particularly in his calling: *When thou tillest the ground, it shall not henceforth yield unto thee its strength*. (2) Settlement on the earth is here denied him: *A fugitive and a vagabond shalt thou be in the earth*. By this he was condemned, [1] To perpetual disgrace and reproach among men. [2] To perpetual disquietude and horror in his own mind. His own guilty conscience should haunt him wherever he went, and make him *Magormissabib*, a *terror round about*. What rest can those find, what settlement, that carry their own disturbance with them in their bosoms wherever they go? Those must needs be fugitives that are thus tossed.

This was the sentence passed upon Cain; and even in this there was mercy mixed, inasmuch as he was not immediately cut off, but had space given him to repent; for God is long-suffering to us-ward, not willing that any should perish.

Verses 13–15

A further account of the proceedings against Cain.

I. Here is Cain's complaint of the sentence passed upon him, as hard and severe. Some make him to speak the language of despair. There is forgiveness with the God of pardons for the greatest sins and sinners; but those forfeit it who despair of it. Just now Cain made nothing of his sin, but now he is in the other extreme: Satan drives his vassals from presumption to despair. He thinks himself rigorously dealt with when really he is favourably treated; and he cries out of wrong when he has more reason to wonder that he is out of hell. Now, to justify this complaint, Cain descants upon the sentence. 1. He sees himself excluded by it from the favour of his God. 2. He sees himself expelled from all the comforts of this life, and concludes that, being a fugitive, he is, in effect, *driven out this day from the face of the earth*. 3. He sees himself exposed by it to the hatred and ill-will of all mankind: *It shall come to pass that everyone that finds me shall slay me*. Wherever he wanders, he goes in peril of his life, at least he thinks so; and, like a man in debt, thinks everyone he meets a bailiff. There were none alive but his near relations; yet even of them he is justly afraid who had himself been so barbarous to his brother. He sees the whole creation armed against him.

II. Here is God's confirmation of the sentence; for when he judges he will overcome, *v.* 15. 1. How Cain is protected from wrath by this declaration, notified, we may suppose, to all that little world which was then in being: *Whosoever slayeth Cain, vengeance shall be taken on him seven-fold*, because thereby the sentence he was under (that he should be a fugitive and a vagabond) would be defeated. God having said in Cain's case, *Vengeance is mine, I will repay*, it would have been a daring usurpation for any man to take the sword out of God's hand. 2. *The Lord set a mark upon Cain*, to distinguish him from the rest of mankind and to notify that he was the man that murdered his brother.

Verses 16–18

A further account of Cain, and what became of him after he was rejected of God.

I. He tamely submitted to that part of his sentence by which he was hidden from God's face; for (*v.* 16) *he went out from the presence of the Lord*, that is, he willingly renounced God and religion, and was content to forego its privileges, so that he might not be under its precepts. Cain went out now from the presence of the Lord, and we never find that he came into it again, to his comfort.

II. He endeavoured to confront that part of the sentence by which he was made a fugitive and a vagabond; for,

1. He chose his land. He went and *dwelt on the east of Eden,* somewhere distant from the place where Adam and his religious family resided. But his attempt to settle was in vain; for the land he dwelt in was to him *the land of Nod* (that is, of *shaking* or *trembling*), because of the continual restlessness and uneasiness of his own spirit. Note, Those that depart from God cannot find rest anywhere else. After Cain went out from the presence of the Lord, he never rested. "*Return therefore to thy rest, O my soul,* to thy rest in God; else thou art for ever restless."

2. He built a city for a habitation, *v.* 17. *He was building a city,* so some read it, ever building it, but, a curse being upon him and the work of his hands, he could not finish it. (1) Cain's defiance of the divine sentence. God said he should be a *fugitive and a vagabond.* Had he repented and humbled himself, this curse might have been turned into a blessing. (2) See what was Cain's choice, after he had forsaken God; he pitched upon a settlement in this world, as his rest for ever. (3) See what method Cain took to defend himself against the terrors with which he was perpetually haunted. He undertook this building, to divert his thoughts from the consideration of his own misery, and to drown the clamours of a guilty conscience with the noise of axes and hammers. Thus many baffle their convictions by thrusting themselves into a hurry of worldly business. (4) See how wicked people often get the start of God's people, and out-go them in outward prosperity. Cain and his cursed race dwell in a city, while Adam and his blessed family dwell in tents.

3. His family also was built up. Here is an account of his posterity, at least the heirs of his family, for seven generations.

Verses 19-22

Some particulars concerning Lamech, the seventh from Adam in the line of Cain.

Though he sinned, in marrying two wives, yet he was blessed with children by both, and those such as lived to be famous in their generation, not for their piety but for their ingenuity. They were not only themselves men of business, but men that were serviceable to the world, and eminent for the invention, or at least the improvement, of some useful arts. 1. Jabal was a famous shepherd. 2. Jubal was a famous musician, and particularly an organist, and the first that gave rules for the noble art or science of music. When Jabal had set them in a way to be rich, Jubal put them in a way to be merry. Jabal was their Pan and Jubal their Apollo. 3. Tubalcain was a famous smith, who greatly improved the art of working in brass and iron, for the service both of war and husbandry. He was their Vulcan. Even those who are destitute of the knowledge and grace of God may be endued with many excellent and useful accomplishments, which may make them famous and serviceable in their generation. Common gifts are given to bad men, while God chooses to himself the foolish things of the world.

Verses 23-24

By this speech of Lamech, which is here recorded, and probably was much talked of in those times, he further appears to have been a wicked man, as Cain's accursed race generally were. He owns himself a man of a fierce and cruel disposition, that would lay about him without mercy, and kill all that stood in his way. His wives, knowing what manner of spirit he was of, how apt both to give and to resent provocation, were afraid lest somebody or other would be the death of him. "Never fear," says he, "I defy any man to set upon me; whosoever does, let me alone to make my part good with him; I will slay him, be he a man or a young man."

Verses 25-26

This is the first mention of Adam in the story of this chapter. No question, the murder of Abel, and the impenitence and apostasy of Cain, were a very great grief to him and Eve, and the more because their own wickedness did now correct them and their backslidings did reprove them. But here we have that which was a relief to our first parents in their affliction.

I. God gave them to see the re-building of their family, which was sorely shaken and weakened by that sad event. For, 1. They saw their seed, *another seed instead of Abel, v.* 25. Observe God's kindness and tenderness towards his people, in his providential dealings with them; when he takes away one comfort from them, he gives them another instead of it, which may prove a greater blessing to them than that was in which they thought their lives were bound up. Those that slay God's servants hope by this means to wear out the saints of the Most High; but they will be deceived. Christ shall still see his seed; God can out of stones raise up children for him, and make the blood of the martyrs the seed of the church. This son, by a prophetic spirit, they called *Seth* (that is, *set, settled,* or *placed*), because, in his seed, mankind should continue to the end of time, and from him the Messiah should descend. While Cain, the head of the apostasy, is made a wanderer, Seth, from whom the true church was to come, is one fixed. In Christ and his church is the only true settlement. 2. They saw their seed's seed, *v.* 26. *To Seth was born a son called Enos.*

II. God gave them to see the reviving of religion in their family: *Then began men to call upon the name of the Lord, v.* 26. It is small comfort to a good man to see his children's children, if he do not, withal, see peace upon Israel, and those that come of him walking in the truth. 1. The worshippers of God began to stir up themselves to do more in religion than they had done. Now men began to worship God, not only in their closets and families, but in public and solemn assemblies. 2. The worshippers of God began to distinguish themselves. The margin reads it, *Then began men to be called by the name of the Lord,* or to call themselves by it.

CHAPTER 5

We have here an account, I. Concerning Adam, ver. 1–5. II. Seth, ver. 6–8. III. Enos, ver. 9–11. IV. Cainan, ver. 12–14. V. Mahalaleel, ver. 15–17. VI. Jared, ver. 18–20. VII. Enoch, ver. 21–24. VIII. Methuselah, ver. 25–27. IX. Lamech and his son Noah, ver. 28–32. All scripture, being given by inspiration of God, is profitable, though not all alike profitable.

Verses 1-5

The first words of the chapter are the title or argument of the whole chapter: it is *the book of the generations of Adam.* The genealogy begins with Adam himself.

I. His creation, *v.* 1, 2, where we have a brief rehearsal of what was before related concerning the creation of man. Observe here, 1. That *God created man.* Man is not his own maker, therefore he must not be his own master; but the Author of his being must be the director of his motions and the centre of them. 2. That there was a day in which God created man. He was not from eternity, but of yesterday. 3. That God made him in his own likeness, righteous and holy, and therefore, undoubtedly, happy. 4. That God created them male and female (*v.* 2), for their mutual comfort as well as for the preservation and increase of their kind.

II. The birth of his son *Seth*, v. 3. That which is most observable here concerning Seth is that Adam begat him *in his own likeness, after his image*. Adam was made in the image of God; but, when he was fallen and corrupt, he begat a son in his own image.

Verses 6–20

We have here all that the Holy Ghost thought fit to leave upon record concerning five of the patriarchs before the flood. Seth, Enos, Cainan, Mahalaleel, and Jared. There is nothing observable concerning any of these particularly, though we have reason to think they were men of eminence, both for prudence and piety, in their day.

I. Concerning each of them, except Enoch, it is said, *and he died*. It is implied in the numbering of the years of their life that their life, when those years were numbered and finished, came to an end; and yet it is still repeated, *and he died*, to show that death passed upon all men without exception. Such a one was a strong healthy man, but he died; such a one was a great and rich man, but he died; such a one was a wise politic man, but he died; such a one was a very good man, perhaps a very useful man, but he died, &c.

II. That which is especially observable is that they all lived very long. Long life to the pious patriarchs was a blessing and made them blessings.

Verses 21–24

The accounts here run on for several generations without anything remarkable, or any variation but of the names and numbers; but at length there comes in one that must not be passed over so, of whom special notice must be taken, and that is *Enoch*, the seventh from Adam: the rest, we may suppose, did virtuously, but he excelled them all, and was the brightest star of the patriarchal age. It is but little that is recorded concerning him; but this little is enough to make his name great, greater than the name of the other Enoch, who had a city called by his name. Here are two things concerning him:—

I. His gracious conversation in this world, which is twice spoken of: *Enoch walked with God after he begat Methuselah* (v. 22), and again, *Enoch walked with God*, v. 24.

1. The nature of his religion and the scope and tenor of his conversation: he *walked with God*, which denotes, (1) True religion; what is godliness, but walking with God? The ungodly and profane are without God in the world, they walk contrary to him: but the godly walk with God, which presupposes reconciliation to God, for two cannot *walk together except they be agreed* (Amos iii. 3). To walk with God is to set God always before us, and to act as those that are always under his eye. It is to live a life of communion with God both in ordinances and providences. It is to make God's word our rule and his glory our end in all our actions. It is to comply with his will, to concur with his designs, and to be workers together with him. (2) Eminent religion. He was entirely dead to this world, and did not only walk after God, as all good men do, but he walked with God, as if he were in heaven already. (3) Activity in promoting religion among others. Executing the priest's office is called *walking before God*, 1 Sam. ii. 30, 35, and see Zech. iii. 7. Enoch, it should seem, was a priest of the most high God. Now the Holy Spirit instead of saying, Enoch *lived*, says, Enoch *walked with God*; for it is the life of a good man to walk with God. This was, [1] The business of Enoch's life. [2] It was the joy and support of his life.

II. His glorious removal to a better world. As he did not live like the rest, so he did not die like the rest (v. 24): *He was not, for God took him;* that is,

as it is explained (Heb. xi. 5), *He was translated that he should not see death, and was not found, because God had translated him.*

Whenever a good man dies, God takes him, fetches him hence, and receives him to himself. The apostle adds concerning Enoch that, *before his translation, he had this testimony, that he pleased God.* Those whose conversation in the world is truly holy shall find their removal out of it truly happy.

Verses 25–27

Methuselah signifies, *he dies*. However, this is observable, that the longest liver that ever was carried death in his name, that he might be reminded of its coming surely, though it came slowly.

Verses 28–32

The first mention of Noah, of whom we shall read much in the following chapters.

I. His name, with the reason of it: *Noah* signifies *rest*; his parents gave him that name, with a prospect of his being a more than ordinary blessing to his generation.

II. His children, Shem, Ham, and Japheth. It should seem that Japheth was the eldest (*ch.* x. 21), but Shem is put first because on him the covenant was entailed, as appears by *ch.* ix. 26, where God is called the *Lord God of Shem*. To him, it is probable, the birth-right was given, and from him, it is certain, both Christ the head, and the church the body, were to descend. Therefore he is called *Shem*, which signifies a *name*, because in his posterity the name of God should always remain, till he should come out of his loins whose name is above every name; so that in putting Shem first Christ was, in effect, put first, who in all things must have the pre-eminence.

Chapter 6

The most remarkable thing we have upon record concerning the old world is the destruction of it by the universal deluge, the account of which commences in this chapter, wherein we have, I. The abounding iniquity of that wicked world, ver. 1–5, and ver. 11, 12. II. The righteous God's just resentment of that abounding iniquity, and his holy resolution to punish it, ver. 6, 7. III. The special favour of God to his servant Noah. 1. In the character given of him, ver. 8–10. 2. In the communication of God's purpose to him, ver. 13, 17. 3. In the directions he gave him to make an ark for his own safety, ver. 14–16. 4. In the employing of him for the preservation of the rest of the creatures, ver. 18–21. Lastly, Noah's obedience to the instructions given him, ver. 22.

Verses 1–2

Now here we have an account of two things which occasioned the wickedness of the old world:—1. The increase of mankind: *Men began to multiply upon the face of the earth.* This was the effect of the blessing (*ch.* i. 28), and yet man's corruption so abused and perverted this blessing that it was turned into a curse. The more sinners the more sin. Infectious diseases are most destructive in populous cities; and sin is a spreading leprosy. 2. Mixed marriages (v. 2): *The sons of God* (that is, the professors of religion) *married the daughters of men*, that is, those that were profane, and strangers to God and godliness. The posterity of Seth did not keep by themselves, as they ought to have done. They intermingled themselves with the excommunicated race of Cain: *They took them wives of all that they chose.* But what was amiss in these marriages? (1) They chose only by the eye: *They saw that they were fair*, which was all they looked at. (2) They followed the choice which their own corrupt affections made. But, (3) That which proved of such bad consequence to them was that they *married strange wives, were unequally yoked with unbelievers*, 2 Cor. vi. 14. The bad will sooner debauch the good than the good reform the bad.

Verse 3

This comes in here as a token of God's displeasure. I. God's resolution not always to strive with man by his Spirit. Note, 1. The blessed Spirit strives with sinners, by the convictions and admonitions of conscience, to turn them from sin to God. 2. If the Spirit be resisted, quenched, and striven against, though he strive long, he will not strive always, Hos. iv. 17. II. The reason of this resolution: *For that he also is flesh*, that is, incurably corrupt, and carnal, and sensual. Note, 1. It is the corrupt nature, and the inclination of the soul towards the flesh, that oppose the Spirit's strivings and render them ineffectual. 2. None lose the Spirit's strivings but those that have first forfeited them. III. A reprieve granted, notwithstanding: *Yet his days shall be one hundred and twenty years*. Note, The time of God's patience and forbearance towards provoking sinners is sometimes long, but always limited: reprieves are not pardons.

Verses 4–5

A further account of the corruption of the old world. I. The temptation they were under to oppress and do violence. They were *giants*, and they were *men of renown*. 1. With their great bulk, as the sons of Anak, Num. xiii. 33. 2. With their great name, as the king of Assyria, Isa. xxxvii. 11. Note, Those that have so much power over others as to be able to oppress them have seldom so much power over themselves as not to oppress. II. The charge exhibited and proved against them, *v*. 5. Now what did God take notice of ? 1. He observed all the streams of sin that flowed along in men's lives, and the breadth and depth of those streams. The oppressors were *mighty men and men of renown*; and, *then, God saw that the wickedness of man was great*. Note, The wickedness of a people is great indeed when the most notorious sinners are men of renown among them. Wickedness is then great when great men are wicked. Note, All the sins of sinners are known to God the Judge. 2. He observed the fountain of sin that was in men's hearts. Anyone might see that *the wickedness of man was great*, for they declared their sin as Sodom; but God's eye went further: *He saw that every imagination of the thoughts of his heart was only evil continually*. (1) The thoughts of the heart were so. (2) The imagination of the thoughts of the heart was so, that is, their designs and devices were wicked. They did not do evil through mere carelessness, but they did evil deliberately and designedly, contriving how to do mischief.

Verses 6–7

Here is, I. God's resentment of man's wickedness. He did not see it as an unconcerned spectator, but as one injured and affronted by it; he saw it as a tender father sees the folly and stubbornness of a rebellious and disobedient child, which not only angers him, but grieves him. 1. This language does not imply any passion or uneasiness in God (nothing can create disturbance to the Eternal Mind), but it expresses his just and holy displeasure against sin and sinners. Does God thus hate sin ? And shall we not hate it ? Has our sin grieved him to the heart ? And shall not we be grieved and pricked to the heart for it ? 2. It does not imply any change of God's mind, but it expresses a change of his way. But, now that man had apostatized, he could not do otherwise than show himself displeased; so that the change was in man, not in God. God repented that he had made man; but we never find him repenting that he redeemed man.

II. God's resolution to destroy man for his wicked-

ness, *v*. 7. We do but mock God in saying that we are sorry for our sin, and that it grieves us to the heart, if we continue to indulge it. The original word is very significant: *I will wipe off man from the earth* (so some), as dirt or filth is wiped off from a place which should be clean. Those forfeit their lives that do not answer the end of their living. God took up this resolution concerning man after his Spirit had been long striving with him in vain. None are ruined by the justice of God but those that hate to be reformed by the grace of God.

Verses 8–10

We have here Noah distinguished from the rest of the world, and a peculiar mark of honour put upon him. 1. When God was displeased with the rest of the world, he favoured Noah: there being one good man, he found him out, and smiled upon him. He was made a vessel of God's mercy. God made him greater and more truly honourable than all the giants that were in those days, who became mighty men and men of renown. Those are highly favoured whom God favours. 2. Noah kept his integrity: *Noah was a just man, v*. 9. This character of Noah comes in here either, (1) As the reason of God's favour to him. God loves those that love him: or, (2) As the effect of God's favour to him. It was God's good-will to him that produced this good work in him. He was a very good man, but he was no better than the grace of God made him, 1 Cor. xv. 10. Now observe his character. [1] He *was a just man*, that is, justified before God by faith in the promised seed; for he was an *heir of the righteousness which is by faith*, Heb. xi. 7. God has sometimes chosen the foolish things of the world, but he never chose the knavish things of it. [2] He was *perfect*, not with a sinless perfection, but a perfection of sincerity; and it is well for us that by virtue of the covenant of grace, upon the score of Christ's righteousness, sincerity is accepted as our gospel perfection. [3] He *walked with God*. He lived a life of communion with God. God looks down with an eye of favour upon those who sincerely look up to him with an eye of faith. It is easy to be religious when religion is in fashion; but it is an evidence of strong faith and resolution to swim against a stream to heaven, and to appear for God when no one else appears for him.

Verses 11–12

The wickedness of that generation is here again spoken of. 1. All kinds of sin was found among them, for it is said (*v*. 11) that the earth was, (1) *Corrupt before God*. (2) *The earth was also filled with violence* and injustice towards men. Wickedness, as it is the shame of human nature, so it is the ruin of human society. Take away conscience and the fear of God, and men become beasts and devils to one another. Sin fills the earth with violence, and so turns the world into a wilderness, into a cock-pit. 2. The proof and evidence of it were undeniable; for *God looked upon the earth*, and was himself an eye-witness of the corruption that was in it. 3. That which most aggravated the matter was the universal spreading of the contagion: *All flesh had corrupted his way*. When wickedness has become general then universal ruin is not far off; while there is a remnant of praying people in a nation, to empty the measure as it fills, judgments may be kept off a great while.

Verses 13–21

It appears indeed that Noah *found grace in the eyes of the Lord*.

I. God here makes Noah the *man of his counsel*, communicating to him his purpose to destroy this wicked world by water, as, afterwards, he told

Abraham his resolution concerning Sodom (*ch.* xviii. 17). *The secret of the Lord* was with *his servants the prophets* (Amos iii. 7), by a spirit of revelation, informing them particularly of his purposes; it is with all believers by a spirit of wisdom and faith, enabling them to understand.

1. God told Noah, in general, that he would destroy the world (*v.* 13). Noah, it is likely, in preaching to his neighbours, had warned them, and now God seconds his endeavours.

2. He told him, particularly, that he would destroy the world by a flood of waters: *And behold, I, even I, do bring a flood of waters upon the earth, v.* 17. The reasons, we may be sure, were wise and just, though to us unknown. God has many arrows in his quiver, and he may use which he please. He intimates the certainty of the judgment: *I, even I,* will do it.

II. God here makes Noah the *man of his covenant,* another Hebrew periphrasis of a friend (*v.* 18): *But with thee will I establish my covenant.* 1. The covenant of providence, that the course of nature shall be continued to the end of time, notwithstanding the interruption which the flood would give to it. This promise was immediately made to Noah and his sons, *ch.* ix. 8, &c. They were as trustees for all this part of the creation. 2. The covenant of grace, that God would be to him a God and that out of his seed God would take to himself a people.

III. God here makes Noah a monument of sparing mercy. Singular piety shall be recompensed with distinguishing salvations.

1. God directs Noah to *make an ark, v.* 14–16. This ark was like the hulk of a ship, fitted not to sail upon the waters (there was no occasion for that, when there should be no shore to sail to), but to float upon the waters, waiting for their fall. God chose to employ him in making that which was to be the means of his preservation, both for the trial of his faith and obedience and to teach us that none shall be saved by Christ but those only that *work out their salvation.* We cannot do it without God, and he will not without us. God gave him very particular instructions concerning this building. (1) It must be made of *gopher-wood.* (2) He must make it three stories high within. (3) He must divide it into cabins, with partitions, places fitted for the several sorts of creatures, so as to lose no room. (4) Exact dimensions were given him. Those that work for God must take their measures from him and carefully observe them. (5) He must *pitch it within and without* —without, to shut off the rain, and to prevent the water from soaking in—within, to take away the bad smell of the beasts when kept close. (6) He must make a little window towards the top, to let in light. (7) He must make a door in the side of it, by which to go in and out.

2. God promises Noah that he and his shall be preserved alive in the ark (*v.* 18): *Thou shalt come into the ark.* Observe, (1) The care of good parents; they are solicitous not only for their own salvation, but for the salvation of their families, and especially their children. (2) The happiness of those children that have godly parents. Their parents' piety often procures them temporal salvation, as here; ·and it furthers them in the way to eternal salvation, if they improve the benefit of it.

IV. God here makes Noah a great blessing to the world, and herein makes him an eminent type of the Messiah. 1. God made him a preacher to the men of that generation. 2. God made him a saviour to the inferior creatures, to keep the several kinds of them from perishing and being lost in the deluge, *v.* 19–21. (1) He was to provide shelter for them, that they might not be drowned. (2) He was to provide sustenance for them, that they might not be starved, *v.* 21. Herein also he was a type of Christ, to whom

it is owing that the world stands, by whom all things consist, and who preserves mankind from being totally cut off and ruined by sin. Noah saved those whom he was to rule, so does Christ, Heb. v. 9.

Verse 22

Noah's care and diligence in building the ark may be considered, 1. As an effect of his faith in the word of God. 2. As an act of obedience to the command of God. His neighbours would ridicule him for his credulity, and he would be the song of the drunkards; his building would be called *Noah's folly.* But these, and a thousand such objections, Noah by faith got over. He did all exactly according to the instructions given him, and, having begun to build, did not leave off till he had finished it; so did he, and so must we do. 3. We must prepare to meet the Lord in his judgments on earth, especially prepare to meet him at death and in the judgment of the great day, build upon Christ the Rock (Matt. vii. 24), go into Christ the Ark. 4. Every blow of his axes and hammers was a call to repentance, a call to them to prepare arks too.

CHAPTER 7

In this chapter we have the performance of what was foretold in the foregoing chapter, both concerning the destruction of the old world and the salvation of Noah. Now here we see what was the end thereof, the end of his care and of their carelessness. We have, in this chapter, I. God's gracious call to Noah to come into the ark (ver. 1). II. Noah's obedience to this heavenly vision, ver. 5, an account of which is repeated (ver. 13–16), to which is added God's tender care to shut him in. III. The coming of the threatened deluge (ver. 10); the causes of it (ver. 11, 12); the prevalency of it, ver. 17–20. IV. The dreadful desolations that were made by it. V. The continuance of it in full sea, before it began to ebb, one hundred and fifty days, ver. 24.

Verses 1–4

I. A gracious invitation of Noah and his family into a place of safety, *v.* 1.

1. The call itself is very kind, like that of a tender father to his children, to come indoors, when he sees night or a storm coming. God does not bid him *go* into the ark, but *come* into it, implying that God would go with him, would lead him into it, accompany him in it, and in due time bring him safely out of it. It was this that made Noah's ark, which was to him not only a refuge, but a palace. This call to Noah was a type of the call which the gospel gives to poor sinners. Christ is an ark already prepared, in whom alone we can be safe when death and judgment come.

2. The reason for this invitation is a very honourable testimony to Noah's integrity. Observe, (1) Those are righteous indeed that are righteous before God, who searches the heart, and cannot be deceived in men's characters. (2) God takes notice of and is pleased with those that are righteous before him: *The Lord knows those that are his.* (3) God, that is a witness to, will shortly be a witness for, his people's integrity. (4) God is, in a special manner, pleased with those that are good in bad times and places. (5) Those that keep themselves pure in times of common iniquity God will keep safe in times of common calamity.

II. Here are necessary orders given concerning the brute-creatures that were to be preserved alive with Noah in the ark, *v.* 2, 3. They were not capable of receiving the warning, therefore man is charged with the care of them: being under his dominion, they must be under his protection.

III. Here is notice given of the now imminent approach of the flood. 1. "It shall be seven days *yet,* before I do it." God grants them a reprieve of seven days longer, but all in vain; these seven days were trifled away, after all the rest; they continued secure and sensual until the day that the flood came. 2. "It shall be *but* seven days." While Noah told them of the judgment at a distance, they were tempted to put off their repentance, because the vision was for a great while to come; but now he is ordered to tell them that it is at the door.

Verses 5–10

Here is Noah's ready obedience to the commands that God gave him. Observe, 1. He went into the ark, upon notice that the flood would come after seven days, though probably as yet there appeared no visible sign of its approach. He went into it by faith in this warning that it would come quickly, though he did not see that the second causes had yet begun to work. In every step he took, he walked by faith, and not by sense. 2. He took all his family along with him, his wife, his sons, and his sons' wives, that by them, not only his family, but the world of mankind, might be built up. 3. The brute creatures readily went in with him.

Verses 11–12

The date of this great event; this is carefully recorded, for the greater certainty of the story.

The years of the old world are reckoned, not by the reigns of the giants, but by the lives of the patriarchs; saints are of more account with God than princes. Noah was now a very old man, even as men's years went then. Note, 1. The longer we live in this world the more we see of the miseries and calamities of it. 2. Sometimes God exercises his old servants with extraordinary trials of obedient patience. The oldest of Christ's soldiers must not promise themselves a discharge from their warfare till death discharge them. Still they must gird on their harness, and not boast as though they had put it off.

II. The second causes that concurred to this deluge.

1. In the self-same day that Noah was fixed in the ark, the inundation began. See what was done on that day, that fatal day to the world of the ungodly. (1) *The fountains of the great deep were broken up.* The waters of the sea returned to cover the earth, as they had done at first, *ch.* i. 9. (2) *The windows of heaven were opened,* and *the waters which were above the firmament* were poured out upon the world. The rain, which ordinarily descends in drops, then came down in streams, or *spouts,* as they call them in the Indies, where clouds have been often known to *burst,* as they express it there, when the rain descends in a much more violent torrent than we have ever seen in the greatest shower.

2. Now learn from this, (1) That all the creatures are at God's disposal, and that he makes what use he pleases of them, whether *for correction, or for mercy.* (2) That God often makes that which *should be for our welfare to become a trap,* Ps. lxix. 22. Nothing is more needful nor useful than water, both the springs of the earth and the showers of heaven; and yet now nothing was more hurtful, nothing more destructive: every creature is to us what God makes it. (3) That it is impossible to escape the righteous judgments of God when they come against sinners with commission.

Verses 13–16

Here is repeated what was related before of Noah's entrance into the ark, with his family and the creatures that were marked for preservation.

I. It is thus repeated for the honour of Noah, whose faith and obedience herein shone so brightly.

II. Notice is here taken of the beasts going in *each after his kind,* according to the phrase used in the history of the creation (*ch.* i. 21–25), and that this preservation was as a new creation: a life remarkably protected is, as it were, a new life.

III. It is added, *The Lord shut him in, v.* 16. As Noah continued his obedience to God, so God continued his care of Noah. God shut the door, 1. To secure him, and keep him safe in the ark. 2. To exclude all others. Hitherto the door of the ark stood open, and if any, even during the last seven days, had repented and believed, for aught I know they might have been welcomed into the ark; but now the door was shut.

IV. There is much of our gospel duty and privilege to be seen in Noah's preservation in the ark. Observe then, 1. It is our great duty, in obedience to the gospel call, by a lively faith in Christ, to come into that way of salvation which God has provided for poor sinners. When Noah came into the ark, he quitted his own house and lands; so must we quit our own righteousness and our worldly possessions, whenever they come into competition with Christ. Noah must, for a while, submit to the confinements and inconveniences of the ark, in order to his preservation for a new world; so those that come into Christ to be saved by him must deny themselves, both in sufferings and services. 2. Those that come into the ark themselves should bring as many as they can in with them, by good instructions, by persuasions, and by a good example. There is room enough in Christ for all comers. 3. Those that by faith come into Christ, the ark, shall by the power of God be shut in, and kept as in a stronghold *by the power of God,* 1 Pet. i. 5.

Verses 17–20

I. How long the flood was increasing—*forty days, v.* 17. The profane world, who believed not that it would come, probably when it came flattered themselves with hopes that it would soon abate; but it prevailed. The gradual approaches of God's judgments, which are designed to bring sinners to repentance, are often abused to the hardening of them in their presumption.

II. To what degree they increased: they rose so high that not only the low flat countries were deluged, but to make sure work, and that none might escape, the tops of the highest mountains were overflowed—*fifteen cubits,* that is, seven yards and a half. Thus the refuge of lies was swept away. There is no place on earth so high as to set men out of the reach of God's judgments, Jer. xlix. 16; Obad. 3, 4.

III. What became of Noah's ark when the waters thus increased: *It was lifted up above the earth (v.* 17), *and went upon the face of the waters, v.* 18. Observe, 1. The waters which broke down everything else bore up the ark. 2. The more the waters increased the higher the ark was lifted up towards heaven. Thus sanctified afflictions are spiritual promotions.

Verses 21–24

I. The general destruction of all flesh by the waters of the flood.

1. All the cattle, fowl, and creeping things, died, except the few that were in the ark. The destruction of the creatures was their deliverance from the bondage of corruption, which deliverance the whole creation now groans after, Rom. viii. 21, 22.

2. All the men, women, and children, that were in the world (except what were in the ark) died. Now, (1) We may easily imagine what terror and consternation seized on them when they saw themselves surrounded. (2) We may suppose that they tried all ways and means possible for their preservation, but all in vain. Those that are not found in Christ, the ark, are certainly undone.

Let us now pause awhile and consider this tremendous judgment ! Eliphaz appeals to this story as a standing warning to a careless world (Job xxii. 15, 16), *Hast thou marked the old way, which wicked men have trodden, who were cut down out of time,* and sent into eternity, *whose foundation was overflown with the flood?*

II. The special preservation of Noah and his family. Observe, 1. Noah lives. When all about him were monuments of justice, thousands falling on his right hand and ten thousands on his left, he was a monument of mercy. We have reason to think that, while the long-suffering of God waited, Noah not only preached to, but prayed for, that wicked world, and would have turned away the wrath; but his prayers return into his own bosom, and are answered only in his own escape, which is plainly referred to, Ezek. xiv. 14, *Noah, Daniel, and Job, shall but deliver their own souls.* 2. He but lives. Noah remains alive, and this is all; he is, in effect, buried alive—cooped up in a close place. But he comforts himself with this, that he is in the way of duty and in the way of deliverance.

CHAPTER 8

In the close of the foregoing chapter we left the world in ruins. Now the scene alters, the brighter side of that cloud which there appeared so black and dark; for, though God contend long, he will not contend for ever, nor be always wrath. We have here, I. The earth made anew, by the recess of the waters, and the appearing of the dry land. 1. The increase of the waters is stayed, ver. 1, 2. 2. They begin sensibly to abate, ver. 3. 3. After sixteen days' ebbing, the ark rests, ver. 4. 4. After sixty days' ebbing, the tops of the mountains appeared, ver. 5. 5. After forty days' ebbing, and twenty days before the mountains appeared, Noah began to send out his spies, a raven and a dove, to gain intelligence, ver. 6–12. 6. Two months after the appearing of the tops of the mountains, the waters had gone, and the face of the earth was dry (ver. 13), though not dried so as to be fit for man till almost two months after, ver. 14. II. Man placed anew upon the earth 1. Noah's discharge and departure out of the ark, ver. 15–19. 2. His sacrifice of praise, which he offered to God upon his enlargement, ver. 20. 3. God's acceptance of his sacrifice, and the promise he made thereupon not to drown the world again, ver. 21, 22. And thus, at length, mercy rejoices against judgment.

Verses 1–3

I. An act of God's grace: *God remembered Noah and every living thing.* This is an expression after the manner of men; for not any of his creatures (Luke xii. 6), much less any of his people, are forgotten of God, Isa. xlix. 15, 16. God's remembering Noah was the return of his mercy to mankind, of whom he would not make a full end. Noah himself, though one that had found grace in the eyes of the Lord, yet seemed to be forgotten in the ark, and perhaps began to think himself so; for we do not find that God had told him how long he should be confined and when he should be released. Very good men have sometimes been ready to conclude themselves forgotten of God, especially when their afflictions have been unusually grievous and long. Perhaps Noah, though a great believer, yet when he found the flood continuing so long after it might reasonably be presumed to have done its work, was tempted to fear lest he that shut him in would keep him in, and began to expostulate. *How long wilt thou forget me?* But at length God returned in mercy to him, and this is expressed by remembering him.

II. An act of God's power over wind and water, both of which are at his beck, though neither of them is under man's control.

1. He commanded the wind, and said to that, *Go*, and it went, in order to the carrying off of the flood: *God made a wind to pass over the earth.* See here, (1) What was God's remembrance of Noah: it was his relieving him. (2) What a sovereign dominion God has over the winds. Even stormy winds fulfil his word, Ps. cxlviii. 8. Now God sent a wind, a drying wind, such a wind as God sent to divide the Red Sea before Israel, Exod. xiv. 21.

2. He commanded the waters, and said to them, *Come*, and they came. (1) He took away the cause. Note, As God has a key to open, so he has a key

to shut up again, and to stay the progress of judgments by stopping the causes of them: and the same hand that brings the desolation must bring the deliverance. He that wounds is alone able to heal. See Job xii. 14, 15. (2) Then the effect ceased; not all at once, but by degrees. God usually works deliverance for his people gradually, that the day of small things may not be despised, nor the day of great things despaired of, Zech. iv. 10. See Prov. iv. 18.

Verses 4–5

Here we have the effects and evidences of the ebbing of the waters. 1. The ark rested. This was some satisfaction to Noah, to feel the house he was in upon firm ground, and no longer movable. It rested upon a mountain, whither it was directed, not by Noah's prudence (he did not steer it), but by the wise and gracious providence of God, that it might rest the sooner. Note, God has times and places of rest for his people after their tossings; and many a time he provides for their seasonable and comfortable settlement without their own contrivance and quite beyond their own foresight. 2. The tops of the mountains were seen, like little islands, appearing above the water. We must suppose that they were seen by Noah and his sons; for there were none besides to see them. It is probable that they had looked through the window of the ark every day, like the longing mariners, after a tedious voyage, to see if they could discover land. They felt ground above forty days before they saw it, according to Dr. Lightfoot's computation, whence he infers that, if the waters decreased proportionably, the ark drew eleven cubits in water.

Verses 6–12

An account of the spies which Noah sent forth to bring him intelligence from abroad, a raven and a dove.

I. That though God had told Noah particularly when the flood would come, yet he did not give him a particular account by revelation at what times, and by what steps, it should *go away*, 1. Because the knowledge of the former was necessary to his preparing the ark, but the knowledge of the latter would serve only to gratify his curiosity, and the concealing of it from him would be the needful exercise of his faith and patience. And, 2. He could not foresee the flood, but by revelation; but he might, by ordinary means, discover the decrease of it.

II. That though Noah by faith expected his enlargement, and by patience waited for it, yet he was inquisitive concerning it, as one that thought it long to be thus confined. *He that believes does not make haste* to run before God, but he does make haste to go forth to meet him, Isa. xxviii. 16. Particularly, 1. Noah sent forth a raven through the window of the ark, which went forth, as the Hebrew phrase is, *going forth and returning*, that is, flying about, but returning to the ark for rest; probably not in it, but upon it. This gave Noah little satisfaction; therefore, 2. He sent forth a dove, which returned the first time with no good news, but probably wet and dirty; but, the second time, she brought an olive-leaf in her bill, which appeared to be first plucked off, a plain indication that now the trees, the fruit-trees, began to appear above water. Note here, (1) That Noah sent forth the dove the second time seven days after the first time, and the third time was after seven days too; and probably the first sending of her out was seven days after the sending forth of the raven. This intimates that it was done on the sabbath day, which, it should seem, Noah religiously observed in the ark. (2) The dove is an emblem of a gracious soul, which finding no rest for its foot, no solid peace or satisfaction in this world, returns to Christ as to its ark. The carnal heart, like the raven, takes up with the world, and feeds on the carrions it finds there. And as Noah put forth his hand, and took the dove, and pulled her in to him, into the ark, so Christ will graciously preserve, and help, and welcome, those that fly to him for rest. (3) The olive-branch, which was an emblem of peace, was brought, not by the raven, a bird of prey, nor by a gay and proud peacock, but by a mild, patient, humble, dove. It is a dove-like disposition that brings into the soul earnests of rest and joy. (4) Some make these things an allegory. The law was first sent forth like the raven, but brought no tidings; therefore, in the fulness of time, God sent forth his gospel, as the dove, in the likeness of which the Holy Spirit descended, and this presents us with an olive-branch and brings in a better hope.

Verses 13–14

1. The ground dry (v. 13), that is, all the water carried off it, of which, upon the first day of the first month (a joyful new-year's-day it was), Noah was himself an eyewitness. He *removed the covering of the ark* to give him a prospect of the earth about it; and a most comfortable prospect he had. For behold, behold and wonder, *the face of the ground was dry*. Note, (1) It is a great mercy to see ground about us. Noah was more sensible of it than we are; for mercies restored are much more affecting than mercies continued. (2) The divine power which now renewed the face of the earth can renew the face of an afflicted troubled soul and of a distressed persecuted church. 2. The ground dried (v. 14), so as to be a fit habitation for Noah. Note, God consults our benefit rather than our desires. We would go out of the ark before the ground is dried: and perhaps, if the door be shut, are ready to remove the covering. God's time of showing mercy is certainly the best time, when the mercy is ripe for us and we are ready for it.

Verses 15–19

I. Noah's dismission out of the ark, v. 15–17. Observe, 1. Noah did not stir till God bade him. Those only go under God's protection that follow God's direction and submit to his government. 2. Though God detained him long, yet at last he gave him his discharge. 3. God had said, *Come into the ark*, which intimated that God went in with him; now he says, not *Come forth*, but *Go forth*, which intimates that God, who went in with him, stayed with him all the while, till he sent him out safely.

II. Noah's departure when he had his dismission. When he found himself preserved there, not only for a new life, but for a new world, he saw no reason to complain of his long confinement. Now observe, 1. Noah and his family came out alive. 2. Noah brought out all the creatures that went in with him, except the raven and the dove, which, probably, were ready to meet their mates at their coming out. Noah was able to give a very good account of his charge; for of all that were given to him he had lost none.

Verses 20–22

I. Noah's thankful acknowledgment of God's favour to him, in completing the mercy of his deliverance, v. 20. 1. He *built an altar*. God is pleased with free-will offerings, and praises that wait for him. Noah was now turned out into a cold and desolate world, where, one would have thought, his first care would have been to build a house for himself; but, behold, he begins with an altar for God: God, that is the first, must be first served; and he begins well that begins with God. 2. He offered a sacrifice upon his altar, *of every clean beast, and of every clean fowl*. Here observe, (1) He offered only those that were clean. (2) Though his stock of cattle was so small, and that rescued from ruin at so great an expense of care and pains, yet he did not grudge to give God his dues out of it. Serving God with our little is the way to make it more; and we must never think that wasted with which God is honoured. (3) See here the antiquity of religion: the first thing we find done in the new world was an act of worship, Jer. vi. 16. We are now to express our thankfulness, not by burnt-offerings, but by the sacrifices of praise and the sacrifices of righteousness, by pious devotions and a pious conversation.

II. God's gracious acceptance of Noah's thankfulness.

1. God was well pleased with the performance, v. 21. He *smelt a sweet savour*, or, as it is in the Hebrew, *a savour of rest*, from it. He was well pleased with Noah's pious zeal, and these hopeful beginnings of the new world. Having caused his anger to rest upon the world of sinners, he here caused his love to rest upon this little remnant of believers.

2. Hereupon, he took up a resolution never to drown the world again. Good security is here given, and that which may be relied upon.

(1) That this judgment should never be repeated. Noah might think, "To what purpose should the world be repaired, when, in all probability, for the wickedness of it, it will quickly be in like manner ruined again?" "No," says God, "it never shall." *Neither will I again smite any more every living thing.* "I will no more take this severe method; for," *First*, "He is rather to be pitied, for it is all the effect of sin dwelling in him; and it is but what might be expected from such a degenerate race: he is called a *transgressor from the womb*, and therefore it is not strange that he deals so very treacherously," Isa. xlviii. 8. Thus God *remembers that he is flesh*. *Secondly*, "He will be utterly ruined, for, if he be dealt with according to his deserts, one flood must succeed another till all be destroyed." See here, 1. That outward judgments, though they may terrify and restrain men, yet cannot of themselves sanctify and renew them; the grace of God must work with those judgments. 2. That God's reasons of mercy are all drawn from himself, not from any thing in us.

(2) That the course of nature should never be discontinued (v. 22): "*While the earth remaineth*, and man upon it, there shall be *summer and winter* (not all winter as had been this last year), *day and night*," not all night, as probably it was ·while the rain was descending. It is plainly intimated that this earth is not to remain always. As long as it does remain God's providence will carefully preserve the regular succession of times and seasons, and cause each to know its place. To this we owe it that the world stands, and the wheel of nature keeps its track. See here how changeable the times are and yet how unchangeable. *First*, The course of nature always changing—*day and night, summer and winter*, counter-changed. *Secondly*, Yet never changed. It is constant in this inconstancy. These seasons have never ceased, nor shall cease, while the sun continues such a steady measurer of time and the moon such a *faithful witness in heaven*. This is *God's covenant of the day and of the night*, the stability of which is mentioned for the confirming of our faith in the covenant of grace, which is no less inviolable, Jer. xxxiii. 20, 21.

CHAPTER 9

Both the world and the church were now again reduced to a family, the family of Noah, of the affairs of which this chapter gives us an account. Here is, I. The covenant of providence settled with Noah and his sons, ver. 1–11. In this covenant 1. God promises them to take care of their lives, so that, (1) They should replenish the earth, ver. 1, 7. (2) They should be safe from the insults of the brute-creatures, ver. 2. (3) They should be allowed to eat flesh; only they must not eat blood, ver. 3, 4. (4) The world should never be drowned again, ver. 8–11. 2. God requires of them to take care of one another's lives and of their own, ver. 5, 6. II. The seal of that covenant, namely, the rainbow, ver. 12–17. III. A story concerning Noah and his sons, 1. Noah's sin and shame, ver. 20, 21. 2. Ham's impudence and impiety, ver. 22. 3. The pious modesty of Shem and Japheth, ver. 23. 4. The curse of Canaan, and the blessing of Shem and Japheth, ver. 24–27. IV. The age and death of Noah, ver. 28, 29.

Verses 1–7

In general, *God blessed Noah and his sons* (v. 1), that is, he assured them of his good-will to them and his gracious intentions concerning them. We read (*ch.* viii. 20) how *Noah blessed God*, by his altar and sacrifice.

Now here we have the *Magna Charta—the great charter* of this new kingdom of nature which was now to be erected, and incorporated, the former charter having been forfeited and seized.

I. The grants of this charter are kind and gracious to men.

1. A grant of lands of vast extent, and a promise of a great increase of men to occupy and enjoy them. The first blessing is here renewed: *Be fruitful, and multiply, and replenish the earth* (v. 1). Now, (1) God sets the whole earth before them, tells them it is all their own, *while it remains*, to them and their heirs. Though it is not a paradise, but a wilderness rather; yet it is better than we deserve. Blessed be God, it is not hell. (2) He gives them a blessing, so that in a little time all the habitable parts of the earth should be more or less inhabited. Though death should still reign, yet the earth should never again be dispeopled as now it was, but still replenished, Acts xvii. 24–6.

2. A grant of power over the inferior creatures, *v.* 2. Man in innocence ruled by love, fallen man rules by fear. Now this grant remains in force, and thus far we have still the benefit of it. Now here see, (1) That God is a good Master, and provides, not only that we may live, but that we may live comfortably, in his service; not for necessity only, but for delight. (2) That every *creature of God is good*, and nothing to be refused, 1 Tim. iv. 4.

II. The precepts and provisos of this charter are no less kind and gracious, and instances of God's good-will to man. The Jewish doctors speak so often of the seven precepts of Noah, or of the sons of Noah, which they say were to be observed by all nations, that it may not be amiss to set them down. The first against the worship of idols. The second against blasphemy, and requiring to bless the name of God. The third against murder. The fourth against incest and all uncleanness. The fifth against theft and rapine. The sixth requiring the administration of justice. The seventh against eating of flesh with the life.

1. Man must not prejudice his own life by eating that food which is unwholesome and prejudicial to his health (v. 4); they must not be greedy and hasty in taking their food; they must not be barbarous and cruel to the inferior creatures. During the continuance of the law of sacrifices, in which the blood made *atonement for the soul* (Lev. xvii. 11), signifying that the life of the sacrifice was accepted for the life of the sinner, blood must not be looked upon as a common thing, but must be *poured out before the Lord* (2 Sam. xxiii. 16). But, now that the great and true sacrifice has been offered, the obligation of the law ceases with the reason of it.

2. Man must not take away his own life: *Your blood of your lives will I require, v.* 5. Our lives are not so our own as that we may quit them at our own pleasure, but they are God's.

3. The beasts must not be suffered to hurt the life

of man. This was confirmed by the law of Moses (Exod. xxi. 28), and I think it would not be unsafe to observe it still. Thus God showed his hatred of the sin of murder, that men might hate it the more, and not only punish, but prevent it.

4. Wilful murderers must be put to death. This is the sin which is here designed to be restrained by the terror of punishment. (1) God will punish murderers. One time or other, in this world or in the next, he will both discover concealed murders, which are hidden from man's eyes, and punish avowed and justified murders, which are too great for man's hand. (2) The magistrate must punish murderers (*v.* 6). There are those who are ministers of God for this purpose, to be a protection to the innocent, by being a terror to the malicious and evildoers, and they must not *bear the sword in vain*, Rom. xiii. 4. It is a sin *which the Lord would not pardon* in a prince (2 Kings xxiv. 3, 4), and which therefore a prince should not pardon in a subject. To this law there is a reason annexed: *For in the image of God made he man* at first. Man is a creature to his Creator, and therefore ought to be so to us. God put honour upon him, let not us then put contempt upon him. Such remains of God's image are still even upon fallen man as that he who unjustly kills a man defaces the image of God and does dishonour to him.

Verses 8–11

Here is, I. The general establishment of God's covenant with this new world, and the extent of that covenant, *v.* 9, 10. Here observe, 1. That God is graciously pleased to deal with man in the way of a covenant, wherein God greatly encourages man's duty and obedience. 2. That all God's covenants with man are of his own making: *I, behold, I.* 3. That God's covenants are established more firmly than the pillars of heaven or the foundations of the earth, and cannot be disannulled. 4. That God's covenants are made with the covenanters and with their seed; the promise is to them and their children.

II. The particular intention of this covenant. It was designed to secure the world from another deluge: *There shall not any more be a flood.* It is owing to God's goodness and faithfulness, not to any reformation of the world, that it has not often been deluged, and that it is not deluged now. As the old world was ruined to be a monument of justice, so this world remains to this day, a monument of mercy, according to the oath of God, that the waters of Noah should no more return to cover the earth, Isa. liv. 9. If the sea should flow but for a few days, as it does twice every day for a few hours, what desolation would it make ! Let us give him the glory of his mercy in promising and of his truth in performing.

Verses 12–17

Articles of agreement among men are usually sealed. God therefore, being *willing more abundantly to show to the heirs of promise the immutability of his councils*, has confirmed his covenant by a seal (Heb. vi. 17). The seal of this covenant of nature was natural enough; it was the *rainbow*. Now, concerning this seal of the covenant, observe, 1. This seal is affixed with repeated assurances of the truth of that promise of which it was designed to be the ratification: *I do set my bow in the cloud* (v. 13); it *shall be seen in the cloud* (v. 14), that the eye may affect the heart and confirm the faith; and it shall be *the token of the covenant* (v. 12, 13), *and I will remember my covenant, that the waters shall no more become a flood, v.* 15. 2. The rainbow appears when the clouds are most disposed to wet, and returns after the rain; when we have most reason to fear the rain prevailing. Thus God obviates our fears. 3. The thicker the cloud the brighter the bow in the cloud. Thus, as threatening afflictions abound, encouraging consolations much more abound, 2 Cor. i. 5. 4. The rainbow appears when one part of the sky is clear, which intimates mercy remembered in the midst of wrath; and the clouds are hemmed as it were with the rainbow, that they may not overspread the heavens, for the bow is coloured rain or the edges of a cloud gilded. A bow bespeaks terror, but this bow has neither string nor arrow, and a bow alone will do little execution. It is a bow, but it is directed upwards, not towards the earth; for the seals of the covenant were intended to comfort, not to terrify.

Verses 18–23

Here is, I. Noah's family and employment. The business Noah applied himself to was that of *a husbandman*, Heb. *a man of the earth*, that is, a man dealing in the earth, that kept ground in his hand, and occupied it. Noah was by his calling led to trade in the fruits of the earth. He *began to be a husbandman*, that is, he returned to his old employment, from which he had been diverted by the building of the ark first, and probably afterwards by the building of a house on dry land for himself and family. For this good while he had been a carpenter, but now he began again to be a husbandman.

II. Noah's sin and shame: *He planted a vineyard*; and, when he had gathered his vintage, probably he appointed a day of mirth and feasting in his family, and had his sons and their children with him, to rejoice with him in the increase of his house as well as in the increase of his vineyard; and perhaps he appointed this feast with a design, at the close of it, to bless his sons. At this feast he *drank of the wine*. But he drank too liberally, for he was *drunk*. Observe, how he came now to be overtaken in this fault. It was his sin, and a great sin, so much the worse for its being so soon after a great deliverance; but God left him to himself, and has left this miscarriage of his upon record, to teach us, 1. That the fairest copy that ever mere man wrote since the fall had its blots and false strokes. 2. That sometimes those who, with watchfulness and resolution, have, by the grace of God, kept their integrity in the midst of temptation, have, through security and carelessness, and neglect of the grace of God, been surprised into sin, when the hour of temptation has been over. 3. That we have need to be very careful, when we use God's good creatures plentifully, lest we use them to excess. Now the consequence of Noah's sin was shame. He was made naked to his shame, as Adam when he had eaten forbidden fruit. Observe here the great evil of the sin of drunkenness. (1) It discovers men. What infirmities they have, they betray when they are drunk, and what secrets they are entrusted with are then easily got out of them. Drunken porters keep open gates. (2) It disgraces men, and exposes them to contempt. Men say and do that when drunk which when they are sober they would blush at the thoughts of, Hab. ii. 15, 16.

III. Ham's impudence and impiety: He *saw the nakedness of his father, and told his two brethren, v.* 22. 1. He pleased himself with the sight. Perhaps Ham had sometimes been himself drunk. It is common for those who walk in false ways themselves to rejoice at the false steps which they sometimes see others make. But charity rejoices not in iniquity. 2. *He told his two brethren* in a scornful deriding manner, that his father might seem vile unto them. It is very wrong, (1) To make a jest of sin (Prov. xiv. 9). And, (2) To publish the faults of any, especially of parents, whom it is our duty to honour.

IV. The pious care of Shem and Japheth to cover their poor father's shame, *v.* 23. 1. There is a mantle of love to be thrown over the faults of all, 1 Pet. iv. 8.

2. Besides this, there is a robe of reverence to be thrown over the faults of parents.

Verses 24–27

I. Noah comes to himself. He *awoke from his wine*.

II. The spirit of prophecy comes upon him, and, like dying Jacob, he tells his sons what shall befall them, *ch.* xlix. 1.

1. He pronounces a curse on Canaan the son of Ham (*v.* 25). The particular curse is, *A servant of servants* (that is, the meanest and most despicable servant) *shall he be,* even *to his brethren.* Note, (1) God often visits the iniquity of the fathers upon the children, when the children inherit the fathers' wicked dispositions,and imitate the fathers' wicked practices, and do nothing to cut off he entail of the curse. (2) Disgrace is justly put upon those that put disgrace upon others, especially that dishonour and grieve their own parents.

2. He entails a blessing upon Shem and Japheth.

(1) He blesses Shem, or rather blesses God for him. Observe, [1] He calls the Lord *the God of Shem.* All blessings are included in this. Shem is sufficiently recompensed for his respect to his father by this, that the Lord himself puts this honour upon him, *to be his God.* [2] He gives to God the glory of that good work which Shem had done. When we see men's good works we should glorify, not them, but *our* Father, Matt. v. 16. It is an honour and a favour to be employed for God and used by him in doing good. [3] He foresees that God's gracious dealings with Shem and his family would be evidence to all the world that he was the God of Shem. [4] It is intimated that the church should be built up and continued in the posterity of Shem; for of him came the Jews, who were, for a great while, the only professing people God had in the world.

(2) He blesses Japheth, and, in him, *the isles of the Gentiles,* which were peopled by his seed: *God shall enlarge Japheth, and he shall dwell in the tents of Shem, v.* 27. Now, Some make this to belong wholly to Japheth, and to denote either, *First,* His outward prosperity, that his seed should be so numerous and so victorious that they should be masters of the tents of Shem, which was fulfilled when the people of the Jews, the most eminent of Shem's race, were tributaries to the Grecians first and afterwards to the Romans, both of Japheth's seed. Or, *Secondly,* It denotes the conversion of the Gentiles, and the bringing of them into the church; and then we should read it, *God shall persuade Japheth* (for so the word signifies), and then, being so persuaded, *he shall dwell in the tents of Shem,* that is, Jews and Gentiles shall be united together in the gospel fold. Note, It is God only that can bring those again into the church who have separated themselves from it. Souls are brought into the church, not by force, but by persuasion, Ps. cx. 3. They are persuaded by reason to be religious.

Verses 28–29

Here see, 1. How God prolonged the life of Noah; this long life was a further reward of his signal piety, and a great blessing to the world. 2. How God put a period to his life at last. Noah lived to see two worlds, but, being an heir of the righteousness which is by faith, when he died he went to see a better than either.

CHAPTER 10

This chapter shows the origin of nations; and yet perhaps there is no nation but that of the Jews that can be confident from which of these seventy fountains (for so many there are here) it derives its streams. Through the want of early records, the mixtures o f people, the revolutions of nations, and distance of time, the knowledge of the lineal descent of the present inhabitants of the earth is lost. I. Of the posterity of Japheth, ver. 2–5. II. The posterity of Ham (ver. 6–20), and in this particular notice is taken of Nimrod, ver. 8–10. III. The posterity of Shem, ver. 21, &c.

Verses 1–5

The posterity of Japheth were allotted to the isles of the Gentiles (*v.* 5), which were divided among them, and probably this island of ours among the rest; all places beyond the sea from Judæa are called *isles* (Jer. xxv. 22), and this directs us to understand that promise (Isa. xlii. 4), *the isles shall wait for his law*, of the conversion of the Gentiles to the faith of Christ.

Verses 6–14

That which is observable and improvable in these verses is the account here given of Nimrod, v. 8–10. He is here represented as a great man in his day: he was resolved to tower above his neighbours. The same spirit that actuated the giants before the flood now revived in him. There are some in whom ambition and affectation of dominion seem to be bred in the bone. Nothing on this side hell will humble and break the proud spirits of some men. Now,

I. Nimrod was a great hunter; with this he began, and for this became famous to a proverb. 1. Some think he did good with his hunting, served his country by ridding it of the wild beasts which infested it. 2. Others think that under pretence of hunting he gathered men under his command, in pursuit of another game he had to play, which was to make himself master of the country. Note, Great conquerors are but great hunters. Alexander and Cæsar would not make such a figure in scripture-history as they do in common history. Nimrod was a mighty hunter *against* the Lord, so the LXX; that is, (1) He set up idolatry. That he might set up a new government, he set up a new religion. *Babel was the mother of harlots.* Or, (2) He carried on his oppression and violence in defiance of God himself.

II. Nimrod was a great ruler: *The beginning of his kingdom was Babel, v.* 10. Some way or other, by arts or arms, he got into power, and so laid the foundations of a monarchy. If Nimrod and his neighbours began, other nations soon learned to incorporate under one head for their common safety and welfare, which, however it began, proved so great a blessing to the world that things were reckoned to go ill indeed when there *was no king in Israel.*

III. Nimrod was a great builder. Probably he was architect in the building of Babel, and there he began his kingdom; but, when his project to rule all the sons of Noah was baffled by the confusion of tongues, *out of that land he went forth into Assyria* (so the margin reads it, *v.* 11) *and built Nineveh, &c.*

Verses 15–20

Observe here, 1. The account of the posterity of Canaan, of the families and nations that descended from him, and of the land they possessed, very pleasantly situated. Canaan here has a better land than either Shem or Japheth, and yet they have a·better lot, for they inherit the blessing.

Verses 21–32

Two things especially are observable in this account of the posterity of Shem:—

I. The description of Shem, *v.* 21. We have not only his name, *Shem*, which signifies *a name*, but two titles to distinguish him by:—

1. He was *the father of all the children of Eber.* Eber was his great grandson; but why should he be called the father of all *his* children, rather than of all Arphaxad's, or Salah's, &c.? Probably because

Abraham and his seed, God's covenant-people, not only descended from Heber, but from him were called *Hebrews; ch.* xiv. 13, *Abram the Hebrew.* The holy tongue being commonly called from him the *Hebrew*, it is probable that he retained it in his family, in the confusion of Babel, as a special token of God's favour to him. Now, when the inspired penman would give Shem an honourable title, he calls him *the father of the Hebrews.* As Ham, though he had many sons, is disowned by being called *the father of Canaan*, so Shem, though he had many sons, is dignified with the title of *the father of Eber*, on whose seed the blessing was entailed. Goodness is true greatness.

2. He was *the brother of Japheth the elder.* The sacred historian had mentioned it as Shem's honour that he was the father of the Hebrews; but, lest Japheth's seed should therefore be looked upon as for ever shut out from the Church, he here reminds us that he *was the brother of Japheth*, not in birth only, but in blessing; for *Japheth was to dwell in the tents of Shem.*

Chapter 11

We have, in this chapter, I. The dispersion of the sons of men at Babel (ver. 1–9), where we have, 1. Their presumptuous design to build a city and a tower, ver. 1–4. 2. The righteous judgment of God upon them by confounding their language, and so scattering them, ver. 5–9. II. The pedigree of the sons of God down to Abraham (ver. 10–26), with a general account of his family, and removal out of his native country, ver. 27, &c.

Verses 1–4

The close of the foregoing chapter tells us that *by* the sons of Noah, or *among* the sons of Noah, *the nations were divided in the earth after the flood*, that is, were distinguished into several tribes, and it was either appointed by Noah, or agreed upon among his sons, which way each several tribe or colony should steer its course. But the sons of men, it should seem, were loth to disperse into distant places; they thought the more the merrier and the safer, and therefore they contrived to keep together, thinking themselves wiser than either God or Noah. Now here we have,

I. The advantages which befriended their design of keeping together, 1. They were all of *one language, v.* 1. Now, while they all understood one another, they would be the more likely to love one another, and the more capable of helping one another, and the less inclinable to separate one from another. 2. They found a very convenient commodious place to settle in (*v.* 2), *a plain in the land of Shinar*, a spacious plain, able to *contain* them all, and a *fruitful* plain, able, according as their present numbers were, to support them all.

II. The method they took to bind themselves to one another, and to settle together in one body. Instead of coveting to enlarge their borders by a peaceful departure under the divine protection, they contrived to fortify them. Their unanimous resolution is, *Let us build ourselves a city and a tower.* Observe here,

1. How they excited and encouraged one another to set about this work. They said, *Go to, let us make brick* (*v.* 3), and again, (*v.* 4), *Go to, let us build ourselves a city;* by mutual excitements they made one another more daring and resolute.

2. What materials they used in their building. The country, being plain, yielded neither stone nor mortar, yet this did not discourage them from their undertaking, but they made brick to serve instead of stone, and slime or pitch instead of mortar. What shift those will make that are resolute in their purposes: were we but thus zealously affected in a good thing, we should not stop our work so often as we do,

under pretence that we want conveniences for carrying it on.

3. For what ends they built. Three things, it seems, they aimed at in building this tower:—

(1) It seems designed for an affront to God himself; for they would build a tower *whose top might reach to heaven*, which bespeaks a defiance of God, or at least a rivalship with him.

(2) They hoped hereby to make themselves a name, and to give posterity to know that there had been such men as they in the world. They would leave this monument of their pride and ambition, and folly. We do not find in any history the name of so much as one of these Babel-builders.

(3) They did it to prevent their dispersion. It is probable that the hand of ambitious Nimrod was in all this. He aimed at universal monarchy, in order to which, under pretence of uniting for their common safety, he contrives to keep them in one body, that, having them all under his eye, he might not fail to have them under his power. It is God's prerogative to be universal monarch, Lord of all, and King of kings; the man that aims at it offers to step into the throne of God, who will not give his glory to another.

Verses 5–9

We have here the quashing of the project of the Babel-builders.

I. The cognizance God took of the design that was on foot. God is incontestibly just and fair in all his proceedings against sin and sinners, and condemns none unheard. They were the sons of *Adam*, so it is in the Hebrew; nay, of that Adam, that sinful disobedient Adam, whose children are by nature children of disobedience. Pious Eber is not found among this ungodly crew; for he and his are called the children of God.

II. The counsels and resolves of the Eternal God concerning this matter.

1. He suffered them to proceed a good way in their enterprise before he put a stop to it, that they might have space to repent.

2. God had tried, by his commands and admonitions, to bring them off from this project, but in vain; therefore he must take another course to keep the world in some order and to tie the hands of those that will not be checked by law. Now observe here, The mercy of God, in moderating the penalty, and not making it proportionable to the offence; for *he deals not with us according to our sins*. He does not say, "*Let us go down* now in thunder and lightning, and consume those rebels in a moment." No; only, "*Let us go down*, and scatter them." They deserved death, but are only banished or transported; for the patience of God is very great towards a provoking world. Three things were done:—

1. Their language was confounded. Those unhappy controversies which are strifes of words, and arise from our misunderstanding one another's language, for aught I know are owing to this confusion of tongues.

2. Their building was stopped: *They left off to build the city*. This was the effect of the confusion of their tongues; for it not only incapacitated them for helping one another, but probably struck such a damp upon their spirits that they could not proceed, since they saw, in this, the hand of the Lord gone out against them. It is wisdom to leave off that which we see God fights against.

3. The builders were scattered abroad upon the face of the whole earth, *v.* 8, 9. They departed in companies, after their families, and after their tongues (*ch.* x. 5, 20, 31), to the several countries and places allotted to them. They left behind them a perpetual memorandum of their reproach, in the name given to the place. It was called *Babel, con-*

fusion. Those that aim at a great name commonly come off with a *bad* name. The children of men were now finally scattered, and never did, nor ever will, come all together again, till the great day, when the Son of man shall sit upon the throne of his glory, and all nations shall be gathered before him, Matt. xxv. 31, 32.

Verses 10–26

We have here a genealogy, not an endless genealogy, for here it ends in Abram, the friend of God, and leads further to Christ, the promised seed, who was the son of Abram, and from Abram the genealogy of Christ is reckoned (Matt. i. 1, &c.). 1. Nothing is left upon record concerning those of this line but their names and ages, the Holy Ghost seeming to hasten through them to the story of Abram. How little do we know of those that have gone before us in this world, even those that lived in the same places where we live, as we likewise know little of those that are our contemporaries in distant places! we have enough to do to mind the work of our own day, and let God alone to *require that which is past*, Eccl. iii. 15. 2. There was an observable gradual decrease in the years of their lives. Shem reached to 600 years, which yet fell short of the age of the patriarchs before the flood; the next three came short of 500; the next three did not reach to 300; after them we read not of any that attained to 200, except Terah; and, not many ages after this, Moses reckoned seventy, or eighty, to be the utmost men ordinarily arrive at. 3. Eber, from whom the Hebrews were denominated, was the longest-lived of any that was born after the flood, which perhaps was the reward of his singular piety and strict adherence to the ways of God.

Verses 27–32

Here begins the story of Abram, whose name is famous, henceforward, in both Testaments.

I. His country: *Ur of the Chaldees.* This was the land of his nativity, an idolatrous country, where even the children of Eber themselves had degenerated. Note, Those who are, through grace, heirs of the land of promise, ought to remember what was the land of their nativity, what was their corrupt and sinful state by nature, the rock out of which they were hewn.

II. His relations, mentioned for his sake, and because of their interest in the following story. 1. His father was *Terah*, of whom it is said (Josh. xxiv. 2) that he served other gods, on the other side of the flood, so early did idolatry gain footing in the world, and so hard is it even for those that have some good principles to swim against the stream. We have, 2. Some account of his brethren. (1) *Nahor*, out of whose family both Isaac and Jacob had their wives. (2) *Haran*, the father of Lot, of whom it is here said (*v.* 28) *that he died before his father Terah*. Note, Children cannot be sure that they shall survive their parents; for death does not go by seniority, taking the eldest first. *The shadow of death is without any order*, Job x. 22. It is likewise said that he died *in Ur of the Chaldees*, before the happy removal of the family out of that idolatrous country. 3. His wife was *Sarai*, who, some think, was the same with Iscah, the daughter of Haran. Abram himself says of her that she was the daughter of his father, but not the daughter of his mother, *ch.* xx. 12. She was ten years younger than Abram.

III. His departure out of Ur of the Chaldees, with his father Terah, his nephew Lot, and the rest of his family, in obedience to the call of God, of which we shall read more, *ch.* xii. 1, &c. This chapter leaves them in Haran, or Charran, a place about midway between Ur and Canaan, where they dwelt till

Terah's head was laid, probably because the old man was unable, through the infirmities of age, to proceed in his journey. Many reach to Charran, and yet fall short of Canaan; they are not far from the kingdom of God, and yet never come thither.

CHAPTER 12

Henceforward Abram and his seed are almost the only subject of the sacred history. In this chapter we have, I. God's call of Abram to the land of Canaan, ver. 1–3. II. Abram's obedience to this call, ver. 4, 5. III. His welcome to the land of Canaan, ver. 6–9. IV. His journey to Egypt, with an account of what happened to him there. Abram's flight and fault, ver. 10–13. Sarai's danger and deliverance, ver. 14–20.

Verses 1–3

We have here the call by which Abram was removed out of the land of his nativity, into the land of promise, and which was designed both to try his faith and obedience and also to separate him and set him apart for God, and for special services. We may be somewhat helped to the knowledge of the circumstances of the call by Stephen's speech, Acts vii. 2, where we are told, 1. That the God of glory appeared in such displays of his glory as left Abram no room to doubt the divine authority of this call. God spoke to him afterwards in divers manners; but this first time, when the correspondence was to be settled, he appeared to him as *the God of glory,* and spoke to him. 2. That this call was given him in Mesopotamia, before he dwelt in Charran. Some think that Haran was in Chaldea, and so was still a part of Abram's country, or that Abram, having stayed there five years, began to call it his country, and to take root there, till God let him know this was not the place he was intended for. Note, If God loves us, and has mercy in store for us, he will not suffer us to take up our rest anywhere short of Canaan, but will graciously repeat his calls, till the good work begun be performed, and our souls repose in God only. In the call itself we have a precept and a promise.

I. A trying precept: *Get thee out of thy country, v.* 1.

1. By this precept he was tried whether he loved his native soil and dearest friends, and whether he could willingly leave all, to go along with God. His country had become idolatrous, his kindred and his father's house were a constant temptation to him, and he could not continue with them without danger of being infected by them. This command which God gave to Abram is much the same with the gospel call by which all the spiritual seed of faithful Abram are brought into covenant with God. For, (1) Natural affection must give way to divine grace. (2) Sin, and all the occasions of it, must be forsaken, and particularly bad company; we must abandon all the idols of iniquity which have been set up in our hearts, willingly parting with that which is dearest to us, when we cannot keep it without hazard of our integrity. (3) The world, and all our enjoyments in it, must be looked upon with a holy indifference; we must no longer look upon it as our country, or home, but as our inn, and must accordingly sit loose to it, live above it, and get out of it in affection.

2. By this precept he was tried whether he could trust God further than he saw him; for he must leave his own country, to go to a *land that God would show him.* He does not say, "It is a land that I will give thee," but merely, "a land that I will show thee." He must follow God with an implicit faith, though he had no particular securities given him that he should be no loser by leaving his country, to follow God.

II. Here is an encouraging promise, nay, it is a complication of promises, many, and exceedingly great and precious. Note, All God's precepts are attended with promises to the obedient. If we obey the command, God will not fail to perform the promise. Here are six promises:—

1. *I will make of thee a great nation.* When God took him from his own people, he promised to make him the head of another; he cut him off from being the branch of a wild olive, to make him the root of a good olive. This promise was, (1) A great relief to Abram's burden; for he had now no child. Note, God knows how to suit his favours to the wants and necessities of his children. He that has a plaster for every sore will first provide one for that which is most painful. (2) A great trial to Abram's faith; for his wife had been long barren.

2. *I will bless thee.* Leave thy father's house, and I will give thee a father's blessing.

3. *I will make thy name great.* By deserting his country, he lost his name there. Having no child, he feared he should have no name; but God will make him a great nation, and so make him a great name.

4. *Thou shalt be a blessing;* that is, (1) "Thy happiness shall be a sample of happiness, so that those who would bless their friends shall only pray that God would make them like Abram"; as Ruth iv. 11. (2) "Thy life shall be a blessing to the places where thou shalt sojourn."

5. *I will bless those that bless thee and curse him that curseth thee.* This made it a kind of a league, offensive and defensive, between God and Abram.

6. *In thee shall all the families of the earth be blessed.* This was the promise that crowned all the rest; for it points to the Messiah, in whom *all the promises are yea and amen.* Note, (1) Jesus Christ is the great blessing of the world, the greatest that ever the world was blessed with. He is a family blessing, by him salvation is brought to the house (Luke xix. 9).

Verses 4–5

I. Abram's removal out of his country, out of Ur first and afterwards out of Haran, in compliance with the call of God. He *went out, not knowing whither he went* (Heb. xi. 8), but knowing whom he followed.

II. His age when he removed: he was *seventy-five years old,* an age when he should rather have had rest and settlement; but, if God will have him to begin the world again now in his old age, he will submit. Here is an instance of an old convert.

III. The company and cargo that he took with him.

1. He took his wife, and his nephew Lot, with him. Note, It is very comfortable when husband and wife agree to go together in the way to heaven. Lot also, his kinsman, was influenced by Abram's good example, who was perhaps his guardian after the death of his father, and he was willing to go along with him too.

2. They took all their effects with them—*all their substance* and movable goods, *that they had gathered.* To have thrown away his substance, because God had promised to bless him, would have been to tempt God, not to trust him.

IV. Here is their happy arrival at their journey's end: *They went forth to go into the land of Canaan;* so they did before (*ch.* xi. 31), and then took up short, but now they held on their way, and, by the good hand of their God upon them, to the land of Canaan they came, where by a fresh revelation they were told that this was the land God promised to show them.

Verses 6–9

One would have expected that Abram having had such an extraordinary call to Canaan some great event should have followed upon his arrival there.

Little notice is taken of him for God will have him to live by faith.

I. How little comfort he had in the land he came to; for, 1. He had it not to himself: He found the country peopled and possessed by Canaanites, who were likely to be but bad neighbours and worse landlords. 2. He had not a settlement in it. All good people must look upon themselves as strangers and sojourners in this world, and by faith sit loose to it as a strange country. We must be journeying, and going on still from strength to strength, as having not yet attained.

II. How much comfort he had in the God he followed.

1. God spoke to him good words and comfortable words: *Unto thy seed will I give this land.* Enemies may part us and our tents, us and our altars, but not us and our God. Mercies to the children are mercies to the parents. "I will give it, not to thee, but to thy seed"; it is a grant in reversion to his seed, which Abram understood also as a grant to himself, for he looked for a heavenly country, Heb. xi. 16.

2. Abram *built an altar unto the Lord who appeared to him, and called on the name of the Lord, v. 7, 8.* Thus he returned God's visit, and kept up his correspondence with heaven, as one that resolved it should not fail on his side. Wherever he had a tent God had an altar, and that an altar sanctified by prayer. The *souls he had gotten in Haran,* being discipled, must be further taught. The way of family worship is a good old way, is no novel invention, but the ancient usage of all the saints. Wherever we go, let us not fail to take our religion along with us.

Verses 10-13

Here is, 1. A famine in the land of Canaan, *a grievous famine,* and a very sore trial it was; it tried what he would think. Nothing short of a strong faith could keep up good thoughts of God under such a providence. Now he was tried whether he could preserve an unshaken confidence that the God who brought him to Canaan would maintain him there, and whether he could rejoice in him as the God of his salvation when the fig-tree did not blossom, Hab. iii. 17, 18. It is possible for a man to be in the way of duty, and in the way to happiness, and yet meet with great troubles and disappointments.

II. Abram's removal into Egypt, upon occasion of this famine. See how wisely God provides that there should be plenty in one place when there was scarcity in another. We must not expect needless miracles. When he must, for a time, quit Canaan, he chooses to go to Egypt, which lay south-west, the contrary way, that he might not so much as seem to look back. See Heb. xi. 15, 16.

III. A great fault which Abram was guilty of, in denying his wife, and pretending that she was his sister. The scripture is impartial in relating the misdeeds of the most celebrated saints, which are recorded, not for our imitation, but for our admonition, that he *who thinks he stands may take heed lest he fall.* 2. That which was at the bottom of it was a jealous timorous fancy he had that some of the Egyptians would be so charmed with the beauty of Sarai that, if they should know he was her husband, they would find some way or other to take him off, that they might marry her. The grace Abram was most eminent for was faith; and yet he thus fell through unbelief and distrust of the divine Providence, even *after God had appeared to him twice.* Alas! what will become of the willows, when the cedars are thus shaken?

Verses 14-20

Here is, I. The danger Sarai was in of having her chastity violated by the king of Egypt. They recommended her to the king, and she was presently taken into Pharaoh's house, as Esther into the seraglio of Ahasuerus (Esth. ii. 8), in order to her being taken into his bed.

II. The deliverance of Sarai from this danger. For if God did not deliver us we should soon be ruined. He deals not with us according to our deserts.

1. God chastised Pharaoh, and so prevented the progress of his sin. Those are happy chastisements that hinder us in a sinful way, and effectually bring us to our duty.

2. Pharaoh reproved Abram, and then dismissed him with respect.

(1) The reproof was calm, but very just: *What is this that thou hast done?* Pharaoh reasons with him: *Why didst thou not tell me that she was thy wife?* intimating that, if he had known this, he would not have taken her into his house. We have often found more of virtue, honour, and conscience, in some people than we thought they possessed; and it ought to be a pleasure to us to be thus disappointed, as Abram was here, who found Pharaoh to be a better man than he expected. Charity teaches us to hope the best.

(2) The dismission was kind and very generous. He restored him his wife without offering any injury to her honour. *Pharaoh commanded his men concerning him.* He appointed them, when Abram was disposed to return home, after the famine, to conduct him safely out of the country, as his convoy.

Observe a resemblance between this deliverance of Abram out of Egypt and the deliverance of his seed thence: 430 years after Abram went into Egypt on occasion of a famine they went thither on occasion of a famine also; he was fetched out with great plagues on Pharaoh, so were they. For God's care of his people is the same *yesterday, to-day, and for ever.*

Chapter 13

In this chapter we have a further account concerning Abram. I. In general, of his condition and behaviour in the land of promise. 1. His riches, ver. 1, 3, 4, 18. 2. His riches, ver. 2. 3. His devotion, ver. 4, 18. II. A particular account of a quarrel that happened between him and Lot. 1. The unhappy occasion of their strife, ver. 5, 6. III. The making up of the quarrel, by the prudence of Abram, ver. 8, 9. IV. Lot's departure from Abram to the plain of Sodom, ver. 10-13. V. God's appearance to Abram, to confirm the promise of the land of Canaan to him, ver. 14, &c.

Verses 1-4

1. Abram's return out of Egypt, *v.* 1. He came himself and brought all his with him back again to Canaan.

II. His wealth: *He was very rich, v.* 2. He was very *heavy,* so the Hebrew word signifies; for *riches are a burden.* There is a burden of care in getting them, fear in keeping them, temptation in using them, guilt in abusing them, sorrow in losing them, and a burden of account, at last, to be given up concerning them. God, in his providence, sometimes makes good men rich men, and teaches them how to abound, as well as how to suffer want. Though it is hard for a rich man to get to heaven, yet it is not impossible, Mark x. 23, 24. Outward prosperity, if well managed, furnishes an opportunity of doing so much the more good.

III. His removal to Beth-el, *v.* 3, 4. Thither he went, not only because there he had formerly had his tent, but because there he had formerly had his altar. Long afterwards God sent Jacob to this same place on that errand (*ch.* xxxv. 1). We have need to be reminded of our solemn vows; and perhaps the place where they were made may help to bring them afresh to mind, and it may therefore do us good to visit it.

IV. His devotion there. His altar was gone, so that he could not offer sacrifice; but *he called on the name of the Lord*, as he had done, *ch.* xii. 8. Abram did not leave his religion behind him in Egypt, as many do in their travels.

Verses 5–9

An unhappy falling out between Abram and Lot, who had hitherto been inseparable companions.

I. The occasion of their quarrel was their riches. Riches are often an occasion of strife and contention. Poverty and travail, wants and wanderings, could not separate between Abram and Lot; but riches did. Friends are soon lost; but God is a friend from whose love neither the height of prosperity nor the depth of adversity shall separate us.

II. The strife began between *the herdsmen of Abram's cattle and the herdsmen of Lot's cattle, v.* 7. They strove which should have the better pasture or the better water.

III. The aggravation of the quarrel was that *the Canaanite and the Perizzite dwelt then in the land*; this made the quarrel, 1. Very dangerous. 2. Very scandalous. The quarrels of professors are the reproach of profession, and give occasion, as much as anything, to the enemies of the Lord to blaspheme.

IV. The making up of this quarrel was very happy. It is best to preserve the peace, that it be not broken; but the next best is, if differences do happen, with all speed to accommodate them. The motion for staying this strife was made by Abram.

1. His petition for peace was very affectionate: *Let there be no strife, I pray thee.* Abram knew how to turn away wrath with a soft answer; he made the first overture of reconciliation. The people of God should always approve themselves a peaceable people; whatever others are for, they must be for peace.

2. His plea for peace was very cogent. (1) "Let there be no strife *between me and thee.* Let the Canaanites and Perizzites contend about trifles; but let not thee and me fall out, who know better things, and look for a better country." The remembrance of old friendships should quickly put an end to new quarrels which at any time happen. (2) Let it be remembered that *we are brethren.* We are rational creatures, and should be ruled by reason. We are men, and not brutes, men, and not children. We are brethren. Men of the same nature, of the same kindred and family, of the same religion, companions in obedience, companions in patience.

3. His proposal for peace was very fair. "Why should we quarrel for room, while there is room enough for us both?" He offers him a sufficient share of the land they were in. He gives him his choice, and offers to take up with his leavings: *If thou wilt take the left hand, I will go to the right.* There was all the reason in the world that Abram should choose first; yet he recedes from his right. It is a noble conquest to be willing to yield for the sake of peace; it is the conquest of ourselves, and our own pride and passion, Matt. v.

Verses 10–13

The choice that Lot made when he parted from Abram. Abram having offered him the choice, without compliment he accepted it, and made his election. Passion and selfishness make men rude.

I. How much he had an eye to the goodness of the land. He *beheld all the plain of Jordan*, the flat country in which Sodom stood, that it was admirably *well watered everywhere.* It would yield him a comfortable settlement, and in such a fruitful soil he should certainly thrive, and grow very rich: and this was all he looked at. But what came of it? Why, the next news we hear of him is that he is in the briars among them, he and his carried captive. At last, God fired the town over his head, and forced

him to the mountain for safety who chose the plain for wealth and pleasure. Sensual choices are sinful choices, and seldom speed well. In all our choices this principle should overrule us, That that is best for us which is best for our souls.

II. *But the men of Sodom were wicked, v.* 13. Some sinners are the worse for living in a good land. So the Sodomites were. Filthy Sodomites dwell in a city, in a fruitful plain, while faithful Abram and his pious family dwell in tents upon the barren mountains. Now Lot's coming to dwell among the Sodomites may be considered a great mercy to them, and a likely means of bringing them to repentance; for now they had a prophet among them and a preacher of righteousness, and, if they had hearkened to him, they might have been reformed, and the ruin prevented.

Verses 14–18

An account of a gracious visit which God paid to Abram, to confirm the promise to him and his.

I. When it was that God renewed and ratified the promise: 1. After the quarrel was over. 2. After Abram's humble self-denying condescensions to Lot for the preserving of peace. 3. After he had lost the comfortable society of his kinsman, and his heart was saddened, then God came to him with these good words and comfortable words. Lot perhaps had the better land, yet Abram had the better *title.* Lot had the paradise, such as it was, but Abram had the promise.

II. The promises themselves with which God now comforted and enriched Abram. Two things he assures him of—a good land, and a numerous issue to enjoy it.

1. Here is the grant of a good land, a land famous above all lands, for it was to be the holy land, and Immanuel's land. Note, That which God has to show us is infinitely better and more desirable than anything that the world has to offer to our view. He secures this land to him and his seed for ever (*v.* 15).

2. Here is the promise of a numerous issue to replenish this good land, so that it should never be lost for want of heirs (*v.* 16). The same God that provides the inheritance provides the heirs.

We are told what Abram did when God had thus confirmed the promise to him, *v.* 18. 1. He *removed his tent.* In compliance with God's will herein, *he removes his tent*, conforming himself to the condition of a pilgrim. 2. He *built there an altar*, in token of his thankfulness to God.

CHAPTER 14

We have four things in the story of this chapter. I. A war with the king of Sodom and his allies, ver. 1–11. II. The captivity of Lot in that war, ver. 12. III. Abram's rescue of Lot from that captivity, ver. 13–16. IV. Abram's return from the expedition (ver. 17). Here we have that promise to Abram in part fulfilled, that God would make his name great.

Verses 1–12

An account of the first war that ever we read of in scripture.

I. The parties engaged in it. The invaders were four kings, two of them no less than kings of Shinar and Elam (that is, Chaldea and Persia). The invaded were the kings of five cities that lay near together in the plain of Jordan, namely, Sodom, Gomorrah, Admah, Zeboiim, and Zoar.

II. The occasion of this war was the revolt of the five kings from under the government of Chedorlaomer. Twelve years they served him. Small joy they had of their fruitful land, while thus they were tributaries to a foreign power, and could not call what they had their own. In the thirteenth year, beginning to be weary of their subjection, they rebelled, denied their tribute, and attempted to shake off the yoke and retrieve their ancient liberties. In the fourteenth year, after some pause and preparation, Chedorlaomer, in conjunction with his allies, set himself to chastise and reduce the rebels.

III. The progress and success of the war. The four kings laid the neighbouring countries waste and enriched themselves with the spoil of them (v. 5–7). 1. The forces of the king of Sodom and his allies were routed. 2. The cities were plundered, v. 11. 3. Lot was carried captive, v. 12. They took Lot among the rest, and his goods. Many an honest man fares the worse for his wicked neighbours. It is therefore our wisdom to separate ourselves and so deliver ourselves, Rev. xviii. 4. Note, When we go out of the way of our duty we put ourselves from under God's protection, and cannot expect that the choices which are made by our lusts should issue to our comfort.

Verses 13–16

We have here an account of the only military action we ever find Abram engaged in, and this he was prompted to, not by his avarice or ambition, but purely by a principle of charity; it was not to enrich himself, but to help his friend.

I. The tidings brought him of his kinsman's distress. 1. He is here called *Abram the Hebrew*, that is, the son and follower of Heber, in whose family the profession of the true religion was kept up in that degenerate age. 2. The tidings were brought by one that had escaped with his life for a prey.

II. The preparations he made for this expedition. This shows that Abram was, 1. A great man, who had so many servants depending upon him. 2. A good man, who not only served God himself, but instructed all about him in the service of God. 3. A wise man, for, though he was a man of peace, yet he disciplined his servants for war. Though our holy religion teaches us to be for peace, yet it does not forbid us to provide for war.

III. His allies and confederates in this expedition. He prevailed with his neighbours, *Aner, Eshcol, and Mamre*, to go along with him. Those who depend on God's help, yet, in times of distress, ought to make use of men's help, as Providence offers it; else they tempt God.

IV. His courage and conduct were very remarkable. 1. There was a great deal of bravery in the enterprise itself, considering the disadvantages he lay under. What could one family of husbandmen and shepherds do against the armies of four princes, who now came fresh from blood and victory? Religion tends to make men, not cowardly, but truly valiant. The true Christian is the true hero. 2. There was a great deal of policy in the management of it. Note, Honest policy is a good friend both to our safety and to our usefulness. The serpent's head (provided it be nothing akin to the old serpent) may well become a good Christian's body, especially if it have a dove's eye in it, Matt. x. 16.

V. His success was very considerable, v. 15, 16. He defeated his enemies, and rescued his friends; and we do not find that he sustained any loss.

1. He rescued his kinsman; twice here he is called his *brother Lot*. The remembrance of the relation that was between them, both by nature and grace, made him forget the little quarrel that had been between them. Note, (1) We ought to be ready, whenever it is in the power of our hands, to succour and relieve those that are in distress. (2) Though others have been wanting in their duty to us, yet we must not therefore deny our duty to them. Some have said that they can more easily forgive their

enemies than their friends; but we shall see ourselves obliged to forgive both.

2. He rescued the rest of the captives, for Lot's sake, though they were strangers to him and such as he was under no obligation to at all. Note, As we have opportunity we must do good to all men.

Verses 17–20

This paragraph begins with the mention of the respect which the king of Sodom paid to Abram, but, before a particular account is given of this, the story of Melchizedek is briefly related.

I. Who he was. He was *king of Salem* and *priest of the most high God*; and other glorious things are said of him, Heb. vii. 1, &c. 1. Rabbinical writers conclude that Melchizedek was Shem the son of Noah. But why should his name be changed? And how came he to settle in Canaan? 2. Many Christian writers have thought that this was an appearance of the Son of God himself. He appeared to him as a righteous king, owning a righteous cause, and giving peace. It is difficult to imagine that any mere man should be said to *be without father, without mother, and without descent, having neither beginning of days nor end of life*, Heb. vii. 3. 3. The most commonly received opinion is that Melchizedek was a Canaanitish prince, that reigned in Salem, and kept up the true religion there; but, if so, why should his name occur here only in all the story of Abram? The *Arabic Catena* gives this account of Melchizedek, That he was the son of Heraclim, the son of Peleg, the son of Eber, and that his mother's name was Salathiel, the daughter of Gomer, the son of Japheth, the son of Noah.

II. What he did. 1. He *brought forth bread and wine*, for the refreshment of Abram and his soldiers, and in congratulation of their victory. This he did as a king. 2. As priest of the most high God, he blessed Abram, which we may suppose a greater refreshment to Abram than his bread and wine were. Thus God, having raised up his Son Jesus, has sent him to bless us, as one having authority; and those whom he blesses are blessed indeed.

III. What he said, v. 19, 20. Two things were said by him:—1. He blessed Abram from God. Observe the titles he here gives to God, which are very glorious. (1) *The most high God.* (2) *Possessor of heaven and earth*, that is, rightful owner, and sovereign Lord, of all the creatures, because he made them. 2. He blessed God for Abram (v. 20): and *blessed be the most high God*.

IV. What was done to him: *Abram gave him tithes of all*, that is, of the spoils, Heb. vii. 4. This may be looked upon, 1. As a gratuity presented to Melchizedek, by way of return for his tokens of respect. 2. As an offering vowed and dedicated to the most high God, and therefore put into the hands of Melchizedek his priest. (1) When we have received some signal mercy from God, it is very fit that we should express our thankfulness by some special act of pious charity. (2) That the tenth of our increase is a very fit proportion to be set apart for the honour of God and the service of his sanctuary. (3) That Jesus Christ, our great Melchizedek, is to have homage done him, and to be humbly acknowledged by every one of us as our king and priest; and not only the tithe of all, but all we have, must be surrendered and given up to him.

Verses 21–24

We have here an account of what passed between Abram and the king of Sodom.

I. The king of Sodom's grateful offer to Abram (v. 21): *Give me the soul, and take thou the substance*; so the Hebrew reads it. Here he fairly begs the persons, but as freely bestows the goods on Abram.

II. Abram's generous refusal of this offer. He not only resigned the persons to him, but he restored all the goods too. He would not take *from a thread to a shoe-latchet*. What are all the ornaments and delights of sense to one that has God and heaven ever in his eye ?

1. Abram ratifies this resolution with a solemn oath. The ceremony used in this oath: *I have lifted up my hand*. In religious swearing we appeal to God's knowledge of our truth and sincerity and imprecate his wrath if we swear falsely, and the *lifting up of the hand* is very significant and expressive of both.

2. He backs his refusal with a good reason: *Lest thou shouldest say, I have made Abram rich*, which would reflect reproach, (1) Upon the promise and covenant of God. And, (2) Upon the piety and charity of Abram. The people of God must, for their credit's sake, take heed of doing anything that looks mean or mercenary, or that savours of covetousness and self-seeking.

CHAPTER 15

In this chapter we have a solemn treaty between God and Abram concerning a covenant that was to be established between them. In the former chapter we had Abram in the field with kings; here we find him in the mount with God; and, though there he looked great, yet, methinks, here he looks much greater. The covenant to be settled between God and Abram was a covenant of promises; accordingly, here is, I. A general assurance of God's kindness and good-will to Abram, ver. 1. II. A particular declaration of the purposes of his love concerning him, in two things:—1. That he would give him a numerous issue, ver. 2–6. 2. That he would give him Canaan for an inheritance, ver. 7–21. The promised seed and the promised land, comforts indeed to this great believer, were both typical of those two invaluable blessings, Christ and heaven.

Verse 1

The time when God made this treaty with Abram. 1. After that famous act of generous charity which Abram had done, in rescuing his friends and neighbours out of distress, and that, *not for price nor reward*. 2. After that victory which he had obtained over four kings.

II. The manner in which God conversed with Abram: which supposes Abram awake, and some visible appearance of the Shechinah, or some sensible token of the presence of the divine glory.

III. The gracious assurance God gave him of his favour to him.

1. He called him by name—*Abram*. God's good word does us good when it is spoken by his Spirit to us in particular. The word says, *Ho, every one* (Isa. lv. 1), the Spirit says, *Ho, such a one*.

2. He cautioned him against being disquieted and confounded: *Fear not, Abram*. Let the sinners in Sion be afraid, but fear not, Abram.

3. He assured him of safety and happiness, that he should for ever be, (1) As safe as God himself could keep him. Not only the God of Israel, but a God to Israel. (2) As happy as God himself could make him: I will be *thy exceedingly great reward*; not only thy rewarder, but thy reward. Abram had generously refused the rewards which the king of Sodom offered him.

Verses 2–6

The assurance given to Abram of a numerous offspring which should descend from him.

1. Abram's repeated complaint, *v.* 2, 3. This was that which gave occasion to this promise. The great affliction that sat heavy upon Abram was the want of a child. Though we must never complain of God, yet we have leave to complain to him, and it is some ease to a burdened spirit to open its case to a faithful and compassionate friend: such a friend God is. Now his complaint is four-fold:—1. That he had no

child (*v.* 3). 2. That he was never likely to have any, intimated in that, *I go*, or "*I am going, childless*, going into years, going down the hill apace." 3. That his servants were for the present and were likely to be to him instead of sons. 4. That the want of a son was so great a trouble to him that it took away the comfort of all his enjoyments: "All is nothing to me, if I have not a son." But, If we suppose that Abram, herein, had an eye to the promised seed, the importunity of his desire was very commendable: all was nothing to him, if he had not an assurance of his relation to the Messiah, of which God had already encouraged him to maintain the expectation. "This, and the other, I have; but what will all this avail me, if I go Christless ?"

II. God's gracious answer to this complaint. 1. God gave him an express promise of a son, *v.* 4. This that is born in thy house *shall not be thy heir*, as thou fearest, but one that shall *come forth out of thy own bowels shall be thy heir*. 2. To affect him the more with this promise, he took him out, and showed him the stars, and then tells him, *So shall thy seed be*, *v.* 5. (1) So numerous; the stars seem innumerable to a common eye: Abram feared he should have no child at all. (2) So illustrious, resembling the stars in splendour. Abram's seed, according to his flesh, were like the dust of the earth (*ch.* xiii. 16), but his spiritual seed are like the stars of heaven, not only numerous, but glorious, and very precious.

III. Abram's firm belief of the promise God now made him, and God's favourable acceptance of his faith, *v.* 6. See how the apostle magnifies this faith of Abram, and makes it a standing example, Rom. iv. 19–21. *God counted it to him for righteousness;* that is, upon the score of this he was accepted of God, and, as the rest of the patriarchs, by faith he *obtained witness that he was righteous*, Heb. xi. 4. This is urged in the New Testament to prove that we are justified by faith without the works of the law (Rom. iv. 3; Gal. iii. 6). All believers are justified as Abram was, and it was his faith that was *counted to him for righteousness*.

Verses 7–11

The assurance given to Abram of the land of Canaan for an inheritance.

I. God declares his purpose concerning it, *v.* 7. Those that are sure of an interest in the promised seed will see no reason to doubt of a title to the promised land. If Christ is ours, heaven is ours. When he believed the former promise (*v.* 6) then God explained and ratified this to him. Three things God here reminds Abram of, for his encouragement concerning the promise of this good land:—

1. What God is in himself: *I am the Lord Jehovah*. "I can give it to thee, whatever opposition may be made, though by the sons of Anak." God never promises more than he is able to perform, as men often do.

2. What he had done for Abram. He had brought him out of Ur of the Chaldees. The Jewish writers have a tradition that Abram was cast into a fiery furnace for refusing to worship idols, and was miraculously delivered. A foundation mercy, the beginning of mercy, peculiar mercy to Abram, and therefore a pledge and earnest of further mercy, Isa. lxvi. 9.

3. What he intended to do yet further for him: "*I brought thee* hither, on purpose *to give thee this land to inherit it*, not only to possess it, but to possess it as an inheritance, which is the sweetest and surest title." The great thing God designs in all his dealings with his people is to bring them safely to heaven.

II. Abram desires a sign: *Whereby shall I know that I shall inherit it ?, v.* 8. 1. For the strengthening and confirming of his own faith; he believed (*v.* 6), but here he prays, *Lord, help me* against *my unbelief. Now* he believed, but he desired a sign to be treasured up against an hour of temptation. 2. For the ratifying of the promise to his posterity, that they also might be brought to believe it.

III. God directs Abram to make preparations for a sacrifice, intending by that to give him a sign, and Abram makes preparation accordingly (*v.* 9–11). Those that would receive the assurances of God's favour, and would have their faith confirmed, must attend instituted ordinances, and expect to meet with God in them. Abram took as God appointed him, though as yet he knew not how these things should become a sign to him. This was not the first instance of Abram's implicit obedience. He divided the beasts in the midst, according to the ceremony used in confirming covenants, Jer. xxxiv. 18, 19, where it is said, They cut *the calf in twain, and passed between the parts.* While God's appearing to own his sacrifice was deferred, Abram continued waiting, and his expectations were raised by the delay; when *the fowls came down upon the carcases* to prey upon them, *Abram drove them away* (*v.* 11). When vain thoughts, like these fowls, come down upon our sacrifices, we must drive them away, and *attend on God without distraction.*

Verses 12–16
A full and particular discovery made to Abram of God's purposes concerning his seed.
I. The time when God came to him with this discovery: *When the sun was going down,* or *declining,* about the time of the *evening oblation.* God often keeps his people long in expectation of the comforts he designs them, for the confirmation of their faith; but though the answers of prayer, and the performance of promises, come slowly, yet they come surely.
II. The preparatives for this discovery. 1. *A deep sleep fell upon Abram,* not a common sleep through weariness or carelessness, but a divine ecstasy. The doors of the body were locked up, that the soul might be private and retired, and might act the more freely. 2. With this sleep, *a horror of great darkness fell upon him.* This great darkness, which brought horror with it, was designed, (1) To strike an awe upon the spirit of Abram, and to possess him with an holy reverence. Holy fear prepares the soul for holy joy; the spirit of bondage makes way for the spirit of adoption. (2) To be a specimen of the methods of God's dealings with his seed. They must first be in the horror and darkness of Egyptian slavery, and then enter with joy into the good land.
III. The prediction itself. Several things are here foretold.
1. The suffering state of Abram's seed for a long time, *v.* 13. He must know that the promised seed should be a persecuted seed. Now we have here,
(1) The particulars of their sufferings. [1] They shall be strangers. Thus the heirs of heaven are first strangers on earth. [2] They shall be servants. The Canaanites serve under a curse, the Hebrews under a blessing. [3] They shall be sufferers. Those whom they serve shall afflict them; see Exod. i. 11.
(2) The continuance of their sufferings—*four hundred years.* This was a long time, but a limited time.
2. The judgment of the enemies of Abram's seed: *That nation whom they shall serve,* even the Egyptians, *will I judge, v.* 14. Though God may suffer persecutors and oppressors to trample upon his people a great while, yet he will certainly reckon with them at last; for his *day is coming,* Ps. xxxvii. 12, 13.
3. The deliverance of Abram's seed out of Egypt. That great event is here foretold: *afterwards shall they come out with great substance.* It is here promised, (1) That they should be enlarged. The destruction

of oppressors is the redemption of the oppressed. (2) That they should be enriched. God took care they should have, not only a good land to go to, but a good stock to carry with them.
4. Their happy settlement in Canaan, *v.* 16. They shall not only come out of Egypt, but *they shall come hither again,* hither to the land of Canaan, wherein thou now art.
5. Abram's peaceful quiet death and burial, before these things should come to pass, *v.* 15. Note, Good men are sometimes greatly favoured by being *taken away from the evil to come,* Isa. lvii. 1. Let this satisfy Abram, that, for his part,
(1) He shall *go to his fathers in peace.* Note, [1] Even the friends and favourites of Heaven are not exempted from the stroke of death. [2] Good men die willingly; they are not fetched, they are not forced, but they go. [3] At death we go to our fathers, godly fathers that have gone before us to the state of the blessed, Heb. xii. 23. Outward peace, to the last, is promised to Abram, peace and truth in his days, whatever should come afterwards (2 Kings xx. 19); peace with God, and everlasting peace, are sure to all the seed.
(2) He shall be *buried in a good old age.* He shall not only die in peace, but die in honour. Old age is a blessing, a great opportunity for usefulness.

Verses 17–21
The covenant ratified (*v.* 17); the sign which Abram desired was given.
1. The *smoking furnace* signified the affliction of his seed in Egypt.
2. The *burning lamp* denotes comfort in this affliction; and this God showed to Abram, at the same time that he showed him the *smoking furnace.* (1) Light denotes deliverance out of the furnace. (2) The lamp denotes direction in the smoke. God's word was their lamp: this word to Abram was so, it was a light shining in a dark place. (3) The burning lamp denotes the destruction of their enemies who kept them so long in the furnace.
3. The passing of these between the pieces was the confirming of the covenant God now made with him. It is probable that the furnace and lamp, which passed between the pieces, burnt and consumed them, and so completed the sacrifice, and testified God's acceptance of it, as of Gideon's (Judges vi. 21). 1. So it intimates, (1) That God's covenants with man are made by sacrifice (Ps. l. 5), by Christ, the great sacrifice: no agreement without atonement. (2) God's acceptance of our spiritual sacrifices is an earnest of further favours.
II. The covenant repeated and explained: *Unto thy seed have I given this land, v.* 18. Here is,
1. A rehearsal of the grant. God's promises are God's gifts, and are so to be accounted. The possession is as sure, in due time, as if it were now actually delivered to them. What God has promised is as sure as if it were already done; hence, it is said, *He that believes hath everlasting life* (John iii. 36), for he shall as surely go to heaven as if he were there already.
2. A recital of the particulars granted, such as is usual in the grants of lands. The land granted is here described in its utmost extent because it was to be a type of the heavenly inheritance, where there is room enough: in our father's house are many mansions.

CHAPTER 16

Hagar is the person mostly concerned in the story of this chapter, an obscure Egyptian woman. Probably she was one of those maid-servants whom the king of Egypt bestowed upon Abram, ch. xii. 16. Concerning her, we have four things in this chapter:—

I. Her marriage to Abram her master, ver. 1–3. II. Her mis-behaviour towards Sarai her mistress, ver. 4–6. III. Her discourse with an angel that met her in her flight, ver. 7–14. IV. Her delivery of a son, ver. 15, 16.

Verses 1–3

We have here the marriage of Abram to Hagar, who was his secondary wife. It seems to have proceeded from an irregular desire to build up families for the speedier peopling of the world and the church. Certainly it must not be so now. Christ has reduced this matter to the first institution, and makes the marriage uinon to be between one man and one woman only.

I. The maker of this match was Sarai herself. It is the policy of Satan to tempt us by our nearest and dearest relations. It would have been much more for Sarai's interest if Abram had kept to the rule of God's law instead of being guided by her foolish projects.

II. The inducement to it was Sarai's barrenness. She used this as an argument with Abram to marry his maid; and he was prevailed upon by this argument to do it.

Abram's compliance with Sarai's proposal, we have reason to think, was from an earnest desire of the promised seed, on whom the covenant should be entailed. God had told him that his heir should be a son of his body, but had not yet told him that it should be a son by Sarai; therefore he thought, "Why not by Hagar, since Sarai herself proposed it?" Fleshly wisdom, as it anticipates God's time of mercy, so it puts us out of God's way. This would be happily prevented if we would ask counsel of God by the word and-by prayer, before we attempt that which is important and suspicious.

Verses 4–6

The immediate bad consequences of Abram's unhappy marriage to Hagar. A great deal of mischief it made quickly. When we do not well both sin and trouble lie at the door. See it in this story.

I. Sarai is despised, and thereby provoked and put into a passion, *v.* 4. Hagar thinks herself a better woman than Sarai, more favoured by Heaven, and likely to be better beloved by Abram, and therefore she will not submit as she has done. 2. We justly suffer by those whom we have sinfully indulged, and it is a righteous thing with God to make those instruments of our trouble whom we have made instruments of our sin.

II. Abram is clamoured upon, and cannot be easy while Sarai is out of humour; she unjustly charges him with the injury (*v.* 5). She rashly appeals to God in the case: *The Lord judge between me and thee*; as if Abram had refused to right her. When passion is upon the throne, reason is out of doors, and is neither heard nor spoken. 2. Those are not always in the right who are most loud and forward in appealing to God. Rash and bold imprecations are commonly evidences of guilt and a bad cause.

III Hagar is afflicted, and driven from the house, *v.* 6. She herself had first given the provocation, by despising her mistress.

Verses 7–9

The first mention we have in scripture of an angel's appearance.

I. How the angel arrested her in her flight, *v.* 7. She was making towards her own country, towards Egypt. It were well if our afflictions would make us think of our home. But Hagar was now out of the way of her duty, and going further astray. 2. God suffers those that are out of the way to wander awhile, that when they see their folly, they may be the better disposed to return. Hagar was not stopped till she was in the wilderness. God brings us into a wilderness, and there meets us, Hos. ii. 14.

II. How he examined her, *v.* 8. Observe,

1. He called her *Hagar, Sarai's maid.* Though she was Abram's wife, yet he calls her *Sarai's maid*, to humble her. Note, Though civility teaches us to call others by their highest titles, yet humility and wisdom teach us to call ourselves by the lowest. Sarai's maid ought to be in Sarai's tent, and not wandering in the wilderness and sauntering by a fountain of water.

2. The questions the angel put to her were proper and very pertinent. (1) *"Whence comest thou?"* Consider that thou art running away from duty. (2) *"Whither wilt thou go? Thou art running thyself into sin, in Egypt, and into danger, in the wilderness."* Note, Those who are forsaking God and their duty would do well to remember not only *whence they have fallen*, but *whither they are falling.*

3. Her answer was honest, and a fair confession: *I flee from the face of my mistress.*

4. How he sent her back, with suitable and compassionate counsel: *"Return to thy mistress, and submit thyself under her hand, v.* 9.

Verses 10–14

We may suppose that the angel having given Hagar that good counsel (*v.* 9) to *return to her mistress* she immediately promised to do so, and was setting her face homeward; and then the angel went on to encourage her with an assurance of the mercy God had in store for her and her seed: for God will meet those with mercy that are returning to their duty. *I said, I will confess, and thou forgavest*, Ps. xxxii. 5.

I. A prediction concerning her posterity given her for her comfort in her present distress. Note, It is a great comfort to women with child to think that they are under the particular cognizance and care of the divine Providence. Now, 1. The angel assures her of a safe delivery, and that of a *son*, which Abram desired. She was saved in child-bearing, not only by providence, but by promise. 2. He names her child, which is an honour both to her and it: Call him *Ishmael, God will hear*; and the reason is, because the Lord has heard. Even where there is little cry of devotion, the God of pity sometimes graciously hears the cry of affliction. Tears speak as well as prayers. 3. He promises her a numerous offspring, *v.* 10. It is supposed that the Turks at this day descend from Ishmael; and they are a great people. He gives a character of the child she should bear. He *will be a wild man*; *a wild ass of a man* (so the word is), rude and bold, and fearing no man—untamed, untractable, living at large, and impatient of service and restraint. *His hand against every man* —this is his *sin; and every man's hand against him*— this is his *punishment.* Note, Those that have turbulent spirits have commonly troublesome lives. And yet, he should live in safety. Note, Many that are much exposed by their own imprudence are yet strangely preserved by the divine Providence, so much better is God to them than they deserve.

II. Hagar's pious reflection upon this gracious appearance of God to her, *v.* 13, 14. Observe in what she said,

1. Her awful adoration of God's omniscience and providence, with application of it to herself: *Thou God seest me*; this should be, with her, his name for ever. *God is* (as the ancients expressed it) *all eye.* He that sees all sees me, as David (Ps. cxxxix. 1), *O Lord, thou hast searched me, and known me.* It is a proper word for a penitent:—"Thou seest the sincerity and seriousness of my return and repentance."

2. Her humble admiration of God's favour to her: *"Have I also here looked after him that seeth me?"*

Probably she knew not who it was that talked with her till he was departing and then she looked after him, with a reflection like that of the two disciples, Luke xxiv. 31, 32. Not only in Abram's tent and at his altar, but *here* also, in this wilderness? Here, where I never expected it, where I was out of the way of my duty? *Lord, how is it?*" John xiv. 22.

III. The name which this gave to the place: *Beer-lahai-roi, The well of him that liveth and seeth me, v.* 14. This was the place where the God of glory manifested the special care he took of a poor woman in distress.

Verses 15–16

It is here taken for granted that Hagar did as the angel commanded her, returning to her mistress and then, in the fulness of time, she brought forth her son.

CHAPTER 17

This chapter contains articles of agreement covenanted and concluded upon between the Father of mercies, on the one part, and Abram, the father of the faithful, on the other part. Abram is therefore called "the friend of God," not only because he was the man of his counsel, but because he was the man of his covenant; both these secrets were with him. Mention was made of this covenant (ch. xv. 18), but here it is put into the form of a covenant. Here are, I. The circumstances of the making of this covenant, the time and manner (ver. 1), and the posture Abram was in, ver. 3. II. The covenant itself. 1. That he should be the father of many nations (ver. 4, 6), and, in token of this, his name was changed, ver. 5. 2. That God would be a God to him and his seed, and would give them the land of Canaan, ver. 7, 8. And the seal of this part of the covenant was circumcision, ver. 9–14. 3. That he should have a son by Sarai, and, in token thereof, her name was changed, ver. 15, 16. This promise Abram received, ver. 17. And his request for Ishmael (ver. 18) was answered, ver. 19–22. III. The circumcision of Abram and his family, according to God's appointment, ver. 23, &c.

Verses 1–3

Here is, I. The time when God made Abram this gracious visit: full thirteen years after the birth of Ishmael. There are some special comforts which are not the daily bread, no, not of the best saints, but they are favoured with them now and then. On this side heaven they have convenient food, but not a continual feast. So long the promise of Isaac was deferred. Perhaps to correct Abram's over-hasty marrying of Hagar.

II. The way in which God made this covenant with him: *The Lord appeared to Abram,* in the *shechinah,* some visible display of God's immediate glorious presence with him.

III. The posture Abram put himself into upon this occasion: *He fell on his face while God talked with him, v.* 3. 1. As one overcome by the brightness of the divine glory. 2. As one ashamed of himself, and blushing to think of the honours done to one so unworthy.

IV. The general scope and summary of the covenant laid down as the foundation on which all the rest was built; it is no other than the covenant of grace still made with all believers in Jesus Christ, *v.* 1.

1. What we may expect God to be to us: *I am the Almighty God.* By this name he chose to make himself known to Abram rather than by his name *Jehovah,* Exod. vi. 3. He used it to Jacob, *ch.* xxxv. 11. They called him by this name, *ch.* xxviii. 3; xliii. 14; xlviii. 3. After Moses, *Jehovah* is more frequently used, and this, *El-shaddai,* very rarely; it bespeaks the almighty power of God, either, (1) As an avenger, or, (2) As a benefactor. He is a God that is enough; or, as our old English translation reads it here very significantly, *I am God all-sufficient.*

2. What God requires that we should be to him. The covenant is mutual: *Walk before me, and be thou perfect.* Observe, (1) That to be religious is to walk before God in our integrity. It is to be *inward*

with him, in all the duties of religious worship, for in them particularly we walk before God (1 Sam. ii. 30). I know no religion but sincerity. (2) That upright walking with God is the condition of our interest in his all-sufficiency.

Verses 4–6

The covenant of grace is a covenant of God's own making; this he glories in (*as for me*), and so may we.

I. It is promised to Abram that he should be a *father of many nations*; that is, (1) That his seed after the flesh should be very numerous. 2. That all believers in every age should be looked upon as his spiritual seed, and that he should be called, not only *the friend of God,* but *the father of the faithful.*

II. In token of this his name was changed from *Abram, a high father,* to *Abraham, the father of a multitude.* This was, 1. To put an honour upon him. 2. To encourage and confirm his faith.

Verses 7–14

Here is, I. The continuance of the covenant, intimated in three things:—1. It is established; not to be altered nor revoked. 2. It is entailed; it is a covenant, not with Abraham only but with his seed after him, not only his seed after the flesh, but his spiritual seed. 3. It is everlasting in the evangelical sense and meaning of it. The covenant of grace is everlasting.

II. The contents of the covenant: it is a covenant of promises. Here are two which indeed are all-sufficient:—1. That God would be their God, *v.* 7, 8. What God is himself, that he will be to his people: his wisdom theirs, to guide and counsel them; his power theirs, to protect and support them; his goodness theirs, to supply and comfort them. 2. That Canaan should be their everlasting possession, *v.* 8. It must be looked upon as a type of heaven's happiness, that everlasting rest which remains for the people of God, Heb. iv. 9. Canaan is here said to be the land wherein Abraham was a stranger; and the heavenly Canaan is a land to which we are strangers, for it does not yet appear what we shall be.

III. The token of the covenant, and that is circumcision, for the sake of which the covenant is itself called the *covenant of circumcision,* Acts vii. 8. It is called a sign and seal (Rom. iv. 11), for it was, 1. A confirmation to Abraham and his seed of those promises which were God's part of the covenant. (1) Circumcision was a bloody ordinance; for all things by the law were purged with blood, Heb. ix. 22. See Exod. xxiv. 8. But, the blood of Christ being shed, all bloody ordinances are now abolished; circumcision therefore gives way to baptism. (2) It was peculiar to the males, though the women were also included in the covenant, for the man is the head of the woman. (3) It was the flesh of the foreskin that was to be cut off, because it is by ordinary generation that sin is propagated. Christ having not yet offered himself for us, God would have man to enter into covenant by the offering of some part of his own body. It is a secret part of the body; for the true circumcision is that of the heart, 1 Cor. xii. 23, 24. (4) The ordinance was to be administered to children when they were eight days old. (5) The children of the strangers, of whom the master of the family was the true domestic owner, were to be circumcised (*v.* 12, 13), which looked favourably upon the Gentiles, who should in due time be brought into the family of Abraham, by faith. See Gal. iii. 14. (6) The contempt of circumcision was a contempt of the covenant; if the parents did not circumcise their children, it was at their peril, as in the case of Moses, Exod. iv. 24, 25.

Verses 15–22

I. The promise made to Abraham of a son by *Sarai*, for *she also shall be a mother of nations, and kings of people shall be of her, v.* 16. Note, 1. God reveals the purposes of his good-will to his people by degrees. God had told Abram long before that he should have a son, but never till now that he should have a son by *Sarai*. 2. The blessing of the Lord makes fruitful, and adds no sorrow with it, no such sorrow as was in Hagar's case. 3. Civil government and order are a great blessing to the church. It is promised, not only that *people*, but *kings of people*, should be of her; not a headless rout, but a well-modelled well-governed society.

II. The ratification of this promise was the change of *Sarai's* name into *Sarah* (*v.* 15). *Sarai* signifies *my princess*, as if her honour were confined to one family only. *Sarah* signifies *a princess*—namely, of *multitudes*.

III. Abraham's joyful, thankful, entertainment of this gracious promise, *v.* 17. Upon this occasion he expressed, 1. Great humility: He *fell on his face*. 2. Great joy: He *laughed*. It was a laughter of delight, not of distrust. There is the joy of faith as well as the joy of fruition. 3. Great admiration: *Shall a child be born to him that is a hundred years old?*

IV. Abraham's prayer for Ishmael: *O that Ishmael might live before thee !* v. 18. This he speaks, not as desiring that Ishmael might be preferred before the son he should have by Sarah; but, dreadful lest he should be abandoned and forsaken of God. Though we ought not to prescribe to God, yet he gives us leave, in prayer, to be humbly free with him, and particular in making known our requests, Phil. iv. 6. It is the duty of parents to pray for their children, for all their children, as Job, who offered burnt offerings according to the number of them all, Job i. 5. The great thing we should desire of God for our children is that they may live before him, that is, that they may be kept in covenant with him, and may have grace to walk before him in their uprightness.

V. God's answer to his prayer; and it is an answer of peace.

1. Common blessings are secured to Ishmael (*v.* 20): *As for Ishmael*, whom thou art in so much care about, *I have heard thee*; he shall find favour for thy sake; *I have blessed him*. His posterity shall be numerous: *I will multiply him exceedingly*, more than his neighbours. They shall be considerable: *Twelve princes shall he beget.*

2. Covenant blessings are reserved for Isaac, and appropriated to him, *v.* 19, 21. (1) God repeats to him the promise of a son by Sarah. (2) He names that child—calls him *Isaac, laughter*, because Abraham rejoiced in spirit when this son was promised him. God's mercies promised shall in due time be our *exceeding* joy. Christ will be laughter to those that look for him. (3) He entails the covenant upon that child.

Verses 23–27

We have here Abraham's obedience to the law of circumcision. He himself and all his family were circumcised, so receiving the token of the covenant and distinguishing themselves from other families, that had no part nor lot in the matter. 1. It was an implicit obedience. 2. It was a speedy obedience: *In the self-same day, v.* 23, 26. Sincere obedience is not dilatory, Ps. cxix. 60. 3. It was a universal obedience: He did not circumcise his family and excuse himself, but set them an example. Ishmael is blessed, and therefore circumcised.

CHAPTER 18

We have an account in this chapter of another interview between God and Abraham. Here is, I. The kind visit which God made him. II. The matters discoursed of between them. 1. The purposes of God's love concerning Sarah, ver. 9–15. 2. The purposes of God's wrath concerning Sodom. (1) The discovery God made to Abraham of his design to destroy Sodom, ver. 16–22. (2) The intercession Abraham made for Sodom, ver. 23, &c.

Verses 1–8

This appearance of God to Abraham seems to have had in it freedom and familiarity, and therefore resembles that great visit when the Word would be made flesh, and appear as one of us.

I. How Abraham expected strangers, and how richly his expectations were answered (*v.* 1). God graciously visits those in whom he has first raised the expectation of him. Those that have been forward to entertain strangers have entertained angels, to their unspeakable honour and satisfaction. Where we see no cause to suspect ill, charity teaches us to hope well and to show kindness accordingly. It is better to feed five drones, or wasps, than to starve one bee.

II. How Abraham entertained those strangers, and how kindly his entertainment was accepted. Forgetting his age and gravity, he *ran to meet them* in the most obliging manner, and with all due courtesy. Religion does not destroy, but improve, good manners, and teaches us to honour all men. It becomes those whom God has blessed with plenty to be liberal and open-hearted. His entertainment, though it was very free, was yet plain and homely. His dining-room was an arbour under a tree. His feast was a joint or two of veal, and some cakes baked on the hearth. Here were no dainties, but good, plain, wholesome food, though Abraham was very rich and his guests were very honourable. He and his wife were busy, in accommodating their guests with the best they had. Sarah herself is cook and baker; Abraham runs to fetch the calf, brings out the milk and butter, and thinks it not below him to wait at table. Hearty friendship will stoop to anything but sin. Christ himself has taught us to wash one another's feet, in humble love.

Verses 9–15

These heavenly guests return his kindness. He receives angels, and has angels' rewards, a gracious message from heaven, Matt. x. 41.

I. Care is taken that Sarah should be within hearing. The women did not sit at meat with men, at least not with strangers, but confined themselves to their own apartments; therefore Sarah is here out of sight: but she must not be out of hearing. *Where is Sarah thy wife?* say the angels. *Behold, in the tent*, says Abraham. "Where should she be else? There she is in her place, as she uses to be." Those are most likely to receive comfort from God and his promises that are in their place and in the way of their duty, Luke ii. 8.

II. The promise is then renewed and ratified, that she should have a son (*v.* 10). Note, 1. The same blessings which others have from common providence believers have from the promise, which makes them very sweet and very sure. 2. The spiritual seed of Abraham owe their life, and joy, and hope, and all, to the promise. They are born by the word of God, 1 Pet. i. 23.

III. Sarah thinks this too good news to be true, and therefore cannot as yet find her heart to believe it: *Sarah laughed within herself, v.* 12—a laughter of doubting and mistrust. The great objection which Sarah could not get over was her age: "*I am waxed old*, and past child-bearing in the course of nature." Human improbability often sets up in contradiction to the divine promise. It is hard to cleave to the first Cause, when second causes frown.

IV. The angel reproves the indecent expressions of her distrust, *v.* 13, 14. God gave this reproof to Sarah by Abraham her husband. To him he said, *Why did Sarah laugh?* Our unbelief and distrust are a great offence to the God of heaven. He justly takes it ill to have the objections of sense set up in contradiction to his promise, as Luke i. 18. *Is any thing too hard for the Lord?*

V. Sarah foolishly endeavours to conceal her fault (*v.* 15): *She denied, saying, I did not laugh*; she told this lie, because *she was afraid.* There seems to be in Sarah a retraction of her distrust. Now she perceived, by laying circumstances together, that it was a divine promise which had been made concerning her, she renounced all doubting distrustful thoughts about it. There was withal a sinful attempt to cover a sin with a lie. It is a shame to do amiss, but a greater shame to deny it.

Verses 16–22

The messengers from heaven had now despatched one part of their business, which was an errand of grace to Abraham and Sarah, but now they have before them work of another nature. Sodom is to be destroyed.

I. The honour Abraham did to his guests: *He went with them to bring them on the way*, as one that was loth to part with such good company, and was desirous to pay his utmost respects to them.

II. The honour they did to him; for those that honour God he will honour. God communicated to Abraham his purpose to destroy Sodom.

1. But why must Abraham be of the cabinet-council? The Jews suggest that because God had granted the land of Canaan to Abraham and his seed therefore he would not destroy those cities which were a part of that land, without his knowledge and consent. But God here gives two other reasons:—

(1) Abraham must know, for he is a friend and a favourite. Those who by faith live a life of communion with God cannot but know more of his mind than other people. They have a better insight than others into what is present (Hos. xiv. 9; Ps. cvii. 43), and a better foresight of what is to come.

(2) Abraham must know, for he will teach his household. Those that expect family blessings must make conscience of family duty. If our children be the Lord's they must be nursed for him; if they wear his livery, they must be trained up in his work. Abraham made it his care and business to promote practical religion in his family. He did not fill their heads with matters of nice speculation, or doubtful disputation; but he taught them to keep *the way of the Lord, and to do judgment and justice*, that is, to be serious and devout in the worship of God and to be honest in their dealings with all men. Abraham was in care that his household after him should keep the way of the Lord, that religion might flourish in his family when he was in his grave.

2. God's friendly talk with Abraham. He tells him of the evidence there was against Sodom. Some sins, and the sins of some sinners, cry aloud to heaven for vengeance. Men are apt to suggest that his way is not equal; but let them know that his judgments are the result of an eternal counsel, and are never rash or sudden resolves. Perhaps the decree is here spoken of as not yet peremptory, that room and encouragement might be given to Abraham to make intercession for them. Thus God looked to see if there were any to intercede; Isa. lix. 16.

Verses 23–33

Communion with God is kept up by the word and by prayer. In the word God speaks to us; in prayer we speak to him. God had revealed to Abraham his purposes concerning Sodom; now from this Abraham takes occasion to speak to God on Sodom's behalf. Note, God's word then does us good when it furnishes us with matter for prayer and excites us to it.

I. The solemnity of Abraham's address to God on this occasion: *Abraham drew near, v.* 23. The expression intimates, 1. A holy concern: *He engaged his heart* to approach to God, Jer. xxx. 21. 2. A holy confidence: He drew near *with an assurance of faith.*

II. The general scope of this prayer. It is the first solemn prayer we have upon record in the Bible; and it is a prayer for the sparing of Sodom. Though sin is to be hated, sinners are to be pitied and prayed for. God delights not in their death, nor should we desire, but deprecate, the woeful day. 1. He begins with a prayer that the righteous among them might be spared, having an eye particularly to just Lot. 2. He improves this into a petition that all might be spared for the sake of the righteous that were among them, God himself countenancing this request.

III. The particular graces eminent in this prayer. 1. Here is great faith; and it is the prayer of faith that is the prevailing prayer. (1) Note, [1] The righteous are mingled with the wicked in this world. Among the best there are, commonly, some bad, and among the worst some good: even in Sodom, one Lot. [2] Though the righteous be among the wicked, yet the righteous God will not, certainly he will not, destroy the righteous with the wicked.

(2) That the righteous shall not *be as the wicked, v.* 25. Though they may suffer with them, yet they do not suffer like them.

2. Here is great humility.

(1) A deep sense of his own unworthiness (*v.* 27): *Behold now, I have taken upon me to speak unto the Lord, who am but dust and ashes*; and again, *v.* 31. He speaks as one amazed at his own boldness. Note, The access we have to the throne of grace, and the freedom of speech allowed us, are just matter of humble wonder, 2 Sam. vii. 18.

(2) An awful dread of God's displeasure. But he with whom we have to do is *God and not man*; and, however he may seem, is not really *angry with the prayers of the upright* (Ps. lxxx. 4), for they are *his delight* (Prov. xv. 8), and he is pleased when he is wrestled with.

3. Here is great charity. (1) A charitable opinion of Sodom's character: as bad as it was, he thought there were several good people in it. It becomes us to hope the best of the worst places. Of the two it is better to err in that extreme. (2) A charitable desire of Sodom's welfare: he used all his interest at the throne of grace for mercy for them.

4. Here are great boldness and believing confidence. Suppose there be fifty, *v.* 24. He advanced upon God's concessions, again and again.

IV. The success of the prayer. God's general goodwill appears in this, that he consented to spare the wicked for the sake of the righteous. See what great blessings good people are to any place. His particular favour to Abraham appeared in this, that he did not leave off granting till Abraham left off asking. Such is the power of prayer.

CHAPTER 19

The contents of this chapter is the history of Sodom's ruin, and Lot's rescue from that ruin. We read (ch. xviii) of God's coming to take a view of the present state of Sodom. Now here we have the result of that enquiry. I. It was found, upon trial, that Lot was very good (ver. 1–3), and it did not appear that there was any more of the same character. II. It was found that the Sodomites were very wicked and vile, ver. 4–11. III. Special care was therefore taken for the securing of Lot and his family, in a place of safety, ver. 12–23. IV. Mercy having rejoiced therein, justice shows itself in the ruin of Sodom and the death of Lot's wife (ver. 24–26), with a general repetition of the story, ver. 27–29. V. A foul sin that Lot was guilty of, in committing incest with his two daughters, ver. 30, &c.

Verses 1–3

Observe here, 1. There was but one good man in Sodom, and these heavenly messengers soon found him out. 2. Lot sufficiently distinguished himself from the rest of his neighbours, at this time, which plainly set a mark upon him. He that did not act like the rest must not fare like the rest. (1) Lot sat in the gate of Sodom at even. (2) He was hospitable, and very free and generous in his invitations and entertainments. He courted these strangers to his house, and to the best accommodations he had, and gave them all the evidences that he could of his sincerity. When the angels accepted his invitation, he treated them nobly. Note, Good people should be (with prudence) generous people.

Verses 4–11

Now it appeared, beyond contradiction, that the cry of Sodom was no louder than there was cause for.

I. That they were all wicked, *v.* 4. Wickedness had become universal, and they were unanimous in any vile design.

II. That they had arrived at the highest pitch of wickedness; they were *sinners before the Lord exceedingly* (ch. xiii. 13); for, 1. It was the most unnatural and abominable wickedness that they were now set upon, a sin that still bears their name, and is called *Sodomy*. Those that have become impudent in sin generally prove impenitent in sin; and it will be their ruin. Those have hard hearts indeed that sin with a high hand, Jer. vi. 15. 3. When Lot interposed, with all the mildness imaginable, to check the rage and fury of their lust, they were most insolently rude and abusive to him. Being greatly disturbed at their vile attempt, he unadvisedly and unjustifiably offered to prostitute his two daughters to them, *v.* 8. It is true, of two evils we must choose the less; but of two sins we must choose neither, nor ever do evil that good may come of it. They threaten him, and lay violent hands upon him.

III. That nothing less than the power of an angel could save a good man out of their wicked hands. 1. They rescue Lot, *v.* 10. The saints, at death, are pulled like Lot into a house of perfect safety, and the door shut for ever against those that pursue them. 2. They chastise the insolence of the Sodomites: *They smote them with blindness, v.* 11. Yet these Sodomites, after they were struck blind, continued seeking the door, to break it down, till they were tired. No judgments will, of themselves, change the corrupt natures and purposes of wicked men. If their minds had not been blinded as well as their bodies, they would have said, as the magicians, *This is the finger of God*, and would have submitted.

Verses 12–14

We have here the preparation for Lot's deliverance.

I. Notice is given him of the approach of Sodom's ruin: *We will destroy this place, v.* 13.

II. He is directed to give notice to his friends and relations, that they, if they would, might be saved with him (*v.* 12). Note, Those who through grace are themselves delivered out of a sinful state should do what they can for the deliverance of others, especially their relations. 2. The offer of great favour. They ask what relations he had there, that, whether righteous or unrighteous, they might be saved with him. Note, Bad people often fare the better in this world for the sake of their good relations. It is good being akin to a godly man.

III. He applies himself accordingly to his sons-in-

law, *v.* 14. Observe, 1. The fair warning that Lot gave them: *Up, get you out of this place.* 2. The slight they put upon this warning: *He seemed to them as one that mocked.* They thought, perhaps, that the assault which the Sodomites had just now made upon his house had disturbed his head. Those who lived a merry life, and made a jest of everything, made a jest of this warning, and so they perished in the overthrow.

Verses 15–23

Here is, I. The rescue of Lot out of Sodom, Ezek. xiv. 14. Early in the morning his own guests, in kindness to him, turned him out of doors, and his family with him, *v.* 15. His daughters that were married perished with their unbelieving husbands; but those that continued with him were preserved with him.

1. With what a gracious violence Lot was brought out of Sodom, *v.* 16. It seems he did not make so much haste as the case required. It might have been fatal to him if the angels had not *laid hold of his hand, and brought him forth*, and saved him with fear, Jude 23. The salvation of the most righteous men must be attributed to God's mercy, not to their own merit. We are saved by grace.

2. With what a gracious vehemence he was urged to make the best of his way, when he was *brought forth, v.* 17. He must not hanker after Sodom: *Look not behind thee.* He must not loiter by the way: *Stay not in all the plain.* He must not take up short of the place of refuge appointed him: *Escape to the mountain.* Such as these are the commands given to those who through grace are delivered out of a sinful state. (1) Return not to sin and Satan, for that is looking back to Sodom. (2) Rest not in self and the world, for that is staying in the plain. And, (3) Reach towards Christ and heaven, for that is escaping to the mountain, short of which we must not take up.

II. The fixing of a place of refuge for him. The mountain was first appointed for him to flee to, but, 1. He begged for a city of refuge, one of the five that lay together, called *Bela*, ch. xiv. 2, 18–20. It was Lot's weakness to think a city of his own choosing safer than the mountain of God's appointing. Could not he that saved him from greater evils save him from the less? He insists much in his petition upon the smallness of the place: *It is a little one, is it not?* This gave a new name to the place; it was called *Zoar, a little one.* 2. God granted him his request, though there was much infirmity in it, *v.* 21, 22. See what favour God showed to a true saint, though weak. (1) Zoar was spared, to gratify him.

III. It is taken notice of that the sun had risen when Lot entered into Zoar; for when a good man comes into a place he brings light along with him, or should do.

Verses 24–25

Then, when Lot had got safely into Zoar, then this ruin came; for good men are taken away from the evil to come. *Then*, when the sun had risen bright and clear, promising a fair day, then this storm arose, to show that it was not from natural causes. It was a strange punishment, Job xxxi. 3. Never was the like before nor since. It was a judgment that laid all waste: *It overthrew the cities*, and destroyed all the inhabitants of them, the plain, and all that grew upon the ground, *v.* 25. It was an utter ruin, and irreparable. That fruitful valley remains to this day a great lake, or dead sea; it is called *the Salt Sea*, Num. xxxiv. 12. It is about thirty miles long and ten miles broad; it has no living creature in it; it is not moved by the wind; the smell of it is offensive; things do not easily sink in it. The Greeks call it

Asphaltites, from a sort of pitch which it casts up. Jordan falls into it, and is lost there. It was a punishment that answered to their sin. Those that went after strange flesh were destroyed by strange fire, Jude 7. It is often referred to in the scripture, and made a pattern of the ruin of Israel (Deut. xxix. 23), of Babylon (Isa. xiii. 19), of Edom (Jer. xlix. 18), of Moab and Ammon (Zeph. ii. 9).

Verse 26

This also is written for our admonition. Our Saviour refers to it (Luke xvii. 32), *Remember Lot's wife.* As by the example of Sodom the wicked are warned to turn from their wickedness, so by the example of Lot's wife the righteous are warned not to turn from their righteousness. See Ezek. iii. 18, 20.

I. The sin of Lot's wife: *She looked back from behind him.* She disobeyed an express command. Probably she hankered after her house and goods in Sodom, and was loth to leave them. Christ intimates this to be her sin (Luke xvii. 31, 32); she too much regarded her *stuff.* Her looking back evinced an inclination to go back; and therefore our Saviour uses it as a warning against apostasy from our Christian profession. We have all renounced the world and the flesh, and have set our faces heavenward; we are in the plain, upon our probation; and it is at our peril if we return into the interests we profess to have abandoned.

II. The punishment of Lot's wife for this sin. Though she was a monument of distinguishing mercy in her deliverance out of Sodom, yet God did not connive at her disobedience. Since it is such a dangerous thing to look back, let us always press forward, Phil. iii. 13, 14.

Verses 27–29

I. Here is Abraham's pious regard to God in this event. *He got up early* to look towards Sodom; and, to intimate that his design herein was to see what became of his prayers. We must direct our prayer as a letter, and then look up for an answer, direct our prayer as an arrow, and then look up to see whether it reach the mark, Ps. v. 3.

II. Here is God's favourable regard to Abraham, *v.* 29. As before, when Abraham prayed for Ishmael, God heard him for Isaac, so now, when he prayed for Sodom, he heard him for Lot. *He remembered Abraham, and,* for his sake, *sent Lot out of the overthrow.* Note, God will certainly give an answer of peace to the prayer of faith, in his own way and time; though, for a while, it seem to be forgotten, yet, sooner or later, it will appear to be remembered.

Verses 30–38

Here is, I. The great trouble and distress that Lot was brought into after his deliverance, *v.* 30. 1. He was frightened out of Zoar, durst not dwell there; probably because he found it as wicked as Sodom, and therefore concluded it could not long survive it. Note, Settlements and shelters of our own choosing, and in which we do not follow God, commonly prove uneasy to us. 2. He was forced to betake himself to the mountain, and to take up with a cave for his habitation there. Observe, (1) He was now glad to go to the mountain, the place which God had appointed for his shelter. (2) He that, awhile ago, could not find room enough for himself and his stock in the whole land, but must jostle with Abraham, and get as far from him as he could, is now confined to a hole in a hill, where he has scarcely room to turn himself, and there he is solitary and trembling.

II. The great sin that Lot and his daughters were guilty of, when they were in this desolate place. It is a sad story.

1. His daughters laid a very wicked plot to bring him to sin; and theirs was, doubtless, the greater guilt. (1) Some think that their pretence was plausible. Their father had no sons, they had no husbands, nor knew they where to have any of the holy seed, whilst if they had children by others, their father's name would not be preserved in them. But, (2) Whatever their pretence was, it is certain that their project was very wicked and vile, and an impudent affront to the very light and law of nature.

2. Lot himself, by his own folly and unwariness, was wretchedly overcome, and suffered himself so far to be imposed upon by his own children as, two nights together, to be drunk, and to commit incest, *v.* 33, &c. *Lord, what is man!* What are the best of men, when God leaves them to themselves! (1) The peril of security. Lot, who kept himself sober and chaste in Sodom, was yet, in the mountain, where he was alone, and as he thought quite out of the way of temptation, shamefully overtaken. Let him therefore that thinks he stands, stands high and stands firm, *take heed lest he fall.* No mountain, on this side the holy hill above, can set us out of the reach of Satan's fiery darts. (2) The peril of drunkenness. It is not only a great sin itself, but it is the inlet of many sins; it may prove the inlet of the worst and most unnatural sins.

3. In the close we have an account of the birth of the two sons, or grandsons (call them which you will), of Lot, Moab and Ammon, the fathers of two nations, neighbours to Israel, and which we often read of in the Old Testament; both together are called *the children of Lot,* Ps. lxxxiii. 8.

Lastly, Observe, that, after this, we never read any more of Lot, but from the silence of the scripture concerning him henceforward we may learn that drunkenness, as it makes men forgetful, so it makes them forgotten.

Chapter 20

We are here returning to the story of Abraham; yet that part of it which is here recorded is not to his honour. The fairest marbles have their flaws, and, while there are spots in the sun, we must not expect anything spotless under it. The scripture, it should be remarked, is impartial in relating the blemishes even of its most celebrated characters. We have here, I. Abraham's sin in denying his wife, and Abimelech's sin thereupon in taking her, ver. 1, 2. II. God's discourse with Abimelech in a dream, upon this occasion, wherein he shows him his error (ver. 3), accepts his plea (ver. 4–6), and directs him to make restitution, ver. 7. III. Abimelech's discourse with Abraham, wherein he chides him for the cheat he had put upon him (ver. 8–10), and Abraham excuses it as well as he can, ver. 11–13. IV. The good issue of the story, in which Abimelech restores Abraham his wife (ver. 14–16), and Abraham, by prayer, prevails with God for the removal of the judgment Abimelech was under, ver. 17, 18.

Verses 1–2

Here is, 1. Abraham's removal from Mamre. We are not told upon what occasion he removed. His sin in denying his wife had here a two-fold aggravation:—(1) He had been guilty of this same sin before, and had been reproved for it. Note, It is possible that a good man may, not only fall into sin, but relapse into the same sin, through the surprise and strength of temptation and the infirmity of the flesh. (2) Sarah, as it should seem, was now with child of the promised seed; he ought therefore to have taken particular care of her now, as Judg. xiii. 4.

Verses 3–7

It appears by this that God revealed himself by dreams even to those who were out of the pale of the church and covenant.

I. God gives him notice of his danger (*v.* 3), his danger of *sin,* telling him that the woman is a man's wife, so that if he take her he will wrong her husband; his danger of death for this sin: *Thou art a dead man.* If thou art a bad man, certainly thou art a dead man.

II. He pleads ignorance that Abraham and Sarah had agreed to impose upon him, and not to let him know that they were any more than brother and sister, *v.* 6. His heart condemns him not, 1 John iii. 21. If our consciences witness to our integrity, and if, however we may have been cheated into a snare, we have not knowingly and wittingly sinned against God, it will be our rejoicing in the day of evil.

III. God gives a very full answer to what he had said.

He allows his plea, and admits that what he did he did in the integrity of his heart: *Yea, I know it, v.* 6. Note, It is matter of comfort to those that are honest that God knows their honesty, and will acknowledge it, though perhaps men that are prejudiced against them either cannot be convinced of it or will not own that they are.

He charges him to make restitution: *Now therefore,* now that thou art better informed, *restore the man his wife, v.* 7. Note, Ignorance will excuse no longer than it continues. If we have entered upon a wrong course through ignorance this will not excuse our knowingly persisting in it. Lev. v. 3–5.

Verses 8–13

Abimelech, being thus warned of God in a dream, takes the warning, and, as one truly afraid of sin and its consequences, he rises early to obey the directions given him.

I. He has a caution for his servants, *v.* 8.

II. He has a chiding for Abraham.

1. The serious reproof which Abimelech gave to Abraham, *v.* 9, 10. His reasoning with Abraham upon this occasion was very strong, and yet very mild. Nothing could be said better; he does not reproach him, not insult over him, does not say, "Is this your profession? I see, though you will not swear, you will lie. If these be prophets, I will beg to be freed from the sight of them:" but he fairly represents the injury Abraham had done him, and calmly signifies his resentment of it. (1) He calls that sin which he now found he had been in danger of, a great sin. (2) He looks upon it that both himself and his kingdom would have been exposed to the wrath of God if he had been guilty of this sin, though ignorantly. Note, The sins of kings often prove the plagues of kingdoms: rulers should therefore, for their people's sake, dread sin. (3) He charges Abraham with doing that which was not justifiable, in disowning his marriage. (4) He takes it as a very great injury to himself and his family that Abraham had thus exposed them to sin: "*What have I offended thee?* If I had been thy worst enemy, thou couldst not have done me a worse turn, nor taken a more effectual course to be revenged on me." (5) He challenges him to assign a cause for his suspecting them as a dangerous people. What reason hadst thou to think that if we had known her to be thy wife thou wouldst have been exposed to any danger by it?" Note, A suspicion of our goodness is justly reckoned a greater affront than a slight upon our greatness.

2. The poor excuse that Abraham made for himself.

(1) He pleaded the bad opinion he had of the place, *v.* 11. "*Surely the fear of God is not in this place,* and then they will slay me." There are many places and persons that have more of the fear of God in them than we think they have: perhaps they are not called by our dividing name, they do not wear our badges, they do not tie themselves to that which we have an opinion of; and therefore we conclude they have not the fear of God in their hearts, which is very injurious both to Christ and Christians, and makes us obnoxious to God's judgment, Matt. vii. 1. Uncharitableness and censoriousness are sins that are the cause of many other sins. Men would not do ill if they did not first think ill.

(2) He excused it from the guilt of a downright lie by making it out that, in a sense, she was his sister, *v.* 12. But those to whom he said, *She is my sister,* understood that she was so his sister as not to be capable of being his wife; so that it was an equivocation, with an intent to deceive.

(3) He clears himself from the imputation of an affront designed against Abimelech by alleging that it had been his practice before, according to an agreement between him and his wife, when they first became sojourners (*v.* 13).

Verses 14–18

Here is, I. The kindness which Abimelech showed to Abraham. See how unjust Abraham's jealousies were. 1. He gives him his royal licence to dwell where he pleased in his country. 2. He gives him his royal gifts. These he gave when he restored Sarah, by way of satisfacton for the wrong he had offered to do, in taking her to his house. The law appointed that when restitution was made something should be added to it. Lev. vi. 5.

II. The kindness of a prophet which Abraham showed to Abimelech: he *prayed for him, v.* 17, 18. God healed Miriam, when Moses, whom she had most affronted, prayed for her (Num. xii. 13), and was reconciled to Job's friends when Job, whom they had grieved, prayed for them (Job xlii. 8–10). Note, The prayers of good men may be a kindness to great men, and ought to be valued.

CHAPTER 21

In this chapter we have, I. Isaac, the child of promise born into Abraham's family, ver. 1–8. II. Ishmael, the son of the bond-woman, cast out of it, ver. 9–21. III. Abraham's league with his neighbour Abimelech, ver. 22–32. IV. His devotion to his God, ver. 33.

Verses 1–8

Few under the Old Testament were brought into the world with such expectation as Isaac was, not for the sake of any great personal eminence at which he was to arrive, but because he was to be, in this very thing, a type of Christ, that seed which the holy God had so long promised and holy men so long expected.

I. The fulfilling of God's promise in the conception and birth of Isaac, *v.* 1, 2. 1. Isaac was born according to the promise. He was born *at the set time of which God had spoken, v.* 2. Note, God is always punctual to his time; though his promised mercies come not at the time we set, they will certainly come at the time he sets, and that is the best time. 2. It was not by the power of common providence, but by the power of a special promise, that Isaac was born. Note, True believers, by virtue of God's promises, are enabled to do that which is above the power of human nature, for *by them they partake of a divine nature,* 2 Pet. i. 4.

II. Abraham's obedience to God's precept concerning Isaac.

1. He named him, as God commanded him, *v.* 3. *Isaac, laughter.* There was good reason for the name, for, (1) When Abraham received the promise of him he laughed for joy, *ch.* xvii. 17. (2) When Sarah received the promise she laughed with distrust and diffidence. (3) Isaac was himself, afterwards, laughed at by Ishmael (*v.* 9), and perhaps his name bade him expect it. (4) The promise which he was the heir of, was to be the joy of all the saints in all ages.

III. The impressions which this mercy made upon Sarah.

1. It filled her with joy (*v.* 6): "*God has made me to laugh;* he has given me both cause to rejoice and a heart to rejoice." Thus the mother of our Lord, Luke i. 46, 47. Whatever is the matter of our joy,

God must be acknowledged as the author of it, unless it be the *laughter of the fool*. It adds to the comfort of any mercy to have our friends rejoice with us in it: *All that hear will laugh with me*; for laughing is catching. See Luke i. 58.

2. It filled her with wonder, *v.* 7. "The thing was so highly improbable, so near to impossible, that if anyone but God had said it we could not have believed it." Note, God's favours to his covenant-people are such as surpass both their own and others' thoughts and expectations. Who would have said that God should send his Son to die for us, his Spirit to sanctify us, his angels to attend us ? Who would have said that such great sins should be pardoned?

IV. A short account of Isaac's infancy: *The child grew, v.* 8. He grew so as not always to need milk, but was able to bear strong meat, and then he was weaned. See Heb. v. 13, 14. Abraham made a feast on the day that he was weaned because God's blessing upon the nursing of children, and the preservation of them through the perils of the infant age, are signal instances of the care and tenderness of the divine providence. See Ps. xxii. 9, 10; Hos. xi. 1.

Verses 9–13

The casting out of Ishmael is here considered of, and resolved on.

I. Ishmael himself gave the occasion by some affronts he gave to Isaac his little brother. Sarah herself was an eye-witness of the abuse. Ishmael is here called the *son of the Egyptian*, because, as some think, the 400 years' affliction of the seed of Abraham by the Egyptians began now, *ch.* xv. 13. Ishmael was fourteen years older than Isaac; and it argued a base disposition in Ishmael to be abusive to a child that was no way a match for him.

II. Sarah made the motion: *Cast out this bondwoman, v.* 10. This seems to be spoken in some heat, yet it is quoted (Gal. iv. 30) as if it had been spoken by a spirit of prophecy; and it is the sentence passed on all hypocrites and carnal people, though they have a place and a name in the visible church.

III. Abraham was averse to it: *The thing was very grievous in Abraham's sight, v.* 11. 1. It grieved him that Ishmael had given such a provocation. 2. It grieved him that Sarah insisted upon such a punishment. "Might it not suffice to correct him ? would nothing less serve than to expel him ?"

IV. God determined it, *v.* 12, 13. The covenant seed of Abraham must be a peculiar people, a people by themselves, distinguished, not mingled with those that were out of covenant; for this reason Ishmael must be separated. The casting out of Ishmael should not be his ruin, *v.* 13. He shall be a *nation, because he is thy seed*. It is presumption to say that all those who are left out of the external dispensation of God's covenant, are therefore excluded from all his mercies. Though he was chased out of the church, he was not *chased out of the world*. *I will make him a nation.* Note, 1. Nations are of God's making: he founds them, he forms them, he fixes them. 2. Many are full of the blessings of God's providence that are strangers to the blessings of his covenant.

Verses 14–21

Here is, I. The casting out of the bondwoman and her son from the family of Abraham, *v.* 14. Abraham's obedience to the divine command in this matter was speedy—*early in the morning*. It was also submissive; it was contrary to his own inclination, to do it; yet as soon as he perceives that it is the mind of God he makes no objections, but silently does as he is bidden.

II. Their wandering in the wilderness, missing their way to the place Abraham designed them for a settlement.

1. They were reduced to great distress there. Their provisions were spent, and Ishmael was sick. Hagar is in tears, and sufficiently mortified. She despairs of relief, counts upon nothing but *the death of the child* (*v.* 15, 16).

2. In this distress, God heard *the voice of the lad, v.* 17. An angel was sent to comfort Hagar, and it was not the first time that she had met with God's comforts in a wilderness (*ch.* xvi. 13). (1) The angel assures her *God has heard the voice of the lad where he is*, though he is in a wilderness (for, wherever we are, there is a way open heaven-ward); therefore *lift up the lad, and hold him in thy hand, v.* 18. (2) He repeats the promise concerning her son, that he should be *a great nation*, as a reason why she should bestir herself to help him. (3) He directs her to a present supply (*v.* 19): and then *she saw a well of water*. Note, Many that have reason enough to be comforted go mourning from day to day. There is a well of water by them in the covenant of grace, but they are not aware of it till the same God that opened their eyes to see their wound opens them to see their remedy, John xvi. 6, 7. Now the apostle tells us that those things concerning Hagar and Ishmael are ἀλληγορούμενα (Gal. iv. 24), they are to be allegorized; this then will serve to illustrate the folly, [1] Of those who, like the unbelieving Jews, seek for righteousness by the law and the carnal ordinances of it, and not by the promise made in Christ. [2] Of those who seek for satisfaction and happiness in the world and the things of it. Those that forsake the comforts of the covenant and communion with God wander endlessly in pursuit of satisfaction, and, at length, sit down short of it.

III. The settlement of Ishmael, at last, in the wilderness of Paran (*v.* 20, 21), a wild place, fittest for a wild man; and such a one he was, *ch.* xvi. 12. Observe, 1. He had some tokens of God's presence: *God was with the lad*. 2. By trade he was an archer. 3. He matched among his mother's relations; she took him a wife out of Egypt: as great an archer as he was, he did not think he could take his aim well, in the business of marriage, if he proceeded without his mother's advice and consent.

Verses 22–32

We have here an account of the treaty between Abimelech and Abraham. His friendship is valued, is courted, though a stranger, though a tenant at will to the Canaanites and Perizzites.

I. The league is proposed by Abimelech, and Phichol his prime-minister of state and general of his army.

1. The inducement to it was God's favour to Abraham (*v.* 22): "*God is with thee in all that thou doest*, and we cannot but take notice of it." It is good being in favour with those that are in favour with God. *We will go with you, for we have heard that God is with you.* We do well for ourselves if we have fellowship with those that have fellowship with God, 1 John i. 3.

2. The tenor of it was, in general, that there should be a firm and constant friendship between the two families. He would have his son, and his son's son, and his land likewise, to have the benefit of it.

II. It is consented to by Abraham, with a particular clause inserted about a well. In Abraham's part of this transaction observe,

1. He was ready to enter into this league with Abimelech, finding him to be a man of honour and conscience, and that had the fear of God before his eyes.

2. He prudently settled the matter concerning a well, about which Abimelech's servants had quarrelled with him. Wells of water, it seems, were choice goods

in that country. Abraham mildly told Abimelech of it, *v.* 25; and no more can be expected from an honest man than that he be ready to do right as soon as he knows that he has done wrong.

3. He made a very handsome present to Abimelech, *v.* 27. The interchanging of kind offices is the improving of love: that which is mine is my friend's.

4. He ratified the covenant by an oath, and registered it by giving a new name to the place (*v.* 31), *Beer-sheba*, the *well of the oath.*

Verses 33–34

He sojourned many days, as many as would consist with his character, as Abraham the *Hebrew*, or *passenger.* 2. There he made, not only a constant practice, but an open profession, of his religion: *There he called on the name of the Lord, the everlasting God*, probably in the grove he planted, which was his oratory or house of prayer. Christ prayed in a garden, on a mountain. In calling the Lord, we must eye him as *the everlasting God. The everlasting God*, who was, before all worlds, and will be, when time and days shall be no more. See Isa. xl. 28.

CHAPTER 22

We have here the famous story of Abraham's offering up his son Isaac, that is, his offering to offer him. Here is, I. The strange command which God gave to Abraham, ver. 1, 2. II. Abraham's strange obedience to this command, ver. 3–10. III. The strange issue of this trial. 1. The sacrificing of Isaac was countermanded, ver. 11, 12. 2. Another sacrifice was provided, ver. 13, 14. 3. The covenant was renewed with Abraham hereupon, ver. 15–19. Lastly, an account of some of Abraham's relations, ver. 20, &c.

Verses 1–2

Here is the trial of Abraham's faith. It was made to appear that he loved God better than his father; now that he loved him better than his son.

I. Now, perhaps, he was beginning to think the storms had all blown over; but, after all, this encounter comes, which is sharper than any yet.

II. The author of the trial: *God* tempted him, not to draw him to sin but to discover his graces, how strong they were, that they might be *found to praise, and honour, and glory*, 1 Pet. i. 7. Thus God tempted Job, that he might appear not only a good man, but a great man. *God did tempt Abraham;* he did *lift up Abraham*, so some read it; as a scholar that improves well is lifted up, when he is put into a higher form.

III. The trial itself. Probably he expected some renewed promise like those, *ch.* xv. 1, and xvii. 1. But, to his great amazement, that which God has to say to him is, in short, *Abraham, Go kill thy son.* Every word here is a sword in his bones: the trial is steeled with trying phrases.

1. The person to be offered. (1) "*Take thy son,* not thy bullocks and thy lambs." "No, *I will take no bullock* out of thy house" (Ps. l. 9). "I must have thy son." "Take *Isaac*, him, by name, *thy laughter,* that *son indeed*," *ch.* xvii. 19. That son *whom thou lovest*. In the Hebrew it is expressed more emphatically, and, I think, might very well be read thus: *Take now that son of thine, that only one of thine, whom thou lovest, that Isaac.*

2. The place: *In the land of Moriah*, three days' journey off; so that he might have time to consider it, that it might be a service the more reasonable and the more honourable.

3. The manner: *Offer him for a burnt-offering.* He must not only kill his son, but kill him as a sacrifice.

Verses 3–10

Abraham's obedience to this severe command. *Being tried, he offered up Isaac*, Heb. xi. 17.

I. The difficulties which he broke through in this act of obedience. 1. It seemed directly against an antecedent law of God, which forbids murder, under a severe penalty, *ch.* ix. 5, 6. 2. How would it consist with natural affection to his own son ? 3. God gave him no reason for it. When Ishmael was to be cast out, a just cause was assigned, but here Isaac must die, and Abraham must kill him, and neither the one nor the other must know why or wherefore. If Isaac had been to die a martyr for the truth, or his life had been the ransom of some other life more precious, it would have been another matter. But the case is not so: he is a dutiful, obedient, hopeful son. "Lord, what profit is there in his blood ?" 4. How would this consist with the promise ? Was it not said that in *Isaac shall thy seed be called*? 5. How should he ever look Sarah in the face again ? 6. What would the Egyptians say, and the Canaanites and the Perizzites who dwelt then in the land ? It would be an eternal reproach to Abraham, and to his altars. "Welcome nature, if this be grace."

II. The several steps of obedience.

1. He rises early, *v.* 3, for the command was peremptory, and would not admit a debate. Note, those that do the will of God heartily will do it speedily.

2. He gets things ready for a sacrifice.

3. It is very probable that he said nothing about it to Sarah.

4. He carefully looked about him, to discover the place appointed for this sacrifice, when he said (*v.* 5), "We will go yonder, where you see the light, and worship."

5. He left his servants at some distance off (*v.* 5), lest they should interpose in his strange oblation. Thus, when Christ was entering upon his agony in the garden, he took only three of his disciples with him, and left the rest at the garden door.

6. He obliged Isaac to carry the wood while he himself carried the fatal knife and fire, *v.* 6.

7. Without any ruffle or disorder, he talks it over with Isaac, as if it had been but a common sacrifice, that he was going to offer, *v.* 7, 8.

(1) It was a very affecting question that Isaac asked him, as they were going together: *My father*, said Isaac; it was a melting word, which, one would think, would strike deeper into the breast of Abraham than his knife could into the breast of Isaac. Yet he keeps his temper, and keeps his countenance, to admiration; he calmly waits for his son's question, and this is it: *Behold the fire and the wood, but where is the lamb?* [1] A trying question to Abraham. How could he endure to think that Isaac was himself the lamb? So it is, but Abraham, as yet, dares not tell him so. [2] It is a teaching question to us all, that, when we are going to worship God, we should seriously consider. Where is the heart? Is that ready to be offered up to God, to ascend to him as a burnt-offering?

(2) It was a very prudent answer which Abraham gave him: *My son, God will provide himself a lamb.* This was the language, either, [1] Of his obedience. Or, [2] Of his faith. A sacrifice was provided instead of Isaac. Thus, *First*, Christ, the great sacrifice of atonement, was of God's providing. *Secondly*, All our sacrifices of acknowledgment are of God's providing too. It is he that prepares the heart, Ps. x. 17. The broken and contrite spirit is a sacrifice of God (Ps. li. 17), of his providing.

8. He goes on with a holy wilfulness, after many a weary step, and with a heavy heart he arrives at length at the fatal place, builds the altar, the saddest that ever he built, lays the wood in order for Isaac's funeral pile, and now tells him the amazing news: "Isaac, thou art the lamb which God has provided." Isaac, for aught that appears, is as willing as Abraham; we do not find that he attempted to make his

escape or made any resistance. Yet it is necessary that a sacrifice be bound. But with what heart could tender Abraham tie those guiltless hands, which perhaps had often been lifted up to ask his blessing, and stretched out to embrace him, and were now the more straitly bound with the cords of love and duty ! However, it must be done. Having bound him, he lays him upon the altar, and his hand upon the head of his sacrifice; and now, we may suppose, with floods of tears, he gives, and takes, the final farewell of a parting kiss. With a fixed heart, and an eye lifted up to heaven, he takes the knife, and stretches out his hand. Be astonished, O heavens ! at this; and wonder, O earth ! Here is an act of faith and obedience, which deserves to be a spectacle to God, angels, and men. Now this obedience of Abraham in offering up Isaac is a lively representation, (1) Of the love of God to us, in delivering up his only-begotten Son to suffer and die for us, as a sacrifice. It *pleased the Lord* himself to *bruise him.* See Isa. liii. 10; Zech. xiii. 7. (2) Of our duty to God, in return for that love. We must tread in the steps of this faith of Abraham. God, by his word, calls us to part with all for Christ.

Verses 11–14

Hitherto this story has been very melancholy, and seemed to hasten towards a most tragical period; but here the sky suddenly clears up, the sun breaks out, and a bright and pleasant scene opens. The same hand that had wounded and cast down here heals and lifts up.

I. Isaac is rescued, *v.* 11, 12. The command to offer him was intended only for trial, therefore the order is countermanded: *Lay not thy hand upon the lad.* The more imminent the danger is, the more wonderful and the more welcome is the deliverance.

II. Abraham is not only approved, but applauded. *Now know I that thou fearest God.* The best evidence of our fearing God is our being willing to serve and honour him with that which is dearest to us.

III. Another sacrifice is provided instead of Isaac, *v.* 13. God must be acknowledged with thankfulness for the deliverance of Isaac. Abraham's words must be made good: *God will provide himself a lamb.* Reference must be had to the promised Messiah, the blessed seed. (1) Christ was sacrificed in our stead, as this ram instead of Isaac, and his death was our discharge. (2) Though that blessed seed was lately promised, and now typified by Isaac, yet the offering of him up should be suspended: and in the mean time the sacrifice of beasts should be accepted, as this ram was, as a pledge of that expiation which should one day be made by that great sacrifice. And it is observable that the temple, the place of sacrifice, was afterwards built upon this Mount Moriah (2 Chron. iii. 1); and Mount Calvary, where Christ was crucified, was not far off.

IV. A new name is given to the place, and for the encouragement of all believers, cheerfully to trust in God: *Jehovah-jireh, The Lord will provide* (*v.* 14), probably alluding to what he had said (*v.* 8), *God will provide himself a lamb.*

Verses 15–19

Abraham's obedience was graciously accepted; but this was not all: here we have it recompensed. Observe, 1. God is pleased to make mention of Abraham's obedience as the consideration of the covenant; and he speaks of it with an encomium: *Because thou hast done this thing, and hast not withheld thy son, thine only son, v.* 16. 2. God now confirmed the promise with an oath. It was said and sealed before; but now it is sworn: *By myself have I sworn*; for he could swear by no greater, Heb. vi. 13. He did (to speak with reverence) even pawn his own

life and being upon it (*As I live*), that by all those immutable things, in which it was impossible for God to lie, he and his might have strong consolation. 3. The particular promise here renewed is that of a numerous offspring: *Multiplying, I will multiply thee, v.* 17. What a figure does the seed of Abraham make in history ! How numerous, how illustrious, were his known descendants, who, to this day, triumph in this, that they have Abraham to their father ! 4. The promise, doubtless, points at the Messiah, and the grace of the gospel. This is the oath sworn to our father Abraham, which Zacharias refers to, Luke i. 73, &c. And so here is a promise, (1) Of the great blessing of the Spirit: *In blessing, I will bless thee,* namely, with that best of blessings, the gift of the Holy Ghost. (2) Of the increase of the church, that believers, his spiritual seed, should be numerous as the stars of heaven. (3) Of spiritual victories. Probably Zacharias refers to this part of the oath (Luke i. 74), *That we, being delivered out of the hand of our enemies, might serve him without fear.* But the crown of all is the last promise. (4) Of the incarnation of Christ: *In thy seed,* one particular person that shall descend from thee (for he speaks not of many, but of one, as the apostle observes, Gal. iii. 16), *shall all the nations of the earth be blessed.*

Verses 20–24

This is recorded here to show that though Abraham saw his own family highly dignified with peculiar privileges, yet he was glad to hear of the increase and prosperity of their families.

CHAPTER 23

Here is, I. Abraham a mourner for the death of Sarah, ver. 1, 2. II. Abraham a purchaser of a burying-place for Sarah. 1. The purchase humbly proposed by Abraham, ver. 3, 4. 2. Fairly treated of, and agreed to, with a great deal of mutual civility and respect, ver. 5–16. 3. The purchase-money paid, ver. 16. 4. The promises conveyed and secured to Abraham, ver. 17, 18, 20. 5. Sarah's funeral, ver. 19.

Verses 1–2

We have here, 1. Sarah's age, *v.* 1. 2. Her death, *v.* 2. She died in the land of Canaan, where she had been above sixty years a sojourner. 3. Abraham's mourning for her. Two words are used: he came both to *mourn* and to *weep.* Tears are a tribute due to our deceased friends. When the body is sown, it must be watered. But we must not sorrow as those that have no hope; for we have a good hope through grace both concerning them and concerning ourselves.

Verses 3–15

Here is, I. The humble request which Abraham made to his neighbours, the Hittites, for a burying-place among them, *v.* 3, 4. The convenient diversion which this affair gave, for the present, to Abraham's grief: *He stood up from before his dead.* There must be a time of standing up from before their dead, and ceasing to mourn. Weeping must not hinder sowing. The death of our relations should effectually remind us that we are not at home in this world. When they are gone, say, "We are going."

II. The generous offer which the children of Heth made to him, *v.* 5, 6. They compliment him, 1. With a title of respect: *Thou art a prince of God among us.* 2. With a tender of the best of their burying-places. Note, Even the light of nature teaches us to be civil and respectful towards all, though they be strangers and sojourners.

III. The particular proposal which Abraham made to them, *v.* 7–9. He returns them his thanks. Though a great man, an old man, and now a mourner, yet he stands up, and bows himself humbly before them, *v.* 7. Note, Religion teaches good manners; and those abuse it that place it in rudeness and clownishness.

IV. The present which Ephron made to Abraham of his field: *The field give I thee, v.* 10, 11. Abraham thought he must be entreated to sell it; but, upon the first mention of it, without entreaty, Ephron freely gives it. Some men have more generosity than they are thought to have.

V. Abraham's modest and sincere refusal of Ephron's kind offer, *v.* 12, 13. Abundance of thanks he returns him for it (*v.* 12), but resolves to give him money for the field, even the full value of it. Abraham was rich in silver and gold (*ch.* xiii. 2) and was able to pay for the field, and therefore would not take advantage of Ephron's generosity. Note, Honesty, as well as honour, forbids us to sponge upon our neighbours.

VI. The price of the land fixed by Ephron but not insisted on: *The land is worth four hundred shekels of silver* (about fifty pounds of our money), *but what is that between me and thee? v.* 14, 15. He would rather oblige his friend than have so much money in his pocket. When we are tempted to be high in demanding our rights, or hard in denying a kindness, we should answer the temptation with this question: "What is that between me and my friend?"

Verses 16–20

We have here the conclusion of the treaty between Abraham and Ephron about the burying-place. The bargain was publicly made before all the neighbours, *in the presence and audience of the sons of Heth, v.* 16, 17. Abraham, thereupon, takes possession, and buries Sarah in the cave which was in the purchased field. It is worth noting, (1) That a burying-place was the first spot of ground Abraham possessed in Canaan. Note, When we are entering into the world it is good to think of our going out of it; for, as soon as we are born, we begin to die. (2) That it was the only piece of land he ever possessed, though the country was all his own in reversion. Abraham sought a better country, that is, a heavenly. Abraham is content to be still flitting, while he lives, but secures a place where, when he dies, his flesh may rest in hope.

CHAPTER 24

Marriages and funerals are the changes of families, and the common news among the inhabitants of the villages. In the foregoing chapter we had Abraham burying his wife, here we have him marrying his son. These stories concerning his family, with their minute circumstances, are largely related, while the histories of the kingdoms of the world then in being, with their revolutions, are buried in silence. Here is, I. Abraham's care about the marrying of his son, ver. 1–9. II. His servant's journey into Abraham's country, to seek a wife for his young master among his own relations, ver. 10–14. III. The kind providence which brought him acquainted with Rebekah, whose father was Isaac's cousin-german, ver. 15–28. IV. The treaty of marriage with her relations, ver. 29–49. V. Their consent obtained, ver. 50–60. VI. The happy meeting and marriage between Isaac and Rebekah, ver. 61, &c.

Verses 1–9

Three things we may observe here concerning Abraham:—

I. The care he took of a good son, to get him married, well married. Now Abraham's pious care concerning his son was, (1) That he should not marry a daughter of Canaan, but one of his kindred. He saw that the Canaanites were degenerating into great wickedness. (2) That yet he should not leave the land of Canaan, to go himself among his kindred, not even for the purpose of choosing a wife, lest he should be tempted to settle there.

II. The charge he gave to a good servant, probably Eliezer of Damascus, one of whose conduct, fidelity, and affection to him and his family, he had had long experience. He trusted him with his great affair, and not Isaac himself, because he would not have Isaac go at all into that country, but marry there by proxy; and no proxy so fit as this *steward of his house.* 1. The servant must be bound by an oath to do his utmost to get a wife for Isaac from among his relations, *v.* 2–4. 2. He must be clear of this oath if, when he had done his utmost, he could not prevail.

III. The confidence he put in a good God, who, he doubts not, will give his servant success in this undertaking, *v.* 7. He remembers also the promise God had made and confirmed to him that he would give Canaan to his seed, and thence infers that God would own him in his endeavours to match his son, not among those devoted nations, but to one that was fit to be the mother of such a seed. God's promises, and our own experiences, are sufficient to encourage our dependence upon God, and our expectations from him, in all the affairs of this life.

Verses 10–28

Abraham's servant is not named, yet much is here recorded to his honour.

I. How faithful Abraham's servant approved himself to his master. Having received his charge, he with all expedition set out on his journey, with an equipage suitable to the object of his negotiation (*v.* 10).

II. How devoutly he acknowledged God in this affair, like one of that happy household which Abraham had *commanded to keep the way of the Lord,* &c., *ch.* xviii. 19. He arrived early in the evening (after many days' journeying) at the place of his destination, and reposed himself by a well of water, to consider how he might manage his business for the best. And,

1. He acknowledges God by a particular prayer (*v.* 12–14), wherein, (1) He petitions for prosperity and good success in this affair: *Send me good speed, this day.* Those that would have good speed must pray for it. (2) He pleads God's covenant with his master Abraham: *O God of my master Abraham, show kindness to him.* He desires that his master's wife might be a humble and industrious woman, bred up to care and labour, and willing to put her hand to any work that was to be done; and that she might be of a courteous disposition, and charitable to strangers. When he came to seek a wife for his master, he did not go to the playhouse or the park, and pray that he might meet one there, but to *the well of water,* expecting to find one there well employed.

2. God owns him by a particular providence. The answer to this prayer was, (1) Speedy—*before he had made an end of speaking* (*v.* 15). (2) Satisfactory: the first that came to draw water was, and did, in everything, according to his own heart. [1] She was so well qualified that in all respects she answered the characters he wished for in the woman that was to be his master's wife, handsome and healthful, humble and industrious, very courteous and obliging to a stranger, and having all the marks of a good disposition. When she came to the well (*v.* 16), she went down and *filled her pitcher, and came up* to go home with it. She did not stand to gaze upon the strange man and his camels, but minded her business, and would not have been diverted from it but by an opportunity of doing good. [2] Providence so ordered it that she did that which exactly answered to his sign, and was wonderfully the counterpart of his proposal: she not only gave him drink, but, which was more than could have been expected, she offered her services to give his camels drink, which was the very sign he proposed. Rebekah hereby, quite beyond her expectation at this time, was brought into the line of Christ and the covenant. There may

be a great deal of obliging kindness in that which costs but little: our Saviour has promised a reward for a cup of cold water, Matt. x. 42. [3] Upon enquiry he found, to his great satisfaction, that she was a near relation to his master, and that the family she was of was considerable, and able to give him entertainment, *v.* 23–25.

3. He acknowledges God in a particular thanksgiving. He first paid his respects to Rebekah, in gratitude for her civility (*v.* 22). Having done this, he turns his wonder (*v.* 21) into worshipping. He had prayed for good speed (*v.* 12), and now that he had sped well he gives thanks. What we win by prayer we must wear with praise. He thinks himself very happy, that he was led to the *house of his master's brethren*, those of them that had come out of Ur of the Chaldees. They were not idolators, but worshippers of the true God, and inclinable to the religion of Abraham's family.

Verses 29–53

We have here the making up of the marriage between Isaac and Rebekah.

I. The very kind reception given to Abraham's servant by Rebekah's relations. 1. The invitation was kind: *Come in, thou blessed of the Lord, v.* 31. Perhaps because they heard from Rebekah (*v.* 28) of the gracious words which proceeded out of his mouth. Note, Those that are blessed of God should be welcome to us. It is good owning those whom God owns. 2. The entertainment was kind, *v.* 32, 33. Particular care was taken of the camels; for a *good man regardeth the life of his beast*, Prov. xii. 10.

II. The full account which he gave them of his errand, and the court he made to them for their consent respecting Rebekah.

1. How intent he was upon his business; though he had come off a journey, and come to a good house, he would *not eat, till he had told his errand, v.* 33.

2. How ingenious he was in the management of it. (1) He gives a short account of his master's family, *v.* 34–36. Two things he suggests, to recommend his proposal:—[1] That his master Abraham, through the blessing of God, had a very good estate; and, [2] That he had settled it all upon Isaac, for whom he was now a suitor.

(2) He tells them the charge his master had given him, to fetch a wife for his son from among his kindred, with the reason of it, *v.* 37, 38. The highest degrees of divine affection must not divest us of natural affection.

(3) He relates to them the wonderful concurrence of providences, to countenance and further the proposal, plainly showing the finger of God in it.

(4) They freely and cheerfully close with the proposal upon a very good principle (*v.* 50): "*The thing proceedeth from the Lord*, Providence smiles upon it, and we have nothing to say against it."

(5) Abraham's servant makes a thankful acknowledgment of the good success he had met with, *He worshipped the Lord, v.* 52. God sent his angel before him, and so gave him success, *v.* 7, 40. But when he has the desired success, he worships God, not the angel.

Verses 54–61

Rebekah is here taking leave of her father's house. Rebekah's relations, from natural affection and according to the usual expression of kindness in that case, solic: her to stay some time among them, *v.* 55. They had consented to the marriage, and yet were loth to part with her. Rebekah herself determined the matter. Rebekah consented, not only to go, but to go immediately. Hereupon she is sent away with Abraham's servant; with suitable attendants; with hearty good wishes. Now that she was going to be a wife, they prayed that she might be a mother both of a numerous and of a victorious progeny.

Verses 62–67

Isaac and Rebekah are, at length, happily brought together.

I. Isaac was well employed when he met Rebekah: *He went out to meditate*, or pray, *in the field, at the even-tide, v.* 62, 63. He went to take the advantage of a silent evening and a solitary field for meditation and prayer, those divine exercises by which we converse with God and our own hearts. Note, 1. Holy souls love retirement. It will do us good to be often left alone, walking alone and sitting alone; and, if we have the art of improving solitude, we shall find we are never less alone than when alone. 2. Meditation and prayer ought to be both our business and our delight when we are alone. The exercises of devotion should be the refreshment and entertainment of the evening, to relieve us from the fatigue occasioned by the care and business of the day, and to prepare us for the repose and sleep of the night. Some think Isaac was now praying for good success in this affair that was depending, and now, when he sets himself, as it were, upon his watchtower, to see what God would answer him, as the prophet (Hab. ii. 1), *he sees the camels coming.*

II. Rebekah behaved herself very becomingly, when she met Isaac: understanding who he was, she *alighted off her camel* (*v.* 64), and *took a veil, and covered herself* (*v.* 65), in token of humility, modesty, and subjection.

III. They were brought together to their mutual comfort, *v.* 67. Observe here, 1. What an affectionate son he was to his mother: it was about three years since her death, and yet he was not, till now, comforted concerning it. 2. What an affectionate husband he was to his wife.

CHAPTER 25

The sacred historian, in this chapter, I. Takes his leave of Abraham, with an account, 1. Of his children by another wife, ver. 1–4. 2. Of his last will and testament, ver. 5, 6. 3. Of his age, death, and burial, ver. 7–10. II. He takes his leave of Ishmael, with a short account. 1. Of his children, ver. 12–16. 2. Of his age and death, ver. 17, 18. III. He enters upon the history of Isaac. 1. His prosperity, ver. 11. 2. The conception and birth of his two sons, with the oracle of God concerning them, ver. 19–26. 3. Their different characters, ver. 27, 28. 4. Esau's selling his birthright to Jacob, ver. 29–34.

Verses 1–10

Abraham lived, after the marriage of Isaac, thirty-five years, and all that is recorded concerning him during that time lies here in a very few verses. We hear no more of God's extraordinary appearances to him or trials of him; for all the days, even of the best and greatest saints, are not eminent days, some slide on silently, and neither come nor go with observation; such were these last days of Abraham.

I. An account of his children by Keturah, another wife whom he married after the death of Sarah.

II. The disposition which Abraham made of his estate, *v.* 5, 6. After the birth of these sons, he set his house in order, with prudence and justice. 1. He made Isaac his heir, as he was bound to do, in justice to Sarah his first and principal wife, and to Rebekah who married Isaac upon the assurance of it, *ch.* xxiv. 36. God having already made him the heir of the promise, Abraham therefore made him heir of his estate. 2. He gave portions to the rest of his children, both to Ishmael, though at first he was sent empty away, and to his sons by Keturah. It was justice to provide for them; parents that do not imitate him in this are worse than infidels. It was prudence to settle them in places distant from Isaac, that they might not pretend to divide the inheritance with him, nor be in any way a care or expense to him. Observe, He did this *while he yet lived*, lest it should not be done, or not so well done, afterwards.

III. The age and death of Abraham, *v.* 7, 8. He lived 175 years, just 100 years after he came to Canaan; so long he was a sojourner in a strange country. 1. He *gave up the ghost*. His life was not extorted from him, but he cheerfully resigned it; into the hands of the Father of spirits he committed his spirit. 2. He *died in a good old age, an old man*; so God had promised him. His death was his discharge from the burdens of his age. It was also the crown of the glory of his old age. 3. He was *full of years*, or full of *life*. He did not live till the world was weary of him, but till he was weary of the world; he had had enough of it, and desired no more. A good man, though he should not die old, dies full of days, satisfied with living here, and longing to live in a better place. 4. He *was gathered to his people*. His body was gathered to the congregation of the dead, and his soul to the congregation of the blessed. Death gathers us to our people. Those that are our people while we live, whether the people of God or the children of this world, are the people to whom death will gather us.

IV. His burial, *v.* 9, 10. 1. Who buried him: *His sons Isaac and Ishmael*. It was the last office of respect they had to pay to their good father. Some distance there had formerly been between Isaac and Ishmael; but it seems either that Abraham had himself brought them together while he lived, or at least that his death reconciled them. 2. Where they buried him: in his own burying-place, which he had purchased, and in which he had buried Sarah.

Verses 11–18

Immediately after the account of Abraham's death, Moses begins the story of Isaac (*v.* 11), and tells us where he dwelt and how remarkably God blessed him. But he presently digresses from the story of Isaac, to give a short account of Ishmael, forasmuch as he also was a son of Abraham, and God had made some promises concerning him. 1. Concerning his children. He had twelve sons, *twelve princes* they are called (*v.* 16), heads of families, which in process of time became nations, distinct tribes, numerous and very considerable. They peopled *Arabia*. The names of his twelve sons are recorded. Midian and Kedar we often read of in scripture. And some very good expositors have taken notice of the signification of those three names which are put together (*v.* 14), as containing good advice to us all, *Mishma, Dumah,* and *Massa*, that is, *hear, keep silence*, and *bear*; we have them together in the same order, Jam. i. 19, *Be swift to hear, slow to speak, slow to wrath*. The posterity of Ishmael had not only tents in the fields, wherein they grew rich in times of peace; but they had towns and castles (*v.* 16), wherein they fortified themselves in time of war. 2. Concerning himself. Here is an account of his age: He *lived* 137 *years* (*v.* 17), which is recorded to show the efficacy of Abraham's prayer for him (*ch.* xvii. 18), *O that Ishmael might live before thee !* Here is also an account of his death; he too *was gathered to his people*; but it is not said that he was *full of days*, though he lived to so great an age. He died with his friends about him, which is comfortable.

Verses 19–28

We have here an account of the birth of Jacob and Esau, the twin sons of Isaac and Rebekah: their entrance into the world was (which is not usual) one of the most considerable parts of their story. Isaac seems not to have been a man of action, nor much tried,

but to have spent his days in quietness and silence. Now concerning Jacob and Esau we are here told,

I. That they were prayed for. Their parents, after they had been long childless, obtained them by prayer, *v.* 20, 21. *Isaac was forty years old when he was married*. He was sixty years old when his sons were born (*v.* 26), so that, after he was married, he had no child for twenty years. But, 1. He prayed. He prayed *for* his wife; some read it *with* his wife. Note, Husbands and wives should pray together. The Jews have a tradition that Isaac, at length, took his wife with him to Mount Moriah, where God had promised that he would multiply Abraham's seed (*ch.* xxii. 17), and there, in his prayer with her and for her, pleaded the promise made in that very place. 2. God heard his prayer, and was entreated of him.

II. That they were prophesied of before they were born, and great mysteries were wrapped up in the prophecies which went before of them, *v.* 22, 23. Now Rebekah being with child of these two sons, observe here,

1. How she was perplexed in her mind concerning her present case: *The children struggled together within her*. This struggle between Jacob and Esau in the wcmb represents the struggle that is maintained between the kingdom of God and the kingdom of Satan. A holy war is better than the peace of the devil's palace.

2. What course she took for her relief: *She went to enquire of the Lord*. It is a great relief to the mind to spread our case before the Lord, and ask counsel at his mouth. *Go into the sanctuary*, Ps. lxxiii. 17.

3. The information given her, upon her enquiry, which expounded the mystery: *Two nations are in thy womb*, *v.* 23. She was now pregnant, not only with two children, but two nations, which should not only in their manners and dispositions greatly differ from each other, but in their interests clash and contend with each other; and the issue of the contest should be that the elder should serve the younger, which was fulfilled in the subjection of the Edomites, for many ages, to the house of David, till they revolted, 2 Chron. xxi. 8. In the struggle between grace and corruption in the soul, grace, the younger, shall certainly get the upper hand at last.

III. That when they were born there was a great difference between them.

1. There was a great difference in their bodies, *v.* 25. Esau, when he was born, was rough and hairy, as if he had been already a grown man, whence he had his name Esau, *made*, reared already. This was an indication of a very strong constitution, and gave cause to expect that he would be a very robust, daring, active man. But Jacob was smooth and tender as other children. It is God's usual way to choose the weak things of the world, and to pass by the mighty, 1 Cor. i. 26, 27.

2. There was a manifest contest in their births.

3. They were very unlike in the temper of their minds, and the way of living they chose, *v.* 27. (1) Esau was a man for this world. He was a man addicted to his sports, for he was a cunning hunter. He was a man of the field, like Nimrod and Ishmael. (2) Jacob was a man for the other world. He was not cut out for a statesman, nor did he affect to look great, but he was *a plain man, dwelling in tents*, an honest man that always meant well, and dealt fairly, that preferred the true delights of solitude and retirement to all the pretended pleasure of busy noisy sports: he dwelt in tents, [1] As a shepherd. He was attached to that safe and silent employment of keeping sheep, to which also he bred up his children, *ch.* xlvi. 34. Or, [2] As a student. He frequented the tents of Melchizedek, or Heber, as some understand it, to be taught by them divine things. And this was that son of Isaac on whom the covenant was entailed.

4. Their interest in the affections of their parents was likewise different. They had but these two children, and, it seems, one was the father's darling and the other the mother's, *v.* 28. (1) Isaac loved to have his son active. Esau knew how to please him, and showed a great respect for him, by treating him often with venison. (2) Rebekah was mindful of the oracle of God, which had given the preference to Jacob, and therefore she preferred him in her love.

Verses 29—34

We have here a bargain made between Jacob and Esau about the birthright, which was Esau's by providence but Jacob's by promise. It was a spiritual privilege, such a birthright as had then the blessing annexed to it, and the entail of the promise.

I. Jacob's pious desire of the birthright, which yet he sought to obtain by indirect courses. For this he is to be commended, that he coveted earnestly the best gifts; yet in this he cannot be justified, that he took advantage of his brother's necessity to make him a very hard bargain (*v.* 31): *Sell me this day thy birthright.* Note, Plain men that have their conversation in simplicity and godly sincerity, and without worldly wisdom, are often found wisest of all for their souls and eternity. Jacob's wisdom appeared in two things:—1. He chose the fittest time. 2. Having made the bargain, he made it sure, and got it confirmed by Esau's oath: *Swear to me this day,* *v.* 33.

II. Esau's profane contempt of the birthright, and the foolish sale he made of it. He is called *profane Esau* for it (Heb. xii. 16), because *for one morsel of meat he sold his birthright,* as dear a morsel as ever was eaten since the forbidden fruit; and he lived to regret it when it was too late. Note, There are those that are penny-wise and pound-foolish, cunning hunters that can out-wit others and draw them into their snares, and yet are themselves imposed upon by Satan's wiles and led captive by him at his will. Observe the instances of Esau's folly.

1. His appetite was very strong, *v.* 29, 30. Poor Jacob had got some bread and pottage (*v.* 34) for his dinner, when Esau came from hunting, hungry and weary. Give me (says he) some of *that red, that red,* as it is in the original. The gratifying of the sensual appetite is that which ruins thousands of precious souls: surely, if Esau was hungry and faint, he might have got a meal's meat cheaper than at the expense of his birthright.

2. His reasoning was very weak (*v.* 32): *Behold, I am at the point to die;* and, if he were, would nothing serve to keep him alive but this pottage? If the famine were now in the land (*ch.* xxvi. 1), as Dr. Lightfoot conjectures, we cannot suppose Isaac so poor, or Rebekah so bad a housekeeper, but that he might have been supplied with food convenient, in other ways. Note, It is egregious folly to part with our interest in God, and Christ, and heaven, for the riches, honours, and pleasures, of this world, as bad a bargain as his that sold a birthright for a dish of broth.

3. Repentance was hidden from his eyes (*v.* 34): *He did eat and drink,* pleased his palate, and then carelessly rose up and went his way, without any show of regret. Thus Esau despised his birthright.

CHAPTER 26

In this chapter we have, I. Isaac in adversity, by reason of a famine which, 1. Obliges him to change his quarters, ver. 1. But, 2. God visits him with direction and comfort, ver. 2–5. 3. He foolishly denies his wife, ver. 6–11. II. Isaac in prosperity, ver. 12–14. And, 1. The Philistines were envious, ver. 14–17. 2. He continued industrious, ver. 18–23. 3. God encouraged him, ver. 24, 25. 4. The Philistines, at length, made a covenant with him, ver. 26–33. 5. The disagreeable marriage of his son Esau, ver. 34, 35.

Verses 1–5

I. God tried Isaac by his providence. Now there is *a famine in the land,* *v.* 1. What shall he think of the promise when the promised land will not find him bread? Yes, Isaac will still cleave to the covenant. Note, The intrinsic worth of God's promises cannot be lessened in a believer's eye by any cross providences.

II. He directed him under this trial by his word. Isaac must go for supply. He set out for Egypt, whither his father went in the like strait, but he takes Gerar in his way. 1. God bade him stay where he was, and *not go down into Egypt: Sojourn in this land,* *v.* 2, 3. There was a famine in Jacob's days, and God bade him *go down into Egypt* (*ch.* xlvi. 3, 4), a famine in *Isaac's* days, and God made him *not to go down,* a famine in Abraham's days, and God left him to his liberty. This variety in the divine procedure some ground upon the different characters of these three patriarchs. Abraham was a man of very high attainments, and intimate communion with God; and to him all places and conditions were alike. Isaac was a very good man, but not cut out for hardship; therefore he is forbidden to go to Egypt. Jacob was inured to difficulties, strong and patient; and therefore he must go down into Egypt. Thus God proportions his people's trials to their strength. "*Abraham obeyed my voice;* do thou do so too, and the promise shall be sure to thee." Abraham's obedience is here celebrated, to his honour; for by it he obtained a good report both with God and men.

Verses 6–11

Isaac had now set up his staff in Gerar, the country in which he was born (*v.* 6), yet there he enters into temptation to deny his wife, and to give out that she was his sister.

I. How he sinned, *v.* 7. Because his wife was handsome, he fancied the Philistines would find some way or other to take him off, that some of them might marry her; and therefore she must pass for his sister.

II. How he was detected, and the cheat discovered, by the king himself. Abimelech (not the same that was in Abraham's days, *ch.* xx, for this was nearly 100 years after that, but this was the common name of the Philistine kings) saw Isaac more familiar with Rebekah than he knew he would be with his sister (*v.* 8): he saw him sporting with her, or *laughing;* it is the same word with that from which Isaac had his name. Nowhere may a man more allow himself to be innocently merry than with his own wife and children. Abimelech charged him with the fraud (*v.* 9), showed him what might have been the bad consequences of it (*v.* 10), and then, to convince him how groundless and unjust his jealousy of them was, took him and his family under his particular protection, forbidding any injury to be done to him or his wife upon pain of death, *v.* 11.

Verses 12–25

I. The tokens of God's good-will to Isaac. 1. His corn multiplied strangely, *v.* 12. He had no land of his own, but took land of the Philistines, and sowed it; and (be it observed for the encouragement of poor tenants, that occupy other people's lands, and are honest and industrious) God blessed him with a great increase. He reaped *a hundred fold* that *same year* when there was a famine in the land. 2. His cattle also increased, *v.* 14. And then, 3. He had *great store of servants,* whom he employed and maintained.

II. The tokens of the Philistines' ill-will to him. They *envied him,* *v.* 14. That is a bad principle indeed which makes men *grieve at the good of others,* as if it must needs be ill with me because it is well with my neighbour. Because they had not flocks of their own to water at the wells, they would not leave them for the use of others; so absurd a thing is malice. The king of Gerar began to look upon him with a jealous eye. Isaac's house was like a court and therefore he must go further off. A wise and a good man will rather retire into obscurity, like Isaac here into a valley, than sit high to be the butt of envy and ill-will.

III. His constancy and continuance in his business still.

1. He kept up his husbandry, and continued industrious to find wells of water, and he set himself to make the best of the country he had come into, which it is every man's prudence to do.

(1) He opened the wells that his father had digged (v. 18). Note, In our searches after truth, that fountain of living water, it is good to make use of the discoveries of former ages, which have been clouded by the corruptions of later times. Enquire for the old way, the wells which our fathers digged, which the adversaries of truth have stopped up.

(2) His servants dug new wells, v. 19. Note, Though we must use the light of former ages, it does not therefore follow that we must rest in it, and make no advances. We must still be building upon their foundation.

(3) In digging his wells he met with much opposition, v. 20, 21. Those that open the fountains of truth must expect contradiction. The first two wells which they dug were called *Esek* and *Sitnah, contention* and *hatred.*

(4) At length he removed to a quiet settlement. He preferred quietness to victory. Note, Those that follow peace, sooner or later, shall find peace. This well they called *Rehoboth, enlargements,* room enough: in the two former wells we may see what the earth is, *straitness* and *strife.* This well shows us what heaven is; it is *enlargement* and *peace,* room enough there, for there are many mansions.

2. He continued firm to his religion, and kept up his communion with God. He came weary and uneasy to Beer-sheba. *Fear not,* says God to him, *I am with thee, and will bless thee.* Those may remove with comfort that are sure of God's presence with them wherever they go. *There he built an altar, and called upon the name of the Lord,* v. 25.

Verses 26–33

We have here the contests that had been between Isaac and the Philistines issuing in a happy peace and reconciliation.

I. Abimelech pays a friendly visit to Isaac, in token of the respect he had for him, v. 26.

II. Isaac prudently and cautiously questions his sincerity in this visit, v. 27.

III. Abimelech professes his sincerity, in this address to Isaac, and earnestly courts his friendship, v. 28, 29. Isaac complained they had *hated him, and sent him away.* No, said Abimelech, *we sent thee away in peace.* He acknowledges the tokens of God's favour to him, and makes this the ground of their desire, to be in league with him: *The Lord is with thee, and thou art the blessed of the Lord.*

IV. Isaac entertains him and his company, and enters into a league of friendship with him, v. 30, 31. Note, Religion teaches us to be neighbourly, and, as much as in us lies, to *live peaceably with all men.*

V. Providence smiled upon what Isaac did; for the same day that he made this covenant with Abimelech his servants brought him the tidings of a well of water they had found, v. 32, 33.

Verses 34–35

Here is, 1. Esau's foolish marriage—foolish, in marrying Canaanites, who were strangers to the blessing of Abraham, for which he is called *profane;* for hereby he intimated that he neither desired the blessing nor dreaded the curse of God. 2. The grief and trouble it created to his tender parents. It grieved them that he married the daughters of Hittites, who had no religion among them.

CHAPTER 27

In this chapter we return to the typical story of the struggle between Esau and Jacob. Esau had profanely sold the birthright to Jacob. Thus this story is explained, Heb. xii. 16, 17, "Because he sold the birthright, when he would have inherited the blessing he was rejected." We have here, I. Isaac's purpose to entail the blessing upon Esau, ver. 1–5. II. Rebekah's plot to procure it for Jacob, ver. 6–17. III. Jacob's successful management of the plot, and his obtaining the blessing, ver. 18–29. IV. Esau's resentment of this, in which, 1. His great importunity wit his father to obtain a blessing, ver. 30–40. 2. His great enmity to his brother for defrauding him of the first blessing, ver. 41, &c.

Verses 1–5

Here is, I. Isaac's design to make his will, and to declare Esau his heir.

II. The directions he gave to Esau, pursuant to this design. He calls him to him, v. 1. For Esau, though he had greatly grieved his parents by his marriage, yet they had not expelled him, but made the best of it. Parents that are justly offended at their children yet must not be implacable towards them.

1. He tells him upon what considerations he resolved to do this now (v. 2).

2. He bids him to get things ready for the solemnity of executing his last will and testament, by which he designed to make him his heir, v. 3, 4. Esau must go a hunting, and bring some venison, which his father will eat of, and then bless him. Prayer is the work of the soul, and not of the lips only; as the soul must be employed in blessing God (Ps. ciii. 1), so it must be in blessing ourselves and others: the blessing will not come to the heart if it do not come from the heart.

Verses 6–17

Rebekah is here contriving to procure for Jacob the blessing which was designed for Esau.

I. The end was good. God had said it should be so, that the elder should *serve the younger;* and therefore Rebekah resolves it shall be so. But,

II. The means were bad, and no way justifiable. If it was not wrong to Esau to deprive him of the blessing (he himself having forfeited it by selling the birthright), yet it was a wrong to Isaac, taking advantage of his infirmity, to impose upon him; it was a wrong to Jacob too, whom she taught to deceive. It would likewise expose him to endless scruples about the blessing, if h should obtain it thus fraudulently. If Rebekah had gone to Isaac, and put him in remembrance of that which God had said concerning their sons,—if she further had shown him how Esau had forfeited the blessing both by selling his birthright and by marrying strange wives, it is probable that Isaac would have been prevailed upon to confer the blessing upon Jacob.

Verses 18–29

Observe here, I. The art and assurance with which Jacob managed this intrigue. Who would have thought that his plain man could have played his part so well in a design of this nature? Note, Lying is soon learnt. I wonder how honest Jacob could so readily turn his tongue to say (v. 19), *I am Esau thy firstborn.* How could he say, *I have done as thou badest me,* when he had received no command from his father, but was doing as his mother bade him? How could he say, *Eat of my venison,* when he knew it came, not from the field, but from the fold? But especially I wonder how he could have the assurance to father it upon God, and to use his name in the cheat (v. 20):

The Lord thy God brought it to me. Is this Jacob? Is this Israel, indeed, without guile? It is certainly written, not for our imitation, but for our admonition.

II. The success of this management. Jacob with some difficulty gained his point, and obtained the blessing.

1. Isaac was at first dissatisfied, and would have discovered the fraud if he could have trusted his own ears; for *the voice was Jacob's voice, v.* 22. His voice is Jacob's voice, but his hands are Esau's. He speaks the language of a saint, but does the works of a sinner; but the judgment will be, as here, by the hands.

2. At length he yielded to the power of the cheat, *because the hands were hairy (v.* 23), not considering how easy it was to counterfeit that circumstance; and now Jacob carries it on dexterously. That which in some small degree extenuates the crime of Rebekah and Jacob is that the fraud was intended, not so much to hasten the fulfilling, as to prevent the thwarting, of the oracle of God: the blessing was just going to be put upon the wrong head, and they thought it was time to bestir themselves. Now let us see how Isaac gave Jacob his blessing, *v.* 26–9. (1) He embraces him, in token of a particular affection to him. (2) He praised him. *He smelt the smell of his raiment, and said, See, the smell of my son is as the smell of a field which the Lord hath blessed.* (3) He rpayed for him, and therein prophesied concerning him. Three things Jacob is here blessed with:—[1] Plenty (*v.* 28). [2] Power (*v.* 29). [3] Prevalence with God, and a great interest in Heaven: *"Cursed be every one that curseth thee and blessed be he that blesseth thee."*

Verses 30–40

Here is, I. The covenant-blessing denied to Esau. He that made so light of the birthright *would now have inherited the blessing.* Observe, 1. How carefully he sought it. When he understood that Jacob had obtained it surreptitiously, he *cried with a great and exceedingly bitter cry, v.* 34. Those that will not so much as ask and seek now, will knock shortly, and cry, *Lord, Lord.* Slighters of Christ will then be humble suitors to him. 2. How he was rejected. Isaac, when first made sensible of the imposition that had been practised on him, *trembled exceedingly, v.* 33. But he soon recovers himself, and ratifies the blessing he had given to Jacob: *I have blessed him, and he shall be blessed.* Having found himself more than ordinarily filled with the Holy Ghost when he gave the blessing to Jacob, he perceived that God did, as it were, say Amen to it. Now, (1) Jacob was hereby confirmed in his possession of the blessing. (2) Isaac hereby acquiesced in the will of God, though it contradicted his own expectation and affection. (3) Esau hereby was cut off from the expectation of that special blessing which he thought to have preserved to himself when he sold his birthright. The Jews, like Esau, hunted *after the law of righteousness (v.* 31), yet missed of the blessing of righteousness, *because they sought it by the works of the law (v.* 32); while the Gentiles, who, like Jacob, sought it by faith in the oracle of God, obtained it by force, with that violence which the kingdom of heaven suffers. See Matt. xi. 12. Those who undervalue their spiritual birthright, and can afford to sell it for a morsel of meat, forfeit spiritual blessings. Those that will part with their wisdom and grace, with their faith and a good conscience, for the honours, wealth, or pleasures, of this world, however they may pretend a zeal for the blessing, have already judged themselves unworthy of it.

II. Here is a common blessing bestowed upon Esau.

1. This he desired: *Bless me also, v.* 34. *Hast thou*

not reserved a blessing for me?, v. 36. It is the folly of most men that they are willing to take up with any good (Ps. iv. 6), as Esau here, who desired but a second-rate blessing, a blessing separated from the birthright. As if he had said, "I will take up with any: though I have not the blessing of the church, yet let me have some blessing."

2. This he had; and let him make his best of it, *v.* 39, 40.

(1) It was promised him, [1] That he should have a competent livelihood—*the fatness of the earth, and the dew of heaven.* Note, Those that come short of the blessings of the covenant may yet have a very good share of outward blessings. [2] That by degrees he should recover his liberty. He shall serve, but he shall not starve; and, at length after much skirmishing, he shall break the yoke of bondage, and wear the marks of freedom. This was fulfilled (2 Kings viii. 20, 22) when the Edomites revolted.

(2) Yet it was far short of Jacob's blessing. For him God had reserved some better thing. In Jacob's blessing *the dew of heaven* is put first, as that which he most valued. In Esau's *the fatness of the earth* is put first, for it was this that he had the principal regard to. Jacob shall have dominion over his brethren: hence the Israelites often ruled over the Edomites. But the great difference is that there is nothing in Esau's blessing that points to Christ, nothing that brings him or his into the church and covenant of God, without which the fatness of the earth will stand him in little stead.

Verses 41–46

Here is, I. The malice Esau bore to Jacob upon account of the blessing which he had obtained, *v.* 41. Esau's hatred of Jacob was, 1. A causeless hatred. He hated him for no other reason but because his father blessed him and God loved him. 2. It was a cruel hatred. Nothing less would satisfy him than to slay his brother. 3. It was a politic hatred. He expected his father would soon die, and then titles must be tried and interests contested between the brothers, which would give him a fair opportunity for revenge.

II. The method Rebekah took to prevent the mischief.

1. She gave Jacob warning of his danger, and advised him to withdraw for a while, and shift for his own safety. Observe here, (1) What Rebekah feared—lest she *should be deprived of them both in one day (v.* 45). (2) What Rebekah hoped—that, if Jacob for a while kept out of sight, the affront which his brother resented so fiercely would by degrees go out of mind.

2. She impressed Isaac with an apprehension of the necessity of Jacob's going among her relations upon another account, which was to take a wife, *v.* 46.

CHAPTER 28

We have here, I. Jacob parting with his parents, to go to Padan-aram; the charge his father gave him (ver. 1, 2), the blessing he sent him away with (ver. 3, 4), and his obedience to the orders given him (ver. 5, 10), and the influence this had upon Esau, ver. 6–9. II. Jacob meeting with God, and his communion with him by the way. And there, 1. His vision of the ladder, ver. 11, 12. 2. The gracious promises God made him, ver. 13–15. 3. The impression this made upon him, ver. 16–19. 4. The vow he made to God, upon this occasion, ver. 20, &c.

Verses 1–5

Jacob had no sooner obtained the blessing than immediately he was forced to flee from his country.

Now *Jacob fled into Syria,* Hos. xii. 12. He was blessed with plenty of corn and wine, and yet he went away poor, was blessed with government, and yet went out to service, a hard service. This was, 1. Perhaps to correct him for his dealing fraudulently with his father. The blessing shall be confirmed to him, and yet he shall smart for the indirect course he took to obtain it. However, 2. It was to teach us that those who inherit the blessing must expect persecution; those who have peace in Christ shall have tribulation in the world, John xvi. 33. Now Jacob is here dismissed by his father.

I. With a solemn charge: *He blessed him, and charged him, v.* 1, 2. Note, Those that have the blessing must keep the charge annexed to it, and not think to separate what God has joined. If Jacob be an heir of promise, he must *not take a wife of the daughters of Canaan*; those that profess religion should not marry those that are irreligious.

II. With a solemn blessing, *v.* 3, 4. He had before blessed him unwittingly; now he does it designedly, for the greater encouragement of Jacob in that melancholy condition to which he was now removing. This blessing is more express and full than the former; it is an entail of the blessing of Abraham. It is a gospel blessing, Gal. iii. 14. It is a blessing from God Almighty, by which name God appeared to the patriarchs, Exod. vi. 3.

1. The promise of heirs: *God make thee fruitful, and multiply thee, v.* 3. (1) And never was such a multitude of people so often gathered into one assembly as the tribes of Israel were in the wilderness, and afterwards. (2) Through his loins should descend from Abraham that person in whom all the families of the earth should be blessed, for all things in heaven and earth are united in Christ (Eph. i. 10).

2. The promise of an inheritance for those heirs: *That thou mayest inherit the land of thy sojournings, v.* 4. Canaan was hereby entailed upon the seed of Jacob, exclusive of the seed of Esau. He is here told that he should inherit the land wherein he sojourned. Those have the best enjoyment of present things that sit most loose to them. This was the better country, which Jacob, with the other patriarchs, had in his eye, when he confessed himself "a stranger and pilgrim upon the earth," Heb. xi. 13.

Away he went to Padan-aram, *v.* 5.

Verses 6–9

This passage concerning Esau comes in in the midst of Jacob's story, either, 1. To show the influence of a good example. Esau, though the greater man, now begins to think Jacob the better man, and disdains not to take him for his pattern in this particular instance of marrying with a daughter of Abraham. Or, 2. To show the folly of an after-wit. Esau did well, but he did it when it was too late. He *saw that the daughters of Canaan pleased not his father,* and he might have seen that long ago if he had consulted his father's judgment as much as he did his palate. And how did he now mend the matter? Why, truly, so as to make bad worse. He married a daughter of Ishmael, the son of the bond-woman, who was cast out. He did it only to please his father, not to please God. He rested in a partial reformation.

Verses 10–15

We have here Jacob upon his journey towards Syria, in a very desolate condition. The first night, he had made a long day's journey from Beersheba to Bethel, and there he had,

I. A hard lodging (*v.* 11), the *stones for his pillows,* and the heavens for his canopy and curtains.

II. In his hard lodging he had a pleasant dream. Any Israelite indeed would be willing to take up with Jacob's pillow, provided he might but have Jacob's dream. Then, and there, he *heard the words of God, and saw the visions of the Almighty.* It was the best night's sleep he ever had in his life.

1. The encouraging vision Jacob saw, *v.* 12. He saw a ladder which reached from earth to heaven, the angels ascending and descending upon it, and God himself at the head of it. Now this represents:—

(1) The providence of God, by which there is a constant correspondence kept up between heaven and earth. Providence does its work gradually, and by steps. The wisdom of God is at the upper end of the ladder, directing all the motions of second causes to the glory of the first Cause. This vision gave very seasonable comfort to Jacob, letting him know that he had both a good guide and a good guard, in his going out and coming in. (2) The mediation of Christ. He is this ladder, the foot on earth in his human nature, the top in heaven in his divine nature: or the former in his humiliation, the latter in his exaltation. If God dwell with us, and we with him, it is by Christ. We have no way of getting to heaven, but by this ladder: if we climb up any other way we are thieves and robbers. To this vision our Saviour alludes when he speaks of the angels of God *ascending and descending upon the Son of man* (John i. 51).

2. The encouraging words Jacob heard.

(1) The former promises made to his father were repeated and ratified to him, *v.* 13, 14. In general, God intimated to him that he would be the same to him that he had been to Abraham and Isaac. [1] The land of Canaan is settled upon him. [2] It is promised him that his posterity should multiply exceedingly as the dust of the earth. [3] It is added that the Messiah should come from his loins, in whom all the families of the earth should be blessed.

(2) Fresh promises were made him. [1] Jacob was apprehensive of danger from his brother Esau; but God promises to keep him. [2] He had now a long journey before him, had to travel alone, in an unknown road, to an unknown country; but, *behold, I am with thee,* says God. [3] He knew not, but God foresaw, what hardships he should meet with in his uncle's service, and therefore promises to preserve him in all places. [4] He was now going as an exile into a place far distant, but God promises him to bring him back again to this land. [5] He seemed to be forsaken of all his friends, but God here gives him this assurance, *I will not leave thee.* Note, Whom God loves he never leaves.

Verses 16–22

Behold his sleep was sweet to him. Here is much of Jacob's devotion on this occasion.

I. He expressed a great surprise at the tokens he had of God's special presence with him in that place: *Surely the Lord is in this place and I knew it not, v.* 16. Note, God can give undeniable demonstrations of his presence, satisfaction not communicable to others, but convincing to themselves. No place excludes divine visits (*ch.* xvi. 13, *here also*); wherever we are, in the city or in the desert, in the house or in the field, in the shop or in the street.

II. It struck an awe upon him (*v.* 17): *He was afraid.* He said, *How dreadful is this place!* What he saw there at this time was, as it were, *the house of God,* and *the gate of heaven.*

III. He took care to preserve the memorial of it two ways: 1. He set up the stone for a pillar (*v.* 18), because he had not time now to build an altar here, as Abraham did in the places where God appeared to him, *ch.* xii. 7. He therefore *poured oil on the top of this stone,* as an earnest of his building an altar when he should have conveniences for it, as afterwards he did, in gratitude to God for this vision, *ch.* xxxv. 7. 2. He gave a new name to the place, *v.* 19. It had been called *Luz, an almond-tree*; but he will have it henceforward called *Beth-el, the house of God.*

IV. He made a solemn vow upon this occasion, *v.* 20–22. When God ratifies his promises to us, it is proper for us to repeat our promises to him. Now in this vow observe, 1. Jacob's faith. God had said (*v.* 15), *I am with thee, and will keep thee.* Jacob takes hold of this, and infers, "I depend upon it." 2. Jacob's modesty and great moderation in his desires. He will cheerfully content himself with bread to eat, and raiment to put on. Nature is content with a little, and grace with less. 3. Jacob's piety, and his regard to God, which appear here, (1) In what he desired, that God would be with him and keep him. (2) In what he designed. His resolution is, [1] In general, to cleave to the Lord, as his God in covenant: *Then shall the Lord be my God.* [2] In particular, that he would perform some special acts of devotion, in token of his gratitude. *First,* "This pillar shall keep possession here till I come back in peace, and then an altar shall be erected here to the honour of God." *Secondly,* "The house of God shall not be unfurnished, nor his altar without a sacrifice: *Of all that thou shalt give me I will surely give the tenth unto thee,* to be spent either upon God's altars or upon his poor," both which are his receivers in the world.

Chapter 29

This chapter gives us an account of God's providence concerning Jacob. I. How he was brought in safety to his journey's end, ver. 1-14. II. How he was comfortably disposed of in marriage, ver. 15-30. III. How his family was built up in the birth of four sons, ver. 31-35.

Verses 1-8

1. We are here told how cheerfully he proceeded in his journey after the sweet communion he had with God at Beth-el: *Then Jacob lifted up his feet;* so the margin reads it, *v.* 1. 2. How happily he arrived at his journey's end. Providence brought him to the very field, where his uncle's flocks were to be watered, and there he met with Rachel, who was to be his wife. (1) The divine Providence is to be acknowledged in all the little circumstances which concur to make a journey, or other undertaking, comfortable and successful. If we meet seasonably with those that can direct us we must not say that it was by chance, but that it was by Providence, and that God therein favoured us. (2) What is here said of the constant care of the shepherds concerning their sheep (*v.* 2, 3, 7, 8) may serve to illustrate the tender concern which our Lord Jesus, the great Shepherd of the sheep, has for his flock, the church; for he is the good Shepherd, that knows his sheep, and is known of them, John x. 14. (3) When all the shepherds came together with their flocks, then, like loving neighbours, at watering-time, they watered their flocks together. (4) It becomes us to speak civilly and respectfully to strangers. The law of kindness in the tongue has a commanding power, Prov. xxxi. 26.

Verses 9-14

Here we see, 1. Rachel's humility and industry: *She kept her father's sheep* (*v.* 9). 2. Jacob's tenderness and affection. When he understood that this was his kinswoman he was wonderfully anxious to serve her (*v.* 10). 3. It is groundless conceit which some of the Jewish writers have, that Jacob, when he kissed Rachel, wept because he had been set upon in his journey by Eliphaz the eldest son of Esau, at the command of his father, and robbed of all his money and jewels, which his mother had given him when she sent him away. It was plain that it was his passion for Rachel, and the surprise of this happy meeting, that drew these tears from his eyes. 4. Laban, though none of the best-humoured men, bade him welcome, was satisfied in the account he gave of himself, and of the reason of his coming in such poor circumstances.

Verses 15-30

Here is, I. The fair contract made between Laban and Jacob, during the month that Jacob spent there as a guest, *v.* 14. Now Jacob had a fair opportunity to make known to Laban the affection he had for his daughter Rachel; and, having no worldly goods in his hand with which to endow her, he promises him seven years' service, upon condition that, at the end of the seven years, he would bestow her upon him for his wife.

II. Jacob's honest performance of his part of the bargain, *v.* 20. Jacob honestly served out his seven years. *They seemed to him but a few days, for the love he had to her,* as if it were more his desire to earn her than to have her.

III. The base cheat which Laban put upon him when he was out of his time: he put Leah into his arms instead of Rachel, *v.* 23. This was Laban's sin; he wronged both Jacob and Rachel. It is easy to observe here how Jacob was paid in his own coin. He had cheated his own father when he pretended to be Esau, and now his father-in-law cheated him.

IV. The excuse and atonement Laban made for the cheat. 1. The excuse was frivolous: *It must not be so done in our country, v.* 26. There was no such custom of his country as he pretends; only he banters Jacob with it, and laughs at his mistake. 2. His compounding the matter did but make bad worse: *We will give thee this also, v.* 27. Hereby he drew Jacob into the sin, and snare, and disquiet, of multiplying wives, which remains a blot in his escutcheon. Honest Jacob did not design it. He could not refuse Rachel, for he had espoused her; still less could he refuse Leah, for he had married her. The polygamy of the patriarchs was, in some measure, excusable in them, because though there was a reason against it as ancient as Adam's marriage (Mal. ii. 15), yet there was no express command against it; it was in them a sin of ignorance. It will by no means justify the like practice now, when God's will is plainly made known, that one man and one woman only must be joined together, 1 Cor. vii. 2. Dr. Lightfoot makes Leah and Rachel to be figures of the two churches, the Jews under the law and the Gentiles under the gospel: the younger the more beautiful, and more in the thoughts of Christ when he came in the form of a servant; but the other, like Leah, first embraced.

Verses 31-35

We have here the birth of four of Jacob's sons, all by Leah. Observe, 1. That Leah, who was less beloved, was blessed with children, when Rachel was denied that blessing, *v.* 31. 2. The names she gave her children were expressive of her respectful regards both to God and to her husband. She called her first-born *Reuben* (*see a son*), with this pleasant thought, *Now will my husband love me;* and her third son *Levi* (*joined*), with this expectation, *Now will my husband be joined unto me, v.* 34. She thankfully acknowledges the kind providence of God in it: *The Lord hath looked upon my affliction, v.* 32. "*The Lord hath heard that I was hated, he has therefore given me this son.*" Her fourth she called *Judah* (*praise*), saying, *Now will I praise the Lord, v.* 35. And this was he of whom, as concerning the flesh, Christ came. He descended from him whose name was praise, for he is our praise. Is Christ formed in my heart ? *Now will I praise the Lord.*

Chapter 30

In this chapter we have an account of the increase, I. Of Jacob's family. Eight children more we find registered in this chapter; II. Of Jacob's estate. He makes a new bargain with Laban, ver. 25-34. And in this six years' further service he did to Laban God wonderfully blessed him, so that his stock of cattle became very considerable, ver. 35-43.

Verses 1–13

We have here the bad consequences of that strange marriage which Jacob made with the two sisters. Here is,

I. An unhappy disagreement between him and Rachel (v. 1, 2), occasioned, not so much by her own barrenness as by her sister's fruitfulness.

1. Rachel frets. She *envied her sister*, v. 1. Envy is grieving at the good of another, than which no sin is more offensive to God, nor more injurious to our neighbour and ourselves.

2. Jacob chides, and most justly. He loved Rachel, and therefore reproved her for what she said amiss, v. 2. Note, Faithful reproofs are products and instances of true affection, Ps. cxli. 5; Prov. xxvii. 5, 6. He was angry, not at the person, but at the sin; he expressed himself so as to show his displeasure. It was a very grave and pious reply which Jacob gave to Rachel's peevish demand: *Am I in God's stead?* The Chaldee paraphrases it well, *Dost thou ask sons of me? Oughtest thou not to ask them from before the Lord?* The Arabic reads it, "*Am I above God? Can I give thee that which God denies thee?*"

II. An unhappy agreement between him and the two handmaids.

1. At the persuasion of Rachel, he took Bilhah her handmaid to wife, that, according to the usage of those times, his children by her might be adopted and owned as her mistress's children, v. 3, &c. She would rather have children by reputation than none at all, children that she might fancy to be her own, and call her own, though they were not so. She takes a pleasure in giving them names that carry in them nothing but marks of emulation with her sister, as if she had overcome her, (1) At law. She calls the first son of her handmaid *Dan* (*judgment*), saying, "*God hath judged me*" (v. 6), that is, "given sentence in my favour." (2) In battle. She calls the next *Naphtali* (*wrestlings*), saying, *I have wrestled with my sister, and have prevailed* (v. 8); as if all Jacob's sons must be born men of contention.

2. At the persuasion of Leah, he took Zilpah her handmaid to wife also, v. 9. Two sons Zilpah bore to Jacob, whom Leah looked upon herself as entitled to, in token of which she called one *Gad* (v. 11), promising herself a little *troop* of children. The other she called *Asher* (*happy*), thinking herself happy in him. There was much amiss in the contest and competition between these two sisters, yet God brought good out of this evil. Thus Jacob's family was replenished with twelve sons, heads of the thousands of Israel, from whom the celebrated twelve tribes descended and were named.

Verses 14–24

I. Reuben, a little lad, five or six years old, playing in the field, found *mandrakes, dudaim*. It is uncertain what they were, either fruits or flowers that were very pleasant to the smell. There are products of the earth in the exposed fields, as well as in the planted protected gardens, that are very valuable and useful. It is a laudable custom of the devout Jews, when they find pleasure, suppose in eating an apple, to lift up their hearts, and say, "Blessed be he that made this fruit pleasant!" Or, in smelling a flower, "Blessed be he that made this flower sweet." Some think these mandrakes were jessamine flowers. Whatever they were, Rachel could not see them in Leah's hands, where the child had placed them, but she must covet them. The learned bishop Patrick very well suggests here that the true reason of this contest between Jacob's wives for his company, and their giving him their maids to be his wives, was the earnest desire they had to fulfil the promise made to Abraham that his seed should be as the stars of heaven for multitude. And he thinks it would have been below

the dignity of this sacred history to take such particular notice of these things if there had not been some such great consideration in them. Leah was now blessed with two sons; the first she called *Issachar* (*a hire*), reckoning herself well repaid for her mandrakes. The other she called *Zebulun* (*dwelling*), owning God's bounty to her: *God has endowed me with a good dowry*, v. 20. She reckons a family of children not a bill of charges, but a good dowry, Ps. cxiii. 9. Mention is made (v. 21) of the birth of a daughter, *Dinah*, because of the following story concerning her, *ch.* xxxiv.

II. Rachel fruitful at last (v. 22). Rachel called her son *Joseph*, which in Hebrew is akin to two words of a contrary signification, *Asaph* (*abstulit*), *He has taken away my reproach*, and *Jasaph* (*addidit*), *The Lord shall add to me another son.*

Verses 25–36

I. Jacob's thoughts of home. He faithfully served his time out with Laban, even his second apprenticeship. He retained his affection for the land of Canaan, not only because it was the land of his nativity, and his father and mother were there, whom he longed to see, but because it was the land of promise.

II. Laban's desire of his stay, v. 27. In love to himself, not to Jacob or to his wives or children, Laban endeavours to persuade him to continue his chief shepherd. Churlish selfish men know how to give good words when it is to serve their own ends. Laban found that his stock had wonderfully increased with Jacob's good management, and he owns it, with very good expressions of respect both to God and Jacob: *I have learned by experience that the Lord has blessed me for thy sake.*

III. The new bargain they came upon. Laban's craft and covetousness took advantage of Jacob's plainness, honesty, and goodnature. Jacob accordingly makes a proposal.

1. He shows what reason he had to insist upon so much, considering, (1) That Laban was bound in gratitude to do well for him. Yet here observe how he speaks, like himself, very modestly. Humble saints take more pleasure in doing good than in hearing of it again. (2) That he himself was bound in duty to take care of his own family.

2. He is willing to refer himself to the providence of God, which, he knew, extends itself to the smallest things, even the colour of the cattle; and he will be content to have for his wages the sheep and goats of such and such a colour, speckled, spotted, and brown, which should hereafter be brought forth, v. 32, 33. Laban was willing to consent to this bargain because he thought if the few he had that were now speckled and spotted were separated from the rest, which by agreement was to be done immediately, the body of the flock which Jacob was to tend, being of one colour, either all black or all white, would produce few or none of mixed colours, and so he should have Jacob's service for nothing, or next to nothing.

Verses 37–43

Now Jacob's contrivances were, 1. To set peeled sticks before the cattle where they were watered, that, looking much at those unusual party-coloured sticks, by the power of imagination they might bring forth young ones in like manner party-coloured, v. 37–39. Probably this custom was commonly used by the shepherds of Canaan, who coveted to have their cattle of this motley colour. When he began to have a stock of ring-straked and brown, he contrived to set them first, and to put the faces of the rest towards them, with the same design as in the former contrivance. Thus *Jacob increased exceedingly* (v. 43), and grew very rich in a little time. Those who, while their beginning is small, are humble and honest, contented and industrious, are in a likely way to see their latter end greatly increasing. He that is faithful in a little shall be entrusted with more. He that is faithful in that which is another man's shall be entrusted with something of his own. Jacob, who had been a just servant, became a rich master.

CHAPTER 31

Jacob was a man of great devotion and integrity, yet he had more trouble and vexation than any of the patriarchs. Here is, I. His resolution to return, ver. 1–16. II. His clandestine departure, ver. 17–21. III. Laban's pursuit of him in displeasure, ver. 22–25. IV. The hot words that passed between them. ver. 26–42. V. Their amicable agreement at last, ver. 43, &c.

Verses 1–16

Jacob is here taking up a resolution immediately to quit his uncle's service, to take what he had and go back to Canaan. This resolution he took.

I. Upon a just provocation; for Laban and his sons had become very ill-natured towards him.

1. Laban's sons showed their ill-will in what they said, v. 1.

2. Laban himself said little, but his countenance was not towards Jacob as it used to be; and Jacob could not but take notice of it, v. 2, 5. He was but a churl at the best, but now he was more churlish than formerly.

II. By divine direction and under the convoy of a promise: *The Lord said unto Jacob, Return, and I will be with thee,* v. 3. He came thither by orders from Heaven, and there he would stay till he was ordered back. It is our duty to set ourselves under God's guidance, both in our going out and in our coming in. Jacob was also encouraged by what is said in v. 13, *I am the God of Beth-el.* This was the place where the covenant was renewed with him. *Now arise* (v. 13) *and return,* (1) To thy devotions in Canaan, the solemnities of which had perhaps been much intermitted while he was with Laban. (2) To thy comforts in Canaan: *Return to the land of thy kindred.*

III. With the knowledge and consent of his wives.

He sent for Rachel and Leah to him to the field (v. 4), that he might confer with them more privately. Husbands that love their wives will communicate their purposes and intentions to them. Where there is a mutual affection there will be a mutual confidence. He told them of the command God had given him, in a dream, to return to his own country (v. 13), that they might not suspect his resolution to arise from inconstancy, or any disaffection to their country or family, but might see it to proceed from a principle of obedience to his God.

His wives cheerfully consented to his resolution. They were willing to go along with their husband, and put themselves with him under the divine direction: *Whatsoever God hath said unto thee do.*

Verses 17–24

Here is, I. Jacob's flight from Laban. It was honestly done to take no more than his own with him, the *cattle of his getting,* v. 18. He took what Providence gave him, and was content with that. Yet Rachel was not so honest as her husband; she *stole her father's images* (v. 19) and carried them away with her. The Hebrew calls them *teraphim.* Some think they were only little representations of the ancestors of the family, in statues or pictures, which Rachel had a particular fondness for, and was desirous to have with her, now that she was going into another country. It should rather seem that they were images

for a religious use, *penates, household-gods,* either worshipped or consulted as oracles; and we are willing to hope that she took them away out of a design hereby to convince her father of the folly of his regard to those as gods which could not secure themselves, Isa. xlvi. 1, 2.

II. Laban's pursuit of Jacob. Tidings were brought him, on the third day, that Jacob had fled; he immediately raises the whole clan. Seven days' journey he marched in pursuit of him, v. 23. But the truth is, bad men are more vehement in their anger than in their love. God interposed in the quarrel, rebuked Laban and sheltered Jacob, charging Laban not to *speak unto him either good or bad* (v. 24). The same Hebraism we have, ch. xxiv. 50. God comes to him, and with one word ties his hands, though he does not turn his heart. The safety of good men is very much owing to the hold God has of the consciences of bad men and the access he has to them.

Verses 25–35

We have here the reasoning, not to say the rallying, that took place between Laban and Jacob at their meeting, in that mountain which was afterwards called *Gilead,* v. 25.

I. The high charge which Laban exhibited against him. He accuses him,

1. As a renegade that had unjustly deserted his service. To represent Jacob as a criminal, he will have it thought that he intended kindness to his daughters (v. 27, 28). It is common for bad men, when they are disappointed in their malicious projects, to pretend that they designed nothing but what was kind and fair.

2. As a thief, v. 30. *Wherefore hast thou stolen my gods?* Foolish man! to call those his gods that could be stolen! Could he expect protection from those that could neither resist nor discover their invaders? Enemies may steal our goods, but not our God.

II. Jacob's apology for himself. 1. As to the charge of stealing away his own wives he clears himself by giving the true reason. He feared lest Laban would by force take away his daughters, and so oblige him, by the bond of his affection to his wives, to continue in his service. 2. As to the charge of stealing Laban's gods he pleads not guilty, v. 32. He not only did not take them himself (he was not so fond of them), but he did not know that they were taken.

III. The diligent search Laban made for his gods (v. 33–35). We do not find that he searched Jacob's flocks for stolen cattle; but he searched his furniture for stolen gods. Laban, after all his searches, missed of finding his gods, and was baffled in his enquiry with a sham; but our God will not only be found of those that seek him, but they shall find him their bountiful rewarder.

Verses 36–42

I. The power of provocation. Jacob's natural temper was mild and calm, yet Laban's unreasonable carriage towards him put him into a heat that transported him into some vehemence, v. 36, 37.

II. The comfort of a good conscience. Those that in any employment have dealt faithfully, if they cannot obtain the credit of it with men, yet shall have the comfort of it in their own bosoms.

III. The character of a good servant, and particularly of a faithful shepherd. 1. He was very careful, so that, through his oversight or neglect, the ewes did not cast their young. 2. He was very honest, and took none of that for his own eating which was not allowed him. 3. He was very laborious, v. 40. He stuck to his business, all weathers.

IV. The character of a hard master. Laban had been such an one to Jacob. Those are bad masters,

1. Who exact from their servants, that which is unjust, by obliging them to make good that which is not damaged by any default of theirs. This Laban did, v. 39. 2. Those also are bad masters who deny to their servants that which is just and equal. This Laban did, v. 41. It was unreasonable for him to make Jacob serve for his daughters, when he had in reversion so great an estate secure to him by the promise of God himself.

V. The care of providence for the protection of injured innocence, v. 42. God took cognizance of the wrong done to Jacob, and repaid him whom Laban would otherwise have sent empty away. Jacob speaks of God the God of Abraham, and the fear of Isaac; for Abraham was dead, and had gone to that world where perfect love casts out fear; but Isaac was yet alive, sanctifying the Lord in his heart, as his fear and his dread.

Verses 43–55

We have here the compromising of the matter between Laban and Jacob. Laban had nothing to say in reply to Jacob's remonstrance: he could neither justify himself nor condemn Jacob, but was convicted by his own conscience of the wrong he had done him.

I. He turns it off with a profession of kindness for Jacob's wives and children (v. 43): *These daughters are my daughters*. When he cannot excuse what he has done, he does, in effect, own what he should have done; he should have treated them as his own, but he had counted them as strangers, v. 15.

II. He proposes a covenant of friendship between them, to which Jacob readily agrees, without insisting upon Laban's submission, much less his restitution. Peace and love are such valuable jewels that we can scarcely buy them too dearly. Better sit down losers than go on in strife.

1. The substance of this covenant. Jacob left it wholly to Laban to settle it. (1) That Jacob should be a good husband to his wives. Jacob had never given him any cause to suspect that he would be any other than a kind husband; yet, as if he had, he was willing to come under this engagement. (2) That he should never be a bad neighbour to Laban, v. 52. It was agreed that Jacob should forgive and forget all the wrongs he had received.

2. The ceremony of this covenant. It was made and ratified with great solemnity, according to the usages of those times. (1) A pillar was erected (v. 45), and a heap of stones raised (v. 46), to perpetuate the memory of the thing. (2) A sacrifice was offered (v. 54), a sacrifice of peace-offerings. Our peace with God is that which puts true comfort into our peace with our friends. If parties contend, the reconciliation of both to him will facilitate their reconciliation one to another. (3) They did eat bread together (v. 46), jointly partaking of the feast upon the sacrifice, v. 54. Covenants of friendship were anciently ratified by the parties eating and drinking together. It was in the nature of a love-feast. (4) They solemnly appealed to God concerning their sincerity herein, [1] As a witness (v. 49): *The Lord watch between me and thee*. When we are out of one another's sight, let this be a restraint upon us, that wherever we are we are under God's eye. [2] As a Judge, v. 53. *The God of Abraham* (from whom Jacob descended), *and the God of Nahor* (from whom Laban descended), *the God of their father* (the common ancestor, from whom they both descended), *judge betwixt us*. God's relation to them is thus expressed to intimate that they worshipped one and the same God, upon which consideration there ought to be no enmity between them. (5) They gave a new name to the place, v. 47, 48. Laban called it in Syriac, and Jacob in Hebrew, *the heap of witness*; and (v. 49) it was called

Mizpah, a watch-tower. These names are applicable to the seals of the gospel covenant, which are witnesses to us if we be faithful, but witnesses against us if we be false. The name Jacob gave this heap (*Galeed*) stuck by it, not the name Laban gave it. In all this rencounter, Laban was noisy and full of words, affecting to say much; Jacob was silent, and said little.

Lastly, After all this angry parley, they part friends, v. 55.

CHAPTER 32

We have here Jacob still upon his journey towards Canaan. Never did so many memorable things occur in any march as in this of Jacob's little family. By the way he meets, I. With good tidings from his God, ver. 1, 2. II. With bad tidings from his brother, to whom he sent a message to notify his return, ver. 3–6. In his distress, 1. He divides his company, ver. 7, 8. 2. He makes his prayer to God, ver. 9–12. 3. He sends a present to his brother, ver. 13–23. 4. He wrestles with the angel, ver. 24–32.

Verses 1–2

1. Here is Jacob's convoy in his journey (v. 1): *The angels of God met him*, in a visible appearance, whether in a vision by day or in a dream by night, as when he saw them upon the ladder (*ch.* xxviii. 12), is uncertain. They had invisibly attended him all along, but now they appeared to him, because he had greater dangers before him than those he had hitherto encountered. God will have us, when we are in peace, to provide for trouble, and, when trouble comes, to live upon former observations and experiences; for *we walk by faith, not by sight*. God's people, at death, are returning to Canaan, to their Father's house; and then the angels of God will meet them. 2. The comfortable notice he took of this convoy, v. 2. *This is God's host*. To preserve the remembrance of this favour, Jacob gave a name to the place from it, *Mahanaim, two hosts*, one on either side, or one in the front and the other in the rear, to protect him from Laban behind and Esau before, that they might be a complete guard. Thus he is *compassed* with God's favour. Perhaps in allusion to this the church is called *Mahanaim, two armies*, Cant. vi. 13. Here were Jacob's family, which made one army, representing the church militant and itinerant on earth; and the angels, another army, representing the church triumphant and at rest in heaven.

Verses 3–8

He takes occasion to remind himself of the enemies he had, particularly Esau. It is probable that Rebekah had sent him word of Esau's settlement in Seir, and of the continuance of his enmity to him. What shall poor Jacob do? He longs to see his father, and yet he dreads to see his brother.

I. He sends a very kind and humble message to Esau. Acts of civility may help to slay enmities. 1. He calls Esau his lord, himself his servant, to intimate that he did not insist upon the prerogatives of the birthright and blessing he had obtained for himself. 2. He gives him a short account of himself, that he was not a fugitive and a vagabond, and that he was not a beggar, nor did he come home, as the prodigal son, destitute of necessaries and likely to be a charge to his relations. And, 3. He courts his favour: *I have sent, that I might find grace in thy sight*.

II. He receives a very formidable account of Esau's warlike preparations against him (v. 6), *He comes to meet thee, and four hundred men with him*. 1. He remembers the old quarrel, and will now be avenged on him for the birthright and blessing, and, if possible, defeat Jacob's expectations from both. Angry men have good memories. 2. He envies Jacob what little estate he had, and, though he himself was now possessed of a much better, yet nothing will serve him but to feed his eyes upon Jacob's ruin, and fill his fields with Jacob's spoils. 3. He concludes it easy to destroy him, now that he was upon the road, a poor weary traveller, unfixed, and (as he thinks) unguarded. 4. He resolves to do it suddenly, and before Jacob had come to his father, lest he should interpose and mediate between them. Out he marches, spurred on with rage; four hundred men he had with him, armed, and now breathing nothing but threatenings and slaughter. The tenth part of these were enough to cut off poor Jacob, and his guiltless helpless family, root and branch. Jacob, though a man of great faith, yet was now greatly afraid. Note, A lively apprehension of danger may very well consist with a humble confidence in God's power and promise. Christ himself, in his agony, was sorely amazed.

III. He puts himself into the best posture of defence that his present circumstances will admit. It was absurd to think of making resistance, all his contrivance is to make an escape, v. 7, 8. He divided his company, not as Abraham (*ch.* xiv. 15), for fight, but for flight.

Verses 9–12

Our rule is to call upon God in the time of trouble; we have here an example to this rule, and the success encourages us to follow this example. In his distress he sought the Lord, and he heard him. Times of fear should be times of prayer; whatever frightens us should drive us to our knees, to our God. Now it is worth while to enquire what there was extraordinary in this prayer, that it should gain the petitioner all this honour.

I. The request itself is one, and very express: *Deliver me from the hand of my brother,* v. 11.

II. The pleas are many, and very powerful; never was cause better ordered, Job xxiii. 4. He offers up his request with great faith, fervency, and humility.

1. He addresses himself to God as the God of his fathers, v. 9. Such was the humble self-denying sense he had of his own unworthiness that he did not call God his own God, but a God in covenant with his ancestors. God's covenant with our fathers may be a comfort to us when we are in distress.

2. He produces his warrant: *Thou saidst unto me, Return unto thy country.* We may be going whither God calls us, and yet may think our way hedged up with thorns. If God be our guide, he will be our guard.

3. He humbly acknowledges his own unworthiness to receive any favour from God (v. 10): *I am not worthy;* it is an unusual plea. Christ never commended any of his petitioners so much as him who said, *Lord, I am not worthy* (Matt. viii. 8), and her who said, *Truth, Lord, yet the dogs eat of the crumbs which fall from their master's table,* Matt. xv. 27. Now observe, (1) How magnificently and honourably he speaks of the mercies of God to him. (2) How meanly and humbly he speaks of himself, disclaiming all thought of his own merit: "*I am not worthy of the least of all thy mercies,* much less am I worthy of so great a favour as this I am now suing for." *I am less than all thy mercies;* so the word is. Those are best prepared for the greatest mercies that see themselves unworthy of the least.

4. He thankfully owns God's goodness to him in his banishment, and how much it had outdone his expectations: "*With my staff I passed over this Jordan,* poor and desolate, like a forlorn and despised pilgrim"; "*and now I have become two bands,* now I am surrounded with a numerous and comfortable retinue of children and servants."

5. He urges the extremity of the peril he was in: *Lord, deliver me from Esau, for I fear him,* v. 11. The people of God have not been shy of telling God their fears. The fear that quickens prayer is itself pleadable.

6. He insists especially upon the promise God had made him (v. 9): *Thou saidst, I will deal well with thee,* and again, in the close (v. 12): *Thou saidst, I will surely do thee good.* The best we can say to God in prayer is what he has said to us.

Verses 13–23

Jacob, having piously made God his friend by a prayer, is here prudently endeavouring to make Esau his friend by a present. He had prayed to God to deliver him from the hand of Esau, nor did his prayer make him presume upon God's mercy, without the use of means. When we have prayed to God for any mercy, we must second our prayers with our endeavours. To pacify Esau,

I. Jacob sent him a very noble present of cattle, to the number of 580 in all, v. 13–15. It was a present that he thought would be acceptable to Esau, who had traded so much in hunting wild beasts that perhaps he was but ill furnished with tame cattle with which to stock his new conquests. Peace and love, though purchased dearly, will prove a good bargain to the purchaser. Jacob forgives and forgets.

II. He sent him a very humble message, which he ordered his servants to deliver in the best manner, v. 17, 18. They must call Esau their *lord,* and Jacob his *servant;* they must tell him the cattle they had was a small present which Jacob had sent him. They must especially take care to tell him that Jacob was coming after (v. 18–20), that he might not suspect he had fled through fear. If Jacob will seem not to be afraid of Esau, Esau, it may be hoped, will not be a terror to Jacob.

Verses 24–32

We have here the remarkable story of Jacob's wrestling with the angel and prevailing, which is referred to, Hos. xii. 4. Very early in the morning, a great while before day, Jacob had helped his wives and his children over the river, and he desired to be private, and was left alone, that he might again more fully spread his cares and fears before God in prayer. While Jacob was earnest in prayer, *stirring up himself to take hold on God,* an angel takes hold on him. Some think this was the *angel of his presence* (Isa. lxiii. 9), one of those that attend on the *shechinah,* or the divine Majesty. Others think it was Michael our prince, the eternal Word, the angel of the covenant. Observe,

I. How Jacob and this angel engaged, v. 24. Jacob was now full of care and fear about the interview he expected, next day, with his brother, and God himself seemed to oppose his entrance into the land of promise. We are told by the prophet (Hos. xii. 4) how *Jacob wrestled:* he *wept, and made supplication;* prayers and tears were his weapons.

II. What was the success of the engagement. 1. Jacob kept his ground; though the struggle continued long, the angel *prevailed not against him* (v. 25), that is, this discouragement did not shake his faith, nor silence his prayer. It was not in his own strength that he wrestled, nor by his own strength that he prevailed, but in and by strength derived from Heaven. Note, We cannot prevail with God but in his own strength. It is his Spirit that intercedes in us, and *helps our infirmities,* Rom. viii. 26. 2. The angel put out Jacob's thigh. Some think that Jacob felt little or no pain from this hurt; it is probable that he did not, for he did not so much as halt till the struggle was over (v. 31), and, if so, this was an evidence of a divine touch indeed, which wounded and healed at the same time. 3. The angel, by an admirable condescension, mildly requests Jacob to let him go (v. 26), as God said to Moses (Exod. xxxii. 10), *Let me alone.* Thus he would put an honour on Jacob's faith and prayer, and further try his constancy. 4. Jacob persists in his holy importunity:

I will not let thee go, except thou bless me. The credit of a conquest will do him no good without the comfort of a blessing. In begging this blessing he owns his inferiority, though he seemed to have the upper hand in the struggle. 5. The angel puts a perpetual mark of honour upon him, by changing his name (*v.* 27, 28): "Thou art a brave combatant" (says the angel), "a man of heroic resolution; what is thy name?" "Jacob," says he, *a supplanter*; so *Jacob* signifies: "Well," says the angel, "thou shalt be called *Israel, a prince with God.*" Jacob is here knighted in the field, as it were, and has a title of honour which will remain, to his praise, to the end of time. Yet this was not all; having power with God, he shall have power with men too. 6. He dismisses him with a blessing, *v.* 29. Instead of telling him his name, he gave him his blessing, which was the thing he wrestled for. An interest in the angel's blessing is better than an acquaintance with his name. The tree of life is better than the tree of knowledge. 7. Jacob gives a new name to the place; he calls it *Peniel,* the *face of God* (*v.* 30). The name he gives to the place preserves and perpetuates, not the honour of his valour or victory, but only the honour of God's free grace. "In this place I saw God face to face, and my life was preserved"; not, "It was my praise that I came off a conqueror, but it was God's mercy that I escaped with my life." 8. The memorandum Jacob carried of this in his bones: *He halted on his thigh* (*v.* 31). The honour and comfort he obtained by this struggle were abundantly sufficient to countervail the damage, though he went limping to his grave. Notice is taken of the sun's rising upon him when he passed over *Penuel;* for it is sunrise with that soul that has communion with God. The inspired penman mentions a traditional custom which the seed of Jacob had, never to eat of that sinew, or muscle, in any beast, by which the hip-bone is fixed in its cup: thus they preserved the memorial of this story.

Chapter 33

We read, in the former chapter, how Jacob had power with God, and prevailed; here we find what power he had with men too, and how his brother Esau was mollified, and, on a sudden, reconciled to him. Here is, I. A very friendly meeting between Jacob and Esau, ver. 1–4. II. Their conference at their meeting, in which they vie with each other in civil and kind expressions. Their discourse is, 1. About Jacob's family, ver. 5–7. 2. About the present he had sent, ver. 8–11. 3. About the progress of their journey, ver. 12–15. III. Jacob's settlement in Canaan, his house, ground, and altar, ver. 16–20.

Verses 1–4

Here, I. Jacob discovered Esau's approach, *v.* 1. Some think that his lifting up his eyes denotes his cheerfulness and confidence, in opposition to a dejected countenance; having by prayer committed his case to God, he went on his way, *and his countenance was no more sad,* 1 Sam. i. 18.

II. He put his family into the best order he could to receive him. Observe what a different figure these two brothers made. Esau is attended with a guard of 400 men, and looks big; Jacob is followed by a cumbersome train of women and children that are his care, and he looks tender and solicitous for their safety; and yet Jacob had the birthright, and was to have the dominion, and was every way the better man. Jacob, at the head of his household, set a better example than Esau at the head of his regiment.

III. At their meeting, the expressions of kindness were interchanged in the best manner that could be between them.

1. Jacob bowed to Esau, *v.* 3. Though he feared Esau as an enemy, yet he did obeisance to him as an elder brother. Many preserve themselves by humbling themselves: the bullet flies over him that stoops.

2. Esau embraced Jacob (*v.* 4): *He ran to meet him,* not in passion, but in love; and, as one heartily reconciled to him. If there was not some wonderful change wrought upon the spirit of Esau at this time, I see not how wrestling Jacob could be said to obtain such power with men as to denominate him a *prince.* God has the hearts of all men in his hands, and can turn them when and how he pleases, by a secret, silent, but resistless power. He can, of a sudden, convert enemies into friends, as he did two Sauls, one by restraining grace (1 Sam. xxvi. 21, 25), the other by renewing grace, Acts ix. 21, 22.

They both wept. Jacob wept for joy, to be thus kindly received by his brother, and Esau perhaps wept for grief and shame.

Verses 5–15

We have here the discourse between the two brothers at their meeting. They converse,

I. About Jacob's retinue, *v.* 5–7. Eleven or twelve little ones, the eldest of them not fourteen years old, followed Jacob closely: *Who are these?* says Esau. Jacob returns a serious answer: They are *the children which God hath graciously given thy servant.* Jacob speaks of his children as God's gifts; they are a *heritage of the Lord,* Ps. cxxviii. 3; cxii. 9; cvii. 41.

II. About the present he had sent him.

1. Esau modestly refused it because he had enough, and did not need it, *v.* 9. It is a good thing for those that have much to know that they have enough, though they have not so much as some others have. Even Esau can say, *I have enough.*

2. Jacob affectionately urges him to accept it, and prevails, *v.* 10, 11. Jacob sent it, through fear (*ch.* xxxii. 20), but, the fear being over, he now importunes his acceptance of it for love, to show that he desires his brother's friendship, and did not merely dread his wrath. It is a very high compliment that he passes upon him: *I have seen thy face, as though I had seen the face of God.* The meaning is that Jacob saw God's favour to him in Esau's: it was a token for good to him that God had accepted his prayers. The competency he had of this world's goods: *God has dealt graciously with me.* "And *I have enough*; I have *all,*" so the word is. Esau's enough was much, but Jacob's enough was all. He has all in prospect; he will have all shortly, when he comes to heaven: upon this principle Jacob urged Esau, and he took his present.

III. About the progress of their journey. 1. Esau offers himself to be his guide and companion, in token of sincere reconciliation, *v.* 12. Esau has become fond of Jacob's company, courts him to Mount Seir: let us never despair of any, nor distrust God in whose hand all hearts are. Yet Jacob saw cause modestly to refuse this offer (*v.* 13, 14), wherein he shows a tender concern for his own family and flocks, like a good shepherd and a good father. He must consider the children, and the flocks with young, and not lead the one, nor drive the other, too fast. This prudence and tenderness of Jacob ought to be imitated by those that have the care and charge of young people in the things of God. They must not be over-driven, at first, by heavy tasks in religious services, but led, as they can bear, having their work made as easy to them as possible. Christ, the good Shepherd, does so, Isa. xl. 11. 2. Esau offers some of his men to be his guard and convoy, *v.* 15. (1) Jacob is humble, and needs it not for state. (2) Jacob is under the divine protection, and needs it not for safety.

Verses 16–20

Here, 1. Having in a friendly manner parted with Esau, who had gone to his own country (*v.* 16), he comes to a place where, it should seem, he rested for some time. The place was afterwards known by the name of Succoth, a city in the tribe of Gad, on the other side Jordan (it signifies *booths*), that when his posterity afterwards dwelt in houses of stone, they might remember that *the Syrian ready to perish* was their father, who was glad of booths (Deut. xxvi. 5). 2. He comes to Shechem; we read it, to *Shalem, a city of Shechem*. After a perilous journey, in which he had met with many difficulties, he came safely, at last, into Canaan. Here, (1) He buys a field, *v.* 19. Though the land of Canaan was his by promise, yet, the time for taking possession not having yet come, he is content to pay for his own. (2) He builds an altar, *v.* 20. [1] In thankfulness to God. [2] That he might keep up the worship of God, in his family. Where we have a tent God must have an altar, where we have a house he must have a church in it. He dedicated this altar to the honour of *El-elohe-Israel—God, the God of Israel*. God had lately called him by the name of *Israel*, and now he calls God *the God of Israel*; though he is styled *a prince with God*, God shall still be a prince with him, his Lord and his God.

CHAPTER 34

At this chapter begins the story of Jacob's afflictions in his children, which are recorded to show, 1. The vanity of this world. That which is dearest to us may prove our great vexation. 2. The common griefs of good people. Jacob's sons, though they were his grief in some things, yet were all taken into covenant with God. In this chapter we have, I. Dinah debauched, ver. 1–5. II. A treaty of marriage between her and Shechem who had defiled her, ver. 6–19. III. The circumcision of the Shechemites pursuant to that treaty, ver. 20–24. IV. The perfidious and bloody revenge which Simeon and Levi took upon them, ver. 25–31.

Verses 1–5

Dinah, Jacob's only daughter, is reckoned now but fifteen or sixteen years of age when she here occasioned so much mischief. Observe, 1. Her vain curiosity. She went to *see*, yet that was not all, she went to be *seen* too; she went to see the daughters of the land, but, it may be, with some thoughts of the sons of the land too. I doubt she went to get an acquaintance with those Canaanites, and to learn their way. 2. The loss of her honour by this means (*v.* 2). Dinah went abroad to look about her; but, if she had looked about her as she ought, she would not have fallen into this snare. 3. The court Shechem made to her, after he had defiled her. 4. The tidings brought to poor Jacob, *v.* 5. The good man *held his peace*, as one astonished, that knows not what to say. He had left the management of his affairs very much (too much I doubt) to his sons, and he would do nothing without them. Note, Things never go well when the authority of a parent runs low in a family.

Verses 6–17

Jacob's sons, when they heard of the injury done to Dinah, showed a very great resentment of it, influenced perhaps rather by jealousy for the honour of their family than by a sense of virtue. Many are concerned at the shamefulness of sin that never lay to heart the sinfulness of it. It is here called *folly in Israel* (*v.* 7). Note, 1. Uncleanness is folly; for it sacrifices the favour of God, peace of conscience, and all the soul can pretend to that is sacred and honourable, to a base and brutish lust. 2. This folly is most shameful in *Israel*, in a family of Israel, where God is known and worshipped.

Hamor came to treat with Jacob himself, but he turns him over to his sons; and here we have a particular account of the treaty, in which the Canaanites were more honest than the Israelites. I. Hamor and Shechem fairly propose this match, in order to a coalition in trade. Shechem is deeply in love with Dinah; he will have her upon any terms,

v. 11, 12. His father not only consents, but solicits for him, and gravely insists upon the advantages that would follow from the union of the families, *v.* 9, 10. II. Jacob's sons basely pretend to insist upon a coalition in religion, when really they designed nothing less. Jacob's sons meditate only revenge. The Shechemites must be circumcised; not to make them holy (they never intended that), but to make them sore, that they might become an easier prey to their sword. 1. The pretence was specious. 2. The intention was malicious, as appears by the sequel of the story; all they aimed at was to prepare them for the day of slaughter. Religion is never more injured, nor are God's sacraments more profaned, than when they are thus used for a cloak of maliciousness.

Verses 18–24

1. Hamor and Shechem gave consent themselves to be circumcised, *v.* 18, 19. To this perhaps they were moved by what they might have heard of the sacred and honourable intentions of this sign, in the family of Abraham, which, it is probable, they had some confused notions. Note, Many who know little of religion, yet know so much of it as makes them willing to join themselves with those that are religious. Jacob's sons were industrious thriving people, and promised themselves and their neighbours advantage by an alliance with them; it would improve ground and trade, and bring money into their country. Now, (1) It was bad enough to marry upon this principle. (2) It was worse to be circumcised upon this principle. There are many with whom gain is godliness, and who are more governed and influenced by their secular interest than by any principle of their religion.

Verses 25–31

Simeon and Levi, two of Jacob's sons, young men not much above twenty years old, cutting the throats of the Shechemites, and thereby breaking the heart of their good father.

I. The barbarous murder of the Shechemites. 1. Slaying the inhabitants of Shechem—*all the males*, Hamor and Shechem particularly, with whom they had been treating in a friendly manner but the other day, yet with a design upon their lives. Note, As nothing secures us better than true religion, so nothing exposes us more than religion only pretended to. But Simeon and Levi were most unrighteous. (1) It was true that Shechem had *wrought folly against Israel*, in defiling Dinah; but it ought to have been considered how far Dinah herself had been accessory to it. (2) It was true that Shechem had done ill; but he was endeavouring to atone for it, and was as honest and honourable, *ex post facto—after the deed*, as the case would admit. (3) It was true that Shechem had done ill; but what was that to all the Shechemites? Must the innocent fall with the guilty? (4) But that which above all aggravated the cruelty was the most perfidious treachery that was in it. 2. Seizing the prey of Shechem, and plundering the town. The Shechemites were willing to gratify the sons of Jacob by submitting to the penance of circumcision, upon this principle, *Shall not their cattle and their substance be ours?* (*v.* 23), and see what was the issue; instead of making themselves masters of the wealth of Jacob's family, Jacob's family become masters of their wealth.

II. Here is Jacob's resentment of this bloody deed of Simeon and Levi, *v.* 30. Two things he bitterly complains of:—1. The reproach they had brought upon him thereby: What will they say of us and our religion? 2. The ruin they had exposed him to. What could be expected, but that the Canaanites, who were numerous and formidable, would confederate against him, and he and his little family would become an easy prey to them? Note, When sin is in the house, there is reason to fear ruin at the door. One would think this should have made them to relent, but, instead of this, they justify themselves, and give him this insolent reply, *Should he deal with our sister as with a harlot?*

CHAPTER 35

In this chapter we have three communions and three funerals. I. Three communions between God and Jacob. 1. God ordered Jacob to Beth-el, ver. 1–5. 2. Jacob built an altar at Beth-el, to the honour of God that had appeared to him, ver. 6, 7. 3. God appeared to him again, and confirmed the change of his name and the covenant with him (ver. 9–13), of which appearance Jacob made a grateful acknowledgment, ver. 14, 15. II. Three funerals. 1. Deborah's, ver. 8. 2. Rachel's, ver. 16–20. 3. Isaac's, ver. 27–29. Here is also Reuben's incest (ver. 22), and an account of Jacob's sons, ver. 23–26.

Verses 1–5

I. God reminds Jacob of his vow at Beth-el, and sends him thither to perform it, *v.* 1. Jacob had said in the day of his distress, *If I come again in peace, this stone shall be God's house*, ch. xxviii. 22. Seven or eight years it was now since he came to Canaan; he had purchased ground there, and had built an altar in remembrance of God's last appearance to him when he called him *Israel* (*ch.* xxxiii. 19, 20); but still Beth-el is forgotten. Note, 1. As many as God loves he will remind of neglected duties, one way or other, by conscience or by providences. 2. When we have vowed a vow to God, it is best not to defer the payment of it (Eccles. v. 4), yet better late than never. In Beth-el, the house of God, we should desire to dwell, Ps. xxvii. 4. That should be our home, not our inn. God reminds him not expressly of his vow, but of the occasion of it: *When thou fleddest from the face of Esau.*

II. Jacob commands his household to prepare for this solemnity; not only for the journey and remove, but for the religious services that were to be performed, *v.* 2, 3. Observe the commands he gives his household, like Abraham, ch. xviii. 19. 1. They must *put away the strange gods.* Strange gods in Jacob's family! Strange things indeed! Could such a family, that was taught the good knowledge of the Lord, admit them? In those families where there is a face of religion, and an altar to God, yet many times there is much amiss, and more strange gods than one would suspect. 2. They must be clean, and *change their garments.* Simeon and Levi had their hands full of blood, it concerned them particularly to wash, and to put off their garments that were so stained. These were but ceremonies, signifying the purification and change of the heart. What are clean clothes, and new clothes, without a clean heart, and a new heart? 3. They must go with him to Bethel, *v.* 3.

III. His family surrendered all they had that was idolatrous or superstitious, *v.* 4. Jacob took care to bury their images, that they might not afterwards find them and return to them.

IV. He removes without molestation from Shechem to Bethel, *v.* 5. *The terror of God was upon the cities.* Note, The way of duty is the way of safety. While there was sin in Jacob's house, he was afraid of his neighbours; but now that the strange gods were put away, and they were all going together to Bethel, his neighbours were afraid of him.

Verses 6–15

Jacob and his retinue having safely arrived at Bethel, we are here told what passed there.

I. There he built an altar (*v.* 7), and offered sacrifice upon it. With these sacrifices he joined praises for former mercies. And he called the place (that is, *the altar*) *El-beth-el, the God of Bethel.* Note, The comfort which the saints have in holy ordinances is not so much from *Bethel, the house of God,* as from *El-beth-el, the God of the house.* The ordinances are but empty things if we do not meet with God in them.

II. There he buried Deborah, Rebekah's nurse, *v.* 8. Rebekah probably was dead, but her old nurse (of whom mention is made *ch.* xxiv. 59) survived her. Honour was done to this nurse, at her death, by Jacob's family, though she was not related to them, and though she was aged. Family afflictions may come even when family reformation and religion are on foot.

III. There God appeared to him (*v.* 9), to own his altar, to answer to the name by which he had called him, *The God of Bethel* (*v.* 7), and to comfort him under his affliction, *v.* 8. He renewed and ratified the covenant with him, by the name *El-Shaddai. I am God Almighty, God all-sufficient* (*v.* 11), able to make good the promise in due time. Two things are promised, 1. That he should be the father of a great nation. 2. That he should be the master of a good land (*v.* 12). He shall not have children without an estate, which is often the case of the poor, nor an estate without children, which is often the grief of the rich; but both. These two promises had a spiritual signification, for, without doubt, Christ is the promised seed, and heaven is the promised land. He then went up from him, or *from over him*, in some visible display of glory, which had hovered over him while he talked with him, *v.* 13.

IV. There Jacob erected a memorial of this, *v.* 14. He set up a pillar. In token of his intending it for a sacred memorial of his communion with God, he poured oil and the other ingredients of a drink-offering upon it. His vow was, *This stone shall be God's house*, that is, shall be set up for his honour, as houses to the praise of their builders.

Verses 16–20

We have here the story of the death of Rachel, the beloved wife of Jacob. 1. She fell in travail by the way, not able to reach to Bethlehem, the next town, though they were near it. Her travail was to the life of the child, but to her own death. Her dying is here called *the departing of her soul.* Note, The death of the body is but the departure of the soul to the world of spirits. Her dying lips called her new-born son *Ben-oni, The son of my sorrow.* But Jacob, because he would not renew the sorrowful remembrance of the mother's death every time he called his son by his name, changed his name, and called him *Benjamin, The son of my right hand*; that is, "very dear to me, set on my right hand for a blessing, the support of my age, like the staff in my right hand." Jacob buried her near the place where she died. If the soul be at rest after death, it matters little where the body lies. Jacob set up a pillar upon her grave, so that it was known, long after, to be Rachel's sepulchre (1 Sam. x. 2), and Providence so ordered it that this place afterwards fell in the lot of Benjamin.

Verses 21–29

Here is, 1. Jacob's removal, *v.* 21. Immediately after the story of Rachel's death he is here called *Israel* (*v.* 21, 22), and not often so afterwards: the Jews say, "The historian does him this honour here because he bore that affliction with such admirable patience and submission to Providence." 2. The sin of Reuben. A piece of abominable wickedness it was that he was guilty of (*v.* 22). Though perhaps Bilhah was the greater criminal, and it is probable was abandoned by Jacob for it, yet Reuben's crime was so provoking that, for it, he lost his birthright and blessing, *ch.* xlix. 4. This was Reuben's sin, but it was Jacob's affliction. 3. A complete list of the sons of Jacob, now that Benjamin the youngest was born. This is the first time we have the names of these heads of the twelve tribes together. 4. The visit which Jacob made to his father Isaac at Hebron. Probably he did this now upon the death of Rebekah, by which Isaac was left solitary. 5. The age and death of Isaac are here recorded. Isaac, a mild quiet man, lived the longest of all the patriarchs. Particular notice is taken of the amicable agreement of Esau and Jacob, in solemnizing their father's funeral (*v.* 29), to show how wonderfully God had changed Esau's mind since he vowed his brother's murder immediately after his father's death, *ch.* xxvii. 41.

Chapter 36

In this chapter we have an account of the posterity of Esau, who, from him, were called Edomites. 1. Because he was the son of Isaac, for whose sake this honour is put upon him. 2. Because the Edomites were neighbours to Israel. 3. It is to show the performance of the promise to Abraham, that he should be "the father of many nations," and of that answer which Rebekah had from the oracle she consulted, "Two nations are in thy womb," and of the blessing of Isaac, "Thy dwelling shall be the fatness of the earth." We have here, I. Esau's wives, ver. 1–5. II. His remove to Mount Seir, ver. 6–8. III. The names of his sons, ver. 9–14. IV. The dukes who descended of his sons, ver. 15–19. V. The dukes of the Horites, ver. 20–30. VI. The kings and dukes of Edom, ver. 31–43. This chapter is abridged, 1 Chron. i. 35, &c.

Verses 1–8

1. Concerning Esau himself, *v.* 1. He is called *Edom* (and again, *v.* 8), that name by which was perpetuated the remembrance of the foolish bargain he made, when he sold his birthright for *that red, that red pottage*. 2. Concerning his wives, and the children they bore him in the land of Canaan. 3. Concerning his removal to Mount Seir, which was the country God had given him for a possession, when he reserved Canaan for the seed of Jacob. God owns it, long afterwards: *I gave to Esau Mount Seir* (Deut. ii. 5; Josh. xxiv. 4), which was the reason why the Edomites must not be disturbed in their possession. He wholly withdrew to Mount Seir, took with him what came to his share of his father's personal estate, and left Canaan to Jacob, not only because he had the promise of it, but because Esau perceived that if they should continue to thrive as they had begun there would not be room for both.

Verses 9–19

Observe here, 1. That only the names of Esau's sons and grandsons are recorded, only their names, not their history. Nor does the genealogy go any further than the third and fourth generation. It is only the pedigree of the Israelites, who were to be the heirs of Canaan, and of whom were to come the promised seed, and the holy seed, that is drawn out to any length, as far as there was occasion for it, even of all the tribes till Canaan was divided among them, and of the royal line till Christ came. 2. That these sons and grandsons of Esau are called *dukes*, or captains, that had soldiers under them; for Esau and his family lived *by the sword, ch.* xxvii. 40. Esau's sons were dukes when Jacob's sons were but plain shepherds, *ch.* xlvii. 3. This is not a reason why such titles should not be used among Christians; but it is a reason why men should not overvalue themselves, or others, for the sake of them. 3. Esau increases, and is enriched first. God's promise to Jacob began to work late, but the effect of it remained longer, and it had its complete accomplishment in the spiritual Israel.

Verses 20–30

In the midst of this genealogy of the Edomites here is inserted the genealogy of the Horites, those Canaanites, or Hittites (compare *ch.* xxvi. 34), that were the natives of Mount Seir. This comes in here, not only to give light to the story, but to be a standing reflection upon the Edomites for intermarrying with

them. Esau having sold his birthright, and lost his blessing, and entered into alliance with the Hittites, his posterity and the sons of Seir are here reckoned together.

Verses 31–42

By degrees, it seems, the Edomites wormed out the Horites, obtained full possession of the country, and had a government of their own. 1. They were ruled by kings, and seem to have come to the throne by election, and not by lineal descent. These kings reigned in *Edom before there reigned any king over the children of Israel*. Esau's blood becomes royal long before any of Jacob's did. We may suppose it was a great trial to the faith of God's Israel to hear of the pomp and power of the kings of Edom, while they were bond-slaves in Egypt; but those that look for great things from God must be content to wait for them; God's time is the best time. 2. They were afterwards governed by dukes, again here named, who, I suppose, ruled all at the same time in several places in the country. We read of the dukes of Edom (Exod. xv. 15), yet, long afterwards, of their kings again. 3. Mount Seir is called *the land of their possession*, *v.* 43. While the Israelites dwelt in the house of bondage, and their Canaan was only the land of promise, the Edomites dwelt in their own habitations, and Seir was in their possession. Note, The children of this world have their all in hand, and nothing in hope (Luke xvi. 25); while the children of God have their all in hope, and next to nothing in hand. But, all things considered, it is better to have Canaan in promise than Mount Seir in possession.

Chapter 37

At this chapter begins the story of Joseph, who, in every subsequent chapter but one to the end of this book, makes the greatest figure. His story is so remarkably divided between his humiliation and his exaltation that we cannot avoid seeing something of Christ in it, who was first humbled and then exalted. It also shows the lot of Christians, who must through many tribulations enter into the kingdom. In this chapter we have, I. The malice his brethren bore against him. 1. Because he informed his father of their wickedness, ver. 1, 2. 2. Because his father loved him, ver. 3, 4. 3. Because he dreamed of his dominion over them, ver. 5–11. II. The mischiefs his brethren designed and did to him. 1. The kind visit he made them gave an opportunity, ver. 12–17. 2. They designed to slay him, but determined to starve him, ver. 18–24. 3. They changed their purpose, and sold him for a slave, ver. 25–28. 4. They made their father believe that he was torn in pieces, ver. 29–35. 5. He was sold into Egypt to Potiphar, ver. 36. And all this was working together for good.

Verses 1–4

The story of Jacob's family: *These are the generations of Jacob*. His is not a bare barren genealogy as that of Esau (*ch.* xxxvi. 1), but a memorable useful history. Here is, 1. Jacob a sojourner with his father Isaac, who was yet living, *v.* 1. 2. Joseph a shepherd, *feeding the flock with his brethren*, *v.* 2. Though he was his father's darling, yet he was not brought up in idleness or delicacy. Those that are trained up to do nothing are likely to be good for nothing. 3. Joseph, beloved by his father (*v.* 3), was the greatest comfort of his old age. Jacob proclaimed his affection to him by dressing him finer than the rest of his children: He *made him a coat of divers colours*. 4. Joseph hated by his brethren, (1) Because his father loved him; when parents make a difference, children soon take notice of it, and it often occasions feuds and quarrels in families. (2) Because he *brought to his father their evil report*. Jacob's sons did that, when they were from under his eye, which they durst not have done if they had been at home with him; but Joseph gave his father an account of their bad carriage.

Verses 5–11

Here, I. Joseph relates the prophetical dreams he had, *v.* 6, 7, 9, 10. His dreams were, 1. That his brethren's sheaves all bowed to his, intimating upon what occasion they should be brought to do homage to him, namely, in seeking to him for corn; their empty sheaves should bow to his full one. 2. That the sun, and moon, and eleven stars, did obeisance to him, *v.* 9. Joseph was more of a prophet than a politician, else he would have kept this to himself, when he could not but know that his brethren did already hate him and that this would but the more exasperate them.

II. His brethren take it very ill, and are more and more enraged against him (*v.* 8): *Shalt thou indeed reign over us?* How scornfully they resented it: "*Shalt thou*, who art but one, *reign over us*, who are many? Thou, who art the youngest, over us who are older?"

III. His father gives him a gentle rebuke for it, yet observes the saying, *v.* 10, 11. Probably he checked him for it. He insinuated that it was but an idle dream. Jacob, like Mary (Luke ii. 51), kept these things in his heart, and no doubt remembered them long afterwards, when the event answered to the prediction.

Verses 12–22

Here is, I. The kind visit which Joseph, in obedience to his father's command, made to his brethren, who were feeding the flock at Shechem, many miles off. See in Joseph an instance, 1. Of dutifulness to his father. Though he was his father's darling, yet he was willing to be his father's servant. How readily does he wait his father's orders! 2. Of kindness to his brethren. Though he knew they hated him and envied him, yet he made no objections against his father's commands. Joseph was sent by his father to Shechem, to see whether his brethren were well there, and whether the country had not risen upon them and destroyed them, in revenge of their barbarous murder of the Shechemites some years before.

II. The bloody and malicious plot of his brethren against him, who rendered good for evil: it was not in a heat, or upon a sudden provocation, that they thought to slay him, but from malice prepense, and in cold blood. The more there is of a project and contrivance in a sin the worse it is; it is bad to do evil, but worse to devise it. How scornfully they reproached him for his dreams (*v.* 19): *This dreamer cometh*; and (*v.* 20), *We shall see what will become of his dreams.* This shows what it was that fretted and enraged them. They could not endure to think of doing homage to him. How they agreed to cover the murder with a lie: *We will say, Some evil beast hath devoured him.*

III. Reuben's project to deliver him, *v.* 21, 22. Reuben, of all the brothers, had most reason to be jealous of Joseph, for he was the first-born, yet he proves his best friend. Reuben made a proposal which they thought would effectually answer their intention of destroying Joseph, and yet which he designed should answer his intention of rescuing Joseph out of their hands and restoring him to his father. But God overruled all to serve his own purpose of making Joseph an instrument to save much people alive.

Verses 23–30

We have here the execution of their plot against Joseph. 1. They stripped him, each striving to seize the envied coat of many colours, *v.* 23. Thus, in imagination, they degraded him from the birthright, of which perhaps this was the badge. Thus our Lord Jesus was stripped of his seamless coat, and thus his suffering saints have first been industriously divested of their privileges and honours, and then made the off-scouring of all things. 2. They went

about to starve him, throwing him into a dry pit, to perish there with hunger. Where envy reigns pity is banished, and humanity itself is forgotten, Prov. xxvii. 4. Is this he to whom his brethren must do homage? Note, God's providences often seem to contradict his purposes, even when they are serving them. 3. They slighted him when he was in distress, and were not grieved for the affliction of Joseph; they *sat down to eat bread, v.* 25. They felt no remorse of conscience for the sin; if they had, it would have spoiled their appetite for their meat, and the relish of it. They were now pleased to think how they were freed from the fear of their brother's dominion over them. 4. They sold him. A caravan of merchants very opportunely passed by, and Judah made the motion that they should sell Joseph to them, to be carried far enough off into Egypt, where, in all probability, he would be lost, and never heard of more. (1) Judah proposed it in compassion to Joseph (*v.* 26): "*What profit is it if we slay our brother?* (2) They acquiesced in it, because they thought that if he were sold for a slave he would never be a lord. Reuben thought himself undone, because the child was sold: *I, whither shall I go? v.* 30. He being the eldest, his father would expect from him an account of Joseph; but, as it proved, they would all have been undone if he had not been sold.

Verses 31–36

I. Joseph would soon be missed, great enquiry would be made for him, and therefore his brethren have a further design, to make the world believe that Joseph was torn in pieces by a wild beast; and this they did, 1. To clear themselves, that they might not be suspected to have done him any mischief. Note, When the devil has taught men to commit one sin, he then teaches them to conceal it with another, theft and murder with lying and perjury; but he that covers his sin shall not prosper long. 2. To grieve their good father. It seems designed by them on purpose to be revenged upon him for his distinguishing love of Joseph. They sent him Joseph's coat of many colours with one colour more than it had had, a bloody colour, *v.* 32. They pretended they had found it in the fields, and Jacob himself must be scornfully asked, *Is this thy son's coat?* Now let those that know the heart of a parent suppose the agonies of poor Jacob. Sleeping or waking, he imagines he sees the wild beast setting upon Joseph. He fancies how the beast tore him limb from limb, and left no remains of him, but the coat of many colours. Now, (1) Endeavours were used to comfort him. His sons basely pretended to do it (*v.* 35); but miserable hypocritical comforters were they all. Had they really desired to comfort him, they might easily have done it, by telling him the truth, "Joseph is alive, he is indeed sold into Egypt, but it will be an easy thing to send thither and ransom him." But (2) It was all in vain: *Jacob refused to be comforted, v.* 35.

II. The Ishmaelites and Midianites having bought Joseph only to make their market of him, here we have him sold again to Potiphar, *v.* 36. How soon was the land of Egypt made a house of bondage to the seed of Jacob! Jacob little thought that ever his beloved Joseph would be thus bought and sold for a servant.

CHAPTER 38

This chapter gives us an account of Judah and his family. If we were to form a character of him by this story, we should not say, "Judah, thou art he whom thy brethren shall praise," ch. xlix. 8. We have, in this chapter, I. Judah's marriage and issue, and the untimely death of his two eldest sons, ver. 1–11. II. Judah's incest with his daughter-in-law Tamar, without his knowing it, ver. 12–23. III. His confusion, when it was discovered, ver. 24–26. IV. The birth of his twin sons, in whom his family was built up, ver. 27, &c.

Verses 1–11

Here is, 1. Judah's foolish friendship with a Canaanite-man. 2. His foolish marriage with a Canaanite-woman, a match made, not by his father, who, it should seem, was not consulted, but by his new friend Hirah, *v.* 2. 3. Three sons he had by her, Er, Onan, and Shelah. Judah married too young, and very rashly; he also married his sons too young, when they had neither wit nor grace to govern themselves, and the consequences were very bad. (1) His first-born, *Er*, was notoriously wicked; he was so *in the sight of the Lord*, that is, in defiance of God and his law. (2) The next son, *Onan*, was, according to the ancient usage, married to the widow, to preserve the name of his deceased brother that died childless. The custom of marrying the brother's widow was afterwards made one of the laws of Moses, Deut. xxv. 5. Onan, though he consented to marry the widow, yet, to the great abuse of his own body, of the wife that he had married, and of the memory of his brother that was gone, refused to raise up seed unto his brother. (3) *Shelah*, the third son, was reserved for the widow (*v.* 11), yet with a design that he should not marry so young. However, Tamar acquiesced for the present, and waited the issue.

Verses 12–23

It is a very ill-favoured story that is here told concerning Judah. He was unjust to his daughter-in-law, either through negligence or design, in not giving her his surviving son, and this exposed her to temptation.

I. Tamar wickedly prostituted herself as a harlot to Judah, that, if the son might not, the father might raise up seed to the deceased. Bishop Patrick thinks it probable that she hoped Shelah, who was by right her husband, might have come along with his father, and that he might have been allured to her embraces. 1. She took an opportunity for it, when Judah had a time of mirth and feasting with his sheep-shearers. 2. She exposed herself as a harlot *in an open place*, *v.* 14. It should seem, it was the custom of harlots, in those times, to cover their faces, that, though they were not ashamed, yet they might seem to be so. The sin of uncleanness did not then go so barefaced as it does now.

II. Judah was taken in the snare, and though it was ignorantly that he was guilty of incest with his daughter-in-law (not knowing who she was), yet he was wilfully guilty of fornication: whoever she was, he knew she was not his wife, and therefore not to be touched. Observe, 1. Judah's sin began in the eye (*v.* 15): *He saw her.* We have need to make a covenant with our eyes, and to turn them from beholding vanity, lest the eye infect the heart. 2. It added to the scandal that the hire of a harlot (than which nothing is more infamous) was demanded, offered, and accepted—*a kid from the flock*, a goodly price at which her chastity and honour were valued! Nay, had the consideration been thousands of rams, and ten thousand rivers of oil, it had not been a valuable consideration. The favour of God, the purity of the soul, the peace of conscience, and the hope of heaven, are too precious to be exposed to sale at any such rates. 3. It turned to the reproach of Judah that he left his jewels in pawn for a kid.

III. He lost his jewels by the bargain; he sent the kid, according to his promise, to redeem his pawn, but the supposed harlot could not be found. Judah sits down content to lose his signet and his bracelets, and forbids any further enquiry, *lest we be shamed*, 23. He expresses no concern about the sin, to get that pardoned, only about the shame, to prevent that.

Verses 24–30

I. Judah's rigour against Tamar, when he heard she was an adulteress. She was, in the eye of the law, Shelah's wife, and therefore her being with child by another was looked upon as an injury and reproach to Judah's family: *Bring her forth therefore*, says Judah, the master of the family, and *let her be burnt*; not burnt to death, but burnt in the cheek or forehead, stigmatized for a harlot. Note, It is a common thing for men to be severe against those very sins in others in which yet they allow themselves; and so, in judging others, they condemn themselves, Rom. ii. 1; xiv. 22.

II. Judah's shame, when it was made to appear that he was the adulterer. She produced *the ring and the bracelets* in court, which justified the fathering of the child upon Judah, *v.* 25, 26. He owns that a perpetual mark of infamy should be fastened rather upon him, who had been so much accessory to it.

III. The building up of Judah's family in the birth of Pharez and Zarah, from whom descended the most considerable families of the illustrious tribe of Judah. The four eldest sons of Jacob fell under very foul guilt, Reuben and Judah under the guilt of incest, Simeon and Levi under that of murder; yet they were patriarchs, and from Levi descended the priests, from Judah the kings and Messiah. Thus they became examples of repentance, and monuments of pardoning mercy.

CHAPTER 39

At this chapter we return to the story of Joseph. We have him here, I. A servant, a slave in Potiphar's house (ver. 1), and yet there greatly honoured and favoured. 1. By the providence of God, which made him, in effect, a master, ver. 2–6. 2. By the grace of God, which made him more than a conqueror over a strong temptation to uncleanness, ver. 7–12. II. We have him here a sufferer, falsely accused (ver. 13–18), imprisoned (ver. 19, 20), and yet his imprisonment made both honourable and comfortable by the tokens of God's special presence with him, ver. 21–23.

Verses 1–6

I. Joseph was sold to an officer of Pharaoh, with whom he might get acquainted with public persons and public business, and so be fitted for the preferment for which he was designed. What God intends men for he will be sure, some way or other, to qualify them for.

II. Joseph blessed, wonderfully blessed, even in the house of his servitude.

1. God prospered him, *v.* 2, 3. Though, at first, we may suppose that his hand was put to the meanest services, even in those appeared his ingenuity and industry; a particular blessing of Heaven attended him, which, as he rose in his employment, became more and more discernible. Joseph's brethren had stripped him of his coat of many colours, but they could not strip him of his virtue and prudence. Joseph was separated from his brethren, but not from his God; banished from his father's house, but *the Lord was with him*, and this comforted him.

2. His master preferred him, and by degrees made him steward of his household, *v.* 4. It is the wisdom of those that are in any sort of authority to countenance and employ those with whom it appears that the presence of God is, Ps. ci. 6. Potiphar knew what he did when he put all into the hands of Joseph.

3. God favoured his master for his sake (*v.* 5): *He blessed the Egyptian's house*, though he was an Egyptian, a stranger to the true God, *for Joseph's sake*. Good men are the blessings of the places where they live.

Verses 7–12

I. A most shameful instance of impudence and immodesty in Joseph's mistress, the shame and scandal of her sex, perfectly lost to all virtue and honour.

1. Her sin began in the eye: She *cast her eyes upon Joseph* (v. 7), who *was a goodly person, and well-favoured, v. 6*. We have great need to make a covenant with our eyes (Job xxxi. 1), lest the eye infect the heart.

2. She was daring and shameless in the sin.

3. She was urgent and violent in the temptation. She *spoke to him day by day, v.* 10. Now this was, (1) Great wickedness in her, and (2) A great temptation to Joseph.

II. Here is a most illustrious instance of virtue and resolved chastity in Joseph, who, by the grace of God, was enabled to resist and overcome this temptation; and, all things considered, his escape was as great an instance of the divine power as the deliverance of the three children out of the fiery furnace.

1. The temptation he was assaulted with was very strong. The tempter was his mistress, a person of quality, whom it was his place to obey and his interest to oblige, whose favour would contribute more than anything to his preferment. On the other hand, it was at his utmost peril if he slighted her, and made her his enemy. Opportunity favoured the temptation. The tempter was in the house with him; his business led him to be, without any suspicion, where she was.

2. His resistance of the temptation was very brave, and the victory truly honourable.

(1) He would not wrong his master. He would not offend his God. This is the chief argument with which he strengthens his aversion to the sin. *How can I do this?* not only, How shall I? or, How dare I? but, *How can I? Id possumus, quod jure possumus—We can do that which we can do lawfully.* Three arguments Joseph urges upon himself. *First,* He considers who he was that was tempted. "*I;* others may perhaps take their liberty, but *I* cannot." *Secondly,* What the sin was to which he was tempted: *This great wickedness.* Others might look upon it as a small matter, a peccadillo, a trick of youth; but Joseph had another idea of it. Let sin appear sin (Rom. vii. 13), call it by its own name, and never go about to lessen it. *Thirdly,* Against whom he was tempted to sin—*against God,* against his nature and his dominion, against his love and his design. Those that love God do for this reason hate sin.

(2) By steadfastness of resolution. The grace of God enabled him to overcome the temptation by avoiding the tempter. He would not stay so much as to parley with the temptation, but flew out from it with the utmost abhorrence; he left his garment, as one escaping for his life. Note, It is better to lose a good coat than a good conscience.

Verses 13–18

Joseph's mistress, having tried in vain to make him a criminal, now endeavours to represent him as one; so to be revenged on him for his virtue. Chaste and holy love will continue, though slighted; but sinful love, like Amnon's to Tamar, is easily changed into sinful hatred. She accused him to his fellow servants (v. 13–15) and gave him a bad name among them. She accused him to his master, who had power in his hand to punish him. Observe, 1. What an improbable story she tells, but it was told to be revenged upon his virtue, a most malicious lie. And yet, 2. She manages it so as to incense her husband against him, reflecting upon him for bringing this Hebrew servant among them.

Verses 19–23

Here is, 1. Joseph wronged by his master. He believed the accusation, and there is no remedy, he is condemned to perpetual imprisonment, v. 19, 20. He should be shut up among the king's prisoners,

the state-prisoners. Potiphar, it is likely, chose that prison because it was the worst. He was committed to the king's prison, that he might thence be preferred to the king's person. 2. Joseph was at a distance from all his friends, but *the Lord was with Joseph, and showed him mercy, v.* 21. No gates nor bars can shut out his gracious presence from his people; for he has promised that he will never leave them. Those that have a good conscience in a prison have a good God there. Joseph is not long a prisoner before he becomes a little ruler. God *gave him favour in the sight of the keeper of the prison.* Note, God can raise up friends for his people even where they little expect to find them. The keeper saw that God was with him and that every thing prospered under his hand; and therefore entrusted him with the management of the affairs of the prison, *v.* 22, 23.

CHAPTER 40

In this chapter things are working, though slowly, towards Joseph's advancement. I. Two of Pharaoh's servants are committed to prison, and there to Joseph's care, and so become witnesses of his extraordinary conduct, ver. 1–4. II. They dreamed each of them a dream, which Joseph interpreted (ver. 5–19), and the event verified the interpretation (ver. 20–22), and so they became witnesses of his extraordinary skill. III. Joseph recommends his case to one of them, whose preferment he foresaw (ver. 14, 15), but in vain, ver. 23.

Verses 1–4

We should not have had this story of Pharaoh's butler and baker recorded in scripture if it had not been serviceable to Joseph's preferment. Observe, 1. Two of the great officers of Pharaoh's court, having offended the king, are committed to prison. Many conjectures there are concerning the offence of these servants of Pharaoh; some make it no less than an attempt to take away his life, others no more than the casual lighting of a fly into his cup and a little sand into his bread. 2. The *captain of the guard* himself, who was Potiphar, charged Joseph with them (v. 4), which intimates that he began now to be reconciled to him, and perhaps to be convinced of his innocence, though he durst not release him for fear of disobliging his wife.

Verses 5–19

I. The special providence of God, which filled the heads of these two prisoners with unusual dreams, such as made extraordinary impressions upon them, and carried with them evidences of a divine origin, both in one night.

II. The impression which was made upon these prisoners by their dreams (v. 6): *They were sad.*

III. Joseph's great tenderness and compassion towards them. He enquired with concern, *Wherefore look you so sadly to-day? v.* 7. Joseph was their keeper, and was now a prisoner with them, and had been a dreamer too. Communion in sufferings helps to work compassion towards those that do suffer. It is some relief to those that are in trouble to be taken notice of.

IV. The dreams themselves, and the interpretation of them. *There is no interpreter* here in the prison, *v.* 8. Joseph hereupon directed them which way to look: *Do not interpretations belong to God?* Joseph suggests, "If interpretations belong to God, he is a free agent, and may communicate the power to whom he pleases, and therefore tell me your dreams." Now, 1. The chief butler's dream was a happy presage of his enlargement, and re-advancement, within three days; and so Joseph explained it to him, *v.* 12, 13. 2. The chief baker's dream portended his ignominious death, *v.* 18, 19. The happy interpretation of the other's dream encouraged him to relate his. It was not Joseph's fault that he brought him no better tidings. Ministers are but interpreters, they cannot make the thing otherwise than it is.

V. The improvement Joseph made of this opportunity to get a friend at court, *v.* 14, 15. He modestly bespoke the favour of the chief butler, whose preferment he foretold: *But think of me when it shall be well with thee.* What a modest representation he makes of his own case, *v.* 15. He does not reflect upon his brethren that sold him. Nor does he reflect on the wrong done him in this imprisonment by his mistress that was his prosecutrix, and his master that was his judge; but mildly avers his own innocence. When we are called to vindicate ourselves we should carefully avoid, as much as may be, speaking ill of others. Let us be content to prove ourselves innocent, and not be fond of upbraiding others with their guilt.

Verses 20-23

The verifying of Joseph's interpretation of the dreams, on the very day prefixed. The chief butler and baker were both advanced, one to his office, the other to the gallows, and both at the three days' end.

Some observe the resemblance between Joseph and Christ in this story. Joseph's fellow-sufferers were like the two thieves that were crucified with Christ— the one saved, the other condemned. One of these, when Joseph said to him, *Remember me when it shall be well with thee,* forgot him; but one of those, when he said to Christ, *Remember me when thou comest into thy kingdom,* was not forgotten.

CHAPTER 41

Two things Providence is here bringing about:—I, The advancement of Joseph. II. The maintenance of Jacob and his family in a time of famine. 1. Pharaoh's dreams, ver. 1–8. 2. The recommendation of Joseph to him for an interpreter, ver. 9–13. 3. The interpretation of the dreams, and the prediction of seven years of plenty and seven years of famine in Egypt, with the prudent advice given to Pharaoh thereupon, ver. 14–36. 4. The preferment of Joseph to a place of the highest power and trust in Egypt, ver. 37–45. 5. The accomplishment of Joseph's prediction, and his fidelity to his trust, ver. 46, &c.

Verses 1-8

Observe, 1. The delay of Joseph's enlargement. It was not till *the end of two full years* (*v.* 1). There is a time set for the deliverance of God's people; that time will come, though it seem to tarry; and, when it comes, it will appear to have been the best time. 2. The means of Joseph's enlargement, which were Pharaoh's dreams, here related. If we were to look upon them as ordinary dreams, we might observe from them the follies and absurdities of a roving working fancy, tame cows as beasts of prey (nay, more ravenous than any, eating up those of their own kind), and ears of corn as devouring one another. Foolish dreams related can make no better than foolish talk. But these dreams which Pharaoh dreamed carried their own evidence with them that they were sent of God; and therefore, when he awoke, his spirit was troubled, *v.* 8. His magicians were puzzled, the rules of their art failed them. This was to make Joseph's performance by the Spirit of God the more admirable. Compare with this story, Dan. ii. 27; iv. 7; v. 8. Joseph's own dreams were the occasion of his troubles, and now Pharaoh's dreams were the occasion of his enlargement.

Verses 9-16

Here is, 1. The recommending of Joseph to Pharaoh for an interpreter. The chief butler did it more in compliment to Pharaoh, to oblige him, than in gratitude to Joseph, or in compassion for his case. The story he had to tell was, in short, That there was an obscure young man in the king's prison, who had

very properly interpreted his dream, and the chief baker's (the event corresponding in each with the interpretation), and that he would recommend him to the king his master for an interpreter. Note, God's time for the enlargement of his people will appear at last to be the fittest time. If the chief butler had at first used his interest for Joseph's enlargement, and had obtained it, it is probable that upon his release he would have gone back to *the land of the Hebrews* again, which he spoke of so feelingly (*ch.* xl. 15), and then he would neither have been so blessed himself, nor such a blessing to his family, as afterwards he proved. But staying two years longer, and coming out now upon this occasion, at last, to interpret the king's dreams, way was made for his very great preferment. 2. The introducing of Joseph to Pharaoh. It is done with all possible expedition, and Joseph is brought in, perhaps almost as much surprised as Peter was, Acts xii. 9. Pharaoh immediately, without enquiring who or whence he was, tells him his business, that he expected he should interpret his dream, *v.* 15. To which Joseph makes him a very modest decent reply (*v.* 16), in which, (1) He gives honour to God. "It is not in me, God must give it." (2) He shows respect to Pharaoh, and hearty good will to him and his government, in supposing that the interpretation would be an answer of peace.

Verses 17-32

I. Pharaoh relates his dream. He dreamt that he stood upon the bank of the river Nile, and saw the kine, both the fat ones and the lean ones, come out of the river.

II. Joseph interprets his dream, and tells him that it signified seven years of plenty now immediately to ensue, which should be succeeded by as many years of famine. Observe, 1. The two dreams signified the same thing, but the repetition was to denote the certainty, the nearness, and the importance of the event, *v.* 32. 2. Yet the two dreams had a distinct reference to the two things wherein we most experience plenty and scarcity, namely, grass and corn. The plenty and scarcity of grass for the cattle were signified by the fat kine and the lean ones; the plenty and scarcity of herb for the service of man by the full ears and the thin ones. 3. See what changes the comforts of this life are subject to. After great plenty may come great scarcity. 4. See the goodness of God in sending the seven years of plenty before those of famine, that provision might be made accordingly. With what wonderful wisdom has Providence, that great housekeeper, ordered the affairs of this numerous family from the beginning hitherto! Great variety of seasons there have been, and the produce of the earth is sometimes more and sometimes less; yet, take one time with another, what was miraculous concerning the manna is ordinarily verified in the common course of Providence, *He that gathers much has nothing over, and he that gathers little has no lack,* Exod. xvi. 18. 5. See the perishing nature of our worldly enjoyments. The great increase of the years of plenty was quite lost and swallowed up in the years of famine; and the overplus of it, which seemed very much, yet did but just serve to keep men alive, *v.* 29–31. Observe, God revealed this beforehand to Pharaoh, who, as king of Egypt, was to be the father of his country, and to make prudent provision for them.

Verses 33-45

I. The good advice that Joseph gave to Pharaoh, which was, 1. That in the years of plenty he should lay up for the years of famine, buy up corn when it was cheap, that he might both enrich himself and supply the country when it would be dear and scarce. 2. Because that which is everybody's work commonly proves nobody's work, he advises Pharaoh to appoint officers who should make it their business, and to select some one person to preside in the affair, v. 33.

II. The great honour that Pharaoh did to Joseph. 1. He gave him an honourable testimony: He is *a man in whom the Spirit of God is*; and this puts a great excellency upon any man; such men ought to be valued, v. 38. He is a nonsuch for prudence: *There is none so discreet and wise as thou art*, v. 39. Now he is abundantly recompensed for the disgrace that had been done him. 2. He put him into an honourable office; not only employed him to buy up corn, but made him prime-minister of state, comptroller of the household. 3. He put upon him all the marks of honour imaginable, to recommend him to the esteem and respect of the people as the king's favourite, and one whom he delighted to honour. He gave him a new name, to show his authority over him, and yet such a name as bespoke the value he had for him. *Zaphnath-paaneah—A revealer of secrets.* He married him honourably to a prince's daughter. Where God had been liberal in giving wisdom and other merits, Pharaoh was not sparing in conferring honours.

Verses 46–57

Observe here, I. The building of Joseph's family in the birth of two sons, Manasseh and Ephraim, v. 50–52. In the names he gave them, he owned the divine Providence giving this happy turn to his affairs. He was made *fruitful in the land of his affliction.* It had been the land of his affliction, and in some sense it was still so, for it was not Canaan, the land of promise. His distance from his father was still his affliction. The afflictions of the saints promote their fruitfulness. *Ephraim* signifies *fruitfulness*, and *Manasseh forgetfulness*, for these two often go together; when Jeshurun waxed fat, he forgot God his Maker.

II. The accomplishment of Joseph's predictions. Pharaoh had great confidence in the truth of them. The seven plenteous years came (v. 47), and, at length, they were ended, v. 53. Years of plenty will end, therefore, Whatever thy hand finds to do, do it; and gather in gathering time. *The seven years of dearth began to come*, v. 54. This famine, it seems, was not only in Egypt, but in other lands, in *all lands*, that is, all the neighbouring countries. It is here said that *in the land of Egypt there was bread.*

III. The performance of Joseph's trust. He was found faithful to it, as a steward ought to be. 1. He was diligent in laying up, while the plenty lasted, v. 48, 49. 2. He was prudent and careful in giving out, when the famine came, and kept the markets low by furnishing them at reasonable rates out of his stores. The people in distress cried to Pharaoh. He sent them to his treasurer, Go to Joseph. Joseph, no doubt, with wisdom and justice fixed the price of the corn he sold, so that the country might not be oppressed, nor advantage taken of their prevailing necessity. And let the price be determined by that golden rule of justice, to do as we would be done by.

Chapter 42

In this and the following chapters we have the fulfilling of the dreams which Joseph himself had dreamed, that his father's family should do homage to him. The story is very largely and particularly related of what passed between Joseph and his brethren, because it is very instructive, and it gave occasion for the removal of Jacob's family into Egypt, on which so many great events afterwards depended. We have, in this chapter, I. The humble application of Jacob's sons to Joseph to buy corn, ver. 1–6. II. The fright Joseph put them into, for their trial, ver. 7–20. III. The conviction they were now under of their sin concerning Joseph long before, ver. 21–24. IV. Their return to Canaan with corn, and the great distress their good father was in upon hearing the account of their expedition, ver. 25, &c.

Verses 1–6

Though Jacob's sons were all married they were still incorporated in one society, under the conduct and presidency of their father Jacob.

I. The orders he gave them to go and buy corn in Egypt, v. 1, 2. Observe, 1. The famine was grievous in the land of Canaan. It is observable that all the three patriarchs, to whom Canaan was the land of promise, met with famine in that land, which was not only to try their faith, whether they could trust God though he should starve them, but to teach them to seek the better country, that is, the heavenly, Heb. xi. 14–16. 2. Still, when there was famine in Canaan, there was corn in Egypt. Thus Providence orders it, that one place should be a succour and supply to another; for we are all brethren. 3. *Jacob saw that there was corn in Egypt.* 4. He reproved his sons for delaying to provide corn for their families. *Why do you look one upon another?* 5. He quickened them to go to Egypt: *Get you down thither.*

II. Their obedience to these orders, v. 3. They *went down to buy corn*; they did not send their servants, but very prudently went themselves, to lay out their own money. Let none think themselves too great nor too good to take pains. Benjamin went not with them, for he was his father's darling. To Egypt they came, and, having a considerable cargo of corn to buy, they were brought before Joseph himself, *they bowed down themselves before him*, v. 6. Now their empty sheaves did obeisance to his full one.

Verses 7–20

We may well wonder that Joseph, during the twenty years that he had now been in Egypt, never made an excursion to Canaan, to visit his aged father, when he was in the borders of Egypt, that lay next to Canaan. It is a probable conjecture that his whole management of himself in this affair was by special direction from Heaven, that the purpose of God concerning Jacob and his family might be accomplished. When Joseph's brethren came, he knew them by many a satisfactory token, but they knew not him, little thinking to find him there, v. 8. Joseph had an eye to his dreams, in his carriage towards his brethren, and aimed at the bringing of his brethren to repentance for their former sins.

I. He showed himself very rigorous and harsh with them. He charged them with bad designs against the government (v. 9), treated them as dangerous persons, saying, You are spies. Now why was Joseph thus hard upon his brethren? We may be sure it was not from a spirit of revenge. It was to bring them to repentance. It was to get out of them an account of the state of their family, which he longed to know. Not seeing his brother Benjamin with them, perhaps he began to suspect that they had made away with him too, and therefore gives them occasion to speak of their father and brother.

II. They, hereupon, were very submissive. They spoke to him with all the respect imaginable: *Nay, my lord* (v. 10)—a great change since they said, *Behold, this dreamer comes.* They very modestly deny the charge: *We are no spies.* They tell him their business, that they came to buy food.

III. He clapped them all up in prison for three days, v. 17.

IV. He concluded with them, at last, that one of them should be left as a hostage, and the rest should go home and fetch Benjamin. It was a very encouraging word he said to them (v. 18): *I fear God;* as if he had said, "You may assure yourselves I will do you no wrong; I dare not, for I know that, high as I am, there is one higher than I." Note, With those that fear God we have reason to expect fair dealing. The fear of God will be a check upon those that are in power, to restrain them from abusing their power to oppression and tyranny. Those that have no one else to stand in awe of ought to stand in awe of their own consciences. See Neh. v. 15, *So did not I, because of the fear of God.*

Verses 21–28

I. The penitent reflection Joseph's brethren made upon the wrong they had formerly done to him, *v.* 21. They talked the matter over in the Hebrew tongue, not suspecting that Joseph, whom they took for a native of Egypt, understood them, much less that he was the person they spoke of.

They remembered with regret the barbarous cruelty wherewith they persecuted him. Now see here, 1. The office of conscience. As time will not wear out the guilt of sin, so it will not blot out the records of conscience. 2. The benefit of afflictions; they often prove the happy and effectual means of awakening conscience.

II. Joseph's tenderness towards them upon this occasion. This represents the tender mercies of our God towards repenting sinners. See Jer. xxxi. 20, *Since I spoke against him I do earnestly remember him still.* See Judg. x. 16.

III. The imprisonment of Simeon, *v.* 24. He chose him for the hostage probably because he remembered him to have been his most bitter enemy, or because he observed him now to be least humbled and concerned.

IV. The dismission of the rest of them. They came for corn, and corn they had; and not only so, but every man had his money restored in his sack's mouth.

1. It was really a merciful event; for I hope they had no wrong done to them when they had their money given them back, but a kindness; yet they were thus terrified by it. Guilty consciences are apt to take good providences in a bad sense. If they had been robbed of their money, they could not have been worse frightened than they were now when they found their money in their sacks.

2. They knew that the Egyptians abhorred a Hebrew (*ch.* xliii. 32), and therefore, since they could not expect to receive any kindness from them, they concluded that this was done with a design to pick a quarrel with them, because the lord of the land had charged them as spies. Their own consciences also were awake, and their sins set in order before them; and this put them into confusion. When men's spirits are sinking every thing helps to sink them.

Verses 29–38

1. The report which Jacob's sons made to their father of the great distress they had been in in Egypt; how they had been suspected, and threatened, and obliged to leave Simeon a prisoner there, till they should bring Benjamin with them thither. 2. The deep impression this made upon the good man. The very bundles of money which Joseph returned, in kindness to his father, frightened him (*v.* 35); for he concluded it was done with some mischievous design. (1) He has very melancholy apprehensions concerning the present state of his family. Jacob gives up Joseph for gone, and Simeon and Benjamin as being in danger; and he concludes, *All these things are against me.* It proved otherwise, that all these were for him, were working together for his good and the good of his family. Through our ignorance and mistake, and the weakness of our faith, we often apprehend that to be against us which is really for us. (2) He is at present resolved that Benjamin shall not go down. No, Jacob's present thoughts are, *My son shall not go down with you.* He plainly intimates a distrust of them, remembering that he never saw Joseph since he had been with them.

CHAPTER 43

Here the story of Joseph's brethren is carried on, I. Their melancholy parting with their father Jacob in Canaan, ver. 1–14. II. Their pleasant meeting with Joseph in Egypt, ver. 15, &c.

Verses 1–10

1. Jacob urges his sons to go and buy more corn in Egypt, *v.* 1, 2. The famine continued; and the corn they had bought was all spent. 2. Judah urges him to consent that Benjamin should go down with them. Judah's conscience had lately smitten him for what he had done a great while ago against Joseph (*ch.* xlii. 21); and, as an evidence of the truth of his repentance he would make some amends for the irreparable injury he had done him by doubling his care concerning Benjamin.

Verses 11–14

I. Jacob's persuasibleness. He would be ruled by reason. *"If it must be so now, take your brother.* If no corn can be had but upon those terms, we may as well expose him to the perils of the journey as suffer ourselves and families, and Benjamin amongst the rest, to perish for want of bread." Constancy is a virtue, but obstinacy is not.

II. Jacob's prudence and justice, which appeared in three things:—1. He sent back the money which they had found in the sacks' mouths, with this discreet construction of it, *Peradventure it was an oversight.* Though we get it by oversight, if we keep it when the oversight is discovered, it is kept by deceit. 2. He sent double money, as much again as they took the time before, upon supposition that the price of corn might have risen, or to show a generous spirit, that they might be the more likely to find generous treatment with *the man, the lord of the land.* 3. He sent a present of such things as the land afforded, and as were scarce in Egypt— *balm and honey,* &c. (*v.* 11), the commodities that Canaan exported, *ch.* xxxvii. 25. Honey and spice will never make up the want of bread-corn. The famine was sore in Canaan, and yet they had balm and myrrh, &c. We may live well enough upon plain food without dainties; but we cannot live upon dainties without plain food. Let us thank God that that which is most needful and useful is generally most cheap and common.

III. Jacob's piety appearing in his prayer: *God Almighty give you mercy before the man! v.* 14. Jacob had formerly turned an angry brother into a kind one with a present and a prayer; and here he betakes himself to the same tried method, and it sped well.

Verses 15–25

Jacob's sons, having got leave to take Benjamin with them, went down the second time into Egypt to buy corn. If we should ever know what a famine of the word means, let us not think it much to travel as far for spiritual food as they did for corporal food. Now here we have an account of what passed between them and Joseph's steward. *They were afraid, because they were brought into Joseph's house, v.* 18. Now they thought they should be reckoned with about the money in the sacks' mouths, and should be charged as cheats. They therefore laid the case before the steward, and, as a substantial proof of their honesty, before they were charged with taking back their money they produced it. The steward encouraged them (*v.* 23): *Peace be to you, fear not.* He directs them to look at the divine Providence in the return of their money: *Your God, and the God of your father, has given you treasure in your sacks.* Hereby he silences their further enquiry about it. "Ask not how it came thither; Providence brought it to you, and let that satisfy you." It appears by what he said that, by his good master's instructions, he was brought to the knowledge of the true God, the God of the Hebrews.

Verses 26–34

I. The great respect that Joseph's brethren paid to him. When they brought him the present, *they bowed themselves before him* (v. 26); and again, when they gave him an account of their father's health, *they made obeisance*, and called him, *Thy servant our father*, v. 28. Thus were Joseph's dreams fulfilled more and more.

II. The great kindness that Joseph showed to them, while they little thought it was a brotherly kindness. Here is,

1. His kind enquiry concerning Jacob: *Is he yet alive?*

2. The kind notice he took of Benjamin, his own brother. (1) He put up a prayer for him: *God be gracious unto thee, my son*, v. 29. (2) He shed some tears for him, v. 30. Tears of tenderness and affection are no disparagement at all, even to great and wise men.

3. When his weeping had subsided so that he could refrain himself, he sat down to dinner with them, treated them nobly, and yet contrived every thing to amuse them.

He ordered three tables to be spread, one for his brethren, another for the Egyptians that dined with him (for so different were their customs that they did not care to eat together), another for himself, who durst not own himself a Hebrew, and yet would not sit with the Egyptians.

He placed his brethren according to their seniority (v. 33).

He gave them a very plentiful entertainment, sent messes to them from his own table, v. 34. This was the more generous in him, and the more obliging to them, because of the present scarcity of provisions. Their cares and fears were now over, and they ate their bread with joy, concluding they were now upon good terms with the man, the lord of the land. Joseph gave them to understand that Benjamin was his favourite; for his mess was *five times as much as any of theirs*.

Chapter 44

Joseph, having entertained his brethren, dismissed them; but here we have them brought back in a greater fright than any they had been in yet. Observe, I. What method he took both to humble them further and also to try their affection to his brother Benjamin, by which he would be able to judge of the sincerity of their repentance for what they had done against himself, of which he was desirous to be satisfied before he manifested his reconciliation to them. This he contrived to do by bringing Benjamin into distress, ver. 1–17. II. The good success of the experiment; he found them all heartily concerned, and Judah particularly, both for the safety of Benjamin and for the comfort of their aged father, ver. 18, &c.

Verses 1-17

Joseph heaps further kindnesses upon his brethren, fills their sacks, returns their money, and sends them away full of gladness; but he also exercises them with further trials. Joseph ordered his steward to put a fine silver cup which he had (and which, it is likely, was used at his table when they dined with him) into Benjamin's sack's mouth, that it might seem as if he had stolen it from the table, and put it there himself, after his corn was delivered to him.

I. How the pretended criminals were pursued and arrested, on suspicion of having stolen a silver cup. The steward charged them with ingratitude.

II. How they pleaded for themselves. They solemnly protested their innocence, and offered to submit to the severest punishment if they should be found guilty, v. 9, 10.

III. How the theft was fastened upon Benjamin. In his sack the cup was found. They dare not arraign

Joseph's justice, nor so much as suggest that perhaps he that had put their money in their sacks' mouths had put the cup there; but they throw themselves upon Joseph's mercy.

IV. Here is their humble submission, v. 16. 1. They acknowledge the righteousness of God: *God hath found out the iniquity of thy servants*, perhaps referring to the injury they had formerly done to Joseph, for which they thought God was now reckoning with them. 2. They surrender themselves prisoners to Joseph: *We are my lord's servants*. Now Joseph's dreams were accomplished to the utmost.

V. Joseph, with an air of justice, gives sentence that Benjamin only should be kept in bondage, and the rest should be dismissed; for why should any suffer but the guilty? It is plain he intended hereby to try the affection of his brethren to Benjamin and to their father. If they had gone away contentedly, and left Benjamin in bonds, no doubt Joseph would soon have released and promoted him, and sent notice to Jacob, and would have left the rest of his brethren justly to suffer for their hard-heartedness; but they proved to be better affected to Benjamin than he feared. Those that had sold Joseph would not now abandon Benjamin. The worst may mend in time.

Verses 18–34

We have here a most ingenious and pathetic speech which Judah made to Joseph on Benjamin's behalf, to obtain his discharge. Perhaps Judah was a better friend to Benjamin than the rest were, or the rest chose him for their spokesman, because he had a greater command of language than any of them.

I. A great deal of unaffected art, and unstudied unforced rhetoric, there is in this speech. 1. He addresses himself to Joseph with a great deal of respect and deference. 2. He represented Benjamin as one well worthy of his compassionate consideration (v. 20); he was *a little one*, compared with the rest of them; the youngest, brought up tenderly with his father. It made the case the more pitiable that he alone was left of his mother, and his brother was dead, namely, *Joseph*. 3. He urged it very closely that Joseph had himself constrained them to bring Benjamin with them. Was he not brought to Egypt, in obedience, purely in obedience, to the command of Joseph? and would he not show him some mercy? 4. The great argument he insisted upon was the insupportable grief it would be to his aged father if Benjamin should be left behind in servitude: *"If he should leave his father, his father would die;* much more if now he be left behind, never more to return to him."* This therefore Judah presses with a great deal of earnestness: *"His life is bound up in the lad's life"* (v. 30). 5. Judah, in honour to the justice of Joseph's sentence, and to show his sincerity in this plea, offers himself to become a bondsman instead of Benjamin, v. 33. Neither Jacob nor Benjamin needed an intercessor with Joseph; for he himself loved them.

II. Upon the whole matter let us take notice, 1. How prudently Judah suppressed all mention of the crime that was charged upon Benjamin. 2. What good reason dying Jacob had to say, *Judah, thou art he whom thy brethren shall praise* (ch. xlix. 8), for he excelled them all in boldness, wisdom, eloquence, and especially tenderness for their father and family. 3. Judah's faithful adherence to Benjamin, now in his distress, was recompensed long after by the constant adherence of the tribe of Benjamin to the tribe of Judah, when all the other ten tribes deserted it. 4. How fitly does the apostle, when he is discoursing of the mediation of Christ, observe, that *our Lord sprang out of Judah* (Heb. vii. 14); for, like his father Judah, he not only *made intercession for the transgressors*, but he became a surety for them.

CHAPTER 45

It is a pity that this chapter and the foregoing should be parted, and read asunder. There we had Judah's intercession for Benjamin. Joseph let him go on without interruption, heard all he had to say, and then answered it all in one word, "I am Joseph." Now he found his brethren humbled for their sins, mindful of himself (for Judah had mentioned him twice in his speech), respectful to their father, and very tender to their brother Benjamin. It was to Joseph's brethren as clear shining after rain, nay, it was to them as life from the dead. Here is, I. Joseph's discovery of himself to his brethren, ver. 1–15. II. The orders Pharaoh, hereupon, gave to fetch Jacob and his family down to Egypt, and Joseph's despatch of his brethren, accordingly, back to his father with those orders, ver. 16–24. III. The joyful tidings of this brought to Jacob, ver. 25, &c.

Verses 1–15

Judah and his brethren were waiting for an answer.

I. Joseph ordered all his attendants to withdraw, *v.* 1. The private conversations of friends are the most free. Thus Christ graciously manifests himself and his loving-kindness to his people, out of the sight and hearing of the world.

II. Tears were the preface or introduction to his discourse, *v.* 2. These were tears of tenderness and strong affection.

III. He very abruptly tells them who he was: *I am Joseph.* They knew him only by his Egyptian name, *Zaphnath-paaneah*, his Hebrew name being lost and forgotten in Egypt; but now he teaches them to call him by that. Thus when Christ would convince Paul he said, *I am Jesus*; and when he would comfort his disciples he said, *It is I, be not afraid.* Thus when Christ manifests himself to his people he encourages them to draw near to him with a true heart.

IV. He endeavours to assuage their grief for the injuries they had done him, by showing them that God had brought much good out of it (*v.* 5): *Be not grieved, nor angry with yourselves.* Sinners must grieve for their sins; but true penitents should be greatly affected when they see God thus bringing good out of evil. Now he tells them how long the famine was likely to last—*five years*; yet (*v.* 6) what a capacity he was in of being kind to his relations and friends. *God sent me before you, v.* 5, 7. 1. God's Israel is the particular care of God's providence. 2. Providence looks a great way forward, and has a long reach. The psalmist praises God for this (Ps. cv. 17): *He sent a man before them, even Joseph.* God sees his work from the beginning to the end, but we do not, Eccl. iii. 11. 3. God often works by contraries. Those that put Christ to death were many of them saved by his death. 4. God must have all the glory. *It was not you that sent me hither, but God, v.* 8. They must not be proud of it, because it was God's doing, and not theirs.

V. He promises to take care of his father and all the family during the rest of the years of famine. 1. His brethren must hasten to Canaan, and must inform Jacob that his son Joseph was *lord of all Egypt* (*v.* 9). If any thing would make him young again, this would. 2. He is very earnest that his father and all his family should come to him to Egypt: *Come down unto me, tarry not, v.* 9. He allots his dwelling in Goshen. He promises to provide for him: *I will nourish thee, v.* 11. Our Lord Jesus being, like Joseph, exalted to the highest honours and powers of the upper world, it is his will that all that are his should be with him where he is, John xvii. 24.

VI. Endearments were interchanged between him and his brethren. He began with the youngest, his own brother Benjamin, who was but about a year old when Joseph was separated from his brethren. After he had embraced Benjamin he, in like manner, caressed them all (*v.* 15); and then *his brethren talked with him.*

Verses 16–24

I. The kindness of Pharaoh to Joseph, and to his relations for his sake: he bade his brethren welcome (*v.* 16), though it was a time of scarcity, and they were likely to be a charge to him. He engaged Joseph to send for his father down to Egypt, and promised to furnish them with all conveniences both for his removal thither and his settlement there. If the good of all the land of Egypt would suffice him, he was welcome to it all, so that they need not *regard their stuff, v.* 20. What they had in Canaan he reckoned but stuff, in comparison with what he had for them in Egypt.

II. The kindness of Joseph to his father and brethren. Pharaoh was respectful to Joseph, in gratitude, because he had been an instrument of much good to him. Joseph likewise was respectful to his father and brethren. He gave them waggons and provisions for the way, both going and coming. To his brethren he gave two suits apiece of good clothes, to Benjamin five suits, and money besides in his pocket, *v.* 22. To his father he sent a very handsome present of the varieties of Egypt, *v.* 23. He dismissed them with a seasonable caution: *See that you fall not out by the way, v.* 24. Now Joseph, having forgiven them all, lays this obligation upon them, not to upbraid one another. This charge our Lord Jesus has given to us, *that we love one another.* For, 1. We are brethren, we have all one Father. 2. We are his brethren, and we shame our relation to him *who is our peace*, if we fall out. 3. We are guilty, *verily guilty*, and, instead of quarrelling with one another, have a great deal of reason to fall out with ourselves.

Verses 25–28

We have here the good news brought to Jacob.

The relation of it, at first, sunk his spirits. To hear that *Joseph is alive* is too good news to be true; he faints, for he believes it not. Note, We faint, because we do not believe. Jacob had easily believed his son formerly when they told him, *Joseph is dead*; but he can hardly believe them now that they tell him, *Joseph is alive.* Weak and tender spirits are influenced more by fear than hope. But at length Jacob is convinced of the truth of the story, especially when he sees the waggons which were sent to carry him (for seeing is believing). He says nothing of Joseph's glory, of which they told him; it was enough to him that Joseph was alive.

CHAPTER 46

Jacob is here removing to Egypt in his old age, forced thither by a famine, and invited thither by a son. Here, I. God sends him thither, ver. 1–4. II. All his family goes with him, ver. 5–27. III. Joseph bids him welcome, ver. 28–34.

Verses 1–4

Jacob has here a very great concern before him.

I. How he acknowledged God in this way. He *came to Beersheba*, from Hebron, where he now dwelt; and there *he offered sacrifices to the God of his father Isaac, v.* 1. Abraham called on God there (*ch.* xxi. 33), so did Isaac (*ch.* xxvi. 25). In his devotion, 1. He had an eye to God as the God of his father Isaac, that is, a God in covenant with him. 2. He *offered sacrifices*, (1) By way of thanksgiving for the late blessed change of the face of his family, for the good news he had received concerning Joseph, and for the hopes he had of seeing him. (2) By way of petition for the presence of God with him in his intended journey. (3) By way of consultation. The heathen consulted their oracles by sacrifice. Jacob would not go till he had asked God's leave.

II. How God directed his paths: *In the visions of*

the night God spoke unto him, v. 2. If we speak to him as we ought, he will not fail to speak to us. What has God to say to him?

1. He renews the covenant with him: *I am God, the God of thy father* (v. 3).

2. He encourages him to make this removal of his family: *Fear not to go down into Egypt*. We must always rejoice with trembling. Jacob had many careful thoughts about this journey, which God took notice of. (1) He was old. It was a long journey. (2) He feared lest his sons should be tainted with the idolatry of Egypt, and forget the God of their fathers, or enamoured with the pleasures of Egypt, and forget the land of promise.

3. He promises him comfort in the removal. (1) That he should multiply in Egypt. (2) That he should have God's presence with him: *I will go down with thee into Egypt*. (3) That neither he nor his should be lost in Egypt. Though Jacob died in Egypt, yet this promise was fulfilled, [1] In the bringing up of his body to be buried in Canaan. [2] In the bringing up of his seed to be settled in Canaan. Whatever low or darksome valley we are called into at any time, we may be confident, if God go down with us into it, that he will surely bring us up again. If he go with us down to death, he will surely bring us up again to glory. (4) That living and dying, his beloved Joseph should be a comfort to him: *Joseph shall put his hand upon thine eyes*.

Verses 5–27

Old Jacob is here flitting. Little did he think of ever leaving Canaan; he expected, no doubt, *to die in his nest*, and to leave his seed in actual possession of the promised land: but Providence orders it otherwise. It is good to be ready, not only for the grave, but for whatever may happen betwixt us and the grave. We have here a particular account of the names of Jacob's family, *his sons' sons*, most of whom are afterwards mentioned as heads of houses in the several tribes. When Jacob himself removed to a land of plenty, he would not leave any of his children behind him to starve in a barren land. It was now 215 years since God had promised Abraham to make him a great nation (*ch*. xii. 2); and yet that branch of his seed on which the promise was entailed had increased only to seventy. When God pleases, *a little one shall become a thousand*, Isa. lx. 22.

Verses 28–34

I. The joyful meeting between Jacob and his son Joseph, in which observe,

1. Jacob's prudence in sending Judah before him to Joseph, to give him notice of his arrival in Goshen.

2. Joseph's filial respect to him. He went in his chariot to meet him, and, in the interview, showed, (1) How much he honoured him. (2) How much he loved him. Time did not wear out the sense of his obligations, but his tears which he shed abundantly upon his father's neck, for joy to see him, were real indications of the sincere and strong affection he had for him.

3. Jacob's great satisfaction in this meeting.

II. Joseph's prudent care concerning his brethren's settlement. Time was when they were contriving to get rid of him; now he is contriving to settle them to their satisfaction and advantage: this is rendering good for evil. Now, 1. He would have them to live *in the land of Goshen*, which lay nearest to Canaan, and which perhaps was more thinly peopled by the Egyptians, and well furnished with pastures for cattle. He desired they might live separately, that they might be in the less danger both of being infected by the vices of the Egyptians and of being insulted by the malice of the Egyptians. 2. He would have them to

continue shepherds, and not to be ashamed to own that as their occupation before Pharaoh. It is better to be the credit of a mean post than the shame of a high one.

CHAPTER 47

In this chapter we have instances, I. Of Joseph's presenting his brethren first and then his father to Pharaoh (ver. 1–10), settling them in Goshen (ver. 11, 12), and paying his respects to his father when he sent for him, ver. 27–31. II. Of Joseph's justice between prince and people in a very critical affair, selling Pharaoh's corn to his subjects with reasonable profits to Pharaoh, ver. 13, &c. Thus he approved himself wise and good, both in his private and in his public capacity.

Verses 1–12

I. The respect which Joseph, as a subject, showed to his prince. Though he had had particular orders from him to send for his father down to Egypt, yet he would not suffer him to settle till he had given notice of it to Pharaoh, v. 1.

II. The respect which Joseph, as a brother, showed to his brethren.

1. Though he was a great man, and they were comparatively mean and despicable, especially in Egypt, yet he owned them. Every branch of the tree is not a top branch; but, because it is a lower branch, is it therefore not of the tree? Our Lord Jesus, like Joseph here, is not *ashamed to call us brethren*.

2. They being strangers and no courtiers, he introduced some of them to Pharaoh. Being presented to Pharaoh, according to the instructions which Joseph had given them, they tell him, (1) What was their business—that they were shepherds, v. 3. Note, All that have a place in the world should have an employment in it according to their capacity. Magistrates should enquire into the occupation of their subjects, as those that have the care of the public welfare; for idle people are as drones in the hive, unprofitable burdens of the commonwealth. (2) What was their business in Egypt—to sojourn there for a time, while the famine so prevailed in Canaan.

3. He obtained for them a grant of a settlement in the land of Goshen, v. 5, 6. This was an instance of Pharaoh's gratitude to Joseph. He offered them preferment as shepherds over his cattle.

III. The respect Joseph, as a son, showed to his father.

1. He presented him to Pharaoh, v. 7. And here, (1) Pharaoh asks Jacob a common question: *How old art thou? v.* 8. A question usually put to old men, for it is natural to us to admire old age and to reverence it (Lev. xix. 32).

(2) Jacob gives Pharaoh an uncommon answer, v. 9. He speaks as becomes a patriarch, with an air of seriousness, for the instruction of Pharaoh. Observe here, [1] He calls his life *a pilgrimage*, looking upon himself as a stranger in this world, and a traveller towards another world: this earth his inn, not his home. [2] He reckons his life by *days*. [3] The character he gives of them is, *First*, That they were few. *Secondly*, That they were evil. Jacob's life, particularly, had been made up of evil days; and the pleasantest days of his life were yet before him. *Thirdly*, That they were short of the days of his fathers, not so many, not so pleasant, as their days.

(3) Jacob both addresses himself to Pharaoh and takes leave of him with a blessing (v. 7): *Jacob blessed Pharaoh*, and again, v. 10, he prayed for him, as one having the authority of a prophet and a patriarch.

Verses 13–26

Joseph now returns to the management of that great trust which Pharaoh had lodged in his hand. It would have been pleasing enough to him to have gone and lived with his father and brethren in Goshen;

but his employment would not permit it. In Joseph's transactions with the Egyptians observe,

I. The great extremity that Egypt, and the parts adjacent, were reduced to by the famine. 1. See here what a dependence we have upon God's providence. If its usual favours are suspended but for a while, we die, we perish, we all perish. All our wealth would not keep us from starving if the rain of heaven were but withheld for two or three years. See how much we lie at God's mercy, and let us keep ourselves always in his love. 2. See how much we smart by our own improvidence. If all the Egyptians had done for themselves in the seven years of plenty as Joseph did for Pharaoh, they had not been now in these straits.

II. The price they had come up to, for their supply, in this exigency. 1. They parted with all their money which they had hoarded up, *v.* 14. Silver and gold would not feed them; they must have corn. 2. When the money failed, they parted with all their cattle, those for labour, as the horses and asses, and those for food, as the flocks and the herds, *v.* 17. Pharaoh saw in reality what he had before seen in vision, nothing but lean kine. 3. When they had sold their stocks off their land, it was easy to persuade themselves to sell their land too; for what good would that do them, when they had neither corn to sow it nor cattle to eat of it? They therefore sold that next, for a further supply of corn. 4. When their land was sold, so that they had nothing to live on, they must of course sell themselves, that they might live purely upon their labour. Note, *Skin for skin, and all that a man hath,* even liberty and property (those darling twins), *will he give for his life;* for life is sweet.

III. The method which Joseph took to accommodate the matter between prince and people. 1. For their lands, he needed not come to any bargain with them while the years of famine lasted; but when these were over he came to an agreement, which it seems both sides were pleased with, that the people should occupy and enjoy the lands, as he thought fit to assign them, and should have seed to sow them with out of the king's stores, for their own proper use and behoof, yielding and paying only a fifth part of the yearly profits as a chief rent to the crown. This became a standing law, *v.* 26. It is observable how faithful Joseph was to him that appointed him. He did not put the money into his own pocket, nor entail the lands upon his own family; but converted both entirely to Pharaoh's use. 2. For their persons, he removed them to cities, *v.* 21. He transplanted them. How hard soever this seems to have been upon them, they themselves were at this time sensible of it as a very great kindness, and were thankful they were not worse used: *Thou hast saved our lives,* v. 25.

IV. The reservation he made in favour of the priests. They were maintained on free cost, so that they needed not to sell their lands, *v.* 22.

Verses 27–31

1. The comfort Jacob lived in (*v.* 27, 28); while the Egyptians were impoverished in their own land, Jacob was replenished in a strange land. 2. The care Jacob died in. At last *the time drew nigh that Israel must die,* v. 29. Now Jacob's care was about his burial, (1) He would be buried in Canaan, because it was the land of promise, and because it was a type of heaven, that better country which he that said these things declared plainly that he was in expectation of, Heb. xi. 14. He aimed at a good land, which would be his rest and bliss on the other side death. (2) He would have Joseph sworn to bring him thither to be buried (*v.* 29, 31). (3) When this was done *Israel bowed himself upon the bed's head,* yielding himself, as it were, to the stroke of death.

CHAPTER 48

The time drawing nigh that Israel must die, he takes leave of his grand-children by Joseph. God's gifts and graces shine forth much more in some saints than in others upon their death-beds. In this chapter, I. Joseph, hearing of his father's sickness, goes to visit him, and takes his two sons with him, ver. 1, 2. II. Jacob solemnly adopts his two sons, and takes them for his own, ver. 3–7. III. He blesses them, ver. 8–16. IV. He explains and justifies the crossing of his hands in blessing them, ver. 17–20. V. He leaves a particular legacy to Joseph, ver. 21, 22.

Verses 1–7

I. Joseph goes to see his aged father, *v.* 1. Visiting the sick, to whom we lie under obligations, or may have opportunity of doing good, either for body or soul, is our duty. Joseph took his own sons with him, that they might receive their dying grandfather's blessing. Manasseh and Ephraim would never forget what passed at this time.

II. Jacob, upon notice of his son's visit, prepared himself as well as he could to entertain him, *v.* 2. Note, It is very good for sick and aged people to be as lively and cheerful as they can, that they may not faint in the day of adversity. *Strengthen thyself,* as Jacob here, and God will strengthen thee.

III. In recompense to Joseph for all his attentions to him, he adopted his two sons. In this charter of adoption there is, 1. A particular recital of God's promise to him, to which this had reference: "*God blessed me* (*v.* 3), and let that blessing be entailed upon them." 2. An express reception of Joseph's sons into his family: "Thy sons are mine (*v.* 5), not only my grandchildren, but as my own children." He explains this at *v.* 16, *Let my name be named upon them, and the name of my fathers.* Thus the aged dying patriarch teaches these young persons not to look upon Egypt as their home, nor to incorporate themselves with the Egyptians, but to take their lot with the people of God, as Moses afterwards in the like temptation, Heb. xi. 24–26. Those are worthy of double honour who, through God's grace, break through the temptations of worldly wealth and preferment, to embrace religion in disgrace and poverty. Mention is made of the death and burial of Rachel, Joseph's mother, and Jacob's best beloved wife (*v.* 7), referring to that story, *ch.* xxxv. 19. Those that were to us as our own souls are dead and buried; and shall we think it much to follow them in the same path?

Verses 8–22

Here is, I. The blessing with which Jacob blessed the two sons of Joseph, which is the more remarkable because the apostle makes such particular mention of it (Heb. xi. 21).

1. Jacob was blind with age, *v.* 10. Jacob, like his father before him, when he was old, was dim-sighted. Note, (1) Those that have the honour of age must therewith be content to take the burden of it. (2) The eye of faith may be very clear even when the eye of the body is very much clouded.

2. Jacob was very fond of Joseph's sons. With what satisfaction does Jacob say here (*v.* 11), *I had not thought to see thy face* (having many years given him up for lost), *and, lo, God has shown me also thy seed!*

3. Before he entails his blessing, he recounts his experiences of God's goodness to him. (1) He had *fed him all his life long unto this day,* v. 15. Note, As long as we have lived in this world we have had continual experience of God's goodness to us, in providing for the support of our natural life. He that has fed us *all our life long* surely will not fail us at last. (2) He had by this angel *redeemed him from all evil,* v. 16.

4. When he confers the blessing and name of Abraham and Isaac upon them he recommends the

pattern and example of Abraham and Isaac to them, *v.* 15. He calls God the *God before whom his fathers Abraham and Isaac walked*, that is, in whom they believed, whom they observed and obeyed.

5. In blessing them, he *crossed hands.* Joseph placed them so that Jacob's right hand should be put on the head of Manasseh the elder, *v.* 12, 13. But Jacob would put it on the head of Ephraim the younger, *v.* 14. But Jacob gave him to understand that he knew what he did, and that he did it not by mistake, nor in a humour, nor from a partial affection to one more than the other, but from a spirit of prophecy, and in compliance with the divine counsels. Manasseh should be great, but truly Ephraim should be greater. Joshua was of that tribe, so was Jeroboam. The tribe of Manasseh was divided, one half on one side Jordan, the other half on the other side, which made it the less powerful and considerable. In the foresight of this, *Jacob crossed hands.* Note, Grace observes not the order of nature, nor does God prefer those whom we think fittest to be preferred, but as it pleases him. It is observable how often God, by the distinguishing favours of his covenant, advanced the younger above the elder, Abel above Cain, Shem above Japheth, Abraham above Nahor and Haran, Isaac above Ishmael, Jacob above Esau; Judah and Joseph were preferred before Reuben, Moses before Aaron, David and Solomon before their elder brethren. See 1 Sam. xvi. 7.

II. The particular tokens of his favour to Joseph. He left with him the promise of their return out of Egypt, as a sacred trust: *I die, but God shall be with you, and bring you again, v.* 21. These words of Jacob furnish us with comfort in reference to the death of our friends. He will bring us to the land of our fathers, the heavenly Canaan, whither our godly fathers have gone before us. If God be with us while we stay behind in this world, and will receive us shortly to be with those that have gone before to a better world, we ought not to sorrow as those that have no hope.

CHAPTER 49

This chapter is a prophecy. Jacob is here upon his death-bed, making his will. The twelve sons of Jacob were, in their day, men of renown, but the twelve tribes of Israel, which descended and were denominated from them, were much more renowned. In the prospect of this their dying father says something remarkable of each son, or of the tribe that bore his name. Here is, I. The preface, ver. 1, 2. II. The prediction concerning each tribe, ver. 3–28. III. The charge repeated concerning his burial, ver. 29–32. IV. His death, ver. 33.

Verses 1–4

I. The preface to the prophecy, in which, 1. The congregation is called together. It was a comfort to Jacob, now that he was dying, to see all his children about him. His calling upon them once and again to gather together intimated a precept to them to unite in love and all make one people. 2. A general idea is given of the intended discourse (*v.* 1): *That I may tell you that which shall befall you* (not your persons, but your posterity) *in the latter days.* 3. Attention is demanded (*v.* 2): "*Hearken to Israel your father*; let Israel, that has prevailed with God, prevail with you."

II. The prophecy concerning Reuben. He begins with him (*v.* 3, 4), for he was the first-born; but by committing uncleanness with his father's wife he forfeited the prerogatives of the birthright. He shall have all the privileges of a son, but not of a first-born. No judge, prophet, nor prince, is found of that tribe, nor any person of renown except Dathan and Abiram, who were noted for their impious rebellion against Moses. Reuben himself seems to have lost all that influence upon his brethren to which his birthright entitled him; for *when he spoke unto them they would*

not hear, ch. xlii. 22. The character fastened upon Reuben, for which he is laid under this mark of infamy, is that he was *unstable as water.* 1. His virtue was unstable; he had not the government of himself and his own appetites. Men do not thrive because they do not fix. 2. His honour consequently was unstable; it departed from him, and became as water spilt upon the ground. Note, Those that throw away their virtue must not expect to save their reputation.

Verses 5–7

Observe, 1. The character of Simeon and Levi: they were brethren in disposition; but, unlike their father, they were passionate and revengeful, fierce and uncontrollable; their swords, which should have been only weapons of defence, were (as the margin reads it, *v.* 5) *weapons of violence.* It is not in the power of parents, no, not by education, to form the dispositions of their children; Jacob bred his sons to every thing that was mild and quiet, and yet they proved to be thus furious. 2. A proof of this is the murder of the Shechemites, which Jacob deeply resented at the time (*ch.* xxxiv. 30) and still continued to resent. Simeon and Levi would not be advised by their aged and experienced father; no, they would be governed by their own passion rather than by his prudence. 3. Jacob's protestation against this barbarous act of theirs: *O my soul, come not thou into their secret.* Hereby he professes not only his abhorrence of such practices in general, but his innocence particularly in that matter. 4. His abhorrence of those brutish lusts that led them to this wickedness: *Cursed be their anger.* He does not curse their persons, but their lusts. We ought carefully to distinguish between the sinner and the sin, so as not to love the sin for the sake of the person, nor to hate the person for the sake of the sin. 5. A token of displeasure which he foretells their posterity should lie under for this: *I will divide them.* The Levites were scattered throughout all the tribes, and Simeon's lot lay not together. This curse was afterwards turned into a blessing to the Levites; but the Simeonites, for Zimri's sin (Num. xxv. 14), had it bound on.

Verses 8–12

Glorious things are here said of Judah. Judah's name signifies *praise*, in allusion to which he says, *Thou art he whom thy brethren shall praise, v.* 8. It is prophesied that, 1. The tribe of Judah should be victorious and successful in war. 2. It should be superior to the rest of the tribes; not only in itself more numerous and illustrious, but having a dominion over them: Judah was the *lawgiver*, Ps. lx. 7. That tribe led the van through the wilderness, and in the conquest of Canaan, Judges i. 2. 3. It should be a strong and courageous tribe, and so qualified for command and conquest: *Judah is a lion's whelp, v.* 9. The lion is the king of beasts; when he seizes his prey none can resist him. By this is foretold that the tribe of Judah should become very formidable, and should not only obtain great victories, but should peaceably and quietly enjoy what was obtained by those victories —that they should make war, not for the sake of war, but for the sake of peace. Judah is compared, not to a lion *rampant*, always tearing, always raging, always ranging; but to a lion *couchant*, enjoying the satisfaction of his power and success, without creating vexation to others: this is to be truly great. 4. It should be the royal tribe, and the tribe from which Messiah the Prince should come: *The sceptre shall not depart from Judah, till Shiloh come, v.* 10. Jacob here foresees and foretells, (1) That the sceptre should come into the tribe of Judah, which was fulfilled in David, on whose family the crown was entailed. (2) That Shiloh should be of this tribe—his seed, that promised seed, in whom the earth should be blessed: *that peaceable and prosperous one*, or *the Saviour*, so others translate it, he shall come of Judah. (3) That after the coming of the sceptre into the tribe of Judah it should continue in that tribe. Till the captivity, all along from David's time, the sceptre was in Judah, and subsequently the governors of Judea were of that tribe, or of the Levites that adhered to it (which was equivalent), till Judea became a province of the Roman Empire, just at the time of our Saviour's birth, and was at that time taxed as one of the provinces, Luke ii. 1. And at the time of his death the Jews expressly owned, *We have no king but Caesar*. Hence it is undeniably inferred against the Jews that our Lord Jesus is he that should come. 5. It should be a very fruitful tribe, especially that it should abound with milk for babes, and *wine to make glad the heart of strong men* (*v.* 11). Much of what is here said concerning Judah is to be applied to our Lord Jesus. In him there is plenty of all that which is nourishing and refreshing to the soul, and which maintains and cheers the divine life in it; in him we may have wine and milk, the riches of Judah's tribe, without money and without price, Isa. lv. 1.

Verses 13–21

Jacob's prophecy concerning six of his sons.

I. Concerning Zebulun (*v.* 13), that his posterity should have their lot upon the seacoast, and should be merchants, and mariners, and traders at sea. This was fulfilled when, two or three hundred years after, the land of Canaan was divided by lot, and the *border of Zebulun went up towards the sea*, Josh. xix. 11.

II. Concerning Issachar, *v.* 14, 15. That the men of that tribe should be strong and industrious, fit for labour and inclined to labour, particularly the toil of husbandry, like the ass, that patiently carried his burden, and, by using himself to it, makes it the easier. Issachar submitted to two burdens, tillage and tribute. It was a tribe that took pains, and, thriving thereby, was called upon for rents and taxes.

III. Concerning Dan, *v.* 16, 17. What is said concerning Dan has reference either, To that tribe in general, that though Dan was one of the sons of the concubines yet he should by art, and policy, and surprise, gain advantages against his enemies, like a serpent suddenly biting the heel of the traveller. Dan shall be incorporated by as good a charter as any of the other tribes. Some, like Dan, may excel in the subtlety of the serpent, as others, like Judah, in the courage of the lion; and both may do good service to the cause of God against the Canaanites.

Thus was Jacob going on with his discourse; but now he relieves himself with those words which come in as a parenthesis (*v.* 18), *I have waited for thy salvation, O Lord!*

IV. Concerning Gad, *v.* 19. He alludes to his name, which signifies a *troop*, foresees the character of that tribe, that it should be a warlike tribe, and so we find (1 Chron. xii. 8); the *Gadites were men of war fit for the battle*. He foresees that the situation of that tribe on the other side Jordan would expose it to the incursions of its neighbours, the Moabites and Ammonites; and he foretells that the troops of their enemies should, in many skirmishes, overcome them; yet he assures them that they should *overcome at the last*, which was fulfilled when, in Saul's time and David's, the Moabites and Ammonites were wholly subdued: see 1 Chron. v. 18, &c. Note, *Vincimur in praelio, sed non in bello—We are foiled in a battle, but not in a campaign*. Grace in the soul is often foiled in its conflicts, but the cause is God's and grace will in the issue come off conqueror, yea *more than conqueror*, Rom. viii. 37.

V. Concerning Asher (*v.* 20), that it should be a very rich tribe, replenished not only with bread for necessity, but with fatness, and *dainties*, and these exported out of Asher to other tribes, perhaps to other lands.

VI. Concerning Naphtali (*v.* 21), a tribe that carries struggles in its name; it signifies *wrestling*, and the blessing entailed upon it signifies prevailing; it is *a hind let loose*. This tribe was, 1. As the loving hind, friendly and obliging. 2. As the loosened hind, zealous for their liberty. 3. As the swift hind (Ps. xviii. 33), quick in despatch of business. Note, Among God's Israel there is to be found a great variety of dispositions, contrary to each other, yet all contributing to the beauty and strength of the body, Judah like a lion, Issachar like an ass, Dan like a serpent, Naphtali like a hind.

Verses 22–27

He closes with the blessings of his best beloved sons, Joseph and Benjamin; with these he will breathe his last.

I. The blessing of Joseph, which is very large and full. He is compared (*v.* 22) to *a fruitful bough*, or young tree; for God had made him fruitful in the land of his affliction; he owned it, *ch*. xli. 52. His two sons were as branches of a vine, or other spreading plants, *running over the wall*.

1. The providences of God concerning Joseph, *v.* 23, 24. Here observe (1) Joseph's straits and troubles, *v.* 23. Though he now lived at ease and in honour, Jacob reminds him of the difficulties he had formerly waded through. He had had many enemies, here called *archers*, being skilful to do mischief. His brethren, in his father's house, thought they had been the death of him. His mistress in the house of Potiphar impudently assaulted his chastity and shot arrows against which there is little fence but the hold God has in the consciences of the worst of men. Doubtless he had enemies in the court of Pharaoh, that envied his preferment, and sought to undermine him. (2) Joseph's strength and support under all these troubles (*v.* 24): *His bow abode in strength*, that is, his faith did not fail. The *arms of his hands were made strong*, that is, his other graces did their part, his wisdom, courage, and patience, which are better than weapons of war. (3) The spring and fountain of this strength it was *by the hands of the mighty God*. All our strength for the resisting of temptations, and the bearing of afflictions, comes from God: his grace is sufficient, and his strength is perfected in our weakness. (4) The state of honour and usefulness to which he was subsequently advanced. Herein Joseph was a type, [1] Of Christ. [2] Of the church in general.

2. The promises of God to Joseph. Our experiences of God's power and goodness in strengthening us hitherto are our encouragements still to hope for help from him. We may build much upon our *Eben-ezers*. Observe the blessings conferred on Joseph. *Blessings of heaven above* (rain in its season, and fair weather in its season, and the benign influences of the heavenly bodies); *blessings of the deep that lieth under* this earth, which, compared with the upper world, is but a great deep, with subterraneous mines and springs. Eminent and transcendent blessings, which *prevail above the blessings of my progenitors*, *v.* 26. Durable and extensive blessings: *Unto the utmost bounds of the everlasting hills*, including all the productions of the most fruitful hills, and lasting as long as they last, Isa. liv. 10.

II. The blessing of Benjamin (*v.* 27): He *shall raven as a wolf*; it is plain by this that Jacob was guided in what he said by a spirit of prophecy, and not by natural affection; else he would have spoken with more tenderness of his beloved son Benjamin, concerning whom he only foresees and foretells this, that his posterity should be a warlike tribe, strong and daring, and that they should enrich themselves with the spoils of their enemies—that they should be active and busy in the world, and a tribe as much feared by their neighbours as any other. Blessed Paul was of this tribe (Rom. xi 1; Phil. iii. 5); and he did in the morning of his day, devour the prey as a persecutor, but, in the evening, divided the spoil as a preacher.

Verses 28–33

I. The summing up of the blessings of Jacob's sons, *v.* 28. Though Reuben, Simeon, and Levi were put under the marks of their father's displeasure, yet he is said to *bless them every one according to his blessing;* for none of them were rejected as Esau was.

II. The solemn charge Jacob gave them concerning his burial, which is a repetition of what he had before given to Joseph. See how he speaks of death: *I am to be gathered unto my people, v.* 29. Though it separates us from our children and our people in this world, it gathers us to our fathers and to our people in the other world.

III. The death of Jacob, *v.* 33: as one cheerfully composing himself to rest, now that he was weary. *I will lay me down, and sleep.* He freely resigned his spirit into the hand of God, the Father of spirits: *He yielded up the ghost.* His separated soul went to the assembly of the souls of the faithful, which, after they are delivered from the burden of the flesh, are in joy and felicity: he was *gathered to his people.*

CHAPTER 50

Here is, I. The preparation for Jacob's funeral, ver. 1–6. II. The funeral itself, ver. 7–14. III. The settling of a good understanding between Joseph and his brethren after the death of Jacob, ver. 15–21. IV. The age and death of Joseph, ver. 22–26. Thus the book of Genesis, which began with the origin of light and life, ends with nothing but death and darkness; so sad a change has sin made.

Verses 1–6

Joseph is here paying his last respects to his deceased father. 1. With tears and kisses, and all the tender expressions of a filial affection, he takes leave of the deserted body, *v.* 1. The departed soul is out of the reach of our tears and kisses, but it is proper to show our respect to the poor body, of which we look for a glorious and joyful resurrection. 2. He ordered the body to be embalmed (*v.* 2), not only because he died in Egypt, and that was the manner of the Egyptians, but because he was to be carried to Canaan. 3. He observed the ceremony of solemn mourning for him, *v.* 3. Even the Egyptians, many of them out of the great respect they had for Joseph, put themselves into mourning for his father. 4. He asked and obtained leave of Pharaoh to go to Canaan, thither to attend the funeral of his father, *v.* 4–6. He promised to return: *I will come again.* When we return to our own houses from burying the bodies of our relations, we say, "We have left them behind"; but, if their souls have gone to our heavenly Father's house, we may say with more reason, "They have left us behind."

Verses 7–14

We have here an account of Jacob's funeral. He dies in honour, and is followed to the grave by all his children. 1. It was a stately funeral. He was attended to the grave, not only by his own family, but by the courtiers, and all the great men of the kingdom, who, in token of their gratitude to Joseph, showed this respect to his father for his sake, and did him honour at his death. Good old Jacob had conducted himself so well among them as to gain universal esteem.

Note, Professors of religion should endeavour, by wisdom and love, to remove the prejudices which many may have conceived against them because they do not know them. 2. It was a sorrowful funeral (*v.* 10, 11). The solemn mourning for Jacob gave a name to the place, *Abel-Mizraim, the mourning of the Egyptians,* which served for a testimony against the next generation of the Egyptians, who oppressed the posterity of this Jacob to whom their ancestors showed such respect.

Verses 15–21

We have here the settling of a good correspondence between Joseph and his brethren, now that their father was dead. When Providence has removed the parents by death, the best methods ought to be taken for the preserving of acquaintance and love, that unity may continue even when that centre of unity is taken away.

I. Joseph's brethren humbly make their court to him for his favour. 1. While their father lived, they thought themselves safe under his shadow; but now that he was dead they feared the worst from Joseph. A guilty conscience exposes men to continual frights. Those that would be fearless must keep themselves guiltless. 2. They humbled themselves before him, confessed their fault, and begged his pardon. *Forgive the trespass. We are thy servants.* 3. They pleaded their relation to Jacob and to Jacob's God. (1) To Jacob, urging that he directed them to make this submission. *Thy father did command.* (2) To Jacob's God. They plead (*v.* 17), *We are the servants of the God of thy father;* not only children of the same Jacob, but worshippers of the same Jehovah.

II. Joseph, with a great deal of compassion, confirms his reconciliation and affection to them; his compassion appears, *v.* 17. *He wept when they spoke to him.* These were tears of sorrow for their suspicion of him, and tears of tenderness upon their submission. In his reply, 1. He directs them to look up to God in their repentance (*v.* 19): *Am I in the place of God?* "Make your peace with God, and then you will find it an easy matter to make your peace with me." 2. He extenuates their fault, from the consideration of the great good which God wonderfully brought out of it, which, though it should not make them the less sorry for their sin, yet might make him the more willing to forgive it (*v.* 20). God often brings good out of evil, and promotes the designs of his providence even by the sins of men; not that he is the author of sin, far be it from us to think so; but his infinite wisdom so overrules events, that, in the issue, that ends in his praise which in its own nature had a direct tendency to his dishonour; as the putting of Christ to death, Acts ii. 23. 3. He assures them of the continuance of his kindness to them: *Fear not; I will nourish you, v.* 21.

Verses 22–26

I. The prolonging of Joseph's life in Egypt: he lived to be *a hundred and ten years old, v.* 22.

II. The building up of Joseph's family: he lived to see his great-grand-children by both his sons (*v.* 23), and probably he saw his two sons solemnly owned as heads of distinct tribes, equal to any of his brethren.

III. The last will and testament of Joseph published in the presence of his brethren, when he saw his death approaching. To those of them who yet survived, and to the sons of those who were gone, who stood up in their fathers' stead, he said this. 1. He comforted them with the assurance of their return to Canaan in due time: *I die, but God will surely visit you, v.* 24. He bids them be confident: *God will bring you out of this land,* and therefore, (1) They must not look upon it as their rest for ever; they must set their hearts upon the land of promise, and call that their home. (2) They must not fear sinking, and being ruined there. "*God will bring you* in triumph *out of this land* at last." 2. For a confession of his own faith, and a confirmation of theirs, he charges them to keep him unburied till they should be settled in the land of promise, *v.* 25. He makes them promise him with an oath that they would bury him in Canaan.

IV. The death of Joseph, and the reservation of his body for a burial in Canaan, *v.* 26. He was *put in a coffin in Egypt,* but not buried till his children had received their inheritance in Canaan, Josh. xxiv. 32.

THE SECOND BOOK OF MOSES, CALLED

EXODUS

Moses, having, in the first book of his history, preserved and transmitted the records of the church, while it existed in private families, comes, in this second book, to give us an account of its growth into a great nation. The beginning of the former book shows us how God formed the world for himself; the beginning of this shows us how he formed Israel for himself, and both to show forth his praise, Isa. xliii. 21. There we have the creation of the world in history, here the redemption of the world in type. The Greek translators called this book Exodus (which signifies a *departure* or *going out*) because it begins with the story of the going out of the children of Israel from Egypt. The forming of Israel into a people was a new creation. This book gives us, I. The accomplishment of the promises made before to Abraham (ch. i.–xix.), and then, II. The establishment of the ordinances which were afterwards observed by Israel, ch. xx.–xl. Moses, in this book, begins, like Caesar, to write his own Commentaries. But henceforward the penman is himself the hero, and gives us the history of those things of which he was himself an eye- and ear-witness, *et quorum pars magna fuit—and in which he bore a conspicuous part.* There are more types of Christ in this book than perhaps in any other book of the Old Testament; for Moses wrote of him, John v. 46. The way of man's reconciliation to God, and coming into covenant and communion with him by a Mediator, is here variously represented; and it is of great use to us for the illustration of the New Testament, now that we have that to assist us in the explication of the Old.

CHAPTER 1

We have here, I. God's kindness to Israel, in multiplying them exceedingly, ver. 1–7. II. The Egyptians' wickedness to them, 1. Oppressing and enslaving them, ver. 8–14. 2. Murdering their children, ver. 15–22. Thus whom the court of heaven blessed the country of Egypt cursed, and for that reason.

Verses 1–7

1. A recital of the names of the *twelve patriarchs*, as they are called, Acts vii. 8. 2. The account which was kept of the number of Jacob's family, when they went down into Egypt. Notice is here taken of this that their increase in Egypt might appear the more wonderful. 3. The death of Joseph, *v.* 6. *All that generation* by degrees wore off. Perhaps all Jacob's sons died much about the same time; for there was not more than seven years' difference in age between the eldest and the youngest of them, except Benjamin. 4. The strange increase of Israel in Egypt, *v.* 7. Here are four words used to express it: They *were fruitful*, and *increased abundantly*. They *multiplied* and *waxed exceedingly mighty*. This wonderful increase was the fulfilment of the promise long before made unto the fathers.

Verses 8–14

The land of Egypt here, at length, becomes to Israel a house of bondage, though hitherto it had been a happy shelter and settlement for them.

I. The obligations they lay under to Israel upon Joseph's account were forgotten: *There arose a new king*, after several successions in Joseph's time, *who knew not Joseph, v.* 8. If we work for men only, our works, at furthest, will die with us; if for God, they will follow us, Rev. xiv. 13.

II. Reasons of state were suggested for their dealing hardly with Israel, *v.* 9, 10. 1. They are represented as more and mightier than the Egyptians; certainly they were not so, but the king of Egypt, when he resolved to oppress them, would have them thought so, and looked on as a formidable body. 2. Hence it is inferred that if care were not taken to keep them under they would become dangerous to the government. Observe, The thing they feared was lest they should *get them up out of the land*, probably having heard them speak of the promise made to their fathers that they should settle in Canaan. 3. It is therefore proposed that a course be taken to prevent their increase: *Come on, let us deal wisely with them, lest they multiply.*

III. The method they took to suppress them, and

check their growth, *v.* 11, 13, 14. 1. They took care to keep them poor, by charging them with heavy taxes. 2. By this means they took an effectual course to make them slaves. The Israelites, it should seem, were much more industrious laborious people than the Egyptians, and therefore Pharaoh took care to find them work, both in building and in husbandry, and this was exacted from them with the utmost rigour and severity. They had *taskmasters* set over them, directed *to afflict them with their burdens.* They made them *serve with rigour*, so that their lives became bitter to them, intending hereby, (1) To break their spirits. (2) To ruin their health and shorten their days, and so diminish their numbers. (3) To discourage them from marrying, since their children would be born to slavery. And it is to be feared that the oppression they were under brought over many of them to join with the Egyptians in their idolatrous worship. However, they were kept a distinct body, unmingled with the Egyptians, and by their other customs separated from them, which was *the Lord's doing, and marvellous.*

IV. The wonderful increase of the Israelites: *The more they afflicted them the more they multiplied*, sorely to the grief and vexation of the Egyptians. The blood of the martyrs was the seed of the church.

Verses 15–22

The Egyptians' indignation at Israel's increase, notwithstanding the many hardships they put upon them, drove them at length to the most barbarous and inhuman methods of suppressing them, by the murder of their children. Pharaoh and Herod sufficiently proved themselves agents for that *great red dragon, who stood to devour the man-child as soon as it was born*, Rev. xii. 3, 4. Pilate delivered Christ to be crucified, after he had confessed that he found no fault in him. It is well for us that, though man can kill the body, this is all he can do.

I. The midwives were commanded to murder them. Observe, 1. The orders given them, *v.* 15, 16. It added much to the barbarity of the intended executions that the *midwives* were appointed to be the executioners. Pharaoh's project was secretly to engage the midwives to stifle the men-children as soon as they were born, and then to lay it upon the difficulty of the birth, or some mischance common in that case, Job iii. 11. 2. Their pious disobedience to this impious command, *v.* 17. *They feared God*, regarded his law, and dreaded his wrath more than

Pharaoh's, and therefore saved the men-children alive. 3. Their justifying themselves in this disobedience, when they were charged with it as a crime, *v.* 18. They gave a reason for it, that they came too late to do it, for generally the children were born before they came, *v.* 19. Some of the ancient Jews expound it thus, *Ere the midwife comes to them they pray to their Father in heaven, and he answereth them, and they do bring forth.* 4. The recompence God gave them for their tenderness towards his people: *He dealt well with them, v.* 20. In particular, *he made them houses (v.* 21), built them up into families, blessed their children, and prospered them in all they did.

II. When this project did not take effect, Pharaoh gave public orders to all his people to drown all the male children of the Hebrews, *v.* 22.

Chapter 2

This chapter begins the story of Moses, that man of renown, famed for his intimate acquaintance with Heaven and his eminent usefulness on earth, and the most remarkable type of Christ, as a prophet, saviour, lawgiver, and mediator, in all the Old Testament. In this chapter we have, I. The perils of his birth and infancy, ver. 1–4. II. His preservation through those perils, and the preferment of his childhood and youth, ver. 5–10. III. The pious choice of his riper years, which was to own the people of God. 1. He offered them his service at present, if they would accept it, ver. 11–14. 2. He retired, that he might reserve himself for further service hereafter, ver. 15–22. IV. The dawning of the day of Israel's deliverance, ver. 23, &c.

Verses 1–4

Moses was a Levite, both by father and mother. Jacob left Levi under marks of disgrace (Gen. xlix. 5); and yet, soon after, Moses appears a descendant from him, that might typify Christ, who came in the likeness of sinful flesh and was made a curse for us. This tribe began to be distinguished from the rest by the birth of Moses, as afterwards it became remarkable in many other instances.

I. How he was hidden. The parents of Moses had Miriam and Aaron, both older than he, born to them before this edict came out. Probably the mother of Moses was full of anxiety in the expectation of his birth, now that this edict was in force. Yet this child proves the glory of his father's house. Just at the time when Pharaoh's cruelty rose to this height the deliverer was born. Note, When men are projecting the church's ruin God is preparing for its salvation. 1. His parents observed him to be a *goodly child,* more than ordinarily beautiful; he was *fair to God,* Acts vii. 20. 2. Therefore they were the more solicitous for his preservation, because they looked upon this as an indication of some kind purpose of God concerning him, and a happy omen of something great. *Three months* they hid him in some private apartment of their own house. Herein Moses was a type of Christ, who, in his infancy, was forced to abscond, and in Egypt too (Matt. ii. 13), and was wonderfully preserved, when many innocents were butchered. Duty is ours, events are God's. Faith in God will set us above the ensnaring fear of man.

II. How he was exposed. At three months' end they put him in an ark of bulrushes by the *river's brink (v.* 3), and set his little sister at some distance to watch what would become of him, and into whose hands he would fall, *v.* 4. God put it into their hearts to do this, to bring about his own purpose, that Moses might by this means be brought into the hands of Pharaoh's daughter. Moses seemed quite abandoned by his friends; his own mother durst not own him: but now the Lord took him up and protected him, Ps. xxvii. 10.

Verses 5–10

Here is, I. Moses saved from perishing. He lay in a bulrush-basket by the river's side. Had he been left to lie there, he must have perished in a little time with hunger, if he had not been sooner washed into the river or devoured by a crocodile. Had he fallen into any other hands than those he did fall into, either they would not, or durst not, have done otherwise than have thrown him straightway into the river; but Providence brings no less a person thither than Pharaoh's daughter, just at that juncture, guides her to the place where this poor forlorn infant lay, and inclines her heart to pity it, which she dares do when none else durst. Never did poor child cry so seasonably, so happily, as this did. God often raises up friends for his people even among their enemies. Pharaoh cruelly seeks Israel's destruction, but his own daughter charitably compassionates a Hebrew child, and not only so, but, beyond her intention, preserves Israel's deliverer.

II. Moses well provided with a good nurse, no less than his own dear mother, *v.* 7–9. Pharaoh's daughter thinks it convenient that he should have a Hebrew nurse, and the sister of Moses, with art and good management, introduces the mother into the place of a nurse, to the great advantage of the child; for mothers are the best nurses.

III. Moses preferred to be the son of Pharaoh's daughter (*v.* 10). The tradition of the Jews is that Pharaoh's daughter had no child of her own, and that she was the only child of her father, so that when he was adopted for her son he stood fair for the crown. Those whom God designs for great services he finds out ways to qualify and prepare beforehand. Moses, by having his education in a court, is the fitter to be a prince and *king in Jeshurun;* by having his education in a learned court (for such the Egyptian then was) is the fitter to be an historian; and by having his education in the court of Egypt is the fitter to be employed, in the name of God, as an ambassador to that court.

IV. Moses named. Pharaoh's daughter called him *Moses, Drawn out of the water,* so it signifies in the Egyptian language. The calling of the Jewish lawgiver by an Egyptian name is a happy omen to the Gentile world, and gives hopes of that day when it shall be said, *Blessed be Egypt my people,* Isa. xix. 25. And his tuition at court was an earnest of the performance of that promise, Isa. xlix. 23. *Kings shall be thy nursing fathers, and queens thy nursing mothers.*

Verses 11–15

Moses had now passed the first forty years of his life in the court of Pharaoh, preparing himself for business; and now it was time for him to enter upon action, and,

I. He boldly owns and espouses the cause of God's people: *When Moses was grown he went out unto his brethren, and looked on their burdens, v.* 11. The best exposition of these words we have from an inspired pen, Heb. xi. 24–26, where we are told that by this he expressed, 1. His holy contempt of the honours and pleasures of the Egyptian court; he *refused to be called the son of Pharaoh's daughter.* 2. His tender concern for his poor brethren in bondage, with whom (though he might easily have avoided it) he *chose to suffer affliction.*

II. He gives a specimen of the great things he was afterwards to do for God and his Israel in two little instances, related particularly by Stephen (Acts vii. 23, &c.).

1. Moses killed the Egyptian who smote the Hebrew (*v.* 11, 12); probably it was one of the Egyptian taskmasters, whom he found abusing his Hebrew slave. The Jews' tradition is that he did not slay him with any weapon, but, as Peter slew Ananias and Sapphira, with the word of his mouth.

2. Moses was afterwards to be employed in governing Israel, and, as a specimen of this, we have him

here trying to end a controversy between two Hebrews.

(1) The unhappy quarrel which Moses observed between two Hebrews, *v.* 13. When God raises up instruments of salvation for the church they will find enough to do, not only with oppressing Egyptians to restrain them, but with quarrelsome Israelites, to reconcile them.

(2) The way he took of dealing with them; he marked him that caused the division, that did the wrong, and mildly reasoned with him: *Wherefore smitest thou thy fellow?* Moses endeavoured to make them friends, a good office. The reproof Moses gave on this occasion may still be of use, *Wherefore smitest thou thy fellow?*

(3) The ill success of his attempt (*v.* 14): *He said, Who made thee a prince?* A man needs no great authority for the giving of a friendly reproof, it is an act of kindness; yet this man needs will interpret it an act of dominion, and represents his reprover as imperious and assuming. Thus when people dislike good discourse, or a seasonable admonition, they will call it *preaching,* as if a man could not speak a word for God and against sin but he took too much upon him. He upbraids him with what he had done in killing the Egyptian: *Intendest thou to kill me?* If the Hebrews had taken the hint, and come in to Moses as their head and captain, it is probable that they would have been delivered now; but, despising their deliverer, their deliverance was justly deferred, and their bondage prolonged forty years, as afterwards their despising Canaan kept them out of it forty years more. We must take heed of being prejudiced against the ways and people of God by the follies and peevishness of some particular persons that profess religion. Christ himself was set at nought by the builders, and is still rejected by those he would save.

(4) The flight of Moses to Midian, in consequence.. God ordered it for wise and holy ends. Things were not yet ripe for Israel's deliverance. Moses is to be further fitted for the service, and therefore is directed to withdraw for the present. God guided Moses to Midian because the Midianites were of the seed of Abraham. And through this country he was afterwards to lead Israel. Hither he came, and sat down by a well, tired and thoughtful, at a loss, and waiting to see which way Providence would direct him. It was a great change with him, since he was but the other day at ease in Pharaoh's court: thus God tried his faith.

Verses 16–22

Moses here gains a settlement in Midian, just as his father Jacob had gained one in Syria, Gen. xxix. 2, &c. Events that seem inconsiderable, and purely accidental, afterwards appear to have been designed by the wisdom of God for very good purposes. A casual transient occurrence has sometimes occasioned the greatest and happiest turns of a man's life.

I. Concerning the seven daughters of Reuel the priest or prince of Midian. 1. They were humble, and very industrious, they *drew water for their father's flock, v.* 16. Idleness can be no one's honour. 2. They were modest, and would not ask this strange Egyptian to come home with them till their father sent for him. Modesty is the ornament of woman.

II. Concerning Moses. He was taken for an Egyptian (*v.* 19). 1. How ready he was to help Reuel's daughters to water their flocks. Those that have had a liberal education yet should not be strangers to servile work, because they know not what necessity Providence may put them in of working for themselves, or what opportunity Providence may give them of being serviceable to others. He loved to be doing good. Wherever the Providence of God casts us we should desire and endeavour to be useful; and, when we cannot do the good we would, we must

be ready to do the good we can. 2. How well he was paid for his serviceableness. When the young women acquainted their father, he sent to invite him to his house, and made much of him, *v.* 20. Moses soon recommended himself to the esteem and good affection of this prince of Midian, who took him into his house, and, in process of time, married one of his daughters to him (*v.* 21), by whom he had a son, whom he called *Gershom, a stranger there* (*v.* 22). Now this settlement of Moses in Midian was designed by Providence, (1) To shelter him for the present. (2) It was also designed to prepare him for the great services he was further designed for. His manner of life in Midian would be of use of him, [1] To inure him to hardship and poverty. [2] To inure him to contemplation and devotion. Egypt accomplished him as a scholar, a gentleman, a statesman, a soldier, but yet he lacked one thing, in which the court of Egypt could not befriend him. He must know what it was to live a life of communion with God; and in this he would be greatly furthered by the solitude and retirement of a shepherd's life in Midian. By the former he was prepared to rule in Jeshurun, but by the latter he was prepared to converse with God in Mount Horeb, near which mount he had spent much of his time.

Verses 23–25

Here is, 1. The continuance of the Israelites' bondage in Egypt, *v.* 23. Probably the murdering of their infants did not continue. The Egyptians now were content with their increase, finding that Egypt was enriched by their labour; so that they might have them for slaves, they cared not how many they were. When one Pharaoh died, another rose up in his place that was governed by the same maxims, and was as cruel to Israel as his predecessors. 2. The preface to their deliverance at last. (1) *They cried, v.* 23. Now, at last, they began to think of God under their troubles, and to return to him from the idols they had served, Ezek. xx. 8. But before God unbound them he put it into their hearts to cry unto him, as it is explained, Num. xx. 16. (2) *God heard, v.* 24, 25. [1] *God heard their groaning.* He knows the burdens they groan under and the blessings they groan after. [2] *God remembered his covenant.* (3) *God looked upon the children of Israel.* Moses looked upon them and pitied them (*v.* 11); but now God looked upon them and helped them. (4) *God had a respect unto them,* a favourable respect to them as his own.

CHAPTER 3

I. The discovery God was pleased to make of his glory to Moses at the bush, to which Moses was forbidden to approach too near, ver 1–5. II. A general declaration of God's grace and good will to his people, who were beloved for their fathers' sakes, ver. 6. III. A particular notification of God's purpose concerning the deliverance of Israel out of Egypt. 1. He assures Moses it should now be done, ver. 7–9. 2. He gives him a commission to act in it as his ambassador both to Pharaoh (ver. 10) and to Israel, ver. 16. 3. He answers the objection Moses made of his own unworthiness, ver. 11, 12. 4. He gives him full instructions what to say both to Pharaoh and to Israel, ver. 13–18. 5. He tells him beforehand what the issue would be, ver. 19, &c.

Verses 1–6

The years of the life of Moses are remarkably divided into three forties: the first forty he spent as a prince in Pharaoh's court, the second a shepherd in Midian, the third a king in Jeshurun. He had now finished his second forty, when he received his commission to bring Israel out of Egypt. Note, Sometimes it is long before God calls his servants out to that work which of old he designed them for, and has been graciously preparing them for.

I. How this appearance of God to him found him employed. He was keeping the flock (tending sheep) near Mount Horeb, *v.* 1. This was a poor employment for a man of his parts and education. It was the lot of Moses, who foresaw nothing to the contrary but that he should die, as he had lived a great while, a poor despicable shepherd. When we are alone, the Father is with us. Moses saw more of God in a desert than ever he had seen in Pharaoh's court.

II. What the appearance was. To his great surprise he saw a bush burning, when he perceived no fire either from earth or heaven to kindle it, and, which was more strange, it did not consume, *v.* 2. It was an extraordinary manifestation of the divine presence and glory. 1. He saw a flame of fire. When Israel's deliverance out of Egypt was promised to Abraham, he saw a burning lamp, which signified the light of joy which that deliverance should cause (Gen. xv. 17); but now it shines brighter, as a flame of fire. 2. This fire was not in a tall and stately cedar, but in a bush, *a thorny bush,* so the word signifies. 3. *The bush burned,* and yet *was not consumed.*

III. The curiosity Moses had to enquire into this extraordinary sight: *I will turn aside and see, v.* 3.

IV. The invitation he had to draw near, yet with a caution not to come too near, nor rashly.

1. God gave him a gracious call, to which he returned a ready answer, *v.* 4. When he turned aside, God called to him. *Draw nigh to God, and he will draw nigh to you.* God called him by name, *Moses, Moses.* The word of the Lord always went along with the glory of the Lord, for every divine vision was designed for divine revelation, Job iv. 16, &c.; xxxiii. 14–16. Divine calls are effectual when we return an obedient answer to them, as Moses here, "*Here am I, what saith my Lord unto his servant?*"

2. God gave him a needful caution. He must draw near, but not too near. His conscience must be satisfied, but not his curiosity. He must express his reverence, and his readiness to obey: *Put off thy shoes from off thy feet,* as a servant. Putting off the shoe was then what putting off the hat is now, a token of respect and submission.

V. The solemn declaration God made of his name, by which he would be known to Moses: *I am the God of thy father, v.* 6. Abraham was dead, and yet God is the God of Abraham; therefore Abraham's soul lives, to which God stands in relation; and, to make his soul completely happy, his body must live again in due time. By these words it appears that God remembered his covenant, *ch.* ii. 24.

VI. The solemn impression this made upon Moses: He *hid his face,* as one both ashamed and afraid to look upon God. He was not afraid of a burning bush till he perceived that God was in it.

Verses 7–10

Now, after forty years of Israel's bondage and Moses's banishment, when we may suppose both he and they began to despair, at length the time has come, even the year of the redeemed.

Here is, I. The notice God takes of the afflictions of Israel (*v.* 7, 9): *Seeing I have seen,* not only, *I have surely seen,* but I have strictly observed and considered the matter. Three things God took cognizance of:—1. *Their sorrows, v.* 7. It is likely they were not permitted to make a remonstrance of their grievances to Pharaoh. But God observed their tears. 2. Their cry: *I have heard their cry* (*v.* 7), *it has come unto me, v.* 9. 3. The tyranny of their persecutors: *I have seen the oppression, v.* 9.

II. The promise God makes of their speedy deliverance and enlargement: *I have come down to deliver them, v.* 8. When God does something very extraordinary he is said to *come down* to do it, as Isa. lxiv. 1. This deliverance was typical of our redemption by Christ, in which the eternal Word did indeed come down from heaven to deliver us. He

promises also their happy settlement in the land of Canaan, that they should exchange bondage for liberty, poverty for plenty, labour for rest.

III. The commission he gives to Moses in order hereunto, *v.* 10. He is not only sent as a prophet to Israel, but he is sent as an ambassador to Pharaoh, to treat with him; and he is sent as a prince to Israel, to conduct and command them. The same hand that now fetched a shepherd out of a desert, to be the planter of a Jewish church, afterwards fetched fishermen from their ships, to be the planters of the Christian church.

Verses 11–15

God, having spoken to Moses, allows him also a liberty of speech.

I. He objects his own insufficiency for the service he was called to (*v.* 11): *Who am I?* He thinks himself unworthy of the honour. He thinks he wants courage. He thinks he wants skill, and therefore cannot bring forth the children of Israel out of Egypt; they are unarmed, undisciplined, quite dispirited. 1. Moses was incomparably the fittest of any man living for this work, eminent for learning, wisdom, experience, valour, faith, holiness; and yet he says, *Who am I?* Note, The more fit any person is for service commonly the less opinion he has of himself: see Judges ix. 8, &c. 2. The difficulties of the work were indeed very great. Yet Moses is the man that does it at last; for God gives grace to the lowly.

II. God answers this objection, *v.* 12. 1. He promises him his presence: *Certainly I will be with thee,* and that is enough. 2. He assures him of success, and that the Israelites should serve God upon this mountain.

III. He begs instructions for the executing of his commission, and desires to know by what name God would at this time make himself known, *v.* 13.

1. He supposes the children of Israel would ask him, *What is his name?* This they would ask either, (1) To perplex Moses. Or (2) For their own information.

2. He desires instructions what answer to give them: "*What shall I say to them?* What name shall I vouch to them for the proof of my authority?"

IV. Two names God would now be known by:—

1. A name that denotes what he is in himself (*v.* 14): *I am that I am.* This explains his name *Jehovah,* and signifies, (1) That he is self-existent; he has his being of himself, and has no dependence upon any other. Being self-existent, he cannot but be self-sufficient, and therefore all-sufficient, and the inexhaustible fountain of being and bliss. (2) That he is eternal and unchangeable. (3) That we cannot by searching find him out. Let Israel know this, *I AM hath sent me unto you.*

2. A name that denotes what he is to his people. *The Lord God of your fathers hath sent me unto you* (*v.* 15): Thus God had made himself known to him (*v.* 6), and thus he must make him known to them, (1) That he might revive among them the religion of their fathers. (2) That he might raise their expectations of the speedy performance of the promises made unto their fathers. God will have this to be his name for ever, and it has been, is, and will be, his name, by which his worshippers know him, and distinguish him from all false gods; see 1 Kings xviii. 36.

Verses 16–22

Moses is here more particularly instructed in his work, and informed beforehand of his success. 1. He must deal with the elders of Israel, and raise their expectations of a speedy removal to Canaan, *v.* 16, 17. His success with the elders of Israel would be good; so he is told (*v.* 18): *They shall hearken to thy voice,* and not thrust thee away as they did forty years ago.

2. He must deal with the king of Egypt (*v.* 18), he and the elders of Israel, and in this they must not begin with a demand, but with a humble petition. *We beseech thee, let us go.* Moreover, they must only beg leave of Pharaoh to go as far as Mount Sinai to worship God. If he would not give them leave to go and sacrifice at Sinai, justly did they go without leave to settle in Canaan. As to his success with Pharaoh, Moses is here told, (1) That petitions would not prevail with him: *I am sure he will not let you go,* *v.* 19. (2) That plagues should compel him to it: *I will smite Egypt,* and then he will *let you go, v.* 20. (3) That his people should furnish them at their departure with abundance of plate and jewels, to their great enriching: *I will give this people favour in the sight of the Egyptians, v.* 21, 22.

CHAPTER 4

This chapter, I. Continues and concludes God's discourse with Moses at the bush concerning this great affair of bringing Israel out of Egypt. 1. Moses objects the people's unbelief (ver. 1), and God answers that objection by giving him a power to work miracles, (1) To turn his rod into a serpent, and then into a rod again, ver. 2–5. (2) To make his hand leprous, and then whole again, ver 6–8. (3) To turn the water into blood, ver. 9. 2. Moses objects his own slowness of speech (ver. 10), and begs to be excused (ver. 13); but God answers this objection, (1) By promising him his presence, ver. 11, 12. (2) By joining Aaron in commission with him, ver. 14–16. (3) By putting an honour upon the very staff in his hand, ver. 17. II. It begins Moses's execution of his commission. 1. He obtains leave of his father-in-law to return into Egypt, ver. 18. 2. He receives further instructions and encouragements from God, ver. 19, 21–23. 3. He hastens his departure, and takes his family with him, ver. 20. 4. He meets with some difficulty in the way about the circumcising of his son, ver. 24–26. 5. He has the satisfaction of meeting his brother Aaron, ver. 27, 28. 6. He produces his commission before the elders of Israel, to their great joy, ver. 29–31. And thus the wheels were set a-going towards that great deliverance.

Verses 1–9

I. Moses objects that in all probability the people would not *hearken to his voice* (*v.* 1), that is, they would not take his bare word, unless he showed them some sign. If there should be some gainsayers among them who would question his commission, how should he deal with them?

II. God empowers him to work miracles, directs him to three particularly, two of which were now immediately wrought for his own satisfaction.

1. The rod in his hand is made the subject of a miracle, a double miracle: it is but thrown out of his hand and it becomes a serpent; he resumes it and it becomes a rod again, *v.* 2–4. Here was an honour put upon Moses, that this change was wrought upon his throwing it down and taking it up, without any spell, or charm, or incantation: his being empowered thus to act under God, out of the common course of nature and providence, was a demonstration of his authority, under God, to settle a new dispensation of the kingdom of grace. There was a significance in the miracle itself. Pharaoh had turned the rod of government into the serpent of oppression, from which Moses had himself fled into Midian; but by the agency of Moses the scene was altered again.

2. His hand itself is next made the subject of a miracle. He puts it once into his bosom, and takes it out leprous; he puts it again into the same place, and takes it out well, *v.* 6, 7. This signified, (1) That Moses, by the power of God, should bring sore diseases upon Egypt, and that, at his prayer, they should be removed. (2) That whereas the Israelites in Egypt had become leprous, polluted by sin, by being taken into the bosom of Moses they should be cleansed and cured. (3) That Moses was not to work miracles by his own power.

3. He is directed, when he shall come to Egypt, to turn some of the water of the river into blood, *v.* 9.

Verses 10–17

Moses still continues backward to the service for which God had designed him; now we can no longer impute it to his humility and modesty, but must own that there was too much of cowardice, slothfulness, and unbelief in it.

I. How Moses endeavours to excuse himself.

1. He pleads that he was no good spokesman: *O my lord! I am not eloquent, v.* 10. God is pleased sometimes to make choice of those as his messengers who have fewest of the advantages of art or nature. Christ's disciples were no orators, till the Spirit made them such.

2. When this plea was overruled, and all his excuses were answered, he begged that God would send somebody else on this errand and leave him to keep sheep in Midian (*v.* 13).

II. How God condescends to answer all his excuses. Though *the anger of the Lord was kindled against him* (*v.* 14), yet he continued to reason with him, till he had overcome him.

1. To balance the weakness of Moses, he here reminds him of his own power, *v.* 11. *Who has made man's mouth? Have not I the Lord?* Moses knew that God made man, but he must be reminded now that God made man's mouth, and of His power in general over the other faculties. The perfections of our faculties are his work, he makes the *seeing*; he formed the eye (Ps. xciv. 9); he opens the understanding, the eye of the mind, Luke xxiv. 45.

2. To encourage him in this great undertaking, he repeats the promise of his presence, not only in general, *I will be with thee* (*ch.* iii. 12), but in particular, "*I will be with thy mouth,* so that the imperfection in thy speech shall be no prejudice to thy message." If others spoke more gracefully, none spoke more powerfully.

3. He joins Aaron in commission with him. He promises that Aaron shall meet him opportunely, and that he will be glad to see him, they having not seen one another (it is likely) for many years, *v.* 14. He directs him to make use of Aaron as his spokesman, *v.* 16, that their natural affection one to another might strengthen their union in the joint execution of their commission. Christ sent his disciples two and two, and some of the couples were brothers. The tongue of Aaron, with the head and heart of Moses, would make one completely fit for this embassy. God promises, *I will be with thy mouth, and with his mouth.* Even Aaron, that could speak well, yet could not speak to purpose unless God was with his mouth.

4. He bids him take the rod with him in his hand (*v.* 17). The rod he carried as a shepherd must be his staff of authority, and must be to him instead both of sword and sceptre.

Verses 18–23

I. Moses obtains leave of his father-in-law to return into Egypt, *v.* 18.

II. He receives from God further encouragements and directions in his work. And, 1. He assures Moses that the coasts were clear. Whatever new enemies he might make by his undertaking, his old enemies were *all dead, all that sought his life, v.* 19. 2. He orders him to do the miracles, not only before the elders of Israel, but before Pharaoh, *v.* 21. 3. That Pharaoh's obstinacy might be no surprise nor discouragement to him, God tells him before that he would *harden his heart.* 4. Words are put into his mouth with which to address Pharaoh, *v.* 22, 23. (1) He must deliver his message in the name of the great Jehovah: *Thus saith the Lord*; this is the first time *that* preface is used by any man which afterwards is used so frequently by all the prophets. (2) He must let Pharaoh know Israel's relation to God, and God's concern for Israel. (3) He must demand a discharge for them: "*Let my son go:* not only my servant whom thou hast no right to detain, but my son whose liberty and honour I am very jealous for." (4) He must threaten Pharaoh with the death of the first-born of Egypt, in case of a refusal: *I will slay thy son, even thy firstborn.*

III. Moses addresses himself to this expedition.

Verses 24–31

Moses is here going to Egypt, and we are told,

I. How God met him in anger, *v.* 24–26. This is a very difficult passage.

1. The sin of Moses, which was neglecting to circumcise his son. This was probably the effect of his being unequally yoked with a Midianite, who was too indulgent of her child.

2. God's displeasure against him. Omissions are sins. God takes notice of, and is much displeased with, the sins of his own people. If they neglect their duty, let them expect to hear of it by their consciences, and perhaps to feel from it by cross providences.

3. The speedy performance of the duty for the neglect of which God had now a controversy with him. His son must be circumcised; Moses is unable to circumcise him; therefore, in this case of necessity, Zipporah does it.

4. The release of Moses thereupon: *So he let him go*; and all was well: only Zipporah cannot forget the fright she was in, and, upon this occasion (it is probable), he sent them back to his father-in-law.

II. How Aaron met him in love, *v.* 27, 28. God sent Aaron to meet him, and directed him where to find him, in the wilderness, that lay towards Midian. He met him *in the mount of God*, the place where God had met with him. They embraced one another as a pledge of their hearty concurrence in the work to which they were jointly called. Moses informed his brother of the commission he had received, *v.* 28.

III. How the elders of Israel met him in faith and obedience. When Moses and Aaron first opened their commission in Egypt they met with a better reception than they promised themselves, *v.* 29–31. *The people believed*, as God had foretold (*ch.* iii. 18). *They bowed their heads and worshipped.*

CHAPTER 5

Moses and Aaron are here dealing with Pharaoh, to get leave of him to go and worship in the wilderness. I. They demand leave in the name of God (ver. 1), and he answers their demand with a defiance of God, ver. 2. II. They beg leave in the name of Israel (ver. 3), and he answers their request with further orders to oppress Israel, ver. 4–9. These cruel orders were, 1. Executed by the task-masters, ver. 10–14. 2. Complained of to Pharaoh, but in vain, ver. 15–19. 3. Complained of by the people to Moses (ver. 20, 21), and by him to God, ver. 22, 23.

Verses 1–2

Moses and Aaron are now to deal with Pharaoh.

I. Their demand is piously bold: *Thus saith the Lord God of Israel, Let my people go, v.* 1. Moses, in treating with the elders of Israel, is directed to call God *the God of their fathers*; but, in treating with Pharaoh, they call him *the God of Israel*, and it is the first time we find him called so in scripture: he is called *the God of Israel*, the *person* (Gen. xxxiii. 20); but here it is Israel, the *people*. They are just beginning to be formed into a people when God is called their God. In this great name they deliver their message: *Let my people go.*

II. Pharaoh's answer is impiously bold: *Who is the Lord, that I should obey his voice? v.* 2. He will not treat about it, nor so much as bear the mention of it. How scornfully he speaks of the God of Israel: "*Who is Jehovah?* I neither know him nor care for him, neither value him nor fear him."

Ignorance and contempt of God are at the bottom of all the wickedness that is in the world. How proudly he speaks of himself: "*That I should obey his voice.* Shall I, that rule the Israel of God, obey the God of Israel?" Here is the core of the controversy: God must rule, but man will not be ruled.

Verses 3–9

Finding that Pharaoh had no veneration at all for God, Moses and Aaron next try whether he had any compassion for Israel.

I. Their request is very humble and modest, *v.* 3. They make no complaint of the rigour they were ruled with. What they ask is very reasonable, only for a short vacation, while they went three days' journey into the desert, "*We will sacrifice unto the Lord our God,* as other people do to theirs."

II. Pharaoh's denial of their request is very barbarous and unreasonable, *v.* 4–9.

1. That the people were idle, and that therefore they talked of going to sacrifice. The cities they built for Pharaoh were witnesses that they were not idle. The malice of Satan has often represented the service and worship of God as fit employment for those only that have nothing else to do.

2. His resolutions hereupon were most barbarous. (1) Moses and Aaron themselves must get to *their burdens* (*v.* 4); they must share in the common slavery of their nation. (2) The usual tale of bricks must be exacted, without the usual allowance of straw to mix with the clay, or to burn the bricks with.

Verses 10–14

Pharaoh's orders are here put in execution; straw is denied, and yet the work not diminished. 1. The Egyptian task-masters were very severe. These task-masters insisted upon the daily tasks, as when there was straw, *v.* 13. 2. The people hereby were dispersed throughout all the land of Egypt, to gather stubble, *v.* 12. 3. The Israelite-officers were used with particular harshness, *v.* 14. What a miserable thing slavery is, and what reason we have to be thankful to God that we are a free people, and not oppressed. Liberty and property are valuable jewels in the eyes of those whose services and possessions lie at the mercy of an arbitrary power. What strange steps God sometimes takes in delivering his people. The lowest ebbs go before the highest tides; and very cloudy mornings commonly introduce the fairest days, Deut. xxxii. 36.

Verses 15–23

It was a great strait that the head-workmen were in.

I. How justly they complained to Pharaoh: They *came and cried unto Pharaoh, v.* 15. *Thy servants are beaten* and yet *the fault is in thy own people*, the task-masters, who deny us what is necessary for carrying on our work. But what did they get by this complaint? It did but make bad worse. Pharaoh taunted them (*v.* 17); when they were almost killed with working, he told them they were idle. It is well for us that men are not to be our judges, but a God who knows what the principles are on which we act.

II. How unjustly they complained of Moses and Aaron: *The Lord look upon you, and judge, v.* 21. This was not fair. Moses and Aaron had given sufficient evidence of their hearty good will to the liberties of Israel; and yet, because things succeed not immediately they are reproached as accessories to their slavery. Now what did Moses do in this strait? 1. He returned to the Lord (*v.* 22), to acquaint him with it. When we find ourselves, at any time, perplexed and embarrassed in the way of our duty, we ought to have recourse to God by faithful and fervent prayer. If we retreat, let us retreat to him, and no further. 2. Now he asks, (1) *Wherefore hast thou so evil entreated this people?* (2) *Why is it thou hast sent me?* Thus, [1] He complains of his ill success: "Pharaoh has done evil to this people, and not one step seems to be taken towards their deliverance." Or, [2] He enquires what was further to be done: *Why hast thou sent me?* that is, "What other method shall I take in pursuance of my commission?"

CHAPTER 6

Witness this chapter, in which, I. God satisfies Moses himself in an answer to his complaints in the close of the foregoing chapter, ver. 1. II. He gives him fuller instructions than had yet been given him what to say to the children of Israel, for their satisfaction (ver. 2–8), but to little purpose, ver. 9. III. He sends him again to Pharaoh, ver. 10, 11. But Moses objects against that (ver. 12), upon which a very strict charge is given to him and his brother to execute their commission with vigour, ver. 13. IV. Here is an abstract of the genealogy of the tribes of Reuben and Simeon, to introduce that of Levi, that the pedigree of Moses and Aaron might be cleared (ver. 14–25), and then the chapter concludes with a repetition of so much of the preceding story as was necessary to make way for the following chapter.

Verses 1–9

Here, I. God silences Moses's complaints with the assurance of success in this negotiation, repeating the promise made him in *ch.* iii. 20, *After that, he will let you go. Then the Lord said unto Moses,* for the quieting of his mind, "*Now shalt thou see what I will do to Pharaoh*" (*v.* 1). See Ps. xii. 5, *Now will I arise.* Note, Man's extremity is God's opportunity of helping and saving. God takes the work into his own hands. *With a strong hand,* that is, being forced to it by a strong hand, *he shall let them go.*

II. He gives him further instructions, that both he and the people of Israel might be encouraged to hope for a glorious issue of this affair. Take comfort,

1. From God's name, Jehovah, *v.* 2, 3. God would now be known by his name *Jehovah,* that is, (1) A God performing what he had promised. (2) A God perfecting what he had begun. In the history of the creation, God is never called Jehovah till the heavens and the earth were finished, Gen. ii. 4. When the salvation of the saints is completed in eternal life, then he will be known by his name Jehovah (Rev. xxii. 13); in the meantime they shall find him, for their strength and support, *El-shaddai, a God all-sufficient,* a God that is enough.

2. From his covenant: *I have established my covenant, v.* 4. We may venture our all upon this bottom.

3. From his compassions (*v.* 5): *I have heard the groaning of the children of Israel.*

4. From his present resolutions, *v.* 6–8. *I will bring you out. I will rid you. I will redeem you. I will bring you into the land of Canaan,* and *I will give it to you.*

5. From his gracious intentions in all these: (1) He intended their happiness: *I will take you to me for a people.* (2) He intended his own glory: *You shall know that I am the Lord.* But regardless of God's promises (*v.* 9): *They hearkened not unto Moses for anguish of spirit.* By indulging ourselves in discontent and fretfulness, we deprive ourselves of the comfort we might have drawn from God's word and from his providence, and must thank ourselves if we go comfortless.

Verses 10–13

I. God sends Moses the second time to Pharaoh (*v.* 11) upon the same errand as before, to command him, at his peril, that he *let the children of Israel go.*

II. Moses makes objections. He pleads, 1. The unlikelihood of Pharaoh's hearing: "*Behold the children of Israel have not hearkened unto me*; they give no heed, no credit, to what I have said; how then can I expect that Pharaoh should hear me?" If God's professing people hear not his messengers, how can it be thought that his professed enemy should? 2. He pleads the unreadiness and infirmity of his own speaking: *I am of uncircumcised lips.* To this objection God had given a sufficient answer for the sufficiency of grace can supply the defects of nature at any time.

III. God again joins Aaron in commission with Moses, and puts an end to the dispute by interposing his own authority, and giving them both a solemn charge. Moses himself has need to be charged, and so has Timothy, 1 Tim. vi. 13; 2 Tim. iv. 1.

Verses 14–30

I. We have here a genealogy, not an endless one, such as the apostle condemns (1 Tim. i. 4), for it ends in those two great patriots Moses and Aaron, and comes in here to show that they were Israelites, bone of their bone and flesh of their flesh whom they were sent to deliver. The heads of the houses of three of the tribes are here named, agreeing with the accounts we had, Gen. xlvi. Dr. Lightfoot thinks that Reuben, Simeon, and Levi, are thus dignified here by themselves because they were left under marks of infamy by their dying father, and therefore Moses would put this particular honour upon them, to magnify God's mercy in their repentance and remission. The two former seem rather to be mentioned only for the sake of a third, which was Levi, from whom Moses and Aaron descended, and all the priests of the Jewish church. Observe here, 1. That Kohath, from whom Moses and Aaron, and all the priests, derived their pedigree, was a younger son of Levi, *v.* 16. 2. That Aaron married Elisheba, daughter of Amminadab, one of the chief of the fathers of the tribe of Judah; for the tribes of Levi and Judah often intermarried, *v.* 23.

II. In the close of the chapter Moses returns to his narrative, from which he had broken off somewhat abruptly (*v.* 13), and repeats, 1. The charge God had given him to deliver his message to Pharaoh (*v.* 29): *Speak all that I say unto thee,* as a faithful ambassador. 2. His objection against it, *v.* 30. Note, Those that have at any time spoken unadvisedly with their lips ought often to reflect upon it with regret, as Moses seems to do here.

CHAPTER 7

In this chapter, I. The dispute between God and Moses finishes, and Moses applies himself to his commission, in obedience to God's command, ver. 1–7. II. The dispute between Moses and Pharaoh begins, and a famous trial of skill it was. Moses, in God's name, demands Israel's release; Pharaoh denies it. The contest is between the power of the great God and the power of a proud prince. 1. Moses confirms the demand he had made to Pharaoh, by a miracle, turning his rod into a serpent; but Pharaoh hardens his heart against this conviction, ver. 8–13. 2. He chastises his disobedience by a plague, the first of the ten, turning the waters into blood; but Pharaoh hardens his heart against this correction, ver. 14, &c.

Verses 1–7

Here, I. God encourages Moses to go to Pharaoh. 1. He clothes him with great power and authority (*v.* 1): *I have made thee a god to Pharaoh;* that is, my representative in this affair, as magistrates are called *gods,* because they are God's vicegerents. He was authorized to speak and act in God's name and stead. Moses was a god, but he was only a *made* god, not essentially one by nature; he was no god but by commission. He was a god, but he was a god only to Pharaoh; the living and true God is a God to all the world. 2. He again nominates him an assistant, his brother Aaron, a notable spokesman: "He shall be *thy prophet.* Thou shalt, as a god, inflict and remove the plagues, and Aaron, as a prophet, shall denounce them, and threaten Pharaoh with them."

3. He tells him that Pharaoh would not hearken to him, and yet the work should be done at last. The Egyptians, who would not know the Lord, should be made to know him.

II. Moses and Aaron apply themselves to their work without further objection: *They did as the Lord commanded them*, v. 6. Their obedience was celebrated by the Psalmist (Ps. cv. 28), *They rebelled not against his word*, namely, Moses and Aaron, whom he mentions, v. 26. Thus Jonah, though at first he was very averse, at length went to Nineveh.

Verses 8–13

The first time that Moses made his application to Pharaoh, he produced his instructions only; now he is directed to produce his credentials, and does accordingly. 1. Pharaoh will say, *Show a miracle*; not with any desire to be convinced, but with the hope that none will be wrought. 2. Orders are therefore given to turn the rod into a serpent, according to the instructions, *ch.* iv. 3. Aaron cast his rod to the ground, and instantly it became a serpent, v. 10. This was proper, not only to affect Pharaoh with wonder, but to strike a terror upon him. 3. This miracle, though too plain to be denied, is enervated, and the conviction of it taken off, by the magicians' imitation of it, v. 11, 12. Moses had been originally instructed in the learning of the Egyptians, and was suspected to have improved himself in magical arts in his long retirement; the magicians are therefore sent for, to vie with him. Their rods became serpents, some think, by the power of God, for the hardening of Pharaoh's heart; others think, by the power of evil angels. Note, God suffers the lying spirit to do strange things, that the faith of some may be tried and manifested (Deut. xiii. 3; 1 Cor. xi. 19). In this contest, Moses plainly gains the victory. The serpent which Aaron's rod was turned into swallowed up the others, which was sufficient to have convinced Pharaoh on which side the right lay. But Pharaoh was not wrought upon by this. The magicians having produced serpents, he had this to say, that the case between them and Moses was disputable.

Verses 14–25

Here is the first of the ten plagues, the turning of the water into blood, which was, 1. A dreadful plague, and very grievous. Fish was food (Num. xi. 5), but the changing of the waters was the death of the fish; it was a pestilence in that element (v. 21): *The fish died. He slew their fish*; and when another destruction of Egypt, long afterwards, is threatened, the disappointment of those that make sluices and ponds for fish is particularly noticed, Isa. xix. 10. It was a righteous plague, and justly inflicted upon the Egyptians. For, (1) Nilus, the river of Egypt, was their idol; they and their land derived so much benefit from it that they served and worshipped it more than the Creator. God punished them, and turned that into blood which they had turned into a god. Note, That creature which we idolize God justly removes from us, or embitters to us. He makes that a scourge to us which we make a competitor with him. Egypt had a great dependence upon their river (Zech. xiv. 18), so that in smiting the river they were warned of the destruction of all the productions of their country, till it came at last to their first-born; and this red river proved a direful omen of the ruin of Pharaoh and all his forces in the Red Sea. One of the first miracles Moses wrought was turning water into blood, but one of the first miracles our Lord Jesus wrought was turning water into wine; for the law was given by Moses, and it was a dispensation of death and terror; but grace and truth, which, like wine, make glad the heart, came by Jesus Christ.

I. Moses is directed to give Pharaoh warning of this plague. "Pharaoh's heart is hardened (v. 14), therefore go and try what this will do to soften it," v. 15. Moses is directed to meet him by the river's brink, whither God foresaw he would come in the morning to pay his morning devotions to the river. There Moses must be ready to give him a new summons to surrender, and, in case of a refusal, to tell him of the judgment that was coming upon that very river on the banks of which they were now standing. Notice is thus given him of it beforehand, that they might have no colour to say it was a chance, or to attribute it to any other cause, but that it might appear to be done by the power of the God of the Hebrews. That God warns before he wounds; for he is *long-suffering, not willing that any should perish, but that all should come to repentance*.

II. Aaron (who carried the mace) is directed to summon the plague by smiting the river with his rod, v. 19, 20. See here the almighty power of God. Every creature is that to us which he makes it to be, water or blood. See the mutability of all things under the sun, and what changes we may meet with in them. A river, at the best, is transient; but divine justice can quickly make it malignant. See what mischievous work sin makes. If the things that have been our comforts prove our crosses, we must thank ourselves: it is sin that turns our waters into blood.

III. Pharaoh endeavours to confront the miracle, because he resolves not to humble himself under the plague. He sends for the magicians, and, by God's permission, they ape the miracle with their enchantments (v. 22), and this serves Pharaoh for an excuse not to set his heart to this also (v. 23), and a pitiful excuse it was. Could they have turned the river of blood into water again, this would have been something to the purpose; then they would have proved their power, and Pharaoh would have been obliged to them as his benefactors.

IV. The Egyptians, in the meantime, are seeking for relief against the plague, digging round about the river for water to drink, v. 24. Probably they found some, with much ado, God remembering mercy in the midst of wrath; for he is full of compassion, and would not let the subjects smart too much for the obstinacy of their prince.

V. The plague continued seven days (v. 25), and, in all that time, Pharaoh's proud heart would not let him so much as desire Moses to intercede for the removal of it.

CHAPTER 8

Three more of the plagues of Egypt are related in this chapter, I. That of the frogs, which is, 1. Threatened, ver. 1–4. 2. Inflicted, ver. 5, 6. 3. Mimicked by the magicians, ver. 7. 4. Removed, at the humble request of Pharaoh (ver. 8–14), who yet hardens his heart, and, notwithstanding his promise while the plague was upon him (ver. 8), refuses to let Israel go, ver. 15. II. The plague of lice (ver. 16, 17), by which, 1. The magicians were baffled (ver. 18, 19), and yet, 2. Pharaoh was hardened, ver. 19. III. That of flies. 1. Pharaoh is warned of it before (ver. 20, 21), and told that the land of Goshen should be exempt from this plague, ver. 22, 23. 2. The plague is brought, ver. 24. 3. Pharaoh treats with Moses about the release of Israel, and humbles himself, ver. 25–29. 4. The plague is thereupon removed (ver. 31), and Pharaoh's heart hardened, ver. 32.

Verses 1–15

Pharaoh is here first threatened and then plagued with frogs, as afterwards, in this chapter, with lice and flies, little despicable inconsiderable animals, and yet by their vast numbers rendered sore plagues to the Egyptians. Some have thought that the power of God is shown as much in the making of an ant as in the making of an elephant; so is his providence in serving his own purposes by the least creatures as effectually as by the strongest, that he might humble Pharaoh's pride, and chastise his insolence. What a mortification must it needs be to this haughty monarch to see himself brought to his knees, and forced to submit by such despicable means! As to the plague of frogs we may observe,

I. How it was threatened. Moses is here directed to give notice to Pharaoh of another judgment coming upon him, in case he continue obstinate. Note, God does not punish men for sin unless they persist in it. The plague threatened, in case of refusal, was formidably extensive.

II. How it was inflicted. Pharaoh not being at all nclined to yield to the summons, Aaron is ordered to give the signal of battle. Shoals of frogs invade the land, and the Egyptians cannot check their progress. Compare this with that prophecy of an army of locusts and caterpillars, Joel ii. 2, &c.; and see Isa. xxxiv. 16, 17.

III. How the magicians were permitted to imitate it, *v.* 7. They also brought up frogs, but could not remove those that God sent. The magicians intended to deceive, but God intended by them to destroy those that would be deceived.

IV. How Pharaoh relented under this plague: it was the first time he did so, *v.* 8. He begs of Moses to intercede for the removal of the frogs, and promises fair that he will let the people go.

V. How Moses fixes the time with Pharaoh, and then prevails with God by prayer for the removal of the frogs. Pharaoh sets the time for *to-morrow, v.* 10. In answer to the prayer of Moses, the frogs that came up one day perished the next, or the next but one.

VI. What was the issue of this plague (*v.* 15): *When Pharaoh saw there was a respite,* without considering either what he had lately felt or what he had reason to fear, he hardened his heart. Note, 1. Till the heart is renewed by the grace of God, the impressions made by the force of affliction do not abide; the convictions wear off, and the promises that were extorted are forgotten. 2. God's patience is shamefully abused by impenitent sinners. He graciously allows them a truce, in order to the making of their peace. They take that opportunity to rally again the baffled forces of an obstinate infidelity. See Eccles. viii. 11; Ps. lxxviii. 34, &c.

Verses 16–19

Here is a short account of the plague of lice.

I. How this plague of lice was inflicted on the Egyptians, *v.* 16, 17. The frogs were produced out of the waters, but these lice out of *the dust of the earth.* The second woe was past, but behold the third woe came very quickly.

II. How the magicians were baffled by it, *v.* 18. They attempted to imitate it, but they could not. This forced them to confess themselves overpowered: *This is the finger of God* (*v.* 19). Sooner or later God will extort, even from his enemies, an acknowledgment of his own sovereignty and overruling power. It is certain they must all (as we say) knock under at last, as Julian the apostate did, when his dying lips confessed, *Thou hast overcome me, O thou Galilean!* God will not only be too hard for all opposers, but will force them to own it.

III. How Pharaoh, notwithstanding this, was made more and more obstinate (*v.* 19). Note, Those that are not made better by God's word and providences are commonly made worse by them.

Verses 20–32

Here is the story of the plague of flies.

I. How it was threatened, like that of frogs, before it was inflicted. Moses is directed (*v.* 20) to rise early in the morning, to meet Pharaoh when he came forth to the water. Moses must *stand before Pharaoh,* proud as he was, and tell him that which was in the highest degree humbling, must challenge him (if he refused to release his captives) to engage with an army of flies, which would obey God's orders if Pharaoh would not.

II. How the Egyptians and the Hebrews were to be remarkably distinguished in this plague, *v.* 22, 23. Pharaoh must be made to know that *God is the Lord in the midst of the earth;* and by this it will be known beyond dispute. Observe how it is repeated: *I will put a division between my people and thy people, v.* 23. Note, The Lord knows those that are his, and will make it appear, perhaps in this world, certainly in the other, that he has set them apart for himself. A day will come when you shall *return and discern between the righteous and the wicked* (Mal. iii. 18), *the sheep and the goats* (Matt. xxv. 32; Ezek. xxxiv. 17), though now intermixed.

III. How it was inflicted, the day after it was threatened: *There came a grievous swarm of flies* (*v.* 24).

IV. How Pharaoh, upon this attack, entered into a treaty with Moses and Aaron about a surrender of his captives: but observe with what reluctance he yields.

1. He is content they should sacrifice to their God, provided they would do it in the land of Egypt, *v.* 25. But Moses will not accept his concession; he cannot do it, *v.* 26. He insists: *We will go three days' journey into the wilderness, v.* 27. Those that would offer an acceptable sacrifice to God must retire from the distractions of the world. Israel cannot keep the feast of the Lord either among the brick-kilns or among the flesh-pots of Egypt. Though they were in the utmost degree of slavery to Pharaoh, yet, in the worship of God, they must observe his commands and not Pharaoh's.

2. When this proposal is rejected, he consents for them to go into the wilderness, provided they do not go *very far away.* We observe here a struggle between Pharaoh's convictions and his corruptions; his convictions said, "Let them go"; his corruptions said, "Yet not very far away": but he sided with his corruptions against his convictions, and this was his ruin. This proposal Moses so far accepted as that he promised the removal of this plague upon it, *v.* 29.

The issue of all was that God graciously removed the plague (*v.* 30, 31), but Pharaoh perfidiously returned to his hardness, and *would not let the people go, v.* 32. His pride would not let him part with such a flower of his crown as his dominion over Israel was, nor his covetousness with such a branch of his revenue as their labours were.

CHAPTER 9

In this chapter we have an account of three more of the plagues of Egypt. I. Murrain among the cattle, which was fatal to them, ver. 1–7. II. Boils upon man and beast, ver. 8–12. III. Hail, with thunder and lightning. 1. Warning is given of this plague, ver. 13–21. 2. It is inflicted, to their great terror, ver. 22–26. 3. Pharaoh, in a fright, renews his treaty with Moses, but instantly breaks his word, ver. 27, &c.

Verses 1–7

Here is, I. Warning given or another plague, namely, the murrain of beasts. 1. *Let my people go, v.* 1. They are my people, therefore let them go. 2. He describes the plague that should come, if he refused, *v.* 2, 3. *The hand of the Lord is upon the cattle,* many of which should die by a sort of pestilence. *To-morrow* it shall be done. We know not what any day will bring forth, and therefore we cannot say what we will do to-morrow, but it is not so with God.

II. The plague itself inflicted. The cattle died, *v.* 6. The Egyptians afterwards, and (some think) now, worshipped their cattle; it was among them that the Israelites learned to make a god of a calf: in this therefore the plague here spoken of meets with them.

III. The distinction put between the cattle of the Egyptians and the Israelites' cattle, according to the word of God: Not *one of the cattle of the Israelites died*, *v*. 6, 7.

Verses 8–12

Concerning the plague of boils and blains.

I. When they were not wrought upon by the death of their cattle, God sent a plague that seized their own bodies, and touched them to the quick. If less judgments do not do their work, God will send greater.

II. The signal by which this plague was summoned. Sometimes God shows men their sin in their punishment; they had oppressed Israel in the furnaces, and now the ashes of the furnace are made as much a terror to them as ever their task-masters had been to the Israelites.

III. The plague itself was very grievous—these eruptions were inflammations, like Job's. This is afterwards called the *botch of Egypt* (Deut. xxviii. 27).

IV. The magicians themselves were struck with these boils, *v*. 11. Thus they were punished for helping to harden Pharaoh's heart. God will severely reckon with those that strengthen the hands of the wicked in their wickedness.

V. Pharaoh continued obstinate, for now *the Lord hardened* his heart, *v*. 12. Before, he had hardened his own heart, and resisted the grace of God; and now God justly gave him up to his own heart's lusts.

Verses 13–21

Here is, I. A general declaration of the wrath of God against Pharaoh for his obstinacy. Though God has hardened his heart (*v*. 12), yet Moses must repeat his applications to him. God would likewise show forth a pattern of long-suffering, and how he waits to be gracious to a *rebellious and gainsaying people*. Six times the demand had been made in vain, yet Moses must make it the seventh time: *Let my people go*, *v*. 13. A most dreadful message Moses is here ordered to deliver to him, whether he will hear or whether he will forbear. "I will send my plagues *upon thy heart*, not only temporal plagues upon thy body, but spiritual plagues upon thy soul." He must tell him that he is to remain in history a standing monument of the justice and power of God's wrath (*v*. 14): *"For this cause have I raised thee up* to the throne at this time, and made thee to stand the shock of the plagues hitherto, *to show in thee my power."* Every thing concurred to signalise this, that God's name (that is, his incontestable sovereignty, his irresistible power, and his inflexible justice) might be declared throughout all the earth, not only to all places, but through all ages while the earth remains. Pharaoh was a great king; God's people were poor shepherds at the best, and now poor slaves; and yet Pharaoh shall be ruined if he exalt himself against them, for it is considered as exalting himself against God.

II. A particular prediction of the plague of hail (*v*. 18), and a gracious advice to Pharaoh and his people to send for their servants and cattle out of the field, that they might be sheltered from the hail, *v*. 19. See here what care God took, not only to distinguish between Egyptians and Israelites, but between some Egyptians and others. *Some believed the things that were spoken*, and they feared, and housed their servants and cattle (*v*. 20), like Noah (Heb. xi. 7), and it was their wisdom. Even among the servants of Pharaoh there were some that trembled at God's word.

Verses 22–35

The threatened plague of hail is here summoned:

I. What desolations it made upon the earth. It killed both men and cattle, and battered down, not only the herbs, but the trees, *v*. 25. The corn that was above ground was destroyed, and that only preserved which as yet had not come up, *v*. 31, 32. Notice is here taken (*v*. 26) of the land of Goshen's being preserved from receiving any damage by this plague.

II. What a consternation it put Pharaoh in. He humbled himself to Moses in the language of a penitent, *v*. 27, 28. He condemns himself and his land: *"I and my people are wicked*, and deserve what is brought upon us."* He begs the prayers of Moses: *"Entreat the Lord* for me, that this direful plague may be removed."* And, *lastly*, he promises to yield up his prisoners: *I will let you go*. Moses, hereupon, becomes an intercessor for him with God. Though he had all the reason in the world to think that he would immediately repent of his repentance, and told him so (*v*. 30), yet he promises to be his friend in the court of heaven. Note, Even those whom we have little hopes of, yet we should continue to pray for, and to admonish, 1 Sam. xii. 23. The place Moses chose for his intercession. Peace with God makes men thunderproof, for thunder is the voice of their Father. The success of it. 1. He prevailed with God, *v*. 33. But, 2. He could not prevail with Pharaoh: *He sinned yet more, and hardened his heart*, *v*. 34, 35. Note, Little credit is to be given to confessions upon the rack.

CHAPTER 10

The eighth and ninth of the plagues of Egypt, that of locusts and that of darkness, are recorded in this chapter. I. Concerning the plague of locusts, 1. God instructs Moses in the meaning of these amazing dispensations of his providence, ver. 1, 2. 2. He threatens the locusts, ver. 3–6. 3. Pharaoh, at the persuasion of his servants, is willing to treat again with Moses (ver. 7–9), but they cannot agree, ver. 10, 11. 4. The locusts come, ver. 12–15. 5. Pharaoh cries Peccavi—I have offended (ver. 16, 17), whereupon Moses prays for the removal of the plague, and it is done, but Pharaoh's heart is still hardened, ver. 18–20. II. Concerning the plague of darkness, 1. It is inflicted, ver. 21–23. 2. Pharaoh again treats with Moses about a surrender, but the treaty breaks off in a heat, ver. 24, &c.

Verses 1–11

I. Moses is instructed. These plagues are standing monuments of the greatness of God, the happiness of the church, and the sinfulness of sin, and standing monitors to the children of men in all ages not to *provoke the Lord to jealousy* nor to *strive with their Maker*.

II. Pharaoh is reproved (*v*. 3): *Thus saith the Lord God of the poor*, despised, persecuted Hebrews, *How long wilt thou refuse to humble thyself before me?* Those that will not humble themselves God will humble.

III. The plague of locusts is threatened, *v*. 4–6. The hail had broken down the fruits of the earth, but these locusts should come and devour them. Moses, when he had delivered his message, not expecting any better answer than he had formerly, *turned himself and went out from* Pharaoh, *v*. 6. Thus Christ appointed his disciples to depart from those who would not receive them, and to *shake off the dust of their feet for a testimony against them*.

IV. Pharaoh's attendants, his ministers of state, or privy-counsellors, interpose, to persuade him to come to some terms with Moses, *v*. 7. The Israelites had become a burdensome stone to the Egyptians, and now, at length, the princes of Egypt were willing to be rid of them, Zech. xii. 3.

V. A new treaty is, hereupon, set on foot between Pharaoh, and Moses, in which Pharaoh consents for the Israelites to go into the wilderness to do sacrifice; but the matter in dispute was who should go, *v*. 8. 1. Moses insists that they should take their whole families, and all their effects, along with them, *v*. 9. 2. Pharaoh will by no means grant this: he will allow the men to go, pretending that this was all they desired, though this matter was never yet mentioned in any of the former treaties; but, for the *little ones*, he resolves to keep them as hostages, to oblige them to return, *v.* 10, 11. 3. The treaty, hereupon, breaks off abruptly.

Verses 12–20

I. The invasion of the land by the locusts— *God's great army*, Joel ii. 11. The locusts obey the summons, and fly upon the wings of the wind, the east wind, and *caterpillars without number*, as we are told, Ps. cv. 34, 35. A formidable army of horse and foot might more easily have been resisted than this host of insects.

II. The desolations they made in it (*v.* 15): They *covered the face of the earth*, and *ate up the fruit* of it. Herbs grow *for the service of man*; yet, when God pleases, those contemptible insects shall not only be fellow-consumers with him, but shall plunder him, and eat the bread out of his mouth.

III. Pharaoh's admission, hereupon, *v.* 16, 17. 1. Pharaoh confesses his fault: *I have sinned against the Lord your God, and against you.* He now sees his own folly in the slights and affronts he had put on God and his ambassadors, and *seems*, at least, to repent of it. 2. He begs pardon, not of God, as penitents ought, but of Moses. 3. He entreats Moses and Aaron to pray for him. Pharaoh desires their prayers *that this death* only might be taken away, not *this sin*: he deprecates the plague of locusts, not the plague of a hard heart, which yet was much the more dangerous.

IV. The removal of the judgment, upon the prayer of Moses, *v.* 18, 19. This was, 1. As great an instance of the power of God as the judgment itself. An east wind brought the locusts, and now a west wind carried them off. Note, Whatever point of the compass the wind is in, it is fulfilling God's word, and turns about by his counsel. 2. It was a proof of the authority of Moses, and a ratification of his commission. 3. It was also as strong an argument for their repentance as the judgment itself; for by this it appeared that God is ready to forgive, and swift to show mercy.

V. Pharaoh's return to his impious resolution again not to let the people go (*v.* 20).

Verses 21–29

Here is, I. The plague of darkness. Observe particularly concerning this plague, 1. That it was a total darkness. They *saw not one another*. Hell is *utter darkness*. The light of *a candle shall shine no more at all in thee*, Rev. xviii. 23. 2. That it was darkness which *might be felt* (*v.* 21). 3. No doubt it astonished and terrified them. The tradition of the Jews is that in this darkness they were terrified by the apparitions of evil spirits, or rather by dreadful sounds and murmurs which they made, or (which is no less frightful) by the horrors of their own consciences. 4. It continued three days, *six nights* (says bishop Hall) *in one*. Spiritual darkness is spiritual bondage; while Satan blinds men's eyes that they see not, he binds their hands and feet that they work not for God, nor move towards heaven. They *sit in darkness*. Never was mind so blinded as Pharaoh's, never was air so darkened as Egypt's. The Egyptians **by their** cruelty would have extinguished the lamp of Israel, and quenched their coal; justly therefore does God put out their lights.

II. Here is the impression made upon Pharaoh by this plague. 1. It awakened him so far that he renewed the treaty with Moses and Aaron, and now, at length, consented that they should take their little ones with them, only he would have their cattle left in pawn, *v.* 24. Moses resolves not to abate in

his terms: *Our cattle shall go with us, v.* 26. Moses gives a very good reason why they must take their cattle with them; they must go to do sacrifice, and therefore they must take wherewithal. 2. Yet it exasperated him so far that, when he might not make his own terms, he broke off the conference abruptly. Moses is dismissed in anger, forbidden the court upon pain of death. Moses takes him at his word (*v.* 29): *I will see thy face no more.* So that, after this interview, Moses came no more, till he was sent for.

CHAPTER 11

We have in this chapter, I. The instructions God had given to Moses, which he was now to pursue (ver. 1, 2), together with the interest Israel and Moses had in the esteem of the Egyptians, ver. 3. II. The last message Moses delivered to Pharaoh, concerning the death of the first-born, ver. 4–8. I.I. A repetition of the prediction of Pharaoh's hardening his heart (ver. 9), and the event answering to it, ver. 10.

Verses 1–3

Here is, I. The high favour Moses and Israel were in with God. Moses longed to see an end of this dreadful work, to see Egypt no more plagued and Israel no more oppressed. The Israelites were favourites of Heaven. This was the last day of their servitude; they were about to go away, and their masters, who had abused them in their work, would now have defrauded them of their wages, and have sent them away empty. Though the patient Israelites were content to lose their wages, yet God would not let them go without them.

II. The high favour Moses and Israel were in with the Egyptians, *v.* 3. 1. Even the people that had been hated and despised now came to be respected. 2. *The man Moses was very great.* How could it be otherwise when they saw what power he was clothed with, and what wonders were wrought by his hand? Thus the apostles, though otherwise despicable men, came to be magnified, Acts v. 13. Those that honour God he will honour. Though Pharaoh hated Moses, there were those of Pharaoh's servants that respected him. Thus in Caesar's household, even Nero's, there were some that had an esteem for blessed Paul, Phil. i. 13.

Verses 4–10

Warning is here given to Pharaoh of the last and conquering plague which was now to be inflicted. This was the *death of all the first-born in Egypt* at once, which had been first threatened (*ch.* iv. 23, *I will slay thy son, thy first-born*), but is last executed. If the death of their cattle had humbled and reformed them, their children would have been spared. The extent of this plague is described, *v.* 5. The prince that was to succeed in the throne was not too high to be reached by it, nor were the slaves at the mill too low to be taken notice of. When Moses had thus delivered his message, it is said, *He went out from Pharaoh in a great anger*, though he was the meekest of all the men of the earth. Probably he expected that the very threatening of the death of the first-born would have induced Pharaoh to comply. But it had not that effect; his proud heart would not yield, no, not to save all the first-born of his kingdom. Moses, hereupon, was provoked to a holy indignation, being grieved (as our Saviour afterwards) for the *hardness of his heart*, Mark iii. 5. Note, It is a great vexation to the spirits of good ministers to see people deaf to all the fair warnings given them, and running headlong upon ruin, notwithstanding all the kind methods taken to prevent it. Thus Ezekiel went in *the bitterness of his spirit* (Ezek. iii. 14), because God had told him that the house of Israel would not hearken to him, *v.* 7. To be angry at nothing but sin is the way not to sin in anger.

CHAPTER 12

I. Not one of all the ordinances of the Jewish church was more eminent than that of the passover, nor is any one more frequently mentioned in the New Testament. The ordinance consisted of three parts:—1. The killing and eating of the paschal lamb, ver. 1–6, 8–11. 2. The sprinkling of the blood upon the door-posts, spoken of as a distinct thing (Heb. xi. 28), and peculiar to this first passover (ver. 7), with the reason for it, ver. 13. 3. The feast of unleavened bread for seven days following, ver. 14–20. This institution is communicated to the people, and they are instructed in the observance, (1) Of this first passover, ver. 21–23. (2) Of the after passovers, ver. 24–27. And the Israelites' obedience to these orders, ver. 28. II. Not one of all the providences of God concerning the Jewish church was more illustrious, or is more frequently mentioned, than the deliverance of the children of Israel out of Egypt. 1. The firstborn of the Egyptians are slain, ver. 29, 30. 2. Orders are given immediately for their discharge, ver. 31–33. 3. They begin their march. (1) Loaded with their own effects, ver. 34. (2) Enriched with the spoils of Egypt, ver. 35, 36. (3) Attended with a mixed multitude, ver. 37, 38. (4) Put to their shifts for present supply, ver. 39.

Verses 1–20

Moses and Aaron here *receive of the Lord* what they were afterwards to *deliver to the people* concerning the ordinance of the passover, to which is prefixed an order for a new style to be observed in their months (*v.* 1, 2): *This shall be to you the beginning of months.* They had hitherto begun their year from the middle of September, but henceforward they were to begin it from the middle of March, at least in all their ecclesiastical computations. Note, It is good to begin the day, and begin the year, and especially to begin our lives, with God. This new calculation began the year with the spring, which *reneweth the face of the earth*, and was used as a figure of the coming of Christ, Cant. ii. 11, 12. While Moses was bringing the ten plagues upon the Egyptians, he was directing the Israelites to prepare for their departure at an hour's warning. Their amazement and hurry, it is easy to suppose, were great; yet now they must apply themselves to the observance of a sacred rite, to the honour of God.

I. God appointed that on the night wherein they were to go out of Egypt they should, in each of their families, *kill a lamb*, or that two or three families, if they were small, should join for a lamb. The lamb was to be got ready four days before, and that afternoon they were to *kill it* (*v.* 6) as a religious ceremony, acknowledging God's goodness to them, not only in preserving them from, but in delivering them by, the plagues inflicted on the Egyptians.

II. The lamb so slain they were to eat, roasted, with unleavened bread and bitter herbs, because they were to eat it *in haste* (*v.* 11), and to leave none of it until the morning; for God would have them to depend upon him for their daily bread. He that led them would feed them.

III. Before they ate the flesh of the lamb, they were to sprinkle the blood upon the door-posts, *v.* 7. By this their houses were to be distinguished from the houses of the Egyptians.

IV. This was to be annually observed as a feast of the Lord in their generations, to which the *feast of unleavened bread* was annexed, during which, for seven days, they were to eat no bread but what was unleavened, in remembrance of their being confined to such bread, of necessity, for many days after they came out of Egypt, *v.* 14–20.

1. The paschal lamb was typical. Christ is *our Passover*, 1 Cor. v. 7. (1) It was to be a *lamb*; and Christ is *the Lamb of God* (John i. 29), often in the Revelation called the *Lamb*, meek and innocent as a lamb, dumb before the shearers. (2) It was to be a *male of the first year* (*v.* 5), in its prime; Christ offered up himself in the midst of his days, not in infancy with the babes of Bethlehem. (3) It was to be *without blemish* (*v.* 5), denoting the purity of the Lord Jesus, a Lamb *without spot*, 1 Pet. i. 19. (4) It was to be set

apart four days before (*v.* 3, 6), denoting the designation of the Lord Jesus to be a Saviour. It is very observable that as Christ was crucified at the passover, so he solemnly entered into Jerusalem four days before, the very day that the paschal lamb was set apart. (5) It was to be slain, and *roasted with fire* (*v.* 6–9), denoting the exquisite sufferings of the Lord Jesus, even unto death, the death of the cross. (6) It was to be killed by the whole congregation. Christ suffered in the *end of the world* (Heb. ix. 26), by the hand of the Jews, the whole multitude of them (Luke xxiii. 18), and for the good of all his spiritual Israel. (7) Not *a bone of it must be broken* (*v.* 46), which is expressly said to be fulfilled in Christ (John xix. 33, 36), denoting the unbroken strength of the Lord Jesus.

2. The sprinkling of the blood was typical. (1) It was not enough that the blood of the lamb was shed, but it must be sprinkled, denoting the application of the merits of Christ's death to our souls; we must *receive the atonement*, Rom. v. 11. (2) It was to be sprinkled with *a bunch of hyssop* (*v.* 22) *dipped in the basin*. Faith is the bunch of hyssop by which we apply the promises to ourselves. (3) It was to be sprinkled upon the *door-posts*, denoting the open profession we are to make of faith in Christ, and obedience to him. (4) It was to be sprinkled upon the *lintel* and the *side-posts*, but not upon the *threshold* (*v.* 7), which cautions us to take heed of trampling under foot the blood of the covenant, Heb. x. 29. (5) The blood, thus sprinkled, was a means of the preservation of the Israelites from the destroying angel, who had nothing to do where the blood was.

3. The solemn eating of the lamb was typical of our gospel-duty to Christ. (1) The paschal lamb was killed, not to be looked upon only, but to be fed upon; so we must by faith make Christ ours, as we do that which we eat, and we must receive spiritual strength and nourishment from him, as from our food: see John vi. 53–55. (2) It was to be all eaten; those that by faith feed upon Christ must feed upon a whole Christ; they must take Christ and his yoke, Christ and his cross, as well as Christ and his crown. (3) It was to be eaten immediately, not deferred till morning, *v.* 10. *To-day* Christ is offered, and is to be accepted while it is called to-day. (4) It was to be eaten *with bitter herbs* (*v.* 8), in remembrance of the bitterness of their bondage in Egypt. Christ will be sweet to us if sin be bitter. (5) It was to be eaten in a departing posture (*v.* 11); when we feed upon Christ by faith we must absolutely forsake the rule and dominion of sin, and we must forsake all for Christ, and reckon it no bad bargain, Heb. xiii. 13, 14.

4. The feast of unleavened bread was typical of the Christian life, 1 Cor. v. 7, 8. Having received Christ Jesus the Lord, (1) We must keep a feast in holy joy, continually delighting ourselves in Christ Jesus. If true believers have not a continual feast, it is their own fault. (2) It must be a feast of unleavened bread, kept in charity, without the leaven of malice, and in sincerity, without the leaven of hypocrisy.

Verses 21–28

I. Moses is here, as a faithful steward in God's house.

1. That this night, when the first-born were to be destroyed, no Israelite must *stir out of doors till morning*. They must not go out of the doors, lest they should straggle and be out of the way when they should be summoned to depart.

2. That hereafter they should carefully teach their children the meaning of this service, *v.* 26, 27.

(1) The question which the children would ask: "*What mean you by this service?* What is the meaning of all this care and exactness about eating this lamb,

and this unleavened bread, more than about common food?" It concerns us all rightly to understand the meaning of those holy ordinances wherein we worship God, what is the nature and what the end of them.

(2) The answer which the parents were to return to this question (v. 27): *You shall say, It is the sacrifice of the Lord's passover*, that is, "By the killing and sacrificing of this lamb, we keep in remembrance the work of wonder and grace which God did for our fathers, when," [1] "To make way for our deliverance out of bondage" He slew the first-born of the Egyptians; and, [2] "Though there were *with us, even with us, sins against the Lord our God*, yet God graciously appointed and accepted the family-sacrifice of a lamb, as, of old, the ram instead of Isaac, and in every house where the lamb was slain the first-born were saved." The word *pesach* signifies a *leap*, or *transition*; it is a passing over; for the destroying angel passed over the houses of the Israelites, and did not destroy their first-born. It was designed to look forward as an earnest of the great sacrifice of the Lamb of God in the fulness of time, instead of us and our first-born. *Christ our passover was sacrificed for us*, his death was our life, and thus he was the *Lamb slain from the foundation of the world*, from the foundation of the Jewish church: Moses kept the passover by faith in Christ, for Christ was *the end of the law for righteousness*.

II. The people received these instructions with reverence and ready obedience. 1. They *bowed the head and worshipped* (v. 27). 2. They *went away and did* as they were commanded, v. 28. Here was none of that discontent and murmuring among them which we read of, *ch.* v. 20, 21. The plagues of Egypt had done them good, and raised their expectations of a glorious deliverance, which before they despaired of; and now they went forth to meet it in the way appointed.

Verses 29–36

Here we have, I. The Egyptians' sons, even their first-born, slain, v. 29, 30. If Pharaoh would have taken the warning which was given him of this plague, and would thereupon have released Israel, what a great many dear and valuable lives might have been preserved! But see what obstinate infidelity brings upon men. It reached from the throne to the dungeon. Prince and peasant stand upon the same level before God's judgments, for there is no respect of persons with him; see Job xxxiv. 19, 20. Let us learn hence, (1) To tremble before God, and to be *afraid of his judgments*, Ps. cxix. 120. (2) To be thankful to God for the daily preservation of ourselves and our families.

II. Now Pharaoh's pride is abased, and he yields to all that Moses had insisted on: *Serve the Lord as you have said* (v. 31), and *take your flocks as you have said*, v. 32. 1. They are commanded to depart: *Rise up and get you forth*, v. 31. Pharaoh had told Moses he should *see his face no more*; but now he sent for him. That he sent them out, not as men hated but as men feared, is plainly discovered by his humble request to them (v. 32): "*Bless me also*; let me have your prayers, that I may not be plagued for what is past, when you are gone." 2. They are hired to depart by the Egyptians; they cried out (v. 33), *We be all dead men*. When the Egyptians urged them to be gone, it was easy for them to say that the Egyptians had kept them poor, that they could not undertake such a journey with empty purses, but that, if they would give them wherewithal to bear their charges, they would be gone. The Israelites might receive and keep what they thus borrowed, or rather required, of the Egyptians, as justly as servants receive wages from their masters for work done, and sue for it if it be detained.

Verses 37–42

Here is the departure of the children of Israel out of Egypt. Pharaoh was now in a good mind; but they had reason to think he would not long continue so, and therefore it was no time to linger. We have here an account, 1. Of their number, about 600,000 men (v. 37), besides women and children, which, I think, we cannot suppose to make less than 1,200,000 more. What a vast increase was this, to arise from seventy souls in little more than 200 years' time! 2. Of their retinue (v. 38): *A mixed multitude went up with them*, hangers on to that great family, some perhaps willing to leave their country, because it was laid waste by the plagues, others went out of curiosity, to see the solemnities of Israel's sacrifice to their God, which had been so much talked of, and expecting to see some glorious appearances of their God to them in the wilderness. Probably the greatest part of this mixed multitude were but a rude unthinking mob, that followed the crowd they knew not why; we afterwards find that they proved a snare to them (Num. xi. 4), and it is probable that when, soon afterwards, they understood that the children of Israel were to continue forty years in the wilderness, they quitted them, and returned to Egypt. 3. Of their effects. They had with them *flocks and herds*, even *very much cattle*. 4. Of the provision made for the camp, which was very poor and slender. They brought some dough with them out of Egypt in their knapsacks, v. 34. They had prepared to bake, the next day, in order to their removal, understanding it was very near; but, being hastened away sooner than they thought of, by some hours, they took the dough as it was, unleavened; when they came to Succoth, their first stage, they baked unleavened cakes, and, though these were of course insipid, yet the liberty they were brought into made this the most joyful meal they had ever eaten in their lives. It was just 430 years from the promise made to Abraham (as the apostle explains it, Gal. iii. 17) at his first coming into Canaan. So long the promise of a settlement lay dormant and unfulfilled, but now, at length, it revived. The first passover-night was a night of the Lord *much to be observed*; but the last passover-night, in which Christ was betrayed (and in which the passover, with the rest of the ceremonial institutions, was superseded and abolished), was a night of the Lord *much more to be observed*, when a yoke heavier than that of Egypt was broken from off our necks, and a land better than that of Canaan set before us. That was a temporal deliverance to be celebrated *in their generation*; this is an eternal redemption to be celebrated in the praises of glorious saints, *world without end*.

Verses 43–51

Some further precepts are here given concerning the passover, as it should be observed in times to come.

I. *All the congregation of Israel must keep it*, v. 47. All that share in God's mercies should join in thankful praises for them. The New Testament passover, the Lord's supper, ought not to be neglected by any who are capable of celebrating it. 1. No stranger that was uncircumcised might be admitted to eat of it, v. 43, 45, 48. We must be born again by the word ere we can be nourished by it. Nor shall any partake of the benefit of Christ's sacrifice, or feast upon it, who are not first circumcised in heart, Col. ii. 11. 2. Any stranger that was circumcised might be welcome to eat of the passover, even *servants*, v. 44. If in sincerity and with that zeal which the thing requires and deserves, we give up ourselves to God, we shall, with ourselves, give up all we have to him, and do our utmost that all ours may be his too. Here is an early indication of favour to the poor

Gentiles, that the stranger, if circumcised, stands upon the same level with the home-born Israelite. It was their dedication to God, not their descent from Abraham, that entitled them to their privileges.

II. *In one house shall it be eaten* (v. 46), that they might rejoice together, and edify one another in the eating of it.

The chapter concludes with a repetition of the whole matter, that the children of Israel did as they were bidden, and God did for them as he promised (v. 50, 51).

CHAPTER 13

In this chapter we have, I. The commands God gave to Israel, 1. To sanctify all their firstborn to him, ver. 1, 2. 2. To be sure to remember their deliverance out of Egypt (ver. 3, 4), and, in remembrance of it, to keep the feast of unleavened bread, ver. 5–7. 3. To transmit the knowledge of it with all possible care to their children, ver. 8–10. 4. To set apart unto God the firstlings of their cattle (ver. 11–13). II. The care God took of Israel, when he had brought them out of Egypt. 1. Choosing their way for them, ver. 17, 18. 2. Guiding them in the way, ver. 20–22. And III. Their care of Joseph's bones, ver. 19.

Verses 1–10

Care is here taken to perpetuate the remembrance,

I. Of the preservation of Israel's firstborn. God here lays claim in particular to the firstborn of the Israelites, by right of protection: *Sanctify to me all the firstborn.* God, who is the first and best, should have the first and best, and to him we should resign that which is most dear to us, and most valuable. The firstborn were the joy and hope of their families. Therefore *they shall be mine,* says God. It is the *church of the firstborn* that is sanctified to God, Heb. xii. 23. Christ is the *firstborn among many brethren* (Rom. viii. 29), and, by virtue of their union with him, all that are born again, and born from above, are accounted as firstborn. There is an *excellency of dignity and power* belonging to them; and, *if children, then heirs.*

II. The remembrance of their coming out of Egypt must also be perpetuated: "*Remember this day* (v. 3). Remember it by a good token, as the most remarkable day of your lives, the birthday of your nation, or the day of its coming of age, to be no longer under the rod." Thus the day of Christ's resurrection is to be remembered, for in it we were raised up with Christ out of death's *house of bondage.*

1. They must be sure to *keep the feast of unleavened bread,* v. 5–7. It was not enough that they remembered it, but they must celebrate the memorial of it in that way which God had appointed. Observe, How strict the prohibition of leaven is (v. 7); not only no leaven must be eaten, but none must be seen, no, not in all their quarters. Accordingly, the Jews' usage was, before the feast of the passover, to cast all the leavened bread out of their houses: they burnt it, or buried it, or broke it small and scattered it in the wind; they searched diligently with lighted candles in all the corners of their houses, lest any leaven should remain.

2. They must instruct their children in the meaning of it, and relate to them the story of their deliverance out of Egypt, v. 8. When they were celebrating the ordinance, they must explain it.

Verses 11–16

I. Further directions concerning the dedicating of their firstborn to God. 1. The firstlings of their cattle were to be dedicated to God, as part of their possessions. 2. The firstborn of their children were to be redeemed, and by no means sacrificed, as the Gentiles sacrificed their children to Moloch. The price of the redemption of the firstborn was fixed by the law (Num. xviii. 16) at *five shekels.*

II. Further directions concerning the catechising of their children, and all those of the rising generation,

from time to time, in this matter. Note, 1. Children should be directed and encouraged to ask their parents questions concerning the things of God. 2. We should all be able to show cause for what we do in religion. As sacraments are sanctified by the word, so they must be explained and understood by it. God's service is reasonable, and it is then acceptable when we perform it intelligently, knowing what we do and why we do it. Mercies to our fathers are mercies to us; we reap the benefit of them. Much more reason have we to say that in the death and resurrection of Jesus Christ we were redeemed.

Verses 17–22

Here is, I. The choice God made of their way, v. 17, 18. He was their guide. Moses gave them direction, but as he received it from the Lord. There were two ways from Egypt to Canaan. One was a short cut from the north of Egypt to the south of Canaan, perhaps about four or five days' journey; the other was much further about, through the wilderness, and that was the way in which God chose to lead his people Israel, v. 18. 1. There were many reasons why God led them *through the way of the wilderness of the Red Sea.* The Egyptians were to be drowned in the Red Sea. The Israelites were to be humbled and proved in the wilderness, Deut. viii. 2. Matters must be settled between them and their God, laws must be given, ordinances instituted, covenants sealed, and the original contract ratified. God's way is the right way, though it seem *about.* If we think he leads not his people the nearest way, yet we may be sure he leads them the best way, and so it will appear when we come to our journey's end. 2. There was one reason why God did not lead them the nearest way, because they were not as yet fit for war, much less for war with the Philistines, v. 17. Their spirits were broken with slavery; it was not easy for them to turn their hands of a sudden from the trowel to the sword. The Philistines were formidable enemies, too fierce to be encountered by raw recruits. God is said to bring Israel out of Egypt as the eagle *brings up her young ones* (Deut. xxxii. 11), teaching them by degrees to fly. Orders being thus given which way they should go, we are told, (1) That they went up themselves, not as a confused rout, but in good order, rank and file: they *went up harnessed,* v. 18. (2) That they took the *bones of Joseph* along with them (v. 19). Joseph had particularly appointed that his bones should be carried up when God should visit them (Gen. l. 25, 26). They might think, "Joseph's bones must rest at last, and then we shall."

II. Here is the guidance they were blessed with in the way: *The Lord went before them,* the shechinah (or appearance of the divine Majesty, which was typical of Christ) or a previous manifestation of the eternal Word, which, in the fulness of time, was to be *made flesh,* and *dwell among us.* Christ was with the church in the wilderness, 1 Cor. x. 9. Note, Those whom God brings into a wilderness he will not leave nor lose there, but will take care to lead them through it. Those who made the glory of God their end, and the word of God their rule, the Spirit of God the guide of their affections, and the providence of God the guide of their affairs, may be confident that *the Lord goes before them,* as truly as he went before Israel in the wilderness, though not so sensibly; we must live by faith. 1. They all saw an appearance from heaven of a pillar, which in the bright day appeared cloudy, and in the dark night appeared fiery. God gave them this ocular demonstration of his presence, in compassion to the infirmity of their faith. 2. They had sensible effects of God's going before them in this pillar. For, (1) It led the way in that wilderness, in which there was no road, no track, of which they had no maps, through which they had no guides. When they marched, this pillar went before them, at the rate that they could follow. (2) It sheltered them by day from the heat. (3) It gave them light by night and at all times made the wilderness they were in less frightful.

III. These were constant standing miracles (*v.* 22): He *took not away the pillar of cloud*. It never left them, till it brought them to the borders of Canaan. It was a cloud which the wind could not scatter. There was something spiritual in this pillar of cloud and fire. Some make this cloud a type of Christ. The cloud of his human nature was a veil to the light and fire of his divine nature. Christ is our way, the light of our way and the guide of it.

Chapter 14

The departure of the children of Israel out of Egypt (which was indeed the birth of the Jewish church) is made yet more memorable. Witness the records of this chapter, the contents whereof, together with a key to it, we have, Heb. xi. 29. Here is, I. The extreme danger that Israel was in at the Red Sea. 1. Notice was given of it to Moses, ver. 1–4. 2. The cause of it was Pharaoh's pursuit of them, ver. 5–9. 3. Israel was in consternation, ver. 10–12. 4. Moses endeavours to encourage them, ver. 13, 14. II. The wonderful deliverance that God wrought. 1. Moses is instructed concerning it, ver. 15–18. 2. Lines that could not be forced are set between the camp of Israel and Pharaoh's camp, ver. 19, 20. 3. By the divine power the Red Sea is divided (ver. 21), and is made, (1) A lane to the Israelites, who marched safely through it, ver. 22, 29. But (2) To the Egyptians it was made, [1] An ambush into which they were drawn, ver. 23–25. And, [2] A grave in which they were all buried, ver. 26–28. III. The impressions this made upon the Israelites, ver. 30, 31.

Verses 1–9

I. Instructions given to Moses concerning Israel's motions and encampments. That there might be no scruple nor dissatisfaction about it, Moses is told before, 1. Whither they must go, *v.* 1, 2. They had got to the edge of the wilderness (*ch.* xiii. 20), and a stage or two more would have brought them to Horeb, the place appointed for their serving God; but, instead of going forward, they are ordered to turn short off, on the right hand from Canaan, and to march towards the Red Sea. 2. Moses shall know, (1) That Pharaoh has a design to ruin Israel, *v.* 3. (2) That therefore God has a design to ruin Pharaoh, and he takes this way to effect it, *v.* 4.

II. Pharaoh's pursuit of Israel, in which, while he gratifies his own malice and revenge, he is furthering the accomplishment of God's counsels concerning him. *It was told him that the people fled, v.* 5. Now, hereupon,

1. He reflects upon it with regret that he had connived at their departure. He and his servants were now angry with themselves for it: *Why have we done thus?* (1) It vexed them that Israel had their liberty, that they had lost the profit of their labours, and the pleasure of chastising them. Note, The liberty of God's people is a heavy grievance to their enemies, Esther v. 12, 13; Acts v. 17, 23. (2) It aggravated the vexation that they themselves had consented to it. Thus God makes men's envy and rage against his people a torment to themselves, Ps. cxii. 10.

2. He resolves, if possible, either to reduce them or to be revenged on them; in order to this, he levies an army, musters all his force of chariots and horsemen, *v.* 17, 18, and thus he doubts not but he shall re-enslave them, *v.* 6, 7. It is said (*v.* 8), The children of Israel went out with a great deal of courage. *But the Egyptians* (*v.* 9) *pursued after them.* Note, Those that in good earnest set their faces heaven-ward, and will live godly in Christ Jesus, must expect to be set upon by Satan's temptations and terrors. He will not tamely part with any out of his service, nor go out without raging, Mark ix. 26.

Verses 10–14

We have here, I. The fright that the children of Israel were in when they perceived that Pharaoh

pursued them, *v.* 10. They knew very well the strength and rage of the enemy, and their own weakness. On the one hand was Pi-hahiroth, a range of craggy rocks impassable; on the other hand were Migdol and Baalzephon; before them was the sea; behind them were the Egyptians: so that there was no way open for them but upwards, and thence their deliverance came. 1. Some of them cried out unto the Lord; their fear set them praying, and that was a good effect of it. God brings us into straits that he may bring us to our knees. 2. Others of them cried out against Moses; their fear set them murmuring, *v.* 11, 12. How inexcusable was their distrust! They here express, (1) A sordid contempt of liberty, preferring servitude before it, only because it was attended with some difficulties. A generous spirit would have said, "Better live God's freemen in the open air of a wilderness than the Egyptians' bondmen in the smoke of the brick-kilns." (2) Base ingratitude to Moses, who had been the faithful instrument of their deliverance. They had as soon forgotten the miracles of mercy as the Egyptians had forgotten the miracles of wrath; and they, as well as the Egyptians, hardened their hearts, at last, to their own ruin; as Egypt after ten plagues, so Israel after ten provocations, of which this was the first (Num. xiv. 22), were sentenced to die in the wilderness.

II. The seasonable encouragement that Moses gave them in this distress, *v.* 12, 14. He answered not these fools according to their folly. Instead of chiding them, he comforts them, and with an admirable presence and composure of mind stills their murmuring, with the assurance of a speedy and complete deliverance: *Fear you not.* Note, It is our duty and interest, when we cannot get out of our troubles, yet to get above our fears, so that they may only serve to quicken our prayers and endeavours, but may not prevail to silence our faith and hope. He directs them to leave it to God, in a silent expectation of the event: "*Stand still,* and think not to save yourselves either by fighting or flying; wait God's orders. God is now about to work for you.

Verses 15–20

I. Direction given to Israel's leader.

1. What he must do himself. He must, for the present, leave off praying, and apply himself to his business (*v.* 15): *Wherefore cryest thou unto me?* But is God displeased with Moses for praying? No, he asks this question, *Wherefore cryest thou unto me?* (1) To satisfy his faith. "Wherefore shouldst thou press thy petition any further, when it is already granted? *I have accepted thy prayer*." (2) To quicken his diligence. Moses had something else to do besides praying; he was to command the hosts of Israel, and it was now requisite that he should be at his post.

2. What he must order Israel to do. *Speak to them, that they go forward.* Moses had bidden them stand still, and expect orders from God; and now orders are given. They thought they must have been directed either to the right hand or to the left. "No," says God, "speak to them to go forward, directly to the sea-side"; as if there had lain a fleet of transport-ships ready for them to embark in.

3. What he might expect God to do. Let the children of Israel go as far as they can upon dry ground, and then God will divide the sea, and open a passage for them through it, *v.* 16–18.

II. A guard set upon Israel's camp where it now lay most exposed, which was *in the rear, v.* 19, 20. *The angel of God,* whose ministry was made use of in the pillar of cloud and fire, went from *before the camp of Israel,* where they did not now need a guide (there was no danger of missing their way through the sea, nor needed they any other word of command than to go forward), and it came behind them, where now they needed a guard and so was a wall of partition between them.

Verses 21–31

We have here the history of that work of wonder which is so often mentioned both in the Old and New Testament, the dividing of the Red Sea before the children of Israel. It was the terror of the Canaanites (Josh. ii. 9, 10), the praise and triumph of the Israelites, Ps. cxiv. 3; cvi. 9; cxxxvi. 13, 14. It was a type of baptism, 1 Cor. x. 1, 2. Israel's passage through it was typical of the conversion of souls (Isa. xi. 15).

I. An instance of God's almighty power in the kingdom of nature, in dividing the sea. It was a bay, or gulf, or arm of the sea, two or three leagues over, which was divided, *v.* 21. The natural sign was a strong east wind, signifying that it was done by the power of God, whom the winds and the seas obey.

II. An instance of his wonderful favour to his Israel. They went through the sea to the opposite shore. They *walked upon dry land in the midst of the sea*, *v.* 29. *The waters were a wall to them on their right hand and on their left.* Moses and Aaron, it is probable, ventured first into this untrodden path, and then all Israel after them; and this march through the paths of the great waters would make their march afterwards, through the wilderness, less formidable. Those who had followed God through the sea needed not to fear following him whithersoever he led them.

This was done, and recorded, in order to encourage God's people in all ages to trust in him in the greatest straits. We find the saints, long afterwards, making themselves sharers in the triumphs of this march (Ps. lxvi. 6).

III. An instance of his just and righteous wrath upon his and his people's enemies, the Egyptians. Observe here, 1. How they were infatuated. They were more advantageously provided with chariots and horses, while the Israelites were on foot. 2. How they were troubled and perplexed, *v.* 24, 25. But, *in the morning watch, the Lord looked upon the host of the Egyptians, and troubled them.* (1) They had hectored and boasted as if the day were their own; but now they were troubled and dismayed, struck with a panic-fear. (2) They had driven furiously; but now they drove heavily, and found themselves plunged and embarrassed at every step. As soon as ever the children of Israel had got safely to the shore, the waters returned to their place, and overwhelmed all the host of the Egyptians, *v.* 27, 28. Pharaoh and his servants, who had hardened one another in sin, now fell together, and not one escaped. An ancient tradition says that Pharaoh's magicians, Jannes and Jambres, perished with the rest. God reckoned with Pharaoh for all his proud and insolent conduct towards Moses his ambassador. Come and see the desolations he made, and write it, not in water, but with an iron pen in the rock for ever. This is Pharaoh and all his multitude, Ezek. xxxi. 18.

IV. Here is the notice which the Israelites took of this wonderful work which God wrought for them. Now they were ashamed of their distrusts and murmurings; they would never again quarrel with Moses, nor talk of returning to Egypt. They were now baptized unto Moses in the sea, 1 Cor. x. 2. Being brought thus triumphantly out of Egypt, they did not doubt that they should be in Canaan shortly, having such a God to trust to, and such a mediator between them and him. O that there had been such a heart in them as now there seemed to be! How well were it for us if we were always in as good a frame as we are in sometimes!

CHAPTER 15

In this chapter, I. Israel looks back upon Egypt with a song of praise for their deliverance. Here is, 1. The song itself, ver. 1–19. 2. The solemn singing of it, ver. 20, 21. II. Israel marches forward in the wilderness (ver. 22); and there, 1. Their discontent at the waters of Marah (ver. 23, 24), and the relief granted them, ver. 25, 26. 2. Their satisfaction in the waters of Elim, ver. 27.

Verses 1–21

Having read how that complete victory of Israel over the Egyptians was obtained, here we are told how it was celebrated. Moses, no doubt by divine inspiration, indited this song, and delivered it to the children of Israel, to be sung before they stirred from the place where they saw the Egyptians dead upon the shore. Observe, They expressed their joy in God, and thankfulness to him, by singing. It was a song of faith.

I. The song itself;

1. We may observe respecting this song, that it is, (1) An ancient song, the most ancient that we know of. (2) A most admirable composition, the style lofty and magnificent, the images lively and proper, and the whole very moving. (3) It is a holy song, consecrated to the honour of God, and intended to exalt his name and celebrate his praise, and his only.

2. What Moses chiefly aims at in this song.

(1) He gives glory to God, and triumphs in him; this is first in his intention (*v.* 1): *I will sing unto the Lord.* Israel rejoiced in God, [1] As their own God, and therefore their *strength, song,* and *salvation, v.* 2. [2] *As their father's God.* This they take notice of, because, being conscious in themselves of their own unworthiness and provocations, they had reason to think that what God had now done for them was for their *father's sake*, Deut. iv. 37. [3] As a God of infinite power (*v.* 3). [4] As a God of matchless and incomparable perfection, *v.* 11. This is expressed, *First,* more generally: *Who is like unto thee, O Lord, among the gods!* Egypt was notorious for the multitude of its gods, but the *God of the Hebrews* was too hard for them and baffled them all, Deut. xxxii. 23–39. More particularly, [i] *He is glorious in holiness;* his holiness is his glory. God is *rich in mercy* —this is his treasure, *glorious in holiness*—this is his honour. [ii] *He is fearful in praises.* That which is the matter of our praise, though it is joyful to the servants of God, is dreadful and very terrible to his enemies, Ps. lxvi. 1–3. 3. He is *doing wonders,* wondrous to all, being above the power and out of the common course of nature. They were wonders of power and wonders of grace; in both God was to be humbly adored.

(2) He describes the deliverance they were now triumphing in, because the song was intended, not only to express and excite their thankfulness for the present, but to preserve and perpetuate the remembrance of this work of wonder to after-ages. Two things were to be taken notice of:—

[1] The destruction of the enemy; the waters were divided, *v.* 8. *The floods stood upright as a heap.* Pharaoh and all his hosts were buried in the waters. The proud waters went over the proud sinners. Their sin had made them hard like a stone, and now they justly sink like a stone.

[2] The protection and guidance of Israel (*v.* 13): *Thou in thy mercy hast led forth the people*, led them forth out of the bondage of Egypt, led them forth out of the perils of the Red Sea, *v.* 19.

(3) He sets himself to improve this wonderful appearance of God for them. God having preserved them, they resolve to spare no cost nor pains for the erecting of a tabernacle to his honour, and there they will exalt him. So confident is this Psalmist of the happy issue of the salvation which was so gloriously

begun that he looks upon it as in effect finished already: *"Thou hast guided them to thy holy habitation, v.* 13. Two ways this great deliverance was encouraging:— *First,* It was such an instance of God's power as would terrify their enemies, and quite dishearten them, *v.* 14–16. It had this effect: the Edomites were afraid of them (Deut. ii. 4), so were the Moabites (Num. xxii. 3), and the Canaanites, Josh. ii. 9, 10; *v.* 1. *Secondly,* It was such a beginning of God's favour to them as gave them an earnest of the perfection of his kindness. *Thou shalt bring them in, v.* 17. If he thus *bring them out of Egypt,* notwithstanding their unworthiness, and the difficulties that lay in the way of their escape, doubtless he will bring them into Canaan. *Lastly,* The great ground of the encouragement which they draw from this work of wonder is, *The Lord shall reign for ever and ever, v.* 18. Note, It is the unspeakable comfort of all God's faithful subjects that he will reign eternally, and there shall be no end of his dominion.

II. The solemn singing of this song, *v.* 20, 21. Moses led the psalm, and gave it out for the men, and then Miriam for the women. Famous victories were wont to be applauded by the daughters of Israel (1 Sam. xviii. 6, 7); so was this.

Verses 22–27

It should seem, it was with some difficulty that Moses prevailed with Israel to leave that triumphant shore on which they sang the foregoing song. Now here we are told,

I. That in the wilderness of Shur they had no water, *v.* 22.

II. That at Marah they had water, but it was bitter, so that though they had been three days without water they could not drink it. Now in this distress, 1. The people fretted and quarrelled with Moses, as if he had done ill by them. *What shall we drink?* is all their clamour, *v.* 24. 2. Moses prayed: *He cried unto the Lord, v.* 25. God is the guide of the church's guides; and to him, as the Chief Shepherd, the under-shepherds must upon all occasions apply. 3. God directed Moses to a tree, which he cast into the waters, in consequence of which, all of a sudden, they were made sweet. Some think this wood had a peculiar virtue in it for this purpose, because it is said, *God showed him the tree.* God is to be acknowledged, not only in the creating of things useful for man, but in discovering their usefulness. Some make this tree typical of the cross of Christ, which sweetens the bitter waters of affliction to all the faithful, and enables them to rejoice in tribulation. *There he made a statute and an ordinance,* and settled matters with them. *There he proved them,* that is, there he put them upon the trial, admitted them as probationers for his favour. In short, he tells them, *v.* 26, (1) What he expected from them, and that was, in one word, obedience. They must not think, now that they were delivered from their bondage in Egypt, that they were their own masters; they must look upon themselves as God's servants, because he had *loosed their bonds,* Ps. cxvi. 16; Luke i. 74, 75. (2) What they might then expect from him: *I will put none of these diseases upon thee,* that is, "I will not bring upon thee any of the plagues of Egypt." Let not the Israelites think God would connive at their sins and let them do as they would. No, God is no respecter of persons; a rebellious Israelite shall fare no better than a rebellious Egyptian; and so they found, to their cost, before they got to Canaan.

III. That at Elim they had good water, and enough of it, *v.* 27. Here were twelve wells for their supply, one for every tribe, that they might not strive for water, as their fathers had sometimes done; and, for their pleasure, there were seventy palm-trees.

CHAPTER 16

This chapter gives us an account of the victualling of the camp of Israel. I. Their complaint for want of bread, ver. 1–3. II. The notice God gave them beforehand of the provision he intended to make for them, ver. 4–12. III. The sending of the manna, ver. 13–15. IV. The laws and orders concerning the manna.

Verses 1–12

The host of Israel, it seems, took along with them out of Egypt a month's provisions, which, by the fifteenth day of the second month, was all spent.

I. Their discontent and murmuring upon that occasion, *v.* 2, 3. 1. They count upon being killed in the wilderness—nothing less, at the first appearance of disaster. It argues great distrust of God to talk of nothing but being speedily killed. 2. They invidiously charge Moses with a design to starve them when he brought them out of Egypt. 3. They so far undervalue their deliverance that they wish they had died in Egypt. They would rather die by the fleshpots of Egypt, where they found themselves with provision, than live under the guidance of the heavenly pillar in a wilderness and be provided for by the hand of God! We cannot suppose that they had any great plenty in Egypt, how largely soever they now talk of the flesh-pots; nor could they fear dying for want in the wilderness, while they had their flocks and herds with them. But discontent magnifies what is past, and vilifies what is present, without regard to truth or reason.

II. The care God graciously took for their supply. 1. How God makes known to Moses his kind intentions, that he might not be uneasy at their murmurings, nor be tempted to wish he had let them alone in Egypt. (1) He takes notice of the people's complaints. (2) He promises them a speedy, sufficient, and constant supply, *v.* 4. See what God designed in making this provision for them: *That I may prove them, whether they will walk in my law or no.* [1] Thus he tried whether they would trust him, and walk in the law of faith or no, whether they could rest satisfied with the bread of the day in its day, and depend upon God for fresh supplies tomorrow. [2] Thus he tried whether they would serve him, and be always faithful. 2. How Moses made known these intentions to Israel, as God ordered him. Here Aaron was his prophet, as he had been to Pharaoh. Moses directed Aaron what to *speak to the congregation of Israel (v.* 9). Note, God condescends to give even murmurers a fair hearing. (1) He convinces them of the evil of their murmurings. They thought they reflected only upon Moses and Aaron, but here they are told that God was struck at through their sides. Note, When we murmur against those who are instruments of any uneasiness to us, whether justly or unjustly, we should do well to consider how much we reflect upon God by it; men are but God's hand. (2) He assures them of the supply of their wants, that since they had harped upon the flesh-pots so much they should for once have flesh in abundance that evening, and bread the next morning, and so on every day thenceforward, *v.* 8, 12. Many there are of whom we say that they are better fed than taught; but the Israelites were thus fed, that they might be taught. [1] *By this you shall know that the Lord hath brought you out from the land of Egypt, v.* 6. That they were brought out of Egypt was plain enough; but so strangely sottish and short-sighted were they that they said it was Moses that brought them out, *v.* 3. [2] *By this you shall know that I am the Lord your God, v.* 12. When God plagued the Egyptians, it was to make them know that he was the Lord; when he provided for the Israelites, it was to make them know that he was their God.

3. How God himself manifested his glory, to still

the murmurings of the people, and to put a reputation upon Moses and Aaron, *v.* 10. While Aaron was speaking, *the glory of the Lord appeared in the cloud.*

Verses 13-21

Now they begin to be provided for by the immediate hand of God.

I. He makes them a feast, at night, of delicate fowl. Quails, or pheasants, or some wild fowl, came up, and covered the camp, so tame that they might take up as many of them as they pleased.

II. Next morning he rained manna upon them, which was to be continued to them for their daily bread. 1. That which was provided for them was manna, itself of such a consistency as to serve for nourishing strengthening food, without anything else. They called it *manna, manhu,* "What is this?" 2. They were to gather it every morning (*v.* 21), *the portion of a day in his day, v.* 4. To this daily raining and gathering of manna our Saviour seems to allude when he teaches us to pray, *Give us this day our daily bread.* We are hereby taught, (1) Prudence and diligence in providing food convenient for ourselves and our household. What God graciously gives we must industriously gather. (2) Contentment and satisfaction with a sufficiency. They must gather, *every man according to his eating*; enough is as good as a feast, and more than enough is as bad as a surfeit. (3) Dependence upon Providence: *Let no man leave till morning* (*v.* 19), but let them learn to go to bed and sleep quietly, though they have not a bit of bread in their tent, nor in all their camp, trusting that God, with the following day, will bring them their daily bread." See here the folly of hoarding. The manna that was laid up by some putrefied, and bred worms, and became good for nothing. 3. Let us set ourselves to think, (1) Of that great power of God which fed Israel in the wilderness, and made miracles their daily bread. Never was there such a market of provisions as this, where so many hundred thousand men were daily furnished, without money and without price. Never was there such an open house kept as God kept in the wilderness for forty years together, nor such free and plentiful entertainment given. (2) Of that constant providence of God. The same wisdom, power, and goodness that now brought food daily out of the clouds, are employed in the constant course of nature, bringing food yearly out of the earth, and giving us all things richly to enjoy.

Verses 22-31

We have here the setting apart of one day in seven for holy work, and, in order to that, for holy rest, was a divine appointment ever since God created man upon the earth, and the most ancient of positive laws. The double provision which God made for the Israelites, and which they were to make for themselves, on the sixth day: God gave them *on the sixth day the bread of two days, v.* 29. Appointing them to rest on the seventh day, he took care that they should be no losers by it; and none ever will be losers by serving God. On that day they were to fetch in enough for two days, and to prepare it, *v.* 23. The law was very strict, that they must bake and seeth, the day before, and not on the sabbath day. This does not now make it unlawful for us to dress meat on the Lord's day, but directs us to contrive our family affairs so that they may hinder us as little as possible in the work of the sabbath. That which they kept for their food on the sabbath day did not putrefy, *v.* 24. Some, it seems, went out on the seventh day, expecting to find manna (*v.* 27); but they found none, for those that will find must seek in the appointed time. God, upon this occasion, said to Moses, *How long refuse you to keep my commandments? v.* 28. Why did he say this to Moses? He was not

disobedient. No, but he was the ruler of a disobedient people, and God charges it upon him that he might the more warmly charge it upon them, and might take care that their disobedience should not be through any neglect or default of his.

Verses 32-36

God having provided manna to be his people's food in the wilderness, we are here told, 1. How the memory of it was preserved. An omer of this manna was laid up in *a golden pot*, as we are told (Heb. ix. 4), and kept *before the testimony*, or the ark, when it was afterwards made, *v.* 32–34. Note, Eaten bread must not be forgotten. God's miracles and mercies are to be had in everlasting remembrance, for our encouragement to trust in him at all times. 2. How the mercy of it was continued as long as they had occasion for it. The manna never ceased till they came to the borders of Canaan, where there was bread enough and to spare, *v.* 35. The manna is called *spiritual meat* (1 Cor. x. 3), because it was typical of spiritual blessings in heavenly things. Christ himself is the true manna, the bread of life, of which this was a figure, John vi. 49–51. The word of God is the manna by which our souls are nourished, Matt. iv. 4. The comforts of the Spirit are hidden manna, Rev. ii. 17. These come from heaven, as the manna did, and are the support and comfort of the divine life in the soul, while we are in the wilderness of this world. It is to be *gathered*; Christ in the word is to be applied to the soul, and the means of grace are to be used. We must every one of us gather for ourselves, and gather in the morning of our days, the morning of our opportunities, which if we let slip, it may be too late to gather. The manna they gathered must not be hoarded up, but eaten; those that have received Christ must by faith live upon him, and not receive his grace in vain. But those that did eat manna hungered again, died at last, and with many of them God was not well pleased; whereas those that feed on Christ by faith shall never hunger, and shall die no more, and with them God will be for ever well pleased. The Lord evermore give us this bread!

CHAPTER 17

I. The watering of the host of Israel. 1. In the wilderness they wanted water, ver. 1, 2. In their want they chided Moses, ver. 2, 3. 3. Moses cried to God, ver. 4. 4. God ordered him to smite the rock, and fetch water out of that; Moses did so, ver. 5, 6. 5. The place named from it, ver. 7. II. The defeating of the host of Amalek. 1. The victory obtained by the prayer of Moses, ver. 8–12. 2. By the sword of Joshua, ver. 13. A record kept of it, ver. 14, 16. And these things which happened to them are written for our instruction in our spiritual journey and warfare.

Verses 1-7

I. The strait that the children of Israel were in for want of water.

II. Their discontent and distrust in this strait. It is said (*v.* 3), They *thirsted there for water.* This intimates that their passion sharpened their appetites and they were violent and impatient in their desire. See what was the language of this inordinate desire. 1. They challenged Moses to supply them (*v.* 2): *Give us water, that we may drink,* demanding it as a debt. 2. They quarrelled with him for bringing them out of Egypt, as if, instead of delivering them, he designed to murder them. To such a degree their malice against Moses rose that they were *almost ready to stone him, v.* 4. 3. They began to question whether God were with them or not: They *tempted the Lord, saying,* "*Is the Lord among us or not?*" *v.* 7. They question his essential presence—whether there was a God or not; his common providence—whether that God governed the world; and his special promise—whether he would be as good as his word to them. This is called their *tempting God.* They do, in effect, suppose that Moses was an impostor, that long series of miracles which had rescued them, served them, and fed them, a chain of cheats, and the promise of Canaan a banter upon them; it was all so, if *the Lord was not among them*.

III. The course that Moses took, 1. He reproved the murmurers (*v.* 2): *Why chide you with me?* Observe how mildly he answered them. He showed them whom their murmurings reflected upon, and that the reproaches they cast on him fell on God himself: *You tempt the Lord*; that is, "By distrusting his power, you try his patience, and so provoke his wrath." 2. He made his complaint to God (*v.* 4): *Moses cried unto the Lord.* When men unjustly censure us and quarrel with us, it will be a great relief to us to go to God, and by prayer lay the case before him and leave it with him: if men will not hear us, God will. Moses begs of God to direct him what he should do, for he was utterly at a loss.

IV. God's gracious appearance for their relief, *v.* 5, 6. He orders Moses to go on before the people. He must take his rod with him, not to summon some plague to chastise them, but to fetch water for their supply. O the wonderful patience and forbearance of God. If God had only shown Moses a fountain of water in the wilderness, as he did Hagar, that would have been a great favour; but that he might show his power as well as his pity, and make it a miracle of mercy, he gave them water out of a rock. He directed Moses whither to go, and appointed him to take some of the elders to be witnesses of what was done, that they might themselves be satisfied of the certainty of God's presence with them. He promised to meet him there in the cloud of glory, and ordered him to smite the rock; Moses obeyed, and immediately water came out of the rock in great abundance. It is called *a fountain of waters*, Ps. cxiv. 8. This fair water, that came out of the rock, is called *honey and oil* (Deut. xxxii. 13), because the people's thirst made it doubly pleasant; coming when they were in extreme want, it was like honey and oil to them. God can open fountains for our supply where we least expect them, *waters in the wilderness* (Isa. xliii. 20), because he makes a *way in the wilderness*, *v.* 19. Those who, in this wilderness, keep to God's way, may trust him to provide for them. The graces and comforts of the Spirit are compared to *rivers of living water*, John vii. 38, 39; iv. 14. These flow from Christ, who is the rock smitten by the law of Moses, for he was made under the law. Nothing will supply the needs, and satisfy the desires, of a soul, but water out of this rock, this fountain opened. The pleasures of sense are puddle-water; spiritual delights are rock water, so pure, so clear, so refreshing—rivers of pleasure.

V. A new name was, upon this occasion, given to the place, preserving the remembrance of the sin of their murmuring—*Massah, temptation*, because they tempted God; *Meribah, strife*, because they chid with Moses, *v.* 7.

Verses 8–16

Amalek was the first of the nations that Israel fought with, Num. xxiv. 20.

I. Amalek's attempt: They *came out, and fought with Israel*, *v.* 8. The Amalekites were the posterity of Esau, who hated Jacob because of the birthright and blessing, and this was an effort of the hereditary enmity. Consider this, 1. As Israel's affliction. 2. As Amalek's sin; so it is reckoned, Deut. xxv. 17, 18. They basely fell upon their rear, and smote those that were faint and feeble and could neither make resistance nor escape. In vain did they attack a camp guarded and victualled by miracles: verily they knew not what they did.

II. Israel's defence against the aggressors.

1. The post assigned to Joshua, of whom this is the first mention: he is nominated commander-in-chief in this expedition, that he might be trained up to the services he was designed for after the death of Moses.

2. The post assumed by Moses: *I will stand on the top of the hill with the rod of God in my hand*, *v.* 9. Joshua fights, Moses prays, and held up *the rod of God in his hand*. This rod Moses held up to Israel, to animate them; the rod was held up as the banner to encourage the soldiers. Moses also held up this rod to God, by way of appeal to him. Moses was not only a standard-bearer, but an intercessor, pleading with God for success and victory. It is here the praying legion that proves the thundering legion. (1) How Moses was tired (*v.* 12): *His hands were heavy*. We do not find that Joshua's hands were heavy in fighting, but Moses's hands were heavy in praying. The more spiritual any service is the more apt we are to fail and flag in it. (2) What influence the rod of Moses had upon the battle (*v.* 11): *When Moses held up his hand* in prayer (so the Chaldee explains it) *Israel prevailed*, but, *when he let down his hand* from prayer, *Amalek prevailed*. (3) The care that was taken for the support of Moses. When he could not stand any longer he sat down upon a stone (*v.* 12); when he could not hold up his hands, he would have them held up. Moses, the man of God, is glad of the assistance of Aaron his brother, and Hur, who, some think, was his brother-in-law, the husband of Miriam. Moses's hands, thus stayed, were *steady till the going down of the sun*. No doubt it was a great encouragement to the people to see Joshua before them in the field of battle and Moses above them upon the top of the hill: Christ is both to us—our Joshua, the captain of our salvation who fights our battles, and our Moses, who, in the upper world, ever lives making intercession, that our faith fail not.

III. The defeat of Amalek. Victory had hovered awhile between the camps, but Israel carried the day, *v.* 13. Though Joshua fought with great disadvantages —his soldiers undisciplined, ill-armed, long inured to servitude, and apt to murmur; yet by them God wrought a great salvation.

IV. The trophies of this victory set up. 1. Moses took care that God should have the glory of it (*v.* 15); instead of setting up a triumphal arch to the honour of Joshua, he builds an altar to the honour of God, and that which is most carefully recorded is the inscription upon the altar, *Jehovah-nissi—The Lord is my banner*, which probably refers to the lifting up of the rod of God as a banner in this action. The presence and power of Jehovah were the banner under which they enlisted, by which they were animated and kept together, and therefore which they erected in the day of their triumph. 2. God took care that posterity should have the comfort and benefit of it: "*Write this for a memorial*, and then *rehearse it in the ears of Joshua*, let him be entrusted with this memorial, to transmit it to the generations to come." Moses must now begin to keep a diary or journal of occurrences; it is the first mention of writing that we find in scripture, and perhaps the command was not given till after the writing of the law upon the tables of stone: "Write it *in perpetuam rei memoriam—that the event may be had in perpetual remembrance*"; that which is written remains. (1) "Write what has been done. Let ages to come know that God fights for his people, and *he that touches them touches the apple of his eye*." (2) Write what shall be done. [1] That in process of time Amalek shall be totally ruined and rooted out (*v.* 14). Israel will at last undoubtedly triumph in the fall of Amalek. This sentence was executed in part by Saul (1 Sam. xv.), and completely by David (*ch.* xxx.; 2 Sam. i. 1; viii. 12); after his time we never read so much as of the name of Amalek. [2] That in the meantime God would have a continual controversy with him (*v.* 16). This was written for direction to Israel never to make any league with the Amalekites.

CHAPTER 18

This chapter is concerning Moses himself, and the affairs of his own family. I. Jethro his father-in-law brings to him his wife and children, ver. 1–6. II. Moses entertains his father-in-law with great respect (ver. 7), with good discourse (ver. 8–11), with a sacrifice and a feast, ver. 12. III. Jethro advises him (ver. 13–23), and Moses, after some time, takes his counsel (ver. 24–26), and so they part, ver. 27.

Verses 1–6

Jethro comes,

I. To congratulate the happiness of Israel, and particularly the honour of Moses his son-in-law; Jethro could not but hear what all the country rang of, the glorious appearances of God for his people Israel (*v.* 1); and he comes to enquire, and to rejoice with them, as one that had a true respect both for them and for their God. Though he, as a Midianite, was not to share with them in the promised land, yet he shared with them in the joy of their deliverance.

II. To bring Moses's wife and children to him. It seems he had sent them back home to his father-in-law. Jethro, we may suppose, was glad of his daughter's company, and fond of her children, yet he would not keep her from her husband, nor them from their father, *v.* 5, 6. Moses must have his family with him, that while he ruled the church of God he might set a good example of prudence in family-government, 1 Tim. iii. 5. Moses had now a great deal both of honour and care put upon him, and it was fit that his wife should be with him to share with him in both. Notice is taken of the significant names of his two sons. 1. The eldest was called *Gershom* (*v.* 3), *a stranger*. 2. The other he called *Eliezer* (*v.* 4), *My God a help*, as we translate it; it looks back to his deliverance from Pharaoh. I would rather translate it so as to look forward, which the original will bear, *The Lord is my help, and will deliver me* from the sword of Pharaoh.

Verses 7–12

I. The kind greeting that took place between Moses and his father-in-law, *v.* 7. Those that stand high in the favour of God are not thereby discharged from the duty they owe to men. Moses went out to meet Jethro, did *homage to him, and kissed him*. Religion does not destroy good manners. *They asked each other of their welfare.*

II. The narrative that Moses gave his father-in-law of the great things God had done for Israel, *v.* 8.

III. The impressions this narrative made upon Jethro. 1. He congratulated God's Israel: *Jethro rejoiced, v.* 9. He not only rejoiced in the honour done to his son-in-law, but in *all the goodness done to Israel, v.* 9. Note, Public blessings are the joy of public spirits. While the Israelites were themselves murmuring, notwithstanding all God's goodness to them, here was a Midianite rejoicing. 2. He gave the glory to Israel's God (*v.* 10). 3. His faith was hereby confirmed, and he took this occasion to make a solemn profession of it: *Now know I that Jehovah is greater than all gods, v.* 11. Observe, (1) The matter of his faith: that the God of Israel is greater than all pretenders, all false and counterfeit deities. (2) The confirmation and improvement of his faith: *Now know I*; he knew it before, but now he knew it better; his faith grew up to a full assurance, upon this fresh evidence. (3) The ground and reason upon which he built it: *For wherein they dealt proudly, he was above them.* The magicians were baffled, the idols

shaken, Pharaoh humbled, his powers broken, and, in spite of all their confederacies, God's Israel was rescued out of their hands.

IV. The expressions of their joy and thankfulness. They had communion with each other both in a feast and in a sacrifice, *v.* 12. Jethro was cheerfully admitted, though a Midianite, into fellowship with Moses and the elders of Israel, *forasmuch as he also was a son of Abraham*, though of a younger house. 1. They joined in a sacrifice of thanksgiving: *Jethro took burnt offerings for God*, and probably offered them himself, for he was a priest in Midian, and a worshipper of the true God. 2. They joined in a feast of rejoicing, a feast upon the sacrifice.

Verses 13–27

I. The great zeal and industry of Moses as a magistrate.

1. Having been employed to redeem Israel out of the house of bondage, herein he is a further type of Christ, that he is employed as a lawgiver and a judge among them. (1) He was to answer enquiries, and to explain the laws of God that were already given them, concerning the sabbath, the manna, &c., beside the laws of nature, relating both to piety and equity, *v.* 15. Moses made them *know the statutes of God and his laws, v.* 16. His business was, not to make laws, but to make known God's laws; his place was but that of a servant. (2) He was to decide controversies, judging between a man and his fellow, *v.* 16. And, if the people were as quarrelsome one with another as they were with God, no doubt he had a great many causes brought before him.

2. Such was the business Moses was called to, and it appears that he did it, (1) With great consideration. (2) With great condescension to the people, who stood *by him, v.* 14. (3) With great constancy and closeness of application.

II. The great prudence and consideration of Jethro as a friend.

1. He disliked the method that Moses took, and was so free with him as to tell him so, *v.* 14, 17, 18. He thought it was too much business for Moses to undertake alone. There may be overdoing even in well-doing.

2. He advised him to such a model of government as would better answer the intention, which was, (1) That he should reserve to himself all applications to God (*v.* 19): *Be thou for them to God-ward*; that was an honour in which it was not fit any other should share with him, Num. xii. 6–8. Also whatever concerned the whole congregation in general must pass through his hand, *v.* 20. But, (2) That he should appoint judges in the several tribes and families, who should try causes between man and man, and determine them, which would be done with less noise, and more despatch, than in the general assembly wherein Moses himself presided. Yet, (3) An appeal might lie, if there were just cause for it, from these inferior courts to Moses himself. *Every great matter they shall bring unto thee, v.* 22.

3. He adds two qualifications to his counsel: (1) That great care should be taken in the choice of the persons who should be admitted into this trust (*v.* 21); they must *be able men*, &c. It was requisite that they should be men of the very best character, [1] For judgment and resolution—*able men*. Clear heads and stout hearts make good judges. [2] For piety and religion—*such as fear God*. Conscientious men, that dare not do a base thing, though they could do it ever so secretly and securely. [3] For integrity and honesty—*men of truth*. [4] For noble and generous contempt of worldly wealth—*hating covetousness*. (2) That he should attend God's direction in the case (*v.* 23): *If thou shalt do this thing, and God command thee so.*

Now Moses did not despise this advice but he *hearkened to the voice of his father-in-law, v.* 24.

III. Jethro's return to his own land, *v.* 27. It is supposed he returned to his own land, *v.* 27. It is (mentioned 1 Sam. xv. 6) were the posterity of Jethro (compare Judges i. 16), and they are there taken under special protection, for the kindness their ancestor here showed to Israel.

CHAPTER 19

This chapter introduces the solemnity of the giving of the law upon Mount Sinai. We have here, I. The circumstances of time and place, ver. 1, 2. II. The covenant between God and Israel settled in general. The gracious proposal God made to them (ver. 3–6), and their consent to the proposal, ver. 7, 8. III. Notice given three days before of God's design to give the law out of a thick cloud, ver. 9. Orders given to prepare the people to receive the law (ver. 10–13), and care taken to execute those orders, ver. 14, 15. IV. A terrible appearance of God's glory upon Mount Sinai, ver. 16–20. V. Silence proclaimed.

Verses 1–8

Here is, I. The date of that great charter by which Israel was incorporated. 1. The time when it bears date (*v.* 1)—*in the third month* after they came out of Egypt. 2. The place whence it bears date—from *Mount Sinai,* the highest in all that range of mountains. Thus God put contempt upon cities, and palaces, and magnificent structures, setting up his pavilion on the top of a high mountain, in a waste and barren desert, there to carry on this treaty. It is called *Sinai,* from the multitude of thorny bushes that overspread it.

II. The charter itself. Moses was called up to the mountain and was employed as the messenger of the covenant: *Thus shalt thou say to the house of Jacob, and tell the children of Israel, v.* 3. Now observe, 1. That the maker, and first mover, of the covenant, is God himself. In all our dealings with God, free grace anticipates us with the blessings of goodness, and all our comfort is owing, not to our knowing God, but rather to our being *known of him,* Gal. iv. 9. 2. That the matter of the covenant is kind and gracious, and such as gives them the greatest privileges and advantages imaginable. (1) He reminds them of what he had done for them, *v.* 4. *I bore you on eagles' wings,* a high expression of the wonderful tenderness God had shown for them. It is explained, Deut. xxxii. 11, 12. It denotes great speed. God not only came upon the wing for their deliverance, but he hastened them out, as it were, upon the wing. He did it with the strength as well as with the swiftness of an eagle. Egypt, that iron furnace, was the nest in which these young ones were hatched, where they were first formed as the embryo of a nation; when, by the increase of their numbers, they grew to some maturity, they were carried out of that nest. Other birds carry their young in their talons, but the eagle (they say) upon her wings, so that even those archers who shoot flying cannot hurt the young ones, unless they first shoot through the old one. *I brought you unto myself.* They were brought not only into a state of liberty and honour, but into covenant and communion with God. This, this was the glory of their deliverance, as it is of ours by Christ, that he died, *the just for the unjust, that he might bring us to God.* This God aims at in all the gracious methods of his providence and grace, to bring us back to himself, from whom we have revolted, and to bring us home to himself, in whom alone we can be happy. Some have well observed that the *Old Testament church* is said to be borne upon eagles' wings, but the *New Testament church* is said to be gathered by the Lord Jesus, *as a hen gathers her chickens under her wings* (Matt. xxiii. 37), denoting the grace and compassion of that dispensation, and the admirable condescension and humiliation of the redeemer. (2) He tells them plainly (*v.* 5), that they should *obey his voice in deed and keep his covenant.*

Being thus saved by him, that which he insisted upon was that they should be ruled by him. (3) He assures them of the honour he would put upon them, and the kindness he would show them, in case they did thus keep his covenant (*v.* 5, 6): *Then you shall be a peculiar treasure to me.* [1] God here asserts his sovereignty over, and propriety in, the whole visible creation: *All the earth is mine.* [2] He appropriates Israel to himself, as a people dear unto him. *You shall be a peculiar treasure.* By giving them divine revelation, instituted ordinances, and promises inclusive of eternal life, by sending his prophets among them, and pouring out his Spirit upon them, he distinguished them from, and dignified them above, all people.

III. Israel's acceptance of this charter, and consent to the conditions of it. 1. Moses faithfully delivered God's message to them (*v.* 7): He *laid before their faces all those words.* His laying it to their faces denotes his laying it to their consciences. 2. They readily agreed to the covenant proposed. *All that the Lord hath spoken we will do.* 3. Moses, as a mediator, returned the words of the people to God, *v.* 8. Thus Christ, the Mediator between us and God, as a prophet reveals God's will to us, and then as a priest offers up to God our spiritual sacrifices. Thus he is that blessed *days-man who lays his hand upon us both.*

Verses 9–15

Here, I. God intimates to Moses his purpose of coming down upon Mount Sinai, in some visible appearance of his glory, in *a thick cloud* (*v.* 9). God would come down *in the sight of all the people* (*v.* 11); though they should see no manner of similitude, yet they should see so much as would convince them that God was among them of a truth. Thus the correspondence was to be first settled by a sensible appearance of the divine glory, which was afterwards to be carried on more silently by the ministry of Moses. In like manner, the Holy Ghost descended visibly upon Christ at his baptism, and all that were present heard God speak to him (Matt. iii. 17), that afterwards, without the repetition of such visible tokens, they might believe him. So likewise the Spirit descended in cloven tongues upon the apostles (Acts ii. 3), that they might be believed.

II. He orders Moses to make preparation for this great solemnity, giving him two days' time for it.

1. He must *sanctify the people* (*v.* 10). "Sanctify *them,*" that is, "Call them off from their worldly business, and call them to religious exercises, meditation and prayer, that they may receive the law from God's mouth with reverence and devotion. Let them be *ready,*" *v.* 11. Wandering thoughts must be gathered in, impure affections abandoned, disquieting passions suppressed, nay, and all cares about secular business, for the present, dismissed and laid by, that our hearts may be *engaged to approach unto God.* In token of their cleansing they must wash their *clothes* (*v.* 10), and they did so (*v.* 14); not that God regards our clothes; but while they were washing their clothes he would have them think of washing their souls by repentance. It becomes us to appear in clean clothes when we wait upon great men; so clean hearts are required in our attendance on the great God, who sees them as plainly as men see our clothes.

2. He must *set bounds about the mountain, v.* 12, 13. Probably he drew a line, or ditch, round at the foot of the hill, which none were to pass upon pain of death. This was to intimate, That humble awful reverence which ought to possess the minds of all those that worship God.

3. He must order the people to attend upon the summons that should be given (*v.* 13): "*When the trumpet soundeth long* then let them take their places

at the foot of the mount, and so sit down at God's feet." No one man's voice could have reached so many, but the voice of God did.

Verses 16–25

Now, at length, comes that memorable day. Never was there such a sermon preached, before nor since, as this which was here preached to the church in the wilderness. For,

I. The preacher was God himself (v. 18): *The Lord descended in fire* and (v. 20), *The Lord came down upon Mount Sinai*. The *shechinah*, or glory of the Lord, appeared in the sight of all the people.

II. The pulpit (or throne rather) was mount Sinai, hung with a *thick cloud* (v. 16), covered with *smoke* (v. 18), and made to *quake* greatly.

III. The congregation was called together by the *sound of a trumpet, exceedingly loud* (v. 16), and *waxing louder and louder, v. 19.*

IV. Moses brought the hearers to the place of meeting, *v. 17*. He that had led them out of the bondage of Egypt now led them to receive the law from God's mouth. Moses, at the head of an assembly worshipping God, was as truly great as Moses at the head of an army in the field.

V. The introductions to the service were *thunders and lightnings, v. 16*. Thunder and lightning have natural causes, but the scripture directs us in a particular manner to take notice of the power of God, and his terror, in them.

VI. Moses is God's minister, who is spoken to, to command silence, and keep the congregatoin in order: *Moses spoke, v. 19*. God stilled his fear by his distinguishing favour to him, in calling him up to the top of the mount (v. 20), by which also he tried his faith and courage. Neither the priests nor the people should offer to force the lines that were set, to *come up unto the Lord*, but Moses and Aaron only, the men whom God delighted to honour. Observe, what it was that God forbade them— breaking through to gaze; enough was provided to awaken their consciences, but they were not allowed to gratify their vain curiosity. They might see, but not gaze. It is at our peril if we break the bounds that God has set us, and intrude upon that which he has not allowed us.

Chapter 20

All things being prepared for the solemn promulgation of the divine law, we have, in this chapter, I. The ten commandments, as God himself spoke them upon Mount Sinai (ver. 1–17). II. The impressions made upon the people thereby, ver. 18–21. III. Some particular instructions which God gave privately to Moses, to be by him communicated to the people, relating to his worship, ver. 22, &c.

Verses 1–11

Here is, I. The preface of the law-writer, Moses: *God spoke all these words, v. 1*. The law of the ten commandments is, 1. A law of God's making. 2. It is a law of his own speaking. God has many ways of speaking to the children of men (Job xxxiii. 14); he never spoke, at any time, upon any occasion, as he spoke the ten commandments. This law God had given to man before (it was written in his heart by nature); but sin had so defaced that writing that it was necessary, in this manner, to revive the knowledge of it.

II. The preface of the Law-maker: *I am the Lord thy God, v. 2*. Herein, 1. God asserts his own authority to enact this law in general. 2. He proposes himself as the sole object of that religious worship which is enjoined in the first four of the commandments. They are here bound to obedience by a threefold cord. (1) Because God *is the Lord*. He that gives being may give law; and therefore he is able to bear us out in our

obedience, to reward it, and to punish our disobedience. (2) He was their God, a God in covenant with them, their God by their own consent. Though that covenant of peculiarity is now no more, yet there is another, by virtue of which all that are baptized are taken into relation to him as their God, and are therefore unjust, unfaithful, and very ungrateful, if they obey him not. (3) He had *brought them out of the land of Egypt*. By redeeming them, he acquired a further right to rule them; they owed their service to him to whom they owed their freedom. And thus Christ, having rescued us out of the bondage of sin, is entitled to the best service we can do him, Luke i. 74.

III. The law itself. The first four of the ten commandments, which concern our duty to God (commonly called *the first table*), we have in these verses. It was fit that those should be put first, because man had a Maker to love before he had a neighbour to love; and justice and charity are acceptable acts of obedience to God only when they flow from the principles of piety. It cannot be expected that he should be true to his brother who is false to his God.

1. The first commandment concerns the object of our worship, Jehovah, and him only (v. 3): *Thou shalt have no other gods before me*. The Egyptians, and other neighbouring nations, had many gods, the creatures of their own fancy, strange gods, *new gods*. The sin against this commandment which *we* are most in danger of is giving the glory and honour to any creature which are due to God only. Pride makes a god of self, coveteousness makes a god of money, sensuality makes a god of the belly, whatever is esteemed or loved, feared or served, delighted in or depended on, more than God, that (whatever it is) we do in effect make a god of. In the last words, *before me*, it is intimated, (1) That we cannot have any other God but he will certainly know it. (2) That it is a sin that dares him to his face, which he cannot, which he will not, overlook.

2. The second commandment concerns the ordinances of worship, or the way in which God will be worshipped.

(1) The prohibition: we are here forbidden to worship even the true God by images, v. 4, 5. The Jews (at least after the captivity) thought themselves forbidden by this commandment to make any image or picture whatsoever. Hence the very images which the Roman armies had in their ensigns are called *an abomination* to them (Matt. xxiv. 15), especially when they were set up *in the holy place*. It is called the changing of the truth of God into a lie (Rom. i. 25), for an image is a teacher of lies; it insinuates to us that God has a body, whereas he is an infinite spirit, Hab. ii. 18. It also forbids us to make images of God in our fancies, as if he were a man as we are. Our religious worship must be governed by the power of faith, not by the power of imagination.

(2) The reasons to enforce this prohibition (v. 5, 6), which are, [1] God's jealousy in the matters of his worship: "*I the Lord* Jehovah, and *thy God, am a jealous God*, especially in things of this nature." [2] The punishment of idolaters. God looks upon them as haters of him. He will *visit it upon the children*. Nor is it an unrighteous thing with God (if the parents died in their iniquity, and the children tread in their steps, and keep up false worships, because they received them by tradition from their fathers), when the measure is full, and God comes by his judgments to reckon with them. Though he bear long with an idolatrous people, he will not bear always, but by the fourth generation, at furthest, he will begin to visit. [3] The favour God would show to his faithful worshippers: *Keeping mercy for thousands* of persons, thousands of generations *of those that love me, and keep my commandments*. As the first commandment requires the inward worship

of love, desire, joy, hope, and admiration, so the second requires the outward worship of prayer and praise, and solemn attendance on God's word. Those that truly love God will make it their constant care to keep his commandments, particularly those that relate to his worship. Those that love God, and keep those commandments, shall receive grace to keep his other commandments. Gospel worship will have a good influence upon all manner of gospel obedience. This mercy shall extend to thousands, much further than the wrath threatened to those that hate him.

3. The third commandment concerns the manner of our worship.

(1) A strict prohibition: *Thou shalt not take the name of the Lord thy God in vain.* We take God's name in vain, [1] By hypocrisy, making a profession of God's name, but not living up to that profession. Those that name the name of Christ, but do not depart from iniquity, name it in vain. [2] By covenant-breaking; if we make promises to God, binding our souls with those bonds to that which is good, and yet perform not to the Lord our vows, we take his name in vain (Matt. v. 23). [3] By rash swearing, mentioning the name of God as a by-word, to no purpose at all, or to no good purpose. [4] By false swearing. One part of the religious regard the Jews were taught to pay to their God was to *swear by his name,* Deut. x. 20. But they affronted him, instead of doing him honour, if they called him to be witness to a lie.

(2) A severe penalty: *The Lord will not hold him guiltless;* magistrates, who punish other offences, may not think themselves concerned to take notice of this, because it does not immediately offer injury either to private property or the public peace. The sinner may perhaps hold himself guiltless. God will *not hold him guiltless,* and they will find it a fearful thing to fall into the hands of the living God.

4. The fourth commandment concerns the time of worship. God is to be served and honoured daily, but one day in seven is to be particularly dedicated to his honour and spent in his service.

(1) The command itself (*v.* 8): *Remember the sabbath day to keep it holy;* and (*v.* 10), *In it thou shalt do no manner of work.* We read of God's blessing and sanctifying a seventh day from the beginning (Gen. ii. 3), so that this was not the enacting of a new law, but the reviving of an old law. [1] They are told what is the day they must religiously observe—*a seventh, after six days' labour;* whether this was the seventh by computation from the first seventh, or from the day of their coming out of Egypt, or both, is not certain. [2] How it must be observed. *First,* As a day of rest; they were to do no manner of work on this day in their callings or worldly business. *Secondly,* As a holy day, set apart to the honour of the holy God, and to be spent in holy exercises. God, by blessing it, had made it holy; they, by solemnly blessing him, must keep it holy. [3] Who must observe it: *Thou, and thy son, and thy daughter;* the wife is not mentioned, because she is supposed to be one with the husband and present with him. God takes notice of what we do, particularly what we do on sabbath days, though we should be where we are strangers. [4] A particular memorandum put upon this duty: *Remember it.* It is intimated that the sabbath was instituted and observed before; but in their bondage in Egypt they had let fall the observance of it. Some think it denotes the preparation we are to make for the sabbath; we must think of it before it comes, that, when it does come, we may keep it holy.

(2) The reasons of this command. [1] We have time enough for ourselves on the other six days: *Six days must thou labour* and time enough to tire ourselves. On the seventh day let us serve God. On the

seventh it will be a kindness to us to be obliged to rest. [2] This is God's day: it is the *sabbath of the Lord thy God,* not only instituted by him, but consecrated to him. [3] It is designed for a memorial of the creation of the world, and therefore to be observed to the glory of the Creator. By the sanctification of the sabbath, the Jews declared that they worshipped the God that made the world, and so distinguished themselves from all other nations, who worshipped gods which they themselves made. [4] God has given us an example of rest, after six days' work: he *rested the seventh day.* [5] He has himself *blessed the sabbath day and sanctified it.* He has put blessings into it, which he has encouraged us to expect from him in the religious observance of that day. It is *the day which the Lord hath made,* let us not do what we can to unmake it.

Verses 12–17

We have here the laws of the second table, as they are commonly called, the last six of the ten commandments, comprehending our duty to ourselves and to one another, and constituting a comment upon the second great commandment, *Thou shalt love thy neighbour as thyself.*

I. The fifth commandment concerns the duties we owe to our relations; those of children to their parents are alone specified: *Honour thy father and thy mother,* which includes, 1. A decent respect to their persons, an inward esteem of them outwardly expressed upon all occasions in our conduct. 2. Obedience to their lawful commands; so it is expounded (Eph. vi. 1–3): "*Children, obey your parents,*" from a principle of love. Though you have said, "We will not," yet afterwards repent and obey, Matt. xxi. 29. 3. Submission to their rebukes, instructions, and corrections; not only to the good and gentle, but also to the froward, out of conscience towards God. Endeavouring, in every thing, to be the comfort of their parents, and to make their old age easy to them, maintaining them if they stand in need of support, which our Saviour makes to be particularly intended in this commandment, Matt. xv. 4–6. The reason annexed to this commandment is a promise: *That thy days may be long in the land which the Lord thy God giveth thee.* He here, in the beginning of the second table, mentions his bringing them into Canaan. A long life in that good land is promised particularly to obedient children.

II. The sixth commandment concerns our own and our neighbour's life (*v.* 13): "*Thou shalt not kill;* thou shalt not do any thing hurtful or injurious to the health, ease, and life, of thy own body, or any other person's unjustly." It does not forbid killing in lawful war, or in our own necessary defence, but it forbids all malice and hatred to the person of any (for *he that hateth his brother is a murderer*), and all personal revenge arising therefrom; also all rash anger upon sudden provocations, and hurt said or done, or aimed to be done, in passion: of this our Saviour expounds this commandment, Matt. v. 22.

III. The seventh commandment concerns our own and our neighbour's chastity: *Thou shalt not commit adultery, v.* 14. This is put before the sixth by our Saviour (Mark x. 19): *Do not commit adultery, do not kill;* for our chastity should be as dear to us as our lives, and we should be as much afraid of that which defiles the body as of that which destroys it.

IV. The eighth commandment concerns our own and our neighbour's wealth, estate, and goods: *Thou shalt not steal, v.* 15. This command forbids us to rob ourselves of what we have by sinful spending, or of the use and comfort of it by sinful sparing, and to rob others by removing the ancient landmarks, invading our neighbour's rights, taking his goods from his person, or house, or field, forcibly or clandestinely, over-reaching in bargains, not restoring what is borrowed or found, withholding just debts, rents, or wages, and (which is worst of all) to rob the public in the coin or revenue, or that which is dedicated to the service of religion.

V. The ninth commandment concerns our own and our neighbour's good name: *Thou shalt not bear false witness*, v. 16. This forbids, 1. Speaking falsely in any matter, lying, equivocating, and any way devising and designing to deceive our neighbour. 2. Speaking unjustly against our neighbour, to the prejudice of his reputation. 3. Bearing false witness against him, laying to his charge things that he knows not, slandering, backbiting, tale-bearing, aggravating what is done amiss and making it worse than it is, and any way endeavouring to raise our own reputation upon the ruin of our neighbour's.

VI. The tenth commandment strikes at the root: *Thou shalt not covet*, v. 17. The foregoing commands implicitly forbid all desire of doing that which will be an injury to our neighbour; this forbids all inordinate desire of having that which will be a gratification to ourselves. St. Paul, when the grace of God caused the scales to fall from his eyes, perceived that this law, *Thou shalt not covet*, forbade all those irregular appetites and desires which are the beginnings of all the sin that is committed by us.

Verses 18–21

I. The extraordinary terror with which the law was given. It was designed to give a sensible discovery of the glorious majesty of God, to prepare the soul for the comforts of the gospel. Thus was the law given by Moses in such a way as might humble men, that the *grace and truth which came by Jesus Christ* might be the more welcome.

II. The impression which this made upon the people: 1. *They removed, and stood afar off*, v. 18. 2. *They entreated that the word should not be so spoken to them any more* (Heb. xii. 19), but begged that God would speak to them by Moses, v. 19. Hereby also they teach us to acquiesce in that method which Infinite Wisdom takes, of speaking to us by men like ourselves.

III. The encouragement Moses gave them, by explaining the design of God in his terror (v. 20): *Fear not*, that is, "Think not that the thunder and fire are designed to consume you." They were intended, 1. To prove them, to try how they would like dealing with God immediately, without a mediator. 2. To keep them to their duty, and prevent their sinning against God. He encourages them, saying, *Fear not*, and yet tells them that God thus spoke to them, *that his fear might be before their face*. We must not fear with amazement, but we must always have in our minds a reverence of God's majesty, a dread of his displeasure, and an obedient regard to his sovereign authority over us: this fear will quicken us to our duty and make us circumspect in our walking.

IV. The progress of their communion with God by the mediation of Moses, v. 21. While the people continued to stand afar off, *Moses drew near unto the thick darkness*; he *was made to draw near*. Some of the rabbis suppose God sent an angel to take him by the hand, and lead him up.

Verses 22–26

Moses having gone into *the thick darkness, where God was*, God there spoke in his hearing only, privately and without terror, all that follows hence to the end of *ch.* xxiii., which is mostly an exposition of the ten commandments; and he was to transmit it by word of mouth first, and afterwards in writing, to the people. The laws in these verses related to God's worship.

I. They are here forbidden to make images for worship (v. 22, 23).

1. This repetition of the second commandment comes in here as pointing to that which might properly be inferred from God's speaking to them as he had done. He had given them sufficient demonstration of his presence among them; they needed not to make images of him, as if he were absent.

2. Though they pretended to worship them but as representations of God, yet really they made them rivals with God, which he would not endure.

II. They are here directed in making altars for worship.

1. To make their altars very plain, either of *earth* or of *unhewn stone*, v. 24, 25. That they might not be tempted to think of a graven image, they must not so much as hew into shape the stones that they made their altars of, but pile them up as they were, in the rough. Plainness should be accepted as the best ornament of the external services of religion, and gospel-worship should not be performed with external pomp and gaiety. The beauty of holiness needs no paint.

2. To make their altars very low (v. 26), so that they might not go up by steps to them. That the higher the altar was, and the nearer heaven, the more acceptable the sacrifice was, was a foolish fancy of the heathen, who therefore chose high places; in opposition to this, and to show that it is the elevation of the heart, not of the sacrifice, that God looks at, they were here ordered to make their altars low.

III. They are here assured of God's gracious acceptance of their devotions, wherever they were paid according to his will (v. 24). Under the gospel, when men are encouraged to pray everywhere, this promise revives in its full extent, that, wherever God's people meet in his name to worship him, he will be *in the midst of them*. There he will come unto them, and will bless them, and more than this we need not desire for the beautifying of our solemn assemblies.

CHAPTER 21

The laws recorded in this chapter relate to the fifth and sixth commandments; and though they are not accommodated to our constitution, nor are the penalties annexed binding on us, yet they are of great use for the explanation of the moral law, and the rules of natural justice. Here are several enlargements, I. Upon the fifth commandment, which concerns particular relations. 1. The duty of masters. 2. The punishment of disobedient children. II. Upon the sixth commandment, which forbids all violence offered to the person of a man. 1. Concerning murder, ver. 12–14. 2. Man-stealing, ver. 16. 3. Assault and battery, ver. 18, 19. 4. Correcting a servant, ver. 20, 21. 5. Hurting a woman with child, ver. 22, 23. 6. The law of retaliation, ver. 24, 25. 7. Maiming a servant, ver. 26, 27. 8. An ox goring, ver. 28–32. 9. Damage by opening a pit, ver. 33, 34. 10. Cattle fighting, ver. 35, 36.

Verses 1–11

The first verse is the general title of the laws contained in this and the two following chapters, most of them relating to matters between man and man. These laws are called *judgments*, because they are framed in infinite wisdom and equity, and because their magistrates were to give judgment according to them. God delivered them privately to Moses, and he was to communicate them to the people. He begins with the laws concerning servants, commanding mercy and moderation towards them.

I. A law concerning men-servants, sold, either by themselves or their parents, through poverty, or by the judges, for their crimes; even those of the latter sort (if Hebrews) were to continue in slavery but seven years at the most. At the seven years' end the servant should either go out free (v. 2, 3), or his servitude should thenceforward be his choice, v. 5, 6.

1. By this law God taught, (1) The Hebrew servants generosity, and a noble love of liberty, for they were

the Lord's freemen. Thus Christians, being *bought with a price, and called unto liberty*, must not be the servants of men, nor of the lusts of men, 1 Cor. vii. 23. He likewise taught, (2) The Hebrew masters not to trample upon their poor servants.

2. This law will be further useful to us to illustrate the right God has to the children of believing parents, as such, and the place they have in his church.

II. Concerning maid-servants, whom their parents, through extreme poverty, had sold, when they were very young, to such as they hoped would marry them when they grew up; if they did not, yet they must not sell them to strangers, but rather study how to make them amends for the disappointment; if they did, they must maintain them handsomely, *v.* 7–11.

Verses 12–21

I. A law concerning murder. He had lately said, *Thou shalt not kill*; 1. For the punishing of wilful murder (*v.* 12): *Whoso sheddeth man's blood, by man shall his blood be shed.* 2. For the relief of such as killed by accident, when a man, without intent of hurt to any, happens to kill another. In this case God provided cities of refuge for the protection of those whose infelicity it was, but not their fault, to occasion the death of another, *v.* 13. With us, who know no avengers of blood but the magistrates, the law itself is a sufficient sanctuary.

II. Concerning rebellious children. It is here made a capital crime, to be punished with death, for children either, 1. To strike their parents (*v.* 15). Or, 2. To curse their parents (*v.* 17). The undutiful behaviour of children towards their parents is a very great provocation to God our common Father; and, if men do not punish it, he will.

III. Here is a law against man-stealing (*v.* 16): *He that steals a man* (that is, a person, man, woman, or child), with design to sell him to the Gentiles (for no Israelite would buy him), was adjudged to death by this statute.

IV. Care is here taken that satisfaction be made for hurt done to a person, though death do not ensue, *v.* 18, 19. He that did the hurt must be accountable for damages, and pay, not only for the cure, but for the loss of time.

V. Direction is given what should be done if a servant died by his master's correction. If he died under his hand, he should be punished for his cruelty, at the discretion of the judges, upon consideration of circumstances, *v.* 20.

Verses 22–36

I. The particular care which the law took of women with child, that no hurt should be done them which might occasion their miscarrying. On this occasion comes in that general law of retaliation which our Saviour refers to, Matt. v. 38, *An eye for an eye*. Now, 1. The execution of this law is not hereby put into the hands of private persons. The tradition of the elders seems to have put this corrupt gloss upon it, in opposition to which our Saviour commands us to forgive injuries, and not to meditate revenge, Matt. v. 39. 2. God often executes it in the course of his providence, making the punishment, in many cases, to answer to the sin, as Judges i. 7; Isa. xxxiii. 1; Hab. ii. 13; Matt. xxvi. 52. 3. Magistrates ought to have an eye to this rule in punishing offenders, and doing right to those that are injured. Consideration must be had of the nature, quality, and degree of the wrong done, that reparation may be made to the party injured, and others deterred from doing the like.

II. The care God took of servants. If their masters maimed them, though it was only striking out a tooth, that should be their discharge, *v.* 26, 27.

III. *Does God take care for oxen?* Yes, it appears by the following laws in this chapter that he does, *for our sakes*, 1 Cor. ix. 9, 10. The Israelites are here directed what to do,

1. In case of hurt done by oxen, or any other brute-creature. (1) As an instance of God's care of the life of man. If an ox killed any man, woman, or child, the ox was to be *stoned* (*v.* 28). Thus God would keep up in the minds of his people a rooted abhorrence of the sin of murder and every thing that was barbarous. (2) To make men careful that none of their cattle might do hurt, but that, by all means possible, mischief might be prevented.

2. In case of hurt done to oxen, or other cattle. (1) If they fall into a pit, and perish there, he that opened the pit must make good the loss, *v.* 33, 34. Mischief done in malice is the great transgression; but mischief done through negligence is not without fault. (2) If cattle fight, and one kill another, the owners shall equally share in the loss, *v.* 35. In the wilderness where they lay closely encamped, and had their flocks and herds among them, such mischiefs as these last mentioned were likely enough to occur.

CHAPTER 22

The laws of this chapter relate, I. To the eighth commandment, concerning theft (ver. 1–4), trespass by cattle (ver. 5), damage by fire (ver. 6), trusts (ver. 7–13), borrowing cattle (ver. 14, 15), or money, ver. 25–27. II. To the seventh commandment. Against fornication (ver. 16, 17), bestiality, ver. 19. III. To the first table, forbidding witchcraft (ver. 18), idolatry, ver. 20. Commanding to offer the firstfruits, ver. 29, 30. IV. To the poor, ver. 21–24. V. To the civil government, ver. 28. VI. To the peculiarity of the Jewish nation, ver. 31.

Verses 1–6

Here are the laws,

I. Concerning theft, which are these:—1. If a man steal any cattle (in which the wealth of those times chiefly consisted), and they be found in his custody, he must restore double, *v.* 4. 2. If he had killed or sold the sheep or ox he had stolen, and thereby persisted in his crime, he must restore *five oxen for an ox, and four sheep for a sheep* (*v.* 1) 3. If he was not able to make restitution, he must be sold for a slave, *v.* 3. 4. If a thief broke a house in the night, and was killed in the doing of it, his blood was upon his own head.

II. Concerning trespass, *v.* 5. He that wilfully put his cattle into his neighbour's field must make restitution of the best of his own.

III. Concerning damage done by fire, *v.* 6. He that designed only the burning of thorns might become accessory to the burning of corn, and should not be held guiltless. Men must suffer for their carelessness, as well as for their malice.

Verses 7–15

I. Concerning trusts, *v.* 7–13. If a man deliver goods, and if a special confidence be reposed in the person they are lodged with, in case these goods be stolen or lost, perish or be damaged, if it appear that it was not by any fault of the trustee, the owner must stand to the loss, otherwise he that has been false to his trust must be compelled to make satisfaction. This teaches us, 1. It is unjust and base, and that which all the world cries shame on, to betray a trust. 2. That there is such a general failing of truth and justice upon earth as gives too much occasion to suspect men's honesty whenever it is their interest to be dishonest. The religion of an oath is very ancient, and a plain indication of the universal belief of a God, and a providence, and a judgment to come.

II. Concerning loans, *v.* 14, 15. If a man (suppose) lent his team to his neighbour, if the owner was with it, or was to receive profit for the loan of it, whatever harm befell the cattle the owner must stand to the loss of: but if the owner was so kind to the borrower as to lend it to him gratis, then, if any harm happened, the borrower must make it good.

Verses 16–24

I. A law that he who debauched a young woman should be obliged to marry her, v. 16, 17. This law puts an honour upon marriage and shows likewise how improper a thing it is that children should marry without their parents' consent.

II. A law which makes witchcraft a capital crime, v. 18.

III. Unnatural abominations are here made capital; such beasts in the shape of men as are guilty of them are unfit to live (v. 19): *Whosoever lies with a beast shall die.*

IV. Idolatry is also made capital, v. 20.

V. A caution against oppression. Because those who were empowered to punish other crimes were themselves most in danger of this, God takes the punishing of it into his own hands.

1. Strangers must not be abused (v. 21), not wronged in judgment by the magistrates, not imposed upon in contracts, nor must any advantage be taken of their ignorance or necessity; no, nor must they be taunted, trampled upon, treated with contempt, or upbraided with being strangers. Note, (1) Humanity is one of the laws of religion. Those that are strangers to us are known to God, and he preserves them, Ps. cxlvi. 9. (2) Those that profess religion should study to oblige strangers, that they may thereby recommend religion.

2. Widows and fatherless must not be abused (v. 22): *You shall not afflict them,* that is, You shall comfort and assist them. Their condition must be considered, who have lost those that should deal for them, and protect them. It is a great comfort to those who are injured and oppressed by men that they have a God to go to who will do more than *give them the hearing.*

Verses 25–31

Here is, I. A law against extortion in lending. This law, in the strictness of it, seems to have been peculiar to the Jewish state; but, in the equity of it, it obliges us to show mercy to those of whom we might take advantage, and to be content to share, in loss as well as profit. It seems as lawful to receive interest for my money, which another takes pains with and improves, but runs the hazard of, in trade, as it is to receive rent for my land, which another takes pains with and improves, but runs the hazard of, in husbandry. They must not take a poor man's bed-clothes in pawn; but, if they did, must restore them by bed-time, v. 26, 27.

II. A law against the contempt of authority (v. 28): *Thou shalt not revile the gods,* that is, the *judges* and *magistrates,* for their executing these laws; they must do their duty, whoever suffer by it.

III. A law concerning the offering of their first-fruits to God, v. 29, 30. It was appointed before (ch. xiii.), and it is here repeated: *The firstborn of thy sons shalt thou give unto me*; and much more reason have we to give ourselves, and all we have, to God, who *spared not his own Son, but delivered him up for us all.* The first ripe of their corn they must not delay to offer. Let not young people delay to offer to God the first-fruits of their time and strength.

IV. A distinction put between the Jews and all other people: *You shall be holy men unto me*; and one mark of that honourable distinction is appointed in their diet, which was, that they should not *eat any flesh that was torn of beasts* (v. 31), not only because it was unwholesome, but because it was paltry to eat the leavings of the beasts of prey.

CHAPTER 23

This chapter continues and concludes the acts that passed in the first session (if I may so call it) upon Mount Sinai. Here are, I. Some laws relating especially to the ninth commandment, against bearing false witness (ver. 1), and giving false judgment, ver. 2, 3, 6–8. Also a law of doing good to our enemies (ver. 4, 5), and not oppressing strangers, ver. 9. II. Some laws peculiar to the Jew. The sabbatical year (ver. 10, 11), the three annual feasts (ver. 14–17), with some laws pertaining thereto. III. Gracious promises of the completing of the mercy God had begun for them, upon condition of their obedience. That God would conduct them through the wilderness (ver. 20–24), that he would prosper all they had (ver. 25, 26), that he would put them in possession of Canaan, ver. 27–31. But they must not mingle themselves with the nations, ver. 32, 33.

Verses 1–9

I. Cautions concerning judicial proceedings.

1. The witnesses are here cautioned that they neither occasion an innocent man to be indicted, by raising a false report of him, nor assist in the prosecution of an innocent man, by *putting their hand* in swearing as witnesses against him, v. 1. Bearing false witness has in it all the guilt of lying, perjury, malice, theft, murder. There is scarcely any one act of wickedness that a man can possibly be guilty of which has in it a greater complication of villainies than this has. Yet the former part of this caution is to be extended to common conversation; so that slandering and backbiting are a species of falsewitness-bearing. A man's reputation lies as much at the mercy of every company as his estate or life does at the mercy of a judge or jury; so that he who raises, or spreads, a false report against his neighbour, sins as much against the laws of truth, justice, and charity, as a false witness does.

2. The judges are here cautioned not to pervert judgment. (1) They might not be overruled, either by might or multitude, to go against their consciences in giving judgment, v. 2. The junior upon the bench voted first, that he might not be swayed nor overruled by the authority of the senior. We must enquire what we ought to do, not what the majority do; because we must be judged by our Master, not by our fellow-servants, and it is too great a compliment to be willing to go to hell for company. (2) They must not pervert judgment, no, not in favour of a poor man, v. 3. Let them not therefore fare the worse for being poor. They must dread the thoughts of assisting or abetting a bad cause (v. 7). Judges themselves are accountable to the great judge. They must not oppress a stranger, v. 9. Though aliens might not inherit lands among them, yet they must have justice done them, must peaceably enjoy their own, and be redressed if they were wronged, though they were strangers to the commonwealth of Israel.

II. Commands concerning neighbourly kindnesses. We must be ready to do all good offices, as there is occasion, for anybody, yea even for those that have done us ill offices, v. 4, 5. The command of loving our enemies, is not only a *new,* but an *old* commandment, Prov. xxv. 21, 22. Infer hence, 1. If we must do this kindness for an enemy, much more for a friend. 2. If it be wrong not to prevent our enemy's loss and damage, how much worse is it to occasion harm and loss to him, or anything he has. 3. If we must bring back our neighbours' cattle when they go astray, much more must we endeavour, by prudent admonitions and instructions, to bring back our neighbours themselves, when they go astray in any sinful path, see Jam. v. 19, 20. And, if we must endeavour to help up a fallen ass, much more should we endeavour to help up a sinking spirit, *saying to those that are of a fearful heart, Be strong.*

Verses 10–19

Here is, I. The institution of the sabbatical year, v. 10, 11. Every seventh year the land was to rest;

they must not plough nor sow it at the beginning of the year, and then they could not expect any great harvest at the end of the year. Now this was designed, 1. To show what a plentiful land that was into which God was bringing them. 2. To remind them of their dependence upon God their great landlord, and their obligation to use the fruit of their land as he should direct. Afterwards we find that their disobedience to this command was a forfeiture of the promises, 2 Chron. xxxvi. 21. 3. To teach them a confidence in the divine Providence.

II. The repetition of the law of the fourth commandment concerning the weekly sabbath, *v.* 12. Some have endeavoured to take away the observance of the sabbath, by pretending that every day must be a sabbath day.

III. All manner of respect to the gods of the heathen is here strictly forbidden, *v.* 13. A general caution is prefixed to this, which has reference to all these precepts: *In all things that I have said unto you, be circumspect.*

IV. Their solemn religious attendance on God in the place which he should choose is here strictly required, *v.* 14–17. Thrice a year all their males must come together in a holy convocation. They must come together *before the Lord* (*v.* 17) to pay their homage to him. They must not *appear before God empty, v.* 15. Some free-will offering or other they must bring, and, as they were not allowed to come empty-handed, so we must not come to worship God empty-hearted; our souls must be filled with grace, with pious and devout affections, holy desires towards him, and dedications of ourselves to him. The passover, pentecost, and feast of tabernacles, in spring, summer, and autumn, were the three times appointed for their attendance.

V. Some particular directions are here given about the three feasts, though not so fully as afterwards. 1. As to the passover, it was not to be offered with leavened bread, nor was the fat of it to remain until the morning, lest it should become offensive, *v.* 18. 2. At the feast of pentecost, when they were to begin their harvest, they must bring *the first of their first-fruits* to God, by the pious presenting of which the whole harvest was sanctified, *v.* 19. 3. At the feast of *ingathering, as it is called* (*v.* 16), they must give God thanks for the harvest-mercies they had received, and must depend upon him for the next harvest, and must not think to receive benefit by that superstitious usage of some of the Gentiles, who, it is said, at the end of their harvest, *seethed a kid in its dam's milk,* and sprinkled that milk-potage, in a magical way, upon their gardens and fields, to make them more fruitful next year.

Verses 20–33

Three gracious promises are here made to Israel, to engage them to their duty and encourage them in it.

I. It is here promised that they should be guided and kept in their way through the wilderness to the land of promise: *Behold, I send an angel before thee* (*v.* 20), *my angel* (*v.* 23), a created angel, say some, a minister of God's providence, employed in conducting and protecting the camp of Israel. Others suppose it to be the Son of God, the angel of the covenant; and we may as well suppose him God's messenger, and the church's Redeemer, before his incarnation, as *the Lamb slain from the foundation of the world.* It is promised that this blessed angel should *keep them in the way.* It is also promised that he should bring them into the place which God had not only designed but prepared for them: and thus Christ has prepared a place for his followers.

II. It is promised that they should have a comfortable settlement in the land of Canaan. Observe, 1. How reasonable the conditions of this promise are—

only that they should serve their own God, who was indeed the only true God. 2. How rich the particulars of this promise are. (1) The comfort of their food. He shall *bless thy bread and thy water.* (2) The continuance of their health: "*I will take sickness away,* either prevent it or remove it." (3) The increase of their wealth. Their cattle should not be barren. (4) The prolonging of their lives to old age: "*The number of thy days I will fulfil,* and they shall not be cut off in the midst by untimely deaths." Thus hath godliness the *promise of the life that now is.*

III. It is promised that they should conquer and subdue their enemies, the present occupants of the land of Canaan, who must be driven out to make room for them. Hosts of hornets made way for the hosts of Israel; such mean creatures can God make use of for the chastising of his people's enemies, as in the plagues of Egypt. When God pleases, hornets can drive out Canaanites, as well as lions could, Josh. xxiv. 12. The precept annexed to this promise is that they should not make any friendship, nor have any familiarity, with idolaters, *v.* 32, 33. Idolaters must not so much as sojourn in their land, unless they renounced their idolatry. Note, Those that would be kept from bad courses must keep from bad company.

CHAPTER 24

I. Moses comes down to the people, acquaints them with the laws he had received, and takes their consent to those laws (ver. 3), writes the laws, and reads them to the people, who repeat their consent (ver. 4–7), and then by sacrifice, and the sprinkling of blood, ratifies the covenant between them and God, ver. 5, 6, 8. II. He returns to God again, to receive further directions. When he was dismissed from his former attendance, he was ordered to attend again, ver. 1, 2. He did so with seventy of the elders, to whom God made a discovery of his glory, ver. 9–11. Moses is ordered up into the mount (ver. 12, 13); the rest are ordered down to the people, ver. 14. The cloud of glory is seen by all the people on the top of mount Sinai (ver. 15–17), and Moses is there with God forty days and forty nights, ver. 18.

Verses 1–8

Moses is directed to bring Aaron and his sons, and the seventy elders of Israel, that they might be witnesses of the glory of God, and that their testimony might confirm the people's faith. They must all be very reverent: *Worship you afar off, v.* 1.

In the following verses, we have the solemn covenant made between God and Israel, and the exchanging of the ratifications.

I. Moses told the people the words of the Lord, *v.* 3. He laid before them all the precepts, general and particular, in the foregoing chapters; and fairly put it to them whether they were willing to submit to these laws or no.

II. The people unanimously consented to the terms proposed, without reservation or exception: *All the words which the Lord hath said will we do.*

This is the tenor of the covenant. That, if they would observe the foregoing precepts, God would perform the foregoing promises. "Obey, and be happy."

1. How it was engrossed in the book of the covenant: *Moses wrote the words of the Lord* (*v.* 4)

2. How it was sealed by the blood of the covenant, that Israel might receive strong consolations from the ratifying of God's promises to them, and might lie under strong obligations from the ratifying of their promises to God. The covenant must be made by sacrifice (Ps. l. 5), because, since man has sinned, and forfeited his Creator's favour, there can be no fellowship by covenant till there be first friendship and atonement by sacrifice.

(1) In preparation therefore [1] Moses builds an altar, to the honour of God, which was principally intended in all the altars that were built, and which was the first thing to be looked at in the covenant they were now to seal. [2] He erects twelve pillars, according to the number of the tribes. These were

to represent the people, the other party to the covenant; and we may suppose that they were set up against the altar, and that Moses, as mediator, passed to and fro between them. Probably each tribe set up and knew its own pillar, and their elders stood by it. [3] He appointed sacrifices to be offered upon the altar (v. 5), burnt-offerings and peace-offerings, which yet were designed to be expiatory.

(2) Preparation being thus made, the ratifications were very solemnly exchanged. [1] The blood of the sacrifice which the people offered was (part of it) sprinkled upon the altar (v. 6), which signifies the people's dedicating themselves, their lives, and beings, to God, and to his honour. [2] The blood of the sacrifice which God owned and accepted was (the remainder of it) sprinkled either upon the people themselves (v. 8) or upon the pillars that represented them, which signified God's graciously conferring his favour upon them. Thus our Lord Jesus, the Mediator of the new covenant (of whom Moses was a type), having offered up himself a sacrifice upon the cross, that his blood might be indeed the blood of the covenant, sprinkles it upon the altar in his intercession (Heb. ix. 12), and sprinkles it upon his church by his word and ordinances and the influences and operations of the Spirit of promise, by whom we are sealed. He himself seemed to allude to this solemnity when, in the institution of the Lord's supper, he said, *This cup is the New Testament* (or covenant) *in my blood.* Compare with this, Heb. ix. 19, 20.

Verses 9–11

God here gives to their representatives some special tokens of his favour to them, and admits them nearer to him than they could have expected. Observe, 1. They saw the God of Israel (v. 10), that is, they had some glimpse of his glory, in light and fire, though they saw *no manner of similitude*, and his being *no man hath seen nor can see*, 1 Tim. vi. 16. They saw the place where the God of Israel stood (so the LXX.), something that came near a similitude, but was not; whatever they saw, it was certainly something of which no image or picture could be made, and yet enough to satisfy them that God was with them of a truth. Nothing is described but that which was under his feet; for our conceptions of God are all below him, and fall infinitely short of being adequate. At the bottom of the brightness, and as the footstool or pedestal of it, they saw a most rich and splendid pavement, as it had been of sapphires, azure or sky-coloured. 2. *Upon the nobles* (or elders) *of Israel, he laid not his hand*, v. 11. Though they were men, the dazzling splendour of his glory was so moderated that they were able to bear it. 3. *They saw God, and did eat and drink.* They had not only their lives preserved, but their vigour, courage, and comfort; it cast no damp upon their joy, but rather increased and elevated it.

Verses 12–18

The public ceremony of sealing the covenant being over, Moses is called up to receive further instructions. I. He is called up into the mount, and there he remains six days at some distance. "Come up, and *I will give thee a law, that thou mayest teach them.*" Having received these orders, 1. He appointed Aaron and Hur to be as lords-justices in his absence, to keep the peace and good order in the congregation, v. 14. 2. He took Joshua up with him into the mount, v. 13. Joshua was his minister, and it would be a satisfaction to him to have him with him as a companion, during the six days that he tarried in the mount, before God called to him. Joshua was to be his successor, and therefore thus he was honoured before the people, above the rest of the elders, that they might afterwards the more readily take him for their governor; and

thus he was prepared for service, by being trained up in communion with God. 3. A cloud covered the mount six days, a visible token of God's special presence there. During these six days Moses stayed waiting upon the mountain for a call into the presence-chamber, v. 15, 16. II. He is called up into a cloud on the seventh day, probably on the sabbath day, v. 16. Now, 1. The thick cloud opened in the sight of all Israel, and the glory of the Lord broke forth *like devouring fire*, v. 17. 2. The entrance of Moses into the cloud was very wonderful: *Moses went into the midst of the cloud*, v. 18, sure that he who called him would protect him. 3. His continuance in the cloud was no less wonderful; he was there *forty days and forty nights*. When Moses was called *into the midst of the cloud* he left Joshua without, who continued to eat and drink daily while he waited for Moses's return, but thenceforward Moses fasted.

CHAPTER 25

At this chapter begins an account of the orders and instructions God gave to Moses upon the mount for the erecting and furnishing of a tabernacle to the honour of God. We have here, I. Orders given for a collection to be made among the people for this purpose, ver. 1–9. II. Particular instructions, 1. Concerning the ark of the covenant, ver. 10–22. 2. The table of showbread, ver. 23–30. 3. The golden candlestick, ver. 31, &c.

Verses 1–9

We may suppose that when Moses went into the midst of the cloud, and abode there so long, he saw and heard very glorious things relating to the upper world, but there were things which it was not lawful nor possible to utter.

In these verses God tells Moses his intention in general, that the children of Israel should build him a sanctuary, for he designed to *dwell among them* (v. 8). God had chosen the people of Israel. As their King, he had already given them laws for the government of themselves, and their dealings one with another, with some general rules for religious worship. I. He orders a royal palace to be set up among them for himself, here called *a sanctuary*, or *holy place*, or *habitation*, of which it is said (Jer. xvii. 12), *A glorious high throne from the beginning is the place of our sanctuary.* This sanctuary is to be considered, 1. As ceremonial, consonant to the other institutions of that dispensation, which consisted in carnal ordinances (Heb. ix. 10); hence it is called a *worldly sanctuary*, Heb. ix. 1. (1) There he manifested his presence among them, a sign or token of his presence, that, while they had that in the midst of them, they might never again ask, *Is the Lord among us or not?* And, because in the wilderness they dwelt in tents, even this royal palace was ordered to be a tabernacle too, that it might move with them. (2) There he ordered his subjects to attend him with their homage and tribute. Thither they must bring their sacrifices, and there all Israel must meet, to pay their joint respects to the God of Israel. 2. As typical; the holy places made with hands were the *figures of the true*, Heb. ix. 24. The body of Christ, in and by which he made atonement, was the *greater and more perfect tabernacle*, Heb. ix. 11. The *Word was made flesh, and dwelt among us*, as in a tabernacle. II. When Moses was to erect this palace, it was requisite that he should first be instructed where he must have the materials, and where he must have the model. 1. The people must furnish him with the materials, not by a tax imposed upon them, but by a voluntary contribution. (1) *Speak unto the children of Israel that they bring me an offering.* Since we live upon him, we must live to him.

(2) This offering must be given willingly, and with the heart. We should ask, not only, "What must we do?" but, "What may we do for God?"

(3) The particulars are here mentioned which they must offer (*v.* 3–7), all of them things that there would be occasion for in the tabernacle. Some observe that here was gold, silver, and brass, provided, but no iron; that is the military metal, and this was to be a house of peace.

2. God himself would furnish him with the model: *According to all that I show thee, v.* 9.

Verses 10–22

The first thing which is here ordered to be made is the ark with its appurtenances, the furniture of the most holy place, and the special token of God's presence, for which the tabernacle was erected to be the receptacle.

I. The ark itself was a chest, or coffer, in which the two tables of the law were to be honourably deposited, and carefully kept. If the Jewish cubit was, as some learned men compute, three inches longer than our half-yard (twenty-one inches in all), this chest or cabinet was about fifty-two inches long, thirty-one broad, and thirty-one deep. It was overlaid within and without with thin plates of gold. It had a crown, or cornice, of gold, round it, with rings and staves to carry it with; and in it he must put the testimony, *v.* 10–16. The tables of the law are called the *testimony* because God did in them testify his will. The gospel of Christ is also called a testimony or witness, Matt. xxiv. 14. It is observable, 1. That the tables of the law were carefully preserved in the ark for the purpose, to teach us to make much of the word of God, and to hide it in our hearts, in our innermost thoughts, as the ark was placed in the holy of holies. 2. That this ark was the chief token of God's presence, which teaches us that the first and great evidence and assurance of God's favour is the putting of his law in the heart. God dwells where that rules, Heb. viii. 10. 3. That provision was made for the carrying of this ark about with them in all their removals, which intimates to us that, wherever we go, we should take our religion along with us, always bearing about with us the love of the Lord Jesus, and his law.

II. The mercy-seat was the covering of the ark or chest, made of solid gold, exactly to fit the dimensions of the ark, *v.* 17, 21.

III. The cherubim of gold were fixed to the mercy-seat, and of a piece with it, and spread their wings over it, *v.* 18. It is supposed that these cherubim were designed to represent the holy angels, who always attended the *shechinah*, or divine Majesty, not by any effigies of an angel, but some emblem of the angelical nature, probably some one of those four faces spoken of, Ezek. i. 10. Whatever the faces were, they looked one towards another, and both downward towards the ark, while their wings were stretched out so as to touch one another. The apostle calls them *cherubim of glory shadowing the mercy-seat*, Heb. ix. 5. God is said to dwell *between the cherubim*, on the mercy-seat (Ps. lxxx. 1), and thence he here promises, for the future, to meet with Moses, and to *commune with him, v.* 22. In allusion to this mercy-seat, we are said to come boldly to *the throne of grace* (Heb. iv. 16); for we *are not under the law*, which is covered, *but under grace*, which is displayed; its wings are stretched out, and we are invited to come under the shadow of them, Ruth ii. 12.

Verses 23–30

Here is, 1. A table ordered to be made of wood overlaid with gold, which was to stand, not in the holy of holies (nothing was in that but the ark with its appurtenances), but in the outer part of the tabernacle, called the *sanctuary*, or *holy place*, Heb.

ix. 2, 23, &c. There must also be the usual furniture of the sideboard, dishes and spoons, &c., and all *of gold, v.* 29. 2. This table was to be always spread, and furnished with the show-bread (*v.* 30) or *bread of faces*, twelve loaves, one for each tribe, set in two rows, six in a row; see the law concerning them, Lev. xxiv. 6, &c. In the royal palace it was fit that there should be a royal table. Some make the twelve loaves to represent the twelve tribes. As the ark signified God's being present with them, so the twelve loaves signified their being presented to God. This bread was designed to be, (1) A thankful acknowledgment of God's goodness to them, in giving them their daily bread, manna in the wilderness, where he prepared a table for them, and, in Canaan, the corn of the land. Christ has taught us to pray every day for the bread of the day. (2) A token of their communion with God. This bread on God's table being made of the same corn with the bread on their own tables, God and Israel did, as it were, eat together, as a pledge of friendship and fellowship; he supped with them, and they with him. (3) A type of the spiritual provision which is made in the church, by the gospel of Christ, for all that are made priests to our God. *In our Father's house there is bread enough and to spare*, a loaf for every tribe.

Verses 31–40

I. The next thing ordered to be made for the furnishing of God's palace was a rich stately candlestick, all of pure gold. The particular directions here given concerning it show, 1. That it was a great ornament; it had many branches drawn from the main shaft, which had not only their bowls (to put the oil and the kindled wick in) for necessity, but knops and flowers for ornament. 2. That it was very convenient, and admirably contrived both to scatter the light and to keep the tabernacle clean from smoke and snuffs. 3. That it was very significant. The tabernacle had no windows by which to let in the light of the day, all its light was candle-light. Yet God left not himself without witness, nor them without instruction; the commandment was a lamp, and the law a light, and the prophets were branches from that lamp, which gave light in their several ages to the Old Testament church. The church is still dark, as the tabernacle was, in comparison with what it will be in heaven; but the word of God is the candlestick, *a light shining in a dark place* (2 Pet. i. 19), and a dark place indeed the world would be without it. The Spirit of God, in his various gifts and graces, is compared to the *seven lamps* which *burn before the throne*, Rev. iv. 5. The churches are golden candlesticks, the lights of the world, *holding forth the word of life* as the candlestick does the light, Phil. ii. 15, 16. Ministers are to light the lamps, and snuff them (*v.* 37), by opening the scriptures.

II. There is in the midst of these instructions an express caution given to Moses, to take heed of varying from his model: *Make them after the pattern shown thee, v.* 40.

CHAPTER 26

Moses here receives instructions, I. Concerning the inner curtains of the tent or tabernacle, and the coupling of those curtains, ver. 1–6. II. Concerning the outer curtains which were of goats' hair, to strengthen the former, ver. 7–13. III. Concerning the case or cover which was to secure it from the weather, ver. 14. IV. Concerning the boards which were to be reared up to support the curtains, with their bars and sockets, ver. 15–30. V. The partition between the holy place and the most holy, ver. 31–35. VI. The veil for the door, ver. 36, 37.

Verses 1–6

I. The house must be a *tabernacle* or *tent*. God manifested his presence among them thus in a tabernacle, 1. In compliance with their present condition in the wilderness, that they might have him with them wherever they went. 2. That it might represent the state of God's church in this world, it is a *tabernacle-state*, Ps. xv. 1. *We have here no continuing city*; being strangers in this world, and travellers towards a better, we shall never be fixed till we come to heaven.

II. The curtains of the tabernacle must correspond to a divine pattern. 1. They were to be very rich, the best of the kind, *fine twined linen*; and colours very pleasing, *blue*, and *purple*, and *scarlet*. 2. They were to be embroidered with cherubim (*v.* 1), to intimate that the angels of God pitch their tents round about the church, Ps. xxxiv. 7. 3. There were to be two hangings, five breadths in each, sewed together, and the two hangings coupled together with golden clasps, or tacks, so that it might be all one tabernacle, *v.* 6. Thus the churches of Christ and the saints, though they are many, are yet one, being *fitly joined together* in holy love, and by the *unity of the Spirit*, so growing into one *holy temple* in the Lord, Eph. ii. 21, 22; iv. 16.

Verses 7–14

Moses is here ordered to make a double covering for the tabernacle, that it might not rain in. 1. There was to be a covering of hair camlet curtains, which were somewhat larger every way than the inner curtains, because they were to enclose them, and probably were stretched out at some little distance from them, *v.* 7, &c. These were coupled together with brass clasps. 2. Over this there was to be another covering, and that a double one (*v.* 14), one of *rams' skins dyed red*, probably dressed with the wool on; another of *badgers' skins*, so we translate it, but it should rather seem to have been some strong sort of leather (but very fine), for we read of the best sort of shoes being made of it, Ezek. xvi. 10. Now observe here that the outside of the tabernacle was coarse and rough, the beauty of it was in the inner curtains. Those in whom God dwells must labour to be better than they seem to be. Let our adorning be that of the hidden man of the heart, which God values, 1 Pet. iii. 4.

Verses 15–30

Very particular directions are here given about the boards of the tabernacle, which were to bear up the curtains, as the stakes of a tent which had need to be strong, Isa. liv. 2. These boards had tenons which fell into the mortises that were made for them in silver bases. God took care to have every thing strong, as well as fine, in his tabernacle. The boards were coupled together with gold rings at top and bottom (*v.* 24), and kept firm with bars that ran through golden staples in every board (*v.* 26), and the boards and bars were all richly gilded, *v.* 29.

Verses 31–37

Two veils are here ordered to be made, 1. One for a partition between the holy place and the most holy, which not only forbade any to enter, but forbade them so much as to look into the holiest of all, *v.* 31, 33. Under this dispensation, divine grace was veiled, but now we behold it with open face, 2 Cor. iii. 18. The apostle tells us (Heb. ix. 8, 9) what was the meaning of this veil; it intimated that the ceremonial law *could not make the comers thereunto perfect*, nor would the observance of it bring men to heaven; the *way into the holiest of all was not made manifest while the first tabernacle was standing; life and immortality* lay concealed till they were *brought to light by the gospel*, which was therefore signified by the rending of this veil at the death of Christ, Matt. xxvii. 51. We have now *boldness to enter into the holiest*, in all acts of devotion, *by the blood of Jesus*, yet such as obliges us to a holy reverence and a humble sense of our distance. 2. Another veil was for the outer door of the tabernacle, *v.* 36, 37. Through this first veil the priests went in every day to minister in the holy place, but not the people, Heb. ix. 6. This veil, which was all the defence the tabernacle had against thieves and robbers, might easily be broken through, for it could be neither locked nor barred, and the abundance of wealth in the tabernacle, one would think, might be a temptation; but by leaving it thus exposed, (1) The priests and Levites would be so much the more obliged to keep a strict watch upon it, and, (2) God would show his care of his church on earth, though it is weak and defenceless, and continually exposed. A curtain shall be (if God please to make it so) as strong a defence to his house as gates of brass and bars of iron.

CHAPTER 27

In this chapter directions are given, I. Concerning the brazen altar for burnt-offerings, ver. 1–8. II. Concerning the court of the tabernacle, with the hangings of it, ver. 9–19. III. Concerning oil for the lamp, ver. 20, 21.

Verses 1–8

As God intended in the tabernacle to manifest his presence among his people, so there they were to pay their devotions to him, not in the tabernacle itself (into that only the priests entered as God's domestic servants), but in the court before the tabernacle. There an altar was ordered to be set up, to which they must bring their sacrifices. Moses is here directed about, 1. The dimensions of it; it was square, *v.* 1. 2. The horns of it (*v.* 2), which were for ornament and for use; the sacrifices were *bound with cords to the horns of the altar*, and to them malefactors fled for refuge. 3. The materials; it was of wood overlaid with brass, *v.* 1, 2. 4. The appurtenances of it (*v.* 3), which were all of brass. 5. The grate, which was let into the hollow of the altar, about the middle of it, in which the fire was kept, and the sacrifice burnt. 6. The staves with which it must be carried, *v.* 6, 7. And, *lastly*, he is referred to the pattern shown him, *v.* 8.

Now this brazen altar was a type of Christ dying to make atonement for our sins. To the horns of this altar poor sinners fly for refuge when justice pursues them, and they are safe in virtue of the sacrifice there offered.

Verses 9–19

Before the tabernacle there was to be a court or yard, enclosed with hangings of the finest linen that was used for tents. This court, according to the common computation of cubits, was fifty yards long, and twenty-five broad. Pillars were set up at convenient distances, in sockets of brass, the pillars filleted with silver, and silver tenter-hooks in them, on which the linen hangings were fastened: the hanging which served for the gate was finer than the rest, *v.* 16. Thanks be to God, now, under the gospel, the enclosure is taken down. God's will is that men *pray everywhere*; and there is room for all that in every place call on the name of Jesus Christ.

Verses 20–21

Here is an order given for the keeping of the lamps constantly burning in it; in every candlestick there should be a burning and shining light; candlesticks without candles are as *wells without water* or as *clouds without rain*. Now, 1. The people were to provide the oil. 2. The priests were to light the lamps, and to tend them; thus it is the work of ministers, by the preaching and expounding of the scriptures (which are as a lamp), to enlighten the church, God's tabernacle upon earth.

CHAPTER 28

In this and the following chapter care is taken about the priests that were to minister in this holy place. In this chapter, I. God pitches upon the persons who should be his servants, ver. 1. II. He appoints their livery; answerable to the glory of the house which was now to be erected, ver. 2–5. 1. He appoints the garments of his head-servants, the high priest. (1) An ephod and girdle, ver. 6–14. (2) A breast-plate of judgment (ver. 15–29), in which must be put the urim and thummim, ver. 30. (3) The robe of the ephod, ver. 31–35. (4) The mitre, ver. 36–39. 2. The garments of the inferior priests, ver. 40–43. And these also were shadows of good things to come.

Verses 1–5

I. The priests nominated: *Aaron and his sons, v.* 1. Moses, who had hitherto officiated, and is therefore reckoned among the *priests of the Lord* (Ps. xcix. 6), had enough to do as their prophet to consult the oracle for them, and as their prince to judge among them; but was well pleased to see his brother Aaron invested in this office. Aaron, who had humbly served as a prophet to his younger brother Moses, and did not decline the office (*ch.* vii. 1), is now advanced to be a priest, a high priest, to God. Because it was requisite that those who ministered at the altar should give themselves wholly to the service, and because that which is everybody's work will soon come to be nobody's work, God here chose from among them one to be a family of priests, the father and his four sons; and from Aaron's loins descended all the priests of the Jewish church, of whom we read so often, both in the Old Testament and in the New.

II. The priests' garments appointed, *for glory and beauty, v.* 2. The garments appointed were, 1. Four which both the high priest and the inferior priests wore, namely, the linen breeches, the linen coat, the linen girdle which fastened it to them, and the bonnet or turban; that which the high priest wore is called *a mitre.* 2. Four more, which were peculiar to the high priest, namely, the ephod, with the curious girdle of it, the breast-plate of judgment, the long robe with the bells and pomegranates at the bottom of it, and the golden plate on his forehead. Our adorning, now under the gospel, is not to be of gold, and pearl, and costly array, but the *garments of salvation, and the robe of righteousness,* Isa. lxi. 10; Ps. cxxxii. 9, 16.

Verses 6–14

Directions are here given concerning the ephod, which was the outmost garment of the high priest. *Linen* ephods were worn by the inferior priests, 1 Sam. xxii. 18. Samuel wore one when he was a child (1 Sam ii. 18), and David when he danced before the ark (2 Sam. vi. 14); but this which the high priest only wore was called a *golden ephod,* because there was a great deal of gold woven into it. It was a short coat without sleeves, buttoned closely to him, with a curious girdle of the same stuff (*v.* 6–8); the shoulder-pieces were buttoned together with two precious stones set in gold, one on each shoulder, on which were engraven the names of the *children of Israel, v.* 9–12.

Verses 15–30

The most considerable of the ornaments of the high priest was this breast-plate, a rich piece of cloth, curiously wrought with gold and purple, &c., two spans long and a span broad, so that, being doubled, it was a span square, *v.* 16. This was fastened to the ephod with wreathen chains of gold (*v.* 13, 14, 22, &c.) both at top and bottom, so that *the breast-plate might not be loosed from the ephod, v.* 28. The ephod was the garment of service; the breast-plate of judgment was an emblem of honour: these two must by no means be separated. In this breast-plate,

I. The tribes of Israel were recommended to God's favour in twelve precious stones, *v.* 17–21, 29. Aaron was to bear their names for a *memorial before the Lord continually,* being *ordained for men,* to represent them in things pertaining to God, herein typifying our great high priest, who always appears in the presence of God for us. 1. Though the people were forbidden to come near, yet by the high priest, who had their names on his breast-plate, they entered into the holiest; so believers, even while they are here on this earth, not only *enter into the holiest,* but by faith are made to *sit with Christ in heavenly places,* Eph. ii. 6. 2. The name of each tribe was engraven in a precious stone, to signify how precious, in God's sight, believers are and how honourable, Isa. xliii. 4. They shall be his in the day he *makes up his jewels,* Mal. iii. 1. 3. The high priest had the names of the tribes both on his shoulders and on his breast, intimating both the power and the love with which our Lord Jesus intercedes for those that are his. He not only bears them up in his arms with an almighty strength, but he bears them *upon his heart, as the expression here is* (*v.* 29), *carries them in his bosom* (Isa. xl. 11), with the most tender affection.

II. The urim and thummim, by which the will of God was made known in doubtful cases, were put in this breast-plate, which is therefore called the *breast-plate of judgment, v.* 30. *Urim* and *thummim* signify *light* and *integrity*: I think the words may be read thus, *And thou shalt give,* or *add,* or *deliver, to the breastplate of judgment, the illuminations and perfections, and they shall be upon the heart of Aaron*; that is, "He shall be endued with a power of knowing and making known the mind of God in all difficult doubtful cases, relating either to the civil or ecclesiastical state of the nation." Their government was a theocracy: God was their King, the high priest was, under God, their ruler, the urim and thummim were his cabinet-council; probably Moses wrote upon the breast-plate, or wove into it, these words, *urim* and *thummim,* to signify that the high priest, having on him this breast-plate, and asking counsel of God in any emergency relating to the public, should be directed to take those measures, and give that advice, which God would own. The answer was given either by a voice from heaven or rather by an impulse upon the mind of the high priest, which last is perhaps intimated in that expression, *He shall bear the judgment of the children of Israel upon his heart.* This oracle was of great use to Israel; Joshua consulted it (Num. xxvii. 21), and, it is likely, the judges after him. It was lost in the captivity, and never regained after. But it was a shadow of good things to come, and the substance is Christ. He is our oracle, by him God in these last days makes known himself and his mind to us, Heb. i. 2; John i. 18. Divine revelation centres in him, and comes to us through him.

Verses 31–39

1. Direction given concerning *the robe of the ephod, v.* 31–35. This was next under the ephod, and reached down to the knees, and was without sleeves. The hole on the top, through which the head was put, was carefully bound about, that it might not tear in the putting on. Round the skirts of the robe were hung golden bells, and the representations of pomegranates made of yarn of divers colours. The pomegranates added to the beauty of the robe, and the sound of the bells gave notice to the people in the outer court when he went into the holy place to burn incense, that they might then apply themselves to the devotions at the same time. Some make the bells of the holy robe to typify the sound of the gospel of Christ in the world, giving notice of his entrance within the veil for us. The adding of the pomegranates, which are a fragrant fruit, denotes

the sweet savour of the gospel. 2. Concerning the golden plate fixed upon Aaron's forehead, on which must be engraven, *Holiness to the Lord* (v. 36, 37), Aaron must hereby be reminded that God is holy, and that his priests must be holy. Aaron must have this upon his forehead, that he may *bear the iniquity of the holy things* (v. 38), and that *they may be accepted before the Lord.* Herein he was a type of Christ, the great Mediator between God and man, through whom it is that we have to do with God. (1) Through him what is amiss in our services is pardoned. In many things we come short of our duty, so that we cannot but be conscious to ourselves of much iniquity cleaving even to our holy things. But Christ, our high priest, bears this iniquity, bears it for us so as to bear it from us, and through him it is forgiven to us and not laid to our charge. (2) Through him what is good is accepted; our persons, our performances, are pleasing to God upon the account of Christ's intercession, and not otherwise, 1 Pet. ii. 5. Having *such a high priest*, we come *boldly to the throne of grace*, Heb. iv. 14–16. 3. The rest of the garments are but named (v. 39). The embroidered coat of fine linen was the innermost of the priestly garments; it reached to the feet, and the sleeves to the wrists, and was bound to the body with a girdle or sash of needle-work. The mitre, or diadem, was of linen, such as kings anciently wore in the east, typifying the kingly office of Christ.

Verses 40–43

We have here, 1. Particular orders about the vestments of the inferior priests. They were to have coats, and girdles, and bonnets, of the same materials with those of the high priest; but there was a difference in shape between their bonnets and his mitre. Theirs, as his, were to be *for glory and beauty* (v. 40), yet all this glory was nothing compared with the glory of grace, this beauty nothing to the beauty of holiness, of which these holy garments were typical. 2. A general rule concerning the garments both of the high priest and of the inferior priests, that they were to be put upon them, at first, when they were consecrated, and then they were to wear them in all their ministrations, but not at other times (v. 43). To us these garments typify, (1) The righteousness of Christ; if we appear not before God in this, we shall *bear iniquity and die.* (2) *The armour of God* prescribed, Eph. vi. 13.

CHAPTER 29

Particular orders are given in this chapter, I. Concerning the consecration of the priests, and the sanctification of the altar, ver. 1–37. II. Concerning the daily sacrifice, ver. 38–41, to which gracious promises are annexed that God would own and bless them in all their services, ver. 42, &c.

Verses 1–37

I. The law concerning the consecration of Aaron and his sons to the priests' office.

1. The ceremonies wherewith it was to be done were very fully and particularly appointed, because nothing of this kind had been done before. Now,

(1) The work to be done was the consecrating of the persons whom God had chosen to be priests, by which they devoted and gave up themselves to the service of God and God declared his acceptance of them; and the people were made to know that they *glorified not themselves* to be made priests, but were *called of God*, Heb. v. 4, 5. Note, All that are to be employed for God are to be sanctified to him. The person must first be accepted, and then the performance.

(2) The person to do it was Moses, by God's appointment. By God's special appointment he now did the priest's work, and therefore that which was the priest's part of the sacrifice was here ordered to be his, v. 26.

(3) The place was at the *door of the tabernacle of meeting*, v. 4. They were consecrated at the door, for they were to be door-keepers.

(4) It was done with many ceremonies.

[1] They were to be washed (v. 4), signifying that those must be clean who *bear the vessels of the Lord*, Isa. lii. 11. Those that would *perfect holiness* must *cleanse themselves from all filthiness of flesh and spirit*, 2 Cor. vii. 1; Isa. i. 16–18.

[2] They were to be clothed with the holy garments (v. 5, 6, 8, 9), to signify that it was not sufficient for them to put away the pollutions of sin, but they must put on the graces of the Spirit, be *clothed with righteousness*, Ps. cxxxii. 9.

[3] The high priest was to be anointed with the *holy anointing oil* (v. 7), that the church might be filled and delighted with the sweet savour of his administrations and in token of the pouring out of the Spirit upon him, to qualify him for his work.

[4] Sacrifices were to be offered for them. The covenant of priesthood, as all other covenants, must be *made by sacrifice.*

First, There must be a sin-offering, to make atonement for them, v. 10–14. It was used as other sin-offerings were; only, whereas the flesh of other sin-offerings was eaten by the priests (Lev. x. 18), in token of the priest's taking away the sin of the people, this was appointed to be all burnt without the camp (v. 14), to signify the imperfection of the legal dispensation.

Secondly, There must be a burnt-offering, a ram wholly burnt, to the honour of God, in token of the dedication of themselves wholly to God and to his service, as living sacrifices, kindled with the fire and ascending in the flame of holy love, v. 15–18.

Thirdly, There must be a peace-offering; it is called the *ram of consecration*, because there was more in this peculiar to the occasion than in the other two. In the burnt-offering God had the glory of their priesthood, in this they had the comfort of it; and, in token of a mutual covenant between God and them, [i] The blood of the sacrifice was divided between God and them (v. 20, 21); part of the blood was *sprinkled upon the altar round about*, and part put upon them, upon their bodies (v. 20), and upon their garments, v. 21. The blood of Christ, and the graces of the Spirit, which constitute and complete the beauty of holiness, recommend us to God; we read of robes *made white with the blood of the lamb.* [ii] The *flesh of the sacrifice*, with the meat-offering annexed to it, was likewise divided between God and them, that (to speak with reverence) God and they might feast together, in token of friendship and fellowship. Their eating of the things wherewith *the atonement was made* signified their *receiving the atonement*, as the expression is (Rom. v. 11), their thankful acceptance of the benefit of it, and their joyful communion with God thereupon, which was the true intent and meaning of a feast upon a sacrifice.

2. The time that was to be spent in this consecration: *Seven days shalt thou consecrate them*, v. 35. Though all the ceremonies were performed on the first day, yet, (1) They were not to look upon their consecration as completed till the seven days' end, which put a distance between this and their former state, and obliged them to enter upon their work with a pause, giving them time to consider the weight and seriousness of it. (2) Every day of the seven, in this first consecration, a bullock was to be offered for a sin-offering (v. 36), which was to intimate to them, [1] That though atonement was made, and they had the comfort of it, yet they must still keep up a penitent sense of sin and often repeat the confession of it. [2] That those sacrifices which were thus offered day by day to make atonement could not make the *comers thereunto perfect*, for then they would have

ceased to be offered, as the apostle argues, Heb. x. 1, 2. They must therefore expect the *bringing in of a better hope*.

3. This consecration of the priests was a *shadow of good things to come*. (1) Our Lord Jesus is the great high-priest of our profession, clothed with the holy garments, even with glory and beauty, sanctified by his own blood, not that of bullocks and rams (Heb. ix. 12), *made perfect*, or consecrated, *through suffer-ings*, Heb. ii. 10. (2) All believers are spiritual priests, to offer spiritual sacrifices (1 Pet. ii. 5), washed in the blood of Christ. It is through Christ, the great sacri-fice, that they are dedicated to this service.

II. The consecration of the altar, which seems to have been coincident with that of the priests, and the sin-offerings which were offered every day for seven days together had reference to the altar as well as the priests, v. 36, 37. The altar was also *sanctified*, not only set apart itself to a sacred use, but made so holy as to *sanctify the gifts* that were offered upon it, Matt. xxiii. 19. Christ is our altar; for our sakes he sanctified himself, that we and our performances might be sanctified and recommended to God, John xvii. 19.

Verses 38–46

I. The daily service appointed. A lamb was to be offered upon the altar every morning, and a lamb every evening, each with a meat-offering, both made by fire, as a *continual burnt-offering throughout their generations*, v. 38–41. Now, 1. This typified the con-tinual intercession which Christ ever lives to make, in virtue of his satisfaction, for the continual sancti-fication of his church: though he offered himself *once for all*, yet that one offering thus becomes a continual offering. 2. This teaches us to offer up to God the spiritual sacrifices of prayer and praise every day, morning and evening, in humble acknowledg-ment of our dependence upon him and our obliga-tions to him. Prayer-time must be kept up as duly as meat-time.

II. Great and precious promises made of God's favour to Israel, and the tokens of his special presence with them. It is constancy in religion that brings in the comfort of it. If we do our part, God will do his, and will mark and fit that for himself which is in sincerity given up to him.

Chapter 30

Moses is, in this chapter, further instructed, I. Concerning the altar of incense, ver. 1–10. II. Concerning the ransom-money which the Israelites were to pay, when they were numbered, ver. 11–16. III. Concerning the laver of brass, which was set for the priests to wash in, ver. 17–21. IV. Concerning the making up of the anointing oil, and the use of it, ver. 22–33. V. Concerning the incense and perfume which were to be burned on the golden altar, ver. 34, &c.

Verses 1–10

I. The orders given concerning the altar of incense are, 1. That it was to be made of wood, and covered with gold, with horns at the corners, a golden cornice round it, with rings and staves of gold, for the con-venience of carrying it, *v.* 1–5. The measure of the altar of incense in Ezekiel's temple is double to what it is here (Ezek. xli. 22), and it is there called *an altar of wood*, and there is no mention of gold, to signify that the incense in gospel times should be spiritual, the worship plain, and the service of God enlarged. 2. That it was to be placed before the mercy-seat, which was within the veil, *v.* 6. For though he that ministered at the altar could not see the mercy-seat, the veil interposing, yet he must look towards it, and direct his incense that way, to teach us that though we cannot with our bodily eyes see the throne of grace, yet we must in prayer by faith set ourselves before it, direct our prayer, and look up. 3. That Aaron was

to burn sweet incense upon this altar, every morning and every evening, intended, not only to take away the ill smell of the flesh that was burnt daily on the brazen altar, but to show the acceptableness of his people's services. As by the offerings on the brazen altar satisfaction was made for what had been done displeasing to God, so, by the offering on this, what they did well was, as it were, recommended to the divine acceptance; for our two great concerns with God are to be acquitted from guilt and accepted as righteous in his sight.

II. This incense-altar typified, 1. The mediation of Christ. The brazen altar in the court was a type of Christ dying on earth; the golden altar in the sanctuary was a type of Christ interceding in heaven. This altar was before the mercy-seat, for Christ always appears in the presence of God for us: he is our *advocate with the father* (1 John ii. 1), and his inter-cession is unto God of a sweet-smelling savour. This altar had a crown fixed to it; for Christ inter-cedes as a king. 2. The devotions of the saints. When the priest was burning incense the people were praying (Luke i. 10), to signify that prayer is the true incense. The lamps were dressed or lighted at the same time that the incense was burnt, to teach us that the reading of the scriptures (which are our light and lamp) is a part of our daily work, and should ordinar-ily accompany our prayers and praises. When we speak to God we must hear what God says to us, and thus the communion is complete. And, if the heart and life be not holy, even *incense is an abomina-tion* (Isa. i. 13), and he that offers it is *as if he blessed an idol*, Isa. lxvi. 3.

Verses 11–16

Moses is here ordered to levy money upon the people by way of poll, so much a head, for the service of the tabernacle. This he must do when he numbered the people. Some think that it refers only to the first numbering of them. Others think that it was afterwards repeated upon any emergency and always when the people were numbered. But many of the Jewish writers are of opinion that it was to be an annual tribute. This was that tribute-money which Christ paid, for fear of offending his adversaries (Matt. xvii. 27). Now, 1. The tribute to be paid was *half a shekel*. The rich were not to give more, nor the poor less (*v.* 15), to intimate that the souls of the rich and poor are alike precious, and that God is *no respecter of persons*, Acts x. 34. In other offerings men were to give according to their ability; but this, which was the *ransom of the soul*, must be alike for all. 2. This tribute was to be paid as a *ransom of the soul, that there might be no plague among them*. 3. This money that was raised was to be employed in the service of the tabernacle (*v.* 16); with it they bought sacrifices, flour, incense, wine, oil, fuel, salt, priests' garments. Note, Those that have the benefit of God's tabernacle among them must be willing to defray the expenses of it.

Verses 17–21

Orders are here given, 1. For the making of a laver, or font, of brass, a large vessel, that would contain a good quantity of water, which was to be set near the door of the tabernacle, *v.* 18. 2. For the using of this laver. Aaron and his sons must wash their hands and feet at this laver every time they went in to minister, every morning, at least, *v.* 19–21. This was designed, (1) To teach them purity in all their ministrations. He only shall *stand in God's holy place* that has *clean hands and a pure heart*, Ps. xxiv. 3, 4. And, (2) It was to teach us, who are daily to attend upon God, daily to renew our repent-ance for sin. *Cleanse your hands and purify your hearts*, and then *draw nigh to God*, Jam. iv. 8.

Verses 22–38

Directions are here given for the composition of the holy anointing oil and the incense that were to be used in the service of the tabernacle. 1. The holy anointing oil is here ordered to be made up; the ingredients, and their quantities, are prescribed, *v.* 23–25. It was to be compounded *secundum artem—after the art of the apothecary* (*v.* 25); the spices were to be infused in the oil, and then strained out, leaving an admirable sweet smell in the oil. With this oil God's tent and all the furniture of it were to be anointed; it was to be used also in the consecration of the priests, *v.* 26–30. Solomon was anointed with it (1 Kings i. 39), and some other of the kings; and all the high priests. Christ's name is said to be *as ointment poured forth* (Cant. i. 3), and the good name of Christians better than *precious ointment*, Eccles. vii. 1. 2. The incense which was burned upon the golden altar was prepared of sweet spices likewise, though not so rare and rich as those of which the anointing oil was compounded, *v.* 34, 35. 3. Concerning both these preparations the same law is here given (v. 32, 33, 37, 38), that the like should not be made for any common use.

Chapter 31

God is here drawing towards a conclusion of what he had to say to Moses upon the mount, where he had now been with him forty days and forty nights; and yet no more is recorded of what was said to him in all that time than what we have read in the six chapters foregoing. In this, I. He appoints what workmen should be employed in the building and furnishing of the tabernacle, ver. 1–11. II. He repeats the law of the sabbath, and the religious observance of it, ver. 12–17. III. He delivers to him the two tables of the testimony at parting, ver. 18.

Verses 1–11

A great deal of fine work God had ordered to be done about the tabernacle; the materials the people were to provide, but who must put them into form? Moses himself was learned in all the learning of the Egyptians, but he knew not how to engrave or embroider. We may suppose that there were some very ingenious men among the Israelites; but, having lived all their days in bondage in Egypt, we cannot think they were any of them instructed in these curious arts. They knew how to make brick and work in clay, but to work in gold and in cutting diamonds was what they had never been brought up to. They had no goldsmiths or jewellers but what must be made out of masons and bricklayers? *Who was sufficient for these things?* But God takes care of this matter also.

I. He nominates the persons that were to be employed. 1. Bezaleel was to be the architect, or master workman, *v.* 2. He was of the tribe of Judah, a tribe that God delighted to honour; the grandson of Hur, probably that Hur who had helped to hold up Moses's hands (*ch.* xvii.). 2. Aholiab, of the tribe of Dan, is appointed next to Bezaleel, and partner with him, *v.* 6. Aholiab was of the tribe of Dan, which was one of the less honourable tribes, that the tribes of Judah and Levi might not be lifted up, as if they were to engross all the preferments. Hiram, who was the head workman in the building of Solomon's temple, was also of the tribe of Dan, 2 Chron. ii. 14. 3. There were others that were employed by and under these in the several operations about the tabernacle, *v.* 6.

II. He qualifies these persons for the service (*v.* 3): *I have filled him with the Spirit of God; and* (*v.* 6) *in the hearts of all that are wise-hearted I have put wisdom*. Note, 1. Skill in common arts and employments is the gift of God; from him are derived both the faculty and the improvement of the faculty. He teaches the husbandman discretion (Isa. xxviii. 26), and the tradesmen too; and he must have the praise of it. 2. God dispenses his gifts variously, one gift to one,

another to another, and all for the good of the whole body, both of mankind and of the church. Moses was fittest of all to govern Israel, but Bezaleel was fitter than he to build the tabernacle. 3. Those whom God calls to any service he will either find, or make, fit for it. The work that was to be done here was to make the tabernacle and the utensils of it, which are here particularly reckoned up, *v.* 7, &c. And for this the persons employed were enabled to *work in gold, and silver, and brass*. When Christ sent his apostles to rear the gospel tabernacle, he poured out his Spirit upon them, to enable them to speak with tongues the wonderful works of God; not to work upon metal, but to work upon men; so much more excellent were the gifts, as the tabernacle to be pitched was a *greater and more perfect tabernacle*, as the apostle calls it, Heb. ix. 11.

Verses 12–18

I. A strict command for the sanctification of the sabbath day, *v.* 13–17. The law of the sabbath had been given them before any other law, by way of preparation (*ch.* xvi. 23); it had been inserted in the body of the moral law, in the fourth commandment; it had been annexed to the judicial law (*ch.* xxiii. 12); and here it is added to the first part of the ceremonial law, because the observance of the sabbath is indeed the hem and hedge of the whole law; where no conscience is made of that, farewell both godliness and honesty; for, in the moral law, it stands in the midst between the two tables. *Verily*, or *nevertheless, my sabbaths you shall keep*. Though they must hasten the work, yet they must not make more haste than good speed; they must not break the law of the sabbath in their haste: even tabernacle-work must give way to the sabbath-rest.

1. The nature, meaning, and intention, of the sabbath, by the declaration of which God puts an honour upon it, and teaches us to value it. Divers things are here said of the sabbath. (1) *It is a sign between me and you* (*v.* 13), and again (*v.* 17). The institution of the sabbath was a sign that he had distinguished them from all other people. God, by sanctifying this day among them, let them know that he sanctified them, and set them apart for himself and his service. (2) *It is holy unto you* (*v.* 14), that is, "It is designed for your benefit as well as for God's honour"; *the sabbath was made for man*. (3) It is the *sabbath of rest, holy to the Lord, v.* 15. It is separated from common use, and designed for the honour and service of God. (4) It was to be observed *throughout their generations*, in every age, *for a perpetual covenant, v.* 16.

2. The law of the sabbath. They must keep it (*v.* 13, 14, 16), keep it as a treasure, as a trust.

3. The reason of the sabbath; for God's laws are not only backed with the highest authority, but supported with the best reason. God's own example is the great reason, *v.* 17.

4. The penalty to be inflicted for the breach of this law: "Every one that *defileth the sabbath*, by doing *any work therein* but works of piety and mercy, *shall be cut off from among his people* (*v.* 14); *he shall surely be put to death, v.* 15.

II. The delivering of the two tables of testimony to Moses. 1. The ten commandments which God had spoken upon Mount Sinai in the hearing of all the people were now written, *in perpetuam rei memoriam—for a perpetual memorial*, because that which is written remains. 2. They were written in *tables of stone*. The law was written in *tables of stone*, to denote the perpetual duration of it. 3. They were written *with the finger of God*, that is, by his will and power immediately. It is God only that can write his law in the heart; by his Spirit, which is the *finger of God*, he writes his will in the *fleshy tables of the heart*, 2 Cor. iii. 3. 4. They were written in two tables, being designed to direct us in our duty both towards God and towards man. 5. They are called *tables of testimony*, because this written law testified both the will of God concerning them and his goodwill towards them, and would be a testimony against them if they were disobedient.

CHAPTER 32

It is a very lamentable interruption which the story of this chapter gives to the record of the establishment of the church, and of religion among the Jews. Things went on admirably well towards that happy settlement: God had shown himself very favourable, and the people also had seemed to be pretty tractable. Moses had now almost completed his forty days upon the mount, and, we may suppose, was pleasing himself with the thoughts of the very joyful welcome he should have to the camp of Israel at his return, and the speedy setting up of the tabernacle among them. But, behold, the measures are broken, and the sin of Israel turns away those good things from them, and puts a stop to the current of God's favours; the sin that did the mischief (would you think it?) was worshipping a golden calf. The marriage was ready to be solemnized between God and Israel, but Israel plays the harlot, and so the match is broken, and it will be no easy matter to piece it again. Here is, I. The sin of Israel, and of Aaron particularly, in making the golden calf for a god (ver. 1–4), and worshipping it, ver. 5, 6. II. The notice which God gave of this to Moses, who was now in the mount with him (ver. 7, 8), and the sentence of his wrath against them, ver. 9, 10. III. The intercession which Moses immediately made for them in the mount (ver. 11–13), and the prevalency of that intercession, ver. 14. IV. His coming down from the mount, when he became an eye-witness of their idolatry (ver. 15–19), in abhorrence of which, and as an expression of just indignation, he broke the tables (ver. 19), and burnt the golden calf, ver. 20. V. The examination of Aaron about it, ver. 21–24. VI. Execution done upon the ring-leaders in the idolatry, ver. 25–29. VII. The further intercession Moses made for them, to turn away the wrath of God from them (ver. 30–32), and a reprieve granted thereupon, reserving them for a further reckoning, ver. 33, &c.

Verses 1–6

While Moses was in the mount, receiving the law from God, the people had time to meditate upon what had been delivered, but there were those among them that were contriving how to break the laws they had already received. On the thirty-ninth day of the forty, the plot broke out of rebellion against the Lord.

I. A tumultuous address which the people made to Aaron, who was entrusted with the government in the absence of Moses: *Up, make us gods, which shall go before us, v.* 1.

1. See the ill effect of Moses's absence from them.

2. See the fury and violence of a multitude when they are influenced and corrupted by such as lie in wait to deceive.

(1) They were weary of waiting for the promised land. They are for hastening to the land *flowing with milk and honey*, and cannot stay to take their religion along with them. We must first wait for God's law before we catch at his promises.

(2) They were weary of waiting for the return of Moses. *As for this Moses, the man that brought us up out of Egypt, we wot not what has become of him. Observe*, [1] How slightly they speak of his person— *this Moses*. Thus ungrateful are they to Moses, who had shown such a tender concern for them, and thus do they walk contrary to God. If he tarried long, it was because God had a great deal to say to him, for their good; he resided upon the mount as their ambassador, and he would certainly return as soon as he had finished the business he went upon; and yet they make this the colour for their wicked proposal. Misinterpretations of our Redeemer's delays are the occasion of a great deal of wickedness. Our Lord Jesus has gone up into the mount of glory, where he is appearing in the presence of God for us, but out of our sight; the heavens must contain him, must conceal him, that we may live by faith. Weariness in waiting betrays us to a great many temptations. Israel here, if they could but have stayed one day longer, would have seen what had become of Moses.

(3) They were weary of waiting for a divine institution of religious worship among them. They were told that they must *serve God in this mountain*, but, because that was not appointed them so soon as they wished, they would set their own wits on work to devise signs of God's presence with them, and would glory in them, and have a worship of their own invention, probably such as they had seen among the Egyptians. To say, *Moses is lost, make us a god*, was the greatest absurdity imaginable. *Make us gods, which shall go before us! Gods!* How many would they have? Is not one sufficient? *Make us gods!* and what good would gods of their own making do them?

II. Here is the demand which Aaron makes of their jewels thereupon: *Bring me your golden ear-rings, v.* 2. We do not find that he said one word to discountenance their proposal, but seemed to approve the motion, and showed himself not unwilling to humour them in it. One would hope he designed, at first, only to make a jest of it, and, by setting up a ridiculous image among them, to expose the motion, and show them the folly of it. Some charitably suppose that when Aaron told them to break off their ear-rings, and bring them to him, he did it with design to crush the proposal, believing that though their coveteousness would have let them *lavish gold out of the bag* to make an idol of (Isa. xlvi. 6), yet their pride would not have suffered them to part with their golden ear-rings.

III. Here is the making of the golden calf, *v.* 3, 4. 1. The people brought in their ear-rings to Aaron, whose demand of them, instead of discouraging the motion, perhaps did rather gratify their superstition, and beget in them a fancy that the gold taken from their ears would be the most acceptable, and would make the most valuable god. 2. Aaron melted down their rings, and, having a mould prepared for the purpose, poured the melted gold into it, and then produced it in the shape of an ox or calf. Some think that Aaron chose this figure, for a sign or token of the divine presence, because he thought the head and horns of an ox a proper emblem of the divine power, and yet, being so plain and common a thing, he hoped the people would not be so sottish as to worship it. But it is probable that they had learnt of the Egyptians thus to represent the Deity, for it is said (Ezek. xx. 8), *They did not forsake the idols of Egypt*, and (ch. xxiii. 8), *Neither left she her whoredoms brought from Egypt. Thus they changed their glory into the similitude of an ox* (Ps. cvi. 20), and proclaimed their own folly, beyond that of other idolaters, who worshipped the host of heaven.

IV. Having made the calf in Horeb, they *worshipped the graven image*, Ps. cvi. 19. Aaron, seeing the people fond of their calf, was willing yet further to humour them, and he built an altar before it, and proclaimed a feast to the honour of it (*v.* 5), a feast of dedication. Yet he calls it *a feast to Jehovah*; for, brutish as they were, they did not imagine that this image was itself a god, but they made it for a representation of the true God, whom they intended to worship in and through this image. The people are forward enough to celebrate this feast (*v.* 6): *They rose up early on the morrow*, to show how well pleased they were with the solemnity, and, according to the ancient rites of worship, they offered sacrifice to this new-made diety, and then feasted upon the sacrifice; thus having, at the expense of their ear-rings, made their god, they endeavour, at the expense of their beasts, to make this god propitious. Now, 1. It was strange that any of the people, especially so great a number of them, should do such a thing. Had they not, but the other day, in this very place, heard the voice of the Lord God speaking to them out of the midst of the fire, *Thou shalt not make to thyself any graven image?* Nay, had they not themselves solemnly entered into covenant with God, and promised that all that which he had said unto them they *would do, and would be obedient*? *ch.* xxiv. 7. *They made a calf in Horeb*, the very place where the law was given. It was otherwise with those that received the gospel; they immediately *turned from idols*, 1 Thess. i. 9. 2. It was especially strange that Aaron should be so deeply implicated in this sin, that he should make the calf, and proclaim the feast! Is this Aaron, who had been with Moses in the mount (*ch.* xix. 24; xxiv. 9), and knew that there was no manner of similitude seen there, by which they might make an image? Is he aiding and abetting in this rebellion against the Lord? How was it possible that he should ever do so sinful a thing? Either he was strangely surprised into it, and did it when he was half asleep, or he was frightened into it by the outrages of the rabble. The Jews have a tradition that his colleague Hur opposing it the people fell upon him and stoned him (and therefore we never read of him after) and that this frightened Aaron into a compliance.

Verses 7–14

Here, I. God acquaints Moses with what was doing in the camp while he was absent, *v.* 7, 8. God says to Moses concerning this sin, 1. That they had *corrupted themselves*. Sin is the corruption or depravation of the sinner, and it is a self-corruption. 2. That they had *turned aside out of the way*. Sin is a deviation from the way of our duty into a by-path. 3. That they had turned aside quickly after the law was given them and they had promised to obey it. 4. He tells him particularly what they had done: *They have made a calf, and worshipped it*. Those sins which are concealed from our governors are naked and open before God. We could not bear to see the thousandth part of that provocation which God sees every day and yet keeps silence. 5. He seems to disown them, in saying to Moses, They are *thy people whom thou broughtest up out of the land of Egypt*. Those that corrupt themselves not only shame themselves, but even make God himself ashamed of them and of his kindness to them. 6. He sends him down to them with all speed: *Go, get thee down*.

II. He expresses his displeasure against Israel for this sin, *v.* 9, 10. 1. He gives this people their true character: "*It is a stiff-necked people*." The righteous God sees, not only what we do, but what we are. 2. He declares what was their just desert—that his wrath should *wax hot against them*. Sin exposes us to the wrath of God; and that wrath, if it be not allayed by divine mercy, will burn us up as stubble. 3. He holds out inducements to Moses not to intercede for them: *Therefore, let me alone*. Thus he would put an honour upon prayer, intimating that nothing but the intercession of Moses could save them from ruin.

III. Moses earnestly intercedes with God on their behalf (*v.* 11–13): he besought the Lord his God. If God would not be called *the God of Israel*, yet he hoped he might address him as *his own God*. He wisely took the hint which God gave him when he said, *Let me alone*, which, though it seemed to forbid his interceding, did really encourage it, by showing what power the prayer of faith has with God. Observe, 1. His prayer (*v.* 12): *Turn from thy fierce wrath*; not as if he thought God was not justly angry, but he begs that he would not be so greatly angry as to consume them. 2. His pleas. He fills his mouth with arguments, not to move God, but to express his own faith and to excite his own fervency in prayer. He urges, (1) God's interest in them, the great things he had already done for them. God had said to Moses (*v.* 7), They are *thy people, whom thou broughtest up out of Egypt*; but Moses humbly

turns them back upon God again: "They are *thy people*, thou art their Lord and owner; I am but their servant. *Thou broughtest them forth out of Egypt*. I was but the instrument in thy hand. "Thou *broughtest them out of Egypt*, though they were unworthy, and had there served the gods of the Egyptians, Josh. xxiv. 15. If thou didst that for them, notwithstanding their sins in Egypt, wilt thou undo it for their sins of the same nature in the wilderness?" (2) He pleads the concern of God's glory (*v.* 12): *Wherefore should the Egyptians say, For mischief did he bring them out?* He cannot bear to hear God reflected on, and therefore this he insists upon, *Lord, what will the Egyptians say?* If a people so strangely saved should be suddenly ruined, what would the world say of it, especially the Egyptians, who have such an implacable hatred both to Israel and to the God of Israel? They would say, "God was either weak, and could not, or fickle, and would not, complete the salvation he began." *What will the Egyptians say?* We ought always to be careful that the name of God and his doctrine be not blasphemed through us. (3) He pleads God's promise to the patriarchs that he would multiply their seed, and give them the land of Canaan. God's promises are to be our pleas in prayer.

IV. God graciously abated the rigour of the sentence, and *repented of the evil he thought to do* (*v.* 14). See here, 1. The power of prayer; God suffers himself to be prevailed with by the humble believing importunity of intercessors. 2. The compassion of God towards poor sinners, and how ready he is to forgive.

Verses 15–20

I. The favour of God to Moses, in trusting him with the two tables of the testimony, which, though of common stone, were far more valuable than all the precious stones that adorned the breastplate of Aaron.

II. The familiarity between Moses and Joshua. While Moses was in the cloud, as in the presence-chamber, Joshua continued as near as he might. When Moses came down he came with him, and not till then. Joshua, who was a military man, feared there was *a noise of war in the camp*, and then he would be missed; but Moses, having received notice of it from God, better distinguished the sound, and was aware that it was *the voice of those that sing*.

III. The great and just displeasure of Moses against Israel, for their idolatry. He resented it as an offence to God, and the scandal of his people. Moses was the meekest man on the earth, and yet when he saw *the calf, and the dancing*, his *anger waxed hot*. Note, It is no breach of the law of meekness to show our displeasure at the wickedness of the wicked. It becomes us to be cool in our own cause, but warm in God's. 1. To convince them that they had forfeited and lost the favour of God, *he broke the tables*, *v.* 19, that the sight of it might the more affect them, and fill them with confusion, when they saw what blessings they had lost. 2. To convince them that they had betaken themselves to a God that could not help them, he *burnt the calf* (*v.* 20), melted it down, and then filed it to dust; and, that the powder to which it was reduced might be taken notice of throughout the camp, he strewed it upon that water of which they all drank. That it might appear that *an idol is nothing in the world* (1 Cor. viii. 4), he reduced this to atoms, that it might be as near nothing as could be.

Verses 21–29

Moses, having shown his just indignation against the sin of Israel by breaking the tables and burning the calf, now proceeds to reckon with the sinners and to call them to an account, herein acting as the representative of God. Now,

I. He begins with Aaron, as God began with Adam, because he was the principal person, though not first in the transgression, but drawn into it. Observe here,

1. The just reproof Moses gives him, v. 21. And having prevailed with God for him, to save him from ruin, he here expostulates with him, to bring him to repentance. He puts Aaron upon considering, (1) What he had done to this people: *Thou hast brought so great a sin upon them.* The people, as the first movers, might be said to bring the sin upon Aaron; but he being a magistrate, who should have suppressed it, and yet aiding and abetting it, might truly be said to bring it upon them, because he hardened their hearts and strengthened their hands in it. (2) What moved him to it: *What did this people unto thee?* Men can but tempt us to sin; they cannot force us. Men can but frighten us; if we do not comply, they cannot hurt us.

2. The frivolous excuse Aaron makes for himself. (1) He deprecates the anger of Moses only, whereas he should have deprecated God's anger in the first place: *Let not the anger of my lord wax hot, v.* 22. (2) He lays all the fault upon the people: *They are set on mischief, and they said, Make us gods.* It is natural to us to endeavour thus to transfer our guilt. Sin is a brat that nobody is willing to own. (3) It is well if he did not intend a reflection upon Moses, as accessory to the sin, by staying so long on the mount, in repeating, without need, that invidious surmise of the people, *As for this Moses, we know not what has become of him, v.* 23. (4) He extenuates and conceals his own share in the sin, and childishly insinuates that when he cast the gold into the fire it came out in this shape; but not a word of his graving and fashioning it, *v.* 24.

II. The people are next to be judged for this sin. The approach of Moses turned their dancing into trembling. Those that hectored Aaron into a compliance with them in their sin durst not look Moses in the face.

1. How they were exposed to shame by their sin: *The people were naked* (v. 25), not so much because they had some of them lost their ear-rings, but because they had lost their integrity. It was a shame to them, and a perpetual blot, that they *changed their glory into the similitude of an ox.* Thus were they *made naked,* stripped of their ornaments, and exposed to contempt.

2. The course that Moses took to roll away this reproach, not by concealing the sin, or putting any false colour upon it, but by punishing it, and so bearing a public testimony against it.

(1) By whom vengeance was taken—by the children of Levi (v. 26, 28); not by the immediate hand of God himself, as on Nadab and Abihu, but by the sword of man, to teach them that idolatry was an *iniquity to be punished by the judge,* being a *denial of the God that is above,* Job. xxxi. 28; Deut. xiii. 9. The innocent must be culled out to be the executioners of the guilty. Now here we are told, [1] How the Levites were called out to this service. *Moses clad himself with zeal* as with a robe, and summoned all those to appear forthwith that were on God's side, against the golden calf. *Who is on the Lord's side?* The interest of sin and wickedness is the devil's interest, and all wicked people side with that interest; the interest of truth and holiness is God's interest, with which all godly people side; and it is a case that will not admit a neutrality. [2] How they were commissioned for this service (v. 27): *Slay every man his brother,* that is, "Slay all those that you know to have been active for the making and worshipping of the golden calf, though they were your own nearest relations, or dearest friends." Yet, it should seem, they were to slay those only whom they found *abroad in the streets* of the camp; for it might be hoped that those

who had retired into their tents were ashamed of what they had done, and were upon their knees, repenting.

(2) On whom vengeance is taken: *There fell of the people that day about* 3,000 *men, v.* 28. Probably these were but few, in comparison with the many that were guilty; but these were the men that headed the rebellion, and were therefore picked out, to be made examples of, for terror to all others.

Verses 30–35

Moses, having executed justice upon the principal offenders, is here dealing both with the people and with God.

I. With the people, to bring them to repentance, *v.* 30.

1. When some were slain, lest the rest should imagine that, because they were exempt from the capital punishment, they were therefore looked upon as free from guilt, Moses here tells the survivors, *You have sinned a great sin.* To affect them with the greatness of their sin he intimates to them what a difficult thing it would be to make up the quarrel which God had with them for it. The malignity of sin appears in the price of pardons.

2. Yet it was some encouragement to the people (when they were told that they had *sinned a great sin*) to hear that Moses would *go up unto the Lord to make atonement* for them. Christ, the great Mediator, went upon greater certainty than this, for he had laid in the bosom of the Father, and perfectly knew all his counsels.

II. He intercedes with God for mercy. Observe,

1. How pathetic his address was. *Moses returned unto the Lord,* not to receive further instructions about the tabernacle. Moses in this address expresses, (1) His great detestation of the people's sin, *v.* 31. *Oh! this people have sinned a great sin.* God had first told him of it (v. 7), and now he tells God of it, by way of lamentation. He does not go about to excuse or extenuate the sin; but what he had said to them by way of conviction he says to God by way of confession: *They have sinned a great sin;* he came not to make apologies, but to make atonement. (2) His great desire of the people's welfare (v. 32): *Yet now* it is not too great a sin for infinite mercy to pardon, and therefore *if thou wilt forgive their sin.* It is an abrupt expression, If thou wilt forgive, is as much as, "O that thou wouldest forgive!" as Luke xix. 42, *If thou hadst known* is, *O that thou hadst known.* "But *if not, blot me, I pray thee, out of the book which thou hast written*"; that is, "If they must be cut off, let me be cut off with them, and cut short of Canaan; if all Israel must perish, I am content to perish with them; let not the land of promise be mine by survivorship." Thus he expresses his tender affection for the people, and is a type of the good Shepherd, that *lays down his life for the sheep* (John x. 11), who was to be *cut off from the land of the living for the transgression of my people,* Isa. liii. 8; Dan. ix. 26. He is also an example of public-spiritedness to all, especially to those in public stations.

2. Observe how prevalent his address was. God would not take him at his word; no, he will not blot any out of his book but those that by their wilful disobedience have forfeited the honour of being enrolled in it (v. 33). This was also an intimation of mercy to the people. Further, in answer to the address of Moses, (1) God promises to go on with his intention of giving them the land of Canaan. Therefore he sends Moses back to them to lead them, though they were unworthy of him, and promises that his angel should go before them. (2) Yet he threatens to remember this sin against them when hereafter he should see cause to punish them for other sins. The Jews have a saying, grounded on this, that henceforward no judgment fell upon Israel but there was

in it an ounce of the powder of the golden calf. Stephen says that when they *made a calf, and offered sacrifice to the idol, God turned, and gave them up to worship the host of heaven* (Acts vii. 41, 42); so that the strange addictedness of that people to the sin of idolatry was a just judgment upon them for making and worshipping the golden calf, and a judgment they were never quite freed from till the captivity of Babylon. See Rom. i. 23–25. Aaron was not plagued, but the people; for his was a sin of infirmity, theirs a presumptuous sin.

CHAPTER 33

In this chapter we have a further account of the mediation of Moses between God and Israel, for the making up of the breach that sin had made between them. I. He brings a very humbling message from God to them (ver. 1–3, 5), which helps to prepare them for mercy, ver. 4, 6. II. He settles a correspondence between God and them, ver. 7–11. III. He is earnest with God in prayer, and prevails, 1. For a promise of his presence with the people, ver. 12–17. 2. For a sight of his glory for himself, ver. 18, &c.

Verses 1–6

Here is, I. The message which God sent by Moses to the children of Israel. 1. He applies to them a mortifying name, by giving them their just character —*a stiff-necked people, v.* 3, 5. God would have brought them under the yoke of his law, and into the bond of his covenant, but their necks were too stiff to bow to them. Note, God judges of men by the temper of their minds. We know what man does; God knows what he is: we know what proceeds from man; God knows what is in man, and nothing is more displeasing to him than stiff-neckedness. 2. He tells them what they deserved. Had he dealt with them according to their sins, he had taken them away with a swift destruction. 3. He bids them *depart and go up hence* to the land of Canaan, *v.* 1. 4. Though he promises to make good his covenant with Abraham, in giving them Canaan, yet he denies them the extraordinary tokens of his presence. *"I will send an angel before thee,* for thy protector, otherwise the evil angels would soon destroy thee; but *I will not go up in the midst of thee, lest I consume thee"* (*v.* 2, 3). Justice said, "Cut them off, and consume them." Mercy said, *"How shall I give thee up, Ephraim?"* Hos. xi. 8. Well, says God, *put off thy ornaments, that I may know what to do with thee;* that is, "Put thyself into the posture of a penitent, that mercy may rejoice against judgment," *v.* 5. Note, Calls to repentance are plain indications of mercy designed.

II. The people's melancholy reception of this message. 1. *They mourned* (*v.* 4), for their sin which had provoked God to withdraw from them, and mourned for this as the sorest punishment of their sin. Note, Of all the bitter fruits and consequences of sin, that which true penitents most lament, and dread most, is God's departure from them. 2. In token of great shame and humiliation, those that were undressed did *not put on their ornaments* (*v.* 4), and those that were dressed *stripped themselves of their ornaments, by the mount;* as some read it, *at a distance from the mount* (*v.* 6), standing afar off like the publican, Luke xviii. 13.

Verses 7–11

Here is, I. One mark of displeasure put upon them for their further humiliation: *Moses took the tabernacle,* the tent wherein he gave audience, heard causes, and enquired of God, the *guild-hall* (as it were) of their camp, and *pitched it without, afar off from the camp* (*v.* 7), to signify to them that they had rendered themselves unworthy of it, and that, unless peace was made, it would return to them no more.

II. Many encouragements given them, notwithstanding, to hope that God would yet be reconciled to them.

1. Though the tabernacle was removed, yet every one that was disposed to seek the Lord was welcome to follow it, *v.* 7. A place was appointed for them to go to *without the camp,* to solicit God's return to them. When God designs mercy, he stirs up prayer.

2. Moses undertook to mediate between God and Israel. He *went out to the tabernacle,* the place of treaty, probably pitched between them and the mount (*v.* 8), and he *entered into the tabernacle, v.* 9.

3. The people seemed to be in a very good mind and well disposed towards a reconciliation. (1) When Moses went out to go to the tabernacle, the people *looked after him* (*v.* 8), in token of their respect to him whom before they had slighted, and their entire dependence upon his mediation. (2) When they saw the cloudy pillar, that symbol of God's presence, they all *worshipped, every man at his tent door, v.* 10. Their worshipping in their tent doors declared plainly that they were not ashamed publicly to own their respect to God and Moses, as they had publicly worshipped the calf.

4. God was, in Moses, reconciling Israel to himself, and manifested himself very willing to be at peace. (1) God met Moses at the place of treaty, *v.* 9. If our hearts go forth towards God to meet him he will graciously come down to meet us. (2) God *talked with Moses* (*v.* 9), *spoke to him face to face, as a man speaks to his friend* (*v.* 11), which intimates that God revealed himself to Moses, not only with greater clearness and evidence of divine light than to any other of the prophets, but also with greater expressions of particular kindness and grace. *Moses turned again into the camp,* but, because he intended speedily to return to the tabernacle of the congregation, he left Joshua there, for it was not fit that the place should be empty, so long as the cloud of glory *stood at the door* (*v.* 9).

Verses 12–23

Moses, having returned to the door of the tabernacle, becomes a humble and importunate supplicant there for two very great favours.

I. He is very earnest with God for a grant of his presence with Israel in the rest of their march to Canaan, notwithstanding their provocations. Observe how admirably Moses orders this cause before God: how he pleads, and how he speeds.

1. How he pleads. (1) He insists upon the commission God had given him to *bring up this people, v.* 12. This he begins with: "Lord, it is thou thyself that employest me; and wilt thou not own me? (2) He improves the interest he himself had with God, and pleads God's gracious expressions of kindness to him: *Thou hast said, I know thee by name. Now, therefore,* says Moses, if it be indeed so, that *I have found grace in thy sight, show me thy way, v.* 13. By this therefore he takes hold on God: "Lord, if ever thou wilt do anything for me, do this for the people." Thus our Lord Jesus, in his intercession, presents himself to the Father, as one in whom he is always well pleased, and so obtains mercy for us with whom he is justly displeased; and we are *accepted in the beloved.* (3) He insinuates that the people also, though most unworthy, yet were in some relation to God: *"Consider that this nation is thy people,* a people that thou hast done great things for, redeemed to thyself, and taken into covenant with thyself; Lord, they are thy own, do not leave them." The offended father considers this, "My child is foolish and froward, but he is my child, and I cannot abandon him." (4) He expresses the great value he had for the presence of God. When God said, *My presence shall go with thee,* he caught at that word, as that which he could not live and move without: *If thy presence go not with me, carry us not up hence," v.* 15. (5) He concludes with an argument taken

from God's glory (v. 16): "*Wherein shall it be known
to the nations that I and thy people have found grace
in thy sight, so as to be separated from all people
upon earth?* How will it appear that we are indeed
thus honoured? *Is it not in that thou goest with us?*"

2. Observe how he speeds. He obtained an assurance of God's favour, (1) To himself (v. 14): *I will
give thee rest.* Moses never entered Canaan, and
yet God made good his word that he would give
him rest, Dan. xii. 13. (2) To the people for his sake.
Gracious generous souls think it not enough to get to
heaven themselves, but would have all their friends
go thither too. God grants as long as he asks, *gives
liberally*, and *does not upbraid* him. See the power of
prayer, and be quickened hereby to ask, and seek,
and knock, and to *continue instant in prayer*, to *pray
always and not to faint.* See, in type, the prevalency of
Christ's intercession, which he ever lives to make for
all those that come to God by him, and the ground
of that prevalency. It is purely his own merit, not
any thing in those for whom he intercedes; it is because *thou hast found grace in my sight.* And now
the matter is settled, God is perfectly reconciled to
them, his presence in the pillar of cloud returns to
them and shall continue with them; all is well again,
and henceforth we hear no more of the golden calf.

II. Having gained this point, he next begs *a sight
of God's glory*, and is heard in this matter also.

1. The humble request Moses makes: *I beseech
thee, show me thy glory*, v. 18. Moses had wonderfully
prevailed with God for one favour after another,
and the success of his prayers emboldened him to go
on still to seek God; the more he had the more he
asked! "*Show me thy glory; make me to see it*
(so the word is); "make it some way or other visible,
and enable me to bear the sight of it." Not that he
was so ignorant as to think God's essence could be
seen with bodily eyes; but, having hitherto only
heard a voice out of a pillar of cloud or fire, he
desired to see some representation of the divine glory,
such as God saw fit to gratify him with. Some think
that Moses desired a sight of God's glory as a token
of his reconciliation, and an earnest of that presence
which he had promised them; but he knew not what
he asked.

2. The gracious reply God made to this request.
(1) He denied that which was not fit to be granted,
and which Moses could not bear: *Thou canst not see
my face*, v. 20. A full discovery of the glory of God
would quite overpower the faculties of any mortal
man in this present state, and overwhelm him, even
Moses himself. There is a knowledge and enjoyment of God which must be waited for in another
world, when we shall *see him as he is*, 1 John iii. 2.
In the meantime let us adore the height of what we
do know of God, and the depth of what we do not.
(2) He granted that which would be abundantly
satisfying. [1] He should hear what would please
him (v. 19): *I will make all my goodness pass before
thee.* He had given him wonderful instances of his
goodness in being reconciled to Israel; but that was
only goodness in the stream; he would show him
goodness in the spring—*all his goodness.* This was a
sufficient answer to his request. "Show me thy glory,"
says Moses. "I will show thee my goodness," says
God. Note, God's goodness is his glory; and he
will have us to know him by the glory of his mercy
more than by the glory of his majesty. It is never said
"I will be angry at whom I will be angry," for his
wrath is always just and holy; but *I will show mercy
on whom I will show mercy*, for his grace is always free.
He never damns by prerogative, but by prerogative
he saves. [2] He should see what he could bear, and
what would suffice him. *First*, Safe in a *cleft of the
rock*, v. 21, 22. *That rock was Christ*, 1 Cor. x. 4.
And it is only through Christ that we have *the know-

ledge of the glory of God.* None can see his glory
to their comfort but those who stand upon this rock,
and take shelter in it. *Secondly*, He should see more
of God than any ever saw on earth, but not so much
as those see who are in heaven. That sight of God
Moses might not have, but such a sight as we have of
a man who has gone past us, so that we only see his
back, and have (as we say) a blush of him. When we
see what God has done in his works, observe the
goings of our God, our King, we see (as it were) his
back-parts. If we faithfully improve the discoveries
God gives us of himself while we are here, a brighter
and more glorious scene will shortly be opened to us;
for *to him that hath shall be given.*

<h1 style="text-align:center">CHAPTER 34</h1>

God, having in the foregoing chapter intimated to Moses his
reconciliation to Israel, here gives proofs of it, proceeding to settle
his covenant and communion with them. I. The orders he gives
to Moses to come up to the mount, the next morning, and bring
two tables of stone with him, ver. 1–4. II. His meeting him
there, and the proclamation of his name, ver. 5–9. III. The
instructions he gave him there, and his converse with him for
forty days together, without intermission, ver. 10–28. IV. The
honour he put upon him when he sent him down with his face
shining, ver. 29–35. In all this God dealt with Moses as a public
person, and mediator between him and Israel, and a type of the
great Mediator.

Verses 1–4

The treaty that was on foot between God and Israel
being broken off abruptly, by their worshipping the
golden calf, when peace was made all must be begun
anew.

I. Moses must prepare for the renewing of the
tables, v. 1. Thus, in the first writing of the law
upon the heart of man in innocency, both the tables
and the writing were the work of God; but when
those were broken and defaced by sin, and the divine
law was to be preserved in the scriptures, God therein
made use of the ministry of man, and Moses first.
But the prophets and apostles did only hew the tables,
as it were; the writing was God's still, for *all scripture
is given by inspiration of God.* Observe, When God
was reconciled to them, he ordered the tables to be
renewed, and wrote his law in them, which plainly
intimates to us, 1. That even under the gospel of
peace and reconciliation by Christ (of which the
intercession of Moses was typical) the moral law
should continue to bind believers. When our Saviour,
in his sermon on the mount, expounded the moral
law, and vindicated it from the corrupt glosses with
which the scribes and Pharisees had broken it (Matt.
v. 19), he did in effect renew the tables, and make
them like the first, that is, reduce the law to its
primitive sense and intention. 2. That the best evidence of the pardon of sin and peace with God is the
writing of the law in the heart. 3. That, if we would
have God to write the law in our hearts, we must
prepare our hearts for the reception of it.

II. Moses must attend again on the top of mount
Sinai, and present himself to God there, v. 2. Moses,
accordingly, *rose up early* (v. 4), to go to the place
appointed. It is good to be early at our devotions.
The morning is perhaps as good a friend to the graces
as it is to the muses.

Verses 5–9

No sooner had Moses got to the top of the mount
than God gave him the meeting (v. 5): *The Lord
descended*, by some sensible token of his presence,
and manifestation of his glory. He descended *in the
cloud.* His making a cloud his pavilion intimated
that, though he made known much of himself, yet
there was much more concealed.

I. How God proclaimed his name (v. 6, 7): he
did it *in transitu—as he passed by him.* Fixed views
of God are reserved for the future state; the best we

have in this world are transient. God now was performing what he had promised Moses, the day before, that his glory should pass by, *ch.* xxxiii. 22. He *proclaimed the name of the Lord*, by which he would make himself known. He had made himself known to Moses in the glory of his self-existence and self-sufficiency when he proclaimed that name, *I am that I am*; now he makes himself known in the glory of his grace, and goodness, and all-sufficiency to us. This is prefixed before the display of his mercy, to teach us to think and to speak even of God's grace and goodness with great seriousness and a holy awe. His greatness and goodness illustrate and set off each other. Many words are here heaped up, to acquaint us with, and convince us of, God's goodness. 1. He is *merciful*. This bespeaks his tender compassion, like that of a father to his children. 2. He is *gracious*. His mercy is grace, free grace; this teaches us to be not only pitiful, but courteous, 1 Pet. iii. 8. 3. He is *long-suffering*, that is, he is slow to anger, and delays the execution of his justice; he waits to be gracious, and lengthens out the offers of his mercy. 4. He is *abundant in goodness and truth*. It bespeaks promised goodness, goodness and truth put together, goodness engaged by promise, and his faithfulness pledged for the security of it. 5. He keepeth *mercy for thousands*. 6. He *forgiveth iniquity, transgression, and sin*. Pardoning mercy is specified, because it is this which opens the door to all other gifts of his divine grace.

II. How Moses received this declaration which God made of himself, and of his grace and mercy. It should seem as if Moses accepted this as a sufficient answer to his request that God would *show him his glory*. Now we are here told,

1. What impression it made upon him: *Moses made haste, and bowed his head*, v. 8.

2. What improvement he made of it. He immediately grounded a prayer upon it (v. 9); and a most earnest affectionate prayer it is, (1) For the presence of God with his people Israel in the wilderness: "*I pray thee, go among us*, for thy presence is all in all to our safety and success." (2) For pardon of sin: "*O pardon our iniquity and our sin*, else we cannot expect thee to go among us." And, (3) For the privileges of a peculiar people: "Take us for *thy inheritance*." These things God had already promised, and given Moses assurances of, and yet he prays for them, not as doubting the sincerity of God's grants, but as one solicitous for the ratification of them. Those who have some good hopes, through grace, that their sins are pardoned, must yet continue to pray for pardon, for the renewing of their pardon, and the clearing of it more and more to their souls. Thus Moses, like a man of a truly public spirit, intercedes even for the children that should be born. But it is a strange plea he urges: *For it is a stiff-necked people*. God had given this as a reason why he would not go along with them, *ch.* xxxiii. 3. "Yea," says Moses, "the rather go along with us; for the worse they are the more need they have of thy presence and grace to make them better."

Verses 10–17

Reconciliation being made, a covenant of friendship is here settled between God and Israel. The traitors are not only pardoned, but preferred and made favourites again. Well may the assurances of this be ushered in with a *behold*, a word commanding attention and admiration: *Behold, I make a covenant*.

1. God's part of this covenant, what he would do for them, v. 10, 11. (1) In general: *Before all thy people, I will do marvels*. Marvels indeed, for they were without precedent, *such as have not been done in all the earth*. They were the joy of Israel, and the confirmation of their faith: *Thy people shall see, and own the work of the Lord*. And they were the

terror of their enemies: *It is a terrible thing that I will do*. Nay, even God's own people should see them with astonishment. 2. In particular: *I drive out before thee the Amorite*.

II. Their part of the covenant: *Observe that which I command thee*, We cannot expect the benefit of the promises unless we make conscience of the precepts.

Thou shalt worship no other gods (v. 14), not give divine honour to any creature, or any name whatsoever, the creature of fancy. Those cannot worship God aright who do not worship him alone. That they might not be tempted to worship other gods, they must not join in affinity or friendship with those that did (v. 12). *Make no covenant with the inhabitants of the land*. If God, in kindness to them, drove out the Canaanites, they ought, in duty to God, not to harbour them. They must particularly take heed of intermarrying with them, v. 15, 16. If they espoused their children, they would be in danger of espousing their gods. That they might not be tempted to make molten gods, they must utterly destroy those they found and all that belong to them, the altars and groves (v. 13).

Verses 18–27

Several appointments relating to their solemn feasts. When they had made the calf, they proclaimed a feast in honour of it; now, that they might never do so again, they are here charged with the observance of the feasts which God had instituted. Note, Men need not be drawn from their religion by the temptation of mirth, for we serve a Master that has abundantly provided for the joy of his servants.

I. Once a week they must rest (v. 21), *even in earing time, and in harvest*, the most busy times of the year. Harvest-work will prosper the better for the religious observance of the sabbath day in harvest time.

II. Thrice a year they must feast (v. 23); they must then appear *before the Lord God, the God of Israel*. The country would be left exposed to the insults of their neighbours; and what would become of the poor women and children, and sick and aged, that were left at home? Trust God with them (v. 24): *Neither shall any man desire thy land*; not only they shall not invade it, but they shall not so much as think of invading it. The way of duty is the way of safety.

III. The three feasts are here mentioned, with their appendages. 1. The passover, and the feast of unleavened bread, in remembrance of their deliverance out of Egypt; and to this is annexed the law of the redemption of the first-born, v. 18–20. This feast was instituted, *ch.* xii. 13, and urged again, *ch.* xxiii. 15. 2. The feast of weeks, that is, that of pentecost, seven weeks after the passover; and to this is annexed the law of the first-fruits. 3. The feast of in-gathering at the year's end, which was the feast of tabernacles (v. 22): of these also he had spoken before, *ch.* xxiii. 16.

IV. These laws are here repeated to show that *not one jot or tittle of the law should pass away*. And in the close, 1. Moses is ordered to write these words (v. 27), that the people might be the better acquainted with them by a frequent perusal, and that they might be transmitted to the generations to come. We can never be thankful enough to God for the written word. 2. He is told that according to the tenor of these words God would make a covenant with Moses and Israel; not with Israel immediately, but with them in Moses as mediator.

Verses 28–35

I. The continuance of Moses in the mount, where he was miraculously sustained, v. 28. When we are weary of an hour or two spent in attendance upon God and adoration of him, we should think how many days and nights Moses spent with him. So long he continued without meat and drink (and probably without sleep too), for, 1. The power of God supported him, that he did not need it. 2. He had meat to eat which the world knew not of, for it was his meat and drink to hear the word of God and pray. When God would treat his favourite Moses, it was not with meat and drink, but with his light, law and love, with the knowledge of himself and his will. As Moses, so Elijah and Christ, fasted forty days and forty nights.

II. The coming down of Moses from the mount, greatly enriched and miraculously adorned.

1. He came down enriched with the best treasure; for he brought in his hands the two tables of the law.

2. He came down adorned with the best beauty; for the *skin of his face shone*, v. 29.

(1) This may be looked upon, [1] As a great honour done to Moses, that the people might never again question his mission. He carried his credentials in his very countenance, The Israelites could not look him in the face but they must there read his commission. Yet, after this, they murmured against him. [2] It was also a great favour to the people, and an encouragement to them, that God put this glory upon him, who was their intercessor, thereby giving them assurance that he was accepted, and they through him. [3] It was the effect of his sight of God. When we have been in the mount with God, we should let our *light shine before men*, that all we converse with may *take knowledge of us that we have been with Jesus*, Acts iv. 13.

(2) Concerning the shining of Moses's face observe here, [1] Moses was not aware of it himself: *He wist not that the skin of his face shone*, v. 29. Whatever beauty God puts upon us, we should still be filled with such a humble sense of our own unworthiness, and manifold infirmities, as will make us even overlook and forget that which makes our faces shine. [2] Aaron and the children of Israel saw it, and *were afraid*, v. 30. Probably they doubted whether it were a token of God's favour or of his displeasure; being conscious of guilt, they feared the worst. [3] Moses put a *veil upon his face*, when he perceived that it shone, v. 33, 35. This teaches us all a lesson of modesty and humility. [4] When Moses *went in before the Lord*, to speak with him in the tabernacle of meeting, he *put off the veil*, v. 34. Then there was no occasion for it, and, before God, every man does and must appear unveiled. This signified also, as it is explained (2 Cor. iii. 16), that when a soul turns to the Lord the veil shall be taken away, that with open face it may behold his glory.

CHAPTER 35

What should have been said and done upon Moses's coming down the first time from the mount now at last, when with great difficulty reconciliation was made, begins to be said and done. I. Moses gives Israel those instructions, received from God, which required immediate observance. 1. Concerning the sabbath, ver. 1–3. 2. Concerning the contribution that was to be made for the erecting of the tabernacle, ver. 4–9. 3. Concerning the framing of the tabernacle and the utensils of it, ver. 10–19. II. The people bring in their contributions, ver. 20–29. III. The head-workmen are nominated, ver. 30, &c.

Verses 1–19

The erecting and furnishing of the tabernacle being the work to which they were now immediately to apply themselves, here is particular mention of the orders given concerning it.

I. All the congregation is summoned to attend (v. 1).

II. Moses gave them in charge all that which God had commanded him. Both sides having reposed

a trust in him, he was true to the trust; yet he was faithful as a servant only, but *Christ as a Son*, Heb. iii. 5, 6.

III. He begins with the law of the sabbath, *Six days shall work be done*, work for the tabernacle, *but on the seventh day* you must not strike a stroke. It is a sabbath of rest. It is a *sabbath of sabbaths* (so some read it), more honourable and excellent than any of the other feasts, and should survive them all. A *sabbath of sabbatism*, so others read it, being typical of that sabbatism or rest, both spiritual and eternal, which *remains for the people of God*, Heb. iv. 9. It is a sabbath and a little sabbath, so some of the Jews would have it read; not only observing the whole day as a sabbath, but an hour before the beginning of it, and an hour after the ending of it, *a little sabbath*, to show how glad they are of the approach of the sabbath and how loth to part with it.

IV. He orders preparation to be made for the setting up of the tabernacle. Two things were to be done:—

1. All that were able must contribute: *Take you from among you an offering*, v. 5. The rule is, *Whosoever is of a willing heart let him bring*. It was not to be a tax imposed upon them, but a benevolence or voluntary contribution, to intimate to us, (1) That God has not made our yoke heavy. (2) That God loves a cheerful giver, and is best pleased with the free-will offering. Those services are acceptable to him that come from the willing heart of a willing people, Ps. cx. 3.

2. All that were skilful must work: *Every wise-hearted among you shall come, and make*, v. 10. See how God dispenses his gifts variously; and, *as every man hath received the gift, so he must minister*, 1 Pet. iv. 10. Those that were rich must bring in materials to work on; those that were ingenious must serve the tabernacle with their ingenuity; as they needed one another, so the tabernacle needed them both, 1 Cor. xii. 7–21.

Verses 20–29

I. The offerings that were brought for the service of the tabernacle (v. 21, &c.). 1. It is intimated that they brought their offerings immediately. No season will be more convenient than the present season. 2. It is said that *their spirits made them willing* (v. 21), *and their hearts*, v. 29. 3. When it is said that as many as were willing-hearted brought their offerings (v. 22), it should seem as if there were some who were not, who loved their gold better than their God, and would not part with it, no, not for the service of the tabernacle. They are for the true religion, provided it be cheap and will cost them nothing. 4. The offerings were of divers kinds, according as they had. Those that had not precious stones to bring brought goats' hair, and rams' skins. Two mites from a pauper were more pleasing than so many talents from a Dives. God has an eye to the heart of the giver more than to the value of the gift. 5. Many of the things they offered were their ornaments, bracelets, and rings, and tablets or lockets (v. 22); and even the women parted with these. If we think those gospel rules concerning our clothing too strict (1 Tim. ii. 9, 10; 1 Pet. iii. 3, 4), I fear we should scarcely have done as these Israelites did. These rich things that they offered, we may suppose, were mostly the spoils of the Egyptians. Who would have thought that even the wealth of Egypt should have been so well employed? Let every man give *according as God hath prospered him*, 1 Cor. xvi. 2. Extraordinary successes should be acknowledged by extraordinary offerings. But then great care must be taken that Egypt's gods mingle not with Egypt's gold.

II. The work that was done for the service of the tabernacle (v. 25): *The women did spin with their hands.* Some spun fine work, of blue and purple; others coarse work, of goats' hair, and yet theirs also is said to be done in wisdom, *v.* 26. As it is not only rich gifts, so it is not only fine work that God accepts. Notice is here taken of the good women's work for God, as well as of Bezaleel's and Aholiab's. Mary's anointing of Christ's head shall be told for a memorial (Matt. xxvi. 13); and a record is kept of the women that laboured in the gospel tabernacle (Phil. iv. 3), and were helpers to Paul in Christ Jesus, Rom. xvi. 3. The poor may relieve the poor, and those that have nothing but their limbs and senses may be very charitable in the labour of love.

Verses 30-35

Here is the divine appointment of the master-workmen, that there might be no strife for the office. God is the God of order and not of confusion. 1. Those whom God called by name to this service he *filled with the Spirit of God*, to qualify them for it, *v.* 30, 31. Skill in secular employments is God's gift, and comes from above, Jam. i. 17. Thus when the apostles were appointed to be master-builders in setting up the gospel tabernacle they were *filled with the Spirit of God in wisdom and understanding*. 2. They were appointed, not only to devise, but to work (*v.* 32). 3. They were not only to devise and work themselves, but they were to teach others, *v.* 34. Not only had Bezaleel power to command, but he was to take pains to instruct. Those that rule should teach; and those to whom God has given knowledge should be willing to communicate it for the benefit of others, not coveting to monopolize it.

Chapter 36

In this chapter, I. The work of the tabernacle is begun, ver. 1–4. II. A stop is put to the people's contributions, ver. 5–7. III. A particular account is given of the making of the tabernacle itself; the fine curtains of it, ver. 8–13. The coarse ones, ver. 14–19. The boards, ver. 20–30. The bars, ver. 31–34. The partition veil, ver. 35, 36. And the hanging for the door, ver. 37, &c.

Verses 1-7

I. The workmen set in without delay. Then they wrought, *v.* 1. When God had qualified them for the work, then they applied themselves to it. They began when Moses called them, *v.* 2. Those are to be called to the building of the gospel tabernacle whom God has by his grace made in some measure fit for the work and free to engage in it. Ability and willingness (with resolution) are the two things to be regarded in the call of ministers. The materials which the people had contributed were delivered by Moses to the workmen, *v.* 3. Precious souls are the materials of the gospel tabernacle; they are *built up a spiritual house*, 1 Pet. ii. 5. To this end they are to offer themselves a free-will offering to the Lord, for his service (Rom. xv. 16), and they are then committed to the care of his ministers, as builders, to be framed and wrought upon by their edification and increase in holiness, till they all come, like the curtains of the tabernacle, *in the unity of the faith to be a holy temple*, Eph. ii. 21, 22; iv. 12, 13. II. The contributions restrained. The people continued to bring *free offerings every morning*, *v.* 3. Now observe, 1. The honesty of the workmen. When they had cut out their work, and found how their stuff held out, they went in a body to Moses to tell him that there needed no more contributions, *v.* 4, 5. They were men of integrity, that scorned to do so mean a thing as to sponge upon the people, and enrich themselves with that which was offered to the Lord. Those are the greatest cheats that cheat the public. 2. The liberality of the people. A rare instance! Most need a spur to quicken their charity; few need a bridle to check it, yet these did.

Verses 8-13

The first work they set about was the framing of the house, not made of timber or stone, but of curtains curiously embroidered and coupled together. This served to typify the state of the church in this world, the palace of God's kingdom among men. It is mean and mutable, and in a militant state; shepherds dwelt in tents, and God is the Shepherd of Israel; soldiers dwelt in tents, and the Lord is a man of war, and his church marches through an enemy's country, and must fight its way. The kings of the earth enclose themselves in cedar (Jer. xxii. 15), but the ark of God was lodged in curtains only. Yet there is a beauty in holiness; the curtains were embroidered, so is the church adorned with the gifts and graces of the Spirit, that *raiment of needle-work*, Ps. xlv. 14.

Verses 14-34

1. The shelter and special protection that the church is under are signified by the curtains of hair-cloth, which were spread over the tabernacle, and the covering of rams' skins and badgers' skins over them, *v.* 14–19. God has provided for his people a *shadow from the heat, and a covert from storm and rain*, Isa. iv. 6. Those that dwell in God's house shall find, be the tempest ever so violent, or the dropping ever so continual, it does not rain in. 2. The strength and stability of the church, though it is but a tabernacle, are signified by the boards and bars with which the curtains were borne up, *v.* 20–34.

Verses 35-38

1. There was a veil made for a partition between the holy place and the most holy, *v.* 35, 36. This signified the darkness and distance of that dispensation, compared with the New Testament, which shows us the glory of God more clearly and invites us to draw near to it. 2. There was a veil made for the door of the tabernacle, *v*, 37, 38. At this door the people assembled, though forbidden to enter; for, while we are in this present state, we must get as near to God as we can.

Chapter 37

Bezaleel and his workmen are still busy, making, I. The ark with the mercy-seat and the cherubim, ver. 1–9. II. The table with its vessels, ver. 10–16. III. The candlestick with its appurtenances, ver. 17–24. IV. The golden altar for incense, ver. 25–28. V. The holy oil and incense, ver. 29.

Verses 1-9

I. Moses had recorded so fully the instructions given him upon the mount for the making of all these things. Why then are so many chapters taken up with this narrative? We must consider, 1. That Moses wrote primarily for the people of Israel, to whom it would be of great use to read and hear often of these divine and sacred treasures with which they were entrusted. The great things of God's law and gospel we need to have inculcated upon us again and again. 2. Moses would thus show the great care which he and his workmen took to make every thing exactly according to the pattern shown him in the mount. Having before given us the original, he here gives us the copy, that we may compare them, and observe how exactly they agree. II. In these verses we have an account of the making of the ark, with its glorious and most significant appurtenances, the mercy-seat and the cherubim. Consider these three together, and they represent the glory of a holy God, the sincerity of a holy heart, and the communion that is between them, in and by a Mediator.

Verses 10-24

Here is, 1. The making of the table on which the show-bread was to be continually placed. God is a good householder, that always keeps a plentiful table. Is the world his tabernacle? His providence in it spreads a table for all the creatures: he *provides food for all flesh.* Is the church his tabernacle? His grace in it spreads a table for all believers, furnished with the bread of life. But observe how much the dispensation of the gospel exceeds that of the law. Though here was a table furnished, it was only with *show-bread,* bread to be looked upon, not to be fed upon, while it was on this table, and afterwards only by the priests; but to the table which Christ has spread in the new covenant all real Christians are invited guests; and to them it is said, *Eat, O friends, come eat of my bread.* What the law gave but a sight of at a distance, the gospel gives the enjoyment of, and a hearty welcome to. 2. The making of the candlestick, all beaten work of pure gold only, *v.* 17, 22. The Bible is a golden candlestick; it is of pure gold, Ps. xix. 10. From it light is diffused to every part of God's tabernacle.

Verses 25–29

Here is, 1. The making of the golden altar, on which incense was to be burnt daily, which signified both the prayers of saints and the intercession of Christ. The rings and staves, and all the appurtenances of this altar, were overlaid with gold, as all the vessels of the table and candlestick were of gold, for these were used in the holy place. 2. The preparing of the incense which was to be burnt upon this altar, and with it the holy anointing oil (*v.* 29).

CHAPTER 38

Here is an account, I. Of the making of the brazen altar (ver. 1–7), and the laver, ver. 8. II. The preparing of the hangings for the enclosing of the court in which the tabernacle was to stand, ver. 9–20. III. A summary of the gold, silver, and brass, that was contributed to, and used in, the preparing of the tabernacle, ver. 21, &c.

Verses 1–8

Bezaleel having finished the gold-work, which, though the richest, yet was ordered to lie most out of sight, in the tabernacle itself, here goes on to prepare the court, which lay open to the view of all. Two things the court was furnished with, and both made of brass:—

I. An altar of burnt-offering, *v.* 1–7. On this all their sacrifices were offered.

II. A laver, to hold water for the priests to wash in when they went in to minister, *v.* 8. This is here said to be made of the *looking-glasses* (or mirrors) of the women that assembled at the door of the tabernacle.

1. It should seem these women were eminent and exemplary for devotion. Anna was such a one long afterwards, who *departed not from the temple, but served God with fastings and prayers night and day,* Luke ii. 37.

2. These women parted with their mirrors for the use of the tabernacle. Rather than the workmen should want brass, or not have of the best, they would part with their mirrors, though they could not do well without them.

3. These mirrors were used for the making of the laver. Either they were artfully joined together, or else molten down and cast anew.

Verses 9–20

The walls of the court, or church yard, were like the rest curtains or hangings, made according to the appointment, *ch.* xxvii. 9, &c. This represented the state of the Old Testament church: it was a garden enclosed; the worshippers were then confined to a little compass. But the enclosure being of curtains only intimated that the confinement of the church in one particular nation was not to be perpetual.

The dispensation itself was a tabernacle-dispensation' movable and mutable, and in due time to be taken down and folded up, when the place of the tent should be enlarged and its cords lengthened, to make room for the Gentile world, as is foretold, Isa. liv. 2, 3.

Verses 21–31

Here we have a breviat of the account which, by Moses's appointment, the Levites took and kept of the gold, silver, and brass, that was brought in for the tabernacle's use, and how it was employed. Ithamar the son of Aaron was appointed to draw up this account, and was thus by less services trained up and filled for greater, *v.* 21. Bezaleel and Aholiab must bring in the account (*v.* 22, 23), and Ithamar must audit it, and give it in to Moses. And it was thus:—1. All the gold was a free will offering. 2. The silver was levied by way of tax; every man was assessed half a shekel, a kind of poll-money.

CHAPTER 39

This chapter gives us an account of the finishing of the work of the tabernacle. I. The last things prepared were the holy garments. The ephod and its curious girdle, ver. 1–5. The onyx-stones for the shoulders, ver. 6, 7. The breastplate with the precious stones in it, ver. 8–21. The robe of the ephod, ver. 22–26. The coats, bonnets, and breeches, for the inferior priests, ver. 27–29. And the plate of the holy crown, ver. 30, 31.

Verses 1–31

In this account of the making of the priests' garments, according to the instructions given (*ch.* xxviii), we may observe, 1. That the priests' garments are called here *clothes of service, v.* 1. It is said of those that are arrayed in white robes that they *are before the throne of God, and serve him day and night in his temple,* Rev. vii. 13, 15. 2. That all the six paragraphs here, which give a distinct account of the making of these holy garments, conclude with those words, *as the Lord commanded Moses, v.* 5, 7, 21, 26, 29, 31. It is an intimation to all the Lord's ministers to make the word of God their rule in all their ministrations, and to act in observance of and obedience to the command of God. 3. That these garments, in conformity to the rest of the furniture of the tabernacle, were very rich and splendid; the church in its infancy was thus taught, thus pleased, with the rudiments of this world. 4. That they were all shadows of good things to come, but the substance is Christ, and the grace of the gospel; when therefore the substance has come, it is a jest to be fond of the shadow. (1) Christ is our great high-priest; when he undertook the work of our redemption, he put on the clothes of service. (2) True believers are spiritual priests. The clean linen with which all their clothes of service must be made is *the righteousness of saints* (Rev. xix. 8).

Verses 32–43

I. The builders of the tabernacle made very good despatch. It was not much more than five months from the beginning to the finishing of it.

II. They punctually observed their orders, and did not in the least vary from them. They did it *according to all that the Lord commanded Moses, v.* 32, 42.

III. They brought all their work to Moses, and submitted it to his inspection and censure, *v.* 33. Though they knew how to do the work better than Moses, Moses had a better and more exact idea of the model than they had, and therefore they could not be well pleased with their own work, unless they had his approbation.

IV. Moses, upon search, found all done according to the rule, *v.* 43. Behold they had done it according to the pattern shown him, for the same Being that showed him the pattern guided their hand in the work.

V. Moses blessed them. 1. He commended them, and signified his approbation of all they had done. He did not find fault where there was none, as some do, who think they disparage their own judgment if they do not find something amiss in the best and most accomplished performance. In all this work it is probable there might have been found here and there a stitch amiss, and a stroke awry, but Moses was too candid to notice small faults where there were no great ones. 2. He not only praised them, but prayed for them.

CHAPTER 40

In this chapter, I. Orders are given for the setting up of the tabernacle and the fixing of all the appurtenances of it in their proper places (ver. 1-8), and the consecrating of it (ver. 9-11), and of the priests, ver. 12-15. II. Care is taken to do all this as it was appointed to be done, ver. 16-33. III. God takes possession of it by the cloud, ver. 34, &c.

Verses 1–15

The materials and furniture of the tabernacle had been viewed severally and approved, and now they must be put together. 1. The time for doing this is fixed to *the first day of the first month* (v. 2). It is good to begin the year with some good work. Let him that is the first have the first; and let the things of his kingdom be first sought. In Hezekiah's time we find they began to sanctify the temple *on the first day of the first month,* 2 Chron. xxix. 17. Moses is particularly ordered to set up the tabernacle itself first, in which God would dwell and would be served (v. 2), then to put the ark in its place, and draw the veil before it (v. 3), then to fix the table, and the candlestick, and the altar of incense, without the veil (v. 4, 5), and to fix the hanging of the door before the door. Then in the court he must place the altar of burnt offering, and the laver (v. 6, 7); and, lastly, he must set up the curtains of the court, and a hanging for a court-gate. 2. He directs Moses, when he had set up the tabernacle and all the furniture of it, to consecrate it and them; by anointing them with the oil which was prepared for the purpose, ch. xxx. 25, &c. Everything was sanctified when it was put in its proper place. As everything is beautiful in its season, so is everything in its place. 3. He directs him to consecrate Aaron and his sons.

Verses 16–33

When the tabernacle and the furniture of it were prepared, they set it up in the midst of their camp, while they were in the wilderness.

Here we have an account of that new year's day's work. That which was to be veiled he veiled (v. 21), and that which was to be used he used immediately. What he did he did by special warrant and direction from God, rather as a prophet, or law-giver, than as a priest. He set the wheels a-going, and then left the work in the hands of the appointed ministry. (1) When he had placed the table, he set the show-bread in order upon it (v. 23). (2) As soon as he had fixed the candlestick, *he lighted the lamps before the Lord,* v. 25. (3) The golden altar being put in its place, immediately he *burnt sweet incense thereon* (v. 27). (4) The altar of burnt-offering was no sooner set up in the court of the tabernacle than he had a *burnt-offering, and a meat-offering, ready to offer upon it,* v. 29. (5) At the laver likewise, when he had fixed that, Moses himself washed his hands and feet.

Verses 34–38

As when, in the creation, God had finished this earth, which he designed for man's habitation, he made man, and put him in possession of it, so when Moses had finished the tabernacle, which was designed for God's dwelling-place among men, God came and took possession of it. Where God has a throne and an altar in the soul, there is a living temple. Accordingly, when God descended to take possession of his house, the *cloud covered it* on the outside, and *the glory of the Lord filled it* within.

I. *The cloud covered the tent.* This cloud was intended to be, 1. A token of God's presence constantly visible day and night (v. 38) to all Israel, even to those that lay in the remotest corners of the camp, that they might never again make a question of it, *Is the Lord among us, or is he not?* 2. A concealment of the tabernacle, and the glory of God in it. God did indeed dwell among them, but he dwelt in a cloud. 3. A protection of the tabernacle. They had sheltered it with one covering upon another, but, after all, the cloud that covered it was its best guard. Those that dwell in the house of the Lord are safe under the divine protection, Ps. xxvii. 4, 5. 4. A guide to the camp of Israel in their march through the wilderness, v. 36, 37. While the cloud continued on the tabernacle, they rested; when it removed, they removed and followed it, as being purely under divine direction.

II. *The glory of the Lord filled the tabernacle,* v. 34, 35. It was in light and fire, and (for aught we know) no otherwise, than that the *shechinah* made itself visible; for *God is light.*

THE THIRD BOOK OF MOSES, CALLED

LEVITICUS

There is nothing historical in all this book of Leviticus except the account which it gives us of the consecration of the priesthood (ch. viii, ix), of the punishment of Nadab and Abihu, by the hand of God, for offering strange fire (ch. x.), and of Shelomith's son, by the hand of the magistrate, for blasphemy, ch. xxiv. All the rest of the book is taken up with the laws, chiefly the ecclesiastical laws, which God gave to Israel by Moses, concerning their sacrifices and offerings, their meats and drinks, and divers washings, and the other peculiarities by which God set that people apart for himself, and distinguished them from other nations, all which were shadows of good things to come, which are realized and superseded by the gospel of Christ. We call the book *Leviticus*, from the Septuagint, because it contains the laws and ordinances of the *levitical priesthood* (as it is called, Heb. vii. 11), and the ministrations of it. The Levites were principally charged with these institutions, both to do their part and to teach the people theirs. We read, in the close of the foregoing book, of the setting up of the tabernacle, which was to be the place of worship; and, as that was framed according to the pattern, so must the ordinances of worship be, which were there to be administered.

CHAPTER 1

This book begins with the laws concerning sacrifices, of which the most ancient were the burnt-offerings, about which God gives Moses instructions in this chapter. I. If it was a bullock out of the herd, ver. 3–9. II. If it was a sheep or goat, a lamb or kid, out of the flock, ver. 10–13. III. If it was a turtle-dove or a young pigeon, ver. 14–17. And whether the offering was more or less valuable in itself, if it was offered with an upright heart, according to these laws, it was accepted of God.

Verses 1–2

Observe here, 1. It is taken for granted that people would be inclined to bring offerings to the Lord. Revealed religion supposes natural religion to be an ancient and early institution, since the fall had directed men to glorify God by sacrifice, which was an implicit acknowledgment of their having received all from God as creatures, and their having forfeited all to him as sinners. Provision is made that men should not indulge their own fancies, nor become vain about their sacrifices, lest, while they pretended to honour God, they should really dishonour him. Everything therefore is directed to be done so that the sacrifices might be most significant both of the great sacrifice of atonement which Christ was to offer in the fulness of time and of the spiritual sacrifices of acknowledgment which believers should offer daily. God gave those laws to Israel by Moses. By other prophets God sent messages to his people, but by Moses he gave them laws. As soon as ever the shechinah had taken possession of its new habitation, God talked with Moses from the mercy-seat, while he attended without the veil, or rather at the door, hearing a voice only. The tabernacle was set up to be a place of communion between God and Israel; there, where they performed their services to God, God revealed his will to them. The moral law was given with terror from a burning mountain in thunder and lightning; but the remedial law of sacrifice was given more gently from a mercy-seat, because that was typical of the grace of the gospel, which is the ministration of life and peace.

Verses 3–9

If a man were rich and could afford it, it is supposed that he would bring his burnt-sacrifice, with which he designed to honour God, out of his herd of larger cattle. 1. The beast to be offered must be a male, and without blemish, and the best he had in his pasture. 2. The owner must offer it voluntarily. What is done in religion, so as to please God, must be done by no other constraint than that of love. 3. It must be offered at the door of the tabernacle, where the brazen altar of burnt-offerings stood, which

sanctified the gift. He must offer it at the door, as one unworthy to enter, and acknowledging that there is no admission for a sinner into covenant and communion with God, but by sacrifice. 4. The offerer must put his hand upon the head of his offering, *v.* 4, signifying thereby, (1) The transfer of all his right to, and interest in, the beast to God. (2) An acknowledgment that he deserved to die, and would have been willing to die if God had required it. (3) A dependence upon the sacrifice, as an instituted type of the great sacrifice on which the iniquity of us all was to be laid. Though the burnt-offerings had not respect to any particular sin, as the sin-offering had, yet they were to make atonement for sin in general. 5. The sacrifice was to be killed by the priests or Levites, before the Lord, that is, in a devout religious manner. 6. The priests were to *sprinkle the blood upon the altar* (*v.* 5); for, the blood being the life, it was this that made atonement for the soul. 7. The beast was to be flayed and decently cut up, and divided into its several joints or pieces, and then all the pieces, with the head and the fat were to be burnt together upon the altar, *v.* 6–9. 8. This is said to be *an offering of a sweet savour*, or *savour of rest, unto the Lord*. The burning of flesh is unsavoury in itself; but this, as an act of obedience to a divine command, and a type of Christ, was well pleasing to God: he was reconciled to the offerer. Christ's offering of himself to God is said to be of *a sweet-smelling savour* (Eph. v. 2), and the spiritual sacrifices of Christians are said to be *acceptable to God, through Christ*, 1 Pet. ii. 5.

Verses 10–17

Here we have the laws concerning the burnt-offerings, which were of the flock or of the fowls. Those of the middle rank, that could not well afford to offer a bullock, would bring a sheep or a goat; and those that were not able to do that should be accepted of God if they brought a turtle-dove or a pigeon. It is observable that those creatures were chosen for sacrifice which were most mild and gentle, harmless and inoffensive, to typify the innocence and meekness that were in Christ, and to teach the innocence and meekness that should be in Christians. Directions are here given, 1. Concerning the burnt-offerings of the flock, *v.* 10. The method of managing these is much the same with that of the bullocks. 2. Concerning those of the fowls. They must be either turtle-doves or *pigeons*, and, if so, they must be young pigeons. The poor man's turtle-doves, or young pigeons, are here said to be *an offering of a sweet-smelling savour*, as much as that of an ox or bullock that hath horns or hoofs. Yet, after all, to *love God with all our heart, and to love our neighbour as ourselves, is better than all burnt-offerings and sacrifices,* Mark xii. 33.

CHAPTER 2

In this chapter we have the law concerning the meat-offering. I. The matter of it; whether of raw flour with oil and incense (ver. 1), or baked in the oven (ver. 4), or upon a plate (ver. 5, 6), or in a frying pan, ver. 7. II. The management of it, of the flour (ver. 2, 3), of the cakes, ver. 8–10. III. Some particular rules concerning it, That leaven and honey must never be admitted (ver. 11, 12), and salt never omitted in the meat-offering, ver. 13. IV. The law concerning the offering of firstfruits in the ear, ver. 14, & c.

Verses 1–10

The law of this chapter concerns those meat-offerings that were offered by themselves, whenever a man saw cause thus to express his devotion. The first offering we read of in scripture was of this kind (Gen. iv. 3): *Cain brought of the fruit of the ground an offering.*

I. This sort of offering was appointed, 1. In condescension to the poor, and their ability, that those who themselves lived only upon bread and cakes might offer an acceptable offering to God out of that which was their own coarse and homely fare. 2. As a proper acknowledgment of the mercy of God to them in their food. This was like a quit-rent, by which they testified their dependence upon God, their thankfulness to him, and their expectations from him. Those that now, with a grateful charitable heart, deal out their bread to the hungry, offer unto God an acceptable meat-offering.

II. The laws of the meat-offerings were these:—1. The ingredients must always be fine flour and oil, two staple commodities of the land of Canaan, Deut. viii. 8. Oil was to them then in their food what butter is now to us. 2. If it was flour unbaked, besides the oil it must have frankincense put upon it, which was to be burnt with it (*v.* 1, 2), for the perfuming of the altar. 3. If it was prepared, this might be done in various ways; the offerer might bake it, or fry it, or mix the flour and oil upon a plate. The law was very exact even about those offerings that were least costly. 4. It was to be presented by the offerer to the priest, which is called *bringing it to the Lord* (*v.* 8). 5. Part of it was to be burnt upon the altar, for a memorial, that is, in token of their mindfulness of God's bounty to them, in giving them all things richly to enjoy. 6. The remainder of the meat-offering was to be given to the priests, *v.* 3, 10. Thus God provided that those who served at the altar should live upon the altar, and live comfortably.

Verses 11–16

I. Leaven and honey are forbidden to be put in any of their meat-offerings. 1. The leaven was forbidden in remembrance of the unleavened bread they ate when they came out of Egypt. 2. Honey was forbidden, though Canaan flowed with it. Some think the chief reason why these two things, leaven and honey, were forbidden, was because the Gentiles used them very much in their sacrifices, and God's people must not learn or use the way of the heathen. Some make this application of this double prohibition: leaven signifies grief and sadness of spirit (Ps. lxxiii. 21), *My heart was leavened*; honey signifies sensual pleasure and mirth.

II. Salt is required in all their offerings, *v.* 13. The altar was the table of the Lord; and therefore, salt being always set on our tables, God would have it always used at his. It is called *the salt of the covenant,* because, as men confirmed their covenants with each other by eating and drinking together, at all which collations salt was used, so God, by accepting his people's gifts and feasting them upon his sacrifices,

supping with them and they with him (Rev. iii. 20), did confirm his covenant with them. Among the ancients salt was a symbol of friendship. The salt for the sacrifice was not brought by the offerers, but was provided at the public charge, as the wood was, Ezra vii. 20–22. And there was a chamber in the court of the temple called *the chamber of salt,* in which they laid it up. Christianity is the salt of the earth.

III. Directions are given about the first-fruits. 1. The oblation of their first-fruits at harvest, of which we read, Deut. xxvi. 2. These were offered to the Lord, not to be burnt upon the altar, but to be given to the priests as perquisites of their office, *v.* 12. 2. A meat-offering of their first-fruits. The former was required by the law; this was a free-will offering, *v.* 14–16. (1) Be sure to bring the first ripe and full ears, not such as were small and half-withered. (2) These green ears must be dried by the fire, that the corn, such as it was, might be beaten out of them. (3) Oil and frankincense must be put upon it. Thus wisdom and humility must soften and sweeten the spirits and services of young people. God takes a particular delight in the first ripe fruits of the Spirit and the expressions of early piety and devotion. (4) It must be used as other meat-offerings, *v.* 16, compare *v.* 9. He shall *offer all the frankincense; it is an offering made by fire.* Holy love to God is the fire by which all our offerings must be made; else they are not of a sweet savour to God. Frankincense denotes the mediation and intercession of Christ, by which all our services are perfumed and recommended to God's gracious acceptance.

CHAPTER 3

In this chapter we have the law concerning the peace-offerings, whether they were, I. Of the herd, a bullock, or a heifer, ver. 1–5. Or, II. Of the flock, either a lamb (ver. 6–11) or a goat, ver. 12–17.

Verses 1–5

The burnt-offerings were purely expressive of adoration, and therefore were wholly burnt. But the peace-offerings had regard to God as a benefactor to his creatures, and the giver of all good things to us; and therefore these were divided between the altar, the priest, and the owner. Peace signifies, 1. Reconciliation, concord, and communion. And so these were called *peace-offerings,* because in them God and his people did, as it were, feast together, in token of friendship. 2. It signifies prosperity and all happiness: *Peace be to you* was as much as, *All good* be to you; and so the peace-offerings were offered either, (1) By way of supplication or request for some good that was wanted and desired. Or, (2) By way of thanksgiving for some particular mercy received. It is called *a peace-offering of thanksgiving,* for so it was sometimes; as in other cases *a vow, ch.* vii. 15, 16. The sacrifice of praise shall please the Lord better than an ox.

Verses 6–17

Directions are here given concerning the peace-offering, if it was a sheep or a goat. Turtle-doves or young pigeons, which might be brought for whole burnt-offerings, were not allowed for peace-offerings, because they have not fat considerable enough to be burnt upon the altar. The laws concerning a lamb or goat offered for a peace offering are much the same with those concerning a bullock.

CHAPTER 4

This chapter is concerning the sin-offering, which was properly intended to make atonement for a sin committed through ignorance, I. By the priest himself, ver. 1–12. Or, II. By the whole congregation, ver. 13–21. Or, III. By a ruler, ver. 22–26. Or, IV. By a private person, ver. 27, &c.

Verses 1–12

Here begin the statutes of another session, another day. From the throne of glory between the cherubim God delivered these orders. Burnt-offerings, meat-offerings, and peace-offerings, it should seem, had been offered before the giving of the law upon Mount Sinai.

I. The general case we have supposed, *v.* 2. Here observe, 1. Concerning sin in general, that it is described to be against *any of the commandments of the Lord*; for *sin is the transgression of the law*, the divine law. It is said likewise, *if a soul sin*, for it is not sin if it be not some way or other the soul's act; hence it is called the *sin of the soul* (Mic. vi. 7), and it is the soul that is injured by it, Prov. viii. 36. 2. Concerning the sins for which those offerings were appointed. (1) They are supposed to be overt acts; for, had they been required to bring a sacrifice for every sinful thought or word, the task had been endless. Atonement was made for those in the gross, on the day of expiation, once a year; but these are said to be done against the commandments. (2) They are supposed to be sins of commission, things which ought not to be done. (3) They are supposed to be sins committed through ignorance. But if the offender were either ignorant of the law, as in divers instances we may suppose many were (so numerous and various were the prohibitions), or were surprised into the sin unawares, relief was provided by the remedial law of the sin-offering.

II. The law begins with the case of the anointed priest, that is, the high priest, provided he should sin through ignorance; for *the law made men priests who had infirmity*. Though his ignorance was of all others least excusable, yet he was allowed to bring his offering. Now the law concerning the sin-offering for the high priest is, 1. That he must bring a bullock without blemish for a sin-offering (*v.* 3), as valuable an offering as that for the whole congregation (*v.* 14). 2. The hand of the offerer must be laid upon the head of the offering (*v.* 4), with a solemn penitent confession of the sin he had committed, putting it upon the head of the sin-offering, ch. xvi. 21. 3. The bullock must be killed, and a great deal of solemnity there must be in disposing of the blood; for it was *the blood that made atonement*, and *without shedding of blood* there was *no remission*, *v.* 5–7. Some of the blood of the high-priest's sin-offering was to be *sprinkled seven times before the veil*, with an eye towards the mercy-seat, though it was veiled: some of it was to be put upon the horns of the golden altar, because at that altar the priest himself ministered; and thus was signified the putting away of that pollution which from his sins did cleave to his services. When this was done the remainder of the blood was poured at the foot of the brazen altar. By this rite, the sinner acknowledged that he deserved to have his blood thus poured out like water. It likewise signified the pouring out of the soul before God in true repentance, and typified our Saviour's *pouring out his soul unto death*. 4. The fat of the inwards was to be burnt upon the altar of burnt-offering, *v.* 8–10. By this the intention of the offering and of the atonement made by it was directed to the glory of God, who, having been dishonoured by the sin, was thus honoured by the sacrifice.

Verses 13–21

This is the law for expiating the guilt of a national sin, by a sin-offering. If the leaders of the people, through mistake concerning the law, caused them to err, when the mistake was discovered an offering must be brought, that wrath might not come upon the whole congregation. 1. It is possible that the church may err, and that her guides may mislead her. It is here supposed that the whole congregation may sin, and sin through ignorance. God will always

have a church on earth; but he never said it should be infallible, or perfectly pure from corruption on this side heaven. 2. When a sacrifice was to be offered for the whole congregation, the elders were to lay their hands upon the head of it (three of them at least), as representatives of the people and agents for them. 3. The blood of this sin-offering, as of the former, was to be *sprinkled seven times before the Lord*, *v.* 17. It was not to be poured out there, but sprinkled only; for the cleansing virtue of the blood of Christ was then and is still sufficiently signified and represented by sprinkling, Isa. lii. 15. It was to be sprinkled seven times. Seven is a number of perfection, because when God had made the world in six days he rested the seventh; so this signified the perfect satisfaction Christ made, and the complete cleansing of the souls of the faithful by it; see Heb. x. 14. When the offering is completed, it is said, *atonement is made, and the sin shall be forgiven*, *v.* 20. The promise of remission is founded upon the atonement.

Verses 22–26

Observe here, 1. That God takes notice of and is displeased with the sins of rulers. 2. The sin of the ruler which he committed through ignorance is supposed afterwards to come to his knowledge (*v.* 23), which must be either by the check of his own conscience or by the reproof of his friends. 3. The sin-offering for a ruler was to be *a kid of the goats*, not a bullock, as for the priest and the whole congregation; nor was the blood of his sin-offering to be brought into the tabernacle, as of the other two, but it was all bestowed upon the brazen altar (*v.* 25); nor was the flesh of it to be burnt, as that of the other two, without the camp, which intimated that the sin of a ruler, though worse than that of a common person, yet was not so heinous, nor of such pernicious consequence, as the sin of the high priest, or of the whole congregation. 4. It is promised that the atonement shall be accepted and the sin forgiven (*v.* 26), that is, if he repent and reform.

Verses 27–35

I. Here is the law of the sin-offering for a common person, which differs from that for a ruler only in this, that a private person might bring either a kid or a lamb, a ruler only a kid; and that for a ruler must be a male, for the other a female. 1. The case supposed: *If any one of the common people sin through ignorance*, *v.* 27. If they sin through ignorance, they must bring a sin-offering. We have all need to pray with David to be cleansed from *secret faults*, the errors which we ourselves do not understand or are not aware of, Ps. xix. 12. 2. That the sins of ignorance committed by a single obscure person did require a sacrifice. 3. That a sin-offering was not only admitted, but accepted, even from one of the common people, and an atonement made by it, *v.* 31, 35. Here rich and poor, prince and peasant, meet together; they are both alike welcome to Christ upon the same terms. See Job xxxiv. 19.

II. From all these laws concerning the sin-offerings we may learn, 1. To hate sin, and to watch against it. 2. To value Christ, the great and true sin-offering, whose blood cleanses from all sin, which it was not possible that the *blood of bulls and of goats should take away*. And perhaps there was some allusion to this law concerning sacrifices for sins of ignorance in that prayer of Christ's, just when he was offering up himself a sacrifice, *Father, forgive them, for they know not what they do.*

CHAPTER 5

This chapter, and part of the next, concern the trespass-offering. The difference between this and the sin-offering lay not so much in the sacrifices themselves as in the occasions of the offering of them. They were both intended to make atonement for sin; but the former was more general, this applied to some particular instances. Observe what is here said, I. Concerning the trespass. If a man sin, 1. In concealing his knowledge, when he is adjured, ver. 1. 2. In touching an unclean thing, ver. 2, 3. 3. In swearing, ver. 4. 4. In embezzling the holy things, ver. 14–16. 5. In any sin of infirmity, ver. 17–19. Some other cases there are, in which these offerings were to be offered, ch. vi. 2–4; xiv. 12; xix. 21; Num. vi. 12. II. Concerning the trespass-offerings, 1. Of the flock, ver. 5, 6. 2. Of fowls, ver. 7–10. 3. Of flour, ver. 11–13; but chiefly a ram without blemish, ver. 15, &c.

Verses 1–6

I. The offences here supposed are, 1. A man's concealing the truth when he was sworn as a witness to speak the truth, the whole truth, and nothing but the truth. Judges among the Jews had power to adjure not only the witnesses, as with us, but the person suspected, as appears by the high priest adjuring our Saviour, who thereupon answered, though before he stood silent, Matt. xxvi. 63, 64. Now (*v.* 1), *If a soul sin* (that is, a person, for the soul is the man), if he *hear the voice of swearing* (that is, if he be adjured to testify what he knows, if in such a case he refuses to give evidence, or gives it but in part, *he shall bear his iniquity.* Let all that are called out at any time to bear testimony think of this law, and be free and open in their evidence, and take heed of prevaricating. An oath of the Lord is a sacred thing, and not to be dallied with. 2. A man's touching anything that was ceremonially unclean, *v.* 2, 3. If a man, polluted by such touch, came into the sanctuary inconsiderately, or if he neglected to wash himself according to the law, then he was to look upon himself as under guilt, and must bring his offering. 3. Rash swearing. If a man bind himself by an oath that he will do or not do such a thing, and the performance of his oath afterwards proves either unlawful or impracticable, by which he is discharged from the obligation, yet he must bring an offering to atone for his folly in swearing so rashly.

II. Now in these cases, 1. The offender must confess his sin and bring his offering (*v.* 5, 6); and the offering was not accepted unless it was accompanied with a penitential confession and a humble prayer for pardon. 2. The priest must *make an atonement for him.*

Verses 7–13

Provision is here made for the poor of God's people, and the pacifying of their consciences under the sense of guilt. Those that were not able to bring a lamb might bring for a sin-offering a pair of *turtle doves* or *two young pigeons*; nay, if any were so extremely poor that they were not able to procure these, they might bring a pottle of fine flour, and this should be accepted. Thus the expense of the sin-offering was brought lower than that of any other offering, to teach us that no man's poverty shall ever be a bar in the way of his pardon. No man shall say that he had not wherewithal to bear the charges of a journey to heaven.

I. If the sinner brought two doves, one was to be offered for a sin-offering and the other for a burnt-offering, *v.* 7. Observe, 1. Before he offered the burnt-offering, which was for the honour and praise of God, he must offer the sin-offering, to make atonement. 2. After the sin-offering, which made atonement, came the burnt-offering, as an acknowledgment of the great mercy of God in appointing and accepting the atonement.

II. If he brought fine flour, a handful of it was to be offered, but without either oil or frankincense (*v.* 11), not only because this would make it too costly for the poor, but because it was a sin-offering, and therefore, to show the loathsomeness of the sin for which it was offered, it must not be made grateful either to the taste by oil or to the smell by frankincense.

Verses 14–19

Here we have the law concerning those that were properly and peculiarly *trespass-offerings*, which were offered to atone for trespass done against a neighbour. Now injuries done to another may be either in holy things or in common things; of the former we have the law in these verses; of the latter in the beginning of the next chapter. Now if a man did alienate or convert to his own use any thing that was dedicated to God, unwittingly, he was to bring this sacrifice; as suppose he had ignorantly made use of the tithes, or first-fruits, or first-born of his cattle, or had eaten any of those parts of the sacrifices which were appropriated to the priests; this was a trespass. If it was done presumptuously, and in contempt of the law, the offender died without mercy, Heb. x. 28. But in case of negligence and ignorance this sacrifice was appointed. The trespasser must bring an offering to the Lord, which, in all those that were purely trespass-offerings, must be a *ram without blemish.* He must likewise make restitution to the priest, according to a just estimation of the thing which he had so alienated, adding a fifth part to it.

CHAPTER 6

The first seven verses of this chapter might fitly have been added to the foregoing chapter, being a continuation of the law of the trespass-offering, and then at ver. 8 he comes to appoint the several rites and ceremonies concerning, 1. The burnt-offering, ver. 8–13. II. The meat-offering (ver. 14–18), particularly that at the consecration of the priest, ver. 19–23. III. The sin-offering, ver. 24, &c.

Verses 1–7

The latter part of the law of the trespass-offering.

I. The trespass supposed, *v.* 2, 3. Though all the instances relate to our neighbour, yet it is called a *trespass against the Lord.* He that speaks evil of his brother is said to speak evil of the law, and consequently of the Law-maker, Jam. iv. 11. The trespasses specified are, 1. Denying a trust: *If a man lie unto his neighbour in that which was delivered him to keep*, or, which is worse, which was lent him for his use. 2. Defrauding a partner: *If a man lie in fellowship*, claiming a sole interest in that wherein he has but a joint-interest. 3. Disowning a manifest wrong: *If a man* has the front to *lie in a thing taken away by violence*, which ordinarily cannot be hid. 4. Deceiving in commerce, or, as some think, by false accusation. 5. Detaining what is found, and denying it (*v.* 3).

II. The trespass-offering appointed. 1. *In the day of his trespass-offering* he must make satisfaction to his brother. Let him faithfully restore all that he has got by fraud or oppression, with a fifth part added. 2. He must *then come and offer his gift*, must *bring his trespass-offering to the Lord* whom he had offended; and the priest must make an atonement for him, *v.* 6, 7.

Verses 8–13

Moses was directed to give instructions to the priests; he must *command Aaron and his sons*, *v.* 9.

In these verses we have the law of the burnt-offering, as far as it was the peculiar care of the priests. The daily sacrifice of a lamb, which was offered morning and evening for the whole congregation, is here chiefly referred to.

I. The priest must take care of the ashes of the burnt-offering, that they may be decently disposed of, *v.* 10, 11. He must clear the altar of them every morning, and put them on the east side of the altar, which was furthest from the sanctuary; this he must do in his linen garment, which he always wore when he did any service at the altar; and then he must put on other garments, and must *carry the ashes into a clean place without the camp.* The priest himself must not only kindle the fire, but clean the hearth, and carry out the ashes. God's servants must think nothing below them but sin.

II. The priest must take care of the fire upon the altar. *The fire shall ever be burning upon the altar, it shall never go out, v.* 13. Though we be not always sacrificing, yet we must keep the fire of holy love always burning; and thus we must pray always.

Verses 14–23

The meat-offering was either that which was offered by the people or that by the priests at their consecration.

I. As to the common meat-offering,

1. Only a handful of it was to be burnt upon the altar; all the rest was allowed to the priests for their food.

2. The laws concerning the eating of it were, (1) That it must be *eaten unleavened, v.* 16. (2) It must be eaten in *the court of the tabernacle* (here called the *holy place*). (3) The males only must eat of it, *v.* 18. (4) The priests only that were clean might eat of it.

II. As to the consecration meat-offering, which was offered for the priests themselves, it was to be *wholly burnt, and none of it eaten, v.* 23. The Jewish writers say that the high priest was bound to offer it every day of his life, from the day in which he was anointed. Josephus says, "The high priest sacrificed twice every day at his own charges, and this was his sacrifice." The meat-offering of the priest was to be baked as if it were to be eaten, and yet it must be wholly burnt.

Verses 24–30

We have here so much of the law of the sin-offering as did peculiarly concern the priests that offered it. As, 1. That it must be killed *in the place where the burnt-offering was killed* (*v.* 25). 2. That the priest who offered it for the sinner was (with his sons, or other priests, *v.* 29) to eat the flesh of it, after the blood and fat had been offered to God, in the *court of the tabernacle, v.* 26. 3. The blood of the sin-offering was with great reverence to be washed out of the clothes on which it happened to light (*v.* 27). 4. The vessel in which the flesh of the sin-offering was boiled must be broken if it were an earthen one, and, if a brazen one, well washed, *v.* 28.

CHAPTER 7

Here is, I. The law of the trespass-offering (ver. 1–7), with some further directions concerning the burnt-offering and the meat-offering, ver. 8–10. II. The law of the peace-offering. The eating of it (ver. 11–21), on which occasion the prohibition of eating fat or blood is repeated (ver. 22–27), and the priests' share of it, ver. 28–34. III. The conclusion of those institutions, ver. 35, &c.

Verses 1–10

Observe here, 1. Concerning the trespass-offering, that, being much of the same nature with the sin-offering, it was to be governed by the same rules, *v.* 6. When the blood and fat were offered to God to make atonement, the priests were to eat the flesh, as that of the sin-offering, in the holy place. The Jews have a tradition (as we have it from the learned bishop Patrick) concerning the sprinkling of the blood of the trespass-offering *round about upon the altar,* "That there was a scarlet line which went round about the altar exactly in the middle, and the blood of the burnt-offerings was sprinkled round about above the line, but that of the trespass-offerings and peace-offerings round about below the line." It seems the offerer was not himself to have any share of his trespass-offering, as he was to have of his peace-offering; but it was all divided between the altar and the priest. They offered peace-offerings in thankfulness

for mercy, and then it was proper to feast; but they offered trespass-offerings in sorrow for sin, and then fasting was more proper, in token of holy mourning, and a resolution to abstain from sin. 2. Concerning the burnt-offering it is here appointed that the priest that offered it should have the skin (*v.* 8), which no doubt he might make money of. 3. Concerning the meat-offering, if it was dressed, it was fit to be eaten immediately; and therefore the priest that offered it was to have it, *v.* 9.

Verses 11–34

I. The nature and intention of the peace-offerings are here more distinctly opened. They were offered either, 1. In thankfulness for some special mercy received, such as recovery from sickness, preservation in a journey, deliverance at sea, redemption out of captivity. Or, 2. In performance of some vow which a man made when he was in distress (*v.* 16). Or, 3. In supplication for some special mercy, here called a *voluntary offering.* This accompanied a man's prayers, as the former did his praises.

II. The rites and ceremonies about the peace-offerings are enlarged upon.

1. If the peace-offering was offered for a thanksgiving, a meat-offering must be offered with it, cakes of several sorts, and wafers (*v.* 12), and (which was peculiar to the peace-offerings) leavened bread must be offered. Unleavened bread was less grateful to the taste, and therefore, though enjoined in the passover for a particular reason, yet in other festivals leavened bread, which was lighter and more pleasant, was appointed, that men might feast at God's table as well as at their own.

2. The flesh of the peace-offerings, both that which was the priest's share and that which was the offerer's, must be eaten quickly, and not kept long, either raw, or dressed, cold. Though they were not obliged to eat it in the holy place, as those offerings that are called most holy, but might take it to their own tents and feast upon it there, yet God would by this law make them to know a difference between that and other meat. (1) Because God would not have that holy flesh to be in danger of putrefying. (2) Because God would not have his people to be niggardly and sparing, and distrustful of providence. (3) The flesh of the peace-offerings was God's treat, and therefore God orders it to be used generously for the entertainment of their friends, and charitably for the relief of the poor.

3. But the flesh, and those that eat it, must be pure. (1) The flesh must *touch no unclean thing;* if it did, it must not be eaten, but burnt, *v.* 19. (2) It must not be eaten by any unclean person. When a person was upon any account ceremonially unclean it was at his peril if he presumed to eat of the flesh of the peace-offerings, *v.* 20, 21. If any dare to partake of the table of the Lord under the pollution of sin unrepented of, and so profane sacred things, they eat and drink *judgment to themselves,* as those did that ate of the peace-offerings in their uncleanness, 1 Cor. xi. 29.

4. The eating of blood and the fat of the inwards is here again prohibited; and the prohibition is annexed as before to the law of the peace-offerings, *ch.* iii. 17. To eat of the flesh of that which died of itself, or was torn of beasts, was unlawful; but to eat of the fat of such was doubly unlawful, *v.* 24. The prohibition of blood is more general (*v.* 26, 27), because the fat was offered to God only by way of acknowledgment, but the blood *made atonement for the soul,* and so typified Christ's sacrifice much more than the burning of the fat did; to this therefore a greater reverence must be paid, till these types had their accomplishment in the offering up of the body of Christ once for all.

5. The priest's share of the peace-offerings is here prescribed. Jesus Christ is our great peace-offering; for he made himself a sacrifice, not only to atone for sin, and so to save us from the curse, but to purchase a blessing for us, and all good. By our joyfully partaking of the benefits of redemption we *feast upon the sacrifice*, to signify which the Lord's supper was instituted.

Verses 35–38

Here is the conclusion of these laws concerning the sacrifices. They are to be considered, 1. As a grant to the priests, v. 35, 36. 2. As a statute for ever to the people, that they should bring these offerings according to the rules prescribed, and cheerfully give the priests their share out of them. God *commanded the children of Israel to offer their oblations*, v. 38. Note, The solemn acts of religious worship are commanded. The observance of the laws of Christ cannot be less necessary than the observance of the laws of Moses was.

CHAPTER 8

This chapter gives us an account of the solemn consecration of Aaron and his sons to the priest's office. I. It was done publicly, ver. 1–4. II. It was done exactly according to God's appointment, ver. 5. 1. They were washed and dressed, ver. 6–9, 13. 2. The tabernacle and the utensils of it were anointed, and then the priests, ver. 10–12. 3. A sin-offering was offered for them, ver. 14–17. 4. A burnt-offering, ver. 18–21. 5. The ram of consecration, ver. 22–30. 6. The continuance of this solemnity for seven days, ver. 31, &c.

Verses 1–13

God had given Moses orders to consecrate Aaron and his sons to the priests' office, when he was with him the first time upon Mount Sinai, Exod. xxviii. and xxix.

I. The orders repeated. The tabernacle was newly set up, which, without the priests, would be as a candlestick without a candle; the law concerning sacrifices was newly given, but could not be observed without priests. Aaron and his sons were near relations to Moses, and therefore he would not consecrate them till he had further orders, lest he should seem too forward to bring honour into his family.

II. The congregation called together, *at the door*, that is, in the court *of the tabernacle*, v. 4. It was done thus publicly, 1. Because it was a solemn transaction between God and Israel, and therefore it was fit that both sides should appear, to own the appointment, at the door of the tabernacle of meeting. 2. The spectators of the solemnity could not but be possessed, by the sight of it, with a great veneration for the priests and their office. It was strange that any of those who were witnesses of what was here done should afterwards say, as some of them did, *You take too much upon you, you sons of Levi.*

III. The Commission read, v. 5. Moses, who was God's representative in this solemnity, produced his orders before the congregation: *This is the thing which the Lord commanded to be done.* The priesthood he delivered to them was that which he had received from the Lord.

IV. The ceremony performed according to the divine ritual. 1. Aaron and his sons were *washed with water* (v. 6), to signify that they ought now to purify themselves from all sinful dispositions and inclinations, and ever after to keep themselves pure. 2. They were clothed with the holy garments, Aaron with his (v. 7–9), which typified the dignity of Christ our great high priest, and his sons with theirs (v. 13), which typified the decency of Christians, who are spiritual priests. Christ wears the breast-plate of judgment and the holy crown; for the church's high priest is her prophet and king. All believers are clothed with the robe of righteousness, and girt with

the girdle of truth, resolution, and close application; and their heads are *bound*, as the word here is, with the bonnet or diadem of beauty, the beauty of holiness. 3. The high priest was anointed. The tabernacle, and all its utensils, had some of the anointing oil put upon them with Moses's finger (v. 10), so had the altar (v. 11); but he poured it out more plentifully upon the head of Aaron (v. 12), so that it ran down to the *skirts of his garments*, because his unction was to typify the anointing of Christ with the Spirit, which was not given by measure to him.

Verses 14–30

Sacrifices of each kind must be offered for the priests, that they might with the more tenderness and concern offer the gifts and sacrifices of the people, with compassion on the ignorant, and on *those that were out of the way*, remembering that they themselves had had sacrifices offered for them, being *compassed with infirmity*. 1. A bullock, the largest sacrifice, was offered for a sin-offering (v. 14). Ministers, that are to declare the remission of sins to others, should give diligence to get it made sure to themselves in the first place that their own sins are pardoned. Those to whom is *committed the ministry of reconciliation* must first be reconciled to God themselves. 2. A ram was offered for a burnt-offering, v. 18–21. By this they gave to God the glory of this great honour which was now put upon them, and returned him praise for it, as Paul thanked Christ Jesus for *putting him into the ministry*, 1 Tim. i. 12. 3. Another ram, called the *ram of consecration*, was offered for a peace-offering, v. 22, &c. All the ceremonies about this offering, as those before, were appointed by the express command of God.

Verses 31–36

Moses, having done his part of the ceremony, now leaves Aaron and his sons to do theirs.

I. They must boil the flesh of their peace-offering, and eat it in the court of the tabernacle, and what remained they must burn with fire, v. 31, 32.

II. They must not stir out of the court of the tabernacle for seven days, v. 33. The priesthood being a good warfare, they must thus learn to endure hardness, and to disentangle themselves from the affairs of this life, 2 Tim. ii. 3, 4. The work lasted seven days; for it was a kind of creation: and this time was appointed in honour of the sabbath, which, probably, was the last day of the seven, for which they were to prepare during the six days. They attended to *keep the charge of the Lord*: we have every one of us a charge to keep, an eternal God to glorify, an immortal soul to provide for, needful duty to be done, our generation to serve; and it must be our daily care to keep this charge, for it is the charge of the Lord our Master. *Lastly*, We are told (v. 36) that *Aaron and his sons did all that was commanded*. But after all the ceremonies that were used in their consecration there was one point of ratification which was reserved to be the honour and establishment of Christ's priesthood, which was this, that they were *made priests without an oath*, but Christ *with an oath* (Heb. vii. 21), for neither such priests nor their priesthood could continue, but Christ's is a perpetual and unchangeable priesthood.

CHAPTER 9

Aaron and his sons, having been solemnly consecrated to the priesthood, are in this chapter entering upon the execution of their office, the very next day after their consecration was completed. I. Moses appoints a meeting between God and his priests, as the representatives of his people, ordering them to attend him, and assuring them that he would appear to them, ver. 1–7. II. The meeting is held according to the appointment. 1. Aaron attends on God by sacrifice, offering a sin-offering and a burnt-offering for himself (ver. 8–14), and then the offerings for the

people, whom he blessed in the name of the Lord, ver. 15–22.
2. God signifies his acceptance, (1) Of their persons, by showing
them his glory, ver. 23. (2) Of their sacrifices, by consuming
them with fire from heaven, ver. 24.

Verses 1–7

Orders are here given for another solemnity upon
the eighth day. The priests had not so much as one
day's respite from service, but were busily employed
the very next day; for their consecration was the
filling of their hands. Now, 1. Moses raises their
expectation of a glorious appearance of God to
them this day (*v.* 4): "*To day the Lord will appear to
you* that are the priests." We are not now to expect
such appearances; we Christians walk more by faith,
and less by sight, than they did. But we may be sure
that God draws nigh to those who draw nigh to him,
and that the offerings of faith are really acceptable to
him, though, the sacrifices being spiritual, the tokens
of the acceptance are, as it is fit they should be,
spiritual likewise. 2. He puts both priests and people
upon preparing to receive this favour which God
designed them. *Aaron and his sons,* and *the elders
of Israel,* are all summoned to attend, *v.* 1. (1) Aaron
is ordered to prepare his offerings: *A young calf for
a sin-offering, v.* 2. The Jewish writers suggest that
a *calf* was appointed for a sin-offering to remind him
of his sin in making the golden calf. (2) Aaron must
direct the people to get theirs ready. (3) Aaron must
offer his own first, and then the people's, *v.* 7. [1] The
high priest made atonement for himself, as one that
was joined with sinners; but we have a high priest
that was separated from sinners, and needed no
atonement. When Messiah the prince was cut off
as a sacrifice, it was not for himself; for he knew no
sin. [2] He must *make an atonement for the people,*
by offering their sacrifices. He must *make atonement
as the Lord commanded.* See here the mercy of God,
that he not only allows an atonement to be made,
but commands it. No room therefore is left to doubt
but that the atonement which is commanded will be
accepted.

Verses 8–22

These being the first offerings that ever were
offered by the levitical priesthood, according to the
newly-enacted law of sacrifices, the manner of offering them is particularly related. 1. Aaron with his
own hands *slew the offering* (*v.* 8), and did the work
of the inferior priests. Therefore, as Moses before,
so Aaron now offered some of each of the several
sorts of sacrifices that were appointed. 2. He offered
these *besides the burnt-sacrifice of the morning,*
which was every day offered first, *v.* 17. When Aaron
had done all that on his part was to be done about the
sacrifices he *lifted up his hand towards the people,
and blessed them, v.* 22. Aaron *lifted up his hands*
in blessing them, to intimate whence he desired and
expected the blessing to come, even from heaven,
which is God's throne. Aaron could but crave a
blessing, it is God's prerogative to command it.
Aaron, when he had blessed, came down; Christ,
when he blessed, went up.

Verses 23–24

We are not told what Moses and Aaron went into
the tabernacle to do, *v.* 23. Some of the Jewish
writers say, "They went in to pray for the appearance
of the divine glory." But, when they came out, they
both joined in blessing the people, who stood expecting the promised appearance of the divine glory;
and it was now (when Moses and Aaron concurred in
praying) that they had what they waited for. Note,
God's manifestations of himself, of his glory and
grace, are commonly given in answer to prayer.
The glory of God appeared, not while the sacrifices
were in offering, but when the priests prayed, which

intimates that the prayers and praises of God's
spiritual priests are more pleasing to God than all
burnt-offerings and sacrifices.

I. *The glory of the Lord appeared unto all the
people, v.* 23. What the appearance of it was we are
not told; no doubt it was such as carried its own
evidence along with it. Those that dwell in God's
house with an eye of faith may *behold the beauty of
the Lord.*

II. *There came a fire out from before the Lord,
and consumed the sacrifice, v.* 24. Whether this fire
came from heaven, or out of the most holy place, or
from that visible appearance of the glory of God
which all the people saw, it was a manifest token of
God's acceptance of their service.

1. This fire did consume (or, as the word is, *eat up*)
the present sacrifice. (1) It signified the turning
away of God's wrath from them. Its fastening upon
the sacrifice, and consuming that, signified God's
acceptance of that as an atonement for the sinner.
(2) It signified God's entering into covenant and
communion with them.

2. This fire did, as it were, take possession of the
altar. This also was a figure of good things to come.
The Spirit descended upon the apostles in *fire* (Acts
ii. 3). And the descent of this holy fire into our souls
to kindle in them pious and devout affections towards
God, and such a holy zeal as burns up the flesh and
the lusts of it, is a certain token of God's gracious
acceptance of our persons and performances.

III. We are here told how the people were affected
with this discovery of God's glory and grace; they
received it, 1. With the highest joy: *They shouted*;
so stirring up themselves and one another to a holy
triumph. 2. With the lowest reverence: *They fell on
their faces,* humbly adoring the majesty of that God
who vouchsafed thus to manifest himself to them.

CHAPTER 10

The story of this chapter is as sad an interruption to the institutions
of the levitical law as that of the golden calf was to the account
of the erecting of the tabernacle. Here is, I. The sin and death
of Nadab and Abihu, the sons of Aaron, ver. 1, 2. II. The
quieting of Aaron under this sore affliction, ver. 3. III. Orders
given and observed about the funeral and mourning, ver. 4–7.
IV. A command to the priests not to drink wine when they went
in to minister, ver. 8–11. V. The care Moses took that they should
go on with their work, ver. 12, &c.

Verses 1–2

Here is, I. The great sin that Nadab and Abihu
were guilty of. But what was their sin? All the
account here given of it is that they *offered strange
fire before the Lord, which he commanded them not*
(*v.* 1), and the same, Num. iii. 4. 1. Nadab and
Abihu were so proud of the honour they were newly
advanced to, and so ambitious of doing the highest
and most honourable part of their work immediately,
that though the service of this day was extraordinary,
and done by particular direction from Moses, yet
without receiving orders, they took their censers,
and they would enter into the tabernacle and burn
incense. And then their *offering strange fire* is the
same with *offering strange incense,* which is expressly
forbidden, Exod. xxx. 9. 2. Presuming thus to burn
incense of their own without order, no marvel that
they made a further blunder, and instead of taking
of the fire from the altar, which was newly kindled
from before the Lord and which henceforward must
be used in offering both sacrifice and incense (Rev.
viii. 5), they took common fire, probably from that
with which the flesh of the peace-offerings was
boiled, and this they made use of in burning incense;
not being holy fire, it is called *strange fire.* 3. Incense
was always to be burned by only one priest at a
time, but here they would both go in together to do
it. 4. They did it rashly, and with precipitation. They

snatched their censers, without due reverence, when all the people *fell upon their faces*, before the *glory of the Lord.* 5. There is reason to suspect that they were drunk when they did it, because of the law which was given upon this occasion, *v.* 8. They had been feasting upon the peace-offerings, and the drink-offerings, and so their heads were light. 6. No doubt it was done presumptuously.

II. The dreadful punishment of this sin: *There went out fire from the Lord, and devoured them, v.* 2.

But why did the Lord deal thus severely with them? Were they not the sons of Aaron, the saint of the Lord, nephews to Moses, the great favourite of heaven? 1. The sin was greatly aggravated. It was a manifest contempt of Moses, and the divine law that was given by Moses. Hitherto it had been expressly observed concerning every thing that was done that they did it *as the Lord commanded Moses*, in opposition to which it is here said they did that *which the Lord commanded them not*, but they did it of their own heads. God was now teaching his people obedience, and to do every thing by rule, as becomes servants; for priests therefore to break rules and disobey was such a provocation as must by no means go unpunished. 2. Their punishment was a piece of necessary justice, now at the first settling of the ceremonial institutions. And no doubt this exemplary piece of justice at first prevented many irregularities afterwards. Thus Ananias and Sapphira were punished, when they presumed to lie to the Holy Ghost, that newly-descended fire.

Verses 3–7

We may well think that when Nadab and Abihu were struck with death, all about them were struck with horror. Moses was composed, though it touched him in a very tender part. He kept possession of his own soul.

I. He endeavours to pacify Aaron under this sad dispensation, *v.* 3.

1. What it was that Moses suggested to his poor brother upon this occasion: *This is it that the Lord spoke.* What was it that God spoke? It was this (the Lord by his grace speak it to all our hearts!) *I will be sanctified in those that come nigh me*, whoever they are, and *before all the people I will be glorified.* What was there in this to quiet Aaron? Two things:— (1) This must silence him, that his sons deserved their death; for they were thus cut off from their people because they did not sanctify and glorify God. (2) This must satisfy him, that the death of his sons redounded to the honour of God, and his impartial justice would for it be adored throughout all ages.

2. What good effects this had upon him: *Aaron held his peace*, that is, he patiently submitted to the holy will of God in this sad providence. When God corrects us or ours for sin, it is our duty to be silent under the correction, not to quarrel with God, arraign his justice, or charge him with folly, but to acquiesce in all that God does; not only bearing, but accepting, the punishment of iniquity. The most effectual arguments to quiet a gracious spirit under afflictions are those that are fetched from God's glory. Far be it from him that he should honour his sons more than God, or wish that God's name, or house, or law, should be exposed to reproach or contempt for the preserving of the reputation of his family.

II. Moses gives orders about the dead bodies. It was not fit that they should be left to lie where they fell. But Moses takes care of this matter, that though they died by the hand of justice in the act of sin, yet they should be decently buried, and they were so, *v.* 4, 5. They carried them out of the camp to be buried. It was a very awful affecting sight to the people. The names of Nadab and Abihu had become very great and honourable among them.

Nadab and Abihu (who had been in the mount with God, Exod. xxiv. 1) were looked upon as the great favourites of heaven, and the hopes of their people; and now on a sudden, when the tidings of the event had scarcely reached their ears, to see them both carried out dead, with the visible marks of divine vengeance upon them, as sacrifices to the justice of God, they could not choose but cry out, *Who is able to stand before this holy Lord God?* 1 Sam. vi. 20.

III. He gives directions about the mourning.

1. That the priests must not mourn. But here it was forbidden both to Aaron and his sons, because, (1) They were now actually in waiting, doing a great work, which must by no means cease (Neh. vi. 3); and it was very much for the honour of God that their attendance on him should take place of their respects to their nearest relations, and that all services should give way to those of their ministry. (2) Their brethren were cut off for their transgression by the immediate hand of God, and therefore they must not mourn for them lest they should seem to countenance the sin, or impeach the justice of God in the punishment. It was very hard, no doubt, for Aaron and his sons to restrain themselves upon such an extraordinary occasion from inordinate grief, but reason and grace mastered the passion, and they bore the affliction with an obedient patience. Happy those who thus are themselves under God's government, and have their passions under their own government.

2. The people must mourn: *Let the whole house of Israel bewail the burning which the Lord has kindled.* The congregation must lament, not only the loss of their priests, but especially the displeasure of God which appeared in it.

Verses 8–11

Aaron having been very observant of what God said to him by Moses, now God does him the honour to speak to him immediately (*v.* 8): *The Lord spoke unto Aaron. Do not drink wine, nor strong drink, when you go into the tabernacle*, and this at his peril, *lest you die, v.* 9. Probably they had seen the ill effect of it in Nadab and Abihu, and therefore must take warning by them. Observe here, 1. The prohibition itself: *Do not drink wine nor strong drink.* At other times they were allowed (it was not expected that every priest should be a Nazarite), but during the time of their ministration they were forbidden it. This was one of the laws in Ezekiel's temple (Ezek. xliv. 21), and so it is required of gospel ministers that they be *not given to wine*, 1 Tim. iii. 3. 2. The penalty annexed to the prohibition: *Lest you die; lest you die* when you are in drink, *and so that day come upon you unawares*, Luke xxi. 34. Or, "Lest you do that which will make you liable to be cut off by the hand of God." 3. The reasons assigned for this prohibition. They must needs be sober, else they could not duly discharge their office; they will be in danger of *erring through wine*, Isa. xxviii. 7. They must be sure to keep sober, (1) That they might themselves be able to distinguish, in their ministrations, between that which was sacred and that which was common, and might never confound them, *v.* 10. (2) That they might be able to teach the people (*v.* 11), for that was a part of the priests' work (Deut. xxxiii. 10); and those that are addicted to drunkenness are very unfit to teach people God's statutes, both because those that live after the flesh can have no experimental acquaintance with the things of the Spirit, and because such teachers pull down with one hand what they build up with the other.

Verses 12–20

Moses is here directing Aaron to go on with his service after this interruption. Afflictions should rather quicken us to our duty than take us off from it. Observe (*v.* 12), He spoke unto Aaron and to his sons *that were left.* The notice taken of their survivorship intimates, 1. That Aaron should take comfort under the loss of two of his sons, from this consideration, that God had graciously spared him the other two. 2. That God's sparing them should be an engagement upon them to proceed in his service, and not to fly off from it. Here were four priests consecrated together, two were taken away, and two left; therefore the two that were left should endeavour to fill up the places of those that were gone, by double care and diligence in the services of the priesthood.

I. Moses repeats the directions he had formerly given them about eating their share of the sacrifices, *v.* 12–14, 15.

II. He enquires concerning one deviation from the appointment, which it seems had happened upon this occasion, which was this:—There was a goat to be sacrificed as a *sin-offering for the people, ch.* ix. 15. Now the law of the sin-offerings was that if the blood of them was brought into the holy place, as that of the sin-offerings for the priest was, then the flesh was to be burnt without the camp. Now the blood of this goat was not brought into the holy place, and yet, it seems, it was burnt without the camp. Moses charged the fault upon Eleazar and Ithamar (*v.* 16), but it is probable that what they did was by Aaron's direction, and therefore he apologized for it. He makes his affliction his excuse, *v.* 19. *Such things have befallen me,* such sad things, which could not but go near his heart, and make it very heavy. He was a high priest *taken from among men,* and could not put off natural affection when he put on the holy garments. He held his peace (*v.* 3), yet his sorrow was stirred. He makes this an excuse for his varying from the appointment about the sin-offering. He could not have eaten it but in his mourning, and with a sorrowful spirit; and would this have been accepted? The acquiescence of Moses in this excuse: *He was content, v.* 20. Perhaps he thought it justified what they had done. God had provided that what could not be eaten might be burnt.

Chapter 11

The ceremonial law is described by the apostle (Heb. ix. 9, 10) to consist, not only "in gifts and sacrifices," but "in meats, and drinks, and divers washings" from ceremonial uncleanness, the laws concerning which begin with this chapter, which puts a difference between some sorts of flesh-meat and others, allowing some to be eaten as clean and forbidding others as unclean. But there is "another kind of flesh of beasts," concerning which the law directs here (ver. 1–8), "another of fishes" (ver. 9–12), "another of birds" (ver. 13–19), and "another of creeping things," which are distinguished into two sorts, flying creeping things (ver. 20–28) and creeping things upon the earth, ver. 29–43. And the law concludes with the general rule of holiness, and reasons for it, ver. 44, &c.

Verses 1–8

Now that Aaron was consecrated a high priest over the house of God, God spoke to him with Moses, and appointed them both as joint-commissioners to deliver his will to the people. It was particularly required of the priests that they should put a difference between clean and unclean, and teach the people to do so. They might eat flesh, but not all kinds of flesh; some they must look upon as unclean and forbidden to them, others as clean and allowed them. But what reason can be given for this law? Most of the meats forbidden as unclean are such as were really unwholesome, and not fit to be eaten; and those of them that we think wholesome enough, and use accordingly, as the rabbit, the hare, and the swine, perhaps in those countries, and to their bodies, might be hurtful. The Lord is for the body, and it is not only folly, but sin against God to prejudice our health for the pleasing of our appetite. It should

seem there had been, before this, some difference between the Hebrews and other nations in their food, kept up by tradition; for the Egyptians and they would not eat together, Gen. xliii. 32. The learned observe further, That most of the creatures which by this law were to be abominated as unclean were such as were had in high veneration among the heathen, not so much for food as for divination and sacrifice to their gods; and therefore those are here mentioned as unclean, and an abomination, which yet they would not be in any temptation to eat, that they might keep up a religious loathing of that for which the Gentiles had a superstitious value. The swine, with the later Gentiles, was sacred to Venus, the owl to Minerva, the eagle to Jupiter, the dog to Hecate, &c., and all these are here made unclean. As to the beasts, there is a general rule laid down, that those which both part the hoof and chew the cud were clean, and those only: these are particularly mentioned in the repetition of this law (Deut. xiv. 4, 5), where it appears that the Israelites had variety enough allowed them, and needed not to complain of the confinement they were under. Those beasts that did not both *chew the cud and divide the hoof* were unclean, by which rule the flesh of swine, and of hares, and of rabbits, was prohibited to them, though commonly used among us. Of all the creatures here forbidden as unclean, none has been more dreaded and detested by the pious Jews than swine's flesh. Many were put to death by Antiochus because they would not eat it. Some suggest that the prohibition of these beasts as unclean was intended to be a caution to the people against the bad qualities of these creatures. We must not be filthy nor wallow in the mire as swine, nor be timorous and faint-hearted as hares, nor dwell in the earth as rabbits; let not man that is in honour make himself like these beasts that perish.

Verses 9–19

Here is, 1. A general rule concerning fishes, which were clean and which not. All that had fins and scales they might eat, and only those odd sorts of water-animals that have not were forbidden, *v.* 9, 10. Concerning the prohibited fish it is said, *They shall be an abomination to you* (*v.* 10–12), that is, "You shall count them unclean, and not only not eat of them, but keep at a distance from them." Thus God's spiritual Israel, as they are dignified above others by the gospel-covenant of adoption and friendship, so they must be mortified more than others by the gospel-commands of self-denial and bearing the cross. 2. Concerning fowls here is no general rule given, but a particular enumeration of those fowls that they must abstain from as unclean, which implies an allowance of all others. Of the fowls here forbidden, (1) Some are birds of prey, as the eagle, vulture, &c., and God would have his people to abhor every thing that is barbarous and cruel, and not to live by blood and rapine. Doves that are preyed upon were fit to be food for man and offerings to God; but kites and hawks that prey upon them must be looked upon as an abomination to God and man. (2) Others of them are solitary birds, that abide in dark and desolate places, as the owl and the pelican (Ps. cii. 6), and the cormorant and raven (Isa. xxxiv. 11); for God's Israel should not be a melancholy people, nor affect sadness and constant solitude. (3) Others of them feed upon that which is impure, as the stork on serpents, others of them on worms; and we must not only abstain from all impurity ourselves, but from communion with those that allow themselves in it. (4) Others of them were used by the Egyptians and other Gentiles in their divinations. Some birds were reckoned fortunate, others ominous; and their soothsayers had great regard to the flights of these birds, all which therefore must be an abomination to

God's people, who must not learn the way of the heathen.

Verses 20–42

Here is the law, 1. Concerning flying insects, as flies, wasps, bees, &c.; these they might not eat (*v.* 20), nor indeed are they fit to be eaten; but there were several sorts of locusts which in those countries were very good meat, and much used: John Baptist lived upon them in the desert, and they are here allowed them, *v.* 21, 22. 2. Concerning the creeping things on the earth; these were all forbidden (*v.* 29, 30), and again, *v.* 41, 42. Dust is the meat of the creeping things, and therefore they are not fit to be man's meat. 3. Concerning the dead carcases of all these unclean animals. (1) Every one that touched them was to be unclean until the evening, *v.* 24–28. It was a *ceremonial* uncleanness they contracted, which for the time forbade them to come into the tabernacle, or to eat of any of the holy things, or so much as to converse familiarly with their neighbours. But the uncleanness continued only till the evening. And we must learn, by daily renewing our repentance every night for the sins of the day, to cleanse ourselves from the pollution we contract by them, that we may not lie down in our uncleanness. (2) Even the vessels, or other things they fell upon, were thereby made unclean until the evening (*v.* 32), and if they were earthen vessels they must be broken, *v.* 33. We ought as industriously to preserve our precious souls from the pollutions of sin, and as speedily to cleanse them when they are polluted, as they were to preserve and cleanse their bodies and household goods from those ceremonial pollutions.

Verses 43–47

Here is, I. The exposition of this law, or a key to let us into the meaning of it. It was not intended merely for a bill of fare, or as the directions of a physician about their diet, but God would hereby teach them to sanctify themselves and to be holy, *v.* 44. These *rudiments of the world* were their tutors and governors (Gal. iv. 2, 3), to bring them to that which is the revival of our first state in Adam and the earnest of our best state with Christ, that is, *holiness*, without which no man shall see the Lord. This is indeed the great design of all the ordinances, that by them we may sanctify ourselves and learn to be holy. Even this law concerning their food, which seemed to stoop so very low, aimed thus high. *Without holiness no man shall see the Lord.* If it was such a provocation for a man to eat swine's flesh himself, much more it must be so to offer swine's blood at God's altar; see Prov. xv. 8.

II. The reasons of this law. 1. *I am the Lord your God, v.* 44. "Therefore you are bound to do thus, in pure obedience." 2. *I am holy, v.* 44, and again, *v.* 45. If God be holy, we must be so, else we cannot expect to be accepted of him. All these ceremonial restraints were designed to teach us that we must not *fashion ourselves according to our former lusts in our ignorance,* 1 Pet. 1. 14. 3. *I am the Lord that bringeth you out of the land of Egypt, v.* 45. He that had done more for them than for any other people might justly expect more from them.

III. The conclusion of this statute: *This is the law of the beasts, and of the fowl,* &c., *v.* 46, 47. This law was to them a statute for ever, that is, as long as that economy lasted; but under the gospel we find it expressly repealed by a voice from heaven to Peter (Acts x. 15), as it had before been virtually set aside by the death of Christ, with the other ordinances that *perished in the using.* And now we are sure that *meat commends us not to God* (1 Cor. viii. 8), and that *nothing is unclean of itself* (Rom. xiv. 14), nor does that defile a man which goes into his mouth, but that which comes out from the heart, Matt. xv. 11. Let us therefore, 1. Give thanks to God that we are not under this yoke, but that to us every creature of God is allowed as good. 2. *Stand fast in the liberty wherewith Christ has made us free.* 3. Be strictly and conscientiously temperate in the use of the good creatures God has allowed us. Nature is content with little, grace with less, but lust with nothing.

CHAPTER 12

After the laws concerning clean and unclean food come the laws concerning clean and unclean persons; and the first is in this chapter concerning the ceremonial uncleanness of women in child-birth, ver. 1–5. And concerning their purification from that uncleanness, ver. 6, &c.

Verses 1–5

The law here pronounces women lying-in ceremonially unclean. The Jews say, "The law extended even to an abortion, if the child was so formed as that the sex was distinguishable." 1. There was some time of strict separation immediately after the birth. During these days she was separated from her husband and friends, and those that necessarily attended her were ceremonially unclean, which was one reason why the males were not circumcised till the eighth day, because they participated in the mother's pollution during the days of her separation. 2. There was also a longer time appointed for their purifying. During this time they were only separated from the sanctuary and forbidden to eat of the passover, or peace-offerings, or, if a priest's wife, to eat of any thing that was holy to the Lord. If sin had not entered, nothing but purity and honour had attended all the productions of that great blessing, *Be fruitful and multiply.* The exclusion of the woman for so many days from the sanctuary, and all participation of the holy things, signified that our original corruption would have excluded us for ever from the enjoyment of God and his favours if he had not graciously provided for our purifying.

Verses 6–8

A woman that had lain in, when the time set for her return to the sanctuary had come, must bring her offerings, *v.* 6. 1. A *burnt-offering*; a lamb if she was able; if poor, a pigeon. This she was to offer in thankfulness to God for his mercy to her, in bringing her safely through the pains of child-bearing and all the perils of child-bed, and in desire and hopes of God's further favour both to her and to the child. When a child is born there is joy and there is hope, and therefore it was proper to bring this offering. But, besides this, 2. She must offer a *sin-offering,* which must be the same for poor and rich, a turtle-dove or a young pigeon; for, whatever difference there may be between rich and poor in the sacrifices of acknowledgment, that of atonement is the same for both. This sin-offering was intended either, (1) To complete her purification from that ceremonial uncleanness which, though it was not in itself sinful, yet was typical of moral pollution; or, (2) To make atonement for that which was really sin, either an inordinate desire of the blessing of children or discontent or impatience under the pains of child-bearing. According to this law, we find that the mother of our blessed Lord, though he was not conceived in sin as others, yet *accomplished the days of purification,* and then presented her son to the Lord, being a first-born, and brought her own offering, *a pair of turtle-doves,* Luke ii. 22–24. So poor were Christ's parents that they were not able to bring a lamb for a burnt-offering; and so early was Christ *made under the law, to redeem those that were under it.*

CHAPTER 13

The next ceremonial uncleanness is that of the leprosy, concerning which the law was very large and particular; we have the discovery of it in this chapter, and the cleansing of the leper in the next. Scarcely any one thing in all the levitical law takes up so much room as this. I. Rules are here given by which the priest must judge whether the man had the leprosy or no, according as the symptom was that appeared. 1. If it was a swelling, a scab, or a bright spot, ver. 1–17. 2. If it was a bile, ver. 18–23. 3. If it was an inflammation, ver. 24–28. 4. If it was in the head or beard, ver. 29–37. 5. If it was a bright spot, ver. 38, 39. 6. If it was in a bald head, ver. 40–44. II. Direction is given how the leper must be disposed of, ver. 45, 46. III. Concerning the leprosy in garments, ver. 47, &c.

Verses 1–17

I. Concerning the plague of leprosy we may observe in general, That it was rather an uncleanness than a disease; or, at least, so the law considered it, and therefore employed not the physicians but the priests about it. Christ is said to cleanse lepers, not to cure them. We do not read of any that died of the leprosy, but it rather buried them alive, by rendering them unfit for conversation with any but such as were infected like themselves. It is said to have begun first in Egypt, whence it spread into Syria. The Jews retained the idolatrous customs they had learnt in Egypt, and therefore God justly caused this with some others of the diseases of Egypt to follow them. Yet we read of Naaman the Syrian, who was a leper, 2 Kings v. 1. There were other breakings-out in the body which did very much resemble the leprosy, but were not it, which might make a man sore and loathsome and yet not ceremonially unclean. The judgment of it was referred to the priests. Lepers were looked upon as stigmatized by the justice of God, and therefore it was left to his servants the priests, who might be presumed to know his mark best, to pronounce who were lepers and who were not. It was a figure of the moral pollution of men's minds by sin, which is the leprosy of the soul, defiling to the conscience, and from which Christ alone can cleanse us; for herein the power of his grace infinitely transcends that of the legal priesthood, that the priest could only convict the leper (for by the law is the knowledge of sin), but Christ can cure the leper, he can take away sin. *Lord, if thou wilt, thou canst make me clean,* which was more than the priests could do, Matt. viii. 2. It is a work of great importance, but of great difficulty, to judge of our spiritual state: we have all cause to suspect ourselves, being conscious to ourselves of sores and spots, but whether clean or unclean is the question.

II. Several rules are here laid down by which the judgment of the priest must be governed. 1. If the sore was but *skin-deep,* it was to be hoped it was not the *leprosy,* v. 4. But, if it was *deeper than the skin,* the man must be pronounced unclean, v. 3. The infirmities that consist with grace do not sink deep into the soul, but *the mind* still *serves the law of God,* and the *inward man delights in it,* Rom. vii. 22, 25. But if the matter be really worse than it shows, and the inwards be infected, the case is dangerous. 2. If the sore *be at a stay,* and does not *spread,* it is no leprosy, v, 5, 6. But if it *spread much abroad,* and continue to do so after several inspections, the case is bad, v. 7, 8. If men do not grow worse, but a stop be put to the course of their sins and their corruptions be checked, it is to be hoped they will grow better; but if sin gets ground, and they become worse every day, they are going downhill. 3. If there was *proud raw flesh* in the rising, the priest needed not to wait any longer, it was certainly a leprosy, v. 10, 11. Nor is there any surer indication of the badness of a man's spiritual state than the heart's rising in self-conceit, confidence in the flesh, and resistance of the reproofs of the word and strivings

of the Spirit. 4. If the eruption, whatever it was, *covered all the skin* from head to foot, it was no leprosy (v. 12, 13); for it was an evidence that the vitals were sound and strong, and nature hereby helped itself, throwing out what was burdensome and pernicious. There is hope in the small-pox when they come out well: so if men freely confess their sins, and hide them not, there is no danger comparable to theirs that cover their sins. Some gather this from it, that there is more hope of the profane than of hypocrites. The publicans and harlots went into the kingdom of heaven before scribes and Pharisees. In one respect, the sudden breakings-out of passion, though bad enough, are not so dangerous as malice concealed. Others gather this, that, if we judge ourselves, we shall not be judged; if we see and own that there is *no health in us, no soundness in our flesh,* by reason of sin, we shall *find grace in the eyes of the Lord.* 5. The priest must take time in making his judgment, and not give it rashly.

Verses 18–37

The priest is here instructed what judgment to make if there was any appearance of a leprosy, either, 1. In an old ulcer or bile, that has been healed, v. 18, &c. When old sores, that seemed to be cured, break out again, it is to be feared there is a leprosy in them; such is the danger of those who, having escaped the pollutions of the world, are again *entangled therein and overcome.* Or, 2. In a burn by accident, for this seems to be meant, v. 24, &c. The burning of strife and contention often proves the occasion of the rising up and breaking out of that corruption which witnesses to men's faces that they are unclean.

Verses 38–46

I. Provisos that neither a *freckled skin* nor a *bald head* should be mistaken for a leprosy, v. 38–41. Every deformity must not forthwith be made a ceremonial defilement.

II. A particular brand set upon the leprosy if at any time it did appear in a *bald head: The plague is in his head, he is utterly unclean,* v. 44. If the leprosy of sin have seized the head, if the judgment be corrupted, and wicked principles which countenance and support wicked practices, be embraced, it is an *utter uncleanness.* Soundness in the faith keeps the leprosy from the head.

III. Directions what must be done with the convicted leper. When the priest, upon mature deliberation, had solemnly pronounced him unclean,

1. He must pronounce himself so, v. 45. He must put himself into the posture of a mourner and cry, *Unclean, unclean.* He must therefore, (1) Humble himself under the mighty hand of God, not insisting upon his cleanness when the priest had pronounced him unclean. He must signify this by *rending his clothes, uncovering* his head, and *covering his upper lip,* all tokens of shame and confusion of face, and very significant of that self-loathing and self-abasement which should fill the hearts of penitents, the language of which is self-judging. (2) He must give warning to others to take heed of coming near him. Wherever he went, he must cry to those he saw at a distance, "I am *unclean, unclean,* take heed of touching me." Not that the leprosy was catching, but by the touch of a leper ceremonial uncleanness was contracted. And this was all that the law could do. The law only shows us our disease; the gospel shows us our help in Christ.

2. He must then be shut out of the camp, and afterwards, when they came to Canaan, out of the city, town, or village, where he lived, and *dwell alone* (v. 46), associating with none but those that were lepers like himself.

Verses 47–59

This is the law concerning the plague of leprosy in a garment, whether linen or woollen. A leprosy in a garment, with discernible indications of it, is a thing which to us now is altogether unaccountable. The process was much the same with that concerning a leprous person. The garment suspected to be tainted was not to be burnt immediately, but it must be *shown to the priest.* If, upon search, it was found that there was a *leprous spot* it must be *burnt.* If the cause of the suspicion was gone, it must be *washed,* and then might be used, *v.* 58.

Chapter 14

The former chapter directed the priests how to convict a leper of ceremonial uncleanness. The remedy here is only adapted to the ceremonial part of his disease; but the authority Christ gave to his ministers was to cure the lepers, and so to cleanse them. We have here, I. The solemn declaration of the leper's being clean, ver. 1–9. II. The sacrifices which he was to offer to God eight days after, ver. 10–32. III. The management of a house in which appeared signs of a leprosy, ver. 33–53. And the conclusion and summary of this whole matter, ver. 54, &c.

Verses 1–9

I. It is supposed that the plague of the leprosy was not an incurable disease. Uzziah's indeed continued to the day of his death, but Miriam's lasted only seven days: we may suppose that it often wore off in process of time.

II. The judgment of the cure, as well as that of the disease, was referred to the priest. He must go out of the camp to the leper, to see whether his leprosy was healed, *v.* 3. It was in mercy to the poor lepers that the priests particularly had orders to attend them. When the leper was shut out, and could not go to the priests, it was well that the priests might come to him. *Is any sick? Let him send for the elders,* the ministers, Jam. v. 14. If we apply it to the spiritual leprosy of sin, it intimates that when we withdraw from those who walk disorderly, that they may be ashamed, we must not count them as enemies, but admonish them as brethren, 2 Thess. iii. 15. And also that when God by his grace has brought those to repentance who were shut out of communion for scandal, they ought with tenderness, and joy, and sincere affection, to be received in again. Thus Paul orders concerning the excommunicated Corinthian that when he had given evidences of his repentance they should forgive him, and comfort him, and *confirm their love towards him,* 2 Cor. ii. 7, 8.

III. If it was found that the leprosy was healed, the priest must declare it with a particular solemnity. The leper or his friends were to get ready two birds caught for this purpose (any sort of wild birds that were clean), and cedar-wood, and scarlet, and hyssop. 1. A preparation was to be made of blood and water, with which the leper must be sprinkled. One of the birds was to be killed over an earthen cup of spring water, so that the blood of the bird might discolour the water. 2. The living bird, with a little scarlet wool, and a bunch of hyssop, must be fastened to a cedar stick, dipped in the water and blood, which must be so sprinkled upon him that was to be cleansed, *v.* 6, 7. The cedar-wood signified the restoring of the leper to his strength and soundness, for that is a sort of wood not apt to putrefy. The scarlet wool signified his recovering a florid colour again, for the leprosy made him white as snow. And the hyssop intimated the removing of the disagreeable scent which commonly attended the leprosy. The cedar the stateliest plant, and hyssop the meanest, are here used together in this service (see 1 Kings iv. 33). The leper must be sprinkled *seven times,* to signify a complete purification, in allusion to which David prays, *Wash me throughly,* Ps. li. 2. Naaman was directed to wash *seven times,* 2 Kings v. 10. 3. The living bird was then to be let loose in the open field, to signify that the leper, being cleansed, was now no longer under restraint and confinement, but might take his liberty to go where he pleased. But this being signified by the flight of a bird towards heaven was an intimation to him henceforward to seek the things that are above, and not to spend this new life to which God had restored him merely in the pursuit of earthly things. Those whose souls before *bowed down to the dust* (Ps. xliv. 25), in grief and fear, now fly in the open firmament of heaven, and soar upwards upon the wings of faith and hope, and holy love and joy. 4. The priest must, upon this, pronounce him clean. Those are clean indeed whom Christ pronounces so, and they need not regard what men say of them. But, though Christ was the *end of the law for righteousness,* yet being in the days of his flesh *made under the law,* which as yet stood unrepealed, he ordered those lepers whom he had cured miraculously to go and *show themselves to the priest,* and *offer for their cleansing according to the law,* Matt. viii. 4; Luke v. 14. 5. When the leper was pronounced clean, he must wash his body and his clothes, and shave *off all his hair* (v. 8), must still tarry seven days out of the camp, and on the seventh day must do it again, *v.* 9. The priest having pronounced him clean from the disease, he must make himself as clean as ever he could from all the remains of it, and from all other defilements.

Verses 10–20

Observe, I. To complete the purification of the leper, on the eighth day, after the former solemnity performed without the camp, he was to attend *at the door of the tabernacle,* and was there to be *presented to the Lord,* with his offering, *v.* 11. Observe here, 1. That the mercies of God oblige us to present ourselves to him, Rom. xii. 1. 2. When God has restored us to the liberty of ordinances again, after restraint by sickness, distance, or otherwise, we should take the first opportunity of testifying our respect to God, and our affection to his sanctuary.

II. Three lambs the cleansed leper was to bring, with a meat-offering, and a log of oil, which was about half a pint. Now, 1. Most of the ceremony peculiar to this case was about the trespass-offering, the lamb for which was offered first, *v.* 12. The Jews say that the leper stood without the gate of the tabernacle and the priest within, and thus the ceremony was performed through the gate, signifying that now he was admitted with other Israelites to attend in the courts of the Lord's house again, and was as welcome as ever; though perhaps the name might stick by him as long as he lived (as we read of one who probably was cleansed by our Lord Jesus, who yet afterwards is called *Simon the leper,* Matt. xxvi. 6). Cleansed lepers are as welcome to the blood and the oil as consecrated priests. 2. Besides this there must be a sin-offering and a burnt-offering, a lamb for each, *v.* 19, 20. By each of these offerings, it is said, the priests shall *make an atonement for him.* (1) His moral guilt shall be removed. (2) His ceremonial pollution shall be removed, which had kept him from the participation of the holy things. And this is called *making an atonement for him,* because our restoration to the privileges of God's children, typified hereby, is owing purely to the great propitiation. The burnt-offering, besides the atonement that was made by it, was a thankful acknowledgment of God's mercy to him: and the more immediate the hand of God was both in the sickness and in the cure the more reason he had thus to give glory to him, and thus, as our Saviour speaks (Mark i. 44), to *offer for his cleansing* all *those things which Moses commanded for a testimony unto them.*

Verses 21–32

We have here the gracious provision which the law made for the cleansing of *poor lepers*. If they were not able to bring three lambs, and three tenth-deals of flour, they must bring one lamb, and one tenth-deal of flour, and, instead of the other two lambs, two turtle-doves or two young pigeons, *v.* 21, 22. Here see, 1. That the poverty of the person concerned would not excuse him if he brought no offerings at all. Let none think that because they are poor God requires no service from them, since he has considered them, and demands that which it is in the power of the poorest to give. "*My son, give me thy heart*, and with that the *calves of thy lips* shall be accepted instead of the *calves of the stall.*" 2. That God expected from those who were poor only according to their ability. If there be first a willing mind and an honest heart, two pigeons, when they are the utmost a man is able to get, are as acceptable to God as two lambs.

Verses 33–53

This is the law concerning the leprosy in a house. The leprosy in a house is as unaccountable as the leprosy in a garment. Now, 1. It is supposed that even in Canaan itself, the land of promise, their houses might be infected with a leprosy. 2. It is likewise taken for granted that the owner of the house will make the priest acquainted with it, as soon as he sees the least cause to suspect the leprosy in his house. Sin, where that reigns in a house, is a plague there, as it is in a heart. And masters of families should be aware and afraid of the first appearance of gross sin in their families, and put away the iniquity, whatever it is, far from their tabernacles, Job xxii. 23. 3. If the priest, upon search, found that the leprosy had got into the house, he must try to cure it, by taking out that part of the building that was infected, *v.* 40, 41. This was like cutting off a gangrened limb for the preservation of the rest of the body. 4. If yet it remained in the house, the whole house must be pulled down, and all the materials carried to the dunghill, *v.* 44, 45. 5. If the taking out the infected stones cured the house, and the leprosy did not spread any further, then the house must be cleansed; not only aired, that it might be healthful, but purified from the ceremonial pollution, that it might be fit to be the habitation of an Israelite. The ceremony of its cleansing was much the same with that of cleansing a leprous person, *v.* 49, &c. And the same care should we take to reform whatever is amiss in our families, that we and our houses may serve the Lord; see Gen. xxxv. 2.

Verses 54–57

This is the conclusion of this law concerning the leprosy. We may see in this law, 1. The gracious care God took of his people Israel. When Naaman the Syrian was cured of his leprosy he was not bidden to show himself to the priest, though he was cured in Jordan, as the Jews that were cured by our Saviour were. 2. The religious care we ought to take of ourselves, to keep our minds from the dominion of all sinful affections and dispositions, which are both their disease and their defilement, that we may be fit for the service of God.

CHAPTER 15

In this chapter we have laws concerning other ceremonial uncleannesses contracted either by bodily disease like that of the leper, or some natural incidents, and this either, I. In men, ver. 1–18. Or, II. In women, ver. 19–33. We need not be at all curious in explaining these antiquated laws, it is enough if we observe the general intention; but we have need to be very cautious lest sin take occasion by the commandment to become more exceedingly sinful.

Verses 1–18

We have here the law concerning the ceremonial uncleanness that was contracted by running issues in men, which was, usually, the effect of a dissolute life. A vile disease for vile deserts. Now whoever had this disease upon him, 1. He was himself unclean, *v.* 2. He must not dare to come near the sanctuary. 2. He made every person and thing unclean that he touched, or that touched him, *v.* 4–12. This signified the contagion of sin, the danger we are in of being polluted by conversing with those that are polluted. 3. When he was cured of the disease, yet he could not be cleansed from the pollution without a sacrifice, for which he was to prepare by bathing in spring water, *v.* 13–15. This signified the great gospel duties of faith and repentance, and the great gospel privileges of the application of Christ's blood to our souls for our justification and his grace for our sanctification.

Verses 19–33

This is concerning the ceremonial uncleanness which women lay under from their issues. This made the woman unclean (*v.* 25) and every thing she touched unclean, *v.* 26, 27. And if she was cured, and found by seven days' trial that she was perfectly free from her issue of blood, she was to be cleansed by the offering of two turtle-doves or two young pigeons, to make an atonement for her, *v.* 28, 29.

By these laws they were taught that they were *purified unto God a peculiar people*, and were intended by the holy God for a kingdom of priests, a holy nation. They were also taught to preserve the honour of their purity, and to keep themselves from all sinful pollutions. In all these laws there seems to be a special regard had to the honour of the tabernacle, to which none must approach in their uncleanness, that they *defile not my tabernacle*. Thus they were taught never to draw near to God but with an awful humble sense of their distance and danger.

Let us bless God that we are not under the yoke of these carnal ordinances, that, as nothing can destroy us, so nothing can defile us, but sin. Those may now partake of the Lord's supper who durst not then eat of the peace-offerings. Let us all see how indispensably necessary real holiness is to our future happiness, and get our hearts purified by faith, that we may see God.

CHAPTER 16

In this chapter we have the institution of the annual solemnity of the day of atonement, or expiation, which had as much gospel in it as perhaps any of the appointments of the ceremonial law, as appears by the reference the apostle makes to it, Heb. ix. 7, &c. This is concerning the stated sacrifice, in which the whole nation was interested. The whole service of the day is committed to the high priest. I. He must never come into the most holy place but upon this day, ver. 1, 2. II. He must come dressed in linen garments, ver. 4. III. He must bring a sin-offering and a burnt-offering for himself (ver. 3), offer his sin-offering (ver. 6–11), then go within the veil with some of the blood of his sin-offering, burn incense, and sprinkle the blood before the mercy-seat, ver. 12–14. IV. Two goats must be provided for the people, lots cast upon them, and, 1. One of them must be a sin-offering for the people (ver. 5, 7–9), and the blood of it must be sprinkled before the mercy-seat (ver. 15–17), and then some of the blood of both the sin-offerings must be sprinkled upon the altar, ver. 18, 19. 2. The other must be a scape-goat (ver. 10), the sins of Israel must be confessed over him, and then he must be sent away into the wilderness (ver. 20–22), and he that brought him away must be ceremonially unclean, ver. 26. V. The burnt-offerings were then to be offered, the fat of the sin-offerings burnt on the altar, and their flesh burnt without the camp, ver. 23–25, 27, 28. VI. The people were to observe the day religiously by a holy rest and holy mourning for sin; and this was to be a statute for ever, ver. 29, &c.

Verses 1–4

Here is, I. The date of this law concerning the day of atonement: it was *after the death of the two sons of Aaron* (*v.* 1), which we read, *ch.* x. 1. 1. Lest Aaron should fear that any remaining guilt of that sin should cleave to his family, he is directed how to make atonement for his house. 2. The priests being warned by the death of Nadab and Abihu to approach to God with reverence and godly fear, directions are here given how the nearest approach might be made.

II. The design of this law. One intention of it was to preserve a veneration for the most holy place, within the veil, where the *Shechinah*, or divine glory, was pleased to dwell between the cherubim. Within the veil none must ever come but the high priest only, and he but on one day in the year. But see what a blessed change is made by the gospel of Christ; all good Christians have now *boldness to enter into the holiest*, through the veil, every day (Heb. x. 19, 20); and we *come boldly* (not as Aaron must, with fear and trembling) to the *throne of grace*, or mercy-seat, Heb. iv. 16. The objects of faith the more they are conversed with the more do they manifest of their greatness and goodness: now therefore we are welcome to come at all times into the *holy place not made with hands*. Then Aaron must not come near at all times, *lest he die*; we now must come near at all times that we may live: it is distance only that is our death.

III. The person to whom the work of this day was committed, and that was the high priest only: *Thus shall Aaron come into the holy place*, v. 3.

IV. The attire of the high priest in this service. He was not to be dressed up in his rich garments, he was not to put on the ephod, with the precious stones in it, but only the linen clothes which he wore in common with the inferior priests, v. 4. That meaner dress did best become him on this day of humiliation.

Verses 5–14

The Jewish writers say that for seven days before the day of expiation the high priest was to dwell in a chamber of the temple, that he might prepare himself. During those seven days he himself did the work of the inferior priests. 1. He was to begin the service of the day very early with the usual morning sacrifice, after he had first washed his whole body before he dressed himself, and his hands and feet again afterwords. He then burned the daily incense, dressed the lamps, and offered the extraordinary sacrifice appointed (Num. xxix. 8). 2. He must now put off his rich robes, bathe himself, put on the linen garments, and present unto the Lord his own bullock, which was to be a sin-offering for himself and his house, v. 6. 3. He must then cast lots upon the two goats, which were to make (both together) one sin-offering for the congregation. One of these goats must be slain, in token of a satisfaction to be made to God's justice for sin, the other must be sent away, in token of the remission or dismission of sin by the mercy of God. Both must be presented together to God (v. 7) before the lot was cast upon them, and afterwards the scape-goat by itself, v. 10. Some think that goats were chosen for the sin-offering because, by the disagreeableness of their smell, the offensiveness of sin is represented. 4. The next thing to be done was to kill the bullock for the sin-offering for himself and his house, v. 11. 5. He took a censer of burning coals and a dish full of the sweet incense and then went into the holy of holies, set the coals down upon the floor, and scattered the incense upon them, so that the room was immediately filled with smoke. The Jews say that he was to go in *side-ways*, that he might not look directly upon the ark where the divine glory was, then he must come out *backwards*, out of reverence to the divine majesty; and, after a short prayer, he was to show himself to the people. 6. He then fetched the blood of the bullock and took that in with him the second time into the holy of holies, which was now filled with the smoke of the incense, and sprinkled with his finger of that blood towards the mercy-seat, once over against the top of it and then seven times towards the lower part of it, v. 14.

Verses 15–19

When the priest had come out from sprinkling the blood of the bullock before the mercy-seat, 1. He must next kill the goat which was the sin-offering for the people (v. 15) and go the third time into the holy of holies, to sprinkle the blood of the goat, as he had done that of the bullock; and thus he was to *make atonement for the holy place* (v. 16). God, being reconciled to them, might continue with them. 2. He must then do the same for the outward part of the tabernacle that he had done for the inner room. The reason intimated is *because the tabernacle remained among them in the midst of their uncleanness*, v. 16. God would hereby show them how much their hearts needed to be purified. 3. He must then put some of the blood, both of the bullock and of the goat mixed together, upon the horns of the altar that is before the Lord, v. 18, 19.

Verses 20–28

The high priest having presented unto the Lord the expiatory sacrifices, by the sprinkling of their blood, 1. He is next to confess the sins of Israel, with both his hands upon the head of the scape-goat (v. 20, 21); and whenever hands were imposed upon the head of any sacrifice it was always done with confession. In the latter and more degenerate ages of the Jewish church they had a set form of confession prepared for the high priest. By this confession he must *put the sins of Israel upon the head of the goat*. 2. The goat was then to be sent away immediately by the hand of a fit person into a wilderness, a land not inhabited; and God allowed them to make this construction of it, that the sending away of the goat was the sending away of their sins, by a free and full remission: *He shall bear upon him all their iniquities*, v. 22. The later Jews had a custom to tie one shred of scarlet cloth to the horns of the goat and another to the gate of the temple, or to the top of the rock where the goat was lost, and they concluded that if it turned white, as they say it usually did, the sins of Israel were forgiven, as it is written, *Though your sins have been as scarlet, they shall be as wool*: and they add that for forty years before the destruction of Jerusalem by the Romans the scarlet cloth never changed colour at all, which is a fair confession that, having rejected the substance, the shadow stood them in no stead. 3. The high priest must then put off his linen garments in the tabernacle, and leave them there, the Jews say never to be worn again by himself or any other, for they made new ones every year; and he must bathe himself in water, put on his rich clothes, and then offer both his own and the people's burnt-offerings, v. 23, 24. When we have the comfort of our pardon God must have the glory of it. 4. The flesh of both those sin-offerings whose blood was taken within the veil was to be all burnt at a distance without the camp, to signify both our putting away sin by true repentance, and the spirit of burning, and God's putting it away by a full remission, so that it shall never rise up in judgment against us. 5. He that took the scape-goat into the wilderness, and those that burned the sin-offering, were to be looked upon as ceremonially unclean, and must not come into the camp till they had washed their clothes and bathed their flesh in water, which signified the defiling nature of sin. 6. When all this was done, the high priest went again into the most holy place to fetch his censer, and so returned to his own house with joy, because he had done his duty, and died not.

Verses 29–34

I. We have here some additional directions in reference to this great solemnity, particularly,

1. The day appointed for this solemnity. It must be observed yearly on *the tenth day of the seventh month, v.* 29.

2. The duty of the people on this day. (1) They must rest from all their labours: *It shall be a sabbath of rest, v.* 31. (2) They must afflict their souls. They must refrain from all bodily refreshments and delights, in token of inward humiliation and contrition of soul for their sins. They all fasted on this day from food (except the sick and children), and laid aside their ornaments.

3. The perpetuity of this institution: *It shall be a statute for ever, v.* 29, 34. It must not be intermitted any year, nor ever let fall till that constitution should be dissolved, and the type should be superseded by the antitype. The annual repetition of the sacrifices showed that there was in them only a faint and feeble effort towards making atonement; it could be done effectually only by the *offering up of the body of Christ once for all*, and that once was sufficient; that sacrifice needed not to be repeated.

II. Let us see what there was of gospel in all this.

1. Here are typified the two great gospel privileges of the remission of sin and access to God, both which we owe to the mediation of our Lord Jesus. Here then let us see,

(1) The expiation of guilt which Christ made for us. He is himself both the maker and the matter of the atonement; for he is, [1] The priest, the high priest, that *makes reconciliation for the sins of the people*, Heb. ii. 17. No man was to be with the high priest when he made atonement (*v.* 17); for our Lord Jesus was to *tread the wine-press alone*, and of the people there must be *none with him* (Isa. lxiii. 3); therefore, when he entered upon his sufferings, *all his disciples forsook him and fled*, for if any of them had been taken and put to death with him it would have looked as if they had assisted in making the atonement. But, whereas the atonement which the high priest made pertained only to the congregation of Israel, Christ is the propitiation, not for their sins only, that are Jews, but for the sins of the whole Gentile world. And in this also Christ infinitely excelled Aaron, that Aaron needed to offer sacrifice for his own sin first, of which he was to make confession upon the head of his sin-offering; but our Lord Jesus had no sin of his own to answer for. [2] As he is the high priest, so he is the sacrifice with which atonement is made; for he is all in all in our reconciliation to God. Thus he was prefigured by the two goats, which both made one offering: the slain goat was a type of Christ dying for our sins, the scape-goat a type of Christ rising again for our justification. *First*, The atonement is said to be completed by putting the sins of Israel upon the head of the goat. They deserved to have been abandoned and sent into a land of forgetfulness, but that punishment was here transferred to the goat that bore their sins, with reference to which God is said to have laid upon our Lord Jesus (the substance of all these shadows) *the iniquity of us all* (Isa. liii. 6), and he is said to have *borne our sins*, even the punishment of them, *in his own body upon the tree*, 1 Pet. ii. 24. *Secondly*, The consequence of this was that all the iniquities of Israel were *carried into a land of forgetfulness*. Thus Christ, the Lamb of God, *takes away the sin of the world*, by taking it upon himself, John i. 29. And, when God forgives sin, he is said to remember it no more (Heb. viii. 12), *to cast it behind his back* (Isa. xxxviii. 17), *into the depths of the sea* (Mic. vii. 19), and to separate it *as far as the east is from the west*, Ps. ciii. 12.

(2) The entrance into heaven which Christ made for us is here typified by the high priest's entrance into the most holy place. This the apostle has expounded (Heb. ix. 7, &c.), and he shows, [1] That heaven is the holiest of all, but not of that building, and that the way into it by faith, hope, and prayer, through a Mediator, was not then so clearly manifested as it is to us now by the gospel. [2] That Christ our high priest entered into heaven at his ascension once for all. [3] That he entered *by his own blood* (Heb. ix. 12), sprinkling his blood, as it were, before the mercy-seat, where it speaks better things than the blood of bulls and goats could do. Hence he is said to appear in the midst of the throne as *a lamb that had been slain*, Rev. v. 6. The intercession of Christ is there set forth before God as incense, as *this incense*. And as the high priest interceded for himself first, then for his household, and then for all Israel, so our Lord Jesus, in the xviith of St. John, recommended himself first to his Father, then his disciples who were his household, and then all that should believe on him through their word, as all Israel.

2. Here are likewise typified the two great gospel duties of faith and repentance, by which we are qualified for the atonement, and come to be entitled to the benefit of it. (1) By faith we must put our hands upon the head of the offering, relying on Christ as the Lord our Righteousness, pleading his satisfaction as that which was alone able to atone for our sins and procure us a pardon. *"Thou shalt answer, Lord, for me."* (2) By repentance we must afflict our souls; not only fasting for a time from the delights of the body, but inwardly sorrowing for our sins, and living a life of self-denial and mortification.

CHAPTER 17

In this chapter we have two prohibitions necessary for the preservation of the honour of that atonement. I. That no sacrifice should be offered by any other than the priests, nor anywhere but at the door of the tabernacle, and this upon pain of death, ver. 1–9. II. That no blood should be eaten, and this under the same penalty, ver. 10, &c.

Verses 1–9

This statute obliged all the people of Israel to bring all their sacrifices to God's altar, to be offered there.

I. How it stood before. 1. It was allowed to all people to build altars, and offer sacrifices to God, where they pleased. 2. This liberty had been an occasion of idolatry. The Israelites themselves had learned in Egypt to sacrifice to demons. And some of them, it should seem, practised it even since the God of Israel had so gloriously appeared for them, and with them.

II. How this law settled it. It is hard to construe this as a temporary law, when it is expressly said to be a *statute for ever* (*v.* 7); and therefore it should seem rather to forbid only the killing of beasts for sacrifice anywhere but at God's altar. They must not offer sacrifice, as they had done, *in the open field* (*v.* 5), no, not to the true God, but it must be brought to the priest, to be offered on the altar of the Lord. If any should transgress this law, and offer sacrifice anywhere but at the tabernacle, 1. The guilt was great: *Blood shall be imputed to that man; he hath shed blood, v.* 4. Idolatrous sacrifices were looked upon, not only as adultery, but as murder: he that *offereth them is as if he slew a man*, Isa. lxvi. 3. 2. The punishment should be severe: *That man shall be cut off from among his people.*

III. How this law was observed. 1. While the Israelites kept their integrity they had a tender and very jealous regard to this law, as appears by their zeal against the altar which was erected by the two tribes and a half, which they would by no means have left standing if they had not been satisfied that it was never designed, nor should ever be used, for sacrifice or offering, Josh. xxii. 12, &c. 2. The breach of this law was for many ages the corruption of the Jewish church, witness that complaint which so often occurs in the history even of the good kings, *Howbeit the high places were not taken away*; and it was an inlet to the grossest idolatries.

IV. How the matter stands now, and what use we are to make of this law. 1. It is certain that the spiritual sacrifices we are now to offer are not confined to any one place. We have now no temple nor altar that sanctifies the gift, nor does the gospel unity lie in one place, but in one heart, and the *unity of the spirit*. 2. Christ is our altar, and the *true tabernacle* (Heb. viii. 2; xiii. 10); in Him God dwells among us, and it is in him that our sacrifices are acceptable to God, and in him only, 1 Pet. ii. 5.

Verses 10–16

We have here, A repetition and confirmation of the law against eating blood. We have met with this prohibition twice before in the levitical law (*ch.* iii. 17; vii. 26), besides the place it had in the precepts of Noah, Gen. ix. 4. But here, 1. The prohibition is repeated again and again, and reference had to the former laws to this purport (*v.* 12). A great stress is laid upon it, as a law which has more in it than at first view one would think. 2. It is made binding, not only on the *house of Israel*, but on the *strangers that sojourned among them* (*v.* 10). 3. The penalty annexed to this law is very severe (*v.* 10). 4. A reason is given for this law (*v.* 11): because *it is the blood that makes atonement for the soul*. The sinner deserved to die; therefore the sacrifice must die. Now, the blood being so—that ordinarily beasts were killed for man's use by the drawing out of all their blood—God appointed the sprinkling or pouring out of the blood of the sacrifice upon the altar to signify that the life of the sacrifice was given to God instead of the sinner's life, and as a ransom or counter-price for it; therefore *without shedding of blood there was no remission*, Heb. ix. 22. For this reason they must eat no blood, and, (1) It was then a very good reason; for God would by this means preserve the honour of that way of atonement which he had instituted. But, (2) This reason is now superseded, which intimates that the law itself was ceremonial, and is now no longer in force: the blood of Christ who has come is that alone which makes atonement for the soul, and of which the blood of the sacrifices was an imperfect type. The blood, provided it be so prepared as not to be unwholesome, is now allowed for the nourishment of our bodies, because it is no longer appointed to make an atonement for the soul.

CHAPTER 18

Here is, I. A general law against all conformity to the corrupt usages of the heathen, ver. 1–5. II. Particular laws, 1. Against incest, ver. 6–18. 2. Against beastly lusts, and barbarous idolatries, ver. 19–23. III. The enforcement of these laws from the ruin of the Canaanites, ver. 24–30.

Verses 1–5

After divers ceremonial institutions, God here returns to the enforcement of moral precepts. The former are still of use to us as types, the latter still binding as laws. We have here, 1. The sacred authority by which these laws are enacted: *I am the Lord your God* (*v.* 2, 4, 30). 2. A strict caution to take heed of retaining the relics of the idolatries of Egypt, where they had dwelt, and of receiving the infection of the idolatries of Canaan, whither they were now going, *v.* 3. If we keep God's commandments in sincerity, though we come short of sinless perfection, we shall find that the way of duty is the way of comfort, and will be the way to happiness. It is the description

of the *righteousness which is by the law, the man that doeth them shall live ἐν αὐτοῖς*—in *them* (Rom. x. 5), and is urged to prove that *the law is not of faith*, Gal. iii. 12. The alteration which the gospel has made is in the last word: still *the man that does them shall live*, but not live *in them*; for the law could not give life, because we could not perfectly keep it. He shall owe his life to the grace of Christ, and not to the merit of his own works; see Gal. iii. 21, 22.

Verses 6–18

These laws relate to the seventh commandment.

I. That which is forbidden as to the relations here specified is *approaching to them to uncover their nakedness, v.* 6.

1. It is chiefly intended to forbid the marrying of any of these relations. Marriage is a divine institution, intended for the comfort of human life, and the decent and honourable propagation of the human race, such as became the dignity of man's nature above that of the beasts. These prohibitions, besides their being enacted by an incontestable authority, are in themselves highly reasonable and equitable. (1) By marriage two were to become one flesh, therefore those that before were in a sense one flesh by nature could not, without the greatest absurdity, become one flesh by institution. (2) Marriage puts an equality between husband and wife. The inequality between master and servant, noble and ignoble, is founded in consent and custom, and there is no harm done if that be taken away by the equality of marriage; but the inequality between parents and children, uncles and nieces, aunts and nephews, either by blood or marriage, is founded in nature, and cannot without confusion be taken away by the equality of marriage. (3) No relations that are equals are forbidden, except brothers and sisters, by the whole blood or half blood, or by marriage. The making use of the ordinance of marriage for the patronising of incestuous mixtures is so far from justifying them, or extenuating their guilt, that it adds the guilt of profaning an ordinance of God, and prostituting that to the vilest of purposes which was instituted for the noblest ends. But,

2. Uncleanness, committed with any of these relations out of marriage, is likewise forbidden here.

II. The relations forbidden are most of them plainly described; and it is generally laid down as a rule that what relations of a man's own he is bound up from marrying the same relations of his wife he is likewise forbidden to marry, for they two are one. That law which forbids marrying a brother's wife (*v.* 16) had an exception peculiar to the Jewish state, that, if a man died without issue, his brother or next of kin should marry the widow, and raise up seed to the deceased (Deut. xxv. 5), for reasons which held good only in that commonwealth.

Verses 19–30

I. A law to preserve the honour of the marriage-bed, that it should not be unseasonably used (*v.* 19), nor invaded by an adulterer, *v.* 20.

II. A law against that which was the most unnatural idolatry, causing their children to *pass through the fire to Moloch, v.* 21. Moloch (as some think) was the idol in and by which they worshipped the sun, that great fire of the world; and therefore in the worship of it they made their own children either sacrifices to this idol, burning them to death before it, or devotees to it, causing them to pass between two fires, as some think, or to be thrown through one, to the honour of this pretended deity, imagining that the consecrating of but one of their children in this manner to Moloch would procure good fortune for all the rest of their children.

III. A law against unnatural lusts, sodomy and bestiality, sins not to be named nor thought of without the utmost abhorrence imaginable, v. 22, 23. Other sins level men with the beasts, but these sink them much lower.

IV. Arguments against these and the like abominable wickedness. 1. Sinners defile themselves with these abominations. All sin is defiling to the conscience, but these are sins that have a peculiar turpitude in them. 2. *The souls that commit them shall be cut off, v.* 29. Fleshly lusts war against the soul, and will certainly be the ruin of it if God's mercy and grace prevent not. For these and the like sins the Canaanites were to be destroyed.

V. The chapter concludes with a sovereign antidote against this infection: *Therefore you shall keep my ordinance that you commit not any one of these abominable customs, v.* 30. A close and constant adherence to God's ordinances is the most effectual preservative from the infection of gross sin. It is the grace of God only that will secure us, and that grace is to be expected only in the use of the means of grace.

Chapter 19

I. The laws of this chapter, which were peculiar to the Jews, are, 1. Concerning their peace-offerings, ver. 5–8. 2. Concerning the gleanings of their fields, ver. 9, 10. 3. Against mixtures of their cattle, seed, and cloth, ver. 19. 4. Concerning their trees, ver. 23–25. 5. Against some superstitious usages, ver. 26–28. But, II. Most of these precepts are binding on us, for they are expositions of most of the ten commandments. 1. Here is the preface to the ten commandments, "I am the Lord," repeated fifteen times. 2. A sum of the ten commandments. All the first table in this, "Be you holy," ver. 2. All the second table in this, "Thou shalt love thy neighbour" (ver. 18), and an answer to the question, "Who is my neighbour?" ver. 33, 34. 3. Something of each commandment. (1) The first commandment implied in that which is often repeated here, "I am your God." And here is a prohibition of enchantment (ver. 26) and witchcraft (ver. 31), which make a god of the devil. (2) Idolatry, against the second commandment, is forbidden, ver. 4. (3) Profanation of God's name, against the third, ver. 12. (4) Sabbath-sanctification is pressed, ver. 3, 30. (5) Children are required to honour their parents (ver. 3), and the aged, ver. 32. (6) Hatred and revenge are here forbidden, against the sixth commandment, ver. 17, 18. (7) Adultery (ver. 20–22), and whoredom, ver. 29. (8) Justice is here required in judgment (ver. 15), theft forbidden (ver. 11), fraud and withholding dues (ver. 13), and false weights, ver. 35, 36. (9) Lying, ver. 11. Slandering, ver. 14. Tale-bearing, and false-witness bearing, ver. 16. (10) The tenth commandment laying a restraint upon the heart, so does that (ver. 17), "Thou shalt not hate thy brother in thy heart." And here is a solemn charge to observe all these statutes, ver. 37. Now these are things which need not much help for the understanding of them, but require constant care and watchfulness for the observing of them. "A good understanding have all those that do these commandments."

Verses 1–10

Moses is ordered to deliver the summary of the laws *to all the congregation of the children of Israel* (v. 2). Many of the precepts here given they had received before, but it was requisite that they should be repeated, that they might be remembered. In these verses it is required,

I. That Israel be a holy people, because the God of Israel is a holy God, v. 2. And this is now the law of Christ. *You shall be holy, for I am holy,* 1 Pet. i. 15, 16. Israel was sanctified by the types and shadows (*ch.* xx. 8), but we are *sanctified by the truth,* or substance of all those shadows, John xvii. 17; Tit. ii. 14.

II. That children be obedient to their parents: "*You shall fear every man his mother and his father,*" v. 3. 1. The fear here required includes inward reverence and esteem, outward expressions of respect, obedience to the lawful commands of parents, care and endeavour to please them and make them easy, and to avoid everything that may offend and grieve them, and incur their displeasure. The Jewish doctors ask, "What is this fear that is owing to a father?" And they answer, "It is not to stand in his way nor

to sit in his place, not to contradict what he says nor to carp at it, not to call him by his name, either living or dead, but 'My Father,' or 'Sir'; it is to provide for him if he be poor, and the like." 2. Children, when they grow up to be men, must not think themselves discharged from this duty: every man, though he be a wise man, and a great man, yet must reverence his parents, because they are his parents. 3. The mother is put first, which is not usual, to show that the duty is equally owing to both. 4. It is added, *and keep my sabbaths.* If God provides by his law for the preserving of the honour of parents, parents must use their authority over their children for the preserving of the honour of God, particularly the honour of his sabbaths. The ruin of young people has often been observed to begin in the contempt of their parents and the profanation of the sabbath day. 5. The reason added to both these precepts is, "*I am the Lord your God;* the Lord of the sabbath and the God of your parents."

III. That God only be worshipped, and not by images (v. 4): "*Turn you not to idols,* to Elilim, to vanities, things of no power, no value, gods that are no gods. You are the work of God's hands, be not so absurd as to worship gods *the work of your own hands.*"

IV. That the sacrifices of their peace-offerings should always be offered, and eaten, according to the law, v. 5–8.

V. That they should leave the gleanings of their harvest and vintage for the poor, v. 9, 10. When they gathered in their corn, they must leave some standing in the corner of the field; the Jewish doctors say, "It should be a sixtieth part of the field"; and they must also leave the gleanings and the small clusters of their grapes, which at first were overlooked.

Verses 11–18

We are taught here,

I. To be honest and true in all our dealings, v. 11. Whatever we have in the world, we must see to it that it be honestly come by, for we cannot be truly rich, nor long rich, with that which is not.

II. To maintain a very reverent regard to the sacred name of God (v. 12).

III. Neither to take nor keep anyone's right from him, v. 13. We must not take that which is none of our own, either by fraud or robbery; nor detain that which belongs to another. Let the day-labourer have his wages as soon as he has done his day's work, if he desire it.

IV. To be particularly tender of the credit and safety of those that cannot help themselves, v. 14. 1. The credit of the deaf: *Thou shalt not curse the deaf;* that is, not only those that are naturally deaf, that cannot hear at all, but also those that are absent, and at present out of hearing. 2. The safety of the blind we must likewise be tender of, and not put a stumbling-block before them; for this is to add affliction to the afflicted. This prohibition implies a precept to help the blind, and remove stumbling-blocks out of their way. The Jewish writers, thinking it impossible that any should be so barbarous as to put a *stumbling-block in the way of the blind,* understood it figuratively, that it forbids giving bad counsel to those that are simple and easily imposed upon, by which they may be led to do something to their own prejudice.

V. Judges and all in authority are here commanded to give verdict and judgment without partiality (v. 15). *Thou shalt not respect the person of the poor,* Exod. xxiii. 3. Whatever may be given to a poor man as an alms, yet let nothing be awarded him as his right but what he is legally entitled to, nor let his poverty excuse him from any just punishment for a fault. The Jews say, "Judges were obliged by this law to be so impartial as not to let one of the contending parties sit while the other stood, nor permit one to say what he pleased and bid the other be short"; see James ii. 1–4.

VI. We are all forbidden to do anything injurious to our neighbour's good name (v. 16), either, 1. In common conversation: *Thou shalt not go up and down as a tale-bearer.* The word used for a tale-bearer signifies a *pedlar,* or *petty chapman,* the interlopers of trade; for tale-bearers pick up ill-natured stories at one house and utter them at another, and commonly barter slanders by way of exchange. See this sin condemned, Prov. xi. 13; xx. 19; Jer. ix. 4, 5; Ezek. xxii. 9. Or, 2. In witness-bearing: Neither *shalt thou stand* as a witness *against the blood of thy neighbour,* if his blood be innocent. The Jewish doctors put this further sense upon it: "He that can by his testimony clear one that is accused is obliged by this law to do it"; see Prov. xxiv. 11, 12.

VII. We are commanded to rebuke our neighbour in love (v. 17): 1. Rather rebuke him than hate him for an injury done to thyself. If we apprehend that our neighbour has any way wronged us, we must not conceive a secret grudge against him, and estrange ourselves from him. We must rather endeavour to convince our brother of the injury, reason the case fairly with him. This is the rule our Saviour gives in the case, Luke xvii. 3. 2. Therefore rebuke him for his sin against God, because thou lovest him. Note, Friendly reproof is a duty we owe to one another, and we ought both to give it and take it in love. *Let the righteous smite me, and it shall be a kindness,* Ps. cxli. 5.

VIII. We are here required to put off all malice, and to put on brotherly love, v. 18. 1. We must be ill-affected to none. 2. We must be well-affected to all: *Thou shalt love thy neighbour as thyself.* We must do to our neighbour as we would be done to ourselves (Matt. vii. 12), putting *our souls into his soul's stead,* Job xvi. 4, 5. Nay, we must in many cases deny ourselves for the good of our neighbour, as Paul, 1 Cor. ix. 19, &c. Herein the gospel goes beyond even that excellent precept of the law; for Christ, by laying down his life for us, has taught us even to *lay down our lives for the brethren,* in some cases (1 John iii. 16), and so to love our neighbour better than ourselves.

Verses 19–29

I. A law against mixtures, v. 19. God in the beginning made the cattle *after their kind* (Gen. i. 25), and we must acquiesce in the order of nature God hath established, believing that is best and sufficient, and not covet monsters. The sowing of mingled corn and the wearing of linsey-woolsey garments are forbidden, either as superstitious customs of the heathen or to intimate how careful they should be not to mingle themselves with the heathen nor to weave any of the usages of the Gentiles into God's ordinances. Ainsworth suggests that it was to lead Israel to the simplicity and sincerity of religion.

II. A law for punishing adultery committed with one that was a bondmaid that was espoused, v. 20–22. It was for the honour of marriage, though but begun by betrothing, that the crime should be punished; but it was for the honour of freedom that it should not be punished as the debauching of a free woman was, so great was the difference then made between bond and free (Gal. iv. 30); but the gospel of Christ knows no such distinction, Col. iii. 11.

III. A law concerning fruit trees, that for the first three years after they were planted, if they should happen to be so forward as to bear in that time, yet no use should be made of the fruit, v. 23–25. It was therefore the practice of the Jews to pluck off the fruit, as soon as they perceived it knit, from their young trees, as gardeners do sometimes, because their early bearing hinders their growing. If any did come to perfection, it was not to be used in the service either of God or man; but what they bore the fourth year was to be holy to the Lord, either given to the priests, or eaten before the Lord with joy, as their second tithe was, and thenceforward it was all their own. This law in the case of fruit trees seems to be parallel with that in the case of animals, that no creature should be accepted as an offering till it was past eight days old, nor till that day were children to be circumcised; see *ch.* xxii. 27. God would have the first-fruits of their trees, but, because for the first three years they were as inconsiderable as a lamb or a calf under eight days old, therefore God would not have them, for it is fit he should have every thing at its best; and yet he would not allow them to be used, because his first-fruits were not as yet offered: they must therefore be accounted as uncircumcised, that is, as an animal under eight days old, not fit for any use.

IV. A law against the superstitious usages of the heathen, v. 26–28. 1. Eating upon the blood, as the Gentiles did, who gathered the blood of their sacrifices into a vessel for their demons (as they fancied) to drink. The blood of God's sacrifices was to be sprinkled on the altar, and then poured at the foot of it, and conveyed away. 2. Enchantment and divination, and a superstitious observation of the times, some days and hours lucky and others unlucky. Curious arts of this kind, it is likely, had been of late invented by the Egyptian priests. It would be unpardonable in those *to whom were committed the oracles of God* to ask counsel of the devil, and yet worse in Christians to whom *the Son of God is manifested,* who has *destroyed the work of the devil.* For Christians to have their nativities cast, and their fortunes told them, to use spells and charms for the cure of diseases and the driving away of evil spirits, to be affected with the falling of the salt, a hare crossing the way, cross days, or the like, is an intolerable affront to the Lord Jesus, a support of paganism and idolatry, and a reproach both to themselves and to that worthy name by which they are called. 3. There was a superstition even in trimming themselves used by the heathen, which must not be imitated by the people of God: *You shall not round the corners of your heads.* Those that worshipped the hosts of heaven, in honour of them, cut their hair so that their heads might resemble the celestial globe; but, as the custom was foolish in itself, so, being done with respect to their false gods, it was idolatrous. 4. The rites and ceremonies by which they expressed their sorrow at their funerals must not be imitated, v. 28. They must not make cuts or prints in their flesh for the dead; for the heathen did so to pacify the infernal deities. Christ by his sufferings has altered the property of death, and made it a true friend to every true Israelite; and now, as there needs nothing to make death propitious to us, so we sorrow not as those that have no hope. *Lastly,* The prostituting of their daughters to uncleanness, which is here forbidden (v. 29), seems to have been practised by the heathen in their idolatrous worships.

Verses 30–37

I. A law for the preserving of the honour of the time and place appropriated to the service of God, v. 30. 1. Sabbaths must be religiously observed. 2. The sanctuary must be reverenced. Though now there is no place holy by divine institution, as the tabernacle and temple then were, yet this law obliges us to respect the solemn assemblies of Christians for religious worship, as being held under a promise of Christ's special presence in them.

II. A caution against all communion with those that were in league with familiar spirits: "*Regard them not, seek not after them*, be not in fear of any evil from them nor in hopes of any good from them."

III. A charge to young people to show respect to the aged: *Thou shalt rise up before the hoary head*, v. 32. Those whom God has honoured with the common blessing of long life we ought to honour. Those who in age are wise and good are worthy of double honour; their credit and comfort must be carefully consulted, and their counsels asked and hearkened to, Job xxxii. 6, 7. Note, Religion teaches good manners, and obliges us to give honour to those to whom honour is due.

IV. A charge to the Israelites to be very tender of strangers, v. 33, 34. "*Thou shalt not vex a stranger*, but *love him as thyself*, and as one of thy own people." Strangers are God's particular care, as the widow and the fatherless are, because it is his honour to help the helpless, Ps. cxlvi. 9. It argues a generous disposition, and a pious regard to God, as a common Father, to be kind to strangers. But here is a reason added peculiar to the Jews: "*For you were strangers in the land of Egypt*. God then favoured you, therefore do you now favour the strangers."

V. Justice in weights and measures is here commanded. That there should be no cheat in them, v. 35. That they should be very exact, v. 36.

VI. The chapter concludes with a general command (v. 37): *You shall observe all my statutes, and do them.*

CHAPTER 20

In this chapter we have, I. Many particular crimes that are made capital. 1. Giving their children to Molech, ver. 1-5. 2. Consulting witches, ver. 6, 27. 3. Cursing parents, ver. 9. 4. Adultery, ver. 10. 5. Incest, ver. 11, 12, 14, 17, 19-21. 6. Unnatural lusts, ver. 13, 15, 16, 18. II. General commands given to be holy, ver. 7, 8, 22-26.

Verses 1-9

I. Three sins are in these verses threatened with death:—

1. Parents abusing their children, by sacrificing them to Molech, v. 2, 3. It was not enough to tell them they might spare their children, but they must be told, (1) That the criminal himself should be put to death as a murderer: *The people of the land shall stone him with stones* (v. 2), which was looked upon as the worst capital punishment among the Jews. (2) That all his aiders and abetters should be cut off likewise by the righteous hand of God. If his neighbours concealed him, and would not come in as witnesses against him,—if the magistrates connived at him, and would not pass sentence upon him, rather pitying his folly than hating his impiety,—God himself would reckon with them, v. 4, 5.

2. Children's abusing their parents, by cursing them, v. 9. If children should speak ill of their parents, or wish ill to them, or carry it scornfully or spitefully towards them, it was an iniquity to be punished by the judges, who were employed as conservators both of God's honour and of the public peace, which were both attacked by this unnatural insolence.

3. Persons abusing themselves by consulting such as have *familiar spirits*, v. 6. By this, as much as any thing, a man diminishes, disparages, and deceives himself, and so abuses himself. What greater madness can there be than for a man to go to a liar for information, and to an enemy for advice? Those do so who turn after those that deal in the black art, and know the depths of Satan.

II. In the midst of these particular laws comes in that general charge, v. 7, 8, where we have,

1. The duties required; and they are two: (1) That in our principles, affections, and aims, we be holy:

Sanctify yourselves and be you holy. (2) That in all our actions, and in the whole course of our conversation, we be obedient to the laws of God: *You shall keep my statutes.* Make the tree good, and the fruit will be good.

2. The reasons to enforce these duties. (1) "*I am the Lord your God*; therefore be holy, that you may resemble him whose people you are, and may be pleasing to him. Holiness becomes his house and household." (2) *I am the Lord who sanctifieth you.* God sanctifieth them by peculiar privileges, laws, and favours, which distinguished them from all other nations, and dignified them as a people set apart for God. He gave them his word and ordinances to be means of their sanctification, and his good Spirit to instruct them.

Verses 10-21

Sins against the seventh commandment are here ordered to be severely punished.

I. Lying with another man's wife was made a capital crime. The adulterer and the adulteress that had joined in the sin must fall alike under the sentence: they shall both be *put to death*, v. 10.

II. Incestuous connections, whether by marriage or not.

III. The unnatural lusts of sodomy and bestiality (sins not to be mentioned without horror) were to be punished with death.

Verses 22-27

The last verse is a particular law, which comes in after the general conclusion, as if omitted in its proper place: it is for the putting of those to death that dealt with familiar spirits, v. 27. Those that are in league with the devil have in effect made a covenant with death.

The rest of these verses repeat and inculcate what had been said before.

I. Their dignity. They had the *Lord for their God*, v. 24. They were his, his care, his choice, his treasure.

II. Their duty; this is inferred from their dignity. God had done more for them than for others, and therefore expected more from them than from others.

III. Their danger. They were going into an infected place (v. 24): *You shall inherit their land*, a land *flowing indeed with milk and honey*, which they would have the comfort of if they kept their integrity; but, withal, it was a land full of idols, idolatries, and superstitious usages, which they would be apt to fall in love with, having brought from Egypt with them a strange disposition to take that infection.

CHAPTER 21

This chapter is a law obliging priests with the utmost care and jealousy to preserve the dignity of their priesthood. I. The inferior priests are here charged both concerning their mourning and concerning their marriages and their children, ver. 1-9. II. The high priest is restrained more than any of them, ver. 10-15. III. Neither the one nor the other must have any blemish, ver. 16, &c.

Verses 1-9

It was before appointed that the priests should teach the people the statutes God had given concerning the *difference between clean and unclean*, ch. x. 10, 11. Now here it is provided that they should themselves observe what they were to teach the people. The priests were to draw nearer to God than any of the people, and to be more intimately conversant with sacred things, and therefore it was required of them that they should keep at a greater distance than others from every thing that was defiling.

I. They must take care not to disparage themselves in their mourning for the dead. "It made a man ceremonially unclean to come within six feet of a dead corpse"; nay, it is declared (Num. xix. 14) that all who come into the tent where the dead body lies shall be unclean seven days. 1. The priests should never put themselves under this incapacity of coming into the sanctuary, unless it were for one of their nearest relations, *v*. 1-3. 2. They must not be extravagant in the expressions of their mourning. Their mourning must not be either, (1) Superstitious, according to the manner of the heathen, who cut off their hair, and let out their blood, in honour of the imaginary deities which presided (as they thought) in the congregation of the dead, that they might engage them to be propitious to their departed friends. Nor, (2) Must it be passionate or immoderate. Note, God's ministers must be examples to others of patience under affliction, particularly that which touches in a very tender part, the death of their near relations.

II. They must take care not to degrade themselves in their marriage, *v*. 7. A priest must not marry a woman of ill fame, that either had been guilty or was suspected to have been guilty of uncleanness.

III. Their children must be afraid of doing any thing to disparage them (*v*. 9): *If the daughter of any priest play the whore*, her crime is great; she not only polluteth but *profaneth herself*: other women have not that honour to lose that she has, who, as one of a priest's family, has eaten of the holy things, and is supposed to have been better educated than others.

Verses 10-15

More was expected from a priest than from other people, but more from the high priest than from other priests, because upon his head the *anointing oil was poured*. It is called the *crown of the anointing oil of his God* (*v*. 12); for the anointing of the Spirit is, to all that have it, a *crown of glory*, and a *diadem of beauty*. The high priest being thus dignified,

I. He must not defile himself at all for the dead, no, not for his nearest relations, *his father or his mother*, much less his child or brother, *v*. 11. Our Lord Jesus, the great high priest of our profession, touched the dead body of Jairus's daughter, the bier of the widow's son, and the grave of Lazarus, to show that he came to alter the property of death, and to take off the terror of it, by breaking the power of it. Now that it cannot destroy it does not defile.

II. He might not marry a widow (as other priests might), much less one divorced, or a harlot, *v*. 13, 14. The reason of this was to put a difference between him and other priests in this matter.

III. He might not profane his seed among his people, *v*. 15. It may be a caution to him in disposing of his children; he must not profane his seed by marrying them unsuitably. Ministers' children are profaned if they be unequally yoked with unbelievers.

Verses 16-24

The priesthood being confined to one particular family, and entailed upon all the male issue of that family throughout their generations, it was very likely that some or other in after-ages that were born to the priesthood would have natural blemishes and deformities.

I. The law concerning priests that had blemishes was, 1. That they might *live upon the altar* (*v*. 22): *He shall eat* of the sacrifices with the other priests, even the *most holy things*, such as the show-bread and the sin-offerings, as well as the *holy things*, such as the tithes and first-fruits, and the priests' share of the peace-offerings. The blemishes were such as they could not help, and therefore, though they might not work, they must not starve. 2. Yet they must not *serve at the altar*, at either of the altars, nor be admitted to attend or assist the other priests in offering sacrifice of burning incense, *v*. 17, 21, 23. It was

for the credit of the sanctuary that none should appear there who were any way disfigured, either by nature or accident.

II. Under the gospel, 1. Those that labour under any such blemishes as these have reason to thank God that they are not thereby excluded from offering spiritual sacrifices to God; nor, if otherwise qualified for it, from the office of the ministry. There is many a healthful beautiful soul lodged in a crazy deformed body. Yet, 2. We ought to infer hence how incapable those are to serve God acceptably whose minds are blemished and deformed by any reigning vice. Those are unworthy to be called Christians, and unfit to be employed as ministers, that are spiritually blind, and lame, and crooked, whose sins render them scandalous and deformed, so as that the offerings of the Lord are abhorred for their sakes.

CHAPTER 22

In this chapter we have divers laws concerning the priests and sacrifices, all for the preserving of the honour of the sanctuary. I. That the priests should not eat of the holy things in their uncleanness, ver. 1-9. II. That no stranger who did not belong to some family of the priests should eat of the holy things (ver. 10-13), and, if he did it unwittingly, he must make restitution, ver. 14-16. III. That the sacrifices which were offered must be without blemish, ver. 17-25. IV. That they must be more than eight days old (ver. 26-28), and that the sacrifices of thanksgiving must be eaten the same day they were offered, ver. 29, &c.

Verses 1-9

Those that had a natural blemish, though they were forbidden to do the priests' work, were yet allowed to eat of the holy things: and the Jewish writers say that "to keep them from idleness they were employed in the wood-room, to pick out that which was worm-eaten, that it might not be used in the fire upon the altar; they might also be employed in the judgment of leprosy": but,

I. Those that were under any ceremonial uncleanness, which possibly they contracted by their own fault, might not so much as eat of the holy things while they continued in their pollution.

II. As to the design of this law we may observe, 1. This obliged the priests carefully to preserve their purity, and to dread every thing that would defile them. 2. This impressed the people with a reverence for the holy things.

Verses 10-16

The holy things were to be eaten by the priests and their families.

I. Here is a law that no stranger should eat of them, that is, no person whatsoever but the priests only, and those that pertained to them, *v*. 10. The priests are charged with this care, not to *profane the holy things* by permitting the strangers to eat of them (*v*. 15) or *suffer them to bear the iniquity of trespass* (*v*. 16). Note, We must not only be careful that we do not bear iniquity ourselves, but we must do what we can to prevent others bearing it.

II. Here is an explanation of the law, showing who were to be looked upon as belonging to the priest's family, and who not. 1. Sojourners and hired servants abode not in the house for ever; they were in the family, but not of it; and therefore they might not eat of the holy things (*v*. 10): but the servant that was born in the house or bought with money, being a heirloom to the family, though a servant, yet might eat of the holy things, *v*. 11. 2. As to the children of the family, concerning the sons there could be no dispute, they were themselves priests, but concerning the daughters there was a distinction. While they continued in their father's house they might eat of the holy things; but, if they married such as were not priests, they lost their right (*v*. 12). 3. Here is a demand of restitution to be made by him that had no right to the holy things, and yet should eat of them unwittingly, *v.* 14.

III. This law might be dispensed with in a case of necessity, as it was when David and his men ate of the show-bread, 1 Sam. xxi. 6. And our Saviour justifies them, and gives a reason for it, which furnishes us with a lasting rule in all such cases, that *God will have mercy and not sacrifice*, Matt. xii. 3, 4, 7. Rituals must give way to morals.

Verses 17–33

Here are four laws concerning sacrifices:—
I. Whatever was offered in sacrifice to God should be without blemish, otherwise it should not be accepted. Moreover a difference is made between what was brought as a free-will offering and what was brought as a vow, *v.* 23. According to this law great care was taken to search all the beasts that were brought to be sacrificed, that there might, to a certainty, be no blemish in them. The heathen priests were many of them not so strict in this matter, but would receive sacrifices for their gods that were ever so scandalous; but let strangers know that the God of Israel would not be so served. It is an instruction to us to offer to God the best we have in our spiritual sacrifices. If our devotions are ignorant, and cold, and trifling, and full of distractions, we offer *the blind, and the lame, and the sick, for sacrifice.*
II. That no beast should be offered in sacrifice before it was eight days old, *v.* 26, 27. It was provided before that the firstlings of their cattle, which were to be dedicated to God, should not be brought to him till after the eighth day, Exod. xxii. 30. Here it is provided that no creature should be offered in sacrifice till it was eight days old complete. Sooner than that it was not fit to be used at men's tables, and therefore not at God's altar.
III. That the dam and her young should not both be killed in one day, whether in sacrifice or for common use, *v.* 28. It looked ill-natured towards the species to kill two generations at once, as if one designed the ruin of the kind.
IV. That the flesh of their thank-offerings should be eaten on the same day that they were sacrificed, *v.* 29, 30. This is a repetition of what we had before, *ch.* vii. 15; xix. 6, 7. The chapter concludes with such a general charge as we have often met with, to *keep God's commandments*, and not to *profane his holy name*, *v.* 31, 32.

CHAPTER 23

Hitherto the levitical law has been chiefly conversant about holy persons, holy things, and holy places; in this chapter we have the institution of holy times. I. The weekly feast of the sabbath, ver. 3. II. The yearly feasts, 1. The passover, and the feast of unleavened bread (ver. 4–8), to which was annexed the offering of the sheaf of firstfruits, ver. 9–14. 2. Pentecost, ver. 15–22. 3. The solemnities of the seventh month. The feast of trumpets on the first day (ver. 23–25), the day of atonement on the tenth day (ver. 26–32), and the feast of tabernacles on the fifteenth, ver. 33, &c.

Verses 1–3

Here is, I. A general account of the holy times which God appointed (*v.* 2), and it is only his appointment that can make time holy; for he is the Lord of time, and as soon as ever he had set its wheels a-going it was he that sanctified and blessed one day above the rest, Gen. ii. 3. Man may by his appointment make a good day (Esth. ix. 19), but it is God's prerogative to make a holy day. Now, concerning the holy times here ordained, observe, 1. They are called *feasts*. The day of atonement, which was one of them, was a fast; yet, because most of them were appointed for joy and rejoicing, they are in the general called feasts. Some read it, *These are my assemblies*, but I would rather read it, These are *my solemnities*; and, reading it so here, the day of atone-

ment was as great a solemnity as any of them. 2. They are the feasts of the Lord (*my feasts*). 3. They were proclaimed; for they were not to be observed by the priests only that attended the sanctuary, but by all the people. 4. They were to be sanctified and solemnized with holy convocations, that the services of these feasts might appear the more honourable and august, and the people the more unanimous in the performance of them.
II. A repetition of the law of the sabbath in the first place. Though the annual feasts were made more remarkable by the general attendance at the sanctuary, yet these must not eclipse the brightness of the sabbath, *v.* 3. Christ appointed the New Testament sabbath to be a holy convocation, by meeting his disciples once and again (and perhaps oftener) on the first day of the week. "Whether you have opportunity of sanctifying it in a holy convocation or not, yet let it be *the sabbath of the Lord in all your dwellings.* Put a difference between that day and other days in your families.

Verses 4–14

Here again the feasts are called the *feasts of the Lord*, because he appointed them. They were most of them times of joy and rejoicing. The weekly sabbath is so, and all their yearly solemnities, except the day of atonement. God would thus teach them that wisdom's ways are pleasantness, and engage them to his service by encouraging them to be cheerful in it and to sing at their work. Seven days were days of strict rest and holy convocations; the first day and the seventh of the feast of unleavened bread, the day of pentecost, the day of the feast of trumpets, the first day and the eighth of the feast of tabernacles, and the day of atonement: here were six for holy joy and one only for holy mourning.
I. A repetition of the law of the passover, which was to be observed on the fourteenth day of the first month, in remembrance of their deliverance out of Egypt and the distinguishing preservation of their first-born, mercies never to be forgotten.
II. An order for the offering of a sheaf of the first-fruits, upon the second day of the feast of unleavened bread; the first is called the *sabbath*, because it was observed as a sabbath (*v.* 11), and, on the morrow after, they had this solemnity. A sheaf or handful of new corn was brought to the priest, who was to heave it up, in token of his presenting it to the God of Heaven, and to wave it to and fro before the Lord, as the Lord of the whole earth, and this should be accepted for them as a thankful acknowledgment of God's mercy to them in clothing their fields with corn, and of their dependence upon God, and desire towards him, for the preserving of it to their use. And the offering of this sheaf of first-fruits in the name of the whole congregation did, as it were, sanctify to them their whole harvest. We find that when they came into Canaan the manna ceased upon the very day that the sheaf of first-fruits was offered; they had eaten of the old corn the day before (Josh. v. 11), and then on this day they offered the first-fruits, by which they became entitled to the new corn too (*v.* 12), so that there was no more occasion for manna. This sheaf of first-fruits was typical of our Lord Jesus, who has risen from the dead as the *first-fruits of those that slept*, 1 Cor. xv. 20. They were not to eat of their new corn till God's part was offered to him out of it (*v.* 14), for we must always begin with God, begin our lives with him, begin every day with him, begin every meal with him, begin every affair and business with him; *seek first the kingdom of God.*

Verses 15–22

Here is the institution of the feast of *pentecost*, or *weeks*, as it is called (Deut. xvi. 9), because it was observed fifty days, or seven weeks, after the passover. It is also called the *feast of harvest*, Exod. xxiii. 16. For as the presenting of the sheaf of first-fruits was an introduction to the harvest, and gave them liberty to put in the sickle, so they solemnized the finishing of their corn-harvest at this feast. 1. Then they offered a handful of ears of barley, now they offered *two loaves of wheaten bread*, v. 17. This was leavened. At the passover they ate unleavened bread, but now at pentecost it was leavened, because it was an acknowledgment of God's goodness to them in their ordinary food, which was leavened. 2. With that sheaf of first-fruits they offered only one lamb for a burnt-offering, but with these loaves of first-fruits they offered seven lambs, two rams, and one bullock, all for a burnt-offering, so giving glory to God, as the Lord of their harvest. They offered likewise a kid for a sin-offering, and lastly, two lambs for a sacrifice of peace-offerings, to beg a blessing upon the corn they had gathered in. 3. That one day was to be kept with a holy convocation, v. 21. It was one of the days on which all Israel was to meet God and one another, at the place which the Lord should choose. Some suggest that whereas seven days were to make up the feast of unleavened bread there was only one day appointed for the feast of pentecost, because this was a busy time of the year with them, and God allowed them speedily to return to their work in the country. This annual feast was instituted in remembrance of the giving of the law upon Mount Sinai, the fiftieth day after they came out of Egypt. But the period and perfection of this feast was the pouring out of the Spirit upon the apostles on the day of this feast (Acts ii. 1), in which the law of faith was given, fifty days after Christ our passover was sacrificed for us.

To the institution of the feast of pentecost is annexed a repetition of that law by which they were required to leave the gleanings of their fields, and the corn that grew on the ends of the butts, for the poor, v. 22. It also taught them that the joy of harvest should express itself in charity to the poor.

Verses 23–32

I. The institution of the feast of trumpets, on the first day of the seventh month, v. 24, 25. That which is here made peculiar to this festival is that it was *a memorial of blowing of trumpets*. They blew the trumpet every new moon (Ps. lxxxi. 3), but in the new moon of the seventh month it was to be done with more than ordinary solemnity; for they began to blow at sun-rise and continued till sun-set. Now, 1. This is here said to be a *memorial*, perhaps of the sound of the trumpet upon Mount Sinai when the law was given, which must never be forgotten. 2. The Jewish writers suppose it to have a spiritual signification. Now at the beginning of the year they were called by this sound of trumpet to shake off their spiritual drowsiness, to search and try their ways, and to amend them: the day of atonement was the ninth day after this; and thus they were awakened to prepare for that day, by sincere and serious repentance. 3. It was typical of the preaching of the gospel, by which joyful sound souls were to be called in to serve God and keep a spiritual feast to him.

II. A repetition of the law of the day of atonement, that is, so much of it as concerned the people. 1. They must on this day rest from all manner of work. The reason is: *For it is a day of atonement*. He that would do the work of a day of atonement in its day, as it should be done, had need lay aside the thoughts of every thing else. 2. They must afflict their souls, and this upon pain of being cut off by the hand of God, v. 27, 29, 32. They must mortify the body, and deny the appetites of it. 3. The entire day must

be observed: *From even to even you shall afflict your souls* (v. 32).

Verses 33–44

We have here, I. The institution of the feast of tabernacles, which was one of the three great feasts at which all the males were bound to attend, and celebrated with more expressions of joy than any of them.

1. As to the directions for regulating this feast, observe, (1) It was to be observed five days after the day of atonement. We may suppose, though they were not all bound to attend on the day of atonement, as on the three great festivals, yet that many of the devout Jews came up so many days before the feast of tabernacles as to enjoy the opportunity of attending on the day of atonement. The afflicting of their souls on the day of atonement prepared them for the joy of the feast of tabernacles. The more we are grieved and humbled for sin, the better qualified we are for the comforts of the Holy Ghost. (2) It was to continue eight days, the first and last of which were to be observed as sabbaths. (3) During the first seven days of this feast all the people were to leave their houses, and the women and children in them, and to dwell in booths made of the boughs of thick trees, particularly palm trees, v. 40, 42. (4) They were to *rejoice before the Lord God* during all the time of this feast, v. 40. The tradition of the Jews is that they were to express their joy by dancing, and singing hymns of praise to God, with musical instruments.

2. As to the design of this feast,
(1) It was to be kept in remembrance of their dwelling in tents in the wilderness.
(2) It was a feast of in-gathering, so it is called, Exod. xxiii. 16.

II. The summary and conclusion of these institutions.

1. God appointed these feasts (v. 37, 38), *besides the sabbaths and your free-will offerings*. God's institutions leave room for free-will offerings. The feasts of the Lord, declared unto us, are not so numerous, nor the observance of them so burdensome and costly, as theirs then were, but more spiritual and significant, and surer sweeter earnests of the everlasting feast, at the last in-gathering.

Chapter 24

In this chapter we have, I. A repetition of the laws concerning the lamps and the show-bread, ver. 1–9. II. A violation of the law against blasphemy, with the imprisonment, trial, condemnation, and execution, of the blasphemer, ver. 10–14, with ver. 23. III. The law against blasphemy reinforced (ver. 15, 16), with sundry other laws, ver. 17, &c.

Verses 1–9

Care is here taken, and orders are given, for the decent furnishing of the candlestick and table in God's house.

I. The lamps must always be kept burning. 1. The people were to provide oil (v. 2), the best, *pure olive-oil, beaten*, probably it was double-strained. Ministers are as burning and shining lights in Christ's church, but it is the duty of people to provide comfortably for them, as Israel for the lamps. Scandalous maintenance makes a scandalous ministry. 2. The priests were to tend the lamps; they must snuff them, clean the candlestick, and supply them with oil, morning and evening, v. 3, 4. Thus it is the work of the ministers of the gospel to *hold forth that word of life*, not to set up new lights, but, by expounding and preaching the word, to make the light of it more clear and extensive.

II. The table must always be kept spread. This

was appointed before, Exod. xxv. 30. 1. There was a loaf for every tribe, for *in our Father's house there is bread enough.* Even after the revolt of the ten tribes this number of loaves was continued (2 Chron. xiii. 11), for the sake of those few of each tribe that retained their affection to the temple and continued their attendance on it. 2. A handful of frankincense was put in a golden saucer. When the bread was removed, and given to the priests, this frankincense was burnt upon the golden altar for a memorial instead of the bread, as a humble acknowledgment, and all the loaves were consigned to the priests. 3. Every sabbath it was renewed. Christ's ministers should provide new bread for his house every sabbath day, the production of their fresh studies in the scripture, that *their proficiency may appear to all,* II Tim. iv. 1, 5.

Verses 10–23

Evil manners, we say, beget good laws. We have here an account of the evil manners of a certain nameless mongrel Israelite, and the good laws occasioned thereby.

I. The offender was the son of an Egyptian father and an Israelitish mother (*v.* 10); his mother was of the tribe of Dan, *v.* 11. This notice is taken of his parentage either, 1. To intimate what occasioned the quarrel he was engaged in. The Jews say, "He offered to set up his tent among the Danites in the right of his mother, but was justly opposed by some or other of that tribe, and informed that his father being an Egyptian he had no part nor lot in the matter, but must look upon himself as a stranger." Or, 2. To show the common ill effect of such mixed marriages.

II. The occasion of the offence was contention: He *strove with a man of Israel.*

III. The offence itself was blasphemy and cursing, *v.* 11. 1. He *blasphemed the name of the Lord.* It is probable that finding himself aggrieved by the divine appointment, which separated between the Israelites and strangers, he impudently reproached both the law and the Law-maker, and set him at defiance. 2. He cursed either God himself or the person with whom he strove.

IV. The caution with which he was proceeded against for this sin. Moses himself would not give judgment hastily, but committed the offender into custody, till he had consulted the oracle in this case. They waited to know what was *the mind of the Lord,* whether he was to be put to death by the hand of the magistrate or to be left to the judgment of God.

V. Sentence passed upon this offender by the righteous Judge of heaven and earth himself: *Let all the congregation stone him, v.* 14.

VI. A standing law made upon this occasion for the stoning of blasphemers, *v.* 15, 16. Magistrates are the guardians of both tables, and ought to be as jealous for the honour of God against those that speak contemptuously of his being and government as for the public peace and safety against the disturbers of them.

VII. A repetition of some other laws annexed to this new law. 1. That murder should be punished with death (*v.* 17, and again *v.* 21). 2. That maimers should in like manner be punished by the law of retaliation, *v.* 19, 20. This law we had before, Exod. xxii. 4, 5. And it was more agreeable to that dispensation, in which were revealed the rigour of the law and what sin deserved, than to the dispensation we are under, in which are revealed the grace of the gospel and the remission of sins: and therefore our Saviour has set aside this law (Matt. v. 38, 39), not to restrain magistrates from executing public justice, but to restrain us all from returning personal injuries and to oblige us to forgive as we are and hope to be forgiven. 3. That hurt done wilfully to a neighbour's

cattle should be punished by making good the damage, *v.* 18, 21. 4. That strangers, as well as native Israelites, should be both entitled to the benefit of this law, so as not to suffer wrong, and liable to the penalty of this law in case they did wrong.

CHAPTER 25

The law of this chapter concerns the lands and estates of the Israelites in Canaan, the occupying and transferring of which were to be under the divine direction, as well as the management of religious worship; for, as the tabernacle was a holy house, so Canaan was a holy land. God appointed, I. That every seventh year should be a year of rest from occupying the land, a sabbatical year, ver. 1–7. II. That every fiftieth year should be a year of jubilee, that is, 1. A year of release of debts and mortgages, and return to the possession of their alienated lands, ver. 8–17. Particular directions are given, (1) Concerning the sale and redemption of lands, ver. 23–28. (2) Of houses in cities and villages, with a proviso for Levite-cities, ver. 29–34. 2. A year of release of servants and bond-slaves. (1) Here is inserted a law for the kind usage of poor debtors, ver. 35–38. (2) Then comes the law for the discharge of all Israelites that were sold for servants, in the year of jubilee, if they were not redeemed before. [1] If they were sold to Israelites, ver. 39–46. And [2] If sold to proselytes, ver. 47–55.

Verses 1–7

The law of Moses laid a great deal of stress upon the sabbath; that law not only revived the observance of the weekly sabbath, but, for the further advancement of the honour of them, added the institution of a sabbatical year: *In the seventh year shall be a sabbath of rest unto the land, v.* 4. This sabbatical year began in September, at the end of harvest, the seventh month of their ecclesiastical year: and the law was, 1. That at the seed-time, which immediately followed the end of their in-gathering, they should sow no corn in their land, and that they should not in the spring dress their vineyards, and consequently that they should not expect either harvest or vintage the next year. 2. That what their ground did produce of itself they should not claim any property or use in, otherwise than from hand to mouth, but leave it for the poor, servants, strangers, and cattle, *v.* 5–7. It must be a sabbath of rest to the land; they must neither do any work about it, nor expect any fruit from it; all annual labours must be intermitted in the seventh year, as much as daily labours on the seventh day. It was a kindness to their land to let it rest sometimes, and would keep it *in heart* (as our husbandmen express it) for posterity, whose satisfaction God would have them to consult, and not to use the ground as if it were designed only for one age. 3. This year of rest typified the spiritual rest which all believers enter into through Christ, our true Noah, who giveth us comfort and rest *concerning our work, and the toil of our hands, because of the ground which the Lord hath cursed,* Gen. v. 29.

Verses 8–22

The general institution of the jubilee, *v.* 8, &c.

1. When it was to be observed: after *seven sabbaths of years* (*v.* 8).

2. How it was to be proclaimed, with sound of trumpet in all parts of the country (*v.* 9), both to give notice to all persons of it, and to express their joy and triumph in it; and the word *jobel,* or *jubilee,* is supposed to signify some particular sound of the trumpet distinguishable from any other. The trumpet was sounded in the close of the day of atonement. When their peace was made with God, then liberty was proclaimed.

3. What was to be done in that year extraordinary; besides the common rest of the land, which was observed every sabbatical year (*v.* 11, 12), and the release of personal debts (Deut. xv. 2, 3), there was to be the legal restoration of every Israelite to all the property, and all the liberty, which had been alienated from him since the last jubilee.

(1) The property which every man had in his dividend of the land of Canaan could not be alienated any longer than till the year of jubilee. Now this was no wrong to the purchaser, because the year of jubilee was fixed, and every man knew when it would come, and made his bargain accordingly. They shall not have power to sell, but only to make leases for any term of years, not going beyond the next jubilee. By this means it was provided, That the distinction of tribes should be kept up; that none should grow exorbitantly rich, by laying *house to house, and field to field* (Isa. v. 8), but should rather apply themselves to the cultivating of what they had than the enlarging of their possessions.

(2) The liberty which every man was born to, if it were sold or forfeited, should likewise return at the year of jubilee: *You shall return every man to his family, v. 10. Those that were sold into other families thereby became strangers to their own; but in this year of redemption they were to return.

II. A law upon this occasion against oppression in buying and selling of land; neither the buyer nor the seller must overreach, *v. 14–17*. It must be settled what the clear yearly value of the land was, and then how many years' purchase it was worth till the year of jubilee. It is easy to observe that the nearer the jubilee was the less must the value of the land be. *According to the fewness of the years thou shalt diminish the price.*

III. Assurance given them that they should be no losers, but great gainers, by observing these years of rest. It is promised, 1. That they should be safe: *You shall dwell in the land in safety, v. 18*, and again *v. 19*. The word signifies both outward safety and inward security and confidence of spirit. 2. That they should be rich: *You shall eat your fill.* 3. That they should not want food convenient that year in which they did neither sow nor reap: *I will command my blessing in the sixth year, and it shall bring forth fruit for three years, v. 21*. It was intended for an encouragement to all God's people, in all ages, to trust him in the way of duty, and to cast their care upon him.

Verses 23–38

Here is, I. A law concerning the real estates of the Israelites in the land of Canaan, and the transferring of them. No land should be sold for ever from the family to whose lot it fell in the division of the land. And the reason given is, *The land is mine, and you are strangers and sojourners with me, v. 23*. If a man was constrained through poverty to sell his land for the subsistence of his family, yet, if afterwards he was able, he might redeem it before the year of jubilee (*v. 24, 26, 27*), and the price must be settled according to the number of years since the sale and before the jubilee. If the person himself was not able to redeem it, his next kinsman might (*v. 25*): *The redeemer thereof, he that is near unto him, shall come and shall redeem,* so it might be read. The kinsman is called *Goel*, the redeemer (Num. v. 8; Ruth iii. 9), to whom belonged the right of redeeming the land. And this typified Christ, who assumed our nature, that he might be our *kinsman*. If the land was not redeemed before the year of jubilee, then it should return of course to him that had sold or mortgaged it: *In the jubilee it shall go out, v. 28*. This was a figure of the free grace of God towards us in Christ, by which we are restored to the favour of God, and become entitled to paradise, from which our first parents were expelled for disobedience. A difference was made between houses in walled cities, and lands in the country, or houses in country villages. Houses in walled cities were more the fruits of their own industry than land in the country, which was the immediate gift of God's bounty; and therefore, if a man sold a house in a city, he might redeem it any

time within a year after the sale, but otherwise it was confirmed to the purchaser for ever, and should not return, no, not at the year of the jubilee, *v. 29, 30*. This provision was made to encourage strangers and proselytes to come and settle among them. Though they could not purchase land in Canaan to them and their heirs, yet they might purchase houses in walled cities. A clause is added in favour of the Levites, by way of exception from these rules.

II. A law for the relief of the poor, and the tender usage of poor debtors, and these are of more general and perpetual obligation than the former.

1. The poor must be relieved, *v. 35*. Here is, (1) Our brother's poverty and distress supposed. All men are to be looked upon and treated as brethren, for *we have all one Father*, Mal. ii. 10. (2) Our duty enjoined: *Thou shalt relieve him.* By sympathy, pitying the poor; by service, doing for them; and by supply, giving to them according to their necessity and thy ability.

2. Poor debtors must not be oppressed: *If thy brother be waxen poor,* and have occasion to borrow money of thee for the necessary support of his family, *take thou no usury of him,* either for money or victuals, *v. 36, 37*.

Verses 39–55

We have here the laws concerning servitude, designed to preserve the honour of the Jewish nation as a free people, and rescued by a divine power out of the house of bondage, into the glorious liberty of God's sons, his first-born. Now the law is,

I. That a native Israelite should never be made a bondman for perpetuity. If he was sold for debt, or for a crime, by the house of judgment, he was to serve but six years, and to go out the seventh; this was appointed, Exod. xxi. 2. But if he sold himself through extreme poverty, having nothing at all left him to preserve his life, and if it was to one of his own nation that he sold himself, in such a case it is here provided, 1. That he should not *serve as a bond-servant* (*v. 39*), nor be *sold with the sale of a bondman* (*v. 42*). He shall serve thee as a *hired servant,* whom the master has the use of only. God had redeemed them out of Egypt, and therefore they must never be exposed to sale as bondmen. 2. That while he did serve he should not be ruled with rigour, as the Israelites were in Egypt, *v. 43*. Both his work and his usage must be such as were fitting for a son of Abraham. 3. That at the year of jubilee he should *go out free,* he *and his children,* and should *return to his own family, v. 41*. For ten days before the jubilee-trumpet sounded, the servants that were to be discharged by it did express their great joy by feasting, and wearing garlands on their heads.

II. That they might purchase bondmen of the heathen nations that were round about them for the year of jubilee should give no discharge to them, *v. 44, 46*.

III. That if an Israelite sold himself for a servant to a wealthy proselyte that sojourned among them care should be taken that he should have the same advantages as if he had sold himself to an Israelite, and in some respects greater. 1. That he should not serve as a bondman, but as a hired servant. Also he was to go free at the year of jubilee, *v. 54*. 2. That he should have this further advantage that he might be redeemed again before the year of jubilee, *v. 48, 49*.

CHAPTER 26

This chapter is a solemn conclusion of the main body of the levitical law. The precepts that follow in this and the following book are repetitions and explications. Now this chapter contains a general enforcement of all those laws by promises of reward in case of obedience, and threatenings of punishment for disobedience, the former to work upon hope, the latter on fear, those two handles of the soul, by which it is taken hold of and managed. Here is, I. A repetition of two or three of the principal commandments, ver. 1, 2. II. An inviting promise of all good things, if they would but keep God's commandments, ver. 3–13. III. A terrible threatening of ruining judgments which would be brought upon them if they were refractory and disobedient, ver. 14–39. IV. A gracious promise of mercy to those of them that would repent and reform, ver. 40, &c. Deut. xxviii. is parallel to this.

Verses 1–13

Here is, I. The inculcating of those precepts of the law which were of the greatest consequence, and by which especially their obedience would be tried, *v.* 1, 2. They are the abstract of the second and fourth commandments. 1. "Be sure you never worship images, nor ever make any sorts of images or pictures for a religious use," *v.* 1. Next to God's being, unity, and universal influence, it is necessary that we know and believe that he is an infinite Spirit; and therefore to represent him by an image in the making of it, to confine him to an image in the consecrating of it, and to worship him by an image in bowing down to it, *changes his truth into a lie* and *his glory into shame*, as much as any thing. 2. "Be sure you keep up a great venêration for sabbaths and religious assemblies," *v.* 2. As nothing tends more to corrupt religion than the use of images in devotion, so nothing contributes more to the support of it than *keeping the sabbaths* and *reverencing the sanctuary.* These make up very much of the instrumental part of religion, by which the essentials of it are kept up.

II. Great encouragements given them to live in constant obedience to all God's commandments. Human governments enforce their laws with penalties to be inflicted for the breach of them; but God will be known as *the rewarder of those that seek and serve him.* 1. Plenty and abundance of the fruits of the earth. Before they had reaped their corn and threshed it, the vintage would be ready; and, before they had finished their vintage, it would be high time to begin their sowing. The plenty should be so great that they should *bring forth the old* to be given away to the poor *because of the new*, to make room for it in their barns. 2. Peace under the divine protection: "*You shall dwell in your land safely* (*v.* 5); both really safe, and safe in your own apprehensions; you shall lie down to rest in the power and promise of God, and not only none shall hurt you, but none shall so much as *make you afraid*," *v.* 6. See Ps. iv. 8. 3. Victory and success in their wars abroad, while they had peace and tranquillity at home, *v.* 7, 8. 4. The increase of their people: *I will make you fruitful and multiply you*, *v.* 9. 5. The favour of God, which is the fountain of all good: *I will have respect unto you, v.* 9. If the eye of our faith be unto God, the eye of his favour will be unto us. 6. Tokens of his presence in and by his ordinances: *I will set my tabernacle among you, v.* 11. 7. The grace of the covenant, as the fountain and foundation, the sweetness and security, of all these blessings: *I will establish my covenant with you, v.* 9. Let them perform their part of the covenant, and God would not fail to perform his. All covenant-blessings are summed up in the covenant-relation (*v.* 12): *I will be your God, and you shall be my people*; and they are all grounded upon their redemption: *I am your God*, because *I brought you forth out of the land of Egypt, v.* 13.

Verses 14–39

After God had set the blessing before them he here sets the curse before them, the death and evil which would make them miserable if they were disobedient. I. How their sin is described, which would bring all this misery upon them. Not sins of ignorance and infirmity; God had provided sacrifices for those. Not the sins they repented of and forsook; but the sins that were presumptuously committed, and

obstinately persisted in. Two things would certainly bring this ruin upon them:—

1. A contempt of God's commandments (*v.* 14). Their sin is supposed to begin in mere carelessness, and neglect, and omission. (1) *Despising God's statutes*, both the duties enjoined and the authority enjoining them, thinking meanly of the law and the Law-maker. (2) *Abhorring his judgments*, their very souls abhorring them. Those that turn from it will turn against it, and their hearts will rise at it. (3) *Breaking his covenant.* When men have come to such a pitch of impiety as to despise and abhor the commandment, the next step will be to disown God, and all relation to him. Those that reject the precept will come at least to renounce the covenant.

2. A contempt of his corrections. Even their disobedience would not have been their destruction if they had not been obstinate and impenitent in it, notwithstanding the methods God took to reclaim them. Three ways this is expressed:—(1) "*If you will not for all this hearken to me,*" *v.* 18, 21, 27. (2) *If you walk contrary to me, v.* 21, 23, 27. All sinners walk contrary to God, to his truths, laws, and counsels; but those especially that are incorrigible under his judgments. (3) *If you will not be reformed by these things.* God's design in punishing is to reform, by giving men sensible convictions of the evil of sin, and obliging them to seek unto him for relief: this is the primary intention; but those that will not be reformed by the judgments of God must expect to be ruined by them.

II. How the misery is described which their sin would bring upon them, under two heads:—

1. God himself would be against them; and this is the root and cause of all their misery. Those that cast off God deserve that he should cast them off. Those that are obstinate and incorrigible, when they have weathered one storm must expect another more violent.

2. The whole creation would be at war with them. (1) Temporal judgments threatened. [1] Diseases of body, which should be epidemical. [2] Famine and scarcity of bread. [3] Your choice men shall die in battle, and *those that hate you shall reign over you*, and justly, since you are not willing that the God that loved you should reign over you, 2 Chron. xii. 8. [4] Wild beasts, lions, bears, and wolves, which should increase upon them. [5] Captivity, or dispersion: *I will scatter you among the heathen* (*v.* 33), *in your enemies' land, v.* 34. Never were any people so incorporated and united among themselves as they were; but for their sin God would scatter them, so that they should be lost among the heathen, from whom God had graciously distinguished them, but with whom they had wickedly mingled themselves. [6] The utter ruin and desolation of their land, which should be so remarkable that their very enemies themselves, who had helped it forward, should in the review be astonished at it, *v.* 32. *First*, Their cities should be waste. *Secondly*, Their sanctuaries should be a desolation. *Thirdly*, The country itself should be desolate, not tilled or husbanded (*v.* 34, 35). [7] The destruction of their idols: *I will destroy your high places, v.* 30. Those that will not be parted from their sins by the commands of God shall be parted from them by his judgments; since they would not destroy their high places, God would.

(2) Spiritual judgments are here threatened. These should seize the mind; for he that made the mind can, when he pleases, make his sword approach to it. It is here threatened, [1] That they should find no acceptance with God: *I will not smell the savour of your sweet odours, v.* 31. [2] That they should have no courage in their wars, but should be quite dispirited and disheartened. [3] That they should have no hope of the forgiveness of their sins (*v.* 39).

Verses 40–46

Here the chapter concludes with gracious promises of the return of God's favour to them upon their repentance, that they might not (unless it were their own fault) *pine away in their iniquity*. As bad as things are, they may be mended. *Yet there is hope in Israel*.

I. How the repentance which would qualify them for this mercy is described, v. 40, 41. The instances of it are three:—1. Confession, by which they must give glory to God, and take shame to themselves. They must in their confession put sin under its worst character, as *walking contrary to God*. 2. Remorse and godly sorrow for sin: *If their uncircumcised heart be humbled*. An impenitent, unbelieving, unhumbled heart, is called an *uncircumcised* heart, the heart of a Gentile that is a stranger to God, rather than the heart of an Israelite in covenant with him. True circumcision is *of the heart* (Rom. ii. 29), without which the circumcision of the flesh avails nothing, Jer. ix. 26. A humble heart under humbling providences prepares for deliverance and true comfort. 3. Submission to the justice of God in all his dealings; if they then *accept of the punishment of their iniquity* (v. 41 and again v. 43), that is, if they justify God and condemn themselves, then they are penitents indeed.

II. How the mercy which they should obtain upon their repentance is described. 1. They should not be abandoned: *Though they have despised my judgments, yet, for all that, I will not cast them away*, v. 43, 44. He speaks as a tender Father that cannot find in his heart to disinherit a son that has been very provoking. 2. They should be remembered: *I will remember the land* with favour, which is grounded upon the promise before, *I will remember my covenant* (v. 42), which is repeated, v. 45. God is said *to remember the covenant* when he performs the promises of it, purely for his faithfulness' sake. The word covenant is thrice repeated, to intimate that God is ever mindful of it and would have us to be so. When those that have walked contrary to God in a way of sin return to him by sincere repentance, though he has walked contrary to them in a way of judgment he will return to them in a way of special mercy, pursuant to the covenant of redemption and grace. None are so ready to repent as God is to forgive upon repentance, through Christ, who is given for a covenant.

CHAPTER 27

Having given laws concerning instituted services, here he directs concerning vows and voluntary services, the free-will offerings of their mouth. Perhaps some devout serious people among them might be so affected with what Moses had delivered to them in the foregoing chapter as in a pang of zeal to consecrate themselves, or their children, or estates to him. Here is, I. The law concerning what was sanctified to God, persons (ver. 2–8), cattle, clean or unclean (ver. 9–13), houses and lands (ver. 14–25), with an exception of firstlings, ver. 26, 27. II. Concerning what was devoted, ver. 28, 29. III. Concerning tithes, ver. 30, &c.

Verses 1–13

This is part of the law concerning singular vows, extraordinary ones, which though God did not expressly insist on, yet, if they were consistent with and conformable to the general precepts, he would be well pleased with.

I. The case is here put of persons vowed to God by a singular vow, v. 2. If a man consecrated himself, or a child, to the service of the tabernacle, to be employed there in some inferior office, as sweeping the floor, carrying out ashes, running errands, or the like, *the person* so consecrated *shall be for the Lord*, that is, "God will graciously accept the good will." *Thou didst well that it was in thy heart*, 2 Chron. vi. 8. But forasmuch as he had no occasion to use their service about the tabernacle, a whole tribe being

appropriated to the use of it, those that were thus vowed were to be redeemed, and the money paid for their redemption was employed for the repair of the sanctuary, or other uses of it, as appears by 2 Kings xii. 14, where it is called, in the margin, the *money of the souls of his estimation*. A book of rates is accordingly provided, by which the priests were to go in their estimation. The poor shall be valued according to their ability, v. 8. Something they must pay, that they might learn not to be rash in vowing to God. Yet not more than their ability, but that they might not ruin themselves and their families by their zeal.

II. The case is put of beasts vowed to God.

Verses 14–25

The law concerning real estates dedicated to the service of God by a singular vow.

I. Suppose a man, in his zeal for the honour of God, should *sanctify his house to God* (v. 14), the house must be valued by the priest, and the money got by the sale of it was to be converted to the use of the sanctuary, which by degrees came to be greatly enriched with *dedicated things*, 1 Kings xv. 15. If the owner be inclined to redeem it himself, he must not have it so cheap as another, but must add a fifth part to the price, for he should have considered before he had vowed it, v. 15.

II. Suppose a man should sanctify some part of his land to the Lord, giving it to pious uses, then a difference must be made between land that came to the donor by descent and that which came by purchase, and accordingly the case altered.

Verses 26–34

I. A caution given that no man should make such a jest of sanctifying things to the Lord as to sanctify any firstling to him, for that was his already by the law, v. 26.

II. Things or persons devoted are here distinguished from things or persons that were only sanctified. 1. Devoted things were most holy to the Lord, and could neither revert nor be alienated, v. 28. 2. Devoted persons were to be put to death, v. 29. Not that it was in the power of any parent or master thus to devote a child or a servant to death; but it must be meant of the public enemies of Israel.

III. A law concerning tithes, which were paid for the service of God before the law, as appears by Abraham's payment of them (Gen. xiv. 20), and Jacob's promise of them, Gen. xxviii. 22. It is here appointed, That they should pay tithe of all their increase, their corn, trees, and cattle, v. 30, 32. And we are taught in general to *honour the Lord with our substance* (Prov. iii. 9), and in particular to support and maintain his ministers, and to be *ready to communicate* to them, Gal. vi. 6; 1 Cor. ix. 11. And how this may be done in a fitter and more equal proportion than that of the tenth, which God himself appointed of old, I cannot see.

IV. The last verse seems to have reference to this whole book, of which it is the conclusion: *These are the commandments which the Lord commanded Moses, for the children of Israel*. Many of these commandments are moral, and of perpetual obligation; others of them, which were ceremonial and peculiar to the Jewish economy, have notwithstanding a spiritual significance, and are instructive to us who are furnished with a key to let us into the mysteries contained in them. Upon the whole matter, we may see cause to bless God that *we have not come to Mount Sinai*, Heb. xii. 18. 1. That we are not under the *dark shadows* of the law, but enjoy the clear light of the gospel, which shows us *Christ the end of the law for righteousness*, Rom. x. 4. The doctrine of our reconciliation to God by a Mediator is not clouded with the smoke of burning sacrifices, but cleared by the knowledge of *Christ and him crucified.* 2. That we are not under the *heavy yoke* of the law, and the carnal ordinances of it (as the apostle calls them, Heb. ix. 10), imposed till the time of reformation, a yoke which *neither they nor their fathers were able to bear* (Acts xv. 10), but under the sweet and easy institutions of the gospel, which pronounces those the *true wor-*

shippers that worship the Father in spirit and truth, by Christ only, and in his name, who is our priest, temple, altar, sacrifice, purification, and all. *Having boldness to enter into the holiest by the blood of Jesus, let us draw near with a true heart, and in full assurance of faith,* worshipping God with so much the more cheerfulness and humble confidence, still saying, *Blessed be God for Jesus Christ!*

THE FOURTH BOOK OF MOSES, CALLED

NUMBERS

The titles of the five books of Moses, which we use in our Bibles, are all borrowed from the Greek translation of the Seventy, the most ancient version of the Old Testament that we know of. But the title of this book only we turn into English; in all the rest we retain the Greek word itself. This book was thus entitled because of the numbers of the children of Israel, so often mentioned in this book, and so well worthy to give a title to it, because it was the remarkable accomplishment of God's promise to Abraham that his seed should be as the stars of heaven for multitude. It also relates to two numberings of them, one at Mount Sinai (ch. i.), the other in the plains of Moab, thirty-nine years after, ch. xxvi. The book is almost equally divided between histories and laws, intermixed.

We have here, I. The histories of the numbering and marshalling of the tribes (ch. i.-iv.), the dedication of the altar and Levites (ch. vii., viii.), their march (ch. ix., x.), their murmuring and unbelief, for which they were sentenced to wander forty years in the wilderness (ch. xi.-xiv.), the rebellion of Korah (ch. xvi., xvii.), the history of the last year of the forty (ch. xx.-xxvi), the conquest of Midian, and the settlement of the two tribes (ch. xxxi., xxxii.), with an account of their journeys, ch. xxxiii. II. Divers laws about the Nazarites, &c. (ch. v., vi.); and again about the priests' charge, &c. (ch. xviii., xix.), feasts (ch. xxviii., xxix.), and vows (ch. xxx.), and relating to their settlement in Canaan, ch. xxvii., xxxiv., xxxv., xxxvi. An abstract of much of this book we have in a few words in Ps. xcv. 10, *Forty years long was I grieved with this generation*; and an application of it to ourselves in Heb. iv. 1, *Let us fear lest we seem to come short*. Many considerable nations were now in being, that dwelt in cities and fortified towns, of which no notice is taken, no account kept, by the sacred history: but very exact records are kept of the affairs of a handful of people, that dwelt in tents, and wandered strangely in a wilderness, because they were the children of the covenant. *For the Lord's portion is his people, Jacob is the lot of his inheritance.*

CHAPTER 1

Israel was now to be formed into a commonwealth, or rather a kingdom; for "the Lord was their King" (1 Sam. xii. 12), their government a theocracy, and Moses under him was king in Jeshurun, Deut. xxxiii. 5. Now, for the right settlement of this holy state, next to the institution of good laws was necessary the institution of good order; an account therefore must be taken of the subjects of this kingdom, which is done in this chapter, where we have, I. Orders given to Moses to number the people, ver. 1-4. II. Persons nominated to assist him herein, ver. 5 16. III. The particular number of each tribe, as it was given in to Moses, ver. 17-43. IV. The sum total of all together, ver. 44-46. V. An exception of the Levites, ver. 47, &c.

Verses 1-16

I. We have here a commission issued out for the numbering of the people of Israel; and David, long after, paid dearly for doing it without a commission. Here is,

1. The date of this commission, *v.* 1. (1) The place: it is given at God's court *in the wilderness of Sinai*, from his royal palace, *the tabernacle of the congregation*. (2) The time: *In the second year* after they came up out of Egypt; we may call it the second year of that reign. The laws in Leviticus were given in the first month of that year; these orders were given in the beginning of the second month.

2. The directions given for the execution of it, *v.* 2, 3. (1) None were to be numbered but the males, and those only such as were fit for war. (2) Nor were any to be numbered who through age, or bodily infirmity, blindness, lameness, or chronical diseases, were unfit for war. (3) The account was to be taken *according to their families*, that it might not only be known how many they were, and what were their names, but of what tribe and family, or clan, nay, of what particular house every person was; or, reckoning it the muster of an army, to what regiment every man belonged, that he might know his place himself and the government might know where to find him. They were numbered a little before this, when their poll-money was paid for the service of the tabernacle, Exod. xxxviii. 25, 26. But it should seem they were not then registered *by the house of their fathers*, as now they were.

3. Commissioners are named for the doing of this work. Moses and Aaron were to preside (*v.* 3),

and one man of every tribe, that was renowned in his tribe, and was presumed to know it well, was to assist in it.

II. Why was this account ordered to be taken and kept? For several reasons. 1. To prove the accomplishment of the promise made to Abraham, that God would *multiply his seed exceedingly*, which promise was renewed to Jacob (Gen. xxviii. 14), that *his seed should be as the dust of the earth*. 2. It was to intimate the particular care which God himself would take of his Israel. God is called the *Shepherd of Israel*, Ps. lxxx. 1. Now the shepherds always kept count of their flocks, and delivered them by number to their under-shepherds, that they might know if any were missing; in like manner God numbers his flock. 3. It was to put a difference between the true-born Israelites and the mixed multitude that were among them; none were numbered but Israelites. 4. It was in order to their being marshalled into several districts, for the more easy administration of justice, and their more regular march through the wilderness.

Verses 17-43

We have here the speedy execution of the orders given for the numbering of the people. It was begun the same day that the orders were given, *The first day of the second month*; compare *v.* 18 with *v.* 1.

In the particulars here left upon record, we may observe, 1. That the numbers are registered in words at length (as I may say), and not in figures; to every one of the twelve tribes it is repeated, for the greater ceremony and solemnity of the account, that they were numbered *by their generations, after their families, by the house of their fathers, according to the number of the names*. Thus every man might know who were his relations or next of kin, on which some laws we have already met with did depend. 2. That they all end with hundreds, only Gad with fifty (*v.* 25), but none of the numbers descend to units or tens. 3. That Judah is the most numerous of them all, more than double to Benjamin and Manasseh, and almost 12,000 more than any other tribe, *v.* 27. It was Judah whom *his brethren must praise* because from him Messiah the Prince was to descend. Judah was to lead the van through the wilderness, and therefore was furnished accordingly with greater strength than any other tribe.

Verses 44–46

We have here the sum total at the foot of the account; they were in all 600,000 fighting men, and 3,550 over. Some think that when this was their number some months before (Exod. xxxviii. 26) the Levites were reckoned with them, but now that tribe was separated for the service of God, yet so many more had by this time attained to the age of twenty years as that still they were the same number, to show that whatever we part with for the honour and service of God it shall certainly be made up to us one way or other.

Verses 47–54

Care is here taken to distinguish from the rest of the tribes the tribe of Levi, which, in the matter of the golden calf, had distinguished itself, Exod xxxii. 26. Note, Singular services shall be recompensed with singular honours.

I. It was the honour of the Levites that they were made guardians of the spiritualities; to them was committed the care of the tabernacle and the treasures thereof, both in their camps and in their marches. 1. When they moved the Levites were to take down the tabernacle, to carry it and all that belonged to it, and then to set it up again in the place appointed, *v.* 50, 51. It was for the honour of the holy things that none should be permitted to see them, or touch them, but those only who were called of God to the service. 2. When they rested the Levites were to *encamp round about the tabernacle* (*v.* 50, 53), that they might be near their work, and resident upon their charge, always ready to attend, and that they might be a guard upon the tabernacle, to preserve it from being either plundered or profaned.

II. It was their further honour that as Israel, being a holy people, was not *reckoned among the nations,* so they, being a holy tribe, were not reckoned among other Israelites, but numbered afterwards by themselves, *v.* 49.

CHAPTER 2

The thousands of Israel, having been mustered in the former chapter, in this are marshalled, and a regular disposition is made of their camp, by a divine appointment. Here is, I. A general order concerning it, ver. 1, 2. II. Particular directions for the posting of each of the tribes, in four distinct squadrons, three tribes in each squadron. 1. In the van-guard on the east were posted Judah, Issachar, and Zebulun, ver. 3–9. 2. In the right wing, southward, Reuben, Simeon, and Gad, ver. 10–16. 3. In the rear, westward, Ephraim, Manasseh, and Benjamin, ver. 18–24. 4. In the left wing, northward, Dan, Asher, and Napthali, ver. 25–31. 5. The tabernacle in the centre, ver. 17. III. The conclusion of this appointment, ver. 32, &c.

Verses 1–2

Here is the general appointment given both for their orderly encampment where they rested and their orderly march when they moved. 1. They all dwelt in tents, and when they marched carried all their tents along with them. 2. Those of a tribe were to pitch together, *every man by his own standard.* Those that are of kin to each other should, as much as they can, be acquainted with each other; and the bonds of nature should be improved for the strengthening of the bonds of Christian communion. 3. Every one must know his place and keep in it. 4. Every tribe had its standard, flag, or ensign, and it should seem every family had some particular ensign of their father's house. It is uncertain how these standards were distinguished: some conjecture that the standard of each tribe was of the same colour with the precious stone in which the name of that tribe was written in

the high priest's ephod. Some of them say the four principal standards were, Judah a lion, Reuben a man, Joseph an ox, and Dan an eagle, making the appearances in Ezekiel's vision to allude to it. 5. They were to pitch about the tabernacle, which was to be in the midst of them, as the tent or pavilion of a general in the centre of an army. That they might be a guard and defence upon the tabernacle and the Levites on every side. 6. Yet they were to pitch afar off, in reverence to the sanctuary. It is supposed (from Josh. iii. 4) that the distance between the nearest part of the camp and the tabernacle was 2,000 cubits, that is, 1,000 yards, little more than half a measured mile with us.

Verses 3–34

We have here the particular distribution of the twelve tribes into four squadrons, three tribes in a squadron, one of which was to lead the other two. 1. God himself appointed them their place, to prevent strife and envy among them. If God in his providence advance others above us, and abase us, we ought to be as well satisfied in his doing it in that way as if he did it, as this was done here, by a voice out of the tabernacle. And as far as our place comes to be our choice our Saviour has given us a rule in Luke xiv. 8, *Sit not down in the highest room*; and another in Matt. xx. 27, *He that will be chief, let him be your servant.* Those that are most humble and most serviceable are really most honourable. 2. Every tribe had a captain, a prince, or commander-in-chief, whom God himself nominated, the same that had been appointed to number them, *ch.* i. 5. Most of them have *El, God,* at one end or other of their names. *Nethaneel, the gift of God; Eliab, my God a Father; Elizur, my God a rock; Shelumiel, God my peace; Eliasaph, God has added; Elishama, my God has heard; Gamaliel, God my reward; Pagiel, God has met me.* 3. Those tribes were placed together under the same standard that were nearest of kin to each other; Judah, Issachar, and Zebulun, were the three younger sons of Leah, and they were put together; and Issachar and Zebulun would not grudge to be under Judah, since he was his younger brethren. Reuben and Simeon would not have been content in their place. Therefore Reuben, Jacob's eldest son, is made chief of the next squadron; Simeon, no doubt, is willing to be under him, and Gad, the son of Zilpah, Leah's handmaid, is fitly added to them in Levi's room: Ephraim, Manasseh, and Benjamin, are all the posterity of Rachel. Dan, the eldest son of Bilhah, is made a leading tribe, though the son of a concubine, that more abundant honour might be bestowed on that which lacked; and it was said, *Dan should judge his people,* and to him were added the two younger sons of the handmaids. Thus unexceptionable was the order in which they were placed. 4. The tribe of Judah was in the first post of honour, encamped towards the rising sun, and in their marches led the van, not only because it was the most numerous tribe, but chiefly because from that tribe Christ was to come. Judah was the first of the twelve sons of Jacob that was blessed. He therefore being first in blessing, though not in birth, is put first, to teach children how to value the smiles of their godly parents and dread their frowns. 5. The tribe of Levi pitched closely about the tabernacle, within the rest of their tribes, *v.* 17. They must defend the sanctuary, and then the rest of the tribes must defend them. Civil powers should protect the religious interests of a nation, and be a defence upon that glory. 6. The camp of Dan, though posted in the left wing when they encamped, was ordered in their march to bring up the rear, *v.* 31. They were the most numerous, next to Judah, and therefore were ordered into a post which, next to the front, required the most strength.

CHAPTER 3

This chapter and the next are concerning the tribe of Levi, which was to be mustered and marshalled by itself. The Levites are in this chapter considered, I. As attendants on, and assistants to, the priests in the temple-service. And so we have an account, 1. Of the priests themselves (ver. 1–4) and their work, ver. 10. 2. Of the gift of the Levites to them (ver. 5–9), in order to which they are mustered (ver. 14–16), and the sum of them taken, ver. 39. Each particular family of them is mustered, has its place assigned and its charge, the Gershonites (ver. 17–26), the Kohathites (ver. 27–32), the Merarites, ver. 33–39. II. As equivalents for the first-born, ver. 11–13. 1. The first-born are numbered, and the Levites taken instead of them, as far as the number of the Levites went, ver. 40–45. 2. What first-born there were more than the Levites were redeemed, ver. 46, &c.

Verses 1–13

I. The family of Aaron is confirmed in the priests' office, *v.* 10. They had been called to it before, and consecrated; here they are appointed to *wait on their priests' office*: the apostle uses this phrase (Rom. xii. 7), *Let us wait on our ministry.* The office of the ministry requires a constant attendance and great diligence; so frequent are the returns of its work, and yet so transient its favourable opportunities, that it must be waited on. *The stranger that cometh nigh shall be put to death*, which forbids the invading of the priests' office by any other person whatsoever; none must come nigh to minister but Aaron and his sons only, all others are strangers. It also lays a charge on the priests, as door-keepers in God's house, to take care that none should come near who were forbidden by the law.

II. A particular account is given of this family of Aaron; what we have met with before concerning them is here repeated. The two younger: Eleazar and Ithamar ministered *in the sight of Aaron.* They kept under their father's eye, and took instruction from him in all they did, because probably Nadab and Abihu got out of their father's sight when they offered strange fire.

III. A grant is made of the Levites to be assistants to the priests in their work: *Give the Levites to Aaron, v.* 9. Aaron was to have a greater propriety in, and power over, the tribe of Levi than any other of the princes had in and over their respective tribes. Here is, 1. The service for which the Levites were designed: they were to *minister to the priests* in their ministration to the Lord (*v.* 6), and to *keep Aaron's charge* (*v.* 7). The Levites killed the sacrifices, and then the priests needed only to sprinkle the blood and burn the fat: the Levites prepared the incense, the priests burnt it. They were to keep, not only Aaron's charge, but the *charge of the whole congregation.* 2. The consideration upon which the Levites were demanded; they were taken instead of the first-born.

Verses 14–39

The Levites being granted to Aaron to minister to him, they are here delivered to him by tale, that he might know what he had, and employ them accordingly.

I. By what rule they were numbered: *Every male from a month old and upward, v.* 15. The rest of the tribes were numbered only from twenty years old and upwards, and of them those only that were *able to go forth to war*; but into the number of the Levites they must take in both infants and infirm; being exempted from the war, it was not insisted upon that they should be of age and strength for the wars. Though it appears afterwards that little more than a third part of the Levites were fit to be employed in the service of the tabernacle (about 8,000 out of 22,000, *ch.* iv. 47, 48), yet God would have them all numbered as retainers to his family.

II. How they were distributed into three classes, according to the number of the sons of Levi, Gershon, Kohath and Merari, and these subdivided into several families, *v.* 17–20.

1. Concerning each of these three classes we have an account, (1) Of their number. (2) Of their post about the tabernacle on which they were to attend. The Gershonites pitched behind the tabernacle, westward, *v.* 23. The Kohathites on the right hand, southward, *v.* 29. The Merarites on the left hand, northward, *v.* 35. And, to complete the square, Moses and Aaron, with the priests, encamped in the front, eastward, *v.* 38. (3) Of their chief or head. As each class had its own place, so each had its own prince. (4) Of their charge, when the camp moved. The Gershonites were charged with the custody and carriage of all the curtains and hangings and coverings of the tabernacle and court (*v.* 25, 26), the Kohathites of all the furniture of the tabernacle—the ark, altar, table, &c. (*v.* 31, 32), the Merarites of the heavy carriage, boards, bars, pillars, &c., *v.* 36, 37.

2. Here we may observe, (1) That the Kohathites, though they were the second house, yet were preferred before the elder family of the Gershonites. Besides that Aaron and the priests were of that family, they were more numerous, and their post and charge more honourable, which probably was ordered to put an honour upon Moses, who was of that family. Yet, (2) The posterity of Moses were not at all dignified or privileged, but stood upon the level with other Levites.

III. The sum total of the numbers of this tribe. They are computed in all 22,000, *v.* 39. That which is especially observable here is that the tribe of Levi was by much the least of all the tribes.

Verses 40–51

Here is the exchange made of the Levites for the first-born. 1. The first-born were numbered from a month old, *v.* 42, 43. Bishop Patrick is decidedly of opinion that none were numbered but those only that were born since their coming out of Egypt, when the first-born were sanctified, Exod. xiii. 2. If there were 22,000 first-born males, we may suppose as many females, and all these brought forth in the first year after they came out of Egypt, we must hence infer that in the last year of their servitude, even when it was in the greatest extremity, there were abundance of marriages made among the Israelites; they were not discouraged by the present distress, but married in faith, expecting that God would shortly visit them with mercy, and that their children, though born in bondage, should live in liberty and honour. They were not only kept alive, but greatly increased, in a barren wilderness. 2. The number of the first-born, and that of the Levites, by a special providence, came pretty near to each other. 3. The small number of first-born which exceeded the number of the Levites (273 in all) were to be redeemed, at five shekels apiece, and the redemption money given to Aaron; for it would not do well to have them added to the Levites.

CHAPTER 4

In the former chapter an account was taken of the whole tribe of Levi, in this we have an account of those of that tribe who were in the prime of their time for service, betwixt thirty and fifty years old. I. The serviceable men of the Kohathites are ordered to be numbered, and their charges are given them, ver. 2–20. II. Of the Gershonites, ver. 24–28. III. Of the Merarites, ver. 29–33. IV. The numbers of each, and the sum total at last, are recorded, ver. 34, &c.

Verses 1–20

We have here a second muster of the tribe of Levi. As that tribe was taken out of all Israel to be God's peculiar, so the middle-aged men of that tribe were taken from among the rest to be actually employed in the service of the tabernacle.

I. Who were to be taken into this number. All the

males from thirty years old to fifty. The service of God requires the best of our strength, and the prime of our time, which cannot be better spent than to the honour of him who is the first and best. And a man may make a good soldier much sooner than a good minister.

1. They were not to be employed till they were thirty years old. They were entered as probationers at twenty-five years old (*ch.* viii. 24), and in David's time, when there was more work to be done, at twenty (1 Chron. xxiii. 24, and so Ezra iii. 8); but they must be five years learning and waiting, and so fitting themselves for service; in David's time they were ten years in preparation, from twenty to thirty. John Baptist began his public ministry, and Christ his, at thirty years old. This gives us two good rules:— (1) That ministers must not be novices, 1 Tim. iii. 6. It is a work that requires ripeness of judgment and great steadiness. (2) That they must learn before they teach, serve before they rule, and must *first be proved*, 1 Tim. iii. 10.

2. They were discharged at fifty years old from the toilsome part of the service, particularly that of carrying the tabernacle.

II. How their work is described. They are said to *enter into the host*, or warfare, *to do the work in the tabernacle*. Those that enter into the ministry must look upon themselves as entered into the *host*, and approve themselves *good soldiers*, 2 Tim. ii. 3. Now, as to the sons of Kohath in particular, here is,

1. Their service appointed them, in the removes of the tabernacle. Afterwards, when the tabernacle was fixed, they had other work assigned them; but this was the work of the day, which was to be done in its day. Now the Kohathites were to carry all the holy things of the tabernacle. (1) Aaron, and his sons the priests, must pack up the things which the Kohathites were to carry, as here directed, *v.* 5, &c. (2) All the holy things must be covered, the ark and table with three coverings, all the rest with two. Even the ashes of the altar, in which the holy fire was carefully preserved and raked up, must have a purple cloth spread over them, *v.* 13. Even the brazen altar, though in the court of the sanctuary it stood open to the view of all, yet was covered in the carriage of it. This signified the darkness of that dispensation. That which is now brought to light by the gospel, and revealed to babes, was then hidden from the wise and prudent. They saw only the coverings, not the holy things themselves (Heb. x. 1); but now Christ has *destroyed the face of the covering*, Isa. xxv. 7. (3) When all the holy things were covered, then the Kohathites were to carry them on their shoulders.

2. Eleazar, now the eldest son of Aaron, is appointed overseer of the Kohathites in this service (*v.* 16).

3. Great care must be taken to preserve the lives of these Levites, by preventing their irreverent approach to the most holy things: *Cut you not off the Kohathites, v.* 18. (1) The Kohathites must not see the holy things till the priests had covered them, *v.* 20. And, (2) When the holy things were covered, they might not touch them, at least not the ark, called here *the holy thing*, upon pain of death, *v.* 15. Thus were the Lord's ministers themselves then kept in fear, and that was a dispensation of terror, as well as darkness; but now, through Christ, the case is altered: we have *seen with our eyes*, and our *hands have handled, the word of life* (1 John i. 1), and we are encouraged to *come boldly to the throne of grace*.

Verses 21–33

We have here the charge of the other two families of the Levites, which, though not so honourable as the first, yet was necessary, and was to be done regularly. 1. The Gershonites were charged with

all the drapery of the tabernacle, the curtains, and hangings, and the coverings of badgers' skins, *v.* 22–26. 2. The Merarites were charged with the heavy carriage, the boards and bars, the pillars and sockets, the pins and cords, and these were delivered to them by name, *v.* 31, 32.

Verses 34–49

We have here a particular account of the numbers of the three families of the Levites respectively, that is, of the effective men, between thirty years old and fifty. The whole number of the able men of the tribe of Levi who entered into God's host to war his warfare was but 8,580, whereas the able men of the other tribes that entered into the host of Israel to war their warfare were many more. The least of the tribes had almost four times as many able men as the Levites, and some of them more than eight times as many; for those that are engaged in the service of this world, and war after the flesh, are many more than those that are devoted to the service of God, and *fight the good fight of faith*.

CHAPTER 5

In this chapter we have, I. An order, pursuant to the laws already made, for the removing of the unclean out of the camp, ver. 1–4. II. A repetition of the laws concerning restitution, in case of wrong done to a neighbour (ver. 5–8), and concerning the appropriating of the hallowed things to the priests, ver. 9, 10. III. A new law made concerning the trial of a wife suspected of adultery, by the waters of jealousy, ver. 11, &c.

Verses 1–10

I. A command for the purifying of the camp, by turning out from within its lines all those that were ceremonially unclean, by issues, leprosies, or the touch of dead bodies, until they were cleansed according to the law, *v.* 2, 3.

1. These orders are executed immediately, *v.* 4. The camp was now newly-modelled and put in order, and therefore, to complete the reformation of it, it is next to be cleansed. God's tabernacle was now fixed in the midst of their camp, and therefore they must be careful to keep it clean. The person, the place, *in the midst of which God dwells*, must not be defiled; for, if it be, he will be affronted, offended, and provoked to withdraw, 1 Cor. iii. 16, 17.

2. This expulsion of the unclean out of the camp was to signify, (1) What the governors of the church ought to do: they must *separate between the precious and the vile*, and purge out scandalous persons. It is for the glory of Christ and the edification of his church that those who are openly and incorrigibly profane and vicious should be put out and kept from Christian communion till they repent. (2) What God himself will do in the great day: he will *throughly purge his floor*, and *gather out of his kingdom all things that offend*. As here the unclean were shut out of the camp, so into the new Jerusalem *no unclean thing shall enter*, Rev. xxi. 27.

II. A law concerning restitution, in case of wrong done to a neighbour. 1. He must *confess his sin*, confess it to God, confess it to his neighbour, and so take shame to himself. 2. He must bring a sacrifice, a *ram of atonement, v.* 8. Satisfaction must be made for the offence done to God, whose law is broken, as well as for the loss sustained by our neighbour; restitution in this case is not sufficient without faith and repentance. 3. Yet the sacrifices would not be accepted till full amends were made to the party wronged, not only the principal, but a fifth part added to it, *v.* 7. If the party wronged was dead, and he had no near kinsman who was entitled to the debt, it must be given to the priest, *v.* 8. Note, Some work of piety or charity is a piece of necessary justice to be done by those who are conscious to themselves that they have done wrong, but know not how otherwise to make restitution.

III. A general rule concerning hallowed things given upon this occasion, that, whatever was given to the priest, *his it shall be, v.* 9, 10.

Verses 11–31

We have here the law concerning the solemn trial of a wife whose husband was jealous of her.

I. What was the case supposed: That a man had some reason to suspect his wife to have committed adultery, *v.* 12–14. The sin of adultery is justly represented as an exceedingly sinful sin. It is committing a trespass against the husband, robbing him of his honour, alienating his right, introducing a spurious breed into his family to share with his children in his estate, and violating her covenant with him. Hence, 1. Let all wives be admonished not to give any the least occasion for the suspicion of their chastity. 2. Let all husbands be admonished not to entertain any causeless or unjust suspicions of their wives. If charity in general, much more conjugal affection, teaches to *think no evil*, 1 Cor. xiii. 5.

II. What was the course prescribed in this case, that, if the suspected wife was innocent, she might not continue under the reproach and uneasiness of her husband's jealousy, and, if guilty, her sin might find her out, and others might hear, and fear, and take warning. Her husband must *bring her to the priest*, with the witnesses that could prove the ground of his suspicion, and desire that she might be put upon her trial. If she confessed, saying, "I am defiled," she was not put to death, but was divorced and lost her dowry; if she said, "I am pure," then they proceeded. God will find out some way or other to clear the innocency of the innocent, and to bring forth their righteousness as the light. To *the pure all things are pure*, but *to the defiled nothing* is so, Tit. i. 15.

CHAPTER 6

In this chapter we have, I. The law concerning Nazarites, 1. What it was to which the vow of a Nazarite obliged him, ver. 1–8. 2. A remedial law in case a Nazarite happened to be polluted by the touch of a dead body, ver. 9–12. 3. The solemnity of his discharge when his time was up, ver. 13–21. II. Instructions given to the priests how they should bless the people, ver. 22, &c.

Verses 1–21

After the law for the discovery and shame of those that by sin had made themselves vile, there follows this for the direction and encouragement of those who by their eminent piety and devotion had made themselves honourable. There were those who went under the character of *Nazarites*, and were celebrated by that title as persons professing greater strictness and zeal in religion than other people. Joseph is called a Nazarite among his brethren (Gen. xlix. 26).

I. The general character of a Nazarite: it is a person *separated unto the Lord, v.* 2. Some were Nazarites for life, either by divine designation, as Samson (Judg. xiii. 5), and John Baptist (Luke i. 15), or by their parents' vow concerning them, as Samuel, 1 Sam. i. 11. Of these this law speaks not. Others were so for a certain time, and by their own voluntary engagement, and concerning them rules are given by this law. A woman might bind herself with the vow of a Nazarite, under the limitations we find, *ch.* xxx. 3. The Nazarites were, 1. Devoted to the Lord during the time of their Nazariteship, and, it is probable, spent much of their time in the study of the law, in acts of devotion, and instructing others. 2. They were separated from common persons and common things. 3. They separated themselves by vowing a vow. Every Israelite was bound by the divine law to love God with all his heart, but the

Nazarites by their own act and deed bound themselves to some religious observances, as fruits and expressions of that love, which other Israelites were not bound to. Christ was called in reproach a Nazarene, so were his followers: but he was no Nazarite according to this law; he drank wine, and touched dead bodies, yet in him this type had its accomplishment, for in him all purity and perfection met; and every true Christian is a spiritual Nazarite, separated by vow unto the Lord.

II. The particular obligations that the Nazarites lay under.

1. They must have nothing to do with *the fruit of the vine, v.* 3, 4. They must drink no wine nor strong drink, nor eat grapes, no, not the kernel nor the husk; they might not so much as eat a raisin. Those who gave the Nazarites wine to drink did the tempter's work (Amos ii. 12), persuading them to that forbidden fruit. That it was reckoned a perfection and praise not to drink wine appears from the instance of the Rechabites, Jer. xxxv. 6. They were to *drink no* wine, (1) That they might be examples of temperance and mortification. Drinking *a little wine for the stomach's sake* is allowed, to help that, 1 Tim. v. 23. But drinking much wine for the *palate's sake*, to please that, does by no means become those who profess to walk·not *after the flesh, but after the Spirit*. (2) That they might be qualified to employ themselves in the service of God. They must not drink, lest they should *forget the law* (Prov. xxxi. 5), lest they should *err through wine* Isa. xxviii. 7. Let all Christians oblige themselves to be very moderate in the use of wine and strong drink; for, if the love of these once gets the mastery of a man, he becomes a very easy prey to Satan.

2. They must not *cut their hair, v.* 5. They must neither poll their heads nor shave their beards; this was that mark of Samson's Nazariteship which we often read of in his story. Now, (1) This signified a noble neglect of the body and the ease and ornament of it, which became those who, being separated to God, ought to be wholly taken up with their souls, to secure their peace and beauty. (2) Some observe that long hair is spoken of as a badge of subjection (1 Cor. xi. 5, &c.); so that the long hair of the Nazarites denoted their subjection to God, and their putting themselves under his dominion.

3. They must not come near any dead body, *v.* 6, 7.

4. All *the days of their separation* they must be *holy to the Lord, v.* 8.

III. The provision that was made for the cleansing of a Nazarite, if he happened unavoidably to contract a ceremonial pollution by the touch of a dead body. He must be purified from the ceremonial pollution he had contracted, as others must, upon the seventh day, *v.* 9. Nay, more was required for the purifying of the Nazarite than of any other person that had touched a dead body; he must bring a sin-offering and a burnt-offering, and an atonement must be *made for him, v.* 10, 11. This teaches us that sins of infirmity, and the faults we are overtaken in by surprise, must be seriously repented of, and that an application must be made of the virtue of Christ's sacrifice to our souls for the forgiveness of them every day, 1 John ii. 1, 2.

IV. The law for the solemn discharge of a Nazarite from his vow, when he had completed the time he fixed to himself. The Jews say that the time of a Nazarite's vow could not be less than thirty days; and if a man said, "I will be a Nazarite but for two days," yet he was bound for thirty; but it should seem Paul's vow was for only seven days (Acts xxi. 27). When the time of the vowed separation was out, he was to be made free, 1. Publicly, *at the door of the tabernacle (v.* 13). 2. It was to be done with sacrifices, *v.* 14. He must bring one of each sort of the instituted offerings. (1) A burnt-offering. (2) A sin-offering. (3) A peace-offering, in thankfulness to God, who had enabled him to fulfil his vow. (4) To these were added the meat-offerings and drink-offerings. (5) Part of the peace-offering, with a cake and wafer, was to be waved for a wave-offering (*v.* 19, 20); and this was a gratuity to the priest, who had it for his pains, after it had been first presented to God. (6) Besides all this, he might bring his free-will offerings, *such as his hand shall get, v.* 21. And, to grace the solemnity, it was common upon this occasion to have their friends to be at *charges with them,* Acts xxi. 24. *Lastly,* One ceremony more was appointed, which was like the cancelling of the bond when the condition is performed, and that was the *cutting off of his hair,* which had been suffered to grow all the time of his being a Nazarite, and burning it in the fire over which the peace-offerings were boiling, *v.* 18. This intimated that his full performance of his vow was acceptable to God in Christ the great sacrifice, and not otherwise.

Verses 22–27

Here, I. The priests, among other good offices which they were to do, are appointed solemnly to bless the people in the *name of the Lord, v.* 23. Though the priest of himself could do no more than beg a blessing, yet being an intercessor by office, and doing that in his name who commands the blessing, the prayer carried with it a promise, and he pronounced it as one having authority with his hands lifted up and his face towards the people. Now, 1. This was a type of Christ's errand into the world, which was to *bless us* (Acts iii. 26), as the high priest of our profession. 2. It was a pattern to gospel ministers, the masters of assemblies, who are in like manner to dismiss their solemn assemblies with a blessing. The same that are God's mouth to his people, to teach and command them, are his mouth likewise to bless them.

II. A form of blessing is here prescribed them. Here observe, 1. That the blessing is commanded upon each particular person: *The Lord bless thee.* If we take the law to ourselves, we may take the blessing to ourselves, as if our names were inserted. 2. That the name *Jehovah* is three times repeated in it, and each with a different accent in the original. 3. That the favour of God is all in all in this blessing, for that is the fountain of all good. (1) *The Lord bless thee!* (2) *The Lord make his face shine upon thee,* alluding to the shining of the sun upon the earth, to enlighten and comfort it, and to renew the face of it. (3) *The Lord lift up his countenance upon thee.* This is to the same purport with the former, and it seems to allude to the smiles of a father upon his child, or of a man upon his friend whom he takes pleasure in. 4. That the fruits of this favour conveyed by this blessing are protection, pardon, and peace. (1) Protection from evil, *v.* 24. The Lord *keep thee.* (2) Pardon of sin, *v.* 25. The Lord be *gracious* or *merciful,* unto thee. (3) Peace (*v.* 26), including all that good which goes to make up a complete happiness.

III. God here promises to ratify and confirm the blessing: *They shall put my name upon the children of Israel, v.* 27.

CHAPTER 7

God having set up house (as it were) in the midst of the camp of Israel, the princes of Israel here come visiting. I. They brought presents, 1. Upon the dedication of the tabernacle, for the service of that, ver. 1–9. 2. Upon the dedication of the altar, for the use of that, ver. 10–88. And, II. God graciously signified his acceptance of them, ver. 89. The two foregoing chapters were the records of additional laws which God gave to Israel, this is the history of the additional services which Israel performed to God.

Verses 1–9

The offering of the princes to the service of the tabernacle.

I. When it was; not till it was *fully set up, v.* 1. When all things were done both about the tabernacle itself, and the camp of Israel which surrounded it.

II. Who it was that offered: *The princes of Israel, heads of the house of their fathers, v.* 2.

III. What was offered: six waggons, with each of them a yoke of oxen to draw them, *v.* 3.

IV. How the offering was disposed of, and what use was made of it: the waggons and oxen were given to the Levites, to be used in carrying the tabernacle. 1. The Gershonites, that had the light carriage, the curtains and hangings, had but two waggons, and two yoke of oxen (*v.* 7). 2. The Merarites, that had the heavy carriage, and that which was most unwieldy, the boards, pillars, sockets, &c., had four waggons, and four yoke of oxen allotted them (*v.* 8). Observe here, How God wisely and graciously ordered the most strength to those that had the most work. Each had waggons *according to their service.* 3. The Kohathites, that had the most sacred carriage, had no waggons at all, because they were to carry their charges upon their shoulders (*v.* 9), with a particular care and veneration.

Verses 10–89

We have here an account of the great solemnity of dedicating the altars, both that of burnt-offerings and that of incense; they had been sanctified before, when they were anointed (Lev. viii. 10, 11), but now they were handselled, as it were, by the princes, with their free-will offerings. They began the use of them with rich presents, great expressions of joy and gladness, and extraordinary respect to those tokens of God's presence with them. Now observe here,

I. That the princes and great men were first and forwardest in the service of God. It is justly expected that those who have more than others should do more good than others with what they have, else they are unfaithful stewards, and will not make up their *account with joy.*

II. The offerings they brought were very rich and valuable.

1. They brought some things to remain for standing service, twelve large silver dishes, each about sixty ounces weight, as many large silver cups, or bowls, of about thirty-five ounces—the former to be used for the meat-offerings, the latter for the drink-offerings—the former for the flesh of the sacrifices, the latter for the blood. The golden spoons being filled with incense were intended, it is probable, for the service of the golden altar, for both the altars were anointed at the same time.

2. They brought some things to be used immediately, offerings of each sort. Hereby they signified their thankful acceptance of, and cheerful submission to, all those laws concerning the sacrifices which God had lately by Moses delivered to them. And, though it was a time of joy and rejoicing, yet it is observable that still in the midst of their sacrifices we find a *sin-offering.*

3. They brought their offerings each on a separate day, in the order that they had been lately put into, so that the solemnity lasted twelve days.

4. All their offerings were exactly the same, though it is probable that neither the princes nor the tribes were all alike rich; but thus it was intimated that all the tribes of Israel had an equal share in the altar, and an equal interest in the sacrifices that were offered upon it.

5. Nahshon, the prince of the tribe of Judah, offered first, because God had given that tribe the first post of honour in the camp; and the rest of the tribes acquiesced.

6. Though the offerings were all the same, yet the account of them is repeated at large for each tribe, in the same words. We find Christ taking particular notice of what was cast into the treasury, Mark xii. 41. Though what is offered be but little, yet if it be according to our ability it shall be recorded.

7. The sum total is added at the foot of the account (v. 84–88), to show how much God was pleased with the mention of his freewill-offerings, and what a great deal they amounted to in the whole, when every prince brought in his quota!

8. God signified his gracious acceptance of these presents that were brought him, by speaking familiarly to Moses, as a man speaks to his friend, from off the mercy-seat (v. 89, *ch.* xii. 8); and in speaking to him he did in effect speak to all Israel, showing them this token for good, Ps. ciii. 7.

CHAPTER 8

This chapter is concerning the lamps or lights of the sanctuary. I. The burning lamps in the candlestick, which the priests were charged to tend, ver. 1–4. II. The living lamps (if I may so call them), the Levites, who as ministers were burning and shining lights. The ordination of the priests we had an account of, Lev. viii. Here we have an account of the ordination of the Levites, the inferior clergy. 1. How they were purified, ver. 5–8. 2. How they were parted with by the people, ver. 9, 10. 3. How they were presented to God in lieu of the first-born, ver. 11–18. 4. How they were consigned to Aaron and his sons, to be ministers to them, ver. 19. 5. How all these orders were duly executed, ver. 20–22. And, lastly, The age appointed for their ministration, ver. 23, &c.

Verses 1–4

Directions were given long before this for the making of the golden candlestick (Exod. xxv, 31), and it was made according to the pattern shown to Moses in the mount, Exod. xxxvii. 17. But now it was that the lamps were first ordered to be lighted, when other things began to be used. Observe, 1. Who must light the lamps; Aaron himself, he *lighted the lamps*, v. 3. As the people's representative to God, he thus did the office of a servant in God's house, lighting his Master's candle. The scripture is *a light shining in a dark place*, 2 Pet. i. 19. Now the work of ministers is to light these lamps, by expounding and applying the word of God. The priest lighted the middle lamp from the fire of the altar, and the rest of the lamps he lighted one from another, which (says Mr. Ainsworth) signifies that the fountain of all light and knowledge is in Christ, who has the *seven spirits of God* figured by the *seven lamps of fire* (Rev. iv. 5), but that in the expounding of scripture one passage must borrow light from another. He also supposes that, *seven* being a number of perfection, by the seven branches of the candlestick is shown the full perfection of the scripture, which are able to make us wise to salvation. 2. To what end the lamps were lighted. They were not lighted like tapers in an urn, to burn to themselves, but to give light to the other side of the tabernacle, for therefore candles are lighted, Matt. v. 15. Therefore we have light, that we may give light.

Verses 5–26

We read before of the separating of the Levites from among the children of Israel when they were numbered, and the numbering of them by themselves (*ch.* iii. 6, 15), that they might be employed in the service of the tabernacle. Now here we have directions given for their solemn ordination (v. 6), and the performance of it, v. 20. All Israel must know that they took not this honour to themselves, but were called of God to it; nor was it enough that they were distinguished from their neighbours, but they must be solemnly devoted to God. Note, All that are employed for God must be dedicated to him, according as the degree of the employment is. Christians must be baptized, ministers must be ordained; we must first give ourselves unto the Lord, and then our services. Observe, in what method this was done:

I. The Levites must be cleansed, and were so. The rites and ceremonies of their cleansing were to be performed, 1. By themselves. Those must be clean that bear the vessels of the Lord. 2. By Moses. He must *sprinkle the water of purifying upon them*, which was prepared by divine direction. It is our duty to cleanse ourselves, and God's promise that he will cleanse us.

II. The Levites, being thus prepared, must be brought before the Lord in a solemn assembly of all Israel, and the *children of Israel* must put their hands *upon them* (v. 10), so transferring their interest in them and in their service (to which, as a part, the whole body of the people was entitled) to God and to his sanctuary. This imposition of hands by the children of Israel upon the Levites did not make them ministers of the sanctuary, but only signified the people's parting with that tribe out of their militia, and civil incorporations, in order to their being made ministers by Aaron, who was to offer them before the Lord.

III. Sacrifices were to be offered for them, a sin-offering first (v. 12), and then a burnt-offering, to make an *atonement for the Levites*. See here, 1. That we are all utterly unworthy and unfit to be admitted into and employed in the service of God, till atonement be made for sin, and thereby our peace made with God. 2. That it is by sacrifice, by Christ the great sacrifice, that we are reconciled to God, and made fit to be offered to him. It is by him that Christians are sanctified to the work of their Christianity, and ministers to the work of their ministry.

IV. The Levites themselves were *offered before the Lord for an offering of the children of Israel*, v. 11. Aaron gave them up to God, as being first given up by themselves, and by the children of Israel.

V. God here declares his acceptance of them: *The Levites shall be mine*, v. 14. All whom God owns he employs; angels themselves have their services.

VI. They are then given as a gift to Aaron and his sons (v. 19), yet so as that the benefit accrued to the children of Israel. 1. The Levites must act under the priests as attendants on them. Aaron offers them to God (v. 11), and then God gives them back to Aaron, v. 19. Our hearts, our children, our estates, are never more ours, more truly, more comfortably ours, than when we have offered them up to God. 2. They must act for the people. God's ministers, while they keep within the sphere of their office and conscientiously discharge the duty of it, must be looked upon as some of the most useful servants of their country.

VII. The time of their ministration is fixed. 1. They were to enter upon the service at twenty-five years old, v. 24. A very good age for ministers to begin their public work at. 2. They were to have a writ of ease at fifty years old; then they were to return from the warfare, as the phrase is (v. 25), not cashiered with disgrace, but preferred rather to the rest which their age required, to be loaded with the honours of their office, as hitherto they had been with the burdens of it. If God's grace provide that men shall have ability according to their work, man's prudence should take care that men have work only according to their ability. The aged are most fit for trusts, and to keep the charge; the younger are most fit for work, and to do the service.

CHAPTER 9

This chapter is, I. Concerning the great ordinance of the passover; 1. Orders given for the observance of it, at the return of the year, ver. 1–5. 2. Provisos added in regard to such as should be ceremonially unclean, or otherwise disabled, at the time when the passover was to be kept, ver. 6–14. II. Concerning the great favour of the pillar of cloud, which was a guide to Israel through the wilderness, ver. 15, &c.

Verses 1–14

Here we have,

I. An order given for the solemnization of the passover, the day twelvemonth after they came out of Egypt, on the fourteenth day of the first month of the second year, some days before they were numbered, for that was done in the beginning of the second month. Observe, 1. God gave particular orders for the keeping of this passover. And, for aught that appears, after this they kept no passover till they came to Canaan, Josh. v. 10. This was an early indication of the abolishing of the ceremonial institutions at last. The ordinance of the Lord's supper (which came in the room of the passover) was not thus intermitted or set aside in the first days of the Christian church, though those were days of greater difficulty and distress than Israel knew in the wilderness; nay, in the times of persecution, the Lord's supper was celebrated more frequently than afterwards. The Israelites in the wilderness could not forget their deliverance out of Egypt. All the danger was when they came to Canaan. However, because the first passover was celebrated in a hurry it was the will of God that at the return of the year, when they were more composed, and better acquainted with the divine law, they should observe it again, that their children might more distinctly understand the solemnity and the better remember it hereafter. 2. Moses faithfully transmitted to the people the orders given him, *v.* 4. 3. The people observed the orders given them, *v.* 5. They kept the passover even in the wilderness. Thus is God's Israel provided for in a desert.

II. Instructions given concerning those that were ceremonially unclean when they were to eat the passover. The law of the passover required every Israelite to eat of it. They must therefore wash, and then *compass God's altar.* Now, *Certain men were defiled by the dead body of a man* (*v.* 6), and they lay under that defilement seven days (*ch.* xix. 11), and in that time might not eat of the holy things, Lev. vii. 20. This was not their iniquity, but their infelicity.

The directions which God gave in this case, and in other similar cases, explanatory of the law of the passover. This disagreeable accident produced good laws. Those that happened to be ceremonially unclean at the time when the passover should be eaten were allowed to eat it that day month, when they were clean; so were those that happened to be *in a journey afar off, v.* 10, 11.

Verses 15–23

We have here the history of the cloud; not a natural history: *who knows the balancings of the clouds?* but a divine history of a cloud that was appointed to be the visible sign and symbol of God's presence with Israel.

I. When the tabernacle was finished this cloud, which before had hung on high over their camp, settled upon the tabernacle, and covered it, to show that God manifests his presence with his people in and by his ordinances.

II. That which appeared as a cloud by day appeared as a fire by night. And thus are we taught to *set God always before us,* and to see him near us both night and day. Something of the nature of that divine revelation which the Old Testament church was governed by might also be signified by these visible signs of God's presence, the cloud denoting the darkness and the fire the terror of that dispensation, in comparison with the more clear and comfortable discoveries God has made of his glory in the face of Jesus Christ.

III. This pillar of cloud and fire directed and determined all the motions, marches, and encampments, of Israel in the wilderness. And the guidance of this cloud is spoken of as signifying the guidance of the blessed Spirit. We are not now to expect such sensible tokens of the divine presence and guidance as this was, but the promise is sure to all God's spiritual Israel that he will *guide them by his counsel* (Ps. lxxiii. 24), *even unto death* (Ps. xlviii. 14), that all the children of God shall be *led by the Spirit of God* (Rom. viii. 14). In our affections and actions we must follow the direction of his word and Spirit; all the motions of our souls must be guided by the divine will; at the commandment of the Lord our hearts should always move and rest.

CHAPTER 10

In this chapter we have, I. Orders given about the making and using of silver trumpets, which seems to have been the last of all the commandments God gave upon Mount Sinai, and one of the least, yet not without its significance, ver. 1–10. II. The history of the removal of Israel's camp from Mount Sinai, and their orderly march into the plains of Paran, ver. 11–28. III. Moses's treaty with Hobab, his brother-in-law, ver. 29–32. IV. Moses's prayer at the removing and resting of the ark, ver. 33, &c.

Verses 1–10

We have here directions concerning the public notices that were to be given to the people upon several occasions by sound of trumpet. The trumpets were to be sounded for the *calling of assemblies, v.* 2. Thus they are told to blow the trumpet in Zion for the calling of a solemn assembly together, to sanctify a fast, Joel ii. 15. But, that the trumpet might not *give an uncertain sound,* they are directed, if only the princes and elders were to meet, to blow but one of the trumpets; but, if the body of the people were to be called together, both trumpets must be sounded. For the *journeying of the camps,* to give notice when each squadron must move. When the trumpets were blown for this purpose, they must *sound an alarm* (*v.* 5), a broken, quavering, interrupted sound, which was proper to excite and encourage the minds of people in their marches against their enemies; whereas a continued equal sound was more proper for the calling of the assembly together (*v.* 7): yet when the people were called together to deprecate God's judgments we find an alarm sounded, Joel ii. 1. At the first sounding, Judah's squadron marched, at the second Reuben's, at the third Ephraim's, at the fourth Dan's, *v.* 5, 6. For the animating and encouraging of their armies, when they went out in battle (*v.* 9). For the solemnizing of their sacred feasts, *v.* 10. One of their feasts was called *a memorial of the blowing of trumpets,* Lev. xxiii. 23, &c. Holy work should be done with holy joy.

Verses 11–28

Here is, I. A general account of the removal of the camp of Israel from Mount Sinai, before which mountain it had lain now about a year, in which time and place a great deal of memorable business was done. Observe, 1. The signal given (*v.* 11): *The cloud was taken up.* 2. The march begun: *They took their journey according to the commandment of the Lord,* and just as the cloud led them, *v.* 13. Some think that mention is thus frequently made in this and the foregoing chapter of the *commandment of the Lord,* guiding and governing them in all their travels, to obviate the calumny and reproach which were afterwards thrown upon Israel, that they tarried so long in the wilderness, because they had lost themselves there, and could not find the way out. Note, Those that have given up themselves to the direction of God's word and Spirit steer a steady course, even when they seem to be bewildered. 3. The place they rested in, after three days' march:

They went *out of the wilderness of Sinai*, and rested *in the wilderness of Paran*.

II. A particular draft of the order of their march, according to the late model. 1. Judah's squadron marched first, *v.* 14–16. The leading standard, now lodged with that tribe, was an earnest of the sceptre which in David's time should be committed to it, and looked further to the captain of our salvation, of whom it was likewise foretold that *unto him should the gathering of the people be.* 2. Then came those two families of the Levites which were entrusted to carry the tabernacle. 3. Reuben's squadron marched forward next, taking place after Judah, *according to the commandment of the Lord, v.* 18–20. 4. Then the Kohathites followed with their charge, the sacred furniture of the tabernacle, *in the midst of the camp,* the safest and most honourable place, *v.* 21. 5. Ephraim's squadron followed next after the ark (*v.* 22–24). 6. Dan's squadron followed last, *v.* 25–27. It is called the *rearward,* or *gathering host,* of all the camps, because it gathered up all that were left behind; not the women and children (these we may suppose were taken care of by the heads of their families in their respective tribes), but all the unclean, the mixed multitude, and all that were weak and feeble, and cast behind in their march.

Verses 29–36

Here is, I. An account of what passed between Moses and Hobab, now upon this advance which the camp of Israel made towards Canaan. Some think that Hobab was the same with Jethro, Moses's father-in-law, and that the story, Exod. xviii., should come in here; it seems more probably that Hobab was the son of Jethro, and that when the father, being aged, went to his own land (Exod. xviii. 27), he left his son Hobab with Moses. Now this Hobab stayed contentedly with Israel while they encamped at Mount Sinai, near his own country; but, now that they were removing, he was for going back to his own country and kindred, and his father's house. Here is, 1. The kind invitation Moses gives him to go forward with them to Canaan, *v.* 29. Note, Those that are bound for the heavenly Canaan should invite and encourage all their friends to go along with them. 2. Hobab's inclination, and present resolution, to go back to his own country, *v.* 30. He was indeed a son of Abraham's loins (for the Midianites descended from Abraham by Keturah), but not an heir of Abraham's faith (Heb. xi. 8), else he would not have given Moses this answer. 3. The great importunity Moses used with him to alter his resolution, *v.* 31, 32. He urges, That he might be serviceable to them: *We are to encamp in the wilderness* (a country well known to Hobab), *and thou mayest be to us instead of eyes.*

We do not find any reply that Hobab here made to Moses, and therefore we hope that his silence gave consent, and he did not leave them. And we find (Judg. i. 16; 1 Sam. xv. 6) that his family was no loser by it.

II. An account of the communion between God and Israel in this removal. They left *the mount of the Lord* (*v.* 33), that Mount Sinai where they had seen his glory and heard his voice. But when they left the *mount of the Lord* they took with them the *ark of the covenant of the Lord,* by which their stated communion with God was to be kept up. For,

1. By it God did *direct their paths.* The ark of the covenant went before them, some think in *place,* at least in this removal; others think only in *influence.* The ark (that is, the God of the ark) is said to *search out a resting place* for them.

2. By it they did *in all ways acknowledge God.* Moses, as the mouth of the congregation, lifted up a prayer, both at the removing and at the resting of the ark; and it is an example to us to begin and end every day's journey, and every day's work, with prayer.

(1) Here is his prayer when the ark set forward: *Rise up, Lord, and let thy enemies be scattered, v.* 35. Note, [1] There are those in the world that are enemies to God, and haters of him: secret and open enemies; enemies of his truths, his laws, his ordinances, his people. [2] The scattering and defeating of God's enemies is a thing to be earnestly desired, and believingly expected, by all the Lord's people.

(2) His prayer when the ark rested, *v.* 36. [1] That God would cause his people to rest. So some read it, "*Return, O Lord, the many thousands of Israel,* return them to their rest again after this fatigue." [2] That God himself would take up his rest among them. So we read it: *Return to the thousands of Israel,* the *ten thousand thousand,* so the word is. The welfare and happiness of the Israel of God consist in the continual presence of God among them.

Chapter 11

Hitherto things had gone pretty well in Israel; little interruption had been given to the methods of God's favour to them since the matter of the golden calf; the people seemed teachable in marshalling and purifying the camp, the princes devout and generous in dedicating the altar, and there was good hope that they would be in Canaan presently. But at this chapter begins a melancholy scene. I. Their murmurings kindled a fire among them, which yet was soon quenched by the prayer of Moses, ver. 1–3. II. No sooner was the fire of judgment quenched than the fire of sin breaks out again, 1. The people fret for want of flesh, ver. 4–9. 2. Moses frets for want of help, ver. 10–15. Now, (1) God promises to gratify them both, to appoint help for Moses (ver. 16, 17), and to give the people flesh, ver. 18–23. And, (2) He presently makes good both these promises. For [1] The Spirit of God qualifies the seventy elders for the government, ver. 24–30. [2] The power of God brings quails to feast the people, ver. 31, 32. Yet, [3] The justice of God plagued them for their murmurings, ver. 33, &c.

Verses 1–3

I. The people's sin. They *complained, v.* 1. The law discovered sin, but could not destroy it; checked it, but could not conquer it. They *complained.* When they were furnished with so much matter for thanksgiving, one may justly wonder where they found any matter for complaint.

II. God's just resentment of the affront given to him by this sin: *The Lord heard it,* and his *anger was kindled.*

III. The judgment wherewith God chastised them for this sin. We read of their murmurings several times, when they came first out of Egypt, Exod. xv., and xvi., and xvii. But we do not read of any plagues inflicted on them for their murmurings, as there were now; for now they had had great experience of God's care of them, and therefore now to distrust him was so much the more inexcusable.

IV. Their cry to Moses, who was their tried intercessor, *v.* 2. *When he slew them, then they sought him,* and made their application to Moses to stand their friend.

V. The prevalence of Moses's intercession for them: *When Moses prayed unto the Lord* God had respect to him and his offering, and *the fire was quenched.*

VI. A new name given hereupon to the place, to perpetuate the shame of a murmuring people. The place was called *Taberah,* a *burning* (*v.* 3), that others might hear, and fear, and take warning not to sin as they did.

Verses 4–15

These verses represent things sadly unhinged and out of order in Israel, both the people and the prince uneasy.

I. Here is the people fretting, and speaking against God himself.

1. Who were the criminals? (1) The *mixed multitude* began, they *fell a-lusting*, v. 4. The rabble that came with them out of Egypt, expecting only the land of promise, but not a state of probation in the way to it. These were the scabbed sheep that infected the flock, the leaven that leavened the whole lump. (2) Even *the children of Israel* took the infection, as we are informed, *v.* 4.

2. What was the crime? (1) They magnified the plenty and dainties they had had in Egypt (*v.* 5), as if God had done them a great deal of wrong in taking them thence. They *remember the cucumbers, and the melons, and the leeks, and the onions, and the garlick* (precious stuff indeed to be fond of!), but they do not remember the brick-kilns and the task-masters, the voice of the oppressor and the smart of the whip. (2) They were sick of the good provision God had made for them, *v.* 6. It was bread from heaven, angels' food. While they lived on manna, they seemed to be exempted from the curse which sin has brought on man, that in the *sweat of his face should he eat bread.* And yet they speak of the manna with such scorn, as if it were not good enough to be meat for swine: *Our soul is dried away.* (3) They could not be satisfied unless they had flesh to eat. (4) They distrusted the power and goodness of God as insufficient for their supply: *Who will give us flesh to eat?* taking it for granted that God could not. (5) They were eager and importunate in their desires; they *lusted a lust*, so the word is, lusted greatly and greedily, till they wept again for vexation. (6) Flesh is good food, and may lawfully be eaten; yet they are said to lust after evil things. What is lawful of itself becomes evil to us when it is what God does not allot to us and yet we eagerly desire it.

II. Moses himself, though so meek and good a man, is uneasy upon this occasion: *Moses also was displeased.* Now, 1. It must be confessed that the provocation was very great. These murmurings of theirs reflected great dishonour upon God, and Moses laid to heart the reproaches cast on him. 2. Yet Moses came short of his duty both to God and Israel in these expostulations. (1) He undervalues the honour God had put upon him. (2) He complains too much of a sensible grievance, and lays too near his heart a little noise and fatigue. (3) He magnifies his own performances, that *all the burden of the people lay upon him.* (4) He is not so sensible as he ought to be of the obligation he lay under, by virtue of the divine commission and command, to do the utmost he could for his people. (5) He takes too much to himself when he asks, *Whence should I have flesh to give them* (*v.* 13), as if he were the housekeeper, and not God. (6) He speaks distrustfully of the divine grace when he despairs of being *able to bear all this people, v.* 14. (7) It was worst of all passionately to wish for death, and desire to be killed out of hand. Is this Moses? Is this the meekest of all the men on the earth? The best have their infirmities, and fail sometimes in the exercise of that grace for which they are most eminent. *Lord, lead us not into temptation.*

Verses 16–23

God's gracious answer to both the foregoing complaints:

I. Provision is made for the redress of the grievances Moses complains of. If he find the weight of government lie too heavy upon him, though he was a little too passionate in his remonstrance, yet he shall be eased, not by being discarded from the government himself, but by having assistants appointed him.

1. Moses is directed to nominate the persons, *v.* 16. The number he is to choose is seventy men, according to the number of the souls that went down into Egypt.

2. God promises to qualify them.

II. Even the humour of the discontented people shall be gratified too, that every mouth may be stopped. They are ordered to *sanctify themselves* (*v.* 18), that is, to put themselves into a posture to receive such a proof of God's power as should be a token both of mercy and judgment.

1. God promises (shall I say?)—he threatens rather, that they shall have their fill of flesh, and, if they have not a better government of their appetites than now it appears they have, they shall be surfeited with it (*v.* 19, 20).

2. Moses objects the improbability of making good this word, *v.* 21, 22. It is an objection like that which the disciples made, Mark viii. 4, *Whence can a man satisfy these men?* He objects the number of the people, as if he that provided bread for them all could not, by the same unlimited power, provide flesh too. He reckons it must be the flesh either of beasts or fishes, little thinking that the flesh of birds, little birds, should serve the purpose.

3. God gives a short but sufficient answer to the objection in that question, *Has the Lord's hand waxed short? v.* 23. God here brings Moses to this first principle, sets him back in his lesson, to learn the ancient name of God, *The Lord God Almighty.*

Verses 24–30

The performance of God's word to Moses, that he should have help in the government of Israel.

I. Here is the case of the seventy privy-counsellors in general. Moses, though a little disturbed by the tumult of the people, yet was thoroughly composed by the communion he had with God, and soon came to himself again. 1. He did his part; he presented the seventy elders before the Lord, round the tabernacle (*v.* 24), that they might there stand ready to receive the grace of God, in the place where he manifested himself. 2. God was not wanting to do his part. *He gave of his Spirit to the seventy elders,* (*v.* 25).

II. Here is the particular case of two of them, *Eldad* and *Medad*, probably two brothers.

1. They were nominated by Moses to be assistants in the government, but they *went not out unto the tabernacle* as the rest did, *v.* 26.

2. The Spirit of God found them out in the camp, where they were hidden among the stuff, and there they prophesied, that is, they exercised their gift of praying, preaching, and praising God, in some private tent. There was a special providence in it that these two should be absent, for thus it appeared that it was indeed a divine Spirit which the elders were actuated by, and that Moses gave them not that Spirit, but God himself.

3. Information of this was given to Moses (*v.* 27): *Eldad and Medad do prophesy in the camp.* Whoever the person was that brought the tidings, he seems to have looked upon it as an irregularity.

4. Joshua moved to have them silenced: *My lord Moses, forbid them, v.* 28. It is probable that Joshua himself was one of the seventy. He does not desire that they should be punished for what they had done, but only restrained for the future.

5. Moses rejected the motion, and reproved him that made it (*v.* 29): "*Enviest thou for my sake?*" Though Joshua was Moses's particular friend and confidant, though he said this out of a respect to Moses, whose honour he was very loth to see lessened by the call of those elders, yet Moses reproved him. We must not be forward to condemn and silence those that differ from us, as if they did not follow Christ because they do not follow *him with us*, Mark ix. 38. Shall we reject those whom Christ has owned, or restrain any from doing good because they

are not in everything of our mind? Moses was of another spirit; so far from silencing these two, and quenching the Spirit in them, he wishes *all the Lord's people were prophets*, that is, that he would *put his Spirit upon them*.

6. The elders, now newly ordained, immediately entered upon their administration (*v.* 30); when their call was sufficiently attested by their prophesying, they went with Moses to the camp, and applied themselves to business.

Verses 31–35

God, having performed his promise to Moses by giving him assessors in the government. He here performs his promise to the people by giving them flesh. Observe, 1. How the people were gratified with flesh in abundance: *A wind* (a south-east wind, as appears, Ps. lxxviii. 26) *brought quails, v.* 31. It is uncertain what sort of animals they were; the psalmist calls them *feathered fowl, or fowl of wing.* The learned bishop Patrick inclines to agree with some modern writers, who think they were *locusts*, a delicious sort of food well known in those parts, the rather because they were brought with a wind, lay in heaps, and were dried in the sun for use. Whatever they were, they answered the intention, they served for a month's feast for Israel, such an indulgent Father was God to his froward family. 2. How greedy they were of this flesh that God sent them. They *flew upon the spoil* with an insatiable appetite, not regarding what Moses had told them from God, that they would surfeit upon it, *v.* 32. 3. How dearly they paid for their feasts, when it came into the reckoning: *The Lord smote them with a very great plague* (*v.* 33), some bodily disease, which probably was the effect of their surfeit, and was the death of many of them. The remembrance of this is preserved in the name given to the place, *v.* 34. Moses called it *Kibroth-hattaavah*, the *graves of lusters* or *of lust*.

CHAPTER 12

In the foregoing chapter we had the vexation which the people gave to Moses; in this we have his patience tried by his own relations. I. Miriam and Aaron, his own brother and sister, affronted him, ver. 1–3. II. God called them to an account for it, ver. 4–9. III. Miriam was smitten with a leprosy for it, ver. 10. IV. Aaron submits, and Moses meekly intercedes for Miriam, ver. 11–13. V. She is healed, but put to shame for seven days, ver. 14–16. And this is recorded to show that the best persons and families have both their follies and their crosses.

Verses 1–3

Here is, I. The unbecoming passion of Aaron and Miriam: they *spoke against Moses, v.* 1. It should seem that Miriam began the quarrel, and Aaron, not having been employed or consulted in the choice of the seventy elders, was for the present somewhat disgusted, and so was the sooner drawn in to take his sister's part. Two things they quarrelled with Moses about:—1. About his marriage: some think a late marriage with a Cushite or Arabian; others because of Zipporah, whom on this occasion they called, in scorn, an Ethiopian woman, and who, they insinuated, had too great an influence upon Moses in the choice of these seventy elders. 2. About his government; not the mismanagement of it, but the monopolizing of it (*v.* 2): "*Hath the Lord spoken only by Moses?*"

II. The wonderful patience of Moses under this provocation. He, *as a deaf man, heard not.* When God's honour was concerned, as in the case of the golden calf, no man more zealous than Moses; but, when his own honour was touched, no man more meek: as bold as a lion in the cause of God, but as mild as a lamb in his own cause. Sometimes the unkindness of our friends is a greater trial of our meekness than the malice of our enemies.

Verses 4–9

Moses did not resent the injury done him, nor complain of it to God, nor make any appeal to him; but God resented it. The more silent we are in our own cause the more is God engaged to plead it. The accused innocent needs to say little if he knows the judge himself will be his advocate.

I. The cause is called, and the parties are summoned forthwith to attend at the door of the tabernacle, *v.* 4, 5.

II. Aaron and Miriam were made to know that great as they were they must not pretend to be equal to Moses, nor set up as rivals with him, *v.* 6–8. 1. It was true that God put a great deal of honour upon the prophets. God *made himself known to them*, either by dreams when they were asleep, or by visions when they were awake, and by them made himself known to others. Now he does it not by dreams and visions, as of old, but by the *Spirit of wisdom and revelation.* 2. Yet the honour put upon Moses was far greater (*v.* 7): *My servant Moses is not so,* he excels them all. To recompense Moses for his meekly and patiently bearing the affronts which Miriam and Aaron gave him, God not only cleared him, but praised him. (1) Moses was a man of great integrity and tried fidelity. He is *faithful in all my house.* This is put first in his character, because grace excels gifts, love excels knowledge, and sincerity in the service of God puts a greater honour upon a man and recommends him to the divine favour more than learning, abstruse speculations, and an ability to *speak with tongues.* (2) Moses was therefore honoured with clearer discoveries of God's mind, and a more intimate communion with God, than any other prophet whatsoever.

Now let Miriam and Aaron consider who it was that they insulted: *Were you not afraid to speak against my servant Moses?*

III. God, having thus shown them their fault and folly, next shows them his displeasure (*v.* 9): *The anger of the Lord was kindled against them.* But indeed it was indication enough of his displeasure that he departed, and would not so much as hear their excuse. The removal of God's presence from us is the surest and saddest token of God's displeasure against us. Woe unto us if he depart; and he never departs till we by our sin and folly drive him from us.

Verses 10–16

Here is, I. God's judgment upon Miriam (*v.* 10): *The cloud departed from off* that part of *the tabernacle,* in token of God's displeasure, and presently Miriam became leprous. Her foul tongue (says Bishop Hall) is justly punished with a foul face. While Moses needs a veil to hide his glory, Miriam needs one to hide her shame. Miriam was struck with a leprosy, but not Aaron, because she was first in the transgression, and God would put a difference between those that mislead and those that are misled. Aaron as priest was to be the judge of the leprosy. He was struck through her side, and could not pronounce her leprous without blushing and trembling, knowing himself to be equally obnoxious.

II. Aaron's submission hereupon (*v.* 11, 12); he humbles himself to Moses, confesses his fault, and begs pardon. He that but just now joined with his sister in speaking against Moses is here forced for himself and his sister to make a penitent address to him. In his submission, 1. He confesses his own and his sister's sin, *v.* 11. 2. He begs Moses's pardon: *Lay not this sin upon us.* 3. He recommends the deplorable condition of his sister to Moses's compassionate consideration (*v.* 12): *Let her not be as one dead.*

III. The intercession made for Miriam (*v.* 13): He

cried unto the Lord with a loud voice, because the cloud, the symbol of his presence, was removed and stood at some distance, and to express his fervency in this request, *Heal her now, O Lord, I beseech thee.* So Miriam here was healed by the prayer of Moses, whom she had abused.

IV. The accommodating of this matter so as that mercy and justice might meet together. 1. Mercy takes place so far as that Miriam shall be healed; Moses forgives her, and God will. See 2 Cor. ii. 10. But, 2. Justice takes place so far as that Miriam shall be humbled (v. 14): *Let her be shut out from the camp seven days.*

V. The hindrance that this gave to the people's progress: *The people journeyed not till Miriam was brought in again, v.* 15. God did not remove the cloud, and therefore they did not remove their camp. This was intended, 1. As a rebuke to the people, who were conscious to themselves of having sinned after the similitude of Miriam's transgression, in speaking against Moses. 2. As a mark of respect to Miriam. If the camp had removed during the days of her suspension, her trouble and shame had been the greater. Those that are under censure and rebuke for sin ought to be treated with a great deal of ten-derness, and not be over-loaded, no, not with the shame they have deserved, not *counted as enemies* (2 Thess. iii. 15), but *forgiven and comforted,* 2 Cor. ii. 7. Sinners must be cast out with grief and penitents taken in with joy.

Chapter 13

It is a memorable and very melancholy story which is related in this and the following chapter, of the turning back of Israel from the borders of Canaan, when they were just ready to set foot in it, and the sentencing of them to wander and perish in the wilder-ness for their unbelief and murmuring. It is referred to Ps. xcv. 7, &c., and improved for warning to Christians, Heb. iii. 7, &c. In this chapter we have, I. The sending of twelve spies before them into Canaan, ver. 1–16. II. The instructions given to these spies, ver. 17–20. III. Their executing their commission according to their instructions, and their return from the search, ver. 21–25. IV. The report they brought back to the camp of Israel, ver. 26, &c.

Verses 1–20

Here we have, I. Orders given to send spies to search out the land of Canaan. It is here said, God directed Moses to send them (v. 1, 2), but it appears (Deut. i. 22) that the motion came originally from the people; they came to Moses, and said, *We will send men before us.* They would not take God's word that it was a good land. How absurd was it for them to send to spy out a land which God himself had spied out for them. But thus we ruin ourselves by giving more credit to the reports and representations of sense than to divine revelation; we walk by sight, not by faith. The people making this motion to Moses, he consulted God in the case, who bade him gratify the people in this matter, and send spies before them: "Let them walk in their own counsels."

II. The persons nominated that were to be employed in this service (v. 4, &c.), one of each tribe, that it might appear to be the act of the people in general. This was designed for the best, but it proved to have this ill effect that the quality of the persons occasioned the evil report they brought up to be the more credited and the people to be the more influenced by it. Some think that they are all named for the sake of two good ones that were among them, Caleb and Joshua. Notice is taken of the change of Joshua's name upon this occasion, v. 16. The name by which he was generally called and known in his own tribe was *Oshea,* but Moses called him *Joshua,* and now he ordered others to call him so. *Oshea* signifies a prayer for salvation, *Save thou; Joshua* signifies a promise of salvation, *He will save,* in answer to that prayer: so near is the relation between prayers and promises. Prayers prevail for promises, and promises

direct and encourage prayers. *Jesus* is the same name with *Joshua,* and it is the name of our Lord Christ, of whom Joshua was a type as successor to Moses, Israel's captain, and conqueror of Canaan. Joshua was the saviour of God's people from the powers of Canaan, but Christ is their Saviour from the powers of hell.

III. The instructions given to those spies. They were sent into the land of Canaan to take account of its present state, v. 17. Two heads of enquiry were given them: 1. Concerning the land itself: *See* whether it be *good or bad,* and (v. 20) *whether it be fat or lean.* Moses himself was well satisfied that Canaan was a very good land, but he sent these spies to bring an account of it for the satisfaction of the people. 2. Concerning the inhabitants—their number, few or many,—their size and stature, whether strong able-bodied men or weak.

IV. Moses dismisses the spies with this charge, *Be of good courage,* intimating that they should bring an encouraging account to the people and make the best of everything.

Verses 21–25

We have here a short account of the survey which the spies made of the promised land. 1. They went quite through it, from Zin in the south, to Rehob, near Hamath, in the north, v. 21. See *ch.* xxxiv. 3, 8. They divided themselves into several companies, and so passed unsuspected, as wayfaring men. 2. They took particular notice of Hebron (v. 22), probably because near there was the field of Machpelah, where the patriarchs were buried (Gen. xxiii. 19). To this sepulchre they made a particular visit, and found the adjoining city in the possession of the sons of Anak. Where the bodies of their ancestors kept possession for them the giants kept possession against them. 3. They brought a bunch of grapes with them, and some other of the fruits of the land, as a proof of the extraordinary goodness of the country. The place whence they took it was called the *valley of the cluster,* that famous cluster which was to Israel both the earnest and the specimen of all the fruits of Canaan.

Verses 26–33

At length the messengers return, but they agree not in their report.

I. The major part discourage the people from going forward to Canaan.

1. Observe their report. (1) They could not deny but that the land of Canaan was a very fruitful land: the bunch of grapes they brought with them was an ocular demonstration of it, v. 27. And yet afterwards they contradict themselves, when they say (v. 32), *It is a land that eateth up the inhabitants thereof;* some think that there was a great plague in the country at the time they surveyed it. They invidiously im-puted it to the unwholesomeness of the air, and thence took occasion to disparage the country. But (2) They represented the conquest of it as altogether im-practicable, and that it was to no purpose to attempt it. Nothing served their ill purpose more than a description of the giants, on whom they lay a great stress. They gave it in as their judgment, *We are not able to go up against them* (v. 31), and therefore must think of taking some other course.

2. Now, even if they had been to judge only by human probabilities, they could not have been ex-cused from the imputation of cowardice. Were not the hosts of Israel very numerous? Effective men, well marshalled and modelled, closely embodied, and entirely united in interest and affection. Moses, their commander-in-chief, was wise and brave; and if the people had put on resolution, and behaved them-selves valiantly, what could have stood before them?

3. But, though they deserved to be posted for cowards, this was not the worst, the scripture brands them for unbelievers. (1) They had tokens of God's presence with them. The Canaanites were stronger than Israel; suppose they were, but were they stronger than the God of Israel? Their cities are walled against us, but can they be walled against heaven? Besides this, (2) They had had very great experience of the length and strength of God's arm, lifted up and made bare on their behalf. Were not the Egyptians as much stronger than they as the Canaanites were? And yet, without a sword drawn by Israel or a stroke struck, the chariots and horsemen of Egypt were quite routed and ruined; the Amalekites were discomfited. (3) They had particular promises made them of victory and success in their wars against the Canaanites. God had given Abraham all possible assurances that he would put his seed into possession of that land, Gen. xv. 18; xvii. 8. He had expressly promised them by Moses that he would *drive out the Canaanites* from *before them* (Exod. xxxiii. 2), and that he would do it *by little and little*, Exod. xxiii. 30. And after all this, for them to say, *We are not able to go up against them*, was in effect to say, "God himself is not able to make his words good."

II. Caleb encouraged them to go forward, though he was seconded by Joshua only (*v.* 30): *Caleb stilled the people.* Caleb signifies *all heart*, and he answered his name, was hearty himself, and would have made the people so if they would have hearkened to him. 1. He speaks very confidently of success: *We are well able to overcome them*, as strong as they are. 2. He animates the people to go on, and, his lot lying in the van, he speaks as one resolved to lead them on with bravery: "*Let us go up at once. Let us go up and possess it.*"

CHAPTER 14

This chapter gives us an account of that fatal quarrel between God and Israel upon which, for their murmuring and unbelief, he swore in his wrath that they should not enter into his rest. Here is, I. The mutiny and rebellion of Israel against God, upon the report of the evil spies, ver. 1–4. II. The fruitless endeavour of Moses and Aaron, Caleb and Joshua, to still the tumult, ver. 5–10. III. Their utter ruin justly threatened by an offended God, ver. 11, 12. IV. The humble intercession of Moses for them, ver. 13–19. V. A mitigation of the sentence in answer to the prayer of Moses; they shall not all be cut off, but the decree goes forth ratified with an oath, published to the people, again and again repeated, that this whole congregation should perish in the wilderness, and none of them enter Canaan but Caleb and Joshua only, ver. 20–35. VI. The present death of the evil spies, ver. 36–39. VII. The rebuke given to those who attempted to go forward notwithstanding, ver. 40–45. And this is written for our admonition, that we "fall not after the same example of unbelief."

Verses 1–4

What mischief the evil spies made by their unfair representation.

I. How the people fretted themselves: *They lifted up their voices and cried* (*v.* 1); giving credit to the report of the spies rather than to the word of God. Those that cried when nothing hurt them deserved to have something given them to cry for.

II. How they flew in the face of their governors—*murmured against Moses and Aaron*, and in them reproached the Lord, *v.* 2, 3. The congregation of elders began the discontent (*v.* 1). 1. They look back with a causeless discontent. They wish that they had died in Egypt. Never were so many months spent so pleasantly as these which they had spent since they came out of Egypt. How base were the spirits of these degenerate Israelites, who desired rather to die in the wilderness. 2. They look forward with a groundless despair, taking it for granted (*v.* 3) that if they went on they must fall by the sword. And here is a most wicked blasphemous reflection upon God himself, as if he had brought them hither

on purpose that their wives and children, those poor innocents, should be a prey.

III. How they came at last to this desperate resolve, that, instead of going forward to Canaan, they would go back again to Egypt. *Were it not better for us to return to Egypt? Let us make a captain and return to Egypt.* 1. It was the greatest folly in the world to wish themselves in Egypt, or to think that if they were there it would be better with them than it was. 2. It was a most senseless, ridiculous thing to talk of returning thither through the wilderness. We are uneasy at that which is, complain of our place and lot, and we would shift; but is there any place or condition in this world that has not something in it to make us uneasy if we are disposed to be so? The way to better our condition is to get our spirits into a better frame; and instead of asking, "Were it not better to go to Egypt?" ask, "Were it not better to be content, and make the best of that which is?"

Verses 5–10

The friends of Israel here interpose to save them if possible from ruining themselves, but in vain.

I. The best endeavours were used to still the tumult.

1. The clamour and noise of the people were so great that Moses and Aaron could not be heard; and, therefore, to gain audience in the sight of all the assembly, they fell on their faces, thus expressing, (1) Their humble prayers to God to still the tumult of the people. (2) The great trouble and concern of their own spirits. They fall down as men astonished and even thunderstruck, amazed to see a people throw away their own mercies. What they said to the people Moses relates in the repetition of this story, Deut. i. 29, 30, *Be not afraid; the Lord your God shall fight for you.*

2. Caleb and Joshua did their part: they rent their clothes in a holy indignation at the sin of the people, and a holy dread of the wrath of God, which they saw ready to break out against them. No reasoning could be more pertinent and pathetic than theirs was (*v.* 7–9), and they spoke as with authority.

(1) They assured them of the goodness of the land they had surveyed, and that it was really worth venturing for.

(2) They made nothing of the difficulties that seemed to lie in the way of their gaining the possession of it: *Fear not the people of the land, v.* 9. Whatever formidable ideas have been given you of them, the lion is not so fierce as he is painted. *They are bread for us*, that is, "they are set before us rather to be fed upon than to be fought with." Though the Canaanites dwell in walled cities, they are naked: *Their defence has departed from them.* The other spies took notice of their strength, but these of their wickedness, and thence inferred that God had forsaken them, and therefore *their defence had departed*.

(3) They showed them plainly that all the danger they were in was from their own discontents, and that they would succeed against all their enemies if they did not make God their enemy.

II. It was all to no purpose; they were deaf to this fair reasoning; nay, they were exasperated by it, and grew more outrageous: *All the congregation bade stone them with stones, v.* 10. Caleb and Joshua knew they appeared for God and his glory, and therefore doubted not but God would appear for them and their safety. And they were not disappointed, for immediately *the glory of the Lord appeared*, to the terror and confusion of those that were for stoning the servants of God.

Verses 11–19

When the glory of the Lord *appeared in the tabernacle* we may suppose that Moses took it for a call to him immediately to come and attend there. Now here we are told what God said to him there.

1. He showed him the great evil of the people's sin, v. 11. Two things God justly complains of to Moses:—(1) Their sin. They *provoke me*, or (as the word signifies) they *reject, reproach, despise* me, for *they will not believe me*. It was their unbelief that made this a day of provocation in the wilderness, Heb. iii. 8. (2) Their continuance in it: *How long will they do so?* The more God has done for us the greater is the provocation if we distrust him.

2. He showed him the sentence which justice passed upon them for it, v. 12. What remains now but that I should make a full end of them? They wish to die; and let them die, and neither root nor branch be left of them.

II. The humble intercession Moses made for them.

1. The prayer of his petition is, in one word, *Pardon. I beseech thee, the iniquity of this people* (v. 19), that is, "Do not bring upon them the ruin they deserve." This was Christ's prayer for those that crucified him, *Father, forgive them.*

2. The pleas are many, and strongly urged.

(1) He insists most upon the plea that is taken from the glory of God, v. 13–16. "If this people that have made so great a noise be all consumed, if their mighty pretensions come to nothing, and their light go out in a snuff, it will be told with pleasure in Gath, and published in the streets of Askelon; and what construction will the heathen put upon it? It will be impossible to make them understand it as an act of God's justice, but they will impute it to the failing of God's power.

(2) He pleads God's proclamation of his name at Horeb (v. 17, 18); *Let the power of the Lord be great.* To enforce this petition, he refers to the word which God had spoken: *The Lord is long-suffering and of great mercy.* God's goodness had there been spoken of as his glory; God gloried in it, Exod. xxxiv. 6, 7. Now here he prays that upon this occasion he would glorify it. He does not ask that they may not be corrected, but that they may not be disinherited.

(3) He pleads past experience: *As thou hast forgiven this people from Egypt, v.* 19. Moses looks upon it as a good plea, *Lord, forgive, as thou hast forgiven.* It will be no more a reproach to thy justice, nor any less the praise of thy mercy, to forgive now, than it has been formerly.

Verses 20–35

God's answer to the prayer of Moses, which sings both of mercy and judgment.

I. The extremity of the sentence is receded from (v. 20). See what countenance and encouragement God gives to our intercessions for others, that we may be public-spirited in prayer. Here is a whole nation rescued from ruin by the effectual fervent prayer of one righteous man.

II. The glorifying of God's name is, in the general, resolved upon, v. 21. Moses in his prayer had shown a great concern for the glory of God. All the world shall see how God hates sin even in his own people, and will reckon for it, and yet how gracious and merciful he is, and how slow to anger. Thus when our Saviour prayed, *Father, glorify thy name*, he was immediately answered, *I have glorified it, and will glorify it yet again*, John xii. 28.

III. The sin of this people which provoked God to proceed against them is here aggravated, v. 22, 27. 1. They tempted God—tempted his power. They tempted his justice, whether he would resent their provocations and punish them or no. 2. They murmured against him. This is much insisted on, v. 27. 3. They did this after they had seen God's miracles in Egypt and in the wilderness, v. 2. 4. They

had repeated the provocations ten times, that is, very often.

IV. The sentence passed upon them for this sin. 1. That they should not see the promised land (v. 23), nor *come into it*, v. 30. The promise of God should be fulfilled to their posterity, but not to them. 2. That they should immediately *turn back into the wilderness*, v. 25. Their next remove should be a retreat. 3. That all those who had now grown up to men's estate should die in the wilderness, not all at once, but by degrees. They wished that they might die in the wilderness, and God said *Amen* to their passionate wish. 4. That in pursuance of this sentence they should wander to and fro in the wilderness, like travellers that have lost themselves, for forty years. (1) That hereby they might be brought to repentance, and find mercy with God in the other world, whatever became of them in this. (2) That they might sensibly feel what a dangerous thing it is for God's covenant-people to break with him. For God never leaves any till they first leave him. (3) That a new generation might in this time be raised up, which could not be done all of a sudden. And the children, being brought up under the tokens of God's displeasure against their fathers, might take warning not to tread in the steps of their fathers' disobedience.

V. The mercy that was mixed with this severe sentence.

1. Mercy to Caleb and Joshua, that though they should wander with the rest in the wilderness, yet they, and they only of all that were now above twenty years old, should survive the years of banishment, and live to enter Canaan. Caleb only is spoken of (v. 24), and a particular mark of honour put upon him, both, (1) In the character given of him: he had *another spirit*, different from the rest of the spies, an *after-spirit*, which furnished him with second thoughts, and he *followed the Lord fully*, kept close to his duty, and went through with it, though deserted and threatened; and, (2) In the recompence promised to him: *Him will I bring in due time into the land whereinto he went.* When Caleb is again mentioned (v. 30) Joshua stands with him, compassed with the same favours and crowned with the same honours, having stood with him in the same services.

2. Mercy to the children even of these rebels. They should have a seed preserved, and Canaan secured to that seed: *Your little ones*, now under twenty years old, *which you*, in your unbelief, *said should be a prey, them will I bring in, v.* 31.

Verses 36–45

Here is, I. The sudden death of the ten evil spies. While the sentence was passing upon the people, before it was published, they *died of the plague before the Lord, v.* 36, 37. 1. They sinned themselves, in bringing up a slander upon the land of promise. Note, Those greatly provoke God who misrepresent religion, cast reproach upon it, and raise prejudices in men's minds against it, or give occasion to those to do so who seek occasion. 2. They *made Israel to sin*. They designedly *made all the congregation murmur* against God.

II. The special preservation of Caleb and Joshua: *They lived still, v.* 38.

III. The publication of the sentence to all the people, v. 36. He told them all what the decree was which had gone forth concerning them, and which could not be reversed, that they must all die in the wilderness, and Canaan must be reserved for the next generation.

IV. The foolish fruitless attempts of some of the Israelites to enter Canaan, notwithstanding the sentence.

1. They were now eager to go forward towards Canaan, v. 40. They were up early, mustered all

their force, got together in a body, and begged of Moses to lead them on against the enemy. But, though God was glorified by this recantation of theirs, they were not benefited by it, because it came too late.

2. Moses utterly disallows their motion, and forbids the expedition they were meditating: *Go not up*, *v.* 41–43. He gives them warning of the danger: *"The Canaanites are before you* to attack you, and *the Lord is not among you* to protect you and fight for you, and therefore look to yourselves *that you be not smitten before your enemies."* Those that are out of the way of their duty are from under God's protection, and go at their peril.

3. They venture notwithstanding. Never was people so perverse and so desperately resolved in every thing to walk contrary to God. God bade them go, and they would not; he forbade them, and they would.

4. The expedition speeds accordingly, *v.* 45. The enemy had posted themselves upon the top of the hill, to make good that pass against the invaders, and, being informed by their scouts of their approach, sallied out upon them, and defeated them, and it is probable that many of the Israelites were killed.

CHAPTER 15

This chapter, which is mostly concerning sacrifice and offering, comes in between the story of two rebellions (one ch. xlv., the other ch. xvi.), to signify that these legal institutions were typical of the gifts which Christ was to receive even for the rebellious, Ps. lxviii. 18. In the foregoing chapter, upon Israel's provocation, God had determined to destroy them, and in token of his wrath had sentenced them to perish in the wilderness. But, upon Moses's intercession, he said, "I have pardoned"; and, in token of that mercy, in this chapter he repeats and explains some of the laws concerning offerings, to show that he was reconciled to them. Here is, I. The law concerning the meat-offerings and drink-offerings (ver. 1–12) both for Israelites and for strangers (ver. 13–16), and a law concerning the heave-offerings of the first of their dough, ver. 17–21. II. The law concerning sacrifices for sins of ignorance, ver. 22–29. III. The punishment of presumptuous-sins (ver. 30, 31), and an instance given in the sabbath-breaker, ver. 32–36. IV. A law concerning fringes, for memorandums, upon the borders of their garments, ver. 37, &c.

Verses 1–21

I. Full instructions given concerning the meat-offerings and drink-offerings, which were appendages to all the sacrifices of animals. The beginning of this law is very encouraging: *When you come into the land of your habitation which I give unto you,* then you shall do so and so, *v.* 2. This was a plain intimation, not only that God was reconciled to them, but that he would secure the promised land to their seed. Now the intent of this law is to direct what proportion the meat-offering and drink-offering should bear to the several sacrifices to which they were annexed.

II. Natives and strangers are here set upon a level, in this as in other matters (*v.* 13–16): *"One law shall be for you and for the stranger* that is proselyted to the Jewish religion." Now, 1. This was an invitation to the Gentiles to become proselytes, and to embrace the faith and worship of the true God. In civil things there was a difference between strangers and true-born Israelites, but not in the things of God. 2. This was an obligation upon the Jews to be kind to strangers, and not to oppress them, because they saw them owned and accepted of God. Communion in religion should slay all enmities. It was a happy presage of the calling of the Gentiles, and of their admission into the church. If the law made so little difference between Jew and Gentile, much less would the gospel make, which broke down the partition-wall, and reconciled both to God in one sacrifice, without the observance of the legal ceremonies.

III. A law for the offering of the first of their dough unto the Lord. This, as the former, goes upon the comfortable supposition of their having *come into the promised land, v.* 18. They must not only offer

him the first-fruits and tenths of the corn in their fields, but when they had it in their houses, in their kneading troughs, when it was almost ready to be set upon their tables, God must have a further tribute, part of their dough must be heaved or offered up to God (*v.* 20, 21), and the priest must have it for the use of his family. Thus they must own their dependence upon God for their daily bread. Christ has taught us to pray not, *Give us this year our yearly harvest,* but *Give us this day our daily bread.*

Verses 22–29

We have here the laws concerning sacrifices for sins of ignorance; the Jews understand it of idolatry, or false worship, through the error of their teachers. If they had failed in the offerings they must bring an offering of atonement, though the omission had been through forgetfulness or mistake. 1. The case is put of a national sin, committed through ignorance, and become customary through a vulgar error (*v.* 24). Now, if there should appear to have been a general neglect of that appointment, then a sacrifice must be offered for the whole congregation. It is likewise supposed to be the case of a particular person. Thus atonement shall be made *for the soul that sins, when he sins through ignorance, v.* 28. Sins committed ignorantly shall be forgiven, through Christ the great sacrifice, who, when he offered up himself once for all upon the cross, seemed to explain the intention of his offering in that prayer, *Father, forgive them, for they know not what they do.* And Paul seems to allude to this law concerning sins of ignorance (1 Tim. i. 13), *I obtained mercy, because I did it ignorantly and in unbelief.* And it looked favourably upon the Gentiles that this law of atoning for sins of ignorance is expressly made to extend to those who were strangers to the commonwealth of Israel (*v.* 29), but supposed to be *proselytes of righteousness.* Thus the blessing of Abraham comes upon the Gentiles.

Verses 30–36

Here is, I. The general doom passed upon presumptuous sinners. Those are to be reckoned presumptuous sinners that sin *with a high hand,* as the original phrase is (*v.* 30), that is, that fight against God, and dare him to do his worst, see Job xv. 25. It imputes folly to Infinite Wisdom, and iniquity to the righteous Judge of heaven and earth; such is the malignity of wilful sin. The sentence passed on such is dreadful. There remains no sacrifice for those sins; the law provided none.

II. A particular instance of presumption in the sin of sabbath-breaking. The offence was the gathering of sticks on the sabbath day (*v.* 32), which, it is probable, were designed to make a fire of, whereas they were commanded to bake and seethe what they had occasion for the day before, Exod. xvi. 23. It appears by the context to have been done presumptuously, and in affront both of the law and to the Law-maker. It seems, even common Israelites, though there was much amiss among them, yet would not contentedly see the sabbath profaned. The law had already made the profanation of the sabbath a capital crime (Exod. xxxi. 14, *ch.* xxxv. 2); but they were in doubt, either concerning the offence (whether this that he had done should be deemed a profanation or no) or concerning the punishment, what death he should die. Sentence was passed; the prisoner was adjudged a sabbath-breaker, according to the intent of that law, and as such he must be put to death; and to show how great the crime was, and how displeasing to God, and that others might hear and fear and not do in like manner presumptuously, that death is appointed him which was looked upon as most terrible: He must be *stoned with stones, v.* 35. Note, God is jealous for the honour of his sabbaths, and will not hold those guiltless, whatever men do, that profane them. Execution was done pursuant to the sentence. *v.* 36. He was *stoned* to death *by the congregation.* As many as could were employed in the execution, that those, at least, might be afraid of breaking the sabbath, who had thrown a stone at this sabbath-breaker. This intimates that the open profanation of the sabbath is a sin which ought to be punished and restrained by the civil magistrate, who, as far as overt acts go, is keeper of both tables. See Neh. xiii. 17. One would think there could be no great harm in gathering a few sticks, on what day soever it was, but God intended the exemplary punishment of him that did so for a standing warning to us all, to make conscience of keeping holy the sabbath.

Verses 37–41

Provision had been just now made by the law for the pardon of sins of ignorance and infirmity; now here is an expedient provided for the preventing of such sins. They are ordered to make fringes upon the borders of their garments, which were to be memorandums to them of their duty. The sign appointed is a fringe of silk, and a blue riband bound on the top of it to keep it tight, *v.* 38. Our Saviour, being made under the law, wore these fringes; hence we read of the hem or border of his garment, Matt. ix. 20. These borders the Pharisees enlarged, that they might be thought more holy and devout than other people. Many look upon their ornaments to feed their pride, but they must look upon these ornaments to awaken their consciences to a sense of their duty.

After the repetition of some ceremonial appointments, the chapter closes with that great and fundamental law of religion, *Be holy unto your God.*

CHAPTER 16

The date of the history contained in this chapter is altogether uncertain. Probably these mutinies happened after their removal back again from Kadesh-barnea. Presently after new laws given follows the story of a new rebellion. Here is, I. A daring and dangerous rebellion raised against Moses and Aaron, by Korah, Dathan, and Abiram, ver. 1–15. 1. Korah and his accomplices contend for the priesthood against Aaron, ver. 3. Moses reasons with them, and appeals to God for a decision of the controversy, ver. 4–11. 2. Dathan and Abiram quarrel with Moses, and refuse to obey his summons, which greatly grieves him, ver 12–15. II. A solemn appearance of the pretenders to the priesthood before God, and a public appearance of the glory of the Lord. III. The deciding of the controversy, and the crushing of the rebellion, by the cutting off of the rebels. IV. A new insurrection of the people, ver. 41–43. 1. God stayed the insurrection by a plague, ver. 45. 2. Aaron stayed the plague by offering incense, ver. 46–50. The manner and method of recording this story plainly shows the ferment to have been very great.

Verses 1–11

Here is, I. An account of the rebels, who and what they were, men of distinction and quality, that made a figure. Korah was the ring-leader: he formed and headed the faction. With him joined Dathan and Abiram, chief men of the tribe of Reuben, the eldest son of Jacob. Probably Korah was disgusted both at the preferment of Aaron to the priesthood and the constituting of Elizaphan to the head of the Kohathites (*ch.* iii. 30); and perhaps the Reubenites were angry that the tribe of Judah had the first post of honour in the camp. And, these being themselves *men of renown*, they seduced into the conspiracy *two hundred and fifty princes of the assembly* (*v.* 2).

II. The rebels' remonstrance, *v.* 3. That which they quarrel with is the settlement of the priesthood upon Aaron and his family. 1. They proudly boast of the holiness of the congregation, and the presence of God in it. Small reason they had to boast of the people's purity, or of God's favour, as the people had been so frequently and so lately polluted with sin. 2. They unjustly charge Moses and Aaron with taking the honour they had to themselves, whereas it was evident, beyond contradiction, that they were called of God to it, Heb. v. 4. See here, (1) What spirit levellers are of, and those that despise dominions, and resist the powers that God has set over them; they are proud, envious, ambitious, turbulent, wicked, and unreasonable men. (2) What usage even the best and most useful men may expect.

III. Moses's conduct when this remonstrance was published against him.

1. He *fell on his face* (*v.* 4), as before, *ch.* xiv. 5. He applied to God, by prayer, for direction what to say and to do upon this sad occasion.

2. He agrees to refer the case to God, and leave it to him to decide it, as one well assured of the goodness of his title, and yet well content to resign, if God thought fit, to gratify this discontented people with another nomination.

3. He argues the case fairly with them, to still the mutiny with fair reasoning, if possible, before the appeal came to God's tribunal, for then he knew it would end in the confusion of his complainants.

(1) He calls them *the sons of Levi, v.* 7, and again *v.* 8. Levites, and yet rebels.

(2) He retorts their charge upon themselves. They had unjustly charged Moses and Aaron with taking too much upon them, though they had done no more than what God put upon them; nay, says Moses, *You take too much upon you, you sons of Levi.*

(3) He shows them the privilege they had as Levites, which was sufficient for them, they needed not to aspire to the honour of the priesthood, *v.* 9, 10.

(4) He convicts them of the sin of undervaluing those privileges: *Seemeth it a small thing unto you?*

(5) He interprets their mutiny to be a rebellion against God (*v.* 11); while they pretended to assert the holiness and liberty of the Israel of God, they really took up arms against the God of Israel: *You are gathered together against the Lord.*

Verses 12–22

Here is, I. The insolence of Dathan and Abiram, and their treasonable remonstrance. Moses had heard what Korah had to say, and had answered it; now he summons Dathan and Abiram to bring in their complaints (*v.* 12); but they would not obey his summons. They send their articles of impeachment against Moses; and the charge runs very high. 1. They charge him with having done them a great deal of wrong in bringing them out of Egypt, invidiously calling that *a land flowing with milk and honey, v.* 13. 2. They charge him with a design upon their lives, that he intended to *kill them in the wilderness.* 3. They charge him with a design upon their liberties, that he meant to enslave them, by *making himself a prince over them.* A prince over them! Was he not a tender father to them? nay, their devoted servant for the Lord's sake? 4. They charge him with cheating them, raising their expectations of a good land, and then defeating them (*v.* 14): *Thou hast not brought us,* as thou promisedst us, *into a land that floweth with milk and honey*; and pray whose fault was that? He had brought them to the borders of it, and was just ready, under God, to put them in possession of it; but they thrust it away from them, and shut the door against themselves; so that it was purely their own fault that they were not now in Canaan, and yet Moses must bear the blame.

II. Moses's just resentment of their insolence, *v.* 15. In this discomposure,

1. He appeals to God concerning his own integrity; God was his witness, (1) That he never got any thing by them: *I have not taken one ass from them,* not only

not by way of bribery and extortion, but not by way of recompence or gratuity for all the good offices he had done them. He got more in his estate when he kept Jethro's flock than when he came to be king in Jeshurun. (2) That they never lost any thing by him: *Neither have I hurt any one of them.*

2. He begs of God to plead his cause, and clear him, by showing his displeasure at the incense which Korah and his company were to offer, with whom Dathan and Abiram were in confederacy. Lord, says he, *Respect not thou their offering.*

III. Issue joined between Moses and his accusers. 1. Moses challenges them to appear with Aaron next morning, at the time of offering up the morning incense, and refer the matter to God's judgment, *v.* 16, 17. 2. Korah accepts the challenge, and makes his appearance with Moses and Aaron *at the door of the tabernacle*, to make good his pretensions, *v.* 18, 19. They *took every man his censer.* Perhaps these were some of the censers which these heads of families had made use of at their family-altars.

IV. The judgment set, and the Judge taking the tribunal, and threatening to give sentence against the whole congregation. 1. The *glory of the Lord appeared, v.* 19. The same glory that appeared to install Aaron in his office at first (Lev. ix. 23) now appeared to confirm him in it, and to confound those that oppose him. 2. God threatened to *consume them all in a moment,* and, in order to that, bade Moses and Aaron stand from among them, *v.* 21.

V. The humble intercession of Moses and Aaron for the congregation, *v.* 22. 1. Their posture was importuning: they *fell on their faces*, prostrating themselves before God, as supplicants in good earnest, that they might prevail for sparing mercy. Though the people had treacherously deserted them, and struck in with those that were in arms against them, yet they approved themselves faithful to the trusts reposed in them, as shepherds of Israel, who were to stand in the breach when they saw the flock in danger. Note, If others fail in their duty to us, this does not discharge us from our duty to them, nor take off the obligations we lie under to seek their welfare. 2. Their prayer was a pleading prayer, and it proved a prevailing one. Observe in the prayer, (1) The title they give to God: *The God of the spirits of all flesh.* See what man is; he is a spirit in flesh, a soul embodied, a creature wonderfully compounded of heaven and earth. See what God is; he is the God of the spirits of all mankind. (2) The argument they insist on; it is much the same with that which Abraham urged in his intercession for Sodom (Gen. xviii. 23): *Wilt thou destroy the righteous with the wicked?* Such is the plea here: *Shall one man sin and wilt thou be wroth with all the congregation?*

Verses 23-34

We have here the determining of the controversy with Dathan and Abiram, who rebelled against Moses, as in the next paragraph the determining of the controversy with Korah and his company, who would be rivals with Aaron. It should seem that Dathan and Abiram had set up a spacious tabernacle in the midst of the tents of their families, where they kept court, met in council, and hung out their flag of defiance against Moses; it is here called the *tabernacle of Korah, Dathan and Abiram, v.* 24, 27.

I. Public warning is given to the congregation to withdraw immediately from the tents of the rebels. 1. God bids Moses speak to this purport, *v.* 24. This was in answer to Moses's prayer. He had begged that God would not *destroy the whole congregation.* God never promised to save by miracles those that would not save themselves by means. Moses that had prayed for them must preach this to them, and warn them to *flee from this wrath to come.* 2. Moses

accordingly repairs to the head-quarters of the rebels, leaving Aaron at the door of the tabernacle, *v.* 25. Dathan and Abiram had contumaciously refused to come up to him (*v.* 12), yet he humbly condescends to go down to them, to try if he could yet convince and reclaim them. 3. Proclamation is made that all manner of persons, as they tendered their own safety, should forthwith *depart from the tents of these wicked men* (*v.* 26).

II. The congregation takes the warning, but the rebels themselves continue obstinate, *v.* 27. 1. God, in mercy, inclined the people to forsake the rebels. 2. God, in justice, left the rebels to the obstinacy and hardness of their own hearts. They impudently *stood in the doors of their tents,* as if they would outface God himself, and dare him to his worst.

III. Sentence is solemnly pronounced upon them by Moses in the name of the Lord, and the decision of the controversy is put upon the execution of that sentence by the almighty power of God.

IV. Execution is immediately done. It appeared that God and his servant Moses understood one another very well; for, as soon as ever Moses had spoken the word, God did the work, the earth *clave asunder* (*v.* 31), *opened her mouth, and swallowed them all up,* them and theirs (*v.* 32), and then *closed upon them, v.* 33. This judgment was, 1. Unparalleled. 2. It was very terrible to the sinners themselves to go down alive into their own graves. 3. It was severe upon their poor children, though we cannot particularly tell how bad they might be to deserve it or how good God might be otherwise to them to compensate it, yet of this we are sure in general, that Infinite Justice did them no wrong.

V. All Israel is alarmed at the judgment: *They fled at the cry of them, v.* 34. Note, Others' ruins should be our warnings.

Verses 35-40

We must now look back to the door of the tabernacle, where we left the pretenders to the priesthood, with their censers in their hands ready to offer incense; and here we find,

I. Vengeance taken on them, *v.* 35. This punishment was no less strange or dreadful, and in it it appeared, 1. That *our God is a consuming fire.* 2. That it is at our peril if we meddle with that which does not belong to us. God is jealous of the honour of his own institutions, and will not have them invaded. Had they been content with their office as Levites, which was sacred and honourable, and better than they deserved, they might have lived and died with joy and reputation.

II. Care is taken to perpetuate the remembrance of this vengeance. Orders are given about their censers, 1. That they be secured, because they are hallowed. Eleazar is charged with this, *v.* 37. Now Eleazar is ordered to scatter the fire, with the incense that was kindled with it, in some unclean place without the camp, to signify God's abhorrence of their offering as a polluted thing: *The sacrifice of the wicked is an abomination to the Lord.* But he is to gather up the censers out of the mingled burning, God's fire and theirs, because *they are hallowed.* 2. That they be used in the service of the sanctuary. They must be beaten into *broad plates for a covering of the brazen altar, v.* 38-40. These pretenders thought to have ruined the altar, by laying the priesthood in common again; but, to show that Aaron's office was so far from being shaken by their impotent malice that it was rather confirmed by it, their censers, which offered to rival his, were used both for the adorning and for the preserving of the altar at which he ministered. These censers were preserved *in terrorem,* that others might hear and fear, and do no more presumptuously.

Verses 41–50

Here is, I. A new rebellion raised the very next day against Moses and Aaron. *On the morrow* (v. 41) the body of the people mutinied. 1. Though they were so lately terrified by the sight of the punishment of the rebels. The same sins were re-acted and all these warnings slighted. 2. Though they were so lately saved from sharing in the same punishment. Their charge runs very high: *You have killed the people of the Lord.* Could anything have been said more unjustly and maliciously? It was plain enough that Moses and Aaron had no hand in their death (they did what they could to save them), so that in charging them with murder they did in effect charge God himself with it. The terrors of his judgments as they were here executed on the disobedient, shows how necessary the grace of God is to the effectual change of men's hearts and lives. Love will do what fear could not.

II. God's speedy appearance against the rebels. When they had *gathered against Moses and Aaron,* perhaps with a design to depose or murder them, they *looked towards the tabernacle,* as if their misgiving consciences expected some frowns thence, and, *behold, the glory of the Lord appeared* (v. 42), for the protection of his servants, and the confusion of his and their accusers and adversaries.

III. The intercession which Moses and Aaron made for them. 1. They both *fell on their faces,* humbly to intercede with God for mercy. This they had done several times before, upon similar occasions; and, though the people had basely requited them for it, yet, God having graciously accepted them, they still have recourse to the same method. This is praying always. 2. Moses, perceiving that the *plague had begun in the congregation* of the rebels, sent Aaron by an act of his priestly office to make atonement for them, v. 46. And Aaron readily went and burned incense between the living and the dead. By this it appeared, (1) That Aaron was a very good man, and a man that had a true love for the children of his people, though they hated and envied him. (2) That Aaron was a very bold man—bold to venture into the midst of an enraged rabble, bold to venture into the midst of the infection. To save their lives he put his own into his hand, not counting it dear to him, so that he might but fulfil his ministry. (3) That Aaron was a man of God, and *ordained for men, in things pertaining to God.* His call to the priesthood was hereby abundantly confirmed and set above all contradiction. (4) That Aaron was a type of Christ, who came into the world to make an atonement for sin.

IV. The result and issue of the whole matter. God showed them what he could do by his power, and what he might do in justice, but then showed them what he would do in his love and pity: he would, notwithstanding all this, preserve them a people to himself in and by a mediator.

Chapter 17

Enough had been done in the chapter before to quash all pretensions of the families of the tribe of Levi that would set up in competition with Aaron, but the princes of the rest of the tribes began to murmur. If the head of a tribe must be a priest, why not the head of some other tribe than that of Levi? He that searches the heart knew this thought to be in the breast of some of them, and before it broke out into any overt act graciously anticipated it, to prevent bloodshed; and it is done by miracle in this chapter, not a miracle of wrath, as before, but of grace. I. The matter is put upon trial by the bringing of twelve rods, one for each prince, before the Lord, ver. 1–7. II. Upon trial, the matter is determined by the miraculous blossoming of Aaron's rod, ver. 8, 9. III. The decision of the controversy is registered by the preservation of the rod, ver. 10, 11. IV. The people acquiesce in it with some reluctance, ver. 12, 13.

Verses 1–7

Here we have, I. Orders given for the bringing in of a rod for every tribe that God by a miracle might make it known on whom he had conferred the honour of the priesthood. 1. It seems then the priesthood was a preferment worth seeking and striving for, even by the princes of the tribes. 2. It seems there were those who would not acquiesce in the divine appointment, but would make an interest in opposition to it. God will rule, but Israel will not be ruled; and this is the quarrel. 3. It is an instance of the grace of God that, having wrought divers miracles to punish sin, he would work one more on purpose to prevent it. The directions are, (1) That twelve rods or staves should be brought in. It is probable that they were all made of the almond-tree. It should seem they were but twelve in all, with Aaron's, for, when Levi comes into the account, Ephraim and Manasseh make but one, under the name of Joseph. (2) That the name of each prince should be written upon his rod. (3) That they should be laid up in the tabernacle, for one night, before the testimony, that is, before the ark, which, with its mercy-seat, was a symbol, token, or testimony, of God's presence with them. (4) They were to expect that the rod of the tribe, or prince, whom God chose to the priesthood, should bud and blossom, v. 5.

II. The preparing of the rods accordingly. The princes brought them in, and *Moses laid them up before the Lord.*

Verses 8–13

Here is, I. The final determination of the controversy concerning the priesthood by a miracle, v. 8, 9. The rods or staves were brought out from the most holy place where they were laid up, and publicly produced before the people; and, while all the rest of the rods remained as they were, Aaron's rod only, of a dry stick, became a living branch, budded, and blossomed, and yielded almonds. This was miraculous, and took away all suspicion of a fraud, as if in the night Moses had taken away Aaron's rod, and put a living branch of an almond tree in the room, of it; for no ordinary branch would have buds, blossoms, and fruits upon it, all at once. Now,

1. This was a plain indication to the people that Aaron was chosen to the priesthood. Bishop Hall here observes that fruitfulness is the best evidence of a divine call, and that the plants of God's setting, and the boughs cut off from them, will flourish. See Ps. xcii. 12–14. The trees of the Lord, though they seem dry trees, are full of sap.

2. It was a very proper sign to represent the priesthood itself, which was hereby confirmed to Aaron. (1) That it should be fruitful and serviceable to the church of God. (2) That there should be a succession of priests. Here were not only almonds for the present, but buds and blossoms promising more hereafter. (3) That yet this priesthood should not be perpetual, but in process of time, like the branches and blossoms of a tree, should fail and wither.

3. It was a type and figure of Christ and his priesthood. He was to *grow up before God,* as this before the ark, *like a tender plant, and a root out of a dry ground,* Isa. liii. 2.

II. The record of this determination, by the preserving of the rod before the testimony, *in perpetuam rei memoriam—that it might be had in perpetual remembrance,* v. 10, 11. 1. The design of God in all his providences is to take away sin, and to prevent it. 2. What God does for the taking away of sin is done in real kindness to us, *that we die not.* All the bitter potions he gives, and all the sharp methods he uses with us, are for the cure of a disease which otherwise would be fatal.

III. The outcry of the people hereupon (v. 12, 13): *Behold, we die, we perish, we all perish. Shall we be consumed with dying?* This may be considered as the

language either, 1. Of a repining people quarrelling
with the judgments of God, which, by their own pride
and obstinacy, they had brought upon themselves.
They seem to speak despairingly, as if God was a hard
Master, that sought advantage against them. Or,
2. Of a repenting people. We submit to the divine
will in this appointment; we will not contend any
more, lest we all perish.

CHAPTER 18

Aaron being now fully established in the priesthood in this
chapter God gives him full instructions concerning his office or
rather repeats those which he had before given him. He tells
him, I. What must be his work and the care and charge committed to him, and what assistance he should have from the
Levites in that work, ver. 1-7. II. What should be his and the
Levites' wages for this work. 1. The perquisites or fees peculiar
to the priests, ver. 8-19. 2. The settled maintenance of the
Levites, ver. 20-24. III. The portion which must be paid to the
priests out of the Levites' maintenance, ver. 25-32. Thus every
one knew what he had to do, and what he had to live upon.

Verses 1-7

The coherence of this chapter with that foregoing is very observable.

I. The people, in the close of that chapter, had
complained of the difficulty and peril that there were
in drawing near to God. Now, in answer to this
complaint, God here gives them to understand by
Aaron that the priests should come near for them
as their representatives.

II. A great deal of honour God had now lately
put upon Aaron. Now God comes to him to remind
him of the burden that was laid upon him, and the
duty required from him as a priest. He would see
reason to receive the honours of his office with
reverence and holy trembling, when he considered
how great was the charge committed to him.

1. God tells him of the danger that attended his
dignity, *v.* 1. (1) That both the priests and Levites
(*thou, and thy sons, and thy father's house*) should
bear the iniquity of the sanctuary; that is, if the
sanctuary were profaned by the intrusion of strangers,
or persons in their uncleanness, the blame should
lie upon the Levites and priests, who ought to have
kept them off. (2) That the priests should themselves
bear the iniquity of the priesthood; that is, if they
either neglected any part of their work or permitted
any other persons to invade their office, and take
their work out of their hands, they should bear the
blame of it.

2. He tells him of the duty that attended his dignity.
(1) That he and his sons must *minister before the
tabernacle of witness* (*v.* 2); that is (as bishop Patrick
explains it), *before the most holy place*, in which the
ark was, on the outside of the veil of that tabernacle,
but within the door of the tabernacle of the congregation. They were to attend the golden altar,
the table, and candlestick, which no Levite might
approach to. *You shall serve, v.* 7. Not, "You
shall rule". Ministers must remember that they are
ministers, that is, servants, of whom it is required
that they be humble, diligent, and faithful. (2) That
the Levites must assist him and his sons, and minister
to them in all the *service of the tabernacle* (*v.* 2-4),
though they must by no means come nigh the vessels
of the sanctuary. (3) That both priests and Levites
must carefully watch against the profanation of sacred
things. The Levites must *keep the charge of the
tabernacle*. And the priests must *keep the charge of
the sanctuary* (*v.* 5), must instruct the people, and
admonish them concerning the due distance they were
to keep.

Verses 8-19

The priest's service is called a *warfare*; and who
goes a-warring at his own charges? As they were well

employed, so they were well provided for. Those
that *served at the altar lived upon the altar*, So those
that preach the gospel should *live upon the gospel*,
and live comfortably, 1 Cor. ix. 13, 14. Scandalous
maintenance makes scandalous ministers. Now
observe, 1. That much of the provision that was
made for them arose out of the sacrifices which they
themselves were employed to offer. 2. Their maintenance was such as left them altogether *disentangled
from the affairs of this life*. Thus provision is made
that a gospel ministry should continue till Christ
comes, by an ordinance for ever. *Lo, I am with you*
(that is their maintenance and support) *always, even
to the end of the world*.

Verses 20-32

A further account of the provision that was made
both for the Levites and for the priests, out of the
country.

I. They must have *no inheritance in the land*; only
cities to dwell in were afterwards allowed them, but
no ground to occupy. God dispenses his favours
variously. The Levites have the honour of attending
the tabernacle, which is denied the Israelites; but
then the Israelites have the honour of inheritances in
Canaan, which is denied the Levites.

II. But they must both have tithes of the land.
Besides the first-fruits which were appropriated to
the priests, the tithe also was appropriated. 1. The
Levites had the tithes of the people's increase (*v.* 21).
The Levites were the smallest tribe of the twelve,
and yet, besides all other advantages, they had a
tenth part of the yearly profits, without the trouble
and expense of ploughing and sowing. 2. The priests
had the tenths of the Levites' tithes settled upon
them. The order for this Moses is directed to give
to the Levites, whom God would have to pay it
with cheerfulness, rather than the priests to demand
it with authority. (1) The Levites were to give God
his dues out of their tithes, as well as the Israelites
out of their increase. Those that are employed to
assist the devotions of others must be sure to pay
their own, as a heave-offering to the Lord. Prayers
and praises lifted up to God, or rather the heart lifted
up in them, are now our heave-offerings. (2) This was
to be given to *Aaron the priest* (*v.* 28), and to his
successors the high priests, to be divided and disposed
of in such proportions as they should think fit among
the inferior priests.

CHAPTER 19

This chapter is only concerning the preparing and using of the
ashes which were to impregnate the water of purification. The
people had complained of the strictness of the law, which forbade
their near approach to the tabernacle, ch. xvii. 13. In answer to
this complaint, they are here directed to purify themselves, so as
that they might come as far as they had occasion without fear.
Here is, I. The method of preparing these ashes, by the burning
of a red heifer, with a great deal of ceremony, ver. 1-10. II. The
way of using them. 1. They were designed to purify persons from
the pollution contracted by a dead body, ver. 11-16. 2. They
were to be put into running water (a small quantity of them),
with which the person to be cleansed must be purified, ver. 17-22.
And that this ceremonial purification was a type and figure of
the cleansing of the conscience of believers from the pollutions
of sin appears by the apostle's discourse, Heb. ix. 13, 14, where he
compares the efficacy of the blood of Christ with the sanctifying
virtue that was in "the ashes of a heifer sprinkling the unclean."

Verses 1-10

We have here the divine appointment concerning
the solemn burning of a red heifer to ashes, and the
preserving of the ashes, that of them might be made,
not a beautifying, but a purifying, water, for that
was the utmost the law reached to; it offered not to
adorn as the gospel does, but to cleanse only.

I. There was a great deal of care employed in
the choice of the heifer that was to be burnt, much
more than in the choice of any other offering, *v.* 2.

It must not only be without blemish, typifying the spotless purity and sinless perfection of the Lord Jesus, but it must be a red heifer, because of the rarity of the colour, that it might be the more remarkable. And it must be one on which never came yoke, which was not insisted on in other sacrifices, but thus was typified the voluntary offer of the Lord Jesus, when he said, *Lo, I come.* He was bound and held with no other cords than those of his own love.

II. There was to be a great deal of ceremony in the burning of it. The care of doing it was committed to Eleazar. By him that was next to Aaron in dignity. Now,

1. The heifer was to be slain without the camp, as an impure thing, which bespeaks the insufficiency of the methods prescribed by the ceremonial law to take away sin.

2. Eleazar was to *sprinkle the blood directly before the door of the tabernacle,* and looking steadfastly towards it, *v.* 4. This made it in some sort an expiation; for the sprinkling of the blood before the Lord was the chief solemnity in all the sacrifices of atonement.

3. The heifer was to be *wholly burnt, v.* 5. The priest was to cast into the fire, while it was burning, cedarwood, hyssop, and scarlet, which were used in the cleansing of lepers (Lev. xiv. 6, 7), that the ashes of these might be mingled with the ashes of the heifer, because they were designed for purification.

4. The ashes of the heifer (separated as well as they could from the ashes of the wood wherewith it was burnt) were to be carefully gathered up by the hand of a clean person, and laid up for the use of the congregation, as there was occasion (*v.* 9).

5. All those that were employed in this service were made ceremonially unclean by it; even Eleazar himself, though he did but sprinkle the blood, *v.* 7. All the sacrifices which were offered for sin were therefore looked upon as impure, because the sins of men were laid upon them, as all our sins were upon Christ, who therefore is said to be *made sin for us,* 2 Cor. v. 21.

Verses 11–22

Directions are here given concerning the use and application of the ashes which were prepared for purification.

I. In what cases there needed a purification with these ashes. No other is mentioned here than the ceremonial uncleanness that was contracted by the touch of a dead body, or of the bone or grave of a dead man, or being in the tent or house where a dead body lay, *v.* 11, 14–16. The law could not conquer death, nor abolish it and alter the property of it, as the gospel does by bringing life and immortality to light, and so introducing a better hope. Since our Redeemer was dead and buried, death is no more destroying to the Israel of God, and therefore dead bodies are no more defiling; but while the church was under the law, the pollution contracted by dead bodies could not but form in their minds melancholy and uncomfortable notions concerning death, while believers now through Christ can triumph over it. *O grave! where is thy victory?* Where is thy pollution?

II. How the ashes were to be used and applied in these cases. 1. A small quantity of the ashes must be put into a cup of spring water, and mixed with the water, which thereby was made, as it is here called, a *water of separation,* because it was to be sprinkled on those who were separated or removed from the sanctuary by their uncleanness. As the ashes of the heifer signified the merit of Christ, so the running water signified the power and grace of the blessed Spirit, who is compared to rivers of living water; and it is by his operation that the righteousness of Christ is applied to us for our cleansing. 2. This

water must be applied by a bunch of hyssop dipped in it, with which the person or thing to be cleansed must be sprinkled (*v.* 18), in allusion to which David prays, *Purge me with hyssop.* Faith is the bunch of hyssop wherewith the conscience is sprinkled and the heart purified. The blood of Christ is said to be the *blood of sprinkling* (Heb. xii. 24), and with it we are said to be *sprinkled from an evil conscience* (Heb. x. 22), that is, we are freed from the uneasiness that arises from a sense of our guilt. And it is foretold that Christ, by his baptism, shall *sprinkle many nations,* Isa. lii. 15.

CHAPTER 20

At this chapter begins the history of the fortieth year (which was the last year) of the Israelites' wandering in the wilderness. And since the beginning of their second year, when they were sentenced to perform their quarantine in the desert, there to wear away the tedious revolution of forty years, there is little recorded concerning them till this last year, which brought them to the borders of Canaan, and the history of this year is almost as large as the history of the first year. This chapter gives an account of, I. The death of Miriam, ver. 1. II. The fetching of water out of the rock, in which observe, 1. The distress Israel was in, for want of water, ver. 2. 2. Their discontent and murmuring in that distress, ver. 3–5. 3. God's pity and power engaged for their supply with water out of the rock, ver. 6–9. 4. The infirmity of Moses and Aaron upon this occasion, ver. 10, 11. 5. God's displeasure against them, ver. 12, 13. III. The negotiation with the Edomites. Israel's request (ver. 14–17), and the repulse the Edomites gave them, ver. 18–21. IV. The death of Aaron the high priest upon Mount Hor, the instalment of Eleazar in his room, and the people's mourning for him, ver. 22, &c.

Verses 1–13

After thirty-eight years' tedious marches, or rather tedious rests, in the wilderness, backward towards the Red Sea, the armies of Israel now at length set their faces towards Canaan again, and had come not far off from the place where they were when, by the righteous sentence of divine Justice, they were made to begin their wanderings. Hitherto they had been led about as in a maze of labyrinth. They were now brought into the right way again; they abode in Kadesh (*v.* 1).

I. Here dies Miriam, the sister of Moses and Aaron, and as it should seem older than either of them. She must have been so if she was that sister that was set to watch Moses when he was put into the ark of bulrushes, Exod. ii. 4. *Miriam died there, v.* 1. She was a prophetess, and had been an instrument of much good to Israel, Mic. vi. 4. When Moses and Aaron with their rod went before them, to work wonders for them, Miriam with her timbrel went before them in praising God for these wondrous works (Exod. xv. 20), and therein did them real service; yet she had once been a murmurer (*ch.* xii. 1), and must not enter Canaan.

II. Here there is another Meribah.

1. *There was no water for the congregation, v.* 2. It is probable that for some time they had been in a country where they were supplied in an ordinary way, and when common providence supplied them it was fit that the miracle should cease. But in this place it fell out that there was no water, or not sufficient for the congregation.

2. Hereupon they murmured, mutinied (*v.* 2), *gathered themselves together,* and took up arms *against Moses and Aaron.* (1) They wished they had died as malefactors by the hands of divine justice, rather than thus seem for a while neglected by the divine mercy. (2) They were angry that they were brought out of Egypt, and led through this wilderness. The present want was of water only, yet, now that they are disposed to find fault, it shall be looked upon as an insufferable hardship put upon them that they have not vines and figs.

3. Moses and Aaron made them no reply, but retired to the door of the tabernacle to know God's mind in this case, *v.* 6.

4. God appeared, to determine the matter; not on his tribunal of justice, to sentence the rebels according to their deserts. But he appeared, (1) On his throne of glory, to silence their unjust murmuring (v. 6). Note, A believing sight of the glory of the Lord would be an effectual check to our lusts and passions, and would keep our mouths as with a bridle. (2) On his throne of grace, to satisfy their just desires. It was requisite that they should have water. Moses must a second time in God's name command water out of a rock for them, to show that God is as able as ever to supply his people with good things. (3) He bids him speak to the rock, which would do as it was bidden, to shame the people who had been so often spoken to, and would not hear nor obey. (4) He promises that the rock should give forth water (v. 8), and it did so (v. 11).

5. Moses and Aaron acted improperly in the management of this matter, so much so that God in displeasure told them immediately that they should not have the honour of bringing Israel into Canaan, v. 10–12.

(1) It is uncertain what it was in this management that was so provoking to God. The fault was complicated. *First*, God bade them *speak to the rock*, and they spoke *to the people*, and *smote the rock*, which at this time they were not ordered to do, but they thought speaking would not do. *Secondly*, They assumed too much of the glory of this work of wonder to themselves: *Must we fetch water?* as if it were done by some power or worthiness of theirs. *Thirdly*, Unbelief was the great transgression (v. 12): *You believed me not*. Dr. Lightfoot's notion of their unbelief is that they doubted whether now at last, when the forty years had expired, they should enter Canaan, and whether they must not for the murmurings of the people be condemned to another period of toil, because a new rock was now opened for their supply, which they took for an indication of their longer stay. *Fourthly*, They said and did all in heat and passion. *Fifthly*, That which aggravated all the rest, and made it the more provoking, was that it was public, *before the eyes of the children of Israel*, to whom they should have been examples of faith, and hope, and meekness.

(2) From the whole we may learn, [1] That the best of men have their failings. [2] That God judges not as man judges concerning sins.

Lastly, The place is hereupon called *Meribah*, v. 13. It is called *Meribah-Kadesh* (Deut. xxxii. 51), to distinguish it from the other Meribah. It is the *water of strife*; to perpetuate the remembrance of the people's sin, and Moses's, and yet of God's mercy, who supplied them with water, and owned and honoured Moses notwithstanding.

Verses 14–21

We have here the application made by Israel to the Edomites. The nearest way to Canaan from the place where Israel now lay encamped was through the country of Edom.

I. Moses sends ambassadors to treat with the king of Edom for leave to pass through his country. 1. They are to claim kindred with the Edomites. Both nations descended from Abraham and Isaac, their common ancestors. 2. They are to give a short account of the history and present state of Israel. And in this there was a double plea: (1) Israel had been abused by the Egyptians, and therefore ought to be pitied and succoured by their relations. (2) Israel had been wonderfully saved by the Lord, and therefore ought to be countenanced and favoured (v. 16). 3. They are humbly to beg a passport through their country. 4. They are to give security for the good behaviour of the Israelites in this march.

II. The ambassadors returned with a refusal,

v. 18. Edom, that is, the king of Edom, threatened, if they attempted to enter his country, it should be at their peril. This was owing, 1. To their jealousy of the Israelites. 2. It was owing to the old enmity which Esau bore to Israel. If they had no reason to fear damage by them, yet they were not willing to show so much kindness to them. Esau hated Jacob because of the blessing.

Verses 22–29

The chapter began with the funeral of Miriam, and it ends with the funeral of her brother Aaron.

I. God bids Aaron die, v. 24. 1. There is something of displeasure in these orders. Aaron must not enter Canaan, because he had failed in his duty at the waters of strife. The mention of this, no doubt, went to the heart of Moses, who knew himself, perhaps, at that time, to be the guiltier of the two. 2. There is much of mercy in them. Aaron, though he dies for his transgression, is not put to death as a malefactor, by a plague, or fire from heaven, but dies with ease and in honour. He is not *cut off from his people*, as the expression usually is concerning those that die by the hand of divine justice, but he is *gathered to his people*, as one that died in the arms of divine grace. 3. There is much of type and significancy in them. Aaron must not enter Canaan, to show that the Levitical priesthood could make nothing perfect: that must be done by the bringing in of a better hope.

II. Aaron submits, and dies in the method and manner appointed, and, for aught that appears, with as much cheerfulness as if he had been going to bed.

1. He puts on his holy garments to take his leave of them, and goes up with his brother and son to the top of Mount Hor, and probably some of the elders of Israel with him, v. 27. His going up the hill to die signified that the death of saints (and Aaron is called *the saint of the Lord*) is their ascension; they rather go up than go down to death.

2. Moses, whose hands had first clothed Aaron with his priestly garments, now strips him of them; for, in reverence to the priesthood, it was not fit that he should die in them.

3. Moses immediately puts the priestly garments upon Eleazar his son, clothes him with his father's robe, and *strengthens him with his girdle*, Isa. xxii. 21. Now, (1) This was a great comfort to Moses, a happy earnest and indication to the church of the care God would take that as one generation of ministers and Christians (spiritual priests) passes away another generation should come up instead of it. (2) It was a great satisfaction to Aaron to see his son, who was dear to him, thus preferred, and his office, which was dearer, thus preserved and secured. (3) It was a great kindness to the people.

CHAPTER 21

The armies of Israel now begin to emerge out of the wilderness, and to come into a land inhabited, to enter upon action, and take possession of the frontiers of the land of promise. I. The defeat of Arad the Canaanite, ver. 1–3. II. The chastisement of the people with fiery serpents for their murmurings, and the relief granted them upon their submission by a brazen serpent, ver. 4–9. III. Several marches forward, and some occurrences, by the way ver. 10–20. IV. The celebrated conquest of Sihon king of the Amorites (ver. 21–32), and of Og king of Bashan (ver. 33–35), and possession taken of their land.

Verses 1–3

1. The descent which Arad the Canaanite made upon the camp of Israel, hearing that they came *by way of the spies*; for, though the spies which Moses had sent thirty-eight years before then passed and repassed unobserved, yet their coming, and their errand, it is likely, were afterwards known to the Canaanites, gave them an alarm, and induced

them to keep an eye upon Israel. 2. His success at first in this attempt. His advance-guards picked up some straggling Israelites, and took them prisoners, *v.* 1. 3. Israel's humble address to God upon this occasion, *v.* 2. It was a temptation to them to murmur as their fathers did, and to despair of getting possession of Canaan; but God, who thus tried them by his providence, enabled them by his grace to quit themselves well in the trial, and to trust in him for relief. 4. The victory which the Israelites obtained over the Canaanites, *v.* 3. A strong party was sent out, probably under the command of Joshua, which not only drove back these Canaanites, but followed them to their cities and utterly destroyed them, and so returned to the camp. *Vincimur in praelio, sed non in bello—We lose a battle, but we finally triumph.* What is said of the tribe of Gad is true of all God's Israel, a troop may overcome them, but they shall overcome at the last.

Verses 4–9

I. The fatigue of Israel by a long march round the land of Edom, because they could not obtain passage through it the nearest way: *The soul of the people was much discouraged because of the way,* *v.* 4.

II. Their unbelief and murmuring upon this occasion, *v.* 5. They have *bread enough and to spare*; and yet they complain *there is no bread*, because, though they eat angels' food, yet they are weary of it; manna itself is loathed, and called *light bread*, fit for children, not for men and soldiers. What will those be pleased with whom manna will not please? Let not the contempt which some cast upon the word of God cause us to value it the less: it is the bread of life, substantial bread, and will nourish those who by faith feed upon it to eternal life, whoever calls it light bread.

III. The righteous judgment which God brought upon them for their murmurings, *v.* 6. He sent *fiery serpents among them*, which bit or stung many of them to death. The wilderness through which they had passed was all along infested with those fiery serpents, as appears, Deut. viii. 15. But hitherto God had wonderfully preserved his people from receiving hurt by them, till now that they murmured. These serpents are called *fiery*, from their colour, or from their rage, or from the effects of their bitings. They in their pride had lifted themselves up against God and Moses, and now God humbled and mortified them, by making these despicable animals a plague to them.

IV. Their repentance and supplication to God under this judgment, *v.* 7. They confess their fault: *We have sinned*. It is to be feared that they would not have owned the sin if they had not felt the smart. They beg the prayers of Moses for them. Afflictions often change men's sentiments concerning God's people, and teach them to value those prayers which, at a former period, they had scorned. Moses, to show that he had heartily forgiven them, blesses those who had cursed him, and *prays for those who had despitefully used him*. Herein he was a type of Christ, who interceded for his persecutors, and a pattern to us to go and do likewise, and thus to show that we *love our enemies*.

V. The wonderful provision which God made for their relief. God ordered Moses to make the representation of a fiery serpent, which he did, in brass, and set it up on a very long pole, so that it might be seen from all parts of the camp, and every one that was stung with a fiery serpent was healed by looking up to this serpent of brass. The people prayed that God would *take away the serpents from them* (*v.* 7), but God saw fit not to do this: for he gives effectual relief in the best way, though not in

our way. The Jews themselves say that it was not the sight of the brazen serpent that cured them, but, in looking up to it, they looked up to God as the Lord that healed them. But there was much of gospel in this appointment. Our Saviour has told us so (John iii. 14, 15), that *as Moses lifted up the serpent in the wilderness so the Son of man must be lifted up, that whosoever believeth in him should not perish.* Observe then a resemblance,

1. Between their disease and ours. The devil is the old serpent, a fiery serpent, hence he appears (Rev. xii. 3) as a *great red dragon*. Sin is the biting of this fiery serpent; it is painful to the startled conscience, and poisonous to the seared conscience. Satan's temptations are called his *fiery darts*, Eph. vi. 16.

2. Between their remedy and ours. (1) It was God himself that devised and prescribed this antidote against the fiery serpents; so our salvation by Christ was the contrivance of Infinite Wisdom; God himself has found the ransom. (2) It was a very unlikely method of cure; so our salvation by the death of Christ is *to the Jews a stumbling-block and to the Greeks foolishness.* (3) That which cured was shaped in the likeness of that which wounded. So Christ, though perfectly free from sin himself, yet was *made in the likeness of sinful flesh* (Rom. viii. 3), so like that it was taken for granted that this man was a sinner, John ix. 24. (4) The brazen serpent was lifted up; so was Christ. He was lifted up upon the cross (John xii. 33, 34), for he was made a spectacle to the world. He was lifted up by the preaching of the gospel. The word here used for a *pole* signifies a *banner*, or *ensign*, for Christ crucified *stands for an ensign of the people*, Isa. xi. 10. Some make the lifting up of the serpent to be a figure of Christ's triumphing over Satan, the old serpent, whose head he bruised, when in his cross he made an open show of the principalities and powers which he had spoiled and destroyed, Col. ii. 15.

3. Between the application of their remedy and ours. They looked and lived, and we, if we believe, shall not perish; it is by faith that we look unto Jesus, Heb. xii. 2. *Look unto me, and be you saved,* Isa. xlv. 22. Whoever looked up to this healing sign, though from the outmost part of the camp, though with a weak and weeping eye, was certainly healed; so whosoever believes in Christ, though as yet but weak in faith, shall not perish.

Verses 10–20

We have here an account of the several stages and removals of the children of Israel, till they came into the plains of Moab, out of which they at length passed over Jordan into Canaan, as we read in the beginning of Joshua. Natural motions are quicker the nearer they are to their centre. The Israelites were now drawing near to the promised rest, and now they *set forward*, as the expression is, *v.* 10. It were well if we would do thus in our way to heaven, and the nearer we come to heaven be so much the more active and abundant in the work of the Lord. Two things especially are observable:

1. The wonderful success which God blessed his people with, near the brooks of Arnon, *v.* 13–15. They had now compassed the land of Edom. It is well that there are more ways than one to Canaan. The enemies of God's people may retard their passage, but cannot prevent their entrance into the promised rest. Care is taken to let us know that the Israelites in their march religiously observed the orders which God gave them to use no hostility against the Moabites (Deut. ii. 9), because they were the posterity of righteous Lot.

2. The wonderful supply which God blessed his people with at *Beer* (*v.* 16), which signifies the *well*

or *fountain*. Hitherto we have found, when they were supplied with water, they asked it in unjust discontent, and God gave it in just displeasure; but here we find, (1) That God gave it in love (*v.* 16): *Gather the people together*, to be witnesses of the wonder, and joint-sharers in the favour, *and I will give them water*. Before they prayed, God granted. (2) That they received it with joy and thankfulness, which made the mercy doubly sweet to them, *v.* 17. Then they sang this song, to the glory of God and the encouragement of one another, *Spring up, O well!* Thus they pray that it may spring up, for promised mercies must be fetched in by prayer. As the brazen serpent was a figure of Christ, who is lifted up for our cure, so is this well a figure of the Spirit, who is poured forth for our comfort, and from whom flow to us *rivers of living waters*, John vii. 38. (3) That whereas before the remembrance of the miracle was perpetuated in the names given to the places, which signified the people's strife and murmuring, now it was perpetuated in a song of praise. *The princes digged the well*—the seventy elders; with their staves they made holes in the soft sandy ground, and God caused the water miraculously to spring up in the holes which they made. God promised to give them water, but they must open the ground to receive it, and give it vent. God's favours must be expected in the use of such means as lie within our power, but still the excellency of the power is of God.

Verses 21–35

An account of the victories obtained by Israel over Sihon and Og.

I. Israel sent a peaceable message to Sihon king of the Amorites (*v.* 21), but received an unpeaceable return. Sihon's army was routed, and not only so, but all his country came into the possession of Israel, *v.* 24, 25. This seizure is justified, 1. Against the Amorites themselves, for they were the aggressors, and provoked the Israelites to battle. 2. Against the Moabites, who had formerly been the lords-proprietors of this country. (1) The justification itself is that though it was true this country had belonged to the Moabites, yet the Amorites had taken it from them some time before, and were now in full and quiet possession of it, *v.* 26. This country being designed in due time for Israel, it is beforehand put into the hand of the Amorites, who little think that they have it but as trustees till Israel come of age, and then must surrender it. We understand not the vast reaches of Providence, but known unto God are all his works, as appears in this instance. (2) For proof of the allegation, he refers to the authentic records of the country, for so their proverbs or songs were, one of which he quotes some passages out of (*v.* 27–30), which sufficiently proves what is vouched for, namely, [1] That such and such places that are here named, though they had been in the possession of the Moabites, had by right of war become the dominion of Sihon king of the Amorites. [2] That the Moabites were utterly disabled and even Chemosh their god had given them up, as unable to rescue them out of the hands of Sihon, *v.* 29.

II. Og king of Bashan, instead of being warned by the fate of his neighbours to make peace with Israel, is instigated by it to make war with them, which proves in like manner to be his destruction. Og was also an Amorite, and more likely to prevail, because of his own gigantic strength and stature. Here observe, 1. That the Amorite begins the war (*v.* 33). His country was very rich and pleasant. Bashan was famous for the best timber (witness the oaks of Bashan), and the best breed of cattle, witness the bulls and kine of Bashan, and the lambs and rams of that country, which are celebrated, Deut. xxxii. 14. 2. That God interests himself in the cause, bids Israel

not to fear this threatening force. Giants are but worms before God's power. 3. That Israel not only routs the enemies' army, but gains the enemies' country, which afterwards was part of the inheritance of the two tribes and a half that were first seated on the other side Jordan.

CHAPTER 22

At this chapter begins the famous story of Balak and Balaam, their attempt to curse Israel, and the baffling of that attempt; God's people are long afterwards told to remember what Balak the king of Moab consulted, and what Balaam the son of Beor answered him, that they might know the righteousness of the Lord, Mic. vi. 5. In this chapter we have, I. Balak's fear of Israel, and the plot he had to get them cursed, ver. 1–4. II. The embassy he sent to Balaam, a conjurer, to fetch him for that purpose, and the disappointment he met with in the first embassy, ver. 5–14. III. Balaam's coming to him upon his second message, ver. 15–21. IV. The opposition Balaam met with by the way, ver. 22–35. V. The interview at length between Balak and Balaam, ver. 36, &c.

Verses 1–14

The children of Israel have at length finished their wanderings in the wilderness out of which they went up (*ch.* xxi. 18), and are now encamped in the plains of Moab near Jordan, where they continued till they passed through Jordan under Joshua, after the death of Moses.

I. The fright which the Moabites were in upon the approach of Israel, *v.* 2–4. Notwithstanding the old friendship between Abraham and Lot, the Moabites resolved to ruin Israel if they could, and therefore they will take it for granted, without any ground for the suspicion, that Israel resolves to ruin them. These fears they communicated to their neighbours, the elders of Midian, that some measures might be concerted between them for their common safety. They had reason to court Israel's friendship, and to come in to their assistance; but having forsaken the religion of their father Lot, and being sunk into idolatry, they hated the people of the God of Abraham.

II. The project which the king of Moab formed to get the people of Israel cursed, that is, to set God against them. He trusted more to his arts than to his arms, and had a notion that if he could get but some prophet or other, with his powerful charms, to imprecate evil upon them, and to pronounce a blessing upon himself and his forces, then, though otherwise too weak, he should be able to deal with them. This notion arose, 1. Out of the remains of some religion; for it owns a dependence upon some visible sovereign powers that rule in the affairs of the children of men. 2. Out of the ruins of the true religion; for if the Midianites and Moabites had not wretchedly degenerated from the faith and worship of their pious ancestors, Abraham and Lot, they could not have imagined it possible to do any mischief with their curses to a people who alone adhered to the service of the true God, from whose service they had themselves revolted.

III. The court which he made to Balaam the son of Beor, a famous conjurer, to engage him to curse Israel. This Balaam lived a great way off, in that country whence Abraham came, and where Laban lived. And to gain him, 1. He makes him his friend. 2. In effect he makes him his god, by the great power he attributes to his word.

IV. The restraint God lays upon Balaam, forbidding him to curse Israel. He lodges the messengers, and takes a night's time to consider what he shall do, and to receive instructions from God, *v.* 8. In the night God comes to him, probably in a dream, and enquires what business those strangers had with him. He knows it, but he will know it from him. Balaam gives him an account of their errand (*v.* 9–11), and God thereupon charges him not to go with them, nor attempt to curse that blessed people, *v.* 12. Balaam is charged not only not to go to Balak, but not to offer to curse this people, which he might have attempted at a distance; and the reason is given: *They are blessed.*

V. The return of the messengers without Balaam. 1. Balaam is not faithful in returning God's answer to the messengers, *v.* 13. He only tells them, *The Lord refuseth to give me leave to go with you.* He did not tell them, as he ought to have done, that Israel was a blessed people, and must by no means be cursed.

Verses 15–21

A second embassy sent to Balaam, to fetch him over to curse Israel.

I. The temptation Balak laid before Balaam. Now he tempted him with honours, laid a bait not only for his covetousness, but for his pride and ambition. See how artfully Balak managed the temptation. 1. The messengers he sent were *more*, and *more honourable*, *v.* 15. 2. The request was very urgent. This powerful prince becomes a suitor to him: "*Let nothing, I pray thee, hinder thee* (*v.* 16), no, not God, nor conscience, nor any fear either of sin or shame.*" 3. The proffers were high: "*I will promote thee to very great honour* among the princes of Moab."

II. Balaam's seeming resistance of, but real yielding to, this temptation. We may here discern in Balaam a struggle between his convictions and his corruptions. 1. His convictions charged him to adhere to the command of God, and he spoke their language, *v.* 18. Nor could any man have said better: "*If Balak would give me his house full of silver and gold, and that is more than he can give or I can ask, I cannot go beyond the word of the Lord my God.*" 2. His corruptions at the same time strongly inclined him to go contrary to the command. He seemed to refuse the temptation, *v.* 18. But even then he expressed no abhorrence of it, as Christ did when he had the kingdoms of the world offered him (*Get thee hence, Satan*), and as Peter did when Simon Magus offered him money: *Thy money perish with thee.* But it appears (*v.* 19) that he had a strong inclination to accept the proffer; for he would further attend, to know what God would say to him, hoping that he might alter his mind and give him leave to go. This was a vile reflection upon God Almighty, as if he could change his mind. Note, It is a very great affront to God, and a certain evidence of the dominion of corruption in the heart, to beg leave to sin.

III. The permission God gave him to go, *v.* 20. God came to him, probably by an angel, and told him he might, if he pleased, go with Balak's messengers. *So he gave him up to his own heart's lust.* Note, As God sometimes denies the prayers of his people in love, so sometimes he grants the desires of the wicked in wrath.

Verses 22–35

An account of the opposition God gave to Balaam in his journey towards Moab.

I. Here is God's displeasure against Balaam for undertaking this journey: God's *anger was kindled because he went, v.* 22. Note, 1. The sin of sinners is not to be thought the less provoking to God because he permits it. 2. Nothing is more displeasing to God than malicious designs against his people; he that touches them touches the apple of his eye.

II. The way God took to let Balaam know his displeasure against him: *An angel stood in the way for an adversary.*

1. Balaam had notice given him of God's displeasure, by the ass, and this *did not startle him.* The *ass saw the angel, v.* 23. How vainly did Balaam boast that he was a man whose *eyes were open*, and that he *saw the visions of the Almighty* (ch. xxiv. 3, 4),

when the ass he rode on saw more than he did, his eyes being blinded with covetousness and ambition. Let none be puffed up with a conceit of visions and revelations, when even an ass saw an angel; to save both herself and her senseless rider, (1) She *turned aside out of the way, v.* 23. Balaam should have taken the hint of this, and considered whether he was not out of the way of his duty; but, instead of this, he *beat her into the way again.* Thus those who by wilful sin are running headlong into perdition are angry at those that would prevent their ruin. (2) She had not gone much further before she saw the angel again, and then, to avoid him, *ran up to a wall*, and *crushed her rider's foot, v.* 24, 25. The crushing of Balaam's foot, though it was the saving of his life, provoked him so much that he smote his ass the second time. (3) Upon the next encounter with the angel, the ass fell down under Balaam, *v.* 26, 27. Balaam the third time smote his ass, though she had now done him the best piece of service that ever she did him, saving him from the sword of the angel, and by her falling down teaching him to do likewise. (4) When all this would not work upon him, God opened the mouth of the ass, and she spoke to him once and again; and yet neither did this move him. Here Mr. Ainsworth observes that the devil, when he tempted our first parents to sin, employed a subtle serpent, but that God, when he would convince Balaam, employed a silly ass, a creature dull and sottish to a proverb. [1] The ass complained of Balaam's cruelty (*v.* 28): *What have I done unto thee, that thou hast smitten me?* Note, The righteous God will not see the meanest and weakest abused; but either they shall be enabled to speak in their own defence or he will some way or other speak for them. His brutish head-strong passion so blinded him that he could not observe or consider the strangeness of the thing. Nothing besots men worse than unbridled anger. [2] The ass reasoned with him, *v.* 30. God enabled not only a dumb creature to speak, but a dull creature to speak to the purpose.

2. Balaam at length had notice of God's displeasure by the angel, and this did startle him. When God opened his eyes *he saw the angel* (*v.* 31), and then he himself *fell flat upon his face.* God has many ways of breaking and bringing down the hard and unhumbled heart. (1) The angel reproved him for his outrageousness (*v.* 32, 33): *Wherefore hast thou smitten thy ass?* (2) Balaam then seemed to relent (*v.* 34): "*I have sinned*, sinned in undertaking this journey, sinned in pushing on so violently"; but he excused it with this, that he saw not the angel; yet, now that he did see him, he was willing to go back again. Here is no sign that his heart is turned, but, if his hands are tied, he cannot help it. Thus many leave their sins only because their sins have left them. There seems to be a reformation of the life, but what will this avail if there be no renovation of the heart? (3) The angel however continued his permission: "*Go with the men, v.* 35. Go, if thou hast a mind to be made a fool of, and to be shamed before Balak, and all the princes of Moab. *Go, only the word that I shall speak unto thee, that thou shalt speak*, whether thou wilt or no," for this seems not to be a precept but a prediction of the event, that he should not only not be able to curse Israel, but should be forced to bless them.

Verses 36–41

We have here the meeting between Balak and Balaam, confederate enemies to God's Israel; but here they seem to differ in their expectations of the success. 1. Balak speaks of it with confidence, not doubting but to gain his point now that Balaam had come. 2. Balaam speaks doubtfully of the issue, and bids Balak not depend too much upon him (*v.* 38): "*Have I now any power at all to say any thing?*

Gladly would I curse Israel; but I must not, I cannot, God will not suffer me." 3. They address themselves with all speed to the business. Balaam is nobly entertained over night, a sacrifice of thanksgiving is offered to the gods of Moab, for the safe arrival of this welcome guest, and he is treated with a feast upon the sacrifice, *v.* 40. And the next morning, that no time might be lost, Balak takes Balaam in his chariot to the high places of his kingdom. And now Balaam is really as solicitous to please Balak as ever he had pretended to be to please God.

CHAPTER 23

In this chapter we have Balak and Balaam busy at work to do Israel a mischief, and, for aught that appears, neither Moses nor the elders of Israel know any thing of the matter, but God baffles the attempt, without any intercession or contrivance of theirs. Here is, I. The first attempt to curse Israel. 1. The preparation made for it by sacrifice, ver. 1–3. 2. The contrary instruction God gave Balaam, ver. 4, 5. 3. The blessing Balaam was compelled to pronounce upon Israel, instead of a curse, ver. 7–10. 4. The great disappointment of Balak, ver. 11, 12. II. The second attempt, in the same manner made, and in the same manner frustrated, ver. 13–26. III. Preparations made for a third attempt (ver. 27–30), the issue of which we have in the next chapter.

Verses 1–12

I. Great preparation made for the cursing of Israel. That which was aimed at was to engage the God of Israel to forsake them, and either to be on Moab's side or to stand neutral, as if he would *eat the flesh of bulls or drink the blood of goats.* Ridiculous nonsense, to think that these would please God, and gain his favour, when there could be in them no exercise either of faith or obedience! Yet, it should seem, they offered these sacrifices to the God of heaven, the supreme *Numen— Divinity*, and not to any of their local deities.

II. The turning of the curse into a blessing, by the overruling power of God, in love to Israel, which is the account Moses gives of it, Deut. xxiii. 5.

1. God puts the blessing into the mouth of Balaam. While the sacrifices were burning, Balaam retired: he *went solitary*, into some dark grove on the top of the high place, *v.* 3, marg. Thus much he knew, that solitude gives a good opportunity for communion with God. But Balaam retired with a peradventure only, having some thoughts that God might meet him; but being conscious to himself of guilt, and knowing that God had lately met him in anger, he had reason to speak doubtfully: *Peradventure the Lord will come to meet me, v.* 3. But, whatever he intended, God designed to serve his own glory by him, and therefore *met Balaam, v.* 4. God would constrain him to utter such a confession, to the honour of God and Israel, as should render those for ever inexcusable who should appear in arms against them. When Balaam was aware that God met him, he boasted of his performances: *I have prepared seven altars, and offered upon every altar a bullock and a ram.* However, though the sacrifice was an abomination, God took the occasion of Balaam's expectation to *put a word into his mouth* (*v.* 5).

2. Balaam pronounces the blessing in the ears of Balak. He pronounces Israel safe and happy, and so blesses them.

(1) He pronounces them safe, and out of the reach of his envenomed darts. [1] He owns that the design was to curse them, that Balak sent for him out of his own country, and that he came, with that intent, *v.* 7. [2] He owns the design defeated, and his own inability to accomplish it. He could not so much as give them an ill word or an ill wish: *How shall I curse those whom God has not cursed? v.* 8. Not that therefore he would not do it, but therefore he could not do it. This is a fair confession, *First,* Of the weakness and impotency of his own magic skill. *Secondly,* It is a confession of the sovereignty and dominion of

the divine power. He owns that he could do no more than God would suffer him to do. *Thirdly,* It is a confession of the inviolable security of the people of God.

(2) He pronounces them happy in three things:—

[1] Happy in their peculiarity, and distinction from the rest of the nations: *From the top of the rock I see him, v.* 9. And it seems to have been a great surprise to him that whereas, it is probable, they were represented to him as a rude and disorderly rabble, that infested the countries round about in rambling parties, he saw them a regular incorporated camp, in which appeared all the marks of discipline and good order. Note, It is the duty and honour of those that are dedicated to God to be separated from the world. Those who make conscience of peculiar duties may take the comfort of peculiar privileges.

[2] Happy in their numbers, not so few and despicable as they were represented to him, but an innumerable company, which made them both honourable and formidable (*v.* 10): *Who can count the dust of Jacob?* The number of the people was the thing that Balak was vexed at (*ch.* xxii. 3). He takes notice of the number, *First,* Of the *dust of Jacob;* that is, the people of Jacob, concerning whom it was foretold that they should be as the dust for number, Gen. xxviii. 14. *Secondly,* Of the *fourth part of Israel,* alluding to the form of their camp, which was cast into four squadrons, under four standards.

[3] Happy in their end: *Let me die the death of the righteous* Israelites, that are in covenant with God, and let my *last end, or future state, be like theirs, or my recompence,* namely, in the other world. Here, *First,* It is taken for granted that death is the end of all men; the righteous themselves must die: and it is good for us to think of this with application, as Balaam himself does here, speaking of his own death. *Secondly,* He goes upon the supposition of the soul's immortality, and a different state on the other side death, to which this is a noble testimony, and an evidence of its being anciently known and believed. *Thirdly,* He pronounces the righteous truly blessed, not only while they live, but when they die. *Fourthly,* He shows his opinion of religion to be better than his resolution; there are many who desire to die the death of the righteous, but do not endeavour to live the life of the righteous. Gladly would they have their end like theirs, but not their way. They would be saints in heaven, but not saints on earth. Now,

III. We are told, 1. How Balak fretted at it, *v.* 11. He pretended to honour the Lord with his sacrifices, and to wait for the answer God would send him; and yet, when it did not prove according to his mind, he forgot God. 2. How Balaam was forced to acquiesce in it. He submits because he cannot help it.

Verses 13–30

Here is, I. Preparation made the second time, as before, for the cursing of Israel. 1. The place is changed, *v.* 13. 2. The sacrifices are repeated, new altars are built, a bullock and a ram offered on every altar, and Balak attends his sacrifice as closely as ever, *v.* 14, 15. 3. Balaam renews his attendance on God, and God meets him the second time, and puts another word into his mouth, not to reverse the former, but to ratify it, *v.* 16, 17.

II. A second conversion of the curse into a blessing by the overruling power of God; and this blessing is both larger and stronger than the former, and quite cuts off all hopes of altering it. Balak having been so forward to ask what the Lord had spoken (*v.* 17), Balaam now addresses himself particularly to him (*v.* 18): *Rise up, Balak, and hear.*

1. Two things Balaam in this discourse informs Balak of:—

(1) That he had no reason to hope that he should ruin Israel.

[1] It would be to no purpose to attempt to ruin them.

First, Because God is unchangeable. He never changes his mind, and therefore never recalls his promise.

Secondly, Because Israel are at present unblamable. There was no idolatry among them, which is in a particular manner called iniquity and perverseness. Balaam knew that nothing would separate between them and God but sin.

Thirdly, Because the power of both was irresistible. They had the presence of God with them. They had the joy of that presence, and were always made to triumph in it.

[2] From all this he infers that it was to no purpose for him to think of doing them a mischief by all the arts he could use, *v.* 23. The curses of hell can never take place against the blessings of heaven.

(2) Balaam shows him that he had more reason to fear being ruined by them, for they were likely to make bloody work among his neighbours; and, if he and his country escaped, it was not because he was too great for them to meddle with, but because he fell not within their commission, *v.* 24.

2. Now what was the issue of this disappointment?

(1) Balak and Balaam were both of them sick of the cause. Balak is now willing to have his conjurer silenced. If thou canst not curse them, I beseech thee not to bless them. Balaam is still willing to own himself overruled, and appeals to what he had said in the beginning of this enterprise (*ch.* xxii. 38): *All that the Lord speaketh, that I must do, v.* 26.

(2) Yet they resolve to make another attempt. The place to which Balak now took Balaam was the top of Peor, the most eminent high place in all his country, where, it is probable, Baal was worshipped, and it was thence called *Baal-peor*.

CHAPTER 24

This chapter continues and concludes the history of the defeat of the counsels of Balak and Balaam against Israel, not by might, nor by power, but by the Spirit of the Lord of hosts. In this chapter we are told, I. What the blessing was into which that intended curse was turned, ver. 1–9. II. How Balak dismissed Balaam from his service thereupon, ver. 10–13. III. The predictions Balaam left behind him concerning Israel, and some of the neighbouring nations, ver. 14, &c.

Verses 1–9

The blessing itself which Balaam here pronounces upon Israel is much the same with the two we had in the foregoing chapter; but the introduction to it is different.

I. The method of proceeding here varies. Balaam laid aside the enchantments which he had hitherto depended on, used no spells, or charms, or magic arts, finding they did him no service; it was to no purpose to deal with the devil for a curse, when it was plain that God was determined immovably to bless, *v.* 1. He did not now retire into a solitary place as before, but set his face directly towards the wilderness where Israel lay encamped. Now *the Spirit of God came upon him,* that is, the Spirit of prophecy. He used a different preface now from what he had used before (*v.* 3, 4), yet savouring very much (as some think) of pride and vain-glory, taking all the praise of this prophecy to himself, and magnifying himself as one of the cabinet-council of heaven. When he attempted to curse Israel, he owns, he was in a mistake, but now he began to see his error, and yet still he remained blinded by covetousness and ambition, those foolish and hurtful lusts. Many have their eyes open that have not their hearts open, are enlightened, but not sanctified.

II. Yet the blessing is for substance the same with those before. Several things he admires in Israel:—

1. Their beauty (*v.* 5): *How goodly are thy tents,*

O Jacob! Though they dwelt not in stately palaces, but in coarse and homely tents, and these, no doubt, sadly weather-beaten, yet Balaam sees a beauty in those tents, because of their admirable order, according to their tribes, *v.* 2. Nothing recommends religion more to the good opinion of those that look upon it at a distance than the unity and harmony of its professors, Ps. cxxxiii. 1.

2. Their fruitfulness and increase. This may be intended by those similitudes (*v.* 6) of the valleys, gardens, and trees, as well as by those expressions (*v.* 7), *He shall pour the water out of his buckets;* that is, God shall water them with his blessing like rain from heaven, and then his *seed shall be in many waters.*

3. Their honour and advancement. As the multitude of the people is the honour of the prince, so the magnificence of the prince is the honour of the people; Balaam therefore foretells that their *king shall be higher than Agag.* Agag, it is probable, was the most potent monarch in those parts.

4. Their power and victory, *v.* 8. (1) He looks back upon what they had done, or rather what had been done for them: *God brought them forth out of Egypt;* this he had spoken of before, *ch.* xxiii. 22. (2) He looks down upon their present strength. (3) He looks forward to their future conquests.

5. Their courage and security: *He lay down as a lion, as a great lion, v.* 9. Lions do not retire into places of shelter to sleep, but lie down anywhere, knowing that none dares meddle with them.

6. Their interest, and influence upon their neighbours. Their friends, and those in alliance with them, were happy.

Verses 10–14

We have here the conclusion of this vain attempt to curse Israel, and the total abandonment of it. 1. Balak made the worst of it. He broke out into a rage against Balaam (*v.* 10). He forbade him his presence, expelled him his country, upbraided him with the preferments he had designed to bestow upon him, but now would not (*v.* 11). 2. Balaam made the best of it. (1) He endeavours to excuse the disappointment. Balak could not say that he had cheated him, since he had given him fair notice of the check he found himself under. (2) He endeavours to atone for it, *v.* 14. He will gratify his curiosity with some predictions concerning the nations about him. He will satisfy him with an assurance that, whatever this formidable people should do to his people, it should not be till the latter days. He will put him into a method of doing Israel a mischief without the ceremonies of enchantment and execration. Since he could not have leave from God to curse them, he puts him in a way of getting help from the devil to tempt them.

Verses 15–25

The office of prophets was both to bless and to prophesy in the name of the Lord.

I. He personates a true prophet admirably well, God permitting and directing him to do so, because, whatever he was, the prophecy itself was a true prophecy. *He saw the vision of the Almighty,* but not so as to be *changed into the same image.* He calls God the *Most High,* and the *Almighty.* Yet he had no true fear of him, love to him, or faith in him, so far may a man go towards heaven, and yet come short.

II. Here is his prophecy concerning him that should be the crown and glory of his people Israel, who is, 1. David, the type under whom the forces of Israel should *do valiantly, v.* 18. This was fulfilled when David smote Moab, 2 Sam. viii. 2. And at the same time the Edomites likewise were brought into obedience to Israel, *v.* 14. But, 2. Our Lord Jesus, the promised Messiah, is chiefly pointed at in the antitype, and of him it is an illustrious prophecy; it was the will of God that notice should thus be given of his coming, a great while before, not only to the people of the Jews, but to other nations, because his gospel and kingdom were to extend themselves so far beyond the borders of the land of Israel. It is here foretold, (1) That his coming should not be yet for a great while: "*I shall see him, but not now*; I do see him in vision, but at a very great distance, through the interposing space of 1,500 years at least. (2) That he shall come out of Jacob, and Israel, as a star and a sceptre, the former denoting his glory and lustre, as the *bright and morning star*, the latter his power and authority; it is *he that shall have dominion*. (3) That his kingdom shall be universal, and victorious over all opposition, which was typified by David's victories over Moab and Edom. Christ shall be king, not only of Jacob and Israel, but of all the world.

III. Here is his prophecy concerning the Amalekites and Kenites, part of whose country, it is probable, he had now in view. 1. The Amalekites were now the *chief of the nations* (*v.* 20). Here Balaam confirms that doom of Amalek which Moses had read (Exod. xvii. 14, 16). 2. The Kenites were now the securest of the nations; their situation was such as that nature was their engineer, and had strongly fortified them: "*Thou puttest thy nest* (like the eagle) *in a rock, v.* 21. Thou thinkest thyself safe, and yet the *Kenites shall be wasted* (*v.* 22) and gradually brought to decay, till they be carried away captive by the Assyrians," which was done at the captivity of the ten tribes. Even a nest in a rock will be no perpetual security.

IV. Here is a prophecy that looks as far forward as the Greeks and Romans, for theirs is supposed to be meant by the *coast of Chittim, v.* 24.

1. The introduction to this parable; this article of his prophecy is very observable (*v.* 23): *Alas! who shall live when God doeth this?* Either, (1) These events are so distant, and so far off to come, that it is hard to say *who shall live till they come*. Or, (2) They will be so dismal, and make such desolations, that scarcely any will escape or be left alive.

2. The prophecy itself is observable. Both Greece and Italy lie much upon the sea, and therefore their armies were sent forth mostly in ships. Now he seems here to foretell, (1) That the forces of the Grecians should humble and bring down the Assyrians, who were united with the Persians, which was fulfilled when the eastern country was overrun by Alexander. (2) That theirs and the Roman forces should afflict the Hebrews, or Jews, who were called *the children of Eber*; this was fulfilled in part when the Grecian empire was oppressive to the Jewish nation, but chiefly when the Roman empire ruined it. But, (3) That Chittim, that is, the Roman empire, in which the Grecian was at length swallowed up, should itself perish when the stone cut out of the mountain without hands shall consume all these kingdoms, and particularly the *feet of iron and clay*, Dan. ii. 34. Thus (says Dr. Lightfoot) Balaam, instead of cursing the church, curses Amalek the first, and Rome the last enemy of the church.

CHAPTER 25

Israel, having escaped the curse of Balaam, here sustains a great deal of damage and reproach by the counsel of Balaam, who, it seems, before he left Balak, put him into a more effectual way than that which Balak thought of to separate between the Israelites and their God. None are more fatally bewitched than those that are bewitched by their own lusts. Here is, I. The sin of Israel; they were enticed by the daughters of Moab both to whoredom and to idolatry, ver. 1–3. II. The punishment of this sin by the hand of the magistrate (ver. 4, 5) and by the immediate hand of God, ver. 9. III. The pious zeal of Phinehas in slaying

Zimri and Cozbi, two impudent sinners, ver. 6, 8, 14, 15. IV. God's commendation of the zeal of Phinehas, ver. 10–13. V. Enmity put between the Israelites and the Midianites, their tempters, as at first between the woman and the serpent, ver. 16, &c.

Verses 1–5

I. The sin of Israel, to which they were enticed by the daughters of Moab and Midian; they were guilty both of corporal and spiritual whoredoms, for *Israel joined himself unto Baal-peor, v.* 3. Not all, nor the most, but very many, were taken in this snare. Now concerning this observe, That whoredom and idolatry went together. They first defiled and debauched their consciences, by committing lewdness with the women, and then were easily drawn, in complaisance to them, and in contempt of the God of Israel, to bow down to their idols. And they were more likely to do so if, as it is commonly supposed, and seems probable by the joining of them together, the uncleanness committed was a part of the worship and service performed to Baal-peor. It was a great aggravation of the sin that *Israel abode in Shittim*, where they had the land of Canaan in view, and were just ready to enter and take possession of it.

II. God's just displeasure against them for this sin. Israel's whoredoms did that which all Balaam's enchantments could not do. 1. A plague immediately broke out. Epidemical diseases are the just punishments of epidemical sins; one infection follows the other. 2. The ringleaders are ordered to be put to death by the hand of public justice, which will be the only way to stay the plague (*v.* 4). The judges must first order them to be *slain with the sword* (*v.* 5), and their dead bodies must be hanged up, that the stupid Israelites might be possessed with a sense of the evil of the sin.

Verses 6–15

Here is a remarkable contest between wickedness and righteousness, and righteousness carries the day, as no doubt it will at last.

I. Never was vice more daring than it was in Zimri, *a prince of a chief house* in the tribe of Simeon. He publicly appeared leading a Midianitish harlot in the sight of Moses, and all the good people of Israel. It was an affront to the justice of the nation, and bade defiance to that. It was an affront to the religion of the nation, and put a contempt upon that.

II. Never was virtue more daring than it was in Phinehas. Being aware of the insolence of Zimri, in a holy indignation at the offenders he rises up from his prayers, takes his sword or half-pike, follows those impudent sinners into their tent, and stabs them both, *v.* 7, 8. It is not at all difficult to justify Phinehas in what he did; for, being now heir-apparent to the highpriesthood, no doubt he was one of those judges of Israel whom Moses had ordered, by the divine appointment, to slay all those whom they knew to have joined themselves to Baal-peor. God testified his acceptance of the pious zeal of Phinehas. He put an honour upon Phinehas. Though he did no more than it was his duty to do as a judge, yet because he did it with extraordinary zeal against sin, and did it when the other judges, out of respect to Zimri's character as a prince, were afraid, God showed himself particularly well pleased with him, and it *was counted to him for righteousness*, Ps. cvi. 31. Phinehas, upon this occasion, though a young man, is pronounced his country's patriot and best friend, *v.* 11. The priesthood is entailed by covenant upon his family. It was designed for him before, but now it was confirmed to him.

Verses 16–18

God had punished the Israelites for their sin with a plague; as a Father he corrected his own children with a rod. The mischief which the Midianites did to Israel by enticing them to whoredom must be remembered and punished with as much severity as that which the Amalekites did in fighting with them when they came out of Egypt, Exod. xvii. 14.

CHAPTER 26

This book is called Numbers, from the numberings of the children of Israel, of which it gives an account. Once they were numbered at Mount Sinai, in the first year after they came out of Egypt, which we had an account of, ch. i. and ii. And now a second time they were numbered in the plains of Moab, just before they entered Canaan, and of this we have an account in this chapter. We have, I. Orders given for the doing of it, ver. 1–4. II. A register of the families and numbers of each tribe (ver. 5–50), and the sum total, ver. 51. III. Direction given to divide the land among them, ver. 52–56. IV. The families and numbers of the Levites by themselves, ver. 57–62. V. Notice taken of the fulfilling of the threatening in the death of all those that were first numbered (ver. 63–65), and to this there seems to have been a special regard in the taking and keeping of this account.

Verses 1–4

Moses did not number the people but when God commanded him. David in his time did it without a command, and paid dearly for it. God now appointed him to take the sum of them. Eleazar was joined in commission with him, as Aaron had been before, by which God confirmed his succession. They were now to go by the same rule that they had gone by in the former numbering, counting those only that were able to go forth to war, for this was the service now before them.

Verses 5–51

This is the register of the tribes as they were now enrolled, in the same order that they were numbered in *ch.* i.

I. The account that is here kept of the families of each tribe, which must not be understood of such as we call families, those that live in a house together, but such as were the descendants of the several sons of the patriarchs. The families of the twelve tribes are thus numbered:—Of Dan but one, for Dan had but one son, and yet that tribe was the most numerous of all except Judah, *v.* 42, 43. Zebulun was divided into three families, Ephraim into two, Issachar into four, Naphtali into four, and Reuben into four; Judah, Simeon, and Asher had five families apiece, Gad and Benjamin seven apiece, and Manasseh eight. Benjamin brought ten sons into Egypt (Gen. xlvi. 21), but three of them, it seems, either died childless or their families were extinct, for here we find seven only of those names preserved.

II. The numbers of each tribe. In this account we may observe, 1. That all the three tribes that were encamped under the standard of Judah, who was the ancestor of Christ, had increased. 2. That none of the tribes had increased so much as that of Manasseh, which in the former account was the smallest of all the tribes, only 32,200, while here it is one of the most considerable. 3. That none of the tribes decreased so much as Simeon did; from 59,300, it sunk to 22,000, little more than a third part of what it was. Some conjecture that most of those 24,000 who were cut off by the plague for the iniquity of Peor were of that tribe; for Zimri, who was a ringleader in that iniquity, was a prince of that tribe.

III. In the account of the tribe of Reuben mention is made of the rebellion of Dathan and Abiram, who were of that tribe, in confederacy with Korah a Levite, *v.* 9–11.

Verses 52–56

If any ask why such a particular account is kept of the tribes, and families, and numbers, of the people of Israel, here is an answer for them; as they were

multiplied, so they were portioned, not by common providence, but by promise; and, for the support of the honour of divine revelation, God will have the fulfilling of the promise taken notice of both in their increase and in their inheritance.

Verses 57–62

Levi was God's tribe, a tribe that was to have no inheritance with the rest in the land of Canaan, and therefore was not numbered with the rest, but by itself; so it had been numbered in the beginning of this book at Mount Sinai, and therefore came not under the sentence passed upon all that were then numbered, that none of them should enter Canaan but Caleb and Joshua; for of the Levites that were not numbered with them, nor were to go forth to war, Eleazar and Ithamar, and perhaps others who were above twenty years old then (as appears, *ch.* iv. 16, 28), entered Canaan; and yet this tribe, now at its second numbering, had increased but 1,000, and was still one of the smallest tribes.

Verses 63–65

That which is observable in this conclusion of the account is the execution of the sentence passed upon the murmurers (*ch.* xiv. 29), that not one of those who *were numbered from twenty years old and upwards* should enter Canaan, except Caleb and Joshua. In the muster now made it appeared that there was not one man numbered now that was numbered then except Caleb and Joshua, *v.* 64, 65. Herein appeared, 1. The righteousness of God, and his faithfulness to his threatenings, when once the *decree has gone forth*. 2. The goodness of God to this people, notwithstanding their provocations. And, though the number fell a little short of what it was at Mount Sinai, yet those now numbered had this advantage, that they were all middle-aged men, between twenty and sixty, in the prime of their time for service; and during the thirty-eight years of their wandering and wasting in the wilderness they had an opportunity of acquainting themselves with the laws and ordinances of God.

CHAPTER 27

Here is, I. The case of Zelophehad's daughters determined, ver. 1–11. II. Notice given to Moses of his death approaching, ver. 12–14. III. Provision made of a successor in the government, 1. By the prayer of Moses, ver. 15–17. 2. By the appointment of God, ver. 18, &c.

Verses 1–11

Mention is made of the case of these daughters of Zelophehad in the chapter before, *v.* 33. It was a singular case, and the like did not at this time occur in all Israel, that the head of a family had no sons, but daughters only. Their case is again debated (*ch.* xxxvi.) upon another article of it; and, according to the judgments given in their case, we find them put in possession, Josh., xvii. 3, 4. One would suppose that their personal character was such as added weight to their case.

Here is, I. Their case stated by themselves, and their petition upon it presented to the highest court of judicature. We find not that they had any advocate to speak for them, but they managed their own cause ingeniously enough, which they could do the better because it was plain and honest, and spoke for itself.

1. What is it they petition for? That they might have a possession in the land of *Canaan, among the brethren of their father, v.* 4. God had said to Moses (*ch.* xxvi. 53) that the land of Canaan was to be divided among those that were now numbered; these daughters knew that they were not numbered, and therefore by this rule must expect no inheritance. If they had had a brother, they would not have applied to Moses for an order to inherit with him. But,

having no brother, they beg for a possession. There is a debt which children owe to the memory of their parents, required by the fifth commandment: *Honour thy father and mother.*

2. What their plea is: That their father did not die under any attainder which might be thought to have corrupted his blood and forfeited his estate, but he *died in his own sin* (*v.* 3), chargeable only with the common iniquities of mankind, for which to his own Master he was to stand or fall, but laid not himself open to any judicial process before Moses and the princes.

II. Their case determined by the divine oracle. 1. The petition is granted (*v.* 7). 2. The point is settled for all future occasions. These daughters of Zelophehad consulted, not only their own comfort and the credit of their family, but the honour and happiness of their sex likewise; for on this particular occasion a general law was made that, in case a man had no son, his estate should go to his daughters (*v.* 8); not to the eldest as the eldest son, but to them all in co-partnership, share and share alike. "If a man have no issue at all his estate shall go to his brethren; if no brethren, then to his father's brethren; and, if there be no such, then to his next kinsman."

Verses 12–14

1. God tells Moses of his fault, his speaking unadvisedly with his lips at the waters of strife, where he did not express, so carefully as he ought to have done, a regard to the honour both of God and Israel, *v.* 14. 2. He tells Moses of his death. Notice is given him of it in such a manner as might best serve to sweeten and mollify the sentence, and reconcile him to it. (1) Moses must die, but he shall first have the satisfaction of seeing the land of promise, *v.* 12. (2) Moses must die, but death does not *cut him off*, it only gathers him to his people, brings him to rest with the holy patriarchs that had gone before him. (3) Moses must die, but only as Aaron died before him, *v.* 13. And Moses had seen how easily and cheerfully Aaron had put off the priesthood first and then the body; let not Moses therefore be afraid of dying; it was but to be *gathered to his people*, as Aaron was gathered.

Verses 15–23

Here, I. Moses prays for a successor. Envious spirits do not love their successors, but Moses was not one of these. We should concern ourselves, both in our prayers and in our endeavours, for the rising generation, that religion may flourish. In this prayer Moses expressed, 1. A tender concern for the people of Israel: *That the congregation of the Lord be not as sheep which have no shepherd.* 2. A believing dependence upon God, as the *God of the spirits of all flesh.* Moses prays to God, not to send an angel but to *set a man over the congregation*, that is, to nominate and appoint one whom he would qualify and own as ruler of his people Israel.

II. God, in answer to his prayer, appoints him a successor, even Joshua, who had long since signalized himself by his courage in fighting Amalek, his humility in ministering to Moses, and his faith and sincerity in witnessing against the report of the evil spies.

1. God directs Moses how to secure the succession to Joshua. (1) He must ordain him: *Lay thy hand upon him, v.* 18. This was done in token of Moses's transferring the government to him, as the laying of hands on the sacrifice put the offering in the place and stead of the offerer; also in token of God's conferring the blessing of the Spirit upon him, which Moses obtained by prayer. It is said (Deut. xxxiv. 9), *Joshua was full of the spirit of wisdom, for Moses had laid his hands on him.* This rite of imposing hands we find used in the New Testament in the setting

apart of gospel ministers, denoting a solemn designation of them to the office and an earnest desire that God would qualify them for it and own them in it. It is the offering of them to Christ and his church for living sacrifices. (2) He must present him to Eleazar and the people, set him before them, that they might know him to be designed of God for this great trust and consent to that designation. (3) He must *give him a charge, v.* 19. (4) He must *put some of his honour upon him, v.* 20. (5) He must appoint Eleazar the high priest, with his breastplate of judgment, to be his privy-council (*v.* 21). This was a direction to Joshua. Though he was full of the Spirit, and had all this honour put upon him, yet he must do nothing without asking counsel of God, not leaning to his own understanding. Thus the government of Israel was now purely divine, for both the designation and direction of their princes were entirely so.

2. Moses does according to these directions, *v.* 22, 23. He cheerfully ordained Joshua, (1) Though it was a present lessening to himself, and amounted almost to a resignation of the government. (2) Though it might appear a perpetual slur upon his family, first to ordain Eleazar high priest, and then Joshua, one of another tribe, chief ruler, while his own children had no preferment at all, but were left in the rank of common Levites, this was such an instance of self-denial and submission to the will of God as was more his glory than the highest advancement of his family could have been.

CHAPTER 28

Now that the people were numbered, orders given for the dividing of the land, and a general of the forces nominated and commissioned, one would have expected that the next chapter should begin the history of the campaign. It contains the ordinances of worship, and provides that now, as they were on the point of entering Canaan, they should be sure to take their religion along with them, and not forget this, in the prosecution of their wars, ver. 1, 2. The laws are here repeated and summed up concerning the sacrifices that were to be offered, I. Daily, ver. 3–8. II. Weekly, ver. 9, 10. III. Monthly, ver. 11–15. IV. Yearly. 1. At the passover, ver. 16–25. 2. At pentecost, ver. 26–31. And the next chapter is concerning the annual solemnities of the seventh month.

Verses 1–8

Here is, I. A general order given concerning the offerings of the Lord, which were to be brought in their season, *v.* 2. God saw fit now to repeat the law of sacrifices, 1. Because this was a new generation of men, that were most of them unborn when the former laws were given. 2. Because they were now entering upon war, and might be tempted to think that while they were engaged in that they should be excused from offering sacrifices. *Inter arma silent leges—law is little regarded amidst the clash of arms.* They were peculiarly concerned to keep their peace with God when they were at war with their enemies. 3. Because possession was now to be given them of the land of promise, that land flowing with milk and honey, where they would have plenty of all good things. "Now" (says God), "when you are feasting yourselves, forget not to offer the bread of your God."

II. The particular law of the daily sacrifice, a lamb in the morning and a lamb in the evening, which, for the constancy of it duly as the day came, is called a *continual burnt-offering* (*v.* 3), which intimates that when we are bidden to *pray always, and to pray without ceasing*, it is intended that at least every morning and every evening we offer up our solemn prayers and praises to God.

Verses 9–15

The new moons and the sabbaths are often spoken of together, as great solemnities in the Jewish church.

Now we have here the sacrifices appointed, 1. For the sabbaths. Every sabbath day the offering must be doubled. 2. For the new moons. Some suggest that, as the sabbath was kept with an eye to the creation of the world, so the new moons were sanctified with an eye to the divine providence, which *appoints the moon for seasons*, guiding the revolutions of time by its changes.

Verses 16–31

The appointment of the passover sacrifices; not that which was the chief, the paschal lamb (sufficient instructions had formerly been given concerning that), but those which were to be offered upon the seven days of unleavened bread, which followed it, *v.* 17–25. The first and last of those seven days were to be sanctified as sabbaths, by a holy rest and a holy convocation, and on each of the seven days they were to be liberal in their sacrifices, in token of their great and constant thankfulness for their deliverance out of Egypt. The sacrifices are likewise appointed which were to be offered at the feast of pentecost, here called the *day of the first-fruits, v.* 26. In the feast of unleavened bread they offered a *sheaf of their first-fruits* of barley (which with them was first ripe) to the priest (Lev. xxiii. 10), as an introduction to the harvest; but now, about seven weeks after, they were to bring a *new meat-offering to the Lord*, at the end of harvest. It was at this feast that *the Spirit was poured out* (Acts ii. 1, &c.), and thousands were converted by the preaching of the apostles, and were presented to Christ, to be *a kind of first-fruits of his creatures.*

CHAPTER 29

This chapter appoints the offerings that were to be made by fire unto the Lord in the three great solemnities of the seventh month. I. In the feast of trumpets on the first day of that month, ver. 1–6. II. In the day of atonement on the tenth day, ver. 7–11. III. In the feast of tabernacles on the fifteenth day and the seven days following, ver. 12–38. And then the conclusion of these ordinances, ver. 39, 40.

Verses 1–11

There were more sacred solemnities in the seventh month than in any other month of the year, not only because it had been the first month till the deliverance of Israel out of Egypt, but because still it continued the first month in the civil reckonings of the jubilees and years of release, and also because it was the time of vacation between harvest and seedtime, when they had most leisure to attend the sanctuary. 1. We have here the appointment of the sacrifices that were to be offered on the first day of the month, the day of *blowing the trumpets*, which was a preparative for the two great solemnities of holy mourning on the day of atonement and of holy joy in the feast of tabernacles. On the *day of atonement* itself, besides all the services of that day, which we had the institution of, Lev. xvi., here are burnt-offerings ordered to be offered, *v.* 8–10.

Verses 12–40

Soon after the day of atonement, that day in which men were to afflict their souls, followed the feast of the tabernacles, in which they were to rejoice before the Lord; for, those that *sow in tears* shall soon *reap in joy*. To the former laws about this feast, which we had, Lev. xxiii. 34, &c., here are added directions about the *offerings made by fire*, which they were to offer unto the Lord during the *seven days of that feast*, Lev. xxiii. 36. Observe here, 1. Their days of rejoicing were to be days of sacrifices. 2. All the days of their dwelling in booths they must offer sacrifices. 3. The sacrifices for each of the seven days, though differing in nothing but the number of the bullocks, are severally and particularly appointed. 4. The

number of the bullocks (which were the most costly part of the sacrifice) decreased every day. The multitude of their sacrifices should end in one great sacrifice, infinitely more worthy than all of them. It was on the last day of the feast, after all these sacrifices had been offered, that our Lord Jesus stood and cried to those who still thirsted after righteousness (being sensible of the insufficiency of these sacrifices to justify them) *to come unto him and drink*, John vii. 37. 5. The meat-offerings and drink-offerings attended all the sacrifices. 6. Every day there must be a sin-offering presented, as we observed in the other feasts. 7. Even when all these sacrifices were offered, yet the continual burnt-offering must not be omitted either morning or evening, but each day this must be offered first in the morning and last in the evening. No extraordinary services should jostle out our stated devotions. 8. Though all these sacrifices were required to be presented by the body of the congregation, at the common charge, yet, besides these, particular persons were to glorify God with their vows and their free-will offerings, *v.* 39.

CHAPTER 30

In this chapter we have a law concerning vows, which had been mentioned in the close of the foregoing chapter. I. Here is a general rule laid down that all vows must be carefully performed, ver. 1, 2. II. Some particular exceptions to this rule. 1. That the vows of daughters should not be binding unless allowed by the father, ver. 3–5. Nor, 2. The vows of wives unless allowed by the husband, ver. 6, &c.

Verses 1–2

This law was delivered to the heads of the tribes that they might instruct those who were under their charge.

1. The case supposed is that a person vows a vow unto the Lord, making God a party to the promise. The matter of the vow is supposed to be something lawful: no man can be by his own promise bound to do that which he is already by the divine precept prohibited from doing. He that vows is here said to *bind his soul with a bond*. It is a vow to God, who is a Spirit, and to him the soul, with all its powers, must be bound. A promise to a man is a bond upon the estate, but a promise to God is a bond upon the soul. 2. The command given is that these vows be conscientiously performed.

Verses 3–16

It is here taken for granted that all such persons as are *sui juris*—at their own disposal, and are likewise of sound understanding and memory, are bound to perform whatever they vow that is lawful and possible; but, if the person vowing be under the dominion and at the disposal of another, the case is different. Two cases much alike are here put and determined:—

I. The case of a daughter in her father's house. The rule is general, If a man vow, he must pay. But for a daughter it is express: her vow is nugatory or in suspense till her father knows it, and (it is supposed) knows it from her; for, when it comes to his knowledge, it is in his power either to ratify or nullify it. But in favour of the vow, 1. Even his silence shall suffice to ratify it: If he *hold his peace*, her *vows shall stand, v.* 4. *Qui tacet, consentire videtur—Silence gives consent.* But, 2. His protestation against it shall perfectly disannul it, because it is possible that such vow may be prejudicial to the affairs of the family. She showed her good-will in making the vow, and, if her intentions therein were sincere, she shall be accepted, and to obey her father shall be accounted better than sacrifice.

II. The case of a wife is much the same. As for a woman that is a widow or divorced, she has neither father nor husband to control her, so that, whatever vows she binds her soul with, they shall *stand against her* (v. 9), it is at her peril if she run back.

CHAPTER 31

This chapter belongs to "the book of the wars of the Lord," in which it is probable it was inserted. It is the history of a holy war, a war with Midian. Here is, I. A divine command for the war, ver. 1, 2. II. The undertaking of the war, ver. 3-6. III. The glorious success of it, ver. 7-12. IV. Their triumphant return from the war. 1. The respect Moses paid to the soldiers, ver. 13. 2. The rebuke he gave them for sparing the women, ver. 14-18. 3. The directions he gave them for the purifying of themselves and their effects, ver. 19-24. 4. The distribution of the spoil they had taken, one half to the soldiers, the other to the congregation, and a tribute to the Lord out of each, ver. 25-47. 5. The free-will offering of the officers, ver. 48, &c.

Verses 1-6

Here, I. The Lord of hosts gives orders to Moses to make war upon the Midianites. The Midianites were the posterity of Abraham by Keturah, Gen. xxv. 2. Some of them settled south of Canaan, among whom Jethro lived, and they retained the worship of the true God; but these were settled east of Canaan, and had fallen into idolatry, neighbours to, and in confederacy with, the Moabites. They made themselves obnoxious by sending their bad women among them to draw them to whoredom and idolatry. This was the provocation, this was the quarrel. For this (says God) *avenge Israel of the Midianites*, v. 2. 1. God would have the Midianites chastised. Israel's quarrel with Amalek, that fought against them, was not avenged till long after: but their quarrel with Midian, that debauched them, was speedily avenged, for they were looked upon as much the more dangerous and malicious enemies. 2. God would have it done by Moses, in his life time, that he who had so deeply resented that injury might have the satisfaction of seeing it avenged.

II. Moses gives orders to the people to prepare for this expedition, v. 3.

III. A detachment is drawn out accordingly for this service, 1,000 *out of every tribe*, 12,000 in all, a small number in comparison with what they could have sent. But God would teach them that it is all one to him *to save by many or by few*, 1 Sam. xiv. 6.

IV. Phinehas the son of Eleazar is sent along with them. The war being a holy war, Phinehas was their common head. He therefore took with him the holy instruments or vessels, probably the breastplate of judgment, by which God might be consulted in any emergency.

Verses 7-12

Here is, 1. The descent which this little army of Israelites made upon the country of Midian. It is very probable that they first published their manifesto, showing the reasons of the war, and requiring them to give up the ringleaders of the mischief to justice; for such afterwards was the *law* (Deut. xx. 10), and such the *practice*, Judg. xx. 12, 13. 2. The execution (the military execution) they did in this descent. (1) They *slew all the males* (v. 7), that is, all they met with as far as they went; they put them all to the sword, and gave no quarter. (2) They *slew the kings of Midian*, the same that are called *elders of Midian* (ch. xxii. 4), and *dukes of Sihon*, Josh. xiii. 21. Five of these princes are here named, one of whom is *Zur*, probably the same Zur whose daughter Cozbi was, *ch.* xxv. 15. (3) They slew Balaam. Whatever was the occasion of his being there, God's over-ruling providence brought him thither, and there his just vengeance found him. (4) They took all the *women and children captives, v. 9*. (5) They *burnt their cities and goodly castles* (v. 10). (6) They plundered the country, and carried off all the cattle and valuable goods, and so returned to the camp of Israel laden with a very rich booty, v. 9, 11, 12.

Verses 13-24

The triumphant return to the army of Israel from the war with Midian, and here,

I. They were met with great respect, v. 13.

II. They were severely reproved for saving the women alive. The execution having reference to that crime, their drawing them in to the worship of Peor, it was easy to conclude that the women, who were the principal criminals, must not be spared. "It is dangerous to let them live; they will be still tempting the Israelites to uncleanness, and so your captives will be your conquerors and a second time your destroyers."

III. They were obliged to purify themselves, according to the ceremony of the law, and to abide without the camp seven days, till their purification was accomplished. Thus God would preserve in their minds a dread and detestation of murder.

IV. They must likewise purify the spoil they had taken, the captives (v. 19) and all the goods, v. 21-23. What would bear the fire must pass through the fire, and what would not must be washed with water.

Verses 25-47

The distribution of the spoil which was taken in this expedition against Midian.

I. The prey is ordered to be divided into two parts, one for the 12,000 men that undertook the war, and the other for the congregation. The prey that was divided seems to have been only the captives and the cattle; as for the plate, and jewels, and other goods, every man kept what he took, as is intimated, v. 50-53. That only was distributed which would be of use for the stocking of that good land into which they were going.

II. God was to have a tribute out of it, as an acknowledgment of his sovereignty over them in general, and that he was their king to whom *tribute was due*.

Verses 48-54

Here is a great example of piety and devotion in the officers of the army. They came to Moses as their general and commander-in-chief, and very humbly and respectfully addressed themselves to him, calling themselves his *servants*. 1. The pious notice they take of God's wonderful goodness to them in this late expedition, in preserving not only their own lives, but the lives of all the men of war that they had under their charge; so that, upon the review of their muster-roll, it appeared there was not one missing, v. 49. They looked upon it as a mercy to themselves that none of those under their charge miscarried. Instead of coming to Moses to demand a recompence for the good service they had done in *avenging the Lord of Midian*, or to set up trophies of their victory for the immortalizing of their own names, they bring an oblation to *make atonement for their souls*.

CHAPTER 32

In this chapter we have, I. The humble request of the tribes of Reuben and Gad for an inheritance on that side Jordan where Israel now lay encamped, ver. 1-5. II. Moses's misinterpretation of their request, ver. 6-15. III. Their explication of it, and stating it aright, ver. 16-19. IV. The grant of their petition under the provisos and limitations which they themselves proposed, ver. 20, &c.

Verses 1-15

Israel's tents were now pitched in the plains of Moab. While they were at a pause, the disposal of the conquests they had already made was here settled, not by any particular order or appointment of God, but at the special instance and request of two of the tribes, to which Moses consented.

I. Here is a motion made by the Reubenites and

Gadites, that the land which they had lately possessed themselves of, and which in the right of conquest belonged to Israel in common, might be assigned to them in particular for their inheritance. Two things common in the world induced these tribes to make this choice and this motion upon it, the *lust of the eye* and the *pride of life*, 1 John ii. 16. 1. The *lust of the eye*. This land which they coveted was not only beautiful for situation, and pleasant to the eye, but it was good for food, food for cattle; and they had a great multitude of cattle, above the rest of the tribes. Now they, having these large stocks, coveted land proportionable. 2. Perhaps there was something of the *pride of life* in it. Reuben was the first-born of Israel, but he had lost his birthright. He here catches at the first lot, though it was out of Canaan, and far off from the tabernacle. The tribe of Gad descended from the first-born of Zilpah, and were like pretenders with the Reubenites; and Manasseh too was a first-born, but knew he must be eclipsed by Ephraim his younger brother, and therefore he also coveted to get precedency.

II. Moses's dislike of this motion, and the severe rebuke he gives to it, as a faithful prince and prophet.

1. It must be confessed that, *prima facie—at first sight*, the thing looked ill, especially the closing words of their petition: *Bring us not over Jordan, v.* 5. It seemed to proceed from a bad principle, a contempt of the land of promise. There seemed also to be covetousness in it; for that which they insisted on was that it was convenient for their cattle. It argued likewise a neglect of their brethren, as if they cared not what became of Israel, while they themselves were well provided for.

2. Moses is therefore very warm upon them. (1) He shows them what he apprehended to be evil in this motion, that it would discourage the heart of their brethren, *v.* 6, 7. (2) He reminds them of the fatal consequences of the unbelief and faint-heartedness of their fathers, when they were just ready to enter Canaan, as they themselves now were. He recites the story very particularly (*v.* 8–13). (3) He gives them fair warning of the mischief that would be likely to follow upon this separation which they were about to make from the camp of Israel; they would be in danger of bringing wrath upon the whole congregation, and hurrying them all back again into the wilderness (*v.* 14, 15).

Verses 16–27

We have here the accommodating of the matter between Moses and the two tribes, about their settlement on this side Jordan. After some consultation, they return with this proposal, that their men of war should go and assist their brethren in the conquest of Canaan, and they would leave their families and flocks behind them in this land: and thus they might have their request, and no harm would be done.

I. Their proposal is very fair and generous, and such as, instead of disheartening, would rather encourage their brethren. 1. That their *men of war*, who were fit for service, would go *ready armed before the children of Israel* into the land of Canaan. 2. That they would leave behind them their families and cattle (which would otherwise be but the incumbrance of their camp), and so they would be the more serviceable to their brethren, *v.* 16. 3. That they would not return to their possessions till the conquest of Canaan was completed, *v.* 18. 4. That yet they would not expect any share of the land that was yet to be conquered (*v.* 19).

II. Moses thereupon grants their request, upon consideration that they would adhere to their proposals. 1. He insists much upon it that they should never lay down their arms till their brethren laid down theirs. They promised to go armed *before the*

children of Israel, v. 17. "Nay," says Moses, "you shall go armed *before the Lord, v.* 20, 21. It is God's cause more than your brethren's. 2. Upon this condition he grants them this land for their possession. But, 3. He warns them of the danger of breaking their word: "If you fail, you *sin against the Lord* (*v.* 23), and not against your brethren only, and *be sure your sin will find you out.*" Note, Sin will, without doubt, find out the sinner sooner or later. It concerns us therefore to find our sins out, that we may repent of them and forsake them, lest our sins find us out to our ruin and confusion.

III. They unanimously agree to the provisos and conditions of the grant, and do, as it were, give bond for performance, by a solemn promise: *Thy servants will do as my lord commandeth, v.* 25.

Verses 28–42

1. Moses settles this matter with Eleazar, and with Joshua who was to be his successor, knowing that he himself must not live to see it perfected, *v.* 28–30. He gives them an estate upon condition, leaving it to Joshua, if they fulfilled the condition, to declare the estate absolute. Hereupon they repeat their promise to adhere to their brethren, *v.* 31, 32. 2. Moses settles them in the land they desired. Here is the first mention of the half tribe of Manasseh coming in with them for a share. Concerning the settlement of these tribes observe, (1) They built the cities, that is, repaired them. (2) They changed the names of them (*v.* 38). Nebo and Baal were names of their gods, which they were forbidden to make mention of (Exod. xxiii. 13), and which, by changing the names of these cities, they endeavoured to bury in oblivion.

CHAPTER 33

In this chapter we have, I. A particular account of the removals and encampments of the children of Israel, from their escape out of Egypt to their entrance into Canaan, forty-two in all, with some remarkable events that happened at some of those places, ver. 1–49. II. A strict command given them to drive out all the inhabitants of the land of Canaan, which they were now going to conquer and take possession of, ver. 50–56. So that the former part of the chapter looks back upon their march through the wilderness, the latter looks forward to their settlement in Canaan.

Verses 1–49

This is a review and brief rehearsal of the travels of the children of Israel through the wilderness.

I. Now the account was kept: *Moses wrote their goings out, v.* 2. It may be of good use to private Christians, but especially to those in public stations, to preserve in writing an account of the providences of God concerning them, the constant series of mercies they have experienced, especially those turns and changes which have made some days of their lives more remarkable. Our memories are deceitful and need this help, that we may *remember all the way which the Lord our God has led us in this wilderness,* Deut. viii. 2.

II. What the account itself was. It began with their departure out of Egypt, continued with their march through the wilderness, and ended in the plains of Moab, where they now lay encamped.

1. Some things are observed here concerning their departure out of Egypt, which they are reminded of upon all occasions, as a work of wonder never to be forgotten. They *went forth with their armies* (*v.* 1), rank and file, as an army with banners. They did not steal away clandestinely (Isa. lii. 12), but in defiance of their enemies, to whom God had made them such a burdensome stone that they neither could, nor would, nor durst, oppose them.

2. Concerning their travels towards Canaan. Observe, (1) They were continually upon the remove.

Such is our state in this world; we have here no continuing city. (2) Most of their way lay through a wilderness, uninhabited, untracked, unfurnished even with the necessaries of human life, which magnifies the wisdom and power of God, by whose wonderful conduct and bounty the thousands of Israel not only subsisted for forty years in that desolate place, but came out at least as numerous and vigorous as they went in. At first they pitched *in the edge of the wilderness* (v. 6), but afterwards in the heart of it; by less difficulties God prepares his people for greater. (3) They were led to and fro, forward and backward, as in a maze or labyrinth, and yet were all the while under the direction of the pillar of cloud and fire. The way which God takes in bringing his people to himself is always the best way, though it does not always seem to us the nearest way.

Verses 50-56

While the children of Israel were in the wilderness their total separation from all other people kept them out of the way of temptation to idolatry. But now that they were to pass over Jordan they were entering again into that temptation, and therefore, 1. They are here strictly charged utterly to destroy all the remnants of idolatry. 2. They were assured that, if they did so, God would by degrees put them in full possession of the land of promise, v. 53, 54. 3. They were threatened that, if they spared either the idols or the idolaters, they should be beaten with their own rod and their sin would certainly be their punishment. If we do not drive sin out, sin will drive us out; if we be not the death of our lusts, our lusts will be the death of our souls.

CHAPTER 34

In this chapter God directs Moses, and he is to direct Israel, I. Concerning the bounds and borders of the land of Canaan, ver. 1–15. II. Concerning the division and distribution of it to the tribes of Israel, ver. 16, &c.

Verses 1-15

We have here a particular draft of the line by which the land of Canaan was meted, and bounded, on all sides. There was a much larger possession promised them, which in due time they would have possessed if they had been obedient, reaching even to the river Euphrates, Deut. xi. 24. And even so far the dominion of Israel did extend in David's time and Solomon's, 2 Chron. ix. 26. But this which is here described is Canaan only, which was the lot of the nine tribes and a half, for the other two and a half were already settled, v. 14, 15. Now concerning the limits of Canaan observe,

I. That it was limited within certain bounds: 1. That they might know whom they were to dispossess, and how far the commission which was given them extended (ch. xxxiii. 53), that they should *drive out the inhabitants*. 2. That they might know what to expect the possession of themselves.

II. That it lay comparatively in a very little compass: as it is here bounded, it is reckoned to be but about 160 miles in length and about fifty in breadth; perhaps it did not contain more than half as much ground as England, and yet this is the country which was promised to the father of the faithful and was the possession of the seed of Israel. This was that little spot of ground in which alone, for many ages, *God was known, and his name was great*, Ps. lxxvi. 1. See here then, 1. How small a part of the world God has for himself. 2. How small a share of the world God often gives to his own people.

III. It is observable what the bounds and limits of it were. 1. Canaan was itself a *pleasant land* (so it is called Dan. viii. 9), and yet it bordered upon wilderness and seas, and was surrounded with divers melancholy prospects. 2. Many of its borders were its defences and natural fortifications. 3. The border reached to the *river of Egypt* (v. 5), that the sight of that country which they could look into out of their own might remind them of their bondage there, and their wonderful deliverance thence. 4. Their border is here made to begin at the *Salt Sea* (v. 3), and there it ends, v. 12. That pleasant fruitful vale in which these cities stood became a lake, which was never stirred by any wind, bore no vessels, was replenished with no fish, no living creature of any sort being found in it, therefore called the *Dead Sea*. 5. Their western border was the *Great Sea* (v. 6), which is now called the *Mediterranean*.

Verses 16-29

God here appoints commissioners for the dividing of the land to them. The conquest of it is taken for granted, though as yet there was never a stroke struck towards it. 1. The principal commissioners, who were of the *quorum*, were Eleazar and Joshua (v. 17). 2. Besides these, that there might be no suspicion of partiality, a prince of each tribe was appointed to inspect this matter, and to see that the tribe he served for was in no respect injured.

CHAPTER 35

Orders having been given before for the dividing of the land of Canaan among the lay-tribes (as I may call them), care is here taken for a competent provision for the clergy, the tribe of Levi, which ministered in holy things. I. Forty-eight cities were to be assigned them, with their suburbs, some in every tribe, ver. 1–8. II. Six cities out of these were to be for cities of refuge, for any man that killed another unawares, ver. 9–15. In the law concerning these observe, 1. In what case sanctuary was not allowed, namely, that of wilful murder, ver. 16–21. 2. In what cases it was allowed, ver. 22–24. 3. What was the law concerning those that took shelter in these cities of refuge, ver. 25, &c.

Verses 1-8

The laws about the tithes and offerings had provided very plentifully for the maintenance of the Levites; but it was not to be thought, nor indeed was it for the public good, that when they came to Canaan they should all live about the tabernacle, as they had done in the wilderness, and therefore care must be taken to provide habitations for them, in which they might live comfortably and usefully. It is this which is here taken care of.

I. Cities were allotted them, with their suburbs, v. 2. They were not to have any ground for tillage. 1. Cities were allotted them, that they might live near together, and converse with one another about the law, and that in doubtful cases they might consult one another. 2. These cities had suburbs annexed to them for their cattle (v. 3), a thousand cubits from the wall was allowed them for out-houses to keep their cattle in, and then two thousand more for fields to graze their cattle in, v. 4, 5.

II. These cities were to be assigned them out of the possessions of each tribe, v. 8. 1. That each tribe might thus make a grateful acknowledgment to God. 2. That each tribe might have the benefit of the Levites dwelling among them, to *teach them the good knowledge of the Lord*.

III. The number allotted them was forty-eight in all, four out of each of the twelve tribes, one with another.

Verses 9-34

We have here the orders given concerning the cities of refuge. In this part of the constitution there is a great deal both of good law and pure gospel.

I. Here is a great deal of good law, in the case of murder and manslaughter.

1. That wilful murder should be punished with death, and in that case no sanctuary should be

allowed, no ransom taken, nor any commutation of the punishment accepted. Where wrong has been done restitution must be made; and, since the murderer cannot restore the life he has wrongfully taken away, his own must be exacted from him in lieu of it, not (as some have fancied) to satisfy the manes or ghost of the person slain, but to satisfy the law and the justice of a nation, and to be a warning to all others not to do likewise. Not only the prosecution, but the execution, of the murderer, is committed to the next of kin, who, as he was to be the redeemer of his kinsman's estate if it were mortgaged, so he was to be the *avenger of his blood if he were murdered* (*v.* 19): *The avenger of blood himself shall slay the murderer.*

2. But if the homicide was not voluntary, nor done designedly, if it was *without enmity, or lying in wait* (*v.* 22), not *seeing* the person or not *seeking his harm* (*v.* 23), which our law calls chance-medley, or homicide *per infortunium—through misfortune*, in this case there were cities of refuge appointed for the man-slayer to flee to. By our law this incurs a forfeiture of goods, but a pardon is granted of course upon the special matter found. Concerning the cities of refuge the law was, (1) That, if a man killed another, in these cities he was safe, and under the protection of the law, till he had his trial *before the congregation*, that is, before the judges in open court. (2) If, upon trial, it were found to be wilful murder, the city of refuge should no longer be a protection to him; it was already determined: *Thou shalt take him from my altar, that he may die*, Exod. xxi. 14. (3) But if it were found to be by error or accident, and that the stroke was given without any design upon the life of the person slain or any other, then the man-slayer should continue safe in *the city of refuge*, and the avenger of blood might not meddle with him, *v.* 25. There he was to remain in banishment from his own house and patrimony *till the death of the high priest*. Now, [1] By the preservation of the life of the man-slayer God would teach us that men ought not to suffer for that which is rather their unhappiness than their crime. [2] By the banishment of the man-slayer from his own city, and his confine-ment to the city of refuge, God would teach us to conceive a dread and horror of the guilt of blood, and to be very careful of life. [3] By the limiting of the time of the offender's banishment to the death of the high priest, an honour was put upon that sacred office. The cities of refuge being all of them Levites' cities, and the high priest being the head of that tribe, those that were confined to them might properly be looked upon as his prisoners, and so his death must be their discharge.

II. Here is a great deal of good gospel couched under the type and figure of the cities of refuge; and to them the apostle seems to allude when he speaks of our *fleeing for refuge to the hope set before us* (Heb. vi. 18), and being *found in Christ*, Phil. iii. 9. 1. There were several cities of refuge, and they were so appointed in several parts of the country that the man-slayer, wherever he dwelt in the land of Israel, might in half a day reach one or other of them; so, though there is but one Christ appointed for our refuge, yet, wherever we are, he is a refuge at hand, a very present help, for *the word is nigh us* and Christ in the word. 2. The man-slayer was safe in any of these cities; so in Christ believers that flee to him, and rest in him, are protected from the wrath of God and the curse of the law. *There is no condemnation to those that are in Christ Jesus*, Rom. viii. 1. 3. They

were all Levites' cities; it was a kindness to the poor prisoner that the Levites would comfort and encourage him, and bid him welcome; so it is the work of gospel ministers to bid poor sinners welcome to Christ, and to assist and counsel those that through grace are in him. 4. Even strangers and sojourners, though they were not native Israelites, might take the benefit of these cities of refuge, *v.* 15. So in Christ Jesus no difference is made between Greek and Jew. 5. Even the suburbs or borders of the city were a sufficient security to the offender, *v.* 26, 27. So there is virtue even in the hem of Christ's garment for the healing and saving of poor sinners.

Chapter 36

We have in this chapter the determination of another question that arose upon the case of the daughters of Zelophehad. God had appointed that they should inherit, ch. xxvii. 7. Now here, I. An inconvenience is suggested, in case they should marry into any other tribe, ver. 1–4. II. It is prevented by a divine appoint-ment that they should marry in their own tribe and family (ver. 5–7), and this is settled for a rule in like cases (ver. 8, 9); and they did marry accordingly to some of their own relations (ver. 10–12), and with this the book concludes, ver. 13.

Verses 1–4

We have here the humble address which the heads of the tribe of Manasseh made to Moses and the princes, on occasion of the order lately made con-cerning the daughters of Zelophehad. 1. They fairly recite the former order made in this case, and do not move to have that set aside, but are very willing to acquiesce in it (*v.* 2). 2. They represent the in-convenience which might, possibly, follow hereupon, if the daughters of Zelophehad should see cause to marry into any other tribes, *v.* 3. Two things they aimed at in their representation:—(1) It would break in upon the divine appointment if such a considerable part of the lot of Manasseh should, by their marriage, be transferred to any other tribe. (2) To prevent contests and quarrels among posterity. If those of other tribes should come among them perhaps it might occasion some contests.

Verses 5–13

Here is, I. The matter settled by express order from God between the daughters of Zelophehad and the rest of the tribe of Manasseh. The petition is assented to, and care taken to prevent the incon-venience feared: *The tribe of the sons of Joseph hath said well, v.* 5. 1. They are not determined to any particular persons; there was choice enough in the family of their father: *Let them marry to whom they think best.* As children must preserve the authority of their parents, and not marry against their minds, so parents must consult the affections of their children in disposing of them, and not compel them to marry such as they cannot love. Forced marriages are not likely to prove blessings. 2. Yet they are confined to their own relations, that their inheritance may not go to another family.

II. The law, in this particular case, was made perpetual.

III. The submission of the daughters of Zelophehad to this appointment.

IV. The conclusion of this whole book, referring to the latter part of it. Whatever new condition God is by his providence bringing us into, we must beg of him to teach us the duty of it, and to enable us to do it, that we may do the work of the day in its day, of the place in its place.

THE FIFTH BOOK OF MOSES, CALLED

DEUTERONOMY

This book is a repetition of very much both of the history and of the laws contained in the three foregoing books. There is no new history in it but that of the death of Moses in the last chapter. But the former laws are repeated and commented upon, explained and enlarged, and some particular precepts added to them, with copious reasonings for the enforcing of them. The Greek interpreters call it *Deuteronomy*, which signifies the *second law*, or a *second edition of the law*, not with amendments, for there needed none, but with additions, for the further direction of the people in divers cases not mentioned before. Now, I. It was much for the honour of the divine law that it should be thus repeated. II. There might be a particular reason for the repeating of it now; the men of that generation to which the law was first given were all dead, and a new generation had sprung up, to whom God would have it repeated by Moses himself, that, if possible, it might make a lasting impression upon them. Now that they were just going to take possession of the land of Canaan, Moses must read the articles of agreement to them, that they might know upon what terms and conditions they were to hold and enjoy that land. III. It would be of great use to the people to have those parts of the law thus gathered up and put together which did more immediately concern them and their practice; for the laws which concerned the priests and Levites, and the execution of their offices, are not repeated. The great and needful truths of the gospel should be often pressed upon people by the ministers of Christ. *To write the same things* (says Paul, Phil. iii. 1) *to me indeed is not grievous, but for you it is safe.* What God has spoken once we have need to hear twice, to hear many times, and it is well if, after all, it be duly perceived and regarded. The gospel is a kind of Deuteronomy, a second law, a remedial law, a spiritual law, a law of faith.

This book of Deuteronomy begins with a brief rehearsal of the most remarkable events that had befallen the Israelites since they came from Mount Sinai. In the fourth chapter we have a most pathetic exhortation to obedience. In the twelfth chapter, and so on to the twenty-seventh, are repeated many particular laws, which are enforced (ch. xxvii. and xxviii.) with promises and threatenings, blessings and curses, formed into a covenant, ch. xxix. and xxx. Care is taken to perpetuate the remembrance of these things among them (ch. xxxi.), particularly by a song (ch. xxxii.), and so Moses concludes with a blessing, ch. xxxiii. All this was delivered by Moses to Israel in the last month of his life. When our Saviour would answer the devil's temptations with, *It is written*, he fetched all his quotations out of this book, Matt. iv. 4, 7, 10.

CHAPTER 1

The first part of Moses's farewell sermon to Israel begins with this chapter, and is continued to the latter end of the fourth chapter. In the first five verses of this chapter we have the date of the sermon, the place where it was preached (ver. 1, 2, 5), and the time when, ver. 3, 4. The narrative in this chapter reminds them, I. Of the promise God made them of the land of Canaan, ver. 6–8. II. Of the provision made of judges for them, ver. 9–18. III. Of their unbelief and murmuring upon the report of the spies, ver. 19–33. IV. Of the sentence passed upon them for it, and the ratification of that sentence, ver. 34, &c.

Verses 1–8

We have here, I. The date of this sermon which Moses preached to the people of Israel. 1. The place where they were now encamped was *in the plain, in the land of Moab* (v. 1, 5), where they were just ready to enter Canaan, and engage in a war with the Canaanites. Yet he discourses not to them concerning military affairs, but concerning their duty to God. 2. The time was near the end of the fortieth year since they came out of Egypt. Now that a new and more pleasant scene was to be introduced, as a token for good, Moses repeats the law to them.

II. The discourse itself. In general, Moses spoke unto them *all that the Lord had given him in commandment* (v. 3). He begins his narrative with their removal from Mount Sinai (v. 6), and relates here, 1. The orders which God gave them to decamp, and proceed in their march (v. 6, 7): *You have dwelt long enough in this mount.* Thither God brought them to humble them, and by the terrors of the law to prepare them for the land of promise. Though God brings his people into spiritual trouble and affliction of mind, he knows when they have dwelt long enough in it, and will certainly find a time, to advance them from the terrors of the spirit of bondage to the comforts of the spirit of adoption. See Rom. viii. 15. 2. The prospect which he gave them of a happy and early settlement in Canaan. When God commands us to go forward in our Christian course he sets the heavenly Canaan before us for our encouragement.

Verses 9–18

Moses here reminds them of the happy constitution of their government, which was such as might make them all safe and easy if it was not their own fault. In this part of his narrative he insinuates to them,

I. That he greatly rejoiced in the increase of their numbers. He owns the accomplishment of God's promise to Abraham (v. 10): *You are as the stars of heaven for multitude* (v. 11): *God make you a thousand times more.* We are not straitened in the power and goodness of God, why should we be straitened in our own faith and hope, which ought to be as large as the promise? larger they need not be. They might become a thousand times more than they were now when they were now ten thousand times more than they were when they went down into Egypt.

II. That he was not ambitious of monopolizing the honour of the government, and ruling them himself alone, as an absolute monarch, v. 9.

III. That he was not desirous to prefer his own creatures, or such as should have a dependence upon him; for he leaves it to the people to choose their own judges, to whom he would grant commissions. He directs them to *take wise men and understanding*, whose personal merit would recommend them.

IV. That he was in this matter very willing to please the people. And they agreed to the proposal. The government they quarrelled with was what they themselves had consented to.

V. That he aimed to edify them as well as to gratify them; for,

1. He appointed men of good characters (v. 15), *wise men and men known*, men that would be faithful to their trust and to the public interest.

2. He gave them a good charge, v. 16, 17. (1) He charges them to be diligent and patient. Hear both sides, hear them fully, hear them carefully; for nature has provided us with two ears. The ear of the learner is necessary to the tongue of the learned, Isa. l. 4. (2) To be just and impartial. No faces must be known in judgment, but unbribed unbiassed equity must always pass sentence. (3) To be resolute and courageous. You are God's vicegerents, you act for him, and therefore must act like him; you are his representatives, but, if you judge unrighteously, you misrepresent him.

3. He allowed them to bring all difficult cases to him, and he would always be ready to hear and determine, and to make both the judges and the people easy.

Verses 19–46

Moses here makes a large rehearsal of the fatal turn which was given to their affairs by their own sins. It was a memorable story; we read it Num. xiii. and xiv., but divers circumstances are found here which are not related there.

I. He reminds them of their march from Horeb to Kadesh-barnea (v. 19), through *that great and terrible wilderness*. This he takes notice of to make them sensible of the great goodness of God to them, in guiding them through so great a wilderness. The remembrance of our dangers should make us thankful for our deliverances.

II. He shows them how fair they stood for Canaan at that time, v. 20, 21. He lets them see how near they were to a happy settlement when they put a bar in their own door.

III. He lays the blame of sending the spies upon them, which did not appear in Numbers; there it is said (ch. xiii. 1, 2) that the Lord directed the sending of them, but here we find that the people first desired it, and God, in permitting it, gave them up to their counsels: *You said, We will send men before us*, v. 22. Moses had given them God's word (v. 20, 21) but they could not find in their hearts to rely upon that: human policy goes further with them than divine wisdom, and they will needs light a candle to the sun.

IV. He repeats the report which the spies brought of the goodness of the land which they were sent to survey, v. 24, 25. Yet they represented the difficulties of conquering it as insuperable (v. 28).

V. He tells them what pains he took with them to encourage them, when their brethren had said so much to discourage them (v. 29). He assured them that God was present with them. And for proof of his power over their enemies he refers them to what they had seen done in Egypt. And for proof of God's goodwill to them he refers them to what *they had seen in the wilderness* (v. 31, 33), through which they had been guided with as much care and tenderness as were ever shown to any child borne in the arms of a nursing father. And was there any room left to distrust this God?

VI. He charges them with the sin which they were guilty of upon this occasion. 1. Disobedience, and rebellion against God's law. 2. Invidious reflections upon God's goodness. 3. An unbelieving heart at the bottom of all this: *You did not believe the Lord your God*, v. 32.

VII. He repeats the sentence passed upon them. 1. They were all condemned to die in the wilderness, and none of them must be suffered to enter Canaan except Caleb and Joshua, v. 34–38. It was not the breach of any of the commands of the law that shut them out of Canaan, no, not the golden calf, but their disbelief of that promise which was typical of gospel grace, to signify that no sin will ruin us but unbelief, which is a sin against the remedy. 2. Moses himself afterwards fell under God's displeasure for a hasty word which they provoked him to speak: *The Lord was angry with me for your sakes*, v. 37. 3. Yet here is mercy mixed with wrath. (1) That, though Moses might not bring them into Canaan, Joshua should (v. 38): (2) That, though this generation should not enter into Canaan, the next should, v. 39.

VIII. He reminds them of their foolish and fruitless attempt to get this sentence reversed when it was too late. 1. They tried it by their reformation in this particular; whereas they had refused to go up against the Canaanites, now they would go up. But this, which looked like a reformation, proved but a further rebellion. They were chased and destroyed. 2. They tried by their prayers and tears to get the sentence reversed: *They returned and wept before the Lord*, v. 45. These were tears of repentance and humiliation *before* God. But their weeping was all to no purpose. *The Lord would not hearken to your voice*, because you would not hearken to his.

CHAPTER 2

Moses, in this chapter, proceeds in the rehearsal of God's providences concerning Israel in their way to Canaan, yet preserves not the record of any thing that happened during their tedious march back to the Red Sea, in which they wore out almost thirty-eight years, but makes his narrative to begin again when they faced about towards Canaan (ver. 1–3), and drew towards the countries that were inhabited, concerning which God here gives them direction, I. What nations they must not give any disturbance to. 1. Not to the Edomites, ver. 4–8. 2. Not to the Moabites (ver. 9), of the antiquities of whose country, with that of the Edomites, he gives some account, ver. 10–12. And here comes in an account of their passing the river Zered, ver. 13–16. 3. Not to the Ammonites, of whose country here is some account given, ver. 17–23. II. What nations they should attack and conquer. They must begin with Sihon, king of the Amorites, ver. 24, 25. And accordingly, 1. They had a fair occasion of quarrelling with him, ver. 26–32. 2. God gave them a complete victory over him, ver. 33, &c.

Verses 1–7

I. A short account of the long stay of Israel in the wilderness: *We compassed Mount Seir many days*, v. 1. Nearly *thirty-eight* years they wandered in the deserts of Seir; probably in some of their rests they stayed several years.

II. Orders given them to turn towards Canaan.

III. A charge given them not to annoy the Edomites.

1. They must not offer any hostility to them as enemies: *Meddle not with them*, v. 4, 5.

2. They must trade with them as neighbours, buy meat and water of them, and pay for what they bought, v. 6. Religion must never be made a cloak for injustice.

Verses 8–23

It is observable here that Moses, speaking of the Edomites (v. 8), calls them our brethren, the children of Esau. Though they had been unkind to Israel, in refusing them a peaceable passage through their country, yet he calls them brethren. Now in these verses we have,

I. The account which Moses gives of the origin of the Moabites, Edomites, and Ammonites. Here he tells us how they came to those countries in which Israel found them; they were not the *aborigines*, or first planters. But, 1. The Moabites dwelt in a country which had belonged to a numerous race of giants, called *Emim* (that is, *terrible ones*), as tall as the Anakim, and perhaps more fierce, v. 10, 11. 2. The Edomites in like manner dispossessed the Horim from Mount Seir, and took their country (v. 12 and again v. 22), of which we read, Gen. xxxvi. 20. 3. The Ammonites likewise got possession of a country that had formerly been inhabited by giants, called *Zamzummim, crafty men*, or *wicked men* (v. 20, 21), probably the same that are called *Zuzim*, Gen. xiv. 5. He illustrates these remarks by an instance older than any of these; the Caphtorim (who were akin to the Philistines, Gen. x. 14) drove the Avim out of their country, and took possession of it, *v.* 23. The learned bishop Patrick supposes these Avites, being expelled hence, to have settled in Assyria, and to be the same people we read of under that name, 2 Kings xvii. 31.

II. The advances which Israel made towards Canaan. They *passed by the way of the wilderness of Moab* (*v.* 8), and then went over the brook or vale of Zered (*v.* 13), and there Moses takes notice of the fulfilling of the word which God had spoken concerning them, that none of those that were numbered at Mount Sinai should see the land that God had promised, Num. xiv. 23.

III. The caution given them not to meddle with the Moabites or Ammonites, whom they must not disseize, nor so much as disturb in their possessions: *Distress them not, nor contend with them*, *v.* 9. But why must not the Moabites and Ammonites be meddled with? 1. Because they were the *children of Lot* (*v.* 9, 19), righteous Lot who kept his integrity in Sodom. 2. Because the land they were possessed of was what God had given them, and he did not design it for Israel.

Verses 24–37

God having tried the self-denial of his people in forbidding them to meddle with the Moabites and Ammonites, and they having quietly passed by those rich countries, and, though superior in number, not made any attack upon them, here he recompenses them for their obedience by giving them possession of the country of Sihon king of the Amorites.

I. God gives them commission to seize upon the country of Sihon king of Heshbon, *v.* 24, 25. This was then God's way of disposing of kingdoms, but such particular grants are not now either to be expected or pretended.

II. Moses sends to Sihon a message of peace, and only begs a passage through his land, with a promise to give his country no disturbance, but the advantage of trading for ready money with so great a body, *v.* 26–29.

III. Sihon began the war (*v.* 32).

IV. Israel was victorious. 1. They put all the Amorites to the sword, men, women, and children (*v.* 33, 34). They died, not as Israel's enemies, but as sacrifices to divine justice, in the offering of which sacrifices Israel was employed, as a kingdom of priests. 2. They took possession of all they had; their cities (*v.* 34), their goods (*v.* 35), and their land, *v.* 36.

CHAPTER 3

Moses, in this chapter, relates, I. The conquest of Og, king of Bashan, and the seizing of his country, ver. 1–11. II. The distribution of these new conquests to the two tribes and a half, ver. 12–17 under certain provisos and limitations, ver. 18–20. III. The encouragement given to Joshua to carry on the war which was so gloriously begun, ver. 21, 22. IV. Moses's request to go over into Canaan (ver. 23–25), with the denial of that request, but the grant of an equivalent, ver. 26, &c.

Verses 1–11

Another brave country delivered into the hand of Israel, that of Bashan.

I. How they got the mastery of Og, a very formidable prince, 1. He was very strong, for he was of the remnant of the giants (*v.* 11). When God pleads his people's cause he can deal with giants as with grasshoppers. No man's might can secure him against the Almighty. The army of Og was very powerful, for he had the command of sixty fortified cities, besides unwalled towns, *v.* 5. 2. He was very bold and daring. He trusted to his own strength, and so was hardened to his destruction. God bade Moses not fear him, *v.* 2. If Moses himself was so strong in faith as not to need

the caution, yet it is probable that the people needed it, and for them these fresh assurances are designed: "*I will deliver him into thy hand.*"

II. How they got possession of Bashan, a very desirable country. They took all the cities (*v.* 4), and all the spoil of them, *v.* 7. They made them all their own, *v.* 10. So that now they had in their hands all that fruitful country which lay east of Jordan, from *the river Arnon unto Hermon*, *v.* 8.

Verses 12–20

Having shown how this country which they were now in was conquered, in these verses he shows how it was settled upon the Reubenites, Gadites, and half tribe of Manasseh, which we had the story of before, Num. xxxii. 1. Moses specifies the particular parts of the country that were allotted to each tribe, especially the distribution of the lot to the half tribe of Manasseh, the subdividing of which tribe is observable. 2. He repeats the condition of the grant which they had already agreed to, *v.* 18–20. That they should send a strong detachment over Jordan to lead the van in the conquest of Canaan, who should not return to their families till they had seen their brethren in as full possession of their respective allotments as they themselves were now in of theirs. A good man cannot rejoice much in the comforts of his family unless withal he sees *peace upon Israel*, Ps. cxxviii. 6.

Verses 21–29

Here is, I. The encouragement which Moses gave to Joshua, who was to succeed him in the government, *v.* 21, 22. He commanded him not to fear. Two things he would have him consider for his encouragement:—1. What God had done. Joshua had seen what a total defeat God had given by the forces of Israel to these two kings. He must not only infer thence that thus the Lord can do with them all, for his arm is not shortened, but thus he will do, for his purpose is not changed; he that has begun will finish. 2. What God had promised. The *Lord your God he shall fight for you*; and that cause cannot but be victorious which the Lord of hosts fights for.

II. The prayer which Moses made for himself, and the answer which God gave to that prayer.

1. His prayer was that, if it were God's will, he might go before Israel over Jordan into Canaan. *Let me go over and see the good land.* Not, "Let me go over and be a prince and a ruler there"; he seeks not his own honour, is content to resign the government to Joshua; but, "Let me go to be a spectator of thy kindness to Israel, to see what I believe concerning the goodness of the land of promise."

2. God's answer to this prayer had in it a mixture of mercy and judgment, that he might sing unto God of both.

(1) There was judgment in the denial of his request, and that in something of anger too: *The Lord was wroth with me for your sakes*, *v.* 26. But how was he wroth with Moses *for the sake of Israel*? Either, [1] For that sin which they provoked him to; see Ps. cvi. 32, 33. Or, [2] The removal of Moses at that time, when he could so ill be spared, was a rebuke to all Israel, and a punishment of their sin. Though Moses, being one of the wrestling seed of Jacob, did not seek in vain, yet he had not the thing itself which he sought for. God may accept our prayers, and yet not grant us the very thing we pray for.

(2) Here is mercy mixed with this wrath in several things:—[1] God quieted the spirit of Moses, *Let it suffice thee*. With this word, no doubt, a divine power went to reconcile Moses to the will of God, and to bring him to acquiesce in it. If God does not by his providence give us what we desire, yet, if by his grace he makes us content without it, it comes to the

same. [2] He put an honour upon his prayer in directing him not to insist upon this request: *Speak no more to me of this matter*. [3] He promised him a sight of Canaan *from the top of Pisgah*, v. 27. Though he should not have the possession of it, he should have the prospect of it; not to tantalize him, but such a sight of it as would yield him true satisfaction, and would enable him to form a very clear and pleasing idea of that promised land. [4] He provided him a successor, one who should support the honour of Moses and carry on and complete that glorious work which the heart of Moses was so much upon, the bringing of Israel to Canaan, and settling them there (v. 28).

CHAPTER 4

In this chapter we have, I. A most earnest and pathetic exhortation to obedience, backed with arguments, repeated again and again, and set before them in the most moving and affectionate manner imaginable, ver. 1–40. II. The appointing of the cities of refuge on that side Jordan, ver. 41–43. III. The particular description of the place where Moses delivered the following repetition of the law, ver. 44, &c.

Verses 1–40

This most lively and excellent discourse is often repeated.

I. In general, it is the use and application of the foregoing history. This use we should make of the review of God's providences concerning us, we should by them be quickened and engaged to duty and obedience.

II. The scope and drift of his discourse is to persuade them to keep close to God and to his service, and not to forsake him for any other god.

1. See here how he charges and commands them, and shows them *what the Lord requires of them*.

(1) He demands their diligent attention to the word of God: *Hearken, O Israel*. He means, not only that they must now give him the hearing, but that whenever the book of the law was read to them, or read by them, they should be attentive to it.

(2) He charges them to preserve the divine law pure and entire among them, v. 2. Keep it pure, and do not add to it; keep it entire, and do not diminish from it.

(3) He charges them to keep God's *commandments* (v. 2), to *do them* (v. 5, 14), to *keep and do them* (v. 6), to *perform the covenant*, v. 13. Hearing must be in order to doing, knowledge in order to practice.

(4) He charges them to be very strict and careful in their observance of the law (v. 9): *Only take heed to thyself, and keep thy soul diligently*; and (v. 15), *Take you therefore good heed unto yourselves*; and again (v. 23), *Take heed to yourselves*.

(5) He charges them particularly to take heed of the sin of idolatry. Two sorts of idolatry he cautions them against:—[1] The worship of images, however by them they might intend to worship the true God, as they had done in the golden calf, so changing the *truth of God into a lie* and his *glory into shame*. The second commandment is expressly directed against this, and is here enlarged upon, v. 15–18. To represent an infinite Spirit by an image, and the great Creator by the image of a creature, is the greatest affront we can put upon God and the greatest cheat we can put upon ourselves. As an argument against their making images of God, he urges it very much upon them that when God made himself known to them at Horeb he did it by a voice of words which sounded in their ears, to teach them that *faith comes by hearing*, and God in the word is nigh us; but no image was presented to their eye, for to see God as he is is reserved for our happiness in the other world, and to see him as he is not will do us hurt and no good in this world. You saw *no similitude* (v. 12), *no manner of similitude*, v. 15. [2] The worship of the

sun, moon, and stars, is another sort of idolatry which they are here cautioned against, v. 19. This was the most ancient species of idolatry and the most plausible. And the plausibleness of it made it the more dangerous. *When thou seest the sun, moon, and stars*, thou wilt so admire their height and brightness, their regular motion and powerful influence, that thou wilt be strongly tempted to give that glory to them which is due to him that made them. It seems there was need of a great deal of resolution to arm them against this temptation, so weak was their faith in an invisible God and an invisible world. These pretended deities, the *sun, moon, and stars*, were only blessings which the Lord their God had imparted to all nations. It is absurd to worship them, for they are man's servants, were made and ordained to give light on earth.

(6) He charges them to teach their children to observe the laws of God: *Teach them to thy sons, and thy sons' sons* (v. 9), *that they may teach their children*, v. 10.

(7) He charges them never to forget their duty: *Take heed lest you forget the covenant of the Lord your God*, v. 23.

2. Let us see now what are the motives or arguments with which he backs these exhortations.

(1) He urges the greatness, glory, and goodness, of God. Did we consider what a God he is with whom we have to do, we should surely make conscience of our duty to him and not dare to sin against him. He reminds them here that the Lord Jehovah is the *one only living and true God*. All the deities of the heathen were counterfeits and usurpers; nor did any of them so much as pretend to be universal monarchs in heaven and earth, but only local deities. The Israelites, who worshipped no other than the supreme *Numen—Divinity*, were for ever inexcusable if they either changed their God or neglected him. Take heed of offending him, for he must have your entire affection and adoration, and will by no means endure a rival. Even in the New Testament we find the same argument urged upon us as a reason why we should serve *God with reverence* (Heb. xii. 28, 29), because though he is our God, and a rejoicing light to those that serve him faithfully, yet he is a consuming fire to those that trifle with him. Yet he is *a merciful God*, v. 31. It comes in here as an encouragement to repentance, but might serve as an inducement to obedience, and a consideration proper to prevent their apostasy.

(2) He urges their relation to this God, his authority over them and their obligations to him. He is the *Lord God of your fathers* (v. 1), so that you are his by inheritance: your fathers were his, and you were born in his house. "He is the *Lord your God* (v. 2), so that you are his by your own consent. He is the *Lord my God* (v. 5), so that I treat with you as his agent and ambassador."

(3) He urges the wisdom of being religious: *For this is your wisdom in the sight of the nations*, v. 6. Great things may justly be looked for from those who are guided by divine revelation, and unto whom are committed the oracles of God.

(4) He urges the singular advantages which they enjoyed by virtue of the happy establishment they were under, v. 7, 8. Our communion with God (which is the highest honour and happiness we are capable of in this world) is kept up by the word and prayer; in both these Israel were happy above any people under heaven. The law of God is far more excellent than the law of nations. No law so consonant to natural equity and the unprejudiced dictates of right reason, so consistent with itself in all the parts of it, and so conducive to the welfare and interest of mankind, as the scripture-law is, Ps. cxix. 128. Those that magnify the law shall be magnified by it.

(5) He urges God's glorious appearances to them at Mount Sinai, when he gave them this law. This he insists much upon. Take heed *lest thou forget the day that thou stoodest before the Lord thy God in Horeb, v.* 10. By what we see of God sufficient ground is given us to believe him to be a Being of infinite power and perfection, but no occasion given us to suspect him to have a body such as we have. What they heard at Mount Sinai (*v.* 12): "*The Lord spoke unto you* with an intelligible voice, in your own language, and you heard it." God manifests himself to all the world in the works of creation, without speech or language, and yet their voice is heard (Ps. xix. 1–3); but to Israel he made himself known by speech and language, condescending to the weakness of the church's infant state.

(6) He urges God's gracious appearances for them, in bringing them out of Egypt, from the iron furnace, where they laboured in the fire, forming them into a people, and then taking them to be his own people, a *people of inheritance* (*v.* 20); this he mentions again, *v.* 34, 37, 38. They were designed for a happy settlement in Canaan, *v.* 38.

(7) He urges God's righteous appearance against them sometimes for their sins. He specifies particularly the matter of Peor, *v.* 3, 4. This had happened very lately: their eyes had seen but the other day the sudden destruction of those that joined themselves to Baal-peor and the preservation of those that clave to the Lord, from which they might easily infer the danger of apostasy from God and the benefit of adherence to him.

(8) He urges the certain advantage of obedience.

(9) He urges the fatal consequences of their apostasy from God, that it would undoubtedly be the ruin of their nation. This he enlarges upon, *v.* 25–31. Here observe, *First,* That whatever place we are in we may *thence seek the Lord our God,* though ever so remote from our own land or from his holy temple. There is no part of this earth that has a gulf fixed between it and heaven. *Secondly,* Those, and those only, shall find God to their comfort, who seek him with all their heart. *Thirdly,* Afflictions are sent to engage and quicken us to see God, and, by the grace of God working with them, many are thus reduced to their right mind.

Now let all these arguments be laid together, and then say whether religion has not reason on its side. None cast off the government of their God but those that have first abandoned the understanding of a man.

Verses 41–49

Here is, 1. The nomination of the cities of refuge on that side Jordan where Israel now lay encamped. Three cities were appointed for that purpose, one in the lot of Reuben, another in that of Gad, and another in that of the half tribe of Manasseh, *v.* 41–43. 2. The introduction to another sermon that Moses preached to Israel, which we have in the following chapters. Probably it was preached the next sabbath day after, when the congregation attended to receive instruction. He had in general exhorted them to obedience in the former chapter; here he comes to repeat the law which they were to observe, for he demands a universal but not an implicit obedience. How can we do our duty if we do not know it? Here therefore he sets the law before them as the rule they were to work by.

CHAPTER 5

In this chapter we have the second edition of the ten commandments. I. The general intent of them; they were in the nature of a covenant between God and Israel, ver. 1–5. II. The particular precepts are repeated (ver. 6–21), with the double delivery of them, both by word and writing, ver. 22. III. The settling of the correspondence thenceforward between God and Israel, by the mediation and ministry of Moses. 1. It was Israel's humble petition that it might be so, ver. 23–27. 2. It was God's gracious grant that it should be so, ver. 28–31. And hence he infers the obligation they were under to obedience, ver. 32, 33.

Verses 1–5

Here, 1. Moses summons the assembly. He *called all Israel.* 2. He demands attention. 3. He refers them to the covenant made with them in Horeb, as that which they must govern themselves by. See the wonderful condescension of divine grace in turning the command into a covenant. Observe, (1) The parties to this covenant. "The covenant was made with us, or our immediate parents that represented us, before Mount Sinai, and transacted for us." (2) The publication of this covenant. God himself did, as it were, read the articles to them (*v.* 4): He *talked with you face to face; word to word,* so the Chaldee. (3) The mediator of the covenant: *Moses stood between God and them,* at the foot of the mount (*v.* 5). Herein Moses was a type of Christ, who *stands between God and man, to show us the word of the Lord,* a blessed days-man, that has laid his hand upon us both, so that we may both hear from God and speak to him without trembling.

Verses 6–22

Here is the repetition of the ten commandments, in which observe, 1. Though they had been spoken before, and written, yet they are again rehearsed. 2. There is some variation here from that record (Exod. xx.). 3. The most considerable variation is in the fourth commandment. In Exod. xx. the reason annexed is taken from the creation of the world; here it is taken from their deliverance out of Egypt, because that was typical of our redemption by Jesus Christ, in remembrance of which the Christian sabbath was to be observed: *Remember that thou wast a servant, and God brought thee out, v.* 15. And therefore, (1) "It is fit that thy servants should be favoured by the sabbath-rest; for thou knowest the heart of a servant, and how welcome one day's ease will be after six days' labour." (2) "It is fit that thy God should be honoured by the sabbath-work, and the religious services of the day, in consideration of the great things he has done for thee." In the resurrection of Christ we were brought into the glorious liberty of the children of God, *with a mighty hand and an outstretched arm*: therefore, by the gospel-edition of the law, we are directed to observe the first day of the week, in remembrance of that glorious work of power and grace. 4. It is added in the fifth commandment, *That it may go well with thee,* which addition the apostle quotes, and puts first (Eph. vi. 3), *that it may be well with thee, and that thou mayest live long.* 5. The last five commandments are connected or coupled together, which they are not in Exodus: *Neither shalt thou commit adultery, neither shalt thou steal,* &c., which intimates that God's commands are all of a piece. 6. That these commandments were given with a great deal of awful solemnity, *v.* 22.

Verses 23–33

I. Moses reminds them of the agreement of both the parties that were now treating, in the mediation of Moses.

1. Here is the consternation that the people were put into by that extreme terror with which the law was given. They owned that they could not bear it any more: "*This great fire will consume us*; this dreadful voice will be fatal to us; we shall certainly die if we hear it any more," *v.* 25.

2. Their earnest request that God would henceforward speak to them by Moses, with a promise that they would hear what he said as from God himself, and do it, *v.* 27.

3. God's approbation of their request. He appoints

Moses to be his messenger to them, to receive the law from his mouth and to communicate it to them, v. 31. God should henceforward speak to us by men like ourselves, by Moses and the prophets, by the apostles and the evangelists, and, if we believe not these, neither should we be persuaded though God should speak to us as he did to Israel at Mount Sinai.

II. Hence he infers a charge to them to observe and do all that God had commanded them, v. 32, 33.

CHAPTER 6

Moses, in this chapter, goes on with his charge to Israel, to be sure to keep up their religion in Canaan. It is much the same with ch. iv. I. His preface is a persuasive to obedience, ver. 1–3. II. He lays down the great principles of obedience. The first truth to be believed, That God is one, ver. 4. The first duty to be done, To love him with all our heart, ver. 5. III. He prescribes the means for keeping up religion, ver. 6–9. IV. He cautions them against those things which would be the ruin of religion—abuse of plenty (ver. 10–12), inclination to idolatry (ver. 14, 15), and gives them some general precepts, ver. 13, 16–18. V. He directs them what instructions to give their children, ver. 20, &c.

Verses 1–3

Observe here, 1. That Moses taught the people all that, and that only, which God commanded him to teach them, v. 1. Thus Christ's ministers are to teach his churches *all that he has commanded*, and neither more nor less, Matt. xxviii. 20. 2. That the end of their being taught was that they might do as they were taught (v. 1), might *keep God's statutes* (v. 2), and *observe to do them*, v. 3. 3. That Moses carefully endeavoured to fix them for God and godliness, now that they were entering upon the land of Canaan.

Verses 4–16

Here is, I. A brief summary of religion, containing the first principles of faith and obedience, v. 4, 5. These two verses the Jews reckon one of the choicest portions of scripture: they write it in their phylacteries, and think themselves not only obliged to say it at least twice every day, but very happy in being so obliged, having this saying among them, *Blessed are we, who every morning and evening say, Hear, O Israel, the Lord our God is one Lord.*

1. What we are here taught to believe concerning God: That *Jehovah our God is one Jehovah.* (1) That the God whom we serve is Jehovah, a Being infinitely and eternally perfect, self-existent, and self-sufficient. (2) That he is the one only living and true God; he only is God, and he is but one. The firm belief of this self-evident truth would effectually arm them against all idolatry, which was introduced by that fundamental error, that there are gods many. Happy they that have this one Lord for their God; for they have but one master to please, but one benefactor to seek to. It is better to have one fountain than a thousand cisterns, one all-sufficient God than a thousand insufficient ones.

2. What we are here taught concerning the duty which God requires of man. It is all summed up in this as its principle, *Thou shalt love the Lord thy God with all thy heart.* Did ever any prince make a law that his subjects should love him? Yet such is the condescension of the divine grace that this is made the first and great commandment of God's law, that we love him, and that we perform all other parts of our duty to him from a principle of love. With an intelligent love; for so it is explained, Mark xii. 33. To love him with all the heart, and with all the understanding, we must know him, and therefore love him as those that see good cause to love him.

II. Means are here prescribed for the maintaining and keeping up of religion in our hearts and houses, that it might not wither and go to decay. And they are these:—1. Meditation: *These words which I com-*

mand thee shall be in thy heart, v. 6. 2. The religious education of children (v. 7): "*Thou shalt teach them diligently to thy children;* and by communicating thy knowledge thou wilt increase it." Take all occasions to discourse with those about thee of divine things; not of unrevealed mysteries, or matters of doubtful disputation, but of the plain truths and laws of God, and the things that belong to our peace. The more conversant we are with them the more we shall admire them and be affected with them, and may thereby be instrumental to communicate divine light and heat. God appointed them, at least for the present, to write some select sentences of the law, that were most weighty and comprehensive, upon their walls, or in scrolls of parchment to be worn about their wrists; and some think that hence the phylacteries so much used among the Jews took rise. Christ blames the Pharisees, not for wearing them, but for affecting to have them broader than other people's, Matt. xxiii. 5. It was prudently and piously provided by the first reformers of the English church that then, when Bibles were scarce, some select portions of scripture should be written on the walls and pillars of the churches, which the people might make familiar to them.

III. A caution is here given not to forget God in a day of prosperity and plenty, v. 10–12. He raises their expectations of the goodness of their God, taking it for granted that he would bring them into the good land that he had promised (v. 10), that they should no longer dwell in tents as shepherds and poor travellers, but should settle in great and goodly cities, should no longer wander in a barren wilderness, but should enjoy houses well furnished and gardens well planted (v. 11), *Cities which thou buildest not, houses which thou filledst not, &c.*

IV. Some special precepts and prohibitions are here given, 1. They must upon all occasions give honour to God (v. 13). Swear by his name in all treaties and covenants with the neighbouring nations, and do not compliment them so far as to swear by their gods. They must take heed of dishonouring God by *tempting him* (v. 16): "You shall not in any exigence distrust the power, presence, and providence of God."

Verses 17–25

I. Moses charges them to keep God's commandments themselves: *You shall diligently keep God's commandments, v.* 17–19.

II. He charges them to instruct their children in the commands of God, not only that they might in their tender years intelligently and affectionately join in religious services, but that afterwards they might in their day keep up religion, and convey it to those that should come after them. Now,

1. Here is a proper question which it is supposed the children would ask (v. 20): "*What mean the testimonies and the statutes?* What is the meaning of the feasts we observe, the sacrifices we offer, and the many peculiar customs we keep up?" Observe, (1) All divine institutions have a certain meaning, and there is something great designed in them. (2) It concerns us to know and understand the meaning of them, that we may perform a reasonable service, and may not *offer the blind for sacrifice.*

2. Here is a full answer put into the parents' mouths to be given to this good question. Did the children ask the meaning of God's laws? Let them be told that they were to be observed, (1) In a grateful remembrance of God's former favours to them, especially their deliverance out of Egypt, v. 21–23. (2) As the prescribed condition of his further favours (v. 24): *The Lord commanded us all these statutes for our good.* Could we perfectly fulfil but that one command of loving God with all our heart, soul,

and might, and could we say, "We have never done otherwise," this would be so our righteousness as to entitle us to the benefits of the covenant of innocency; had we continued in every thing that is written in the book of the law to do it, the law would have justified us. But this we cannot pretend to, therefore our sincere obedience shall be accepted through a Mediator.

CHAPTER 7

Moses in this chapter exhorts, Israel I. In general, to keep God's commandments, ver. 11, 12. II. In particular to keep themselves pure from all communion with idolaters. 1. They must utterly destroy the seven devoted nations, ver. 1, 2, 16, 24. 2. They must by no means marry with the remainders of them, ver. 3, 4. 3. They must deface and consume their altars and images, and not so much as take the silver and gold of them to their own use, ver. 5, 25, 26. To enforce this charge, he shows that they were bound to do so, (1) In duty. Considering [1] Their election to God, ver. 6. [2] The reason of that election, ver. 7, 8. [3] The terms they stood upon with God, ver, 9. 10. (2) In interest. It is here promised, [1] In general, that, if they would serve God, he would bless and prosper them, ver. 12-15. [2] In particular, that if they would drive out the nations, that they might not be a temptation to them, God would drive them out, that they should not be any vexation to them, ver. 17, &c.

Verses 1–11

I. A very strict caution against all friendship and fellowship with idols and idolaters.

1. These devoted nations are here named and numbered (v. 1). They are specified that Israel might know the bounds and limits of their commission. The confining of this commission to the nations here mentioned plainly intimates that after-ages were not to draw this into a precedent; this will not serve to justify those barbarous laws which give no quarter. If God cast them out, Israel must not take them in, no, not as tenants, nor tributaries, nor servants. The iniquity of the Amorites was now full, and the longer it had been in the filling the sorer was the vengeance when it came at last. The people of these abominations must not be mingled with the holy seed, lest they corrupt them. Thus we must deal with our lusts that war against our souls; God has delivered them into our hands by that promise, *Sin shall not have dominion over you*, unless it be your own faults; let not us then make covenants with them, nor show them any mercy, but mortify and crucify them, and utterly destroy them.

2. They must make no marriages with those of them that escaped the sword, v. 3, 4. There is more ground of fear in mixed marriages that the good will be perverted than of hope that the bad will be converted. One of the Chaldee paraphrases adds here, as a reason of this command (v. 3), *For he that marries with idolaters does in effect marry with their idols.*

3. They must destroy all the relics of their idolatry, v. 5. Their altars and pillars, their groves and graven images, all must be destroyed, both in a holy indignation against idolatry and to prevent infection.

II. Here are very good reasons to enforce this caution.

1. The choice which God had made of this people for his own, v. 6.

2. The freeness of that grace which made this choice. God fetched the reason of it purely from himself, v. 8. All that God loves he loves freely, Hos. xiv. 4.

3. The tenor of the covenant into which they were taken; it was in short this, That as they were to God so God would be to them.

Verses 12–26

I. The caution against idolatry is repeated, and against communion with idolaters. Here is also a repetition of the charge to destroy the images, v. 25, 26. The idols which the heathen had worshipped were an abomination to God, and therefore must be so to them: all that truly love God hate what he hates.

II. The promise of God's favour to them if they would be obedient is enlarged upon. All possible assurance is here given them. Let us be constant in our duty, and we cannot question the constancy of God's mercy. If they would keep themselves pure from the idolatries of Egypt, God would keep them clear from the *diseases of Egypt*, v. 15. It seems to refer not only to those plagues of Egypt by the force of which they were delivered, but to some other epidemical country disease (as we call it), which they remembered the prevalence of among the Egyptians, and by which God had chastised them for their national sins. Let them not be disheartened by the slow progress of their arms, nor think that the Canaanites would never be subdued if they were not expelled the first year; no, they must be *put out by little and little*, and not *all at once*, v. 22. Note, We must not think that, because the deliverance of the church and the destruction of its enemies are not effected immediately, therefore they will never be effected. God will do his own work in his own method and time, and we may be sure that they are always the best. Thus corruption is driven out of the hearts of believers *by little and little*. The work of sanctification is carried on gradually; but that judgment will at length be brought forth into a complete victory.

CHAPTER 8

Moses had charged parents in teaching their children to whet the word of God upon them (ch. vi. 7) by frequent repetition of the same things over and over again; and here he himself takes the same method of instructing the Israelites as his children, frequently inculcating the same precepts and cautions. In this chapter Moses gives them, I. General exhortations to obedience, ver. 1, 6. II. A review of the great things God had done for them in the wilderness, as a good argument for obedience, ver. 2-5, and ver. 15, 16. III. A prospect of the good land into which God would now bring them, ver. 7-9. IV. A necessary caution against the temptations of a prosperous condition, ver. 10-14, and 17, 18. V. A fair warning of the fatal consequences of apostasy from God, ver. 19, 20.

Verses 1–9

The charge here given them is the same as before, to keep and do all God's commandments. He directs them,

I. To look back upon the wilderness through which God had now brought them. Now that they had come of age, and were entering upon their inheritance, they must be reminded of the discipline they had been under during their minority and the method God had taken to train them up for himself. The wilderness was the school in which they had been for forty years boarded and taught, under tutors and governors; and this was a time to bring it all to remembrance. Here let us set up our Ebenezer.

1. They must remember the straits they were sometimes brought into, (1) For the mortifying of their pride. (2) For the manifesting of their perverseness. God thereby proved them whether they would trust his promises, the word which he commanded to a thousand generations, and, in dependence on his promises, obey his precepts.

2. They must remember the supplies which were always granted them. Though God has appointed bread for the strengthening of man's heart, and that is ordinarily made the staff of life, yet God can, when he pleases, command support and nourishment without it, and make something else, very unlikely, to answer the intention as well. We might live upon air if it were sanctified for that use by *the word of God*. Our Saviour quotes this scripture in answer to that temptation of Satan, *Command that these stones be made bread.* "What need of that?" says Christ; "my heavenly Father can keep me alive without bread," Matt. iv. 3, 4. It may be applied spiritually; the *word of God*, as it is the revelation of

God's will and grace duly received and entertained by faith, is the food of the soul. The life which is supported by that is the life of the man, and not only that life which is supported by bread. The manna typified Christ, *the bread of life*. He is *the Word of God*; by him we live.

3. They must also remember the rebukes they had been under, *v.* 5. During these years of their education they had been kept under a strict discipline, and not without need. They were chastened that they might not be condemned, chastened with the rod of men. Not as a man wounds and slays his enemies whose destruction he aims at, but as a man chastens his son whose happiness and welfare he designs: so did their God chasten them; he chastened and taught them, Ps. xciv. 12.

II. He directs them to look forward to Canaan, into which God was now bringing them. Look which way we will, both our reviews and our prospects will furnish us with arguments for obedience.

Verses 10–20

Moses, having mentioned the great plenty they would find in the land of Canaan, finds it necessary to caution them against the abuse of that plenty, which was a sin they would be the more prone to now that they came into that vineyard of the Lord, immediately out of a barren desert.

I. He directs them to the duty of a prosperous condition, *v.* 10. Whatever they had the comfort of, God must have the glory of. As our Saviour has taught us to bless before we eat (Matt. xiv. 19, 20), so we are here taught to bless after meat. This is our *Hosanna—God bless*; this is our *Hallelujah—Blessed be God. In every thing we must give thanks.* From this law the religious Jews took up a laudable usage of blessing God, not only at their solemn meals, but upon other occasions; if they drank a cup of wine they lifted up their hands and said, *Blessed be he that created the fruit of the vine to make glad the heart.* If they did but smell at a flower, they said, *Blessed be he that made this flower sweet.*

II. He arms them against the temptations of a prosperous condition. 1. "Then take heed of pride." When the estate rises, the mind is apt to rise with it, in self-conceit, self-conplacency, and self-confidence. 2. "Then take heed of forgetting God." When men grow rich they are tempted to think religion a needless thing. They are happy without it, think it a thing below them and too hard upon them. Their dignity forbids them to stoop, and their liberty forbids them to serve.

CHAPTER 9

The design of Moses in this chapter is to convince the people of Israel of their utter unworthiness to receive from God those great favours that were now to be conferred upon them. I. He assures them of victory over their enemies, ver. 1–3. II. He cautions them not to attribute their successes to their own merit, but to God's justice, which was engaged against their enemies, and his faithfulness, which was engaged to their fathers, ver. 4–6. III. To make it evident that they had no reason to boast of their own righteousness, he mentions their faults. In general, they had been all along a provoking people, ver. 7–24. In particular, 1. In the matter of the golden calf, the story of which he largely relates, ver. 8–21. 2. He mentions some other instances of their rebellion, ver. 22, 23. And, 3. Returns, at ver. 25, to speak of the intercession he had made for them at Horeb, to prevent their being ruined for the golden calf.

Verses 1–6

The call to attention (*v.* 1), *Hear, O Israel*, intimates that this was a new discourse.

I. Moses represents to the people the formidable strength of the enemies which they were now to encounter, *v.* 1. This representation is much the same with that which the evil spies had made (Num. xiii. 28, 33), but made with a very different intention:

that was designed to drive them from God and to discourage their hope in him; this to drive them to God and to engage their hope in him.

II. He assures them of victory, by the presence of God with them, notwithstanding the strength of the enemy, *v.* 3.

III. He cautions them not to entertain the least thought of their own righteousness, as if that had procured them this favour at God's hand. Note, Our gaining possession of the heavenly Canaan, as it must be attributed to God's power and not to our own might, so it must be ascribed to God's grace and not to our own merit.

IV. He intimates to them the true reasons why God would take this good land out of the hands of the Canaanites, and settle it upon Israel.

Verses 7–29

That they might have no pretence to think that God brought them to Canaan *for their righteousness*, Moses here shows them what a miracle of mercy it was that they had not long ere this been destroyed in the wilderness: "*Remember, and forget not, how thou provokedst the Lord thy God* (*v.* 7); so far from purchasing his favour, thou hast many a time laid thyself open to his displeasure." They had been a provoking people ever since they came out of Egypt, *v.* 7. Though the Mosaic history records little more than the occurrences of the first and last year of the forty, yet it seems by this general account that the rest of the years were not much better, but one continued provocation.

Now let them lay all this together, and it will appear that whatever favour God should hereafter show them, in subduing their enemies and putting them in possession of the land of Canaan, it was not for their righteousness. It is good for us often to remember against ourselves, with sorrow and shame, our former sins, and to review the records conscience keeps of them, that we may see how much we are indebted to free grace, and may humbly own that we never merited at God's hand any thing but wrath and the curse.

CHAPTER 10

Moses, in this chapter, sets before them God's great mercy to them, notwithstanding their provocations. I. He mentions divers tokens of God's favour and reconciliation to them, never to be forgotten. (1) The renewing of the tables of the covenant, ver. 1–5. (2) Giving orders for their progress towards Canaan, ver. 6, 7. (3) Choosing the tribe of Levi for his own, ver. 8, 9. (4) And continuing the priesthood after the death of Aaron, ver. 6. (5) Owning and accepting the intercession of Moses for them, ver. 10, 11. II. Hence he infers what obligations they lay under to fear, and love, and serve God, ver. 12, &c.

Verses 1–11

There were four things in and by which God showed himself reconciled to Israel and made them truly great and happy.

I. He gave them his law, gave it to them in writing, as a standing pledge of his favour. Note, God's putting his law in our hearts, and writing it in our inward parts, furnish the surest evidence of our reconciliation to God and the best earnest of our happiness in him. God will send his law and gospel to those whose hearts are prepared as arks to receive them. Christ is the ark in which now our salvation is kept safely, that it may not be lost as it was in the first Adam, when he had it in his own hand. These two tables, thus engraven, were faithfully laid up in the ark. *And there they be*, said Moses, pointing it is probable towards the sanctuary, *v.* 5. That good thing which was committed to him, he transmitted to them, and left it pure and entire in their hands; now let them look to it at their peril. Thus we may say to the rising generation, "God has entrusted us with Bibles, sabbaths, sacraments, &c., as tokens of his presence and favour, and there they be; we lodge them with you," 2 Tim. i. 13, 14.

II. He led them forward towards Canaan, though they in their hearts turned back towards Egypt, and he might justly have chosen their delusions, *v.* 6, 7.

III. He appointed a standing ministry among them, to deal for them in holy things. Note, A settled ministry is a great blessing to a people, and a special token of God's favour. Under the law, a succession in the ministry was kept up, by an entail of the office on a certain tribe and family. But now, under the gospel, when the effusion of the Spirit is more plentiful and powerful, the succession is kept up by the Spirit's operation on men's hearts, qualifying men for, and inclining men to, that work, some in every age.

IV. He accepted Moses as an advocate or intercessor for them, and therefore constituted him their prince and leader (*v.* 10, 11): *The Lord hearkened to me and said, Arise, go before the people.* It was a mercy to them that they had such a friend, so faithful both to him that appointed him and to those for whom he was appointed.

Verses 12–22

A most pathetic exhortation to obedience.

I. We are here most plainly directed in our duty to God, to our neighbour, and to ourselves.

1. We are here taught our duty to God. We must *fear the Lord our God*, *v.* 12, and again *v.* 20. Fear him as a great God, and Lord, and love him as a good God and Father and benefactor. We must *serve him* (*v.* 20), *serve him with all our heart and soul* (*v.* 12), and what we do for him we must do cheerfully and with a good will. We must *keep his commandments and his statutes*, *v.* 13.

2. We are here taught our duty to our neighbour (*v.* 19): *Love the stranger*; and, if the stranger, much more our brethren, as ourselves. Two arguments are here urged to enforce this duty:—(1) God's common providence, which extends itself to all nations of men, they being all *made of one blood*. God *loveth the stranger* (*v.* 18), that is, he gives to all life, and breath, and all things, even to those that are Gentiles, and *strangers to the commonwealth of Israel* and to Israel's God. (2) The afflicted condition which the Israelites themselves had been in, when they were strangers in Egypt. Those that have themselves been in distress, and have found mercy with God, should sympathize most feelingly with those that are in the like distress and be ready to show kindness to them. The people of the Jews conceived a rooted antipathy to the Gentiles, and this brought a final ruin upon themselves.

3. We are here taught our duty to ourselves (*v.* 16): *Circumcise the foreskin of your hearts*, that is, "Cast away from you all corrupt affections and inclinations, which hinder you from fearing and loving God. The circumcision of the heart makes it ready to yield to God, and draw in his yoke.

II. We are here most pathetically persuaded to our duty. Let but reason rule us, and religion will.

1. Consider the greatness and glory of God, and therefore fear him, and from that principle serve and obey him.

2. Consider the goodness and grace of God, and therefore love him, and from that principle serve and obey him. His goodness is his glory as much as his greatness.

Chapter 11

With this chapter Moses concludes his preface to the repetition of the statutes and judgments which they must observe to do. He repeats the general charge (ver. 1), and, having in the close of the foregoing chapter begun to mention the great things God had done among them, in this, I. He specifies several of the great works God had done before their eyes, ver. 2–7. II. He sets before

them, for the future, life and death, the blessing and the curse, according as they did, or did not, keep God's commandments. III. He directs them what means to use that they might keep in mind the law of God, ver. 18–21. Concludes all with solemnly charging them to choose which they would have, the blessing or the curse, ver. 26, &c.

Verses 1–7

Thou shalt *keep his charge*, that is, the oracles of his word and ordinances of his worship, with which they were entrusted and for which they were accountable. It is a phrase often used concerning the office of the priests and Levites, for all Israel was a kingdom of priests, a holy nation. Observe the connection of these two: *Thou shalt love the Lord*, and *keep his charge*, since love will work in obedience, and that only is acceptable obedience which flows from a principle of love. 1 John v. 3.

Verses 8–17

Still Moses urges the same subject, as loth to conclude till he had gained his point. "*If thou wilt enter into life*, if thou wilt enter into Canaan, a type of that life, and find it a good land indeed to thee, keep the commandments: *Keep all the commandments which I command you this day*; love God, and serve him with all your heart."

He does not go about to teach them the art of war, how to draw the bow, and use the sword, and keep ranks, that they might be strong, and go in and possess the land; no, but let them keep God's commandments, and their religion, while they are true to it, will be their strength and secure their success. Sin tends to the shortening of the days of particular persons and to the shortening of the days of a people's prosperity; but obedience will be a lengthening out of their tranquillity. Note, The better God has provided, by our outward condition, for our ease and convenience, the more we should abound in his service: the less we have to do for our bodies the more we should do for God and our souls. To awaken them to take heed, Moses here tells them plainly that if they should *turn aside to other gods*, 1. They would provoke the wrath of God against them. 2. Good things would be turned away from them; the heaven would withhold its rain, and then of course the earth would not yield its fruit.

Verses 18–25

I. Moses repeats the directions he had given for the guidance and assistance of the people in their obedience. Let us all be directed by the three rules here given:—1. Let our hearts be filled with the word of God: *Lay up these words in your heart and in your soul.* 2. Let our eyes be fixed upon the word of God. Bind these words for a sign *upon your hand*, which is always in view (Isa. xlix. 16), *and as frontlets between your eyes*. 3. Let our tongues be employed about the word of God. Let it be the subject of our familiar discourse, wherever we are; especially with our children.

II. He repeats the assurances he had before given them, in God's name, of prosperity and success if they were obedient. Nothing contributes more to the making of a nation considerable abroad, valuable to its friends and formidable to its enemies, than religion reigning in it; for who can be against those that have God for them? And he is certainly for those that are sincerely for him, Prov. xiv. 24.

Verses 26–32

Moses concludes his general exhortation to obedience.

I. He sums up all his arguments for obedience in two words, *the blessing and the curse* (*v.* 26), taking hold of hope and fear, those two handles of the soul, by which it is caught, held, and managed.

II. He appoints a public and solemn proclamation to be made of the blessing and curse which he had set before them, upon the two mountains of Gerizim and Ebal, *v.* 29, 30. We have more particular directions for this solemnity in *ch.* xxvii. 11, &c., and an account of the performance of it, Josh. viii. 33, &c. It was to be done, and was done, immediately upon their coming into Canaan, that when they first took possession of that land they might know upon what terms they stood.

CHAPTER 12

Moses at this chapter comes to the particular statutes which he had to give in charge to Israel, and he begins with those which relate to the worship of God, and particularly those which explain the second commandment, about which God is in a special manner jealous. I. They must utterly destroy all relics and remains of idolatry, ver. 1–3. II. They must keep close to the tabernacle, ver. 4, 5. The former precept was intended to prevent all false worship, the latter to preserve the worship God had instituted.

Verses 1–4

From those great original truths, That there is a God, and that there is but one God, arise those great fundamental laws, That that God is to be worshipped, and he only, and that therefore we are to have no other God before him: this is the first commandment, and the second is a guard upon it, or a hedge about it. To prevent a revolt to false gods, we are forbidden to worship the true God in such a way and manner as the false gods were worshipped in, and are commanded to observe the instituted ordinances of worship that we may adhere to the proper object of worship. For this reason Moses is very large in his exposition of the second commandment. What is contained in this and the four following chapters mostly refers to that.

I. They are here charged to abolish and extirpate all those things that the Canaanites had served their idol-gods with, *v.* 2, 3. The places that had been used, and were now to be levelled, were enclosures for their worship on *mountains and hills* (as if the height of the ground would give advantage to the ascent of their devotions), and under green trees, either because pleasant or because awful. He begins the statutes that relate to divine worship with this, because there must first be an abhorrence of that which is evil before there can be a steady adherence to that which is good, Rom. xii. 9. The kingdom of God must be set up, both in persons and places, upon the ruins of the devil's kingdom; for they cannot stand together, nor can there be any communion between Christ and Belial.

II. They are charged not to transfer the rites and usages of idolaters into the worship of God; no, not under colour of beautifying and improving it (*v.* 4).

Verses 5–32

There is not any one particular precept (as I remember) in all the law of Moses, so largely pressed and inculcated as this, by which they are all tied to bring their sacrifices to that one altar which was set up in the court of the tabernacle, and there to perform all the rituals of their religion; for, as to moral services, then, no doubt, as now, men might pray everywhere, as they did in their synagogues. The command to do this, and the prohibition of the contrary, are here repeated. 1. Because of the strange proneness there was in the hearts of the people to idolatry and superstition. 2. Because of the great use which the observance of this appointment would be to preserve among them unity and brotherly love, that, meeting all in one place, they might continue both of one way and of one heart. 3. Because of the significance of this appointment. They must keep to one place, in token of their belief of those two great truths, which we find together (1 Tim. ii. 5), That

there is one God, and *one Mediator between God and man.*

Let us now reduce this long charge to its proper heads.

I. It is here promised that when they were settled in Canaan, when they had *rest from their enemies, and dwelt in safety,* God would choose a certain place, which he would appoint to be the centre of their unity, to which they should bring all their offerings, *v.* 10, 11. He does not appoint the place now, as he had appointed Mounts Gerizim and Ebal, for the pronouncing of the blessings and curses (*ch.* xi. 29), but reserves the doing of it till hereafter, that hereby they might be made to expect further directions from heaven, and a divine conduct, after Moses should be removed. The ark was the token of God's presence, and where that was put there God put his name, and that was his habitation. The place which God first chose for the ark to reside in was Shiloh; and, after that place had sinned away its honours, we find the ark at Kirjath-jearim and other places; but at length, in David's time, it was fixed at Jerusalem, and God said concerning Solomon's temple, more expressly than ever he had said concerning any other place, *This I have chosen for a house of sacrifice,* 2 Chron. vii. 12. Compare 2 Chron. vi. 5. Now, under the gospel, we have no temple that sanctifies the gold, no altar that sanctifies the gift, but Christ only; and, as to the places of worship, the prophets foretold that *in every place* the spiritual *incense should be offered,* Mal. i. 11. And our Saviour has declared that those are accepted as true worshippers who worship God in sincerity and truth, without regard either to this mountain or Jerusalem, John iv. 23.

II. They are commanded to bring all their burnt-offerings and sacrifices to this place that God would choose (*v.* 6 and again *v.* 11).

III. They are commanded to feast upon their hallowed things before the Lord, with holy joy. If we glorify God, we edify ourselves, and cultivate our own minds, through the grace of God, by the increase of our knowledge and faith, the enlivening of devout affections, and the confirming of gracious habits and resolutions: thus is the soul nourished. Now while they were before the Lord they must rejoice, *v.* 12. It is the will of God that we should serve him with gladness; none displeased him more than those that *covered his altar with tears,* Mal. ii. 13. See what a good Master we serve, who has made it our duty to sing at our work.

It should seem that while they were in the wilderness they did not eat the flesh of any of those kinds of beasts that were used in sacrifice, but what was killed at the door of the tabernacle, and part of it presented to God as a peace-offering, Lev. xvii. 3, 4. But when they came to Canaan, where they must live at a great distance from the tabernacle, they might kill what they pleased for their own use of their flocks and herds, without bringing part to the altar. They must not eat blood (*v.* 16, and again, *v.* 23). When they could not bring the blood to the altar, to pour it out there before the Lord, as belonging to him, they must pour it out upon the earth, as not belonging to them, because it was the life, and therefore, as an acknowledgment, belonged to him who gives life, and, as an atonement, belonged to him to whom life is forfeited. Bishop Patrick thinks one reason why they were forbidden thus strictly the eating of blood was to prevent the superstitions of the old idolaters about the blood of their sacrifices, which they thought their demons delighted in, and by eating of which they imagined that they had communion with them.

Never was there a better governor than Moses, and one would think never a better opportunity of keeping up good order and discipline than now among the people of Israel, when they lay so closely encamped under the eye of their governor; and yet it seems there was much amiss and many irregularities had crept in among them. But (says Moses) when you come to Canaan, you *shall not do as we do here*. Note, When the people of God are in an unsettled condition, that may be tolerated and dispensed with which would by no means be allowed at another time. Moses was now about to lay down his life and government, and it was a comfort to him to foresee that Israel would be better in the next reign than they had been in his.

CHAPTER 13

In this chapter he cautions them against the rise of idolatry from among themselves; they must take heed lest any should draw them to idolatry. I. By the pretence of prophecy, ver. 1-5. II. By the pretence of friendship and relation, ver. 6-11. III. By the pretence of numbers, ver. 12-18.

Verses 1-5

Here is, I. A very strange supposition, *v.* 1, 2. 1. It is strange that there should arise any among themselves, especially any pretending to vision and prophecy, who should instigate them to *go and serve other gods*. Could an Israelite ever be guilty of such impiety? We see it in our own day and therefore may think it the less strange; multitudes that profess both learning and religion yet exciting both themselves and others, not only to worship God by images, but to give divine honour to saints and angels. So here, 2. It is to fortify them against the danger of impostures and lying wonders (2 Thess. ii. 9).

II. A very necessary charge given,

1. Not to yield to the temptation: "*Thou shalt not hearken to the words of that prophet, v.* 3. Not only thou shalt not do the thing he tempts thee to, but thou shalt not so much as patiently hear the temptation, but reject it with the utmost disdain and detestation. Keep close to your duty, and you keep out of harm's way. God never leaves us till we leave him.

2. Not to spare the tempter, *v.* 5. The infection must be kept from spreading by cutting off the gangrened limb, and putting away the mischief-makers. Such dangerous diseases as these must be taken in time.

Verses 6-11

Further provision is made by this branch of the statute against receiving the infection of idolatry from those that are near and dear to us. Satan tempted Adam by Eve and Christ by Peter.

Verses 12-18

Here the case is put of a city revolting from its allegiance to the God of Israel, *and serving other gods.*

I. The crime is supposed to be committed, 1. By one of the cities of Israel, that lay within the jurisdiction of their courts. The city that is here supposed to have become idolatrous is one that formerly worshipped the true God, but had now withdrawn to other gods, which intimates how great the crime is. 2. It is supposed to be committed by the generality of the inhabitants of the city. 3. They are supposed to be drawn to idolatry by *certain men, the children of Belial*. Belial is put for *the devil* (2 Cor. vi. 15), and the children of Belial are his children.

II. The cause is ordered to be tried with a great deal of care (*v.* 14): *Thou shalt enquire and make search.*

III. If the crime were proved, and the criminals were incorrigible, the city was to be wholly destroyed. If there were a few righteous men in it, no doubt they would remove themselves and their families out of such a dangerous place. The faithful worshippers

of the true God must take all occasions to show their just indignation against idolatry, much more against atheism, infidelity, and irreligion. They might think it impolitic, and against the interest of their nation, to ruin a whole city for a crime relating purely to religion, and that they should be more sparing of the blood of Israelites: "Fear not that" (says Moses), "God will multiply you the more; the body of your nation will lose nothing by the letting out of this corrupt blood." Though idolaters may escape punishment from men (nor is this law in the letter of it binding now, under the gospel), yet the Lord our God will not suffer them to escape his righteous judgments.

CHAPTER 14

Moses in this chapter teaches them, I. To distinguish themselves from their neighbours by a singularity, 1. In their mourning, ver. 1, 2. 2. In their meat, ver. 3-21. II. To devote themselves unto God, and, in token of that, to give him his dues out of their estates, the yearly tithe, and that every third year, for the maintenance of their religious feasts, the Levites, and the poor, ver. 22, &c.

Verses 1-21

Moses here tells the people of Israel,

I. How God had dignified them, as a peculiar people, with three distinguishing privileges. 1. Here is election: *The Lord hath chosen thee, v.* 2. He did not choose them because they were by their own dedication and subjection a peculiar people to him above other nations, but he chose them that they might be so by his grace. 2. Here is adoption (*v.* 1): "*You are the children of the Lord your God*, formed by him into a people, owned by him as his people, nay, his family, *a people near unto him*, nearer than any other." 3. Here is sanctification (*v.* 2): "*Thou art a holy people*, separated and set apart for God, devoted to his service, designed for his praise, governed by a holy law, graced by a holy tabernacle, and the holy ordinances relating to it."

II. How they ought to distinguish themselves by a sober singularity from all the nations that were about them. *Be you the children of the Lord your God:* so the Seventy read it, as a command, that is, "Carry yourselves as becomes the children of God, and do nothing to disgrace the honour and forfeit the privileges of the relation." In two things particularly they must distinguish themselves:—

1. In their mourning: *You shall not cut yourselves, v.* 1. This forbids (as some think), not only their cutting themselves at their funerals, either to express their grief or with their own blood to appease the infernal deities, but their wounding and mangling themselves in the worship of their gods, as Baal's prophets did (1 Kings xviii. 28). They are forbidden to disturb and afflict their own minds with inordinate grief for the loss of near and dear relations. We that have a God to hope in, and a heaven to hope for, must bear up ourselves with that hope under every burden of this kind.

2. They must be singular in their meat. Observe,

(1) Many sorts of flesh which were wholesome enough, and which other people did commonly eat, they must religiously abstain from as unclean. [1] Concerning beasts, here is a more particular enumeration of those which they were allowed to eat than was in Leviticus. [2] Concerning fish there is only one general rule given, that whatsoever had not fins and scales (as shell-fish and eels, besides leeches and other animals in the water that are not proper food) was *unclean and forbidden, v.* 9, 10. [3] No general rule is given concerning fowl, but those are particularly mentioned that were to be unclean to them, and there are few or none of them which are here forbidden that are now commonly eaten.

[4] They are further forbidden, *First*, To eat the flesh of any creature that died of itself, because the blood was not separated from it, and, besides the ceremonial uncleanness which it lay under (from Lev. xi. 39), it is not wholesome food. *Secondly*, To *seethe a kid in its mother's milk*, either to gratify their own luxury, supposing it a dainty bit, or in conformity to some superstitious custom of the heathen.

(2) Now as to all these precepts concerning their food, [1] It is plain in the law itself that they belonged only to the Jews, and were not moral, nor of perpetual use, because not of universal obligation; for what they might not eat themselves they might give to a stranger, or they might sell it to an alien, a mere Gentile, that came into their country for trade, *v.* 21. [2] It is plain in the gospel that they are now antiquated and repealed. For *every creature of God is good, and nothing now to be refused*, or *called common and unclean*, 1 Tim. iv. 4.

Verses 22–29

We have here a part of the statute concerning tithes. The productions of the ground were twice tithed, so that, putting both together, a fifth part was devoted to God out of their increase, and only four parts of five were for their own common use. The first tithe was for the maintenance of their Levites. But it is the second tithe that is here spoken of, which was to be taken out of the remainder when the Levites had had theirs.

I. They are here charged to separate it, and set it apart for God: *Thou shalt truly tithe all the increase of thy seed, v.* 22.

II. They are here directed how to dispose of it when they had separated it. This second tithe may be disposed of,

1. In works of piety, for the first two years after the year of release.

2. Every third year this tithe must be disposed of at home in works of charity (*v.* 28, 29): *Lay it up within thy own gates*, and let it be given to the poor. "Thither let them come, and eat and be satisfied."

CHAPTER 15

In this chapter Moses gives orders, I. Concerning the release of debts, every seventh year (ver. 1–6), with a caution that this should be no hindrance to charitable lending, ver. 7–11. II. Concerning the release of servants after seven years' service, ver. 12–18. III. Concerning the sanctification of the firstlings of cattle to God, ver. 19, &c.

Verses 1–11

Here is, I. A law for the relief of poor debtors. Every seventh year was a year of release, in which the ground rested from being tilled and servants were discharged from their services; and, among other acts of grace, this was one, that those who had borrowed money, and had not been able to pay it before, should this year be released from it; and though, if they were able, they were afterwards bound in conscience to repay it, yet thenceforth the creditor should never recover it by law. Many good expositors think it only forbids the exacting of the debt in the year of release, because, no harvest being gathered in that year, it could not be expected that men should pay their debts then, but that afterwards it might be sued for and recovered: so that the release did not extinguish the debt, but only stayed the process for a time. But others think it was a release of the debt for ever, and this seems more probable. The law is not that the creditor shall not receive the debt if the debtor, or his friends for him, can pay it; but he shall not exact it by a legal process. The reasons of this law are, 1. To put an honour upon the sabbatical year: *Because it is called the Lord's release, v.* 2. 2. It was to prevent the falling of any Israelite into

extreme poverty: so the margin reads (*v.* 4), *To the end there shall be no poor among you.* 3. God's security is here given by a divine promise that, whatever they lost by their poor debtors, it should be made up to them in the blessing of God upon all they had and did, *v.* 4–6.

II. Here is a law in favour of poor borrowers, that they might not suffer damage by the former law. 1. It is taken for granted that there would be poor among them, who would have occasion to borrow (*v.* 7), and that there would never cease to be some such objects of charity (*v.* 11). 2. In such a case we are here commanded to lend or give, according to our ability and the necessity of the case: *Thou shalt not harden thy heart, nor shut thy hand, v.* 7. Thou shalt *open thy hand wide unto him*, to *lend him sufficient, v.* 8. Sometimes there is as much charity in prudent lending as in giving, as it obliges the borrower to industry and honesty and may put him into a way of helping himself. When we have an occasion of charitable lending, if we cannot trust the borrower, we must trust God, and lend, hoping for nothing again in this world, but expecting it will be recompensed in the resurrection of the just, Luke vi. 35; xiv. 14.

III. Here is a command to give cheerfully whatever we give in charity: *Thy heart shall not be grieved when thou givest, v.* 10.

Verses 12–18

Here is, I. A repetition of the law that had been given concerning Hebrew servants who had sold themselves for servants, or were sold by their parents through extreme poverty, or were sold by the court of judgment for some crime committed. The law was, 1. That they should serve but six years, and in the seventh should go out free, *v.* 12. Compare Exod. xxi. 2. And, if the year of jubilee happened before they served out their time, that would be their discharge. 2. That if, when their six years' service had expired, they had no mind to go out free, but would rather continue in service, they must lay themselves under an obligation to serve for ever, that is, for life, by having *their ears bored to the door-posts, v.* 16, 17.

II. Here is an addition to this law, requiring them to put some small stock into their servants' hands to set up with for themselves, when they sent them out of their service, *v.* 13, 14.

Verses 19–23

Here is, 1. A repetition of the law concerning the firstlings of their cattle. 2. An addition to that law, for the further explication of it, directing them what to do with the firstlings, (1) That were females: "Thou shalt *do no work with the* female *firstlings of the cow*, nor shear those of the sheep" (*v.* 19). (2) But what must they do with that which was blemished, ill-blemished? *v.* 21. Were it male or female, it must not be brought near the sanctuary, nor used either for sacrifice or for holy feasting, for it would not be fit to honour God with. What a mercy is it that we are not under this yoke! We are not dieted as they were; we make no difference between a first calf, or lamb, and the rest that follow. Let us therefore realize the gospel meaning of this law, devoting ourselves and the first of our time and strength to God, as a kind of first-fruits of his creatures.

CHAPTER 16

In this chapter we have, I. A repetition of the laws concerning the three yearly feasts; in particular, that of the passover, ver. 1–8. That of pentecost, ver. 9–12. That of tabernacles, ver. 13–15. And the general law concerning the people's attendance on them, ver. 16, 17. II. The institution of an inferior magistracy, and general rules of justice given to those that were called into office, ver. 18–20. III. A caveat against groves and images, ver. 21, 22.

Verses 1–17

Much of the communion between God and his people Israel was kept up, and a face of religion preserved in the nation, by the three yearly feasts, the institution of which, and the laws concerning them, we have several times met with already; and here they are repeated.

I. The law of the passover, so great a solemnity that it made the whole month, in the midst of which it was placed, considerable: *Observe the month Abib, v.* 1. Though one week only of this month was to be kept as a festival, yet their preparations before must be so solemn, and their reflections upon it and improvements of it afterwards so serious, as to amount to an observance of the whole month. The laws concerning it are, 1. That they must be sure to sacrifice the passover in the place that God should choose (*v.* 2), and in no other place, *v.* 5–7. 2. That they must eat unleavened bread for seven days, and no leavened bread must be seen in all their coasts, *v,* 3, 4, 8. The gospel meaning of this feast of unleavened bread the apostle gives us, 1 Cor. v. 7. *Christ our passover being sacrificed for us,* and we having participated in the blessed fruits of that sacrifice to our comfort, *let us keep the feast* in a holy conversation, free from *the leaven of malice* towards our brethren and hypocrisy towards God, and *with the unleavened bread of sincerity* and love.

II. Seven weeks after the passover the feast of pentecost was to be observed. They must *bring an offering unto God, v.* 10. It is here called a *tribute of a freewill-offering.* The law did not determine the *quantum,* but it was left to every man's generosity to bring what he chose, and whatever he brought he must give cheerfully, it is therefore called a *free-will offering.*

III. They must keep the feast of tabernacles, *v.* 13–15. When we rejoice in God ourselves we should do what we can to assist others also to rejoice in him, by comforting the mourners and supplying the necessitous, that even *the stranger, the fatherless, and the widow may rejoice with us.* See Job xxix. 13. Those that make God their joy may *rejoice in hope,* for he is faithful that has promised.

IV. The laws concerning the three solemn feasts are summed up (*v.* 16, 17). The general commands concerning them are, 1. That all the males must then make their personal appearance before God. 2. That none must appear before God empty, but every man must bring some offering or other.

Verses 18–22

Here is, I. Care taken for the due administration of justice among them, that controversies might be determined, matters in variance adjusted, the injured redressed, and the injurious punished. While they were encamped in the wilderness, they had *judges and officers* according to their numbers, rulers of thousands and hundreds, Exod. xviii. 25. When they came to Canaan, they must have them according to their towns and cities, in all their gates; for the courts of judgment sat in the gates.

II. Care taken for the preventing of all conformity to the idolatrous customs of the heathen, *v.* 21, 22. They must not plant a grove, nor so much as a tree, near God's altar, lest they should make it look like the altars of the false gods. Nothing tends more to corrupt and debauch the minds of men, than representing and worshipping by an image that God who is an infinite and eternal Spirit.

CHAPTER 17

The charge of this chapter is, I. Concerning the purity and perfection of all those animals that were offered in sacrifice, ver. 1. II. Concerning the punishment of those that worshipped idols,

ver. 2–7. III. Concerning appeals from the inferior courts to the great sanhedrin, ver. 8–13. IV. Concerning the choice and duty of a king, ver. 14, &c.

Verses 1–7

Here is, I. A law for preserving the honour of God's worship, by providing that no creature that had any blemish should be offered in sacrifice to him, *v.* 1. The Old Testament sacrifices in a special manner were types of Christ, who is a *Lamb without blemish or spot* (1 Pet. i. 19). In the latter times of the Jewish church, when by the captivity in Babylon they were cured of idolatry, yet they were charged with profaneness in the breach of this law, with *offering the blind, and the lame, and the sick for sacrifice,* Mal. i. 8.

II. A law for the punishing of those that worshipped false gods. That which was the most ancient and plausible idolatry is specified, worshipping the sun, moon, and stars; and, if that was so detestable a thing, much more was it so to worship stocks and stones, or the representations of mean and contemptible animals. How heinous and dangerous soever the crime is, yet they must not punish any for it, unless there were good proof against them, by two witnesses at least. So great a punishment as death, so great a death as stoning, must be inflicted on the idolater, whether man or woman, for the infirmity of the weaker sex would be no excuse, *v.* 5. The hands of the witnesses, in this as in other cases, must be first upon him, that is, they must cast the first stone at him, thereby avowing their testimony, and solemnly imprecating the guilt of his blood upon themselves if their evidence were false. This custom might be of use to deter men from false-witness bearing.

Verses 8–13

Courts of judgment were ordered to be erected in every city (*ch.* xvi. 18), and they were empowered to hear and determine causes according to law, both those which we call pleas of the crown and those between party and party; and we may suppose that ordinarily they ended the matters that were brought before them, and their sentence was definitive; but, 1. It is here taken for granted that sometimes a case might come into their court too difficult for those inferior judges to determine. These difficult cases, which hitherto had been brought to Moses, according to Jethro's advice, were, after his death, to be brought to the supreme power, wherever it was lodged, whether in a judge (when there was such an extraordinary person raised up and qualified for that great service, as Othniel, Deborah, Gideon, &c.) or in the high-priest (when he was by the eminency of his gifts called of God to preside in public affairs, as Eli), or, if no single person were marked by heaven for this honour, then in the priests and Levites.

Verses 14–20

After the laws which concerned subjects fitly followed the laws which concern kings; for those that rule others must themselves remember that they are under command. Here are laws given,

I. To the electors of the empire, what rules they must go by in making their choice, *v.* 14, 15. 1. It is here supposed that the people would, in process of time, be desirous of a king, whose royal pomp and power would be thought to make their nation look great among their neighbours. 2. They are directed in their choice. If they will have a king over them, as God foresaw they would (though it does not appear that ever the motion was made till almost 400 years after), then they must, (1) Ask counsel at God's mouth, and make him king whom God shall choose. Accordingly, when the people desired a king, they applied to Samuel a prophet of the Lord; and afterwards David, Solomon, Jeroboam, Jehu, and others, were chosen by the prophets. (2) They must not choose a foreigner under pretence of strengthening their alliances, lest a strange king should introduce strange customs or usages.

II. Laws are here given to the prince that should be elected for the due administration of the government.

1. He must carefully avoid every thing that would divert him from God and religion. Riches, honours, and pleasures are the three great hindrances of godliness (*the lusts of the flesh, the lusts of the eye, and the pride of life*), especially to those in high stations: against these therefore the king is here warned.

2. He must carefully apply himself to the law of God, and make that his rule. This must be to him better than all riches, honours, and pleasures, than many horses or many wives, better than thousands of gold and silver.

(1) He must write himself a copy of the law out of the original, which was in the custody of the priests that attended the sanctuary, *v.* 18. Note, It is of great use for each of us to write down what we observe as most affecting and edifying to us, out of the scriptures and good books, and out of the sermons we hear. A prudent pen may go far towards making up the deficiencies of the memory, and the furnishing of the treasures of the good householder with things new and old.

(2) His writing and reading were all nothing if he did not reduce to practice what he wrote and read, *v.* 19, 20. Let him know, what dominion his religion must have over him, and what influence it must have upon him. *First,* It must possess him with a very reverent and awful regard to the divine majesty and authority. *Secondly,* It must engage him to a constant observance of the law of God, and a conscientious obedience to it, as the effect of that fear. *Thirdly,* It must keep him humble. How much soever he is advanced, let him keep his spirit low, and let the *fear of his God prevent the contempt of his brethren.*

CHAPTER 18

In this chapter, I. The rights and revenues of the church are settled, and rules given concerning the Levites' ministration and maintenance, ver. 1–8. II. The caution against the idolatrous abominable customs of the heathen is repeated, ver. 9–14. III. A promise is given them of the spirit of prophecy to continue among them, and to centre at last in Christ the great prophet, ver. 15–18. IV. Wrath threatened against those that despise prophecy (ver. 19) or counterfeit it (ver. 20), and a rule given for the trial of it, ver. 21, 22.

Verses 1–8

Magistracy and ministry are two divine institutions of admirable use for the support and advancement of the *kingdom of God among men.* Laws concerning the former we had in the close of the foregoing chapter, directions are in this given concerning the latter. Land marks are here set between the estates of the priests and those of the people.

I. Care is taken that the priests entangle not themselves with the affairs of this life, nor enrich themselves with the wealth of this world; they have better things to mind.

II. Care is likewise taken that they want not any of the comforts and conveniences of this life. Though God, who is a Spirit, is their inheritance, it does not therefore follow that they must live upon the air. The people must provide for them. They must have their *due from the people, v.* 3. Their maintenance must not depend upon the generosity of the people, but they must be by law entitled to it.

Verses 9–14

One would not think there had been so much need as it seems there was to arm the people of Israel against the infection of the idolatrous customs of the Canaanites. After many cautions, they are here charged not to do after the abominations of those nations, *v.* 9.

I. Some particulars are specified; as, 1. The consecrating of their children to Moloch, an idol that represented the sun, by making them to *pass through the fire,* and sometimes consuming them as sacrifices in the fire, *v.* 10. See the law against this before, Lev. xviii. 21. 2. Using arts of divination, to get the unnecessary knowledge of things to come, *enchantments, witchcrafts, charms,* &c.

II. Some reasons are given against their conformity to the customs of the Gentiles. 1. Because it would make them abominable to God. 2. Because these abominable practices had been the ruin of the Canaanites, of which ruin they were not only the witnesses but the instruments. 3. Because they were *better taught, v.* 13, 14. It is an argument like that of the apostle against Christians walking as the Gentiles walked (Eph. iv. 17, 18, 20): *You have not so learned Christ.*

Verses 15–22

I. The promise of the great prophet, with a command to receive him, and hearken to him.

1. Some think it is the promise of a succession of prophets, that should for many ages be kept up in Israel. Besides the priests and Levites, their ordinary ministers, whose office it was to teach Jacob God's law, they should have prophets, extraordinary ministers, to reprove them for their faults, remind them of their duty, and foretell things to come, judgments for warning and deliverances for their comfort.

2. Whether a succession of prophets be included in this promise or not, we are sure that it is primarily intended as a promise of Christ, and it is the clearest promise of him that is in all the law of Moses. It is expressly applied to our Lord Jesus as the Messiah promised (Acts iii. 22; vii. 37), and the people had an eye to this promise when they said concerning him, *This is of a truth that prophet that should come into the world* (John vi. 14); and it was his Spirit that spoke in all the other prophets, 1 Pet. i. 11. It is also a charge and command given to all people to hear and believe, hear and obey, this great prophet here promised: *Unto him you shall hearken* (*v.* 15); and whoever will not hearken to him shall be surely and severely reckoned with for his contempt (*v.* 19): *I will require it of him.*

II. Here is a caution against false prophets. Whatever is directly repugnant to sense, to the light and law of nature, and to the plain meaning of the written word, we may be sure is not that which the Lord has spoken; nor that which gives countenance and encouragement to sin, or has a manifest tendency to the destruction of piety or charity.

CHAPTER 19

The laws which Moses had hitherto been repeating and urging mostly concerned the acts of religion and devotion towards God; but here he comes more fully to press the duties of righteousness between man and man. This chapter relates, I. To the sixth commandment, "Thou shalt not kill," ver. 1–13. II. To the eighth commandment, "Thou shalt not steal," ver. 14. III. To the ninth commandment, "Thou shalt not bear false witness," ver. 15, &c.

Verses 1–13

It was one of the precepts given to the sons of Noah that *whoso sheddeth man's blood by man shall his blood be shed,* that is, by the avenger of blood, Gen. ix. 6. Now here we have the law settled between blood and blood, between the blood of the murdered and the blood of the murderer, and effectual provision made,

I. That the cities of refuge should be a protection to him that slew another casually, so that he should not die for that as a crime which was not his voluntary act, but only his unhappiness.

1. The appointing of three cities in Canaan for this purpose. The country was to be divided into three districts, and a city of refuge in the centre of each, so that every corner of the land might have one within reach.

2. The use to be made of these cities, *v.* 4–6. (1) It is supposed that it might so happen that a man might be the death of his neighbour without any design upon him either from a sudden passion or malice prepense, but purely by accident, as by the flying off of an axe-head, which is the instance here given, with which every case of this kind was to be compared, and by it adjudged. (2) It is supposed that the relations of the person slain would be forward to avenge the blood. Though the law did not allow the avenging of any other affront or injury with death, yet the avenger of blood, the blood of a relation, shall have great allowances made for the heat of his heart upon such a provocation as that, and his killing the man-slayer, though he was so by accident only, should not be accounted murder if he did it before he got to the city of refuge. (3) It is provided that, if an avenger of blood should be so unreasonable as to demand satisfaction for blood shed by accident only, then the city of refuge should protect the slayer.

3. The appointing of three cities more for this use in case God should hereafter enlarge their territories and the dominion of their religion, that all those places which came under the government of the law of Moses in other instances might enjoy the benefit of that law in this instance, *v.* 8–10.

II. It is provided that the cities of refuge should be no sanctuary or shelter to a wilful murderer, but even thence he should be fetched, and delivered to the avenger of blood, *v.* 11–13. Before the Reformation, there were some churches and religious houses (as they called them) that were made sanctuaries for the protection of all sorts of criminals that fled to them, wilful murderers not excepted, so that (as Stamford says, in his *Pleas of the Crown, lib.* II, *c.* xxxviii.) the government follows not Moses but Romulus, and it was not till about the latter end of Henry VIII's time that this privilege of sanctuary for wilful murder was taken away.

Verses 14–21

Here is a statute for the preventing of frauds and perjuries; for the divine law takes care of men's rights and properties, and has made a hedge about them.

I. A law against frauds, *v.* 14. 1. Here is an implicit direction given to the first planters of Canaan to fix land marks, according to the distribution of the land to the several tribes and families by lot. 2. An express law to posterity not to remove those land-marks. It forbids, (1) The invading of any man's right, and taking to ourselves that which is not our own, by any fraudulent arts or practices, as by forging, concealing, destroying, or altering deeds and writings (which are our land marks, to which appeals are made), or by shifting hedges, meer-stones, and boundaries. (2) It forbids the sowing of discord among neighbours, and doing any thing to occasion strife and law-suits.

II. A law against perjuries, which enacts two things:—1. That a single witness should never be admitted to give evidence in a criminal cause, so as that sentence should be passed upon his testimony, *v.* 15. 2. That a false witness should incur the same punishment which was to have been inflicted upon the person he accused, *v.* 16–21.

CHAPTER 20

This chapter settles the militia, and establishes the laws and ordinances of war, I. Relating to the soldiers. 1. Those must be encouraged that were drawn up to battle, ver. 1–4. 2. Those must be dismissed and sent back again whose private affairs called for their attendance at home (ver. 5–7), or whose weakness and timidity unfitted them for service in the field, ver. 8, 9. II. Relating to the enemies they made war with. 1. The treaties they must make with the cities that were far off, ver. 10–15. 2. The destruction they must make of the people into whose land they were going, ver. 16–18. 3. The care they must take, in besieging cities, not to destroy the fruit trees, ver. 19, 20.

Verses 1–9

Israel was at this time to be considered rather as a camp than as a kingdom, entering upon an enemy's country, and not yet settled in a country of their own; and, besides the war they were now entering upon in order to their settlement, even after their settlement they could neither protect nor enlarge their coast without hearing the alarms of war. It was therefore needful that they should have directions given them in their military affairs.

I. Those that were disposed to fight must be encouraged and animated against their fears. 1. The presence of God with them: "*The Lord thy God is with thee,* and therefore thou art not in danger, nor needest thou be afraid." See Isa. xli. 10. 2. The experience they and their fathers had had of God's power and goodness in *bringing them out of the land of Egypt,* in defiance of Pharaoh and all his hosts. *Let not your hearts be tender* (so the word is), to receive all the impressions of fear, but let a believing confidence in the power and promise of God harden them. *Fear not, and do not make haste* (so the word is), for he that believeth doth not make more haste than good speed. "Do not make haste either rashly to anticipate your advantages or basely to fly off upon every disadvantage." The giving of this encouragement by a priest, one of the Lord's ministers, intimates, (1) That it is very fit that armies should have chaplains, not only to pray for them, but to preach to them, both to reprove that which would hinder their success and to raise their hopes of it. (2) That it is the work of Christ's ministers to encourage his good soldiers in their spiritual conflicts with the world and the flesh, and to assure them of a conquest, yea, more than a conquest, through Christ that loved us.

II. Those that were indisposed to fight must be discharged. 1. The Jewish writers agree that this liberty to return was allowed only in those wars which were made voluntarily (as bishop Patrick expresses it), not those which were made by the divine command against Amalek and the Canaanites, in which every man was bound to fight.

2. If a man's indisposition to fight arose from the weakness and timidity of his own spirit, he had leave to return from the war, *v.* 8. It was partly in kindness to them that they had their discharge (for, though shamed, they were eased); but much more in kindness to the rest of the army, who were hereby freed from the incumbrance of such as were useless and unserviceable, while the danger of infection from their cowardice and flight was prevented.

III. It is here ordered that, when all the cowards were dismissed, then captains should be nominated (*v.* 9), for it was in a special manner necessary that the leaders and commanders should be men of courage.

Verses 10–20

They are here directed what method to take in dealing with the cities (these only are mentioned, *v.* 10, but doubtless the armies in the field, and the nations they had occasion to deal with, are likewise intended) upon which they made war. They must not make a descent upon any of their neighbours till they had first given them fair notice, by a public manifesto, or remonstrance, stating the ground of their quarrel with them.

I. Even to the proclamation of war must be subjoined a tender of peace, if they would accept of it upon reasonable terms. They must first proclaim peace to them. Let this show, 1. God's grace in dealing with sinners: though he might most justly and easily destroy them, yet, having no pleasure in their ruin, he proclaims peace, and beseeches them to be reconciled. 2. Let it show us our duty in dealing with our brethren: if any quarrel happen, let us not only be ready to hearken to the proposals of peace, but forward to make such proposals. We should never make use of the law till we have first tried to accommodate matters in variance amicably, and without expense and vexation. *We* must be for peace, whoever are for war.

II. If the offers of peace were not accepted, then they must proceed to push on the war.

III. The nations of Canaan are excepted from the merciful provisions made by this law. Remnants might be left of the cities that were very far off (*v.* 15), because by them they were not in so much danger of being infected with idolatry, but of the cities which were given to Israel for an inheritance no remnants must be left of their inhabitants (*v.* 16), because, since it could not be expected that they should be cured of their idolatry, if they were left with that plague-sore upon them they would be in danger of infecting God's Israel, who were too apt to take the infection.

IV. Care is here taken that in the besieging of cities there should not be any destruction made of fruit trees, *v.* 19, 20. The intent of many of the divine precepts is to restrain us from destroying that which is our life and food. Armies and their commanders are not allowed to make what desolation they please in the countries that are the seat of war. No fruit tree is to be destroyed unless it be barren, and cumber the ground. "Nay," they maintain, "whoso wilfully breaks vessels, tears clothes, stops wells, pulls down buildings, or destroys meat, transgresses this law: *Thou shalt not destroy.*"

CHAPTER 21

In this chapter provision is made, I. For the putting away of the guilt of blood from the land, when he that shed it had fled from justice, ver. 1–9. II. For the preserving of the honour of a captive maid, ver. 10–14. III. For the securing of the right of a firstborn son, though he were not a favourite, ver. 15–17. IV. For the restraining and punishing of a rebellious son, ver. 18–21. V. For the maintaining of the honour of human bodies, which must not be hanged in chains, but decently buried, even the bodies of the worst malefactors, ver. 22, 23.

Verses 1–9

Care had been taken by some preceding laws for the vigorous and effectual prosecution of a wilful murderer (*ch.* xix. 11, &c.), the putting of whom to death was the putting away of the guilt of blood from the land; but if this could not be done, the murderer not being discovered, they must not think that the land was in no danger of contracting any pollution because it was not through any neglect of theirs that the murderer was unpunished; no, a great solemnity is here provided for the putting away of the guilt, as an expression of their dread and detestation of that sin.

I. The case supposed is that *one is found slain, and it is not known who slew him, v.* 1.

II. Directions are given concerning what is to be done in this case. The priests were to pray to God for the country and nation, that God would be merciful to them, and not bring upon them the judgments which the connivance at the sin of murder would deserve.

Verses 10–14

By this law a soldier is allowed to marry his captive if he pleased. For the hardness of their hearts Moses gave them this permission, lest, if they had not had liberty given them to marry such, they should have taken liberty to defile themselves with them, and by such wickedness the camp would have been troubled. The man is supposed to have a wife already, and to take this wife for a secondary wife, as the Jews called them. This indulgence of men's inordinate desires, in which their hearts walked after their eyes, is by no means agreeable to the law of Christ, which therefore in this respect, among others, far exceeds in glory the law of Moses.

Verses 15–17

This law restrains men from disinheriting their eldest sons out of mere caprice, and without just provocation.

I. The case here put (*v.* 15) is very instructive. 1. It shows the great mischief of having more wives than one, which the law of Moses did not restrain. 2. It shows how Providence commonly sides with the weakest. For the first-born son is here supposed to be *hers that was hated*; it was so in Jacob's family: because *the Lord saw that Leah was hated*, Gen. xxix. 31.

II. The law in this case is still binding on parents; they must give their children their right without partiality. In the case supposed, the eldest son, though the son of the less-beloved wife, must have his birthright privilege, which was a double portion of the father's estate, because he was the beginning of his strength. No son should be abandoned by his father till he manifestly appear to be abandoned of God, which is hard to say of any while there is life.

Verses 18–23

Here is, I. A law for the punishing of a rebellious son. Having in the former law provided that parents should not deprive their children of their right, it was fit that it should next be provided that children withdraw not the honour and duty which are owing to their parents.

1. How the criminal is here described. He is a *stubborn and rebellious son, v.* 18. No child was to fare the worse for the weakness of his capacity, the slowness or dullness of his understanding, but for his wilfulness and obstinacy. He is particularly supposed (*v.* 20) to be a *glutton or a drunkard.* This intimates either, (1) That these were sins which his parents did in a particular manner warn him against. Or, (2) That his being a *glutton and a drunkard* was the cause of his insolence and obstinacy towards his parents. When men take to drink they forget the law, they forget all law (Prov. xxxi. 5), even that fundamental law of honouring parents.

2. How this criminal is to be proceeded against. His own father and mother are to be his prosecutors, *v.* 19, 20.

II. A law for the burying of the bodies of malefactors that were hanged, *v.* 22. Of such as were stoned to death, it was usual, by order of the judges, to hang up the dead bodies upon a post for some time, as a spectacle to the world, to express the ignominy of the crime. Now it is here provided that, whatever time of the day they were thus hanged up, at sun set they should be taken down and buried. Now, 1. God would thus preserve the honour of human bodies and tenderness towards the worst of criminals. 2. Yet it is plain there was something ceremonial in it; by the law of Moses the touch of a dead body was defiling, and therefore dead bodies must not be left hanging up in the country, because, by the same rule, this would defile the land. 3. *He that is hanged is accursed of God,* that is, it is the highest degree of disgrace and reproach that can be done to a man, and proclaims him under the curse of God as much as any external punishment can. Those that see him thus hang between heaven and earth will conclude him abandoned of both and unworthy of either; and therefore let him not hang all night, for that would carry it too far.

CHAPTER 22

The laws of this chapter provide, I. For the preservation of charity and good neighbourship, in the care of strayed or fallen cattle, ver. 1–4. II. For the preservation of order and distinction, that men and women should not wear one another's clothes (ver. 5), and that other needless mixtures should be avoided, ver. 9–11. III. For the preservation of birds, ver. 6, 7. IV. Of life, ver. 8. V. Of the commandments, ver. 12. VI. Of the reputation of a wife abused, if she were innocent (ver. 13–19), but for her punishment if guilty, ver. 20, 21. VII. For the preservation of the chastity of wives, ver. 22. Virgins betrothed (ver. 23–27), or not betrothed, ver. 28, 29. And, lastly, against incest, ver. 30.

Verses 1–4

The kindness that was commanded to be shown in reference to an enemy (Exod. xxiii. 4, &c.) is here required to be much more done for, a neighbour, though he were not an Israelite. 1. That strayed cattle should be brought back, either to the owner or to the pasture out of which they had gone astray, v. 1, 2. If such care must be taken of a neighbour's ox or ass going astray, much more of himself going astray from God and his duty; we should do our utmost to convert him (Jam. v. 19), and restore him, considering ourselves, Gal. vi. 1. 2. That lost goods should be brought to the owner, v. 3. The Jews say, "He that found the lost goods was to give public notice of them three or four times."

Verses 5–12

Here are several laws in these verses which seem to stoop very low, and to take cognizance of things mean and minute.

I. The distinction of sexes by the apparel is to be kept up, for the preservation of our own and our neighbour's chastity, v. 5. 1. Some think it refers to the idolatrous custom of the Gentiles: in the worship of Venus, women appeared in armour, and men in women's clothes. 2. It forbids the confounding of the dispositions and affairs of the sexes. 3. Probably this confounding of garments had been used to gain opportunity of committing uncleanness, and is therefore forbidden.

II. In taking a bird's nest, the dam must be let go, v. 6, 7. But *doth God take care* for birds? 1 Cor. ix. 9. Yes, certainly; and perhaps to this law our Saviour alludes. Luke xii. 6, *Are not five sparrows sold for two farthings, and not one of them is forgotten before God?* This law, 1. Forbids us to be cruel to the brute creatures, or to take a pleasure in destroying them. 2. It teaches us compassion to those of our own kind, and to abhor the thought of everything that looks barbarous, and cruel, and ill-natured, especially towards those of the weaker and tender sex, who always ought to be treated with the utmost respect, in consideration of the sorrows wherein they bring forth children.

III. In building a house, care must be taken to make it safe, that none might receive mischief by falling from it, v. 8. The roofs of their houses were flat for people to walk on. They must compass them with battlements, which (the Jews say) must be three feet and a half high. See here, 1. How precious men's lives are to God, who protects them, not only by his providence, but by his law. 2. How precious, therefore, they ought to be to us, and what care we should take to fence, or remove, every thing by which life may be endangered, to cover draw-wells, keep bridges in repair, and the like.

IV. Odd mixtures are here forbidden, v. 9, 10. Much of this we met with before, Lev. xix. 19. There appears not any thing at all of moral evil in these things, and therefore we now make no conscience of sowing wheat and rye together, ploughing with horses and oxen together, and of wearing linsey-woolsey garments; but hereby is forbidden either, 1. A conformity to some idolatrous customs of the heathen. Or, 2. That which is contrary to the plainness and purity of an Israelite. They must not gratify their own vanity and curiosity by putting those things together which the Creator in infinite wisdom had made asunder.

V. The law concerning fringes upon their garments, and memorandums of the commandments, which we had before (Num. xv. 38, 39), is here repeated, v. 12. By these they were distinguished from other people, so that it might be said, upon the first sight, There goes an Israelite.

Verses 13–30

These laws relate to the seventh commandment, laying a restraint by laying a penalty upon those fleshly lusts which war against the soul.

I. If a man, lusting after another woman, to get rid of his wife slander her and falsely accuse her, upon the disproof of his slander he must be punished, v. 13–19. The nearer any are in relation to us the greater sin it is to belie them and blemish their reputation.

II. If the woman that was married as a virgin was not found to be one she was to be stoned to death at her father's door, v. 20, 21. Now, 1. This gave a powerful caution to young women to flee fornication, since, however concealed before, so as not to mar their marriage, it would very likely be discovered afterwards, to their perpetual infamy and utter ruin. 2. It is intimated to parents that they must by all means possible preserve their children's chastity, by giving them good advice and admonition, setting them good examples, keeping them from bad company, praying for them, and laying them under needful restraints.

III. If any man, single or married, lay with a married woman, they were both to be put to death, v. 22. This law we had before, Lev. xx. 10.

IV. If a damsel were betrothed and not married, she was from under the eye of her intended husband, and therefore she and her chastity were taken under the special protection of the law.

CHAPTER 23

The laws of this chapter provide, I. For the preserving of the purity and honour of the families of Israel, by excluding such as would be a disgrace to them, ver. 1–8. II. For the preserving of the purity and honour of the camp of Israel when it was abroad, ver. 9–14. III. For the encouraging and entertaining of slaves who fled, to them, ver. 15, 16. IV. Against whoredom, ver. 17, 18. V. Against usury, ver. 19, 20. VI. Against the breach of vows, ver. 21–23. VII. What liberty a man might take in his neighbour's field and vineyard, and what not, ver. 24, 25.

Verses 1–8

Interpreters are not agreed what is here meant by *entering into the congregation of the Lord*, which is here forbidden to eunuchs and to bastards, Ammonites and Moabites, for ever, but to Edomites and Egyptians only till the third generation. 1. Some think they are hereby excluded from communicating with the people of God in their religious services. 2. Others think they are hereby excluded from bearing office in the congregation. 3. Others think they are excluded only from marrying with Israelites. With the daughters of these nations (though out of the nations of Canaan), it should seem, the men of Israel might marry, if they were completely proselyted to the Jewish religion; but with the men of these nations the daughters of Israel might not marry, nor could the men be naturalized, otherwise than as here provided.

Verses 9–14

Israel was now encamped, and this vast army was just entering upon action, which was likely to keep them together for a long time, and therefore it was fit to give them particular directions for the good ordering of their camp. And the charge is in one word to be *clean*. They must take care to keep their camp pure from moral, ceremonial, and natural pollution.

I. From moral pollution (v. 9): *When the host goes forth against thy enemy* then look upon thyself as in a special manner engaged to *keep thyself from every evil thing*. 1. The soldiers themselves must take heed of sin, for sin takes off the edge of valour; guilt makes men cowards. Soldiers must keep themselves from the idols, or accursed things, they found in the camps they plundered. 2. Even those that tarried at home must at that time especially keep from every wicked thing. Times of war should be times of reformation, else how can we expect God should hear and answer our prayers for success? Ps. lxvi. 18. See 1 Sam. vii. 3.

II. From ceremonial pollution. By this trouble and reproach, which even involuntary pollutions exposed men to, they were taught to keep up a very great dread of all fleshly lusts.

III. From natural pollution; the camp of the Lord must have nothing offensive in it, v. 12–14. If there must be this care taken to preserve the body clean and sweet, much more should we be solicitous to keep the mind so. This is the reason here given: *For the Lord thy God walketh* by his ark, the special token of his presence, *in the midst of thy camp*; with respect to that external symbol this external purity is required, which teaches us to preserve inward purity of soul, in consideration of the eye of God, which is always upon us.

Verses 15–25

Orders are here given about five several things which have no relation one to another:—

I. The land of Israel is here made a sanctuary, or city of refuge, for servants that were wronged and abused by their masters, and fled thither for shelter from the neighbouring countries, v. 15, 16. 1. It is an honourable thing to shelter and protect the weak, provided they be not wicked. The angel bid Hagar return to her mistress, and Paul sent Onesimus back to his master Philemon, because they had neither of them any cause to go away, nor was either of them exposed to any danger in returning. 2. If it appeared that the servant was abused, they must not only protect him, but, supposing him willing to embrace their religion, they must give him all the encouragement that might be to settle among them.

II. The land of Israel must be no shelter for the unclean; no whore, no Sodomite, must be suffered to live among them (v. 17, 18), neither a whore nor a whoremonger. No houses of uncleanness must be kept either by men or women.

III. The matter of usury is here settled, v. 19, 20. 1. They must not lend upon usury to an Israelite. It was seldom or never that they had occasion to borrow any great sums, only what was necessary for the subsistence of their families when the fruits of their ground had met with any disaster, or the like. Where the borrower gets, or hopes to get, it is just that the lender should share in the gain; but to him that borrows for his necessary food pity must be shown, and we must lend, hoping for nothing again, if we have wherewithal to do it, Luke vi. 35. 2. They might lend upon usury to a stranger, who was sup-

posed to live by trade, and (as we say) by turning the penny, and therefore got by what he borrowed, and came among them in hopes to do so. By this it appears that usury is not in itself oppressive; for they must not oppress a stranger, and yet might exact usury from him.

IV. The performance of the vows wherewith we have bound our souls is here required. 1. We are here left at our liberty whether we will make vows or no. God had already signified his readiness to accept a free-will offering thus vowed, though it were but a little fine flour (Lev. ii. 4, &c.). But lest the priests, who had the largest share of those vows and voluntary offerings, should sponge upon the people, by pressing it upon them as their duty to make such vows, beyond their ability and inclination, they are here expressly told that it should not be reckoned a sin in them if they did not make any such vows. 2. We are here laid under the highest obligations, when we have made a vow, to perform it, and to perform it speedily.

V. Allowance is here given, when they passed through a cornfield or vineyard, to pluck and eat of the corn or grapes that grew by the road side. Now, 1. This law intimated to them what great plenty of corn and wine they should have in Canaan. 2. It provided for the support of poor travellers, to relieve the fatigue of their journey. 3. It teaches us not to insist upon property in a small matter, of which it is easy to say, *What is that between me and thee?* 4. It used them to hospitality.

CHAPTER 24

In this chapter we have, I. The toleration of divorce, ver. 1–4. II. A discharge of new-married men from the war, ver. 5. III. Laws concerning pledges, ver. 6, 10–13, 17. IV. Against man-stealing, ver. 7. V. Concerning the leprosy, ver. 8, 9. VI. Against the injustice of masters towards their servants, ver. 14, 15. Judges in capital causes (ver. 16), and civil concerns, ver. 17, 18. VII. Of charity to the poor, ver. 19, &c.

Verses 1–4

This is that permission which the Pharisees erroneously referred to as a precept, Matt. xix. 7, *Moses commanded to give a writing of divorcement*. It was not so; our Saviour told them that he only suffered it lest, if they had not had liberty to divorce their wives, they should have ruled them with rigour, and, it may be, have been the death of them. It is probable that divorces were in use before (they are taken for granted, Lev. xxi. 14), and Moses thought it needful here to give some rules concerning them. 1. That a man might not divorce his wife unless he *found some uncleanness in her*, v. 1. It was not sufficient to say that he did not like her, or that he liked another better, but he must show cause for his dislike. 2. That it must be done, not by word of mouth, for that might be spoken hastily, but by writing, and that put in due form, and solemnly declared, before witnesses, to be his own act and deed, which was a work of time, and left room for consideration, that it might not be done rashly. 3. That the husband must give it into the hand of his wife, and send her away, which some think obliged him to endow her. 4. That being divorced it was lawful for her to marry another husband, v. 2. The divorce had dissolved the bond of marriage as effectually as death could dissolve it; so that she was free to marry again as if her first husband had been naturally dead. 5. That if her second husband died, or divorced her, then still she might marry a third, but her first husband should never take her again (v. 3, 4). The Jewish writers say that this was to prevent a most vile and wicked practice which the Egyptians had of changing wives.

Verses 5–13

Here is, I. Provision made for the preservation and confirmation of love between new-married people, *v.* 5. This fitly follows upon the laws concerning divorce, which would be prevented if their affection to each other were well settled at first. If the husband were much abroad from his wife the first year, his love to her would be in danger of cooling, and of being drawn aside to others whom he would meet with abroad; therefore his service to his country in war, embassies, or other public business that would call him from home, shall be dispensed with, *that he may cheer up the wife that he has taken.* 1. It is of great consequence that love be kept up between husband and wife. 2. One of the duties of that relation is to cheer up one another under the cares and crosses that happen, as helpers of each other's joy; for a cheerful heart does good like a medicine.

II. A law against man-stealing, *v.* 7. It was not death by the law of Moses to steal cattle or goods; but to steal a child, or a weak and simple man, or one that a man had in his power, and to make merchandize of him, this was a capital crime. It was taking away a man's liberty, the liberty of a freeborn Israelite, which was next in value to his life.

III. A memorandum concerning the leprosy, *v.* 8, 9. The laws concerning it must be carefully observed. The laws concerning it we had, Lev. xiii. 14.

IV. Some necessary orders given about pledges for the security of money lent. 1. They must not take the millstone for a pledge (*v.* 6), for with that they ground the corn that was to be bread for their families, and so it forbids the taking of any thing for a pledge by the want of which a man was in danger of being undone. Consonant to this is the ancient common law of England, which provides that no man be distrained of the utensils or instruments of his trade or profession, as the axe of a carpenter, or the books of a scholar. That creditor who cares not though his debtor and his family starve so he may but get his money, goes contrary, not only to the law of Christ, but even to the law of Moses too. 2. They must not go into the borrower's house to fetch the pledge. It is provided that he shall take not what he pleases, but what the borrower can best spare. A poor man's bed-clothes should never be taken for a pledge, *v.* 12, 13. This we had before, Exod. xxii. 26, 27. If they were taken in the morning, they must be brought back again at night, which is in effect to say that they must not be taken at all.

Verses 14–22

I. Masters are commanded to be just to their poor servants, v. 14, 15. 1. They must not oppress them. "For *thou wast a bondman* in the land where thou wast a stranger (*v.* 18), and thou knowest what a grievous thing it is to be oppressed by a taskmaster, and therefore, *thou shalt not oppress a servant.*" 2. They must be faithful and punctual in paying them their wages. He that works by daywages is supposed to live from hand to mouth, and cannot have to-morrow's bread for his family till he is paid for this day's labour.

II. Magistrates and judges are commanded to be just in their administrations.

III. The rich are commanded to be kind and charitable to the poor. Many ways they are ordered to be so by the law of Moses. The particular instance of charity here prescribed is that they should not be greedy in gathering in their corn, and grapes, and olives, so as to be afraid of leaving any behind them, but be willing to overlook some, and let the poor have the gleanings, *v.* 19–22.

CHAPTER 25

Here is, I. A law to moderate the scourging of malefactors, ver. 1–3. II. A law in favour of the ox that treads out the corn, ver. 4. III. For the disgracing of him that refused to marry his brother's widow, ver. 5–10. IV. For the punishment of an immodest woman, ver. 11, 12. V. For just weights and measures, ver. 13–16. VI. For the destroying of Amalek, ver. 17, &c.

Verses 1–4

I. A direction to the judges in scourging malefactors, *v.* 1–3. A great many precepts we have met with which have not any particular penalty annexed to them, the violation of most of which, according to the constant practice of the Jews, was punished by scourging. The directions here given for the scourging of criminals are, 1. That it be done solemnly; not tumultuously through the streets, but in open court before the judges' face, and with so much deliberation as that the stripes might be numbered. The Jews say that while execution was in doing the chief justice of the court read with a loud voice Deut. xxviii. 58, 59, and xxix. 9, and concluded with those words (Ps. lxxviii. 38), *But he, being full of compassion, forgave their iniquity.* Thus it was made a sort of religious act, and so much the more likely to reform the offender himself and to be a warning to others. 2. That it be done in proportion to the crime. 3. That how great soever the crime were the number of stripes should never exceed *forty*, *v.* 3. Forty *save one* was the common usage, as appears, 2 Cor. xi. 24. They abated one for fear of having miscounted or because they would never go to the utmost rigour, or because the execution was usually done with a whip of three lashes, so that thirteen stripes (each one being counted for three) made up thirty-nine, but one more by that reckoning would have been forty-two.

II. A charge to husbandmen not to hinder their cattle from eating when they were working, if meat were within their reach, *v.* 4.

Verses 5–12

Here is, I. The law settled concerning the marrying of a brother's widow. It appears from the story of Judah's family that this had been an ancient usage (Gen. xxxviii. 8). The case put is a case that often happens, of a man's dying without issue, while his brethren were yet so young as to be unmarried. Now in this case, 1. The widow was not to marry again into any other family, unless all the relations of her husband did refuse her, that the estate she was endowed with might not be alienated. 2. The husband's brother, or next of kin, must marry her, partly out of respect to her, who, having forgotten her own people and her father's house, should have all possible kindness shown her by the family into which she was married; and partly out of respect to the deceased husband, that though he was dead and gone he might not be forgotten, nor lost out of the genealogies of his tribe; for the first-born child, which the brother or next kinsman should have by the widow, should be denominated from him that was dead, and entered in the genealogy as his child, *v.* 5, 6. But, 3. If the brother, or next of kin, declined to do this good office to the memory of him that was gone, what must be done in that case? Why, (1) He shall not be compelled to do it, *v.* 7. (2) Yet he shall be publicly disgraced for not doing it.

II. A law for the punishing of an immodest woman, *v.* 11, 12.

Verses 13–19

Here is, I. A law against deceitful weights and measures: they must not only not use them, but they must not have them, for, if they had them, they would be strongly tempted to use them. They must not have a great weight and measure to buy by and a small one to sell by, for that was to cheat both ways. But *thou shalt have a perfect and just weight, v.* 15.

II. A law for the rooting out of Amalek.
1. The mischief Amalek did to Israel must be here

remembered, *v.* 17, 18. They had no occasion at all to quarrel with Israel nor did they give them any notice, by a manifesto or declaration of war; but took them at an advantage, when they had just come out of the house of bondage, and, for aught that appeared to them, were only going to *sacrifice to God in the wilderness.*

2. This mischief must in due time be revenged, *v.* 19. It was nearly 400 years after this that Saul was ordered to put this sentence in execution (1 Sam. xv.), and was rejected of God because he did not do it effectually.

CHAPTER 26

With this chapter Moses concludes the particular statutes which he thought fit to give Israel in charge at his parting with them; what follows is by way of sanction and ratification. In this chapter, I. Moses gives them a form of confessions to be made by him that offered the basket of his first-fruits, ver. 1–11. II. The protestation and prayer to be made after the disposal of the third year's tithe, ver. 12–15 . III. He binds on all the precepts he had given them, 1. By the divine authority: "Not I, but the Lord thy God has commanded thee to do these statutes," ver. 16. 2. By the mutual covenant between God and them, ver. 17, &c.

Verses 1–11

Here is, I. A good work ordered to be done, and that is the presenting of a basket of their first-fruits to God every year, *v.* 1, 2. When a man went into the field or vineyard at the time when the fruits were ripening, he was to mark that which he observed most forward, and to lay it by for first-fruits, wheat, barley, grapes, figs, pomegranates, olives, and dates, some of each sort must be put in the same basket, with leaves between them, and presented to God in the place which he should choose. Now from this law we may learn, 1. To acknowledge God as the giver of all those good things which are the support and comfort of our natural life. 2. To deny ourselves. What is first ripe we are most fond of; those that are nice and curious expect to be served with each fruit at its first coming in. 3. To give to God the first and best we have. Those that consecrate the days of their youth, and the prime of their time, to the service and honour of God, bring him their first-fruits.

II. Good words put into their mouths to be said in the doing of this good work. Two things they must own for this purpose:—1. The meanness of their common ancestor: *A Syrian ready to perish was my father, v.* 5. Jacob is here called an *Aramite,* or *Syrian,* because he lived twenty years in Padan-Aram. 2. The miserable condition of their nation in its infancy. They sojourned in Egypt as strangers, they served there as slaves (*v.* 6).

Verses 12–15

Concerning the disposal of their tithe the third year we had the law before, *ch.* xiv. 28, 29. The second tithe, which in the other two years was to be spent in extraordinaries at the feasts, was to be spent the third year at home, in entertaining the poor.

I. They must make a solemn protestation to this purport, *v.* 13, 14. 1. That no hallowed things were hoarded up: "*I have brought them away out of my house,* nothing now remains there but my own part." 2. That the poor, and particularly poor ministers, poor strangers, and poor widows, had had their part according to the commandment. 3. That none of this tithe had been misapplied to any common use, much less to any ill use. The Jews say that this protestation of their integrity was to be made with a low voice, because it looked like a self-condemnation, but that the foregoing confession of God's goodness was to be made with a loud voice to his glory. He that durst not make this protestation must bring his *trespass-offering,* Lev. v. 15.

II. To this solemn protestation they must add a *solemn prayer* (*v.* 15), not particularly for themselves, but for *God's people Israel;* for in the common peace and prosperity every particular person prospers and has peace.

Verses 16–19

Two things Moses here urges to enforce all these precepts:—1. That they were the commands of God, *v.* 16. They were not the dictates of his own wisdom, nor were they enacted by any authority of his own, but infinite wisdom framed them, and the power of the King of kings made them binding to them: *The Lord thy God commands thee.* 2. That their covenant with God obliged them to keep these commands.

CHAPTER 27

Moses having very largely and fully set before the people their duty and having in the close of the foregoing chapter laid them under the obligation both of the command and the covenant, he comes in this chapter to prescribe outward means, I. For the helping of their memories. They must write all the words of this law upon stones, ver. 1–10. II. For the moving of their affections, that they might not be indifferent to the law as a light thing. When they came into Canaan, the blessings and curses which were the sanctions of the law, were to be solemnly pronounced in the hearing of all Israel, who were to say Amen to them, ver. 11–26.

Verses 1–10

Here is, I. A general charge to the people to keep God's commandments. This is pressed upon them, with all authority. *Moses with the elders of Israel,* the rulers of each tribe (*v.* 1), and again, *Moses and the priests the Levites* (*v.* 9), commanded their people to *keep God's law.*

II. A particular direction to them with great solemnity to register *the words of this law,* as soon as they came into Canaan. There was a solemn ratification of the covenant between God and Israel at Mount Sinai, when an altar was erected, with twelve pillars, and the book of the covenant was produced, Exod. xxiv. 4. That which is here appointed is a somewhat similar solemnity.

1. They must set up a monument on which they must *write the words of this law.*

2. They must also set up an altar. By the words of the law which were written upon the plaster, God *spoke to them;* by the altar, and the sacrifices offered upon it, they spoke to God; and thus was communion kept up between them and God.

Verses 11–26

There were, it seems, in Canaan, that part of it which afterwards fell to the lot of Ephraim (Joshua's tribe), two mountains that lay near together, with a valley between, one called *Gerizim* and the other *Ebal.* On the sides of these two mountains, which faced one another, all the tribes were to be drawn up, six on one side and six on the other. Then when silence was proclaimed, and attention commanded, one of the priests pronounced with a loud voice one of the curses here following, and all the people that stood on the side and foot of Mount Ebal said *Amen;* then the contrary blessing was pronounced, "Blessed is he that doth not so or so," and then those that stood on the side, and at the foot, of Mount Gerizim, said *Amen.*

I. Something is to be observed, in general, concerning this solemnity, which was to be done but once, but would be talked of to posterity. 1. God appointed which tribes should stand upon Mount Gerizim and which on Mount Ebal (*v.* 12, 13). The six tribes that were appointed for blessing were all the children of the free women, for to such the promise belongs, Gal. iv. 31. Levi is here put among the rest, to teach ministers to apply to themselves the blessing and curse which they preach to others, and by faith to set their own *Amen* to it. 2. Of those tribes that were to say *Amen* to the blessings it is said, *They stood to bless the people*, but of the other, *They stood to curse*, not mentioning the people, as loth to suppose that any of this people whom God had taken for his own should lay themselves under the curse. 3. The Levites or priests, such of them as were appointed for that purpose, were to pronounce the curses as well as the blessings. 4. The curses are here expressed, but not the blessings. In Christ's sermon upon the mount, which was the true Mount Gerizim, we have blessings only, Matt. v. 3, &c. 5. To each of the curses the people were to say *Amen*. The Jews have a saying to encourage people to say *Amen* to the public prayers, *Whosoever answereth* Amen, *after him that blesseth, he is as he that blesseth*. But how could they say *Amen* to the curses? When they said *Amen*, they did in effect say, not only, *It is certain it shall be so*, but, *It is just it should be so*.

II. Let us now observe what are the particular sins against which the curses are here denounced.

1. Sins against the second commandment. This flaming sword is set to keep that commandment first, *v.* 15. Those are here cursed, not only that worship images, but that make them or keep them, if they be such (or like such) as idolators used in the service of their gods.

2. Against the fifth commandment, *v.* 16. The contempt of parents is a sin so heinous that it is put next to the contempt of God himself.

3. Against the eighth commandment. The curse of God is here fastened, (1) Upon an unjust neighbour that *removes the land marks, v.* 17. See *ch.* xix. 14. (2) Upon an unjust counsellor. (3) Upon an unjust judge, that *perverteth the judgment of the stranger, fatherless, and widow*, whom he should protect and vindicate, *v.* 19.

4. Against the seventh commandment. Incest is a cursed sin, with a *sister, a father's wife, or a mother-in-law, v.* 20, 22, 23.

5. Against the sixth commandment. Two of the worst kinds of murder are here specified:—(1) Murder unseen, when a man does not set upon his neighbour as a fair adversary, giving him an opportunity to defend himself, but *smites him secretly* (*v.* 24), as by poison or otherwise, when he sees not who hurts him. See Ps. x. 8, 9. (2) Murder under colour of law. Cursed therefore is he that will be hired, or bribed, to accuse, or to convict, or to condemn, and so *to slay, an innocent person, v.* 25. See Ps. xv. 5.

6. The solemnity concludes with a general curse upon him *that confirmeth not all the words of this law to do them, v.* 26. By our obedience to the law we set our seal to it, and so confirm it, as by our disobedience we do what lies in us to disannul it, Ps. cxix. 126.

CHAPTER 28

This chapter is a very large exposition of two words in the foregoing chapter, the blessing and the curse. I. He describes the blessings that should come upon them if they were obedient; personal, family, and especially national, both in that capacity especially they are here treated with, ver. 1–14. II. He more largely describes the curses which would come upon them if they were disobedient; such as would be, 1. Their extreme vexation, ver. 15–44. 2. Their utter ruin and destruction at last, ver. 45–68. This chapter is much to the same purport with Lev. xxvi, setting before them life and death, good and evil; and the promise, in the close of that chapter, of their restoration, upon their repentance, is here likewise more largely repeated, ch. xxx.

Verses 1–14

The blessings are here put before the curses, to intimate, 1. That God is slow to anger, but swift to show mercy: he has said it, and sworn, that he would much rather we would obey and live than sin and die. 2. That obedience pleases best which comes from a principle of delight in God's goodness.

The particulars of this blessing.

I. It is promised that the providence of God should prosper them in all their outward concerns. These blessings are said to *overtake them, v.* 2. Thus in the great day the blessing will overtake the righteous that say, *Lord, when saw we thee hungry and fed thee?* Matt. xxv. 37.

1. Several things are enumerated in which God by his providence would bless them:—(1) They should be safe and easy; a blessing should rest upon their persons wherever they were, *in the city or in the field, v.* 3. Their persons should be protected, and the affair they went about should succeed well. (2) Their families should be built up in a numerous issue. (3) They should be rich, and have an abundance of all the good things of this life. A blessing is promised, *First*, On all they had without doors, corn and cattle in the field (*v.* 4, 11), their cows and sheep particularly. *Secondly*, On all they had within doors, the basket and the store (*v.* 5), the store-houses or barns, *v.* 8. We depend upon God and his blessing, not only for our yearly corn out of the field, but for our daily bread out of our basket and store, and therefore are taught to pray for it every day. (4) They should have success in all their employments, God would own their industry, and *bless the work of their hand* (*v.* 12). (5) They should have honour among their neighbours (*v.* 1). Two things should help to make them great among the nations:—*First*, Their wealth (*v.* 12): "*Thou shalt lend to many nations* upon interest" (which they were allowed to take from the neighbouring nations), "but thou shalt not have occasion to borrow." *Secondly*, Their power (*v.* 13): "*The Lord shall make thee the head*, to give law to all about thee, to exact tribute, and to arbitrate all controversies." Religion among them, and the blessing of God upon them, would make them formidable to all their neighbours, terrible as an army with banners. (6) They should be victorious over their enemies, and prosper in all their wars.

2. From the whole we learn (though it were well if men would believe it) that religion and piety are the best friends to outward prosperity. Though temporal blessings do not take up so much room in the promises of the New Testament as they do in those of the Old, yet it is enough that our Lord Jesus has given us his word (and surely we may take his word) that if we *seek first the kingdom of God, and the righteousness thereof, all other things* shall be added to us, as far as Infinite Wisdom sees good; and who can desire them further? Matt. vi. 33.

II. It is likewise promised that the grace of God should *establish them a holy people, v.* 9. This establishment of their religion would be the establishment of their reputation (*v.* 10).

Verses 15–44

Having viewed the bright side of the cloud, which is towards the obedient, we have now presented to us the dark side, which is towards the disobedient. If we do not keep God's commandments, we not only come short of the blessing promised, but we lay ourselves under the curse, which is as comprehensive of all misery as the blessing is of all happiness.

I. The equity of this curse. It is not a curse causeless, nor for some light cause; God seeks not occasion against us, nor is he apt to quarrel with us. That which is here mentioned as bringing the curse is, 1. Despising God, refusing to *hearken to his voice* (*v.* 15), which bespeaks the highest contempt imaginable. 2. Disobeying him, *not doing his commandments*. 3. Deserting him. God never casts us off till we first cast him off.

II. The extent and efficacy of this curse.

1. In general, it is declared, "*All these curses shall come upon thee* from above, *and shall overtake thee;* though thou endeavour to escape them." There is no

running from God but by running to him, no fleeing from his justice but by fleeing to his mercy. See Ps. xxi. 7, 8. To those whose *mind and conscience are defiled* everything else is so, Tit. i. 15. This curse is just the reverse of the blessing in the former part of the chapter.

2. Many particular judgments are here enumerated, which would be the fruits of the curse. Note, God's judgments can reach the minds of men, to fill them with darkness and horror, as well as their bodies and estates; and those are the sorest of all judgments which make men a terror to themselves, and their own destroyers.

Verses 45–68

One would have thought that enough had been said to possess them with a dread of that *wrath of God* which is *revealed from heaven against the ungodliness and unrighteousness of men.* But to show how deep the treasures of that wrath are, and that still there is more and worse behind, Moses, when one would have thought that he had concluded this dismal subject, begins again, and adds to this roll of curses many similar words; as Jeremiah did to his, Jer. xxxvi. 32. Here, in this latter part, he foretells their last destruction by the Romans and their dispersion thereupon. And the present deplorable state of the Jewish nation, and of all that have incorporated themselves with them, by embracing their religion, does so fully and exactly answer to the prediction in these verses that it serves for an incontestable proof of the truth of prophecy, and consequently of the divine authority of the scripture. And, this last destruction being here represented as more dreadful than the former, it shows that their sin, in rejecting Christ and his gospel, was more heinous. Under this last destruction now for above 1600 years they continue incurably averse to the Lord Jesus.

I. It is amazing to think that a people so long the favourites of Heaven should be so perfectly abandoned and cast off, that a people so closely incorporated should be so universally dispersed, and yet that a people so scattered in all nations should preserve themselves distinct and not mix with any, but like Cain be fugitives and vagabonds, and yet marked to be known.

II. The destruction threatened is described. Moses is here upon the same melancholy subject that our Saviour is discoursing of to his disciples in his farewell sermon (Matt. xxiv.), namely, The destruction of Jerusalem and the Jewish nation.

1. Five things are here foretold as steps to their ruin:—

(1) That they should be invaded by a foreign enemy (v. 49, 50): A *nation from far,* namely, the Romans, *as swift as the eagle* hastening to the prey. Our Saviour makes use of this similitude, in foretelling this destruction, that *where the carcase is there will the eagles be gathered together,* Matt. xxiv. 28. And bishop Patrick observes that the ensign of the Roman armies was an eagle.

(2) That the country should be laid waste, and all the fruits of it eaten up by this army of foreigners, which is the natural consequence of an invasion, especially when it is made, as that by the Romans was, for the chastisement of rebels.

(3) That their cities should be besieged, and that such would be the obstinacy of the besieged, and such the vigour of the besiegers, that they would be reduced to the last extremity, and at length fall into the hands of the enemy, *v.* 52.

(4) That multitudes of them should perish, so that they should become *few in number, v.* 62.

(5) That the remnant should be scattered throughout the nations. This completes their woe: *The Lord shall scatter thee among all people, v.* 64.

2. Upon the whole matter, (1) The accomplishment of these predictions upon the Jewish nation shows that Moses spoke by the Spirit of God. (2) Let us all hence learn to stand in awe and not to sin. I have heard of a wicked man, who, upon reading the threatenings of this chapter, was so enraged that he tore the leaf out of the Bible, as Jehoiakim cut Jeremiah's roll; but to what purpose is it to deface a copy, while the original remains upon record in the divine counsels, by which it is unalterably determined that *the wages of sin is death,* whether men will hear or whether they will forbear?

CHAPTER 29

The first words of this chapter are the contents of it, "These are the words of the covenant" (ver. 1), that is, these that follow. Here is, I. A recital of God's dealings with them, in order to the bringing of them into this covenant, ver. 2–8. II. A solemn charge to them to keep the covenant, ver. 9. III. An abstract of the covenant itself, ver. 12, 13. IV. A specification of the persons taken into the covenant, ver. 10, 11, 14, 15. V. An intimation of the great design of this covenant against idolatry, in a parenthesis, ver. 16, 17. VI. A most solemn and dreadful denunciation of the wrath of God against such persons as promise themselves peace in a sinful way, ver. 18–28. VII. The conclusion of this treaty, with a distinction between things secret and things revealed, ver. 29.

Verses 1–9

Now that Moses had largely repeated the commands which the people were to observe as their part of the covenant, and the promises and threatenings which God would make good (according as they behaved themselves) as his part of the covenant, the whole is here summed up in a federal transaction. The covenant formerly made is here renewed, and Moses, who was before, is still, the mediator of it (*v.* 1): *The Lord commanded Moses to make it.* It is probable that some now living, though not of age to be mustered, were of age to consent for themselves to the covenant made at Horeb, and yet it is here renewed. But the far greater part were a new generation, and therefore the covenant must be made afresh with them, for it is fit that the covenant should be renewed to the children of the covenant.

I. It is usual for indentures to begin with a recital; this does so, with a rehearsal of the great things God had done for them, 1. As an encouragement to them to believe that God would indeed be to them a God, for he would not have done so much for them if he had not designed more, to which all he had hitherto done was but a preface. 2. As an engagement upon them to be to him an obedient people, in consideration of what he had done for them.

II. For the proof of what he here advances he appeals to their own eyes (*v.* 2): *You have seen all that the Lord did.* Their own senses were incontestable evidence of the matter of fact: *Keep therefore the words of this covenant, v.* 9.

III. These things he specifies, to show the power and goodness of God in his appearances for them. 1. Their deliverance out of Egypt, *v.* 2, 3. 2. Their conduct through the wilderness for forty years, *v.* 5, 6. There they were led, and clad, and fed, by miracles. By these miracles they were made to know that the Lord was God, and by these mercies that he was their God. 3. The victory they had lately obtained over Sihon and Og, and that good land which they had taken possession of, *v.* 7, 8.

IV. By way of inference from these memoirs, Moses laments their stupidity: *Yet the Lord has not given you a heart to perceive, v.* 4. Note, 1 The hearing ear, the seeing eye, and the understanding heart, are the gift of God. 2 God gives not only food and raiment, but wealth and large possessions, to many to whom he does not give grace. Many enjoy the gifts who have not hearts to perceive the giver, nor the true intention and use of the gifts. 3 God's readiness to do us good in other things is a plain evidence that if we have not grace, that best of gifts, it is our own fault and not his.

Verses 10–29

It appears by the length of the sentences here, and by the copiousness and pungency of the expressions, that Moses, now that he was drawing near to the close of his discourse, was very zealous, and very desirous to impress what he said upon the minds of this unthinking people. To bind them the faster to God and duty, he here concludes a bargain (as it were) between them and God, an everlasting covenant. He requires not their explicit consent, but lays the matter plainly before them, and then leaves it between God and their own consciences.

I. The parties to this covenant. 1. It is the Lord their God they are to covenant with, v. 12. 2. They are all to be taken into covenant with him. They were all summoned to attend (v. 2). (1) Even their great men, the captains of their tribes, their elders and officers, must not think it any disparagement to put their necks under the yoke of this covenant, and to draw in it. (2) Not the men only, but their wives and children, must come into this covenant, v. 11. (3) Not the men of Israel only, but the stranger that was in their camp, provided he was so far proselyted to their religion as to renounce all false gods. This was an early indication of favour to the Gentiles, and of the kindness God had in store for them. (4) Not the freemen only, but the hewers of wood and drawers of water, the meanest drudge they had among them. (5) Not only those that were now present before God in this solemn assembly, but those also that were not here with them were taken into covenant (v. 15). That is, [1] Those that tarried at home were included; though detained either by sickness or necessary business. [2] The generations to come are included. And so, taking this covenant as a typical dispensation of the covenant of grace, it is a noble testimony to the Mediator of that covenant, who is *the same yesterday, to-day, and for ever.*

II. The summary of this covenant. All the precepts and all the promises of the covenant are included in the covenant-relation between God and them, v. 13.

III. The principal design of the renewing of this covenant at this time was to fortify them against temptations to idolatry. Idolaters were like drunkards, violently set upon their idols themselves and industrious to draw others in with them. Revellings commonly accompanied their idolatries (1 Pet. iv. 3), so that this speaks a woe to drunkards. Drunkenness is a sin that hardens the heart, and debauches the conscience, as much as any other, a sin to which men are strangely tempted themselves even when they have lately felt the mischiefs of it, and to which they are strangely fond of drawing others.

Idolatry would be the ruin of their nation; it would bring plagues upon the land that connived at this root of bitterness and received the infection; as far as the sin spread, the judgment should spread likewise. We are forbidden curiously to enquire into the secret counsels of God. A full answer is given to that question, *Wherefore has the Lord done thus to this land?* sufficient to justify God and admonish us. But if any ask further why God would be at such a vast expense of miracles to form such a people, whose apostasy and ruin he plainly foresaw, why he did not by his almighty grace prevent it, or what he intends yet to do with them, let such know that these are questions which cannot be answered. See Acts i. 7; John xxi. 22; Col. ii. 18. We are directed and encouraged diligently to enquire into that which God has made known: things *revealed belong to us and to our children.* Note, 1. Though God has kept much of his counsel secret, yet there is enough re-vealed to satisfy and save us. He has *kept back nothing that is profitable for us.* 2. We ought to acquaint ourselves, and our children too, with the things of God that are revealed. We are not only allowed to search into them, but are concerned to do so. They are things which we and ours are closely interested in. They are the rules we are to live by, the grants we are to live upon; and therefore we are to learn them diligently ourselves, and to teach them diligently to our children. 3. All our knowledge must be in order to practise, for this is the end of all divine revelation, not to furnish us with curious subjects of speculation and discourse, with which to entertain ourselves and our friends, *but that we may do all the words of this law,* and be blessed in our deed.

Chapter 30

One would have thought that the threatenings in the close of the foregoing chapter had made a full end of the people of Israel, and had left their case for ever desperate; but in this chapter we have a plain intimation of the mercy God had in store for them in the latter days, so that mercy at length rejoices against judgment, and has the last word. Here we have, I. Exceedingly great and precious promises made to them, upon their repentance and return to God, ver. 1–10. II. The righteousness of faith set before them in the plainness and easiness of the commandment that was now given them, ver. 11–14. III. A fair reference of the whole matter to their choice, ver. 15, &c.

Verses 1–10

These verses may be considered either as a conditional promise or as an absolute prediction.

I. They are chiefly to be considered as a conditional promise, and so they belong to all persons and all people, and not to Israel only; and the design of them is to assure us that the greatest sinners, if they repent and be converted, shall have their sins pardoned, and be restored to God's favour. This is the purport of the covenant of grace, it leaves room for repentance in case of misdemeanour, and promises pardon upon repentance. Now observe here,

1. How the repentance is described which is the condition of these promises. (1) It begins in *serious consideration, v. 1.* "Thou shalt call to mind that which thou hadst forgotten or not regarded." Note, Consideration is the first step towards conversion. Isa. xlvi. 8, *Bring to mind, O you transgressors.* The prodigal son came to himself first, and then to his father. That which they should call to mind is the blessing and the curse. If sinners would but seriously consider the happiness they have lost by sin and the misery they have brought themselves into, and that by repentance they may escape that misery and recover that happiness, they would not delay to *return to the Lord their God.* The prodigal *called to mind the blessing and the curse* when he considered his present poverty and the plenty of bread *in his father's house,* Luke xv. 17. (2) It consists in sincere conversion. The effect of the consideration cannot but be godly sorrow and shame, Ezek. vi. 9; vii. 16. But that which is the life and soul of repentance, and without which the most passionate expressions are but a jest, is *returning to the Lord our God, v. 2.* If thou turn (v. 10) *with all thy heart and with all thy soul.* (3) It is evidenced by a constant obedience to the holy will of God. [1] This obedience must be with an eye to God: Thou shalt *obey his voice* (v. 8), and hearken to it, v. 10. [2] It must be sincere, and cheerful, and entire: *With all thy heart, and with all thy soul, v. 2.* [3] It must be from a principle of love, and that love must be *with all thy heart and with all thy soul, v. 6.*

2. What the favour is which is promised upon this repentance. Though they are brought to God by their trouble and distress, in the nations whither they were driven (v. 1), yet God will graciously accept of them notwithstanding; for on this errand afflictions

are sent, to bring us to repentance. *Undique ad cœlos tantundem est viæ—From every place there is the same way to heaven.* It is here promised, (1) That God would have compassion upon them, as proper objects of his pity, *v.* 3. (2) That he would *turn their captivity, and gather them from the nations whither they were scattered* (*v.* 3), though ever so remote, *v.* 4. (3) That he would *bring them into their land again*, *v.* 5. Note, Penitent sinners are not only delivered out of their misery, but restored to true happiness in the favour of God.

II. This may also be considered as a prediction of the repentance and restoration of the Jews: *When all these things shall have come upon thee* (*v.* 1), the blessing first, and after that the curse, then the mercy in reserve shall take place. Though their hearts were wretchedly hardened, yet the grace of God could soften and change them; and then, though their case was deplorably miserable, the providence of God would redress all their grievances. Now, 1. It is certain that this was fulfilled in their return from their captivity in Babylon. It was a wonderful instance of their repentance and reformation that Ephraim, who had been joined to idols, renounced them, and said, *What have I to do any more with idols?* That captivity effectually cured them of idolatry; and then God planted them again in their own land and did them good. But, 2. Some think that it is yet further to be accomplished in the conversion of the Jews who are now dispersed, their repentance for the sin of their fathers in crucifying Christ, their return to God through him, and their accession to the Christian church.

Verses 11–14

Moses here urges them to obedience from the consideration of the plainness and easiness of the command.

I. This is true of the law of Moses. They could never plead in excuse of their disobedience that God had enjoined them that which was either unintelligible or impracticable, impossible to be known or to be done (*v.* 11): *It is not hidden from thee.* That is, 1. "It is not too high for thee; thou needest not send messengers to heaven (*v.* 12), to enquire what thou must do to please God; nor needest thou go *beyond sea* (*v.* 13), as the philosophers did, that travelled through many and distant regions in pursuit of learning." 2. "It is not too *hard* nor *heavy* for thee": so the Septuagint reads it, *v.* 11. "There is that in thee which *consents to the law that it is good*, Rom. vii. 16. Thou hast therefore no reason to complain of any insuperable difficulty in the observance of it."

II. This is true of the gospel of Christ, to which the apostle applies it, and makes it the language of the *righteousness which is of faith*, Rom. x. 6–8. This is God's commandment now under the gospel that we *believe in the name of his Son Jesus Christ*, 1 John iii. 23. But the word is nigh us, and Christ in that word; so that if we believe with the heart that the promises of the incarnation and resurrection of the Messiah are fulfilled in our Lord Jesus, and receive him accordingly, and confess him with our mouth, we have then Christ with us, and we shall be saved. He is near, very near, that justifies us. The law was plain and easy, but the gospel much more so.

Verses 15–20

Moses here concludes with a very bright light, and a very strong fire, that, if possible, what he had been preaching of might find entrance into the understanding and affections of this unthinking people.

I. He states the case very fairly. 1. Every man covets to obtain life and good, and to escape death and evil, desires happiness and dreads misery. "Well," says he, "I have shown you the way to obtain all the happiness you can desire and to avoid all misery. Be obedient, and all shall be well, and nothing amiss." 2. Every man is moved and governed in his actions by hope and fear, hope of good and fear of evil, real or apparent. "Now," says Moses, "I have tried both ways; if you will be either drawn to obedience by the certain prospect of advantage by it, or driven to obedience by the no less certain prospect of ruin in case you be disobedient—if you will be wrought upon either way, you will be kept close to God and your duty; but, if you will not, you are utterly inexcusable."

II. Having thus stated the case, he fairly puts them to their choice, with a direction to them to choose well.

III. In the last verse, He shows them, in short, what their duty is, *to love God*, and to love him as *the Lord*, a Being most amiable, and as *their God*, a God in covenant with them. *He is thy life, and the length of thy days.*

CHAPTER 31

In this chapter Moses, having finished his sermon, I. Encourages both the people who were now to enter Canaan (ver. 1–6), and Joshua who was to lead them, ver. 7, 8, 23. And, II. He takes care for the keeping of these things always in their remembrance after his decease, 1. By the book of the law which was, (1) Written. (2) Delivered into the custody of the priests, ver. 9, and 24–27. (3) Ordered to be publicly read every seventh year, ver. 10–13. 2. By a song which God orders Moses to prepare for their instruction and admonition. (1) He calls Moses and Joshua to the door of the tabernacle, ver. 14, 15. (2) He foretells the apostasy of Israel in process of time, and the judgments they would thereby bring upon themselves, ver. 16–18. (3) He prescribes the following song to be a witness against them, ver. 19–21. (4) Moses wrote it, ver. 22. And delivered it to Israel, with an intimation of the design of it, as he had received it from the Lord, ver. 28, &c.

Verses 1–8

Loth to part (we say) *bids oft farewell.* Moses does so to the children of Israel; not because he was loth to go to God, but because he was loth to leave them, fearing that when he had left them they would leave God. Here he calls them together to give them a word of encouragement. It was a discouragement to them that Moses was to be removed at a time when he could so ill be spared: though Joshua would continue to fight for them in the valley, they would want Moses to intercede for them on the hill, as he did, Exod. xvii. 10. 1. He is 120 *years old*, and it is time for him to think of resigning his honour and returning to his rest. 2. He is under a divine sentence: *Thou shalt not go over Jordan.*

I. He encourages the people; and never could any general animate his soldiers upon such good grounds as those on which Moses here encourages Israel. 1. He assures them of the constant presence of God with them (*v.* 3): *The Lord thy God that has led thee and kept thee hitherto will go over before thee.* This is applied by the apostle to all God's spiritual Israel, for the encouragement of their faith and hope; unto us is this gospel preached, as well as unto them. *He will never fail thee, nor forsake thee*, Heb. xiii. 5. 2. He commends Joshua to them for a leader, one whose conduct, and courage, and sincere affection to their interest, they had had long experience of; and one whom God had ordained and appointed to be their leader, and therefore, no doubt, would own and bless, and make a blessing to them. See Num. xxvii. 18. 3. He ensures their success. Two things might encourage their hopes of this:—(1) The victories they had already obtained over Sihon and Og (*v.* 4), from which they might infer the power of God, that he could do what he had done, and the purpose of God, that he would finish what he had begun to do. (2) The command God had given them to destroy the Canaanites (*ch.* vii. 2; xii. 2), and from which they might infer that no doubt he would put it into the power of their hands to do it.

II. He encourages Joshua, *v.* 7, 8. Observe, 1. Joshua was an experienced general, and a man of approved gallantry and very well pleased to be admonished by Moses to be strong and of good courage. 2. He gives him this charge *in the sight of all Israel*, that they might be the more observant of him whom they saw thus solemnly inaugurated. 3. He gives him the same assurances of the divine presence, and consequently of a glorious success, that he had given the people.

Verses 9–13

The law was given by Moses; so it is said, John i. 17. He was not only entrusted to deliver it to that generation, but to transmit it to the generations to come; and here it appears that he was faithful to that trust.

I. *Moses wrote this law, v.* 9. 1. That those who had heard it might often review it themselves, and call it to mind. 2. That it might be the more safely handed down to posterity. Note, The church has received abundance of advantage from the writing, as well as from the preaching, of divine things; faith comes not only by hearing, but by reading. The same care that was taken of the law, thanks be to God, is taken of the gospel too; soon after it was preached it was written, that it might reach to those on whom the ends of the world shall come.

II. Having written it, he committed it to the care and custody of the priests and elders. He delivered one authentic copy to the priests, to be laid up by the ark (*v.* 26), there to remain as a standard by which all other copies must be tried.

III. He appointed the public reading of this law in a general assembly of all Israel every seventh year. The pious Jews (it is very probable) read the law daily in their families, and *Moses of old time was read in the synagogue every sabbath day*, Acts. xv. 21. But once in seven years, that the law might be the more magnified and made honourable, it must be read in a general assembly. Now here it gives direction,

1. When this solemn reading of the law must be, that the time might add to the solemnity; it must be done, (1) In the year of release. In that year the land rested, so that they could the better spare time to attend this service. Servants who were then discharged, and poor debtors who were then acquitted from their debts, must know that, having the benefit of the law, it was justly expected they should yield obedience to it, and therefore give up themselves to be God's servants, because he had loosed their bonds. The year of release was typical of gospel grace, which therefore is called the *acceptable year of the Lord*; for our remission and liberty by Christ engage us to keep his commandments, Luke i. 74, 75. (2) At the feast of tabernacles in that year. In that feast they were particularly required to *rejoice before God*, Lev. xxiii. 40.

2. To whom it must be read: To *all Israel* (*v.* 11), *men, women, and children, and the strangers, v.* 12. The women and children were not obliged to go up to the other feasts, but to this only in which the law was read.

3. By whom it must be read: *Thou shalt read it* (*v.* 11), "Thou, O Israel," by a proper person appointed for that purpose; or, "Thou, O Joshua," their chief ruler; accordingly we find that he did read the law himself, Josh. viii. 34, 35. So did Josiah, 2 Chron. xxxiv. 30, and Ezra, Neh. viii. 3.

4. For what end it must be thus solemnly read. That the present generation might hereby keep up their acquaintance with the law of God, *v.* 12. They must hear, that they may learn, and *fear God, and observe to do their duty*. See here what we are to aim

at in hearing the word; we must hear, that we may learn and grow in knowledge; and every time we read the scriptures we shall find that there is still more and more to be learned out of them.

Verses 14–21

Here, I. Moses and Joshua are summoned to attend the divine majesty at the door of the tabernacle, *v.* 14. Moses is told again that he must shortly die. He must also bring Joshua with him to be presented to God for a successor, and to receive his commission and charge.

II. God graciously gives them the meeting: *He appeared in the tabernacle* (as the shechinah used to appear) *in a pillar of a cloud, v.* 15.

III. He tells Moses that, after his death, the covenant which he had taken so much pains to make between Israel and their God would certainly be broken. 1. That Israel would *forsake God, v.* 16. Worshipping the gods of the Canaanites would undoubtedly be counted a violation of the covenant. Thus still those are revolters from Christ, who either make a god of their money by allowing covetousness to reign, or a god of their belly by allowing sensuality to reign. Those that *turn to other gods* (*v.* 18) forsake their own mercies. 2. That then God would forsake Israel; and justly does he cast those off who had so unjustly cast him off (*v.* 17). Those that have sinned away their God will find that thereby they pull all mischiefs upon their own heads.

IV. He directs Moses to deliver them a song, in the composing of which he should be divinely inspired, and which should remain a standing testimony for God as faithful to them in giving them warning. The wisdom of man has devised many ways of conveying the knowledge of good and evil, by laws, histories, prophecies, proverbs, and, among the rest, by songs; each has its advantages. And the wisdom of God has in the scripture made use of them all, that ignorant and careless men might be left inexcusable. 1. This song, if rightly improved, might be a means to prevent their apostasy. 2. If this song did not prevent their apostasy, yet it might help to bring them to repentance. When their troubles come upon them, this *song shall not be forgotten*, but may serve as a glass to show them their own faces, that they may humble themselves, and return to him from whom they have revolted. Note, Those for whom God has mercy in store he may leave to fall, yet will provide means for their recovery. Medicines are prepared beforehand for their cure.

Verses 22–30

Here, I. The charge is given to Joshua, which God had said (*v.* 14) he would give him. Joshua had now heard from God so much of the wickedness of the people whom he was to have the conduct of as could not but be a discouragement to him: "Nay," says God, "how bad soever they are, thou shalt go through thy undertaking, for *I will be with thee*. Therefore *be of good courage.*"

II. The solemn delivery of the book of the law to the Levites, to be deposited in the side of the ark, is here again related (*v.* 24–26). Only they are here directed where to treasure up this precious original, not in the ark (there only the two tables were preserved), but in another box *by the side of the ark*. It is probable that this was the very book that was found in the house of the Lord (having been somehow or other misplaced) in the days of Josiah (2 Chron. xxxiv. 14).

III. The song which follows in the next chapter is here delivered to Moses, and by him to the people. 1. He declares what little joy he had had of them while he was with them, *v.* 27. Their rebellions against himself he makes no mention of: these he had long since forgiven and forgotten; but they must be made to hear of their rebellions against God, that they may be ever repented of and never repeated. 2. What little hopes he had of them now that he was leaving them. *I know that after my death you will utterly corrupt yourselves.* Thus our Lord Jesus, a little before his death, foretold the rise of false Christs and false prophets (Matt. xxiv. 24), notwithstanding which, and all the apostasies of the latter times, we may be confident that *the gates of hell shall not prevail against the church,* for the *foundation of God stands sure.*

CHAPTER 32

In this chapter we have, I. The song which Moses, by the appointment of God, delivered to the children of Israel. 1. The preface, ver. 1, 2. 2. A high character of God, and, in opposition to that, a bad character of the people of Israel, ver. 3–6. 3. A rehearsal of the great things God had done for them, and in opposition to that an account of their ill carriage towards him, ver. 7–18. 4. A prediction of the wasting destroying judgments which God would bring upon them for their sins, ver. 19–33. 5. A promise of the destruction of their enemies and oppressors at last, and the glorious deliverance of a remnant of Israel, ver. 36–43. II. The exhortation with which Moses delivered this song to them, ver. 44–47. III. The orders God gives to Moses to go up to Mount Nebo and die, ver. 48, &c.

Verses 1–6

Here is, I. A commanding preface or introduction to this song of Moses, *v.* 1, 2. He begins, 1. With a solemn appeal to heaven and earth concerning the truth and importance of what he was about to say, and the justice of the divine proceedings against a rebellious and backsliding people. Heaven and earth will be witnesses against sinners, witnesses of the warning given them and of their refusal to take the warning (see Job xx. 27). 2. He begins with a solemn application of what he was about to say to the people (*v.* 2): *My doctrine shall drop as the rain.* "It shall be a beating sweeping rain to the rebellious"; so one of the Chaldee paraphrasts expounds the first clause. Rain is sometimes sent for judgment, and the word of God, while to some it is so refreshing —a *savour of life unto life,* is to others terrifying. It shall be as a sweet and comfortable dew to those who are rightly prepared to receive it. Observe, (1) The subject of this song is doctrine; he had given them a song of praise and thanksgiving (Exod. xv.), but this is a song of instruction, for in psalms, and hymns, and spiritual songs, we are not only to give glory to God, but to *teach and admonish one another,* Col. iii. 16. Hence many of David's psalms are entitled *Maschil—to give instruction.* (2) This doctrine is fitly compared to rain and showers which come from above, to make the earth fruitful. (3) He promises that his doctrine shall drop and distil as the dew, and the small rain, which descend silently and without noise. The word preached is likely to profit when it comes gently, and sweetly insinuates itself into the hearts and affections of the hearers. (4) He bespeaks their acceptance and entertainment of it.

II. An awful declaration of the greatness and righteousness of God, *v.* 3, 4.

1. He begins with this, and lays it down as his first principle. To justify God in his dealings with them; we must abide by it, that God is righteous, even when his *judgments are a great deep,* Jer. xii. 1; Ps. xxxvi. 6.

2. Moses here sets himself to *publish the name of the Lord* (*v.* 3), that Israel might never be such fools as to exchange him for a false god. It will be of great use to us for the preventing of sin, and the preserving of us in the way of our duty, always to keep up high and honourable thoughts of God, and to take all occasions to express them: *Ascribe greatness to our God.* Now, when Moses would set forth the greatness of God, he does it, not by explaining his eternity and immensity, or describing the brightness of his glory in the upper world, but by showing the faithfulness of his word, the perfection of his works, and the wisdom and equity of all the administrations of his government; for in these his glory shines most clearly to us, and these are the things revealed concerning him, which *belong to us and our children, v.* 4. (1) *He is the rock.* God is the rock, for he is in himself immutable, immovable, and he is to all that seek him and fly to him an impenetrable shelter, and to all that trust in him an everlasting foundation. (2) *His work is perfect.* His work of creation was so, *all very good;* his works of providence are so, or will be so in due time, and when the mystery of God shall be finished the perfection of his works will appear to all the world. Nothing that God does can be mended, Eccl. iii. 14. God was now perfecting what he had promised and begun for his people Israel. (3) *All his ways are judgment.* The ends of his ways are all righteous, and he is wise in the choice of the means in order to those ends. *Judgment* signifies both *prudence* and *justice.* (4) He is a *God of truth,* whose word we may take and rely upon, for he cannot lie who is faithful to all his promises, nor shall his threatenings fall to the ground. (5) He is *without iniquity,* one who never cheated any that trusted in him, never wronged any that appealed to his justice, nor ever was hard upon any that cast themselves upon his mercy. (6) *Just and right is he.* As he will not wrong any by punishing them more than they deserve, so he will not fail to recompense all those that serve him or suffer for him.

III. A high charge exhibited against the Israel of God, whose character was in all respects the reverse of that of the *God of Israel, v.* 5. 1. *They have corrupted themselves.* 2. *Their spot is not the spot of his children.* Even God's children have their spots, while they are in this imperfect state; for if we say we have no sin, no spot, we deceive ourselves. But the sin of Israel was none of those; it was not an infirmity which they strove against, watched and prayed against, but an evil which their hearts were fully set in them to do. For, 3. They were a *perverse and crooked generation,* that were actuated by a spirit of contradiction, and therefore would do what was forbidden because it was forbidden.

IV. A pathetic expostulation with this provoking people for their ingratitude (*v.* 6): *Do you thus requite the Lord?* 1. He reminds them of the obligations God had laid upon them to serve him, and to cleave to him. He had been a Father to them. And are not our obligations, as baptized Christians, equally great and strong to our Creator that made us, our Redeemer that bought us, and our Sanctifier that has established us? 2. Hence he infers the evil of deserting him and rebelling against him. For, (1) It was base ingratitude. (2) It was prodigious madness.

Verses 7–14

Moses, having in general represented God to them as their great benefactor, in these verses gives particular instances of God's kindness to them and concern for them. 1. Some instances were ancient, and for proof of them he appeals to the records (*v.* 7): *Remember the days of old.* Note, The authentic histories of ancient times are of singular use, and especially the history of the church in its infancy, both the Old Testament and the New Testament church. 2. Others were more modern, and for proof of them he appeals to their fathers and elders that were now alive and with them.

Three things are here enlarged upon as instances of God's kindness to his people Israel.

I. The early designation of the land of Canaan for their inheritance; for herein it was a type and figure of our heavenly inheritance, that it was of old ordained and prepared in the divine counsels, *v.* 8. Observe,

1. When the earth was divided among the sons of men, God had Israel in his thoughts.

2. The reason given for the particular care God took for this people, so long before they were either born or thought of (as I may say), in our world, does yet more magnify the kindness, and make it obliging beyond expression (*v.* 9): *For the Lord's portion is his people.*

II. The forming of them into a people, that they might be fit to enter upon this inheritance, like an heir of age, at the time appointed of the Father. And herein also Canaan was a figure of the heavenly inheritance; for, as it was from eternity proposed and designed for all God's spiritual Israel, so they are, in time (and it is a work of time), fitted and made meet for it, Col. i. 12. A great deal was done to model this people, to cast them into some shape, and to fit them for the great things designed for them in the land of promise.

1. *He found him in a desert land, v.* 10. This refers, no doubt, to the wilderness through which God brought them to Canaan, and in which he took so much pains with them; it is called *the church in the wilderness,* Acts vii. 38. There it was born, and nursed, and educated. (1) Their condition was forlorn. Egypt was to them a desert land, and a waste howling wilderness, for they were bond-slaves in it. (2) Their disposition was very unpromising. So ignorant were the generality of them in divine things, so stupid and unapt to receive the impressions of them, so peevish and humoursome, that they might well be said to be found in a desert land.

2. *He led him about and instructed him.* When God had them in the wilderness he did not bring them directly to Canaan, but made them go a great way about, and so he instructed them. Learners must have time to learn. By this means he tried their faith, and patience, and dependence upon God, and inured them to the hardships of the wilderness, and so instructed them. Every stage had something in it that was instructive. We may well imagine how unfit that people would have been for Canaan had they not first gone through the discipline of the wilderness.

3. *He kept him as the apple of his eye,* with all the care and tenderness that could be, from the malignant influences of an open sky and air, and all the perils of an inhospitable desert. The pillar of cloud and fire was both a guide and a guard to them.

4. He did that for them which the eagle does for her nest of young, *v.* 11, 12. The similitude was touched upon, Exod. xix. 4, *I bore you on eagles' wings;* here it is enlarged upon. The eagle is observed to have a strong affection for her young, by protecting them and making provision for them, by educating them and teaching them to fly. For this purpose she stirs them out of the nest where they lie dozing, flutters over them, to show them how they must use their wings, and then accustoms them to fly upon her wings till they have learnt to fly upon their own. This, by the way, is an example to parents to train up their children to business, and not to indulge them in idleness and the love of ease. God did thus by Israel; when they were in love with their slavery, and loth to leave it, God, by Moses, stirred them up to aspire after liberty. He carried them out of Egypt, led them into the wilderness, and now at length had led them through it.

III. The settling of them in a good land. This was done in part already, in the happy planting of the two tribes and a half, an earnest of what would speedily and certainly be done for the rest of the tribes, with great plenty of all good things. *Honey out of the rock, and oil out of the flinty rock.* Ainsworth

makes the plenty of good things in Canaan to be a figure of the fruitfulness of Christ's kingdom, and the heavenly comforts of his word and Spirit: for the children of his kingdom he has butter and milk, the sincere milk of the word; and strong meat for strong men, with the wine that makes glad the heart.

Verses 15–18
We have here a description of the apostasy of Israel from God, which would shortly come to pass, and to which already they had a disposition. Here are two great instances of their wickedness.

I. Security and sensuality, pride and insolence, and the other common abuses of plenty and prosperity, *v.* 15. They *kicked;* they grew proud and insolent, and *lifted up the heel* even against God himself. They *kicked against the goad,* as an *untamed heifer,* or a *bullock unaccustomed to the yoke,* and in their rage persecuted the prophets, and flew in the face of providence itself.

II. Idolatry was the great instance of their apostasy, and which the former led them to, as it made them sick of their religion, self-willed, and fond of changes. Observe,

1. What sort of gods they chose and offered sacrifice to, when they forsook the God that made them, *v.* 16, 17. Those very services which they should have done to the true God they did, (1) To *strange gods,* that could not pretend to have done them any kindness. (2) To *new gods, that came newly up.* A new god! can there be a more monstrous absurdity? (3) They were such as were no gods at all, their names the invention of men's fancies, and their images the work of men's hands. Nay, (4) They were devils. So far from being *gods,* they really were *destroyers* (so the word signifies), such as aimed to do mischief.

2. What a great affront this was to Jehovah their God. (1) It was justly interpreted a forgetting of him (*v.* 18): *Of the Rock that begat thee thou art unmindful.* (2) It was justly resented as an inexcusable offence.

Verses 19–25
The method of this song follows the method of the predictions in the foregoing chapter.

I. He had delighted in them, but now he would reject them. Note, The nearer any are to God in profession the more noisome are they to him if they are defiled in a sinful way, Ps. cvi. 39, 40.

II. He had given them the tokens of his presence with them and his favour to them; but now he would withdraw and *hide his face from them, v.* 20. His *hiding his face* signifies his great displeasure, but here it denotes also the slowness of God's proceedings against them in a way of judgment. 1. They were froward. 2. They were faithless, and a people that could not be trusted.

III. He had done every thing to make them easy, but now the punishment here answers the sin, *v.* 21. 1. They had provoked God with despicable deities which were not gods at all. 2. God would therefore plague them with despicable enemies. The more base the people were that tyrannised over them the more barbarous they would be (none so insolent as a beggar on horseback).

IV. He had planted them in a good land, and replenished them with all good things; but now he would strip them of all their comforts, and bring them to ruin. The particular judgments here threatened are, 1. Famine. 2. Pestilence. 3. The insults of the inferior creatures: *the teeth of beasts and the poison of serpents, v.* 24. 4. War and the fatal consequences of it, *v.* 25.

Verses 26–38
After many terrible threatenings of deserved wrath and vengeance, we have here surprising intimations

of mercy, undeserved mercy, which rejoices against judgment, and by which it appears that God has *no pleasure in the death of sinners*, but would rather they should *turn and live*.

I. In jealousy for his own honour, he will not *make a full end* of them, v. 26–28. Mercy prevails for the sparing of a remnant and the saving of that unworthy people from utter ruin: *I feared the wrath of the enemy*. It is an expression after the manner of men; it is certain that God fears no man's wrath, but he acted in this matter as if he had feared it. He needed not Moses to plead it with him, but reminded himself of it: *What will the Egyptians say?* How much soever we deserve to be disgraced, God will never *disgrace the throne of his glory*.

II. In concern for their welfare, he earnestly desires their conversion. God delights not to see sinners ruin themselves, but desires they will help themselves; and, if they will, he is ready to help them. It will contribute much to the return of sinners to God, seriously to consider the latter end, or the future state. It is here meant particularly of that which God by Moses had foretold concerning this people in the latter days: but it may be applied more generally.

III. He calls to mind the great things he had done for them formerly, as a reason why he should not quite cast them off. This seems to be the meaning of (v. 30, 31), "How should one Israelite have been too hard for a thousand Canaanites, as they have been many a time, but that God, who is greater than all gods, fought for them!" And so it corresponds with, Isa. lxiii. 10, 11. When he was *turned to be their enemy*, as here, *and fought against them* for their sins, *then he remembered the days of old*, saying, *Where is he that brought them out of the sea?* God would soon have subdued their enemies (Ps. lxxxi. 14), but that the wickedness of Israel delivered them into their hands.

IV. He resolves upon the destruction of those at last that had been their persecutors and oppressors. God will in due time bring down the church's enemies.

1. In displeasure against their wickedness, which he takes notice of, and keeps an account of, v. 34, 35. Some understand it of the sin of Israel, especially their persecuting the prophets, which was laid up in store against them from the *blood of righteous Abel*, Matt. xxiii. 35. However, it teaches us that the wickedness of the wicked is all laid up in store with God.

2. He will do it in compassion to his own people, who, though they had greatly provoked him, yet stood in relation to him, and their misery appealed to his mercy (v. 36). This plainly points at the deliverances God wrought for Israel by the judges out of the hands of those to whom he had sold them for their sins (see Judges ii. 11–18), and how *his soul was grieved for the misery of Israel* (Judges x. 16), and this when they were reduced to the last extremity. God helped them when they could not help themselves.

3. He will do it in contempt and to the reproach of the idol-gods, v. 37, 38. *Where are their gods?* Two ways it may be understood:—(1) That God would do that for his people which the idols they had served could not do for them. Or, (2) That God would do that against his enemies which the idols they had served could not save them from. Sennacherib and Nebuchadnezzar boldly challenged the God of Israel to deliver his worshippers (Isa. xxxvii. 10; Dan. iii. 15), and he did deliver them, to the confusion of their enemies. But the God of Israel challenged Bel and Nebo to deliver their worshippers, to rise up and help them, and to be their protection (Isa. xlvii. 12, 13); but they were so far from helping them that they themselves, that is, their images, which was all that was of them, *went into captivity*, Isa. xlvi. 1, 2.

Verses 39–43

This conclusion of the song speaks three things:—

I. Glory to God, v. 39. The great God here demands the glory, 1. Of a self-existence: *I, even I, am he*. Thus Moses concludes with the name of God by which he was first made to know him (Exod. iii. 14), "*I am that I am.* I am he that I have been, that I will be, that I have promised to be, that I have threatened to be; all shall find me true to my word." The Targum of Uzzielides paraphrases it thus: *When the Word of the Lord shall reveal himself to redeem his people, he shall say to all people, See that I now am what I am, and have been, and I am what I will be,* which we know very well how to apply to him who said to John, *I am he who is, and was, and is to come,* Rev. i. 8. These words, *I, even, I, am he*, we meet with often in those chapters of Isaiah where God is encouraging his people to hope for their deliverance out of Babylon, Isa. xli. 4; xliii. 11, 13, 25; xlvi. 4. 2. Of a sole supremacy. "There *is no god with me*. None to help with me, none to cope with me." See Isa. xliii. 10, 11. 3. Of an absolute sovereignty, a universal agency: *I kill, and I make alive.* 4. Of an irresistible power.

II. Terror to his enemies, v. 40–42. Terror indeed to those that hate him, as all those do that serve other gods, that persist in wilful disobedience to the divine law, and that malign and persecute his faithful servants. In order to alarm such in time to repent. 1. The divine sentence is ratified with an oath (v. 40): He *lifts up his hand to heaven*, the habitation of his holiness; this was an ancient and very significant sign used in swearing, Gen. xiv. 22. The sin of sinners shall be their ruin if they go on in it. 2. Preparation is made for the execution: The *glittering sword is whet.* See Ps. vii. 12. 3. The execution itself will be very terrible.

III. Comfort to his own people (v. 43): *Rejoice, O you nations, with his people.* He concludes the song with words of joy; for in God's Israel there is a remnant whose end will be peace. God's people will rejoice at last, will rejoice everlastingly. Three things are here mentioned as matter of joy:—1. The enlarging of the church's bounds. The apostle applies the first words of this verse to the conversion of the Gentiles. Rom. xv. 10, *Rejoice you Gentiles with his people.* 2. The avenging of the church's controversies upon her adversaries. 3. The mercy God has in store for his church, and for all that belong to it: He will be *merciful to his land, and to his people,* that is, to all everywhere that fear and serve him.

Verses 44–52

Here is, I. The solemn delivery of this song to the children of Israel, v. 44, 45. Moses spoke it to as many as could hear him, while Joshua, in another assembly at the same time, delivered it to as many as his voice would reach. Though they changed their commander, there was no change in the divine command; Joshua, as well as Moses, would be a witness against them if ever they forsook God.

II. An earnest charge to them to mind these and all the rest of the good words that Moses had said to them.

1. The duties he charges upon them are, (1) Carefully to attend to these themselves: "Set your hearts both to the laws, and to the promises and threatenings, the blessings and curses, and now at last to this song." (2) Faithfully to transmit these things to those that should come after them. Those that are good themselves cannot but desire that their children may be so likewise.

2. The arguments he uses to persuade them to make religion their business and to persevere in it are, (1) The vast importance of the things themselves which he had charged upon them (v. 47): "*It is not a*

vain thing, because it is your life. It is not an indifferent thing, but of absolute necessity. (2) The vast advantage it would be of to them: *Through this thing you shall prolong your days* in Canaan, which is a typical promise of that eternal life which Christ has assured us those shall enter into that keep the commandments of God, Matt. xix. 17.

III. Orders given to Moses concerning his death. Now that this renowned witness for God had finished his testimony, he must go up to Mount Nebo and die. Orders were given to Moses that self-same day, *v.* 48. Now that he had done his work, why should he desire to live a day longer? He had indeed formerly prayed that he might go over Jordan, but now he is entirely satisfied, and, as God had bidden him, *saith no more of that matter.* 1. God here reminds him of the sin he had been guilty of, for which he was excluded Canaan (*v.* 51). 2. He reminds him of the death of his brother Aaron (*v.* 50), to make his own the more familiar and the less formidable. 3. He sends him up to a high hill, thence to take a view of the land of Canaan and then die, *v.* 49, 50. The remembrance of his sin might make death terrible, but the sight God gave him of Canaan took off the terror of it, as it was a token of God's being reconciled to him, and a plain indication to him that though his sin shut him out of the earthly Canaan, yet it should not deprive him of that better country which in this world can only be seen, and that with an eye of faith.

CHAPTER 33

Yet Moses has not done with the children of Israel. He had preached them a farewell sermon. After sermon he had given out a psalm, and now nothing remains but to dismiss them with a blessing; that blessing he pronounces in this chapter in the name of the Lord, and so leaves them. I. He pronounces them all blessed in what God had done for them already, especially in giving them his law, ver. 2–5. II. He pronounces a blessing upon each tribe, which is both a prayer for and a prophecy of their felicity. 1. Reuben, ver. 6. 2. Judah, ver. 7. 3. Levi, ver. 8–11. 4. Benjamin, ver. 12. 5. Joseph, ver. 13–17. 6. Zebulun and Issachar, ver. 18, 19. 7. Gad, ver. 20, 21. 8. Dan, ver. 22. 9. Napthali, ver. 23. 10. Asher, ver. 24, 25. III. He pronounces them all in general blessed if they were obedient, ver. 26, &c.

Verses 1–5

The first verse is the title of the chapter: it is a blessing. In the foregoing chapter he had thundered out the terrors of the Lord against Israel for their sin. Now that he might not seem to part in anger, he here subjoins a blessing. Thus Christ's last work on earth was to bless his disciples (Luke xxiv. 50), like Moses here, in token of parting as friends. Moses blessed them, 1. As a prophet—a *man of God.* 2. As a parent to Israel; for so good princes are to their subjects. Jacob upon his death-bed blessed his sons (Gen. xlix. 1), in conformity to whose example Moses here blesses the tribes that were descended from them. He desired their happiness, though he must die and not share in it.

He begins his blessing with a lofty description of the glorious appearances of God to them in giving them the law, and the great advantage they had by it.

I. There was a visible and illustrious discovery of the divine majesty, enough to convince and for ever silence atheists and infidels, to awaken and affect those that were most stupid and careless, and to put to shame all secret inclinations to other gods, *v.* 2. His retinue was glorious; he came with his holy myriads, as Enoch had long since foretold he should come in the last day to judge the world, Jude 14. Hence the law is said to be *given by the disposition of angels,* Acts vii. 53; Heb. ii. 2.

II. He gave them his law, which is, 1. Called *a fiery law,* because it was given them *out of the midst of the fire* (Deut. iv. 33), and because it works like fire; if it be received, it is melting, warming, purifying,

and burns up the dross of corruption; if it be rejected, it hardens, sears, torments, and destroys. The Spirit descended in cloven tongues as of fire; for the gospel also is a fiery law. 2. It is said to *go from his right hand,* to denote the power and energy of the law and the divine strength that goes along with it, that it may not return void. It came as a gift to them, and a precious gift it was, a righthand blessing. 3. It was an instance of the special kindness he had for them: *Yea, he loved the people* (*v.* 3), and therefore, though it was a fiery law, yet it is said to *go for them* (*v.* 2), that is, in favour to them. Note, The law of God written in the heart is a certain evidence of the love of God shed abroad there: we must reckon God's law one of the gifts of his grace. *All his saints are in his hand.* They were in his hand to be covered and protected, used and disposed of, as the seven stars were in the hand of Christ, Rev. i. 16.

III. He disposed them to receive the law which he gave them: *They sat down at thy feet,* as scholars at the feet of their master, in token of reverence, in attendance and humble submission to what is taught; so Israel sat at the foot of Mount Sinai, and promised to hear and do whatever God should say. Every one then stood ready to receive God's words, and did so again when the law was publicly read to them, as Josh. viii. 34.

1. They are taught to speak with great respect of the law, and to call it *the inheritance of the congregation of Jacob.*

2. They are taught to speak with great respect of Moses; and they were the more obliged to keep up his name because he had not provided for the keeping of it up in his family; his posterity were never called the *sons of Moses,* as the priests were the *sons of Aaron.*

Verses 6–7

Here is, I. The blessing of Reuben. Though Reuben had lost the honour of his birthright, yet Moses begins with him; for we should not insult over those that are disgraced, nor desire to perpetuate marks of infamy upon any, *v.* 6. Moses desires and foretells, 1. The preserving of this tribe. Though a frontier tribe on the other side Jordan, yet, "Let it *live,* and not be either ruined by its neighbours or lost among them." And perhaps he refers to those chosen men of that tribe who, having had their lot assigned them already, left their families in it, and were now ready to *go over armed before their brethren,* Num. xxxii. 27. 2. The increase of this tribe: *Let not his men be few;* or, *Let his men be a number. Let Reuben live and not die, though his men be few;* so bishop Patrick thinks it may be rendered. All the Chaldee paraphrasts refer this to the other world: *Let Reuben live in life eternal, and not die the second death,* so Onkelos. *Let Reuben live in this world, and not die that death which the wicked die in the world to come,* so Jonathan and the Jerusalem Targum.

II. The blessing of Judah, which is put before Levi because our *Lord sprang out of Judah.* The blessing (*v.* 7) may refer either, 1. To the whole tribe in general. Moses prays for, and prophesies, the great prosperity of that tribe. It is taken for granted that the tribe of Judah would be both a praying tribe and an active tribe. Or, 2. It may refer in particular to David, as a type of Christ, that God *would hear his prayers,* as that he would give him victory over his enemies, and success in his great undertakings. And that prayer that God would *bring him to his people* seems to refer to Jacob's prophecy concerning Shiloh, That *to him should the gathering of the people be,* Gen. xlix. 10. The tribe of Simeon is omitted in the blessing, because Jacob had left it under a brand, and it had never done any thing, as Levi had done, to retrieve its honour. It was lessened in the wilderness more than any other of the tribes; and Zimri, who was so notoriously guilty in the matter of Peor was of that tribe. Or, because the lot of Simeon was an appendage to that of Judah, that tribe is included in the blessing of Judah.

Verses 8–11

In blessing the tribe of Levi, Moses expresses himself more at large, not so much because it was his own tribe (for he takes no notice of his relation to it) as because it was God's tribe. The blessing of Levi has reference,

I. To the high priest, here called God's *holy one* (v. 8), because his office was holy, in token of which, *Holiness to the Lord* was written upon his forehead. 1. He seems to acknowledge that God might justly have displaced Aaron and his seed, for his sin at Meribah, Num. xx. 12. So many understand it. It seems rather probable to me that, on the contrary, he pleads with God the zeal and faithfulness of Aaron, and his boldness in stemming the tide of the people's murmurings at the other Meribah (Exod. xvii. 7). All the Chaldee paraphrasts agree that it was a trial in which he was *found perfect and faithful*. 2. He prays that the office of the high priest might ever remain: *Let thy thummim and thy urim be with him*. It was given him for some eminent piece of service, as appears, Mal. ii. 5. "Lord, let it never be taken from him." Notwithstanding this blessing, the urim and thummim were lost in the captivity, and never restored under the second temple. *Thummim* signifies *integrity*, and *Urim illumination*: Let these be with thy holy one, that is, "Lord, let the high priest ever be both an upright man and an understanding man." A good prayer to be put up for the ministers of the gospel, that they may have clear heads and honest hearts; light and sincerity make a complete minister.

II. To the inferior priests and Levites, *v.* 9–11. 1. He commends the zeal of this tribe for God when they sided with Moses (and so with God) against the worshippers of the golden calf (Exod. xxxii. 26, &c.). And those who not only keep themselves pure from the common iniquities of the times and places in which they live, but, as they are capable, bear testimony against them, and *stand up for God against the evil-doers*, shall have special marks of honour put upon them. Perhaps Moses may have an eye to the sons of Korah, who refused to join with their father in his gainsaying, Num. xxvi. 11. Also to Phinehas, who *executed judgment*, and *stayed the plague*. 2. He confirms the commission granted to this tribe to minister in holy things, which was the recompense of their zeal and fidelity, *v.* 10. (1) They were to deal for God with the people: "*They shall teach Jacob thy judgments and Israel thy laws*, both as preachers in their religious assemblies, reading and expounding the law (Neh. viii. 7, 8), and as judges, determining doubtful and difficult cases that were brought before them," 2 Chron. xvii. 8, 9. (2) They were to deal for the people with God, in burning incense to the praise and glory of God, and offering sacrifices to make atonement for sin and to obtain the divine favour. This was the work of the priests, but the Levites attended and assisted in it. 3. He prays for them, *v.* 11. (1) That God would prosper them in their estates. *Bless, Lord, his substance. Bless, Lord, his virtue*; so some read it. "Lord, increase thy graces in them, and make them more and more fit for their work." (2) That he would accept them in their services: "*Accept the work of his hands*, both for himself and for the people for whom he ministers." (3) That he would take his part against all his enemies.

Verses 12–17

Here is, I. The blessing of Benjamin, *v.* 12. Benjamin is put next to Levi, because the temple, where the priests' work lay, was just upon the edge of the lot of this tribe; and it is put before Joseph because of the dignity of Jerusalem (part of which was in this tribe) above Samaria, which was in the tribe of Ephraim, and because Benjamin adhered to the house of David, and to the temple of the Lord, when the rest of the tribes deserted both with Jeroboam. 1. Benjamin is here called the *beloved of the lord*, as the father of this tribe was Jacob's beloved son, the *son of his right hand*. Saul the first king, and Paul the great apostle, were both of this tribe. 2. He is here assured of the divine protection: he shall *dwell safely*. 3. It is here intimated that the temple in which God would dwell should be built in the borders of this tribe. Jerusalem the holy city was in the lot of this tribe (Josh. xviii. 28); and though Zion, the city of David, is supposed to belong to Judah, yet Mount Moriah, on which the temple was built, was in Benjamin's lot. God is *therefore* said to dwell *between his shoulders*, because the temple stood on that mount, as the head of a man upon his shoulders.

II. The blessing of Joseph, including both Manasseh and Ephraim. In Jacob's blessing (Gen. xlix.) that of Joseph is the largest, and so it is here; and thence Moses here borrows the title he gives to Joseph (*v.* 16), that he was *separated from his brethren*. His brethren separated him from them by making him a slave, but God distinguished him from them by making him a prince.

1. Great plenty, *v.* 13–16. In general: *Blessed of the Lord be his land*. Those were very fruitful countries that fell into the lot of Ephraim and Manasseh, yet Moses prays they might be watered with the blessing of God.

(1) He enumerates many particulars which he prays may contribute to the wealth and abundance of those two tribes. He prays, [1] For seasonable rains and dews, *the precious things of heaven*; and so precious they are, though but pure water, that without them the fruits of the earth would all fail and be cut off. [2] For plentiful springs, which help to make the earth fruitful, called here *the deep that coucheth beneath*. [3] For the benign influences of the heavenly bodies (*v.* 14), *for the precious fruits* put forth by the quickening heart of the sun, and the cooling moisture of the moon. [4] For the fruitfulness even of their hills and mountains, which in other countries used to be barren (*v.* 15). [5] For the productions of the lower grounds (*v.* 16): *For the precious things of the earth*. Though the earth itself seems a useless worthless lump of matter, yet there are precious things produced out of it, for the support and comfort of human life. Some make these precious things here prayed for to be figures of *spiritual blessings in heavenly things by Christ*, the gifts, graces, and comforts of the Spirit.

(2) He crowns all with the goodwill, or favourable acceptance, of him that *dwelt in the bush* (*v.* 16), that is, of God, that God who appeared to Moses in the bush that burned and was not consumed (Exod. iii. 2), to give him his commission for the bringing of Israel out of Egypt. Though God's glory appeared there but for a while, yet it is said to dwell there: *the goodwill of the shechinah in the bush*; so it might be read, for *shechinah* signifies *that which dwelleth*. Many a time God had appeared to Moses, but now that he is just dying he seems to have the most pleasing remembrance of that which was the first time, when his acquaintance with the visions of the Almighty first began: that was a time of love never to be forgotten. So that, when he prays for the goodwill of him that *dwelt in the bush*, he has an eye to the covenant then and there renewed, on

which all our hopes of God's favour must be bottomed.

2. Great power Joseph is here blessed with, *v.* 17. Here are three instances of his power foretold:— (1) His authority among his brethren: *His glory is like the firstling of his bullock*, or young bull, which is a stately creature, and therefore was formerly used as an emblem of royal majesty. (2) His force against his enemies and victory over them: *His horns are like the horn of a unicorn*, that is, "The forces he shall bring into the field shall be very strong and formidable, and *with them he shall push the people*." (3) The numbers of his people, in which Ephraim, though the younger house, exceeded, Jacob having, in the foresight of the same thing, crossed hands, Gen. xlviii. 18. *They are the ten thousands of Ephraim, and the thousands of Manasseh.*

Verses 18–21

Here we have, I. The blessings of Zebulun and Issachar put together, for they were both the sons of Jacob by Leah, and by their lot in Canaan they were neighbours; it is foretold,

1. That they should both have a comfortable settlement and employment, *v.* 18. Zebulun must rejoice, for he shall have cause to rejoice; and Moses prays that he may have cause in his going out, either to war or to sea, for Zebulun was a *haven of ships*, Gen. xlix. 13. And Issachar must rejoice in his tents, that is, in his business at home, his husbandry, to which the men of that tribe generally confined themselves. Observe here, (1) That the providence of God, as it variously appoints the bounds of men's habitation, some in the city and some in the country, some in the seaports and some in the inland towns, so it wisely disposes men's inclinations to different employments. The genius of some men leads them to a book, of others to the sea, of others to the sword; some are inclined to rural affairs, others to trade, and some have a turn for mechanics; and it is well it is so. *If the whole body were an eye, where were the hearing?* 1 Cor. xii. 17. It was for the common good of Israel that the men of Zebulun were merchants and that the men of Issachar were husbandmen. (2) That whatever our place and business are it is our wisdom and duty to accommodate ourselves to them, and it is a great happiness to be well pleased with them.

2. That they should both be serviceable in their places to the honour of God and the interests of religion in the nation (*v.* 19). It has been often observed that though those that with Zebulun dwell in the haven of ships, which are places of concourse, have commonly more of the *light* of religion, those that with Issachar dwell in tents in the country have more of the *life* and *heat* of it. (1) It is here foretold that both these tribes should grow rich. Zebulun that goes abroad shall *suck of the abundance of the seas*, which are full breasts to the merchants, while Issachar, that tarries at home, shall enrich himself with *treasures hid in the sands*, either the fruits of the earth or the underground treasures of metals and minerals, or (because the word for sand here signifies properly the sand of the sea) the rich things thrown up by the sea, for the lot of Issachar reached to the sea-side. (2) It is foretold, that these tribes, being thus enriched, should *consecrate their gain unto the Lord, and their substance unto the Lord of the whole earth*, Mic. iv. 13.

II. The blessing of the tribe of Gad comes next, *v.* 20, 21. This was one of the tribes that was already seated on that side Jordan where Moses now was.

1. He foretells what this tribe would be, *v.* 20. (1) That it would be enlarged, as at present it had a spacious allotment. We find how this tribe was enlarged by their success in a war which it seems they carried on very religiously against the Hagarites, 1 Chron. v. 19, 20, 22. (2) That it would be a valiant and victorious tribe, would, if let alone, dwell secure and fearless as a lion; but, if provoked, would, like a lion, *tear the arm with the crown of the head*; that is, would pull in pieces all that stood in his way, both the arm (that is, the strength) and the crown of the head (that is, the policy and authority) of his enemies.

2. He commends this tribe for what they had done and were now doing, *v.* 21.

Verses 22–25

Here is, I. The blessing of Dan, *v.* 22. Jacob in his blessing had compared him to a serpent for subtlety; Moses compares him to a lion for courage and resolution: and what could stand before those that had the head of a serpent and the heart of a lion? He is compared to the lions that leaped from Bashan, a mountain noted for fierce lions, whence they came down to leap upon their prey in the plains. A party of them, upon information brought them of the security of Laish, which lay in the furthest part of the land of Canaan from them, surprised it, and soon made themselves masters of it. See Judges xviii. 27. And, the mountains of Bashan lying not far from that city, probably thence they made their descent upon it; and therefore are here said to *leap from Bashan*.

II. The blessing of Naphtali, *v.* 23. He looks upon this tribe with wonder, and applauds it: "O Naphtali, thou art happy, thou shalt be so, mayest thou be ever so!" Jacob had described this tribe to be, generally, courteous obliging people, giving goodly words, as the loving hind, Gen. xlix. 21. Now what should they get by being so? Moses here tells them they should have an interest in the affections of their neighbours, and be satisfied with favour. "The portion of the tribe of Naphtali" (the Jews say) "was so fruitful, and the productions so forward, though it lay north, that those of that tribe were generally the first that brought their first-fruits to the temple; and so they had first the blessing from the priest, which was the blessing of the Lord." Capernaum, in which Christ chiefly resided, lay in this tribe. Be thou *in possession of the sea and the south*; so it may be read, that is, of that sea which shall lie south of thy lot, that was the sea of Galilee, which we so often read of in the gospels, directly north of which the lot of this tribe lay, and which was of great advantage to this tribe, witness the wealth of Capernaum and Bethsaida.

III. The blessing of Asher, *v.* 24, 25. Four things he prays for and prophecies concerning this tribe, which carries blessedness in its name; for Leah called the father of it *Asher*, saying *Happy am I*, Gen. xxx. 13. 1. The increase of their numbers. 2. Their interest in their neighbours: *Let him be acceptable to his brethren*. 3. The richness of their land. (1) Above ground: *Let him dip his foot in oil*, that is, "Let him have such plenty of it in his lot that he may not only anoint his head with it, but, if he please, wash his feet in it." (2) Under ground: *Thy shoes shall be iron and brass*, that is, "Thou shalt have great plenty of these metals (mines of them) in thy own ground. The Chaldee paraphrasts understand this figuratively: "Thou shalt be strong and bright, as iron and brass." 4. The continuance of their strength and vigour: *As thy days, so shall thy strength be*. Many paraphrase it thus, "The strength of thy old age shall be like that of thy youth; thou shalt not feel a decay, nor be the worse for the wearing, but shalt renew thy youth; as if not thy shoes only, but thy bones, were iron and brass." Have they work appointed them? They shall have strength to do it. Have they burdens appointed them? They shall have strength to bear them; and never be *tempted above that they are able*.

Verses 26–29

Moses, the man of God, with his last breath magnifies both the God of Israel and the Israel of God.

I. No God like the God of Israel. None of the gods of the nations were capable of doing that for their worshippers which Jehovah did for his: *There is none like unto the God of Jeshurun, v.* 26. 1. His sovereign power and authority: *He rides upon the heavens.* When he has any thing to do for his people he *rides upon the heavens* to do it; for he does it swiftly and strongly: no enemy can either anticipate or obstruct the progress of him that rides on the heavens. 2. His boundless eternity; he is the eternal God, and his arms are *everlasting, v.* 27. The gods of the heathen were but lately invented, and would shortly perish; but the God of Jeshurun is eternal: he was before all worlds, and will be when time and days shall be no more. See Hab. i. 12.

II. No people like the Israel of God. Having pronounced each tribe happy, in the close he pronounces all together very happy, so happy in all respects that there was no nation under the sun comparable to them (*v.* 29). If Israel honour God as its non-such God, he will favour them so as to make them a non-such people. What is here said of the church of Israel is certainly to be applied to *the church of the first-born*, that are written in heaven. The Christian church is the Israel of God, as the apostle calls it (Gal. vi. 16).

1. Never were people so well seated and sheltered (*v.* 27): *The eternal God is thy refuge.* Or, as the word signifies, "thy *habitation,* or *mansion-house,* in which thou art safe, and easy, and at rest, as a man in his own house." Every Israelite indeed is at home in God; the soul returns to him, and reposes in him as its resting-place (Ps. cxvi. 7), its hiding-place, Ps. xxxii. 7.

2. Never were people so well supported and borne up: *Underneath are the everlasting arms*; that is, the almighty power of God. The everlasting covenant, and the everlasting consolations that flow from it, are indeed everlasting arms, with which believers have been wonderfully sustained, and kept cheerful in the worst of times; divine grace is sufficient for them, 2 Cor. xii. 9.

3. Never were people so well commanded and led on to battle: "*He shall thrust out the enemy from before thee* by his almighty power, which will make room for thee. Thus believers are more than conquerors over their spiritual enemies, through Christ that loved them. The captain of our salvation *thrust out the enemy from before us* when he overcame the world and spoiled principalities and powers on the cross.

4. Never were people so well secured and protected (*v.* 28): *Israel shall then dwell in safety alone.* Those that dwell in God, and make his name their strong tower, *dwell in safety*; the *place of their defence is the munitions of rocks,* Isa. xxxiii. 16. They shall dwell in safety alone. (1) Though alone. Though they contract no alliances with their neighbours. (2) Because alone. They shall dwell in safety as long as they continue pure, and unmixed with the heathen.

5. Never were people so well provided for: *The fountain of Jacob* (that is, the present generation of that people, which is as the fountain to all the streams that shall hereafter descend and be derived from it) shall now presently be fixed upon a good land. *The eye of Jacob* (so it might be read, for the same word signifies a fountain and an eye) *is upon the land of corn and wine,* just before their faces, on the other side the river.

6. Never were people so well helped. If they were in any strait, God himself rode upon the heavens for *their help, v.* 26. And they were *a people saved by the Lord, v.* 29.

7. Never were people so well armed. God himself was the shield of their help by whom they were armed defensively, and he was the *sword of their excellency,* by whom they were armed offensively, and made formidable.

8. Never were people so well assured of victory over their enemies: *They shall be found liars unto thee*; that is, "shall be forced to submit to thee sorely against their will, so that it will be but a counterfeit submission. *If thy enemies be found liars to thee* (so some read it), *thou shalt tread upon their high places.*

CHAPTER 34

Having read how Moses finished his testimony, we are told here how he immediately after finished his life. We have had an account of his dying words, here we have an account of his dying work, and that is work we must all do shortly, and it had need be well done. Here is, I. The view Moses had of the land of Canaan just before he died, ver. 1–4. II. His death and burial, ver. 5, 6. III. His age, ver. 7. IV. Israel's mourning for him, ver. 8. V. His successor, ver. 9. VI. His character, ver. 10, &c.

Verses 1–4

I. Moses climbing upwards towards heaven, as high as the top of Pisgah, there to die; for that was the place appointed, *ch.* xxxii. 49, 50. Israel lay encamped upon the flat grounds in the plains of Moab, and thence he went up, according to order, to the mountain of Nebo, to the highest point or ridge of that mountain, which was called *Pisgah, v.* 1. Pisgah is an appellative name for all such eminences. It should seem Moses went up alone to the top of Pisgah, *alone without help.* When he had made an end of blessing Israel, we may suppose, he solemnly took leave of Joshua, and Eleazar, and the rest of his friends, who probably brought him to the foot of the hill; but then he gave them such a charge as Abraham gave to his servants at the foot of another hill: *Tarry you here while I go yonder and die.* 1. To show that he was willing to die. When he knew the place of his death, he was so far from avoiding it that he cheerfully mounted a steep hill to come at it. 2. To show that he looked upon death as his ascension. The soul of a man, of a good man, when it leaves the body, *goes upwards* (Eccles. iii. 21). When God's servants are sent for out of the world, the summons runs thus, *Go up and die.*

II. Moses looking downward again towards this earth, to see the earthly Canaan into which he must never enter, but therein by faith looking forwards to the heavenly Canaan into which he should now immediately enter. 1. If he went up alone to the top of Pisgah, yet he *was not alone, for the Father was with him,* John xvi. 32. 2. Note, All the pleasant prospects we have of the better country we are beholden to the grace of God for; it is he that gives the *spirit of wisdom* as well as the *spirit of revelation,* the eye as well as the object. 3. He saw it at a distance. Such a sight believers now have, through grace, of the bliss and glory of their future state. The word and ordinances are to them what Mount Pisgah was to Moses. 4. He saw it, but must never enjoy it. Glorious things are spoken of the kingdom of Christ in the latter days, its advancement, enlargement, and flourishing state; we foresee it, but we are not likely to live to see it. Those that shall come after us, we hope, will enter that promised land, which is a comfort to us. 5. Canaan was *Immanuel's land* (Isa. viii. 8), so that in viewing it he had a view of the blessings we enjoy by Christ.

Verses 5–8

Here is, I. The death of Moses (*v.* 5): *Moses the servant of the Lord died.* It bore hard upon Moses himself, when he had gone through all the fatigues of the wilderness, to be prevented from enjoying the pleasures of Canaan. But *the man Moses was very meek*; God will have it so, and he cheerfully submits. 1. He is here called *the servant of the Lord*, not only as a good man (all the saints are God's servants), but as a useful man, eminently useful, who had served God's counsels in bringing Israel out of Egypt, and leading them through the wilderness. 2. Yet he dies. Neither his piety nor his usefulness would exempt him from the stroke of death. God's servants must die that they may rest from their labours, receive their recompense, and make room for others. When God's servants are removed, and must serve him no longer on earth, they go to serve him better, to serve him *day and night in his temple*. He dies *according to the word of the Lord. At the mouth of the Lord*; so the word is. The Jews say, "with a kiss from the mouth of God." Note, The servants of the Lord, when they have done all their other work, must die at last, in obedience to their Master, and be freely willing to go home whenever he sends for them, Acts xxi. 13.

II. His burial, *v.* 6. God takes care of the dead bodies of his servants; as their death is precious, so is their dust, but the covenant with it shall be remembered. He was buried in a valley *over against Beth-peor*. If the soul be at rest with God, the matter is not great where the body rests. The particular place was not known, lest the children of Israel, who were so very prone to idolatry, should have enshrined and worshipped the dead body of Moses, that great founder and benefactor of their nation.

III. His age, *v.* 7. His life was prolonged, 1. To old age. He was 120 years old, which, though far short of the years of the patriarchs, yet much exceeded the years of most of his contemporaries. The years of the life of Moses were three forties. The first forty he lived a courtier, at ease and in honour in Pharaoh's court; the second forty he lived a poor desolate shepherd in Midian; the third forty he lived a king in Jeshurun, in honour and power, but encumbered with a great deal of care and toil. 2. To a good old age: *His eye was not dim* (as Isaac's, Gen. xxvii. 1, and Jacob's, Gen. xlviii. 10), *nor was his natural force abated*.

IV. The solemn mourning that there was for him, *v.* 8. Observe, 1. Who the mourners were: *The children of Israel*. 2. How long they mourned: *Thirty days*. Yet the *ending of the days of weeping and mourning* for Moses is an intimation that, how great soever our losses have been, we must not abandon ourselves to perpetual grief; we must suffer the wound at least to heal up in time. If we hope to go to heaven rejoicing, why should we resolve to go to the grave mourning?

Verses 9–12

A very honourable encomium passed both on Moses and Joshua; each has his praise, and should have. Let God be glorified in both.

I. Joshua is praised as a man admirably qualified for the work to which he was called, *v.* 9. Moses brought Israel to the borders of Canaan and then died and left them, to signify that *the law made nothing perfect*, Heb. vii. 19. It brings men into a wilderness of conviction, but not into the Canaan of rest and settled peace. It is an honour reserved for Joshua (our Lord Jesus, of whom Joshua was a type) to do that for us which *the law could not do, in that it was weak through the flesh*, Rom. viii. 3. Through him we enter into rest, the spiritual rest of conscience and eternal rest in heaven. Two things concurred to clear Joshua's call to this great undertaking:— 1. God fitted him for it: *He was full of the spirit of wisdom*. Conduct is as requisite in a general as courage. 2. Moses, by the divine appointment, had ordained him to it: *He had laid his hands upon him*, so substituting him to be his successor, and praying to God to qualify him for the service to which he had called him.

II. Moses is praised (*v.* 10–12), and with good reason.

1. He was indeed a very great man, especially upon two accounts:—(1) His intimacy with the God of nature: *God knew him face to face*, and so he knew God. See Num. xii. 8. (2) His interest and power in the kingdom of nature. The miracles of judgment he wrought in Egypt before Pharaoh, and his miracles of mercy he wrought in the wilderness before Israel, served to demonstrate that he was a particular favourite of Heaven, and had an extraordinary commission to act as he did on this earth. Never was there any man whom Israel had more reason to love, or whom the enemies of Israel had more reason to fear.

2. He was greater than any other of the prophets of the Old Testament. Though they were men of great interest in heaven and great influence upon earth, yet they were none of them to be compared with this great man; none of them either so evidenced or executed a commission from heaven as Moses did. This encomium of Moses seems to have been written long after his death, yet then there had not arisen any prophet *like unto Moses*. By Moses God gave the law, and moulded and formed the Jewish church; by the other prophets he only sent particular reproofs, directions, and predictions. The last of the prophets concludes with a charge *to remember the law of Moses*, Mal. iv. 4. Christ himself often appealed to the writings of Moses, and vouched him for a witness, as one that *saw his day* at a distance *and spoke of him*. Moses was faithful as a servant, but Christ as a Son. The history of Moses leaves him buried in the plains of Moab, and concludes with the period of his government; but the history of our Saviour leaves him sitting *at the right hand of the Majesty on high*, and we are assured that *of the increase of his government and peace there shall be no end*.

AN EXPOSITION OF

THE BOOK OF JOSHUA

I. We have now before us the history of the Jewish nation in this book and those that follow it to the end of the book of Esther. They were part of the oracles of God, which were committed to the Jews, and were so received and referred to by our Saviour and the apostles.

In the five books of Moses we had a very full account of the rise, advance, and constitution, of the Old-Testament church, the family out of which it was raised, the promise, that great charter by which it was incorporated, the miracles by which it was built up, and the laws and ordinances by which it was to be governed. A nation that had statutes and judgments so righteous, one would think, should have been very holy; and very happy. But, alas! a great part of the history is a melancholy representation of their sins and miseries; if we compare the history of the Christian church with its constitution, we shall find the same cause for wonder, so many have been its errors and corruptions; for neither does the *gospel make any thing perfect* in this world, but leaves us still in expectation of a *better hope* in the future state.

II. We have next before us the *book of Joshua*, so called, perhaps, not because it was written by him, for that is uncertain. Dr. Lightfoot thinks that Phinehas wrote it. Bishop Patrick is clear that Joshua wrote it himself. However that be, it is written concerning him, and, if any other wrote it, it was collected out of his journals or memoirs. It contains the history of Israel under the command and government of Joshua, how he presided as general of their armies, 1. In their entrance into Canaan, ch. i.–v. 2. In their conquest of Canaan, ch. vi.–xii. 3. In the distribution of the land of Canaan among the tribes of Israel, ch. xiii.–xxi. 4. In the settlement and establishment of religion among them, ch. xxii.–xxiv. We may see in it, 1. Much of God and his providence—his power, his justice, his faithfulness, and his kindness to his people Israel, notwithstanding their provocations. 2. Much of Christ and his grace. Though Joshua is not expressly mentioned in the New Testament as a type of Christ, yet all agree that he was a very eminent one. He bore our Saviour's name, as did also another type of him, Joshua the high priest, Zech. vi. 11, 12. The LXX, giving the name of Joshua a Greek termination, calls him all along Ιησους, Jesus, and so he is called Acts vii. 45, and Heb. iv. 8. It signifies, He shall save. Joshua saves God's people from the Canaanites; our Lord Jesus saves them from their sins. Christ, as Joshua, is the captain of our salvation, a leader and commander of the people, to tread Satan under their feet, to put them in possession of the heavenly Canaan, and to give them rest, which (it is said, Heb. iv. 8) Joshua did not.

CHAPTER 1

In this chapter, I. God appoints him to the government in the stead of Moses, gives him an ample commission, full instructions, and great encouragements, ver. 1-9. II. He accepts the government, and addresses himself immediately to the business of it, giving orders to the officers of the people in general, ver. 10, 11, and particularly to the two tribes and a half, ver. 12-15. III. The people agree to it, and take an oath of fealty to him, ver. 16-18.

Verses 1–9

Honour is here put upon Joshua, and great power lodged in his hand, by him that is the fountain of honour and power, and by whom kings reign. God speaks to him (v. 1), probably as he spoke to Moses (Lev. i. 1) *out of the tabernacle of the congregation,* for his greater encouragement, God here speaks to him immediately, some think in a dream or vision (as Job xxxiii. 15). Concerning Joshua's call observe here,

I. The time when it was given him: *After the death of Moses.* As soon as ever Moses was dead, Joshua took upon him the administration, by virtue of his solemn ordination in Moses's life-time. God did not speak to him to go forward towards Canaan till after the thirty days of mourning for Moses were ended; God would give time to the people not only to lament their loss of him, but to repent of their miscarriages towards him.

II. The place Joshua had been in before he was thus preferred. He was Moses's minister, that is, an assistant in business. The LXX translate it ὑπουργος, a workman under his direction. Observe, 1. He had been long bred to business. 2. He was trained up in subjection and under command. Those are fittest to rule that have learnt to obey. 3. He that was to succeed Moses was intimately acquainted with him, that he might take the same measures, walk in the same spirit, having to carry on the same work. 4. He was herein a type of Christ, who might therefore be called Moses's minister, because he was made under the law and fulfilled all the righteousness of it.

III. The call itself that God gave him,

1. The consideration upon which he was called to the government: *Moses my servant is dead, v. 2.* Moses, when he has done his work as a servant, dies and goes to *rest from his labours, and enters into the joy of his Lord.*

2. The call itself. *Now therefore arise.* (1) "Though Moses is dead, the work must go on; therefore arise, and go about it." When God has work to do, he will either find or make instruments fit to carry it on. Moses the *servant* is dead, but God the *Master* is not: he lives for ever. (2) "Because Moses is dead, therefore the work devolves upon thee as his successor." Joshua must arise to finish what Moses began. Thus the latter generations enter into the labours of the former. And thus Christ, our Joshua, does that for us which could never be done by the law of Moses, —justifies (Acts xiii. 39), and *sanctifies,* Romans viii. 3. The life of Moses made way for Joshua, and prepared the people for what was to be done by him. Thus the law was a schoolmaster to bring us to Christ.

3. The particular service he was now called out to: "*Arise, go over* this Jordan, this river which you have in view, and on the banks of which you lie encamped.*" This was a trial to the faith of Joshua. He had no pontoons or bridge of boats by which to convey them over, and yet he must believe that God, who had ordered them over, would open a way for them. Going over Jordan was going into Canaan.

4. The grant of the land of Canaan to the children of Israel is here repeated (v. 2-4): *I do give it them.* To the patriarchs it was promised, *I will give it;* but, now that the fourth generation had expired, the time had come for the performance of the promise (v. 3), *I have given it;* though it be yet unconquered, it is as sure to you as if it were in your hands." Observe, (1) The persons to whom the conveyance is made: *To them, even to the children of Israel* (v. 2), because they are the seed of Jacob, who was called

Israel at the time when this promise was made to him, Gen. xxxv. 10, 12. (2) The land itself that is conveyed: From the river Euphrates eastward, to the Mediterranean Sea westward, *v.* 4. Had they been obedient, God would have given them this and much more. Out of all these countries, and many others, there were in process of time proselytes to the Jewish religion, as appears, Acts ii. 5, &c. (3) The condition is here implied upon which this grant is made, in those words, *as I said unto Moses,* that is, "upon the terms that Moses told you of many a time, *if you will keep my statutes,* you shall go in and possess that good land. Take it under those provisos and limitations, and not otherwise." (4) *"Every place that the sole of your foot shall tread upon* (within the following bounds) shall be your own. Do but set your foot upon it and you have it."

5. The promises God here makes to Joshua for his encouragement. (1) That he should be sure of the presence of God (*v.* 5): *"As I was with Moses,* in bringing Israel out of Egypt and leading them through the wilderness, so I will be with thee to enable thee to settle them in Canaan." What Moses did was done by virtue of the presence of God with him, and, though Joshua had not always the same presence of mind that Moses had, yet, if he had always the same presence of God, he would do well enough. Note, It is a great comfort to the rising generation of ministers and Christians that the same grace which was sufficient for those that went before them shall not be wanting to them if they be not wanting to themselves in the improvement of it. It is repeated here again (*v.* 9). Note, Those that go where God sends them shall have him with them wherever they go. (2) That the presence of God should never be withdrawn from him: *I will not fail thee, nor forsake thee, v.* 5. Moses had assured him of this (Deut. xxxi. 8), that, though he must now leave him, God never would: of this we may be sure, that *the Lord is with us while we are with him.* This promise here made to Joshua is applied to all believers. (3) That he should have victory over all the enemies of Israel (*v.* 5): *There shall not any man* that comes against thee *be able to stand before thee.* Note, There is no standing before those that have God on their side. *If he be for us, who can be against us?* (4) That he should himself have the dividing of this land among the people of Israel, *v.* 6. He should be of good courage, because of the bad character of the people whom he must cause to inherit that land. He knew well what a froward discontented people they were, and how unmanageable they had been in his predecessor's time.

6. The charge or command he gives to Joshua, which is,

(1) That he conform himself in every thing to the law of God, and make this his rule, *v.* 7, 8. God does, as it were, put the book of the law into Joshua's hand; And he is charged, [1] To *meditate therein day and night.* If ever any man's business might have excused him from meditation, and other acts of devotion, one would think Joshua's might at this time. It was a great trust that was lodged in his hands; the care of it was enough to fill him, if he had had ten souls, and yet he must find time and thoughts for meditation. [2] Not to let it depart out of his mouth; that is, all his orders to the people, must be consonant to the law of God; upon all occasions he must *speak according to this rule,* Isa. viii. 20. There was no occasion to make new laws; but *that good thing which was committed to him,* he must carefully and faithfully keep, 2 Tim. i. 14. [3] He must *observe to do according to all this law.* Joshua was a man of great power and authority, yet he must himself be under command and do as he is bidden. No man's dignity or dominion, how great soever, sets him

above the law of God. *First,* He must do what was written. *Secondly,* He must do according to what was written, exactly observing the law as his copy. *Thirdly,* He must do according to all that was written, without exception or reserve. *Fourthly,* He must observe the checks of conscience, the hints of providence, and all the advantages of opportunity. *Fifthly,* He must *not turn from it,* either in his own practice or in any act of government, for virtue is in the mean. *Sixthly,* He must be *strong and courageous.* And, *lastly,* he assures him that then he shall *do wisely* (as it is in the margin) and *make his way prosperous, v.* 7, 8.

(2) That he encourage himself herein with the promise and presence of God, and make these his stay (*v.* 6, 7, 9). Joshua had long since signalized his valour, in the war with Amalek, and in his dissent from the report of the evil spies. Joshua was humble not distrustful of God, but diffident of himself, and of his sufficiency for the work, and therefore God repeats this so often, *"Be strong and of a good courage; Have not I commanded thee?* [1] "I have commanded the work to be done, and therefore it shall be done." It will help very much to animate and embolden us if we keep our eye upon the divine warrant, and hear God saying, *"Have not I commanded thee?* I will therefore help thee, succeed thee, accept thee, reward thee."

Verses 10–13

Joshua, being settled in the government, immediately applies himself to further the work of God among the people over whom God had set him.

I. He issues out orders to the people to provide for a march. The officers of the people that commanded under Joshua in their respective tribes and families attended him for orders, which they were to transmit to the people. What could Joshua have done without officers? We are required to be subject, not only to *the king as supreme, but to governors as to those that are sent by him,* 1 Pet. ii. 13, 14. By these officers, 1. Joshua gives public notice that they were *to pass over Jordan within three days.* Observe with what assurance Joshua says to the people, because God had said it to him, *You shall pass over Jordan, and shall possess* the land. We greatly honour the truth of God when we stagger not at the promise of God. 2. He gives them directions to prepare victuals, not to prepare transport vessels. He that bore them out of Egypt would in like manner bear them into Canaan, Exod. xix. 4. But those that were desirous to have other victuals besides the manna, which had not yet ceased, must prepare it, and have it ready against the time appointed. Perhaps, though the manna did not quite cease till they came into Canaan (*ch.* v. 12), yet since they had come *into a land inhabited* (Exod. xvi. 35), where they might be furnished in part with other provisions, it did not fall so plentifully. See Exod. xix. 10, 11.

II. He reminds the two tribes and a half of the obligations they were under to go over Jordan with their brethren, though they left their possessions and families on this side. It was an act of self-denial, and against the grain; therefore it was needful to produce the agreement which Moses had made with them (*v.* 13): *Remember the word which Moses commanded you.* Though Moses was dead, his commands and their promises were still in full force. He reminds them. 1, Of the advantages they had received in being first settled: *"The Lord your God hath given you rest.* He has given your minds rest; you are not as the rest of the tribes waiting the issue of the war first and then of the lot. He has also given your families rest, giving you this land, this good land." Note, When God by his providence has given us rest we ought to consider what service we may do to our brethren who are unsettled. When God had given David rest (2 Sam. vii. 1), see how restless he was till he had *found out a habitation* for the ark, Ps. cxxxii. 4, 5. 2. He reminds them of their agreement to help their brethren in the wars of Canaan till God had in like manner given them rest, *v.* 14, 15. This was, (1) Reasonable in itself. (2) It was enjoined them by Moses, the servant of the Lord; (3) It was the only expedient they had to save themselves from the guilt of a great sin in settling on that side Jordan, a sin which would one time or other find them out, Num. xxxii. 23. (4) It was the condition of the grant Moses had made them, of *the land of their possession*, as it is here called (*v.* 15). (5) They themselves had covenanted and agreed thereunto (Num. xxxii. 25): *Thy servants will do as my Lord commandeth.*

Verses 16–18

This answer was given by the *officers of all the people* (*v.* 10), as their representatives.

I. They promise him obedience (*v.* 16), as subjects to their prince, as soldiers to their general. Thus the people of Israel here engage themselves to Joshua: "*All that thou commandest us we will readily do,* without murmuring or disputing." We must thus swear allegiance to our Lord Jesus, as the captain of our salvation, and bind ourselves to do what he commands us by his word, and to go where he sends us by his providence. The people had no reason to boast of their obedience to Moses; he had found them a stiff-necked people, Deut. ix. 13. But they meant that they would be as observant of Joshua as they should have been of Moses. Note, We must not so magnify those that are gone as to be wanting in the honour and duty we owe to those that succeed them. Obedience for conscience' sake will continue, though Providence change the hands by which it rules and acts.

II. They pray for the presence of God with him (*v.* 17): "*Only the Lord thy God be with thee,* to bless and prosper thee, and give thee success, *as he was with Moses.*" The best thing we can ask of God for our magistrates is that they may have the presence of God with them. Those that we have reason to think have favour from God should have honour and respect from us. Some understand it as a limitation of their obedience: "We will obey only as far as we perceive the Lord is with thee, but no further. While thou keepest close to God we will keep close to thee; hitherto shall our obedience come, but no further."

III. They pass an act to make it death for any Israelite to disobey Joshua's orders, or *rebel against his commandments, v.* 18. There was a special reason for the making of this law now that they were entering upon the wars of Canaan; for in times of war the severity of military discipline is more necessary than at other times.

IV. It very much heartens those that lead in a good work to see those that follow with a good will. Joshua, though of approved valour, did not take it as an affront, but as a great kindness, for the people to bid him be strong and of a good courage.

Chapter 2

In this chapter we have an account of the scouts that were employed to bring an account to Joshua of the posture of the city of Jericho. Observe here, 1. How Joshua sent them, ver. 1. II. How Rahab received them, and protected them. III. The account she gave them of the present posture of Jericho, and the panic-fear they were struck with upon the approach of Israel, ver. 8–11. IV. The bargain she made with them for the security of herself and her relations, ver. 12–21. V. Their safe return to Joshua, and the account they gave him of their expedition, ver. 22–24. Rahab is twice celebrated in the New Testament as a great believer (Heb. xi. 31) and as one whose faith proved itself by good works, James ii. 25.

Verses 1–7

In these verses we have,

I. The prudence of Joshua, in sending spies to observe this important pass, which was likely to be disputed at the entrance of Israel into Canaan (*v.* 1). *Go view the land, even Jericho.* Moses had sent spies (Num. xiii.); Joshua himself was one of them. Joshua now sent spies, not, as the former were sent, to survey the whole land, but Jericho only. Joshua was particularly careful to take the first step well and not to stumble at the threshold. Observe, 1. Great men must see with other people's eyes, which makes it very necessary that they be cautious in the choice of those they employ. 2. Faith in God's promise ought not to supersede but encourage our diligence in the use of proper means. We do not trust God, but tempt him, if our expectations slacken our endeavours. 3. See how ready these men were to go upon this hazardous enterprise. In obedience to Joshua their general, in zeal for the service of the camp, and in dependence upon the power of God.

II. The providence of God directing the spies to the house of Rahab. How they got over Jordan, we are not told; but into Jericho they came, which was about seven or eight miles from the river, and there seeking for a convenient inn were directed to the house of Rahab, here called a *harlot*, a woman that had formerly been of ill fame, the reproach of which stuck to her name, though of late she had repented and reformed. Rahab the harlot is so called in the New Testament, where both her faith and her good works are praised, to teach us, 1. That the greatness of sin is no bar to pardoning mercy if it be truly repented of in time. We read of publicans and harlots entering into the kingdom of the Messiah, and being welcomed to all the privileges of that kingdom, Matt. xxi. 31. 2. That there are many who before their conversion were very wicked and vile, and yet afterwards come to great eminence in faith and holiness. 3. Even those that through grace have repented of the sins of their youth must expect to bear the reproach of them. God's Israel, for aught that appears, had but one well-wisher in all Jericho, and that was Rahab a harlot. God has often served his own purposes and his church's interests by men of indifferent morals. Had these scouts gone to any other house than this they would certainly have been betrayed. But God knew where they had a friend, though they did not, and directed them thither. Those that faithfully acknowledge God in their ways he will *guide with his eye.* See Jer. xxxvi. 19, 26.

III. The piety of Rahab in receiving and protecting these Israelites. Rahab showed her guests more than common civility; it was *by faith* that she received those with peace against whom her king and country had denounced war, Heb. xi. 31. 1. She bade them welcome to her house; they lodged there, though she knew both whence they came and what their business was. 2. She hid them upon the roof of the house, which was flat, and covered them with stalks of flax (*v.* 6). By these stalks of flax, which she herself had lain in order upon the roof to dry in the sun, in order to the beating of it and making it ready for the wheel, it appears she had one of the good characters of the virtuous woman, Prov. xxxi. 13. 3. When she was examined concerning them, she denied they were in her house. Nor marvel that the king of Jericho sent to enquire after them (*v.* 2, 3). Rahab not only disowned that she knew them, but, that no further search might be made for them in the city, told the pursuers they had gone away again, and in all probability might be overtaken, *v.* 4, 5. Now, (1) We are sure this was a good work: it is canonized by the apostle (James ii. 25), where she is said to be *justified by works*, and this is specified, that *she received the messengers, and sent them out another way*, and she did it by faith, above the fear of man, even of the wrath of the king. She believed, upon the report she had heard of the wonders wrought for Israel, that their God was the only true God, and that therefore their declared design upon Canaan would undoubtedly take effect. Note, Those that by faith take the Lord for their God take his people for their people, and cast in their lot among them. Those that have God for their refuge must shelter his people when there is occasion. *Let my outcasts dwell with thee*, Isa. xvi. 3, 4. And we must be glad of an opportunity of testifying the sincerity and zeal of our love to God by hazardous services to his church and kingdom among men. But, (2) There is that in it which it is not easy to justify, [1] It is plain that she betrayed her country by harbouring the enemies of it. That which justifies her in this is that *she knew the Lord had given Israel this land* (*v.* 9), knew it by the incontestable miracles God had wrought for them, which confirmed that grant; and her obligations to God were higher than her obligations to any other. If she knew *God had given them* this land, it would have been a sin to join with those that hindered them from possessing it. [2] It is plain that she deceived the officers that examined her with an untruth. What shall we say to this? If she had either told the truth or been silent, she would have betrayed the spies, and it does not appear that she had any other way of concealing them than by this ironical direction to the officers to pursue them another way. This case was altogether extraordinary, and therefore cannot be drawn into a precedent. Yet divines generally conceive that it was a sin, which however admitted of this extenuation, that being a Canaanite she was not better taught the evil of lying. However it was in this case, we are sure it is our duty to speak every man the truth to his neighbour, to dread and detest lying, and never to *do evil, that good may come of it*, Rom. iii. 8. But God accepts what is sincerely and honestly intended, though there be a mixture of frailty and folly in it, and is not extreme to mark what we do amiss.

Verses 8–21

The matter is here settled between Rahab and the spies respecting the service she was now to do for them, and the favour they were afterwards to show to her.

I. Having got clear of the officers, she comes up to them to the *roof of the house* where they lay hid. 1. She lets them know that the report of the great things God had done for them had come to Jericho (*v.* 10), to the amazement of everybody. 2. She tells them what impressions the tidings of these things had made upon the Canaanites: Your *terror has fallen upon us* (*v.* 9); *our hearts did melt, v.* 11. If she kept a public house, this would give her an opportunity of understanding the sense of various companies and of travellers from other parts of the country. It would put courage into the most cowardly Israelite to hear how their enemies were dispirited, and it was easy to conclude that those who now fainted before them would infallibly fall before them, it would be an earnest of the accomplishment of all the other promises God had made to them. Let not God's Israel be afraid of their most powerful enemies. 3. She hereupon makes profession of her faith in God and his promise. (1) She believes God's power and dominion over all the world (*v.* 11): "Jehovah your God, whom you worship and call upon, is so far above all gods that he is the only true God; for *he is God in heaven above and in earth beneath*, and is served by all the hosts of both." (2) She believes his promise to his people Israel (*v.* 9): *I know that the Lord hath given you the land.* The most powerful

means of conviction will not of themselves attain the end without divine grace, and by that grace Rahab the harlot, who had only heard of the wonders God had wrought, speaks with more assurance of the truth of the promise made to the fathers than all the elders of Israel had done who were eye-witnesses of those wonders, many of whom perished through unbelief of this promise.

II. She engaged them to take her and her relations under their protection, *v.* 12, 13. Now, 1. It was an evidence of the sincerity and strength of her faith. Those who truly believe the divine revelation concerning the ruin of sinners, and the grant of the heavenly land to God's Israel, will give diligence to flee from the wrath to come, and to lay hold on eternal life, by joining themselves to God and to his people. 2. The provision she made for the safety of her relations, as well as for her own, is a laudable instance of natural affection, and an intimation to us to do all we can for the salvation of the souls of those that are dear to us. 3. Her request that they would swear unto her by Jehovah is an instance of her acquaintance with the only true God, and her faith in him. 4. Her petition is very just and reasonable, that since she had protected them, they should protect her. Note, Those that show mercy may expect to find mercy. Rahab was afterwards advanced to be a princess in Israel, the wife of Salmon, and one of the ancestors of Christ, Matt. i. 5.

III. They solemnly engaged for her preservation in the common destruction (*v.* 14): "*Our life for yours.*" She had pawned her life for theirs, and now they in requital pawn their lives for hers, and (as public persons) with them they pawn the public faith and the credit of their nation. The law of gratitude is one of the laws of nature. Now observe here, 1. The promises they made her. In general, "*We will deal kindly and truly with thee, v.* 14. We will not only be kind in promising now, but kind in outdoing thy demands and expectations." 2. The provisos and limitations of their promises. Though they were in haste, yet we find them very cautious in settling this agreement, not to bind themselves to more than was fit for them to perform. Note, Covenants must be made with care. Those that will be conscientious in keeping their promises will be cautious in making them. Their promise is here accompanied with three provisos. They will protect Rahab, and all her relations always, provided, (1) That she tie the scarlet cord with which she was now about to let them down in the window of her house, *v.* 18. That no soldier might offer any violence to the house that was thus distinguished. This was like the blood sprinkled upon the door-post, which secured the first-born from the destroying angel. The same cord that she made use of for the preservation of these Israelites was to be made use of for her preservation. What we serve and honour God with we may expect he will bless and make comfortable to us. (2) That she should have all those whose safety she had desired in the house with her and keep them there, and that, at the time of taking the town, none of them should dare to stir out of doors, *v.* 18, 19. It was a *reasonable* proviso that, since they were saved purely for Rahab's sake, her house should have the honour of being their castle. It was likewise a *significant* proviso, intimating to us that those who are added to the church that they may be saved must keep close to the society of the faithful. (3) That she should keep counsel (*v.* 14, 20): *If thou utter this our business*, that is, "If thou betray us when we are gone, we will be clear of thy oath." Those are unworthy of *the secret of the Lord* that know not how to keep it to themselves when there is occasion.

IV. She then took effectual care to secure her new friends, and *sent them out another way*, James ii. 25

(*v.* 15), the situation of her house befriending them herein: thus Paul made his escape out of Damascus, 2 Cor. xi. 33. She also directed them which way to go for their own safety, *v.* 16. She directs them to leave the high road, and abscond in the mountains till the pursuers returned. Those that are in the way of God may expect that Providence will protect them, but this will not excuse them from taking all prudent methods for their own safety. Providence must be trusted, but not tempted.

Verses 22–24

We have here the safe return of the spies Joshua had sent, and the great encouragement they brought with them to Israel to proceed in their descent upon Canaan. They might have told them what they had observed of the height and strength of the walls of Jericho, but they were of another spirit, and, depending themselves upon the divine promise, they animated Joshua likewise. 1. Their return in safety was itself an encouragement to Joshua, and a token for good. That they had come back in peace, was such an instance of God's great care concerning them for Israel's sake as might assure the people of the divine guidance and care. He that so wonderfully protected their scouts would preserve their men of war. 2. The report they brought was much more encouraging (*v.* 24): "*All the inhabitants of the country,* though resolved to stand it out, yet *do faint because of us,* they have neither wisdom to yield nor courage to fight," whence they conclude, "*Truly the Lord has delivered into our hands all the land.*" Sinners' frights are sometimes sure presages of their fall. If we resist our spiritual enemies they will flee before us.

CHAPTER 3

This chapter, and that which follows it, give us the history of Israel's passing through Jordan into Canaan. By Joshua's order they marched up to the river's side (ver. 1), and then almighty power led them through it. They passed through the Red Sea unexpectedly, and in their flight by night, but they have notice some time before of their passing through Jordan, and their expectations raised. I. The people are directed to follow the ark, ver. 2–4. II. They are commanded to sanctify themselves, ver. 5. III. The priests with the ark are ordered to lead the van, ver. 6. IV. Joshua is magnified and made commander in chief, ver. 7, 8. V. Public notice is given of what God is about to do for them, ver. 9–13. VI. The thing is done, Jordan is divided, and Israel brought safely through it, ver. 14–17. This was the Lord's doing, and it is marvellous in our eyes.

Verses 1–6

Rahab, in mentioning to the spies the *drying up of the Red Sea* (*ch.* ii. 10), intimates that those on that side the water expected that Jordan, that great defence of their country, would in like manner give way to them. God often *did things for them which they looked not for,* Isa. lxiv. 3. Now here we are told,

I. That they *came to Jordan and lodged there, v.* 1. Though they were not yet told how they should pass the river, they went forward in faith, having been told (*ch.* i. 11) that they should pass it. Let us proceed as far as we can, and depend on divine sufficiency. In this march Joshua led them, and particular notice is taken of his early rising (*ch.* vi. 12; vii. 16; viii. 10), which intimates how little he loved his ease. Those that would bring great things to pass must rise early.

II. That the people were directed to follow the ark.

1. They might depend upon the ark to lead them; that is, upon God himself, of whose presence the ark was an instituted sign and token. It is called here the *ark of the covenant of the Lord their God.* What greater encouragement could they have than this, that the Lord was their God, a God in covenant with them? Here was the *ark of the covenant.* Formerly the ark was carried in the midst of the

camp, but now it went before them to *search out a resting-place* for them (Num. x. 33), and, as it were, to give them livery and seisin of the promised land, and put them in possession of it. In the ark the tables of the law were, and over it the mercy-seat; for the divine law and grace reigning in the heart are the surest pledges of God's presence and favour.

2. They might depend upon the priests and Levites, appointed to carry the ark before them. The work of ministers is to hold forth the word of life, and to take care of the administration of those ordinances which are the tokens of God's presence and the instruments of his power and grace.

3. The people must follow the ark: *Remove from your place and go after it,* (1) Wherever God's ordinances are, there we must be; if they flit, we must remove and go after them. (2) Thus must we walk after the rule of the word and the direction of the Spirit in everything, so shall *peace be upon us,* as it now was upon the Israel of God. They must follow the priests as far as they carried the ark, but no further; so we must follow our ministers only as they follow Christ.

4. In following the ark, they must *keep their distance, v.* 4. They must none of them come within a thousand yards of the ark. (1) They must thus express reverent regard lest its familiarity with them should breed contempt. This charge was agreeable to that dispensation of darkness, bondage, and terror: but we now through Christ have access with boldness. (2) The ark was able to protect itself, and needed not to be guarded by the men of war, but was itself a guard to them. (3) Thus it was the better seen by those that were to be led by it: *That you may know the way by which you must go.* They would all have the satisfaction of seeing it, and would be animated by the sight. *For you have not passed this way heretofore.* It was an untrodden path, especially through Jordan. Our way through the *valley of the shadow of death* is a way we have not gone before. But, if we have the assurance of God's presence, we need not fear.

III. They were commanded to sanctify themselves, for *to-morrow the Lord will do wonders among you, v.* 5. Joshua could tell beforehand what God would do, and when. See what preparation we must make to receive the discoveries of God's glory and the communications of his grace: we must sanctify ourselves; we must separate ourselves from all other cares, devote ourselves to God's honour, and *cleanse ourselves from all filthiness of flesh and spirit.*

IV. The priests were ordered to take up the ark and carry it *before the people, v.* 6. It was the Levites' work ordinarily to carry the ark, Num. iv. 15. And now we may suppose that prayer of Moses used, when the ark set forward (Num. x. 35), *Rise up, Lord, and let thy enemies be scattered.* Magistrates are here instructed to stir up ministers to their work. Ministers must likewise learn to go before in the way of God. They must expect to be most struck at, but they *know whom they have trusted.*

Verses 7–13

God honours Joshua and Joshua honours God. Thus those that honour God he will honour.

I. *v.* 7, 8. 1. It was a great honour God did him that he spoke to him, as he had done to Moses from off the mercy-seat. 2. That he designed to *magnify him in the sight of all Israel.* He had told him before that he would be with him (*ch.* i. 5), but now all Israel shall see it. Those are truly great with whom God is and whom he employs and owns in his service. Pious magistrates are to be highly honoured and esteemed as public blessings, and the more we see of God with them the more we should honour them. By the dividing of Jordan, they shall be convinced that God is in like manner with Joshua in bringing them into Canaan. It was at the banks of Jordan that God began to magnify Joshua, and at the same place he began to magnify our Lord Jesus as Mediator; for John was baptizing at Bethabara, *the house of passage*, and there it was that when our Saviour was baptized it was proclaimed, *This is my beloved Son*. 3. That by him he gave orders to the priests themselves, to stand still at the brink of Jordan while the waters part, *at the presence of the Lord*, Ps. cxiv. 5, 7. God could have divided the river without the priests, but they could not without him.

II. Joshua speaks to the people, and therein honours God.

1. He had commanded them to sanctify themselves, and therefore calls them to *hear the word of God*, for that is the ordinary means of sanctification, John xvii. 17.

2. He now tells them, at length, by what way they should pass over Jordan, by the stopping of its streams (*v.* 13): *The waters of Jordan shall be cut off*. The dividing of the Red Sea is here repeated, to show that God has the same power to finish the salvation of his people that he had to begin it, and that *the word of the Lord* was as truly with Joshua as it was with Moses. The God whom they worshipped was the same God that made the world and it was the same power that was engaged and employed for them.

3. The people having been directed before to follow the ark are here told that it should *pass before them into Jordan*, *v.* 11. Observe, (1) The ark of the covenant must be their guide. Divine grace under the Mosaic dispensation was wrapt up as in a cloud and covered with a veil, while by Christ, our Joshua, it is revealed in the ark of the covenant unveiled. (2) It is called *the ark of the covenant of the Lord of all the earth*. "It is your honour and happiness to have him in covenant with you: if he be yours, all the creatures are at your service, and when he pleases shall be employed for you." (3) They are told that the ark should *pass before them into Jordan*. They might safely venture, even into Jordan itself, if the ark of the covenant led them. Isa. xliii. 2, *When thou passest through the waters I will be with thee, and through the rivers they shall not overflow thee*.

4. From what God was now about to do for them he infers an assurance of what he would yet further do. The dividing of Jordan was intended to be to them, (1) A sure token of God's presence with them. (2) A sure pledge of the conquest of Canaan. If the living God is among you, *expelling he will expel* (so the Hebrew phrase is) *from before you the Canaanites*. The forcing of the lines was a certain presage of the ruin of all their hosts. This assurance which Joshua here gives them was so well grounded that it would enable one Israelite to chase a thousand Canaanites. Note, God's glorious appearances for his church and people ought to be improved by us for the encouragement of our faith and hope for the future. *As for God, his work is perfect*. If Jordan's flood cannot keep them out, Canaan's force cannot turn them out again.

5. He directs them to get twelve men ready, one of each tribe, who must be within call, to receive orders.

Verses 14–17

Here we have a short and plain account of the dividing of the river Jordan.

I. This river was now broader and deeper than usually it was at other times of the year, *v.* 15. The melting of the snow on the mountains of Lebanon, near which this river had its rise, was the occasion that at the time of harvest, barley-harvest, which was the spring of the year, Jordan overflowed all his banks. This great flood magnified the power of God and his kindness to Israel. Let the banks of Jordan be filled to the brink, it is as easy to Omnipotence to divide them, and dry them up, as if they were ever so narrow, ever so shallow.

II. As soon as ever the feet of the priests dipped in the brim of the water the stream stopped immediately, *v.* 15, 16. The waters above swelled, stood on a heap, and ran back, and yet did not spread. The waters on the other side this invisible dam ran down and left the bottom of the river dry. When they passed through the Red Sea, the waters were a wall on either hand, here only on the right-hand. What cannot God do? What will he not do for the perfecting of his people's salvation? When we have finished our pilgrimage through this wilderness, death will be like this Jordan between us and the heavenly Canaan, but the ark of the covenant has prepared us a way through it; it is the last enemy that shall be destroyed.

III. *The people passed over right against Jericho*, which was, 1. An instance of their boldness, and a noble defiance of their enemies. 2. It was an encouragement to them to venture through Jordan, for Jericho was a goodly city and the country about it extremely pleasant. 3. It would increase the confusion and terror of their enemies.

IV. The priests *stood still in the midst of Jordan while all the people passed over*, *v.* 17. There the ark was appointed to be, to show that the same power that parted the waters kept them parted as long as there was occasion. There the priests were appointed to stand still. 1. To try their faith. As they made a bold step when they set the first foot into Jordan, so now they made a bold stand when they tarried longest in Jordan; but they knew they carried their own protection with them. 2. It was to encourage the faith of the people, that they might go triumphantly into Canaan, and *fear no evil*, no, not in this *valley of the shadow of death*, being assured of God's presence, which interposed between them and the proud waters, which otherwise had gone over their souls.

CHAPTER 4

This chapter gives a further account of the miraculous passage of Israel through Jordan. I. Twelve stones set up in Jordan (ver. 9) and other twelve stones taken up out of Jordan, ver. 1–8. II. The march of the people through Jordan's channel, ver. 10–14. III. The closing of the waters again, ver. 15–19. IV. The erecting of the monument in Gilgal, ver. 20–24.

Verses 1–9

How busy Joshua and all the men of war were while they were passing over Jordan, marching into an enemy's country. They had their wives, and children, cattle, and tents, bag and baggage, to convey, by this strange and untrodden path, yet care must be taken to perpetuate the memorial of this wondrous work of God. Note, How much soever we have to do of business we must not omit what we have to do for the glory of God, for that is our best business. Now,

I. God gave orders for the preparing of this memorial. Had Joshua done it without divine direction, it might have looked like a design to perpetuate his own name. Note, God's works of wonder ought to be kept in everlasting remembrance. Some of the Israelites perhaps felt no concern to have it remembered; while others, it may be, had such deep impressions made upon them by it, that they thought there needed no memorial of it to be erected. But God, knowing how apt they had been soon to forget his works, ordered an expedient for the keeping of this in remembrance to all generations. 1. Joshua, as chief captain, must give direction about it (*v.* 1): *When all the people had clean passed over Jordan* God spoke unto Joshua to provide materials for this monument. 2. One man out of each tribe must be employed to prepare materials that each tribe might have the story told them by one of themselves, and each tribe might contribute something to the glory of God thereby (*v.* 2, 4): *Out of every tribe a man.* 3. The stones that must be set up for this memorial are ordered to be taken out of the midst of the channel and as near as might be from the very place where the priests stood *with the ark*, *v.* 3, 5. Let posterity know by this that Jordan was driven back, for these very stones were then fetched out of it. 4. The use of these stones is here appointed for a sign (*v.* 6), a memorial, *v.* 7. They would give occasion to the children to ask their parents in time to come, *How came these stones hither?*

II. According to these orders the thing was done. 1. Twelve stones were taken up out of the midst of Jordan. By these which they were ordered to take up God did, as it were, give them livery and seisin of this good land; it is all their own, let them enter and take possession; therefore what these twelve did the children of Israel are said to do (*v.* 8), because they were the representatives of their respective tribes. When the Lord Jesus, our Joshua, having overcome the sharpness of death and dried up that Jordan, had opened the kingdom of heaven to all believers, he appointed his twelve apostles by the memorial of the gospel to transmit the knowledge of this to remote places and future ages. 2. Other twelve stones were set up *in the midst of Jordan* (*v.* 9), to notify the very place where the ark stood.

Verses 10–19

Joshua pursued the orders God gave him, and did nothing without divine direction, finishing all that *the Lord had commanded* him (*v.* 10).

I. *The people hasted and passed over*, *v.* 10. 1. Some hasted because they were not able to trust God. 2. Others because they were not willing to tempt God to continue the miracle longer than needs must. 3. Others because they were eager to be in Canaan. 4. Those that considered least, yet hasted because others did. He that believeth doth not make haste to *anticipate* God's counsels, but he makes haste to *attend* them, Isa. xxviii. 16.

II. The two tribes and a half led the van, *v.* 12, 13. They were all chosen men, and fit for service, ready armed. And the two tribes had no reason to complain: the post of danger is the post of honour.

III. When all the people had got clear to the other side, the priests with the ark came up out of Jordan. Joshua did not order them out of Jordan till God directed him to do so, *v.* 15–17. How low a condition soever God may at any time bring his priests or people to, let them patiently wait, till by his providence he shall call them up out of it, and let them not be weary of waiting, while they have the tokens of God's presence with them, in the depth of their adversity.

IV. As soon as ever the priests and the ark had come up out of Jordan, the waters of the river, which had stood on a heap, gradually flowed down according to their nature and usual course, *v.* 18. When Israel's turn was served, and the token of God's presence was removed, immediately the water went forward again.

V. Notice is taken of the honour put upon Joshua by all this (*v.* 14): *On that day the Lord magnified Joshua*, both by the fellowship he admitted him to with himself, and by the authority he confirmed him in over both priests and people. The best and surest way to command the respect of inferiors is not by blustering and threatening, but by holiness and love,

and a constant regard to their welfare, and to God's will and honour. Those that are sanctified are truly magnified, and are worthy of double honour.

VI. An account is kept of the time of this great event (*v.* 19): it was *on the tenth day of the first month*, just forty years since they came out of Egypt, wanting five days. God had said in his wrath that they should wander forty years in the wilderness, and at last he brought them into Canaan five days before the forty years were ended, to show how little pleasure God takes in punishing, how swift he is to show mercy. God ordered it so that they should enter Canaan four days before the annual solemnity of the passover, and on the very day when the preparation for it was to begin (Exod. xii. 3), because he would have them then to be reminded of their deliverance out of Egypt.

Verses 20–24

The twelve stones which were *laid down in Gilgal* (*v.* 8) are here set up either one upon another, or one by another in rows; for after they were fixed they are not called *a heap of stones*, but *these stones*.

I. Posterity would enquire into the meaning of them: *Your children shall ask their fathers, What mean these stones?* Note, Those that will be wise when they are old must be inquisitive when they are young. Our Lord Jesus, though he had in himself the fulness of knowledge, has by his example taught children and young people to hear and ask questions, Luke ii. 46.

II. The parents are here directed what answer to give to this enquiry (*v.* 22): "*You shall let your children know* that which you have yourselves learned from the written word and from your fathers." Note, It is the duty of parents to acquaint their children betimes with the word and works of God.

1. They must let their children know that Jordan was driven back before Israel, who *went through it upon dry land*, and that this was the very place where they passed over. Note, God's mercies to our ancestors were mercies to us; and we should revive the remembrance of the great things God did for our fathers *in the days of old*.

2. They must take that occasion to tell their children of the drying up of the Red Sea forty years before: *As the Lord your God did to the Red Sea.* Note, (i) By making the comparison, it appears that God is the same yesterday, to-day, and for ever. (ii) Later mercies should bring to remembrance former mercies, and revive our thankfulness for them. (1) The power of God was hereby magnified. The deliverances of God's people are instructions to all people, and fair warnings not to contend with Omnipotence. (2) The remembrance of this wonderful work should effectually restrain them from the worship of other gods, and constrain them to abide and abound in the service of their own God.

CHAPTER 5

Israel have now got over Jordan. They have now got footing in Canaan, and must apply themselves to the conquest of it, in order to which this chapter tells us, I. How their enemies were dispirited, ver. 1. II. What was done at their first landing to assist and encourage them. 1. The covenant of circumcision was renewed, ver. 2–9. 2. The feast of the passover was celebrated, ver. 10. 3. Their camp was victualled with the corn of the land, whereupon the manna ceased, ver. 11, 12. 4. The captain of the Lord's host himself appeared to Joshua to animate and direct him, ver. 13–15.

Verses 1–9

A vast show, no doubt, the numerous camp of Israel made in the plains of Jericho, where now they had pitched their tents. The *church in the wilderness has now come up from the wilderness.* How terrible she was in the eyes of her enemies we are here told, *v.* 1. How fair and clear she was made in the eyes of her friends, by the rolling away of the reproach of Egypt, we are told in the following verses.

I. Here are impressions the tidings made upon the kings of this land: *Their heart melted* like wax before the fire, *neither was there spirit in them any more*. The kings have till now kept up their spirits pretty well, being in possession, their country populous, and their cities fortified, they should be able to make their part good against the invaders; but when they heard not only that they had come over Jordan, but that they had come over by a miracle, the God of nature manifestly fighting for them, *their hearts failed them* too, and they were now at their wits' end. And, 1. They had reason enough to be afraid; Israel itself was a formidable body, and much more so when God was its head, a God of almighty power. 2. God impressed these fears upon them, and dispirited them, as he had promised (Exod. xxiii. 27).

II. *At that time* (v. 2), when the country about them was in that great consternation, God ordered Joshua to circumcise the children of Israel.

1. The occasion there was for this general circumcision. All that came out of Egypt were circumcised, *v.* 5. But when the edict was made for the destruction of their male infants, the administration of this ordinance was interrupted; many of them were uncircumcised, of whom there was a general circumcision. It is with reference to that general circumcision that this is called a *second*, *v.* 2. Under the government of Moses himself, to have all their children that were born for thirty-eight years together left uncircumcised is unaccountable. Now, (1) Some think circumcision was omitted because it was needless: it was appointed to be a mark of distinction between the Israelites and other nations, and therefore in the wilderness there was no occasion for it. (2) Others think that they did not look upon the precept of circumcision as obligatory till they came to settle in Canaan. (3) Others think that God favourably dispensed with the observance of this ordinance in consideration of the unsettledness of their state. (4) To me it seems to have been a continued token of God's displeasure against them for their unbelief and murmuring. And this was such a significant indication of God's wrath as when Israel had broken the covenant by making the golden calf. Whatever the reason was, it seems that this great ordinance was omitted in Israel for almost forty years together, which is a plain indication that it was not of absolute necessity, nor was to be of perpetual obligation.

2. The orders given to Joshua for this general circumcision (v. 2). Why was this ordered to be done now? (1) Because now the promise of which circumcision was instituted to be the seal was performed. The seed of Israel was brought safely into the land of Canaan. (2) Because now the threatening was fully executed by the expiring of the forty years, therefore now the seal of the covenant is revived again. [1] God would hereby show that the camp of Israel was not governed by the ordinary rules and measures of war, but by immediate direction from God. [2] God would hereby animate his people Israel against the difficulties they were now to encounter, by confirming his covenant with them, which gave them unquestionable assurance of victory and success, and the full possession of the land of promise. [3] God would hereby teach them, and us with them, in all great undertakings to *begin with God*, to make sure of his favour, by offering ourselves to him *a living sacrifice* (for that was signified by the blood of circumcision). [4] The reviving of circumcision, after it had been so long disused, was designed to revive the observance of other institutions. [5] This *second* circumcision, as it is here called, was typical of the spiritual circumcision with which the Israel of God, when they enter into the gospel rest, are circumcised; it points to *Jesus as the true circumciser*, the author of *another circumcision* than that *of the flesh*, commanded by the law, even the *circumcision of the heart* (Rom. ii. 29), called the *circumcision of Christ*, Col. ii. 11.

3. The people's obedience to these orders. Joshua *circumcised the children of Israel* (v. 3), and here they gave an instance of their dutifulness by submitting to this painful institution.

4. (1) Their circumcision rolled away the reproach of Egypt. They were tainted with the idolatry of Egypt, and that was their reproach; but now that they were circumcised it was to be hoped they would be so entirely devoted to God that the reproach would be rolled away. (2) Their coming safely to Canaan rolled away the reproach of Egypt, for it silenced that spiteful suggestion of the Egyptians, that *for mischief they were brought out, the wilderness had shut them in*, Exod. xiv. 3.

Verses 10–12

We may well imagine that the people of Canaan were astonished. Joshua opens the campaign with one act of devotion after another. That is likely to end well which begins with God.

I. A solemn passover kept, at the time appointed by the law, *the fourteenth day of the first month*, and in the same place where they were circumcised, *v.* 10. While they were wandering in the wilderness they were denied the benefit and comfort of this ordinance, but now God comforted them again, and therefore that joyful ordinance is revived. The solemn passover followed immediately after the solemn circumcision; thus, when those that received the word were baptized, immediately we find them *breaking bread*, Acts ii. 41, 42. They kept this passover in the plains of Jericho, as it were in defiance of the Canaanites. He now *prepared a table before them in the presence of their enemies*, Ps. xxiii. 5.

II. Provision made for their camp of the *corn of the land*, and the *ceasing of the manna* thereupon, *v.* 11, 12. Manna was a wonderful mercy to them when they needed it. But it was the mark of a wilderness state; more acceptable to them to eat of the *corn of the land*, and this they are now furnished with.

1. The country people, having retired for safety into Jericho, had left their barns and fields, and all that was in them. And the supply came very seasonably, for, (1) After the passover they were to keep *the feast of unleavened bread*, which they could not do according to the appointment when they had nothing but manna to live upon; now they found old corn enough in the barns of the Canaanites to supply them plentifully for that occasion. (2) On the morrow after the passover-sabbath they were to *wave the sheaf of first-fruits before the Lord*, Lev. xxiii. 10, 11. And this they were particularly ordered to do when they *came into the land which God would give them*: and they were furnished for this with the *fruit of the land that year* (v. 12), which was then growing and beginning to be ripe.

2. Notice is taken of the ceasing of the manna as soon as ever they had eaten the *old corn of the land*, (1) It came just when they needed it, so it continued as long as they had occasion for it and no longer. (2) To teach us not to expect extraordinary supplies when supplies may be had in an ordinary way. Now that they needed it not God withdrew it. He is a wise Father, who knows the necessities of his children, and accommodates his gifts to *them*, not to their humours. The word and ordinances of God are spiritual manna, with which God nourishes his people in this wilderness, but when we come to the heavenly Canaan this manna will cease, for we shall no longer have need of it.

Verses 13–15

We have hitherto found God often speaking to Joshua, but we read not till now of any appearance of God's glory to him; now that his difficulties increased his encouragements were increased in proportion.

I. The time when he was favoured with this vision. It was immediately after he had performed the great solemnities of circumcision and the passover. Note, We may then expect the discoveries of the divine grace when we are found in the way of our duty.

II. The place where he had this vision. It was *by Jericho*. There, it should seem, he was all alone, fearless of danger, because sure of the divine protection. There he was (some think) meditating and praying. Or perhaps to take a view of the city, and contrive how to attack it; when God came and directed him. Note, God will *help those that help themselves*. *Vigilantibus non dormientibus succurrit lex—The law succours those who watch, not those who sleep.* Joshua was in his post as a general, when God came and made himself known as Generalissimo.

III. The appearance itself. Joshua, as is usual with those that are full of thought and care, was looking downwards, his eyes fixed on the ground, when of a sudden he was surprised with the appearance of a man who stood before him at some little distance, which obliged him to lift up his eyes. Now, 1. We have reason to think that this man was the Son of God, the eternal Word, who, before he assumed the human nature for a perpetuity, frequently appeared in a human shape. 2. He here appeared as a soldier, with *his sword drawn in his hand*. To Abraham in his tent he appeared as a traveller; to Joshua in the field as a man of war. Christ will be to his people what their faith expects and desires. He came to encourage him to carry it on with vigour; for Christ's sword drawn in his hand denotes how ready he is for the defence and salvation of his people, who through him shall do valiantly.

IV. The bold question with which Joshua accosted him. This shows, 1. His great courage and resolution. He was not ruffled by the suddenness of the appearance. 2. His great concern for the people and their cause. It should seem, he suspected him for an enemy. Thus apt are we to look upon that as against us which is most for us. The cause between the Israelites and the Canaanites, between Christ and Beelzebub, will not admit of a neutrality. *He that is not with us is against us.*

V. The account he gave of himself, *v.* 14. "Nay, not for your adversaries, you may be sure, but *as captain of the host of the Lord have I now come*, not only for you as a friend, but over you as commander in chief." He, as captain of both, conducts the host of Israel and commands the host of angels to their assistance. Perhaps in allusion to this Christ is called the *captain of our salvation* (Heb. ii. 10), *and a leader and commander to the people*, Isa lv. 4.

VI. He perceived that he was a divine person, and not a man. 1. Joshua paid homage to him: He *fell on his face to the earth and did worship*. Joshua was himself general of the forces of Israel, and yet cheerfully submitted to him as his commander. 2. He begged to receive commands and directions from him: *What saith my Lord unto his servant?* His former question was not more bold and soldier-like than this was pious and saint-like; nor was it any disparagement to the greatness of Joshua's spirit: even crowned heads cannot bow too low before the throne of the Lord Jesus, who is *King of kings*, Ps. ii. 10, 11; lxxii. 10, 11; Rev. xix. 16. Observe, (1) The relation he owns between himself and Christ, that Christ was his Lord and himself his servant and under his command, Christ his Captain and himself a soldier

under him, to do as he is bidden, Matt. viii. 9. (2) The enquiry he makes pursuant to this relation: *What saith my Lord?* which implies an earnest desire to know the will of Christ, and a cheerful readiness and resolution to do it. This temper of mind shows him fit for the post he was in; for those know best how to command that know how to obey.

VII. The further expressions of reverence which this divine captain required from Joshua (*v.* 15): *Loose thy shoe from off thy foot*, in token of reverence and respect (which with us are signified by uncovering the head). We are accustomed to say of a person for whom we have a great affection that we love the very ground he treads upon. Outward expressions of inward reverence well become us, and are required of us. Bishop Patrick well observes here that the very same orders that God gave to Moses at the bush (Exod. iii. 5), he here gives to Joshua; as he had been with Moses so he would be with him, *ch.* i. 5.

CHAPTER 6

Joshua opened the campaign with the siege of Jericho, a city which trusted so much to the strength of its walls as to stand upon its defence. Now here we have the story of the taking of it. I. The directions and assurances which the captain of the Lord's host gave concerning it, ver. 1–5. II. The trial of the people's patient obedience in walking round the city six days, ver. 6–14. III. The wonderful delivery of it into their hands the seventh day, with a solemn charge to them to use it as a devoted thing, ver. 15–21, and ver. 24. IV. The preservation of Rahab and her relations, ver. 22, 23, 25. V. A curse pronounced upon the man that should dare to rebuild this city, ver. 26, 27. An abstract of this story we find among the trophies of faith, Heb. xi. 30.

Verses 1–5

We have here a contest between God and the men of Jericho.

I. Jericho resolves Israel shall *not* be its master, *v.* 1. None went out as deserters or to treat of peace, nor were any admitted in to offer peace.

II. God resolves Israel *shall* be its master, and that quickly. 1. The captain of the Lord's host gives directions how the city should be besieged. No trenches are to be opened, nor any military preparations made; but the ark of God must be carried by the priests round the city once a day for six days together, and seven times the seventh day, attended by the men of war in silence, the priests all the while blowing with trumpets of rams' horns, *v.* 3, 4. This was all they were to do. 2. He assures them that on the seventh day before night they should, without fail, be masters of the town. Upon a signal given, they must all shout, and immediately the wall should fall down, *v.* 5. God appointed this way, (1) To magnify his own power, that he might be *exalted in his own strength* (Ps. xxi. 13), not in the strength of instruments. (2) To put an honour upon his ark, the instituted token of his presence, and to give a reason for the laws by which the people were obliged to look upon it with the most profound veneration and respect. (3) It was likewise to put honour upon the priests, who were appointed upon this occasion to carry the ark and sound the trumpets. (4) It was to try the faith, obedience, and patience, of the people, to try whether they would observe a precept which to human policy seemed foolish to obey and believe a promise which in human probability seemed impossible to be performed. Thus by faith, not by force, the walls of Jericho fell down. (5) It was to encourage the hope of Israel with reference to the remaining difficulties that were before them. The strongest and highest walls cannot hold out against Omnipotence.

Verses 6–16

We have here an account of the cavalcade which Israel made about Jericho, the orders Joshua gave concerning it, as he had received them from the Lord and their punctual observance of these orders.

I. Wherever the ark went the people attended it, v. 9. The armed men went before it to clear the way, pioneers to the ark of God. It is an honour to the greatest men to do any good office to the ark and to serve the interests of religion in their country. The *rereward*, either another body of armed men, or Dan's squadron, which marched last through the wilderness, or, as some think, the multitude of the people who were not armed, followed the ark.

II. Seven priests went immediately before the ark, having trumpets in their hands, with which they were continually sounding, v. 4, 5, 9, 13. 1. They proclaimed war with the Canaanites, and so struck a terror upon them. Thus God's ministers, by the solemn declarations of his wrath against all ungodliness and unrighteousness of men, must blow the trumpet in Zion, that the sinners in Zion may be afraid. 2. They proclaimed God's gracious presence with Israel, and so put life and courage into them.

III. The trumpets they used were not silver trumpets, but trumpets of rams' horns, bored hollow for the purpose. These trumpets were of the basest matter, dullest sound, and least show, that the excellency of the power might be of God. Thus by the foolishness of preaching, fitly compared to the sounding of these rams' horns, the devil's kingdom is thrown down; and the *weapons of our warfare*, though they are not carnal, are yet *mighty through God to the pulling down of strong-holds*, 2 Cor. x. 4, 5.

IV. All the people were commanded to be silent, not to speak a word, nor make any noise (v. 10), that they might the more carefully attend to the sound of the sacred trumpets, which they were now to look upon as the voice of God among them; and it does not become us to speak when God is speaking.

V. They were to do this once a day for six days together and seven times the seventh day, and they did so, v. 14, 15. As promised deliverances must be expected in God's way, so they must be expected in his time.

VI. One of these days must needs be a sabbath day, and the Jews say that it was the last, but this is not certain; however, if he that appointed them to rest on the other sabbath days appointed them to walk on this, that was sufficient to justify them in it; he never intended to bind himself by his own laws, but that when he pleased he might dispense with them. And, besides, the law of the sabbath forbids our own work, which is servile and secular, but this which they did was a religious act. It is certainly no breach of the sabbath rest to do the sabbath work.

VII. They continued to do this during the time appointed, and seven times the seventh day, though they saw not any effect of it. We may suppose the oddness of the thing did at first amuse the besieged. Probably they bantered the besiegers, as those mentioned in Neh. vi. 2, "*What do these feeble Jews?*"

VIII. At last they were to give a shout, and did so, and immediately the walls fell, v. 16. This was a triumphant shout; a shout of prayer, an echo to the sound of the trumpets which proclaimed the promise that God would remember them. And at the end of time, when our Lord shall descend from heaven with a shout, and the sound of a trumpet, Satan's kingdom shall be completely ruined, and not till then, when all opposing rule, principality, and power, shall be effectually and eternally put down.

Verses 17–27

The people had religiously observed the orders given them concerning the besieging of Jericho, and now at length Joshua had told them (v. 16),

"*The Lord hath given you the city*, enter and take possession."

I. The rules they were to observe in taking possession. 1. The city shall be a *cherem*, a devoted thing, it and all therein, to the Lord. No life in it might be ransomed upon any terms. Only, when this severity is ordered, Rahab and her family are excepted: *She shall live and all that are with her*. She had distinguished herself from her neighbours by the kindness she showed to Israel. 2. All the treasure of it, the money and plate and valuable goods, must be consecrated to the service of the tabernacle. God had promised them a land *flowing with milk and honey*, not a land abounding with silver and gold. He would have them to reckon themselves enriched in the enriching of the tabernacle. 3. A particular caution is given them to take heed of meddling with the forbidding spoil; "*In any wise keep yourselves from the accursed thing*; check yourselves, and frighten yourselves from having anything to do with it." He speaks as if he foresaw the sin of Achan, which we have an account of in the next chapter.

II. The entrance that was opened to them into the city by the sudden fall of the walls. That which the inhabitants trusted to for defence proved their destruction. The sudden fall of the wall, no doubt, put the inhabitants into such a consternation that they had no strength nor spirit to make any resistance, but they became an easy prey to the sword of Israel. Thus shall Satan's kingdom fall, nor shall any prosper that harden themselves against God.

III. The execution of the orders given concerning this devoted city. 1. All that breathed were put to the sword. If they had not had a divine warrant under the seal of miracles for this execution, it could not have been justified, nor can it justify the like now, when we are sure no such warrant can be produced. The spirit of the gospel is very different, for Christ came not to destroy men's lives but to save them, Luke ix. 56. Christ's victories were of another nature. 2. The city was *burnt with fire, and all that was in it*, v. 24. 3. All the silver and gold, and all those vessels which were capable of being purified by fire, were brought into the treasury of the house of the Lord.

IV. The preservation of Rahab the harlot, or innkeeper, who *perished not with those that believed not*, Heb. xi. 31. The public faith was engaged for her safety by the two spies. The same persons that she had secured were employed to secure her, v. 22, 23. All her kindred were saved with her. Now being preserved alive, 1. She was left for some time without the camp to be purified from the Gentile superstition, which she was to renounce, and to be prepared for her admission as a proselyte. 2. She was in due time incorporated with the church of Israel, and she and her posterity dwelt in Israel, and her family was remarkable long after. We find her the wife of Salmon, prince of Judah, mother of Boaz, and named among the ancestors of our Saviour, Matt. i. 5.

V. Jericho is condemned to a perpetual desolation, and a curse pronounced upon the man that at any time hereafter should offer to rebuild it (v. 26). The situation of the city was very pleasant, and probably its nearness to Jordan was an advantage to it, which would tempt men to build upon the same spot; but they are here told it is at their peril if they do it. Men build for their posterity, but he that builds Jericho shall have no posterity to enjoy what he builds. This curse did come upon that man who long after rebuilded Jericho (1 Kings xvi. 34), but we are not to think it made the place ever the worse when it was built, or brought any hurt to those that inhabited it. We find Jericho afterwards graced with the presence, not only of those two great prophets Elijah and Elisha, but of our blessed Saviour himself, Luke xviii. 35; xix. 1; Matt. xx. 29.

CHAPTER 7

More than once we have found the affairs of Israel, even when they were in the happiest posture and gave the most hopeful prospects, perplexed and embarrassed by sin, and in this chapter we have another instance of the interruption given to the progress of their arms by sin. But it being only the sin of one person or family, and soon expiated, the consequences were not so mischievous. We have here, I. The sin of Achan in meddling with the accursed thing, ver. 1. II. The defeat of Israel before Ai thereupon, ver. 2–5. III. Joshua's humiliation and prayer on occasion of that sad disaster, ver. 6–9. IV. The directions God gave him for the putting away of the guilt, ver. 10–15. V. The discovery, trial, conviction, condemnation, and execution, of the criminal, ver. 16–26. And by this story it appears that, as the laws, so Canaan itself, "made nothing perfect," the perfection both of holiness and peace to God's Israel is to be expected in the heavenly Canaan only.

Verses 1–5

The story of this chapter begins with a *but*. The *Lord was with Joshua, and his fame was noised through all that country*, so the foregoing chapter ends. *But the children of Israel committed a trespass*, and so set God against them. If we lose our God, we lose our friends, who cannot help us unless God be for us.

I. Achan sinning, *v*. 1. The sin is here said to be *taking of the accursed thing*, in disobedience to the command and in defiance of the threatening, *ch*. vi. 18. In the sacking of Jericho compassion was put off and yielded to the law, but covetousness was indulged. The love of the world is that root of bitterness which of all others is most hardly rooted up. Yet the history of Achan is a plain intimation that he of all the thousands of Israel was the only delinquent in this matter. And yet, though it was a single person that sinned, the children of Israel are said *to commit the trespass*, because one of their body did it, and he was not as yet separated from them, nor disowned by them. They did it, that is, by what Achan did guilt was brought upon the whole society of which he was a member. This should be a warning to us to take heed of sin ourselves, lest by it many be defiled or disquieted (Heb. xii. 15). Many a careful tradesman has been broken by a careless partner. And it concerns us to watch over one another for the preventing of sin.

II. The camp of Israel suffering for the same: *The anger of the Lord was kindled against Israel*; he saw the offence, though they did not, and takes a course to make them see it. 1. Joshua sends a detachment to seize upon the next city that was in their way, and that was Ai. Only 3000 men were sent, advice being brought him by his spies that the place was inconsiderable, and needed no greater force for the reduction of it, *v*. 2, 3. *They are but few* (say the spies), but, as few as they were, they were too many for them. It will awaken our care and diligence in our Christian warfare to consider that *we wrestle with principalities and powers*. 2. The party he sent, in their first attack upon the town, were repulsed with some loss (*v*. 4, 5). It served, (1) To humble God's Israel. (2) To harden the Canaanites, and to make them the more secure. (3) To be an evidence of God's displeasure against Israel, and a call to them to *purge out the old leaven*. And this was principally intended in their defeat. 3. The retreat of this party in disorder put the whole camp of Israel into a fright: *The hearts of the people melted*, not so much for the loss as for the disappointment. To every thinking man among them it appeared an indication of God's displeasure.

Verses 6–9

An account of the deep concern Joshua was in upon this sad occasion.

I. How he grieved: He *rent his clothes* (*v*. 6), in token of great sorrow for this public disaster, and especially a dread of God's displeasure, which was

certainly the cause of it. One of the bravest soldiers that ever was owned that his *flesh trembled for fear of God*, Ps. cxix. 120. As one *humbling himself under the mighty hand of God, he fell to the earth upon his face*. The elders of Israel, being interested in the cause and influenced by his example, prostrated themselves with him, and, in token of deep humiliation, *put dust upon their heads*, not only as mourners, but as penitents. His eye is upon God as displeased, and that troubles him.

II. How he prayed, or pleaded rather, humbly expostulating the case with God, not sullen, as David when *the Lord had made a breach upon Uzzah*, but much affected; his spirit seemed to be somewhat ruffled and discomposed, yet not so as to be put out of frame for prayer; but, by giving vent to his trouble in a humble address to God, he keeps his temper and it ends well. 1. Now he wishes they had all taken up with the lot of the two tribes on the other side Jordan, *v*. 7. Those words, *wherefore hast thou brought us over Jordan to destroy us?* are too like what the murmurers often said (Exod. xiv. 11, 12; xvi. 3; xvii. 3; Num. xiv. 2, 3); but he that searches the heart knew they came from another spirit, and therefore was not extreme to mark what he said amiss. 2. He speaks as one quite at a loss concerning the meaning of this event (*v*. 8). Is the Lord's arm shortened? Note, The methods of Providence are often intricate and perplexing, and such as the wisest and best of men know not what to say to; but *they shall know hereafter*, John xiii. 7. 3. He pleads the danger Israel was now in of being ruined. Thus even good men, when things go against them a little, are too apt to fear the worst. But this comes in here as a plea: "Lord, let not Israel's name, which has been so dear to thee and so great in the world, be cut off." 4. He pleads the reproach that would be cast on God, and that if Israel were ruined his glory would suffer by it. He feared it would reflect on God, his wisdom and power, his goodness and faithfulness; what would the Egyptians say? Note, Nothing is more grievous to a gracious soul than dishonour done to God's name. We cannot urge a better plea than this, Lord, *What wilt thou do for thy great name?* Let God in all be glorified, and then welcome his whole will.

Verses 10–15

God's answer to Joshua's address. And let those that find themselves under the tokens of God's displeasure never complain *of* him, but complain *to* him, and they shall receive an answer of peace. The answer came immediately.

I. God encourages Joshua against his present despondencies: "*Get thee up*, suffer not thy spirits to droop and sink thus; *wherefore liest thou thus upon thy face?*" Now God told him it was enough, he would not have him continue any longer in that melancholy posture, for God delights not in the grief of penitents when they afflict their souls further than as it qualifies them for pardon and peace. Joshua continued his mourning *till eventide* (*v*. 6). It is time for him to lay aside his mourning weeds, and put on his judge's robes, and *clothe himself with zeal as a cloak*. Weeping must not hinder sowing, nor one duty of religion jostle out another.

II. He informs him of the true and only cause of this disaster (*v*. 11): *Israel hath sinned*. The sinner is not named, though the sin is described, but it is spoken of as the act of Israel in general. Observe how the sin is here made to appear exceedingly sinful. 1. *They have transgressed my covenant*, an express precept with a penalty annexed to it. It was agreed that God should have all the spoil of Jericho, and they should have the spoil of the rest of the cities of Canaan; but, in robbing God of his part, they *transgressed this covenant*. 2. *They have even taken of the devoted thing.* 3. They *have also stolen*; they did it clandestinely, as if they could conceal it from the divine omniscience. 4. They have *dissembled* also. Achan joined with the rest in a general protestation of innocency, and kept his countenance, like the adulterous woman that *eats and wipes her mouth, and says, I have done no wickedness.* Nay, 5. They have put the accursed thing *among their own goods*, as if they had as good a title to that as to anything they have. God could at this time have told him who the person was that had done this thing, but he does not, (1) To exercise the zeal of Joshua and Israel, in searching out the criminal. (2) To give the sinner himself space to repent and make confession. But Achan never discovering himself till the lot discovered him evidenced the hardness of his heart, and therefore he found no mercy.

III. He awakens him to enquire further into it, by telling him, 1. That this was the only ground for the controversy so that when this accursed thing was put away he needed not fear. 2. That if this accursed thing were not destroyed they could not expect the return of God's gracious presence. By personal repentance and reformation, we destroy the accursed thing in our own hearts, and, unless we do this, we must never expect the favour of the blessed God.

IV. He directs him in what method to make this enquiry and prosecution. 1. He must *sanctify the people*, now over-night, that is, as it is explained, he must command them to *sanctify themselves*, *v.* 13. And what can either magistrates or ministers do more towards sanctification? They must put themselves into a suitable frame to appear before God and submit to the divine scrutiny. 2. He must bring them all under the scrutiny of the lot (*v.* 14); the tribe which the guilty person was of should first be discovered by lot, then the family, then the household, and last of all the person. The conviction came upon him thus gradually that he might have some space given him to come in and surrender himself; for God is *not willing that any should perish, but that all should come to repentance.* 3. When the criminal was found out he must be put to death *without mercy* (Heb. x. 28). It was *sacrilege*; this was the crime to be thus severely punished, for warning to all people in all ages to take heed how they rob God.

Verses 16–26

I. The discovery of Achan by the lot. In the scrutiny observe, 1. That the guilty tribe was that of Judah, which was, and was to be, of all the tribes, the most honourable and illustrious. The Jews' tradition is that when the tribe of Judah was taken the valiant men of that tribe drew their swords, and professed they would not sheathe them again till they saw the criminal punished and themselves cleared who knew their own innocence. 2. That the guilty person was at length fastened upon, and the language of the lot was, *Thou art the man, v.* 18. It was strange that Achan, being conscious to himself of guilt, when he saw the lot come nearer and nearer to him, had not either the wit to make an escape or the grace to make a confession. See here, (1) The folly of those that promise themselves secrecy in sin: the righteous God has many ways of bringing to light the hidden works of darkness. (2) How much it is our concern, when God is contending with us, to find out what the particular sin is, and pray earnestly with holy Job, *Lord, show me wherefore thou contendest with me.*

II. His arraignment and examination, *v.* 19. Joshua sits judge, and urges him to make a penitent confession, that his soul might be saved by it in the other world. Observe, 1. How he accosts him with the greatest tenderness. He might justly have called him "thief", and "rebel", "Raca", and "thou fool", but he calls him "son"; he might have adjured him to

confess, as the high priest did our blessed Saviour, or threatened him with the torture to extort a confession, but for love's sake he rather beseeches him: *I pray thee make confession.* This is an example to all not to insult over those that are in misery, though they have brought themselves into it by their own wickedness. It is likewise an example to magistrates never to be transported into any indecencies of behaviour or language towards those that have given the greatest provocations. *The wrath of man worketh not the righteousness of God.* 2. What he wishes him to do, to confess the fact. Joshua was to him in God's stead, so that in confessing to him he confessed to God. Note, In confessing sin, as we take shame to ourselves, so we give glory to God as a righteous God, owning him justly displeased with us, and as a good God, who will not improve our confessions as evidences against us, but is faithful and just to forgive when we are brought to own that he would be faithful and just if he should punish. By sin we have injured God in his honour. Christ by his death has made satisfaction for the injury; but it is required that we by repentance show our good will to his honour, and, as far as in us lies, give glory to him.

III. His confession, which now at last, when he saw it was to no purpose to conceal his crime, was free and ingenuous enough, *v.* 20, 21. Here is, 1. A penitent acknowledgment of the fault. 2. A particular narrative of the fact: *Thus and thus have I done.* Note, It becomes penitents, in the confession of their sins to God, to be very particular; not only, "I have sinned," but, "In this and that instance I have sinned." He confesses, (1) To the things taken. In plundering a house in Jericho he found a goodly Babylonish garment; the word signifies a robe, such as princes wore when they appeared in state. "A thousand pities" (thinks Achan) "that it should be burnt; it will serve me many a year for my best garment." Under these pretences he makes bold with this first, but, his hand being thus in, he proceeds to take a bag of money, *two hundred shekels*, that is, one hundred ounces of silver, and a *wedge of gold* which weighed *fifty shekels*, that is, twenty-five ounces. He could not plead that, in taking these, he saved them *from the fire*, but those that make a slight excuse to serve in daring to commit one sin will venture upon the next without such an excuse; for the way of sin is downhill. See what a poor prize it was for which Achan ran this desperate hazard. See Matt. xvi. 26. (2) He confesses the manner of taking them. [1] The sin began in the eye. He saw these fine things, as Eve saw the forbidden fruit, and was strangely charmed with the sight. See what comes of suffering the heart to walk after the eyes, and what need we have to make this covenant with our eyes, that if they wander they shall be sure to weep for it. *Look not thou upon the wine that is red*, upon the woman that is fair. [2] It proceeded out of the heart. He owns, *I coveted them.* Thus lust conceived and brought forth this sin. Those that would be kept from sinful actions must mortify and check in themselves sinful desires. It was not the looking, but the lusting that ruined him. [3] When he had committed it he was very industrious to conceal it. See the *deceitfulness of sin*; that which is pleasing in the commission is bitter in the reflection; at the last it bites like a serpent.

IV. His conviction. God had convicted him by the lot; he had convicted himself by his own confession. Joshua has him further convicted by the searching of his tent, in which the goods were found which he confessed to.

V. His condemnation. Joshua passes sentence upon him (*v.* 25): *Why hast thou troubled us?* Note, Sin is a very troublesome thing, not only to the sinner himself, but to all about him. Now (says Joshua) *God shall trouble thee.* See why Achan was so severely dealt with, not only because he had robbed God, but because he had troubled Israel; over his head he had (as it were) this accusation written, "Achan, *the troubler of Israel*," as Ahab, 1 Kings xviii. 18. Some of the Jewish doctors, from that word which determines the troubling of him to *this day*, infer that therefore he should not be troubled in the world to come; the flesh was destroyed that the spirit might be saved, and, if so, the dispensation was really less severe than it seemed.

VI. His execution.

1. The place of execution. The execution was at a distance, that the camp which was disturbed by Achan's sin might not be defiled by his death.

2. The persons employed in his execution. It was the act of all Israel, v. 24, 25.

3. The partakers with him in the punishment; for *he perished not alone in his iniquity*, ch. xxii. 20. (1) The stolen goods were destroyed with him. (2) All his other goods were destroyed likewise, not only his tent, and the furniture of that, but his *oxen, asses, and sheep*. Those lose their own that grasp at more than their own. (3) His sons and daughters were put to death with him. Some indeed think that they were *brought out* (v. 24) only to be the spectators of their father's punishment. Perhaps his sons and daughters were aiders and abettors in the villainy, had helped to carry off the accursed thing. It is very probable that they assisted in the concealment.

4. The punishment itself that was inflicted on him. He was stoned (some think as a sabbath breaker, supposing that the sacrilege was committed on the sabbath day), and then his dead body was burnt.

5. The pacifying of God's wrath hereby (v. 26): *The Lord turned from the fierceness of his anger*. Take away the cause, and the effect will cease.

VII. The record of his conviction and execution. Care was taken to preserve the remembrance of it, for warning and instruction to posterity. 1. A heap of stones was raised on the place where Achan executed, every one perhaps of the congregation throwing a stone to the heap, in token of his detestation of the crime. 2. A new name was given to the place; it was called the *Valley of Achor*, or *trouble*. The *Valley of Achor* is said to be given for a *door of hope*, because when we put away the accursed thing then there begins to be hope in Israel, Hos. ii. 15; Ezra x. 2.

CHAPTER 8

Here is, I. The glorious progress of their arms in the taking of Ai, before which they had lately suffered disgrace. 1. God encourages Joshua to attack it, with the assurance of success, ver. 1, 2. 2. Joshua gives orders accordingly to the men of war, ver. 3–8. 3. The stratagem succeeds, ver. 9–22. 4. Joshua becomes master of this city, puts all the inhabitants to the sword, burns it, hangs the king, but gives the plunder to the soldiers, ver. 23–29. II. The great solemnity of writing and reading the law before a general assembly of all Israel, drawn up for that purpose upon the two mountains of Gerizim and Ebal, ver. 30–35.

Verses 1–2

It should seem, Joshua was now at a stand and could not think, without fear and trembling, of pushing forward, lest there should be in the camp another Achan; then God spoke to him, either by vision, as before (*ch.* v), as a man of war with his sword drawn, or by the breastplate of judgment. Note, When we have faithfully put away sin, that accursed thing, we may expect to hear from God to our comfort; and God's directing us how to go on in our Christian work and warfare is a good evidence of his being reconciled to us.

I. The encouragement God gives to Joshua to proceed: *Fear not, neither be thou dismayed*, v. 1. Corruptions within the church weaken the hands, and damp the spirits, of her guides and helpers, more than oppositions from without; treacherous Israelites

are to be dreaded more than malicious Canaanites. But God bids Joshua not be dismayed; the same power that keeps Israel from being ruined by their enemies shall keep them from ruining themselves. To animate him, 1. He assures him of success against Ai, tells him it is all his own; but he must take it as God's gift. 2. He allows the people to take the spoil to themselves. Here the spoil was not consecrated to God as that of Jericho.

II. The direction he gives him in attacking Ai. It must not be such a work of time as the taking of Jericho was. Nor was it, as that, to be taken by miracle, but now their own conduct and courage must be exercised; having seen God work for them, they must now bestir themselves. God directs him, 1. To take all the people. 2. To lay an ambush behind the city.

Verses 3–22

We have here an account of the taking of Ai by stratagem. Nothing was dissembled, nothing counterfeited, but a retreat. The enemy ought to have been upon their guard, and to have kept within the defence of their own walls. Common prudence, had they been governed by it, would have directed them not to venture on the pursuit of an army which they saw was so far superior to them in numbers, and leave their city unguarded; but *si populus vult decipi, decipiatur—if the people will be deceived, let them*.

I. There is some difficulty in adjusting the numbers that were employed to effect it. Mention is made (v. 3) of 30,000 that were *chosen and sent away by night*, to whom the charge was given to surprise the city as soon as ever they perceived it was evacuated, v. 4, 7, 8. And yet afterwards (v. 12) it is said, Joshua took 5000 *men and set them to lie in ambush* behind the city, and that *ambush entered the city*, and *set it on fire*, v. 19. Now, 1. Some think there were two parties sent out to lie in ambush, and that Joshua made his open attack upon the city with all the thousands of Israel. But, 2. Others think that all the people were taken only to encamp before the city, and that out of them Joshua chose out 30,000 men to be employed in the action, out of which he sent out 5000 to lie in ambush, which were as many as could be supposed to march *incognito—without being discovered*.

II. Yet the principal parts of the story are plain enough, that a detachment being secretly marched behind the city, on the other side to that on which the main body of the army lay, Joshua, and the forces with him, faced the city; the garrison made a vigorous sally out upon them, whereupon they withdrew, gave ground, and retreated in some seeming disorder towards the wilderness, which being perceived by the men of Ai, they drew out all the force they had to pursue them. This gave a fair opportunity for those that lay in ambush to make themselves masters of the city, whereof when they had given notice by a smoke to Joshua, he, with all his force, returned upon the pursuers, who now, when it was too late, were aware of the snare they were drawn into, and, their retreat being intercepted, they were every man of them cut off.

1. What a brave commander Joshua was. Though an army of Israelites had been repulsed before Ai, yet he resolves to lead them on in person the second time, v. 5. He *went that night into the midst of the valley*, to make the necessary dispositions for an attack. It is the pious conjecture of the learned bishop Patrick that he went into the valley alone, to pray to God. When he had stretched out his spear towards the city (v. 18, a spear almost as fatal and formidable to the enemies of Israel as the rod of Moses was) he never drew back his hand till the work was done. Those that have stretched out their hands against

their spiritual enemies must never draw them back. Joshua conquered by yielding, as if he had himself been conquered; so our Lord Jesus, when he bowed his head and gave up the ghost, seemed as if death had triumphed over him, and as if he and all his interests had been routed and ruined; but in his resurrection he rallied again and gave the powers of darkness a total defeat; he broke the serpent's head, by suffering him to bruise his heel. A glorious stratagem!

2. What an obedient people Israel was. What *Joshua commanded them to do, according to the commandment of the Lord* (v. 8), they did it without murmuring or disputing.

3. What an infatuated enemy the king of Ai was! He did not by his scouts discover those that lay in ambush behind the city, v. 14. From the killing of thirty-six men out of 3000, when Israel made the former attack upon his city, he inferred the total routing of so great an army as now he had to deal with (v. 6): *They flee before us as at the first.* See how the prosperity of fools destroys them and hardens them to their ruin.

4. What a complete victory Israel obtained over them by the favour and blessing of God. Each did his part.

Verses 23–29

We have here an account of the improvement which the Israelites made of their victory over Ai. 1. They put all to the sword. Here it is said (v. 26) that *Joshua drew not his hand back wherewith he stretched out the spear* (v. 18). Some think the spear he stretched out was not to slay the enemies, but to animate and encourage his own soldiers. He kept the inferior post of a standard-bearer, and did not quit it till the work was done. By the spear stretched out, he directed the people to expect their help from God, and to him to give the praise. 2. They plundered the city and took all the spoil to themselves, v. 27. 3. They laid the city in ashes, and left it to remain so, v. 28. Israel must yet dwell in tents, and therefore this city, as well as Jericho, must be burnt. 4. The king of Ai was taken prisoner and hanged, and his dead body thrown at the gate of his own city, *under a heap of stones,* v. 23, 29. It is likely he had been notoriously wicked and vile, and a blasphemer of the God of Israel, perhaps upon occasion of the repulse he had given to the forces of Israel in their first onset.

Verses 30–35

This religious solemnity of which we have here an account comes in somewhat surprisingly in the midst of the history of the wars of Canaan. Here a scene opens of quite another nature; the camp of Israel is drawn out into the field, not to engage the enemy, but to offer sacrifice, to hear the law read, and to say *Amen* to the blessings and the curses. It is a remarkable instance, 1. Of the zeal of Israel for the service of God and for his honour. The business of the war shall stand still, while they make a long march to the place appointed, and there attend this solemnity. The way to prosper is to begin with God, Matt. vi. 33. 2. It is an instance of the care of God concerning his faithful servants and worshippers. Though they were in an enemy's country, as yet unconquered, yet in the service of God they were safe. It was a federal transaction: the covenant was now renewed between God and Israel upon their taking possession of the land of promise, that they might be encouraged in the conquest of it, and might know upon what terms they held it, and come under fresh obligations to obedience. In token of the covenant,

I. They built an altar, and offered sacrifice to God (v. 30, 31), in token of their dedication of themselves to God, as living sacrifices to his honour, in and by a Mediator, who is the altar that sanctifies this gift. This altar was erected on Mount *Ebal.* The curses pronounced on Mount Ebal would immediately have been executed if atonement had not been made by sacrifice. By the sacrifices offered on this altar they did likewise give God the glory of the victories they had already obtained, as Exod. xvii. 15. The altar they built was of rough unhewn stone, according to the law (Exod. xx. 25), for that which is most plain and natural, and least artful and affected, in the worship of God, he is best pleased with.

II. They received the law from God; and this those must do that would find favour with him, and expect to have their offerings accepted. Now here,

1. The law of the ten commandments was written upon stones in the presence of all Israel, as an abridgement of the whole, v. 32. But the stones were plastered, and it was written upon the plaster, Deut. xxvii. 4, 8. It was written, that all might see what it was that they consented to.

2. The blessings and the curses, the sanctions of the law, were publicly read, and the people (we may suppose), according to Moses's appointment, said *Amen* to them, v. 33, 34.

(1) The auditory was very large. [1] The greatest prince was not excused. [2] The poorest stranger was not excluded. This was an encouragement to proselytes, and a happy presage of the kindnesses intended for the poor Gentiles in the latter days.

(2) The tribes were posted, as Moses directed, six towards Gerizim and six towards Ebal. And the ark in the midst of the valley was between them, for it was the *ark of the covenant;* and in it were shut up the close rolls of that law which was copied out and shown openly upon the stones. The covenant was commanded, and the command covenanted. The priests that attended the ark, or some of the Levites that attended them, after the people had all taken their places, and silence was proclaimed, pronounced distinctly the blessings and the curses, as Moses had drawn them up, to which the tribes said *Amen;* and yet it is here only said that they should *bless the people,* for the blessing was that which was first and chiefly intended, and which God designed in giving the law. If they fell under the curse, that was their own fault.

3. The law itself also containing the precepts and prohibitions was read (v. 35), it should seem by Joshua himself.

CHAPTER 9

Here is in this chapter, I. The impolitic confederacy of the kings of Canaan against Israel, ver. 1, 2. II. The politic confederacy of the inhabitants of Gideon with Israel. 1. How it was subtly proposed and petitioned for by the Gibeonites pretending to come from a far country, ver. 3–13. 2. How it was unwarily consented to by Joshua and the Israelites, to the disgust of the congregation when the fraud was discovered, ver. 14–18. 3. How the matter was adjusted to the satisfaction of all sides, by giving these Gibeonites their lives because they had covenanted with them, yet depriving them of their liberties because the covenant was not fairly obtained, ver. 19–27.

Verses 1–2

Hitherto the Canaanites had acted defensively; the Israelites were the aggressors upon Jericho and Ai. But here the kings of Canaan are in consultation to attack Israel, and concert matters for a vigorous effort of their united forces to check the progress of their victorious arms. When they *heard thereof* (v. 1), not only of the conquest of Jericho and Ai, but of the convention of the states of Mount Ebal—when they heard that Joshua, as if he thought himself already completely master of the country, had had all his people together, and had read the laws to them by which they must be governed, and taken their promises to submit to those laws—then they perceived the Israelites were in good earnest, and thought it was high time for them to bestir themselves. Though they were many kings of different nations, Hittites, Amorites, Perizzites, &c., doubtless of different interests, and that had often been at variance one with another, yet they determined, *nemine contradicente—unanimously*, to unite against Israel.

Verses 3–14

I. The Gibeonites desire to make peace with Israel, being alarmed by the tidings they heard of the destruction of Jericho, *v.* 3. Other people heard those tidings, and were irritated thereby to make war upon Israel; but the Gibeonites heard them and were induced to make peace with them. The same sun softens wax and hardens clay. These four united cities (mentioned *v.* 17) seem to have been governed by elders, or senators (*v.* 11), who consulted the common safety more than their own personal dignity. The inhabitants of Gibeon did well for themselves.

II. The method they took to compass it. They knew that all the inhabitants of the land of Canaan were to be cut off, and therefore there was no way of saving their lives from the sword of Israel unless they could, by disguising themselves, make Joshua believe that they came from some very far country, which the Israelites were not commanded to make war upon nor forbidden to *make peace with*, but were particularly appointed to *offer peace to*, Deut. xx. 10, 15. This therefore is the only game they have to play, and observe,

1. They play it very artfully and successfully. Never was any such thing more craftily managed.

(1) They come under the character of ambassadors from a foreign state, which they thought would please the princes of Israel, and make them proud of the honour of being courted by distant countries.

(2) They pretended to have undergone the fatigues of a very long journey, and produced what passed for an ocular demonstration of it. Now they here pretended that their provision, when they brought it from home, was fresh and new, but now it appeared to be old and dry. Their shoes and clothes were worse than those of the Israelites in forty years, and their bread was mouldy, *v.* 4, 5, and again, *v.* 12, 13.

(3) When they were suspected, and more strictly examined as to whence they came, they industriously declined telling the name of their country, till the agreement was settled. [1] The men of Israel suspected a fraud (*v.* 7): "*Peradventure you dwell among us*, and then we may not, we must not, make any league with you." [2] Joshua put the questions to them, *Who are you? and whence come you?* [3] They would not tell whence they came; but still repeat the same thing: *We have come from a very far country*, *v.* 9.

(4) They profess a respect for the God of Israel, the more to ingratiate themselves with Joshua, and we charitably believe they were sincere in this profession: *We have come because of the name of the Lord thy God* (*v.* 9).

(5) They fetch their inducements from what had been done some time before in Moses's reign, the plagues of Egypt and the destruction of Sihon and Og (*v.* 9, 10), but prudently say nothing of the destruction of Jericho and Ai because they will have it supposed that they came from home long before those conquests were made.

(6) They make a general submission—*We are your servants*; and humbly sue for a general agreement—*Make a league with us*, *v.* 11. But,

2. There is a mixture of good and evil in their conduct. (1) Their falsehood cannot be justified, nor ought it to be drawn into a precedent. It is observable that when they had once said, *We have come from a far country* (*v.* 6), they found themselves necessitated to say it again (*v.* 9), and to say what was utterly false concerning their bread, their bottles, and their clothes (*v.* 12, 13), for one lie is an inlet to another, and that to a third, and so on. But, (2) Their faith and prudence are to be greatly commended. Our Lord commended even the unjust steward, because he had done wisely and well for himself, Luke xvi. 8. In submitting to Israel, they submitted to the God of Israel, which implied a renunciation of the god they had served. They did not stay till Israel had besieged their cities; then it would have been too late to capitulate; but when they were at some distance they desired conditions of peace. The way to avoid a judgment is to meet it by repentance. Let us imitate these Gibeonites, and make our peace with God in the rags of humiliation, godly sorrow, and mortification, so our iniquity shall not be our ruin. Let us be servants to Jesus, our blessed Joshua, and make a league with him and the Israel of God, and we shall live.

Verses 15–21

Here is, I. The treaty soon concluded with the Gibeonites, *v.* 15. The thing was not done with much formality, but in short, 1. They agreed to let them live, and more the Gibeonites did not ask. 2. This agreement was made not by Joshua only, but by the princes of the congregation in conjunction with him. 3. It was ratified by an oath; they swore unto them, not by any of the gods of Canaan, but by the God of Israel only, *v.* 19. 4. Nothing appears to have been culpable in all this but that it was done rashly. Making use of their senses only, but not their reason, *they received the men* (as the margin reads it) *because of their victuals*, upon the view and taste of their bread. But *they asked not counsel at the mouth of the Lord*. Joshua himself was not altogether without blame herein. Note, We make more haste than good speed in any business when we stay not to take God along with us, and by the word and prayer to consult him.

II. The fraud soon discovered, by which this league was procured. *A lying tongue is but for a moment*, and truth will be the daughter of time. Within three days they found, to their great surprise, that the cities which these ambassadors had treated for were very near them, but one night's footmarch from the camp at Gilgal, ch. x. 9.

III. The disgust of the congregation at this. They did indeed submit to the restraints which this league laid upon them, and smote not the cities of the Gibeonites, neither slew the persons nor seized the prey; but it vexed them to have their hands thus tied, and they *murmured against the princes* (*v.* 18).

IV. The prudent endeavour of the princes to pacify the discontented congregation doubtless disposed the people to acquiesce.

1. They resolved to spare the lives of the Gibeonites, for so they had expressly sworn to do (*v.* 15), to let them live. (1) The oath was lawful. (2) The oath being lawful, both the princes and the people for whom they transacted were bound by it, bound in conscience, bound in honour to the God of Israel, by whom they had sworn, and whose name would have been blasphemed by the Canaanites if they had violated this oath. The princes would keep their word, [1] Though they lost by it. A citizen of Zion *swears to his own hurt and changes not*, ·Ps. xv. 4. [2] Though the people were uneasy at it, and their discontent might have ended in a mutiny, yet the princes would not violate their engagement to the Gibeonites; we must never be overawed, either by majesty or multitude, to do a sinful thing, and go against our consciences. [3] Though they were drawn into this league by a wile, and might have had a very plausible pretence to declare it null and void, yet they adhered to it. Let this convince us all how religiously we ought to perform our promises, and

make good our bargains; and what conscience we ought to make of our words when they are once given. If a covenant obtained by so many lies and deceits might not be broken, shall we think to evade the obligation of those that have been made with all possible honesty and fairness?

2. Though they spared their lives, yet they seized their liberties, and sentenced them to be *hewers of wood and drawers of water to the congregation, v.* 21. By this proposal the discontented congregation was pacified.

Verses 22–27

The matter is here settled between Joshua and the Gibeonites.

I. Joshua reproves them for their fraud, *v.* 22. And they excuse it as well as they can, *v.* 24. 1. Joshua gives the reproof very mildly: *Wherefore have you beguiled us?* 2. They make the best excuse for themselves, that the thing would bear, *v.* 24. They considered that God's sovereignty is incontestable, his justice inflexible, his power irresistible, and therefore resolved to try what his mercy was, and found it was not in vain to cast themselves upon it. They do not go about to justify their lie, but in effect beg pardon for it, pleading it was purely to save their lives that they did it.

II. Joshua condemns them to servitude, as a punishment of their fraud (*v.* 23), and they submit to the sentence (*v.* 25), and for aught that appears both sides are pleased.

1. Joshua pronounces them perpetual bondmen. Observe how the judgment is given against them. (1) Their servitude is made a curse to them. (2) Yet this curse is turned into a blessing; they must be servants, but it shall be for *the house of my God.* The princes would have them slaves *unto all the congregation* (*v.* 21), but Joshua mitigates the sentence, both in honour to God and in favour to the Gibeonites. Even servile work becomes honourable when it is done for the house of our God and the offices thereof. [1] They were hereby excluded from the liberties and privileges of true-born Israelites. [2] They were hereby employed in such services as required their personal attendance upon *the altar of God in the place which he should choose* (*v.* 27), which would bring them to the knowledge of the law of God. [3] This would be a great advantage to the priests and Levites to have so many, and those mighty men, constant attendants upon them, and engaged by office to do all the drudgery of the tabernacle. A great deal of wood must be hewed for fuel for God's house. And a great deal of water must be drawn for the divers washings which the law prescribed. [4] They were herein servants to the congregation too; for whatever promotes and helps forward the worship of God is real service to the commonwealth. Gibeonites were afterwards called *Nethinim,* men given to the Levites, as the Levites were to the priests (Num. iii. 9), to minister to them in the service of God. [5] This may be looked upon as typifying the admission of the Gentiles into the gospel church.

2. They submit to this condition, *v.* 25. *Do as it seemeth right unto thee.* Accordingly the matter was determined. And thus Israel's bondmen became the Lord's freemen, for his service in the meanest office is liberty, and his work is its own wages. Let us, in like manner, submit to our Lord Jesus, and refer our lives to him. If he appoint us to bear his cross, and draw in his yoke, and serve at his altar, this shall be afterwards neither shame nor grief to us.

Chapter 10

We have in this chapter an account of the conquest of the kings and kingdoms of the southern part of the land of Canaan, as, in the next chapter, of the reduction of the northern parts. In this chapter we have an account, I. Of the routing of their forces in the field, in which observe, 1. Their confederacy against the Gibeonites, ver. 1–5. 2. The Gibeonites' request to Joshua to assist them, ver. 6. 3. Joshua's speedy march under divine encouragement for their relief, ver. 7–9. 4. The defeat of the armies of these confederate kings, ver. 10, 11. 5. The miraculous prolonging of the day by the standing still of the sun, in favour of the conquerors, ver. 12–14. II. Of the execution of the kings that escaped out of the battle, ver. 15–27. III. Of the taking of the particular cities, and the total destruction of all that were found in them. Makkedah, ver. 28. Libnah, ver. 29, 30. Lachish, ver. 31, 32, and the king of Gezer that attempted its rescue, ver. 33. Eglon, ver. 34, 35. Hebron, ver. 36, 37. Debir, ver. 38, 39. And the bringing of all that country into the hands of Israel, ver. 40–42. And, lastly, the return of the army to their headquarters, ver. 43.

Verses 1–6

Joshua and the hosts of Israel were made masters of Jericho by a miracle, of Ai by stratagem, and of Gibeon by surrender, and that was all. Those among them that were impatient of delays, it is probable, complained of Joshua's slowness, and asked why they did not immediately penetrate into the heart of the country, before the enemy could rally their forces. Thus Joshua's prudence, perhaps, was censured as slothfulness, cowardice, and want of spirit. But, 1. Canaan was not to be conquered in a day. God had said that *by little and little* he would drive out the Canaanites, Exod. xxiii. 30. 2. Joshua waited for the Canaanites to be the aggressors.

After Israel had waited awhile for an occasion to make war upon the Canaanites, a fair one offers itself. 1. Five kings combine against the Gibeonites. Adonizedec king of Jerusalem was the first mover and ringleader of this confederacy. It seems he was a bad man, and an implacable enemy to the posterity of that Abraham to whom his predecessor, Melchizedek, was such a faithful friend. *Come,* says he, *and help me, that we may smite Gibeon.* This he resolves to do, either, (1) In policy, that he might retake the city, because it was a strong city, and of great consequence to his country in whose hands it was; or, (2) In passion, that he might chastise the citizens for making peace with Joshua, pretending that they had perfidiously betrayed their country. 2. The Gibeonites send notice to Joshua of the distress and danger they are in, *v.* 6. They think Joshua obliged to help them, (1) In conscience, because they were his servants. (2) In honour, because the ground of their enemies' quarrel with them was the respect they had shown to Israel. When our spiritual enemies set themselves in array against us, and threaten to swallow us up, let us, by faith and prayer, apply to Christ, our Joshua, for strength and succour, as Paul did, and we shall receive the same answer of peace, *My grace is sufficient for thee,* 2 Cor. xii. 8, 9.

Verses 7–14

Here, I. Joshua resolves to assist the Gibeonites, and God encourages him in this resolve. 1. He ascended from Gilgal (*v.* 7), determined to relieve Gibeon. He knew that when they embraced the faith and worship of the God of Israel they came to trust under the shadow of his wings (Ruth ii. 12), and therefore, as his servants, he was bound to protect them. 2. God animated him for his undertaking, (*v.* 8): *Fear not,* that is, (1) "Doubt not of the goodness of thy cause and the clearness of thy call." (2) "Dread not the power of the enemy; *I have delivered them into thy hand.*"

II. Joshua applies himself to execute this resolve, and God assists him in the execution. Here we have,

1. The great industry of Joshua, and the power of God working with it for the defeat of the enemy. In this action, Joshua showed his goodwill in the haste he made for the relief of Gibeon (*v.* 9). Now that things were ripe for execution no man more expeditious than Joshua, who before had seemed slow. He marched all night, resolving not to give sleep to his eyes, nor slumber to his eye-lids, till he

had accomplished this enterprise. Let the *good soldiers of Jesus Christ* learn hence to *endure hardness, in following the Lamb whithersoever he goes,* and not think themselves undone if their religion lose them now and then a night's sleep; it will be enough to rest when we come to heaven. But why needed Joshua to put himself and his men so much to the stretch? Had not God promised him that without fail he would *deliver the enemies into his hand*? It is true he had; but God's promises are intended, not to slacken and supersede, but to quicken and encourage our endeavours. *The Lord discomfited them before Israel.* Israel did what they could, and yet God did all.

2. The great faith of Joshua, and the power of God crowning it with the miraculous arrest of the sun, that the day of Israel's victories might be prolonged, and so the enemy totally defeated. The hailstones had their rise no higher than the clouds, but, to show that Israel's help came from above the clouds, the sun itself, who by his constant motion serves the whole earth, by halting when there was occasion served the Israelites, and did them a kindness. *The sun and moon stood still in their habitation, at the light of thy arrows* which gave the signal, Hab. iii. 11.

(1) Now, *First,* It looked great for Joshua to say, *Sun, stand thou still.* His ancestor Joseph had indeed dreamed that the sun and moon did homage to him; but who would have thought that, after it had been fulfilled in the figure, it should be again fulfilled in the letter to one of his posterity? He bids the sun stand still upon Gibeon, the place of action and the seat of war, intimating that what he designed in this request was the advantage of Israel against their enemies; it is probable that the sun was now declining, and here he mentions the valley of Ajalon, which was near to Gibeon, because there he was at that time. *Secondly,* It was bold indeed to say so before Israel, and argues a very strong assurance of faith.

(2) The wonderful answer to this prayer. No sooner said than done (*v.* 13): *The sun stood still, and the moon staid.* The same God that rules in heaven above rules at the same time on this earth, and, when he pleases, even *the heavens shall hear the earth,* as here. Concerning this great miracle it is here said, [1] *That it continued a whole day,* that is, the sun continued as long again above the horizon as otherwise it would have done. [2] That hereby the people had full time to avenge themselves of their enemies, and to give them a total defeat. Note, Sometimes God completes a great salvation in a little time, and makes but one day's work of it. This is said to be written *in the book of Jasher,* a collection of state-poems, in which the poem made upon this occasion was preserved among the rest. Those words, *Sun, stand thou still upon Gibeon, and thou moon in the valley of Ajalon,* sounding metrical, are supposed to be taken from the narrative of this event as it was found in the book of Jasher. The sun, the eye of the world, must be fixed for some hours upon Gibeon and the valley of Ajalon, as if to contemplate the great works of God there for Israel, and so to engage the children of men to look that way, and to *enquire of this wonder done in the land,* 2 Chron. xxxii. 31. He would hereby convince and confound those idolaters that worshipped the sun and moon and gave divine honours to them, by demonstrating that they were subject to the command of the God of Israel. This miracle signified that in the latter days, when the light of the world was tending towards a night of darkness, the *Sun of righteousness,* even our Joshua, should arise (Mal. iv. 2), give check to the approaching night, and be the true light.

Verses 15–27

The five kings were all routed. And now Joshua thought, his work being done, he might go with his army into quarters, but he soon finds he has more work cut out for him. The victory must be pursued, that the spoils might be divided.

I. The forces that had dispersed themselves must be followed. He directs his men to pursue the common soldiers, as much as might be, to prevent their escaping to the garrisons. The result of this vigorous pursuit was, 1. That a very great slaughter was made of the enemies of God and Israel. And, 2. The field was cleared of them, so that none remained but such as got into fenced cities. 3. *None moved his tongue against any of the children of Israel, v.* 21. This expression intimates, (1) Their perfect safety and tranquillity. They were not threatened by any danger at all after their victory, no, not so much as the barking of a dog. (2) Their honour and reputation; no man had any reproach to cast upon them, nor an ill word to give them.

II. The kings that had hidden themselves must now be called to an account, as rebels against the Israel of God.

1. How they were secured. The cave which they fled to, and trusted in for a refuge, became their prison, in which they were clapped up, till Joshua sat in judgment on them, *v.* 18.

2. How they were triumphed over. Joshua ordered them to be brought forth out of the cave, set before him as at the bar, and their names called over, *v.* 22, 23. And when they either were bound and cast upon the ground, unable to help themselves, or threw themselves upon the ground, humbly to beg for their lives, he called for the general officers and great men, and commanded them to trample upon these kings, and set their feet upon their necks. The thing does indeed look barbarous, thus to insult over men in misery, who had suddenly fallen from the highest pitch of honour into this disgrace. Certainly it ought not to be drawn into a precedent, for the case was extraordinary. (1) God would hereby, by this public act of justice done upon these ringleaders of the Canaanites in sin, possess his people with the greater dread and detestation of those sins of *the nations that God cast out from before them,* which they would be tempted to imitate. (2) He would hereby have the promise by Moses made good (Deut. xxxiii. 29), *Thou shalt tread upon their high places.* (3) He would hereby encourage the faith and hope of his people Israel in reference to the wars that were yet before them. Therefore Joshua said (*v.* 25): *Fear not, nor be dismayed.* [1] "Fear not these things, nor any of theirs." [2] "Fear not any other kings, who may at any time be in confederacy against you, for you see these brought down, whom you thought formidable." (4) He would hereby give a type and figure of Christ's victories over the powers of darkness, and believers' victories through him. All the enemies of the Redeemer shall be *made his footstool,* Ps. cx. 1. Sooner or later we shall see all things put under him (Heb. ii. 8), and *principalities and powers* made a show of, Col. ii. 15.

3. How they were put to death. Joshua smote them with the sword, and then hanged up their bodies till evening, when they were taken down, and thrown *into the cave in which they had hidden themselves, v.* 26, 27. If these five kings had humbled themselves in time, and had begged peace instead of waging war, they might have saved their lives.

Verses 28–43

I. Here is a particular account of the several cities which he immediately made himself master of. 1. The cities of three of the kings whom he had conquered in the field he went and took possession of, Lachish (*v.* 31, 32), Eglon (*v.* 34, 35), and Hebron, *v.* 36, 37. The other two, Jerusalem and Jarmuth, were not taken at this time. 2. Three other cities, and royal cities too, he took: Makkedah (*v.* 28), Libnah (*v.* 29, 30) and Debir, *v.* 38, 39. 3. One king that brought in his forces for the relief of Lachish, Horam king of Gezer, was cut off with all his forces, *v.* 33.

II. The country which was hereby reduced and brought into Israel's hands (*v.* 40–42) lay south of Jerusalem, and afterwards fell, for the most part, to the lot of the tribe of Judah. Observe in his narrative,

1. The great speed Joshua made in taking these cities.

2. The great severity Joshua used towards those he conquered. He gave no quarter to man, woman, nor child, put to the sword *all the souls* (*v.* 28, 30, 32, 35, &c.), *utterly destroyed all that breathed* (*v.* 40), and *left none remaining.* God would hereby, (1) Manifest his hatred of the idolatries and other abominations which the Canaanites had been guilty of. (2) He would hereby magnify his love to his people Israel.

3. The great success of this expedition. The Lord *fought for Israel, v.* 42. They could not have gotten the victory if God had not undertaken the battle.

CHAPTER 11

This chapter continues and concludes the history of the conquest of Canaan; of the reduction of the southern parts we had an account in the foregoing chapter, after which we may suppose Joshua allowed his forces some breathing-time; now here we have the story of the war in the north, and the happy success of that war. I. The confederacy of the northern crowns against Israel, ver. 1–5. II. The encouragement which God gave to Joshua to engage them, ver. 6. III. His victory over them, ver. 7–9. IV. The taking of their cities, ver. 10–15. V. The destruction of the Anakim, ver. 21, 22. VI. The general conclusion of the story of this war, ver. 16–20, 23.

Verses 1–9

We are here entering upon the story of another campaign that Joshua made. In respect of miracles it was inferior to it in glory. The wonders God then wrought for them were to animate and encourage them to act vigorously themselves. Thus the war carried on by the preaching of the gospel against Satan's kingdom was at first forwarded by miracles; but, the war being by them sufficiently proved to be of God, the managers of it are now left to the ordinary assistance of divine grace in the use of the sword of the Spirit, and must not expect hailstones nor the standing still of the sun. In this story we have,

I. The Canaanites taking the field against Israel. They were the aggressors. Note, Sinners bring ruin upon their own heads, so that *God will be justified when he speaks*, and they alone shall bear the blame for ever. Now, 1. Several nations joined in this confederacy, some *in the mountains* and some *in the plains, v.* 2. They here unite against Israel as against a common enemy. Thus are *the children of this world* more unanimous, and therein *wiser, than the children of light.* The oneness of the church's enemies should shame the church's friends out of their discords and divisions and engage them to be one. 2. The head of this confederacy was *Jabin king of Hazor* (*v.* 1). When they had all drawn up their forces together, they were a very great army; they had horses and chariots very many, which we do not find the southern kings had.

II. The encouragement God gave to Joshua to give them the meeting, even upon the ground of their own choosing (*v.* 6): *Be not afraid because of them.* Joshua was remarkable for his courage—it was his master grace, and yet it seems he had need to be again and again cautioned not to be afraid. For his encouragement, 1. God assures him of success, and fixes the hour: *To-morrow about this time.* 2. He appoints him to *hough their horses, hamstring* them, *lame* them, and *burn their chariots*, not only that Israel might not use them hereafter, but they might not fear them now. Let Israel look upon their chariots but as rotten wood designed for the fire, and their horses of war as disabled things, scarcely good enough for the cart.

III. Joshua's march against these confederate forces, *v.* 7. He *came upon them suddenly*, and surprised them in their quarters.

IV. His success, *v.* 8. He obtained the honour and advantage of a complete victory; he smote them and chased them, in the several ways they took in their flight.

V. His obedience to the orders given him, in destroying the horses and chariots (*v.* 9), which was an instance, of his care to keep up in the people the like confidence in God, by taking that from them which they would be tempted to trust too much to. This was *cutting off a right hand.*

Verses 10–14

We have here the same improvement made of this victory as was made of that in the foregoing chapter. 1. The destruction of Hazor is particularly recorded, because in it, and by the king thereof, this daring design against Israel was laid, *v.* 10, 11. 2. The rest of the cities of that part of the country are spoken of only in general, that Joshua got them all into his hands, but did not burn them as he did Hazor, for Israel was to dwell in *great and goodly cities which they builded not* (Deut. vi. 10) and in these among the rest.

Verses 15–23

We have here the conclusion of this whole matter.

I. A short account is here given of what was done in four things:—1. The obstinacy of the Canaanites in their opposition to the Israelites. It is intimated that other cities might have made as good terms for themselves, without ragged clothes and clouted shoes, if they would have humbled themselves, but they never so much as *desired conditions of peace.* To punish them for all their other follies, God left them to this, to make those their enemies whom they might have made their friends. 2. The constancy of the Israelites in prosecuting this war (*v.* 18): *Joshua made war a long time*; some reckon it five years, others seven, that were spent in subduing this land. 3. The conquest of the Anakim at last, *v.* 21, 22. Either this was done as they met with them where they were dispersed, as some think, or rather it should seem the Anakim had retired to their fastnesses, and so were hunted out and cut off at last, after all the rest of Israel's enemies. The mountains of Judah and Israel were the habitations of those mountains of men; but not their height, nor the strength of their caves, nor the difficulty of the passes to them, could secure, no, not these mighty men, from the sword of Joshua. The cutting off of the sons of Anak is particularly mentioned because these had been such a terror to the spies forty years before, and their bulk and strength had been thought an insuperable difficulty in the way of the reducing of Canaan, Num. xiii. 28, 33. Giants are dwarfs to Omnipotence; yet this struggle with the Anakim was reserved for the latter end of the war, when the Israelites had become more expert in the arts of war, and had had more experience of the power and goodness of God. Note, God sometimes reserves the sharpest trials of his people by affliction and temptation for the latter end of their days. Death, that tremendous son of Anak, is the last enemy that is to be encountered; but it is *to be destroyed*, 1 Cor. xv. 26. 4. The end and issue of this long war. The Canaanites were rooted out: *Joshua took all that land, v.* 16, 17. And we may suppose the people dispersed themselves and their families into the countries they had conquered, at least those that lay nearest to the headquarters at Gilgal.

II. That which was now done is here compared with that which had been said to Moses. It is here observed in the close, 1. That all the precepts God had given to Moses relating to the conquest of Canaan were obeyed on the people's part, at least while Joshua lived. Joshua was himself a great commander, and yet nothing was more his praise than his obedience. Joshua, in his zeal for the Lord of hosts, spared neither the idols nor the idolaters. Saul's disobedience, or rather his partial obedience, to the command of God, for the utter destruction of the Amalekites, cost him his kingdom. 2. That all the promises God had given to Moses relating to his conquest were accomplished *on his part, v.* 23. God had promised to drive out the nations before them (Exod. xxxiii. 2; xxxiv. 11), and to *bring them down*, Deut. ix. 3. And now it was done.

CHAPTER 12

This chapter is a summary of Israel's conquests. I. Their conquests under Moses, on the other side Jordan. And here the abridgement of that history, ver. 1–6. II. Their conquests under Joshua, on this side Jordan, westward. 1. The country they reduced, ver. 7, 8. 2. The kings they subdued, thirty-one in all, ver. 9–24. And this comes in here as a preface to the history of the dividing of Canaan, that all that might be put together which they were now to make a distribution of.

Verses 1–6

Joshua, or whoever else is the historian, before he comes to sum up the new conquests Israel had made, in these verses recites their former conquests in Moses's time, under whom they became masters of the great and potent kingdoms of Sihon and Og. Joshua's services and achievements are confessedly great, but let not those under Moses be overlooked and forgotten. Here is, 1. A description of this conquered country (*v.* 1): *From the river Arnon* in the south, to *Mount Hermon* in the north. In particular, here is a description of the kingdom of Sihon (*v.* 2, 3), and that of Og, *v.* 4, 5. Moses had described this country very particularly (Deut. ii. 36; iii. 4, &c.), and this description here agrees with his. King Og is said to dwell at Ashtaroth and Edrei (*v.* 4), probably because they were both his royal cities; he had palaces in both. But Israel took both from him, and made one grave to serve him that could not be content with one palace. 2. The distribution of this country. Moses assigned it to the two tribes and a half, at their request, and divided it among them (*v.* 6), of which we had the story at large, Num. xxxii. The dividing of it when it was conquered by Moses is here mentioned as an example to Joshua what he must do now that he had conquered the country on this side Jordan. Moses, in his time, gave to one part of Israel a very rich and fruitful country, but it was on the outside of Jordan; but Joshua gave to all Israel the holy land, the mountain of God's sanctuary, within Jordan.

Verses 7–24

We have here a breviate of Joshua's conquests.
I. The limits of the country he conquered. It lay between Jordan on the east and the Mediterranean Sea on the west, and extended from Baal-gad near Lebanon in the north to Halak, which lay upon the country of Edom in the south, *v.* 7. The boundaries are more largely described, Num. xxxiv. 2, &c. God had been as good as his word, and had given them possession of all he had promised them by Moses.
II. The various kinds of land that were found in this country, which contributed both to its pleasantness and to its fruitfulness, *v.* 8. There were mountains, not craggy, and rocky, and barren, but fruitful hills, such as put forth *precious things* (Deut. xxxiii. 15). And valleys, not mossy and boggy, but *covered with corn*, Ps. lxv. 13. There were plains, and springs to

water them; and even in that rich land there were wildernesses too, or forests.
III. The several nations that had been in possession of this country—Hittites, Amorites, Canaanites, &c., all of them descended from Canaan, the accursed son of Ham, Gen. x. 15–18. Seven nations they are called (Deut. vii. 1), and so many are there reckoned up, but here six only are mentioned, the Girgashites being either lost or left out, though we find them, Gen. x. 16 and xv. 21. Either they were incorporated with some other of these nations, or, as the tradition of the Jews is, upon the approach of Israel under Joshua they all withdrew and went into Africa.
IV. A list of the kings that were conquered and subdued by the sword of Israel, the kings of Jericho and Ai, the king of Jerusalem and the princes of the south that were in confederacy with him, and then those of the northern association. This shows what a very fruitful country Canaan then was, which could support so many kingdoms.

CHAPTER 13

At this chapter begins the account of the dividing of the land of Canaan among the tribes of Israel by lot. The preserving of this distribution would be of great use to the Jewish nation, who were obliged by the law to keep up this first distribution, and not to transfer inheritances from tribe to tribe, Num. xxxvi. 9. It is likewise of use to us for the explaining of other scriptures: the learned know how much light the geographical description of a country gives to the history of it. In this chapter, I. God informs Joshua what parts of the country that were intended in the grant to Israel yet remained unconquered, ver. 1–6. II. He appoints him, notwithstanding, to make a distribution of what was conquered, ver. 7. III. To complete this account, here is a repetition of the distribution Moses had made of the land on the other side Jordan; in general (ver. 8–14), in particular, the lot of Reuben (ver. 15–23), of Gad (ver. 24–28), of the half tribe of Manasseh, ver. 29–33.

Verses 1–6

I. God puts Joshua in mind of his old age, *v.* 1. 1. It is said that Joshua was *old and stricken in years*, and he and Caleb were at this time the only old men among the thousands of Israel, none except them of all those who were numbered at Mount Sinai being now alive. Joshua had not the same strength and vigour in his old age that Moses had; all that come to old age do not find it alike good. 2. God takes notice of it to him: *God said to him, Thou art old.* (1) As a reason why he should now lay by the thoughts of pursuing the war. As he had entered into the labours of Moses, so let others enter into his, and bring forth the top-stone, the doing of which was reserved for David long after. (2) As a reason why he should speedily apply himself to the dividing of that which he had conquered. That work must be done, and done quickly; he being *old and stricken in years*, and not likely to continue long, let him make this his concluding piece of service to God and Israel.
II. He gives him a particular account of the land that yet remained unconquered, which was intended for Israel, and which, in due time, they should be masters of if they did not put a bar in their own door. Divers places are here mentioned, some in the south, as the country of the Philistines, governed by five lords, and the land that lay towards Egypt (*v.* 2, 3), some westward, as that which lay towards the Sidonians (*v.* 4), some eastward, as all Lebanon (*v.* 5), some towards the north, as that in the entering in of Hamath, *v.* 5.
III. He promises that he would make the Israelites masters of all those countries that were yet unsubdued, though Joshua was old. God will do his own work in his own time (*v.* 6): *I will drive them out.* This promise that he would drive them out from before the children of Israel plainly supposes it as the condition of the promise that the children of Israel must themselves attempt their extirpation, else they could

not be said to be driven out before them; if afterwards Israel, through sloth, or cowardice, sit still and let them alone, they must blame themselves, and not God, if they be not driven out. We must work out our salvation, and then God will work in us and work with us.

Verses 7–33

I. Orders given to Joshua to assign to each tribe its portion of this land, including that which was yet unsubdued.

1. The land must be divided among the several tribes, and they must not always live in common, as now they did.

2. That it must be divided for an inheritance, though they got it by conquest. (1) The promise of it came to them as an inheritance from their fathers; the land of promise pertained to the children of promise. (2) The possession of it was to be transmitted by them, as an inheritance to their children.

3. That Joshua must not divide it by his own will. Though he was a very wise, just, and good man, it must not be left to him to give what he pleased to each tribe; but he must do it by lot, which referred the matter wholly to God, and to his determination. Joshua must have the honour of dividing the land, (1) Because he had undergone the fatigue of conquering it. (2) That he might be herein a type of Christ, who has not only conquered for us the gates of hell, but has opened to us the gates of heaven, and, having purchased the eternal inheritance for all believers, will in due time put them all in possession of it.

II. An account is here given of the distribution of the land on the other side Jordan among the Reubenites, and Gadites, and half the tribe of Manasseh.

1. How this account is introduced. It comes in, (1) As the reason why this land within Jordan must be divided only to the nine tribes and a half, because the other two and a half were already provided for. (2) As a pattern to Joshua in the work he had now to do. (3) As an inducement to Joshua to hasten the dividing of this land, that the nine tribes and a half might not be kept any longer than was necessary out of their possession, since their brethren of the two tribes and a half were so well settled in theirs.

2. The particulars of this account.

(1) Here is a general description of the country that was given to the two tribes and a half, *which Moses gave them, even as Moses gave them, v.* 8. The repetition implies a ratification of the grant by Joshua. Here we have, [1] The fixing of the boundaries of this country, by which they were divided from the neighbouring nations, *v.* 9, &c. Israel must know their own and keep to it. [2] An exception of one part of this country from Israel's possession, though it was in their grant, namely, the Geshurites and the Maachathites, *v.* 13.

(2) A very particular account of the inheritances of these two tribes and a half. This is very fully and exactly set down in order that posterity might, in reading this history, be the more affected with the goodness of God to their ancestors, and also that the limits of every tribe being punctually set down in this authentic record disputes might be prevented.

[1] We have here the lot of the tribe of Reuben, Jacob's first-born, who, though he had lost the dignity and power which pertained to the birthright, yet, it seems, had the advantage of being first served. The separation of this tribe from the rest, by the river Jordan, was that which Deborah lamented; and the preference they gave to their private interests was what she censured, Judges v. 15, 16. In this tribe lay Heshbon and Sibmah, famed for their fruitful fields and vineyards. This tribe, with that of Gad, was sorely shaken by Hazael king of Syria (2 Kings x. 33), and afterwards dislodged and carried

into captivity, twenty years before the general captivity of the ten tribes by the king of Assyria, 1 Chron. v. 26.

[2] The lot of the tribe of Gad, *v.* 24–28. This lay north of Reuben's lot; the country of Gilead lay in this tribe, so famous for its balm and the cities of Jabesh-Gilead and Ramoth-Gilead which we often read of in scripture. Succoth and Penuel, which we read of in the story of Gideon, were in this tribe. Sharon, famous for roses, was in this tribe. And within the limits of this tribe lived those Gadarenes that loved their swine better than their Saviour, fitter to be called *Girgashites* than *Israelites*.

[3] The lot of the half-tribe of Manasseh, *v.* 29–31. Bashan, the kingdom of Og, was in this allotment, famous for the best timber, witness the oaks of Bashan—and the best breed of cattle, witness the bulls and rams of Bashan. This tribe lay north of Gad, reached to Mount Hermon, and had in it part of Gilead. Mizpeh was in this half-tribe, and Jephthah was one of its ornaments; so was Elijah, for in this tribe was Thisbe, whence he is called the Tishbite; and Jair was another. In the edge of the tribe stood Chorazin, honoured with Christ's wondrous works, but ruined by his righteous woe for not improving them.

[4] To the tribe of Levi *Moses gave no inheritance* (*v.* 14, 33), for so God had appointed, Num. xviii. 20. Their habitations must be scattered in all the tribes, and their maintenance brought out of all the tribes, Deut. x. 9; xviii. 2.

CHAPTER 14

Here is, I. The general method that was taken in dividing the land, ver. 1–5. II. The demand Caleb made of Hebron, as his by promise, and therefore not to be put into the lot with the rest, ver. 6–12. And Joshua's grant of that demand, ver. 13–15. This was done at Gilgal, which was as yet their headquarters.

Verses 1–5

The historian now comes to tell us what they did with the countries in the land of Canaan. They were not conquered to be left desert. Canaan would have been subdued in vain if it had not been inhabited. Yet every man might not go and settle where he pleased. God had given Moses directions how this distribution should be made. See Num. xxvi. 53, &c.

I. The managers of this great affair were Joshua the chief magistrate, Eleazar the chief priest, and ten princes, one of each of the tribes, that were now to have their inheritance, whom God himself had nominated (Num. xxxiv. 17, &c.).

II. The tribes among whom this dividend was to be made were nine and a half. Not the tribe of Levi; this was to be otherwise provided for. Joseph made two tribes, Manasseh and Ephraim, pursuant to Jacob's adoption of Joseph's two sons, and so the number of the tribes was kept up to twelve, though Levi was taken out, which is intimated here (*v.* 4).

III. The rule by which they went was the lot, *v.* 2. *The disposal* of that is *of the Lord*, Prov. xvi. 33. It was here used in an affair of weight, and which could not otherwise be accommodated to universal satisfaction, and it was used in a solemn religious manner as an appeal to God, by consent of parties.

Verses 6–15

Before the lot was cast into the lap for the determining of the portions of the respective tribes, the particular portion of Caleb was assigned to him. He was now, except Joshua, not only the oldest man in all Israel, but was twenty years older than any of them, for all that were above twenty years old when he was forty were dead in the wilderness; it was fit therefore that this phoenix of his age should have some particular marks of honour put upon him in the dividing of the land.

I. Caleb here presents his petition, or rather makes his demand, to have Hebron given him for a possession (*this mountain* he calls it, *v.* 12), and not to have that put into the lot with the other parts of the country. To justify his demand, he shows that God had long since, by Moses, promised him *that very mountain*.

1. To enforce his petition, (1) He brings the children of Judah, that is, the heads and great men of that tribe, along with him, to present it. (2) He appeals to Joshua himself concerning the truth of the allegations upon which he grounded his petition: *Thou knowest the thing, v.* 6.

2. In his petition he sets forth,

(1) The testimony of his conscience concerning the spying out of the land. [1] That he made his report as it was in his heart, as we find he did, Num. xiii. 30; xiv. 7–9. He did not do it merely to please Moses, or to keep the people quiet, much less from a spirit of contradiction to his fellows, but from a full conviction of the truth of what he said and a firm belief of the divine promise. [2] That herein he *wholly followed the Lord his God*, and therefore it was not vain-glory in him to speak of it, any more than it is for those who have *God's Spirit witnessing with their spirits* that they are the children of God humbly and thankfully to tell others for their encouragement what God has done for their souls. [3] That he did this when all his brethren and companions in that service, except Joshua, did otherwise.

(2) The experience he had had of God's goodness to him ever since to this day. [1] That he was kept alive in the wilderness, not only notwithstanding the common perils and fatigues of that tedious march, but though all that generation of Israelites, except himself and Joshua, were one way or other cut off by death. With what a grateful sense of God's goodness to him does he speak it! (*v.* 10). *Now behold* (behold and wonder) *the Lord hath kept me alive these forty and five years*, thirty-eight years in the wilderness, through the plagues of the desert, and seven years in Canaan through the perils of war! Note, The longer we live the more sensible we should be of God's goodness to us in keeping us alive, his care in prolonging our frail lives, his patience in prolonging our forfeited lives. [2] That he was fit for business, now that he was in Canaan. Though eighty-five years old, yet as hearty and lively as when he was forty (*v.* 11): *As my strength was then, so is it now*. This was the fruit of the promise, and out-did what was said; for God not only gives what he promises, but he gives more: life by promise shall be life, and health, and strength, and all that which will make the promised life a blessing and comfort.

(3) The promise Moses had made him in God's name that he should have *this mountain, v.* 9. This was the place from which, more than any other, the spies took their report, for here they met with the sons of Anak (Num. xiii. 22), the sight of whom made such an impression upon them, *v.* 33. We may suppose that Caleb, observing what stress they laid upon the difficulty of conquering Hebron, a city garrisoned by the giants, bravely desired to have that city which they called *invincible* assigned to himself for his own portion: "I will undertake to deal with that, and, if I cannot get it for my inheritance, I will be without." He chose this place only because it was the most difficult to be conquered. And, to show that his soul did not decay any more than his body, now forty-five years after he adheres to his choice and is still of the same mind.

(4) The hopes he had of being master of it, though the sons of Anak were in possession of it (*v.* 12): *If the Lord will be with me, then I shall be able to drive them out*. The city of Hebron Joshua had already

reduced (*ch.* x. 37), but the mountain which belonged to it, and which was inhabited by the sons of Anak, was yet unconquered. Here, [1] He seems to speak doubtfully of God's being with him from a humble sense of his own unworthiness. [2] But he expresses without the least doubt his assurance that if God were with him he should be able to dispossess the sons of Anak. Herein Caleb answered his name, which signifies *all heart*.

II. Joshua grants his petition (*v.* 13): *Joshua blessed him*, commended his bravery, applauded his request, and gave him what he asked. Hebron was settled on Caleb and his heirs (*v.* 14), *because he wholly followed the Lord God of Israel*. Hebron had been the city of Arba, a great man among the Anakim (*v.* 15); we find it called *Kirjatharba* (Gen. xxiii. 2), as the place where Sarah died. Hereabouts Abraham, Isaac, and Jacob lived most of their time in Canaan, and near to it was the cave of Machpelah, where they were buried, which perhaps had led Caleb hither when he went to spy out the land, and had made him covet this rather than any other part for his inheritance. It was one of the cities belonging to the priests (Josh. xxi. 13), and a *city of refuge*, Josh. xx. 7. When Caleb had it, he contented himself with the country about it, and cheerfully gave the city to the priests, the Lord's ministers. It was a royal city, and, in the beginning of David's reign, the metropolis of the kingdom of Judah; thither the people resorted to him, and there he reigned seven years.

CHAPTER 15

In this chapter we have the lot of the tribe of Judah, which in this, as in other things, had the precedency. I. The borders or bounds of the inheritance of Judah, ver. 1–12. II. The particular assignment of Hebron and the country thereabout to Caleb and his family, ver. 13–19. III. The names of the several cities that fell within Judah's lot, ver. 20–63.

Verses 1–12

Judah and Joseph were the two sons of Jacob on whom Reuben's forfeited birthright devolved. Judah had the dominion entailed on him, and Joseph the double portion, and therefore these two tribes were first seated, Judah in the southern part of the land of Canaan and Joseph in the northern part.

In these verses, we have the borders of the lot of Judah, which, as the rest, is said to be *by their families*, that is, with an eye to the number of their families. And it intimates that Joshua and Eleazar, and the rest of the commissioners, when they had by lot given each tribe its portion, did afterwards subdivide those larger portions, and assign to each family its inheritance, and then to each household. 1. The eastern border was all, and only, the Salt Sea, *v.* 5. 2. The southern border was that of the land of Canaan in general, as will appear by comparing *v.* 1–4 with Num. xxxiv. 3–5. So that this powerful and warlike tribe of Judah guarded the frontiers of the whole land, on that side which lay towards their old sworn enemies the Edomites. 3. The northern border divided it from the lot of Benjamin. In this, mention is made of *the stone of Bohan* a Reubenite (*v.* 6), who died in the camp at Gilgal, and was buried not far off under this stone. The valley of Achor likewise lies upon this border (*v.* 7), to remind the men of Judah of the trouble which Achan, one of their tribe, gave to the congregation of Israel. This northern line touched closely upon Jerusalem (*v.* 8), so closely as to include in the lot of this tribe Mount Zion and Mount Moriah, though the greater part of the city lay in the lot of Benjamin. 4. The west border went near to the great sea at first (*v.* 12), but afterwards the lot of the tribe of Dan took off a good part of Judah's lot on that side. Judah's inheritance had its boundaries determined.

Verses 13–19

The historian seems pleased with every occasion to make mention of Caleb because he had honoured God.

I. The grant Joshua made him of the mountain of Hebron for his inheritance is here repeated (*v.* 13).

II. Caleb having obtained this grant, we are told,

1. How he signalized his own valour in the conquest of Hebron (*v.* 14): *He drove thence the three sons of Anak*, he and those that he engaged to assist him in this service.

2. How he encouraged the valour of those about him in the conquest of Debir, *v.* 15, &c. It seems, though Joshua had once made himself master of Debir (*ch.* x. 39), yet the Canaanites had regained the possession in the absence of the army, so that the work had to be done a second time; and when Caleb had completed the reduction of Hebron, which was for himself and his own family, to show his zeal for the public good, as much as for his own private interest, he pushes on his conquest to Debir.

The proffer that Caleb made of his daughter, and a good portion with her, to any one that would undertake to reduce that city. Caleb's family was not only honourable and wealthy, but religious. The place was bravely taken by Othniel, a nephew of Caleb, whom probably Caleb had thoughts of when he made the proffer, *v.* 17. Othniel married his cousin-german Achsah, Caleb's daughter. The historian gives us an account of Achsah's portion. Some land she obtained by Caleb's free grant. He *gave her a south land, v.* 19. Land indeed, but *a south land*, dry, and apt to be parched. She obtained more upon her request. When her father brought her home to the house of her husband, she *lighted off her ass*, in token of respect and reverence to her father. She was sure that, since she married not only with her father's consent, but in obedience to his command, he would not deny her his blessing. She asks only for the *water*, without which the ground she had would be of little use either for tillage or pasture, but she means the field in which the springs of water were. Achsah gained her point; her father gave her what she asked, and perhaps more, for *he gave her the upper springs and the nether springs*, two fields so called from the springs that were in them, as we commonly distinguish between the higher field and the lower field.

From this story we learn it is no breach of the tenth commandment moderately to desire those comforts and conveniences of this life which we see attainable in a fair and regular way. Husbands and wives should mutually advise, and jointly agree, about that which is for the common good of their family. Parents must never think that lost which is bestowed upon their children for their real advantage.

Verses 20–63

We have here a list of the several cities that fell within the lot of the tribe of Judah.

I. The cities are here named, and numbered in several classes. Here are, 1. Some that are said to be the uttermost cities *towards the coast of Edom, v.* 21–32. Here are thirty-eight named, and yet said to be *twenty-nine* (*v.* 32), because nine of these were afterwards transferred to the lot of Simeon. 2. Others that are said to be *in the valley* (*v.* 33) are counted to be fourteen, yet fifteen are named; but it is probable that Gederah and Gederathaim were two parts of one and the same city. 3. Then sixteen are named without any head of distinction, *v.* 37–41, and nine more, *v.* 42–44. 4. Then the three Philistine-cities, Ekron, Ashdod, and Gaza, *v.* 45–47. 5. Cities *in the mountains*.

II. Now here, 1. We do not find Bethlehem, which was afterwards the city of David, and was ennobled by the birth of our Lord Jesus in it. But that city was but *little among the thousands of Judah* (Mic. v. 2), except that it was thus dignified. Christ came to give honour to the places he was related to, not to receive honour from them. 2. Jerusalem is said to continue in the hands of the Jebusites (*v.* 63), *for the children of Judah could not drive them out*, through their sluggishness, stupidity, and unbelief. 3. Among the cities of Judah (in all 114) we meet with Libnah, which in Joram's days revolted, and probably set up for a free independent state (2 Kings viii. 22), and Lachish, where king Amaziah was slain (2 Kings xiv. 19); it led the dance in idolatry (Mic. i. 13); it was the *beginning of sin to the daughter of Zion*. Many of the cities of this tribe occur in the history of David's troubles. Adullam, Ziph, Keilah, Maon, Engedi, Ziklag, here reckoned in this tribe, were places near which David had most of his haunts.

CHAPTER 16

It is a pity that this and the following chapter should be separated, for both of them give us the lot of the children of Joseph, Ephraim and Manasseh, who, next to Judah, were to have the post of honour, and therefore had the first and best portion in the northern part of Canaan, as Judah now had in the southern part. In this chapter we have, I. A general account of the lot of these two tribes together, ver. 1–4. II. The borders of the lot of Ephraim in particular, ver. 5–10. That of Manasseh following in the next chapter.

Verses 1–4

Though Joseph was one of the younger sons of Jacob, yet he was his eldest by his most just and best beloved wife Rachel, was himself *his best beloved son*. His posterity were very much favoured by the lot. Their portion lay in the very heart of the land of Canaan. It extended from Jordan in the east (*v.* 1) to the sea, the Mediterranean Sea, in the west, and the fruitfulness of the soil answered the blessings both of Jacob and Moses, Gen. xlix. 25, 26, and Deut. xxxiii. 13, &c. The portions allotted to Ephraim and Manasseh are not so particularly described as those of the other tribes; we have only the limits and boundaries of them, not the particular cities in them.

Verses 5–10

Here, 1. The border of the lot of Ephraim is set down, by which it was divided on the south from Benjamin and Dan, who lay between it and Judah, and on the north from Manasseh; for east and west it reached from Jordan to the great sea. 2. Some separate cities are spoken of, that lay not within these borders, at least not if the line was drawn direct, but lay within the lot of Manasseh (*v.* 9), which might better be read, *and there were separate cities for the children of Ephraim among the inheritance of the children of Manasseh*. 3. A brand is put upon the Ephraimites, that they did not drive out the Canaanites from Gezer (*v.* 10), putting them under tribute. It shows that they spared them out of covetousness, that they might be profited by their labours, and by dealing with them for their tribute they were in danger of being infected with their idolatry; yet some think that, when they brought them under tribute, they obliged them to renounce their idols. Samaria, built by Omri after the burning of the royal palace of Tirzah, was in this tribe, and was long the royal city of the kingdom of the ten tribes; not far from it were Shechem, and the mountains Ebal and Gerizim, and Sychar, near which was Jacob's well, where Christ talked with the woman of Samaria. We read much of Mount Ephraim in the story of the Judges, and of a city called *Ephraim*, it is probable in this tribe, to which Christ retired, John xi. 54. The whole kingdom of the ten tribes is often, in the prophets, especially in Hosea, called *Ephraim*.

CHAPTER 17

The half tribe of Manasseh comes next to be provided for; and here we have, I. The families of that tribe that were to be portioned, ver. 1–6. II. The country that fell to their lot, ver. 7–13. III. The joint request of the two tribes that descended from Joseph, for the enlargement of their lot, and Joshua's answer to that request, ver. 14–18.

Verses 1–6

Manasseh was itself but one half of the tribe of Joseph, and yet was divided and subdivided. 1. It was divided into two parts, one already settled on the other side Jordan, consisting of those who were the posterity of Machir, *v.* 1. This Machir was born to Manasseh in Egypt; there he had signalized himself as a man of war, probably in the contests between the Ephraimites and the men of Gath, 1 Chron. vii. 21. 2. That part on this side Jordan was subdivided into ten families, *v.* 5. Here is, (1) The claim which the daughters of Zelophehad made, grounded upon the command God gave to Moses concerning them, *v.* 4. They had themselves, when they were young, pleaded their own cause before Moses, and obtained the grant of an inheritance with their brethren, and now they would not lose the benefit of that grant for want of speaking to Joshua. (2) The assignment of their portions according to their claim. Joshua knew very well what God had ordered in their case, and did not object that they having not served in the wars of Canaan there was no reason why they should share in the possessions of Canaan, but readily *gave them an inheritance among the brethren of their father*.

Verses 7–13

We have here a short account of the lot of this half tribe. It reached from Jordan on the east to the great sea on the west; on the south it lay all along contiguous to Ephraim, but on the north it abutted upon Asher and Issachar. Some things are particularly observed concerning this lot:—1. That there was great communication between this tribe and that of Ephraim. The city of Tappuah belonged to Ephraim, but the country adjoining to Manasseh (*v.* 8); there were likewise many cities of Ephraim that lay within the border of Manasseh (*v.* 9), of which before, *ch.* xvi. 9. 2. That Manasseh likewise had cities with their appurtenances in the tribes of Issachar and Asher (*v.* 11), God so ordering it, that though every tribe had its peculiar inheritance, which might not be alienated from it, yet they should thus intermix one with another, as became those who, though of different tribes, were all one Israel. 3. That they suffered the Canaanites to live among them, contrary to the command of God, serving their own ends by conniving at them, for they made them tributaries, *v.* 12, 13. The most remarkable person of this half tribe in after-time was Gideon, whose great actions were done within this lot.

Verses 14–18

I. The children of Joseph quarrel with their lot. Joshua makes them know that in the discharge of his office, as a public person, he had no more regard to his own tribe than to any other. Two things they suggest, 1. That they were very numerous, through the blessing of God upon them (*v.* 14): *I am a great people, for the Lord has blessed me*; and we have reason to hope that he that hath sent mouths will send meat. 2. That a good part of that country which had now fallen to their lot was in the hands of the Canaanites, and that they were

formidable enemies, who brought into the field of battle *chariots of iron* (*v.* 16), that is, chariots with long scythes fastened to the sides of them, or the axletree, which made great destruction of all that came in their way, mowing them down like corn.

II. Joshua endeavours to reconcile them to their lot. He owns they were a *great people*, and being two tribes ought to have more than *one lot only* (*v.* 17), but tells them that what had fallen to their share would be a sufficient lot for them both, if they would but work and fight. "If thou hast many mouths to be filled, thou hast twice as many hands to be employed; earn, and then eat." 1. He bids them work for more (*v.* 15): "*Get thee up to the woodcountry*, which is within thy own border, and let all hands be set to work to cut down the trees, rid the rough lands, and make them, with art and industry, good arable ground." Note, Many wish for larger possessions who do not cultivate and make the best of what they have. 2. He bids them fight for more (*v.* 17, 18), when they pleaded that they could not come at the woodlands he spoke of because in the valley between them and it there were Canaanites whom they durst not enter the lists with.

CHAPTER 18

In this chapter we have, I. The setting up of the tabernacle at Shiloh, ver. 1. II. The stirring up of the seven tribes that were yet unsettled to look after their lot, and the putting of them in a method for it, by Joshua, ver. 2–7. III. The distributing of the land into seven lots, by certain men employed for that purpose, ver. 8, 9. IV. The determining of these seven portions to the seven tribes yet unprovided for by lot, ver. 10. V. The particular lot of the tribe of Benjamin, the borders of it, ver. 11–20. And the cities contained in it, ver. 21–28. The other six tribes we shall find well provided for in the next chapter.

Verse 1

In the midst of the story of the dividing of the land comes in this account of the setting up of the tabernacle, which had hitherto continued in its old place in the centre of their camp; but now that three of the four squadrons that used to surround it in the wilderness were broken and diminished, it was time to think of removing the tabernacle itself into a city. Many a time the priests and Levites had taken it down, carried it, and set it up again in the wilderness, according to the directions given them (Num. iv. 5, &c.); but now they must do it for good and all.

I. The place to which the tabernacle was removed, and in which it was set up. It was *Shiloh*, a city in the lot of Ephraim, but lying close upon the lot of Benjamin. This place was pitched upon, 1. Because it was in the heart of the country. It had been in the midst of their camp in the wilderness, and therefore must now be in the midst of their nation. 2. The setting up of the tabernacle in Shiloh gave them a hint that in that Shiloh which Jacob spoke of all the ordinances of this worldly sanctuary should have their accomplishment in a greater and more perfect tabernacle, Heb. ix. 1, 11.

II. The solemn manner of doing it: *The whole congregation assembled together* to attend the solemnity, to do honour to the ark of God, as the token of his presence. It was a good presage of a comfortable settlement to themselves in Canaan, when their first care was to see the ark well settled as soon as they had a safe place ready to settle it in. Here the ark continued about 300 years, till the sins of Eli's house forfeited the ark, lost it and ruined Shiloh, and its ruins were long after made use of as warnings to Jerusalem. *Go, see what I did to Shiloh*, Jer. vii. 12; Ps. lxxviii. 60.

Verses 2–10

I. Joshua reproves those tribes which were yet unsettled that they did not bestir themselves to gain a settlement in the land which God had given them. Joshua reasons (v. 3): *How long are you slack?* 1. They were too well pleased with their present condition. The spoil of the cities they had taken served them to live plentifully upon for the present, and they banished the thoughts of time to come. 2. They were slothful and dilatory. Note, Many are diverted from real duties, and debarred from real comforts, by seeming difficulties. God by his grace has given us a title to a good land, the heavenly Canaan, but we are *slack to take possession*; we enter not into that rest, as we might by faith, and hope, and holy joy; we live not in heaven, as we might by setting our affections on things above and having our conversation there.

II. He puts them in a way to settle themselves.

1. The land that remained must be surveyed, an account taken of the cities, and the territories belonging to them, v. 4. These must be divided into seven equal parts. The Levites were to have no temporal estate. Gad and Reuben, with half of the tribe of Manasseh, were already fixed, and needed not to have any further care taken of them. Now, (1) The surveyors were three men out of each of the seven tribes that were to be provided for (v. 4). (2) The survey was accordingly made, and brought in to Joshua, v. 8, 9. [1] The faith and courage of the persons employed: abundance of Canaanites remained in the land, and all raging against Israel, *as a bear robbed of her whelps.* [2] The good providence of God in protecting them from the many deaths they were exposed to, and bringing them all safely again to the host at Shiloh.

2. When it was surveyed, and reduced to seven lots, then Joshua would, by appeal to God, and direction from him, determine which of these lots should belong to each tribe (v. 6). *That I may cast lots for you here* at the tabernacle (because it was a sacred transaction) *before the Lord our God.*

Verses 11–28

We have here the lot of the tribe of Benjamin, which Providence cast next to Joseph on the one hand, because Benjamin was own and only brother to Joseph, and was little Benjamin (Ps. lxviii. 27), that needed the protection of great Joseph. And it was next to Judah on the other hand, that this tribe might hereafter unite with Judah in an adherence to the throne of David and the temple at Jerusalem. Here we have, 1. The exact borders and limits of this tribe. The western border is said to *compass the corner of the sea southward* (v. 14). Bishop Patrick thinks the meaning is that it ran along in a parallel line to the great sea, though at a distance. 2. The particular cities in this tribe, not all, but the most considerable. Twenty-six are here named. Jericho is put first, though dismantled, and forbidden to be rebuilt as a city with gates and walls. Gilgal, where Israel first encamped when Saul was made king (1 Sam. xi. 15), was in this tribe. It was afterwards a very profane place. Hos. ix. 15, *All their wickedness is in Gilgal.* Beth-el was in this tribe, a famous place.

CHAPTER 19

In the description of the lots of Judah and Benjamin we have an account both of the borders that surrounded them and of the cities contained in them. In that of Ephraim and Manasseh we have the borders, but not the cities; in this chapter Simeon and Dan are described by their cities only, and not their borders, because they lay very much within Judah, especially the former; the rest have both their borders described and their cities named, especially frontiers. Here is, I. The lot of Simeon, ver. 1–9. II. Of Zebulun, ver. 10–16. III. Of Issachar, ver. 17–23. IV. Of Asher, ver. 24–31. V. Of Naphtali, ver. 32–39. VI. Of Dan, ver. 40–48. Lastly, The inheritance assigned to Joshua himself and his own family, ver. 49–51.

Verses 1–9

Simeon's lot was drawn after Judah's, Joseph's, and Benjamin's, because Jacob had put that tribe under disgrace. Not one person of note, neither judge nor prophet, was of this tribe, that we know of. I. The situation of their lot was within that of Judah (v. 1) and was taken from it, v. 9. 1. The men of Judah did not oppose the taking away of the cities again, which by the first distribution fell within their border, when they were convinced that they had more than their proportion. 2. That which was thus taken off from Judah to be put into a new lot Providence directed to the tribe of Simeon. The cities of Simeon were scattered in Judah. This brought them into a confederacy with the tribe of Judah (Judg. i. 3), and afterwards was a happy occasion of the adherence of many of this tribe to the house of David, at the time of the revolt of the ten tribes to Jeroboam.

II. The cities within their lot are here named. Beersheba, or Sheba, for these names seem to refer to the same place, is put first. Ziklag, which we read of in David's story, is one of them.

Verses 10–16

This is the lot of Zebulun, who, though born of Leah after Issachar, yet was blessed by Jacob and Moses before him. 1. The lot of this tribe was washed by the great sea on the west, and by the sea of Tiberias on the east, answering Jacob's prophecy (Gen. xlix. 13), *Zebulun shall be a haven of ships*, trading ships on the great sea and fishing ships on the sea of Galilee. 2. Though there were some places in this tribe which were made famous in the Old Testament, especially *Mount Carmel*, yet it was made much more illustrious in the New Testament; for within the lot of this tribe was Nazareth, where our blessed Saviour spent so much of his time on earth, and that coast of the sea of Galilee on which Christ preached so many sermons and wrought so many miracles.

Verses 17–23

The lot of Issachar ran from Jordan in the east to the great sea in the west, Manasseh on the south, and Zebulun on the north. Places in this tribe were, 1. Jezreel, in which was Ahab's palace, and near it Naboth's vineyard. 2. Shunem, where lived the good Shunamite that entertained Elisha. 3. The river Kishon, on the banks of which, in this tribe, Sisera was beaten by Deborah and Barak. 4. The mountains of Gilboa, on which Saul and Jonathan were slain, which were not far from Endor, where Saul consulted the witch. 5. The valley of Megiddo, where Josiah was slain near Hadad-rimmon, 2 Kings xxiii. 29; Zech. xii. 11.

Verses 24–31

The lot of Asher lay upon the coast of the great sea. We read not of any famous person of this tribe but Anna the prophetess, who was a constant resident in the temple at the time of our Saviour's birth, Luke ii. 36. But close adjoining to this tribe were the celebrated seaport towns of Tyre and Sidon.

Verses 32–39

Naphtali lay furthest north of all the tribes, bordering on Mount Libanus. The city of Leshem, or Laish, lay on the utmost edge of it to the north, and therefore when the Danites had made themselves masters of it, and called it *Dan*, the length of Canaan from north to south was reckoned from Dan to Beersheba. It was in the lot of this tribe, near the waters of Merom, that Joshua fought and routed Jabin, *ch.* xi. 1, &c. In this tribe stood Capernaum and Bethsaida, on the north end of the sea of Tiberias, in which Christ did so many mighty works.

Verses 40-48

Dan, though commander of one of the four squadrons of the camp of Israel, in the wilderness, that which brought up the rear, yet was last provided for in Canaan, and his lot fell in the southern part of Canaan, between Judah on the east and the land of the Philistines on the west, Ephraim on the north and Simeon on the south. Providence ordered this numerous and powerful tribe into a post of danger, as best able to deal with those vexatious neighbours the Philistines, and so it was found in Samson. Japho, or Joppa was in this lot.

Verses 49-51

Here is an account of the particular inheritance assigned to Joshua. 1. He was last served, though the eldest and greatest man of all Israel. In all he did he sought the good of his country, and not any private interest of his own. He was content to be unfixed till he saw them all settled. 2. He had his lot *according to the word of the Lord.* It is probable that, when God by Moses told Caleb what inheritance he should have (*ch.* xiv. 9), he gave the like promise to Joshua. 3. He chose it in Mount Ephraim, which belonged to his own tribe. 4. The *children of Israel* are said to *give it to him* (*v.* 49), which bespeaks his humility, that he would not take it to himself without the people's consent and approbation. 5. It was a city that must be built before it was fit to be dwelt in.

CHAPTER 20

This short chapter is concerning the cities of refuge, which we often read of in the writings of Moses; but this is the last time that we find mention of them, for now that matter was thoroughly settled. Here is, I. The law God gave concerning them, ver. 1–6. II. The people's designation of the particular cities for that use, ver. 7–9. And this remedial law was a figure of good things to come.

Verses 1-6

Many things were by the law of Moses ordered to be done when they came to Canaan and this among the rest, the appointing of sanctuaries for the protecting of those that were guilty of casual murder. It was for the interest of the land that the blood of an innocent person, whose hand only was guilty but not his heart, should not be shed, no, not by the avenger of blood: of this law, which was so much for their advantage, God here reminds them. 1. Orders are given for the appointing of these cities (*v.* 2), Deut. xix. 3. Yet it is probable that it was not done till after the Levites had their portion assigned them, because the cities of refuge were all to be Levites' cities. As soon as ever God had given them cities of rest, he bade them appoint cities of refuge, to which none of them knew but they might be glad to escape. And it intimates what God's spiritual Israel have and shall have, in Christ and heaven, not only rest to repose themselves in, but refuge to secure themselves in. 2. Instructions are given for the using of these cities. The laws in this matter we had before, Num. xxxv. 10, &c., where they were opened at large. It is provided that if upon trial it appeared that the murder was done purely by accident, and not by design, either upon an old grudge or a sudden passion, then the slayer should be sheltered from the avenger of blood in any one of these cities, *v.* 4–6. By this law he was entitled to a dwelling in that city, but was confined to it, as a prisoner at large.

Verses 7-9

We have here the nomination of the cities of refuge in the land of Canaan. 1. They are said to *sanctify* these cities, that is the original word for *appointed*, *v.* 7. Not that any ceremony was used to signify the consecration of them, only they did by a public

act of court solemnly declare them cities of refuge, and as such sacred to the honour of God, as the protector of exposed innocency. 2. These cities (as those also on the other side Jordan) stood in the three several parts of the country, so conveniently that a man might (they say) in half a day reach some one of them from any corner of the country. 3. They were all Levites' cities, which put an honour upon God's tribe, making them judges in those cases wherein divine Providence was so nearly concerned, and protectors to oppressed innocency. If he must be confined, it shall be to a Levite-city, where he may, if he will, improve his time. 4. These cities were upon hills to be seen afar off, for though therefore his way at last was uphill, yet this would comfort him, that he would be in his place of safety quickly. 5. Some observe a significancy in the names of these cities with application to Christ our refuge. *Kedesh* signifies *holy*, and our refuge is the holy Jesus. *Shechem, a shoulder*, and the government is upon his shoulder. *Hebron, fellowship*, and believers are called into the fellowship of Christ Jesus our Lord. *Bezer, a fortification*, for he is a stronghold to all those that trust in him. *Ramoth, high* or *exalted*, for him hath God exalted with his own right hand. *Golan, joy* or *exultation*, for in him all the saints are justified, and shall glory. *Lastly*, Besides all these, the horns of the altar, wherever it was, were a refuge to those who took hold of them, if the crime were such as that sanctuary allowed. This is implied in that law (Exod. xxi. 14), that a wilful murderer shall be taken from God's altar to be put to death.

CHAPTER 21

It had been often said that the tribe of Levi should have "no inheritance with their brethren," no particular part of the country assigned them, as the other tribes had, but it appears, by the provision made for them in this chapter, that they were no losers, by their being dispersed. We have here, I. The motion they made to have their cities assigned them, according to God's appointment, ver. 1, 2. II. The nomination of the cities accordingly out of the several tribes, and the distribution of them to the respective families of this tribe, ver. 3–8. III. A catalogue of the cities, forty-eight in all, ver. 9–42. IV. A receipt entered in full of all that God had promised to his people Israel, ver. 43–45.

Verses 1-8

Here is, I. The Levites' petition presented to this general convention of the states, now sitting at Shiloh, *v.* 1, 2. Observe, 1. They had not their lot assigned them till they made their claim. They build their claim upon a very good foundation, not their own merits nor services, but the divine precept: "*The Lord commanded by the hand of Moses to give us cities,* commanded you to grant them, which implied a command to us to ask them." Note, The maintenance of ministers is not an arbitrary thing, left purely to the good-will of the people, who may let them starve if they please; no, as the God of Israel commanded that the Levites should be well provided for, so has the Lord Jesus, the King of the Christian church, ordained that *those who preach the gospel should live of the gospel* (1 Cor. ix. 14). 2. They did not make their claim till all the rest of the tribes were provided for, and then they did it immediately. They were willing to be served last, and they fared never the worse for it. Let not God's ministers complain if at any time they find themselves postponed in men's thoughts and cares, but let them make sure of the favour of God and the honour that comes from him, and then they may well enough afford to bear the slights and neglects of men.

II. The Levites' petition granted immediately, without any dispute. 1. The children of Israel are said to give the cities for the Levites. God had appointed how many they should be in all, forty-eight. God had appointed, Num. xxxv. 8, *Every one shall give of his cities to the Levites.* It appears by the following catalogue that the cities they gave to the Levites were generally some of the best and most considerable in each tribe. 2. They gave them *at the commandment of the Lord.* 3. When the forty-eight cities were pitched upon, they were divided into four lots, as they lay next together, and then by lot were determined to the four several families of the tribe of Levi. (1) The family of Aaron, who were the only priests, had for their share the thirteen cities that were given by the tribes of Judah, Simeon, and Benjamin, *v.* 4. (2) The Kohathite-Levites (among whom were the posterity of Moses, though never distinguished from them) had the cities that lay in the lot of Dan, which lay next to Judah, and in that of Ephraim, and the half-tribe of Manasseh, which lay next to Benjamin. So those who descended from Aaron's father joined nearest to Aaron's sons. (3) Gershon was the eldest son of Levi, and therefore, though the younger house of the Kohathites was preferred before his, yet his children had the precedency of the other family of Merari, *v.* 6. (4) The Merarites, the youngest house, had their lot last, and it lay furthest off, *v.* 7.

Verses 9–42

Several things may be observed in this account, besides what was observed in the law concerning it, Num. xxxv.

I. That the Levites were dispersed into all the tribes, and not suffered to live all together in any one part of the country. Christ left his twelve disciples together in a body, but left orders that they should in due time disperse themselves, that they might *preach the gospel to every creature.*

II. That every tribe of Israel was adorned and enriched with its share of Levites' cities in proportion to its compass, even those that lay most remote. 1. To show kindness to, as God appointed them, Deut. xii. 19; xiv. 29. 2. To receive advice and instruction from; when they could not go up to the tabernacle, to consult those who attended there, they might go to a Levites' city, and be taught the good knowledge of the Lord. Thus God set up a candle in every room of his house, to give light to all his family.

III. That there were thirteen cities, and those some of the best, appointed for the priests, the sons of Aaron, *v.* 19. Aaron left but two sons, Eleazar and Ithamar, yet his family was now so much increased, and it was foreseen that it would in process of time grow so numerous, as to replenish all these cities. We read in both Testaments of such numbers of priests that we may suppose none of all the families of Israel that came out of Egypt increased afterwards so much as that of Aaron did; and the promise afterwards to the house of Aaron is, *God shall increase you more and more, you and your children,* Ps. cxv. 12, 14.

IV. That some of the Levites' cities were afterwards famous upon other accounts. Hebron was the city in which David began his reign, and in Mahanaim, another Levites' city (*v.* 38), he lay, and had his headquarters when he fled from Absalom. The first Israelite that ever wore the title of king (namely, Abimelech, the son of Gideon) reigned in Shechem, another Levites' city, *v.* 21.

Verses 43–45

We have here the foregoing history summed up.

I. God had promised to give the seed of Abraham the land of Canaan for a possession, and now at last he performed this promise (*v.* 43): *They possessed it, and dwelt therein.*

II. God had promised to give them rest in that land, and now they had rest round about, rest from

their travel through the wilderness, rest from their wars in Canaan. They now dwelt, not only in habitations of their own, but those quiet and peaceable ones. This rest continued till they by their own sin and folly put thorns into their own beds and their own eyes.

III. God had promised to give them victory and success in their wars, and this promise likewise was fulfilled: *There stood not a man before them, v.* 44. Israel's experience of God's fidelity is here upon record, and is an acquittance under their hands to the honour of God, the vindication of his promise which had been so often distrusted, and the encouragement of all believers to the end of the world: *There failed not any good thing,* no, nor *aught* of any good thing (so full is it expressed), *which the Lord had spoken unto the house of Israel,* but in due time *all came to pass, v.* 45.

Chapter 22

Many particular things we have read concerning the two tribes and a half, though nothing separated them from the rest of the tribes except the river Jordan, and this chapter is wholly concerning them. I. Joshua's dismission of the militia of those tribes from the camp of Israel, in which they had served as auxiliaries, during all the wars of Canaan, and their return thereupon to their own country, ver. 1–9. II. The altar they built on the borders of Jordan, in token of their communion with the land of Israel, ver. 10. III. The offence which the rest of the tribes took at this altar, and the message they sent thereupon, ver. 11–20. IV. The apology which the two tribes and a half made for what they had done, ver. 21–29. V. The satisfaction which their apology gave to the rest of the tribes, ver. 30–34.

Verses 1–9

The war being ended, and ended gloriously, Joshua, as a prudent general, disbands his army, who never designed to make war their trade, and sends them home, to enjoy what they had conquered, and to beat their swords into plough-shares and their spears into pruning-hooks; and particularly the forces of these separate tribes, who had received their inheritance on the other side Jordan. Joshua publicly and solemnly in Shiloh gives them their discharge. It was not done till after Shiloh was made the headquarters (*v.* 2), and the land was begun to be divided before they removed from Gilgal, *ch.* xiv. 6.

It is probable that this army of Reubenites and Gadites, which had led the van in all the wars of Canaan, had sometimes made a step over Jordan, for it was not far, to visit their families, but still these two tribes and a half had their quota of troops ready, 40,000 in all, which, whenever there was occasion, presented themselves at their respective posts, and now attended in a body to receive their discharge. So must we stay on earth till our warfare be accomplished, wait for a due discharge, and not anticipate the time of our removal.

I. Joshua dismisses them to the *land of their possession, v.* 4. Those that were first in the assignment of their lot were last in the enjoyment of it.

II. He dismisses them with their pay; for who goes a warfare at his own charge? *Return with much riches unto your tents, v.* 8. "Go," says Joshua, "go home to your tents," that is, "your houses," which he calls *tents,* because they had been so much used to tents in the wilderness. "Go home *with much riches,* not only cattle, the spoil of the country, but silver and gold, the plunder of the cities, and let your brethren whom you go to, who abode by the stuff, have some share of the spoil: *Divide the spoil with your brethren.*"

III. He dismisses them with a very honourable character. 1. For the readiness of their obedience to their commanders, *v.* 2. 2. For the constancy of their affection and adherence to their brethren: *You have not left them these many days.* 3. For the faithfulness of their obedience to the divine law. They had not only done their duty to Joshua and Israel, but, which was best of all, they had made conscience of their duty to God: *You have kept the charge*, or, as the word is, *You have kept the keeping*, that is, "You have carefully and circumspectly kept the *commandment of the Lord your God*, not only in this particular instance of continuing in the service of Israel to the end of the war, but, in general, you have kept up religion in your part of the camp, a rare and excellent thing among soldiers, and where it is worthy to be praised."

IV. He dismisses them with good counsel, not to cultivate their ground, fortify their cities, and, now that their hands were inured to war and victory, to invade their neighbours, and so enlarge their own territories, but to keep up serious godliness among them in the power of it.

V. He dismisses them with a blessing (*v.* 6), particularly the half tribe of Manasseh, to which Joshua, as an Ephraimite, was somewhat nearer akin than to the other two, and who perhaps were the more loth to depart because they left one half of their own tribe behind them, and therefore, bidding often farewell, and lingering behind, had a second dismission and blessing, *v.* 7. Joshua not only prayed for them as a friend, but blessed them as a father in the name of the Lord, recommending them, their families, and affairs, to the grace of God.

Verses 10–20

I. The pious care of the separated tribes to keep their hold of Canaan's religion. In order to this, they built a great altar on the borders of Jordan, to be a witness for them that they were Israelites, and as such *partakers of the altar of* the Lord, 1 Cor. x. 18. When they came to Jordan (*v.* 10) their relation to the church of God, together with their interest in the communion of saints, is that which they are solicitous to preserve, and therefore without delay, immediately they erected this altar, which served as a bridge to keep up their fellowship with the other tribes in the things of God. This altar was very innocently and honestly designed, but it would have been well if, since it had in it an appearance of evil, and might be an occasion of offence to their brethren, they had consulted the oracle of God about it before they did it, or at least acquainted their brethren with their purpose, and given them the same explication of their altar before, to prevent their jealousy, which they did afterwards, to remove it.

II. The holy jealousy of the other tribes for the honour of God and his altar at Shiloh. Notice was immediately brought to the princes of Israel of the setting up of this altar, *v.* 11. And they were soon apprehensive that the setting up of another altar was an affront to the choice which God had lately made of a place to put his name in, and had a direct tendency to the worship of some other God. Now,

1. Their suspicion was very excusable, for it must be confessed the thing, *prima facie*—*at first sight*, looked ill, and seemed to imply a design to set up and maintain a competitor with the altar at Shiloh.

2. Their zeal, upon this suspicion, was very commendable, *v.* 12. They all gathered together, and Shiloh was the place of their rendezvous, because it was in defence of the divine charter lately granted to that place that they now appeared; their resolution was as became a kingdom of priests, who, being devoted to God and his service, did not *acknowledge their brethren* nor *know their own children*, Deut. xxxiii. 9. They would immediately *go up to war against them* if it appeared they had revolted from God, and were in rebellion against him.

3. Their prudence in the prosecution of this zealous resolution is no less commendable. They resolve here not to send forth their armies, to wage war,

till they had first sent their ambassadors to enquire into the merits of the cause, and these men of the first rank, one out of each tribe, and Phinehas at the head of them to be their spokesman, *v.* 13, 14.

4. The ambassadors' management of this matter bespeaks much both of zeal and prudence.

(1) The charge they draw up against their brethren is indeed very high, and admits no other excuse than that it was in their zeal for the honour of God, and was now intended to justify the resentments of the congregation at Shiloh and to awaken the supposed delinquents to clear themselves.

(2) The aggravation of the crime charged upon their brethren is somewhat far-fetched: Is *the iniquity of Peor too little for us? v.* 17. The building of this altar seemed but a small matter, but it might lead to an iniquity as bad as that of Peor, and therefore must be crushed in its first rise.

(3) The reason they give for their concerning themselves so warmly in this matter is very sufficient. They were obliged to it, in their own necessary defence, by the law of self-preservation: "For, if you revolt from God to-day, who knows but to-morrow his judgments may break in upon the *whole congregation* (*v.* 18), as in the case of Achan? *v.* 20. He sinned, and we all smarted for it.

(4) The offer they make is very fair and kind (*v.* 19), that if they thought the land of their possession unclean, for want of an altar, and therefore could not be easy without one, rather than they should set up another in competition with that at Shiloh they should be welcome to come back to the land *where the Lord's tabernacle was*, and settle there, and they would very willingly straiten themselves to make room for them.

Verses 21–29

Their reply to the warm remonstrance of the ten tribes is very fair and ingenuous. They do not retort their charge, nor reproach them for their rash and hasty censures, but give them a soft answer which turns away wrath. They demur not to their jurisdiction, nor plead that they were not accountable to them for what they had done, nor bid them mind their own business, but, by a free and open declaration of their sincere intention in what they did, free themselves from the imputation they were under, and set themselves right in the opinion of their brethren.

I. They solemnly protest against any design to use this altar for sacrifice or offering, and therefore were far from setting it up in competition with the altar at Shiloh, or from entertaining the least thought of deserting that. They had indeed set up that which had the shape and fashion of an altar, but they had not dedicated it to a religious use. To gain credit to this protestation here is,

1. A solemn appeal to God concerning it, with which they begin their defence, intending thereby to give glory to God first, and then to give satisfaction to their brethren, *v.* 22. (1) A profound awe and reverence of God are expressed in the form of their appeal: *The Lord God of gods, the Lord God of gods, he knows.* This brief confession of their faith would help to obviate and remove their brethren's suspicion of them, as if they intended to desert the God of Israel, and worship other gods. (2) It is a great confidence of their own integrity which they express in the matter of their appeal. Nothing but a clear conscience would have thus imprecated divine justice to avenge the rebellion if there had been any.

2. A sober apology presented to their brethren: *Israel, he shall know.*

3. A serious abjuration or renunciation of the design which they were suspected to be guilty of. With this they conclude their defence (*v.* 29): "*God forbid that we should rebel against the Lord. We have as*

great a value and veneration for the altar of the Lord at Shiloh as any of the tribes of Israel have, and are as firmly resolved to adhere to it and constantly to attend it; we have the same concern that you have for the purity of God's worship and the unity of his church; far be it, far be it from us, to think of turning away from following God."

II. They fully explain their true intent and meaning in building this altar. In their vindication, they make it out that the building of this altar was so far from being a step towards a separation from their brethren, and from the altar of the Lord at Shiloh, that, on the contrary, it was really designed for a pledge and preservative of their communion with their brethren and with the altar of God, and a token of their resolution to *do the service of the Lord before him* (v. 27), and to continue to do so.

1. They gave an account of the fears they had lest, in process of time, their posterity, being seated at such a distance from the tabernacle, should be looked upon and treated as strangers to the commonwealth of Israel (v. 24). Those that are cut off from public ordinances are likely to lose all religion, and will by degrees cease from fearing the Lord. Though the form and profession of godliness are kept up by many without the life and power of it, yet the life and power of it will not long be kept up without the form and profession. You take away grace if you take away the means of grace.

2. The project they had to prevent this, v. 26-28. "Therefore, to secure an interest in the altar of God to those who shall come after us, and to prove their title to it, *we said, Let us build an altar, to be a witness between us and you*," that, having this copy of the altar in their custody, it might be produced as an evidence of their right to the privileges of the original.

Verses 30-34

We have here the good issue of this controversy, which, if there had not been on both sides a disposition to peace, as there was on both sides a zeal for God, might have been of ill consequence; for quarrels about religion, for want of wisdom and love, often prove the most fierce and most difficult to be accommodated.

I. The ambassadors were exceedingly pleased when the separate tribes had given in a protestation of the innocency of their intentions in building this altar. 1. The ambassadors did not call in question their sincerity in that protestation. 2. They did not upbraid them with the rashness and unadvisedness of this action. 3. Much less did they go about to fish for evidence to make out their charge, because they had once exhibited it, but were glad to have their mistake rectified, and were not at all ashamed to own it. Proud and peevish spirits, when they have passed an unjust censure upon their brethren, though ever so much convincing evidence be brought of the injustice of it, will stand to it, and can by no means be persuaded to retract it.

II. The congregation was abundantly satisfied when their ambassadors reported to them their brethren's apology for what they had done.

III. The separate tribes were gratified, and, since they had a mind to preserve among them this pattern of the altar of God, though there was not likely to be that occasion for it which they fancied, yet Joshua and the princes let them have their humour, and did not give orders for the demolishing of it. Only care was taken that they having explained the meaning of their altar, that it was intended for no more than a testimony of their communion with the altar at Shiloh, this explanation should be recorded, by giving a name to it signifying so much (v. 34); they called it *Ed, a witness* to that, and no more, a witness of the relation they stood in to God and Israel.

CHAPTER 23

In this and the following chapter we have two farewell sermons, which Joshua preached to the people of Israel a little before his death. Had he designed to gratify the curiosity of succeeding ages, he would rather have recorded the method of Israel's settlement in their new conquests, but that which he intended in the registers of this book was to entail on posterity a sense of religion and their duty to God; and therefore, he here transmits to his reader the methods he took to persuade Israel to be faithful to their covenant with their God. In this chapter we have, I. A convention of the states called (ver. 1, 2). II. Joshua's speech to them at the opening, or perhaps at the concluding, of the sessions, to hear which was the principal design of their coming together. In it, 1. Joshua reminds them of what God had done for them (ver. 3, 4, 9, 14), and what he was ready to do yet further, ver. 5, 10. 2. He exhorts them carefully and resolutely to persevere in their duty to God, ver. 6, 8, 11. III. He cautions them against all familiarity with their idolatrous neighbours, ver. 7. IV. He gives them fair warning of the fatal consequences of it, if they should revolt from God and turn to idols, ver. 12, 13, 15, 16.

Verses 1-10

As to the date of this edict of Joshua,

I. No mention at all is made of the place where this general assembly was held; some think it was at Timnath-serah, Joshua's own city, where he lived, and whence, being old, he could not well remove. It is more probable this meeting was at Shiloh, where the tabernacle of meeting was.

II. There is only a general mention of the time when this was done. It was *long after the Lord had given them rest*, but it is not said how long, v. 1. It was, 1. So long as that Israel had time to feel the comforts of their rest and possessions in Canaan, and to enjoy the advantages of that good land. 2. So long as that Joshua had time to observe which way their danger lay of being corrupted, namely, by their intimacy with the Canaanites that remained, against which he is therefore careful to arm them.

III. The persons to whom Joshua made this speech: *To all Israel, even their elders, &c.* So it might be read, v. 2.

IV. Joshua's circumstances when he gave them this charge: He *was old and stricken in age* (v. 1), probably it was in the last year of his life, and he lived to be 110 years old, *ch.* xxiv. 29. *I am old and stricken in age.* He uses it, 1. As an argument with himself to give them this charge, because being old he could expect to be but a little while with them, to advise and instruct them. 2. As an argument with them to give heed to what he said. He was old and experienced, and he had grown old in their service, and had spent himself for their good, and therefore was to be the more regarded by them.

V. The discourse itself.

1. He puts them in mind of the great things God had done for them, now in his days. For the proof of this he appeals to their own eyes (v. 3): "*You have seen all that the Lord your God has done*; not what I have done, or what you have done but what God himself has done by me and for you." (1) Many great and mighty nations (as the rate of nations then went) were driven out from as fine a country as any was at that time upon the face of the earth, to make room for Israel. (2) They were not only driven out, they were subdued before them, which made the possessing of their land so much the more glorious. (3) They had not only conquered the Canaanites, but were put in full possession of their land (v. 4).

2. He assures them of God's readiness to carry on and complete this glorious work in due time. He tells them what little need they had to be in care about the numbers of their forces (v. 10): *One man of you shall chase a thousand*, as Jonathan did, 1 Sam. xiv. 13. "The Lord your God, *he it is that fighteth for you*; and how many do you reckon him for?"

3. He hereupon most earnestly charges them to adhere to their duty, to go on and persevere in the

good ways of the Lord wherein they had so well set out. He exhorts them,

(1) To be very courageous (v. 6): "God fighteth for you against your enemies, do you therefore *behave yourselves valiantly* for him."

(2) To be very cautious. [1] They must not acquaint themselves with idolaters, nor come among them to visit them or be present at any of their feasts or entertainments, for they could not contract any intimacy nor keep up any conversation with them, without danger of infection. [2] They must not show the least respect to any idol, nor *make mention of the name of their gods*, but endeavour to bury the remembrance of them in perpetual oblivion, that the worship of them may never be revived. [3] They must not countenance others in showing respect to them. They must not only not swear by them themselves, but they must not cause others to swear by them, which supposes that they must not make any covenants with idolaters, because they, in the confirming of their covenants, would swear by their idols; never let Israelites admit such an oath.

(3) To be very constant (v. 8): *Cleave unto the Lord your God*, that is, "delight in him, depend upon him, devote yourselves to his glory, and continue to do so to the end."

Verses 11–16

Here, I. Joshua directs them what to do, that they might persevere in religion, v. 11. Would we cleave to the Lord, and not forsake him, 1. We must always stand upon our guard, for many a precious soul is lost and ruined through carelessness: "Take heed therefore, *take good heed to yourselves*, to your *souls* (so the word is). 2. What we do in religion we must do from a principle of love, not by constraint or from a slavish fear of God, but of choice and with delight. "*Love the Lord your God,* and you will not leave him."

II. He urges God's fidelity to them as an argument why they should be faithful to him (v. 14): "*I am going the way of all the earth,* I am old and dying. Now that I am near my end it is proper to look back upon the years that are past; you know that *not one thing hath failed of all the good things which the Lord spoke concerning you*" (and he spoke a great many); see *ch.* xxi. 45.

III. He gives them fair warning what would be the fatal consequences of apostasy (v. 12, 13, 15, 16): "If you go back, know for a certainty it will be your ruin."

1. How he describes the apostasy which he warns them against. The first step would be (v. 12) growing intimate with idolaters. The next step would be intermarrying with them. And the consequence of that would be (v. 16) *serving other gods* (which were pretended to be the ancient deities of the country) and bowing down to them.

2. How he describes the destruction which he warns them of. He tells them, (1) That these remainders of the Canaanites would be snares and traps to them, both to draw them to sin and also to draw them into foolish bargains, unprofitable projects, and all manner of inconveniences. (2) That the anger of the Lord would be kindled against them. Their making leagues with the Canaanites would not only give those idolaters the opportunity of doing them a mischief, and be the fostering of snakes in their bosoms, but it would likewise provoke God to become their enemy, and would kindle the fire of his displeasure against them. (3) That all the threatenings of the word would be fulfilled, as the promise had been, for the God of eternal truth is faithful to both (v. 15): "*As all good things have come upon you* according to the promise, so long as you have kept close to God, so all evil things will come upon you according to the threatening, if you forsake him."

CHAPTER 24

This chapter concludes the life and reign of Joshua, in which we have, I. The great care and pains he took to confirm the people of Israel in the true faith and worship of God, that they might, after his death, persevere therein. In order to this he called another general assembly of the heads of the congregation of Israel (ver. 1) and dealt with them. 1, By way of narrative, recounting the great things God had done for them and their fathers, ver. 2–13. 2. By way of charge to them, in consideration thereof, to serve God, ver. 14. 3. By way of treaty with them, wherein he aims to bring them, (1) To make religion their deliberate choice; and they did so, with reasons for their choice, ver. 15–18. (2) To make it their determinate choice, and to resolve to adhere to it, ver. 19–24. 4. By way of covenant upon that treaty, ver. 25–28. II. The conclusion of this history, with, 1. The death and burial of Joshua (ver. 29, 30) and Eleazar (ver. 33), and the mention of the burial of Joseph's bones upon that occasion, ver. 32. 2. A general account of the state of Israel at that time, ver. 31.

Verses 1–14

Joshua thought he had taken his last farewell of Israel in the solemn charge he gave them in the foregoing chapter, when he said, *I go the way of all the earth;* but God graciously continuing his life longer than expected, he was desirous to improve it for the good of Israel. He summons them together again, that he might try what more he could do to engage them for God.

I. The place appointed for their meeting is *Shechem*, not only because that lay nearer to Joshua than Shiloh, and therefore more convenient now that he was infirm and unfit for travelling, but because it was the place where Abraham, the first trustee of God's covenant with this people, settled at his coming to Canaan, and where God appeared to him (Gen. xii. 6, 7), and near which stood Mounts Gerizim and Ebal, where the people had renewed their covenant with God at their first coming into Canaan, Josh. viii. 30.

II. They presented themselves not only before Joshua, but before God, in this assembly. Joshua ordered the ark of God to be brought by the priests to Shechem, which, they say, was about ten miles from Shiloh, and to be set down in the place of their meeting, which is therefore called (v. 26) *the sanctuary of the Lord*, the presence of the ark making it so at that time. We have not now any such sensible tokens of the divine presence, but are to believe that *where two or three are gathered together* in Christ's name he is as really in the midst of them as God was where the ark was, and they are indeed presenting themselves before him.

III. Joshua spoke to them in God's name, and as from him, in the language of a prophet (v. 2): "*Thus saith the Lord.*" Note, The word of God is to be received by us as his, whoever is the messenger that brings it, whose greatness cannot add to it, nor his meanness diminish from it.

1. The doctrinal part is a history of the great things God had done for his people, and for their fathers before them. (1) He brought Abraham out of Ur of the Chaldees, v. 2, 3. Abraham, who afterwards was the friend of God and the great favourite of heaven, was bred up in idolatry, and lived long in it, till God by his grace snatched him as a brand out of that burning. Hence Abraham's justification is made by the apostle an instance of God's *justifying the ungodly*, Rom. iv. 5. (2) He brought him to Canaan, and built up his family, led him through the land to Shechem, where they now were, multiplied his seed by Ishmael, who begat twelve princes, but at last gave him Isaac the promised son, and in him multiplied his seed. When Isaac had two sons, Jacob and Esau, God provided for Esau elsewhere in Mount Seir, that the land of Canaan might be reserved entire for the seed of Jacob, and the posterity of Esau might not pretend to a share in it. (3) He delivered the seed of Jacob out of Egypt with a high hand (v. 5, 6), and rescued them out of the hands of

Pharaoh and his host at the Red Sea, *v.* 6, 7. The same waters were the Israelites' guard and the Egyptians' grave, and this in answer to prayer; for, though we find in the story that they in that distress murmured against God (Exod. xiv. 11, 12), notice is here taken of their *crying to God*; he graciously accepted those that prayed to him, and overlooked the folly of those that quarrelled with him. (4) He protected them in the wilderness, where they are here said, not to *wander*, but to *dwell for a long season, v.* 7. (5) He gave them the land of the Amorites, on the other side Jordan (*v.* 8), and there defeated the plot of Balak and Balaam against them, so that Balaam could not curse them as he desired, and therefore Balak durst not fight them as he designed, and as, because he designed it, he is here said to have done it. (6) He brought them safely and triumphantly into Canaan, delivered the Canaanites into their hand (*v.* 11), *sent hornets before them*, when they were actually engaged in battle with the enemy, which with their stings tormented them and with their noise terrified them, so that they became a very easy prey to Israel. *Lastly,* They were now in the peaceable possession of a good land, and lived comfortably upon the fruit of other people's labours, *v.* 13.

2. The application of this history of God's mercies to them is by way of exhortation to fear and serve God, in gratitude for his favour, and that it might be continued to them, *v.* 14. It should seem by this charge, which is repeated (*v.* 23), that there were some among them that privately kept in their closets the images or pictures of these dunghill-deities, which came to their hands from their ancestors, as heir-looms of their families, though, it may be, they did not worship them; these Joshua earnestly urges them to throw away: "Deface them, destroy them, lest you be tempted to serve them."

Verses 15–28

Never was any treaty carried on with better man-agement, nor brought to a better issue, than this of Joshua with the people, to engage them to serve God.

I. Would it be any obligation upon them if they made the service of God their choice?—he here puts them to their choice, because it would have a great influence upon their perseverance in religion if they embraced it with the reason of men and with the resolution of men. These two things he here brings them to.

1. He brings them to embrace their religion ration-ally and intelligently, for it is a reasonable service. Accordingly,

(1) Joshua fairly puts the matter to their choice, *v.* 15. Here, [1] He proposes the candidates that stand for the election. The Lord, Jehovah, on one side, and on the other side either the gods of their ancestors, or the *gods of their neighbours*, the Amorites, *in whose land they dwelt*, which would insinuate them-selves into the affections of those that were com-plaisant and fond of good fellowship. [2] He supposes there were those to whom, upon some account or other, it would *seem evil to serve the Lord*. There are prejudices and objections which some people raise against religion. It seems evil to them, hard and unreasonable, to be obliged to deny themselves, mortify the flesh, take up their cross, &c. [3] He refers it to themselves: "*Choose you whom you will serve*, choose this day, now that the matter is laid thus plainly before you, speedily bring it to a head, and do not stand hesitating." Elijah, long after this, referred the decision of the controversy between Jehovah and Baal to the consciences of those with whom he was treating, 1 Kings xviii. 21. Joshua's putting the matter here to this issue plainly intimates two things:—*First,* That it is the will of God we should

every one of us make religion our serious and de-liberate choice. *Secondly,* That religion has so much self-evident reason and righteousness on its side that it may safely be referred to every man that allows himself a free thought either to choose or refuse it; for the merits of the cause are so plain that no con-siderate man can do otherwise but choose it. [4] He directs their choice in this matter by an open declara-tion of his own resolutions: "*But as for me and my house*, whatever you do, *we will serve the Lord*, and I hope you will all be of the same mind."

(2) The matter being thus put to their choice, they immediately determine it by a free, rational, and in-telligent declaration, for the God of Israel, against all competitors whatsoever, *v.* 16–18. *We will also serve the Lord* (*v.* 18). They give very substantial reasons for their choice, to show that they did not make it purely in compliance to Joshua, but from a full conviction of the reasonableness and equity of it.

2. He brings them to embrace their religion reso-lutely, and to express a full purpose of heart to cleave to the Lord. Now that he has them in a good mind he follows his blow, and drives the nail to the head, that it might, if possible, be a nail in a sure place. Fast bind, fast find.

(1) In order to this he sets before them the difficulties of religion, and that in it which might be thought discouraging (*v.* 19, 20): *You cannot serve the Lord, for he is a holy God. He will not forgive*, And, *if you forsake him, he will do you hurt*. Certainly Joshua does not intend hereby to deter them from the service of God as impracticable and dangerous. But, [1] He perhaps intends to represent here the suggestions of seducers, who tempted Israel from their God, with insinuations that he was a hard master, his work impossible to be done, and he not to be pleased. It is probable that this was then commonly objected against the Jewish religion. Or, [2] He thus expresses his godly jealousy over them, and his fear concern-ing them, that, notwithstanding the profession they now made of zeal for God and his service, they would afterwards draw back. Or, [3] He resolves to let them know the worst of it. "*You cannot serve the Lord*, except you put away all other gods." Thus, though our Master has assured us that *his yoke is easy*, yet lest we should grow remiss and careless, he has also told us that the gate is strait, and the way narrow, that leads to life, that we may therefore strive to enter, and not seek only. Or, [4] Joshua thus urges on them the seeming discouragements which lay in their way, that he might sharpen their resolutions.

(2) Notwithstanding this statement of the difficulties of religion, they declare a firm and fixed resolution to continue and persevere therein (*v.* 21): "*Nay, but we will serve the Lord.*"

II. The service of God being thus made their deliberate choice, Joshua binds them to it by a solemn covenant, *v.* 25. Moses had twice publicly ratified this covenant between God and Israel, at Mount Sinai (Exod. xxiv.) and in the plains of Moab, Deut. xxix. 1. Joshua had likewise done it once (*ch.* viii. 31, &c.) and now the second time. Now to give it the formalities of a covenant, 1. He calls witnesses, no other than themselves (*v.* 22): *You are witnesses that you have chosen the Lord.* 2. He put it in writing, and inserted it, as we find it here, in the sacred canon: He *wrote it in the book of the law* (*v.* 26). He *set up a great stone under an oak*, as a monument of this covenant, and perhaps wrote an inscription upon it (by which stones are made to speak) signifying the intention of it.

Verses 29–33

We have here, 1. The burial of Joseph, *v.* 32. He died about 200 years before in Egypt, but *gave commandment concerning his bones,* that they should not rest in their grave until Israel had rest in the land of promise; now therefore the children of Israel, who had brought this coffin full of bones with them out of Egypt, carried it along with them in all their marches through the wilderness and kept it in their camp till Canaan was perfectly reduced. Now at last they deposited his bones in that piece of ground which his father gave him near Shechem, Gen. xlviii. 22. Probably the sermon in this chapter served both for Joseph's funeral sermon and his own farewell sermon. 2. The death and burial of Joshua, *v.* 29, 30. He is here called the *servant of the Lord,* the same title that was given to Moses (*ch.* i. 1) when mention was made of his death. Joshua's burying-place is here said to be *on the north side of the hill Gaash,* or the *quaking hill*; the Jews say it was so called because it trembled at the burial of Joshua, to upbraid the people of Israel with their stupidity in that they did not lament the death of that great and good man as they ought to have done. 3. The death and burial of Eleazar the chief priest, who, it is probable, died about the same time that Joshua did, as Aaron in the same year with Moses, *v.* 33. He was buried in a hill that pertained to Phinehas his son. 4. A general idea given us of the state of Israel at this time, *v.* 31. While Joshua lived, religion was kept up among them under his care and influence; but soon after he and his contemporaries died it went to decay. How well is it for the gospel church that Christ, our Joshua, is still with it, by his Spirit, and will be always, even *unto the end of the world*!

AN EXPOSITION OF
THE BOOK OF JUDGES

This is called in the Hebrew *Shepher Shoptim*, the *Book of Judges*, which the Syriac and Arabic versions enlarge upon, and call it, *The Book of the Judges of the Children of Israel*. The LXX. entitles it only Κριταί, *Judges*. It is the history of the *commonwealth of Israel*, during the government of the judges from Othniel to Eli. It contains the history (according to Dr. Lightfoot's computation) of 299 years, reckoning to Othniel of Judah forty years, to Ehud of Benjamin eighty years, to Barak of Naphtali forty years, to Gideon of Manasseh forty years, to Abimelech his son three years, to Tola of Issachar twenty-three, to Jair of Manasseh twenty-two, to Jephtha of Manasseh six, to Ibzan of Judah seven, to Elon of Zebulun ten, to Abdon of Ephraim eight, to Samson of Dan twenty, in all 299. The judges here appear to have been of eight several tribes; that honour was thus diffused, until at last it centred in Judah. Eli and Samuel, the two judges that fall not within this book, were of Levi. It seems, there was no judge of Reuben or Simeon, Gad or Asher. The history of these judges in their order we have in this book to the end of *ch.* xvi. And then in the last five chapters we have an account of some particular memorable events which happened, as the story of Ruth did (Ruth i. 1) *in the days when the Judges ruled*, but it is not certain in which judge's days. Now as to the state of the commonwealth of Israel during this period, I. They do not appear here either so great or so good as one might have expected the character of such a peculiar people would be, that were governed by such laws and enriched by such promises. We find them wretchedly corrupted, and wretchedly oppressed by their neighbours about them. Yet, II. We may hope that though the historian in this book enlarges most upon their provocations and grievances, yet there was a face of religion upon the land; and, however there were those among them that were drawn aside to idolatry, yet the tabernacle-service, according to the law of Moses, was kept up, and there were many that attended it. III. It should seem that in these times each tribe had very much its government in ordinary within itself, and acted separately, without one common head, or council, which occasioned many differences among themselves, and kept them from being or doing anything considerable. IV. The government of the judges was not constant, but occasional when it is said that after Ehud's victory *the land rested eighty years*, and after Barak's *forty*, it is not certain that they lived, much less that they governed, so long; but they and the rest were raised up and animated by the Spirit of God to do particular service to the public when there was occasion, to *avenge Israel of their enemies* and to purge Israel of their idolatries, which are the two things principally meant by their judging Israel. Yet Deborah, as a prophetess, was attended for judgment by all Israel, before there was occasion for her agency in war, *ch.* iv. 4. V. During the government of the judges, God was in a more especial manner Israel's king; so Samuel tells them when they were resolved to throw off this form of government, 1 Sam. xii. 12. Four of the judges of Israel are canonized (Heb. xi. 32), Gideon, Barak, Samson, and Jephtha. The learned bishop Patrick thinks the prophet Samuel was the penman of this Book.

CHAPTER 1

This chapter gives us a particular account what sort of progress the several tribes of Israel made in the reducing of Canaan after the death of Joshua. He did (as we say) break the neck of that great work, and put it into such a posture that they might easily have perfected it in due time, if they had not been wanting to themselves; wherein they came short, we are told. I. The united tribes of Judah and Simeon did bravely. 1. God appointed Judah to begin, ver. 1, 2. 2. Judah took Simeon to act in conjunction with him, ver. 3. 3. They succeeded in their enterprises against Bezek (ver. 4–7), Jerusalem (ver. 8), Hebron and Debir (ver. 9–15), Hormah, Gaza, and other places, ver. 17–19. 4. Yet where there were chariots of iron their hearts failed them, ver. 19. Mention is made of the Kenites settling among them, ver. 16. II. The other tribes, in comparison with these, acted a cowardly part. 1. Benjamin failed, ver. 21. 2. The house of Joseph did well against Beth-el (ver. 22–26), but in other places did not improve their advantages, nor Manasseh (ver. 27, 28), nor Ephraim, ver. 29. 3. Zebulun spared the Canaanites, ver. 30. 4. Asher truckled worse than any of them to the Canaanites, ver. 31, 32. 5. Naphtali was kept out of the full possession of several of his cities, ver. 33. 6. Dan was straitened by the Amorites, ver. 34–36. No account is given of Issachar, nor of the two tribes and a half on the other side of Jordan.

Verses 1–8

I. The children of Israel consult the oracle of God for direction which of all the tribes should first attempt to clear their country of the Canaanites. The question they ask is, *Who shall go up first? v.* 1. By this time, we may suppose, they were so multiplied that the places they were in possession of began to be too strait for them. Whether each tribe was ambitious of being first, and so strove for the honour of it, or whether each was afraid of being first, and so strove to decline it, does not appear.

II. God appointed that Judah should go up first, and promised him success (*v.* 2): "*I have delivered the land into his hand*, to be possessed, and therefore will

deliver the enemy that keeps him out of possession, into his hand, to be destroyed." And why must Judah be first in this undertaking? 1. Judah was the most numerous and powerful tribe. 2. Judah was first in dignity, and therefore must be first in duty. Judah was the tribe out of which our Lord was to spring: so that in Judah, Christ, the Lion of the tribe of Judah, went before them. Christ engaged the powers of darkness first, and foiled them, which animates us for our conflicts; and it is in him that we are *more than conquerors*.

III. Judah hereupon prepares to go up, but courts his brother and neighbour the tribe of Simeon to join forces with him, *v.* 3. The strongest should not despise but desire the assistance even of those that are weaker. Judah was the most considerable of all the tribes, and Simeon the least considerable, and yet Judah begs Simeon's friendship, and prays an aid from him; the head cannot say to the foot, *I have no need of thee*, for we are *members one of another*.

IV. The confederate forces of Judah and Simeon take the field: *Judah went up* (*v.* 4), and Simeon with him, *v.* 3. Caleb, it is probable, was commander-in-chief of this expedition. It should seem by what follows (*v.* 10, 11), that he was not yet in possession of his own allotment. It was happy for them that they had such a general as, according to his name, was all heart.

V. God gave them great success. Whether they invaded the enemy, or the enemy first gave them the alarm, *the Lord delivered them into their hand, v.* 4. Now, 1. We are told how the army of the Canaanites was routed in the field, in or near Bezek, the place where they drew up, which afterwards Saul made the place of a general rendezvous (1 Sam. xi. 8); they slew 10,000 men, which blow, if followed, could not but be a very great weakening to those that were already brought so very low. 2. How their king was taken and mortified. His name was Adoni-bezek, which signifies, *lord of Bezek*. He was taken prisoner after the battle, and we are here told how they used him; they cut off his thumbs, to disfit him for fighting, and his great toes, that he might not be able to run away, *v.* 6. It had been barbarous thus to triumph over a man in misery, and that lay at their mercy, but that he was a devoted Canaanite, and one that had in like manner abused others. Here observe, (1) What a great man this Adoni-bezek had been, yet now himself a prisoner and reduced to the extremity of meanness and disgrace. (2) What desolations he had made among his neighbours: he had wholly subdued seventy kings. "Judah," says Dr. Lightfoot, "in conquering Adoni-bezek, did, in effect, conquer seventy kings." (3) How justly he was treated as he had treated others. (4) How honestly he owned the righteousness of God herein: *As I have done, so God has requited me.*

VI. Particular notice is taken of the conquest of Jerusalem, *v.* 8.

Verses 9–20

A further account of that glorious and successful campaign which Judah and Simeon made. 1. The lot of Judah was pretty well cleared of the Canaanites, yet not thoroughly. Those that *dwelt in the mountain* (the mountains that were round about Jerusalem) were driven out (*v.* 9, 19), but those in the valley kept their ground against them, having *chariots of iron*, such as we read of, Josh. xvii. 16. They had iron chariots, and therefore it was thought not safe to attack them: but had not Israel God on their side, *whose chariots are thousands of angels* (Ps. lxviii. 17). Yet they suffered their fears to prevail against their faith, they could not trust God under any disadvantages, but meanly withdrew their forces, when with one bold stroke they might have completed their victories. 2. Caleb was put in possession of Hebron, which, though given him by Joshua ten or twelve years before, yet being employed in public service, for the settling of the tribes, which he preferred before his own private interests, it seems he did not till now make himself master of; so well content was that good man to serve others, while he left himself to be served last. Yet now the men of Judah all came in to his assistance for the reducing of Hebron (*v.* 10), slew the sons of Anak, and put him in possession of it, *v.* 20. They gave Hebron unto Caleb. And now Caleb, that he might return the kindness of his countrymen, is impatient to see Debir reduced and put into the hands of the men of Judah, to expedite which he proffers his daughter to the person that will undertake to command in the siege of that important place, *v.* 11, 12. Othniel bravely undertakes it, and wins the town and the lady (*v.* 13). 3. Simeon got ground of the Canaanites in his border, *v.* 17, 18. In the eastern part of Simeon's lot, they destroyed the Canaanites in Zephath, and called it *Hormah—destruction.* In the western part they took Gaza, Askelon, and Ekron, cities of the Philistines; they gained present possession of the cities, but, not destroying the inhabitants, the Philistines in process of time recovered the cities, and proved inveterate enemies to the Israel of God, and no better could come of doing their work by the halves. 4. The Kenites gained a settlement in the tribe of Judah, choosing it there rather than in any other tribe, because it was the strongest, and there they hoped to be safe and quiet, *v.* 16. These were the posterity of Jethro. They had at first seated themselves in the *city of palm-trees*, that is, Jericho, a city which never was to be rebuilt, and

therefore the fitter for those who *dwelt in tents*, and did not mind building. But afterwards they removed into the wilderness of Judah. This respect Israel showed them, to let them fix where they pleased, being a quiet people, who, wherever they were, were content with a little. Those that molested none were molested by none. *Blessed are the meek, for thus they shall inherit the earth.*

Verses 21–36

We are here told upon what terms the rest of the tribes stood with the Canaanites that remained.

I. Benjamin neglected to drive the Jebusites out of that part of the city of Jerusalem which fell to their lot, *v.* 21. Judah had set them a good example, and gained them great advantages by what they did (*v.* 9), but they did not follow the blow for want of resolution.

II. 1. The house of Joseph bestirred themselves a little to get possession of Beth-el, *v.* 22. That city is mentioned in the tribe of Benjamin, Josh. xviii. 22. Yet it is spoken of there (*v.* 13), as a city in the borders of that tribe, and, it should seem, the line went through it, so that one half of it only belonged to Benjamin, the other half to Ephraim. In this account of the expedition of the Ephraimites against Beth-el observe,

(1) Their interest in the divine favour: *The Lord was with them*, and would have been with the other tribes if they would have exerted their strength.

(2) The prudent measures they took to gain the city. They sent spies to observe what part of the city was weakest, *v.* 23. These spies got very good information from a man who showed them a private way into the town. It seems, he would not join himself to the people of Israel, and therefore he removed after a colony of the Hittites, which had gone into Arabia and settled there upon Joshua's invasion of the country; with them this man chose to dwell, and built a city, and in the name of it preserved the ancient name of his native city, *Luz, an almond-tree*, preferring this before its new name, which carried religion in it, *Bethel—the house of God.*

(3) Their success. The spies brought or sent notice of the intelligence they had gained to the army, which improved their advantages, surprised the city, and put them all to the sword, *v.* 25.

2. Besides this achievement, it seems, the children of Joseph did nothing remarkable.

III. Zebulun, perhaps inclining to the sea-trade, for it was foretold that it should be a haven for ships, neglected to reduce Kitron and Nahalol (*v.* 30), and only made the inhabitants of those places tributaries to them.

IV. Asher quitted itself worse than any of the tribes (*v.* 31, 32), not only in leaving more towns than any of them in the hands of the Canaanites, but in submitting to the Canaanites instead of making them tributaries.

V. Naphtali also permitted the Canaanites to live among them (*v.* 33), only by degrees they got them so far under as to exact contributions from them.

VI. Dan was so far from extending his conquests where his lot lay that, wanting spirit to make head against the Amorites, he was forced by them to retire into the mountains and inhabit the cities there, but durst not venture into the valley, where, it is probable, the chariots of iron were, *v.* 34. In Jacob's blessing Judah is compared to a lion, Dan to a serpent; now observe how Judah with his lion-like courage prospered and prevailed, but Dan with all his serpentine subtlety could get no ground; craft and artful management do not always effect the wonders they pretend to.

Upon the whole matter it appears that the people of Israel were generally very careless both of their duty and interest in this thing; they did not what they might have done to expel the Canaanites and make room for themselves. The same thing that kept their fathers forty years out of Canaan kept them now out of the full possession of it, and that was unbelief. Distrust of the power and promise of God lost them their advantages, and ran them into a thousand mischiefs.

CHAPTER 2

I. A particular message which God sent to Israel by an angel, and the impression it made upon them, ver. 1–5. II. A general idea of the state of Israel during the government of the judges. 1. Their adherence to God while Joshua and the elders lived, ver. 6–10. 2. Their revolt afterwards to idolatry, ver. 11–13. 3. God's displeasure against them, and his judgments upon them for it, ver. 14, 15. 4. His pity towards them, shown in raising them up deliverers, ver. 16–18. 5. Their relapse into idolatry after the judgment was over, ver. 17–19. 6. The full stop God in anger put to their successes, ver. 20–23.

Verses 1–5

It was the privilege of Israel that they had particular messages sent them from heaven, as there was occasion, for reproof, for correction, and for instruction. Besides the written word which they had before them to read, they often *heard a word behind them, saying, This is the way*, Isa. xxx. 21. Here begins that way of God's dealing with them. In these verses we have a very awakening sermon that was preached to them when they began to cool in their religion.

I. The preacher was an *angel of the Lord* (*v.* 1). Such extraordinary messengers we sometimes find in this book employed in the raising up of the judges that delivered Israel, as Gideon and Samson; and now, to show how various are the good offices they do for God's Israel, here is one sent to preach to them, to prevent their falling into sin and trouble.

II. The persons to whom this sermon was preached were *all the children of Israel, v.* 4. A great congregation for a great preacher! The place is called *Bochim* (*v.* 1), because it gained that name upon this occasion. All Israel needed the reproof and warning here given.

III. The sermon itself is short, but very close. God here tells them plainly, 1. What he had done for them, *v.* 1. He had brought them out of Egypt, a land of slavery and toil, into Canaan, a land of rest, liberty, and plenty. 2. What he had promised them: *I said, I will never break my covenant with you.* 3. What were his just and reasonable expectations from them (*v.* 2): that being taken into covenant with God they should make no league with the Canaanites, who were both his enemies and theirs,—that having set up his altar they should throw down their altars, lest they should be a temptation to them to serve their gods. 4. How they had in this very thing, which he had most insisted on, disobeyed him: "But you have not in so small a matter obeyed my voice." 5. How they must expect to smart by and by for this their folly, *v.* 3. Those deceive themselves who expect advantage by friendship with those that are enemies to God.

IV. The good success of this sermon is very remarkable: The people *lifted up their voice and wept, v.* 4. But this was not enough; they wept, but we do not find that they reformed, that they went home and destroyed all the remains of idolatry and idolaters among them. Many are melted under the word that harden again before they are cast into a new mould. However, this general weeping, 1. Gave a new name to the place (*v.* 5): they called it *Bochim, Weepers*. 2. It gave occasion for a solemn sacrifice: They *sacrificed there unto the Lord*, having (as is supposed) met at Shiloh, where God's altar was.

Verses 6–23

The angel had foretold that the Canaanites and

their idols would be a snare to Israel; now the historian undertakes to show that they were so, and, that this may appear the more clear, he looks back a little, and takes notice, 1. Of their happy settlement in the land of Canaan. Joshua, having distributed this land among them, dismissed them to the quiet and comfortable possession of it (*v.* 6). 2. Of their continuance in the faith and fear of God's holy name as long as Joshua lived, *v.* 7. 3. Of the death and burial of Joshua, which gave a fatal stroke to the interests of religion among the people, *v.* 8, 9. 4. Of the rising of a new generation, *v.* 10. They were so entirely devoted to the world, so intent upon the business of it or so indulgent of the flesh in ease and luxury, that they never minded the true God and his holy religion, and so were easily drawn aside to false gods and their abominable superstitions.

A general idea of the series of things in Israel during the time of the judges,

I. The people of Israel forsook the God of Israel. In general, *they did evil*, nothing could be more evil, that is, more provoking to God, nor more prejudicial to themselves, and it was *in the sight of the Lord*. In particular, 1. They *forsook the Lord* (*v.* 12, and again *v.* 13); this was one of the two great evils they were guilty of, Jer. ii. 13. They had been joined to the Lord in covenant, but now they forsook him, as a wife *treacherously departs from her husband*. 2. When they forsook the only true God they did not turn atheists, nor were they such fools as to say, *There is no God*; but they followed other gods: so much remained of pure nature as to own a God, yet so much appeared of corrupt nature as to multiply gods, and take up with any, and to follow the fashion, not the rule, in religious worship. *Baalim* signifies *lords*, and *Ashtaroth blessed ones*, both plural, for when they forsook Jehovah, who is one, they had gods many and lords many.

II. The God of Israel was hereby provoked to anger, and delivered them up into the hand of their enemies, *v.* 14. 15. 1. The scale of victory turned against them. God would rather give the success to those that had never known nor owned him than to those that had done both, but had now deserted him. 2. The balance of power then turned against them of course.

III. The God of infinite mercy took pity on them in their distresses, though they had brought themselves into them by their own sin and folly, and wrought deliverance for them. Here observe, 1. The inducement of their deliverance. It came purely from God's pity and tender compassion; the reason was fetched from within himself. It is not so much the burden of sin as the burden of affliction that they are said to groan under. It is true they deserved to perish for ever under his curse, yet, this being the day of his patience and our probation, he does not stir up all his wrath. 2. The instruments of their deliverance. God raised up judges from among themselves, as there was occasion, men to whom God gave extraordinary qualifications to reform and deliver Israel, and whose great attempts he crowned with wonderful success: *The Lord was with the judges* when he raised them up, and so they became saviours. Observe, (1) In the days of the greatest degeneracy and distress of the church there shall be some whom God will make fit to redress its grievances and set things to rights. (2) God endues men with wisdom and courage, gives them hearts to act and venture. All that are in any way the blessings of their country must be looked upon as the gifts of God.

IV. The degenerate Israelites were not effectually and thoroughly reformed, no, not by their judges, *v.* 17–19. They had been espoused to God, but broke the marriage-covenant, and went a-whoring after these gods. Idolatry is spiritual adultery. *They* corrupted themselves more than their fathers, strove to outdo them in multiplying strange gods and inventing profane and impious rites of worship, as it were in contradiction to their reformers.

V. God's just resolution hereupon was still to continue the rod over them. After Joshua's death, little was done for a long time against the Canaanites: Israel indulged them, and grew familiar with them, and therefore God would not drive them out any more, *v.* 21. God chose their delusions, Isa. lxvi. 4. Thus men cherish and indulge their own corrupt appetites and passions, and therefore God justly leaves them to themselves under the power of their sins, which will be their ruin. *So shall their doom be; they themselves have decided it.*

CHAPTER 3

I. A general account of Israel's enemies is premised, and of the mischief they did them, ver. 1–7. II. A particular account of the brave exploits done by the first three of the judges. 1. Othniel, whom God raised up to fight Israel's battles against the king of Mesopotamia, ver. 8–11. 2. Ehud, who was employed in rescuing Israel out of the hands of the Moabites, ver. 12–30. 3.Shamgar, who signalized himself in an encounter with the Philistines, ver. 31.

Verses 1–7

We are here told what remained of the old inhabitants of Canaan. 1. There were some of them that kept together in united bodies, unbroken (*v.* 3): *The five lords of the Philistines*, namely, Ashdod, Gaza, Askelon, Gath, and Ekron, 1 Sam. vi. 17. There was a particular nation called *Canaanites*, that kept their ground with the Sidonians, upon the coast of the great sea. And in the north the Hivites held much of Mount Lebanon. But, besides these, 2. There were everywhere in all parts of the country some scatterings of the nations (*v.* 5), Hittites, Amorites, &c.

Now concerning these remnants of the natives observe,

I. How wisely God permitted them to remain. It is mentioned in the close of the foregoing chapter as an act of God's justice, that he let them remain for Israel's correction. But here another construction is put upon it, and it appears to have been an act of God's *wisdom*, that he let them remain for Israel's real advantage, that those who *had not known the wars of Canaan* might *learn war*, *v.* 1, 2. Because their country lay very much in the midst of enemies it was therefore necessary they should be well disciplined, that they might defend their coasts when invaded, and might hereafter enlarge their coast as God had promised them.

II. How wickedly Israel mingled themselves with those that did remain. 1. They joined in marriage with the Canaanites (*v.* 6), though they could not advance either their honour or their estate by marrying with them. 2. Thus they were brought to join in worship with them; they served their *gods* (*v.* 6), *Baalim and the groves* (*v.* 7), that is, the images that were worshipped in groves of thick trees, which were a sort of natural temple. In such unequal matches there is more reason to fear that the bad will corrupt the good than to hope that the good will reform the bad, as there is in laying two pears together, the one rotten and the other sound. When they inclined to worship other gods they *forgot the Lord their God.*

Verses 8–11

We now come to the records of the government of the particular judges, the first of which was Othniel, in whom the story of this book is knit to that of Joshua. In this short narrative of Othniel's government we have,

I. The distress that Israel was brought into for their sin, *v.* 8. God being justly displeased with them laid them open to the nations, set them to sale as goods he would part with, and the first that laid hands on them was Chushan-rishathaim, king of that Syria which lay between the two great rivers of Tigris and Euphrates, thence called *Mesopotamia*, which signifies *in the midst of rivers*. Aiming to enlarge his dominions, he invaded the two tribes first on the other side Jordan that lay next him, and afterwards, perhaps by degrees, penetrated into the heart of the country, and as far as he went put them under contribution, exacting it with rigour, and perhaps quartering soldiers upon them.

II. Their return to God in this distress: *When he slew them, then they sought him* whom before they had slighted. The *children of Israel*, even the generality of them, *cried unto the Lord*, *v.* 9. Those who in the day of their mirth had cried to Baalim and Ashtaroth now that they are in trouble cry to the Lord.

III. God's return in mercy to them for their deliverance. 1. The deliverer was Othniel, who married Caleb's daughter, one of the old stock that had *seen the works of the Lord*. He was now, we may suppose, far advanced in years, when God raised him up to this honour. 2. Whence he had his commission, not of man, nor by man; but *the Spirit of the Lord came upon him* (*v.* 10), the spirit of wisdom and courage to qualify him for the service, and a spirit of power to excite him to it. 3. What method he took. He first judged Israel, reproved them, and reformed them, and then went out to war. This was the right method. Let sin at home be conquered, and then enemies abroad will be the more easily dealt with. Thus let Christ be our Judge and Law-giver, and then *he will save us*, and on no other terms, Isa. xxxiii. 22. 4. What good success he had. He prevailed to break the yoke of the oppression, for it is said, *The Lord delivered Chushan-rishathaim into his hand.* 5. The happy consequence of Othniel's good services. The land had rest, forty years; and the benefit would have been perpetual if they had kept close to God and their duty.

Verses 12–30

Ehud is the next of the judges whose achievements are related in this history, and here is an account of his actions.

I. When Israel sins again God raises up a new oppressor, *v.* 12–14. Perhaps they thought they might make the more bold with their old sins because they saw themselves in no danger from their old oppressor; the powers of that kingdom were weakened and brought low. But God *strengthened Eglon king of Moab against them*. This oppressor lay nearer to them than the former, and therefore would be the more mischievous to them. The king of Moab took to his assistance the Ammonites and Amalekites (*v.* 13), and this strengthened him; and we are here told how they prevailed. 1. They beat them in the field: They *went and smote Israel* (*v.* 13), not only those tribes that lay next them on the other side Jordan, but those also within Jordan, for they made themselves masters of *the city of palm-trees*, near the place where Jericho had stood, for that was so called (Deut. xxxiv. 3). 2. They made them to serve (*v.* 14), that is, exacted tribute from them, either the fruits of the earth in kind or money in lieu of them.

II. When Israel prays again God raises up a new deliverer (*v.* 15), named *Ehud*.

1. That he was a Benjamite. The city of palm-trees lay within the lot of this tribe, by which it is probable that they suffered most, and therefore stirred first to shake off the yoke. The weakest of all the tribes, yet out of it God raised up this deliverer.

2. That he was left-handed, as it seems many of that tribe were, *ch.* xx. 16. Benjamin signifies *the*

son of the right hand, and yet multitudes of them were left-handed; for men's natures do not always answer their names. God chose this left-handed man to be the man of his right hand, whom he would *make strong for himself*, Ps. lxxx. 17. It was *God's right hand* that gained Israel the victory (Ps. xliv. 3), not the right hand of the instruments he employed.

3. We are here told what Ehud did for the deliverance of Israel out of the hands of the Moabites.

(1) He put to death Eglon the king of Moab; I say, *put him to death*, not murdered or assassinated him, but as a judge, or minister of divine justice, executed the judgments of God upon him.

[1] He had a fair occasion of access to him. Being an ingenious active man, and fit to stand before kings, his people chose him to carry a present in the name of all Israel, over and above their tribute, to their great lord the king of Moab, that they might find favour in his eyes, *v.* 15. Ehud went on his errand to Eglon, offered his present with the usual ceremony and expressions of dutiful respect, the better to colour what he intended and to prevent suspicion.

[2] It should seem, from the first, he designed to be the death of him. That he compassed and imagined the death of this tyrant appears by the preparation he made of a weapon for the purpose, a short dagger, which might easily be concealed under his clothes (*v.* 16). This he wore on his right thigh, that it might be the more ready to his left hand, and might be the less suspected.

[3] He contrived how to be alone with him, which he might the more easily be now that he had not only made himself known to him, but ingratiated himself by the present. He begged a private audience, and obtained it in a withdrawing-room, here called a *summer parlour*. He told the king he had a secret errand to him, who thereupon ordered all his attendants to withdraw, *v.* 19.

[4] When he had him alone he soon dispatched him. Ehud demands his attention to *a message from God* (*v.* 20), and that message was a dagger. The message was delivered, not to his ear, but immediately, and literally, to his heart, into which the fatal knife was thrust, and was left there, *v.* 21, 22. Eglon signifies a *calf*, and he fell like a fatted calf, by the knife, an acceptable sacrifice to divine justice. No such commissions are now given, and to pretend to them is to blaspheme God, and make him patronize the worst of villainies.

[5] Providence wonderfully favoured his escape, when he had done the execution. The tyrant fell silently, without any shriek or out-cry, which might have been overheard by his servants at a distance. The heroic executioner of this vengeance shut the doors after him, took the key with him, and passed through the guards with an air of innocence, and boldness, and unconcernedness. The servants that attended in the antechamber, coming to the door of the inner parlour, when Ehud had gone, to know their master's pleasure, and finding it locked and all quiet, concluded he had lain down to sleep. Thus by their care not to disturb his sleep they lost the opportunity of revenging his death. The servants at length opened the door, and found their master had *slept indeed his long sleep, v.* 25. Ehud by this means made his escape to Sierath, *a thick wood, v.* 26.

(2) Ehud, having slain the king of Moab, gave a total rout to the forces of the Moabites that were among them, and so effectually shook off the yoke of their oppression. [1] He raised an army immediately in Mount Ephraim, at some distance from the headquarters of the Moabites, and headed them himself, *v.* 27. The trumpet he blew was indeed a jubilee-trumpet, proclaiming liberty, and a joyful sound it

was to the oppressed Israelites, who for a long time had heard no other trumpets than those of their enemies. [2] Like a pious man, and as one that did all this in faith, he took encouragement himself, and gave encouragement to his soldiers, from the power of God engaged for them (*v.* 28): "*Follow me, for the Lord hath delivered your enemies into your hands.*" [3] Like a politic general, he first secured the fords of Jordan, set strong guards upon all those passes, to cut off the communications. He then fell upon them, and put them all to the sword: *There escaped not a man* of them. The consequence of this victory was that the power of the Moabites was wholly broken in the land of Israel. The country was cleared of these oppressors, and *the land had rest eighty years, v.* 30.

Verse 31

The other side of the country which lay south-west was in that time infested by the Philistines, against whom Shamgar made head. 1. It seems Israel needed deliverance, for *he delivered Israel*; how great the distress was, Deborah afterwards related in her song (*ch.* v. 6), that *in the days of Shamgar the high-ways were unoccupied*, &c. 2. God raised him up to deliver them, as it should seem, while Ehud was yet living. So inconsiderable were the enemies for number that it seems the killing of 600 of them amounted to a deliverance of Israel, and so many he slew with an ox-goad, or, as some read it, *a plough shure*. He that has the residue of the Spirit could, when he pleased, make ploughmen judges and generals, and fishermen apostles. It is no matter how weak the weapon is if God direct and strengthen the arm. An ox-goad, when God pleases, shall do more than Goliath's sword.

CHAPTER 4

The history of Deborah and Barak. I. Israel revolted from God, ver. 1. II. Israel oppressed by Jabin, ver. 2, 3. III. Israel judged by Deborah, ver. 4, 5. IV. Israel rescued out of the hands of Jabin. 1. Their deliverance is concerted between Deborah and Barak, ver. 6, 9. 2. Barak takes the field, ver 10. Sisera, Jabin's general, meets him, ver. 12, 13. Deborah encourages him, ver. 14. And God gives him a complete victory, ver. 15, 16. The general forced to flee, ver. 17. And where he expected shelter he had his life stolen from him by Jael while he was asleep (ver. 18–21), which completes Barak's triumph (ver. 22) and Israel's deliverance, ver. 23, 24.

Verses 1–3

I. Israel backsliding from God: They again *did evil in his sight*. See in this, 1. The strange strength of corruption, which hurries men into sin notwithstanding the most frequent experience of its fatal consequences. 2. The common ill effects of a long peace. The land had rest eighty years, which should have confirmed them in their religion; but, on the contrary, it made them secure and wanton. 3. The great loss which a people sustains by the death of good governors. *They did evil, because Ehud was dead.*

II. Israel oppressed by their enemies. When they forsook God, he forsook them; and then they became an easy prey to every spoiler. Jabin reigned in Hazor, as another of the same name, and perhaps his ancestor, had done before him, whom Joshua routed and slew, and burnt his city, Josh. xi. 1, 10. But it seems, in process of time, the city was rebuilt. Jabin, and his general Sisera, did mightily oppress Israel. That which aggravated the oppression was, that these Canaanites had formerly been conquered and subdued by Israel, were of old sentenced to be their servants (Gen. ix. 25), and might now have been under their feet if their own slothfulness, cowardice, and unbelief, had not suffered them thus to get ahead.

III. Israel returning to their God: They *cried unto the Lord*, when distress drove them to him, and they saw no other way of relief.

Verses 4–9

The year of the redeemed at length came, when Israel was to be delivered out of the hands of Jabin.

I. The preparation of the people for their deliverance, by the prophetic conduct and government of Deborah, *v.* 4, 5. Her name signifies a *bee*; and she answered her name by her industry, sagacity, and great usefulness to the public, her sweetness to her friends and sharpness to her enemies. She is said to be *the wife of Lapidoth*; but, the termination not being commonly found in the name of a man, some make this the name of a place: she was *a woman of Lapidoth*. Others take it appellatively, Lapidoth signifies *lamps*. The Rabbis say she had employed herself in making wicks for the lamps of the tabernacle. Or she was a woman of *illuminations*, or of *splendours*, one that was extraordinarily knowing and wise. Concerning her we are here told, 1. That she was intimately acquainted with God; she was *a prophetess.* 2. That she was entirely devoted to the service of Israel. She judged Israel at the time that Jabin oppressed them. She judged, not as a princess, by any civil authority conferred upon her, but as a prophetess, and as God's mouth to them. It is said she *dwelt*, or, as some read it, she *sat* under a palm-tree, called ever after from her *the palm-tree of Deborah.* Either she had her house under that tree or she had her judgment-seat in the open air, under the shadow of that tree, which was an emblem of the justice she sat there to administer, which will thrive and grow against opposition, as palms under pressures.

II. The project laid for their deliverance. She was not herself fit to command an army in person, being a woman; but she nominated one that was fit, Barak of Naphtali. He could do nothing without her head, nor she without his hands; but both together made a complete deliverer, and effected a complete deliverance.

1. By God's direction, she orders Barak to raise an army, and engage Jabin's forces, that were under Sisera's command, *v.* 6, 7. Barak, it may be, had been meditating some great attempt against the common enemy. But two things discouraged him: (1) He wanted a commission to levy forces; this therefore Deborah here gives him under the broad seal of heaven, which, as a prophetess, she had a warrant to affix to it: "*Hath not the Lord God of Israel commanded it? Go and draw towards Mount Tabor.*" [1] She directs him what number of men to raise—10,000. [2] Whence he should raise them—only out of his own tribe, and that of Zebulun next adjoining. And, [3] She orders him where to make his rendezvous —at Mount Tabor, in his own neighbourhood. (2) When he had an army raised, he knew not how he should have an opportunity of engaging the enemy. "Well," says Deborah, "*I will draw unto thee Sisera and his army.*" She gave him an express promise of success: *I will* (that is, God will, in whose name I speak) *deliver them into thy hand.*

2. At Barak's request, she promises to go along with him to the field of battle. (1) Barak insisted much upon the necessity of her presence, which would be to him better than a council of war (*v.* 8): "*If thou wilt go with me* to direct and advise me, and in every difficult case to let me know God's mind, *then I will go* with all my heart, and not fear the chariots of iron; otherwise not." Nothing would be a greater satisfaction to him than to have the prophetess with him to animate the soldiers and to be consulted as an oracle upon all occasions. (2) Deborah promised to go with him, *v.* 9. No toil nor peril shall discourage her from doing the utmost that becomes her for the service of her country. Deborah was the weaker vessel, yet had the stronger faith. But though she agrees to go with Barak, if he

insists upon it, she gives him a hint proper enough to move a soldier not to insist upon it: "*The journey thou undertakest shall not be for thy honour*; not so much for thy honour as if thou hadst gone by thyself; for *the Lord shall sell Sisera into the hands of a woman*"; that is, [1] The world would ascribe the victory to the hand of Deborah. [2] God would complete the victory by the hand of Jael, which would be some eclipse to his glory. But Barak values the good success of his enterprise more than his honour; and therefore will by no means drop his request.

Verses 10–16

I. Barak beats up for volunteers, and soon has his quota of men ready. *v.* 10. Though the tribes of Zebulun and Naphtali were chiefly depended on, yet it appears by Deborah's song that some had come in to him from other tribes (Manasseh and Issachar), and more were expected that came not, from Reuben, Dan, and Asher, *ch.* v. 14–17. The 11th verse, concerning the removal of Heber, one of the families of the Kenites, out of the wilderness of Judah, in the south, comes in for the sake of what was to follow concerning the exploit of Jael, a wife of that family.

II. Sisera takes the field with a very numerous and powerful army (*v.* 12, 13). Sisera's confidence was chiefly in his chariots; therefore particular notice is taken of them, 900 *chariots of iron*, which, with the scythes fastened to their axle-trees, when they were driven into an army of footmen, did terrible execution.

III. Deborah gives orders to engage the enemy, *v.* 14. Josephus says that when Barak saw Sisera's army drawn up, and attempting to surround the mountain on the top of which he and his forces lay encamped, his heart quite failed him, but Deborah animated him to make a descent upon Sisera, "*The Lord hath delivered Sisera into thy hand.*" It was well for Barak that he had Deborah with him; for she made up what was defective, 1. In his conduct, by telling him, *This is the day.* 2. In his courage, by assuring him of God's presence.

IV. God himself routs the enemy's army, *v.* 15. It was not so much the bold and surprising alarm which Barak gave their camp that dispirited and dispersed them, but God's terror seized their spirits. *The stars*, it seems, fought against them, *ch.* v. 20. Josephus says that a violent storm of hail which beat in their faces drove them back; so that they became a very easy prey to the army of Israel, and Deborah's words were made good: "*The Lord has delivered them into thy hand.*"

V. Barak pursues the scattered forces, even to their general's headquarters at Harosheth (*v.* 16), and spares none whom God had delivered into his hand to be destroyed: *There was not a man left.*

Verses 17–24

We have seen the army of the Canaanites totally routed.

I. The fall of their general, Sisera, captain of the host. Let us trace the steps of this mighty man's fall.

1. He quitted his chariot, and took to his feet, *v.* 15, 17. How miserable doth Sisera look now he is dismounted! He who but lately trusted to his arms with so much assurance must now trust to his heels only with so little.

2. He fled for shelter to the tents of the Kenites, having no stronghold, nor any place of his own in reach to retire to. And that which encouraged him to go thither was that at this time there was peace between his master and the house of Heber. Sisera thought he might therefore be safe among them.

3. Jael invited him in, and bade him very welcome. Probably she stood at the tent door, to enquire what news from the army, and what was the success of

the battle which was fought not far off. (1) She invited him in. Perhaps she stood waiting for an opportunity to show kindness to any distressed Israelite, if there should be occasion for it. (2) She made very much of him, and seemed mighty careful to have him easy, as her invited guest. We must suppose she kept her tent as quiet as she could, and free from noise, that he might sleep the sooner and the faster. And now was Sisera least safe when he was most secure.

4. When he lay fast asleep she drove a long nail through his temples, so fastened his head to the ground, and killed him, *v.* 21. It was a divine warrant that justified her in the doing of it; and therefore, since no such extraordinary commissions can now be pretended, it ought not in any case to be imitated. The laws of friendship and hospitality must be religiously observed, and we must abhor the thought of betraying any whom we have invited and encouraged to put a confidence in us. And, as to this act of Jael (like that of Ehud in the chapter before), we have reason to think she was conscious of such a divine impulse upon her spirit to do it as did abundantly satisfy herself that it was well done. He that thought to destroy Israel with his many iron chariots is himself destroyed with one iron nail.

II. The glory and joy of Israel hereupon. 1. Barak their leader finds his enemy dead, (*v.* 22), and no doubt, he was very well pleased to find his work done so well to his hand, and so much to the glory of God and the confusion of his enemies. 2. Israel is completely delivered out of the hands of Jabin king of Canaan, *v.* 23, 24. They not only shook off his yoke by this day's victory, but they afterwards prosecuted the war against him, till they had destroyed him.

CHAPTER 5

The triumphal song which was composed and sung upon occasion of that glorious victory which Israel obtained over the forces of Jabin king of Canaan and the happy consequences of that victory. I. It begins with praise to God, ver. 2, 3. II. The substance of this song transmits the memory of this great achievement. 1. Comparing God's appearances for them on this occasion with his appearances to them on Mount Sinai, ver. 4, 5. 2. Magnifying their deliverance from the calamitous condition they had been in, ver. 6–8. 3. Calling those to join in praise that shared in the success, ver. 9–13. 4. Reflecting honour upon those tribes that were forward and active in that war, and disgrace on those that declined the service, ver. 14–19, 23. 5. Taking notice how God himself fought for them, ver. 20–22. 6. Celebrating particularly the honour of Jael, that slew Sisera, ver. 24–30. It concludes with a prayer to God, ver. 31.

Verses 1–5

I. God is praised by a song, which is, 1. A very natural expression of rejoicing. *Is any merry? Let him sing*; and holy joy is the very soul and root of praise and thanksgiving. 2. A very proper expedient for perpetuating the remembrance of great events. Neighbours would learn this song one of another and children of their parents; and *one generation* would thus *praise God's works to another*, and *declare his mighty acts*, Ps. cxlv. 4, &c.

II. Deborah herself penned this song, as appears by *v.* 7. 1. She used her gifts as a prophetess in composing the song, and the strain throughout is very fine and lofty, the images are lively, the expressions elegant, and an admirable mixture there is in it of sweetness and majesty. 2. We may suppose she used her power as a princess, in obliging the conquering army of Israel to learn and sing this song. She had been the first wheel in the action, and now is so in the thanksgiving.

1. She begins with a general Hallelujah: *Praise* (or *bless*, for that is the word) *you the Lord, v.* 2. The design of the song is to give glory to God; this therefore is put first, to explain and direct all that follows, like the first petition of the Lord's prayer, *Hallowed be thy name.*

2. She calls to the great ones of the world, that sit at the upper end of its table, to attend to her song, and take notice of the subject of it: *Hear, O you kings! give ear, O you princes!* (1) She would have them know that horses and chariots are vain things for safety. (2) She would have them to join with her in praising the God of Israel, and no longer to praise their counterfeit deities. (3) She would have them take warning by Sisera's fate, and not dare to offer any injury to the people of God.

3. She looks back upon God's former appearances, and compares this with them. What God is doing should bring to our mind what he has done; for he is the same yesterday, to-day, and for ever (*v.* 4): *Lord, when thou wentest out of Sair.* This may be understood either, (1) Of the appearances of God's power and justice against the enemies of Israel to subdue and conquer them. God had led his people Israel from the country of Edom; he brought down under their feet Sihon and Og, striking them and their armies with such terror and amazement that they seemed apprehensive heaven and earth were coming together. Or it notes the glorious displays of the divine majesty, and the surprising effects of the divine power, enough to make the earth tremble, the heavens drop like snow before the sun, and the mountains to melt. Or, (2) It is meant of the appearances of God's glory and majesty to Israel, when he gave them his law at Mount Sinai. It was then literally true, *the earth trembled, and the heavens dropped, &c.* The Chaldee paraphrase applies it to the giving of the law, but has a strange descant on those words, *the mountains melted. Tabor, Hermon, and Carmel, contended among themselves: one said, Let the divine majesty dwell upon me; the other said, Let it dwell upon me; but God made it to dwell upon Mount Sinai, the meanest and least of all the mountains.* I suppose it means the least valuable, because barren and rocky.

Verses 6–11

I. Deborah describes the distressed state of Israel under the tyranny of Jabin. *From the days of Shamgar,* who did something towards the deliverance of Israel from the Philistines, to the days of Jael, the present day, in which Jael has so signalized herself, the country has been in a manner desolate. 1. No trade. All commerce ceased, and the highways were unoccupied; no caravans of merchants, as formerly. 2. No travelling. 3. No tillage. The fields must needs be laid waste and unoccupied when the inhabitants of the villages were obliged to take shelter for themselves and their families in walled and fenced cities. 4. No administration of justice. There was war in the gates where their courts were kept, *v.* 8. 5. No peace to him that went out nor to him that came in. The gates through which they passed and repassed were infested by the enemy; nay, the places of drawing water were alarmed by the archers—a mighty achievement to terrify the drawers of water. 6. Neither arms nor spirit to help themselves with, not a *shield nor spear seen among forty thousand, v.* 8.

II. She shows in one word what it was that brought all this misery upon them: *They chose new gods, v.* 8. It was their idolatry that provoked God to give them up thus into the hands of their enemies.

III. She takes notice of God's great goodness to Israel in raising up such as should redress these grievances. Herself first (*v.* 7): *Till that I Deborah arose,* to restrain and punish those who disturbed the public peace. Thus she became a mother in Israel, a nursing mother, such was the affection she bore to her people. Under her there were other governors of Israel (*v.* 9). Of these governors she says, *My heart is towards them.*

IV. She calls upon those who had a particular share in the advantages of this great salvation, to offer up particular thanks to God for it, *v.* 10, 11. 1. *You that ride on white asses,* that is, the nobility and gentry. Let such as are by this salvation restored, not only to their liberty as other Israelites, but to their dignity, speak God's praises. 2. Let those that *sit in judgment* be sensible of it, and thankful that the sword of justice is not struck out of their hand by the sword of war. 3. Let those that *walk by the way,* and meet with none there to make them afraid, speak of the goodness of God in ridding the roads of those banditti that had so long infested them. 4. Let those that have not their wells taken from them, or stopped up, nor are in danger of being caught by the enemy when they go forth to draw, *rehearse the acts of the Lord,* not Deborah's acts, nor Barak's, but the Lord's, taking notice of his hand making peace in their borders. Observe in these acts of his, (1) Justice executed on his daring enemies. (2) Kindness shown to his trembling people, *the inhabitants of the villages,* who lay most open to the enemy. It is the glory of God to protect those that are most exposed, and to help the weakest.

Verses 12–23

I. Deborah stirs up herself and Barak to celebrate this victory in the most solemn manner. 1. Deborah, as a prophetess, must do it by a song, to compose and sing which she excites herself: *Awake, awake,* and again, *awake, awake.* 2. Barak, as a general, must do it by a triumph: *Lead thy captivity captive.* Though the army of Sisera was cut off in the field, and no quarter given, yet we may suppose in the prosecution of the victory, when the war was carried into the enemy's country, many not found in arms were seized and made prisoners of war.

II. She gives good reason for this praise and triumph, *v.* 13. 1. The Israelites had become few and inconsiderable, and yet to them God gave dominion over nobles. As long as any of God's Israel remain (and a remnant God will have in the worst of times) there is hope, be it ever so small a remnant, for God can make him that remains, though it should be but one single person, triumph over the most proud and potent. 2. Deborah was herself of the weaker sex, and the sex that from the fall had been sentenced to subjection, and yet the Lord authorized her to rule over the mighty men of Israel, who willingly submitted to her direction, and enabled her to triumph over the mighty men of Canaan.

III. She makes particular remarks on the several parties concerned in this great action, taking notice who fought against them, who fought for them, and who stood neutral.

1. Who fought against them. Jabin and Sisera had been mentioned in the history, but here it appears, (1) That Amalek was in league with Jabin. Ephraim is here said to act against Amalek (*v.* 14), probably intercepting and cutting off some forces of the Amalekites that were upon their march to join Sisera. (2) That others of the kings of Canaan, who had somewhat recovered themselves since their defeat by Joshua, joined with Jabin, and strengthened his army with their forces. These kings *came and fought, v.* 19. It is said of these kings that *they took no gain of money,* they were not mercenary troops hired into the service of Jabin.

2. Who fought for them. The several tribes that assisted in this great exploit are here spoken of with honour.

(1) Ephraim and Benjamin, those tribes among whom Deborah herself lived, bestirred themselves, and did bravely. Herein Benjamin had set them a good example among his people. "Ephraim moved *after thee, Benjamin*"; though Benjamin was the junior tribe, and much inferior, especially at this time, to Ephraim, both in number and wealth, yet when they led Ephraim followed.

(2) The ice being broken by Ephraim and Benjamin, Machir (the half-tribe of Manasseh beyond Jordan) and Zebulun sent in men that were very serviceable to this great design.

(3) Issachar did good service too; though he *saw that rest was good,* and therefore *bowed his shoulder to bear,* which is the character of that tribe (Gen. xlix. 15), yet they disdained to bear the yoke of Jabin's tribute, and now preferred the generous toils of war to a servile rest.

(4) Zebulun and Naphtali were the most bold and active of all the tribes, not only out of a particular affection to Barak their countryman, but because, they lying nearest to Jabin, the yoke of oppression lay heavier on their necks than on those of any other tribe.

(5) The stars from heaven appeared, or acted at least, on Israel's side (*v.* 20): *The stars in their courses,* according to the order and direction of him who is the great Lord of their hosts, *fought against Sisera,* by their malignant influences, or by causing the storms of hail and thunder which contributed so much to the rout of Sisera's army.

(6) The river of Kishon fought against their enemies. It swept away multitudes of those that hoped to make their escape through it, *v.* 21. Ordinarily, it was but a shallow river, and yet now, probably by the great rain that fell, it was so swollen, and the stream so deep and strong, that those who attempted to pass it were drowned.

(7) Deborah's own soul fought against them; she speaks of it with a holy exultation (*v.* 21): *O, my soul, thou hast trodden down strength.*

3. In this great engagement she observes who stood *neutral,* and did not side with Israel as might have been expected. No mention is made of Judah nor Simeon among the tribes concerned, because they, lying so very remote from the scene of action, had not an opportunity to appear.

(1) Reuben basely declined the service, *v.* 15, 16. Two things hindered them from engaging:—[1] Their divisions. Not only for their division from Canaan by the river Jordan, which needed not to have hindered them had they been hearty in the cause, but it means either that they were divided among themselves, could not agree who should go or who should lead, or that they were divided in their opinion of this war from the rest of the tribes, and thought the attempt either not justifiable or not practicable. [2] Their business in the world: *Reuben abode among the sheepfolds,* a warmer and safer place than the camp, pretending they could not conveniently leave the sheep they tended.

(2) Dan and Asher did the same, *v.* 17. These two lay on the seacoast, and [1] Dan pretended he could not leave his ships but they would be exposed, and therefore *I pray thee have me excused.* [2] Asher pretended he must stay at home to repair the breaches which the sea had in some places made upon his land, and to fortify his works against the encroachments of it, or he abode in his creeks, or small havens, where his trading vessels lay to attend them.

(3) But above all Meroz is condemned, and a curse pronounced upon the inhabitants of it, *Because they came not to the help of the Lord, v.* 23. Probably this was some city that lay near the scene of action, and therefore the inhabitants had a fair opportunity of showing their obedience to God and their concern for Israel, and of doing good service to the common cause; but they basely declined it, for fear of Jabin's iron chariots, being willing to sleep in a whole skin. God looks upon those as against him that are not with him. This city of Meroz seems to have been at this time a considerable place, since something great was expected from it.

Verses 24–31

Deborah here concludes this triumphant song,

I. With the praises of Jael, her sister-heroine, whose valiant act had completed and crowned the victory. Her poetry is finest and most florid here in the latter end of the song. How honourably does she speak of Jael (*v.* 24), who preferred her peace with the God of Israel before her peace with the king of Canaan. *Blessed shall she be above women in the tent.* Those whose lot is cast in the tent, in a very low and narrow sphere of activity, if they serve God in that according to their capacity, shall in no wise lose their reward.

II. She concludes all with a prayer to God, 1. For the destruction of all his foes: "*So*, so shamefully, so miserably, *let all thy enemies perish, O Lord.*" 2. For the exaltation and comfort of all his friends. "But let those that love him, and heartily wish well to his kingdom among men, *be as the sun when he goeth forth in his strength.*"

The victory here celebrated with this song was of such happy consequence to Israel that for the best part of one age they enjoyed the peace which it opened the way to: *The land had rest forty years.*

CHAPTER 6

Nothing that occurred in the quiet and peaceable times of Israel is recorded; the forty years' rest after the conquest of Jabin is passed over in silence; and here begins the story of another distress and another deliverance, by Gideon, the fourth of the judges. I. The calamitous condition of Israel, by the inroads of the Midianites, ver. 1 6. II. The message God sent them by a prophet, ver. 7–10. III. The raising up of Gideon to be their deliverer. 1. A commission which God sent him and confirmed by a sign, ver. 11–24. 2. The first-fruits of his government in the reform of his father's house, ver. 25–32. 3. The preparations he made for a war with the Midianites, ver. 33–40.

Verses 1–6

I. Israel's sin renewed: *They did evil in the sight of the Lord, v.* 1.

II. Israel's troubles repeated. This would follow of course; let all that sin expect to suffer; let all that return to folly expect to return to misery. Now as to this trouble, 1. It arose from a very despicable enemy. God delivered them into the hand of Midian (*v.* 1), that joined to Moab (Num. xxii. 4), a people that all men despised as uncultivated and unintelligent; a people that Israel had formerly subdued, and in a manner destroyed (see Num. xxxi. 7), and yet by this time so magnified, that they were capable of being made a very severe scourge to Israel. 2. It arose to a very formidable height (*v.* 2): *The hand of Midian prevailed,* purely by their multitude. God had promised to increase Israel as the sand on the sea shore; but their sin stopped their growth and diminished them, and then their enemies, though otherwise every way inferior to them, overpowered them with numbers. Here we have, (1) The Israelites imprisoned, or rather imprisoning themselves, in dens and caves, *v.* 2. This was owing purely to their own timorousness and faint-heartedness, that they would rather fly than fight; it was the effect of a guilty conscience. (2) The Israelites impoverished, greatly impoverished, *v.* 6. The Midianites made frequent incursions into the land of Canaan. This fruitful land was a great temptation to them. They came up against them (*v.* 3), pitched their camps among them (*v.* 4), and penetrated through the heart of the country as far as Gaza on the western side, *v.* 4. They let the Israelites alone to sow their ground, but towards harvest they came and seized all, and ate up and destroyed it, both grass and corn, and when they went away took with them the sheep and oxen. Now here we may see, [1] The justice of God in the punishment of their sin. [2] The consequence of God's departure from a people; when he goes all good goes and all mischiefs break in.

III. Israel's sense of God's hand revived at last. Seven years, year after year, did the Midianites make these inroads upon them, each we may suppose worse than the other (*v.* 1), until at last, all other succours failing, *Israel cried unto the Lord* (*v.* 6).

Verses 7–10

I. The cognizance God took of the cries of Israel, when at length they were directed towards him. Thus would he show how ready he is to forgive, how swift he is to show mercy, and how inclinable to hear prayer.

II. The method God took of working deliverance for them.

1. Before he sent an angel to raise them up a saviour he sent a prophet to reprove them for sin, and to bring them to repentance, *v.* 8. His errand was to convince them of sin, that, in their crying to the Lord, they might confess that with sorrow and shame, and not spend their breath in only complaining of their trouble. Note, (1) We have reason to hope God is designing mercy for us if we find he is by his grace preparing us for it. (2) The sending of prophets to a people, and the furnishing of a land with faithful ministers, is a token for good, and an evidence that God has mercy in store for them.

2. We have here the heads of the message which this prophet delivered to Israel, in the name of the Lord.

(1) He sets before them the great things God had done for them (*v.* 8, 9). [1] He brought them out of Egypt, where otherwise they would have continued in perpetual poverty and slavery. [2] He *delivered them out of the hands of all that oppressed them*; this is mentioned to intimate that the reason why they were not now delivered out of the hands of the oppressing Midianites was not for want of any power or goodwill in God. [3] He put them in quiet possession of this good land; this not only aggravated their sin, and affixed the brand of base ingratitude to it, but it justified God, and cleared him from blame upon account of the trouble they were now in.

(2) He shows the easiness and equity of God's demands and expectations from them (*v.* 10): "*I am the Lord your God*, to whom you lie under the highest obligations, *fear not the gods of the Amorites.*"

(3) He charges them with rebellion against God, who had laid this injunction upon them: *But you have not obeyed my voice.*

Verses 11–24

It is not said what effect the prophet's sermon had upon the people, but we may hope it had a good effect, and that some of them at least repented and reformed upon it; for here, immediately after, we have the dawning of the day of their deliverance, by the effectual calling of Gideon to take upon him the command of their forces against the Midianites.

I. The person to be commissioned for this service was Gideon, the son of Joash, *v.* 14. The father kept up in his own family the worship of Baal (*v.* 25), which we may suppose this son, as far as was in his power, witnessed against. He was of the half tribe of Manasseh that lay in Canaan, of the family of Abiezer; the eldest house of that tribe, Josh. xvii. 2.

II. The person that gave him the commission was an *angel of the Lord.* This angel is here called *Jehovah,* the incommunicable name of God (*v.* 14, 16), and he said, *I will be with thee.*

1. This divine person appeared here to Gideon, and it is observable how he found him, (1) Retired —all alone. God often manifests himself to his people when they are out of the noise and hurry of this world. (2) Employed in threshing wheat, with a *staff* or *rod,* probably because he had but little to thresh, he needed not the oxen to tread it out. The

work he was about was an emblem of that greater work to which he was now to be called, as the disciples' fishing was. From threshing corn he is fetched to thresh the Midianites, Isa. xli. 15. (3) Distressed; he was threshing his wheat, not in the threshing-floor, the proper place, but *by the wine-press*, in some private unsuspected corner, for fear of the Midianites.

2. Let us now see what passed between the angel and Gideon, who knew not with certainty, till after he was gone, that he was an angel, but supposed he was a prophet.

(1) The angel accosted him with respect, and assured him of the presence of God with him, *v.* 12. By this word, [1] He gives him his commission. [2] He inspires him with all necessary qualifications for the execution of his commission. [3] He assures him of success; for, *if God be for us, who can* prevail *against us?*

(2) Gideon gave a very melancholy answer to this joyful salutation (*v.* 13 : *O my Lord! if the Lord be with us why then has all this befallen us?* Gideon, as if not conscious to himself of anything great or encouraging in his own spirit, fastens only on the assurance the angel had given him of God's presence. The angel spoke in particular to him: *The Lord is with thee*; but he expostulates for all: *If the Lord be with us*, herding himself with the thousands of Israel, and admitting no comfort but what they might be sharers in, so far is he from the thoughts of monopolising it, though he had so fair an occasion given him. Gideon was a mighty man of valour, but as yet weak in faith. This was his weakness. We must not expect that the miracles which were wrought when a church was in the forming, and some great truth in the settling, should be continued and repeated when the formation and settlement are completed: no, nor that the mercies God showed to our fathers that served him, and kept close to him, should be renewed to us, if we degenerate and revolt from him.

(3) The angel gave him a very effectual answer to his objections, by giving him a commission to deliver Israel out of the hands of the Midianites, and assuring him of success therein, *v.* 14. Now the angel is called *Jehovah*, for he speaks as one having authority, and not as a messenger. [1] There was something extraordinary in the look he now gave to Gideon. He looked upon him, and smiled at the objections he made, but girded and clothed him with such power as would shortly enable him to answer them himself, and make him ashamed that ever he had made them. It was a speaking look, like Christ's upon Peter (Luke xxii. 61), a powerful look, a look that strangely darted new light and life into Gideon's breast. [2] But there was much more in what he said to him. *First*, He commissioned him to appear and act as Israel's deliverer. Such a one the few thinking people in the nation, and Gideon among the rest, were now expecting to be raised up, and now Gideon is told, "Thou art the man: *Go in this thy might*, this might wherewith thou art now threshing wheat; go and employ it to a nobler purpose; *I will make thee a thresher of men*." "Go, not in thy might, but go in *this* thy might, this which thou hast now received, *go in the strength of the Lord God*, that is, the strength with which thou must strengthen thyself." *Secondly*, He assured him of success. *Thou shalt save Israel from the hand of the Midianites*, and so shalt not only be an eye-witness, but a glorious instrument, of such wonders as thy *fathers told thee of*. Gideon, we may suppose, looked as one astonished at this strange and surprising power conferred upon him.

(4) Gideon made a very modest objection against this commission (*v.* 15): *O my Lord! wherewith shall I save Israel?* This question bespeaks him either, [1] Distrustful of God and his power. Or, [2] In-

quisitive concerning the methods he must take: "Lord, I labour under all imaginable disadvantages for it; if I must do it, thou must put me in the way." Or rather, [3] Humble, self-diffident, and self-denying. The angel had honoured him, but see how meanly he speaks of himself: "My family is comparatively poor in Manasseh and I am the least, that have the least honour and interest, *in my father's house*; what can I pretend to do? I am utterly unfit for the service, and unworthy of the honour." God delights to advance the humble.

(5) This objection was soon answered by a repetition of the promise that God would be with him, *v.* 16. "*Surely I will be with thee*, to direct and strengthen thee, and be assured *thou shalt smite the Midianites as one man*, as easily as if they were but one man and as effectually. All the thousands of Midian shall be as if they had but one neck, and thou shalt have the cutting of it off."

(6) Gideon desires to have his faith confirmed touching this commission. He therefore humbly begs of this divine person, whoever he was, [1] That he would give him a sign, *v.* 17. Now, under the dispensation of the Spirit, we are not to expect signs before our eyes, such as Gideon here desired, but must earnestly pray to God that, if *we have found grace in his sight*, he would show us a sign in our heart, by the powerful operations of his Spirit there, *fulfilling the work of faith*. [2] That he would give him a further and longer opportunity of conversation with him, *v.* 18. Upon the angel's promise to stay to dinner with him, he intended, *First*, To testify his grateful and generous respects to this stranger, and, in him, to God who sent him. Out of the little which the Midianites had left him he would gladly spare enough to entertain a friend, especially a messenger from heaven. *Secondly*, To try who and what this extraordinary person was. What he brought out is called his *present*, *v.* 18. It is the same word that is used for a meat-offering. If he ate of it as common meat, he would suppose him to be a man, a prophet; if otherwise, as it proved, he should know him to be an angel.

(7) The angel ordered him to take the flesh and bread out of the basket, and lay it upon a hard and cold rock, and to pour out the broth upon it, which, if he brought it hot, would soon be cold there; and *Gideon did so* (*v.* 20), believing that the angel appointed it with an intention to give him a sign. [1] He turned the *meat into an offering made by fire, of a sweet savour*. [2] He brought fire *out of the rock*, to consume this sacrifice. Hereby he gave him a sign that he had *found grace in his sight*. This acceptance of his sacrifice evidenced the acceptance of his person, and confirmed his commission. [3] He *departed out of his sight* immediately.

(8) Gideon, though no doubt he was confirmed in his faith by the indications was put into a great fright till God removed his fears. [1] Gideon speaks peril to himself (*v.* 22): *When he perceived that he was an angel* he cried out, *Alas! O Lord! God* be merciful to me, I am undone, for *I have seen an angel*. In this world of sense, it is a very awful thing to have any sensible conversation with that world of spirits to which we are so much strangers. Gideon's courage failed him now. [2] God speaks peace to him, *v.* 23. The Lord had *departed out of his sight*, *v.* 21. But though he must no longer walk by sight he might still live by faith. For the Lord said to him, "*Peace be unto thee, thou shalt not die.*"

3. The memorial of this vision which Gideon set up was a monument in the form of an altar, of use to preserve the remembrance of the vision, which was known by the name *Jehovah-shalom* (*v.* 24)—*The Lord peace*. This is, (1) The title of the Lord that spoke to him. Or, (2) The substance of what he said to

him: "*The Lord spoke peace.*" Or, (3) A prayer grounded upon what he had said, so the margin understands it, *The Lord send peace,* that is, rest from the present trouble, for still the public welfare lay nearest his heart.

Verses 25-32

I. Orders are given to Gideon to begin his government with the reformation of his father's house, *v.* 25, 26. The same night after he had seen God, when he was full of thoughts concerning what had passed, *the Lord said unto him* in a dream, *Do so and so.* Bid God welcome, and he will come again. Gideon is appointed, 1. To throw down Baal's altar, which it seems his father had, either for his own house or perhaps for the whole town. He must likewise *cut down the grove that was by it.* 2. To erect an altar to God, *to Jehovah his God.* God directs him to the place where he should build it, on the *top of the rock.* The word here used for the rock on which the altar was to be built signifies a fortress, or stronghold, erected, some think, to secure them from the Midianites. On this altar, (1) He was to offer sacrifice. Two bullocks he must offer: his father's *young bullock, and the second bullock of seven years old.* The former, we may suppose, he was to offer for himself, the latter *for the sins of the people* whom he was to deliver. (2) Baal's grove, or image, or whatever it was that was the sanctity or beauty of his altar, must not only be burnt, but must be used as fuel for God's altar. God ordered Gideon to do this, [1] To try his zeal for religion, which it was necessary he should give proofs of before he took the field. [2] That some steps might hereby be taken towards Israel's reformation, which must prepare the way for their deliverance. Sin, the cause, must be taken away, else how should the trouble, which was but the effect, come to an end?

II. Gideon was *obedient to the heavenly vision,* *v.* 27. He that was to command the Israel of God must first *save his people from their sins,* and then save them from their enemies. 1. He had servants of his own, whom he could confide in. 2. He did not scruple taking his father's bullock and offering it to God without his father's consent, because God, who expressly commanded him to do so, had a better title to it than his father had, and it was the greatest real kindness he could do to his father to prevent his sin. 3. He expected to incur the displeasure of his father's household by it; while he was sure of the favour of God, he feared not the anger of men. Yet, 4. To prevent their resistance in the doing of it he prudently chose to do it by night.

III. He was brought into peril of his life for doing it, *v.* 28-30. 1. It was soon discovered what was done, for the men of the city *rose early in the morning* to say their matins at Baal's altar. 2. It was soon discovered who had done it. 3. Gideon being found guilty of the fact, these degenerate Israelites require his own father to deliver him up: *Bring out thy son, that he may die.*

IV. He was rescued out of the hands of his persecutors by his own father, *v.* 31.

1. There were those that stood against Gideon, that would have him put to death. Notwithstanding the heavy judgments they were at this time under for their idolatry, yet they hated to be reformed. 2. Yet then *Joash stood for him*; he was one of the chief men of the city.

(1) This Joash had patronised Baal's altar, yet now protects him that had destroyed it, [1] Out of natural affection to his son. If Joash had a kindness for Baal, yet he had a greater kindness for his son. Or, [2] Out of a care for the public peace. The mob grew riotous, and, he feared, would grow more so, and therefore, as some think, he bestirred himself to repress the tumult. Or, [3] Out of a conviction that Gideon had

done well. Let us do our duty, and then trust God with our safety.

(2) Two things Joash urges:—[1] That it was absurd for them to plead for Baal. It is bad to commit sin, but it is great wickedness indeed to plead for it, especially to plead for Baal, that idol, whatever it is, which possesses that room in the heart which God should have. [2] That it was needless for them to plead for Baal. If he were not a god, as was pretended, they could have nothing to say for him; if he were, he was able to plead for himself.

(3) Gideon's father hereupon gave him a new name (*v.* 32); he called him *Jerubaal*: "Let Baal plead; let him plead against him if he can; if he have anything to say for himself against his destroyer, let him say it."

Verses 33-40

I. The descent which the enemies of Israel made upon them, *v.* 33. A vast number of Midianites, Amalekites, and Arabians, made their headquarters in the valley of Jezreel, in the heart of Manasseh's tribe, not far from Gideon's city. But it proved that *the measure of their iniquity was full* and the year of recompence had come; they must now *make an end to spoil* and *must be spoiled,* and they are *gathered as sheaves to the floor* (Mic. iv. 12, 13), for Gideon to thresh.

II. The preparation which Gideon makes to attack them in their camp, *v.* 34, 35. 1. God by his Spirit put life into Gideon: *The Spirit of the Lord clothed Gideon* (so the word is), clothed him as a robe, to put honour upon him, clothed him as a coat of mail, to put defence upon him. Whom God calls to his work he will qualify and animate for it. 2. Gideon with his trumpet put life into his neighbours, God working with him. (1) The men of Abiezer, though lately enraged against him for throwing down the altar of Baal, and though they had condemned him to death as a criminal, were now convinced of their error, and bravely came in to his assistance. (2) Distant tribes, even Asher and Naphtali, which lay most remote, though strangers to him, obeyed his summons, *v.* 35.

III. The signs which God gratified him with, for the confirming both of his own faith and that of his followers. Observe, 1. His request for a sign (*v.* 36, 37): "Let me by this *know that thou wilt save Israel by my hand,* let *a fleece of wool,* spread in the open air, be *wet with the dew,* and let the ground about it be dry." The purport of this is, *Lord, I believe, help thou my unbelief.* When he repeated his request for a second sign, the reverse of the former, he did it with a very humble apology, deprecating God's displeasure, because it looked so like a peevish humoursome distrust of God. God's favour must be sought with great reverence, a due sense of our distance, and a religious fear. 2. God's gracious grant of his request. See how tender God is of true believers though they be weak. Gideon would have *the fleece wet* and the *ground dry*; but then, lest any should object, "It is natural for wool, if ever so little moisture fall, to drink it in and retain it, and therefore there was nothing extraordinary in this," though the quantity wrung out was sufficient to obviate such an objection, yet he desires that next night the ground might be wet and the fleece dry, and it is done, so willing is God to *give to the heirs of promise strong consolation* (Heb. vi. 17, 18), even by two immutable things. He suffers himself, not only to be prevailed with by their importunities, but even to be prescribed to by their doubts and dissatisfactions. Is Gideon desirous that the dew of divine grace might descend upon himself in particular? He sees the fleece wet with dew to assure him of it. Does he desire that God will be as the dew to all Israel? Behold, all the ground is wet.

CHAPTER 7

Gideon in the field, commanding the army of Israel, and routing the army of the Midianites. I. What direction God gave to Gideon for the modelling of his army, by which it was reduced to 300 men, ver. 1, 8. II. What encouragement God gave to Gideon to attack the enemy, by sending him secretly into their camp to hear a Midianite tell his dream, ver. 9–15. III. How he formed his attack upon the enemy's camp with his 300 men, not to fight them, but to frighten them, ver. 16–20. IV. The success of this attack; it put them to flight, and gave them a total rout.

Verses 1–8

I. Gideon applies himself to do the part of a good general. He pitched near a famous well, that his army might not be distressed for want of water, and gained the higher ground, which possibly might be some advantage to him, for the Midianites *were beneath him in the valley*. Note, Faith in God's promises must not slacken, but rather quicken, our endeavours.

II. The army consisted of 32,000 men, a small army in comparison with what Israel might have raised, and a very small one in comparison with what the Midianites had now brought into the field; Gideon was ready to think them too few, but God tells him they are *too many*, v. 2. He would hereby silence and exclude boasting. This is the reason here given by him who knows the pride that is in men's hearts: *Lest Israel vaunt themselves against me*.

Two ways God took to lessen their numbers:— 1. He ordered all that would own themselves timorous and faint-hearted to be dismissed, v. 3. One would have thought there would be scarcely one Israelite to be found that against such an enemy as the Midianites, and under such a leader as Gideon, would own himself fearful; yet above two parts of three took advantage of this proclamation, and filed off. Some think the oppression they had been under so long had broken their spirits, others, more probably, that consciousness of their own guilt had deprived them of their courage. Sin stared them in the face, and therefore they durst not look death in the face. 2. He directed the cashiering of all that remained except 300 men, and he did it by a sign: *The people are yet too many* for me to make use of, v. 4. But God saith they are yet *too many*, which may help us to understand those providences which sometimes seem to weaken the church and its interests. Gideon is ordered to bring his soldiers to the watering, probably to the well of Harod (v. 1) and the stream that ran from it. Now some, and no doubt the most, would kneel down on their knees to drink, and put their mouths to the water as horses do. Others, it may be, would not make such a formal business of it, but as a dog laps with his tongue, a lap and away, so they would hastily take up a little water in their hands, and cool their mouths with that, and be gone. Three hundred and no more there were of this latter sort, that drank in haste, and by those God tells Gideon he would rout the Midianites, v. 7. (1) Men that were hardy, that could endure long fatigue, without complaining of thirst or weariness. (2) Men that were hasty, that thought it long till they were engaged with the enemy, preferring the service of God and their country before their necessary refreshment. It was a great trial to the faith and courage of Gideon, when God bade him let all the rest of the people but these 300 *go every man to his place*. Thus strangely was Gideon's army purged, and modelled, and reduced instead of being recruited. Let us see how this little despicable regiment, on which the stress of the action must lie, was accoutred and fitted out. Every soldier turns sutler: They *took victuals in their hands* (v. 8), left their bag and baggage behind, and every man burdened himself with his own provision, which was a trial of their faith, whether they could trust God when they had no more provisions with them than they could carry, and a trial of their diligence, whether they could carry as much as they had occasion for. This was indeed living from hand to mouth. Every soldier turns trumpeter as if they had been going rather to a game than to a battle.

Verse 9–15

Gideon's army being diminished as we have found it was, he must either fight by faith or not at all; God therefore here provides recruits for his faith, instead of recruits for his forces.

I. He furnishes him with a good foundation to build his faith upon. Nothing but a word from God will be a footing for faith. 1. A word of command to warrant the action. *Arise, get thee down* with this handful of men *unto the host*. 2. A word of promise to assure him of the success. *I have delivered it into thy hand*; it is all thy own. This *word of the Lord* came to him the same night, when he was greatly agitated and full of care how he should come off; *in the multitude of his thoughts within him these comforts did delight his soul*.

II. He furnishes him with a good prop to support his faith with. 1. He orders him to be his own spy, and now in the dead of the night to go down privately into the host of Midian, and see what intelligence he could gain: "*If thou fear to go down* to fight, go first only with thy own servant (v. 10) and *hear what they say*" (v. 11); and it is intimated to him that he should hear that which would greatly strengthen his faith. He must take with him *Phurah his servant*, probably one of the ten that had helped him to break down the altar of Baal. 2. Being so, he orders him the sight of something that was discouraging. It was enough to frighten him to discern, perhaps by moonlight, the vast numbers of the enemy (v. 12), the men like grasshoppers for multitude, and they proved no better than grasshoppers for strength and courage; the camels one could not count, any more than the sand. But, 3. He causes him to hear that which was to him a very good omen. He overheard two soldiers of the enemy, that were comrades, talking. (1) One of them tells his dream: He saw a barley-cake come rolling down the hill into the camp of the Midianites, and "methought this rolling cake struck one of our tents with such violence that it overturned the tent, forced down the stakes, and broke the cords at one blow, and buried its inhabitants," v. 13. (2) The other undertakes to interpret this dream, *This is nothing else save the sword of Gideon*, v. 14. Gideon, who had threshed corn for his family, and made cakes for his friend (*ch.* vi. 11–19), was fitly represented by a cake,—that he and his army were as inconsiderable as a cake made of a little flour, as contemptible as a barley-cake, hastily got together as a cake suddenly baked upon the coals, and as unlikely to conquer this great army as a cake to overthrow a tent. It was an evidence that the enemy was quite dispirited, and that the name of Gideon had become so formidable to them that it disturbed their sleep.

Lastly, Gideon was exceedingly encouraged. He was very well pleased to hear himself compared to a barley-cake, when it proved to effect such great things. He gave God the glory of it; and in a short ejaculation thanked God for the victory he was now sure of, and for this encouragement to expect it. He gave his friends a share in the encouragements he had received: *Arise*, prepare to march presently; *the Lord has delivered Midian into your hand*.

Verses 16–22

I. The alarm which Gideon gave to the hosts of Midian in the dead time of the night; for it was intended that those who had so long been a terror to Israel should themselves be routed and ruined purely by terror.

Gideon, 1. Divided his army, small as it was, into three battalions (v. 16), one of which he himself commanded (v. 19). 2. He ordered them all to do as he did, v. 17. Such is the word of command which our Lord Jesus, the captain of our salvation, gives his soldiers; for he has *left us an example*, with a charge to follow it: *As I do, so shall you do*. 3. He made his descent in the night, when they were secure and least expected it, and when the smallness of his army would not be discovered. In the night all frights are most frightful. He accoutred his army with every man a trumpet in his right hand, and an earthen pitcher, with a torch in it, in his left. The fewness of his men favoured his design. Three ways Gideon contrived to strike a terror upon this army, (1) With a great noise. Every man must blow his trumpet in the most terrible manner he could and clatter an earthen pitcher to pieces at the same time. (2) With a great blaze. The lighted torches were hid in the pitchers, and then, being taken out all together of a sudden, would make a glaring show. Perhaps with these they set some of the tents on the outside of the camp on fire. (3) With a great shout. Every man must cry, *For the Lord and for Gideon*, so some think it should be read in v. 18, for there the sword is not in the original, but it is in v. 20, *The sword of the Lord and of Gideon*. The sword of the Lord is all in all to the success of the sword of Gideon, yet the sword of Gideon must be employed always in subserviency and subordination to God.

This method here taken of defeating the Midianites may be alluded to, as typifying the destruction of the devil's kingdom in the world by the preaching of the everlasting gospel, the sounding of that trumpet, and the holding forth of that light out of earthen vessels, 2 Cor. iv. 6, 7. Thus God chose the *foolish things of the world to confound the wise*, a barley-cake to overthrow the tents of Midian, that the *excellency of the power might be of God only*; the gospel is a sword, not in the hand, but in the mouth.

II. The wonderful success of this alarm. Gideon's soldiers observed their orders, and *stood every man in his place round about the camp* (v. 21), sounding his trumpet to excite them to fight one another, and holding out his torch to light them to their ruin. Observe how the design took effect. 1. They feared the Israelites. *All the host* immediately took the alarm; they had reason to suspect that it was a very great army which was to be ushered in with all those trumpeters and torch-bearers. But there was more of a supernatural power impressing this terror upon them. God himself gave it the setting on. See the power of imagination, and how much it may become a terror at some times, as at other times it is a pleasure. 2. They fell foul upon one another: *The Lord set every man's sword against his fellow*, v. 22. God often makes the enemies of his church instruments to destroy one another. 3. They fled for their lives.

Verses 23–25

We have here the prosecution of this glorious victory. 1. Gideon's soldiers that had been dismissed got together again, and vigorously pursued those whom they had not courage to face. Those who were fearful and afraid to fight (v. 3) now took heart, when the worst was over, and were ready enough to divide the spoil, though backward to make the onset. 2. The Ephraimites, upon a summons from Gideon, came in unanimously, and secured the passes over Jordan, by the several fords, to cut off the enemies' retreat into their own country. 3. Two of the chief commanders of the host of Midian were taken and slain by the Ephraimites on this side Jordan, v. 25. Their names perhaps signified their

nature, *Oreb* signifies a *raven*, and *Zeeb* a *wolf* (*corvus* and *lupus*).

CHAPTER 8

This chapter further accounts of Gideon's victory over the Midianites, with the story of his life and government. I. Gideon prudently pacifies the Ephraimites, ver. 1–3. II. He bravely pursues the Midianites, ver. 4, 10–12. III. He justly chastises the insolence of the men of Succoth and Penuel (ver. 5–9), and ver. 13–17. IV. He honourably slays the two kings of Midian, ver. 18–21. V. After all this he modestly declines the government of Israel, ver. 22, 23. VI. He foolishly gratified the superstitious humour of his people, by setting up an ephod in his own city, ver. 24–27. VII. He kept the country quiet for forty years, ver. 28. VIII. He died in honour, and left a numerous family behind him, ver. 29–32. IX. Both he and his God were soon forgotten by ungrateful Israel, ver. 33–35.

Verses 1–3

No sooner were the Midianites, the common enemy, subdued, than the children of Israel were ready to quarrel among themselves. The Ephraimites, when they brought the heads of Oreb and Zeeb to Gideon as general, picked a quarrel with him and grew very hot upon it.

I. Their accusation was very peevish and unreasonable: *Why didst thou not call us when thou wentest to fight with the Midianites?* v. 1. Ephraim was very jealous of Manasseh, lest that tribe should at any time eclipse the honour of theirs. How unjust was their quarrel with Gideon! But, 1. Gideon was called of God, and neither took the honour to himself nor did he himself dispose of honours, but left it to God to do all. So that the Ephraimites in this quarrel, reflected upon the divine conduct. 2. Why did not the Ephraimites offer themselves willingly to the service? The case itself called them, they needed not wait for a call from Gideon. Cowards will seem valiant when the danger is over, but those consult their reputation who try not their courage when danger is near.

II. Gideon's answer was intended not so much to justify himself as to please and pacify them, v. 2, 3. He answers them, 1. With a great deal of meekness, and he won as true honour by this command which he had over his own passion as by his victory over the Midianites. 2. With a great deal of modesty, magnifying their performances above his own: *Is not the gleaning of the grapes of Ephraim*, who picked up the stragglers of the enemy, and cut off those of them that escaped, *better than the vintage of Abiezer* —a greater honour to them, and better service to the country, than the first attack Gideon made upon them? The improving of a victory is often more honourable, and of greater consequence, than the winning of it. Gideon shows us, (1) That humility of deportment is the best way to remove envy. (2) It is likewise the surest method of ending strife. Now what was the issue of this controversy? The Ephraimites had *chidden with him sharply* (v. 1), but Gideon's *soft answer turned away their wrath*, Prov. xv. 1.

Verses 4–17

I. Gideon, as a valiant general, pursuing the remaining Midianites, and, it seems, the two kings of Midian, being better provided than the rest for an escape, with 15,000 men got over Jordan before the passes could be secured by the Ephraimites, and made towards their own country. Gideon thinks he does not fully execute his commission to save Israel if he lets them escape.

1. His firmness was very exemplary under the greatest disadvantages and discouragements. (1) He took none with him but his 300 men. He expected more from 300 men, supported by a particular promise, than from so many thousands supported only by their own valour. (2) They were *faint, and yet pursuing*. (3) Though he met with discouragement from

those of his own people. If those that should be our helpers in the way of our duty prove hindrances to us, let not this drive us off from it. (4) He made a very long march by *the way of those that dwelt in tents* (*v.* 11). Now he found it an advantage to have his 300 men such as could bear hunger, and thirst, and toil.

2. His success was very encouraging to resolution and industry in a good cause. He routed the army (*v.* 11), and took the two kings prisoners, *v.* 12.

II. Here is Gideon, as a righteous judge, chastising the insolence of the disaffected Israelites, the men of Succoth, and the men of Penuel.

1. Their crime was great. Gideon, with a handful of feeble folk was pursuing the common enemy, to complete the deliverance of Israel. His way led him through the city of Succoth first and afterwards of Penuel. He only begs some necessary food for his soldiers that were ready to faint for want, and he does it very humbly and importunately: *Give, I pray you, loaves of bread unto the people that follow me, v.* 5. The request would have been reasonable if they had been but poor travellers in distress. Nothing could be more just than that their brethren should furnish them with the best provisions their city afforded. But the princes of Succoth neither *feared God nor regarded man.* For, (1) In contempt of God, they refused to answer the just demands of him whom God had raised up to save them, and were very willing to believe that the remaining forces of Midian, which they had now seen march through their country, would be too hard for him. (2) The bowels of their compassion were shut up against their brethren; they were as destitute of love as they were of faith, and would not give morsels of bread (so some read it) to those that were ready to perish. The men of Penuel gave the same answer to the same request, defying *the sword of the Lord and of Gideon, v.* 8.

2. The warning he gave them of the punishment of their crime was very fair. (1) He did not punish it immediately because he would not seem to do it in a heat of passion. But, (2) He told them how he would punish it (*v.* 7, 9), to show the confidence he had of success in the strength of God, and that they might upon second thoughts repent of their folly, sending after him succours and supplies. God gives notice of danger, and space to repent, that sinners may *flee from the wrath to come.*

3. The warning being slighted, the punishment, though very severe, was really very just.

(1) The princes of Succoth were first made examples. And he punished them with thorns and briers, but, it should seem, not unto death. With these, [1] He tormented their bodies. [2] He instructed their minds: With these *he taught the men of Succoth, v.* 16. The correction he gave them was intended, not for destruction, but wholesome discipline, to make them wiser and better for the future. *He made them know* (so the word is), made them know themselves and their folly, God and their duty. Note, Many are taught with the briers and thorns of affliction that would not learn otherwise.

(2) The doom of the men of Penuel comes next. [1] He *beat down their tower,* in which they trusted, perhaps scornfully advising Gideon and his men rather to secure themselves in that than to pursue the Midianites. [2] He *slew the men of the city* that were most insolent and abusive, for terror to the rest, and *so he taught the men of Penuel.*

Verses 18–21

The kings of Midian must now be reckoned with. 1. They are indicted for the murder of Gideon's brethren some time ago at Mount Tabor. When the children of Israel, for fear of the Midianites, made

themselves *dens in the mountains* (*ch.* vi. 2), those young men, it is likely, took shelter in that mountain, where they were found by these two kings, and most basely and barbarously slain in cold blood. 2. Being found guilty of this murder by their own confession by him must *their blood be shed,* though they were kings. 3. The execution is done by Gideon himself with his own hand, because he was the *avenger of blood;* he bade his son slay them. But, (1) The young man himself desired to be excused *because he was yet a youth.* (2) The prisoners themselves desired that Gideon would excuse it (*v.* 21), "Thou art at thy full strength; he has not yet come to it; therefore be thou the executioner."

Verses 22–28

I. Gideon's laudable modesty, after his great victory, in refusing the government which the people offered him. 1. It was honest in them to offer it: *Rule thou over us, for thou hast delivered us, v.* 22. 2. It was honourable in him to refuse it: *I will not rule over you, v.* 23. What he did was with a design to serve them, not to rule them—to make them safe, easy, and happy, not to make himself great or honourable. "*The Lord shall* still *rule over you,* and constitute your judges by the special designation of his own Spirit, as he has done." This intimates, (1) His modesty, and the mean opinion he had of himself and his own merits. (2) His piety, and the great opinion he had of God's government.

II. Gideon's irregular zeal to perpetuate the remembrance of this victory by an ephod made of the choicest of the spoils. 1. He asked the men of Israel to give him the ear-rings of their prey. 2. He himself added the spoil he took from the kings of Midian. 3. Of this he made an ephod, *v.* 27. (1) It was plausible enough, and might be well intended to preserve a memorial of so divine a victory in the judge's own city. But it was a very unadvised thing to make that memorial to be an ephod, a sacred garment. I would gladly put the best construction that can be upon the actions of good men, and such a one we are sure Gideon was. But we have reason to suspect that this ephod had, as usual, a teraphim annexed to it (Hos. iii. 4), and that, having an altar already built by divine appointment (*ch.* vi. 26), which he erroneously imagined he might still use for sacrifice, he intended this for an oracle, to be consulted in doubtful cases. So the learned Dr. Spencer supposes. Each tribe having now very much its government within itself, they were too apt to covet their religion among themselves. We read very little of Shiloh, and the ark there, in all the story of the Judges. Note, Many are led into false ways by one false step of a good man. The beginning of sin, particularly of idolatry and will-worship, *is as the letting forth of water,* so it has been found in the fatal corruptions of the church of Rome; therefore *leave it off before it be meddled with.* (2) It became a snare to Gideon himself, abating his zeal for the house of God in his old age, and much more to his house, who were drawn by it into sin, and it proved the ruin of the family.

III. Gideon's happy agency for the repose of Israel, *v.* 28. Gideon, though he would not assume the honour and power of a king, governed as a judge, and did all the good offices he could for his people; so that *the country was in quietness forty years.* Hitherto the times of Israel had been reckoned by forties. Othniel judged forty years, Ehud eighty—just two forties, Barak forty, and now Gideon forty, providence so ordering it to bring in mind the forty years of their wandering in the wilderness. After these, Eli ruled forty years (1 Sam. iv. 18), Samuel and Saul forty (Acts xiii. 21), David forty, and Solomon forty. Forty years is about an age.

Verses 29-35

The conclusion of the story of Gideon. 1. He lived privately, but retired to the house he had lived in before his elevation. Thus that brave Roman who was called from the plough upon a sudden occasion to command the army when the action was over returned to his plough again. 2. His family was multiplied. 3. He died in honour, in a good old age. 4. After his death the people corrupted themselves, and went all to naught. As soon as ever Gideon was dead they *went a whoring after Baalim*, v. 33. False worships made way for false deities. They now chose a new god (*ch.* v. 8), a god of a new name, *Baalberith* (a goddess, say some); Berith, some think, was Berytus, the place where the Phoenicians worshipped this idol. The name signifies *the Lord of a covenant*. Perhaps he was so called because his worshippers joined themselves by covenant to him, in imitation of Israel's covenanting with God; for the devil is God's ape. In this revolt of Israel to idolatry they showed, (1) Great ingratitude to God (*v.* 34): *They remembered not the Lord.* (2) Great ingratitude to Gideon, *v.* 35. Israel showed not kindness to Gideon's family. No wonder if those who forget their God forget their friends.

CHAPTER 9

The apostasy of Israel after the death of Gideon is punished by intestine broils among themselves. It is an account of the usurpation and tyranny of Abimelech, who was base son to Gideon; so we must call him, and not more modishly his natural son: he was so unlike him. I. How he thrust himself into the government at Shechem. II. How his doom was read in a parable by Jotham, Gideon's youngest son, ver. 7-21. III. What strifes there were between Abimelech and his friends the Shechemites, ver. 22-41. IV. How this ended in the ruin of the Shechemites (ver. 42-49), and of Abimelech himself, ver. 50-57.

Verses 1-6

We are here told by what arts Abimelech got into authority, and made himself great. His mother perhaps had instilled into his mind some towering ambitious thoughts, and the name his father gave him, carrying royalty in it, might help to blow up these sparks. He had no call from God to this honour as his father had, nor was there any present occasion for a judge to deliver Israel as there was when his father was advanced.

I. How craftily he got his mother's relations into his interests. Shechem was a city in the tribe of Ephraim, of great note. Joshua had held his last assembly there. If that city would but appear for him, and set him up, he thought it would go far in his favour. None would have dreamed of making such a one king, if he had not dreamed of it himself. And see here, 1. How he wheedled them into the choice, *v.* 2, 3. He basely suggested that Gideon having left seventy sons, they were designing to keep the power which their father had in their hands. "Now," says he, "you had better have one king than more." *Remember that I am your bone and your flesh.* The plot took wonderfully. The magistrates of Shechem were pleased to think of their city being a royal city and the metropolis of Israel, and therefore they *inclined to follow him; for they said, "He is our brother*, and his advancement will be our advantage." 2. How he got money from them to bear the charges of his pretensions (*v.* 4): *They gave him seventy pieces of silver;* money out of the house of Baal-berith, that is, out of the public treasury, which, out of respect to their idol, they deposited in his temple to be protected by him. How unfit was he to reign over Israel, because unlikely to defend them, who, instead of restraining and punishing idolatry, thus early made himself a pensioner to an idol! 3. What soldiers he enlisted. He hired into

his service vain and light persons, the scum and scoundrels of the country, men of broken fortunes, giddy heads, and profligate lives.

II. How cruelly he got his father's sons out of the way.

1. The first thing he did with the rabble he headed was to kill all his brethren at once, publicly, and in cold blood, threescore and ten men, one only escaping, all slain upon one stone. (1) The power of ambition what beasts it will turn men into! (2) The peril of honour and high birth.

2. Way being thus made for Abimelech's election, the men of Shechem proceeded to choose him king, *v.* 6. God was not consulted whether they should have any king at all, much less who it should be. But, (1) The Shechemites aided and abetted him in the murder of his brethren (*v.* 24), and then they *made him king. Pretium sceleris tulit hic diadema—His wickedness was rewarded with a diadem.* (2) The rest of the Israelites were so very sottish as to sit by unconcerned. It is for this that they are charged with ingratitude (*ch.* viii. 35): *Neither showed they kindness to the house of Jerubbaal.*

Verses 7-21

Only Jotham, the youngest son of Gideon, who by a special providence escaped the common ruin of his family (*v.* 5), dealt plainly with the Shechemites. Jotham did not go about to raise an army out of the other cities of Israel but he contents himself with giving a faithful reproof to the Shechemites, and fair warning of the fatal consequences.

I. His preface is very serious: "*Hearken unto me, you men of Shechem, that God may hearken unto you*", v. 7.

II. His parable is very ingenious—that when the trees were disposed to choose a king the government was offered to those valuable trees the olive, the fig tree, and the vine, but they refused it, choosing rather to serve than rule, to do good than bear sway. But the same tender being made to the bramble he accepted it with vain-glorious exultation.

1. He hereby applauds the generous modesty of Gideon, and the other judges who were before him, and perhaps of the sons of Gideon, who had declined accepting the state and power of kings when they might have had them, and likewise shows that it is in general the temper of all wise and good men to decline preferment and to choose rather to be useful than to be great. (1) There was no occasion at all for the trees to choose a king. Nor was there any occasion for Israel to talk of setting a king over them; for *the Lord was their king.* (2) When they had it in their thoughts to choose a king they did not offer the government to the stately cedar, or the lofty pine, which are only for show and shade, and not otherwise useful till they are cut down, but to the fruit trees, the vine and the olive. Those that bear fruit for the public good are justly respected and honoured. (3) The reason which all these fruit trees gave for their refusal was much the same. The olive pleads (*v.* 9), *Should I leave my fatness?* And the vine (*v.* 13), *Should I leave my wine*, wherewith both God and man are served and honoured? for oil and wine were used both at God's altars and at men's tables. And *shall I leave my sweetness, saith the fig tree, and my good fruit* (*v.* 11), *and go to be promoted over the trees?* or, as the margin reads it, *go up and down for the trees?* It is intimated, [1] That government involves a man in a great deal both of toil and care. [2] That those who are preferred to places of public trust and power must resolve to forego all their private interests and advantages, and sacrifice them to the good of the community. [3] That those who are advanced to honour and dignity are in great danger of losing their fatness and fruitfulness. Preferment is apt to make men proud and slothful, and

thus spoil their usefulness, for which reason those that desire to do good are afraid of being too great.

2. He hereby exposes the ridiculous ambition of Abimelech, whom he compares to the bramble or thistle, *v.* 14. The bramble is a worthless plant, not to be numbered among the trees, useless and fruitless, nay, hurtful and vexatious, scratching and tearing, and doing mischief; it began with the curse, and its end is to be burned. Such a one was Abimelech, and yet chosen to the government *by the trees, by all the trees.* Let us not think it strange if we see *folly set in great dignity* (Eccles. x. 6), and the *vilest men exalted* (Ps. xii. 8), and men blind to their own interest in the choice of their guides.

III. His application is very close and plain. In it, 1. He reminds them of the many good services his father had done for them, *v.* 17. 2. He aggravates their unkindness to his father's family. They had not *done to him according to the deserving of his hands, v.* 16. Gideon had left many sons that were an honour to his name and family, and these they had barbarously murdered; one son he had left was *the son of his maid-servant,* whom all that had any respect to Gideon's honour would endeavour to conceal, yet him they made their king. 3. He leaves it to the event to determine whether they had done well. (1) If they prospered long in this villainy, he would give them leave to say they had done well, *v.* 19. But, (2) If they had, as he was sure they had, dealt basely and wickedly in this matter, let them never expect to prosper, *v.* 20.

Jotham, having given them this admonition, made a shift to escape with his life, *v.* 21. But, for fear of Abimelech, he lived in exile, in some remote obscure place.

Verses 22–49

Three years Abimelech reigned, after a sort, without any disturbance; it is not said, He judged Israel, or did any service at all to his country, but so long he enjoyed the title and dignity of a king. But the triumphing of the wicked is short. The ruin of these confederates in wickedness was from the righteous hand of the God. *He sent an evil spirit between Abimelech and the Shechemites* (*v.* 23), that is, they grew jealous one of another and ill-affected one to another. This was from God. He permitted the devil, that great mischief-maker, to sow discord between them, and he is *an evil spirit,* whom God not only keeps under his check, but sometimes serves his own purposes by. Their own lusts were evil spirits; they are devils in men's own hearts; from them come wars and fightings. These God gave them up to, and so might be said to *send the evil spirits between them.* When men's sin is made their punishment, though God is not the author of the sin, yet the punishment is from him. The Shechemites that countenanced Abimelech's pretensions, aided and abetted him in his bloody project, and avowed the fact by making him king after he had done it, must fall with him, and fall first.

I. The Shechemites began to affront Abimelech. 1. They *dealt treacherously with him, v.* 23. It is not said, They repented of their sin in owning him. 2. They aimed to seize him when he was at Arumah (*v.* 41), his country seat. Expecting him to come to town, they *set liers in wait for him* (*v.* 25). Those who were thus posted, he not coming, took the opportunity of robbing travellers. 3. They entertained one Gaal, and set him up as their head in opposition to Abimelech, *v.* 26. This Gaal is said to be the son of *Ebed,* which signifies *a servant.* As Abimelech was by the mother's side, so he by the father's, the son of a servant. Here was one bramble contesting with another. He was a bold ambitious man, so he went over to them to blow the coals, and they *put their confidence*

in him. 4. They did all the despite they could to Abimelech's name, *v.* 27. They *went into the house of their god,* to solemnize their feast of ingathering, and there *they did eat, and drink, and cursed Abimelech,* praying to their idol to destroy him. That very temple whence they had fetched money to set him up with did they now meet in to curse him and contrive his ruin. 5. They pleased themselves with Gaal's vaunted defiance of Abimelech, *v.* 28, 29. They loved to hear that impudent upstart speak scornfully, (1) Of Abimelech. (2) Of his good father likewise, Gideon: *Is not he the son of Jerubbaal?* (3) Of his prime minister of state, *Zebul his officer, and ruler of the city.* Gaal aimed not to recover Shechem's liberty, only to change their tyrant: "*O that this people were under my hand!*" This pleased the Shechemites, who were now as sick of Abimelech as ever they had been fond of him. Men of no conscience will be men of no constancy.

II. Abimelech turned all his force upon them, and, in a little time, quite ruined them. Observe the steps of their overthrow.

1. The Shechemites' counsels were betrayed to Abimelech by Zebul his confidant, the ruler of the city, who continued hearty for him. *His anger was kindled,* (*v.* 30). He thinks it best that he should march his forces by night into the neighbourhood. How could the Shechemites hope to speed in their attempt when the ruler of their city was in the interests of their enemy?

2. Gaal, that headed their faction, having been betrayed by Zebul, Abimelech's confidant, was most wretchedly bantered by him. "It is but *the shadow of the mountains* which thou takest to be an army." By this he intended, (1) To ridicule him. (2) To detain him, while the forces of Abimelech were coming up. Then Zebul took another way to banter him, upbraiding him with what he had said but a day or two before, in contempt of Abimelech (*v.* 38). Now Zebul, in Abimelech's name, challenges him: *Go out, and fight with them,* if thou darest.

3. Abimelech routed Gaal's forces that sallied out of the town, *v.* 39, 40.

4. Zebul that night expelled Gaal, and the party he had brought with him into Shechem, out of the city (*v.* 41), sending him to the place whence he came.

5. Abimelech, the next day, set upon the city, and quite destroyed it, for their treacherous dealings with him. He resolved to follow his blow, and effectually to chastise their treachery. (1) He had intelligence brought him that the people of Shechem had come out *into the field, v.* 42, to plough and sow. Others think they went out into the field of battle; though Gaal was driven out, they would not lay down their arms. (2) He himself, with a strong detachment, cut off the communication between them and the city, and then sent two companies of his men, who were too strong for them, and they put them all to the sword, and *ran upon those that were in the fields and slew them.* (3) He then fell upon the city itself, and sowed it with salt, that it might remain a lasting monument of the punishment of perfidiousness. Yet Abimelech prevailed not to make its desolations perpetual; for it was afterwards rebuilt, and became so considerable a place that all Israel came thither to make Rehoboam king, 1 Kings xii. 1.

6. Those that retired into a stronghold of their idol-temple were all destroyed there. These are called *the men of the tower of Shechem* (*v.* 46, 47), some castle that belonged to the city, but lay at some distance from it. But that which they hoped would be for their welfare proved to them a snare and a trap, as those will certainly find that run to idols for shelter. All that were in it were either burnt or stifled with the smoke. What inventions men have to destroy one another! Whence come these cruel wars and

fightings but from their lusts? About 1000 men and women perished in these flames, many of whom, it is probable, were no way concerned in the quarrel between Abimelech and the Shechemites, yet, in this civil war, they came to this miserable end; for men of factious turbulent spirits *perish not alone in their iniquity*, but involve many more, that follow them in their simplicity, in the same calamity with them.

Verses 50–57

Thebez was a small city, probably not far from Shechem, dependent upon it, and in confederacy with it.

I. Abimelech attempted the destruction of this city (*v.* 50), and drove all the inhabitants of the town into the castle, or citadel, *v.* 51.

II. In the attempt he was himself destroyed, having his brains knocked out with a piece of a millstone, *v.* 57. Three circumstances are worthy of observation in the death of Abimelech:—1. That he was slain with a stone, as he had slain his brethren all *upon one stone*. 2. That he had his skull broken. Vengeance aimed at that guilty head which had worn the usurped crown. 3. That the stone was cast upon him by a woman, *v.* 53. Nothing troubled him so much as this, that it should be said, A woman slew him. See, (1) His foolish pride, in laying so much to heart this little circumstance of his disgrace. Here was no care taken about his precious soul, no concern what would become of that, no prayer to God for his mercy; but very solicitous he is to patch up his shattered credit, when there is no patching his shattered skull. "O let it never be said that such a mighty man as Abimelech was killed by a woman!" (2) His foolish project to avoid this disgrace; nothing could be more ridiculous; his own servant must run him through, not to rid him the sooner out of his pain, but *that men say not, A woman slew him.*

III. The issue of all is that Abimelech being slain, 1. Israel's peace was restored, and an end was put to this civil war. 2. God's justice was glorified (*v* 56, 57). Though wickedness may prosper awhile, it will not prosper always.

CHAPTER 10

I. The peaceable times Israel enjoyed under the two judges, Tola and Jair, ver. 1–5. II. The troublesome times that ensued. 1. Israel's sin that brought them into trouble, ver. 6. 2. The trouble itself, ver. 7–9. III. Their repentance and humiliation, their prayers and reformation, and the mercy they found with God, ver. 10–16. IV. Preparation made for their deliverance out of the hand of their oppressors, ver. 17, 18.

Verses 1–5

Quiet and peaceable were the reigns of these two judges, Tola and Jair, who make but a small figure and take up but a very little room in this history. But no doubt they were both *raised up of God* to serve their country in the quality of judges, not pretending, as Abimelech had done, to the grandeur of kings, nor, like him, taking the honour they had to themselves, but being called of God to it. 1. Concerning Tola it is said that he arose after Abimelech to defend Israel, *v.* 1. God animated this good man to appear for the reforming of abuses, the putting down of idolatry, the appeasing of tumults, and the healing of the wounds given to the state by Abimelech's usurpation. 2. Jair was a Gileadite, so was his next successor Jephthah, both of that half tribe of Manasseh which lay on the other side of Jordan. That which is chiefly remarkable concerning this Jair is the increase and honour of his family: *He had thirty sons, v.* 4. And, (1) They had good preferments, for they *rode on thirty ass colts*; that is, they were judges itinerant, who, as deputies to their father, rode from place to place in their several circuits to administer justice. (2) They had good possessions,

every one a city, out of those that were called, from their ancestor of the same name with their father, *Havoth-jair—the villages of Jair*; yet they are called *cities*. Villages are cities to a contented mind.

Verses 6–9

While those two judges, Tola and Jair, presided in the affairs of Israel, things went well, but afterwards,

I. Israel returned to their idolatry. 1. They worshipped many gods; not only their old demons Baalim and Ashtaroth, which the Canaanites had worshipped, but, as if they would proclaim their folly to all their neighbours, they served the gods of Syria, Zidon, Moab, Ammon, and the Philistines. It looks as if the chief trade of Israel had been to import deities from all countries. It is hard to say whether it was more impious or impolitic to do this. Those nations which by their wicked arts they sought to make their friends by the righteous judgments of God became their enemies and oppressors. 2. They did not so much as admit the God of Israel to be one of those many deities they worshipped, but quite cast him off. Those that think to serve both God and Mammon will soon come entirely to forsake God, and to serve Mammon only. If God have not all the heart, he will soon have none of it.

II. God renewed his judgments upon them, bringing them under the power of oppressing enemies. God had appointed that, if any of the cities of Israel should revolt to idolatry, the rest should make war upon them and cut them off, Deut. xiii. 12, &c. God brought the neighbouring nations upon them, to chastise them for their apostasy. The oppression of Israel by the Ammonites, the posterity of Lot, was, 1. Very long. It continued eighteen years. 2. Very grievous. They began with those tribes that lay next them on the other side Jordan, here called *the land of the Amorites* (*v.* 8) because the Israelites had so wretchedly degenerated, and had made themselves so like the heathen, that they had become, in a manner, perfect Amorites (Ezek. xvi. 3). But by degrees they pushed forward, came over Jordan, and invaded Judah, and Benjamin, and Ephraim (*v.* 9), three of the most famous tribes of Israel, yet thus insulted when they had forsaken God, and unable to make head against the invader.

Verses 10–18

I. A humble confession which Israel make to God in their distress, *v.* 10. They confess their omissions, for in them their sin began— "We have forsaken our God," and their commissions—"We have served Baalim, and herein have done foolishly, treacherously, and very wickedly."

II. A humbling message which God thereupon sends to Israel, whether by an angel (as *ch.* ii. 1) or by a prophet (as *ch.* vi. 8) is not certain. Now in this message, 1. He upbraids them with their great ingratitude, reminds them of the great things he had done for them. God had in justice corrected them, and in mercy delivered them, and therefore might reasonably expect that either through fear or through love they would adhere to him and his service. 2. He shows them how justly he might now abandon them to ruin, by abandoning them to the *gods that they had served*. To awaken them to a thorough repentance and reformation, he lets them see, (1) Their folly in serving Baalim. "*Go, and cry unto the gods which you have chosen*" (*v.* 14), try what they can do for you now. It is necessary, in true repentance, that there be a full conviction of the utter insufficiency of all those things to help us. We must be convinced that the pleasures of sense on which we have doted cannot be our satisfaction, nor the wealth of the world which we have coveted be our portion, that we cannot be happy or easy anywhere but in God. (2) Their misery and danger in forsaking God.

III. A humble submission which Israel hereupon made to God's justice, with a humble application to his mercy, *v.* 15. They not only repeat their confession, *We have sinned*, but, 1. They surrender themselves to God's justice: *Do thou unto us whatsoever seemeth good unto thee.* 2. They supplicate for God's mercy.

IV. A blessed reformation set on foot hereupon. They brought forth fruits meet for repentance (*v.* 16): *They put away the gods of strangers* (as the word is), strange gods, and they *served the Lord*. This is true repentance not only for sin, but from sin.

V. God's gracious return in mercy to them, which is expressed here very tenderly (*v.* 16): *His soul was grieved for the misery of Israel.* As he is pleased to put himself into the relation of a father to his people that are in covenant with him, so he is pleased to represent his goodness to them by the compassions of a father towards his children; for, as he is the Father of lights, so he is the Father of mercies.

VI. Things are now working towards their deliverance from the Ammonites' oppression, *v.* 17, 18. God had said, "I will deliver you no more"; but now they are not what they were, they are other men, they are new men, and now he will deliver them. 1. The Ammonites are hardened to their own ruin. They gathered together in one body, that they might be destroyed at one blow, Rev. xvi. 16. 2. The Israelites are animated to their own rescue. They assembled likewise, *v.* 17. During their eighteen years' oppression, as in their former servitudes, they were run down by their enemies, because they would not incorporate; each family, city, or tribe, would stand by itself, and act independently, and so they all became an easy prey to the oppressors, for want of a due sense of a common interest to cement them: but, whenever they got together, they did well; so they did here. When God's Israel become as one man to advance a common good and oppose a common enemy what difficulty can stand before them?

CHAPTER 11

The history of Jephthah, that by faith did great things (Heb. xi. 32). I. The disadvantages of his origin, ver. 1–3. II. The Gileadites' choice of him to be commander-in-chief against the Ammonites, ver. 4–11. III. His treaty with the king of Ammon about the rights of the two nations, that the matter might be determined, if possible, without bloodshed, ver. 12–28. IV. His war with the Ammonites, which he enters upon with a solemn vow (ver. 29–31), prosecutes with bravery (ver. 32), and ends with a glorious victory, ver. 33. V. The straits he was brought into at his return to his own house by the vow he had made, ver. 34–40.

Verses 1–3

The princes and people of Gilead we left, in the close of the foregoing chapter, consulting about the choice of a general. Now all agreed that Jephthah, the Gileadite, was a mighty man of valour, and very fit for that purpose, none so fit as he, but he lay under three disadvantages:—1. He was *the son of a harlot* (*v.* 1), of *a strange woman* (*v.* 2), an Ishmaelite, say the Jews. If his mother was a harlot, that was not his fault, however, it was his disgrace. Men ought not to be reproached with any of the infelicities of their parentage or extraction. The son of a harlot, if born again, born from above, shall be accepted of God, and be as welcome as any other to the glorious liberties of his children. 2. He had been driven from his country by his brethren. His father's legitimate children, insisting upon the rigour of the law, thrust him out from having any inheritance with them, without any consideration of his extraordinary qualifications, which merited a dispensation, and would have made him a mighty strength and ornament of their family. God often humbles those whom he designs to exalt, and makes that *stone the head of the corner*

which the builders refused; so Joseph, Moses, and David, the three most eminent of the shepherds of Israel, were all thrust out by men, before they were called of God to their great offices. 3. He had, in his exile, headed a rabble, *v.* 3. Being driven out by his brethren, his great soul would not suffer him either to dig or beg, but by his sword he must live; those that were reduced to such straits, and animated by such a spirit, enlisted themselves under him. *Vain men* they are here called, that is, men that had run through their estates and had to seek for a livelihood. These went out with him, not to rob or plunder, but to hunt wild beasts. This is the man that must save Israel.

Verses 4–11

I. The distress which the children of Israel were in upon the Ammonites' invasion of their country, *v.* 4.

II. The court which the elders made to Jephthah hereupon to come and help them. They did not write or send a messenger to him, but went themselves to fetch him. They know him to be a bold man, and inured to the sword, and therefore he must be the man. See how God prepares men for the service he designs them for, and makes their troubles work for their advancement. If Jephthah had not been put to his shifts by his brethren's unkindness, he would not have had such occasion as this gave him to exercise and improve his martial genius, and so to signalize himself and become famous. An army without a general is like a body without a head. Any community would humbly beg the favour of being commanded rather than that every man should be his own master. Blessed be God for government, for a good government.

III. The objections Jephthah makes against accepting their offer: *Did you not hate me, and expel me? v.* 7. Jephthah was very willing to serve his country, but he thought fit to give them a hint of their former unkindness to him, that they might repent of their sin in using him so ill. Thus Joseph humbled his brethren before he made himself known to them. Many slight God and good men till they come to be in distress, and then they are desirous of God's mercy and good men's prayers.

IV. Their urgency with him to accept the government they offer him, *v.* 8. Let this instance be, 1. A caution to us not to despise or trample upon any because they are mean. Make no man our enemy, because we know not how soon our distresses may be such as that we may be highly concerned to make him our friend. 2. An encouragement to men of worth that are slighted or ill-treated. Let them bear it with meekness and cheerfulness, and leave it to God to make their light shine out of obscurity.

V. The bargain he makes with them. God had forgiven Israel the affronts they had put upon him (*ch.* x. 16), and therefore Jephthah will forgive. 1. He puts to them a fair question, *v.* 9. "Now if, by the blessing of God, I come home a conqueror, tell me plainly *shall I be your head?* If I deliver you, under God, shall I, under him, reform you?" The same question is put to those who desire salvation by Christ. "If he save you, will you be willing that he shall rule you? for on no other terms will he save you. If he make you happy, shall he make you holy? If he be your helper, shall he be your head?" 2. They immediately give him a positive answer (*v.* 10): "We will *do according to thy words*; command us in war, and thou shalt command us in peace." Thus was the original contract ratified between Jephthah and the Gileadites, which all Israel, it should seem, agreed to afterwards, for it is said (*ch.* xii. 7), *he judged Israel.* He hereupon went with them (*v.* 11) to the place where they were all assembled (*ch.* x. 17), and there by common consent they *made him head and captain.* Jephthah, to obtain this little honour, was willing to expose his life for them (*ch.* xii. 3), and shall we be discouraged in our Christian warfare by any of the difficulties we may meet with in it, when Christ himself has promised *a crown of life to him that overcometh*?

VI. Jephthah's pious acknowledgment of God in this great affair (*v.* 11): *He uttered all his words before the Lord in Mizpeh,* that is, upon his elevation, he immediately retired to his devotions, and in prayer spread the whole matter before God. He utters before God all his thoughts and cares in this matter; for God gives us leave to be free with him. 1. "Lord, the people have made me their head; wilt thou confirm the choice, and own me as thy people's head under thee and for thee?" "Lord," said Jephthah, "I will not accept the government unless thou give me leave." 2. Thus Jephthah opened the campaign with prayer. That was likely to end gloriously which began thus piously.

Verses 12–28

The treaty between Jephthah, now judge of Israel, and the king of the Ammonites.

I. Jephthah, as one having authority, sent to the king of Ammon, who in this war was the aggressor, to demand his reasons for invading the land of Israel. Now this fair demand shows, 1. That Jephthah did not delight in war, though he was a mighty man of valour, but was willing to prevent it by a peaceable accommodation. War should be the last remedy, not to be used till all other methods of ending matters in variance have been tried. This rule should be observed in going to law. The sword of justice, as well as the sword of war, must not be appealed to till the contending parties have first endeavoured by gentler means to understand one another, and to accommodate matters in variance, 1. Cor. vi. 1. 2. That Jephthah did delight in equity, and designed no other than to do justice.

II. The king of the Ammonites now gives in his demand, which he should have published before he had invaded Israel, *v.* 13. His pretence is, "Israel took away my lands long since; now therefore restore those lands."

III. Jephthah gives a very full and satisfactory answer to this demand, showing that the Ammonites had no title to this country that lay between the rivers Arnon and Jabbok, now in the possession of the tribes of Reuben and Gad.

1. That Israel never took any land away either from the Moabites or Ammonites. He puts them together because they were brethren, the children of Lot, near neighbours, and of united interests, having the same god, Chemosh, and perhaps sometimes the same king. The lands in question Israel took away from Sihon king of the Amorites. If the Amorites, before Israel came into that country, had taken these lands from the Moabites or Ammonites, as it should seem they had (Num. xxi. 26; Josh. xiii. 25), Israel was not concerned to enquire into that or answer for it. 2. That they were so far from invading the property of any other nations than the devoted posterity of cursed Canaan (one of the branches of which the Amorites were, Gen. x. 16) that they would not so much as force a passage through the country either of the Edomites, the seed of Esau, or of the Moabites, the seed of Lot. 3. That in that war in which they took this land out of the hands of Sihon king of the Amorites he was the aggressor, and not they, *v.* 19, 20. They sent a humble petition to him for leave to go through his land, willing to give him any security for their good behaviour in their march. But Sihon not only denied them this courtesy, but he mustered all his forces, and fought against Israel (*v.* 20). Israel therefore, in their war with him, stood in their own just and necessary defence, and therefore, having routed his army, might justly, in further revenge of the injury, seize his country as forfeited. Thus Israel came to the possession of this country and it is very unreasonable for the Ammonites to question their title.

4. He pleads a grant from the crown, and claims under that, *v.* 23, 24. God gave them the land by an express and particular conveyance, such as vested the title in them, which they might make good against all the world. Deut. ii. 24, *I have given into thy hand Sihon and his land.* To corroborate this plea, he urges an argument *ad hominem—directed to the man*: *Wilt thou possess that which Chemosh thy god giveth thee?* Not that Jephthah thought Chemosh a god, only he is *thy god,* and the worshippers even of those dunghill deities that could do neither good nor evil yet thought themselves beholden to them for all they had (Hos. ii. 12). "Now," says Jephthah, "we have as good a title to our country as you have to yours."

5. He pleads prescription. (1) Their title had not been disputed when they first entered upon it, *v.* 25. (2) Their possession had never yet been disturbed, *v.* 26. He pleads that they had kept this country as their own now about 300 years, and the Ammonites in all that time had never attempted to take it from them. So that, supposing their title had not been clear at the first, yet, no claim having been made for so many generations, the entry of the children of Ammon, without doubt, was barred for ever. A title so long unquestioned shall be presumed unquestionable.

6. By these arguments Jephthah justifies himself and his own cause and condemns the Ammonites: "*Thou doest me wrong to war against me,* and must expect to speed accordingly," *v.* 27. The children of Israel, in the days of their prosperity and power (for some such days they had in the times of the judges) had conducted themselves very inoffensively to all their neighbours. The king of the Ammonites, when he would seek an occasion of quarrelling with them, was forced to look 300 years back for a pretence.

7. For the deciding of the controversy, he puts himself upon God and his sword, and the king of Ammon joins issue with him (*v.* 27, 28): *The Lord the Judge be judge this day.*

Neither Jephthah's apology, nor his appeal, wrought upon the king of the children of Ammon; they had found the sweets of the spoil of Israel, in the eighteen years wherein they had oppressed them (*ch.* x. 8), and hoped now to make themselves masters of the tree with the fruit of which they had so often enriched themselves.

Verses 29–40

We have here Jephthah triumphing, but troubled and distressed by an unadvised vow.

I. Jephthah's victory was clear. 1. God gave him an excellent spirit, and he improved it bravely, *v.* 29. The Spirit of the Lord came upon him, and very much advanced his natural faculties, enduing him with power from on high. Hereby God confirmed him in his office, and assured him of success in his undertaking. Thus animated, he loses no time, but with an undaunted resolution takes the field. 2. God gave him eminent success, and he bravely improved that too (*v.* 32). Having routed their forces in the field, he pursued them to their cities. But it does not appear that he utterly destroyed the people, nor that he offered to make himself master of the country. Though others' attempting wrong to us will justify us in the defence of our own right, yet it will not authorize us to do them wrong.

II. Jephthah's vow is dark, and much in the clouds. When he was going out from his own house upon this hazardous undertaking, in prayer to God for his presence with him he makes a secret but solemn vow or religious promise to God, that, if God would graciously bring him back a conqueror, whosoever or whatsoever should first come out of his house to meet him it should be devoted to God, and offered up for a burnt-offering. At his return, tidings of his victory coming home before him, his own and only daughter meets him with the seasonable expressions of joy. This puts him into a great confusion; but there was no remedy: after she had taken some time to lament her own infelicity, she cheerfully submitted to the performance of his vow. Now,

1. There are several good lessons to be learnt out of this story. (1) That there may be remainders of distrust and doubting even in the hearts of true and great believers. A fond conceit he had that he could not promise himself a victory unless he proffered something considerable to be given to God in lieu of it. (2) That yet it is very good, when we are in the pursuit or expectation of any mercy, to make vows to God of some instance of acceptable service to him, not as a purchase of the favour we desire, but as an expression of our gratitude to him and the deep sense we have of our obligations to render according to the benefit done to us. (3) That we have great need to be very cautious and well advised in the making of such vows, lest, by indulging a present emotion even of pious zeal, we entangle our own consciences. (4) That what we have solemnly vowed to God we must conscientiously perform, if it be possible and lawful, though it be ever so difficult and grievous to us. (5) That it well becomes children obediently and cheerfully to submit to their parents in the Lord, and particularly to comply with their pious resolutions for the honour of God and the keeping up of religion in their families, though they be harsh and severe, as the Rechabites, who for many generations religiously observed the commands of Jonadab their father in forbearing wine, and Jephthah's daughter here, who, for the satisfying of her father's conscience, and for the honour of God and her country, yielded herself as one devoted (*v.* 36). (6) That our friends' grievances should be our griefs. Where she went to bewail her hard fate the virgins, her companions, joined with her in her lamentations, *v.* 38. Those are unworthy the name of friends that will only rejoice with us, and not weep with us. (7) That heroic zeal for the honour of God and Israel, though alloyed with infirmity and indiscretion, is worthy to be had in perpetual remembrance. It well became the daughters of Israel by an annual solemnity to preserve the honourable memory of Jephthah's daughter, who made light even of her own life.

2. Yet there are some difficult questions that do arise upon this story.

(1) It is hard to say what Jephthah did to his daughter in performance of his vow. [1] Some think he only shut her up totally to sequester her from all the affairs of this life, and consequently from marriage, and to employ her wholly in the acts of devotion all her days. That which countenances this opinion is that she is *said to bewail her virginity* (*v.* 37, 38) and that *she knew no man, v.* 39. [2] It seems more probable that he offered her up for a sacrifice, according to the letter of his vow, misunderstanding that law which spoke of persons devoted by the curse of God as if it were to be applied to such as were devoted by men's vows (Lev. xxvii. 29, *None devoted shall be redeemed, but shall surely be put to death*). Since he had made such a vow, he thought better to kill his daughter than break his vow, and let Providence bear the blame, that brought her forth to meet him.

(2) But, supposing that Jephthah did sacrifice his daughter, the question is whether he did well. [1] Some justify him in it, and think he did well, and as became one that preferred the honour of God before that which was dearest to him in this world. But, [2] Most condemn Jephthah; he did ill to make so rash a vow, and worse to perform it. He could not be bound by his vow to that which God had forbidden by the letter of the sixth commandment: *Thou shalt not kill.* God had forbidden human sacrifices, so that it was (says Dr. Lightfoot) in effect a sacrifice to Moloch.

CHAPTER 12

I. Jephthah's rencounter with the Ephraimites, and the blood shed on that unhappy occasion (ver. 1–6), and the conclusion of Jephthah's life and government, ver. 7. II. A short account of three other of the judges of Israel: Ibzan (ver. 8–10), Elon (ver. 11, 12), Abdon, ver. 13–15.

Verses 1–7

I. The unreasonable displeasure of the men of Ephraim against Jephthah, because he had not called them in to his assistance against the Ammonites, that they might share in the triumphs and spoils, *v.* 1. Pride was at the bottom of the quarrel. Proud men think all the honours lost that go beside themselves, and then *who can stand before envy*? The anger of the Ephraimites at Jephthah was, 1. Causeless and unjust. Why *didst thou not call us to go with thee*? For a good reason. Because it was the men of Gilead that had made him their captain, not the men of Ephraim, so that he had no authority to call them. 2. It was cruel and outrageous. They get together in a tumultuous manner, pass over Jordan as far as Mizpeh in Gilead, where Jephthah lived, and no less will satisfy their fury but they will burn his house and him in it. Those resentments that have the least reason for them have commonly the most rage in them. Barbarous men take a pleasure in adding affliction to the afflicted.

II. Jephthah's warm vindication of himself. Whether they would be pacified or no, Jephthah takes care.

1. To justify himself, *v.* 2, 3. He makes it out that they had no cause at all to quarrel with him, for, (1) It was not in pursuit of glory that he had engaged in this war, but for the necessary defence of his country. (2) He had invited the Ephraimites to come and join with him, but they had declined the service. He had more cause to quarrel with them for deserting the common interests of Israel in a time of need. It is no new thing for those who are themselves most culpable to be most clamorous in accusing the innocent. (3) The enterprise was very hazardous. The honour they envied was bought dearly enough; they needed not to grudge it to him; few of them would have ventured so far for it. (4) He does not take the glory of the success to himself but gives it all to God: "*The Lord delivered them into my hands.* If God was pleased so far to make use of me for his glory, why should you be offended at that?"

2. When this just answer (though not so soft an answer as Gideon's) did not prevail to turn away their wrath, he took care both to defend himself from their fury and to chastise their insolence with the sword, by virtue of his authority as Israel's judge. (1) The Ephraimites had not only quarrelled with Jephthah, but, when his neighbours and friends appeared to take his part, they had abused them. "Who cares for you? All your neighbours know what you are, no better than fugitives and vagabonds, separated from your brethren, and driven hither into a corner." It is an ill thing to fasten names or characters of reproach upon persons or countries, as is common, especially upon those that lie under outward disadvantages: it often occasions quarrels that

prove of ill consequence, as it did here. (2) This affront raises the Gileadites' blood, and the indignity done to themselves, as well as to their captain, must be revenged. [1] They routed them in the field, *v.* 4. [2] The Gileadites, who perhaps were better acquainted with the passages of Jordan than the Ephraimites were, secured them with strong guards, who were ordered to slay every Ephraimite that offered to pass the river. Here was, *First*, Cruelty. There needed not this severity to cut off all that escaped. Shall the sword devour for ever? *Secondly*, Cunning enough in the discovery of them. It seems the Ephraimites, though they spoke the same language with other Israelites, yet had got a custom in the dialect of their country to pronounce the Hebrew letter *Shin* like *Samech*. Those that first used *s* for *sh*, did it either because it was shorter or because it was finer, and their children learnt to speak like them, so that you might know an Ephraimite by it; as in England we know a west-country man or a north-country man, nay, perhaps a Shropshire man, and a Cheshire man, by his pronunciation. *Thou art a Galilean, and thy speech betrays thee.* If they took a man that they suspected to be an Ephraimite, but he denied it, they bade him say *Shibboleth*; but either he *could not*, or he did not, pronounce it aright, but said *Sibboleth*, and so was known to be an Ephraimite, and was slain immediately. *Shibboleth* signifies a *river or stream*: "Ask leave to go over Shibboleth, the river."

3. The punishment of these proud and passionate Ephraimites, which in several instances answered to their sin. (1) They were proud of the honour of their tribe, but how soon were they brought to be ashamed or afraid to own their country! *Art thou an Ephraimite?* No, now rather of any tribe than that. (2) They had gone in a rage over Jordan to burn Jephthah's house with fire, but now they came back to Jordan as sneakingly as they had passed it furiously, and were cut off from ever returning to their own houses. (3) They had upbraided the Gileadites with the infelicity of their country, lying at such a distance, and now they suffered by an infirmity peculiar to their own country, in not being able to pronounce *Shibboleth*. (4) They had called the Gileadites, unjustly, fugitives, and now they really and in good earnest became fugitives themselves. He that rolls the stone of reproach unjustly upon another, let him expect that it will justly return upon himself.

III. The end of Jephthah's government. He judged Israel but six years, and then died, *v.* 7. Perhaps the death of his daughter sunk him so that he never looked up afterwards, but it shortened his days, and he went to his grave mourning.

Verses 8–15

We have here a short account of the short reigns of three more of the judges of Israel, the first of whom governed but seven years, the second ten, and the third eight.

I. Ibzan of Bethlehem, most probably Bethlehem of Judah, David's city, not that in Zebulun, which is only mentioned once, Josh. xix. 15. He ruled but seven years, but by the number of his children, and his disposing of them all in marriage himself it appears that he lived long. That which is remarkable concerning him is, 1. That he had many children, sixty in all. 2. That he had an equal number of each sex, thirty sons and thirty daughters, a thing which does not often happen in the same family, yet, in the great family of mankind, he that at first made two, male and female, by his wise providence preserves a succession of both in some sort of equality as far as is requisite to the keeping up of the generations of men upon earth. 3. That he took care to marry them all. The Jews say, Every father owes three

things to his son: to teach him to read the law, give him a trade, and get him a wife.

II. Elon of Zebulun, in the north of Canaan, was next raised up to preside in public affairs, to administer justice, and to reform abuses. Ten years he continued a blessing to Israel, and then died, *v.* 11, 12. Dr. Lightfoot computes that in the beginning of his time the forty years' oppression by the Philistines began (spoken of *ch.* xiii. 1), and about that time Samson was born.

III. Abdon, of the tribe of Ephraim, succeeded, and in him that illustrious tribe begins to recover its reputation. This Abdon was famous for the multitude of his offspring (*v.* 14): he had forty sons and thirty grandsons, all of whom he lived to see grown up. It was a satisfaction to him thus to see his children's children, but he did not see peace upon Israel, for by this time the Philistines had begun to break in upon them.

It is very strange that in the history of all these judges, some of whose actions are very particularly related, there is not so much as once mention made of the high priest, or any other priest or Levite, appearing either for counsel or action in any public affair, from Phinehas (Judges xx. 28) to Eli, which may well be computed 250 years; only the names of the high priests at that time are preserved, 1 Chron. vi. 4–7; and Ezra vii. 3–5. How can this strange obscurity of that priesthood for so long a time, now in the beginning of its days, agree with that mighty splendour with which it was introduced and the figure which the institution of it makes in the law of Moses? Surely it intimates that the institution was chiefly intended to be typical, and that the great benefits that seemed to be promised by it were to be chiefly looked for in its antitype, the everlasting priesthood of our Lord Jesus, in comparison of the superior glory of which that priesthood had no glory, 2 Cor. iii. 10.

Chapter 13

Samson, the last of the judges of Israel whose story is recorded in this book, and next before Eli. The figure he makes in this history is vastly different from that of his predecessors. We never find him at the head either of a court or of an army, never upon the throne of judgment nor in the field of battle, yet, in his own proper person, a great patriot of his country, and a terrible scourge and check to its enemies and oppressors. The history of the rest of the judges commences from their advancement to that station, but Samson's begins with his birth. I. The occasion of raising up this deliverer was the oppression of Israel by the Philistines, ver. 1. II. His birth is foretold by an angel to his mother, ver. 2–5. III. She relates the prediction to his father, ver. 6, 7. IV. They both together have it again from the angel (ver. 8–14), whom they treat with respect (ver. 15–18), and who, to their great amazement, discovers his dignity at parting, ver. 19–23. V. Samson is born, ver. 24, 25.

Verses 1–7

The first verse gives us a short account of the great distress that Israel was in, which gave occasion for the raising up of a deliverer. They did evil, as they had done, *in the sight of the Lord*. The enemies God now sold them to were the Philistines, their next neighbours, an inconsiderable people in comparison with Israel (they had but five cities of any note), and yet, when God made use of them as the staff in his hand, they were very oppressive and vexatious. And this trouble lasted longer than any yet: it continued forty years, though probably not always alike violent. When Israel was in this distress Samson was born; and here we have his birth foretold by an angel. Observe,

I. His extraction. He was of the tribe of Dan, *v.* 2. *Dan* signifies a *judge* or *judgment*, Gen. xxx. 6. The lot of the tribe of Dan lay next to the country of the Philistines, and therefore one of that tribe was most fit to be made a bridle upon them. His parents had been long childless. Many eminent persons were born of mothers that had been kept a great while in the want of the blessing of children, as Isaac, Joseph, Samuel, and John Baptist, that the mercy might be the more acceptable when it did come.

II. The glad tidings brought to his mother, that she should have a son. The messenger was an *angel of the Lord* (v. 3), yet appearing as a man, with the aspect and garb of a prophet, or man of God. It was not so much for the sake of Manoah and his wife, obscure Danites, that this extraordinary message was sent, but for Israel's sake, whose deliverer he was to be, and not only so but for the Messiah's sake, whose type he was to be, and whose birth must be foretold by an angel, as his was. The angel, in the message he delivers, 1. Takes notice of her affliction: *Behold now, thou art barren and bearest not.* "Now thou art barren, but thou shalt not be always so," as she feared, "not long so." 2. He assures her that she should *conceive and bear a son* (v. 3) and repeats the assurance, v. 5. To show the power of a divine word, the strongest man that ever was was a child of promise. 3. He appoints that the child should be a Nazarite from his birth, and therefore that the mother should be subject to the law of the Nazarites (though not under the vow of a Nazarite) and should *drink no wine or strong drink* so long as this child was to have its nourishment from her, either in the womb or at the breast, v. 4, 5. Other judges had corrected their apostasies from God, but Samson must appear as one, more than any of them, consecrated to God; and, notwithstanding what we read of his faults, we have reason to think that being a Nazarite of God's making he did exemplify, not only the ceremony, but the substance of that *separation to the Lord* in which the Nazariteship did consist, Num. vi. 2. The mother of this deliverer must therefore deny herself, and not eat any unclean thing; what was lawful at another time was now to be forborne. Women with child ought conscientiously to avoid whatever they have reason to think will be any way prejudicial to the health or good constitution of the fruit of their body. And perhaps Samson's mother was to refrain from wine and strong drink, not only because he was designed for a Nazarite, but because he was designed for a man of great strength, which his mother's temperance would contribute to. 4. He foretells the service which this child should do to his country: *He shall begin to deliver Israel.* Observe, *He shall begin* to deliver Israel. This intimated that the oppression of the Philistines should last long. He shall only *begin* to deliver Israel, which intimates that the trouble should still be prolonged. Now herein Samson was a type of Christ, (1) As a Nazarite to God, a Nazarite from the womb. For, though our Lord Jesus was not a Nazarite himself, yet he was typified by the Nazarites, as being perfectly pure from all sin, not so much as conceived in it, and entirely devoted to his Father's honour. (2) As a deliverer of Israel; for he is Jesus a Saviour, who saves his people from their sins. But with this difference: Samson did only begin to deliver Israel (David was afterwards raised up to complete the destruction of the Philistines), but our Lord Jesus is both Samson and David too, both the *author and finisher of our faith*.

III. The report which Manoah's wife, in a transport of joy, brings in all haste to her husband, of this surprising message, v. 6, 7. 1. Of the messenger. It was a man of God, v. 6. His countenance she could describe; it was very awful: he had such a majesty in his looks, that according to the idea she had of an angel he had the very countenance of one. But his name she can give no account of, nor to what tribe or city of Israel he belonged. She was abundantly satisfied that he was a servant of God; his person and message she thought carried their own evidence along with them, and she enquired no further. 2. Of the message. She gives him a particular account both of the promise and of the precept (v. 7), that he also might believe the promise. Thus should yoke-fellows communicate to each other their experiences of communion with God, that they may be helpful to each other in *the way that is called holy*.

Verses 8–14
An account of a second visit which the angel of God made to Manoah and his wife.

I. Manoah earnestly prayed for it, v. 8. 1. He takes it for granted that this child of promise shall in due time be given them, and speaks without hesitation of *the child that shall be born. Blessed are those that have not seen and yet*, as Manoah here, *have believed.* 2. All his care is *what they should do to the child* that should be born. Note, Good men are more solicitous and desirous to know the duty that is to be done by them than to know the events that shall occur concerning them; for duty is ours, events are God's. 3. He therefore prays to God to send the same blessed messenger again, to give them further instructions concerning the management of this Nazarite, fearing lest his wife's joy for the promise might have made her forget some part of the precept, in which he was desirous to be fully informed, and lie under no mistake. Would we have God's messengers, the ministers of his gospel, to bring a word proper for us, and for our instruction? *Entreat the Lord* to send them to us, to teach us, Rom. xv. 30, 32.

II. God graciously granted it: *God hearkened to the voice of Manoah*, v. 9.

1. The angel appears the second time also to the wife, when she is sitting alone, probably tending the flocks. Solitude is often a good opportunity of communion with God; good people have thought themselves never less alone than when alone, if God be with them.

2. She goes in all haste to call her husband, doubtless humbly beseeching the stay of this blessed messenger till she should return and her husband with her, v. 10, 11. The man of God is very willing she should call her husband, John iv. 16. Manoah is not disgusted that the angel did not this second time appear to him, but very willingly goes after his wife to the man of God. If the wife will lead, let not the husband think it any disparagement to him to follow her in that which is virtuous and praiseworthy.

3. Manoah having come to the angel, and being satisfied by him that he was the same that had appeared to his wife, does, with all humility, (1) Welcome the promise (v. 12): *Now let thy words come to pass;* this was the language, not only of his desire, but of his faith, like that of the blessed Virgin, Luke i. 38. "*Be it according to thy word.* Lord, I lay hold on what thou hast said, and depend upon it; *let it come to pass.*" (2) Beg that the prescriptions given might be repeated: *How shall we order the child?* The directions were given to his wife, but he looks upon himself as concerned to assist her in the careful management of this promised seed, according to order; for the utmost care of both the parents, and their constant joint endeavour, are little enough to be engaged for the good ordering of children that are devoted to God and to be brought up for him. Let not one devolve it on the other, but both do their best. Those to whom God has given children must be very careful how they order them, and what they do unto them, that they may drive out the foolishness that is *bound up in their hearts*, form their minds and manners well betimes, and *train them in the way wherein they should go*. Herein pious parents will beg divine assistance. "Lord, teach us how we may order our children, that they may be Nazarites, and living sacrifices to thee."

4. The angel repeats the directions he had before given (v. 13, 14). There is need of a good deal both of caution and observation, for the right ordering both of ourselves and of our children. Those that would preserve themselves pure must keep at a distance from that which borders upon sin or leads to it. When she was with child of a Nazarite, she must not eat *any unclean thing*; so those *in whom Christ is formed* must carefully *cleanse themselves from all filthiness of flesh and spirit,* and do nothing to the prejudice of that new man.

Verses 15–23

I. What further passed between Manoah and the angel at this interview. It was in kindness to him that while the angel was with him it was concealed from him that he was an angel. We could not bear the sight of the divine glory unveiled. God having determined to speak to us by men like ourselves, prophets and ministers, even when he spoke by his angels, or by his Son, they appeared in the likeness of men, and were taken but for men of God. Now,

1. The angel declined to accept his treat, and appointed him to turn it into a sacrifice. Manoah begged he would take some refreshment with him (v. 15), but the angel told him (v. 16) he would *not eat of his bread,* any more than he would of Gideon's, but directed him to offer it to God, *ch.* vi. 20, 21. Though we cannot live without meat and drink, yet we eat and drink to the glory of God, and so turn even our common meals into sacrifices.

2. The angel declined telling him his name. Manoah desired to know his name (v. 17), and of what tribe he was, *"That when thy sayings come to pass, we may do thee honour."* What Manoah asked for instruction in his duty he was readily told (v. 12, 13), but what he asked to gratify his curiosity was denied. God has in his word given us full directions concerning our duty, but he never designed to answer all the enquiries of a speculative head. We must never indulge a vain curiosity in our enquiries concerning these things, Col. ii. 18. *Nescire velle quæ Magister maximus docere non vult erudita inscitia est—To be willingly ignorant of those things which our great Master refuses to teach us is to be at once ignorant and wise.*

3. The angel assisted and owned their sacrifice. Thus we must bring our hearts to God as living sacrifices, and submit them to the operation of his Spirit. Prayer is the ascent of the soul to God. But it is Christ in the heart by faith that makes it an offering of a sweet-smelling savour: without him our services are offensive smoke, but, in him, acceptable flame. We may apply it to Christ's sacrifice of himself for us; he ascended in the flame of his own offering, for *by his own blood he entered in once into the holy place,* Heb. ix. 12.

II. An account of the impressions which this vision made upon Manoah and his wife. 1. In Manoah's reflection upon it there is *great fear, v.* 22. He had spoken with great assurance of the son they should shortly be the joyful parents of (v. 8, 12), and yet is now put into confusion. *We shall surely die.* It was a vulgar opinion generally received among the ancient Jews that it was present death to see God or an angel; and this notion quite overcame his faith for the present, as it did Gideon's, *ch.* vi. 22. 2. In his wife's reflection upon it there is great faith, v. 23. Here the weaker vessel was the stronger believer, which perhaps was the reason why the angel chose once and again to appear to her. Yoke-fellows should piously assist each other's faith and joy as there is occasion. None could argue better than Manoah's wife does here: *We shall surely die,* said her husband; "Nay," said she, "the tokens of his favour which we have received forbid us to think that he designs our

destruction. Had he thought fit to kill us, (1) He would not have accepted our sacrifice. (2) He would not have shown us all these things, nor would he have given us these exceedingly great and precious promises of a son that shall be a Nazarite and a deliverer of Israel." Note, Hereby it appears that God designs not the death of sinners that he has accepted the great sacrifice which Christ offered up for their salvation. And let those good Christians who have had communion with God in the word and prayer, to whom he has graciously manifested himself, take encouragement thence in a cloudy and dark day. "God would not have done what he has done for my soul if he had designed to forsake me, and leave me to perish at last; for his work is perfect, nor will he mock his people with his favours." Learn to reason as Manoah's wife did.

Verses 24–25

1. Samson's birth. The woman that had been long barren bore a son, according to the promise. 2. His name, *Samson,* has been derived, by some, from *Shemesh, the sun,* turned into a diminutive, *sol exiguus —the sun in miniature,* perhaps because, being born like Moses to be a deliverer, he was like him exceedingly fair, his face shone like a little sun, because of his great strength. The sun is compared to a *strong man* (Ps. xix. 5). A little sun, because the glory of, and a light to, his people Israel, a type of Christ, the Sun of righteousness. 3. His childhood. He far outgrew other children of his age; it appeared that the Lord blessed him, qualified him, both in body and mind, for something great and extraordinary. 4. His youth. When he grew up a little *the Spirit of the Lord began to move him, v.* 25. The Spirit of God moved Samson in the camp of Dan to oppose the incursions of the Philistines; there Samson, when a child, appeared among them, and signalized himself by some very brave actions, excelling them all in manly exercises and trials of strength: and probably he showed himself more than ordinarily zealous against the enemies of his country.

CHAPTER 14

The idea which this chapter gives us of Samson is not what one might have expected concerning one who, by the special designation of heaven, was a Nazarite to God and a deliverer of Israel; and yet really he was both. Here is, I. Samson's courtship of a daughter of the Philistines, and his marriage to her, ver. 1–5, 7, 8. II. His conquest of a lion, and the prize he found in the carcase of it, ver. 5, 6, 8, 9. III. Samson's riddle proposed to his companions (ver. 10–14) and unriddled by the treachery of his wife, ver. 15–18. IV. The occasion this gave him to kill thirty of the Philistines (ver. 19) and to break off his new alliance, ver. 20.

Verses 1–9

I. Samson, under the extraordinary guidance of Providence, seeks an occasion of quarrelling with the Philistines, by joining in affinity with them—a strange method, but the truth is Samson was himself a riddle, a paradox of a man, and did that which was really great and good, by that which was seemingly weak and evil.

1. As the negotiation of Samson's marriage was a common case, we may observe, (1) That it was foolish to set his affections upon a daughter of the Philistines. Shall one that is not only an Israelite, but a Nazarite, devoted to the Lord, covet to become one with a worshipper of Dagon? Shall one marked for a patriot of his country match among those that are its sworn enemies? His parents did well to dissuade him from yoking himself thus unequally with unbelievers. *"Is there never a woman among the daughters of thy brethren,* or, if none of our tribe, *never a one among all thy people,* never an Israelite, that pleases thee, or that thou canst think worthy of thy affection, that thou shouldest marry a Philistine?"

(2) If there had not been a special reason for it, it certainly would have been improper in him to insist upon his choice, and in them to agree to it at last. This Nazarite, in his subjection to his parents, asking their consent, and not proceeding till he had it, was an example to all children.

2. But this treaty of marriage is expressly said to be *of the Lord*, v. 4. Not only that God afterwards overruled it to serve his designs against the Philistines, but that he put it into Samson's heart to make this choice, that he *might have occasion against the Philistines*. It should seem, the way in which the Philistines oppressed Israel was, not by great armies, but by the clandestine incursions of their giants and small parties of their plunderers. In the same way therefore Samson must deal with them; let him but by this marriage get among them, and he would be a *thorn in their sides*.

II. Samson, by a special providence, is animated and encouraged to attack the Philistines. God prepared him for it by two occurrences:—

1. By enabling him, in one journey to Timnath, to *kill a lion*, v. 5, 6. (1) Samson's encounter with the lion was hazardous. It was a young lion, one of the fiercest sort, that set upon him, roaring for his prey. He was all alone in the vineyards, whither he had rambled from his father and mother, probably to eat grapes. Had Samson met with this lion in the way, he might have had more reason to expect help both from God and man than here in the solitary vineyards, out of his road. But there was a special providence in it, and the more hazardous the encounter was, (2) The victory was so much the more illustrious. It was obtained without any difficulty: he strangled the lion, and tore his throat as easily as he would have strangled a kid. Christ engaged the roaring lion, and conquered him in the beginning of his public work (Matt. iv. 1, &c.), and afterwards spoiled principalities and powers, triumphing over them *in himself*. He was *exalted in his own strength*. He did not boast of it, did *not so much as tell his father nor mother* that which many a one would soon have published through the whole country. Modesty and humility make up the brightest crown of great performances.

2. By providing him, the next journey, with honey in the carcase of this lion, v. 8, 9. When he came down the next time he found the carcase of the lion; the birds or beasts of prey, it is likely, had eaten the flesh, and in the skeleton a swarm of bees had knit, and made a hive of it, and had not been idle, but had there laid up a good stock of honey, which was one of the staple commodities of Canaan. Samson, having a better title than any man to the hive, seizes the honey with his hands. This supposes an encounter with the bees; but he that dreaded not the lion's paws had no reason to fear *their* stings. By dislodging the bees he was taught not to fear the multitude of the Philistines; though they *compassed him about like bees*. Of the honey he here found, (1) He ate himself, asking no questions for conscience' sake. John Baptist, that Nazarite of the New Testament, lived upon wild honey. (2) He gave to his parents, and they did eat; he did not eat all himself. He let his parents share with him. Let those that by the grace of God have found sweetness in religion themselves communicate their experience to their friends and relations, and invite them to come and share with them. He told not his parents whence he had it, lest they should scruple eating it. Honey is honey still, though in a dead lion.

Verses 10–20

An account of Samson's wedding feast and the occasion it gave him to fall foul upon the Philistines.

I. Samson conformed to the custom of the country in making a festival of his nuptial solemnities, which continued seven days, v. 10. It is no part of religion to go contrary to the innocent usages of the places where we live: nay, it is a reproach to religion when those who profess it give just occasion to others to call them covetous, sneaking, and morose. A good man should strive to make himself, in the best sense, a good companion.

II. His wife's relations paid him the accustomed respect of the place upon that occasion, and brought him thirty young men to keep him company during the solemnity, and to attend him as his grooms-men (v. 11): *When they saw him*, they brought these, seemingly to be his companions, but really to be a guard upon him, or spies to observe him.

III. Samson, to entertain the company, propounds a riddle to them, and lays a wager with them that they cannot find it out in seven days, v. 12–14. The usage, it seems, was very ancient upon such occasions. Now, 1. Samson's riddle was his own invention, for it was his own achievement that gave occasion for it: *Out of the eater came forth meat, and out of the strong came forth sweetness.* Read my riddle, what is this? This riddle is applicable to many of the methods of divine providence and grace. When God, by an overruling providence, brings good out of evil to his church and people,—when that which threatened their ruin turns to their advantage,—when their enemies are made serviceable to them, and the wrath of men turns to God's praise,—then comes *meat out of the eater* and *sweetness out of the strong*. See Phil. i. 12.

IV. His companions, when they could not expound the riddle themselves, obliged his wife to get from him the exposition of it, v. 15. If she would not use means with the bridegroom to let them into the meaning of it, they would *burn her and her father's house with fire*. Could anything be more brutish?

V. His wife, by unreasonable importunity, obtains from him a key to his riddle. It was *on the seventh day*, that is, the seventh day of the week (as Dr. Lightfoot conjectures), but the fourth day of the feast, that they solicited her to entice her husband (v. 15), and she did it, 1. With great art and management (v. 16). 2. With great success. At last, being quite wearied with her importunity, he told her what was the meaning of his riddle, and though we may suppose she promised secrecy, and that if he would but let her know she would tell nobody, she immediately told it to the *children of her people*; nor could he expect better from a Philistine. The riddle is at length *unriddled* (v. 18): *What is sweeter than honey*, or a better meat? Prov. xxiv. 13. *What is stronger than a lion*, or a greater devourer? Samson generously owns they had won the wager. But he thought fit to tell them: *If you had not ploughed with my heifer*, made use of your interest with my wife, *you would not have found out my riddle*. Satan, in his temptations, could not do us the mischief he does if he did not plough with the heifer of our own corrupt nature.

VI. Samson pays his wager to these Philistines with the spoils of others of their countrymen, v. 19.

VII. This proves a good occasion of weaning Samson from his new relations. He found how his companions had abused him and how his wife had betrayed him, and therefore *his anger was kindled*, v. 19. And, meeting with this ill usage among them, he *went up to his father's house*. It were well for us if the unkindnesses we meet with from the world, and our disappointments in it, had but this good effect upon us, to oblige us by faith and prayer to return to our heavenly Father's house and rest there. The inconveniences that occur in our way should make us love home and long to be there.

CHAPTER 15

Samson, when he courted an alliance with the Philistines, did but seek an occasion against them, ch. xiv. 4. I. From the perfidiousness of his wife and her father, he took occasion to burn their corn, ver. 1–5. II. From the Philistines' barbarous cruelty to his wife and her father, he took occasion to smite them with a great slaughter, ver. 6–8. III. From the treachery of his countrymen, who delivered him bound to the Philistines, he took occasion to kill 1000 of them with the jaw-bone of an ass, ver. 9–17. IV. From the distress he was then in for want of water, God took occasion to show him favour in a seasonable supply, ver. 18–20.

Verses 1–8

I. Samson's return to his wife, whom he had left in displeasure; when time had a little cooled his resentments, he came back to her, *visited her with a kid, v.* 1. It was intended as a token of reconciliation, and perhaps was then so used. When differences happen between near relations, let those be ever reckoned the wisest that are most forward to forgive and forget injuries.

II. The repulse he met with. Her father forbade him to come near her; for truly he had married her to another, *v.* 2. He endeavours, 1. To justify himself in this wrong: *I verily thought that thou hadst utterly hated her.* 2. He endeavours to pacify Samson by offering him his younger daughter. Samson scorned his proposal; he knew better things than *to take a wife to her sister,* Lev. xviii. 18.

III. The revenge Samson took upon the Philistines for this abuse. He looks upon himself as a public person, and the affront as done to the whole nation of Israel. Now the way Samson took to be revenged on them was by setting their cornfields on fire, which would be a great weakening and impoverishing to the country, *v.* 4, 5. 1. The method he took to do it was very strange. He sent 150 couple of foxes, tied tail to tail, into the cornfields; every couple had a stick of fire between their tails, with which, being terrified, they ran into the corn for shelter, and so set fire to it; thus the fire would break out in many places at the same time. We never find Samson, in any of his exploits, making use of any person whatsoever, either servant or soldier. By the meanness and weakness of the animals he employed, he designed to put contempt upon the enemies he fought against. This stratagem is often alluded to to show how the church's adversaries have often united in a fire-brand, some cursed project or other, to waste the church of God, and particularly to kindle the fire of division in it. 2. The mischief he hereby did to the Philistines was very great. It was in the time of wheat harvest (*v.* 1), so that the straw being dry it soon burnt the shocks of corn that were cut, and *the standing corn, and the vineyards and olives.*

IV. The Philistines' outrage against Samson's treacherous wife and her father. Understanding that they had provoked Samson to do this mischief to the country, the rabble set upon them and burnt them with fire, perhaps in their own house, *v.* 6. The Philistines had threatened Samson's wife that, if she would not get the riddle out of him, they would *burn her and her father's house with fire,* ch. xiv. 15. She, to save herself and oblige her countrymen, betrayed her husband. The very thing that she feared, and sought by sin to avoid, came upon her; she and her father's house were burnt with fire. The mischief we seek to escape by any unlawful practices we often pull upon our own heads.

V. The occasion Samson took hence to do them a yet greater mischief, which touched their bone and their flesh, *v.* 7, 8. "I have Israel's cause to plead as a public person, and for the wrongs done to them *I will be avenged on you.*" So he *smote them hip and thigh with a great stroke,* so the word is. And, when he had done, he retired, to a natural fortress in the top of the rock Etam, where he waited to see whether the Philistines would be tamed by the correction he had given them.

Verses 9–17

I. Samson violently pursued by the Philistines. They pitched in Judah, and spread themselves up and down the country, to find out Samson, whom they heard had come this way, *v.* 9. Here was an army sent against one man, for indeed he was himself an army. Thus a whole band of men was sent to seize our Lord Jesus, that blessed Samson, though a tenth part would have served now that his hour had come, and ten times as many would have done nothing if he had not yielded.

II. Samson basely betrayed and delivered up by the men of Judah, *v.* 11. Of Judah were they? Degenerate branches of that valiant tribe! Perhaps they were disaffected to Samson because he was not of their tribe. Out of a foolish fondness for their forfeited precedency, they would rather be oppressed by Philistines than rescued by a Danite. Often has the church's deliverance been obstructed by such jealousies and pretended points of honour. Sin dispirits men, nay, it infatuates them, and hides from their eyes the things that belong to their peace. Probably Samson went into the border of that country to offer his service, *supposing his brethren would have understood how that God by his hand would deliver them,* as Moses did, Acts vii. 25. They begged of him that he would suffer them to bind him, and deliver him up to the Philistines. Cowardly unthankful wretches!

III. Samson tamely yielding to be bound by his countrymen, and delivered into the hands of his enraged enemies, *v.* 12, 13. He patiently submitted, 1. That he might give an example of great meekness, mixed with great strength and courage; as one that had rule over his own spirit, he knew how to yield as well as how to conquer. 2. That, by being delivered up to the Philistines, he might have an opportunity of making a slaughter among them. Justly is their misery prolonged who, to oblige their worst enemies, thus abuse their best friend. Never were men so infatuated except those who thus treated our blessed Saviour.

IV. Samson making his part good even when he was delivered fast pinioned with two new cords. The Philistines, when they had him among them, *shouted against him* (*v.* 14), so triumphing in their success, and insulting over him. When they shouted against him as a man run down, confident that all was their own, then the *Spirit of the Lord came upon him.* Thus fired, 1. He presently got clear of his bonds. The two new cords, upon the first struggle he gave, broke, and were *melted* (as the original word is) from off his hands, no doubt to the great amazement and terror of those that shouted against him, whose shouts were hereby turned into shrieks. Observe, *Where the Spirit of the Lord is there is liberty,* and those who are free indeed who are thus freed. This typified the resurrection of Christ by the power of the Spirit of holiness. In it he loosed the bands of death, and its cords, the graveclothes, fell from his hands without being loosed, as Lazarus's were, because it was impossible that the mighty Saviour should be holden of them; and thus he triumphed over the powers of darkness that shouted against him, as if they had him sure. 2. He made a great destruction among the Philistines, who all gathered about him to make sport with him, *v.* 15. See how poorly he was armed: he had no better weapon than the jaw-bone of an ass, and yet what execution he did with it! he never laid it out of his hand till he had with it laid 1,000 Philistines dead upon the spot. Had it been the jaw-bone of a lion, especially that which he himself had slain, it might have helped to heighten his fancy and to make him think himself the more formidable; but to take the bone of that despicable animal was to do wonders by *the foolish things of the world,* that the *excellency of the power might be of God and not of man.*

V. Samson celebrating his own victory, since the men of Judah would not do even that for him. He composed a short song, which he sang to himself. The burden of this song was, *With the jaw-bone of an ass, heaps upon heaps, have I slain a thousand men, v.* 16. The same word in Hebrew (*chamor*) signifies both an *ass* and a *heap,* so that this is an elegant paronomasia, and represents the Philistines falling as tamely as asses. He also gave a name to the place, to perpetuate the Philistines' disgrace, *v.* 17. *Ramath-lehi,* the *lifting up of the jaw-bone.*

Verses 18–20

I. The distress which Samson was in after this great performance (*v.* 18). He found himself reduced to the last extremity for want of water and ready to faint. Josephus says, It was designed to chastise him for not making mention of God and his hand in his memorial of the victory he had obtained, but taking all the praise to himself: *I have slain a thousand men.*

II. His prayer to God in this distress. Those that forget to attend God with their praises may perhaps be compelled to attend him with their prayers. Afflictions are often sent to bring unthankful people to God. Two things he pleads with God in this prayer, 1. He owns himself God's servant in what he had been doing: He calls his victory a *deliverance,* a *great* deliverance; for, if God had not helped him, he had not only not conquered the Philistines, but had been swallowed up by them. Note, Past experiences of God's power and goodness are excellent pleas in prayer for further mercy. 2. His being now exposed to his enemies: *Lest I fall into the hands of the uncircumcised,* and then they will triumph, will *tell it in Gath, and in the streets of Ashkelon.*

III. The seasonable relief God sent him. God heard his prayer, and sent him water. I rather incline to our marginal reading: *God clave a hollow place that was in Lehi:* the place of his action was, from the jaw-bone, called *Lehi;* even before the action we find it so called, *v.* 9, 14. And there God caused water to spring up in abundance. Of this fair water he drank, and his spirits revived. We should be more thankful for the mercy of water did we consider how ill we can spare it.

IV. The memorial of this, in the name Samson gave to this upstart fountain, *Enhakkore, the well of him that cried,* thereby keeping in remembrance both his own distress and God's favour to him. Many a spring of comfort God opens to his people, which may fitly be called by this name; it is *the well of him that cried.* Samson had given a name to the place which denoted him great and triumphant— *Ramath-lehi,* the *lifting up of the jaw-bone;* but here he gives it another name, which denotes him needy and dependent.

V. The continuance of Samson's government after these achievements, *v.* 20. At length Israel submitted to him whom they had betrayed. It was a mercy to Israel that, though they were oppressed by a foreign enemy, yet they had a judge that preserved order and kept them from ruining one another. Twenty years his government continued, but of the particulars we have no account, save of the beginning of his government in this chapter and the end of it in the next.

CHAPTER 16

Samson's name signifies a little sun; we have seen this sun rising very bright, and we take it for granted that the middle of the day was proportionably illustrious, while he judged Israel twenty years; but this chapter gives us such an account of his evening as did not commend his day. This little sun set under a cloud, and yet, just in the setting, darted forth one such strong and glorious beam as made him even then a type of Christ, conquering by death. I. Samson greatly endangered by his familiarity with one harlot, and hardly escaping, ver. 1–3. II. Samson quite ruined by his familiarity with another harlot, Delilah. Observe, 1. How he was betrayed to her by his own lusts, ver. 4. 2. How he was betrayed by her to his sworn enemies, the Philistines, who, (1) By her means got it out of him at last where his great strength lay, ver. 5–17. (2) Then robbed him of his strength, ver. 18–20. (3) Then seized him, blinded him, imprisoned him, abused him, and, at a solemn festival, made a show of him, ver. 21–25. But, lastly, he avenged himself of them by pulling down the theatre upon their heads, and so dying with them, ver. 26–31.

Verses 1–3

1. Samson's sin, *v.* 1. His taking a Philistine to wife, in the beginning of his time, was in some degree excusable, but to join himself to a harlot that he accidentally saw among them was a profanation of his honour as an Israelite, as a Nazarite. *Tell it not in Gath.* 2. Samson's danger. Notice was sent to the magistrates of Gaza, perhaps by the treacherous harlot herself, that Samson was in the town, *v.* 2. The gates of the city were thereupon shut, guards set, all kept quiet, that Samson might suspect no danger. Now they thought they had him in prison, and doubted not but to be the death of him the next morning. O that all those who indulge their sensual appetites in drunkenness, uncleanness, or any fleshly lusts, would see themselves thus surrounded by their spiritual enemies! 3. Samson's escape, *v.* 3. He rose at midnight, perhaps roused by the checks of his own conscience. He arose with a penitent abhorrence (we hope) of the sin he was now committing, and of himself because of it, and with a pious resolution not to return to it. It was bad that he lay down without such checks; but it would have been worse if he had lain still under them. He makes immediately towards the gate, stays not to break open the gates, but plucks up the posts, takes them, gates and bar and all, *up to the top of a hill,* in disdain of their attempt to secure him with gates and bars, proof of the great strength God had given him and a type of Christ's victory over death and the grave. He not only rolled away the stone from the door of the sepulchre, and so came forth himself, but carried away the gates of the grave, bar and all, and so left it, ever after, an open prison to all that are his.

Verses 4–17

The burnt child dreads the fire; yet Samson, that has more than the strength of a man, in this comes short of the wisdom of a child; for, though he had been more than once brought into the highest degree of mischief and danger by the love of women and lusting after them, yet he would not take warning, but is here again taken in the same snare, and this third time pays for all. This bad woman, that brought Samson to ruin, is here named *Delilah,* an infamous name, fitly used to express the person that by flattery or falsehood brings destruction on those to whom kindness is pretended.

I. The affection Samson had for Delilah: he loved her, *v.* 4. Whether she was an Israelite or a Philistine is not certain. If an Israelite, which is scarcely probable, yet she had the heart of a Philistine.

II. The interest which the lords of the Philistines made with her to betray Samson, *v.* 5. 1. That which they told her they designed was to humble him, or afflict him; they would promise not to do him any hurt, only they would disable him not to do them any. 2. That which they desired was to know where his great strength lay, and by what means he might be bound. They engaged Delilah to get it out of him, telling her what a kindness it would be to them, and perhaps assuring her it should not be improved to any real mischief, either to him or her. 3. For this they bid high, promised to give her each of them 1,100 pieces of silver, 5,500 in all. With this she was hired to betray one she pretended to love.

III. The arts by which he put her off from time to time. She asked him *where his great strength lay*, and whether it were possible for him to be bound and afflicted (*v.* 6), pretending that she thought it was impossible he should be bound otherwise than by her charms.

1. When she urged him very much, he told her, (1) That he might be bound with *seven green withs*, *v.* 7. The experiment was tried (*v.* 8), but he *broke the withs* as easily *as a thread of tow is broken when it toucheth the fire, v.* 9. (2) When she still continued her importunity (*v.* 10) he told her that with two new ropes he might be so cramped and hampered that he might be as easily dealt with as any other man, *v.* 11. This experiment failed: the *new ropes* broke from off his arm *like a thread, v.* 12. (3) He then told her that the weaving of the seven locks of his head would make a great alteration in him, *v.* 13. This came nearer the matter than any thing he had yet said. His strength appeared to be very much in his hair, when, upon the trial of this, purely by the strength of his hair, he carried away the *pin of the beam* and *the web*.

2. In the making of all these experiments, it is hard to say whether there appears more of Samson's weakness or Delilah's wickedness. (1) Could any-thing be more wicked than her restless and unreason-able importunity with him to discover a secret which she knew would endanger his life. What could be more base and disingenuous, more false and treacher-ous, than to lay his head in her lap, as one whom she loved, and at the same time to design the betraying of him to those by whom he was mortally hated? (2) Could anything be more weak than for him to continue a parley with one who, he so plainly saw, was aiming to do him a mischief?

IV. The disclosure he at last made of this great secret; and, if the disclosure proved fatal to him, he must thank himself, who had not power to keep his own counsel from one that manifestly sought his ruin. Delilah signifies a *consumer*; she was so to him. Observe, 1. How she teased him, telling him she would not believe he loved her, unless he would gratify her in this matter (*v.* 15): *How canst thou say, I love thee, when thy heart is not with me?* She con-tinued many days vexatious to him with her impor-tunity, so that he had no pleasure of his life with her (*v.* 16). 2. How she conquered him (*v.* 17): He *told her all his heart.* God left him to himself to do this foolish thing, to punish him for indulging himself in the lusts of uncleanness. *No razor should come upon his head, ch.* xiii. 5. His consecration to God was to be his strength. Therefore the badge of his consecration was the pledge of his strength; if he lose the former, he knows he forfeits the latter. "If I be shaven, I shall no longer be a Nazarite, and then my strength will be lost." The making of his bodily strength to depend so much on his hair, which could have no natural influence upon it either one way or other, teaches us to magnify divine institutions, and to expect God's grace, and the continuance of it, only in the use of those means of grace wherein he has appointed us to attend upon him, the word, sacraments, and prayer.

Verses 18–21

The fatal consequences of Samson's folly in be-traying his own strength. Observe, 1. What care Delilah took to make sure of the money for herself. It would have grieved one's heart to have seen one of the bravest men in the world sold and bought, as a *sheep for the slaughter.* 2. What course she took to deliver him up to them according to the bargain.

See what a treacherous method she took (*v.* 19): She *made him sleep upon her knees.* See the fatal conse-quences of security. Satan ruins men by rocking them asleep, flattering them into a good opinion of their own safety, and so bringing them to mind nothing and fear nothing, and then he robs them of their strength and honour and leads them captive at his will. When he was asleep she had a person ready to cut off his hair, which he did so silently and so quickly that it did not awake him. 3. What little concern he himself was in at it, *v.* 20. He could not but miss his hair as soon as he awoke, and yet said, "*I will shake myself as at other times* after sleep." He soon found in himself some change, and yet *wist not that the Lord had departed from him*: he did not consider that this was the reason of the change. Note, Many have lost the favourable presence of God and are not aware of it; they have provoked God to withdraw from them, but are not sensible of their loss. 4. What improvement the Philistines soon made of their advantages against him, *v.* 21. The Philistines took him when God had departed from him. If we sleep in the lap of our lusts, we shall certainly wake in the hands of the Philistines. It is probable they had promised Delilah not to kill him, but they took an effectual course to disable him. The first thing they did, when they had him in their hands and found they could manage him, was to *put out his eyes*, by *applying fire to them*, says the Arabic version. They considered that his eyes would never come again, as perhaps his hair might, and that the strongest arms could do little without eyes to guide them, and therefore, if now they blind him, they for ever blind him. His eyes were the inlets of his sin: he saw the harlot at Gaza, and went in unto her (*v.* 1), and now his punishment began there. *They brought him down to Gaza*, that there he might appear in weakness where he had lately given such proofs of his strength (*v.* 3). They *bound him with fetters of brass* who had before been held in the cords of his own iniquity, and he did *grind in the prison.* Poor Samson, how hast thou fallen! How is thy honour laid in the dust!

Verses 22–31

Though the last stage of Samson's life was in-glorious there was honour in his death. No doubt he greatly repented of his sin, for that God was re-conciled to him appears, 1. By the return of the sign of his Nazariteship (*v.* 22): *His hair began to grow again, as when he was shaven*, that is, to be as thick and as long as when it was cut off. It seems to have been extraordinary, and designed for a special in-dication of the return of God's favour to him upon his repentance. 2. By the use God made of him for the destruction of the enemies of his people, and that at a time when it would be most for the vindica-tion of the honour of God, and not immediately for the defence and deliverance of Israel. Observe,

I. How insolently the Philistines affronted the God of Israel, 1. By the sacrifices they offered to Dagon, his rival. This Dagon they call their *god*, a god of their own making, represented by an image, the upper part of which was in the shape of a man, the lower part of which was in the shape of a fish, purely the creature of fancy; yet it served them to set up in opposition to the true and living God. It was only such a dunghill-deity as Dagon that was fit to be made a patron of the villainy. 2. By the sport they made with Samson, God's champion, they reflected on God himself. They made one another laugh to see how, being blind, he stumbled and blundered. They said, *Where is now thy God?* Being a penitent, his godly sorrow makes him patient, and he accepts the indignity as the punishment of his iniquity.

II. How justly the God of Israel brought sudden destruction upon them by the hands of Samson.

Thousands of the Philistines had got together, to attend their lords in the sacrifices and joys of this day, and to be the spectators of this comedy. They were all slain. Observe,

1. Who were destroyed: All the *lords of the Philistines* (v. 27), who had by bribes corrupted Delilah to betray Samson to them. Samson had been drawn into sin by the Philistine women, and now a great slaughter is made among them.

2. When they were destroyed. (1) When they were merry, secure, and jovial, and far from apprehending themselves in any danger. (2) It was when they were praising Dagon their god. (3) It was when they were making sport with an Israelite, a Nazarite, and insulting over him, persecuting him whom God had smitten. Those know not what they do, nor whom they affront, that make sport with a good man.

3. How they were destroyed. Samson pulled the house down upon them. (1) He gained strength to do it by prayer, v. 28. That strength which he had lost by sin he, like a true penitent, recovers by prayer. He prayed to God to remember him and strengthen him this once, thereby owning that his strength for what he had already done he had from God, and begged it might be afforded to him once more, to give them a parting blow. Samson died praying, so did our blessed Saviour; but Samson prayed for vengeance, Christ for forgiveness. (2) He gained opportunity to do it by leaning on the two pillars which were the chief supports of the building. The vast concourse of people that were upon the roof contributed to the fall of it. Few could escape being either stifled or crushed to death. Now in this, [1] The Philistines were greatly mortified. All their lords and great men were killed; the temple of Dagon (as many think the house was) was pulled down, and Dagon buried in it. [2] Samson may very well be justified, and brought in not guilty of any sinful murder either of himself or the Philistines. Nor was he *felo de se*, or *a self-murderer*, in it; for it was not his own life that he aimed at. [3] God was glorified in pardoning Samson's great transgressions, of which this was an evidence. [4] Christ was plainly typified. He pulled down the devil's kingdom, as Samson did Dagon's temple; and, when he died, he obtained the most glorious victory over the powers of darkness. Then when his arms were stretched out upon the cross, as Samson's to the two pillars, he gave a fatal shake to the gates of hell, and, *through death, destroyed him that had the power of death, that is, the devil* (Heb. ii. 14, 15), and herein exceeded Samson, that he not only died with the Philistines, but rose again to triumph over them.

Lastly, The story of Samson concludes, 1. With an account of his burial. 2. With the repetition of the account we had before of the continuance of his government: *He judged Israel twenty years.*

CHAPTER 17

What is related in the rest of the chapters to the end of this book was done soon after the death of Joshua, in the days of Phinehas the son of Eleazar, ch. xx. 28. But it is cast here that it might not interrupt the history of the Judges. That it might appear how happy the nation was in the judges it is here shown how unhappy they were when there was none. I. Then idolatry began in the family of Micah, ch. xvii. II. Then it spread itself into the tribe of Dan, ch. xviii. III. Then villainy was committed in Gibeah of Benjamin, ch. xix. IV. Then that whole tribe was destroyed for countenancing it, ch. xx. V. Then strange expedients were adopted to keep up that tribe, ch. xxi. In this chapter we are told how Micah an Ephraimite furnished himself, 1. With an image for his god, ver. 1–6. 2. With a Levite, such a one as he was, for his priest, ver. 7–13.

Verses 1–6

I. Micah and his mother quarrelling. 1. The son robs the mother. The old woman had hoarded, with long scraping and saving, a great sum of money,

1,100 pieces of silver. It is likely she intended, when she died, to leave it to her son. 2. The mother curses the son, or whoever had taken her money. See what mischief the love of money makes, how it destroys the duty and comfort of every relation. Outward losses drive good people to their prayers, but bad people to their curses.

II. Micah and his mother reconciled. 1. The son was so terrified with his mother's curses that he restored the money. 2. The mother was so pleased with her son's repentance that she recalled her curses, and turned them into prayers for her son's welfare: *Blessed be thou of the Lord, my son.*

III. Micah and his mother agreeing to turn their money into a god, and set up idolatry in their family. And though this was only the worship of the true God by an image, against the *second* commandment, yet this opened the door to the worship of other gods, Baalim and the groves, against the *first and great* commandment. Observe,

1. The mother's contrivance of this matter. When the silver was restored she pretended she had *dedicated it to the Lord* (v. 3) before it was stolen. "Come," said she to her son, "the money is mine, but thou hast a mind to it; let it be neither mine nor thine, but let us both agree to make it into an image for a religious use." Probably this old woman was one of those that came out of Egypt, and would have such images made as she had seen there; and perhaps told her son that this way of worshipping God by images was, to her knowledge, the old religion.

2. The son's compliance with her. It should seem, when she first proposed the thing he stumbled at it, knowing what the second commandment was. But, when the images were made, Micah, by his mother's persuasion, was not only well reconciled to them, but greatly pleased. But observe how the old woman's covetousness prevailed, in part, above her superstition. She had wholly dedicated the silver to make the graven and molten images (v. 3), but, when it came to be done, she made less than a fifth part serve, even 200 *shekels*, v. 4. Now observe,

(1) What was the corruption here introduced, v. 5. The man Micah had *a house of gods, a house of God*, so the LXX, for so he thought it, as good as that at Shiloh, and better, because his own, for people love to have their religion under their girdle, to manage it as they please. *A house of error*, so the Chaldee, for really it was so, a deviation from the way of truth and an inlet to all deceit. He made *teraphim*, little images which he might advise with as there was occasion, and receive informations, directions, and predictions from. Thus, while the honour of Jehovah was pretended (v. 3), yet, his institution being relinquished, these Israelites unavoidably lapsed into downright idolatry and demon-worship. Some room or apartment in the house of Micah was appointed for the temple or house of God; an ephod, or holy garment, was provided for his priest to officiate in, in imitation of those used at the tabernacle of God, and one of his sons he consecrated, probably the eldest, to be his priest. Here idolatry began, and it spread like a fretting leprosy. Dr. Lightfoot would have us observe that as 1,100 pieces of silver were here devoted to the making of an idol, which ruined religion, especially in the tribe of Dan, so 1,100 pieces of silver were given by each Philistine lord for the ruin of Samson.

(2) What was the cause of this corruption (v. 6): *There was no king in Israel*, no judge or sovereign prince to take cognizance of the setting up of these images. Every man did that which was *right in his own eyes*, and then they soon did that which was *evil in the sight of the Lord*. See what a mercy government is, and what reason there is that not only *prayers and intercessions, but giving of thanks, should be made*

for kings and all in authority, 1. Tim. ii. 1, 2. Nothing contributes more, under God, to the support of religion in the world, than the due administration of those two great ordinances, magistracy and ministry.

Verses 7–13

An account of Micah's furnishing himself with a Levite for his chaplain. I. By his mother's side he was of the family of Judah, and lived at Bethlehem. Thence he went to *sojourn where he could find a place*, and in his travels came to the house of Micah in Mount Ephraim, *v.* 8. Some think it was his unhappiness that he was under a necessity of removing, because he was neglected and starved, at Bethlehem. Israel's forsaking God began with forsaking the Levites. It is a sign religion is going to decay when good ministers are neglected and at a loss for a livelihood.

II. What bargain Micah made with him. Micah courts him into his family (*v.* 10), and promises him, 1. Good preferment: *Be unto me a father and a priest*. He asks not for his credentials. He might serve for a priest to a graven image, like Jeroboam's priest of the *lowest of the people*, 1 Kings xii. 31. No marvel if those who can make any thing serve for a god can also make any thing serve for a priest. 2. A tolerable maintenance. He will allow him *meat, and drink, and clothes, a double suit*, so the word is in the margin, a better and a worse, one for every day's wear and one for holy days, and ten shekels, about twenty-five shillings, a year for spending money—a poor salary in comparison of what God provided for the Levites that behaved well; but those that forsake God's service will never better themselves, nor find a better master. The ministry is the best calling but the worst trade in the world.

III. The Levite's settlement with him (*v.* 11): He was *content to dwell with the man*; though his work was superstitious and his wages were scandalous. Micah, thinking himself holier than any of his neighbours, presumed to consecrate this Levite, *v.* 12.

IV. Micah's satisfaction in this (*v.* 13): *Now know I that the Lord will do me good.* 1. He thought it was a sign of God's favour to him and his images that he had so opportunely sent a Levite to his door. 2. He thought now that the error of his priesthood was amended all was well, though he still retained his graven and molten image. Note, Many deceive themselves into a good opinion of their state by a partial reformation. They think they are as good as they should be, because, in some one particular instance, they are not so bad as they have been. 3. He thought the making of a Levite into a priest was a very meritorious act, which really was a presumptuous usurpation. 4. He thought that having a Levite in the house with him would of course entitle him to the divine favour. Having a Levite to be their priest, amounts to no security at all that God will do them good, unless they be good themselves, and make a good use of these advantages.

CHAPTER 18

How idolatry crept into the family of Micah we read in the preceding chapter, how it was translated thence into the tribe of Dan we have an account in this chapter. The tribe of Dan had their lot assigned them last of all the tribes, and a considerable city in the utmost corner of Canaan northward was added to it. Now here we are told, I. How they sent spies to bring them an account of the place, who, by the way, got acquainted with Micah's priest, ver. 1–6. II. What an encouraging report these spies brought back, ver. 7–10. III. What forces were sent to conquer Laish, ver. 11–13. IV. How they, by the way, plundered Micah of his gods, ver. 14–26. V. How easily they conquered Laish, ver. 27–29, and, when they had it, set up the graven image in it, ver. 30, 31.

Verses 1–6

1. The eye which these Danites had upon Laish, not the whole tribe of Dan, but one family of them, to whose lot, in the subdivision of Canaan, that city fell. Hitherto this family had sojourned with their brethren, who had taken possession of their lot, which lay between Judah and the Philistines, and had declined going to their own city, because there was *no king in Israel* to rule over them, *v.* 1. But at length necessity forced them to arouse themselves, and they began to think of an inheritance to dwell in. 2. They sent *five men to search the land* (*v.* 2). The men they sent were men of valour, who, if they fell into their enemies' hands, knew how to look danger in the face. 3. The acquaintance which their spies got with Micah's priest. It seems, they had known this Levite formerly, he having in his rambles been sometimes in their country. They knew him again by his voice, *v.* 3. They, understanding that he had an oracle in his custody, desired he would tell them whether they should prosper in their present undertaking, *v.* 5. They seem to have had a greater opinion of Micah's teraphim than of God's urim; for they had passed by Shiloh, and, for aught that appears, had not enquired there of God's high priest, but Micah's shabby Levite shall be an oracle to them. He made them believe he had an answer from God encouraging them to go on, and assuring them of good success (*v.* 6).

Verses 7–13

I. The observation which the spies made upon the city of Laish, *v.* 7. Never was place so ill governed and so ill guarded, which would make it a very easy prey to the invader.

1. It was ill governed, for every man might be as bad as he would, and there was no magistrate, no *heir of restraint* (as the word is), so that by the most impudent immoralities they provoked God's wrath, and by all manner of mutual mischiefs weakened and consumed one another. See here, (1) What the office of magistrate is. They are to be *heirs of restraint*, for the restraining of that which is evil. They are *possessors of restraint*, entrusted with their authority for this end, that they may check and suppress every thing that is vicious and be *a terror to evil doers*. It is only God's grace that can renew men's depraved minds and turn their hearts; but the magistrate's power may restrain their bad practices and tie their hands, so that the wickedness of the wicked may not be either so injurious or so infectious as otherwise it would be. (2) See what method must be used for the restraint of wickedness. Sinners must be put to shame, that those who will not be restrained by the shamefulness of the sin before God and their own consciences may be restrained by the shamefulness of the punishment before men. All ways must be tried to dash sin out of countenance and cover it with contempt, to make people ashamed of their idleness, drunkenness, cheating, lying, and other sins, by making reputation always appear on virtue's side. (3) See how miserable, and how near to ruin, those places are that either have no magistrates or none that bear the sword to any purpose.

2. It was ill guarded. The people of Laish were careless, quiet, and secure, their gates left open, their walls out of repair, because under no apprehension of danger in any way. It was a sign that the Israelites, through their sloth and cowardice, were not now such a terror to the Canaanites as they were when they first came among them, else the city of Laish, which probably knew itself to be assigned to them, would not have been so very secure. And, *lastly*, they had *no business with any man*, which bespeaks either the idleness or the independency they affected: they scorned to be either in subjection to or alliance with any of their neighbours. They cared for nobody and therefore nobody cared for them. Such as these were the men of Laish.

II. The encouragement which they consequently gave to their countrymen that sent them to prosecute their design upon this city, v. 8–10. 1. They represent the place as desirable (v. 9), better than the mountainous country into which they were crowded by the Philistines. 2. They represent it as attainable. They do not at all question but, with God's blessing, they may soon get possession of it; for *the people are secure*, v. 10.

III. The Danites' expedition against Laish. This particular family of them, to whose lot that city fell, now at length make towards it, v. 11–13. The military men were but 600 in all. It was strange that none of their brethren of their own tribe came in to their assistance; but it was long after Israel came to Canaan before there appeared among them anything of a public spirit. It appears (by v. 21) that these 600 were the whole number that went to settle there, for they had their families and effects with them, their *little ones and cattle*. The second day's march brought them to Mount Ephraim, near Micah's house (v. 13), and there we must pause awhile.

Verses 14–26

The Danites had sent out their spies to find out a country for them. Now that they came to the place they oblige them with a further discovery—they can tell them where there are gods: "Here, *in these houses*, there are an ephod, and teraphim, and a great many fine things for devotion, such as we have not the like in our country; *now therefore consider what you have to do*, v. 14. We consulted them, and had a good answer from them; they are worth having, and, if we can but make ourselves masters of these gods, we may the better hope to prosper, and make ourselves masters of Laish." So far they were in the right, that it was desirable to have God's presence with them, but wretchedly mistaken when they took these images (which were fitter to be used in a puppet-play than in acts of devotion) for tokens of God's presence. The place they were going to settle in being so far from Shiloh, they thought they had more need of a *house of gods* among themselves than Micah had that lived so near to it. Being determined to take these gods along with them, we are here told how they stole the images, cajoled the priest, and frightened Micah from attempting to rescue them.

I. The five men that knew the house and the avenues to it, and particularly the chapel, went in and fetched out the images, with the ephod, and teraphim, and all the appurtenances, while the 600 kept the priest in talk at the gate, v. 16–18. See what little care this sorry priest took of his gods. See how impotent these sorry gods were, that could not keep themselves from being stolen. O the sottishness of these Danites! They must have *gods to go before them*, not of their own making indeed, but, which was as bad, of their own stealing. Their idolatry began in theft, a proper prologue for such an opera. In order to the breaking of the second commandment, they begin with the eighth, and take their neighbour's goods to make them their gods.

II. They set upon the priest, and flattered him into a good humour, not only to let the gods go, but to go himself along with them; for without him they knew not well how to make use of the gods. Observe, 1. How they tempted him, v. 19. They assured him of better preferment with them than what he now had. 2. How they won him. A little persuasion served: *His heart was glad*, v. 20. He takes the images with him, and carries the infection of the idolatry into a whole city. If ten shekels won him (as Bishop Hall expresses it), eleven would lose him; for what can hold those that have made shipwreck of a good conscience? *The hireling flees because he is a hireling*.

III. They frightened Micah back when he pursued

them to recover his gods. His neighbours got together, and pursued the robbers, who, having their children and cattle before them (v. 21), could make no great haste. The pursuers called after them, desiring to speak a word with them; those in the rear turned about and asked Micah what he would have, v. 23. He argues with them, and pleads his right, which he thought should prevail; but they, in answer, plead their might, which, it proved, did prevail.

1. He insists upon the wrong they had certainly done him (v. 24): "*You have taken away my gods*, my images of God. I made them myself." What a folly was it for him to call those his *gods* which he had made, when he only that made us is to be worshipped by us as a God!

2. They insist upon the mischief they would certainly do him if he prosecuted his demand. They would not hear reason, nor do justice, nor so much as offer to pay him the prime cost he had been at upon those images. They would not so much as give him good words, but resolved to justify their robbery with murder if he did not immediately let fall his claims, v. 25. Micah has not courage enough to venture his life for the rescue of his gods, so little opinion has he of their being able to protect him and bear him out, and therefore tamely gives them up (v. 26). If the loss of our idols cure us of the love of them, and make us say, *What have we to do any more with idols?* the loss will be unspeakable again. See Isa. ii. 20; xxx. 22.

Verses 27–31

I. Laish conquered by the Danites. They proceeded on their march, and, because they met with no disaster, perhaps concluded they had not done amiss in robbing Micah. Many justify themselves in their impiety by their prosperity. Observe, 1. The people of Laish were quiet and secure, which made them a very easy prey to this little handful of men that came upon them, v. 27. 2. What a complete victory they obtained over them: They *put all the people to the sword*, and burnt down so much of the city as they thought fit to rebuild (v. 27, 28). 3. How the conquerors settled themselves in their room, v. 28, 29. They built the city, or much of it, anew and *called the name of it Dan*, to be a witness for them that, though separated so far off from their brethren, they were nevertheless Danites by birth.

II. Idolatry immediately set up there. God had graciously performed his promise, in putting them in possession of that which fell to their lot. But the first thing they do after they are settled is to break his statutes. As soon as they began to settle themselves they *set up the graven image* (v. 30), perversely attributing their success to that idol. Their Levite, who officiated as priest, is at length *named here*— *Jonathan, the son of Gershom, the son of Manasseh*. The word *Manasseh*, in the original, has the letter נ, *n*, set over the head, which, some of the Jewish rabbis say, is an intimation that it should be left out, and then *Manasseh* will be *Moses*, and this Levite, they say, was grandson to the famous Moses, who indeed had a son named Gershom. The vulgar Latin reads it *Moses*. And if indeed Moses had a grandson that was rakish, and was picked up as a fit tool to be made use of in the setting up of idolatry, it is not the only instance of the unhappy degenerating of the posterity of great and good men. Children's children are not always the crown of old men. But the learned Bishop Patrick takes this to be an idle conceit of the rabbis, and supposes this Jonathan to be of some other family of the Levites. How long these corruptions continued we are told in the close. The posterity of this Jonathan continued to act as priests to this family of Dan that was seated as Laish. These images continued till Samuel's time, for so long *the* ark of God was at Shiloh; and it is probable that in his time effectual care was taken to suppress and abolish this idolatry. See how dangerous it is to admit an infection, for spiritual distempers are not so soon cured as caught.

CHAPTER 19

The three remaining chapters of this book contain a most tragical story of the wickedness of the men of Gibeah, patronised by the tribe of Benjamin. This seems to have been when there was no king, no judge, in Israel (ver. 1, and ch. xxi. 25). These iniquities, the Danites' idolatry, and the Benjamites' immorality, let in that general apostasy, ch. iii. 7. The abuse of the Levite's concubine is here related. I. Her adulterous elopement from him, ver. 1, 2. II. His reconciliation to her, and the journey he took to fetch her home, ver. 3. III. Her father's kind entertainment of him, ver. 4–9. IV. The abuse he met with at Gibeah, 1. He was neglected by the men of Gibeah (ver. 10–15) and entertained by an Ephraimite that sojourned among them, ver. 16–21. 2. They set upon him in his quarters, as the Sodomites did on Lot's guests, ver. 22–24. 3. They villainously forced his concubine to death, ver. 25–28. V. The course he took to send notice of this to all the tribes of Israel, ver. 29, 30.

Verses 1–15

This Levite was of Mount Ephraim, *v.* 1. He married a wife of Bethlehem-Judah. It does not appear that he had any other wife, and the margin calls her *a wife, a concubine, v.* 1.

I. This Levite's concubine played the whore and eloped from her husband, *v.* 2. The Chaldee reads it only that she *carried herself insolently to him,* or *despised him,* and, he being displeased at it, *she went away from him,* and was received and entertained at her father's house. When she treacherously departed from her husband to embrace the bosom of a stranger, her father ought not to have countenanced her sin. Children's ruin is often owing very much to parents' indulgence.

II. The Levite went himself to court her return. She is addressed in the kindest manner by her injured husband, who takes a long journey on purpose to beseech her to be reconciled, *v.* 3. It is part of the character of the wisdom from above that it is gentle and easy to be entreated. He spoke *friendly* to her, or *comfortably* (for so the Hebrew phrase of *speaking to the heart* commonly signifies), which intimates that she was in sorrow, penitent for what she had done amiss.

III. Her father made him very welcome. 1. He entertains him kindly, *rejoices to see him* (*v.* 3), treats him generously for three days, *v.* 4. And the Levite, to show that he was perfectly reconciled, accepted his kindness, and we do not find that he upbraided him or his daughter with what had been amiss. It becomes all, but especially Levites, to forgive as God does. Every thing among them gave a hopeful prospect of their living comfortably together for the future. 2. He is very earnest for his stay, as a further demonstration of his hearty welcome. The affection he had for him, and the pleasure he took in his company, proceeded, (1) From a civil regard to him as his son-in-law and an ingrafted branch of his own house. Note, Love and duty are due to those to whom we are related by marriage as well as to those who are bone of our bone. (2) From a pious respect to him as a Levite, a servant of God's house. [1] He engages him to stay as long as he possibly could. The Levite, though nobly treated, was very urgent to be gone. A good man's heart is where his business is. It is a sign a man has either little to do at home, or little heart to do what he has to do, when he can take pleasure in being long abroad where he has nothing to do. [2] He forces him to stay till the afternoon of the fifth day, and this, as it proved, was unkind, *v.* 8, 9. Had they set out early, they might have reached some better lodging-place than that which they were now constrained to take up with, nay, they might have got to Shiloh.

IV. In his return home he was forced to lodge at Gibeah, a city in the tribe of Benjamin, afterwards called *Gibeah of Saul,* which lay on his road towards Shiloh and Mount Ephraim. When night came they could not pursue their journey. 1. The servant proposed that they should lodge in Jebus, afterwards Jerusalem, but as yet in the possession of Jebusites. If they had done so, it is probable they would have had much better usage than they met with in Gibeah of Benjamin. Debauched and profligate Israelites are worse and much more dangerous than Canaanites themselves. 2. Having passed by Jebus they stopped at Gibeah (*v.* 13–15); there they sat down in the street, nobody offering them a lodging. This traveller, though a Levite (and to those of that tribe God had particularly commanded his people to be kind upon all occasions), met with very cold entertainment at Gibeah: *No man took them into his house.*

Verses 16–21

When the Levite, and his wife, and servant, were beginning to fear that they must lie in the street all night (and as good have laid in a den of lions) they were at length invited into a house, and we are here told,

I. Who that kind man was that invited them. 1. He was a man of Mount Ephraim, and only sojourned in Gibeah, *v.* 16. Of all the tribes of Israel, the Benjamites had most reason to be kind to poor travellers, for their ancestor, Benjamin, was born upon the road, his mother being then upon a journey, and very near to this place, Gen. xxxv. 16, 17. Yet they were hard-hearted to a traveller in distress, while an honest Ephraimite had compassion on him, and, no doubt, was the more kind to him, when, upon enquiry, he found that he was his countryman, of Mount Ephraim likewise. 2. He was an old man, one that retained some of the expiring virtue of an Israelite. The rising generation was entirely corrupted; if there was any good remaining among them, it was only with those that were old and going off. 3. He was coming home from his work out of the field at eventide. The rest had given themselves up to sloth and luxury, and no marvel there was among them, as in Sodom, abundance of uncleanness, when there was among them, as in Sodom, abundance of idleness, Ezek. xvi. 49.

II. How free and generous he was in his invitation. He did not stay till they applied to him to beg for a night's lodging. Thus our good God answers before we call. Note, A charitable disposition expects only opportunity, not importunity, to do good, and will succour upon sight, unsought unto. Charity is not apt to distrust, but *hopeth all things* (1 Cor. xiii. 7).

Verses 22–30

I. The great wickedness of the men of Gibeah. The sinners are here called *sons of Belial,* that is, ungovernable men, men that would endure no yoke, children of the devil (for he is Belial), resembling him, and joining with him in rebellion against God and his government.

1. They made a rude and insolent assault, in the night, upon the habitation of an honest man, that not only lived peaceably among them, but kept a good house and was a blessing and ornament to their city.

2. They had a particular spite at the strangers that were within their gates, that only desired a night's lodging among them, contrary to the laws of hospitality, which all civilized nations have accounted sacred, and which the master of the house pleaded with them (*v.* 23).

3. They designed in the most filthy and abominable manner (not to be thought of without horror and detestation) to abuse the Levite. *Bring him forth that we may know him.* Now, (1) This was the sin of Sodom, and is thence called *Sodomy.* What did it avail them that they had the ark of God in Shiloh when they had Sodom in their streets—God's law

in their fringes, but the devil in their hearts? (2) This was the punishment of their idolatry, that sin to which they were, above all others, most addicted. He gave them up to these vile affections, by which they dishonoured themselves as they had by their idolatry dishonoured him and turned his glory into shame, Rom. i. 24, 28.

4. They were deaf to the reproofs and reasonings of the good man of the house, who, being well acquainted (we may suppose) with the story of Lot and the Sodomites, set himself to imitate Lot, *v.* 23, 24. Compare Gen. xix. 6–8. But in one thing he conformed too far to Lot's example in offering them his daughter to do what they would with. He had not power thus to prostitute his daughter, nor ought he to have done this evil that good might come. But *they would not hearken to him, v.* 25. Headstrong lusts are like the deaf adder that stoppeth her ear; they sear the conscience and make it insensible.

5. They got the Levite's wife among them, and abused her to death, *v.* 25. They slighted the old man's offer of his daughter to their lust.

II. The notice that was sent of this wickedness to all the tribes of Israel. The poor abused woman made towards her husband's lodgings as soon as ever the approach of the daylight obliged these sons of Belial to let her go (for these works of darkness hate and dread the light), *v.* 25. Down she fell at the door, with her hands on the threshold, and in that posture of a penitent, with her mouth in the dust, she expired. There he found her (*v.* 26, 27), soon perceived she was dead (*v.* 28), took up her dead body, waived his purpose of going to Shiloh, and went directly home. There was no king in Israel to appeal to, and demand justice from. He has therefore no other way left him than to appeal to the people: let the community be judge. To each of the tribes, in their respective meetings, he sent by special messengers a remonstrance of the wrong that was done him, in all its aggravating circumstances, and with it a piece of his wife's dead body (*v.* 29), to represent their barbarous usage of his wife. All that saw the pieces of the dead body, and were told how the matter was, expressed the same sentiments upon it. 1. That the men of Gibeah had been guilty of a very heinous piece of wickedness, the like to which had never been known before in Israel, *v.* 30. 2. That a general assembly of all Israel should be called, to debate what was fit to be done for the punishment of this wickedness, that a stop might be put to this threatening inundation of debauchery, and the wrath of God might not be poured upon the whole nation for it. We have here the three great rules by which those that sit in council ought to go in every arduous affair. (1) Let every man retire into himself, and weigh the matter impartially and fully in his own thoughts, and seriously and calmly consider it, without prejudice on either side, before he speaks upon it. (2) Let them freely talk it over, and every man take advice of his friend, know his opinion and his reasons, and weigh them. (3) Then let every man speak his mind, and give his vote according to his conscience. In the multitude of such counsellors there is safety.

CHAPTER 20

Into the book of the wars of the Lord the story of this chapter must be brought, but it looks as sad and uncomfortable as any article in all that history; for there is nothing in it that looks in the least bright or pleasant. And yet this happened soon after the glorious settlement of Israel in the land of promise, upon which one would have expected everything to be prosperous and serene. In this chapter we have, I. The Levite's cause heard in a general convention of the tribes, ver. 1–7. II. A unanimous resolve to avenge his quarrel upon the men of Gibeah, ver. 8–11. III. The Benjamites appearing in defence of the criminals, ver. 12–17. IV. The defeat of Israel in the first and second day's battle, ver. 18–25. V. Their humbling themselves before God upon that occasion, ver. 26–28. VI. The total rout they gave

the Benjaminites in the third engagement, by a stratagem, by which they were all cut off, except 600 men, ver. 29–48.

Verses 1–11

I. A general meeting of all the congregation of Israel to examine the matter concerning the Levite's concubine, and to consider what was to be done upon it, *v.* 1, 2. They came together by the consent and agreement, as it were, of one common heart, fired with a holy zeal for the honour of God and Israel. 1. The place of their meeting was *Mizpeh*; they gathered together unto the Lord there, for Mizpeh was so very near to Shiloh that their encampment might very well be supposed to reach from Mizpeh to Shiloh. Shiloh was a small town, and therefore, when there was a general meeting of the people to present themselves before God, they chose Mizpeh for their headquarters. 2. The persons that met were all Israel, from Dan in the north to Beersheba in the south, with the land of Gilead (that is, the tribes on the other side Jordan), all *as one man,* so unanimous were they in their concern for the public good. In this assembly of all Israel, the chief (or corners) of the people (for rulers are the cornerstones of the people, that keep all together) presented themselves as the representatives of the rest. They rendered themselves at their respective posts, at the head of the thousands and hundreds, the fifties and tens, over which they presided; for so much order and government, we may suppose, at least, they had among them, though they had no general or commander-in-chief. So that here was, (1) A general congress of the states for counsel. (2) A general rendezvous of the militia for action, all that drew sword and were men of war (*v.* 17).

II. Notice given to the tribe of Benjamin of this meeting (*v.* 3): *They heard that the children of Israel had gone up to Mizpeh.* But the notice they had of this meeting rather hardened and exasperated them than awakened them to think of the things that belonged to their peace and honour.

III. A solemn examination of the crime charged upon the men of Gibeah. The Levite gives a particular account of the matter. He concludes his declaration with an appeal to the judgment of the court (*v.* 7): *You are all children of Israel,* and therefore you *know law and judgment,* Esther i. 13, therefore give your advice and counsel what is to be done.

IV. The resolution they came to hereupon, which was that, being now together, they would not disperse till they had seen vengeance taken upon this wicked city, which was the reproach and scandal of their nation. Observe, 1. Their zeal against the lewdness that was committed. They would not return to their houses, how much soever their families and their affairs at home wanted them, till they had vindicated the honour of God and Israel. 2. Their prudence in sending out a considerable body of their forces to fetch provisions for the rest, *v.* 9, 10. 3. Their unanimity in these counsels, and the execution of them. The resolution was voted, *Nemine contradicente—Without a dissenting voice* (*v.* 8). This was their glory and strength, that the several tribes had no separate interests when the common good was concerned.

Verses 12–17

I. The fair and just demand which the tribes of Israel, now encamped, sent to the tribe of Benjamin, to deliver up the malefactors of Gibeah to justice, *v.* 12, 13. The Israelites were zealous against the wickedness that was committed, yet they were discreet in their zeal, and did not think it would justify them in falling upon the whole tribe of Benjamin unless they, by refusing to give up the criminals, and protecting them against justice, should make themselves guilty, *ex post facto—as accessories after the fact.*

II. The wretched obstinacy and perverseness of the men of Benjamin, who seem to have been as unanimous and zealous in their resolutions to stand by the criminals as the rest of the tribes were to punish them, so little sense had they of their honour, duty, and interest. They took it ill that the other tribes should meddle with their concerns; they would not do that which they knew was their duty because they were reminded of it by their brethren, by whom they scorned to be taught and controlled.

2. They were so prodigiously vain and presumptuous as to make head against the united force of all Israel. How could they expect to prosper when they fought against justice, and consequently against the just God himself, against those that had the high priest and the divine oracle on their side, and so acted in downright rebellion against the sacred and supreme authority of the nation. It should seem they depended upon the skill of their men to make up what was wanting in numbers, especially a regiment of slingers, 700 men, who, though left-handed, were so dexterous at slinging stones that they would not be a hair's breadth beside their mark, *v.* 16. But these good marksmen were very much out in their aim when they espoused this bad cause.

Verses 18–25

The defeat of the men of Israel in their first and second battle with the Benjamites.

I. Before their first engagement they asked counsel of God concerning the order of their battle and were directed, and yet they were sorely beaten. The whole army lay siege to Gibeah, *v.* 19. The Benjamites advance to raise the siege, the army prepares to give them a warm reception (*v.* 20), and turns upon them to fight them, *v.* 20. But between the Benjamites that attacked them in the front with incredible fury, and the men of Gibeah that sallied out upon their rear, they were put into confusion and lost 22,000 men, *v.* 21.

II. Before their second engagement they again *asked counsel of God*, and more solemnly than before; for they *wept before the Lord until evening* (*v.* 23). Also at this time they did not ask who should go up first, but whether they should go up at all. God bade them go up; he allowed the attempt for, though Benjamin was their brother, he was a gangrened member of their body and must be cut off. Upon this they encouraged themselves, perhaps more in their own strength than in the divine commission, and made a second attempt upon the forces of the rebels, in the same place where the former battle was fought (*v.* 22). But they were this second time repulsed, with the loss of 18,000 men, *v.* 25. But what shall we say to these things, that so just and honourable a cause should thus be put to the worst once and again? Were they not fighting God's battles against sin? 1. God's judgments are a great deep, and his way is in the sea. We may be sure of the righteousness, when we cannot see the reasons, of God's proceedings. 2. God would hereby show them, and us in them, that *the race is not to the swift nor the battle to the strong*, that we are not to confide in numbers, which perhaps the Israelites did with too much assurance. We must never lay the weight on an arm of flesh, which only the Rock of ages will bear. 3. God designed hereby to correct Israel for their sins. They did well to show such a zeal against the wickedness of Gibeah: but *were there not with them, even with them, sins against the Lord their God?* Some think it was a rebuke to them for not witnessing against the idolatry of Micah and the Danites. 4. God would hereby teach us not to think it strange if a good cause should suffer defeat for a while, nor to judge of the merits of it by the success of it. The interest of grace in the heart, and of religion in the world, may be foiled, and suffer great loss, and seem to be quite run down, but judgment will be brought forth to victory at last. *Vincimur in praelio, sed non in bello—We are foiled in a battle, but not in the whole campaign.* Right may fall, but it shall arise.

Verses 26–48

A full account of the complete victory which the Israelites obtained over the Benjamites in the third engagement: the righteous cause was victorious at last.

I. How the victory was obtained. Two things they had trusted too much to in the former engagements —the goodness of their cause and the superiority of their numbers. It was true that they had both right and strength on their side, which were great advantages; but they depended too much upon them, to the neglect of those duties to which now, this third time, when they see their error, they apply themselves.

1. They were previously so confident of the goodness of their cause that they thought it needless to address themselves to God for his presence and blessing. They took it for granted that God would bless them, nay, perhaps they concluded that he owed them his favour. Before they only consulted God's oracle, *Who shall go up first?* And, *Shall we go up?* But now they implored his favour, fasted and prayed, and *offered burnt-offerings and peace-offerings* (*v.* 26), to make an atonement for sin and an acknowledgment of their dependence upon God. And when they were in this frame, and thus sought the Lord, then he not only ordered them to go up against the Benjamites the third time, but gave them a promise of victory: *Tomorrow I will deliver them into thy hand, v.* 28.

2. They were previously so confident of the greatness of their strength that they thought it needless to use any art, to lay an ambush, or form a stratagem, not doubting but to conquer purely by a strong hand; but now they saw it was requisite to use some policy, as if they had an enemy to deal with them that had been superior in number; accordingly, they set *liers in wait* (*v.* 29), and gained their point, as their fathers did before Ai (Josh. viii).

(1) Observe the method they took. The body of the army faced the city of Gibeah, as they had done before, advancing towards the gates, *v.* 30. The Benjamites, the body of whose army was now quartered at Gibeah, sallied out upon them, and charged them with great bravery. The besiegers gave back, retired with precipitation, as if their hearts failed them upon the sight of the Benjamites. But, when the Benjamites were all drawn out of the city, the ambush seized the city (*v.* 37), gave a signal to the body of the army (*v.* 38, 40), which immediately turned upon them (*v.* 41), and, it should seem, another considerable party that was posted at Baal-tamar came upon them at the same time (*v.* 33); so that the Benjamites were quite surrounded, which put them into the greatest consternation that could be. A sense of guilt now disheartened them. Every man's hand was against them.

(2) Observe in this story, [1] That the Benjamites, in the beginning of the battle, were confident that the day was their own. Sometimes God suffers wicked men to be lifted up in successes and hopes, that their fall may be the sorer. See how short their joy is, and their triumphing but for a moment. [2] Evil was near them and they did not know it, *v.* 34. [3] Though the men of Israel played their parts so well in this engagement, yet the victory is ascribed to God (*v.* 35). They *trode down the men of Benjamin with ease* when God fought against them, *v.* 43.

II. How the victory was prosecuted and improved in a military execution done upon these sinners against their own souls. 1. Gibeah itself, that nest of lewdness, was destroyed in the first place. 2. The army in the field was quite routed and cut off. 3. Those that escaped from the field were pursued, and cut off in their flight. 4. Even those that tarried at home were involved in the ruin. So that of all the tribe of Benjamin, for aught that appears, there remained none alive but 600 men that took shelter in the rock Rimmon, and lay close there four months, *v.* 47.

This affair of Gibeah is twice spoken of by the prophet Hosea as the beginning of the corruption of Israel and a pattern to all that followed (Hos. ix. 9): *They have deeply corrupted themselves as in the days of Gibeah;* and (Hos. x. 9), *Thou hast sinned from the days of Gibeah*; and it is added that *the battle in Gibeah against the children of iniquity did not* (that is, did not *at first*) overtake them.

CHAPTER 21

The ruins of the tribe of Benjamin we read of in the foregoing chapter; now here we have, I. The lamentation which Israel made over these ruins, ver. 1–4, 6, 15. II. The provision they made for the repair of them out of the 600 men that escaped, for whom they procured wives. 1. Of the virgins of Jabesh-Gilead, ver. 5, 7–14. 2. Of the daughters of Shiloh, ver. 16–25.

Verses 1–15

I. The ardent zeal which the Israelites had expressed against the wickedness of the men of Gibeah, as it was countenanced by the tribe of Benjamin. 1. While the general convention of the states was gathering together, they bound themselves with the great execration, which they called the *Cherum,* utterly to destroy all those cities that should not send in their representatives, for they would look upon such refusers as having no indignation at the crime committed, no concern for the securing of the nation from God's judgments by the administration of justice, nor any regard to the authority of a common consent, by which they were summoned to meet. 2. When they had met and heard the cause they made another solemn oath that none of all the thousands of Israel then present, nor any of those whom they represented (not intending to bind their posterity), should, if they could help it, *marry a daughter* to a Benjamite, *v.* 1. This was made an article of the war, not with any design to extirpate the tribe, but because in general they would treat those who were then actors and abettors of this villainy in all respects as they treated the devoted nations of Canaan, whom they were not only obliged to destroy, but with whom they were forbidden to marry.

II. The deep concern which the Israelites did express for the destruction of the tribe of Benjamin when it was accomplished. Observe,

1. The tide of their anger at Benjamin's crime did not run so high and so strong before but the tide of their grief for Benjamin's destruction ran as high and as strong after: *They repented for Benjamin their brother, v.* 6, 15. They did not repent of their zeal against the sin. But they repented of the sad consequences of what they had done, that they had carried the matter further than was either just or necessary. It would have been enough to destroy all they found in arms; they needed not to have cut off the husbandman and shepherds, the women and children. Note, (1) There may be over-doing in well-doing. Great care must be taken in the government of our zeal, lest that which seemed supernatural in its causes prove unnatural in its effects. That is no good divinity which swallows up humanity. Many a war is ill ended which was well begun. (2) Even necessary justice is to be done with compassion. God does not punish with delight, nor should men. (3) Strong passions make work for repentance. What we say and do in a heat our calmer thoughts commonly wish undone again. Now,

2. How did they express their concern? (1) By

their grief for the breach that was made. They came to the house of God, for thither they brought all their doubts, all their counsels, all their cares, and all their sorrows. *There is one tribe lacking.* Benjamin become a Benoni, the son of the right hand a son of sorrow! In this trouble they built an altar, to atone for their folly in the pursuit of victory, and to implore the divine favour in their present strait. Every thing that grieves us should bring us to God. (2) By their amicable treaty with the poor distressed refugees that were hidden in the rock Rimmon, to whom they sent an act of indemnity, assuring them, upon the public faith, that they would now no longer treat them as enemies, but receive them as brethren, *v.* 13. (3) By the care they took to provide wives for them, that their tribe might be built up again, and the ruins of it repaired. All heads were at work to find out ways and means for the rebuilding of this tribe. While the poor distressed Benjamites that were hidden in the rock feared their brethren were contriving to ruin them, they were at the same time upon a project to prefer them. Four hundred virgins that were marriageable were found in Jabesh-Gilead, and these were married to so many of the surviving Benjamites, *v.* 14. Perhaps the alliance now contracted between Benjamin and Jabesh-Gilead made Saul, who was a Benjamite, the more concerned for that place (1 Sam. xi. 4), though then inhabited by new families.

Verses 16–25

We have here the method that was taken to provide the 200 Benjamites that remained with wives.

I. At Shiloh, in the fields, all the young ladies of that city met to dance, in honour of a *feast of the Lord,* probably the feast of tabernacles (*v.* 19), for that feast was the only season wherein the Jewish virgins were allowed to dance, and that not so much for their own recreation as to express their holy joy, as David when he danced before the ark. The dancing was very modest and chaste. However their dancing thus in public made them an easy prey to those that had a design upon them.

II. The elders of Israel gave authority to the Benjamites to *lie in wait in the vineyards* and catch every man a wife for himself, and carry them straight away to their own country, *v.* 20, 21. Here was a very preposterous way of match-making, when both the mutual affection of the young people and the consent of the parents must be presumed to come after; the case was extraordinary, and may by no means be drawn into a precedent. Overhasty marriages often occasion a leisurely repentance; and what comfort can be expected from a match made either by force or fraud?

III. They undertook to pacify the fathers of these young women. The oath they were bound by, not to give their daughters to Benjamites, might perhaps stick with some of them, whose consciences were tender. The necessity was urgent (*v.* 22): *We reserved not to each man his wife,* owning now that they did ill to destroy all the women, and desiring to atone for their too rigorous construction of their vow to destroy them by the most favourable construction of their vow not to match with them.

Lastly, In the close of all we have, 1. The settling of the tribe of Benjamin again. The few that remained returned to the inheritance of that tribe, *v.* 23. And soon after from among them sprang Ehud, who was famous in his generation, the second judge of Israel, *ch.* iii. 15. 2. The disbanding and dispersing of the army of Israel, *v.* 24. They did not set up for a standing army, nor pretend to make any alterations or establishments in the government; but, when the affair was over for which they were called together, they quietly departed in God's peace, every man to his family.

AN EXPOSITION, WITH PRACTICAL OBSERVATIONS, ON

THE BOOK OF RUTH

This short history of the domestic affairs of one particular family fitly follows the book of Judges (the events related here happening in the days of the judges), and fitly goes before the books of Samuel, because in the close it introduces David. It relates not miracles nor laws, wars nor victories, nor the revolutions of states, but the affliction first and afterwards the comfort of Naomi, the conversion first and afterwards the preferment of Ruth. The design of this book is, I. To lead to providence, to show us how conversant it is about our private concerns. See 1 Sam. ii. 7, 8; Ps. cxiii. 7–9. II. To lead to Christ, who descended from Ruth, and part of whose genealogy concludes the book, whence it is fetched into Matt. i. In the conversion of Ruth the Moabitess, and the bringing of her into the pedigree of the Messiah, we have a type of the calling of the Gentiles in due time into the fellowship of Christ Jesus our Lord. The afflictions of Naomi and Ruth we have an account of, *ch.* i. Instances of their industry and humility, *ch.* ii. The bringing of them into an alliance with Boaz, *ch.* iii. And their happy settlement thereby, *ch.* iv. And let us remember the scene is laid in Bethlehem, the city where our Redeemer was born.

CHAPTER 1

In this chapter we have Naomi's afflictions. I. As a distressed housekeeper, forced by famine to remove into the land of Moab, ver. 1, 2. II. As a mournful widow and mother, bewailing the death of her husband and her two sons, ver. 3–5. III. As a careful mother-in-law, desirous to be kind to her two daughters, ver. 6–18. IV. As a poor woman sent back to the place of her first settlement, ver. 19–22.

Verses 1–5

The first words give all the date we have of this story. It was *in the days when the judges ruled* (v. 1). It must have been towards the beginning of the judges' time, for Boaz, who married Ruth, was born of Rahab, who received the spies in Joshua's time. Some think it was in the days of Ehud, others of Deborah; the learned Bishop Patrick inclines to think it was in the days of Gideon, because in his days only we read of a famine by the Midianites' invasion, Judges vi. 3, 4.

I. A famine in the land, in the land of Canaan, that land *flowing with milk and honey*. This was one of the judgments which God had threatened to bring upon them for their sins, Lev. xxvi. 19, 20. When the land had rest, yet it had not plenty; even in Bethlehem, which signifies *the house of bread*, there was scarcity. A *fruitful land is turned into barrenness*, to correct and restrain the luxury and wantonness of those that dwell therein.

II. An account of one particular family distressed in the famine; it is that of *Elimelech*. His name signifies *my God a king*. His wife was *Naomi*, which signifies my *amiable* or *pleasant one*. But his son's names were *Mahlon* and *Chilion*, *sickness* and *consumption*, perhaps because weakly children.

III. The removal of this family from Bethlehem into the country of Moab on the other side Jordan, for subsistence, because of the famine, *v.* 1, 2. It seems there was plenty in the country of Moab when there was scarcity of bread in the land of Israel. Thither Elimelech goes, to sojourn for a time, during the dearth, as Abraham, on a similar occasion, went into Egypt, and Isaac into the land of the Philistines. Now here, 1. Elimelech's care to provide for his family, and his taking his wife and children with him, were without doubt commendable. But, 2. I see not how his removal into the country of Moab, upon this occasion, could be justified. The seed of Israel were now fixed, and ought not to remove into the territories of the heathen. What reason had Elimelech to go more than any of his neighbours? If he could not be content with the short allowance that his neighbours took up with, if he could not live in hope that there would come years of plenty again in due time, or could not with patience wait for those years, it was his fault, and he did by it dishonour

God and the good land he had given them, *weaken the hands of his brethren*, with whom he should have been willing to take his lot, and set an ill example to others. It is an evidence of a discontented, distrustful, unstable spirit, to be weary of the place in which God hath set us, and to be for leaving it immediately whenever we meet with any uneasiness or inconvenience in it. Or, if he would remove, why to the country of Moab? If he had made enquiry, it is probable he would have found plenty in some of the tribes of Israel, those, for instance, on the other side Jordan, that bordered on the land of Moab; if he had had that zeal for God and that affection for his brethren which became an Israelite, he would not have persuaded himself so easily to go and sojourn among Moabites.

IV. The marriage of his two sons to two of the daughters of Moab after his death, *v.* 4. All agree that this was ill done. The Chaldee says, *They transgressed the decree of the word of the Lord in taking strange wives*. It does not appear that the women they married were proselyted to the Jewish religion, for Orpah is said to return to her gods (*v.* 15). It is a groundless tradition of the Jews that Ruth was the daughter of Eglon king of Moab.

V. The death of Elimelech and his two sons, and the disconsolate condition Naomi was thereby reduced to. Her husband died (*v.* 3) and her two sons (*v.* 5) soon after their marriage, and the Chaldee says, *Their days were shortened*, because they transgressed the law in marrying strange wives. When Naomi had lost her husband she put so much the more confidence in her sons. How disconsolate the spirit of poor Naomi, when the woman was *left of her two sons and her husband*; When *these two things, loss of children and widowhood, come upon her in a moment, by whom shall she be comforted?* Isa. xlvii. 9; li. 19. It is God alone who has wherewithal to comfort those who are thus cast down.

Verses 6–18

I. The good affection Naomi bore to the land of Israel, *v.* 6. Though the country of Moab had afforded her shelter and supply in a time of need, yet she did not intend it should be her rest for ever; no land should be that but the holy land, in which the sanctuary of God was.

1. God, at last, returned in mercy to his people. At length God graciously *visited his people in giving them bread*. Plenty is God's gift, and it is his visitation which by bread, the staff of life, *holds our souls in life*. Though this mercy be the more striking when it come after famine, yet if we have constantly enjoyed it, and never known what famine meant, we are not to think it the less valuable.

2. Naomi at last has good news brought her of plenty in Bethlehem, and then she can think of no other than returning thither again. Though there be a reason for our being in bad places, yet, when the reason ceases, we must by no means continue in them. Forced absence from God's ordinances, and forced presence with wicked people, are great afflictions; but when the force ceases, and such a situation is continued of choice, then it becomes a great sin. The land of Moab had now become a melancholy place to her. Now she will go to Canaan again. Earth is embittered to us, that heaven may be endeared.

II. The good affection which her daughters-in-law, and one of them especially, bore to her, and her generous return of their good affection.

1. They were both so kind as to accompany her, some part of the way at least, when she returned towards the land of Judah. By this we see both that Naomi, as became an Israelite, had been very kind to them and had won their love, and that Orpah and Ruth had a just sense of her kindness. They had dwelt together in unity, though *those* were dead by whom the relation between them came. Though they retained an affection for the gods of Moab (*v.* 15), and Naomi was still faithful to the God of Israel, yet that was no hindrance to either side from love and kindness, and all the good offices that the relation required. Mothers-in-law and daughters-in-law are too often at variance (Matt. x. 35), and therefore it is the more commendable if they live in love.

2. When they had gone a little way with her, Naomi, with a great deal of affection, urged them to go back (*v.* 8, 9): *Return each to her mother's house.* Naomi suggests that their own mothers would be more agreeable to them than a mother-in-law, especially when their own mothers had houses and their mother-in-law was not sure she had a place to lay her head in which she could call her own. She dismisses them,

(1) With commendation.

(2) With prayer. It is very proper for friends, when they part, to part with prayer. She sends them home with her blessing; and the blessing of a mother-in-law is not to be slighted. In this blessing she twice mentions the name *Jehovah*, Israel's God, and the only true God, that she might direct her daughters to look up to him as the only fountain of all good. That they might be happy in marrying again: *The Lord grant that you may find rest, each of you in the house of her husband.*

(3) She dismissed them with great affection: *She kissed them*, wished she had somewhat better to give them, but silver and gold she had none. However, this parting kiss shall be the seal of a true friendship.

3. The two young widows could not think of parting with their good mother-in-law, so much had the good conversation of that pious Israelite won upon them. "*Surely we will return with thee unto thy people*, and take our lot with thee." It is a rare instance of affection to a mother-in-law and an evidence that they had, for her sake, conceived a good opinion of the people of Israel. Even Orpah, who afterwards went back to her gods, now seemed resolved to go forward with Naomi.

4. Naomi sets herself to dissuade them from going along with her, *v.* 11–13.

(1) Naomi urged her afflicted condition. If she had had any sons in Canaan, or any near kinsmen, whom she could have expected to marry the widows it might have been some encouragement to them to hope for a comfortable settlement at Bethlehem. The greatest grievance of that poor condition to which she was reduced was that she was not in a capacity to do for them as she would. She laments most the trouble that redounded to them from it. A gracious generous spirit can better bear its own burden than it can bear to see it a grievance to others, or others in

any way drawn into trouble by it. Naomi could more easily want herself than see her daughters want.

(2) Did Naomi do well thus to discourage her daughters from going with her, when, by taking them with her, she might save them from the idolatry of Moab and bring them to the faith and worship of the God of Israel? Naomi, no doubt, desired to do so. But, [1] If they did come with her, she would not have them to come upon her account. Those that take upon them a profession of religion only in complaisance to their relations, to oblige their friends, or for the sake of company, will be converts of small value and of short continuance. [2] If they did come with her, she would have them to make it their deliberate choice, and to sit down first and count the cost, as it concerns those to do that may take up a profession of religion. It is good for us to be told the worst. Our Saviour took this course with him who, in the heart of zeal, spoke that bold word, *Master, I will follow thee whithersoever thou goest.* "Come, come," says Christ, "canst thou fare as I fare? *The Son of man has not where to lay his head;* know this, and then consider whether thou canst find in thy heart to take thy lot with him," Matt. viii. 19, 20. Thus Naomi deals with her daughters-in-law. Thoughts ripened into resolves by serious consideration are likely to be kept always in the imagination of the heart, whereas what is soon ripe is soon rotten.

5. Orpah was easily persuaded to yield to her own corrupt inclination, and to go back to her country, her kindred, and her father's house, now when she stood fair for an effectual call from it. They both *lifted up their voice and wept again* (*v.* 14), being much affected with the tender things that Naomi had said. But it had a different effect upon them: to Orpah the representation Naomi had made of the inconveniences they must count upon if they went forward to Canaan sent her back to the country of Moab, but, on the contrary, it strengthened Ruth's resolution. (1) *Orpah kissed her mother-in-law*, that is, took an affectionate leave of her, bade her farewell for ever. Orpah's kiss showed she had an affection for Naomi and was loth to part from her; yet she did not love her well enough to leave her country for her sake. Thus many have a value and affection for Christ, and yet come short of salvation by him, because they cannot find in their hearts to forsake other things for him. They love him and yet leave him, because they do not love him enough, but love other things better. Thus the young man that went away from Christ went away sorrowful, Matt. xix. 22. But, (2) *Ruth clave unto her.* Whether, when she came from home, she was resolved to go forward with her or no does not appear.

6. Naomi persuades Ruth to go back, urging, as a further inducement, her sister's example: Now, *return thou after thy sister*, that is, "If ever thou wilt return, return now. This is the greatest trial of thy constancy; stand this trial, and thou art mine for ever."

7. Ruth puts an end to the debate by a most solemn profession of her immovable resolution never to forsake her, nor to return to her own country, and her old relations again, *v.* 16, 17.

(1) Nothing could be said more fine, more brave, than this. She seems to have had another spirit, and another speech, now that her sister had gone, and it is an instance of the grace of God inclining the soul to the resolute choice of the better part. [1] She begs of her mother-in-law to say no more against her going: *Entreat me not to leave thee, or to return from following after thee.* [2] She is very particular in her resolution to cleave to her and never to forsake her; and she speaks the language of one resolved for God and heaven. *First*, She will travel with her: *Whither thou goest I will go*, though to a country I never saw, though far from my own country, yet with thee every road shall be pleasant. *Secondly,*

She will dwell with her: "*Where thou lodgest I will lodge*, though it be in a cottage, nay, though it be no better a lodging than Jacob had when he had the stones for his pillow. *Thirdly*, She will twist interests with her: *Thy people shall be my people. Fourthly*, She will join in religion with her. Thus she determined to be hers—*usque ad aras—to the very altars*: "*Thy God shall be my God.*" *Fifthly*, She will gladly die in the same bed: *Where thou diest will I die. Sixthly*, She will desire to be buried in the same grave, and to lay her bones by hers: *There will I be buried*, not desiring to have so much as her dead body carried back to the country of Moab, in token of any remaining kindness for it; but, Naomi and she having joined souls, she desires they may mingle dust, in hopes of rising together, and being together for ever in the other world. [3] She backs her resolution to adhere to Naomi with a solemn oath: *The Lord do so to me, and more also* (which was an ancient form of imprecation), *if aught but death part thee and me.*

(2) This is a pattern of a resolute convert to God and religion. Thus must we be at a point. [1] We must take the Lord for our God. "This God is *my God for ever and ever*; I have avouched him for mine." [2] When we take God for our God we must take his people for our people in all conditions; though they be a poor despised people, yet, if they be his, they must be ours. [3] Having cast in our lot among them, we must be willing to take our lot with them and to fare as they fare.

8. Naomi is hereby silenced (*v.* 18): *When she saw that Ruth was steadfastly minded to go with her* (which was the very thing she aimed at in all that she had said, to make her of a steadfast mind in going with her), when she saw that she had gained her point, she was well satisfied, and *left off speaking to her.*

Verses 19–22

Naomi and Ruth, after many a weary step, came at last to Bethlehem. And they came very seasonably, *in the beginning of the barley-harvest*, which was the first of their harvests, that of wheat following after. And now they had opportunity to provide for winter.

I. The discomposure of the neighbours upon this occasion (*v.* 19): *All the city was moved about them.* Her old acquaintance gathered about her, to enquire concerning her state, and to bid her welcome to Bethlehem again. Or perhaps they were *moved about her*, lest she should be a charge to the town, she looked so bare. And they said, *Is this Naomi?* Those with whom she had formerly been intimate were surprised to see her in this condition; she was so much broken and altered with her afflictions. *Is this Naomi?* The generality asked it in compassion and commiseration: "Is this she that lived so plentifully, and kept so good a house, and was so charitable to the poor? Afflictions will make great and surprising changes in a little time. When we see how sickness and old age alter people, change their countenance and temper, we may think of what the Bethlehemites said: "*Is this Naomi?*" God, by his grace, fit us for all such changes, especially the great change!

II. The composure of Naomi's spirit. If some upbraided her with her poverty, she was not moved against them, as she would have been if she had been poor and proud: *Call me not Naomi, call me Mara*, &c. "*Naomi* signifies *pleasant* or *amiable*; but all my pleasant things are laid waste; call me *Mara*, *bitter* or *bitterness*, for I am now a woman of a sorrowful spirit."

1. The change of her state, and how it is described, with a pious regard to the divine providence, and without any passionate murmurings or complaints. She now *came home again empty*, a widow and childless, and probably had sold her goods, and of all the effects she took with her brought home no more

than the clothes on her back. (2) She acknowledges the hand of God, his mighty hand, in the affliction. "It is the Lord that has *brought me home again empty*; it is the Almighty that has afflicted me." Note, Nothing conduces more to satisfy a gracious soul under an affliction than the consideration of the hand of God in it. He that empties us of the creature knows how to fill us with himself.

2. The compliance of her spirit with this change: "*Call me not Naomi*, for I am no more pleasant, either to myself or to my friends; *but call me Mara*, a name more agreeable to my present state." If God deal bitterly with her, she will accommodate herself to the dispensation, and is willing to be called *Mara, bitter*. An affliction rightly borne does us good. *Tribulation works patience.*

CHAPTER 2

I. Ruth's humility and industry in gleaning corn, Providence directing her to Boaz's field, ver. 1–3. II. The great favour which Boaz showed to her in many instances, ver. 4–16. III. The return of Ruth to her mother-in-law, ver. 18–23.

Verses 1–3

Naomi had now gained a settlement in Bethlehem among her old friends; and here we have an account,

I. Of her rich kinsman, Boaz, *a mighty man of wealth, v.* 1. The Chaldee reads it, *mighty in the law.* He carries might in his name, *Boaz—in him is strength*; and he was of the family of Elimelech, that family which was now reduced and brought so low.

II. Of her poor daughter-in-law, Ruth. 1. Her condition was very low and poor, which was a great trial to the faith and constancy of a young proselyte. Naomi and her daughter-in-law have no way of getting necessary food but by gleaning corn. 2. Her character, in this condition, was very good (*v.* 2). She is *not mindful of the country from which she came out*, otherwise she had now a fair occasion to return. The God of Israel shall be her God, and, though he slay her, yet will she trust in him and never forsake him. *Let me go to the field, and glean ears of corn.* Let Ruth be remembered, who is a great example, (1) Of humility. When Providence had made her poor she did not say, "To glean, which is in effect to beg, I am ashamed." She does not tell her mother she was never brought up to live upon crumbs. Though she was not brought up to it, she is brought down to it, and is not uneasy at it. (2) Of industry. "*Let me go and glean ears of corn*, which will turn to some good account." A disposition to diligence bodes well both for this world and the other. We must not be shy of any honest employment, though it be mean, ἐργον ουδεν ὀνειδος—*No labour is a reproach.* (3) Of regard to her mother. Though she was but her mother-in-law, she is dutifully observant of her. (4) Of dependence upon Providence, intimated in that, I will *glean after him in whose sight I shall find grace.* She knows not which way to go, nor whom to enquire for, but will trust Providence to raise her up some friend or other that will be kind to her. And it did well for Ruth; for when she went out alone, without guide or companion, to glean, *her hap was to light on the field of Boaz, v.* 3. To her it seemed casual but Providence directed her steps to this field. Many a great affair is brought about by a little turn, which seemed fortuitous to us, but was directed by Providence with design.

Verses 4–16

Now Boaz himself appears, and a great deal of decency appears in his carriage:

I. Towards his own servants, and those that were employed for him in reaping and gathering in his corn. Harvest-time is busy time, many hands must then be at work. Boaz is here an example of a good master.

1. He had a servant that was set over the reapers, *v.* 6.

2. Yet he came himself to his reapers, to see how the work went forward. It was for the encouragement of his servants. who would go on the more cheerfully in their work when their master countenanced them so far as to make them a visit.

3. Kind and pious salutations were interchanged between Boaz and his reapers.

(1) He said to them, *The Lord be with you*; and they replied, *The Lord bless thee, v.* 4. Hereby they expressed, [1] Their mutual respect to each other. Things are likely to go on well in a house where there is such goodwill as this between master and servants. [2] Their joint-dependence upon the divine providence. They express their kindness to each other by praying one for another.

(2) Let us hence learn to use, [1] Courteous salutations, as expressions of a sincere goodwill to our friends. [2] Pious ejaculations, lifting up our hearts to God for his favour, in such short prayers as these. Only we must take heed that they do not degenerate into formality.

4. He took an account from his rearers concerning a stranger he met with in the field, and gave necessary orders concerning her, that they should not touch her (*v.* 9) nor reproach her, *v.* 15. He also ordered them to be kind to her, and *let fall some of the handfuls on purpose for her.*

II. Boaz was very kind to Ruth, and showed her a great deal of favour, induced to it by the account he had of her, and what he observed concerning her.

1. The steward gave to Boaz a very fair account of her, proper to recommend her to his favour, *v.* 6, 7. (1) That she was a stranger, and therefore one of those that by the law of God were to *gather the gleanings of the harvest*, Lev. xix. 9, 10. (2) That she was allied to his family; she came back with Naomi, the wife of Elimelech, a kinsman of Boaz. (3) That she was a proselyte, for she came out of the country of Moab to settle in the land of Israel. (4) That she was very modest, and had not gleaned till she had asked leave. (5) That she was very industrious, and had continued close to her work from morning even until now. Now, in the heat of the day, she tarried a little in the booth that was set up in the field for shelter.

2. Boaz was hereupon extremely civil to her. (1) He ordered her to attend his reapers in every field they gathered in and not to glean in the field of another, for she should not need to go anywhere else to better herself (*v.* 8). (2) He charged all his servants to be very tender of her and respectful to her. She was a stranger, and it is probable her language, dress, and mien differed much from theirs. (3) He bade her welcome to the entertainment he had provided for his own servants. He ordered her, not only to drink of the water which was drawn for them, but at *meal-time to come and eat of their bread* (*v.* 14), yea, and she should be welcome to their sauce too: *Come, dip thy morsel in the vinegar*, to make it savoury. And he himself, happening to be present when the reapers sat down to meat, *reached her parched corn* to eat. (4) He commended her for her dutiful respect to her mother-in-law, whom, though he did not know her by sight, yet he had heard of (*v.* 11). But that which especially he commended her for was that she had left her own country, and had become a proselyte to the Jewish religion. (5) He prayed for her (*v.* 12): *The Lord recompense thy work*. Those that by faith come under the wings of the divine grace may be sure of a full recompence of reward for their so doing. The Jews describe a proselyte to be one that is *gathered under the wings of the divine majesty*. (6) He encouraged her to go on in her gleaning. Boaz ordered his servants to let her glean among the sheaves and not to reproach her.

3. Ruth received his favours with a great deal of humility and gratitude. She paid all possible respect to him, and gave him honour, according to the usage of the country (*v.* 10): *She fell on her face, and bowed herself to the ground.* She humbly owned herself unworthy of his favours: "*I am a stranger* (*v.* 10) and *not like one of thy handmaids* (*v.* 13). She begs the continuance of his good-will. When Boaz gave her her dinner with his reapers she only ate so much as would suffice her, and immediately rose up to glean, *v.* 14, 15.

Verses 17–23

I. Ruth finishes her day's work, *v.* 17. 1. She took care not to lose time, for she gleaned until evening. 2. She took care not to lose what she had gathered, but threshed it herself, that she might the more easily carry it home, and might have it ready for use. Ruth had gathered it ear by ear, but, when she had put it all together, it was an ephah of barley, about four pecks.

II. She paid her respects to her mother-in-law and *showed her what she had gleaned*, that she might see she had not been idle. She gave her an account of her day's work, and how a kind providence had favoured her in it. Naomi asked her where she had been: *Where hast thou gleaned to-day?* Ruth gave her a particular account of the kindness she had received from Boaz (*v.* 19) and the hopes she had of further kindness from him, he having ordered her to attend his servants throughout all the harvest, *v.* 21. Naomi prayed heartily for him that had been her daughter's benefactor, even before she knew who it was (*v.* 19), *Blessed be he*, whoever he was, *that did take knowledge of thee*, shooting the arrow of prayer at a venture. She now remembered the former kindnesses Boaz had shown to her husband and sons, and joins those to this: he has not *left off his kindness to the living and to the dead*. She acquainted Ruth with the relation their family was in to Boaz: *The man is near of kin to us.* Observe the chain of thought here, and in it a chain of providences, bringing about what was designed concerning Ruth. Ruth names Boaz as one that had been kind to her. Naomi bethinks herself who that should be, and presently recollects herself: "*The man is near of kin to us;* now that I hear his name, I remember him very well." She appointed Ruth to continue her attendance in the fields of Boaz (*v.* 22): "*Let them not meet thee in any other field*, for that will be construed a contempt of his courtesy." Has the Lord dealt bountifully with us? Let us not be found in any other field, nor seek for happiness and satisfaction in the creature. Ruth dutifully observed her mother's directions; she continued to glean, to the end, not only of barley-harvest, but of the wheat-harvest, which followed it, that she might gather food in harvest to serve for winter, Prov. vi. 6–8.

CHAPTER 3

I. The directions Naomi gave to her daughter-in-law how to claim Boaz for her husband, ver. 1–5. II. Ruth's punctual observance of those directions, ver. 6, 7. III. The kind and honourable treatment Boaz gave her, ver 8–12. IV. Her return to her mother-in-law, ver. 16–18.

Verses 1–5

I. Naomi's care for her daughter's comfort is without doubt very commendable. She is full of contrivance how to get her well married. Her wisdom projected that for her daughter which her daughter's modesty forbade her to project for herself, *v.* 1. This she did, 1. In justice to the dead, to raise up seed to those that were gone, and so to preserve the family from being extinct. 2. In kindness and gratitude to her daughter-in-law, who had conducted herself very dutifully and respectfully to her. "*My daughter*" (said she, looking upon her in all respects as her own), "*shall I not seek rest for thee*," that is, a settlement in the married state. A married state is, or should be, a state of rest to young people. Wandering affections are then fixed, and the heart must be at rest. It is at rest in the house of a husband, and in his heart, *ch.* i. 9. Those are giddy indeed that marriage does not compose.

II. The course she took in order to her daughter's preferment was very extraordinary and looks suspicious. If there was any thing improper in it, the fault must lie upon Naomi, who put her daughter upon it, and who knew, or should know, the laws and usages of Israel better than Ruth. 1. It was true that Boaz, being near of kin to the deceased, and (for aught that Naomi knew to the contrary) the nearest of all now alive, was obliged by the divine law to marry the widow of Mahlon, who was the eldest son of Elimelech, and was dead without issue (*v.* 2). "Why should we not remind him of his duty?" 2. It was a convenient time to remind him of it, now that he had got so much acquaintance with Ruth by her constant attendance on his reapers during the whole harvest, which was now ended. It was a good opportunity to apply to him when he made a winnowing-feast at his threshing-floor (*v.* 2). 3. Naomi thought Ruth the most proper person to do it herself; and perhaps it was the usage in that country that in this case the woman should make the demand; so much is intimated by the law, Deut. xxv. 7–9. "*Wash thyself and anoint thee*, put on thy raiment, and go down to the floor," whither, it is probable, she was invited to the supper there made; but she must not make herself known, that is, not make her errand known till the company had dispersed and Boaz had retired. But, 4. Her coming to lie down at his feet, when he was asleep in his bed, had such an appearance of evil, that we know not well how to justify it. All agree that it is not to be drawn into a precedent; neither our laws nor our times are the same that were then; yet I am willing to make the best of it. If Boaz was, as they presumed, the next kinsman, she was his wife before God (as we say), and there needed but little ceremony to complete the nuptials; and Naomi did not intend that Ruth should approach to him any otherwise than as his wife. She knew Boaz to be a grave sober man, a virtuous and religious man, and one that feared God. She knew Ruth to be a modest woman, *chaste, and a keeper at home*, Tit. ii. 5. Naomi herself designed nothing but what was honest and honourable. If what she advised had been then as indecent and immodest (according to the usage of the country), as it seems now to us, we cannot think that Naomi would have had so little wisdom as to put her daughter upon it, and have alienated the affections of so grave and good a man as Boaz from her. We must therefore think that the thing did not look so ill then as it does now. We may be sure, if Ruth had apprehended any evil in that which her mother advised her to, she was a woman of too much virtue and too much sense to promise as she did (*v.* 5): *All that thou sayest unto me I will do.*

Verses 6–13

I. Boaz's good management of his common affairs. It is probable, according to the common usage, 1. When his servants winnowed, he was with them to prevent carelessness in the winnowing. 2. When he had more than ordinary work to be done, he treated his servants with extraordinary entertainments, and, for their encouragement, did *eat and drink with them*. 3. When Boaz had supped with his workmen, and been awhile pleasant with them, he *went to bed in due time*, so early that by midnight he had his first sleep (*v.* 8). 4. He had his bed or couch laid *at the end of the heap of corn*; he was like his father Jacob, a plain man, that, when there was occasion, could

make his bed in a barn, and, if need were, sleep contentedly in the straw.

II. Ruth's good assurance in the management of her affair. When he awaked in the night, and perceived there was somebody at his feet, and enquired who it was, she told him her name and then her errand (*v.* 9), that she came to put herself under his protection, as the person appointed by the divine law to be her protector: "*Thou art he that has a right to redeem* a family and an estate from perishing, and therefore *let this ruin be under thy hand*: and *spread thy skirt over me*—be pleased to espouse me and my cause."

III. The good acceptance Ruth gained with Boaz. He knew her demand was just and honourable, and treated her accordingly. Boaz knew it was not any sinful lust that brought her thither, and therefore bravely maintained both his own honour and hers.

(1) He commended her, spoke kindly to her, called her his *daughter*, and spoke honourably of her, as a woman of eminent virtue. It was very kind to leave her own country and come along with her mother to the land of Israel, to dwell with her, and help to maintain her. For this he had blessed her (*ch.* ii. 12); but now he says, Thou hast *shown more kindness in the latter end than at the beginning* (*v.* 10), in that she consulted not her own fancy, but her husband's family, in marrying again.

(2) He promised her marriage (*v.* 11): "*Fear not* that I will slight thee, or expose thee; no, *I will do all that thou requirest*, for it is the same that the law requires, from the next of kin, and I have no reason to decline it, *for all the city of my people doth know that thou art a virtuous woman*," *v.* 11.

(3) He made his promise conditional, and could not do otherwise, for it seems there was a kinsman that was nearer than he, to whom the right of redemption did belong, *v.* 12. He would himself propose it to the other kinsman, and know his mind. If the other kinsman refused to do the kinsman's part, he would do it, would marry the widow, redeem the land, and so repair the family. Bishop Hall thus sums up this matter: "Boaz, instead of touching her as a wanton, blesseth her as a father, encourageth her as a friend, promiseth her as a kinsman, rewards her as a patron, and sends her away laden with hopes and gifts, no less chaste, more happy, than she came."

Verses 14–18

I. How Ruth was dismissed by Boaz. 1. With a charge to keep counsel (*v.* 14): *Let it not be known that a woman came into the floor*, and lay all night so near to Boaz. 2. He dismissed her with a good present of corn, which would be very acceptable to her poor mother at home, and an evidence for her that he had not sent her away in dislike, which Naomi might have suspected if he had sent her away empty. He gave it to her in her *veil*, or *apron*, or *mantle*, gave it to her by measure.

II. How she was welcomed by her mother-in-law. She asked her, "*Who art thou, my daughter?* Art thou a bride or no? Must I give thee joy?" So Ruth told her how the matter stood (*v.* 17), whereupon her mother, 1. Advised her to be satisfied in what was done: *Sit still, my daughter, till thou know how the matter will fall* (*v.* 18). 2. She assured her that Boaz, having undertaken this matter, would approve himself a faithful careful friend: *He will not be at rest till he have finished the matter.*

CHAPTER 4

Verses 1–8

1. Boaz calls a court immediately. It is probable he was himself one of the elders (or aldermen) of the city. But why was Boaz so hasty, why so fond of the match? Ruth was not rich, but a poor stranger. But that which made Boaz in love with her, and solicitous to expedite the affair, was that all her neighbours agreed she was a virtuous woman. He will therefore bring it to a conclusion immediately. It was not court-day, but he got ten men of the elders of the city to meet him in the town hall over the gate, where public business used to be transacted, *v.* 2. So many, it is probable, by the custom of the city, made a full court. 2. He summons his rival to come and hear the matter that was to be proposed to him (*v.* 1). 3. He proposes to the other kinsman the redemption of Naomi's land, which, it is probable, had been mortgaged for money to buy bread with when the famine was in the land (*v.* 3): "*Naomi has a parcel of land to sell.*" This he gives the kinsman legal notice of (*v.* 4), that he might have the refusal of it. 4. The kinsman seemed forward to redeem the land till he was told that, if he did that, he must marry the widow, and then he flew off. "*I cannot redeem it for myself.* I will not meddle with it upon these terms, lest I mar my own inheritance." The land, he thought, would be an improvement of his inheritance, but not the land with the woman; that would mar it. 5. The right of redemption is fairly resigned to Boaz. If this nameless kinsman lost a good bargain, a good estate, and a good wife too, he may thank himself for not considering it better, and Boaz will thank him for making his way clear to that which he valued and desired above any thing. In those ancient times it was not the usage to pass estates by writings, as afterwards (Jer. xxxii. 10, &c.), but by some sign or ceremony, as with us by livery and seisin, as we commonly call it, that is, the delivery of seisin, seisin of a house by giving the key, of land by giving turf and a twig. The ceremony here used was, he that surrendered *plucked off his shoe* and gave it to him to whom he made the surrender, intimating thereby that, whatever right he had to tread on go upon the land, he conveyed and transferred it, upon a valuable consideration, to the purchaser: this was a *testimony in Israel, v.* 7. And it was done in this case, *v.* 8.

Verses 9–12

Boaz now sees his way clear to perform his promise made to Ruth that he would do the kinsman's part, but in the gate of his city, before the elders and all the people, publishes a marriage-contract between himself and Ruth the Moabitess, and therewith the purchase of all the estate that belonged to the family of Elimelech. Now concerning this marriage it appears,

I. That it was solemnized, or at least published, before many witnesses, *v.* 9, 10. 1. "That I have bought the estate. Whoever has it, or any part of it, mortgaged to him, let him come to me and he shall have his money." 2. "That I have purchased the widow to be my wife." He had no portion with her; what jointure she had was encumbered, and he could not have it without giving as much for it as it was worth, and therefore he might well say he purchased her. He designed, in marrying her, to preserve the memory of the dead, that the name of Mahlon, though he left no son to bear it up, by this means might be preserved. And observe that because Boaz did this honour to the dead, as well as this kindness to the living, God did him the honour to bring him into the genealogy of the Messiah, by which his family was dignified above all the families of Israel; while the other kinsman, that was so much afraid of diminishing himself, and marring his inheritance, by marrying the widow, has his name, family, and inheritance, buried in oblivion and disgrace. Our Lord Jesus is our *Goel*, our *Redeemer*, our everlasting Redeemer. He looked, like Boaz, with compassion on the deplorable state of fallen mankind. At a vast expense he redeemed the heavenly inheritance for us, which by sin was mortgaged, and forfeited into the hands of divine justice, and which we should never have been able to redeem.

II. That it was attended with many prayers. The elders and all the people, when they witnessed to it, wished well to it, and blessed it, *v.* 11, 12.

1. The senior elder, it is likely, made this prayer, and the rest of the elders, with the people, joined in it, and therefore it is spoken of as made by them all; for in public prayers, though but one speaks, we must all pray. Marriages ought to be blessed, and accompanied with prayer. We ought to desire and pray for the welfare and prosperity one of another.

2. Now here, (1) They prayed for Ruth, *The Lord make the woman that has come into thy house like Rachel and Leah*, that is, "God make her a good wife and a fruitful mother." (2) They prayed for Boaz. They desired that the wife might be a blessing in the private affairs of the house, and the husband a blessing in the public business of the town, that she in her place, and he in his, might be wise, virtuous, and successful. (3) They prayed for the family: "*Let thy house be like the house of Pharez,*" that is, "let it be very numerous, let it greatly increase and multiply as the house of Pharez did." The Bethlehemites were of the house of Pharez. Now they prayed that the family of Boaz, which was one branch of that stock, might in process of time become as numerous and great as the whole stock now was.

Verses 13–22

I. Ruth a wife. Boaz took her, with the usual solemnities, to his house, and *she became his wife* (*v.* 13). Boaz had prayed that this pious proselyte might receive a full reward of her courage and constancy from the God of Israel, *under whose wings she had come to trust*; and now he became an instrument of that kindness, which was an answer to his prayer, and helped to make his own words good.

II. Ruth a mother: *The Lord gave her conception*; for *the fruit of the womb is his reward*, Ps. cxxvii. 3.

III. Ruth still a daughter-in-law, and the same that she always was, to Naomi, who was so far from being forgotten that she was a principal sharer in these new joys. Prayer to God attended the marriage (*v.* 11), and praise to him attended the birth of the child. What a pity it is that such pious language should either be disused among Christians or degenerate into a formality. "*Blessed be the Lord* that has sent thee this grandson," *v.* 14, 15. They say of Ruth that she loved Naomi, and therefore was better to her than seven sons. The bonds of love prove stronger than those of nature, so here there was a daughter-in-law better than an own child. (1) The child is named by the neighbours, *v.* 17. The good women would have it called *Obed, a servant*, either in remembrance of the meanness and poverty of the mother or in prospect of his being hereafter a servant, and very serviceable, to his grandmother. (2) The child is nursed by the grandmother. Grandmothers are often the most fond.

IV. Ruth is hereby brought in among the ancestors of David and Christ, which was the greatest honour. The genealogy is here drawn from Pharez, through Boaz and Obed, to David and so leads towards the Messiah.

AN EXPOSITION, WITH PRACTICAL OBSERVATIONS, OF

THE FIRST
BOOK OF SAMUEL

This book, and that which follows it, bear the name of Samuel in the title, not because he was the penman of them, but because the first book begins with a large account of him, his birth and childhood, his life and government; and the rest of these two volumes that are denominated from him contains the history of the reigns of *Saul* and *David*, who were both anointed by him. And, because the history of these two kings takes up the greatest part of these books, the Vulgar Latin calls them the *First* and *Second Books of the Kings*, and the two that follow the *Third* and *Fourth*, which the titles in our English Bibles take notice of with an *alias: otherwise called the First Book of the Kings*, &c. The LXX calls them the first and second Book *of the Kingdoms*. These two books contain the history of the last two of the judges, *Eli* and *Samuel*, who were not, as the rest, men of war, but priests (and so much of them is an appendix to the book of judges), and of the first two of the kings, *Saul* and *David*, and so much of them is an entrance upon the history of the kings. This first book gives us a full account of Eli's fall and Samuel's rise and good government, *ch.* i.–viii. Of Samuel's resignation of the government and Saul's advancement and maladministration, *ch.* ix.–xv. The choice of David, his struggles with Saul, Saul's ruin at last, and the opening of the way for David to the throne, *ch.* xvi.–xxxi.

CHAPTER 1

The history of Samuel here begins even before he was born. The story of Samuel introduces him as a child of prayer. Samson's birth was foretold by an angel to his mother; Samuel was asked of God by his mother. Samuel's mother was Hannah, the principal person concerned in the story of this chapter. I. Here is her affliction — she was childless, and this affliction aggravated by her rival's insolence, but in some measure balanced by her husband's kindness, ver. 1–8. II. The prayer and vow she made to God under his affliction, in which Eli the high priest at first censured her, but afterwards encouraged her, ver. 9–19. III. The birth and nursing of Samuel, ver. 19–23. IV. The presenting of him to the Lord, ver. 24–28.

Verses 1–8

We have here an account of the state of the family into which Samuel the prophet was born. His father's name was Elkanah, a Levite, and of the family of the Kohathites (the most honourable house of that tribe) as appears, 1 Chron. vi. 33, 34. His ancestor Zuph was an Ephrathite, that is, of Bethlehem-Judah, which was called *Ephrathah*, Ruth i. 2. There this family of the Levites was first seated, but one branch of it, in process of time, removed to Mount Ephraim, from which this Elkanah descended. This Elkanah lived at Ramah, or Ramathaim, which signifies *the double Ramah*, the higher and lower town.

I. It was a devout family. All the families of Israel should be so, but Levites' families in a particular manner. Ministers should be patterns of family religion. Elkanah went up at the solemn feasts to the tabernacle at Shiloh, to *worship and to sacrifice to the Lord of hosts*. Probably Samuel the prophet was the first that used this title of God, for the comfort of Israel, when in his time their hosts were few and feeble and those of their enemies many and mighty; then it would be a support to them to think that the God they served was Lord of hosts, of all the hosts both of heaven and earth. Elkanah was a country Levite, and, for aught that appears, had not any place or office which required his attendance at the tabernacle, but he went up as a common Israelite, with his own sacrifices, to encourage his neighbours and set them a good example. And that which made it the more commendable in him was, 1. That there was a general decay and neglect of religion in the nation. 2. That Hophni and Phinehas, the sons of Eli, were the men that were now chiefly employed in the service of the house of God; and they were men that conducted themselves very ill in their place, yet Elkanah went up to sacrifice. If the priests did not do their duty, he would do his.

II. Yet it was a divided family, and the division of it carried with them both guilt and grief.

1. The original cause of this division was Elkanah's marrying two wives, which was a transgression of the original institution of marriage, to which our Saviour reduces it. Matt. xix. 5, 8, *From the beginning it was not so.* It made mischief in Abraham's family, and Jacob's, and here in Elkanah's.

2. That which followed upon this error was that the two wives could not agree. They had different blessings: Peninnah, like Leah, was fruitful and had many children, which should have made her easy and thankful, though she was but a second wife, and was less beloved; Hannah, like Rachel, was childless indeed, but she was very dear to her husband. But they were of different tempers: Peninnah could not bear the blessing of fruitfulness, but she grew haughty and insolent; Hannah could not bear the affliction of barrenness, but she grew melancholy and discontented: and Elkanah had a difficult part to act between them.

(1) Elkanah kept up his attendance at God's altar notwithstanding this unhappy difference in his family, and took his wives and children with him, that, if they could not agree in other things, they might agree to worship God together. If the devotions of a family prevail not to put an end to its divisions, yet let not the divisions put a stop to the devotions.

(2) He did all he could to encourage Hannah, and to keep up her spirits under her affliction, *v.* 4, 5. At the feast he offered peace-offerings, to supplicate for peace in his family. [1] He studied to show his love so much the more because she was afflicted, insulted, and low-spirited. [2] He showed his great love to her by the share he gave her of his peace-offerings. Thus we should testify our affection to our friends and relations, by abounding in prayer for them.

(3) Peninnah was extremely peevish and provoking. [1] She upbraided Hannah with her affliction, despised her because she was barren, and gave her taunting language, as one whom Heaven did not favour. [2] She envied the interest she had in the love of Elkanah. [3] She did this most when they *went up to the house of the Lord*, perhaps because then they were more together than at other times, or because then Elkanah showed his affection most to Hannah. That which she designed was to make her fret, perhaps in hopes to break her heart, that she might possess her husband's heart solely.

(4) Hannah (poor woman) could not bear the provocation: *She wept, and did not eat, v. 7.* Yet it was her infirmity so far to give way to the sorrow of the world as to unfit herself for holy joy in God. Those that are of a fretful spirit, and are apt to lay provocations too much to heart, are enemies to themselves, and strip themselves very much of the comforts both of life and godliness.

(5) Elkanah said what he could to her to comfort her. *Hannah, why weepest thou?* Those that by marriage are made one flesh ought thus far to be of one spirit, too, to share in each other's troubles, so that one cannot be easy while the other is uneasy. He intimates that nothing should be wanting on his part to balance her grief: "*Am not I better to thee than ten sons?* Thou knowest thou hast my entire affection, and let that comfort thee." Note, We ought to take notice of our comforts, to keep us from grieving excessively for our crosses; for our crosses we deserve, but our comforts we have forfeited. If we would keep the balance even, we must look at that which is for us, as well as at that which is against us, else we are unjust to Providence and unkind to ourselves.

Verses 9–18

Elkanah had gently reproved Hannah for her inordinate grief, and here we find the good effect of the reproof.

I. It brought her to her meat. She ate and drank, *v. 9.* She did not harden herself in sorrow, nor grow sullen when she was reproved for it. It is as great a piece of self-denial to control our passions as it is to control our appetites.

II. It brought her to her prayers. "Instead of binding the burden thus upon my own shoulders, had I not better ease myself of it, and cast it upon the Lord by prayer?" If ever she will make a more solemn address than ordinary to the throne of grace upon this errand, now is the time. They are at Shiloh, at the door of the tabernacle, where God had promised to meet his people, and which was the *house of prayer.* They had recently offered their peace-offerings. Now concerning Hannah's prayer,

1. The warm and lively devotion there was in it, which appeared in several instances, for our direction in prayer. (1) She improved the present grief and trouble of her spirit for the exciting and quickening of her pious affections in prayer: *Being in bitterness of soul, she prayed, v. 10.* This good use we should made of our afflictions, they should make us the more lively in our addresses to God. Our blessed Saviour himself, *being in an agony, prayed more earnestly,* Luke xxii. 44. (2) She mingled tears with her prayers. It was not a dry prayer: she wept sore. (3) She was very particular, and yet very modest, in her petition. She begged a child, a man-child, that it might be fit to serve in the tabernacle. (4) She made a solemn vow, or promise, that if God would give her a son she would *give him up to God, v. 11.* He would be by birth a Levite, and so devoted to the service of God, but he should be by her vow a Nazarite, and his very childhood should be sacred. Note further, it is very proper, when we are in pursuit of any mercy, to bind our own souls with a bond. Not that hereby we can pretend to merit the gift, but thus we are qualified for it and for the comfort of it. In hope of mercy, let us promise duty. (5) She spoke all this so softly that none could hear her. Her lips moved, but *her voice was not heard, v. 13.* She trusted God's knowledge of the heart. Thoughts are words to him.

2. The hard censure she fell under for it. Eli was now high priest, and judge in Israel; he sat upon a seat in the temple, to oversee what was done there, *v. 9.* The tabernacle is here called the *temple,* because it was now fixed, and served all the purposes of a

temple. There Eli sat to receive addresses and give direction, and somewhere (it is probable in a private corner) he espied Hannah at her prayers, and by her unusual manner fancied she was drunken, and spoke to her accordingly (*v. 14*): *How long wilt thou be drunken?*—the very imputation that Peter and the apostles fell under when the Holy Ghost *gave them utterance,* Acts ii. 13. Perhaps in this degenerate age it was no strange thing to see drunken women at the door of the tabernacle. When a disease is epidemical every one is suspected to be tainted with it. She had been reproved by Elkanah because she would not eat and drink, and now to be reproached by Eli as if she had eaten and drunk too much was very hard.

3. Hannah's humble vindication of herself from this crime with which she was charged. (1) In justice to herself she expressly denies the charge. "No, my lord, it is not as you suspect; I have drunk neither wine nor strong drink, not any at all, *count not thy handmaid for a daughter of Belial.*" Note, The very manner of her speaking in her own defence was sufficient to demonstrate that she was not drunk. (2) In justice to him, she gives an account of her present behaviour. She had been more than ordinarily fervent in prayer to God, and this, she tells him, was the true reason of the transport and disorder she seemed to be in.

4. The atonement Eli made for his rash unfriendly censure, by a kind and fatherly benediction, *v. 17.* He now encouraged Hannah's devotions as much as before he had discountenanced them; and intimated that he was satisfied of her innocency by those words, *Go in peace. The God of Israel grant thee thy petition, whatever it is, that thou hast asked of him.*

5. The great satisfaction of mind with which Hannah now went away, *v. 18.* She went her way and did eat of what remained of the peace-offerings *and her countenance was no more sad.* Whence came this sudden happy change? She had by prayer committed her case to God and left it with him, and now she was no more perplexed about it. She had prayed for herself, and Eli had prayed for her; and she believed that God would either give her the mercy she had prayed for or make up the want of it to her some other way. Prayer is heart's ease to a gracious soul.

Verses 19–28

I. The return of Elkanah and his family to their own habitation, when the days appointed for the feast were over, *v. 19.* They had a journey before them, and a family of children to take with them, and yet they would not stir till they had worshipped God together. Prayer and provender do not hinder a journey.

II. The birth and name of this desired son. At length the Lord remembered Hannah, for she conceived and bore a son. This son the mother called *Samuel, v. 20.* Some make the etymology of this name to be much the same with that of *Ishmael—heard of God,* because the mother's prayers were remarkably heard, and he was an answer to them. Others, because of the reason she gives for the name, make it to signify *asked of God.* Mercies in answer to prayer are to be remembered with peculiar expressions of thankfulness, as Ps. cxvi. 1, 2. How many seasonable deliverances and supplies may we call *Samuels, asked of God!* He was asked of God and was at the same time dedicated to him.

III. The close attendance Hannah gave to the nursing of him, not only because he was dear to her, but because he was devoted to God. Hannah, though she felt a warm regard for the courts of God's house, begged leave of her husband to stay at home; for the women were not under any obligation to go up to the three yearly feasts, as the men were. However Hannah had been accustomed to go, but now desired to be excused, 1. Because she would not be so long absent from her nursery. God will have mercy and not sacrifice. Those that are detained from public ordinances by the nursing and tending of little children may take comfort from this instance, and believe that, if they do that with an eye to God, he will graciously accept them therein. 2. Because she would not go up to Shiloh till her son was big enough, not only to be taken thither, but to be left there; for, if once she took him thither, she thought she could never find in her heart to bring him back again.

IV. The solemn entering of this child into the service of the sanctuary. Some think it was as soon as he was weaned from the breast, which, the Jews say, was not till he was three years old. Others think it was not till he was weaned from childish things, at eight or ten years old. It is said (*v.* 24), *The child was young.* Observe how she presented her child, 1. With a sacrifice; no less than three bullocks, with a meat-offering for each, *v.* 24. A bullock, perhaps, for each year of the child's life. Or one for a burnt-offering, another for a sin-offering, and the third for a peace-offering. 2. With a grateful acknowledgment of God's goodness in answer to prayer. This she makes to Eli, because he had encouraged her to hope for an answer of peace (*v.* 26, 27): "*For this child I prayed.*" 3. With a full surrender of all her interest in this child unto the Lord (*v.* 28): *I have lent him to the Lord as long as he liveth.* (1) Whatever we give to God, it is what we have first asked and received from him. *Of thy own, Lord, have we given thee,* 1 Chron. xxix. 14, 16. (2) Whatever we give to God may upon this account be said to be *lent* to him. When by baptism we dedicate our children to God, let us remember that they were his before by a sovereign right, and that that they are ours still so much the more to our comfort.

Lastly, The child Samuel did his part beyond what could have been expected from one of his years; for of him that seems to be spoken, *He worshipped the Lord there,* that is, *he said his prayers.* Little children should learn betimes to worship God. Their parents should instruct them in his worship and bring them to it, put them upon engaging in it as well as they can, and God will graciously accept them and teach them to do better.

CHAPTER 2

I. Hannah's song of thanksgiving to God for giving her Samuel, ver. 1–10. II. Their return to their family, with Eli's blessing, ver. 11, 20. The increase of their family, ver. 21. Samuel's growth and improvement (ver. 11, 18, 21, 26), and the care Hannah took to clothe him, ver. 19. III. The great wickedness of Eli's sons, ver. 12–17, 22. IV. The over-mild reproof that Eli gave them, ver. 23–25. V. The justly dreadful message God sent him by a prophet, ver. 27–36.

Verses 1–10

We have here Hannah's thanksgiving, dictated, not only by the spirit of prayer, but by the spirit of prophecy. Observe in general, 1. When she had received mercy from God she owned it, with thankfulness to his praise. Praise is our rent, our tribute. We are unjust if we do not pay it. 2. The mercy she had received was an answer to prayer, and therefore she thought herself especially obliged to give thanks for it. 3. Her thanksgiving is here called a prayer: *Hannah prayed;* for thanksgiving is an essential part of prayer. *Her voice was not heard;* but in her thanksgiving she spoke, that all might hear her. She made her supplication *with groanings that could not be uttered,* but now her lips were opened to *show forth God's praise.* Three things we have in this thanksgiving:

I. Hannah's triumph in God, in his glorious perfections, and the great things he had done for her, *v.* 1–3.

1. What great things she says of God. She takes little notice of the particular mercy she was now rejoicing in. She overlooks the gift, and praises the giver; whereas most forget the giver and fasten only on the gift. Four of God's glorious attributes Hannah here celebrates, (1) His unspotted purity. *There is none holy as the Lord.* (2) His almighty power: *Neither is there any rock like our God.* (3) His unsearchable wisdom: *The Lord,* the Judge of all, *is a God of knowledge.* (4) His unerring justice: *By him actions are weighed.*

2. How she solaces herself in these things. What we give God the glory of we may take the comfort of. Hannah does so, (1) In holy joy: *My heart rejoiceth in the Lord*; not so much in her son as in her God. (2) In holy triumph: "*My horn is exalted*; not only is my reputation saved by my having a son, but greatly raised by having such a son." *My horn is exalted* means this, "My praises are very much elevated to an unusual strain." *My mouth is enlarged,* that is, "Now I have wherewith to answer those that reproached me."

3. How she herewith silences those that set up themselves as rivals with God and rebels against him (*v.* 3): *Talk no more so exceedingly proudly.*

II. The notice she takes of the wisdom and sovereignty of the divine providence, in its disposals of the affairs of the children of men.

1. The strong are soon weakened and the weak are soon strengthened, when God pleases, *v.* 4. On the one hand, if he speak the word, *the bows of the mighty men are broken*; they are disarmed, disabled to do as they have before done and as they have designed to do. On the other hand, if the Lord speak the word, those who stumble through weakness, who were so feeble that they could not go straight or steady, are *girded with strength*, in body and mind, and are able to bring great things to pass.

2. The rich are soon impoverished, and the poor strangely enriched on a sudden, *v.* 5. *Riches flee away* (Prov. xxiii. 5), and leave those miserable who, when they had them, placed their happiness in them. To those that have been full and free poverty and slavery must needs be doubly grievous. But, on the other hand, sometimes Providence so orders it that *those who are hungry cease*, that is, cease to hire out themselves for bread as they have done. It may be understood of the same person; those that were rich God makes poor. and after awhile makes rich again, as Job; he gave, he takes away, and then gives again, Let not the rich be proud and secure, for God can soon make them poor; let not the poor despond and despair, for God can in due time enrich them again.

3. Empty families are replenished and numerous families diminished and made few. *The barren hath borne seven,* meaning herself, for, though at present she had but one son, yet that one being a Nazarite, devoted to God and employed in his immediate service, he was to her as good as seven. Or it is the language of her faith. Now that she had one she hoped for more, and was not disappointed.

4. God is the sovereign Lord of life and death (*v.* 6): *The Lord killeth and maketh alive.* Nothing is too hard for God to do, no, not the quickening of the dead, and putting life into dry bones.

5. Advancement and abasement are both from him. He brings some low and lifts up others (*v.* 7), humbles the proud and gives grace and honour to the lowly, lays those in the dust that would vie with the God above them and trample upon all about them (Job xl. 12, 13), but lifts up those with his salvation that humble themselves before him, Jam. iv. 10. Joseph, and Daniel, Moses and David, were thus strangely advanced, from a prison to a palace, from a sheep-hook to a sceptre.

6. A reason is given for all these dispensations which obliges us to acquiesce in them, how surprising soever they are: *For the pillars of the earth are the Lord's.* (1) If we understand this literally, it intimates God's almighty power, which cannot be controlled. He upholds the whole creation, founded the earth, and still sustains it by the word of his power. What cannot he do in the affairs of families and kingdoms, far beyond our conception and expectation, *who hangs the earth upon nothing?* Job xxvi. 7. But, (2) If we understand it figuratively, it intimates his incontestable sovereignty, which cannot be disputed. The princes and great ones of the earth, the directors of states and governments, are the *pillars of the earth,* Ps. lxxv. 3. On these hinges the affairs of the world seem to turn, but they are the Lord's, Ps. xlvii. 9. From him they have their power, and therefore he may advance whom he pleases; and who may say, *What doest thou?*

III. A prediction of the preservation and advancement of all God's faithful friends, and the destruction of all his and their enemies. Having testified her joyful triumph in what God had done, and is doing, she concludes with joyful hopes of what he would do, v. 9, 10. Pious affections in those days rose many times to the height of prophecy. This prophecy may refer, 1. More immediately to the government of Israel by Samuel, and by David whom he was employed to anoint. Israel (that in the time of the judges had made so small a figure and had much ado to subsist) should now shortly become great and considerable, and give law to all its neighbours. An extraordinary change that was; and the birth of Samuel was, as it were, the dawning of that day. But, 2. We have reason to think that this prophecy looks further, to the kingdom of Christ, and the administration of that kingdom of grace, of which she now comes to speak, having spoken so largely of the kingdom of providence. And here is the first time that we meet with the name *Messiah,* or *his Anointed.* The ancient expositors, both Jewish and Christian, make it to look beyond David, to the Son of David. Glorious things are here spoken of the kingdom of the Mediator. Concerning that kingdom we are here assured, (1) That all the loyal subjects of it shall be carefully and powerfully protected (v. 9): *He will keep the feet of his saints.* If he will keep their feet, much more their head and hearts. Or he will keep their feet, that is, he will secure the ground they stand on, and establish their goings; he will set a guard of grace upon their affections and actions, that their feet may neither wander out of the way nor stumble in the way. (2) That all the powers engaged against it shall not be able to effect the ruin of it. (3) That all the enemies of it will certainly be broken and brought down: *The wicked shall be silent in darkness,* v. 9. (4) That the conquests of this kingdom shall extend themselves to distant regions: *The Lord shall judge the ends of the earth.* David's victories and dominions reached far, but the *uttermost parts of the earth* are promised to the Messiah for his *possession* (Ps. ii. 8). (5) That the power and honour of Messiah the prince shall grow and increase more and more: *He shall give strength unto his king,* for the accomplishing of his great undertaking (Ps. lxxxix. 21, and see Luke xxii. 43), strengthen him to go through the difficulties of his humiliation, and in his exaltation he will *lift up the head* (Ps. cx. 7), lift up the horn, the power and honour, of his *anointed,* and *make him higher than the kings of the earth,* Ps. lxxxix. 27.

Verses 11–26

In these verses we have the good character of Elkanah's family, and the bad character of Eli's family.

I. Let us see how well things went in Elkanah's family and how much better than formerly. 1. Eli dismissed them from the house of the Lord, when they had entered their little son there, with a blessing, v. 20. If Hannah had then had many children, it would not have been such a generous piece of piety to part with one out of many for the service of the tabernacle; but when she had but one, to present him to the Lord was such an act of heroic piety as should by no means lose its reward. As when Abraham had offered Isaac he received the promise of a numerous issue (Gen. xxii. 16, 17), so did Hannah, when she had presented Samuel unto the Lord a living sacrifice. 2. They returned to their own habitation. This is twice mentioned, v. 11, and again v. 20. 3. They kept up their constant attendance at the house of God with their *yearly sacrifice,* v. 19. They did not think that their son's ministering there would excuse them. We may suppose they went thither to see their child oftener than once a year, for it was not ten miles from Ramah; but their annual visit is taken notice of because then they brought their yearly sacrifice, and then Hannah fitted up her son (and some think oftener than once a year) with a new suit of clothes, *a little coat* (v. 19) and everything belonging to it. 4. The child Samuel did very well. Four separate times he is mentioned in these verses, and two things we are told of:—(1) The service he did to the Lord. He did well indeed, for he *ministered to the Lord* (v. 11, 18). Perhaps he attended immediately on Eli's person. He could light a candle, or hold a dish, or run on an errand, or shut a door; and, because he did this with a pious disposition of mind it is called *ministering to the Lord.* (2) The blessing he received from the Lord. He *grew before the Lord,* as a tender plant (v. 21), *grew on* (v. 26) in strength and stature, and especially in wisdom and understanding. *He was in favour with the Lord and with man.* What is here said of Samuel is said of our blessed Saviour, that great example, Luke ii. 52.

II. Let us now see how ill things went in Eli's family, though seated at the very door of the tabernacle. The nearer the church the further from God.

1. The abominable wickedness of Eli's sons (v. 12): *The sons of Eli were sons of Belial.* It is emphatically expressed. *They knew not the Lord.* They were resident at the fountain-head both of magistracy and ministry, and yet they were *sons of Belial,* and their honour, power, and learning, made them so much the worse. It is hard to say which dishonours God more, idolatry or profaneness, especially the profaneness of the priests.

(1) They profaned the offerings of the Lord, and made a gain to themselves, or rather a gratification of their own luxury, out of them. [1] They robbed the offerers, and seized for themselves some of their part of the sacrifice of the peace-offerings. The priests had for their share the *wave-breast* and the *heave shoulder* (Lev. vii. 34), but these did not content them. [2] They stepped in before God himself, and encroached upon his right too. *As if it were a small thing to weary men, they wearied my God also,* Isa. vii. 13. The effect was, *First,* That God was displeased: *The sin of the young men was very great before the Lord,* v. 17. *Secondly,* That religion suffered by it: *Men abhorred the offerings of the Lord.* In the midst of this sad story comes in the repeated mention of Samuel's devotion. *But Samuel ministered before the Lord,* as an instance of the power of God's grace, in preserving him pure and pious in the midst of this wicked crew; and this helped to keep up the sinking credit of the sanctuary in the minds of the people.

(2) They debauched the women that came to worship at the door of the tabernacle, v. 22.

2. The reproof which Eli gave his sons for this their wickedness: *Eli was very old* (*v.* 22) and could not himself inspect the service of the tabernacle as he had done, but left all to his sons, who, because of the infirmities of his age, slighted him, and did what they would. It should seem he did not so much as reprove them till he heard of their debauching the women, and then he thought fit to give them a check. Now concerning the reproof he gave them observe,

(1) That it was very just and rational. That which he said was very proper. [1] He tells them that the matter of fact was too plain to be denied and too public to be concealed: "*I hear of your evil dealings by all this people,*" *v.* 23. [2] He shows them the bad consequences of it, that they not only sinned, but made Israel to sin, and would have the people's sin to answer for as well as their own. [3] He warns them of the danger they brought themselves into by it, *v.* 25. He intimates to them what God afterwards told him, that the *iniquity* would not be *purged with sacrifice nor offering, ch.* iii. 14.

(2) It was too mild and gentle. He should have rebuked them sharply. Their crimes deserved sharpness; their temper needed it; the softness of his dealing with them would but harden them the more. What he said was right, but it was not enough.

3. Their obstinacy against this reproof. They *hearkened not to their father*, though he was also a judge. Samuel's tractableness is again mentioned (*v.* 26), to shame their obstinacy: *The child Samuel grew*. God's grace is his own; he denied it to the sons of the high priest and gave it to the child of an obscure country Levite.

Verses 27–36

Eli reproved his sons too gently, and did not threaten them as he should, and therefore God sent a prophet to him to reprove him sharply. The message is sent to Eli himself, because God would bring him to repentance and save him; not to his sons, whom he had determined to destroy.

I. He reminds him of the great things God had done for the house of his fathers and for his family. He appeared to Aaron in Egypt (Exod. iv. 27), in the house of bondage, as a token of further favour which he designed for him, *v.* 27. He advanced him to the priesthood, entailed it upon his family, and thereby dignified it above any of the families of Israel.

II. He exhibits a high charge against him and his family. His children did wickedly, and he connived at it, and thereby involved himself in the guilt; the indictment therefore runs against them all, *v.* 29. 1. His sons had impiously profaned the holy things of God: "*You kick at my sacrifice which I have commanded.*" 2. Eli had bolstered them up in it, by not punishing their insolence and impiety: "Thou for thy part *honourest thy sons above me.*" 3. They had all shared in the gains of the sacrilege. It is to be feared that Eli himself, though he disliked and reproved the abuses they committed, yet did not forbear to eat of the roast meat they sacrilegiously got, *v.* 15.

III. He declares the cutting off of the entail of the high priesthood from his family (*v.* 30): *I said, indeed, that thy house, and the house of thy father* Ithamar (for from that younger son of Aaron Eli descended), *should walk before me for ever*. Upon what occasion the dignity of the high priesthood was transferred from the family of Eleazar to that of Ithamar does not appear; but it seems this had been done, and Eli stood fair to have that honour perpetuated to his posterity. But observe, the promise carried its own condition along with it: *They shall walk before me for ever*, that is, "they shall have the

honour, provided they faithfully do the service." *Walking before God* is the great condition of the covenant, Gen. xvii. 1. Let them set me before their face, and I will set them before my face continually (Ps. xli. 12), otherwise not. But now the Lord says, *Be it far from me*. "Now that you cast me off you can expect no other than that I should cast you off; you will not walk before me as you should, and therefore you shall not."

IV. He gives a good reason for this revocation, taken from a settled and standing rule of God's government, according to which all must expect to be dealt with (like that by which Cain was tried, Gen. iv. 7): *Those that honour me I will honour, and those that despise me shall be lightly esteemed*. The way to be truly great is to be truly good. If we humble and deny ourselves in anything to honour God, and have a single eye to him in it, we may depend upon this promise, he will put the best honour upon us. See John xii. 26.

V. He foretells the particular judgments which should come upon his family, to its perpetual ignominy.

1. That their power should be broken (*v.* 31): *I will cut off thy arm, and the arm of thy father's house*. They should be stripped of all their authority, should be deposed, and have no influence upon the people as they had had.

2. That their lives should be shortened. It is twice spoken: "*There shall not be an old man in thy house for ever*"; and again (*v.* 33), "*All the increase of thy house*, from generation to generation, *shall die in the flower of their age.*"

3. That all their comforts should be embittered. (1) The comfort they had in the sanctuary, in its wealth and prosperity: *Thou shalt see an enemy in my habitation*. This was fulfilled in the Philistines' invasions and the mischiefs they did to Israel (*ch.* xiii. 19). (2) The comfort of their children: "*The man of thine whom I shall not cut off by an untimely death*" shall live to be a blot and burden to the family. Grief for a dead child is great, but for a bad child often greater.

4. That their substance should be wasted and they should be reduced to extreme poverty (*v.* 26): "*He that is left alive in thy house* shall have little joy of his life, for want of a livelihood; he shall come and crouch to the succeeding family for a subsistence." (1) He shall beg for the smallest alms—*a piece of silver* (and the word signifies the *least* piece) and *a morsel of bread*. Want is the just punishment of wantonness. Those who could not be content without dainties and varieties are brought, they or theirs, to want necessaries. (2) He shall beg for the meanest office: *Put me into somewhat belonging to the priesthood* (as it is in the original); *make me as one of the hired servants*, the fittest place for a prodigal. Plenty and power are forfeited when they are abused. This, it is probable, was fully accomplished when Abiathar, who was of Eli's race, was deposed by Solomon for treason, and he and his turned out of office in the temple (1 Kings ii. 26, 27).

5. That God would shortly begin to execute these judgments in the death of Hophni and Phinehas, the sad tidings of which Eli himself should live to hear: *This shall be a sign to thee, v.* 34.

VI. In the midst of all these threatenings against the house of Eli, here is mercy promised to Israel (*v.* 35): *I will raise me up a faithful priest*. 1. This was fulfilled in Zadok, of the family of Eleazar, who came into Abiathar's place in the beginning of Solomon's reign, and was faithful to his trust. If some betray their trust, yet others shall be raised up that will be true to it. God's work shall never fall to the ground for want of hands to carry it on. 2. It has its full accomplishment in the priesthood of Christ.

CHAPTER 3

In the foregoing chapter we had Samuel a young priest, though by birth a Levite only, for he ministered before the Lord in a linen ephod; in this chapter we have him a young prophet, God revealing himself to him, and in him reviving, if not commencing, prophecy in Israel. I. God's first manifestation of himself in an extraordinary manner to Samuel, ver. 1–10. II. The message he sent by him to Eli, ver. 11–14. III. The faithful delivery of that message to Eli, and his submission to the righteousness of God in it, ver. 15–18. IV. The establishment of Samuel to be a prophet in Israel, ver. 19–21.

Verses 1–10

We are here told, 1. How industrious Samuel was in serving God. It was an aggravation of the wickedness of Eli's sons that the child Samuel shamed them. They rebelled against the Lord, but Samuel ministered to him; they slighted their father's admonitions, but Samuel was observant of them; he ministered before Eli, under his eye and direction. Those are fittest to rule who have learnt to obey. 2. How scarce a thing prophecy then was, which made the call of Samuel to be the greater surprise to himself and the greater favour to Israel: *The word of the Lord was precious in those days.* It was precious, for what there was (it seems) was private: *There was no open vision.* Perhaps the impiety and impurity that prevailed in the tabernacle, and no doubt corrupted the whole nation, had provoked God, as a token of his displeasure, to withdraw that spirit of prophecy.

The manner of God's revealing himself to Samuel is here related very particularly, for it was uncommon. I. Eli had retired. Samuel had waited on him to his bed (v. 2): *Eli had laid down in his place.* II. Samuel had laid down to sleep, in some closet near to Eli's room, ready within call if the old man should want any thing in the night. When his own sons were a grief to him, his little servitor was his joy. *Samuel had laid down ere the lamp of God went out, v. 3.* III. God called him by name, and he took it for Eli's call, and ran to him, v. 4, 5. Here we have an instance, 1. Of Samuel's industry, and readiness to wait on Eli. "Here am I," said he—a good example to servants, to come when they are called; and to the younger, not only to submit to the elder, but to be careful and tender of them. 2. Of his unacquaintedness with the visions of the Almighty, that he took that to be only Eli's call which was really the call of God. Such mistakes as these we make oftener than we think. God calls to us by his word, and we take it to be only the call of the minister, and answer it accordingly; he calls to us by his providences, and we look only at the instruments. Eli assured him he did not call him, but mildly bade him lie down again. So *Samuel went and lay down.* IV. The same call was repeated, and the same mistake made, a second and third time, v. 6–9. 1. God continued to call the child *yet again* (v. 6), and *again the third time, v.* 8. 2. Samuel was still ignorant that it was the Lord that called him (v. 7): *Samuel did not yet know the Lord.* The witness of the Spirit in the hearts of the faithful is often thus mistaken, by which means they lose the comfort of it; and the strivings of the Spirit with the consciences of sinners are likewise often mistaken, and so the benefit of their convictions is lost. Samuel went to Eli this second and third time, and he tells Eli, with great assurance, "*Thou didst call me* (v. 6–8), it could be no one else." But there was a special providence in it, that he should go thus often to Eli; for hereby, at length, *Eli perceived that the Lord had called the child, v.* 8. This would be a mortification to him, and he would apprehend it to be a step towards his family's being degraded, that when God had something to say he should choose to say it to the child Samuel, his servant that waited on him, and not to him.

V. At length Samuel was put into a posture to receive a message from God. 1. Eli, perceiving that it was the voice of God that Samuel heard, gave him instructions what to say, v. 9. The instruction was, when God called the next time, to say, *Speak, Lord, for thy servant heareth.* We may expect that God will speak to us, when we set ourselves to hearken to what he says, Ps. lxxxv. 8; Hab. ii. 1. When we come to read the word of God, and to attend on the preaching of it, we should come thus disposed, submitting ourselves to the commanding light and power of it: *Speak, Lord, for thy servant heareth.* 2. It should seem that God spoke the fourth time in a way somewhat different from the other; now *he stood and called,* which intimates that there was now some visible appearance of the divine glory to Samuel. This satisfied him that it was not Eli that called. Now also the call was doubled—*Samuel, Samuel,* as if God delighted in the mention of his name. 3. Samuel said, as he was taught, *Speak, for thy servant heareth.* Samuel did not now rise and run as before when he thought Eli called, but lay still and listened. The more sedate and composed our spirits are the better prepared they are for divine discoveries. All must be silent when he speaks. But observe, Samuel left out one word; he did not say, *Speak, Lord,* but only, *Speak, for thy servant heareth,* perhaps, as Bishop Patrick suggests, out of uncertainty whether it was God that spoke to him or no.

Verses 11–18

I. The message which, after all this introduction, God delivered to Samuel concerning Eli's house. The message is short, not nearly so long as that which the man of God brought, *ch.* ii. 27. But it is a sad message, to ratify the message in the former chapter, and to bind on the sentence there pronounced.

1. Concerning the sin: it is the *iniquity that he knoweth, v.* 13. The man of God told him of it, and many a time his own conscience had told him of it. *His sons made themselves vile, and he restrained them not.* Or, as it is in the Hebrew, he *frowned not upon them.*

2. Concerning the punishment: it is *that which I have spoken concerning his house, v.* 12 and 13. When that sentence began to be executed it would be very dreadful and amazing to all Israel (*v.* 11): *Both the ears of every one that heareth it shall tingle.* Every Israelite would be struck with terror and astonishment to hear of the slaying of Eli's sons, the breaking of Eli's neck, and the dispersion of Eli's family. "The *iniquity of Eli's house shall not be purged with sacrifice nor offering for ever.* No atonement shall be made for the sin, nor any abatement of the punishment." This was the imperfection of the legal sacrifices, that there were iniquities which they did not reach, which they would not purge; but *the blood of Christ cleanseth from all sin,* and secured all those that by faith are interested in it from that eternal death which is the wages of sin.

II. The delivery of this message to Eli.

1. Samuel's modest concealment of it, *v.* 15. (1) He *lay till the morning,* and we may well suppose he lay awake pondering on what he had heard. (2) *He opened the doors of the house of the Lord,* in the morning, as he used to do, being up first in the tabernacle. That he should do so at other times was an instance of extraordinary towardliness in a child, but that he should do so this morning was an instance of great humility. God had highly honoured him above all the children of his people, yet he was not proud of the honour, but, as cheerfully as ever, went and opened the doors of the tabernacle. (3) *He feared to show Eli the vision,* because he was afraid to grieve and trouble the good old man.

2. Eli's careful enquiry into it, *v.* 16, 17. As soon as ever he heard Samuel's stirring he called for him, probably to his bedside. He had reason enough to fear that the message prophesied no good concerning him, but evil; and yet, because it was a message from God, he could not contentedly be ignorant of it. A good man desires to be acquainted with all the will of God, whether it make for him or against him.

3. Samuel's faithful delivery of his message at last (*v.* 18); *He told him every whit.*

4. Eli's pious acquiescence in it. He did not question Samuel's integrity, was not cross with him, nor had he any thing to object against the equity of the sentence. *It is the Lord, let him do what seemeth him good. It is the Lord,* with whom there is no unrighteousness, who never did nor ever will do any wrong to any of his creatures, nor exact more than their iniquity deserves. *"Let him do what seemeth him good. I have nothing to say against his proceedings."*

Verses 19–21

Samuel being thus brought acquainted with the visions of God,

I. God did him honour. Having begun to favour him, he carried on and crowned his own work in him: *Samuel grew, for the Lord was with him, v.* 19. God honoured Samuel; 1. By further manifestations of himself to him: *The Lord revealed himself again to Samuel in Shiloh, v.* 21. 2. By fulfilling what he spoke by him: *God did let none of his words fall to the ground, v.* 19. Whatever Samuel said, as a prophet, it proved true, and was accomplished in its season.

II. Israel did him honour. They all knew and owned *that Samuel was established to be a prophet, v.* 20. 1. He grew famous. 2. He grew useful and very serviceable to his generation. He that began betimes to *be good* soon came to *do* good.

CHAPTER 4

The predictions concerning the ruin of Eli's house begin to be fulfilled. I. The disgrace Israel sustained in an encounter with the Philistines, ver. 1, 2. II. Their foolish project to fortify themselves by bringing the ark of God into their camp upon the shoulders of Hophni and Phinehas (ver. 3, 4), which made them secure (ver. 5) and struck a fear into the Philistines, but such a fear as roused them, ver. 6–9. III. The fatal consequences: Israel was beaten, and the ark taken prisoner, ver. 10, 11. IV. The tidings brought to Shiloh, and the sad reception of those tidings. 1. The city was put into confusion, ver. 12, 13. 2. Eli fell, and broke his neck, ver. 14–18. 3. Upon hearing what had occurred his daughter-in-law fell in labour, bore a son, but died immediately, ver. 19–22.

Verses 1–9

I. A war entered into with the Philistines, *v.* 1. It was an attempt to throw off the yoke of their oppression, and would have succeeded better if they had first repented and reformed, and so begun their work at the right end.

II. The defeat of Israel in that war, *v.* 2. Israel, who were the aggressors, were smitten, and had 4,000 men killed upon the spot. Sin, the accursed thing, was in the camp, and gave their enemies all the advantage against them they could wish for.

III. The measures they concerted for another engagement. 1. They quarrelled with God for appearing against them (*v.* 3): *Wherefore has the Lord smitten us?* They expostulate boldly with God about it, are displeased at what God has done, and dispute the matter with him. 2. They imagined that they could oblige him to appear for them the next time by bringing the ark into their camp. They sent to Shiloh for the ark, and Eli had not courage enough to detain it, but sent his ungodly sons, Hophni and Phinehas, along with it, or at least permitted them to go. See here, (1) The profound veneration the people had for the ark. "O send for that, and it will do wonders for us." The ark was, by institution, a

visible token of God's presence. They thought that, by paying a great respect to this sacred chest, they should prove themselves to be Israelites and engage God Almighty to appear in their favour. It is common for those that have estranged themselves from the vitals of religion to discover a great fondness for the rituals and external observances of it. And yet indeed they did but make an idol of the ark, and looked upon it to be as much an image of the God of Israel as those idols which the heathen worshipped were of their gods. (2) Their egregious folly in thinking that the ark, if they had it in their camp, would certainly *save them out of the hand of their enemies,* and bring victory back to their side. What good would the ark do them, the shell without the kernel? Instead of honouring God by what they did, they really affronted him. If there had been nothing else to invalidate their expectations from the ark, how could they expect it should bring a blessing when Hophni and Phinehas were the men that carried it?

IV. The great joy there was in the camp of Israel when the ark was brought into it (*v.* 5): *They shouted, so that the earth rang again.* Now they thought themselves sure of victory.

V. The consternation into which the bringing of the ark into the camp of Israel put the Philistines. The two armies lay so near encamped that the Philistines heard the shout the Israelites gave on this great occasion. They soon understood what it was they triumphed in (*v.* 6), and were afraid of the consequences. For, 1. It had never been done before in their days: *God has come into their camp,* and therefore *woe unto us* (*v.* 7), and again, *woe unto us, v.* 8. See what gross notions they had of the divine presence, as if the God of Israel were not as much in the camp before the ark came thither, which may very well be excused in them, since the notions the Israelites themselves had of that presence were no better. 2. When it had been done in the days of old, it had wrought wonders: *These are the gods that smote the Egyptians with all the plagues in the wilderness,* 4. 8. Here they were as much out in their history as in their divinity: the plagues of Egypt were inflicted before the ark was made and before Israel came into the wilderness. Yet, it should seem, they scarcely believed themselves when they spoke thus formidably of *these mighty gods,* but only bantered; they stirred up one another to fight so much the more stoutly.

Verses 10–11

Here is a short account of the issue of this battle.

I. Israel was smitten, the army dispersed and totally routed. 1. Though they had the better cause, were the people of God, yet they failed of success, for *their rock had sold them.* A good cause often suffers for the sake of the bad men that undertake it. 2. Though they had the greater confidence, and were the more courageous. The ark in the camp will add nothing to its strength when there is an Achan in it.

II. The ark itself was taken by the Philistines; and Hophni and Phinehas were *both slain, v.* 11. 1. The slaughter of the priests, considering their bad character, was no great loss to Israel, but it was a dreadful judgment upon the house of Eli. The word which God had spoken was fulfilled in it (*ch.* ii. 34). But, 2. The taking of the ark, was a very great judgment upon Israel, and a certain token of God's hot displeasure against them. Now they are made to see their folly in trusting to their external privileges when they had by their wickedness forfeited them, and fancying that the ark would save them when God had departed from them.

Verses 12–18

Tidings are here brought to Shiloh of the fatal issue of their battle with the Philistines. Bad news flies fast. Thither therefore an express posted away immediately; it was a man of Benjamin; the Jews fancy it was Saul. *He rent his clothes, and put earth upon his head*, by these signs to proclaim the sorrowful news. He went straight to Shiloh with it.

I. How the city received it. *Eli sat in the gate* (v. 13, 18), but the messenger passed him by, and told it in the city, with all the aggravating circumstances; and now *both the ears of every one that heard it tingled*, as was foretold, *ch*. iii. 11. Their hearts trembled, and every face gathered blackness. *All the city cried out* (v. 13), and well they might, for it was a particular loss to Shiloh, and the ruin of that place; for, though the ark was soon rescued out of the hands of the Philistines, yet it never returned to Shiloh again. This abandoning of Shiloh Jerusalem is long afterwards reminded of, and told to take warning by. Jer. vii. 12, "*Go see what I did to Shiloh*."

II. What a fatal blow it was to old Eli. 1. With what fear he expected the tidings. Though old, and blind, and heavy, yet he could not keep his chamber when he was sensible the glory of Israel lay at stake, but placed himself by the way side, to receive the first intelligence; for *his heart trembled for the ark of God*, v. 13. He also apprehended imminent danger. Israel had forfeited the ark (his own sons especially) and now the threatening comes to his mind, that he should *see an enemy in God's habitation* (*ch*. ii. 32); and perhaps his own heart reproached him for not using his authority to prevent the carrying of the ark into the camp. All good men lay the interests of God's church nearer their hearts than any secular interest or concern of their own. How can we be easy if the ark be not safe? 2. With what grief he received the tidings. Though he could not see, he could hear the *tumult* and *crying of the city*, and perceived it to be the voice of lamentation. He is told there is an express come from the army, who relates the story to him very distinctly, having himself been an eye-witness of it, *v*. 16, 17. The account of the defeat of the army, and the slaughter of a great number of the soldiers, was very grievous to him as a judge; but the tidings of the death of his two sons, who, he had reason to fear, died impenitent, touched him in a tender part as a father. He does not interrupt the narrative with any passionate lamentations for his sons, like David for Absalom, but waits for the end of the story, not doubting but that the messenger, being an Israelite, would, without being asked, say something of the ark; and if he could but have said, "Yet the ark of God is safe, and we are bringing that home," his joy for that would have overcome his grief for all the other disasters. When the messenger concludes his story with, *The ark of God is taken*, he is struck to the heart, and, it should seem, he swooned away, and died immediately. His heart was broken first, and then his neck. Thus were the folly and wickedness of those sons of his, whom he had indulged, his ruin at last. Yet we must observe, to Eli's praise, that it was the loss of the ark that was his death, not the slaughter of his sons.

Verses 19–22

Another melancholy story, that carries on the desolations of Eli's house, and the sorrowful feeling which the tidings of the ark's captivity excited. It is concerning the wife of Phinehas, one of those ungracious sons of Eli that had brought all this mischief on Israel.

I. She was a woman of a very tender spirit. She was near her time. When she heard of the death of her father-in-law whom she reverenced, and her husband whom, bad as he was, she loved, but especially of the loss of the ark, *she travailed, for her pains came* thickly *upon her* (v. 19), and though she had strength to bear the child, she, soon after, fainted and died, being very willing to let life go when she had lost the greatest comforts of her life.

II. She was a woman of a very gracious spirit. Her concern for the death of her husband and father-in-law was an evidence of her natural affection; but her much greater concern for the loss of the ark was an evidence of her pious and devout affection to God and sacred things. *She said, The glory has departed from Israel*.

1. The women that attended her *said unto her, Fear not*, now the worst is past, *for thou hast borne a son* (and perhaps it was her first-born), *but she answered not, neither did she regard it*. What is it to one that is lamenting the loss of the ark? Small comfort could she have of a child born in Israel, in Shiloh, when the ark is lost, and is a prisoner in the land of the Philistines.

2. This made her give her child a name which should perpetuate the remembrance of the calamity and her sense of it. She orders them to call it *I-chabod*, that is, *Where is the glory?* Or, *Alas for the glory!* or, *There is no glory* (v. 21), which she thus explains with her dying lips (v. 22): "*The glory has departed from Israel; for the ark of God is taken*." If God go, the glory goes, and all good goes.

CHAPTER 5

It is now time to enquire what has become of the ark of God; but we find not any motion made, so little was there of zeal or courage left. "It is gone, and let it go." Unworthy they were of the name of Israelites that could thus tamely part with the glory of Israel. God would therefore take the work into his own hands. I. How the Philistines triumphed over the ark, ver. 1, 2. and II. How the ark triumphed over the Philistines, 1. Over Dagon their god, ver. 3–5. 2. Over the Philistines themselves, who were sorely plagued with emerods, the men of Ashdod first (ver. 6, 7), then the men of Gath (ver. 8, 9), and lastly those of Ekron, which forced them at length upon a resolution to send the ark back to the land of Israel.

Verses 1–5

I. The Philistines' triumph over the ark, which they were the more pleased to be now masters of because before the battle they were possessed with a great fear of it, *ch*. iv. 7. When they had it in their hands God restrained them, that they did not offer any violence to it, but carefully carried it to a place of safety. They carried it to Ashdod, one of their five cities, and that in which Dagon's temple was; there they placed the ark of God, *by Dagon* (v. 2), either, 1. As a sacred thing, which they designed to pay some religious respect to, in conjunction with Dagon; for the gods of the heathen were never looked upon as averse to partners. Though the nations would not change their gods, yet they would multiply them and add to them. But they were mistaken in the God of Israel when, in putting his ark by Dagon's image, they intended to do him honour; for he is not worshipped at all if he is not worshipped alone. Or rather, 2. They placed it there as a trophy of victory, in honour of Dagon their god. (1) God will show of how little account the ark of the covenant is if the covenant itself be broken and neglected; even sacred signs are not things that either he is tied to or we can trust to. (2) For a time, God may have so much the more glory, in reckoning with those that thus affront him, and get him honour upon them. Having punished Israel, that betrayed the ark, by giving it into the hands of the Philistines, he will next deal with those that abused it, and will fetch it out of their hands again.

II. The ark's triumph over Dagon. Once and again Dagon was made to fall before it. The next morning, when the worshippers of Dagon came to pay their devotions to his shrine, they found their triumphing short, Job xx. 5.

1. Dagon had *fallen upon his face to the earth before the ark*, v. 3. Great care was taken, in setting

up the images of their gods, to fix them. The prophet takes notice of it, Isa. xli. 7, *He fastened it with nails that it should not be moved*; and again, Isa. xlvi. 7. And yet Dagon's fastenings stood him in no stead. The kingdom of Satan will certainly fall before the kingdom of Christ, error before truth, profaneness before godliness, and corruption before grace in the hearts of the faithful. When the interests of religion seem to be run down and ready to sink, yet even then we may be confident that the day of their triumph will come.

2. The priests, finding their idol on the floor, make all the haste they can, before it be known, to set him in his place again. A sorry silly thing it was to make a god of, which, when it was down, wanted help to get up again; and sottish wretches those were that could pray for help from that idol that needed, and in effect implored, their help. How could they attribute their victory to the power of Dagon when Dagon himself could not keep his own ground before the ark? But they are resolved Dagon shall be their god still, and therefore set him in his place.

3. The next night Dagon fell the second time, *v.* 4. The head and hands were *cut off upon the threshold*, so that nothing remained but the stump, or, as the margin reads it, *the fishy part of* Dagon; for (as many learned men conjecture) the upper part of this image was in a human shape, the lower in the shape of a fish, as mermaids are painted. The misshapen monster is by this fall made to appear, (1) Very ridiculous, and worthy to be despised. A pretty figure Dagon made now, when the fall had anatomized him, and shown how the human part and the fishy part were artificially put together. (2) Very impotent, and unworthy to be prayed to or trusted in; for his losing his head and hands proved him utterly destitute both of wisdom and power, and for ever disabled either to advise or act for his worshippers.

4. The threshold of Dagon's temple was ever looked upon as sacred, and not to be trodden on, *v.* 5. Some think that reference is had to this superstitious usage of Dagon's worshippers in Zeph. i. 9, where God threatens to punish those who, in imitation of them, leaped over the threshold. Instead of despising Dagon, for the threshold's sake that beheaded him, they were almost ready to worship the threshold because it was the block on which he was beheaded.

Verses 6–12

The downfall of Dagon (if the people had made a good use of it, and had been brought by it to repent of their idolatries and to humble themselves before the God of Israel and seek his face) might have prevented the vengeance which God here proceeds to take upon them for the indignities done to his ark. *He destroyed them.* At Gath it is called *a great destruction* (*v.* 9), *a deadly destruction*, *v.* 11. And it is expressly said (*v.* 12) that those who were *smitten with the emerods were the men that died not* by the other *destruction*, which probably was the pestilence. Those that were not destroyed *he smote with emerods* (*v.* 6), *in their secret parts* (*v.* 9), so grievous that (*v.* 12) the *cry went up to heaven*, that is, it might be heard a great way off, and perhaps, in the extremity of their pain and misery, they cried, not to Dagon, but to the God of heaven. The emerods was both a painful and shameful disease. By it God would humble their pride, and put contempt upon them, as they had done upon his ark. The disease was epidemical, and perhaps, among them, a new disease. *Ashdod was smitten, and the coasts thereof*, the country round. The men of Ashdod were soon aware that it was *the hand of God, the God of Israel, v.* 7. Thus they were constrained to acknowledge his power and dominion, and confess themselves

within his jurisdiction, and yet they would not renounce Dagon and submit to Jehovah; but rather, now that he touched their bone and their flesh, they were ready to curse him to his face, and instead of making their peace with him, and courting the stay of his ark upon better terms, they desired to get clear of it. Carnal hearts, when they smart under the judgments of God, would rather, if it were possible, put him far from them than enter into covenant and communion with him, and make him their friend. Thus the men of Ashdod resolve, *The ark of the God of Israel shall not abide with us.* It is resolved to change the place of its imprisonment. It was agreed that it should be carried to Gath, *v.* 8. Some superstitious conceit they had that the fault was in the place, and that the ark would be better pleased with another lodging, further off from Dagon's temple; and therefore, instead of returning it, as they should have done, to its own place, they contrive to send it to another place. *Gath* is pitched upon, a place famed for a race of giants, but their strength and stature are no fence against the pestilence and the emerods: the men of that city were smitten, *both great and small* (*v.* 9), both dwarfs and giants, all alike to God's judgments. They were all at last weary of the ark, and very willing to get rid of it. It was sent from Gath to Ekron, and, coming by order of council, the Ekronites could not refuse it, but were much exasperated against their great men for sending them such a fatal present (*v.* 10): *They have sent it to us to slay us and our people.* A general assembly is instantly called, to advise about *sending the ark again to its place, v.* 11. While they are consulting about it, the hand of God is doing execution; and their contrivances to evade the judgment do but spread it. Many drop down dead among them. Many more are raging ill of the emerods, *v.* 12. What shall they do?

CHAPTER 6

The return of the ark to the land of Israel, I. How the Philistines dismissed it, by the advice of their priests (ver. 1–11), with rich presents to the God of Israel, to make an atonement for their sin (ver. 3–5), and yet with a project to bring it back, unless Providence directed the kine, contrary to their inclination, to go to the land of Israel, ver. 8, 9. II. How the Israelites entertained it. 1. With great joy and sacrifices of praise, ver. 12–18. 2. With an over-bold curiosity to look into it, for which many of them were struck dead, ver. 19–21.

Verses 1–9

The ark was *in the country of the Philistines seven months.* So long as they carried it captive, they should find it a curse to them. 1. Seven months Israel was punished with the absence of the ark, that special token of God's presence. A melancholy time no doubt, but they had this to comfort themselves with, that, wherever the ark is, *the Lord is in his holy temple*, and by faith and prayer we may have access with boldness to him there. We may have God nigh unto us when the ark is at a distance. 2. Seven months the Philistines were punished with the presence of the ark; so long it was a plague to them, because they would not send it home sooner. Note, Sinners lengthen out their own miseries by obstinately refusing to part with their sins. But at length it is determined that the ark must be sent back.

I. The priests and the diviners are consulted about it, *v.* 2. They were supposed to be best acquainted both with the rules of wisdom and with the rites of worship and atonement, and therefore it was proper to ask them, *What shall we do to the ark of Jehovah?*

II. They give their advice very fully, and seem to be very unanimous in it. 1. They urge it upon them that it was absolutely necessary to send the ark back, from the example of Pharaoh and the Egyptians, *v.* 6. 2. They advise that, when they sent it back, they should send a trespass-offering with it, v. 3. They knew the God of Israel was a jealous God, and those with whom he had such a quarrel must *in any wise return him a trespass-offering*, and they could not expect to be healed upon any other terms. But when they began to contrive what that satisfaction should be, they became wretchedly vain in their imaginations. 3. They direct that this trespass-offering should be an acknowledgment of the punishment of their iniquity. They must make images of the *emerods*, that is, of the swellings and sores with which they had been afflicted, so making the reproach of that shameful disease perpetual by their own act and deed (Ps. lxxviii. 66), also images of the *mice that had marred the land*, owning thereby the almighty power of the God of Israel, who could chastise and humble them, even in the day of their triumph, by such small and despicable animals. These images must be made of gold, the most precious metal, to intimate that they would gladly purchase their peace with the God of Israel at any rate. The *golden emerods* must be, in number, five, according to the *number of the lords*, who, it is likely, were all afflicted with them, and were content thus to own it; it was advised that the *golden mice* should be five too. 4. They encourage them to hope that hereby they would take an effectual course to get rid of the plague: *You shall be healed*, v. 3. "Let them therefore send back the ark, and then," say they, "*It shall be known to you why his hand is not removed from you*, that is, by this it will appear whether it is for your detaining the ark that you are thus plagued; for, if it be, upon your delivering it up the plague will cease." 5. Yet they put them in a way to make a further trial whether it was the hand of the God of Israel that had smitten them with these plagues or no. They must, in honour of the ark, put it on a new cart or carriage, to be drawn by two milch-cows (v. 7), unused to draw, and inclined to home. They must have no one to lead or drive them, but must take their own way, which, in all reason, one might expect, would be home again; and yet, unless the God of Israel, after all the other miracles he has wrought, will work one more, and by an invisible power lead these cows, contrary to their mutual instinct and inclination, to the land of Israel, and particularly to Beth-shemesh, they will retract their former opinion, and will believe it was not the hand of God that smote them, but it was a chance that *happened to them*, v. 8, 9.

Verses 10–18

I. How the Philistines dismissed the ark, v. 10, 11. They were made as glad to part with it as ever they had been to take it. 1. They received no money or price for the ransom of it, as they hoped to do, even beyond a king's ransom. 2. They gave jewels of gold, as the Egyptians did to the Israelites, to be rid of it.

II. How the kine brought it to the land of Israel, v. 12. They *took the straight way to Beth-shemesh*, the next city of the land of Israel, and a priests' city, *and turned not aside*. This was a wonderful instance of the power of God over the brute-creatures that cattle unaccustomed to the yoke should go the straight road to Beth-shemesh, a city eight or ten miles off, never miss the way, never turn aside into the fields to feed themselves, nor turn back home to feed their calves.

III. How it was welcomed to the land of Israel: *The men of Beth-shemesh were reaping their wheat-harvest*, v. 13. They were going on with their worldly business, and were in no care about the ark. God will in his own time effect the deliverance of his church, not only though it be fought against by its enemies, but though it be neglected by its friends. The same invisible hand that directed the kine to the land of Israel brought them into the field of Joshua, for the sake of the great stone in that field, which was convenient to put the ark upon, and which is spoken of, v. 14, 15, 18. 1. When the reapers *saw the ark, they rejoiced* (v. 13). Though they had not zeal and courage enough to attempt the rescue or ransom of it, yet, when it did come, they bade it heartily welcome. 2. They offered up the kine for a burnt-offering, to the honour of God, and made use of the wood of the cart for fuel, v. 14. Probably the Philistines intended these, when they sent them, to be a part of their trespass-offering, to make atonement, v. 3, 7. 3. They deposited the ark, with a chest of jewels that the Philistines presented, upon the great stone in the open field, a cold lodging for the ark of the Lord and a very mean one; yet better so than in Dagon's temple, or in the hands of the Philistines. As the burning of the cart and cows that brought home the ark might be construed to signify their hopes that it should never be carried away again out of the land of Israel, so the setting of it upon a great stone might signify their hopes that it should be established again upon a firm foundation. The church is built upon a rock. 4. They offered the sacrifices of thanksgiving to God, some think upon the great stone, more probably upon an altar of earth made for the purpose, v. 15. This accidental bringing of the ark hither was an indication of its designed settlement there, in process of time. It was one of those cities which were assigned out of the lot of Judah to the *sons of Aaron* Josh. xxi. 16. Whither should the ark go but to a priests' city? And it was well they had those of that sacred order ready to take down the ark and to offer the sacrifices. 5. The lords of the Philistines returned to Ekron, much affected, we may suppose, with what they had seen of the glory of God and the zeal of the Israelites, and yet not reclaimed from the worship of Dagon.

Verses 19–21

1. The sin of the men of Beth-shemesh: *They looked into the ark of the Lord*, v. 19. We were all ruined by an ambition of forbidden knowledge. That which made this looking into the ark a great sin was that it proceeded from a very low and mean opinion of the ark. It may be they presumed upon the present mean circumstances the ark was in, newly come out of captivity, and unsettled. It is an offence to God if we think meanly of his ordinances because of the meanness of the manner of their administration. Had they looked with an understanding eye upon the ark, and not judged purely by outward appearance, they would have thought that the ark never shone with greater majesty than it did now. 2. Their punishment for this sin: *He smote the men of Beth-shemesh, many of them, with a great slaughter.* Josephus says only seventy were smitten. 3. The terror that was struck upon the men of Beth-shemesh by this severe stroke. They said, as well they might, *Who is able to stand before this holy Lord God*? v. 20. To stand before God to worship him (blessed be his name) is not impossible; we are through Christ invited, encouraged, and enabled to do it, but to stand before God to contend with him we are not able. 4. Their desire, hereupon, to be rid of the ark. They asked, *To whom shall he go up from us?* v. 20. They sent messengers to the elders of Kirjath-jearim, a strong city further up in the country, and begged of them to come and fetch the ark up thither, v. 21. It lay in the way from Beth-shemesh to Shiloh, so that when they sent to them to fetch it, we may suppose, they intended that the elders of Shiloh should fetch it thence, but God intended otherwise. Thus was it sent from town to town, and no care taken of it by the public, a sign that there was no king in Israel.

CHAPTER 7

I. The eclipsing of the glory of the ark, by its privacy in Kirjath-jearim for many years, ver. 1, 2. II. The appearing of the glory of Samuel in his public services for the good of Israel, to whom he was raised up to be a judge, and he was the last that bore that character. We have him here active, 1. In the reformation of Israel from their idolatry, ver. 3, 4. 2. In the reviving of religion among them, ver. 5, 6. 3. In praying for them against the invading Philistines (ver. 7–9), over whom God, in answer to his prayer, gave them a glorious victory, ver. 10, 21. 4. In erecting a thankful memorial of that victory, ver. 12, 5. In the improvement of that victory, ver. 13, 14. 6. In the administration of justice, ver. 15–17.

Verses 1–2

Here we must attend the ark to Kirjath-jearim, to hear not a word more of it except once (*ch.* xiv. 18), till David fetched it thence, about forty years after, 1 Chron. xiii. 6.

I. The men of Beth-shemesh have by their own folly made that a burden which might have been a blessing.

1. The men of Kirjath-jearim cheerfully bring it among them, *v.* 1. Their neighbours the Beth-shemites, were not more glad to get rid of it than they were to receive it, knowing very well that what slaughter the ark had made at Beth-shemesh was not an act of arbitrary power, but of necessary justice, and those that suffered by it must blame themselves, not the ark.

2. They carefully provided for its decent entertainment among them, with true affection, with respect and reverence.

(1) They provided a proper place to receive it, in the house of Abinadab, which stood upon the highest ground, and, probably, was the best house in their city. The men of Beth-shemesh left it exposed upon a stone in the open field, but the men of Kirjath-jearim gave it house-room. God will find out a resting-place for his ark; if some thrust it from them, yet the hearts of others shall be inclined to receive it. It is no new thing for God's ark to be thrust into a private house.

(2) They provided a proper person to attend it: *They sanctified Eleazar his son to keep it*; not the father, because he was aged and infirm. His business was to keep the ark, not only from being seized by malicious Philistines, but from being touched or looked into by too curious Israelites. He was to keep the room clean and decent in which the ark was, that it might not look like a neglected thing. It does not appear that this Eleazar was of the tribe of Levi, much less of the house of Aaron. We may suppose that some devout Israelites would come and pray before the ark, and those that did so he was there ready to attend and assist. For this purpose they set him apart for it in the name of all their citizens. This was irregular, but was excusable because of the present distress.

II. Yet we are very loth to leave it here, wishing it well at Shiloh again, but that is made desolate (Jer. vii. 14), it must lie by the way for want of some public-spirited men to bring it to its proper place. 1. The time of its continuance here was long. Above forty years it lay in a remote, obscure, private place, unfrequented and almost unregarded (*v.* 2). It was very strange that all the time that Samuel governed, the ark was never brought to its place in the holy of holies, an evidence of the decay of holy zeal among them. God suffered it to be so, to punish them for their neglect when it was in its place. 2. Twenty years of this time had passed before the house of Israel was sensible of the want of the ark. The Septuagint read it somewhat more clearly than we do; *and it was twenty years, and* (that is, when) *the whole house of Israel looked up again after the Lord.* While it was absent from the tabernacle, the token of God's special presence was wanting, nor could they keep the day of atonement as it should be kept. They were content with the altars without the ark; so easily can formal professors rest satisfied in a round of external performances, without any tokens of God's presence or acceptance. But at length they bethought themselves, and began to lament after the Lord, stirred up to it, it is probable, by the preaching of Samuel, with which an extraordinary working of the Spirit of God set in. A general disposition to repentance and reformation now appears throughout all Israel. True repentance and conversion begin in lamenting after the Lord. It was better with the Israelites when they wanted the ark, and were lamenting after it, than when they had the ark, and were prying into it, or priding themselves in it.

Verses 3–6

We may well wonder where Samuel was and what he was doing all this while, but his labours among his people are not mentioned till there appears the fruit of them. When he perceived that they began to *lament after the Lord* he struck while the iron was hot, and two things he endeavoured to do for them,

I. He endeavoured to separate between them and their idols, for *there* reformation must begin. He *spoke to all the house of Israel* (*v.* 3), going, as it should seem, from place to place, an itinerant preacher (for we find not that they were gathered together till *v.* 5), and wherever he came this was his exhortation, "*If you do indeed return to the Lord*, then know, 1. That you must renounce and abandon your idols. Put away Baalim, the strange gods, and Ashtaroth, the strange goddess," for such also they had. Ashtaroth is particularly named because it was the best-beloved idol. True repentance strikes at the darling sin, and will with a peculiar zeal and resolution put away that, the sin which most *easily besets us.* 2. That you must make a solemn business of returning to God, and do it with a serious consideration and a steadfast resolution, for both are included in *preparing the heart*, directing, disposing, establishing, the heart unto the Lord. 3. That you must be wholly for God, for him and no other, *serve him only*, else you do not serve him at all so as to please him. Take this course, and *he will deliver you out of the hand of the Philistines*. This was the purport of Samuel's preaching, and it had a wonderfully good effect (*v.* 4): *They put away Baalim and Ashtaroth*, not only quitted the worship of them, but destroyed their images, demolished their altars, and quite abandoned them.

II. He endeavoured to engage them for ever to God and his service.

1. He summons all Israel, at least by their elders, as their representatives, to meet him at Mizpeh (*v.* 5), and there he promises to pray for them. When we come together in religious assemblies, we must remember that it is as much our business there to join in public prayers as it is to hear a sermon.

2. They obey his summons, and not only come to the meeting, but conform to the intentions of it, and appear there very well disposed, *v.* 6.

(1) *They drew water and poured it out before the Lord*, signifying, [1] Their humiliation and contrition for sin, owning themselves as water spilt upon the ground, which cannot be gathered up again (2 Sam. xiv. 14). The Chaldee reads it, *They poured out their hearts in repentance before the Lord.* [2] Their earnest prayers and supplications to God for mercy. [3] Their universal reformation; they thus expressed their willingness to part with all their sins, and to retain no more of the relish or savour of them than the vessel does of the water that is poured out of it. [4] Some think it signifies their joy in the hope of God's mercy, which Samuel had assured them of.

(2) *They fasted*, abstained from food, afflicted their souls, so expressing repentance.

(3) They made a public confession: *We have sinned against the Lord*, so giving glory to God and taking shame to themselves.

3. Samuel judged them at that time in Mizpeh, that is, he assured them, in God's name, of the pardon of their sins, upon their repentance, and that God was reconciled to them. It was a judgment of absolution. Whereas before he acted only as a prophet, now he began to act as a magistrate, to prevent their relapsing into those sins which now they seemed to have renounced.

Verses 7–12

I. The Philistines invade Israel (*v.* 7), taking umbrage from that general meeting for repentance and prayer as if it had been a rendezvous for war. 1. How evil sometimes seems to come out of good! The religious meeting of the Israelites at Mizpeh brought trouble upon them from the Philistines. When sinners begin to repent and reform, they must expect that Satan will muster all his force against them, and set his instruments on work to the utmost to oppose and discourage them. But, 2. How good is, at length, brought out of that evil. Israel could never be threatened more seasonably than at this time, when they were repenting and praying, nor could they have been better prepared to receive the enemy.

II. Israel cleaves closely to Samuel, as their best friend, under God, in this distress; though he was no military man, nor ever celebrated as a mighty man of valour, yet, they engaged Samuel's prayers for them: *Cease not to cry unto the Lord our God for us, v.* 8. They were here unarmed, unprepared for war, come together to fast and pray, not to fight; prayers and tears therefore being all the weapons many of them are now furnished with, to these they have recourse.

III. Samuel intercedes with God for them, and does it *by sacrifice, v.* 9. Samuel's sacrifice without his prayer would have been an empty shadow, his prayer without the sacrifice would not have been so prevalent, but both together teach us what great things we may expect from God in answer to those prayers which are made with faith in Christ's sacrifice. It was a burnt-offering, which was offered purely for the glory of God. It was but one sucking lamb that he offered; for it is the integrity and intention of the heart that God looks at, more than the bulk or number of the offerings. Samuel was no priest, but he was a Levite and a prophet; the case was extraordinary, and what he did was by special direction, and therefore accepted of God.

IV. God gave a gracious answer to Samuel's prayer (*v.* 9): *The Lord heard him.* He was himself a *Samuel, asked of God*, and many a Samuel, then a mercy in answer to prayer, God gave him. The prayer of Samuel was honoured; for at the very time when he was offering up his sacrifice, and his prayer with it, the battle began, and turned immediately against the Philistines. As in a former engagement with the Philistines God had justly chastised their presumptuous confidence in the presence of the ark, on the shoulders of two profane priests, so now he graciously accepted their humble dependence upon the prayer of faith from the mouth and heart of a pious prophet.

V. Samuel erected a thankful memorial of this victory, to the glory of God and for the encouragement of Israel, *v.* 12. He set up an *Eben-ezer, the stone of help.* The place where this memorial was set up was the same where, twenty years before, the Israelites were smitten before the Philistines, for that was beside Eben-ezer, *ch.* iv. 1. The reason he gives for the name is, *Hitherto the Lord hath helped us*, in which he speaks thankfully of what was past, and yet he speaks somewhat doubtfully for the future: "Hitherto things have done well, but what God may

yet do with us we know not, *that* we refer to him; but let us praise him for what he has done." *Having obtained help from God. I continue hitherto*, says blessed Paul, Acts xxvi. 22.

Verses 13–17

It appears (2 Chron. xxxv. 18) that in the days of Samuel the prophet the people of Israel kept the ordinance of the passover with more than ordinary devotion, notwithstanding the distance of the ark and the desolations of Shiloh. Here we are only told how instrumental he was, 1. In securing the public peace (*v.* 13): *In his days the Philistines came no more into the coast of Israel.* Samuel was a protector and deliverer to Israel, not by dint of sword, as Gideon, nor by strength of arm, as Samson, but by the power of prayer to God and carrying on a work of reformation among the people. Religion and piety are the best securities of a nation. 2. In recovering the public rights, *v.* 14. By his influence Israel had the courage to demand the cities which the Philistines had unjustly taken from them. It is added, *There was peace between Israel and the Amorites*, that is, the Canaanites, the remains of the natives. 3. In administering public justice (*v.* 15, 16): *He judged Israel.* Even after Saul was made king he promised them (*ch.* xii. 23), *I will not cease to teach you the good and the right way.* He kept courts at Beth-el, Gilgal, and Mizpeh, all in the tribe of Benjamin; but his constant residence was at Ramah, his father's city, and there he judged Israel. 4. In keeping up the public exercises of religion; for there, where he lived, he built an altar to the Lord, not in contempt of the altar that was at Nob, or Gibeon. He did as the patriarchs did, he built an altar where he lived, both for the use of his own family and for the good of the country that resorted to it.

CHAPTER 8

Israel's good days seldom continue long. I. Samuel decaying, ver. 1. II. His sons degenerating, ver. 2, 3. III. Israel discontented with the present government and anxious to see a change. For, 1. They petition Samuel to set a king over them, ver. 4, 5. 2. Samuel brings the matter to God, ver. 6. 3. God directs him what answer to give them, by way of reproof (ver. 7, 8), setting forth the consequence of a change of the government, and how uneasy they would soon be under it, ver. 9–18. 4. They insist upon their petition, ver. 19, 20. 5. Samuel promises them, from God, that they shall shortly be gratified, ver. 21, 22.

Verses 1–3

Two sad things we find here, but not strange things:—1. A good and useful man growing old and unfit for service (*v.* 1): *Samuel was old*, and could not judge Israel, as he had done. He is not reckoned to be past sixty years of age now, perhaps not so much; but he was a man betimes, was full of thoughts and cares when he was a child. The fruits that are the first ripe keep the worst. He had spent his strength and spirits in the fatigue of public business, and now, if he think to shake himself as at other times, he finds he is mistaken, old age has cut his hair. Those that are in the prime of their time ought to be busy in doing the work of life. 2. The children of a good man turning aside, and not treading in his steps. We have reason to think that Samuel gave them their commissions, not because they were his sons, but because, for aught that yet appeared, they were men very fit for the trust. But, alas! *his sons walked not in his ways* (*v.* 3), and, when their character was the reverse of his, their relation to so good a man, which otherwise would have been their honour, was really their disgrace. When Samuel's sons were made judges, and settled at a distance from him, then they discovered themselves. Many that have done well in a state of subjection have been spoiled by preferment and power. Honours change men's minds, and too often for the worse. It does not appear that

Samuel's sons were so profane and vicious as Eli's sons; but, whatever they were in other respects, they were corrupt judges, they *turned aside after lucre*, after *the mammon of unrighteousness*, so the Chaldee reads it. In determining controversies, they had an eye to the bribe, not to the law, and enquired who bid highest, not who had right on his side.

Verses 4–22

We have here the starting of a matter perfectly new and surprising, which was the setting up of kingly government in Israel.

I. The address of the elders to Samuel in this matter (*v.* 4, 5). They came to him to his house at Ramah with their address, which contained,

1. A remonstrance of their grievances: in short, *Thou art old, and thy sons walk not in thy ways.* (1) It was true that Samuel was old; yet it made him the more wise and experienced, and, upon that account, the fitter to rule. (2) It was true that his sons did not walk in his ways; the more was his grief, but they could not say it was his fault: he had not, like Eli, indulged them in their badness, but was ready to receive complaints against them.

2. A petition for the redress of these grievances, by setting a king over them: *Make us a king to judge us like all the nations.* Thus far it was well, that they did not rise up in rebellion against Samuel and set up a king for themselves. But it appears by what followed that it was an evil proposal and ill made, and was displeasing to God. They must have a king to judge them with external pomp and power, like *all the nations.* A poor prophet in a mantle, though conversant in the visions of the Almighty, looked mean in the eyes of those who judged by outward appearance; but a king in a purple robe, with his guards and officers of state, would look great: and such a one they must have.

II. Samuel's resentment of this address, *v.* 6. 1. It cut him to the heart. Probably it was a surprise to him. It *displeased him when they said, Give us a king to judge us*, because that reflected upon God and his honour. 2. It drove him to his knees; he gave them no answer for the present, but took time to consider of what they proposed, and prayed unto the Lord for direction what to do.

III. The instruction God gave him concerning this matter. He tells him,

1. That which would be an allay to his displeasure. Samuel was much disturbed at the proposal: but God tells him he must not think it either hard or strange. (1) He must not think it hard that they had put this slight upon him, for they had herein put a slight upon God himself. If God interest himself in the indignities that are done us, we may well afford to bear them patiently. Samuel must not complain that they were weary of his government, for really they were weary of God's government. The government of Israel had hitherto been a Theocracy, a divine government; their judges had their call and commission immediately from God; the affairs of their nation were under his peculiar direction. (2) He must not think it strange for they do as they always have done. They had always been rude to their governors, witness Moses and Aaron.

2. He tells him that which would be an answer to their demand. Samuel would not have known what to say if God had not instructed him, but he gives them, with assurance, the answer God sent them.

(1) He must tell them that *they shall have a king. Hearken to the voice of the people, v.* 7, and again, *v.* 9. God bade Samuel humour them in this matter, [1] That they might be beaten with their own rod, and might feel, to their cost, the difference between his government and the government of a king. [2] To prevent something worse. If they were not gratified,

they would either rise in rebellion against Samuel or universally revolt from their religion and admit the gods of the nations, that they might have kings like them.

(2) But he must tell them, withal, that when they have a king they will soon have enough of him, and will, when it is too late, repent of their choice.

IV. Samuel's faithful delivery of God's mind to them, *v.* 10. He *told them all the words of the Lord*, how ill he resented it, that he construed it a rejecting of him, and compared it with their serving other gods. He lays before them, very particularly, what would be, not the right of a king in general, but *the manner of the king that should reign over them*, according to the pattern of the nations, *v.* 11.

1. If they will have such a king as the nations have, let them consider, (1) That a king must have a great retinue, a multitude of attendants. And whence must he have these? "Why, he will take your sons, and will *appoint them for himself," v.* 11. They must wait upon him, *ear his ground, and reap his harvest* (*v.* 12), and count it their preferment too, *v.* 16. (2) He must keep a great table. (3) He must needs have a standing army, for guards and garrisons. (4) "You may expect that he will have great favourites, whom, having dignified and ennobled, he must enrich out of your inheritances (*v.* 14). How will you like that?" (5) "He must have great revenues to maintain his grandeur and power. He will take the tenth of the fruits of your ground (*v.* 15), and your cattle," *v.* 17.

2. These would be their grievances. When they complained to God he *would not hear them, v.* 18.

V. The people's obstinacy in their demand, *v.* 19, 20. "*We will have a king over us*, whatever God or Samuel say to the contrary; we will have a king, whatever it cost us, and whatever inconvenience we bring upon ourselves or our posterity by it." They were quite deaf to reason and blind to their own interest. They could not stay God's time. God had intimated to them in the law that, in due time, Israel should have a king (Deut. xvii. 14, 15). Could they but have waited ten or twelve years longer they would have had David, a king of God's giving in mercy, and all the calamities that attended the setting up of Saul would have been prevented.

VI. The dismissing of them with an intimation that very shortly they should have what they asked. 1. *Samuel rehearsed all their words in the ears of the Lord, v.* 21. It bespeaks a holy familiarity, to which God graciously admits his people: they speak in the ears of the Lord, as one friend whispers with another. 2. God gave direction that they should have a king, since they were so inordinately set upon it (*v.* 22): "*Make them a king*, and let them make their best of him." *So he gave them up to their own hearts' lusts.* Samuel sent them home for the present, *every man to his city*; for the designation of the person must be left to God; they had now no more to do.

CHAPTER 9

Most governments began in the ambition of the prince to rule, but Israel's in the ambition of the people to be ruled. God having, in the law, undertaken to choose their king (Deut. xvii. 15), they all sit still, till they hear from heaven, and that they do in this chapter, which begins the story of Saul, their first king, and, by strange steps of Providence, brings him to Samuel to be anointed privately, and so to be prepared for an election by lot, and a public commendation to the people, which follows in the next chapter. Here is, I. A short account of Saul's parentage and person, ver. 1, 2. II. A large and particular account of the bringing of him to Samuel, to whom he had been before altogether a stranger. 1. God, by revelation, had told Samuel to expect him, ver. 15, 16. 2. God, by providence, led him to Samuel. (1) Being sent to seek his father's asses, he was at a loss, ver. 3–5. (2) By the advice of his servant, he determined to consult Samuel, ver. 6–10. (3) By the direction of the young maidens, he found him out, ver. 11–14. (4) Samuel, being informed of God concerning him (ver. 17), treated him with respect, ver. 27.

Verses 1–2

We are here told, 1. What a good family Saul was of, *v.* 1. He was of the tribe of Benjamin; so was the New Testament Saul, who also was called *Paul*, and he mentions it as his honour, for Benjamin was a favourite, Rom. xi. 1; Phil. iii. 5. That tribe, though fewest in number, was first in dignity. His father was *Kish, a mighty man of power*, or, as the margin reads it, *in substance*; in spirit bold, in body strong, in estate wealthy. 2. What a good figure Saul made, *v.* 2. No mention is here made of his wisdom or virtue, his learning or piety, or any of the accomplishments of his mind, but that he was a tall, proper, handsome man, that had a good face, a good shape, and a good presence, graceful and well proportioned: *Among all the children of Israel there was not a goodlier person than he.* He was taller by the head and shoulders than any of the people. When God chose a king after his own heart he pitched upon one that was not at all remarkable for the height of his stature, nor any thing in his countenance but the innocence and sweetness that appeared there, *ch.* xvi. 7, 12. But when he chose a king after the people's heart, who aimed at nothing so much as stateliness and grandeur, he pitched upon this huge tall man, who, if he had no other good qualities, yet would look great.

Verses 3–10

I. A great man rising from small beginnings. It does not appear that Saul had any preferment at all, or was in any post of honour or trust, till he was chosen king of Israel.

II. A great event arising from small occurrences. How low does the history begin! Having to trace Saul to the crown, we find him first employed as meanly as any we meet with called out to preferment.

1. Saul's father sends him with one of his servants to seek some asses that he had lost. Saul and his servants travelled far (probably on foot) in quest of the asses, but in vain: they found them not. He missed what he sought, but he met with the kingdom, of which he never dreamed.

2. When he could not find them, he determined to return to his father (*v.* 5), in consideration of his father's tender concern for him.

3. His servant proposed that, since they were now at Ramah, they should call on Samuel, and take his advice in this important affair. They were close by the city where Samuel lived, and that put it into their heads to consult him (*v.* 6). *He is a man of God, and an honourable man.* This was the honour of Samuel, as a man of God, that *all he saith comes surely to pass.* They agreed to consult him concerning *the way that they should go; peradventure he can show us.* Most people would rather be told their fortune than told their duty, how to be rich than how to be saved. If it were the business of the men of God to direct for the recovery of lost asses, they would be consulted much more than they are now that it is their business to direct for the recovery of lost souls. Saul was thoughtful what present they should bring to the man of God. They could not present him with loaves and cakes (1 Kings xiv. 3), for their bread was spent; but the servant bethought himself that he had in his pocket the fourth part of a shekel. "That will do," says Saul; "*let us go*," *v.* 10. He came to him as a fortune-teller, rather than as a prophet, and therefore thought the fourth part of a shekel was enough to give him. Most people love a cheap religion, and like it best when they can devolve the expense of it on others. The historian here takes notice of the name then given to the prophets: they called them *Seers*, or *seeing men* (*v.* 9), not but that the name *prophet* was then used, and applied to such persons, but that of seers was more in use. Those that are prophets must first be seers; those who undertake to speak to others of the things of God must have an insight into those things themselves.

Verses 11–17

I. Saul, by an ordinary enquiry, is directed to Samuel, *v.* 11–14. Gibeah of Saul was not twenty miles from Ramah where Samuel dwelt, and was near to Mizpeh where he often judged Israel.

1. The maid-servants of Ramah, whom they met with at the places of drawing water, could give him and his servant intelligence concerning Samuel. (1) That there was a sacrifice that day in the high place. Samuel had built an altar at Ramah (*ch.* vii. 17), and here we have him making use of that altar. (2) That Samuel came that day to the city. (3) That this was just the time of their meeting to feast before the Lord upon the sacrifice. (4) That the people would not eat till Samuel came, because *he* must bless the sacrifice. [1] As a common meal. Or, [2] As a religious assembly. When the sacrifice was offered it was requisite that it should in a particular manner be blessed, as is the Christian eucharist.

2. Saul and his servant followed the directions given them, and very opportunely met Samuel going to the high place, the synagogue of the city, *v.* 14.

II. Samuel, by an extraordinary revelation, is informed concerning Saul. He was a seer, and therefore must see this in a way peculiar to himself.

1. God had told him, the day before, that he would, at this time, send him the man that should serve the people of Israel for such a king as they wished to have. He *told him in his ear*, that is, privately, by a secret whisper to his mind, or perhaps by a still small voice. The Hebrew phrase is, *He uncovered the ear of Samuel.* When God will manifest himself to a soul, he uncovers the ear, says, *Ephphatha, Be opened*; he takes *the veil from off the heart*, 2 Cor. iii. 16. Though God had, in displeasure, granted their request for a king, yet here he speaks tenderly of Israel. (1) He calls them again and again his people; though a peevish and provoking people, yet mine still. (2) He sends them a man to be captain over them. (3) He does it with a gracious respect to them and to their cry: *I have looked upon my people*, and *their cry has come unto me.*

2. When Saul came up towards him in the street God again whispered Samuel in the ear (*v.* 17): *Behold the man whom I spoke to thee of*; That he might be fully satisfied, God told him expressly, *That is the man* that shall *restrain* (for magistrates are heirs of restraint) *my people Israel.*

Verses 18–27

Providence having at length brought Samuel and Saul together, we have here an account of what passed between them in the gate, at the feast, and in private.

I. In the gate of the city; passing through that, Saul found him (*v.* 18), and asked him the way to Samuel's house. Samuel answered him, "*I am the seer*, the person you enquire for," *v.* 19. Samuel knew him before he knew Samuel. 1. Samuel obliges him to stay with him till the next day. Saul had nothing in his mind but to find his asses, but Samuel would take him off from that care, and dispose him to the exercises of piety; and therefore bids him *go to the high place.* 2. He satisfies him about his asses (*v.* 20): *Set not thy mind on them*, be not in further care about them; *they are found.* By this Saul might perceive that he was a prophet. 3. He surprises him with an intimation of preferment before him: "*On whom is all the desire of Israel?* Is it not a king that they are set upon, and there is never a man in Israel that will suit them as thou wilt." 4. To this strange intimation Saul returns a very modest answer, *v.* 21. Samuel, he thought, did but banter him, because he was a tall man, but a very unlikely man to be a king; *I am a Benjamite, my family the least,* probably a younger house, not in any place of honour, or trust, no, not in their own tribe.

II. At the public feast; thither Samuel took him and his servant. Samuel treats him not as a common person, but a person of quality and distinction, to prepare both him and the people for what was to follow. Two marks of honour he put upon him:— 1. He set him *in the best place.* 2. He presented him with the *best dish.* And what should this precious dish be for the king-elect? It was a plain shoulder of mutton (*v.* 23, 24). The right shoulder of the peace-offerings was to be given to the priests, who were God's receivers (Lev. vii. 32); the next in honour to that was the left shoulder, which probably was always allotted to those that sat at the upper end of the table, and was wont to be Samuel's mess at other times; so that his giving it to Saul now was an implicit resignation of his place to him.

III. What passed between them in private. Both that evening and early the next morning Samuel communed with Saul upon the flat roof of the house, *v.* 25, 26. We may suppose Samuel now told him the whole story of the people's desire of a king, the grounds of their desire, and God's grant of it. Early in the morning he sent him towards home, brought him part of the way, bade him send his servant before, that they might be private (*v.* 27), and there, as we find in the beginning of the next chapter, he anointed him, and therein showed him the *word of the Lord.*

CHAPTER 10

I. The anointing of Saul then and there, ver. 1. The signs Samuel gave him, ver. 2–6. And instructions, ver. 7–8. II. The accomplishment of those signs to the satisfaction of Saul, ver. 9–13. III. His return to his father's house, ver. 14–16. IV. His public election by lot, and solemn inauguration, ver. 17–25. V. His return to his own city, ver. 26, 27.

Verses 1–8

Samuel is here executing the office of a prophet, giving Saul full assurance from God that he should be king.

I. He *anointed him* and *kissed him, v.* 1. This was not done in a solemn assembly, but it was done by divine appointment, which made up the want of all external solemnities. 1. Samuel, by anointing Saul, assured him that it was God's act to make him king: *Is it not because the Lord hath anointed thee?* 2. By kissing him, he assured him of his own approbation of the choice, though it abridged his power and eclipsed his glory and the glory of his family. It was likewise a kiss of homage and allegiance; hereby he not only owns him to be king, but his king, and in this sense we are commanded to *kiss the Son,* Ps. ii. 12. He reminds him, (1) Of the nature of the government to which he is called. He was anointed to be a captain, a commander in war, which bespeaks care, and toil, and danger. (2) Of the origin of it: *The Lord hath anointed thee.* By him he ruled, and therefore must rule for him, in dependence on him, and with an eye to his glory. (3) Of the end of it. It is over his inheritance, to take care of that, protect it, and order all the affairs of it for the best, as a steward whom a great man sets over his estate.

II. For his further satisfaction he gives him some signs, which should come to pass immediately this very day. 1. He should presently meet with some that would bring him intelligence from home of the care his father's house was in concerning him, *v.* 2. These he would meet hard by Rachel's sepulchre. Here two men would meet him, and would tell him the asses were found. 2. He should next meet with others going to Bethel, where, it should seem, there was a high place for religious worship, and these men were

bringing their sacrifices thither, *v.* 3, 4. It is supposed that those kids and loaves, and the bottle of wine which the three men had with them, were designed for sacrifice, with the meat-offerings and drink-offerings that were to attend the sacrifice; yet Samuel tells Saul that they will give him two of their loaves, and he must take them. It would be construed a fit present for a prince; and, as such, Saul must receive it the first present that was brought to him, by such as knew not what they did, nor why they did it, but God put it into their hearts, which made it the more fit to be a sign to him. 3. The most remarkable sign of all would be his joining with a company of prophets that he should meet with, under the influence of a spirit of prophecy, which should at that time come upon him. What God works in us by his Spirit serves much more for the confirming of faith than any thing wrought for us by his providence. He here (*v.* 5, 6) tells him, (1) Where this would happen: *At the hill of God,* where there was a *garrison of the Philistines.* After they were subdued in the beginning of his time they got ground again, so far as to force this garrison into that place, and thence God raised up the man that should chastise them. There was a place that was called the *hill of God,* because of one of the schools of the prophets built upon it; and such respect did even Philistines themselves pay to religion that a garrison of their soldiers suffered a school of God's prophets to live peaceably by them, and did not disturb the public exercises of their devotion. (2) Upon what occasion; he should meet *a company of prophets with music before them, prophesying,* and with them he should join himself. These prophets employed themselves in the study of the law, in instructing their neighbours, and in the acts of piety, especially in praising God. What a pity was it that Israel should be weary of the government of such a man, who had, as a man of God, settled the schools of the prophets! These prophets had been at the high place, probably offering sacrifice, and now they came back singing psalms. Saul should find himself strongly moved to join with them, and should be turned thereby *into another man* from what he had been while he lived in a private capacity.

III. He directs him to proceed in the administration of his government as Providence should lead him, and as Samuel should advise him. 1. He must follow Providence in ordinary cases (*v.* 7): "*Do as occasion shall serve thee.* Take such measures as thy own prudence shall direct thee." But, 2. In an extra-ordinary strait that would hereafter befall him at Gilgal, and would be the most critical juncture of all, when he would have special need of divine aids, he must wait for Samuel to come to him, and must tarry *seven days* in expectation of him, *v.* 8. How his failing in this matter proved his fall we find afterwards, *ch.* xiii. 11.

Verses 9–16

Saul has now taken his leave of Samuel, much amazed.

I. What occurred by the way, *v.* 9. Those signs which Samuel had given him came to pass very punctually; but that which gave him the greatest satisfaction of all was this, he found immediately that God had given him *another heart.* A new fire was kindled in his breast. Seeking the asses is quite out of his mind, and he thinks of nothing but fighting the Philistines, redressing the grievances of Israel, making laws, administering justice, and providing for the public safety; these are the things that now fill his head. He has no longer the heart of a husband-man, which is low, and mean, and narrow, and concerned only about his corn and cattle; but the heart of a statesman, a general, a prince. Whom God calls to any service he will make fit for it.

II. What occurred when he came near home. They came to *the hill* (v. 10), that is, to *Gibeah*, or *Geba*, which signifies *a hill*. He met with the prophets as Samuel had told him, and the Spirit of God came upon him, strongly and suddenly (so the word signifies), but not so as to rest and abide upon him. However, for the present, it had a strange effect upon him; for he immediately joined with the prophets in their devotion. *He prophesied among them.*

1. His prophesying was publicly taken notice of, v. 11, 12. He was now among his acquaintance, who, when they saw him among the prophets, called one another to come and see a strange sight. This would prepare them to accept him as a king. Now, (1) They all wondered to see Saul among the prophets: *What is this that has come to the son of Kish;* Though this school of the prophets was near his father's house, yet he had never associated with them. Now to see him prophesying among them was a surprise to them, as it was long after when his namesake, in the New Testament, preached that gospel which he had before persecuted, Acts ix. 21. Where God gives another heart it will soon show itself. (2) One of them, that was wiser than the rest, asked, *"Who is their father, or instructor? Is it not God? Are they not all taught of him? Do they not all owe their gifts to him? And is he limited? Cannot he make Saul a prophet, as well as any of them, if he please?"* Or, *"Is not Samuel their father?"* (3) It became a proverb, commonly used in Israel, when they would express their wonder at a bad man's either becoming good, or at least being found in good company, *Is Saul among the prophets?*

2. His being anointed was kept private. When he had done prophesying, (1) He went straight *to the high place* (v. 13), to give God thanks for his mercies to him and to pray for the continuance of those mercies. But, (2) He industriously concealed from his relations what had passed. His uncle, who met with him either at the high place or as soon as he came home, examined him, v. 14. Saul owned, for his servant knew it, that they had been with Samuel, and that he told them the asses were found, but said not a word of *the kingdom*, v. 14, 15. This was an instance, [1] Of his humility. [2] Of his prudence. Had he been forward to proclaim it, he would have been envied, and he knew not what difficulty that might have created him.

Verses 17–27

Saul's nomination to the throne is here made public, in a general assembly of the elders of Israel, the representatives of their respective tribes at Mizpeh. The people having met in a solemn assembly, in which God was in a peculiar manner present (and therefore, it is said they were *called together unto the Lord*, v. 17), Samuel acts for God among them.

I. He reproves them for casting off the government of a prophet, and desiring that of a captain. 1. He shows them (v. 18) how happy they had been under the divine government; when God ruled them, he *delivered them out of the hand of those that oppressed them*, and what would they desire more? 2. He likewise shows them (v. 19) what an affront they had put upon God. *"You have this day rejected your God;* you have in effect done it: so he construes it, and he might justly, for your so doing, reject you."

II. He puts them upon choosing their king by lot. Benjamin is taken out of all the tribes (v. 20), and out of that tribe Saul the son of Kish, v. 21. By this method it would appear to the people, as it already appeared to Samuel, that Saul was appointed of God to be king; for *the disposal of the lot is of the Lord.*

III. It is with much ado, and not without further enquiries of the Lord, that Saul is at length produced.

When the lot fell upon him, every one expected he should answer to his name at the first call, but, instead of that, none of his friends could find him (v. 21), he had *hidden himself among the stuff* (v. 22). 1. He withdrew, in hopes that, upon his not appearing, they would proceed to another choice. We may suppose he was at this time really averse to take upon him the government, (1) Because he was conscious to himself of unfitness for so great a trust. (2) Because it would expose him to the envy of his neighbours. (3) Because he understood, by what Samuel had said, that the people sinned in asking a king. (4) Because the affairs of Israel were at this time in a bad posture; the Philistines were strong, the Ammonites threatening: and he must be bold indeed that will set sail in a storm. 2. But the congregation, believing that choice well made which God himself made, would leave no way untried to find him out on whom the lot fell.

IV. Samuel presents him to the people, and they accept him. He needed not to mount the bench, or scaffold, to be seen; for he was taller than any of them by *head and shoulders*, v 23. "Look you," said Samuel, "what a king God has chosen for you, just such a one as you wished for; *there is none like him among all the people*, that has so much majesty in his countenance and such a graceful stateliness in his mien; he is in the crowd like a cedar among the shrubs." The people hereupon signified their approbation of the choice, and their acceptance of him; they *shouted and said, Let the king live*, that is, "Let him long reign over us in health and prosperity."

V. Samuel settles the original contract between them, and leaves it upon record, v. 25. He fixed the land marks between them, that neither might encroach upon the other. Let them rightly understand one another at first, and let the agreement remain in black and white, which will tend to preserve a good understanding between them ever after.

VI. The convention was dissolved when the solemnity was over: *Samuel sent every man to his house. Saul also went home to Gibeah*, to his father's house, not puffed up with the name of a kingdom under him. At Gibeah ha had no palace, no throne, no court, yet thither he goes. If he must be a king, as one mindful of the rock out of which he was hewn, he will make his own city the royal city, nor will he be ashamed (as too many are when they are preferred) of his mean relations.

1. How did the people stand affected to their new king? The generality of them, it should seem, did not show themselves much concerned: They *went every man to his own house*. But, (1) There were some so faithful as to attend him: *A band of men whose hearts God had touched*, v. 26. A small company went with him to Gibeah, as his life-guard. They were those *whose hearts God had touched*, in this instance, to do their duty. (2) There were others so spiteful as to affront him; children of Belial, men that would endure no yoke. Thus differently are men affected to our exalted Redeemer. God hath set him king upon the holy hill of Sion. There is a remnant *whose hearts God has touched*, whom he has *made willing in the day of his power*. But there are others who despise him, who ask, *How shall this man save us?*

2. How did Saul resent the bad conduct of those that were disaffected to his government? *He held his peace*. Margin, *He was as though he had been deaf.*

CHAPTER 11

I. The great extremity to which the city of Jabesh-Gilead, on the other side of Jordan, was reduced by the Ammonites, ver. 1–3. II. Saul's great readiness to come to their relief, whom he here signalized himself, ver. 4–10. III. The good success of his attempt, by which God signalized him, ver. 11. IV. Saul's tenderness, notwithstanding this, towards those that had opposed him, ver. 12, 13. V. The public confirmation and recognition of his election to the government, ver. 14, 15.

Verses 1–4

The Ammonites were bad neighbours to those tribes of Israel that lay next them, though descendants from just Lot, and, for that reason, dealt civilly with by Israel. See Deut. ii. 19. The city of Jabesh-Gilead had been, some ages ago, destroyed by Israel's sword of justice, for not appearing against the wickedness of Gibeah (Judges xxi. 10); and now being replenished again, probably by the posterity of those that then escaped the sword, it is in danger of being destroyed by the Ammonites, as if some bad fate attended the place. Nahash, king of Ammon (1 Chron. xix. 1), laid siege to it.

I. The besieged beat a parley (v. 1): "*Make a covenant with us, and we will* surrender upon terms, and *serve thee.*" They had lost the virtue of Israelites, else they would not have thus lost the valour of Israelites, nor tamely yielded to serve an Ammonite.

II. The besiegers offer them base and barbarous conditions; they will spare their lives, and take them to be their servants, upon condition that they shall *put out their right eyes, v.* 2. The Gileadites were content to part with their liberty and estates. But their abject concessions make the Ammonites more insolent in their demands. 1. They must torment them, and put them to pain, exquisite pain, for so the thrusting out of an eye would do. 2. They must disable them for war, for in those times they fought with shields in their left hands, which covered their left eye, so that a soldier without his right eye was in effect blind.

III. The besieged desire, and obtain, seven days' time to consider of this proposal, v. 3. Nahash, not imagining it possible that, in so short a time, they should have relief, and being very secure of the advantages he thought he had against them, in a bravado gave them seven days, that the reproach upon Israel, for not rescuing them, might be greater, and his triumphs the more illustrious.

IV. Notice is sent of this to Gibeah. They said they would send messengers *to all the coasts of Israel* (v. 3), which made Nahash the more secure, for that, he thought, would be a work of time. But the messengers, either of their own accord or by order from their masters, went straight to Gibeah, and, not finding Saul within, told their news to the people, who fell a-weeping upon hearing it, v. 4.

Verses 5–11

What is here related turns very much to the honour of Saul, and shows the happy fruits of that other spirit with which he was endued.

I. His humility. Though he was anointed king, and accepted by his people, yet he did not think it below him to know the state of his own flocks, but went himself to see them, and came in the evening, with his servants, *after the herd out of the field, v.* 5. Like Paul, he worked with his hands; for, if he neglect his domestic affairs, how must he maintain himself and his family?

II. His concern for his neighbours. When he perceived them in tears, he asked, "*What ails the people that they weep?* Let me know, that, if it be a grievance which can be redressed, I may help them, and that, if not, I may weep with them."

III. His zeal for the safety and honour of Israel. When he heard of the insolence of the Ammonites, and the distress of a city, a mother in Israel, *the Spirit of God came upon him,* and put great thoughts into his mind, *and his anger was kindled greatly, v.* 6. He was angry at the insolence of the Ammonites, angry at the mean and sneaking spirit of the men of Jabesh-Gilead, angry to see his neighbours weep-

ing, when it was fitter for them to be preparing for war.

IV. The authority and power he exerted upon this important occasion. He soon let Israel know that he had a care for the public, and knew how to command men into the field, as well as how to drive cattle out of the field, v. 5, 7. He sent a summons to all the coasts of Israel, and ordered all the military men forthwith to appear in arms at a general rendezvous in Bezek. Observe, 1. His modesty, in joining Samuel in commission with himself. He would not execute the office of a king without a due regard to that of a prophet. 2. His mildness in the penalty threatened against those that should disobey his orders. He hews a yoke of oxen in pieces, and sends the pieces to the several cities of Israel, threatening, with respect to him who should decline the public service, not, "Thus shall it be done to *him,*" but, "Thus shall it be done to his *oxen.*" The effect of this summons was that the militia, or trained bands, of the nation, *came out as one man,* and the reason given is, because *the fear of the Lord fell upon them.* Those that fear God will make conscience of their duty to all men, particularly to their rulers.

V. His prudent proceedings in this great affair, v. 8. He numbered those that came in to him, that he might know his own strength, and how to distribute his forces in the best manner. In this muster, it seems, Judah, though numbered by itself, made no great figure; for it was but an eleventh part of the whole number, 30,330, though the rendezvous was at Bezek, in that tribe.

VI. His faith and confidence and his courage and resolution, in this enterprise. He now sends back this assurance (in which, it is probable, Samuel encouraged him): "*To-morrow,* by such an hour, before the enemy can pretend that the seven days have expired, *you shall have deliverance, v.* 9. Be you ready to do your part, and we will not fail to do ours. Do you sally out upon the besiegers, while we surround them." Saul knew he had a just cause, a clear call, and God on his side, and therefore doubted not of success. This was good news to the besieged Gileadites. When they heard it they were glad, relying on the assurances that were sent to them. And they sent into the enemies' camp (v. 10) to tell them that next day they would be ready to meet them, which the enemies understood as an intimation that they despaired of relief, and so were made the more secure by it.

VII. His industry and close application to this business. When the Spirit of the Lord comes upon men it will make them expert even without experience. A vast army (especially in comparison with the present usage) Saul had now at his foot, and a long march before him, nearly sixty miles, and over Jordan too. No cavalry in his army, but all infantry, which he divides into three battalions, v. 11. With what incredible swiftness he flew to the enemy. He was better than his word, for he promised help next day, *by that time the sun was hot (v.* 9), but brought it before day, *in the morning-watch, v.* 11. With what incredible bravery he flew upon the enemy. Betimes in the morning he was in the midst of their host; and his men, being marched against them in three columns, surrounded them on every side, so that they could have neither heart nor time to make head against them.

Lastly, To complete his honour, God crowned all these virtues with success. Jabesh-Gilead was rescued, and the Ammonites were totally routed.

Verses 12–15

We have here the improvement of the glorious victory which Saul had obtained.

I. The people took this occasion to show their

jealousy for the honour of Saul, and their resentment of the indignities done him. The sons of Belial that would not have him to reign over them should be brought forth and slain, *v.* 12. They had not courage thus to move for the prosecution of those that opposed him when he himself looked mean, but, now that his victory made him look great, nothing would serve but they must be put to death.

II. Saul took this occasion to give further proofs of his clemency, for, without waiting for Samuel's answer, he himself quashed the motion (*v.* 13): *There shall not a man be put to death this day.* 1. Because it was a day of joy and triumph: *To-day the Lord has wrought salvation in Israel*; and, since God has been so good to us all, let us not be harsh to one another. 2. Because he hoped they were by this day's work brought to a better temper, were now convinced that this man, under God, could save them, now honoured him whom before they had despised; and, if they are but reclaimed, he is secured from receiving any disturbance by them, and therefore his point is gained. If an enemy be made a friend, that will be more to our advantage than to have him slain.

III. Samuel took this occasion to call the people together *before the Lord in Gilgal, v.* 14, 15. 1. That they might publicly give God thanks for their late victory. 2. That they might confirm Saul in the government, more solemnly than had been yet done, that he might not retire again to his obscurity.

CHAPTER 12

Samuel's speech when he resigned the government into the hands of Saul, in which, I. He clears himself from all suspicion or imputation of mismanagement, while the administration was in his hands, ver. 1–5. II. He reminds them of the great things God had done for them and for their fathers, ver. 6–13. III. He sets before them good and evil, the blessing and the curse, ver. 14, 15. IV. He awakens them to regard what he said to them, by calling to God for thunder, ver. 16–19. V. He encourages them with hopes that all should be well, ver. 20–25. This is his farewell sermon to that august assembly and Saul's coronation sermon.

Verses 1–5

I. Samuel gives them a short account of the late revolution, and of the present posture of their government, by way of preface to what he had further to say to them, *v.* 1, 2. 1. For his own part, he had spent his days in their service: "*I have walked before you*, as a guide to direct you, as a shepherd that leads his flock (Ps. lxxx. 1), *from my childhood unto this day.*" "And now my best days are done: *I am old and grey-headed*"; therefore they were the more unkind to cast him off, yet therefore he was the more willing to resign. 2. As for his sons, "*Behold*" (says he), "*they are with you*", you may, if you please, call them to an account for any thing they have done amiss. 3. As for their new king, Samuel had gratified them in setting him over them (*v.* 1). Now that you have made yourselves like the nations in your civil government, and have cast off the divine administration in that, take heed lest you make yourselves like the nations in religion and cast off the worship of God.

II. He solemnly appeals to them concerning his own integrity in the administration of the government (*v.* 3): *Witness against me, whose ox have I taken?*

1. His design in this appeal. By this he intended, (1) To convince them of the injury they had done him in setting him aside. (2) To preserve his own reputation. Those that heard of Samuel's being rejected as he was, would be ready to suspect that certainly he had done some evil thing, or he would never have been so ill treated. (3) As he designed hereby to leave a good name behind him, so he designed to leave his successor a good example before him; let him write after his copy, and he will write fair.

2. In the appeal itself observe,

(1) What it is that Samuel here acquits himself from. [1] He had never taken that which was not his own, ox or ass, had never distrained their cattle for tribute, fines, or forfeitures, nor used their service without paying for it. [2] He had never defrauded those with whom he dealt, nor oppressed those that were under his power. [3] He had never taken bribes to pervert justice.

(2) How he calls upon those that had slighted him to bear witness concerning his conduct: "*Here I am; witness against me.*"

III. Upon this appeal he is honourably acquitted. All he desired was that they should do him justice, and that they did (*v.* 4).

IV. This honourable testimony borne to Samuel's integrity is left upon record to his honour (*v.* 5): "*The Lord is witness*, who searcheth the heart, *and his anointed is witness*, who trieth overt acts"; and the people agree to it: "*He is witness.*"

Verses 6–15

Samuel, having sufficiently secured his own reputation, instead of upbraiding the people upon it with their unkindness to him, sets himself to instruct them in the way of their duty.

I. He reminds them of the great goodness of God to them and to their fathers, gives them an abstract of the history of their nation, that, by the consideration of the great things God had done for them, they might be for ever engaged to love him and serve him. He not only puts them in mind of what God had done for them in their days, but of what he had done of old, in the days of their fathers, because the present age had had the benefit of God's former favours. 1. He reminds them of their deliverance out of Egypt. 2. He reminds them of the miseries and calamities which their fathers brought themselves into by forgetting God and serving other gods, *v.* 9. 3. He reminds them of their fathers' repentance and humiliation before God for their idolatries: *They said, We have sinned, v.* 10. 4. He reminds them of the glorious deliverances God had wrought for them, the victories he had blessed them with, and their happy settlements, many a time, after days of trouble and distress, *v.* 11. He specifies some of their judges, Gideon and Jephthah, great conquerors in their time. 5. At last he puts them in mind of God's late favour to the present generation, in gratifying them with a king, when they would prescribe to God by such a one to save them out of the hand of Nahash king of Ammon, *v.* 12, 13. Now it appears that this was the immediate occasion of their desiring a king: Nahash threatened them; they desired Samuel to nominate a general; he told them that God was commander-in-chief in all their wars and they needed no other, that what was wanting in them should be made up by his power: *The Lord is your king.* But they insisted on it, *Nay, but a king shall reign over us.* "And now," said he, "you have a king, a king of your own asking—let that be spoken to your shame; but a king of God's making—let that be spoken to his honour and the glory of his grace."

II. He shows them that they are now upon their good behaviour, they and their king. Let them not think that they had now cut themselves off from all dependence upon God.

1. Their obedience to God would certainly be their happiness, *v.* 14. If they would not revolt from God to idols, but would persevere in their allegiance to him, then they and their king should certainly be happy. (1) "You shall continue in the way of your duty to God, which will be your honour and comfort." (2) "You shall continue under the divine guidance and protection": *You shall be after the Lord*, so it is in the original, that is, "he will go before you to lead and prosper you, and make

your way plain. *The Lord is with you while you are with him."*

2. Their disobedience would as certainly be their ruin (*v.* 15).

Verses 16–25

Two things Samuel here aims at:—

I. To convince the people of their sin in desiring a king. They were now rejoicing before God in and with their king (*ch.* xi. 15), and offering to God the sacrifices of praise, which they hoped God would accept; and this perhaps made them think that there was no harm in their asking a king.

1. The expression of God's displeasure against them for asking a king. At Samuel's word, God sent prodigious thunder and rain upon them, at a season of the year when, in that country, the like was never seen or known before, *v.* 16–18. Thunder and rain have natural causes and sometimes terrible effects. But Samuel made it to appear that this was designed by the almighty power of God on purpose to convince them that they had done very *wickedly in asking a king.* He spoke to them of it (*v.* 16, 17): *Stand and see this great thing.* If what he said in a *still small voice* did not reach their hearts, nor his doctrine which dropped as the dew, they shall hear God speaking to them in dreadful claps of thunder and the great rain of his strength. Samuel, that son of prayer, was still famous for success in prayer. He intimated to them that how serene and prosperous soever their condition seemed to be now that they had a king, like the weather in wheat-harvest, yet, if God pleased, he could soon change the face of their heavens.

2. The impressions which this made upon the people. It startled them very much, as well it might. (1) *They greatly feared the Lord and Samuel.* (2) They owned their sin and folly in desiring a king: *We have added to all our sins this evil, v.* 19. (3) They earnestly begged Samuel's prayers (*v.* 19): *Pray for thy servants, that we die not.* They were apprehensive of their danger from the wrath of God, and could not expect that he should hear their prayers for themselves, and therefore they entreat Samuel to pray for them. Now they see their need of him whom awhile ago they slighted.

II. To confirm the people in their religion, and engage them for ever to cleave unto the Lord. The design of his discourse is much the same with Joshua's, *ch.* xxiii. and xxiv.

1. He would not that the terrors of the Lord should frighten them from him, for they were intended to frighten them to him (*v.* 20): *"Fear not; though you have done all this wickedness,* and though God is angry with you for it, yet do not therefore abandon his service, nor *turn from following him." Fear not,* that is, "despair not, fear not with amazement, the weather will clear up after the storm. Fear not; for, though God will frown upon his people, yet he will not forsake them (*v.* 22) *for his great name's sake*; do not you forsake him then."

2. He cautions them against idolatry: *"Turn not aside* from God and the worship of him" (*v.* 20 and again *v.* 21); "for if you turn aside from God, whatever you turn aside to, you will find it is a vain thing, that can never answer your expectations, but will certainly deceive you if you trust to it; it is a broken reed, a broken cistern."

3. He comforts them with an assurance that he would continue his care and concern for them, *v.* 23. They asked him only to pray for them, but he promised to do more for them, not only to pray for them, but to teach them; though they were not willing to be under his government as a judge, he would not therefore deny them his instructions as a prophet.

4. He concludes with an earnest exhortation to practical religion and serious godliness, *v.* 24, 25.

Chapter 13

While Samuel was joined in commission with Saul things went well, ch. xi. 7. But, now that Saul began to reign alone, all went to decay, and Samuel's words began to be fulfilled: "You shall be consumed, both you and your king". I. Saul appears here a very silly prince. 1. Infatuated in his counsels, ver. 1–3. 2. Invaded by his neighbours, ver. 4, 5. 3. Deserted by his soldiers, ver. 6, 7. 4. Disordered in his own spirit, and sacrificing in confusion, ver. 8–10. 5. Chidden by Samuel, ver. 11–13. 6. Rejected of God from being king, ver. 14. II. The people appear here a very miserable people. 1. Disheartened and dispersed, ver. 6, 7. 2. Diminished, ver. 15, 16. 3. Plundered, ver. 17, 18. 4. Disarmed, ver. 19–23.

Verses 1–7

The people of Israel offended God else he would not have left them, as here it appears he did; for,

I. Saul was very weak and impolitic, and did not order his affairs with discretion. *Saul reigned one year,* and nothing happened that was considerable, it was a year of no action; but in his second year he did as follows:—1. He chose a band of 3,000 men, of whom he himself commanded 2,000, and his son Jonathan 1,000, *v.* 2. The rest of the people he dismissed to their tents. If he intended these only for the guard of his person and his honorary attendants, it was impolitic to have so many, if for a standing army, in apprehension of danger from the Philistines, it was no less impolitic to have so few; and perhaps the confidence he put in this select number, and his disbanding the rest of that brave army with which he had lately beaten the Ammonites (*ch.* xi. 8–11), was looked upon as an affront to the kingdom, excited general disgust, and was the reason he had so few at his call when he had occasion for them. 2. He ordered his son Jonathan to surprise and destroy the garrison of the Philistines that lay near him in Geba, *v.* 3. 3. When he had thus exasperated the Philistines, then he began to raise forces, which, if he had acted wisely, he would have done before. As many as thought fit came to Saul to Gilgal, *v.* 4. But now the generality, we may suppose, drew back (either in dislike of Saul's politics or in dread of the Philistines' power).

II. Never did the Philistines appear in such a formidable body as they did now, upon this provocation which Saul gave them. If Saul had asked counsel of God before he had given the Philistines this provocation, he and his people might the better have borne this threatening trouble which they had now brought on themselves by their own folly.

III. Never were the people of Israel so faint-hearted, so sneaking, so very cowardly, as they were now. Some considerable numbers, it may be, came to Saul to Gilgal; but, hearing of the Philistines' numbers and preparations, their spirits sunk within them, some think because they did not find Samuel there with Saul. Now that they saw the Philistines making war upon them, and Samuel not coming in to help them, they knew not what to do; *men's hearts failed them for fear.* And, 1. Some absconded. Thousands of degenerate Israelites tremble at the approach of a great crowd of Philistines. Guilt makes men cowards. 2. Others fled (*v.* 7): They *went over Jordan to the land of Gilead,* as far as they could from the danger, and to a place where they had lately been victorious over the Ammonites. 3. Those that stayed with Saul *followed him trembling,* expecting no other than to be cut off, and having their hands and hearts very much weakened by the desertion of so many of their troops.

Verses 8–14

I. Saul's offence in offering sacrifice before Samuel came. Samuel, when he anointed him, had ordered him to tarry for him seven days in Gilgal, *ch.* x. 8. Perhaps that order was lately repeated with reference to this particular occasion. This order Saul broke. 1. He presumed to offer sacrifice without Samuel. 2. He determined to engage the Philistines without Samuel's directions. So self-sufficient Saul was that he thought it not worth while to stay for a prophet of the Lord either to pray for him or to advise him. (1) He did not send any messenger to Samuel, to know his mind. (2) When Samuel came he rather seemed to boast of what he had done than to repent of it; for he *went forth to salute him*, as his brother-sacrificer. He went out to *bless him*, so the word is, as if he now thought himself a complete priest. (3) He charged Samuel with breach of promise: *Thou camest not within the days appointed* (v. 11). (4) When he was charged with disobedience he justified himself in what he had done, and gave no sign at all of repentance for it. See what excuses he made, *v.* 11, 12. He would have this act of disobedience pass, [1] For an instance of his prudence. [2] For an instance of his piety. He would be thought very devout, and in great care not to engage the Philistines till he had by prayer and sacrifice engaged God on his side: "*The Philistines*," said he, "*will come down upon me, before I have made my supplication to the Lord*, and then I am undone." And yet, lastly, He owns it went against his conscience to do it: *I forced myself and offered a burnt-offering*.

II. The sentence passed upon Saul for this offence. 1. He shows him the aggravations of his crime, and charges him with being an enemy to himself, and his interest—*Thou hast done foolishly*, and a rebel to God and his government—"*Thou hast not kept the commandment of the Lord thy God*, that commandment wherewith he intended to try thy obedience." Sin is folly, and sinners are the greatest fools. 2. He reads him his doom (*v.* 14): He shows that there is no sin little, because no little god to sin against; but that every sin is a forfeiture of the heavenly kingdom, for which we stood fair. Saul lost his kingdom for want of two or three hours' patience.

Verses 15–23

1. Samuel departs in displeasure. Saul has set up for himself, and now he is left to himself: *Samuel gat him from Gilgal* (v. 15). Yet in going up to Gibeah of Benjamin, which was Saul's city, he intimated that he had not quite abandoned him. 2. Saul goes after him to Gibeah, and there musters his army, and finds his whole number to be but 600 men, *v.* 15, 16. 3. The Philistines ravage the country. The body of their army lay in an advantageous pass at Michmash, but thence they sent out three separate parties or detachments that took several ways, to plunder the country. By these the land of Israel was both terrified and impoverished, and the Philistines were animated and enriched. 4. The Israelites that take the field with Saul are unarmed, having only slings and clubs, not a sword or spear among them all, except what Saul and Jonathan themselves have, *v.* 19, 22. (1) How politic the Philistines were! They put down all the smiths' shops, transplanted the smiths into their own country, and forbade any Israelite, under severe penalties, to exercise the trade or mystery of working in brass or iron. They must go to some or other of their garrisons, to have all their iron-work done, and no more might an Israelite do than use a file (*v.* 20, 21). (2) How impolitic Saul was, that did not, in the beginning of his reign, set himself to redress this grievance. (3) How slothful and mean-spirited the Israelites were, that suffered the Philistines thus to impose upon them and had no thought nor spirit to help themselves. If they had not been dispirited, they could not have been disarmed, but it was sin that made them naked to their shame.

CHAPTER 14

I. Jonathan (ver. 1–3), with his armour-bearer only, made a brave attack upon the Philistines, encouraging himself in the Lord his God, ver. 4–7. He challenged them (ver. 8–12), and, upon their acceptance of the challenge, charged them with such fury, or rather such faith, that he put them to flight, and set them one against another (ver. 13–15), which gave opportunity to Saul and his forces, with other Israelites, to follow the blow, and gain a victory, ver. 16–23. II. The host of Israel troubled and perplexed by the rashness and folly of Saul, who adjured the people to eat no food till night, which 1. Brought Jonathan to a *præmunire*, ver. 24–30. 2. Was a temptation to the people, when the time of their fast had expired, to eat with the blood, ver. 31–35. Jonathan's error, through ignorance, had like to have been his death, but the people rescued him, ver. 36–46. III. In the close we have a general account of Saul's exploits (ver. 47, 48) and of his family, ver. 49–52.

Verses 1–15

I. Of the goodness of God in restraining the Philistines, who had a vast army of valiant men in the field, from falling upon that little handful of timorous trembling people that Saul had with him.

II. Of the weakness of Saul, who seems here to have been quite at a loss, and unable to help himself. 1. He pitched his tent under a tree, and had but 600 men with him, *v.* 2. He durst not stay in Gibeah, but got into some obscure place, in the uttermost part of the city, under a pomegranate-tree, under *Rimmon*. 2. Now he sent for a priest, and the ark, a priest from Shiloh, and the ark from Kirjath-jearim, *v.* 3, 18. Samuel, the Lord's prophet, had forsaken him, but he thinks he can make up that loss by commanding Ahiah, the Lord's priest, to attend him. He will also have the ark brought in hopes that this would make up the deficiency of his forces; one would have supposed that they would never bring the ark into the camp again, since, the last time, it not only did not save them, but did itself fall into the Philistines' hands. But it is common for those that have lost the substance of religion to be most fond of the shadows of it, as here is a deserted prince courting a deserted priest.

III. Of the bravery and piety of Jonathan, the son of Saul, who was much fitter than the father to wear the crown. "A sweet imp (says Bishop Hall) out of a crab-stock."

1. He resolved to go *incognito—unknown to any one*, into the camp of the Philistines. The way of access to the enemies' camp is described (*v.* 4, 5) as being peculiarly difficult, and their natural entrenchments impregnable, yet this does not discourage him; the strength and sharpness of the rocks do but harden and whet his resolution. Great and generous souls are animated by opposition and take a pleasure in breaking through it.

2. He encouraged his armour-bearer, a young man that attended him, to go along with him in this daring enterprise, (*v.* 6): "*Come, and let us* put our lives in our hands, *and go over to the* enemies' *garrison*, and try what we can do to put them into confusion." (1) They are uncircumcised. Fear not, we shall do well enough with them, for they are not under the protection of God's covenant as we are. If such as are enemies to us are also strangers to God, we need not fear them. (2) "God is able to make us two victorious over their unnumbered regiments. *There is no restraint in the Lord to save by many or by few.*" This is a truth easily granted in general, and yet it is not so easy to apply it to a particular case; when we are but few to believe that God can not only save us, but save by us, this is an instance of faith, which, wherever it is, shall obtain a good report. (3) Who knows but he that can use us for his glory will do it? *It may be the Lord will work for us.* An active faith will venture far in God's cause upon an *it may be*. Jonathan's armour-bearer, or esquire, as if he had learned to carry, not his arms only, but his heart,

promised to stand by him and to follow him whither-soever he went, *v.* 7.

3. How bold soever his resolution was, he resolved to follow Providence in the execution of it. "Come" (says he to his confidant), "we will discover ourselves to the enemy, as those that are not afraid to look them in the face (*v.* 8), and then, if they be so cautious as to bid us stand, we will advance no further, taking it for an intimation of Providence that God would have us act defensively (*v.* 9); but if they challenge us, and the first sentinel we meet bid us march on, we will push forward, and make as brisk an onset, assuredly gathering thence that it is the will of God we should act offensively, and then not doubting but he will *stand by us*," *v.* 10. And upon this issue he puts it, firmly believing, (1) That God has the governing of the hearts and tongues of all men. Jonathan knew God could discover his mind to him as surely by the mouth of a Philistine as by the mouth of a priest. (2) That God will, some way or other, direct the steps of those that *acknowledge him in all their ways*.

4. Providence gave him the sign he expected, and he answered the signal. He and his armour-bearer did not surprise the Philistines when they were asleep, but discovered themselves to them by day light, *v.* 11. The guards of the Philistines, (1) Disdained them, *Behold, the Hebrews come forth out of their holes.* (2) They defied them (*v.* 12): *Come, and we will show you a thing.* They bantered them. This greatly em-boldened Jonathan. With it he encouraged his ser-vant; he had spoken with uncertainty (*v.* 6): *It may be the Lord will work for us*; but now he speaks with assurance (*v.* 12). *The Lord has delivered them into the hand of Israel.* His faith being thus strengthened, no difficulty can stand before him; he climbs up the rock upon all fours (*v.* 13), though he has nothing to cover him, nor any but his own servant to second him, nor any human probability of any thing but death before him.

5. The wonderful success of this daring enterprise. The Philistines, instead of falling upon Jonathan, to slay him, or take him prisoner, fell before him (*v.* 13) unaccountably, upon the first blow he gave. They fall, that is, (1) They were many of them slain by him and his armour-bearer, *v.* 14. It was God's right hand and his arm that got him this victory. (2) The rest were put to flight, and fell foul upon one another (*v.* 15): *There was trembling in the host.* It is called *a trembling of God.* He that made the heart knows how to make it tremble. To complete the confusion, even the earth quaked, and made them ready to fear that it would sink under them.

Verses 16–23

I. The Philistines were, by the power of God, set against one another. They melted away like snow before the sun, and *went on beating down one another* (*v.* 16), for (*v.* 20) *every man's sword was against his fellow.* Now, God showed them the folly of their confidence, by making their own swords and spears the instruments of their destruction, and more fatal in their own hands than if they had been in the hands of Israel.

II. The Israelites were hereby animated against them.

1. Notice was soon taken of it by the watchmen of Saul, those that stood sentinel at Gibeah, *v.* 16.

2. Saul began to enquire of God, but soon de-sisted. He called for the ark (*v.* 18), desiring to know whether it would be safe for him to attack the Phil-istines, upon the disorder they perceived them to be in. Many will consult God about their safety that would never consult him about their duty. But, perceiving by his scouts that the noise in the enemy's camp increased, he commanded the priest that officia-ted to break off abruptly: "*Withdraw thy hand* (*v.* 19), consult no more, wait no longer for an answer. It is rather a prohibition to his enquiring of the Lord, either, (1) Because now he thought he did not need an answer, the case was plain enough. Or, (2) Be-cause he was in such haste to fight a falling enemy that he would not stay to make an end of his devotions.

3. He, and all the little force he had, made a vigorous attack upon the enemy; and all the people *were cried together* (so the word is, *v.* 20), for want of the silver trumpets wherewith God appointed them to sound an alarm in the day of battle, Num. x. 9. They summoned them by shouting, and their number was not so great but that they might soon be got together.

4. Every Hebrew, even those from whom one would least have expected it, now turned his hand against the Philistines. (1) Those that had deserted and gone over to the enemy, and were among them, now fought against them, *v.* 21. Such as had been taken prisoners by them, were as goads in their sides. (2) Those that had fled their colours, and hid them-selves in the mountains, returned to their posts, and joined in with the pursuers (*v.* 22). It was not much to their praise to appear now, but it would have been more their reproach if they had not appeared. Thus all hands were at work against the Philistines, yet it is said (*v.* 23), it was the Lord that saved Israel that day. He did it by them, for without him they could do nothing.

Verses 24–35

An account of the distress of the children of Israel, even in the day of their triumphs.

I. Saul forbade the people, under the penalty of a curse, to taste any food that day, *v.* 24. He did it with a good intention, lest the people, who perhaps had been kept for some time at short allowance, when they found plenty of victuals in the deserted camp of the Philistines, should fall greedily upon that, and so lose time in pursuing the enemy. And yet his making this severe order was unwise; for, if it gained time, it lost strength, for the pursuit. It was impious to enforce the prohibition with a curse and an oath. Had he no penalty less than an anathema wherewith to support his military discipline?

II. The people observed his order. 1. The soldiers were tantalized; for, in their pursuit of the enemy, it happened that they went through a wood so full of wild honey that it dropped from the trees upon the ground, yet, for fear of the curse, they did not so much as taste the honey, *v.* 25, 26. 2. Jonathan fell under the curse through ignorance. He heard not of the charge his father had given; for, having bravely forced the lines, he was then following the chase. He, not knowing any peril in it, took up a piece of honey-comb upon the end of his staff, and sucked it (*v.* 27), and was sensibly refreshed by it. He thought no harm, nor feared any, till one of the people acquainted him with the order, and then he found himself in a snare. Many a good son has been distressed by the rashness of an inconsiderate father. Jonathan, for his part, lost the crown he was heir to by his father's folly. 3. The soldiers were faint, and grew feeble, in the pursuit of the Philistines. Jonathan foresaw this would be the effect of it; their spirits would flag, and their strength would fail, for want of sustenance. 4. The worst effect of all was that at evening, when the restraint was taken off and they returned to their food again, they were so greedy and eager upon it that they ate the flesh with the blood, expressly contrary to the law of God, *v.* 32. Two hungry meals, we say, make the third a glutton; it was so here. Saul, being informed of it, reproved them for the sin (*v.* 33). To put a stop to this irregu-larity, Saul ordered them to set up a great stone before him, and let all that had cattle to kill, for their present use, bring them thither, and kill them under his eye upon that stone (v. 33), and the people did so (v. 34), so easily were they restrained and reformed when their prince took care to do his part.

III. On this occasion Saul built an altar (v. 35), that he might offer sacrifice, either by way of acknowledgment of the victory or by way of atonement for the sin. *The same was the first altar that he built.* Saul was turning aside from God, and yet now he began to build altars, being most zealous (as many are) for the form of godliness when he was denying the power of it. See Hos. viii. 14, *Israel has forgotten his Maker, and buildeth temples.*

Verses 36–46

I. Saul's boasting against the Philistines. He proposed to pursue them all night, and *not leave a man of them*, v. 36. Here he showed much zeal, but little discretion; for his army, thus fatigued, could as ill spare a night's sleep as a meal's meat. Only the priest thought it convenient to go on with the devotions that were broken off abruptly (v. 19), and to consult the oracle: *Let us draw near hither unto God.* Princes and great men have need of such about them as will thus be their remembrancers, wherever they go, to take God along with them. And, when the priest proposed it, Saul could not for shame reject the proposal, but *asked counsel of God* (v. 37).

II. His falling foul on his son Jonathan: for, while he is prosecuted, the Philistines make their escape.

1. God, by giving an intimation of his displeasure, put Saul upon searching for an accursed thing. Saul swears by his Maker that whoever was the Achan that troubled the camp, by eating the forbidden fruit, should certainly die, though it were Jonathan himself. (v. 39).

2. Jonathan was discovered by lot to be the offender. Saul would have lots cast between himself and Jonathan on the one side, and the people on the other, perhaps because he was as confident of Jonathan's innocency in this matter as of his own, v. 40. Jonathan at length was taken (v. 42), Providence designing hereby to countenance and support a lawful authority, reserving another way to bring off one that had done nothing worthy of death.

3. Jonathan ingenuously confesses the fact, and Saul, with an angry curse, passes sentence upon him. Jonathan denies not the truth, only he thinks it hard that he must *die for it*, v. 43. He might very fairly have pleaded his ignorance of the law, but he submitted to the necessity with a great and generous mind: "God's and my father's will be done". It is as brave to yield in some cases as it is in other cases to fight. Saul is not mollified by his filial submission nor the hardness of his case; but with another imprecation he gives judgment upon Jonathan (v. 44): "*God do so and more also* to me if I do not execute the law upon thee, *for thou shalt surely die, Jonathan.*" (1) He passed this sentence too hastily, without consulting the oracle. Jonathan had a very good plea in arrest of the judgment. What he had done was not *malum in se—bad in itself*; and, as for the prohibition of it, he was ignorant of that, so that he could not be charged with rebellion or disobedience. (2) He did it in fury. Had Jonathan been worthy to die, yet it would have become a judge, much more a father, to pass sentence with tenderness and compassion. Justice is debased when it is administered with wrath and bitterness. (3) He backed it with a curse upon himself if he did not see the sentence executed; and this curse did return upon his own head. Jonathan escaped, but God did so to Saul, and more also; for he was rejected of God and made anathema. Let none upon any occasion dare to use such imprecations as these, lest God say Amen to

them, and *make their own tongues to fall upon them*, Ps. lxiv. 8. Yet we have reason to think that Saul's bowels yearned towards Jonathan, so that he really punished himself, and very justly, when he seemed so severe upon Jonathan. By all these vexatious accidents God did likewise correct him for his presumption in offering sacrifice without Samuel.

4. The people rescued Jonathan out of his father's hands, v. 45. Hitherto they had expressed themselves very observant of Saul. What seemed good to him they acquiesced in, v. 36, 40. But, when Jonathan is in danger, Saul's word is no longer a law to them, but with the utmost zeal they oppose the execution of his sentence: "*Shall Jonathan die*—that blessing, that darling, of his country? Shall that life be sacrificed to a punctilio of law and honour which was so bravely exposed for the public service, and to which we owe our lives and triumphs? No, we will never stand by and see him thus treated whom God delights to honour." It is good to see Israelites zealous for the protection of those whom God has made instruments of public good. "*As the Lord liveth there shall not* only not his head, but not *a hair of his head fall to the ground*"; they did not rescue him by violence, but by reason and resolution; and Josephus says they made their prayer to God that he might be loosed from the curse. They plead for him that *he has wrought with God this day*; that is, "he has owned God's cause, and God has owned his endeavours, and therefore his life is too precious to be thrown away upon a nicety."

5. The design against the Philistines is quashed by this incident (v. 46): *Saul went up from following them*, and so an opportunity was lost of completing the victory.

Verses 47–52

A general account of Saul's court and camp. 1. Of his court and family, the names of his sons and daughters (v. 49), and of his wife and his cousin-german that was general of his army, v. 50. There is mention of another wife of Saul's (2 Sam. xxi. 8), Rizpah, a secondary wife, and of the children he had by her. 2. Of his camp and military actions. (1) How he levied his army: *When he saw any strong valiant man*, that was remarkably fit for service, he *took him unto him* (v. 52), as Samuel had told them the manner of the king would be (ch. viii. 11). (2) How he employed his army. He guarded his country against the insults of its enemies on every side, and prevented their incursions, v. 47, 48. But the enemies he struggled most with were the Philistines, with whom he had *sore war all his days*, v. 52.

CHAPTER 15

The final rejection of Saul from being king, I. The commission God gave him to destroy the Amalekites, with a command to do it utterly, ver. 1–3. II. Saul's preparation for this expedition, ver. 4–6. III. His success, and partial execution of this commission, ver. 7–9. IV. His examination before Samuel, and sentence passed upon him, notwithstanding the many frivolous pleas he made to excuse himself, ver. 10–31. V. The slaying of Agag, ver. 32, 33. VI. Samuel's final farewell to Saul, ver. 34, 35.

Verses 1–9

I. Samuel, in God's name, solemnly requires Saul to be obedient to the command of God, and plainly intimates that he was now about to put him upon a trial, in one particular instance, whether he would be obedient, or no, v. 1. 1. He reminds him of what God had done for him: "*The Lord sent me to anoint thee to be a king.*" God gave thee thy power, and therefore he expects thou shouldst use thy power for him. Men's preferment, instead of releasing them from their obedience to God, obliges them so much the more to it. 2. He tells him, in general, that, in consideration of this, whatever God commanded him to do he was bound to do it: *Now therefore hearken to the voice of the Lord.*

II. He appoints him a particular piece of service, in which he must now show his obedience to God more than in any thing he had done yet. He also gives him a reason for the command, that the severity he must use might not seem hard: *I remember that which Amalek did to Israel, v.* 2. God had an ancient quarrel with the Amalekites, for the injuries they did to his people Israel, Exod. xvii. 8, &c., and the crime is aggravated, Deut. xxv. 18. This is the work that Saul is now appointed to do (*v.* 3): "*Go and smite Amalek.* Israel is now strong, now go and make a full riddance of that nation."

III. Saul hereupon musters his forces, and makes a descent upon the country of Amalek. Saul numbered them in *Telaim,* which signifies *lambs.* He numbered them *like lambs* (so the vulgar Latin), numbered them *by the paschal lambs* (so the Chaldee), allowing ten to a lamb, a way of numbering used by the Jews in the later times of their nation. Saul drew all his forces to the *city of Amalek.*

IV. He gave friendly advice to the Kenites to separate themselves from the Amalekites among whom they dwelt. The Kenites were of the family and kindred of Jethro, Moses's father-in-law, a people that dwelt in tents, which made it easy for them, upon every occasion, to remove to other lands not appropriated. Many of them, at this time, dwelt among the Amalekites, fortified by nature, for *they put their nest in a rock,* being hardy people that could live any where, and affected fastnesses. Num. xxiv. 21. Saul must not waste them. 1. He acknowledges the kindness of their ancestors to Israel, when they came out of Egypt. Jethro and his family had been very helpful and serviceable to them in their passage through the wilderness, had been to them instead of eyes, and this is remembered to their posterity many ages after. Thus a good man leaves the divine blessing for an inheritance to his children's children; those that come after us may be reaping the benefit of our good works when we are in our graves. 2. He desires them to remove their tents from among the Amalekites.

V. Saul prevailed against the Amalekites, for it was rather an execution of condemned malefactors than a war with contending enemies. They were idolaters, and were guilty of many other sins, for which they deserved to fall under the wrath of God; yet, when God would reckon with them, he fastened upon the sin of their ancestors in abusing his Israel as the ground of his quarrel.

VI. Yet he did his work by halves, *v.* 9. 1. He *spared Agag,* because he was a king like himself, and perhaps in hope to get a great ransom for him. 2. He spared the best of the cattle, and destroyed only the refuse, that was good for little. Many of the people, we may suppose, made their escape, and took their effects with them into other countries, and therefore we read of Amalekites after this.

Verses 10–23

Saul is here called to account by Samuel concerning the execution of his commission against the Amalekites.

I. What passed between God and Samuel, in secret, upon this occasion, *v.* 10, 11. 1. God determines Saul's rejection, and acquaints Samuel with it: *It repenteth me that I have set up Saul to be king.* Repentance in God is not, as it is in us, a change of his mind, but a change of his method or dispensation. He does not alter his will, but wills an alteration. The change was in Saul: *He has turned back from following me;* this construction God put upon the partiality of his obedience, and the prevalency of his covetousness. And hereby he did himself make God

his enemy. 2. Samuel laments and deprecates it. *It grieved Samuel* that Saul had forfeited God's favour, and that God had resolved to cast him off; and he *cried unto the Lord all night.* The rejection of sinners is the grief of good people; God delights not in their death, nor should we.

II. What passed between Samuel and Saul in public. Samuel, being sent of God to him with these heavy tidings, went, as Ezekiel, in *bitterness of soul,* to meet him. But Samuel was informed that Saul had set up a triumphal arch, or some monument of his victory, at Carmel, a city in the mountains of Judah, seeking his own honour more than the honour of God, and also that he had marched in great state to Gilgal, for this seems to be intimated in the manner of expression: *He has gone about, and passed on, and gone down,* with a great deal of pomp and parade. There Samuel gave him the meeting, and,

1. Saul makes his boast to Samuel of his obedience: "*Blessed be thou of the Lord,* for thou sentest me upon a good errand, in which I have had great success, and *I have performed the commandment of the Lord.*" It is very likely, if his conscience had not charged him with disobedience, he would not have been so forward to proclaim his obedience; for by this he hoped to prevent Samuel's reproving him. Thus sinners think, by justifying themselves, to escape being *judged of the Lord;* whereas the only way to do that is by *judging ourselves.*

2. Samuel convicts him by a plain demonstration of his disobedience. "Hast thou performed the commandment of the Lord? *What means then the bleating of the sheep?*" *v.* 14. Samuel appeals to them as witnesses against him. The noise the cattle made would be a *witness against him.*

3. Saul insists upon his own justification against this charge, *v.* 15. The fact he cannot deny; the sheep and oxen were brought from the Amalekites. But, (1) It was not his fault, for *the people spared them;* as if they durst have done it without the express orders of Saul, when they knew it was against the express orders of Samuel. Sin is a brat that nobody cares to have laid at his doors. It is the sorry subterfuge of an impenitent heart, that will not confess its guilt, to lay the blame on those that were tempters, or partners, or only followers in it. (2) It was with a good intention: "It was *to sacrifice to the Lord thy God.*" This was a false plea, for both Saul and the people designed their own profit in sparing the cattle. But, if it had been true, it would still have been frivolous, for God hates robbery for burnt-offering.

4. Samuel overrules, or rather overlooks, his plea, and proceeds, in God's name, to give judgment against him. (1) He reminds Saul of the honour God had done him in making him king (*v.* 17), *when he was little in his own sight.* Those that are advanced to honour and wealth ought often to remember their mean beginnings, that they may never think highly of themselves, but always study to do great things for the God that has advanced them. (2) He lays before him the plainness of the orders he was to execute (*v.* 18): *The Lord sent thee on a journey;* so easy was the service, and so certain the success, that it was rather to be called a *journey* than a *war.* Had he denied himself, and set aside the consideration of his own profit so far as to have destroyed all that belonged to Amalek, he would have been no loser by it at last, nor have gone this *warfare on his own charges.* And therefore, (3) He shows him how inexcusable he was in aiming to make a profit of this expedition, and to enrich himself by it (*v.* 19): "*Wherefore then didst thou fly upon the spoil,* and convert that to thy own use which was to have been destroyed for God's honour?" *Thou didst not obey the voice of the Lord.*

5. Saul repeats his vindication of himself, as that

which, in defiance of conviction, he resolved to abide by, v. 20, 21. He denies the charge (v. 20): "*Yea, I have obeyed*, I have done all I should do"; for he had done all which he thought he needed to do, so much wiser was he in his own eyes than God himself. As to the spoil, he owns it should have been *utterly destroyed*. But he thought that would be wilful waste; the cattle of the Midianites were taken for a prey in Moses's time (Num. xxxi. 32, &c.), and why not the cattle of the Amalekites now? Better they should be a prey to the Israelites than to the fowls of the air and the wild beasts; and therefore he connived at the people's carrying it away for *sacrifice to the Lord* here at Gilgal, whither they were now bringing them.

6. Samuel gives a full answer to his apology, since he did insist upon it, v. 22, 23. He appeals to his own conscience: *Has the Lord as great delight in sacrifices as in obedience?* Here we are plainly told. (1) That humble, sincere, and conscientious obedience to the will of God is more pleasing and acceptable to him than *all burnt-offerings and sacrifices*. A careful conformity to moral precepts recommends us to God more than all ceremonial observances, Mic. vi. 6–8; Hos. vi. 6. Obedience was the law of innocency, but sacrifice supposes sin come into the world and is but a feeble attempt to take that away which obedience would have prevented. It is much easier to bring a bullock or lamb to be burnt upon the altar than to bring *every high thought into obedience* to God and the will subject to his will. (2) That nothing is so provoking to God as disobedience, setting up our wills in competition with his. This is here called *rebellion* and *stubbornness*, and is said to be as bad as *witchcraft* and *idolatry*, v. 23. It is as bad to set up other gods as to live in disobedience to the true God. It was disobedience that made us all sinners (Rom. v. 19), and this is the malignity of sin, that it is the *transgression of the law*, and consequently it is *enmity to God*, Rom. viii. 7.

7. He reads his doom: in short, "*Because thou hast rejected the word of the Lord*, hast *despised it* (so the Chaldee), hast *made nothing of it* (so the LXX.), therefore he has *rejected thee*, despised and made nothing of thee, but cast thee off *from being king*." Those are unfit and unworthy to rule over men who are not willing that God should rule over them.

Verses 24–31

Saul is at length brought to put himself into the dress of a penitent; but it is too evident that he only acts the part of a penitent, and is not one in deed.

I. How poorly he expressed his repentance. It was with much ado that he was made sensible of his fault, and not till he was threatened with being deposed. This touched him in a tender part. Then he began to relent, and not till then. 1. He made his application to Samuel only, and seemed most solicitous to stand right in his opinion only to preserve his reputation with the people, because they all knew Samuel to be a prophet, and the man that had been the instrument of his preferment. Thinking it would please Samuel, and be a sort of bribe to him, he puts it into his confession: *I have transgressed the commandment of the Lord and thy word*; as if he had been in God's stead, he also applies to Samuel for forgiveness (v. 25): *I pray thee, pardon my sin*; as if any could forgive sin but God only. The most charitable construction we can put upon this of Saul is to suppose that he looked upon Samuel as a sort of mediator between him and God, and intended an address to God in his application to him. 2. He excused his fault even in the confession of it, and that is never the fashion of a true penitent (v. 24): I did it because *I feared the people, and obeyed their voice*. 3. All his care was to save his credit, and preserve his interest in the people, lest they should revolt from him, or at least despise him. Therefore he courts Samuel with so much earnestness (v. 25); he feared that if Samuel forsook him the people would do so too.

II. How little he got by these thin shows of repentance. 1. Samuel repeated the sentence passed upon him, so far was he from giving any hopes of the repeal of it, v. 26, the same with v. 23. 2. He illustrates the sentence by a sign. When Samuel was turning from him he tore his clothes to detain him (v. 27). Samuel put a construction upon this accident which none but a prophet could do. He made it to signify the *rending of the kingdom* from him (v. 28), and that, like this, was his own doing. "He hath rent it from thee, and *given it to a neighbour better than thou*," namely, to David, who afterwards, upon occasion, cut off the skirt of Saul's robe (1 Sam. xxiv. 4), upon which Saul said (1 Sam. xxiv. 20), *I know that thou shalt surely be king*, perhaps remembering this sign, the tearing of the skirt of Samuel's mantle. 3. He ratified it by a solemn declaration of its being irreversible (v. 29): *The Strength of Israel will not lie*.

Verses 32–35

Samuel, as a prophet, is here set over kings, Jer. i. 10.

I. He destroys king Agag.

1. How Agag's present vain hopes were frustrated: He *came delicately*, in a stately manner, to show that he was a king. Having escaped the sword of Saul, that man of war, he thought he was in no danger from Samuel, an old prophet, a man of peace.

2. How his former wicked practices were now punished. Samuel calls him to account, not only for the sins of his ancestors, but his own sins: *Thy sword has made women childless*, v. 33.

II. He deserts king Saul, takes leave of him (v. 34), and *never came any more to see him* (v. 35). He looked upon him as rejected of God, and therefore he forsook him. Yet he *mourned for Saul*, thinking it a very lamentable thing that a man who stood so fair for great things should ruin himself so foolishly.

CHAPTER 16

At this chapter begins the story of David. Here, I. Samuel is appointed and commissioned to anoint a king among the sons of Jesse at Bethlehem, ver. 1–5. II. All his elder sons are passed by and David the youngest is pitched upon and anointed, ver. 6–13. III. Saul growing melancholy, David is pitched upon to relieve him by music, ver. 14–23.

Verses 1–5

Samuel had retired to his own house in Ramah, with a resolution not to appear any more in public business, but to addict himself wholly to the instructing and training up of the sons of the prophets, over whom he presided, as we find, *ch.* xix. 20.

I. God reproves him for continuing so long to mourn for the rejection of Saul. "Mourn not for Saul, for I *have provided me a king*. The people provided themselves a king and he proved bad, now I will provide myself one, *a man after my own heart*."

II. He sends him to Bethlehem, to anoint one of the sons of Jesse, a person probably not unknown to Samuel. *Fill thy horn with oil*.

III. Samuel objects the peril of going on this errand (v. 2): *If Saul hear it, he will kill me*. By this it appears, 1. That Saul had grown very wicked and outrageous since his rejection, else Samuel would not have mentioned this. What impiety would he not be guilty of who durst kill Samuel? 2. That Samuel's faith was not so strong as one would have expected, else he would not have thus feared the rage of Saul.

IV. God orders him to cover his design with a sacrifice: *Say, I have come to sacrifice*; and it was true he did, and it was proper that he should, when he came to anoint a king, *ch.* xi. 15. Let him give notice of a sacrifice, and invite Jesse (who, it is probable, was the principal man of the city) and his family to come to the feast upon the sacrifice; and, says God, *I will show thee what thou shalt do.* Those that go about God's work in God's way shall be directed step by step.

V. Samuel went accordingly to Bethlehem, not in pomp, or with any retinue, only a servant to lead the heifer which he was to sacrifice; yet *the elders of Bethlehem trembled at his coming,* fearing it was an indication of God's displeasure against them and that he came to denounce some judgment for the iniquities of the place. They asked him, "*Comest thou peaceably?*" "*I come peaceably,* for *I come to sacrifice,* not with a message of wrath against you, but with the methods of peace and reconciliation; and therefore you may bid me welcome and need not fear my coming; therefore *sanctify yourselves,* and prepare to join with me in the sacrifice, that you may have the benefit of it."

VI. He had a particular regard to Jesse and his sons, for with them his private business lay, with which, it is likely, he acquainted Jesse at his first coming, and took up his lodging at his house. Samuel assisted them in their family preparations for the public sacrifice, and, it is probable, chose out David, and anointed him, at the family-solemnities, before the sacrifice was offered or the holy feast solemnized. Perhaps he offered private sacrifices, like Job, *according to the number of them all* (Job i. 5), and, under colour of that, called for them all to appear before him.

Verses 6–13

I. How all the elder sons, who stood fairest for the preferment, were passed by.

1. Eliab, the eldest, was privately presented first to Samuel, probably none being present but Jesse only, and Samuel thought he must needs be the man: *Surely this is the Lord's anointed,* v. 6. When God would please the people with a king he chose a comely man; but, when he would have one after his own heart, he should not be chosen by the outside. *The Lord looks on the heart,* that is, (1) He knows it. We can tell how men look, but he can tell what they are. God looks on the heart, and sees the thoughts and intents. (2) He judges men by it. Let us reckon that to be true beauty which is within, and judge of men, as far as we are capable, by their minds, not their mien.

2. When Eliab was set aside, Abinadad and Shammah, and, after them, four more of the sons of Jesse, seven in all, were presented to Samuel, as likely for his purpose; but Samuel, who now attended more carefully than he did at first to the divine direction, rejected them all: *The Lord has not chosen these,* v. 8, 10.

II. How David at length was pitched upon. He was the youngest of all the sons of Jesse; his name signifies *beloved,* for he was a type of the beloved Son. Observe, 1 How he was in the fields, *keeping the sheep* (v. 11), and was left there, though there was a sacrifice and a feast at his father's house. David was taken *from following the ewes to feed Jacob* (Ps. lxxviii. 71), as Moses from keeping the flock of Jethro. We should think a military life, but God saw a pastoral life (which gives advantage for contemplation and communion with heaven), the best preparative for kingly power, at least for those graces of the Spirit which are necessary to the due discharge of that trust which attends it. 2. How earnest Samuel was to have him sent for: "*We will not sit down* to meat *till he come hither*; for, if all the rest be rejected, this must be he." 3. What appearance he made when he did come. No notice is taken of his clothing. No doubt that was according to his employment, mean and coarse, as shepherds' coats

commonly are, but he had a very honest look, not stately, as Saul's, but sweet and lovely: *He was ruddy, of a beautiful countenance, and goodly to look to* (v. 12). Though he was so far from using any art to help his beauty, that his employment exposed it to the sun and wind, his modest blush, when he was brought before Samuel made him look much the handsomer. 4. The anointing of him. The Lord told Samuel in his ear (as he had done, *ch.* ix. 15) that this was he whom he must anoint, signifying thereby, (1) A divine designation to the government entailed upon him, to come to him in due time. (2) A divine communication of gifts and graces, to fit him for the government, and make him a type of him who was to be the Messiah, the anointed One, who received the Spirit, not by measure, but without measure. He is said to be anointed *in the midst of his brethren.* Bishop Patrick reads it, *He anointed him from the midst of his brethren,* that is, he singled him out from the rest, and privately anointed him, but with a charge to keep his own counsel, and not to let his own brethren know it, as by what we find (*ch.* xvii. 28), it should seem, Eliab did not. Dr. Lightfoot reckons that he was about twenty-five, and that his troubles lasted but five years. 5. The happy effects of this anointing: The *Spirit of the Lord came upon David from that day forward, v.* 13. The anointing of him was not an empty ceremony, but a divine power went along with that instituted sign, and he found himself inwardly advanced in wisdom, and courage, and concern for the public, though not at all advanced in his outward circumstances. Some think that his courage, by which he slew the lion and the bear, and his extraordinary skill in music, were the effects and evidences of the Spirit's coming upon him. Samuel, having done this, went to Ramah in safety, and we never read of him again but once (*ch.* xix. 18), till we read of his death; now he retired to die in peace, since his eyes had seen the sceptre brought into the tribe of Judah.

Verses 14–23

Saul falling and David rising.

I. Here is Saul made a terror to himself (v. 14): *The Spirit of the Lord departed from him.* He lost all his good qualities. This was the effect of his rejecting God, and an evidence of his being rejected by him. The consequence of this was that *an evil spirit from God troubled him.* Those that drive the good Spirit away from them do of course become a prey to the evil spirit. He grew fretful, and peevish, and discontented, timorous and suspicious, ever and anon starting and trembling.

II. Here is David made a physician to Saul, and by this means brought to court, a physician that helped him against the worst of diseases, when none else could. 1. The means they all advised him to for his relief was music (v. 16): "Let us have a *cunning player on the harp* to attend thee." Saul's servants did not amiss to send for music as a help to cheer up the spirits, if they had but withal sent for a prophet to give him good counsel. 2. One of his servants recommended David to him, as a fit person to be employed in the use of these means, little imagining that he was the man whom Samuel meant when he told Saul of a neighbour of his, better than he, who should have the kingdom, *ch.* xv. 28. Though David, after he was anointed, returned to his country business, yet the workings of the Spirit signified by the oil could not be hid, but made him shine in obscurity so that all his neighbours observed with wonder the great improvements of his mind on a sudden. David, even in his shepherd's garb, has become an oracle, a champion, and every thing that is great. His fame reached the court soon, for Saul was inquisitive after such young men, *ch.* xiv. 52. When the Spirit of God comes upon a man he will make his face to shine. 3. David is hereupon sent for to court. (1) His father was very willing to part with him, sent him very readily, and a present with him to Saul, *v.* 20. The present was, according to the usage of those times, bread and wine (compare, *ch.* x. 3, 4.) therefore acceptable because expressive of the homage and allegiance of him that sent it. (2) Saul became very kind to him (*v.* 21), *loved him greatly*, and designed to *make him his armour-bearer*, and asked his father's leave to keep him in his service (*v.* 22): *Let David, I pray thee, stand before me.* David's music was Saul's physic. Music has a natural tendency to compose and exhilarate the mind, when it is disturbed and saddened. On some it has a greater influence and effect than on others, and, probably, Saul was one of those. It made his spirit sedate, and allayed those tumults by which the devil had advantage against him. Music cannot work upon the devil, but it may shut up the passages by which he had access to the mind. Saul found, even after he had conceived an enmity to David, that no one else could do him the same service (*ch.* xix. 9, 10).

CHAPTER 17

David is the man whom God now delights to honour, for he is a man after his own heart. In the court he was only Saul's physician; but in the camp Israel's champion; there he fairly fought, and beat Goliath of Gath. I. What a noble figure Goliath made, and how daringly he challenged the armies of Israel, ver. 1–11. II. What a mean figure David made, when Providence brought him to the army, ver. 12–30. III. The unparalleled bravery wherewith David undertook to encounter this Philistine, ver. 31–39. IV. The pious resolution with which he attacked him, ver. 40–47. V. The glorious victory he obtained over him with a sling and a stone, and the advantage which the Israelites thereby gained against the Philistines, ver. 48–54. VI. The great notice which was hereupon taken of David at court, ver. 55–58.

Verses 1–11

It was not long ago that the Philistines were soundly beaten, but here we have them making head again.

I. How they *defied Israel with their armies, v.* 1. They made a descent upon the Israelites' country, and possessed themselves, as it should seem, of some part of it, for they encamped in a place *which belonged to Judah.* The Philistines (it is probable) had heard that Samuel had fallen out with Saul and forsaken him, and that Saul had grown melancholy and unfit. Saul mustered his forces, and faced them, *v.* 2, 3. The evil spirit, for the present, had left Saul, *ch.* xvi. 23. David's harp having given him some relief, perhaps the alarms and affairs of the war prevented the return of the distemper. Business is a good antidote against melancholy. David had returned to Bethlehem to keep his father's sheep; this was a rare instance, in a young man that stood so fair for preferment, of humility and affection to his parents.

II. How they defied Israel with their champion Goliath, hoping by him to recover their reputation and dominion. Perhaps the army of the Israelites was superior in number and strength to that of the Philistines, which made the Philistines decline a battle, and stand at bay with them, desiring rather to put the issue upon a single combat, in which, having such a champion, they hoped to gain the victory. Now concerning this champion,

1. His prodigious size. He was of the sons of Anak, who at Gath kept their ground in Joshua's time (Josh. xi. 22). He was in height *six cubits and a span, v.* 4. The learned Bishop Cumberland has made it out that the scripture-cubit was above twenty-one inches and a span was half a cubit, by which computation Goliath wanted but eight inches of four yards in height, eleven feet and four inches, a monstrous stature.

2. His armour. *A helmet of brass on his head,*

a coat of mail, made of brass plates laid over one another, like the scales of a fish; and, because his legs would lie most within the reach of an ordinary man, he wore brass boots, and had a large corselet of brass about his neck. The coat is said to weigh 5,000 shekels. But some think it should be translated, not the *weight* of the coat, but the *value* of it, was 5,000 shekels. His offensive weapons were extraordinary, of which his spear only is here described, *v.* 7. It was like a weaver's beam. His arm could manage that which an ordinary man could scarcely heave. His shield only, was carried before him by his esquire, probably for state; for he that was clad in brass little needed a shield.

3. His challenge. The Philistines having chosen him for their champion, to save themselves from the hazard of a battle, he here throws down the gauntlet, and bids defiance to the armies of Israel, *v.* 8–10. He came into the valley that lay between the camps, and, his voice probably being as much stronger than other people's as his arm was, he cried so as to make them all hear him, *Give me a man, that we may fight together.* He looked upon Israel with disdain and defies them to find a man among them bold enough to enter the list with him. (1) He upbraids them with their folly in drawing an army together. (2) He offers to put the war entirely upon the issue of the duel he proposes: "If your champion kill me, we will be your servants; if I kill him, you shall be ours." This, says Bishop Patrick, was only a bravado. The Chaldee paraphrase brings him in boasting that he was the man that had killed Hophni and Phmehas and taken the ark prisoner.

4. The terror this struck upon Israel: *Saul and all his army were greatly afraid, v.* 11. The people would not have been dismayed but that they observed Saul's courage failed him; and it is not to be expected that, if the leader be a coward, the followers should be bold. Jonathan must sit still, because the honour of engaging Goliath is reserved for David.

Verses 12–30

Forty days the two armies lay encamped facing one another, and perhaps there were frequent skirmishes between small detached parties. All this while, morning and evening, did the insulting champion appear in the field and repeat his challenge. All this while David is keeping his father's sheep, but at the end of forty days Providence brings him to the field to win and wear the laurel which no other Israelite dares venture for.

I. The state of his family. His father was old (*v.* 12). David's three elder brethren, who perhaps envied his place at the court, got their father to send for him home, and let them go to the camp, where they hoped to signalize themselves and eclipse him (*v.* 13, 14), while David himself returned to the care, and toil, and (as it proved, *v.* 34) the peril, of *keeping his father's sheep.*

II. The orders his father gave him to go and visit his brethren in the camp. He must carry some bread and cheese to his brethren, ten loaves with some parched corn for themselves (*v.* 17) and ten cheeses for a present to their colonel, *v.* 18. David must still be the drudge of the family, though he was to be the greatest ornament of it. He had not so much as an ass at command to carry his load, but must take it on his back, and yet run to the camp. He must observe how his brethren fared, whether they were not reduced to short allowance, whom they associate with, and what sort of life they lead.

III. David's dutiful obedience, so well had he learnt to obey before he pretended to command. God's providence brought him to the camp very seasonably, when both sides had set the battle in array, *v.* 21. Both sides were now preparing to fight.

1. How brisk and lively David was, *v.* 22. Though he had come a long journey with a great load, he *ran into the army*, to see what was doing there, and to pay his respects to his brethren.

2. How bold and daring the Philistine was, *v.* 23. Now that the armies were drawn out into a line of battle he appeared first to renew his challenge.

3. How timorous and faint-hearted the men of Israel were. Upon his approach, they *fled from him and were greatly afraid, v.* 24.

4. How high Saul bid for a champion. Whoever will do it shall have as good preferment as he can give him, *v.* 25.

5. How much concerned David was to assert the honour of God and Israel against the impudent challenges of this champion. Two considerations, it seems, fired David with a holy indignation:—(1) That the challenger was one that was uncircumcised, a stranger to God and out of covenant with him. (2) That the challenged were the armies of the living God, devoted to him, employed by him and for him, so that the affronts offered to them reflected upon the living God himself, and *that* he could not bear. When therefore some had told him what was the reward proposed for killing the Philistine (*v.* 27) he asked others (*v.* 30), with the same resentment, which he expected would at length come to Saul's ear.

6. How he was browbeaten and discouraged by his eldest brother Eliab, *v.* 28. (1) As the fruit of Eliab's jealousy. He was the eldest brother, and David the youngest. Eliab was now vexed that his younger brother should speak those bold words against the Philistine which he himself durst not say. He would rather that Goliath should triumph over Israel than that David should be the man that should triumph over him. Eliab intended, in what he said, to represent him to those about him as an idle proud lad. He gives them to understand that his business was only to keep sheep, and falsely insinuates that he was a careless unfaithful shepherd. David could not escape this hard character from his own brother. (2) As a trial of David's meekness, patience, and constancy. A short trial it was, and he approved himself well in it; for, [1] he bore the provocation with admirable temper (*v.* 29): "*What have I now done?*" He had right and reason on his side, and knew it, and therefore with a soft answer turned away his brother's wrath. This conquest of his own passion was in some respects more honourable than his conquest of Goliath. [2] He broke through the discouragement with admirable resolution. He would not be driven off from his thoughts of engaging the Philistine by the ill-will of his brother.

Verses 31–39

David is at length presented to Saul for his champion (*v.* 31) and he bravely undertakes to fight the Philistine (*v.* 32). A little shepherd, come but this morning from keeping sheep, has more courage than all the mighty men of Israel, and encourages them. Two things David had to do with Saul:—

I. To get clear of the objection Saul made against his undertaking. "Alas!" says Saul, "thou hast a good heart to it, but art by no means an equal match for this Philistine." David, in reasoning with him, argues from experience; though he was but a youth, and never in the wars, yet perhaps he had done as much as the killing of Goliath came to, for he had had, by divine assistance, spirit enough to subdue a lion once and another time a bear that robbed him of his lambs, *v.* 34–36. To these he compares this uncircumcised Philistine, looks upon him to be as much a ravenous beast as either of them, and therefore doubts not but to deal as easily with him; and hereby he gives Saul to understand that he was not

so inexperienced in hazardous combats as he took him to be.

1. He tells his story like a man of spirit. When David kept sheep, (1) He approved himself very careful and tender of his flock. He could not see a lamb in distress but he would venture his life to rescue it. This temper made him fit to be a king, to whom the lives of subjects should be dear and their blood precious (Ps. lxxii. 14), and fit to be a type of Christ, the good Shepherd, who *gathers the lambs in his arms and carries them in his bosom* (Isa. xl. 11), and who not only ventured, but *laid down his life for his sheep.* (2) He approved himself very bold and brave in the defence of his flock. "Thy servant *slew both the lion and the bear.*"

2. He applies his story like a man of faith. He owns (*v.* 37) it was *the Lord that delivered him from the lion and the bear*; to him he gives the praise of that great achievement, and thence he infers, *He will deliver me out of the hand of this Philistine.* Thus David took off Saul's objection against his undertaking, and gained a commission to fight the Philistine.

II. To get clear of the armour wherewith Saul would, by all means, have him dressed up when he went upon this great action (*v.* 38). David, being not yet resolved which way to attack his enemy, *girded on his sword*, but he found the armour would but encumber him, and would be rather his burden than his defence, and therefore he desires leave of Saul to put them off again. "I have never been accustomed to such accoutrements as these."

Verses 40–47

I. The preparations made on both sides for the encounter. The Philistine was already fixed, as he had been daily for the last forty days. Well might he go with his armour, for he had sufficiently proved it. But what arms and ammunition is David furnished with? Truly none but what he brought with him as a shepherd; no breastplate, nor corselet, but his plain shepherd's coat; no spear, but his staff; no sword nor bow, but his sling; no quiver, but his scrip; nor any arrows, but, instead of them, five smooth stones picked up out of the brook, *v.* 40. By this it appeared that his confidence was purely in the power of God.

II. The conference which precedes the encounter.

1. How very proud Goliath was, (1) With what scorn he looked upon his adversary, *v.* 42. He took notice of his person, that he was but a youth, not come to his strength, *ruddy and of a fair countenance*, fitter to accompany the virgins of Israel in their dances than to lead on the men of Israel in their battles. He took notice of his array with great indignation (*v.* 43), "*Am I a dog, that thou comest to me with staves?*" (2) With what confidence he presumed upon his success. He cursed David by his gods. "*Come unto me, and I will give thy flesh to the fowls of the air*, it will be a tender and delicate feast for them."

2. How very pious David was. His speech savours nothing of ostentation, but God is all in all in it, *v.* 45–47. (1) He derives his authority from God: "*I come to thee in the name of the Lord*, by the special grace of his covenant," *the God of the armies of Israel.* The name of God David relied on, as Goliath did on his sword and spear. (2) He depends for success upon God, *v.* 46. David speaks with as much assurance as Goliath had done, but upon better ground; it is his faith that says, "*This day will the Lord deliver thee into my hand*, and not only thy carcase, but the carcases of the host of the Philistines, shall be given to the birds and beasts of prey." (3) He devotes the praise and glory of all to God. [1] All the world should be made to know that there is a God, and that the God of Israel is the one only living and true God, and all other pretended deities

are vanity and a lie. [2] All Israel shall *know that the Lord saveth not with sword and spear* (v. 47), but can, when he pleases, save without either and against both, Ps. xlvi. 9. David addresses himself to this combat rather as a priest that was going to offer a sacrifice to the justice of God than as a soldier that was going to engage an enemy of his country.

Verses 48–58

1. The engagement between the two champions, v. 48. To this engagement the Philistine advanced with a great deal of state and gravity; if he must encounter a pigmy, yet it shall be like a stalking mountain, overlaid with brass and iron, *to meet David.* David advanced with no less activity and cheerfulness, as one that aimed more to do execution than to make a figure: He *hasted, and ran,* being lightly clad, to *meet the Philistine.* We may imagine with what tenderness and compassion the Israelites saw such a pleasing youth as this throwing himself into the mouth of destruction, but he knew whom he had believed and for whom he acted. 2. The fall of Goliath in this engagement. He was in no haste, because in no fear, but confident that he should soon at one stroke cleave his adversary's head; but, while he was preparing to do it solemnly, David did his business effectually, without any parade: he slang a stone which hit him in the forehead, and, in the twinkling of an eye, fetched him to the ground, v. 49. Goliath knew there were famous slingers in Israel (Judges xx. 16), yet was either so forgetful or presumptuous as to go with the beaver of his helmet open. To complete the execution, David drew Goliath's own sword, a two-handed weapon for David, and with it *cut off his head,* v. 51. David's victory over Goliath was typical of the triumphs of the son of David over Satan and all the powers of darkness, whom he *spoiled, and made a show of them openly* (Col. ii. 15), and we through him are *more than conquerors.* 3. The defeat of the Philistines' army hereupon. They relied wholly upon the strength of their champion, and therefore, when they saw him slain, they did not, as Goliath had offered, throw down their arms and surrender themselves servants to Israel (v. 9), but took to their heels, being wholly dispirited, and thinking it to no purpose to oppose one before whom such a mighty man had fallen: *They fled* (v. 51), and this put life into the Israelites, who *shouted and pursued them.* They seized all the baggage, plundered the tents (v. 53), and enriched themselves with the spoil. 4. David's disposal of his trophies, v. 54. He brought the head of the Philistine to Jerusalem, to be a terror to the Jebusites, who held the strong-hold of Sion. *His armour he laid up in his tent;* only the sword was preserved behind the ephod in the tabernacle, as consecrated to God, *ch.* xxi. 9. 5. The notice that was taken of David. Saul had forgotten him, being melancholy and mindless, and little thinking that his musician would have spirit enough to be his champion. Abner was a stranger to him, but brought him to Saul (v. 57), and he gave a modest account of himself, v. 58. And now he was introduced to the court with much greater advantages than before, in which he owned God's hand performing all things for him.

CHAPTER 18

I. The improvement of his triumphs; he soon became, 1. Saul's constant attendant, ver. 2. 2. Jonathan's covenant friend, ver. 1, 3, 4. 3. The darling of his country, ver. 5, 7, 16. **II.** The allays of his triumphs. 1. Saul hated him, and sought to kill him himself, ver. 8–11. 2. He feared him, and contrived how he might have some mischief done him, ver. 12–17. He proposed to marry his daughter to him; but, (1) Cheated him of the eldest to provoke him, ver. 19), and, (2) Gave him the younger, upon conditions which would endanger his life, ver. 20–25. But David performed his conditions bravely (ver. 26, 27), and grew to be more and more esteemed, ver. 28–30.

Verses 1–5

David was anointed to the crown to take it out of Saul's hand, and over Jonathan's head, and yet here we find,

I. That Saul, who was now in possession of the crown, reposed a confidence in him, God so ordering it, that he might by his preferment at court be prepared for future service. Saul now took David home with him, and would not suffer him to return again to his retirement, v. 2. *Saul set him over the men of war* (v. 5), not that he made him general (Abner was in that post), but perhaps captain of the lifeguard. He employed him in the affairs of government; and *David went out whithersoever Saul sent him.* Those that hope to rule must first learn to obey.

II. That Jonathan, who was heir to the crown, entered into covenant with him, God so ordering it, that David's way might be the clearer when his rival was his friend. 1. Jonathan conceived an extraordinary kindness and affection for him (v. 1): *The soul of Jonathan was* immediately *knit unto the soul of David.* Jonathan had formerly set upon a Philistine army with the same faith and bravery with which David had now attacked a Philistine giant; so that there was between them a very near resemblance. None had so much reason to dislike David as Jonathan had, because he was to put him by the crown, yet none regards him more. 2. He testified his love to David by a generous present he made him, v. 4. He takes care to put him speedily into the habit of a courtier (for he gave him a robe) and of a soldier, for he gave him, instead of his staff and sling, a sword and bow, and, instead of his shepherd's scrip, a girdle, either a belt or a sash; the same that he himself had worn and he stripped himself of them to dress David in them. Saul's would not fit him, but Jonathan's did. Their bodies were of a size, a circumstance which well agreed with the suitableness of their minds. David is seen in Jonathan's clothes, that all may take notice he is a Jonathan's second self. Our Lord Jesus has thus shown his love to us, that he stripped himself to clothe us, emptied himself to enrich us; nay, he did more than Jonathan, he clothed himself with our rags, whereas Jonathan did not put on David's. 3. He endeavoured to perpetuate this friendship. They made a covenant with each other, v. 3.

III. That both court and country agree to bless him. And it was certainly a great instance of the power of God's grace in David that he was able to bear all this respect and honour flowing in upon him on a sudden without being lifted up above measure. Those that climb so fast have need of good heads and good hearts.

Verses 6–11

Now begin David's troubles, and they not only tread on the heels of his triumphs, but take rise from them.

I. He was too much magnified by the common people. Some time after the victory Saul went on a triumphant progress through the cities of Israel. And, when he made his public entry into any place, the women had got a song which they sang, the burden of which was, *Saul has slain his thousands, and David his ten thousands.*

II. This mightily displeased Saul, and made him envy David, v. 8, 9. He ought to have considered that they referred only to this late action, and intended not to diminish any of Saul's former exploits. David, in killing Goliath, did in effect slay all the Philistines that were slain that day and defeated the whole army; so that they did but give David his due. But Saul was very wroth, and presently suspected some treasonable design at the bottom of it, *What can he have more but the kingdom?*

III. In his fury he aimed to kill David, *v.* 10, 11.
1. His fits of frenzy returned upon him. Those that indulge themselves in envy and uncharitableness *give place to the devil*, and prepare for the re-entry of the unclean spirit, with seven others more wicked. Saul pretended a religious ecstasy: *He prophesied in the midst of the house*, that is, he had the gestures and motions of a prophet, and humoured the thing well enough to decoy David, that he might be off his guard; and perhaps designing, if he could but kill him, to impute it to a divine impulse but really it was a hellish fury that actuated him. 2. David returns to his harp: *He played with his hand as at other times.* 3. He took this opportunity to aim at the death of David. He had a javelin or dart in his hand, which he projected, endeavouring to slay David, not in a sudden passion, but deliberately. One would think he should have allowed himself to consider the kindness David was now doing him, in relieving him, as no one else could, against the worst of troubles. Compare David, with his harp in his hand, aiming to serve Saul, and Saul, with his javelin in his hand, aiming to slay David; and observe the meekness and usefulness of God's persecuted people and the brutishness and barbarity of their persecutors.
4. David happily avoided the blow twice. He did not throw the javelin at Saul again, though he had both strength and courage enough, and colour of right, to make resistance, yet he did no more than secure himself, by getting out of the way of it.

Verses 12–30

Saul began in open hostility when he threw the javelin at him. His enmity proceeded, and David received the attacks.

I. How Saul expressed his malice against David.
1. He was *afraid of him, v.* 12. He really stood in awe of him, as Herod feared John, Mark vi. 20. Saul was sensible that he had lost the favourable presence of God himself, and that David had it, and for this reason he feared him. The way to be both feared and loved, feared by those to whom we would wish to be a terror and loved by those to whom we would wish to be a delight, is to *behave ourselves wisely.* 2. He removed him from court, and gave him a regiment in the country, *v.* 13, that he might not secure the interest of the courtiers. Yet herein he did impoliticly; for it gave David an opportunity of ingratiating himself with the people, who therefore *loved him* (*v.* 16) because he *went out and came in before them. (v.* 16). 3. He stirred him up to take all occasions of quarrelling with the Philistines (*v.* 17), insinuating to him that he would do good service to his prince and good service to his God, and would qualify himself for the honour he designed him, which was to marry his eldest daughter to him. 4. He did what he could to provoke him by breaking his promise with him, and giving his daughter to another. 5. When he was disappointed in this, he proffered him his other daughter. (1) Perhaps he hoped that she would, even after her marriage to David, take part with her father against her husband. (2) The conditions of the marriage must be that he killed 100 Philistines, and, as proofs that those he had slain were uncircumcised, he must bring in their foreskins. David, in doing this, would make them seek to be revenged on him, which was the thing that Saul desired and designed. *For Saul thought to make David fall by the Philistines, v.* 25. [1] Saul's conscience would not suffer him to aim at David's life himself, but he thought that to expose him designedly to the Philistines had nothing bad in it (*Let not my hand be upon him, but the hand of the Philistines*). [2] Saul pretended extraordinary kindness for David even when he aimed at his ruin: *Thou shalt be my son-in-law*, says he (*v.* 21).

II. How David conducted himself when the tide of Saul's displeasure ran thus high against him.
1. *He behaved himself wisely in all his ways.* He did not complain of hard measure nor make himself the head of a party, but managed all the affairs he was entrusted with as one that made it his business to do real service to his king and country. And then *the Lord was with him* to give him success in all his undertakings.
2. When it was proposed to him to be son-in-law to the king he once and again received the proposal with all possible modesty and humility. (1) How highly he speaks of the honour offered him: *To be son-in-law to the king.* Religion is so far from teaching us to be rude and unmannerly that it does not allow us to be so. We must *render honour to whom honour is due.* (2) How humbly he speaks of himself: *Who am I? Who am I, a poor man, and lightly esteemed?* It well becomes us, however God has advanced us, always to have low thoughts of ourselves.
3. When the slaying of 100 Philistines was made the condition of David's marrying Saul's daughter he readily closed with it (*v.* 26). He would not seem to suspect that Saul designed his hurt by it. He knew God was with him, and therefore, whatever Saul hoped, David did not fear falling by the Philistines, though he must needs expose himself much by such an undertaking as this.
Even after he was married he continued his good services to Israel. When the princes of the Philistines began to move towards another war David was ready to oppose them, and *behaved himself more wisely than all the servants of Saul, v.* 30. The law dispensed with men from going to war the first year after they were married (Deut. xxiv. 5), but David loved his country too well to make use of that dispensation.

III. How God brought good to David out of Saul's project against him. 1. Saul gave him his daughter to be a snare to him, but in this respect that marriage was a kindness to him. 2. Saul thought, by putting him upon dangerous services, to have him taken off, but the more he did against the Philistines the better they loved him, so that *his name was much set by* (*v.* 30), which would make his coming to the crown the more easy.

CHAPTER 19

Immediately after David's marriage, his death was vowed. Four fair escapes of his from the hurtful sword of Saul, the first by the prudent mediation of Jonathan (ver. 1–7), the second by his own quickness (ver. 8–10), the third by Michal's fidelity (ver. 11–17), the fourth by Samuel's protection, and a change, for the present, wrought upon Saul, ver. 18–24.

Verses 1–7

Saul and Jonathan appear here in their different characters, with reference to David.

I. Never was enemy so unreasonably cruel as Saul. His projects to take him off had failed, and therefore he proclaims him an outlaw, and charges all about him, upon their allegiance, to take the first opportunity to kill David. It was strange that he who knew how well Jonathan loved him should expect him to kill him; but he thought that because he was heir to the crown he must needs be as envious at David as himself was.

II. Never was friend so surprisingly kind as Jonathan. He not only continued to delight much in him, though David's glory eclipsed his, but bravely appeared for him now that the stream ran so strongly against him.
1. He took care for his present security by letting him know his danger (*v.* 2).
2. He took pains to pacify his father and reconcile him to David. The next morning he ventured to commune with him concerning David (*v.* 3).

(1) His intercession for David was very prudent. He pleads, [1] The good services David had done to the public, and particularly to Saul. Witness the relief he had given him against his distemper with his harp, and his bold encounter with Goliath, that memorable action, which did, in effect, save Saul's life and kingdom. [2] He pleads his innocency. If he be slain, it is without cause. Jonathan could not entail anything upon his family more pernicious than the guilt of innocent blood.

(2) His intercession, being thus prudent, was prevalent. God inclined the heart of Saul to hearken to the voice of Jonathan. [1] He recalled the bloody warrant for his execution (*v.* 6): *As the Lord liveth, he shall not be slain.* We suppose that he spoke as he thought for the present, but the convictions soon wore off and his corruptions prevailed and triumphed over them. [2] He renewed the grant of his place at court. Jonathan brought him to Saul, and *he was in his presence as in times past* (*v.* 7), hoping that now the storm was over.

Verses 8–10

I. David continues his good services to his king and country. 1. As bold as ever in using his sword for the service of his country, *v.* 8. The war broke out again with the Philistines, which gave David occasion again to signalize himself. 2. As cheerful as ever in using his harp for the service of the prince. When Saul was disturbed with his former fits of melancholy *David played with his hand, v.* 9. He had learned to render good for evil, and to trust God with his safety in the way of his duty.

II. Saul continues his malice against David. He that but the other day had sworn by his Maker that David *should not be slain* now endeavours to slay him himself. Saul's fear and jealousy made him a torment to himself, so that he could not sit in his house without a javelin in his hand, pretending it was for his preservation, but designing it for David's destruction; for he endeavoured to nail him to the wall, running at him so violently that he struck the *javelin into the wall* (*v.* 10).

III. God continues his care of David and still watches over him for good. Saul missed his blow. David was too quick for him and fled, and by a kind providence escaped that night. To these preservations among others, David often refers in his Psalms, when he speaks of God's being his shield and buckler, his rock and fortress, and delivering his *soul from death.*

Verses 11–17

I. Saul's further design of mischief to David. When David had escaped the javelin, Saul sent some of his guards after him to lay wait at the door of his house, and to assassinate him in the morning as soon as he stirred out, *v.* 11.

II. David's wonderful deliverance out of this danger. Michal was the instrument of it, whom Saul gave him to be a snare to him, but she proved his protector and helper. She, knowing her father's great indignation at David, soon suspected the design, and bestirred herself for her husband's safety. 1. She got David out of the danger. She told him how imminent the peril was (*v.* 11): *Tomorrow thou wilt be slain.* David himself was better versed in the art of fighting than of flying, but *Michal let him down through a window* (*v.* 2), and so he *fled and escaped.* 2. She practised a deception upon Saul and those whom he employed to be the instruments of his cruelty. When the doors of the house were opened in the morning, and David did not appear, the messengers would search the house for him, and did so. But Michal told them he was sick in bed (*v.* 14), and, if they would not believe her, they might see, for (*v.* 13) she had put a wooden image in the bed, and wrapped it

up close and warm as if it had been David asleep, not in a condition to be spoken to; the goats' hair about the image was to resemble David's hair, the better to impose upon them. Saul, when he heard it, gave positive orders: *Bring him to me in the bed, that I may slay him, v.* 15. When the messengers were sent again, the cheat was discovered, *v.* 16. But by this time David was safe, and Michal was not then much concerned at the discovery. Saul chid her for helping David to escape (*v.* 17).

Verses 18–24

I. David's place of refuge. Having got away in the night from his own house, he fled not to Bethlehem but ran straight to Samuel and *told him all that Saul had done to him, v.* 18. 1. Because Samuel was the man that had given him assurance of the crown. In flying to Samuel he made God his refuge, trusting in the *shadow of his wings;* where else can a good man think himself safe? 2. Because Samuel, as a prophet, was best able to advise him what to do in this day of his distress. 3. Because with Samuel there was a college of prophets with whom he might join in praising God, and this would be the greatest relief imaginable to him in his present distress. He met with little rest or satisfaction in Saul's court, and therefore went to seek it in Samuel's church.

II. David's protection in this place: *He and Samuel went and dwelt* (*or* lodged) *in Naioth,* where the school of the prophets was, in Ramath. But Saul, having notice of it by some of his spies (*v.* 19), sent officers to seize David, *v.* 20. When they did not bring him he sent more; when they returned not he sent the third time (*v.* 21), and, hearing no tidings of these, he went himself, *v.* 22. How was David delivered, now that he was just ready to fall (like his own lamb formerly) into the mouth of the lions? Not as he delivered his lamb, by slaying the lion, or, as Elijah was delivered, by consuming the messengers with *fire from heaven,* but by turning the lions for the present into lambs.

1. When the messengers came into the congregation where David was among the prophets *the Spirit of God* came upon them, and they joined with the priest in praising God. Instead of seizing David, they themselves were seized. And thus, (1) God secured David; for either they were put into such an ecstasy by the spirit of prophecy, that they could not think of anything else, and so forgot their errand and never minded David, or they were by it put, for the present, into so good a frame that they could not entertain the thought of doing so bad a thing. (2) He put an honour upon the sons of the prophets and the communion of saints, and showed how he can strike an awe upon the worst of men, by the tokens of his presence in the assemblies. See also the benefit of religious societies. (3) He magnified his power over the spirits of men.

2. Saul himself was likewise seized with the spirit of prophecy. One would have thought that so bad a man as he was in no danger of being turned into a prophet, yet he prophesies, as his messengers did, *v.* 23. He stripped off his royal robe and warlike habiliments, because they were either too fine or too heavy for this service, and fell into a trance as it should seem, or into a rapture, which continued all that day and night. Now the proverb recurs, *Is Saul among the prophets?* See *ch.* x. 12.

CHAPTER 20

David, having several times narrowly escaped Saul's fury, begins to consider at last whether it may not be necessary for him to retire into the country and to take up arms in his own defence. But he will not do so daring a thing without consulting his faithful friend Jonathan. I. David complains to Jonathan of his present distress, and engages him to be his friend, ver. 1–8. II. Jonathan faithfully promises to get and give him intelligence how his father stood affected to him, and renews the covenant of friendship with him, ver. 9–23. III. Jonathan, upon trial, finds, to his grief, that his father was implacably enraged against David, ver. 24–34. IV. He gives David notice of this, according to the appointment between them, ver. 35–42.

Verses 1–8

I. While Saul lay bound by his trance at Naioth David escaped to the court, and got to speak with Jonathan. It was happy for him that he had such a friend at court, when he had such an enemy on the throne. If there be those that hate and despise us, let us not be disturbed at that, for there are those also that love and respect us. 1. David appeals to Jonathan himself concerning his innocency, *What have I done?* v. 1. 2. He endeavours to convince him that, notwithstanding his innocency, Saul sought his life. Jonathan, as became a dutiful son, endeavoured to cover his father's shame, as far as was consistent with justice and fidelity to David. David therefore gives him the assurance of an oath concerning his own danger, "*As the Lord liveth*, and as *thy soul liveth, there is but a step between me and death*," v. 3.

II. Jonathan generously offers him his service (v. 4): *Whatsoever thou desirest I will even do it for thee.*

III. David only desires him to satisfy himself, and then to satisfy him whether Saul did really design his death or no. 1. The method of trial he proposed was very natural. The two next days Saul was to dine publicly, upon occasion of the solemnities of the new moon, when extraordinary sacrifices were offered and feasts made upon the sacrifices. At these solemn feasts Saul had either all his children to sit with him, and David had a seat as one of them, or all his great officers, and David had a seat as one of them. However it was, David resolved his seat should be empty. If Saul admitted an excuse for his absence, he would conclude he had changed his mind and was reconciled to him; but if he resented it, and was put into a passion by it, it was easy to conclude he designed him a mischief. 2. The excuse he desired Jonathan to make for his absence, was that he was invited by his elder brother to Bethlehem, his own city, to celebrate with his relations there, because, they had now a yearly sacrifice, and a holy feast upon it, for *all the family*, v. 6. They kept a day of thanksgiving in their family for the comforts they enjoyed, and of prayer for the continuance of them. 3. The arguments he used with Jonathan to persuade him to do this kindness for him were very pressing, v. 8. (1) That he had entered into a league of friendship with him. (2) That he would by no means urge him to espouse his cause if he was not sure that it was a righteous cause. No honest man will urge his friend to do a dishonest thing for his sake.

Verses 9–23

I. Jonathan protests his fidelity to David in his distress. He faithfully promised him that he would let him know how, upon trial, he found his father affected towards him, "If there be *good towards thee*, I will *show it thee*, that thou mayest be easy (v. 12), if evil, I will *send thee away*, that thou mayest be safe" (v. 13); and thus he would help to deliver him from the evil if it were real and from the fear of evil if it were but imaginary. Jonathan adds to his protestations his hearty prayers: "*The Lord be with thee*, to protect and prosper thee, *as he has been* formerly *with my father*, though now he has withdrawn."

II. He provides for the entail of the covenant of friendship with David upon his posterity, v. 14–16. He engages David to be a friend to his family when he was gone (v. 15). The house of David must likewise be bound to the house of Jonathan from generation to generation; he *made a covenant* (v. 16) *with the* *house of David*. This kindness, 1. He calls *the kindness of the Lord*, because it is such kindness as God shows. 2. He secures it by an imprecation (v. 16): *The Lord require it at the hand of David's seed* if they prove so far David's enemies as to deal wrongfully with the posterity of Jonathan, David's friend. Having himself sworn to David, he caused David to swear to him, which David consented to swear by his love to him, which he looked upon as a sacred thing. Jonathan's heart was so much upon it that, when they parted this time, he concluded with a solemn appeal to God: *The Lord be between me and thee for ever* (v. 23). It was in remembrance of this covenant that David was kind to Mephibosheth, 2 Sam. ix. 7; xxi. 7.

III. He settled by what signs and tokens he would give him notice how his father stood affected towards him. David would be missed and would be enquired after, v. 18. On the third day, by which time he would have returned from Bethlehem, he must be at such a place (v. 19), and Jonathan would come towards that place with his bow and arrows to shoot for diversion (v. 20), would send his lad to fetch his arrows, and, if they were shot short of the lad, David must take it for a signal of safety, and not be afraid to show his head (v. 21); but, if he shot beyond the lad, it was a signal of danger, and he must shift for his safety, v. 22.

Verses 24–34

Jonathan is here effectually convinced of that which he was so loth to believe, that his father had an implacable enmity to David, and would certainly be the death of him if it were in his power.

I. David is missed from the feast on the first day, but nothing is said of him. *The king sat upon his seat as at other times* (v. 25), and yet had his heart full of envy and malice against David. When the king came to take his seat Jonathan arose, in reverence to him both as a father and as his sovereign; everyone knew his place, but David's was empty. But that day Saul took no notice that he missed David, but said within himself, "*Surely he is not clean, v.* 26. Some ceremonial pollution has befallen him."

II. He is enquired for the second day, v. 27. Saul asked Jonathan, who he knew was his confidant, *Wherefore cometh not the son of Jesse to meat?*

III. Jonathan makes his excuse, v. 28, 29. 1. That he was keeping the feast in another place, and that he had gone to pay his respects to his relations. He pleads, 2. That he did not go without leave humbly asked and obtained from Jonathan, as his superior officer.

IV. Saul hereupon breaks out into a most extravagant passion, and rages like a lion disappointed of his prey. David was out of his reach, but he falls upon Jonathan for his sake (v. 30, 31). He does in effect call him, 1. A bastard: *Thou son of the perverse rebellious woman.* 2. A traitor: *Thou son of perverse rebellion* (so the word is), that is, "thou perverse rebel." 3. A fool: *Thou hast chosen the son of Jesse* for thy friend *to thy own confusion*, for while he lives *thou shalt never be established.*

V. Jonathan is sorely grieved and put into disorder by his father's barbarous passion, and the more because he had hoped better things, v. 2. His father's reflections upon himself he made no return to. *When thou art the anvil lie thou still.* But his dooming David to die he could not bear: to that he replied with some heart (v. 32), *Wherefore shall he be slain? What has he done?* Generous spirits can much more easily bear to be abused themselves than to hear their friends abused. Saul was now so outrageous that he threw his javelin at Jonathan, v. 33. Jonathan *rose from table*, thinking it high time when his life was struck at, and *would eat no meat.*

Verses 35-42

1. He went at the time and to the place appointed (*v.* 35), within sight of which he knew David lay hid, sent his footboy to fetch his arrows, which he would shoot at random (*v.* 36), and gave David the fatal signal by shooting an arrow beyond the lad (*v.* 37). Finding the coast clear and no danger of a discovery, he presumed upon one minute's personal conversation with David after he had bidden him flee for his life. 2. The most sorrowful parting of these two friends, who, for aught that appears, never came together again but once, and that was by stealth *in a wood*, *ch.* xxiii. 16. They took leave of each other with the greatest affection imaginable, with kisses and tears. The separation of two such faithful friends was equally grievous to them both, but David's case was the more deplorable; for, when Jonathan was returning to his family and friends, David was leaving all his comforts, even those of God's sanctuary.

Chapter 21

David has now quite taken leave of Saul's court, and henceforward to the end of this book he is looked upon and treated as an outlaw and proclaimed a traitor. His troubles are a key to the Psalms. We find David in his flight, I. Imposing upon Ahimelech the priest, to get from him both victuals and arms, ver. 1-9. II. Imposing upon Achish, king of Gath, by feigning himself mad, ver. 10-15. Justly are troubles called temptations, for many are by them drawn into sin.

Verses 1-9

I. David, in distress, flies to the tabernacle of God, now pitched at Nob, supposed to be a city in the tribe of Benjamin. Since Shiloh was forsaken, the tabernacle was often removed, though the ark still remained at Kirjath-jearim. Hither David came in his flight from Saul's fury (*v.* 1), and applied to Ahimelech the the priest. Samuel the prophet could not protect him, Jonathan the prince could not. He therefore has recourse next to Ahimelech the priest. He foresees he must not be an exile, and therefore comes to the tabernacle, 1. To take an affecting leave of it, for he knows now when he shall see it again. 2. To enquire of the Lord there, and to beg direction from him in the way both of duty and safety.

II. Ahimelech the priest, having heard that he had fallen into disgrace at court, looked shy upon him, as most are apt to do upon their friends when the world frowns upon them. He was afraid of incurring Saul's displeasure by entertaining him. *Why art thou alone?* He that was suddenly advanced from the solitude of a shepherd's life to the crowds and hurries of the camp is now as soon reduced to the desolate condition of an exile.

III. David, under pretence of being sent by Saul upon public services, solicits Ahimelech to supply his present wants, *v.* 2, 3.

1. David did not behave like himself. He told Ahimelech a gross untruth, that Saul had ordered him business to despatch, that his attendants were dismissed to such a place, and that he was charged to observe secrecy. This was all false. It was ill done, and proved of bad consequence; for it *occasioned the death of the priests of the Lord*, as David reflected upon it afterwards with regret, *ch.* xxii. 22. David was a man of great faith and courage, and yet now both failed him, and he fell thus foully through fear and cowardice, and both owing to the weakness of his faith.

2. Two things David begged of Ahimelech, *bread* and a *sword*.

(1) He wanted bread: *Five loaves, v.* 3. The priest objected that he had none but hallowed bread, *show-bread*, which had stood a week on the golden table in the sanctuary, and was taken thence for the use of the priests and their families, *v.* 4. David pleads that he and those that were with him, in this case of necessity, might lawfully eat of the hallowed bread, for they were not only able to answer his terms of keeping from women for three days past, but *the vessels* (that is, the bodies) *of the young men were holy*, being *possessed in sanctification and honour at all times*. He pleads that the bread is in a manner common now that what was primarily the religious use of it is over; especially (as our margin reads it) *when there is other bread* (*hot, v.* 6) *sanctified this day in the vessel*, and put in the room of it upon the table. This was David's plea, and the Son of David approves it, and shows from it that mercy is to be preferred to sacrifice, that ritual observances must give way to moral duties, and that that may be done in a case of an urgent providential necessity which may not otherwise be done. He brings it to justify his disciples in plucking the ears of corn on the sabbath day, for which the Pharisees censured them, Matt. xii. 3, 4. Ahimelech hereupon supplies him: *He gave him hallowed bread* (*v.* 6). The show-bread was but twelve loaves in all, yet out of these he gave David five (*v.* 3), though they had no more in the house; but he trusted Providence.

(2) He wanted a sword. It happened that he had now no weapons with him, the reason of which he pretends to be because he came away in haste, *v.* 8. There was not a sword to be found about the tabernacle but the sword of Goliath, which was laid up behind the ephod. Probably David had an eye to that when he asked the priest to help him with a sword; for, that being mentioned, O! says he, *there is none like that, give it to me, v.* 9. Two things we may observe concerning this sword: Whenever he looked upon it, it would be a great support to his faith, by bringing to mind that great instance of the particular care and countenance of the divine providence respecting him. Experiences are great encouragements. He had gratefully given it back to God, dedicating it to him and to his honour as a token of his thankfulness; and now in his distress it stood him greatly in stead.

Thus was David well furnished with arms and victuals; but it fell out very unhappily that there was one of Saul's servants then attending before the Lord, *Doeg* by name, that proved a base traitor both to David and to Ahimelech. He was by birth an Edomite (*v.* 7), and though proselyted to the Jewish religion under Saul, yet he retained the ancient and hereditary enmity of Edom to Israel. He was master of the herds. Some occasion or other he had at this time to wait on the priest, it is said, he was *detained before the Lord*. He would rather have been any where else than before the Lord, and therefore, instead of minding the business he came about, was plotting to do David a mischief and to be revenged on Ahimelech for detaining him.

Verses 10-15

David, though king elect, is here an exile. Thus do God's providences sometimes seem to run counter to his promises. 1. David's flight into the land of the Philistines, where he hoped to remain undiscovered in the camp of Achish king of Gath, *v.* 10. To him David now went directly, as to one he could confide in, as afterwards (*ch.* xxvii. 2, 3). God's persecuted people have often found better usage from Philistines than from Israelites, in the Gentile theatres than in the Jewish synagogues. The king of Judah imprisoned Jeremiah, and the king of Babylon set him at liberty. 2. The disgust which the servants of Achish took at his being there, and their complaint of it to Achish (*v.* 11): "*Is not this David?* Is not this he that has triumphed over the Philistines?" As such, he must be an enemy to our country; and is it safe or honourable for us to protect or entertain such a man? Achish perhaps had intimated to them that it would be policy to entertain David, because he was now an enemy to Saul, and he might be hereafter a friend to them. It is common for the outlaws of a nation to be sheltered by the enemies of that nation. 3. The fright which this put David into. Though he had some reason to put confidence in Achish, yet, when he perceived the servants of Achish jealous of him, he began to be afraid that Achish would be obliged to deliver him up to them, and he was *sorely afraid* (*v.* 12). 4. The course he took to get out of their hands: *He feigned himself mad, v.* 13. It may in some degree be excused, for it is like a stratagem in war, by which he imposed upon his enemies for the preservation of his own life. 5. His escape by this means, *v.* 14, 15. I am apt to think Achish was aware that the delirium was but counterfeit, but, being desirous to protect David (as we find afterwards he was very kind to him, even when the lords of the Philistines favoured him not, *ch.* xxviii. 1, 2; xxix. 6), he pretended to his servants that he really thought he was mad. "I will show him no kindness, but then you shall do him no hurt, for, if he be a madman, he is to be pitied." He therefore *drove him away,* as it is in the title of Ps. xxxiv.

Chapter 22

David, being driven from Achish, returns into the land of Israel to be hunted by Saul. I. David sets up his standard in the cave of Adullam, entertains his relations (ver. 1), enlists soldiers (ver. 2), but removes his aged parents to a more quiet settlement (ver. 3, 4), and has the prophet Gad for his counsellor, ver. 5. Saul resolves to pursue him and find him out, complains of his servants and Jonathan (ver. 6–8), and, finding by Doeg's information that Ahimelech had been kind to David, he ordered him and all the priests that were with him, eighty-five in all, to be put to death, and all that belonged to them destroyed (ver. 9–19) from the barbarous execution of which sentence Abiathar escaped to David, ver. 20–23.

Verses 1–5

I. David shelters himself in the cave of Adullam, *v.* 1. Whether it was a natural or artificial fastness does not appear; it is probable that the access to it was so difficult that David thought himself able, with Goliath's sword, to keep it against all the forces of Saul, while he was waiting to see (as he says here, *v.* 3) what God would do with him. The promise of the kingdom implied a promise of preservation to it, and yet David used proper means for his own safety, otherwise he would have tempted God. He did not do anything that aimed to destroy Saul, but only to secure himself. It was at this time that David penned Psalm cxlii, which is entitled, *A prayer when David was in the cave.*

II. Thither his relations flocked to him, *his brethren and all his father's house,* to be protected by him, to give assistance to him, and to take their lot with him. Now Joab, and Abishai, and the rest of his relations, came to him, to suffer and venture with him.

III. Here he began to raise forces in his own defence, *v.* 2. He found by the late experiments he had made that he could not save himself by flight, and therefore was necessitated to do it by force, wherein he never acted offensively, never offered any violence to his prince nor gave any disturbance to the peace of the kingdom but only used his forces as a guard to his own person. The regiment he had was made up not of great men, nor rich men, nor stout men, no, nor good men, but men *in distress, in debt, and discontented,* men of broken fortunes and restless spirits, that were put to their shifts, and knew not well what to do with themselves. When David had fixed his headquarters in the cave of Adullam, they came and enlisted themselves under him to the number of about 400.

IV. He took care to settle his parents in a place of safety. No such place could he find in all the land of Israel while Saul was so bitterly enraged against him and all that belonged to him for his sake; he therefore goes with them to the king of Moab, and puts them under his protection, *v.* 3, 4. The first thing he does is to find them a quiet habitation, whatever became of himself. With what a humble faith he expects the issue of his present distresses: *Till I know what God will do for me.*

V. He had the advice and assistance of the prophet Gad, who probably was one of the sons of the prophets that were brought up under Samuel, and was by him recommended to David for his chaplain or spiritual guide. He advised him to go into the land of Judah (*v.* 5), as one that was confident of his own innocency, and was well assured of the divine protection, and was desirous, even in his present hard circumstances, to do some service to his tribe and country.

Verses 6–19

The progress of Saul's wickedness. He seems to have laid aside the thoughts of all other business and to have devoted himself wholly to the pursuit of David. He heard at length, by the common fame of the country, that David *was discovered.* Hereupon he called all his servants about him, and sat down under a tree, or grove, in the high place at Gibeah, with his spear in his hand for a sceptre, intimating the present temper of his spirit, or its distemper rather, which was to kill all that stood in his way. In this bloody court of inquisition,

I. Saul seeks for information against David and Jonathan, *v.* 7, 8. Two things he was willing to suspect. 1. That his servant David did *lie in wait* for him and seek his life, which was utterly false. He really sought David's life. 2. That his son Jonathan stirred him up to do so, and was confederate with him in compassing and imagining the death of the king. This also was notoriously false. Saul took it for granted that Jonathan and David were in a plot against him, his crown and dignity and was displeased with his servants that they did not give him information of it, and told them, (1) That they were very unwise, for David would never be able to give them such rewards as he had for them. (2) That they were unfaithful: *You have conspired against me.* (3) That they were very unkind. He thought to work upon their good nature with that word: *There is none of you that is* so much as *sorry for me,* or *solicitous for me,* as some read it.

II. Though he could not learn anything from his servants against David or Jonathan, yet he got information from Doeg against Ahimelech the priest.

1. An indictment is brought against Ahimelech by Doeg, and he himself is evidence against him, *v.* 9, 10, and therefore tells Saul what kindness Ahimelech had shown to David. He had *enquired of God for him* (which the priest used not to do but for public persons and about public affairs) and he had furnished him with *bread and a sword.* All this was true; but it was not the whole truth. He ought to have told Saul further that David had made Ahimelech believe he was then going upon the king's business; so that what service he did to David, however it proved, was designed in honour to Saul, and this would have cleared Ahimelech.

2. Ahimelech is summoned to appear before the king, and upon this indictment he is arraigned. The king sent for him and all the priests who then attended the sanctuary, whom he supposed to be aiding and abetting. Saul arraigns Ahimelech himself with the utmost disdain and indignation (*v.* 12): *Hear now, thou son of Ahitub*; not so much as calling him by his name, much less giving him his title of distinction. Ahimelech holds up his hand at the bar

in these words: "*Here I am, my lord,* ready to hear my charge, knowing I have done no wrong."

3. His indictment is read to him (*v.* 13), that he, as a false traitor, had joined himself with the son of Jesse in a plot to depose and murder the king. "His design" (says Saul) "was to *rise up against me,* and thou didst assist him with victuals and arms." See what bad constructions the most innocent actions are liable to, how unsafe those are that live under a tyrannical government, and what reason we have to be thankful for the happy constitution and administration of the government we are under.

4. To this indictment he pleads, Not guilty, *v.* 14, 15. He owns the fact, but denies that he did it traitorously or maliciously, or with any design against the king. He insists upon the settled reputation David had, as the most faithful of all the servants of Saul, the honour the king had put upon him in marrying his daughter to him, the use the king had often made of him, and the trust he had reposed in him. He pleads that he had been wont to *enquire of God for him* when he was sent by Saul upon any expedition, and did it now as innocently as ever he had done it.

5. Saul himself gives judgment against him (*v.* 16): *Thou shalt surely die, Ahimelech,* as a rebel, *thou and all thy father's house.* What could be more unjust? (1) It was unjust that Saul should himself, himself alone, give judgment in his own cause. (2) That so fair a plea should be overruled and rejected without any reason given. (3) That sentence should be passed so hastily. (4) That the sentences should be passed not only on Ahimelech himself, who was the only person accused by Doeg, but on *all his father's house,* against whom nothing was alleged. (5) That the sentence should be pronounced not for the support of justice, but for the gratification of his brutish rage.

6. He issues a warrant for the immediate execution of this bloody sentence.

(1) He ordered his footmen to be the executioners of this sentence, but they refused, *v.* 17. [1] Never was the command of a prince more barbarously given: *Turn and slay the priests of the Lord.* He seems well pleased with this opportunity of being revenged on the priests of the Lord, since God himself was out of his reach. [2] Never was the command of a prince more honourably disobeyed. The footmen had more sense and grace than their master. They would not offer to fall upon the priests of the Lord, such a reverence had they for their office, and such a conviction of their innocence.

(2) He ordered Doeg (the accuser) to be the executioner, and he obeyed. The most bloody tyrants have found out instruments of their cruelty as barbarous as themselves. Doeg is no sooner commanded to fall upon the priests than he does it willingly enough, and, meeting with no resistance, slays with his own hand (for aught that appears) on that same day eighty-five priests that were of the age of ministration, between twenty and fifty, for they *wore a linen ephod* (*v.* 18), and perhaps appeared at this time before Saul in their habits, and were slain in them. Doeg, by Saul's order no doubt, having murdered the priests, went to their city Nob, and put all to the sword there (*v.* 19), *men, women, and children,* and the cattle too. How deplorable was the state of religion at this time in Israel! To see their priests weltering in their own blood, and the heirs of the priesthood too, and the city of the priests made a desolation, so that the altar of God must needs be neglected for want of attendants, and this by the unjust and cruel order of their own king to satisfy his brutish rage—this could not but go to the heart of all pious Israelites, and make them wish a thousand times they had been satisfied with the government of Samuel and his sons.

Verses 20–23

1. The escape of Abiathar, the son of Ahimelech, out of the desolations of the priests' city. Probably when his father went to appear, upon Saul's summons, he was left at home to attend the altar, by which means he escaped the first execution, and, before Doeg and his bloodhounds came to Nob, he had intelligence of the danger, and had time to shift for his own safety. And whither should he go but to David? *v.* 20. 2. David's resentment of the melancholy tidings he brought. David greatly lamented the calamity itself, but especially his being accessory to it: *I have occasioned the death of all the persons of thy father's house, v.* 22. 3. The protection he granted to Abiathar. *With me thou shalt be in safeguard, v.* 23. David, having now time to recollect himself, speaks with assurance of his own safety, and promises that Abiathar shall have the full benefit of his protection. David had now not only a prophet, but a priest, a high-priest, with him, to whom he was a blessing and they to him, and both a happy omen of his success. Yet it appears (by *ch.* xxviii. 6) that Saul had a high priest too, for he preferred Ahitub the father of Zadok, of the family of Eleazar (1 Chron. vi. 8), even those that hate the power of godliness yet will not be without the form.

CHAPTER 23

Saul, having made himself drunk with the blood of the priests of the Lord, is here, in this chapter, seeking David's life, who appears doing good, and suffering ill. I. The good service he did to his king and country, in rescuing the city of Keilah out of the hands of the Philistines, ver. 1–6. II. The danger he was thereby brought into and his deliverance, by divine direction, from that danger, ver. 7–13. III. David in a wood, and his friend Jonathan visiting him there and encouraging him, ver. 14–18. IV. The information which the Ziphites brought to Saul of David's haunts, and the expedition Saul made, in pursuit of him, ver. 19–25. The narrow escape David had of falling into his hands, ver. 26–29.

Verses 1–6

The prophet Gad ordered David to go into the land of Judah, *ch.* xxii. 5. Since Saul neglected the public safety, he might take care of it, notwithstanding the ill treatment that was given him.

I. Tidings are brought to David that the Philistines had made a descent upon the city of Keilah and plundered the country thereabouts, *v.* 1. The way for any country to be quiet is to let God's church be quiet in it. If Saul fight against David, the Philistines shall fight against his country.

II. David is forward enough to come in for their relief. 1. David's generosity and public-spiritedness. He was concerned for the safety of his country and could not sit still to see that ravaged: though Saul, whose business it was to guard the borders of his land, hated him and sought his life. 2. David's piety and regard to God. He enquired of the Lord by the prophet Gad: *Shall I go and smite these Philistines?*

III. God appointed him once and again to go against the Philistines, and promised him success: *Go, and smite the Philistines, v.* 2. His men opposed it, *v.* 3. To satisfy them, therefore, he *enquired of the Lord again,* and now received, not only a full commission, which would warrant him to fight though he had no orders from Saul (*Arise, go down to Keilah*), but also a full assurance of victory: *I will deliver the Philistines into thy hand, v.* 4.

IV. He went accordingly against the Philistines, routed them, and rescued Keilah, (*v.* 5), and it should seem he made a sally into the country of the Philistines, for he carried off their cattle by way of reprisal for the wrong they did to the men of Keilah in robbing their threshing-floors,

Verses 7–13

I. Saul contriving within himself the destruction of David (*v.* 7, 8). Was it not told him that he had bravely relieved Keilah and delivered it out of the hands of the Philistines? This should have put Saul upon considering what honour should be done to David. But, instead of that, he catches at it as an opportunity of doing David a mischief. 1. How Saul abused the *God of Israel. God hath delivered him into my hand*; as if he who was rejected of God were in this instance favoured by him. He impiously connects God with his cause, because he thought he had gained one point. 2. How Saul abused the Israel of God, in making them the servants of his malice against David. He called all the people together to march to Keilah, pretending to oppose the Philistines, but intending to besiege David and his men.

II. David consulting with God concerning his own preservation. No sooner is the ephod brought to him than he makes use of it: *Bring hither the ephod.* We have the scriptures, those lively oracles, in our hands; let us take advice from them in doubtful cases. "Bring hither the Bible."

1. David's address to God upon this occasion is, (1) Very solemn and reverent. Twice he calls God the *Lord God of Israel*, and thrice calls himself his *servant*, *v.* 10, 11. "Lord, direct me in this matter, about which I am now at a loss." If he had asked the men (the magistrates or elders) of Keilah themselves what they would do in that case, they could not have told him, not knowing their own minds, or they might have told him they would protect him, and yet afterwards have betrayed him; but God could tell him infallibly: "When Saul besieges their city, and demands of them that they surrender thee into his hands, they will deliver thee up rather than stand the shock of Saul's fury."

2. David, having thus far notice given him of his danger, quitted Keilah, *v.* 13. His followers had now increased in number to 600; with these he went out, not knowing whither he went, but resolving to follow Providence. This broke Saul's measures. He thought God had delivered David into his hand, but it proved that God delivered him out of his hand, as a bird out of the snare of the fowler.

Verses 14–18

I. David abode in a *wilderness, in a mountain* (*v.* 14), *in a wood, v.* 15. He did not draw up his forces against Saul, surprise him by some stratagem or other, and so avenge his own quarrel and put an end to the calamities of the country under Saul's tyrannical government. He keeps God's way, waits God's time, and is content to secure himself in woods and wilderness. What shall we say to this? Let it reconcile even great and active men to privacy and restraint, and let it make us long for that kingdom where goodness shall for ever be in glory and holiness in honour.

II. Saul hunting him, as his implacable enemy. He sought him every day, so restless was his malice, *v.* 14.

III. God defending him, as his powerful protector. God delivered him not into Saul's hand, as Saul hoped (*v.* 7).

IV. Jonathan comforting him as his faithful and constant friend. True friendship will not shrink from danger, but can easily venture, will not shrink from condescension, but can easily stoop, and exchange a palace for a wood, to serve a friend. The very sight of Jonathan was reviving to David. 1. As a pious friend he *strengthened his hand in God.* David, though a strong believer, needed the help of his friends for the perfecting of what was lacking in his faith; and herein Jonathan was helpful to him, by reminding him of the promise of God. Jonathan

was not in a capacity of doing anything to strengthen him, but he assured him God would. 2. As a self-denying friend, he took a pleasure in the prospect of David's advancement to that honour which was his own birthright, *v.* 17. "Thou shalt live to be king, and I shall think it preferment enough to be next thee, near thee, though under thee, and will never pretend to be a rival with thee." 3. As a constant friend, he renewed his league of friendship with him, *v.* 18. True love takes delight in repeating its engagements. Our covenant with God should be often renewed, and therein our communion with him kept up. David and Jonathan now parted, and never came together again in this world.

Verses 19–29

1. The Ziphites offer their service to Saul, to betray David to him, *v.* 19, 20. He was sheltering himself in the wilderness of Ziph (*v.* 14, 15), putting the more confidence in the people of that country because they were of his own tribe. But, to ingratiate themselves with Saul, they went to him, and not only informed him where David quartered (*v.* 19), but invited him to come into their country and promised to deliver him into his hand, *v.* 20. 2. Saul thankfully receives their information, and gladly lays hold of the opportunity of hunting David in their wilderness. He likewise insinuates the little concern that the generality of his people showed for him. "You have compassion on me, which others have not." It was strange that Saul did not go down with them immediately, but the Ziphites had laid their spies upon all the places where he was likely to be discovered, and therefore Saul thought himself sure of his prey. 3. The imminent peril that David was now brought into. Upon intelligence that the Ziphites had betrayed him, he retired from the hill of Hachilah to the wilderness of Maon (*v.* 24), and at this time he penned the 54th Psalm, as appears by the title, wherein he calls the Ziphites *strangers*, though they were Israelites, because they used him barbarously; but he puts himself under the divine protection: He "*Behold, God is my helper*, and then all shall be well." Saul pursued him closely (*v.* 25), till he came so near him that there was but a mountain between them (*v.* 26), David and his men on one side of the mountain flying and Saul and his men on the other side pursuing. But this mountain was an emblem of the divine Providence coming between David and the destroyer, like the pillar of cloud between the Israelites and the Egyptians. David was concealed by this mountain and Saul confounded by it. Saul hoped with his numerous forces to enclose David, but the ground did not prove convenient for his design, and so it failed. A new name was given to the place in remembrance of this (*v.* 28): *Selah-hammahlekoth—the rock of division*, because it divided between Saul and David. 4. The deliverance of David out of this danger. Providence gave Saul a diversion, when he was just ready to lay hold of David; notice was brought him that the Philistines were *invading the land* (*v.* 27). He found himself under a necessity of *going against the Philistines* (*v.* 28), and by this means David was delivered. As this Saul was diverted, so another Saul was converted, just then when he was *breathing out threatenings and slaughter against the saints of the Lord*, Acts. ix. 1. 5. David having thus escaped, took shelter in some natural fortresses, which he found in the wilderness of En-gedi, *v.* 29.

CHAPTER 24

David had a fair opportunity to destroy Saul, and, to his honour, he did not make use of it; and his sparing Saul's life was as great an instance of God's grace in him as the preserving of his own life was of God's providence over him. I. How maliciously Saul sought David's life, ver. 1, 2. II. How generously David saved

Saul's life (when he had him at an advantage) and only cut off the skirt of his robe, ver. 3–8. III. How pathetically he reasoned with Saul, upon this, to bring him to a better temper towards him, ver. 9–15. IV. The good impression this made upon Saul for the present, ver. 16–22.

Verses 1–8

I. Saul renews his pursuit of David, *v.* 1, 2. Hearing that he is *in the wilderness of En-gedi*, he draws out 3,000 choice men, and goes in pursuit of him *upon the rocks of the wild goats*.

II. Providence brings Saul alone into the same cave wherein David and his men had hidden them-selves, *v.* 3. In those countries there were very large caves in the sides of the rocks or mountains, partly natural, but probably much enlarged by art for the sheltering of sheep from the heat of the sun; hence we read of places where the flocks did rest at noon (Cant. i. 7), and this cave seems to be spoken of as one of the sheep-cotes. Saul, passing by, turned in himself alone. He turned aside to *cover his feet*, that is, to sleep awhile.

III. David's servants stir him up to kill Saul now that he has so fair an opportunity to do it, *v.* 4. Saul now lay at his mercy. How apt we are to misunderstand, 1. The promises of God. God had assured David that he would deliver him from Saul, and his men interpret this as a warrant to destroy Saul. 2. The providences of God. Because it was now in his power to kill him, they concluded he might lawfully do it.

IV. David *cut off the skirt of his robe*, but soon repented that he had done this because it was an affront to Saul's royal dignity.

V. He reasons strongly both with himself and with his servants against doing Saul any hurt. 1. He reasons with himself (*v.* 6): *The Lord forbid that I should do this thing*. He considered Saul now, not as his enemy but as God's anointed (that is, the person whom God had appointed to reign as long as he lived, and who, as such, was under the particular protection of the divine law). 2. He reasons with his servants: *He suffered them not to rise against Saul, v.* 7. Thus did he render good for evil and was herein both a type of Christ, who saved his persecutors, and an example to all Christians.

VI. He followed Saul out of the cave, and, though he would not take the opportunity to slay him, yet he wisely took the opportunity, if possible, to slay his enmity, by convincing him that he was not such a man as he took him for. 1. Even in showing his head now he testified that he had an honourable opinion of Saul. 2. His behaviour was very respectful: He *stooped with his face to the earth, and bowed himself*.

Verses 9–15

David's warm and pathetic speech to Saul to persuade him to be reconciled.

I. He calls him *father* (*v.* 11), for he was not only, as king, the father of his country, but he was, in particular, his father-in-law.

II. He lays the blame of his rage against him upon his evil counsellors: *Wherefore hearest thou men's words? v.* 9.

III. He solemnly protests his own innocence, and that he is far from designing any hurt or mischief to Saul: "*There is neither evil nor transgression in my hand, v.* 11. Perhaps it was about this time that David penned the seventh psalm, concerning the affair of Cush the Benjamite (that is, Saul, as some think).

IV. He produces undeniable evidence to prove the falsehood of the suggestion upon which Saul's malice against him was grounded. David was charged with seeking Saul's hurt: "*See*," says he, "*yea, see the skirt of thy robe, v.* 11. Had that been true of which I am accused, I should now have had thy head in my hand." *The Lord delivered thee*, very surprisingly, *to-day into my hand. Some bade me kill thee*. It was upon a good principle that he refused to do it; by the fear of God he was restrained from it. Such a happy command he had of himself that his nature, in the midst of the greatest provocation, was not suffered to rebel against his principles.

V. He declares it to be his fixed resolution never to be his own avenger: "*The Lord avenge me of thee*, that is, deliver me out of thy hand; but, whatever comes of it, *my hand shall not be upon thee*" (*v.* 12). Bad men will do bad things; according as men's principles and dispositions are, so will their actions be.

VI. He endeavours to convince Saul that as it was a bad thing, so it was a mean thing, for him to give chase to such an inconsiderable person as he was (*v.* 14): *Whom does the king of Israel pursue* with all this care and force? *A dead dog; a flea; one flea*, so it is in the Hebrew. It is below so great a king to enter the lists with one that is so unequal a match for him, one of his own servants, bred a poor shepherd, now an exile, neither able nor willing to make any resistance. What credit would it be to Saul to trample upon a dead dog? What pleasure could it be to him to hunt a flea, a single flea, which (as some have observed), if it be sought, is not easily found, if it be found, is not easily caught, and, if it be caught, is a poor prize, especially for a prince.

VII. He once and again appeals to God as the righteous Judge (*v.* 12 and *v.* 15): *The Lord judge between me and thee*.

Verses 16–22

I. Saul's penitent reply to David's speech. 1. He melted into tears. He speaks as one quite overcome with David's kindness: *Is this thy voice, my son David?* He *lifted up his voice and wept, v.* 16. 2. He ingenuously acknowledges David's integrity and his own iniquity (*v.* 17): *Thou art more righteous than I*. This fair confession was enough to prove David innocent (even his enemy himself being judge), but not enough to prove Saul himself a true penitent. 3. He prays God to recompense David for this his generous kindness to him. *The Lord reward thee good, v.* 19. 4. He prophesies his advancement to the throne (*v.* 20): *I know well that thou shalt surely be king*. He knew it before, by the promise Samuel had made him of it compared with the excellent spirit that appeared in David, which highly aggravated his sin and folly in persecuting him as he did. This acknowledgment which Saul made of David's incontestable title to the crown was a great encouragement to David himself and a support to his faith and hope. 5. He binds David with an oath hereafter to show the same tenderness of his seed and of his name as he had now shown of his person, *v.* 21. This oath he afterwards religiously observed: he supported Mephibosheth, and executed those as traitors that slew Ish-bosheth.

II. Their parting in peace. 1. Saul, for the present, desisted from the persecution. He went home convinced, but not converted; ashamed of his envy of David, yet retaining in his breast that root of bitterness; vexed that, when at last he had found David, he could not at that time find in his heart to destroy him, as he had designed. 2. David continued to shift for his own safety. He knew Saul too well to trust him, and therefore *got him up into the hold*.

CHAPTER 25

The troubles of David. I. Tidings of the death of Samuel could not but trouble him, ver. 1. But, II. The abuse he received from Nabal is more largely recorded in this chapter. 1. The character of Nabal, ver. 2, 3. 2. The humble request sent to him, ver. 4–9. 3. His churlish answer, ver. 10–12. 4. David's angry resentment of it, ver. 13, 21, 22. 5. Abigail's prudent care to prevent the mischief it was likely to bring upon her family, ver. 14–20.

6. Her address to David to pacify him, ver. 23–31. 7. David's favourable reception of her, ver. 32–35. 8. The death of Nabal, ver. 36–38. 9 Abigail's marriage to David, ver. 39–44.

Verse 1

A short account of Samuel's death and burial. 1. Though he was a great man he spent the latter end of his days in retirement and obscurity because Israel had rejected him, for which God thus justly chastised them. 2. Though he was a firm friend to David, for which Saul hated him, yet he died in peace even in the worst of the days of the tyranny of Saul. Though Saul loved him not, yet he feared him, as Herod did John, and feared the people, for all knew him to be a prophet. 3. All Israel lamented him. His personal merits commanded this honour to be done him at his death. His former services to the public, when he judged Israel, made this respect to his name and memory a just debt. The sons of the prophets had lost the founder of their colleges. But Samuel was a constant intercessor for Israel, *ch*. xii. 23. If he go, they part with the best friend they have. 4. They buried him, not in the school of the prophets at Naioth, but in his own house at Ramah, where he was born. 5. David, hereupon, went down to the wilderness of Paran, retiring perhaps to mourn for the death of Samuel. Now that he had lost so good a friend, he apprehended his danger to be greater than ever, and therefore withdrew to a wilderness out of the limits of the land of Israel; and now it was that he *dwelt in the tents of Kedar*, Ps. cxx. 5.

Verses 2–11

The story of Nabal.

I. A short account of a man we should never have heard of if there had not happened some communication between him and David. 1. His name: *Nabal*—*a fool*; so it signifies. 2. His family: He was of the house of Caleb and inherited Caleb's estate; for Maon and Carmel lay near Hebron, which was given to Caleb (Josh. xv. 54, 55; xiv. 14), but he was far from inheriting his virtues. The LXX, and some other ancient versions, read it: He was a dogged man, of a currish disposition, surly and snappish, and always snarling. 3. His wealth: He was very great, that is, very rich (for riches make men look great in the eye of the world), otherwise, to one that takes his measures aright, he really looked very mean. 4. His wife— Abigail, a woman of great understanding. Her name signifies, *the joy of her father*; yet he could not promise himself much joy of her when he married her to such a husband, enquiring more after his wealth than after his wisdom. Many a child is thrown away upon a heap of worldly wealth, married to that, and to nothing else that is desirable. Many an Abigail is tied to a Nabal. 5. His character. He had no sense either of honour or honesty; not of honour, for he was churlish, cross, and ill-humoured; not of honesty, for he was evil in his doings, hard and oppressive.

II. David's humble request to him, that he would send him some victuals for himself and his men.

1. David, it seems, was in such distress that he would be glad to be beholden to him, and did in effect come a begging to his door.

2. He chose a good time to send to Nabal, when he had many hands employed about him in shearing his sheep, for whom he was to make a plentiful entertainment, so that good cheer was stirring. It was usual to make feasts at their sheep-shearings, as appears by Absalom's feast on that occasion (2 Sam. xiii. 24).

3. David ordered his men to deliver their message to him with a great deal of courtesy and respect: "*Go to Nabal, and greet him in my name*", v. 5. *Thus shall you say to him that liveth*: "*Peace be to thee*, all good both to soul and body. *Peace be to thy house and to all that thou hast*." He bids them call him his *son David* (v. 8), intimating that David honoured him as a father.

4. He pleaded the kindness which Nabal's shepherds had received from David and his men. (1) They did not hurt them themselves, were not a terror to them, nor took any of the lambs out of the flock. Yet, considering the character of David's men, men in distress, and debt, and discontented, and the scarcity of provisions in his camp, it was not without a great deal of care and good management that they were kept from plundering. (2) They protected them from being hurt by others. Nabal's servants, to whom he appealed, went further (v. 16): *They were a wall unto us, both by night and day*. David's soldiers were a guard to Nabal's shepherds when the bands' of the *Philistines robbed the threshing-floors* (ch. xxiii. 1) and would have robbed the sheepfolds. From those plunderers Nabal's flocks were protected by David's care, and therefore he says, *Let us find favour in thy eyes*.

5. He was very modest in his request. "Give whatsoever comes to thy hand, and we will be thankful for it." David demands not what he wanted as a debt, either by way of tribute as he was a king, or by way of contribution as he was a general, but asks it as a boon to a friend, that was his humble servant.

III. Nabal's churlish answer to this modest petition, v. 10, 11. Nabal not only denied him, but abused him. 1. He speaks scornfully of David as an insignificant man, not worth taking notice of. The Philistines could say of him, *This is* David *the king of the land*, that *slew his ten thousands* (ch. xxi. 11), yet Nabal his near neighbour, and one of the same tribe, affects not to know him, or not to know him to be a man of any merit or distinction: *Who is David? And who is the son of Jesse?* 2. He upbraids him with his present distress, and takes occasion from it to represent him as a bad man, that was fitter to be set in the stocks for a vagrant than to have any kindness shown him. How naturally does he speak the churlish clownish language of those that hate to give alms! David was reduced to this distress, not by any fault but purely by the good services he had done to his country and the honours which his God had put upon him; and yet he was represented as a fugitive and runagate. 3. He insists much upon the property he had in the provisions of his table, and will by no means admit anybody to share in them. We mistake if we think we are absolute lords of what we have and may do what we please with it. No, we are but stewards, and must use it as we are directed, remembering it is not our own, but his that entrusted us with it.

Verses 12–17

I. The report made to David of the abuse Nabal had given to his messengers (v. 12): *They turned their way*. They showed their displeasure by breaking off abruptly from such a churl. Christ's servants, when they are thus abused, must leave it to him to plead his own cause and wait till he appear in it.

II. David's hasty resolution hereupon. He girded on his sword, and ordered his men to do so too. 1. He repented of the kindness he had done to Nabal, and looked upon it as thrown away upon him. He said, "*Surely in vain have I kept all that this fellow hath in the wilderness*." 2. He determined to destroy Nabal and all that belonged to him, v. 22. Here David did not act like himself. His resolution was bloody, to cut off all the males of Nabal's house. The ratification of his resolution was passionate: *So, and more also do God to the enemies of David. Is this thy voice, O David?* Is this he who but the other day spared him who sought his life, and yet now will not spare anything that belongs to him who has only put an affront upon his messengers? He who at other times used to be calm and considerate is now put into such a heat by a few hard words that nothing will atone for them but the blood of a whole family. What are the best of men, when God leaves them to themselves? From Nabal he expected kindness, and therefore the affront he gave him was a surprise to him, found him off his guard, and, by a sudden and unexpected attack, put him for the present into disorder. What need have we to pray, *Lord, lead us not into temptation!*

III. The account given of this matter to Abigail by one of the servants, who was more considerate than the rest, *v.* 14. Abigail, being a woman of good understanding, took cognizance of the matter, even from her servant, who, 1. Did David justice in commending him and his men for their civility to Nabal's shepherds, *v.* 15, 16. "The men were very good to us, and, though they were themselves exposed, yet they protected us and were a wall unto us." 2. He did Nabal no wrong in condemning him for his rudeness to David's messengers: *He railed on them* (*v.* 14), *he flew upon them* (so the word is) with an intolerable rage; "for," say they, "it is his usual practice," *v.* 17. 3. He did Abigail and the whole family a kindness in making her sensible what was likely to be the consequence. Something therefore must be done to pacify David.

Verses 18–31

An account of Abigail's prudent management for the preserving of her husband and family from the destruction that was just coming upon them. Wisdom in such a case as this was better than weapons of war. 1. It was her wisdom that what she did she did quickly, and without delay. Those that desire conditions of peace must send when the enemy is yet a great way off, Luke xiv. 32. 2. It was her wisdom that what she did she did herself, being a woman of great prudence and very happy address.

Abigail must endeavour to atone for Nabal's faults.

I. By a most generous present, Abigail atones for his denial of their request. Abigail prepares the very best the house afforded and abundance of it (*v.* 18), not only *bread* and *flesh*, but *raisins* and *figs*. Nabal grudged them *water*, but she took *two bottles* (*casks* or *rundlets*) *of wine*, loaded her asses with these provisions, and sent them before. Abigail not only lawfully, but laudably, disposed of all these goods of her husband's without his knowledge, because it was for the necessary defence of him and his family, which otherwise would have been inevitably ruined. Husbands and wives, for their common good and benefit, have a joint-interest in their worldly possessions; but if either waste, or unduly spend in any way, it is a robbing of the other.

II. By a most obliging demeanour, and charming speech, she atones for the abusive language which Nabal had given them. She met David upon the march, big with resentment, and meditating the destruction of Nabal (*v.* 20); but with all possible expressions of complaisance and respect she humbly begs his favour, and solicits him to pass by the offence.

1. She speaks to him all along with deference and respect. She does not upbraid him with the heat of his passion, but endeavours to bring him to a better temper.

2. She takes the blame of the ill-treatment of his messengers upon herself: "*Upon me, my lord, upon me, let this iniquity be,*" *v.* 24. Abigail here discovered the sincerity and strength of her conjugal affection and concern for her family: whatever Nabal was, he was her husband.

3. She excuses her husband's fault by imputing it to his natural weakness and want of understanding (*v.* 25). He is simple, but not spiteful. Forgive him, for he knows not what he does.

4. She pleads her own ignorance of the matter: "*I saw not the young men,* else they should have had a better answer."

The very mentioning of what he was about to do, to shed blood and to avenge himself, was enough to work upon such a tender gracious spirit as David had; and it should seem, by his reply (*v.* 33), that it affected him. She applauds David for the good services he had done against the common enemies of his country. "*My lord fighteth the battles of the Lord* against the Philistines, and therefore he will leave it to God to fight his battles against those that affront him," *v.* 28. She foretells the glorious issue of his present troubles. She speaks with assurance, (1) That God would keep him safe: *The soul of my lord shall be bound in the bundle of life with the Lord thy God,* that is, God shall *hold thy soul in life* (as the expression is, Ps. lxvi. 9) as we hold those things which are bundled up or which are precious to us, Ps. cxvi. 15. The Jews understand this not only of the *life that now is,* but of that *which is to come,* and therefore use it commonly as an inscription on their gravestones. "Here we have laid the body, but trust that *the soul is bound up in the bundle of life, with the Lord our God.*" (2) That God would make him victorious over his enemies. "*The Lord will certainly make my lord a sure house,* therefore *forgive this trespass.*" She is confident that if he pass by the offence it will afterwards be no grief to him; but, on the contrary, it would yield him unspeakable satisfaction that his wisdom and grace had got the better of his passion.

Verses 32–35

As an ear-ring of gold, and an ornament of fine gold, so is a wise reprover upon an obedient ear, Prov. xxv. 12. Abigail was a wise reprover of David's passion, and he gave an obedient ear to the reproof, according to his own principle (Ps. cxli. 5): *Let the righteous smite me, it shall be a kindness.*

I. David gives God thanks for sending him this happy check to a sinful way (*v.* 32): *Blessed be the Lord God of Israel, who sent thee this day to meet me.* God is to be acknowledged in all the kindnesses that our friends do us either for soul or body.

II. He gives Abigail thanks for interposing so opportunely between him and the mischief he was about to do: *Blessed be thy advice, and blessed be thou, v.* 33.

III. He seems very apprehensive of the great danger he was in, which magnified the mercy of his deliverance. He speaks of the sin as very great. He was coming to shed blood, a sin of which when in his right mind he had a great horror, witness his prayer, *Deliver me from blood-guiltiness.*

IV. He dismissed her with an answer of peace, *v.* 35. He does, in effect, own himself overcome by her eloquence: "*I have hearkened to thy voice,* and will not prosecute the intended revenge, for I *have accepted thy person,* am well pleased with thee and what thou hast said."

Verses 36–44

We are now to attend Nabal's funeral and Abigail's wedding.

I. Nabal's funeral.

1. *Nabal dead drunk, v.* 36. Abigail came home, and, it should seem, he had so many people and so much plenty about him that he neither missed her nor the provisions she took to David. *He was very drunk,* a sign he was *Nabal, a fool,* that could not use his plenty without abusing it, could not be pleasant with his friends without making a beast of himself. There is not a surer sign that a man has but little wisdom, not a surer way to ruin the little he has, than drinking to excess. Nabal, that never thought

he could bestow too little in charity, never thought he could bestow too much in luxury.

2. Nabal again dead with melancholy, *v.* 37. Next morning, when he had come to himself a little, his wife told him how near to destruction he had brought himself and his family by his own rudeness, and with what difficulty she had interposed to prevent it; and, upon this *his heart died within him and he became as a stone.* He grew sullen, and said little, ashamed of his own folly.

3. Nabal, at last, dead indeed: *About ten days after,* when he had been kept so long under this pressure and pain, *the Lord smote him that he died* (*v.* 38).

II. Abigail's wedding. David was charmed with the beauty of her person, and the uncommon prudence of her conduct and address. He courted by proxy, his affairs, perhaps, not permitting him to come himself. She received the address with great modesty and humility (*v.* 41), reckoning herself unworthy of the honour. She agreed to the proposal, went with his messengers, took a retinue with her agreeable to her quality, and *she became his wife,* *v.* 42. She married him in faith, not questioning but that, though now he had not a house of his own, yet God's promise to him would at length be fulfilled.

Lastly, On this occasion we have some account of David's wives. 1. One that he had lost before he married Abigail, Michal, Saul's daughter, his first, and the wife of his youth, to whom he would have been constant if she would have been so to him, but Saul had given her to another (*v.* 44), in token of his displeasure against him and disclaiming the relation of a father-in-law to him. 2. Another that he married besides Abigail (*v.* 43), and, as should seem, before her, for she is named first, *ch.* xxvii. 3. David was carried away by the corrupt custom of those times. When David could not keep his first wife he thought that would excuse him if he did not keep to his second. But we deceive ourselves if we think to make others' faults a cloak for our own.

CHAPTER 26

David's troubles from Saul here begin again. I. The Ziphites informed him where David was (ver. 1), and thereupon he marched out with a considerable force in quest of him, ver. 2, 3. II. David gained intelligence of his motions (ver. 4), and took a view of his camp, ver. 5. III. He and one of his men ventured into his camp in the night and found him and all his guards fast asleep, ver. 6, 7. IV. David, though much urged to it by his companions, would not take away Saul's life, but only carried off his spear and his cruse of water, ver. 8–12. V. He produced these as a further witness for him that he did not design any ill to Saul, and reasoned with him upon his conduct, ver. 13–20. VI. Saul was hereby convinced of his error, and once more desisted from persecuting David, ver. 21–25.

Verses 1–5

1. Saul gets information of David's movements and acts offensively. The Ziphites came to him and told him where David now was, in the same place where he was when they formerly betrayed him, *ch.* xxiii. 19. For aught we know, Saul would have continued in the same good mind that he was in (*ch.* xxiv. 17), and would not have given David this fresh trouble, if the Ziphites had not put him on. Saul readily caught at the information, and went down with an army to the place where David hid himself, *v.* 2.

2. David gets information of Saul's movements and acts defensively. He sought only his own safety, not Saul's ruin; therefore he *abode in the wilderness* (*v.* 3), curbing the bravery of his own spirit by a silent retirement, showing more true valour than he could have done by an irregular resistance. (1) He had spies who informed him of Saul's descent, for he would not believe that Saul would deal so basely with him till he had the utmost evidence of it. (2) He

observed with his own eyes how Saul was encamped, *v.* 5.

Verses 6–12

I. David's bold adventure into Saul's camp in the night, accompanied only by his kinsman, Abishai, the son of Zeruiah. Like Gideon, he ventured through the guards, with a special assurance of the divine protection.

II. The posture he found the camp in: *Saul lay sleeping in the trench,* or, as some read it, *in his chariot, and in the midst of his carriages,* with *his spear stuck in the ground* by him, and all the soldiers, even those that were appointed to stand sentinel, were *fast asleep,* *v.* 12. Something extraordinary there was in it that they should all be asleep together, and so fast asleep that David and Abishai walked and talked among them, and yet none of them stirred. How helpless do Saul and all his forces lie, all, in effect, disarmed and chained! and yet nothing is done to them; they are only rocked asleep.

III. Abishai's request to David for a commission to dispatch Saul with the spear that stuck at his bolster. It was a special providence which gave him this opportunity; he ought not therefore to let it slip.

IV. David's generous refusal to suffer any harm to be done to Saul, and in it a resolute adherence to his principles of loyalty, *v.* 9. No man could do it and be guiltless. The thing he feared was guilt and his concern respected his innocence more than his safety. He resolved to wait till God shall think fit to avenge him on Saul, and he will by no means *avenge himself* (*v.* 10). Thus bravely does he prefer his conscience to his interest and trusts God with the issue.

He and Abishai carried away the spear and cruse of water which Saul had by his bedside (*v.* 12).

Verses 13–20

David having got safely from Saul's camp himself, and having brought with him proofs sufficient that he had been there, posts himself conveniently, so that they might hear him and yet not reach him (*v.* 13), and then begins to reason with them upon what had passed.

I. He reasons ironically with Abner, and keenly banters him. Abner got up and enquired who called, and disturbed the king's repose. "It is I," said David, and then he upbraids him with his sleeping when he should have been upon his guard. David, to put him into confusion, told him, 1. That he had lost his honour (*v.* 15). 2. That he deserved to lose his head (*v.* 16): "*You are all worthy to die,* by martial law, for being off your guard, when you had the king himself asleep in the midst of you. *Ecce signum—Behold this token.* See where the king's spear is, in the hand of him whom the king himself is pleased to count his enemy. Those that took away this might as easily and safely have taken away his life. Now see who are the king's best friends, you that neglected him and left him exposed or I that protected him when he was exposed.

II. He reasons seriously and affectionately with Saul. By this time he was so well awake as to hear what was said, and to discern who said it (*v.* 17): *Is this thy voice, my son David?* He had given his wife to another and yet calls him *son,* thirsted after his blood and yet is glad to hear his voice. And now David has as fair an opportunity of reaching Saul's conscience as he had just now of taking away his life.

1. He complains of the very melancholy condition he was brought into by the enmity of Saul against him. Two things he laments: —(1) That he was driven from his master and from his business: "*My lord pursues after his servant, v.* 18. Instead of being owned as a servant, I am pursued as a rebel. (2) That

he was driven from his God and from his religion; he was constrained to live among the worshippers of strange gods and was thereby thrust into temptation to join with them in their idolatrous worship. If David had not been a man of extraordinary grace, and firmness to his religion, the ill usage he met with from his own prince and people, who were Israelites and worshippers of the true God, would have prejudiced him against the religion they professed and have driven him to communicate with idolators.

2. He insists upon his own innocency: *What have I done or what evil is in my hand? v.* 18.

3. He endeavours to convince Saul that his pursuit of him is not only wrong, but mean, and much below him. He compares himself to a partridge, a very innocent harmless bird, which, when attempts are made upon its life, flies if it can, but makes no resistance. And would Saul bring the flower of his army into the field only to hunt one poor partridge? "Let us join in making our peace with God, reconciling ourselves to him, which may be done, by sacrifice; and then I hope the sin will be pardoned, whatever it is, and the trouble, which is so great a vexation both to thee and me, will come to an end." See the right method of peace-making; let us first make God our friend by Christ the great Sacrifice, and then all other enmities shall be slain, Eph. ii. 16; Prov. xvi. 7. He decently lays the blame upon the evil counsellors who advised the king to that which was dishonourable and dishonest, and insists upon it that they be removed from about him and forbidden his presence, as men cursed before the Lord.

Verses 21–25

I. Saul's penitent confession of his fault and folly in persecuting David and his promise to do so no more. He acknowledges he has done very wrong to persecute him, that he has therein acted against God's law (*I have sinned*), and against his own interest (*I have played the fool*), in pursuing him as an enemy who would have been one of his best friends. He invites him to court again: *Return, my son David.* He promises him that he will not persecute him as he has done, but protect him: *I will no more do thee harm.*

II. David's improvement of Saul's convictions and confessions and the evidence he had to produce of his own sincerity. He desired that one of the footmen might fetch the spear (*v.* 22), and then (*v.* 23), 1. He appeals to God as judge of the controversy: *The Lord render to every man his righteousness.* 2. He reminds Saul again of the proof he had now given of his respect to him from a principle of loyalty: *I would not stretch forth my hand against the Lord's anointed,* intimating to Saul that the anointing oil was his protection, for which he was indebted to the Lord and ought to express his gratitude to him. 3. Not relying much upon Saul's promises, he puts himself under God's protection, and begs his favour (*v.* 24): *"Let my life be much set by in the eyes of the Lord,* how light soever thou makest of it."

III. Saul's prediction of David's advancement. He commends him (*v.* 25): *Blessed be thou, my son David.* He foretells his victories, and his elevation at last: *Thou shalt do great things.* The princely qualities which appeared in David—his generosity in sparing Saul, his military authority in reprimanding Abner for sleeping, his care of the public good, and the signal tokens of God's presence with him—convinced Saul that he would certainly be advanced to the throne at last, according to the prophecies concerning him.

Lastly, A palliative cure being thus made of the wound, they parted friends. Saul returned to Gibeah. *David went on his way.* And, after this parting, it does not appear that ever Saul and David saw one another again.

CHAPTER 27

David was a man after God's own heart, and yet he had his faults, which are recorded, not for our imitation, but for our admonition. I. We find, to his praise, that he prudently took care of his own safety and his family's (ver. 2–4) and valiantly fought Israel's battles against the Canaanites (ver. 8–9), yet, II. We find to his dishonour, I. That he began to despair of his deliverance, ver. 1. 2. That he deserted his own country, and went to dwell in the land of the Philistines, ver. 1, 5–7. 3. That he imposed upon Achish with an equivocation, if not a lie, concerning his expedition, ver. 10–12.

Verses 1–7

I. The prevalence of David's fear, which was the effect of the weakness of his faith (*v.* 1). In a melancholy mood, he draws this dark conclusion: *I shall one day perish by the hand of Saul.* But, *O thou of little faith: wherefore dost thou doubt?* Though he had no reason to trust Saul's promises, had he not all the reason in the world to trust the promises of God? Unbelief is a sin that easily besets even good men. *Lord, increase our faith.*

II. The resolution he came to hereupon. Now that Saul had, for this time, returned to his place, he determined to take this opportunity of retiring into the Philistines' country. David was no friend to himself in taking this course. God had appointed him to set up his standard *in the land of Judah,* ch. xxii. 5. How could he expect the protection of the God of Israel if he went out of the borders of the land of Israel?

III. The kind reception he had at Gath. Achish bade him welcome, partly out of generosity, being proud of entertaining so brave a man, partly out of policy, hoping to engage him for ever to his service, and that his example would invite many more to desert and come over to him. No doubt he gave David a solemn promise of protection, which he could rely upon when he could not trust Saul's promises.

IV. Saul's desisting from the further prosecution of him (*v.* 4). Saul sought no more for him, contenting himself with his banishment.

V. David's removal from Gath to Ziklag.

1. David's request for leave to remove was prudent and very modest, *v.* 5. (1) It was really prudent. David knew what it was to be envied in the court of Saul, and had much more reason to fear in the court of Achish, and therefore declines preferment there. In a town of his own he might have the more free exercise of his religion, and keep his men better to it, and not have his righteous soul vexed, as it was at Gath, with the idolatries of the Philistines. (2) As it was presented to Achish it was very modest. He does not prescribe to him what place he should assign him. *"Why should thy servant dwell in the royal city,* to crowd thee, and disoblige those about thee?"

2. The grant which Achish made to him, upon that request, was very generous and kind (*v.* 6, 7): *Achish gave him Ziklag.* Hereby, (1) Israel recovered their ancient right; for Ziklag was in the lot of the tribe of Judah (Josh. xv. 31), and afterwards, out of that lot, was assigned, with some other cities, to Simeon, Josh. xix. 5. But either it was never subdued, or the Philistines had, in some struggle with Israel, made themselves masters of it. (2) David gained a commodious settlement, not only at a distance from Gath, but bordering upon Israel. Though we do not find that he augmented his forces at all while Saul lived (for, *ch.* xxx. 10, he had but his *six hundred* men), yet, immediately after Saul's death, that was the rendezvous of his friends.

Verses 8–12

An account of David's actions while he was in the land of the Philistines, a fierce attack he made, his success in it, and the representation he gave of it to Achish. 1. We may acquit him of injustice and cruelty in this action because those people whom he cut off were such as heaven had long since doomed to destruction. The Amalekites were to be all cut off. Probably the Geshurites and Gezrites were branches of Amalek. Saul was rejected for sparing them, David makes up the deficiency of his obedience before he succeeds him. 2. Yet we cannot acquit him of dissimulation with Achish in the account he gave him of this expedition. (1) David, it seems, was not willing that he should know the truth, and therefore spared none to carry tidings to Gath (v. 11), not because he was ashamed of what he had done as a bad thing, but because he was afraid, if the Philistines knew it, they would be apprehensive of danger to themselves or their allies by harbouring him among them and would expel him from their coasts. (2) He hid it from Achish with an equivocation not at all becoming his character. Being asked which way he had made his sally, he answered, *Against the south of Judah, v.* 13. It was true he had invaded those countries that lay south of Judah, but he made Achish believe he had invaded those that lay south in Judah, the Ziphites for example, that had once and again betrayed him; so Achish understood him, and thence inferred that he *had made his people Israel to abhor him,* and so rivetted himself in the interest of Achish.

CHAPTER 28

Preparations are herein making for that war which will put an end to the life and reign of Saul, and so make way for David to the throne. In this war, I. The Philistines are the aggressors and Achish their king makes David his confidant, ver. 1, 2. The Israelites prepare to receive them, and Saul their king makes the devil his privy counsellor, and thereby fills the measure of his iniquity. 1. The despairing condition which Saul was in, ver. 3–6. 2. The application he made to a witch, to bring him up Samuel, ver. 7–14. 3. His discourse with the apparition, ver. 15–19. The damp it struck upon him, ver. 20–25.

Verses 1–6

I. The design of the Philistines against Israel. They resolved to *fight them.*

II. The expectation Achish had of assistance from David in this war. "If I protect thee, I may demand service from thee"; and he will think himself happy if he may have such a man as David on his side. David gave him an ambiguous answer: "We will see what will be done; it will be time enough to talk of that hereafter; but *surely thou shalt know what thy servant can do*" (v. 2). Thus he keeps himself free from a promise to serve him and yet keeps up his expectation of it.

III. The drawing of the armies, on both sides, into the field (v. 4): *The Philistines pitched in Shunem,* which was in the tribe of Issachar, a great way north from their country. On some of the adjacent mountains of Gilboa Saul mustered his forces, and prepared to engage the Philistines.

IV. The terror Saul was in: He *saw the host of the Philistines,* more numerous, better armed, and in better heart, than his own were. Had he kept close to God, he needed not have been afraid at the sight of an army of Philistines; now his interest failed, his armies dwindled and looked mean, and, which was worse, his spirits failed him. Now he remembered the guilty blood of the Amalekites which he had spared, and the innocent blood of the priests which he had spilt. His sins were set in order before his eyes, which robbed him of all his courage. In this distress *Saul enquired of the Lord, v.* 6. He enquired in such a manner that it was as if he had *not enquired at all.* Therefore it is said (1 Chron. x. 14), *He enquired not of the Lord;* for he did it faintly and coldly, and with a secret design, if God did not answer him, to consult the devil. He did not enquire in faith, but

with a double unstable mind. Could he that hated and persecuted Samuel and David, who were both prophets, expect to be answered by prophets? Could he that had slain the high priest, expect to be answered by Urim? Or could he that had sinned away the Spirit of grace, expect to be answered by dreams?

V. The mention of some things that had happened a good while ago, to introduce the following story, v. 3. 1. The death of Samuel. Samuel was dead, which made the Philistines the more bold and Saul the more afraid. 2. Saul's edict against witchcraft. He had put the laws in execution against *those that had familiar spirits,* who must not be *suffered to live,* Exod. xxii. 18. Some think that he did this while he was under Samuel's influence. Perhaps when Saul was himself troubled with an evil spirit he suspected that he was bewitched, and, for that reason, cut off all that had familiar spirits. Many seem zealous against sin, when they themselves are any way hurt by it (they will inform against swearers if they swear at them, or against drunkards if in their drink they abuse them), who otherwise have no concern for the glory of God, nor any dislike of sin as sin.

Verses 7–14

I. Saul seeks for a witch, v. 7. When God *answered him not,* if he had humbled himself by repentance and persevered in seeking God, who knows but that at length he might have been entreated for him? but, since he can discern no comfort either from heaven or earth (Isa. viii. 21, 22), he resolves to knock at the gates of hell, and to see if any there will befriend him and give him advice: *Seek me a woman that has a familiar spirit, v.* 7. His servants presently recommended one to him at Endor. To her he resolves to apply. Herein he is chargeable, 1. With contempt of the God of Israel. 2. With contradiction to himself.

II. He hastens to her, but goes by night, and in disguise, only with two servants, and probably on foot, v. 8. Those that are led captive by Satan are forced, 1. To disparage themselves. Never did Saul look so mean as when he went sneaking to a sorry witch to know his fortune. 2. To dissemble. Such is the power of natural conscience that even those who do evil blush and are ashamed to do it.

III. He tells her his errand and promises her impunity. 1. All he desires of her is to bring up one from the dead. It was necromancy, or divination by the dead, that he hoped to serve his purpose by. This was expressly forbidden by the law (Deut. xviii. 11). *Bring me up him whom I shall name, v.* 8. It was generally taken for granted that souls exist after death, and that great knowledge was attributed to separate souls. But to think that any good souls would come up at the beck of an evil spirit, or that God would suffer him to reap any real advantage by a cursed diabolical invention, was very absurd. 2. She signifies her fear of the law, and her suspicion that this stranger came to draw her into a snare (v. 9): *Thou knowest what Saul has done.* How sensible she is of danger from the edict of Saul, and what care she is in to guard against it; but not at all apprehensive of the obligations of God's law and the terrors of his wrath. She considered what *Saul* had done, not what *God* had done, against such practices, and feared a snare laid for her life more than a snare laid for her soul. 3. Saul promises with an oath not to betray her, v. 10. But he promised more than he could perform when he said, *There shall no punishment happen to thee;* for he that could not secure himself could much less secure her from divine vengeance.

IV. Samuel, who was lately dead, is the person whom Saul desired to have some talk with. 1. As soon as Saul had given the witch the assurance she desired she applied to her witchcrafts, and asked, *Whom shall I bring up to thee? v.* 11. 2. Saul desires to speak with Samuel: *Bring me up Samuel.* Samuel had anointed him to the kingdom and had formerly been his faithful friend and counsellor. While Samuel was living at Ramah, not far from Gibeah of Saul, and presided there in the school of the prophets, we never read of Saul's going to him to consult him (it would have been well for him if he had)! Saul said, *Bring me up Samuel,* and the very next words are, *When the woman saw Samuel (v.* 12). The witch, upon sight of the apparition, was aware that her client was Saul (*v.* 12): "*Why hast thou deceived me* with a disguise; for thou art Saul, the very man that I am afraid of above any man?" Had she believed that it was really Samuel whom she saw, she would have had more reason to be afraid of him, who was a good prophet, than of Saul, who was a wicked king. Saul bade her not to be afraid of him and enquired *what she saw? v.* 13. *O,* says the woman, *I saw gods* (that is, a spirit) *ascending out of the earth.* Poor gods that ascend *out of the earth;* But she speaks the language of the heathen, who had their infernal deities and had them in veneration. If Saul had thought it necessary to his conversation with Samuel that the body of Samuel should be called out of the grave, he would have taken the witch with him to Ramah, where his sepulchre was; but the design was wholly upon his soul, which yet, if it became visible, was expected to appear in the usual resemblance of the body; and God permitted the devil, to answer the design that those who would not *receive the love of the truth* might be *given up to strong delusions and believe a lie.* Saul, it seems, was not permitted to see any manner of similitude himself, but he must take the woman's word for it, that she saw *an old man covered with a mantle, or robe,* the habit of a judge, which Samuel had sometimes worn. Saul, perceiving, by the woman's description, that it was Samuel, *stooped with his face to the ground* in reverence to Samuel, though he saw him not.

Verses 15–19.

The conference between Saul and Satan. Saul came in disguise (*v.* 8), but Satan soon discovered him, *v.* 12. Satan comes in disguise, in the disguise of Samuel's mantle, and Saul cannot discover him. Such is the disadvantage we labour under, in wrestling with *the rulers of the darkness of this world,* that they know us, while we are ignorant of their wiles and devices.

I. The spectre, or apparition, personating Samuel, asks why he is sent for (*v.* 15): *Why hast thou disquieted me to bring me up?*

II. Saul makes his complaint to this counterfeit Samuel, mistaking him for the true; and a most doleful complaint it is: "*I am sorely distressed,* and know not what to do, *for the Philistines make war against me.* But, alas! *God has departed from me.*" He does not, like a penitent, own the righteousness of God in this; but, like a man enraged, flies out against God as unkind and flies off from him: *Therefore I have called thee;* as if Samuel, a servant of God, would favour those whom God frowned upon, or as if a dead prophet could do him more service than the living ones.

III. It is cold comfort which this evil spirit in Samuel's mantle gives to Saul, and is manifestly intended to drive him to despair and self-murder. Had it been the true Samuel he would have told him to repent and make his peace with God, and recall David from his banishment, that he might hope in this way to find mercy with God; but, instead of that, he represents his case as helpless and hopeless, serving him as he did Judas, to whom he was first a tempter and then a tormentor, persuading him first to sell his master and then to hang himself. 1. He upbraids him with his present distress (*v.* 16). 2. He upbraids him with the anointing of David to the kingdom, *v.* 17. Yet, to make him believe that he was Samuel, the apparition affirmed that it was God who spoke by him. The devil knows how to speak with an air of religion, and can teach *false apostles to transform themselves into the apostles of Christ* and imitate their language. 3. He upbraids him with his disobedience to the command of God in not destroying the Amalekites, *v.* 18. Satan had helped him to palliate and excuse that sin when Samuel was dealing with him to bring him to repentance, but now he aggravates it, to make him despair of God's mercy.

4. He foretells his approaching ruin, *v.* 19. (1) That his army should be routed by the Philistines. (2) That he and his sons should be slain in the battle: *To-morrow thou and thy sons shall be with me,* that is, in the state of the dead, separate from the body.

Verses 20–25

How Saul received this terrible message from the ghost he consulted. He desired to be told *what he should do (v.* 15), but was only told what he had not done and what should be done to him.

I. How he sunk under the load, *v.* 20. He was indeed unfit to bear it, having *eaten nothing all the day before,* nor *that night.* He came fasting from the camp, and continued fasting; not for want of food, but for want of an appetite. *He fell all along on the earth,* as if the archers of the Philistines had already hit him, *and there was no strength in him* to bear up against these heavy tidings. Now he had enough of consulting witches, and found them miserable comforters.

II. With what difficulty he was persuaded to take so much relief as was necessary to carry him back to his post in the camp. The witch was very importunate with him to take some refreshment, that he might be able to get clear from her house, fearing that if he should be ill, especially if he should die there, she should be punished for it as a traitor, though she had escaped punishment as a witch. 1. She showed herself very importunate with him to take some refreshment. She had a fat calf at hand (and the word signifies one that was made use of in treading out the corn, and therefore could the worse be spared); this she prepared for his entertainment, *v.* 24. 2. He showed himself very averse to it: *He refused, and said, I will not eat (v.* 23). Had he laboured only under a defect of animal spirits, food might have helped him; but, alas! his case was out of the reach of such succours. What are dainty meats to a wounded conscience? 3. The woman at length, with the help of his servants, overpersuaded him, against his inclination and resolution, to take some refreshment. Saul was somewhat revived so that he and his servants *rose up and went away* before it was light (*v.* 25), that they might hasten to their business. Josephus here much admires the bravery and magnanimity of Saul, that, though he was assured he should lose both his life and honour, yet he would not desert his army, but resolutely returned to the camp, and stood ready for an engagement.

Chapter 29

In this chapter we find how David, who kept close to God, when he was in a strait was extricated and brought off by the providence of God, without any contrivance of his own. We have him, I. Marching with the Philistines, ver. 1, 2. II. Excepted against by the lords of the Philistines, ver. 3–5. III. Happily dismissed by Achish from that service which did so ill become him, and which yet he knew not how to decline, ver. 6–11.

Verses 1–5

I. The great strait that David was in. The two armies of the Philistines and the Israelites were encamped and ready to engage, v. 1. Achish, who had been kind to David, had obliged him to come himself and bring the forces he had into his service. David came accordingly, and, upon a review of the army, was found with Achish, in the post assigned him in the rear, v. 2. 1. If, when the armies engaged, he should retire, he would fall under the indelible reproach, not only of cowardice and treachery, but of base ingratitude to Achish. 2. If he should, as was expected from him, fight for the Philistines against Israel, he would incur the imputation of being an enemy to the Israel of God and a traitor to his country, would make his own people hate him, and unanimously oppose his coming to the crown. If Saul should be killed (as it proved he was) in this engagement, the fault would be laid at David's door, as if he had killed him. So that on each side there seemed to be both sin and scandal. Into this strait he brought himself by his own unadvisedness, in quitting the land of Judah. Therefore, though God might justly have left him in this difficulty, to chastise him for his folly, yet, because his heart was upright with him, he would *not suffer him to be tempted above what he was able, but with the temptation made a way for him to escape*, 1 Cor. x. 13.

II. A door opened for his deliverance out of this strait. God inclined the hearts of the princes of the Philistines to oppose his being employed in the battle, and to insist upon his being dismissed. 1. It was a proper question which they asked, upon the mustering of the forces, "*What do these Hebrews here? v. 3.* It was an honourable testimony which Achish, on this occasion gave to David. He looked upon him as a refugee, that fled from a wrongful prosecution in his own country, and had put himself under his protection, whom therefore he was obliged, in justice, to take care of, and thought he might in prudence employ. 2. Yet the princes are peremptory in it, that he must be sent home. (1) Because he had been an old enemy to the Philistines; witness what was sung in honour of his triumphs over them: *Saul slew his thousands, and David his ten thousands*, v. 5. (2) Because he might be a most dangerous enemy to them, and do them more mischief than all Saul's army could (v. 4): "He may *in the battle be an adversary to us*, and surprise us with an attack in the rear."

Verses 6-11

Achish was but one of five, though the chief, and the only one that had the title of king; accordingly, in a council of war held on this occasion, he was over-voted, and obliged to dismiss David, though he was extremely fond of him.

I. The discharge Achish gives him is very honourable, and not a final discharge, but only from the present service. 1. He signifies the great pleasure and satisfaction he had taken in him and in his conversation: *Thou art good in my sight as an angel of God*, v. 9. 2. He gives him a testimonial of his good behaviour, v. 6. It is very full and in obliging terms: "*Thou hast been upright*, and thy whole conduct has been *good in my sight*, and *I have not found evil in thee*." 3. He lays all the blame of his dismission upon the princes, who would by no means suffer him to continue in the camp. 4. He orders him to be gone early, as soon as it was light (v. 10).

II. His reception of this discourse is very complimental; but, I fear, not without some degree of dissimulation. He seemed anxious to serve him when he was at this juncture really anxious to leave him.

III. God's providence ordered it wisely and graciously for him. For, besides that the snare was broken it proved a happy hastening of him to the relief of his own city, which sorely wanted him, though he did not know it. Thus the disgrace which the lords of the Philistines put upon him proved, in more ways than one, an advantage to him. *The steps of a good man are ordered by the Lord, and he delighteth in his way.* What he does with us we know not now, but we shall know hereafter, and shall see it was all for good.

CHAPTER 30

When David was dismissed from the army of the Philistines he did not go over to the camp of Israel, but, being expelled by Saul, observed an exact neutrality, and silently retired to his own city Ziklag, leaving the armies ready to engage. I. What a melancholy posture he found the city in, all laid waste by the Amalekites, and what distress it occasioned him and his men, ver. 1–6. II. He enquired of God, and took out a commission from him (ver. 7, 8), pursued the enemy (ver. 9, 10), gained intelligence from a straggler (ver. 11–15), attacked and routed the plunderers (ver. 16, 17), and recovered all that they had carried off, ver. 18–20. III. What method he observed in the distribution of the spoil, ver. 21–31.

Verses 1-6

I. The descent which the Amalekites made upon Ziklag in David's absence. They surprised the city when it was left unguarded, plundered it, burnt it, and carried all the women and children captives, v. 1, 2. They intended, by this, to revenge the like havoc that David had lately made of them and their country, *ch. xxvii. 8.* 1. How wonderfully God inclined the hearts of these Amalekites to carry the women and children away captives, and not to kill them.

II. The confusion and consternation that David and his men were in when they found their houses in ashes and their wives and children gone into captivity. Three days' march they had from the camp of the Philistines to Ziklag, and now that they came thither weary, but hoping to find rest in their houses and joy in their families, behold a black and dismal scene was presented to them (v. 3), which made them all weep (David himself not excepted), though they were men of war, *till they had no more power to weep*, v. 4.

III. The mutiny and murmuring of David's men against him (v. 6): *David was greatly distressed*, for, in the midst of all his losses, his own people spoke of stoning him, 1. Because they looked upon him as the occasion of their calamities, by the provocation he had given the Amalekites, and his indiscretion in leaving Ziklag without a garrison in it. 2. Because now they began to despair of that preferment which they had promised themselves in following David. They hoped ere this to have been all princes; and now find themselves all beggars. Saul had driven him from his country, the Philistines had driven him from their camp, the Amalekites had plundered his city, his wives were taken prisoners, and now, to complete his woe, his own familiar friends, in whom he trusted, whom he had sheltered, and who did eat of his bread, instead of sympathising with him, *lifted up the heel against him*, and threatened to stone him. Great faith must expect such severe exercises. Things are sometimes at the worst with the church and people of God just before they begin to mend.

IV. David's pious dependence upon the divine providence and grace in this distress: *But David encouraged himself in the Lord his God*. His men fretted at their loss. *The soul of the people was bitter*, so the word is. Their own discontent and impatience added *wormwood and gall* to the affliction and misery, and made their case doubly grievous. But David bore it better, though he had more reason than any of them to lament it; they gave liberty to their passions, but he set his graces on work, and by encouraging himself in God, while they dispirited each other, he kept his spirit calm and sedate. It was David's practice, and he had the comfort of it, *What time I am afraid I will trust in thee*. When he was at his wits' end he was not at his faith's end.

Verses 7–20

I. He enquired of the Lord both concerning his duty—*Shall I pursue after this troop?* and concerning the event—*Shall I overtake them? v.* 8. David had no room to doubt but that his war against these Amalekites was just, and he had an inclination strong enough to set upon them when it was for the recovery of that which was dearest to him in this world; and yet he would not go about it without asking counsel of God, thereby owning his dependence upon God and submission to him.

II. He went himself in person, and took with him all the force he had in pursuit of the Amalekites, *v.* 9, 10. See how quickly the mutiny among the soldiers was quelled by his patience and faith. When they *spoke of stoning him* (*v.* 6), if he had spoken of hanging them, or had ordered that the ringleaders of the faction should immediately have their heads struck off, though it would have been just, yet it might have been of pernicious consequence to his interest in this critical juncture. All his men were willing to go along with him in pursuit of the Amalekites, and he needed them all; but he was forced to drop a third part of them by the way; 200 out of 600 were so fatigued with their long march, that they could not pass the brook Besor. 1. A great trial of David's faith, whether he could go on, in dependence upon the word of God, when so many of his men failed him. When we are disappointed and discouraged in our expectations from second causes, then to go on with cheerfulness, confiding in the divine power, this is giving glory to God, by believing against hope, in hope. 2. A great instance of David's tenderness to his men, that he would by no means urge them beyond their strength, though the case itself was so very urgent. The son of David thus considers the frame of his followers, who are not all alike strong and vigorous in their spiritual pursuits and conflicts; but, where we are weak, there he is kind; nay, more, there he is strong, 2 Cor. xii. 9, 10.

III. Providence threw one in their way that gave them intelligence of the enemy's motions, and guided theirs; a poor Egyptian lad, scarcely alive. 1. His master's cruelty to him. He had got out of him all the service he could, and when the lad fell sick he barbarously left him to perish in the field. Justly did Providence make this poor servant, that was thus basely abused, instrumental towards the destruction of a whole army of Amalekites and his master among the rest. 2. David's compassion to him. Though he had reason to think he was one of those that had helped to destroy Ziklag, yet, finding him in distress, be generously relieved him, not only with *bread and water* (*v.* 11), but with *figs and raisins, v.* 12. Though the Israelites were in haste, and had no great plenty for themselves, yet they would not *forbear to deliver one that was drawn unto death*, nor say, *Behold, we knew it not*, Prov. xxiv. 11, 12. 3. The intelligence David received from this poor Egyptian when he had come to himself. He gave an account concerning his party. (1) What they had done (*v.* 14): *We made an invasion*, &c. (2) Whither they had gone, *v.* 15. This he promised David to inform him of upon condition he would spare his life and protect him from his master, who, if he could hear of him again (he thought), would add cruelty to cruelty. Such an opinion this poor Egyptian had of the obligation of an oath that he desired no greater security for his life than this: *Swear unto me by God*, not by the gods of Egypt or Amalek, but by the one supreme God.

IV. David, being directed to the place where they lay, securely celebrating their triumphs, fell upon them, and, as he used to pray, *saw his desire upon his enemies.* 1. The spoilers were cut off. The Amalekites, finding the booty was rich were making themselves very merry with it, *v.* 16. In this posture David surprised them, which made the conquest of them, and the blow he gave them, the more easy. 2. The spoil was recovered and brought off, and nothing was lost, but a great deal gotten. (1) They retrieved all their own (*v.* 18, 19): *David rescued his two wives*; this is mentioned particularly, because this pleased David more than all the rest of his achievements. (2) They took all that belonged to the Amalekites besides (*v.* 20): *Flocks and herds.* Those who lately spoke of stoning him now cried him up, because they got by him more than they had then lost. Thus are the world and its sentiments governed by interest.

Verses 21–31

An account of the distribution of the spoil which was taken from the Amalekites. David disposed of the spoil as one that knew that justice and charity must govern us in the use we make of whatever we have in this world.

I. David was just and kind to those who abode by the stuff. He saluted them; *he asked them of peace* (so the word is), bade them be of good cheer, they should lose nothing by staying behind; for of this they seemed afraid, as perhaps David saw by their countenances.

1. There were those that opposed their coming in to share in the spoil; some of David's soldiers, probably the same that spoke of stoning him, spoke now of defrauding their brethren; they are called wicked men and *men of Belial, v.* 22. These made a motion that the 200 men who abode by the stuff should only have their wives and children given them, but none of their goods.

2. David would by no means admit this, but ordered that those who tarried behind should come in for an equal share in the spoils with those that went to the battle, *v.* 23, 24. God's mercy to us should make us merciful to one another. It was true they tarried behind; but, [1] It was not for want of goodwill to the cause or to their brethren, but because they had not strength to keep up with them. [2] Though they tarried behind now, they had formerly engaged many times in battle and done their part as well as the best of their brethren. [3] Even now they did good service, for they abode by the stuff, to guard that which somebody must take care of, else that might have fallen into the hands of some other enemy. Every post of service is not alike a post of honour, yet those that are in any way serviceable to the common interest, though in a meaner station, ought to share in the common advantages, as in the natural body every member has its use and therefore has its share of the nourishment. Thus he settled the matter for the time to come, made it a statute of his kingdom (a statute of distributions, *primo Davidus—in the first year of David's reign*), an ordinance of war (*v.* 25), that *as his part is that goes down to the battle*, and hazards his life in the high places of the field, so shall his be that guards the carriages.

II. David was generous and kind to all his friends. When he had given every one his own with interest there was a considerable overplus; probably the spoil of the tents of the Amalekites consisted much in plate and jewels (Judges viii. 24, 26), and these he thought fit to make presents of to his friends, even the *elders of Judah, v.* 26. Several places are here named to which he sent of these presents, all of them in or near the tribe of Judah. The first place named is *Bethel.* Thither David sent the first and best, to those that attended there, for his sake who is the first and best. *Hebron* is named last (*v.* 31), the largest share, having an eye upon that place as fittest for his head-quarters, 2 Sam. ii. 1. In David's sending these presents observe, 1. His generosity. He aimed not to enrich himself, but to serve his country. It becomes gracious souls to be generous. 2. His gratitude. He sent presents to *all the places where he and his men were wont to haunt* (v. 31), that is, to all that he had received kindness from, that had sheltered him and sent him intelligence or provisions. 3. His piety. He calls his present *a blessing*; for no present we give to our friends will be a comfort to them but as it is made so by the blessing of God: it intimates that his prayers for them accompanied his present. 4. His policy. He sent these presents among his countrymen to engage them to be ready to appear for him upon his accession to the throne, which he now saw at hand.

CHAPTER 31

In this chapter we have Saul conquered and worse than a captive. The very same day, perhaps, that David was triumphing over the Amalekites, were the Philistines triumphing over Saul. One is set over against the other, that men may see what comes of trusting in God and what comes of forsaking him. We left Saul ready to engage the Philistines, with a shaking hand and an aching heart, having had his doom read him from hell, which he would not regard when it was read him from heaven. I. His army routed, ver. 1. II. His three sons slain, ver. 2. III. Himself wounded (ver. 3), and slain by his own hand, ver. 4. The death of his armour-bearer (ver. 5) and all his men, ver. 6. IV. His country possessed by the Philistines, ver. 7. His camp plundered, and his dead body deserted, ver. 8. His fall triumphed in, ver. 9. His body publicly exposed (ver. 10) and with difficulty rescued by the men of Jabesh-Gilead, ver. 11–13. Thus fell the man that was rejected of God.

Verses 1–7

The day of recompense has now come, in which Saul should descend into battle and perish, *ch.* xxvi. 10.

I. He sees his soldiers fall about him, v. 1. The best of the troops were put into disorder, and multitudes slain.

II. He sees his sons fall before him. The victorious Philistines pressed most forcibly upon the king of Israel and those about him. His sons were next him, and they were all three slain before his face. Jonathan, that wise, valiant, good man, who was as much David's friend as Saul was his enemy, yet falls with the rest. Duty to his father would not permit him to stay at home, or to retire when the armies engaged. If the family must fall, Jonathan, that is one of it, must fall with it. He would hereby make David's way to the crown the more clear and open. For, though Jonathan himself would have cheerfully resigned all his title yet it is very probable that many of the people would have made use of his name for the support of the house of Saul, or at least would have come in but slowly to David. If Ish-bosheth (who was now left at home as one unfit for action, and so escaped) had so many friends, what would Jonathan have had, who had been the darling of the people and had never forfeited their favour? This would have embarrassed David.

III. Saul is sorely wounded by the Philistines and then slain by his own hand. The archers hit him (v. 3), so that he could neither fight nor fly, and therefore must inevitably fall into their hands. 1. He was desirous to die by the hand of his own servant rather than by the hand of the Philistines, lest they should abuse him as they had abused Samson. As he lived, so he died, proud and jealous, and a terror to himself and all about him. Those are in a deplorable condition indeed who leap into a hell before them, to escape a hell within them. 2. When he could not obtain that favour he became his own executioner. His armour-bearer would not run him through, for, having a profound reverence for the king his master, he could not do him any hurt

IV. His armour-bearer who refused to kill him refused not to die with him, but *fell likewise upon his sword*, v. 5. The Jews say that Saul's armour-bearer was Doeg.

V. The country was put into such confusion by the rout of Saul's army that the inhabitants of the neighbouring cities (*on that side Jordan*, as it might be read) quitted them, and the Philistines, for a time, had possession of them, till things were settled in Israel (v. 7).

Verses 8–13

The scripture makes no mention of the souls of Saul and his sons, but of their bodies only.

I. How they were basely abused by the Philistines. The day after the battle, when they had recovered their fatigue, they came to strip the slain, and, among the rest, found the bodies of Saul and his three sons, v. 8. Saul might have saved himself the fatal thrust and have made his escape; for the pursuers (in fear of whom he slew himself) came not to the place where he was till the next day. Finding Saul's body, 1. They cut off his head. They intended it in general, for a reproach to Israel, who promised themselves that a crowned and an anointed head would save them from the Philistines, and a particular reproach to Saul, who was taller by the head than other men (which perhaps he was wont to boast of), but was now shorter by the head. 2. They stripped him of his armour (v. 9), and sent that to be set up as a trophy of their victory, in the house of Ashtaroth their goddess (v. 10); and we are told, 1 Chron. x. 10, that they fastened his head in the temple of Dagon. 3. They sent expresses throughout their country, and ordered public notice to be given in the houses of their gods of the victory they had obtained (v. 9), that public rejoicings might be made and thanks given to their gods. 4. They fastened his body and the bodies of his sons (as appears, v. 12) to the wall of *Beth-shan*, a city that lay not far from Gilboa and very near to the river Jordan. Hither the dead bodies were dragged and here hung up in chains, to be devoured by the birds of prey.

II. How they were bravely rescued by the men of Jabesh-Gilead. Little more than the river Jordan lay between Beth-shan and Jabesh-Gilead, and Jordan was in that place passable by its fords; a bold adventure was therefore made by the valiant men of that city, who in the night passed the river, took down the dead bodies, and gave them decent burial, v. 11, 13. This they did, 1. Out of a common concern for the honour of Israel, or the land of Israel, which ought not to be defiled by the exposing of any dead bodies, and especially of the crown of Israel, which was thus profaned by the uncircumcised. 2. Out of a particular sense of gratitude to Saul, for his zeal and forwardness to rescue them from the Ammonites when he first came to the throne, *ch.* xi. They buried the bodies, when, by burning over them, they had sweetened them (or, if they burnt them, they buried the bones and ashes), under a tree, which serves for a gravestone and monument. They *fasted seven days*; thus they lamented the death of Saul and the present distracted state of Israel, and perhaps joined prayers with their fasting for the re-establishment of their shattered state.

This book began with the birth of Samuel, but now it ends with the burial of Saul, the comparing of which two together will teach us to prefer the honour that comes from God before any of the honours which this world pretends to have the disposal of.

THE SECOND
BOOK OF SAMUEL

This book is the history of the reign of king David. We had in the foregoing book an account of his designation to the government, and his struggles with Saul, which ended at length in the death of his persecutor. This book begins with his accession to the throne, and is entirely taken up with the affairs of the government during the forty years he reigned, and therefore is entitled by the LXX. *The Third Book of the Kings.* It gives us an account of David's triumphs and his troubles. I. His triumphs over the house of Saul (*ch.* i.–iv.), over the Jebusites and Philistines (*ch.* v.), at the bringing up of the ark (*ch.* vi. and vii), over the neighbouring nations that opposed him (*ch.* viii.–x.); and so far the history is what we might expect from David's character. But his cloud has a dark side. II. We have his troubles, the causes of them, his sin in the matter of Uriah (*ch.* xi. and xii.), the troubles themselves from the sin of Amnon (*ch.* xiii.), the rebellion of Absalom (*ch.* xiv.–xix.), and of Sheba (*ch.* xx.), and the plague in Israel for his numbering the people (*ch.* xxiv.), besides the famine of the Gibeonites, *ch.* xxi. His song we have (*ch.* xxii.), and his words and worthies, *ch.* xxiii. Many things in his history are very instructive but for the hero it must be confessed that his honour shines brighter in his Psalms than in his Annals.

CHAPTER 1

We are now to look towards the rising sun, and to enquire where David is, and what he is doing. In this chapter we have, I. Tidings brought him to Ziklag of the death of Saul and Jonathan, by an Amalekite, who undertook to give him a particular narrative of it, ver. 1–10. II. David's sorrowful reception of these tidings, ver. 11, 12. III. Justice done upon the messenger, who boasted that he had helped Saul to dispatch himself, ver. 13–16. IV. An elegy which David penned upon this occasion, ver. 17–27.

Verses 1–10

I. David settling again in Ziklag, his own city, after he had rescued his family and friends out of the hands of the Amalekites (*v.* 1): He *abode in Ziklag.* There he was ready to receive those that came into his interests; not men in distress and debt, as his first followers were, but persons of quality in their country, *mighty men, men of war,* and *captains of thousands* (as we find, 1 Chron. xii. 1, 8, 20); such came day by day to him.

II. Intelligence brought him thither of the death of Saul. It was strange that he did not leave some spies about the camp, to bring him early notice of the issue of the engagement, a sign that he desired not Saul's woeful day, nor was impatient to come to the throne. 1. The messenger presents himself to David as an express, in the posture of a mourner for the deceased prince and a subject to the succeeding one. He came with his clothes rent, and made obeisance to David (*v.* 2), pleasing himself with the fancy that he had the honour to be the first that did him homage as his sovereign, but it proved he was the first that received from him sentence of death as his judge. 2. He gives him a general account of the issue of the battle and he told him very distinctly that the army of Israel was routed, many slain, and, among the rest, Saul and Jonathan, *v.* 4. He named only Saul and Jonathan, because he knew David would be most solicitous to know their fate; for Saul was the man whom he most feared and Jonathan the man whom he most loved. 3. He gives him a more particular account of the death of Saul. He therefore asks, *How knowest thou that Saul and Jonathan are dead?* in answer to which the young man tells him a very ready story, putting it past doubt that Saul was dead, for he himself had been not only an eye-witness of his death, but an instrument of it. He says nothing, in his narrative, of the death of Jonathan, but accounts only for Saul, thinking (as David understood it well enough, *ch.* iv. 10) that he should be welcome for that, and rewarded as one that brought good tidings.

The account he gives of this matter is, (1) Very particular. That he happened to go to the place where Saul was (*v.* 6), that he found Saul endeavouring to run himself through with his own spear, none of his attendants being willing to do it for him. He therefore called this stranger to him (*v.* 7). Understanding that he was an Amalekite (neither one of his subjects nor one of his enemies), he begs this favour from him (*v.* 9): *Stand upon me, and slay me.* "Hereupon," saith our young man, "*I stood upon him, and slew him*" (*v.* 10) at which word, perhaps, he observed David look upon him with some show of displeasure, and therefore he excuses himself in the next words: "*For I was sure he could not live.*" (2) It is doubtful whether this story be true. But most interpreters think that it was false, and that, though he might happen to be present, yet he was not assisting in the death of Saul, but told David so in expectation that he would reward him for it, as having done him a piece of good service. (3) However he produced that which was proof sufficient of the death of Saul, the crown that was upon his head and the bracelet that was on his arm. These fell into the hands of this Amalekite. The tradition of the Jews is that this Amalekite was the son of Doeg, and that Doeg, who they suppose was Saul's armour-bearer, before he slew himself gave Saul's crown and bracelet (the ensigns of his royalty) to his son, and bade him carry them to David, to curry favour with him.

Verses 11–16

I. David's reception of these tidings. So far was he from falling into a transport of joy, as the Amalekite expected, that he fell into a passion of weeping, *rent his clothes* (*v.* 11), *mourned and fasted* (*v.* 12), not only for his people Israel and Jonathan his friend, but for Saul his enemy. This he did, not only as a man of honour, but as a good man and a man of conscience, that had forgiven the injuries Saul had done him and bore him no malice. He knew it, before his son wrote it (Prov. xxiv. 17, 18), that if we *rejoice when our enemy falls the Lord sees it, and it displeases him;* and that *he who is glad at calamities shall not go unpunished,* Prov. xvii. 5. By what he did when he heard of Saul's death, we may perceive that his natural temper was very tender, and that he was kindly affected even to those that hated him.

II. The reward he gave to him that brought him the tidings. Instead of preferring him, he put him to death, judged him out of his own mouth, as a murderer of his prince, and ordered him to be forth-with executed for the same. David herein did not do unjustly. The man was an Amalekite. This, lest he should have mistaken it in his narrative, he made him own a second time, *v.* 13. He did himself confess the crime, so that the evidence was, by the consent of all laws, sufficient to convict him; for every man is presumed to make the best of himself. If he did as he said, he deserved to die for treason (*v.* 14), doing that which, it is probable, he heard Saul's own armour-bearer refuse to do; if not, yet by boasting of it to David, he showed what opinion he had of him, that he would rejoice in it, as one altogether like himself, which was an intolerable affront to him who had himself once and again refused to *stretch forth his hand against the Lord's anointed.*

Verses 17–27

When David had rent his clothes, mourned, and wept, and fasted, for the death of Saul, one would think he had made full payment of the debt of honour he owed to his memory; yet this is not all: we have here a poem he wrote on that occasion. By this elegy he designed both to express his own sorrow for this great calamity and to impress the like on the minds of others, who ought to lay it to heart. Those might gain information by poems that would not read history.

I. The orders David gave with this elegy (*v.* 18): *He bade them teach the children of Judah the use of the bow,* either, 1. The bow used in war. David hereby showed his authority over and concern for the armies of Israel, and set himself to rectify the errors of the former reign. But we find that the companies which had now come to David to Ziklag were armed with bows (1 Chron. xii. 2); therefore, 2. Some understand it either of some musical instru-ment called *a bow* (to which he would have the mournful ditties sung) or of the elegy itself. *He bade them teach the children of Judah Kesheth, the bow,* that is, this song, which was so entitled for the sake of Jonathan's bow, the achievements of which are here celebrated. It is *written in the book of Jasher,* there it was kept upon record, and thence transcribed into this history. That book was probably a collection of state-poems; what is said to be written in that book (Josh. x. 13) is also poetical, a fragment of an his-torical poem.

II. The elegy itself. It is not a divine hymn, nor given by inspiration of God to be used in divine service, nor is there any mention of God in it; but it is a human composition, and therefore was inserted, not in the book of Psalms but in the book of Jasher, which, being only a collection of common poems, is long since lost. This elegy proves David to have been,

1. A man of an excellent spirit, in four things:—

(1) He was very generous to Saul, his sworn enemy. [1] He conceals his faults; and, though there was no preventing their appearance in his history, yet they should not appear in this elegy. Charity teaches us to make the best we can of everybody and to say nothing of those of whom we can say no good, especially when they are gone. *De mortuis nil nisi bonum—Say nothing but good concerning the dead.* [2] He celebrates that which was praiseworthy in him. That he was *anointed with oil* (*v.* 21), the sacred oil, which signified his elevation to, and qualification for, the government. That he was a man of war, a *mighty man* (*v.* 19–21), that he had often been vic-torious over the enemies of Israel and *vexed them whithersoever he turned,* 1 Sam. xiv. 47. Though his sun set under a cloud, time was when it shone brightly. That take him with Jonathan he was a man of a very agreeable temper, that recommended himself to the affections of his subjects (*v.* 23): *Saul and Jonathan were lovely and pleasant.* Jonathan was always so,

and Saul was so as long as he concurred with him. Take them together, and in the pursuit of the enemy, never were men more bold, more brave; they were *swifter than eagles and stronger than lions.* They were lovely and pleasant one to another, Jonathan a dutiful son, Saul an affectionate father; and therefore dear to each other in their lives, and *in their death they were not divided,* but kept close together in the stand they made against the Philistines, and fell together in the same cause.

(2) He was very grateful to Jonathan. He lamented him for what he had been: "*Very pleasant hast thou been unto me;* but that pleasantness is now over, and *I am distressed for thee.*" He had reason to say that Jonathan's love to him was wonderful; surely never was the like, for a man to love one who he knew was to take the crown over his head, and to be so faithful to his rival. [1] That nothing is more delightful in this world than a true friend, that is wise and good, that kindly receives and returns our affection, and is faithful to us in all our true interests. [2] That nothing is more distressful than the loss of such a friend; it is parting with a piece of one's self. The more we love the more we grieve.

(3) He was deeply concerned for the honour of God; for this is what he has an eye to when he fears lest *the daughters of the uncircumcised,* that are out of covenant with God, should triumph over Israel, and the God of Israel, *v.* 20. Good men are touched in a very sensible part by the reproaches of those that reproach God.

(4) He was deeply concerned for the public welfare. It was the beauty of Israel that was slain (*v.* 19) and the honour of the public that was disgraced. David hoped God would make him instrumental to repair those losses and yet laments them.

2. A man of a fine imagination, as well as a wise and holy man. (1) The embargo he would fain lay upon fame is elegant (*v.* 20): *Tell it not in Gath.* It grieved him to the heart to think that it would be proclaimed in the cities of the Philistines. (2) The curse he entails on the mountains of Gilboa, the theatre on which this tragedy was acted: *Let there be no dew upon you, nor fields of offerings, v.* 21. This is the reproach David fastens upon the mountains of Gilboa, which, having been stained with royal blood, thereby forfeited celestial dews.

CHAPTER 2

Saul is dead, now therefore David arises. I. By direction from God he went up to Hebron, and was there anointed king, ver. 1–4. II. He returned thanks to the men of Jabesh-Gilead for burying Saul, ver. 5–7. III. Ish-bosheth, the son of Saul, is set up in opposition to him, ver. 8–11. IV. A warm encounter happens between David's party and Ish-bosheth's, in which, 1. Twelve of each side engaged hand to hand and were all slain, ver. 12–16. 2. Saul's party was beaten, ver. 17. 3. Asahel, on David's side, was slain by Abner, ver. 18–23. 4. Joab, at Abner's request, sounds a retreat, ver. 24–28. 5. Abner makes the best of his way (ver. 29), and the loss on both sides is computed, ver. 30–32. So that here we have an account of a civil war in Israel, which, in process of time, ended in the complete settlement of David on the throne.

Verses 1–7

When Saul and Jonathan were dead, though David knew himself anointed to be king, yet he did not immediately send messengers through all the coasts of Israel to summon all people to come in and swear allegiance to him. Many had come in to his assistance from several tribes while he continued at Ziklag, as we find (1 Chron. xii. 1–22), and with such a force he might have come in by conquest. But he that will rule with meekness will not rise with violence.

I. The direction he sought and had from God in this critical juncture, *v.* 1. He doubted not of success, yet he used proper means, both divine and human. 1. David, according to the precept, *acknowledged*

God in his way. He enquired of the Lord by the breastplate of judgment, which Abiathar brought to him. We must apply to God not only when we are in distress, but even when the world smiles upon us and second causes work in favour of us. His enquiry was, *Shall I go up to any of the cities of Judah?* Though Ziklag be in ruins, he will not quit it without direction from God. "If I stir hence, *Shall I go to one of the cities of Judah?*" 2. God, according to the promise, directed his path, bade him go up, told him whither, unto Hebron, a priests' city, one of the cities of refuge, so it was to David, and an intimation that God himself would be to him a little sanctuary.

II. The care he took of his family and friends in his removal to Hebron. 1. He took his wives with him (*v.* 2), that, as they had been companions with him in tribulation, they might be so in the kingdom. It does not appear that as yet he had any children; his first was born in Hebron, *ch.* iii. 2. 2. He took his friends and followers with him, *v.* 3. They had accompanied him in his wanderings, and therefore, when he gained a settlement, they settled with him.

III. The honour done him by the men of Judah: They *anointed him king over the house of Judah, v.* 4. The tribe of Judah had often stood by itself more than any other of the tribes. In Saul's time it was numbered by itself as a distinct body (1 Sam. xv. 4) and those of this tribe had been accustomed to act separately. They did so now; yet they did it for themselves only; they did not pretend to anoint him king *over all Israel* (as Judg. ix. 22), but only *over the house of Judah.* He was first anointed king in *reversion,* then *in possession* of one tribe only, and at last of all the tribes. Thus the kingdom of the Messiah, the Son of David, is set up by degrees; he is Lord of all by divine designation, but *we see not yet all things put under him,* Heb. ii. 8.

IV. The respectful message he sent to the men of Jabesh-Gilead, to return them thanks for their kindness to Saul. Still he studies to honour the memory of his predecessor, and thereby to show that he was far from aiming at the crown from any principle of ambition or enmity to Saul, but purely because he was called of God to it. "Saul was your lord," says David, "and therefore you did well to show him this kindness and do him this honour." He prays to God to bless them for it, and to recompense it to them: *Blessed are you. The Lord show kindness and truth to you* (*v.* 6). He promises to make them amends for it: *I also will requite you.* He does not turn them over to God for a recompense that he may excuse himself from rewarding them. Good wishes are good things, and instances of gratitude, but they are too cheap to be rested in where there is an ability to do more.

Verses 8–17

I. A rivalship between two kings—David, whom God made king, and Ish-bosheth, whom Abner made king. One would have thought David would come to the throne without any opposition, since all Israel knew how manifestly God had designated him to it; but such a spirit of contradiction is there, in the devices of men, to the counsels of God, that such a weak and silly thing as Ish-bosheth, who was not thought fit to go with his father to the battle, shall yet be thought fit to succeed him in the government, rather than David shall come peaceably to it. 1. Abner was the person who set up Ish-bosheth in competition with David, perhaps in his zeal for the lineal succession, or rather in his affection to his own family and relations (for he was Saul's uncle), and because he had no other way to secure to himself the post of honour he was in, as captain of the host. Ish-bosheth would never have set up himself if Abner had not set him up, and made a tool of him to serve his own purposes. 2. Mahanaim, the place where he first

made his claim, was on the other side Jordan, where it was thought David had the least interest, and being at a distance from his forces they might have time to strengthen themselves. But, having set up his standard there, the unthinking people of all the tribes of Israel (that is, the generality of them) submitted to him (*v.* 9), and Judah only was entirely for David.

II. An encounter between their two armies.

1. It does not appear that either side brought their whole force into the field, for the slaughter was but small, *v.* 30, 31. It is likely, David would not suffer them to act offensively, choosing rather to wait till the thing would do itself or rather till God would do it for him, without the effusion of Israelitish blood. The men of Israel stand neuter, and sit down tamely under Ish-bosheth, for so many years. *Wise men, mighty men, men of valour, expert in war,* and not of double heart, and yet for seven years together, most of them seemed indifferent in whose hand the public administration was.

2. In this battle Abner was the aggressor. David sat still to see how the matter would fall, but the house of Saul, and Abner at the head of it, gave the challenge.

The seat of the war was Gibeon. Abner chose it because it was in the lot of Benjamin, where Saul had the most friends; yet, since he offered battle, Joab, David's general, would not decline it, but there joined issue with him, and met him *by the pool of Gibeon, v.* 13. David's cause, being built upon God's promise, feared not the disadvantages of the ground. The pool between gave both sides time to deliberate. The engagement was at first proposed by Abner, and accepted by Joab, to be between twelve and twelve of a side. (1) It should seem this trial of skill began in sport. Abner made the motion (*v.* 14): *Let the young men arise and play before us,* as gladiators. He meant, "Let them *fight* before us," when he said, "Let them *play* before us." Joab, having been bred up under David, had so much wisdom as not to make such a proposal, yet had not resolution enough to resist and gainsay it when another made it; for he stood upon a point of honour, and thought it a blemish to his reputation to refuse a challenge, and therefore said, *Let them arise.* Twelve of each side were accordingly called out as champions to enter the lists, a double jury of life and death, and the champions on Abner's side seem to have been most forward, for they took the field first (*v.* 15). But, (2) However it began, it ended in blood (*v.* 16): They thrust *every man his sword into his fellow's side* (spurred on by honour, not by enmity); so they *fell down together,* that is, all the twenty-four were slain. The wonderful obstinacy of both sides was remembered in the name given to the place: *Helkath-hazzurim— the field of rocky men,* men that were not only strong in body, but of firm and unshaken constancy, that stirred not at the sight of death. The whole army at length engaged, and Abner's forces were routed, *v.* 17.

Verses 18–24

The contest between Abner and Asahel. Asahel, the brother of Joab and cousin-german to David, was one of the principal commanders of David's forces, and was famous for swiftness in running: he was *as light of foot as a wild roe* (*v.* 18); this he got the name of by swift pursuing, not swift flying. He was not comparable to Abner as a skilful experienced soldier.

I. How rash he was in aiming to make Abner his prisoner. He pursued after him, and no other, *v.* 19. Proud of his relation to David and Joab, his own swiftness, and the success of his party, no less a trophy of victory would now serve the young warrior than Abner himself, either slain or bound, which he thought would put an end to the war and effectually open David's way to the throne.

II. How generous Abner was in giving him notice of the danger he exposed himself to, and advising him not to *meddle to his own hurt*, 2 Chron. xxv. 19. 1. He bade him content himself with a less prey (*v.* 21). 2. He begged of him not to put him upon the necessity of slaying him in his own defence, which he was very loth to do, but must do rather than be slain by him, *v.* 22.

III. How fatal Asahel's rashness was to him. He refused to turn aside, thinking that Abner spoke so courteously because he feared him; but what came of it? Abner, as soon as he came up to him, gave him his death's wound with a back stroke (*v.* 23): *He smote him with the hinder end of his spear*, from which he feared no danger. Joab and Abishai, instead of being disheartened were exasperated by it, pursued Abner with so much the more fury (*v.* 24), and overtook him at last about sunset, when the approaching night would oblige them to retire.

Verses 25–32

I. Abner, being conquered, meanly begs for a cessation of arms. He rallied the remains of his forces on the top of a hill (*v.* 25), as if he would have made head again, but becomes a humble supplicant to Joab for a little breathing-time, *v.* 26. He that was most forward to fight was the first that had enough of it. He that made a jest of bloodshed (*Let the young men arise and play before us, v.* 14) is now shocked at it, when he finds himself on the losing side. Then it was but playing with the sword; now, *Shall the sword devour for ever?* Now he can appeal to Joab himself concerning the miserable consequences of a civil war: *Knowest thou not that it will be bitterness in the latter end?* Now he begs of Joab to sound a retreat, and pleads that they were brethren, who ought not thus to bite and devour one another. How easy it is for men to use reason when it makes for them who would not use it if it made against them. If Abner had been the conqueror, we should not have had him complaining of the voraciousness of the sword and the miseries of a civil war, nor pleading that both sides were brethren.

II. Joab, though a conqueror, generously grants it, and sounds a retreat, knowing very well his master's mind and how averse he was to the shedding of blood.

III. The armies being separated, both retired to the places whence they came, and both marched in the night, Abner to Mahanaim, on the other side Jordan (*v.* 29), and Joab to Hebron, where David was, *v.* 32. Asahel's funeral is here mentioned; the rest they buried in the field of battle, but he was carried to Bethlehem, and buried in the sepulchre of his father, *v.* 32.

CHAPTER 3

I. The gradual advance of David's interest, ver. 1. II. The building up of his family, ver. 2–5. III. Abner's quarrel with Ish-bosheth, and his treaty with David, ver. 6–12. IV. The preliminaries settled, ver. 13–16. V. Abner's undertaking and attempt to bring Israel over to David, ver. 17–21. VI. The treacherous murder of Abner by Joab, when he was carrying on this matter, ver. 22–27. VII. David's great concern and trouble for the death of Abner, ver. 28–39.

Verses 1–6

I. The struggle that David had with the house of Saul before his settlement in the throne was completed, *v.* 1. The length of this war tried the faith and patience of David. The house of Saul waxed weaker and weaker, lost places, lost men, sunk in its reputation, and was foiled in every engagement. But the house of David grew stronger. Many deserted the declining cause of Saul's house. The contest between grace and corruption in the hearts of be-

lievers, who are sanctified but in part, may fitly be compared to this recorded here. There is a long war between them, the flesh lusting against the spirit and the spirit against the flesh; but, as the work of sanctification is carried on, corruption, like the house of Saul, grows weaker and weaker; while grace, like the house of David, grows stronger and stronger, till it come to a perfect man, and judgment be brought forth unto victory.

II. The increase of his own house. Here is an account of six sons he had by six several wives, in the seven years he reigned in Hebron. It was David's fault thus to multiply wives, contrary to the law (Deut. xvii. 17), and it was a bad example to his successors. We read not that any of these sons came to be famous (three of them were infamous, Amnon, Absalom, and Adonijah). His son by Abigail is called *Chileab* (*v.* 3), whereas (1 Chron. iii. 1) he is called *Daniel*. His first name was *Daniel—God has judged me* (namely, against Nabal), but David's enemies reproached him, and said, "It is Nabal's son, and not David's," as he grew up, he became, in his countenance and features, extremely like David, upon which he gave him the name of *Chileab*, which signifies, *like his father*, or the father's picture. Absalom's mother is said to be the daughter of Talmai, king of Geshur, a heathen prince. Perhaps David thereby hoped to strengthen his interest, but the issue of the marriage was one that proved his grief and shame. The last is called *David's wife*, which therefore, some think, was Michal, his first and most rightful wife, called here by another name: and, though she had no child after she mocked David, she might have had before.

Verses 7–21

I. Abner breaks with Ish-bosheth, upon a little provocation which Ish-bosheth unadvisedly gave him. 1. Ish-bosheth accused Abner of no less a crime than debauching one of his father's concubines, *v.* 7. 2. Abner resented the charge very strongly. He lets Ish-bosheth know, (1) That he scorned to be reproached with it by him, and would not take reproof at his hands. Proud men will not bear to be reproved, especially by those whom they think they have obliged. (2) That he would certainly be revenged on him, *v.* 9, 10. With the utmost degree of arrogance and insolence he lets him know that, as he had raised him up, so he could pull him down again and would do it. Abner's ambition made him zealous for Ish-bosheth, and now his revenge made him as zealous for David. If he had sincerely regarded God's promise to David, and acted with an eye to that, he would have been steady and uniform in his counsels. If Ish-bosheth had had the spirit of a man, especially of a prince, he might have answered him that his merits were the aggravation of his crimes, that he would not be served by so base a man. But he was conscious to himself of his own weakness, and therefore said not a word.

II. Abner treats with David. We must suppose that he began to grow weary of Ish-bosheth's cause, and sought an opportunity to desert it. He *sent messengers to David*, to tell him that he was at his service. Note, God can find out ways to make those serviceable to the kingdom of Christ who yet have no sincere affection for it and who have vigorously set themselves against it. Enemies are sometimes made a footstool, not only to be trodden upon, but to ascend by. The earth helped the woman.

III. David enters into a treaty with Abner, but upon condition that he shall procure him the restitution of Michal his wife, *v.* 13. 1. David showed the sincerity of his conjugal affection to his first and most rightful wife; neither her marrying another, nor his, had alienated him from her. Many waters could not quench that love. 2. He testified his respect to the house of Saul. He cannot be pleased with the honours of the throne unless he have Michal, Saul's daughter, to share with him in them, so far is he from bearing any malice to the family of his enemy. Abner sent him word that he must apply to Ish-bosheth, which he did (*v.* 14), pleading that he had purchased her at a dear rate, and she was wrongfully taken from him. Ish-bosheth durst not deny his demand, but took her from Phaltiel, to whom Saul had married her (*v.* 15), and Abner conducted her to David, not doubting but that then he should be doubly welcome when he brought him a wife in one hand and a crown in the other. Her latter husband was loth to part with her, but there was no remedy: he must thank himself: for when he took her he knew that another had a right to her. If any disagreement has separated husband and wife, as they expect the blessing of God let them be reconciled, and come together again; let all former quarrels be forgotten, and let them live together in love, according to God's holy ordinance.

IV. Abner uses his interest with the elders of Israel to bring them over to David, knowing that whichever way they went the common people would follow of course. No man can pretend to greater personal merit than David nor to less than Ish-bosheth. You have tried them both, *Detir digniori—Give the crown to him that best deserves it.* Let David be your king. God, having promised, by David's hand, to save Israel, it is both your duty, in compliance with God's will, and your interest, in order to your victories over your enemies, to submit to him; and it is the greatest folly in the world to oppose him.

V. David concludes the treaty with Abner. Abner reported to David the sense of the people and the success of his communications with them, *v.* 19. He came now with a retinue of twenty men, and David entertained them with a *feast* (*v.* 20) in token of reconciliation and joy and as a pledge of the agreement between them: it was a feast upon a covenant, like that, Gen. xxvi. 30.

Verses 22–39

The murder of Abner by Joab, and David's deep resentment of it.

I. Joab very insolently fell foul upon David for treating with Abner. He was informed that Abner was just gone (*v.* 22, 23), and that a great many kind things had passed between David and him. He chides David, and reproaches him to his face (*v.* 24, 25): *What hast thou done?* As if David were accountable to him for what he did: "*Why hast thou sent him away,* when thou mightest have made him a prisoner? He came as a spy, and will certainly betray thee." We find no answer that David gave him, not because he feared him, as Ish-bosheth did Abner (*v.* 11), but because he despised him.

II. Joab very treacherously sent for Abner back, and, under colour of a private conference with him, barbarously killed him with his own hand. That he made use of David's name, under pretence of giving him some further instructions, is intimated in that, *but David knew it not, v.* 26. Abner very innocently returned to Hebron, and, when he found Joab waiting for him at the gate, turned aside with him to speak with him, and there Joab murdered him (*v.* 27), and it is intimated (*v.* 30) that Abishai was privy to the design, and was aiding and abetting. Abner had maliciously, and against the convictions of his conscience, opposed David. He had now basely deserted Ish-bosheth and betrayed him, under pretence of regard to God and Israel, but really from a principle of pride, and revenge, and impatience of control. It is as certain that Joab was unrighteous, and, in what he did, did wickedly. Abner had indeed

slain his brother Asahel, and Joab and Abishai pretended herein to be the avengers of his blood (*v.* 27, 30); but Abner slew Asahel in an open war. He did it likewise, in his own defence, and not till he had given him fair warning but Joab here shed *the blood of war in peace*, 1 Kings ii. 5. That which was at the bottom of Joab's enmity to Abner made it much worse. Joab was now general of David's forces; but, if Abner should come into his interest, he would possibly be preferred before him, being a senior officer, and more experienced in the art of war. He did it treacherously, and under pretence of speaking peaceably to him, Deut. xxvii. 24. Had he challenged him, he would have done like a soldier; but to assassinate him was done villainously and like a coward. Abner was now actually in his master's service, so that, through his side, he struck at David himself. It was a great aggravation of the murder that he did it in the gate, openly and avowedly, as one that was not ashamed.

III. David laid deeply to heart and in many ways expressed his detestation of this execrable villainy.

1. He washed his hands from the guilt of Abner's blood. *I and my kingdom are guiltless before the Lord for ever, v.* 28.

2. He entailed the curse for it upon Joab and his family (*v.* 29): "*Let it rest on the head of Joab.*" A resolute punishment of the murderer himself would better have become David than this passionate imprecation of God's judgments upon his posterity.

3. He called upon all about him, even Joab himself, to lament the death of Abner (*v.* 31). When he could not call him a saint or a good man, he said nothing of that, but what was true he gave him the praise of, though he had been his enemy, that he was *a prince and a great man.* (1) Let them all lament it. A public loss must be every man's grief, for every man shares in it. Thus David took care that honour should be done to the memory of a man of merit, to animate others. (2) Let Joab, in a particular manner, lament it, which he has less heart but more reason to do than any of them.

4. David himself followed the corpse as chief mourner, and made a funeral oration at the grave. He attended the bier (*v.* 31) *and wept at the grave, v.* 32. Because he had been a man of bravery in the field, and might have done great service in the public counsels at this critical juncture, all former quarrels are forgotten and David is a true mourner for his fall. What he said over the grave fetched tears from the eyes of all that were present: *Died Abner as a fool dieth?* (1) He speaks as one vexed that Abner was fooled out of his life, imposed upon by a colour of friendship, slain by surprise. The wisest and stoutest of men have no fence against treachery. To see Abner, who thought himself the main hinge on which the great affairs of Israel turned, made a fool of by a base rival, and falling on a sudden a sacrifice to his ambition and jealousy—this stains the pride of all glory, and should put one out of conceit with worldly grandeur. Or, (2) He speaks as one boasting that Abner did not fool himself out of his life: "*Died Abner as a fool dies?* No, he did not, not as a criminal, a traitor or felon." *Died Abner as Nabal died?* so the LXX read it. Nabal died as he lived, like himself, like a sot: but Abner's fate was such as might have been the fate of the wisest and best man in the world.

5. He fasted all that day, and would by no means be persuaded to eat any thing till night, *v.* 34.

6. He bewailed it that he could not with safety do justice on the murderers, *v.* 30. He was weak, his kingdom was newly planted, and a little shake would overthrow it. Joab's family had a great interest, were bold and daring, and to make them his enemies now might be of bad consequence. David contents himself

as a private person, to leave them to the judgment of God: *The Lord shall reward the doer of evil according to his wickedness.* Now this is a diminution, (1) To David's greatness. (2) To David's goodness. He ought to have done his duty, and trusted God with the issue. *Fiat justitia, ruat coelum—Let justice be done, though the heavens should fall asunder.* If the law had had its course against Joab, perhaps the murder of Ish-bosheth, Amnon, and others, would have been prevented. It was carnal policy and cruel pity that spared Joab.

CHAPTER 4

The removal of Ish-bosheth. I. Two of his own servants slew him, and brought his head to David, ver. 1-8. II. David, instead of rewarding them, put them to death for what they had done, ver. 9-12.

Verses 1-8

I. The weakness of Saul's house. 1. As for Ish-bosheth, his hands were feeble, *v.* 1. All the strength they ever had was from Abner's support, and now that he was dead he had no spirit left in him. He sees himself forsaken by his friends and at the mercy of his enemies. 2. As for Mephibosheth, who in the right of his father Jonathan had a prior title, his feet were lame, and he was unfit for any service, *v.* 4. He was but five years old when his father and grandfather were killed. His nurse, hearing of the Philistines' victory, was apprehensive that they would immediately aim at her young master, who was now next heir to the crown. She fled with the child in her arms, and, making more haste than good speed, she fell with the child, and by the fall some bone was broken or put out, and not well set, so that he was lame of it as long as he lived.

II. The murder of Saul's son.

1. Who were the murderers: *Baanah and Rechab, v.* 2, 3. They were brothers, Ish-bosheth's own servants, employed under him, so much the more base and treacherous was it in them to do him a mischief. They were Benjamites, of his own tribe. They were of the city of Beeroth; the inhabitants, upon some occasion or other, perhaps upon the death of Saul, retired to Gittaim. There the Beerothites were when this was written.

2. How the murder was committed, *v.* 5-7. Ish-bosheth was a sluggish man, loved his ease and hated business: and when he should have been, at this critical juncture, at the head of his forces in the field, or at the head of his counsels in a treaty with David, he was lying upon his bed and sleeping, for his hands were feeble (*v.* 1), and so were his head and heart. The treachery of Baanah and Rechab. They came into the house, under pretence of fetching wheat for the victualling of their regiments. The king's corn-chamber and his bed-chamber lay near together, which gave them an opportunity, when they were fetching wheat, to murder him as he lay on the bed.

3. The murderers triumphed in what they had done. As if they had performed some very glorious action they made a present of Ish-bosheth's head to David (*v.* 8). Not that they had any regard either to God or to David's honour; they aimed at nothing but to make their own fortunes and to get preferment in David's court.

Verses 9-12

Justice done upon the murderers of Ish-bosheth.

I. Sentence passed upon them. There needed no evidence, their own tongues witnessed against them; they were so far from denying the fact that they gloried in it. David therefore shows them the heinousness of the crime. Ish-bosheth was a righteous person, he had done them no wrong, nor designed them any. David owns Ish-bosheth an honest man, though he had created him a great deal of trouble unjustly. The manner of it much aggravated the crime. To slay him in his own house and upon his bed, when he was in no capacity of making any opposition, this is treacherous and barbarous. He quotes a precedent (*v.* 10): he had put him to death who had brought him the tidings of the death of Saul, because he thought it would be good tidings to David. He ratifies the sentence with an oath (*v.* 9): *As the Lord liveth, who hath redeemed my soul out of all adversity.* He expresses himself thus resolutely, to prevent the making of any intercession for the criminals by those about him, and thus piously to intimate that his dependence was upon God for the putting of him in possession of the promised throne, and that he would not be beholden to any man to help him to it by any indirect or unlawful practices. Hereupon he signs a warrant for the execution of these men, *v.* 12. If wicked men smite Ish-bosheth, they deserve to die for taking God's work out of his hand.

II. Execution done. The murderers were put to death according to law, to be monuments of David's justice. But what a confusion was this to the two murderers! What a horrid disappointment! And such those will meet with who think to serve the interests of the Son of David by any immoral practices, by war and persecution, fraud and rapine, who, under colour of religion, murder princes, break solemn contracts, lay countries waste, *hate their brethren, and cast them out, and say, Let the Lord be glorified, kill them, and think they do God good service.* However men may canonize such methods of serving the church and the catholic cause, Christ will let them know, another day, that Christianity was not intended to destroy humanity; and those who thus think to merit heaven shall not escape the damnation of hell.

CHAPTER 5

In this chapter, I. David anointed king by all the tribes, ver. 1-5. II. Making himself master of the stronghold of Zion, ver. 6-10. III. Building himself a house and strengthening himself in his kingdom, ver. 11, 12. IV. His children that were born after this, ver. 13-16. V. His victories over the Philistines, ver. 17-25.

Verses 1-5

I. The humble address of all the tribes to David, beseeching him to take upon him the government and owning him for their king. Judah had submitted to David as their king above seven years ago, and their ease and happiness, under his administration, encouraged the rest of the tribes to make their court to him. What numbers came from each tribe, with what zeal and sincerity they came, and how they were entertained for three days at Hebron, when they were all of one heart to make David king, we have a full account, 1 Chron. xii. 23-40. Here we have the grounds they went upon in making David king. 1. Their relation to him was some inducement: "*We are thy bone and thy flesh*" (*v.* 1), not only thou art our bone and our flesh, not a stranger, unqualified by the law to be king (Deut. xvii. 15), but we are thine. Thou wilt be as glad as we shall be to put an end to this long civil war; and thou wilt take pity on us, protect us, and do thy utmost for our welfare." Those who take Christ for their king may thus plead with him: *We are thy bone and thy flesh, thou hast made thyself in all things like unto thy brethren* (Heb. ii. 17); therefore be thou our ruler, and let this ruin be under thy hand," Isa. iii. 6. 2. His former good services to the public were a further inducement (*v.* 2). 3. The divine appointment was the greatest inducement of all.

II. The public and solemn inauguration of David, *v.* 3. A convention of the states was called; all the elders of Israel came to him; the contract was settled, the *pacta conventa—covenants*, sworn to, and subscribed on both sides. He obliged himself to protect them as their judge in peace and captain in war; and they obliged themselves to obey him. He *made a league* with them to which God was a witness: it was *before the Lord.* Hereupon he was, for the third time, anointed king. His advances were gradual, that his faith might be tried and that he might gain experience. And thus his kingdom typified that of the Messiah, which was to come to its height by degrees; for *we see not yet all things put under him* (Heb. ii. 8), but we shall see it, 1 Cor. xv. 25.

III. A general account of his reign and age. He was thirty years old when he began to reign, upon the death of Saul, *v.* 4. At that age the Levites were at first appointed to begin their administration, Num. iv. 3. About that age the Son of David entered upon his public ministry, Luke iii. 23. Then men come to their full maturity of strength and judgment. He reigned, in all, forty years and six months, of which seven years and a half in Hebron and thirty-three years in Jerusalem, *v.* 5. Hebron had been famous, Josh. xiv. 15. It was a priest's city. But Jerusalem was to be more so, and to be the holy city.

Verses 6–10

If Salem, the place of which Melchizedec was king, was Jerusalem (as seems probable from Ps. lxxvi. 2), it was famous in Abraham's time. Joshua, in his time, found it the chief city of the south part of Canaan, Joshua x. 1–3. It fell to Benjamin's lot (Joshua xviii. 28), but joined close to Judah's, Joshua xv. 8. The children of Judah had taken it (Judges i. 8), but the children of Benjamin suffered the Jebusites to dwell among them (Judges i. 21), and they grew so upon them that it became a *city of Jebusites,* Judges xix. 11. Now the very first exploit David did, after he was anointed king over all Israel, was to gain Jerusalem out of the hand of the Jebusites, which, because it belonged to Benjamin, he could not well attempt till that tribe, which long adhered to Saul's house (1 Chron. xii. 29), submitted to him.

I. The Jebusites' defiance of David and his forces. They said, *Except thou take away the blind and the lame, thou shalt not come in hither, v.* 6. They sent David this provoking message, because they could not believe that *ever an enemy would enter into the gates of Jerusalem,* Lam. iv. 12. They confided either, 1. In the protection of their gods, which David, in contempt, had called *the blind and the lame,* for *they have eyes and see not, feet and walk not.* Or, 2. In the strength of their fortifications, which they thought were made so impregnable by nature or art, or both, that the blind and the lame were sufficient to defend them against the most powerful assailant. The stronghold of Zion they especially depended on, as that which could not be forced.

II. David's success against the Jebusites. Their pride and insolence, instead of daunting him, animated him, and when he made a general assault he gave this order to his men: *"He that smiteth the Jebusites, let him also throw down into the ditch,* or gutter, *the lame and the blind,* which are set upon the wall to affront us and our God." David, having gained the fort, said that these images, which could not protect their worshippers, should never have any place there more.

III. His fixing his royal seat in Sion. He himself dwelt in the fort and he built houses round about for his attendants and guards (*v.* 9) from Millo (the townhall, or state-house) and inward. He proceeded and prospered in all he set his hand to, grew great in honour, strength, and wealth, more and more honourable in the eyes of his subjects and formidable in the eyes of his enemies; for *the Lord God of hosts was with him.*

Verses 11–15

I. David's house built, a royal palace, fit for the reception of the court he kept and the homage that was paid to him, *v.* 11. Hiram, king of Tyre, a wealthy prince, when he sent to congratulate David on his accession to the throne, offered him workmen to build him a house. David thankfully accepted the offer, and Hiram's workmen built David a house to his mind. Many have excelled in arts and sciences who were strangers to the covenants of promise. Yet David's house was never the worse, nor the less fit to be dedicated to God, for being built by the sons of the stranger. It is prophesied of the gospel church, *The sons of the strangers shall build up thy walls, and their kings shall minister unto thee,* Isa. lx. 10.

II. David's government settled and built up, *v.* 12. 1. His kingdom was established, there was nothing to shake it. He that made him king established him, because he was to be a type of Christ, with whom God's hand should be established. 2. It was exalted in the eyes both of its friends and enemies. Never had the nation of Israel looked so great or made such a figure as it began now to do. God did not make Israel his subjects for his sake, that he might be great, and rich, and absolute: but he made him their king for their sake, that he might lead, and guide, and protect them.

III. David's family multiplied and increased. All the sons that were born to him after he came to Jerusalem are here mentioned together, eleven in all, besides the six that were born to him before in Hebron, *ch.* iii. 2, 5. It is said that he *took more concubines and wives, v.* 13. Shall we praise him for this? We praise him not; we justify him not; nor can we scarcely excuse him. The bad example of the patriarchs might make him think there was no harm in it, and he might hope it would strengthen his interest, by multiplying his alliances, and increasing the royal family. But one vine by the side of the house, with the blessing of God, may send boughs to the sea and branches to the rivers. David had many wives, and yet that did not keep him from coveting his neighbour's wife and defiling her; for men that have once broken the fence will wander endlessly.

Verses 17–25

The particular service for which David was raised up was to *save Israel out of the hand of the Philistines, ch.* iii. 18. Two great victories obtained over the Philistines we have here an account of, by which David not only balanced the disgrace and retrieved the loss Israel had sustained in the battle wherein Saul was slain, but went far towards the total subduing of those vexatious neighbours.

I. In both these actions the Philistines were the aggressors. 1. In the former they *came up to seek David* (*v.* 17), because they *heard that he was anointed king over Israel.* They therefore try to crush his government in its infancy, before it was well settled. They took counsel together, but were *broken in pieces,* Isa. viii. 9, 10. 2. In the latter they *came up yet again,* hoping to recover what they had lost in the former engagement, their hearts being hardened to their destruction, *v.* 22. 3. In both they *spread themselves in the valley of Rephaim,* which lay very near Jerusalem. That city they hoped to make themselves masters of before David had completed the fortifications. Their spreading themselves intimates that they were very numerous.

II. In both, David, though forward enough to go forth against them yet entered not upon action till he had *enquired of the Lord* by the breast-plate of judgment, *v.* 19, and again, *v.* 23. His enquiry was twofold:—1. Concerning his duty: *"Shall I go up?"* Achish had been kind to him in his distress, and had protected him. "Now," says David, "ought not

I, in remembrance of that, rather to make peace with them than to make war with them?" "No," says God, "they are Israel's enemies, *go up.*" 2. Concerning his success. His conscience asked the former question, *Shall I go up?* His prudence asked this, *Wilt thou deliver them into my hand?* Hereby he owns his dependence on God for victory. Yea, says God, *I will doubtless do it.* If God send us, he will bear us out and stand by us. The assurance God has given us of victory over our spiritual enemies, that he will tread Satan under our feet shortly, should animate us in our spiritual conflicts. David had now a great army at command and in good heart, yet he relied more on God's promise than his own force.

III. In the former of these engagements David routed the army of the Philistines by dint of sword (*v.* 20): he *smote them*; and when he had done, 1. He gave his God the glory. He called the place *Baalperazim, the master of the breaches*, because, God having broken in upon their forces, he soon had the mastery of them. 2. He put their gods to shame. They brought the images of their gods into the field as their protectors, in imitation of the Israelites bringing the ark into their camp; but, being put to flight, they could not stay to carry off their images, for they were a *burden to the weary beasts* (Isa. xlvi. 1), and therefore they left them to fall with the rest of their baggage into the hands of the conqueror. David and his men converted to their own use the rest of the plunder, but the images they burnt, as God had appointed (Deut. vii. 5). Bishop Patrick well observes here that when the ark fell into the Philistines' hands it consumed them, but when these images fell into the hands of Israel, they could not save themselves from being consumed.

IV. In the latter of these engagements God gave David some sensible tokens of his presence with him, bade him not fall upon them directly, as he had done before, but *fetch a compass behind them, v.* 23. 1. God appoints him to draw back, as *Israel stood still to see the salvation of the Lord.* 2. He promised him to charge the enemy himself, by an invisible host of angels, *v.* 24. "Thou shalt hear the *sound of a going*, like the march of an army in the air, *upon the tops of the mulberry trees.*" God's grace must quicken our endeavours. The sound of the going was, (1) A signal to David when to move; it is comfortable going out when God goes before us. And, (2) Perhaps it was an alarm to the enemy, and put them into confusion. Hearing the march of an army against their front, they retreated with precipitation, and fell into David's army which lay behind them in their rear. (3) The success of this is briefly set down, *v.* 25. David observed his orders, waited till God moved, and stirred then, but not till then. He smote the Philistines, even to the borders of their own country. When the kingdom of the Messiah was to be set up, the apostles that were to beat down the devil's kingdom must not attempt anything till they received the promise of the Spirit, who *came with a sound from heaven as of a rushing mighty wind* (Acts ii. 2), which was typified by this sound of the going on the tops of the mulberry trees; and, when they heard that, they must bestir themselves, and did so; they went forth conquering and to conquer.

CHAPTER 6

David, having humbled the Philistines, is here bringing up the ark to his own city, that it might be near him, and be an ornament and strength to his new foundation. I. An attempt to do it, which failed and miscarried. The design was well laid, ver. 1, 2. But, 1. They were guilty of an error in carrying it in a cart, ver. 3-5. 2. They were punished for that error by the sudden death of Uzzah (ver. 6, 7), which was a great terror to David (ver. 8, 9) and put a stop to his proceedings, ver. 10, 11. II. The great joy and satisfaction with which it was at last done, ver. 12-15. And, 1. The good understanding between David and his people, ver. 17-19. 2. The uneasiness between David and his wife upon that occasion, ver. 16, 20-23. And, when we consider that the ark was both the token of God's presence and a type of Christ, we shall see that this story is very instructive.

Verses 1-5

The ark was lodged in Kirjath-jearim, immediately after its return out of its captivity among the Philistines (1 Sam. vii. 1, 2). Once Saul called for it, 1 Sam. xiv. 18. That which in former days had made so great a figure is as a neglected thing for many years. Perpetual visibility is no mark of the true church. God is graciously present with the souls of his people even when they want the external tokens of his presence. But now that David is settled in the throne the honour of the ark begins to revive.

I. Here is honourable mention made of the ark. Because it had not been spoken of a great while, now it is described (*v.* 2): *the ark of God whose name is called by the name of the Lord of hosts that dwelleth between the cherubim.* Let us learn hence, 1. To think and speak highly of God. He is the name above every name, *the Lord of hosts*, that has all the creatures in heaven and earth, at his command, and yet is pleased to dwell between the cherubim, over the propitiatory or mercy-seat, graciously manifesting himself to his people, reconciled in a Mediator, and ready to do them good. 2. To think and speak honourably of holy ordinances, which are to us, as the ark was to Israel, the token of God's presence (Matt. xxviii. 20), and the means of our communion with him, Ps. xxvii. 4. Christ is our ark.

II. Here is an honourable attendance given to the ark upon the removal of it. David made the motion (1 Chron. xiii. 1-3). All the chosen men of Israel are called together to grace the solemnity, to pay their respect to the ark, and to testify their joy in its restoration. This would help to inspire the young people of the nation, who perhaps had scarcely heard of the ark, with a great veneration for it.

III. Here are great expressions of joy upon the removal of the ark, *v.* 5. As secret worship is better the more secret it is, so public worship is better the more public it is; and we have reason to rejoice when restraints are taken off, and the ark of God finds welcome in the city of David, and has not only the protection and support, but the countenance and encouragement, of the civil powers; for joy of this they *played before the Lord.* Dr. Lightfoot supposes that, upon this occasion, David penned the 68th Psalm, because it begins with that ancient prayer of Moses at the removing of the ark, *Let God arise, and let his enemies be scattered*; and notice is taken there (*v.* 25) of the *singers and players on instruments* that attended, and (*v.* 27) of the princes of several of the tribes; and perhaps those words in the last verse, *O God, thou art terrible out of thy holy places*, were added upon occasion of the death of Uzzah.

IV. Here is an error that they were guilty of in this matter, that they carried the ark in a cart or carriage, whereas the priests should have carried it upon their shoulders, *v.* 3. The Kohathites that had the charge of the ark had no waggons assigned them, because *their service was to bear it upon their shoulders*, Num. vii. 9. The ark was no such heavy burden but that they might, among them, have carried it as far as Mount Sion upon their shoulders, they needed not to put it in a cart like a common thing. It was no excuse for them that the Philistines had done so and were not punished for it; they knew no better. Philistines may cart the ark with impunity; but, if Israelites do so, they do it at their peril. And it mended the matter very little that it was a new cart; old or new, it was not what God had appointed.

Verses 6-11

Uzzah struck dead for touching the ark, when it

was upon its journey towards the city of David, a sad providence, which damped their mirth, stopped the progress of the ark, and, for the present, dispersed this great assembly, which had come together to attend it, and sent them home in a fright.

I. Uzzah's offence seems very small. He and his brother Ahio, the sons of Abinadab, in whose house the ark had long been lodged, having been used to attend it, undertook to drive the cart in which the ark was carried, this being perhaps the last service they were likely to do it; for others would be employed about it when it came to the city of David. Ahio went before, to clear the way, and, if need were, to lead the oxen. Uzzah followed close to the side of the cart. It happened that the oxen shook it, *v.* 6. The critics are not agreed about the signification of the original word: *They stumbled* (so our margin); *they kicked* (so some), perhaps against the goad with which Uzzah drove them; *they stuck in the mire*, so some. By some accident or other the ark was in danger of being overthrown. Uzzah thereupon laid hold of it, to save it from falling. Uzzah was a Levite, but priests only might touch the ark. The law was express concerning the Kohathites, that, though they were to carry the ark by the staves, yet *they must not touch any holy thing, lest they die*, Num. iv. 15.

II. His punishment for this offence seems very great (*v.* 7). There he sinned, and there he died, *by the ark of God*; even the mercy-seat would not save him. Why was God thus severe with him? 1. The touching of the ark was forbidden to the Levites expressly under pain of death—*lest they die*. 2. God saw the presumption and irreverence of Uzzah's heart. Perhaps he affected to show, before this great assembly, how bold he could make with the ark, having been so long acquainted with it. 3. David afterwards owned that Uzzah died for an error they were all guilty of, which was carrying the ark in a cart. But Uzzah was singled out to be made an example, perhaps because he had been most forward in advising that way of conveyance. 4. God would hereby strike an awe upon the thousands of Israel, would convince them that the ark was never the less venerable for its having been so long in mean circumstances, and thus he would teach them to rejoice with trembling, and always to treat holy things with reverence and holy fear.

III. David's feelings on the infliction of this stroke were keen, and perhaps not altogether as they should have been. 1. He was displeased. *David's anger was kindled*. It is the same word that is used for God's displeasure, *v.* 7. Because God was angry, David was angry and out of humour. The death of Uzzah was indeed an eclipse to the glory of a solemnity, but he ought nevertheless to have subscribed to the righteousness and wisdom of God in it, and not to have been displeased at it. When we lie under God's anger we must keep under our own. 2. He was afraid, *v.* 9. It should seem he was afraid with amazement; for he said, *How shall the ark of the Lord come to me?* As if God was so extremely tender of his ark that there was no dealing with it; and therefore better for him to keep it at a distance. He should rather have said, "Let the ark come to me, and I will take warning by this to treat it with more reverence." David therefore will not bring the ark into his own city (*v.* 10) till he is better prepared for its reception. 3. He took care to perpetuate the remembrance of this stroke by a new name he gave to the place: *Perez-uzzah, the breach of Uzzah, v.* 8. He had been lately triumphing in the breach made upon his enemies, and called the place *Baal-perazim, a place of breaches*. But here is a breach upon his friends. The memorial of this stroke would be a warning to posterity to take heed of all rashness and irreverence in dealing about holy things. 4. He lodged the ark in a good house, the house of Obed-edom a Levite,

which happened to be near the place where this disaster happened, and there, (1) It was kindly entertained and welcomed, and continued there *three months, v.* 10, 11. Obed-edom knew what slaughter the ark had made among the Philistines and the Bethshemites. He saw Uzzah struck dead for touching it, and perceived that David himself was afraid of meddling with it; yet he opens his doors to it without fear, knowing it was a *savour of death unto death* only to those that treated it ill. (2) It paid well for its entertainment: *The Lord blessed Obed-edom and all his household.* The same hand that punished Uzzah's proud presumption rewarded Obed-edom's humble boldness, and made the ark to him a *savour of life unto life*. The ark is a guest which none shall lose by that bid it welcome. It is good living in a family that entertains the ark, for all about it will fare the better for it.

Verses 12–19

The second attempt to bring the ark home to the city of David; and this succeeded, though the former miscarried.

I. The blessing with which the house of Obed-edom was blessed was an evidence that God was reconciled to them, and his anger was turned away. If God be at peace with them, they can cheerfully go on with their design. 1. It was an evidence that the ark was not such a burdensome stone as it was taken to be, but, on the contrary, happy was the man that had it near him. Christ is indeed a *stone of stumbling, and a rock of offence*, to those that are disobedient; but to those who believe he is a *corner-stone, elect, precious*, 1 Pet. ii. 6–8.

II. How David managed the matter now. 1. He ordered those whose business it was to carry it on their shoulders. This is implied here (*v.* 13) and expressed 1 Chron. xv. 15. 2. At their first setting out he offered sacrifices to God (*v.* 13) by way of atonement for their former errors. 3. He himself attended the solemnity with the highest expressions of joy that could be (*v.* 14): *He danced before the Lord with all his might*; he leaped for joy. His dancing was not artificial, by any certain rule or measure, but was a natural expression of his great joy and exultation of mind. 4. All the people triumphed in this advancement of the ark (*v.* 15): *They brought it up* into the royal city *with shouting*, and *with sound of trumpet*. 5. The ark was safely brought to, and honourably deposited in, the place prepared for it, *v.* 17. They set it in *the midst of the tabernacle*, or tent, *which David had pitched for it.* As soon as ever it was lodged, he offered burnt-offerings and peace-offerings, in thankfulness to God and in supplication to God for the continuance of his favour. 6. The people were then dismissed with great satisfaction. He sent them away, (1) With a gracious prayer: *He blessed them in the name of the Lord of hosts* (*v.* 18). He testified his desire for their welfare by this prayer, and let them know they had a king that loved them. (2) With a generous treat; for so it was, rather than a distribution of alms.

Verses 20–23

David, having dismissed the congregation with a blessing, *returned to bless his household* (*v.* 20), to offer up his family thanksgiving for this national mercy.

Never did David return to his house with so much pleasure and satisfaction as he did now that he had got the ark into his neighbourhood; and yet even this joyful day concluded with some uneasiness, occasioned by his wife. Michal was not pleased with his dancing before the ark. When he came home she scolded him. She thought he degraded himself in dancing before the ark.

I. When she saw David in the street dancing before the Lord she *despised him in her heart*, v. 16. She thought this mighty zeal of his for the ark of God, and the transport of joy he was in upon its coming home, was unbecoming so great a soldier, and statesman, and monarch.

II. When he came home in the very best disposition she went out to meet him with her reproaches.

1. How she taunted him (v. 20): *"How glorious was the king of Israel to-day*. What a figure didst thou make to-day in the midst of the mob!"* That which displeased her was his affection to the ark, but she basely represents his conduct, in dancing before the ark, as lewd and immodest. We have no reason to think that this was true in fact. David, no doubt, observed decorum, and governed his zeal with discretion. To disparage one who had shown such affection for her that he would not accept a crown unless he might have her restored to him (*ch.* iii. 13), was a most base and wicked thing, and showed her to have more of Saul's daughter in her than of David's wife or Jonathan's sister.

2. How he replied to her reproach.

(1) He designed to honour God (v. 21): *It was before the Lord*, and with an eye to him. Whatever invidious construction she was pleased to put upon it, he had the testimony of his conscience for him that he sincerely aimed at the glory of God. Here he reminds her indeed of the setting aside of her father's house, to make way for him to the throne, that she might not think herself the most proper judge of propriety: *"God chose me before thy father, and appointed me to be ruler over Israel*, and, if the expressions of a warm devotion to God were looked upon as mean and unfashionable in thy father's court, yet *I will play before the Lord*, and thereby bring them into reputation again. [1] If we can approve ourselves to God in what we do in religion, and do it as before the Lord, we need not value the censures and reproaches of men. [2] The more we are vilified for well-doing the more resolute we should be in it, and hold our religion the faster.

(2) He designed thereby to humble himself: *"I will be base in my own sight*, and will think nothing too mean to stoop to for the honour of God."

(3) He doubted not but even this would turn to his reputation among those whose reproach Michal pretended to fear: *Of the maid-servants shall I be had in honour*. She unjustly reproached David for his devotion. *Those that honour God he will honour*; but those that despise him, and his servants and service, *shall be lightly esteemed.*

Chapter 7

The ark is David's care as well as his joy. I. His consultation with Nathan about building a house for it; he signifies his purpose to do it (ver. 1, 2), and Nathan approves his purpose, ver. 3. II. His communion with God about it. 1. A gracious message God sent him about it, ver. 4–17. 2. A very humble prayer which David offered up to God in return to that gracious message, thankfully accepting God's promises to him, and earnestly praying for the performance of them, ver. 18–29.

Verses 1–3

I. David at rest. *He sat in his house* (v. 1), quiet and undisturbed, having no occasion to take the field. He had not been long at rest, nor was it long before he was again engaged in war; but at present he enjoyed a calm, and he was in his element when he was sitting in his house, meditating in the law of God.

II. David's thought of building a temple for the honour of God. He had built a palace for himself and a city for his servants; and now he thinks of building a habitation for the ark. 1. Thus he would make a grateful return for the honours God put upon him. *What shall I render unto the Lord?* 2. Thus he would improve the present calm, and make a good use of the rest God had given him. David considered (v. 2) the stateliness of his own habitation (*I dwell in a house of cedar*), and compared with that the meanness of the habitation of the ark (*the ark dwells within curtains*), and thought this incongruous, that he should dwell in a palace and the ark in a tent. David had been uneasy till he found out *a place for the ark* (Ps. cxxxii. 4, 5), and now he is uneasy till he finds out a better place. Gracious grateful souls cannot enjoy their own accommodations while they see the church of God in distress and under a cloud. David can take little pleasure in a house of cedar for himself, unless the ark have one.

III. His communicating this thought to Nathan the prophet. David told him, that by him he might know the mind of God. It was certainly a good work, but it was uncertain whether it was the will of God that David should have the doing of it.

IV. Nathan's approbation of it: *Go, do all that is in thy heart; for the Lord is with thee*, v. 3. Nathan easily gathered what was in his heart, and bade him go on and prosper. We ought to do all we can to encourage and promote the good purposes and designs of others, and put in a good word, as we have opportunity, to forward a good work. Nathan spoke this, not in God's name, but as from himself; not as a prophet, but as a wise and good man.

Verses 4–17

A full revelation of God's favour to David, the notices and assurances of which God sent him by Nathan the prophet. The design of it is to take him off from his purpose of building the temple and it was therefore sent, 1. By the same hand that had given him encouragement to do it, lest, if it had been sent by any other, Nathan should be despised and insulted and David should be perplexed. 2. The same night, that Nathan might not continue long in an error nor David have his head any further filled with thoughts of that which he must never bring to pass.

I. David's purpose to build God a house is superseded. God took notice of that purpose, for he knows what is in man; and he was well pleased with it, as appears 1 Kings viii. 18, *Thou didst well that it was in thy heart*; yet he forbade him to go on with his purpose (v. 5): *"Shalt thou build me a house?* No, *thou shalt not* (as it is explained in the parallel place, 1 Chron. xvii. 4); there is other work appointed for thee to do, which must be done first." David is a man of war, and he must enlarge the borders of Israel, by carrying on his conquests. David is a sweet psalmist, and he must prepare psalms for the use of the temple when it is built, and settle the courses of the Levites; but his son's genius will better suit for building the house, and he will have a better treasure to bear the charge of it, and therefore let it be reserved for him to do. *As every man hath received the gift, so let him minister*. The building of a temple was to be a work of time, and preparation made for it; but it was a thing that had never been spoken of till now. God tells him, 1. That hitherto he had never had a house built for him (v. 6), a tabernacle had served hitherto, and it might serve awhile longer. God regards not outward pomp in his service; his presence was as surely with his people when the ark was in a tent as when it was in a temple. Christ, like the ark, when here on earth walked in a tent or tabernacle, for he *went about doing good*, and dwelt not in any house of his own, till he ascended on high, to the mansions above, in his Father's house, and there he sat down. The church, like the ark, in this world is ambulatory, dwells in a tent, because its present state is both pastoral and military; its continuing city is to come. David, in his psalms, often calls the tabernacle a temple (as Ps. v. 7; xxvii. 4; xxix. 9; lxv. 4; cxxxviii. 2), because it answered the intention of a temple, though it was made but of curtains. 2. That he had never given any orders or directions, or the least intimation, to any of the sceptres of Israel, that is, to any of the judges, 1 Chron. xvii. 6 (for rulers are called *sceptres*, Ezek. xix. 14, the great Ruler is called so, Num. xxiv. 17), concerning the building of the temple, *v.* 7.

II. David is reminded of the great things God had done for him. 1. He had raised him from a very mean and low condition: *He took him from the sheep-cote.* 2. He had given him success and victory over his enemies (*v.* 9): "*I was with thee whithersoever thou wentest*, to protect thee when pursued, to prosper thee when pursuing." 3. He had crowned him not only with power and dominion in Israel, but with honour and reputation among the nations about: *I have made thee a great name.*

III. A happy establishment is promised to God's Israel, *v.* 10, 11. This comes in a parenthesis, before the promises made to David himself, to let him understand that what God designed to do for him was for Israel's sake, that they might be happy under his administration, and to give him the satisfaction of foreseeing peace upon Israel, when it was promised him that he should *see his children's children*, Ps. cxxviii. 6. Two things are promised:—1. A quiet place: Canaan should be clearly their own without any ejection or molestation. 2. A quiet enjoyment of that place: *The children of wickedness* (meaning especially the Philistines, who had been so long a plague to them) *shall not afflict them any more.*

IV. Blessings are entailed upon the family and posterity of David. David had purposed to build God a house, and, in requital, God promises to *build him a house, v.* 11.

1. Some of these promises relate to Solomon, his immediate successor, and to the royal line of Judah. (1) That God would advance him to the throne. (2) That he would settle him in the throne: *I will establish his kingdom* (*v.* 12), *the throne of his kingdom, v.* 13. (3) That he would employ him in that good work of building the temple, which David had only the satisfaction of designing: *He shall build a house for my name, v.* 13. (4) That he would take him into the covenant of adoption (*v.* 14, 15): *I will be his father, and he shall be my son.* We need no more to make us and ours happy than to have God to be a Father to us and them. The promise here speaks *as unto sons.* [1] That his Father would correct him when there was occasion; for *what son is he whom the Father chasteneth not?* Not a stroke, or wound, but a gentle touch. [2] That yet he would not disinherit him (*v.* 15): The revolt of the ten tribes from the house of David was their correction for iniquity, but the constant adherence of the other two to that family, perpetuated the mercy of God to the seed of David, though that family was cut short, yet it was not cut off, as the house of Saul was.

2. Others of them relate to Christ, who is often called *David* and the *Son of David*, that Son of David to whom these promises pointed and in whom they had their full accomplishment. He was of the *seed of David*, Acts. xiii. 23. That promise, *I will be his Father, and he shall be my Son,* is expressly applied to Christ by the apostle, Heb. i. 5. But the establishing of his house, and his throne, and his *kingdom, for ever* (*v.* 13, and again, and a third time, *v.* 16, *for ever*), can be applied to no other than Christ and his kingdom. David's house and kingdom have long since come to an end; it is only the Messiah's kingdom that is everlasting, and *of the increase of his government and peace there shall be no end.* Now, (1) This message Nathan faithfully delivered to David (*v.* 17); though, in forbidding him to build the temple, he contradicted his own words. (2) These promises God faithfully performed to David and his seed in due time.

Verses 18–29

The solemn address David made to God, in answer to the gracious message God had sent him.

I. The place he retired to: He *went in before the Lord*, that is, into the tabernacle where the ark was, which was the token of God's presence; before *that* he presented himself.

II. The posture he put himself into: He *sat before the Lord.* 1. It denotes the posture of his body. Kneeling or standing is certainly the most proper gesture to be used in prayer. *David went in, and took his place before the Lord*, so it may be read; but, when he prayed, he stood up as the manner was. Or he *went in and continued before the Lord*, stayed some time silently meditating, before he began his prayer, and then remained longer than usual in the tabernacle. Or, 2. It may denote the frame of his spirit at this time.

III. The prayer itself, which is full of the breathings of pious and devout affection towards God.

1. He speaks very humbly of himself and his own merits. So he begins as one astonished: *Who am I, O Lord God; and what is my house? v.* 18. He had low thoughts, (1) Of his personal merits: *Who am I?* He was upon all accounts a very considerable and valuable man. His endowments both of body and mind were extraordinary. Yet, when he comes to speak of himself before God, he says, "*Who am I?* A man not worth taking notice of." (2) Of the merits of his family: *What is my house?* His house was of the royal tribe, and descended from the prince of that tribe; and yet, like Gideon, he thinks his family poor in Judah and himself *the least in his father's house*, Judges vi. 15. All our attainments must be looked upon as God's vouchsafements.

2. He speaks very highly and honourably of God's favours to him. (1) In what he had done for him: "*Thou hast brought me hitherto*, to this great dignity and dominion. Hitherto thou hast helped me." (2) In what he had yet further promised him. God had done great things for him already, and yet, as if those had been nothing, he had promised to do much more, *v.* 19. We must own, as David here, [1] That it is far beyond what we could expect: *Is this the manner of men?* that is, *First,* Can man expect to be so dealt with by his Maker? He is brought near to God, purchased at a high rate, taken into covenant and communion with God; could this ever have been thought of? *Secondly,* Do men usually deal thus with one another? No, the way of our God is far above the manner of men. Though he be high, he has respect to the lowly; and is this the manner of men? Though he is offended by us, he beseeches us to be reconciled, waits to be gracious, multiplies his pardons: and is this the manner of men? [2] That beyond this there is nothing we can desire: "*And what can David say more unto thee? v.* 20. What can I ask or wish for more? *Thou, Lord, knowest thy servant,* knowest what will make me happy, and what thou hast promised is enough to do so." The promise of Christ includes all. What can we say more for ourselves in our prayers than he has said for us in his promises?

3. He ascribes all to the free grace of God (*v.* 21), both the great things he had done for him and the great things he had made known to him.

4. He adores the greatness and glory of God (*v.* 22): *Thou art great, O Lord God! for there is none like thee.* God's gracious condescension to him, and the honour he had put upon him, did not at all abate his awful veneration for the divine Majesty; for the nearer any are brought to God the more they see of his glory, and the dearer we are in his eyes the greater he should be in ours.

5. He expresses a great esteem for the Israel of God, *v.* 23, 24. As there was none among the gods

to be compared with Jehovah, so none among the nations to be compared with Israel, considering,

(1) The works he had done for them. He went to redeem them, applied himself to it as a great work, went about it with solemnity. The redemption of Israel, as described here, was typical of our redemption by Christ in that, [1] They were redeemed from the nations and their gods; so are we from all iniquity and all conformity to this present world. Christ came to save his people from their sins. [2] They were redeemed to be a peculiar people unto God, purified and appropriated to himself, that he might make himself a great name and do for them great things.

(2) The covenant he had made with them, *v.* 24. It was, [1] Mutual: "They to be a people to thee, and thou to be a God to them; all their interests consecrated to thee, and all thy attributes engaged for them." [2] Immutable: "Thou hast confirmed them." He that makes the covenant makes it sure and will make it good.

6. He concludes with humble petitions to God. (1) He grounds his petitions upon the message which God had sent him (*v.* 27): "Thou hast of thy own good will given me the promise that thou wilt build me a house, else I could never have found in my heart to pray such a prayer as this," too great for me to beg, but not too great for thee to give. (2) He builds his faith and hopes to speed upon the fidelity of God's promise (*v.* 25): "*Thou art that God* (thou art *he*, even *that God*, the *Lord of hosts*, and *God of Israel*, or *that God whose words are true*, that God whom one may depend upon); and *thou hast promised this goodness unto thy servant*, which I am therefore bold to pray for." (3) Thence he fetches the matter of his prayer, and refers to that as the guide of his prayers. [1] He prays for the performance of God's promise (*v.* 25): "I desire no more, and I expect no less." Thus we must turn God's promises into prayers, and then they shall be turned into performances; for, with God, saying and doing are not two things, as they often are with men. [2] He prays for the glorifying of God's name (*v.* 26): *Let thy name be magnified for ever.* This ought to be the summary and centre of all our prayers, the Alpha and the Omega of them. Begin with *Hallowed be thy name*, and end with *Thine is the glory for ever.* "Whether I be magnified or no, *let thy name be magnified.*" [3] He prays for his house, for to that the promise has special reference, *First*, That it might be happy (*v.* 29): *Let it please thee to bless the house of thy servant. Secondly*, That the happiness of it might remain: "Let it be *established before thee* (*v.* 26); let it *continue for ever before thee*," *v.* 29. He longs 1. That none of his might ever forfeit it, but that they might walk before God, which would be their establishment. 2. That his kingdom might have its perfection and perpetuity in the kingdom of the Messiah. When Christ for ever sat down on the right hand of God (Heb. x. 12), and received all possible assurance that his seed and throne shall be as the days of heaven, this prayer of David the son of Jesse for his seed was abundantly answered, that it might *continue before God for ever*.

CHAPTER 8

David having sought first the kingdom of God, settled the ark as soon as he was himself well settled. Here is an account, I. Of his conquests. He triumphed, 1. Over the Philistines, ver. 1. 2. Over the Moabites, ver. 2. 3. Over the king of Zobah, ver. 3, 4. 4. Over the Syrians, ver 5–8, 13. 5. Over the Edomites, ver. 14. II. Of the presents that were brought him and the wealth he got from the nations he subdued, which he dedicated to God, ver. 9–12. III. Of his court, the administration of his government (ver. 15), and his chief officers, ver. 16–18. This gives us a general idea of the prosperity of David's reign.

Verses 1–8

David has now commission given him to make war

for the avenging of Israel's quarrels and the recovery of their rights; for as yet they were not in full possession of that country to which by the promise of God they were entitled.

I. He quite subdued the Philistines, *v.* 1. They had long been vexatious and oppressive to Israel. Saul got no ground against them; but David completed Israel's deliverance out of their hands, which Samson had begun long before, Judges xiii. 5. *Methegammah* was *Gath* (the chief and royal city of the Philistines) and the towns belonging to it, among which there was a constant garrison kept by the Philistines on the hill Ammah (2 Sam. ii. 24), which was *Metheg*, a *bridle* (so it signifies) or *curb* upon the people of Israel; this David took out of their hand and used it as a curb upon them.

II. He smote the Moabites, and made them tributaries to Israel, *v.* 2. He divided the country into three parts, two of which he destroyed, the third part he spared, to till the ground and be servants to Israel. Now Balaam's prophecy was fulfilled, *A sceptre shall arise out of Israel, and shall smite the corners of Moab.* The Moabites continued tributaries to Israel till after the death of Ahab, 2 Kings iii. 4, 5. Then they rebelled and were never reduced.

III. He smote the Syrians or Aramites. Of them there were two distinct kingdoms, as we find them spoken of in the title of the 60th Psalm: *Aram Nahuralm,—Syria of the rivers*, whose head city was Damascus (famed for its rivers, 2 Kings v. 12), and *Arum Zobah*, which joined to it, but extended to Euphrates. These were the two northern crowns. 1. David began with the Syrians of Zobah, *v.* 3, 4. As he went to settle his border at the river Euphrates (for so far the land conveyed by the divine grant to Abraham and his seed did extend, Gen. xv. 18), the king of Zobah opposed him, being himself possessed of those countries which belonged to Israel; but David routed his forces, and took his chariots and horsemen.

IV. In all these wars, 1. David was protected: *The Lord preserved him whithersoever he went.* 2. He was enriched. He took the shields of gold which the servants of Hadadezer had in their custody (*v.* 7) and much brass from several cities of Syria (*v.* 8), which he was entitled to by the ancient entail of these countries on the seed of Abraham.

Verses 9–14

1. The court made to David by the king of Hamath, who, it seems was at this time at war with the king of Zobah. He, hearing of David's success against his enemy, sent his own son ambassador to him (*v.* 9, 10) to beg his friendship. And David lost nothing by taking this little prince under his protection; for the wealth he had from the countries he conquered by way of spoil he had from this by way of present or gratuity: *Vessels of silver and gold.* Better get by composition than by compulsion. 2. The offering David made to God of the spoils of the nations. He dedicated all to the Lord, *v.* 11, 12. This crowned all his victories, and made them far to outshine Alexander's or Cæsar's, that they sought their own glory, but he aimed at the glory of God. All the precious things he was master of were dedicated things, that is, they were designed for the building of the temple. Their gods of gold David burnt (2 Sam. v. 21), but their vessels of gold he dedicated. Thus in the conquest of a soul, by the grace of the Son of David, what stands in opposition to God must be destroyed, every lust mortified and crucified, but what may glorify him must be dedicated and the property of it altered. 3. The reputation he got, in a particular manner, by his victory over the Syrians and their allies the Edomites. *He got himself a name.* Something extraordinary there was in that action,

which turned very much to his honour, yet he is careful to transfer the honour to God. 4. His success against the Edomites. They all became David's servants, *v.* 13. The Edomites continued long tributary to the kings of Judah, as the Moabites were to the kings of Israel, till, in Joram's time, they revolted (2 Chron. xxi. 8) as Isaac had there foretold that Esau should, in process of time, break the yoke from off his neck. Thus David by his conquests, (1) Secured peace to his son, that he might have time to build the temple. And, (2) Procured wealth for his son, that he might have wherewith to build it. God employs his servants variously, some in the spiritual battles, others in the spiritual buildings; and one prepares work for the other, that God may have the glory of all. All David's victories were typical of the success of the gospel against the kingdom of Satan, in which the Son of David rode forth, conquering and to conquer.

Verses 15–18

David was not so engaged in his wars abroad as to neglect the administration of the government at home.

I. His care extended itself to all the parts of his dominion: *He reigned over all Israel* (*v.* 15).

II. He did justice with an unbiassed unshaken hand: *He executed judgment unto all his people.* This intimates, 1. His industry and close application to business, his easiness of access and readiness to admit all addresses and appeals made to him. 2. His impartiality and the equity of his proceedings, in administering justice. See Ps. lxxii. 1, 2.

III. He kept good order and good officers in his court. David being the first king that had an established government (for Saul's reign was short and unsettled) he had the modelling of the administration. In Saul's time we read of no other great officer than Abner, that was captain of the host. But David appointed more officers. 1. Two military officers: Joab that was general of the forces in the field, and Banaiah that was over the Cherethites and Pelethites, who were either the city train-bands (*archers and slingers,* so the Chaldee), or rather the life-guards, or standing force, that attended the king's person, the prætorian band, the militia. They were ready to do service at home, to assist in the administering of justice, and to preserve the public peace. 2. Two ecclesiastical officers: *Zadok and Ahimelech were priests,* that is, they were most employed in the priests' work under Abiathar, the high priest. 3. Two civil officers: one that was recorder, or remembrancer, to put the king in mind of business in its season (he was prime minister of state, yet not entrusted with the custody of the king's conscience, as they say of our lord chancellor, but only of the king's memory); another that was scribe, or secretary of state, that drew up public orders and despatches, and recorded judgments given. 4. David's sons, as they grew up to be fit for business, were made chief rulers. They were chief about the king (so it is explained, 1 Chron. xviii. 17), employed near him, that they might be under his eye. David made his sons chief rulers; but all believers, Christ's spiritual seed, are better preferred, for they are *made to our God kings and priests,* Rev. i. 6.

CHAPTER 9

The kindness David showed to Jonathan's seed for his sake. I. The kind of enquiry he made after the remains of the house of Saul, and his discovery of Mephibosheth, ver. 1–4. II. The kind reception he gave to Mephibosheth, when he was brought to him, ver. 5–8. III. The kind provision he made for him and his, ver. 9–13.

Verses 1–8

I. David's enquiry after the remains of the ruined house of Saul, *v.* 1. This was a great while after his accession to the throne, for it should seem that Mephibosheth, who was but five years old when Saul died, had now a son born, *v.* 12. David had too long forgotten his obligations to Jonathan, but now, at length, they are brought to his mind.

1. He sought an opportunity to do good. *Is there any yet left of the house of Saul, that I may show him kindness? v.* 3. "Is there any, not only to whom I may do justice (Num. v. 8), but to whom I may show kindness?" The most necessitous are the least clamorous.

2. Those he enquired after were the remains of the house of Saul, to whom he would show kindness for Jonathan's sake. He was desirous to show kindness to the house of Saul, not only because he trusted in God and feared not what they could do unto him, but because he was of a charitable disposition, and forgave what they had done to him. We must not be backward to do any office of love and goodwill to those that have done us many an injury. 1 Pet. iii. 9,—*but, contrariwise, blessing.* This is the way to overcome evil, and to find mercy for ourselves and ours, when we or they need it. Jonathan was David's sworn friend, and therefore he would show kindness to his house. The kindness we have promised we must conscientiously perform, though it should not be claimed. God is faithful to us; let us not be unfaithful to one another. Though there be not a solemn league of friendship tying us to this constancy of love, yet there is a sacred law of friendship no less obliging, that to him that is in misery pity should be shown by his friend, Job. vi. 14. *A brother is born for adversity.* Friendship obliges us to take cognizance of the families and surviving relations of those we have loved.

3. The kindness he promised to show them he calls the *kindness of God*; not only great kindness, but, (1) Kindness in pursuance of the covenant that was between him and Jonathan, to which God was a witness. See 1 Sam. xx. 42. (2) Kindness after God's example; for we must be merciful as he is. Jonathan's request to David was (1 Sam. xx. 14, 15), "*Show me the kindness of the Lord, that I die not,* and the same to my seed."

II. Information given him concerning Mephibosheth, the son of Jonathan. Ziba was an old retainer to Saul's family, and knew the state of it. He informed the king that Jonathan's son was living, but *lame* (how he came to be so we read before, *ch.* iv. 4), and that he lived in obscurity, probably among his mother's relations in Lo-debar, in Gilead, on the other side Jordan, where he was *forgotten, as a dead man out of mind.*

III. The bringing of him to court. The king sent (Ziba, it is likely) to bring him up to Jerusalem with all convenient speed, *v.* 5. Thus he eased Machir of his trouble, and perhaps recompensed him for what he had laid out on Mephibosheth's account. This Machir appears to have been a very generous free-hearted man, and to have entertained Mephibosheth, not out of any disaffection to David or his government, but in compassion to the reduced son of a prince, for afterwards we find him kind to David himself when he fled from Absalom. He is named (*ch.* xvii. 27) among those that furnished the king with what he wanted at Mahanaim.

1. Mephibosheth presented himself to David. Lame as he was, *he fell on his face, and did homage, v.* 6. David had thus made his honours to Mephibosheth's father, Jonathan, when he was next to the throne (1 Sam. xx. 41, *he bowed himself to him three times*), and now Mephibosheth, in like manner, addresses him, when affairs are so completely reversed.

2. David received him with all the kindness that could be. (1) He spoke to him as one surprised, but

pleased to see him. (2) He bade him not be afraid: *Fear not*, *v.* 7. He assures him that he sent for him, not with any bad design upon him, but to show him kindness. (3) He gives him, by grant from the crown, *all the land of Saul his father*, that is, his paternal estate, which was forfeited by Ish-bosheth's rebellion and added to his own revenue. True friendship will be generous. (4) Though he had thus given him a good estate, sufficient to maintain him, yet for Jonathan's sake (whom perhaps he saw some resemblance of in Mephibosheth's face), he will take him to be a constant guest at his own table, where he will be comfortably fed. Though Mephibosheth was lame and unsightly, and does not appear to have had any great fitness for business, yet, for his good father's sake, David took him to be one of his family.

3. Mephibosheth accepts this kindness with great humility and self-abasement. How does he magnify David's kindness! It would have been easy to lessen it if he had been so disposed.

Verses 9–13

The matter is here settled concerning Mephibosheth. 1. This grant of his father's estate is confirmed to him, and Ziba called to be a witness to it (*v.* 9); and, it should seem, Saul had a very good estate, fields and vineyards to bestow, 1 Sam. xxii. 7. Be it ever so much, Mephibosheth is now master of it all. 2. The management of the estate is committed to Ziba. How unfaithful Ziba was to him we shall find afterwards, *ch.* xvi. 3. Now because David was a type of Christ, his Lord and son, his root and offspring, let his kindness to Mephibosheth serve to illustrate the kindness and love of God our Saviour towards fallen man, which yet he was under no obligation to, as David was to Jonathan. Man was convicted of rebellion against God, and, like Saul's house, under a sentence of rejection from him, was not only brought low and impoverished, but lame and impotent, made so by the fall. The Son of God enquires after this degenerate race, and comes to seek and save them. To those of them that humble themselves before him, and commit themselves to him, he restores the forfeited inheritance, he entitles them to a better paradise than that which Adam lost, and takes them into communion with himself, sets them with his children at his table, and feasts with the dainties of heaven.

Chapter 10

A war David had with the Ammonites and the Syrians their allies. I. David sent a friendly embassy to Hanun king of the Ammonites, ver. 1, 2. II. He, upon a base surmise that it was ill intended, abused David's ambassadors, ver. 3, 4. III. David resenting it (ver. 5), the Ammonites prepared for war against him, ver. 6. IV. David carried the war into their country, sent against them Joab and Abishai, who addressed themselves to the battle with a great deal of conduct and bravery, ver. 7–12. V. The Ammonites, and the Syrians their allies, were totally routed, ver. 13, 14. VI. The forces of the Syrians, which rallied again, were a second time defeated, ver. 15–19.

Verses 1–5

I. The great respect David paid to his neighbour, the king of the Ammonites, *v.* 1, 2. 1. The inducement to it was some kindness he had formerly received from Nahash the deceased king. He *showed kindness to me*, says David (*v.* 2). If David received kindness, he resolves gratefully to return it. 2. The particular instance was sending an embassy to condole with him on his father's death. *David sent to comfort him.* It is a comfort to children, when their parents are dead, to find that their parents' friends are theirs, and that they intend to keep up an acquaintance with them.

II. The great affront which Hanun the king of the Ammonites put upon David in his ambassadors.

1. He hearkened to the spiteful suggestions of his princes, who insinuated that David's ambassadors, under pretence of being comforters, were sent as spies, *v.* 3. False men are ready to think others as false as themselves. Bishop Patrick's note on this is that "there is nothing so well meant but it may be ill interpreted, and is wont to be so by men who love nobody but themselves." 2. Entertaining this vile suggestion, he basely abused David's ambassadors, like a man of a sordid villainous spirit, that was fitter to rake a kennel than to wear a crown. They and their reputation were under the special protection of the law of nations; they put a confidence in the Ammonites, and came among them unarmed; yet Hanun used them like rogues and vagabonds, and worse, *shaved off the one half of their beards, and cut off their garments in the midst*, to expose them to the contempt and ridicule of his servants.

III. David's tender concern for his servants that were thus abused. He sent to meet them and directed them to stay at Jericho, a private place, where they would not have occasion to come into company, till that half of their beards which was shaved off had grown to such a length that the other half might be decently cut to it, *v.* 5. The Jews wore their beards long, reckoning it an honour to appear aged and grave. Let us learn not to lay too much to heart unjust reproaches; after awhile they will wear off themselves, and turn only to the shame of their authors, while the injured reputation in a little time grows again, as these beards did. God will *bring forth thy righteousness as the light*, therefore *wait patiently for him*, Ps. xxxvii. 6, 7.

Verses 6–14

I. The preparation which the Ammonites made for war, *v.* 6. They found themselves an unequal match, and were forced to hire forces of other nations into their service.

II. The speedy descent which David's forces made upon them, *v.* 7. When David heard of their military preparations, he sent Joab with a great army to attack them, *v.* 7. It was David's prudence to carry the war into their country, and fight them at the entering in of the gate of their capital city, *Rabbah*, as some think, or *Medeba*, a city in their borders, before which they pitched to guard their coast, 1 Chron. xix. 7.

III. Preparations made on both sides for an engagement. 1. The enemy disposed themselves into two bodies, one of Ammonites, which, being their own, were posted at the gate of the city; the other of Syrians, whom they had taken into their pay, and who were therefore posted at a distance in the field, to charge the forces of Israel in the flank or rear, while the Ammonites charged them in the front, *v.* 8. 2. Joab, like a wise general, accordingly divided his forces: the choicest men he took under his own command, to fight the Syrians. The rest of the forces he put under the command of Abishai his brother, to engage the Ammonites, *v.* 10.

IV. Joab's speech before the battle, *v.* 11, 12. 1. He prudently concerts the matter with Abishai his brother. He supposes the worst, that one of them should be obliged to give back; and in that case, upon a signal given, the other should send a detachment to receive it. Christ's soldiers should thus strengthen one another's hands in their spiritual warfare. The strong must succour and help the weak. Those that through grace are conquerors over temptation must counsel, and comfort, and pray for, those that are tempted. *When thou art converted, strengthen thy brethren*, Luke xxii. 32. 2. He bravely encourages himself, and his brother, and the rest of the officers and soldiers. When Joab saw the front of the battle was against him, both before and behind, instead of giving orders to make an honourable retreat, he animated his men to charge so much more furiously: *Be of good courage and let us play the men*, not for pay and preferment, for honour and fame, but *for our people, and for the cities of our God*, for the public safety and welfare, in which the glory of God is so much interested. *God and our country* was the word. 3. He piously leaves the issue with God. When we make conscience of doing our duty we may, with the greatest satisfaction, leave the event with God.

V. The victory Joab obtained over the confederate forces of Syria and Ammon, *v.* 13, 14. The Syrians were first routed by Joab, and then the Ammonites by Abishai; the Ammonites seem not to have fought at all, but, upon the retreat of the Syrians, to have fled into the city.

Verses 15–19

1. A new attempt of the Syrians to recover their lost honour and to check the progress of David's victorious arms. 2. The defeat of this attempt by the vigilance and valour of David, who, in a pitched battle, routed the Syrians (*v.* 18). Their general was killed in the battle, and David came home in triumph. 3. The consequence of this victory over the Syrians. (1) David gained several tributaries, *v.* 19. *The kings*, or petty princes, that had been subject to Hadarezer, when they saw how powerful David was, very wisely *made peace with Israel*, whom they found they could not make war with, *and served them*, since they were able to give them protection. Thus the promise made to Abraham (Gen. xv. 18), and repeated to Joshua (*ch.* i. 4), that the borders of Israel should extend to the river Euphrates, was performed, at length. (2) The Ammonites lost their old allies: *The Syrians feared to help the children of Ammon*.

CHAPTER 11

The scripture is faithful in relating the faults even of those whom it most applauds, which is an instance of the sincerity of the penmen, and an evidence that it was not written to serve any party: and even such stories as these "were written for our learning", that "he that thinks he stands may take heed lest he fall," and that others' harms may be our warning. Those are very great sins, and greatly aggravated, which here we find David guilty of. I. He committed adultery with Bath-sheba, the wife of Uriah, ver. 1–5. II. He endeavoured to father the spurious brood upon Uriah, ver. 6–13. III. When that project failed, he plotted the death of Uriah by the sword of the children of Ammon, and effected it, ver. 14–25. IV. He married Bath-sheba, ver. 26, 27. Is this David? Let him that readeth understand what the best of men are when God leaves them to themselves.

Verses 1–5

I. David's glory, in pursuing the war against the Ammonites, *v.* 1. Rabbah, their metropolis, made a stand, and held out a great while. To this city Joab laid close siege, and it was at the time of this siege that David fell into sin.

II. David's shame, in being himself conquered, and led captive by his own lust. The sin he was guilty of was adultery, against the letter of the seventh commandment.

1. Observe the occasions which led to this sin. (1) Neglect of his business. When he should have been abroad with his army in the field, fighting the battles of the Lord, he devolved the care upon others, and he himself *tarried still at Jerusalem*, *v.* 1. Had he been now at his post at the head of his forces, he would have been out of the way of this temptation. When we are out of the way of our duty we are in the way of temptation. (2) Love of ease, and the indulgence of a slothful temper: *He came off his bed at evening-tide*, *v.* 2. Idleness gives great advantage to the tempter. Standing waters gather filth. The bed of sloth often proves the bed of lust. (3) A wandering eye: *He saw a woman washing herself*, probably from some ceremonial pollution, according to the law.

2. The steps of the sin. When he saw her, lust immediately conceived, and, (1) He enquired who she was (*v.* 3), perhaps intending only, if she were unmarried, to take her to wife. (2) The corrupt desire growing more violent, though he was told she was a wife, and whose wife she was, yet he sent messengers for her, and then, it may be, intended only to please himself with her company and conversation. But, (3) When she came *he lay with her*, she too easily consenting, because he was a great man, and famed for his goodness too.

3. The aggravations of the sin. (1) He was now in years, fifty at least. (2) He had many wives and concubines of his own. (3) Uriah, whom he wronged, was one of his own worthies, hazarding his life in the high places of the field for the honour and safety of him and his kingdom, where he himself should have been. (4) Bath-sheba, whom he debauched, was a lady of good reputation. The adulterer not only wrongs and ruins his own soul, but, as much as he can, another's soul too. (5) David was a king, whom God had entrusted with the sword of justice and the execution of the law upon other criminals, particularly upon adulterers. I can think but of one excuse for it, which is that it was done but once; it was far from being his practice; it was by the surprise of a temptation that he was drawn into it. He was not one of those of whom the prophet complains that *they were as fed horses, neighing every one after his neighbour's wife* (Jer. v. 8); but this once God left him to himself. But by this instance we are taught what need we have to pray every day, *Father, in heaven, lead us not into temptation*, and to watch, that we enter not into it.

Verses 6–13

Uriah, we may suppose, had now been absent from his wife some weeks. The situation of his wife would *bring to light the hidden works of darkness*; and when Uriah, at his return, should find how he had been abused, and by whom, it might well be expected, 1. That he would prosecute his wife, according to law, and have her stoned to death. This Bath-sheba was apprehensive of when she sent to let David know she was with child, intimating that he was concerned to protect her. 2. It might also be expected that since he could not prosecute David by law for an offence of this nature he would take his revenge another way, and raise a rebellion against him. To prevent this double mischief, David endeavours to father the child which should be born upon Uriah himself, and therefore sends for him home to stay a night or two with his wife.

I. How the plot was laid. Uriah must come home from the army under pretence of bringing David an account *how the war prospered*, and how they went on with the siege of Rabbah, *v.* 7. David, having had as much conference with Uriah as he thought requisite to cover the design, sent him to his house. When that project failed the first night, and Uriah, being weary of his journey and more desirous of sleep than meat, lay all night in the guard-chamber, the next night *he made him drunk* (*v.* 13). It is a very wicked thing, upon any design whatsoever, to make a person drunk. Robbing a man of his reason is worse than robbing him of his money.

II. How this plot was defeated by Uriah's firm resolution not to lie in his own bed. "Joab, and all the mighty men of Israel, lie hard and uneasy, and much exposed to the weather and to the enemy; and shall I go and take my ease and pleasure at my own house?" No, he protests he will not do it. Now, (1) This was in itself a generous resolution, and showed Uriah to be a man of a public spirit, bold and hardy, and mortified to the delights of sense. (2) It might have been of use to awaken David's conscience, and make his heart to smite him for what he had done.

Verses 14–27

When David's project of fathering the child upon Uriah himself failed, so that, in process of time, Uriah would certainly know the wrong that had been done him, the devil put it into David's heart to take him off. That innocent, valiant, gallant man, who was ready to die for his prince's honour, must die by his prince's hand. See how fleshly lusts war against the soul, and what devastations they make in that war; how they blind the eyes, harden the heart, sear the conscience, and deprive men of all sense of honour and justice. The devil, having, as a poisonous serpent, put it into David's heart to murder Uriah, as a subtle serpent he puts it into his head how to do it.

I. Orders are sent to Joab to set Uriah in the front of the hottest battle, and then to desert him, and abandon him to the enemy, *v.* 14, 15. 1. It was deliberate. 2. He sent the letter by Uriah himself, than which nothing could be more base and barbarous, to make him accessory to his own death. 3. Advantage must be taken of Uriah's own courage and zeal for his king and country, which deserve the greatest praise and recompence, to betray him the more easily to his fate. 4. Many must be involved in the guilt. Joab, the general, and all that retire from Uriah when they ought in conscience to support and second him, became guilty of his death. 5. Uriah cannot thus die alone: the party he commands is in danger of being cut off with him. 6. It will be the triumph and joy of the Ammonites, the sworn enemies of God and Israel.

II. Joab executes these orders. In the next assault that is made upon the city Uriah has the most dangerous post assigned him, and he is slain in it, *v.* 16, 17. It was strange that Joab would do such a thing merely upon a letter, without knowing the reason. But, 1. Perhaps he supposed Uriah had been guilty of some great crime. 2. Joab had been guilty of blood, and we may suppose it pleased him very well to see David himself falling into the same guilt.

III. He sends an account of it to David. An express is despatched away immediately with a report of this last disgrace and loss which they had sustained, *v.* 18. He slyly orders the messenger to soothe it with telling him that Uriah the Hittite was dead also. The messenger delivered this message agreeably to orders, *v.* 22–24. He makes the besieged to sally out first upon the besiegers (*they came out unto us into the field*), represents the besiegers as doing their part with great bravery (*we were upon them even to the entering of the gate*—we forced them to retire into the city with precipitation), and so concludes with a slight mention of the slaughter made among them by some shot from the wall: *Some of the king's servants are dead*, and particularly *Uriah the Hittite*, an officer of note, stood first in the list of the slain.

IV. David receives the account with a secret satisfaction, *v.* 25.

V. He marries the widow in a little time. She submitted to the ceremony of mourning for her husband as short a time as custom would admit (*v.* 26), and then David took her to his house as his wife, and she bore him a son. The whole *matter of Uriah* (as it is called, 1 Kings xv. 5), the adultery, falsehood, murder, and this marriage at last, it was all displeasing to the Lord. God sees and hates sin in his own people. Nay, the nearer any are to God in profession the more displeasing to him their sins are. Let none therefore encourage themselves in sin by the example of David; for those that sin as he did will fall under the displeasure of God as he did.

CHAPTER 12

The foregoing chapter gave us the account of David's sin; this gives us the account of his repentance. Though he fell, he was not utterly cast down, but, by the grace of God, recovered himself, and found mercy with God. I. His conviction, by a message Nathan brought him from God, which was a parable that obliged him to condemn himself (ver. 1–6), and the application of the parable, in which Nathan charged him with the sin (ver. 7–9) and pronounced sentence upon him, ver. 10–12. II. His repentance and remission, with a proviso, ver. 13, 14. III. The sickness and death of the child, and his behaviour while it was sick and when it was dead (ver. 15–23), in both which David gave evidence of his repentance. IV. The birth of Solomon, and God's gracious message concerning him, in which God gave an evidence of his reconciliation to David, ver. 24, 25. V. The taking of Rabbah (ver. 26–31), which is mentioned as a further instance that God did not deal with David according to his sins.

Verses 1–14

It seems to have been a great while after David had been guilty of adultery with Bath-sheba before he was brought to repentance for it. For, when Nathan was sent to him, the child was born (*v.* 14). What shall we think of David's state all this while? We may well suppose his comforts and the exercises of his graces suspended, and his communion with God interrupted; during all that time, it is certain, he penned no psalms, his harp was out of tune, and his soul like a tree in winter, that has life in the root only.

I. The messenger God sent to him. He sent a prophet — Nathan, his faithful friend and confidant, to instruct and counsel him, *v.* 1. Though God may suffer his people to fall into sin, he will not suffer them to lie still in it. He sends after us before we seek after him, else we should certainly be lost. Nathan was the prophet by whom God had sent him notice of his kind intentions towards him (*ch.* vii. 4), and now, by the same hand, he sends him this message of wrath.

II. The message Nathan delivered to him.

1. He fetched a compass with a parable, which seemed to David as a complaint made to him against one of his subjects that had wronged his poor neighbour. (1) Nathan represented to David a grievous injury which a rich man had done to an honest neighbour that was not able to contend with him: *The rich man had many flocks and herds* (*v.* 2); the poor man had one lamb only. This poor man had but one lamb, a ewe-lamb, a little ewe-lamb, having not wherewithal to buy or keep more. But it was a *cade*-lamb (as we call it); *it grew up with his children*, *v.* 3. He was fond of it, and it was familiar with him at all times. The rich man, having occasion for a lamb to entertain a friend with, took the poor man's lamb from him by violence and made use of that (*v.* 4), either out of covetousness, because he grudged to make use of his own, or rather out of luxury, because he fancied the lamb that was thus tenderly kept, and ate and drank like a child, must needs be more delicate food than any of his own and have a better relish. (2) In this he showed him the evil of the sin he had been guilty of in defiling Bath-sheba. He had many wives and concubines, whom he kept at a distance, as rich men keep their flocks in their fields. Marriage is a remedy against fornication, but marrying many is not; for, when once the law of unity is transgressed, the indulged lust will hardly stint itself. Observe that this evil disposition is called a traveller, for in the beginning it is only so, but, in time, it becomes a guest, and, in conclusion, is master of the house. (3) By this parable he drew from David a sentence against himself. For David supposing it to be a case in fact, and not doubting the truth of it when he had it from Nathan himself, gave judgment immediately against the offender, and confirmed it with an oath, *v.* 5, 6. [1] That, for his injustice in taking away the lamb, he should restore

fourfold, according to the law (Exod. xxii. 1), *four sheep for a sheep.* [2] That for his tyranny and cruelty, and the pleasure he took in abusing a poor man, he should be put to death.

2. He closed in with him, at length, in the application of the parable. In plain terms, "*Thou art the man* who hast done this wrong, and a much greater, to thy neighbour." Did he deserve to die who took his neighbour's lamb? and dost not thou who hast taken thy neighbour's wife? Now he speaks immediately from God, not as a petitioner for a poor man, but as an ambassador from the great God, with whom is no respect of persons.

(1) God, by Nathan, reminds David of the great things he had done and designed for him, anointing him to be king, and preserving him to the kingdom (*v.* 7). He had given him the house of Israel and Judah. The wealth of the kingdom was at his service and everybody was willing to oblige him.

(2) He charges him with a high contempt of the divine authority, in the sins he had been guilty of: *Wherefore hast thou* (presuming upon thy royal dignity and power) *despised the commandment of the Lord? v.* 9. [1] The murder of Uriah is twice mentioned: "*Thou hast killed Uriah with the sword. Thou hast slain him with the sword of the children of Ammon,* those uncircumcised enemies of God and Israel." [2] The marrying of Bath-sheba is likewise twice mentioned, because he thought there was no harm in that (*v.* 9): *Thou hast taken his wife to be thy wife,* and again, *v.* 10. To marry her whom he had before defiled, and whose husband he had slain, was an affront upon the ordinance of marriage, making that not only to palliate, but in a manner to consecrate, such villainies.

(3) He threatens an entail of judgments upon his family for this sin (*v.* 10): "*The sword shall never depart from thy house,* not in thy time nor afterwards, but, for the most part, thou and thy posterity shall be engaged in war." Can the mercy and the sword consist with each other? Yes, those may lie under great and long afflictions who yet shall not be excluded from the grace of the covenant. The reason given is, *Because thou hast despised me.* It is particularly threatened, [1] That his children should be his grief: *I will raise up evil against thee out of thy own house.* [2] That his wives should be his shame, that by an unparalleled piece of villainy they should be publicly debauched before all Israel, *v.* 11, 12.

3. David's penitent confession of his sin hereupon. *I have sinned against the Lord, v.* 13.

4. His pardon declared, upon this penitent confession, but with a proviso. When David said *I have sinned,* and Nathan perceived that he was a true penitent,

(1) He did, in God's name, assure him that his sin was forgiven: "*The Lord also has put away thy sin* out of the sight of his avenging eye; *thou shalt not die,*" that is, "not die eternally, nor be for ever put away from God, as thou wouldest have been if he had not put away the sin." "*The sword shall not depart from thy house,* but, [1] It shall not cut thee off, thou shalt come to thy grave in peace." [2] "Though thou shalt all thy days be *chastened of the Lord,* yet thou *shalt not be condemned with the world.*"

(2) Yet he pronounces a sentence of death upon the child, *v.* 14. Behold the sovereignty of God! The guilty parent lives, and the guiltless infant dies. [1] David had, by his sin, wronged God in his honour; he had *given occasion to the enemies of the Lord to blaspheme.* There is this great evil in the scandalous sins of those that profess religion, and relation to God, that they furnish the enemies of God and religion with matter for reproach and blasphemy, Rom. ii. 24. [2] God will therefore vindicate his

honour by showing his displeasure against David for this sin, and letting the world see that though he loves David he hates his sin; and he chooses to do it by the *death of the child.*

Verses 15–25

Nathan, having delivered his message, stayed not at court, but went home, probably to pray for David, to whom he had been preaching. David named one of his sons by Bath-sheba *Nathan,* in honour of this prophet (1 Chron. iii. 5), and it was that son of whom Christ, the great prophet, lineally descended, Luke iii. 31. When Nathan retired, David, it is probable, retired likewise, and penned the 51st Psalm, in which (though he had been assured that his sin was pardoned) he prays earnestly for pardon, and greatly laments his sin; for then will true penitents be ashamed of what they have done when God is *pacified towards them,* Ezek. xvi. 63.

I. The child's illness: *The Lord struck* it, *and it was very sick.*

II. David's humiliation under this token of God's displeasure, and the intercession he made with God for the life of the child (*v.* 16, 17): *He fasted, and lay all night upon the earth.* This was an evidence of the truth of his repentance. For, 1. Hereby it appeared that he was willing to bear the shame of his sin, for this child would be a continual memorandum of it, therefore he was so far from desiring its death, as most in such circumstances do, that he prayed earnestly for its life. 2. A very tender compassionate spirit appeared in this towards little children, even their own; and this was another sign of a broken contrite spirit. Those that are penitent will be pitiful. 3. He discovered, in this, a great concern for another world, which is an evidence of repentance. Nathan had told him that certainly the child should die; yet, while it is in the reach of prayer, he earnestly intercedes with God for it, chiefly (as we may suppose) that its soul might be safe and happy in another world, and that his sin might not come against the child, and that it might not fare the worse for that in the future state.

III. The death of the child: It *died on the seventh day* (*v.* 18), when it was seven days old, and therefore not circumcised, which David might perhaps interpret as a further token of God's displeasure, that it died before it was brought under the seal of the covenant; yet he does not therefore doubt of its being happy, for the benefits of the covenant do not depend upon the seals.

IV. David's wonderful calmness and composure of mind when he understood the child was dead.

1. What he did. (1) He laid aside the expressions of his sorrow, washed and anointed himself, and called for clean linen, that he might decently appear before God in his house. (2) *He went up to the tabernacle and worshipped,* like Job when he heard of the death of his children. (3) *Then he went to his own house* and refreshed himself, as one who found benefit by his religion in the day of his affliction.

2. The reason he gave for what he did. His servants thought it strange that he should afflict himself so for the sickness of the child and yet take the death of it so easily, and asked him the reason of it (*v.* 21), in answer to which he gives this plain account of his conduct, (1) That while the child was alive he thought it his duty to importune the divine favour towards it, *v.* 22. When our relations and friends have fallen sick, the prayer of faith has prevailed much; while there is life there is hope, and, while there is hope, there is room for prayer. (2) That now the child was dead he thought it as much his duty to be satisfied in the divine disposal concerning it (*v.* 23): *Now, wherefore should I fast?* Two things checked his

grief:—[1] *I cannot bring him back again*; and again, *He shall not return to me.* Those that are dead are out of the reach of prayer; nor can our tears profit them. [2] *I shall go to him. First,* To him to the grave. Note, The consideration of our own death should moderate our sorrow at the death of our relations. *Secondly,* To him to heaven, to a state of blessedness, which even the Old Testament saints had some expectation of. This may comfort us when our children are removed from us by death, they are better provided for, both in work and wealth, than they could have been in this world. We shall be with them shortly, to part no more.

V. The birth of Solomon. Though David's marrying Bath-sheba had displeased the Lord, yet he was not therefore commanded to divorce her. Bath-sheba, no doubt, was greatly afflicted with the sense of her sin, and the tokens of God's displeasure. But, God having restored to David the joys of his salvation, he comforted her with the same comforts with which he himself was comforted of God (*v.* 24). 1. Inasmuch as, by his providence, he gave them a son. They called him *Solomon—peaceful,* because his birth was a token of God's being at peace with them, because of the prosperity which was entailed upon him, and because he was to be a type of Christ, the prince of peace. David had very patiently submitted to the will of God in the death of the other child, and now God made up the loss of that, abundantly to his advantage, in the birth of this. 2. Inasmuch as, by his grace, he particularly owned and favoured that son: *The Lord loved him* (*v.* 24 and 25), ordered him, by the prophet Nathan, to be called *Jedidiah—Beloved of the Lord.*

Verses 26–31

An account of the conquest of Rabbah, and other cities of the Ammonites. Though this comes in here after the birth of David's child, yet it is most probable that it was effected a good while before, and soon after the death of Uriah, perhaps during the days of Bath-sheba's mourning for him. Observe, 1. That God was very gracious in giving David this great success against his enemies. Justly might he have made his sword, thenceforward, a plague to David and his kingdom; yet he breaks it and makes David's sword victorious, even before he repents, that this *goodness of God might lead him to repentance.* 2. That Joab acted very honestly and honourably; for when he had taken *the city of waters,* the royal city, where the palace was, and from which 'the rest of the city was supplied with water (and therefore, upon the cutting off of that, would be obliged speedily to surrender), he sent to David to come in person to complete this great action, that he might have the praise of it, *v.* 26–28. 3. That David was both too haughty and too severe upon this occasion, and neither so humble nor so tender as he should have been. (1) He seems to have been too fond of the crown of the king of Ammon, *v.* 30. Because it was of extraordinary value, by reason of the precious stones with which it was set, David would have it set upon his head, though it would have been better to have cast it at God's feet, and at this time to have put his own mouth in the dust, under guilt. (2) He seems to have been too harsh with his prisoners of war, *v.* 31. Taking the city by storm, after it had obstinately held out against a long and expensive siege, if he had put all whom he found in arms to the sword in the heat of battle, it would have been severe enough; but to kill them afterwards in cold blood, and by cruel tortures, with saws and harrows, tearing them to pieces, did not become him who, when he entered upon the government, promised to sing of mercy as well as judgment, Ps. ci. 1.

Chapter 13

The righteous God had lately told David, by Nathan the prophet, that, to chastise him for his sin in the matter of Uriah, he would "raise up evil against him out of his own house", ch. xii. 11. And here, we find the evil beginning to rise; henceforward he was followed with one trouble after another. Adultery and murder were David's sins, and those sins among his children (Amnon defiling his sister Tamar, and Absalom murdering his brother Amnon) were the beginnings of his punishment. In this chapter we have, I. Amnon ravishing Tamar, assisted in his plot to do it by Jonadab his kinsman, and villainously executing it, ver. 1–20. II. Absalom murdering Amnon for it, ver. 21–39. Both were great griefs to David, and the more because he was unwittingly made accessory to both, by sending Tamar to Amnon and Amnon to Absalom.

Verses 1–20

A particular account of the abominable wickedness of Amnon in ravishing his sister. Amnon's character, we have reason to think, was bad in other things; if he had not forsaken God, he would never have been given up to these vile affections.

I. The devil, as an unclean spirit, put it into his heart to lust after his sister Tamar. Beauty is a snare to many; it was so to her. Amnon's lust was, 1. Unnatural in itself. Such a spirit of contradiction there is in man's corrupt nature that still it desires forbidden fruit, and the more strongly it is forbidden the more greedily it is desired. 2. It was very uneasy to him. He was so vexed that he could not gain an opportunity to solicit her chastity that he *fell sick, v.* 2.

II. The devil, as a subtle serpent, put it into his head how to compass this wicked design. Amnon had a friend, a subtle man, cunning to carry on an intrigue of this nature, *v.* 3.

1. He took notice that Amnon looked ill, and, being a subtle man, concluded that he was love-sick (*v.* 4). *Being the king's son,* "Thou hast the power of a prince to command what thou wantest and wishest for: use that power, therefore, and gratify thyself."

2. Amnon having the impudence to own his wicked lust, miscalling it *love* (*I love Tamar*), Jonadab put him in a way to compass his design, *v.* 5. Amnon is already sick, but goes about; he must take upon him to be so ill as not to be able to get up. The best dish from the king's table cannot please him; but, if he can eat anything, it must be from his sister Tamar's fair hand.

3. Amnon followed these directions, and thus got Tamar within his reach. David was always fond of his children, and concerned if anything ailed them; he no sooner hears that Amnon is sick than he comes himself to visit him. At parting, the indulgent father asks, "Is there anything thou hast a mind to, that I can procure for thee?" "Yes, Sir," says the dissembling son, "my stomach is weak, and I know not of any thing I can eat, unless it be a cake of my sister Tamar's making, and I cannot be satisfied that it is so unless I see her make it, and it will do me the more good if I eat it at her hand." David saw no reason to suspect any mischief intended. He therefore immediately orders Tamar to go and attend her sick brother, *v.* 7.

4. Having got her to him, he contrives to have her alone. Tamar has not the least thought of that which his polluted breast is full of; and therefore she makes no scruple of being alone with him *in the inner chamber, v.* 10. And now the mask is thrown off, the meat is thrown by, and the wicked wretch calls her *sister,* and yet impudently courts her to *come and lie with him, v.* 11.

III. The devil, as a strong tempter, deafens his ear to all the reasonings with which she resisted his assaults and would have persuaded him to desist. 1. She calls him *brother,* reminding him of the nearness of the relation, which made it unlawful for him to marry her, much less to debauch her. It was expressly forbidden (Lev. xviii. 9) under a severe penalty, Lev. xx. 17. 2. She entreats him not to force her, which intimates that she would never consent to it in any degree. 3. She lays before him the great wickedness of it. 4. She represents to him the shame of it. 5. To divert him from his wicked purpose she intimates to him that probably the king, rather than he should die for love of her, would dispense with the divine law and let him marry her: not as if she thought he had such a dispensing power, or would pretend to it; but she was confident that, upon notice given to the king by himself of this wicked desire, he would take an effectual course to protect her from him. But all her arts and all her arguments availed not. His proud spirit cannot bear a denial; but her honour, and all that was dear to her, must be sacrificed to his outrageous lust, *v.* 14. It is to be feared that Amnon, though young, had long lived a lewd life, for a man could not of a sudden arrive at such a pitch of wickedness.

IV. The devil, as a tormentor and betrayer, immediately turns his love of her into hatred (*v.* 15).

1. He basely turned her out of doors by force. To dismiss her thus as if she had done some wicked thing, obliged her, in her own defence, to proclaim the wrong. We may learn from it the mischievous consequences of sin (at last, it bites like a serpent); sins, sweet in the commission, afterwards become odious and painful, and the sinner's own conscience makes them so to himself. But to hate the person he had abused showed that his conscience was terrified, but his heart not at all humbled.

2. What becomes of the poor victim? (1) She bitterly lamented the injury she had received, as it was a stain to her honour, though no real blemish to her virtue. She tore her fine clothes in token of her grief, and put ashes upon her head, loathing her own beauty and ornaments, because they had occasioned Amnon's unlawful love; and she went on crying for another's sin, *v.* 19. (2) She retired to her brother Absalom's house, because he was her own brother, and there she lived in solitude and sorrow, in token of her modesty and detestation of uncleanness. Absalom spoke kindly to her, bade her pass by the injury for the present, designing himself to revenge it, *v.* 20.

Verses 21–29

What Solomon says of the beginning of strife is as true of the beginning of all sin, it is as the letting forth of water. One mischief begets another.

I. How David resented the tidings of Amnon's sin. But was it enough for him to be angry? He ought to have punished his son for it, and have put him to open shame.

II. How Absalom resented it. He resolves already to do the part of a judge in Israel; and, since his father will not punish Amnon, he will, from a principle, not of justice or zeal for virtue, but of revenge, because he reckons himself affronted in the abuse done to his sister.

1. The design conceived: *Absalom hated Amnon* (*v.* 22). Absalom's hatred of his brother's crime would have been commendable, and he might justly have prosecuted him for it by a due course of law, for example to others, and the making of some compensation to his injured sister; but to hate his person, and design his death by assassination, was to put a great affront upon God, by offering to repair the breach of his seventh commandment by the violation of his sixth, as if they were not all alike sacred. *But he that said, Do not commit adultery, said also, Do not kill,* James ii. 11.

2. The design concealed. He said nothing to Amnon. If Absalom had reasoned the matter with Amnon, he might have convinced him of his sin and brought him to repentance. Two full years Absalom nursed this root of bitterness, *v.* 24. It may be, at first, he did not intend to kill his brother, and only waited for an occasion to disgrace him or do him some other mischief; but in time his hatred ripened to this, that he would be no less than the death of him.

3. The design laid. (1) Absalom has a feast at his house in the country, as Nabal had, on occasion of his sheep-shearing, *v.* 23. (2) To this feast he invites the king his father, and all the princes of the blood (*v.* 24), that he might make himself the more respected among his neighbours. The king would not go himself, because he would not put him to the expense of his entertainment, *v.* 25. Absalom got leave for Amnon, and all the rest of the king's sons, to come and grace his table in the country, *v.* 26, 27. Absalom had so effectually concealed his enmity to Amnon that David saw no reason to suspect any design upon him in that particular invitation.

4. The design executed, *v.* 28, 29. (1) Absalom's entertainment was very plentiful; for he resolves that they shall all be merry with wine. But, (2) The orders he gave to his servants concerning Amnon, that they should mingle his blood with his wine, were very barbarous. He would have Amnon slain *when his heart was merry with wine,* not giving him time to say, *Lord. have mercy upon me.* His servants must be employed to do it, and so be involved in the guilt. He was to give the word of command—*Smite Amnon;* and then they must *kill him.* He did it in the presence of *all the king's sons,* of whom it is said (*ch.* viii. 18) that they were *chief rulers;* so that it was an affront to public justice and to the king his father, whom they represented. There is reason to suspect that Absalom did this, not only to revenge his sister's quarrel, but to make way for himself to the throne, which he was ambitious of, and which he would stand fair for if Amnon the eldest son was taken off. When the word of command was given Absalom's servants failed not to execute it, being buoyed up with an opinion that their master, being now next heir to the crown, would save them from harm. Now the threatened sword is drawn in David's house which should not depart from it. *First,* His eldest son falls by it. *Secondly,* All his sons flee from it, and come home in terror, not knowing how far their brother Absalom's bloody design might extend.

Verses 30–39

I. The fright that David was put into by a false report brought to Jerusalem that Absalom had *slain all the king's sons,* *v.* 30. This false news gave as much affliction to David, for the present, as if it had been true, *v.* 31.

II. The rectifying of the mistake in two ways:—
1. By the sly suggestions of Jonadab, David's nephew, who could tell him, *Amnon only is dead,* and not all the king's sons (*v.* 32, 33), and could tell him too that it was done by the appointment of Absalom, and designed from the day Amnon forced his sister Tamar. It is well if Jonadab was not as guilty of Amnon's death as he was of his sin; such friends do those prove who are hearkened to as counsellors to do wickedly: he that would not be so kind as to prevent Amnon's sin would not be so kind as to prevent his ruin, when, it should seem, he might have done both. 2. By the safe return of all the king's sons except Amnon. They bring the certain sad news that Absalom had murdered their brother Amnon. That Amnon was dead, and slain by his own brother in such a treacherous barbarous manner, was enough to put the king and court, the king and kingdom, into real mourning. Sorrow is never more reasonable than when there is sin in the case.

III. Absalom's flight from justice. He was now as much afraid of the king's sons as they were of him; they fled from his malice, he from their justice. No part of the land of Israel would shelter him. He therefore made the best of his way to his mother's relations, and was entertained by his grandfather *Talmai, king of Geshur* (v. 37), and there he was protected *three years* (v. 38).

IV. David's uneasiness for his absence. He mourned for Amnon a good while (v. 37), but time wore off his detestation of Absalom's sin; instead of loathing him as a murderer, he *longs to go forth to him*, v. 39.

Chapter 14

How Absalom threw himself out of his royal father's protection and favour we read in the foregoing chapter. In this chapter we have the arts that were used to bring him and his father together again, here recorded to show the folly of David in sparing him and indulging him in his wickedness, for which he was soon after severely corrected by his unnatural rebellion. I. Joab, by bringing a feigned issue to be tried before him, in the case of a poor widow of Tekoah, gains from him a judgment in general, That the case might be so as that the putting of a murderer to death ought to be dispensed with, ver. 1–20. II. Upon the application of this, he gains from him an order to bring Absalom back to Jerusalem, while yet he was forbidden the court, ver. 21–24. III. At length he was introduced by Joab into the king's presence, and the king was thoroughly reconciled to him, ver. 25–33.

Verses 1–20

I. Joab's design to get Absalom recalled out of banishment, v. 1. 1. As a courtier. Joab, finding how David stood affected, undertook this good office. 2. As a friend to Absalom. He plainly foresaw that his father would at length be reconciled to him, and therefore thought he should make both his friends if he were instrumental to bring it about. 3. As a statesman, and one concerned for the public welfare. He knew how much Absalom was the darling of the people, and, if David should die while he was in banishment, it might occasion a civil war, for it is probable that though all Israel loved his person, yet they were much divided upon his case. 4. As one who was himself a delinquent, by the murder of Abner. Whatever favour he could procure to be shown to Absalom would corroborate his reprieve.

II. His contrivance to do it by laying somewhat of a parallel case before the king so dexterously that the king took it for a real case, and gave judgment upon it, as he had done upon Nathan's parable.

1. The person he employed is not named, but she is said to be *a woman of Tekoah*. It is said, She was *a wise woman*, one that had a quicker wit and a readier tongue than most of her neighbours, v. 2. The truth of the story would be the less suspected when it came, as was supposed, from the person's own mouth.

2. The character she put on was that of a disconsolate widow, v. 2. Joab knew such a one would have an easy access to the king, who was always ready to comfort the mourners.

3. It was a case of compassion which she had to represent to the king, the judgment of all the inferior courts being against her. She tells the king that she had buried her husband (v. 5),—that she had two sons that were the support and comfort of her widowed state,—that these two fell out and fought, and one of them unhappily killed the other (v. 6),—that, for her part, she was desirous to protect the manslayer, yet the other relations insisted upon it that the surviving brother should be put to death according to law, that, by destroying the heir the inheritance might be theirs: and thus they would cut off, (1) Her comfort: "*They shall quench my coal*, deprive me of the only support of my old age, and put a period to all my joy in this world, which is reduced to this one coal." (2) Her husband's memory: "His family

will be quite extinct, and they will *leave* him *neither name nor remainder*," v. 7.

4. The king promised her his favour and a protection for her son. (1) Upon the representation of her case he promised to consider of it and to give orders about it, v. 8. (2) The woman was not content with this, but begged that he would immediately give judgment in her favour. (3) Being thus pressed, he made a further promise that she should not be injured nor insulted by her adversaries, but he would protect her from all molestation, v. 10. (4) Yet this does not content her, unless she can get her son's pardon, and protection for him too. Parents are not easy, unless their children be safe, safe for both worlds: "*Let not the avenger of blood destroy my son* (v. 11), for I am undone if I lose him; as good take my life as his." "*Remember* how *the Lord thy God* spared Cain, forgave thee the blood of Uriah, and let the king, that has found mercy, show mercy." (5) This importunate widow, by pressing the matter thus closely, obtains at last a full pardon for her son, ratified with an oath as she desired. Whether David did well thus to undertake the protection of a murderer, whom the cities of refuge would not protect, I cannot say. But there was room enough for a favourable judgment: he had slain his brother, but he *hated him not in time past*; it was upon a sudden provocation, and, for aught that appeared, it might be done in his own defence.

5. The case being thus adjudged in favour of her son, it is now time to apply it to the king's son, Absalom. The mask here begins to be thrown off, and another scene opened. The king is surprised, but not at all displeased, to find his humble petitioner become an advocate for the prince his son. She begs his pardon, and his patience, for what she had further to say (v. 12). (1) She supposes Absalom's case to be, in effect, the same with that which she had put as her son's; and therefore, if the king would protect her son, though he had slain his brother, much more ought he to protect his own, and to *fetch home his banished*, v. 13. It is true, Absalom's case differed very much from that which she had put. Absalom did not slay his brother upon a hasty passion. Absalom was not an only son, as hers was; David had many more. But David was himself too well affected to the cause to be critical, and was more desirous than she could be to bring that favourable judgment to his own son which he had given concerning hers. (2) She reasons with the king, to persuade him to recall Absalom out of banishment, give him his pardon, and take him into his favour again. [1] She pleads the interest which the people of Israel had in him. [2] She pleads man's mortality (v. 14): "*We must needs die.* Amnon must have died, some time, if Absalom had not killed him; and, if Absalom be now put to death for killing him, that will not bring him to life again." [3] She pleads God's mercy and his clemency towards poor guilty sinners, v. 14. Here are two great instances of the mercy of God to sinners: *First*, The patience he exercises towards them. His law is broken, yet he does not immediately take away the life of those that break it. *Secondly*, The provision he has made for their restoration to his favour, that though by sin they have banished themselves from him, yet they might not be expelled, or cast off, for ever. Poor banished sinners are likely to be for ever expelled from God if some course be not taken to prevent it. It is against the mind of God that they should be so, for he is not willing that any should perish.

6. She concludes her address with high compliments to the king, and strong expressions of her assurance that he would do what was just and kind both in the one case and in the other (v. 15–17). (1) She would not have troubled the king thus, but

that the people made her afraid. Understanding it of Absalom's case, she gives the king to understand, what he did not know before, that the nation was disgusted at his severity towards Absalom to such a degree that she was really afraid it would occasion a general mutiny or insurrection. (2) She applied to him with a great confidence in his wisdom and clemency. What this woman says by way of compliment the prophet says by way of promise (Zech. xii. 8), that, when *the weak shall be as David, the house of David shall be as the angel of the Lord*.

7. The hand of Joab is suspected by the king, and acknowledged by the woman, to be in all this, *v.* 18–20. (1) The king soon suspected it. (2) The woman very honestly owned it: *"Thy servant Joab bade me.* She speaks the truth as it was, and gives us an example to do likewise, and never to tell a lie for the concealing of a well-managed scheme. *Dare to be true; nothing can need a lie.*

Verses 21–27

I. Orders given for the bringing back of Absalom. Joab, having received these orders, 1. Returns thanks to the king for doing him the honour to employ him in an affair so universally grateful, *v.* 22. 2. Delays not to execute David's orders; he brought Absalom to Jerusalem, *v.* 23. I see not how David can be justified in suspending the execution of the ancient law (Gen. ix. 6), *Whoso sheds man's blood, by man shall his blood be shed.* God's laws were never designed to be like cobwebs, which catch the little flies, but suffer the great ones to break through. But, though he allowed him to return to his own house, he forbade him the court, and would not see him himself, *v.* 24. He put him under this interdict, (1) For his own honour, that he might not seem to forgive him too easily. (2) For Absalom's greater humiliation.

II. Occasion taken hence to give an account of Absalom. Nothing is said of his wisdom and piety, nothing of his devotion. All that is here said of him is, 1. That he was a very handsome man (*v.* 25), a poor commendation for a man that had nothing else in him valuable. Handsome are those that handsome do. Many a polluted deformed soul dwells in a fair and comely body; witness Absalom's, that was polluted with blood, and deformed with unnatural disaffection to his father and prince. In his body there was no blemish, but in his mind nothing but wounds and bruises. 2. That he had a very fine head of hair, not as the hair of a Nazarite (he was far from that strictness), but as the hair of a beau. He let it grow till it was a burden to him, and was heavy on him, nor would he cut it as long as ever he could bear it; as pride feels no cold, so it feels no heat, and that which feeds and gratifies it is not complained of, though very uneasy. He did poll it at certain times, that it might be seen how much it excelled other men's, and it weighed 200 shekels, which some reckon to be three pounds and two ounces of our weight; and with the oil and powder, especially if powdered (as Josephus says the fashion then was) with gold dust, it is not at all incredible that it should weigh so much. This fine hair proved his halter, *ch.* xviii. 9. 3. That his family began to be built up. It is probable that it was a good while before he had a child; and then it was that, despairing of having one, he set up that pillar which is mentioned, *ch.* xviii. 18, to bear up his name; but afterwards he had three sons and one daughter, *v.* 27.

Verses 28–33

Three years Absalom had been an exile from his father-in-law, and now two years a prisoner at large in his own house, and, in both, better dealt with than he deserved; yet his spirit was still unhumbled. He thinks himself sorely wronged that he is not restored to all his places at court. He longed to see the king's face, pretending it was because he loved him, but really because he wanted an opportunity to supplant him. He cannot do his father a mischief till he is reconciled to him; this therefore is the first branch of his plot; this snake cannot sting again till he be warmed in his father's bosom. He gained this point, not by promises of reformation, but by insults and injuries. 1. By his insolent carriage towards Joab, he brought him to mediate for him. A person in Absalom's circumstances should have sent to Joab a kindly message, but instead of this, he bids his servants set Joab's cornfields on fire (*v.* 30). Strange that Absalom should think, by doing Joab a mischief, to prevail with him to do him a kindness. Yet by this means he brings Joab to him, *v.* 31. And now Joab (perhaps frightened at the surprising boldness and fury of Absalom, and apprehensive that he had made an interest in the people strong enough to bear him out, not only puts up with this injury, but goes on his errand to the king. 2. By his insolent message to the king, he recovered his place at court, to see the king's face, that is, to become a privy counsellor, Esther i. 14. (1) His message was haughty and imperious, and very unbecoming either a son or a subject, *v.* 32. He undervalued the favour that had been shown him in recalling him from banishment, and restoring him to his own house, and that in Jerusalem. He defies the king's justice: "Let him kill me, if he can find it in his heart." (2) Yet with this message he carried his point, *v.* 33. David's strong affection for him construed all this to be the language of a great respect to his father, and an earnest desire of his favour, when, alas! it was far otherwise. Absalom, by the posture of his body, testified his submission to his father: *He bowed himself on his face to the ground*; and David, with a kiss, sealed his pardon.

Chapter 15

Absalom's name signifies "the peace of his father," yet he proves his greatest trouble. The sword entailed upon David's house had hitherto been among his children, but now it begins to be drawn against himself; had he done justice upon the murderer, he would have prevented the traitor. The story of Absalom's rebellion begins with this chapter. I. The arts Absalom used to insinuate himself into the people's affections, ver. 1–6. II. His open avowal of his pretensions to the crown at Hebron, whither he went under colour of a vow, and the strong party that appeared for him there, ver. 7–12. III. The notice brought of this to David, and his flight from Jerusalem thereupon, ver. 13–18. In his flight we are told, 1. What passed between him and Ittai, ver. 19–22. 2. The concern of the country for him, ver. 23. 3. His conference with Zadok, ver. 24–29. 4. His tears and prayers upon this occasion, ver. 30, 31. 5. Matters concerted by him with Hushai, ver. 32–37.

Verses 1–6

Absalom is no sooner restored to his place at court than he aims to be on the throne. If he had had any sense of gratitude he would have studied how to oblige his father, and make him easy; but, on the contrary, he meditates how to undermine him, by stealing the hearts of the people from him. Two things recommend a man to popular esteem—greatness and goodness.

I. Absalom looks great, *v.* 1. He had learned of the king of Geshur (what was not allowed to the kings of Israel) to multiply horses, which made him look desirable, while his father, on his mule, looked despicable. The people desired a king like the nations. Samuel had foretold that this would be *the manner of the king*: He shall *have chariots and horsemen, and some shall run before his chariots* (1 Sam. viii. 11); and this is Absalom's manner. Fifty footmen running before him would highly gratify his pride and the people's foolish fancy. David thinks that this parade is designed only to grace his court, and connives at it.

II. Absalom will seem very good too, but with a very bad design. Had he proved himself a good son and a good subject he would have shown himself worthy of future honours, after his father's death. Those that know how to obey well know how to rule. Those are good indeed that are good in their own place, not that pretend how good they would be in other people's places.

1. He wishes that he were a judge in Israel, v. 4. He that should himself have been judged to death for murder has the impudence to aim at being a judge of others. We read not of Absalom's wisdom, virtue, or learning in the laws, yet he wishes he were judge. Those are commonly most ambitious of preferment that are least fit for it; the best qualified are the most modest and self-diffident.

2. He takes a very bad course for the accomplishing of his wish. He wants to be such a judge that every man who has any cause shall come to him: in all causes he must preside. To gain the power he aims at, he endeavours to instil into the people's minds,

(1) A bad opinion of the present administration, as if the affairs of the kingdom were altogether neglected, and no care taken about them. "*There is no man deputed of the king to hear thee.* The king is himself old, and past business, or so taken up with his devotions that he never minds business; his sons are so addicted to their pleasures that, though they have the name of chief rulers, they take no care of the affairs committed to them." Every appellant shall be made to believe that he will never have justice done him, unless Absalom be viceroy or lord-justice. It is the way of turbulent, factious, aspiring men, to reproach the government they are under.

(2) A good opinion of his own fitness to rule. That the people might say, "O that Absalom were a judge!" he recommends himself to them, [1] As very diligent. [2] As very inquisitive and prying, and desirous to be acquainted with everyone's case. [3] As very familiar and humble. If any Israelite offered to do obeisance to him he took him and embraced him as a friend. No man's conduct could be more condescending, while his heart was as proud as Lucifer's.

Verses 7–12

The breaking out of Absalom's rebellion, which he had long been contriving. The same restless spirit was still working, and still they were given to change: as fond now of a new man as then of a new model. Absalom's plot being now ripe for execution,

I. The place he chose for the rendezvous of his party was Hebron, where he was born, and where his father began his reign and continued it several years. Everyone knew Hebron to be a royal city; and it lay in the heart of Judah's lot, in which tribe, probably, he thought his interest strong.

II. The pretence he had both to go thither and to invite his friends to him there was to offer a sacrifice to God, in performance of a vow he had made during his banishment, v. 7, 8. Under this pretence, 1. He got leave of his father to go to Hebron. David would be well pleased to hear that his son, being brought back, remembered his vow, and resolved to perform it. David was overjoyed to hear that Absalom inclined to *serve the Lord,* and therefore readily gave him leave to go to Hebron, and to go thither with solemnity. 2. He got a good number of sober substantial citizens to go along with him, v. 11. He knew that it was to no purpose to tempt them into his plot: they were inviolably firm to David. But he drew them in to accompany him, that the common people might think that they were in his

interest, and that David was deserted by some of his best friends. When religion is made a stalking-horse, and sacrifice a shoeing-horn, to sedition and usurpation it is not to be wondered at if some that were well affected to religion, as these followers of Absalom here, are imposed upon by the fallacy, and drawn in to give countenance to that, with their names, which in their heart they abhor, not having known the depths of Satan.

III. The project he laid was to get himself proclaimed king throughout all the tribes of Israel upon a signal given, v. 10. Spies were sent abroad, to be ready in every country to receive the notice with satisfaction and acclamations of joy. Some would conclude that David was dead, others that he had resigned: many, if they had rightly understood the matter, would have abhorred the thought of it.

IV. The person he especially courted and relied upon in this affair was Ahithophel, a politic thinking man that had been David's counsellor. But, upon some disgust of David's against him, or his against David, he was banished and lived privately in the country. A fitter tool Absalom could not find in all the kingdom than one that was so great a statesman, and yet was disaffected to the present ministry. While Absalom was offering his sacrifices, in performance of his pretended vow, he sent for this man.

V. The party that joined with him proved at last very considerable. The people increased continually with Absalom, which made the conspiracy strong and formidable. Everyone whom he had complimented and caressed not only came himself, but made all the interest he could for him, so that he wanted not for numbers.

Verses 13–23

I. The notice brought to David of Absalom's rebellion, v. 13. The matter was bad enough, and yet it seems to have been made worse to him, for he was told that *the hearts of the men of Israel* (that is, the generality of them, at least the leading men) were *after Absalom.* It is the wisdom of princes to make sure of the hearts of their subjects; for, if they have them, they have their purses, and arms, and all, at their service.

II. The alarm this gave to David, and the resolutions he came to thereupon. We may well imagine him thunderstruck, when he heard that the son he loved so dearly, was so unnaturally and ungratefully in arms against him. David did not call a council, but, consulting only with God and his own heart, determined immediately to quit Jerusalem, v. 14. He took up this strange resolve, either, 1. As a penitent submitting to the rod, and lying down under God's correcting hand. Or, 2. As a politician. Jerusalem was a great city, but not tenable. It was too large to be garrisoned by so small a force as David had now with him. He had reason to fear that the generality of the inhabitants were too well affected to Absalom to be true to him. And he had such a kindness for Jerusalem that he was loth to make it the seat of war, and expose it to the calamities of a siege.

III. His hasty flight from Jerusalem. 1. He went out of Jerusalem himself on foot, while his son Absalom had chariots and horses. 2. He took his household with him, his wives and children, that he might protect them in this day of danger, and that they might be a comfort to him in this day of grief. 3. He took his life-guard with him, the Cherethites and Pelethites, who were under the command of Benaiah, and the Gittites, who were under the command of Ittai, v. 18. These Gittites seem to have been, by birth, Philistines, in David's service, having known him at Gath, and being greatly in love with him for his virtue and piety, and having embraced the Jews' religion. David made them *his bodyguard,* and they adhered to him in his distress. 4. As many as would, of the people of Jerusalem, he took with him, and made a halt at some distance from the city, to draw them up, *v.* 17. He compelled none. Christ enlists none but volunteers.

IV. His discourse with Ittai the Gittite, who commanded the Philistine-proselytes.

1. David dissuaded him from going along with him, *v.* 19, 20. (1) He would try whether he was hearty for him, and not inclined to Absalom. He therefore bids him return to his post in Jerusalem, and serve the new king. (2) If he was faithful to David, yet David would not have him exposed to the perils he now counted upon. "*Should I make thee go up and down with us?* No, return with thy brethren." Generous souls are more concerned at the share others have in their troubles than at their own. Ittai shall therefore be dismissed with a blessing: *Mercy and truth be with thee.* David's dependence was upon the mercy and truth of God for comfort and happiness, both for himself and his friends; see Ps. lxi. 7.

2. Ittai bravely resolved not to leave him, *v.* 21. Where David is, *whether in life or death*, safe or in peril, there will this faithful friend of his be; and he confirms this resolution with an oath, that he might not be tempted to break it. Thus should we cleave to the Son of David with full purpose of heart that *neither life nor death shall separate us from his love.*

V. The common people's sympathy with David in his affliction. When he and his attendants *passed over the brook Kidron* (the very same brook that Christ passed over when he entered upon his sufferings, John xviii. 1), *towards the way of the wilderness*, which lay between Jerusalem and Jericho, *all the country wept with a loud voice, v.* 23. To see a prince thus reduced, forced from his palace and in fear of his life, with a small retinue seeking shelter in a desert, to see the city of David, which he himself won, built, and fortified, made an unsafe abode for David himself.

Verses 24–30

I. The fidelity of the priests and Levites and their firm adherence to David and his interest. Zadok and Abiathar, and all the Levites, if he go, will accompany him, and take the ark with them, that, by it, they may ask counsel of God for him, *v.* 24.

II. David's dismission of them back into the city, *v.* 25, 26. Abiathar was high priest (1 Kings ii. 35), but Zadok was his assistant, and attended the ark most closely, while Abiathar was active in public business, *v.* 24. Therefore David directs his speech to Zadok. 1. He is very solicitous for the safety of the ark: "By all means *carry the ark back into the city*, surely Absalom, bad as he is, will do that no harm." 2. He is very desirous to return to the enjoyment of the privileges of God's house. 3. He is very submissive to the holy will of God concerning the issue of this dark dispensation. See him here patiently awaiting the event: "*Behold, here am I*, as a servant expecting orders"; and see him willing to commit himself to God concerning it: "*Let him do to me as seemeth good to him.* I have nothing to object. All is well that God does. *Let him do what he will.*" That we may not complain of what is, let us see God's hand in all events; and, that we may not be afraid of what shall be, let us see all events in God's hand.

III. The confidence David put in the priests that they would serve his interest to the utmost of their power in his absence. He calls Zadok a *seer* (*v.* 27). One friend that is a seer, in such an exigency as this, was worth twenty that were not so quick-sighted. 1. Whom they should send to him—their two sons, Ahimaaz and Jonathan. 2. Whither they should send. He would encamp *in the plain of the wilderness* till he heard from them (*v.* 28), and then would move

according to the information and advice they should send him.

IV. The melancholy posture that David and his men put themselves into, when, at the beginning of their march, they went up the *mount of Olives, v.* 30.

1. David himself went bare-foot, as a prisoner or a slave, for mortification, and went weeping. He could not but weep to think that one who came out of his bowels, and had so often lain in his arms, should thus lift up the heel against him. There was much of the displeasure of his God in it. His sin was *ever before him* (Ps. li. 3), but never so plain nor ever appearing so black as now. He never wept thus when Saul hunted him: but a wounded conscience makes troubles lie heavily, Ps. xxxviii. 4.

2. When David wept all his company wept likewise, being much affected with his grief and willing to share in it.

Verses 31–37

Nothing, it seems, appeared to David more threatening in Absalom's plot than that Ahithophel was in it; for one good head, in such a design, is worth a thousand good hands. Absalom was himself no politician, but he had got one entirely in his interest that was. If therefore he can be baffled, Absalom is as good as routed and the head of the conspiracy cut off. This David endeavours to do.

I. By prayer. When he heard that Ahithophel was in the plot he lifted up his heart to God in this short prayer: *Lord, turn the counsel of Ahithophel into foolishness, v.* 31. David prayed not against Ahithophel's person, but against his counsel.

II. By policy. We must second our prayer with our endeavours, else we tempt God. Now he penned the third Psalm, as appears by the title; and some think that his singing this was the worship he now paid to God. Just now Providence brought Hushai, the person that should be instrumental to befool Ahithophel. He came to condole with David on his present trouble, with his coat rent and earth upon his head; but David resolved to employ him as a spy upon Absalom, and sent him to Jerusalem, to wait for Absalom's arrival, as a deserter from David, and to offer him his service, *v.* 34. How this gross dissimulation, which David put Hushai upon, can be justified, as a stratagem in war, I do not see. The best that can be made of it is that Absalom, if he rebel against his father, must stand upon his guard against all mankind, and, if he will be deceived, let him be deceived. David recommended Hushai to Zadok, and Hushai, thus instructed, came to Jerusalem (*v.* 37), whither also Absalom soon after came with his forces.

CHAPTER 16

I. We are to follow David in his melancholy flight; and there we find him, 1. Cheated by Ziba, ver. 1–4. 2. Cursed by Shimei, ver. 5–14. II. We meet Absalom in his triumphant entry; and there we find him, 1. Cheated by Hushai, ver. 15–19. 2. Counselled by Ahithophel to go in unto his father's concubines, ver. 20–23.

Verses 1–4

We read before how kind David was to Mephibosheth the son of Jonathan, how he prudently entrusted his servant Ziba with the management of his estate, while he generously entertained him at his own table, *ch.* ix. 10, but, it seems, Ziba is not content to be manager, he longs to be master, of Mephibosheth's estate. Now, he thinks, is his time to make himself so; if he can procure a grant of it from the crown, whether David or Absalom get the better it is all one to him, he hopes he shall secure his prey. 1. He made David a handsome present of provisions, which was the more welcome because it came seasonably (*v.* 1). David inferred from this that Ziba was a very discreet and generous man, and well affected to him, when, in all, he designed nothing but to make his own market and to get Mephibosheth's estate settled upon himself. Whatever Ziba intended in this present, God's providence sent it to David for his support very graciously. God makes use of bad men for good purposes to his people, and sends them meat by ravens. 2. Having by his present insinuated himself into David's affection, the next thing is to incense him against Mephibosheth, which he does by a false accusation, representing him as ungratefully designing to recover the crown to his own head, now that David and his son were contending for it. David enquires for him as one of his family, which gives Ziba occasion to tell this false story of him, *v.* 3. David gives credit to the calumny, without further enquiry, convicts Mephibosheth of treason, seizes his lands as forfeited, and grants them to Ziba, a rash judgment, and which afterwards he was ashamed of, when the truth came to light, *ch.* xix. 29. Having by his wiles gained his point, Ziba secretly laughed at the king's credulity.

Verses 5–14

David bore Shimei's curses much better than he had borne Ziba's flatteries. By the latter he was brought to pass a wrong judgment on another, by the former to pass a right judgment on himself. The world's smiles are more dangerous than its frowns.

I. How insolent and furious Shimei was, and how his malice took occasion from David's present distress to be so much the more outrageous. David, in his flight, had come to Bahurim, a city of Benjamin in or near which this Shimei lived, who, being of the house of Saul (with the fall of which all his hopes of preferment fell), had an implacable enmity to David, unjustly looking upon him as the ruin of Saul and his family only because, by the divine appointment, he succeeded Saul, *v.* 5. 1. Why he took this opportunity to give vent to his malice. (1) Because now he thought he might do it safely. (2) Because now it would be most grievous to David, would add affliction to his grief, and pour vinegar into his wounds. (3) Because now he thought that Providence justified his reproaches, and that David's present afflictions proved him to be as bad a man as he was willing to represent him. Job's friends condemned him upon this false principle. 2. How his malice was expressed. (1) *He cast stones at David* (*v.* 6), as if his king had been a dog. *He cast dust* (*v.* 13), which, probably, would blow into his own eyes, like the curses he threw, which, being causeless, would return upon his own head. Thus, while his malice made him odious, the impotency of it made him ridiculous and contemptible. (2) What he said. With the stones he shot his arrows, even bitter words (*v.* 7, 8). What was done long since to the house of Saul was the only thing which he could recollect, and with this he upbraided David because it was the thing that he himself was a loser by. No man could be more innocent of the blood of the house of Saul than David was. Once and again he spared Saul's life, while Saul sought his. The blood of the house of Saul is here most unjustly charged upon David, [1] As that which gave him his character, and denominated him a bloody man and a man of Belial, *v.* 7. [2] As that which brought the present trouble upon him: *The Lord has returned upon thee the blood of the house of Saul.* See how forward malicious men are to press God's judgments into the service of their own passion and revenge. [3] As that which would now be his utter ruin; for he endeavours to make him despair of ever recovering his throne again.

II. See how patient and submissive David was under this abuse. The sons of Zeruiah, Abishai particularly, resented the affront keenly, as well they might:

Why should this dead dog be suffered to *curse the king? v.* 9. If David will but give them leave, they will put these lying cursing lips to silence, and take off his head. But the king would by no means suffer it: *What have I to do with you? So let him curse.* Thus Christ rebuked the disciples who, in zeal for his honour, would have commanded fire from heaven on the town that affronted him, Luke ix. 55. Let us see with what considerations David quieted himself. 1. The chief thing that silenced him was that he had deserved this affliction. 2. He observes the hand of God in it: *The Lord hath said unto him, Curse David* (*v.* 10), and again, *So let him curse, for the Lord hath bidden him, v.* 11. As it was Shimei's sin, it was not from God, but from the devil and his own wicked heart. David looked above the instrument of his trouble to the supreme director, as Job, when the plunderers had stripped him, acknowledged, *The Lord hath taken away.* Nothing more proper to quiet a gracious soul under affliction than an eye to the hand of God in it. 3. He quiets himself under the less affliction with the consideration of the greater (*v.* 11): *My son seeks my life, much more may this Benjamite.* 4. He comforts himself with hopes that God would, in some way or other, bring good to him out of his affliction: *The Lord will requite me good for his cursing.* We may depend upon God as our paymaster, not only for our services, but for our sufferings. David, at length, is housed at Bahurim (*v.* 14), where he meets with refreshment and is hidden from this strife of tongues.

Verses 15–23

Absalom had notice sent him speedily by some of his friends at Jerusalem that David had withdrawn, and with what a small retinue he had gone; Absalom might take possession of Jerusalem when he pleased. Accordingly he came without delay (*v.* 15), extremely elevated, no doubt, with this success at first. The most celebrated politicians of that age were Ahithophel and Hushai. The former Absalom brings with him to Jerusalem (*v.* 15), the other meets him there (*v.* 16), so that he cannot but think himself sure of success. But miserable counsellors were they both; for,

I. Hushai would never counsel him to do wisely. He was really his enemy, and designed to betray him. 1. Hushai complimented him upon his accession to the throne, as if he had been abundantly satisfied in his title, and well pleased that he had come to the possession, *v.* 16. 2. Absalom was surprised to find *him* who was known to be David's intimate friend and confidant. 3. Hushai confirmed him in the belief that he was hearty for him. It was true, he loved his father; but he had had his day, and it was over; and why should he not love his successor as well? Thus he pretended to give reasons for a resolution he abhorred.

II. Ahithophel counselled him to do wickedly, and so did as effectually betray him as he did who was designedly false to him; for those that advise men to sin certainly advise them to their hurt; and that government which is founded in sin is founded in the sand.

1. It seems, Ahithophel was noted as a deep politician; his counsel was as if a man had enquired at the oracle of God, *v.* 23. Let us observe from this account of Ahithophel's fame for policy, (1) That many excel in worldly wisdom who are utterly destitute of heavenly grace, because those who set up for oracles themselves are apt to despise the oracles of God. (2) That frequently the greatest politicians act most foolishly for themselves.

2. His policy in this case defeated its own aim. (1) The wicked counsel Ahithophel gave to Absalom. Finding that David had left his concubines to keep the house, he advised him to *lie with them* (*v.* 21), because it would give assurance to all Israel,

[1] That he was in good earnest in his pretensions. No doubt he resolved to make himself master of all that belonged to his predecessor when he began with his concubines. [2] That he was resolved never to make peace with his father upon any terms. Having drawn the sword, he did, by this provocation, throw away the scabbard, which would strengthen the hands of his party and keep them firmly to him. This was Ahithophel's cursed policy, which bespoke him rather *an oracle of the devil than of God.*

(2) Absalom's compliance with this counsel. It entirely suited his lewd and wicked mind, and he delayed not to put it in execution, *v.* 22. Yet, in this, the word of God was fulfilled in the letter of it: God had threatened, by Nathan, that, for defiling Bath-sheba, David should have his own wives publicly debauched (*ch.* xii. 11, 12), and some think that Ahithophel, in advising it, designed to be revenged on David for the injury done to Bath-sheba, who was his grand-daughter: for she was the daughter of Eliam (*ch.* xi. 3), who was the son of Ahithophel, *ch.* xxiii. 34.

CHAPTER 17

The contest between David and Absalom is now hastening towards a crisis. It must be determined by the sword. I. Absalom calls a council of war, in which Ahithophel urges despatch (ver. 1–4), but Hushai recommends deliberation (ver. 5–13); and Hushai's counsel is agreed to (ver. 14), for vexation at which Ahithophel hangs himself, ver. 23. II. Secret intelligence is sent to David (but with much difficulty) of their proceedings, ver. 15–21. III. David marches to the other side Jordan (ver. 22–24), and there his camp is victualled by some of his friends in that country, ver. 27–29. IV. Absalom and his forces march after him into the land of Gilead on the other side Jordan, ver. 25, 26.

Verses 1–14

Absalom is now in peaceable possession of Jerusalem; the palace-royal is his own. His good father reigned in Hebron, and only over the tribe of Judah, above seven years, and was not hasty to destroy his rival; his government was built upon a divine promise, and therefore he waited patiently in the meantime. But the young man, Absalom, not only hastens from Hebron to Jerusalem, but is impatient there till he has destroyed his father, and cannot be content with his throne till he has his life.

David and all that adhered to him must be cut off. None durst mention his personal merits, and the great services done to his country. None durst propose that his banishment should suffice. It is past dispute that David must be destroyed; all the question is how he may be destroyed.

I. Ahithophel advises that he be pursued immediately, this very night, with a flying army, that the king only be smitten and his forces dispersed, and then the people that were now for him would fall in with Absalom. Nothing could be more fatal to David than the taking of these measures. It was probable enough that upon a fierce attack, especially in the night, the small force he had would be put into confusion and disorder, and it would be an easy thing to *smite the king only.* Compare with this the plot of Caiaphas (that second Ahithophel) against the Son of David to crush his interest by destroying him. Let that *one man die for the people,* John xi. 50.

II. Hushai advises that they be not too hasty in pursuing David, but take time to draw up all their force against him, and to overpower him with numbers, as Ahithophel had advised to take him by surprise. Now Hushai, in giving this counsel, really intended to serve David and his interest, that he might have time to send him notice of his proceedings, and that David might gain time to gather an army and to remove into those countries beyond Jordan, in which, lying more remote, Absalom had probably least interest.

1. Absalom gave Hushai a fair invitation to advise

him. All the elders of Israel approved of Ahithophel's counsel, yet God overruled the heart of Absalom not to proceed upon it, till he had consulted Hushai (*v.* 5): *Let us hear what he saith.*

2. Hushai gave very plausible reasons for what he said.

(1) He argued against Ahithophel's counsel, and undertook to show the danger of following his advice. [1] He insisted much upon it that David was a great soldier, a man of great conduct, courage, and experience, and not so weary and weak-handed as Ahithophel imagines. His retiring from Jerusalem must be imputed, not to his cowardice, but his prudence. [2] His attendants, though few, were mighty men (*v.* 8), valiant men (*v.* 10), men of celebrated bravery and versed in all the arts of war. [3] They were all exasperated against Absalom, who was the author of all this mischief, were chafed in their minds, and would fight with the utmost fury; there would be no standing before them, especially for such raw soldiers as Absalom's generally were. [4] He suggested that probably David and some of his men would lie in ambush, in some pit, or other close place, and fall upon Absalom's soldiers, and the defeat, though but of a small party, would dispirit all the rest, especially their own consciences at the same time accusing them of treason against one that, they were sure, was not only God's anointed, *but a man after his own heart, v.* 9.

(2) He offered his own advice, and gave his reasons; and, [1] He counselled that which he knew would gratify Absalom's proud vainglorious humour, though it would not be really serviceable to his interest. *First,* He advised that all Israel should be gathered together, that is, the militia of all the tribes. *Secondly,* He advised that Absalom go to battle in his own person, as if he looked upon him to be a better soldier than Ahithophel. [2] He counselled that which seemed to secure the success, at last, infallibly without running any hazard. For, if they could raise such vast numbers as they promised themselves, wherever they found David they could not fail to crush him. *First,* If in the field, they should cut off all his men with him, *v.* 12. Perhaps Absalom was better pleased with the design, of cutting off all the men that were with him, having a particular antipathy to some of David's friends. Thus Hushai gained his point by humouring his revenge, as well as his pride. *Secondly,* If in a city, they need not fear conquering him, for they should have hands enough, if occasion were, to draw the city itself into its river with ropes, *v.* 13.

(3) By all these arts, Hushai gained not only Absalom's approbation of his advice, but the unanimous concurrence of this great council of war; they all agreed that the counsel of Hushai was better than the counsel of Ahithophel, *v.* 14.

Verses 15–21

Hushai tells the priests what had passed in council, *v.* 15. But, it should seem, he was not sure but that yet Ahithophel's counsel might be followed, and was therefore jealous lest, if he made not the best of his way, the king would be *swallowed up, and all the people that were with him, v.* 16. Such strict guards did Absalom set upon all the avenues to Jerusalem that they had much ado to get this necessary intelligence to David. 1. The young priests that were to be the messengers were forced to retire secretly out of the city, by *En-rogel.* 2. Instructions were sent to them by a poor simple young woman, who probably went to that well under pretence of fetching water, *v.* 17. 3. Yet, by the vigilance of Absalom's spies, they were discovered, and information was brought to Absalom of their motions: *A lad saw them and told him, v.* 18. 4. They, being aware that they were discovered, sheltered themselves in a friend's house in Bahurim, where David had refreshed himself but just before, *ch.* xvi. 14. There they were happily hidden in a well, which now, in summer time, perhaps was dry, *v.* 18. The woman of the house very ingeniously covered the mouth of the well with a cloth, on which she spread corn to dry, so that the pursuers were not aware that there was a well; else they would have searched it, *v.* 19. Being thus preserved, they brought their intelligence very faithfully to David (*v.* 21), with this advice of his friends, that he should not delay to pass over Jordan, near to which, it seems, he now was.

Verses 22–29

I. The transporting of David and his forces over Jordan. He, and all that were with him, went over in the night, but none deserted him. Having got over Jordan, he marched many miles forward to Mahanaim, a Levites' city in the tribe of Gad. This city, which Ish-bosheth had made his royal city (*ch.* ii. 8), David now made his headquarters, *v.* 24. And now he had time to raise an army wherewith to oppose the rebels and give them a warm reception.

II. The death of Ahithophel, *v.* 23. He died by his own hands, *felo de se—a suicide.* He hanged himself for vexation that his counsel was not followed; for thereby, 1. He thought himself slighted, and an intolerable slur cast upon his reputation for wisdom. 2. He thought himself endangered and his life exposed. He concluded that, because his counsel was not followed, Absalom's cause would certainly miscarry, and then, whoever would find David's mercy, he concluded that he, who was the greatest criminal, and had particularly advised him to lie with his father's concubines, must be sacrificed to his justice. Now, as David had prayed, Ahithophel's counsel was *turned into foolishness to himself.*

III. Absalom's pursuit of his father. Not content that he had driven his good father to the utmost corner of his kingdom, he resolved to chase him out of the world. Absalom made one Amasa his general (*v.* 25), whose father was by birth Jether, an Ishmaelite (1 Chron. ii. 17), but by religion Ithra (as he is here called), an Israelite. Amasa was in the same relation to David that Joab was.

IV. The friends David met with in this distant country. Even Shobi, a younger brother of the royal family of the Ammonites, was kind to him, *v.* 27. We should, as we have opportunity, *do good to all men,* for *he that watereth shall be watered also himself,* when there is occasion. Machir, the son of Ammiel, was he that maintained Mephibosheth (*ch.* ix. 4), till David eased him of that charge, and is now repaid for it by that generous man, who, it seems, was the common patron of distressed princes. Barzillai we shall hear of again. These, compassionating David and his men, now that they were weary with a long march, brought him furniture for his house, *beds and basins,* and provision for his table, *wheat and barley,* &c., *v.* 28, 29. In token of their dutiful affection to him they brought in plenty of all that which he had occasion for. Let us learn hence to be generous and open-handed, according as our ability is, to all in distress. God sometimes makes up to his people that comfort from strangers which they are disappointed of in their own families.

CHAPTER 18

This chapter puts a period to Absalom's rebellion and life, and so makes way for David to his throne again. I. David's preparations to engage the rebels, ver. 1–5. II. The total defeat of Absalom's party, ver. 6–8. III. The death of Absalom, and his burial, ver. 9–18. IV. The bringing of the tidings to David, who tarried at Mahanaim, ver. 19–32. V. His bitter lamentation for Absalom, ver. 33.

Verses 1–8

David raised an army here, and reinforcements were sent him from all the coasts of Israel, at least from the neighbouring tribes.

I. His army numbered and marshalled, *v.* 1, 2. Josephus says they were, in all, about 4,000. These he divided into regiments and companies, to each of which he appointed proper officers, and then disposed them, as is usual, into the right wing, the left wing, and the centre, two of which he committed to his two old experienced generals, Joab and Abishai, and the third to his new friend Ittai. Good order and good conduct may sometimes be as serviceable in an army as great numbers.

II. Himself over-persuaded not to go in person to the battle. David's true friends would not let him go, remembering what they had been told of Ahithophel's design to *smite the king only.* David showed his affection to them by being willing to venture with them (*v.* 2), and they showed theirs to him by opposing it. He might be more serviceable to them by tarrying in the city, with a reserve of his forces there, whence he might send them recruits. That may be a post of real service which yet is not a post of danger.

III. The charge he gave concerning Absalom, *v.* 5. When the army was drawn out, rank and file, Josephus says, he encouraged them, and prayed for them, but withal bade them all take heed of doing Absalom any hurt. Absalom would have David only smitten. David would have Absalom only spared. Each did his utmost, and showed how bad it is possible for a child to be to the best of fathers and how good it is possible for a father to be to the worst of children; as if it were designed to be a resemblance of man's wickedness towards God and God's mercy towards man. Deal gently with a traitor? Of all traitors, with a son? Must the cause of the quarrel be the motive of mercy? But was not this done in type of that immeasurable mercy of the true King and Redeemer of Israel, who prayed for his persecutors, for his murderers, *Father, forgive them. Deal gently with them for my sake.* When God sends an affliction to correct his children, it is with this charge, "Deal gently with them for my sake"; for he knows our frame.

IV. A complete victory gained over Absalom's forces. The battle was fought *in the wood of Ephraim* (*v.* 6), so called from some memorable action of the Ephraimites there, though it lay in the tribe of Gad. David thought fit to meet the enemy with his forces at some distance, before they came up to Mahanaim, lest he should bring that city into trouble which had so kindly sheltered him. The cause shall be decided by a pitched battle. Josephus represents the fight as very obstinate, but the rebels were at length totally routed and 20,000 of them slain, *v.* 7. Now they see what it is to take counsel *against the Lord and his anointed,* and to think of *breaking his bands asunder.* And that they might see that God fought against them, 1. They are conquered by a few, an army, in all probability, much inferior to theirs in number. 2. By that flight with which they hoped to save themselves they destroyed themselves. The pits and bogs, the stumps and thickets, and, as the Chaldee paraphrast understands it, the wild beasts of the wood, were probably the death of multitudes of the dispersed distracted Israelites.

Verses 9–18

Here is Absalom quite at a loss, at his wit's end first, and then at his life's end. Though they were forbidden to meddle with him, he durst not look them in the face; but, finding they were near him, he clapped spurs to his mule and made the best of his way, through thick and thin, and so rode headlong upon his own destruction.

I. He is hanged by the neck. Riding furiously, neck or nothing, *under the thick boughs of a great oak* which hung low and had never been cropped, either the twisted branches, or some one forked bough of the oak, caught hold of his head by his long hair, which had been so much his pride, and was now justly made a halter for him, and there he hung. His *mule went away* from *under him*, as if glad to get clear of such a burden. He hung *between heaven and earth*, as unworthy of either, as abandoned of both.

II. He is caught alive by one of the servants of David, who goes directly and tells Joab in what posture he found that arch-rebel, *v.* 10. Joab chides the man for not dispatching him (*v.* 11), the man, though zealous enough against Absalom, justified himself in not doing it. Those that love the treason hate the traitor. Joab could not deny this, nor blame the man for his caution.

III. He is so pitifully mangled as he hangs there, and receives his death in such a manner as to see all its terrors and feel all its pain. 1. Joab throws three darts into his body; while he broke the order of a too indulgent father, he did real service both to his king and country, and would have endangered the welfare of both if he had not done it. 2. Joab's young men, ten of them, smite him, before he is dispatched, *v.* 15. Joab hereupon sounds a retreat, *v.* 15. The danger is over, now that Absalom is slain; the people will soon return to their allegiance to David; and therefore no more blood shall be spilt.

IV. His body is disposed of disgracefully (*v.* 17, 18): They *cast it into a great pit in the wood*; they would not bring it to his father (for that circumstance would but have added to his grief), nor would they preserve it to be buried, but threw it into the next pit with indignation. Now where is the beauty he had been so proud of and for which he had been so much admired? Where are his aspiring projects, and the castles he had built in the air? His thoughts perish, and he with them. To aggravate the ignominy of Absalom's burial, the historian takes notice of a pillar he had erected in the valley of Kidron, near Jerusalem, to be a monument for himself (*v.* 18), at the foot of which, it is probable, he designed to be buried. What care do many people take about the disposal of their bodies, when they are dead, that have no care at all what shall become of their precious souls! Absalom had three sons (*ch.* xiv. 27), but, it seems, now he had none. His care was to have his name kept in remembrance, and it is so, to his everlasting dishonour.

Verses 19–33

I. How David was informed of it. He stayed behind at the city of Mahanaim. Absalom's scattered forces all made homeward towards Jordan, which was the contrary way from Mahanaim, so that his watchmen could not perceive how the battle went, till an express came on purpose to bring advice of the issue, which the king sat in the gate expecting to hear, *v.* 24.

1. Cushi was the man Joab ordered to carry the tidings (*v.* 21), an *Ethiopian*, so his name signifies, and some think that he was a black that waited on Joab.

2. Ahimaaz, the young priest (one of those who brought David intelligence of Absalom's motions, *ch.* xvii. 17), was very forward to be the messenger of these tidings. Thus he desired that he might have the pleasure and satisfaction of bringing the king, whom he loved, this good news. Joab knew David better than Ahimaaz did, and that the tidings of Absalom's death would spoil the acceptableness of all the rest; and he loves Ahimaaz too well to let him be the messenger of those tidings (*v.* 20). How-

ever, when Cushi was gone, Ahimaaz begged hard for leave to run after him, and with great importunity obtained it, *v.* 22, 23. Perhaps it was in tenderness to the king that he desired it. He knew he could get there before Cushi, and therefore was willing to prepare the king, by a vague and general report, for the plain truth which Cushi was ordered to tell him. If bad news must come, it is best that it come gradually, and will be the better borne.

3. They are both discovered by the watchman on the gate of Mahanaim, Ahimaaz first (*v.* 24), for, though Cushi had the lead, Ahimaaz soon outran him; but presently after Cushi appeared, *v.* 26. When he hears it is Ahimaaz he concludes he brings good news, *v.* 27. Ahimaaz, it seems, was so famous for running that he was known by it at a distance, and so eminently good that it is taken for granted, if he be the messenger, the news must needs be good.

4. Ahimaaz cries at a distance, "Peace, there is peace." And, when he comes near, he tells him the news more particularly, "They are all cut off *that lifted up their hand against the king*"; and, as became a priest, while he gives the king the joy of it, he gives God the glory of it. *"Blessed be the Lord thy God, that has done this for thee, as thy God, pursuant to the promises made to uphold thy throne," ch.* vii. 16. When he said this, *he fell down upon his face*, not only in reverence to the king, but in humble adoration of God, whose name he praised for this success. By directing David thus to give God thanks for his victory, he prepared him. The more our hearts are fixed and enlarged in thanksgiving to God for our mercies the better disposed we shall be to bear the afflictions mixed with them. Poor David is so much a father that he forgets he is a king, and therefore cannot rejoice in the news of a victory, till he know whether the *young man Absalom be safe*. Ahimaaz soon discerned, what Joab intimated to him, that the death of the king's son would make the tidings of the day very unwelcome. "When Joab sent the king's servant (namely, *Cushi) and me thy servant*, to bring the news, *I saw a great tumult*, but I have nothing to say about it. Cushi is better able to inform you than I am. I will not be the messenger of evil tidings; nor will I pretend to know that which I cannot give a perfect account of."

5. Cushi, the slow post, proves the sure one, and besides the confirmation of the news of the victory which Ahimaaz had brought—*The Lord has avenged thee of all those that rose up against thee* (*v.* 31)— he satisfied the king's enquiry concerning Absalom, *v.* 32. *Is he safe?* says David. "Yes," says Cushi, "he is safe in his grave"; but he tells the news so discreetly that, how unwelcome soever the message is, the messenger can have no blame. *"The enemies of my lord the king*, whoever they are, *and all that rise against thee to do thee hurt, be as that young man is."*

II. How David received the intelligence. He forgets all the joy of his deliverance, and is quite overwhelmed with the sorrowful tidings of Absalom's death, *v.* 33. *"O my son Absalom! my son, my son Absalom! Would God I had died for thee. O Absalom! my son, my son!"*

CHAPTER 19

We left David's army in triumph and yet David himself in tears: now here we have, I. His return to himself, by the persuasion of Joab, ver. 1–8. II. His return to his kingdom from his present banishment. 1. The men of Israel were forward of themselves to bring him back, ver. 9, 10. 2. The men of Judah were dealt with by David's agents to do it (ver. 11–14) and did it, ver. 15. III. At the king's coming over Jordan, Shimei's treason is pardoned (ver. 16–23), Mephibosheth's failure is excused (ver. 24–30), and Barzillai's kindness is thankfully owned, and recompensed to his son, ver. 31–39. IV. The men of Israel quarrelled with the men of Judah, for not calling them to the ceremony of the king's restoration.

Verses 1–8

Soon after the messengers had brought the news Joab and his victorious army followed.

I. What a disappointment it was to them to find the king in tears for Absalom's death, which they construed as a token of his displeasure against them for what they had done, whereas they expected him to have met them with joy and thanks for their good services: *It was told Joab*, v. 1. The report of it ran through the army (v. 2), *how the king was grieved for his son.* They were loth to blame the king, for *whatever he did used to please them* (*ch.* iii. 36), but they took it as a great mortification to them. *Their victory was turned into mourning*, v. 2. *They stole into the city as men ashamed*, v. 3. In compliment to their sovereign, they would not rejoice in that which they perceived so afflictive to him.

II. How plainly and vehemently Joab reproved David for this indiscreet management of himself in this critical juncture. David never more needed the hearts of his subjects than now. Joab magnifies the services of David's soldiers: *"This day they have saved thy life. Thou hast shamed their faces."* What can be more absurd than to love thy enemies and to hate thy friends? He advises him to present himself immediately at the head of his troops, to smile upon them, welcome them home, congratulate their success, and return them thanks for their services.

III. How prudently and mildly David took the reproof and counsel given him, v. 8. He shook off his grief, anointed his head, and washed his face, that he might not appear unto men to mourn, and then made his appearance in public in the gate, which was as the guildhall of the city. Hither the people flocked to him to congratulate his and their safety, and all was well.

Verses 9–15

It is strange that David did not immediately march back to Jerusalem. Could not he himself go back with the victorious army he had with him in Gilead? He could, but he would go back as a prince, with the consent and unanimous approbation of the people, and not as a conqueror forcing his way. He would go back in honour, and like himself, not at the head of his forces, but in the arms of his subjects; for the prince that has wisdom and goodness enough to make himself his people's darling, without doubt, looks greater and makes a much better figure than the prince that has strength enough to make himself his people's terror.

I. The men of Israel (that is, the ten tribes) were the first that talked of it, v. 9, 10. David had formerly helped them, had fought their battles, subdued their enemies, and done them much service, and therefore it was a shame that he should continue banished from their country who had been so great a benefactor to it. Absalom had now disappointed them. "We were foolishly sick of the cedar, and chose the branch to reign over us; but we have had enough of him: he is consumed, and we narrowly escaped being consumed with him. Let us therefore return to our allegiance, and think of bringing the king back." Perhaps this was all the strife among them, not a dispute whether the king should be brought back, or no (all agreed it was to be done), but whose fault it was that it was not done.

II. The men of Judah were not so forward as the rest. David had intelligence of the good disposition of all the rest towards him, but nothing from Judah. David would not return till he knew the sense of his own tribe. That his way home might be the more clear, 1. He employed Zadok and Abiathar, the two chief priests, to treat with the elders of Judah, and to excite them to give the king an invitation back to his house, even to his house, which was the glory of their tribe, v. 11, 12. Perhaps they were so sensible of the greatness of the provocation they had given to David, by joining with Absalom, that they were afraid to bring him back, despairing of his favour; he therefore warrants his agents to assure them of it, with this reason: "*You are my brethren, my bone and my flesh*, and therefore I cannot be severe with you." 2. He particularly courted into his interest Amasa, who had been Absalom's general, but was his own nephew as well as Joab, v. 13. He owns him for his kinsman, and promises him that, if he will appear for him now, he will make him captain-general of all his forces in the room of Joab. But, if David did wisely for himself in designating Amasa for this post (Joab having now grown intolerably haughty), he did not do kindly by Amasa in letting his design be known, for it occasioned his death by Joab's hand, *ch.* xx. 10. 3. The point was hereby gained. He bowed the heart of the men of Judah to pass a vote for the recall of the king, v. 14. God's providence, by the priests' persuasions and Amasa's interest, brought them to this resolve. David stirred not till he received this invitation, and then he came as far back as Jordan, at which river they were to meet him, v. 15.

Verses 16–23

David, in his flight, remembered God particularly *from the land of Jordan* (Ps. xlii. 6), and now that land, more than any other, was graced with the glories of his return. David's soldiers furnished themselves with accommodations for their passage over this river, but, for his own family, *a ferry-boat* was sent on purpose, v. 18. Two remarkable persons met him on the banks of Jordan, both of whom had abused him wretchedly when he was in his flight.

I. Ziba, who by accusing his master had obtained from the king a grant of his estate, *ch.* xvi. 4, imposing upon his credulity, to draw him in to do a thing so unkind to the son of his friend Jonathan. He comes now to meet the king (v. 17), that he may obtain favour, and so come off the better when Mephibosheth shall shortly undeceive him, and clear himself, v. 26.

II. Shimei, who had railed at him, and cursed him, *ch.* xvi. 5, thinks it his interest to make his peace with him. Shimei, to recommend himself to the king, 1. Came with good company, with the men of Judah. 2. He brought a regiment of the men of Benjamin with him, offering his own and their service to the king. 3. What he did he hastened to do. He did it publicly. The offence was public, therefore the submission ought to be so. He owns his crime: *Thy servant doth know that I have sinned.* He begs the king's pardon: *Let not the king impute iniquity to thy servant*, that is, deal with me as I deserve. A motion made for judgment against him (v. 21) was made by Abishai, who would have ventured his life to have been the death of Shimei when he was cursing, *ch.* xvi. 9. David rejected Abishai's motion with displeasure: *What have I to do with you, you sons of Zeruiah?* The less we have to do with those who are of an angry revengeful spirit, and who put us upon doing what is harsh and rigorous, the better. It is the glory of kings to forgive those that humble and surrender themselves: *Satis est protrâsse leoni—It suffices the lion that he has laid his victim prostrate.* His joy inclined him to forgive. Yet this was not all; his experience of God's mercy in restoring him to his kingdom, his exclusion from which he attributed to his sin, inclined him to show mercy to Shimei. Shemei hereupon had his pardon signed and sealed with an oath.

Verses 24–30

The day of David's return was a day of bringing

to remembrance. Among other things, after the case of Shimei, that of Mephibosheth comes to be enquired into, and he himself brings it on.

I. He went down in the crowd *to meet the king* (v. 24), and, as a proof of the sincerity of his joy in the king's return, we are here told what a true mourner he was for the king's banishment. He was never trimmed, nor put on clean linen, but wholly neglected himself, as one abandoned to grief for the king's affliction and the kingdom's misery.

II. When the king came to Jerusalem he made his appearance before him (v. 25); and when the king asked him why he, being one of his family, had stayed behind, and not accompanied him in his exile, he opened his case fully to the king. 1. He complained of Ziba, his servant, who should have been his friend, but had been in two ways his enemy; for, first, he had hindered him from going along with the king, by taking the ass himself which he was ordered to make ready for his master (v. 26), basely taking advantage of his lameness and his inability to help himself; and, secondly, he had accused him to David of a design to usurp the government, v. 27. 2. He gratefully acknowledged the king's great kindness to him when he and all his father's house lay at the king's mercy, v. 28. 3. He referred his cause to the king's pleasure, depending on the king's wisdom, and his ability to discern between truth and falsehood, and disclaiming all pretensions of his own merit.

III. David hereupon recalls the sequestration of Mephibosheth's estate; being deceived in his grant, he revokes it, and confirms his former settlement of it: "*I have said, Thou and Ziba divide the land* (v. 29), that is, Let it be as I first ordered it (*ch.* ix. 10); the property shall still be vested in thee, but Ziba shall have the occupancy: he shall till the land, paying thee a rent." Thus Mephibosheth is where he was; no harm is done, only Ziba goes away unpunished for his false and malicious information against his master.

IV. Mephibosheth drowns all his cares about his estate in his joy for the king's return (v. 30): "*Yea, let him take all*, the presence and favour of the king shall be to me instead of all."

Verses 31–39

Barzillai, the Gileadite, who had a noble seat at Rogelim, not far from Mahanaim, was the man who, of all the nobility and gentry of that country, had been most kind to David in his distress. If Absalom had prevailed, it is likely he would have suffered for his loyalty; but now he and his shall be no losers by it.

I. Barzillai's great respect to David as his rightful sovereign: He *provided him with much sustenance*, for himself and his family, *while he lay at Mahanaim*, v. 32. God had given him a large estate, *for he was a very great man*, and, it seems, he had a large heart to do good with it: what else but that is a large estate good for?

II. The kind invitation David gave him to court (v. 33): *Come thou over with me.* He invited him, 1. That he might have the pleasure of his company and the benefit of his counsel. 2. That he might have an opportunity of returning his kindness: "*I will feed thee with me.*"

III. Barzillai's reply to this invitation, wherein, 1. He admires the king's generosity in making him this offer, lessening his service, and magnifying the king's return for it.

2. He declines accepting the invitation. He begs his majesty's pardon for refusing so generous an offer: but, (1) He is old, and unfit to remove at all, especially to court. (2) He is dying, and must begin to think of his long journey, his removal out of the world, v. 37.

3. He desires the king to be kind to his son Chimham: *Let him go over with my lord the king*, and have

preferment at court. What favour is done to him Barzillai will take as done to himself.

IV. David's farewell to Barzillai. 1. He sends him back into his country with a kiss and a blessing (v. 39), signifying that in gratitude for his kindness he would love him and pray for him, and with a promise that whatever request he should at any time make to him he would be ready to oblige him (v. 38): *Whatsoever thou shalt think of*, when thou comest home to *ask of me*, that *will I do for thee*. 2. He takes Chimham forward with him, and leaves it to Barzillai to choose him his preferment: I will *do to him what shall seem good to thee*, v. 38. And, it should seem, Barzillai begged a country seat for him near Jerusalem, for, long after, we read of a place near Beth-lehem, David's city, which is called *the habitation of Chimham*, allotted to him, probably, not out of the crown-lands or the forfeited estates, but out of David's paternal estate.

Verses 40–43

David came over Jordan attended and assisted only by the men of Judah; but when he had advanced as far as Gilgal, the first stage on this side Jordan, *half the people of Israel* (that is, of their elders and great men) had come to kiss his hand, but found they came too late to witness the solemnity of his first entrance. This occasioned a quarrel between them and the men of Judah, and the beginning of further mischief. Here is, 1. The complaint which the men of Israel brought to the king against the men of Judah (v. 41), that they had performed the ceremony of bringing the king over Jordan, and not given them notice, as if they were not so well affected to the king, whereas the king himself knew that they had spoken of it before the men of Judah thought of it, v. 11. 2. The excuse which the men of Judah made for themselves, v. 42. (1) They plead relation to the king: "*He is near of kin to us*", and therefore in a matter of mere ceremony, as this was, we may claim precedency. (2) They deny the insinuated charge of self-seeking in what they had done: "*Have we eaten at all of the king's cost?* No, we have all borne our own charges. *Hath he given us any gift?* No, we have no design to engross the advantages of his return; you have come time enough to share in them." 3. The men of Israel's vindication of their charge, v. 43. They pleaded, "*We have ten parts in the king*" (Judah having Simeon only, whose lot lay within his, to join with him), "and therefore it is a slight upon us that our advice was not asked about *bringing back the king*."

CHAPTER 20

No sooner is one of David's troubles over than another arises, I. Before he reaches Jerusalem a new rebellion is raised by Sheba, ver. 1, 2. II. His first work, when he comes to Jerusalem, is to condemn his concubines to perpetual imprisonment, ver. 3. III. Amasa, whom he entrusts to raise an army against Sheba, is too slow in his motions, which puts him into a fright, ver. 4–6. IV. One of his generals barbarously murders the other, when they are taking the field, ver. 7–13. V. Sheba is at length shut up in the city of Abel (ver. 14, 15), but the citizens deliver him up to Joab, and so his rebellion is crushed, ver. 16–22. The chapter concludes with a short account of David's great officers, ver. 23–26.

Verses 1–3

David, in the midst of his triumphs, has to see his kingdom disturbed and his family disgraced.

I. His subjects revolting from him at the instigation of a *man of Belial*, whom they followed when they forsook the *man after God's own heart*. We must not think it strange, while we are in this world, if the end of one trouble be the beginning of another. A broken bone, when it is set, must have time to knit. The ringleader of this rebellion was Sheba, a Benjamite by birth (v. 1), who had his habitation in Mount Ephraim, v. 21. Shimei and he were both of Saul's tribe, and both retained the ancient grudge of that house. The occasion of it was that foolish quarrel, which we read of in the close of the foregoing chapter, between the elders of Israel and the elders of Judah, about bringing the king back. "If the king will suffer himself to be engrossed by the men of Judah, let him and them make their best of one another, and we will set up one for ourselves." This was proclaimed by Sheba (*v.* 1), who probably was a man of note, and had been active in Absalom's rebellion; the disgusted Israelites took the hint, and *went up from after David to follow Sheba* (*v.* 2). The perverting of words is the subverting of peace; and much mischief is made by forcing invidious constructions upon what is said and written and drawing consequences that were never intended. The men of Judah said, *The king is near of kin to us.* "By this," say the men of Israel, "you mean that *we have no part in him*"; whereas they meant no such thing.

II. His concubines imprisoned for life, and he himself under a necessity of putting them in confinement, because they had been defiled by Absalom, *v.* 3. Those whom he had loved must now be loathed.

Verses 4–13

We have here Amasa's fall just as he began to rise. He had been Absalom's general, and came over into David's interest, upon a promise that he should be general of his forces instead of Joab.

I. Amasa has a commission to raise forces for the suppressing of Sheba's rebellion, and is ordered to raise them with all possible expedition, *v.* 4. Amasa is sent to assemble the men of Judah within three days; but he finds them so backward and unready that he cannot do it within the time appointed (*v.* 5).

II. Upon Amasa's delay, Abishai, the brother of Joab, is ordered to take the guards and standing forces, and with them to pursue Sheba (*v.* 6, 7), for nothing could be of more dangerous consequence than to give him time. David gives these orders to Abishai, because he resolves to mortify Joab. Joab, without orders, though in disgrace, goes along with his brother.

III. Joab, near Gibeon, meets with Amasa, and barbarously murders him, *v.* 8–10. 1. He did subtilely, and with contrivance, and not upon a sudden provocation. He girded his coat about him, that it might not hang in his way, and girded his belt upon his coat, that his sword might be the readier to his hand; he also put his sword in a sheath too big for it, that, whenever he pleased, it might, upon a little shake, fall out, as if it fell by accident, and so he might take it into his hand, unsuspected, as if he were going to return it into the scabbard. 2. He did it treacherously, and under pretence of friendship, that Amasa might not be upon his guard. He called him *brother*. 3. He did it impudently, not in a corner, but at the head of his troops. He did it in contempt and defiance of David and the commission he had given to Amasa.

IV. Joab immediately resumes his general's place, and takes care to lead the army on in pursuit of Sheba. He knew how many favoured him rather than Amasa, who had been a traitor. What man of Judah would not be for his old king and his old general? But one would wonder with what face a murderer could pursue a traitor. Care is taken to remove the dead body out of the way, and to cover it with a cloth, *v.* 12, 13. Wicked men think themselves safe in their wickedness if they can but conceal it from the eye of the world: if it be hidden, it is with them as if it were never done.

Verses 14–22

I. The rebel, when he had rambled over all the tribes of Israel, and found them not so willing, upon second thoughts, to follow him, at length entered Abel-Beth-maacah, a strong city in the north. His adherents were mostly Berites, of Beeroth in Benjamin, *v.* 14.

II. Joab drew up all his force against the city, besieged it, battered the wall, and made it almost ready for a general storm, *v.* 15.

III. A discreet good woman of the city of Abel brings this matter to a good issue, so as to satisfy Joab and yet save the city.

1. Her treaty with Joab by which he is engaged to raise the siege, upon condition that Sheba be delivered up. It seems, none of all the men of Abel offered to treat with Joab. But this one woman with her wisdom saved the city. Souls know no difference of sex. Though the man be the head, it does not therefore follow that he has the monopoly of the brains, and therefore he ought not, by any salique law, to have the monopoly of the crown. Many a masculine heart, and more than masculine, has been found in a female breast; nor is the treasure of wisdom the less valuable for being lodged in the weaker vessel. In the treaty between this nameless heroine and Joab,

(1) She gains his audience and attention, *v.* 16, 17.

(2) She reasons with him on behalf of her city, and very ingeniously. [1] That it was a city famous for wisdom (*v.* 18), as we translate it. [2] That the inhabitants were generally peaceable and faithful in Israel, *v.* 19. [3] That it was a mother in Israel, a guide and nurse to the towns and country about; and that it was a part of *the inheritance of the Lord.* [4] That they expected him to offer them peace before he made an attack upon them, according to that known law of war, Deut. xx. 10.

(3) Joab and Abel's advocate soon agree that Sheba's head shall be the ransom of the city. "Our quarrel is not with your city. Our quarrel is only with the traitor that is harboured among you; deliver him up, and we have done." A great deal of mischief would be prevented if contending parties would but understand one another. The single condition of peace is the surrender of the traitor. It is so in God's dealings with the soul, when it is besieged by conviction and distress: sin is the traitor; the beloved lust is the rebel; part with that, cast away the transgression, and all shall be well.

2. Her treaty with the citizens. She went to them in her wisdom and persuaded them to cut off Sheba's head. Joab hereupon raised the siege, and marched back to Jerusalem, with the trophies rather of peace than victory.

Verses 23–26

Here is an account of the state of David's court after his restoration. Joab retained the office of general. Benaiah, as before, was captain of the guards. Here is one new office erected, that of *treasurer* or one *over the tribute*, for it was not till towards the latter end of his time that David began to raise taxes.

CHAPTER 21

The date of the events of this chapter is uncertain. I incline to think that they happened as they are here placed, after Absalom's and Sheba's rebellion, and towards the latter end of David's reign. The people were numbered just after the three years' famine for the Gibeonites, for that which is threatened as "three" years' famine (1 Chron. xxi. 12) is called "seven" years (2 Sam. xxiv. 12, 13), three more, with the year current, added to those three. We have here. I. The Gibeonites avenged, 1. By a famine in the land, ver. 1. 2. By the putting of seven of Saul's posterity to death (ver. 2–9), care, however, being taken of their dead bodies, and of the bones of Saul, ver. 10–14. II. The giants of the Philistines slain in several battles, ver. 15–22.

Verses 1–9

I. The injury which Saul had, long before this, done to the Gibeonites. The Gibeonites were of the remnant of the Amorites (*v.* 2), who by a stratagem had made peace with Israel, and had the public faith pledged to them, Joshua ix., where it was agreed (v. 23) that they should have their lives secured, but be deprived of their lands and liberties, that they and theirs should be tenants in villainage to Israel. Saul, under colour of zeal for the honour of Israel, that it might not be said that they had any of the natives among them, aimed to root them out, and, in order to do that, slew many of them. It may be, he designed, by this severity towards the Gibeonites, to atone for his clemency towards the Amalekites. That which made this an exceedingly sinful sin was that he not only shed innocent blood, but therein violated the solemn oath by which the nation was bound to protect them.

II. We find the nation of Israel chastised with a sore famine, long after, for this sin of Saul. 1. Even in the land of Israel, that fruitful land, and in the reign of David, that glorious reign, there was a famine, great drought, and scarcity of provisions, the consequence of it, for three years together. 2. David enquired of God concerning it. Though he was himself a prophet, he must consult the oracle, and know God's mind in his own appointed way. 3. God was ready in his answer, though David was slow in his enquiries: *It is for Saul.* Time does not wear out the guilt of sin; nor can we build hopes of impunity upon the delay of judgments.

III. We have vengeance taken upon the house of Saul for the turning away of God's wrath from the land, which, at present, smarted for his sin.

1. David, probably by divine direction, referred it to the Gibeonites themselves to prescribe what satisfaction should be given them for the wrong that had been done them, v. 3.

2. They desired that seven of Saul's posterity might be put to death, and David granted their demand. (1) They required no *silver, nor gold,* v. 4. The Gibeonites had now a fair opportunity to get a discharge from their servitude. But they did not insist on this; though the covenant was broken on the other side. it should not be broken on theirs. They were *Nethinim,* given to God and his people Israel, and they would not seem weary of the service. (2) They required no lives but of Saul's family. (3) They would not impose it upon David to do this execution: *Thou shalt not for us kill any man* (v. 4), but we will do it ourselves, *we will hang them up unto the Lord* (v. 6), that, if there were any hardship in it, they might bear the blame, and not David or his house. (4) They did not require this out of malice against Saul or his family (had they been revengeful, they would have moved it themselves long before), but out of love to the people of Israel, whom they saw plagued for the injury done to them. (5) The nomination of the persons they left to David, who took care to secure Mephibosheth for Jonathan's sake, that, while he was avenging the breach of one oath, he might not himself break another (v. 7). (6) The place, time, and manner, of their execution, all added to the solemnity of their being sacrificed to divine justice. [1] They were hanged up, as anathemas, under a peculiar mark of God's displeasure; for the law had said, *He that is hanged is accursed of God,* Deut. xxi. 23; Gal. iii. 13. [2] They were hanged up in Gibeah of Saul (v. 6), to show that it was for his sin that they died.

Verses 10–14

I. Saul's sons not only hanged, but hanged in chains, their dead bodies left hanging, and exposed, till the judgment ceased, which their death was to turn away, by the sending of rain upon the land. They died as sacrifices, and thus they were, in a manner, offered up, not consumed all at once by fire, but gradually by the air.

II. Their dead bodies watched by Rizpah, the mother of two of them, v. 10. It was a great affliction to her, now in her old age, to see her two sons, who, we may suppose, had been a comfort to her, and were likely to be the support of her declining years, cut off in this dreadful manner. None know what sorrows they are reserved for. She may not see them decently interred, but they shall be decently attended. She attempts not to violate the sentence passed upon them, that they should hang there till God sent rain; she neither steals nor forces away their dead bodies, though the divine law might have been cited to bear her out; but she patiently submits, pitches a tent of sackcloth near the gibbets, where, with her servants and friends, she protects the dead bodies from birds and beasts of prey. Thus she let the world know that her sons died, not for any sin of their own, not as stubborn and rebellious sons. But they died for their father's sin, and therefore her mind could not be alienated from them by their hard fate. Though there is no remedy, but they must die, yet they shall die pitied and lamented.

III. The solemn interment of their dead bodies, with the bones of Saul and Jonathan, in the burying-place of their family. David was so far from being displeased at what Rizpah had done that he was himself stirred up by it to do honour to the house of Saul, and to these branches of it among the rest; thus it appeared that it was not out of any personal disgust to the family that he delivered them up, but that he was obliged to do it for the public good. 1. He now bethought himself of removing the bodies of Saul and Jonathan from the place where the men of Jabesh-Gilead had decently, but privately and obscurely, interred them, *under a tree,* 1 Sam. xxxi. 12, 13. 2. With them he buried the bodies *of those that were hanged;* for, when God's anger was turned away, they were no longer to be looked upon as a curse, v. 13, 14. When *water dropped upon them out of heaven* (v. 10), that is, when God sent rain to water the earth, they were taken down, for then it appeared *that God was entreated for the land.*

Verses 15–22

The story of some conflicts with the Philistines, which happened, as it should seem, in the latter end of David's reign. Though he had so subdued them that they could not bring any great numbers into the field, yet, as long as they had any giants among them to be their champions, they took all occasions to disturb the peace of Israel.

I. David himself was engaged with one of the giants. The Philistines began the war yet again, v. 15. David, though old, desired not a writ of ease from the public service, but he *went down* in person to fight *against the Philistines.* But he found age had cut his hair, and, after a little toil, he *waxed faint.* His body could not keep pace with his mind. The champion of the Philistines was soon aware of his advantage, perceived that David's strength failed him, and, being himself strong and well-armed, *he thought to slay David;* but God was not in his thoughts, and therefore in that very day they all perished. David was rescued by Abishai, who came seasonably in to his relief, v. 17. When *Abishai succoured him,* gave him a cordial, it may be, to relieve his fainting spirits, or appeared as his second, *he* (namely, David, so I understand it) *smote the Philistine and killed him;* for it is said (v. 22) that David had himself a hand in slaying the giants. David fainted, but he did not flee; though his strength failed him, he bravely kept his ground, and then God sent him this help in the time of need. Christ, in his agonies, was strengthened by an angel. In spiritual conflicts, even strong saints sometimes wax faint; then Satan attacks them furiously; but those that stand their ground and resist him shall be relieved, and made more than conquerors.

II. The rest of the giants fell by the hand of David's servants. 1. Saph was slain by Sibbechai, one of David's worthies, *v.* 18. 1 Chron. xi. 29. 2. Another, who was brother to Goliath, was slain by Elhanan, who is mentioned *ch.* xxiii. 24. 3. Another, who was of very unusual bulk, who had more fingers and toes than other people (*v.* 20), and such an unparalleled insolence that, though he had seen the fall of other giants, yet he defied Israel, was slain by *Jonathan the son of Shimea.* Shimea had one son named *Jonadab* (2 Sam. xiii. 3), whom I should have taken for the same with this Jonathan, but that the former was noted for subtlety, the latter for bravery. These giants were probably the remains of the sons of Anak, who, though long feared, fell at last. It is folly for the strong man to *glory in his strength.* David's servants were no bigger nor stronger than other men; yet thus, by divine assistance, they mastered one giant after another. The most powerful enemies are often reserved for the last conflict. David began his glory with the conquest of one giant, and here concludes with the conquest of four. Death is a Christian's last enemy, and a son of Anak; but, through him that triumphed for us, we hope to be more than conquerors at last, even over that enemy.

CHAPTER 22

This chapter is a psalm, a psalm of praise; we find it afterwards inserted among David's psalms (Ps. xviii.) with some little variation. We have it here as it was first composed for his own harp; but there we have it as it was afterwards delivered to the chief musician for the service of the church. The inspired historian, having largely related David's deliverances in this and the foregoing book, and one particularly in the close of the foregoing chapter, thought fit to record this sacred poem as a memorial of all that had been before related. Some think that David penned this psalm when he was old, upon a general review of the mercies of his life and the many wonderful preservations God had blessed him with, from first to last. We should, in our praises, look as far back as we can, and not suffer time to wear out the sense of God's favours. I. The title of the psalm, ver. 1. II. The psalm itself, in which, 1. He gives glory to God. 2. He takes comfort in him; and he finds matter for both, (1) In the experience he had of God's former favours. (2) In the expectations he had of his further favours.

Verse 1

I. It has often been the lot of God's people to have many enemies, and to be in imminent danger of falling into their hands. David was a man after God's heart, but not after men's heart: many were those that hated him, and sought his ruin. Let not those whom God loves marvel if the world hate them.

II. Those that trust God in the way of duty shall find him a present help to them in their greatest dangers. We shall never be delivered from all our enemies till we get to heaven; and to that heavenly kingdom God will preserve all that are his, 2 Tim. iv. 18.

III. Those that have received many signal mercies from God ought to give him the glory of them. Every new mercy in our hand should put a new song into our mouth, even praises to our God.

IV. We ought to be speedy in our thankful returns to God: *In the day that God delivered him he sang this song.*

Verses 2–51

I. How David adores God, and gives him the glory of his infinite perfections. There is none like him, nor any to be compared with him (*v.* 32): *Who is God, save the Lord?* All others that are adored as deities are counterfeits and pretenders. *Who is a rock, save our God?* They are dead, but *the Lord liveth, v.* 47. God will finish his work, and his word is tried, and what we may trust.

II. How he triumphs in the interest he has in this God, and his relation to him, which he lays down as the foundation of all the benefits he has received from him: *He is my God*; as such he cries to him (*v.* 7), and cleaves to him (*v.* 22); "and, if *my God*, then *my rock*" (*v.* 2), that is "my strength and my power (*v.* 33), the rock under which I take shelter, the rock on which I build my hope," *v.* 3. Whatever is my strength and support, he is *the God of the rock of my salvation* (*v.* 47). David often hid himself in a rock (1 Sam. xxiv. 2), but God was his chief hiding-place. "He is my fortress, in which I am safe and think myself so—*my high tower,* or stronghold, in which I am out of the reach of real evils—the *tower of salvation* (*v.* 51), which can never be scaled, nor battered, nor undermined. Salvation itself saves me. Christ is spoken of as the *horn of salvation* in the house of David, Luke i. 69. "Am I burdened, and ready to sink? *The Lord is my stay* (*v.* 19), by whom I am supported. Am I in the dark, benighted, at a loss? *Thou art my lamp, O Lord!* to show me my way, and thou wilt dispel *my darkness,*" *v.* 29. If we sincerely take the Lord for our God, all this, and much more, he will be to us, all we need and can desire.

III. What improvement he makes of his interest in God. If he be mine, 1. *In him will I trust* (*v.* 3). 2. *On him I will call* (*v.* 4), for *he is worthy to be praised.* 3. *To him will I give thanks* (*v.* 50), and that publicly.

IV. The full account he gives to others, of the great things God had done for him. This takes up most of the song. He gives God the glory both of his deliverances and of his successes.

1. He magnifies the great salvations God had wrought for him. To magnify the salvation, he observes,

(1) That the danger was very great and threatening out of which he was delivered. Men *rose up against him* (*v.* 40, 49) that *hated him* (*v.* 41), a *violent man* (*v.* 49), namely, Saul, who was malicious and vigorous in his pursuit. This is expressed figuratively, *v.* 5, 6. So violently did the waves of death beat upon him, so strongly did the cords and snares of death hold him, that he could not help himself, any more than a man in the grave can.

(2) That his deliverance was an answer to prayer, *v.* 7. He has here left us a good example, when we are in distress, to cry unto God with importunity, as children in a fright cry to their parents.

(3) That God appeared in a singular and extra-ordinary manner for him and against his enemies. The expressions are borrowed from the descent of the divine Majesty upon Mount Sinai, *v.* 8, 9, &c.

(4) That God manifested his particular favour and kindness to him in these deliverances (*v.* 20). *He delivered me, because he delighted in me.* The deliverance came not from common providence, but covenant-love. Herein he was a type of Christ, whom God upheld because he *delighted in him,* Isa. xlii. 1, 2.

2. He magnifies the great successes God had crowned him with. He had not only preserved but prospered him. He was blessed, (1) With liberty and enlargement. He was *brought into a large place* (*v.* 20). (2) With military skill, and strength, and swiftness. Though he was bred up to the crook, he was well instructed in the arts of war and qualified for the toils and perils of it. God, having called him to fight his battles, qualified him for the service. (3) With victory over his enemies, not only Saul and Absalom, but the Philistines, Moabites, Ammonites, Syrians, and other neighbouring nations, whom he subdued and made tributaries to Israel. His wonderful victories are here described, *v.* 38–43. (4) With advancement to honour and power. God *made his way perfect* (*v.* 33), gave him success in all

his undertakings, *set him upon his high places* (v. 34), denoting both safety and dignity. God's gentleness, his grace and tender mercy, *made him great* (v. 36).

V. The comfortable reflections he makes upon his own integrity, which God, by those wonderful deliverances, had graciously owned and witnessed to, *v.* 21–25. He means especially his integrity with reference to Saul and Ish-bosheth, Absalom and Sheba, and those who either opposed his coming to the crown or endeavoured to dethrone him. They falsely accused him and misrepresented him, but he had the testimony of his conscience for him that he was not an ambitious aspiring man, a false and bloody man, as they called him. His conscience witnessed for him, 1. That he had made the word of God his rule, and had kept to it, *v.* 32. Wherever he was, God's judgments were before him as his guide; whithersoever he went, he took his religion along with him. 2. That he had carefully avoided the by-paths of sin. He had not wickedly departed from his God. He could not say but that he had taken some false steps, but he had not deserted God, nor forsaken his way. Sins of infirmity he could not acquit himself from, but the grace of God had kept him from presumptuous sins. David reflected with more comfort upon his victories over his own iniquity than upon his conquest of Goliath and all the hosts of the uncircumcised Philistines. If a great man be a good man, his goodness will be much more his satisfaction than his greatness.

VI. The comfortable prospects he has of God's further favour. As he looks back, so he looks forward, with pleasure, and assures himself of the kindness God has in store for all the saints, for himself, and also for his seed.

1. For all good people, *v.* 26–28. He takes occasion here to lay down God's procedure with the children of men:

(1) That he will do good to those that are upright in their hearts. [1] God's mercy and grace will be the joy of those that are merciful and gracious. [2] God's uprightness, his justice and faithfulness, will be the joy of those that are upright, just, and faithful, both towards God and man. [3] God's purity and holiness will be the joy of those that are pure and holy. On the other hand,

(2) That those who turn aside to crooked ways he will *lead forth with the workers of iniquity*, as he says in another psalm.

2. For himself. He foresaw that his conquests and kingdom would be yet further enlarged, *v.* 45, 46.

3. For his seed: He *showeth mercy to his Messiah* (v. 51), not only to David himself, but to that seed of his for evermore. David was himself anointed of God, therefore he doubted not but God would show mercy to him, that mercy which he had promised not to take from him nor from his posterity (*ch.* vii. 15, 16); on that promise he depends, with an eye to Christ, who alone is his *seed for evermore*, whose throne and kingdom still continue, and will to the end. Thus all his joys and all his hopes terminate, as ours should, in the great Redeemer.

CHAPTER 23

The historian is now drawing towards a conclusion of David's reign, and gives an account here, I. Of some of his last words, which seem to have reference to his seed, spoken of in the foregoing chapter, ver. 1–7. II. Of the great men that were employed under him, the first three (ver. 8–17), two of the next three (ver. 18–23), and then the thirty, ver. 24–29.

Verses 1–7

The last will and testament of king David, after he had settled the crown upon Solomon and his treasures upon the temple which was to be built.

I. He is described, 1. By the meanness of his

origin: He was *the son of Jesse.* 2. The height of his elevation: He *was raised up on high,* as one favoured of God, and designed for something great, raised up as a prince, and as a prophet, to see further; for, (1) He was *the anointed of the God of Jacob,* and so was serviceable to the people of God in their civil interests, the protection of their country and the administration of justice among them. (2) He was *the sweet psalmist of Israel,* and so was serviceable to them in their religious exercises.

II. It is an account of his communion with God.

1. What God said to him both for his direction and for his encouragement as a king, and to be, in like manner, of use to his successors.

(1) Who spoke: *The Spirit of the Lord, the God of Israel,* and *the Rock of Israel,* which some think is an intimation of the Trinity of persons in the Godhead—the Father *the God of Israel,* the Son *the Rock of Israel,* and *the Spirit* proceeding from the Father and the Son, *who spoke by the prophets,* and particularly by David. David here avows his divine inspiration, that in his psalms, and in this composition, *The Spirit of God spoke by him.* This puts an honour upon the book of Psalms, and recommends them to our use in our devotions, that they are words which the Holy Ghost teaches.

(2) What was spoken. Here seems to be a distinction made between what the Spirit of God spoke *by* David, which includes all his psalms, and what the Rock of Israel spoke *to* David, which concerned himself and his family. Those whose office it is to teach others their duty must be sure to learn and do their own. Now that which is here said (v. 3, 4) may be considered, [1] With application to David, and his royal family. And so here is, *First,* The duty of magistrates enjoined them. When a king was spoken to from God he was not to be complimented with the height of his dignity and the extent of his power, but to be told his duty. *He must be just, ruling in the fear of God*; and so must all inferior magistrates in their places. Let rulers remember that they rule over men—not over beasts. They rule over men that have their follies and infirmities, and therefore must be borne with. It is not enough that they do no wrong, but they must not suffer wrong to be done. They must rule in the fear of God. They must also endeavour to promote the fear of God (that is, the practice of religion) among those over whom they rule. *He that* rules *in the fear of God shall be as the light of the morning, v.* 4. Light is sweet and pleasant, and he that does his duty shall have the comfort of it; his rejoicing will be the testimony of his conscience. Light is bright, and a good prince is illustrious; his justice and piety will be his honour. Light is a blessing, nor are there any greater and more extensive blessings to the public than princes that *rule in the fear of God.* As *the light of the morning,* which is most welcome after the darkness of the night. See Is. lxviii, 8, which were also some of the last words of David, and seem to refer to those recorded here. [2] With application to Christ, the Son of David, and then it must all be taken as a prophecy, and the original will bear it: *There shall be a ruler among men,* or over men, that *shall be just,* and *shall rule in the fear of God,* that is, shall order the affairs of religion and divine worship according to his Father's will; and he shall be as *the light of the morning,* &c., for he is the light of the world, and *as the tender grass,* for he is the *branch of the Lord,* and the *fruit of the earth,* Isa. iv. 2. God, by the Spirit, gave David the foresight of this, to comfort him under the many calamities of his family and the melancholy prospects he had of the degeneracy of his seed.

2. What comfortable use he made of this which God spoke to him, and what were his devout meditations on it, by way of reply, *v.* 5.

(1) Trouble supposed: *Although my house be not so with God*, and *although he make it not to grow*. David's family was not so with God as is described (v. 3, 4), and as he could wish, not so good, not so happy; it had not been so while he lived; he foresaw it would not be so when he was gone, that his house would be neither so pious nor so prosperous as one might have expected the offspring of such a father to be. This was what David's heart was upon concerning his children, that they might be right with God, faithful to him and zealous for him.

(2) Comfort ensured: *Yet he hath made with me an everlasting covenant*. Whatever trouble a child of God may have the prospect of, still he has some comfort or other to balance it (2. Cor. iv. 8, 9). God has made a covenant of grace with us in Jesus Christ, and we are here told, *First*, That it is an *everlasting* covenant, from everlasting in the contrivance and counsel of it, and to everlasting in the continuance and consequences of it. *Secondly*, That it is *ordered*, well ordered in all things, admirably well, to advance the glory of God and the honour of the Mediator, together with the holiness and comfort of believers. *Thirdly*, That the promised mercies are sure on the performance of the conditions. *Fourthly*, That it is *all our salvation*. Nothing but this will save us, and this is sufficient: it is this only upon which our salvation depends. *Fifthly*, That therefore it must be *all our desire*.

3. Here is the doom of the sons of Belial read, v. 6, 7. They shall be thrust away as thorns—rejected, abandoned. Now this is intended, [1] As a direction to magistrates to use their power for the punishing and suppressing of wickedness. Let them *thrust away the sons of Belial*; see Ps. ci. 8. Or, [2] As a caution to magistrates, and particularly to David's sons and successors, to see that they be not themselves sons of Belial (as too many of them were), for then neither the dignity of their place nor their relation to David would secure them from being thrust away by the righteous judgments of God.

Verses 8–38

I. The catalogue which his historian has here left upon record of the great soldiers that were in David's time is intended, 1. For the honour of David, who trained them up in the arts and exercises of war, and set them an example of conduct and courage. 2. For the honour of those worthies themselves, who were instrumental to bring David to the crown, settle and protect him in the throne, and enlarge his conquests. 3. To excite those that come after to a generous emulation. 4. To show how much religion contributes to the inspiring of men with true courage. David, both by his psalms and by his offerings for the service of the temple, greatly promoted piety among the grandees of the kingdom (1 Chron. xxix. 6), and, when they became famous for piety, they became famous for bravery.

II. Now these mighty men are here divided into three ranks:

1. The first three, who had done the greatest exploits and thereby gained the greatest reputation—Adino (v. 8), Eleazar (v. 9, 10), and Shammah (v. 11, 12). The exploits of this brave triumvirate are here recorded. They signalized themselves in the wars of Israel against their enemies, especially the Philistines. (1) Adino slew 800 at once with his spear. (2) Eleazar defied the Philistines, as they by Goliath, had defied Israel, but with better success and greater bravery: for when the men of Israel had gone away, he not only kept his ground, but *arose, and smote the Philistines*, on whom God struck a terror equal to the courage with which this great hero was inspired. His hand was weary, and yet it clave to his sword; as long as he had any strength remaining he held

his weapon and followed his blow. Thus, in the service of God, we should keep up the willingness and resolution of the spirit, notwithstanding the weakness and weariness of the flesh—faint, yet pursuing (Judg. viii. 4), the hand weary, yet not quitting the sword. (3) Shammah met with a party of the enemy, that were foraging, and routed them, v. 11, 12. But observe, both concerning this exploit and the former, it is here said, *The Lord wrought a great victory*.

2. The next three were distinguished from, and dignified above, the thirty, but attained not to the first three, v. 23. Of this second triumvirate two only are named, Abishai and Benaiah, whom we have often met with in the story of David.

(1) A brave action of these three in conjunction. They attended David in his troubles in the cave of Adullam (v. 13), suffered with him, and therefore were afterwards preferred by him. When David and his brave men who attended him, who had acted so vigorously against the Philistines, were driven to shelter themselves in caves and strongholds, the Philistines put a garrison even in Bethlehem itself, v. 13, 14. [1] How earnestly David longed for the water of the well of Bethlehem. It was harvest-time; the weather was hot; he was thirsty; perhaps good water was scarce, and therefore he earnestly wished, "O that I could but have one draught of the water of the well of Bethlehem!" With the water of that well he had often refreshed himself when he was a youth. Other water might quench his thirst as well, but he had a fancy for that above any. [2] How bravely his three mighty men, Abishai, Benaiah, and another not named, ventured through the camp of the Philistines, upon the very mouth of danger, and fetched water from the well of Bethlehem, without David's knowledge, v. 16. How much they valued their prince, and with what pleasure they could run the greatest hazards and undergo the greatest hardships in his service! And shall not we covet to approve ourselves to our Lord Jesus by a ready compliance with every intimation of his will given us by his word, Spirit, and providence? How little they feared the Philistines! [3] How self-denyingly David, when he had this far-fetched dear-bought water, *poured it out before the Lord*, v. 17. Thus he would cross his own foolish fancy, and punish himself for entertaining and indulging it. Thus he would honour God and give glory to him. The water purchased at this rate he thought too precious for his own drinking and fit only to be poured out to God as a drink-offering. Bishop Patrick speaks of some who think that David hereby showed that it was not material water he longed for, but the Messiah, who had the water of life, who, he knew, should be born at Bethlehem, which the Philistines therefore should not be able to destroy.

(2) The brave actions of two of them on other occasions. Abishai slew 300 men at once, v. 18, 19. Benaiah did many great things. [1] He slew two Moabites that were lion-like men, so bold and strong, so fierce and furious. [2] He slew a lion in a pit, either in his own defence, as Samson, or perhaps in kindness to the country, a lion that had done mischief. It being in a time of snow, he was more stiff and the lion more fierce and ravenous, and yet he mastered him. [3] He slew an Egyptian, on what occasion it is not said; he was well armed, but Benaiah attacked him with no other weapon than a walking staff, dexterously wrested his spear out of his hand, and slew him with it, v. 21. For these and similar exploits David preferred him to be captain of the life-guard or standing forces, v. 23.

3. Inferior to the second three, but of great note, were the thirty-one here mentioned by name, v. 24, &c. The surnames here given them are taken, as

it should seem, from the places of their birth or habitation, as many surnames with us originally were. From all parts of the nation, the most wise and valiant were picked up to serve the king. Several of those who are here named we find captains of the twelve courses which David appointed, one for each month in the year, 1 Chron. xxvii.

Christ, the Son of David, has his worthies too, who, like David's, are influenced by his example, fight his battles against the spiritual enemies of his kingdom, and in his strength are more than conquerors. Christ's apostles were his immediate attendants, did and suffered great things for him, and at length came to reign with him. They are mentioned with honour in the New Testament, as these in the Old, especially, Rev. xxi. 14. Nay, all the good soldiers of Jesus Christ have their names better preserved than even these worthies have; for they are written in heaven.

CHAPTER 24

The last words of David were good, but in this chapter we read of some of his last works, which were none of the best; yet he repented, and so finished well. We have here, I. His sin, which was numbering the people in the pride of his heart, ver. 1–9. II. His conviction of the sin, and repentance for it, ver. 10. III. The judgment inflicted upon him for it, ver. 11–15. IV. The staying of the judgment, ver. 16, 17. V. The erecting of an altar in token of God's reconciliation to him and his people, ver. 18–25.

Verses 1–9

I. The orders which David gave to Joab to number the people of Israel and Judah, v. 1, 2. Two things here seem strange:—1. The sinfulness of this. What harm was there in it? (1) Some think the fault was that he numbered those that were under twenty years old if they were but of stature and strength able to bear arms, and that this was the reason why this account was not enrolled, because it was illegal, 1 Chron. xxvii. 23, 24. (2) Others think the fault was that he did not require the half-shekel, which was to be paid for the service of the sanctuary whenever the people were numbered, as a *ransom for their souls*, Exod. xxx. 12. (3) Others think that he did it with a design to impose a tribute upon them for himself, to be put into his treasury. But nothing of this appears, nor was David ever a raiser of taxes. (4) This was the fault, that he had no orders from God to do it. (5) Some think that it was an affront to the ancient promise which God made to Abraham, that his seed should be innumerable as the dust of the earth; it savoured of distrust of that promise. (6) That which was the worst thing in numbering the people was that David did it in the pride of his heart, which was Hezekiah's sin in showing his treasures to the ambassadors. [1] It was a proud conceit of his own greatness in having the command of so numerous a people. [2] It was a proud confidence in his own strength. By publishing among the nations the number of his people, he thought to appear the more formidable.

2. The spring from which it is here said to arise is yet more strange, v. 1. It is not strange that *the anger of the Lord should be kindled against Israel*. But that, in this displeasure, he should move David to number the people is very strange. We are sure that God is not the author of sin; he tempts no man: we are told (1 Chron. xxi. 1) that *Satan provoked David to number Israel*. Satan, as an enemy, suggested it for a sin, as he put it into the heart of Judas to betray Christ. God, as righteous Judge, permitted it, with a design, from this sin of David, that princes may from these instances learn, when the judgments of God are abroad, to suspect that their sins are the ground of the controversy, and may therefore repent and reform themselves.

II. The opposition which Joab made to these orders.

Even he was aware of David's folly and vain-glory in this design. There was no occasion to tax them, nor to enlist them, nor to make any distribution of them. They were all easy and happy; and Joab wished both that their number might increase and that the king, though old, might live to see their increase, and have the satisfaction of it. *"But why doth my lord the king delight in this thing?* What need is there of doing it?" *Pauperis est numerare pecus—Leave it to the poor to count their flocks.* Joab was aware of David's vanity herein, but he himself was not.

III. The orders executed notwithstanding. *The king's word prevailed*, v. 4. Joab, according to order, applied himself with some reluctancy to this unpleasing task, and took the captains of the host to help him. The sum total was, at length, brought to the king at Jerusalem, v. 9. Whether the numbers answered David's expectation or no we are not told, nor whether the account fed his pride or mortified it.

Verses 10–17

I. Here is David's penitent reflection upon and confession of his sin in numbering the people. When the account was finished and laid before him, that very night his conscience was awakened. 1. He was convinced of his sin: *His heart smote him* before the prophet came to him (I think it should not be read *for* (v. 11), but *and when David was up*, so it is in the original), his conscience showed him the evil of what he had done. 2. He confessed it to God and begged earnestly for the forgiveness of it. He owned that he had *done foolishly, very foolishly*, because he had done it in the pride of his heart.

II. The just and necessary correction which he suffered for this sin, David had been full of tossings to and fro all night under the sense of his sin, *and he arose in the morning* designing to speak with Gad his seer concerning it. God directed the prophet Gad what to say to him (v. 11),

1. Three things are taken for granted, (1) That David must be corrected for his fault. Of the seven things that God hates, pride is the first, Prov. vi. 17. (2) The punishment must answer to the sin. (3) It must be such a punishment as the people must have a large share in, *for God's anger was kindled against Israel*, v. 1. Though it was David's sin that immediately opened the sluice, the sins of the people all contributed to the deluge.

2. As to the punishment that must be inflicted,

(1) David is told to choose what rod he will be beaten with, v. 12, 13. His heavenly Father must correct him, but, to show that he does not do it willingly, he gives David leave to make choice whether it shall be by war, famine, or pestilence, that he might the more patiently bear the rod when it was a rod of his own choosing. The prophet bids him advise with himself, and then tell him what answer he should *return to him that sent him*.

(2) He objects only against the judgments of the sword, and, for the other two, he refers the matter to God, but intimates his choice of the pestilence (v. 14). [1] He begs that he may *not fall into the hand of man.* [2] He casts himself upon God: *Let us fall now into the hand of the Lord, for his mercies are great.* David refers it to God which of these shall be the scourge, and God chooses the shortest, that he may the sooner testify his being reconciled. But some think that David, by these words, intimates his choice of the pestilence. That is a judgment to which David himself, and his own family, lie as open as the meanest subject, but not so either to famine or sword, and therefore David, tenderly conscious of his guilt, chooses that. But David, a penitent, dares cast himself into God's hand, knowing he shall find that *his mercies are great.* Good men, even when they are under God's frowns, yet will entertain no other

than good thoughts of him. *Though he slay me, yet will I trust in him.*

(3) A pestilence is accordingly sent (*v.* 15), which lasted from morning to the third day (so Mr. Poole), or only to the evening of the first day, the time appointed for the evening sacrifice, so Bishop Patrick and others.

III. God's gracious relaxation of the judgment, when it began to be inflicted upon Jerusalem (*v.* 16): *The angel stretched out his hand upon Jerusalem.* Perhaps there was more wickedness, especially more pride (and that was the sin now chastised), in Jerusalem than elsewhere, therefore the hand of the destroyer is stretched out upon that; but then *the Lord repented him of the evil,* and said to the destroying angel, *It is enough; stay now thy hand,* and *let mercy rejoice against judgment.* This was on Mount Moriah. Dr. Lightfoot observes that in the very place where Abraham, by a countermand from heaven, was stayed from slaying his son, this angel, by a like countermand, was stayed from destroying Jerusalem.

IV. David's renewed repentance for his sin upon this occasion, *v.* 17. He saw the angel (God opening his eyes for that purpose), saw his sword stretched out to destroy, a flaming sword, saw him ready to sheath it upon the orders given him to stay proceedings; seeing all this, he spoke to the *Lord, and said, Lo, I have sinned.* How he criminates himself, as if he could never speak ill enough of his own fault: "*I have sinned, and I have done wickedly;* mine is the crime, and therefore on me be the cross." How he intercedes for the people, whose bitter lamentations made his heart to ache, and his ears to tingle: *These sheep, what have they done?* Let this remind us of the grace of our Lord Jesus, who gave himself for our sins and was willing that God's hand should be against him, that we might escape. The shepherd was smitten that the sheep might be spared.

Verses 18–25

I. A command sent to David to erect an altar in the place where he saw the angel, *v.* 18. This was to intimate to David, 1. That God was now thoroughly reconciled to him; *for, if the Lord had been pleased to kill him, he would not have accepted an offering,* and therefore would not have ordered him to *build an altar.* God's encouraging us to offer to him spiritual sacrifices is evidence of his reconciling us to himself. 2. That peace is made between God and sinners by sacrifice, even by Christ the great propitiation, of whom all the legal sacrifices were types. 3. That when God's judgments are graciously stayed we ought to acknowledge it with thankfulness to his praise.

II. The purchase which David made of the ground. It seems the owner was a Jebusite, Araunah by name, proselyted no doubt to the Jewish religion, though by birth a Gentile, and therefore allowed, not only to dwell among the Israelites, but to have a possession of his own in a city, Lev. xxv. 29, 30. The piece of ground was a threshing-floor, a mean place, *yet* thus dignified—a place of labour, *therefore* thus dignified.

1. David went in person to the owner, to treat with him. See his justice, that he would not so much as use this place though the proprietor was an alien, though he himself was a king, and though he had express orders from God to rear an altar there, till he had bought it and paid for it. God *hates robbery for burnt-offering.* See his humility, though a king, he went himself (*v.* 19), and lost no honour by it. Araunah, when he saw him, *bowed himself to the ground before him, v.* 20. Great men will never be the less respected for their humility, but the more.

2. Araunah, when he understood his business (*v.* 21), generously offered him, not only the ground to build his altar on, but *oxen for sacrifices,* and other things that might be of use to him in the service (*v.* 22), and all this *gratis,* and a good prayer into the bargain: *The Lord thy God accept thee!* This he did, (1) Because he had a generous spirit with a great estate. *He gave as a king* (*v.* 23); though an ordinary subject, he had the spirit of a prince. In the Hebrew it is, *He gave, even the king to the king,* whence it is supposed that Araunah had been king of the Jebusites in that place. (2) Because he highly esteemed David, though his conqueror. (3) Because he had an affection for Israel, and earnestly desired that *the plague might be stayed;* and the honour of its being stayed at *his threshing-floor,* he would account a valuable consideration.

3. David resolved to pay the full value of it, and did so, *v.* 24. He will not offer that to God which costs him nothing. He thanked him, paid him *fifty shekels of silver* for the floor and the oxen for the present service, and afterwards 600 shekels of gold for the ground adjoining, to build the temple on.

III. The building of the altar, and the offering of the proper sacrifices upon it (*v.* 25), burnt-offerings to the glory of God's justice and peace-offerings to the glory of his mercy.

AN EXPOSITION, WITH PRACTICAL OBSERVATIONS, OF

THE FIRST
BOOK OF KINGS

The Bible began with the story of patriarchs, and prophets, and judges, men whose converse with heaven was more immediate, the record of which strengthens our faith, but is not so easily accommodated to our case, now that we expect not visions, as the subsequent history of affairs like ours under the direction of common providence; and here also we find, though not many types and figures of the Messiah, yet great expectations of him; for not only prophets, but kings, desired to see the great mysteries of the gospel, Luke x. 24.—The two books of Samuel are introductions to the books of the Kings, as they relate the origin of the royal government in Saul and of the royal family in David. These two books give us an account of David's successor, Solomon, the division of his kingdom, and the succession of the several kings both of Judah and Israel, with an abstract of their history down to the captivity. And as from the book of Genesis we may collect excellent rules of economics, for the good governing of families, so from these books we may collect rules of politics, for the directing of public affairs. There is in *these* books special regard had to the house and lineage of David, from which Christ came. Some of his sons trod in his steps, and others did not. The characters of the kings of Judah may be thus briefly given:— David the devout, Solomon the wise, Rehoboam the simple, Abijah the valiant, Asa the upright, Jehoshaphat the religious, Jehoram the wicked, Ahaziah the profane, Joash the backslider, Amaziah the rash, Uzziah the mighty, Jotham the peaceable, Ahaz the idolater, Hezekiah the reformer, Manasseh the penitent, Amon the obscure, Josiah the tender-hearted, Jehoahaz, Jehoiakim, Jehoiachin, and Zedekiah, all wicked, and such as brought ruin quickly on themselves and their kingdom. The number of the good and bad is nearly equal, but the reigns of the good were generally long and those of the bad short. In this *first* book we have, I. The death of David, *ch.* i. and ii. II. The glorious reign of Solomon, and his building the temple (*ch.* iii.-x.), but the cloud his sun set under, *ch.* xi. III. The division of the kingdoms in Rehoboam, and his reign and Jeroboam's, *ch.* xii.-xiv. IV. The reigns of Abijah and Asa over Judah, Baasha and Omri over Israel, *ch.* xv. and xvi. V. Elijah's miracles, *ch.* xvii.-xix. VI. Ahab's success against Benhadad, his wickedness and fall, *ch.* xx.-xxii. And in all this history it appears that kings, though gods to us, are men to God, mortal and accountable.

CHAPTER 1

In this chapter we have, I. David declining in his health, ver. 1–4. II. Adonijah aspiring to the kingdom, ver. 5–10. III. Nathan and Bath-sheba contriving to secure the succession to Solomon, and prevailing for an order from David for that purpose, ver. 11–31. IV. The anointing of Solomon accordingly, and the people's joy therein, ver. 32–40. V. The effectual stop this put to Adonijah's usurpation, and the dispersion of his party, ver. 41–49. VI Solomon's dismission of Adonijah upon his good behaviour, ver. 50–53.

Verses 1–4

David under the infirmities of old age. 1. It would have troubled one to see David so infirm. He was old, and his natural heat was so wasted that no clothes could keep him warm, *v.* 1. 2. It would have troubled one to see his physicians so weak and unskilful that they knew no other way of relieving him than by outward applications. *They covered him with clothes,* which where there is any inward heat, will keep it in, and so increase it; but, where it is not, they have none to communicate, no, not even royal clothing. They foolishly prescribed nuptials. His prophets should have been consulted as well as his physicians in an affair of this nature. That Abishag was married to David before she lay with him, and was his secondary wife, appears from its being imputed as a great crime to Adonijah that he desired to marry her (*ch.* ii. 22) after his father's death.

Verses 5–10

David had much affliction in his children. Amnon and Absalom had both been his grief; the one his first-born, the other his third, 2 Sam. iii. 2, 3. His second, whom he had by Abigail, we will suppose he had comfort in; his fourth was Adonijah (2 Sam. iii. 4) born in Hebron. He was a comely person, next in age, and (as it proved) next in temper, to Absalom, *v.* 6. In his father's eyes he had been a jewel, but was now a thorn.

I. His father had made a fondling of him, *v.* 6. He had not displeased him at any time. It was the son's fault that he was displeased at reproof whereby he lost the benefit of it; and it was the father's fault that, because he saw it displeased him, he did not reprove him; and now he justly smarted for indulging him.

II. He, in return, made a fool of his father. Because he was old, and confined to his bed, he *exalted himself,* and said, *I will be king, v.* 5. 1. He looked upon the days of mourning for his father to be at hand, and therefore he prepared to succeed him, though he knew that by the designation both of God and David Solomon was to be the man, 1 Chron. xxii. 9; xxiii. 1. 2. He looked upon his father as superannuated and good for nothing, and therefore he entered immediately upon the possession of the throne. His father is not fit to govern, for he is old and past ruling; nor Solomon, for he is young, and not yet able to rule; and therefore Adonijah will take the government upon him. 3. In pursuance of this ambitious project, (1) He got a great retinue (*v.* 5), *chariots and horsemen,* both for state and strength, to wait on him, and to fight for him. (2) He made great interest with no less than Joab, the general of the army, and Abiathar the high priest, *v.* 7. They were old men, who had been faithful to David in the most difficult and troublesome of his times, men of sense and experience, who, one would think, would not easily be wheedled. But God, in this matter, left them to themselves, perhaps to correct them for some former misconduct with a scourge of their own making. We are told (*v.* 8) who those were that were of such approved fidelity to David that Adonijah had not the confidence so much as to propose his project to them—Zadok, Benaiah, and Nathan. (3) He prepared a great entertainment (*v.* 9) at En-rogel, not far from Jerusalem; his guests were the king's sons, and the king's servants, whom he feasted and caressed to bring them over to his party; but Solomon was not invited, either because he despised him or because he despaired of him, *v.* 10. Some think that Adonijah slew these sheep and oxen, even fat ones, for sacrifice, and that it was a religious feast he made, beginning his usurpation with a show of devotion which he might do the more plausibly when he had the high priest himself on his side.

Verses 11–31

The effectual endeavours that were used by Nathan and Bath-sheba to obtain from David a ratification of Solomon's succession, for the crushing of Adonijah's usurpation. 1. David himself knew not what was doing. 2. Bath-sheba lived retired, and knew nothing of it either, till Nathan informed her. 3. Solomon, it is likely, knew of it, but was as a deaf man that heard not. Though he had years, and wisdom above his years, yet we do not find that he stirred to oppose Adonijah, but quietly composed himself and left it to God and his friends to order the matter. How then is the design brought about?

I. Nathan the prophet alarms Bath-sheba by acquainting her with the case, and puts her in a way to get an order from the king for the confirming of Solomon's title. He was concerned, because he knew God's mind, and David's and Israel's interest; it was by him that God had named Solomon *Jedidiah* (2 Sam. xii. 25), and therefore he could not sit still and see the throne usurped, which he knew was Solomon's right by the will of him from whom promotion cometh. Nathan applied to Bath-sheba, as one that had the greatest concern for Solomon, and could have the freest access to David. He informed her of Adonijah's attempt (*v.* 11), and that it was not with David's consent or knowledge. He suggested to her that not only Solomon was in danger of losing the crown, but that he and she too were in danger of losing their lives if Adonijah prevailed. Now, says Nathan, let me *give thee counsel how to save thy own life and the life of thy son, v.* 12. He directs her (*v.* 13) to go to the king, to remind him of his word and oath, that Solomon should be his successor; and to ask him in the most humble manner, *Why doth Adonijah reign?* He thought David was not so cold but this would warm him. Conscience, as well as a sense of honour, would put life into him upon such an occasion as this; and he promised (*v.* 14) that, while she was reasoning with the king upon this matter, he would come in and second her, as if he came accidentally.

II. Bath-sheba, according to Nathan's advice and direction, loses no time, but immediately makes her application to the king, to intercede for her life. She knew she should be welcome at any time. Her address to the king, on this occasion, is very discreet. 1. She reminded him of his promise made to her, and confirmed with a solemn oath, that Solomon should succeed him, *v.* 17. She knew how fast this would hold such a conscientious man as David was. 2. She informed him of Adonijah's attempt, which he was ignorant of (*v.* 18). She told him who were Adonijah's guests, and who were in his interest, and added, but *"Solomon thy servant has he not called,"* which plainly shows he looks upon him as his rival, and aims to undermine him, *v.* 19. 3. She pleads that it is very much in his power to obviate this mischief (*v.* 20): *The eyes of all Israel are upon thee,* not only as a *king,* but as a *prophet.* All Israel knew that David was not only himself *the anointed of the God of Jacob,* but that the *Spirit of the Lord spoke by him* (2 Sam. xxiii. 1, 2), and therefore waiting for and depending upon a divine designation, in a matter of such importance, David's word would be an oracle and a law to them. 4. She suggested the imminent

peril which she and her son would be in if this matter was not settled in David's lifetime, *v.* 21.

III. Nathan the prophet, according to his promise, seasonably stepped in, and seconded her, while she was speaking, before the king had given his answer. The king is told that Nathan the prophet has come, and he is sure to be always welcome to the king. He *bowed himself with his face to the ground, v.* 23. He deals a little more plainly with the king than Bath-sheba had done. 1. He makes the same representation of Adonijah's attempt as Bathsheba had made (*v.* 25, 26), adding that his party had already got to such a height of assurance as to shout, *God save king Adonijah,* as if king David were already dead. They had not invited him to their feast (*Me thy servant has he not called*), thereby intimating that they resolved not to consult either God or David in the matter. 2. He makes David sensible how much he was concerned to clear himself from having a hand in it: *Hast thou said, Adonijah shall reign after me?* (*v.* 24), and again (*v.* 27): *Is this thing done by my lord the king?* If it be, he is not so faithful either to God's word or to his own as we all took him to be; if it be not, it is high time that we witness against the usurpation, and declare Solomon his successor." Thus he endeavoured to incense David against them, that he might act the more vigorously for the support of Solomon's interest.

IV. David, hereupon, made a solemn declaration of his firm adherence to his former resolution, that Solomon should be his successor. Bath-sheba is called in (*v.* 28), and to her, as acting for and on behalf of her son, the king gives these fresh assurances. 1. He repeats his former promise and oath, owns that he had *sworn unto her by the Lord God of Israel that Solomon should reign after him, v.* 30. 2. He ratifies it with another, because the occasion called for it: *As the Lord liveth, that hath redeemed my soul out of all distress, even so will I certainly do this day,* without dispute, without delay. His form of swearing seems to be what he commonly used on solemn occasions, for we find it in 2 Sam. iv. 9. And it carries in it a grateful acknowledgment of the goodness of God to him. Perhaps he speaks thus, on this occasion, for the encouragement of his son and successor to trust in God in the distresses he also might meet with.

V. Bath-sheba receives these assurances (*v.* 31), with hearty good wishes for the king's health: *Let him live.* So far was she from thinking that he lived too long that she prayed he might live for ever, if it were possible, to adorn the crown he wore and to be a blessing to his people.

Verses 32–40

The effectual care David took both to secure Solomon's right and to preserve the public peace, by crushing Adonijah's project.

I. The express orders he gave for the proclaiming of Solomon. The persons he entrusted with this affair were Zadok, Nathan, and Benaiah, men of power and interest whom David had always found faithful to him. David orders them forthwith, with all possible solemnity, to proclaim Solomon. They must take with them *the servants of their lord,* the lifeguards, and all the servants of the household. They must set Solomon on the mule the king used to ride. 1. Zadok and Nathan, the two ecclesiastical persons, must, in God's name, anoint him king. 2. The great officers, civil and military, are ordered to give public notice of this, and to express the public joy upon this occasion by sound of trumpet, by which the law of Moses directed the gracing of great solemnities; to this must be added the acclamations of the people: "*Let king Solomon live.*" 3. They must then bring him in state to the city of David, and he must sit upon the throne of his father, as his viceroy, to despatch public business during his weakness and be his successor after his death: *He shall be king in my stead.* It would be a great satisfaction to David himself, and to all parties concerned, to have this done immediately, that upon the demise of the king there might be no dispute, or agitation, in the public affairs.

II. The great satisfaction which Benaiah, in the name of the rest, professed in these orders. The king said, "Solomon shall reign for me, and reign after me." "Amen" (says Benaiah heartily); "as the king says, so say we; and since we can bring nothing to pass without the concurrence of a propitious providence, *The Lord God of my lord the king say so too!*" *v.* 36. This is the language of his faith in that promise of God on which Solomon's government was founded. To this he adds a prayer for Solomon (*v.* 37), that God would be with him as he had been with David, and make his throne greater. He knew David was not one of those that envy their children's greatness, and that therefore he would not be disquieted at this prayer, nor take it as an affront, but would heartily say *Amen* to it.

III. The immediate execution of these orders, *v.* 38–40. No time was lost, but Solomon was brought in state to the place appointed, and there Zadok anointed him by the direction of Nathan the prophet and David the king, *v.* 39. In the tabernacle, where the ark was now lodged, was kept, among other sacred things, the holy oil for many religious services, thence Zadok took a *horn of oil*, which denotes both power and plenty and therewith anointed Solomon. The people, hereupon, express their great joy and satisfaction in the elevation of Solomon, surround him with their Hosannas—*God save king Solomon*, and attend him with their music and shouts of joy, *v.* 40.

Verses 41–53

I. The tidings of Solomon's inauguration brought to Adonijah and his party, in the midst of their jollity: *They had made an end of eating*, and, it should seem, it was a great while before they made an end, for all the affair of Solomon's anointing was ordered and finished while they were at dinner, glutting themselves. When *they made an end of eating*, and were preparing themselves to proclaim their king, and bring him in triumph into the city, they *heard the sound of the trumpet* (*v.* 41). Joab was an old man, and was alarmed at it, but Adonijah was very confident that the messenger, being a *worthy man, brought good tidings*, *v.* 42. "*Verily*, the best tidings I have to bring you is that *Solomon is made king*, so that your pretensions are all quashed." He relates to them, 1. With what great solemnity *Solomon* was *made king* (*v.* 44, 45), and that he was now *sitting on the throne of the kingdom*, *v.* 46. 2. With what general satisfaction Solomon was made king. The people were pleased: *The king's servants* attended him with an address of congratulation upon this occasion, *v.* 47. They *blessed king David*. They also prayed for Solomon, that God would make his name better than his father's, which it might well be when he had his father's foundation to build upon. A child, on a giant's shoulders, is higher than the giant himself. The king himself was pleased: He *bowed himself upon the bed*, not only to signify his acceptance of his servants' address, but to offer up his own address to God (*v.* 48).

II. The effectual crush which this gave to Adonijah's attempt. It spoiled the sport of his party, dispersed the company, and obliged every man to shift for his own safety.

III. The terror Adonijah himself was in and the course he took to secure himself. He had despised Solomon as not worthy to be his guest (*v.* 10), but now he dreads him as his judge: He *feared because of Solomon*. He *took hold on the horns of the altar*,

which was always looked upon as a sanctuary or place of refuge (Exod. xxi. 14), intimating hereby that he durst not stand a trial, but threw himself upon the mercy of his prince, in suing for which he relied upon no other plea than the mercy of God, which was manifested in the institution and acceptance of the sacrifices that were offered on that altar and the remission of sin thereupon.

IV. His humble address to Solomon for mercy. By those who brought Solomon tidings where he was, he sent a request for his life (*v.* 15): *Let king Solomon swear to me that he will not slay his servant.*

V. The orders Solomon gave concerning him. He discharged him upon his good behaviour, *v.* 52, 53. He considered that Adonijah was his brother, and that it was the first offence. Thus the Son of David receives those to mercy that have been rebellious: if they will return to their allegiance, and be faithful to their Sovereign, their former crimes shall not be mentioned against them; but, if still they continue in the interests of the world and the flesh, this will be their ruin.

CHAPTER 2

I. The conclusion of David's reign with his life, 1. The charge he gives to Solomon upon his death-bed, in general, to serve God (ver. 1–4), in particular, concerning Joab, Barzillai, and Shimei, ver. 5–9. 2. His death and burial, and the years of his reign, ver. 10, 11. II. The beginning of Solomon's reign, ver. 12. Though he was to be a prince of peace, he began his reign with some remarkable acts of justice, 1. Upon Adonijah, whom he put to death for his aspiring pretensions, ver. 13–25. 2. Upon Abiathar, whom he deposed from the high priesthood for siding with Adonijah, ver. 26, 27. 3. Upon Joab, whom he put to death for his late treasons and former murders, ver. 28–35. 4. Upon Shimei, whom, for cursing David, he confined to Jerusalem (ver. 36–38), and three years after, for transgressing the rules, put to death, ver. 39–46.

Verses 1–11

David, that great and good man, is here a dying man (*v.* 1), and a dead man, *v.* 10. It is well there is another life after this, for death stains all the glory of this, and lays it in the dust.

I. The charge and instructions which David, when he was dying, gave to Solomon, his son and declared successor. He feels himself declining, and is not backward to own it, *I go the way of all the earth*, *v.* 2. Heb. *I am walking in it.* Death is a way; not only a period of this life, but a passage to a better. Even the sons and heirs of heaven must *go the way of all the earth*, they must needs die; but they walk with pleasure in this way, *through the valley of the shadow of death*, Ps. xxiii. 4. Prophets, and even kings, must go this way to brighter light and honour than prophecy or sovereignty. David is going this way, and therefore gives Solomon directions what to do.

1. He charges him, in general, to keep God's commandments and to make conscience of his duty, *v.* 2–4. He prescribes to him, (1) A good rule to act by—the divine will: "Govern thyself by that." David's charge to him is to *keep the charge of the Lord* his God. (2) A good spirit to act with: *Be strong and show thyself a man*, though in years but a child. (3) Good reasons for all this. *That the Lord may continue* and so confirm *his word which he spoke concerning me.* Let each, in his own age, successively, keep God's charge, and then God will be sure to continue his word. We never let fall the promise till we let fall the precept. God had promised David that the Messiah should come from his loins, and that promise was absolute: but the promise that there should not fail him *a man on the throne of Israel* was conditional —if his seed behave themselves, as they should. If Solomon, in his day, fulfil the condition, he does his part towards the perpetuating of the promise. The condition is that he walk before God in all his institutions, in sincerity, with zeal and resolution.

2. He gives him directions concerning some particular persons, what to do with them. (1) Concerning Joab, *v.* 5. David was now conscious to himself that he had not done well to spare him, when he had made himself once and again obnoxious to the law, by the murder of Abner first and afterwards of Amasa, both of them great men, *captains of the hosts of Israel.* He slew them treacherously (*shed the blood of war in peace*), and injuriously to David: *Thou knowest what he did to me* therein. It aggravated Joab's crime that he was neither ashamed of the sin nor afraid of the punishment, but daringly wore the girdle and shoes that were stained with innocent blood, in defiance of the justice both of God and the king. David refers him to Solomon's wisdom (*v.* 6), with an intimation that he left him to his justice. (2) Concerning Barzillai's family, to whom he orders him to be kind for Barzillai's sake, who, we may suppose, by this time, was dead, *v.* 7. The kindnesses we have received from our friends must not be buried either in their graves or ours, but our children must return them to theirs. (3) Concerning Shimei, *v.* 8, 9. *He cursed me with a grievous curse;* the more grievous because he insulted him when he was in misery and poured vinegar into his wounds. His case is left with Solomon as one that knew what was fit to be done and would do as he found occasion. His turbulent spirit will soon give thee an occasion, which thou shouldst not fail to take, for the bringing of his *hoary head to the grave with blood.* This proceeded not from personal revenge, but a prudent zeal for the honour of the government and the covenant God had made with his family, the contempt of which ought not to be unpunished.

II. David's death and burial (*v.* 10): He *was buried in the city of David*, not in the burying place of his father, as Saul was, but in his own city, which he was the founder of. There were set the thrones, and there the tombs, of the house of David. His epitaph may be taken from 2 Sam. xxiii. 1. Here lies *David the son of Jesse, the man who was raised up on high, the anointed of the God of Jacob, and the sweet psalmist of Israel*, adding his own words (Ps. xvi. 9), *My flesh also shall rest in hope.*

Verses 12–25

I. Solomon's accession to the throne, *v.* 12. He came to it much more easily and peaceably than David did, and much sooner saw his government established. It is happy for a kingdom when the end of one good reign is the beginning of another, as it was here.

II. His just and necessary removal of Adonijah his rival, in order to the establishment of his throne. 1. Adonijah's treasonable project, which was to marry Abishag, David's concubine, not because he was in love with her, but because, by her, he hoped to renew his claim to the crown, which might stand him in stead. Absalom thought his pretensions much supported by lying with his father's concubines. Adonijah flatters himself that if he may succeed him in his bed, especially with the best of his wives, he may by that means step up to succeed him in his throne. 2. The means he used to compass this. He durst not make suit to Abishag immediately, but he engaged Bath-sheba to be his friend in this matter, who would be forward to believe it a matter of love, and not apt to suspect it a matter of policy. Bath-sheba was surprised to see Adonijah in her apartment, and asked him if he did not come with a design to do her a mischief, because she had been instrumental to crush his late attempt. "No," says he, "I come *peaceably* (*v.* 13), and to beg a favour" (*v.* 14), that she would use the great interest she had in her son to gain his consent, that he might marry Abishag

(*v.* 16, 17). He would represent himself as an object of compassion, that had been deprived of a crown, and therefore might well be gratified in a wife. Thus he pretends to be well pleased with Solomon's accession to the throne, when he is doing all he can to give him disturbance. *His words were smoother than butter, but war was in his heart.*

3. Bath-sheba's address to Solomon on his behalf. She promised to speak to the king for him (*v.* 18) and did so, *v.* 19. Solomon received her with all the respect that was due to a mother, though he himself was a king: He *rose up to meet her, bowed himself to her*, and caused her *to sit on his right hand*, according to the law of the fifth commandment. She tells him her errand at last (*v.* 21): *Let Abishag be given to Adonijah thy brother.* It was strange that she did not suspect the treason, but more strange that she did not abhor the incest, that was in the proposal. But either she did not take Abishag to be David's wife, because the marriage was not consummated, or she thought it might be dispensed with to gratify Adonijah, in consideration of his tame submission to Solomon.

4. Solomon's just and judicious rejection of the request. Solomon convinces his mother of the unreasonableness of the request, and shows her the tendency of it, which, before, she was not aware of. His reply is somewhat sharp: "*Ask for him the kingdom also*, *v.* 22. To ask that he may succeed the king in his bed is, in effect, to ask that he may succeed him in his throne; for that is it he aims at." He convicts and condemns Adonijah for his pretensions, and both with an oath. He convicts him out of his own mouth, *v.* 23. He condemns him to die immediately. He *shall be put to death this day*, *v.* 24. It was plain enough that Adonijah aimed at the crown, and Solomon could not be safe while he lived. Ambitious turbulent spirits commonly prepare for themselves the instruments of death. Many a head has been lost by catching at a crown.

Verses 26–34

Abiathar and Joab were both aiding and abetting in Adonijah's rebellious attempt, and it is probable were at the bottom of this new motion made by Adonijah for Abishag, and it should seem Solomon knew it, *v.* 22. This was, in both, an intolerable affront both to God and to the government, and the worse because of their high station and the great influence their examples might have upon many. They are both equally guilty of the treason, but, in the judgment passed upon them, a difference is made and with good reason.

I. Abiathar, in consideration of his old services, is only degraded, *v.* 26, 27. 1. Solomon convicts him, and by his great wisdom finds him guilty. 2. He calls to mind the respect he had formerly shown to David his father, and that he had both ministered to him in holy things (*had borne before him the ark of the Lord*), and also had tenderly sympathized with him in his afflictions. 3. For this reason he spares Abiathar's life, but deposes him from his offices, and confines him to his country seat at Anathoth, forbids him the court, the city, the tabernacle, the altar, and all intermeddling in public business. 4. The depriving of Abiathar was the fulfilling of the threatening against the house of Eli (1 Sam. ii. 30), for he was the last high priest of that family.

II. Joab, in consideration of his old sins, is put to death.

1. His guilty conscience sent him to the horns of the altar. He heard that Adonijah was executed and Abiathar deposed, and therefore, fearing his turn would be next, he fled for refuge to the altar.

2. Solomon ordered him to be put to death there for the murder of Abner and Amasa; for these were the crimes upon which he thought fit to ground the sentence, rather than upon his treasonable adherence to Adonijah. On this he grounds the sentence that he *fell upon two men more righteous and better than he*, that had done him no wrong nor meant him any, and, had they lived, might probably have done David better service. For these crimes, (1) He must die, and die by the sword of public justice. (2) He must die at the altar, rather than escape. Joab resolved not to stir from the altar (*v.* 30). Benaiah made a scruple of either killing him there or dragging him thence; but Solomon knew the law, that the altar of God should give no protection to wilful murderers. In case of such sins as the blood of beasts would atone for the altar was a refuge, but not in Joab's case. He therefore orders him to be executed there. The holiness of any place should never countenance the wickedness of any person. Those who, by a lively faith, take hold on Christ and his righteousness, with a resolution, if they perish, to perish there, shall find in him a more powerful protection than Joab found at the horns of the altar. Benaiah slew him (*v.* 34), with the solemnity, no doubt, of a public execution.

3. Solomon pleased himself with this act of justice not as it gratified any personal revenge, but as it was the fulfilling of his father's orders and a real kindness to himself and his own government. Peace was hereby secured (*v.* 33) upon David. Upon *his seed, his house, and his throne*, shall there be *peace for ever from the Lord.* Now that such a turbulent man as Joab is removed there shall be peace. Solomon, in this blessing of peace upon his house and throne, piously looks upward to God as the author of it and forward to eternity as the perfection of it. "It shall be peace from the Lord, and peace for ever from the Lord." The Lord of peace himself give us that peace which is everlasting.

Verses 35–46

I. The preferment of Benaiah and Zadok, two faithful friends to Solomon and his government, *v.* 35. Joab being put to death, Benaiah was advanced to be general of the forces in his room, and, Abiathar being deposed, Zadok was made high priest in his room, and therein was fulfilled that word of God, when he threatened to cut off the house of Eli (1 Sam. ii. 35), *I will raise me up a faithful priest, and will build him a sure house.*

II. The course that was taken with Shimei. He is sent for, by a messenger, from his house at Bahurim, expecting perhaps no better than Adonijah's doom, being conscious of his enmity to the house of David; but Solomon knows how to make a difference of crimes and criminals. David had promised Shimei his life for his time. Solomon is not bound by that promise, yet he will not go directly contrary to it. 1. He confines him to Jerusalem, and forbids him, upon any pretence whatsoever, to go out of the city any further than the brook Kidron, *v.* 36, 37, lest he should make mischief among his neighbours, but took him to Jerusalem, where he kept him prisoner at large. He has his life upon easy terms: he shall live if he will but be content to live at Jerusalem. 2. Shimei submits to the confinement, and thankfully takes his life upon those terms. Two of his servants ran from him to the land of the Philistines, *v.* 39. Thither he pursued them, and thence brought them back to Jerusalem, *v.* 40. Solomon takes the forfeiture. Information is given him that Shimei has transgressed, *v.* 41. Had he represented to Solomon the urgency of the occasion, and begged leave to go, perhaps Solomon might have given him leave; but to presume either upon his ignorance or his connivance

was to affront him in the highest degree. He condemns him for his former crime, cursing David, and throwing stones at him in the day of his affliction. He gives orders for the execution of Shimei immediately, *v.* 46.

CHAPTER 3

Solomon's reign looked bloody in the foregoing chapter, but the necessary acts of justice must not be called cruelty; in this chapter it appears with another face. We must not think the worse of God's mercy to his subjects for his judgments on rebels. We have here, I. Solomon's marriage to Pharaoh's daughter, ver. 1. II. A general view of his religion, ver. 2–4. III. A particular account of his prayer to God for wisdom, and the answer to that prayer, ver. 5–15. IV. A particular instance of his wisdom, in deciding the controversy between the two harlots, ver. 16–28. And very great he looks here, both at the altar and on the bench, and therefore on the bench because at the altar.

Verses 1–4

I Something that was unquestionably good, for which Solomon is to be praised and in which he is to be imitated. 1. He *loved the Lord, v.* 3. Particular notice was taken of God's love to him, 2 Sam. xii. 24. He had his name from it: *Jedidiah—beloved of the Lord.* And here we find he returned that love, as John, the beloved disciple, was most full of love. Solomon was a wise man, a rich man, a great man; yet the brightest encomium of him is that which is the character of all the saints, even the poorest, He *loved the Lord. He loved the worship of the Lord,* so the Chaldee; all that love God love his worship, love to hear from him and speak to him, and so to have communion with him. 2. He *walked in the statutes of David his father*, that is, in the statutes that David gave him, *ch.* ii. 2, 3; 1 Chron. xxviii. 9, 10, or in God's statutes, which David his father walked in before him; he kept close to God's ordinances. Those that truly *love God* will make conscience of *walking in his statutes.* 3. He was very free and generous in what he did for the honour of God. We must never think that wasted which is laid out in the service of God.

II. Here is something concerning which it may be doubted whether it was good or no. 1. His marrying Pharaoh's daughter, *v.* 1. We will suppose she was proselyted, otherwise the marriage would not have been lawful; yet, if so, surely it was not advisable. Some think that he did this with the advice of his friends, that she was a sincere convert (for the gods of the Egyptians are not reckoned among the strange gods which his strange wives drew him in to the worship of, *ch.* xi. 5, 6), and that the book of Canticles and the 45th Psalm were penned on this occasion, by which these nuptials were made typical of the mystical espousals of the church to Christ, especially the Gentile church. 2. His worshipping in the high places, and thereby tempting the people to do so too, *v.* 2, 3. Abraham built his altars on mountains (Gen. xii. 8; xxii. 2), and worshipped in a grove, Gen. xxi. 33. Thence the custom was derived, and was proper, till the divine law confined them to one place, Deut. xii. 5, 6. David kept to the ark, and did not care for the high places, but Solomon, though in other things he *walked in the statutes of his father*, in this came short of him. He showed thereby a great zeal for sacrificing, but to obey would have been better.

Verses 5–15

An account of a gracious visit which God paid to Solomon, and the communion he had with God.

I. The circumstances of this visit, *v.* 5. 1. The place. It was in Gibeon; that was the great high place, because there the tabernacle and the brazen altar were, 2 Chron. i. 3. There Solomon offered his great sacrifices, and there God owned him. The nearer we come to the rule in our worship the more reason we have to expect the tokens of God's presence. 2. The time. It was by night, the night after he had offered that generous sacrifice, *v.* 4. The more we abound in God's work the more comfort we may expect in him; if the day has been busy for him, the night will be easy in him. Silence and retirement befriend our communion with God. 3. The manner. It was in a dream, when he was asleep, his senses locked up, that God's access to his mind might be the more free and immediate. In this way God used to speak to the prophets (Num. xii. 6) and to private persons, for their own benefit, Job xxxiii. 15, 16. These divine dreams were plainly distinguishable from those in which there are divers vanities, Eccl. v. 7.

II. The gracious offer God made him, *v.* 5. He saw the glory of God shine about him, and heard a voice saying, *Ask what I shall give thee.*

III. The pious request Solomon hereupon made to God. He readily laid hold of this offer. Solomon prayed in his sleep, God's grace assisting him; yet it was a lively prayer. The grace of God wrought in him these gracious desires.

1. He acknowledges God's great goodness to his father David, *v.* 6. God's favours are doubly sweet when we observe them transmitted to us through the hands of those that have gone before us.

2. He owns his own insufficiency for the discharge of that great trust to which he is called, *v.* 7, 8. And here is a double plea to enforce his petition for wisdom:—(1) That his place required it, as he was successor to David. (2) That he wanted it. As one that had a humble sense of his own deficiency, he pleads, *"Lord, I am but a little child. I know not how to go out or come in* as I should, nor to do so much as the common daily business of the government." Paul's question (*Who is sufficient for these things?*) is much like Solomon's here, *Who is able to judge this thy so great a people? v.* 9. Absalom, who was a fool, wished himself a judge; Solomon, who was a wise man, trembles at the undertaking and suspects his own fitness for it.

3. He begs of God to give him wisdom (*v.* 9): *Give therefore thy servant an understanding heart.* Thus his good father prayed, and thus he pleaded. Ps. cxix. 125, *I am thy servant, give me understanding.* An understanding heart is God's gift, Prov. ii. 6. We must pray for it (James i. 5), and pray for it with application to our particular calling.

4. The favourable answer God gave to his request. It was a pleasing prayer (*v.* 10): *The speech pleased the Lord.* Those are accepted of God who prefer spiritual blessings to temporal. But that was not all; it was a prevailing prayer, and prevailed for more than he asked. (1) God gave him wisdom, *v.* 12. Such an insight, and such a foresight, never was prince so blessed with. (2) He gave him riches and honour over and above into the bargain (*v.* 13). These also are God's gift, and, as far as is good for them, are promised to all that *seek first the kingdom of God and the righteousness thereof,* Matt. vi. 33. Let young people learn to prefer grace to gold in all that they choose, because *godliness has the promise of the life that now is,* but *the life that now is* has not *the promise of godliness.* But, if we make sure of wisdom and grace, these will either bring outward prosperity with them or sweeten the want of it. God promised Solomon riches and honour absolutely, but long life upon condition (*v.* 14). *If thou wilt walk in my ways, as David did, then I will lengthen thy days.* He failed in the condition; and therefore, though he had riches and honour, he did not live so long to enjoy them as in the course of nature he might have done. [1] The way to obtain spiritual blessings is to be importunate for them, to wrestle with God in prayer for them, as Solomon did for wisdom, asking that

only, as the *one thing needful.* [2] The way to obtain temporal blessings is to be indifferent to them and to refer ourselves to God concerning them. Solomon had wisdom given him because he did ask it and wealth because he did not ask it.

5. The grateful return Solomon made for the visit God was pleased to pay him, *v.* 15. He awoke, we may suppose in a transport of joy; being satisfied of God's favour, he began to think *what he should render to the Lord.* He had made his prayer at the high place at Gibeon, and there God had graciously met him; but he comes to Jerusalem to give thanks *before the ark of the covenant,* blaming himself, as it were, that he had not prayed there, the ark being the token of God's presence, and wondering that God had met him anywhere else. God's passing by our mistakes should persuade us to amend them. There he, (1) Offered a great sacrifice to God. (2) He made a great feast upon the sacrifice, that those about him might rejoice with him in the grace of God.

Verses 16–28

An instance is here given of Solomon's wisdom. The proof is fetched, not from the mysteries of state, though there no doubt he excelled, but from the trial of a cause between party and party.

I. The case opened, not by lawyers, but by the parties themselves, though they were women. These two women were harlots. It is probable the cause had been heard in the inferior courts, before it was brought before Solomon, the judges being unable to determine it. These two women, who lived in a house together, were each of them delivered of a son within three days of one another, *v.* 17, 18. One of them overlaid her child, and, in the night, exchanged it with the other (*v.* 19, 20), who was soon aware of the cheat put upon her, and appealed to public justice to be righted, *v.* 21.

II. The difficulty of the case. The question was, Who was the mother of this living child? Both mothers were vehement in their claim, and showed a deep concern about it. Neither will own the dead child, though it would be cheaper to bury that than to maintain the other: but it is the living one they strive for. The neighbours, though it is probable that some of them were present at the birth and circumcision of the children, yet had not taken so much notice of them as to be able to distinguish them.

III. The determination of it. Solomon, having patiently heard what both sides had to say, sums up the evidence, *v.* 23. Solomon calls for a sword, and gives orders to divide the living child between the two contenders. It proved an effectual discovery of the truth. Some think that Solomon did himself discern it, before he made this experiment, by the countenances of the women and their way of speaking. To find out the true mother, he could not try which the child loved best, and must therefore try which loved the child best; both pretended to a motherly affection, but their sincerity will be tried when the child is in danger. (1) She that knew the child was not her own, but in contending for it stood upon a point of honour, was well content to have it divided. (2) She that knew the child was her own, rather than the child should be butchered, gives it up to her adversary. How feelingly does she cry out, *O, my lord! give her the living child, v.* 26. "Let me see it hers, rather than not see it at all." By this tenderness towards the child it appeared that she was not the careless mother that had overlaid the dead child, but was the true mother of the living one, that could not endure to see its death, having compassion on the son of her womb.

IV. We are told what a great reputation Solomon got among his people by this and other instances of his wisdom, which would have a great influence upon the ease of his government: *They feared the king* (v. 28), *for they saw that the wisdom of God was in him*, that is, that wisdom with which God had promised to endue him.

CHAPTER 4

An instance of the wisdom God granted to Solomon we had in the close of the foregoing chapter. In this we have an account of his wealth and prosperity. I. The magnificence of his court, his ministers of state (ver. 1–6), and the purveyors of his household (ver. 7–19), and their office, ver. 27, 28. II. The provisions for his table, ver. 22, 23. III. The extent of his dominion, ver. 21–24. IV. The numbers, case, and peace, of his subjects, ver. 20–25. V. His stables, ver. 26. VI. His great reputation for wisdom and learning, ver. 29–34.

Verses 1–19

I. Solomon upon his throne (v. 1): *So king Solomon was king*, that is, he was confirmed and established king *over all Israel*.

II. The great officers of his court. It is observable, 1. That several of them are the same that were in his father's time. Zadok and Abiathar were then priests (2 Sam. xx. 25), Jehoshaphat was then recorder, Benaiah, in his father's time, was a principal man in military affairs. 2. The rest were priests' sons. His prime-minister of state was *Azariah the son of Zadok the priest*. Two others of the first rank were the sons of Nathan the prophet, v. 5.

III. The purveyors for his household, whose business it was to send in provisions from several parts of the country, that thus, 1. His house might always be well furnished at the best hand. 2. That thus he himself, and those who immediately attended him, might the more closely apply themselves to the business of the state, not troubled about much serving. 3. That thus all the parts of the kingdom might be equally benefited by the taking off of the commodities that were the productions of their country and the circulating of the coin. Industry would hereby be encouraged, and consequently wealth increased, even in those tribes that lay most remote from the court. 4. The dividing of this trust into so many hands was prudent, that no man might be continually burdened with the care of it nor grow exorbitantly rich with the profit of it.

Verses 20–28

Such a kingdom, and such a court, surely never any prince had, as Solomon's.

I. Such a kingdom. The account here given of it is such as fully answers the prophecies which we have concerning it in Ps. lxxii., which is a psalm for Solomon, but with references to Christ. 1. The territories of his kingdom were large and its tributaries many; so it was foretold that he should *have dominion from sea to sea*, Ps. lxxii. 8–11. Solomon reigned over all the neighbouring kingdoms, who were his subjects by constraint. All the princes from the river Euphrates, north-east to the border of Egypt south-west, added to his wealth by serving him, and bringing him presents, v. 21. He had *peace on all sides*, v. 24. 2. The subjects of his kingdom, and its inhabitants, were many and cheerful. (1) They were numerous and the country was exceedingly populous (v. 20): *Judah and Israel were many*, and that good land was sufficient to maintain them all. (2) They were easy, they dwelt safely. They dwelt every man under *his vine and fig tree*. Solomon invaded no man's property, but what they had they could call their own: he protected every man in the possession and enjoyment of his property. (3) They were cheerful in the use of their plenty, *eating and drinking, and making merry*, v. 20. Go where you would, you might see all the marks of plenty, peace, and satisfaction. The spiritual peace, and joy, and holy security, of all

the faithful subjects of the Lord Jesus were typified by this. *The kingdom of God is not*, as Solomon's was, *meat and drink*, but, what is infinitely better, *righteousness, and peace, and joy in the Holy Ghost*.

II. Such a court Solomon kept as can scarcely be paralleled. Ahasuerus, once in his reign, made a great feast, to *show the riches of his kingdom*, Esther i. 3, 4. But it was much more the honour of Solomon that he kept a constant table not of dainties but substantial food, for the entertainment of those who came to hear his wisdom. Thus Christ fed those whom he taught, 5,000 at a time, more than ever Solomon's table would entertain at once: and all believers have in him a continual feast. Herein he far outdoes Solomon, that he feeds all his subjects, not with the bread that perishes, but *with that which endures to eternal life*.

Verses 29–34

Solomon's wisdom was more his glory than his wealth.

I. The fountain of his wisdom: *God gave it him*, v. 29.

II. The fulness of it: *He had wisdom and understanding, exceeding much*. It is called *largeness of heart*; for the heart is often put for the intellectual powers. He was very free and communicative, had the gift of utterance as well as wisdom, was as free of his learning as he was of his meat, and grudged neither to any that were about him. The greatness of Solomon's wisdom is illustrated by comparison. Chaldea and Egypt were nations famous for learning; thence the Greeks borrowed theirs; but the greatest scholars of these nations came short of Solomon, v. 30. *Solomon excelled them all* (v. 30), he outdid them and confounded them; his counsel was much more valuable.

III. The fame of it. It was talked of *in all nations round about*.

IV. The fruits of it; by these the tree is known: he did not bury his talent, but showed his wisdom, 1. In his compositions. It appears by what he spoke, or dictated to be written from him, (1) That he was a moralist, and a man of great prudence, for he spoke 3,000 *proverbs*, wise sayings, apophthegms, of admirable use for the conduct of human life. Whether those proverbs of Solomon that we have were any part of the 3,000 is uncertain. (2) That he was a poet and a man of great wit: *His songs were 1,005*, of which one only is extant, because that only was divinely inspired, which is therefore called his *Song of songs*. (3) That he was a natural philosopher, and a man of great learning and insight into the mysteries of nature. From his own and others' observations and experience, he wrote both of plants and animals (v. 33).

2. In his conversation. There came persons from all parts to *hear the wisdom of Solomon*, v. 34. But,

Lastly, Solomon was, herein, a type of Christ, *in whom are hidden all the treasures of wisdom and knowledge*, and hidden for use; for he is *made of God to us wisdom*.

CHAPTER 5

The great work which Solomon was raised up to do was the building of the temple. In this chapter we have an account of the preparations he made for that and his other buildings. Gold and silver his good father had prepared in abundance, but timber and stones he must get ready; and about these we have him treating with Hiram king of Tyre. I. Hiram congratulated him on his accession to the throne, ver. 1. II. Solomon signified to him his design to build the temple and desired him to furnish him with workmen, ver. 2–6. III. Hiram agreed to do it, ver. 7–9. IV. Solomon's work was accordingly well done and Hiram's workmen were well paid, ver. 10–18.

Verses 1–9

The amicable correspondence between Solomon and Hiram. Tyre was a famous trading city, that lay close upon the sea, in the border of Israel. It is here said of Hiram the king that he was *ever a lover of David*; and we have reason to think he was a worshipper of the true God, and had himself renounced, though he could not reform, the idolatry of his city.

I. Hiram's embassy of compliment to Solomon, *v.* 1.

II. Solomon's embassy of business to Hiram, sent, it is likely, by messengers of his own. Solomon, in his letter to Hiram, acquaints him,

1. With his design to build a temple to the honour of God. Solomon tells Hiram, who was himself no stranger to the affair, (1) That David's wars were an obstruction to him, that he could not build this temple, though he designed it, *v.* 3. (2) That peace gave him an opportunity to build it, and therefore he resolved to set about it immediately: *God has given me rest* both at home and abroad, and there is no adversary (*v.* 4), no *Satan* (so the word is), no instrument of Satan to oppose it, or to divert us from it.

2. With his desire that Hiram would assist him herein. Lebanon was the place whence timber must be had, a noble forest in the north of Canaan, particularly expressed in the grant of that land to Israel —*all Lebanon*, Joshua xiii. 5, so that Solomon was proprietor of all its productions. But Solomon owned that though the trees were his the Israelites had not *skill to hew timber*, like the Sidonians, who were Hiram's subjects. Solomon courts Hiram to send him workmen, and promises (*v.* 6) both to *assist* them (*my servants shall be with thy servants*, to work under them), and to *pay* them (*unto thee will I give hire for thy servants*); for the labourer, even in churchwork, though it be indeed its own wages, *is worthy of his hire.* The evangelical prophet seems to allude to this story, Isa. lx, where he prophesies, (1) That the *sons of strangers* (such were the Tyrians and Sidonians) shall *build up the wall* of the gospel temple, *v.* 10. (2) That the *glory of Lebanon* shall be brought to it to *beautify it*, *v.* 13.

3. Hiram's reception of, and return to, this message.

(1) He received it with great satisfaction to himself: He *rejoiced greatly* (*v.* 7) that Solomon trod in his father's steps. In this Hiram's generous spirit rejoiced. With what pleasure Hiram speaks of Solomon's wisdom and the extent of his dominion. Let us learn not to envy others either those secular advantages or those endowments of the mind wherein they excel us.

(2) He answered it with great satisfaction to Solomon, granting him what he desired, and showing himself very forward to assist him in this great and good work to which he was laying his hand. We have here his articles of agreement with Solomon. [1] He deliberated upon the proposal, before he returned an answer (*v.* 8). Those do not lose time who take time to consider. [2] He descended to particulars in the articles. Solomon had spoken of hewing the trees (*v.* 6), and Hiram agrees to what he desired concerning that (*v.* 8); but nothing had been said concerning carriage, he therefore undertakes to bring all the timber down from Lebanon by sea, a coasting voyage. Solomon must appoint the place where the timber shall be delivered, and thither Hiram will undertake to bring it and be responsible for its safety. As the Sidonians excelled the Israelites in timberwork, so they did in sailing; for Tyre and Sidon were *situate at the entry of the sea* (Ezek. xxvii. 3): they therefore were fittest to take care of the watercarriage. And, [3] If Hiram undertake for the work, he justly expects that Solomon shall undertake for the wages: "*Thou shalt accomplish my desire in giving food for my household* (*v.* 9), not only for the workmen, but for my own family." If Tyre supply Israel with craftsmen, Israel will supply Tyre with corn, Ezek.

xxvii. 17. Thus, by the wise disposal of Providence, one country has need of another.

Verses 10–18

I. The performance of the agreement between Solomon and Hiram. 1. Hiram delivered Solomon the timber, according to his bargain, *v.* 10. 2. Solomon conveyed to Hiram the corn which he had promised him, *v.* 11.

II. The confirmation of the friendship that was between them hereby. It is wisdom to strengthen our friendship with those whom we find to be honest and fair, lest new friends prove not so firm and so kind as old ones.

III. The labourers whom Solomon employed in preparing materials for the temple. 1. Some were Israelites, who were employed felling trees and helping to square them, in conjunction with Hiram's servants; for this he appointed 30,000, but employed only 10,000 at a time, so that for one month's work they had two months' vacation, both for rest and for the despatch of their own affairs at home, *v.* 13, 14. It was temple service, yet Solomon takes care that they shall not be overworked. 2. Others were captives of other nations, who were to bear burdens and to hew stone (*v.* 15). 3. There were some employed as directors and overseers (*v.* 16), 3,300 that ruled over the people, for preparation was now to be made, not only for the temple, but for all the rest of Solomon's buildings, at Jerusalem, and here in the forest of Lebanon, and in other places of his dominion, of which see *ch.* ix. 17–19.

IV. The laying of the foundation of the temple; for that is the building his heart is chiefly upon, and therefore he begins with that, *v.* 17, 18. It should seem, Solomon was himself present, and president, at the founding of the temple, and that the first stone was laid with some solemnity. *Solomon commanded and they brought costly stones* for the foundation; though, being out of sight, worse might have served. That sincerity which is our gospel perfection obliges us to lay our foundation firm and to bestow most pains on that part of our religion which lies out of the sight of men.

CHAPTER 6

Great and long preparation had been making for the building of the temple, and here, at length, comes an account of the building of it; a noble piece of work it was, in its spiritual significancy, one of the glories of the church. I. The time when it was built (ver. 1), and how long it was in the building, ver. 37, 38. II. The silence with which it was built, ver. 7. III. The dimensions of it, ver. 2, 3. IV. The message God sent to Solomon, when it was in the building, ver. 11–13. V. The particulars: windows (ver. 4), chambers (ver. 5, 6, 8–10), the walls and flooring (ver. 15–18), the oracle (ver. 19–22), the cherubim (ver. 23–30), the doors (ver. 31–35), and the inner court, ver. 36.

Verses 1–10

I. The temple is called *the house of the Lord* (*v.* 1), because it was, 1. Directed and modelled by him. Infinite Wisdom was the architect, and gave David the plan or pattern by the Spirit. 2. Dedicated and devoted to him and to his honour, to be employed in his service, for he manifested his glory in it in a way agreeable to that dispensation. This gave it its *beauty of holiness*, that it was *the house of the Lord*, which far transcended all its other beauties.

II. The time when it began to be built is exactly set down. 1. It was just 480 years after the bringing of the children of Israel out of Egypt. Allowing forty years to Moses, seventeen to Joshua, 299 to the Judges, forty to Eli, forty to Samuel and Saul, forty to David, and four to Solomon before he began the work, we have just the sum of 480. David's tent, which was clean and convenient, though it was neither stately nor rich, is called the *house of the Lord* (2 Sam. xii. 20), and served as well as Solomon's temple; yet, when God gave Solomon great wealth, he put it into his heart thus to employ it, and graciously accepted him, chiefly because it was to be a shadow of good things to come, Heb. ix. 9. 2. It was in the fourth year of Solomon's reign, the first three years being taken up in settling the affairs of his kingdom, that he might not find any embarrassment from them in this work. It is not time lost which is spent in composing ourselves for the work of God, and disentangling ourselves from everything which might distract or divert us.

III. The materials are brought in, ready for their place (v. 7), so ready that there was *neither hammer nor axe heard in the house while it was in building*. It was to be the temple of the God of peace, and therefore no iron tool must be heard in it. Quietness and silence both become and befriend religious exercises: God's work should be done with as much care and as little noise as may be. The temple was thrown down with axes and hammers, and those that threw it down roared *in the midst of the congregation* (Ps. lxxiv. 4, 6); but it was built up in silence. Clamour and violence often hinder the work of God, but never further it.

IV. The dimensions are laid down (v. 2, 3) according to the rules of proportion. Some observe that the length and breadth were just double to that of the tabernacle.

V. An account of the windows (v. 4): They were *broad within, and narrow without*, Marg. Such should be the eyes of our mind be, reflecting nearer on ourselves than on other people, looking much within, to judge ourselves, but little without, to censure our brethren.

VI. The chambers are described (v. 5, 6), which served as vestries, in which the utensils of the tabernacle were carefully laid up, and where the priests dressed. Care was taken that the beams should not be fastened in the walls to weaken them, v. 6. Let not the church's strength be impaired under pretence of adding to its beauty or convenience.

Verses 11–14

I. The word God sent to Solomon, when he was engaged in building the temple. He assured him that if he would proceed and persevere in obedience to the divine law, and keep in the way of duty and the true worship of God, the divine loving-kindness should be drawn out both to himself (*I will perform my word with thee*) and to his kingdom. This word God sent him probably by a prophet, 1. That by the promise he might be encouraged and comforted in his work. An eye to the promise will carry us cheerfully through our work; and those who wish well to the public will think nothing too much that they can do to secure and perpetuate to it the tokens of God's presence. 2. That, by the condition annexed, he might be awakened to consider that though he built the temple ever so strong the glory of it would soon depart, unless he and his people continued *to walk in God's statutes*.

II. The work Solomon did for God: *So he built the house* (v. 14), *so* animated by the message God had sent him, *so* admonished not to expect that God should own his building unless he were obedient to his laws. The strictness of God's government will never drive a good man from his service, but quicken him in it. Solomon built and finished, he went on with the work, and God went along with him till it was completed.

Verses 15–38

I. We have a particular account of the details of the building.

1. The wainscot of the temple. It was of cedar (v. 15), which was strong and durable, and of a very sweet smell. The wainscot was curiously carved with knops (like eggs or apples) and flowers, v. 18.

2. The gilding. It was not like ours, washed over, but *the whole house*, all the inside of the temple (v. 22), even the floor (v. 30), he *overlaid with gold*, and the most holy place with *pure gold*, v. 21.

3. The oracle, or *speaking-place, the holy of holies*, so called because thence God spoke to Moses, and perhaps to the high priest. In this place *the ark of the covenant was to be set*, v. 19. Solomon made everything new, except the ark, which was still the same that Moses made, with its mercy-seat and cherubim; that was the token of God's presence, which is always the same with his people whether they meet in tent or temple, and changes not with their condition.

4. The cherubim. Besides those at the ends of the mercy-seat, which covered the ark, (1) Solomon set up two more, very large ones, with wings made of olive-wood, and all overlaid with gold, v. 23, &c. (2) He carved cherubim upon all the walls of the house, v. 29. The heathen set up images of their gods and worshipped them; but these were designed to represent the servants and attendants of the God of Israel, the holy angels, not to be themselves worshipped.

5. The doors. The folding doors that led into the oracle were but a fifth part of the wall (v. 31), those into the temple were a fourth part (v. 33); but both were beautified with cherubim engraven on them, v. 32, 35.

6. The inner court, in which the brazen altar was at which the priests ministered. This was separated from the court where the people were by a low wall, three rows of hewn stone tipped with a cornice of cedar (v. 36), that over it the people might see what was done and hear what the priests said to them.

7. The time spent in this building. It was but seven years and a half from the founding to the finishing of it, v. 38.

II. Let us now see what was typified by this temple. 1. Christ is the true temple; he himself spoke of the temple of his body, John ii. 21. God himself prepared him his body, Heb. x. 5. *In him dwelt the fulness of the Godhead*, as the Shechinah in the temple. In him meet all God's spiritual Israel. Through him we have access with confidence to God. 2. Every believer is a living temple, in whom the Spirit of God dwells, 1 Cor. iii. 16. Even the body is such by virtue of its union with the soul, 1 Cor. vi. 19. We are not only wonderfully made by the divine providence, but more wonderfully made anew by the divine grace. This living temple is built upon Christ as its foundation and will be perfected in due time. 3. The gospel church is the mystical temple; it grows to a *holy temple in the Lord* (Eph. ii. 21), enriched and beautified with the gifts and graces of the Spirit, as Solomon's temple with gold and precious stones. Only Jews built the tabernacle, but Gentiles joined with them in building the temple. Even strangers and foreigners are built up *a habitation of God*, Eph. ii. 19, 22. The temple was divided into the holy place and the most holy, the courts of it into the outer and inner; so there are the visible and the invisible church. The door into the temple was wider than that into the oracle. Many enter into profession that come short of salvation. The top-stone of the gospel church will, at length, be brought forth with shoutings, and it is a pity that there should be the clashing of axes and hammers in the building of it. Angels are ministering spirits, attending the church on all sides and all the members of it. 4. Heaven is the everlasting temple. There the church will be fixed, and no longer movable. The streets of the new Jerusalem, in allusion to the flooring of the temple, are said to be *of pure gold*, Rev. xxi. 21. The cherubim there always attend the throne of glory. The temple was uniform, and in heaven there is the perfection of beauty and harmony.

In Solomon's temple there was no noise of axes and hammers. Everything is quiet and serene in heaven; all that shall be stones in that building must in the present state of probation and preparation be fitted and made ready for it, hewn and squared by divine grace, and so made meet for a place there.

CHAPTER 7

In this chapter we have, I. Solomon's fitting up several buildings for himself and his own use, ver. 1–12. II. His furnishing the temple which he had built for God, 1. With two pillars, ver. 13–22. 2. With a molten sea, ver. 23–26. 3. With ten basins of brass (ver. 27–37), and ten lavers upon them, ver. 38, 39. 4. With all the other utensils of the temple, ver. 40–50. 5. With the things that his father had dedicated, ver. 51. The particular description of these things was not needless when it was written, nor is it now useless.

Verses 1–12

Never had any man so much of the spirit of building as Solomon had, nor to better purpose; he began with the temple, built for God first, and then all his other buildings were comfortable. 1. He built a house for himself (*v.* 1), *where he dwelt*, *v.* 8. His father had built a good house; but it was no reflection upon his father for him to build a better. Much of the comfort of this life is connected with an agreeable house. He was thirteen years building this house, whereas he built the temple in little more than seven years. He was in no haste for his own palace, but impatient till the temple was finished and fit for use. 2. He built *the house of the forest at Lebanon* (*v.* 2), supposed to be a country seat, so called from the trees that encompassed it. Express notice is taken of his buildings, not only in Jerusalem, but in Lebanon (*ch.* ix. 19), and we read of the tower of Lebanon, which looks towards Damascus (Cant. vii. 4), which probably was part of this house. A particular account is given of this house, that being built in Lebanon, a place famed for cedars, the pillars, and beams, and roof, were all cedar (*v.* 2, 3), and, being designed for pleasant prospects, there were three tiers of windows on each side, *light against light* (*v.* 4, 5), or, as it may be read, *prospect against prospect*. 3. He built piazzas before one of his houses, either that at Jerusalem or that in Lebanon, which were very famous—a porch of pillars (*v.* 6). He himself speaks of Wisdom's building her house, and *hewing out her seven pillars* (Prov. ix. 1). 4. At his house where he dwelt in Jerusalem he built a great hall, or porch of judgment, where was set the throne, or king's bench, for the trial of causes, in which he himself was appealed to, and this was richly wainscoted with cedar, from the floor to the roof, *v.* 7. He had there also *another court within the porch*, nearer his house, of similar work, for his attendants to walk in, *v.* 8. 5. He built a house for his wife, where she kept her court, *v.* 8. It is said to be *like the porch*, because built of cedar like it.

Verses 13–47

We have here an account of the brasswork about the temple. There was no iron about the temple, though we find David preparing for the temple *iron for things of iron*, 1 Chron. xxix. 2. I. The brazier whom Solomon employed to preside in this part of the work was Hiram, or Huram (2 Chron. iv. 11), who was by his mother's side an Israelite, of the tribe of Naphtali, by his father's side a man of Tyre, *v.* 14. If he had the ingenuity of a Tyrian, and the affection of an Israelite to the house of God, it was happy that the blood of the two nations mixed in him, for thereby he was qualified for the work to which he was designed. As the tabernacle was built with the wealth of Egypt, so the temple with the wit of Tyre. II. All the brazen vessels were of *bright brass* (*v.* 45), *good* brass, so the Chaldee, that which was strongest and looked finest.

III. The place where all the brazen vessels were cast was the plain of Jordan, because the ground there was stiff and clayey, fit to make moulds of for the casting of the brass (*v.* 46), and Solomon would not have this dirty smoky work done in or near Jerusalem. IV. The quantity was not accounted for. The vessels *were exceedingly numerous*, and it would have been an endless thing to keep the account of them; *neither was the weight of the brass*, when it was delivered to the workmen, searched or enquired into; so honest were the workmen, and such great plenty of brass they had, that there was no danger of wanting. V. Some particulars of the brass-work are described.

1. Two brazen pillars were set up *in the porch of the temple* (*v.* 21), between the temple and the court of the priests, purely for ornament. (1) What an ornament they were we may gather from the account here given of the curious work that was about them, chequer-work, chain-work, net-work, lily-work, and pomegranates in rows, and all of bright brass. (2) Their significancy is intimated in the names given them (*v.* 21): *Jachin—he will establish*; and *Boaz—in him is strength*. Some think they were intended for memorials of the pillar of cloud and fire which led Israel through the wilderness: I rather think them designed for memorandums to the priests and others that came to worship at God's door, [1] To depend upon God for strength and establishment in all their religious exercises. When we come to wait upon God, and find our hearts wandering and unfixed, then by faith let us fetch in help from heaven: *Jachin—God will fix this roving mind. Boaz—in him is our strength*, who works in us both to will and to do. *I will go in the strength of the Lord God*. Spiritual strength and stability are to be had at the door of God's temple, where we must wait for the gifts of grace in the use of the means of grace. [2] It was a memorandum to them of the strength and establishment of the temple of God among them. But, with respect to this temple, when it was destroyed particular notice was taken of the destroying of these pillars (2 Kings xxv. 13, 17), which had been the tokens of its establishment, and would have been so if they had not forsaken God.

2. A brazen sea, a very large vessel, above five yards in diameter, and which contained above 500 barrels of water for the priests' use, in washing themselves and the sacrifices, and keeping the courts of the temple clean, *v.* 23, &c. It stood raised upon the figures of twelve oxen in brass. The Gibeonites, or Nethinim, who were to draw water for the house of God, had the care of filling it. Some think Solomon made the images of oxen to support this great cistern in contempt of the golden calf which Israel had worshipped, that (as Bishop Patrick expresses it) the people might see there was nothing worthy of adoration in those figures; they were fitter to make posts of than to make gods of.

3. Ten bases, or stands, or settles, of brass, on which were put ten lavers, to be filled with water for the service of the temple, because there would not be room at the molten sea for all that had occasion to wash there. The bases on which the lavers were fixed are very largely described here, *v.* 27, &c. They were curiously adorned and set upon wheels, that the lavers might be removed as there was occasion; but ordinarily they stood in two rows, five on one side of the court and five on the other, *v.* 39. Each laver contained forty baths, that is, about ten barrels, *v.* 38.

4. Besides these, there was a vast number of brass pots made to boil the flesh of the peace-offerings in, which the priests and offerers were to feast upon before the Lord (see 1 Sam. ii. 14); also shovels, wherewith they took out the ashes of the altar. Some

think the word signifies *flesh-hooks*, with which they took meat out of the pot. The basins also were made of brass, to receive the blood of the sacrifices.

Verses 48–51

1. The making of the gold work of the temple, which it seems was done last, for with it the work of the house of God ended. All within doors was gold, and all made new (except the ark, with its mercy-seat and cherubim), the old being either melted down or laid by—the golden altar, table, and candlestick, with all their appurtenances. The altar of incense was still *one*, for Christ and his intercession are so: but he made ten golden tables, 2 Chron. iv. 8, and *ten golden candlesticks* (v. 49), intimating the much greater plenty both of spiritual food and heavenly light which the gospel blesses us with than the law of Moses did or could afford. Even the hinges of the door were of gold (v. 50). 2. The bringing in of the dedicated things, which David had devoted to the honour of God, *v.* 51. What was not expended in the building and furniture was laid up in the treasury, for repairs, exigencies, and the constant charge of the temple-service. What the parents have dedicated to God the children ought by no means to alienate or recall, but should cheerfully devote what was intended for pious and charitable uses, that they may, with their estates, inherit the blessing.

CHAPTER 8

The building and furniture of the temple were very glorious, but the dedication of it exceeds in glory as much as prayer and praise exceed the casting of metal and the graving of stones. The temple was designed for the keeping up of the correspondence between God and his people; and here we have an account of the solemnity of their first meeting there. I. The representatives of all Israel were called together (ver. 1, 2), to keep a feast to the honour of God, for fourteen days, ver. 65. II. The priests brought the ark into the most holy place, and fixed it there, ver. 3–9. III. God took possession of it by a cloud, ver. 10, 11. IV. Solomon, with thankful acknowledgments to God, informed the people touching the occasion of their meeting, ver. 12–21. V. In a long prayer he recommended to God's gracious acceptance all the prayers that should be made in or towards this place, ver. 22–53. VI. He dismissed the assembly with a blessing and an exhortation, ver. 54–61. VII. He offered abundance of sacrifices, on which he and his people feasted, and so parted, with great satisfaction, ver. 62–66. These were Israel's golden days, days of the Son of man in type.

Verses 1–11

The temple, though richly beautified, yet while it was without the ark was like a body without a soul, or a candlestick without a candle, or a house without an inhabitant. All the cost and pains bestowed on this stately structure are lost if God do not accept them. When therefore *all the work* is ended (*ch.* vii. 51), the *one thing needful* is the bringing in of the ark. This must crown the work.

I. Solomon presides in this service, as David did in the bringing up of the ark to Jerusalem. This great assembly he summons (v. 1), *at the feast in the seventh month* (v. 2), namely, the feast of tabernacles, which was appointed on the fifteenth day of that month, Lev. xxiii. 34. David, like a very *good* man, brings the ark to a *convenient* place, near him; Solomon, like a very *great* man, brings it to a *magnificent* place. Let children proceed in God's service where their parents left off.

II. All Israel attend the service, their judges and the chief of their tribes and families, all their officers, civil and military, and the heads of their clans. These came together, on this occasion, 1. To do honour to Solomon, and to return him the thanks of the nation for all the good offices he had done. 2. To do honour to the ark. Public mercies call for public acknowledgments. Those that appeared before the Lord did not appear empty, for they all sacrificed sheep and oxen innumerable, *v.* 5.

III. The priests do their part of the service. In the wilderness, the Levites were to carry the ark, but here (it being the last time that the ark was to be carried) the priests themselves did it, as they were ordered to do when it surrounded Jericho. We are here told, 1. What was in the ark, nothing but the two tables of stone (v. 9), a treasure far exceeding all the dedicated things both of David and Solomon. The pot of manna and Aaron's rod were *by* the ark, but not *in* it. 2. What was brought up with the ark (v. 4): *The tabernacle of the congregation*. It is probable that both that which Moses set up in the wildernèss, which was in Gibeon, and that which David pitched in Zion, were brought to the temple, to which they did, as it were, surrender all their holiness, merging it in that of the temple, which must henceforward be the place where God must be sought unto. Thus will all the church's holy things on earth, that are so much its joy and glory, be swallowed up in the perfection of holiness above. 3. Where it was fixed in its place, the place appointed for its rest after all its wanderings (v. 6): *In the oracle of the house*, whence they expected God to speak to them, even in the most holy place, which was made so by the presence of the ark, *under the wings of the* great *cherubim* which Solomon set up (ch. vi. 27), signifying the special protection of angels, under which God's ordinances and the assemblies of his people are taken.

IV. God graciously owns what is done and testifies his acceptance of it, v. 10, 11. The priests might come into the most holy place till God manifested his glory there; but, thenceforward, none might, at their peril, approach the ark, except the high priest, on the day of atonement. Therefore it was not till the priests had come out of the oracle that the *Shechinah* took possession of it, in a cloud, which filled not only the most holy place, but the temple, so that the priests who burnt incense at the golden altar could not bear it. By this visible emanation of the divine glory, 1. God put an honour upon the ark, and owned it as a token of his presence. The glory of it had been long diminished and eclipsed by its frequent removes, the meanness of its lodging, and its being exposed too much to common view; but God will now show that it is as dear to him as ever, and he will have it looked upon with as much veneration as it was when Moses first brought it into his tabernacle. 2. He testified his acceptance of the building and furnishing of the temple as good service done to his name and his kingdom among men. 3. He struck an awe upon this great assembly; and, by what they saw, confirmed their belief of what they read in the books of Moses concerning the glory of God's appearances to their fathers. 4. He showed himself ready to hear the prayer Solomon was now about to make. But the glory of God appeared in a cloud, a dark cloud, to signify, (1) The darkness of that dispensation in comparison with the light of the gospel. (2) The darkness of our present state in comparison with the vision of God, which will be the happiness of heaven, where the divine glory is unveiled.

Verses 12–21

I. Solomon encourages the priests. The disciples of Christ *feared when they entered into the cloud*, though it was a *bright cloud* (Luke ix. 34), so did the priests when they found themselves wrapped in a thick cloud. To silence their fears, 1. He reminds them that this was a token of God's presence (v. 12). It is an indication of his favour; for he had said, *I will appear in a cloud*, Lev. xvi. 2. Where God dwells in light faith is swallowed up in vision and fear in love. 2. He himself bids it welcome, as worthy of all acceptation (v. 13): "*Surely I come*," says God.

"*Amen,*" says Solomon. "*Even so, come, Lord.* The house is thy own, entirely thy own, *I have surely built it for thee.*" It is Solomon's joy that God has taken possession; and it is his desire that he would keep possession. Let not the priests therefore dread that in which Solomon so much triumphs.

II. He instructs the people. He spoke briefly to the priests, but *turned his face about* (*v.* 14) from them *to the congregation* that stood in the outer court, and addressed himself to them largely.

1. He blessed them. When they saw the dark cloud enter the temple they blessed themselves, being astonished at it and afraid lest the thick darkness should be utter darkness to them. Solomon *blessed them*, that is, he pacified them, and freed them from the consternation they were in.

2. He informed them concerning this house which he had built and was now dedicating.

(1) He began his account with a thankful acknowledgment of the good hand of his God upon him hitherto: *Blessed be the Lord God of Israel, v.* 15. What we have the pleasure of, God must have the praise of. He thus engaged the congregation to lift up their hearts in thanksgivings to God. Solomon here blessed God, [1] For his promise which he *spoke with his mouth to David.* [2] For the performance, that he had now *fulfilled it with his hand.* We have then the best sense of God's mercies, when we compare what God does with what he has said.

(2) Solomon is now making a solemn surrender or dedication of this house unto God. Here is a recital of the special causes and considerations moving Solomon to build this house. [1] He recites the want of such a place. *I chose no city to build a house in for my name;* therefore there is occasion for the building of this. [2] He recites David's purpose to build such a place. God chose the person first that should rule his people (*I chose David, v.* 16) and then put it into *his heart to build a house* for God's name, *v.* 17. [3] He recites God's promise concerning himself. God approved his father's purpose (*v.* 18): *Thou didst well, that it was in thy heart.* What he had done was not of his own head, nor for his own glory, but the work itself was according to his father's design and his doing it was according to God's designation. [4] He recites what he himself had done, and with what intention: *I have built a house,* not for my own name, but *for the name of the Lord God of Israel* (*v.* 20), and *set there a place for the ark, v.* 21. The more we do for God the more we are indebted to him; for our sufficiency is of him, and not of ourselves.

Verses 22–53

Solomon having made a general surrender of this house to God, which God had signified his acceptance of by taking possession, next followed Solomon's prayer, his request that this temple may be deemed and taken, not only for a house of sacrifice but a *house of prayer for all people*; and herein it was a type of the gospel church; see Isa. lvi. 7, compared with Matt. xxi. 13.

I. Solomon did not appoint one of the priests to do it, nor one of the prophets, but did it himself, *in the presence of all the congregation of Israel, v.* 22. 1. It was well that he was able to do it, a sign that he learnt to pray well, and knew how to express himself to God in a suitable manner, *pro re nata—on the spur of the occasion,* without a prescribed form. 2. It was well that he was not shy of performing divine service before so great a congregation. Solomon, in all his other glory, even on his ivory throne, looked not so great as he did now.

II. The posture in which he prayed was very reverent, and expressive of humility, seriousness, and fervency in prayer. 1. He *kneeled down,* as appears, *v.* 54, where he is said to *rise from his knees;* compare 2 Chron. vi. 13. Kneeling is the most proper posture for prayer, Eph. iii. 14. Mr. Herbert says, "Kneeling never spoiled silk stockings." 2. *He spread forth his hands towards heaven,* and (as it should seem by *v.* 54) continued so to the end of the prayer, hereby expressing his desire towards, and expectations from, God, as a *Father in heaven.* He spread forth his hands, as it were to offer up the prayer from an open enlarged heart and to present it to heaven, and also to receive thence, with both arms, the mercy which he prayed for.

III. The prayer itself was very long, and perhaps much longer than is here recorded. It is not making long prayers, but making them for a pretence, that Christ condemns. In this prayer Solomon does,

1. Give glory to God. This he begins with, as the most proper act of adoration. (1) He gives him the praise of what he is, the best of masters to his people: "*Who keepest covenant and mercy with thy servants;* doing that for them of which thou hast not given them an express promise, provided they *walk before thee with all their hearts.*" (2) He gives him thanks for what he had done, in particular, for his family (*v.* 24): "*Thou hast kept with thy servant David,* as with thy other servants, *that which thou promisedst him.*"

2. He sues for grace and favour from God.

(1) That God would perform to him and his the mercy which he had promised, *v.* 25, 26. Hitherto God has helped, 2. Cor. i. 10. Solomon repeats the promise (*v.* 25): *There shall not fail thee a man to sit on the throne,* not omitting the condition, *so that thy children take heed to their way;* for we cannot expect God's performance of the promise but upon our performance of the condition. And then he humbly begs this entail (*v.* 26): *Now, O God of Israel! let thy word be verified.*

(2) That God would have respect to this temple, that he would graciously own it. To this purpose,

[1] He premises, *First,* A humble admiration of God's gracious condescension (*v.* 27): "*But will God indeed dwell on the earth?* Can we imagine that a Being infinitely high, and holy, and happy, will stoop so low as to let it be said of him that he *dwells upon the earth?*" *Secondly,* A humble acknowledgment of the incapacity of the house he had built, though very capacious, to contain God: "*The heaven of heavens cannot contain thee,* this house is too little, too mean to be the residence of him that is infinite in being and glory."

[2] This premised, he prays in general, *First,* That God would graciously hear and answer the prayer he was now praying, *v.* 28. It was a humble prayer, an earnest prayer, a prayer made in faith: "Lord, *hearken to it, have respect to it,* not as the prayer of Israel's king but as the prayer of thy servant." *Secondly,* That God would in like manner hear and answer all the prayers that should, at any time hereafter, be made in or towards this house which he had now built, "*Hear it in heaven, that* is indeed *thy dwelling-place,* and, *when thou hearest, forgive.*" None but priests might come into that place; but when they worshipped in the courts of the temple, it must be with an eye towards it, as an instituted medium of their worship, helping the weakness of their faith, and typifying the mediation of Jesus Christ, who is the true temple.

[3] More particularly, he here puts divers cases:

First, If God were appealed to by an oath for the determining of any controverted right between man and man, and the oath were taken before this altar, he prayed that God would, in some way or other, discover the truth, and judge between the contending parties, *v.* 31, 32. He prayed that, in difficult matters, this throne of grace might be a throne of judgment.

Secondly, If the people of Israel were groaning under any national calamity, or any particular Israelite under any personal calamity, he desired that the prayers they should make in or towards this house might be heard and answered.

a. In case of public judgments, he could not, he would not, ask that their prayer might be answered unless they did also *turn from their sin* (*v*. 35) and *turn again to God* (*v*. 33), that is, unless they did truly repent and reform. But if they did thus qualify for mercy he prays, (*a*) That God would hear from heaven. (*b*) That he would forgive their sin. (*c*) That he would *teach them the good way wherein they should walk*, by his Spirit, with his word and prophets; and thus they might be both profited by their trouble, and prepared for deliverance, which then comes in love when it finds us brought back to the good way of God and duty. (*d*) That he would then remove the judgment, and redress the grievance, in the mercy prayed for.

b. In case of personal afflictions, *v*. 38–40. He does not mention particulars, so numerous, so various, are the grievances of the children of men. He supposes that the complainants themselves would very sensibly feel their own burden. They *shall know every man the plague of his own heart*, and shall spread their hands, that is, spread their case, as Hezekiah spread the letter, in prayer, towards this house; whether the trouble be of body or mind, they shall represent it before God. He refers all cases of this kind, that should be brought hither, to God. (*a*) To his omniscience. (*b*) To his justice: *Give to every man according to his ways;* and he will not fail to do so, by the rules of grace, not the law, for then we should all be undone. (*c*) To his mercy: *Hear, and forgive, and do* (*v*. 39), *that they may fear thee all their days*, *v*. 40.

c. The case of the stranger that is not an Israelite is next mentioned, a proselyte that comes to the temple to pray to the God of Israel, being convinced of the folly and wickedness of worshipping the gods of his country. He begged that God would accept and answer the proselyte's prayer (*v*. 43): *Do according to all that the stranger calleth to thee for*. Thus early, thus ancient, were the indications of favour towards the *sinners of the Gentiles*: as there was then *one law for the native and for the stranger* (Exod. xii. 49), so there was one gospel for both.

d. The case of an army going forth to battle is next recommended by Solomon to the divine favour. It is supposed that the army is encamped at a distance, somewhere a great way off, sent by divine order *against the enemy*, *v*. 44.

e. The case of poor captives is the last that is here mentioned as a proper object of divine compassion. (*a*) He supposes that Israel will sin. He knew them, and himself, and the nature of man. (*b*) He supposes that, if Israel revolt from God, God will be *angry with them*, and *deliver them into the hand of their enemies*, to be carried captive into a strange country, *v*. 46. (*c*) He then supposes that they will bethink themselves, will repent and humble themselves, saying, *We have sinned and have done perversely* (*v*. 47), and *in the land of their enemies will return to God*, whom they had forsaken in their own land. (*d*) He supposes that in their prayers they will look towards their own land, the holy land, Jerusalem, the holy city, and the temple, the holy house, and directs them so to do (*v*. 48). (*e*) He prays that then God would *hear their prayers, forgive their sins, plead their cause*, and incline their enemies to *have compassion on them*, *v*. 49, 50.

Lastly, No place now, under the gospel, can be imagined to add any acceptableness to the prayers made in or towards it, as the temple then did. That was a shadow: the substance is Christ; whatever we ask in his name, it shall be given us.

Verses 54–61

Solomon, after his sermon in Ecclesiastes, gives us the conclusion of the whole matter; so he does here, after this long prayer; it is called his *blessing the people*, *v*. 55.

I. He gives God the glory of the great things he had done for Israel, *v*. 56. He stood up to *bless the congregation* (*v*. 55), but began with blessing God. He blesses God who has given, he does not say wealth, and honour, and power, and victory, to Israel, but *rest*, as if that were a blessing more valuable than any of those. 1. He refers to the *promises given by the hand of Moses*, as he did (*v*. 15, 24) to those which were made to David. There were promises given by Moses, as well as precepts. 2. He does, as it were, write a receipt in full on the back of these bonds: *There has not failed one word of all his good promises*.

II. He blesses himself and the congregation, expressing his earnest desire and hope of these four things: 1 The presence of God with them. This great congregation was now shortly to be scattered, and it was not likely that they would ever be all together again in this world. Solomon therefore dismisses them with this blessing: *"The Lord be present with us*, and that will be comfort enough when we are absent from each other. *The Lord our God be with us, as he was with our fathers* (*v*. 57); *let him not leave us*, let him be to us today, and to ours for ever, what he was to those that went before us." 2. The power of his grace upon them: *"Let him be with us*, and continue with us, not that he may enlarge our coasts and increase our wealth, but *that he may incline our hearts to himself, to walk in all his ways and to keep his commandments*," *v*. 58. 3. An answer to the prayer he had now made: *"Let these my words be nigh unto the Lord our God day and night*, *v*. 59. Let a gracious return be made to every prayer that shall be made here, and that will be a continual answer to this prayer." What Solomon asks here for his prayer is still granted in the intercession of Christ.

III. He solemnly charges his people to continue and persevere in their duty to God. Having spoken to God for them, he here speaks from God to them, and those only would fare the better for his prayers that were made better by his preaching.

Verses 62–66

We read before that Judah and Israel were very cheerful under their own vines and fig-trees; here we have them so in God's courts.

I. They had abundant joy and satisfaction while they attended at God's house, for there, 1. Solomon offered a great sacrifice, 22,000 oxen and 120,000 sheep, enough to have drained the country of cattle if it had not been a very fruitful land. All these sacrifices could not be offered in one day, but in the several days of the feast. 2. He kept a feast, the feast of tabernacles, as it should seem, after the feast of dedication, and both together lasted fourteen days (*v*. 65).

II. They carried this joy and satisfaction with them to their own houses. God's goodness was the matter of their joy, so it should be of ours at all times.

Chapter 9

In this chapter we have, I. The answer which God, in a vision, gave to Solomon's prayer, and the terms he settled with him, ver. 1–9. II. The interchanging of gr[?]eful kindnesses between Solomon and Hiram, ver. 10–14. III. F[?]s workmen and buildings, ver. 15–24. IV. His devotion, ver. 25. V. His trading navy, ver. 26–28.

Verses 1–9

God had given a real answer to Solomon's prayer, and tokens of his acceptance of it, immediately, by the *fire from heaven* which consumed the sacrifices (as we find, 2 Chron. vii. 1); but here we have a more express and distinct answer to it.

I. In what way God gave him this answer. He appeared to him, as he had done at Gibeon, in the beginning of his reign, in a dream or vision, *v.* 2. The comparing of it with that intimates that it was the very night after he had finished the solemnities of his festival, for so that was, 2 Chron. i. 6, 7.

II. The purport of this answer. 1. He assures him of his special presence in the temple he had built, in answer to the prayer he had made (*v.* 3): *I have hallowed this house.* Solomon had dedicated it, but it was God's prerogative to hallow it—to sanctify or consecrate it. 2. He shows him that he and his people were for the future *upon their good behaviour.* Let them not be secure now, as if they might live as they please now that they have the *temple of the Lord* among them, Jer. vii. 4. "*If thou wilt walk before me as David did, in integrity of heart and uprightness, then I will establish the throne of thy kingdom,* and not otherwise," for on that condition the promise was made, Ps. cxxxii. 12. "But know thou, and let thy family and kingdom know it, and be admonished by it, that *if you shall altogether turn from following me*" Israel, though a holy nation, will be cut off (*v.* 7), by one judgment after another. "The temple, though a holy house, which God himself has *hallowed for his name,* shall be abandoned and laid desolate (*v.* 8, 9): *This house which is high.*" Those that *now pass by it are astonished* at the bulk and beauty of it; but, if you forsake God, its height will make its fall the more amazing. God gave Solomon fair warning of this, now that he had newly built and dedicated it, that he and his people might not be high-minded, but fear.

Verses 10–14

Solomon and Hiram, their fair and friendly parting when the work was done. 1. Hiram made good his bargain to the utmost. So far was he from envying Solomon's growing greatness and reputation, that he helped to magnify him. 2. Solomon, no doubt, made good his bargain, and gave Hiram *food for his household,* as was agreed, *ch.* v. 9. But here we are told that he gave him twenty cities (small ones we may suppose, like those mentioned here, *v.* 19) *in the land of Galilee, v.* 11. Hiram came to see these cities, and did not like them (*v.* 12): *They pleased him not.* He called the country the land of *Cabul,* a Phœnician word (says Josephus) which signifies *displeasing, v.* 13. He therefore returned them to Solomon (as we find, 2 Chron. viii. 2), who repaired them, and then *caused the children of Israel to inhabit them.* The country was truly valuable, and so were the cities in it, but not agreeable to Hiram's genius. The Tyrians were merchants, trading men, that lived in fine houses, and became rich by navigation, but knew not how to value a country that was fit for corn and pasture. Hiram desired Solomon to gratify him by becoming his partner in trade, as we find he did, *v.* 27. Some take delight in husbandry, and wonder what pleasure sailors can take on a rough sea; others take as much delight in navigation, and wonder what pleasure husbandmen can take in a dirty country, like the land of Cabul.

Verses 15–28

A further account of Solomon's greatness.

I. His buildings. He raised a great levy both of men and money, because he projected a great deal of building, which would both employ many hands and put him to a vast expense, *v.* 15. He raised it, not for war (as other princes), which would spend the blood of his subjects, but for building, which would require only their labour and purses. Perhaps David observed Solomon's genius to lie towards building, and foresaw he would have his head and hands full of it, when he penned that song of degrees for Solomon, which begins, *Except the Lord build the house, those labour in vain that build it* (Ps. cxxvii. 1). And Solomon verily began his work at the right end, for he built God's house first, and finished that before he began his own; and then God blessed him, and he prospered in all his other buildings. The further order in Solomon's buildings is observable. God's house first for religion, then his own for his own convenience, then a house for his wife, to which she removed as soon as it was ready for her (*v.* 24), then Milo, the town-house or guild-hall, then the wall of Jerusalem, the royal city, then some cities of note and strength in the country, which were decayed and unfortified, Hazor, Megiddo, &c.

II. His workmen and servants. In doing such great works, he must needs employ abundance of workmen. 1. Solomon employed those who remained of the conquered nations in all the slavish work, *v.* 20, 21. 2. He employed Israelites in the more creditable services (*v.* 22, 23): *Of them he made no bondmen,* for they were God's freemen, and honoured their relation to God as a kingdom of priests.

III. His piety and devotion (*v.* 25): *Three times in a year* he offered burnt-offerings extraordinary (namely, at the three yearly feasts, the passover, pentecost, and feast of tabernacles) in honour of the divine institution. It is said, He offered *on the altar which he himself built.* He took care to build it, and then, 1. He himself made use of it. Many will assist the devotions of others that neglect their own. 2. He himself had the benefit and comfort of it.

IV. His merchandise. He built a fleet of trading ships at Ezion-geber (*v.* 26), a port on the coast of the Red Sea, the furthest stage of the Israelites when they wandered in the wilderness, Num. xxxiii. 35. The fleet traded to Ophir in the East Indies, supposed to be that which is now called *Ceylon.* Gold was the commodity traded for, substantial wealth. It should seem, Solomon had before been Hiram's partner, or put a venture into his ships, which made him a rich return of 120 talents (*v.* 14), which encouraged him to build a fleet of his own. Solomon sent his own servants as factors, and merchants, and supercargoes, but hired Tyrians for sailors, for they had *knowledge of the sea, v.* 27. Thus one nation needs another, Providence so ordering it that there may be mutual commerce and assistance; for not only as Christians, but as men, we are members one of another. The fleet brought home to Solomon 420 *talents of gold, v.* 28. Solomon got much by his merchandise, but, it should seem, David got much more by his conquests. What were Solomon's 420 *talents* to David's 100,000 *talents of gold*? 1 Chron. xxii. 14; xxix. 4. Solomon got much by his merchandise, and yet he has directed us to a better trade, within reach of the poorest, having assured us from his own experience of both that the *merchandise of wisdom is better than the merchandise of silver and the gain thereof than fine gold,* Prov. iii. 14.

CHAPTER 10

Still Solomon looks great, and everything in this chapter adds to his magnificence. We read nothing indeed of his charity, yet, no question, many poor were relieved from the abundance of his table. A church he had built, never to be equalled; schools or colleges he need not build any, his own palace is an academy. I. What abundance of wisdom there was there appears from the application the queen of Sheba made to him, and the great satisfaction she had in her entertainment there (ver. 1–13), and others likewise, ver. 24. II. What abundance of wealth there was there appears here by the gold imported, with other things, yearly (ver. 14, 15), and in a triennial return, ver. 22. Gold presented (ver. 25), and gold used in targets and shields (ver. 16, 17), and vessels, ver. 21. A stately throne made, ver. 18–20. His chariots and horsemen, ver. 26. His trade with Egypt, ver. 28, 29. And the great plenty of silver and cedars among his people, ver. 27. So that, putting all together, "king Solomon exceeded all the kings of the earth for riches, and for wisdom." Yet what was he to the King of kings? Where Christ is, by his word and Spirit, "Behold, a greater than Solomon is there."

Verses 1–13

An account of the visit which the queen of Sheba made to Solomon, no doubt when he was in the height of his piety and prosperity. Our Saviour calls her *the queen of the south*, for Sheba lay south of Canaan. The common opinion is that it was in Africa; and the Christians in Ethiopia, to this day, are confident that she came from their country, and that Candace was her successor, who is mentioned Acts viii. 27. But it is more probable that she came from the south part of Arabia.

I. On what errand the queen of Sheba came—not to treat of trade or commerce, but, 1. To satisfy her curiosity; for she had heard of his fame, especially for wisdom. 2. To receive instruction from him. She came to *hear his wisdom*, and thereby to improve her own (Matt. xii. 42), that she might be the better able to govern her own kingdom by his maxims of policy. But that which she chiefly aimed at was to be instructed in the things of God.

II. With what equipage she came, with a very great retinue, agreeable to her rank. Yet she came not as one begging, but brought enough abundantly to recompense Solomon for his attention to her, nothing mean or common, but gold, and precious stones, and spices, because she came to trade for wisdom.

III. What entertainment Solomon gave her. He despised not the weakness of her sex, but made her welcome and all her train, gave her liberty to put all her questions, to *commune with him of all that was in her heart* (v. 2) and gave her a satisfactory answer to *all her questions* (v. 3), whether natural, moral, political, or divine. But he informed her no doubt, with particular care, concerning God, and his law and instituted worship.

IV. How she was affected with what she saw and heard in Solomon's court. Divers things are here mentioned which she admired, the buildings and furniture of his palace, the provision that was made every day for his table, the orderly sitting of his servants, every one in his place, and the ready attendance of his ministers. But, above all these, the first thing mentioned is his wisdom (v. 4), and the last thing mentioned, which crowned all, is his piety, the *ascent by which he went up to the house of the Lord*.

V. How she expressed herself upon this occasion. 1. She owned her expectation far out-done, though it was highly raised by the report she heard, v. 6, 7. She is far from repenting her journey or calling herself a *fool* for undertaking it, but acknowledges it was well worth her while to come so far for the sight of that which she could not believe the report of. Those who, through grace, are brought to experience the delights of communion with God will say that the one-half was not told them of the pleasures of Wisdom's ways and the advantages of her gates. Glorified saints, much more, will say that it was a true report which they heard of the happiness of heaven, but that the thousandth part was not told them, 1 Cor. ii. 9. 2. She pronounced those happy that constantly attended him, and waited on him at table: "*Happy are thy men, happy are these thy servants* (v. 8); they may improve their own wisdom by hearing thine." 3. She blessed God, the giver of Solomon's wisdom and wealth, and the author of his advancement, who had made him king. "He has made thee king, not that thou mayest live in pomp and pleasure, and do what thou wilt, but *to do judgment and justice*."

VI. How they parted. 1. She made a noble present to Solomon of *gold and spices*, v. 10. The present of gold and spices which the wise men of the east brought to Christ was signified by this, Matt. ii. 11. Thus she paid for the wisdom she had learned and did not think she bought it dearly. Let those that

are taught of God give him their hearts, and the present will be more acceptable than this of gold and spices. The almug-trees are here spoken of (v. 11, 12) as extraordinary, because perhaps much admired by the queen of Sheba. 2. Solomon was not behind-hand with her: *He gave her whatsoever she asked*, patterns, we may suppose, of those things that were curious, by which she might make the like; or perhaps he gave her his precepts of wisdom and piety in writing, *besides that which he gave her of his royal bounty*, v. 13.

Verses 14–29

A further account of Solomon's prosperity.

I. How he increased his wealth. 1. Besides the gold that came from Ophir (*ch*. ix. 28), he brought so much into his country from other places that the whole amounted, every year, to 666 *talents* (v. 14). 2. He received a great deal in customs from the merchants, and in land-taxes from the countries his father had conquered and made tributaries to Israel, v. 15. 3. He was Hiram's partner in a Tharshish fleet, of Tyre, which imported once in three years, not only gold, and silver, and ivory, substantial goods and serviceable, but apes and peacocks, v. 22. 4. He had presents made him, every year, from the neighbouring princes and great men, because they had often occasion to consult him as an oracle, and sent him these presents by way of recompence for his advice in politics. 5. He traded to Egypt for horses and linen-yarn (or, as some read it, *linen-cloth*), the staple commodities of that country, and had his own merchants or factors whom he employed in this traffic and who were accountable to him, v. 28, 29.

II. What use he made of his wealth.

1. He laid out his gold in fine things for himself, which he might the better be allowed to do when he had before laid out so much in fine things for the house of God. (1) He made 200 targets, and 300 shields, of beaten gold (v. 16, 17), not for service, but for state, to be carried before him when he appeared in pomp. Solomon had *shields* and *targets* carried before him, to signify that he took more pleasure in using his power for the defence and protection of the good, to whom he would be a praise. (2) He made a stately throne, on which he sat, to give laws to his subjects, audience to ambassadors, and judgment upon appeals, v. 18–20. It was made of ivory, or elephants' teeth, which was very rich; and yet, as if he had so much gold that he knew not what to do with it, he *overlaid that with gold*, the best gold. (3) He made all his drinking vessels, and all the furniture of his table, even at his country seat, of pure gold, v. 21.

2. He made it circulate among his subjects, so that the kingdom was as rich as the king; for he had no separate interests of his own to consult, but sought the welfare of his people. Solomon was instrumental to bring so much gold into the country, and disperse it, that *silver was nothing accounted of*, v. 21. If *gold in abundance* would make silver to seem so despicable, shall not wisdom, and grace, and the foretastes of heaven, which are far better than gold, make earthly wealth seem much more despicable?

Now let us remember, 1. That this was he who, when he was *setting out in the world*, did not ask for the wealth and honour of it, but asked for a *wise and understanding heart*. 2. That this was he who, having tasted all these enjoyments, wrote a whole book to show the vanity of all worldly things and the folly of setting our hearts upon them, and to recommend to us the practice of serious godliness, which, through the grace of God, is within our reach, when the thousandth part of Solomon's greatness is a thousand times more than we can ever be so vain as to promise ourselves in this world.

CHAPTER 11

Hitherto we have read nothing of Solomon but what was great and good; but the lustre both of his goodness and of his greatness is here sullied and eclipsed, and his sun sets under a cloud. I. The glory of his piety is stained by his departure from God and his duty, in his latter days, marrying strange wives and worshipping strange gods, ver. 4–8. II. The glory of his prosperity is stained by God's displeasure against him and the fruits of that displeasure.

Verses 1–8

Solomon's defection and degeneracy.

I. Let us enquire into the occasions and particulars of it. *There was no king like Solomon who was beloved of his God, yet even him did outlandish women cause to sin.* There is the summary of his apostasy.

1. He doted on strange women, *many strange women.* (1) He gave himself to women, which his mother had particularly cautioned him against. Prov. xxxi. 3, *Give not thy strength unto women* (perhaps alluding to Samson, who lost his strength by giving information of it to a woman). His father David's fall began with the lusts of the flesh. The love of women has *cast down many wounded* (Prov. vii. 26) and *many* (says Bishop Hall) *have had their head broken by their own rib.* (2) He took many women, so many that, at last, they amounted to 700 wives and 300 concubines, 1,000 in all. Divine wisdom has appointed one woman for one man, and those who do not think one enough will not think two or three enough. (3) They were strange women, Moabites, Ammonites, &c., of the nations which God had particularly forbidden them to inter-marry with, *v.* 2. Some think it was in policy that he married these foreigners, by them to get intelligence of the state of those countries. (4) To complete the mischief, *Solomon clave unto these in love, v.* 2. Solomon was master of a great deal of knowledge, but to what purpose, when he had no better a government of his appetites?

2. He was drawn by them to the worship of strange gods, as Israel to Baal-peor by the daughters of Moab. *His wives turned away his heart after other gods, v.* 3, 4. (1) He grew cool and indifferent in his own religion and remiss in the service of the God of Israel: *His heart was not perfect with the Lord his God* (*v.* 4), nor did he *follow him fully* (*v.* 6), like David. *He was not perfect,* because he was not *constant.* (2) He tolerated and maintained his wives in their idolatry and made no scruple of joining with them in it. He built chapels for their gods (*v.* 7, 8), maintained their priests, and occasionally did himself attend their altars, making a jest of it, asking, "What harm is there in it? Are not all religions alike?" which (says Bishop Patrick) has been the *disease of some great wits.* These high places continued here, not utterly demolished, till Josiah's time, 2 Kings xxiii. 13. This is the account here given of Solomon's apostasy.

II. Let us now pause a while, and lament Solomon's fall; and we must justly stand and wonder at it.

1. How strange, (1) That Solomon, in his old age, should be ensnared with fleshly lusts, youthful lusts. (2) That so wise a man as Solomon was, so famed for a quick understanding and sound judgment, should suffer himself to be made such a fool of by these foolish women. (3) That one who had so often and so plainly warned others of the danger of the love of women should himself be so wretchedly bewitched with it; it is easier to see a mischief, and to show it to others, than to shun it ourselves. (4) That so good a man, so zealous for the worship of God, should do these sinful things.

2. What shall we say to all this? (1) Let him that thinks he stands take heed lest he fall. We see how weak we are of ourselves, without the grace of God; let us therefore live in a constant dependence on that grace. (2) See the danger of a prosperous condition,

and how hard it is to overcome the temptations of it. Solomon, like Jeshurun, waxed fat and then kicked. (3) See what need those have to stand upon their guard who have made a great profession of religion, and shown themselves forward and zealous in devotion, because the devil will set upon them most violently, and, if they misbehave, the reproach is the greater. It is the evening that commends the day; let us therefore fear, lest, having run well, we seem to come short.

Verses 9–13

I. God's anger against Solomon for his sin. The thing he did *displeased the Lord* for there was in his sin, 1. The most base ingratitude that could be. God's appearing to Solomon was such a sensible confirmation of his faith as should have for ever prevented his worshipping *any other god.* 2. The most wilful disobedience. This was the very thing concerning which *God had commanded him—that he should not go after other gods,* yet he was not restrained by such an express admonition, *v.* 10.

II. The message he sent him hereupon (*v.* 11): *The Lord said unto Solomon* (it is likely by a prophet) that he must expect to smart for his apostasy. And here, 1. The sentence is just, that, since he had revolted from God, part of his kingdom should revolt from his family. Sin brings ruin upon families, cuts off entails, alienates estates, and lays men's honour in the dust. 2. Yet the mitigations of it are very kind, for David's sake (*v.* 12, 13), that is, for the sake of the promise made to David. The kingdom shall be rent from Solomon's house, but, (1) Not immediately. Solomon shall not live to see it done, but it shall be rent *out of the hand of his son,* a son that was born to him by one of his strange wives, for his mother was an Ammonitess (1 Kings xiv. 31). (2) Not wholly. One tribe, that of Judah, the strongest and most numerous, shall remain to the house of David (*v.* 13), for Jerusalem's sake, which David built, and for the sake of the temple there, which Solomon built; these shall not go into other hands.

Upon this message which God graciously sent to Solomon, to awaken his conscience and bring him to repentance, we have reason to hope that he humbled himself before God, confessed his sin, begged pardon, and returned to his duty, that he then published his repentance in the book of Ecclesiastes. That penitential sermon was as true an indication of a heart broken for sin and turned from it as David's penitential psalms were, though of another nature. God's grace in his people works variously. Thus, though Solomon fell, *he was not utterly cast down*; what God had said to David concerning him was fulfilled: *I will chasten him with the rod of men, but my mercy shall not depart from him,* 2 Sam. vii. 14, 15. Though God may suffer those whom he loves to fall into sin, he will not suffer them to lie still in it.

Verses 14–25

An account of two adversaries that appeared against him, inconsiderable, and that could not have done anything worth taking notice of if Solomon had not first made God his enemy. What hurt could Hadad or Rezon have done to so great and powerful a king as Solomon was if he had not, by sin, made himself mean and weak? And then those little people menace and insult him.

I. Both these adversaries God stirred up, *v.* 14, 23. Though they themselves were moved by principles of ambition or revenge, God made use of them to serve his design of correcting Solomon.

II. Both these adversaries had the origin of their enmity to Solomon and Israel laid in David's time, and in his conquests of their respective countries, *v.* 15, 24. Solomon had the benefit and advantage of his father's successes both in the enlargement of his dominion and the increase of his treasure, and would never have known anything but the benefit of them if he had kept closely to God; but now he finds evils to balance the advantages.

1. Hadad, an Edomite, was an adversary to Solomon. (1) What induced him to bear Solomon a grudge. David had conquered Edom, 2 Sam. viii. 14. Joab put all the males to the sword, *v.* 15, 16. A terrible execution he made, avenging on Edom their old enmity to Israel. From this general slaughter, while Joab was burying the slain, Hadad, a branch of the royal family, then a little child, was taken and preserved by some of the king's servants, and conveyed to Egypt, *v.* 17. They halted by the way, in Midian first, and then in Paran, where they furnished themselves with men to attend them, that their young master might go into Egypt with an equipage agreeable to his quality. There he was kindly sheltered by Pharaoh, as a distressed prince, and so recommended himself that he married the queen's sister (*v.* 19), and by her had a child, which the queen herself conceived such a kindness for that she brought him up in Pharaoh's house, among the king's children. (2) What enabled him to do Solomon a mischief. Upon the death of David and Joab, he returned to his own country, in which, it should seem, he settled and remained quiet while Solomon continued wise and watchful for the public good, but from which he had opportunity of making inroads upon Israel when Solomon, having sinned away his wisdom as Samson did his strength, forfeited the divine protection. What vexation Hadad gave to Solomon we are not here told, but only how loth Pharaoh was to part with him and how earnestly he solicited his stay (*v.* 22): *What hast thou lacked with me?* "Nothing," says Hadad; "but let me go to my own country, my native air, my native soil."

2. Rezon, a Syrian, was another adversary to Solomon. When David conquered the Syrians, he headed the remains, lived at large by spoil and rapine, till Solomon grew careless, and then he got possession of Damascus, reigned there (*v.* 24) and over the country about (*v.* 25), and he created troubles to Israel, probably in conjunction with Hadad, all the days of Solomon (namely, after his apostasy).

Verses 26–40

Here is the first mention of that infamous name *Jeroboam the son of Nebat, that made Israel to sin,* an adversary to Solomon. God had expressly told (*v.* 11) that he would give the greatest part of his kingdom to his servant, and Jeroboam was the man.

I. Of his extraction, *v.* 26. He was of the tribe of Ephraim, the next in honour to Judah. His mother was a widow.

II. Of his elevation. It was Solomon's wisdom, when he had work to do, to employ proper persons in it. Jeroboam was ruler of the burden, or tribute, that is, either of the taxes or of the militia of the house of Joseph. Observe a difference between David, and both his predecessor and his successor: when Saul saw a *valiant man he took him to himself* (1 Sam. xiv. 52); when Solomon saw an *industrious* man he preferred him.

III. Of his designation to the government of the ten tribes after the death of Solomon. The Jews say that when he was employed by Solomon in building Millo he took opportunities of reflecting upon Solomon as oppressive to his people, and suggesting that which would alienate them from his government. Solomon made him ruler over the tribes of Joseph, and, as he was going to take possession of his government, he was told by a prophet in God's name that he should be king, which emboldened him to aim high, and in some instances to oppose the king. 1. The prophet by whom this message was sent was

Ahijah of Shiloh; we shall read of him again, *ch.* xiv. 2. It seems, Shiloh was not so perfectly forsaken and forgotten of God but that, in remembrance of the former days, it was blessed with a prophet. 2. The sign by which it was represented to him was the rending of a garment into twelve pieces, and giving him ten, *v.* 30, 31. The prophets, both true and false, used such signs, even in the New Testament, as Agabus, Acts xxi. 10, 11. 3. The message itself, which is very particular. (1) He assures him that he shall be king over ten of the twelve tribes of Israel, *v.* 31. (2) He tells him the reason; not for his good character or deserts, but for the chastising of Solomon's apostasy: "Because he, and his family, and many of his people with him, *have forsaken me, and worshipped other gods*," *v.* 33. Jeroboam did not deserve so good a post, but Israel deserved so bad a prince. (3) He limits his expectations to the ten tribes only, and to them in reversion after the death of Solomon, lest he should aim at the whole and give immediate disturbance to Solomon's government. He is here told, [1] That two tribes (called here *one tribe*, because little Benjamin was in a manner lost in the thousands of Judah) should remain sure to the house of David, and he must never make any attempt upon them. He must not think that David was rejected, as Saul was. The house of David must be supported and kept in reputation, for all this, because out of it the Messiah must arise. *Destroy it not,* for that *blessing is in it.* [2] That Solomon must keep possession during his life, *v.* 34, 35. Jeroboam therefore must not offer to dethrone him, but wait with patience till his day shall come to fall. Children that do not tread in their parents' steps yet often fare the better in this world for their good parents' piety. (4) He gives him to understand that he will be upon his good behaviour. "If thou wilt *do what is right in my sight, I will build thee a sure house*, and not otherwise" (*v.* 38).

IV. Jeroboam's flight into Egypt, *v.* 40. In some way or other Solomon came to know of all this, probably from Jeroboam's own talk of it. 1. Solomon foolishly sought to kill his successor. 2. Jeroboam prudently withdrew into Egypt.

Verses 41–43

We have here the conclusion of Solomon's story, and in it, 1. Reference is had to another history then extant, but since lost, *the Book of the Acts of Solomon*, *v.* 41. Probably this book was written by a chronologer whom Solomon employed to write his annals, out of which the sacred writer extracted what God saw fit to transmit to the church. 2. A summary of the years of his reign (*v.* 42): His reign was as long as his father's, but not his life. Sin shortened his days. 3. His death and burial, and his successor, *v.* 43. (1) He followed his fathers to the grave, slept with them, and was buried in David's burying-place. (2) His son followed him in the throne.

CHAPTER 12

The glory of the kingdom of Israel was in its height and perfection in Solomon; it was long in coming to it, but it soon declined, and began to sink and wither in the very next reign. I. Rehoboam's accession to the throne and Jeroboam's return out of Egypt, ver. 1, 2. II. The people's petition to Rehoboam for the redress of grievances, and the rough answer he gave, by the advice of his young counsellors, ver. 3–15. III. The revolt of the ten tribes and their setting up Jeroboam, ver. 16–20. IV. Rehoboam's attempt to reduce them and the prohibition God gave to that attempt, ver. 21–24. V. Jeroboam's establishment of his government upon idolatry, ver. 25–33. Thus did Judah become weak, being deserted by their brethren, and Israel, by deserting the house of the Lord.

Verses 1–15

Solomon had 1,000 wives and concubines, yet we read but of one son he had to bear up his name, and he a fool. Sin is a bad way of building up a family. Rehoboam was the son of the wisest of men, yet did not inherit his father's wisdom. Neither wisdom nor grace runs in the blood. Solomon's court was a mart of wisdom and the rendezvous of learned men, and Rehoboam was the darling of the court; and yet all was not sufficient to make him a wise man.

I. The people desired a treaty with him at Shechem, and he condescended to meet them there. 1. Their pretence was to make him king, but the design was to unmake him. They would give him a public inauguration in another place than the city of David, that he might not seem to be king of Judah only. 2. The place was ominous: at *Shechem*, where Abimelech set up himself (Judges ix.); yet it had been famous for the convention of the states there, Joshua xxiv. 1. Rehoboam knew of the threatening, that the kingdom should be rent from him, and hoped by going to Shechem, and treating there with the ten tribes, to prevent it: yet it proved the most impolitic thing he could do, and hastened the rupture.

II. The representatives of the tribes addressed him, praying to be eased of the taxes they were burdened with. The meeting being appointed, they sent for Jeroboam out of Egypt to come and be their speaker. In their address, 1. They complain of the last reign: *Thy father made our yoke grievous, v.* 4. They complain not of his father's idolatry, so careless and indifferent were they in the matters of religion, as if God or Moloch were all one, so they might but live at ease and pay no taxes. Yet the complaint was groundless and unjust. Never did people live more at ease than they did, nor in greater plenty. Did they pay taxes? It was to advance the strength and magnificence of their kingdom. If Solomon's buildings cost them money, they cost them no blood, as war would do. Factious spirits will never want something to complain of. I know nothing in Solomon's administration that could make the people's yoke grievous, unless perhaps the women were connived at in oppressing them. 2. They demand relief from him, and on this condition will continue in their allegiance to the house of David.

III. Rehoboam consulted with those about him concerning the answer he should give to this address. 1. The grave experienced men of his council advised him by all means to give the petitioners a kind answer, and that he would redress all their grievances. The way to rule is to serve, to do good, and stoop to do it, to become all things to all men and so win their hearts. 2. The young men of his council were hot and haughty, and they advised him to return a severe and threatening answer to the people's demands. It was an instance of Rehoboam's weakness, (1) That he did not prefer aged counsellors, but had a better opinion of the young men that had grown up with him and with whom he was familiar, *v.* 8. It is of great consequence to young people, setting out in the world, on whom they depend upon for advice. If they reckon those that feed their pride, and further them in their pleasures, their best friends, they are already marked for ruin. (2) That he did not prefer moderate counsels, but was pleased with those that advised him to double the taxes. These young counsellors thought the old men expressed themselves but dully, *v.* 7. The old men did not undertake to put words into Rehoboam's mouth, but the young men will furnish him with very quaint and pretty phrases: *My little finger shall be thicker than my father's loins*, &c. That is not always the best sense that is best worded.

IV. He answered the people according to the counsel of the young men, *v.* 14, 15. He affected to be haughty and imperious, and fancied he could carry all before him with a high hand.

1. How Rehoboam was infatuated in his counsels.

(1) He owned their reflections upon his father's government to be true: *My father made your yoke heavy;* and therein he was unjust to his father's memory. (2) He fancied himself better able to manage them, and impose upon them, than his father was. (3) He threatened not only to squeeze them by taxes, but to chastise them by cruel laws. (4) He gave this provocation to a people that by long ease and prosperity were made wealthy, and strong, and proud, to a people that were now disposed to revolt, and had one ready to head them.

2. How God's counsels were hereby fulfilled. It was *from the Lord, v.* 15. He left Rehoboam to his own folly, and *hid from his eyes* the *things which belonged to his peace*. Those that lose the kingdom of heaven throw it away, as Rehoboam did his, by their own wilfulness and folly.

Verses 16–24

The rending of the kingdom of the ten tribes from the house of David, to effect which,

I. The people were bold and resolute in their revolt. *What portion have we in David? v.* 16. Had they enquired who gave Rehoboam this advice, and taken a course to remove those evil counsellors from about him, the rupture might have been prevented. Thus to rebel against the seed of David, whom God had advanced to the kingdom (entailing it on his seed), and to set up another king in opposition to that family, was a great sin; see 2 Chron. xiii. 5–8. (And it is here mentioned to the praise of the tribe of Judah that they *followed the house of David* (*v.* 17, 20), and found Rehoboam better than his word, nor did he rule with the rigour which at first he threatened.)

II. Rehoboam was imprudent in the further management of this affair. 1. He was very unadvised in sending Adoram, who was *over the tribute*, to treat with them, *v.* 18. The very sight of him, whose name was odious among them, exasperated them, and made them outrageous. 2. Some think he was also unadvised in quitting his ground, and making so much haste to Jerusalem, for thereby he deserted his friends and gave advantage to his enemies, who had gone to their tents indeed (*v.* 16) in disgust, but did not offer to make Jeroboam king till Rehoboam had gone, *v.* 20.

III. God forbade his attempt to recover by the sword what he had lost. The thing must rest as it is, and therefore God forbids the battle. 1. It was brave in Rehoboam to design the reducing of the revolters by force. His courage came to him when he had come to Jerusalem, *v.* 21. Judah and Benjamin (who feared the Lord and the king, and meddled not with those that were given to change) presently raised an army of 180,000 men, for the recovery of their king's right to the ten tribes, and were resolved to stand by him. 2. It was more brave in Rehoboam to desist when God, by a prophet, ordered him to lay down his arms. To proceed in this war would be not only to *fight against their brethren* (*v.* 24), whom they ought to love, but to fight against their God, to whom they ought to submit. Rehoboam and his people *hearkened to the word of the Lord*, disbanded the army, and acquiesced. (1) They regarded the command of God though sent by a poor prophet. (2) They consulted their own interest, concluding that though they had all the advantages, even that of right, on their side, yet they could not prosper if they fought in disobedience to God.

Verses 25–33

The beginning of the reign of Jeroboam. He built Shechem first and then Penuel—beautified and fortified them, but he formed another project for the establishing of his kingdom which was fatal to the interests of religion in it.

I. That which he designed was by some effectual means to secure those to himself who had now chosen him for their king, and to prevent their return to the house of David, *v.* 26, 27. 1. He was jealous of the people, afraid that, some time or other, they would kill him and go again to Rehoboam. Jeroboam could not put any confidence in the affections of his people, for what is got by usurpation cannot be enjoyed nor kept with any security. 2. He was distrustful of the promise of God, but he would contrive ways and means, and sinful ones too, for his own safety. A practical disbelief of God's all-sufficiency is at the bottom of all our treacherous departures from him.

II. The way he took to do this was by keeping the people from going up to Jerusalem to worship.

1. Jeroboam apprehended that, if the people continued to do this, they would in time return to the house of David, allured by the magnificence both of the court and of the temple. If they cleave to their old religion, they will go back to their old king.

2. He therefore dissuaded them from going up to Jerusalem, pretending to consult their ease: "*It is too much for you* to go so far to worship God, *v.* 28. Why should we now be tied to one place any more than in Samuel's time?"

3. He provided for the assistance of their devotion at home. Upon consultation with some of his politicians, he set up two golden calves, as tokens or signs of the divine presence, and some are so charitable as to think they were made to represent the mercy-seat and the cherubim over the ark; but more probably he adopted the idolatry of the Egyptians, in whose land he had sojourned for some time and who worshipped their god Apis under the similitude of a bull or calf. He intended, no doubt, by these to represent, or rather make present, not any false god, as Moloch or Chemosh, but the true God only, the God of Israel, the God that brought them up out of the land of Egypt, as he declares, *v.* 28. So that it was no violation of the first commandment, but the second. He set up two, by degrees to break people off from the belief of the unity of the godhead, which would pave the way to the polytheism of the Pagans.

4. The people complied with him herein, and were fond enough of the novelty: They *went to worship before the one, even unto Dan* (*v.* 30). Those that thought it much to go to Jerusalem, to worship God according to his institution, made no difficulty of going twice as far, to Dan, to worship him according to their own inventions. God had sometimes dispensed with the law concerning worshipping in one place, but never allowed the worship of him by images.

5. Having set up the gods, he fitted up accommodations for them. (1) He made a house of high-places, or of altars, one temple at Dan, we may suppose, and another at Beth-el (*v.* 31), and in each many altars. (2) He made priests of the lowest of the people; and the lowest of the people were good enough to be priests to his calves, and too good. He made priests out of every corner of the country. Thus were they dispersed as the Levites, but *were not of the sons of Levi.* But the priests of the high-places, or altars, he ordered to reside in Beth-el, as the priests at Jerusalem (*v.* 32), to attend the public service. (3) The feast of tabernacles, which God had appointed on the fifteenth day of the seventh month, he adjourned to the fifteenth day of the eighth month (*v.* 32), *the month which he devised of his own heart*, to show his power in ecclesiastical matters, *v.* 33. (4) He himself assuming a power to make priests, no marvel if he undertook to do the priests' work with his own hands: *He offered upon the altar.* He did it himself to get the reputation of a devout man.

And thus, [1] Jeroboam sinned himself, yet perhaps excused himself that he did not do so ill as Solomon did, who worshipped other gods. [2] He *made Israel to sin*, drew them off from the worship of God and entailed idolatry upon their seed.

CHAPTER 13

Jeroboam attending his altar at Beth-el, when he received a testimony from God against his idolatry and apostasy. This was sent to him by a prophet, a man of God that lived in Judah. I. What passed between him and the new king. 1. The prophet threatened Jeroboam's altar (ver. 1, 2), and gave him a sign (ver. 3), which immediately came to pass, ver. 5. 2. The king threatened the prophet, and was himself made another sign, by the withering of his hand (ver. 4), and the restoring of it upon his submission and the prophet's intercession, ver. 6. 3. The prophet refused the kindness offered him thereupon, ver. 7–10. II. What passed between him and the old prophet. 1. The old prophet fetched him back by a lie, and gave him entertainment, ver. 11–19. 2. He, for accepting it, in disobedience to the divine command, is threatened with death, ver. 20–22. And, 3. The threatening is executed, for he is slain by a lion (ver. 23, 24), and buried at Beth-el, ver. 25–32. 4. Jeroboam is hardened in his idolatry, ver. 32, 34. "Thy judgments, Lord, are a great deep."

Verses 1–10

I. A messenger sent to Jeroboam, to signify to him God's displeasure against his idolatry, *v.* 1. The army of Judah that aimed to ruin him was countermanded, and might not draw a sword against him (*ch.* xii. 24); but a prophet of Judah is sent to reclaim him from his evil way, and is sent in time, while he is but dedicating his altar, before his heart is hardened, for God delights not in the death of sinners, but would rather they would turn and live.

II. The message delivered in God's name, not whispered, but cried with a loud voice, denoting both the prophet's courage, and his earnestness. It was directed, not to Jeroboam nor to the people, but to the altar. Yet, in threatening the altar, God threatened the founder and worshippers, who might conclude, "If God's wrath fasten upon the lifeless guiltless altar, how shall we escape?" That which was foretold concerning the altar (*v.* 2) was that, in process of time, a prince of the house of David, Josiah by name, should pollute this altar by sacrificing the idolatrous priests themselves upon it, and burning the bones of dead men. Let Jeroboam know and be sure, 1. That the altar he now consecrated should be desecrated. 2. That the *priests of the high places* he now made should themselves be made sacrifices to the justice of God. 3. That this should be done by a branch *of the house of David*. It was about 356 years ere this prediction was fulfilled, yet it was spoken of as sure and nigh at hand, for a thousand years with God are but as one day.

III. A sign is given for the confirming of the truth of this prediction, that the altar should be shaken to pieces by an invisible power and the ashes of the sacrifice scattered (*v.* 3), which came to pass immediately, *v.* 5. This was, 1. A proof that the prophet was sent of God, *who confirmed the word with this sign following*, Mark xvi. 20. 2. A present indication of God's displeasure against these idolatrous sacrifices. 3. It was a reproach to the people, whose hearts were harder than these stones and rent not under the word of the Lord. 4. It was a specimen of what should be done to it in the accomplishment of this prophecy by Josiah; it was now rent, in token of its being then ruined.

IV. Jeroboam's hand withered, which he stretched out to seize or smite the man of God, *v.* 4. Jeroboam's inability to pull in his hand made him a spectacle to all about him, that they might see and fear. If God, in justice, harden the hearts of sinners, so that the hand they had stretched out in sin they cannot pull in again by repentance, that is a spiritual judgment, represented by this, and much more dreadful.

V. The sudden healing of the hand that was

suddenly dried up, upon his submission, v. 6. That word of God which should have touched his conscience humbled him not, but this which *touched his bone and his flesh* brings down his proud spirit. He looks for help now, 1. Not from his calves, but from God only, from his power and his favour. 2. Not by his own sacrifice or incense, but by the prayer and intercession of the prophet, whom he had just now threatened and aimed to destroy. But observe, He did not desire the prophet to pray that his sin might be pardoned, and his heart changed, only that *his hand might be restored.* The prophet immediately addresses himself to God for him. God put this further honour upon him, that at his word he recalled the judgment and by another miracle healed the withered hand, that by the goodness of God Jeroboam might be led to repentance, and, if he were not broken by the judgment, yet might be melted by the mercy. With both he seemed affected for the present, but the impressions wore off.

VI. The prophet's refusal of Jeroboam's kind invitation, in which observe, 1. That God forbade his messenger to eat or drink in Beth-el (v. 9), to show his detestation of their execrable idolatry and apostasy from God. 2. That Jeroboam was so affected with the cure of his hand that he was willing to express his gratitude to the prophet and pay him for his prayers, v. 7. 3. That the prophet, though hungry and weary, and perhaps poor, in obedience to the divine command refused both the entertainment and the reward proffered him.

Verses 11–22

The man of God had honestly and resolutely refused the king's invitation, though he promised him a reward; yet he was over-persuaded by an old prophet to come back with him, and dine in Beth-el, contrary to the command given him. Here we find how dearly his dinner cost him.

I. The old prophet's wickedness. I cannot but call him a false prophet. Perhaps he was trained up among the sons of the prophets, in one of Samuel's colleges not far off, whence he retained the name of a prophet, but, growing worldly and profane, the spirit of prophecy had departed from him. If he had been a good prophet he would have reproved Jeroboam's idolatry. 1. Whether he had any good design in fetching back the man of God is not certain. One may hope that he did it in compassion to him, concluding he wanted refreshment. I suppose it was done with a bad design, for false prophets have ever been the worst enemies to the true prophets, usually aiming to destroy them, but sometimes, as here, to debauch them and draw them from their duty. But, 2. It is certain that he took a very bad method to bring him back. When the man of God had told him, "I may not, and therefore I will not, return to eat bread with thee," he wickedly pretended that he had an order from heaven to fetch him back.

II. The good prophet's weakness, in suffering himself to be thus imposed upon: *He went back with him,* v. 19. He that had resolution enough to refuse the invitation of the king, who promised him a reward, could not resist the insinuations of one that pretended to be a prophet. The message delivered to the man of God was strange. Judgment is given upon it: "Thou shalt never reach thy own house, but shalt be a carcase quickly, nor shall thy dead body be brought to *the place of thy father's sepulchres,* to be interred." Yet it was more strange that the old prophet himself should be the messenger. The message could not but affect him the more when he himself had the delivering of it, and had so strong an impression made upon his spirit by it that he cried out, as one in an agony, v. 21. Perhaps it had a good effect upon him. Those who preach God's wrath to others have hard hearts indeed if they fear it not themselves.

Verses 23–34

I. The death of the deceived disobedient prophet. The old prophet that had deluded him, furnished him with an ass to ride home on; but by the way a lion set upon him, and killed him, v. 23, 24. Did he think this old prophet's house safer to eat in than other houses at Beth-el, when God had forbidden him to eat in any? That was to refine upon the command, and make himself wiser than God. Nothing is more provoking to him than disobedience to an express command. God is displeased at the sins of his own people, and no man shall be protected in disobedience by the sanctity of his profession, the dignity of his office, his nearness to God, or any good services he has done for him.

II. The wonderful preservation of his dead body, which was a token of God's mercy remembered in the midst of wrath. The lion that gently strangled him, or tore him, did not devour his dead body, nor so much as tear the ass, v. 24, 25, 28. Nay, what was more, he did not set upon the old prophet when he came to take up the corpse.

III. The care which the old prophet took of his burial. The case was indeed very lamentable that so good a man, a prophet so faithful, and so bold in God's cause, should, for one offence, die as a criminal, while an old lying prophet lives at ease and an idolatrous prince in pomp and power. We cannot judge of men by their sufferings, nor of sins by their present punishments; with some the flesh is destroyed that the spirit may be saved.

IV. The charge which the old prophet gave his sons concerning his own burial, that they should be sure to bury him in the same grave where the man of God was buried (v. 3): "*Lay my bones beside his bones.*" Though he was a lying prophet, yet he desired to *die the death of a* true prophet. "Gather not my soul with the sinners of Beth-el, but with the man of God." He does honour to the deceased prophet, as one whose *word* would not fall to the ground, though *he* did. It was foretold that men's bones should be burnt upon Jeroboam's altar: "Lay mine (says he) close to his, and then they will not be disturbed"; and it was, accordingly, their security, as we find, 2 Kings xxiii. 18. No mention is made here of the inscription on the prophet's tomb; but it is spoken of 2 Kings xxiii. 17, where Josiah asks, *What title is that?* and is told, *It is the sepulchre of the man of God that came from Judah, who proclaimed these things which thou hast done.*

V. The obstinacy of Jeroboam in his idolatry (v. 33): *He returned not from his evil way;* some hand was found that durst repair the altar God had rent, and then Jeroboam offered sacrifice on it again. Various methods had been used to reclaim him, but neither threats nor signs, neither judgments nor mercies, wrought upon him, so strangely was he wedded to his calves.

CHAPTER 14

The kingdom divided into that of Judah and that of Israel. I. The prophecy of the destruction of Jeroboam's house, ver. 7–16. The sickness of his child was the occasion of it (ver. 1–6), and the death of his child the earnest of it (ver. 17, 18), together with the conclusion of his reign, ver. 19, 20. II. The history of the declension and diminution of Rehoboam's house and kingdom (ver. 21–28) and the conclusion of his reign, ver. 29–31.

Verses 1–6

Jeroboam persisted in his contempt of God and religion.

I. His child fell sick, v. 1. It is probable that he was his eldest son, and heir-apparent to the crown; for at his death all the kingdom went into mourning for him, *v.* 13. *At that time*, when Jeroboam prostituted and profaned the priesthood (*ch.* xiii. 33), his child sickened.

II. He sent his wife in disguise to enquire of Ahijah the prophet *what should become of the child, v.* 2, 3.

1. Jeroboam's great desire, under this affliction, is to know *what shall become of the child*, whether he will live or die. (1) It would have been more prudent if he had desired to know what means they should use for the recovery of the child, but by this instance, and those of Ahaziah (2 Kings i. 2) and Benhadad (2 Kings viii. 8), it should seem they had then such a foolish notion of fatality as took them off from all use of means; for, if they were sure the patient would live, they thought means needless; if he would die, they thought them useless. (2) It would have been more pious if he had begged the prophet's prayers, and cast away his idols from him; then the child might have been restored to him, as his hand was. But most people would rather be told their fortune than their faults or their duty.

2. That he might know the child's doom, he sent to Ahijah the prophet, who lived obscurely and neglected in Shiloh, blind through age, yet still blest with the visions of the Almighty, which need not bodily eyes, but are rather favoured by the want of them, the eyes of the mind being then most intent and least diverted. Jeroboam sent not to him for advice about the setting up of his calves, or the consecrating of his priests, but had recourse to him in his distress, when the gods he served could give him no relief. He sent to Ahijah, because he had *told him he should be king, v.* 2. "He was once the messenger of good tidings, surely he will be so again." Those that by sin disqualify themselves for comfort, and yet expect their ministers, because they are good men, should speak peace and comfort to them, greatly wrong both themselves and their ministers.

3. He sent his wife to enquire of the prophet, because she could best put the question without naming names, or making any other description than this, "Sir, I have a son ill; will he recover or not?" It would have been much fitter for her to have stayed at home to tend him than go to Shiloh to enquire what would become of him. If she go, she must go *incognito—in disguise*, not only to conceal herself from her own court and the country through which she passed, but also to conceal herself from the prophet himself, that he might only answer her question concerning her son, and not enter upon the unpleasing subject of her husband's defection.

III. God gave Ahijah notice of the approach of Jeroboam's wife, and that she came in disguise, and full instructions what to say to her (*v.* 5), which enabled him, as she came in at the door, to call her by her name, to her great surprise, and so to discover to all about him who she was (*v.* 6): *Come in, thou wife of Jeroboam, why feignest thou thyself to be another?*

Verses 7–20

I. The prophet anticipates the enquiry concerning the child, and foretells the ruin of Jeroboam's house for the wickedness of it.

1. God calls himself the *Lord God of Israel*. Though Israel had forsaken God, God had not cast them off. He is Israel's God, and therefore will take vengeance on him who did them the greatest mischief he could do them, debauched them and drew them away from God.

2. He upbraids Jeroboam with the great favour he had bestowed upon him, in making him king over God's chosen Israel, and taking the kingdom *from the house of David*, to bestow it upon him.

3. He charges him with his impiety and apostasy, and his idolatry particularly: *Thou hast done evil above all that were before thee, v.* 9. Jeroboam's

calves, though pretended to be set up in honour of the God of Israel, yet are here called *other gods*, or *strange gods*, because by them he *changed the truth of God into a lie* and represented him as altogether different from what he is, and because many of the ignorant worshippers terminated their devotion in the image, and did not at all regard the God of Israel.

4. He foretells the utter ruin of Jeroboam's house, *v.* 10, 11. See this fulfilled, *ch.* xv. 29.

5. He foretells the immediate death of the sick child, *v.* 12, 13.

(1) In mercy to him, lest, if he live, he be infected with the sin, and so involved in the ruin, of his father's house. Observe the character given of him: *In him was found some good thing towards the Lord God of Israel, in the house of Jeroboam*. The divine image in miniature has a peculiar beauty and lustre in it. He only, of all Jeroboam's family, shall die in honour, shall be buried, and shall be lamented as one that lived desired. This hopeful child dies first of all the family, for God often *takes those soonest whom he loves best*. Heaven is the fittest place for them; this earth is not worthy of them.

(2) In wrath to the family. It was a sign the family would be ruined when *he* was taken by whom it might have been reformed.

6. He foretells the setting up of another family to rule over Israel, *v.* 14. This was fulfilled in Baasha of Issachar, who conspired against Nadab the son of Jeroboam, in the second year of his reign, and murdered him and all his family.

7. He foretells the judgments which should come upon the people of Israel for conforming to the worship which Jeroboam had established. It is here foretold, *v.* 15, (1) That they should never be easy, not rightly settled in their land, but continually *shaken like a reed in the water*. After they left the house of David, the government never continued long in one family, but one undermined and destroyed another. (2) That they should, ere long, be totally expelled out of their land. This was fulfilled in the captivity of the ten tribes by the king of Assyria.

II. Jeroboam's wife has nothing to say against the word of the Lord, but she goes home with a heavy heart to their house in *Tirzah*, a *sweet delightful place*, so the name signifies, famed for its beauty, Cant. vi. 4. 1. *The child died* (*v.* 17), and justly did all Israel mourn, for the loss of so hopeful a prince. 2. Jeroboam himself died soon after, *v.* 20, when he had reigned twenty-two years, and left his crown to a son who lost it, and his life, too, and all the lives of his family, within two years after.

Verses 21–31

Judah's story and Israel's are intermixed. Jeroboam out-lived Rehoboam, four or five years, yet his history is despatched first, that the account of Rehoboam's reign may be laid together; and a sad account it is.

I. Here is no good said of the king. All the account we have of him here is, 1. That he was forty-one years old when he began to reign. 2. That he reigned seventeen years in Jerusalem, *the city where God put his name*, where he had opportunity enough to know his duty, if he had but had a heart to do it. 3. That his mother was Naamah, an Ammonitess; this is twice mentioned, *v.* 21, 31. Probably she was daughter to Shobi the Ammonite, who was kind to David (2 Sam. xvii. 27), and David was too willing to requite him by matching his son into his family. 4. That he had continual war with Jeroboam (*v.* 30), which could not but be a perpetual uneasiness to him. 5. That when he had reigned but seventeen years he died, and left his throne to his son.

II. Here is much evil said of the subjects, both as to their character and their condition.

1. It is a most sad account that is here given of their apostasy from God, v. 22–24. Judah, the only professing people God had in the world, *did evil in his sight*. Their fathers had been bad enough, especially in the times of the judges, but they did abominable things, *above all that their fathers had done*. Nothing less than the *pouring out of the Spirit from on high* will keep God's Israel in their allegiance to him. (1) They became *vain in their imaginations* concerning God, and *changed his glory into an image*, for they built themselves *high places, images, and groves* (v. 23), profaning God's name by affixing to it their images, and God's ordinances by serving their idols with them. (2) They were given up to vile affections (as those idolaters Rom. i. 26, 27), for there were *sodomites in the land* (v. 24), *men with men working that which is unseemly*, and not to be thought of, much less mentioned, without abhorrence and indignation. They dishonoured God by one sin and then God left them to dishonour themselves by another.

2. See here how weak and poor they were; and this was the consequence of the former. Shishak, king of Egypt, came against them, and so far, either by force or surrender, made himself master of Jerusalem itself that he took away the treasures both of the temple and of the exchequer, of the house of the Lord and of the king's house, which David and Solomon had amassed, v. 25, 26. He also took away the golden shields that were made but in his father's time, v. 26. These the king of Egypt carried off as trophies of his victory; and, instead of them, Rehoboam made brazen shields. This was an emblem of the diminution of his glory. Sin makes the gold become dim, changes the most fine gold, and turns it into brass.

CHAPTER 15

In this chapter we have the history, I. Of two of the kings of Judah, Abijam, the days of whose reign were few and evil (ver. 1–8), and Asa, who reigned well and long, ver. 9–24. II. Of two of the kings of Israel, Nadab the son of Jeroboam, and Baasha the destroyer of Jeroboam's house, ver. 25–34.

Verses 1–8

A short account of the short reign of Abijam, the son of Rehoboam king of Judah. He makes a better figure, 2 Chron. xiii, where we have an account of his war with Jeroboam. There he is called *Abijah—My father is the Lord*, because no wickedness is there laid to his charge. But here, where we are told of his faults, *Jah*, the name of God, is taken away from his name, and he is called *Abijam*.

I. Few particulars are related concerning him. 1. Here began his reign in the beginning of Jeroboam's eighteenth year; for Rehoboam reigned but seventeen, *ch.* xiv. 21. Jeroboam indeed survived Rehoboam, but Rehoboam's Abijah lived to succeed him and to be a terror to Jeroboam, while Jeroboam's Abijah (whom we read of *ch.* xiv. 1) died before him. 2. He reigned scarcely three years, for he died before the end of Jeroboam's twentieth year, v. 9. Being made proud and secure by his great victory over Jeroboam (2 Chron. xiii. 21), God cut him off, to make way for his son Asa, who would be a better man. 3. *His mother's name was Maachah, the daughter of Abishalom*, that is, Absalom, David's son, as I am the rather inclined to think. 4. He carried on his father's wars with Jeroboam. As there was continual war between Rehoboam and Jeroboam, not set battles but frequent encounters, especially upon the borders, so there was between Abijam and Jeroboam (v. 7), till Jeroboam, with a great army, invaded him, and then Abijam, not being forbidden to act in his own defence, routed him, so that he compelled him to be quiet during the rest of his reign, 2 Chron. xiii. 20.

II. But, in general, we are told, 1. That he was not like David, had no hearty affection for the ordinances of God, though, to serve his purpose against Jeroboam, he pleaded his possession of the temple and priesthood, as that upon which he valued himself, 2 Chron. xiii. 10–12. He seemed to have zeal, but he wanted sincerity; he began pretty well, but he fell off, and *walked in all the sins of his father*. 2. That yet it was for David's sake that he was advanced, and continued upon the throne; it was *for his sake* (v. 4, 5) that God thus *set up his son after him*; not for his own sake, nor for the sake of his father, in whose steps he trod, *but for the sake of David*, whose example he would not follow. It aggravates the sin of a degenerate seed that they fare the better for the piety of their ancestors and owe their blessings to it, and yet will not imitate it.

Verses 9–24

A short account of the reign of Asa; we shall find a more copious history of it 2 Chron. xiv, xv and xvi.

I. The length of it: *He reigned forty-one years in Jerusalem*, v. 10. In the account we have of the kings of Judah we find the number of the good kings and the bad ones nearly equal; but then we may observe, to our comfort, that the reign of the good kings was generally long, but that of the bad kings short.

II. The general good character of it (v. 11): *Asa did that which was right in the eyes of the Lord*, and that is right indeed which is so in God's eyes. He did *as did David his father*, kept close to God, though he was not a prophet, or psalmist, as David was. If we come up to the graces of those that have gone before us it will be our praise with God, though we come short of their gifts.

III. The particular instances of Asa's piety. His times were times of reformation.

1. He removed that which was evil. Immorality he first struck at: *He took away the sodomites out of the land*, suppressed the brothels; for how can either prince or people prosper, while those cages of unclean and filthy birds, more dangerous than pest-houses, are suffered to remain? Then he proceeded against idolatry: *He removed all the idols*, even those *that his father had made*, v. 12. When it appeared that Maachah his mother, or rather his grandmother (but called his *mother* because she had the educating of him in his childhood), had an idol in a grove, he would by no means connive at her idolatry. Reformation must begin at home. Asa, in everything else, will honour and respect his mother; he loves her well, but he loves God better, and (like the Levite, Deut. xxxiii. 9) readily forgets the relation when it comes in competition with his duty. If she be an idolater, (1) Her idol shall be destroyed, publicly exposed to contempt, defaced, and burnt to ashes *by the brook Kidron*. (2) She shall be deposed. He removed her from being queen, or from the queen, that is, from conversing with his wife; he banished her from the court, and confined her to an obscure and private life.

2. He re-established that which was good (v. 15): He *brought into the house of God the dedicated things* which he himself had vowed out of the spoils of the Ethiopians he had conquered. When those who, in their infancy, were by baptism devoted to God, make it their own act and deed to join themselves to him and vigorously employ themselves in his service, this is bringing in the dedicated things which they and their fathers have dedicated.

IV. The policy of his reign. He built cities himself, to encourage the increase of his people (v. 23) and to invite others to him by the conveniences of habitation.

V. The faults of his reign. In both the things for which he was praised he was found defective. The fairest characters are not without some *but* or other in them. 1. Did he take away the idols? That was well; *but the high places were not removed* (v. 14); therein his reformation fell short. It was not well that Asa, when his hand was in, did not remove these. *Nevertheless his heart was perfect with the Lord.* This affords us a comfortable note, That those may be found honest and upright with God, and be accepted of him, who yet, in some instances, come short of doing the good they might and should do. The perfection which is made the indispensable condition of the new covenant is not to be understood of sinlessness (then we were all undone), but sincerity. 2. Did he bring in the dedicated things? That was well; but he afterwards alienated the dedicated things, when he took the gold and silver out of the house of God and sent them as a bribe to Benhadad, to hire him to break his league with Baasha, and, by making an inroad upon his country, to give him a diversion from the building of Ramah, v. 18, 19. Here he sinned, (1) In tempting Ben-hadad to break his league, and so to violate the public faith. If he did wrong in doing it, as certainly he did, Asa did wrong in persuading him to do it. (2) In that he could not trust God, who had done so much for him, to free him out of this strait, without using such indirect means to help himself. (3) In taking the gold out of the treasury of the temple, which was not to be made use of but on extraordinary occasions. The project succeeded. Ben-hadad made a descent upon the land of Israel, which obliged Baasha to retire with his whole force from Ramah (v. 20, 21), which gave Asa a fair opportunity to demolish his works there, and the timber and stones served him for the building of some cities of his own, v. 22. But, though the design prospered, we find it was displeasing to God; and though Asa valued himself upon the policy of it, and promised himself that it would effectually secure his peace, he was told by the prophet that he had done foolishly, and that *thenceforth he should have wars*; see 2 Chron. xvi. 7–9.

VI. The troubles of his reign. For the most part he prospered; but, 1. Baasha king of Israel was a very troublesome neighbour to him. This was the effect of the division of the kingdoms, that they were continually vexing one another, which made them both an easier prey to the common enemy. 2. In his old age he was himself afflicted with the gout.

VII. The conclusion of his reign. He reigned long, but finished at last with honour, and left his throne to a successor no way inferior to him.

Verses 25–34

The miserable state of Israel, while the kingdom of Judah was happy under Asa's good government. It was threatened that there should be as *a reed shaken in the water* (ch. xiv. 15), and so they were, when, during the single reign of Asa, the government of their kingdom was in six or seven different hands. Jeroboam was upon the throne in the beginning of his reign and Ahab at the end of it, and between them were Nadab, Baasha, Elah, Zimri, Tibni, and Omri, undermining and destroying one another. This they got by deserting the house both of God and of David. 1. The ruin and extirpation of the family of Jeroboam, according to the word of the Lord by Ahijah. His son Nadab succeeded him. If the death of his brother Ahijah had had a due influence upon him to make him religious, and the honour done him at his death had engaged him to follow his good example, his reign might have been long and glorious; but he *walked in the way of his father* (v. 26), kept up the worship of his calves, and forbade his subjects to go up to Jerusalem to worship, *sinned and made Israel to sin*, and therefore God brought ruin upon him quickly, in the second year of his reign. He was besieging Gibbethon, a city which the Philistines had taken from the Danites, and there did Baasha, with others, conspire against him and kill him (v. 27), and so little interest had he in the affections of his people that his army chose his murderer for his successor. Baasha *slew him*, and *reigned in his stead*, v. 28. And the first thing he did when he came to the crown was to *cut off all the house of Jeroboam*. 2. The elevation of Baasha. He shall be tried awhile, as Jeroboam was. Twenty-four years he reigned (v. 33), but *walked in the way of Jeroboam* (v. 34), though he had seen the end of that way.

CHAPTER 16

This chapter relates wholly to the kingdom of Israel, and the revolutions of that kingdom. I. The ruin of Baasha's family, after it had been but twenty-six years a royal family, foretold by a prophet (ver. 1–7), and executed by Zimri, one of his captains, ver. 8–14. II. The seven days' reign of Zimri, and his sudden fall, ver. 15–20. III. The struggle between Omri and Tibni, and Omri's prevalency, and his reign, ver. 21–28. IV. The beginning of the reign of Ahab, ver. 29–33. V. The rebuilding of Jericho, v. 34. All this while, in Judah, things went well.

Verses 1–14

I. The ruin of the family of Baasha foretold. He was a man likely enough to have raised and established his family—active, politic, and daring; but he was an idolater, and this brought destruction upon his family.

1. God sent him warning of it before. (1) That, if he were thereby wrought upon to repent and reform, the ruin might be prevented. (2) That, if not, the destruction when it did come, whoever might be instruments of it, was the punishment of sin.

2. The warning was sent by *Jehu the son of Hanani*. The father was a seer, or prophet, at the same time (2 Chron. xvi. 7), and was sent to Asa king of Judah; but the son, who was young and more active, was sent on this longer and more dangerous expedition to Baasha king of Israel. This *Jehu* continued long in his usefulness, for we find him reproving Jehoshaphat (2 Chron. xix. 2) above forty years after, and writing the annals of that prince, 2 Chron. xx. 34.

(1) He reminds Baasha of the great things God had done for him (v. 2). God puts power into bad men's hands, which he makes to serve his good purposes, notwithstanding the bad use they make of it.

(2) He charges him with high crimes and misdemeanours. [1] That he had caused *Israel to sin* and brought them to pay to dunghill-deities the homage due to him only. [2] That he had himself *provoked God to anger with the work of his hands*, that is, by worshipping images, the *work of men's hands*. [3] That he had *destroyed the house of Jeroboam* (v. 7), *because he killed him*, namely, Jeroboam's son and all his, and is justly punished for the malice and ambition which actuated and governed him in all he did.

(3) He foretells the same destruction to come upon his family which he himself had been employed to bring upon the family of Jeroboam, v. 3, 4.

II. A reprieve granted for some time, so long that Baasha himself dies in peace, and is buried with honour in his own royal city (v. 6), so far is he from being a prey either to the dogs or to the fowls, which yet was threatened to his house, v. 4.

III. Execution done at last. Baasha's son Elah, like Jeroboam's son, Nadab, reigned two years, and then was slain by Zimri, one of his own soldiers, as Nadab was by Baasha; so like was his house made to that of Jeroboam, as was threatened, v. 3.

1. As then, so now, the king himself was first slain, but Elah fell more ingloriously than Nadab. Nadab was slain in the field of action and honour, he and his army then besieging Gibbethon (ch. xv. 27). Elah should have been with them to command in chief, but he loved his own ease and therefore stayed behind

to take his pleasure; and, when he was *drinking himself drunk in his servant's house*, Zimri killed him, *v.* 9, 10. Death comes easily upon men when they are drunk. Besides the chronic diseases which men frequently bring themselves into by hard drinking, and which cut them off in the midst of their days, men in that condition are more easily overcome by an enemy, as Amnon by Absalom, and are liable to more bad accidents, being unable to help themselves.

2. As then, so now, the whole family was cut off, and rooted out. The first thing Zimri did was to *slay all the house of Baasha*; thus he held by cruelty what he got by treason.

Verses 15–28

Zimri, and Tibni, and Omri, are here striving for the crown. Proud aspiring men ruin one another, and involve others in the ruin. These confusions end in the settlement of Omri.

I. How he was chosen, as the Roman emperors often were, by the army in the field, now encamped before Gibbethon, that they might without delay avenge the death of Elah upon Zimri. The siege of Gibbethon is quitted (Philistines are sure to gain when Israelites quarrel) and Zimri is prosecuted.

II. How he conquered Zimri, who is said to have reigned seven days (*v.* 15), so long before Omri was proclaimed king and himself proclaimed traitor. Tirzah was a beautiful city, but not fortified, so that Omri soon made himself master of it (*v.* 17), forced Zimri into the palace, which being unable to defend, and yet unwilling to surrender, he burnt, and himself in it, *v.* 18.

III. How he struggled with Tibni, and at length got clear of him: *Half of the people followed this Tibni* (*v.* 21), probably those who were in Zimri's interest. The contest between these two lasted some years, and it was in the twenty-seventh year of Asa that Omri was first elected (*v.* 15), but it was not till the thirty-first year of Asa that he began to reign without a rival; then Tibni died, it is likely in battle, *and Omri reigned*, *v.* 22.

IV. How he reigned when he was at length settled on the throne. 1. He made himself famous by building Samaria, which, ever after, was the royal city of the kings of Israel. He bought the ground for *two talents of silver*. It was called *Samaria*, or *Shemeren* (as it is in the Hebrew), from Shemer, the former owner, *v.* 24. The kings of Israel changed their royal seats, Shechem first, then Tirzah, now Samaria; but the kings of Judah were constant to Jerusalem, the city of God. 2. He made himself infamous by his wickedness; for *he did worse than all that were before him*, *v.* 25. He went further than they had done in *establishing iniquity by a law*. Jeroboam caused Israel to sin by temptation, example, and allurement; but Omri did it by compulsion.

Verses 29–34

The beginning of the reign of Ahab, of whom we have more particulars recorded than of any of the kings of Israel.

I. He exceeded all his predecessors in wickedness, *did evil above all that were before him* (*v.* 30), and, as if it were done with a particular enmity both to God and Israel, to affront him and ruin them, it is said, *He did more to provoke the Lord God of Israel to anger than all the kings of Israel that were before him*, *v.* 33.

II. He married a wicked woman, *Jezebel* (*v.* 31), a zealous idolater, extremely imperious and malicious in her natural temper, addicted to witchcrafts and whoredoms (2. Kings ix. 22), and every way vicious. What mischiefs she did, and what mischief at last befell her (2 Kings ix. 33), we shall find in the following story.

III. He set up the worship of Baal and served the god of the Sidonians, Jupiter, a deified hero of the Phœnicians. In honour of this mock deity, whom they called *Baal—lord*, 1. Ahab built a temple in Samaria, the royal city, because the temple of God was in Jerusalem, the royal city of the other kingdom. 2. He reared an altar in that temple, on which to offer sacrifice to Baal. 3. He made a grove about his temple.

IV. One of his subjects, in imitation of his presumption, ventured to build Jericho, in defiance of the curse Joshua had long since pronounced on him that should attempt it, *v.* 34. He built for his children, but his eldest son died when he began, and youngest when he finished, and all the rest (it is supposed) between. None ever hardened his heart against God and prospered.

CHAPTER 17

Never was Israel so blessed with a good prophet as when it was so plagued with a bad king. Never was king so bold to sin as Ahab; never was prophet so bold to reprove and threaten as Elijah, whose story begins in this chapter and is full of wonders. He only, of all the prophets, had the honour of Enoch, the first prophet, to be translated, that he should not see death, and the honour of Moses, the great prophet, to attend our Saviour in his transfiguration. Other prophets prophesied and wrote, he prophesied and acted, but wrote nothing; but his actions cast more lustre on his name than their writings did on theirs. I. His prediction of a famine in Israel, through the want of rain, ver. 1. II. The provision made for him in that famine, 1. By the ravens at the brook Cherith, ver. 2–7. 2. When that failed, by the widow at Zarephath, who received him in the name of a prophet and had a prophet's reward; for (1) He multiplied her meal and her oil, ver. 8–16. (2) He raised her dead son to life, ver. 17–24. Thus his story begins with judgments and miracles, designed to awaken that stupid generation that had so deeply corrupted themselves.

Verses 1–7

The history of Elijah begins somewhat abruptly. Elijah drops (so to speak) out of the clouds, as if, like Melchisedek, he were without father, without mother, and without descent, which made some of the Jews fancy that he was an angel sent from heaven; but the apostle has assured us that he was a man *subject to like passions as we are* (James v. 17). 1. The prophet's name: *Elijahu—"My God Jehovah is he"* (so it signifies), "is he who sends me and will own me and bear me out, is he to whom I would bring Israel back and who alone can effect that great work." 2. His country: He was *of the inhabitants of Gilead*, on the other side Jordan, either of the tribe of Gad or the half of Manasseh, for Gilead was divided between them. We need not enquire whence men are, but what they are: if it be a good thing, no matter though it come out of Nazareth. He is called a *Tishbite* from Thisbe. The beginning of his story:—

I. How he foretold a famine with which Israel should be punished for their sins. He proclaimed it to the king, in whose power it was to reform the land, and so to prevent the judgment. Unless he repented and reformed this judgment would be brought upon his land. There should be *neither dew nor rain for some years*. He prayed earnestly *that it might not rain*; and, according to his prayers, the heavens became as brass, till he *prayed again that it might rain*. Elijah lets Ahab know, 1. That *the Lord Jehovah* is the *God of Israel*, whom he had forsaken. 2. That he is a *living God*, and not like the gods he worshipped, which were dead and dumb idols. 3. That he himself was God's servant in office, and a messenger sent from him. 4. That, notwithstanding the present peace and prosperity of the kingdom of Israel, God was displeased with them for their idolatry and would chastise them for it by the want of rain, which would effectually prove their impotency, and the folly of those who left the living God, to make their court to such as could do neither good nor evil. 5. He lets

Ahab know what interest he had in heaven: It shall be *according to my word.*

II. How he was himself taken care of in that famine. 1. How he was hidden. God bade him go *and hide himself by the brook Cherith, v.* 3. For the present, in obedience to the divine command, he went and dwelt all alone in some obscure unfrequented place, probably among the reeds of the brook. If Providence calls us to solitude and retirement, it becomes us to acquiesce; when we cannot be useful we must be patient, and when we cannot work for God we must sit still quietly for him. 2. How he was fed. When the woman, the church, is *driven into the wilderness,* care is taken that she be fed and nourished there, a time, times, and half a time, that is, three years and a half, which was just the time of Elijah's concealment. See Rev. xii. 6, 14. Elijah must drink of the brook, and the ravens were appointed to *bring him meat (v.* 4) and did so, *v.* 6. Here, (1) The provision was plentiful, and good, and constant, bread and flesh twice a day, daily bread and food convenient. It ill becomes God's servants, especially his servants the prophets, to be nice and curious about their food and to affect dainties and varieties; instead of envying those who have daintier fare, we should think how many there are, better than we, who live comfortably upon coarser fare and would be glad of our leavings. (2) The caterers were very unlikely; the *ravens* brought it to him. Obadiah would gladly have entertained Elijah; but he was a man by himself, a figure of John the Baptist, whose meat was locusts and wild honey. If it be asked whence the ravens had this provision, how and where it was cooked, and whether they came honestly by it, we must answer, as Jacob did (Gen. xxvii. 20), *The Lord our God brought it to them.* But why ravens? [1] They are birds of prey, more likely to have taken his meat from him, or to have picked out his eyes (Prov. xxx. 17); but thus Samson's riddle is again unriddled, *Out of the eater comes forth meat.* [2] They are unclean creatures. *Every raven after his kind* was, by the law, forbidden to be eaten (Lev. xi. 15), yet Elijah did not think the meat they brought ever the worse for that, but ate and gave thanks, asking no question for conscience' sake. [3] Ravens feed on insects and carrion themselves, yet they brought the prophet man's meat and wholesome food. [4] Ravens could bring but a little, and broken meat, yet Elijah was thankful that he was fed, though not feasted. [5] Ravens neglect their own young ones, and do not feed them; yet when God pleases they shall feed his prophet. [6] Ravens are themselves fed by special providence (Job xxxviii. 41; Ps. cxlvii. 9), and now they fed the prophet.

Thus does Elijah, for a great while, *eat his morsels alone,* and his provision of water, which he has in an ordinary way from the brook, fails him before that which he has by miracle. The powers of nature are limited, but not the powers of the God of nature. Elijah's brook dried up *(v.* 7) *because there was no rain.*

Verses 8–16

An account of the further protection Elijah was taken under. When the brook was dried up Jordan was not; why did not God send him thither? Surely because he would show that he has a variety of ways to provide for his people and is not tied to any one.

I. The place he is sent to, to *Zarephath,* or *Sarepta,* a city of Sidon, out of the borders of the land of Israel, *v.* 9. Our Saviour takes notice of this as an early and ancient indication of the favour of God designed for the poor Gentiles, in the fulness of time, Luke iv. 25, 26. *Many widows were in Israel in the days of Elias,* yet he is sent to honour and bless with his presence a city of Sidon, a Gentile city, and so

becomes (says Dr. Lightfoot) *the first prophet of the Gentiles.* Elijah was hated and driven out by his countrymen; therefore, lo, he turns to the Gentiles, as the apostles were afterwards ordered to do, Acts xviii. 6. But why to a city of Sidon? Perhaps because the worship of Baal came lately thence with Jezebel, who was a Sidonian *(ch.* xvi. 31). Jezebel was Elijah's greatest enemy; yet, to show her the impotency of her malice, God will find a hiding-place for him even in her country.

II. The person that is appointed to entertain him, a poor widow woman, destitute and desolate. It is God's way, and it is his glory, to make use of the *weak and foolish things of the world* and put honour upon them.

III. The provision made for him there. Providence brought the widow woman to meet him very opportunely at the gate of the city *(v.* 10).

1. Her case and character: (1) She had nothing to live upon but a handful of meal and a little oil. When she has eaten the little she has, for aught she yet sees, she must die for want, she and her son, *v.* 12. She had no fuel but the sticks she gathered in the streets. To her Elijah was sent, that he might still live upon Providence as much as he did when the ravens fed him. It was in compassion to the low estate of his handmaiden that God sent the prophet to her, not to beg of her, but to board with her, and he would pay well for his table. (2) She was very humble and industrious. He found her gathering sticks, and preparing to bake her own bread, *v.* 10, 12. (3) She was very charitable and generous. When this stranger desired her to go and fetch him some water to drink, she readily went, at the first word, *v.* 10, 11. She objected not to the present scarcity of it, nor asked him what he would give her, nor hinted that he was a stranger, an Israelite, but left off gathering the sticks for herself to fetch water for him. (4) It was a great trial for her faith and obedience when, having told the prophet how low her stock of meal and oil was and that she had but just enough for herself and her son, he bade her *make a cake for him,* and make *his* first, and then *prepare for herself and her son.* Elijah, it is true, made mention of *the God of Israel (v.* 14), but what was that to a Sidonian? Or if she had a veneration for the name *Jehovah,* and valued the God of Israel as the true God, yet what assurance had she that this stranger was his prophet or had any warrant to speak in his name? It was easy for a hungry vagrant to impose upon her. But she gets over all these objections, and obeys the precept in dependence upon the promise. Those that deal with God must deal upon trust; seek first his kingdom, and then other things shall be added. But surely the increase of this widow's faith, to such a degree as to enable her thus to deny herself and to depend upon the divine promise, was as great a miracle in the kingdom of grace as the increase of her oil was in the kingdom of providence.

2. The care God took of her guest: *The barrel of meal wasted not, nor did the cruse of oil fail,* but still as they took from them more was added to them by the divine power, *v.* 16. Never did corn or olive so increase in the growing (says Bishop Hall) as these did in the using; but the *multiplying of the seed sown* (2 Cor. ix. 10) in the common course of providence is an instance of the power and goodness of God not to be overlooked as common. The meal and the oil multiplied, not in the hoarding, but in the spending. (1) This was a maintenance for the prophet. Still miracles shall be his daily bread. Hitherto he had been fed with bread and flesh, now he was fed with bread and oil, which they used as we do butter. (2) It was a maintenance for *the poor widow and her son,* and a recompence to her for entertaining the prophet. Christ has promised to those

who open their doors to him that he will come in to them, and *sup with them,* and *they with him,* Rev. iii. 20. It is promised to those that trust in God that they *shall not be ashamed in the evil time, but in the days of famine they shall be satisfied,* Ps. xxxvii. 19.

Verses 17–24

A further recompence made to the widow for her kindness to the prophet; her son, when dead, is restored to life.

I. The sickness and death of the child. For aught that appears he was her only son, the comfort of her widowed estate. 1. She was nurse to a great prophet, was employed to sustain him, and had strong reason to think the Lord would do her good; yet now she loses her child. 2. She was herself nursed by miracle, and in the midst of all this satisfaction she was thus afflicted.

II. Her pathetic complaint to the prophet of this affliction. 1. She expresses herself passionately: *What have I to do with thee, O thou man of God?* The death of her child was now a surprise to her, and it is hard to keep our spirits composed when troubles come upon us suddenly and unexpectedly, and in the midst of our peace and prosperity. She calls him *a man of God,* and yet quarrels with him as if he had occasioned the death of her child. "Wherein have I offended thee, or been wanting in my duty? *Show me wherefore thou contendest with me.*" 2. Yet she expresses herself penitently: "*Hast thou come to call my sin to* thy *remembrance,* as the cause of the affliction?" Perhaps she knew of Elijah's intercession against Israel, and, being conscious of her former worshipping of Baal the god of the Sidonians, she apprehends he had made intercession against her.

III. The prophet's address to God upon this occasion. He gave no answer to her expostulation, but brought it to God, and laid the case before him, not knowing what to say to it himself. He took the dead child from the mother's bosom to his own bed, *v.* 19. Probably he had taken a particular kindness to the child. He retired to his chamber, and, 1. He humbly reasons with God concerning the death of the child, *v.* 20. 2. He earnestly begs of God to restore the child to life again, *v.* 21. We do not read before this of any that were raised to life; yet Elijah, by a divine impulse, prays for the resurrection of this child, which yet will not warrant us to do the like. David expected not, by fasting and prayer, to bring his child back to life (2 Sam. xii. 23), but Elijah had a power to work miracles, which David had not. He *stretched himself upon the child,* to effect the restoration of the child—he would if he could put life into him by his own breath and warmth. He is very particular in his prayer: *I pray thee let this child's soul come into him again,* which plainly supposes the existence of the soul in a state of separation from the body, and consequently its immortality, which Grotius thinks God designed by this miracle to give intimation and evidence of, for the encouragement of his suffering people.

IV. The resurrection of the child, and the great satisfaction it gave to the mother: the child revived, *v.* 22. See the power of prayer and the power of him that hears prayer, who *kills and makes alive.* Elijah brought him to his mother, who, we may suppose, could scarcely believe her own eyes. The good woman hereupon cries out, *Now I know that thou art a man of God*; though she knew it before, by the increase of her meal, yet the death of her child she took so unkindly that she began to question it; but now she was abundantly satisfied that he had both the power and goodness of a man of God. Thus the death of the child was for the glory of God and the honour of his prophet.

CHAPTER 18

It does not appear that either the increase of the provision or the raising of the child had caused Elijah to be taken notice of at Zarephath. The days appointed for his concealment being finished, he is now commanded to show himself to Ahab, and to expect rain upon the earth, ver. 1. I. His interview with Obadiah, one of Ahab's servants, by whom he sends notice to Ahab of his coming, ver. 2–16. II. His interview with Ahab himself, ver. 17–20. III. His interview with all Israel upon Mount Carmel, in order to a public trial of titles between the Lord and Baal; a most distinguished solemnity it was, in which, 1. Baal and his prophets were confounded. 2. God and Elijah were honoured, ver. 21–39. IV. The execution he did upon the prophets of Baal, ver. 40. V. The return of the mercy of rain, at the word of Elijah, ver. 41–46.

Verses 1–16

I. The sad state of Israel at this time, upon two accounts:

1. *Jezebel cut off the prophets of the Lord* (*v.* 4), *slew them, v.* 13. Being an idolater, she was a persecutor, and made Ahab one. Even in those bad times there were some good people that feared God and served him, and some good prophets that assisted them in their devotions. The priests and the Levites had all gone to Judah and Jerusalem (2 Chron. xi. 13, 14), but, instead of them, God raised up these prophets, who read and expounded the law in private meetings, or in the families that retained their integrity; they had not the spirit of prophecy as Elijah, nor did they offer sacrifice, or burn incense, but taught people to live well, and keep close to the God of Israel. These Jezebel aimed to extirpate, and put many of them to death, which was as much a public calamity as a public iniquity, and threatened the utter ruin of religion's poor remains in Israel. Those few that escaped the sword were forced to abscond, and hide themselves in caves, where they were buried alive and cut off, though not from life, yet from usefulness, which is the end and comfort of life.

(1) There was one very good man, who was a great man at court, *Obadiah,* who answered his name—*a servant of the Lord,* one who feared God and was faithful to him, and yet was steward of the household to Ahab. He *feared the Lord greatly* (*v.* 3), and he *feared the Lord from his youth* (*v.* 12). [1] It was strange that so wicked a man as Ahab would prefer him; certainly it was because he was a man of celebrated honesty, industry, and ingenuity, and one in whom he could repose a confidence, whose eyes he could trust as much as his own, as appears here, *v.* 5. [2] It was strange that so good a man as Obadiah would accept of preferment in a court so addicted to idolatry and all manner of wickedness. Obadiah would not have accepted the place if he could not have had it without bowing the knee to Baal. Obadiah therefore could with a good conscience enjoy the place. Those that fear God need not go out of the world, bad as it is.

(2) This great good man used his power for the protection of God's prophets. He hid 100 of them in two caves, when the persecution was hot, and *fed them with bread and water, v.* 4. See how wonderfully God raises up friends for his ministers and people, for their shelter in difficult times, even where one would least expect them.

2. When Jezebel cut off God's prophets God cut off the necessary provisions by the extremity of the drought. Perhaps Jezebel persecuted God's prophets under pretence that they were the cause of the judgment, because Elijah had foretold it. But God made them know the contrary, for the famine continued till Baal's prophets were sacrificed, and so great a scarcity of water there was that the king himself and Obadiah went in person throughout the land to seek for grass for the cattle, *v.* 5, 6. Ahab's care was not to *lose all the beasts,* many being already lost; but he took no care about his soul, not to lose that; he took

a deal of pains to seek grass, but none to seek the favour of God, fencing against the effect, but not enquiring how to remove the cause. The land of Judah lay close to the land of Israel, yet we find no complaint there of the want of rain; for *Judah yet ruled with God.*

II. The steps taken towards redressing the grievance, by Elijah's appearing again upon the stage, to act as a *Tishbite,* a *converter* or *reformer* of Israel, for so (some think) that title of his signifies. Turn them again to the Lord God of hosts, from whom they have revolted, and all will be well quickly; this must be Elijah's doing. See Luke i. 16, 17.

1. Ahab had made diligent search for him (*v.* 10), had offered rewards to any one that would discover him. It should seem, he made this diligent search for him, not so much that he might punish him for what he had done in denouncing the judgment as that he might oblige him to undo it again, by recalling the sentence.

2. God, at length, ordered Elijah to present himself to Ahab, because the time had now come when he would *send rain upon the earth* (*v.* 1), or rather *upon the land.* Above two years he had lain hid with the widow at Zarephath, after he had been concealed one year by the brook Cherith; so that the third year of his sojourning there, here spoken of (*v.* 1), was the fourth of the famine, which lasted in all three years and six months, as we find, Luke iv. 25; James v. 17.

3. Elijah first surrendered, or rather discovered, himself to Obadiah. He knew, by the Spirit, where to meet him.

(1) Obadiah saluted him with great respect, fell on his face, and humbly asked, *Art thou that my lord Elijah? v.* 7. As he had shown the tenderness of a father to the sons of the prophets, so he showed the reverence of a son to this father of the prophets; and by this made it appear that he did indeed *fear God greatly.*

(2) Elijah, in answer to him, [1] Transfers the title of honour he gave him to Ahab: "Call him thy lord, not me;" that is a fitter title for a prince than for a prophet, *who seeks not honour from men.* Prophets should be called *seers,* and *shepherds,* and *watchmen,* and *ministers,* rather than *lords,* as those that mind duty more than dominion. [2] He bids Obadiah go and tell the king that he is there to speak with him: *Tell thy lord, Behold, Elijah* is forth-coming, *v.* 8.

(3) Obadiah begs to be excused from carrying this message to Ahab, for it might prove as much as his life was worth. He thought Elijah was not in good earnest when he bade him tell Ahab where he was, but intended only to expose the impotency of his malice; for he knew Ahab was not worthy to receive any kindness from the prophet and it was not fit that the prophet should receive any mischief from him. He is sure Ahab would be so enraged that he would put him to death for making a fool of him, or for not laying hands on Elijah himself, when he had him in his reach, *v.* 12. He pleads that he did not deserve to be thus exposed, and put in peril of his life: *What have I said amiss? v.* 9. Nay (*v.* 13), *Was it not told my lord how I hid the prophets?* He mentions this to convince Elijah that though he was Ahab's servant he was not in his interest. He that had protected so many prophets, he hoped, should not have his own life hazarded by so great a prophet.

(4) Elijah satisfied him that he might with safety deliver this message to Ahab, by assuring him, with an oath, that he would, this very day, present himself to Ahab, *v.* 15.

(5) Notice is hereby soon brought to Ahab that Elijah had sent him a challenge to meet him immediately at such a place, and Ahab accepts the challenge: *He went to meet Elijah, v.* 16. We may suppose it was a great surprise to Ahab to hear that Elijah, whom he had so long sought and not found, was now found without seeking. He went in quest of grass, and found him from whose word, at God's mouth, he must expect rain. Yet his guilty conscience gave him little reason to hope for it, but, rather, to fear some other more dreadful judgment.

Verses 17–20

The meeting between Ahab and Elijah, as bad a king as ever the world was plagued with and as good a prophet as ever the church was blessed with. 1. Ahab, like himself, basely accused Elijah. He durst not strike him, remembering that Jeroboam's hand withered when it was stretched out against a prophet, but gave him bad language, which was no less an affront to him that sent him. *Art thou he that troubleth Israel? v.* 17. How unlike was this to that with which his servant Obadiah saluted him (*v.* 7): *Art thou that my lord Elijah?* Obadiah feared God greatly; Ahab had sold himself to work wickedness; and both discovered their character by the manner of their address to the prophet. It has been the lot of the best and most useful men to be called and counted *the troublers of the land,* and to be run down as public grievances. Even Christ and his apostles were thus misrepresented, Acts xvii. 6. 2. Elijah boldly returned the charge upon the king, and proved it upon him, that he was *the troubler of Israel, v.* 18. Those that procure God's judgments do the mischief, not he that merely foretells them and gives warning of them, that the nation may repent and prevent them. *I would have healed Israel, but they would not be healed.* Ahab is the troubler, who follows Baalim, those accursed things. 3. As one having authority immediately from the King of kings, he ordered a convention of the states to be forthwith summoned to meet at Mount Carmel, where there had been an altar built to God, *v.* 30. Thither all Israel must come, to give Elijah the meeting; and the prophets of Baal who were dispersed all the country over, with those of the groves who were Jezebel's domestic chaplains, must there make their personal appearance. 4. Ahab issued out writs accordingly, for the convening of this great assembly (*v.* 20), either because he feared Elijah and durst not oppose him, or because he hoped Elijah would bless the land, and speak the word that they might have rain, and upon those terms they would be all at his beck.

Verses 21–40

Ahab and the people expected that Elijah would, in this solemn assembly, *bless the land,* and pray for rain; but he had other work to do first. The people must be brought to repent and reform, and then they may look for the removal of the judgment, but not till then. Deserters must not look for God's favour till they return to their allegiance. Elijah might have looked for rain seventy times seven times, and not have seen it, if he had not thus begun his work at the right end. God's cause is so incontestably just that it need not fear to have the evidences of its equity searched into and weighed.

I. Elijah reproved the people for mixing the worship of God and the worship of Baal together. Not only some Israelites worshipped God and others Baal, but the same Israelites sometimes worshipped one and sometimes the other. This he calls (*v.* 21) *halting between two opinions,* or *thoughts.* They worshipped God to please the prophets, but worshipped Baal to please Jezebel and curry favour at court. "There can be but one God, but one infinite and but one supreme: there needs but one God, one omnipotent, one all-sufficient. What occasion for addition to that which is perfect? Now if, upon trial, it appears that Baal is that one infinite omnipotent Being, that one supreme Lord and all-sufficient benefactor, you ought to renounce Jehovah and cleave to Baal only: but, if Jehovah be that one God, Baal is a cheat, and you must have no more to do with him." Those halt between, that are unresolved under their convictions, unstable and unsteady in their purposes, promise fair, but do not perform, begin well, but do not hold on, that are inconsistent with themselves, or indifferent and lukewarm in that which is good. *Their heart is divided* (Hos. x. 2), whereas God will have all or none. We are fairly put to our choice *whom we will serve,* Joshua xxiv. 15. To this fair proposal which Elijah here makes, the people knew not what to say: *They answered him not a word.*

II. He proposed to bring the matter to a fair trial; and Baal had all the external advantages on his side. The king and court were all for Baal; so was the body of the people. The managers of Baal's cause were 450 men (*v.* 22), besides 400 more, their supporters or seconds, *v.* 19. The manager of God's cause was but one man, lately a poor exile, hardly kept from starving; so that God's cause has nothing to support it but its own right. However, it is put to this experiment, "Let each side prepare a sacrifice, and pray to its God, and *the God that answereth by fire, let him be God*; if neither shall thus answer, let the people turn Atheists; if both, let them continue to *halt between two.*" It is an instance of the courage of Elijah that he durst stand alone in the cause of God against such powers and numbers; and the issue encourages all God's witnesses and advocates never to fear the face of man.

III. The people join issue with him: *It is well spoken,* v. 24. Ahab and the prophets of Baal durst not oppose for fear of the people. If, in this trial, they could but bring it to a drawn battle, their other advantages would give them the victory. Let it go on therefore to a trial.

IV. The prophets of Baal try first, but in vain, with their god. Elijah allows it to them (*v.* 25), gives them the lead for their greater confusion.

1. How importunate and noisy the prophets of Baal were in their applications to him. They got their sacrifices ready; and they cried as one man, and with all their might, *O Baal! hear us, O Baal! answer us.* How senseless, how brutish, were they in their addresses to Baal! (1) Like fools, *they leaped upon the altar,* as if they would themselves become sacrifices with their bullock. *They leaped up and down* to please their deity. (2) Like madmen they *cut themselves in pieces with knives and lancets* (v. 28) for vexation that they were not answered, or in a sort of prophetic fury, hoping to obtain the favour of their god by offering to him their own blood. God expressly forbade his worshippers to cut themselves, Deut. xiv. 1.

2. How sharp Elijah was upon them, *v.* 27. He stood by them, and patiently heard them for so many hours praying to an idol, yet with secret indignation and disdain; and at noon bantered them: "*Cry aloud, for he is a god,* a goodly god that cannot be made to hear without all this clamour." Baal's prophets were so far from being convinced and put to shame by the just reproach Elijah cast upon them that it made them the more violent and led them to act more ridiculously.

3. How deaf Baal was to them. Elijah did not interrupt them, but let them go on till they were tired, and quite despaired of success, which was not *till the time of the evening sacrifice,* v. 29.

V. Elijah soon obtains from his God an answer by fire.

1. He fitted up an altar. He would not make use of theirs, which had been polluted with their prayers to Baal, but, finding the ruins of an altar there, which had formerly been used in the service of the Lord, he chose to repair that (*v.* 30), to intimate to them that he was not about to introduce any new religion, but to revive the faith and worship of their fathers' God. He repaired this altar with *twelve stones, according to the number of the twelve tribes,* v. 31. Though ten of the tribes had revolted to Baal, he would look upon them as belonging to God still, by virtue of the ancient covenant with their fathers.

2. Having built his altar *in the name of the Lord* (v. 32), he prepared his sacrifice, v. 33. *Behold the bullock and the wood; but where is the fire?* Gen. xxii. 7, 8. *God will provide himself fire.* If we, in sincerity, offer our hearts to God, he will, by his grace, kindle a holy fire in them. Elijah was no priest, nor were his attendants Levites. Carmel had neither tabernacle nor temple, yet never was any sacrifice more acceptable to God than this.

3. He ordered abundance of water to be poured upon his altar, for which he had prepared a trench for its reception (*v.* 32). Twelve barrels of water (probably sea-water, for the sea was near, and so much fresh water in this time of drought was too precious for him to be so prodigal of it) he poured upon this sacrifice, to prevent the suspicion of any fire under.

4. He then solemnly addressed himself to God by prayer before his altar, humbly beseeching him to *turn to ashes his burnt-offering* and to testify his acceptance of it. His prayer was not long, but it was very grave and composed, and showed his mind to be calm and sedate, and far from the heats and disorders that Baal's prophets were in, *v.* 36, 37. He addressed himself to God as "*the God of Abraham, Isaac, and Israel,*" reminding people of their relation both to God and to the patriarchs. Two things he pleads here: (1) The glory of God: "Lord, hear me, and answer me, *that it may be known that thou art God in Israel.*" (2) The edification of the people: "*That they may know that thou art the Lord, turning their heart back again to thee,* in order to thy return in a way of mercy to them."

5. God immediately answered him by fire, v. 38. While he was yet speaking, *the fire of the Lord fell, consumed the sacrifice and the wood, licked up all the water in the trench.* But this was not all; to complete the miracle, the fire consumed the *stones of the altar, and* the very *dust.* Moses's altar and Solomon's were consecrated by the fire from heaven; but this was destroyed, because no more to be used. We may well imagine what a terror the fire struck on guilty Ahab and all the worshippers of Baal.

VI. What was the result of this fair trial. The prophets of Baal had failed. Elijah had, by the most convincing and undeniable evidence, proved his claims on behalf of the God of Israel. And now, 1. The people, as the jury, gave in their verdict upon the trial, and they are all agreed in it: *They fell on their faces,* and all, as one man, said, "Jehovah, he is the God, and not Baal; *Jehovah, he is the God*" (*v.* 39), whence, one would think, they should have inferred, "If he be the God, he shall be our God, and we will serve him only." Some, we hope, had their hearts thus turned back, but the generality of them were convinced only, not converted, yielded to the truth of God, that he is the God, but consented not to his covenant, that he should be theirs. 2. The prophets of Baal, as criminals, are seized, condemned, and executed, according to law, v. 40. Elijah (acting still by an extraordinary commission, which is not to be drawn into a precedent) orders them all to be slain immediately as the troublers of the land. These were the 450 prophets of Baal; the 400 prophets of the groves (who, some think, were Sidonians), though summoned (*v.* 19), yet, as it should seem, did not attend, and so escaped this execution, but it proved they were reserved to be the instruments of

Ahab's destruction, some time after, by encouraging him to go up to Ramoth-Gilead, *ch.* xxii. 6.

Verses 41-46

Israel being thus far reformed that they had acknowledged the Lord to be God, God thereupon opened the bottles of heaven, and poured out blessings upon his land, that very evening.

I. Elijah sent Ahab to *eat and drink*. Ahab had continued fasting all day, either religiously, it being a day of prayer, or for want of leisure, it being a day of great expectation; but now let him *eat and drink*, for, though others perceive no sign of it, Elijah, by faith, hears *the sound of abundance of rain*, v. 41.

II. He himself retired to pray and to give thanks for God's answer by fire, now hoping for an answer by water. 1. He withdrew to a strange place, to the *top of Carmel*, which was very high and very private. Hence we read of those that *hide themselves in the top of Carmel*, Amos ix. 3. There he would be alone. Those who are called to appear and act in public for God must yet find time to be private with him and keep up their converse with him in solitude. 2. He put himself into a strange posture. He cast himself down on his knees upon the earth, in token of humility, and *put his face between his knees*.

III. He ordered his servant to bring him notice as soon as he discerned a cloud arising out of the sea, the Mediterranean Sea, which he had a large prospect of from the top of Carmel. The sailors at this day call it *Cape Carmel*. Six times his servant goes to the point of the hill and sees nothing, brings no good news to his master; yet Elijah continues praying, but still sends his servant to see if he can discover any hopeful cloud, while he keeps his mind close and intent in prayer, and abides by it, as one that has taken up his father Jacob's resolution, *I will not let thee go except thou bless me.*

IV. A little cloud at length appeared, no bigger than a man's hand, which presently overspread the heaven's and watered the earth, v. 44, 45. Great blessings often arise from small beginnings, and showers of plenty from a cloud of a span long.

V. Elijah hereupon hastened Ahab home, and attended him himself. Ahab rode in his chariot, at ease and in state, v. 45. Elijah ran on foot before him. If Ahab had paid the respect to Elijah that he deserved he would have taken him into his chariot, as the eunuch did Philip, that he might honour him before the elders of Israel, and confer with him further about the reformation of the kingdom. But his corruptions got the better of his convictions, and he was glad to get clear of him, as Felix of Paul, when he dismissed him, and adjourned his conference with him to a more convenient season.

CHAPTER 19

We left Elijah at the entrance of Jezreel, still appearing publicly, and all the people's eyes upon him. In this chapter we have him again absconding, and driven into obscurity, at a time when he could ill be spared. When people will not learn it is just with God to remove their teachers into corners. Now observe, I. How he was driven into banishment by the malice of Jezebel his sworn enemy, ver. 1-3. II. How he was met, in his banishment, by the favour of God, his covenant friend. 1. How God fed him, ver. 4-8. 2. How he conversed with him, and manifested himself to him (ver. 9, 11-13), heard his complaint (ver. 10-14), directed him what to do (ver. 15-17), and encouraged him, ver. 18. III. How his hands were strengthened, at his return out of banishment, by the joining of Elisha with him, ver. 19-21.

Verses 1-8

One would have expected, after such a public and sensible manifestation of the glory of God that now they would all, as one man, return to the worship of the God of Israel and take Elijah for their guide and oracle. But he is neglected whom God honoured; no respect is paid to him, no care taken of him, nor

any use made of him, but, on the contrary, the land of Israel is now made too hot for him. 1. Ahab incensed Jezebel against him. That queen-consort, it seems, was in effect queen-regent, as she was afterwards when she was queen-dowager, an imperious woman that managed king and kingdom and did what she would. Ahab's conscience would not let him persecute Elijah, but he told Jezebel all that Elijah had done (v. 1), not to convince, but to exasperate her. It is not said he told her what *God* had done, but what *Elijah* had done, as if he, by some spell or charm, had brought fire from heaven, and the hand of the Lord had not been in it. Especially he represented to her that he had slain the prophets. 2. Jezebel sent him a threatening message (v. 2), that she had vowed and sworn to be the death of him within twenty-four hours. But how came she to send him word of her design, and so to give him an opportunity of making his escape? I think that though she desired nothing more than his blood, yet, at this time, she durst not meddle with him *for fear of the people, all counting him a prophet*, a great prophet, and therefore sent this message to him merely to frighten him and get him out of the way. 3. Elijah, hereupon, fled for his life, it is likely by night, and came to Beersheba, v. 3. Where was the courage with which he had lately confronted Ahab and all the prophets of Baal? He could not but know that he might be very serviceable to Israel at this juncture, and had all the reason in the world to depend upon God's protection while he was doing God's work; yet he fled. In his former danger God had bidden him hide himself (ch. xvii. 3), therefore he supposed he might do so now. 4. From Beer-sheba he went forward into the wilderness, that vast howling wilderness in which the Israelites wandered. Beer-sheba was so far distant from Jezreel, and within the dominion of so good a king as Jehoshaphat, that he could not but be safe there; yet, as if his fears haunted him even when he was out of the reach of danger, he could not rest there, but went a day's journey into the desert. Yet perhaps he retired thither not so much for his safety as that he might be wholly retired from the world, in order to a more free and intimate communion with God. *He left his servant at Beer-sheba*, perhaps because he would not expose his servant, who was young and tender, to the hardships of the wilderness. 5. Being wearied with his journey, he grew cross (like children when they are sleepy) and *wished he might die*, v. 4. Those that are, in this manner, forward to die are not in the fittest frame for dying. Jezebel has sworn his death, and therefore he, in a fret, prays for it, runs from death to death, yet with this difference, he wishes to die by the hand of the Lord. He would rather die in the wilderness than as Baal's prophet died, according to Jezebel's threatening (v. 2), lest the worshippers of Baal should triumph and blaspheme the God of Israel. He pleads, "It is enough. I have done enough, and suffered enough. I am weary of living." He pleads, "*I am not better than my fathers.*" But is this *Elijah*? Can that great and gallant spirit shrink thus? God thus left him to himself, to show that when he was bold and strong it was *in the Lord and the power of his might*, but of himself he was *no better than his fathers* or brethren. 6. God, by an angel, fed him in that wilderness, into the wants and perils of which he had wilfully thrown himself. Elijah, in a pet, wished to die; God needed him not, yet he designed further to employ and honour him, and therefore sent an angel to *keep him alive*. Our case would be bad sometimes if God should take us at our word and grant us our foolish passionate requests. Having prayed that he might die, he *laid down and slept* (v. 5), wishing it may be to die in his sleep, but he is awakened and finds himself not only well provided for with bread and water (v. 6), but attended by an angel, who guarded him when he slept, and twice called him to his food when it was ready for him, *v.* 5, 7. Wherever God's children are, as they are still upon their Father's ground, so they are still under their Father's eye and care. They may lose themselves in a wilderness, but God has not lost them. 7. He was carried, in the strength of this meat, to Horeb, *the mount of God, v.* 8. Thither the Spirit of the Lord led him, probably beyond his own intention, that he might have communion with God in the same place where Moses had. The angel bade him eat the second time, because of the greatness *of the journey* that was *before him, v.* 7. Note God knows what he designs us for, that we be furnished with *grace sufficient.* He that appoints what the voyage shall be will victual the ship accordingly. See how many different ways God took to keep Elijah alive; he fed him by ravens, with multiplied meals—then by an angel—and now, to show that *man lives not by bread alone,* he kept him alive forty days without meat, continually traversing the mazes of the desert, a day for a year of Israel's wanderings; yet he neither needs food nor desires it.

Verses 9–18

Here is, I. Elijah housed in a cave at Mount Horeb, which is called *the mount of God,* because on it God had formerly manifested his glory. And perhaps this was the same cave, or cleft of a rock, in which Moses was hidden when the Lord *passed by before him and proclaimed his name,* Exod. xxxiii. 22.

II. The visit God paid to him there and the enquiry he made concerning him: *The word of the Lord came to him.* We cannot go anywhere to be out of the reach of God's eye, his arm, and his word. John saw visions of the Almighty when he was in banishment in the isle of Patmos, Rev. i. 9. The question God puts to the prophet is, *What doest* thou *here, Elijah? v.* 9, and again *v.* 13. This is a reproof, 1. For his fleeing hither. "What brings thee so far from home? Dost thou flee from Jezebel?" Lay the emphasis upon the pronoun *thou.* "What *thou*!" 2. For his fixing here. "What doest thou here, in this cave? Is this a place for a prophet of the Lord to lodge in? Is this a time for such men to retreat, when the public has such need of them?"

III. The account he gives of himself, in answer to the question put to him (*v.* 10), and repeated, in answer to the same question, *v.* 14.

1. He excuses his retreat. God knew, and his own conscience witnessed for him, that as long as there was any hope of doing good he had been *very jealous for the Lord God of Hosts;* but now that he had *laboured in vain,* and all his endeavours were to no purpose, he thought it was time to give up the cause.

2. He complains of the people, their obstinacy in sin. "*The children of Israel have forsaken thy covenant,* and that is the reason I have forsaken them; who can stay among them, to see everything that is sacred ruined and run down?" He had often been, of choice, their advocate, but now he is necessitated to be their accuser, before God. He charges them (1) With having forsaken God's covenant; though they retained circumcision, the sign and seal of it, yet they had quitted his worship and service, which was the intention of it. (2) With having *thrown down his altars,* not only deserted them and suffered them to go to decay, but, in their zeal for the worship of Baal, wilfully demolished them. These separate altars, though breaking in upon the unity of the church, yet, being erected and attended by those that sincerely aimed at the glory of God, God owned them for his altars, as well as that at Jerusalem, and the putting of them down is charged upon Israel as a crying sin. (3) *They have slain thy prophets with the sword,* who, it is probable, ministered at those altars. Jezebel, a

foreigner, slew them (*ch.* xviii. 4), but the crime is charged upon the body of the people because the generality of them were *consenting to their death,* and pleased with it.

3. He gives the reasons why he retired into this desert and took up his residence in this cave. (1) It was because he could not appear to any purpose: "*I only am left.* What can one do against thousands?" (2) It was because he could not appear with any safety: "*They seek my life to take it away*'; and I had better spend my life in a useless solitude than lose my life in a fruitless endeavour to reform those that hate to be reformed."

IV. God's manifestation of himself to him. Did he come hither to meet with God? Moses was put into the cave when God's glory passed before him; but Elijah was called out of it: *Stand upon the mount before the Lord, v.* 11. He *saw no manner of similitude,* any more than Israel did when God *talked to them in Horeb.* But, 1. He heard a strong wind, and saw the terrible effects of it, for it rent the mountains and tore the rocks. 2. He felt the shock of an earthquake. 3. He saw an eruption of fire, *v.* 12. But, 4. At last he perceived a *still small voice,* in which *the Lord was,* that is, by which he spoke to him, and not out of the wind, or the earthquake, or the fire. Those struck an awe upon him, but God chose to make known his mind to him in whispers soft, not in those dreadful sounds. When he perceived this, (1) *He wrapped his face in his mantle,* as one afraid to look upon the glory of God. Elijah hid his face in token of shame for having been such a coward as to flee from his duty when he had such a God of power to stand by him in it. The wind, and earthquake, and fire, did not make him cover his face, but the still voice did. Gracious souls are more affected by the tender mercies of the Lord than by his terrors. (2) He stood at the entrance of the cave, ready to hear what God had to say to him. Elijah being now called to revive that law, especially the first two commandments of it, is here taught how to manage it; he must not only awaken and terrify the people with amazing signs, like the earthquake and fire, but he must endeavour, with a still small voice, to convince and persuade them. Faith comes by hearing the word of God; miracles do but make way for it.

V. The orders God gives him to execute. He repeats the question he had put to him before, "*What doest thou here?* This is not a place for thee now." Elijah gives the same answer (*v.* 14), complaining of Israel's apostasy from God and the ruin of religion among them. To this God gives him a reply. He sends him back with directions to appoint Hazael king of Syria (*v.* 15), Jehu king of Israel, and Elisha his successor in the eminency of the prophetical office (*v.* 16), which is intended as a prediction that by these God would chastise the degenerate Israelites, plead his own cause among them, and *avenge the quarrel of his covenant, v.* 17. Elisha, with the *sword of the Spirit,* shall terrify and wound the consciences of those who escape Hazael's sword of war and Jehu's sword of justice.

VI. The comfortable information God gives him of the number of Israelites who retained their integrity, though he thought he was left alone (*v.* 18): *I have left 7,000 in Israel* (besides Judea) *who have not bowed the knee to Baal.* In times of the greatest degeneracy and apostasy God has always had, and will have, a remnant faithful to him, some that keep their integrity and do not go down the stream. It is God's work to preserve that remnant, and distinguish them from the rest, for without his grace they could not have distinguished themselves. God's faithful ones are often his hidden ones (Ps. lxxxiii. 3), and the visible church is scarcely visible, the wheat lost in the chaff and the gold in the dross, till the sifting, refining, separating day comes. *The Lord knows those that are his*, though we do not; he sees in secret. There are more good people in the world than some wise and holy men think there are. When we come to heaven, as we shall miss a great many whom we thought to meet there, so we shall meet a great many whom we little thought to find there. God's love often proves larger than man's charity and more extensive.

Verses 19–21

Elisha was named last in the orders God gave to Elijah, but he was first called, for by him the other two were to be called. He must come in Elijah's room; yet Elijah rejoices to think that he shall leave the work of God in such good hands. Concerning the call of Elisha observe, 1. That it was an unexpected surprising call. Elijah found him *in the field*, not reading, nor praying, nor sacrificing, but *ploughing*, *v.* 19. Though a great man (as appears by his feast, *v.* 21), master of the ground, and oxen, and servants, yet he did not think it any disparagement to lay his hand to the plough. An honest calling in the world does not at all put us out of the way of our heavenly calling, any more than it did Elisha, who was taken from following the plough to feed Israel and to sow the *seed of the word*, as the apostles were taken from fishing to catch men. 2. That it was a powerful call. Elijah did but *cast his mantle upon him* (*v.* 19), in token of friendship, that he would take him under his care and tuition as he did under his mantle, in token of his being clothed with the spirit of Elijah (now he put some of his honour upon him, as Moses on Joshua, Num. xxvii. 20); but, when Elijah went to heaven, he had the mantle entire, 2 Kings ii. 13. And immediately he *left the oxen* to go as they would, and *ran after Elijah*. An invisible hand touched his heart, and unaccountably inclined him by a secret power, without any external persuasions, to quit his husbandry and give himself to the ministry. Elisha came to a resolution presently, but begged a little time, not to *ask* leave, but only to *take* leave, of his parents. Elijah bade him go back and do it. He will not force him, nor take him against his will; let him sit down and count the cost, and make it his own act. The efficacy of God's grace preserves the native liberty of man's will, so that those who are good are good of choice and not by constraint, not pressed men, but volunteers. 3. That it was a pleasant and acceptable call to him, which appears by the farewell-feast he made for his family (*v.* 21). It was a discouraging time for prophets to set out in. A man that had consulted with flesh and blood would not be fond of Elijah's mantle, nor willing to wear his coat; yet Elisha cheerfully, and with a great deal of satisfaction, leaves all to accompany him. 4. That it was an effectual call. Elijah did not stay for him, lest he should seem to compel him, and he soon arose, went after him, and not only associated with him, but *ministered to him* as his servitor, *poured water on his hands*, 2 Kings iii. 11. Those that would be fit to teach must have time to learn; and those that hope hereafter to rise and rule must be willing at first to stoop and serve.

CHAPTER 20

This chapter is the history of a war between Ben-hadad king of Syria and Ahab king of Israel, in which Ahab was victorious. We read nothing of Elijah or Elisha in all this story; Jezebel's rage it is probable, had abated, and the persecution of the prophets began to cool, which gleam of peace Elijah improved. He appeared not at court, but, being told how many thousands of good people there were in Israel more than he thought of, employed himself, as we may suppose, in founding schools of prophets, in several parts of the country, to be nurseries of religion, that they might help to reform the nation when the throne and court would not be reformed. While he was thus busied, God favoured the nation with the successes we here read of, which were the more remarkable because obtained against Ben-hadad king of Syria, whose successor, Hazael, was ordained to be a scourge to Israel. They must shortly suffer by the Syrians, and yet now triumphed over them, that, if possible, they might be led to repentance by the goodness of God. Here is, I. Ben-hadad's descent upon Israel, and his insolent demand, ver. 1–11. II. The defeat Ahab gave him, encouraged and directed by a prophet, ver. 12–21. III. The Syrians rallying again, and the second defeat Ahab made gave them, ver. 22–30. IV. The covenant of peace Ahab made with Ben-hadad, when he had him at his mercy (ver. 31–34), for which he is reproved and threatened by a prophet, ver. 35–43.

Verses 1–11

I. The threatening descent which Ben-hadad made upon Ahab's kingdom, and the siege he laid to Samaria, his royal city, *v.* 1. David in his time had quite subdued the Syrians and made them tributaries to Israel, but Israel's apostasy from God makes them formidable again. Asa had tempted the Syrians to invade Israel once (*ch.* xv. 18–20), and now they did it of their own accord. It is dangerous bringing a foreign force into the country: posterity may pay dearly for it.

II. The treaty between these two kings.

1. Ben-hadad's proud spirit sends Ahab a very insolent demand, *v.* 2, 3. A parley is sounded to let Ahab know that he will raise the siege upon condition that Ahab becomes his vassal and not only pay him a tribute but make over his title to Ben-hadad, and hold all at his will, even his wives and children.

2. Ahab's poor spirit sends Ben-hadad a very disgraceful submission. *I am thine, and all that I have*, *v.* 4. See the effect of sin. (1) If he had not by sin provoked God to depart from him, Ben-hadad could not have made such a demand. If God may not rule us, our enemies shall. A rebel to God is a slave to all besides. (2) If he had not by sin wronged his own conscience, and set that against him, he could not have made such a mean surrender. Guilt dispirits men, and makes them cowards.

3. Ben-hadad's proud spirit rises upon his submission, and becomes yet more insolent and imperious, *v.* 5, 6. (1) Ben-hadad is as covetous as he is proud, and cannot go away unless he have the possession as well as the dominion. (2) He is as spiteful as he is haughty. Had he come himself to select what he had a mind for, it would have shown some respect to a crowned head; but he will send his servants to insult the prince: *Whatsoever is pleasant in thy eyes they shall take away*. (3) He is as unreasonable as he is unjust, and will construe the surrender Ahab made for himself as made for all his subjects too.

4. Ahab's poor spirit begins to rise too, upon this growing insolence; and, if it becomes not bold, yet it becomes desperate, and he will rather hazard his life than give up all thus. (1) Now he takes advice of his privy-council, who encourage him to stand it out. (2) Yet he expresses himself very modestly in his denial, *v.* 9.

5. Ben-hadad proudly swears the ruin of Samaria.

6. Ahab sends him a decent rebuke to his assurance, dares not defy his menaces, only reminds him of the uncertain turns of war (*v.* 11).

Verses 12–21

The treaty between the besiegers and the besieged being broken off abruptly, we have here an account of the battle that ensued.

I. The Syrians, the besiegers, had their directions from a drunken king, who gave orders over his cups, as he was *drinking* (*v.* 12), *drinking himself drunk* (*v.* 16) *with the kings in the pavilions*, and this at noon. Had he not been very secure he would not have sat to drink; and, had he not been intoxicated, he would not have been so very secure. Security and sensuality went together in the old world, and Sodom, Luke xvii. 26, &c. Ben-hadad's drunkenness was the forerunner of his fall, as Belshazzar's was, Dan. v. In his drink, 1. He orders the town to be invested. 2. When the besieged made a sally he gave orders to take them alive (*v.* 18), not to kill them, which might have been done more easily and safely, but to seize them, which gave them an opportunity of killing the aggressors.

II. The Israelites, the besieged, had their directions from an inspired prophet, one of the prophets of the Lord, whom Ahab had hated and persecuted.

1. Behold, and wonder, that God should send a prophet with a kind and gracious message to so wicked a prince as Ahab was; but he did it, (1) For his people Israel's sake. (2) That he might magnify his mercy, in doing good to one so evil and unthankful, might either bring him to repentance or leave him the more inexcusable. (3) That he might mortify the pride of Ben-hadad and check his insolence. He enquired not for a prophet of the Lord, but God sent one to him unasked, for he waits to be gracious.

2. Two things the prophet does: (1) He animates Ahab with an assurance of victory, which was more than all the elders of Israel could give him (*v.* 8), though they promised to stand by him. He is informed what use he ought to make of this blessed turn of affairs: "*Thou shalt know that I am Jehovah,* the sovereign Lord of all." (2) He instructs him what to do for the gaining of this victory. [1] He must not stay till the enemy attacked him, but must sally out upon them and surprise them in their trenches. [2] The persons employed must be the *young men of the princes of the provinces,* the pages, the footmen, who were few in number, only 232, utterly unacquainted with war, and the unlikeliest men that could be thought of for such a bold attempt. [3] Ahab must himself so far testify his confidence in the word of God as to command in person, though, in the eye of reason, he exposed himself to the utmost danger by it. Yet, [4] He is allowed to make use of what other forces he has at hand, to follow the blow, when these young men have broken the ice. All he had in Samaria, or within call, were but 7,000 men, *v.* 15. It is observable that it is the same number with theirs that had not *bowed the knee to Baal* (*ch.* xix. 18), though, it is likely, not the same men.

III. The issue was accordingly. The proud Syrians were beaten, and the poor despised Israelites were more than conquerors. See how God *takes away the spirit of princes,* and makes himself *terrible to the kings of the earth.* Now where are the silver and gold he demanded of Ahab? Where are the handfuls of Samaria's dust?

Verses 22–30

An account of another successful campaign which Ahab, by divine aid, made against the Syrians, in which he gave them a greater defeat than in the former. Strange! Ahab idolatrous and yet victorious, a persecutor and yet a conqueror! God has wise and holy ends in suffering wicked men to prosper.

I. Ahab is admonished by a prophet to prepare for another war, *v.* 22. The prophet told him they would renew their attempt at the return of the year, hoping to retrieve the honour they had lost and be avenged for the blow they had received. He therefore bade him strengthen himself. It concerns us always to expect assaults from our spiritual enemies, and therefore to mark and see what we do.

II. Ben-hadad is advised by those about him concerning the operations of the next campaign. 1. They advised him to *change his ground, v.* 23. They took it for granted that it was not Israel, but Israel's gods, that beat them, but they speak very ignorantly of Jehovah—that he was *many,* whereas he is one and his name one—that he was *their* God only, a local deity, peculiar to that nation, whereas he is the

Creator and ruler of all the world. 2. They advised him to change his officers (*v.* 24, 25), not to employ the kings, who were commanders by birth, but captains rather, who were commanders by merit, who were inured to war.

III. Both armies take the field. Ben-hadad, with his Syrians, encamps near Aphek, in the tribe of Asher. Ahab, with his forces, posted himself at some distance over against them, *v.* 27. The disproportion of numbers was very remarkable. *The children of Israel,* who were cantoned in two battalions, looked like *two little flocks of kids,* their numbers small, their equipage mean, and the figure they made contemptible; *but the Syrians filled the country* with their numbers, their noise, their chariots, their carriages, and their baggage.

IV. Ahab is encouraged to fight the Syrians, notwithstanding their advantages and confidence. A man of God is sent to him, to tell him that this numerous army shall *all be delivered into his hand* (*v.* 28), but not for his sake; be it known to him, he is utterly unworthy for whom God will do this.

V. After the armies had faced one another seven days they engaged, and the Syrians were totally routed. Ben-hadad, who thought his city Aphek would hold out against the conquerers, finding it thus unwalled, and the remnant of his forces dispirited and dispersed, had nothing but secrecy to rely upon for safety, and therefore hid himself in *a chamber within a chamber,* lest the pursuers should seize him. See how the greatest confidence often ends in the greatest cowardice.

Verses 31–43

An account of what followed upon the victory which Israel obtained over the Syrians.

I. Ben-hadad's tame and mean submission. His servants, seeing him and themselves reduced to the last extremity, advised that they should surrender at discretion, and make themselves prisoners and petitioners to Ahab for their lives, *v.* 31. The servants will put their lives in their hands, and venture first. They had heard that the God of Israel proclaimed his name *gracious and merciful,* and they concluded their kings would make their God their pattern. This encouragement poor sinners have to repent and humble themselves before God. "Have we not heard that the God of Israel is a merciful God? Have we not found him so? Let us therefore rend our hearts and return to him." Joel ii. 13. That is evangelical repentance which flows from an apprehension of the mercy of God in Christ; *there is forgiveness with him.* Two things Ben-hadad's servants undertake to represent to Ahab: 1. Their master a penitent; for they *girded sackcloth on their loins,* as mourners, and *put ropes on their heads,* as condemned criminals going to execution. Many pretend to repent of their wrong-doing, when it does not succeed, who, if they had prospered in it, would have justified it and gloried in it. 2. Their master a beggar, a beggar for his life: *Thy servant Ben-hadad saith,* "*I pray thee, let me live,*" *v.* 32. What a great change is here, (1) In his condition! How has he fallen from the height of power and prosperity to the depths of disgrace and distress. (2) In his temper—in the beginning of the chapter hectoring, swearing, and threatening, and none more high in his demands, but here crouching and whining and none more low in his requests!

II. Ahab's foolish acceptance of his submission, and the league he suddenly made with him upon it. He was proud to be thus courted by him whom he had feared. *Is he yet alive? He is my brother,* brother-king, though not brother-Israelite; and Ahab valued himself more upon his royalty than on his religion. "*Is he thy brother, Ahab?* Did he use thee like a brother when he sent thee that barbarous message? *v.* 5, 6. Would he have called thee brother if he had been the conqueror? Would he now have called himself *thy servant* if he had not been reduced to the utmost strait? Canst thou suffer thyself to be thus imposed upon by a forced and counterfeit submission?" Ben-hadad, upon his submission, shall not only be honourably conveyed (he *took him up into the chariot*), but treated with as an ally (*v.* 34): he *made a covenant with him*, not consulting God's prophets, or the elders of the land. He might now have demanded some of Ben-hadad's cities, but was content with the restitution of his own. He might now have demanded the stores, and treasures, and magazines of Damascus, but was content with a poor liberty, at his own expense, to build streets there. With this covenant he sent him away, without so much as reproving him for his blasphemous reflections upon the God of Israel, for whose honour Ahab had no concern.

III. The reproof given to Ahab for his clemency to Ben-hadad and his covenant with him. It was given him by a prophet, in the name of the Lord, the Jews say by Micaiah, and not unlikely, for Ahab complains of him (*ch.* xxii. 8) that he used to *prophesy evil concerning him*. This prophet designed to reprove Ahab by a parable. To make his parable the more plausible, he finds it necessary to put himself into the posture of a wounded soldier. 1. With some difficulty he gets himself wounded, for he would not wound himself with his own hands. He commanded one of his brother prophets to smite him, and this in God's name (*v.* 35), but finds him not so willing to give the blow as he is to receive it. We cannot but think it was from a good principle he declined it. Good men can much more easily receive a wrongful blow than give one; yet because he disobeyed an express command of God (which was so much the worse if he was himself a prophet), like that other disobedient prophet (*ch.* xiii. 24), he was presently *slain by a lion, v.* 36. This was intended to intimate to Ahab that if a good prophet were thus punished for sparing his friend and God's, when God said, *Smite;* of much sorer punishment should a wicked king be thought worthy, who spared his enemy and God's, when God said, *Smite.* The next he met with made no difficulty of smiting him and did it so that he *wounded him, v.* 37. He fetched blood with the blow, probably in his face. 2. Wounded as he was, and disguised with ashes that he might not be known to be a prophet, he made his application to the king in a story wherein he charged himself with such a crime as the king was now guilty of in sparing Ben-hadad, and waited for the king's judgment upon it. The case in short is this—A prisoner taken in the battle was committed to his custody by a man with this charge, *If he be missing, thy life shall be for his life, v.* 39. The prisoner has made his escape through his carelessness. Can the chancery in the king's breast relieve him against his captain, who demands his life in lieu of the prisoner's? "By no means," says the king, "thou shouldst either not have undertaken the trust or been more careful and faithful to it; there is no remedy, thou hast forfeited thy bond, and execution must go out upon it: *So shall thy doom be, thou thyself hast decided it.*" Now the prophet has what he would have, puts off his disguise, and is known by Ahab himself to be a prophet (*v.* 41) and plainly tells him, "*Thou art the man.* Out of thy own mouth art thou judged. God delivered into thy hands one plainly marked for destruction both by his own pride and God's providence, and thou hast wittingly and willingly dismissed him, and so hast been false to thy trust." 3. We are told how Ahab resented this reproof. He *went to his house heavy and displeased* (*v.* 43), enraged at the prophet, exasperated against God, and yet vexed at himself.

CHAPTER 21

Ahab is still the unhappy subject of the sacred history; from the great affairs of his camp and kingdom this chapter leads us into his garden, and gives us an account of some ill things relating to his domestic affairs. I. Ahab is sick for Naboth's vineyard, ver. 1–4. II. Naboth dies by Jezebel's plot, that the vineyard may escheat to Ahab, ver. 5–14. III. Ahab goes to take possession, ver. 15–16. IV. Elijah meets him, and denounces the judgments of God against him for his injustice, ver. 17–24. V. Upon his humiliation a reprieve is granted, ver. 25–29.

Verses 1–4

1. Ahab coveting his neighbour's vineyard, which unhappily lay near his palace and conveniently for a kitchen-garden. Ahab sets his eye and heart on this vineyard, *v.* 2. It will be a pretty addition to his demesne, and nothing will serve him but it must be his own. Yet he is not such a tyrant as to take it by force, but fairly proposes either to give Naboth the full value of it in money or a better vineyard in exchange. To desire a convenience to his estate was not evil, but to desire anything inordinately is a fruit of selfishness. 2. The repulse he met with in this desire. Naboth would by no means part with it (*v.* 3): *The Lord forbid it me.* Canaan was in a peculiar manner God's land; the Israelites were his tenants; and this was one of the conditions of their leases, that they should not alienate any part of that which fell to their lot, unless in case of extreme necessity, and then only till the year of jubilee, Lev. xxv. 28. Now Naboth foresaw that, if his vineyard were sold to the crown, it would never return to his heirs, no, not in the jubilee. He would gladly oblige the king, but he must obey God rather than men, and therefore in this matter desires to be excused. Some conceive that Naboth looked upon his earthly inheritance as an earnest of his lot in the heavenly Canaan, and therefore would not part with the former, lest it should amount to a forfeiture of the latter. 3. Ahab's great discontent and uneasiness hereupon. He was as before (*ch.* xx. 43) *heavy and displeased* (*v.* 4), grew melancholy upon it, threw himself upon his bed, would not eat nor admit company to come to him. He cursed the squeamishness of Naboth's conscience. Nor could he bear the disappointment; it cut him to the heart to be crossed in his desires, and he was perfectly sick for vexation. He had all the delights of Canaan, that pleasant land, at command, the wealth of a kingdom, the pleasures of a court, and the honours and powers of a throne; and yet *all this avails him nothing* without Naboth's vineyard.

Verses 5–16

Nothing but mischief is to be expected when Jezebel enters into the story—*that cursed woman,* 2 Kings ix. 34.

I. Under pretence of comforting her afflicted husband, she feeds his pride and passion, and blows the coals of his corruptions. He told her what troubled him (*v.* 6), yet invidiously concealed Naboth's reason for his refusal, representing it as peevish, when it was conscientious—*I will not give it thee,* whereas he said, *I may not.* What! says Jezebel (*v.* 7), *Dost thou govern Israel? Arise, and eat bread.* "*Dost thou govern Israel,* and shall any subject thou hast deny thee anything thou hast a mind to? If thou knowest not how to support the dignity of a king, let me alone to do it; give me but leave to make use of thy name, and I will soon *give thee the vineyard of Naboth*; right or wrong, it shall be thy own shortly, and cost thee nothing."

II. In order to gratify him, she projects and compasses the death of Naboth.

1. Had she aimed only at his land, her false witnesses might have sworn him out of that by a forged deed, but Naboth must die.

(1) Never were more wicked orders given by any prince than those which Jezebel sent to the magistrates of Jezreel, *v.* 8–10. She borrows the privy-seal, but the king shall not know what she will do with it. She makes use of the king's name; in short, she commands them, upon their allegiance, to put Naboth to death. She must have looked upon the elders of Jezreel as men perfectly lost to everything that is honest and honourable when she expected these orders should be obeyed. [1] It must be done under colour of religion: "*Proclaim a fast;* pretend to be afraid that there is some great offender among you undiscovered, for whose sake God is angry with your city; and at last let Naboth be fastened upon as the suspected person, probably because he does not join with his neighbours in their worship." [2] It must be done *under colour of justice* too, and with the formalities of a legal process. The crime they must lay to his charge was *blaspheming God and the king*— a complicated blasphemy.

(2) Never were wicked orders more wickedly obeyed than these were by the magistrates of Jezreel. They did *as it was written in the letters* (*v.* 11, 12), neither made any difficulty of it, nor met with any difficulty in it, but cleverly carried on the villainy. They stoned Naboth to death (*v.* 13), and, as it should seem, his sons with him, or after him.

2. Let us take occasion (1) To stand amazed at the wickedness of the wicked, and the power of Satan in the children of disobedience. (2) To lament the hard case of oppressed innocency. (3) To commit the keeping of our lives and comforts to God, for innocency itself will not always be our security. (4) To rejoice in the belief of a judgment to come, in which such wrong judgments as these will be called over.

III. Naboth being taken off, Ahab takes possession of his vineyard. 1. The elders of Jezreel sent notice to Jezebel very unconcernedly, sent it to her as a piece of agreeable news, *Naboth is stoned and is dead, v.* 14. 2. Jezebel, jocund enough that her plot succeeded so well, brings notice to Ahab that *Naboth is not alive, but dead*; therefore, says she, *Arise, take possession of his vineyard, v.* 15. He might have taken possession by one of his officers, but so pleased is he with this accession to his estate that he will make a journey to Jezreel himself to enter upon it; and it should seem he went in state too, as if he had obtained some mighty victory, for Jehu remembers long after that he and Bidkar attended him at this time, 2 Kings ix. 25.

Verses 17–29

I. The very bad character that is given of Ahab (*v.* 25, 26), which comes in here to justify God in the heavy sentence passed upon him, and to show that though it was passed upon occasion of his sin in the matter of Naboth, yet God would not have punished him so severely if he had not been guilty of many other sins, especially idolatry. He was wholly given up to sin, and, upon condition he might have the pleasures of it, he would take the wages of it, which is death, Rom. vi. 23. It was no excuse of his crimes that *Jezebel his wife stirred him up* to do wickedly, and made him, in many respects, worse then otherwise he would have been.

II. The message with which Elijah was sent to him, when he went to take possession of Naboth's vineyard, *v.* 17–19.

1. Hitherto God kept silence, but now Ahab is reproved and his *sin set in order before his eyes.* (1) The person sent is Elijah. (2) The place is Naboth's vineyard and the time just when he is taking possession of it; then, and there, must his doom be read him. Now he is pleasing himself with his ill-gotten wealth, and giving direction for the turning of this vineyard into a flower-garden.

2. What passed between him and the prophet.

(1) Ahab vented his wrath against Elijah, fell into a passion at the sight of him, and, instead of humbling himself before the prophet, as he ought to have done (2 Chron. xxxvi. 12), was ready to fly in his face. *Hast thou found me, O my enemy? v.* 20. This shows, [1] That he hated him. The last time we found them together they parted very good friends, *ch.* xviii. 46. Then Ahab had countenanced the reformation, and therefore then all was well between him and the prophet; but now he had relapsed, and was worse than ever. His conscience told him he had made God his enemy, and therefore he could not expect Elijah should be his friend. [2] That he feared him: *Hast thou found me?* Never was poor debtor or criminal so confounded at the sight of the officer that came to arrest him.

(2) Elijah denounced God's wrath against Ahab: *I have found thee* (says he, *v.* 20), *because thou hast sold thyself to work evil.* [1] Elijah finds the indictment against him, and convicts him upon the notorious evidence of the fact (*v.* 19): *Hast thou killed, and also taken possession?* [2] He passes judgment upon him. He told him from God that his family should be ruined and rooted out (*v.* 21) and all his posterity cut off. "*Thy blood, even thine*, though it be royal blood, though it swell thy veins with pride and boil in thy heart with anger, shall ere long be an entertainment for the dogs," which was fulfilled, *ch.* xxii. 38.

III. Ahab's humiliation under the sentence passed upon him, and the favourable message sent him thereupon. 1. Ahab was a kind of penitent. The message Elijah delivered to him in God's name put him into a fright for the present, so that he *rent his clothes* and *put on sackcloth, v.* 27. Ahab put on the garb and guise of a penitent, and yet his heart was unhumbled and unchanged. 2. He obtained hereby a reprieve, which I may call a kind of pardon. Though it was but an outside repentance (lamenting the judgment only, and not the sin), though he did not leave his idols, nor restore the vineyard to Naboth's heirs, yet, because he did hereby give some glory to God, God took notice of it, and bade Elijah take notice of it: *Seest thou how Ahab humbles himself? v.* 29. This teaches us to take notice of that which is good even in those who are not so good as they should be: let it be commended as far as it goes. This gives a reason why wicked people sometimes prosper long; God is rewarding their external services with external mercies. This encourages all those that truly repent and unfeignedly believe the holy gospel. If a pretending partial penitent shall go to his house reprieved, doubtless a sincere penitent shall *go to his house justified.*

CHAPTER 22

It was promised in the close of the foregoing chapter that the ruin of his house should not come in his days, but his days were soon at an end. His war with the Syrians at Ramoth-Gilead is that which we have an account of in this chapter. I. His preparations for that war. He consulted, 1. His privy-council, ver. 1–3. 2. Jehoshaphat, ver. 4. 3. His prophets. (1) His own, who encouraged him to go on this expedition (ver. 5, 6), Zedekiah particularly, ver. 11, 12. (2) A prophet of the Lord, Micaiah, who was desired to come by Jehoshaphat (ver. 7, 8), was sent for (ver. 9, 10–13, 14), upbraided Ahab with his confidence in the false prophets (ver. 15), but foretold his fall in this expedition (ver. 16–18), and gave him an account how he came to be thus imposed upon by his prophets, ver. 19–23. He is abused by Zedekiah (ver. 24, 25), and imprisoned by Ahab, ver. 26–28. II. The battle itself, in which, 1. Jehoshaphat is exposed. But, 2. Ahab is slain, ver. 29–40. In the close of the chapter we have a short account, (1) Of the good reign of Jehoshaphat king of Judah, ver. 41–50. (2) Of the wicked reign of Ahaziah king of Israel, ver. 51–53.

Verses 1–14

As a reward for his professions of repentance and humiliation, though the time drew near when he should descend into battle and perish, yet we have him blessed with a three years' peace (*v.* 1) and an honourable visit made him by Jehoshaphat king of Judah, *v.* 2. The Jews have a fabulous conceit, that when Ahab humbled himself for his sin, and lay in sackcloth, he sent for Jehoshaphat to come to him, to chastise him; and that he stayed with him for some time, and gave him so many stripes every day. This is a groundless tradition. He came now, it is probable, to consult him about the affairs of their kingdoms. The Syrians durst not give Ahab any disturbance. But,

I. Ahab here meditates a war against the Syrians, and advises concerning it with those about him, *v.* 3. The king of Syria gave him the provocation; when he lay at his mercy, he promised to restore him his cities (*ch.* xx. 34), and Ahab foolishly took his word. Ben-hadad is one of those princes that think themselves bound by their word no further and no longer than it is for their interest. Whether any other cities were restored we do not find, but Ramoth-Gilead was not, a considerable city in the tribe of Gad, on the other side Jordan, a Levites' city, and one of the cities of refuge. Ahab blames himself, and his people, that they did not bestir themselves to recover it out of the hands of the Syrians, and to chastise Ben-hadad's violation of his league.

II. He engages Jehoshaphat, and draws him in, to join with him in this expedition, for the recovery of Ramoth-Gilead, *v.* 4. But it is strange that Jehoshaphat will go so entirely into Ahab's interests as to say, *I am as thou art, and my people as thy people.* I hope not; Jehoshaphat and his people are not so wicked and corrupt as Ahab and his people. Too great a complaisance to evil-doers has brought many good people, through unwariness, into a dangerous fellowship with *the unfruitful works of darkness.* Jehoshaphat had like to have paid dearly for his compliment when, in battle, he was taken for Ahab. Yet some observe that in joining with Israel against Syria he atoned for his father's fault in joining with Syria against Israel, *ch.* xv. 19, 20.

III. At the special instance and request of Jehoshaphat, he asks counsel of the prophets concerning this expedition. Ahab thought it enough to consult with his statesmen, but Jehoshaphat moves that they should *enquire of the word of the Lord, v.* 5. Whithersoever a good man goes he ought to take his religion along with him, and not be ashamed to own it, no, not when he is with those who have no kindness for it.

IV. Ahab's 400 prophets (*prophets of the groves* they called them), agreed to encourage him in this expedition and to assure him of success, *v.* 6. He put the question to them: *Shall I go or shall I forbear?* But they knew which way his inclination was and designed only to humour the two kings. To please Jehoshaphat, they made use of the name *Jehovah*: He shall *deliver it into the hand of the king.* To please Ahab they said, *Go up.* "Thou shalt certainly recover Ramoth-Gilead." Zedekiah, a leading man among these prophets, illustrated his false prophecy with a sign, *v.* 11. He made himself a pair of iron horns, representing the two kings, and their honour and power (both of which were signified by horns, exaltation and force), and with these the Syrians must be pushed. All the prophets agreed, as one man, that Ahab should return from this expedition a conqueror, *v.* 12.

V. Jehoshaphat cannot relish this sort of preaching; it is not like what he was used to. The false prophets cannot so mimic the true but that he who had spiritual senses exercised could discern the fallacy, and therefore he enquired for a *prophet of the Lord besides, v.* 7.

VI. Ahab has another, but one he hates, Micaiah by name, a true prophet, and one that knew God's

mind. And yet, 1. He hated him, and was not ashamed to own to the king of Judah that he did so, and to give this for a reason, He *doth not prophesy good concerning me, but evil.* And whose fault was that? If Ahab had done well, he would have heard nothing but good from heaven. Those are wretchedly hardened in sin, and are ripening apace for ruin, who hate God's ministers because they deal plainly with them. 2. He had imprisoned him. We may suppose that this was he that reproved him for his clemency to Ben-hadad (*ch.* xx. 38, &c.) and for so doing was cast into prison, where he had lain these three years. This was the reason why Ahab knew where to find him so readily, *v.* 9. He was bound, but *the word of the Lord was not.* Jehoshaphat gave too gentle a reproof to Ahab for expressing his indignation against a faithful prophet: *Let not the king say so, v.* 8. Such sinners as Ahab must be rebuked sharply. However he so far yielded to the reproof that, for fear of provoking Jehoshaphat to break off from his alliance with him, he orders Micaiah to be sent for with all speed, *v.* 9. The two kings sat each in their robes and chairs of state, in the gate of Samaria, ready to receive this poor prophet, and to hear what he had to say. They were attended with a crowd of flattering prophets, that could not think of prophesying anything but what was very sweet and very smooth to two such glorious princes now in confederacy.

VII. Micaiah is pressed by the officer that fetches him to follow the cry, *v.* 13. But Micaiah, who knows better things, protests, and backs his protestation with an oath, that he will deliver his message from God with all faithfulness, whether it be pleasing or displeasing to his prince (*v.* 14): "*What the Lord saith to me, that will I speak.*"

Verses 15–28

I. We are told how faithfully he delivered his message. In three ways he delivers his message, and all displeasing to Ahab:

1. He spoke as the rest of the prophets had spoken, but ironically: *Go, and prosper, v.* 15. Ahab put the same question to him that he had put to his own prophets, seeming desirous to know God's mind, when, like Balaam, he was strongly bent to do his own, which Micaiah plainly took notice of when he bade him go, but he spoke by way of derision; as if he had said, go then, and take what follows. In answer to this Ahab adjured him to tell him the truth, and not to jest with him (*v.* 16).

2. Being thus pressed, he plainly foretold that the king would be cut off in this expedition, and his army scattered, *v.* 17. He saw them in a vision, dispersed upon the mountains, as sheep that had no one to guide them. This intimates, (1) That Israel should be deprived of their king, who was their shepherd. (2) That they would make a dishonourable retreat. *Let them return every man to his house in peace,* no great losers by the death of their king. Thus Micaiah, in his prophecy, testified what he had seen and heard. Now Ahab finds himself aggrieved, turns to Jehoshaphat and appeals to him whether Micaiah had not manifestly a spite against him, *v.* 18.

3. He informed the king how it was that all his prophets encouraged him to proceed, that God permitted Satan by them to deceive him into his ruin, and he by vision knew of it. God is a great king above all kings, and has a throne above all the thrones of earthly princes. The rise and fall of princes, the issues of war, and all the great affairs of state, which are the subject of the consultations of wise and great men, are no more above God's direction than the meanest concerns of the poorest cottages are below his notice. It is not without the divine permission that the devil deceives men, and even thereby God serves his own purposes. Thus Micaiah gave Ahab

fair warning, not only of the danger of proceeding in this war, but of the danger of believing those that encouraged him to proceed.

II. We are told how he was abused for delivering his message thus faithfully. 1. Zedekiah, a wicked prophet, impudently insulted him in the face of the court, *smote him on the cheek*, to silence him and stop his mouth. To strike within the verge of the court, especially in the king's presence, is looked upon by our law as a high misdemeanour; yet this wicked prophet gives this abuse to a prophet of the Lord. Micaiah, though he returns not his blow leaves Ahab to be convinced of his error by the event: *Thou shalt know when thou hidest thyself in an inner chamber*, v. 25. It is likely Zedekiah went with Ahab to the battle, and took his horns of iron with him to encourage the soldiers, to see with pleasure the accomplishment of his prophecy, and return in triumph with the king; but, the army being routed, he fled among the rest from the sword of the enemy, sheltered himself as Ben-hadad had done in *a chamber within a chamber* (ch. xx. 30), lest he should perish. 2. Ahab, that wicked king, committed him to prison (v. 27), to be fed with bread and water, coarse bread and puddle-water, till he should return, not doubting but that he should return a conqueror, and then he would put him to death for a false prophet (v. 27)— hard usage for one that would have prevented his ruin! Micaiah put it upon the issue, and called all the people to be witnesses that he did so: "*If thou return in peace, the Lord has not spoken by me, v. 28.* Let me incur the reproach and punishment of a false prophet, if the king come home alive."

Verses 29–40

I. The two kings march with their forces to Ramoth-Gilead, v. 29. That Jehoshaphat, that pious prince, who had desired to enquire by a *prophet of the Lord*, discrediting Ahab's prophets, should yet proceed, after so fair a warning, is matter of astonishment. But by the easiness of his temper he was carried away with the delusion of his friends. He gave too much heed to Ahab's prophets, because it was 400 to one that they should succeed.

II. Ahab adopts a contrivance by which he hopes to secure himself and expose his friend (v. 30): "*I will disguise myself*, and go in the habit of a common soldier, but let *Jehoshaphat put on his robes*, to appear in the dress of a general." He pretended thereby to do honour to Jehoshaphat, but he intended, 1. To make a liar of a good prophet. Thus he hoped to elude the danger. 2. To make a fool of a good king, whom he did not cordially love. How can it be expected that he should be true to his friend that has been false to his God?

III. Jehoshaphat, having more piety than policy, put himself into the post of honour, though it was the post of danger, and was thereby brought into peril of his life, but God graciously delivered him. The king of Syria charged his captains to level their force, not against the king of Judah, for with him he had no quarrel, but against the king of Israel only (v. 31). Some think that he designed only to have him taken prisoner. Whatever was the reason, the officers, seeing Jehoshaphat in his royal habit, took him for the king of Israel, and surrounded him. 1. By his danger God let him know that he was displeased with him for joining in confederacy with Ahab. 2. By his deliverance God let him know that, though he was displeased with him, yet he had not deserted him. Some of the captains that knew him perceived their mistake, and so retired from the pursuit of him.

IV. Ahab receives his mortal wound in the battle. Let no man think to hide himself from God's judg-

ment. The Syrian that shot him *drew a bow at a venture*, not aiming particularly at any man, yet God so directed the arrow that, 1. He hit the right person. 2. He hit him in the right place, *between the joints of the harness*, the only place about him where this arrow of death could find entrance.

V. The army is dispersed by the enemy and sent home by the king. Ahab himself lived long enough to see that part of Micaiah's prophecy accomplished that all Israel should be scattered *upon the mountains of Gilead* (v. 17).

VI. The royal corpse is brought to Samaria and buried there (v. 37). Now Naboth's blood was avenged (ch. xxi. 19), and that word of David was fulfilled (Ps. lxviii. 23), *That thy foot may be dipped in the blood of thy enemies, and the tongue of thy dogs in the same.*

Lastly, The story of Ahab is here concluded in the usual form, v. 39, 40. Among his works mention is made of an ivory house, so called because many parts of it were inlaid with ivory; perhaps it was intended to vie with the stately palace of the kings of Judah, which Solomon built.

Verses 41–53

I. A short account of the reign of Jehoshaphat king of Judah, of which we have a much fuller narrative in the book of Chronicles, and of the greatness and goodness of that prince, neither of which was lessened or sullied by anything but his intimacy with the house of Ahab. His confederacy with Ahab in war we have already found dangerous to him, and his confederacy with Ahaziah his son in trade sped no better. He offered to go partner with him in a fleet of merchant-ships, that should fetch gold from Ophir. But, while they were preparing to set sail, they were disabled by a storm (*broken at Ezion-geber*). When Ahaziah desired a second time to be a partner with him, *Jehoshaphat would not*. The rod of God, expounded by the word of God, had effectually broken him off from his confederacy with that ungodly unhappy prince. Now Jehoshaphat's reign appears here to have been none of the longest, but one of the best. 1. It was none of the longest, for he reigned but twenty-five years (v. 42), but these twenty-five, added to his father's happy forty-one, give us a grateful idea of the flourishing condition of the kingdom of Judah, and of religion in it. 2. Yet it was one of the best, both in respect of piety and prosperity. (1) He did well: He *did that which was right in the eyes of the Lord* (v. 43). Yet the *high places were not taken away*, no, not out of Judah and Benjamin, though those tribes lay so near Jerusalem that they could not pretend, as some other of the tribes, the inconveniency of lying remote. (2) His affairs did well. He prevented the mischiefs which had attended their wars with the kingdom of Israel, establishing a lasting peace (v. 44); he put a deputy, or viceroy, in Edom, so that that kingdom was tributary to him (v. 47), and therein the prophecy concerning Esau and Jacob was fulfilled, that *the elder should serve the younger*. He pleased God, and God blessed him with strength and success.

II. The beginning of the story of Ahaziah the son of Ahab, v. 51–53. His reign was very short, not two years. Some sinners God makes quick work with. It is a very bad character that is here given him. He not only kept up Jeroboam's idolatry, but the worship of Baal likewise; though he had heard of the ruin of Jeroboam's family, and had seen his own father drawn into destruction by the prophets of Baal, who had often been proved false prophets, yet he followed the example of his wicked father and the counsel of his more wicked mother Jezebel, who was still living.

THE SECOND
BOOK OF KINGS

This second book of the Kings (which the LXX., numbering from Samuel, called the *fourth*) is a continuation of the former book; and, some think, might better have been made to begin with the fifty-first verse of the foregoing chapter, where the reign of Ahaziah begins. The former book had an illustrious beginning, in the glories of the kingdom of Israel, when it was entire; this has a melancholy conclusion, in the desolations of the kingdoms of Israel first, and then of Judah. But, as Elijah's mighty works were very much the glory of the former book, towards the latter end of it, so were Elisha's the glory of this, towards the beginning of it. These prophets out-shone their princes; and therefore, as far as they go, the history shall be accounted for in them. Here is, I. Elijah fetching fire from heaven and ascending in fire to heaven, *ch.* i and ii. II. Elisha working many miracles, both for prince and people, Israelites and foreigners, *ch.* iii.–vii. III. Hazael and Jehu anointed, the former for the correction of Israel, the latter for the destruction of the house of Ahab and the worship of Baal, *ch.* viii.–x. IV. The reign of several of the kings, both of Judah and Israel, *ch.* xi.–xvi. V. The captivity of the ten tribes, *ch.* xvii. VI. The good and glorious reign of Hezekiah, *ch.* xviii.–xx. VII. Manasseh's wicked reign, and Josiah's good one, *ch.* xxi.–xxiii. VIII. The destruction of Jerusalem by the king of Babylon, *ch.* xxiv.–xxv. This history, in the several passages of it, confirms that observation of Solomon, *That righteousness exalts a nation, but sin is the reproach of any people.*

CHAPTER 1

We here find Ahaziah, the genuine son and successor of Ahab, on the throne of Israel. His reign continued not two years; he died by a fall in his own house. I. The message which he sent to the god of Ekron, ver. 2. II. The message he received from the God of Israel, ver. 3–8. III. The destruction of the messengers he sent to seize the prophet, once and again, ver. 9–12. IV. His compassion to, and compliance with, the third messenger, upon his submission, and the delivery of the message to the king himself, ver. 13–16. V. The death of Ahaziah, ver. 17, 18. In the story we may observe how great the prophet looks and how little the prince.

Verses 1–8

Ahaziah, the wicked king of Israel, under God's rebukes both by his providence and by his prophet, by his rod and by his word.

I. He is crossed in his affairs. How can those expect to prosper that *do evil in the sight of the Lord*, and *provoke him to anger*? When he rebelled against God, and revolted from his allegiance to him, Moab rebelled against Israel, and revolted from the subjection they had long paid to the kings of Israel, *v.* 1.

II. He is seized with sickness in body, not from any inward cause, but by a severe accident. *He fell down through a lattice.* Ahaziah would not attempt to reduce the Moabites, lest he should perish in the field of battle: but he is not safe, though he tarry at home. Royal palaces do not always yield firm footing.

III. In his distress he sends messengers to enquire of the god of Ekron whether he should recover or no, *v.* 2. 1. His enquiry was very foolish: *Shall I recover?* Even nature itself would rather have asked, "What means may I use that I may recover?" 2. His sending to Baal-zebub was very wicked. Baal-zebub, which signifies *the lord of a fly*, was one of their Baals that perhaps gave his answers, either by the power of the demons or the craft of the priests, with a humming noise, like that of a great fly, or that had (as they fancied) rid their country of the swarms of flies wherewith it was infested, or of some pestilential disease brought among them by flies. In the New Testament *the prince of the devils* is called *Beel-zebub* (Matt. xii. 24).

IV. Elijah, by direction from God, meets the messengers, and turns them back with an answer that shall save them the labour of going to Ekron.

1. He faithfully reproves his sin (*v.* 3): *Is it not because there is not* (that is, because you think there

is not) a God in Israel *that you go to enquire of Baal-zebub, the god of Ekron*, a despicable town of the Philistines (Zech. ix. 7), long since vanquished by Israel? (1) The sin was bad enough, giving that honour to the devil which is due to God alone. (2) The construction which Elijah, in God's name, puts upon it, makes it much worse: "It is because you think not only that the God of Israel is not able to tell you, but that there is no God at all in Israel, else you would not send so far for a divine answer."

2. He plainly reads his doom: Go, tell him *he shall surely die, v.* 4.

V. The message being delivered to him by his servants, he enquires of them by whom it was sent to him, and concludes, by their description of him, that it must be Elijah, *v.* 7, 8. His dress was the same that he had seen him in, in his father's court. He was clad in a hairy garment, and had a leathern girdle about him, was plain and homely in his garb.

Verses 9–18

I. The king issues out a warrant for the apprehending of Elijah. If the God of Ekron had told him he should die, it is probable he would have taken it quietly; but now that a prophet of the Lord tells him so, reproving him for his sin and reminding him of the God of Israel, he cannot bear it.

II. The captain that was sent with his fifty soldiers found Elijah on the top of a hill (some think Carmel), and commanded him, in the king's name, to surrender himself, *v.* 9. Elijah was now so far from absconding, as formerly, into the close recesses of a cave, that he makes a bold appearance on the top of a hill; experience of God's protection makes him more bold. The captain calls him *a man of God*. Had he really looked upon him as a prophet, he would not have attempted to make him his prisoner; and, had he thought him entrusted with the word of God, he would not have pretended to command him with the word of a king.

III. Elijah calls for fire from heaven, to consume this haughty daring sinner, to prove his mission. It was not long since Elijah had fetched fire from heaven, to consume the sacrifice (1 Kings xviii. 38), but, they having slighted that, now the fire falls, not on the sacrifice, but on the sinners themselves, *v.* 10. 1. What an interest the prophets had in heaven;

what the Spirit of God in them demanded the power of God effected. Elijah did but speak, and it was done. 2. What an interest heaven had in the prophets! God was always ready to plead their cause, and avenge the injuries done to them. Doubtless Elijah did this by a divine impulse, and yet our Saviour would not allow the disciples to draw it into a precedent, Luke ix. 54. "No," says Christ, "by no means, *you know not what manner of spirit you are of*," that is, (1) "You do not consider *what manner of spirit*, as disciples, you are called to, and how different from that of the Old Testament dispensation; it was agreeable enough to that dispensation of terror for Elias to call for fire, but the dispensation of the Spirit and of grace will by no means allow of it." (2) "You are not aware what manner of spirit you are, upon this occasion, actuated by, and how different from that of Elias: he did it in holy zeal, you in passion; he was concerned for God's glory, you for your own reputation only."

IV. Ahaziah sends, a second time, to apprehend Elijah (*v.* 11), as if he were resolved not to be baffled by omnipotence itself. Another captain is ready with his fifty. This is as impudent and imperious as the last, and more in haste. "*Come down quickly*, and do not trifle, the king's business requires haste." Elijah relents not, but calls for another flash of lightning, which instantly lays this captain and his fifty dead upon the spot.

V. The third captain humbled himself and cast himself upon the mercy of God and Elijah. He took warning by the fate of his predecessors, and, instead of summoning the prophet down, fell down before him, and begged for his life and the lives of his soldiers, acknowledging their own evil deserts and the prophet's power (*v.* 13, 14): *Let my life be precious in thy sight*.

VI. Elijah does more than grant the request of this third captain. God is as ready to show mercy to those that repent and submit to him; never any found it in vain to cast themselves upon the mercy of God. This captain, not only has his life spared, but is permitted to carry his point: Elijah, being so commanded by the angel, *goes down with him to the king*, *v.* 15. He comes boldly to the king, and tells him to his face what he had before sent to him (*v.* 16), that he shall surely and shortly die; he mitigates not the sentence, either for fear of the king's displeasure or in pity to his misery. The God of Israel has condemned him, let him send to see whether the god of Ekron can deliver him. So thunderstruck is Ahaziah with this message, when it comes from the prophet's own mouth, that neither he nor any of those about him durst offer him any violence, nor so much as give him an affront; but out of that den of lions he comes unhurt, like Daniel.

Lastly, The prediction is accomplished in a few days. Ahaziah died (*v.* 17), and, dying childless, left his kingdom to his brother Jehoram.

CHAPTER 2

I. The translation of Elijah. In the close of the foregoing chapter we had a wicked king leaving the world in disgrace, here we have a holy prophet leaving it in honour. Here is, 1. Elijah taking leave of his friends, the sons of the prophets, and especially Elisha, who kept close to him, and walked with him through Jordan, ver. 1–10. 2. Elijah taken into heaven by the ministry of angels (ver. 11), and Elisha's lamentation of the loss this earth had of him, ver. 12. II. The manifestation of Elisha, as a prophet in his room. 1. By the dividing of Jordan, ver. 13, 14. 2. By the respect which the sons of the prophets paid him, ver. 15–18. 3. By the healing of the unwholesome waters of Jericho, ver. 19–22. 4. By the destruction of the children of Bethel that mocked him, ver. 23–25.

Verses 1–8

Elijah's times, and the events concerning him, are as little dated as those of any great man in scripture; we are not told of his age, nor in what year of Ahab's

reign he first appeared, nor in what year of Jehoram's he disappeared, and therefore cannot conjecture how long he flourished; it is supposed about twenty years in all.

I. God had determined to take him up into heaven by a whirlwind, *v.* 1. It is not for us to say why God would put such a peculiar honour upon Elijah above any other of the prophets; he was a man *subject to like passions as we are*, knew sin, and yet never tasted death. We may suppose that herein, 1. God looked back upon his past services, which were eminent and extraordinary, and intended a recompence for those and an encouragement to the sons of the prophets to tread in the steps of his zeal and faithfulness, and to witness against the corruptions of the age they lived in. 2. He looked down upon the present dark and degenerate state of the church, and would thus give a very sensible proof of another life after this, and draw the hearts of the faithful few upward towards himself, and that other life. 3. He looked forward to the evangelical dispensation, and, in the translation of Elijah, gave a type and figure of the ascension of Christ and the *opening of the kingdom of heaven to all believers*. Elijah had, by faith and prayer, conversed much with heaven, and now he is taken thither, to assure us that if we have our conversation in heaven, while we are here on earth, we shall be there shortly, the soul shall (and that is the man) be happy there, there for ever.

II. Elisha had determined, as long as he continued on earth to cleave to him, and not to leave him. Elijah seemed desirous to shake him off, would have had him stay behind at Gilgal, at Bethel, at Jericho, *v.* 2, 4, 6. Some think out of humility; he knew what glory God designed for him, but would not seem to glory in it. In vain does Elijah entreat him to tarry here and tarry there; he resolves to tarry nowhere behind his master, till he goes to heaven, and leaves him behind on this earth. "Whatever comes of it, *I will not leave thee*;" and why so? 1. Because he desired to be edified by his holy heavenly converse as long as he stayed on earth. 2. Because he desired to be satisfied concerning his departure, and to see him when he was taken up, that his faith might be confirmed and his acquaintance with the invisible world increased.

III. That Elijah, before his departure, visited the schools of the prophets and took leave of them. It seems that there were such schools in many of the cities of Israel, probably even in Samaria itself. Here we find *sons of the prophets*, and considerable numbers of them, even at Bethel, where one of the calves was set up, and at Jericho, which was lately built in defiance of a divine curse. At Jerusalem, and in the kingdom of Judah, they had priests and Levites, and the temple-service, the want of which, in the kingdom of Israel, God graciously made up by those colleges, where men were trained up and employed in the exercises of religion and devotion.

IV. That the sons of the prophets had intelligence that he was now shortly to be removed; and, 1. They told Elisha of it, both at Bethel (*v.* 3) and at Jericho (*v.* 5): *Knowest thou that the Lord will take away thy master from thy head today?* Elisha knew it too well and *sorrow had filled his heart* upon this account (as the disciples in a like case, John xvi. 6), and therefore he did not need to be told of it, did not care for hearing of it. *I know it; hold you your peace.* He speaks with an awful silence expecting the event: *I know it; be silent*, Zech. ii. 13. 2. They went themselves to be witnesses of it at a distance, though they might not closely attend (*v.* 7): *Fifty of them stood to view afar off*, intending to satisfy their curiosity, but God so ordered it that they might be eye-witnesses of the honour heaven did to that prophet, who was *despised and rejected of men*.

V. That the miraculous dividing of the river Jordan was the preface to Elijah's translation into the heavenly Canaan, as it had been to the entrance of Israel into the earthly Canaan, *v.* 8. He must go on to the other side Jordan to be translated, because it was his native country, and that he might be near the place where Moses died, and that thus honour might be put on that part of the country which was most despised. God would magnify Elijah in his exit, as he did Joshua in his entrance, by the dividing of this river, Joshua iii. 7. When God will take up his faithful ones to heaven death is the Jordan which, immediately before their translation, they must pass through, and they find a way through it, a safe and comfortable way; the death of Christ has divided those waters, that the ransomed of the Lord may pass over.

Verses 9–12

I. Elijah makes his will, and leaves Elisha his heir, now anointing him to be prophet in his room, more than when he *cast his mantle upon him*, 1 Kings xix. 19.

1. Elijah, being greatly pleased with the constancy of Elisha's affection and attendance, bade him ask what he should do for him, what blessing he should leave him at parting.

2. Elisha, having this fair opportunity to enrich himself with the best riches, prays for a *double portion of his spirit*. He asks not for wealth, nor honour, nor exemption from trouble, but to be qualified for the service of God and his generation; he asks, (1) For the Spirit, not that the gifts and graces of the Spirit were in Elijah's power to give, therefore, he says not, "Give me the Spirit" (he knew very well it was God's gift), but, "*Let it be upon me*, intercede with God for this for me." (2) For *his* spirit, because he was to be a prophet in his room, to carry on his work, to father the sons of the prophets and face their enemies, because he had the same difficulties to encounter. (3) For a *double portion of his spirit*; he does not mean double to what Elijah had, but double to what the rest of the prophets had, from whom so much would not be expected as from Elisha, who had been brought up under Elijah.

3. Elijah promised him that which he asked, but under two provisos, *v.* 10. (1) Provided he put a due value upon it and esteem it highly: this he teaches him to do by calling it *a hard thing*, not too hard for God to do, but too great for him to expect. (2) Provided he kept close to his master, even to the last, and was observant of him: *If thou see me when I am taken from thee, it shall be* so, otherwise not.

II. Elijah is carried up to heaven in a fiery chariot, *v.* 11. Like Enoch, he was translated, *that he should not see death*; and was (as Mr. Cowley expresses it) *the second man that leaped the ditch where all the rest of mankind fell, and went not downward to the sky.* Let it suffice that we are here told,

1. What his Lord, when he came, found him doing. He was talking with Elisha, instructing and encouraging him, directing him in his work, and quickening him to it, for the good of those whom he left behind. He was not meditating nor praying, as one wholly taken up with the world he was going to, but engaged in edifying discourse, as one concerned about the kingdom of God among men.

2. What convoy his Lord sent for him—*a chariot of fire and horses of fire*, that he may ride in state, may ride in triumph, like a prince, like a conqueror, yea, *more than a conqueror*. The angels are called in scripture *cherubim* and *seraphim*, and their appearance here, though it may seem below their dignity, answers to both those names; for (1) *Seraphim* signifies *fiery*, and God is said to make them *a flame of fire*, Ps. civ. 4. (2) *Cherubim* (as many think) signifies *chariots*, and they are called *the chariots of*

God (Ps. lxviii. 17). The chariot and horses appeared like fire, not for burning, but brightness, not to torture or consume him, but to render his ascension conspicuous and illustrious in the eyes of those that stood afar off to view it. Elijah had burned with holy zeal for God and his honour, and now with a heavenly fire he was refined and translated.

3. How he was separated from Elisha. This chariot parted them both asunder.

4. Whither he was carried. He *went up by a whirlwind into heaven*. Elijah had once, in a passion, wished he might die; yet God was so gracious to him as to honour him with this singular privilege, that he should never see death; and by this instance, and that of Enoch, (1) God showed how men should have left the world if they had not sinned, not by death, but by a translation. (2) He gave a glimpse of that life and immortality which are brought to light by the gospel, and the *opening of the kingdom of heaven to all believers*, as then to Elijah. It was also a figure of Christ's ascension.

III. Elisha pathetically laments the loss of that great prophet. 1. He saw it; by which he was assured of the grant of his request for a double portion of Elijah's spirit. He looked steadfastly towards heaven, whence he was to expect that gift, as the disciples did, Acts i. 10. He saw it awhile, but the vision was presently out of his sight; and *he saw him no more*. 2. He rent his own clothes, in token of the sense he had of his own and the public loss. Though Elijah had gone triumphantly to heaven, yet this world could ill spare him. Surely their hearts are hard whose eyes are dry when God, by taking away faithful useful men, calls for weeping and mourning. Though Elijah's departure made way for Elisha's eminency, yet he lamented the loss of him, for he loved him, and could have served him for ever. 3. He gave him a very honourable character. He himself had lost the guide of his youth: *My father, my father*. The public had lost its best guard; he was *the chariot of Israel, and the horsemen thereof*. He would have brought them all to heaven, as in this chariot, if it had not been their own fault.

Verses 13–18

What followed immediately after the translation of Elijah.

I. The tokens of God's presence with Elisha, and the marks of his elevation into Elijah's room.

1. He was possessed of Elijah's mantle, the badge of his office, which, we may suppose, he put on and wore for his master's sake, *v.* 13. When Elijah went to heaven he left his mantle as a legacy to Elisha, and, as it was a token of the descent of the Spirit upon him, it was more than if he had bequeathed to him thousands of gold and silver. Elisha took it up as a significant garment to be worn. He that then so cheerfully obeyed the summons of it, and became Elijah's servant, is now dignified with it, and becomes his successor.

2. He was possessed of Elijah's power to divide Jordan, *v.* 14. Having parted with his father, he returns to his sons in the schools of the prophets. Jordan was between him and them; it had been divided to make way for Elijah to his glory; he will try whether it will divide to make way for him to his business. Elijah's last miracle shall be Elisha's first. In dividing the waters, (1) He made use of Elijah's mantle, as Elijah himself had done (*v.* 8), to signify that he designed to keep to his master's methods. (2) He applied to Elijah's God: *Where is the Lord God of Elijah?* He does not ask, "Where is Elijah?" "The God that owned, and protected, and provided for Elijah, and many ways honoured him, especially now at last, where is he? Lord, am not I promised Elijah's spirit? Make good that promise." The words which

next follow in the original, *aph-his*—*even he*, which we join to the following clause, *when he also had smitten the waters*, some make an answer to this question, *Where is Elijah's God?* "*He is in being still, and nigh at hand.* We have lost Elijah, but we have not lost Elijah's God. He *has not forsaken the earth*; it is even he that is still with me." Those that walk in the spirit and steps of their godly faithful predecessors shall certainly experience the same grace that they experienced; Elijah's God will be Elisha's too. The Lord God of the holy prophets is the same yesterday, today, and for ever; and what will it avail us to have the mantles of those that are gone, their places, their books, if we have not their spirit, their God?

3. He was possessed of Elijah's interest in the sons of the prophets, *v.* 15. Some, who had placed themselves conveniently near Jordan, to see what passed, were surprised to see Jordan divided before Elisha in his return, and took that as a convincing evidence that *the spirit of Elijah did rest upon him.* Accordingly they went to meet him, to congratulate him on his safe passage through fire and water, and the honour God had put upon him; and they *bowed themselves to the ground before him.* They were trained up in the schools; Elisha was taken from the plough; yet when they perceived that God was with him, and that this was *the man whom he delighted to honour*, they readily submitted to him as their head and father, as the people to Joshua when Moses was dead, Joshua i. 17. Whomsoever God honours, we must.

II. The needless search which the sons of the prophets made for Elijah. 1. They suggested that possibly he was dropped, either alive or dead, upon some mountain, or in some valley, *v.* 16. Some of them perhaps started this as a demurrer to the choice of Elisha: "Let us first be sure that Elijah has quite gone." 2. Elisha consented not till they overcame him with importunity, *v.* 17. They urged him till he was ashamed to oppose it any further, lest he should be thought wanting in his respect to his old master or loth to resign the mantle again. 3. The issue made them ashamed of their proposal. Their messengers, after they had tired themselves with fruitless search, returned and gave Elisha an opportunity of upbraiding his friends with their folly: *Did I not say unto you, Go not? v.* 18. Traversing hills and valleys will never bring us to Elijah, but the imitation of his holy faith and zeal will, in due time.

Verses 19–25

Elisha wrought more miracles than Elijah. Some reckon them in number just double. Two are recorded in these verses—a miracle of mercy to Jericho and a miracle of judgment to Bethel, Ps. ci. 1.

I. Here is a blessing upon the waters of Jericho, which was effectual to heal them. Jericho was built in disobedience to a command, but even within those walls that were built by iniquity we find a nursery of piety. Hither Elisha came, to confirm the souls of the disciples with a more particular account of Elijah's translation than their spies, who saw at a distance, could give them. Here he stayed while the fifty men were searching for him. And, 1. The men of Jericho represented to him their grievance, *v.* 19. They had not applied to Elijah concerning the matter, perhaps because he was not so easy of access as Elisha was. The situation was pleasant and afforded a good prospect; but they had neither wholesome water to drink nor fruitful soil to yield them food. Some think that it was not all the ground about Jericho that was barren and had bad water, but some one part only. 2. He soon redressed their grievance. Prophets should endeavour to make every place they come to, some way or other, the better for them, endeavouring to sweeten bitter spirits, and to make barren souls

fruitful, by the due application of the word of God. Elisha will heal their waters; but, (1) They must furnish him with salt in a new cruse, *v.* 20. If salt had been proper to season the water, yet what could so small a quantity do towards it and what the better for being in a new cruse? But thus those that would be helped must be employed and have their faith and obedience tried. God's works of grace are wrought, not by any operations of ours, but in observance of his institutions. (2) He cast the salt *into the spring of the waters*, and so healed the streams and the ground they watered. Thus the way to reform men's lives is to renew their hearts; let those be seasoned with the salt of grace, for *out of them are the issues of life.* Purify the heart and that will cleanse the hands. (3) He did not pretend to do this by his own power, but in God's name: *Thus saith the Lord, I have healed these waters.* By doing them this kindness with a *Thus saith the Lord*, they would be made the more willing, hereafter, to receive from him a reproof, admonition, or command, with the same preface. (4) The cure was lasting, and not for the present only: *The waters were healed unto this day, v.* 22.

II. A curse upon the children of Bethel. At Bethel there was another school of prophets. Thither Elisha went next, and the scholars welcomed him with all possible respect, but the townsmen were abusive to him. One of Jeroboam's calves was at Bethel; this they were proud of, and hated those that reproved them. We may suppose it was their usual practice to jeer the prophets as they went along the streets, to call them by some nickname or other, and, if possible, drive them out of their town. Had the abuse done to Elisha been the first offence of that kind, it is probable that it would not have been so severely punished. But *mocking the messengers of the Lord*, and *misusing the prophets*, was one of the *crying sins of Israel*, as we find, 2 Chron. xxxvi. 16. 1. An instance of that sin. The little *children of Bethel*, the boys and girls that were playing in the streets, went out to meet him, gathered about him and mocked him, as if he had been a fool. *Go up, thou bald head, go up, thou bald head.* It was his character as a prophet that they designed to abuse. The honour God had crowned him with should have been sufficient to cover his bald head and protect him from their scoffs. These children said as they were taught; they had learned of their idolatrous parents to call foul names and give bad language, especially to prophets. These young cocks, as we say, crowed after the old ones. 2. A specimen of that ruin which came upon Israel at last, for misusing God's prophets, and of which this was intended to give them fair warning. Elisha heard their taunts, a good while, with patience; but at length he *turned and looked upon them*, to try if a grave and severe look would put them out of countenance, but they *were not ashamed*, and therefore he *cursed them in the name of the Lord*, to punish the dishonour done to God. His summons was immediately obeyed; two she-bears came out of an adjacent wood, and presently killed forty-two children, *v.* 24. The prophet must be justified, for he did it by divine impulse. He intended hereby to punish the parents and to make them afraid of God's judgments. Let parents, that would have comfort in their children, train them up well. In vain do we look for good from those children whose education we have neglected; and in vain do we grieve for those miscarriages which our care might have prevented.

CHAPTER 3

The public affairs of Israel, in which we find Elisha concerned. I. The general character of Jehoram, king of Israel, ver. 1–3. II. A war with Moab, in which Jehoram and his allies were engaged, ver. 4–8. III. The straits which the confederate army were reduced to in their expedition against Moab, and their consulting Elisha in that distress, with the answer of peace he gave them, ver. 9–19. IV. The glorious issue of this campaign (ver. 20–25) and the barbarous method the king of Moab took to oblige the confederate army to retire, ver. 26, 27. The house of Ahab is doomed to destruction.

Verses 1–5

Jehoram, the son of Ahab, and brother of Ahaziah, is here upon the throne of Israel; and, though he was a bad man, yet two commendable things are here recorded of him:

I. That he removed his father's idols. He did evil in many things, but not like his father Ahab or his mother Jezebel, *v.* 2. Perhaps Jehoshaphat, though by his alliance with the house of Ahab he made his own family worse, did something towards making Ahab's better. Jehoram *put away the image of Baal*, resolving to worship the God of Israel only, and consult none but his prophets. So far was well, yet it did not prevent the destruction of Ahab's family. 1. He only put away the image of Baal *which his father had made*. He did not destroy the worship of Baal among the people, for Jehu found it prevalent, *ch.* x. 19. It was well to reform his family, but he ought to have used his power for the reforming of his kingdom. 2. When he put away the image of Baal, he adhered to the worship of the calves, that politic sin of Jeroboam, *v.* 3. *He departed not therefrom*, by which the division between the two tribes was supported. Those do not truly reform, who only part with the sins that they lose by, but continue their affection to the sins that they get by. 3. He only *put away* the image of Baal, he did not break it in pieces, as he ought to have done.

II. That he did what he could to recover his brother's losses. As he had something more of the religion of an Israelite than his father, so he had something more of the spirit of a king than his brother. Moab rebelled against Israel immediately upon the death of Ahab, *ch.* i. 1. And we do not find that Ahaziah made any attempt to chastise or reduce them. The tribute which the king of Moab paid was a very considerable branch of the revenue of the crown of Israel: 100,000 *lambs, and* 100,000 *wethers, v.* 4. Taxes were then paid not so much in money as in the commodities of the country. The revolt of Moab was a great loss to Israel, yet Ahaziah sat still in sloth and ease. But an upper chamber in his house proved as fatal to him as the high places of the field could have been (*ch.* i. 2), and the breaking of his lattice let into his throne a man of a more active genius.

Verses 6–19

Jehoram has no sooner got the sceptre into his hand than he takes the sword to reduce Moab.

I. The concerting of this expedition between Jehoram king of Israel and Jehoshaphat king of Judah. Jehoram levied an army (*v.* 6), and such an opinion he had of the godly king of Judah that, 1. He courted him to be his confederate: *Wilt thou go with me against Moab?* And he gained him. Judah and Israel, though unhappily divided from each other, yet can unite against Moab a common enemy. Jehoshaphat treats with Israel as a sister-kingdom. Those are no friends to their own peace and strength who can never find in their hearts to forgive and forget an old injury. 2. He consulted him as his confidant, *v.* 8. He took advice of Jehoshaphat, who had more wisdom and experience than himself, which way they should make their descent upon the country of Moab; and he advised that they should not march against them the nearest way, over Jordan, but go round *through the wilderness of Edom*, that they might take the king of Edom (who was tributary to him) and his forces along with them.

II. The great straits that the army of the confederates was reduced to in this expedition. Before they saw the face of an enemy they were all in danger of perishing for want of water, *v.* 9. The king of Israel sadly lamented the present distress, and the imminent danger. It was he that had *called these kings together*; yet he charges it upon Providence, and reflects upon that as unkind.

III. Jehoshaphat's good motion to ask counsel of God in this exigency, *v.* 11. The place they were now in could not but remind them of the *wonders of which their fathers told them*, the waters fetched out of the rock. The thought of this, we may suppose, encouraged Jehoshaphat to ask, *Is there not here a prophet of the Lord*, like unto Moses? It was well that Jehoshaphat enquired of the Lord now, but it would have been much better if he had done it sooner, before he steered this course; so the distress might have been prevented.

IV. Elisha recommended as a proper person for them to consult with, *v.* 11. We may suppose it was by special direction from heaven that Elisha attended the war, as *the chariot of Israel and the horsemen thereof*. A servant of the king of Israel knew of his being there when the King himself did not. Probably it was such a servant as Obadiah was to his father Ahab, one that *feared the Lord*; to such a one Elisha made himself known, not to the kings.

V. The application which the kings made to Elisha. They went down to him to his quarters, *v.* 12. He that humbled himself was thus exalted, and looked great, when three kings came to knock at his door, and beg his assistance.

VI. The entertainment which Elisha gave them. 1. He was very plain with the wicked king of Israel (*v.* 13): "*What have I to do with thee? Get thee to the prophets of thy father and mother*, whom thy hast countenanced and maintained in thy prosperity, and let them help thee now in thy distress. The world and the flesh have ruled you, let them help you; why should God be *enquired of by* you?" Ezek. xiv. 3. Elisha tells him to his face, in a holy indignation at his wickedness, that he can scarcely find in his heart to *look towards him* or to *see him, v.* 14. Jehoram is to be respected as a prince. Elisha, as a subject, will honour him, but as a prophet he will cause him to know his iniquity. Jehoram has so much self-command as to take this plain dealing patiently; he cares not now for hearing of the prophets of Baal, but is a humble suitor to the God of Israel and his prophet, representing the present case as very deplorable and humbly recommending it to the prophet's compassionate consideration. In effect, he owns himself unworthy, but let not the other kings be ruined for his sake. 2. Elisha showed a great respect to the godly king of Judah, *regarded his presence*, and, for his sake, would *enquire of the Lord* for them all. 3. He composed himself to receive instructions from God, yet his zeal for the present indisposed him for prayer and the operations of the Spirit, which required a mind very calm and sedate. He therefore called for a musician (*v.* 15), a devout musician, one accustomed to play upon his harp and sing psalms to it. Elisha being refreshed, and having the tumult of his spirits laid by this divine music, *the hand of the Lord came upon him*, and his visit did him more honour than that of three kings. 4. God, by him, gave them assurance that the issue of the present distress would be comfortable and glorious. (1) They should speedily be supplied with water, *v.* 16, 17. To try their faith and obedience, he bids them *make the valley full of ditches* to receive the water. Elijah, by prayer, obtained water out of the clouds, but Elisha fetches it nobody knows whence. The spring of these waters shall be as secret as the head of the Nile. God is not tied to second causes.

Ordinarily it is by a plentiful rain that God *confirms his inheritance* (Ps. lxviii. 9), but here it is done without rain, at least without rain in that place. (2) That supply should be an earnest of victory (v. 18): *"This is but a light thing in the sight of the Lord;* you shall not only be saved from perishing, but shall return in triumph." It is promised that they shall be masters of the rebellious country.

Verses 20–27

I. We have here the divine gift of both those things which God had promised by Elisha—water and victory, and the former not only a pledge of the latter, but a means of it.

1. It relieved their armies, which were ready to perish, v. 20. And this relief came just at the time of the *offering of the morning sacrifice* upon the altar at Jerusalem. We now cannot pitch upon any hour more acceptable than another, because our high priest is always appearing for us, to present and plead his sacrifice. That time God chose for the hour of mercy to put an honour upon the daily sacrifice, which had been despised. God answered Daniel's prayer just at the *time of the evening sacrifice* (Dan. ix. 21).

2. It deceived their enemies, who were ready to triumph, promising themselves that it would be easy dealing with an army fatigued by so long a march through the wilderness of Edom.

(1) How easily they were drawn into their own delusions. [1] They saw the water in the valley where the army of Israel encamped, and conceited it was blood (v. 22), because they knew the valley to be dry, and could not imagine it should be water. The sun shone upon it, probably the sky was red and lowering, making the water look red, which made them willing to believe *This is blood.* [2] If their camp was thus full of blood, they conclude, "Certainly the kings have fallen out and they have *slain one another*" (v. 23). "*Now therefore, Moab, to the spoil.*"

(2) How fatally they thereby ran upon their own destruction. They rushed carelessly into the camp of Israel, to plunder it, but were undeceived when it was too late. The Israelites, animated by the assurances Elisha had given them of victory, fell upon them with the utmost fury, routed them, and pursued them into their own country (v. 24), which they laid waste (v. 25), destroyed the cities, marred the ground, stopped up the wells, felled the timber, and left only the royal city standing, in the walls of which they made great breaches with their battering engines.

II. In the close of the chapter we are told what the king of Moab did when he found himself reduced to the last extremity. 1. He attempted that which was bold and brave. He got together 700 choice men, and with them sallied out upon the intrenchments of the king of Edom, who, being but a mercenary in this expedition, would not, he hoped, make any great resistance if vigorously attacked, and so he might make his escape that way. But it would not do; even the king of Edom proved too hard for him, and obliged him to retire, v. 26. 2. This failing, he did that which was brutish and barbarous; he took his own son, his eldest son, that was to succeed him, than whom nothing could be more dear to himself and his people, and *offered him for a burnt-offering upon the wall,* v. 27. He designed by this, (1) To obtain the favour of Chemosh his god, which, being a devil, delighted in blood and murder, and the destruction of mankind. (2) To terrify the besiegers, and oblige them to retire. Therefore he did it *upon the wall,* in their sight, that they might see what desperate courses he resolved to take rather than surrender, and how dearly he would sell his city and life.

CHAPTER 4

Great service Elisha had done for the three kings: to his prayers and prophecies they owed their lives and triumphs. One would have expected that the next chapter would tell us what honours and what dignities were conferred on Elisha for this. No, the wise man delivered the army, but no man remembered the wise man, Eccles. ix. 15. Or, if he had preferment offered him, he declined it: he preferred the honour of doing good in the schools of the prophets before that of being great in the courts of princes. God magnified him, and that sufficed him—for we have him here employed in working no fewer than five miracles. I. He multiplied the poor widow's oil, ver. 1–7. II. He obtained for the good Shunammite the blessing of a son in her old age, ver. 8–17. III. He raised that child to life when it was dead, ver. 18–37. IV. He healed the deadly pottage, ver. 38–41. V. He fed 100 men with twenty small loaves, ver. 42–44.

Verses 1–7

Elisha's miracles were for use, not for show; this recorded here was an act of real charity. Such also were the miracles of Christ, not only great wonders, but great favours to those for whom they were wrought.

I. Elisha readily receives a poor widow's complaint. She was a prophet's widow. It seems, the prophets had wives as well as the priests. Marriage is honourable in all, and not inconsistent with the most sacred professions. Now, by the complaint of this poor woman (v. 1), we are given to understand, 1. That her husband, being *one of the sons of the prophets,* was well known to Elisha. 2. That he had the reputation of a godly man. He was one that kept his integrity in a time of general apostasy, one of the 7,000 that had not bowed the knee to Baal. 3. That he was dead. Those that were clothed with the spirit of prophecy were not thereby armed against the stroke of death. 4. That he died poor, and in debt more than he was worth. He did not contract his debts by prodigality, and luxury, and riotous living, for he was one that feared the Lord. Yet it may be the lot of those that fear God to be in debt, and insolvent, through afflictive providences, losses by sea, or bad debts, or their own imprudence, for the *children of light* are not always *wise for this world.* Perhaps this prophet was impoverished by persecution: when Jezebel ruled, prophets had much ado to live, and especially if they had families. 5. That the creditors were very severe with her. Two sons she had to be the support of her widowed state, and their labour is reckoned *assets* in her hand; that must go therefore, and they must be bondmen for seven years (Exod. xxi. 2) to work out this debt. In this distress the poor widow goes to Elisha, in dependence upon the promise that the seed of the righteous shall not be forsaken.

II. He effectually relieves this poor widow's distress, and puts her in a way both to pay her debt and to maintain herself and her family. He did not give her some small matter for her present provision, but set her up in the world to sell oil, and put a stock into her hand to begin with.

1. He directed her what to do, considered her case: *What shall I do for thee?* Elisha therefore enquired what she had to make money of, and found she had nothing to sell but one pot of oil, v. 2. If she had not had this pot of oil, the divine power could have supplied her; but, having this, it will work upon this, and so teach us to make the best of what we have. The prophet, knowing her to have credit among her neighbours, bids her borrow of them *empty vessels* (v. 3). He directs her to shut the door upon herself and her sons, while she filled all those vessels out of that one. The oil was to be multiplied in the pouring, as the other widow's meal in the spending. The way to increase what we have is to use it; to him that hath shall be given.

2. She did it firmly believing the divine power and goodness, and in obedience to the prophet. They

were all amazed to find their pot, like a fountain of living water, always flowing, and yet always full.

3. The oil continued flowing as long as she had any empty vessels to receive it. He gives above what we ask: were there more vessels, there is enough in God to fill them—enough for all, enough for each.

4. The prophet directed her what to do with the oil she had, *v.* 7. (1) She must sell the oil to those that were rich, and could afford to bestow it on themselves. (2) She must pay her debt with the money she received for her oil. It is one of the fundamental laws of our religion that we render to all their due, for conscience' sake. (3) The rest must not be laid up, but she and her children must live upon the money received, with which they must put themselves into a capacity of getting an honest livelihood. [1] Let those that are poor and in distress be encouraged to trust God. *Verily thou shalt be fed,* though not feasted. It is true we cannot now expect miracles, yet we may expect mercies, if we wait on God and seek to him. [2] Let those whom God has blessed with plenty use it for the glory of God and under the direction of his word.

Verses 8–17

The giving of a son to such as were old, and had been long childless, was an ancient instance of the divine power and favour; we find it here among the wonders wrought by Elisha.

I. The kindness of the Shunammite woman to Elisha. Shunem lay in the road between Samaria and Carmel, a road that Elisha often travelled, as we find *ch.* ii. 25. *There* lived *a great woman,* who was very hospitable. So famous a man as Elisha could not pass and repass unobserved. Probably this pious matron, having notice of his being there, constrained him to dine with her, *v.* 8. He was modest and loth to be troublesome, so that it was not without some difficulty that he was first drawn into an acquaintance there; but afterwards, whenever he went that way, he called. She suggests, 1. That the stranger she would invite was *a holy man of God,* who therefore would do good to their family. 2. That the kindness she intended him would be no great charge to them; she would build him only a little chamber. The furniture shall be very plain; a bed, and a table, a stool, and a candlestick, all that was needful for his convenience. Elisha seemed highly pleased with these accommodations.

II. Elisha's gratitude for this kindness. 1. He offered to use his interest for her in the king's court (*v.* 13): "*Wouldst thou be spoken for to the king, or the captain of the host,* for an office for thy husband, civil or military? Wherein can I serve thee?" But she needs not any good offices of this kind to be done for her: *I dwell* (says she) *among my own people,* that is, "We are well off as we are, and do not aim at preferment." Some years after this we find this Shunammite had occasion to be spoken for to the king, though now she needed it not, *ch.* viii. 3, 4. 2. He did use his interest for her in the court of heaven. Elisha consulted with his servant what kindness he should do for her. Gehazi reminded him that she was childless, had a great estate, but no son to leave it to, and was past hopes of having any, her husband being old. If Elisha could obtain this favour from God for her, it would be the removal of that which at present was her only grievance. He sent for her immediately. She very humbly and respectfully *stood in the door* (*v.* 15), according to her accustomed modesty, and then he assured her that within a year she should bring forth a son, *v.* 16. The event, within the time limited, confirmed the truth of the promise: *She bore a son* at the season that Elisha spoke of, *v.* 17.

Verses 18–37

We may well suppose that, after the birth of this son, the prophet was doubly welcome to the good Shunammite. He had thought himself indebted to her, but henceforth, as long as she lives, she will think herself in his debt, and that she can never do too much for him. We may also suppose that the child was very dear to the prophet, as the son of his prayers, and very dear to the parents, as the son of their old age.

I. The sudden death of the child. A child of promise, a child of prayer, and given in love, yet taken away. But how admirably does the prudent pious mother guard her lips under this surprising affliction! She had heard of the raising of the widow's son of Sarepta, and that the spirit of Elijah rested on Elisha; and such confidence had she of God's goodness that she was very ready to believe that he who so soon took away what he had given would restore what he had now taken away. In this faith she makes no preparation for the burial of her dead child, but for its resurrection; for she *lays him on the prophet's bed* (*v.* 21), expecting that he will stand her friend. *O woman! great is thy faith.*

II. The sorrowful mother's application to the prophet on this sad occasion; for it happened very opportunely that he was now at the college upon Mount Carmel, not far off.

1. She begged leave of her husband to go to the prophet, yet not acquainting him with her errand, lest he should not have faith enough to let her go, *v.* 22. See how this husband and wife vied with each other in showing mutual regard; she was so dutiful to him that she would not go till she had acquainted him with her journey, and he so kind to her that he would not oppose it, though she did not think fit to acquaint him with her business. 2. She made all the haste she could to the prophet (*v.* 24), and he, seeing her at a distance, sent his servant to enquire whether anything was amiss, *v.* 25, 26. The answer was general: *It is well.* Gehazi was not the man that she came to complain to, and therefore she put him off with this. Note, When God calls away our dearest relations by death it becomes us quietly to say, "It is well both with us and them;" it is well, for all is well that God does; all is well with those that are gone if they have gone to heaven, and all well with us that stay behind if by the affliction we are furthered in our way thither. 3. When she came to the prophet she humbly reasoned with him concerning her present affliction. Elisha waited to hear from her, since he might not know immediately from God, what was the cause of her trouble. What she said was very pathetic. She appealed to the prophet, (1) Concerning her indifference to this mercy which was now taken from her: "*Did I desire a son of my lord?* No, thou knowest I did not; it was thy own proposal, not mine; I did not fret for the want of a son, as Hannah, nor beg, as Rachel, *Give me children or else I die.*" (2) Concerning her entire dependence upon the prophet's word, pleading with the prophet for the raising of the child to life again: "*I said, Do not deceive me,* and I know thou wilt not."

III. The raising of the child to life again. We may suppose that the woman gave Elisha a more express account of the child's death, and he gave her a more express promise of his resurrection, than is here related, where we are briefly told,

1. That Elisha sent Gehazi to go in all haste to the dead child, gave him his staff, and bade him lay that on the face of the child, *v.* 29. Bishop Hall suggests that it was done out of human conceit, and not by divine instinct, and therefore it failed of the effect; God will not have such great favours made too cheap, nor shall they be too easily come by, lest they be undervalued.

2. The woman resolved not to go back without the prophet himself (v. 30): *I will not leave thee*. She had no great expectation from the staff, she would have the hand, and she was in the right of it.

3. The prophet, by earnest prayer, obtained from God the restoring of this dead child to life again. He found the child dead upon his own bed (v. 32), *and shut the door upon them twain*, v. 33.

(1) How closely the prophet applied himself to this great operation, perhaps being sensible that he had tempted God too much in thinking to effect it by the staff in Gehazi's hand. [1] He *prayed unto the Lord* (v. 33), probably as Elijah had done, *Let this child's soul come into him again*. Christ raised the dead to life as one having authority—*Damsel, arise—Young man, I say unto thee, Arise—Lazarus, come forth* (for he was powerful and faithful as a Son, the Lord of life), but Elijah and Elisha did it by petition, as servants. [2] He *lay upon the child* (v. 34), as if he would communicate to him some of his vital heat or spirits. He first *put his mouth to the child's mouth*, as if, in God's name, he would breathe into him the breath of life; then *his eyes to the child's eyes*, to open them again to the light of life; then *his hands to the child's hands*, to put strength into them. He then *returned, and walked in the house*, as one full of care and concern, and wholly intent upon what he was about. Then he went upstairs again, and, the second time, *stretched himself upon the child*, v. 35.

(2) How gradually the operation was performed. At the first application, *the flesh of the child waxed warm* (v. 34), which gave the prophet encouragement to continue instant in prayer. After a while, *the child sneezed seven times*, which was an indication, not only of life, but liveliness.

(3) How joyfully the child was restored alive to his mother (v. 36, 37), and all parties concerned *were not a little comforted*, Acts xx. 12.

Verses 38–44

Elisha in his place, in his element, among the sons of the prophets, teaching them, and, as a father, providing for them. There was a dearth in the land, for the wickedness of those that dwelt therein, the same that we read of, *ch.* viii. 1. It continued seven years, just as long again as that in Elijah's time.

I. He made hurtful food to become safe and wholesome. 1. The sons of the prophets being all to attend, he ordered his servant to provide food for their bodies, while he was breaking to them the bread of life for their souls. He orders only that pottage should be seethed for them of herbs, v. 38. The sons of the prophets should be examples of temperance and mortification. 2. One of the servitors, who was sent to gather herbs, by mistake brought in that which was noxious, and shred it into the pottage: *wild gourds* they are called, v. 39. Some think it was *coloquintida*, a herb strongly cathartic, and dangerous. 3. The guests complained to Elisha of the unwholesomeness of their food. They cried out, *There is death in the pot*, v. 40. 4. Elisha immediately cured the bad taste and prevented the bad consequences of this unwholesome pottage; as before he had healed the bitter waters with salt, so now the bitter broth with meal, v. 41. Now all was well, not only no death, but no harm in the pot.

II. He made a little food to go a great way. 1. Elisha had a present brought him of twenty barley-loaves and some ears of corn (v. 42), a present in a special manner valuable, when there was a dearth in the land. 2. Having freely received, he freely gave, ordering it all to be set before the sons of the prophets, reserving none for himself, none for hereafter. It well becomes the fathers of the prophets to be liberal to the sons of the prophets. 3. Though

the loaves were little, yet with twenty of them he satisfied 100 men, v. 43, 44. His servant thought that to set so little meat before so many men was but to shame his master; but he, in God's name, pronounced it a full meal for them, and so it proved; they did eat, and left thereof, not because their stomachs failed them, but because the bread increased in the eating.

CHAPTER 5

Two more of Elisha's miracles are recorded in this chapter. I. The cleansing of Naaman, a Syrian, a stranger, from his leprosy, 1. The badness of his case, ver. 1. 2. The providence that brought him to Elisha, the intelligence given him by a captive maid, ver. 2–4. A letter from the king of Syria to the king of Israel, to introduce him, ver. 5–7. And the invitation Elisha sent him, ver. 8. 3. The method prescribed for his cure, his submission to that method, and his cure thereby, ver. 9–14. 4. The grateful acknowledgments he made to Elisha hereupon, ver. 15–19. II. The smiting of Gehazi, his own servant, with that leprosy. 1. Gehazi's sins, which were belying his master to Naaman (ver. 20–24), and lying to his master when he examined him, ver. 25. 2. His punishment for these sins. Naaman's leprosy was entailed on his family, ver. 26, 27. And, if Naaman's cure was typical of the calling of the Gentiles, as our Saviour seems to make it (Luke iv. 27), Gehazi's stroke may be looked upon as typical of the blinding and rejecting of the Jews, who envied God's grace to the Gentiles, as Gehazi envied Elisha's favour to Naaman.

Verses 1–8

Our Saviour's miracles were intended for the lost sheep of the house of Israel, yet one, like a crumb, fell from the table to a woman of Canaan; so this one miracle Elisha wrought for Naaman, a Syrian; for God does good to all, and will have all men to be saved.

I. The great affliction Naaman was under, in the midst of all his honours, v. 1. He was very acceptable to his prince, was his favourite, and prime-minister of state; a mighty man of valour, but he was a leper, a burden to himself. Every man has some *but* or other in his character, something that blemishes and diminishes him. Naaman was as great as the world could make him, and yet (as Bishop Hall expresses it) the basest slave in Syria would not change skins with him.

II. The notice that was given him of Elisha's power, by a little maid that waited on his lady, v. 2, 3. This maid was, by birth, an Israelite, providentially carried captive into Syria, into Naaman's family, where she published Elisha's fame to the honour of Israel and Israel's God. The unhappy dispersing of the people of God has sometimes proved the happy occasion of the diffusion of the knowledge of God, Acts viii. 4. This little maid, as became a true-born Israelite, consulted the honour of her country, and could give an account, though but a girl, of the famous prophet they had among them. As became a good servant, she desired the health and welfare of her master. *Elisha* had *not cleansed any leper in Israel* (Luke iv. 27), yet this little maid inferred that he *could* cure her master, and that he *would* do it, though he was a Syrian.

III. The application which the king of Syria hereupon made to the king of Israel on Naaman's behalf. See what Naaman did upon this little hint. 1. He would not send for the prophet to come to him, but such honour would he pay to one that had so much of a divine power with him as to be able to cure diseases that he would go to him himself. 2. He would not go *incognito*—*in disguise*, though his errand proclaimed his loathsome disease, but went in state, and with a great retinue, to do the more honour to the prophet. 3. He would not go empty-handed, but took with him gold, silver, and raiment, to present to his physician. 4. He would not go without a letter to the king of Israel from the king his master, who did himself earnestly desire his recovery.

IV. The alarm this gave to the king of Israel, v. 7. He apprehended there was in this letter, 1. A great affront upon God, and therefore he rent his clothes, according to the custom of the Jews when they heard or read that which they thought blasphemous; and what less could it be than to attribute to him a divine power? "*Am I a God, to kill* whom I will, and *make alive* whom I will? No, I pretend not to such an authority." 2. A bad design upon himself. He appeals to those about him for this: "*See how he seeketh a quarrel against me;* he requires me to recover the leper, and if I do not, though I cannot, he will make that a pretence to wage war with me," which he suspects the rather because Naaman is his general. If he had bethought himself of Elisha, and his power, he would easily have understood the letter, and have known what he had to do.

V. The proffer which Elisha made of his services. Hearing on what occasion the king had rent his clothes, he sent to him to let him know that if his patient would come to him he should not lose his labour (*v.* 8): *He shall know that there is a prophet in Israel* who can do that which the king of Israel dares not attempt, which the prophets of Syria cannot pretend to.

Verses 9–14

The cure of Naaman's leprosy.

I. The short and plain direction which the prophet gave him, with assurance of success. Naaman, with all his retinue, attended at Elisha's door as a beggar for an alms. Naaman expected to have his compliment returned, but Elisha gave him his answer without any formality, would not go to the door to him, lest he should seem too much pleased with the honour done him, but sent a messenger to him, saying, *Go wash in Jordan seven times,* and promising him that if he did so his disease should be cured. The promise was express: *Thou shalt be clean.* The method prescribed was plain: *Go wash in Jordan.* It was intended as a sign of the cure, and a trial of his obedience. Those that will be helped of God must do as they are bidden.

II. Naaman's disgust at the method prescribed, because it was not what he expected. Two things disgusted him:

1. That Elisha, as he thought, put a slight upon his person, in sending him orders by a servant, and not coming to him himself, *v.* 11. Being big with the expectation of a cure, he had been fancying how this cure would be wrought: "*He will surely come out to me,* that is the least he can do to me, a peer of Syria, to me that have so often been victorious over Israel. *He will stand,* and *call on the name of his God,* and name me in his prayer, and then he will *wave his hand over the place,* and so effect the cure." And, because the thing was not done just thus, he fell into a passion. He scorns to be healed, unless he be humoured.

2. That Elisha, as he thought, put a slight upon his country. He took it hard that he must be sent to wash in Jordan, a river of Israel, when he thought *Abana and Pharpar, rivers of Damascus, better than all the waters of Israel. May I not wash in them and be clean?* He might wash in them and be clean from dirt, but not wash in them and be clean from leprosy. Jordan was the river appointed, and, if he expected a cure from the divine power, he ought to acquiesce in the divine will, without asking why or wherefore. Naaman talked himself into such a heat (as passionate men usually do) that he turned away from the prophet's door in a rage, ready to swear he would never have anything more to say to Elisha; and who then would be the loser?

III. The modest advice which his servants gave him, to observe the prophet's prescriptions, with a tacit reproof of his resentments, *v.* 13. "*If the prophet had bidden thee do some great thing,* had ordered thee into a tedious course of physic, *Wouldst thou not have done it?* No doubt thou wouldst. And wilt thou not submit to so easy a method as this, *Wash and be clean?*" The reproof was very modest and respectful, very rational and considerate. If the servants had stirred up their master's angry resentment, and offered to avenge his quarrel upon the prophet, how mischievous would the consequences have been! They reasoned with him, (1) From his earnest desire of a cure: *Wouldst thou not do* anything? Note, When diseased sinners come to this, that they are content to do anything, to submit to anything, to part with anything, for a cure, then, and not till then, there begin to be some hopes of them. Then they will take Christ on his own terms when they are made willing to have Christ upon any terms. (2) From the easiness of the method prescribed: *Wash and be clean.* Note, The methods prescribed for the healing of the leprosy of sin are so plain that we are utterly inexcusable if we do not observe them. It is but, "Believe, and be saved"—"Repent, and be pardoned" —"Wash, and be clean."

IV. The cure effected, in the use of the means prescribed, *v.* 14. Naaman, upon second thoughts, yielded to make the experiment. *His flesh came again, like the flesh of a child,* to his great surprise and joy.

Verses 15–19

Of the ten lepers that our Saviour cleansed, the only one that *returned to give thanks* was a *Samaritan,* Luke xvii. 16. This Syrian did so, and here expresses himself.

I. Convinced of the power of the God of Israel, not only that he is God, but that he is God alone, and that indeed *there is no God in all the earth but in Israel* (*v.* 15). Had he seen other lepers cleansed, perhaps the sight would not have convinced him, but the mercy of the cure affected him more than the miracle of it. Those are best able to speak of the power of divine grace who have themselves experienced it.

II. Grateful to Elisha the prophet: "Therefore, for his sake whose servant thou art, I have a present for thee, silver, and gold, and raiment, whatever thou wilt please to accept." But Elisha generously refused the fee, not because he did not need it, for he was poor enough, but he would not be beholden to this Syrian. It would be much for the honour of God to show this new convert that the servants of the God of Israel were taught to look upon the wealth of this world with a holy contempt, which would confirm him in his belief that *there was no God but in Israel.* See 1 Cor. ix. 18; 2 Cor. xi. 9.

III. Proselyted to the worship of the God of Israel. He will not only offer a sacrifice to the Lord, in thanks for his present cure, but he resolves he will never offer sacrifice to any other gods, *v.* 17. It was a happy cure of his leprosy which cured him of his idolatry, a more dangerous disease. But, 1. In one instance he over-did it, that he would not only worship the God of Israel, but he would have clods of earth out of the prophet's garden to *make an altar of, v.* 17. He that awhile ago had spoken very slightingly of the waters of Israel (*v.* 12) now is in another extreme, and over-values the earth of Israel, supposing that an altar of that earth would be most acceptable to him. 2. In another instance he under-did it, that he reserved to himself a liberty to bow in the house of Rimmon, in complaisance to the king his master, and according to the duty of his place at court (*v.* 18), *in this thing* he must be excused. If, in covenanting with God, we make a reservation for any known sin, which we will continue to indulge ourselves in, that reservation is a defeasance of his covenant. We must cast away all our transgressions and not except any house of Rimmon. If we ask for a dispensation to go on in any sin for the future, we mock God, and deceive ourselves.

Verses 20–27

Elisha, a holy prophet, a man of God, has but one servant, and he proves a base fellow. One would have expected that Elisha's servant should be a saint (even Ahab's servant, Obadiah, was), but even Christ himself had a Judas among his followers.

I. Gehazi's sin. 1. The love of money, that root of all evil, was at the bottom of it. His master contemned Naaman's treasures, but he coveted them, *v.* 20. His heart (says Bishop Hall) was packed up in Naaman's chests, and he must run after him to fetch it. 2. He blamed his master for refusing Naaman's present, envied and grudged his kindness and generosity to this stranger. 3. When Naaman alighted from his chariot to meet him (*v.* 21), he told him a deliberate lie, that his master sent him to him. 4. He abused his master, and basely misrepresented him to Naaman as one that had soon repented of his generosity. His story of the two sons of the prophets was as silly as it was false; if he would have begged a token for two young scholars, surely less than a talent of silver might serve them. 5. There was danger of his alienating Naaman from that holy religion which he had espoused, and lessening his good opinion of it. 6. His seeking to conceal what he had unjustly got added much to his sin. He hid it, till he should have an opportunity of laying it out, *v.* 24. He denied it: He *went in, and stood before his master*, ready to receive his orders. His master asked him where he had been. "Nowhere, sir" (said he), "out of the house."

II. The punishment of this sin. Elisha immediately called him to an account for it.

1. How he was convicted. He thought to impose upon the prophet, but was soon given to understand that the Spirit of prophecy could not be deceived, and that it was in vain to lie to the Holy Ghost. Elisha could tell him, (1) What he had done, though he had denied it. "Thou sayest thou wentest nowhere, but *went not my heart with thee?*" *v.* 26. (2) What he designed, though he kept that in his own breast. He could tell him the very thoughts and intents of his heart, that he was projecting, now that he had got these two talents, to purchase ground and cattle, to leave Elisha's service, and to set up for himself. "*Is it a time to receive money?* Is this an opportunity of enriching thyself? Couldst thou find no better way of getting money than by belying thy master and laying a stumbling-block before a young convert?"

2. How he was punished for it: *The leprosy of Naaman shall cleave to thee, v.* 27. He *went out from his presence a leper as white as snow.* Thus he is stigmatised and made infamous, and carries the mark of his shame wherever he goes. What was Gehazi profited, though he gained his two talents, when thereby he lost his health, his honour, his peace, his service, and, if repentance prevented not, his soul for ever? See Job xx. 12, &c.

CHAPTER 6

I. A further account of the wondrous works of Elisha. 1. His making iron to swim, ver. 1–7. 2. His disclosing to the king of Israel the secret counsels of the king of Syria, ver. 8–12. 3. His saving himself out of the hands of those who were sent to apprehend him, ver. 13–23. II. The besieging of Samaria by the Syrians and the great distress the city was reduced to, ver. 24–33.

Verses 1–7

1. Concerning the sons of the prophets, and their condition and character. The college here spoken of seems to be that at Gilgal, and it was near Jordan; and, probably, wherever Elisha resided as many as could of the sons of the prophets flocked to him for the advantage of his instructions, counsels, and prayers. Everyone would covet to dwell with him and be near him.

1. Their number increased so that they wanted room: *The place is too strait for us* (*v.* 1)—a good hearing, for it is a sign many are added to them. Elisha's miracles doubtless drew in many.

2. They were humble men. It becomes the sons of the prophets, who profess to look for great things in the other world, to be content with mean things in this.

3. They were poor men. Poverty is no bar to prophecy.

4. They were industrious men, and willing to take pains. Let no man think an honest employment either a burden or disparagement.

5. They were men that had a great value and veneration for Elisha. (1) They would not go about to build at all without his leave, *v.* 2. (2) They would not willingly go to fell timber without his company: "*Go with thy servants*" (*v.* 3). Good disciples desire to be always under good discipline.

6. They were honest men, and men that were in care to give all men their own. When one of them, accidentally fetching too fierce a stroke, threw off his axe-head into the water, he cries out with deep concern, *Alas, master! For it was borrowed, v.* 5. It is likely this prophet was poor, and had not wherewithal to pay for the axe, which made the loss of it so much the greater trouble.

II. Concerning the father of the prophets, Elisha. 1. That he was a man of great condescension and compassion; he went with the sons of the prophets to the woods, when they desired his company, *v.* 3. 2. That he was a man of great power; he could make iron to swim, contrary to its nature (*v.* 6). God's grace can thus raise the stony iron heart which has sunk into the mud of this world, and raise up affections naturally earthly, to things above.

Verses 8–12

Here we have Elisha, with his spirit of prophecy, serving the king, as before helping the sons of the prophets.

I. How the king of Israel was informed by Elisha of all the designs of his enemy, the king of Syria, *v.* 8–10. 1. The enemies of God's Israel are politic in their devices, and restless in their attempts, against him. 2. All those devices are known to God, even those that are deepest laid. He knows not only what men do, but what they design, and has many ways of countermining them. 3. It is a great advantage to us to be warned of our danger, that we may stand upon our guard against it. The work of God's prophets is to give us warning. The king of Israel would regard the warnings Elisha gave him of his danger by the Syrians, but not the warnings he gave him of his danger by his sins.

II. How the king of Syria resented this. He suspected treachery among his senators, and that his counsels were betrayed, *v.* 11. But one of his servants, that had heard, by Naaman and others, of Elisha's wondrous works, concludes it must needs be that gave this intelligence to the king of Israel, *v.* 12.

Verses 13–23

I. The great force which the king of Syria sent to seize Elisha. He found out where he was, at Dothan (*v.* 13), which was not far from Samaria; thither he sent a great host, who were to come upon him by night, and to bring him dead or alive, *v.* 14. Thus he hoped to make sure of him, especially coming upon him by surprise.

II. The grievous fright which the prophet's servant was in, when he perceived the city surrounded by the

Syrians, and the effectual course which the prophet took to pacify him and free him from his fears. 1. What a consternation he was in. He ran straight to Elisha, to bring him an account of it: "*Alas, master!*" (said he), "*what shall we do? We are undone:* it is to no purpose to think either of fighting or flying, we must fall into their hands." Had he considered that he was embarked with his master, by whom God had done great things, and whom he would not now leave to *fall into the hands of the uncircumcised,* he would not have been thus at a loss. If he had only said, *What shall I do?* it would have been the more excusable. 2. How his master quieted him, (1) By word. What he said to him (*v.* 16) is spoken to all the faithful servants of God, when *without are fightings and within are fears:* "*Fear not* with that fear which has torment and amazement, *for those that are with us,* to protect us, *are more than those that are against us,* to destroy us—angels unspeakably more numerous—God infinitely more powerful." When we are magnifying the causes of our fear we ought to possess ourselves with clear, and great, and high thoughts of God and the invisible world. *If God be for us,* we know what follows, Rom. viii. 31. (2) By vision, *v.* 17. [1] It seems Elisha was much concerned for the satisfaction of his servant, newly come into his service. [2] He saw himself safe, and wished no more than that his servant might see what he saw, a guard of angels round about him. [3] For the satisfaction of his servant there needed no more than the opening of his eyes; *that* therefore he prayed for, and obtained for him: *Lord, open his eyes that he may see.* The eyes of his body were open, and with them he saw the danger. "Lord, open the eyes of his faith, that with them he may see the protection we are under." The opening of our eyes will be the silencing of our fears. In the dark we are most apt to be frightened. The clearer sight we have of the sovereignty and power of heaven the less we shall fear the calamities of this earth.

III. The shameful defeat which Elisha gave to the host of Syrians who came to seize him. 1. He prayed to God to smite them with blindness, and they were all struck blind, immediately, not stone-blind, but their sight was so altered that they could not know the persons and places they were before acquainted with, *v.* 18. They were so confounded that those among them whom they depended upon for information did not know this place to be Dothan nor this person to be Elisha, but *groped at noon day as in the night.* 2. When they were thus bewildered and confounded he led them to Samaria (*v.* 19), promising that he would show them the man whom they sought, and he did so. He did not lie to them when he told them, *This is not the way, nor is this the city* where Elisha is; for he had now come out of the city. 3. When he had brought them to Samaria he prayed to God so to open their eyes that they might see where they were (*v.* 20), *and behold,* to their great terror, *they were in the midst of Samaria,* where, it is probable, there was a standing force sufficient to cut them all off, or make them prisoners of war. 4. When he had them at his mercy he made it appear that he was influenced by a divine goodness as well as a divine power. (1) He took care to protect them from the danger into which he had brought them, and was content to show them what he could have done: *My father shall I smite them?* And, again, as if he longed for the assault, *Shall I smite them?* But the prophet would by no means suffer him to meddle with them; they were brought hither to be convinced and shamed, not to be killed, *v.* 22. They were not his prisoners; they were God's prisoners and the prophet's, and therefore he must do them no harm. (2) He took care to provide for them; he ordered the

king to treat them handsomely and then dismiss them fairly, which he did, *v.* 23. [1] It was the king's praise that he was so obsequious to the prophet, contrary to his inclination, and, as it seemed, to his interest, 1 Sam. xxiv. 19. So willing was he to oblige Elisha that he *prepared great provision* for them, for the credit of his court and the country and of Elisha. [2] It was the prophet's praise that he was so generous to his enemies. The great duty of loving enemies, and doing good to those that hate us, was both commanded in the Old Testament (Prov. xxv. 21, 22, *If thy enemy hunger, feed him,* Exod. xxiii. 4, 5) and practised, as here by Elisha.

IV. The good effect this had, for the present, upon the Syrians. They *came no more into the land of Israel* (*v.* 23). The most glorious victory over an enemy is to turn him into a friend.

Verses 24-33

This last paragraph of this chapter begins a new story.

I. The siege which the king of Syria laid to Samaria. The Syrians had soon forgotten the kindnesses they had lately received in Samaria, and without any provocation, sought the destruction of it, *v.* 24. The country was plundered and laid waste when this capital city was brought to the last extremity, *v.* 25. The dearth which had of late been in the land was probably the occasion of the emptiness of their stores, so that, while the sword devoured without, the famine within was more grievous , for the Syrians designed not to storm the city, but to starve it. So great was the scarcity that an ass's head was sold for five pounds, and a small quantity of coarse corn, then called *dove's dung,* no more of it than the quantity of six eggs, for five pieces of silver. How contemptible money is, when, in time of famine, it is so freely parted with for anything that is eatable.

II. The sad complaint which a poor woman had to make to the king, in the extremity of the famine. He was *passing by upon the wall* to give orders for the mounting of the guard, when a woman of the city cried to him, *Help, my lord, O king!* v. 26. He returns but a melancholy answer (*v.* 27): *If the Lord do not help thee, whence shall I?* Some think it was a *quarrelling* word, but it rather seems to be a *quieting* word: "Let us be content, and make the best of our affliction, looking up to God, for, till he help us, I cannot help thee." 1. He laments the emptiness of the floor and the wine-press. 2. He acknowledges himself disabled to help, unless God would help them. However, though he cannot help her, he is willing to hear her (*v.* 28): "*What ails thee?* Is there anything singular in thy case, or dost thou fare worse than thy neighbours?" Truly yes; she and one of her neighbours had made a barbarous agreement, that, all provisions failing, they should boil and eat her son first and then her neighbour's; hers was eaten and now her neighbour hid hers, *v.* 28, 29.

III. The king's indignation against Elisha upon this occasion. He lamented the calamity, *rent his clothes, and had sackcloth upon his flesh* (*v.* 30), as one heartily concerned for the misery of his people, and that it was not in his power to help them; but he did not lament his own iniquity, nor the iniquity of his people. Instead of vowing to pull down the calves at Dan and Beth-el, he swears *the death of Elisha,* v. 31. Why? What has Elisha done? His head is the most innocent and valuable in all Israel. Thus in the days of the persecuting emperors, when the empire groaned under any extraordinary calamity, the fault was laid on the Christians, and they were doomed to destruction. *Christianos ad leones—Away with the Christians to the lions.*

IV. The foresight Elisha had of the king's design against him, *v.* 32. He sat in his house well composed, and the elders with him. He told the elders there was an officer coming from the king to cut off his head, and bade them stop him at the door, for the king his master was just following him, to revoke the order.

V. The king's passionate speech, when he came to prevent the execution of his edict for the beheading of Elisha. He seems to have been in a struggle between his convictions and his corruptions.

CHAPTER 7

Relief is here brought to Samaria and her king. I. It is foretold by Elisha, and an unbelieving lord shut out from the benefit of it, ver. 1, 2. II. It is brought about, 1. By an unaccountable fright into which God put the Syrians (ver. 6), which caused them to retire precipitately, ver. 7. 2. By the seasonable discovery which four lepers made of this (ver. 3–5), and the account which they gave of it to the court, ver. 8–11. 3. By the cautious trial which the king made of the truth of it, ver. 12–15. III. The event answered the prediction both in the sudden plenty (ver. 16), and the death of the unbelieving lord (ver. 17–20).

Verses 1–2

I. Elisha foretells that within twenty-four hours they shall have plenty, v. 1. The king of Israel despaired of it and grew weary of waiting: then Elisha foretold it, when things were at the worst. Man's extremity is God's opportunity of magnifying his own power; his time to appear for his people is when *their strength is gone*, Deut. xxxii. 36. The king said, *Why shall I wait for the Lord any longer?* "Well," said Elisha, "*now hear you the word of the Lord*, hear what he says: tomorrow corn shall be sold at the usual rate in the gate of Samaria." 2. The consequence of that shall be great plenty. This would, in time, follow of course, but that corn should be thus cheap in so short a time was quite beyond what could be thought of.

II. A peer of Israel that happened to be present openly declared his disbelief of this prediction, v. 2. He was a courtier whom the king had an affection for, on whom the king leaned, and in whom he reposed much confidence.

III. The just doom passed upon him for his infidelity, that he should see this great plenty for his conviction, and yet not eat of it to his comfort.

Verses 3–11

I. How the siege of Samaria was raised in the evening, at the edge of night (v. 6, 7), not by might or power, but by the Spirit of the Lord of hosts, striking terror upon the spirits of the besiegers. Here was not a sword drawn against them, but, 1. *The Lord made them to hear a noise of chariots and horses.* The Syrians that besieged Dothan had their *sight* imposed upon, *ch.* vi. 18. These had their *hearing* imposed upon. Whether the noise was really made in the air by the ministry of angels, or whether it was only a sound in their ears, is not certain; whichsoever it was, it was from God, who both *brings the wind out of his treasures*, and *forms the spirit of man within him*. Notices from the invisible world are either very comfortable or very dreadful, according as men are at peace with God or at war with him. 2. Hearing this noise, they concluded the king of Israel had certainly procured assistance from some foreign power: *He has hired against us the kings of the Hittites and the kings of the Egyptians.* 3. Hereupon they all fled with incredible precipitation, as for their lives, left their camp as it was: even their horses, that might have hastened their flight, they could not stay to take with them, v. 7. Those that will not fear God he can make to fear at the shaking of a leaf.

II. How the Syrians' flight was discovered by four leprous men. Samaria was delivered, and did not know it. The watchmen on the walls were not aware of the retreat of the enemy, so silently did they steal

away. But Providence employed four lepers to be the intelligencers, who had their lodging without the gate, being excluded from the city, as ceremonially unclean: the Jews say they were Gehazi and his three sons. 1. How these lepers reasoned themselves into a resolution to make a visit in the night to the camp of the Syrians, v. 3, 4. They were ready to perish for hunger; none passed through the gate to relieve them. They therefore determine to go over to the enemy, and throw themselves upon their mercy: perhaps they would save them alive, as objects of compassion. According to this resolution, they went, in the beginning of the night, to the camp of the Syrians, and, to their great surprise, found it wholly deserted, not a man to be seen or heard in it, v. 5. 2. How they reasoned themselves into a resolution to bring tidings of this to the city. They feasted in the first tent they came to (v. 8) and then began to think of enriching themselves with the plunder; but they corrected themselves (v. 9): "*We do not well to conceal these good tidings from the community we are members of, therefore let us bring them the news.* Though it awake them from sleep, it will be *life from the dead* to them." According to this resolution, they returned to the gate, and acquainted the sentinel with what they had discovered (v. 10), who straightway brought the intelligence to court (v. 11), and it was not the less acceptable for being first brought by lepers.

Verses 12–20

I. The king's jealousy of a stratagem in the Syrian's retreat, v. 12. He feared that they had withdrawn into an ambush, to draw out the besieged, that they might fall on them with more advantage.

II. The course they took to prevent their falling into a snare. They sent out spies to see what had become of the Syrians, and found they had all fled indeed, commanders as well as common soldiers. They could track them by the garments, which they threw off, and left by the way, for their greater expedition, v. 15. He that gave this advice seems to have been very sensible of the deplorable condition the people were in (v. 13). He advised to send five horsemen, but, it should seem, there were only two horses fit to be sent, and those chariot-horses, v. 14.

III. The plenty that was in Samaria, from the plunder of the camp of the Syrians, v. 16. God determined that the besieging of Samaria, which was intended for its ruin, should turn to its advantage, and that Israel should now be enriched with the spoil of the Syrians as of old with that of the Egyptians. The word of Elisha fulfilled to a tittle: *A measure of fine flour was sold for a shekel;* those that spoiled the camp had not only enough to supply themselves with, but an overplus to sell at an easy rate for the benefit of others, and so even *those that tarried at home did divide the spoil*, Ps. lxviii. 12; Isa. xxxiii. 23.

IV. The death of the unbelieving courtier, that questioned the truth of Elisha's word. This lord, 1. Was preferred by the king to the *charge of the gate* (v. 17), to keep the peace, and to see that there was no tumult or disorder in dividing and disposing of the spoil. 2. Was trodden to death by the people in the gate, either by accident, the crowd being exceedingly great, or perhaps designedly, because he abused his power. However it was, God's justice was glorified, and the word of Elisha was fulfilled. He saw the plenty, corn cheap without *opening windows in heaven*, and therein saw his own folly in prescribing to God; but he did not eat of the plenty he saw. This event is compared with the prediction (v. 18–20), that we might take special notice of it, and might learn, (1) How deeply God resents our distrust of him, of his power, providence, and promise. (2) How uncertain life and the enjoyments of it are. Honour and power cannot secure men from sudden and inglorious deaths. He whom the king leaned upon the people trod upon.

CHAPTER 8

The passages of story recorded in this chapter oblige us to look back. I. We read before of a Shunammite woman that was a kind benefactor to Elisha; now here we are told how she fared the better for it, afterwards, in the advice Elisha gave her, and the favour the king showed her for his sake, ver. 1–6. II. We read before of the designation of Hazael to be king of Syria (1 Kings xix. 15), and here we have an account of his elevation to that throne by killing his master, ver. 7–15. III. We read before of Jehoram's reigning over Judah in the room of his father Jehoshaphat (1 Kings xxii. 50), now here we have a short and sad history of his short and wicked reign (ver. 16–24), and the beginning of the history of the reign of his son Ahaziah, ver. 25–29.

Verses 1–6

I. The wickedness of Israel punished with a long famine, one of God's sore judgments often threatened in the law. The famine in Samaria was soon relieved by the raising of the siege, but neither that judgment nor that mercy had a due influence upon them. If less judgments do not prevail to bring men to repentance, he will send greater and longer. This famine continued seven years, as long again as that in Elijah's time; for, if men will walk contrary to him, he will heat the furnace yet hotter.

II. The kindness of the good Shunammite to the prophet rewarded by the care that was taken of her in that famine. 1. She had notice given her of this famine before it came, that she might provide accordingly, and was directed to remove to some other country; anywhere but in Israel she would find plenty. 2. Providence gave her a comfortable settlement in *the land of the Philistines*, who, though subdued by David, yet were not wholly rooted out. It seems the famine was peculiar to the land of Israel, and other countries that joined close to them had plenty at the same time, which plainly showed the immediate hand of God in it.

III. Her petition to the king at her return, favoured by the seasonableness of her application to him. 1. When the famine was over she *returned out of the land of the Philistines*. 2. At her return she found herself kept out of the possession of her own estate, it being either confiscated to the exchequer, or usurped in her absence by some of the neighbours. 3. She made her application to the king himself for redress. 4. She found the king talking with Gehazi about Elisha's miracles, *v.* 4. The law did not forbid all conversation with lepers, but only dwelling with them. There being then no priests in Israel, perhaps the king, or someone appointed by him, had the inspection of lepers, and passed the judgment upon them, which might bring him acquainted with Gehazi. 5. This happy coincidence befriended both Gehazi's narrative and her petition. (1) It made the king ready to believe Gehazi's narrative when it was thus confirmed by the persons most nearly concerned: "*This is the woman, and this her son;* let them speak for themselves," *v.* 5. (2) It made him ready to grant her request; for who would not be ready to favour one whom heaven had thus favoured, and to support a life which was given once and again by miracle? In consideration of this the king gave orders that her land should be restored to her and all the profits that were made of it in her absence. It is not enough for those in authority that they do no wrong themselves, but they must support the right of those that are wronged.

Verses 7–15

I. We may enquire what brought Elisha to Damascus, the chief city of Syria. Perhaps he went to pay a visit to Naaman his convert, and to confirm him in his choice of the true religion, which was the more needful now because he was now out of his place (for Hazael is supposed to be captain of the host); either

he resigned it or was turned out of it, because he would not bow heartily, in the house of Rimmon. Some think he went to Damascus upon account of the famine, or rather he went thither in obedience to the orders God gave Elijah, 1 Kings xix. 15, "*Go to Damascus to anoint Hazael*, thou, or thy successor."

II. We may observe that Benhadad, a great king, rich and mighty, lay sick. No honour, wealth, or power, will secure men from the common diseases and disasters of human life; palaces and thrones lie as open to sickness and death as the meanest cottage.

III. We may wonder that the king of Syria, in his sickness, should make Elisha his oracle.

1. Notice was soon brought him that *the man of God* (for by that title he was well known in Syria since he cured Naaman) had come to Damascus, *v.* 7. "Never in better time," says Benhadad. "*Go, and enquire of the Lord by him.*" In his health he *bowed in the house of Rimmon*, but now that he is sick he distrusts his idol, and sends to enquire of the God of Israel. This is the more observable, (1) Because it was not long since a king of Israel had, in his sickness, sent to enquire of the god of Ekron (*ch.* i. 2), as if there had been no God in Israel. (2) Because it was not long since this Benhadad had sent a great force to treat Elisha as an enemy (*ch.* vi. 14), yet now he courts him as a prophet.

2. To put an honour upon the prophet, (1) He sends *to* him, and does not send *for* him, as if, with the centurion, he thought himself not worthy that the man of God should come under his roof. (2) He sends to him by Hazael, his prime-minister of state, and not by a common messenger. (3) He sends him a noble present, *of every good thing of Damascus*, as much as loaded forty camels (*v.* 9), bidding him welcome to Damascus. It is probable that Elisha accepted it, though he refused Naaman's. (4) He orders Hazael to call him *his son Ben-hadad*, conforming to the language of Israel, who called the prophets *fathers*. (5) He puts an honour upon him as one acquainted with the secrets of heaven, when he enquires of him, *Shall I recover?*

IV. What passed between Hazael and Elisha is especially remarkable.

1. Elisha answered his enquiry concerning the king, that he might recover, the disease was not mortal, but that he should die another way (*v.* 10), not a natural but a violent death.

2. He looked Hazael in the face with an unusual concern, till he made Hazael blush and himself weep, *v.* 11.

3. When Hazael asked him why he wept he told him what a great deal of mischief he foresaw he would do to the Israel of God (*v.* 12). Elisha wept to think that ever Israelites should be thus abused. See what havoc war makes, what havoc sin makes, and how the nature of man is changed by the fall, and stripped even of humanity itself.

4. Hazael was greatly surprised at this prediction (*v.* 13): *What*, says he, *Is thy servant a dog, that he should do this great thing?* This great thing he looks upon to be, (1) An act of great power, not to be done but by a crowned head. (2) An act of great barbarity, which could not be done but by one lost to all honour and virtue. It is possible for a wicked man, under the convictions and restraints of natural conscience, to express great abhorrence of a sin, and yet afterwards to be well reconciled to it.

5. In answer to this Elisha only told him *he should be king over Syria*; then he would have power to do it, and then he would find in his heart to do it.

V. What mischief Hazael did to his master hereupon. 1. He basely cheated his master, and belied the prophet (*v.* 14): *He told me thou shouldst certainly recover.* This was an injury to the king, who lost the benefit of this warning to prepare for death and an injury to Elisha, who would be counted a false prophet. 2. He barbarously murdered his master, and so made good the prophet's word, *v.* 15. He dipped a thick cloth in cold water, and stifled him. Hazael, who was Benhadad's confidant, was his murderer, and, some think, was not suspected, nor did the truth ever come out but by the pen of this inspired historian.

Verses 16–24

A brief account of the life and reign of Jehoram, one of the worst of the kings of Judah, but the son and successor of Jehoshaphat, one of the best. A nation is sometimes justly punished with the miseries of a bad reign for not improving the blessings and advantages of a good one.

Concerning Jehoram,

I. The general idea here given of his wickedness (*v.* 18): *He did as the house of Ahab,* and worse he could not do. Jehoram chose the house of Ahab for his pattern rather than his father's house, and this choice was his ruin.

II. The occasions of his wickedness. His father was a very good man, and no doubt took care to have him taught the good knowledge of the Lord, but, 1. It is certain he did ill to marry him to the daughter of Ahab. Those that are ill-matched are already half-ruined. 2. He did not do well to make him king in his own life-time. It is said here (*v.* 16) that he *began to reign, Jehoshaphat being then king;* hereby he gratified his pride. Jehoshaphat had made this wicked son of his viceroy once, when he went with Ahab to Ramoth-Gilead, from which Jehoshaphat's seventeenth year (1 Kings xxii. 51) is made Jehoram's second (2 Kings i. 17), but afterwards, in his twenty-second year, he made him partner in his government. It has been hurtful to many young men to come too soon to their estates. Samuel got nothing by *making his sons judges.*

III. The rebukes of Providence which he was under for his wickedness. 1. The Edomites revolted, who had been under the government of the kings of Judah ever since David's time, about 150 years, *v.* 20. He attempted to reduce them, and gave them a defeat (*v.* 21), but he could not recover his dominion over them: *Yet Edom revolted* (*v.* 22), and the Edomites were, after this, bitter enemies to the Jews, as appears by the prophecy of Obadiah and Ps. cxxxvii. 7. 2. Libnah revolted. This was a city in Judah, in the heart of his country, a priests' city; the inhabitants of this city shook off his government *because he had forsaken God,* and would have compelled them to do so too, 2 Chron. xxi. 10, 11. In order that they might preserve their religion they set up for a free state. 3. His reign was short. God cut him off in the midst of his days, when he was but forty years old, and had reigned but eight years.

IV. The gracious care of Providence for the keeping up of the kingdom of Judah, and the house of David, notwithstanding the apostasies and calamities of Jehoram's reign (*v.* 19): *Yet the Lord would not destroy Judah.*

V. The conclusion of this impious and inglorious reign, *v.* 23, 24. Nothing peculiar is here said of him; but we are told (2 Chron. xxi. 19, 20) that he *died of sore diseases* and *died without being desired.*

Verses 25–29

As among common persons there are some that we call *little men,* who make no figure, are little regarded, and less valued, so among kings there are some whom, in comparison with others, we may call *little kings.* This Ahaziah was one of these; he looks mean in the history, and in God's account vile, because wicked. Jehoshaphat and Ahab had the same names in their families at the same time, in which they designed to compliment one another. Ahab had two sons, Ahaziah and Jehoram, who reigned successively; Jehoshaphat had a son and grandson named Jehoram and Ahaziah, who, in like manner, reigned successively. Ahaziah king of Israel had reigned but two years, Ahaziah king of Judah reigned but one. We are here told that his relation to Ahab's family was the occasion, 1. Of his wickedness (*v.* 27): *He walked in the way of the house of Ahab,* that idolatrous bloody house: for his mother was Ahab's daughter (*v.* 26). When men choose wives for themselves they must remember they are choosing mothers for their children, and are concerned to choose accordingly. 2. Of his fall. Joram, his mother's brother, courted him to join with him for the recovery of Ramoth-Gilead, an attempt fatal to Ahab; so it was to Joram his son, for in that expedition he was wounded (*v.* 28), and returned to Jezreel to be cured, leaving his army there in possession of the place. Ahaziah likewise returned, but went to Jezreel to see how Jehoram did, *v.* 29.

CHAPTER 9

Hazael and Jehu were designed to be the instruments of God's justice in destroying the house of Ahab. Elijah was told to appoint them to this service; but, upon Ahab's humiliation, a reprieve was granted, and so it was left to Elisha to appoint them. Hazael's elevation to the throne of Syria we read of in the foregoing chapter; and we must now attend Jehu to the throne of Israel; for him that escapeth the sword of Hazael, as Joram and Ahaziah did, Jehu must slay. I. A commission is sent to Jehu by the hand of one of the prophets, to take upon him the government, and destroy the house of Ahab, ver. 1–10. II. His speedy execution of this commission. 1. He communicates it to his captains, ver. 11–15. 2. He marches directly to Jezreel (ver. 16–20), and there dispatches, (1) Joram king of Israel, ver. 21–26. (2) Ahaziah king of Judah, ver. 27–29. (3) Jezebel, ver. 30–37.

Verses 1–10

The anointing of Jehu to be king. It does not appear that Jehu aimed at the government. Some think that he had been anointed before by Elijah, whom God ordered to do it, but privately, and with an intimation that he must not act till further orders, as Samuel anointed David long before he was to come to the throne: but that is not at all probable, for then we must suppose Elijah had anointed Hazael too.

I. The commission sent.

1. Elisha did not go himself to anoint Jehu, because he was old and unfit for such a journey and so well known that he could not do it privately, therefore he sends *one of the sons of the prophets* to do it, *v.* 1.

2. When he sent him, (1) He put the oil into his hand with which he must anoint Jehu: *Take this box of oil.* Solomon was anointed with *oil out of the tabernacle,* 1 Kings i. 39. That could not now be had, but oil from a prophet's hand was equivalent to oil out of God's house. (2) He put the words into his mouth which he must say (*v.* 3)—*I have anointed thee king, v.* 7–10. (3) He also ordered him, [1] To do it privately, to single out Jehu from the rest of the captains and anoint him *in an inner chamber* (*v.* 2). [2] To do it expeditiously. When he had done it he must *flee and not tarry.*

II. The commission delivered. The young prophet did his business with despatch, was at Ramoth-Gilead presently, *v.* 4. There he found the general officers in a council of war, *v.* 5. With the assurance that became a messenger from God, he called Jehu out from the rest as one having authority: *I have an errand to thee, O captain.* Perhaps Jehu had some intimation of his business; and therefore, that he might not seem too forward to catch at the honour, he asked, *To which of all us?* When the prophet had him alone he anointed him, *v.* 6.

1. He invests him with the royal dignity: *Thus saith the Lord God of Israel*, whose messenger I am, in his name *I have anointed thee king over the people of the Lord*. He reminds him that he was made king, (1) *By the God of Israel*; from him he must see his power derived, for him he must use it, and to him he must be accountable. (2) *Over the Israel of God*. Though the people of Israel had forfeited all the honour of relationship to God, yet they are here called the *people of the Lord*, for he had a right to them. Jehu must look upon the people he was made king of as the *people of the Lord*, God's freemen, not to be abused or tyrannised over, *God's people*, and therefore to be ruled for him, and according to his laws.

2. He instructs him in his present service, which was to destroy all the house of Ahab (*v.* 7), not that he might clear his own way to the throne, but that he might execute the judgments of God upon that guilty and obnoxious family. He calls Ahab his *master*: "But thou art under higher obligations to thy Master in heaven than to thy master Ahab. He has determined that *the whole house of Ahab shall perish*, and *by thy hand*; fear not danger; his command will secure and prosper thee." That he might intelligently do this execution on the house of Ahab, he tells him, (1) What was their crime. That they were idolaters was bad enough, but the controversy God has with them is for their being persecutors, not so much their *throwing down God's altars* as their *slaying his prophets with the sword*. This was the sin that brought on Jerusalem its first destruction (2 Chron. xxxvi. 16) and its final one, Matt. xxiii. 37, 38. Jezebel's whoredoms and witchcrafts were not so provoking as her persecuting the prophets, killing some and driving the rest into corners and caves, 1 Kings xviii. 4. (2) What was their doom. They were sentenced to utter destruction; and he is particularly directed to throw Jezebel to the dogs, *v.* 10.

Verses 11–15

Jehu, after some pause, returned to his place at the board, taking no notice of what had passed, but, as it should seem, designing, for the present, to keep it to himself.

I. With what contempt the captains speak of the young prophet (*v.* 11): "*Wherefore came this mad fellow to thee?* What business had he with thee?" They thought the prophets were fools and the *spiritual men were mad*, Hos. ix. 7. Those that have no religion commonly speak with disdain of those that are religious, and look upon them as mad. They said of our Saviour, *He is beside himself*, of John Baptist, *He has a devil*, of St. Paul, *Much learning has made him mad*. The highest wisdom is thus represented as folly, and those that best understand themselves are looked upon as beside themselves. Perhaps Jehu intended it for a rebuke to his friends when he said, "*You know the man* to be a prophet, why then do you call him a mad fellow?" Thus he thought to put them off, but they urged him to tell them. "It is false," say they, "we cannot conjecture what was his errand, and therefore tell us." Being thus pressed to it, he told them that the prophet had *anointed him king*, and it is probable showed them the oil upon his head, *v.* 12.

II. With what respect they compliment the new king upon the first notice of his advancement, *v.* 13. In token of their subjection and allegiance to him, they put their garments under him, that he might stand *on the top of the stairs*, in sight of the soldiers, who, upon the first intimation, came together to grace the solemnity.

III. With what caution Jehu proceeded. He had the army with him. Joram had left it, and had gone home badly wounded. Jehu's good conduct appears in two things:—1. That he complimented the captains, and would do nothing without their advice and consent. 2. That he contrived to surprise Joram; and, in order thereto, to come upon him with speed. The suddenness of an attack sometimes turns to as good an account as the force of it.

Verses 16–29

From Ramoth-Gilead to Jezreel was more than one day's march; about the mid-way between them the river Jordan must be crossed.

I. Joram's watchman discovers him first at a distance, him and his retinue, and gives notice to the king of the approach of a company, whether of friends or foes he cannot tell. But the king sent first one messenger, and then another, to bring him intelligence, *v.* 17–19. Each messenger asked the same question: "*Is it peace?* are you for us or for our adversaries?" Each had the same answer: *What hast thou to do with peace? Turn thee behind me*, *v.* 18, 19. The watchman gave notice that the messengers were taken prisoners, and at length observed that the leader of this troop drove like Jehu, who it seems was noted for driving furiously. A man of such a violent temper was fittest for the service to which Jehu was designated.

II. Joram himself goes out to meet him, and takes Ahaziah king of Judah along with him, neither of them equipped for war, as not expecting an enemy, but in haste to have their curiosity satisfied.

1. The place where Joram met Jehu was ominous: *In the portion of Naboth the Jezreelite*, *v.* 21. The very sight of that ground was enough to make Joram tremble and Jehu triumph; for Joram had the guilt of Naboth's blood fighting against him and Jehu had the force of Elijah's curse fighting for him.

2. Joram's demand was still the same: "*Is it peace, Jehu?* Is all well? Dost thou come home thus flying from the Syrians or more than a conqueror over them?"

3. Jehu's reply was very startling. He answered him with a question: *What peace* canst thou expect, *so long as the whoredoms of thy mother Jezebel and her witchcrafts are so many?* Observe, (1) He charges upon him his mother's wickedness. She stands impeached for whoredom, corporal and spiritual, for witchcraft likewise, enchantments and divinations, used in honour of her idols; and these multiplied, for those that abandon themselves to wicked courses know not where they will stop. (2) Upon that account he throws him off from all pretensions to peace: "What peace can come to that house in which there is so much wickedness unrepented of?" The way of sin can never be the way of peace, Isa. lvii. 21. No peace so long as sin is persisted in; but, as soon as it is repented of and forsaken there is peace.

4. The execution was done immediately. When Joram heard of his mother's crimes his heart failed him; he presently concluded the long-threatened day of reckoning had now come, and cried out, "*There is treachery, O Ahaziah!* Jehu is our enemy, and it is time for us to shift for our safety." Both fled, and, (1) Joram king of Israel was slain presently, *v.* 24. Jehu dispatched him with his own hands. He died a criminal, under the sentence of the law, which Jehu, the executioner, pursues in the disposal of the dead body. Naboth's vineyard was hard by, which put him in mind of that circumstance of the doom Elijah passed upon Ahab, "*I will requite thee in this plat, said the Lord* (*v.* 25, 26), *for the blood of Naboth* himself, and *for the blood of his sons*." That very piece of ground which he, with so much pride and pleasure, had made himself master of at the expense of the guilt of innocent blood, now became the theatre on which his son's dead body lay exposed a spectacle to the world. (2) Ahaziah king of Judah

was pursued, and slain in a little time, and not far off, *v.* 27, 28. Though he was now in Joram's company, he would not have been slain but that he was joined with the house of Ahab both in affinity and in iniquity.

Verses 30-37

The greatest delinquent in the house of Ahab was Jezebel: it was she that introduced Baal, slew the Lord's prophets, contrived the murder of Naboth, stirred up her husband first, and then her sons, to do wickedly; a *cursed woman* she is here called (*v.* 34). Three reigns her reign had lasted, but now, at length, her day had come to fall. So that Jezebel's destruction may be looked upon as typical of the destruction of idolaters and persecutors.

I. Jezebel daring the judgment. She heard that Jehu had slain her son, and slain him for her whoredoms and witchcrafts, and thrown his dead body into the portion of Naboth, and that he was now coming to Jezreel. She posted herself in a window, at the entering of the gate, to affront Jehu and set him at defiance. 1. Instead of hiding herself, as one afraid of divine vengeance, she exposed herself to it and scorned to flee. 2. Instead of humbling herself, and putting herself into close mourning for her son, she *painted her face, and tired her head*, that she might appear like herself, that is (as she thought), great and majestic, hoping thereby to daunt Jehu. There is not a surer presage of ruin than an unhumbled heart under humbling providences. 3. Instead of trembling before Jehu, the instrument of God's vengeance, she thought to make him tremble with that threatening question, *Had Zimri peace, who slew his master?* (1) She took no notice of the hand of God gone out against her family, but flew in the face of him that was only the sword in his hand. (2) She pleased herself with the thought that what Jehu was now doing would certainly end in his own ruin, and that he would not have peace in it. (3) She quoted a precedent, to deter him from the prosecution of this enterprise: "*Had Zimri peace?* No, he had not; he came to the throne by blood and treachery, and within seven days was constrained to burn the palace over his head and himself in it: and canst thou expect to fare any better?" But Zimri had no warrant for what he did, but was incited to it merely by his own ambition and cruelty; whereas Jehu was anointed by one of the sons of the prophets, and did this by order from heaven, which would bear him out.

II. Jehu demanding aid against her. He looked up to the window, not daunted at the menaces of her impudent but impotent rage, and cried, *Who is on my side? Who? v.* 32. When reformation-work is set on foot, it is time to ask, "Who sides with it?"

III. Her own attendants delivering her up to his just revenge. Two or three chamberlains looked out to Jehu with such a countenance as encouraged him to believe they were on his side, and to them he called immediately to throw her down, which was one way of stoning malefactors, casting them headlong from some steep place. Thus was vengeance taken on her for the stoning of Naboth. They threw her down, *v.* 33. Thus she was most shamefully put to death, dashed against the wall and the pavement.

IV. The very dogs completing her shame and ruin, according to the prophecy. Jehu bethought himself of showing so much respect to Jezebel's sex and quality as to bury her. As bad as she was, she was a daughter, a king's daughter, a king's wife, a king's mother: *Go and bury her, v.* 34. While he was eating and drinking, the dogs had devoured her dead body. The hungry dogs had no respect to the dignity of her extraction; a king's daughter was no more to them than a common person. When notice was brought of this to Jehu, he remembered the threatening (1 Kings xxi. 23), *The dogs shall eat Jezebel by the wall*

of Jezreel. Jezebel's name nowhere remained, but as stigmatised in sacred writ: they could not so much as say, "This is Jezebel's dust, This is Jezebel's grave."

CHAPTER 10

I. A further account of Jehu's execution of his commission. He cut off, 1. All Ahab's sons, ver. 1-10. 2. All Ahab's kindred, ver. 11-14, 17. 3. Ahab's idolatry: his zeal against this he took Jonadab to be witness to (ver. 15, 16), summoned all the worshippers of Baal to attend (ver. 18-23), and slew them all (ver. 24, 25), and then abolished that idolatry, ver. 26-28. II. A short account of the administration of his government. 1. The old idolatry of Israel, the worship of the calves, was retained, ver. 29-31. 2. This brought God's judgments upon them by Hazael, with which his reign concludes, ver. 32-36.

Verses 1-14

Jehu knew the whole house of Ahab must be cut off.

I. He got the heads of all the sons of Ahab cut off by their own guardians at Samaria. These sons of Ahab were now at Samaria, a strong city, perhaps brought thither upon occasion of the war with Syria, as a place of safety, or upon notice of Jehu's insurrection; with them were the rulers of Jezreel, that is, the great officers of the court, who went to Samaria to secure themselves or to consult what was to be done. Jehu did not think fit to bring his forces to Samaria to destroy them, but, that the hand of God might appear the more remarkably in it, made their guardians their murderers. 1. He sent a challenge to their friends to stand by them, *v.* 2, 3. Not that he desired they should do this, or expected they would, but thus he upbraided them with their cowardice and utter inability to contest with the divine counsels. 2. Hereby he gained from them a submission. They prudently reasoned with themselves: "*Behold, two kings stood not before him,* but fell as sacrifices to his rage; *how then shall we stand?*" *v.* 4. Therefore they sent him a surrender of themselves: "*We are thy servants,* thy subjects, and *will do all that thou shalt bid us.*" 3. This was improved so far as to make them the executioners of those whom they had the tuition of (*v.* 6). These elders of Jezreel had been wickedly obsequious to Jezebel's order for the murder of Naboth, 1 Kings xxi. 11. She gloried, it is likely, in the power she had over them; and now the same base spirit makes them as pliable to Jehu and as ready to obey his orders for the murder of Ahab's sons. When the heads were presented to Jehu, he upbraided those that were the executioners, yet owned the hand of God in it. (1) He seems to blame those that had been the executioners of this vengeance. "I slew but one; they have slain all these. Let not the people of Samaria, nor any of the friends of the house of Ahab, ever reproach me for what I have done, when their own elders, and the very guardians of the orphans, have done this." But, (2) He resolves all into the righteous judgment of God (*v.* 10): *The Lord hath done that which he spoke by Elijah.*

II. He proceeded to destroy all that remained of the house of Ahab, not only those that descended from him, but those that were in any relation to him. Having done this in Jezreel, he did the same in Samaria (*v.* 17), *slew all that remained to Ahab in Samaria.* This was bloody work, and is not now, in any case, to be drawn into a precedent. Let the guilty suffer, but not the guiltless for their sakes.

III. Providence bringing the brethren of Ahaziah in his way, as he was going on with this execution, he slew them likewise, *v.* 12-14. 1. They were branches of Ahab's house, being descended from Athaliah, and therefore fell within his commission. 2. They were tainted with the wickedness of the house of Ahab. 3. They were now going to make their court to the princes of the house of Ahab, to *salute the children of the king and the queen,* Joram and Jezebel, which showed that they were linked to them in affection as well as in affinity.

Verses 15–28

I. Courting the friendship of a good man, *Jehonadab the son of Rechab, v.* 15, 16. This Jehonadab, though mortified to the world and meddling little with the business of it (as appears by his charge to his posterity, which they religiously observed 300 years after, not to drink wine nor dwell in cities, Jer. xxxv. 6, &c.), yet, upon this occasion, went to meet Jehu, that he might encourage him in the work to which God had called him. Jehonadab, though no prophet, priest, or Levite, was generally respected for that life of self-denial and devotion which he lived: Jehu, though a soldier, knew him and honoured him. When he met him (though it is likely he drove now as furiously as ever) he stopped to speak to him. 1. Jehu saluted him; he *blessed him* (so the word is), paid him respect. 2. Jehu professed that *his heart was right with him,* that he had a true affection for his person and a veneration for the crown of his Nazariteship, and desired to know whether he had the same affection for him: *Is thy heart right?* Jehonadab gave him his word (*It is*), and gave him his hand as a pledge of his heart. 3. Jehu took him up into his chariot and took him along with him to Samaria. All sober people would think the better of Jehu when they saw Jehonadab in the chariot with him. This was not the only time in which the piety of some has been made to serve the policy of others, and designing men have strengthened themselves by drawing good men into their interests. Jehonadab is a stranger to the arts of fleshly wisdom, and therefore, if Jehu be a servant of God and an enemy to Baal, he will be his faithful friend. "Come then" (says Jehu), "come with me, *and see my zeal for the Lord.*" This is commonly taken as giving cause to suspect that the zeal he pretended for the Lord was really zeal for himself and his own advancement. For, (1) He boasted of it, and spoke as if God and man were mightily indebted to him for it. (2) He desired it might be seen and taken notice of, like the Pharisees, who did all to be seen of men. Jehonadab went with him, and, it is likely, animated and assisted him in the further execution of his commission (*v.* 17), destroying all Ahab's friends in Samaria. A man may hate cruelty and yet love justice.

II. Contriving the destruction of all the worshippers of Baal. Jehu's project is to cut them all off together. 1. By a wile he brought them together to the temple of Baal. He pretended he would worship Baal more than ever Ahab had done, *v.* 18. He issued a proclamation, requiring the attendance of all the worshippers of Baal to join with him in a sacrifice to Baal (*v.* 19, 20). 2. He took care that none of the servants of the Lord should be among them, *v.* 23. 3. He gave orders for the cutting of them all off, and Jehonadab joined with him therein, *v.* 23. Then the guards were sent in to put them all to the sword. 4. The idolators being thus destroyed, the idolatry itself was utterly abolished. The buildings about the house of Baal were destroyed; all the little images, statues, pictures, or shrines, which beautified Baal's temple, with the great image of Baal himself, were brought out and burnt (*v.* 26, 27), and the temple of Baal was broken down. Thus was the worship of Baal quite destroyed. Thus will God destroy all the gods of the heathen, and, sooner or later, triumph over them all.

Verses 29–36

The account of the reign of Jehu.

I. God's approbation of what Jehu had done. 1. God pronounced that to be right which he had done. The extirpating of idolaters and idolatry was a thing right in God's eyes. 2. God promised him a reward,

that his children of the fourth generation from him should *sit upon the throne of Israel.*

II. Jehu's carelessness in what he was further to do. By this it appeared that his heart was not right with God, that he was partial in his reformation. 1. He did not put away all the evil. He departed from the sins of Ahab, but not from the sins of Jeroboam— discarded Baal, but adhered to the calves. The worship of the calves was a politic idolatry, was begun and kept up for reasons of state, to prevent the return of the ten tribes to the house of David, and therefore Jehu clave to that. True conversion is not only from those sins that are destructive to the secular interest, but from those that support and befriend it, in forsaking which is the great trial whether we can deny ourselves and trust God. 2. He put away evil, but he did not mind that which was good (*v.* 31): *He took no heed to walk in the law of the Lord God of Israel.* He had shown great care and zeal for the rooting out of a false religion; but in the true religion, (1) He was not at all solicitous to please God. (2) He showed no zeal. It seems, he was a man that had little religion himself, and yet God made use of him as an instrument of reformation in Israel.

III. The judgment that came upon Israel in his reign. There was a general decay of piety and increase of profaneness; and therefore it is not strange that the next news we hear is, *In those days the Lord began to cut Israel short, v.* 32. Their neighbours encroached upon them on every side. Hazael king of Syria was, above any other, vexatious and mischievous to them, *smote them in all the coasts of Israel.*

Lastly, The conclusion of Jehu's reign, *v.* 34–36. Because he took no heed to serve God, the memorials of his mighty enterprises and achievements are justly buried in oblivion.

CHAPTER 11

The affairs of the kingdom of Judah. I. Athaliah usurps the government and destroys all the seed-royal, ver. 1. II. Joash, a child of a year old, is wonderfully preserved, ver. 2, 3. III. At six years' end he is produced, and, by the agency of Jehoiada, made king, ver. 4–12. IV. Athaliah is slain, ver. 13–16. V. Both the civil and religious interests of the kingdom are well settled in the hands of Joash, ver. 17–21.

Verses 1–3

God had assured David of the continuance of his family, which is called his *ordaining a lamp for his anointed.* Now here we have David's promised lamp almost extinguished and yet wonderfully preserved.

I. It was almost extinguished by the barbarous malice of Athaliah, the queen-mother, who, when she heard that her son Ahaziah was slain by Jehu, *arose and destroyed all the seed-royal* (*v.* 1), all that she knew to be akin to the crown. She did it, 1. From a spirit of ambition. She thirsted after rule, and thought she could not get to it any other way. 2. From a spirit of revenge and rage against God. The house of Ahab being utterly destroyed, she resolved, as it were, by way of reprisal, to destroy the house of David. Well might she be called Athaliah, *that wicked woman* (2 Chron. xxiv. 7), Jezebel's own daughter.

II. It was wonderfully preserved by the pious care of one of Joram's daughters (who was wife to Jehoiada the priest), who stole away one of the king's sons, Joash by name, and hid him, *v.* 2, 3. The place of his safety was the house of the Lord, one of the chambers belonging to the temple, a place Athaliah seldom troubled. His aunt, by bringing him hither, put him under God's special protection, and so hid him by faith, as Moses was hidden. Now were David's words made good to one of his seed (Ps. xxvii. 5), *In the secret of his tabernacle shall he hide me.* With good reason did this Joash, when he grew up, set himself to repair the house of the Lord, for it had been a sanctuary to him. See the wisdom and care of Providence, and how it prepares for what it designs; and see what blessings those lay up in store for their families that marry their children to those that are wise and good.

Verses 4–12

Six years Athaliah tyrannised. While Jehu was extirpating the worship of Baal in Israel, she was establishing it in Judah, as appears, 2 Chron. xxiv. 7. All this while, Joash lay hid, entitled to a crown and intended for it, and yet buried alive in obscurity. Joash in his seventh year was ready to be shown, having served his first apprenticeship to life and arrived at his first climacterical year. By that time the people had grown weary of Athaliah's tyranny and ripe for a revolution. How that revolution was effected:

I. The manager of this great affair was Jehoiada the priest, probably the high priest. By his birth and office he was a man in authority. By marriage he was allied to the royal family, and, if all the seed-royal were destroyed, his wife, as daughter to Joram, had a better title to the crown than Athaliah had. By his eminent gifts and graces he was fitted to serve his country, and better service he could not do it than to free it from Athaliah's usurpation.

II. The management was very discreet as became so wise and good a man as Jehoiada.

1. He concerted the matter with the *rulers of hundreds and the captains*, the men in office, ecclesiastical, civil, and military; he got them to him to the temple, consulted with them, gave them an oath of secrecy, and *showed them the king's son* (v. 4). What a pleasing surprise it was to them, who feared that the house and lineage of David were quite cut off, to find such a spark as this in the embers.

2. He posted the priests and Levites, who were more immediately under his direction, in the several avenues to the temple, to keep the guard. David had divided the priests into courses. Every sabbath-day morning a new company came into waiting, but the company of the foregoing week did not go out of waiting till the sabbath evening, so that on the sabbath day, when double service was to be done, there was a double number to do it. These Jehoiada employed to attend on this great occasion; he armed them out of the magazines of the temple with David's spears and shields. Two things they were ordered to do: (1) To protect the young king from being insulted. (2) To preserve the holy temple from being profaned by the concourse of people that would come together on this occasion (v. 6).

3. When the guards were fixed, then the king was brought forth, v. 12. Jehoiada, without delay, proceeded to the coronation of this young king. This was done with great solemnity, v. 12. (1) In token of his being invested with kingly power, he *put the crown upon him.* (2) In token of his obligation to govern by law, and to make the word of God his rule, he gave him the testimony, Deut. xvii. 18, 19. (3) In token of his receiving the Spirit, to qualify him for this great work to which he before was called, he anointed him. (4) In token of the people's acceptance of him and subjection to his government, they clapped their hands for joy, and expressed their hearty good wishes to him: *Let the king live;* and thus they made him their king and concurred with the divine appointment. They had reason to bid him welcome to the crown whose right it was, and to pray, *Let him live,* concerning him who came to them as life from the dead and in whom the house of David was to live. With such acclamations of joy and satisfaction must the kingdom of Christ be welcomed into our hearts when his throne is set up there and Satan the usurper is deposed.

Verses 13–16

It was designed when they had finished the solemnity of the king's inauguration, to pay a visit to Atha-

liah, and call her to an account for her murders, usurpation, and tyranny; but, like her mother Jezebel, she went out to meet them, and hastened her own destruction. 1. Hearing the noise, she came in a fright to see what was the matter, v. 13. Jehoiada and his friends proclaimed what they were doing. When she heard the noise it was strange that she was so ill advised as to come herself, and, for aught that appears, to come alone. 2. Seeing what was done she cried out for help. She saw the king's place by the pillar possessed by one to whom the princes and people did homage (v. 14). This made her rend her clothes and cry, "Treason! treason! Come and help against the traitors." 3. Jehoiada gave orders to put her to death as an idolater, a usurper, and an enemy to the public peace. Care was taken, (1) That she should not be killed in the temple. (2) That whoever appeared for her should die with her. She endeavouring to make her escape the back way to the palace, through the stalls, they pursued her, and there killed her, v. 16.

Verses 17–21

Jehoiada had now got over the hardest part of his work, when, by the death of Athaliah, the young prince had his way to the throne cleared of all opposition.

I. The good foundations he laid, by an original contract, v. 17. Now that prince and people were together in God's house, Jehoiada took care that they should jointly covenant with God, and mutually covenant with each other, that they might rightly understand their duty both to God and to one another. 1. He endeavoured to settle and secure the interests of religion among them, by a covenant between them and God. In this covenant, the king stands upon the same level with his subjects and is as much bound as any of them to serve the Lord. By this engagement they renounced Baal, whom many of them had worshipped, and resigned themselves to God's government. By our bonds to God the bonds of every relation are strengthened. They *first gave themselves to the Lord,* and then *to us,* 2 Cor. viii. 5. 2. He then settled both the coronation-oath and the oath of allegiance, the *pacta conventa—covenant,* between the king and the people, by which the king was obliged to govern according to law and to protect his subjects, and they were obliged, while he did so, to obey him and to bear faith and true allegiance to him.

II. The good beginnings he raised on those foundations. 1. Pursuant to their covenant with God they immediately abolished idolatry. Every one, now that they were so well headed, would lend a hand to pull down Baal's temple, his altars, and his images. All his worshippers, it should seem, deserted him; only his priest Mattan stuck to his altar. Though all men forsook Baal, he would not, and there he was slain. Having destroyed Baal's temple, they appointed *officers over the house of God,* to see that the service of God was regularly performed by the proper persons, in due time, and according to the instituted manner. 2. Pursuant to their covenant with one another, (1) The king was brought in state to the royal palace, and sat there on the throne of judgment, *the thrones of the house of David* (v. 19), ready to receive petitions and appeals, which he would refer to Jehoiada to give answers to and to give judgment upon. (2) The people rejoiced, and Jerusalem was in quiet (v. 20).

CHAPTER 12

This chapter gives us the history of the reign of Joash, which does not answer to that glorious beginning of it which we had an account of in the foregoing chapter; he was not so illustrious at forty years old as he was at seven, yet his reign is to be reckoned one of the better sort, and appears much worse in Chronicles

(2 Chron. xxiv) than it does here. Here we are only told, I. That he did well while Jehoiada lived, ver. 1–3. II. That he was careful and active to repair the temple, ver. 4–16. III. That after a mean compact with Hazael (ver. 17, 18) he died ingloriously, ver. 19–21.

Verses 1–3

The general account given of Joash is, 1. That he reigned forty years. 2. That he did that which was right as long as Jehoiada lived to instruct him, *v.* 2. 3. That the *high places were not taken away*, *v.* 3. Up and down the country they had altars both for sacrifice and incense, to the honour of the God of Israel only. These private altars, perhaps, had been more used in the late bad reigns than formerly, because it was not safe to go up to Jerusalem, nor was the temple-service performed as it should have been; and, it may be, Jehoiada connived at them, because he hoped that the reforming of the temple, and putting things into a good posture there, would by degrees draw people from their high places and they would dwindle of themselves.

Verses 4–16

An account of the repairing of the temple in the reign of Joash.

I. Though Solomon built it of the best materials and in the best manner, yet in time it went to decay, and there were *breaches found in it* (*v.* 5). Even temples themselves are the worse for the wearing; but the heavenly temple will never wax old. Yet it was not only the teeth of time that made these breaches, the sons of Athaliah had *broken up the house of God* (2 Chron. xxiv. 7).

II. The king himself was the first and forwardest man that took care for the repair of it. 1. Because he was king, and God expects and requires from those who have power that they use it for the maintenance and support of religion, the redress of grievances, and reparation of decays. 2. Because the temple had been both his nursery and his sanctuary when he was a child, in a grateful remembrance of which he now appeared zealous for the honour of it. Those who have experienced the comfort and benefit of religious assemblies will make the support of them their care, and the prosperity of them their chief joy.

III. The priests were ordered to collect money for these repairs, and to take care that the work was done. 1. He gave them orders for the levying of the money. They must not stay till it was paid in, but they must call for it where they knew it was due, in their respective districts, as redemption-money (by virtue of the law, Exod. xxx. 12), or as estimation-money (by virtue of the law, Lev. xxvii. 2, 3), or as a free-will offering, *v.* 4.

IV. This method did not answer the intention, *v.* 6. Little money was raised. Either the priests were careless, and did not call on the people to pay in their dues, or the people had so little confidence in the priests' management that they were backward to pay money into their hands. But what money was raised was not applied to the proper use: *The breaches of the house were not repaired.*

V. Another method was therefore taken. The king had his heart much set upon having *the breaches of the house repaired*, *v.* 7. His apostasy, at last, gives us cause to question whether he had as good an affection for the service of the temple as he had for the structure. Many have been zealous for building and beautifying churches, and for other forms of godliness, who yet have been strangers to the power of it. However, we commend his zeal. Another course was taken,

1. For raising money, *v.* 9, 10. The money was put into a public chest, and then people brought it in readily and in great abundance. The money that was given, (1) Was dropped into the chest through a hole in the lid, past recall, to intimate

that what has been once resigned to God must never be resumed. (2) The chest was put on the right hand as they went in, which, some think, is alluded to in that rule of charity which our Saviour gives, *Let not thy left hand know what thy right hand doeth.* But, while they were getting all they could for the repair of the temple, they did not break in upon that which was the stated maintenance of the priests, *v.* 16. Let not the servants of the temple be starved under colour of repairing the breaches of it.

2. For laying out the money that was raised.

(1) They did not put it into the hands of the priests, who were not versed in affairs of this nature, having other work to mind, but *into the hands of those that did the work*, or at least *had the oversight of it*, *v.* 11. [1] Carefully, purchasing materials and paying workmen, *v.* 12. [2] Faithfully, such a reputation they got for honesty that there was no occasion to examine their bills or audit their accounts. Those that think it is no sin to cheat the government, cheat the country, or cheat the church, will be of another mind when God shall set their sins in order before them.

(2) They did not lay it out in ornaments for the temple, in vessels of gold or silver, but in necessary repairs first (*v.* 13).

Verses 17–21

When Joash had revolted from God and become both an idolater and a persecutor the hand of the Lord went out against him, and his *last state was worse than his first.*

I. His wealth and honour became an easy prey to his neighbours. Hazael, when he had chastised Israel (*ch.* x. 32), threatened Judah and Jerusalem likewise, took Gath, a strong city (*v.* 17), and thence intended to march with his forces against Jerusalem. Joash had neither spirit nor strength to make head against him, but gave him all the hallowed things, and all the gold that was found both in his exchequer and in the treasures of the temple (*v.* 18), to bribe him to march another way. If he had not forsaken God, and forfeited his protection, his affairs would not have been brought to this extremity. He lost the honour of a prince and a soldier. He impoverished himself and his kingdom. He tempted Hazael to come again, when he could carry home so rich a booty without striking a stroke. And the next year the host of Syria came up against Jerusalem, destroyed the prince, and plundered the city, 2 Chron. xxiv. 23, 24.

II. His life became an easy prey to his own servants. They conspired against him and slew him (*v.* 20, 21), to be avenged on him for murdering the prophet, Jehoiada's son. Thus fell Joash, who began in the spirit and ended in the flesh.

CHAPTER 13

The history of the kings of Israel, and particularly of the family of Jehu. We have here an account of the reign, I. Of his son Jehoahaz, which continued seventeen years. 1. His bad character in general (ver. 1, 2), the trouble he was brought into (ver. 3), and the low ebb of his affairs, ver. 7. 2. His humiliation before God, and God's compassion towards him, ver. 4, 5, and again, ver. 23. 3. His continuance in his idolatry notwithstanding, ver. 6. 4. His death, ver. 8, 9. II. Of his grandson Joash, which continued sixteen years. Here is a general account of his reign (ver. 10–13), but a particular account of the death of Elisha. 1. The kind visit the king made him (ver. 14), the encouragement he gave the king in his wars with Syria, ver. 15–19. 2. His death and burial (ver. 20), and a miracle wrought by his bones, ver. 21. And, lastly, the advantages Joash gained against the Syrians, according to his predictions, ver. 24, 25.

Verses 1–9

A general account of the reign of Jehoahaz, and of the state of Israel during his seventeen years.

I. The glory of Israel turned into shame. How is its crown profaned and its honour laid in the dust!

1. It was the honour of Israel that they worshipped the only living and true God, who is a Spirit, an eternal mind, and had rules by which to worship him of his own appointment; but by *changing the glory of their incorruptible God into the similitude of an ox, the truth of God into a lie*, they lost this honour, and levelled themselves with the nations that worshipped the work of their own hands. We find here that the king *followed the sins of Jeroboam* (v. 2), and the people departed *not from them, but walked therein*, v. 6. 2. It was the honour of Israel that they were taken under the special protection of heaven; God himself was their defence. But here, as often before, we find them stripped of this glory, and exposed to the insults of all their neighbours. They by their sins provoked God to anger, and then he *delivered them into the hands of Hazael and Benhadad, v. 3. Hazael oppressed Israel, v.* 22. Surely never was any nation so often plucked and pillaged by their neighbours as Israel was.

II. Some sparks of Israel's ancient honour appearing in these ashes. For, 1. It was the ancient honour of Israel that they were a praying people: and here we find somewhat of that honour revived; for Jehoahaz their king, in his distress, *besought the Lord* (v. 4), applied for help, not to the calves (what help could they give him?) but to the Lord. 2. It was the ancient honour of Israel that they had *God nigh unto them in all that which they called upon him for* (Deut. iv. 7), and so he was here. Though he might justly have rejected the prayer as an abomination to him, yet *the Lord hearkened unto Jehoahaz*, and to his prayer for himself and for his people (v. 4), and *he gave Israel a saviour* (v. 5), not Jehoahaz himself, for all his days Hazael oppressed Israel (v. 22), but his son, to whom, in answer to his father's prayers, God gave success against the Syrians, so that he recovered the cities which they had taken from his father, v. 25. This gracious answer God gave to the prayer of Jehoahaz in remembrance of his covenant with Abraham (v. 23). See how swift God is to show mercy, how willing to find out a reason to be gracious, else he would not look so far back as that ancient covenant.

Verses 10–19

Joash, the son of Jehoahaz and grandson of Jehu, upon the throne of Israel. Probably the house of Jehu intended some respect to the house of David when they gave this heir-apparent to the crown the same name with him that was then king of Judah.

I. He was none of the worst, and yet, because he kept up that ancient and politic idolatry of the house of Jeroboam, it is said, *He did that which was evil in the sight of the Lord.*

II. The particular account of what passed between him and Elisha:

1. Elisha fell sick, v. 14. (1) It was now about sixty years since he was first called to be a prophet. It was a great mercy to Israel, and especially to the sons of the prophets, that he was continued so long a burning and shining light. (2) All the latter part of his time, from the anointing of Jehu, which was forty-five years before Joash began his reign, we find no mention made of him, or of anything he did, till we find him here upon his death-bed.

2. King Joash visited him in his sickness, and *wept over him, v.* 14. This was an evidence of some good in him, that he had a value and affection for a faithful prophet. When the king heard of Elisha's sickness he came to visit him, and to receive his dying counsel and blessing. He lamented him in the same words with which Elisha had himself lamented the removal of Elijah: *My father, my father.*

3. Elisha gave the king great assurances of his success against the Syrians, Israel's present oppressors, and encouraged him to prosecute the war against

them with vigour. *I die, but God will surely visit you.* He has the residue of the Spirit, and can raise up other prophets to pray for you. He gives him a sign, orders him to *take bow and arrow* (v. 15). God would be the agent, but he must be the instrument. And that he should be successful he gives him a token, by directing him,

(1) To shoot an arrow towards Syria, v. 16, 17. He received the words of command from the prophet: *Put thy hand upon the bow—Open the window—Shoot.* As if he had been a child that never drew a bow before, *Elisha put his hands upon the king's hands*, to signify that in all his expeditions against the Syrians he must look up to God for direction and strength. The trembling hands of a dying prophet, as they signified the concurrence and communication of the power of God, gave this arrow more force than the hands of the king in his full strength. The Syrians had made themselves masters of the country that lay eastward, *ch.* x. 33. Thitherward therefore the arrow was directed, and such an interpretation given by the prophet of the shooting of this arrow as made it, [1] A commission to the king to attack the Syrians. [2] A promise of success therein. It is the *arrow of the Lord's deliverance, even the arrow of deliverance from Syria.*

(2) To *strike with the arrows, v.* 18, 19. The prophet having in God's name assured him of victory over the Syrians, he will now try him and see what improvement he will make of his victories, whether he will push them on with more zeal than Ahab did when Benhadad lay at his mercy. For the trial of this he bids him *smite with the arrows on the ground*: Now show me what thou wilt do to them when thou hast them down. The king showed not that eagerness and flame which one might have expected upon this occasion, but smote thrice, and no more. But, by contemning the sign, he lost the thing signified, sorely to the grief of the dying prophet, who told him he should have smitten five or six times. Not being straitened in the power and promise of God, why should he be straitened in his own expectations and endeavours?

Verses 20–25

I. The sepulchre of Elisha: he died in a good old age, and they buried him. As soon as he was dead, the bands of the Moabites invaded the land—roving skulking bands, that murdered and plundered by surprise. The king was apprehensive of danger only from the Syrians, but, behold, the Moabites invade him. Elisha's dead body communicated life to another dead body, v. 21. This great miracle was a plain indication of another life after this. The neighbours were carrying the dead body of a man to the grave, and, fearing to fall into the hands of the Moabites, a party of whom they saw at a distance near the place where the body was to be interred, they laid the corpse in the next convenient place, which proved to be Elisha's sepulchre. The dead man, upon touching Elisha's bones, revived, and, it is likely, went home again with his friends. Elijah was honoured *in* his departure. Elisha was honoured *after* his departure. God thus dispenses honours as he pleases, but, one way or other, the rest of all the saints will be glorious, Isa. xi. 10.

II. The sword of Joash king of Israel successful against the Syrians. 1. The cause of his success was God's favour (v. 23): *The Lord was gracious to them, had compassion on them* in their miseries and *respect unto them.* It was of the Lord's mercies that they were not consumed, because he would give them space to repent. 2. The effect of his success. He recovered out of the hands of Benhadad the cities of Israel which the Syrians were possessed of, v. 25. Thrice Joash beat the Syrians, just as often as he had struck the ground with the arrows, and then a full stop was put to the course of his victories.

Chapter 14

This chapter continues the history of the succession in the kingdoms both of Judah and Israel. I. In the kingdom of Judah, 1. The entire history of Amaziah's reign. (1) His good character, ver. 1–4. (2) The justice he executed on the murderers of his father, ver. 5, 6. (3) His victory over the Edomites, ver. 7. (4) His war with Joash, and his defeat in that war, ver. 8–14. (5) His fall, at last, by a conspiracy against him, ver. 17–20. 2. The beginning of the history of Azariah, ver. 21, 22. II. In the kingdom of Israel, the conclusion of the reign of Joash (ver. 15, 16), and the entire history of Jeroboam his son, the second of that name, ver. 23–29.

Verses 1–7

Amaziah, the son and successor of Joash.

I. In the temple he acted, in some measure, well, like Joash, but not like David, v. 3. He began well, but did not persevere. It is not enough to do that which our pious predecessors did, merely to keep up the usage, but we must do it *as* they did it, from the same principle of faith and devotion and with the same sincerity and resolution. It is here taken notice of, as before, that *the high places were not taken away, v.* 4.

II. On the bench we have him doing justice on the traitors that murdered his father, not as soon as ever he came to the crown, lest it should occasion some disturbance, but he prudently deferred it till *the kingdom was confirmed in his hand, v.* 5. *The children of the murderers he slew not*, because the law of Moses had expressly provided that the *children should not be put to death for the fathers, v.* 6.

III. In the field we find him triumphing over the Edomites, *v.* 7. Edom had *revolted from under the hand of Judah* in Joram's time, ch. viii. 22. Now he makes war upon them to bring them back to their allegiance. We shall find a larger account of this expedition, 2 Chron. xxv. 5, &c.

Verses 8–14

For several successions after the division of the kingdoms that of Judah suffered much by the *enmity* of Israel. After Asa's time, for several successions, it suffered more by the *friendship* of Israel, and by the alliance and affinity made with them. But now we meet with hostility between them again.

I. Amaziah, upon no provocation, and' without showing any cause of quarrel, challenged Joash into the field (*v.* 8): *Come, let us look one another in the face;* let us try our strength in battle. Hereby he showed himself proud, presumptuous, and prodigal of blood. Some think that he had the vanity to think of subduing the kingdom of Israel, and reuniting it to Judah.

II. Joash sent him a grave rebuke for his challenge, with advice to withdraw it, *v.* 9, 10. 1. He mortifies his pride, by comparing himself to a cedar, a stately tree, and Amaziah to a thistle, a sorry weed, telling him he was so far from fearing him that he despised him, and scorned as much to have anything to do with him, or make any alliance with him, as the cedar would to match his daughter to a thistle. The ancient house of David he thinks not worthy to be named the same day with the house of Jehu, though an upstart. 2. He foretells his fall: *A wild beast trod down the thistle*, and so put an end to his treaty with the cedar; so easily does Joash think his forces can crush Amaziah. 3. He shows him the folly of his challenge. "Thou art proud of the blow thou hast given to Edom, as if that had made thee formidable to all mankind." 4. He counsels him to be content with the honour he has won, and not to hazard that, by grasping at more that was out of his reach.

III. Amaziah persisted in his resolution, and the issue was bad. 1. His army was routed and dispersed,

v. 12. Josephus says, When they were to engage they were struck with such terror that they did not strike a stroke, but every one made the best of his way. 2. He himself was taken prisoner by the king of Israel, and then had enough of *looking him in the face.* 3. The conqueror entered Jerusalem, which tamely opened to him, and yet he broke down their wall (and, as Josephus says, drove his chariot in triumph through the breach), in reproach to them. 4. He plundered Jerusalem, took away all that was valuable, and returned to Samaria, laden with spoils, *v.* 14.

Verses 15–22

Here are three kings brought to their graves in these few verses:—1. Joash king of Israel, *v.* 15, 16. 2. Amaziah king of Judah. Fifteen years he survived his conqueror the king of Israel, *v.* 17. He was slain by his own subjects, who hated him for his maladministration (*v.* 19) and made Jerusalem too hot for him, the ignominious breach made in their walls being occasioned by his folly and presumption. He fled to Lachish. How long he continued concealed or sheltered there we are not told, but, at last, he was there murdered, *v.* 19. 3. Azariah succeeded Amaziah, but not till twelve years after his father's death, for he was but four years old at the death of his father, so that, for twelve years, till he came to be sixteen, the government was in the hands of protectors. He reigned very long (*ch.* xv. 2) and yet the account of his reign is here industriously huddled up, and broken off abruptly (*v.* 22): *He built Elath* which had belonged to the Edomites.

Verses 23–29

An account of the reign of Jeroboam the second.

I. His reign was long, the longest of all the reigns of the kings of Israel: *He reigned forty-one years;* yet his contemporary Azariah, the king of Judah, reigned longer, even fifty-two years. This Jeroboam reigned just as long as Asa had done (1 Kings xv. 10), yet one did that which was good and the other that which was evil. We cannot measure men's characters by the length of their lives or by their outward prosperity.

II. His character was the same with that of the rest of those kings: *He did that which was evil* (*v.* 24), for *he departed not from the sins of Jeroboam*; he kept up the worship of the calves. But a sin is never the less evil in God's sight for its being an ancient usage.

III. Yet he prospered more than most of them, for though, in that one thing, he did evil in the sight of the Lord, yet it is likely, in other respects, there was some good found in him and therefore God owned him, 1. By prophecy. He raised up Jonah the son of Amittai, a Galilean. It is a sign that God has not cast off his people if he continue faithful ministers among them; when Elisha, who strengthened the hands of Joash, was removed, Jonah was sent to encourage his son. It is probable that it was when he was a young man, that God sent him to Nineveh, and that he flew off and fretted as he did; and, if so, this is an undoubted evidence of the forgiveness of his faults and follies, that he was afterwards employed as a messenger of mercy to Israel. A commission amounts to a pardon. 2. By providence. The event was *according to the word of the Lord*: his arms were successful; he *restored the coast of Israel*, recovered those frontier-towns and countries that lay from Hamath in the north to the sea of the plain, *v.* 25. Two reasons why God blessed them with those victories:—(1) Because their distress was very great, which made them the objects of his compassion, *v.* 26. Those that lived in those countries which the enemies were masters of were miserably oppressed and enslaved, and the rest were much impoverished by the frequent incursions the enemy made upon them to plunder them. Let those whose case is pitiable take comfort from the divine pity: we read of God's bowels of mercy (Isa. lxiii. 15; Jer. xxxi. 20) and that he is full of compassion, Ps. lxxxvi. 15. (2) Because he had not as yet said *he would blot out the name of Israel* (v. 27). If this be understood of the dispersion of the ten tribes, he did say it and do it, not long after—if of the utter extirpation of the name of Israel, he never said it, nor will ever do it, for that name still remains under heaven in the *gospel Israel*, and will to the end of time.

IV. Here is the conclusion of Jeroboam's reign. We read (v. 28) of his might, and how he warred. Many prophets there had been in Israel, but none had left any of their prophecies in writing till those of this age began to do it, and their prophecies are part of the canon of scripture. It was in the reign of this Jeroboam that *Hosea* began to prophesy, and he was the first that wrote his prophecies; therefore the word of the Lord by him is called *the beginning of the word of the Lord*, Hos. i. 2. At the same time *Amos* prophesied, and wrote his prophecy, soon afterwards *Micah*, and then *Isaiah*, in the days of Ahaz and Hezekiah. Thus God never left himself without witness.

CHAPTER 15

I. The history of two of the kings of Judah is briefly recorded:— 1. Of Azariah, or Uzziah, ver. 1–7. 2. Of Jotham his son, ver. 32–38. II. The history of many of the kings of Israel that reigned at the same time is given in short, five in succession. 1. Zachariah, the last of the house of Jehu, reigned six months, and then was slain and succeeded by Shallum, ver. 8–12. 2. Shallum reigned one month, and then was slain and succeeded by Menahem, ver. 13–15. 3. Menahem reigned ten years, or tyrannised rather, and then died in his bed, and left his son to succeed him first, and then suffer for him, ver. 16–22. 4. Pekahiah reigned two years, and then was slain and succeeded by Pekah, ver. 23 36. 5. Pekah reigned twenty years, and then was slain and succeeded by Hoshea, the last of all the kings of Israel (ver. 27–31), for things were now hastening towards the final destruction of that kingdom.

Verses 1–7

The reign of Azariah. 1. He began young and reigned long (v. 2), did, for the most part, that which was right, v. 3, only he had not zeal and courage to take away the high places, v. 4. 2. That which is peculiar, v. 5 (that God smote him with a leprosy) is more largely related, with the occasion of it, 2. Chron. xxvi. 16, &c., where we have also a fuller account of the glories of the former part of his reign, as well as of the disgraces of the latter part of it. Here we are told, (1) That he was a leper. (2) God smote him with this leprosy, to chastise him for his presumptuous invasion of the priests' office. (3) That he was a leper *to the day of his death*. Though we have reason to think he repented and the sin was pardoned, yet, for warning to others, he was continued under this mark of God's displeasure. (4) That he *dwelt in a separate house*, as being made ceremonially unclean by the law, to the discipline of which, though a king, he must submit. (5) That his son was his viceroy in the affairs both of his court (for *he was over the house*) and of his kingdom (for he was *judging the people of the land*); and it was both a comfort to him and a blessing to his kingdom that he had such a son to fill up his room.

Verses 8–31

The best days of the kingdom of Israel were while the government was in Jehu's family. In his reign, and the next three reigns, though there were many abominable corruptions and miserable grievances in Israel, yet the crown went in succession, the kings died in their beds, and some care was taken of public affairs; but, now that those days are at an end, the history which we have in these verses of about thirty-three years represents the affairs of that kingdom in the utmost confusion imaginable.

I. These unhappy revolutions—these bad times, as they may truly be called. 1. God had tried the people of Israel both with judgments and mercies, explained and enforced by his servants the prophets, and yet they continued impenitent and unreformed, and therefore God justly brought these miseries upon them. 2. God made good his promise to Jehu, that his sons to the fourth generation after him should sit upon the throne of Israel, which was a greater favour than was shown to any of the royal families either before or after his. Thus God rewarded Jehu for his zeal in destroying the worship of Baal and the house of Ahab; and yet, when the measure of the sins of the house of Jehu was full, God avenged upon it the blood then shed, called *the blood of Jezreel*, Hos. i. 4. 3. All these kings did that which was *evil in the sight of the Lord*, for *they walked in the sins of Jeroboam the son of Nebat*. Though at variance with one another, yet in this they agreed, to keep up idolatry, and the people loved to have it so. 4. Each of these (except one) conspired against his predecessor, and slew him—*Shallum, Menahem, Pekah, and Hoshea*, all traitors and murderers, and yet all kings awhile. One wicked man is often made a scourge to another, and every wicked man, at length, a ruin to himself. 5. The ambition of the great men made the nation miserable. Here is Tiphsah, a city of Israel, barbarously destroyed, with all the coasts thereof, by one of these pretenders (v. 16). 6. While the nation was thus shattered by divisions at home the kings of Assyria, first one (v. 19) and then another (v. 29), came against it and did what they pleased. 7. This was the condition of Israel just before they were quite ruined and carried away captive, for that was in the ninth year of Hoshea, the last of these usurpers. If they had, in these days of confusion and perplexity, humbled themselves before God and sought his face, that final destruction might have been prevented.

II. A short view of the particular reigns.

1. Zachariah, the son of Jeroboam, began to reign in the thirty-eighth year of Azariah, or Uzziah, king of Judah, v. 8. Some of the most critical chronologers reckon that between Jeroboam and his son Zachariah the throne was vacant twenty-two years through the disturbances and dissensions that were in the kingdom. Zachariah was deposed before he was well seated on the throne: he reigned but six months, and then Shallum *slew him before the people*, with the approbation of the people, to whom he had, some way or other, made himself odious; so ended the line of Jehu.

2. But had Shallum peace, who slew his master? No, he had not (v. 13), one month of days measured his reign and then he was cut off. Menaham, either provoked by his crime or animated by his example, soon served him as he had served his master—*slew him and reigned in his stead*, v. 14.

3. Menaham held the kingdom ten years, v. 17. He was so prodigiously cruel to those of his own nation who hesitated a little at submitting to him that he not only ruined a city, but *ripped up all the women with child*, v. 16. By these cruel methods he hoped to frighten all others into his interests; but when the king of Assyria came against him, (1) So little confidence had he in his people that he durst not meet him as an enemy, but was obliged, at a vast expense, to purchase a peace with him. (2) Such need had he of help *to confirm the kingdom in his hand* that he made it part of his bargain that he should assist him against his own subjects that were disaffected to him. Thus he got clear of the king of Assyria for this time; but his army now got so rich a booty with so little trouble that it encouraged them to come again, not long after, when they laid all waste.

4. Pekahiah, the son of Menahem, succeeded his father, but reigned only two years, and then was treacherously slain by Pekah.

5. Pekah, though he got the kingdom by treason, kept it twenty years (*v.* 27), so long it was before his violent dealing returned upon his own head, but it returned at last. This Pekah, son of Remaliah, (1) Made himself more considerable abroad than any of these usurpers, for he was a great terror to the kingdom of Judah, as we find, Isa. vii. 1, &c. (2) He lost a great part of his kingdom to the king of Assyria. By this judgment God punished him for his attempt upon Judah and Jerusalem. (3) Soon after this he forfeited his life to the resentments of his countrymen, who, it is probable, were disgusted at him for leaving them exposed to a foreign enemy, while he was invading Judah, of which Hoshea took advantage and, to gain his crown, seized his life, *slew him, and reigned in his stead.* Surely he was fond of a crown indeed who, at this time, would run such a hazard as a traitor did—a crown which a wise man would not have taken up in the street, yet Hoshea not only ventured *upon* it but ventured *for* it, and it cost him dear.

Verses 32–38

A short account of the reign of Jotham king of Judah, of whom we are told, 1. That he reigned very well, *did that which was right in the sight of the Lord, v.* 34. Josephus gives him a very high character, stating that he was pious towards God, just towards men, and laid out himself for the public good. Though the high places were not taken away, yet to draw people from them, and keep them close to God's holy place, he showed great respect to the temple, and built the higher gate to the temple. If magistrates cannot do all they would for the suppressing of vice and profaneness, let them do so much the more for the support and advancement of piety and virtue. If they cannot pull down the high places of sin, yet let them build and beautify the high gate of God's house. 2. That he died in the midst of his days, *v.* 33. By these accounts it appears that there was none of all the kings of Judah that reached David's age, seventy, the common age of man. Asa's age I do not find. Uzziah lived to be sixty-eight, Manasseh sixty-seven, and Jehoshaphat sixty; and these were the three oldest; many of those that were of note did not reach fifty. This Jotham died at forty-one. 3. That in his days the confederacy was formed against Judah by Rezin and Remaliah's son, the king of Syria and the king of Israel, which appeared so very formidable in the beginning of the reign of Ahaz that, upon notice of it, the heart of that prince was moved and *the heart of the people, as the trees of the wood are moved with the wind,* Isa. vii. 2.

CHAPTER 16

The reign of Ahaz. I. He was a notorious idolater, ver. 1–4. II. With the treasures of the temple, as well as his own, he hired the king of Assyria to invade Syria and Israel, ver. 5–9. III. He took pattern from an idol's altar which he saw at Damascus for a new altar in God's temple, ver. 10–16. IV. He abused and embezzled the furniture of the temple, ver. 17, 18.

Verses 1–4

A general character of the reign of Ahaz. 1. He *did not that which was right like David* (*v.* 2). He had no love for the temple, made no conscience of his duty to God, nor had any regard to his law. He was a reproach to that honourable name and family, which therefore was really a reproach to him. 2. He walked *in the way of the kings of Israel* (*v.* 3), who all worshipped the calves. The kings of Israel pleaded policy and reasons of state for their idolatry, but Ahaz had no such pretence. They were his enemies, and

had proved enemies to themselves too by their idolatry; yet he walked in their way. 3. He *made his sons to pass through the fire,* to the honour of his dunghill-deities. He burnt them (2 Chron. xxviii. 3), and made others pass between two fires, or to be drawn through a flame, in token of their dedication to the idol. 4. He did *according to the abominations of the heathen whom the Lord had cast out.* 5. He *sacrificed in the high places, v.* 4. If his father had but had zeal enough to take them away, the debauching of his sons might have been prevented; but those that connive at sin know not what dangerous snares they lay for those that come after them.

Verses 5–9

1. The attempt of his confederate neighbours, the kings of Syria and Israel, upon him. They thought to make themselves masters of Jerusalem, and to set a king of their own in it, Isa. vii. 6. In this they fell short, but the king of Syria recovered Elath, a considerable port upon the Red Sea, which Amaziah had taken from the Syrians, *ch.* xiv. 22. 2. His project to get clear of them. Having forsaken God, he had neither courage nor strength to make head against his enemies, nor could he, with any boldness, ask help of God; but he made his court to the king of Assyria, and got him to come in for his relief. The sin itself was its own punishment; for, though it is true that he gained his point the king of Assyria hearkened to him, and, to serve his own turn, made a descent upon Damascus, whereby he gave a powerful diversion to the king of Syria (*v.* 9), and obliged him to let fall his design against Ahaz, carrying the Syrians captive to Kir, yet, considering all, he made but a bad bargain; for, to compass this, (1) He enslaved himself (*v.* 7): *I am thy servant and thy son.* (2) He impoverished himself; for he took the silver and gold that were laid up in the treasury both of the temple and of the kingdom, and sent it to the king of Assyria, *v.* 8. I know not what authority he had thus to dispose of the public stock; but it is common for those that have brought themselves into straits by one sin to help themselves out by another.

Verses 10–16

Though Ahaz had himself sacrificed in high places (*v.* 4), yet God's altar had hitherto continued in its place and in use, but here we have it taken away by wicked Ahaz, and another altar, an idolatrous one, put in the room of it.

I. The model of this new altar, taken from one at Damascus, by the king himself, *v.* 10. The king of Assyria having taken Damascus, thither Ahaz went, to congratulate him and to receive his commands. At Damascus he saw an altar that pleased his fancy extremely. He must have an altar just like this: a pattern of it must be taken immediately.

II. The making of it by Urijah the priest, *v.* 11. Whatever pretence he had, it was a most base wicked thing for him that was a chief priest to make this altar, in compliance with an idolatrous prince, for hereby, 1. He prostituted his authority and profaned the crown of his priesthood, making himself a servant to the lusts of men. 2. He betrayed his trust.

III. The dedicating of it. Urijah set it near the brazen altar. The king was exceedingly pleased with it and offered thereon his burnt-offering, &c., *v.* 12, 13. His sacrifices were not offered to the God of Israel, but to the gods of Damascus.

IV. The removal of God's altar, to make room for it. Ahaz removed God's altar to an obscure corner in the north side of the court, and put his own before the sanctuary, in the place of it. His superstitious invention, at first, jostled *with* God's sacred institution, but at length jostled it *out.* Those will soon come to make nothing of God that will not be content to make him their all. Ahaz durst not quite demolish the brazen altar. He pretends to advance it above its institution. The altar was never designed for an oracle, yet Ahaz will have it for that use. The Jews say that, afterwards, of the brass of it he made that famous dial which was called *the dial of Ahaz, ch.* xx. 11.

Verses 17–20

Here is, I. Ahaz abusing the temple, not the building itself, but some of the furniture of it. 1. He defaced the bases on which the lavers were set (1 Kings vii. 28, 29) and took down the molten sea, *v.* 17. These the priests used for washing. 2. He removed *the covert for the sabbath*, erected either in honour of the sabbath or for the convenience of the priests, when, on the sabbath, they officiated in greater numbers than on other days. 3. The king's entry, which led to the house of the Lord, for the convenience of the royal family (perhaps that ascent which Solomon had made, and which the queen of Sheba admired, 1 Kings x. 5), he turned another way, to show that he did not intend to frequent the house of the Lord any more.

II. Ahaz resigning his life in the midst of his days, at thirty-six years of age (*v.* 19) and leaving his kingdom to a better man, Hezekiah his son (*v.* 20), who proved as much a friend to the temple as he had been an enemy to it.

CHAPTER 17

An account of the captivity of the ten tribes finishes the history of that kingdom, after it had continued about 265 years, from the setting up of Jeroboam the son of Nebat. I. A short narrative of this destruction, ver. 1–6. II. Remarks upon it, and the causes of it, ver. 7–23. III. An account of the nations which succeeded them in the possession of their land, and the mongrel religion set up among them, ver. 24–41.

Verses 1–6

The reign and ruin of Hoshea, the last of the kings of Israel, concerning whom observe,

I. That though he forced his way to the crown by treason and murder (as we read *ch.* xv. 30), yet he gained not the possession of it till seven or eight years after.

II. That, though he was bad, yet not so bad as the kings of Israel had been before him (*v.* 2), not so devoted to the calves as they had been. And some say that this Hoshea took off the embargo which the former kings had put their subjects under, forbidding them to go up to Jerusalem to worship. But what shall we think of this dispensation of providence, that the destruction of the kingdom of Israel should come in the reign of one of the best of its kings? If Hoshea was not so bad as the former kings, yet the people were as bad as those that went before them. Their king gave them leave to do better, but they did as bad as ever, which laid the blame of their sin and ruin wholly upon themselves.

III. That the destruction came gradually.

IV. That they brought it upon themselves by the indirect course they took to shake off the yoke of the king of Assyria, *v.* 4. Had the king and the people of Israel applied to God, made their peace with him and their prayers to him, they might have recovered their liberty, ease, and honour; but they withheld their tribute, and trusted to the king of Egypt to assist them in their revolt, which, if it had taken effect, would have been but to change their oppressors. But Egypt became to them the staff of a broken reed.

V. That it was an utter destruction that came upon them. 1. The king of Israel was made a prisoner. 2. The land of Israel was made a prey. The army of the king of Assyria treated the people as traitors to be punished with the sword of justice rather than as

fair enemies. 3. The royal city of Israel was besieged, and at length taken. Three years it held out after the country was conquered. 4. The people of Israel were carried captives into Assyria, *v.* 6. The generality of the people, those that were of any note, were forced away into the conqueror's country, to be slaves and beggars there. Those that forgot God were themselves forgotten. Many of the meaner sort of people were left behind, many of every tribe, who either went over to Judah or became subject to the Assyrian colonies, and their posterity were *Galileans* or *Samaritans*. But thus ended Israel as a nation; now they became *Lo-ammi—not a people*, and *Lo-ruhamah—unpitied*. James writes to the twelve tribes scattered abroad (James i. 1) and Paul speaks of the twelve tribes which *instantly served God day and night* (Acts xxvi. 7); so that though we never read of those that were carried captive, yet a remnant of them did escape, to keep up the name of Israel, till it came to be worn by the gospel church, the spiritual Israel, in which it will ever remain, Gal. vi. 16.

Verses 7–23

The destruction of the kingdom of the ten tribes and the reasons of it assigned. 1. It was *the Lord that removed Israel out of his sight*; whoever were the instruments, he was the author of this calamity. It was *destruction from the Almighty*; the Assyrian was but the *rod of his anger*, Isa. x. 5. But why would God ruin a people that were raised and incorporated, as Israel was, by miracles and oracles? Was it purely an act of sovereignty? No, it was an act of necessary justice. For, 2. They provoked him to do this by their wickedness. Was it God's doing? Nay, it was their own; by their *way and their doings* they *procured all this to themselves*, and it was their own wickedness that did correct them. This is here very movingly laid open as the cause of all the desolations of Israel.

I. What God had done for Israel, to engage them to serve him. 1. He gave them their liberty (*v.* 7). Thus they were bound in duty and gratitude to be his servants, for he had loosed their bonds; nor would he that rescued them out of the hand of the king of Egypt have contradicted himself so far as to deliver them into the hand of the king of Assyria, as he did, if they had not, by their iniquity, betrayed their liberty and sold themselves. 2. He gave them their law, and was himself their king. They could not plead ignorance of good and evil, sin and duty. 3. He gave them *their land*, for he *cast out the heathen from before them* (*v.* 8), to make room for them; and the casting out of them for their idolatries was as fair a warning as could be given to Israel not to do like them.

II. What they had done against God, notwithstanding these engagements which he had laid upon them. 1. They *sinned against the Lord their God* (*v.* 7), they *did those things that were not right* (*v.* 9), but *secretly*. They *sold themselves to do evil in the sight of the Lord*, that is, they wholly addicted themselves to sin, as slaves to the service of those to whom they are sold, and, by their obstinately persisting in sin, so hardened their own hearts that at length it had become morally impossible for them to recover themselves. Though they were guilty of many immoralities, and violated all the commands of the second table, yet nothing is here specified but their idolatry. *This* was the sin that did most easily beset them; this was, of all sins, most provoking to God: it was the spiritual adultery that broke the marriage-covenant, and was the inlet of all other wickedness. They feared other gods (*v.* 7), that is, worshipped them and paid their homage to them, as if they feared their displeasure. They *built themselves high places in all their cities*, *v.* 9. If in any place there was but the tower of the watchmen (a country town that had no walls, but only a tower to shelter the watch in time of danger), or but a lodge for shepherds, it must be honoured with a high place, and that with an altar. If there was a fenced city, it must be further fortified with a high place. They *set them up images and groves—Asherim* (even *wooden images*, so some think the term, which we translate *groves*, should be rendered) or *Ashtaroth* (so others)—directly contrary to the second commandment, *v.* 10. They served idols (*v.* 12), the works of their own hands. They *burnt incense in all the high places*, to the honour of strange gods, for it was to the dishonour of the true God, *v.* 11. Besides the molten images, even the two calves, they *worshipped all the host of heaven—* the sun, moon, and stars. They used divinations and enchantments, that they might receive directions from the gods.

III. What means God used with them, to bring them off from their idolatries, and to how little purpose. Though they had forsaken God's family of priests, he did not leave them without a succession of prophets, who made it their business to teach them the good knowledge of the Lord, but all in vain (*v.* 14).

IV. How God punished them for their sins. He *was very angry with them* (*v.* 18). He afflicted them (*v.* 20) and *delivered them into the hand of spoilers*, in the days of the judges and of Saul, and afterwards in the days of most of their kings, to see if they would be awakened by the judgments of God to consider and amend their ways; but, when all these corrections did not prevail to drive out the folly, God first *rent Israel from the house of David*, under which they might have been happy.

Lastly, Here is a complaint against Judah in the midst of all (*v.* 19): *Also Judah kept not the commandments of God:* though they were not as yet quite so bad as Israel, yet Israel communicated the infection to Judah.

Verses 24-41

When the children of Israel were dispossessed, and turned out of Canaan, the king of Assyria soon transplanted thither the supernumeraries of his own country, who should be servants to him and masters to the Israelites that remained; and here we have an account of these new inhabitants.

I. Concerning the Assyrians that were brought into the land of Israel we are here told, 1. That they possessed Samaria and *dwelt in the cities thereof*, *v.* 24. 2. That at their first coming God *sent lions among them*. They were probably insufficient to people the country, which occasioned *the beasts of the field to multiply against them* (Exod. xxiii. 29); yet, besides the natural cause, there was a manifest hand of God in it. God ordered them this rough welcome to check their pride. 3. That they sent a remonstrance of this grievance to the king their master, setting forth, it is likely, the loss their infant colony had sustained by the lions and the continual fear they were in of them, and stating that they looked upon it to be a judgment upon them for not worshipping the God of the land, which they could not, because they knew not how, *v.* 26. Herein they shamed the Israelites, who were not so ready to hear the voice of God's judgments as they were. Assyrians begged to be taught that which Israelites hated to be taught. 4. That the king of Assyria took care to have them taught *the manner of the God of the land* (*v.* 27, 28), not out of any affection to that God, but to save his subjects from the lions. He sent back one of the priests of the calves, and he came and dwelt among them, to teach them how they should *fear the Lord*. Being thus taught, they made a mongrel religion of it, worshipped the God of Israel for fear and their own idols for

love (*v.* 33): *They feared the Lord*, but they *served their own gods*. If we may credit the traditions of the Jewish doctors, they tell us that Succoth-Benoth was worshipped in a hen and chickens, Nergal in a cock, Ashima in a smooth goat, Nibhaz in a dog, Tartak in an ass, Adrammelech in a peacock, Anammelech in a pheasant. Our own tell us, more probably, that Succoth-Benoth (signifying *the tents of the daughters*) was Venus. Nergal, being worshipped by the Cuthites, or Persians, was *the fire*. Adrammelech and Anammelech were only distinctions of Moloch. This medley superstition is here said to *continue unto this day* (*v.* 41), till the time when this book was written and long after, above 300 years in all, till the time of Alexander the Great, when Manasse drew over many of the Jews to him, and prevailed with the Samaritans to cast away all their idols and to worship the God of Israel only.

II. Concerning the Israelites that were carried into the land of Assyria. When the two tribes were afterwards carried into Babylon, they were cured by it of their idolatry, and therefore, after seventy years, they were brought back with joy; but the ten tribes were hardened in the furnace and therefore were justly lost in it and left to perish. When they were in the hand of their enemies, and stood in need of deliverance, they were so stupid that they did after the former manner (*v.* 40), they served both the true God and false gods, as if they knew no difference. *Ephraim is joined to idols, let him alone.* So they did, and so did the nations that succeeded them.

Chapter 18

When the prophet had condemned Ephraim for lies and deceit he comforted himself that Judah yet "ruled with God, and was faithful with the Most Holy," Hos. xi. 12. This chapter shows us the affairs of Judah in a good posture, that it may appear God has not quite cast off the seed of Abraham, Rom. xi. 1. Hezekiah is here upon the throne, I. Reforming his kingdom, ver. 1–6. II. Prospering in all his undertakings (ver. 7, 8), and this at the same time when the ten tribes were led captive, ver. 9–12. III. Yet invaded by Sennacherib, the king of Assyria, ver. 13. 1 His country put under contribution, ver. 14–16. 2. Jerusalem besieged, ver. 17. 3. God blasphemed, himself reviled, and his people solicited to revolt, in a virulent speech made by Rabshakeh, ver. 18–37. But how well it ended, and how much to the honour and comfort of our great reformer, we shall find in the next chapter.

Verses 1-8

A general account of the reign of Hezekiah.

I. His great piety, which was the more wonderful because his father was one of the worst of the kings, yet he was one of the best. What good there is in any is not of nature, but of grace, which, contrary to nature, grafts into the good olive that which was wild by nature (Rom. xi. 24), and also that grace gets over the greatest difficulties and disadvantages. Ahaz, it is likely, gave his son a bad education as well as a bad example; Urijah his priest perhaps had the tuition of him; his attendants and companions were such as were addicted to idolatry; and yet Hezekiah became eminently good. When God's grace will work what can hinder it?

1. He was a genuine son of David (*v.* 3): *He did that which was right, according to all that David his father did.* Hezekiah was a second David, had such a love for God's word, and God's house, as he had. Let us not be frightened with an apprehension of the continual decay of virtue, as if, when times and men are bad, they must needs, of course, grow worse and worse; that does not follow, for, after many bad kings, God raised up one that was like David himself.

2. He was a zealous reformer of his kingdom (2 Chron. xxix. 3). He found his kingdom very corrupt, the people in all things superstitious. They had always been so, but in the last reign worse than ever. Idolatry had overspread the land; his spirit was stirred against this idolatry and therefore, as soon as

ever he had power in his hands, he set himself to abolish it (*v.* 4). (1) The images and the groves were idolatrous. These he broke and destroyed. (2) The high places, though they had sometimes been used by the prophets upon special occasions and had been hitherto connived at by the good kings, were nevertheless an affront to the temple and gave opportunity for the introducing of idolatrous usages. Hezekiah, therefore, who made God's word his rule, not the example of his predecessors, removed them, made a law for the removal of them, which law was put in execution with vigour. (3) The brazen serpent was originally of divine institution, and yet, because it had been abused to idolatry, he broke it to pieces. It seems, it had been carefully preserved, as a memorial of God's goodness to their fathers in the wilderness, Num. xxi. 9. But when they began to worship the creature more than the Creator, those that would not worship images borrowed from the heathen were drawn in by the tempter to burn incense to the brazen serpent, because that was made by order from God himself and had been an instrument of good to them. But Hezekiah, in his pious zeal for God's honour, not only forbade the people to worship it, but, that it might never be so abused any more, he showed the people that it was *Nehushtan*, nothing else but *a piece of brass*, and that therefore it was an idle wicked thing to burn incense to it; he then broke it to pieces. If any think that the just honour of the brazen serpent was hereby diminished they will find it abundantly made up again, John iii. 14, where our Saviour makes it a type of himself.

3. Two things he was eminent for in his reformation: (1) Courage and confidence in God. In abolishing idolatry, there was danger of disobliging his subjects, and provoking them to rebel; but *he trusted in the Lord God of Israel* to bear him out in what he did and save him from harm. (2) Constancy and perseverance in his duty.

II. His great prosperity, *v.* 7, 8. He was with God, and then God was with him. Finding himself successful, 1. He threw off the yoke of the king of Assyria, which his father had basely submitted to. When he had thrown out the idolatry of the nations he might well throw off the yoke of their oppression. 2. He made a vigorous attack upon the Philistines, and smote them even unto Gaza.

Verses 9–16

The kingdom of Assyria had now grown considerable.

I. Of the success of Shalmaneser, king of Assyria, against Israel, his besieging Samaria (*v.* 9), taking it (*v.* 10), and carrying the people into captivity (*v.* 11), with the reason why God brought this judgment upon them (*v.* 12): *Because they obeyed not the voice of the Lord their God.* This was related in the foregoing chapter, but it is here repeated, 1. As that which stirred up Hezekiah and his people to purge out idolatry, because they saw the ruin which it brought upon Israel. 2. As that which Hezekiah much lamented, but had not strength to prevent. Though the ten tribes had revolted from the house of David, yet being of the seed of Israel he could not be glad at their calamities. 3. As that which laid Hezekiah and his kingdom open to the king of Assyria, and made it much more easy for him to invade the land.

II. Of the attempt of Sennacherib, the succeeding king of Assyria, against Judah. The descent he made upon Judah was a great calamity to that kingdom, by which God would try the faith of Hezekiah and chastise the people, because they did not willingly part with their idols, but kept them up in their hearts. Even times of reformation may prove troublesome times and then the blame is laid upon the reformers.

This calamity will appear great upon Hezekiah if we consider, 1. How much he lost of his country, *v.* 13. The king of Assyria took all or most of the fenced cities of Judah, the frontier-towns and the garrisons. 2. How dearly he paid for his peace. He saw Jerusalem itself in danger of falling into the enemies' hand, and was willing to purchase its safety at the expense, (1) Of a mean submission (*v.* 14). Where was Hezekiah's courage? Where his confidence in God? (2) Of a vast sum of money—300 talents of silver and thirty of gold to be paid as a present ransom. To raise this sum, he was forced not only to empty the public treasures (*v.* 15), but to take the golden plates off from the doors of the temple, and from the pillars, *v.* 16. Though *the temple sanctified the gold* yet, the necessity being urgent, he thought he might make as bold with that as his father David did with the shew-bread. His father Ahaz had plundered the temple in contempt of it, 2 Chron. xxviii. 24. He had repaid with interest what his father took; and now, with all due reverence, he only begged leave to borrow it in an exigency and for a greater good.

Verses 17–37

I. Jerusalem besieged by Sennacherib's army, *v.* 17. He sent three of his great generals with a great host against Jerusalem. Is this the great king, the king of Assyria? Let him never be named with honour that could do such a dishonourable thing as this, to take Hezekiah's money, which he gave him upon condition he should withdraw his army, and then to advance against his capital city.

II. Hezekiah, and his princes and people, railed upon by Rabshakeh, the chief speaker of the three generals, and one that had the most satirical genius. He was instructed what to say by Sennacherib, who intended to pick a new quarrel with Hezekiah. He had promised, upon the receipt of Hezekiah's money, to withdraw his army, and therefore could not for shame make a forcible attack upon Jerusalem immediately; but he sent Rabshakeh to persuade Hezekiah to surrender it, and, if he should refuse, to besiege it, and to take it by storm. Rabshakeh had the impudence to desire audience of the king himself at the conduit of the upper pool, without the walls; but Hezekiah had the prudence to decline a personal treaty, and sent three commissioners to hear what he had to say. One interruption they gave him in his discourse, which was only to desire that he would speak to them now in the Syrian language, and they would consider what he said and report it to the king, and, if they did not give him a satisfactory answer, then he might appear to the people, by speaking *in the Jews' language*, *v.* 26. Hilkiah did not consider what an unreasonable man he had to deal with, else he would not have made this request, for it did but exasperate Rabshakeh, *v.* 27. Against all the rules of decency and honour he menaces the soldiery, persuades them to desert or mutiny, threatens if they hold out to reduce them to the last extremities of famine, and then goes on to persuade Hezekiah, and his princes and people, to surrender the city.

1. He magnifies his master the king of Assyria. Once and again he calls him, *That great king, the king of Assyria*, *v.* 19, 28. But to those who by faith see the King of Kings in his power and glory even the king of Assyria looks mean and little. Ps. lxxxii. 6, 7.

2. He endeavours to make them believe that it will be much for their advantage to surrender. If they would capitulate, seek his favour with a present and cast themselves upon his mercy, he would give them very good treatment, *v.* 31. If they would surrender upon discretion, though they must expect to be prisoners and captives, yet it would really be happy for them to be so. (1) Their imprisonment

would be to their advantage, for they should *eat every man of his own vine* (v. 31); though the property of their estates would be vested in the conquerors, yet they should have the free use of them. (2) Their captivity would be much more to their advantage: *I will take you away to a land like your own land;* and what the better would they be for that, when they must have nothing in it to call their own?

3. That which he aims at especially is to convince them that it is to no purpose for them to stand out: *What confidence is this wherein thou trustest? v.* 19. To the people he says (v. 29), "*Let not Hezekiah deceive you* into your own ruin, for *he shall not be able to deliver you*; you must either bend or break." Three things he supposes Hezekiah might trust to, and he endeavours to make out the insufficiency of these:—(1) His own military preparations: *Thou sayest, I have counsel and strength for the war;* and we find that so he had, 2 Chron. xxxii. 3. But this Rabshakeh turns off with a slight. With the greatest haughtiness he challenges him to produce 2,000 men that know how to manage a horse, and will venture to give him 2,000 horses if he can. He falsely insinuates that Hezekiah has no men fit to be soldiers, *v.* 23. (2) His alliance with Egypt. He supposes that Hezekiah trusts to Egypt for chariots and horsemen (*v.* 24), because the king of Israel had done so, and of this confidence he truly says, It is *a broken reed* (*v.* 21), it will not only fail a man when he leans on it, but *it will run into his hand and pierce it*, Ezek. xxix. 6, 7. So is the king of Egypt, says he. (3) His interest in God, *v.* 22. He supported himself by depending on the power and promise of God; with this he encouraged himself and his people (*v.* 30): *The Lord will surely deliver us*, and again, *v.* 32. This Rabshakeh was sensible was their great stay, and therefore his endeavours to shake this, as David's enemies, who used all the arts they had to drive him from his confidence in God (Ps. iii. 2; xi. 1), and thus did Christ's enemies, Matt. xxvii. 43. Three things Rabshakeh suggested to discourage their confidence in God, [1] That Hezekiah had forfeited God's protection, and thrown himself out of it, by *destroying the high places and the altars, v.* 22. Here he measures the God of Israel by the gods of the heathen, who delighted in the multitude of altars and temples, and concludes that Hezekiah has given a great offence to the God of Israel, in confining his people to one altar. [2] That God had given orders for the destruction of Jerusalem at this time (*v.* 25): *Have I now come up without the lord?* This is all banter and rhodomontade. He made this pretence to terrify the *people that were on the wall.* [3] That if Jehovah, the God of Israel, should undertake to protect them from the king of Assyria, yet he was not able to do it. With this blasphemy he concluded his speech (*v.* 33-35). See here, *First*, His pride. When he conquered a city he reckoned himself to have conquered its gods, and valued himself mightily upon it. *Secondly*, His profaneness. The God of Israel was not a local deity, but the God of the whole earth. The tradition of the Jews is that Rabshakeh was an apostate Jew, which made him so ready in the Jews' language; if so, his ignorance of the God of Israel was the less excusable and his enmity the less strange, for apostates are commonly the most bitter and spiteful enemies, witness Julian.

Lastly, We are told what the commissioners on Hezekiah's part did. 1. They held their peace, not for want of something to say both on God's behalf and Hezekiah's. But the king had commanded them not to answer him, and they observed their instructions. 2. They rent their clothes in detestation of his blasphemy and in grief for the despised afflicted condition of Jerusalem, the reproach of which was a burden to them. 3. They faithfully reported the matter to the king, their master, and *told him the words of Rabshakeh*.

CHAPTER 19

Jerusalem just ready to be swallowed up by the Assyrian army. An account of its glorious deliverance, not by sword or bow, but by prayer and prophecy, and by the hand of an angel. I. Hezekiah, in great concern, sent to the prophet Isaiah, to desire his prayers (ver. 1–5) and received from him an answer of peace, ver. 6, 7. II. Sennacherib sent a letter to Hezekiah to frighten him into a surrender, ver. 8–13. III. Hezekiah thereupon, by a very solemn prayer, recommended his case to God, the righteous Judge, and begged help from him, ver. 14–19. IV. God, by Isaiah, sent him a very comfortable message, assuring him of deliverance, ver. 20–34. V. The army of the Assyrians was all cut off by an angel and Sennacherib himself slain by his own sons, ver. 35–37. And so God glorified himself and saved his people.

Verses 1-7

The contents of Rabshakeh's speech brought to Hezekiah.

I. Hezekiah discovered a deep concern at the dishonour done to God by Rabshakeh's blasphemy. When he heard it he *rent his clothes and covered himself with sackcloth, v.* 1. Royal robes are not too good to be rent, nor royal flesh too good to be clothed with sackcloth, in humiliation for indignities done to God and for the perils and terrors of his Jerusalem. The king was in sackcloth, but many of his subjects were in soft clothing.

II. He *went up to the house of the Lord*, to meditate and pray. He was not considering what answer to return to Rabshakeh, but refers the matter to God. "*Thou shalt answer, Lord, for me.*"

III. He sent to the prophet Isaiah, by honourable messengers, to desire his prayers, *v.* 2-4. Eliakim and Shebna were two of those that had heard the words of Rabshakeh and were able to acquaint Isaiah with the case. The messengers were to go in sackcloth, because they were to represent the king, who was so clothed.

1. Their errand to Isaiah was, "*Lift up thy prayer for the remnant that is left*, that is, for Judah, which is but a remnant now that the ten tribes are gone—for Jerusalem, which is but a remnant now that the defenced cities of Judah are taken." When we desire the prayers of others for us we must not think we are excused from praying for ourselves. When Hezekiah sent to Isaiah to pray for him he himself *went into the house of the Lord* to offer up his own prayers. When the interests of God's church are brought very low, so that there is but a remnant left, then it is time to *lift up our prayer for that remnant.*

2. Two things are urged to Isaiah, to engage his prayers for them:—(1) Their fears of the enemy (*v.* 3). "We are ready to perish; *if thou canst do anything, have compassion upon us and help us.*" (2) Their hopes in God. To him they look, on him they depend, to appear for them. "He has heard and known the blasphemous words of Rabshakeh, and therefore, it may be, he will hear and rebuke them. We hope he will. Help us with thy prayers to bring the cause before him, and then we are content to leave it with him."

IV. God, by Isaiah, sent to Hezekiah, to assure him that he would glorify himself in the ruin of the Assyrians. Hezekiah sent to Isaiah, not to enquire concerning the event, but to desire his assistance in his duty. He encouraged Hezekiah, who was much dismayed: *Be not afraid of the words which thou hast heard;* they are but words (though swelling and fiery words), and words are but wind. He promised to frighten the king of Assyria worse than Rabshakeh had frightened him: "*I will send a blast upon him*" (that pestilential breath which killed his army).

Verses 8-19

Rabshakeh, having delivered his message and received no answer left his army before Jerusalem, under the command of the other generals, and went to the king for further orders. He found him besieging Libnah, a city that had revolted from Judah, *ch.* viii. 22. However, he was now alarmed with the rumour that the king of the Cushites, who bordered upon the Arabians, was coming out against him with a great army, *v.* 9. This made him very desirous to gain Jerusalem with all speed. To take it by force would cost him more time and men than he could well spare, and therefore he renewed his attack upon Hezekiah to persuade him tamely to surrender it.

I. Sennacherib sent a letter to Hezekiah, a railing letter, a blasphemous letter, to persuade him to surrender Jerusalem, *"Let not thy God deceive thee,"* *v.* 10. To terrify Hezekiah, and drive him from his anchor, he magnifies himself and his own achievements. How proudly he boasts, 1. Of the lands he had conquered (*v.* 11): *All lands,* and destroyed utterly! So far was he from destroying all lands that at this time the land of Cush, and Tirhakah its king, were a terror to him. 2. Of the gods he had conquered, *v.* 12. 3. Of the kings he had conquered (*v.* 13), the *king of Hamath and the king of Arpad.* Whether he means the prince or the idol, he means to make himself appear greater than either.

II. Hezekiah was not so haughty as not to receive the letter. When he had read it he was not in such a passion as to write an answer to it in the same provoking language; but he immediately went up to the temple, presented himself, and then *spread the letter before the Lord* (*v.* 14); not as if God needed to have the letter shown to him, but hereby he signified that he acknowledged God in all his ways. In the prayer which Hezekiah prayed over this letter, 1. He adores the God whom Sennacherib had blasphemed (*v.* 15), calls him *the God of Israel,* because Israel was his peculiar people, and *the God that dwelt between the cherubim,* because there was the peculiar residence of his glory upon earth; but he gives glory to him as *the God of the whole earth,* and not, as Sennacherib fancied him to be, *the God of Israel only,* and confined to the temple. 2. He appeals to God concerning the insolence and profaneness of Sennacherib (*v.* 16). 3. He owns Sennacherib's triumphs over the gods of the heathen, but distinguishes between them and the God of Israel (*v.* 17, 18): He has indeed *cast their gods into the fire;* for *they were no gods.* 4. He prays that God will now glorify himself in the defeat of Sennacherib and the deliverance of Jerusalem out of his hands (*v.* 19): *"Now therefore save us;* and let all the world know, and be made to confess, that *thou art the Lord God,* the self-existent sovereign God, *even thou only,* and that all pretenders are vanity and a lie."

Verses 20–34

The gracious answer which God gave to Hezekiah's prayer. In general, God assured him that his prayer was heard, his prayer against Sennacherib, *v.* 20.

I. Confusion and shame to Sennacherib and his forces. It is here foretold that he should be humbled and broken. Sennacherib is here represented,

1. As the scorn of Jerusalem, *v.* 21. He thought himself the terror of the daughter of Zion, that chaste and beautiful virgin, and that by his threats he could force her to submit to him: "But, being a virgin in her Father's house and under his protection, she defies thee, despises thee, laughs thee to scorn. Thy impotent malice is ridiculous; he that sits in heaven laughs at thee, and therefore so do those that abide under his shadow." By this word God intended to silence the fears of Hezekiah and his people.

2. As an enemy to God. Hezekiah pleaded this: "Lord, he has reproached thee," *v.* 16. "He has," saith God, "and I take it as against myself (*v.* 22): *Whom hast thou reproached?* Is it not the Holy One of Israel, whose honour is dear to him, and who has power to vindicate it, which the gods of the heathen have not?"

3. As a proud vainglorious fool, that spoke *great swelling words of vanity,* and *boasted of a false gift,* by his boasts, as well as by his threats, reproaching the Lord. For, (1) He magnified his own achievements out of measure (*v.* 23, 24): *Thou hast said* so and so. What a mighty figure does Sennacherib think he makes! Driving his chariots to the tops of the highest mountains, forcing his way through woods and rivers, breaking through all difficulties, making himself master of all he had a mind to. (2) He took to himself the glory of doing these great things, whereas they were all *the Lord's doing,* *v.* 25, 26. And as for the desolations thou hast made in the earth, and particularly in Judah, thou art but the instrument in God's hand, a mere tool: it is *I that have brought it to pass.* Sennacherib's boasts here are expounded in Isa. x. 13, 14, *By the strength of my hand I have done it, and by my wisdom,* &c.; and they are answered (*v.* 15), *Shall the axe boast itself against him that heweth therewith?*

4. As under the check and rebuke of that God whom he blasphemed. All his motions were, (1) Under the divine cognizance (*v.* 27): *"I know thy abode,* and what thou dost secretly devise and design, the noise and bluster thou makest: I know it all." (2) Under the divine control (*v.* 28): *"I will put my hook in thy nose,* thou great Leviathan (Job xli. 1, 2), *my bridle in thy jaws,* thou great Behemoth. I will restrain thee, manage thee, turn thee where I please, send thee home like a fool as thou camest."

II. Salvation and joy to Hezekiah and his people. This shall be a sign to them of God's favour, and that he is reconciled to them, and *his anger is turned away* (Isa. xii. 1), that a good issue shall be put to their present distress.

1. Provisions were scarce and dear; and what should they do for food? The fruits of the earth were devoured by the Assyrian army, Isa. xxxii. 9, 10, &c. Why, they shall not only dwell in the land, but *verily they shall be fed.* "*Eat you this year that which groweth of itself,* and you shall reap what you did not sow." But the next year was the sabbatical year, when the land was to rest, and they must neither sow nor reap. What must they do that year? Why, *Jehovah-jireh—The Lord will provide.* And then, the third year, their husbandry should return into its former channel, and they should sow and reap as they used to do. 2. The country was laid waste, families were broken up and scattered, and all was in confusion; how should it be otherwise when it was over-run by such an army? As to this, it is promised that *the remnant that has escaped of the house of Judah* shall yet again be planted in their own habitations, shall increase and grow rich, *v.* 30. See how their prosperity is described: it is *taking root downwards,* and *bearing fruit upwards.* Such is the prosperity of the soul: it is taking root downwards by faith in Christ, and then being fruitful in fruits of righteousness. 3. The city was shut up, none went out or came in; but now the remnant in Jerusalem and Zion shall go forth freely, and there shall be none to hinder them, or make them afraid, *v.* 31. Great destruction had been made both in city and country, but in both there was a remnant that typified the saved remnant of Israelites that escaped, which typified the saved remnant of Israelites indeed (as appears by comparing Isa. x. 22, 23, which speaks of this very event, with Rom. ix. 27, 28), and they shall go forth into the glorious liberty of the children of God. 4. The Assyrians were advancing towards Jerusalem, and would in a little time besiege it in form, and it was in great danger of falling into their hands. But it is here promised that, though the enemy had now encamped before the city, yet

they should never *come into the city*, no, nor so much as *shoot an arrow* into it (v. 32, 33),—that he should be forced to retire with shame. 5. The honour and truth of God are engaged for the doing of all this. These are great things, but how will they be effected? Why, *the zeal of the Lord of hosts shall do this*, v. 31. His zeal, (1) For his own honour (v. 34): "I will do it for my own sake, to make myself an everlasting name." God's reasons of mercy are fetched from within himself. (2) For his own truth: "I will do it for my servant David's sake; not for the sake of his merit, but the promise made to him and the covenant made with him, those sure mercies of David."

Verses 35–37

The word was no sooner spoken than the work was done.

I. The army of Assyria was entirely routed. Hezekiah had not force sufficient to sally out upon them and attack their camp, nor would God do it by sword or bow. It was *not by the sword of a mighty man or of a mean man*, that is, not of any man at all, but of an angel, that the Assyrian army was to fall (Isa. xxxi. 8). Josephus says it was done by a pestilential disease, which was instant death to them. The number slain was very great, 185,000 men, and Rabshakeh, it is likely, among the rest. When the besieged *arose, early in the morning, behold they were all dead corpses*, scarcely a living man among them. Some think the 76th Psalm was penned on this occasion, where we read that the *stout-hearted were spoiled and slept their sleep*, their last, their long sleep, v. 5.

II. The king of Assyria was hereby put into the utmost confusion. Ashamed to see himself, after all his proud boasts, thus defeated and disabled *He departed, and went, and returned*; the manner of the expression intimates the great disorder and distraction of mind he was in, v. 36. And it was not long before God cut him off too, by the hands of *two of his own sons*, v. 37. The God of Israel had done enough to convince him that he was the only true God, whom therefore he ought to worship; yet he persists in his idolatry, and seeks to his false god for protection against a God of irresistible power. His sons that murdered him were suffered to escape, and would be looked upon as the more excusable in what they had done if it be true (as Bishop Patrick suggested) that he was now vowing to sacrifice them to his god. His successor was another son, *Esarhaddon*, who did not aim, like his father, to enlarge his conquests, but rather to improve them; for he it was that first sent colonies of Assyrians to inhabit the country of Samaria, as appears, Ezra iv. 2, where the Samaritans say it was *Esarhaddon that brought them thither*.

CHAPTER 20

I. Hezekiah's sickness, and his recovery in answer to prayer, in performance of a promise, in the use of means, and confirmed with a sign, ver. 1–11. II. Hezekiah's sin, and his recovery from that, ver. 12–19. In both of these, Isaiah was God's messenger to him. III. The conclusion of his reign, ver. 20, 21.

Verses 1–11

The historian, having shown us blaspheming Sennacherib destroyed in the midst of the prospects of life, here shows us praying Hezekiah delivered in the midst of the prospects of death.

I. Here is Hezekiah's sickness. *In those days*, that is, in the same year in which the king of Assyria besieged Jerusalem. Some think it was at the time that the Assyrian army was besieging the city or preparing for it. Others think it was soon after the defeat of Sennacherib. Hezekiah, in the midst of his triumphs, is seized with sickness. He was sick of the plague, for we read of the boil or plague-sore,

v. 7. The same disease which was killing to the Assyrians was trying to him. Hezekiah, lately favoured of heaven above most men, yet is sick unto death.

II. Warning brought him to prepare for death. It is brought by Isaiah. The prophet tells him, 1. That his disease is mortal, and, if he be not recovered by a miracle of mercy, will certainly be fatal: *Thou shalt die, and not live.* 2. That therefore he must, with all speed, get ready for death: *Set thy house in order.* Set the heart in order by renewed acts of repentance, and faith, and resignation to God, with cheerful farewells to this world and welcomes to another; and set the house in order, make thy will, settle thy estate, put thy affairs in the best posture thou canst, for the ease of those that shall come after thee.

III. His prayer hereupon: *He prayed unto the Lord*, v. 2. Is any sick? Let him be prayed for, let him be prayed with, and let him pray. Hezekiah had found the prayers of faith bring in answers of peace. He had now received the sentence of death within himself, and, if it was reversible, it must be reversed by prayer. If the sentence was irreversible, yet prayer is one of the best preparations for death, because by it we fetch in strength and grace from God to enable us to finish well. Observe,

1. The circumstances of this prayer. (1) He *turned his face to the wall*, probably as he lay in his bed. This he did perhaps for privacy; he could not retire to his closet as he used to do, but he turned from the company that were about him, to converse with God. Or, as some think, he turned his face towards the temple, to show how willingly he would have gone up thither, to pray this prayer (as he did, ch. xix. 1, 14), if he had been able. (2) He *wept sorely*. Some gather from this that he was unwilling to die. It is in the nature of man to have some dread of the separation of soul and body. There was also something peculiar in Hezekiah's case: he was now in the midst of his usefulness, had begun a good work of reformation, which he feared would, through the corruption of the people, fall to the ground, if he should die. Let Hezekiah's prayer interpret his tears, and in *that* we find nothing that intimates him to have been under any of that fear of death which has either bondage or torment.

2. The prayer itself: "*Remember now, O Lord! how I have walked before thee in truth;* and either spare me to live, that I may continue thus to walk, or, if my work be done, receive me to that glory which thou hast prepared for those that have thus walked." Hezekiah does not pray, "Lord, spare me," or "Lord, take me; God's will be done;" but, *Lord, remember me; whether I live or die, let me be thine.*

IV. The answer which God immediately gave to this prayer of Hezekiah. The prophet had got but to the middle court when he was sent back with another message to Hezekiah (v. 4, 5), to tell him that he should recover. Upon Hezekiah's prayer God did that for him which otherwise he would not have done. God here calls Hezekiah *the captain of his people*, to intimate that he would reprieve him for his people's sake. He calls himself *the God of David*, to intimate that he would reprieve him out of a regard to the covenant made with David. In this answer, 1. God honours his prayers: *I have heard thy prayers, I have seen thy tears.* 2. God exceeds his prayers; he only begged that God would remember his integrity, but God here promises, (1) To restore him from his illness: *I will heal thee.* (2) To restore him to such a degree of health that *on the third day he should go up to the house of the Lord*, to return thanks. (3) To add fifteen years to his life. (4) To deliver Jerusalem from the king of Assyria, v. 6. This was the thing which Hezekiah's heart was upon as much as his own recovery, and therefore the promise of this is here repeated.

V. The means which were to be used for his recovery, *v.* 7. Isaiah was his physician. He ordered an outward application, a very cheap and common thing: "Lay a *lump of figs to the boil*, to ripen it and bring it to a head, that the matter of the disease may be discharged that way." It is our duty, when we are sick, to make use of such means as are proper to help nature, else we do not trust God, but tempt him. Plain and ordinary medicines must not be despised, for many such God has graciously made serviceable to man.

VI. The sign which was given for the encouragement of his faith. 1. He begged it, not in any distrust of the power or promise of God, but because he looked upon the things promised to be very great things and worthy to be so confirmed. Hezekiah asked, *What is the sign*, not that I shall go up to the thrones of judgment or up to the gate, but *up to the house of the Lord?* He desired to recover that he might glorify God *in the gates of the daughter of Zion*. It is not worth while to live for any other purpose than to serve God. 2. It was put to his choice whether the sun should go back or go forward. It is supposed that the degrees were half hours, and that it was just noon when the proposal was made, and the question is, "Shall the sun go back to its place at seven in the morning or forward to its place at five in the evening?" He humbly desired the sun might go back ten degrees, because, though either would be a great miracle, yet, it being the natural course of the sun to go forward, its going back would seem more strange, and would be more significant of Hezekiah's *returning to the days of his youth* (Job. xxxiii. 25) and the lengthening out of the day of his life. It was accordingly done, upon the prayer of Isaiah (*v.* 11): God brought the sun back ten degrees, which appeared to Hezekiah by the going back of the shadow upon the dial of Ahaz, which, it is likely, he could see through his chamber window; and the same was observed upon all other dials, even in Babylon, 2 Chron. xxxii. 31. Whether this retrograde motion of the sun was gradual—which would make the day ten hours longer than usual—or whether it darted back on a sudden, and, after continuing a little while, was restored again to its usual place, so that no change was made in the state of the heavenly bodies (as the learned Bishop Patrick thinks)—we are not told.

Verses 12–21

I. An embassy sent to Hezekiah by the king of Babylon, to congratulate him on his recovery, *v.* 12. The kings of Babylon had hitherto been tributaries to the kings of Assyria, and Nineveh was the royal city. We find Babylon subject to the king of Assyria, *ch.* xvii. 24. But by degrees things were so changed that Assyria became subject to the kings of Babylon. This king of Babylon sent to compliment Hezekiah upon a double account. 1. Upon the account of religion. The Babylonians worshipped the sun, and, perceiving what honour their god had done to Hezekiah, in going back for his sake, they thought themselves obliged to do honour to him likewise. 2. Upon the account of civil interest. If the king of Babylon was now meditating a revolt from the king of Assyria, it was policy to get Hezekiah into his interest. He found himself obliged to Hezekiah, and his God, for the weakening of the Assyrian forces, and had reason to think he could not have a more powerful and valuable ally than one that had so good an interest in the upper world.

II. The kind entertainment Hezekiah gave to these ambassadors, *v.* 13. 1. He was too fond of them. He *hearkened unto them*. Though they were idolaters,

yet he was forward to come into a confederacy with the king their master. 2. He was too fond of showing them his palace, his treasures, and his magazines, that they might see, and might report to their master, what a great king he was.

III. The examination of Hezekiah concerning this matter, *v.* 14, 15. Isaiah, who had often been his comforter, is now his reprover. "Who are these? What is their business?" Hezekiah not only submitted to the examination but made an ingenuous confession: *There is nothing among my treasures that I have not shown them*. Why then did he not bring them to Isaiah, and show him to them who was the best treasure, and who by his prayers had been instrumental in all those wonders which these ambassadors came to enquire into?

IV. The sentence passed upon him for his pride and vanity. The sentence is (*v.* 17, 18), 1. That the treasures he was so proud of should hereafter become a prey. 2. That the king of Babylon, with whom he was so fond of an alliance, should be the enemy that should make a prey of them. The sins of Manasseh, his idolatries and murders, were the cause of that calamity; but it is now foretold to Hezekiah, to convince him of the folly of his pride. Hezekiah was fond of assisting the king of Babylon to rise, and to reduce the exorbitant power of the kings of Assyria; but he is told that his royal seed shall become the king of Babylon's slaves. Babylon will be the ruin of those that are fond of Babylon.

V. Hezekiah's humble and patient submission to this sentence, *v.* 19. It is not only just, but good; for he will bring good out of it, and do me good by the foresight of it.

Lastly, Here is the conclusion of Hezekiah's life and story, *v.* 20, 21. In 2 Chron. *ch.* xxix–xxxii much more is recorded of Hezekiah's work of reformation and it seems that in the civil chronicles there were many things recorded of his might and the good offices he did for Jerusalem, particularly his bringing water by pipes into the city. But this historian leaves him *asleep with his fathers*, and a son in his throne that proved very untoward. Wicked Ahaz was the son of a godly father and the father of a godly son; holy Hezekiah was the son of a wicked father and the father of a wicked son.

CHAPTER 21

A short but sad account of the reigns of two of the kings of Judah, Manasseh and Amon. I. Concerning Manasseh, all the account we have of him here is, 1. That he devoted himself to sin, to all manner of wickedness, idolatry, and murder, ver. 1–9 and ver. 16. 2. That therefore God devoted him, and Jerusalem for his sake, to ruin, ver. 10–18. In the book of Chronicles we have an account of his troubles, and his repentance. II. Concerning Amon we are only told that he lived in sin (ver. 19–22), died quickly by the sword, and left good Josiah his successor, ver. 23–26. By these two reigns Jerusalem was much debauched and much weakened.

Verses 1–9

The beauty of Jerusalem is stained, and all her glory, all her joy, sunk and gone. These verses give such an account of this reign as make it, in all respects, the reverse of the last, and, in a manner, the ruin of it.

I. Manasseh began young. He was but *twelve years old when he began to reign* (*v.* 1), born when his father was about forty-two years old, three years after his sickness. But being young, 1. He was puffed up with his honour, and thinking himself very wise, valued himself upon his undoing what his father had done. 2. He was easily wrought upon and drawn aside by seducers. Those that were enemies to Hezekiah's reformation, and retained an affection for the old idolatries, flattered him, and used his power at their pleasure.

II. He reigned long, longest of any of the kings of Judah, fifty-five years. This was the only very bad reign that was a long one: in the beginning of his reign for some time affairs continued to move in the course that his father left them in, and in the latter end of his reign, after his repentance, religion got head again. Though he reigned long, yet some of this time he was a prisoner in Babylon.

III. He reigned very ill.

1. In general, (1) *He did that which was evil in the sight of the Lord.* (2) *He did after the abominations of the heathen* (v. 2) and as did Ahab (v. 3), nay (v. 9), he *did more evil than did the nations whom the Lord destroyed.*

2. More particularly, (1) He *rebuilt the high places which his father had destroyed,* v. 3. (2) He set up other gods, *Baal* and *Ashtaroth* (which we translate *a grove*), and all the host of heaven, the sun and moon, the other planets, and the constellations; these he worshipped and served (v. 3), gave their names to the images he made, and then did homage to them. To these he built altars (v. 5), and offered sacrifices, no doubt, on these altars. (3) He *made his son pass through the fire,* by which he dedicated him a votary to Moloch, in contempt of the seal of circumcision by which he had been dedicated to God. (4) He made the devil his oracle, and *used enchantments and dealt with familiar spirits* (v. 6) like Saul. Conjurers and fortune-tellers (who pretended, by the stars or the clouds, lucky and unlucky days, good and bad omens, the flight of birds, or the entrails of beasts, to foretell things to come) were his intimates. (5) We find afterwards (v. 16) that he shed innocent blood. The *blood of the prophets* is, in a particular manner, charged upon Jerusalem, and it is probable that he put to death many of them. The tradition of the Jews is that he caused the prophet Isaiah to be sawn asunder; and many think the apostle refers to this in Heb. xi. 37.

3. Three things are here mentioned as aggravations of Manasseh's idolatry:—(1) That he set up his images and altars *in the house of the Lord* (v. 4), in the two courts of the temple (v. 5), in the very house of which God had said to Solomon, *Here will I put my name,* v. 7. (2) That hereby he put a great slight upon the word of God, and his covenant with Israel.

Verses 10–18

Here is the doom of Judah and Jerusalem read. The prophets were sent, in the first place, to teach them the knowledge of God, to remind them of their duty. If they succeeded not in that, their next work was to reprove them for their sins, that they might repent. If in this they prevailed not, but sinners went on frowardly, their next work was to foretell the judgments of God, that the terror of them might awaken those to repentance who would not be made sensible of the obligations of his love.

I. A recital of the crime. The indictment is read upon which the judgment is grounded, v. 11.

II. A prediction of the judgment God would bring upon them for this: *They have done that which was evil,* and therefore *I am bringing evil upon them* (v. 12). It should make a great noise in the world and occasion many speculations. When God lays judgment to the plummet it shall be *the plummet of the house of Ahab,* marking out for the same ruin to which that wretched family was devoted. See Isa. xxviii. 17. *I will wipe it as a man wipes a dish.* The city should be emptied of its inhabitants, which had been the filth of it, as a dish is emptied when it is wiped: "They shall all be carried captive, the *land shall enjoy her sabbaths,* and be laid by as a dish when it is wiped." This should be in order to the purifying, not the destroying, of Jerusalem. The dish shall not be dropped, not broken to pieces, or melted down, but only wiped. Sin is spoken of here as the alpha and omega of their miseries.

This is all we have here of Manasseh; he stands convicted and condemned; but in the book of Chronicles we hear of his repentance, and acceptance with God. He was buried, it is likely by his own order, *in the garden of his own house* (v. 18); for, being truly humbled for his sins, he judged himself *no more worthy to be called a son,* a son of David, and therefore not worthy to have even his dead body buried *in the sepulchres of his fathers.* And better it is, and more honourable, for a sinner to die repenting, and be buried in a garden, than to die impenitent, and be buried in the abbey.

Verses 19–26

The short and inglorious reign of Amon, the son of Manasseh—a son not born till he was forty-five years old. 1. His reign was very wicked: *He forsook the God of his fathers* (v. 22), disobeyed the commands given to his fathers. He trod in the steps of his father's idolatry, and revived that which he, in the latter end of his days, had put down. 2. His end was very tragical. He having rebelled against God, his own servants *conspired against him and slew him,* when he had reigned but two years, v. 23. Two things the people of the land did, by their representatives, (1) They did justice on the traitors that had slain the king, and put them to death; for, though he was a *bad* king, he was *their* king, and it was a part of their allegiance to him to avenge his death. (2) They did a kindness to themselves in *making Josiah his son king in his stead,* encouraged, it may be, by the indications he gave, even in his early days, of a good disposition. Now they made a happy change from one of the worst to one of the best of all the kings of Judah.

CHAPTER 22

The story of the reign of good king Josiah. Here, after his general character (ver. 1, 2), we have a particular account of the respect he paid, I. To God's house, which he repaired, ver. 3–7. II. To God's book, which he was much affected with the reading of, ver. 8–11. III. To God's messengers, whom he thereupon consulted, ver. 12–14, and by whom he received from God an answer threatening Jerusalem's destruction (ver. 15–17), but promising favour to him (ver. 18–20), upon which he set about that glorious work of reformation which we have an account of in the next chapter.

Verses 1–10

Concerning Josiah we are here told,

I. That he was very young when he began to reign (v. 1), only eight years old. Our English Israel had once a king that was such a child, Edward VI. Josiah, being young, had not received any bad impressions from the example of his father and grandfather, but soon saw their errors, and God gave him grace to take warning by them. See Ezek. xviii. 14, &c.

II. That he *did that which was right in the sight of the Lord,* v. 2. See the sovereignty of divine grace—the father passed by and left to perish in his sin, the son a chosen vessel. Nothing is too hard for that grace to do. There are errors on both hands, but God kept him in the right way; he fell neither into superstition nor profaneness.

III. That he took care for the repair of the temple. This he did in the eighteenth year of his reign, v. 3. Compare 2 Chron. xxxiv. 8. He began much sooner to *seek the Lord* (as appears, 2 Chron. xxxiv. 3), but it is to be feared the work of reformation went slowly on and met with much opposition. He sent Shaphan, the secretary of state, to Hilkiah the high priest, to take an account of the money that was collected for this use by the door-keepers (v. 4), for, it seems, they took much the same way of raising the money that Joash took, *ch.* xii. 9. This money, so collected, he ordered him to lay out for the repair of the temple, v. 5, 6. And now, it seems, the workmen (as in the days of Joash) acquitted themselves so well that *there was no reckoning made with them* (*v.* 7), which is certainly mentioned to the praise of the workmen.

IV. That, in repairing the temple, *the book of the law* was happily found and brought to the king, *v.* 8, 10. Some think this book was the autograph, or original manuscript, of the five books of Moses, under his own hand; others think it was only an ancient and authentic copy. 1. It seems, this book of the law was lost or missing. Perhaps it was carelessly mislaid and neglected, thrown by into a corner (as some throw their Bibles), by those that knew not the value of it, and forgotten there; or it was maliciously concealed by some of the idolatrous kings who buried it, in hopes it would never see the light again; or, as some think, it was carefully laid up by some of its friends, lest it should fall into the hands of its enemies. Whoever were the instruments of its preservation, we ought to acknowledge the hand of God in it. If this was the only authentic copy of the Pentateuch then in being, we now have reason to thank God, upon our knees, for that happy providence by which Hilkiah found this book at this time, found it when *he sought it not,* Isa. lxv. 1. God's care of the Bible is a plain indication of his interest in it. 2. Whether this was the only authentic copy in being or no, it seems the things contained in it were new both to the king himself and to the high priest; for the king, upon the reading of it, rent his clothes. If the book of the law was lost, it seems difficult to determine what rule *Josiah* went by in doing that which was *right in the sight of the Lord,* and how the priests and people kept up the rites of their religion. I am apt to think that the people generally took up with abstracts of the law, like our abridgments of the statutes, a sort of ritual, directing them in the observances of their religion, but leaving out what they thought fit, and particularly the promises and threatenings (Lev. xxvi and Deut. xxviii &c.). These were the portions of the law which Josiah was so much affected with (*v.* 13), for these were new to him. No summaries, extracts, or collections, out of the Bible (though they may have their use) can be effectual to convey and preserve the knowledge of God and his will like the Bible itself. 3. It was a great instance of God's favour, and a token for good to Josiah and his people, that the book of the law was thus seasonably brought to light, to direct and quicken that blessed reformation which Josiah had begun. The translating of the scriptures into vulgar tongues was the glory, strength, and joy of the Reformation. It is observable that they were about a good work, repairing the temple, when they found the book of the law. Those that do their duty according to their knowledge shall have their knowledge increased. 4. Hilkiah the priest was exceedingly well pleased with the discovery. "O," says he to Shaphan, "rejoice with me, for *I have found the book of the law,* εὑρηκα, εὑρηκα, *I have found, I have found,* that jewel of inestimable value. Here, carry it to the king; it is the richest jewel of his crown. Read it before him. He walks in *the way of David his father.*"

Verses 11–20

The book of the law is not laid up in the king's cabinet as a piece of antiquity, a rarity to be admired, but it is read before the king. Those put the truest honour upon their Bibles that study them and converse with them daily, feed on that bread and walk by that light.

I. The impressions which the reading of the law made upon Josiah. He had long thought the case of his kingdom bad, by reason of the idolatries and impieties that had been found among them, but he never thought it so bad as he perceived it to be by the book of the law now read to him. The rending of his clothes signified the rending of his heart.

II. The application he made to God hereupon: *Go, enquire of the Lord for me, v.* 13.

1. Two things we may suppose he desired to know:— "Enquire, (1) What we shall do; what course we shall take to turn away God's wrath and prevent the judgments which our sins have deserved." (2) "What we may expect and must provide for." He acknowledges, "*Our fathers have not hearkened to the words of this book;* if this be the rule of right, certainly our fathers have been much in the wrong. Certainly *great is the wrath that is kindled against us;* if this be the word of God, as no doubt it is, and he will be true to his word, as no doubt he will be, we are all undone."

2. This enquiry Josiah sent, (1) By some of his great men, who are named, *v.* 12, and again *v.* 14. (2) To Huldah the prophetess, *v.* 14. Miriam helped to lead Israel out of Egypt (Micah vi. 4), Deborah judged them, and now Huldah instructed them in the mind of God, and her being a wife was no prejudice at all to her being a prophetess; *marriage is honourable in all.* It was a mercy to Jerusalem that when Bibles were scarce they had prophets, as afterwards, when prophecy ceased, that they had more Bibles. The king's messengers made Huldah their oracle, probably because her husband had a place at court (for he was keeper of the wardrobe). They had, it is likely, consulted her upon other occasions, and had found that the word of God in her mouth was truth. She was near, for she dwelt at Jerusalem, in the second rank of buildings from the royal palace. The Jews say that she prophesied among the women, the court ladies, who it is probable had their apartments in that place.

III. The answer he received from God to his enquiry. Huldah returned it in the dialect of a prophetess, speaking from him before whom all stand upon the same level—*Tell the man that sent you to me, v.* 15.

1. She let him know what judgments God had in store for Judah and Jerusalem (*v.* 16, 17): *My wrath shall be kindled against this place.*

2. She let him know what mercy God had in store for him. (1) Notice is taken of his great tenderness and concern—*Thy heart was tender.* He received the impressions of God's word, trembled at it and yielded to it. This is tenderness of heart, and thus he *humbled himself before the Lord.* Those that most fear God's wrath are least likely to feel it. (2) A reprieve is granted till after his death (*v.* 20): *I will gather thee to thy fathers.* God promised him he should not live to see it, which would have been but a small reward for his eminent piety if there had not been another world in which he should be abundantly recompensed, Heb. xi. 16. He died in the love and favour of God, which secure such a peace as no circumstances of dying, no, not dying in the field of war, could alter the nature of, or break in upon.

CHAPTER 23

I. The happy continuance of the goodness of Josiah's reign, and the progress of the reformation he began, reading the law (ver. 1, 2), renewing the covenant (ver. 3), cleansing the temple (ver. 4), and rooting out idols and idolatry, with all the relics thereof, in all places, as far as his power reached (ver. 5–20), keeping a solemn passover (ver. 21–23), and clearing the country of witches (ver. 24); and in all this acting with extraordinary vigour, ver. 25. II. The unhappy conclusion of it in his untimely death, as a token of the continuance of God's wrath against Jerusalem, ver. 26–30. III. The more unhappy consequences of his death, in the bad reigns of his two sons Jehoahaz and Jehoiakim, that came after him, ver. 31–37.

Verses 1–3

Josiah had received a message from God that there was no preventing the ruin of Jerusalem, but he did not therefore sit down in despair. Here we have the preparations for reformation. 1. He summoned a general assembly of the states, the elders, the magistrates or representatives of Judah and Jerusalem, to meet him *in the house of the Lord*, with the priests and prophets, the ordinary and extraordinary ministers, that it might become a national act. 2. Instead of making a speech to this convention, he ordered the book of the law to be read to them; nay, it should seem, he read it himself (*v.* 2), as one much affected with it and desirous that they should be so too. Besides the convention of the great men, he had a congregation of the *men of Judah and the inhabitants of Jerusalem* to hear the law read. If the people be but as steadfastly resolved to obey by law as he is to govern by law, the kingdom will be happy. 3. Instead of proposing laws for the confirming of them in their duty, he proposed an association by which they should all jointly engage themselves to God, *v.* 3. The book of the law was the book of the covenant, that, if they would be to God a people, he would be to them a God; they here engage themselves to do their part, not doubting but that then God would do his. The covenanters were, in the first place, the king himself, who stood by his pillar (*ch.* xi. 14) and publicly declared his consent to this covenant. *All the people* likewise *stood to the covenant*.

Verses 4–24

An account of such a reformation as we have not met with in all the history of the kings of Judah, such thorough riddance made of all the abominable things and such foundations laid of a glorious good work. The generality of the people, after all, hated to be reformed.

I. What abundance of wickedness there was, and had been, in Judah and Jerusalem. 1. Even in the house of the Lord, that sacred temple which Solomon built, and dedicated to the honour and for the worship of the God of Israel, there were found vessels, all manner of utensils, for the worship of Baal, *and of the grove* (or *Ashtaroth*), and *of all the host of heaven, v.* 4. Though Josiah had suppressed the worship of idols, yet the utensils made for that worship were all carefully preserved, even in the temple itself. 2. Just *at the entering in of the house of the Lord* was a stable for horses kept for a religious use; they were holy horses, *given to the sun* (*v.* 11), as if he needed them who *rejoiceth as a strong man to run a race* (Ps. xix. 5), making their religion to conform to the poetical fictions of the chariot of the sun. Some say that those horses were to be led forth in pomp every morning to meet the rising sun, others that the worshippers of the sun rode out upon them to adore the rising sun; it should seem that they drew the chariots of the sun, which the people worshipped. 3. Hard *by the house of the Lord* there were *houses of the Sodomites*, where all manner of lewdness and filthiness, even that which was most unnatural, was practised, and under pretence of religion too, in honour of their impure deities. Those that dishonoured their God were justly left thus to dishonour themselves, Rom. i. 24, &c. There were women that *wove hangings for the grove* (*v.* 7), tents which encompassed the image of Venus, where the worshippers committed all manner of lewdness, and this *in the house of the Lord*. 4. There were many idolatrous altars found (*v.* 12), some in the palace, *on the top of the upper chamber of Ahaz*. The roofs of their houses being flat, they made them their high places, and set up altars upon them (Jer. xix. 13; Zeph. i. 5), domestic altars. 5. There was *Tophet, in the valley of the son of Hinnom*, very near Jerusalem, where the image of Moloch (that god of unnatural cruelty, as others were of unnatural uncleanness) was kept, to which some sacrificed their children, burning them in the fire, others dedicated them, making them to pass through

the fire (*v.* 10), *labouring in the very fire*, Hab. ii. 13. It is supposed to have been called *Tophet* from *toph*, a drum, because they beat drums at the burning of the children, that their shrieks might not be heard. 6. There were *high places before Jerusalem*, which *Solomon had built, v.* 13. There were also high places all the kingdom over, from *Geba to Beer-sheba* (*v.* 8), and *high places of the gates, in the entering in of the gate of the governor*. 7. There were idolatrous priests, that officiated at all those idolatrous altars (*v.* 5), chemarim, black men, or that wore black. See Zeph. i. 4. Those that sacrificed to Osiris, or that wept for Tammuz (Ezek. viii. 14), or that worshipped the infernal deities, put on black garments as mourners. 8. There were conjurers and wizards, and such as *dealt with familiar spirits, v.* 24.

II. What a full destruction good Josiah made of all those relics of idolatry. 1. He ordered Hilkiah, and the other priests, to clear the temple. Away with all the vessels that were made for Baal. They must all be burnt, and the ashes of them carried to Bethel. That place had been the common source of idolatry, for there was set up one of the calves. 2. The idolatrous priests were all put down. Those of them that were not of the house of Aaron, or had sacrificed to Baal or other false gods, he put to death, according to the law, *v.* 20. He *slew them upon their own altars*, the most acceptable sacrifice that ever had been offered upon them. Those that were descendants from Aaron, and yet had burnt incense in the high places, but to the true God only, he forbade ever to approach the altar of the Lord; but he allowed them to *eat of the unleavened bread among their brethren*, with whom they were to reside, that unleavened bread (heavy and unpleasant as it was), was better than they deserved, and that would serve to keep them alive. 3. All the images were broken to pieces and burnt. The image of the grove (*v.* 6), some goddess or other, was reduced to ashes, and the *ashes cast upon the graves of the common people* (*v.* 6), the common burying-place of the city. By the law a ceremonial uncleanness was contracted by the touch of a grave, so that in casting them here he declared them most impure. He *filled the places of the groves with the bones of men*; as he carried the ashes of the images to the graves, to mingle them with dead men's bones, so he carried dead men's bones to the places where the images had been, and put them in the room of them, that, both ways, idolatry might be rendered loathsome, and the people kept both from the dust of the images and from the ruins of the places where they had been worshipped. 4. All the wicked houses were suppressed, those nests of impiety that harboured idolaters, the houses of the Sodomites, *v.* 7. The high places were in like manner broken down and levelled with the ground (*v.* 8). Tophet, which, contrary to other places of idolatry, was in a valley, whereas they were on hills or high places, was likewise defiled (*v.* 10), was made the burying-place of the city. Concerning this we have a whole sermon, Jer. xix. 1, 2, &c., where it is said, *They shall bury in Tophet*, and the whole city is threatened to be made like Tophet. 5. The horses that had been given to the sun were taken away and put to common use, and the chariots of the sun he burnt with fire. 6. The workers with familiar spirits and the wizards were put away, *v.* 24.

III. How his zeal extended itself to the cities of Israel that were within his reach. The ten tribes were carried captive and the Assyrian colonies did not fully people the country, so that, it is likely, many cities had put themselves under the protection of the kings of Judah, 2 Chron. xxx. 1; xxxiv. 6. These he here visits, to carry on his reformation.

1. He defiled and demolished Jeroboam's altar at Bethel, with the high place and the grove that be-

longed to it, *v.* 15, 16. The golden calf, it should seem, was gone (*thy calf, O Samaria! has cast thee off*), but the altar was there. This was, (1) Defiled, *v.* 16. Josiah, in his pious zeal, was ransacking the old seats of idolatry, and spied the sepulchres in the mount, in which probably the idolatrous priests were buried. These he opened, took out the bones, and *burnt them upon the altar, v.* 20. Thus he polluted the altar, desecrated it, and made it odious. (2) It was demolished. He broke down the altar and all its appurtenances (*v.* 15), burnt what was combustible, and *stamped it small to powder* and made it *as dust before the wind.*

2. He destroyed all the houses of the high places, all those synagogues of Satan that were *in the cities of Samaria, v.* 19.

3. He carefully preserved the sepulchre of that man of God who came from Judah to foretell this. This was that good prophet who *proclaimed these things against the altar of Bethel,* and yet was himself slain by a lion, but to show that God's displeasure against him went no further than his death, God so ordered it that when all the graves about his were disturbed his was safe (*v.* 17, 18) and no man moved his bones.

IV. We are here told what a solemn passover Josiah and his people kept after all this. When they had cleared the country of the old leaven they then applied themselves to the keeping of the feast. We have not such a particular account of this passover as of that in Hezekiah's time, 2 Chron. xxx. But, in general, we are told that *there was not holden such a passover* in any of the foregoing reigns, no, not *from the days of the judges* (*v.* 22). This passover, it seems, was extraordinary for the number and devotion of the communicants, their sacrifices and offerings, and their exact observance of the laws of the feast. God was pleased to recompense their zeal in destroying idolatry with uncommon tokens of his presence and favour. All this concurred to make it a distinguished passover.

Verses 25–30

I. It is here owned that Josiah was one of the best kings that ever sat upon the throne of David, *v.* 25. As Hezekiah was a nonsuch for faith and dependence upon God in straits (*ch.* xviii. 5), so Josiah was a nonsuch for sincerity and zeal in carrying on a work of reformation. 1. He *turned to the Lord from whom his fathers had revolted.* He did what he could to turn his kingdom also to the Lord. 2. He did this *with his heart and soul.* 3. He did it with *all his heart,* and *all his soul,* and *all his might*—with vigour, and courage, and resolution. 4. He did this *according to all the law of Moses.* In all he did, he walked by rule.

II. Notwithstanding this he was cut off by a violent death in the midst of his days, and his kingdom was ruined within a few years after. Consequent upon such a reformation as this, one would have expected nothing but the prosperity and glory both of king and kingdom; but, quite contrary, we find both under a cloud. 1. Even the reformed kingdom continues marked for ruin. For all this (*v.* 26) *the Lord turned not from the fierceness of his great wrath.* That is certainly true, which God spoke by the prophet (Jer. xviii. 7, 8), that if a nation, doomed to destruction, *turn from the evil* of sin, God will *repent of the evil* of punishment; and therefore we must conclude that Josiah's people, though they submitted to Josiah's power, did not heartily imbibe Josiah's principles. They were turned by force, and did not voluntarily *turn from their evil way,* but still continued their affection for their idols; and therefore he that knows men's hearts would not recall the sentence, which was, That Judah should be removed, as Israel

had been, and Jerusalem itself cast off, *v.* 27. Yet even this destruction was intended to be their effectual reformation; so that we must say that the disease had come to a crisis, and was ready for a cure. 2. As an evidence of this, even the reforming king is cut off in the midst of his usefulness—in mercy to him, that he might not see the evil which was coming upon his kingdom. The king of Egypt waged war with the king of Assyria: so the king of Babylon is now called. Josiah's kingdom lay between them. He therefore thought himself concerned to oppose the king of Egypt, and check the growing, threatening, greatness of his power. Therefore *Josiah went against him,* and was killed in the first engagement, *v.* 29, 30. We must adore God's righteousness in taking away such a jewel from an unthankful people that knew not how to value it. They greatly lamented his death (2 Chron. xxxv. 25), urged to it by Jeremiah, who told them the meaning of it, and what a threatening omen it was.

Verses 31–37

Jerusalem saw not a good day after Josiah was laid in his grave, but one trouble came after another, till within twenty-two years it was quite destroyed. Of the reign of two of his sons here is a short account; the former we find a prisoner and the latter a tributary to the king of Egypt. This king of Egypt having slain Josiah, bent all his force against his family and kingdom.

I. Jehoahaz, a younger son, was first made king by *the people of the land,* probably because he was of a more warlike genius than his elder brother, and likely to make head against the king of Egypt and to avenge his father's death. He did ill, *v.* 32. He did *according to all that his* wicked *fathers had done.* Though he had not time to do much, yet he had chosen his patterns. He was but three months a prince, and was then made a prisoner and lived and died so.

II. Eliakim, another son of Josiah, was made king by the king of Egypt. The crown of Judah had hitherto always descended from a father to a son, and never, till now, from one brother to another. The king of Egypt, having used his power in making him king, further showed it in changing his name; he called him *Jehoiakim,* a name that had reference to Jehovah, for he had no design to make him renounce or forget the religion of his country. Of this Jehoiakim we are here told the king of Egypt made him poor, exacted from him a vast tribute of 100 *talents of silver and a talent of gold* (*v.* 33), which, with much difficulty, he squeezed out of his subjects and gave to Pharaoh, *v.* 35. Notwithstanding the rebukes of Providence he was under, by which he should have been convinced, humbled, and reformed, he *did that which was evil in the sight of the Lord* (*v.* 37).

CHAPTER 24

Things are hastening towards the utter destruction of Jerusalem. We left Jehoiakim on the throne, placed there by the king of Egypt: I. The troubles of his reign, how he was brought into subjection by the king of Babylon (ver. 1–6), and how Egypt also was conquered by Nebuchadnezzar, ver. 7. II. The desolations of his son's reign, which continued but three months; and then he and all his great men, being forced to surrender at discretion, were carried captives to Babylon, ver. 8–16. III. The preparatives of the next reign (which was the last of all) for the utter ruin of Jerusalem, ver. 17–20.

Verses 1–7

We have here the first mention of *Nebuchadnezzar,* king of Babylon (*v.* 1), that head of gold. He was a potent prince, and one that was the terror of the mighty; and yet his name would not have been known in sacred writ if he had not been employed in the destruction of Jerusalem and the captivity of the Jews.

I. He made Jehoiakim his tributary and kept him in subjection three years, v. 1. Nebuchadnezzar began his reign in the fourth year of Jehoiakim. In his eighth year he made him his prisoner, but restored him upon his promise of faithfulness to him. That promise he kept about three years, but then rebelled, probably in hopes of assistance from the king of Egypt.

II. When he rebelled Nebuchadnezzar sent his forces against him to destroy his country, bands of Chaldeans, Syrians, Moabites, Ammonites, who were all now in the service and pay of the king of Babylon (v. 2), and withal retained, and now showed, their ancient enmity to the Israel of God. Two things God intended in suffering Judah to be thus harassed:—
1. The punishment of the sins of Manasseh, which God now visited upon *the third and fourth generation.* So long he waited before he visited them, to see if the nation would repent; but they continued impenitent. Though Manasseh repented, and we have reason to think even the persecutions and murders he was guilty of were pardoned, yet, as they were national sins, they lay still charged upon the land, crying for national judgments. Perhaps some were now living who were aiding and abetting. See what need nations have to lament the sins of their fathers, lest they smart for them.

III. The king of Egypt was likewise subdued by the king of Babylon, and a great part of his country taken from him, v. 7. He dares not *come any more out of his land.* Afterwards he attempted to give Zedekiah some relief, but was obliged to retire, Jer. xxxvii. 7.

IV. Jehoiakim, seeing his country laid waste and himself ready to fall into the enemy's hand, as it should seem, died of a broken heart, in the midst of his days (v. 6).

Verses 8-20

The history of king Jehoiachin's *captivity,* as it is called, Ezek. i. 2. He came to the crown, not to have the honour of wearing it, but the shame of losing it.

I. His reign was short and inconsiderable. He reigned but three months, and then was removed and carried captive to Babylon. Yet this young prince reigned long enough to show that he justly smarted for his fathers' sins, for he trod in their steps (v. 9).

II. The calamities that came upon him, and his family, and people, in the very beginning of his reign, 1. Jerusalem was besieged by the king of Babylon, v. 10, 11. 2. Jehoiachin immediately surrendered; wanting the faith and piety of an Israelite, he had not the resolution of a man, of a soldier, of a prince. He and his royal family delivered themselves up prisoners of war. 3. Nebuchadnezzar rifled the treasuries both of the church and of the state, and carried away the silver and gold of both, v. 13. Now the word of God by Isaiah was fulfilled (ch. xx. 17), *All that is in thy house shall be carried to Babylon.* 4. He carried away a great part of Jerusalem into captivity. There had been some carried away eight years before this, in the first year of Nebuchadnezzar and the third of Jehoiakim, among whom were Daniel and his fellows. See Dan. i. 1, 6. Now he carried off, (1) The young king himself and his family (v. 15), and we find (ch. xxv. 27–29) that for thirty-seven years he continued a close prisoner. (2) All the great men, the princes and officers. (3) All the military men, the *mighty men of valour* (v. 14), *the mighty of the land* (v. 15), *the men of might, even all that were strong and apt for war,* v. 16. (4) All the craftsmen and smiths who made weapons of war. In this captivity Ezekiel the prophet was carried away (Ezek. i. 1, 2).

III. The successor whom the king of Babylon appointed in the room of Jehoiachin. The king of Babylon made Mattaniah king, the son of Josiah; and to let all the world know, that he was his creature,

he changed his name and called him *Zedekiah,* v. 17. This Zedekiah was the last of the kings of Judah. The name which the king of Babylon gave him signifies *The justice of the Lord. He rebelled against the king of Babylon* (v. 20). This was the most foolish thing he could do, and hastened the ruin of his kingdom.

CHAPTER 25

I. The utter destruction of Jerusalem by the Chaldeans, the city besieged and taken (ver. 1–4), the houses burnt (ver. 8, 9), the wall broken down (ver. 10), and the inhabitants carried away into captivity, ver. 11, 12. The glory of Jerusalem was, 1. That it was the royal city, but that glory has now departed, for the prince is made a most miserable prisoner, the seed royal is destroyed (ver. 5–7), and the principal officers are put to death, ver. 18–21. 2. That it was the holy city, where was the testimony of Israel; but that glory has departed, for Solomon's temple is burnt to the ground (ver. 9) and the sacred vessels that remained are carried away to Babylon, ver. 13–17. II. The distraction and dispersion of the remnant that was left in Judah under Gedaliah, ver. 22–26. III. The countenance which, after thirty-seven years' imprisonment, was given to Jehoiachin the captive king of Judah, ver. 27–30.

Verses 1-7

Zedekiah in rebellion against the king of Babylon (ch. xxiv. 20), contriving and endeavouring to shake off his yoke.

I. The king of Babylon's army laid siege to Jerusalem, v. 1. Two years this siege lasted; at first the army retired, for fear of the king of Egypt (Jer. xxxvii. 11), but, finding him not so powerful as they thought, they soon returned.

II. During this siege the famine prevailed (v. 3).

III. At length the city was taken by storm: it was *broken up,* v. 4. The besiegers made a breach in the wall, at which they forced their way into it.

IV. The king, his family, and all his great men, made their escape in the night, by some secret passages, v. 4. Intelligence was given to the Chaldeans of the king's flight, and they soon overtook him, v. 5. 1. He was brought to the king of Babylon, and tried by a council of war for rebelling against him to whom he had sworn fidelity. 2. His *sons were slain before his eyes.* 3. His eyes were put out, by which he was deprived of the light of the sun. Jeremiah prophesied that Zedekiah should be brought to Babylon, Jer. xxxii. 5; xxxiv. 3. Ezekiel prophesied that he should not see Babylon, Ezek. xii. 13. He was brought thither, but, his eyes being put out, he did not see it. Thus he ended his days, before he ended his life. 4. He was *bound in fetters of brass* and so *carried to Babylon.* For his greater disgrace, they led him bound.

Verses 8-21

About a month after (compare v. 8 with v. 3) Nebuzar-adan was sent with orders to complete the destruction of Jerusalem. This space God gave them to repent, after all the foregoing days of his patience, but in vain. 1. The city and temple are burnt, v. 9. That house which David prepared for, and which Solomon built at such a vast expense—that house which had the eye and heart of God perpetually upon it (1 Kings ix. 3) must be turned into ashes. By the burning of the temple God would show how little he cares for the external pomp of his worship when the life and power of religion are neglected. The people trusted to the temple, as if that would protect them in their sins (Jer. vii. 4). It is observable that the second temple was burnt by the Romans the same month, and the same day of the month, that the first temple was burnt by the Chaldeans, which, Josephus says, was the tenth of August. 2. The walls of Jerusalem are demolished (v. 10), as if the victorious army would be revenged on them for having kept them out so long. These walls were never repaired till Nehemiah's time. 3. The residue of the people are carried away captive to Babylon, *v.* 11. Only the poor of the land were left behind (*v.* 12) to till the ground and dress the vineyards for the Chaldeans. Sometimes poverty is a protection; for those that have nothing have nothing to lose. 4. The brazen vessels, and other appurtenances of the temple, are carried away, those of silver and gold being most of them gone before. Those two famous columns of brass, *Jachin* and *Boaz*, which signified the strength and stability of the house of God, were broken to pieces and the brass of them was carried to Babylon, *v.* 13. 5. Several of the great men are slain in cold blood. This completed the calamity: *So Judah was carried away out of their land*, about 860 years after they were put in possession of it by Joshua. Sin kept their fathers forty years out of Canaan, and now turned *them* out.

Verses 22–30

I. The dispersion of the remaining people. The city of Jerusalem was quite laid waste. Some people there were in the land of Judah (*v.* 22) that had weathered the storm, and had *their lives given them for a prey*. The king of Babylon appointed Gedaliah, one of themselves, to be their governor and protector under him, a very good man, and one that would make the best of the bad, *v.* 22. His father Ahikam was one that countenanced and protected Jeremiah when the princes had vowed his death, Jer. xxvi. 24. It is probable that this Gedaliah, by the advice of Jeremiah, had gone over to the Chaldeans, and had conducted himself so well that the king of Babylon entrusted him with the government. He resided not at Jerusalem, but at Mizpah, in the land of Benjamin, a place famous in Samuel's time. Thither those came who had fled from Zedekiah (*v.* 4) and put themselves under his protection (*v.* 23). Gedaliah, though he had not the pomp and power of a sovereign prince, yet might have been a greater blessing to them than many of their kings had been. Yet this hopeful settlement is dashed to pieces, not by the Chaldeans, but by some of themselves. Ishmael, who was of the royal family, envying Gedaliah's advancement and the happy settlement of the people under him, basely slew him and all his friends, both Jews and Chaldeans. The Chaldeans had reason enough to be offended at the murder of Gedaliah; but if those that remained had humbly remonstrated, alleging that it was only the act of Ishmael and his party, those who were innocent of it would not have been punished for it: but contrary to the counsel of Jeremiah, they all went to Egypt, where, it is probable, they mixed with the Egyptians by degrees, and were never heard of more as Israelites. Thus was there a full end made of them by their own folly and disobedience, and Egypt had the last of them, that the last verse of that chapter of threatenings might be fulfilled, Deut. xxviii. 68, *The Lord shall bring thee into Egypt again*. These events are more largely related by the prophet Jeremiah, *ch.* xl. to *ch.* xlv.

II. The reviving of the captive prince. Of Jehoiachin, or Jeconiah, who surrendered himself (*ch.* xxiv. 12), we are here told that as soon as Evil-merodach came to the crown, upon the death of his father Nebuchadnezzar, he released him out of prison (where he had lain thirty-seven years, and was now fifty-five years old), *spoke kindly to him* (*v.* 28), gave him princely clothing instead of his prison-garments, maintained him in his own palace (*v.* 29), and allowed him a pension for himself and his family in some measure corresponding to his rank, *a daily rate for every day as long as he lived*. To have honour and liberty after he had been so long in confinement and disgrace was like the return of the morning after a very dark and tedious night. Let none say that they shall never see good again because they have long seen little but evil; the most miserable know not what blessed turn Providence may yet give to their affairs, Ps. xc. 15. However the death of afflicted saints is to them such a change: it will release them out of their prison, shake off the body, that prison-garment, and it will send them to the throne, to the table, of the King of kings, the glorious liberty of God's children. Evil-merodach thought his father made the yoke of his captives too heavy, and therefore, with the tenderness of a man and the honour of a prince, made it lighter. The Jews say that this Evil-merodach had been himself imprisoned by his own father, when he returned from his madness, for some mismanagement at that time, and that in prison he contracted a friendship with Jehoiachin, in consequence of which, as soon as he had it in his power, he showed him this kindess as a sufferer, as a fellow-sufferer. Some suggest that Evil-merodach had learned from Daniel and his fellows the principles of the true religion. Thirty-six of the seventy years were now past, and now to see their king thus advanced would be a comfortable earnest to the captive people of their own release in due time, in the set time. When therefore we are perplexed, let us not be in despair.

AN EXPOSITION, WITH PRACTICAL OBSERVATIONS, OF

THE FIRST
BOOK OF CHRONICLES

These books of Chronicles are in a great measure repetition; and yet there are no *vain repetitions*. We could ill spare them; for there are many most excellent useful things in them, which we find not elsewhere. Abstracts, abridgments, and references, are of use in divinity as well as law. It is still of use, that *out of the mouth of two witnesses every word may be established*. The penman of these books is supposed to be Ezra, that *ready scribe in the law of the Lord*, Ezra vii. 6. These books are called in the Hebrew *words of days*—journals or annals, because, by divine direction, collected out of some public and authentic records. The collection was made after the captivity. The LXX. call it a book Παραλειπομένων—of *things left*, or overlooked, by the preceding historians. It is the rereward, the gathering host, of this sacred camp, which gathers up what remained, that nothing might be lost. In this first book we have, I. A collection of sacred genealogies, from Adam to David: and they are none of those which the apostle calls *endless genealogies*, but have their use and end in Christ, *ch.* i.–ix. Divers little passages of history are here inserted which we had not before. II. A repetition of the history of the translation of the kingdom from Saul to David, and of the triumph of David's reign, with large additions, *ch.* x.–xxi. III. An original account of the settlement David made of the ecclesiastical affairs, and the preparation he made for the building of the temple, *ch.* xxii.–xxix.

CHAPTER 1

These genealogies, 1. Were then of great use, when they were here preserved, and put into the hands of the Jews after their return from Babylon; for the captivity had put all into confusion, and they, in that dispersion, would be in danger of losing the distinctions of their tribes and families. This therefore revives the ancient landmarks even of some of the tribes that were carried captive into Assyria. 2. They are still of some use for the illustrating of the scripture-story, and especially for the clearing of the pedigrees of the Messiah, that it might appear that our blessed Saviour was, according to the prophecies which went before of him, the son of David, the son of Judah, the son of Abraham, the son of Adam. In this chapter we have an abstract of all the genealogies in the book of Genesis, till we come to Jacob. I. The descents from Adam to Noah and his sons, out of Gen. v., ver. 1–4. II. The posterity of Noah's sons, by which the earth was repeopled, out of Gen. x., ver. 5–23. III. The descents from Shem to Abraham, out of Gen. xi., ver. 24–28. IV. The posterity of Ishmael, and of Abraham's sons by Keturah, out of Gen. xxv., ver. 29–35. V. The posterity of Esau, out of Gen. xxxvi., ver. 36–43.

Verses 1–27

This paragraph has *Adam* for its first word and *Abraham* for its last. Adam was the common father of our flesh, Abraham the common father of the faithful. By the breach which the former made of the covenant of innocency, we were all made miserable; by the covenant of grace made with the latter, we all are, or may be, made happy. We all are, by nature, the seed of Adam, branches of that wild olive. Let us see to it that, by faith, we become the seed of Abraham (Rom. iv. 11, 12), that we be grafted into the good olive and partake of its root and fatness.

I. The first four verses of this paragraph, and the last four, which are linked together by Shem (*v.* 4, 24), contain the sacred line of Christ from Adam to Abraham, and are inserted in his pedigree, Luke iii. 34–38, the order ascending as here it descends.

II. All the verses between repeat the account of the replenishing of the earth by the sons of Noah after the flood. The historian begins with those who were strangers to the church, the sons of Japhet, who were planted in the isles of the Gentiles, those western parts of the world, the countries of Europe. The sons of Ham moved southward towards Africa and those parts of Asia which lay that way. The posterity of Shem, *v.* 17–23, peopled Asia, and spread themselves eastward. The Assyrians, Syrians, Chaldeans, Persians, and Arabians, descended from these. At first the originals of the respective nations

were known; but at this day the nations are so mingled with one another, by the enlargement of commerce and dominion, the transplanting of colonies, the carrying away of captives, and many other circumstances, that no one nation, no, nor the greatest part of any, is descended entire from any one of these fountains. Only this we are sure of, that God has *created of one blood all nations of men*. The great promise of the Messiah (says Bishop Patrick) was translated from Adam to Seth, from him to Shem, from him to Eber, and so to the Hebrew nation, who were entrusted, above all nations, with that sacred treasure, till the promise was performed and the Messiah had come.

Verses 28–54

All nations but the seed of Abraham are already shaken off from this genealogy: they have no part nor lot in this matter. *The Lord's portion is his people*. Not that we are to conclude that therefore no particular persons of any other nation but the seed of Abraham found favour with God. There were many, very many, good people in the world, that lay out of the pale of God's covenant of peculiarity with Abraham, whose names were in the book of life, though not descended from any of the following families written in this book. *The Lord knows those that are his*. But Israel was a chosen nation, elect in type; and no other nation, in its national capacity, was so dignified and privileged as the Jewish nation was. That is the holy nation which is the subject of the sacred story; and therefore we are next to shake off all the seed of Abraham but the posterity of Jacob only.

I. We shall have little to say of the *Ishmaelites*. They were the sons of the bond-woman, that were to be cast out and not to be heirs with the child of the promise. Ishmael's twelve sons are just named here (*v.* 29–31), to show the performance of the promise God made to Abraham that he should become a great nation, and particularly that he should beget twelve princes, Gen. xvii. 20.

II. We shall have little to say of the *Midianites*, who descended from Abraham's children by Keturah. They were *children of the east* and were separated from Isaac, the heir of the promise (Gen. xxv. 6), and therefore they are only named here, *v.* 32.

III. We shall not have much to say of the *Edomites*. They had an inveterate enmity to God's Israel; yet because they descended from Esau, the son of Isaac, we have here an account of their families, and the names of some of their famous men, *v.* 35 to the end.

CHAPTER 2

The register of the children of Israel, that distinguished people, that were to "dwell alone, and not be reckoned among the nations." I. The names of the twelve sons of Israel, ver. 1, 2. II. An account of the tribe of Judah, which has the precedency, not so much for the sake of David as for the sake of the Son of David, our Lord, who sprang out of Judah, Heb. vii. 14. 1. The first descendants from Judah, down to Jesse, ver. 3-12. 2. The children of Jesse, ver. 13-17. 3. The posterity of Hezron, not only through Ram, from whom David came, but through Caleb (ver. 18-20), Segub (ver. 21-24), Jerahmeel (ver. 25-33, and so to ver. 41), and more by Caleb (ver. 42-49), with the family of Caleb, the son of Hur, ver. 50-55.

Verses 1-17

I. The family of Jacob. His twelve sons are here named, that illustrious number so often celebrated almost throughout the whole Bible. At every turn we meet with the twelve tribes that descended from these twelve patriarchs. The personal character of several of them was none of the best (the first four were much blemished), and yet the covenant was entailed on their seed; for it was of grace, free grace, that it was said, *Jacob have I loved—not of works, lest any man should boast.*

II. The family of Judah. That tribe was most praised, most increased, of any of the tribes, and therefore the genealogy of it is the first and largest of them all. In the account of the first branches of that illustrious tree, of which Christ was to be the top branch, we meet, 1. With some that were very bad. Here is Er, Judah's eldest son, that was *evil in the sight of the Lord,* and was cut off, in the beginning of his days, *v.* 3. His next brother, Onan, fared no better. Here is Tamar, with whom Judah, her father-in-law, committed incest, *v.* 4. And here is Achan, called *Achar—a troubler,* that troubled Israel by taking of the accursed thing, *v.* 7. 2. With some that were very wise and good, as Heman and Ethan, Calcol and Dara, who were not perhaps the immediate sons of Zerah, but descendants from him, and are named because they were the glory of their father's house, 1 Kings iv. 31. 3. With some that were very great, as Nahshon, who was prince of Judah when the camp of Israel was formed in the wilderness, and so led the van in that glorious march, and Salman, or Salmon, who was in that post of honour when they entered into Canaan, *v.* 10, 11.

III. The family of Jesse, of which a particular account is kept for the sake of David, and the Son of David, who is *a rod out of the stem of Jesse,* Isa. xi. 1. Hence it appears that David was a seventh son, and that his three great commanders, Joab, Abishai, and Asahel, were the sons of one of his sisters, and Amasa of another.

Verses 18-55

Very few of those to whom this paragraph relates are mentioned anywhere else. 1. Here we find Bezaleel, who was head-workman in building the tabernacle, Exod. xxxi. 2. 2. Hezron was one of the seventy that went down with Jacob into Egypt, Gen. xlvi. 12. The achievements of Jair, here mentioned (*v.* 22, 23), were long after the conquest of Canaan. The pedigree of several of these terminates, not in a person, but in a place or country, as one is said to be *the father of Kirjath-jearim* (*v.* 50), another of Bethlehem (*v.* 51), which was afterwards David's city, because these places fell to their lot in the division of the land. Among all these great families we are glad to find some that were *families of scribes, v.* 55. *Would to God that all the Lord's people were*

prophets—all the families of Israel families of scribes, well instructed to the kingdom of heaven.

CHAPTER 3

Of all the families of Israel none was so illustrious as the family of David. That is the family which was mentioned in the foregoing chapter, ver. 15. Here we have a full account of it. I. David's sons, ver. 1-9. II. His successors in the throne as long as the kingdom continued, ver. 10-16. III. The remains of his family in and after the captivity, ver. 17-24. From this family, "as concerning the flesh, Christ came."

Verses 1-9

We had an account of David's sons, 2 Sam. iii. 2, &c., and v. 14, &c. Some of them were a grief to him, as Amnon, Absalom, and Adonijah; and none imitated his piety or devotion except Solomon, and he came far short of it. One of them, which Bathsheba bore to him, he called Nathan, probably in honour of Nathan the prophet, who reproved him for his sin in that matter and was instrumental to bring him to repentance. It seems he loved him the better for it as long as he lived. It is wisdom to esteem those our best friends that deal faithfully with us. From this son of David our Lord Jesus descended, as appears Luke iii. 31. Here are two Elishamas, and two Eliphelets, *v.* 6, 8. Probably the two former were dead, and therefore David called two more by their names.

Verses 10-24

David having nineteen sons, we may suppose them to have raised many noble families in Israel whom we never hear of in the history. But the scripture gives us an account only of the descendants of Solomon here, and of Nathan, Luke iii. We have here, 1. The great and celebrated names by which the line of David is drawn down to the captivity, the kings of Judah in a lineal succession. Seldom has a crown gone in a direct line from father to son for seventeen descents together, as here. This was the recompence of David's piety. About the time of the captivity the lineal descent was interrupted, and the crown went from one brother to another and from a nephew to an uncle. 2. The less famous, and most of them very obscure names, in which the house of David subsisted after the captivity. The only famous man of that house that we meet with at their return from captivity was Zerubbabel. Salathiel is said to be *the son of* Jeconiah because adopted by him, and because, as some think, he succeeded him in the dignity to which he was restored by Evil-merodach. Otherwise Jeconiah was written childless: he was *the signet God plucked from his right hand* (Jer. xxii. 24), and in his room Zerubbabel was placed, and therefore God saith to him (Hag. ii. 23), *I will make thee as a signet.* The posterity of Zerubbabel here bear not the same names that they do in the genealogies (Matt. i, or Luke iii), but those no doubt were taken from the public registers which the priests kept of all the families of Judah, especially that of David.

CHAPTER 4

In this chapter we have, I. A further account of the genealogies of the tribe of Judah, the most numerous and most famous of all the tribes. The posterity of Shobal the son of Hur (ver. 1-4), of Ashur the posthumous son of Hezron (who was mentioned, ch. ii. 24), with something particular concerning Jabez (ver. 5-10), of Chelub and others (ver. 11-20), of Shelah, ver. 21-23. II. An account of the posterity and cities of Simeon, their conquest of Gedon, and of the Amalekites in Mount Seir, ver. 24-43.

Verses 1-10

One reason, no doubt, why Ezra is here most particular in the register of the tribe of Judah is because it was that tribe which, with its appendages, Simeon, Benjamin, and Levi, made up the kingdom of Judah, which now when this was written, returned out of captivity, when the generality of the other tribes were lost in the kingdom of Assyria. The most remarkable person in this paragraph is Jabez, the founder of one of the families of Aharel, mentioned *v.* 8.

I. The reason of his name: his mother gave him the name with this reason, *Because I bore him with sorrow, v.* 9. Usually the sorrow in bearing is afterwards forgotten *for joy that the child is born*; but here it seems it was remembered when the child came to be circumcised, and care was taken to perpetuate the remembrance of it while he lived. 1. That it might be a continual memorandum to herself, to be thankful to God as long as she lived for bringing her through that sorrow. 2. That it might likewise be a memorandum to him what this world is into which she bore him, a vale of tears, in which he must expect *few days and full of trouble*. It might also remind him to love and honour his mother, and labour, in everything, to be a comfort to her who brought him into the world with so much sorrow.

II. The eminence of his character: *He was more honourable than his brethren*. We have most reason to think it was upon the account of his learning and piety. 1. In learning, because we find that *the families of the scribes dwelt at Jabez* (*ch.* ii. 55), a city which, it is likely, took its name from him. 2. In piety, because we find here that he was a praying man.

III. The prayer he made just when he was setting out in the world. He set himself to acknowledge God in all his ways, put himself under the divine blessing, and protection, and prospered accordingly. Observe,

1. To whom he prayed; he *called on the God of Israel*, a God in covenant with his people, the God with whom Jacob wrestled and prevailed and was thence called Israel.

2. What was the nature of his prayer. (1) As the *margin* reads it, it was a solemn vow—*If thou wilt bless me indeed, &c.*, and then the sense is imperfect, but may easily be filled up from Jacob's vow, or some such like—*then thou shalt be my God*. He does, as it were, give God a blank paper, let him write what he pleases: "Lord, if thou wilt bless me and keep me, do what thou wilt with me, I will be at thy command and disposal for ever." (2) As the *text* reads it, it was the language of a most ardent and affectionate desire: *O that thou wouldst bless me!*

3. What was the matter of his prayer. Four things he prayed for:—(1) That God would bless him indeed: "That, *blessing, thou wilt bless me*, bless me greatly with manifold and abundant blessings." (2) That he would enlarge his coast, that he would prosper his endeavours for the increase of what fell to his lot either by work or war. (3) That God's hand might be with him. God's hand with us, to lead us, protect us, strengthen us, and to work all our works in us and for us, is indeed a hand sufficient for us, all-sufficient. (4) That he would keep him from evil, the evil of sin, the evil of trouble, all the evil designs of his enemies, that they might not hurt him, or grieve him.

4. *God granted him that which he requested*, prospered him remarkably, and gave him success in his undertakings, in his studies, in his worldly business, in his conflicts with the Caananites.

Verses 11–23

1. Here is a whole family of craftsmen that applied themselves to all sorts of manufactures, in which they were ingenious and industrious above their neighbours, *v.* 14. There was a valley where they lived which was, from them, called *the valley of craftsmen*. 2. One of these married the daughter of Pharaoh (*v.* 18), which was the common name of the kings of Egypt. 3. Another is said to be the *father*

of the house of those that wrought fine linen, v. 21. They were the best weavers in the kingdom, and they brought up their children, from one generation to another, to the same business. His posterity inhabited the city of Maseshah, the manufacture or staple commodity of which place was linen-cloth, with which their kings and priests were clothed. 4. Another family had had *dominion in Moab*, but were now in *servitude in Babylon, v.* 22, 23. (1) It was found among the *ancient things* that they had the *dominion in Moab*. Probably in David's time, when that country was conquered, they transplanted themselves thither. (2) Their posterity were now potters and gardeners in Babylon, where they *dwelt with the king for his work*, got a good livelihood and therefore cared not for returning to their own land, after the years of captivity had expired.

Verses 24–43

Some of the genealogies of the tribe of Simeon. Of this tribe it is said that they *increased greatly*, but *not like the children of Judah, v.* 27. 1. The cities allotted them (*v.* 28), of which see Joshua xix. 1, &c. When it is said that they were theirs *unto the reign of David* (*v.* 31) intimation is given that when the ten tribes revolted from the house of David many of the Simeonites quitted these cities, because they lay within Judah, and seated themselves elsewhere. 2. The ground they got elsewhere. It was in the days of Hezekiah that a generation of Simeonites, whose tribe had long crouched and truckled, was animated to make these bold efforts. (1) Some of them attacked a place in Arabia called *the entrance of Gedor*, made themselves masters of it, and dwelt there. This adds to the glory of Hezekiah's pious reign, that, as his kingdom in general prospered, so did particular families. (2) Others of them, to the number of 500, under the command of four brethren, here named, made a descent upon Mount Seir, and smote the Amalekites, and took possession of their country, *v.* 42, 43.

CHAPTER 5

The two tribes and a half that were seated on the other side Jordan. I. Of Reuben, ver. 1–10. II. Of Gad, ver. 11–17. III. Of the half-tribe of Manasseh, ver. 23, 24. IV. Concerning all three acting in conjunction we are told, 1. How they conquered the Hagarites, ver. 18–22. 2. How they were, at length, themselves conquered, and made captives, by the king of Assyria, because they had forsaken God, ver. 25, 26.

Verses 1–17

An extract out of the genealogies,

I. Of the tribe of Reuben, where we have,

1. The reason why this tribe is thus postponed. Reuben the first born of Israel forfeited his birth-right by defiling his father's concubine, Gen. xlix. 4. The advantages of the birthright were dominion and a double portion. Reuben having forfeited these, it was thought too much that both should be transferred to any one, and therefore they were divided. (1) Joseph had the double portion; for two tribes descended from him, Ephraim and Manasseh, each of whom had a child's part (for so Jacob by faith blessed them, Heb. xi. 21; Gen. xlviii. 15, 22), and each of those tribes was as considerable, and made as good a figure, as any one of the twelve, except Judah. But, (2) Judah had the dominion; on him the dying patriarch entailed the sceptre, Gen. xlix. 10. Of him came the chief ruler, David first, and, in the fulness of time, Messiah the Prince, Micah v. 2.

2. The genealogy of the princes of this tribe to Beerah, who was head of this clan when the king of Assyria carried them captive, *v.* 4–6.

3. The enlargement of the coasts of this tribe. They increasing, and their cattle being multiplied, they crowded out their neighbours the Hagarites, and extended their conquests, *v.* 9, 10.

II. Of the tribe of Gad. Some great families of that tribe are here named (v. 12), seven that were the children of Abihail, whose pedigree is carried upwards from the son to the father (v. 14, 15), as that v. 4, 5, is brought downwards from father to son.

Verses 18–26

The heads of the half-tribe of Manasseh, that were seated on the other side Jordan, are named here, v. 23, 24. Their lot, at first, was Bashan only; but afterwards they increased so much in wealth and power that they spread far north, even unto Hermon. Two things only are here recorded concerning these tribes on the other side Jordan, in which they were all concerned. They all shared,

I. In a glorious victory over the Hagarites, so the Ishmaelites were now called, to remind them that they were *the sons of the bond-woman,* that was *cast out.*

1. What a brave army these frontier-tribes brought into the field against the Hagarites, 44,000 men and upwards, all strong, and brave, and skilful in war.

2. What course they took to engage God for them: They *cried to God,* and *put their trust in him,* v. 20. Though they had a powerful army, they relied not on that, but on the divine power. See the like done, 2 Chron. xiii. 14. In our spiritual conflicts, we must look up to heaven for strength; and it is the believing prayer that will be the prevailing prayer.

3. If the battle be the Lord's, there is reason to hope it will be successful.

II. They shared, at length, in an inglorious captivity. Had they kept close to God and their duty, they would have continued to enjoy both their ancient lot and their new conquests; but they *transgressed against the God of their fathers,* v. 25. They lay upon the borders and conversed most with the neighbouring nations, by which means they learned their idolatrous usages and transmitted the infection to the other tribes. These tribes were first placed, and they were first displaced. They would have the best land, not considering that it lay most exposed. But those who are governed more by sense than by reason or faith in their choices may expect to fare accordingly.

Chapter 6

Though Joseph and Judah shared between them the forfeited honours of the birthright, yet Levi was first of all the tribes, dignified and distinguished with an honour more valuable than either the precedence or the double portion, and that was the priesthood. That tribe God set apart for himself; it was Moses's tribe, and perhaps for his sake was thus favoured. Of that tribe we have an account in this chapter. I. Their pedigree, the first fathers of the tribe (ver. 1–3), the line of the priests, from Aaron to the captivity (ver. 4–15), and of some other of their families, ver. 16–30. II. Their work, the work of the Levites (ver. 31–48), of the priests, ver. 49–53. III. The cities appointed them in the land of Canaan, ver. 54–81.

Verses 1–30

The priests and Levites were more concerned than any other Israelites to preserve their pedigree clear and to be able to prove it, because all the honours and privileges of their office depended upon their descent. Very little is here recorded of the genealogies of this sacred tribe. 1. The first fathers of it are here named twice, v. 1, 16. Gershom, Kohath, and Merari, are three names which we were very conversant with in the book of Numbers. Aaron, and Moses, and Miriam, we have known much more of than their names, remembering that God honoured them in making them the instruments of Israel's deliverance and settlement and *figures of him that was to come,* Moses as a prophet and Aaron as a priest. And the mention of Nadab and Abihu cannot but remind us of the terrors of divine justice. 2. The line of Eleazar, the successor of Aaron, is here drawn down to the time of the captivity v. 4–15. It begins with Eleazar, who came out of the house of

bondage in Egypt, and ends with Jehozadak, who went into the house of bondage in Babylon. All these here named were not high priests; for, in the time of the judges, that dignity was, upon some occasion or other, brought into the family of Ithamar, of which Eli was; but in Zadok it returned again to the right line. Of Azariah it is here said (v. 10), *He it is that executed the priest's office in the temple that Solomon built.* It is supposed that this was that Azariah who bravely opposed the presumption of king Uzziah when he invaded the priest's office (2 Chron. xxvi. 17, 18). This was done like a priest, like one that was truly zealous for his God. One of the families of Gershom (that of Libni) is here drawn down as far as Samuel, who had the honour of a prophet added to that of a Levite. One of the families of Merari (that of Mahli) is likewise drawn down for several descents, v. 29, 30.

Verses 31–53

When the Levites were first ordained in the wilderness much of the work then appointed them lay in carrying and taking care of the tabernacle and the utensils of it, while they were in their march through the wilderness. In David's time their number was increased; and, though the greater part of them were dispersed all the nation over, to teach the people the good knowledge of the Lord, yet those that attended the house of God were so numerous that there was not constant work for them all; and therefore David, by special commission and direction from God, new-modelled the Levites, as we shall find in the latter part of this book. Here we are told what the work was which he assigned them.

1. Singing-work, v. 31. David was raised up on high to be the sweet psalmist of Israel (2 Sam. xxiii. 1), not only to pen psalms, but to appoint the singing of them in the house of the Lord, and this he did *after that the ark had rest.* While that was in captivity, obscure, and unsettled, the harps were hung upon the willow-trees: singing was then thought unseasonable, but the harps being resumed, and the songs revived, at the bringing up of the ark, they were continued afterwards. When the service of the ark was much superseded by its rest they had other work cut out for them (for Levites should never be idle) and were employed in the service of song. These singers kept up that service in the tabernacle till the temple was built, and then they *waited on their office* there, v. 32. We have here an account of the three great masters who were employed in the service of the sacred song, with their respective families; for they *waited with their children,* that is, such as descended from them or were allied to them, v. 33. Heman, Asaph, and Ethan, were the three that were appointed to this service, one of each of the three houses of the Levites. 1. Of the house of Kohath was Heman with his family (v. 33), a man of a sorrowful spirit, if it be the same Heman that penned the 88th psalm, and yet a singer. He was the grandson of Samuel the prophet, the son of Joel, of whom it is said that *he walked not in the ways of Samuel* (1 Sam. viii. 2, 3); but it seems, though the son did not, the grandson did. Perhaps David, in making Heman the chief, had some respect to his old friend Samuel. 2. Of the house of Gershom was Asaph, called *his brother,* because in the same office and of the same tribe, though of another family. He was posted on Heman's right hand in the choir, v. 39. Several of the psalms bear his name. It is plain that he was the penman of some psalms; for we read of those that praised the Lord in the words of David and of Asaph. He was a seer as well as a singer, 2 Chron. xxix. 30. His pedigree is traced up here, through names utterly unknown, as high as Levi, v. 39–43. 3. Of the house of Merari was Ethan (v. 44), who was appointed to

Heman's left hand. His pedigree is also traced up to Levi, *v.* 47.

II. There was serving-work, abundance of service to be done *in the tabernacle of the house of God* (*v.* 48), to provide water and fuel,—to wash and sweep, and carry out ashes,—to kill, and flay, and boil the sacrifices; and to all such services there were Levites appointed, those of other families, or perhaps those that were not fit to be singers, that had either no good voice or no good ear. *As everyone has received the gift, so let him minister.*

III. There was sacrificing-work, and that was to be done by the priests only, *v.* 49. They only were to sprinkle the blood and burn the incense; as for *the work of the most holy place*, that was to be done by the high priest only. Each had his work, and they both needed one another and both helped one another in it. Concerning the work of the priests we are here told, they were to *make an atonement for Israel*, to mediate between the people and God; not to magnify and enrich themselves, but to serve the public. They presided in God's house, yet must do as they were bidden, according to all that God commanded.

Verses 54–81

An account of the Levites' cities. They and their possessions were, in a particular manner, the care of the divine providence: as God was their portion, so God was their protection; and a cottage will be a castle to those that abide under the shadow of the Almighty. It is common for cities to have several names. *Sarum* and *Salisbury*, *Salop* and *Shrewsbury*, are more unlike than *Hilen* (*v.* 58) and *Holon* (Joshua xxi. 15), *Ashan* (*v.* 59) and *Ain* (Joshua xxi. 16), *Alemeth* (*v.* 60) and *Almon* (Joshua xxi. 18); and time changes names. In this appointment of cities for the Levites God took care, 1. For Jacob's prediction concerning this tribe, that it should be *scattered in Israel*, Gen. xlix. 7. 2. For the diffusing of the knowledge of himself and his law to all parts of the land of Israel. Every tribe had Levites' cities in it. 3. For a comfortable maintenance for those that ministered in holy things. Some of the most considerable cities of Israel fell to the Levites' lot.

CHAPTER 7

The genealogies, I. Of Issachar, ver. 1–5. II. Of Benjamin, ver. 6–12. III. Of Naphtali, ver. 13. IV. Of Manasseh, ver. 14–19. V. Of Ephraim, ver. 20–29. VI. Of Asher, ver. 30–40.

Verses 1–19

A short view,

I. Of the tribe of Issachar, whom Jacob had compared to a *strong ass, couching between two burdens* (Gen. xlix. 14), an industrious tribe, that minded their country business very closely and *rejoiced in their tents*, Deut. xxxiii. 18. So fruitful their country was that they saw no danger of over-stocking the pasture, and so ingenious the people were that they could find work for all hands. Let no people complain of their numbers, provided they suffer none to be idle. The number of the respective families is here set down, amounting in the whole to above 145,000 men fit for war.

II. Of the tribe of Benjamin. Some account is here given of this tribe, but a much larger in the next chapter. The militia of this tribe scarcely reached to 60,000; but they are said to be *mighty men of valour*, *v.* 7, 9, 11. It was the honour of this tribe that it produced Saul the first king, and more its honour that it adhered to the rightful kings of the house of David when the other tribes revolted.

III. Of the tribe of Naphtali, *v.* 13. The first fathers only of that tribe are named, the very same that we find, Gen. xlvi. 24, only that *Shillem* there is

Shallum here. None of their descendants are named, perhaps because their genealogies were lost.

IV. Of the tribe of Manasseh, that part of it which was seated within Jordan; for of the other part we had some account before, *ch.* v. 23, &c. One of them married an Aramitess, that is, a Syrian, *v.* 14. This was during their bondage in Egypt, so early did they begin to mingle with the nations. The father married a Syrian, Machir; the son of that marriage took to wife a daughter of Benjamin, *v.* 15.

Verses 20–40

An account,

I. Of the tribe of Ephraim. Great things we read of that tribe when it came to maturity. Here we have the disasters of its infancy, while it was in Egypt. 1. The great breach that was made upon the family of Ephraim. The men of Gath, Philistines, giants, slew many of the sons of that family, *because they came down to take away their cattle*, *v.* 21. It is uncertain who were the aggressors here. Some make the men of Gath the aggressors, supposing that they came down into the land of Goshen, to drive away the Ephraimites' cattle, and slew the owners, because they stood up in the defence of them. Others think that the Ephraimites made a descent upon the men of Gath to plunder them. I rather think that the men of Gath came down upon the Ephraimites, because the Israelites in Egypt were shepherds, not soldiers, abounded in cattle of their own, and therefore were not likely to venture their lives for their neighbours' cattle: and the words may be read, *The men of Gath slew them, for they came down to take away their cattle. Ephraim mourned many days*. Nothing brings the aged to the grave with more sorrow than their following the young that descend from them to the grave first, especially if in blood. It was a brotherly friendly office which his brethren did, when *they came to comfort him*. The repair of this breach, in some measure, by the addition of another son to his family in his old age (*v.* 23), like Seth, *another seed instead of that of Abel whom Cain slew*, Gen. iv. 25. When God thus restores comfort to his mourners, *makes glad according to the days wherein he afflicted*, setting the mercies over against the crosses, we ought therein to take notice of the kindness and tenderness of divine Providence; it is as if *it repented God concerning his servants*, Ps. xc. 13, 15. Yet joy that a man was born into his family could not make him forget his grief; for he gives a melancholy name to this son, *Beriah—in trouble*, for he was born when the family was in mourning, when *it went evil with his house*. It is added, as a further honour to the house of Ephraim, that a son of that tribe was employed in the conquest of Canaan, *Joshua the son of Nun*, *v.* 27.

II. Of the tribe of Asher. Some men of note of that tribe are here named. Their militia was not numerous in comparison with some other tribes, only 26,000 men in all; but their princes were *choice and mighty men of valour, chief of the princes* (*v.* 40), and perhaps it was their wisdom that they coveted not to make their trained bands numerous, but rather to have a few serviceable men.

CHAPTER 8

We had some account given us of Benjamin in the foregoing chapter; here we have a larger catalogue of the great men of that tribe. 1. Because of that tribe Saul came, the first king of Israel, ch. x. 1. 2. Because that tribe clave to Judah, inhabited much of Jerusalem, was one of the two tribes that went into captivity, and returned back, ch. ix. 1. Here is, I. Some of the heads of that tribe named, ver. 1–32. II. A more particular account of the family of Saul, ver. 33–40.

Verses 1–32

There is little or nothing of history in all these verses. In this and the foregoing genealogies some *ascend*, others *descend*; some have *numbers* affixed, others *places*; some have historical remarks intermixed, others have not; some are shorter, others longer; some agree with other records, other differ; some, it is likely, were torn, erased, and blotted, others more legible. Those of Dan and Reuben were entirely lost. Many things in these genealogies which to us seem intricate, abrupt, and perplexed, were plain and easy to them then (who knew how to fill up the deficiencies). Many great and mighty nations there were now in being upon earth, and many illustrious men in them, whose names are buried in perpetual oblivion, while the names of multitudes of the Israel of God are here carefully preserved in everlasting remembrance. They are *Jasher, Jeshurun* —*just ones*, and *the memory of the just is blessed*. This tribe of Benjamin was once brought to a very low ebb, in the time of the judges, upon the occasion of the iniquity of Gibeah, when only 600 men escaped the sword of justice; and yet, in these genealogies, it makes as good a figure as almost any of the tribes. Here is mention of one Ehud (*v.* 6), in the preceding verse of one Gera (*v.* 5) and (*v.* 8) of one that descended from him, that *begat children in the country of Moab*, who was the second of the judges of Israel; for he is said to be *the son of Gera* and *a Benjamite* (Judges iii. 15), and he delivered Israel from the oppression of the Moabites by killing the king of Moab. Here is mention of some of the Benjamites that *drove away the inhabitants of Gath* (*v.* 13), perhaps those that had slain the Ephraimites (*ch.* vii. 21) and one of those that did this piece of justice was named *Beriah*. Particular notice is taken of those that *dwelt in Jerusalem* (*v.* 28 and again *v.* 32), that those whose ancestors had had their residence there might thereby be induced, at their return from captivity, to settle there and therefore we find (Neh. xi. 2) *the people blessed those that willingly offered themselves to dwell at Jerusalem*.

Verses 33–40

Among all the genealogies of the tribes there is no mention of any of the kings of Israel after their defection from the house of David, much less of their families; not a word of Jeroboam's house or Baasha's, or Omri's or Jehu's; for they were all idolaters. But of the family of Saul, which was the royal family before the elevation of David, we have here a particular account. 1. Before Saul, Kish and Ner only are named, his father and grandfather, *v.* 33. He was in truth the son of Ner but the grandson of Abiel, as appears by 1 Sam. xiv. 51. 2. After Saul, divers of his sons are named, but the posterity of none of them, save Jonathan only, for the sake of his sincere kindness to David. This genealogy ends in Ulam, whose family became famous in the tribe of Benjamin for the number of its valiant men. Of that one man's posterity, there were at one time 150 archers.

CHAPTER 9

This chapter intimates to us that one end of recording all these genealogies was to direct the Jews, now that they had returned, out of captivity, with whom to incorporate and where to reside; for here we have an account of those who first took possession of Jerusalem after their return from Babylon, and began the rebuilding of it upon the old foundation. I. The Israelites, ver. 2–9. II. The priests, ver. 10–13. III. The Levites and other Nethinim, ver. 14–26. IV. Here is the particular charge of some of the priests and Levites, ver. 27–34. V. A repetition of the genealogy of king Saul, ver. 35–44.

Verses 1–13

The first verse tells us of *the books of the kings of Israel and Judah*. Mentioning Israel and Judah, the historian takes notice of their being *carried away to Babylon for their transgression*. Then follows an account of the first inhabitants, after their return

from captivity, that dwelt in their cities, especially in Jerusalem. 1. The Israelites. That general name is used (*v.* 2) because with those of Judah and Benjamin there were many of Ephraim and Manasseh, and the other ten tribes (*v.* 3), such as had escaped to Judah when the body of the ten tribes were carried captive or returned to Judah upon the revolutions in Assyria, and so went into captivity with them. It was foretold that the *children of Judah and of Israel* should be *gathered together and come up out of the land* (Hosea i. 11), and that they should be one nation again, Ezek. xxxvii. 22. Pieces of metal that have been separated will run together again when melted in the same crucible. Many both of Judah and Israel stayed behind in captivity. 2. The priests, *v.* 10. It was their praise that they came with the first. (1) It is said of one of them that he was *the ruler of the house of God* (*v.* 11) not the chief ruler, for Joshua was then the high priest, but the sagan, the next under him. (2) It is said of many of them that they were *very able men for the service of the house of God, v.* 13. In the house of God there is service to be done, constant service; and it is well for the church when those are employed in that service who are qualified for it, *able ministers of the New Testament*, 2 Cor. iii. 6. The service of the temple required great courage and vigour of mind, as well as strength of body; and therefore they are praised as *mighty men of valour*.

Verses 14–34

The good posture which the affairs of religion were put into immediately upon the return of the people out of Babylon. The late want of ordinances made them very zealous in setting up the worship of God among them; and so they began their worship of God at the right end.

I. Before the house of the Lord was built they had the house of the tabernacle, a plain and movable tent. Those that cannot yet reach to have a temple must not be without a tabernacle, but be thankful for that and make the best of it. Never let God's work be left undone for want of a place to do it in.

II. In allotting to the priests and Levites their respective employments, they had the model that was drawn up by David, and Samuel the seer, *v.* 22. Samuel, in his time, had drawn the scheme of it, and laid the foundation, though the ark was then in obscurity, and David afterwards finished it, and both acted by immediate direction from God.

III. The most of them dwelt at Jerusalem (*v.* 34), yet there were some that dwelt in the villages (*v.* 16, 22), because, it may be, there was not yet room for them in Jerusalem. However they were employed in the service of the tabernacle (*v.* 25).

IV. Many of the Levites were employed as porters at the gates of the house of God, four chief porters (*v.* 26), and, under them, others, to the number of 212, *v.* 22. They had the oversight of the gates (*v.* 23), were keepers of the *thresholds*, as in the margin (*v.* 19), and keepers of the entry. This seemed a mean office; and yet David would rather have it than *dwell in the tents of wickedness*, Ps. lxxxiv. 10. Their office was, 1. To open the doors of God's house every morning (*v.* 27) and shut them at night. 2. To keep off the unclean, and hinder those from thrusting in that were forbidden by the law. 3. To direct and introduce into the courts of the Lord those that came thither to worship. Ministers have work to do of this kind.

V. Here is one Phinehas, a son of Eleazar, that is said to be a *ruler over them in time past* (*v.* 20), not the famous high priest of that name, but an eminent Levite, of whom it is here said that *the Lord was with him*, or (as the Chaldee reads it) *the Word of the Lord was his helper*.

VI. It is said of some of them that *they lodged roundabout the house of God*, v. 27. The Levites pitched about the tabernacle when they marched through the wilderness. Then they were porters in one sense, bearing the burdens of the sanctuary, now porters in another sense, attending the gates and the doors—in both instances keeping the charge of the sanctuary.

VII. Every one knew his charge. Some were entrusted with the ministering vessels, to bring them in and out, v. 28. Others were appointed to prepare the fine flour, wine, oil, &c., v. 29. Others, that were priests, made up the holy anointing oil, v. 30. Others took care of the meat-offerings, v. 31. Others of the shewbread, v. 32. God is the God of order: but that which is everybody's work will be nobody's work.

VIII. The singers *were employed in that work day and night*, v. 33. They were the *chief fathers of the Levites* that made a business of it, not mean singing-men that made a trade of it. They remained in the chambers of the temple, that they might closely and constantly attend it, and were therefore excused from all other services. It should seem, some companies were continually singing, at least at stated hours, both day and night. Thus was God continually praised.

Verses 35–44

These verses are the very same with *ch.* viii. 29–38, giving an account of the ancestors of Saul and the posterity of Jonathan. *There* it is the conclusion of the genealogy of Benjamin; *here* it is an introduction to the story of Saul.

Chapter 10

In this chapter we have, I. The fatal rout which the Philistines gave to Saul's army, and the fatal stroke which he gave himself, ver. 1–7. II. The Philistines' triumph therein, ver. 8–10. III. The respect which the men of Jabesh-Gilead showed the royal corpse, ver. 11, 12. IV. The reason of Saul's rejection, ver. 13, 14.

Verses 1–7

This account of Saul's death is the same which we had, 1 Sam. xxxi. 1, &c. Only let us observe, 1. Princes sin and the people suffer for it. 2. Parents sin and the children suffer for it. When the measure of Saul's iniquity was full, and his day came to fall (which David foresaw, 1 Sam. xxvi. 10), he not only descended into battle and perished himself, but his sons (all but Ishbosheth) perished with him, and Jonathan among the rest, that gracious, generous man; for *all things come alike to all*.

Verses 8–14

I. From the triumph of the Philistines over the body of Saul we may learn, 1. That the greater dignity men are advanced to the greater disgrace they are in danger of falling into. 2. That, if we give not to God the glory of our successes, even the Philistines will rise up in judgment against us and condemn us; for, when they had obtained a victory over Saul, they *sent tidings to their idols*—poor idols, that knew not what was done a few miles off till the tidings were brought them, nor then either! They also put Saul's armour *in the house of their gods*, v. 10.

II. From the triumph of the men of Jabesh-Gilead in the rescue of the bodies of Saul and his sons we learn that there is a respect due to the remains of the deceased. We must treat the dead body as those who remember it has been united to an immortal soul and must be so again.

III. From the divine Justice in the ruin of Saul we may learn, 1. That the sin of sinners will certainly find them out. 2. That no man's greatness can exempt him from the judgments of God.

Chapter 11

In this chapter is repeated, I. The elevation of David to the throne, immediately upon the death of Saul, by common consent, ver. 1–3. II. His gaining the castle of Zion out of the hands of the Jebusites, ver. 4–9. III. The catalogue of the worthies and great men of his kingdom, ver. 10–47.

Verses 1–9

David is here brought to the possession,

I. Of the throne of Israel, after he had reigned seven years in Hebron, over Judah only. In consideration of his relation to them (v. 1), his former good services, and especially the divine designation (v. 2), they anointed him their king: he covenanted to protect them, and they to bear faith and true allegiance to him, v. 3.

II. Of the stronghold of Zion, which was held by the Jebusites till David's time. Whether David had a particular eye upon it as a place fit to make a royal city, or whether he had a promise of it from God, it seems that one of his first exploits was to make himself master of that fort; and, when he had it, he called it the *city of David*, v. 7. To this reference is had, Ps. ii. 6. *I have set my king upon my holy hill of Zion.*

Verses 10–47

An account of David's worthies, the great men of his time that served him and were preferred by him. The first edition of this catalogue we had, 2 Sam. xxiii. 8, &c. This is much the same, only that those named here from v. 41 to the end are added.

I. The connexion of this catalogue with that which is said concerning David, v. 9. *The Lord of hosts was with him, and these were the mighty men which he had.* God was with him and wrought for him, but by men and means and the use of second causes.

II. The title of this catalogue (v. 10): *These are the men who strengthened themselves with him.* In strengthening him they strengthened themselves and their own interest; for his advancement was theirs.

III. That which made all these men honourable was the good service that they did to their king and country; they helped to make David King (v. 10)— a good work. They slew the Philistines, and other public enemies, and were instrumental to save Israel. The honours of Christ's kingdom are prepared for those that *fight the good fight of faith*, that labour and suffer, and are willing to venture all, even life itself, for Christ and a good conscience.

IV. Among all the great exploits of David's mighty men, here is nothing great mentioned concerning David himself but his *pouring out water before the Lord* which he had *longed for*, v. 18, 19. Four very honourable dispositions of David appeared in that action. 1. Repentance for his own weakness. 2. Denial of his own appetite. He longed for the water of the well of Bethlehem; but, when he had it, he would not drink it, because he would not so far humour himself and gratify a foolish fancy. 3. Devotion towards God. That water which he thought too good, too precious, for his own drinking, he *poured out to the Lord* for a *drink-offering*. 4. Tenderness of his servants. It put him into the greatest confusion imaginable to think that three brave men should hazard their lives to fetch water for him.

V. In the wonderful achievements of these heroes the power of God must be acknowledged.

VI. One of these worthies is said to be *an Ammonite* (v. 39), another *a Moabite* (v. 46), and yet the law was that an *Ammonite* and *a Moabite should not enter into the congregation of the Lord*, Deut. xxiii. 3. These, it is likely, had approved themselves so hearty for the interest of Israel that in their case it was thought fit to dispense with that law, and the rather because it was an indication that the Son of David would have worthies among the Gentiles.

CHAPTER 12

It was not all at once, but gradually, that David ascended the throne. His kingdom was to last; and therefore, like fruits that keep longest, it ripened slowly. I. What help came in to him to Ziklag, to make him king of Judah, ver. 1–22. II. What help came in to him in Hebron, to make him king over all Israel, above seven years after, ver. 23–40.

Verses 1–22

An account of those that appeared and acted as David's friends, upon the death of Saul, to bring about the revolution. All the force he had, while he was persecuted, was but 600 men, but, when the time had come that he must begin to act offensively, Providence brought in more to his assistance. Even while he *kept himself close, because of Saul* (v. 1), while he did not appear, to invite or encourage his friends and well wishers to come in to him (not foreseeing that the death of Saul was so near), God was inclining and preparing them to come over to him. Those that trust God to do his work for them in his own way and time shall find his providence outdoing all their forecast and contrivance.

I. Some even of Saul's brethren, of the tribe of Benjamin, and a-kin to him, came over to David, *v.* 2. These Benjamites are described to be men of great dexterity, that were trained up in shooting and slinging, and used both hands alike—ingenious active men. See Judges xx. 16.

II. Some of the tribe of Gad, though seated on the other side Jordan, had such a conviction of David's title and fitness that they *separated themselves from their brethren* to go to David, though he was *in the hold in the wilderness* (v. 8). They were but few, eleven in all, here named, but they added much to David's strength. Those that had hitherto come were most of them men of broken fortunes, distressed, discontented, and soldiers of fortune, that came to him rather for protection than to do him any service, 1 Sam. xxii. 2. But these Gadites were brave men, *men of war, and fit for the battle, v.* 8. They were disciplined men in their own tribe (*v.* 14). What enemies those were that they met with in the valleys, when they had passed Jordan, does not appear; but they put them to flight with their lion-like faces, and pursued them with matchless fury, both *towards the east and towards the west.*

III. Some of Judah and Benjamin came to him, *v.* 16. Their leader was Amasai, whether the same with that Amasa that afterwards sided with Absalom (2 Sam. xvii. 25) does not appear.

1. David's prudent treaty with them, *v.* 17. He was surprised to see them, having been so often in danger by the treachery of the men of Ziph and the men of Keilah, who yet were all men of Judah. No marvel that he meets these men of Judah with caution.

(1) How fairly he deals with them. [1] If they be faithful and honourable, he will be their rewarder. But, [2] If they be false, and come to betray him into the hands of Saul, under colour of friendship, he leaves them to God to be their avenger. Never was man more violently run upon, and run down, than David was (except the Son of David himself), and yet he had the testimony of his conscience that there was no wrong in his hands.

(2) In this appeal observe, [1] He calls God the *God of our fathers*, both his fathers and theirs. Thus he reminded them not to deal ill with him; for they were both descendants from the same patriarchs, and both dependents on the same God. [2] He does not imprecate any fearful judgment upon them.

2. Their hearty closure with him, *v.* 18. Amasai was their spokesman, on whom the *Spirit of the Lord came.* Nothing could be said finer, more lively, or more pertinent to the occasion. *Thine are we, David, and on thy side, thou son of Jesse.* In calling him *son of Jesse* they reminded themselves that he was lineally descended from Nahshon and Salmon, who in their days were princes of the tribe of Judah. Saul called him so in disdain (1 Sam. xx. 27; xxii. 7), but they looked upon it as his honour. *"Peace, peace, be unto thee,* all the good thy heart desires, and *peace be to thy helpers,* among whom we desire to be reckoned, that peace may be on us." He assured him of help from heaven: *"For thy God helpeth thee."* From these expressions of Amasai we may take instruction how to testify our affection and allegiance to the Lord Jesus.

3. David's cheerful acceptance of them into his interest and friendship. *David received them,* and preferred them to be *captains of the band.*

IV. Some of Manasseh likewise joined in with him, *v.* 19. Providence gave them a fair opportunity to do so when he and his men marched through their country upon this occasion. We have the story, 1 Sam. xxix. 4, &c. In his return some great men of Manasseh struck in with David to help him *against the band of Amalekites* who had plundered Ziklag.

Verses 23–40

An account of those who were active in perfecting the settlement of David upon the throne, after the death of Ishbosheth. The quota which every tribe brought in *ready armed to war*, in case there should be any opposition, *v.* 23.

I. Those tribes that lived nearest brought in the fewest—Judah but 6,800 (*v.* 24), Simeon but 7,100 (*v.* 25); whereas Zebulun, that lay remote, brought 50,000, Asher 40,000, and the two tribes and a half on the other side Jordan 120,000. Not as if the adjacent tribes were cold in the cause; but they showed prudence in bringing few, since all the rest lay within call.

II. The Levites themselves, and the priests (called here the Aaronites), appeared very hearty in this cause, and were ready, if there were occasion, to fight for David, as well as pray for him, because they knew he was called of God to the government, *v.* 26–28.

III. Even some of the kindred of Saul came over to David (*v.* 29).

IV. It is said of most of these that they were *mighty men of valour* (*v.* 25, 28, 30), of others that they were *expert in war* (*v.* 35, 36), and of them all that they *could keep rank, v.* 38.

V. Some were so considerate as to bring with them arms.

VI. The men of Issachar were the fewest of all, only 200, and yet as serviceable to David's interest as those that brought in the greatest numbers, these few being in effect the whole tribe. They were weatherwise. They understood public affairs, the temper of the nation, and the tendencies of the present events. We read of *the princes of Issachar*, Judges v. 15. They knew how to rule, and the rest knew how to obey.

VII. It is said of them all that they engaged in this enterprise *with a perfect heart* (*v.* 38).

VIII. The men of Judah, and others of the adjacent tribes, prepared for the victualling of their respective camps when they came to Hebron, *v.* 39, 40.

CHAPTER 13

In this chapter care is taken about religion. I. David consults with the representatives of the people about bringing up the ark out of its obscurity into a public place, ver. 1–4. II. With a great deal of solemnity and joy, it is carried from Kirjath-jearim, ver. 5–8. III. Uzza is struck dead for touching it, ver. 9–14.

Verses 1–8

I. David's pious proposal to bring up the ark of God to Jerusalem, that the royal city might be the holy city, *v.* 1–3.

1. As soon as David was well seated on his throne he had thoughts concerning the ark of God: *Let us bring the ark to us, v.* 3. (1) To do honour to God, by showing respect to his ark, the token of his presence. (2) To have the comfort and benefit of that sacred oracle. "Let us bring it to us, not only that we may be a credit to it, but that it may be a blessing to us." It is the wisdom of those who are setting out in the world to take God's ark with them, to make his oracles their counsellors and his laws their rule.

2. He consulted with the leaders of the people about it, *v.* 1. (1) That he might show respect to the great men of the kingdom and put honour upon them. No prince that is wise will covet to be absolute. (2) That he might be advised by them in the manner of doing it.

3. He would have all the people summoned to attend on this occasion, both for the honour of the ark and for the people's satisfaction and edification, *v.* 2. (1) He calls the common people *brethren,* which bespeaks his humility and condescension. (2) He speaks of the people as a remnant that had escaped: *Our brethren that are left in all the land of Israel.* They had been under scattering providences. (3) He takes care that the priests and Levites especially should be summoned to attend the ark.

4. All this is upon supposition that it is *of the Lord their God.*

5. Thus it was requisite they should amend what had been amiss in the last reign: "For *we enquired not at it in the days of Saul,* and David makes no peevish reflections upon Saul, but, in general, *We enquired not at it,* making himself with others guilty of the neglect.

II. The people's ready agreement to this proposal (*v.* 4): *The thing* was *right in the eyes of all the people.*

III. The solemnity of bringing up the ark, *v.* 5, &c., which we read before, 2 Sam. vi. 1, &c.

Verses 9-14

This breach upon Uzza, which caused all the joy to cease, we had an account of, 2 Sam. vi. 6, &c. Let the sin of Uzza warn us all to take heed of presumption, rashness, and irreverence, in dealing about holy things (*v.* 9), and not to think that a good intention will justify a bad action.

Chapter 14

I. David's kingdom established, ver. 1, 2. II. His family built up, ver. 3-7. III. His enemies, the Philistines, routed in two campaigns, ver. 8-17. This is repeated here from 2 Sam. v. 11, &c.

Verses 1-7

1. There is no man that has such a sufficiency in himself but he has need of his neighbours and has reason to be thankful for their help: David had a very large kingdom, Hiram a very little one; yet David could not build himself a house to his mind unless Hiram furnished him with both workmen and materials, *v.* 1. 2. It is a great satisfaction to a wise man to be settled, and to a good man to see the special providence of God in his settlement. The people had made David king; but he could not be easy till he perceived that *the Lord had confirmed him king over Israel, v.* 2. 3. We must look upon all our advancements as designed for our usefulness. We are blessed in order that we may be blessings. See Gen. xii. 2.

Verses 8-17

This narrative of David's triumph over the Philistines is much the same with that, 2 Sam. v. 17, &c. Let the attack which the Philistines made upon David forbid us to be secure in any settlement or advancement. When we are most easy something or other may come to be a terror or vexation to us. Christ's

kingdom will thus be insulted by the serpent's seed, especially when it makes any advances. Let David's thankful acknowledgment of the hand of God in his successes direct us to bring all our sacrifices of praise to God's altar. *Not unto us, O Lord! not unto us, but to thy name give glory.*

Chapter 15

The bringing in of the ark to the city of David was a very good work; it was attempted, but not perfected; it lay in the house of Obed-edom. Now this chapter gives us an account of the completing of that good work. I. How it was done more regularly than before. 1. A place was prepared for it, ver. 1. 2. The priests were ordered to carry it, ver. 2-15. 3. The Levites had their offices assigned them in attending on it, ver. 16-24. II. How it was done more successfully than before, ver. 25. 1. The Levites made no mistake in their work, ver. 26. 2. David and the people met with no damp upon their joy, ver. 27, 28.

Verses 1-24

Preparation is here made for the bringing of the ark home to the city of David from the house of Obed-edom. 1. David now prepared a place for the reception of the ark, before he brought it to him. He had not time to *build a house,* but he *pitched a tent* for it (*v.* 1), probably according to the pattern shown to Moses in the mount, or as near it as might be, of curtains and boards. Wherever we build for ourselves, we must be sure to make room for God's ark, for a church in the house. 2. David now ordered that the Levites or priests should carry the ark upon their shoulders. The Kohathites carried it in their ordinary marches, and therefore had no waggons allotted them, because their work was to *bear upon their shoulders,* Num. vii. 9. But upon extraordinary occasions, as when they passed Jordan and compassed Jericho, the priests carried it. This rule was express, and yet David himself forgot it, and put the ark upon a cart. David now took care not only to summon the Levites to the solemnity, as he did all Israel (*v.* 3) and had done before (*ch.* xiii. 2), but to see that they assembled (*v.* 4), especially the sons of Aaron, *v.* 11. To them he gives that solemn charge (*v.* 12): *You are the chief of the fathers of the Levites,* therefore do you *bring up the ark of the Lord.* 3. The Levites and Priests sanctified themselves (*v.* 14) and were ready to carry the ark on their shoulders, according to the law, *v.* 15. 4. Officers were appointed to be ready to bid the ark welcome, with every possible expression of joy, *v.* 16. Heman, Asaph, and Ethan, were now first appointed, *v.* 17. They undertook to sound with symbols (*v.* 19), others with psalteries (*v.* 20), others with harps, on the *Sheminith,* or *eighth,* eight notes higher or lower than the rest, according to the rules of concert, *v.* 21. Some that were priests blew with the trumpet (*v.* 24), as was usual at the removal of the ark (Num. x. 8) and at solemn feasts, Ps. lxxxi. 3. And one was appointed for song (*v.* 22), for he was skilful in it, could sing well himself and instruct others.

Verses 25-29

All things being got ready for the carrying of the ark to the city of David, and its reception there, we have here an account of the solemnity of this conveyance thither from the house of Obed-edom.

I. God helped the Levites that carried it. If God did not help us, we could not stir a step. The Levites, remembering the breach upon Uzza, were probably ready to tremble when they took up the ark; but God helped them, silenced their fears, and strengthened their faith. God's ministers that bear the vessels of the Lord have special need of divine help in their ministrations, that God in them may be glorified and his church edified.

II. When they experienced the tokens of God's presence with them they offered sacrifices of praise to him, *v.* 26.

III. There were great expressions of rejoicing used: the sacred music was played, David danced, the singers sang, and the common people shouted, *v.* 27, 28. This we had before, 2 Sam. vi. 14, 15.

CHAPTER 16

This chapter concludes the settlement of the public worship of God during the reign of David. I. The solemnity with which the ark was fixed, ver. 1–6. II. The psalm David gave to be sung on this occasion, ver. 7–36. III. The settling of the stated public worship of God in order thenceforward, ver. 37–43.

Verses 1–6

It was a glorious day when the ark of God was safely lodged in the tent David had pitched for it.

I. The ark had been obscure in a country town, in the fields of the wood; now it was removed to a public place, to the royal city. It had been neglected, as a despised broken vessel; now it was attended with veneration, and God was enquired of by it. This was but a tent, a poor mean dwelling; yet this was the tabernacle, the temple, which David in his psalms often speaks of with so much affection. David, who pitched a tent for the ark and continued steadfast to it, did far better than Solomon, who built a temple for it and yet in his latter end turned his back upon it. The church's poorest times were its purest.

II. Now David was easy in his mind, the ark was fixed, and fixed near him. He takes care, 1. That God shall have the glory of it. (1) By sacrifices (*v.* 1), burnt-offerings in adoration of his perfections, peace-offerings in acknowledgment of his favours. (2) By songs; he appointed Levites to record this story in a song for the benefit of others. 2. That the people shall have the joy of it. They shall fare the better for this day's solemnity; for he gives them all not only a royal treat but also a *blessing in the name of the Lord,* as a father, as a prophet, *v.* 2.

Verses 7–36

The thanksgiving psalm which David, by the Spirit, composed, and delivered to the chief musician, to be sung upon occasion of the public entry the ark made into the tent prepared for it. It is gathered out of several psalms (from the beginning to *v.* 23 is taken from Ps. cv. 1, &c.; and then *v.* 23 to *v.* 34 is the whole 96th psalm, with little variation; *v.* 34 is taken from Ps. cxxxvi. 1 and divers others; and then the last two verses are taken from the close of Ps. cvi.), which some think warrants us to do likewise, and make up hymns out of David's psalms, a part of one and a part of another put together so as may be most proper to express and excite the devotion of Christians. In the midst of our praises we must not forget to pray for the succour and relief of those saints and servants of God that are in distress (*v.* 35): *Save us, gather us, deliver us from the heathen,* those of us that are scattered and oppressed. When we are rejoicing in God's favours to us we must remember our afflicted brethren, and pray for their salvation, and deliverance as our own. We are members one of another; and therefore when we mean, "Lord, save *them,*" it is not improper to say, "Lord, save *us.*" Let us make God the Alpha and Omega of our praises. David begins with (*v.* 8), *Give thanks to the Lord;* he concludes (*v.* 36), *Blessed be the Lord.* And whereas in the place whence this doxology is taken (Ps. cvi. 48) it is added, *Let all the people say, Amen, Hallelujah,* here we find they did according to that directory: *All the people said, Amen, and praised the Lord.*

Verses 37–43

The worship of God is not only to be the work of a solemn day now and then, brought in to grace a triumph; but it ought to be the work of every day. David therefore settles it here for a constancy.

1. At Jerusalem, where the ark was, Asaph and his brethren were appointed to attend, to *minister before the ark continually,* with songs of praise, *as every day's work required, v.* 37. No sacrifices were offered there, nor incense burnt, because the altars were not there, but David's prayers were *directed as incense, and the lifting up of his hands as the evening sacrifice* (Ps. cxli. 2), so early did spiritual worship take place of ceremonial. 2. Yet the ceremonial worship, being of divine institution, must by no means be omitted; and therefore at Gibeon were the altars where the priests attended, for their work was to sacrifice and burn incense, which they did *continually, morning and evening, according to the law of Moses, v.* 39, 40. These must be kept up, because, however in their own nature they were inferior to the moral services of prayer and praise, yet, as they were types of the mediation of Christ, they had a great deal of honour put upon them, and the observance of them was of great consequence. At Gibeon, where the altars were, David also appointed *singers to give thanks to the Lord,* and the burden of all their songs must be, *For his mercy endureth for ever, v.* 41. (1) The people were satisfied, and went home [pleased. (2) David returned to bless his house, resolving to keep up his family worship still, which public worship must not supersede.

CHAPTER 17

This chapter is the same with 2 Sam. vii. It will be worth while to look back upon what was there said upon it. Two things in general we have:—I. God's gracious acceptance of David's purpose to build him a house, and the promise he made thereupon, ver. 1–15. II. David's gracious acceptance of God's good promise to build him a house, and the prayer he made thereupon, ver. 16–27.

Verses 1–15

I. David could not be easy in a house of cedar while the ark was lodged within curtains, *v.* 1. Those that are contriving where to bestow their fruits and their goods would do well to enquire what condition the ark is in, and whether some may not be well bestowed upon it.

II. How ready God's prophets should be to encourage every good purpose (*v.* 2).

III. How little God affects external pomp and splendour in his service. His ark was content with a tabernacle (*v.* 5). He commanded the judges to *feed his people,* but never bade them *build him a house, v.* 6.

IV. How graciously God accepts his people's good purposes, yea, though he himself prevents the performance of them. David must not *build this house, v.* 4. He must prepare for it, but not do it; as Moses must bring Israel within sight of Canaan, but must then leave it to Joshua to put them in possession of it. Yet David must not think that, because he was not permitted to build the temple, 1. His preferment was in vain; no, "*I took thee from the sheep-cote,* though not to be a builder of the temple, yet to be *ruler over my people Israel.*" Nor, 2. Must he think that his good purpose was in vain, and that he should lose the reward of it; he shall be as fully recompensed as if he had done it: "*The Lord will build thee a house,* and annex the crown of Israel to it," *v.* 10. If there be a willing mind, it shall not only be accepted, but thus rewarded. Nor, 3. Must he think that because *he* might not do this good work therefore it would never be done, and that it was in vain to think of it; no, *I will raise up thy seed, and he shall build me a house, v.* 11, 12. Nor, 4. Must he confine his thoughts to the temporal prosperity of his family, but must entertain himself with the prospect of the kingdom of the Messiah, who should descend from his loins, and whose throne should be *established for evermore, v.* 14.

Verses 16–27

David's solemn address to God, in answer to the gracious message he had now received from him. By faith he receives the promises, embraces them, and is persuaded of them, as the patriarchs, Heb. xi. 13. What an example is this to us of humble, believing, fervent prayer! Observe only those few expressions in which the prayer, as we find it here, differs from the record of it in 2 Sam. vii.

I. That which is there expressed by way of question (*Is this the manner of men, O Lord God?*) is here an acknowledgment: "*Thou hast regarded me according to the estate of a man of high degree.*" God, by the covenant-relations into which he admits believers, regards them according to the estate of men of high degree, though they are mean and vile.

II. After the words *What can David say more unto thee*, it is here added, *for the honour of thy servant? v.* 18. The honour God puts upon his servants, by taking them into covenant and communion with himself, is so great that they need not, they cannot, desire to be more highly honoured.

III. It is very observable that what in Samuel is said to be *for thy word's sake* is here said to be *for thy servant's sake, v.* 19. Jesus Christ is both *the Word of God* (Rev. xix. 13) and *the servant of God* (Isa. xlii. 1), and it is for his sake, upon the score of his mediation, that the promises are both made and made good to all believers.

IV. In Samuel, the Lord of hosts is said to be the *God over Israel*; here he is said to be *the God of Israel, even a God to Israel, v.* 24. There were those that were called *gods* of such and such nations, gods of Assyria and Egypt, gods of Hamad and Arpad; but they were no gods to them, for they stood them in no stead at all, were mere ciphers, nothing but a name. But *the God of Israel* is a *God to Israel*; all his attributes and perfections redound to their real benefit and advantage.

V. The closing words in Samuel are, *With thy blessing let the house of thy servant be blessed for ever.* That is the language of a holy desire. But the closing words here are the language of a most holy faith: *For thou blessest, O Lord! and it shall be blessed for ever, v.* 27. David's prayer concludes as God's promise did (*v.* 14) with that which is *for ever.* God's word looks at things eternal, and so should our desires and hopes.

CHAPTER 18

Those that seek first the kingdom of God and the righteousness thereof, as David did, shall have other things added to them. I. His prosperity abroad. He conquered the Philistines (ver. 1), the Moabites (ver. 2), the king of Zobah (ver. 3, 4), the Syrians (ver. 5–8), made the king of Hamath his tributary (ver. 9–11), and the Edomites, ver. 12, 13. II. His prosperity at home. His court and kingdom flourished, ver. 14–17. All this we had an account of before, 2 Sam. viii.

Verses 1–8

After this, it is said (*v.* 1), David did great exploits. After the sweet communion he had had with God by the word and prayer, he went on in his work with extraordinary vigour and courage, *conquering and to conquer.* The Philistines had, for several generations, been vexatious to Israel, but now *David subdued them, v.* 1. Such is the uncertainty of this world that frequently men lose their wealth and power when they think to confirm it. Hadarezer was smitten *as he went to establish his dominion, v.* 3. The Syrians of Damascus were smitten when they came to help Hadarezer.

Verses 9–17

What God blesses us with we must honour him with. It was said before (*v.* 6) and here it is repeated (*v.* 13) that *the Lord preserved David whithersoever he went.* God gives men power, not that they

may look great with it, but that they may do good with it.

CHAPTER 19

The story is here repeated of David's war with the Ammonites and the Syrians their allies, which we read in 2 Sam. x. I. David's civility to the king of Ammon, in sending an embassy of condolence to him on occasion of his father's death, ver. 1, 2. II. His great incivility to David, in the base usage he gave to his ambassadors, ver. 3, 4. III. David's just resentment of it, and the war which broke out thereupon, in which the Ammonites acted with policy in bringing the Syrians to their assistance (ver. 6, 7), Joab did bravely (ver. 8–13), and Israel was once and again victorious, ver. 14–19.

Verses 1–5

It becomes good people to be neighbourly, and especially to be grateful. David will pay respect to Hanun because he is his neighbour; and religion teaches us to be civil and to be ready to do all offices of kindness to those we live among; nor must difference in religion be any obstruction to this. But, besides this, David remembered the kindness which his father showed to him. Those that are base, and design ill themselves, are apt to be jealous and to suspect ill of others without cause. Hanun's servants suggested that David's ambassadors came as spies, as if so great and mighty a man as David needed to do so mean a thing. Yet Hanun, against the law of nations, treated David's ambassadors villainously.

Verses 6–19

The hearts of sinners are hardened to their destruction. The children of Ammon saw that *they had made themselves odious to David* (*v.* 6); it would have been their wisdom to desire conditions of peace, to humble themselves and offer any satisfaction for the injury they had done him. But, instead of this, they prepared for war, and so brought upon themselves, by David's hand, those desolations which he never intended them. The courage of brave men is heightened and invigorated by difficulties. When Joab saw that the battle was set against him before and behind (*v.* 10), instead of meditating a retreat, he doubled his resolution; and not only spoke, but acted, like a gallant man, that had great presence of mind when he saw himself surrounded. He engaged with his brother for mutual assistance (*v.* 12), excited himself and the rest of the officers to act vigorously in their respective posts, and then left the issue to God: *Let the Lord do that which is right in his sight.* The Ammonites did their utmost to make the best of their position: they brought as good a force into the field, yet, having a bad cause, they were put to the worst. Right will prevail and triumph at last. The Syrians, though in no way concerned in the merits of the cause, but serving only as mercenaries to the Ammonites, when they were beaten, thought themselves concerned to retrieve their honour, and therefore called in the assistance of the Syrians on the other side Euphrates; but to no purpose, for still they *fled before Israel* (*v.* 18). The Syrians, finding that Israel was the conquering side, not only broke off their alliance with the Ammonites and would help them no more (*v.* 19), *but made peace with David and became his servants.*

CHAPTER 20

Here is a repetition of the story of David's wars. I. With the Ammonites, and the taking of Rabbah, ver. 1–3. II. With the giants of the Philistines, ver. 4–8.

Verses 1–3

The destruction of Rabbah, the metropolis of their kingdom (*v.* 1), the putting of their king's crown upon David's head (*v.* 2), and the great severity that was used towards the people, *v.* 3. Of this we had a more full account in 2 Sam. xi, xii. While

Joab was besieging Rabbah David fell into that greater sin in the matter of Uriah.

Verses 4–8

The Philistines were nearly subdued (*ch.* xviii. 1); but the giants of Gath were last brought down. In the conflicts between grace and corruption there are some sins which, like these giants, are not mastered without much difficulty and a long struggle. 1. We never read of giants among the Israelites, as we do of giants among the Philistines—giants of Gath, but not giants of Jerusalem. The growth of God's plants is in usefulness, not in bulk. 2. The servants of David, though men of ordinary stature, were too hard for the giants of Gath in every encounter, because they had God on their side. We need not fear great men against us while we have the great God for us. What will a finger more on each hand do, or a toe more on each foot, in contest with Omnipotence?

CHAPTER 21

David's sin, in numbering the people, is here related, because, in the atonement made for that sin, an intimation was given of the spot of ground on which the temple should be built. Here is, I. David's sin, in forcing Joab to number the people, ver. 1–6. II. David's sorrow for what he had done, as soon as he perceived the sinfulness of it, ver. 7, 8. III. The sad dilemma (or trilemma rather) he was brought to, when it was put to him to choose how he would be punished for this sin, and what rod he would be beaten with, ver. 9–13. IV. The woeful havoc which was made by the pestilence in the country, and the narrow escape which Jerusalem had from being laid waste by it, ver. 14–17. V. David's repentance, and sacrifice, upon this occasion, and the staying of the plague thereupon, ver. 18–30. This story we met with, and meditated upon, 2 Sam. xxiv.

Verses 1–6

Numbering the people, one would think, was no bad thing. Why should not the shepherd know the number of his flock? He did it in the pride of his heart; and there is no sin that has in it more of contradiction and therefore more of offence to God than pride. The sin was David's.

I. How active the tempter was in it (*v.* 1): *Satan stood up against Israel, and provoked David* to do it. It is said (2 Sam. xxiv. 1) that *the anger of the Lord was kindled against Israel, and he moved David* to do it. When it is said that he moved David to do it, it must be explained by what is intimated here, that, for wise and holy ends, he permitted the devil to do it. Now, when Satan meant to do Israel a mischief, what course did he take? He did not *move God against them to destroy them*, but he provoked David, the best friend they had, to number them, and so to offend God, and set him against them. The devil does us more mischief by tempting us to sin against our God than he does by accusing us before our God.

II. Joab, the person whom David employed, was an active man in public business; but to this he was perfectly forced, and did it with the greatest reluctance imaginable. No man more forward than he in anything that really tended to the honour of the king or the welfare of the kingdom; but in this matter he would gladly be excused. It was a needless thing. There was no occasion at all for it. It was a dangerous thing. In doing it he might be a cause of trespass to Israel, and might provoke God against them. There was a general disgust at these orders, which confirmed Joab in his dislike of them. He left two tribes unnumbered (*v.* 5, 6), two considerable ones, Levi and Benjamin, and perhaps was not very exact in numbering the rest, because he did not do it with any pleasure, which might be one occasion of the difference between the sums here and 2 Sam. xxiv. 9.

Verses 7–17

David is here under the rod for numbering the people, that rod of correction which drives out the foolishness that is bound up in the heart, the foolishness of pride.

I. How he was corrected. God takes notice of, and is displeased with, the sins of his people; and no sin is more displeasing to him than pride of heart. David must have the people numbered: *Bring me the number of them*, says he, *that I may know it*. But now God numbers them after another manner, and David had another number of them brought, more to his confusion than to his satisfaction, namely, a black bill of mortality. He sees the destroying angel, with his sword drawn against Jerusalem, *v.* 16. Pestilences make the greatest devastations in the most populous places.

II. How he bore the correction. He owned that he had sinned, had done foolishly, and he entreated that, however he might be corrected for it, the iniquity of it might be done away. I submit to the rod, only let me be the sufferer, for I am the sinner. 1. He cast himself upon the mercy of God (though he knew he was angry with him) and did not entertain any hard thoughts of him. However it be, *Let us fall into the hands of the Lord, for his mercies are great, v.* 13. Good men, even when God frowns upon them, think well of him. *Though he slay me, yet will I trust in him.* 2. He expressed a very tender concern for the people, and it went to his heart to see them plagued for his transgression: *These sheep, what have they done?*

Verses 18–30

Upon David's repentance, his peace made with God. When David repented of the sin God repented of the judgment, and ordered the destroying angel to *stay his hand* and *sheath his sword, v.* 27. Direction was given to David to rear an altar in the threshing-floor of Ornan, *v.* 18. The commanding of David to build an altar was a blessed token of reconciliation. David immediately made a bargain with Ornan for the threshing-floor. Ornan generously offered it to him gratis. God testified his acceptance of David's offerings on this altar: He *answered him from heaven by fire, v.* 26. He continued to offer his sacrifices upon this altar. The brazen altar which Moses made was at Gibeon (*v.* 29), and there all the sacrifices of Israel were offered: but David was so terrified at the sight of the sword of the angel that he *could not go thither, v.* 30. The business required haste, when the plague was begun. And therefore God, in tenderness to him, bade him build an altar in that place. The symbols of unity were not so much insisted on as unity itself. When the present distress was over, David, as long as he lived, sacrificed there, though the altar at Gibeon was still kept up. "Here God has graciously met me, and therefore I will still expect to meet with him."

CHAPTER 22

"Out of the eater comes forth meat." It was upon occasion of the terrible judgment inflicted on Israel for the sin of David that God gave intimation of the setting up of another altar, and of the place where he would have the temple to be built. I. Directed him to the place, ver. 1. II. Encouraged and quickened him to the work. 1. He set himself to prepare for the building, ver. 2–5. 2. He instructed Solomon, and gave him a charge concerning this work, ver. 6–16. 3. He commanded the princes to assist him in it, ver. 17–19. There is a great deal of difference between the frame of David's spirit in the beginning of the former chapter and in the beginning of this. There, in the pride of his heart, he was numbering the people; here, in his humility, preparing for the service of God.

Verses 1–5

I. The place fixed for the building of the temple (*v.* 1). The ground was a threshing-floor; for the church of the living God is his floor, his threshing, and *the corn of his floor*, Isa. xxi. 10. Christ's fan is in his hand, thoroughly to purge his floor. This is to be the house because this is the altar. The temple was built for the sake of the altar. There were altars long before there were temples.

II. Preparation made for that building. David must not build it, but he would do all he could towards it: He *prepared abundantly before his death*, v. 5.

1. What induced him to make such preparation. (1) Solomon was young and tender, and not likely to apply with any great vigour to this business at first; so that, unless he found the wheels set a-going, he would be in danger of losing a great deal of time at first. (2) The house must be very stately and sumptuous, strong and beautiful, everything about it the best in its kind, since it was intended for the honour of the Lord of the whole earth, and was to be a type of Christ, in whom all fulness dwells and in whom are hid all treasures. The grandeur of the house would help to affect the worshippers with a holy awe and reverence of God, and would invite strangers to come to see it, as the wonder of the world, who thereby would be brought acquainted with the true God.

2. What preparation he made. In general, he prepared abundantly cedar and stones, iron and brass, v. 2–4. Cedar he had from the Tyrians and the Zidonians. He also got workmen together, *the strangers that were in the land of Israel*.

Verses 6–16

Solomon was *to build a house for the Lord God of Israel*, v. 6.

I. David tells him why he did not do it himself. It was in his mind to do it (v. 7), but God forbade him, because *he had shed much blood*, v. 8. Some think this refers to the blood of Uriah, but that honour was forbidden him before he had shed that blood; therefore it must be meant of the blood he shed in his wars.

II. He gives him the reason why he imposed this task upon him. 1. Because God had nominated him as the man that should do it: *A son shall be born to thee*, that shall be called *Solomon*, and *he shall build a house for my name*, v. 9, 10. 2. Because he would have leisure and opportunity to do it. He should have rest from his enemies abroad and he should have peace and quietness at home; and therefore let him build the house.

III. He delivers him an account of the vast preparations he had made for this building (v. 14), as an encouragement to Solomon to engage cheerfully in the work, for which so solid a foundation was laid. The treasure here mentioned of 100,000 talents of gold, and 1,000,000 talents of silver, amounts to such an incredible sum that most interpreters either allow an error in the copy or think the talent here signifies no more than a plate or piece: *ingots* we call them.

IV. He charges him to keep God's commandments, v. 13. He must not think by building the temple to purchase a dispensation to sin.

V. He encourages him to go about this great work, and to go on in it (v. 13): It is God's work, and it shall come to perfection.

VI. He quickens him not to rest in the preparations he had made, v. 14. He prays for him: *The Lord give thee wisdom and understanding, and give thee charge concerning Israel*, v. 12. He concludes (v. 16), *Up and be going, and the Lord be with thee*.

Verses 17–19

David here engages the princes of Israel to assist Solomon in the great work he had to do. God had given them victory, and rest, and a good land for an inheritance, v. 18. He presses that upon them which should make them zealous in it (v. 19).

CHAPTER 23

David, having given charge concerning the building of the temple, settles the method of the temple-service and puts into order the offices and officers of it. In the late irregular times, and during the wars in the beginning of his reign, though the Levitical ordinances were kept up, yet it was not with the beauty and exactness, that were desirable. Now David, being a prophet, as well as a prince, "set in order the things that were wanting." I. He declared Solomon to be his successor, ver. 1. II. He numbered the Levites, and appointed them to their respective offices, ver. 2–5. III. He took an account of the several families of the Levites, ver. 6–23. IV. He made a new reckoning of them from twenty years old, and appointed them their work, ver. 24–32.

Verses 1–23

David made Solomon king, not to reign with him, or reign under him, but only to reign after him. He did it in a solemn assembly of all the princes of Israel, which made Adonijah's attempt to break in upon Solomon's title and set it aside, the more impudent and ridiculous.

II. The Levites numbered, according to the rule in Moses's time, from thirty years old to fifty, Num. iv. 2, 3. Their number in Moses's time, by this rule, was 8,580 (Num. iv. 47, 48), but the serviceable men of Levi's tribe were now 38,000.

III. The Levites distributed to their respective posts (v. 4, 5), that every hand might be employed (for, of all men, an idle Levite makes the worst figure). The work assigned the Levites was four-fold:—1. Some, and indeed far the greater number, were to set forward the work of the house of the Lord: 24,000, almost two-thirds, were appointed for this service, to attend the priests in killing the sacrifices, washing them, burning them, to have the meat-offerings and drink-offerings ready, to keep all the vessels of the temple clean, and everything in its place. These served 1,000 a week, and so went round in twenty-four courses. Perhaps while the temple was in building some of these were employed to set forward that work, to assist the builders. 2. Others were officers and judges, not in the affairs of the temple, but in the country. They were magistrates, to give the laws of God in charge, to resolve difficulties, and to determine controversies. Of these there were 6,000, in the several parts of the kingdom, that assisted the princes and elders of every tribe in the administration of justice. 3. Others were porters, to guard all the avenues of the house of God, to examine those that desired entrance, and to resist those that would force an entrance. 4. Others were singers and players on instruments, whose business it was to keep up that part of the service; this was a new-erected office.

IV. The Levites mustered into their respective families and kindreds, that an account of them might the better be kept by calling over the roll, which each family might do for itself. In this account of the families of the Levites the posterity of Moses stood upon the level with common Levites, whilst the posterity of Aaron were advanced to the priest's office, to *sanctify the most holy things*, v. 13. The levelling of Moses's family with the rest is an evidence of his self-denial. He was no self-seeking man, as appears from his leaving to his children no marks of distinction, which was a sign that he had the spirit of God and not the spirit of the world. The elevation of Aaron's family above the rest was a recompence for his self-denial. When Moses (his younger brother) was made a god to Pharaoh, and he only his prophet or spokesman, to observe his orders and do as he was bidden, Aaron never disputed it. Because he thus submitted himself, in his own person, to his junior, in compliance with the will of God, God highly exalted his family.

Verses 24–32

I. An alteration made in the computation of the effective men of the Levites—that whereas, in Moses's time, they were not enlisted, or taken into service, till they were thirty-years old, nor admitted as probationers till twenty-five (Num. viii. 24), David ordered, by direction from God, that they should be numbered *for the service of the house of the Lord*, from the age of twenty years and upwards, v. 24. Perhaps the young Levites, having no work appointed them till twenty-five years old, had many of them got a habit of idleness, to prevent which they are set to work, and brought under discipline, at twenty years old. There was no more occasion to carry the tabernacle and the vessels thereof, the service was much easier, and what would not over-work them nor over-load them if they entered upon it at twenty years old. Now it was requisite there should be more hands employed in the temple-service, that every Israelite who brought an offering might find a Levite ready to assist him.

II. The work of the priests was (v. 13): To *sanctify the most holy things, to burn incense before the Lord*, and to *bless in his name*; that work the Levites were not to meddle with, and yet they had work enough to which they were appointed, v. 4, 5. 1. Those that were to *set forward the work of the house of God* (v. 4) were therein to *wait on the sons of Aaron* (v. 28), were to do the drudgery-work of the house of God, to keep the courts and chambers clean, set things in their places. They were to prepare the shew-bread which the priests were to set on the table, to provide the flour and cakes for the meal-offerings, that the priests might have everything ready to their hands. 2. The standards of all weights and measures were kept in the sanctuary; and the Levites had the care of them, to see that they were exact, and to try other weights and measures by them when they were appealed to. 3. The work of the singers was to *thank* and *praise the Lord* (v. 30), at the offering of the morning and evening sacrifices, and other oblations on the sabbaths, new moons, &c., v. 31. Moses appointed that they should blow trumpets over their burnt offerings and other sacrifices, and on their solemn days, Num. x. 10. The sound of the trumpet was awful, and might be affecting to the worshippers, but was not articulate, nor such a reasonable service as this which David appointed, of singing psalms on those occasions. As the Jewish church grew up from its infancy, it grew more and more intelligent in its devotions. 4. The work of the porters (v. 5) was to keep *the charge of the tabernacle and of the holy place*, that none might come nigh but such as were allowed, v. 32.

CHAPTER 24

A more particular account of the distribution of the priests and Levites into their respective classes, for the more regular discharge of the duties of their offices, according to their families. I. Of the priests, ver. 1–19. II. Of the Levites, ver. 20–31.

Verses 1–19

The particular account of these establishments, when Ezra published it, was of great use to direct their church affairs after their return from captivity. The title of this record we have v. 1—*These are the divisions of the sons of Aaron*, the distribution of them in order to the dividing of their work among themselves. 1. This distribution was made for the more regular discharge of the duties of their office. In the mystical body, every member has its use, for the good of the whole, Rom. xii. 4, 5; 1 Cor. xii. 12. 2. It was made by lot, that the disposal thereof might be of the Lord, and so all quarrels and contentions might be prevented. As God is the God of order, so he is the God of peace. 3. The lot was cast publicly, and with great solemnity, in the presence of the king, princes, and priests, that there might be no room for any fraudulent practices or the suspicion of them.

4. What those priests were chosen to was to preside in the affairs of the sanctuary (v. 5), in their several courses and turns. That which was to be determined by the lot was only the precedency, not who should serve but who should serve first, and who next. Of the twenty-four chief men of the priests sixteen were of the house of Eleazar and eight of Ithamar. The method of drawing the lots is intimated (v. 6), one chief household being taken for Eleazar, and one for Ithamar. The sixteen chief names of Eleazar were put in one urn, the eight for Ithamar in another, and they drew out of them alternately, as long as those for Ithamar lasted, and then out of those only for Eleazar, or two for Eleazar, and then one for Ithamar, throughout. 5. Among these twenty-four courses the eighth is that of Abijah or Abia (v. 10), which is mentioned (Luke i. 5) as the course which Zechariah was of, the father of John Baptist, by which it appears that these courses which David now settled, though interrupted perhaps in the bad reigns and long broken off by the captivity, yet continued in succession till the destruction of the second temple by the Romans.

Verses 20–31

Most of the Levites here named were mentioned before, ch. xxiii. 16, &c. But they are here mentioned as heads of the twenty-four courses of Levites who were to attend the twenty-four courses of the priests. The principal fathers cast lots over against their younger brethren; that is, those that were of the elder house came upon the level with those of the younger families, and took their place, not by seniority, but as God by the lot directed. The younger brethren, if they be faithful and sincere, shall be no less acceptable to Christ than the principal fathers.

CHAPTER 25

David, having settled the courses of these Levites that were to attend the priests in their ministrations, proceeds to put those into a method that were appointed to be singers and musicians in the temple. I. The persons that were to be employed, Asaph, Heman, and Jeduthun (ver. 1), their sons (ver. 2–6), and other skilful persons, ver. 7. II. The order in which they were to attend determined by lot, ver. 8–31.

Verses 1–7

I. Singing the praises of God is here called *prophesying* (v. 1–3), not that all those who were employed in this service were honoured with visions of God. Heman indeed is said to be the *king's seer in the words of God* (v. 5); but the psalms they sang were composed by prophets, and many of them were prophetical. In Samuel's time singing the praises of God went by the name of *prophesying* (1 Sam. x. 5; xix. 20).

II. This is here called a *service*, and the persons employed in it *workmen*, v. 1. In our present state of corruption and infirmity, it will not be done as it should be done without labour and struggle.

III. Here were a great variety of musical instruments used, *harps, psalteries, cymbals* (v. 1, 6), and here was one that *lifted up the horn* (v. 5), that is, used wind-music.

IV. The glory and honour of God were principally intended in all this temple-music, whether vocal or instrumental. The intention of the perpetuating of psalmody in the gospel-church, is *to make melody with the heart*, in conjunction with the voice, *unto the Lord*, Eph. v. 19.

V. The order of the king is likewise taken notice of, v. 2 and again v. 6. His taking care for the due and regular observance of divine institutions, both ancient and modern, is an example to all in authority to use their power for the promoting of religion, and the enforcing of the laws of Christ.

VI. The fathers presided in this service, Asaph, Heman, and Jeduthun (v. 1), and the children were *under the hands of their father, v.* 2, 3, 6. It is probable that Heman, Asaph, and Jeduthun, were bred up under Samuel, and had their education in the schools of the prophets which he was the founder and president of; then they were pupils, now they came to be masters. Solomon perfects what David began, so David perfects what Samuel began.

VII. There were others also, besides the sons of these three great men, who are called their *brethren* who were *instructed in the songs of the Lord*, and were cunning or well skilled therein, *v.* 7. They were all Levites and were in number 288. Yet these were but a small number in comparison with the 4,000 whom David appointed thus to *praise the Lord, ch.* xxiii. 5, and were disposed of, all the kingdom over, to preside in the country congregations, in this good work: for, though the sacrifices instituted by the hand of Moses might be offered but at one place, the psalms penned by David might be sung everywhere, 1 Tim. ii. 8.

Verses 8–31

Twenty-four persons are named in the beginning of this chapter as sons of those three great men, Asaph, Heman, and Jeduthun. Ethan was the third (*ch.* vi. 44), but probably he was dead before the establishment was perfected and Jeduthun came in his room. [Or perhaps Ethan and Jeduthun were two names for the same person.] All twenty-four (who were named, *v.* 2–4), were qualified for the service and called to it. In what order must they serve? This was determined by lot.

I. The lot was thrown impartially. They were placed in twenty-four companies, twelve in a company, in two rows, twelve companies in a row, and so they cast lots, *ward against ward*, putting them all upon a level, small and great, teacher and scholar.

II. God determined it as he pleased. The respective merits of the persons are of much more importance than seniority of age or priority of birth.

III. Probably twelve, some for the voice and others for the instrument, made up the concert. Let us learn with one mind and one mouth to glorify God, and that will be the best concern.

CHAPTER 26

An account of the business of the Levites. That tribe had made but a very small figure all the time of the judges, till Eli and Samuel appeared. But when David revived religion the Levites were, of all men, in the greatest reputation. And happy it was that they had Levites who were men fit to support the honour of their tribe. We have here an account, I. Of the Levites that were appointed to be porters, ver. 1–19. II. Of those that were appointed to be treasurers and storekeepers, ver. 20–28. III. Of those that were officers and judges in the country, and were entrusted with the administration of public affairs, ver. 29–32.

Verses 1–19

I. There were porters appointed to attend the temple, who guarded all the avenues that led to it, opened and shut all the outer doors to direct and instruct those who were going to worship in the courts of the sanctuary in the decorum they were to observe, to encourage those that were timorous, to send back the strangers and unclean, and to guard against enemies of the house of God. In allusion to this office, ministers are said to have *the keys of the kingdom of heaven* committed to them (Matt. xvi. 19), that they may admit, and exclude, according to the law of Christ.

II. Of several of those that were called to this service, it is taken notice of that they were *mighty men of valour* (*v.* 6), *strong men* (*v.* 7), *able men* (*v.* 8), and one of them that he was *a wise counsellor* (*v.* 14). Whatever service God calls men to he either finds them fit or makes them so.

III. The sons of Obed-edom were employed in this office, sixty-two of that family. This was he that entertained the ark with reverence and cheerfulness;

and see how he was rewarded for it. 1. He had eight *sons* (*v.* 5), *for God blessed him.* 2. His sons were preferred to places of trust in the sanctuary. They had faithfully attended the ark in their own house, and now were called to attend it in God's house. He that keeps God's ordinances in his own tent is fit to have the custody of them in God's tabernacle, 1 Tim. iii. 4, 5.

IV. It is said of one here that *though he was not the first-born his father made him the chief* (*v.* 10), either because he was very excellent, or because the elder son was very weak.

V. The porters, as the singers, had their post assigned them by lot, so many at such a gate, and so many at such a one, that every one might know his post and make it good, *v.* 13.

Verses 20–28

1. There were *treasures of the house of God.* A great house cannot be well kept without stores of all manner of provisions. These treasures typified the plenty there is in our heavenly Father's house, enough and to spare. In Christ, the true temple, are hid *treasures of wisdom and knowledge*, and *unsearchable riches.* 2. There were *treasures of dedicated things* as a grateful acknowledgment of the divine protection. Abraham gave Melchisedec the *tenth of the spoils*, Heb. vii. 4. In Moses's time the officers of the army, when they returned victorious, brought of their spoils an *oblation to the Lord*, Num. xxxi. 50. Of late this pious custom had been revived; and not only Samuel and David, but Saul, and Abner, and Joab, had dedicated of their spoils to the honour and support of the house of God, *v.* 28.

Verses 29–32

The magistracy is an ordinance of God for the good of the church as truly as the ministry is. And here we are told, 1. That the Levites were employed in the administration of justice in concurrence with the princes and elders of the several tribes, who could not be supposed to understand the law so well as the Levites, who made it their business to study it. None of those Levites who were employed in the service of the sanctuary, none of the singers or porters, were concerned in this outward business; either one was enough to engage the whole man or it was presumption to undertake both. 2. Their charge was both *in all business of the Lord*, and *in the service of kings, v.* 30 and again *v.* 32. They managed the affairs of the country, as well ecclesiastical as civil, took care both of God's tithes and the king's taxes, punished offences committed immediately against God and his honour and those against the government and the public peace, guarded both against idolatry and against injustice, and took care to put the laws in execution against both. 3. There were more Levites employed as judges with the two tribes and a half on the other side Jordan than with all the rest of the tribes; there were 2,700; whereas on the west side of Jordan there were 1,700, *v.* 30, 32. Either those remote tribes were not so well furnished as the rest with judges of their own, or because they, lying furthest from Jerusalem and on the borders of the neighbouring nations, were most in danger of being infected with idolatry, and most needed the help of Levites to prevent it.

CHAPTER 27

The civil list, including the military. I. The twelve captains for every separate month of the year, ver. 1–15. II. The princes of the several tribes, ver. 16–24. III. The officers of the court, ver. 25–34.

Verses 1–15

An account of the regulation of the militia of the kingdom. David was himself a man of war. He contrived to keep up a constant force, and yet not a standing army. 1. He kept up 24,000 constantly in arms. This was a sufficient strength for the securing of the public peace and safety. 2. He changed them every month; so that the whole number of the militia amounted to 288,000, perhaps about a fifth part of the able men of the kingdom. 3. Every course had a commander-in-chief over it. All these twelve great commanders are mentioned among David's worthies and champions, 2 Sam. xxiii. and 1 Chron. xi. Benaiah is here called *a chief priest, v.* 5. But, *cohen* signifying both a *priest* and a *prince*, it might better be translated here *a chief ruler*, or (as in the margin) *a principal officer*. When his wars were over he revived this method, for the peaceable reign of his son Solomon.

Verses 16–34

An account,

I. Of the princes of the tribes. Something of the ancient order instituted by Moses in the wilderness was still kept up, that every tribe should have its prince or chief. Whether these princes were of the nature of lord-lieutenants that guided them in their military affairs, or chief-justices that presided in their courts of judgment, does not appear. Their power, we may suppose, was much less now that all the tribes were united under one king than it had been when, for the most part, they acted separately.

II. Of the numbering of the people, *v.* 23, 24. It is here said, 1. That when David ordered the people to be numbered he forbade the numbering of those under twenty years old. 2. That that account which David took of the people, in the pride of his heart, turned to no good account; for it was never perfected, nor done with exactness, nor was it ever recorded as an authentic account. Joab was disgusted with it, and did it by halves; David was ashamed of it, and willing it should be forgotten, because there fell wrath for it against Israel.

III. Of the officers of the court. 1. The *rulers of the* king's *substance* (as they are called, *v.* 31), such as had the oversight and charge of the king's tillage, his vineyards, his olive-yards, his herds, his camels, his asses, his flocks. Here are officers all for service, agreeable to the simplicity and plainness of those times. David was a great soldier, a great scholar, and a great prince, and yet a great husband of his estate. 2. The attendants on the king's person were such as were eminent for wisdom. His uncle, who was a wise man and a scribe, not only well skilled in politics, but well read in the scriptures, was his counsellor, *v.* 32. Hushai, an honest man, was his companion and confidant.

CHAPTER 28

The account of David's exit, in the beginning of the first book of Kings, does not make his sun nearly so bright as that given in this and the following chapter, where we have his solemn farewell both to his son and his subjects. I. A general convention of the states summoned to meet, ver. 1. II. A solemn declaration of the divine entail both of the crown and of the honour of building the temple upon Solomon, ver. 2–7. III. An exhortation both to the people and to Solomon to make religion their business, ver. 8–10. IV. The model and materials delivered to Solomon for the building of the temple, ver. 11–19. V. Encouragement given him to undertake it and proceed in it, ver. 20, 21.

Verses 1–10

David had *served his generation according to the will of God*, Acts xiii. 36. But now the time draws nigh that he must die, and, as a type of the Son of David, the nearer he comes to his end the more busy he is.

I. He summoned all the great men to attend him, that he might take leave of them all together, *v.* 1. Thus Moses did (Deut. xxxi. 28), and Joshua, *ch.* xxiii. 2; xxiv. 1.

II. He addressed them with a great deal of respect and tenderness. He not only exerted himself to rise from his bed, but he rose out of his chair, and *stood up upon his feet* (*v.* 2), in reverence to God whose will he was to declare, and in reverence to this solemn assembly of the Israel of God, as if he looked upon himself, though *major singulis—greater than any individual among them*, yet *minor universis—less than the whole of them together*. It had been too much his pleasure that they were all his *servants* (*ch.* xxi. 3), but now he calls them his *brethren*, whom he loved, his people, whom he took care of, not his servants, whom he had the command of: *Hear me, my brethren, and my people*.

III. He declared the purpose he had formed to build a temple for God, and God's disallowing that purpose, *v.* 2, 3. He must serve the public with the sword; another must do it with the line and plummet. Times of rest are building times, Acts ix. 31.

IV. He produced his own title first, and then Solomon's, to the crown; both were undoubtedly *jure divino—divine*. 1. Judah was not the eldest son of Jacob, yet God chose that tribe to be the ruling tribe; Jacob entailed the sceptre upon it, Gen. xlix. 10. 2. It does not appear that the family of Jesse was the senior house of that tribe. 3. David was the youngest son of Jesse, yet God liked him to make him king; so it seemed good unto him. 4. Solomon was one of the youngest sons of David, and yet God chose him to sit upon the throne, because he was the likeliest of them all to build the temple, the wisest and best inclined.

V. He opened to them God's gracious purposes concerning Solomon (*v.* 6, 7): *I have chosen him to be my son*. Of him God said, as a figure of him that was to come, 1. *He shall build my house*. Christ is both the founder and the foundation of the gospel temple. 2. *I will establish his kingdom for ever*. This must have its accomplishment in the kingdom of the Messiah, which shall continue in his hands through all the ages of time (Isa. ix. 7; Luke i. 33) and shall then be delivered up to God, even the Father, yet perhaps to be delivered back to the Redeemer for ever. As to Solomon, this promise of the establishment of his kingdom is here made conditional: *If he be constant to do my commandments, as at this day*.

VI. He charged them to adhere steadfastly to God and their duty, *v.* 8. The matter of this charge: *Keep, and seek for all the commandments of the Lord your God*. The Lord was their God; his commandments must be their rule; they must be inquisitive concerning their duty, search the scriptures, take advice, seek the law at the mouth of those whose lips were to keep this knowledge, and pray to God to teach and direct them. God's commandments will not be kept without great care. 2. The solemnity of it. He charged them in the sight of all Israel, "God is witness, and all this congregation is witness, that they have good counsel given them, and fair warning; if they do not take it, it is their fault, and God and man will be witnesses against them." See 1 Tim. v. 21; 2 Tim. iv. 1. 3. The motive to observe this charge. It was the way to be happy, to have the peaceable possession of this good land themselves and to preserve the entail of it upon their children.

VII. He concluded with a charge to Solomon himself, *v.* 9, 10. He was much concerned that Solomon should be religious.

1. The charge he gives him. He was born in God's house and therefore bound in duty to be his, brought up in his house and therefore bound in gratitude. *Thy own friend, and thy father's friend, forsake not*.

2. The arguments to enforce this charge.

(1) Two arguments of general inducement:—[1] That the secrets of our souls are open before God;

he searches all hearts, even the hearts of kings, which to men are unsearchable, Prov. xxv. 3. [2] That we are happy or miserable here, and for ever, according as we do, or do not, serve God. *If we seek him diligently, he will be found of us,* and that is enough to make us happy, Heb. xi. 6. God never casts any off till they have first cast him off.

(2) One argument peculiar to Solomon (*v.* 10): *"Thou art to build a house for the sanctuary;* therefore seek and serve God, that that work may be done from a good principle, in a right manner, and may be accepted."

3. The means prescribed, and they are prescribed to us all. (1) Caution: *Take heed;* beware of everything that looks like, or leads to, that which is evil. (2) Courage: *Be strong, and do it.* We cannot do our work as we should unless we put on resolution, and fetch in strength from divine grace.

Verses 11–21

As for the general charge that David gave his son to seek God and serve him, the book of the law was, in that, his only rule, and there needed no other; but, in building the temple, David was now to give him three things:—1. A model of the building, because it was to be such a building as neither he nor his architects ever saw. Moses had a pattern of the tabernacle shown him in the mount (Heb. viii. 5), so had David of the temple, by the immediate hand of God upon him, *v.* 19. It is said (*v.* 12), *He had this pattern by the Spirit.* The contrivance either of David's devotion or of Solomon's wisdom must not be trusted to in an affair of this nature. The temple must be a sacred thing and a type of Christ; it was a kind of sacrament, and therefore it must not be left to man's art or invention to contrive it, but must be framed by divine institution. This pattern David gave to Solomon, that he might know what to provide and might go by a certain rule. He gave him a table of the courses of the priests, patterns of the vessels of service (*v.* 13), and a pattern of the chariot of the cherubim, *v.* 18. Besides the two cherubim over the mercy-seat, there were two much larger, whose wings reached from wall to wall (1 Kings vi. 23, &c.), and of these David here gave Solomon the pattern, called a *chariot;* for the angels are the chariots of God, Ps. lxviii. 17. 2. Materials for the most costly of the utensils of the temple. That they might not be made any less than the patterns, he weighed out the exact quantity for each vessel both of gold and silver, *v.* 14. In the tabernacle there was but one golden candlestick; in the temple there were ten (1 Kings vii. 49), besides silver ones, which, it is supposed, were hand-candlesticks, *v.* 15. In the tabernacle there was but one table; but in the temple, besides that on which the shew-bread was set, there were ten others for other uses (2 Chron. iv. 8), besides silver tables; for, this house being much larger than that, it would look bare if it had not furniture proportionable. The gold for the altar of incense is particularly said to be *refined gold* (*v.* 18), purer than any of the rest; for that was typical of the intercession of Christ, than which nothing is more pure and perfect. 3. Directions which way to look for help in this great undertaking. God will help thee, and thou must look up to him in the first place (*v.* 20): *The Lord God, even my God,* whom I have chosen and served, who has all along been present with me and prospered me, and to whom, from my own experience of his power and goodness, I recommend thee, he will be with thee, to direct, strengthen, and prosper thee; he will not fail thee nor forsake thee. We may be sure that God, who owned our fathers and carried them through the services of their day, will, in like manner, if we be faithful to him, go along with us in our day, and will never leave us, while he has any work to do

in us or by us. "Good men will help thee, *v.* 21. The priests and Levites will advise thee, and thou mayest consult them. Thou hast good workmen, who are both willing and skilful;" and these are two very good properties in a workman, especially in those that work at the temple. And, *lastly,* "The princes and the people will be so far from opposing or retarding the work that they will be wholly at thy command, every one in his place ready to further it."

CHAPTER 29

David had said what he had to say to Solomon. But he had something more to say to the congregation before he parted with them. I. He pressed them to contribute, according to their ability, towards the building and furnishing of the temple, ver. 1–5. II. They made their presents accordingly with great generosity, ver. 6–9. III. David offered up solemn prayers and praises to God upon that occasion (ver. 10–20), with sacrifices, ver. 21, 22. IV. Solomon was hereupon enthroned, with great joy and magnificence, ver. 23–25. V. David, soon after this, finished his course, ver. 26–30. And it is hard to say which shines brighter here, the setting sun or the rising sun.

Verses 1–9

I. David spoke to the great men of Israel, to engage them to contribute towards the building of the temple. Though David would not impose on them, as a tax, what they should give towards it, he would recommend the present as a fair occasion for a free-will offering, because what is done in works of piety and charity should be done willingly and not by constraint; for God loves a cheerful giver. 1. He would have them consider that Solomon was young, and needed help; but that he was the person whom God had chosen to do this work. 2. That the work was great, and all hands should contribute to the carrying of it on. 3. He tells them what great preparations had been made for this work. He did not intend to throw all the burden upon them, but that they should show their goodwill, by adding to what was done (*v.* 2): *I have prepared with all my might.* 4. He sets them a good example. He had, out of his own share, offered largely for the beautifying and enriching of it, 2,000 talents of gold and 7,000 talents of silver (*v.* 4, 5), and this because he had set his affection on the house of his God. 5. He stirs them up to do as he had done (*v.* 5): *And who then is willing to consecrate his service this day unto the Lord?* We must make the service of God our business, must *fill our hands to the Lord,* so the Hebrew phrase is. The filling of our hands with the service of God intimates that we must serve him only, serve him liberally, and serve him in the strength of grace derived from him.

II. How handsomely they all contributed towards the building of the temple when they were thus stirred up to it. How generous they were appears by the sum total of the contributions, *v.* 7, 8. They gave like princes of Israel. *The people rejoiced:* they were glad of the opportunity of honouring God thus with their substance, and glad of the prospect of bringing this good work to perfection. *David rejoiced with great joy* that his son and successor would have those about him that were so well affected to the house of God, and that this work, upon which his heart was so much set, was likely to go on.

Verses 10–22

I. The solemn address which David made to God: *Wherefore David blessed the Lord before all the congregation.* David's psalms, towards the latter end of the book, are most of them psalms of praise. The nearer we come to the world of everlasting praise the more we should speak the language and do the work of that world. In this address,

1. He adores God, and ascribes glory to him as the God of Israel, *blessed for ever and ever.* Our Lord's

prayer ends with a doxology much like this which David here begins with—*for thine is the kingdom, the power, and the glory.* This is properly praising God—with holy awe and reverence, acknowledging, (1) His infinite perfections. He is the fountain and centre of everything that is bright and blessed. His is the *greatness*; his greatness is immense and incomprehensible. His is the *power*, and it is almighty and irresistible. His is the *glory*; for his glory is his own end and the end of the whole creation. His is the *victory*; he transcends and surpasses all, and is able to conquer and subdue all things to himself. And his is the *majesty*, real and personal, inexpressible and inconceivable. (2) His sovereign dominion, as rightful owner and possessor of all: "*All that is in heaven, and in the earth, is thine: thine is the kingdom*, and all kings are thy subjects; for thou art head, and art to be exalted and worshipped as head above all." (3) His universal influence and agency. All that are rich and honourable among the children of men have their riches and honours from God. What they had returned to him was but a small part of what they had received from him.

2. He acknowledges with thankfulness the grace of God enabling him to contribute so cheerfully towards the building of the temple (*v.* 13, 14): *Now therefore, our God, we thank thee.* It is a great instance of the power of God's grace in us to be able to do the work of God willingly.

3. He speaks very humbly of himself, and his people, and the offerings they had now presented to God. (1) For himself, and those that joined with him, though they were princes, he wondered that God should take such notice of them and do so much for them (*v.* 14): *Who am I, O Lord?* for (*v.* 15) *we are strangers before thee, and sojourners,* poor despicable creatures. *Our days on the earth are as a shadow,* which intimates that our life is a vain life, a dark life, a transient life, and a life that will have its period either in perfect light or perfect darkness. The next words explain it: *There is no abiding,* Heb. vii. 3, *no expectation.* We cannot expect any great matters from it, nor can we expect any long continuance of it, which forbids us to boast of the service we do to God. Alas! it is confined to a scantling of time. (2) As to their offerings, *Lord,* says he, *of thy own have we given thee* (*v.* 14), and again (*v.* 16), *It cometh of thy hand, and is all thy own.* Let him that glories therefore *glory in the Lord.*

4. He appeals to God concerning his own sincerity in what he did, *v.* 17. It is a great satisfaction to a good man to think that God *tries the heart* and *has pleasure in uprightness.* It was David's comfort that God knew with what pleasure he both offered his own and saw the people's offering. He was neither proud of his own good work nor envious of the good works of others.

5. He prays to God both for the people and for Solomon, that both might hold on as they began. In this prayer he addresses God as *the God of Abraham, Isaac, and Jacob,* a God in covenant with them and with us for their sakes. (1) For the people he prays (*v.* 18) that what good God had put into their minds he would always keep there, that they might always have the same thoughts of things as they now seemed to have. Great consequences depend upon what is innermost, and what uppermost, in the imagination of the thoughts of our heart, what we aim at and what we love to think of. If any good have got possession of our hearts, or the hearts of our friends, it is good by prayer to commit the custody of it to the grace of God: "Lord, keep it there, keep it for ever there. Confirm their resolutions. They are in

a good mind; keep them so when I am gone, them and theirs for ever." (2) For Solomon he prays (*v.* 19), *Give him a perfect heart.* He does not pray, "Lord, make him a rich man, a great man, a learned man;" but, "Lord, make him an honest man;" for that is better than all. Yet his building the house would not prove him to have a perfect heart unless he made conscience of keeping God's commandments. It is not helping to build churches that will save us if we live in disobedience to God's law.

II. The cheerful concurrence of this great assembly in this great solemnity. 1. They joined with David in the adoration of God. (*Now bless the Lord your God, v.* 20), which accordingly they did, by *bowing down their heads,* a gesture of adoration. Whoever is the mouth of the congregation, those only have the benefit who join with him, not by *bowing down the head* so much as by *lifting up the soul.* 2. They paid their respects to the king, looking upon him as an instrument in God's hand of much good to them; and, in honouring him, they honoured God. 3. The next day they offered abundance of sacrifices to God (*v.* 21). 4. They feasted and rejoiced before God, *v.* 22. 5. They made Solomon king the second time. He having been before anointed in haste, upon occasion of Adonijah's rebellion, it was thought fit to repeat the ceremony, for the greater satisfaction of the people. They *anointed him to the Lord.*

Verses 23–30

These verses bring king Solomon to his throne and king David to his grave.

I. Here is Solomon rising (*v.* 23): *Solomon sat on the throne of the Lord.* The throne of Israel is called *the throne of the Lord* because not only is he King of all nations, and all kings rule under him, but he was in a peculiar manner King of Israel, 1 Sam. xii. 12. Solomon's kingdom typified the kingdom of the Messiah, and his is indeed *the throne of the Lord.* Solomon prospered; for, 1. His people paid honour to him, as one to whom honour is due: *All Israel obeyed him,* that is, were ready to swear allegiance to him (*v.* 23). God inclined their hearts to do so, that his reign might, from the first, be peaceable. His father was a better man that he, and yet came to the crown with much difficulty, after long delay, and by many and slow steps. David had more faith, and therefore had it more tried. *They submitted themselves* (Heb. *They gave the hand under Solomon*), that is, bound themselves by oath to be true to him (putting the hand under the thigh was a ceremony anciently used in swearing). 2. God put honour upon him; for those that honour him he will honour: *The Lord magnified Solomon exceedingly, v.* 25. None of all the judges or kings of Israel, his predecessors, made such a figure as he did nor lived in such splendour.

II. Here is David's setting, that great man going off the stage. The historian here brings him to the end of his day, leaves him asleep, and draws the curtains about him.

1. He gives a summary account of the years of his reign, *v.* 26, 27.

2. He gives a short account of his death (*v.* 28), that he died *full of days, riches, and honour.* Honoured both of God and man. He had been a man of war from his youth, but was preserved through all the dangers of a military life, lived to a good old age, and died in peace, died in his bed, and yet in the bed of honour. For a fuller account of David's life and reign he refers to the histories or records of those times, which were written by Samuel while he lived, and continued, after his death, by Nathan and Gad, *v.* 29.

AN EXPOSITION, WITH PRACTICAL OBSERVATIONS, OF

THE SECOND
BOOK OF CHRONICLES

This book begins with the reign of Solomon and the building of the temple and continues the history of the kings of Judah thenceforward to the captivity and so concludes with the fall of that illustrious monarchy and the destruction of the temple. That monarchy of the house of David, as it was prior in time, so it was superior in worth and dignity to all those four celebrated ones of which Nebuchadnezzar dreamed. The succession was kept up in a lineal descent throughout the whole monarchy, which continued between 400 and 500 years, and, after a long eclipse, shone forth again in the kingdom of the Messiah, *of the increase of whose government and peace there shall be no end*. We had the story of the house of David before, in the first and second books of Kings, intermixed with that of the kings of Israel, which *there* took more room than that of Judah; but here we have it entire. Much is repeated here which we had before, yet many of the passages of the story are enlarged upon, and divers added, especially relating to the affairs of religion; for it is a church-history. All along the good kings prospered and the wicked kings suffered. The peaceable reign of Solomon we have (*ch.* i.–ix.), the blemished reign of Rehoboam (*ch.* x.–xii.), the short but busy reign of Abijah (*ch.* xiii.), the long and happy reign of Asa (*ch.* xiv.–xvi.), the pious and prosperous reign of Jehoshaphat (*ch.* xvii.–xx.), the impious and infamous reigns of Jehoram and Ahaziah (*ch.* xxi.–xxii.), the unsteady reigns of Joash and Amaziah (*ch.* xxiv., xxv.), the long and prosperous reign of Uzziah (*ch.* xxvi.), the regular reign of Jotham (*ch.* xxvii.), the profane and wicked reign of Ahaz (*ch.* xxviii.), the gracious glorious reign of Hezekiah (*ch.* xxix.–xxxii.), the wicked reigns of Manasseh and Amon (*ch.* xxxiii.), the reforming reign of Josiah (*ch.* xxxiv., xxxv.), the ruining reigns of his sons, *ch.* xxxvi. Put all these together, and the truth of that word of God will appear, *Those that honour me I will honour, but those that despise me shall be lightly esteemed*.

CHAPTER 1

In the foregoing book we read how God magnified Solomon and Israel obeyed him. Now here we have an account, I. How he honoured God by sacrifice (ver. 1–6) and by prayer, ver. 7–12. II. How he honoured Israel by increasing their strength, wealth, and trade, ver. 13–17.

Verses 1–12

I. Solomon's great prosperity, *v.* 1. God being with him, he was *strengthened in his kingdom*.

II. His great piety and devotion.

1. All his great men must thus far be good men that they must join with him in worshipping God. He spoke to the captains and judges, the governors and chief of the fathers, to go with him to Gibeon, *v.* 2, 3. Solomon began his reign with this public pious visit to God's altar, and it was a very good omen. Magistrates are then likely to do well for themselves and their people when they thus take God along with them at their setting out.

2. He offered abundance of sacrifices to God there (*v.* 6). His father David had left him flocks and herds in abundance (1 Chron. xxvii. 29, 31), and thus he gave God his dues out of them. The ark was at Jerusalem (*v.* 4), but the altar was at Gibeon (*v.* 5), and thither he brought his sacrifices.

3. He prayed a good prayer to God: this, with the answer to it, we had before, 1 Kings iii. 5, &c. (1) God bade him ask what he would; not only that he might put him in the right way of obtaining the favours that were intended him, but that he might discover what was in his heart. Men's characters appear in their choices and desires. What wouldst thou *have*? tries a man as much as, What wouldst thou *do*? (2) Like a genuine son of David, he chose spiritual blessings rather than temporal. His petition here is, *Give me wisdom and knowledge*. God gave the faculty of understanding, and to him we must apply for the furniture of it. Two things are here pleaded which we had not in Kings. [1] *Thou hast made me reign in my father's stead, v.* 8. Must I reign in my father's stead? Lord, give me my father's spirit." [2] *Let thy promise to David my father be*

established, *v.* 9. The promise was, *He shall build a house for my name, I will establish his throne, he shall be my son*, and *my mercy shall not depart from him*. "Now, Lord, unless thou give me wisdom, thy house will not be built, nor my throne established; therefore, *Lord, give me wisdom.*"

4. He received a gracious answer to this prayer, *v.* 11, 12. (1) God gave him the wisdom that he asked for because he asked for it. God's grace shall never be wanting to those who sincerely desire to know and do their duty. (2) God gave him the wealth and honour which he did not ask for because he asked not for them. Those that make this world their end come short of the other and are disappointed in this too; but those that make the other world their end shall not only obtain that, and full satisfaction in it, but shall enjoy as much as is convenient of this world in their way.

Verses 13–17

Here is, 1. Solomon's entrance upon the government (*v.* 13): He came *from before the tabernacle, and reigned over Israel*. He would not do any acts of government till he had done his acts of devotion, would not take honour to himself till he had given honour to God—first the tabernacle, and then the throne. 2. The magnificence of his court (*v.* 14): *He gathered chariots and horsemen*. He made silver and gold very cheap and common, *v.* 15. The increase of gold lowers the value of it; but the increase of grace advances its price; the more men have of that the more they value it. *How much better* therefore *is it to get wisdom than gold*! He opened also a trade with Egypt, whence he imported horses and linen-yarn, which he exported again to the kings of Syria, with great advantage no doubt, *v.* 16, 17. This we had before, 1 Kings x. 28, 29.

CHAPTER 2

Solomon's trading, which we read of in the close of the foregoing chapter, and the encouragement he gave both to merchandise and manufactures, were very commendable. But building was the work he was designed for, and to that business he is here applying himself. Here is, I. Solomon's determination to build the temple and a royal palace, and his appointing labourers to be employed herein, ver. 1, 2, 17, 18. II. His request to Huram, king of Tyre to furnish him both with artists and materials, ver. 3–10. III. Huram's obliging answer to, and compliance with, his request, ver. 11–16.

Verses 1–10

Solomon's wisdom was given him, not merely for speculation, nor merely for conversation, to entertain his friends, but for action; and therefore to action he immediately applies himself.

I. His resolution concerning his business (*v.* 1): *He determined to build*, in the first place, *a house for the name of the Lord*. It is fit that he who is the first should be first served—first a temple and then a palace, a house not so much for his own convenience and magnitude, as for the kingdom, for the honour of it among its neighbours and for the decent reception of the people whenever they had occasion to apply to their prince; so that in both he aimed at the public good. We are not born for ourselves, but for God and our country.

II. His embassy to Huram, king of Tyre. The purport of his errand to him is much the same here as we had it 1 Kings v. 2, &c.

1. The reasons why he makes this application to Huram are here more fully represented, (1) He pleads his father's interest in Huram, and the kindness he had received from him (*v.* 3): *As thou didst deal with David, so deal with me*. (2) He represents his design in building the temple: he intended it for a place of religious worship (*v.* 4). The house was built that it might be dedicated to God and used in his service. He mentions various particular services that were there to be performed, for the instruction of Huram. (3) He endeavours to inspire Huram with very great and high thoughts of the God of Israel, by expressing the mighty veneration he had for his holy name: *Great is our God above all gods*, above all idols, above all princes. Therefore, [1] "The house must be great; not in proportion to the greatness of that God to whom it is to be dedicated (for between finite and infinite there can be no proportion), but in some proportion to the great value and esteem we have for this God." [2] "Yet, be it ever so great, it cannot be a habitation for the great God. Let not Huram think that the God of Israel, like the gods of the nations, *dwells in temples made with hands*, Acts xvii. 24. No, the *heaven of heavens cannot contain him*. It is intended only for the convenience of his priests and worshippers, that they may have a fit place wherein to burn sacrifice before him." [3] He looked upon himself, though a mighty prince, as unworthy the honour of being employed in this great work: *Who am I that I should build him a house?*

2. The requests he makes to him are more particularly set down here. (1) He desired Huram would furnish him with a good hand to work (*v.* 7): *Send me a man*. "There are ingenious men in Jerusalem, but not such engravers as are in Tyre; and therefore, since temple-work must be the best in its kind, let me have the best workmen that can be got." (2) With good materials to work on (*v.* 8), cedar and other timber in abundance (*v.* 8, 9); for the house must be *wonderfully great*.

3. Here is Solomon's engagement to maintain the workmen (*v.* 10), to give them so much wheat and barley, so much wine and oil. He did not feed his workmen with bread and water, but with plenty, and everything of the best.

Verses 11–18

I. The return which Huram made to Solomon's embassy, in which he shows a great respect for Solomon and a readiness to serve him. 1. He congratulates Israel on having such a king as Solomon was (*v.* 11):

Because the Lord loved his people, he has made thee king. 2. He blesses God for raising up such a successor to David, *v.* 12. Huram was not only very well affected to the Jewish nation, and well pleased with their prosperity, but worshipped Jehovah, *the God of Israel* (who was now known by that name to the neighbouring nations). Now that the people of Israel kept close to the law and worship of God, and so preserved their honour, the neighbouring nations were as willing to be instructed by them in the true religion as Israel had been, in the days of their apostasy, to be infected with the idolatries and superstitions of their neighbours. 3. He sent him a very ingenious curious workman, that would not fail to answer his expectations in everything, one that had both Jewish and Gentile blood meeting in him; for his mother was an Israelite, his father a Tyrian. 4. He engaged for the timber, as much as he would have occasion for, and undertook to deliver it at Joppa, and withal signified his dependence upon Solomon for the maintenance of the workmen as he had promised, *v.* 15, 16.

II. The orders which Solomon gave about the workmen. He would not employ the free-born Israelites in the drudgery work of the temple itself, not so much as to be overseers of it. In this he employed the strangers who were proselyted to the Jewish religion. There were, at this time, vast numbers of them in the land (*v.* 17), who fell under the law, of the Gibeonites, to be hewers of wood for the congregation. The distribution of them we have here (*v.* 2, and again *v.* 18), in all 150,000. Mr. Fuller suggests that the expedient peculiar to this structure, of framing all beforehand, must needs increase the work.

CHAPTER 3

In this chapter we have, I. The place and time of building the temple, ver. 1, 2. II. The dimensions and rich ornaments of it, ver. 3–9. III. The cherubim in the most holy place, ver. 10–13. IV. The veil, ver. 14. V. The two pillars, ver. 15–17. Of all this we have already had an account, 1 Kings vi, vii.

Verses 1–9

I. The place where the temple was built. It was before determined (1 Chron. xxii. 1). 1. It must be at Jerusalem; for that was the place God had chosen. The royal city must be the holy city. 2. It must be on Mount Moriah, which, some think, was that very place in the land of Moriah where Abraham offered Isaac, Gen. xxii. 2. 3. It must be *where the Lord appeared to David*, and *answered him by fire*, 1 Chron. xxi. 18, 26. There atonement was made once; and therefore, in remembrance of that, there atonement must still be made. 4. It must be in the place which David had prepared, not only which he had purchased with his money, but which he had pitched upon by divine direction. 5. It must be in the threshing-floor of Ornan.

II. The time when it was begun; not till the fourth year of Solomon's reign, *v.* 2. The first three years were employed in the necessary preparations for it, wherein three years would be soon gone, considering how many hands were to be got together and set to work.

III. The dimensions of it, in which Solomon was instructed (*v.* 3), as he was in other things, by his father. *This was the foundation* (so it may be read) *which Solomon laid for the building of the house*. This was the rule he went by, so many cubits the length and breadth, *after the first measure*, that is, according to the measure first fixed, for the dimensions were given by divine wisdom.

IV. The ornaments of the temple. The timber-work was very fine, and yet, within, it was *overlaid with pure gold* (*v.* 4), with *fine gold* (*v.* 5), and that embossed with *palm-trees* and chains. It was gold of *Parvain* (*v.* 6), the best gold. The *beams* and *posts*, the *walls* and *doors*, were *overlaid with gold*, *v.* 7. The most holy place, which was ten yards square, was all *overlaid with fine gold* (*v.* 8), even the *upper chambers*, or rather the *upper floor or roof*—top, bottom, and sides, were all overlaid with gold. Every nail, or screw, or pin, with which the golden plates were fastened to the walls that were overlaid with them, weighed fifty shekels, or was worth so much workmanship and all. A great many precious stones were dedicated to God (1 Chron. xxix. 2, 8), and these were set here and there, where they would show to the best advantage.

Verses 10-17

1. The two cherubim, which were set up in the holy of holies. There were two already over the ark, which covered the mercy-seat with their wings; these were small ones. Now that the most holy place was enlarged, though these were continued (being appurtenances to the ark, which was not to be made new, as all the other utensils of the tabernacle were), yet those two large ones were added. These cherubim are said to be of *image-work* (*v.* 10), to represent the angels who attend the divine Majesty. Each wing extended five cubits, so that the whole was twenty cubits (*v.* 12, 13), which was just the breadth of the most holy place, *v.* 8. They stood on their feet, as servants, their faces inward towards the ark (*v.* 13), that it might appear they were not set there to be adored (for then they would have been made sitting, as on a throne, and their faces towards their worshippers), but rather as themselves attendants on the invisible God. We must not worship angels, but we must worship *with* angels; for we have come into communication with them (Heb. xii. 22), and must do the will of God as the angels do it. Compare 1 Cor. xi. 10 with Isa. vi. 2. 2. The veil that parted between the temple and the most holy place, *v.* 14. This denoted the darkness of that dispensation, and the distance which the worshippers were kept at; but, at the death of Christ, this veil was rent; for through him we are made nigh, and have boldness not only to look, but to enter, into the holiest. On this he wrought cherubim. Heb. *he caused them to ascend*, that is, they were made in raised work, embossed. 3. The two pillars which were set up before the temple. Both together were somewhat above thirty-five cubits in length (*v.* 15), about eighteen cubits high a-piece. See 1 Kings vii. 15, &c., where we took a view of those pillars, *Jachin* and *Boaz*.

CHAPTER 4

A further account of the furniture of God's house. I. Those things that were of brass. The altar for burnt-offerings (ver. 1), the sea and lavers to hold water (ver. 2-6), the plates with which the doors of the court were overlaid (ver. 9), the vessels of the altar, and other things, ver. 10-18. II. Those that were of gold. The candlesticks and tables (ver. 7, 8), the altar of incense (ver. 19), and the appurtenances of each of these, ver. 20-22.

Verses 1-10

David often speaks with much affection both of the *house of the Lord* and of the *courts of our God*.

I. Things in the open court, in the view of all the people, which were very significant.

1. There was the *brazen altar*, *v.* 1. On this all the sacrifices were offered, and it sanctified the gift. This altar was much larger than that which Moses made in the tabernacle; that was five cubits square, this was twenty cubits square. God had greatly enlarged their borders; it was therefore fit that they should enlarge his altars. Our returns should bear some proportion to our receivings. It was ten cubits high, so that the people who worshipped in the courts might see the sacrifices burnt, and their eye might affect their heart with sorrow for sin. And

with the smoke of the sacrifices their hearts might ascend to heaven in holy desires towards God and his favour. In all our devotions we must keep the eye of faith fixed upon Christ, the great propitiation.

2. There was the molten sea, a very large brass pan, in which they put water for the priests to wash in, *v.* 2, 6. (1) There is a fulness of merit in Jesus Christ for all those that by faith apply to him for the purifying of their consciences, that they may serve the *living God*, Heb. ix. 14. (2) Our great gospel duty, which is to cleanse ourselves by true repentance. Our hearts must be sanctified, or we cannot sanctify the name of God. Those that draw nigh to God must *cleanse their hands, and purify their hearts*, James iv. 8.

3. There were *ten lavers* of brass, in which *they washed such things as they offered for the burnt offerings*, *v.* 6. As the priests must be washed, so must the sacrifices. We must not only purify ourselves but carefully put away all those vain thoughts which cleave to our performances themselves and pollute them.

4. The doors of the court were overlaid with brass (*v.* 9), both for strength and beauty, and that they might not be rotted with the weather.

II. There were those things in *the house of the Lord* (into which the priests alone went to minister) that were very significant. All was of gold there. The nearer we come to God the purer we must be, the purer we shall be. 1. There were ten *golden candle-sticks*, according to the form of that one which was in the tabernacle, *v.* 7. The written word is a lamp and a light, shining in a dark place. In Moses's time they had but one candlestick, the Pentateuch; but the additions which, in process of time, were to be made of other books of scripture might be signified by this increase of the number of the candlesticks. Light was growing. The candlesticks are the churches, Rev. i. 20. Moses set up but one, the church of the Jews; but, in the gospel temple, not only believers, but churches, are multiplied. 2. There were ten *golden tables* (*v.* 8), *tables whereon the shew-bread was set*, *v.* 19. To those tables belonged 100 golden basins, or dishes. 3. There was a *golden altar* (*v.* 19), on which they burnt incense.

Verses 11-22

A summary both of the brass-work and the gold-work of the temple. 1. Huram the workman was very punctual: *He finished all that he was to make* (*v.* 11). *Huram his father*, he is called, *v.* 16. Probably it was a sort of a nickname, for the king of Tyre called him *Huram Abi, my father*, he being a great artist and *father of the artificers* in brass and iron. 2. Solomon was very generous. He made *all the vessels in great abundance* (*v.* 18), that some might be laid up for use when others were worn out.

CHAPTER 5

The temple being built and furnished for God, we have here, I. Possession given to him, by bringing in the dedicated things (ver. 1), but especially the ark, the token of his presence, ver. 2-10. II. Possession taken by him, in a cloud, ver. 11-14.

Verses 1-10

This agrees with what we had 1 Kings viii. 2, &c., where an account was given of the solemn introduction of the ark into the new-erected temple. 1. There needed no great solemnity for the bringing in of the dedicated things, *v.* 1. They added to the wealth, and perhaps to the beauty of it; but they could not add to the holiness for it was the *temple that sanctified the gold*, Matt. xxiii. 17. See how just Solomon was both to God and to his father. Whatever David had dedicated to God he put it among the treasures of the temple. When Solomon had made all the vessels of the temple in abundance (*ch.* iv. 18), many of the materials were left, which he would not convert to any other use, but laid up in the treasury for a time of need. 2. But it was fit that the ark should be brought in with great solemnity; and so it was. All the other vessels were made new, and larger, in proportion to the house, than they had been in the tabernacle. But the ark, with the mercy-seat and the cherubim, was the same; for the presence and the grace of God are the same in little assemblies as they are in large ones. Wherever two or three are gathered together in Christ's name there is he as truly present with them as if there were 2,000 or 3,000. The ark was brought in attended by a very great assembly of the elders of Israel, who came to grace the solemnity, *v.* 2–4. It was carried by the priests (*v.* 7), brought into the most holy place, and put under the wings of the great cherubim which Solomon had set up there, *v.* 7, 8. *There they are unto this day* (*v.* 9), not the day when this book was written after the captivity, but when that was written out of which this story was transcribed. The ark was a type of Christ, and, as such, a token of the presence of God. The temple itself, if Christ leave it, is a desolate place, Matt. xxiii. 38. 3. With the ark they brought up the tabernacle and all the *holy vessels that were in the tabernacle*, *v.* 5. 4. This was done with great joy. They kept a holy feast upon the occasion (*v.* 3), and *sacrificed sheep and oxen without number*, *v.* 6. When Christ is formed in a soul, the law written in the heart, the ark of the covenant settled there, so that it becomes the temple of the Holy Ghost, there is true satisfaction in that soul.

Verses 11–14

Solomon, and the elders of Israel, had done what they could to grace the solemnity of the introduction of the ark; but God, by testifying his acceptance of what they did, put the greatest honour upon it. The cloud of glory that filled the house beautified it more than all the gold with which it was overlaid or the precious stones with which it was garnished; and yet that was no glory in comparison with the glory of the gospel dispensation, 2 Cor. iii. 8–10.
I. How God took possession of the temple: He *filled it with a cloud*, *v.* 13. 1. Thus he signified his acceptance of this temple to be the same to him that the tabernacle of Moses was, Exod. xl. 34. 2. Thus he considered the weakness and infirmity of those to whom he manifested himself, who could not bear the dazzling lustre of the divine light. Christ revealed things unto his disciples as they were able to bear them, and in parables, which wrapped up divine things as in a cloud.
II. When he took possession of it. 1. *When the priests had come out of the holy place*, *v.* 11. This is the way of giving possession. All must come out, that the rightful owner may come in. Would we have God dwell in our hearts? We must leave room for him; let everything else give way. 2. When the singers and musicians praised God, then the house was filled with a cloud. This is very observable; it was not when they *offered sacrifices*, but when they *sang the praises of God*, that God gave them this token of his favour; for the sacrifice of praise *pleaseth the Lord* better than that of *an ox or bullock*, Ps. lxix. 31. Where unity is the Lord commands the blessing. God's goodness is his glory, and he is pleased when we give him the glory of it.
III. What was the effect of it. The *priests themselves could not stand to minister, by reason of the cloud* (*v.* 14). The Word was made flesh; and when he comes to his temple, like a refiner's fire, *who may abide the day of his coming*? And *who shall stand when he appeareth*? Mal. iii. 1, 2.

CHAPTER 6

The glory of the Lord, in the vehicle of a thick cloud, having filled the house, Solomon immediately improves the opportunity, and addresses God. I. He makes a solemn declaration of his intention in building this house, to the satisfaction of the people and the honour of God, both of whom he blessed, ver. 1–11. II. He makes a solemn prayer to God that he would please graciously to accept and answer all the prayers that should be made in that house, ver. 12–42. This whole chapter we had before, with very little variation (1 Kings viii. 12–53), to which it may not be amiss here to look back.

Verses 1–11

It is of great consequence, in all our religious actions, that we design well, and that our eye be single. If Solomon had built this temple in the pride of his heart it would not have turned at all to his account. 1. He did it for the glory and honour of God; this was his highest and ultimate end in it. It was *for the name of the Lord God of Israel* (*v.* 10), to be *a house of habitation for him*, *v.* 2. 2. He did it in compliance with the choice God had been pleased to make of Jerusalem, to be the city in which he would record his name (*v.* 6): *I have chosen Jerusalem*. 3. He did it in pursuance of his father's good intentions, which he never had an opportunity to put in execution: *"It was in the heart of David my father to build a house for God;"* the project was his, be it known, to his honour (*v.* 7), and God approved of it, though he permitted him not to put it in execution (*v.* 8), *Thou didst well that it was in thy heart*. Temple-work is often thus done; one sows and another reaps (John iv. 37, 38), one age begins that which the next brings to perfection. Every good piece is not an original. 4. He did it in performance of the word which God had spoken. God had said, *Thy son shall build the house for my name*; and now he had done it, *v.* 9, 10.

Verses 12–41

Solomon had, in the foregoing verses, signed and sealed, as it were, the deed of dedication, by which the temple was appropriated to the honour and service of God. Now here he prays the consecration-prayer, by which it was made a figure of Christ, the great Mediator, through whom we are to offer all our prayers.
I. Here are some doctrinal truths laid down. As, 1. That the God of Israel is a being of incomparable perfection. We cannot describe him; but this we know, there is *none like him in heaven or in earth*, *v.* 14. 2. That he is, and will be, true to every word that he has spoken; and all that serve him in sincerity shall certainly find him both faithful and kind. 3. That he is a being infinite and immense, whom the heaven, and heaven of heavens, cannot contain, and to whose felicity nothing is added by the utmost we can do in his service, *v.* 18. He is infinitely beyond the bounds of the creation and infinitely above the praises of all intelligent creatures. 4. That he, and *he only, knows the hearts of the children of men*, *v.* 30. All men's thoughts, aims, and affections, are naked and open before him; and the imaginations and intents of our hearts cannot be hidden from God, who knows not only what is in the heart, but the heart itself and all the beatings of it. 5. That there is no such thing as a sinless perfection to be found in this life (*v.* 36).
II. Here are some suppositions. 1. He supposed that if doubts and controversies arose between man and man both sides would agree to appeal to God, and lay an oath upon the person whose testimony must decide the matter, *v.* 22. 2. He supposed that, though Israel enjoyed a profound peace and tranquillity, yet troublesome times would come. 3. He supposed that those who had not called upon God at other times, yet, in their affliction, would seek him early and earnestly. Trouble will drive those to God

who have said to him, Depart, v. 24, 26, 28. 4. He supposed that strangers would come from afar to worship the God of Israel and to pay homage to him.

III. Here are petitions. 1. That God would own this house, v. 20. 2. That God would hear and accept the prayers which should be made in or towards that place, v. 21. He prayed that God would hear from his dwelling-place, even from heaven. Heaven is his dwelling-place still, not this temple; and thence help must come. *When thou hearest forgive.* Note, The forgiveness of our sins is that which makes way for all the other answers to our prayers. 3. That God would give judgment according to equity upon all the appeals that should be made to him, v. 23, 30. 4. That God would return in mercy to his people when they repented, and reformed, and sought unto him, v. 25, 27, 38, 39. 5. That God would bid the strangers welcome to this house, and answer their prayers (v. 33). 6. That God would, upon all occasions, own and plead the cause of his people Israel, against all the opposers of it (v. 35): *Maintain their cause;* and again, v. 39. 7. He concludes this prayer with some expressions which he had learned of his good father, and borrowed from one of his psalms. We had them not in the Kings, but here we have them, v. 41, 42. He prayed (v. 41), (1) That God would take possession of the temple, and keep possession, that he would make it his resting-place: *Thou and the ark;* what will the ark do without the God of the ark—ordinances without the God of the ordinances? (2) That he would make the ministers of the temple public blessings: *Clothe them with salvation,* that is, not only save them, but make them instrumental to save others, by offering the sacrifices of righteousness. (3) That the service of the temple might turn abundantly to the joy and satisfaction of all the Lord's people.

CHAPTER 7

God's answer to Solomon's prayer. I. His public answer by fire from heaven, which consumed the sacrifices (ver. 1), with which the priests and people were much affected, ver. 2, 3. By that token of God's acceptance they were encouraged to continue the solemnities of the feast for fourteen days, and Solomon was encouraged to pursue all his designs for the honour of God, ver. 4-11. II. His private answer by word of mouth, in a dream or vision of the night, ver. 12-22. Most of these things we had before, 1 Kings viii. and ix.

Verses 1–11

I. The gracious answer which God immediately made to Solomon's prayer: The *fire came down from heaven and consumed the sacrifice,* v. 1. In this way God testified his acceptance of Moses (Lev. ix. 24), of Gideon (Judges vi. 21), of David (1 Chron. xxi. 26), of Elijah (1 Kings xviii. 38); and, in general, to accept the burnt-sacrifice is, in the Hebrew phrase, to turn it to ashes, Ps. xx. 3. Let us apply this, 1. To the sufferings of Christ. When it pleased the Lord to bruise him, and put him to grief, in that he showed his goodwill to men, having laid on him the iniquity of us all. His death was our life, and he was made sin and a curse that he might inherit righteousness and a blessing. 2. To the sanctification of the Spirit, who descends like fire, burning up our lusts and corruptions, those beasts that must be sacrificed or we are undone, and kindling in our souls a holy fire of pious and devout affections, always to be kept burning on the altar of the heart.

II. The grateful return made to God for this gracious token of his favour.

1. The people *worshipped and praised God,* v. 3. with reverence adoring the glory of God: *They bowed their faces to the ground and worshipped,* thus expressing their awful dread of the divine majesty, their cheerful submission to the divine authority, and the sense they had of their unworthiness to come into God's presence. Even when the fire of the Lord came down they praised him, saying, *He is good, for his mercy endureth for ever.* This is a song never out of season, and for which our hearts and tongues should be never out of tune.

2. The king and all the people offered sacrifices in abundance, v. 4, 5.

3. The priests did their part; they waited on their offices, and the singers and musicians on theirs (v. 6), with the instruments that David made, and the *hymn that David had put into their hand,* as some think it may be read (1 Chron. xvi. 7), or, as we read it, *when David praised by their ministry.*

4. The whole congregation expressed the greatest joy and satisfaction imaginable. They kept the feast of the dedication of the altar seven days, from the second to the ninth; the tenth day was the day of atonement, when they were to afflict their souls for sin, and that was not unseasonable in the midst of their rejoicings; on the fifteenth day began the feast of tabernacles; which continued to the twenty-second, and they did not separate till the twenty-third.

Verses 12–22

God appeared to Solomon in the night, as he did once before (ch. i. 7), and after a day of sacrifice too, as then, and gave him a particular answer to his prayer. We had the substance of it before, 1 Kings ix. 2–9.

I. He promised to own this house for *a house of sacrifice to Israel* and a *house of prayer for all people* (Isa. lvi. 7): *My name shall be there for ever* (v. 12, 16).

II. He promised to answer the prayers of his people that should at any time be made in that place, v. 13–15. 1. National judgments are here supposed (v. 13), famine, and pestilence, and perhaps war, for by the locusts devouring the land may be meant enemies as greedy as locusts, and laying all waste. 2. National repentance, prayer, and reformation, are required, v. 14. 3. National mercy is then promised, that God will forgive their sin, which brought the judgment upon them, and then heal their land, redress all their grievances. Pardoning mercy makes way for healing mercy, Ps. ciii. 3; Matt. ix. 2.

III. He promised to perpetuate Solomon's kingdom, upon condition that he persevered in his duty, v. 17, 18. But he set before him death as well as life, the curse as well as the blessing. 1. He supposed it possible that though they had this temple built to the honour of God, yet they might be drawn aside to worship other gods, v. 19. 2. He threatened it as certain that, if they did so, it would certainly be the ruin of both church and state.

CHAPTER 8

In this chapter we are told, I. What cities Solomon built, ver. 1-6. II. What workmen Solomon employed, ver. 7-10. III. What care he took about a proper settlement for his wife, ver. 11. IV. What a good method he put the temple-service into, ver. 12-16. V. What trading he had with foreign countries, ver. 17, 18.

Verses 1–11

There is a similar account in 1 Kings ix. 10–24.

I. Though Solomon was a man of great learning and knowledge, yet he spent his days, not in contemplation, but in action, in building cities and fortifying them.

II. He employed a great many hands, kept abundance of people to work. A great many strangers there were in Israel, many that remained of the Canaanites; and they were welcome to live there, but not to live and do nothing.

III. When Solomon had begun with building the house of God, and made good work and quick work of that, he prospered in all his undertakings, so that he built all that he desired to build, v. 6. He knew how to set bounds to his desires. He finished all he desired, and then he desires no more.

IV. One reason why Solomon built a palace on purpose for the queen, and removed her and her court to it, was because he thought it by no means proper that she should *dwell in the house of David* (v. 11). She was proselyted, it is likely, to the Jewish religion; but it is a question whether all her servants were. Perhaps they had among them the idols of Egypt. Now, though Solomon had not zeal and courage enough to suppress and punish what was amiss there, yet he so far consulted the honour of his father's memory that he would not suffer that place to be thus profaned where the ark of God had been and where holy David had prayed many a good prayer and sung many a sweet psalm.

Verses 12–18

I. Solomon's devotion. The building of the temple was in order to the service of the temple. Whatever cost he was at in rearing the structure, if he had neglected the worship that was to be performed there, it would all have been to no purpose. When Solomon had built the temple, 1. He kept up the holy sacrifices there, according to the law of Moses, v. 12, 13. Those are spiritual sacrifices that are now required of us, which we are to bring daily and weekly; and it is good to be in a settled method of devotion. 2. He kept up the holy songs there, according to the *law of David*, who is here called *the man of God*, as Moses was, because he was both instructed and authorised of God to make these establishments; and Solomon took care to see them observed *as the duty of every day required*, v. 14. *None departed from the commandment of the king concerning any matter*, v. 15. When the service of the temple was put into this good order, *The house of the Lord was perfected*, v. 16.

II. Solomon's merchandise. He did himself in person visit the sea-port towns of Eloth and Eziongeber. Canaan was a rich country, and yet must send to Ophir for gold; the Israelites were a wise and understanding people, and yet must be beholden to the king of Tyre for *men that had knowledge of the seas*, v. 18. Yet Canaan was God's peculiar land, and Israel God's peculiar people. This teaches us that grace, and not gold, is the best riches, and acquaintance with God and his law the best knowledge.

CHAPTER 9

Solomon here continues to appear great both at home and abroad. 1 Kings x. Nothing is here added; but his defection towards his latter end, which we have there (ch. xi.), is here omitted, and the close of this chapter brings him to the grave with an unstained reputation. I. The honour which the Queen of Sheba did to Solomon, in the visit she made to hear his wisdom, ver. 1–12. II. Many instances given of the riches and splendour of Solomon's court, ver. 13–28. III. The conclusion of his reign, ver. 29–31.

Verses 1–12

This passage of story has been largely considered in the Kings. Our Saviour has proposed it as an example to us in our enquiries after him (Matt. xii. 42). 1. *Those who honour God he will honour*, 1 Sam. ii. 30. Solomon had greatly honoured God, in building, beautifying, and dedicating the temple; all his wisdom and all his wealth were employed for the making of that a consummate piece: and now God made his wisdom and wealth to redound greatly to his reputation. 2. Those who know the worth of true wisdom will grudge no pains nor cost to obtain it. The queen of Sheba put herself to a great deal of trouble and expense to hear the wisdom of Solomon; and yet, learning from him to serve God and do her duty, she thought herself well paid for her pains. Heavenly wisdom is that *pearl of great price* which it is a good bargain to purchase by parting with all that

we have. 3. As every man has received the gift so he ought to minister the same for the edification of others, as he has opportunity. Solomon was communicative of his wisdom and willing to teach others what he knew himself. The queen of Sheba was exceedingly affected to see the propriety with which Solomon's servants attended him and with which both he and they attended in the house of God. 5. Those are happy who have the opportunity of a constant converse with such as are knowing, wise, and good. The queen of Sheba thought Solomon's servants happy who continually *heard his wisdom*; it is observable that the posterity of those who had places in his court thought themselves sufficiently distinguished and dignified when they were called the *children of Solomon's servants* (Ezra ii. 55; Neh. vii. 57). It becomes those that are wise and good to be generous according to their place and power. The queen of Sheba was so to Solomon, Solomon was so to her, v. 9, 12. They both knew how to value wisdom, and therefore were neither of them covetous of their money, but cultivated the acquaintance and confirmed the friendship they had contracted by mutual presents.

Verses 13–30

I. Here is Solomon reigning in wealth and power, in ease and fulness, such as could never since be paralleled by any king whatsoever. The most illustrious of them were famed for their wars, whereas Solomon reigned forty years in profound peace. Some of those that might be thought to vie with Solomon affected retirement, kept people in awe by keeping them at a great distance; but Solomon went much abroad, and appeared in public business. The promise was fulfilled, that God would give him riches, and wealth, and honour, such as no kings *have had, or shall have*, ch. i. 12. 1. Never any prince appeared in public with greater splendour than Solomon did, which to those that judge by the sight of the eye, as most people do, would very much recommend him. He had 200 targets and 300 shields, all of beaten gold, carried before him (v. 15, 16), and sat upon a most stately throne, v. 17–19. *There was not the like in any kingdom.* 2. Never any prince had greater plenty of gold and silver, though there were no gold or silver mines in his own kingdom. 3. Never any prince had such presents brought him by all his neighbours as Solomon had: *All the kings of Arabia, and governors of the country, brought him gold and silver* (v. 14), not as tribute which he extorted from them, but as freewill offerings to procure his favour, or in a way of exchange for some of the productions of his husbandry, corn or cattle. Herein he was a type of Christ, to whom, as soon as he was born, the wise men of the east brought presents, *gold, frankincense, and myrrh* (Matt. ii. 11), and to whom all that are about him must bring presents, Ps. lxxvi. 11; Rom. xii. 1. 4. Never any prince was so renowned for wisdom, so courted, so consulted, so admired (v. 23).

II. Here is Solomon dying, stripped of his pomp, and leaving all his wealth and power, not to one concerning whom he knew not *whether he would be a wise man or a fool* (Eccles. ii. 19), but who he knew would be a fool. This was not only vanity but vexation of spirit, v. 29–31. Though he fell, yet he was not utterly cast down. His sin is not again recorded, because it was repented of, and pardoned, and so became as if it had never been. Scripture-silence sometimes speaks. I am willing to believe that its silence here concerning the sin of Solomon is an intimation that none of the sins he committed were mentioned against him, Ezek. xxxiii. 16. When God pardons sin he *casts it behind his back and remembers it no more*.

CHAPTER 10

This chapter is copied almost verbatim from 1 Kings xii. 1–19. Solomon's defection from God was not repeated, but the defection of the ten tribes from his family is, in this chapter, where we find, I. How foolish Rehoboam was in his treating with them, ver. 1, 5–14. II. How wicked the people were in complaining of Solomon (ver. 2–4) and forsaking Rehoboam, ver. 16–19. III. How just and righteous God was in all this, ver. 15. His counsel was thereby fulfilled.

Verses 1–11

1. The wisest and best cannot give everybody content. Solomon enriched and advanced his kingdom, did all that could be done to make them happy and easy; and yet was indiscreet in burdening them with the imposition of taxes and services. No man is perfectly wise. It is probable that it was when Solomon had declined from God and his duty that his wisdom failed him, and God left him to himself to act in this impolitic manner. Even Solomon's treasures were exhausted by his love of women; and probably it was to maintain them, and their pride, luxury, and idolatry, that he burdened his subjects. 2. Turbulent and ungrateful spirits will find fault with the government, and complain of grievances. Had they not peace in Solomon's time? They were never plundered by invaders, as formerly, never put in fear by the alarms of war, nor obliged to hazard their lives in the high places of the field. Had they not plenty—meat enough, and money enough? And yet they complain that Solomon made their yoke grievous. 3. Many ruin themselves and their interests by trampling upon and provoking their inferiors. Rehoboam thought that because he was king he might assume as much authority as his father had done. But, though he wore his father's crown, he wanted his father's brains. Such a wise man as Solomon may do as he will, but such a fool as Rehoboam must do as he can. Rehoboam paid dearly for threatening, and talking big, and thinking to carry matters with a high hand. A tender consideration of those in subjection, and a forwardness to make them easy, will be the comfort and praise of all in authority, in the church, in the state, and in families. 4. Moderate counsels are generally wisest and best. Gentleness will do what violence will not do. Rehoboam's old experienced counsellors directed him to this method (*v.* 7): "*Be kind to this people, and please them, and speak good words to them,* and thou art sure of them for ever." Good words cost nothing but a little self-denial, and yet they purchase great things.

Verses 12–19

1. When public affairs are in a ferment violent proceedings do but make bad worse. Rough answers (such as Rehoboam here gave) do but stir up anger and bring oil to the flames. 2. Whatever the devices and designs of men are, God is, by all, doing his own work, and fulfilling the word which he has spoken, no iota or tittle of which shall fall to the ground. 3. Worldly wealth, honour, and dominion, are very uncertain things. *Solomon reigned over all Israel,* and, one would think, had done enough to secure the monarchy entire to his family for many ages; and yet he is scarcely cold in his grave before ten of the twelve tribes finally revolt from his son. All the good services he had done for Israel were now forgotten. 4. God often visits the iniquities of the fathers upon the children. Solomon forsakes God, and therefore his son after him, is forsaken by the greatest part of his people. Thus God, by making the penal consequences of sin to last long and visibly to continue after the sinner's death, would give an indication of its malignity, and perhaps some intimation of the perpetuity of its punishment. He that

sins against God not only wrongs his soul, but perhaps wrongs his seed more than he thinks. 5. When God is fulfilling his threatenings, he will take care that, at the same time, promises do not fall to the ground. When Solomon's iniquity is remembered, and for it his son loses ten tribes, David's piety is not forgotten, nor the promise made to him; but for the sake of that his grandson had two tribes preserved to him.

CHAPTER 11

I. Rehoboam's attempt to recover the ten tribes he had lost, and the letting fall of that attempt in obedience to the divine command, ver. 1–4. II. His successful endeavours to preserve the two tribes that remained, ver. 5–12. III. The resort of the priests and Levites to him, ver. 13–17. IV. An account of his wives and children, ver. 18–23.

Verses 1–12

How the ten tribes deserted the house of David we read in the foregoing chapter. They had formerly sat loose to that family (2 Sam. xx. 1, 2), and now they quite threw it off, not considering how much it would weaken the common interest. But thus the *kingdom* must be corrected as well as the *house* of David. 1. Rehoboam at length, like a bold man, raises an army, with a design to reduce the revolters, *v.* 1. Judah and Benjamin were ready to give him the best assistance they could for the recovery of his right. Judah was his own tribe, that owned him some years before the rest did; Benjamin was the tribe in which Jerusalem, or the greatest part of it, stood. 2. Yet, like a conscientious man, when God forbade him to prosecute this design, in obedience to him he let it fall, either because he reverenced the divine authority or because he knew that he should not prosper if he should go contrary to God's command. They *obeyed the words of the Lord*; and though it looked mean, and would turn to their reproach among their neighbours, yet, because God would have it so, they laid down their arms. 3. Like a discreet man, he fortified his own country. Now, his aged and experienced counsellors were hearkened to, and they advised him to submit to the will of God concerning what was lost, and to make it his business to keep what he had. It was probably by their advice that, (1) He fortified his frontiers, and many of the principal cities of his kingdom. (2) He furnished them with good store of victuals and arms, *v.* 11, 12. Because God forbade him to fight he prudently provided against an attack. Those that may not be conquerors, yet may be builders.

Verses 13–23

I. Rehoboam strengthened by the priests and Levites, and all the devout and pious Israelites.

1. Jeroboam set up such a way of worship as obliged them to withdraw from his altar, and he would not allow them to go up to Jerusalem to worship at the altar there; so that he totally *cast them off from executing the priest's office, v.* 14. And very willing he was that room might be made for those mean and scandalous persons whom he *ordained priests for the high places, v.* 15. Compare 1 Kings xii. 31.

2. They thereupon *left their suburbs and possessions, v.* 14. They were driven out of all their cities except those in Judah and Benjamin. But why did they leave their possessions? (1) Because they saw they could do no good among their neighbours, in whom (now that Jeroboam set up his calves), the old proneness to idolatry revived. (2) Because they themselves would be in continual temptation. (3) Because, they had reason to expect persecution from Jeroboam and his sons.

3. They *came to Judah and Jerusalem* (*v.* 14) and *presented themselves to Rehoboam, v.* 13, *margin.*

(1) It was a mercy that when Jeroboam cast them off there were those so near that would bid them welcome. (2) It was an evidence that they loved their work better than their maintenance, in that they *left their suburbs* because they were restrained from serving God there, and cast themselves upon God's providence and the charity of their brethren. Better live upon alms, or die in a prison, with a good conscience, than roll in wealth and pleasure with a prostituted one. (3) Rehoboam and his people bade them welcome. Conscientious refugees will bring a blessing along with them to the countries that entertain them, as they leave a curse behind them with those that expel them.

4. When the priests and Levites came to Jerusalem all the devout pious Israelites of every tribe followed them.

5. They *strengthened the kingdom of Judah* (v. 17) by their piety and their prayers. See Zech. xii. 5. They made him and his people *strong three years*; for so long they *walked in the way of David and Solomon*, their *good* way. But when they forsook that, the best friends they had could no longer help to strengthen them.

II. Rehoboam was weakened by indulging himself in his pleasures. He *desired many wives*, as his father did (v. 23), yet, 1. In *this* he was more wise than his father, that he does not appear to have married strange wives. The wives mentioned here were daughters of Israel, of the family of David. 2. In *this* he was more happy than his father, that he had many sons and daughters; whereas we read not of more than one son that his father had. Several of Rehoboam's sons are here named (v. 19, 20) as men of note, and such active men that he thought it his wisdom to *disperse them throughout the countries of Judah and Benjamin* (v. 23). He could repose confidence in them for the preserving of the public peace and could trust them with fenced cities, that they might stand him in stead in case of an invasion.

Chapter 12

A more full account of the reign of Rehoboam than we had before in Kings. I. Rehoboam and his people did evil in the sight of the Lord, ver. 1. II. God thereupon sold them into the hands of Shishak, king of Egypt, who greatly oppressed them, ver. 2–4. III. God sent a prophet to them, to expound to them the judgment and to call them to repentance, ver. 5. IV. They thereupon humbled themselves, ver. 6. V. God, upon their repentance, turned from his anger (ver. 7, 12) and yet left them under the marks of his displeasure, ver. 8–11. Lastly, Here is a general character of Rehoboam and his reign, with the conclusion of it, ver. 13–16.

Verses 1–12

Israel was disgraced and weakened by being divided into two kingdoms; yet the kingdom of Judah, having both the temple and the royal city, might have done very well if they had continued in the way of their duty.

I. Rehoboam and his people left God, v. 1. He walked in the way of David and Solomon (*ch*. xi. 17), but he grew remiss in the worship of God. As long as he thought his throne tottered he kept to his duty, that he might make God his friend; but, when he found it stood pretty firmly, he thought he had no more occasion for religion; he was safe enough without it.

II. God quickly brought troubles upon them, to recover them to repentance, before their hearts were hardened. It was in the fourth year of Rehoboam that they began to corrupt themselves, and in the fifth year the king of Egypt came up against them with a vast army, took *the fenced cities of Judah, and came against Jerusalem*, v. 2, 3, 4. This great calamity coming upon them so soon after they begun to desert the worship of God, by a hand they had

little reason to suspect (having had a great deal of friendly correspondence with Egypt in the last reign), plainly showed that it was from the Lord, because they had transgressed against him.

III. Lest they should not rightly understand the meaning of this providence, God by the word explains the rod, v. 5. When the princes of Judah had all met at Jerusalem in a council of war, he sent a prophet to them, the same that had brought them an injunction from God not to fight against the ten tribes (*ch*. xi. 2), Shemaiah by name; he told them plainly that the reason why Shishak prevailed against them was because they had forsaken God.

IV. The rebukes both of the word and of the rod being thus joined, the king and princes humbled themselves before God for their iniquity, and patiently accepted the punishment, saying, *The Lord is righteous*, v. 6.

V. Upon the profession they made of repentance God saved them from ruin, and yet left them under some remaining fears of the judgment, to prevent their revolt again.

1. Such a vast and now victorious army as Shishak had what could be expected but that the whole country, and even Jerusalem itself, would in a little time be theirs? But when God saith, *Here shall the proud waves be stayed*, the most threatening force strangely dwindles and becomes impotent. The destroying angel, when he comes to Jerusalem, is forbidden to destroy it: "*My wrath shall not be poured out upon Jerusalem*," v. 7, 12. So ready is the God of mercy to take the first occasion to show mercy.

2. He granted them some deliverance, not complete, but in part. They reformed but partially, and for a little while, soon relapsing again; and, as their reformation was, so was their deliverance. Yet it is said (v. 12), *in Judah things went well*. (1) In respect of piety. *There were good things in Judah* (so it is in the margin), good ministers, good people, good families. (2) In respect of prosperity. In Judah things went ill when all the fenced cities were taken (v. 4), but when they repented their affairs altered and things went well.

3. Yet he left them to smart sorely by the hand of Shishak, both in their liberty and in their wealth.

(1) In their liberty (v. 8): *They shall be his servants that they may know my service, and the service of the kingdoms of the countries.* They complained, it may be, of the strictness of their religion. Let them better themselves if they can; let the neighbouring princes rule them awhile. The more God's service is compared with other services the more reasonable and easy it will appear. Are the laws of temperance thought hard? The effects of intemperance will be much harder. The service of virtue is perfect liberty; the service of lust is perfect slavery.

(2) In their wealth. The king of Egypt plundered both the temple and the exchequer, the treasuries of both which Solomon left very full; but he *took them away*; yea, he *took all*, all he could lay his hands on, v. 9. This was what he came for.

Verses 13–16

The story of Rehoboam's reign concluded. Two things especially are observable. 1. That he was at length well *fixed in his kingdom*, v. 13. He *strengthened himself in Jerusalem*, and there he reigned seventeen years. He had his royal seat in the holy city, which yet was but an aggravation of his impiety—near the temple, but far from God. Frequent skirmishes there were between his subjects and Jeroboam's, such as amounted to *continual wars* (v. 15), but he held his own, and did not so grossly *forsake the law of God* as he had done (v. 1) in his fourth year. 2. That he was never rightly fixed in his religion, v. 14. He did not serve the Lord because he did not seek the Lord. He did not pray, as Solomon did, for wisdom and grace. If we prayed better, we should be every way better. He did evil because he was never determined for that which is good.

CHAPTER 13

A much fuller account of the reign of Abijah, the son of Rehoboam, than we had in the Kings. Here we find him more brave and successful in war than his father was. He reigned but three years, and was chiefly famous for a glorious victory he obtained over the forces of Jeroboam. I. The armies brought into the field on both sides, ver. 3. II. The remonstrance which Abijah made before the battle, setting forth the justice of his cause, ver. 4–12. III. The distress which Judah was brought into by the policy of Jeroboam, ver. 13, 14. IV. The victory they obtained notwithstanding, by the power of God, ver. 15–20. V. The conclusion of Abijah's reign, ver. 21, 22.

Verses 1–12

Abijah's mother was called *Maachah*, the daughter of Absalom, ch. xi. 20; here she is called *Michaiah*, the daughter of Uriel. It is most probable that she was a granddaughter of Absalom, by his daughter Tamar (2 Sam. xiv. 27), and that her immediate father was this Uriel.

I. God gave Abijah leave to engage with Jeroboam; and owned him in the conflict. Jeroboam, it is probable, was now the aggressor, and what Abijah did was in his own necessary defence. Jeroboam claimed the crown of Judah. Against these impudent pretensions it was brave in Abijah to take up arms, and God stood by him. Abijah is allowed to chastise him.

II. Jeroboam's army was double in number to that of Abijah (v. 3), for he had ten tribes, while Abijah had but two. The inferior number however proved victorious.

III. Abijah, before he fought them, reasoned with them, to desist from fighting against the house of David. It is good to try reason before we use force. We must never fly to violent methods till all the arts of persuasion have been tried in vain. War must be the *ultima ratio regum—the last resort of kings.* Fair reasoning may do a great deal of good and prevent a great deal of mischief. Abijah had got with his army into the heart of their country; for he made this speech upon a hill in Mount Ephraim. Two things Abijah undertakes to make out,

1. That he had right on his side, a *jus divinum—a divine right*: "You know that *God gave the kingdom to David and his sons for ever*" (v. 5), by a covenant of salt, a lasting covenant, a covenant made by sacrifice, which was always salted; so Bishop Patrick. All Israel had owned that David was a king of God's making, and that God had entailed the crown upon his family; so that Jeroboam's taking the crown of Israel at first was not justifiable. Abijah shows, (1) That there was a great deal of dishonesty in Jeroboam's first setting himself up: He *rebelled against his lord* (v. 6) who had preferred him (1 Kings xi. 28), and basely took advantage of Rehoboam's weakness. Those that supported him are here called *vain men* (a character perhaps borrowed from Judges xi. 3). (2) That there was a great deal of impiety in his present attempt; for, in fighting against the house of David, he fought *against the kingdom of the Lord.*

2. That he had God on his side. This he insisted much upon, that the religion of Jeroboam and his army was false and idolatrous, but that he and his people, the men of Judah, had the pure worship of the true and living God among them. It appears from the character given of Abijah (1 Kings xv. 3) that he was not himself truly religious, and yet here he encouraged himself in this war chiefly from the religion of his kingdom. Whatever he was otherwise, it should seem that he was no idolater. Whatever corruptions

there were in the kingdom of Judah, the state of religion among them was better than in the kingdom of Israel, with which they were now contending. It was the cause of his kingdom that he was pleading; and, though he was not himself so good as he should have been, yet he hoped that, for the sake of the good men and good things that were in Judah, God would now appear for them. "We *keep his charge*, v. 10, 11. We worship no images, have no priests but what he has ordained, no rites of worship but what he has prescribed. He is our captain, and we may therefore be sure that he is with us, because we are with him, v. 12. And in the day of battle we shall be *remembered before the Lord our God* and *saved from our enemies.*" He concludes with fair warning to his enemies. "*Fight not against the God of your fathers.*"

Verses 13–22

Jeroboam resolved not to heed, and therefore heard as though he heard not. He came to fight, not to dispute. The longest sword, he thought, would determine the matter, not the better cause.

I. Jeroboam, who trusted to his politics, was beaten. He was so far from fair reasoning that he was not for fair fighting. A parley, it is probable, was agreed on, yet Jeroboam basely takes advantage of it, and, while he was treating, *laid his ambushment behind Judah*, against all the laws of arms.

II. Abijah and his people, who trusted in their God, came off conquerors, notwithstanding the disproportion of their strength and numbers.

1. They were brought into a great strait, put into a great fright, for *the battle was before and behind.* A good cause may for a season be involved in embarrassment and distress.

2. In this distress, when danger was on every side, which way should they look but upwards for deliverance? It is an unspeakable comfort that no enemy, no stratagem or ambushment, can cut off our communication with heaven; our way thitherward is always open. (1) *They cried unto the Lord*, v. 14. (2) They *relied on the God of their fathers*, and committed themselves to him, v. 18. The prayer of faith is the prevailing prayer, and this is that by which we overcome the world, *even our faith*, 1 John v. 4. (3) The *priests sounded the trumpets* to put life into their faith. (4) They shouted in confidence of victory: "The day is our own, for God is with us." To the cry of prayer they added the shout of faith, and so became more than conquerors.

3. Thus they obtained a complete victory: *As the men of Judah shouted* for joy in God's salvation, *God smote Jeroboam* and his army with such terror that they fled with the greatest precipitation imaginable, and the conquerors gave no quarter, but the battle was the Lord's, who would thus chastise the idolatry of Israel and own the house of David.

4. The consequence of this was that the children of Israel, though they were not brought back to the house of David, yet, for that time, were *brought under*, v. 18. Many cities were taken, and remained in the possession of the kings of Judah; as Bethel particularly, v. 19.

Lastly, The death both of the conquered and of the conqueror, not long after. 1. Jeroboam never looked up after this defeat, though he survived it two or three years. He could not recover *strength again*, v. 20. 2. Abijah waxed mighty upon it. But soon after his triumphs, death conquered the conqueror.

CHAPTER 14

In this and the two following chapters we have the history of the reign of Asa, a good reign and a long one. I. His piety, ver. 1–5. II. His policy, ver. 6–8. III. His prosperity, and particularly a glorious victory he obtained over a great army of Ethiopians that came out against him, ver. 9–15.

Verses 1–8

I. Asa's general character (*v.* 2): He did *that which was good and right in the eyes of the Lord his God.* 1. He aimed at pleasing God, studied to approve himself to him. 2. He saw God's eye always upon him, and that helped much to keep him to what was good and right.

II. A blessed work of reformation which he set on foot immediately upon his accession to the crown. 1. He removed and abolished idolatry. Since Solomon admitted idolatry, in the latter end of his reign, nothing had been done to suppress it. Strange gods were worshipped and had their altars, images, and groves; and the temple service, though kept up by the priests (*ch.* xiii. 10), was neglected by many of the people. Asa, as soon as he had power in his hands, made it his business to destroy all those idolatrous altars and images (*v.* 3, 5). He hoped by destroying the idols to reform the idolaters, which he aimed at, rather than to ruin them. 2. He revived and established the pure worship of God; and, since the priests did their part in attending God's altars, he obliged the people to do theirs (*v.* 4): *He commanded Judah to seek the Lord God of their fathers, and not the gods of the heathen, and to do the law and the commandments.* In doing this, *the land was quiet before him, v.* 5.

III. The tranquillity of his kingdom, after constant alarms of war during the last two reigns: *In his days the land was quiet ten years* (*v.* 1), no war with the kingdom of Israel. Abijah's victory laid a foundation for Asa's peace, which was the reward of his piety and reformation. Though Abijah had little religion himself, he was instrumental to prepare the way for one that had much.

IV. The improvement he made of that tranquillity: *The land had rest, for the Lord had given him rest.* 1. Asa, takes notice of the rest they had as the gift of God, and as the reward of the reformation begun: *Because we have sought the Lord our God, he has given us rest.* We find by experience that it is good to seek the Lord; it *gives us rest.* 2. He consults with his people, by their representatives, how to make a good use of the peace they enjoyed, and concludes with them, (1) That they must not be idle, but busy. In the years when he had no war he said, "Let us build; still let us be doing." When the *churches had rest* they were *built up,* Acts ix. 31. When the sword is sheathed take up the trowel. (2) In times of peace we must be getting ready for trouble, expect it and lay up in store for it. [1] He fortified his principal cities with *walls, towers, gates, and bars, v.* 7. He speaks as if he expected that trouble would arise, when it would be too late to fortify, and when they would wish they had done it. *So they built and prospered.* [2] He had a good army ready to bring into the field (*v.* 8). Judah and Benjamin were mustered severally; and Benjamin had almost as many soldiers as Judah. These two tribes were differently armed, both offensively and defensively. The men of Judah guarded themselves with targets, the men of Benjamin with shields, the former of which were much larger than the latter, 1 Kings x. 16, 17. The men of Judah fought with spears; the men of Benjamin drew bows, to reach the enemy at a distance.

Verses 9–15

I. Disturbance given to the peace of Asa's kingdom by a formidable army of Ethiopians that invaded them, *v.* 9, 10.

II. The application Asa made to God on occasion of the threatening cloud which now hung over his head, *v.* 11. He that sought God in the day of his prosperity could with holy boldness cry to God in the day of his trouble, and call him *his* God. His prayer is short, but has much in it. 1. He gives to God the glory of his infinite power and sovereignty: *It is nothing with thee to help* and save by many or few. God works in his own strength, not in the strength of instruments. "We do not say, Lord, take our part, for we have a good army for thee to work by; but, take our part, for without thee we have no power." 2. He takes hold of their covenant-relation to God as theirs. *O Lord our God!* 3. He pleads their dependence upon God. He was well prepared for it, yet trusted not to his preparations; but, "Lord, *we rest on thee, and in thy name we go against this multitude,* by warrant from thee, aiming at thy glory, and trusting to thy strength." 4. He interests God in their cause: "*Let not man*" (*mortal man,* so the word is) "*prevail against thee.*" The enemy is a mortal man; make it to appear what an unequal match he is for an immortal God.

III. The glorious victory God gave him over his enemies. 1. God defeated the enemy, and put their forces into disorder (*v.* 12): *The Lord smote the Ethiopians* with terror so that they fled, and knew neither why nor whither. 2. Asa and his soldiers took the advantage God gave them against the enemy. (1) They destroyed them. (2) They took the plunder of their camp. (3) They *smote the cities* that were in league with them, to which they fled for shelter (*v.* 14). (4) They fetched away the cattle out of the enemy's country, in vast numbers, *v.* 15.

CHAPTER 15

Asa and his army were now returning in triumph from the battle, laden with spoils and adorned with the trophies of victory. He knew that the work of reformation, which he had begun in his kingdom, was not perfected; his enemies abroad were subdued, but there were more dangerous enemies at home—idols in Judah and Benjamin. I. The message which God sent to him, by a prophet, to encourage him in the prosecution of reformation, ver. 1–7. II. The life which this message put into that good cause, and their proceedings in pursuance of it. Idols removed, ver. 8. The spoil dedicated to God, ver. 9–11. A covenant made with God, and a law for the punishing of idolaters, ver. 12–15. A reformation at court, ver. 16. Dedicated things brought into the house of God, ver. 18.

Verses 1–7

Here was a prophet sent to Asa and his army, when they returned victorious from the war with the Ethiopians, not to congratulate them on their success, but to quicken them to their duty; this is the proper business of God's ministers. The *Spirit of God came* upon the prophet (*v.* 1), both to instruct him what he should say and to enable him to say it with clearness and boldness.

I. He told them plainly upon what terms they stood with God. Let them not think that, having obtained this victory, all was their own for ever. Let them do well, and it will be well with them, otherwise not. 1. *The Lord is with you while you are with him.* 2. *If you seek him, he will be found of you.* 3. If you forsake him and his ordinances, he is not tied to you, but will certainly forsake you.

II. He set before them the consequence of forsaking God and his ordinances, and that there was no way of having grievances redressed, but by repenting, and returning unto God. When Israel forsook their duty they were over-run with a deluge of atheism, impiety, irreligion, and all irregularity (*v.* 3), and were continually embarrassed with wars, foreign and domestic, *v.* 5, 6. But when their troubles drove them to God they found it not in vain to seek him, *v.* 4. But the question is, What time does this refer to? 1. Some think it looks as far back as the days of the Judges. These were sad times, when they were frequently oppressed by one enemy or other and grievously harassed by Moabites, Midianites, Ammonites, and other nations. When, in their perplexity, they turned to God by repentance, prayer, and reformation, he raised up deliverers for them. 2.

Others think it describes the state of the ten tribes (who were now properly called *Israel*) in the days of Asa. In those times there was no peace, *v.* 5. Their war with Judah gave them frequent alarms; so did the late insurrection of Baasha. They provoked God with all iniquity, and then he *vexed them with all adversity*; yet, *when they turned to God*, he was entreated for them. 3. Others think the whole passage may be read in the future tense: Hereafter *Israel will be without the true God and a teaching priest*, and they will be destroyed by one judgment after another till they *return to God* and *seek him*. See Hos. iii. 4.

III. Upon this he grounded his exhortation to prosecute the work of reformation with vigour (*v.* 7): *Be strong, for your work shall be rewarded.*

Verses 8–19

The good effect the foregoing sermon had upon Asa.

I. He grew more bold for God than he had been. Now he took courage. He saw how necessary a further reformation was, and what assurance he had of God's presence with him in it. Now he ventured to destroy all the abominable idols. He also *renewed the altar of the Lord.*

II. He extended his influence further than before, *v.* 9. He summoned a solemn assembly, and brought the strangers to it, who had come over to him from the ten tribes. Their coming was a great encouragement to him; for the reason of their coming was because *they saw that the Lord his God was with him.* The invitation he gave them to the general assembly was a great encouragement to them. This meeting was held in the third month, probably at the feast of Pentecost, which was in that month.

III. He and his people offered sacrifices to God, as his share of the spoil they had got, *v.* 11. These sacrifices were intended by way of thanksgiving for the favours they had received, and supplication for further favours. Prayers and praises are now our spiritual sacrifices. *He brought into the house of God all the dedicated things, v.* 18. It is honesty to render to God the things that are his.

IV. *They entered into covenant with God*, repenting that they had violated their engagements to him and resolving to do better for the future. It is proper for penitents, for converts, to renew their covenants. 1. What was this covenant. It would help to increase their sense of the obligation, to arm them against temptations, and would be a testimony. And, by joining all together in this covenant, they strengthened the hands one of another. Two things they engaged themselves to:—(1) That they would diligently seek God themselves, seek his precepts, seek his favour. What is religion but seeking God, enquiring after him, applying to him, upon all occasions? (2) That they would, to the utmost of their power, oblige others to seek him, *v.* 13. They agreed that *whosoever would not seek the Lord God of Israel* (that is, an obstinate idolater or an obstinate atheist) he should be put to death. 2. In what manner they made this covenant. (1) With great cheerfulness, and all possible expressions of joy: *They swore unto the Lord* with a loud voice, and they all rejoiced at the oath, *v.* 14, 15. Every honest Israelite was pleased with his own engagements to God, and they were all pleased with one another's. They rejoiced in it as a hopeful expedient to prevent their apostasy from God and a happy indication of God's presence with them. It is an honour and happiness to be in bonds to God. (2) They did it with great sincerity, zeal, and resolution: *They swore to God with all their hearts*, and *sought him with their whole desire.* If God has the heart, we have the joy.

V. The effect of this their solemn covenanting with God. 1. God did well for them: *He* was *found of them, and gave them rest round about* (*v.* 15), so that there was no war for a long time after (*v.* 19), though there were constant bickerings between Judah and Israel upon the frontiers, 1 Kings xv. 16. 2. They did, on the whole, well for him. They carried on the reformation so far that Maachah the queen-mother was deposed for idolatry and her idol destroyed, *v.* 16. Asa knows he must honour God more than his grandmother, and dares not leave an idol in an apartment of his palace while he is destroying idols in the cities of his kingdom. We may suppose Maachah was convinced of her sin and therefore was not put to death. But because she had been an idolater Asa thought fit to divest her of the dignity and authority she had. But the reformation was not complete; the high places were not all taken away, though many of them were, *ch.* xiv. 3, 5. There may be defects in some particular duties where yet the heart, in the main, is upright with God. Sincerity is something less than sinless perfection.

CHAPTER 16

This chapter concludes the history of the reign of Asa. I. Here is a foolish treaty with Benhadad king of Syria, ver. 1–6. II. The reproof which God sent him for it by a prophet, ver. 7–9. III. Asa's displeasure against the prophet for his faithfulness, ver. 10. IV. The sickness, death, and burial of Asa, ver. 11–14.

Verses 1–6

This passage we had before (1 Kings xv. 17, &c.) and Asa was in several ways faulty in it. 1. He did not do well to make a league with Benhadad, a heathen king, *v.* 3. Had he relied more upon his covenant, and his father's, with God, he would not have boasted so much of his league, and his fathers, with the royal family of Syria. 2. If he had had a due regard to the honour of Israel in general, he would have found some other expedient to give Baasha a diversion than by calling in a foreign force, and inviting into the country a common enemy, who, in process of time, might be a plague to Judah too. 3. It was doubtless a sin in Benhadad to break his league with Baasha upon no provocation, but merely through the influence of a bribe; and, if so, certainly it was a sin in Asa to move him to it, especially to hire him to do it. 4. To take silver and gold out of the house of the Lord for this purpose was a great aggravation of the sin. 5. Perhaps Asa intended not that they should carry the matter so far. However the project succeeded. Benhadad gave Baasha a powerful diversion, obliged him to leave off building Ramah and betake himself to the defence of his own country northward, which gave Asa an opportunity, not only to demolish his fortifications, but to sieze the materials and convert them to his own use.

Verses 7–14

I. A plain and faithful reproof given to Asa by a prophet of the Lord, for making this league with Baasha. The reprover was Hanani the seer, the father of Jehu, another prophet, whom we read of 1 Kings xvi. 1; 2 Chron. xix. 2. That which the prophet here charges upon him as the greatest fault is his *relying on the king of Syria and not on the Lord his God, v.* 7. He plainly tells the king that herein he had done foolishly, *v.* 9. It is a foolish thing to lean on a broken reed, when we have the rock of ages to rely upon. To convince him of his folly he shows him,

1. That he acted against his experience, *v.* 8. He, of all men, had no reason to distrust God, who had found him such a present powerful helper. *"What!"* said the prophet, *"Were not the Ethiopians and the Lubim a huge host*, enough to swallow up a kingdom? And yet, *because thou didst rely on the Lord, he*

delivered them into thy hand; and was not he sufficient to help thee against Baasha?" But see how deceitful our hearts are! We trust in God when we have nothing else to trust to, but, when we have other things to stay on, we are apt to stay too much on them.

2. That he acted against his knowledge of God and his providence, *v. 9.* Asa could not trust God and therefore made court to Benhadad.

3. That he acted against his interest. (1) He had lost an opportunity of checking the growing greatness of the king of Syria (v. 7): His *host has escaped out of thy hand*, which otherwise would have joined with Baasha's and fallen with it. (2) He had incurred God's displeasure and henceforth must expect no peace, but the constant alarms of war, *v. 9.*

II. Asa's displeasure at this reproof. Though it came from God by one that was known to be his messenger, yet he was wroth with the seer for telling him of his folly; *he was in a rage with him, v. 10.* 1. In his rage he committed the prophet to the jail, *put him in a prison-house,* as a malefactor, *in the stocks* (so some read it), or into *little-ease.* 2. Having proceeded thus far, *he oppressed some of the people,* probably such as owned the prophet in his sufferings, or were known to be his particular friends.

III. His sickness. Two years before he died *he was diseased in his feet* (*v.* 12), afflicted with the gout in a high degree. He had put the prophet in the stocks, and now God put him in the stocks; so his punishment answered his sin. His making use of physicians was his duty; but trusting to them, and expecting that from them which was to be had from God only, were his sin and folly.

IV. His death and burial. His funeral had something of extraordinary solemnity in it, *v.* 14. They made a very magnificent *burying for him.* This funeral pomp was an expression of the great respect his people retained for him, notwithstanding the failings and infirmities of his latter days. The eminent piety and usefulness of good men ought to be remembered to their praise, though they have had their blemishes. Let their faults be buried in their graves, while their services are remembered over their graves.

Chapter 17

The life and reign of Jehoshaphat, who was one of the best that swayed the sceptre of Judah since David's head was laid. He was the good son of a good father, so that, at this time, grace ran in the blood. I. His accession to and establishment in the throne, ver. 1, 2, 5. II. His personal piety, ver. 3, 4, 6. III. The course he took to promote religion in his kingdom, ver. 7–9. IV. The mighty sway he bore among the neighbours, ver. 10, 11. V. The great strength of his kingdom, both in garrisons and standing forces, ver. 12–19.

Verses 1–9

Concerning Jehoshaphat,

I. What a wise man he was. As soon as he came to the crown he *strengthened himself against Israel, v.* 1. Ahab, an active warlike prince, had been three years upon the throne of Israel. The first thing Jehoshaphat had to do was to check the growing greatness of the king of Israel, which he did so effectually, and without bloodshed, that Ahab soon courted his alliance. Jehoshaphat strengthened himself not to act offensively against Israel or invade them, but only to maintain his own, which he did by fortifying the cities that were on his frontiers, and putting garrisons, stronger than had been, in the cities of Ephraim.

II. What a good man he was. 1. He *walked in the ways of his father David.* In the characters of the kings, David's ways are often made the standard, as 1 Kings xv. 3, 11; 2 Kings xiv. 3; xvi. 2; xviii. 3. Jehoshaphat followed David as far as he followed God and no further. The words here will admit another reading; they run thus: *He walked in the*

ways of David his father (*Hareshonim*), those first ways, or those *ancient ways.* He proposed to himself, for his example, the primitive times of the royal family, those purest times, before the corruptions of the late reigns came in. It is good to be cautious in following the best men, lest we step aside after them. 2. He *sought not to Baalim, but sought to the Lord God of his father, v.* 3, 4. 3. He *walked in God's commandments,* not only worshipped the true God, but worshipped him according to his own institution, *and not after the doings of Israel, v.* 4. 4. *His heart was lifted up in the ways of the Lord* (*v.* 6), or *he lifted up his heart.* He was lively and affectionate in his religion, *fervent in spirit, serving the Lord,* cheerful and pleasant in it; he went on in his work with alacrity, as Jacob, who, after his vision of God at Bethel, *lifted up his feet,* Gen. xxix. 1, margin.

III. What a useful man he was, not only a good man, but a good king. He not only was good himself, but did good. 1. He took away the teachers of lies, so images are called (Hab. ii. 18), the *high places* and *the groves, v.* 6. It is meant of those in which idols were worshipped. 2. He sent forth teachers of truth. When he enquired into the state of religion in his kingdom he found his people generally very ignorant: they *knew not that they did evil.* Jehoshaphat resolves to begin his work at the right end, will not lead them blindfold, no, not into a reformation, but endeavours to have them well taught, knowing that that was the way to have them well cured. In this good work he employed, (1) His princes. He ordered them, in the administration of justice, not only to correct the people when they did ill, but to teach them how to do better, and to give a reason for what they did. (2) The *Levites* and *priests* went *with the princes,* and *taught in Judah,* having the *book of the law with them, v.* 8, 9. They were teachers by office, Deut. xxxiii. 10.

What an abundance of good may be done when Moses and Aaron thus go hand in hand in the doing of it, when princes with their power, and priests and Levites with their scripture learning, agree to teach the people the good knowledge of God and their duty! These itinerant judges and itinerant preachers together were instrumental to diffuse a blessed light throughout the cities of Judah. *They had the book of the law of the Lord with them* for the conviction of the people, that they might see that they had a divine warrant for what they said and delivered to them that only which they received from the Lord.

IV. What a happy man he was. *The Lord was with him* (*v.* 3); *the word of the Lord was his helper* (so the Chaldee paraphrase); *the Lord established the kingdom in his hand, v.* 5. *All Judah brought him presents,* in acknowledgment of his kindness in sending preachers among them. The more there is of true religion among a people the more there will be of conscientious loyalty. Riches and honour in abundance prove to many a hindrance, an occasion of pride, but they had a quite contrary effect upon Jehoshaphat; his abundance was oil to the wheels of his obedience, and the more he had of the wealth of this world the more was his heart *lifted up in the ways of the Lord.*

Verses 10–19

A further account of Jehoshaphat's great prosperity and the flourishing state of his kingdom.

I. He had good interest in the neighbouring princes and nations. Though he was not perhaps so great a soldier as David, nor so great a scholar as Solomon, yet *the fear of the Lord fell so upon them* that they had all a reverence for him, *v.* 10. And, 1. *None of them made war against him.* 2. Many of them brought presents to him (*v.* 11), to secure his friendship.

II. He had very considerable stores laid up in the cities of Judah.

III. He had the militia in good order. Five *lord-lieutenants* are here named, with the numbers of those under their command. It is said of one of these great commanders, *Amasiah*, that *he willingly offered himself unto the Lord* (v. 16), not only to the king, to serve him in this post, but to the Lord, to glorify him in it. It was usual for great generals then to offer of their spoils to the Lord, 1 Chron. xxvi. 26. But this good man offered himself first to the Lord, and then his dedicated things. The armies, we may suppose, were dispersed all the country over, and each man resided for the most part on his own estate; but they appeared often, to be mustered and trained, and were ready at call whenever there was occasion.

But, *lastly*, observe, It was not this formidable army that struck a terror upon the neighbouring nations, but the fear of God which fell upon them when Jehoshaphat reformed his country and set up a preaching ministry in it, v. 10.

CHAPTER 18

The story of this chapter we had just as it is here related in the story of the reign of Ahab king of Israel, 1 Kings xxii. I. The alliance he contracted with Ahab, ver. 1. II. His consent to join with him in his expedition for the recovery of Ramoth-Gilead out of the hands of the Syrians, ver. 2, 3. III. Their consulting with the prophets, false and true, before they went, ver. 4–27. IV. The success of their expedition. Jehoshaphat hardly escaped (ver. 28–32) and Ahab received his death's wound, ver. 33, 34.

Verses 1–3

I. Jehoshaphat growing greater.

II. Not growing wiser, else he would not have joined with Ahab, that degenerate Israelite, who had sold himself to work wickedness. With him he joined in affinity, that is, married his son Jehoram to Ahab's daughter Athaliah.

1. This was the worst match that ever was made by any of the house of David. (1) Perhaps pride made the match. His religion forbade him to marry his son to a daughter of any of the heathen princes that were about him, and, having riches and honour in abundance, he thought it a disparagement to marry him to a subject. A king's daughter it must be, and therefore Ahab's, little considering that Jezebel was her mother. (2) Some think he did it in policy, hoping by this expedient to unite the kingdoms in his son.

2. This match drew Jehoshaphat, (1) Into an intimate familiarity with Ahab. He paid him a visit at Samaria, and Ahab, proud of the honour which Jehoshaphat did him, gave him entertainment, according to the splendour of those times. (2) Into a league with Ahab against the Syrians. Ahab persuaded him to join forces with him in an expedition for the recovery of Ramoth-Gilead, a city in the tribe of Gad, on the other side Jordan. Did not Ahab know that that, and all the other cities of Israel, did of right belong to Jehoshaphat, as heir of the house of David? The feast Ahab made for Jehoshaphat was designed only to wheedle him into this expedition.

Verses 4–27

This is almost word for word the same with 1 Kings xxii. 1. Of the great duty of acknowledging God in all our ways *and enquiring at his word*, whatever we undertake. Jehoshaphat was not willing to proceed till he had done this, v. 4. 2. Of the great danger of bad company even to good men. Jehoshaphat here, in complaisance to Ahab, sits in his robes, and dares not rebuke that false prophet who basely abused the faithful seer nor oppose Ahab who committed him to prison. 3. Of the unhappiness of those who are surrounded with flatterers, especially flattering

prophets, who cry peace to them and prophesy nothing but smooth things. Thus was Ahab cheated into his ruin, and justly; for he hearkened to such, and preferred those that humoured him before a good prophet that gave him fair warning of his danger. 4. Of the power of Satan, by the divine permission, *in the children of disobedience.* One lying spirit can make 400 lying prophets and make use of them to deceive Ahab, v. 21. 5. Of the justice of God in giving those up to strong delusions, to believe a lie, who will not receive the love of the truth, but rebel against it, v. 21. 6. Of the hard case of faithful ministers, whose lot it has often been to be hated, and persecuted, and ill-treated, for being true to their God and just and kind to the souls of men. Micaiah, for discharging a good conscience, was buffeted, imprisoned, and condemned to the bread and water of affliction. But he could with assurance appeal to the issue, as all those may do who are persecuted for their faithfulness, v. 27.

Verses 28–34

1. Good Jehoshaphat exposing himself in his robes, thereby endangered, and yet delivered. We have reason to think that Ahab, while he pretended friendship, really aimed at Jehoshaphat's life, else he would never have advised him to enter into the battle with his robes on, which was but to make himself an easy mark to the enemy. The enemy had soon an eye upon the robes, and vigorously attacked the unwary prince who now, when it was too late, wished himself in the habit of the poorest soldier, rather than in his princely raiment. *The Lord helped him out* of his distress, by *moving the captains to depart from him,* v. 31. God has all men's hearts in his hand, and turns them as he pleases, contrary to their own first intentions, to serve his purposes. Many are moved unaccountably both to themselves and others, but an invisible power moves them. 2. Wicked Ahab disguising himself, thereby as he thought securing himself, and yet slain, v. 33. Jehoshaphat is safe in his robes, Ahab killed in his armour.

CHAPTER 19

A further account of the good reign of Jehoshaphat. I. His return in peace to Jerusalem, ver. 1. II. The reproof given him for his league with Ahab, and his acting in conjunction with him, ver. 2, 3. III. The great care he took thereupon to reform his kingdom, ver. 4. IV. The instructions he gave to his judges, both those in the country towns that kept the inferior courts (ver. 5–7), and those in Jerusalem that sat in the supreme judicature of the kingdom, ver. 8–11.

Verses 1–4

I. The great favour God showed to Jehoshaphat,

1. In bringing him back in safety from his dangerous expedition with Ahab, which had like to have cost him dearly (v. 1): *He returned to his house in peace.* Whenever we return in peace to our houses we ought to acknowledge God's providence in preserving our going out and our coming in. He fared better than he deserved.

2. In sending him a reproof for his affinity with Ahab. It is a great mercy to be told in time wherein we have erred, that we may repent and amend the error before it be too late. The prophet by whom the reproof is sent is Jehu the son of Hanani. The father was an eminent prophet in the last reign, as appeared by Asa's putting him in the stocks for his plain dealing; yet the son was not afraid to reprove another king. The prophet told him plainly that he had done very ill in joining with Ahab: *Shouldst thou love those that hate the Lord?* God was displeased with him for doing this: "*There is wrath upon thee from before the Lord,* and thou must, by repentance, make thy peace with him, or it will be the worse for thee." He did so, and God's anger was turned away. Yet

he took notice of that which was praiseworthy, as it is proper for us to do when we give a reproof (*v.* 3): *"There are good things found in thee;* and therefore, though God be displeased with thee, he does not, he will not, cast thee off."

II. Jehoshaphat took the reproof well, was not wroth with the seer as his father was, but submitted. He *dwelt at Jerusalem* (*v.* 4), minded his own business at home, and would not expose himself by paying any more such visits to Ahab. To atone for the visit he had paid to Ahab, he made a pious profitable visitation of his own kingdom: He *went out through the people* in his own person from Beersheba in the south to Mount Ephraim in the north, and *brought them back to the Lord God of their fathers,* that is, did all he could towards recovering them. His late affinity with the idolatrous house of Ahab had had a bad influence upon his own kingdom. Many were emboldened to revolt to idolatry when they saw even their reforming king so intimate with idolaters; and therefore he thought himself doubly obliged to do all he could to restore them.

Verses 5–11

Jehoshaphat, having done what he could to make his people good, is here providing, if possible, to keep them so by the influence of a settled magistracy. He had sent preachers among them, to instruct them (*ch.* xvii. 7–9), but now he saw it further requisite to send judges among them, to see the laws put in execution, and to be a terror to evil-doers.

I. He erected inferior courts of justice in the several cities of the kingdom, *v.* 5. The judges of these courts were to keep the people in the worship of God, to punish the violations of the law, and to decide controversies between man and man. Here is the charge he gave them (*v.* 6): *Take heed what you do, v.* 6. And again, *"Take heed and do it* (*v.* 7). Mind your business; take heed of making any mistakes." Judges of all men, have need to be cautious, because so much depends upon the correctness of their judgment. *"Let the fear of God be upon you,* and that will be a restraint upon you to keep you from doing wrong and an engagement to you to be active in doing the duty of your place." The powers that be are ordained by God and for him: "*You judge not for man, but for the Lord;* your business is to glorify him, and serve the interests of his kingdom among men." "He is *with you in the judgment,* to take notice what you do and call you to an account if you do amiss."

II. He erected a supreme court at Jerusalem, which was appealed to, in all the difficult causes that occurred in the inferior courts. This court sat in Jerusalem; for *there were set the thrones of judgment;* there they would be under the inspection of the king himself.

1. The causes cognizable in this court were of two kinds, (1) Pleas of the crown, called here *the judgment of the Lord,* because the law of God was the law of the realm. All criminals were charged with the breach of some part of his law and were said to offend against his peace, his crown and dignity. (2) Common pleas, between party and party, called here *controversies* (*v.* 8) and *causes of their brethren* (*v.* 10), differences *between blood and blood* (this refers to Deut. xvii. 8). Since the revolt of the ten tribes all the cities of refuge, except Hebron, belonged to the kingdom of Israel; and therefore, we may suppose, the courts of the temple, or the horns of the altar, were chiefly used as sanctuaries in that case, and hence the trial of homicides was reserved for the court at Jerusalem.

2. The judges of this court were some of *the Levites and priests* that were most learned in the law, eminent for wisdom, and of approved integrity, and some of *the chief of the fathers of Israel,* or persons of age and experience.

3. The two chiefs, or presidents, of this court. Amariah, the high priest, was to preside in ecclesiastical causes. Zebadiah, the prime-minister of that state, was to preside in all civil causes, *v.* 11.

4, The inferior officers of the court. "Some of *the Levites shall be officers before you,*" *v.* 11.

5. They must see to it that they acted from a good principle; they must do all in the *fear of the Lord,* and *with a perfect upright heart, v.* 9. They must act with resolution. "Deal courageously, and fear not the face of man; be bold and daring in the discharge of your duty, and, whoever is against you, God will protect you."

CHAPTER 20

I. The great danger and distress that Jehoshaphat and his kingdom were in from a foreign invasion, ver. 1, 2. II. The pious course he took for their safety, by fasting, and praying, and seeking God, ver. 3–13. III. The assurance which God, by a prophet, immediately gave them of victory, ver. 14–17. IV. Their thankful believing reception of those assurances, ver. 18–21. V. The defeat which God gave to their enemies thereupon, ver. 22–25. VI. A solemn thanksgiving which they kept for their victory, and for the happy consequences of it, ver. 26–30. VII. The conclusion of the reign of Jehoshaphat, ver. 31–37.

Verses 1–13

Jehoshaphat in distress, which was followed by such a glorious deliverance as was an abundant recompence for his piety.

I. A formidable invasion of Jehoshaphat's kingdom by the Moabites and Ammonites, *v.* 1. Jehoshaphat was surprised when the enemy entered his country, *v.* 2. What pretence they had to quarrel with Jehoshaphat does not appear; they are said to come *from beyond the sea,* meaning *the Dead Sea,* where Sodom had stood. The neighbouring nations had feared Jehoshaphat (*ch.* xvii. 10), but perhaps his affinity with Ahab had lessened him in their esteem.

II. The preparation Jehoshaphat made against the invaders. No mention is made of his mustering his forces, which yet it is most probable he did. But his great care was to obtain the favour of God. But he is of the mind of his father David. If we must be corrected, yet *let us not fall into the hands of man.* Consciousness of guilt made him fear. *He set himself to seek the Lord,* and, in the first place, to make him his friend. He *proclaimed a fast throughout all Judah,* appointed a day of humiliation and prayer, that they might join together in confessing their sins and *asking help of the Lord.* The people readily assembled out of all the cities of Judah in the court of the temple to join in prayer (*v.* 4). Jehoshaphat himself was the mouth of the congregation to God. The prayer Jehoshaphat prayed is here recorded. He acknowledges the sovereign dominion of the divine Providence, gives to God the glory of it and takes to himself the comfort of it (*v.* 6): *"Art not thou God in heaven?* Control these heathen then; set bounds to their daring threatening insults." He lays hold on their covenant-relation to God. "Thou that art *God in heaven* art the *God of our fathers* (*v.* 6) and *our God, v.* 7. Whom should we seek to, whom should we trust to, for relief, but to the God we have chosen and served?" "We hold this land by grant from thee. Suffer us not to be *cast out of thy possession." v.* 11. He makes mention of the temple they had built for God's name (*v.* 8), not as if that merited anything at God's hand, for *of his own they gave him,* but it was a token of God's favourable presence with them, *v.* 8, 9. "Lord, when it was built it was intended for the encouragement of our faith at such a time as this. Here thy name is; here we are. Lord, help us, for the glory of thy name." He professes his entire dependence upon God for deliverance. Though he had a great army on foot, and well disciplined, yet he said, "*We have no might against this*

great company**, but *our eyes are upon thee. In thee,
O God! do we put our trust; our souls wait on thee*."

Verses 14–19

God's gracious answer to Jehoshaphat's prayer.
While he was yet speaking God heard: before the
congregation was dismissed they had assurance
given them that they should be victorious; for it is
never in vain to seek God. 1. The spirit of prophecy
came upon a Levite *in the midst of the congregation,*
v. 14. He was of the sons of Asaph, and therefore one
of the singers; on that office God would put an
honour. There needed no sign, the thing itself was
to be performed the very next day, and that would
be confirmation enough to his prophecy. 2. He
encouraged them to trust in God, though the danger
was very threatening (*v.* 15): "*Be not afraid. The
battle is not yours; the battle is God's.*" 3. He gives
them intelligence of the motions of the enemy, and
orders them to march towards them, with particular
directions where they should find them. *To-morrow*
(the day after the fast) *go you down against them,*
v. 16, 17. 4. He assures them that they should be,
not the glorious instruments, but the joyful spectators,
of the total defeat of the enemy: "You shall not need
to strike a stroke; the work shall be done to your
hands; only stand still and see it," *v.* 17. Let but the
Christian soldier go out against his spiritual enemies,
and the God of peace will *tread them under his feet*
and make *him more than a conqueror.* 5. Jehoshaphat and his people received these assurances with
faith, reverence, and thankfulness. They b*owed their
heads,* Jehoshaphat first, and then all the people *fell
before the Lord, and worshipped.* They lifted up their
voices in praise to God, *v.* 19.

Verses 20–30

The foregoing prayer answered and the foregoing
promise performed, in the total overthrow of the
enemies' forces and the triumph of Jehoshaphat's
forces over them.

I. Never was army drawn out to the field of battle
as Jehoshaphat's army was. He had soldiers *ready
prepared for war* (*ch.* xvii. 18), but here is no notice
taken of their military equipment, their swords or
spears, their shields or bows. But Jehoshaphat took
care, 1. That faith should be their armour. As they
went forth, instead of calling them to handle their
arms, he bade them *believe in the Lord God* and give
credit to his word in the mouth of his prophets,
and assured them that then they should *prosper* and
be established, v. 20. 2. That praise and thanksgiving
should be their vanguard, *v.* 21. Jehoshaphat called
a council of war, and it was resolved to appoint
singers to go out before the army to praise God,
with that ancient and good doxology which eternity
itself will not wear thread-bare, *Praise the Lord; for
his mercy endureth for ever.* By this strange advance
towards the field of battle, Jehoshaphat intended to
express his firm reliance upon the word of God.

II. Never was army so unaccountably destroyed
as that of the enemy; not by thunder, or hail, or the
sword of an angel, not by dint of sword, but the Lord
set ambushments against them, as Bishop Patrick
thinks, their own ambushments, whom God struck
with such confusion that they fell upon their own
friends as if they had been enemies, and *everyone
helped to destroy another,* so that *none escaped.*
This God did *when his people began to sing and to
praise* (*v.* 22). When they did but begin the work of
praise God perfected the work of their deliverance.

III. Never was spoil so cheerfully divided, for
Jehoshaphat's army had nothing to do besides; the
rest was done for them. The spoil *was more than they
could carry away* at once, and they were *three days
in gathering it, v.* 25.

IV. Never was victory celebrated with more solemn
and enlarged thanksgivings. They kept a day of
praise in the camp, before they drew their forces
out of the field. On the fourth day they assembled
in a valley, where they blessed God with so much
zeal and fervency that that day's work gave a name to
the place, the valley of *Berechah,* that is, *of blessing,*
v. 26. Yet they did not think this enough, but came
in solemn procession, and Jehoshaphat at the head of
them, to Jerusalem, that the country, as they passed
along, might join with them in their praises, and that
they might give thanks for the mercy where they had
by prayer obtained it, *in the house of the Lord, v.*
27, 28. Public mercies call for public acknowledgments *in the courts of the Lord's house,* Ps. cxvi. 19.

V. Never did victory turn to a better account than
this; for, 1. Jehoshaphat's kingdom was hereby made
to look very great and considerable abroad, *v.* 29.
It begat in the neighbours a reverence of God and a
cautious fear of doing any injury to his people.
2. It was made very easy and quiet at home, *v.* 30.
They were quiet from the fear of insults from their
neighbours, God having given them rest round about.
And, if he give rest, who can give disturbance?

Verses 31–37

The close of the history of Jehoshaphat's reign.
This was the general character of his reign, that he
did that which was right in the sight of the Lord,
kept close to the worship of God himself and did
what he could to keep his people close to it. But
two things are to be lamented:—1. The people still
retained a partiality for the high places, *v.* 33. Those
that were erected to the honour of strange gods were
taken away (*ch.* xvii. 6); but those where the true
God was worshipped, being less culpable, were
thought allowable. 2. Jehoshaphat himself still
retained a partiality for the house of Ahab, because
he had married his son to a daughter of that family,
though he had been plainly reproved for it and had
like to have smarted for it. He joined himself with
him, not in war, as with his father, but in trade, became his partner in a fleet bound for Tarshish, *v.* 35,
36. God sends to him, to show him his error and bring
him to repentance, (1) By a prophet, who foretold the
blasting of his project, *v.* 37. And, (2) By a storm,
which broke the ships in the port before they set sail,
by which he was warned to break off his alliance
with Ahaziah; and it seems he took the warning, for,
when Ahaziah afterwards pressed him to join with
him, he *would not,* 1 Kings xxii. 49.

CHAPTER 21

Jehoram, one of the vilest, succeeded Jehoshaphat, one of the
best. Thus were they punished for not making a better use of
Jehoshaphat's good government, and his reformation, ch. xx. 33.
I. Jehoram's elevation to the throne, ver. 1–3. II. The wicked
course he took to establish himself in it, by the murder of his
brethren, ver. 4. III. The idolatries and other wickedness he was
guilty of, ver. 5, 6, 11. IV. The prophecy of Elijah against him,
ver. 12–15. V. The judgments of God upon him, in the revolt
of his subjects from him (ver. 8–10) and the success of his enemies
against him, ver. 16, 17. VI. His miserable sickness and inglorious exit, ver. 18–20. VII. The preservation of the house of
David notwithstanding, ver. 7.

Verses 1–11

I. Jehoshaphat was a very careful indulgent father
to Jehoram. He had many sons, who are here named
(*v.* 2), and it is said (*v.* 13) that they were better than
Jehoram, and any of them more fit for the crown
than he; and yet, because he was the firstborn (*v.* 3),
his father secured the kingdom for him. His birthright entitled him to a double portion of his father's
estate, Deut. xxi. 17. But if he appeared utterly unfit
for government (the end of which is the good of the
people), and likely to undo all that his father had
done, it would have been better perhaps to have set

him aside, and taken the next that was hopeful, and not inclined as he was to idolatry.

II. Jehoram was a most barbarous brother to his father's sons. As soon as he had settled himself in the throne he slew all his brethren with the sword, either by false accusation, under colour of law, or by assassination. With them he slew divers of the princes of Israel, who adhered to them, or were likely to avenge their death.

III. Jehoram was a most wicked king, who corrupted and debauched his kingdom, and ruined the reformation that his good father and grandfather had carried on: He *walked in the way of the house of Ahab* (*v.* 6), made high places, and did his utmost to set up idolatry again, *v.* 11. 1. As for the inhabitants of Jerusalem, where he kept his court, he easily drew them into his spiritual whoredom. 2. The country people seem to have been brought to it with more difficulty; but those that would not be corrupted by flatteries were driven by force to partake in his abominable idolatries.

IV. When he forsook God and his worship his subjects withdrew from their allegiance to him. 1. Some of the provinces abroad that were tributaries to him did so. The Edomites revolted (*v.* 8), and, though he chastised them (*v.* 9), yet he could not reduce them, *v.* 10. 2. One of the cities of his own kingdom did so. Libnah revolted (*v.* 10) and set up for a free state, as of old it had a king of its own, Joshua xii. 15.

V. God was tender of his covenant with the house of David, and therefore would not destroy the royal family, though it was so wretchedly corrupted and degenerated, *v.* 7.

Verses 12-20

I. A warning from God sent to Jehoram by a writing from Elijah the prophet. By this it appears that Jehoram came to the throne, and showed himself what he was, before Elijah's translation. We will suppose that the time of his departure was at hand, so that he could not go in person to Jehoram; but that, hearing of his great wickedness in murdering his brethren, he left this writing with Elisha, to be sent him by the first opportunity, that it might either be a means to reclaim him or a witness against him. 1. His crimes are plainly charged upon him—his departure from the good ways of God, in which he had been educated (*v.* 12)—his conformity to the ways of the house of Ahab, his setting up and enforcing idolatry in his kingdom—and his murdering his brethren, *v.* 13. 2. Judgment is given against him for these crimes; he is plainly told that his sin should certainly be the ruin, (1) Of his kingdom and family (*v.* 14). His people justly suffer because they had complied with his idolatry, and his wives because they had drawn him to it. (2) Of his health and life. And now, if he had learned to humble himself upon the receipt of his threatening message from Elijah, who knows but he might have obtained at least a reprieve? But it does not appear that he took any notice of it; Elijah seemed to him *as one that mocked*.

II. The threatened judgments brought upon him because he slighted the warning. 1. Jehoram stripped of all his comforts. God *stirred up the spirit of his neighbours* against him. Some occasion or other they took to quarrel with him, invaded his country, but fought against the king's house only; they made directly to that, and *carried away all the substance that was found in it*. They *carried away* his sons; but we find (*ch.* xxii. 1) that they *slew all the eldest*. Now all his sons are slain but one. If he had not been of the house of David, that one would not have escaped. 2. His disease was very grievous. Two years he continued ill, and could get no relief. These sore

diseases seized him just after his house was plundered and his wives and children were carried away. Perhaps his grief and anguish of mind for that calamity might occasion his sickness. To be sick and poor, sick and solitary, but especially to be sick and in sin, sick and destitute of grace to bear the affliction, and of comfort to counter-balance it—is a most deplorable case.

3. He reigned but eight years, and then *departed without being desired, v.* 20. To show what little affection or respect they had for him, they would not *bury him in the sepulchres of the kings*, as thinking him unworthy. This further disgrace they put upon him, that they *made no burning for him, like the burning of his fathers, v.* 19. They did not honour him with any sweet odours or precious spices.

CHAPTER 22

The carrying away of Jehoram's sons and his wives; but one of his sons and one of his wives left to be the shame and plague of his family. I. Ahaziah was the shame of it as a partaker, 1. In the sin, and, 2. In the destruction, of the house of Ahab, ver. 1–9. II. Athaliah was the plague of it, for she destroyed all the seed-royal, and usurped the throne, ver. 10–12.

Verses 1-9

An account of the reign of Ahaziah, a short reign (of one year only). He was called *Jeho-ahaz* (*ch.* xxi. 17); here he is called *Ahaz-iah*, the same name transposed. He is here said to be forty-two years old when he began to reign (*v.* 2), but it is said (2 Kings viii. 26) that he was twenty-two years old. Some make this forty-two to be the age of his mother Athaliah, for in the original it is, *he was the son of forty-two years.*

The history of Ahaziah's reign is briefly summed up in two clauses, *v.* 3, 4.

I. He did wickedly, *walked in the way of the house of Ahab, did evil in the sight of the Lord* like them (*v.* 3, 4), that is, he worshipped the same false gods that they worshipped, Baalim and Ashtaroth. These Baalim encouraged in their worshippers all manner of lewdness and sensuality, which the God of Israel strictly forbade.

II. He was counselled by his mother and her relations to do so. *She was his counsellor* (*v.* 3) and so were *they*, after the death of his father, *v.* 4. The counsel of the ungodly is the ruin of many young persons when they are setting out in the world. This young prince might have had better advice from the princes and the judges, the priests and the Levites, that had been famous in his good grandfather's time for teaching the knowledge of God; but the house of Ahab humoured him, and *he walked after their counsel*.

III. He was counselled by them to his destruction. It was bad enough that they exposed him to the sword of the Syrians, drawing him in to join with Joram king of Israel in an expedition to Ramoth-Gilead, where Joram was wounded, an expedition that was not for his honour. But that was not all: by engaging him in an intimacy with Joram king of Israel, they involved him in the common ruin of the house of Ahab. He came on a visit to Joram (*v.* 6) just at the time that Jehu was executing the judgment of God upon that idolatrous family, and so was cut off with them, *v.* 7–9.

Verses 10-12

1. A wicked woman endeavouring to destroy the house of David, that she might set up a throne for herself upon the ruins of it. Athaliah barbarously cut off all the seed-royal (*v.* 10), perhaps intending to transmit the crown of Judah after herself to some of her own relations. 2. A good woman effectually preserving it from being wholly extirpated. One of

the late king's sons, a child of a year old, was rescued from among the dead, and saved alive by the care of Jehoiada's wife (v. 11, 12).

CHAPTER 23

Six years Athaliah had tyrannised; in this chapter we have her deposed and slain, and Joash, the rightful heir, enthroned. The story before related, 2 Kings xi. 4, &c. I. Jehoiada prepared the people for the king, acquainted them with his design, armed them, and appointed them their posts, ver. 1-10. II. He produced the king to the people, crowned him, and anointed him, ver. 11. III. He slew the usurper, ver. 12-15. IV. He reformed the kingdom, re-established religion, and restored the civil government, ver. 16-21.

Verses 1-11

Imagine the bad position of affairs in Jerusalem during Athaliah's six years' usurpation. After such a dark and tedious night the returning day in this revolution was the brighter and the more welcome. The continuance of David's seed and throne was what God had sworn by his holiness (Ps. lxxxix. 35), and the stream of government here runs again in the right channel. The instrument and chief manager of the restoration is Jehoiada. 1. A man of great prudence, who reserved the young prince for so many years till he was fit to appear in public, who prepared his work beforehand, and then effected it with admirable secrecy and expedition. 2. A man of great interest. The captains joined with him, v. 1. The Levites and the chief of the fathers of Israel came at his call to Jerusalem (v. 2). *The Levites and all Judah did as Jehoiada commanded* (v. 8). 3. A man of great faith. *The king's son shall reign*, must reign, *as the Lord hath said.* 4. A man of great religion. He gave special order that none of the people should come into the house of the Lord, but the priests and Levites only, who were holy, upon pain of death, v. 6, 7. Never let sacred things be profaned, no, not for the support of civil rights. 5. A man of great resolution. When he had undertaken this business he went through with it, *brought out the king, crowned him, and gave him the testimony*, v. 11.

Verses 12-21

I. The people pleased, v. 12, 13. When the king stood at his pillar, whose right it was to stand there, *all the people of the land rejoiced to see a rod sprung out of the stem of Jesse*, Isa. xi. 1.

II. Athaliah slain. She ventured *into the house of the Lord* at that time, and cried, *Treason, treason!* But nobody seconded her, or sided with her. Jehoiada, as protector in the king's minority, ordered her to be slain (v. 14), which was done immediately (v. 15).

III. The original contract agreed to, v. 16. In the *Kings* it is said that Jehoiada made a covenant between the *Lord*, the people, and the king, 2 Kings xi. 17. Here it is said to be between *himself*, the people, and the king; for he, as God's priest, was his representative in this transaction, or a sort of mediator, as Moses was. Let us look upon ourselves and one another as *the Lord's people*, and this will have a powerful influence upon us in the discharge of all our duty both to God and man.

IV. Baal destroyed, v. 17. They would not have done half their work if they had only destroyed the usurper of the *king's* right, and not the usurper of *God's* right—if they had asserted the honour of the throne, and not that of the altar. Down with Baal's house, his altars, his images; down with them all, Deut. xiii. 5, 6.

V. The temple service revived, v. 18, 19. Jehoiada restored *the offices of the house of the Lord.* 1. He appointed the priests to their courses, for the due offering of sacrifices. 2. The singers to theirs, according to the appointment of David. 3. The porters were put in their respective posts as David ordered (v. 19), to take care that none who were ceremonially

unclean should be admitted into the courts of the temple.

VI. The civil government re-established, v. 20. They brought the king in state to his own palace, and set him *upon the throne of the kingdom*, to give law, and give judgment, either in his own person or by Jehoiada his tutor. Thus was this happy revolution perfected.

CHAPTER 24

The history of the reign of Joash. How wonderfully he was preserved for the throne, and placed in it, we read before; now here we are told how he began in the spirit, but ended in the flesh. I. In the beginning of his time, while Jehoiada lived, he did well; particularly, he took care to put the temple in good repair, ver. 1-14. II. In the latter end of his time, after Jehoiada's death, he apostatized from God, and his apostasy was his ruin. 1. He set up the worship of Baal again (ver. 15-18). 2. He put Zechariah the prophet to death because he reproved him for what he had done, ver. 20-22. 3. The judgments of God came upon him for it. The Syrians invaded him, ver. 23, 24. He was struck with sore diseases; his own servants conspired against him and slew him.

Verses 1-14

An account of Joash's good beginnings. 1. It is a happy thing for young people, when they are setting out in the world, to be under the direction of those that are wise and good and faithful to them, as Joash was under the influence of Jehoiada, during whose time he *did that which was right.* Let those that are young reckon it a blessing to have those that will caution them against that which is evil and quicken them to that which is good; and let them reckon it not a mark of weakness to hearken to such. He that will not be counselled cannot be helped. It is especially prudent for young people to take advice in their marriages. 2. Men may go far in the external performances of religion, merely by the power of their education and the influence of their friends, who are not actuated by a living principle of grace in their hearts. 3. In the outward expressions of devotion it is possible that those who have only the form of godliness may out-strip those who have the power of it. Joash is more solicitous and more zealous about the repair of the temple than Jehoiada himself, whom he reproves for his remissness in that matter, v. 6. It is easier to build temples than to be temples to God. 4. The repairing of churches is a good work. When Joash found that money did not come in as he expected in one way he tried another. The throwing of money into a chest, through a hole in the lid of it, was a way that had not been used before, and perhaps the very novelty of the thing made it a successful expedient for the raising of money; a great deal was thrown in and with a great deal of cheerfulness: they all rejoiced, v. 10.

Verses 15-26

A sad account of the degeneracy and apostasy of Joash. God had done great things for him; he had done something for God; but now he proved ungrateful to his God.

I. The occasions of his apostasy. He never was sincere, never acted from principle, but in compliance to Jehoiada, who had helped him to the crown, and because he had been protected in the temple and rose upon the ruins of idolatry; and therefore, when the wind turned, he turned with it. 1. His good counsellor left him, and was by death removed from him. *They buried him among the kings*, with this honourable encomium, that *he had done good in Israel.* Judah is called *Israel* because, the other tribes having revolted from God, they only were Israelites indeed. Jehoiada finished his course with honour; but the little religion that Joash had was all buried in his grave, and, after his death, both king and kingdom miserably degenerated. See how necessary it is that, as our Saviour speaks, we *have salt in ourselves*, that we act in religion from an inward principle, which will carry us on through all changes. Then the loss of a parent, a minister, a friend, will not involve the loss of our religion. 2. Bad counsellors got about him, insinuated themselves into his affections, and, instead of condoling, congratulated him upon the death of his old tutor, as his release from discipline. They tell him he must be priest-ridden no longer, he may do as he pleases: and the princes of Judah were industrious to debauch him, *v.* 17. His father and grandfather were corrupted by the house of *Ahab*, from whom no better could be expected. But that the princes of Judah should be seducers to their king was very sad. And he hearkened to them: their discourse pleased him, and was more agreeable than Jehoiada's dictates used to be.

II. The apostasy itself: *They left the house of God, and served groves and idols*, *v.* 18. The princes had a request to the king that they may set up the groves and idols again which were thrown down in the beginning of his reign, for they hate to be always confined to the dull old-fashioned service of the temple. And he not only gave them leave to do it themselves, but he joined with them.

III. The aggravations of this apostasy. God *sent prophets to them* (*v.* 19) to reprove them. It is the work of ministers to bring people, not to themselves, but to God—to bring those again to him who have gone a-whoring from him. They slighted all the prophets and slew one of the most eminent, *Zechariah the son of Jehoiada*. The people were assembled in the court of the temple when this Zechariah, being filled with the spirit of prophecy, stood up and plainly told the people of their sin and what would be the consequences of it. He did not impeach any particular persons, but reminded them of what was written in the law. "*You transgress the commandments of the Lord*, you know you do so, in serving groves and idols: and why will you so offend God and wrong yourselves?" By the conspiracy of the princes, or some of their party, and *by the commandment of the king*, they stoned him to death immediately, not under colour of law, accusing him as a blasphemer, a traitor, or a false prophet, but in a popular tumult, *in the court of the house of the Lord*. The *person* was sacred—a priest, the *place* sacred—the court of the temple (the inner court, *between the porch and the altar*), the *message* yet more sacred. The reproof was just, the warning fair, both backed with scripture, and the delivery very gentle and tender. The Jews say there were seven transgressions in this; for they killed a priest, a prophet, a judge, they shed innocent blood, and polluted the court of the temple, the sabbath, and the day of expiation: for on that day, their tradition says, this happened. This Zechariah, who suffered martyrdom for his faithfulness to God and his country, was the son of Jehoiada, who had done so much good in Israel, and particularly had been as a father to Joash, *v.* 22. The dying martyr's prophetic imprecation upon his murderers: *The Lord look upon it, and require it!* This came not from a spirit of revenge, but a spirit of prophecy: *He will require it*. This precious blood was quickly reckoned for in the judgments that came upon this apostate prince; it came into the account afterwards in the destruction of Jerusalem by the Chaldeans (*ch.* xxxvi. 16); nay, our Saviour makes the persecutors of him and his gospel answerable for the blood of this Zechariah; so loud, so long, does the blood of the martyrs cry. See Matt. xxiii. 35.

IV. The judgments of God which came upon Joash for this aggravated wickedness of his. 1. A small army of Syrians made themselves masters of Jerusalem, destroyed the princes, plundered the city, and sent the spoil of it to Damascus, *v.* 23, 24. 2. God

smote him with great diseases, of body, or mind, or both. 3. His own servants conspired against him. They slew him in his bed *for the blood of the sons of Jehoiada*, by which it should seem that he did not only slay Zechariah, but others of the sons of Jehoiada for his sake. 4. His people would not bury him in the sepulchres of the kings because he had stained his honour by his mal-administration.

CHAPTER 25

Amaziah's reign, recorded in this chapter, was not one of the worst and yet far from good. Most of the passages in this chapter we had before more briefly related, 2 Kings xiv. Amaziah, I. A just revenger of his father's death, ver. 1–4. II. An obedient observer of the command of God, ver. 5–10. III. A cruel conqueror of the Edomites, ver. 11–13. IV. A foolish worshipper of the gods of Edom and impatient of reproof for it, ver. 14–16. V. Rashly challenging the king of Israel, and smarting for his rashness, ver. 17–24. And, lastly, ending his days ingloriously, ver. 25–28.

Verses 1–13

I. The general character of Amaziah: *He did that which was right in the eyes of the Lord*, worshipped the true God, kept the temple service going, and countenanced religion in his kingdom; but he did not do it *with a perfect heart* (*v.* 2), that is, he was not a man of serious piety or devotion himself. He was no enemy to it, but a cool and indifferent friend. Such is the character of too many in this Laodicean age: they do that which is good, but not with a perfect heart.

II. A necessary piece of justice which he did upon the traitors that murdered his father: he put them to death, *v.* 3. Though they intended to avenge on their king the death of the prophet, *they* presumptuously took God's work out of his hands: and therefore Amaziah did what became him in calling them to an account for it, *v.* 4.

III. An expedition of his against the Edomites. 1. The great preparation he made for this expedition. (1) He mustered his own forces (*v.* 5), and found Judah and Benjamin in all but 300,000 men fit for war, whereas, in Jehoshaphat's time they were four times as many. Sin weakens a people, diminishes them, dispirits them, and lessens their number. (2) He hired auxiliary troops out of the kingdom of Israel, *v.* 6.

2. The command which God sent him by a prophet to dismiss the forces of Israel, *v.* 7, 8. If he made sure of God's presence, the army he had of his own was sufficient. But particularly he must not take in *their* assistance: *For the Lord is not with the children of Ephraim, because they are not with him*, but worship the calves.

3. The objection which Amaziah made against this command, and the satisfactory answer which the prophet gave to that objection, *v.* 9. The king had remitted 100 talents to the men of Israel for advance-money. "Now," says he, "if I send them back, I shall lose that: *But what shall we do for the* 100 *talents?*" This is an objection men often make against their duty: they are afraid of losing by it. "Regard not that," says the prophet: "*The Lord is able to give thee much more than this;* and, thou mayest depend upon it, he will not see thee lose by him." What is it to trust in God, but to be willing to venture the loss of anything for him, in confidence of the goodness of the security he gives us that we shall not lose by him, but that whatever we part with for his sake shall be made up to us in kind or kindness. He is just, and he is good, and he is solvent. The king lost 100 talents by his obedience; and we find just that sum given to his grandson Jotham as a present (*ch.* xxvii. 5); then the principal was repaid, and, for interest, 10,000 measures of wheat and as many of barley.

4. His obedience to the command of God, which is upon record to his honour. *He separated the army of Ephraim, to go home again, v.* 10. And they went home in great anger.

5. His triumphs over the Edomites, *v.* 11, 12. He left dead upon the spot, in the field of battle, 10,000 men; 10,000 more he took prisoners, and barbarously killed them all by throwing them down some steep and craggy precipice. What provocation he had to exercise this cruelty towards them we are not told.

6. The mischief which the disbanded soldiers of Israel did to the cities of Judah, either in their return or soon after, *v.* 13. They were so enraged at being sent home that, if they might not go to share with Judah in the spoil of Edom, they would make a prey of Judah. Several cities that lay upon the borders they plundered, killing 3,000 men that made resistance. But why should God suffer this to be done? Doubtless God intended hereby to chastise those cities of Judah for their idolatries, which were found most in those parts that lay next to Israel.

Verses 14–16

I. The revolt of Amaziah·from the God of Israel to the gods of the Edomites. Egregious folly! Ahaz worshipped the gods of those that had conquered him, for which he had some little colour, *ch.* xxviii. 23. But to worship the gods of those whom he had conquered, who could not protect their own worshippers, was the greatest absurdity that could be. If he had cast the idols down from the rock and broken them to pieces, instead of the prisoners, he would have manifested more of the piety as well as more of the pity of an Israelite; but perhaps for that barbarous inhumanity he was given up to this ridiculous idolatry.

II. The reproof which God sent to him, by a prophet, for this sin. The prophet reasoned with him very fairly and very mildly: *Why hast thou sought the favour of those gods which could not deliver their own people? v.* 15.

III. The check he gave to the reprover, *v.* 16. He could say nothing in excuse of his own folly; but he fell into a passion. 1. He taunted him as meddling with that which did not belong·to him: *Art thou made of the king's counsel?* 2. He silenced him, bade him say not a word more to him. He *said to the seer, See not,* Isa. xxx. 10. 3. He threatened him. He seems to remind him of Zechariah's fate in the last reign, who was put to death for making bold with the king; and bids him take warning by him.

IV. The doom which the prophet passed upon him for this. He had made to say to him by way of instruction and advice; but, finding him obstinate in his iniquity, he forbore. Miserable is the condition of that man with whom the blessed Spirit, by ministers and conscience, *forbears to strive,* Gen. vi. 3. And both the reprovers in the gate and that in the bosom, if long brow-beaten and baffled, will at length forbear. So I *gave them up to their own heart's lusts.*

Verses 17–28

This degenerate prince mortified by his neighbour and murdered by his own subjects.

I. Never was proud prince more thoroughly mortified than Amaziah was by Joash king of Israel.

1. This part of the story (which was as fully related 2 Kings xiv. 8, &c., as it is here)—embracing the foolish challenge which Amaziah sent to Joash (*v.* 17), his haughty scornful answer to it (*v.* 18), with the friendly advice he gave him to sit still and know when he was well off (*v.* 19),—his wilfully persisting in his challenge (*v.* 20, 21) the defeat that was given him (*v.* 22), and the calamity he brought upon himself and his city thereby (*v.* 23, 24),—verifies two of Solomon's proverbs:—(1) That *a man's pride will*

bring him low, Prov. xxix. 23. (2) That he that *goes forth hastily to strive* will probably not know what to do in the end thereof, *when his neighbour has put him to shame,* Prov. xxv. 8.

2. But there are two passages in this story not in the *Kings.* (1) That *Amaziah took advice* before he challenged the king of Israel, *v.* 17. But of whom? Not of the prophet but of his statesmen that would flatter him and bid him go up and prosper. (2) Amaziah's imprudence is here made the punishment of his impiety (*v.* 20).

II. Never was poor prince more violently pursued by his own subjects. *From the time* that he departed from the Lord (so it may be read, *v.* 27) the hearts of his subjects departed from him, and they began to form a design against him in Jerusalem. At length the ferment grew so high, and he perceived the plot to be laid so deeply, that he thought fit to quit his royal city and flee to Lachish, but they sent after him thither, and slew him there.

Chapter 26

An account of the reign of Uzziah (Azariah he was called, 2 Kings xiv. 21; xv. 1, &c.). I. His good character in general, ver. 1–5. II. His great prosperity in his wars, his buildings, and all the affairs of his kingdom, ver. 6–15. III. His presumption in invading the priests' office, for which he was struck with a leprosy, and confined by it (ver. 16–21) even to his death, ver. 22, 23.

Verses 1–15

An account of two things concerning Uzziah:—

I. His piety. In this he was not very eminent or zealous; yet *he did that which was right in the sight of the Lord.* He kept up the pure worship of the true God *as his father* did, and was better than his father, inasmuch as he never worshipped idols as his father did. It is said (*v.* 5), He *sought God in the days of Zechariah,* who, some think, was the son of that Zechariah whom his grandfather Joash slew. This Zechariah was one that *had understanding in the visions of God,* and had great influence with Uzziah.

II. His prosperity.

1. In general, *as long as he sought the Lord,* and minded religion, *God made him to prosper.*

2. Here are several particular instances of his prosperity:—(1) His success in his wars: *God helped him* (*v.* 7), and then he triumphed over the Philistines, demolished the fortifications of their cities, and put garrisons of his own among them, *v.* 6. He obliged the Ammonites to pay him tribute, *v.* 8. (2) The greatness of his fame and reputation. His name was celebrated throughout all the neighbouring countries (*v.* 8) and it was a good name, a name for good things with God and good people. (3) His buildings. While he acted offensively abroad, he did not neglect the defence of his kingdom at home, but *built towers in Jerusalem* and fortified them, *v.* 9. Much of the wall of Jerusalem was in his father's time broken down (*ch.* xxv. 23); and he *built a tower at the corner gate.* But his best fortification of Jerusalem was his close adherence to the worship of God. While he fortified the city, he did not forget the country, but *built towers in the desert* too (*v.* 10), to protect the country people from the inroads of the plunderers, *ch.* xxi. 16. (4) His husbandry. He dealt much in cattle and corn for he *loved husbandry* (*v.* 10). (5) His standing armies. He had, as it should seem, two military establishments. [1] A *host of fighting men* that were to make excursions abroad. These *went out to war by bands, v.* 11. They fetched in spoil from the neighbouring countries by way of reprisal for the depredations they had so often made upon Judah, [2] Another army for *guards and garrisons,* that were ready to defend the country in case it should be invaded, *v.* 12, 13. Uzziah furnished himself with a great armoury (*v.* 14), spears, bows, and slings, shields, helmets, and

habergeons: swords are not mentioned, because it is probable that every man had a sword of his own. Engines were invented, in his time, for annoying besiegers with darts and stones shot from the towers and bulwarks, *v.* 15. What a pity it is that the wars and fightings which come from men's lusts have made it necessary for cunning men to employ their skill in inventing instruments of death.

Verses 16–23

The only blot we find on the name of king Uzziah.

I. His sin was invading the priest's office. The transgression of his predecessors was forsaking the temple of the Lord (*ch.* xxiv. 18), and burning incense upon idolatrous altars, *ch.* xxv. 14. *His* was intruding *into the temple of the Lord* further than was allowed him, and attempting himself to *burn incense upon the altar* of God.

1. That which was at the bottom of his sin was pride of heart (*v.* 16): *When he was strong* (and he was marvellously helped by the good providence of God *till he was so, v.* 15), when he had grown very great and considerable in wealth and power, instead of lifting up the name of God in gratitude his *heart was lifted up to his destruction.*

2. His sin was *going into the temple of the Lord to burn incense*, probably when he himself had some special occasion for supplicating the divine favour. (1) Perhaps he fancied the priests did not do their office so devoutly, as they ought, and he could do it better. Or, (2) He observed that the idolatrous kings did themselves burn incense at the altars of their gods; his father did so, and Jeroboam (1 Kings xiii. 1), and he, being resolved to cleave to God's altar, would try to come as near it as the idolatrous kings did to their altars. But it is called a *transgression against the Lord his God.*

3. He was opposed in this attempt by the chief priest and other priests that attended and assisted him, *v.* 17, 18. They were ready to burn incense for the king, according to the duty of their place; but, when he offered to do it himself, they plainly let him know that he meddled with that which did not belong to him, and that it was at his peril. "*It appertaineth not to thee, O Uzziah*! but *to the priests*, whose birthright it is, as sons of Aaron, and who are consecrated to the service." Aaron and his sons were appointed by the law to burn incense, Exod. xxx. 7. See Deut. xxxiii. 10; 1 Chron. xxiii. 13. David had blessed the people and Solomon and Jehoshaphat had prayed with them and preached to them. Uzziah might have done this, and it would have been to his praise; but, as for burning incense, that service was to be performed by the priests only. Korah and his accomplices, though Levites, paid dearly for offering to burn incense, which was the work of the priests only, Num. xvi. 35. The incense of our prayers must be by faith put into the hands of our Lord Jesus, the great high priest of our profession, else we cannot expect it should be accepted by God, Rev. viii. 3.

4. He fell into a passion with the priests that reproved him (*v.* 19): *Uzziah was wroth*, and would not part with the censer out of his hand.

II. His punishment was an incurable leprosy, which rose up in his forehead while he was contending with the priests. When the leprosy appeared, they were emboldened to thrust him out of the temple; nay, he himself *hasted to go out, because the Lord had smitten him* with a disease which was in a particular manner a token of his displeasure, and which he knew secluded him from common converse with men, much more from the altar of God. 2. It remained a lasting punishment of his transgression; for he continued a *leper to the day of his death, v.* 21. 3. It was a punishment that answered the sin as face does face in a glass. (1) Pride was at the bottom of his transgression,

and thus God humbled him and put dishonour upon him. (2) He invaded the office of the priests in contempt of them, and God struck him with a disease which in a particular manner made him subject to the inspection and sentence of the priests; for to them pertained the *judgment of the leprosy*, Deut. xxiv. 8. (3) He thrust himself into the temple of God, whither the priests only had admission, and for that was thrust out of the very courts of the temple, into which the meanest of his subjects that was ceremonially clean had free access.

CHAPTER 27

A very short account of the reign of Jotham, a pious prosperous prince, of whom one would wish to have known more. I. Of the date and continuance of this reign, ver. 1, 8. II. The general good character of it, ver. 2, 6. III. The prosperity of it, ver. 3–5. IV. The period of it, ver. 7, 9.

Verses 1–9

Concerning Jotham.

I. He reigned well. He *did that which was right in the sight of the Lord*; he *prepared his ways before the Lord his God* (*v.* 6). He walked steadily and constantly in the way of his duty, not like some of those that went before him, who, though they had some good in them, lost their credit by their inconstancy and inconsistency with themselves. Two things are observed here in his character:—1. What was amiss in his father he amended in himself (*v.* 2). 2. What was amiss in his people he could not prevail to amend: *The people did yet corruptly,*

II. He prospered. 1. He built. He began with *the gate of the house of the Lord*, which he repaired, beautifully, and raised. He then *fortified the wall of Ophel, and built cities in the mountains of Judah* (*v.* 3, 4). 2. He conquered. He prevailed against the Ammonites, who had invaded Judah in Jehoshaphat's time, *ch.* xx. 1. 3. He *became mighty* (*v.* 6) in wealth and power, and influence upon the neighbouring nations, who courted his friendship and feared his displeasure; and this he got by *preparing his ways before the Lord his God.*

III. He finished his course too soon, but finished it with honour. He died when he was but forty-one years of age (*v.* 8); but *his wars and his ways*, his wars abroad and his ways at home, were so glorious that they were recorded in the book of the kings of Israel, as well as of the kings of Judah, *v.* 7.

CHAPTER 28

This chapter is the history of the reign of Ahaz the son of Jotham; a bad reign it was. I. His great wickedness, ver. 1–4. II. The trouble he brought by it, ver. 5–8. III. The reproof which God sent by a prophet to the army of Israel for trampling upon their brethren of Judah, and the obedient ear they gave to that reproof, ver. 9–15. IV. The many calamities that followed to Ahaz and his people (ver. 16–21). V. The continuance of his idolatry notwithstanding (ver. 22–25), and so his story ends, ver. 26, 27.

Verses 1–5

Never surely had a man greater opportunity of doing well than Ahaz had, and yet here we have him in these few verses, 1. Wretchedly corrupted and debauched. He had had a good education given him, but *He did not that which was right in the sight of the Lord* (*v.* 1), nay, he did a great deal that was wrong, a wrong to God, to his own soul, and to his people; he walked in the way of the revolted Israelites and the Canaanites, made molten images and worshipped them. He forsook the temple of the Lord and sacrificed and burnt incense on the hills, as if they would place him nearer heaven, and under every green tree, as if they would signify the protection and influence of heaven by their shade and dropping. To complete his wickedness, as one perfectly divested of all natural affection as well as religion, he *burnt his children in the fire to Moloch* (*v.* 3). 2. Wretchedly spoiled. (1) The Syrians insulted him and triumphed over him, beat him in the field and carried away a great many of his people into captivity. (2) The king of Israel, though an idolater, too was made a scourge to him, and *smote him with a great slaughter*.

Verses 6–15

I. Treacherous Judah under the rebukes of God's providence. Never was such bloody work made among them since they were a kingdom, and by Israelites too. It is just with God to make those our plagues whom we make our patterns or make ourselves partners with in sin. A war broke out between Judah and Israel, in which Judah was worsted. 1. There was a great slaughter of men in the field of battle. Vast numbers were slain (v. 6) and some of the first rank, the king's son for one. The kingdom of Israel was not strong at this time, and yet strong enough to bring this great destruction upon Judah. 2. There was a great captivity of *women and children*, v. 8.

II. Even victorious Israel under the rebuke of God's word.

1. The message which God sent them by a prophet, who went out to meet them, not to applaud their valour, but in God's name to tell them of their faults.

(1) He told them how they came by this victory of which they were so proud. *Not for your righteousness*, be it known to you, but *for their wickedness* (Deut. ix. 5) *they are broken off*; therefore *be not you high-minded but fear, lest God also spare not you*, Rom. xi. 20, 21.

(2) He charged them with the abuse of the power God had given them over their brethren. The conquerors are here reproved, [1] For the cruelty of the slaughter they had made in the field. They had indeed *shed the blood of war in war*; they did it from a bad principle of enmity to their brethren and after a bad manner, with a barbarous fury. *The wrath of man worketh not the righteousness of God.* [2] For the imperious treatment they gave their prisoners. "*You now purpose to keep them under*, to use them or sell them as slaves, though they are your brethren and free-born Israelites."

(3) He reminded them of their own sins, by which they also were obnoxious to the wrath of God: *Are there not with you, even with you, sins against the Lord your God?* v. 10. This is intended as a check, [1] To their triumph in their success. "You are sinners, and it ill becomes sinners to be proud; for, if judgment begin thus with those that have *the house of God* among them, what shall be the end of such as worship the calves?" [2] To their severity towards their brethren. It ill becomes sinners to be cruel. You have transgressions enough to answer for already, and need not add this to the rest.

(4) He commanded them to release the prisoners, and to send them home again carefully (v. 11); "for you having sinned, *the fierce wrath of God is upon you*, and there is no other way of escaping it than by showing mercy."

2. The resolution of the princes thereupon not to detain the prisoners. They *stood up against those that came from the war*, though flushed with victory, and told them plainly that they should not bring their captives into Samaria, v. 12, 13.

3. The armed men acquiesced, and left their captives and the spoil to the disposal of *the princes* (v. 14), and herein they showed more truly heroic bravery than they did in taking them. It is a great honour for any man to yield to the authority of reason and religion against his interest. The princes generously sent home the poor captives well accommodated, v. 15.

Verses 16–27

I. The great distress which the kingdom of Ahaz was reduced to for his sin. In general, 1. *The Lord brought Judah low*, v. 19. They had lately been very high in wealth and power; but God found means to bring them down, and make them as despicable as they had been formidable. 2. Ahaz made Judah naked. As his sin debased them, so it exposed them. It made them naked to their shame; for it exposed them to contempt, as a man unclothed. It made them naked to their danger; for it exposed them to assaults, as a man unarmed, Exod. xxxii. 25. Sin strips men. In particular, the Edomites, to be revenged for Amaziah's cruel treatment of them (*ch*. xxv. 12), smote Judah, and carried off many captives, v. 17. The Philistines also insulted them, took and kept possession of several cities and villages that lay near them (v. 18), and so they were revenged for the incursions which Uzziah had made upon them, *ch*. xxvi. 6.

II. The addition which Ahaz made both to the national distress and the national guilt.

1. He added to the distress, by making court to strange kings, in hopes they would relieve him. When the Edomites and Philistines were vexatious to him, *he sent to the kings of Assyria to help him* (v. 16). He pillaged the house of God, and the king's house, and squeezed the princes for money to hire these foreign forces into his service, v. 21. But what did Ahaz get by the king of Assyria? Why, he *came to him*, but he *distressed him*, and *strengthened him not* (v. 20), *helped him not*, v. 21. The forces of the Assyrian quartered upon his country, and so impoverished and weakened it.

2. He added to the guilt, by making court to strange gods, in hopes they would relieve him. (1) He abused the house of God; for he *cut in pieces the vessels* of it, that the priests might not perform the service of the temple for want of vessels; and, at length, he *shut up the doors*, that the people might not attend it, v. 24. (2) He confronted the altar of God, for he *made himself altars in every corner of Jerusalem*; so that, as the prophet speaks, they were like *heaps in the furrows of the fields*, Hos. xii. 11. And in the cities of Judah he erected high places for the people to burn incense to what idols they pleased, as if on purpose to *provoke the God of his fathers*, v. 25. (3) He cast off God himself; for he *sacrificed to the gods of Damascus* (v. 23), because he feared them, thinking that they helped his enemies, and that, if he could bring them into his interest, they would help him. And what comes of it? The gods of Syria befriend Ahaz no more than the kings of Assyria did; they were *the ruin of him and of all Israel*. This sin debauched the people so that the reformation of the next reign could not prevail to cure them of their inclination to idolatry, but they retained that root of bitterness till the captivity in Babylon plucked it up.

For aught that appears, he died impenitent, and therefore died inglorious, for he was not buried in *the sepulchres of the kings*.

CHAPTER 29

A pleasant scene, the good and glorious reign of Hezekiah, in which we shall find more of God and religion than perhaps in any of the good reigns we have yet met with; for he was a very zealous, devout, good man, none like him. In this chapter we have an account of the work of reformation which he set about with vigour immediately after his accession to the crown. I. His exhortation to the priests and Levites, when he put them in possession of the house of God again, ver. 1–11. II. The care and pains which the Levites took to cleanse the temple, and put things in order there, ver. 12–19. III. A solemn revival of God's ordinances that had been neglected, in which atonement was made for the sins of the last reign, and the wheels were set a-going again, to the great satisfaction of king and people, ver. 20–36.

Verses 1–11

I. Hezekiah was *twenty-five years old*. Joash, who came to the crown after two bad reigns, was but seven years old; Josiah, who came after two bad reigns, was but eight, which occasioned the delay of the reformation; but Hezekiah had come to years, and so applied himself immediately to it.

II. His general character. He *did that which was right like David*, v. 2. Of several of his predecessors it had been said that they did that which was right, *but not like David*, not with David's integrity and zeal. But here was one that had as hearty an affection for the ark and law of God as ever David had.

III. His speedy application to the great work of restoring religion. The first thing he did was to *open the doors of the house of the Lord*, v. 3. He found Judah low and naked, yet did not make it his first business to revive the civil interests of his kingdom, but to restore religion. Those that begin with God begin at the right end of their work.

IV. His speech to the priests and Levites. Hezekiah's exhortation to the Levites is very pathetic.

1. He laid before them the desolations of religion and the deplorable state to which it was brought among them (v. 6, 7): *Our fathers have trespassed.* He complained, (1) That the house of God had been deserted: *They have forsaken God, and turned their backs upon his habitation.* (2) That the instituted worship of God there had been let fall. The lamps were not lighted, and incense was not burnt. There are still such neglects as these, and they are no less culpable, when the word is not duly read and opened (for that was signified by the *lighting of the lamps*) and when prayers and praises are not duly offered up, for that was signified by *the burning of incense*.

2. He showed the sad consequences of the neglect and decay of religion among them, v. 8, 9.

3. He declared his own full purpose and resolution to revive religion and make it his business to promote it (v. 10): "*It is in my heart to make a covenant with the Lord God of Israel* (that is, to worship him only, and in that way which he has appointed)." This covenant he would not only make himself, but bring his people into the bond of.

4. He engaged and excited the Levites and priests to do their duty on this occasion. This he begins with (v. 5); this he ends with, v. 11. He called them *Levites* to remind them of their obligation to God, called them his *sons* to remind them of their relation to himself, that he expected that, *as a son with the father, they should serve with him* in the reformation of the land. (1) He told them what was their duty, to sanctify *themselves* first by repenting of their neglects, and renewing their covenants with God, and then to *sanctify the house of God*, as his servants, to make it clean and to set it up for the purposes for which it was made. (2) He stirred them up to do it (v. 11): *Be not deceived*, so the *margin*. Those that by their negligence in the service of God think to mock God, do but deceive themselves. God expected work from them. They were not chosen to be idle, to enjoy the dignity and leave the duty to be done by others, but to serve him and to minister to him.

Verses 12–19

Busy work, good work, and needful work, the cleansing of the house of the Lord.

I. The persons employed in this work were the priests and Levites, who should have kept the temple clean. Several of the Levites are here named, two of each of the three principal houses, Kohath, Gershon, and Merari (v. 12), and two of each of the three families of singers, Asaph, Heman, and Jeduthun, v. 13, 14, because they were more zealous and active than the rest. When God has work to do he will raise up leading men to preside in it. And it is not always that the first in place and rank are most fit for service or most forward to it.

II. The work was *cleansing the house of God*, 1. From the common dirt it had contracted while it was shut up—dust, and cobwebs, and the rust of the vessels. 2. From the idols and idolatrous altars that were set up in it, which, though kept ever so neat, were a greater pollution to it than if it had been made the common sewer of the city. The priests were none of them mentioned as leading men in this work, yet none but they durst go *into the inner part of the house, no, not to cleanse it*, which they did, and perhaps the high priest into the holy of holies, to cleanse that. What filth the priests brought into the court the Levites carried to the brook Kidron.

III. The expedition with which they did this work was remarkable. They began on the first day of the first month, a happy beginning of the new-year, and one that promised a good year. Thus should every year begin with the reformation of what is amiss, and the purging away, by true repentance, of all the defilements contracted the foregoing year. In eight days they cleared and cleansed the temple, and in eight days more the *courts* of the temple, v. 17.

IV. The report they made of it to Hezekiah was very agreeable, v. 18, 19. They knew the good king had set his heart upon God's altar, and longed to be attending that, and therefore they insisted most upon the readiness they had put that into—that the vessels of the altar were scoured and brightened. Those vessels which Ahaz, in his *transgression, had cast away* as vessels in which there was no pleasure, they gathered them together, sanctified them, and laid them in their place *before the altar*.

Verses 20–36

A solemn assembly was called to meet the king at the temple, the very next day (v. 20); and very glad, no doubt, all the good people in Jerusalem were, when it was said, *Let us go up to the house of the Lord*, Ps. cxxii. 1. As soon as Hezekiah heard that the temple was ready for him he lost no time, but was ready for it. He rose early to go up to the house of the Lord, earlier on that day than on other days, to show that his heart was upon his work there.

I. Atonement must be made for the sins of the last reign. They thought it not enough to lament and forsake those sins, but they brought a sin-offering. Even our repentance and reformation will not obtain pardon but in and through Christ, who was made *sin* (that is, a sin-offering) for us. No peace but through his blood, no, not for penitents. 1. The sin-offering was *for the kingdom, for the sanctuary*, and *for Judah* (v. 21), that is, to make atonement for the sins of princes, priests, and people, for they had all corrupted their way. The law of Moses appointed sacrifices to make atonement for the sins of the whole congregation (Lev. iv. 13, 14; Num. xv. 24, 25), that the national judgments which their national sins deserved might be turned away. For this purpose we must now have an eye to Christ the great propitiation, as well as for the remission and salvation of particular persons. 2. The law appointed only one goat for a sin-offering, as on the day of atonement (Lev. xvi. 15) and on such extraordinary occasions as this, Num. xv. 24. But they here offered seven (v. 21), because the sins of the congregation had been very great and long continued in. Seven is a number of perfection. Our great sin-offering is but one, yet that one *perfects* for ever *those that are sanctified*. 3. The king and the *congregation* (that is, the representatives of the congregation) *laid their hands on the heads of the goats* that were for the *sin-offering* (v. 23), thereby owning themselves guilty before God and expressing their desire that the guilt of the sinner might be transferred to the sacrifice. By faith we lay our hands on the Lord Jesus, and so *receive the atonement*, Rom. v. 11. 4. Burnt-offerings were offered with the sin-offerings, *seven bullocks, seven rams,* and *seven lambs.* The intention of the burnt-offerings was to give glory to the God of Israel, whom they owned as the only true God, which it was proper to do at the same time that they were by the sin-offering making atonement for their offences. The blood of those, as well as of the sin-offering, was *sprinkled upon the altar* (*v.* 22), to make reconciliation *for all Israel* (*v.* 24), and not for Judah only. Christ is a propitiation, not for the sins of Israel only, but *of the whole world,* 1 John ii. 1, 2. 5. While the offerings were burning upon the altar the *Levites* sang *the song of the Lord* (*v.* 27), the Psalms composed by David and Asaph (*v.* 30), accompanied by the musical instruments which God by his prophets had commanded the use of (*v.* 25), and which had been long neglected. Even sorrow for sin must not put us out of tune for praising God. 6. The king and all the congregation testified their consent to and concurrence in all that was done, by *bowing their heads* and *worshipping.* This is taken notice of, *v.* 28–40.

II. The solemnities of this day did likewise look forward. The temple service was to be set up again that it might be continually kept up; and this Hezekiah calls them to, *v.* 31. "Now that you have *consecrated yourselves to the Lord*—have both made an atonement and made a covenant by sacrifice, are solemnly reconciled and engaged to him—now *come near, and bring sacrifices.*" Having consecrated ourselves, in the first place, to the Lord, we must bring the sacrifices of prayer, and praise, and alms, to his house. Now, in this work, it was found,

1. That the people were free. Being called to it by the king, they brought in their offerings, though not in such abundance as in the glorious days of Solomon, but according to what they had, considering their poverty and the great decay of piety among them. (1) Some were so generous as to bring burnt-offerings, which were wholly consumed to the honour of God, and of which the offerer had no part. (2) Others brought peace-offerings and thank-offerings, the fat of which was burnt upon the altar, and the flesh divided between the priests and the offerers, *v.* 35.

2. That *the priests were few,* too few for the service, *v.* 34.

3. That the Levites were forward. They had been *more upright in heart to sanctify themselves than the priests* (*v.* 34), were better affected to the work and better prepared and qualified for it. This was their praise, and, in recompence for it, they had the honour to be employed in that which was the priests' work: they *helped them to flay the offerings.* This was not according to the law (Lev. i. 5, 6), but the irregularity was dispensed with in cases of necessity, and thus encouragement was given to the faithful zealous Levites and a just disgrace put upon the careless priests.

4. That all were pleased. The king and all the people rejoiced in this blessed turn of affairs and the new face of religion which the kingdom had put on, *v.* 36. Two things in this matter pleased them:—(1) That it was soon brought about: *The thing was done suddenly,* in a little time, with a great deal of ease, and without any opposition. (2) That the hand of God was plainly in it: *God had prepared the people* by the secret influences of his grace, so that many of those who had in the last reign doted on the idolatrous altars were now as much in love with God's altar.

CHAPTER 30

An account of the solemn passover which Hezekiah kept in the first year of his reign. I. The consultation about it, and the resolution he and his people came to for the observance of it, ver. 2–5. II. The invitation he sent to Judah and Israel to come and keep it, ver. 1, 6–12. III. The joyful celebration of it, ver. 13–27. By this the reformation, set on foot in the foregoing chapter, was greatly advanced and established.

Verses 1–12

I. A passover resolved upon. Shall we revive it? The time has elapsed for this year; the priests are not prepared, *v.* 3. Many, it is likely, were for deferring it; but Hezekiah finding a proviso in the law of Moses that particular persons who were unclean in the first month might keep the passover the fourteenth day of the second month (Num. ix. 11), doubted not but what it might be extended to the congregation. Whereupon they resolved to keep the passover *in the second month.*

II. A proclamation to give notice of this passover and to summon the people to it.

1. An invitation was sent to the ten revolted tribes to stir them up to come and attend this solemnity. Letters were written to Ephraim and Manasseh to invite them to Jerusalem to keep this passover (*v.* 1), with a pious design to bring them back to the Lord God of Israel. "Let them take whom they will for their king," says Hezekiah, "so they will but take him for their God."

(1) The contents of the letters that were despatched upon this occasion, in which Hezekiah discovers a great concern both for the honour of God and for the welfare of the neighbouring kingdom. *"Yield yourselves unto the Lord.* Before you can come into communion with him you must come into covenant with him," *Give the hand to the Lord* (so the word is), that is, "Consent to take him for your God." "The doors of the sanctuary are now opened, and you have liberty to enter; the temple service is now revived, and you are welcome to join in it. You are children of Israel. The God you are called to return to is the God of Abraham, Isaac, and Jacob, a God in covenant with your first fathers. Your late fathers that forsook him and trespassed against him have been given up to desolation; their apostasy and idolatry have been their ruin, as you see (*v.* 7). You yourselves are but a *remnant* narrowly *escaped out of the hands of the kings of Assyria* (*v.* 6). If you return to God in a way of duty, he will return to you in a way of mercy." This he begins with (*v.* 6) and concludes with, *v.* 9. Could anything be expressed more pathetically, more movingly? Could there be a better cause, or could it be better pleaded?

(2) The entertainment which Hezekiah's messengers and message met with. It does not appear that Hoshea, who was now king of Israel, forbade his subjects to accept the invitation. They might go to Jerusalem to worship if they pleased; for, though he did evil, yet *not like the kings of Israel that were before him,* 2 Kings xvii. 2. The generality of them slighted the call and turned a deaf ear to it. The messengers went from city to city, but they *laughed them to scorn, and mocked them* (*v.* 10). The destruction of the kingdom of the ten tribes was now at hand. It was but two or three years after this that the king of Assyria laid siege to Samaria, which ended in the captivity of those tribes. Yet there were some few that accepted the invitation. In the worst of times God has had a remnant; so he had here, many of Asher, Manasseh, and Zebulun (here is no mention of any out of Ephraim, though some of that tribe are mentioned, *v.* 18), *humbled themselves, and came to Jerusalem.*

2. A command was given to the men of Judah to attend this solemnity; and they universally obeyed it, *v.* 12. They did it with one heart, were all of a mind in it, and *the hand of God gave* them that *one heart.*

Verses 13–20

The time appointed for the passover having arrived, a very great congregation came together upon the occasion, *v.* 13.

I. The preparation they made for the passover,

and good preparation it was: *They took away* all *the* idolatrous *altars* that were found, not only in the temple, but *in Jerusalem*, v. 14. The best preparation we can make for the gospel passover is to cast away our iniquities, our spiritual idolatries.

II. The celebration of the passover. In this the people were so forward and zealous that the priests and Levites blushed to see them more ready to bring sacrifices than they were to offer them. This put them upon sanctifying themselves (v. 15).

III. The irregularities they were guilty of in this solemnity. 1. The *Levites killed the passover*, which should have been done by the priests only, v. 17. 2. Many were permitted to eat the passover who were not purified according to the strictness of the law, v. 18. Grotius observes from this that ritual institutions must give way, not only to a public necessity, but to a public benefit and advantage.

IV. Hezekiah's prayer to God for the forgiveness of this irregularity.

1. A short prayer, but to the purpose: *The good Lord pardon every one* in the congregation that has *prepared his heart* to those services, though the ceremonial preparation be wanting. For *this* is the *one thing needful*, that we *seek God*, his favour, his honour, and that we set our hearts to do it. Where this sincerity and fixedness of heart are there may still be many defects and infirmities. These defects need pardoning healing grace; for omissions in duty are sins as well as omissions of duty. The way to obtain pardon for our deficiencies in duty is to seek it of God by prayer.

2. A successful prayer: *The Lord hearkened to Hezekiah* and, in answer to his prayer, *healed the people* (v. 20), not only did not lay their sin to their charge, but graciously accepted their services, for healing denotes not only forgiveness (Isa. vi. 10; Ps. ciii. 3), but comfort and peace, Isa. lvii. 18; Mal. iv. 2.

Verses 21–27

After the passover followed the feast of unleavened bread, which continued seven days. 1. Abundance of sacrifices were offered to God in peace-offerings, by which they both acknowledged and implored the favour of God. 2. Many good prayers were put up to God with the peace-offerings, v. 22. They *made confession to the Lord God of their fathers*, in which the intent and meaning of the peace-offerings were directed and explained. 3. There was a great deal of good preaching. The Levites (whose office it was, Deut. xxxiii. 10) *taught the people the good knowledge of the Lord.* Hezekiah did not himself preach, but he *spoke comfortably to the Levites* that did, attended their preaching, commended their diligence, and assured them of his protection and countenance. 4. They sang psalms every day (v. 21): *The Levites and priests praised the Lord day by day.* 5. Having kept the seven days of the feast in this religious manner they had so much comfort in the service that they *kept other seven days*, v. 23. The case was extraordinary: they had been long without the ordinance; guilt had been contracted by the neglect of it; they had now got a very great congregation together, and were in a devout serious frame; they knew not when they might have such another opportunity, and therefore could not now find in their hearts to separate till they had doubled the time. How unlike those who snuffed at God's service, and said, *What a weariness is it!* Or those who asked, *When will the sabbath be gone?* 6. All this they did *with gladness* (v. 23); they all rejoiced, and particularly *the strangers*, v. 25. *So there was great joy in Jerusalem*, v. 26. Never was the like since the dedication of the temple in Solomon's time. 7. The congregation was at length dismissed with a solemn blessing, v. 27. (1) The

priests pronounced it; for it was part of their office to *bless the people* (Num. vi. 22, 23), in which they were both the people's mouth to God by way of prayer and God's mouth to the people by way of promise; for their blessing included both. What a comfort is it to a congregation to be sent home thus crowned! (2) God said *Amen* to it. The prayer that comes up to heaven will come down again to this earth in showers of blessings.

Chapter 31

A further account of that blessed reformation of which Hezekiah was a glorious instrument, and of the happy advances he made in it. I. All the remnants of idolatry were destroyed and abolished, ver. 1. II. The priests and Levites were set to work again, every man in his place, ver. 2. III. Care was taken for their maintenance. 1. The royal bounty to the clergy, and for the support of the temple service, was duly paid, ver. 3. 2. Orders were given for the raising of the people's quota, ver. 4. 3. The people, thereupon, brought in their dues abundantly, ver. 5–10. 4. Commissioners were appointed for the due distribution of what was brought in, ver. 11–19. Lastly, The general praise of Hezekiah's sincerity in all his undertakings, ver. 20, 21.

Verses 1–10

An account of what was done after the passover. What was wanting in the solemnities of preparation for it before was made up in that which is better, a due improvement of it after

I. They applied themselves with vigour to destroy all the monuments of idolatry, v. 1. This was done immediately after the passover. If our hearts have been made to burn within us at an ordinance, that spirit of burning will consume the dross of corruption. Hoshea king of Israel not forbidding it, their zeal carried them out to the destruction of idolatry even in many parts of his kingdom. At least those that came out of Ephraim and Manasseh to keep the passover (as many did, ch. xxx. 18) destroyed all their own images and groves, and did the like for many more. 2. They destroyed all: though ever so ancient, ever so costly, ever so beautiful, and ever so well patronised, yet they must all be destroyed.

II. Hezekiah revived and restored the courses of the priests and Levites, which David had appointed and which had of late been put out of course, v. 2. And all this in the *gates* or *courts* of *the tents of the Lord.* The temple is here called a tent because the temple privileges are movable things and this temple was shortly to be removed.

III. He appropriated a branch of the revenue of his crown to the maintenance and support of the altar. It was a generous act of piety, wherein he consulted both God's honour and his people's ease, as a faithful servant to him and a tender father to them.

IV. He issued out an order to the inhabitants of Jerusalem first, v. 4, but afterwards extended to the *cities of Judah*, that they should carefully pay in their dues, according to the law, to the priests and Levites.

V. The people thereupon brought in their tithes very readily. What the priests had occasion for, for themselves and their families, they made use of, and the overplus was *laid in heaps*, v. 6. All harvest-time they were increasing these heaps, as the fruits of the earth were gathered in; for God was to have his dues out of them all. When harvest ended they finished their heaps, v. 7. Hezekiah *questioned the priests and Levites* concerning them, why they did not use what was paid in, but hoarded it up thus (v. 9), to which it was answered that they had made use of all they had occasion for, for the maintenance of themselves and their families and for their winter store, and that this was that which was left over and above, v. 10. They did not hoard these heaps for covetousness, but to show what plentiful provision God had made for them. See the acknowledgment which the king and princes made of it, *v.* 8. They gave thanks to God for his good providence, which gave them something to bring, and his good grace, which gave them hearts to bring it.

Verses 11–21

I. Two particular instances of the care of Hezekiah concerning church matters. The tithes and other holy things being brought in, he provided, 1. That they should be carefully laid up, and not left exposed in loose heaps, liable to be wasted and embezzled. He ordered chambers to be made ready in some of the courts of the temple for store-chambers (*v.* 11), and into them the offerings were brought. 2. That they should be faithfully laid out, according to the uses they were intended for. Church treasures are not to be hoarded any longer than till there is occasion for them. Out of the offerings of the Lord distribution was made, (1) To the priests in the cities (*v.* 15), who stayed at home while their brethren went to Jerusalem, and did good there in *teaching the good knowledge of the Lord.* (2) To those that *entered into the house of the Lord*, all the *males from three years old and upwards*; for the male children even at that tender age, were allowed to come into the temple with their parents, and shared with them in this distribution, *v.* 16. (3) Even the Levites from twenty years old and upwards had their share, *v.* 17. (4) The wives and children of the priests and Levites had a comfortable maintenance out of those offerings, *v.* 18. In maintaining ministers, regard must be had to their families.

II. A general character of Hezekiah's services for the support of religion, *v.* 20, 21. 1. His pious zeal reached to all the parts of his kingdom: *Thus he did throughout all Judah.* 2. He sincerely designed to please God, and approved himself to him in all he did: *He wrought that which was good before the Lord his God.*

CHAPTER 32

This chapter concludes the history of the reign of Hezekiah. I. The descent which Sennacherib made upon him, and the care he took to fortify himself, his city, and the minds of his people against that enemy, ver. 1–8. II. The insolent blasphemous letters and messages which Sennacherib sent him, ver. 9–19. III. The real answer God gave to Sennacherib's blasphemies, and to Hezekiah's prayers, in the total rout of the Assyrian army, to the shame of Sennacherib and the honour of Hezekiah, ver. 20–23. IV. Hezekiah's sickness and his recovery from that, his sin and his recovery from that, with the honours that attended him living and dead, ver. 24–33.

Verses 1–8

I. The formidable design of Sennacherib against Hezekiah's kingdom. Sennacherib was now, as Nebuchadnezzar was afterwards, the terror and scourge of that part of the world. He aimed to raise a boundless monarchy for himself upon the ruins of all his neighbours. His predecessor Shalmaneser had lately made himself master of the kingdom of Israel, and carried the ten tribes captives. Sennacherib thought, in like manner, to win Judah for himself. It is observable that, just about this time, Rome, a city which afterwards came to reign more than any other had done *over the kings of the earth*, was built by Romulus. Sennacherib invaded Judah immediately after the re-establishment of religion in it: *After these things he entered into Judah*, *v.* 1. Perhaps he intended to chastise Hezekiah for destroying that idolatry to which he himself was devoted. One would have expected to hear of nothing but perfect peace, and that none durst meddle with a people thus qualified for the divine favour; yet the next news we hear is that a threatening destroying army enters the country, and is ready to lay all waste. The little opposition which Sennacherib met with in entering Judah induced him to imagine that all was his own. He thought to *win all the fenced cities* (*v.* 1), and

purposed to *fight against Jerusalem*, *v.* 2. See 2 Kings xviii. 7, 13.

II. The preparation which Hezekiah made against this storm that threatened him: *He took counsel with his princes*, *v.* 3. With their advice he provided, 1. That the country should give him a cold reception, for he took care that he should find no water in it. All hands were set immediately to work to *stop up the fountains*, and *the brook that ran through the midst of the land*. Such as this is the policy commonly practised now-a-days of destroying the forage before an invading army. 2. That the city should give him a warm reception. In order to do this he repaired the wall, raised towers, and made darts and shields in abundance (*v.* 5), and appointed captains, *v.* 6.

III. The encouragement which he gave to his people to depend upon God in this distress. He gathered them together in a broad open street, and *spoke comfortably to them*, *v.* 6. With what he said he put life into his people, his captains especially, and *spoke to their heart*, as the word is. 1. He endeavoured to keep down their fears: "*Be strong and courageous*"; do not think of surrendering the city or capitulating, but resolve to hold it out to the last man. The prophet had thus encouraged them from God (Isa. x. 24): *Be not afraid of the Assyrians;* and here the king from him. 2. He endeavoured to keep up their faith, in order to the silencing and suppressing of their fears. "Sennacherib has a *multitude with him*, and yet there are *more with us than with him*; for we have God with us, and how many do you reckon him for? With our enemy is an arm of flesh, which he trusts to; but *with us is the Lord*, whose power is irresistible, our God, whose promise, is inviolable, a God in covenant with us, *to help us, and to fight our battles.*" God will raise us above the prevailing fear of man. He that *feareth the fury of the oppressor forgetteth the Lord his Maker*, Isa. li. 12, 13. It is probable that Hezekiah said more concerning the presence of God with them and his power to relieve them. Let the good subjects and soldiers of Jesus Christ rest thus upon his word, and boldly say, *Since God is for us, who can be against us?*

Verses 9–23

This story of the rage and blasphemy of Sennacherib, Hezekiah's prayer, and the deliverance of Jerusalem by the destruction of the Assyrian army, we had more at large in the book of Kings, 2 Kings xviii and xix.

I. Sennacherib has his hands full in besieging Lachish (*v.* 9), but hears that Hezekiah is fortifying Jerusalem and encouraging his people to stand it out; and therefore, before he come in person to besiege it, he sends messengers, and writes letters to frighten Hezekiah and his people into a surrender of the city. He did not treat with Hezekiah as a man of honour, nor propose fair terms to him, but used mean and base artifices, to terrify the common people and persuade them to desert him. He represented Hezekiah as one who designed to betray them *to famine and thirst* (*v.* 11), as one who had exposed them already to the divine displeasure by taking away the high places and altars (*v.* 12). This proud blasphemer compared the great Jehovah, the Maker of heaven and earth, with the dunghill gods of the nations, the work of men's hands, and thought him no more able to deliver his worshippers than they were to deliver theirs (*v.* 19), as if an infinite and eternal Spirit had no more wisdom and power than a stone or the stock of a tree. He boasted of his triumphs over the gods of the nations, that they could none of them protect their people (*v.* 13–15), and thence inferred as if he were inferior to them all, *How much less shall your God deliver you?* All this was intended to frighten the people from their hope in God. Thus they hoped to take the city by weakening the hands of those that should defend it. Satan, in his temptations, aims to destroy our faith in God's all-sufficiency, knowing that he shall gain his point if he can do that; as we keep our ground if our *faith fail not*, Luke xxii. 32.

II. The duty is in the day of distress to pray and cry to Heaven. So Hezekiah did, and the prophet Isaiah, *v.* 20. It was a happy time when the king and the prophet joined thus in prayer.

III. The power and goodness of God. He is able both to control his enemies, be they ever so high, and to relieve his friends, be they ever so low.

1. As the blasphemies of his enemies engage him against them (Deut. xxxii. 27), so the prayers of his people engage him for them. The army of the Assyrians was cut off by the sword of an angel, which triumphed particularly in the slaughter of the mighty men of valour. The king of the Assyrians, having received this disgrace, was cut off by the sword of his own sons.

2. By this work of wonder God was glorified, as the protector of his people. Thus he saved Jerusalem, not only from the hand of Sennacherib, but from the hand *of all others*, *v.* 22; for such a deliverance as this was an earnest of much mercy in store; and he *guided them*, that is, he guarded them, on every side.

Verses 24–33

The story of Hezekiah concluded:

I. His sickness and his recovery from it, *v.* 24. The account of his sickness is but briefly mentioned here; we had a large narrative of it, 2 Kings xx. His disease seemed likely to be mortal. In the extremity of it he prayed. God answered him, and gave him a sign that he should recover, the going back of the sun ten degrees.

II. His sin and his repentance for it, which were also more largely related, 2 Kings xx. 12, &c. The occasion of it was the king of Babylon's sending an honourable embassy to him to congratulate him on his recovery. But here it is added that they came to enquire of *the wonder that was done in the land* (*v.* 31), either the destruction of the Assyrian army or the going back of the sun. The Assyrians were their enemies; they came to enquire concerning their fall, that they might triumph in it. The sun was their god; they came to enquire concerning the favour he had shown to Hezekiah, that they might honour him whom their god honoured, *v.* 31. His sin was that *his heart was lifted up*, *v.* 25. He was proud of the honour God had put upon him in so many instances, the honour his neighbours did him in bringing him presents, and now that the king of Babylon should send an embassy to him to caress and court him: this exalted him above measure. When Hezekiah had destroyed other idolatries he began to idolize himself. Though we cannot render an equivalent, or the payment of a debt, we must render the acknowledgment of a favour. His repentance for this sin: *He humbled himself for the pride of his heart.*

III. Here is the honour done to Hezekiah, while he lived. He had *exceeding much riches and honour* (*v.* 27). Among his great performances, his turning the water-course of Gihon is mentioned (*v.* 30), which was done upon occasion of Sennacherib's invasion, *v.* 3, 4. The water had come into that which is called the *old pool* (Isa. xxii. 11) and the *upper pool* (Isa. vii. 3); but he gathered the waters into a new place, for the greater convenience of the city, called the *lower pool*, Isa. xxii. 9. And, in general, he *prospered in all his works*, for they were good works. The prophet Isaiah wrote his life and reign (*v.* 132), his acts and his goodness or piety. The people *did him honour at his death* (*v.* 33), buried him in the chief of the sepulchres, made as great a burning for him as for Asa, or, which is a much greater honour, made great lamentation for him, as for Josiah.

CHAPTER 33

In this chapter we have the history, I. Of Manasseh, who reigned long. 1. His wretched apostasy from God, and revolt to idolatry and all wickedness, ver. 1–10. 2. His happy return to God in his affliction; his repentance (ver. 11–13), his reformation (ver. 15–17), and prosperity (ver. 14), with the conclusion of his reign, ver. 18–20. II. Of Amon, who reigned wickedly (ver. 21–23), and soon ended his days unhappily, ver. 24, 25.

Verses 1–10

An account of the great wickedness of Manasseh. It is the same almost word for word with that which we had, 2 Kings xxi. 1–9. This foolish young prince, in contradiction to the good example and good education his father gave him, abandoned himself to all impiety, transcribed the abominations of the heathen (*v.* 2), ruined the established religion, unravelled his father's glorious reformation (*v.* 3), profaned the house of God with his idolatry (*v.* 4, 5), dedicated his children to Moloch, and made the devil's lying oracles his guides and his counsellors, *v.* 6. We may here admire the grace of God in speaking to them, and their obstinacy in turning a deaf ear to him, that either their badness did not quite turn away his goodness, but still he waited to be gracious, or that his goodness did not turn them from their badness, but still they hated to be reformed. Corruptions in worship are such diseases of the church as it is very apt to relapse into again even when they seem to be cured. The god of this world has strangely blinded men's minds, and has a wonderful power over those that are led captive by him; else he could not draw them from God, their best friend, to depend upon their sworn enemy.

Verses 11–20

Manasseh by his wickedness undid the good that his father had done; by repentance undid the evil that he himself had done. A memorable instance it is of the riches of God's pardoning mercy and the power of his renewing grace.

I. The occasion of Manasseh's repentance was his affliction. God brought a foreign enemy upon him; the king of Babylon, that courted his father who faithfully served God, invaded him now that he had treacherously departed from God. He is here called *king of Assyria*, because he had made himself master of Assyria, which he would the more easily do for the defeat of Sennacherib's army, and its destruction before Jerusalem. The captain took *Manasseh among the thorns*, in some bush or other, perhaps in his garden, where he had hid himself. Or it is spoken figuratively: he was perplexed in his counsels and embarrassed in his affairs. He was, as we say, in the briers, and knew not which way to extricate himself, and so became an easy prey to the Assyrian captains, who no doubt plundered his house and took away what they pleased, as Isaiah had foretold, 2 Kings xx. 17, 18. What was Hezekiah's pride was their prey. They bound Manasseh, who had been held before with the cords of his own iniquity, and carried him prisoner to Babylon.

II. The expressions of his repentance (*v.* 12, 13): *When he was in affliction* he had time to bethink himself and reason enough too. 1. He was convinced that Jehovah is the only living and true God. Had he been a prince in the palace of Babylon, it is probable he would have been confirmed in his idolatry; but, being a captive in the prisons of Babylon, he was convinced of it and reclaimed from it. 2. He applied to him as *his* God now, renouncing all others, and resolving to cleave to him only, the God of his fathers, and a God in covenant with him. 3. He humbled himself greatly before him. 4. He prayed to him for the pardon of sin and the return of his favour. That is a good prayer, and very pertinent in this case, which we find among the apocryphal books, entitled, *The prayer of Manasses, king of Judah, when he was holden captive in Babylon.*

III. God's gracious acceptance of his repentance: *God was entreated of him, and heard his supplication.* Though affliction drive us to God, he will not therefore reject us if in sincerity we seek him, for afflictions are sent on purpose to bring us to him. Let not great sinners despair, when Manasseh himself, upon his repentance, found favour with God; in whom God *showed forth a pattern of longsuffering,* as 1 Tim. i. 16; Isa. i. 18.

IV. The *fruits meet for repentance* which he brought forth after his return to his own land, *v.* 15, 16. He *took away the strange gods,* the images of them, and that idol (whatever it was) which he had set up with so much solemnity *in the house of the Lord.* He returned to his duty; for he *repaired the altar of the Lord.* He sacrificed thereon peace-offerings to implore God's favour, and thank-offerings to praise him for his deliverance.

V. His prosperity, in some measure, after his repentance. When he returned to God in a way of duty, God returned to him in a way of mercy. Josephus says that all the rest of his time he was so changed for the better that he was looked upon as a very happy man.

Verses 21–25

Concerning Amon,

I. His great wickedness. He did as *Manasseh had done* in the days of his apostasy, *v.* 22. Manasseh, when he *cast out the images,* did not utterly deface and destroy them, according to the law which required Israel to *burn the images with fire,* Deut. vii. 5. How necessary that law was this instance shows; for the *carved images* being only thrown by, and not burnt, Amon knew where to find them, soon set them up, and sacrificed to them It is added, *He trespassed more and more, v.* 23. He *humbled not himself before the Lord, as his father had humbled himself.* He fell like him, but did not get up again like him. It is not so much sin as impenitence in sin that ruins men.

II. His speedy destruction. He reigned but two years and then his servants *conspired against him* and *slew him, v.* 24.

CHAPTER 34

In this chapter we have, I. A general account of Josiah's character, ver. 1, 2. II. His zeal to root out idolatry, ver. 3–7. III. His care to repair the temple, ver. 8–13. IV. The finding of the book of the law and the good use made of it, ver. 14–28. V. The public reading of the law to the people and their renewing their covenant with God thereupon, ver. 29–33. Much of this we had, 2 Kings xxii.

Verses 1–7

Josiah came to the crown when he was very young, only eight years old and he reigned *thirty-one years* (*v.* 1). In the beginning of his reign things went much as they had done in his father's time, because, being a child, he must have left the management of them to others; so that it was not till his twelfth year that the reformation began, *v.* 3. He reigned very well (*v.* 2), approved himself to God, trod in the steps of David, and did not decline either *to the right hand or to the left.* While he was young, about sixteen years old, he *began to seek after God, v.* 3. In the twelfth year of his reign, when it is probable he took the administration of the government entirely into his own hands, he *began to purge his kingdom from the remains of idolatry;* he destroyed the high places, groves, images, altars, all the utensils of idolatry, *v.* 3, 4. He not only cast them out as Manasseh did, but broke them to pieces, and made dust of them. This destruction of idolatry is here said to be in his twelfth year, but it was said (2 Kings

xxiii. 23) to be in his eighteenth year. Something was probably done towards it in his twelfth year; then he began to purge out idolatry, but that good work met with opposition, so that it was not thoroughly done till they had found the book of the law six years afterwards.

Verses 8–13

Orders are given by the king for the repair of the temple, *v.* 8. When he had purged the house of the corruptions of it he began to fit it up for the services that were to be performed in it. Those that truly love God will *love the habitation of his house.* The Levites went about the country and gathered money towards it, which was returned to the three trustees mentioned, *v.* 8. They brought it to Hilkiah the high priest (*v.* 9), and he and they put it into the hands of workmen, both overseers and labourers, *v.* 10, 11. It is observed that the workmen were industrious and honest: They *did the work faithfully* (*v.* 12). It is also intimated that the overseers were ingenious; for it is said that all those were employed to inspect this work who were skilful in *instruments of music;* not that their skill in music could be of any use in architecture, but it was an evidence that they were men of sense and ingenuity. They had need of one another, and the work needed both. Let not the overseers of the work despise the bearers of burdens, nor let those that work in the service grudge at those whose office it is to direct; but let each esteem and serve the other in love, and let God have the glory and the church the benefit of the different gifts and dispositions of both.

Verses 14–28

This whole paragraph we had, just as it is here related, 2 Kings xxii. 8–20, and have nothing to add here to what was there observed. We take occasion to bless God that we have plenty of Bibles, and that they are, or may be, in all hands,—that the book of the law and gospel is not lost, is not scarce. Bibles are jewels, but, thanks be to God, they are not rarities. Were the things contained in the scripture new to us, as they were here to Josiah, surely they would make deeper impressions upon us than commonly they do; but they are not the less weighty, and therefore should not be the less considered by us, for their being well known. We are here directed when we are under convictions of sin, and apprehensions of divine wrath, to enquire of the Lord; so Josiah did, *v.* 21. It concerns us to ask (as they did, Acts ii. 37), *Men and brethren, what shall we do?* and more particularly (as the jailor), *What must I do to be saved?* Acts xvi. 30. Blessed be God, we have the lively oracles to which to apply with these enquiries. We are here encouraged to humble ourselves before God and seek unto him, as Josiah did.

Verses 29–33

An account of the further advances which Josiah made towards the reformation of his kingdom upon the hearing of the law read and the receipt of the message God sent him by the prophetess. Happy the people that had such a king. They were well taught. He did not go about to force them to do their duty, till he had first instructed them in it. He called all the people together, great and small, young and old, rich and poor, high and low. *He that hath ears to hear, let him hear* the words of *the book of the covenant.* The king himself read the book to the people (*v.* 30). The articles of agreement between God and Israel being read, that they might intelligently covenant with God, both king and people with great solemnity did as it were subscribe the articles. He caused *all that were present to stand to it* (*v.* 32), and made them all *to serve, even to serve the Lord their God* (*v.* 33). *All his days they departed not from following the Lord;* he kept them, with much ado, from running into idolatry again. *All his days* were days of restraint upon them; but this intimated that there was in them a *bent to backslide*, a strong inclination to idolatry. Josiah was sincere in what he did, but the generality of the people were averse to it and hankered after their idols still. This God saw, and therefore from that time, when one would have thought the foundations had been laid for a perpetual security and peace, from that very time did the decree go forth for their destruction.

CHAPTER 35

I. To the temple, where we see Josiah's religious care for the due observance of the ordinance of the passover, according to the law, ver. 1-19. II. To the field of battle, where we see his rashness in engaging with the king of Egypt, and how dearly it cost him, ver. 20-23. III. To the grave, where we see him bitterly lamented, ver. 24-27.

Verses 1-19

The destruction which Josiah made of idols and idolatry was more largely related in the *Kings*, and but just mentioned here in the foregoing chapter (*v.* 33); but his solemnizing the passover, which was touched upon there (2 Kings xxiii. 21), is very particularly related here. Many were the feasts of the Lord, appointed by the ceremonial law, but the passover was the chief. In the celebration of it Hezekiah and Josiah, those two great reformers, revived religion in their day. The ordinance of the Lord's supper resembles the passover; and the due observance of that ordinance is an instance and means both of the growing purity and beauty of churches and of the growing piety and devotion of particular Christians.

In the account we had of Hezekiah's passover the great zeal of the people was observable, and the transport of devout affection that they were in; but little of the same spirit appears here. It was more in compliance with the king that they all kept the passover (*v.* 17, 18) than from any great inclination they had to it themselves. Some pride they took in this form of godliness, but little pleasure in the power of it.

I. The king exhorted and directed, quickened and encouraged, the priests and Levites to do their office in this solemnity. Let us see how this good king managed his clergy upon this occasion. 1. He reduced them to the office they were appointed to by the law of Moses (*v.* 6) and the order they were put into by David and Solomon, *v.* 4. 2. He ordered the ark to be put in its place. 3. He charged them to *serve God and his people Israel*, *v.* 3. 4. He charged them to *sanctify themselves*, and *prepare their brethren*, *v.* 6. Ministers' work must begin at home. But it must not end there; they must do what they can to *prepare their brethren* by admonishing, instructing, exhorting, quickening, and comforting them. 5. He *encouraged them to the service*, *v.* 2. He spoke comfortably to them, as Hezekiah did, *ch.* xxx. 22.

II. The king and the princes, influenced by his example, gave liberally for the bearing of the charges of this passover. Josiah, at his own proper cost, furnished the congregation with paschal lambs, and other sacrifices, to be offered during the seven days of the feast. The chief of the priests contributed towards the priests' charges, as Josiah did towards the people's.

III. The priests and Levites performed their office very readily, *v.* 10. The priests and Levites took care to honour God by *eating of the passover* themselves, *v.* 14.

IV. The singers expressed the joy of the congregation, and the porters at the gates took care that there should be no breaking in of anything to defile or disquiet the assembly, nor going out of any from it, that none should steal away till the service was done.

V. The whole solemnity was performed according to the law (*v.* 16, 17), there was none like it since Samuel's time (*v.* 18).

Verses 20-27

It was thirteen years from Josiah's famous passover to his death. During this time things went well in his kingdom, and religion flourished. The next news we hear of Josiah is that he is cut off in the midst of his days and usefulness, before he is full forty years old. We had this sad story, 2 Kings xxiii. 29, 30.

I. Josiah was a very good prince, yet he was to be blamed for his rashness in going out to war against the king of Egypt without cause. It was bad enough, as it appeared in the *Kings*, that he meddled with strife which belonged not to him. But here it looks worse; for the king of Egypt sent ambassadors to him, to warn him against this enterprise, *v.* 21.

1. The king of Egypt argued with Josiah, (1) From principles of justice. If even a *righteous man* engage in an *unrighteous cause*, let him not expect to prosper. (2) From principles of religion: "*God is with me; nay, He commanded me to make haste*, and therefore, it thou retard my motions, thou meddlest with God." It cannot be that the king of Egypt only pretended this, hoping thereby to make Josiah desist, for it is said here (*v.* 22) that the words of Necho were from the mouth of God. Either by a dream, or by a strong impulse which he had reason to think was from God, or by Jeremiah or some other prophet, he had ordered him to make war upon the king of Assyria. (3) From principles of policy: "*That he destroy thee not;* it is at thy peril if thou engage against one that has not only a better army and a better cause, but God on his side."

2. Josiah, whose heart was upright with the Lord his God, in wrath to a hypocritical nation, was so far infatuated as not to hearken to these fair reasonings and desist from his enterprise. He *would not turn his face from him*, but went in person and fought the Egyptian army in the *valley of Megiddo*, *v.* 22. In this matter he walked not in the ways of David his father; for, had it been his case, he would have enquired of the Lord, *Shall I go up? Wilt thou deliver them into my hands?*

II. The people were a wicked people, yet they were to be commended for lamenting the death of Josiah as they did. All Judah and Jerusalem, that stupid senseless people, *mourned for him* (*v.* 24). Elegies were inserted in the collections of state poems; they are written in the Lamentations. It appeared, 1. That they had some respect to their good prince, and that, though they did not cordially comply with him in all his good designs, they could not but greatly honour him. 2. That they had some sense of their own danger now that he was gone. They lamented the death of him that was their defence. Many will shed tears for their troubles, but will not be prevailed upon to part with their sins.

CHAPTER 36

I. A short but sad account of the utter ruin of Judah and Jerusalem within a few years after Josiah's death. 1. The history of it in the unhappy reigns of Jehoahaz for three months (ver. 1-4), Jehoiakim (ver. 5-8) for eleven years, Jehoiachin three months (ver. 9, 10), and Zedekiah eleven years, ver. 11. The destruction was, at length, completed in the slaughter of multitudes (ver. 17), the plundering and burning of the temple and all the palaces, the desolation of the city (ver. 18, 19), and the captivity of the people that remained, ver. 20. 2. Herein sin was punished, Zedekiah's wickedness (ver. 12, 13), the idolatry the people were guilty of (ver. 14), and their abuse of God's prophets, ver. 15, 16. The word of God was herein fulfilled, ver. 21. II. The dawning of the day of their deliverance in Cyrus's proclamation, ver. 22, 23.

Verses 1-10

The destruction of Judah and Jerusalem by degrees. God gives them both time and inducement to repent and waits to be gracious. The history of these reigns was more largely recorded in the last three chapters of the second of *Kings*. 1. Jehoahaz was set up by the people (*v.* 1), but was deposed by Pharaohnecho, and carried a prisoner to Egypt, *v.* 2-4. Of this young prince we hear no more. 2. Jehoiakim was set up by the king of Egypt, and reigned eleven years. How low was Judah brought when the king of Egypt, an old enemy to their land, gave what king he pleased to the kingdom and what name he pleased to the king! *v.* 4. He made Eliakim king, and called him *Jehoiakim*, in token of his authority over him. *Jehoiakim did that which was evil* (*v.* 5), we read of the *abominations which he did* (*v.* 8). We hear no more of the king of Egypt, but the king of Babylon came up against him (*v.* 6), seized him, and bound him with a design to carry him to Babylon; but, it seems, he either suffered him to reign as his vassal, or death released the prisoner before he was carried away. However, the best and most valuable vessels of the temple were now carried away and made use of in Nebuchadnezzar's temple in Babylon (*v.* 7). As the carrying away of these vessels to Babylon began the calamity of Jerusalem, so Belshazzar's daring profanation of them there filled the measure of the iniquity of Babylon; for, when he drank wine in them to the honour of his gods, the handwriting on the wall presented him with his doom, Dan. v. 3, &c. In the reference to the book of the *Kings* concerning this Jehoiakim mention is made of *that which was found in him* (*v.* 8), which seems to be meant of the treachery that was found in him towards the king of Babylon; but some of the Jewish writers understand it of certain private marks or signatures found in his dead body, in honour of his idol, such cuttings as God had forbidden, Lev. xix. 28. 3. Jehoiachin, or Jeconiah, the son of Jehoiakim, attempted to reign in his stead, and reigned long enough to show his evil inclination; but, after three months and ten days, the king of Babylon sent and fetched him away captive, with more of the goodly vessels of the temple.

Verses 11–21

An account of the destruction of the kingdom of Judah and the city of Jerusalem by the Chaldeans. Abraham, God's friend, was called out of that country, from Ur of the Chaldees, when God took him into covenant and communion with himself; and now his degenerate seed were carried into that country again, to signify that they had forfeited all that kindness wherewith they had been regarded for the father's sake.

I. The sins that brought this desolation.

1. Zedekiah, the king in whose days it came, brought it upon himself by his own folly. (1) If he had but made God his friend, that would have prevented the ruin. Jeremiah brought him messages from God, but it is here charged upon him that he *humbled not himself before Jeremiah*, *v.* 12. Because he would not thus make himself a servant to God, he was made a slave to his enemies. (2) If he had but been true to his covenant with the king of Babylon, that would have prevented his ruin; but he *rebelled against him*, though he had sworn to be his faithful tributary, *v.* 13. It was this that provoked the king of Babylon to deal so severely with him as he did. The thing that ruined Zedekiah was not only that he *turned not to the Lord God of Israel*, but that he *stiffened his neck and hardened his heart from turning to him*, and so, in effect, he *would not be healed*, he *would not live*.

2. The great sin that brought this destruction was idolatry. The priests, the chief of the priests, who should have opposed idolatry, were ring-leaders in it.

3. The great aggravation of their sin was the abuse they gave to God's prophets, who were sent to call them to repentance, *v.* 15, 16. (1) God's tender compassion towards them in sending prophets to them. The reason given why God by his prophets did thus strive with them is because *he had compassion on his people and on his dwelling-place*, and would by

these means have prevented their ruin. The methods God takes to reclaim sinners by his word, by ministers, by conscience, by providences, are all instances of his compassion towards them and his unwillingness *that any should perish*. (2) *They mocked the messengers of God, despised his word* in their mouths, and *misused the prophets*, treating them as their enemies. The ill usage they gave Jeremiah who lived at this time, and which we read much of in the book of his prophecy, is an instance of this. This brought wrath upon them without remedy, for it was sinning against the remedy. Nothing is more provoking to God than abuses given to his faithful ministers; for what is done against them he takes as done against himself. *Saul, Saul, why persecutest thou me?* Persecution was the sin that brought upon Jerusalem its final destruction by the Romans. See Matt. xxiii. 34–37.

II. The desolation itself, and some few of the particulars of it, which we had more largely, 2 Kings xxv. 1. Multitudes were put to the sword, even *in the house of their sanctuary* (*v.* 17), whither they fled for refuge, hoping that the holiness of the place would be their protection. The Chaldeans not only paid no reverence to the sanctuary, but showed no natural pity either to the tender sex or to venerable age. 2. All the remaining vessels of the temple, great and small, and all the treasures, sacred and secular, the treasures of God's house and of the king and his princes, were seized, and brought to Babylon, *v.* 18. 3. The temple was burnt, the walls of Jerusalem were demolished, the houses (called here the *palaces*, as Ps. xlviii. 3, so stately, rich, and sumptuous were they) laid in ashes, and all the furniture, called here *the goodly vessels thereof*, destroyed, *v.* 19. 4. The remainder of the people that escaped the sword were carried captives to Babylon (*v.* 20), impoverished, enslaved, insulted, and exposed to all the miseries of a strange and barbarous land. Now they sat down by the rivers of Babylon, with the streams of which they mingled their tears, Ps. cxxxvii. 1. And though there, it should seem, they were cured of idolatry, yet, as appears by the prophet Ezekiel, they were not cured of mocking the prophets. 5. The land lay desolate while they were captives in Babylon, *v.* 21. Now this may be considered, (1) As the just punishment of their former abuse of it. They had served Baal with its fruits; *cursed* therefore *is the ground for their sakes*. Now the land *enjoyed her sabbaths* (*v.* 21); as God had threatened by Moses, Lev. xxvi. 34. (2) Yet we may consider it as giving some encouragement to their hopes that they should, in due time, return to it again. Had others come and taken possession of it, they might have despaired of ever recovering it; but, while it lay desolate, it did, as it were, lie waiting for them again.

Verses 22–23

These last two verses of this book have a double aspect. 1. They look back to the prophecy of Jeremiah, and show how that was accomplished, *v.* 22. God had, by him, promised the restoring of the captives and the rebuilding of Jerusalem, at the end of seventy years; and that time to favour Sion, that set time, came at last. After a long and dark night the day-spring from on high visited them. 2. They look forward to the history of Ezra, which begins with the repetition of these last two verses. They are there the introduction to a pleasant story; here they are the conclusion of a very melancholy one; and so we learn from them that, though God's church be cast down, it is not cast off, though his people be corrected, they are not abandoned, though thrown into the furnace, yet not lost there, nor left there any longer than till the dross be separated. It may be long, but the vision is for an appointed time, and at the end it shall speak and not lie; therefore, though it tarry, wait for it.

THE BOOK OF EZRA

The history of this book is the accomplishment of Jeremiah's prophecy concerning the return of the Jews out of Babylon at the end of seventy years, and a type of the accomplishment of the prophecies of the Apocalypse concerning the deliverance of the gospel church out of the New Testament Babylon. Ezra preserved the records of that great revolution and transmitted them to the church in this book. His name signifies a helper; and so he was to that people. A particular account concerning him we shall meet with, *ch.* vii., where he himself enters upon the stage of action. The book gives us an account, I. Of the Jews' return out of their captivity, *ch.* i., ii. II. Of the building of the temple, the opposition it met with, and yet the perfecting of it at last, *ch.* iii.–vi. III. Of Ezra's coming to Jerusalem, *ch.* vii., viii. IV. Of the good service he did there, in obliging those that had married strange wives to put them away, *ch.* ix., x.

CHAPTER 1

I. The proclamation which Cyrus, king of Persia, issued for the release of all the Jews that he found captives in Babylon, and the building of their temple in Jerusalem, ver. 1–4. II. The return of many, ver. 5, 6. III. Orders given for the restoring of the vessels of the temple, ver. 7–11. And this is the dawning of the day of deliverance.

Verses 1–4

1. What was the state of the captive Jews in Babylon. They were under the power of those that hated them, had nothing they could call their own; no temple, no altar; if they sang psalms, their enemies ridiculed them; and yet they had prophets among them. Some of them were preferred at court, others had comfortable settlements in the country, and they were all borne up with hope that, in due time, they should return to their own land again, in expectation of which they preserved among them the distinction of their families, the knowledge of their religion, and an aversion to idolatry. 2. What was the state of the government under which they were. Nebuchadnezzar carried many of them into captivity in the first year of his reign, which was the fourth of Jehoiakim; he reigned forty-five years, his son Evil-merodach twenty-three, and his grandson Belshazzar three years, which make up the seventy years. It is charged upon Nebuchadnezzar that he *opened not the house of his prisoners*, Isa. xiv. 17. And, if he had shown mercy to the poor Jews, Daniel told him it would have been the *lengthening of his tranquillity*, Dan. iv. 27. But the measure of the sins of Babylon was at length full, and then destruction was brought upon them by Darius the Mede and Cyrus the Persian, which we read of, Dan. v. Darius, being old, left the government to Cyrus, and he was employed as the instrument of the Jews' deliverance, as soon as ever he was master of the kingdom of Babylon, perhaps in a pious regard to the prophecy of Isaiah, where he was expressly named as the man that should do this for God, and for whom God would do great things (Isa. xliv. 28; xlv. 1, &c.). His name (some say) in the Persian language signifies the *sun*, for he brought light and healing to the church of God, and was an eminent type of Christ the *Sun of righteousness*.

I. *The Lord stirred up the spirit of Cyrus.* It is said of Cyrus that he knew not God, nor how to serve him; but God knew him, and how to serve himself by him, Isa. xlv. 4. God governs the world by his influence on the spirits of men, and whatever good is done at any time, it is God that stirs up the spirit to do it, puts thoughts into the mind, gives to the understanding to form a right judgment, and directs the will which way he pleases.

II. The reference it had to the prophecy of Jeremiah, by whom God had not only promised that they should return, but had fixed the time. What Cyrus now did was long since said to be the *confirming of the word of God's servants*, Isa. xliv. 26. Jeremiah, while he lived, was hated and despised; yet thus did Providence honour him long after, that a mighty monarch was influenced to act in pursuance of the word of the Lord by his mouth.

III. The date of this proclamation. It was in his first year, not the first of his reign over Persia, the kingdom he was born to, but the first of his reign over Babylon, the kingdom he had conquered.

IV. The publication of it, both by word of mouth and also in black and white: he put it in writing, that it might be the more satisfactory, and might be sent to those distant provinces where the ten tribes were scattered in Assyria and Media, 2 Kings xvii. 6.

V. The purport of this proclamation of liberty.

1. The preamble shows the causes and considerations by which he was influenced, *v.* 2. His mind was enlightened with the knowledge of *Jehovah*, the God of Israel, as the only *living and true God*, the *God of heaven*, who is the sovereign Lord and disposer of all *the kingdoms of the earth*; of him he says (*v.* 3), He is the God, God alone, God above all. He professes that he does it, (1) In gratitude to God for the favours he had bestowed upon him: *The God of heaven has given me all the kingdoms of the earth*. He means that God had given him all that was given to Nebuchadnezzar, whose dominion, Daniel says, was *to the end of the earth*, Dan. iv. 22; v. 19.

2. He gives free leave to all the Jews that were in his dominions to go up to Jerusalem, and to *build the temple of the Lord* there, *v.* 3.

3. He subjoins a brief for a collection to bear the charges of such as were poor and not able to bear their own, *v.* 4. "Whosoever remaineth, because he has not the means to bear his charges to Jerusalem, *let the men of his place help him.*" Cyrus not only gave his good wishes with those that went (*Their God be with them, v.* 3), but took care also to furnish them with such things as they needed.

Verses 5–11

I. How Cyrus's proclamation succeeded with others. 1. He having given leave to the Jews to go up to Jerusalem, many of them went up accordingly, *v.* 5. The same God that had raised up the spirit of Cyrus to proclaim this liberty raised up their spirits to take the benefit of it; for it was done, *not by might, nor by power, but by the Spirit of the Lord of hosts*, Zech. iv. 6. The temptation perhaps was strong to some of them to stay in Babylon. The discouragements of their return were many and great, the journey long, their wives and children unfit for travelling, their own land was to them a strange land, the road to it an unknown road. Go up to Jerusalem! And what should they do there? It was all in ruins, and in the midst of enemies to whom they would be an easy prey. Many were wrought upon by these considerations to stay in Babylon, at least not to go with the first. But there were some that got over these difficulties, and they were those whose spirits God raised. He, by his Spirit and grace, filled them with a generous ambition of liberty, a gracious affection to their own land, and a desire of the free and public exercise of their religion. The call and offer of the gospel are like Cyrus's proclamation. *Deliverance is preached to the captives*, Luke iv. 18. Those that are bound under the unrighteous dominion of sin, and bound over to the righteous judgment of God, may be made free by Jesus Christ. Whoever will, by repentance and faith, return to God, Jesus Christ has opened the way for him, and let him go up out of the slavery of sin into the *glorious liberty of the children of God*. The offer is general to all. Christ makes it, in pursuance of the grant which the Father has made him of *all power both in heaven and in earth* and of the charge given him to *build God a house*, to set him up a church in the world, a kingdom among men, Many that hear this joyful sound choose to sit still in Babylon, are in love with their sins and will not venture upon the difficulties of a holy life; but some there are that break through the discouragements, and resolve to *build the house of God*, to make heaven of their religion, whatever it cost them. Thus will the heavenly Canaan be replenished, though many perish in Babylon; and the gospel-offer will not be made in vain. 2. Cyrus having given order that their neighbours should help them, they did so, *v.* 6. All those that were about them furnished them with plate and goods to bear the charges of their journey, and to help them in building and furnishing both their own houses and God's temple. As the tabernacle was made of the spoils of Egypt, and the first temple built by the labours of the strangers, so the second by the contributions of the Chaldeans, all intimating the admission of the Gentiles into the church in due time.

II. How this proclamation was seconded by Cyrus himself. To give proof of the sincerity of his affection to the house of God, he not only released the people of God, but restored the vessels of the temple, *v.* 7, 8.

Judah had a prince, even in captivity. Sheshbazzar, supposed to be the same with Zerubbabel, is here called *prince of Judah*; the Chaldeans called him *Sheshbazzar*, which signifies *joy in tribulation*; but among his own people he went by the name of *Zerubbabel—a stranger in Babylon*; so he looked upon himself, and considered Jerusalem his home, though, as Josephus says, he was captain of the life-guard to the king of Babylon. He took care of the affairs of the Jews. To him the sacred vessels were numbered out (*v.* 8), and he took care for their safe conveyance to Jerusalem, *v.* 11.

CHAPTER 2

A catalogue of the several families that returned, ver. 1. I. The leaders, ver. 2. II. The people, ver. 3–35. III. The priests, Levites, and retainers to the temple, ver. 36–63. IV. The sum total, with an account of their retinue, ver. 64–67. V. Their offerings to the service of the temple, ver. 68–70.

Verses 1–35

1. An account was kept in writing of the families that came up out of captivity, and the numbers of each family. This was done for their honour, as part of their recompence for their faith and courage, and their affection to their own land, and to stir up others to follow their good example. The names of all those Israelites indeed that accept the offer of deliverance by Christ shall be found, to their honour, in a more sacred record than this, even in *the Lamb's book of life*. The account that was kept of the families

that came up from the captivity was intended also for the benefit of posterity, that they might know from whom they descended and to whom they were allied. 2. They are called *children of the province*. Judah, which had been an illustrious kingdom, to which other kingdoms had been made provinces, subject to it and dependent on it, was now itself made a province, to receive laws and commissions from the king of Persia and to be accountable to him. 3. They are said to come *every one to his city*, that is, the city appointed them, in which appointment an eye, no doubt, was had to their former settlement by Joshua; and to that, as near as might be, they returned. 4. That the leaders are first mentioned, *v.* 2. Zerubbabel and Jeshua were their Moses and Aaron, the former their chief prince, the latter their chief priest. 5. Some of these several families are named from the persons that were their ancestors, others from the places in which they had formerly resided. Here are two families that are called *the children of Elam* (one *v.* 7, another *v.* 31), and, which is strange, the number of both is the same, 1,254. The children of Bethlehem (*v.* 21) were but 123, though it was David's city; for Bethlehem was *little among the thousands of Judah*, yet there must the Messiah arise, Micah v. 2. Anathoth had been a famous place in the tribe of Benjamin and yet here it numbered but 128 (*v.* 23), which is to be imputed to the divine curse which the men of Anathoth brought upon themselves by persecuting Jeremiah, who was of their city. Jer. xi. 21, 23.

Verses 36–63

An account, I. Of the priests that returned, and they were a considerable number, about a tenth part of the whole company: for the whole were above 42,000 (*v.* 64), and four families of priests made up above 4,200 (*v.* 36–39).

II. Of the Levites. The small number of them, for, taking in both the singers and the porters (*v.* 40–42), they did not make 350.

III. Of the Nethinim, the Gibeonites, *given* (so their name signifies) by Joshua first (Joshua ix. 27), and again by David (Ezra viii. 20), when Saul had expelled them, to be employed by the Levites in the work of God's house as hewers of wood and drawers of water.

IV. Of some that were looked upon as Israelites by birth, and others as priests, and yet could not make out a clear title to the honour. 1. There were some that could not prove themselves Israelites (*v.* 59, 60), a considerable number, who presumed they were of the seed of Jacob, but could not produce their pedigrees, and yet would go up to Jerusalem, having an affection to the house and people of God. 2. There were others that could not prove themselves priests, and yet were supposed to be of the seed of Aaron.

Verses 64–70

I. The sum total of the company that returned out of Babylon. The before mentioned amount not quite to 30,000 (29,818), so that there were above 12,000 who, it is probable, were of the rest of the tribes of Israel, besides Judah and Benjamin. This was more than double the number that were carried captive into Babylon by Nebuchadnezzar, so that, as in Egypt, the time of their affliction was the time of their increase.

II. Their retinue. Their servants were comparatively few (*v.* 65) and their beasts of burden about as many, *v.* 66, 67. But notice is taken of 200 *singing-men and women* whom they had among them, who were intended (as those 2 Chron. xxxv. 25) to excite *their mourning*.

III. Their oblations. It is said (*v.* 68, 69), 1. That they *came to the house of the Lord at Jerusalem*; and yet that house, that holy and beautiful house, was now in ruins. 2. That they offered freely towards the *setting of it up in its place*. That, it seems, was the first house they talked of setting up. Their offering was nothing in comparison with the offerings of the princes in David's time; then they offered by talents (1 Chron. xxix. 7), now by drams, yet these drams, being after their ability, were as acceptable to God as those talents, like the widow's two mites. 3. That they *dwelt in their cities, v.* 70. Though their cities were out of repair, yet, because they were their cities, such as God had assigned them, they were content to dwell in them. Their poverty was a bad cause, but their unity and unanimity were a good effect of it.

Chapter 3

The ground untilled, the cities in ruins, all out of order; but here we have an account of the early care they took about the re-establishment of religion among them. Thus did they lay the foundation well, and begin their work at the right end. I. They set up an altar, and offered sacrifices upon it, kept the feasts, and contributed towards the rebuilding of the temple, ver. 1-7. II. They laid the foundation of the temple with a mixture of joy and sorrow, ver. 8-13.

Verses 1-7

I. A general assembly of the returned Israelites at Jerusalem, in the *seventh month, v.* 1. We may suppose that they came from Babylon in the spring. The seventh month therefore soon came, in which many of the feasts of the Lord were to be solemnized. Such was their zeal for religion that they left all their business in the country, to attend God's altar; and they came *as one man.* Let worldly business be postponed to the business of religion and it will prosper the better.

II. The care which their leading men took to have an altar ready for them to attend upon.

1. Joshua and his brethren the priests, Zerubbabel and his brethren the princes, built *the altar of the God of Israel* (*v.* 2), in the same place where it had stood, *v.* 3. They could not immediately have a temple, but they would not be without an altar. Abraham, wherever he came, *built an altar;* and wherever we come, though we may perhaps want the benefit of the candlestick of preaching, and the showbread of the eucharist, yet, if we bring not the sacrifices of prayer and praise, we are wanting in our duty, for we have an altar that sanctifies the gift ever ready.

2. The reason here given why they hastened to set up the altar: *Fear was upon them, because of the people of the land.* They were in the midst of enemies that bore ill will to them and their religion. *Because* they were so, therefore they set up the altar. Apprehension of danger should stir us up to our duty. This good use we should make of our fears, we should be driven by them to our knees.

III. The sacrifices they offered upon the altar. Let not those that have an altar starve it.

1. They began *on the first day of the seventh month, v.* 6.

2. Having begun, they kept up the *continual burnt-offering* (*v.* 5), *morning and evening, v.* 3. They had known by sad experience what it was to want the comfort of the daily sacrifice to plead in their daily prayers.

3. They observed all the *set feasts of the Lord,* and offered the sacrifices appointed for each, and particularly *the feast of tabernacles, v.* 4, 5. Now that they were beginning to settle in their cities it might serve well to remind them of their fathers dwelling in tents in the wilderness.

4. They offered *every man's free-will offering, v.* 5. The law required much, but they brought more; for, though they had little wealth to support the expense of their sacrifices, they had much zeal, and, we may suppose, spared at their own tables that they might plentifully supply God's altar.

IV. The preparation they made for the building of the temple, *v.* 7. Tyre and Sidon must now, as of old, furnish them with workmen, and Lebanon with timber, orders for both which they had from Cyrus.

Verses 8-13

There was no dispute among the returned Jews whether they should build the temple or no. An account of the beginning of that good work.

I. When it was begun—as soon as ever the season of the year would permit (*v.* 8), and when they had ended the solemnities of the passover. They took little more than half a year for making preparation of the ground and materials.

II. Who began it—Zerubbabel, and Jeshua, and their brethren. Then the work of God is likely to go on well when magistrates, ministers, and people, are hearty for it.

III. They appointed the *Levites to set forward the work* (*v.* 8), and they did it by *setting forward the workmen* (*v.* 9), and strengthening their hands with good and comfortable words.

IV. How God was praised at the laying of the foundation of the temple (*v.* 10, 11); the priests with the trumpets appointed by Moses, and the Levites with the cymbals appointed by David to assist the singing of that everlasting hymn which will never be out of date, and to which our tongues should never be out of tune, *God is good, and his mercy endureth for ever.* Let all the streams of mercy be traced up to the fountain. However it be, yet *God is good to Israel* (Ps. lxxiii. 1), good to us. Let the reviving of the church's interests, when they seemed dead, be ascribed to the continuance of God's mercy for ever, for therefore the church continues.

V. How the people were affected. Different sentiments there were among the people of God, and each expressed himself according to his sentiments, and yet there was no disagreement among them. 1. Those that only knew the misery of having no temple at all praised the Lord with shouts of joy when they saw but the foundation of one laid, *v.* 11. To them even this foundation seemed great, and was as life from the dead. They shouted, so that *the noise was heard afar off.* 2. Those that remembered the glory of the first temple which Solomon built, and considered how far this was likely to be inferior to that, perhaps in dimensions, certainly in magnificence and sumptuousness, *wept with a loud voice, v.* 12. If we date the destruction of the first temple 586 B.C., and the return from Babylon 537 B.C., the foundation of the new temple was laid in 536 B.C., fifty years after the temple was burnt. So that many now alive might remember it standing. These lamented the disproportion between this temple and the former. And, (1) There was some reason for it; and if they turned their tears into the right channel, and bewailed the sin that was the cause of this melancholy change, they did well. (2) Yet it was their infirmity to mingle those tears with the common joys and so to cast a damp upon them. In the harmony of public joys, let not us be jarring strings. They were priests and Levites, who should have known and taught others how to be duly affected under various providences, and not to let the remembrance of former afflictions drown the sense of present mercies. This mixture of sorrow and joy here is a representation of this world. We can scarcely *discern the shouts of joy from the noise of the weeping.*

CHAPTER 4

The good work of rebuilding the temple was no sooner begun than it met with opposition; the Samaritans were enemies to the Jews and their religion, and they set themselves to obstruct it. I. They offered to be partners in the building of it, that they might have it in their power to retard it; but they were refused, ver. 1–3. II. They discouraged them in it, and dissuaded them from it, ver. 4, 5. III. They basely misrepresented the undertaking, and the undertakers, to the king of Persia, by a memorial they sent him, ver. 6–16. IV. They obtained from him an order to stop the building (ver. 17–22), which they immediately put in execution, ver. 23, 24.

Verses 1–5

An instance of the old enmity that was put between the seed of the woman and the seed of the serpent. God's temple cannot be built, but Satan will rage, and the *gates of hell* will *fight against it*. The gospel kingdom was, in like manner, to be set up with much struggling and contention.

I. The *children of the captivity* (v. 1) had newly come out of captivity, were born in captivity, had still the marks of their captivity upon them; though they were not now captives, they were under the control of those whose captives they had lately been. Israel was God's son, his first-born; but by their iniquity the people sold and enslaved themselves, and so became children of the captivity.

II. The opposers of the undertaking are here said to be *the adversaries of Judah and Benjamin*, not the Chaldeans or Persians, but the relics of the ten tribes, and the foreigners that had joined themselves to them, and patched up that mongrel religion we had an account of, 2 Kings xvii. 33. *They feared the Lord, and served their own gods too*. They are called *the people of the land, v. 4*.

III. The opposition they gave had in it much of the subtlety of the old serpent. When they heard that the temple was in building they were immediately aware that it would be a fatal blow to their superstition, and set themselves to oppose it.

1. They offered their service to build with the Israelites only that thereby they might get an opportunity to retard the work, while they pretended to further it. Their offer was plausible enough, and looked kind: "*We will build with you*, will help you to contrive, and will contribute towards the expense; *for we seek your God as you do*," v. 2. This was false, for, though they sought the same God, they did not seek him only, nor seek him in the way he appointed. *The chief of the fathers of Israel* were soon aware that they meant them no kindness, whatever they pretended, but really designed to do them a mischief, and therefore told them plainly, "*You have nothing to do with us*, have no part nor lot in this matter, are not true-born Israelites nor faithful worshippers of God; *you worship you know not what*, John iv. 22. You are none of those with whom we dare hold communion, and therefore we ourselves will build it."

2. When this plot failed they did what they could to divert them from the work and discourage them in it. Those that were cool and indifferent were by these artifices drawn off from the work, which wanted their help, v. 4. Wonder not at the restlessness of the church's enemies in their attempts against the building of God's temple. He whom they serve, and whose work they are doing, is *unwearied* in *walking to and fro through the earth* to do mischief.

Verses 6–16

Cyrus steadfastly adhered to the Jews' interest. His successor was Ahasuerus (v. 6), called also *Artaxerxes* (v. 7), supposed to be the same that in heathen authors is called *Cambyses*, who had never taken such cognizance of the despised Jews as to concern himself for them. To him these Samaritans applied for an order to stop the building of the temple; and they did it in the beginning of his reign, being resolved to lose no time when they thought they had a king for their purpose. See how watchful the church's enemies are to take the first opportunity of doing it a mischief; let not its friends be less careful to do it a kindness.

I. The general purport of the letter which they sent to the king, to inform him of this matter. It is called (v. 6) *an accusation against the inhabitants of Judah and Jerusalem.*

II. The persons concerned in writing this letter. The contrivers are named (v. 7) that plotted the thing, the writers (v. 8) that put it into form, and the subscribers (v. 9) that concurred in it and joined with them. The *rulers take counsel together against the Lord* and his temple. The building of the temple would do them no harm, yet they appear against it with the utmost concern and virulence, perhaps because the prophets of the God of Israel had foretold the *famishing* and *perishing* of all the *gods of the heathen*, Zeph. ii. 11; Jer. x. 11. The people concurred with them in imagining this vain thing. All the several colonies from the cities or countries of Assyria, Chaldea, Persia, &c., whence they came, set their hands, by their representatives, to this letter.

III. A copy of the letter itself, which Ezra inserts here out of the records of the kingdom of Persia.

1. They represent themselves as very loyal to the government, and greatly concerned for the honour and interest of it. *Because we are salted with the salt of the palace* (so it is in the *margin*), we have our salary from the court, and could no more live without it than flesh could be preserved without salt. Now, in consideration of this, "*it is not meet for us to see the king's dishonour*;" and therefore they urge him to stop the building of the temple.

2. They represent the Jews as disloyal, and dangerous to the government, that Jerusalem was *the rebellious and bad city* (v. 12), *hurtful to kings and provinces*, v. 15.

(1) Their history of what was past was invidious, that *within this city sedition had been moved of old time*, and, for *that cause, it was destroyed*, v. 15. There was some colour given for this suggestion by the attempts of Jehoiakim and Zedekiah to shake off the yoke of the king of Babylon. But their efforts to recover their rights would have been justifiable had they taken the right method and made their peace with God first. Though these Jews, and their princes, had been guilty of rebellion, yet it was unjust therefore to fasten this as an indelible brand upon this city. The Jews, in their captivity, had given such specimens of good behaviour as were sufficient, with any reasonable men, to roll away that one reproach.

(2) Their information concerning what was now doing was grossly false in matter of fact. Very careful they were to inform the king that the Jews had *set up the walls of this city*. They had only begun to build the temple, which Cyrus commanded them to do, but, as for the walls, there was nothing done nor designed towards the repair of them, as appears by the condition they were in many years after (Neh. i. 3), all in ruins.

(3) Their prognostics of the consequences were altogether groundless and absurd. They were very confident that if this city should be built, not only the Jews would *pay no toll, tribute, or custom* (v. 13), but that all the countries on this side Euphrates would instantly revolt, drawn in to do so by their example; and, if the prince in possession should connive at this, he would wrong, not only himself, but his successors: *Thou shalt endamage the revenue of the kings*. See how every line in this letter

breathes both the subtlety and malice of the old serpent.

Verses 17–24

I. The orders which the king of Persia gave, in answer to the information sent him by the Samaritans against the Jews. He suffered himself to be imposed upon by their falsehood, but was very willing to gratify them with an order to stay proceedings. He consulted the records concerning Jerusalem, and found that it had indeed rebelled against the king of Babylon, and therefore that it was, as they called it, a *bad city* (*v.* 19), and that in times past kings had reigned there, to whom all the countries on that side the river had been tributaries (*v.* 20). He appointed these Samaritans to stop the building of the city immediately, *v.* 21, 22. Neither they, in their letter, nor he, in his order, make any mention of the temple, and the building of that, because both they and he knew that they had a command from Cyrus to rebuild that. They spoke only of the *city*: "Let not *that* be built," that is, as a city with walls and gates.

II. The use which the enemies of the Jews made of these orders, so fraudulently obtained. The order was only to prevent the walling of the *city*, but, having force and power on their side, they construed it as relating to the *temple*, for it was that to which they had an ill will. The consequence was that *the work of the house of God ceased* for a time, through the power and insolence of its enemies.

Chapter 5

The temple-work at a full stop; but, being God's work, it shall be revived, and here we have an account of the reviving of it. The blessed Spirit, I. Warmed its cool-hearted friends, and excited them to build, ver. 1, 2. II. Cooled its hot-headed enemies, and brought them to better tempers; for, though they secretly disliked the work as much as those in the foregoing chapter, yet, 1. They were more mild towards the builders, ver. 3–5. 2. They were more fair in their representation of the matter to the king, of which we have here an account, ver. 6–17.

Verses 1–2

During this time they had an altar and a tabernacle. But the counsellors that were hired to hinder the work (*ch.* iv. 5) told them that the time had not come for the building of the temple (Hag. i. 2), urging that it was long ere the time came for the building of Solomon's temple; and thus the people were made easy in their own *ceiled houses*, while *God's house lay waste*.

I. They had two good ministers, who, in God's name, earnestly persuaded them to put the wheel of business in motion again. Haggai and Zechariah both began to prophesy in the second year of Darius, as appears, Hag. i. 1; Zech. i. 1. The temple of God among men is to be built not by secular force but by *the word of God*. As the *weapons of our warfare*, so the instruments of our building *are not carnal*, but *spiritual*. It is the business of God's prophets to stir up God's people to that which is good, and to help them in it, to strengthen their hands, and, by suitable considerations fetched from the word of God, to quicken them to their duty and encourage them in it. They prophesied in the name, or (as some read it) *in the cause*, or for the sake, *of the God of Israel*; they spoke by commission from him, and argued from his authority.

II. They had two good magistrates, who were forward and active in this work. Zerubbabel their chief prince, and Jeshua their chief priest, *v.* 2. These great men thought it no disparagement to them, but a happiness, to be taught and prescribed to by the prophets of the Lord, and were glad of their help in reviving this good work. Read the first chapter of the prophecy of Haggai here (for that is the best comment on these two verses) and see what great

things God does by his word, which he magnifies above all his name, and by his Spirit working with it.

Verses 3–17

I. The cognizance which their neighbours soon took of the reviving of this good work. No sooner did the Spirit of God stir up the friends of the temple to appear for it than the evil spirit stirred up its enemies to appear against it. While the people built and ceiled their own houses their enemies gave them no molestation (Hag. i. 4), but when they fell to work again at the temple then the alarm was taken, and all heads were at work to hinder them, *v.* 3, 4. The adversaries are here named: *Tatnai* and *Shethar-boznai*. These, though real enemies to the building of the temple, made some conscience of telling truth. If *all men have not faith* (2 Thess. iii. 2), it is well some have, and a sense of honour. The church's enemies are not all equally wicked and unreasonable.

II. The care which the divine Providence took of this good work (*v.* 5): *The eye of their God was upon the elders of the Jews*, who were active in the work, so that their enemies could not cause them to cease, as they would have done, till the matter came to Darius. They desired they would only cease till they had instructions from the king about it. But they would not so much as yield them that, for *the eye of God was upon them*, even their God. The elders of the Jews saw *the eye of God upon them*, to observe what they did and own them in what they did well, and then they had courage enough to face their enemies and to go on vigorously with their work, notwithstanding all the opposition they met with.

III. The account they sent to the king of this matter.

1. How fully the elders of the Jews gave the Samaritans an account of their proceedings. They put these questions to them:—"By what authority do you do these things, and who gave you that authority?" To this they answered: "*We are the servants of the God of heaven and earth*. The God we worship is not a local deity, and therefore we cannot be charged with making a faction, or setting up a sect, in building this temple, to his honour: but we pay our homage to a God on whom the whole creation depends, and therefore ought to be protected and assisted by all and hindered by none. . . . It was to punish us for our sins that we were, for a time, put out of the possession of this house; not because the gods of the nations had prevailed against our God, but because we had provoked him (*v.* 12), for which he delivered us and our temple into the hands of the king of Babylon. We have the royal decree of Cyrus to justify us."

This is the account they give of their proceedings, not asking what authority they had to examine them, nor upbraiding them with their idolatry, and superstitions, and medley religion. Let us learn hence with meekness and fear to *give a reason of the hope that is in us* (1 Peter iii. 15), rightly to understand, and then readily to declare, what we do in God's service and why we do it.

2. How fairly the Samaritans represented this to the king. They called the temple at Jerusalem the *house of the great God* (*v.* 8); for though the Samaritans had yet gods many and lords many, they owned the God of Israel to be the *great God*, who is above all gods. They told him truly what was done, not stating, as their predecessors did, that they were fortifying the city as if they intended war, but only that they were rearing the temple as those that intended worship, *v.* 8. God's people could not be persecuted if they were not belied, could not be baited if they were not dressed up in bears' skins. Let but the cause of God and truth be fairly stated, and fairly heard, and it will keep its ground.

CHAPTER 6

How solemnly the foundation of the temple was laid, ch. iii. How slowly the building went on, and with how much difficulty, ch. iv and v. But how gloriously the topstone was at length brought forth with shoutings in this chapter. As for God, his work is perfect; it may be slow work, but it will be sure work. We have here, I. A recital of the decree of Cyrus for the building of the temple, ver. 1–5. II. The enforcing of that decree by a new order from Darius for the perfecting of that work, ver. 6–12. III. The finishing of it, ver. 13–15. IV. The solemn dedication of it when it was built (ver. 16–18), and the handselling of it with the celebration of the passover, ver. 19–22.

Verses 1–12

I. The decree of Cyrus for the building of the temple repeated. Search was ordered to be made for it among the records. It was looked for in Babylon (v. 1). But it was not found there. At length it was found at Achmetha, in the province of the Medes, v. 2. It is here inserted, v. 3–5. 1. Here is a warrant for the building of the temple: *Let the house of God at Jerusalem*, yea, *let that house be built* within such and such dimensions, and with such and such materials. 2. A warrant for the taking of the expenses of the building out of the king's revenue, v. 4. We do not find that they had received what was here ordered them, the face of things at court being changed. 3. A warrant for the restoring of the vessels and utensils of the temple, which Nebuchadnezzar had taken away (v. 5), with an order that the priests, the Lord's ministers, should return them all to their places in the house of God.

II. The confirmation of it by a decree of Darius, grounded upon it and in pursuance of it.

1. The decree of Darius is very explicit and satisfactory.

(1) He forbids his officers to do anything in opposition to the building of the temple. The manner of expression intimates that he knew they had a mind to hinder it: *Be you far hence* (v. 6); *let the work of this house of God alone*, v. 7.

(2) He orders them out of his own revenue to assist the builders with money. I. For carrying on the building, v. 8. Herein he pursues the example of Cyrus, v. 4. II. For maintaining the sacrifices there when it was built, v. 9. See here how he gives honour, *First*, To Israel's God, whom he calls once and again the *God of heaven. Secondly*, To his ministers, in ordering his commissioners to give out supplies for the temple service at the appointment of the priests. *Thirdly*, To prayer: *That they may pray for the life of the king.* · (3) He enforces his decree with a penalty (v. 11). (4) He entails a divine curse upon all those kings and people that should ever have any hand in the destruction of this house, v. 12.

2. The heart of kings is in the hand of God, and he turns it which way soever he pleases; what they are he makes them to be, for he is *King of kings*. When God's time has come for the accomplishing of his gracious purposes concerning his church he will raise up instruments to promote them from whom such good service was not expected. *The earth sometimes helps the woman* (Rev. xii. 16), and those are made use of for the defence of religion, who have little religion themselves. The enemies of the Jews, in appealing to Darius, hoped to get an order to suppress them, but, instead of that, they got an order to supply them.

Verses 13–22

I. The Jews' enemies made their friends. When they received this order from the king they came with as much haste to encourage and assist the work as their predecessors had done to put a stop to it, ch. iv. 23.

II. The building of the temple carried on, and finished in a little time, v. 14, 15. Now the *elders of*

the Jews built with cheerfulness. They found themselves bound to it *by the commandment of the God of Israel.* They found themselves shamed into it by the commandment of the heathen kings, Cyrus formerly, Darius now, and Artaxerxes some time after. They found themselves encouraged in it by the prophesying of Haggai and Zechariah. And now the work went on so prosperously that, in four years' time, it was brought to perfection. The gospel church, that spiritual temple, is long in the building, but it will be finished at last, when the mystical body is completed. Every believer is a *living temple, building up himself in his most holy faith.* Much opposition is given to this work by Satan and our own corruptions. We trifle, and proceed in it with many stops and pauses; but he that has *begun the good work* will see it performed, and will *bring forth judgment unto victory.*

III. The dedication of the temple. When it was built, being designed only for sacred uses, *they showed by an example how it should be used*, which (says Bishop Patrick) is the proper sense of the word *dedicate.* They entered upon it with solemnity and probably with a public declaration of the separating of it from common uses and the surrender of it to the honour of God, to be employed in his worship. 1. The persons employed in this service were not only *the priests and Levites* who officiated, but *the children of Israel*, some of each of the *twelve tribes*, though Judah and Benjamin were the chief, and *the rest of the children of the captivity.* 2. The sacrifices that were offered upon this occasion were *bullocks, rams, and lambs* (v. 17), for burnt-offerings and peace-offerings; not to be compared, in number, with what had been offered at the dedication of Solomon's temple, but, being according to their present ability, they were accepted. These hundreds were more to them than Solomon's thousands were to him. 3. This service was performed with joy. 4. When they dedicated the house they settled the household. Though the temple service could not now be performed with so much pomp and plenty as formerly, because of their poverty, yet perhaps it was performed with as much purity and close adherence to the divine institution as ever, which was the true glory of it. No beauty like the beauty of holiness.

IV. The celebration of the passover in the newly-erected temple. Now that they were newly delivered out of their bondage in Babylon it was seasonable to commemorate their deliverance out of their bondage in Egypt. Fresh mercies should put us in mind of former mercies. Now they made a joyful festival of it, it falling out in the next month after the temple was finished and dedicated, v. 19. Notice is here taken, 1. Of the purity of the priests and Levites that *killed the passover*, v. 20. They joined together in their preparations, that they might help one another, so that all of them were pure, to a man. The purity of ministers adds much to the beauty of their ministrations; so does their unity. 2. Of the proselytes that communicated with them in this ordinance: *All such as had separated themselves unto them*, had left their country and the superstitions of it and cast in their lot with the Israel of God, and had *turned from the filthiness of the heathen of the land*, both their idolatries and immoralities, *to seek the Lord God of Israel* as their God, did eat the passover. 3. Of the great pleasure and satisfaction wherewith they *kept the feast of unleavened bread*, v. 22. *The Lord had made them joyful*, had given them both cause to rejoice and hearts to rejoice.

CHAPTER 7

Ezra's precious name at first, in the title of the book, but this chapter introduces him into public action in another reign, that of Artaxerxes. Zerubbabel and Jeshua by this time have grown old, if not gone off; nor do we hear any more of Haggai and Zechariah; they have finished their testimony. What shall become of the cause of God and Israel when these useful instruments are laid aside? Trust God, who has the residue of the Spirit, to raise up others in their room. Ezra here, and Nehemiah in the next book, are as serviceable in their days as those were in theirs. I. An account, in general, of Ezra himself, and of his expedition to Jerusalem for the public good, ver. 1–10. II. A copy of the commission which Artaxerxes gave him, ver. 11–26. III. His thankfulness to God for it, ver. 27, 28.

Verses 1–10

I. Ezra's pedigree. He was one of the sons of Aaron, a priest. Him God chose to be an instrument of good to Israel, that he might put honour upon the priesthood, the glory of which had been much eclipsed by the captivity. He is said to be *the son of Seraiah*, that Seraiah, as is supposed, whom the king of Babylon put to death when he sacked Jerusalem, 2 Kings xxv. 18, 21. If we take the shortest computation, it was seventy-five years since Seraiah died; many reckon it much longer, and, because they suppose Ezra called out in the prime of his time to public service, therefore think that Seraiah was not his immediate parent, but his grandfather or great-grandfather, 1 Chron. vi. 4, &c.

II. His character. Though of the younger house, his personal qualifications made him very eminent. 1. He was a man of great learning, a scribe, a *ready scribe, in the law of Moses, v.* 6. He was very much conversant with the scriptures, especially the writings of Moses, had the words ready and was well acquainted with the sense and meaning of them. It is to be feared that learning ran low among the Jews in Babylon; but Ezra was instrumental to revive it. The Jews say that he collected and collated all the copies of the law he could find out, and published an accurate edition of it, with all the prophetical books, historical and poetical, that were given by divine inspiration, and so made up the canon of the Old Testament, with the addition of the prophecies and histories of his own time. Now that prophecy was about to cease it was time to promote scripture-knowledge, Mal. iv. 4. 2. He was a man of great piety and holy zeal (v. 10): *He had prepared his heart to seek the law of the Lord,* &c. The Chaldeans, among whom he was born and bred, were famed for literature, especially the study of the stars, to which, being a studious man, we may suppose that Ezra was tempted to apply himself. But he got over the temptation; the law of his God was more to him than all the writings of their magicians and astrologers. He *sought the law of the Lord,* that is, he searched the scriptures, and sought the knowledge of God, of his mind and will. He set it before him as his rule. He set himself *to teach Israel the statutes and judgments* of that law. He first learned and then taught. He also first did and then taught. He *prepared his heart* to do all this, or he fixed his heart.

III. His expedition to Jerusalem for the good of his country: *He went up from Babylon* (v. 6), and, in four months' time, came to Jerusalem, v. 8. 1. How kind the king was to him. He *granted him all his request,* whatever he desired to put him into a capacity to serve his country. 2. How kind his people were to him. When he went many more went with him, because they would venture to dwell in Jerusalem when he had gone thither. 3. How kind his God was to him. He obtained this favour from his king and country by *the good hand of the Lord that was upon him,* v. 6, 9.

Verses 11–26

The commission which the Persian emperor granted to Ezra, giving him authority to act for the good of the Jews. The commission runs *Artaxerxes, King of kings.* This however is too high a title for any mortal man to assume; he was indeed king of some kings, but to speak as if he were king of all kings was to usurp *his*

prerogative who hath *all power both in heaven and in earth.* He sends greeting to his trusty and well-beloved Ezra, whom he calls a *scribe of the law of the God of heaven* (v. 12). He reckoned it more his honour to be a *scribe of God's law* than to be a peer or prince of the empire.

I. He gives Ezra leave to go up to Jerusalem, and as many of his countrymen as pleased to go up with him, v. 13.

II. He gives him authority to enquire into the affairs of Judah and Jerusalem, v. 14. The rule of his enquiry was to be *the law of his God, which was in his hand.* He must enquire whether the Jews, in their religion, had and did according to that law—whether the temple was built, the priesthood was settled, and the sacrifices were offered conformably to the divine appointment. If he found anything amiss, he must get it amended, and, like Titus in Crete, must *set in order the things that were wanting,* Titus i. 5. Thus are the Jews restored to their ancient privilege of governing themselves by that law.

III. He entrusts him with the money that was freely given by the king himself and his counsellors, and collected among his subjects, for the service of the house of God, v. 15, 16. Ezra was entrusted, (1) To receive this money and to carry it to Jerusalem. (2) To lay out this money in the best manner, in sacrifices to be offered upon the altar of God (v. 17), and in whatever else he or his brethren thought fit (v. 18), with this limitation only that it should be *after the will of their God.*

IV. He draws him a bill, or warrant rather, upon the *treasurers on that side the river,* requiring them to furnish him with what he had occasion for out of the king's revenues, and to place it to the king's account, v. 20, 22. This was considerately done; for Ezra, having yet to enquire into the state of things, knew not what he should have occasion for and was modest in his demand.

V. He charges him to let nothing be wanting that was requisite to be done in or about the temple for the honour of the God of Israel. In this charge (v. 23), 1. How honourably he speaks of God. He had called him before *the God of Jerusalem;* but here, lest it should be thought that he looked upon him as a local deity, he calls him twice, with great veneration, the *God of heaven.* 2. How strictly he eyes the word and law of God, which, it is likely, he had read and admired: "Whatsoever is *commanded by your God* let it be done, let it be diligently done, with care and speed."

VI. He exempts all the ministers of the temple from paying taxes to the government. From the greatest of the priests to the least of the Nethinim, *it shall not be lawful* for the king's officers *to impose* that *toll, tribute, or custom upon them,* which the rest of the king's subjects paid, v. 24.

VII. He empowers Ezra to nominate and appoint judges and magistrates for all the Jews on that side the river, v. 25, 26. It was a great favour to the Jews to have such nobles of themselves, and especially to have them of Ezra's nomination. 1. All that *knew the laws of Ezra's God* (that is, all that professed the Jewish religion) were to be under the jurisdiction of these judges, which intimates that they were exempted from the jurisdiction of the heathen magistrates. 2. These judges were allowed and encouraged to make proselytes: Let them *teach the laws of God* to *those that do not know them.* They were not allowed to make new laws, but must see the laws of God duly executed; and they were entrusted with the sword in order that they might be *a terror to evil doers.*

Verses 27–28

Two things Ezra blessed God for:—1. For his commission. *Blessed be God* (says he) *that put such a thing as this into the king's heart.* God can put things into men's hearts which would not arise there of themselves, and into their heads too, both by his providence and by his grace, in things *pertaining both to life and godliness.* If any good appear to be in our own hearts, or in the hearts of others, we must own it was God that put it there, and bless him for it. When princes and magistrates act for the suppression of vice, and the encouragement of religion, we must thank God that *put it into their hearts* to do so. 2. For the encouragement he had in pursuance of his commission (*v.* 28): *He has extended mercy to me.* Ezra himself was a man of courage, yet he attributed his encouragement not to his own heart, but to God's hand: "I was strengthened to undertake the services, *as the hand of the Lord my God was upon me,* to direct and support me."

CHAPTER 8

This chapter gives us a more particular narrative of Ezra's journey to Jerusalem. I. The company that went up with him, ver. 1–20. II. The solemn fast which he kept with his company, to implore God's presence with them in this journey, ver. 21–23. III. The care he took of the treasure he had with him, and the charge he gave concerning it to the priests, to whose custody he committed it, ver. 24–30. IV. The care God took of him and his company in the way, ver. 31. V. Their safe arrival at Jerusalem, where they delivered their treasure to the priests (ver. 32–34), their commissions to the king's lieutenants (ver. 36), and offered sacrifices to God (ver. 35).

Verses 1–20

Ezra, having received his commission from the king, beats up for volunteers, as it were, sets up an ensign to assemble the outcasts of Israel and the dispersed of Judah, Isa. xi. 12. "Whoever of the sons of Sion, that *dwell with the daughters of Babylon,* is disposed to go to Jerusalem, now that the temple there is finished and the temple-service set a-going, now is their time."

I. Some offered themselves willingly to go with Ezra. The heads of the several families are here named, for their honour, and the numbers of the males that each brought in, amounting in all to 1,496. Several of their families, or clans, here named, we had before, *ch.* ii.

II. The Levites who went in this company were in a manner pressed into the service. Ezra appointed a general rendezvous of all his company at a certain place upon new-year's day, the first day of the first month, *ch.* vii. 9. There he mustered them, and *found there none of the sons of Levi, v.* 15. Some priests there were, but no others that were Levites. Where was the spirit of that sacred tribe? Ezra had money enough for the service of the temple, but wanted men. Eleven men of understanding, he chooses out of his company, to be employed for the filling up of this lamentable vacancy. Ezra sent them to a proper place, where there was a college of Levites, *the place Casiphia,* probably a street or square in Babylon allowed for that purpose—*Silver Street* one may call it, for *ceseph* signifies *silver.* He sent them to a proper person, to Iddo, the chief president of the college, to urge him to send some of the juniors, *ministers for the house of our God, v.* 17. Though the warning was short, they brought about forty Levites to attend Ezra. Of the Nethinim, the servitors of the sacred college, more appeared forward to go. Of them 220, upon this hasty summons, enlisted themselves, and had the honour to be expressed by name in Ezra's muster-roll, *v.* 20.

Verses 21–23

Ezra has procured Levites, but what will that avail, unless he have God with him?

I. The steadfast confidence he had in God and in his gracious protection. God's servants have his power engaged for them; his enemies have it engaged against them. This Ezra believed with his heart, and with his mouth made confession of it before the king; and therefore he was ashamed to ask of the king a convoy, lest the king, and those about him, suspected either God's power to help his people or Ezra's confidence in that power. Not but that those who depend upon God must use proper means for their preservation, and they need not be ashamed to do so.

II. The solemn application he made to God in that confidence: He *proclaimed a fast, v.* 21. For public mercies public prayers must be made. Their fasting was, 1. To express their humiliation. This he declares to be the meaning of it, "*that we might afflict ourselves before our God* for our sins, and so be qualified for the pardon of them." 2. To excite their supplications. Prayer was always joined with religious fasting. Their errand to the throne of grace was *to seek of God the right way,* that is, to commit themselves to the guidance of the divine Providence, to put themselves under the divine protection, and to beg of God to guide and keep them in their journey and bring them safely to their journey's end.

III. The good success of their doing so (*v.* 23): *We besought our God* by joint-prayer, *and he was entreated of us.*

Verses 24–30

An account of the particular care which Ezra took of the treasure he had with him, that belonged to God's sanctuary, 1. Having committed the keeping of it to God, he committed the keeping of it to proper men, whose business it was to watch it, though without God they would have waked in vain. 2. Having prayed to God to preserve all the substance they had with them, he shows himself especially solicitous for that part of it which belonged to the house of God and was an offering to him. Twelve chief priests, and as many Levites, he appointed to this trust (*v.* 24, 30). Ezra tells them why he put those things into their hands (*v.* 28): *You are holy unto the Lord, the vessels are holy also;* and who so fit to take care of holy things as holy persons? He *weighed to them the silver, the gold, and the vessels* (*v.* 25), because he expected to have it from them again by weight. The charge he gave them with these treasures (*v.* 29): "*Watch you, and keep them,* that they be not lost, nor embezzled, nor mingled with the other articles. Keep them together; keep them by themselves; keep them safely, till you weigh them in the temple, before the great men there."

Verses 31–36

Ezra goes to Jerusalem, but his multitude made his marches slow and his stages short. His God was good, and he acknowledged his goodness: *The hand of our God was upon us.* Even the common perils of journeys oblige us to sanctify our going out with prayer and our returns in peace with praise and thanksgiving; much more in such a dangerous expedition as this was. They were brought in safety to their journey's end, *v.* 32. His companions were devout. As soon as they came to be near the altar they thought themselves obliged to offer sacrifice, whatever they had done in Babylon, *v.* 35. Among their sacrifices they had a sin-offering; for it is the atonement that sweetens and secures every mercy to us. The number of their offerings related to the number of the tribes, twelve bullocks, twelve he-goats, and ninety-six rams, intimating the union of the two kingdoms, according to what was foretold, Ezek. xxxvii. 22. They did not any longer go two tribes one way and ten another, but all the twelve met by their representatives at the same altar. Even the enemies of the Jews became their friends, bowed to Ezra's commission, and, instead of hindering the people of God, furthered them (*v.* 36).

CHAPTER 9

Now that Ezra presided their enemies had either their hearts turned or at least their hands tied; their neighbours were civil, and we hear of no wars nor rumours of wars; all was as well as could be, considering that they were few, and poor, and subjects to a foreign prince. Look at home; nothing of Baal, nor Ashtaroth, nor Moloch, no images, nor groves, nor golden calves, no, nor so much as high places, but the temple service was duly respected and the temple service carefully kept up. Yet all was not well. I. A complaint brought to Ezra of the many marriages that had been made with strange wives, ver. 1, 2. II. The great trouble which he, and others influenced by his example, were in upon this information, ver. 3, 4. III. The solemn confession which he made of this sin to God, ver. 5-15.

Verses 1-4

Ezra saw nothing amiss, but information is brought him that many of the people, and some of the rulers, had married wives out of heathen families, and joined themselves in affinity with strangers.

I. The sin was *mingling with the people of those lands* (*v.* 2), associating with them both in trade and in conversation, and taking *their daughters in marriages* to their sons. They disobeyed the express command of God, which forbade all intimacy with the heathen, and particularly in matrimonial contracts, Deut. vii. 3. They exposed themselves, and much more their children, to the peril of idolatry, the very sin that had once been the ruin of their nation.

II. The persons that were guilty of this sin, not only some of the unthinking people of Israel, that knew no better, but *many of the priests and Levites*, whose office it was to teach the law, and in whom it was a greater crime. Miserable is the case of that people whose leaders debauch them and cause them to err.

III. The information was given to Ezra. It was given by the princes, those of them that had kept their integrity and with it their dignity. They applied to Ezra, hoping that his wisdom, authority, and interest would prevail.

IV. The impression this made upon Ezra (*v.* 3): *He rent his clothes, plucked off his hair*, and *sat down astonished*. It grieved him to the heart to think that a people called by God's name should so grossly violate his law. Sorrow for sin must be great sorrow; such Ezra's was, *as for an only son or a first-born*.

V. The influence which Ezra's grief for this had upon others. Public notice was soon taken of it, and all the devout serious people that were at hand assembled themselves to him. All good people ought to own those that appear and act in the cause of God against vice and profaneness, to stand by them, and do what they can to strengthen their hands.

Verses 5-15

A most pathetic address Ezra makes to Heaven upon this occasion.

I. He made this address—*at the evening sacrifice*, *v.* 5. Then devout people used to come into the courts of the temple to offer up their own prayers. In their hearing Ezra chose to make this confession, that they might be made duly sensible of the sins of their people. The sacrifice, and especially the evening sacrifice, was a type of the great propitiation. Ezra had faith in this penitential address to God; he makes confession with his hand, as it were, upon the head of that great sacrifice, through which *we receive the atonement*.

II. His preparation for this address. 1. He *rose up from his heaviness*, and so far shook off the burden of his grief as was necessary to the lifting up of his heart to God. 2. He *fell upon his knees*, put himself into the posture of a penitent, representing the people for whom he was now an intercessor. 3. He *spread out his hands*, as one affected with what he was going to say, offering it up unto God.

III. The address itself. If we give prayer its full latitude, it is the offering up of pious and devout affections to God. His address is a penitent confession of sin, not his own, but the sin of his people. Though he himself was wholly clear from this guilt, yet he puts himself into the number of the sinners, because he was a member of the same community—*our sins and our trespass*. He owns their sins to have been very great: "*Our iniquities are increased over our heads* (*v.* 6); we are ready to perish in them as in deep waters.*" But let this be the comfort of true penitents that though their sins reach to the heavens God's mercy is *in the heavens*, Ps. xxxvi. 5. They were *not forsaken in their bondage*, but even in Babylon had the tokens of God's presence,—they were a remnant of Israelites left, a few out of many, and those narrowly escaped out of the hands of their enemies, by the favour of the kings of Persia. They had *a nail in his holy place*, that is (as it is explained, *v.* 9), that they had set up the *house of God*. They had their religion settled and the service of the temple in a constant method. This enlightened their eyes and revived their hearts; it was life from the dead to them. "Now," says Ezra, "how ungrateful are we to offend a God that has been so kind to us!" The sin was against an express command: *We have forsaken thy commandments*, *v.* 10. Gen. xxxiv. 14. But, besides that, God had strictly forbidden it. He recites the command, *v.* 11, 12. Nothing could be more express: *Give not your daughters to their sons, nor take their daughters to your sons.* The reason given is because, if they mingled with those nations, they would pollute themselves. It was an unclean land, and they were a holy people. Ezra, in a penitential sense of the great malignity that was in their sin, acknowledged that, though the punishment was very great, it was less than they deserved. He speaks as one much ashamed. With this he begins (*v.* 6), *O my God! I am ashamed and blush, O my God! to lift up my face unto thee.* Sin is a shameful thing. Holy shame is as necessary an ingredient in true and ingenuous repentance as holy sorrow. The sins of others should be our shame, and we should blush for those who do not blush for themselves. The publican, when he went to the temple to pray, hung down his head more than ever, as one ashamed, Luke xviii. 13. True penitents are at a loss what to say. Shall we say, We have *not sinned*, or, *God will not require it?* If we do, *we deceive ourselves, and the truth is not in us.* Shall we say, Have patience with us and we will pay thee all, with *thousands of rams, or our first-born for our transgression?* God will not thus be mocked: he knows we are insolvent. Shall we say, *There is no hope*, and *let come on us what will?* That is but to make bad worse. True penitents should, as Ezra, beg of God to teach them. What shall we say? Say, "I have sinned; I have done foolishly; God be merciful to me a sinner;" and the like. See Hos. xiv. 2. He speaks as one much assured of the righteousness of God. "*Thou art righteous*, wise, just, and good; thou wilt neither do us wrong nor be hard upon us; and therefore behold *we are before thee*, we lie at thy feet, waiting our doom; *we cannot stand before thee*, insisting upon any righteousness of our own, having no plea to support us and therefore we fall down before thee, in our trespass, and cast ourselves on thy mercy. *Do unto us whatsoever seemeth good unto thee*, Judges x. 15. We have nothing to say, nothing to do, but to *make supplication to our Judge*," Job ix. 15. Thus does this good man lay his grief before God and then leave it with him.

CHAPTER 10

That grievance redressed which was lamented in the foregoing chapter. I. How the people's hearts were prepared for the redress of it, ver. 1. II. How it was proposed to Ezra by Shechaniah, ver. 2–4. III. How the proposal was put in execution. 1. The great men were sworn to stand to it, ver. 5. 2. Ezra appeared first in it, ver. 6. 3. A general assembly was called, ver. 7–9. 4. They all, in compliance with Ezra's exhortation, agreed to the reformation, ver. 10–14. 5. Commissioners were appointed to enquire who had married strange wives and to oblige them to put them away, which was done accordingly (ver. 15–17), and a list of the names of those that were found guilty given in, ver. 18–44.

Verses 1–5

I. What good impressions were made upon the people by Ezra's humiliation and confession of sin. No sooner was it noised in the city that their new governor, in whom they rejoiced, was himself in grief, for them and their sin, than presently there *assembled to him a very great congregation*, to mingle their tears with him, *v.* 1. See what a happy influence the good examples of great ones may have upon their inferiors. When Ezra, a scribe, a scholar, a man in authority under the king, so deeply lamented the public corruptions, they concluded that they were indeed very grievous.

II. What a good motion Shechaniah made upon this occasion. The place was *Bochim*—a place of *weepers*; but, for aught that appears, there was a profound silence among them till Shechaniah (one of Ezra's companions from Babylon, *ch.* viii. 3, 5) stood up, and made a speech addressed to Ezra, in which he owns the national guilt, sums up all Ezra's confession in one word, and sets to his seal that it is true: "*We have trespassed against God, and have taken strange wives,*" *v.* 2. It does not appear that Shechaniah was himself culpable in this matter, but his father was guilty, and several of his father's house (as appears *v.* 26), and therefore he reckons himself among the trespassers. *Now there is hope;* now that the disease is discovered it is half-cured. The sin that truly troubles us shall not ruin us. The case is plain; what has been done amiss must be undone again as far as possible. *Let us put away all the wives, and such as are born of them, v.* 3. Ezra despaired of ever bringing the people to it, but Shechaniah, who conversed more with the people than he did, assured him the thing was practicable if they went wisely to work. As to the case of being *unequally yoked with unbelievers,* Shechaniah's counsel will not hold now; such marriages, it is certain, are sinful, and ought not to be made, but they are not null. *Quod fieri non debuit, factum valet—That which ought not to have been done must, when done, abide.*

Our rule, under the gospel is, *If a brother has a wife that believeth not,* and *she be pleased to dwell with him, let him not put her away,* 1 Cor. vii. 12, 13. Shechaniah said to Ezra and the people: Let us covenant, not only that, if we have strange wives ourselves, we will put them away, but that, if we have not, we will do what we can in our places to oblige others to put away theirs.

Verses 6–14

An account of the proceedings concerning the strange wives. Ezra sent orders to all the children of the captivity to attend him at Jerusalem *within three days* (*v.* 7, 8). Within the time limited the generality of the people met at Jerusalem and made their appearance *in the street of the house of God, v.* 9. Ezra gave the charge at this great assize. He found that since their return out of captivity they had *increased the trespass of Israel* by *marrying strange wives,* which would certainly be a means of again introducing idolatry. He called them together that they might *confess their sin to God,* and that they might separate themselves from all idolaters, especially idolatrous wives, *v.* 10, 11. The people submitted not only to Ezra's jurisdiction in general, but to his inquisition and determination in this matter: "*As thou hast said, so must we do,*" *v.* 12.

Verses 15–44

The congregation dismissed, that each in his respective place might gain and give intelligence to facilitate the matter. The commissioners that sat upon this matter. Ezra was president, and with him *certain chief* men *of the fathers* who were qualified with wisdom and zeal above others for this service, *v.* 16. They began *the first day of the tenth month to examine the matter* (*v.* 16), which was but ten days after this method was proposed (*v.* 9), and they finished in three months, *v.* 17. About 113 in all are here named who had married strange wives, and some of them, it is said (*v.* 44), had children by them, which implies that not many of them had, God not crowning those marriages with the blessing of increase. Whether the children were turned off with the mothers, as Shechaniah proposed, does not appear; it should seem not: however, it is probable that the wives which were put away were well provided for, according to their rank.

AN EXPOSITION, WITH PRACTICAL OBSERVATIONS, OF

THE BOOK OF NEHEMIAH

This book continues the history of the *children of the captivity*, the poor Jews, that had lately returned out of Babylon to their own land. At this time not only the Persian monarchy flourished in great pomp and power, but Greece and Rome began to make a figure. Of the affairs of those high and mighty states we have authentic accounts extant; but the sacred and inspired history takes cognizance only of the state of the Jews. Ezra the scribe and Nehemiah the tirshatha, though neither of them ever wore a crown, commanded an army, conquered any country, or was famed for philosophy or oratory, yet both of them, being pious praying men, and very service-able in their day to the interests of religion, were really greater men and more honourable, not only than any of the Roman consuls or dictators, but than Xenophon, or Demosthenes, or Plato himself, who lived at the same time, the bright ornaments of Greece. Nehemiah's agency for the advancing of the settlement of Israel we have a full account of in this book, wherein he records not only the works of his hands, but the workings of his heart, in the management of public affairs. Twelve years, from his twentieth year (*ch.* i. 1) to his thirty-second year (*ch.* xiii. 6), he was governor of Judæa, under Artaxerxes king of Persia, whom Dr. Lightfoot supposes to be the same Artaxerxes as Ezra had his commission from. This book relates, I. Nehemiah's concern for Jerusalem and the commission he obtained from the king to go thither, *ch.* i., ii. II. His building the wall of Jerusalem not-withstanding the opposition he met with, *ch.* iii., iv. III. His redressing the grievances of the people, *ch.* v. IV. His finishing the wall, *ch.* vi. V. The account he took of the people, *ch.* vii. VI. The religious solemnities of reading the law, fasting, and praying, and renewing their covenants, to which he called the people, *ch.* viii.–x. VII. The care he took for the replenishing of the holy city and the settling of the holy tribe, *ch.* xi., xii. VIII. His zeal in reforming various abuses, *ch.* xiii. Some call this the second book of Ezra, not because he was the penman of it, but because it is a continuation of the history of the foregoing book, with which it is connected, *v.* 1. This was the last *historical* book that was written, as Malachi was the last *prophetical* book, of the Old Testament.

CHAPTER 1

Nehemiah at the Persian court, I. Inquisitive concerning the state of the Jews and Jerusalem, ver. 1, 2. II. Informed of their deplorable condition, ver. 3. III. Fasting and praying thereupon (ver. 4), with a particular account of his prayer, ver. 5–11.

Verses 1–4

I. Nehemiah's station at the court of Persia. He was *In Shushan the palace*, or royal city, of the king of Persia, where the court was ordinarily kept (*v.* 1), and (*v.* 11) he was *the king's cup-bearer*. By this place at court he would be the bettter qualified for the service of his country in that post for which God had designed him, as Moses was the fitter to govern for being bred up in Pharaoh's court, and David in Saul's. He would also have the fairer opportunity of serving his country by his interest in the king and those about him. God has his remnant in all places; we read of Obadiah in the house of Ahab, saints in Cæsar's household, and a devout Nehemiah in Shushan the palace. God can make the courts of princes sometimes nurseries and sometimes sanctuaries to the friends and patrons of the church's cause.

II. Nehemiah's tender and compassionate enquiry concerning the state of the Jews in their own land, *v.* 2. It happened that a friend and relation of his came to the court, with some other company, by whom he had an opportunity of informing himself fully how it went with the children of the captivity and what posture Jerusalem, the beloved city, was in. Nehe-miah lived at ease, in honour and fulness, himself, but could not forget that he was an Israelite, nor shake off the thoughts of his brethren in distress, but in spirit (like Moses, Acts vii. 23) he *visited them and looked upon their burdens.* Though he was a great man yet he did not think it below him to take cogniz-ance of his brethren that were low and despised, nor was he ashamed to own his relation to them and concern for them. Though he did not go to settle at Jerusalem himself he did not therefore judge nor despise those that had returned.

III. The melancholy account which is here given him of the present state of the Jews and Jerusalem, *v.* 3. Hanani, the person he enquired of, has this character given of him (*ch.* vii. 2), that he *feared God*

above many, and therefore would not only speak truly, but, when he spoke of the desolations of Jerusalem, would speak tenderly. It is probable that his errand to court at this time was to solicit some favour, some relief or other, that they stood in need of. Now the account he gives is, 1. That the holy seed was miserably trampled on and abused, *in great affliction and reproach,* insulted upon all occasions by their neighbours, and *filled with the scorning of those that were at ease.* 2. That the holy city was exposed and in ruins. *The wall of Jerusalem was* still *broken down, and the gates* were, as the Chaldeans left them, in ruins. This made the condition of the inhabitants both very despicable under the abiding marks of poverty and slavery, and very dangerous, for their enemies might when they pleased make an easy prey of them. The temple was built, the government settled, and a work of reformation brought to some head, but here was one good work yet undone; this was still wanting.

IV. The great affliction this gave to Nehemiah and the deep concern it put him into, *v.* 4. 1. He *wept and mourned.* 2. He *fasted and prayed.*

Verses 5–11

Nehemiah's prayer, a prayer that has reference to all the prayers which he had for some time before been putting up to God day and night, while he con-tinued his sorrows for the desolations of Jerusalem, and withal to the petition he was now intending to present to the king his master for his favour to Jeru-salem.

I. His humble and reverent address to God. It teaches us to draw near to God, 1. With a holy awe of his majesty and glory, remembering that he is the God of heaven, infinitely above us, infinitely excelling all the principalities and powers both of the upper and of the lower world, angels and kings. 2. With a holy confidence in his grace and truth, for he *keepeth covenant and mercy for those that love him,* not only the mercy that is promised, but even more than he promised.

II. His general request for the audience and accept-ance of all the prayers and confessions he now made to God (*v.* 6): "*Let thy ear be attentive to the prayer,* which I *pray before thee.*"

III. His penitent confession of sin; not only Israel has sinned but *I and my father's house have sinned, v.* 6.

IV. The pleas he urges for mercy for his people Israel.

1. He pleads what God had of old said to them. He had said indeed that, if they broke covenant with him, he would *scatter them among the nations,* and that threatening was fulfilled in their captivity: never was people so widely dispersed as Israel was at this time, though at first so closely incorporated; but he had said withal that if they *turned to him* (as now they began to do, having renounced idolatry and kept to the temple service) he would *gather them again.* This he quotes from Deut. xxx. 1–5, and begs leave to put God in mind of it (though the Eternal Mind needs no remembrancer) as that which he guided his desires by, and grounded his faith and hope upon, in praying this prayer. If God were not more mindful of his promises than we are of his precepts we should be undone. Our best pleas therefore in prayer are those that are taken from the promise of God, the *word on which he has caused us to hope,* Ps. cxix. 49.

2. He pleads the relation wherein of old they stood to God: "These are *thy servants and thy people* (*v.* 10), whom thou hast set apart for thyself, and taken into covenant with thee. Wilt thou suffer thy sworn enemies to trample upon and oppress thy sworn servants? If thou wilt not appear for thy people, whom wilt thou appear for?" See Isa. lxiii. 19. As an evidence of their being God's servants he gives them this character (*v.* 11): "*They desire to fear thy name;* they are not only called by thy name, but really have a reverence for thy name; they now worship thee, and thee only, according to thy will, and have an awe of all the discoveries thou art pleased to make of thyself; this they have a desire to do."

3. He pleads the great things God had formerly done for them (*v.* 10).

Lastly, He concludes with a particular petition, that God would prosper him in his undertaking, and give him favour with the king. *Mercy in the sight of this man* is what he prays for, meaning not the king's mercy, but mercy from God in his address to the king. Favour with men is then comfortable when we can see it springing from the mercy of God.

CHAPTER 2

How Nehemiah wrestled with God and prevailed we read in the foregoing chapter; now here we are told how, like Jacob, he prevailed with men also, and so found that his prayers were heard and answered. I. He prevailed with the king to send him to Jerusalem with a commission to build a wall about it, and grant him what was necessary for it, ver. 1–8. II. He prevailed against the enemies that would have obstructed him in his journey (ver. 9–11) and laughed him out of his undertaking, ver. 19, 20. III. He prevailed upon his own people to join with him in this good work, viewing the desolations of the walls (ver. 12–16) and then gaining them to lend every one a hand towards the rebuilding of them, ver. 17, 18.

Verses 1–8

Nehemiah had prayed for the relief of his countrymen. Nearly four months passed, from Chisleu to Nisan (from November to March), before Nehemiah made his application to the king for leave to go to Jerusalem, either because the winter was not a proper time for such a journey, or because it was so long before his month of waiting came, and there was no coming into the king's presence uncalled, Esther iv. 11. Now that he attended the king's table he hoped to have his ear.

I. The occasion which he gave the king to enquire into his cares and griefs, by appearing sad in his presence. He took up the wine and gave it to the king when he called for it, expecting that then he would look him in the face. He had not used to be sad in the king's presence, but conformed to the rules of the court (as courtiers must do), which would admit no sorrows, Esther iv. 2. Good men should do what they can by their cheerfulness to convince the world of the pleasantness of religious ways and to roll away the reproach cast upon them as melancholy; but there is a time for all things, Eccles. iii. 4. Nehemiah now saw cause both to be sad and to appear. so. The miseries of Jerusalem gave him cause to be sad, and his showing his grief would give occasion to the king to enquire into the cause.

II. The kind notice which the king took of his sadness and the enquiry he made into the cause of it (*v.* 2): *Why is thy countenance sad, seeing thou art not sick?*

III. The account which Nehemiah gave the king of the cause of his sadness, which he gave with meekness and fear. He modestly asked, "*Why should not my countenance be sad* as it is *when the city, the place of my fathers' sepulchres, lieth waste?*" He assigns the ruins of Jerusalem as the true cause of his grief.

IV. The encouragement which the king gave him to tell his mind, and the application he thereupon made in his heart to God, *v.* 4. The king had an affection for him, and was not pleased to see him melancholy. It is also probable that he had a kindness for the Jews' religion; he had discovered it before in the commission he gave to Ezra, who was a churchman, and now again in the power he put Nehemiah into, who was a statesman. Wanting therefore only to know how he might be serviceable to Jerusalem, he asks this its anxious friend, "*For what dost thou make request?* Something thou wouldst have; what is it?" Nehemiah immediately *prayed to the God of heaven* that he would give him wisdom to ask properly and incline the king's heart to grant him his request. It was a secret sudden ejaculation; he lifted up his heart to that God who understands the language of his heart: *Lord, give me a mouth and wisdom; Lord, give me favour in the sight of this man.*

V. His humble petition to the king. He asked for a commission to go as governor to Judah, to build the wall of Jerusalem. He also asked for a convoy (*v.* 7), and an order upon the governors, not only to permit and suffer him to pass through their respective provinces, but to supply him with what he had occasion for, with another order upon the keeper of the forest of Lebanon to give him timber for the work that he designed.

VI. The king's great favour to him in asking him *when he would return, v.* 6. He intimated that he was unwilling to lose him. He would spare him awhile, and let him have what clauses he pleased inserted in his commission, *v.* 8. Here was an immediate answer to his prayer. In the account he gives of the success of his petition he takes notice, 1. Of the presence of the queen; she sat by (*v.* 6), which (they say) was not usual in the Persian court, Esther i. 11. 2. Of the power and grace of God. He gained his point *according to the good hand of his God upon him.*

Verses 9–20

I. How Nehemiah was dismissed by the court he was sent from. The king appointed *captains of the army* and *horsemen* to go *with him* (*v.* 9), both for his guard and to show that he was a man whom *the king did delight to honour,* that all the king's servants might respect him accordingly.

II. How he was received by the country he was sent to.

1. By the Jews and their friends at Jerusalem.

(1) While he concealed his errand they took little notice of him. He was at *Jerusalem three days* (*v.* 11), and it does not appear that any of the great men of the city waited on him to congratulate him on his arrival, but he remained unknown.

(2) Though they took little notice of him he took great notice of them and their state. He arose in the night, and viewed the ruins of the walls, probably by moonlight (v. 13), that he might see what was to be done and in what method they must go about it, whether the old foundation would serve, and what there was of the old materials that would be of use. Those that would build up the church's walls must first take notice of the ruins of those walls. Those that would know how to amend must enquire what is amiss, what needs reformation, and what may serve as it is.

(3) When he disclosed his design to the rulers and people they cheerfully concurred with him in it. He did not tell them, at first, what he came about (v. 16), because he would not seem to do it for ostentation, and because, if he found it impracticable, he might retreat the more honourably. But when he had viewed and considered the thing, and probably felt the pulse of the rulers and people, he told them *what God had put into his heart* (v. 12), even to *build up the wall of Jerusalem, v. 17. "Come, therefore, and let us build up the wall."* He did not undertake to do the work without them (it could not be the work of one man), nor did he charge or command imperiously, though he had the king's commission; but in a friendly brotherly way he exhorted and excited them to join with him in this work. To encourage them hereto, he speaks of the design, *First,* As that which owed its origin to the special grace of God. He takes not the praise of it to himself, as a good thought of his own, but acknowledges that God *put it into his heart. Secondly,* As that which owed its progress hitherto to the special providence of God. He produced the king's commission, told them how readily it was granted and how forward the king was to favour his design, in which he saw the hand of his God *good upon him.* They presently came to a resolution, one and all, to concur with him: *Let us rise up and build. So they strengthened their hands,* their own and one another's, *for this good work.* Many a good work would find hands enough to be laid to it if there were but one good head to lead in it.

2. By those that wished ill to the Jews. Sanballat and Tobiah, two of the Samaritans, but by birth the former a Moabite, the latter an Ammonite, when they saw one come armed with a commission from the king to do service to Israel, *were exceedingly grieved* that all their little paltry arts to weaken Israel were thus baffled and frustrated by a fair, and noble, and generous project to strengthen them. When they saw a man come in that manner, who professedly *sought the welfare of the children of Israel,* it vexed them to the heart. When he began to act they set themselves to hinder him, but in vain, v. 19, 20. With what good reason the Jews slighted these discouragements: They bore up themselves with this that they were the *servants of the God of heaven,* the only true and living God, that they were acting for him in what they did, and that therefore he would bear them out and prosper them, though the heathen raged, Ps. ii. 1.

CHAPTER 3

Saying and doing are often two things: many are ready to say, "Let us rise up and build," who sit still and do nothing, like that fair-spoken son who said, "I go, Sir, but went not." The undertakers here were none of those. As soon as they had resolved to build the wall about Jerusalem they lost no time, but set about it. This chapter gives an account of two things:—
I. The names of the builders which are recorded here to their honour, for they were such as herein discovered a great zeal for God and their country. II. The order of the building; they took it before them, and ended where they began. They repaired, 1. From the sheep-gate to the fish-gate, ver. 1, 2. 2. Thence to the old-gate, ver. 3–5. 3. Thence to the valley-gate, ver. 6–12. 4. Thence to the dung-gate, ver. 13, 14. 5. Thence to the gate of the fountain, ver. 15. 6. Thence to the water-gate, ver. 16–26. 7. Thence by the horse-gate to the sheep-gate again, where they began (ver. 27–32), and so they brought their work quite round the city.

Verses 1–32

Several things are observable in the account here given of the buildings of the wall about Jerusalem:—

I. That Eliashib the high priest, with his brethren the priests, led the van in this troop of builders, v. 1. If there be labour in it, who so fit as they to work? if danger, who so fit as they to venture? The priests repaired the *sheep-gate,* so called because through it were brought the sheep that were to be sacrificed in the temple; and therefore the priests undertook the repair of it because the *offerings of the Lord made by fire were* their inheritance. And of this gate only it is said that *they sanctified it* with the word and prayer.

II. That the undertakers were very many, who each took his share, some more and some less, in this work, according as they ability was.

III. That many were active in this work who were not themselves inhabitants of Jerusalem, and therefore consulted purely the public welfare and not any private interest or advantage of their own. Here are the men of Jericho with the first (v. 2), the men of Gibeon and Mizpah (v. 7), and Zanoah, v. 13. Every Israelite should lend a hand towards the building up of Jerusalem.

IV. That several rulers, both of Jerusalem and of other cities, were active in this work, thinking themselves bound in honour to do the utmost that their wealth and power enabled them to do for the furtherance of this good work.

V. Here is a just reproach fastened upon the nobles of Tekoa, that they *put not their necks to the work of their Lord* (v. 5), that is, they would not come under the yoke of an obligation to this service; as if the dignity and liberty of their peerage were their discharge from serving God and doing good.

VI. Two persons joined in repairing *the old gate* (v. 6), and so were co-founders, and shared the honour of it between them. The good work which we cannot compass ourselves we must be thankful to those that will go partners with us in. Some think that this is called the *old gate* because it belonged to the ancient Salem, which was said to be first built by Melchizedek.

VII. Several good honest tradesmen, as well as priests and rulers, were active in this work—*goldsmiths, apothecaries, merchants, v.* 8, 32. They did not think their callings excused them, nor plead that they could not leave their shops to attend the public business, knowing that what they lost would certainly be made up to them by the blessing of God upon their callings.

VIII. Some ladies are spoken of as helping forward this work—*Shallum and his daughters* (v. 12), who, though not capable of personal service, yet having their portions in their own hands, or being rich widows, contributed money for buying materials and paying workmen. St. Paul speaks of some good women that *laboured with him in the gospel,* Phil. iv. 3.

IX. Of some it is said that they repaired *over against their houses* (v. 10, 23, 28, 29), and of one (who, it is likely, was only a lodger) that he repaired *over against his chamber, v.* 30. When a general good work is to be done each should apply himself to that part of it that falls nearest to him and is within his reach. If every one will sweep before his own door, the street will be clean; if everyone will mend one, we shall be all mended. If he that has but a chamber will repair before that, he does his part.

X. Of one it is said that he *earnestly* repaired that which fell to his share (v. 20). It is good to be thus *zealously affected in a good thing*; and it is probable that this good man's zeal provoked very many to take the more pains and make the more haste.

XI. Of one of these builders it is observed that he was *the sixth son* of his father, v. 30. His five elder brethren, it seems, laid not their hands to this work, but he did. In doing that which is good we need not stay to see our elders go before us; if they decline it, it does not therefore follow that we must. Thus the younger brother, if he be the better man, and does God and his generation better service, is indeed the better gentleman; those are most honourable that are most useful.

XII. Some of those that had *first done helped their fellows*, and undertook another share where they saw there was most need. Meremoth repaired, *v.* 4 and again, *v.* 21. And the Tekoites, besides the piece they repaired (*v.* 5), undertook another piece (*v.* 27), which is the more remarkable because their nobles set them a bad example by withdrawing from the service, which, instead of serving them for an excuse to sit still, perhaps made them the more forward to do double work, that by their zeal they might either shame or atone for the covetousness and carelessness of their nobles.

Lastly, Here is no mention of any particular share that Nehemiah himself had in this work. A namesake of his is mentioned, *v.* 16. But did he do nothing? Yes, though he undertook not any particular piece of the wall, yet he did more than any of them, for he had the oversight of them all; half of his servants worked where there was most need, and the other half stood sentinel, as we find afterwards (*ch.* iv. 16), while he himself in his own person walked the rounds, directed and encouraged the builders, set his hand to the work where he saw occasion, and kept a watchful eye upon the motions of the enemy, as we shall find in the next chapter. The pilot need not haul at a rope; it is enough for him to steer.

CHAPTER 4

We left all hands at work for the building of the wall about Jerusalem. But such good work is not wont to be carried on without opposition; now here we are told what opposition was given to it, and what methods Nehemiah took to forward the work, notwithstanding that opposition. I. Their enemies reproached and ridiculed their undertaking, but their scoffs they answered with prayers: they heeded them not, but went on with their work notwithstanding, ver. 1–6. II. They formed a bloody design against them, to hinder them by force of arms, ver. 7, 8, 10–12. To guard against this Nehemiah prayed (ver. 9), set guards (ver. 13), and encouraged them to fight (ver. 14), by which the design was broken (ver. 15), and so the work was carried on with all needful precaution against a surprise, ver. 16–23.

Verses 1–6

Here is, I. The spiteful scornful reflection which Sanballat and Tobiah cast upon the Jews for their attempt to build the wall about Jerusalem. The intelligence was brought to Samaria, that nest of enemies to the Jews, and here we are told how they received the tidings. 1. In heart. They were very angry at the undertaking, and had *great indignation, v.* 1. It vexed them that Nehemiah came to seek the welfare of the children of Israel (*ch.* ii. 10); but, when they heard of this great undertaking for their good, they were out of all patience. 2. In word. They despised it, and made it the subject of their ridicule. "*These feeble Jews*" (*v.* 2), "what will they do for materials? *Will they revive the stones out of the rubbish?* And what mean they by being so hasty? Do they think to make the walling of a city but one day's work, and to keep the feast of dedication with sacrifice the next day? Poor silly people! See how ridiculous they made themselves!" "*If a fox go up*, not with his subtlety, but with his weight, he *will break down their stone wall.*"

II. Nehemiah's humble and devout address to God when he heard of these reflections. He did not answer these fools according to their folly; he did not upbraid them with their weakness, but looked up to God by prayer.

1. He begs of God to take notice of the indignities

that were done them (*v.* 4), and in this we are to imitate him: *Hear, O our God! for we are despised.*

2. He begs of God to avenge their cause and turn the reproach upon the enemies themselves (*v.* 4, 5); and this was spoken rather by a spirit of prophecy than by a spirit of prayer, and is not to be imitated by us who are taught of Christ to *pray for those that despitefully use and persecute us.* Christ himself prayed for those that reproached him: *Father, forgive them.*

III. The vigour of the builders, notwithstanding these reflections, *v.* 6. They made such good speed that in a little time they had run up the wall to half its height, for *the people had a mind to work*; their hearts were upon it, and they would have it forwarded.

Verses 7–15

I. The conspiracy which the Jews' enemies formed against them, to stay the building by slaying the builders. The conspirators were not only Sanballat and Tobiah, but other neighbouring people whom they had drawn into the plot. *They were very wroth. Cursed be their anger, for it was fierce, and their wrath, for it was cruel.* Nothing would serve but they would *fight against Jerusalem, v.* 8. Why, what quarrel had they with the Jews? They hated the Jews' piety, and were therefore vexed at their prosperity and sought their ruin. The hindering of good work is that which bad men aim at and promise themselves; but good work is God's work, and it shall prosper.

II. The discouragements which the builders themselves laboured under. At the very time when the adversaries said, Let us *cause the work to cease*, Judah said, "Let us even let it fall, for we are not able to go forward with it," *v.* 10. They represent the labourers as tired, and the remaining difficulties, even of that first part of their work, the removing of the rubbish, as insuperable, and therefore they think it advisable to desist for the present. Active leading men have many times as much ado to grapple with the fears of their friends as with the terrors of their enemies.

III. The information that was brought to Nehemiah of the enemies' designs, *v.* 12. There were *Jews that dwelt by them*, in the country, who, though they had not zeal enough to bring them to Jerusalem to help their brethren in building the wall, yet, having by their situation opportunity to discover the enemies' motions, had so much honesty and affection to the cause as to give intelligence of them; nay, that their intelligence might be the more credited, they came themselves to give it, and they said it ten times, repeating it as men in earnest, and under a concern, and the report was confirmed by many witnesses. "*Whatever place you turn to, they are against us*, so that you have need to be upon your guard on all sides."

IV. The pious and prudent methods which Nehemiah, hereupon, took to baffle the design, and to secure his work and workmen.

1. It is said (*v.* 14) he *looked*. (1) He looked up, engaged God for him, and put himself and his cause under the divine protection (*v.* 9): *We made our prayer unto our God.* That was the way of this good man, and should be our way; all his cares, all his griefs, all his fears, he spread before God, and thereby made himself easy. This was the first thing he did; before he used any means, he made his prayer to God, for with him we must always begin. (2) He looked about him. Having prayed, he *set a watch against them.* The instructions Christ has given us in our spiritual warfare agree with this example, Matt. xxvi. 41. *Watch and pray.* If we think to secure ourselves by prayer only, without watchfulness, we are slothful and tempt God; if by watchfulness, without prayer, we are proud and slight God; and, either way, we forfeit his protection.

2. Observe, (1) How he posted the guards, *v.* 13. *In the lower places* he set them *behind the wall*, that they might annoy the enemy over it, as a breast-work; but *in the higher places*, where the wall was raised to its full height, he set them upon it, that from the top of it they might throw down stones or darts upon the heads of the assailants: he set them *after their families*, that mutual relation might engage them to mutual assistance. (2) How he animated and encouraged the people, *v.* 14. "Come," says he, "*be not afraid of them*, but behave yourselves valiantly, considering, [1] Whom you fight under. You cannot have a better captain: *Remember the Lord, who is great and terrible;* you think your enemies *great and terrible*, but what are they in comparison with God, especially in opposition to him? He is great above them to control them, and will be terrible to them when he comes to reckon with them." The reigning fear of God is the best antidote against the ensnaring fear of man.

V. The disappointment which this gave to the enemies, *v.* 15. When they found that their design was discovered, and that the Jews were upon their guard, they concluded that it was to no purpose to attempt anything, but that *God had brought their counsel to nought.* They knew they could not gain their point but by surprise, and, if their plot was known, it was quashed. The Jews hereupon *returned everyone to his work*, with so much the more cheerfulness because they saw plainly that God owned it and owned them in the doing of it.

Verses 16–23

When the builders had so far reason to think the design of the enemies broken *as to return to their work*, yet they were not so secure as to lay down their arms. 1. While one half were at work, the other half were under their arms, holding *spears, and shields, and bows*, not only for themselves but for the labourers too, who would immediately quit their work, and betake themselves to their weapons, upon the first alarm, *v.* 16. Thus dividing their time between the trowels and the spears they are said to *work with one hand* and hold their weapons *with the other* (*v.* 17), which cannot be understood literally, for the work would require both hands; but it intimates that they were equally employed in both. 2. Every builder had a sword by his side (*v.* 18). which he could carry without hindering his labour. The word of God is the sword of the Spirit, which we ought to have always at hand and never to seek, both in our labours and in our conflicts as Christians. 3. Care was taken both to get and give early notice of the approach of the enemy, in case they should endeavour to surprise them. Nehemiah kept a trumpeter always by him to sound an alarm upon the first intimation of danger. The work was large, and the builders were dispersed; for in all parts of the wall they were labouring at the same time. Nehemiah continually walked round to oversee the work and encourage the workmen. When they acted as workmen, it was requisite they should be dispersed wherever there was work to do; but when as soldiers it was requisite they should come into close order, and be found in a body. Thus should the labourers in Christ's building be ready to unite against a common foe. 4. The inhabitants of the villages were ordered to lodge within Jerusalem, with their servants, not only that they might be the nearer to their work in the morning, but that they might be ready to help in case of an attack in the night, *v.* 22. 5. Nehemiah himself, and all his men, kept closely to their business. The spears were held up, with the sight of them to terrify the enemy, not only from sun to sun, but from twilight to twilight every day, *v.* 21.

CHAPTER 5

How bravely Nehemiah, as a wise and faithful governor, stood upon his guard against the attacks of enemies abroad, we read in the foregoing chapter. Here we have him no less bold and active to redress grievances at home, and, having kept them from being destroyed by their enemies, to keep them from destroying one another. I. The complaint which the poor made to him of the great hardships which the rich (of whom they were forced to borrow money) put upon them, ver. 1–5. II. The effectual course which Nehemiah took both to reform the oppressors and to relieve the oppressed, ver. 6–13. III. The good example which he himself, as governor, set them of compassion and tenderness, ver. 14–19.

Verses 1–5

Hard times and hard hearts made the poor miserable.

I. The times they lived in were hard. There was a dearth of corn (*v.* 3), probably for want of rain. When the markets are high, and provisions scarce and dear, the poor soon feel it from it, and are pinched by it. That which made the scarcity here complained of the more grievous was that their *sons and their daughters were many, v.* 2. The families that were most necessitous were most numerous. As corn was dear, so the taxes were high; the king's tribute must be paid, *v.* 4. This mark of their captivity still remained upon them. Now, it seems, they had not wherewithal of their own to buy corn and pay taxes, but were necessitated to borrow. Their families came poor out of Babylon; they had been at great expense in building them houses, and had not yet got up their strength, when these new burdens came upon them.

II. The persons they dealt with were hard. Money must be had, but it must be borrowed; and those that lent them money, taking advantage of their necessity, were very hard upon them. 1. They exacted interest from them at twelve per cent, the hundredth part every month, *v.* 11. But if the poor borrow to maintain their families, and we be able to help them, it is certain we ought either to lend freely what they have occasion for, or (if they be not likely to repay it) to give freely something towards it. 2. They forced them to mortgage to them their lands and houses for the securing of the money (*v.* 3), and not only so, but took the profits of them for interest (*v.* 5, compare *v.* 11), that by degrees they might make themselves masters of all they had. Yet this was not the worst. 3. They took their children for bond-servants, to be enslaved or sold at pleasure, *v.* 5. "Our heirs must be their slaves, and *it is not in our power to redeem them.*" This they made a humble remonstrance of to Nehemiah, not only because they saw he was a great man that could relieve them, but a good man that would. Let us lament the hardships which many in the world are groaning under; putting our souls into their souls' stead, and remembering in our prayers and succours those that are burdened, as burdened with them. But let those who show no mercy expect *judgment without mercy.* It was an aggravation of the sin of these oppressing Jews that they were themselves so lately delivered out of the house of bondage, which obliged them in gratitude to *undo the heavy burdens*, Isa. lviii. 6.

Verses 6–13

The foregoing complaint was made to Nehemiah at the time when he had his head and hands as full as possible of the public business about building the wall; yet, perceiving it to be just, he did not reject it. The case called for speedy interposition, and therefore he applied himself immediately to the consideration of it, knowing that, let him build Jerusalem's walls ever so high, so thick, so strong, the city could not be safe while such abuses as these were tolerated.

I. He *was very angry* (v. 6).

II. He *consulted with himself*, v. 7. By this it appears that he did not say or do anything unadvisedly. Before he rebuked the nobles, he consulted with himself what to say, and when, and how.

III. He *rebuked the nobles and rulers*, who were the monied men, and whose power perhaps made them the more bold to oppress. Let no man imagine that his dignity sets him above reproof.

IV. He set a great assembly against them. He called the people together to bear their testimony (which the people will generally be forward to do) against the oppressions and extortions, v. 12. Ezra and Nehemiah were both of them very wise, good, useful men, yet, in cases not unlike, there was a great deal of difference between their management: when Ezra was told of the sin of the rulers in marrying strange wives he rent his clothes, and wept, and prayed, and was hardly persuaded to attempt a reformation, fearing it to be impracticable, for he was a man of a mild tender spirit; when Nehemiah was told of as bad a thing he kindled immediately, reproached the delinquents, incensed the people against them, and never rested till, by all the rough methods he could use, he forced them to reform; for he was a man of a hot and eager spirit. Very holy men may differ much from each other in their natural temper. 2. God's work may be well done and yet different methods taken in the doing of it, which is a good reason why we should neither arraign the management of others nor make our own a standard.

V. He fairly reasoned the case with them, and showed them the evil of what they did. The regular way of reforming men's lives is to endeavour, in the first place, to convince their consciences. He lays it before them, 1. That those whom they oppressed were their brethren. 2. That they were but lately redeemed *out of the hand of the heathen*. The body of the people were so by the wonderful providence of God. "Now," says he, "have we taken all this pains to get their liberty out of the hands of the heathen, and shall their own rulers enslave them?" 3. That it was a great sin thus to oppress the poor (v. 9). 4. That it was a reproach to their profession. "Consider *the reproach of the heathen our enemies;* they will say, These Jews, that profess so much devotion to God, see how barbarous they are one to another." Nothing exposes religion more to the reproach of its enemies than the worldliness and hardheartedness of the professors of it.

VI. He earnestly pressed them not only not to make their poor neighbours any more such hard bargains, but to restore that which they had got into their hands, v. 11. See how familiarly he speaks to them: *Let us leave off this usury*, putting himself in, as becomes reprovers, though far from being any way guilty of the crime. Though he had authority to command, yet, *for love's sake, he rather beseeches.*

VII. He got a promise from them (v. 12): *We will restore them.* He sent for the priests to give them their oath that they would perform this promise. *So let God shake out every man that performeth not this promise*, v. 13. This was a threatening to which the people said *Amen*. With this *Amen* the people *praised the Lord*. This cheerfulness in promising was well, but that which follows was better: *They did according to this promise*, and adhered to what they had done.

Verses 14–19

Nehemiah relates more particularly what his practice was, not in pride or vainglory, but as an inducement both to his successors and to the inferior magistrates to be as tender as might be of the people's ease.

I. He intimates what had been the way of his predecessors, v. 15. He does not name them, because what he had to say of them was not to their honour, and in such a case it is good to spare names. The government allowed them *forty shekels of silver* (so much a day, it is probable); but, besides that, they obliged the people to furnish them with *bread and wine*, and they suffered their servants to squeeze the people, and to get all they could out of them.

II. He tells us what had been his own way.

1. In general, he had not done as the former governors did. The fear of God restrained him from oppressing the people. He was thus generous purely for conscience' sake. Nehemiah, for his part, got nothing, except the satisfaction of doing good: *Neither bought we any land*, v. 16.

2. More particularly, observe (1) How little Nehemiah received of what he might have required. So far was he from extorting more than his due that he never demanded that, but lived upon what he had got in the king of Persia's court and his own estate in Judæa: the reason he gives for this piece of self-denial is, *Because the bondage was heavy upon the people*. In our demands we must consider not only the justice of them, but the ability of those on whom we make them. (2) How much he gave which he might have withheld. [1] His servants' work, v. 16. [2] His own meat, v. 17, 18.

III. He concludes with a prayer (v. 19): *Think upon me, my God, for good*. 1. Nehemiah here mentions what he had *done for this people* to shame the rulers out of their oppressions. 2. He mentions it to God in prayer, not as if he thought he had hereby merited any favour from God, as a debt. "If God do but *think upon me for good*, I have enough."

CHAPTER 6

The cries of oppressed poverty being stilled, the building of the wall goes forward, and in this chapter we find it finished with joy. How the Jews' enemies were baffled in their design to put a stop to it by force we read before, ch. iv. Here we find how their endeavours to drive Nehemiah off from it were frustrated. I. When they courted him to an interview, with design to do him a mischief, he would not stir, ver. 1–4. II. When they would have made him believe his undertaking was represented as seditious and treasonable, ver. 5–9. III. When they hired pretended prophets to advise him to retire, ver. 10–14. IV. Notwithstanding the secret correspondence that was kept up between them and some false and treacherous Jews, the work was finished, ver. 15–19.

Verses 1–9

Two plots upon Nehemiah.

I. A plot to trepan him into a snare. The enemies had an account that all the breaches of the wall were made up, so that they considered it as good as done, though at that time the *doors of the gates* were off the hinges (v. 1); they must therefore now or never, by one bold stroke, take off Nehemiah. 1. With subtlety they courted him to meet them in a village in the lot of Benjamin: "Come, let us meet *together* to consult about the common interests of our provinces." *But they thought to do him a mischief.* 2. He declined the motion. His care was that the work might not cease; he knew it would if he left it ever so little; and *why should it cease while I come down to you?* Four times *I answered them* (says he) *after the same manner*, v. 4.

II. A plot to terrify him from his work. This therefore Sanballat attempts, but in vain. 1. He endeavours to possess Nehemiah with an apprehension that his undertaking to build the walls of Jerusalem was generally represented as factious and seditious, v. 5–7. This is written to him in *an open letter*, as a thing generally known and talked of, and Gashmu will aver it for truth, that Nehemiah was aiming to make himself king and to shake off the Persian yoke. Now Sanballat pretends to inform Nehemiah of this as a friend—"*Let us take counsel together* how to quell the report." He hoped, like Judas, to kiss and kill. Nehemiah not only denied that such things were true, but that they were reported; he was better known than to be thus suspected. 2. Thus he escaped the snare and kept his ground. While we keep a good conscience, let us trust God with our good name.

He lifts up his heart to Heaven in this short prayer: *Now therefore, O God! strengthen my hands.* When, in our Christian work and warfare, we are entering upon any particular services or conflicts, this is a good prayer—"*Now therefore, O God! strengthen my hands.*"

Verses 10–14

The Jews' enemies leave no stone unturned, to take Nehemiah off from building the wall about Jerusalem. Now they try to drive him into the temple for his own safety; let him be anywhere but at his work.

I. How basely the enemies managed this temptation.

1. That which they designed was to bring Nehemiah to do a foolish thing, that they might laugh at him (v. 13): *That I should be afraid*, and so they might have *matter for an evil report*, and *might reproach me*.

2. The tools they made use of were a pretended prophet and prophetess, whom they hired to persuade Nehemiah to quit his work and retire for his own safety. The pretended prophet was Shemaiah, of whom it is said that he was *shut up* in his own house, under pretence of retirement for meditation. Nehemiah went to his house to consult him, v. 10. Other prophets there were, and one prophetess, Noadiah (v. 14), that were in the interest of the Jews' enemies.

3. The pretence was plausible. These prophets suggested to Nehemiah that the enemies would come and slay him, *in the night*. They pretended to be much concerned for his safety. They very gravely advised him to hide himself in the temple till the danger was over. If Nehemiah had been prevailed upon to do this, immediately the people would both have left off their work and thrown down their arms, and everyone would have shifted for his own safety; and then the enemies might easily, and without opposition, have broken down the wall again.

II. Nehemiah vanquished this temptation, and came off conqueror.

1. He immediately resolved not to yield to it, v. 11. "*Should such a man as I flee?* I will not go in. I will rather die at my work than live in an inglorious retreat from it."

2. He was immediately aware of what was the rise of it (v. 12): "*I perceived that God had not sent him*, that he gave this advice, not by any divine direction, but with a design against me." Two things Nehemiah says he dreaded (1) Offending God: *That I should be afraid, and do so, and sin.* Sin is that which above anything we should dread; and a good preservative it is against sin to be afraid of nothing but sin. (2) Shaming himself: *That they might reproach me.*

3. He humbly begs of God to reckon with them for their base designs upon him (v. 14): *My God, think thou upon Tobiah*, and the rest of them, *according to their works.*

Verses 15–19

Nehemiah is here finishing the wall of Jerusalem, and yet still has trouble created by his enemies.

I. Tobiah, and the other adversaries of the Jews, had the mortification to see the wall built up, notwithstanding all their attempts to hinder it. The wall was finished *in fifty-two days*, and we have reason to believe they rested on the sabbaths, v. 15. Many were employed, and what they did they did cheerfully, because they loved it. When the enemies heard that the wall was finished before they thought it was well begun, they were *much cast down in their own*

eyes, v. 16. They envied the prosperity and success of the Jews, grieved to see the walls of Jerusalem built. If it were of God, it was to no purpose to think of opposing it; it would certainly prevail and be victorious.

II. Nehemiah had the vexation notwithstanding this, to see some of his own people treacherously corresponding with Tobiah. Many in Judah were in a strict but secret confederacy with him to advance the interest of his country, though it would certainly be the ruin of their own. They were *sworn unto him*, not as their prince, but as their friend and ally, because both he and his son had married daughters of Israel, *v.* 18. See the mischief of marrying with strangers; for one heathen that was converted by it ten Jews were perverted. They had the impudence to court Nehemiah himself into a friendship with him. They were so false as to betray Nehemiah's counsels to him. Thus were all their thoughts against him for evil, yet God thought upon him for good.

Chapter 7

Nehemiah, having fortified Jerusalem with gates and walls, his next care is, I. To see the city well kept, ver. 1–4. II. To see it well peopled, in order to which he here reviews and calls over the register of the children of the captivity, the families that returned at first, and records it, ver. 5–73. What use he made of it we shall find afterwards, when he brought one of ten to live in Jerusalem, ch. xi. 1.

Verses 1–4

God saith concerning his church (Isa. lxii. 6), *I have set watchmen upon thy walls, O Jerusalem!* This is Nehemiah's care here; for dead walls, without living watchmen, are but a poor defence to a city.

I. He appointed *the porters, singers, and Levites*, in their places to their work. God's worship is the defence of a place, and his ministers, when they mind their duty, are watchmen on the walls.

II. He appointed two governors or consuls, to whom he committed the care of the city, and gave them in charge to provide for the public peace and safety. Hanani, his brother, who came to him with the tidings of the desolations of Jerusalem, was one, a man of approved integrity and affection to his country; the other was Hananiah, who had been ruler of the palace. Of this Hananiah it is said that he was a *faithful man and one that feared God above many, v.* 2.

III. He gave orders about the shutting of the gates and the guarding of the walls, v. 3, 4. The city, in compass, was large. The walls enclosed the same ground as formerly; but much of it lay waste, for the houses were not built; so that Nehemiah walled the city in faith, and with an eye to that promise of the replenishing of it which God had lately made by the prophet, Zech. viii. 3, &c. Though the people were now few, he believed they would be multiplied and therefore built the walls so as to make room for them. The care of Nehemiah for it. He ordered the rulers of the city themselves, 1. To stand by, and see the city-gates shut up and barred every night. 2. To take care that they should not be opened in the morning till they could see that all was clear and quiet. 3. To set sentinels who should, in case of the approach of the enemy, give timely notice to the city of the danger; and, as it came to their turn to watch, they must post themselves *over against their own houses*, because of them, they would be in a particular manner careful. The public safety depends upon everyone's particular care to guard himself and his own family against sin, that common enemy. They were made sensible that *except the Lord kept the city the watchman waked but in vain*, Ps. cxxvii. 1.

Verses 5–73

Another good project of Nehemiah's. He knew very well that the safety of a city, under God, depends more upon the number and valour of the inhabitants than upon the height or strength of its walls; and therefore he thought fit to take an account of the people, that he might find what families had formerly had their settlement in Jerusalem, that he might bring them back, and what families could be influenced by their religion, or by their business, to come and rebuild the houses in Jerusalem and dwell in them. It is the wisdom of the governors of a nation to keep the balance even between the city and country, that the metropolis be not so extravagantly large as to drain and impoverish the country, nor yet so weak as not to be able to protect it.

I. Whence this good design of Nehemiah's came. He owns, *My God put it into my heart, v.* 5.

II. What method he took in prosecution of it.

1. He called the rulers together, and the people, that he might have an account of the present state of their families—their number and strength, and where they were settled.

2. He reviewed the old *register of the genealogy of those who came up at the first,* and compared the present accounts with that; and here we have the repetition of that out of Ezra ii. There are many differences in the numbers between this catalogue and that in Ezra. What differences there are we may suppose to arise either from the mistakes of transcribers, or from the diversity of the copies from which they were taken. Or perhaps one was the account of them when they set out from Babylon with Zerubbabel, the other when they came to Jerusalem. The sum totals are all just the same there and here, except of the singing-men and singing-women, which there are 200, here 245. An account of the offerings which were given towards the work of God, *v.* 70, &c. differs much from that in Ezra ii. 68, 69, and it must be questioned whether it refers to the same contribution; here the tirshatha, or chief governor, who there was not mentioned, begins the offering; and the single sum mentioned there exceeds all those here put together; yet it is probable that it was the same, but that followed one copy of the lists, this another; for the last verse is the same here that it was Ezra ii. 70, and Ezra iii. 1. Blessed be God that our faith and hope are not built upon the niceties of names and numbers, genealogy, and chronology, but on the great things of the law and gospel.

CHAPTER 8

Ezra came up out of Babylon thirteen years before Nehemiah came, yet we have here a piece of good work which he did, that might have been done before, but was not done till Nehemiah came, who was a man of a more lively, active spirit. His zeal set Ezra's learning on work, and then great things were done, as we find here, I. The public and solemn reading and expounding of the law, ver. 1–8. II. The joy which the people were ordered to express upon that occasion, ver. 9–12. III. The solemn keeping of the feast of tabernacles according to the law, ver. 13–18.

Verses 1–8

An account of a solemn religious assembly, and the good work that was done in that assembly.

I. The time of it was the *first day of the seventh month, v.* 2. That was the day of the *feast of trumpets,* which is called a *sabbath,* and on which they were to have a *holy convocation,* Lev. xxiii. 24; Num. xxix. 1. But that was not all: it was on that day that the altar was set up, and they began to offer their burnt-offerings after their return out of captivity, a recent mercy in the memory of many then living.

II. The place was in the *street that was before the water-gate (v.* 1), a spacious broad street, able to contain so great a multitude, which the court of the temple was not; for probably it was not now built nearly so large as it had been in Solomon's time. Sacrifices were to be offered only at the door of the temple, but praying, and praising, and preach-

ing, were, and are, services of religion as acceptably performed in one place as in another. When this congregation thus met in the street of the city no doubt God was with them.

III. The persons that met were all the people, who were not compelled to come, but voluntarily gathered themselves together by common agreement, as one man: not only men came, but women and children. Little ones, as they come to the exercise of reason, must be trained up in the exercises of religion.

IV. The master of this assembly was Ezra the priest.

1. His call to the service was very clear; for being in office as a priest, and qualified as a scribe, the *people spoke to him to bring the book of the law* and read it to them, *v.* 1. 2. His post was very convenient. He stood in a pulpit or tower of wood, *which they made for the word, for the preaching of the word,* that what he said might be the more gracefully delivered and the better heard, and that the eyes of the hearers might be upon him, Luke xx. 20. 3. He had several assistants. Some of these stood with him (*v.* 4), six on his right hand and seven on his left. Others who are mentioned (*v.* 7) seem to have been employed at the same time in other places near at hand, to read and expound to those who could not come within hearing of Ezra.

V. The religious exercises performed in this assembly were not ceremonial, but moral, praying and preaching. Ezra, as president of the assembly, was, 1. The people's mouth to God, and they affectionately joined with him, *v.* 6. He blessed the Lord as the great God, and the people said *Amen, Amen, lifted up up their hands* and *bowed their heads* in reverence. 2. God's mouth to the people, and they attentively hearkened to him. *Ezra brought the law before the congregation, v.* 2. Ministers, when they go to the pulpit, should take their Bibles with them; Ezra did so; thence they must fetch their knowledge. See 2 Chron. xvii. 9. He opened the book with great reverence and solemnity, *in the sight of all the people v.* 5. He and others read in the book of the law, *from morning till noon (v.* 3), and they read *distinctly, v.* 8. Let those that read and preach the word learn also to deliver themselves distinctly, as those who understand what they say and are affected with it themselves, and who desire that those they speak to may understand it, retain it, and be affected with it likewise. *It is a snare for a man to devour that which is holy.* What they read they expounded. It is requisite that those who hear the word should understand it. It is therefore required of those who are teachers by office that they explain the word and give the sense of it. When Ezra opened the book *all the people stood up (v.* 5), thereby showing respect both to Ezra and to the word he was about to read.

Verses 9–12

I. The people were wounded with the words of the law that were read to them. The law shows men their sins, and their misery and danger because of sin. Therefore when they heard it they *all wept (v.* 9): it was a good sign that their hearts were tender, like Josiah's when he heard the words of the law. They wept to think how they had offended God.

II. They were healed and comforted with the words of peace that were spoken to them. It was one of the solemn feasts, on which it was their duty to rejoice; and even sorrow for sin must not hinder our joy in God, but rather lead us to it. Ezra was pleased to see them so affected with the word, but Nehemiah observed to him, and Ezra concurred in the thought, that it was now unseasonable. This day was holy and therefore was to be celebrated with joy and praise, not as if it were *a day to afflict their souls.* They forbade the people to *mourn and weep (v.* 9): *Be not sorry (v.* 10); *hold your peace, neither be you* grieved, *v.* 11. They commanded them to testify their joy, to put *on the garments of praise instead of the spirit of heaviness.* They allowed them, in token of their joy, to feast themselves. But then it must be, 1. With charity to the poor: "*Send portions to those for whom nothing is prepared* that your abundance may supply their want, that they may rejoice with you." 2. It must be with piety and devotion: *The joy of the Lord is your strength.* Holy joy will be oil to the wheels of our obedience.

III. The assembly complied with the directions that were given them. Their weeping was *stilled* (*v.* 11) and they *made great mirth, v.* 12. Those that *sow in tears shall reap in joy;* those that tremble at the convictions of the word may triumph in the consolations of it. They made mirth, not because they had the fat to eat and the sweet to drink, and a great deal of good company, but because they had *understood the words that were declared to them.* The darkness of trouble arises from the darkness of ignorance and mistake. When the words were first declared to them they wept; but, when they understood them, they rejoiced, finding at length precious promises made to those who repented and reformed and that therefore there was hope in Israel.

Verses 13–18

I. The people's renewed attendance upon the word. The next day after, though it was no festival, the chief of them came together again to hear Ezra expound (*v.* 13). Now the priests and the Levites themselves came with *the chief of the people to Ezra,* as it is in the margin, *that they might instruct in the words of the law;* they came to be taught themselves, that they might be qualified to teach others. Now, they being by trial made more sensible than ever of their own deficiencies and his excellencies, on the second day their humility set them at Ezra's feet, as learners of him.

II. The people's ready obedience to the word as soon as they were made sensible of their duty therein. It is probable that Ezra, *after the wisdom of his God that was in his hand* (Ezra vii. 25), when they applied to him for instruction out of the law on the second day of the seventh month, read to them those laws which concerned the feasts of that month, and, among the rest, that of the feast of tabernacles, Lev. xxiii. 34; Deut. xvi. 13. 1. The divine appointment of the feast of tabernacles reviewed, *v.* 14, 15. *They found written in the law* a commandment concerning it. This feast of tabernacles was a memorial of their dwelling in tents in the wilderness, a representation of our tabernacle state in this world. The conversion of the nations to the faith of Christ is foretold under the figure of this feast (Zech. xiv. 16); they shall come to *keep the feast of tabernacles,* as having here no continuing city. The people were themselves to fetch boughs of trees (they of Jerusalem fetched them from the mount of Olives) and to make booths, or arbours, of them, in which they were to lodge. 2. This appointment religiously observed, *v.* 16, 17. (1) They observed the ceremony: *They sat in booths,* which the priests and Levites set up in the courts of the temple; those that had houses of their own set up booths on the roofs of them, or in their courts; and those that had not, set them up in the streets. All their holy feasts, but this especially, were to be celebrated with joy. (2) They attended the reading and expounding of the word of God during all the days of the feast, *v.* 18.

CHAPTER 9

An account of an occasional fast that was kept as a day of humiliation. I. How this fast was observed, ver. 1–3. II. What were the heads of the prayer that was made to God on that occasion, concluding with a solemn resolution of new obedience, ver. 4–38.

Verses 1–3

A general account of a public fast which the children of Israel kept, probably by order from Nehemiah. It was a fast that men appointed, but such *a fast as God had chosen;* for, 1. It was a day *to afflict the soul,* Isa. lviii. 5. Probably they assembled in the courts of the temple, and they there appeared in sackcloth and in the posture of mourners, with earth on their heads, *v.* 1. They were restrained from *weeping, ch,* viii. 9, but now they were directed to weep. 2. It was a day *to loose the bands of wickedness,* and that is the fast that God has chosen, Isa. lviii. 6. Without this, spreading sackcloth and ashes under us is but a jest. 3. It was a day of communion with God. *They fasted to him, even to him* (Zech. vii. 5); for, (1) They spoke to him in prayer. Fasting without prayer is a body without a soul, a worthless carcase. (2) They heard him speaking to them by his word; for they read in the book of the law that, in the glass of the law, we may see our deformities and defilements, and know what to acknowledge and what to amend. The time was equally divided between these two. Three hours they spent in reading, expounding, and applying the scriptures, and three hours in confessing sin and praying; so that they stayed together six hours, and spent all the time in the solemn acts of religion, without saying, *Behold, what a weariness is it!*

Verses 4–38

An account how the work of this fast-day was carried on. 1. The names of the ministers that were employed. They are twice named (*v.* 4, 5). Either they prayed successively, or, as some think, there were eight several congregations at some distance from each other, and each had a Levite to preside in it. 2. The work itself in which they employed themselves. (1) They prayed to God for the pardon of the sins of Israel and God's favour to them. (2) They praised God; for the work of praise is not unseasonable on a fast-day; in all acts of devotion we must aim at this, *to give unto God the glory due to his name.* The summary of their prayers we have here upon record.

I. An awful adoration of God, as a perfect and glorious Being, and the fountain of all beings, *v.* 5, 6. The congregation is called upon to signify their concurrence herewith by standing up; and so the minister directs himself to God, *blessed be thy glorious name.* God is here adored, 1. As the only living and true God: *Thou art Jehovah alone.* 2. As the Creator of all things: *Thou hast made heaven, earth, and seas,* and all that is in them. 3. As the great Protector of the whole creation: "Thou preservest in being all the creatures thou hast given being to." 4. As the object of the creatures' praises: "*The host of heaven,* the world of holy angels, *worshippeth thee, v.* 6. But thy *name is exalted above all blessing and praise.*"

II. A thankful acknowledgment of God's favours to Israel.

1. Many of these are here reckoned up in order before him.

2. The particular instances of God's goodness to Israel here recounted. (1) The call of Abraham, *v.* 7. (2) The covenant God made with him to give the land of Canaan to him and his seed, a type of the better country, *v.* 8. (3) The deliverance of Israel out of Egypt, *v.* 9–11. It was seasonable to remember this now that they were interceding for the perfecting of their deliverance out of Babylon. (4) The conducting of them through the wilderness, by the pillar of cloud and fire, which showed them which way they should go, when they should remove, and when and where they should rest, directed all their stages and all their steps, *v.* 12. It was also a visible token of God's presence with them, to guide and guard them.

(5) The plentiful provision made for them in the wilderness, that they might not perish for hunger: Thou *gavest them bread from heaven*, and *water out of the rock* (v. 15), and, to hold up their hearts, a promise that they should go in and possess the land of Canaan. They had meat and drink, food convenient in the way, and the good land at their journey's end; what would they more? This also is repeated (v. 20, 21) as that which was continued, notwithstanding their provocations: *Forty years didst thou sustain them.* (6) The giving of the law upon Mount Sinai. The Lawgiver was very glorious, v. 13. "Thou didst not only send, but camest down thyself, and *didst speak with them*," Deut. iv. 33. No nation under the sun had such *right judgments, true laws*, and *good statutes*, Deut. iv. 8. And with *the law* and *the sabbath*, he *gave his good Spirit to instruct them*, v. 20. Besides the law given on Mount Sinai, the five books of Moses, which he wrote *as he was moved by the Holy Ghost*, were constant instructions to them. (7) The putting of them in possession of Canaan, that good land, *kingdoms and nations*, v. 22. They were made so numerous as to replenish it (v. 23) and so victorious as to be masters of it (v. 24). (8) God's great readiness to pardon their sins, and work deliverance for them, when they had by their provocations brought his judgments upon themselves. Afterwards, when they were settled in Canaan and sold themselves by their sins into the hands of their enemies, upon their submission and humble request he *gave them saviours* (v. 27), the judges, by whom God wrought many a great deliverance for them when they were on the brink of ruin. (9) The admonitions and fair warnings he gave them by his servants the prophets. When he delivered them from their troubles he *testified against their sins* (v. 28, 29), that they might not misconstrue their deliverances as connivances at their wickedness. The testimony of the prophets was the testimony of the Spirit in the prophets, and it was the Spirit of Christ in them, 1 Peter i. 10, 11. They *spoke as they were moved by the Holy Ghost*, and what they said is to be received accordingly. (10) The lengthening out of his patience and the moderating of his rebukes: *Many years did he forbear them* (v. 30), as loth to punish them, and waiting to see if they would repent; and when he did punish them, he did not *utterly consume them nor forsake them*, v. 31.

III. A penitent confession of sin, their own sins, and the sins of their fathers.

1. They begin with the sins of Israel in the wilderness: *They, even our fathers dealt proudly and hardened their necks*, v. 16. Pride is at the bottom of men's obstinacy and disobedience. When men make no right use either of God's ordinances or of his providences, what can be expected from them? Two great sins are here specified, which they were guilty of in the wilderness—meditating a return, (1) To Egyptian slavery, which, for the sake of the garlick and onions, they preferred before the glorious liberty of the Israel of God attended with some difficulty and inconvenience. (2) To Egyptian idolatry: *They made a molten calf*, and were so sottish as to say, *This is thy God.*

2. They next bewail the provocations of their fathers after they were put in possession of Canaan.

3. They at length come nearer to their own day, and lament the sins which had brought those judgments upon them which they had long been groaning under and were now but in part delivered from. Two things they charge upon themselves and their fathers, as the cause of their troubles:—(1) A contempt of the good law God had given them: They *sinned against thy judgments*, the dictates of divine wisdom, and the demands of divine sovereignty. (2) A contempt of the good land God had given them (v. 35).

Those that would not serve God in their own land were made to serve their enemies in a strange land, as was threatened, Deut. xxviii. 47, 48.

IV. A humble representation of the judgments of God, which they had been and were now under.

1. Former judgments are remembered. They had not taken warning. In the days of the judges their *enemies vexed them* (v. 27); and, when they did evil again, God did again *leave them in the hand of their enemies*.

2. Their present calamitous state is laid before the Lord (v. 36, 37): *We are servants this day.* Freeborn Israelites are enslaved, and the land which they had long held by a much more honourable tenure, they now held by, from, and under, the kings of Persia, whose vassals they were. This, they honestly own, was for their sins. Poverty and slavery are the fruits of sin; it is sin that brings us into all our distresses.

V. Their address to God under these calamities.

1. By way of request, that their trouble might not *seem little*, v. 32. It is the only petition in all this prayer. The trouble was universal; it had come on their *kings, princes, priests, prophets, fathers, and all their people*; they had all shared in the sin (v. 34), and now all shared in the judgment. It was of long continuance: *From the time of the kings of Assyria*, who carried the ten tribes captive, *unto this day*. "Lord, let it not all seem little and not worthy to be regarded, or not needing to be relieved." They do not prescribe to God what he shall do for them, but leave it to him. 2. By way of acknowledgment, notwithstanding, that really it was less than they deserved, v. 33. They own the justice of God in all their troubles.

VI. The result and conclusion of this whole matter. After this long remonstrance of their case was made they came at last to this resolution. "Because of all this, we make a sure covenant with God; in consideration of our frequent departures from God, we will now more firmly than ever bind ourselves to him. Because we have smarted so much for sin, we will now steadfastly resolve against it, that we may not any more withdraw the shoulder." A certain number of the princes, priests, and Levites, were chosen as the representatives of the congregation, to subscribe and seal it for and in the name of the rest.

CHAPTER 10

A particular account of the covenant which in the close of the foregoing chapter was resolved upon, I. The names of those that set their hands and seals to it, ver. 1–27. II. An account of those who signified their consent and concurrence, ver. 28, 29. III. The covenant itself, and the articles of it in general, that they would "keep God's commandments" (ver. 29); in particular, that they would not marry with the heathen (ver. 30), nor profane the sabbath, nor be rigorous with their debtors (ver. 31), and that they would carefully pay their church-dues, for the maintenance of the temple service, ver. 32–39.

Verses 1–31

When Israel was first brought into covenant with God it was done by sacrifice and the sprinkling of blood, Exod. xxiv. But here it was done by the more natural and common way of sealing and subscribing the written articles of the covenant.

I. The names of those public persons who, as the representatives and heads of the congregation, set their hands and seals to this covenant. Nehemiah, who was the governor, signed first. Next to him subscribed twenty-two priests. Next to the priests, seventeen Levites subscribed this covenant, among whom we find all or most of those who were the mouth of the congregation in prayer, *ch.* ix. 4, 5. Those that lead in prayer should lead in every other good work. Next to the Levites, forty-four of the chief of the people gave it under their hands for themselves and all the rest.

II. The concurrence of the rest of the people with them, and the rest of the priests and Levites, who signified their consent to what their chiefs did. With them joined, 1. Their wives and children; for they had transgressed, and they must reform. 2. The proselytes of other nations, *all that had separated themselves from the people of the lands*, their gods and their worship, *unto the law of God*, and the observance of that law. See what conversion is; it is separating ourselves from the course and custom of this world, and devoting ourselves to the conduct of the word of God. And, as there is one law, so there is one covenant, one baptism, for the stranger and for him that is born in the land. The concurrence of the people is expressed, *v.* 29. *They clave to their brethren* one and all.

III. The general purport of this covenant. They laid upon themselves no other burden than this necessary thing, which they were already obliged to by all other engagements of duty, interest, and gratitude—*to walk in God's law, and to do all his commandments, v.* 29.

IV. Some of the particular articles of this covenant, such as were adopted to their present temptations. 1. That they would not intermarry with the heathen, *v.* 30. 2. That they would keep no markets on the sabbath day, or any other day of which the law has said, *You shall do no work therein.* The sabbath is a market day for our souls, but not for our bodies. 3. That they would not be severe in exacting their debts, but would observe the seventh year as a year of release, according to the law, *v.* 31.

Verses 32–39

I. It was resolved, in general, that the temple service should be carefully kept up, that the work of the house of their God should be done in its season, according to the law, *v.* 33. It is likely to go well with our houses when care is taken that the work of God's house may go well. It was likewise resolved that they would never *forsake the house of their God* (*v.* 39), for the house of any other god, or for the high places, as idolaters did, nor forsake it for their farms and merchandises, as those did that were atheistical and profane. Those that forsake the worship of God forsake God.

II. It was resolved, in pursuance of this, that they would liberally maintain the temple service, and not starve it if the people would do theirs, which was to find them materials to work upon. Now here it was agreed and concluded, 1. That a stock should be raised for the furnishing of God's table and altar plentifully. The people therefore agreed to contribute yearly, every one of them, the third part of a shekel, about ten pence a-piece for the bearing of this expense. When everyone will act, and everyone will give, though but little, towards a good work, the whole amount will be considerable. The tirshatha did not impose this tax, but the people made it an ordinance for themselves, and charged themselves with it, *v.* 32, 33. 2. That particular care should be taken to provide wood for the altar, to keep the fire always burning upon it. 3. That all those things which the divine law had appointed for the maintenance of the priests and Levites should be duly paid in, that they might not be under any temptation to neglect it for the making of necessary provision for their families. First-fruits and tenths were then the principal branches of the minister's revenues; and they here resolve to bring in the first fruits justly and to bring in their tenths likewise. This was the law (Num. xviii. 21–28); but these dues had been withheld, in consequence of which God, by the prophet, charges them with *robbing him* (Mal. iii. 8, 9), at the same time encouraging them to be more just to him and his receivers, with a promise that,

if they brought the *tithes into the store-house*, he would *pour out blessings upon them, v.* 10. This therefore they resolved to do, that there might be meat in God's house. "We will do it (say they) *in all the cities of our tillage," v.* 37. *In all the cities of our servitude*, so the LXX, for they were servants in their own land, *ch.* ix. 36. Though they paid great taxes to the kings of Persia, and had much hardship put upon them, they would not make that an excuse for not paying their tithes, but would render to God the things that were his, as well as to Cæsar the things that were his.

CHAPTER 11

Jerusalem was walled round, but it was not as yet fully inhabited. Nehemiah's next care is to bring people into it. I. The methods taken to replenish it, ver. 1, 2. II. The principal persons that resided there, of Judah and Benjamin (ver. 3–9), of the priests and Levites, ver. 10–19. III. The several cities and villages of Judah and Benjamin that were peopled by the rest of their families, ver. 20–36.

Verses 1–19

Jerusalem is called here *the holy city* (*v.* 1), because there the temple was, and God had chosen to put his name there; the holy seed should all have chosen to dwell there, but, on the contrary, they declined. 1. Because a greater strictness was expected from the inhabitants of Jerusalem than from others. Those who care not for being holy themselves are shy of dwelling in a holy city. Or, 2. Because Jerusalem, of all places, was most hated by the heathen their neighbours, which made that the post of danger (as the post of honour usually is) and therefore they were not willing to expose themselves there. Fear of persecution and reproach, keeps many out of the holy city, and makes them backward to appear for God and religion, not considering that, as Jerusalem is threatened and insulted by its enemies, so it is with a special care protected by its God and made a *quiet habitation*, Isa. xxxiii. 20; Ps. xlvi. 4, 5. Or, 3. Because it was more for their worldly advantage to dwell in the country. Jerusalem was no trading city, and therefore there was no money to be got there by merchandise, as there was in the country by corn and cattle.

I. By what means it was replenished. 1. The rulers dwelt there, *v.* 1. That was the proper place for them to reside in, because *there were set the thrones of judgment* (Ps. cxxii. 5). Their dwelling there would invite and encourage others too. *Magnates magnetes—the mighty are magnetic.* 2. There were some that willingly offered themselves to dwell at Jerusalem, nobly foregoing their own secular interest for the public welfare, *v.* 2. They *sought the good of Jerusalem, because of the house of the Lord their God.* 3. They, finding that *yet there was room*, concluded upon a review of their whole body to bring one in ten to dwell in Jerusalem; who they should be was determined by lot, the disposal whereof, all knew, was of the Lord.

II. By what persons it was replenished. 1. Many of the children of Judah and Benjamin dwelt there; for, originally, part of the city lay in the lot of one of those tribes and part in that of the other; but the greater part was in the lot of Benjamin, and therefore here we find of the children of Judah only 468 families in Jerusalem (*v.* 6), but of Benjamin 928, *v.* 7, 8. Though the Benjamites were more in number, yet of the men of Judah it is said (*v.* 6) that they were valiant men, fit for service, and able to defend the city in case of an attack. Judah has not lost its ancient character of a lion's whelp, bold and daring. Of the Benjamites that dwelt in Jerusalem we are here told who was *overseer*, and who was second, *v.* 9. 2. The priests and Levites did many of them settle at Jerusalem. Of those that did the work of the house in their courses here were 822 of one family, 242 of another, and 128 of another, *v.* 12–14. It is said of some of them that they were *mighty men of valour* (*v.* 14). Some of the Levites also came and dwelt at Jerusalem, yet but few in comparison, 284 in all (*v.* 18), with 172 porters (*v.* 19), for much of their work was to *teach the good knowledge of God* up and down the country, for which purpose they were to be scattered in Israel. (1) It is said of one of the Levites that he had *the oversight of the outward business of the house of God, v.* 16. The priests were chief managers of the business within the temple gates; but this Levite was entrusted with the secular concerns of God's house, the collecting of the contributions, the providing of materials for the temple service, and the like. Those who take care of the *outward concerns* of the church, the serving of its tables, are as necessary in their place as those who take care of *its inward concerns*, who give themselves to the word and prayer. (2) It is said of another that he was *the principal to begin the thanksgiving in prayer*. Probably he had a good ear and a good voice, and was a scientific singer, and therefore was chosen to lead the psalm. He was precentor in the temple.

Verses 20–36

Some account of the other cities, in which dwelt *the residue of Israel, v.* 20. It was requisite that Jerusalem should be replenished, yet not so as to drain the country. 1. The Nethinims, the posterity of the Gibeonites, dwelt in Ophel, which was upon the wall of Jerusalem (*ch.* iii. 26). 2. Though the Levites were dispersed through the cities of Judah, yet they had an overseer who resided in Jerusalem, superior of their order and their provincial. 3. Some of the singers were appointed to look after the necessary repairs of the temple, they were *over the business of the house of God, v.* 22. The king of Persia allotted a particular maintenance for them, besides what belonged to them as Levites, *v.* 23. 4. Here is one that was the king's commissioner at Jerusalem. He is said to be *at the king's hand*, or *on the king's part*, in *all matters concerning the people*, to determine controversies that arose between the king's officers and his subjects, to see that what was due to the king from the people was duly paid in and what was allowed by the king for the temple service was duly paid out, and happy it was for the Jews that one of themselves was in this post. 5. An account of the villages, or country towns, which were inhabited by the residue of Israel—the towns in which the children of Judah dwelt (*v.* 25–30), those that were inhabited by the children of Benjamin (*v.* 31–35), and divisions for the Levites among both, *v.* 36.

CHAPTER 12

I. The names of the chief of the priests and the Levites that came up with Zerubbabel, v. 1–9. II. The succession of the high priests, ver. 10, 11. III. The names of the next generation of the other chief priests, ver. 12–21. IV. The eminent Levites that were in Nehemiah's time, ver. 22–26. V. The solemnity of dedicating the wall of Jerusalem, ver. 27–43. VI. The settling of the offices of the priests and Levites in the temple, ver. 44–47.

Verses 1–26

The names, of a great many priests and Levites, that were eminent in their day among the returned Jews. Perhaps it is intended to stir up their posterity, who succeeded them in the priest's office and inherited their dignities and preferments, to imitate their courage and fidelity. The succession of high priests during the Persian monarchy, from Jeshua, who was high priest at the time of the restoration, to Jaddua (or Jaddus), who was high priest when Alexander the Great, after the conquest of Tyre, came to Jerusalem, and paid great respect to this Jaddus, who met him in his pontifical habit, and showed him the prophecy

of Daniel, which foretold his conquests. The next generation of priests, who were chief men, and active in the days of Joiakim, sons of the first set. All those who are mentioned *v.* 1, &c., as eminent in their generation, are again mentioned, though with some variation in several of the names, *v.* 12, &c., except two, as having sons that were likewise eminent in their generation—a rare instance, that twenty good fathers should leave behind them twenty good sons. The next generation of Levites, or rather a latter generation; for those priests who are mentioned flourished in the days of Joiakim the high priest, these Levites in the days of Eliashib, *v.* 22. Then a generation of Levites was *raised up*, who were *recorded chief of the fathers* (*v.* 22), and were eminently serviceable to the interests of the church, and their service not the less acceptable for their being Levites only. Eliashib the high priest being allied to Tobiah (*ch.* xiii. 4), the other priests grew remiss; but then the Levites appeared the more zealous. Those who were now employed in expounding (*ch.* viii. 7) and in praying (*ch.* ix. 4, 5) were all Levites, not priests, regard being had to their personal qualifications more than to their order.

Verses 27–43

The dedication of the wall of Jerusalem.

I. The meaning of this dedication of the wall. It was not done till the city was pretty well replenished, *ch.* xi. It was a solemn thanksgiving to God for his great mercy. They devoted the city in a peculiar manner to God and to his honour, and took possession of it for him and in his name. This city was (as never any other was) a *holy city*, the *city of the great king* (Ps. xlviii. 2 and Matt. v. 35). They put the city and its walls under the divine protection, owning that *unless the Lord kept the city* the walls were *built in vain*.

II. With what solemnity it was performed, under the direction of Nehemiah. The Levites from all parts of the country were summoned to attend. There was a general rendezvous, *v.* 28. 29. They *purified themselves, v.* 30, then the people. Then they purified *the gates and the wall*. This purification was performed by sprinkling the *water of purifying* (or of *separation*, as it is called, Num. xix. 9) on *themselves* and the *people*, the walls and the gates—a type of the blood of Christ, with which our consciences being *purged from dead works*, we become fit to *serve the living God* (Heb. ix. 14). The princes, priests, and Levites, walked round upon the wall in two companies, with musical instruments, to signify the dedication of it all to God (*v.* 36). They had a rendezvous where they divided themselves into two companies. Half of the princes, with several priests and Levites, went on the right hand, Ezra leading their van, *v.* 36. The other half of the princes and priests, who gave thanks likewise, went to the left hand, Nehemiah bringing up the rear, *v.* 38. At length both companies met in the temple, where they joined their thanksgivings, *v.* 40. The crowd of people, it is likely, walked some within the wall and others without. The people *greatly rejoiced, v.* 43. Their shouts, coming from a sincere and hearty joy, are here taken notice of; for God graciously accepts honest zealous services, though there is in them little of part. *The women and children rejoiced;* and their hosannas were not despised.

Verses 44–47

When the solemnities of a thanksgiving day leave such impressions on ministers and people as that both are more careful and cheerful in doing their duty afterwards, then they are indeed acceptable to God. So it was here. 1. The ministers were more careful than they had been of their work, *v.* 45. *The singers kept the ward of their God*, attending in due time to the duty of their office; the *porters*, too, *kept the ward of the purification*, that is, they took care to preserve the purity of the temple. 2. The people were more careful than they had been of the maintenance of their ministers, *v.* 44. Now, (1) Care is here taken for the collecting of their dues. They were modest, and would rather lose their right than call for it themselves. The people were many of them careless and would not bring their dues unless they were called upon; and therefore *some were appointed* whose office it should be to gather into the treasuries, *out of the fields of the cities, the portions of the law for the priests and Levites* (*v.* 44). (2) Care is taken that, being *gathered in*, they might be duly *paid out*, *v.* 47. They gave the singers and porters their daily portion, over and above what was due to them as Levites; for we may suppose that when David and Solomon appointed them their work (*v.* 45, 46), above what was required from them as Levites, they settled a fund for their further encouragement. For the other Levites, the tithes, here called *the holy things*, were duly set apart for them, out of which they paid the priests their tithe according to the law.

CHAPTER 13

Nehemiah, having finished what he undertook for the fencing and filling of the holy city, returned to the king his master, who was not willing to be long without him, as appears, ver. 6. But, after some time, he obtained leave to come back again to Jerusalem, to redress grievances, and purge out some corruptions which had crept in in his absence. I. He turned out from Israel the mixed multitude, the Moabites and Ammonites especially, ver. 1–3. With a particular indignation, he expelled Tobiah out of the lodgings he had got in the court of the temple, ver. 4–9. II. He secured the maintenance of the priests and Levites, ver. 10–14. III. He restrained the profanation of the sabbath day, ver. 15–22. IV. He checked the growing mischief of marrying strange wives, ver. 23–31.

Verses 1–9

Israel was not to mingle with the nations, nor suffer any of them to incorporate with them.

I. The law to this purport happened to be read *on that day, in the audience of the people* (*v.* 1), on the day of the dedication of the wall. They found a law, that the Ammonites and Moabites should not be naturalised, should not settle among them, nor unite with them, *v.* 1. The reason given is because they had been injurious and ill-natured to the Israel of God (*v.* 2), had not shown them common civility, but sought their ruin. This law we have, with this reason, Deut. xxiii. 3–5.

II. The people's ready compliance with this law, *v.* 3. See the benefit of the public reading of the word of God; it discovers to us sin and duty, good and evil, and shows us wherein we have erred. They *separated from Israel all the mixed multitude*, which had of old been a snare to them, for the *mixed multitude fell a-lusting*, Num. xi. 4. These they expelled.

III. The particular case of Tobiah, who was an Ammonite. He had the same enmity to Israel that his ancestors had, the spirit of an Ammonite, witness his indignation at Nehemiah (*ch.* ii. 10).

1. How basely Eliashib the chief priest took this Tobiah in to be a lodger even in the courts of the temple. He was allied to Tobiah (*v.* 4), by marriage first and then by friendship. His grandson had married Sanballat's daughter, *v.* 28. Probably some other of his family had married Tobiah's. It was expressly provided by the law that the high priest should marry *one of his own people*, else he *profanes his seed among his people*, Lev. xxi. 14, 15. In the courts of the temple, out of several little chambers used for store-chambers, he contrived to make a state-room for Tobiah, *v.* 5. That Tobiah the Ammonite should be entertained with respect in Israel, in the courts of God's house, as if to confront God himself; this was next to setting up an idol there. An Ammonite must not *come into the congregation*; and

shall one of the worst and vilest of the Ammonites be courted into the temple itself? Well might Nehemiah add (*v.* 6), *But all this time was not I at Jerusalem.* If he had been there, the high priest durst not have done such a thing.

2. How bravely Nehemiah, the chief governor, threw him out, and all that belonged to him, and restored the chambers to their proper use. When he came to Jerusalem, and was informed by the good people who were troubled at it what an intimacy had grown between their chief priest and their chief enemy, it *grieved him sorely* (*v.* 7, 8). Nehemiah has power and he will use it for God. Tobiah shall be expelled. He fears not his resentments, or Eliashib's, but expels the intruder, by casting forth all his household stuff. Our Saviour thus *cleansed the temple*, that the *house of prayer* might not be a *den of thieves*. And thus those that would expel sin out of their hearts, those living temples, must throw out all those things that are the food and fuel of lust. The temple stores shall be brought in again, and the *vessels of the house of God put in their places*; but the chambers must first be sprinkled with the water of purification, and so cleansed. Thus, when sin is cast out of the heart by repentance, let the blood of Christ be applied to it by faith, and then let it be furnished with the graces of God's Spirit for every good work.

Verses 10–14

Another grievance redressed by Nehemiah.

I. The Levites had been wronged. Their *portions had not been given them, v.* 10. The Levites were so modest as not to sue for them; *for the Levites and singers fled every one to his field.* This comes in as a reason either, 1. Why their payments were withheld. The Levites were non-residents: when they should have been doing their work about the temple, they were at their farms in the country; and therefore the people were little inclined to give them their maintenance. Or rather, 2. It is the reason why Nehemiah soon perceived that their dues had been denied them, because he missed them from their posts. "They have gone to get a livelihood for themselves and their families out of their grounds; for their profession would not maintain them." A scandalous maintenance makes a scandalous ministry.

II. Nehemiah laid the fault upon the rulers. Nehemiah began with the rulers, and called them to an account: "*Why is the house of God forsaken?* *v.* 11. Why are the Levites starved out of it?"

III. He delayed not to bring the dispersed Levites to *their places* again, and set them in *their stations* (as the word is), *v.* 11.

IV. He obliged the people to bring in their tithes, *v.* 12.

V. He provided that just and prompt payment should be made of the Levites' stipends. Commissioners were appointed to see to this (*v.* 13).

VI. Having no recompence from those for whom he did these good services, he looks up to God as his paymaster (*v.* 14): *Remember me, O my God! concerning this.* Nehemiah was a man much in pious ejaculations. He only prays, *Remember me*, not *Reward me*.

Verses 15–22

Another instance of that blessed reformation in which Nehemiah was so active. He revived sabbath-sanctification, and maintained the authority of the fourth commandment.

I. The law of the sabbath was very strict and much insisted on, and with good reason, for religion is never in the throne while sabbaths are trodden under foot. But Nehemiah discovered even in Judah this law was wretchedly violated. 1. The husbandmen trod their winepresses and brought home their corn on that day (*v.* 15), though there was an express command that *in earing-time, and in harvest-time, they should rest* on the sabbaths (Exod. xxxiv. 21). 2. The carriers *loaded their asses with all manner of burdens,* and made no scruple of it, though there was a particular proviso in the law for the cattle resting (Deut. v. 14) and that they should *bear no burden on the sabbath day,* Jer. xvii. 21. 3. The hawkers, and pedlars, and petty chapmen, that were men of Tyre, that famous trading city, *sold all manner of wares* on the sabbath day (*v.* 16).

II. The reformation of it.

1. He testified against those who profaned it, *v.* 15, and again *v.* 21.

2. He reasoned with the rulers concerning it, took the nobles of Judah to task, *v.* 17. He charges them with it: *You do it.* They did not carry corn, nor sell fish, but, they connived at those that did, and did not use their power to restrain them, and so made themselves guilty, as those magistrates do who bear the sword in vain. They set a bad example in other things. If the nobles allowed themselves in sports and recreations, in idle visits and idle talk, on the sabbath day, the men of business, both in city and country, would profane it by their worldly employments, as more justifiable. He reasons the case with them (*v.* 18). If they did not take warning, but returned to the same sins again, they had reason to expect further judgments: *You bring more wrath upon Israel by profaning the sabbath.*

3. He took care to prevent the profanation of the sabbath, as one that aimed only at reformation. If he could reform them, he would not punish them, and, if he should punish them, it was but that he might reform them. This is an example to magistrates to be heirs of restraint, and prudently to use the bit and bridle, that there may be no occasion for the lash. He ordered the gates of Jerusalem to be kept shut from the evening before the sabbath to the morning after, and set his own servants to watch them, that no burdens should be brought in on the sabbath day, nor late the night before, nor early in the morning after, lest sabbath time should be encroached upon, *v.* 19. He threatened those who came with goods to the gates, telling them that, if they came again, he would certainly lay hands on them (*v.* 21). He charged the Levites to take care about the due sanctifying of the sabbath, that they should cleanse themselves in the first place, and so give a good example to the people, and *that they should* some of them *come and keep the gates, v.* 22. Then there is likely to be a reformation, in this and other respects, when magistrates and ministers join their forces. The cure he wrought was lasting. In our Saviour's time, we find the Jews in the other extreme, over-scrupulous in the ceremonial part of Sabbath-sanctification.

4. He concludes this passage with a prayer (*v.* 22).

Verses 23-31

One instance more of Nehemiah's pious zeal for the purifying of his countrymen as a peculiar people to God.

I. They had corrupted themselves by marrying strange wives. This was complained of in Ezra's time, and much done towards a reformation, Ezra ix and x. Nehemiah, like a good governor, enquired into the state of the families of those that were under his charge, that he might reform what was amiss in them, and so heal the streams by healing the springs. He found that many of the Jews had *married wives of Ashdod, of Ammon, and of Moab* (*v.* 23). He talked with the children, and found they were *children of strangers,* for their *speech betrayed them.* The children were bred up with their mothers, and learned of them and their nurses and servants to speak, so that they could not speak the Jews' language, or not purely, but *half in the speech of Ashdod,* or Ammon, or Moab, according as the country was which the mother was a native of.

II. What course Nehemiah took to purge out this corruption.

1. He showed them the evil of it, and the obligation he lay under to witness against it. He quotes a precept, to prove that it was in itself a great sin; and makes them swear to that precept: *You shall not give your daughters unto their sons,* &c., which is taken from Deut. vii. 3. He quotes a precedent, to show the pernicious consequences of it, which made it necessary to be animadverted upon by the government (*v.* 26): *Did not Solomon king of Israel sin by these things?*

2. He showed himself highly displeased at it, that he might awaken them to a due sense of the evil of it: *He contended with them, v.* 25. He showed them how frivolous their excuses were, and argued it warmly with them. When he had silenced them he *cursed them,* that is, he denounced the judgments of God against them, and showed them what their sin deserved. Ezra, in this case, had plucked off his own hair, in holy sorrow for the sin; Nehemiah plucked off their hair, in a holy indignation at the sinners.

3. He obliged them not to take any more such wives, and separated those whom they had taken: *He cleansed them from all strangers,* both men and women (*v.* 30), and made them promise with an oath that they would never do so again, *v.* 25.

4. He took particular care of the priests' families, that they might not lie under this stain, this guilt. He found, upon enquiry, that a branch of the high priest's own family, one of his grandsons, had married a daughter of Sanballat, that notorious enemy of the Jews (*ch.* ii. 10; iv. 1), and so had, in effect, twisted interests with the Samaritans, *v.* 28. It seems this young priest would not put away his wife, and therefore Nehemiah *chased him from him,* deprived him, degraded him, and made him for ever incapable of the priesthood. Josephus says that this expelled priest was Manasseh, and that when Nehemiah drove him away he went to his father-in-law Sanballat, who built him a temple upon Mount Gerizim, like that at Jerusalem, and promised him he should be high priest in it, and that then was laid the foundation of the Samaritans' pretensions, which continued warm to our Saviour's time. Here are Nehemiah's prayers on this occasion. (1) He prays, *Remember them, O my God! v.* 29. "Lord, convince and convert them; put them in mind of what they should be and do, that they may come to themselves." (2) He prays, *Remember me, O my God! v.* 31.

AN EXPOSITION, WITH PRACTICAL OBSERVATIONS, OF

THE BOOK OF ESTHER

God deals not with us according to our folly and weakness. Those Jews who were scattered in the provinces of the heathen were taken care of, as well as those who were gathered in the land of Judæa, and were wonderfully preserved, when doomed to destruction and appointed as sheep for the slaughter. Who drew up this story is uncertain. Mordecai was as able as any man to relate, on his own knowledge, the several passages of it. That he wrote such an account of them as was necessary to inform his people of the grounds of their observing the feast of Purim we are told (*ch.* ix. 20, *Mordecai wrote these things*, and sent them enclosed in letters to all the Jews). It is the narrative of a plot laid against the Jews to cut them all off. The name of God is not found in this book; but the apocryphal addition to it (which is not in the Hebrew, nor was ever received by the Jews into the canon), containing six chapters, begins thus, *Then Mordecai said, God has done these things.* But, though the name of God be not in it, the finger of God is, directing many minute events for the bringing about of his people's deliverance. In such ways as God here took to defeat Haman's plot he will still protect his people. I. How Esther came to be queen and Mordecai to be great at court, who were to be the instruments of the intended deliverance, *ch.* i., ii. II. Upon what provocation, and by what arts, Haman the Amalekite obtained an order for the destruction of all the Jews, *ch.* iii. III. The great distress the Jews were in, *ch.* iv. IV. The defeating of Haman's particular plot against Mordecai's life, *ch.* v.–vii. V. The defeating of his general plot against the Jews, *ch.* viii. VI. The care that was taken to perpetuate the remembrance of this, *ch.* ix., x.

CHAPTER 1

The design of recording the story is to show how way was made for Esther to the crown, in order to her being instrumental to defeat Haman's plot, and this long before the plot was laid, that we may observe and admire the foresight and vast reaches of Providence. Ahasuerus the king, I. In his height feasts all his great men, ver. 1–9. II. In his heat he divorces his queen, because she would not come to him when he sent for her, ver. 10–22. This shows how God serves his own purposes even by the sins and follies of men.

Verses 1–9

Which of the kings of Persia this Ahasuerus was the learned are not agreed. Mordecai is said to have been one of those that were *carried* captive from *Jerusalem* (*ch.* ii. 5, 6), whence it should seem that this Ahasuerus was one of the first kings of that empire. Dr. Lightfoot thinks that he was that Artaxerxes who hindered the building of the temple, who is called also *Ahasuerus* (Ezra iv. 6, 7), after his great-grandfather of the Medes, Dan. ix. 1.

I. Of the vast extent of his dominion. In the time of Darius and Cyrus there were but 120 provinces (Dan. vi. 1); now there were 127, *from India to Ethiopia, v.* 1. It had become an over-grown kingdom, which in time would sink with its own weight.

II. Of the great pomp and magnificence of his court. He made a most extravagant feast *to show the riches of his glorious kingdom and the honour of his excellent majesty, v.* 4. This was vain glory, to no purpose at all. If he had shown the riches of his kingdom as some of his successors did, in contributing towards the building of the temple (Ezra vi. 8; vii. 22), it would have turned to a much better account. Two feasts Ahasuerus made:—1. One for his nobles and princes, which lasted *a hundred and eighty days, v.* 3, 4. 2. Another was made for *all the people, both great and small*, which lasted *seven days in the court of the garden, v.* 5. The tents which were there pitched for the company, were very fine and rich; so were the beds and the pavement under their feet, *v.* 6.

III. Of the good order which in some respects was kept there notwithstanding. Yet the Chaldee paraphrase says that the vessels of the sanctuary were used in this feast, to the great grief of the pious Jews. Two things which are laudable from the account here given:—1. *The drinking was according to the law*, probably some law lately made; *none did compel*, no, not by a continual proposing of it (as Josephus explains it). This caution of a heathen prince, even

when he would show his generosity, may shame many who are called Christians, who think they do not bid their friends welcome, unless they make them drunk, and, under pretence of sending the health round, send the sin round, and death with it. 2. There was no mixed dancing, Vashti feasted the women in her own apartment, *in the royal house, v.* 9. Thus, while the king showed the honour of his majesty, she and her ladies showed the honour of their modesty, which is truly the majesty of the fair sex.

Verses 10–22

Ahasuerus's feast; it ended in heaviness by his own folly. An unhappy falling out between the king and queen, broke off the feast abruptly, and sent the guests away silent and ashamed.

I. It was certainly the king's weakness to send for Vashti into his presence when he was drunk, and in company with gentlemen in the same condition. *When his heart was merry with wine* Vashti must come, well dressed as she was, with *the crown on her head*, that the princes and people might see what a handsome woman she was, *v.* 10, 11. Hereby, 1. He dishonoured himself as a husband, who ought to be to her *a covering of the eyes* (Gen. xx. 16), not to uncover them. 2. It was against the custom of the Persians for the women to appear in public, and he put a great hardship upon her when he did not court, but command her to do so uncouth a thing, and make her a show.

II. *She refused to come* (*v.* 12); though he sent his command by seven honourable messengers, yet she persisted in her denial. Had she come, while it was evident that she did it in pure obedience, it would have been no reflection upon her modesty. Perhaps she refused in a haughty manner, and then it was certainly evil; she *scorned to come at the king's commandment.* What a mortification was this to him!

III. The king thereupon grew outrageous. He that had rule over 127 provinces had no rule over his own spirit, but his *anger burned in him, v.* 12.

IV. Though he was very angry, he would not do anything till he advised with his privy-counsellors. Of these counsellors it is said that they were learned men, for they *knew law* and *judgment*,—that they were wise men, for they *knew the times*,—and that the king put great confidence in them and honour upon them, for they *saw the king's face and sat first in the kingdom, v.* 13, 14.

1. The question proposed to this cabinet-council (*v.* 15): *What shall we do to the queen Vashti according to the law?*

2. The proposal which Memucan made, that Vashti should be divorced for her disobedience. (1) He shows what would be the bad consequences of the queen's disobedience to her husband, if it were passed by. (2) He shows what would be the good consequence of a decree against Vashti that she should be divorced. Therefore they gave this judgment against her, that she *come no more before the king*, and this judgment so ratified as never to be reversed, *v.* 19.

3. The edict that passed according to this proposal, signifying that the queen was divorced for contumacy, according to the law, and that, if other wives were in like manner undutiful to their husbands, they must expect to be in like manner disgraced (*v.* 21, 22): were they better than the queen?

CHAPTER 2

Two things were working towards the deliverance of the Jews from Haman's conspiracy:—I. The advancement of Esther to be queen instead of Vashti. Many others were candidates for the honour (ver. 1–4); but Esther, an orphan, a captive-Jewess (ver. 5–7), recommended herself to the king's chamberlain first (ver. 8–11) and then to the king (ver. 12–17), who made her queen, ver. 18–20. II. The good service that Mordecai did to the king in discovering a plot against his life, ver. 21–23.

Verses 1–20

Vashti being humbled for her height, Esther is advanced for her humility. Observe,

I. The extravagant course that was taken to please the king with another wife instead of Vashti. Josephus says that when his anger was over he would have been reconciled to Vashti but that, by the constitution of the government, the judgment was irrevocable. Therefore, to make him forget her, they contrived how to entertain him first with a great variety of concubines. All the provinces of his kingdom must be searched for fair young virgins, and officers appointed to choose them, *v.* 3. After the king had once taken them to his bed they were looked upon as secondary wives, were maintained by the king accordingly, and might not marry. We may see, by this instance, to what absurd practices those came who were destitute of divine revelation, and who, as a punishment for their idolatry, were given up to vile affections. Having broken through that law of creation which resulted from God's making man, they broke through another law, which was founded upon his making one man and one woman. See what need there was of the gospel of Christ to purify men from the lusts of the flesh and to reduce them to the original institution.

II. The overruling providence of God bringing Esther to be queen. She came in her turn, after several others, and it was found that Esther excelled them all. Concerning Esther,

1. Her origin and character. (1) She was one of the *children of the captivity*, a Jewess and a sharer with her people in their bondage. (2) She was an orphan; her father and mother were both dead (*v.* 7), but, when they had forsaken her, then the Lord took her up, Ps. xxvii. 10. (3) She was a beauty, *fair of form, good of countenance*; so it is in the margin, *v.* 7. Her wisdom and virtue were her greatest beauty, but it is an advantage to a diamond to be well set. (4) Mordecai, her cousin-german, was her guardian, *brought her up, and took her for his own daughter*. Let God be acknowledged in raising up friends for the fatherless and motherless; let it be an encouragement to that pious instance of charity that many who have taken care of the education of orphans have lived to see the good fruit of their care and pains, abundantly to their comfort. Mordecai being Esther's guardian we are told, [1] How tender he was of her,

as if she had been his own child (*v.* 11). [2] How respectful she was to him. Though in relation she was his equal, yet, being in age and dependance his inferior, she honoured him as her father—*did his commandment, v.* 20. She did not *show her people or her kindred*, because Mordecai had charged her that she should not, *v.* 10. He did not bid her tell a lie to conceal her parentage; he only told her not to proclaim her country. She being born in Shushan, and her parents being dead, all took her to be of Persian extraction.

2. Her preferment. Who would have thought that a Jewess, a captive, an orphan, was born to be a queen, an empress! The king's chamberlain honoured her (*v.* 9), and was ready to serve her. The king himself fell in love with her. The more natural beauty is the more agreeable. *The king loved Esther above all the women, v.* 17. Now he needed not to take time to deliberate; he is soon determined to *set the royal crown upon her head, and make her queen, v.* 17. This was done in his seventh year (*v.* 16). He graced the solemnity of her coronation with a *royal feast* (*v.* 18). He also granted a *release to the provinces*, either a remittance of the taxes in arrear or an act of grace for criminals. Esther still *did the commandment of Mordecai, as when she was brought up with him, v.* 20. Mordecai sat *in the king's gate*; that was the height of his preferment: he was one of the porters or door-keepers of the court.

Verses 21–23

This good service which Mordecai did to the government, in discovering a plot against the life of the king, is here recorded, because the mention of it will again occur to his advantage. No step is yet taken towards Haman's design of the Jews' destruction, but several steps are taken towards God's design of their deliverance. God now gives Mordecai an opportunity of doing the king a good turn, that he might have the fairer opportunity afterwards of doing the Jews a good turn. 1. A design was laid against the king by two of his own servants, who sought *to lay hands on him*, not only to make him a prisoner, but to take away his life, *v.* 21. 2. Mordecai got notice of their treason, and, by Esther's means, discovered it to the king, hereby confirming her in and recommending himself to the king's favour. 3. The traitors were hanged, as they deserved, but not till their treason was, upon search, fully proved against them (*v.* 23), and the whole matter was recorded in the king's journals, with a particular remark that Mordecai was the man who discovered the treason.

CHAPTER 3

A very black and mournful scene here opens, which threatens the ruin of all the people of God. I. Haman is made the king's favourite, ver. 1. II. Mordecai refuses to give him the honour he demands, ver. 2–4. III. Haman, for his sake, vows to be revenged upon all the Jews, ver. 5, 6. IV. He, upon a malicious suggestion, obtains an order from the king to have them all massacred upon a certain day, ver. 7–13. V. This order is dispersed through the kingdom, ver. 14, 15.

Verses 1–6

I. Haman advanced by the prince, and adored thereupon by the people. Haman was an Agagite (an Amalekite, says Josephus), probably of the descendants of Agag, a common name of the princes of Amalek, as appears, Num. xxiv. 7. The king took a fancy to him (princes are not bound to give reasons for their favours), made him his favourite, his confidant, his prime-minister of state. It is plain that he was not a man of honour or justice, of any true courage or steady conduct, but proud, and passionate, and revengeful; yet was he promoted, and caressed, and there was none so great as he.

II. Mordecai adhering to his principles with a bold and daring resolution, and therefore refusing to reverence Haman as the rest of the king's servants did, *v.* 2. He was urged to it by his friends. They *spoke daily to him* (*v.* 4), to persuade him to conform, but all in vain: he hearkened not to them, but told them plainly that he was a Jew, and could not in conscience do it. It does not appear that anyone scrupled at conforming to it except Mordecai; and yet his refusal was pious, conscientious, and pleasing to God, for the religion of a Jew forbade him, 1. To give such extravagant honours as were required to any mortal man, especially so wicked a man as Haman was. In the apocryphal chapters of this book (*ch.* xiii. 12–14) Mordecai is brought in thus appealing to God in this matter: *Thou knowest, Lord, that it was neither in contempt nor pride, nor for any desire of glory, that I did not bow down to proud Haman, for I could have been content with goodwill, for the salvation of Israel, to kiss the soles of his feet; but I did this that I might not prefer the glory of man above the glory of God, neither will I worship any but thee.* 2. He especially thought it a piece of injustice to his nation to give such honour to an Amalekite, one of that nation with which God had sworn that he would have perpetual war (Exod. xvii. 16) and concerning which he had given that solemn charge (Deut. xxv. 17), *Remember what Amalek did.*

III. Haman meditating revenge. Some that hoped thereby to curry favour with Haman took notice to him of Mordecai's rudeness, waiting to see whether he would bend or break, *v.* 4. Haman then observed it himself, and was *full of wrath, v.* 5. It is soon resolved that Mordecai must die. Haman thinks his life nothing towards a satisfaction for the affront: thousands of innocent and valuable lives must be sacrificed to his indignation; and therefore he vows the destruction of all the people of Mordecai, for his sake, because his being a Jew was the reason he gave why he did not reverence Haman.

Verses 7–15

Haman doubts not but to find desperate and bloody hands enough to cut all their throats if the king will but give him leave. He obtained leave, and commission to do it.

I. He makes a false and malicious representation of the Jews, and their character, to the king, *v.* 8. He would have the king believe, 1. That the Jews were a despicable people, and that it was not for his credit to harbour them: "*A certain people there is, scattered abroad and dispersed in all the provinces* as fugitives and vagabonds on the earth, and inmates in all countries, the burden and scandal of the places where they live." 2. That they were a dangerous people. "They have laws of their own, and conform not to the statutes of the kingdom, and may be looked upon as disaffected to the government, which may end in a rebellion."

II. He bids leave to destroy them all, *v.* 9. He knew there were many that hated the Jews. *Let it be written* therefore *that they may be destroyed.* Give but orders for a general massacre of all the Jews. If the king will gratify him in this matter, he will make him a present of *ten thousand talents,* which shall be *paid into the king's treasuries.* This, he thought, would obviate the strongest objection that the government must needs sustain loss in its revenues by the destruction of so many of its subjects. No doubt Haman knew how to re-imburse himself out of the spoil of the Jews, which his janizaries were to seize for him (*v.* 13), and so to make them bear the charges of their own ruin.

III. He obtains what he desired, a full commission to do what he would with the Jews, *v.* 10, 11. The king was so bewitched with Haman, that he was

willing to believe the worst concerning the Jews, and therefore he gave them up into his hands, as lambs to the lion: *The people are thine, do with them as it seemeth good unto thee.* So little did he consider how much Haman would gain in the spoil, that he gave him withal the ten thousand talents: *The silver is thine.*

IV. He then consults with his soothsayers to find out a lucky day for the designed massacre, *v.* 7. The resolve was taken up in the first month, in the twelfth year of the king, when Esther had been his wife about five years. The lot fell upon the twelfth month, so that Mordecai and Esther had eleven months for the defeating of the design. Haman, though eager to have the Jews cut off, yet will submit to the laws of his superstition. God's wisdom serves its own purposes by men's folly. Haman has appealed to the lot, and to the lot he shall go, which, by adjourning the execution, gives judgment against him and breaks the neck of the plot.

V. The bloody edict is drawn up, signed, and published, giving orders to the militia of every province to be ready against *the thirteenth day of the twelfth month,* and, on that day, to murder all the Jews, men, women, and children, and seize their effects, *v.* 12–14. No crime is laid to their charge; but die they must, without mercy.

VI. The different temper of the court and city hereupon. The court was very merry upon it: *The king and Haman sat down to drink.* Haman was afraid lest the king's conscience should smite him for what he had done, to prevent which he kept him drinking. This cursed method many take to drown their convictions, and harden their own hearts and the hearts of others in sin. The city was very sad upon it: *The city of Shushan was perplexed,* not only the Jews themselves, but all their neighbours that had any principles of justice and compassion. It grieved them to see men that lived peaceably treated so barbarously. But the king and Haman cared for none of these things.

Chapter 4

Things here begin to work towards a deliverance, and they begin at the right end. I. The Jews' friends lay to heart the danger and lament it, ver. 1–4. II. Matters are concerted between Mordecai and Esther for the preventing of it. 1. Esther enquires into this case, and received a particular account of it, ver. 5–7. 2. Mordecai urges her to intercede with the king for a revocation of the edict, ver. 8, 9. III. Esther objects the danger of addressing the king uncalled, ver. 10–13. IV. Mordecai presses her to venture, ver. 13, 14. V. Esther, after a religious fast of three days, promises to do so (ver. 15–17), and we shall find that she sped well.

Verses 1–4

An account of the general sorrow that there was among the Jews upon the publishing of Haman's bloody edict against them. 1. Mordecai cried bitterly, *rent his clothes, and put on sackcloth, v.* 1, 2. He not only thus vented his grief, but proclaimed it, that all might take notice of it that he was not ashamed to own himself a friend to the Jews, and a fellow-sufferer with them. It was nobly done thus publicly to espouse what he knew to be a righteous cause, and the cause of God, even when it seemed a desperate and a sinking cause. Mordecai knew that Haman's spite was against him primarily, and that it was for his sake that the rest of the Jews were struck at; and therefore it troubled him greatly that his people should suffer for his scruples. But, being able to appeal to God that what he did he did from a principle of conscience, he could with comfort commit his own cause and that of his people to him. Notice is here taken of a law that *none might enter into the king's gate clothed with sackcloth.* None must come near the king in a mourning dress, because he was not willing to hear the complaints of such. Nothing but what was gay and pleasant must appear at court. This obliged Mordecai to keep his distance, and only to come before the gate, not to take his place in the gate. 2. All the Jews in every province laid it much to heart, *v.* 2. They denied themselves the comfort of their tables (for they fasted and mingled tears with their meat and drink), and *they lay in sackcloth and ashes*. 3. Esther the queen, upon a general intimation of the trouble Mordecai was in, *was exceedingly grieved, v.* 4. Mordecai's grief was hers, and the Jews' danger was her distress. Esther sent change of raiment to Mordecai, but because he would make her sensible of the greatness of his grief, and consequently of the cause of it, *he received it not*, but was as one that refused to be comforted.

Verses 5–17

So strictly did the laws of Persia confine the wives, especially the king's wives, that it was not possible for Mordecai to have a conference with Esther, but divers messages are here carried between them by Hatach, whom the king had appointed to attend her.

I. She sent to Mordecai to know more fully what the trouble was which he was now lamenting (*v.* 5) and why it was that he would not put off his sackcloth.

II. Mordecai sent her an authentic account of the whole matter, with a charge to her to intercede with the king: *Mordecai told him all that had happened unto him* (*v.* 7), what a pique Haman had against him for not bowing to him, and by what arts he had procured this edict. He sent her also a true copy of the edict, that she might see what imminent danger she and her people were in, and charged her, if she had any respect for him or any kindness for the Jewish nation, that she should rectify the misinformations with which the king was imposed upon.

III. She sent her case to Mordecai, that she could not, without peril of her life, address the king.

1. The law was express, and all knew it, that whosoever came to the king uncalled should be put to death, unless he was pleased to *hold out the golden sceptre to them*. This made the royal palace little better than a royal prison, and the kings themselves could not but become morose. It was bad for their subjects; for what good had they of a king that they might never have liberty to apply to for the redress of grievances. It is not thus in the court of the King of kings; to the footstool of his throne of grace we may at any time *come boldly*, and may be sure of an answer of peace to the prayer of faith. It was particularly very uncomfortable for their wives (for there was not a proviso in the law to except them).

2. Her case was at present very discouraging. Providence so ordered it that, just at this juncture, she was under a cloud, and the king's affections cooled towards her, for she had been *kept from his presence thirty days*.

IV. Mordecai still insisted upon it that, whatever hazard she might run, she must apply to the king in this great affair, *v.* 13, 14. He suggested to her, 1. That it was her own cause, for that the decree to *destroy all the Jews* did not except her: "*Think not therefore that thou shalt escape in the king's house*, that the palace will be thy protection, and the crown save thy head: no, thou art a Jewess, and, if the rest be cut off, thou wilt be cut off too." 2. That it was a cause which, one way or other, would certainly be carried, and which therefore she might safely venture in. "If thou shouldst decline the service, *enlargement and deliverance will arise to the Jews from another place*." This was the language of a strong faith, which *staggered not at the promise* when the danger was most threatening, but *against hope believed in hope*. 3. That if she deserted her friends now, through cowardice and unbelief, she would have reason to fear that some judgment from heaven would be the ruin of her and her family: "*Thou and thy father's house shall be destroyed*, when the rest of the families of the Jews

shall be preserved." 4. That divine Providence had an eye to this in bringing her to be queen: "*Who knows whether thou hast come to the kingdom for such a time as this?*" We should every one of us consider for what end God has put us in the place where we are, and, when any particular opportunity of serving God and our generation offers itself, we must take care that we do not let it slip. These things Mordecai urges to Esther; and some of the Jewish writers, who are fruitful in invention, add another thing which had *happened to him* (*v.* 7) which he desired she might be told, "that going home, the night before, in great heaviness, upon the notice of Haman's plot, he met three Jewish children coming from school, of whom he enquired what they had learned that day; one of them told him his lesson was, Prov. iii. 25, 26, *Be not afraid of sudden fear*; the second told him his was, Isa. viii. 10, *Take counsel together, and it shall come to nought*; the third told him his was Isa. xlvi. 4, *I have made, and I will bear, even I will carry and will deliver you*.

V. Esther hereupon resolved, whatever it might cost her, to apply to the king, but not till she and her friends had first applied to God. Let them first by fasting and prayer obtain God's favour, and then she should hope to find favour with the king, *v.* 15, 16. She spoke,

1. With the piety and devotion that became an Israelite, for she believed that God's favour was obtained by prayer. She knew it was the practice of good people, in extraordinary cases, to join fasting with prayer. She therefore, (1) Desired that Mordecai would direct the Jews that were in Shushan to *sanctify a fast* and *call a solemn assembly*, to meet in the respective synagogues to which they belonged, and to pray for her, and to keep a solemn fast. (2) She promised that she and her family would sanctify this fast in her apartment of the palace, for she might not come to their assemblies. Those who are confined to privacy may join their prayers with those of the solemn assemblies of God's people; those that are absent in body may be present in spirit.

2. With the courage and resolution that became a queen. "When we have sought God in this matter, *I will go in unto the king* to intercede for my people. *I know it is not according to the king's law*, but it is according to God's law; and therefore I will venture, and, *if I perish, I perish*. I cannot lose my life in a better cause. Better do my duty and die with them." She said not this in despair or passion, but in a holy resolution to do her duty and trust God with the issue.

CHAPTER 5

The last news we had of Haman left him in his cups, ch. iii. 15. Our last news of Queen Esther left her in tears, fasting and praying. Now this chapter brings in, I. Esther in her joys, smiled upon by the king and honoured with his company at her banquet of wine, ver. 1–8. II. Haman upon the fret, because he had not Mordecai's cap and knee, and with great indignation setting up a gallows for him, ver. 9–14.

Verses 1–8

I. Esther's bold approach to the king, *v.* 1. When the time appointed for their fast was finished she lost no time, but on the third day, when the impressions of her devotions were fresh upon her spirit, she addressed the king. Now she *put on her royal apparel*, that she might the better recommend herself to the king, and laid aside her fast-day clothes. In the Apocrypha (Esther xiv. 16), she thus appeals to God: *Thou knowest, Lord, I abhor the sign of my high estate which is upon my head, in the days wherein I show myself*, &c. She stood *in the inner court over against the king*, expecting her doom, between hope and fear.

II. The favourable reception which the king gave her. When he *saw her* she *obtained favour in his sight*.

The apocryphal author and Josephus say that she took two maids with her, on one of whom she leaned, while the other bore up her train,—that her countenance was cheerful and very amiable, but her heart was in anguish,—that the king, lifting up his countenance that shone with majesty, at first looked very fiercely upon her, whereupon she grew pale, and fainted, and bowed herself on the head of the maid that went by her; but then God changed the spirit of the king, and, in a fear, he leaped from his throne, took her in his arms till she came to herself, and comforted her with loving words. Here we are only told,

1. That he protected her from the law, and assured her of safety, by *holding out to her the golden sceptre* (*v.* 2), which she thankfully *touched the top of*, thereby presenting herself to him as a humble petitioner.

2. That he encouraged her address (*v.* 3): *What wilt thou, queen Esther, and what is thy request?* Esther feared that she should perish, but was promised that she should have what she might ask for, though it were *the half of the kingdom.* Let us from this story infer, as our Saviour does from the parable of the unjust judge, an encouragement to *pray always* to our God, *and not faint*, Luke xviii. 6–8. Esther came to a proud imperious man; we come to the God of love and grace. She was not called; we are: the Spirit says, *Come*, and the bride says, *Come*. She had a law against her; we have a promise, many a promise, in favour of us: *Ask, and it shall be given you.* She had no friend to introduce her, or intercede for her, while on the contrary he that was then the king's favourite was her enemy; but we have an advocate with the Father, in whom he is well pleased. *Let us therefore come boldly to the throne of grace.*

3. That all the request she had to make to him, at this time, was that he would please to come to a banquet which she had prepared for him, and bring Haman along with him, *v.* 4, 5. She would endeavour to bring him into a pleasant humour, and soften his spirit, that he might with the more tenderness receive the complaint she had to make to him. She would please him, by making court to Haman his favourite, and inviting him to come whose company she knew he loved and whom she desired to have present when she made her complaint.

4. That he readily came, and ordered Haman to come along with him (*v.* 5). There he renewed his kind enquiry (*What is thy petition?*) and his generous promise, that it should be granted, *even to the half of the kingdom* (*v.* 6), a proverbial expression, by which he assured her that he would deny her nothing in reason.

5. That then Esther thought fit to ask no more than a promise that he would please to accept of another treat, the next day, in her apartment, and Haman with him (*v.* 7, 8), intimating to him that then she would let him know what her business was. The putting of it off thus she knew would be well taken as an expression of the great reverence she had for the king, and her unwillingness to be too pressing upon him.

Verses 9–14

Haman, in whom pride and wrath had so much the ascendant.

I. Puffed up with the honour of being invited to Esther's feast. He was *joyful and glad of heart* at it, *v.* 9. He thought it was because she was exceedingly charmed with his conversation that the next day she had invited him also to come with the king.

II. Mordecai was as determined as ever: *He stood not up, nor moved for him*, *v.* 9. Haman can as ill bear it as ever; nay, the higher he is lifted up, the more impatient is he of contempt and the more enraged at it. Gladly would he have drawn his sword and run Mordecai through for affronting him thus; but he hoped shortly to see him fall with all the Jews, and therefore with much ado prevailed with himself to forbear stabbing him.

III. Meditating revenge, Haman was assisted by his wife and his friends, *v.* 14. For the pleasing of his fancy they advise him to get *a gallows ready*, and have it set up before his own door, that, as soon as ever he could get the warrant signed, there might be no delay of the execution. This is very agreeable to Haman, who has the gallows made and fixed immediately; it must be fifty cubits high, for the greater disgrace of Mordecai and to make him a spectacle to everyone that passed by. They advised him to go early in the morning to the king, and get an order from him for the hanging of Mordecai.

CHAPTER 6

A very surprising scene opens in this chapter. Haman, when he hoped to be Mordecai's judge, was made his page, to his great confusion and mortification; and thus way was made for the defeat of Haman's plot and the deliverance of the Jews. I. The providence of God recommends Mordecai in the night to the king's favour, ver. 1–3. II. Haman, who came to incense the king against him, is employed as an instrument of the king's favour to him, ver. 4–11. III. From this his friends read him his doom, which is executed in the next chapter, ver. 12–14.

Verses 1–3

When Satan put it into the heart of Haman to contrive Mordecai's death, God put it into the heart of the king to contrive Mordecai's honour. The steps which Providence took towards the advancement of Mordecai.

I. *On that night could not the king sleep.* His *sleep fled away* (so the word is); and perhaps, like a shadow, the more carefully he pursued it the further it went from him.

II. When he could not sleep he called to have the book of records, the Journals of his reign, read to him, *v.* 1. But God put it into his heart to call for it, rather than for music or songs, which would have been more likely to compose him to rest.

III. The servant that read to him lighted on that article which concerned Mordecai. Among other things it was found written that Mordecai had discovered a plot against the life of the king which prevented the execution of it, *v.* 2. How Mordecai's good service was recorded we read *ch.* ii. 23, and here it is found upon record.

IV. The king enquired *what honour and dignity had been done to Mordecai* for this, suspecting that this good service had gone unrewarded.

V. The servants informed him that nothing had been done to Mordecai for that eminent service; in the king's gate he sat before, and there he still sat. Humility, modesty, and self-denial, though in God's account of great price, yet commonly hinder men's preferment in the world. Mordecai rises no higher than the king's gate, while proud ambitious Haman gets the king's ear and heart; but, though the aspiring rise fast, the humble stand fast. Mordecai is at this time, by the king's edict, doomed to destruction, with all the Jews, though it is owned that he deserved dignity.

Verses 4–11

It is now morning, and people begin to stir.

I. Haman is so impatient to get Mordecai hanged that he comes early to court, before any other business is brought to get a warrant for his execution (*v.* 4), which he makes sure that he shall have at the first word. He could tell the king that he was so confident of the justice of his request, and the king's favour to him in it, that he had got the gallows ready: one word from the king would complete his satisfaction.

II. The king is so impatient to have Mordecai honoured that he sends to know who is in the court that is fit to be employed in it. Word is brought him that Haman is in the court, *v. 5*. *Let him come in*, says the king, the fittest man to be made use of both in directing and in dispensing the king's favour; and the king knew nothing of any quarrel he had with Mordecai. Haman is brought in immediately, proud of the honour done him in being admitted into the king's bed-chamber *before he was up*. Now Haman thinks he has the fairest opportunity he can wish for to solicit against Mordecai; but the king's heart is as full as his, and it is fit he should speak first.

III. The king asks Haman how he should express his favour to one whom he had marked for a favourite: *What shall be done to the man whom the king delights to honour? v. 6.*

IV. Haman concludes that he himself is the favourite intended, and therefore prescribes the highest expressions of honour that could be bestowed upon a subject. Now Haman thinks he is carving out honour for himself, and therefore does it very liberally, *v. 8, 9*.

V. The king confounds him with a positive order that he should immediately go himself and put all this honour upon Mordecai the Jew, *v. 10*. If the king had but said, as Haman expected, *Thou art the man!* But how is he thunderstruck when the king bids him not to order all this to be done, but to do it himself to Mordecai the Jew, the very man he hated above all men and whose ruin he was now designing!

VI. Haman dares not dispute nor so much as seem to dislike the king's order, but, with the greatest reluctance brings it to Mordecai, who did no more cringe to Haman now than he had done, valuing his counterfeit respect no more than he had valued his concealed malice. The apparel is brought, Mordecai is dressed up, and rides in state through the city, recognized as the king's favourite, *v. 11*.

Verses 12–14

I. How little Mordecai was puffed up with his advancement. He *came again to the king's gate* (*v. 12*); he returned to his place and the duty of it immediately, and minded his business as closely as he had done before.

II. How much Haman was cast down with his disappointment. To wait upon any man, especially Mordecai, and at this time, when he hoped to have seen him hanged, was enough to break such a proud heart.

III. How his doom was read to him by his wife and his friends: "If Mordecai be, as they say he is, *of the seed of the Jews, before whom thou hast begun to fall*, never expect to *prevail against him*; for thou *shalt surely fall before him*," *v. 13*. This Mordecai was *of the seed of the Jews*; *feeble Jews* their enemies sometimes called them; but formidable Jews they sometimes found them. They are a holy seed, a praying seed, in covenant with God, and a seed that the Lord hath all along blessed, and therefore let not their enemies expect to triumph over them.

IV. He was now sent for to the banquet that Esther had prepared, *v. 14*. He thought it seasonable in hopes it would revive his drooping spirits and save his sinking honour.

Chapter 7

The second banquet to which the king and Haman were invited: and there, I. Esther presents her petition to the king for her life and the life of her people, ver. 1–4. II. She plainly tells the king that Haman is the man who designed her ruin and the ruin of all her friends, ver. 5, 6. III. The king thereupon gave orders for the hanging of Haman upon the gallows that he had prepared for Mordecai, which was done accordingly, ver. 7–10.

Verses 1–6

The king in humour, and Haman out of humour, meet at Esther's table.

I. The king urged Esther, a third time, to tell him what her request was, for he longed to know, and repeated his promise that it should be granted, *v. 2*.

II. Esther, at length, surprises the king with a petition for the preservation of herself and her countrymen from death and destruction, *v. 3, 4*. That a friend, a wife, should have occasion to present such a petition was very affecting: *Let my life be given me at my petition, and my people at my request*. To move the king the more she suggests she and her people were bought and sold. They had not sold themselves by any offence against the government, but were sold to gratify the pride and revenge of one man. That it was not their liberty only, but their lives that were sold. "Had we been sold" (says she) "into slavery, I would not have complained; for in time we might have recovered our liberty, though the king would have made but a bad bargain of it. Whatever had been paid for us, the loss of so many industrious hands out of his kingdom would have been more damage to the treasury than the price would countervail." *We are sold* (says she) *to be destroyed, to be slain, and to perish*. She refers to the words of the decree (*ch. iii. 13*), which aimed at nothing short of their destruction.

III. The king stands amazed at the remonstrance, and asks (*v. 5*). "*Who is he, and where is he, that durst presume in his heart to do so?* We sometimes startle at the mention of that evil which yet we ourselves are chargeable with. Ahasuerus is amazed at that wickedness which he himself was guilty of; for he consented to that bloody edict against the Jews. *Thou art the man*, might Esther too truly have said.

IV. Esther plainly charges Haman with it before his face: "Here he is, let him speak for himself, for therefore he is invited: *The adversary and enemy is this wicked Haman* (*v. 6*); it is he that has designed our murder."

V. Haman is apprehensive of his danger: *He was afraid before the king and queen;* and it was time for him to fear when the queen was his prosecutor, the king his judge, and his own conscience a witness against him.

Verses 7–10

I. The king retires in anger. He rose from table in a great passion, and *went into the palace garden* to cool himself and to consider what was to be done, *v. 7*. He blames himself, that he should be such a fool as to doom a guiltless nation to destruction, and his own queen among the rest, upon the base suggestions of a self-seeking man, without examining the truth of his allegations. He condemned Haman whom he had laid in his bosom, that he should be such a villain as to draw him to consent to so wicked a measure.

II. Haman becomes a humble petitioner to the queen for his life. He might easily perceive by the king's hastily flying out of the room that *there was evil determined against him*. How mean Haman looks, when he stands up first and then falls down at Esther's feet, to beg she would save his life and take all he had. How great Esther looks, who of late had been neglected and doomed! Now her sworn enemy owns that he lies at her mercy, and begs his life at her hand. The day is coming when those that hate and persecute God's chosen ones would gladly be beholden to them.

III. The king returns yet more exasperated against Haman.

IV. Those about him were ready to be the instruments of his wrath. The courtiers that adored Haman when he was the rising sun set themselves as much against him now that he is a falling star. As soon as the king spoke an angry word *they covered Haman's face*, as a condemned man; they marked him for execution. Those that are hanged commonly have their faces covered. One of those that had been lately sent to Haman's house, to fetch him to the banquet, informed the king of the gallows which Haman had prepared for Mordecai, *v.* 9.

V. The king gave orders that he should be hanged upon his own gallows, which was done accordingly.

CHAPTER 8

I. His plot was to raise an estate for himself; and all his estate, being confiscated for treason, is given to Esther and Mordecai, ver. 1, 2. II. His plot was to ruin the Jews; and as to that, 1. Esther earnestly intercedes for the reversing of the edict against them, ver. 3–6. 2. It is in effect done by another edict, here published, empowering the Jews to stand up in their own defence against their enemies, ver. 7–14. III. This occasions great joy to the Jews and all their friends, ver. 15–17.

Verses 1-2

1. Esther enriched. Haman was hanged as a traitor, therefore his estate was forfeited to the crown, and the king gave it all to Esther. 2. Mordecai advanced. His procession, this morning, through the streets of the city, was but a sudden blaze of honour; but here we have the more durable preferments to which he was raised. He is owned as the queen's cousin, which till now, though Esther had been four years queen, the king did not know. So humble, so modest, a man was Mordecai, and so far from being ambitious of a place at court, that he concealed his relation to the queen, and her obligations to him as her guardian. Now, at length, *Esther had told what he was to her*, near akin, who took care of her when she was an orphan, and one whom she still respected as a father. All the trust he had reposed in Haman, and all the power he had given him, are here transferred to Mordecai; for the ring which he had taken from Haman he gave to Mordecai, and made this trusty humble man his confidant. The queen makes him her steward, for the management of Haman's estate, *She set Mordecai over the house of Haman*.

Verses 3-14

Haman, the chief enemy of the Jews, was hanged, Mordecai and Esther, their chief friends, were sufficiently protected; but many others there were in the king's dominions that hated the Jews and desired their ruin, and to their rage and malice all the rest of that people lay exposed for the edict against them was still in force.

I. The queen here makes intercession with much affection and importunity. She came, a second time, uncalled into the king's presence (*v.* 3), and was as before encouraged to present her petition, by the king's holding out the golden sceptre to her, *v.* 4. Her petition is that the king, having put away Haman, would put away the mischief of Haman and his device against the Jews. This petition Esther presents with much affection: She *fell down at the king's feet and besought him with tears* (*v.* 3), every tear as precious as any of the pearls with which she was adorned. *If it please the king and if I have found favour in his sight*—and again, "If the thing itself seem right and reasonable before the king, and if I that ask it *be pleasing in his eyes*, let the decree be reversed." She enforces her petition with a pathetic plea: "*For how can I endure to see the evil that shall come upon my people?*"

II. The king here takes a course for the preventing of the mischief that Haman had designed. The king knew, and informed the queen, that, according to the constitution of the Persian government, the former edict could not be revoked (*v.* 8): What is *written in the king's name, and sealed with the king's ring*, may not, under any pretence whatsoever, be reversed. Yet he found an expedient to undo the devices of Haman, and defeat his design, by singing and publishing another decree to authorize the Jews to stand upon their defence, *vim vi repellere, et invasorem*

occidere—to oppose force to force, and destroy the assailant. This would be their effectual security. "*Write for the Jews as it liketh you* (*v.* 8), saving only the honour of our constitution. Let the mischief be put away as effectually as may be without reversing the letters." This edict was to be drawn up and published in the respective languages of all the provinces. The purport of this decree was to commission the Jews, upon the day which was appointed for their destruction, to draw together in a body for their own defence. And, 1. To stand for their life, that, whoever assaulted them, it might be at their peril. 2. They might not only act defensively, but might *destroy, and slay, and cause to perish, all the power of the people that would assault them*. Now, (1) This showed his kindness to the Jews, and sufficiently provided for their safety; for the latter decree would be looked upon as a tacit revocation of the former. But, (2) It shows the absurdity of their constitution that none of the king's edicts might be repealed; for it laid the king here under a necessity of enacting a civil war in his own dominions, between the Jews and their enemies, so that both sides took up arms *by* his authority, and yet *against* his authority.

Verses 15-17

Here is a blessed change, Mordecai in purple and all the Jews in joy. 1. Mordecai in purple, *v.* 15. Having obtained an order for the relief of all the Jews, he was easy, he put on the *royal apparel*. His robes were rich, *blue and white, of fine linen and purple*; so was his coronet: it was *of gold*. These things were marks of the king's favour, and the fruit of God's favour to his church. The *city Shushan* was sensible of its advantage in the preferment of Mordecai, and therefore *rejoiced and was glad*. 2. The Jews in joy, *v.* 16, 17. The Jews, who awhile ago were under a dark cloud, dejected and disgraced, now had *light and gladness, joy and honour, a feast and a good day*. One good effect of this deliverance was that *many of the people of the land*, that were considerate, sober, and well inclined, became Jews, were proselyted to the Jewish religion, renounced idolatry, and worshipped the true God only. *We will go with you, for we have heard*, we have seen, *that God is with you, the shield of your help, and the sword of your excellency*, Deut. xxxiii. 29.

CHAPTER 9

Two royal edicts in force, both given at the court of Shushan, one bearing date the thirteenth day of the first month, appointing that on the thirteenth day of the twelfth month then next ensuing all the Jews should be killed; another bearing date the twenty-third day of the third month, empowering the Jews, on the day appointed for their slaughter, to draw the sword in their own defence. The Jews' cause was to be tried by battle and the day was fixed by authority. Their enemies resolved not to lose the advantages given them by the first edict, in hope to overpower them by numbers; the Jews relied on the goodness of their God and the justice of their cause. I. What a glorious day it was, that year, to the Jews, and the two days following—a day of victory and triumph, both in the city Shushan and in all the rest of the king's provinces, ver. 1–19. II. What a memorable day it was made to posterity, by an annual feast, in commemoration of this great deliverance, called "the feast of Purim", ver. 20–32.

Verses 1-19

A decisive battle fought between the Jews and their enemies, in which the Jews were victorious. Neither side could call the other *rebels*, for they were both supported by the royal authority.

I. The enemies of the Jews were the aggressors.

II. But the Jews were the conquerors. That very day when the king's decree for their destruction was to be put in execution, and which the enemies thought would have been *their* day, proved *God's day*, Ps. xxxvii. 13. *They gathered themselves together in their cities*, embodied, and stood upon their defence, offering violence to none, but bidding defiance to all. If they had not had an edict to warrant them, they durst not have done it, but, being so supported, they strove lawfully. Had they acted separately, each family apart, they would have been an easy prey to their enemies; but acting in concert, and gathering together in their cities, they strengthened one another, and durst face their enemies. All the officers of the king, who, by the bloody edict, were ordered to help forward their destruction (*ch.* iii. 12, 13), conformed to the latter edict and *helped the Jews*, which turned the scale on their side, *v.* 3. The provinces would generally do as the rulers of the provinces inclined, and therefore their favouring the Jews would greatly further them. But why did they help them? Not because they had any kindness for them, but because *the fear of Mordecai fell upon them*, he having manifestly the countenance both of God and the king. *No man could withstand them* (*v.* 2), but *they did what they would to those that hated them*, *v.* 5. So strangely were the Jews strengthened and animated, and their enemies weakened and dispirited, that none of those who had marked themselves for their destruction escaped. On the thirteenth day of the month Adar they slew in the city Shushan 500 men (*v.* 6) and the ten sons of *Haman*, *v.* 10. On the fourteenth day they slew in Shushan 300 more, who had escaped the sword on the former day of execution, *v.* 15. This Esther obtained leave of the king for them to do, for the greater terror of their enemies, and the utter crushing of that malignant party of men. That which justifies them in the execution of so many is that they did it in their own just and necessary defence; they *stood for their lives*, authorized to do so by the law of self-preservation, as well as by the king's decree. The king's commission had warranted them to *take the spoil* of their enemies *for a prey* (*ch.* viii. 11), and a fair opportunity they had of enriching themselves with it. But the Jews would not do so by them, 1. That they might, to the honour of their religion, evidence a holy and generous contempt of worldly wealth, in imitation of their father Abraham, who scorned to enrich himself with the spoils of Sodom. 2. That they might make it to appear that they aimed at nothing but their own preservation, and used their interest at court for the saving of their lives, not for the raising of their estates. 3. Their commission empowered them to destroy the families of their enemies, even the *little ones* and *the women*, *ch.* viii. 11. But their humanity forbade them to do that. They slew none but those they found in arms; and therefore they did not take the spoil, but left it to the women and little ones. Herein they acted with a consideration and compassion well worthy of imitation.

Verses 20–32

To perpetuate the remembrance of it to posterity,

I. The history was written, and copies of it were dispersed among all the Jews in all the provinces of the empire, *both nigh and far*, *v.* 20. Mordecai *wrote all these things*. And if this book be the same that he wrote, as many think it is, what a difference there is between Mordecai's style and Nehemiah's. Nehemiah, at every turn, takes notice of divine Providence and the *good hand of his God* upon him, which is very proper to stir up devout affections in the minds of his readers; but Mordecai never so much as mentions the name of God in the whole story. Nehemiah wrote his book at Jerusalem, where religion was in fashion. Mordecai wrote his at Shushan the palace, where policy reigned more than piety, and he wrote according to the genius of the place. Because there is so little of the language of Canaan in this book, many think it was not written by Mordecai, but was an extract out of the journals of the kings of Persia.

II. A festival was instituted, to be observed yearly from generation to generation by the Jews, in remembrance of this wonderful work which God wrought for them, that *the children who should be born* might know it, and *declare it to their children, that they might set their hope in God*, Ps. lxxviii. 6, 7. Posterity would reap the benefit of this deliverance, and therefore ought to celebrate the memorial of it. Concerning this festival

1. It was observed—every year on *the fourteenth and fifteenth days of the twelfth month*, just a month before the passover, *v.* 21. They kept two days together as thanksgiving days, and did not think them too much to spend in praising God. On the fourteenth day country-Jews rested, and on the fifteenth those in Shushan, and both those days they kept.

2. It was called—*The feast of Purim* (*v.* 26), from *Pur*, a Persian word which signifies *a lot*, because Haman had by lot determined this to be the time of the Jews' destruction, but the Lord, at whose disposal the lot is, had determined it to be the time of their triumph.

3. It was not a divine institution, and therefore it is not called a *holy day*, but a human appointment, by which it was made a *good day*, *v.* 19, 22. (1) The Jews ordained it, and took it upon themselves (*v.* 27), voluntarily *undertook to do as they had begun*, *v.* 23. (2) Mordecai and Esther confirmed their resolve, that it might be the more binding on posterity, and might come well recommended by those great names. They wrote, [1] *With all authority* (*v.* 29), Esther being queen and Mordecai prime-minister of state. [2] *With words of peace and truth*. Though they wrote with authority, they wrote with tenderness,

4. It was to be observed—by *all the Jews*, and by *their seed*, and by all such as *joined themselves to them*, *v.* 27. A concurrence in joys and praises is one branch of the communion of saints.

5. It was to be observed—that the memorial of the great things God had done for his church might never *perish from their seed*, *v.* 28. When Esther, in peril of her life, *came before the king*, he repealed the edict, *v.* 25. This also must be remembered. Good deeds done for the Israel of God ought to be remembered, for the encouragement of others to do the like. The more cries we have offered up in our trouble, and the more prayers for deliverance, the more we are obliged to be thankful to God for deliverance.

6. How it was to be observed. They should make it, (1) A day of cheerfulness, *a day of feasting and joy* (*v.* 22). (2) A day of generosity, *sending portions one to another*, in token of mutual respect, and being knit by this and other public common dangers and deliverances so much the closer to each other in love. (3) A day of charity, sending *gifts to the poor*. Those that have received mercy must, in token of their gratitude, show mercy. Thanksgiving and almsgiving should go together, that, when we are rejoicing and blessing God, the heart of the poor may rejoice with us. They always, at the feast, read the whole story over in the synagogue each day, and put up three prayers to God, in the first of which they praise God for counting them worthy to attend this divine service; in the second they thank him for the miraculous preservation of their ancestors; in the third they praise him that they have lived to observe another festival in memory of it.

CHAPTER 10

This is but a part of a chapter; the rest of it, beginning at ver. 4, with six chapters more, being found only in the Greek, is rejected as apocryphal. In these three verses we have only some short hints, I. Concerning Ahasuerus in the throne, what a mighty prince he was, ver. 1, 2. II. Concerning Mordecai his favourite, what a distinguished blessing he was to his people, ver. 2, 3.

Verses 1–3

I. How great and powerful king Ahasuerus was. He had a vast dominion, both in the continent and among the islands, from which he raised a vast revenue. Besides the usual customs which the kings of Persia exacted (Ezra iv. 13), he laid an additional tribute upon his subjects (*v.* 1): *The king laid a tribute.* Besides this instance of the grandeur of Ahasuerus, many more might be given, that were *acts of his power and of his might.* These however are not recorded here in the sacred story, which is confined to the Jews, and relates the affairs of other nations only as they fell in with their affairs.

II. How great and good Mordecai was. Long had Mordecai sat contentedly in the king's gate, and now at length he is advanced. The declaration of the greatness to which the king advanced Mordecai was *written in the chronicles of the kingdom,* as very memorable, and contributing to the great achievements of the king. He was *great among the Jews* (*v.* 3), not only great above them, but great with them, dear to them, and much respected by them. He was good, for he did good. He did not disown his people the Jews, though they were strangers and captives, dispersed and despised. Still he wrote himself *Mordecai the Jew.* He did not seek his own wealth, or the raising of an estate for himself and his family. His power, his wealth, and all his interest in the king and queen, he improved for the public good. He did not side with any one party of his people against another, but, whatever differences there were among them, he was a common father to them all.

AN EXPOSITION, WITH PRACTICAL OBSERVATIONS, OF

THE BOOK OF JOB

This book of Job stands by itself, is not connected with any other, and is therefore to be considered alone. Many copies of the Hebrew Bible place it after the book of Psalms, and some after the Proverbs, which perhaps has given occasion to some learned men to imagine it to have been written by Isaiah or some of the later prophets. It is most fitly placed first in this collection of divine morals: also, being doctrinal, it is proper to precede and introduce the book of Psalms, which is devotional, and the book of Proverbs, which is practical; for how shall we worship or obey a God whom we know not? As to this book,

I. We are sure that it is given by inspiration of God, though we are not certain who was the penman of it. The Jews, though no friends to Job, because he was a stranger to the commonwealth of Israel, yet, as faithful conservators of the *oracles of God* committed to them, always retained this book in their sacred canon. The history is referred to by one apostle (James v. 11) and one passage (*ch.* v. 13) is quoted by another apostle, with the usual form of quoting scripture, *It is written,* 1 Cor. iii. 19. It seems most probable to me that Elihu was the penman of it, at least of the discourses, because (*ch.* xxxii. 15, 16) he mingles the words of a historian with those of a disputant. If Job wrote it himself, some of the Jewish writers themselves own him a *prophet among the Gentiles*; if Elihu, we find he had a spirit of prophecy which *filled him with matter and constrained him, ch.* xxxii. 18.

II. It is, for the substance of it, a true history, and not a romance, though the dialogues are poetical. No doubt there was such a man as Job; the prophet Ezekiel names him with Noah and Daniel, Ezek. xiv. 14. The narrative we have here of his prosperity and piety, his strange afflictions and exemplary patience, the substance of his conferences with his friends, and God's discourse with him out of the whirlwind, with his return at length to a very prosperous condition, no doubt is exactly true, though the inspired penman is allowed the usual liberty of putting the matter of which Job and his friends discoursed into his own words.

III. It is very ancient, though we cannot fix the precise time either when Job lived or when the book was written. So many, so evident, are its hoary hairs, the marks of its antiquity, that we have reason to think that holy Job was contemporary with Isaac and Jacob; though not coheir with them of the promise of the earthly Canaan, yet a joint-expectant with them of the *better country*, that is, *the heavenly*. Probably he was of the posterity of Nahor, Abraham's brother, whose first-born was *Uz* (Gen. xxii. 21), and in whose family religion was for some ages kept up, as appears, Gen. xxxi. 53, where God is called, not only *the God of Abraham*, but *the God of Nahor*. He lived before the age of man was shortened to seventy or eighty, as it was in Moses's time, before sacrifices were confined to one altar, before the general apostasy of the nations from the knowledge and worship of the true God, and while yet there was no other idolatry known than the worship of the sun and moon, and that punished by the Judges, *ch.* xxxi. 26–28. He lived while God was known by the name of *God Almighty* more than by the name of *Jehovah*; for he is called *Shaddai*—the *Almighty*, above thirty times in this book. He lived while divine knowledge was conveyed, not by writing, but by tradition; for to that appeals are here made, *ch.* viii. 8; xxi. 29; xv. 18; v. 1. And we have therefore reason to think that he lived before Moses, because here is no mention at all of the deliverance of Israel out of Egypt, or the giving of the law. We conclude therefore that we are here got back to the patriarchal age, and, besides its authority, we receive this book with veneration for its antiquity.

IV. We are sure that it is of great use to the church, and to every good Christian, though there are many passages in it dark and hard to be understood. It is a book that finds a great deal of work for the critics; but enough is plain to make the whole profitable and it was all written for our learning.

1. This noble poem presents to us, in very clear and lively characters, these five things among others:—(1) *A monument of primitive theology.* The first and great principles of the light of nature, on which natural religion is founded, are here, in a warm, and long, and learned dispute, not only taken for granted, but by common consent plainly laid down as eternal truths. Were ever the being of God, his glorious attributes and perfections, his unsearchable wisdom, his irresistible power, his inconceivable glory, his inflexible justice, and his incontestable sovereignty, discoursed of with more clearness, fullness, reverence, and divine eloquence, than in this book? The creation of the world, and the government of it, are here admirably described, not as matters of nice speculation, but as laying most powerful obligations upon us to fear and serve, to submit to and trust in, our Creator. Moral good and evil, virtue and vice, were never drawn more to the life (the beauty of the one and the deformity of the other) than in this book; nor the inviolable rule of God's judgment more plainly laid down. These are not questions of the schools to keep the learned world in action. It appears by this book that they are sacred truths of undoubted certainty. (2) It presents us with a *specimen of Gentile piety.* This great saint was out of the pale of the covenant, no Israelite, no proselyte, and yet none like him for religion, nor such a favourite of heaven upon this earth. It was a truth therefore, before St. Peter perceived it, that *in every nation he that fears God and works righteousness is accepted of him,* Acts x. 35. There were *children of God scattered abroad* (John xi. 52) besides the incorporated *children of the kingdom,* Matt. viii. 11, 12. (3) It presents us with *an exposition of the book of Providence.* The prosperity of the wicked and the afflictions of the righteous have always been reckoned two as hard chapters as any in that book; but they are here expounded, and reconciled with the divine wisdom, purity, and goodness. (4) It presents us with *a great example of patience* and close adherence to God in the midst of the sorest calamities. Sir Richard Blackmore's most ingenious pen, in his excellent preface to his paraphrase on this book, makes Job a hero proper for an epic poem; for, says he, "He appears brave in distress and valiant in affliction, maintains his virtue, and with that his character, under the most exasperating provocations that the malice of hell could invent, and thereby gives a most noble example of passive fortitude, a character no way inferior to that of the active hero," &c. (5) It presents us with *an illustrious type of Christ,* the particulars of which we shall endeavour to take notice of as we go along. In general, Job was a great sufferer, was emptied and humbled, but in order to his greater glory. So Christ abased himself, that we might be exalted. The learned Bishop Patrick quotes St. Jerome more than once speaking of Job as a type of Christ, who *for the joy that was set before him endured the cross,* who was persecu'ed, for a time, by men and devils, and seemed forsaken of God too, but was

raised to be an intercessor even for his friends that had added affliction to his misery. When the apostle speaks of the *patience of Job* he immediately takes notice of *the end of the Lord*, that is, of the Lord Jesus (as some understand it), typified by Job, James v. 11.

2. In this book we have, (1) The history of Job's sufferings, and his patience under them (*ch.* i, ii), not without a mixture of human frailty, *ch.* iii. (2) A dispute between him and his friends upon them, in which, [1] The opponents were Eliphaz, Bildad, and Zophar. [2] The respondent was Job. [3] The moderators were, *First*, Elihu, *ch.* xxxii.–xxxvii. *Secondly*, God himself, *ch.* xxxviii.–xli. (3) The issue of all in Job's honour and prosperity, *ch.* xlii. Upon the whole, we learn that *many are the afflictions of the righteous but* that when the Lord *delivers them out of them all the trial of their faith will be found to praise, and honour, and glory.*

CHAPTER 1

The history of Job begins here with an account, I. Of his great piety in general (ver. 1), and in a particular instance, ver. 5. II. Of his great prosperity, ver. 2–4. III. Of the malice of Satan against him, and the permission he obtained to try his constancy, ver. 6–12. IV. Of the surprising troubles that befell him, the ruin of his estate (ver. 13–17), and the death of his children, ver. 18, 19. V. Of his exemplary patience and piety under these troubles, ver. 20–22. In all this he is set forth for an example of suffering affliction, from which no prosperity can secure us, but through which integrity and uprightness will preserve us.

Verses 1–3

Concerning Job,

I. He was a man; therefore subject to like passions as we are. He was *Ish*, a man in authority. The country he lived in was the land of Uz, in the eastern part of Arabia, near Euphrates. God has his remnant in all places. It was the privilege of the land of Uz to have so good a man as Job in it; the worse others were round about him the better he was. His name *Job*, or *Jjob*, some say, signifies *one hated* and counted as an enemy. Others make it to signify one that grieves or groans.

II. He was a very good man, eminently pious, and better than his neighbours: *He was perfect and upright*. It is the judgment of God concerning him, and we are sure that is according to truth. 1. Job was a religious man, *one that feared God*, that is, worshipped him. 2. He was sincere in his religion: He was *perfect*; not sinless, as he himself owns (*ch.* ix. 20): *If I say I am perfect, I shall be proved perverse*. But, having a respect to all God's commandments, aiming at perfection, he was really as good as he seemed to be, his heart was sound and his eye single. 3. He was upright in his dealings both with God and man, was faithful to his promises, steady in his counsels, true to every trust. 4. The fear of God reigning in his heart was the principle that governed his whole conversation. 5. He dreaded the thought of doing what was wrong; with the utmost abhorrence and detestation he *eschewed evil*. *The fear of the Lord is to hate evil* (Prov. viii. 13) and then *by the fear of the Lord men depart from evil*, Prov. xvi. 6.

III. He was prosperous and yet pious. Though it is hard and rare, it is not impossible, for *a rich man to enter into the kingdom of heaven*. He was prosperous, and his prosperity put a lustre upon his piety, and gave him who was so good so much greater opportunity of doing good. 1. He had a numerous family. He was eminent for religion, and yet not a hermit, not a recluse, but the father and master of a family. 2. He had a good estate for the support of his family; his *substance* was considerable, *v*. 3. Riches are called *substance*. Job's substance is described, not by the acres of land he was lord of, but, (1) By his cattle—*sheep and camels, oxen and asses*. As soon as God had made man, and provided for his maintenance by the herbs and fruits, he made him rich and great by giving him *dominion over the creatures*, Gen. i. 28. (2) By his servants. He had a very good household or husbandry, and thus he both had honour and did good. Job's wealth, with his wisdom, entitled him to the honour and power he had in his country, which he describes (*ch.* xxix). Job was upright and *therefore* grew rich; for honesty is the best policy, and piety and charity are ordinarily

the surest ways of thriving. The account of Job's piety and prosperity comes before the history of his great afflictions, to show that neither will secure us from the calamities of human life. Piety will not secure us, as Job's mistaken friends thought, for *all things come alike to all*; prosperity will not, as a careless world thinks, Isa. xlvii. 8.

Verses 4–5

A further account of Job's prosperity and his piety.

I. His great comfort in his children is taken notice of as an instance of his prosperity; for our temporary comforts are borrowed, depend upon others, and are as those about us are. It was a comfort to this good man, 1. To see his children grown up and settled in the world. All his sons were in houses of their own, probably married. 2. To see them thrive in their affairs, and able to feast one another, as well as to feed themselves. 3. To see them in health. 4. Especially to see them live in love, and unity, and mutual good affection, no jars or quarrels among them. 5. It added to his comfort to see the brothers so kind to their sisters, that they sent for them to feast with them. 6. They feasted in their own houses.

II. His great care about his children is taken notice of as an instance of his piety. Observe (*v*. 5) Job's pious concern for the spiritual welfare of his children.

1. He was jealous over them with a godly jealousy; and so we ought to be over ourselves and those that are dearest to us, as far as is necessary to our care and endeavour for their good.

2. As soon as the days of their feasting were over he called them to the solemn exercises of religion.

3. He sent to them to prepare for solemn ordinances, *sent and sanctified them*, ordered them to examine their own consciences and repent of what they had done amiss in their feasting. Thus he kept his authority over them for their good, and they submitted to it, though they had got into houses of their own. Still he was the priest of the family, and at his altar they all attended, valuing their share in his prayers more than their share in his estate. Parents cannot give grace to their children (it is God that sanctifies) but they ought by seasonable admonitions and counsels to further their sanctification.

4. He offered sacrifice for them. Job, like Abraham, had an altar for his family. On this extraordinary occasion, he offered more sacrifices than usual, *according to the number of them all*, one for each child. "For this child I prayed, according to its particular temper, genius, and condition," to which the prayers, as well as the endeavours, must be accommodated. He rose early as one whose heart was upon his work. He required his children to attend the sacrifice.

5. Thus he did *continually*. The acts of repentance and faith must be often renewed, because we often repeat our transgressions. He that serves God uprightly will serve him continually.

Verses 6–12

Job was not only so rich and great, but withal so wise and good, that one would think the mountain of his prosperity stood so strong that it could not be moved; but here we have a thick cloud gathering over his head. The devil, having a great enmity to Job for his eminent piety, begged and obtained leave to torment him. It does not at all derogate from the credibility of Job's story in general to allow that this discourse between God and Satan, in these verses, is parabolical, like that of Micaiah (1 Kings xxii. 19, &c.), and an allegory designed to represent the malice of the devil against good men and the divine check and restraint which that malice is under.

I. Satan among the sons of God (v. 6), an *adversary* (*so Satan* signifies) to God, to men, to all good: he thrust himself into an assembly of the *sons of God* that came to *present themselves before the Lord*. This means either, 1. A meeting of the saints on earth. Professors of religion, in the patriarchal age, were called *sons of God* (Gen. vi. 2); they had then religious assemblies and stated times for them. But there was a Satan among the sons of God; when they came together he is among them, to distract and disturb them. Or, 2. A meeting of the angels in heaven. They are *the sons of God, ch.* xxxviii. 7. Satan was one of them originally.

II. His examination, how he came thither (v. 7): *The Lord said unto Satan, Whence comest thou?* He knew very well whence he came, and with what design he came thither, that as the good angels came to do good he came for a permission to do hurt; but he would, by calling him to an account, show him that he was under check and control.

III. The account he gives of himself and of the tour he had made. I come (says he) *from going to and fro on the earth.* 1. He could not pretend he had been doing any good. 2. He would not own he had been doing any hurt. While we are on this earth we are within his reach, and with so much subtlety, swiftness, and industry, does he penetrate into all the corners of it, that we cannot be in any place secure from his temptations. 3. He yet seems to give some representation of his own character. Perhaps it is spoken proudly. Perhaps it is spoken fretfully, and with discontent. He had been walking to and fro, and could find no rest, but was as much a fugitive and a vagabond as Cain in the land of Nod. Perhaps it is spoken carefully: "I have been hard at work, going to and fro," in quest of an opportunity to do mischief.

IV. The question God puts to him concerning Job (v. 8): *Hast thou considered my servant Job?* How honourably God speaks of Job: "Yonder is *my servant Job*; there is *none like him.*" How closely he gives to Satan this good character of Job: *Hast thou set thy heart to my servant Job?* designing hereby to answer the devil's seeming boast of the interest he had in this earth. Saith God, "Job is my faithful servant." Satan may boast, but he shall not triumph. As if he had said, "Satan, I know thy errand; thou hast come to inform against Job; but *hast thou considered him?*"

V. The devil's base insinuation against Job, in answer to God's encomium of him. He could not deny but that Job feared God, but suggested that he was mercenary in his religion, and therefore a hypocrite (v. 9): *Doth Job fear God for nought?* How impatient the devil was of hearing Job praised, though it was God himself that praised him. Those are like the devil who cannot endure that anybody should be praised but themselves. How slily he censured him as a hypocrite, not asserting that he was so, but only asking, "Is he not so?" This is the common way of slanderers, whisperers, backbiters, to suggest that by way of query which yet they have no reason to think is true. How unjustly he accused him as mercenary, to prove him a hypocrite. It was a great truth that Job did not fear God for nought; he got much by it, for godliness is great gain: but it was a falsehood that he would not have feared God if he

had not got this by it, as the event proved. Job's friends charged him with hypocrisy because he was greatly afflicted, Satan because he greatly prospered.

VI. The complaint Satan made of Job's prosperity, *v.* 10. God's peculiar people are taken under his special protection, they and all that belong to them; divine grace makes a hedge about their spiritual life, and divine providence about their natural life. He had prospered him, not in idleness or injustice but in the way of honest diligence: *Thou hast blessed the work of his hands.* The devil speaks of it with vexation. "I see thou hast *made a hedge about him, round about.*" *The wicked* one *saw it and was grieved*, and argued against Job that the only reason why he served God was because God prospered him so well.

VII. The proof Satan undertakes to give of the hypocrisy and mercenariness of God's religion, if he might but have leave to strip him of his wealth. "Let it be put to this issue," says he (v. 11); "make him poor, frown upon him, turn thy hand against him, and then see where his religion will be; touch what he has and it will appear what he is. How spitefully he speaks of the impression it would make upon Job: "He will not only let fall his devotion, but *even curse thee to thy face.*" God declared Job the best man then living: now, if Satan can prove him a hypocrite, it will follow that God had not one faithful servant among men and that there was no such thing as true and sincere piety in the world, but religion was all a sham, and Satan was king *de facto—in fact*, over all mankind.

VIII. The permission God gave to Satan to afflict Job for the trial of his sincerity. 1. It is matter of wonder that God should give Satan such a permission as this, but he did it for his own glory, the honour of Job, the explanation of Providence, and the encouragement of his afflicted people in all ages. He suffered Job to be tried, as he suffered Peter to be sifted, but took care that *his faith should not fail* (Luke xxii. 32). 2. It is matter of comfort that God has the devil *in a chain.* He could not afflict Job without leave from God first asked and obtained, and then no further than he had leave: "*Only upon himself put not forth thy hand;* meddle not with his body, but only with his estate." It is a limited power that the devil has.

IX. Satan's departure from this meeting of the sons of God. He went forth now, not to go to and fro, rambling through the earth, but with a direct course, to fall upon poor Job, who is carefully going on in the way of his duty, and knows nothing of the matter.

Verses 13–19

A particular account of Job's troubles.

I. Satan brought them upon him on the very day that his children began their course of feasting, at their *elder brother's house* (v. 13).

II. They all come upon him at once; while one messenger of evil tidings was speaking another came, and, before he had told his story, a third, and a fourth, followed immediately. 1. That there might appear a more than ordinary displeasure of God against him in his troubles. 2. That he might not have leisure to consider, and reason himself into a gracious submission, but might be overwhelmed by a complication of calamities.

III. They took from him all that he had, and made a full end of his enjoyments.

1. He had 500 *yoke of oxen*, and 500 *she-asses*, and a competent number of servants to attend them; and all these he lost at once, v. 14, 15. His neighbours the Sabeans, carried off the oxen and asses, and slew the servants that faithfully and bravely did their best to defend them, and *one only escaped.* When Satan has God's permission to do mischief he will

not want mischievous men to be his instruments in doing it.

2. He had 7,000 *sheep*, and shepherds that kept them; and all those he lost at the same time by lightning, v. 16. Job was ready to reproach the Sabeans, and fly out against them for their injustice and cruelty, when the next news immediately directs him to look upwards. *The fire of God has fallen from heaven.* All his sheep and shepherds were not only killed, but consumed by it at once, and one shepherd only was left alive to carry the news to poor Job. This would tempt Job to say, *It is in vain to serve God.* The messenger called the lightning the *fire of God.* How terrible then were the tidings of this destruction, which came immediately from the hand of God!

3. He had 3,000 *camels*, and servants tending them; and he lost them all at the same time by the Chaldeans, who came in three bands, and drove them away, and slew the servants, v. 17. When the way of the wicked prospers, and they carry off their booty, while just and good men are suddenly cut off, God's righteousness is like the great deep, the bottom of which we cannot find, Ps. xxxvi. 6.

4. His dearest and most valuable possessions were his ten children; and, to conclude the tragedy, news is brought him, at the same time, that they were killed and buried in the ruins of the house in which they were feasting, and all the servants that waited on them, except one that came express with the tidings, of it v. 18, 19. This was the greatest of Job's losses, and therefore the devil reserved it for the last, that, if the other provocations failed, this might make him curse God. Our children are pieces of ourselves; it is very hard to part with them, and touches a good man in as tender a part as any. But to part with them all at once, and for them to be all cut off in a moment, who had been so many years his cares and hopes, went to the quick indeed. They all died together. They died suddenly. They died when they were feasting and making merry. Had they died suddenly when they were praying, he might the better have borne it. They were taken away when he had most need of them to comfort him under all his other losses.

Verses 20–22

The devil had done all he desired leave to do against Job, to provoke him to curse God. He whom the rising sun saw the richest of all the men in the east was before night poor to a proverb. If his riches had been, as Satan insinuated, the only principle of his religion, now that he had lost his riches he would certainly have lost his religion; but the account we have, in these verses, of his pious deportment under his affliction, sufficiently proved the devil a liar and Job an honest man.

I. He conducted himself like a man under his afflictions (v. 20), he *arose, and rent his mantle, and shaved his head,* which were the usual expressions of great sorrow, to show that he was sensible of the hand of the Lord that had gone out against him; yet he did not break out into any extravagant passion. He kept his temper, and bravely maintained the possession and repose of his own soul, in the midst of all these provocations. The time when he began to show his feelings was not till he heard of the death of his children, and then he rent his mantle. A worldly unbelieving heart would have said, "Now that the meat is gone it is well that the mouths are gone too." But Job knew better, and would have been thankful if Providence had spared his children, though he had had little or nothing for them, for *Jehovah-jireh—the Lord will provide.*

II. He conducted himself like a wise and good man under his affliction, like *one that feared God* and *eschewed* the *evil* of sin more than that of outward trouble.

1. He humbled himself under the hand of God, and accommodated himself to the providences he was under, as one that knew how to want as well as how to abound.

2. He composed himself with quieting considerations, that he might not be disturbed and put out of the possession of his own soul by these events. He reasons from the common state of human life, which he describes with application to himself: *Naked came I* (as others do) *out of my mother's womb, and naked shall I return thither.* St. Paul refers to this of Job, 1 Tim. vi. 7. *We brought nothing of this world's goods into the world,* we have them from others; and *it is certain that we can carry nothing out,* but must leave them to others. This consideration silenced Job under all his losses. He is but where he was at first. He looks upon himself only as naked, not maimed, not wounded; he was himself still his own man, when nothing else was his own, and therefore but reduced to his first condition. He is but where he must have been at last, and is only unclothed, or unloaded rather, a little sooner than he expected. If we put off our clothes, before we go to bed, it is some inconvenience, but it may be the better borne when it is near bed-time.

3. We may well rejoice to find Job in this good frame, because this was the very thing upon which the trial of his integrity was put. The devil said that he would, under his affliction, curse God; but he blessed him, and so proved himself an honest man.

(1) He acknowledged the hand of God both in the mercies he had formerly enjoyed and in the afflictions he was now exercised with: *The Lord gave, and the Lord has taken away.* The same that gave hath taken away; and may he not do what he will with his own? See how Job looks above instruments, and keeps his eye upon the first Cause.

(2) He adored God in both. When all was gone he fell down and worshipped. Afflictions must not divert us from, but quicken us to, the exercises of religion. Weeping must not hinder sowing, nor hinder worshipping. He gives God thanks for good designed him by his afflictions, for gracious supports under his afflictions, and the believing hopes he had of a happy issue at last.

Lastly, Here is the honourable testimony which the Holy Ghost gives to Job's constancy and good conduct under his afflictions. He passed his trials with applause, v. 22.

CHAPTER 2

Job honourably acquitted upon a fair trial between God and Satan concerning him. One would have thought, this would be conclusive, and that Job would never have his reputation called in question again; but Job is brought upon his trial, a second time. I. Satan moves for another trial, which should touch his bone and his flesh, ver. 1–5. II. God, for holy ends, permits it, ver. 6. III. Satan smites him with a very painful and loathsome disease, ver. 7, 8. IV. His wife tempts him to curse God, but he resists the temptation, ver. 9, 10. V. His friends come to condole with him and to comfort him, ver. 11–13. And in this that good man is set forth for an example of suffering affliction and of patience.

Verses 1–6

Satan will have Job's cause called over again.

I. The court set, and the prosecutor making his appearance (v. 1, 2), as before, ch. i, 6, 7. The angels attended God's throne and Satan among them. He is asked the same question as before, *Whence comest thou?* and answers as before, *From going to and fro in the earth;* as if he had been doing no harm.

II. The judge himself pleading for him (v. 3): "*Hast thou considered my servant Job* better than thou didst, *a perfect and an upright man*; for thou seest he *still holds fast his integrity?*" Satan is condemned for his allegations against Job: "*Thou movedst me against*

him, as an accuser, *to destroy him without cause.*"
How well it is for us that neither men nor devils
are to be our judges, for perhaps they would destroy
us, right or wrong; but our judgment proceeds from
the Lord, whose judgment never errs nor is biassed.
Job is commended for his constancy notwithstanding
the attacks made upon him. *Still he holds fast his
integrity.* Constancy crowns integrity.

III. The accusation further prosecuted, *v.* 4. *Skin
for skin, and all that a man has, will he give for his
life.* Men will not only venture, but give, their
estates to save their lives. Satan grounds upon this
an accusation of Job, slyly representing him, 1. As
unnatural to those about him, and one that laid not
to heart the death of his children and servants. 2. As
wholly selfish, and minding nothing but his own ease
and safety.

IV. A challenge given to make a further trial of
Job's integrity (*v.* 5): "*Put forth thy hand now and
touch his bone and his flesh,* and then *he will curse
thee to thy face,* and let go his integrity." Nothing is
more likely to ruffle the thoughts and put the mind
into disorder than acute pain and distemper of
body. St. Paul himself had much ado to bear a
thorn in the flesh, nor could he have borne it without
special grace from Christ, 2 Cor. xii. 8, 9.

V. A permission granted to Satan to make this
trial, *v.* 6. "*He is in thy hand,* do thy worst with him;
only save his life, or his soul. Afflict him, but not to
death." "Save his soul," that is, "his reason" (or
some), "preserve to him the use of that, for otherwise it will be no fair trial; if in his delirium, he should
curse God, that will be no disproof of his integrity.
It would be the language not of his heart, but of his
distemper."

Verses 7–10

The devil, having got leave to tear and worry
poor Job, presently fell to work with him, as a tormentor first and then as a tempter. Artfully is the
temptation managed with all the subtlety of the old
serpent, who is here playing the same game against
Job that he played against our first parents (Gen. iii).

I. He provokes him to curse God by smiting him
with sore boils, and so making him a burden to
himself, *v.* 7, 8.

1. The disease with which Job was seized was very
grievous: Satan *smote him with boils, sore boils,*
all over him, from head to foot, an erysipelas, perhaps,
in a higher degree.

2. Instead of healing salves, *he took a potsherd,* a
piece of a broken pitcher, *to scrape himself withal.*
A very sad pass this poor man had come to. Even
Lazarus had some ease from the tongues of the dogs
that came and *licked his sores;* but poor Job has no
help afforded him. None of those he had formerly
been kind to had so much gratitude as to minister
to him in his distress, either because the disease
was loathsome and noisome or because they apprehended it to be infectious. Instead of reposing in a
soft and warm bed, he *sat down among the ashes.*
Thus did he humble himself under the mighty hand
of God, and bring his mind to the meanness and
poverty of his condition. The Septuagint reads it,
He sat *down upon a dunghill without the city,* but the
original says no more than that he sat *in the midst
of the ashes.*

II. Satan urges him, by the persuasions of his own
wife, to curse God, *v.* 9. She was spared to him,
when the rest of his comforts were taken away, for
this purpose, to be a troubler and tempter to him.
If Satan leaves anything that he has permission to
take away, it is with a design of mischief. She banters
Job for his constancy in his religion: "*Dost thou still
retain thy integrity?* Art thou so tame and sheepish
as thus to truckle to a God who is so far from

rewarding thy services with marks of his favour that
he strips thee, and scourges thee, without any provocation given? Is this a God to be still loved, and
blessed, and served?" She urges him to renounce his
religion, to blaspheme God, and dare him to do his
worst: *Curse God and die;* be thy own deliverer by
being thy own executioner; end thy troubles by ending
thy life. These are two of the blackest and most
horrid of all Satan's temptations. Nothing is more
contrary to natural conscience than blaspheming
God, nor to natural sense than self-murder.

III. He bravely resists and overcomes the temptation, *v.* 10.

1. He was very indignant at having such a thing
mentioned to him: "What! Curse God? I abhor
the thought of it. *Get thee behind me, Satan.*" In
other cases Job reasoned with his wife with a great
deal of mildness, even when she was unkind to him
(*ch.* xix. 17): *I entreated her for the children's sake
of my own body.* But, when she persuaded him to curse
God, he was much displeased, and showed her
the evil of what she said. In such a pious household
as Job had his wife was one that had been well affected
to religion, but now, when all their estate and comfort were gone, she could not bear the loss with that
temper of mind that Job had. When Peter was a
Satan to Christ he told him plainly, *Thou art an
offence to me.* If those whom we think wise and good
at any time speak that which is foolish and bad, we
ought to reprove them faithfully.

2. He reasoned against the temptation: *Shall
we receive good at the hand of God, and shall we not
receive evil also?* Those whom we reprove we must
endeavour to convince. He argues for, not only
the bearing, but the receiving of evil: *Shall we not
receive evil,* that is, "Shall we not expect to receive it?
If God give us so many good things, shall we be
surprised, or think it strange, if he sometimes afflict
us, when he has told us that prosperity and adversity
are set the one over against the other?" 1 Peter iv. 12.
"Shall we not set ourselves to receive it aright?"
The word signifies to receive as a gift, and denotes
a pious affection and disposition of soul under our
afflictions, accounting them gifts (Phil. i. 29), accepting
them as punishments of our iniquity (Lev. xxvi. 41),
acquiescing in the will of God in them ("Let him do
with me as seemeth him good"). "Shall we receive
so much good as has come to us from the hand of
God during all those years of peace and prosperity,
and shall we not now receive evil, when God thinks
fit to lay it on us?" If we receive so much good for
the body, shall we not receive some good for the soul;
something which, by saddening the countenance,
makes the heart better?

IV. Thus Job still held fast his integrity, and Satan's
design against him was defeated: *In all this did not
Job sin with his lips.* Grace got the upper hand and
he took care that the root of bitterness might not
spring up to trouble him, Heb. xii. 15.

Verses 11–13

An account of the kind visit which Job's three
friends paid him in his affliction. Some, who were his
enemies, triumphed in his calamities, *ch.* xvi. 10;
xix. 18; xxx. 1, &c. But his friends concerned themselves for him, and endeavoured to comfort him.
Three of them are here named (*v.* 11), Eliphaz, Bildad,
and Zophar. These three were eminently wise and
good men, as appears by their discourses. They were
old men, had a great reputation for knowledge,
and much deference was paid to their judgment,
ch. xxxii. 6.

I. Job, in his prosperity, had contracted a friendship
with them. Much of the comfort of this life lies
in acquaintance and friendship with those that are
prudent and virtuous; and he that has a few such

friends ought to value them highly. Job's three friends are supposed to have been all of them of the posterity of Abraham. Eliphaz descended from Teman, the grandson of Esau (Gen. xxxvi. 11), Bildad (it is probable) from Shuah, Abraham's son by Keturah, Gen. xxv. 2. Zophar is thought by some to be the same with Zepho, a descendant from Esau, Gen. xxxvi. 11. The preserving of so much wisdom and piety among those that were strangers to the covenants of promise was a happy presage of God's grace to the Gentiles, when the partition-wall should in the latter days be taken down. Esau was rejected; yet many that came from him inherited some of the best blessings.

II. They continued their friendship with Job in his adversity, when most of his friends had forsaken him, *ch.* xix. 14. They come to share with him in his griefs, as formerly they had come to share with him in his comforts. Many a good lesson is to be learned from the troubles of others; we may look upon them and receive instruction, and be made wise and serious. Some good word may be spoken to them which may help to make them easy. Job's friends came to mourn with him, to mingle their tears with his, and so to comfort him. It is much more pleasant to visit those in affliction to whom comfort belongs than those to whom we must first speak conviction. They were not sent for, but came of their own accord (*ch.* vi. 22). They came with a design to comfort him, and yet proved miserable comforters, through their unskilful management of his case. When they saw him at some distance he was so disfigured and deformed with his sores that *they knew him not, v.* 12. What a change will a sore disease, or oppressing care and grief, make in the countenance, in a little item! *Is this Job?* Observing him thus miserably altered, they did not leave him, in a fright or loathing, but expressed so much the more tenderness towards him. The sight of them revived Job's grief, and set him a weeping afresh, which fetched floods of tears from their eyes. *They rent their clothes, and sprinkled dust upon their heads,* as men that would strip themselves, and abase themselves, with their friend that was stripped and abased. They had many a time, it is likely, sat with him on his couches and at his table, in his prosperity, and were therefore willing to share with him in his grief and poverty because they had shared with him in his joy and plenty. They resolved to stay with him till they saw him mend or end, and therefore took lodgings near him, though he was not now able to entertain them. Every day, for seven days together, they came and sat with him, as his companions in tribulation. They sat with him, but *none spoke a word* to him, only they all attended to the particular narratives he gave of his troubles. By their silence so long they would intimate that what they afterwards said was well considered and digested and the results of many thoughts. We should think twice before we speak once, especially in such a case as this, think long, and we shall be the better able to speak short and to the purpose.

CHAPTER 3

"You have heard of the patience of Job," says the apostle, James v. 11. So we have, and of his impatience too. In this chapter we find him cursing his day. I. Complaining that he was born, ver. 1–10. II. Complaining that he did not die as soon as he was born, ver. 11–19. III. Complaining that his life was now continued when he was in misery, ver. 20–26.

Verses 1–10

Long was Job's heart hot within him; and, while he was musing the fire burned, and the more for being stifled and suppressed. So long Job and his friends sat thinking, but said nothing; *they* were afraid of speaking what they thought, lest they should grieve him, and *he* durst not give vent to his thoughts, lest

he should offend them. Job first gives vent to his thoughts. In short, he cursed the day of his birth, wished he had never been born.

I. The extremity of his troubles and the discomposure of his spirits may excuse it in part, but he can by no means be justified in it. Now he has forgotten the good he was born to, the lean kine have eaten up the fat ones, and he is filled with thoughts of the evil only, and wishes he had never been born. The prophet Jeremiah himself expressed his painful sense of his calamities in language, not much unlike this: *Woe is me, my mother, that thou hast borne me!* Jer. xv. 10. *Cursed be the day wherein I was born,* Jer. xx. 14, &c. There is no condition of life a man can be in in this world but he may in it (if it be not his own fault) so honour God, and work out his own salvation, and make sure a happiness for himself in a better world, that he will have no reason at all to wish he had never been born, but a great deal of reason to say that he had his being to good purpose. Yet it must be owned, if there were not another life after this, so many are the sorrows and troubles of this that we might sometimes be tempted to say that we were *made in vain* (Ps. lxxxix. 47), and to wish we had never been. Let us observe it, to the honour of the spiritual life above the natural, that though many have cursed the day of their first birth, never any cursed the day of their new-birth, nor wished they never had had grace, and the Spirit of grace, given them.

II. Job cursed his day, but he did not curse his God—was weary of his life, and would gladly have parted with that, but not weary of his religion; he resolutely cleaves to that, and will never let it go. The dispute between God and Satan concerning Job was not whether Job had his infirmities, and whether he was subject to like passions as we are (that was granted), but whether he was a hypocrite, who secretly hated God, and, if he were provoked, would show his hatred; and, upon trial, it proved that he was no such man. The particular expressions which Job used in cursing his day are full of poetical fancy, flame, and rapture. We need not be particular in our observations upon them. When he would express his passionate wish that he had never been, he falls foul upon the day, and wishes,

(1) That earth might forget it.

(2) That Heaven might frown upon it: *Let not God regard it from above, v.* 4. Let the gloominess of the day represent Job's condition, whose sun went down at noon.

(3) That all joy might forsake it: *Let no joyful voice come therein* (*v.* 7); let it be a long night, and not *see the eye-lids of the morning* (*v.* 9), which bring joy with them.

(4) That all curses might follow it (*v.* 8): "Let none ever desire to see it, but, on the contrary, *let those curse it that curse the day.* Whatever day any are tempted to curse, let them at the same time bestow one curse upon my birth-day." What a foolish thing it was to wish that his eyes had never seen the light, that so they might not have seen sorrow, which yet he might hope to see through, and beyond which he might see joy!

Verses 11–19

Job, perhaps reflecting upon himself for his folly in wishing he had never been born, follows it, and thinks to mend it, with another, little better, that he had died as soon as he was born. Job here complains of life as a curse, and covets death and the grave as the greatest and most desirable bliss. Surely Satan was deceived in Job when he applied that maxim to him, *All that a man hath will he give for his life;* for never any man valued life at a lower rate than he did.

I. He ungratefully quarrels with life, and is angry that it was not taken from him as soon as it was given him (v. 11, 12): *Why died not I from the womb?* What a weak and helpless creature man is when he comes into the world, and how slender the thread of life is when it is first drawn. What a merciful and tender care divine Providence took of us at our entrance into the world. What a great deal of vanity and vexation of spirit attends human life. If we had not a God to serve in this world, and better things to hope for in another world, considering the faculties we are endued with and the troubles we are surrounded with, we should be strongly tempted to wish that we had *died from the womb.* How much soever life is embittered, we must say, "It was of the Lord's mercies that we died not from the womb, that we were not consumed." Hatred of life is a contradiction to the common sense and sentiments of mankind, and to our own at any other time. When the old man in the fable, being tired with his burden, threw it down with discontent and called for Death, and Death came to him and asked him what he would have with him, he then answered, "Nothing, but to help me up with my burden."

II. He passionately applauds death and the grave, and seems quite in love with them. To desire to die that we may be with Christ, that we may be free from sin, and that we may be *clothed upon with our house which is from heaven,* is the effect and evidence of grace; but to desire to die only that we may be quiet in the grave, and delivered from the troubles of this life, savours of corruption. Job here frets himself with thinking that if he had but died as soon as he was born: I should have been (says he, v. 14) *with kings and counsellors of the earth,* whose pomp, power, and policy, cannot set them out of the reach of death, nor secure them from the grave, nor distinguish theirs from common dust in the grave. Though they filled their houses with silver, yet they were forced to leave it all behind them, no more to return to it. Some, by the *desolate places* which the kings and counsellors are here said *to build for themselves,* understand the sepulchres or monuments they prepared for themselves in their life-time; and by the gold which the princes had, and the silver with which they filled their houses, they understand the treasures which, they say, it was usual to deposit in the graves of great men. Such arts have been used to preserve their dignity, if possible, on the other side death, and to keep themselves from lying with those of inferior rank; but it will not do: death is, and will be, an irresistible leveller. *Death mingles sceptres with spades.* There a *hidden untimely birth* (v. 16), a child that either never saw light or but just opened its eyes and peeped into the world, and, not liking it, closed them again and hastened out of it, lies as soft and easy, lies as high and safe, as kings, and counsellors, and princes, that had gold. "And therefore," says Job, "would I have lain there in the dust, rather than live to lie here in the ashes! *Then should I have lain still, and been quiet,* which now I cannot do, I cannot be, but am still tossing and unquiet; then *I should have slept,* where as now sleep departeth from my eyes; *then had I been at rest,* whereas now I am restless." Now that life and immortality are brought to a much clearer light by the gospel than before good Christians can give a better account than this of the gain of death. But all that poor Job dreamed of was rest and quietness in the grave out of the fear of evil tidings and out of the feeling of sore boils. *Then should I have been quiet.* How finely he describes the repose of the grave. Those that now are troubled will there be out of the reach of trouble (v. 17): *There the wicked cease from troubling.* Those that are now toiled will there see the period of their toils. *There the weary*

are at rest. Those that were here enslaved are there at liberty. Death is the prisoner's discharge, the relief of the oppressed, and the servant's manumission (v. 18).

Verses 20–26

Job here complains that his life was now continued and not cut off.

I. He thinks it hard, in general, that miserable lives should be prolonged (v. 20–22): *Wherefore is light in life given to those that are bitter in soul?* Life is called *light,* because pleasant and serviceable for walking and working. It is candle-light; the longer it burns the shorter it is, and the nearer to the socket. This light is said to be given us. Job reckons that to those who are in misery it is δῶρον ἄδωρον—*gift and no gift,* while the light only serves them to see their own misery. He here speaks of those who long for death, when they have outlived their comforts and usefulness, are burdened with age and infirmities, with pain or sickness, poverty or disgrace, and yet it comes not; while, at the same time, it comes to many who dread it and would put it far from them. The continuance and period of life must be according to God's will, not according to ours. It is not fit that we should be consulted how long we would live and when we would die; our times are in a better hand than our own. *Some dig for it as for hidden treasures,* that is, would give anything for a fair dismission out of this world. It may be a sin to long for death, but I am sure it is no sin to long for heaven.

II. He thinks himself, in particular, hardly dealt with, that he might not be eased of his pain and misery by death. To be thus impatient of life for the sake of the troubles we meet with is not only unnatural in itself, but ungrateful to the giver of life. Grace teaches us, in the midst of life's greatest comforts, to be willing to die, and, in the midst of its greatest crosses, to be willing to live. He had no comfort of his life: *My sighing comes before I eat,* v. 24. His griefs returned as duly as his meals, and affliction was his daily bread. He had no prospect of bettering his condition: *His way was hidden,* and God had *hedged him in,* v. 23. That which made his grief now the more grievous was that he was not conscious either of negligence or security in the day of his prosperity, which might provoke God thus to chastise him. He had kept up such a fear of trouble as was necessary to the maintaining of his guard. He was afraid for his children when they were feasting, lest they should offend God (ch. i. 5), afraid for his servants lest they should offend his neighbours; he took all the care he could of his own health, yet all would not do. He had not been secure, nor indulged himself in ease and softness, yet trouble came. Thus his way was hidden, for he knew not wherefore God contended with him.

CHAPTER 4

Job having given vent to his passion, his friends here come gravely to give vent to their judgment upon his case. The dispute begins, and it soon becomes fierce. The opponents are Job's three friends. Job himself is respondent. Elihu appears, first, as moderator, and at length God himself gives judgment upon the controversy. The question in dispute is whether Job was an honest man or no. Satan durst not pretend that his cursing his day was a constructive cursing of his God; no, he cannot deny but that Job still holds fast his integrity; but Job's friends will needs have it that, if Job were an honest man, he would not have been thus sorely afflicted, and therefore urge him to confess himself a hypocrite in the profession he had made of religion: "No," says Job, "that I will never do; I have offended God, but my heart, notwithstanding, has been upright with him;" and still he holds fast the comfort of his integrity. Eliphaz, who, it is likely, was the senior, begins with him in this chapter, in which, I. He bespeaks a patient hearing, ver. 2. II. He compliments Job with an acknowledgment of the eminence and usefulness of the profession he had made of religion, ver. 3, 4. III. He charges him with hypocrisy in his profession, grounding his charge upon his present troubles and his conduct under them, ver. 5, 6. IV. To make good the inference, he maintains that man's wickedness is that which always brings God's judgments, ver. 7–11. V. He corroborates his assertion by a vision which he had, in which he was reminded of the incontestable purity and justice of God, and the meanness, weakness, and sinfulness of man, ver. 12–21. By all this he aims to bring down Job's spirit and to make him both penitent and patient under his afflictions.

Verses 1–6

I. Eliphaz excuses the trouble he is now about to give to Job by his discourse (*v.* 2): "*If we assay a word with thee*, offer a word of reproof and counsel, wilt thou be grieved and take it ill? We have reason to fear thou wilt; but there is no remedy: *Who can refrain from words?*" With what tenderness he speaks of Job, and his present afflicted condition: "If we tell thee our mind, *wilt thou be grieved?*" We should show ourselves backward to say that which we foresee will be grievous, though ever so necessary. With what assurance he speaks of the truth of what he was about to say: *Who can withhold himself from speaking?* It is foolish pity not to reprove our friends, even our friends in affliction, for what they say or do amiss, only for fear of offending them.

II. He exhibits a twofold charge against Job.

1. As to his particular conduct under this affliction. He charges him with weakness and faint-heartedness.

(1) He takes notice of Job's former serviceableness to the comfort of others. He owns that Job had instructed many, not only his own children and servants. With suitable counsels and comforts he *strengthened the weak hands* for work and service and the spiritual warfare. Those who have abundance of spiritual riches should abound in spiritual charity. But why does Eliphaz mention this here? Perhaps he praises him thus for the good he had done that he might make the intended reproof the more passable with him. He remembers how Job had comforted others as a reason why he might justly expect to be himself comforted. He speaks in pity, lamenting that through the extremity of his affliction he could not apply those comforts to himself which he had formerly administered to others. He mentions it, upbraiding him with his knowledge, and the good offices he had done for others, as if he had said, "Thou that hast taught others, why dost thou not teach thyself?"

(2) He upbraids him with his present low-spiritedness, *v.* 5. "*Now* that *it has come upon thee*, now that *it touches thee, thou faintest, thou art troubled.*" He makes too light of Job's afflictions: "It *touches thee.*" The very word that Satan himself had used, *ch.* i. 11; ii. 5. Had Eliphaz felt but the one-half of Job's affliction, he would have said, "It smites me, it wounds me;" but, speaking of Job's afflictions, he makes a mere trifle of it. He makes too much of Job's resentments. Men in deep distress must have grains of allowance, and a favourable construction put upon what they say.

2. As to his general character before this affliction. He charges him with wickedness and false-heartedness, and this article of his charge was utterly groundless and unjust. How unkindly does he upbraid him with the great profession of religion he had made, as if it had all now come to nothing and proved a sham (*v.* 6): "*Is not this thy fear, thy confidence, thy hope, and the uprightness of thy ways?* Does it not all appear now to be a mere pretence? For, hadst thou been sincere in it, God would not thus have afflicted thee, nor wouldst thou have behaved thus under the affliction." This was the very thing Satan aimed at, to prove Job a hypocrite. When he could not himself do this to God, he endeavoured, by his friends, to do it to Job himself, and to persuade him to confess himself a hypocrite. But, by the grace of God, Job was enabled to hold fast his integrity, and would not bear false witness against himself.

Those that pass rash and uncharitable censures upon their brethren, and condemn them as hypocrites, do Satan's work. This verse is differently read in several editions of our common English Bibles. One of the first, in 1612, has it, "*Is not this thy fear, thy confidence, the uprightness of thy ways, and thy hope?* Does it not appear now that all the religion both of thy devotion and of thy conversation was only in hope and confidence that thou shouldst grow rich by it? If it had been sincere, would it not have kept thee from this despair? It is true, *if thou faint in the day of adversity, thy strength*, thy grace, *is small* (Prov. xxiv. 10); but it does not therefore follow that thou hast no grace, no strength at all." A man's character is not to be taken from a single act.

Verses 7–11

Eliphaz here advances another argument to prove Job a hypocrite, and will have not only his impatience under his afflictions to be evidence against him, but even his afflictions themselves.

I. Good men were never thus ruined. For the proof of this he appeals to Job's own observation (*v.* 7): "*Remember, I pray thee;* and give me an instance of any one that was righteous, and yet was cut off as thou art." If we understand it of a final destruction, his principle is true. None that are righteous perish for ever, 2 Thess. ii. 3. But, if we understand it of any temporal calamity, his principle is not true.

II. Wicked men were often thus ruined. For the proof of this he vouches his own observation (*v.* 8): "*Even as I have seen*, many a time, *those that plough iniquity, and sow wickedness, reap accordingly; by the blast of God they perish, v.* 9." We have reason to think that, whatever profession of religion thou hast made, thou hast but ploughed iniquity and sown wickedness. Some, by iniquity and wickedness, understand wrong and injury done to others. They shall be paid in their own coin. Those who are troublesome shall be troubled. He further describes their destruction (*v.* 9): *By the blast of God they perish.* Some think that in attributing the destruction of sinners to the blast of God, and *the breath of his nostrils*, he refers to the wind which blew the house down upon Job's children. He speaks particularly of tyrants and cruel oppressors, under the similitude of lions, *v.* 10, 11. The Hebrew tongue has five several names for lions, and they are all here used to set forth the terrible tearing power, fierceness, and cruelty, of proud oppressors. The voice of their roaring shall be stopped. God will take away their power to do hurt: *The teeth of the young lions are broken.* They shall not enrich themselves with the spoil of their neighbours. Even *the old lion* is famished, and *perishes for lack of prey.* They shall not leave a succession: *The stout lion's whelps are scattered abroad*, to seek for food themselves, which the old ones used to bring in for them, Nah. ii. 12. Perhaps Eliphaz intended, in this, to reflect upon Job, as if he, being the *greatest of all the men of the east*, had got his estate by spoil, but now his power and estate were gone, and his family was scattered: if so, it was a pity that a man whom God praised should be thus abused.

Verses 12–21

Eliphaz, having undertaken to convince Job of the sin and folly of his discontent and impatience, here vouches a vision which he relates to Job. It would have been well if he had kept to the purport of this vision, which would serve for a ground on which to reprove Job for his murmuring, but not to condemn him as a hypocrite. The people of God had not then any written word to quote, and therefore God sometimes notified to them even common truths by the extraordinary ways of revelation. We

that have Bibles have there (thanks be to God) a
more sure word to depend upon than even visions
and voices, 2 Peter i. 19.

I. This message was sent to Eliphaz *secretly.* Some
of the sweetest communion gracious souls have with
God is in secret, where no eye sees but that of him
who is all eye. God has ways of bringing conviction,
counsel, and comfort, to his people, unobserved by
the world, by private whispers, as powerfully and
effectually as by the public ministry. *He received
a little thereof, v.* 12. We know little in comparison
with what is to be known, and with what we shall
know when we come to heaven. It was brought to
him in the *visions of the night* (*v.* 13), when he had
retired from the world and the hurry of it, and all
about him was composed and quiet. It was prefaced
with terrors: *Fears came upon him, and trembling,
v.* 14. A holy awe and reverence of God and his
majesty being struck upon his spirit, he was thereby
prepared for a divine visit.

II. Concerning this apparition which Eliphaz saw
we are here told (*v.* 15, 16) it was real, and not a
dream. If some have been so knavish as to impose
false visions on others, and some so foolish as to be
themselves imposed upon, it does not therefore
follow but that there may have been apparitions of
spirits, both good and bad. He *could not discern the
form thereof,* so as to frame any exact idea of it in
his own mind, much less to give a description of it.
His conscience was to be awakened and informed,
not his curiosity gratified.

III. The message was delivered in a still small voice,
and this was it (*v.* 17): "*Shall mortal man be more
just than God,* the immortal God? *Shall a man be
thought to be,* or pretend to be, *more pure than his
Maker?*" It is a reproof of Job's murmuring and
discontent: "Shall a man pretend to be more just
and pure than God? more truly to understand, and
more strictly to observe, the rules and laws of equity
than God?"

IV. Eliphaz shows how little the angels themselves
are in comparison with God, *v.* 18. Angels are God's
servants, waiting servants, working servants. If the
world were left to the government of the angels,
and they were trusted with the sole management of
affairs, they would take false steps, and everything
would not be done for the best, as now it is. Angels
are intelligences, but finite ones. Thence he infers
how much less man is, how much less to be trusted
in or gloried in. If there is such a distance between
God and angels, what is there between God and man!
Look upon man in his life, and he is very mean,
v. 19. Take man in his best estate, and he is a very
despicable creature in comparison with the holy
angels, though honourable if compared with the
brutes. Angels are pure spirits; the souls of men
dwell in houses of clay: such the bodies of men are.
Angels are free; human souls are houses, and the
body is a cloud, a clog, to it; it is its cage; it is its
prison. Angels are fixed, but the very *foundation* of
that house of clay in which man dwells *is in the dust.*
We stand but upon the dust; some have a higher heap
of dust to stand upon than others, but still it is the
earth that stays us up and will shortly swallow us up.
Angels are immortal, but man is soon *crushed like
a moth* between one's fingers. A little thing will
destroy his life. He is *crushed before the face of the
moth,* so the word is. Is such a creature as this to be
trusted in, or can any service be expected from him
by that God who puts no trust in angels themselves?
In his death he appears yet more despicable, and unfit
to be trusted. Men are mortal and dying, *v.* 20, 21.
They are dying daily, and continually wasting:
Destroyed from morning to evening. In death all
their excellency passes away; beauty, strength, learning, not only cannot secure them from death, but

must die with them, nor shall their pomp, their
wealth, or power, descend after them. Their wisdom
cannot save them from death. Shall such a mean,
weak, foolish, sinful, dying creature as this pretend
to be *more just than God and more pure than his
Maker?* No, instead of quarrelling with his afflictions,
let him wonder that he is out of hell.

CHAPTER 5

Eliphaz, for the making good of his charge against Job, had
vouched a word from heaven, sent him in a vision. In this
chapter he appeals to those that bear record on earth, to the
saints, the faithful witnesses of God's truth in all ages, ver. 1.
They will testify, 1. That the sin of sinners is their ruin, ver. 2–5.
II. That affliction is the common lot of mankind, ver. 6, 7.
III. That when we are in affliction it is our wisdom and duty to
apply to God, for he is able and ready to help us, ver. 8–16.
IV. That the afflictions which are borne well will end well; and
Job particularly, if he would come to a better temper, might
assure himself that God had great mercy in store for him, ver.
17–27. So that he concludes his discourse in somewhat a better
humour than he began it.

Verses 1–5

So well assured is Eliphaz of the goodness of his
own cause that he moves Job himself to choose the
arbitrators (*v.* 1): *Call now, if there be any that will
answer thee.* "Canst thou produce an instance of
anyone that was really a saint that was reduced to
such an extremity as thou art now reduced to? God
never dealt with any that love his name as he deals
with thee, and therefore surely thou art none of them.
Did ever any good man curse his day as thou dost?"
To which of the saints wilt thou turn? Good people are
called *saints* even in the Old Testament; and therefore
I know not why we should appropriate the title to
those of the New Testament, and not say St. Abraham,
St. Moses, and St. Isaiah, as well as St. Matthew
and St. Mark; and St. David the psalmist, as well as
St. David the British bishop. There are two things
which Eliphaz here maintains, and in which he doubts
not but all the saints concur with him:—

I. That the sin of sinners directly tends to their
own ruin (*v.* 2): *Wrath kills the foolish man,* his own
wrath, and therefore he is foolish for indulging it.
Envy is the rottenness of the bones, and so *slays the
silly one* that frets himself with it. "So it is with
thee," says Eliphaz, "while thou quarrellest with
God thou doest thyself the greatest mischief." Job had
told his wife she spoke as the foolish women; now
Eliphaz tells him he acted as the foolish men, the
silly ones.

II. That their prosperity is short and their destruction certain, *v.* 3–5. He seems here to parallel Job's
case with that which is commonly the case of wicked
people. Job's prosperity was now at an end, and so
has the prosperity of other wicked people quickly
been. Eliphaz foresaw their ruin. Those who looked
only at present things blessed their habitation, and
thought them happy. He saw, at length, what he had
foreseen. His family was undone, and his estate
ruined. In these particulars he plainly and very
invidiously reflects on Job's calamities. His children
were crushed, *v.* 4. This is commonly understood of
the destruction of the families of wicked men, to
oblige them to restore what they have ill-gotten. They
leave it to their children; but the rightful owners will
crush their children, and cast them by due course of
law. His estate was plundered, *v.* 5. Job's was so.
The hungry robbers, the Sabeans and Chaldeans,
ran away with it, and swallowed it; and this, says he,
I have often observed in others. What has been got
by spoil and rapine has been lost in the same way.
The careful owner hedged it about with thorns, and
then thought it safe; but the fence proved insignificant
against the greediness of the spoilers, which will go
through the thorns and briers, and *burn them together,*
Isa. xxvii. 4.

Verses 6–16

Eliphaz, having touched Job, in mentioning the loss of his estate and the death of his children as the just punishment of his sin, that he might not drive him to despair, here begins to encourage him. Now he speaks in the accents of kindness, as if he would atone for the hard words he had given him.

I. He reminds him that no affliction comes by chance, nor is to be attributed to second causes: It *doth not come forth of the dust*, nor *spring out of the ground*, as the grass doth, *v.* 6. If men be bad, they must not lay the blame upon the soil, the climate, or the stars, but on themselves.

II. He reminds him that trouble and affliction are what we have all reason to expect in this world: *Man is brought to trouble* (*v.* 7), not as man, but as sinful man. Such is the frailty of our bodies, and the vanity of our enjoyments, that our troubles arise as naturally *as the sparks fly upwards*. Why then should we be surprised at our afflictions as strange, or quarrel with them as hard.

III. He directs him how to behave himself under his affliction (*v.* 8): *I would seek unto God; surely I would:* so it is in the original. It is easy to say what we would do if we were in such a one's case; but, when it comes to the trial, perhaps it will be found not so easy to do as we say. Good and seasonable advice Eliphaz transfers to himself in a figure: "For my part, the best way I should think I could take, if I were in thy condition, would be to apply to God." We must by prayer fetch in mercy and grace from God, though he contend with us. His favour we must seek when we have lost all we have in the world. *Is any afflicted? let him pray.* It is heart's ease, a salve for every sore. *To God would I commit my cause*, having laid it at his feet, I would lodge it in his hand.

IV. He encourages him thus to seek to God, and commit his cause to him. In general, he *doeth great things* (*v.* 9), great indeed, for he can do anything, he doth do everything, and all according to the counsel of his own will. The works of nature are mysterious; and the wisest philosophers have owned themselves at a loss. The designs of Providence are much more deep and unaccountable, Rom. xi. 33. He doeth great *things without number*; his power is never exhausted, nor will all his purposes ever be fulfilled till the end of time. Now, by the consideration of this, Eliphaz intends to convince Job of his fault and folly in quarrelling with God. He gives some instances of God's dominion and power. God doeth great things in the kingdom of nature: *He gives rain upon the earth* (*v.* 10), put here for all the gifts of common providence, all the *fruitful seasons* by which he *filleth our hearts with food and gladness*, Acts xiv. 17. He doeth great things in the affairs of the children of men, not only enriches the poor and comforts the needy, by the rain he sends (*v.* 10), but, in order to the advancing of those that are low, he *disappoints the devices of the crafty*; for *v.* 11 is to be joined to *v.* 12. God can defeat all the designs of his and his people's enemies. How were the plots of Ahithophel, Sanballat, and Haman baffled! How were the confederacies of Syria and Ephraim against Judah, of Gebal, and Ammon, and Amalek, against God's Israel, the kings of the earth and the princes against the Lord and against his anointed, broken! The learned men of the heathen were befooled by their own vain philosophy. When God infatuates men they are perplexed, and at a loss, even in those things that seem most plain and easy (*v.* 14): *They meet with darkness* even *in the daytime*: nay (as in the margin), *They run themselves into darkness* by the violence and precipitation of their own counsels. See *ch.* xii. 20, 24, 25. He exalts the humble, *v.* 11. The lowly in heart, and those that mourn, he advances, comforts, and makes to *dwell on high*, in the *munitions*

of rocks, Isa. xxxiii. 16. *So the poor*, who began to despair, *has hope.* The experiences of some are encouragements to others to hope the best in the worst of times; for it is the glory of God to send help to the helpless and hope to the hopeless.

Verses 17–27

Eliphaz gives Job a comfortable prospect of the issue of his afflictions, if he did but recover his temper and accommodate himself to them.

I. The seasonable word of caution and exhortation that he gives him (*v.* 17): "*Despise not thou the chastening of the Almighty.* Call it a chastening, which comes from the father's love and is designed for the child's good. Let grace conquer the antipathy which nature has to suffering, and reconcile thyself to the will of God in it." We must never think it a thing below us to come under his discipline, but reckon, on the contrary, that God really magnifies man when he thus *visits and tries him*, *ch.* vii. 17, 18. Do not overlook and disregard it, as if it were only a chance, and the production of second causes, but take great notice of it as the voice of God and a messenger from heaven.

II. The comfortable words of encouragement which he gives him.

1. *Happy is the man whom God correcteth* if he make but a due improvement of the correction. Correction is an evidence of his sonship and a means of his sanctification; it mortifies his corruptions, weans his heart from the world, draws him nearer to God, brings him to his Bible, brings him to his knees, and so is working for him, a far more exceeding and eternal weight of glory. The issue and consequence of it would be very good, *v.* 18. When God makes sores by the rebukes of his providence he binds up by the consolations of his Spirit.

2. In the following verses Eliphaz addresses himself directly to Job, and gives him many precious promises of great and kind things which God would do for him if he did but humble himself under his hand. And, though Job's friends spoke both of God and Job some things that were not right, yet the general doctrines they laid down expressed the pious sense of the patriarchal age, and as St. Paul quoted *v.* 13 for canonical scripture, and as the command *v.* 17 is no doubt binding on us, so these promises must be, received and applied as divine promises, and we may *through patience and comfort of this* part of *scripture have hope.*

(1) It is here promised that as afflictions and troubles recur deliverances shall be graciously repeated, be it ever so often: *In six troubles he shall* be ready to *deliver thee*; *yea, and in seven*, *v.* 19.

(2) Whatever troubles good men may be in, *there shall no evil touch them*; they shall do them no real harm; they may hiss, but they cannot hurt, Ps. xci. 10.

(3) When desolating judgments are abroad, they shall be taken under special protection, *v.* 20.

(4) Whatever is maliciously said against them, it shall not affect them to do them any hurt, *v.* 21. The best men, and the most inoffensive, cannot secure themselves from calumny, reproach, and false accusation. From these a man cannot hide himself, but God can hide him, so that the most malicious slanders shall not disturb his peace nor blemish his reputation.

(5) They shall have a holy security and serenity of mind, arising from their hope and confidence in God. When dangers are most threatening they *shall not be afraid of destruction*, no, not when they see it coming (*v.* 21), nor *of the beasts of the field* when they set upon them, nor of men as cruel as beasts; *at destruction and famine thou shalt laugh* (*v.* 22). Blessed Paul laughed at destruction when he said, *O death! where is thy sting?* when, in the name of all the saints, he defied all the calamities of this

present time to *separate us from the love of God*, concluding that *in all these things we are more than conquerors*, Rom. viii. 35, &c.

(6) Being at peace with God, there shall be a covenant of friendship between them and the whole creation, *v.* 23. "When thou walkest over thy grounds thou shalt not need to fear stumbling, for *thou shalt be at league with the stones of the field*, not to dash thy foot against any of them, nor shalt thou be in danger from *the beasts of the field*, for they shall all be at peace with thee."

(7) Their houses and families shall be comfortable to them, *v.* 24. *That peace is thy tabernacle* (so the word is); peace is the house in which those dwell who dwell in God, and are at home in him. "*Thou shalt visit*" (that is, enquire into the affairs of) "*thy habitation*, and take a review of them, *and shalt not sin*." God will provide a settlement for his people, mean perhaps and movable, a cottage, a tabernacle, but a fixed and quiet habitation. "Thou shalt not sin," or *wander*; that is, as some understand it, "thou shalt not be a fugitive and a vagabond." They shall have wisdom to govern their families aright, to order their affairs with discretion, which is here called *visiting their habitation.* Family piety crowns family peace and prosperity.

(8) Their posterity shall be numerous and prosperous. Job had lost all his children; "but," says Eliphaz, "if thou return to God, he will again build up thy family." It is a comfort to parents to see the prosperity, especially the spiritual prosperity, of their children; if they are truly good, they are truly great, how small a figure soever they may make in the world.

(9) Their death shall be seasonable, and they shall finish their course, at length, with joy and honour, *v.* 26. If the providence of God do not give us long life, yet if the grace of God give us to be satisfied with the time allotted us, we may be said to come to a full age. Our times are in God's hand; it is well they are so, for he will take care that those who are his shall die in the best time: however their death may seem to us untimely, it will be found not unseasonable.

3. In the last verse he recommends these promises to Job, as faithful sayings, which he might be confident of the truth of: "*Lo, this we have searched, and so it is.* We have indeed received these things by tradition from our fathers, but we have diligently studied them, and been confirmed in our belief of them from our own observation and experience; and we are all of a mind that so it is." *Hear it, and know thou it for thy good.* It is not enough to hear and know the truth, but we must improve it, and be made wiser and better by it. *Know it for thyself* (so the word is) not only "This is true," but "this is true concerning me." That is indeed a good sermon to us which does us good.

CHAPTER 6

Eliphaz concluded his discourse with an air of assurance. Job is not convinced by all he had said, but still justifies himself in his complaints and condemns him for the weakness of his arguing. I. He shows that he had just cause to complain as he did of his troubles, and so it would appear to any impartial judge, ver. 2–7. II. He continues his passionate wish that he might speedily be cut off and so be eased of all his miseries, ver. 8–13. III. He reproves his friends for their uncharitable censures of him and their unkind treatment, ver. 14–30. It must be owned that Job, in all this, spoke much that was reasonable, but with a mixture of passion and human infirmity. And in this contest, as indeed in most contests, there was fault on both sides.

Verses 1–7

Eliphaz, in the beginning of his discourse, had been very sharp upon Job, and yet it does not appear that Job gave him any interruption, but when he had concluded, he makes his reply, in which he speaks very feelingly.

I. He represents his calamity, in general, as much heavier than either he had expressed it or they had apprehended it, *v.* 2, 3. He would gladly appeal to a third person, who had just weights and just balances with which to weigh his grief and calamity. He wished that they would set his grief and all the expressions of it in one scale, his calamity and all the particulars of it in the other, and they would find (as he says, *ch.* xxiii. 2) that *his stroke was heavier than his groaning*; for, whatever his grief was, his calamity was *heavier than the sand of the sea*. "Therefore (says he) *my words are swallowed up*;" that is, "Therefore you must excuse both the brokenness and the bitterness of my expressions." He complains that his friends undertook to administer spiritual physic to him before they thoroughly understood his case. He excuses the passionate expressions he had used when he cursed his day. Though he could not himself justify all he had said, yet he thought his friends should not thus violently condemn it. He bespeaks the charitable and compassionate sympathy of his friends with him.

II. He complains of the trouble and terror of mind he was in as the sorest part of his calamity, *v.* 4. Herein he was a type of Christ, who, in his sufferings, complained most of the sufferings of his soul. *Now is my soul troubled*, John xii. 27. *My soul is exceedingly sorrowful*, Matt. xxvi. 38. *My God, my God, why hast thou forsaken me?* Matt. xxvii. 46. Poor Job sadly complains *The arrows of the Almighty are within me.* That which cut him to the heart was to think that the God he loved and served had laid him under these marks of his displeasure. Note, Trouble of mind is the sorest trouble. *A wounded spirit who can bear!* The poison or heat of these arrows is said to drink up his spirit, because it disturbed his reason, shook his resolution, exhausted his vigour, and threatened his life. He saw himself charged by *the terrors of God*, as by an army set in battle-array, and surrounded by them.

III. He reflects upon his friends for their severe censures of his complaints. Their reproofs were causeless. He complained, it is true, now that he was in this affliction, but he never used to complain. He did not *bray when he had grass*, nor *low over his fodder*, *v.* 5. But, now that he was utterly deprived of all his comforts, he must be a stock or a stone, and not have the sense of an ox or a wild ass, if he did not give some vent to his grief. He was forced to eat unsavoury meats, and was so poor that he had not a grain of salt wherewith to season them, nor to give a little taste to the white of an egg, which was now the choicest dish he had at his table, *v.* 6. Food which once he would have scorned to touch was his *sorrowful meat, v.* 7.

Verses 8–13

The troubled sea rages most when it dashes against a rock. Job, instead of unsaying what he had said, says it here again with more vehemence than before.

I. He is still most passionately desirous to die. He could see no end of his trouble but death, and had not patience to wait the time appointed for that. He has a request to make; there is a thing he longs for (*v.* 8): *That it would please God to destroy me, v.* 9. Though Job was extremely desirous of death, and very angry at its delays, yet he did not offer to destroy himself, nor to take away his own life, only he begged *that it would please God to destroy him.*

II. He puts this desire into a prayer, that God would grant him this request.

III. He promises himself effectual relief, and the redress of all his grievances, by the stroke of death (*v.* 10): *Then should I yet have comfort.* If Job had not had a good conscience, he could not have spoken with this assurance of comfort on the other side death.

IV. He challenges death to do its worst. If he could not die without bitter pains yet, in prospect of dying at last, he would make nothing of dying pangs: "*I would harden myself in sorrow. Let him not spare; I desire no mitigation of that pain which will put a happy period to all my pains.*"

V. He grounds his comfort upon the testimony of his conscience for him that he had been faithful and firm to his profession of religion: *I have not concealed the words of the Holy One.*

VI. He justifies himself, in this extreme desire of death, from the deplorable condition he was now in, *v.* 10, 12, and very ingeniously, yet perversely, argues against the encouragements that were given him. "*What is my strength, that I should hope?* You see how I am weakened and brought low, and therefore what reason have I to hope that I should see better days? *Is my strength the strength of stones?* Are my muscles brass and my sinews steel? No, they are not, and therefore I cannot hold out always in this pain and misery, but must needs sink under the load." *What is our strength?* It is depending strength. We have no more strength than God gives us; for in him we live and move. "*What is my end, that I should desire to prolong my life?* What comfort can I promise myself in life, comparable to the comfort I promise myself in death?"

VII. He obviates the suspicion of his being delirious (*v.* 13): *Is not my help in me?* "Do you think wisdom is driven quite from me, and that I am gone distracted? No, I am not mad, most noble Eliphaz, but *speak the words of truth and soberness.*"

Verses 14–21

Eliphaz had been very severe in his censures of Job; and his companions had intimated their concurrence with him. Their unkindness poor Job complains of, as an aggravation of his calamity and a further excuse of his desire to die; for what satisfaction could he expect in this world when those that should have been his comforters thus proved his tormentors?

I. He shows what reason he had to expect kindness from them. His expectation was grounded upon the common principles of humanity (*v.* 14): "*To him that is afflicted pity should be shown from his friend;* and he that does not show that pity *forsakes the fear of the Almighty.*" Inhumanity is impiety and irreligion. *He that withholds compassion from his friend forsakes the fear of the Almighty.* So the Chaldee. When a man is afflicted he will see who are his friends indeed and who are but pretenders.

II. He shows how wretchedly he was disappointed in his expectations from them (*v.* 15): "*My brethren, who should have helped me, have dealt deceitfully as a brook.*" None questioned but that the drift of their discourses would be to comfort Job with the remembrance of his former piety, the assurance of God's favour to him, and the prospect of a glorious issue; but, instead of this, they fall upon him with their reproaches and censures, condemn him as a hypocrite, and pour vinegar instead of oil, into his wounds. We cannot expect too little from the creature nor too much from the Creator. God will out-do our hopes as much as men come short of them. This disappointment which Job met with he here illustrates by the failing of brooks in summer. His expectations from them, which their coming so solemnly to comfort him had raised, he compares to the expectation which the weary thirsty travellers have of finding water in the summer where they have often seen it in great abundance in the winter, *v.* 19. *The troops of Tema and Sheba,* the caravans of the merchants of those countries, whose road lay through the deserts of Arabia, looked and waited for supply of water from those brooks. "Hard by here," says one, "A little further," says another, "when I last travelled this way, there was water enough; we shall have that to refresh us." The disappointment of his expectation is here compared to the confusion which seizes the poor travellers when they find heaps of sand where they expected floods of water. In the winter, when they were not thirsty, there was water enough. Everyone will applaud and admire those that are full and in prosperity. But in the heat of summer, when they needed water, then it failed them; it was consumed (*v.* 17); it was turned aside, *v.* 18. When Job was in prosperity his friends were something to him, but "*Now you are nothing,* now I can find no comfort but in God." You are not what you have been, what you should be, what you pretend to be, what I thought you would have been; *for you see my casting down and are afraid.* You are afraid lest, if you own me, you should be obliged to keep me.

Verses 22–30

Poor Job goes on here to upbraid his friends with their unkindness. If they would but think impartially, and speak as they thought, they could not but own,

I. That though he was necessitous, yet he was not craving, nor burdensome to his friends. Job would be glad to see his friends, but he did not say, *Bring unto me* (*v.* 22), or, *Deliver me, v.* 23. He did not desire to put them to any expense. "Did I send for you to *deliver me out of the hand of the mighty?* No, I never expected you should either expose yourselves to any danger or put yourselves to any charge upon my account." Job's not asking their help did not excuse them from offering it when he needed it and it was in the power of their hands to give it. It often happens that from man, even when we expect little, we have less, but from God, even when we expect much, we have more, Eph. iii. 20.

II. That, though he differed in opinion from them, yet he was not obstinate, but ready to yield to conviction (*v.* 24, 25): *Teach me, and I will hold my tongue;* for I have often found, with pleasure and wonder, *how forcible right words are.* But the method you take will never make proselytes: *What doth your arguing prove?* Your hypothesis is false, your surmises are groundless, your management is weak, and your application peevish and uncharitable.

III. That, though he had been indeed in a fault, yet they ought not to have given him such hard usage (*v.* 26, 27): "*Do you imagine,* or contrive with a great deal of art" (for so the word signifies), "*to reprove words,* some passionate expressions of mine in this desperate condition, as if they were certain indications of reigning impiety and atheism? A little charity would have served to excuse them, and to put a better construction upon them. Shall a man's spiritual state be judged of by some rash and hasty words, which a surprising trouble extorts from him? Is it kind, is it just, to criticise in such a case?" They took advantage of his weakness and the helpless condition he was in: *You overwhelm the fatherless,* a proverbial expression, denoting that which is most barbarous and inhuman. They made pretence of kindness: "*You dig a pit for your friend;* not only you are unkind to me, who am your friend, but, under colour of friendship, you ensnare me." When they came to see and sit with him he thought he might speak his mind freely to them. But this freedom of speech, which their professions of concern for him made him use, had exposed him to their censures, and so they might be said to dig a pit for him.

IV. That, though he had let fall some passionate expressions, yet in the main he was in the right, and that his afflictions, though very extraordinary, did not prove him to be a hypocrite or a wicked man. "*Be content*, and *look upon me*; what do you see in me that bespeaks me either a madman or a wicked man? Let the show of my countenance witness for me that, though I have cursed my day, I do not curse my God. You hear what I have to say: *Is there iniquity in my tongue?* that iniquity that you charge me with? Have I blasphemed God or renounced him? *Return, I pray you*, consider the thing over again without prejudice and you will find *my righteousness is in it*," that is, "I am in the right in this matter; and, though I cannot keep my temper as I should, I keep my integrity."

CHAPTER 7

Job goes on to express the bitter sense he had of his calamities and to justify himself in his desire of death. I. He complains to himself and his friends of his troubles, and the constant agitation he was in, ver. 1–6. II. He turns to God, and expostulates with him (ver. 7, to the end), in which, 1. He pleads the final period which death puts to our present state, ver. 7–10. 2. He passionately complains of the miserable condition he was now in, ver. 11–16. 3. He wonders that God will thus contend with him, and begs for the pardon of his sins and a speedy release out of his miseries, ver. 17–21.

Verses 1–6

Job is here excusing what he could not justify, even his inordinate desire of death. I. Every man must die shortly. "Pray mistake not my desires of death, as if I thought the time appointed of God could be anticipated: no, I know very well that that is fixed; only in such language as this I take the liberty to express my present uneasiness: *Is there not an appointed time* (*a warfare*, so the word is) *to man upon earth?* and *are not his days* here *like the days of a hireling?*" Certainly there is, and it is easy to say by whom the appointment is made, even by him that made us and set us here. We are not to think that we are governed by the blind fate of the Stoics, nor by the blind fortune of the Epicureans, but by the wise, holy, and sovereign counsel of God. Man's life is *a warfare*, and *as the days of a hireling*. We are to look upon ourselves in this world, 1. As soldiers, exposed to hardship and in the midst of enemies; we must serve under command; and, when our warfare is accomplished, we must be disbanded. 2. As day-labourers, that have the work of the day to do in its day and must make up their account at night.

II. He had as much reason, he thought, to wish for death, as a poor servant or hireling that is tired with his work has to wish for the shadows of the evening, when he shall receive his penny and go to rest, *v.* 2. The comparison is plain, the application is somewhat obscure. Exactness of language is not to be expected from one in Job's condition. "*As a servant earnestly desires the shadow, so* and for the same reason I earnestly desire death; for *I am made to possess*, &c." Hear his complaint.

1. His days were useless, and had been so a great while. Every day was a burden to him, because he was in no capacity of doing good, or of spending it to any purpose. But when we are disabled to work for God, if we will but sit still quietly for him, it is all one; we shall be accepted.

2. His nights were restless, *v.* 3, 4. The night relieves the toil and fatigue of the day, not only to the labourers, but to the sufferers. But poor Job could not gain this relief. This made him dread the night as much as the servant desires it.

3. His body was noisome, *v.* 5.

4. His life was hastening apace towards a period, *v.* 6. He thought he had no reason to expect a long life, for he found himself declining fast (*v.* 6): *My days are swifter than a weaver's shuttle*, and he was therefore without hope of being restored to his former prosperity.

Verses 7–16

Job is here begging of God either to ease him or to end him. He represents himself to God,

I. As a dying man, surely and speedily dying (*v.* 7): *O remember that my life is wind.* He recommends himself to God as an object of his pity and compassion, with this consideration, that he was a frail creature and his abode in this world uncertain. *The eye of him that hath* here *seen me shall see me no more* there. Dying is work that is to be done but once. This is illustrated by the plotting out and scattering of a cloud. It is consumed and vanisheth away, is resolved into air and never knits again. Other clouds arise, but the same cloud never returns: so a new generation of the children of men is raised up (*v.* 10): *He shall return no more to his house.* From these premises he might have drawn a better conclusion than this (*v.* 11): *Therefore I will not refrain my mouth; I will speak; I will complain.* Better die praying and praising than die complaining and quarrelling.

II. As a distempered man, sorely and grievously distempered both in body and mind. In this part of his representation he is very peevish: "*Am I a sea, or a whale* (*v.* 12), a raging sea, that must be kept within bounds, or an unruly whale, that must be restrained by force from devouring all the fishes of the sea?" With poor Job, his bed, instead of comforting him, terrified him; and his couch, instead of easing his complaint, added to it. In Job's dreams, though they might partly arise from his distemper, we have reason to think Satan had a hand, for he delights to terrify those whom it is out of his reach to destroy; but Job looked up to God and mistook Satan's representations for the *terrors of God setting themselves in array against him.* We have reason to pray to God that our dreams may neither defile nor disquiet us. He covets to rest in his grave, that bed where there are no tossings to and fro, nor any frightful dreams, *v.* 15, 16. Doubtless this was Job's infirmity; for though a good man would not wish to live always in this world, and would choose strangling and death rather than sin, as the martyrs did, yet he will be content to live as long as pleases God, and will not choose death rather than life, because life is our opportunity of glorifying God and getting ready for heaven.

Verses 17–21

Job here reasons with God,

I. Concerning his dealings with man in general (*v.* 17, 18): *What is man, that thou shouldst magnify him?* We mistake God, and the nature of his providence, if we think it any lessening to him to take notice of the meanest of his creatures. Job owns God's favour to man in general, even when he complains of his own particular troubles. "*What is man*, a poor, mean, weak creature, *that thou*, the great and glorious God, shouldst deal with him as thou dost? What is man, 1. That thou shouldst put such honour upon him, *shouldst magnify him*, by taking him into covenant and communion with thyself? 2. That thou *shouldst set thy heart upon him*, as dear to thee. 3. *That thou shouldst visit him* with thy compassions *every morning.*"

II. Concerning his dealings with him in particular. 1. That he was the butt to God's arrows: "*Thou hast set me as a mark against thee*," *v.* 20. "My case is singular, and none is shot at as I am." 2. That he was a *burden to himself*, ready to sink under the load of his own life. 3. That he had no intermission of his griefs (*v.* 19): "*How long* will it be ere thou cause thy rod to *depart from me*, or abate the rigour of the correction, at least for so long as that I may *swallow down my spittle?*" It should seem, Job's distemper lay much in his throat, and almost choked him, so that he could not swallow his spittle. He complains (*ch.* xxx. 18) that it *bound him about like the collar of his coat.* "Lord," says he, "wilt not thou give me some respite, some breathing time?" *ch.* ix. 18. He ingenuously owns himself guilty before God: *I have sinned.* God had said of him that he was a *perfect and an upright man*; yet he says of himself, *I have sinned.* Those may be upright who yet are not sinless; and those who are sincerely penitent are accepted, through a Mediator, as evangelically perfect. Job maintained, against his friends, that he was not a hypocrite, not a wicked man; and yet he owned to his God that he had sinned. Penitent confessions would drown and silence passionate complaints. He seriously enquires how he may make his peace with God: "*What shall I do unto thee,* having done so much against thee?" In our repentance we must keep up good thoughts of God, as one that delights not in the ruin of his creatures, but would rather they should return and live. "Thou art the Saviour of men; be my Saviour, for I cast myself upon thy mercy." He earnestly begs for the forgiveness of his sins, *v.* 21. The heat of his spirit, as, on the one hand, it made his complaints the more bitter, so, on the other hand, it made his prayers the more lively and importunate; as here: "*Why dost thou not pardon my transgression?*" When the mercy of God pardons the transgression that is committed by us the grace of God takes away the iniquity that reigns in us. Wherever God removes the guilt of sin he breaks the power of sin.

CHAPTER 8

Job's friends are like Job's messengers; the latter followed one another close with evil tidings, the former followed him with harsh censures: both, unawares, served Satan's design; these to drive him from his integrity, those to drive him from the comfort of it. Eliphaz did not reply to what Job had said in answer to him, but left it to Bildad. Eliphaz had undertaken to show that because Job was sorely afflicted he was certainly a wicked man, Bildad is much of the same mind, and will conclude Job a wicked man unless God do speedily appear for his relief. In this chapter he endeavours to convince Job, I. That he had spoken too passionately, ver. 2. II. That he and his children had suffered justly, ver. 3, 4. III. That, if he were a true penitent, God would soon turn his captivity, ver. 5–7. IV. That it was a usual thing for Providence to extinguish the joys and hopes of wicked men as his were extinguished; and therefore that they had reason to suspect him for a hypocrite, ver. 8–19. V. That they would be abundantly confirmed in their suspicion unless God did speedily appear for his relief, ver. 20–22.

Verses 1–7

I. Bildad reproves Job for what he had said (*v.* 2), checks his passion, but (as is too common) with greater passion. Job spoke a great deal of good sense, but Bildad turns it all off with this, *How long wilt thou speak these things*? Bildad compares Job's discourse to a *strong wind.*

II. He justifies God in what he had done. This he had no occasion to do at this time (for Job did not condemn God, as he would have it thought he did), or he might at least have done it without reflecting upon Job's children, as he does here. 1. He is right in general, that *God doth not pervert judgment*, nor ever go contrary to any settled rule of justice, *v.* 3. 2. Yet he takes it for granted that Job's children (the death of whom was one of the greatest of his afflictions) had been guilty of some notorious wickedness, *v.* 4. Job readily owned that God did not pervert judgment; and yet it did not therefore follow either that his children died for some great transgression. It is true that we and our children have sinned against God, but extraordinary afflictions are not always the punishment of extraordinary sins, but sometimes the trial of extraordinary graces; and, in our judgment of another's case we ought to take the more favourable side, as our Saviour directs, Luke xiii. 2–4.

III. He put Job in hope that, if he were indeed upright, as he said he was, he should yet see a good issue of his present troubles: "*Although thy children have sinned against him, and are cast away in their transgression,* yet if thou be pure and upright thyself, and as an evidence of that wilt now seek unto God and submit to him, all shall be well yet," *v.* 5–7. This may be taken two ways, either, 1. As designed to prove Job a hypocrite and a wicked man by the continuance of his afflictions. Herein Bildad was not in the right; for a good man may be afflicted for his trial, not only very sorely, but very long, and yet, if for life, it is in comparison with eternity but for a moment. Or, 2. As designed to direct and encourage Job, that he might not thus run himself into despair, there might yet be hope if he would take the right course. He gives him good hopes that he shall yet again see good days, secretly suspecting, however, that he was not qualified to see them. Let not Job object that he had so little left to begin the world with again that it was impossible he should ever prosper as he had done; no, "Though thy beginning should be ever so small, a little meal in the barrel and a little oil in the cruse, God's blessing shall multiply that to a great increase." This is God's way of enriching the souls of his people with graces and comforts, not *per saltum*—as by a bound, but *per gradum—step by step*.

Verses 8–19

Bildad will not be so bold as to say with Eliphaz that none that were righteous were ever cut off thus (*ch.* iv. 7); yet he takes it for granted that God does ordinarily bring wicked men to shame and ruin in this world, and that, by making their prosperity short, he discovers their piety to be counterfeit. Whether this will certainly prove that all who are thus ruined must be concluded to have been hypocrites he will not say.

I. He proves the certain destruction of all the hopes and joys of hypocrites, by an appeal to antiquity. He insists not on his own judgment and that of his companions: *We are but of yesterday, and know nothing*, *v.* 9. He refers to the testimony of the ancients, *v.* 8. *They will teach thee*, and inform thee (*v.* 10), that all along, in their time, the judgments of God followed wicked men. The learned Bishop Patrick suggests that Bildad being a Shuhite, descended from Shuah one of Abraham's sons by Keturah (Gen. xxv. 2), in this appeal which he makes to history has a particular respect to the rewards which the blessing of God secured to the posterity of faithful Abraham.

II. He illustrates this truth by some similitudes. 1. The hopes and joys of the hypocrite are compared to a rush or flag, *v.* 11–13. It grows up out of the mire and water. The hypocrite cannot gain his hope without some false rotten ground or other out of which to raise it, and with which to support it and keep it alive, any more than the rush can grow without mire. He grounds it on his worldly prosperity, the plausible profession he makes of religion, the good opinion of his neighbours, and his own good conceit of himself, which are no solid foundation on which to build his confidence. It may look green and gay for a while (the rush outgrows the grass), but it is light, and hollow and empty. It withers presently, *before any other herb*, *v.* 12. Even *while it is in its greenness* it is dried away and gone in a little time. *So are the paths of all that forget God* (*v.* 13); they take the same way that the rush does, *for the hypocrite's hope shall perish.*

2. They are compared to *a spider's web*, or *a spider's house* (as it is in the margin), a cobweb, *v.* 14, 15. The hope of the hypocrite is the creature of his own fancy, and arises merely from a conceit of his own

merit and sufficiency. There is a great deal of difference between the work of the bee and that of the
spider. A diligent Christian, like the laborious bee,
fetches in all his comfort from the heavenly dews
of God's word; but the hypocrite, like the subtle
spider, weaves his out of a false hypothesis of his
own concerning God, as if he were altogether such an
one as himself. He is very fond of it, as the spider
of her web; wraps himself in it, calls it his house,
leans upon it, and holds it fast. It is said of the spider
that *she takes hold with her hands, and is in kings'
palaces,* Prov. xxx. 28. So does a carnal worldling
hug himself in the fulness and firmness of his outward
prosperity; he prides himself in that house as his
palace. It will be swept away, as the cobweb with the
besom, when God shall come to purge his house.

3. The hypocrite is here compared to a flourishing
and well-rooted tree, which, though it do not wither
of itself, yet will easily be cut down and its place
know it no more. See this tree fair and flourishing
(*v.* 16) under the protection of his garden-wall and
with the benefit of his garden-soil, taking deep root,
never likely to be overthrown by stormy winds,
for his roots are interwoven with the stones (*v.* 17);
it grows in firm ground, not, as the rush, in mire
and water. Thus does a wicked man, when he prospers in the world, think himself secure. See this tree
felled and forgotten notwithstanding, *destroyed from
his place* (*v.* 18).

Verses 20-22

Bildad sums up what he has to say in a few words,
1. On the one hand, if Job were a perfect upright
man, God would not *cast him away, v.* 20. Though
now he seemed forsaken of God, he would yet return
to him, and his *mouth* should be *filled with laughing, v.*
21. Those that loved him would rejoice with him;
but those that hated him, and had triumphed in his
fall, would be ashamed of their insolence. Now it is
true that *God will not cast away an upright man*;
he may be cast down for a time, but he shall not be
cast away for ever. 2. On the other hand, if he were
a wicked man and an evil-doer, God would not help
him, but leave him to perish in his present distresses
(*v.* 20), and his *dwelling-place* should *come to nought,
v.* 22. It is true that *the dwelling-place of the wicked,*
sooner or later, *will come to nought.* Those only *who
make God their dwelling-place* are safe for ever, Ps. xc.
1; xci. 1. Sin brings ruin on persons and families.
Yet to argue (as Bildad slyly does) that because Job's
family was sunk, and he himself at present seemed
helpless, therefore he certainly was an ungodly
wicked man, was neither just nor charitable.

CHAPTER 9

Job's answer to Bildad's discourse, wherein he speaks honourably of God, humbly of himself, and feelingly of his troubles;
but not one word by way of reflection upon his friends. In this
chapter we have, I. The doctrine of God's justice laid down, ver. 2.
II. The proof of it, from his wisdom, and power, and sovereign
dominion, ver. 3–13. III. The application of it, in which, 1. He
condemns himself, as not able to contend with God, ver. 14–21.
2. He maintains his point, that we cannot judge of men's character
by their outward condition, ver. 22–24. 3. He complains of the
greatness of his troubles, the confusion he was in, and the loss
he was at what to say or do, ver. 25–35.

Verses 1-13

Bildad began with a rebuke to Job for talking so
much, *ch.* viii. 2. Job makes no answer to that, but
in what he next lays down as his principle, that God
never perverts judgment, Job agrees with him: *I
know it is so of a truth, v.* 2. *How should man be just
with God?* Some understand this as a passionate
complaint of God's strictness and severity, and it
cannot be denied that there are, in this chapter, some
peevish expressions. But I take this rather as a pious

confession of man's sinfulness, and his own in particular, that, if God should deal with any of us
according to the desert of our iniquities, we should
certainly be undone.

I. He lays this down for a truth, that man is an
unequal match for his Maker.

1. In dispute (*v.* 3): *If he will contend with him,*
either at law or at any argument, *he cannot answer
him one of a thousand.* When God spoke to Job out
of the whirlwind he asked him a great many questions
(*Dost thou know* this? *Canst thou do* that?) to none
of which Job could give an answer, *ch.* xxxviii, xxxix.
God can lay to our charge a thousand offences,
and we cannot answer him so as to acquit ourselves
from any of them.

2. In combat (*v.* 4): "*Who hath hardened himself
against him and hath prospered?*" You cannot produce
any instance of any daring sinner who has *hardened
himself against God,* who did not find God too hard
for him and pay dearly for his folly.

II. He proves it by showing what a God he is with
whom we have to do: *He is wise in heart,* and therefore
we cannot answer him at law; he is *mighty in strength,*
and therefore we cannot fight it out with him. The
devil promised himself that Job, in the day of his
affliction, would curse God and speak ill of him, but,
instead of that, he sets himself to honour God and
to speak highly of him. The God of nature acts
with an uncontrollable power and does what he
pleases; for all the orders and all the powers of nature
are derived from him and depend upon him. When
he pleases he alters the course of nature, and turned
back its streams, *v.* 4–5. Nothing more firm than the
mountains. When we speak of removing mountains
we mean that which is impossible; yet the divine
power can make them change their seat. He can
level them, and overturn them. Men have much ado
to pass over them, but God, when he pleases, can
make them pass away. Nothing more fixed than the
earth on its axletree; yet God can, when he pleases,
shake the earth out of its place, heave it off its centre,
and make even *its pillars to tremble.* God has power
enough to shake the earth from under that guilty
race of mankind which makes it groan under the
burden of sin, and so to *shake the wicked out of it*
(Chap. xxxviii. 13); yet he continues the earth, and
man upon it, and does not make it, as once, to
swallow up the rebels. Nothing more constant than
the rising sun, it never misses its appointed time;
yet God, when he pleases, can suspend it. Thus great
is God's power; and how great then is his goodness,
which causes his sun to shine even upon the evil and
unthankful, though he could withhold it! Job here
speaks of what God can do; but, if we must understand it of what he has done in fact, all these verses
may perhaps be applied to Noah's flood. As long as
he pleases he preserves the settled course and order
of nature; and this is a continued creation. He himself alone, by his own power, and without the assistance of any other, *Spreads out the heaven* (*v.* 8), not
only did spread them out at first, but still spreads
them out. *He treads upon the waves of the sea;*
that is, he suppresses them and keeps them under,
that they return not to deluge the earth (Ps. civ. 9),
which is given as a reason why we should all fear
God and stand in awe of him, Jer. v. 22. God makes
the constellations; three are named for all the rest
(*v.* 9), *Arcturus, Orion,* and *Pleiades,* and in general
the chambers of the south. The stars he makes to be
what they are to man, and inclines the hearts of men
to observe them, which the beasts are not capable
of doing. Not only those stars which we see and
give names to, but those also in the other hemisphere,
about the antarctic pole, which never come in our
sight, called here *the chambers of the south,* are under
the divine direction and dominion. Consider what

God does in the government of the world, and you will say, He is *wise in heart* and *mighty in strength.* He does many things and great, many and great to admiration, *v.* 10. God is a great God, and *doeth great things,* a wonder-working God; his works of wonder are so many that we cannot number them and so mysterious that we cannot find them out. He acts invisibly and undiscerned, *v.* 11. *"He goes by me* in his operations, *and I see him not, I perceive him not. His way is in the sea,"* Ps. lxxvii. 19. Our finite understandings cannot fathom his counsels, apprehend his motions, or comprehend the measures he takes; we are therefore incompetent judges of God's proceedings, because we know not what he does nor what he designs. The *arcania imperii—secrets of government,* are things above us, which therefore we must not pretend to expound. He acts with an incontestable sovereignty, *v.* 12. What action can be brought against him? Or *who will say unto him, What doest thou?* God is not obliged to give us a reason of what he does. The meaning of his proceedings we know not now; it will be time enough to know hereafter, when it will appear that what seemed now to be done by prerogative was done in infinite wisdom and for the best. He acts with an irresistible power, which no creature can resist, *v.* 13. *If God will not withdraw his anger the proud helpers do stoop under him;* that is, He certainly breaks and crushes those that proudly help one another against him.

Verses 14–21

What Job had said of man's utter inability to contend with God he here applics to himself, and in effect despairs of gaining his favour. It arises from the dark and cloudy apprehensions which at present he had of God's displeasure against him.

I. He durst not dispute with God (*v.* 14): *"If the proud helpers do stoop under him, how much less shall I* (a poor weak creature, so far from being a helper that I am very helpless) *answer him?* What can I say against that which God does?"

II. He durst not insist upon his own justification before God. Though he vindicated his own integrity to his friends, and would not yield that he was a hypocrite and a wicked man, as they suggested, yet he would never plead it as his righteousness before God.

1. He knew so much of God that he durst not stand a trial with him, *v.* 15–19. God knew him better than he knew himself and therefore (*v.* 15), *"Though I were righteous* in my own apprehension, and my own heart did not condemn me, *yet God is greater than my heart,* and knows those secret faults and errors of mine which I do not and cannot understand, and is able to charge me with them, and therefore *I would not answer."* Job will therefore cast himself upon God's mercy, and not think to come off by his own merit. God answers before we call and not because we call, and gives gracious answers to our prayers, but not for our prayers (*v.* 16): *"If I had called, and he had answered,* had given the thing I called to him for, yet, so weak and defective are my best prayers, that *I would not believe he had therein hearkened to my voice;* I could not say that he had *saved with his right hand and answered me"* (Ps. lx. 5), "but that he did it purely for his own name's sake." Job was not conscious to himself of any extraordinary guilt, and yet fell under extraordinary afflictions, *v.* 17, 18. Job was *broken with a tempest.* Job's troubles came so thickly upon him that he had no breathing time, and he was filled with bitterness. And he presumes to say that all this was *without cause,* without any great provocation given. Here, no doubt, *he spoke unadvisedly with his lips;* he reflected on God's goodness in saying that he was not suffered *to take*

his breath (while yet he had such good use of his reason and speech as to be able to talk thus) and on his justice in saying that it was without cause. There is no disputing (said one once to Cæsar) with him that commands legions. Much less is there any with him that has legions of angels at command.

2. He knew so much of himself that he durst not stand a trial, *v.* 21, 20. *"If I go* about to *justify myself,* and to plead a righteousness of my own, my defence will be my offence, and *my own mouth shall condemn me* even when it goes about to acquit me." A good man, who knows the deceitfulness of his own heart, is suspicious of more evil in himself than he is really conscious of, and therefore will by no means think of justifying himself before God. "Though I were free from gross sin, though my conscience should not charge me with any enormous crime, yet would I not believe my own heart so far as to insist upon my innocency nor think my life worth striving for with God."

Verses 22–24

Here Job touches briefly upon the main point now in dispute between him and his friends. They maintained that those who are righteous and good always prosper in this world, and none but the wicked are in misery and distress; he asserted, on the contrary, that it is a common thing for the wicked to prosper and the righteous to be greatly afflicted. "I said it, and say it again, that all things come alike to all." Now, 1. It must be owned that there is very much truth in what Job here means, that temporal judgments, when they are sent abroad, fall both upon good and bad. Let this reconcile God's children to their troubles; they are but trials, designed for their honour and benefit, and, if God be pleased with them, let not them be displeased. On the other hand, the wicked are so far from being made the marks of God's judgments that *the earth is given into their hand, v.* 24, *into the hand of the wicked one* (in the original, the word is singular). The wicked have the earth given them, but the righteous have heaven given them, and which is better—heaven without earth or earth without heaven? Job ought not to have said, *He laughs at it,* for God doth not afflict willingly. When the spirit is heated, either with dispute or with discontent, we need to set a watch before the door of our lips.

Verses 25–35

Job grows more querulous. When we are in trouble we are allowed to complain to God, as the Psalmist often, but must by no means complain of God, as Job here.

I. His complaint here of the passing away of the days of his prosperity is proper enough (*v.* 25, 26): *"My days* (that is, all my good days) *are gone,* never to return, gone of a sudden, gone ere I was aware."

II. His complaint of his present uneasiness is excusable, *v.* 27, 28. He did his endeavour to compose himself as his friends advised him. He would fain *forget his complaints* and praise God. He found he could not do it: *"I am afraid of all my sorrows."*

III. His complaint of God as implacable and inexorable was by no means to be excused. He knew better, and, at another time, would have been far from harbouring any such hard thoughts of God. Good men do not always speak like themselves; but God, who considers their frame and the strength of their temptations, gives them leave afterwards to unsay what was amiss by repentance and will not lay it to their charge.

1. Job seems to speak here, (1) As if he despaired of obtaining from God any relief or redress of his grievances: *"I know that thou wilt not hold me innocent.*

My afflictions have continued so long upon me. *Why then do I labour in vain* to clear myself and maintain my own integrity?" *v.* 29. With men it is often labour in vain for the most innocent to go about to clear themselves. But it is not so in our dealings with God, to whom it was never in vain to commit a righteous cause (*v.* 30, 31): "*If I wash myself with snow-water*, and make my integrity ever so evident, it will be all to no purpose; judgment must go against me. *Thou shalt plunge me in the ditch* (the pit of destruction, so some, or rather the filthy kennel, or sewer), which will make me so offensive in the nostrils of all about me that *my own clothes shall abhor me* and I shall even loathe to touch myself." He saw his afflictions coming from God. Yet these words are capable of a good construction. If we keep our hands ever so clean from the pollutions of gross sin, which fall under the eye of the world,—yet God, who knows our hearts, can charge us with so much secret sin as will for ever take off all our pretensions to purity and innocency, and make us see ourselves odious in the sight of the holy God. Paul, while a Pharisee, made his hands very clean; but when the commandment came and discovered to him his heart-sins, made him know lust, that *plunged him in the ditch*. (2) As if he despaired to have a fair hearing with God. He complains that he was not upon even terms with God (*v.* 32): "*He is not a man, as I am.* I could venture to dispute with a man like myself." *Neither is there any daysman between us.* This complaint that there was not is in effect a wish that there were, and so the LXX read it: *O that there were a mediator between us!* Job would gladly refer the matter, but no creature was capable of being a referee, and therefore he must even refer it still to God himself and resolve to acquiesce in his judgment. Our Lord Jesus is the blessed days-man, who has mediated between heaven and earth. The gospel leaves no room for such a complaint as this. Job knew not how to address God with the confidence with which he was formerly wont to approach him, *v.* 34, 35. "*Let him take his rod away from me*." He means not so much his outward afflictions as *his fear* which *terrified him.*

2. From all this let us pity those that are wounded in spirit, and keep up good thoughts of God in our minds, for hard thoughts of him are the inlets of much mischief.

CHAPTER 10

Job owns that he was full of confusion (ver. 15), he knew not what to say, and perhaps sometimes scarcely knew what he said. In this chapter, I. He complains of the hardships he was under (ver. 1–7), and then comforts himself with this, that he was in the hand of the God that made him, ver. 8–13. II. He complains again of the severity of God's dealings with him (ver. 14–17), and then comforts himself with this, that death would put an end to his troubles, ver. 18–22.

Verses 1–7

I. A passionate resolution to persist in his complaint, *v.* 1. He resolves to give himself some ease by giving vent to his resentments. "*My soul is weary of my life*." He will give vent to the bitterness of his soul by violent words. Job's corruption speaks here, yet grace puts in a word. 1. He will complain, but he will *leave his complaint upon himself*. 2. He will speak, but it shall be the *bitterness of his soul* that he will express, not his settled judgment. If I speak amiss, it is *not I, but sin that dwells in me*, not my soul, but its bitterness.

II. A humble petition to God. He will speak, but the first word shall be a prayer, *v.* 2. 1. That he might be delivered from the sting of his afflictions, which is sin. "Thou dost correct me; I will bear that as well as I can; but O do not condemn me!" It is the comfort of those who are in Christ Jesus, that though they are in affliction, there is *no condemnation*

to them, Rom. viii. 1. "Lord, do not condemn me; my friends condemn me, but do not thou." 2. That he might be made acquainted with the true cause of his afflictions, and that is sin too: Lord, *show me wherefore thou contendest with me*. When God afflicts us he contends with us, and when he contends with us there is always a reason.

III. A peevish expostulation with God concerning his dealings with him.

1. He thinks it unbecoming the goodness of God, and the mercifulness of his nature, to deal so hardly with his creature as to lay upon him more than he can bear (*v.* 3): *Is it good unto thee that thou shouldst oppress? What profit is there in my blood?* Far be it from Job to think that God did him wrong, but he is quite at a loss how to reconcile his providences with his justice, as good men have often been, and must wait until the day shall declare it.

2. He thinks it unbecoming the infinite knowledge of God to put his prisoner thus upon the rack, as it were, by torture, to extort a confession from him, *v.* 4–6. Many things are hidden from eyes of flesh, the most curious and piercing; *there is a path which even the vulture's eye has not seen*: but nothing is, or can be, hidden from the eye of God, to which all things are naked and open. Eyes of flesh see the outward appearance only, but God sees everything truly. Eyes of flesh discover things gradually, but God sees everything at one view. Eyes of flesh are soon tired, but the keeper of Israel neither slumbers nor sleeps, nor does his sight every decay. *God sees not as man sees*, that is, he does not judge as man judges, but *we are sure that the judgment of God is according to truth*. God is not short-sighted, like man, so he is not short-lived (*v.* 5): "*Are thy days as the days of man*, few and evil?" Men grow wiser by experience and must take time for their searches. But it is not so with God; to him nothing is past, nothing future, but everything present.

3. He thinks it looked like an abuse of his omnipotence to keep a poor prisoner in custody, whom he knew to be innocent, only because there was none that could deliver him out of his hand (*v.* 7): *Thou knowest that I am not wicked.* He had already owned himself a sinner, but he here stands to it that he was not devoted to sin, not an enemy to God. I cannot say that I am not wanting, or I am not weak; but through grace, I can say, *I am not wicked*: thou knowest I am not, for *thou knowest I love thee.*

Verses 8–13

I. Job eyes God as his Creator and preserver, and describes his dependence upon him as the author and upholder of his being.

1. God made us, he, and not our parents, who were only the instruments of his power and providence in our production. *He made us, and not we ourselves.* The soul also, which animates the body, is his gift. Job takes notice of both here. (1) The body is *made as the clay* (*v.* 9), cast into shape as the clay is formed into a vessel, according to the skill and will of the potter. The formation of human bodies in the womb is described by an elegant similitude (*v.* 10, *Thou hast poured me out like milk, which is coagulated into cheese*), and by an induction of some particulars, *v.* 11. Though we come into the world naked, yet the body is itself both clothed and armed. The skin and flesh are its clothing; the bones and sinews are its armour, not offensive, but defensive. The vital parts, the heart and lungs, are thus clothed, not to be seen—thus fenced, not to be hurt. The admirable structure of human bodies is an illustrious instance of the wisdom, power, and goodness of the Creator. What a pity it is that these bodies should be instruments of unrighteousness which are capable of being temples of the Holy Ghost! (2) The soul is

the life, the soul is the man, and this is the gift of God: *Thou hast granted me life*, breathed into me the breath of life, without which the body would be but a worthless carcase. God is the Father of spirits: he made us living souls, and endued us with the powers of reason; he gave us *life and favour*, and life is a favour. Now Job was in a better mind than he was when he quarrelled with life as a burden, and asked, *Why died I not from the womb?*

2. God maintains us. Having lighted the lamp of life, he does not leave it to burn upon its own stock, but continually supplies it with fresh oil: *"Thy visitation has preserved my spirit*, kept me alive, protected me from the adversaries of life, and blessed me with the daily supplies it needs and craves."

II. He pleads this with God (*v.* 9): *Remember, I beseech thee, that thou hast made me.* 1. "Thou hast made me, and needest not to examine me by scourging, not to put me upon the rack for the discovery of what is within me." 2. "Thou hast made me, as the clay, by an act of sovereignty; and wilt thou by a like act of sovereignty unmake me again?" 3. "Wilt thou destroy the work of thy own hands? Wilt thou not spare and help me, and stand by *the work of thy own hands?*" Ps. cxxxviii. 8. Job knew not how to reconcile God's former favours and his present frowns, but concludes (*v.* 13), *"These things hast thou hidden in thy heart."*

Verses 14–22

I. Job's passionate complaints. On this harsh and unpleasant string he harps much, in which, though he cannot be justified, he may be excused. If we think it looks ill in him, let it be a warning to us to keep our temper better.

1. He complains of the strictness of God's judgment and the rigour of his proceedings against him, and is ready to call it *summum jus—justice bordering on severity.* (1) That he took all advantages against him: *"If I sin, then thou markest me," v.* 14. (2) That he prosecuted those advantages to the utmost: *Thou wilt not acquit me from my iniquity.* While his troubles continued he could not take the comfort of his pardon, nor hear that voice of joy and gladness; so hard is it to see love in God's heart when we see frowns in his face and a rod in his hand. (3) That, whatever was his character, his case at present was very uncomfortable, *v.* 15. [1] If he be wicked, he is certainly undone in the other world: *If I be wicked, woe to me.* [2] If he be *righteous*, yet he dares not *lift up his head*, dares not answer as before, *ch.* ix. 15. He is so oppressed and overwhelmed with his troubles that he cannot look up with any comfort or confidence.

2. He complains of the severity of the execution. God (he thought) did not only punish him for every failure, but punish him in a high degree, *v.* 16, 17. God *hunted him* as a lion. God was not only strange to him, but *showed himself marvellous upon him*, by bringing him into uncommon troubles and so making him a prodigy, a wonder unto many. That which made his afflictions most grievous was that he felt God's *indignation* in them. It was growing, still growing worse and worse. This he insists much upon; when he hoped the tide would turn, and begin to ebb, still it flowed higher and higher.

3. He complains of his life, and that ever he was born to all this trouble and misery (*v.* 18, 19): "If this was designed for my lot, *why was I brought out of the womb*, and not smothered there, or stifled in the birth?" Mr. Caryl gives this a good turn in favour of Job. "We may charitably suppose," says he, "that that which troubled Job was that he was in a condition of life which (as he conceived) hindered the main end of his life, which was the glorifying of God. He feared lest his troubles should reflect dishonour upon God and give occasion to his enemies

to blaspheme; and therefore he wishes, *O that I had given up the ghost!* A godly man reckons that he lives to no purpose if he do not live to the praise and glory of God." If that was his meaning, it was grounded on a mistake; for we may *glorify the Lord in the fires.*

II. Job's humble requests. He prays, 1. That God would *see his affliction* (*v.* 15). 2. That God would grant him some ease.

CHAPTER 11

Poor Job's wounds were yet bleeding, his sore still runs and ceases not, but none of his friends bring him any oil, any balm; Zophar, the third, pours into them as much vinegar as the two former had done. I. He exhibits a very high charge against Job, as proud and false in justifying himself, ver. 1–4. II. He appeals to God for his conviction (ver. 5) and that Job might be made sensible, 1. Of God's unerring wisdom and his inviolable justice, ver. 6. 2. Of his unsearchable perfections, ver. 7–9. 3. Of his incontestable sovereignty and uncontrollable power, ver. 10. 4. Of the cognizance he takes of the children of men, ver. 11, 12. III. He assures him that, upon his repentance and reformation (ver. 13, 14), God would restore him to his former prosperity and safety (ver. 15–19); but that, if he were wicked it was in vain to expect it, ver. 20.

Verses 1–6

It is sad to see what intemperate passions even wise and good men are sometimes betrayed into by the heat of disputation, of which Zophar here is an instance. Eliphaz began with a very modest preface, *ch.* iv. 2. Bildad was a little more rough upon Job, *ch.* viii. 2. But Zophar falls upon him without mercy. *Should a man full of talk be justified? And should thy lies make men hold their peace?* Is this the way to comfort Job? Does this become one that appears as an advocate for God and his justice?

I. He represents Job otherwise than what he was, *v.* 2, 3. He would have him thought one that loved to hear himself talk; and all this that it might be looked upon as a piece of justice to chastise him. We have read and considered Job's discourses in the foregoing chapters, and have found them full of good sense, that his principles are right, his reasonings strong, and that what there is in them of heat and passion a little charity will excuse and overlook; and yet Zophar here invidiously represents him, 1. As a man that never considered what he said. *Should not the multitude of words be answered?* Truly, sometimes it is no great matter whether it be or no. *Should a man full of talk* (margin, *a man of lips*, that is all tongue, *a mere voice*) *be justified?* Should he be justified in his loquacity, as in effect he is if he be not reproved for it? No, for *in the multitude of words there wanteth not sin.* 2. As a man that made no conscience of what he said—a liar, and one that hoped by the impudence of lies to silence his adversaries (*should thy lies make men hold their peace?*)— one that bantered all mankind. Job was not mad, but spoke the words of truth and soberness, and yet was thus misrepresented.

II. He charges Job with saying that which he had not said (*v.* 4): *Thou hast said, My doctrine is pure.* Job spoke better of God than his friends did. If he had expressed himself unwarily, yet it did not therefore follow but that his doctrine was true. But he charges him with saying, *I am clean in thy eyes.* Job had not said so: he had indeed said, *Thou knowest that I am not wicked* (*ch.* x. 7); but he had also said, *I have sinned.* He had indeed maintained that he was not a hypocrite as they charged him; but to infer thence that he would not own himself a sinner was an unfair insinuation.

III. He appeals to God, and wishes him to appear against Job. Nothing will serve him but that God must immediately appear to silence and condemn him. We are commonly ready with too much assurance to interest God in our quarrels, and to conclude that, if he would but speak, he would take our part and speak for us, as Zophar here: *O that God would speak!* for he would certainly *open his lips against thee*; whereas, when God did speak, he opened his lips for Job against his three friends. Zophar despairs to convince Job himself, and therefore desires God would convince him of two things:—

1. The unsearchable depth of God's counsels. Zophar desires that God himself would show Job so much of the secrets of the divine wisdom as might convince him *that they are* at least *double to that which is*, v. 6. What we know of God is nothing to what we cannot know. What is hidden is more than double to what appears, Eph. iii. 9. God knows a great deal more evil of us than we do of ourselves; so some understand it.

2. The unexceptionable justice of his proceedings. "*God exacteth of thee less than thy iniquity deserves*," or (as some read it), "he *remits thee part of thy iniquity.*"

Verses 7–12

Zophar here speaks concerning God and his greatness and glory, concerning man and his vanity and folly.

I. God is an incomprehensible Being. We that are so little acquainted with the divine nature are incompetent judges of the divine providence; and, when we censure the dispensations of it, we talk of things that we do not understand. Zophar here shows, that God's nature infinitely exceeds the capacities of our understandings: "*Canst thou find out God, find him out to perfection?*" v. 7, 8. We may, by searching find God (Acts xvii. 27); we may apprehend him, but we cannot comprehend him; we may know that he is, but cannot know what he is. This is a good reason why we should always speak of God with humility and caution and never quarrel with him, why we should be thankful for what he has revealed of himself and long to be where we shall see him as he is, 1 Cor. xiii. 9, 10. We cannot fathom God's designs, nor find out the reasons of his proceedings. His judgments are a great deep. Paul attributes such immeasurable dimensions to the divine love as Zophar here attributes to the divine wisdom, and yet recommends it to our acquaintance. Eph. iii. 18, 19, *That you may know the breadth, and length, and depth, and height, of the love of Christ.* God is a sovereign Lord (v. 10): *If he cut off* by death (margin, *If he make a change*, for death is a change; if he make a change in nations, in families, in the posture of our affairs), or *if he gather to himself man's spirit, then who can hinder him?* God is a strict and just observer of the children of men (v. 11): *He knows vain men.* He takes knowledge of the vanity of men (that is, their little sins; so some) their vain thoughts and vain words, and unsteadiness in that which is good. He observes bad men: *He sees* gross *wickedness also. Will he not then consider it?*

II. See here what man is, and let him be humbled, v. 12. God sees vain man that he *would be wise*, would be thought so, *though he is born like a wild ass's colt*, so sottish and foolish, unteachable and untameable. He is a vain creature—*empty;* so the word is. God made him full, but he emptied himself, and now he is *raca*, a creature that has nothing in him. He has become *like the beasts that perish* (Ps. xlix. 20; lxxiii. 22), an idiot, born like an ass, the most stupid animal, an ass's colt, not yet brought to any service. If ever he come to be good for any thing, it is owing to the grace of Christ, who once, in the day of his triumph, served himself by an ass's colt. He is a wilful ungovernable creature. An ass's colt may be made good for something, but the wild ass's colt will never be reclaimed, nor regards the crying of the driver. See Chap. xxxix. 5–7. Yet he is a proud creature and self-conceited. Now is such a creature as this fit to contend with God or call him to an account?

Verses 13–20

Zophar, as the other two, here encourages Job to hope for better times if he would but come to a better temper.

I. He gives him good counsel (v. 13, 14), as Eliphaz did (ch. v. 8), and Bildad, (ch. viii. 5). He must look within, and get his mind changed and the tree made good. He must *prepare his heart*; there the work of conversion and reformation must begin. He must look up, and *stretch out his hands towards God*, that is, must pray to him with earnestness and importunity. To *give the hand to the Lord* signifies to yield ourselves to him and to covenant with him, 2 Chron. xxx. 8. Job had prayed, but Zophar would have him to pray in a better manner, not as an appellant, but as a petitioner and humble suppliant. He must amend what was amiss (v. 14): "*If iniquity be in thy hand* (that is, if there be any sin which thou dost yet live in the practice of) *put it far away.*" The guilt of sin is not removed if the gain of sin be not restored. He must do his utmost to reform his family too: "*Let not wickedness dwell in thy tabernacles;* let not thy house harbour or shelter any wicked persons, any wicked practices, or any wealth gotten by wickedness."

II. He assures him of comfort if he took this counsel, v. 15, &c. "*Then shalt thou lift up thy face towards heaven* without spot; thou mayest come boldly to the throne of grace, and not with that terror and amazement expressed," ch. ix. 34. *Thou shalt be steadfast, and shalt not fear.* Job was full of confusion (ch. x. 15), while he looked upon God as his enemy and quarrelled with him; but Zophar assures him that, if he would submit and humble himself, his mind would be composed. "*Thou shalt forget thy misery;* thou shalt be perfectly freed from the impressions it makes upon thee, and *thou shalt remember it as waters that pass away*, or are poured out of a vessel, which leave no taste or tincture behind them as other liquors do." Job had endeavoured to forget his complaint (ch. ix. 27), but found he could not. Zophar here thinks to please Job. Though now his light was eclipsed it should shine out again, and more brightly than ever (v. 17). Though now he was in a continual fear and terror, he should live in a holy rest and security, and find himself continually safe and easy (v. 18): *Thou shalt be secure, because there is hope.* "*Thou shalt dig about thee*," that is, "Thou shalt be as safe as an army in its intrenchments." Those that submit to God's government are safe both day and night. "*Thou shalt dig in safety*, thou and thy servants for thee, and not be again set upon by the plunderers, who fell upon thy servants at plough," ch. i. 14, 15. It is no part of the promised prosperity that he should live in idleness, but that he should have a calling and follow it, and, when he was about the business of it, should be under the divine protection. "*Thou shalt lie down* (v. 19), not forced to wander where there is no place to lay thy head on, but thou shalt go to bed at bedtime, and not only shall none hurt thee, but none shall make thee afraid nor so much as give thee an alarm." Though now he was slighted, yet he should be courted: "*Many shall make suit to thee*, and think it their interest to secure thy friendship."

III. Zophar concludes with a brief account of the doom of wicked people (v. 20): *But the eyes of the wicked shall fail.* He suspected that Job would not take his counsel, and here tells him what would then come of it, setting death as well as life before him. *When a wicked man dies his expectation perishes*, Prov. xi. 7. *Their hope shall be as a puff of breath* (margin), vanished and gone past recall. Those that will not fly to God will find it in vain to think of flying from him.

CHAPTER 12

Job's answer to Zophar's discourse, in which, as before, he first reasons with his friends (see ch. xiii. 19) and then turns to his God. In this chapter he addresses himself to his friends, and, I. He condemns the judgment they had given of his character, ver. 1–5. II. He contradicts what they had said of the destruction of wicked people in this world, showing that they often prosper, ver. 6–11. III. He consents to what they had said of the wisdom, power, and sovereignty of God, and enlarges upon it, ver. 12–25.

Verses 1–5

The reproofs Job gives to his friends.

I. He upbraids them with their conceit of themselves, and the good opinion they seemed to have of their own wisdom. 1. He represents them as claiming the monopoly of wisdom, *v*. 2. He speaks ironically: "*No doubt you are the people;* you think yourselves fit to dictate and give law to all mankind, and, therefore every top-sail must lower to you, and, right or wrong, we must all say as you say, and you three must be the people, the majority, to have the casting vote. You not only think there are none, but that there will be none, as wise as you, and therefore that *wisdom must die with you*, that all the world must be fools when you are gone, and in the dark when your sun has set." It is folly for us to think that there will be any great irreparable loss of us when we are gone, since God can raise up others, more fit than we are, to do his work. 2. He does himself the justice to put in his claim as a sharer in the gifts of wisdom (*v*. 3). "*But I have understanding (a heart) as well as you;* nay, *I fall not lower than you;*" as it is in the margin. "I am as well able to judge of the methods and meanings of the divine providence, and to construe the hard chapters of it, as you are." He says not this to magnify himself. "*Yea, who knows not such things as these?* What things you have said that are true are plain truths, which many can talk as excellently of as either you or I." But he says it to humble them, and check the value they had for themselves as doctors of the chair.

II. He complains of the great contempt with which they had treated him (*v*. 4): *I am as one mocked.* We are apt to call reproofs reproaches, and to think ourselves mocked when we are but advised and admonished. Yet there was colour for this charge; they came to comfort him, but they vexed him, and therefore he thought they mocked him. They were his *neighbours*, his friends, his companions (so the word signifies), and they were professors of religion, such as *called upon God*, and said that he *answered them.* Job had a God to go to, with whom he could lodge his appeal. The mockers were themselves rich and at ease, and therefore they despised him who had fallen into poverty. It is the way of the world. Those that prosper are praised, but of those that are going down it is said, "Down with them."

Verses 6–11

Job's friends went upon this principle, that wicked people cannot prosper long in this world; *the eyes of the wicked shall fail*, ch. xi. 20. This principle Job here opposes, and maintains that God, in disposing men's outward affairs, acts as a sovereign, reserving the exact distribution of rewards and punishments for the future state.

I. He asserts it as an undoubted truth that wicked people may, and often do, prosper long in this world, *v*. 6. They are *robbers*, and such as provoke God, the worst kind of sinners, blasphemers and persecutors. (Perhaps he refers to the Sabeans and Chaldeans, who had robbed him, and had always lived by spoil and rapine, and yet prospered.) Even *their tabernacles prosper*, those that live with them and those that come after them and descend from them. It seems as if a blessing were entailed upon their families;

and that is sometimes preserved to succeeding generations which was got by fraud. We cannot therefore judge of men's piety by their plenty, nor of what they have in their heart by what they have in their hand.

II. He appeals even to the inferior creatures for the proof of this—the beasts, and fowls, and trees, and even the earth itself; consult these, and they shall tell thee, *v*. 7, 8. Even among the brute creatures the greater devour the less and the stronger prey upon the weaker, and men are as the fishes of the sea, Hab. i. 14. If sin had not entered, we may suppose there would have been no such disorder among the creatures, but the wolf and the lamb would have lain down together. Zophar had made a vast mystery of it, *ch*. xi. 7. "So far from that," says Job, "what we are concerned to know we may learn even from the inferior creatures; for *who knows not from all these? v*. 9. Anyone may easily gather from the book of the creatures that *the hand of the Lord has wrought this*." A wise Providence guides and governs all these things by rules. From God's sovereign dominion over the inferior creatures we should learn to acquiesce in all his disposals of the affairs of the children of men.

III. He resolves all into the absolute propriety which God has in all the creatures (*v*. 10): *In whose hand is the soul of every living thing.* All the creatures, and mankind particularly, derive their being from him. All souls are his; and may he not do what he will with his own? The name *Jehovah* is used here (*v*. 9), and it is the only time that we meet with it in all the discourses between Job and his friends; for God was, in that age, more known by the name of *Shaddai—the Almighty*.

IV. Those words—(*v*. 11), *Doth not the ear try words, as the mouth tastes meat?*—may be taken either as the conclusion to the foregoing discourse or the preface to what follows. The mind of man has as good a faculty of discerning between truth and error, when duly stated, as the palate has of discerning between what is sweet and what is bitter. Job seems to appeal to any man's impartial judgment in this controversy.

Verses 12–25

This is a noble discourse of Job's concerning the wisdom, power, and sovereignty of God. It were well if wise and good men, that differ about minor things, would dwell most upon those great things in which they are agreed. On this subject Job speaks like himself. Here are no passionate complaints, no peevish reflections, but everything masculine and great.

I. He asserts the unsearchable wisdom and irresistible power of God. It is allowed that among men there is *wisdom and understanding*, *v*. 12. But it is to be found only *with the ancient*, who get it by long experience and constant experience; and, when they have got the wisdom, they have lost their strength. But now *with God there are* both *wisdom and strength*, wisdom to design the best and strength to accomplish what is designed. He does not get counsel or understanding, as we do, by observation, but he has it essentially and eternally in himself, *v*. 13. Happy are those who have this God for their God, for they have infinite wisdom and strength engaged for them. Foolish and fruitless are all the attempts of men against him (*v*. 14): *He breaketh down, and it cannot be built again.*

II. He gives an instance, for the proof of this doctrine in nature, *v*. 15. God has the command of the waters, *binds them as in a garment* (Prov. xxx. 4), holds them *in the hollow of his hand* (Isa. xl. 12). 1. Great droughts are sometimes great judgments: *He withholds the waters, and they dry up;* if the heaven be as brass, the earth is as iron. 2. Great wet is sometimes a great judgment. He raises the waters, and *overturns the earth*, the productions of it, the buildings upon it.

III. He gives many instances of it in God's powerful management of the children of men.

1. In general (*v.* 16): *With him are strength and reason* (so some translate it), strength and consistency with himself: it is an elegant word in the original. With him are the very quintessence and extract of wisdom. *With him are power and all that is;* so some read it. He is what he is of himself, and by him and in him all things subsist. Having this strength and wisdom, he knows how to make use, not only of those who are wise and good, but even of those who are foolish and bad, who, one would think, could be made no way serviceable to the designs of his providence: *The deceived and the deceiver are his;* the simplest men that are deceived are not below his notice; the subtlest men that deceive cannot with all their subtlety escape his cognizance.

2. He next descends to the particular instances of the wisdom and power of God in the revolutions of states and kingdoms. Some think that Job here refers to the extirpation of those powerful nations, the Rephaim, the Zuzim, the Emim, and the Horites (mentioned Gen. xiv. 5, 6; Deut. ii. 10, 20), in which perhaps it was particularly noticed how strangely they were infatuated and enfeebled: if so, it is designed to show it is God that does it, and we must therein observe his sovereign dominion, even over those that think themselves most powerful, politic, and absolute. Compare this with that of Eliphaz, *ch.* v. 12, &c. Those that were wise are sometimes strangely infatuated, and in this the hand of God must be acknowledged (*v.* 17): *He leadeth counsellors away spoiled.* His counsel stands, while all their devices are brought to nought. *He maketh the judges fools.* By a work on their minds he deprives them of their qualifications for business, and so they become really fools. Let not the wise man therefore glory in his wisdom, nor the ablest counsellors and judges be proud of their station, but humbly depend upon God for the continuance of their abilities. Even the aged, who seem to hold their wisdom, by prescription, may yet be deprived of it by the infirmities of age, which make them twice children: He *taketh away the understanding of the aged, v.* 20. Those that were high and in authority are strangely brought down, impoverished, and enslaved, and it is God that humbles them (*v.* 18): *He looseth the bond of kings,* and taketh from them the power wherewith they ruled their subjects, unbuckles their belts, so that the sword drops from their side, and then no marvel if the crown quickly drops from their head, on which immediately follows the *girding of their loins with a girdle,* a badge of servitude. Those that were strong are strangely weakened, and it is God that weakens them (*v.* 21) and *overthrows the mighty, v.* 19. Those that were famed for eloquence, and entrusted with public business, are strangely silenced, and have nothing to say (*v.* 20): *He removeth away the speech of the trusty,* so that they cannot speak as they intended and as they used to do, with freedom and clearness, but blunder, and falter, and make nothing of it. Those that were honoured and admired strangely fall into disgrace (*v.* 21): He *poureth contempt upon princes.* That which was secret, and lay hidden, is strangely brought to light and laid open (*v.* 22): *He discovers deep things out of darkness.* Plots closely laid are discovered and defeated; wickedness closely committed and artfully concealed is discovered. Kingdoms have their ebbings and flowings, their waxings and wanings; and both are from God (*v.* 23). *He taketh away the heart of the chief of the people,* their leaders most famed for their martial fire. They are heartless, and ready to flee at the shaking of a leaf. Those that were driving on their

projects with full speed are strangely bewildered and at a loss, wandering like men in a desert (*v.* 24), groping like men in the dark, and staggering like men in drink, *v.* 25. Heaven and earth are shaken, but the Lord sits King for ever, and with him we look for *a kingdom that cannot be shaken.*

CHAPTER 13

Job here comes to make application of what he had said. I. He is very bold with his friends, comparing himself with them, notwithstanding the mortifications he was under, ver. 1, 2, condemning them for their falsehood, their partiality (ver. 4–8), and threatening them with the judgments of God for their so doing (ver. 9–12), desiring them to be silent (ver. 5, 13, 17), and turning from them to God, ver. 3. II. He is very bold with his God. 1. In some expressions his faith is very bold, yet that is not more bold than welcome, ver. 15, 16, 18. But, 2. In other expressions his passion is rather too bold in expostulations with God concerning the deplorable condition he was in (ver. 14, 19, &c.), complaining of the confusion he was in (ver. 20–22), and the loss he was at to find out the sin that provoked God thus to afflict him.

Verses 1–12

Job warmly expresses his resentment of the unkindness of his friends.

I. He comes up with them as one that did not need to be taught by them, *v.* 1, 2. They compelled him, as the Corinthians did Paul, to commend himself and his own knowledge, yet not in a way of self-applause, but of self-justification. Happy are those who not only see and hear, but understand, the greatness, glory, and sovereignty of God. This, he thought, would justify what he had said before (*ch.* xii. 3), which he repeats here (*v.* 2): "*What you know, the same do I know also,* so that I need not come to you to be taught; *I am not inferior unto you* in wisdom."

II. He turns from them to God (*v.* 3): *Surely I would speak to the Almighty.* Job would rather argue with God himself than with his friends.

III. He condemns them for their unjust and uncharitable treatment of him, *v.* 4. They falsely accused him, and that was unjust: *You are forgers of lies.* They framed a wrong hypothesis concerning the divine Providence, as if it did never remarkably afflict any but wicked men in this world, and thence they drew a false judgment concerning Job, that he was certainly a hypocrite. They undertook his cure, and pretended to be his physicians; but they were all *physicians of no value,* "idol-physicians, who can do me no more good than an idol can."

IV. He begs they would be silent and give him a patient hearing, *v.* 5, 6. "*Hold your peace, and it shall be your wisdom,* for thereby you will conceal your ignorance and ill-nature." *Hear now my reasoning.* Perhaps, though they did not interrupt him in his discourse, yet they seemed careless, and did not much heed what he said. He therefore begged that they would not only hear, but hearken.

V. He endeavours to convince them of the wrong they did to God's honour, while they pretended to plead for him, *v.* 7, 8. God and his cause did not need such advocates: "*Will you* think to *contend for God,* as if his justice were clouded and wanted to be cleared up, or as if he were at a loss what to say and wanted you to speak for him? If you were for ever silent, the heavens would declare his righteousness." Under pretence of justifying God in afflicting Job they magisterially condemned him as a hypocrite and a bad man. "This" (says he) "is *speaking wickedly*" (for uncharitableness and censoriousness are wickedness, great wickedness). God's truth needs not our lie, nor God's cause either our sinful policies or our sinful passions.

VI. He endeavours to possess them with a fear of God's judgment, and so to bring them to a better temper. Let them consider whether they could give him a good account of what they did (*v.* 9): "*Is it good that he should search you out?*" It is good to an upright man who means honestly that God should search him. But it is bad to him who looks one way and rows another that God should search him out. The severity of his rebukes and displeasure against them (*v.* 10): "*If you do accept persons, though but secretly and in heart, he will surely reprove you.* You that have great knowledge of God, and profess a fear of him, how dare you talk at this rate and give yourselves so great a liberty of speech?" There is in God a dreadful excellency. His excellencies in themselves are amiable, but considering man's distance from God by nature, and his defection and degeneracy by sin, his excellencies are dreadful. Let them consider themselves, and what an unequal match they were for this great God (*v.* 12): "*Your remembrances* (all that in you for which you hope to be remembered when you are gone) *are like unto ashes,* worthless and weak, and easily trampled on and blown away. *Your bodies are like bodies of clay.* Your remonstrances on God's behalf are no better than dust, and the arguments you accumulate but like so many heaps of dirt."

Verses 13–22

Job here takes fresh hold, fast hold, of his integrity, as one that was resolved not to let it go, nor suffer it to be wrested from him.

I. He entreats his friends and all the company to let him alone, and not interrupt him in what he was about to say (*v.* 13), but diligently to hearken to it, *v.* 17. He would have his own protestation to be decisive, for none but God and himself knew his heart. "Be silent therefore, and let me hear no more of you, but hearken diligently to what I say, and let my own oath for confirmation be an end of the strife."

II. He resolves to adhere to the testimony his own conscience gave of his integrity: "I will speak in my own defence, and *let come on me what will, v.* 13. I hope God will not make my necessary defence to be my offence, as you do. He will justify me (*v.* 18) and then nothing can come amiss to me." He resolves (*v.* 15) that he will *maintain his own ways.* "*If I hold my tongue,* and do not speak for myself, my silence now will for ever silence me, for *I shall* certainly *give up the ghost," v.* 19.

III. He complains of the extremity of pain and misery he was in (*v.* 14): *Wherefore do I take my flesh in my teeth?* That is, "Why do I suffer such agonies? I cannot but wonder that God should lay so much upon me when he knows I am not a wicked man." It would vex the most patient man, when he had lost everything else, to be denied the comfort (if he deserves it) of a good conscience and a good name.

IV. He still depends upon God for—justification and salvation, the two great things we hope for through Christ (*v.* 18): *I have ordered my cause, and,* upon the whole matter, *I know that I shall be justified.* Those whose hearts are upright with God, in walking not after the flesh but after the Spirit, may be sure that through Christ there shall be no condemnation to them, but that, whoever lays anything to their charge, they shall be justified (*v.* 16): *He also shall be my salvation.* He means it not of temporal salvation (he had little expectation of that); but concerning his eternal salvation he was very confident. He knew himself not to be a hypocrite, and therefore concluded he should not be rejected. Sincerity is our evangelical perfection; nothing will ruin us but the want of that. *Though he slay me, yet will I trust in him, v.* 15. This is a high expression of faith. We must rejoice in God when we have nothing else to rejoice in, and cleave to him, yea, though we cannot for the present find comfort in him.

V. He wishes to argue the case even with God himself, if he might but have leave to settle the preliminaries of the treaty, *v.* 20–22. "*Withdraw thy hand far from me;* for, while I am in this extremity, I am fit for nothing." "*Let not thy dread make me afraid*"; "Lord," says Job, "let me not be put into such a consternation of spirit, together with this bodily affliction; for then I must certainly drop the cause, and shall make nothing of it." How can even a good man, much less a bad man, reason with God, so as to be justified before him, when he is upon the rack of pain.

Verses 23–28

I. Job enquires after his sins, and begs to have them discovered to him. *Make me to know my transgressions, v.* 23. His friends were ready enough to tell him how numerous and how heinous they were, *ch.* xxii. 5. "But Lord," says he, "let me know them from thee; *for thy judgment is according to truth,* theirs is not." *That which I see not, teach thou me.* A true penitent is willing to know the worst of himself; and we should all desire to know what our transgressions are, that we may be particular in the confession of them and on our guard against them for the future.

II. He bitterly complains of God's withdrawings from him (*v.* 24): *Wherefore hidest thou thy face?* This must be meant of something more than his outward afflictions; *his soul was also sorely vexed.* God hid his face as one strange to him, displeased with him. Note, The Holy Ghost sometimes denies his favours to the best and dearest of his saints and servants in this world. Evidences for heaven are eclipsed, communications interrupted, and the returns of comfort, for the present, despaired of, Ps. lxxvii. 7–9; lxxxviii. 7, 15, 16. These are grievous burdens to a gracious soul, that values God's loving-kindness as better than life, Prov. xviii. 14. *A wounded spirit who can bear?* Job, by asking here, *Why hidest thou thy face?* teaches us that, when at any time we are under the sense of God's withdrawings, we are to enquire into the reason of them—what is the sin for which he corrects us and what the good he designs us. Job's sufferings were typical of the sufferings of Christ, from whom not only men hid their faces (Isa. liii. 3), but God hid his, witness the darkness which surrounded him on the cross when he cried out, *My God, my God, why hast thou forsaken me?*

III. He humbly pleads with God his own utter inability to stand before him (*v.* 25): "*Wilt thou break a leaf, pursue the dry stubble?*" We ought to have such an apprehension of the goodness and compassion of God as to believe that he will not *break the bruised reed,* Matt. xii. 20.

IV. He sadly complains of God's severe dealings with him. He owns it was for his sins that God thus contended with him, but thinks it hard (*v.* 26): *Thou writest bitter things against me.* Afflictions are bitter things. "Herein *thou makest me to possess the iniquities of my youth,*" that is, "thou punishest me for them, and thereby puttest me in mind of them, and obligest me to renew my repentance for them." Time does not wear out the guilt of sin. God writes bitter things against us to bring forgotten sins to mind, and so to bring us to remorse for them as to break us off from them. "*Thou puttest my feet also in the stocks* to correct me for every false step. Thou *settest a print upon the heels of my feet* no sooner have I trodden wrong, though ever so little, than immediately I smart for it; the punishment treads upon the very heels of the sin." Now, (1) It was not true that God did thus seek advantages against him. But he is so far from this that he deals not with us according to the desert. This therefore was the language of Job's melancholy; his sober thoughts never represented God thus as a hard Master. (2) But we should keep such a strict and jealous eye as this upon ourselves and our own steps, both for the discovery of sin past and the prevention of it for the future.

V. He finds himself wasting away apace under the heavy hand of God, *v.* 28. *He* (that is, man) *as a rotten thing*, the principle of whose putrefaction is in itself, *consumes even like a moth-eaten garment*, which becomes continually worse and worse. While there is so little soundness in the soul, no marvel there is so little soundness in the flesh, Ps. xxxviii. 3.

CHAPTER 14

Job goes on to speak to God and himself. He had reminded his friends of their frailty and mortality (ch. xiii. 12); here he reminds himself of his own, and pleads it with God for some mitigation of his miseries. We have here an account, I. Of man's life, that it is, 1. Short, ver. 1. 2. Sorrowful, ver. 1. 3. Sinful, ver. 4. 4. Stinted, ver. 5, 14. II. Of man's death, that it puts a final period to our present life, to which we shall not again return (ver. 7–12), that it hides us from the calamities of life (ver. 13), destroys the hopes of life (ver. 18, 19), sends us away from the business of life (ver. 20), and keeps us in the dark concerning our relations in this life, how much soever we have formerly been in care about them, ver. 21, 22. III. The use Job makes of all this. 1. He pleads it with God, who, he thought, was too strict and severe with him (ver. 16, 17), begging that, in consideration of his frailty, he would not contend with him (ver. 3), but grant him some respite, ver. 6. 2. He engages himself to prepare for death (ver. 14), and encourages himself to hope that it would be comfortable to him, ver. 15. This chapter is proper for funeral solemnities.

Verses 1–6

We are here led to think,

I. Of the original of human life. God is indeed its great original, for he *breathed into man the breath of life* and in him we live; but we date it from our birth, and thence we must date both its frailty and its pollution. 1. Its frailty: *Man, that is born of a woman, is therefore of few days, v.* 1. This may refer to the first woman, who was called *Eve*, or it may refer to every man's immediate mother. 2. Its pollution (*v.* 4): *Who can bring a clean thing out of an unclean?* Our blood is not only attainted by a legal conviction, but tainted with an hereditary disease. Our Lord Jesus, being made sin for us, is said to be *made of a woman*, Gal. iv..4.

II. Of the nature of human life: it is *a flower*, it is *a shadow, v.* 2. The flower is fading, and all its beauty soon withers and is gone. The shadow is fleeting, and its very being will soon be lost and drowned in the shadows of the night.

III. Of the shortness and uncertainty of human life: Man is *of few days*. Life is here computed, not by months or years, but by days, for we cannot be sure of any day. Man sometimes no sooner comes forth than he *is cut down*—comes forth into the world and enters into the business of it than he is hurried away as soon as he has laid his hand to the plough. If not cut down immediately, yet *he flees as a shadow*, and never continues in one stay.

IV. Of the calamitous state of human life. Man, as he is short-lived, so he is sad-lived. During these few days he is *full of trouble*, not only troubled, but full of trouble, either toiling or fretting, grieving or fearing. When we come to heaven our days will be many, and perfectly free from trouble, and in the mean time faith, hope, and love, balance the present grievances.

V. Of the sinfulness of human life, arising from the sinfulness of the human nature. So some understand that question (*v.* 4), *Who can bring a clean thing out of an unclean?* He intends it as a plea with God for compassion: "Lord, be not extreme to mark my sins of human frailty and infirmity, for thou knowest my weakness. *O remember that I am flesh!*" The Chaldee paraphrase has an observable reading of this verse: *Who can make a man clean that is polluted with sin? Cannot one? that is, God.*

VI. Of the settled period of human life, *v.* 5. Nothing comes to pass by chance, so, not the execution done by a bow drawn at a venture. We are no more governed by the Stoic's blind fate than by the Epicurean's blind fortune. The consideration of our own inability to contend with God, of our own sinfulness and weakness, should engage us to pray, *Lord, enter not into judgment with thy servant.* Thus may we find some relief under great troubles by recommending ourselves to the compassion of that God who knows our frame and will consider it, and our being out of frame too.

Verses 7–15

Job here shows,

I. That death is a removal for ever out of this world. A man cut down by death will not revive again, as a tree cut down will. What hope there is of a tree he shows very elegantly, *v.* 7–9. If the body of the tree be cut down, and only the stem or stump left in the ground, though it seem dead and dry, yet it will shoot out young boughs again, as if it were but newly planted. But man has no such prospect of a return to life. The vegetable life is a cheap and easy thing: the scent of water will recover it. The animal life, in some insects and fowls, is so: the heat of the sun retrieves it. But the rational soul, when once retired, is too great, too noble, a thing to be recalled by any of the powers of nature; it is out of the reach of sun or rain, and cannot be restored but by the immediate operations of Omnipotence itself; for (*v.* 10) *man dieth and wasteth away, yea, man giveth up the ghost, and where is he?* Two words are here used for man:—*Geber, a mighty man*, though mighty, dies; *Adam, a man of the earth*, because earthy, gives up the ghost. After death: *Where is he?* He is not where he was; his place knows him no more; but *is he nowhere?* So some read it. Yes, he is somewhere; and it is a very awful consideration to think where those are that have given up the ghost, and where we shall be when we give it up. It has gone to the world of spirits, gone into eternity, gone to return no more to this world.

II. That yet there will be a return of man to life again in another world, at the end of time, when *the heavens* are *no more.* Then *they shall awake and be raised out of their sleep.* The resurrection of the dead was doubtless an article of Job's creed, as appears, *ch.* xix. 26.

1. A humble petition for a hiding-place in the grave, *v.* 13. It was not only in a passionate weariness of this life that he wished to die, but in a pious assurance of a better life, to which at length he should arise.

2. A holy resolution patiently to attend the will of God both in his death, and in his resurrection (*v.* 14): *If a man die, shall he live again? All the days of my appointed time will I wait till my change come.* Job's friends proving miserable comforters, he set himself to be the more his own comforter. His case was now bad, but he pleases himself with the expectation of a change.

3. A joyful expectation of bliss and satisfaction in this (*v.* 15): Then *thou shalt call, and I will answer thee.* Now, he was under such a cloud that he could not, he durst not, answer (*ch.* ix. 15, 35; xiii. 22); but he comforted himself with this, that there would come a time when God would call and he should answer. "Thou *wilt have a desire to the work of thy hands.* Thou hast mercy in store for me, not only as made by thy providence, but new-made by thy grace; otherwise *he that made them will not save them.*" Grace in the soul is the work of God's own hands, and therefore he will not forsake it in this world (Ps. cxxxviii. 8), but will have a desire to it, to perfect it in the other, and to crown it with endless glory.

Verses 16—22

Job returns to his complaints; and, though he is not without hope of future bliss, he finds it very hard to get over his present grievances.

I. He complains of the particular hardships he apprehended himself under from the strictness of God's justice, *v.* 16, 17. *Therefore* he longed to go hence to that world where God's wrath will be past, because now he was under the continual tokens of it, as a child, under the severe discipline of the rod, longs to be of age. "When shall my change come? *For now thou* seemest to me to *number my steps*, and *watch over my sin*, and *seal it up in a bag*, as bills of indictment are kept safely, to be produced against the prisoner." See Deut. xxxii. 34. 1. Job does right to the divine justice in owning that he smarted for his sins and transgressions, that he had done enough to deserve all that was laid upon him. But, 2. He does wrong to the divine goodness in suggesting that God was extreme to mark what he did amiss, and made the worst of everything. He spoke to this purport, *ch.* xiii. 27, but we are punished less than our iniquities deserve. God does indeed seal and sew up, against the day of wrath, the transgression of the impenitent, but the sins of his people he blots out as a cloud.

II. He complains of the wasting condition of mankind in general. We live in a dying world. 1. We see the decays of the earth itself. (1) Of the strongest parts of it, *v.* 18. Nothing will last always, for we see even mountains moulder and come to nought; they wither and fall as a leaf; rocks wax old and pass away by the continual beating of the sea against them. *The waters wear the stones* with constant dropping, *non vi, sed sæpe cadendo—not by the violence, but by the constancy with which they fall*. On this earth everything is the worse for the wearing. *Tempus edax rerum—Time devours all things*. (2) Of the natural products of it. The things which grow out of the earth, and seem to be firmly rooted in it, are sometimes by an excess of rain washed away, *v.* 19. 2. No marvel then if we see the decays of man upon the earth, for he is of the earth, earthy. Job begins to think his case is not singular, and therefore he ought to reconcile himself to the common lot. How vain it is to expect much from the enjoyments of life: "*Thou destroyest the hope of man*," that is, "puttest an end to all the projects he had framed and all the prospects of satisfaction he had flattered himself with." Death will be the destruction of all those hopes which are built upon worldly confidences and confined to worldly comforts. Hope in Christ, and hope in heaven, death will consummate and not destroy. The consideration of this should moderate our cares concerning our children and families. God will know what comes of them when we are gone. To him therefore let us commit them, with him let us leave them, and not burden ourselves with needless fruitless cares concerning them. It is true wisdom, by making our peace with God in Christ and keeping a good conscience, to treasure up comforts which will support and relieve us against the pains and sorrows of a dying hour.

CHAPTER 15

Perhaps Job thought, if he had not convinced, yet he had at least silenced all his three friends; but, it seems, he had not: in this chapter they begin a second attack upon him. Eliphaz here keeps close to the principles upon which he had condemned Job, and, I. He reproves him for justifying himself, and fathers on him many evil things which are unfairly inferred, ver. 2–13. II. He persuades him to humble himself before God and to take shame to himself, ver. 14–16. III. He reads him a long lecture concerning the woeful estate of wicked people, who harden their hearts against God and the judgments which are prepared for them, ver. 17–35. A good use may be made both of his reproofs (for they are plain) and of his doctrine (for it is sound), though both the one and the other are misapplied to Job.

Verses 1–16

Eliphaz here falls very foul upon Job, because he contradicted what he and his colleagues had said. Several great crimes Eliphaz here charges Job with, only because he would not own himself a hypocrite.

I. He charges him with folly and absurdity (*v.* 2, 3), that, whereas he had been reputed a wise man, he had now quite forfeited his reputation. It is common for angry disputants thus to represent one another's reasonings as impertinent and ridiculous. There is a great deal of vain knowledge, science falsely so called, that is useless, and therefore worthless. This is the knowledge that puffs up, with which men swell in a fond conceit of their own accomplishments. Vain knowledge or unprofitable talk ought to be reproved and checked, especially in a wise man, whom it worst becomes.

II. He charges him with impiety and irreligion (*v.* 4): "*Thou castest off fear*," that is, "the fear of God, and that regard to him which thou shouldst have; and then *thou restrainest prayer*." See what religion is summed up in, fearing God and praying to him, the former the most needful principle, the latter the most needful practice. Those who are prayerless are fearless and graceless. Those who either omit prayer or straiten and abridge themselves in it, quenching the spirit of adoption and denying themselves the liberty they might take in the duty, restrain prayer. This is bad enough, but it is worse to restrain others from prayer, to prohibit and discourage prayer, as Darius, Dan. vi. 7. Eliphaz charges this upon Job. He thought that Job talked of God with such liberty as if he had been his equal, that he had quite thrown off all religious regard to him. This charge was utterly false, and yet wanted not some colour. We ought not only to take care that we keep up prayer and the fear of God, but that we never drop any unwary expressions which may give occasion to those who seek occasion to question our sincerity and constancy in religion. "If this be true" (thinks Eliphaz) "which Job says, that a man may be thus surely afflicted and yet be a good man, then farewell all religion, farewell prayer and the fear of God. *Thy mouth utters thy iniquity— teaches it*," so the word is. "*Thou teachest* others to have the same hard thoughts of God and religion that thou thyself hast." But *thou choosest the tongue of the crafty*, that is, "Thou utterest thy iniquity with some show and pretence of piety, mixing some good words with the bad, as tradesmen do with their wares to help them off." Eliphaz, in his first discourse, had proceeded against Job upon mere surmise (*ch.* iv. 6, 7), but now he has got proof against him from his own discourses (*v.* 6): *Thy own mouth condemns thee, and not I*. But he should have considered that he and his fellows had provoked him to say that which now they took advantage of; and that was not fair.

III. He charges him with intolerable arrogancy and self-conceitedness. It was a just, and reasonable, and modest demand that Job had made (*ch.* xii. 3), *Allow that I have understanding as well as you*; but see how they seek occasion against him: that is misconstrued, as if he pretended to be wiser than any man. "*Art thou the first man that was born? Wast thou made before the hills*, as Wisdom herself was? (Prov. viii. 23, &c.) Dost thou know more of the world than any of us do? No, thou art but of yesterday even as we are," *ch.* viii. 9. In intimacy of acquaintance with God (*v.* 8): "*Hast thou heard the secret of God?*" He also represents him, (1) As assuming to himself such knowledge as none else had: "*Dost thou restrain wisdom to thyself*, as if none were wise besides?" Job had said (*ch.* xiii. 2), *What you know, the same do I know also*. (2) As opposing the stream of antiquity, a venerable name, under the shade of which all contending parties strive to shelter themselves: "*With us are the grey-headed and very aged men* (*v.* 10). We have the fathers on our side."

IV. He charges him with a contempt of the counsels and comforts that were given him by his friends (*v.* 11): *Are the consolations of God small with thee?* Eliphaz takes it ill that Job did not value the comforts which he and his friends administered to him more than it seems he did. He represents this as a slight put upon divine consolations in general, as if they were of small account with him, whereas really they were not. If he had not highly valued them, he could not have borne up as he did under his sufferings.

V. He charges him with opposition to God himself and to religion (*v.* 12, 13): "*Why doth thy heart carry thee away* into such indecent irreligious expressions?" He thought Job's spirit was soured against God, and so turned from what it had been, and exasperated at his dealings with him. Eliphaz wanted candour and charity, else he would not have put such a harsh construction upon the speeches of one that had such a settled reputation for piety and was now in temptation.

VI. He charges him with justifying himself to such a degree as even to deny his share in the common corruption and pollution of the human nature (*v.* 14): *What is man, that he should be clean?* that is, that he should pretend to be so, or that any should expect to find him so. What is *he that is born of a woman, a sinful woman, that he should be righteous?* With these plain truths Eliphaz thinks to convince Job, whereas he had just now said the same (*ch.* xiv. 4): *Who can bring a clean thing out of an unclean?* But does it therefore follow that Job is a hypocrite and a wicked man, which is all that he denied? By no means. Though man, as born of a woman, is not clean, yet, as born again of the Spirit, he is clean. Further to evince this he here shows, (1) That the brightest creatures are imperfect and impure before God, *v.* 15. He takes no complacency in the heavens themselves. How pure soever they seem to us, in his eye they had many a speck and many a flaw: *The heavens are not clean in his sight.* If the stars have no light in the sight of the sun, what light has the sun in the sight of God! See Isa. xxiv. 23. (2) That man is much more so (*v.* 16): *How much more abominable and filthy is man!* If saints are not to be trusted, much less sinners. If the heavens are not pure, which are as God made them, much less man, who is degenerated. Nay, he is abominable and filthy in the sight of God, and if ever he repent he is so in his own sight, and therefore he abhors himself.

Verses 17–35

Eliphaz comes to maintain his own thesis, upon which he built his censure of Job. Those who are wicked are certainly miserable, those who are miserable are certainly wicked, therefore Job was so.

I. His solemn preface (*v.* 17): "*I will show thee* that which is worth hearing, and not reason, as thou dost, with unprofitable talk." He promises to teach him, 1. From his own experience and observation: "*That which I have myself seen,* in divers instances, *I will declare.*" 2. From the wisdom of the ancients (*v.* 18): *Which wise men have told from their fathers.* The wisdom and learning of the moderns are very much derived from those of the ancients. Good children will learn a good deal from their good parents; and what we have learned from our ancestors we must transmit to our posterity.

II. The discourse itself.

1. Those who are wise and good do ordinarily prosper in this world. This he only hints at (*v.* 19), that those were such as had the earth given to them, and to them only; they enjoyed it entirely and peaceably. Job had said, *The earth is given into the hand*

of the wicked, *ch.* ix. 24. "No," says Eliphaz, "it is given into the hands of the saints, and they are not robbed and plundered by strangers making inroads upon them, as thou art by the Sabeans and Chaldeans."

2. Wicked people, and particularly tyrannizing rulers, are subject to continual terrors, and perish very miserably. Even those who impiously dare God's judgments will feel them at last. He speaks in the singular number—*the wicked man.* He meant Job himself, whom he expressly charges both with the tyranny and with the timorousness here described, *ch.* xxii. 9, 10. Here he thinks Job might, in this description, see his own face.

(1) He describes the sinner who lives thus miserably, *v.* 25–28. It is no ordinary sinner, that bids defiance to God, *v.* 25. Tell him of the divine law, and its obligations; he breaks those bonds asunder. Tell him of the divine wrath, and he bids the Almighty do his worst, and will not be controlled by law, or conscience. *He stretches out his hand against God* to show that, if it were in his power, he would ungod him. *He strengthens himself* (*he would be valiant,* so some read it) *against the Almighty.* It is the prodigious madness of presumptuous sinners that they enter the lists with Omnipotence. *He runs upon him,* upon God himself, *even upon his neck,* as a desperate combatant, when he finds himself an unequal match for his adversary, flies in his face, though, at the same time, he falls on his sword's point, or the sharp spike ·of his buckler. He wraps himself up in security and sensuality (*v.* 27): *He covers his face with his fatness.* This signifies both the pampering of his flesh with daily delicious fare and the hardening of his heart hereby against the judgments of God. The fat that covers his face makes him look bold and haughty, and that which covers his flanks makes him lie easy and soft, and feel little; but this will prove poor shelter against the darts of God's wrath. He enriches himself with the spoils of all about him, *v.* 28. *They conceive mischief,* and then they effect it by *preparing deceit,* pretending to protect those whom they design to subdue, and making leagues of peace the more effectually to carry on the operations of war.

(2) The miserable condition of this wicked man, both in spiritual and temporal judgments. His inward peace is continually disturbed. His own conscience accuses him, and with the pangs of that *he travaileth in pain all his days, v.* 20. His sins stare him in the face at every turn. He is vexed at the uncertainty of the continuance of his wealth and power: *The number of years is hidden to the oppressor.* He is under a *certain fearful expectation of judgment. A dreadful sound is in his ears, v.* 21. He knows that God is angry with him and that all the world hates him; he has done nothing to make his peace with either. Again (*v.* 23): *He knows that the day of darkness* (or the *night* of darkness rather) *is ready at his hand,* that it is appointed to him and cannot be put by. 'No marvel that it follows (*v.* 24), *Trouble and anguish shall make him afraid* of worse to come. If at any time he be in trouble, he despairs of getting out (*v.* 22). Such a dread he has of poverty, and such a waste does he discern· upon his estate, that he is already, in his own imagination, *wandering abroad for bread.* How can he prosper when God runs upon him? so some understand that, *v.* 26. Whom God runs *upon* he will certainly run *down.* Many that get much by fraud and injustice, yet do not grow rich: it goes as it comes; it is got by one sin and spent upon another. He is in care to leave what he has got and kept to his children after him. But the branches of his family shall perish. *They shall not be green, v.* 32. *The flame shall dry them up, v.* 30. He shall shake them off as blossoms that never knit, or as the *unripe grape, v.* 33. Many a man's family is ruined by his iniquity. He is in care, when he is in trouble, how to get out of it (not how

to get good by it); but in this also he is crossed (*v.* 30): *He shall not depart out of darkness.* He is in care to secure his partners, but that is in vain too, *v.* 34, 35. *The congregation* of them, the whole confederacy they and all their tabernacles, *shall be desolate.*

(3) Will the prosperity of presumptuous sinners end thus miserably? Then (*v.* 31) *let not him that is deceived trust in vanity.* Those who trust to their sinful ways of getting wealth *trust in vanity*, and *vanity will be their recompence.* Those who trust to their wealth when they have gotten it, especially to the wealth they have gotten dishonestly, trust in vanity; for it will yield them no satisfaction. They will own at length, with the utmost confusion, that *a deceived heart turned them aside*, and that they cheated themselves with *a lie in their right hand.*

CHAPTER 16

Job's reply to that discourse of Eliphaz in the foregoing chapter; it is but the second part of the same song of lamentation with which he had before bemoaned himself, and is set to the same melancholy tune. I. He upbraids his friends with their unkind usage of him, ver. 1–5. II. He represents his own case as very deplorable, ver. 6–16. III. He still holds fast his integrity, concerning which he appeals to God's righteous judgment from the unrighteous censures of his friends, ver. 17–22.

Verses 1–5

Both Job and his friends undervalue one another's sense, and wisdom, and management. The longer the saw of contention is drawn the hotter it grows. Eliphaz had represented Job's discourses as idle, and unprofitable, and Job here gives his the same character. Job here reproves Eliphaz, 1. For needless repetitions (*v.* 2): "*I have heard many such things.*" 2. For unskilful applications. "*Miserable comforters are you all*, who, instead of offering anything to alleviate the affliction add affliction to it, and make it yet more grievous." The patient's case is sad indeed when his medicines are poisons and his physicians his worst disease. 3. For endless impertinence. Job wishes that *vain words might have an end, v.* 3. 4. For obstinacy. *What emboldeneth thee, that thou answerest?* It is a great piece of confidence, to pass a judgment on men's spiritual state upon the view of their outward condition. 5. For the violation of the sacred laws of friendship. This is a cutting reproof, *v.* 4, 5. He desires his friends, in imagination, to suppose themselves in misery like him and him at ease like them. He represents the unkindness of their conduct towards him, by showing what he could do to them if they were in his condition: *I could speak as you do.* He shows them what they should do, by telling them what in that case he would do (*v.* 5): "*I would strengthen you*, and say all I could to assuage your grief, but nothing to aggravate it." What is the duty we owe to our brethren in their affliction? We should say and do all we can to strengthen them, to encourage their confidence in God, to support their sinking spirits, to assuage their grief—the causes of their grief, if possible, or at least their resentment of those causes. Good words cost nothing; but they may be of good service to those that are in sorrow, not only as it is some comfort to them to see their friends concerned for them, but as they may be so reminded of that which, through the prevalency of grief, was forgotten. Though hard words break no bones, yet kind words may help to make broken bones rejoice.

Verses 6–16

Job's complaint is here as bitter as anywhere in all his discourses. Sometimes giving vent to grief gives ease; but, "*Though I speak*" (says Job), "*my grief is not assuaged*, what I speak is so misconstrued as to be turned to the aggravation of my grief." At other times keeping silence makes the trouble the easier and the sooner forgotten; but (says Job) *though I forbear what am I eased?* If he complained he was

censured as passionate; if not, as sullen. If he maintained his integrity, that was his crime; if he made no answer to their accusations, his silence was taken for a confession of his guilt.

I. His family was scattered (*v.* 7). He had company indeed, but such as he would rather have been without, for they seemed to triumph in his desolation.

II. His body was worn away with diseases and pains, *v.* 8. His face was furrowed, not with age, but sickness: *Thou hast filled me with wrinkles.* "They are witnesses *for* me, that my complaint is not causeless."

III. His enemy threatened him (*v.* 9): *He tears me in his wrath.* But who is this enemy? 1. Eliphaz, who showed himself very much exasperated against him, and what he said tore Job's good name and thundered nothing but terror to him. Or, 2. Satan. He was his enemy that hated him, and aimed to make him curse God. It is not improbable that this is the enemy he means. Or, 3. God himself. If we understand it of him, the expressions are indeed as rash as any he used. God hates none of his creatures; but Job's melancholy did thus represent to him the terrors of the Almighty.

IV. All about him were abusive to him, *v.* 10. Herein Job was a type of Christ, as many of the ancients make him: these very expressions are used in the predictions of his sufferings, Ps. xxii. 13, *They gaped upon me with their mouths;* and (Mic. v. 1), *They shall smite the Judge of Israel with a rod upon the cheek*, which was literally fulfilled, Matt. xxvi. 67.

V. God, instead of delivering him out of their hands, as he hoped, delivered him into their hands (*v.* 11): *He hath turned me over into the hands of the wicked.* Herein also Job was a type of Christ, who was delivered into wicked hands, to be crucified and slain, by the *determinate counsel and foreknowledge of God*, Acts ii. 23.

VI. God not only delivered him into the hands of the wicked, but took him into his own hands too (*v.* 12): "*I was at ease* in the comfortable enjoyment of the gifts of God's bounty, yet *he has broken me asunder*, put me upon the rack of pain, and torn me limb from limb." "*He has set me up for his mark*, the butt at which he is pleased to let fly all his arrows." When God set him up for a mark *his archers* presently *compassed him round.* Whoever are our enemies, we must look upon them as God's archers, and see him directing the arrow. *It is the Lord; let him do what seemeth him good.* As if he had no mercy in reserve for him, he does not spare nor abate anything of the extremity. "*He breaketh me with breach upon breach*, follows me with one wound after another." Thus he thought that God ran upon him *like a giant*, whom he could not possibly stand before or confront. Even good men, when they are in great and extraordinary troubles, have much ado not to entertain hard thoughts of God.

VII. He had divested himself of all his honour, and all his comfort. Job, as one truly penitent and truly patient, humbled himself under the mighty hand of God, *v.* 15, 16. He consulted not either his ease or finery in his dress, but sewed sackcloth upon his skin; that clothing he thought good enough for such a defiled distempered body as he had. He insisted not upon any points of honour, but humbled himself under humbling providences: *He defiled his horn in the dust*, and refused the respect that used to be paid to his dignity. "*My face is foul with weeping* so constantly for my sins, for God's displeasure against me, and for my friends' unkindness: this has brought a *shadow of death upon my eyelids.*"

Verses 17–22

Job's condition was very deplorable; but,

I. He had the testimony of his conscience that he

had walked uprightly, and had never allowed himself in any gross sin. None was ever more ready than he to acknowledge his sins of infirmity; but he could not charge himself with any enormous crime, for which he should be made more miserable than other men, *v.* 17. Eliphaz had represented him as a tyrant and an oppressor. "No," says he, "I never did any wrong to any man, but always despised the gain of oppression." Eliphaz had charged him with hypocrisy in religion, but he specifies prayer, the great act of religion, and professes that in that he was pure, though not from all infirmity. It was not like the prayers of the Pharisees, who looked no further than to be seen of men, and to serve a turn.

1. This assertion of his own integrity he backs with a solemn imprecation of shame and confusion to himself if it were not true, *v.* 18. If there were any injustice in his hands, he wished it might not be concealed: *O earth! cover thou not my blood,* that is, "the innocent blood of others, which I am suspected to have shed." If there were any impurity in his prayers, he wished they might not be accepted: *Let my cry have no place.*

II. He could appeal to God's omniscience concerning his integrity, *v.* 19. The witness in our own bosoms for us will stand us in little stead if we have not a witness in heaven for us too; for *God is greater than our hearts,* and we are not to be our own judges. This therefore is Job's triumph, *My witness is in heaven.* It is an unspeakable comfort to a good man, when he lies under the censure of his brethren, that there is a God in heaven who knows his integrity and will clear it up sooner or later.

III. He had a God to go to before whom he might unbosom himself, *v.* 20, 21. "My friends (so they call themselves) scorn me; they set themselves not only to resist me, but to use all their art and eloquence" (so the word signifies) "to run me down." He doubted not but that God did now take cognizance of his sorrows: *My eye pours out tears to God.* Even tears, when sanctified to God, give ease to troubled spirits; and, if men slight our grief, this may comfort us, that God regards them. If he could but now have the same freedom at God's bar that men commonly have at the bar of the civil magistrate, he doubted not but to carry his cause, for the Judge himself was a witness to his integrity. The language of this wish is like that in Isa. l. 7, 8, *I know that I shall not be ashamed, for he is near that justifies me.*

IV. He had a prospect of death which would put a period to all his troubles. Such confidence had he towards God that he could take pleasure in thinking of the approach of death, when he should be determined to his everlasting state, as one that doubted not but it would be well with him then: *When a few years have come* (*the years of number* which are determined and appointed to me) *then I shall go the way whence I shall not return.* To die is to *go the way whence we shall not return.* It is to go a journey from the world of sense to the world of spirits. It is a journey to our long home. We must all of us very certainly go this journey; and it is comfortable to those who keep a good conscience to think of it, for it is the crown of their integrity.

CHAPTER 17

I. Job reflects upon the harsh censures which his friends had passed upon him, and, looking upon himself as a dying man (ver. 1), he appeals to God, and begs of him speedily to appear for him, and right him, because they had wronged him, and he knew not how to right himself, ver. 2–7. But he hopes that, though it should be a surprise, it will be no stumbling-block, to good people, to see him thus abused, ver. 8, 9. II. He reflects upon the vain hopes they had fed him with, ver. 10–16.

Verses 1–9

Job's discourse is broken and he passes suddenly from one thing to another, as is usual with men in trouble.

I. The deplorable condition which he describes to justify his own complaints.

1. He was a dying man, *v.* 1. He had said (*ch.* xvi. 22), "*When a few years have come,* I shall go that long journey." But here he corrects himself. "Why do I talk of years to come? *My breath is already corrupt,* I am a gone man." It concerns us therefore carefully to redeem the days of time, and to spend them in getting ready for the days of eternity. We are expected in our long home: *The graves are ready for me.* He speaks of the *sepulchres of his fathers,* to which he must be gathered.

2. He was a despised man (*v.* 6): "*He*" (that is, Eliphaz, so some, or God) "*has made me a byword of the people,* a laughing-stock to many, and *aforetime I was as a tabret,* that whoever chose might play upon." They made ballads of him; his name became a proverb; it is so still, *As poor as Job.* "*He has* now *made me a by-word,*" a reproach of men, whereas, aforetime, in my prosperity, I was as a tabret, *deliciæ humani generis—the darling of the human race.*

3. He was a man of sorrows, *v.* 7. He wept so much that he had almost lost his sight: *My eye is dim by reason of sorrow,* ch. xvi. 16. He had become a perfect skeleton. "*All my members are as a shadow.* I am not to be called a man, but the *shadow of a man.*"

II. The ill use which his friends made of his miseries. They condemned him as a hypocrite, because he was thus grievously afflicted.

1. Job looks upon himself as basely abused by them. "They are *mockers,* who deride my calamities, because I am thus brought low." They had all promised him that he would be happy if he would take their advice. Now all this he looked upon as flattery, and as designed to vex him so much the more. All this he calls their *provocation, v.* 2.

2. He condemns it. It was a sign that *God had hidden their heart from understanding* (*v.* 4). Those that are void of compassion are so far void of understanding. Where there is not the tenderness of a man one may question whether there be the understanding of a man. *Therefore shalt thou not exalt them.* Those are certainly kept back from honour whose hearts are hidden from understanding. He that thus violates the sacred laws of friendship forfeits the benefit of it, not only for himself, but for his posterity: "*Even the eyes of his children shall fail,* and, when they look for succour and comfort from their own and their father's friends, they shall look in vain as I have done, and be as much disappointed as I am in you." Those that wrong their neighbours may thereby, in the end, wrong their own children.

3. He appeals from them to God (*v.* 3): *Lay down now, put me in a surety with thee.* Those whose hearts condemn them not have confidence towards God, and can with humble and believing boldness beg of him to search and try them. Our English annotations give this reading of the verse: "*Appoint, I pray thee, my surety with thee,* namely, Christ who is with thee in heaven." "Who dares then contend with me? Who shall lay anything to my charge if Christ be an advocate for me?" Rom. viii. 32, 33.

III. The good use which the righteous should make of Job's afflictions from God, from his enemies, and from his friends, *v.* 8, 9. They are *upright men,* honest and sincere, and that act from a steady principle, with a single eye. This was Job's own character (*ch.* i. 1), and probably he speaks of such upright men especially as had been his intimates and associates. They are *the innocent,* not perfectly so, but innocence is what they aim at and press towards. Sincerity is evangelical innocency. They have *clean hands,* kept clean from the gross pollutions of sin, and, when spotted with infirmities, *washed with innocency,* Ps. xxvi. 6. Job's troubles will amaze them: *Upright men shall be astonished at this;* they will wonder to hear that so good a man as Job should be so grievously afflicted in body, name, and estate, that God should lay his hand so heavily upon him, and that his friends, who ought to have comforted him, should add to his grief. They would hereby be animated to confront the corrupt and pernicious inferences which evil men would draw from Job's sufferings, as that God has forsaken the earth, that it is in vain to serve him, and the like. The boldness of the attacks which profane people make upon religion should sharpen the courage and resolution of its friends and advocates. When vice is daring it is no time for virtue, through fear, to hide itself. *The righteous*, instead of drawing back at this frightful spectacle, *shall* with so much the more constancy and resolution *hold on his way* and press forward. Those who keep their eye upon heaven as their end will keep their feet in the paths of religion as their way, whatever difficulties and discouragements they meet with in it. By the sight of other good men's trials, and the experience of his own, he will be made more vigorous and lively in his duty, more warm and affectionate, more resolute and undaunted. The blustering wind makes the traveller gather his cloak the closer about him and gird it the faster.

Verses 10-16

Job's friends had pretended to comfort him with the hopes of his return to a prosperous estate.

I. It was their folly to talk so (*v.* 10): "*Return, and come now*, be convinced that you are in an error, and let me persuade you to be of my mind; *for I cannot find one wise man among you*, that knows how to explain the difficulties of God's providence or how to apply the consolations of his promises." It is our wisdom to comfort ourselves, and others, in distress, with that which will not fail, the promise of God, his love and grace, and a well-grounded hope of eternal life.

II. It would be his folly to heed them.

1. All his measures were already broken and he was full of confusion, *v.* 11, 12. He had had thoughts about enlarging his border, increasing his stock, and settling his children, and many pious thoughts, it is likely, of promoting religion in his country, but he concluded that all these thoughts of his heart were now at an end, and that he should never have the satisfaction of seeing his designs effected. But, if with full purpose of heart we cleave to the Lord, death will not break off that purpose. Job was under a constant uneasiness (*v.* 12): *The thoughts of his heart being broken, they changed the night into day and shortened the light.*

2. All his expectations from this world would very shortly be buried in the grave with him; so that it was a jest for him to think of such mighty things as they had flattered him with the hopes of, *ch.* v. 19, viii. 21; xi. 17. "Alas! you do but make a fool of me." He endeavours not only to reconcile himself to the grave, but to recommend it to himself: "It is my house." The grave is a house; to the wicked it is a prison-house (*ch.* xxiv. 19, 20); to the godly it is *Bethabara, a passage-house* in their way home. "There," says he, "*I have made my bed*." The grave is a bed, for we shall rest in it in the evening of our day on earth, and rise from it in the morning of our everlasting day, Isa. lvii. 2. Let this make good people willing to die; it is but going to bed; they are weary and sleepy, and it is time that they were in their beds. Why should they not go willingly, when their father calls? He saw all his hopes from this world dropping into the grave with him (*v.* 15, 16): "Seeing I must shortly leave the world, *where is now my hope?* How can I expect to prosper who do not expect to live?" He is not hopeless, but his hope is not where they would have it be. "No, that hope which I comfort myself with is something out of sight, not things that are seen, that are temporal, but things not seen, that are eternal."

Chapter 18

In this chapter Bildad makes a second assault upon Job. In his first discourse (ch. viii) he had given him encouragement to hope that all should yet be well with him. He has grown more peevish, and is so far from being convinced by Job's reasonings that he is but more exasperated. I. He sharply reproves Job as haughty and passionate, and obstinate in his opinion, ver. 1-4. II. He enlarges upon the doctrine he had before maintained, concerning the misery of wicked people, ver. 5-21. In this he seems to have an eye to Job's complaints of the miserable condition he was in. "This," says Bildad, "is the condition of a wicked man; and therefore thou art one."

Verses 1-4

Bildad shoots his arrows, even bitter words, against poor Job, little thinking that, though he was a wise and good man, in this instance he was serving Satan's design in adding to Job's affliction.

I. He charges him with idle endless talk, as Eliphaz had done (*ch.* xv. 2, 3): *How long will it be ere you make an end of words? v.* 2. Bildad was weary of hearing others speak, and impatient till it came to his turn. How unbecoming this conduct is in others everyone can see; but few that are guilty of it can see it in themselves. Time was when Job had the last word in all debates (*ch.* xxix. 22): *After my words they spoke not again.* Then he was in power and prosperity; but now that he was impoverished and brought low he could scarcely be allowed to speak at all.

II. With a regardlessness of what was said to him, intimated in that, *Mark, and afterwards we will speak.*

III. With a haughty contempt and disdain of his friends and of that which they offered (*v.* 3): *Wherefore are we counted as beasts?* Job had indeed called them *mockers*, had represented them both as unwise and as unkind, but he did not count them beasts; yet Bildad so represents the matter. His hot spirit was willing to find a pretence to be hard upon Job. Those that incline to be severe upon others will have it thought that others have first been so upon them.

IV. With outrageous passion: *He teareth himself in his anger, v.* 4. Herein he seems to reflect upon what Job had said (*ch.* xiii. 14): *Wherefore do I take my flesh in my teeth?*

V. With a proud and arrogant expectation to give law even to Providence itself: "*Shall the earth be forsaken for thee?* There is no reason that the course of nature should be changed and the settled rules of government violated to gratify the humour of one man. Job, dost thou think the world cannot stand without thee; but that, if thou art ruined, all the world is ruined and forsaken with thee?" To expect that God's counsels should change, his method alter, and his word fail, to please us, is as absurd and unreasonable as to think that *the earth should be forsaken for us and the rock removed out of its place.*

Verses 5-10

The rest of Bildad's discourse is entirely taken up in an elegant description of the miserable condition of a wicked man, in which there is a great deal of truth. But it is not true that all wicked people are made miserable in this world; nor is it true that all who are brought into great distress are *therefore* to be deemed wicked men. Therefore, though Bildad thought the application of it to Job was easy, yet it was not safe nor just.

I. The destruction of the wicked foreseen and foretold, under the similitude of darkness (*v.* 5, 6): *Yea, the light of the wicked shall be put out.* "Yea," says Bildad, "so it is; thou art clouded, and straitened, and made miserable, and no better could be expected; for *the light of the wicked shall be put out*, and therefore thine shall."

II. The destruction represented under the similitude of a beast or bird caught in a snare, or a malefactor arrested and taken into custody in order to his punishment, *v.* 7–10. 1. Satan is preparing for his destruction. He is *the robber that shall prevail against him* (*v.* 9). He *hunts for the precious life.* 2. He is himself preparing for his own destruction by going on in sin, and *so treasuring up wrath against the day of wrath. His own counsels cast him down, v.* 7. He is *cast into a net by his own feet* (*v.* 8). 3. God is preparing for his destruction. The sinner is infatuated to run himself into the snare. *The steps of his strength,* his mighty designs and efforts, *shall be straitened,* so that he shall not compass what he intended; and the more he strives to extricate himself the more will he be entangled. *The gin shall take him by the heel.* He can no more escape the divine wrath that is in pursuit of him than a man, so held, can flee from the pursuer.

Verses 11–21

Bildad describes the destruction itself.

I. The dread of God's wrath (*v.* 11, 12): *Terror shall make him afraid on every side.* The terrors of the sinner's conscience shall haunt him, so that he shall never be easy. His feet will do him no service; they are fast in the snare, *v.* 9. He sees his ruin approaching. He feels himself utterly unable to grapple with it, either to escape it or to bear up under it.

II. Miserable indeed a wicked man's death is, how secure and jovial soever his life was. 1. See him dying, arrested by *the first-born of death*—some disease, or some stroke that has in it a more than ordinary resemblance of death itself. The harbingers of death *devour the strength of his skin,* bring rottenness into his bones and consume them. *His confidence shall then be rooted out of his tabernacle* (*v.* 14), that is, all that he trusted to for his support shall be taken from him. 2. See him dead. (1) He is then brought to *the king of terrors.* Death is terrible to nature; our Saviour himself prayed, *Father, save me from this hour.* But to the wicked it is in a special manner *the king of terrors.* How happy then are the saints, and how much indebted to the Lord Jesus, by whom death is so far abolished, and the property of it altered, that this king of terrors becomes a friend and servant! (2) He is then *driven from light into darkness* (*v.* 18), from the light of this world, and his prosperous condition in it, into darkness. (3) He is then *chased out of the world,* hurried and dragged away by the messengers of death, sorely against his will, chased as Adam out of paradise, for the world is his paradise. All the world is weary of him, and glad to get rid of him. This is death to a wicked man.

III. His family sunk and cut off, *v.* 15. Even the dwelling shall be ruined for the sake of its owner: *Brimstone shall be scattered upon his habitation,* rained upon it as upon Sodom, to the destruction of which this seems to have reference. Some think he here upbraids Job with the burning of his sheep and servants with fire from heaven. The reason is here given: *Because it is none of his;* that is, it was unjustly got. His children shall perish, either with him or after him, *v.* 16. Those who consult the true honour of their family, and the welfare of its branches, will be afraid of withering it by sin. The extirpation of the sinner's family is mentioned again (*v.* 19): *He shall neither have son nor nephew.* Sin entails a curse upon posterity. It is probable that Bildad reflects upon the death of Job's children and servants, as a further proof of his being a wicked man.

IV. His memory buried with him, or made odious; he shall either be forgotten or spoken of with dishonour (*v.* 17): *His remembrance shall perish from the earth.* All his honour shall be lost in the dust, so that *he shall have no name in the street,* departing without being desired.

V. Amazement at his fall, *v.* 20. Those that see it are affrighted. Horrible sins bring strange punishments. Ignorance of God is a wilful ignorance, for there is that to be known of him which is sufficient to leave them for ever inexcusable. They know not God, and then they commit all iniquity.

CHAPTER 19

Job's answer to Bildad's discourse. Though his spirit was grieved and Bildad was very peevish, yet he gave him leave to say all he designed to say, but, when he had done, he gave him a fair answer, in which, I. He complains of unkind usage. And very unkindly he takes it. 1. That his comforters added to his affliction, ver. 2–7. 2. That his God was the author of his afflictions, ver. 8–12. 3. That his relations and friends were strange to him, and shy of him, in his affliction, ver. 13–19. 4. That he had no compassion shown him in his affliction, ver. 20–22. II. He comforts himself with the believing hopes of happiness in the other world though he had so little comfort in this, making a very solemn confession of his faith, with a desire that it might be recorded as an evidence of his sincerity, ver. 23–27. III. He concludes with a caution to his friends not to persist in their hard censures of him, ver. 28, 29. His cheerful views of the future state may shame us Christians, and may serve to silence our complaints, or at least to balance them.

Verses 1–7

Bildad had twice begun with a *How long* (ch. viii. 2; xviii. 2), and therefore Job begins with a *How long* too, *v.* 2. Job had more reason to think those long who assaulted him than they had to think him long who only vindicated himself.

I. They *vexed his soul.* They were his friends; they came to comfort him, but with a great deal of gravity, and affectation of wisdom and piety, they set themselves to rob him of the only comfort he had now left him in a good God, a good conscience, and a good name; and this vexed him to the heart. They *broke him in pieces with words.* They *reproached him* (*v.* 3), gave him a bad character and *made themselves strange to him,* were shy of him now that he was in his troubles, and seemed as if they did not know him. They *magnified themselves against him* (*v.* 5), not only looked shy of him, but insulted him, magnifying themselves to depress him. *They pleaded against him his reproach,* that is, they made use of his affliction as an argument to prove him a wicked man.

II. They had thus abused him often (*v.* 3): *These ten times you have reproached me,* that is, very often. They were not ashamed of what they did, *v.* 3. They had reason to be ashamed of their hard-heartedness, of their uncharitableness, and of their deceitfulness, so ill becoming friends.

III. He answers their harsh censures, by showing them that what they condemned was capable of excuse, which they ought to have considered. The errors of his judgment were excusable (*v.* 4): "*Be it indeed that I have erred,* that I am in the wrong through ignorance or mistake." "But be it so," said Job, "*my error remaineth with myself,*" that is, "I speak according to the best of my judgment, with all sincerity, and not from a spirit of contradiction." *Hast thou faith? Have it to thyself.* Some give this sense of these words: "If I be in an error, it is I that must smart for it; and therefore you need not concern yourselves." The breakings out of his passion, though not justifiable, yet were excusable, considering the vastness of his grief and the extremity of his misery. *Know then that God has overthrown me, v.* 6. Three things he would have them consider:—(1) He was overthrown, and could not help himself, enclosed as in a net, and could not get out. (2) God was the author of it, and that, in it, he fought against him. "I have enough to do to grapple with God's displeasure; let me not have yours also." (3) He could not obtain any hope of the redress of his grievances, *v.* 7. *I cry out of wrong, but I am not heard.*

Verses 8–22

Bildad had perverted Job's complaints by making them the description of the miserable condition of a wicked man; and yet he repeats them here, to move their pity, if they had any left in them.

I. He complains of the tokens of God's displeasure. "*He hath kindled his wrath against me*, which burns and pains me," *v.* 11. Enlightened consciences fear it now, but shall not feel it hereafter. Job's present apprehension was that *God counted him as one of his enemies*; and yet, at the same time, God loved him as his faithful friend. It is a gross mistake, but a very common one, to think that whom God afflicts he treats as his enemies; whereas, on the contrary, *as many as he loves he rebukes and chastens*; it is the discipline of his sons. "*He has stripped me of my glory*, my wealth, honour, power, and all the opportunity I had of doing good. My children were my glory, but I have lost them; and whatever was a crown to my head he has taken it from me, and has laid all my honour in the dust." Did he look down upon his present troubles? He saw God giving them their commission, and their orders to attack him. They are *his troops*, that act by his direction, which *encamp against me, v.* 12. It did not so much trouble him that his miseries came upon him in troops as that they were *God's* troops in whom it seemed as if God fought against him and intended his destruction. Time was when God's hosts encamped round him for safety. Now they surrounded him and *destroyed him on every side, v.* 10. He saw the hand of God cutting off all hope (*v.* 8): "*He hath fenced up my way, that I cannot pass.* I have now no way left to help myself." Hope in this life is a perishing thing, but the hope of good men, when it is cut off from this world, is but removed like a tree, transplanted from this nursery to the garden of the Lord. We shall have no reason to complain if God thus remove our hopes from the sand to the rock, from things temporal to things eternal.

II. He complains of the unkindness of his relations and of all his old acquaintance. In this also he owns the hand of God (*v.* 13): *He has put my brethren far from me*, that is, "He has laid those afflictions upon me which frighten them from me, and make them stand aloof from my sores." Yet this does not excuse Job's relations and friends from the guilt of horrid ingratitude and injustice to him. His kindred and acquaintance, his neighbours, and such as he had formerly been familiar with, who were bound by all the laws of friendship and civility, were *estranged from him, v.* 13. Poor Job was misused by his own family, and some of his worst foes were those of his own house. His own servants slighted him. His maids did not attend him in his illness, but *counted him for a stranger and an alien, v.* 15. Though he was now sickly, yet he was not cross and imperious, but entreated his servants with his mouth, when he had authority to command; and yet they would not be civil to him, neither kind nor just. But, one would think, when all forsook him, the wife of his bosom should have been tender of him: no, because he would not curse God and die, as she persuaded him, she did not care for coming near him, nor took any notice of what he said, *v.* 17. Even the little children who were born in his house, the children of his own servants, despised him (*v.* 18); they let him know that they neither feared him nor loved him.

III. He complains of the decay of his body; all the beauty and strength of that were gone (*v.* 20): *My bone cleaves now to my skin.*

IV. Upon all these accounts he recommends himself to the compassion of his friends. "*Have pity upon me, have pity upon me, O you my friends! Have pity upon me, for the hand of God hath touched me.*" If they would not ease his affliction by their pity, yet they must not be so barbarous as to add to it by their censures and reproaches (*v.* 22): "*Why do you persecute me as God?*" If they did delight in his

calamity, let them be satisfied with his flesh, which was wasted and gone, but let them not wound his spirit. Great tenderness is due to those that are in affliction, especially to those that are troubled in mind.

Verses 23-29

Here is much both of Christ and heaven in these verses: and he that said such things as these *declared plainly that he sought the better country, that is, the heavenly*; as the patriarchs of that age did, Heb. xi. 14. We have here Job's creed, or confession of faith. His belief in God the Father Almighty, the Maker of heaven and earth, and the principles of natural religion, he had often professed: but here we find him no stranger to revealed religion; though the revelation of the promised Seed, and the promised inheritance, was then discerned only like the dawning of the day, yet Job was taught of God to believe in a living Redeemer, and to *look for the resurrection of the dead and the life of the world to come*, for of these, doubtless, he must be understood to speak. These were the things he comforted himself with the expectation of, and not a deliverance from his trouble or a revival of his happiness in this world, as some would understand him. The expressions he here uses, of the Redeemer's *standing at the latter day upon the earth*, of his seeing God, and *seeing him for himself*, are wretchedly forced if they be understood of any temporal deliverance. Job was now under an extraordinary impulse of the blessed Spirit, which raised him above himself, gave him light, and gave him utterance. And some observe that, after this, we do not find in Job's discourses such passionate complaints of God and his providence as before. This hope quieted his spirit, stilled the storm, and, having here cast anchor within the veil, his mind was kept steady from this time forward.

I. Job makes this confession of his faith here. Never did anything come in more pertinently, or to better purpose. His friends reproached him as a hypocrite, but he appeals to his creed, to his faith, to his hope, and to his own conscience, which comforted him with the expectation of a blessed resurrection. *These are not the words of him that has a devil*. He appeals to the coming of the Redeemer, from this wrangle at the bar to the judgment of the bench. Job was now afflicted, and this was his cordial; when he was pressed above measure this kept him from fainting—he believed that he should *see the goodness of the Lord in the land of the living*; not in this world, for that is the land of the dying.

II. With what a solemn preface he introduces it, *v.* 23, 24. He breaks off his complaints abruptly, to triumph in his comforts. That which Job here somewhat passionately wished for God graciously granted him. His words are written; they are printed in God's book; so that, wherever that book is read, there shall this be told for a memorial concerning Job.

III. His confession itself is written, *v.* 25-27.

1. He believes the glory of the Redeemer (*v.* 25): *I know that my Redeemer liveth*, that he is in being and is my life, *and that he shall stand at last upon the earth*. There is a Redeemer provided for fallen man, and Jesus Christ is that Redeemer. The word is *Goël* which is used for the next of kin, to whom, by the law of Moses, the right of redeeming a mortgaged estate did belong, Lev. xxv. 25. Our heavenly inheritance was mortgaged by sin; we are ourselves utterly unable to redeem it; Christ is near of kin to us, the next kinsman that is able to redeem; he has paid our debt, satisfied God's justice for sin, and so has taken off the mortgage and made a new settlement of the inheritance. Our persons also want a Redeemer; we are sold for sin, and sold under sin; our Lord Jesus has wrought out a redemption for us, and proclaims redemption to us, and so he is truly the Redeemer.

Because he lives we shall live also, John xiv. 19. When Job had lost all his wealth and all his friends, yet he was not separated from Christ, nor cut off from his relation to him: "Still he is my Redeemer." That next kinsman adhered to him when all his other kindred forsook him, and he had the comfort of it. *I know* (observe with what an air of assurance he speaks it, as one confident of this very thing), *I know that my Redeemer lives*.

2. He believes the happiness of the redeemed, and his own title to that happiness. He counts upon the corrupting of his body in the grave, and speaks of it with a holy carelessness and unconcernedness: *Though, after my skin they destroy this body*. Job mentions this, that the glory of the resurrection he believed and hoped for might shine the more brightly. The same power that made man's body at first, out of common dust, can raise it out of its own dust. He comforts himself with the hopes of happiness on the other side death and the grave: *After I shall awake* (so the margin reads it), *though this body be destroyed, yet out of my flesh shall I see God*. Soul and body shall come together again. That body which must be destroyed in the grave shall be raised again, a glorious body, *Yet in my flesh I shall see God*. Job speaks of seeing him with eyes of flesh, *in my flesh, with my eyes*; the same body that died shall rise again, a glorified body, a *spiritual body*, 1 Cor. xv. 44. ' Job and God shall come together again: *In my flesh shall I see God. My eyes shall behold him, and not another.*

IV. His creed spoke comfort to himself, but warning and terror to those that set themselves against him. It was a word of caution to them not to proceed and persist in their unkind usage of him, *v.* 28. A living, quickening, commanding, principle of grace in the heart, is the root of the matter, as necessary to our religion as the root to the tree. Love to God and our brethren, faith in Christ, hatred of sin—these are the root of the matter; other things are but leaves in comparison with these. Serious godliness is the one thing needful. We are to believe that many have the root of the matter in them who are not in everything of our mind—who have their follies, and weaknesses, and mistakes—and to conclude that it is at our peril if we persecute any such. Job and his friends differed in some notions concerning the methods of Providence, but they agreed in the root of the matter, the belief of another world. Good men need to be frightened from sin by the terrors of the Almighty, particularly from the sin of rashly judging their brethren, Matt. vii. 1; James iii. 1.

CHAPTER 20

One would have thought that such an excellent confession of faith as Job made would satisfy his friends, but they do not seem to have taken any notice of it, and therefore Zophar attacks him with as much vehemence as before. I. His preface is short, but hot, ver. 2, 3. II. His discourse is long, and all upon one subject, the certain misery of wicked people and the ruin that awaits them. 1. He asserts, in general, that the prosperity of a wicked person is short, and his ruin sure, ver. 4–9. 2. He proves the misery of his condition by many instances—that he should have a diseased body, a troubled conscience, a ruined estate, a beggared family, an infamous name, and that he himself should perish under the weight of divine wrath, ver. 10–29. But the great mistake was that he imagined God never varied from this method, and therefore Job was, without doubt, a very bad man.

Verses 1–9

Here, I. Zophar begins very passionately (*v.* 2): *Therefore do my thoughts cause me to answer.* He takes no notice of what Job had said to move their pity. He excuses his haste with two things:—1. That Job had given him a strong provocation (*v.* 3): "I *have heard the check of my reproach.*" Job's friends, I doubt, had spirits too high to deal with a man in his low condition; and high spirits are impatient of contradiction. They cannot bear a check but they

call it *the check of their reproach*. 2. That his own heart caused him to answer (*v.* 2), for *out of the abundance of the heart the mouth speaks*; but he fathers the instigation (*v.* 3) upon *the spirit of his understanding*.

II. Zophar proceeds to show the ruin and destruction of wicked people, insinuating that because Job was destroyed and ruined he was certainly a wicked man.

1. He appeals, (1) To Job's own knowledge and conviction: "*Knowest thou not this?*" (2) To the experience of all ages. It was known of old that the sin of sinners will be their ruin.

2. It is laid down (*v.* 5): *The triumphing of the wicked is short, and the joy of the hypocrite but for a moment*. Job's friends were loth to own, at first, that wicked people might prosper at all (*ch.* iv. 9), until Job proved it plainly (*ch.* ix. 24; xii. 6), and now Zophar yields it; but lays it down that they will not prosper long.

3. It is illustrated, *v.* 6–9. (1) He supposes his prosperity to be very high, as high as you can imagine, *v.* 6. (2) He is confident that his ruin will accordingly be very great, and his fall the more dreadful for his having risen so high: *He shall perish for ever*, *v.* 7.

Verses 10–22

The instances of the miserable condition of the wicked man in this world are expressed with great fulness.

I. What his wickedness is for which he is punished.

1. The lusts of the flesh, here called *the sins of his youth* (*v.* 11). The forbidden pleasures of sense are said to be *sweet in his mouth* (*v.* 12); he indulges himself in all the gratifications of the carnal appetite, as yielding the satisfaction which *he hides under his tongue*, as the most dainty delicate thing that can be. *He keeps it still within his mouth* (*v.* 13); let him have that, and he desires no more. Or his hiding it and keeping it under his tongue denotes his industrious concealment of his beloved lust.

2. The love of the world and the wealth of it. *He has swallowed down riches* as eagerly as ever a hungry man swallowed down meat. It is that which he desired (*v.* 20). It is *that which he laboured for* (*v.* 18), all ways and methods, *per fas, per nefas*—right or wrong, to be rich. We must *labour*, not *to be rich* (Prov. xxiii. 4), but to be charitable, *that we may have to give* (Eph. iv. 28), not to spend. He expected rivers of sensual delights.

3. Violence and oppression, and injustice in his poor neighbours, *v.* 19. It is charged upon this wicked man, that *he has forsaken the poor*. He has *oppressed* them. He has *violently taken away their houses*.

II. His punishment for this wickedness. *He shall never see the rivers, the floods, the brooks of honey and butter*, with which he hoped to glut himself. The enjoyment sinks far below the raised expectation. He shall be diseased and distempered in his body; and how little comfort a man has in riches if he has not health! The sins of his youth shall *lie down with him in the dust*. He shall be disquieted and troubled in his mind: *Surely he shall not feel quietness in his belly*, *v.* 20. Let none expect to enjoy that comfortably which they have gotten unjustly. Even that wickedness which was sweet in the commission, and was rolled under the tongue as a delicate morsel, becomes bitter in the reflection, and, when it is reviewed, fills him with horror and vexation. It is turned into *the gall of asps*, than which nothing is more bitter, *the poison of asps* (*v.* 16), than which nothing more fatal, and so it will be to him. *In the fulness of his sufficiency*, when he thinks himself most sure of the continuance of his happiness, *he shall be in straits*, through the anxieties and perplexities of his own mind. He shall be dispossessed of his estate; that shall sink and dwindle away to nothing, so that *he shall not rejoice therein, v.* 18. *His children shall seek to please the poor,* while his own hands shall restore them their goods with shame (*v.* 18). Thus, *he shall not save of that which he desired* (*v.* 20), not only he shall not save it all, but he shall save nothing of it. In all this Zophar reflects upon Job, who had lost all and was reduced to the last extremity.

Verses 23–29

Zophar here comes to show their utter ruin at last.

I. Their ruin will take its rise from God's wrath and vengeance, *v.* 23. *God shall cast the fury of his wrath upon him and rain it upon him.* Every word here speaks terror. There is no fence against this, but in Christ, who is the only covert from the storm and tempest, Isa. xxxii. 2. Perhaps Zophar here reflects on the death of Job's children when they were eating and drinking.

II. Their ruin will be inevitable (*v.* 24). *He shall flee from the iron weapon.* If he escape the sword, yet *the bow of steel shall strike him through.*

III. It will be a total terrible ruin. O what *terrors are upon him*!

IV. Sometimes it is a ruin that comes upon him insensibly, *v.* 26. 1. The darkness he is wrapped up in is a hidden darkness, and it is *hid in his secret place,* whither he has retreated and where he hopes to shelter himself; he never retires into his own conscience but he finds himself in the dark and utterly at a loss. He is wasted by a soft gentle fire—the fire needs no blowing, and that is his case; he is ripe for ruin.

V. It is a ruin, not only to himself, but to his family: *It shall go ill with him that is left in his tabernacle,* for the curse shall reach him, and he shall be cut off. *His goods shall flow away* from his family as fast as ever they flowed into it.

VI. It is a ruin which will manifestly appear to be just and righteous, and what he has brought upon himself by his own wickedness; for (*v.* 27) *the heaven shall reveal his iniquity.*

VII. Zophar concludes like an orator (*v.* 29): *This is the portion of a wicked man from God.* Never was any doctrine better explained, or worse applied, than this by Zophar, who intended by all this to prove Job a hypocrite. Let us receive the good explication, and make a better application.

CHAPTER 21

Job's reply to Zophar's discourse, in which he complains less of his own miseries than he had done in his former discourses, and comes closer to the general question that was in dispute between him and them, Whether outward prosperity, and the continuance of it, were a mark of the true church and the true members of it, so that the ruin of a man's prosperity is sufficient to prove him a hypocrite, though no other evidence appear against him: this they asserted, but Job denied. I. His preface here is designed for the moving of their affections, that he might gain their attention, ver. 1–6. II. His discourse is designed for the convincing of their judgments and the rectifying of their mistakes. He owns that God does sometimes hang up a wicked man as it were in chains, in terrorem—as a terror to others, but denies that he always does so; nay, he maintains that commonly he does otherwise, suffering even the worst of sinners to live all their days in prosperity and to go out of the world without any visible mark of his wrath upon them. 1. He describes the great prosperity of wicked people, ver. 7–13. 2. He shows their great impiety, in which they are hardened by their prosperity, ver. 14–16. 3. He foretells their ruin at length, but after a long reprieve, ver. 17–21. 4. He observes a very great variety in the ways of God's providence towards men, even towards bad men, ver. 22–26. 5. He overthrows the ground of their severe censures of him, by showing that the destruction of the wicked is reserved for the other world, and that they often escape to the last in this world (ver. 27, to the end), and in this Job was clearly in the right.

Verses 1–6

Job here recommends himself to the compassionate consideration of his friends. That which he entreats of them is very fair, that they would suffer him to speak (*v.* 3) and not break in upon him. They came to comfort him. "Now," says he, "*let this be to your consolations* (*v.* 2); if you have no other comforts to administer to me, be so just, as to give me a patient hearing. After I have spoken you may go on with what you have to say, and I will not hinder you, no, though you go on to mock me. If you will but give me a fair hearing, I believe I shall say that which will change your note and make you pity me rather than mock me. *Is my complaint to man?* No, if it were I see it would be to little purpose to complain. But my complaint is to God, and to him do I appeal. Let him be Judge between you and me." It was not a common case, but a very extraordinary one. He himself was amazed at it. "*When I remember* that terrible day in which I was on a sudden stripped of all my comforts, that day in which I was stricken with sore boils,—when I remember all the hard speeches with which you have grieved me,—I confess *I am afraid, and trembling takes hold of my flesh,* especially when I compare this with the prosperous condition of many wicked people, and the applauses of their neighbours, with which they pass through the world."

Verses 7–16

All Job's three friends, in their last discourses, had been very copious in describing the miserable condition of a wicked man in this world. "It is true," says Job, "remarkable judgments are sometimes brought upon notorious sinners, but not always; for we have many instances of the great and long prosperity of those that are openly and avowedly wicked; though they are hardened in their wickedness by their prosperity, yet they are still suffered to prosper."

I. He here describes their prosperity in the height, and breadth, and length of it. They live, and are not suddenly cut off by the strokes of divine vengeance. Not only do they live but they *live in prosperity,* 1 Sam. xxv. 6. They are *mighty in power,* are preferred to places of authority and trust. This is the day of God's patience, and, in some way or other, he makes use of their prosperity to serve his own counsels, while it ripens them for ruin. *Their seed is established in their sight.* They are easy and quiet, *v.* 9. Whereas Zophar had spoken of their continual frights and terrors, Job says, *Their houses are safe* both from danger and from the fear of it (*v.* 9). They are rich and thrive in their estates. Of this he gives only one instance, *v.* 10. They are merry and live a jovial life (*v.* 11, 12).

II. He shows how they abuse their prosperity and are confirmed and hardened by it in their impiety, *v.* 14, 15. God suffers them to prosper; but let us not wonder at it, for *the prosperity of fools destroy them,* by hardening them in sin, Prov. i. 32; Ps. lxxiii. 7–9. How light these prospering sinners make of God and religion, as if because they have so much of this world they had no need to look after another. How ill affected they are to God and religion; they abandon them, and cast off the thoughts of them. The world is the portion they have chosen, and take up with, and think themselves happy in; while they have that they can live without God. *We desire not the knowledge of thy ways.* The two great bonds by which we are drawn and held to religion are those of duty and interest. They will not believe it is their duty to be religious: *What is the Almighty, that we should serve him?* How slightly they speak of God: *What is the Almighty?* As if he were a mere name. How hardly they speak of religion. They call it a *service* which they look upon as a task and drudgery. How highly they speak of themselves: "*That we should serve him;* we who are rich and mighty in power, shall we be subject and accountable to him? No, we are lords," Jer. ii. 31. They will not believe it is their interest to be religious: *What profit shall we have if we pray unto him?* Is nothing to be called gain but the wealth and honour of this world? If we obtain the favour of God, and spiritual and eternal blessings, we have no reason to complain of losing by our religion.

III. He shows their folly herein, and utterly disclaims all concurrence with them (*v.* 19): *Lo, their good is not in their hand,* that is, they did not get it without God, and therefore they are very ungrateful to slight him thus. It was *not their might, nor the power of their hand,* that got them this wealth, and therefore they ought to remember God who gave it them. Nor can they keep it without God, and therefore they are very unwise to lose their interest in him and bid him to depart from them. Some give this sense of it: "Their good is in their barns and their bags, hoarded up there; it is not in their hand, to do good to others with it; and then what good does it do them? Therefore," says Job, "*the counsel of the wicked is far from me.* Far be it from me that I should be of their mind, say as they say, do as they do, and take my measures from them. Their *posterity approve their sayings,* though *their way* be *their folly* (Ps. xlix. 13); but I know better things than to walk in their counsel."

Verses 17-26

Job had described the prosperity of wicked people; now,

I. He opposes this to what his friends had maintained concerning their certain ruin in this life. "Tell me *how often* do you see *the candle of the wicked put out?* Do you not as often see it burnt down to the socket, until it goes out of itself? *v.* 17. How often do you see *their destruction come upon them,* or *God distributing sorrows in his anger* among them? Do you not as often see their mirth and prosperity continuing to the last?"

II. He reconciles this to the holiness and justice of God. Though wicked people prosper thus all their days, they are *as stubble and chaff before the stormy wind, v.* 18. They are light and worthless, and of no account either with God or with wise and good men. They are fitted to destruction, and continually lie exposed to it, and in the height of their pomp and power there is but a step between them and ruin. Though they prosper in this world, yet they shall be reckoned with in another world. He shall know it (*v.* 20): *His eyes shall see his destruction* which he would not be persuaded to believe. They *will not see, but they shall see,* Isa. xxvi. 11. The eyes that have been wilfully shut against the grace of God shall be opened to see his destruction. *What pleasure has he in his house after him? v.* 21. Little will the gain of the world profit him that has lost his soul.

III. He resolves this difference which Providence makes between one wicked man and another into the wisdom and sovereignty of God (*v.* 22): *Shall any pretend to teach God knowledge?* Shall we take upon us to tell God how he should govern the world, what sinner he should spare and whom he should punish? So vast is the disproportion between time and eternity that, if hell be the lot of every sinner at last, it makes little difference if one goes singing thither and another sighing. One dies suddenly, *in his full strength,* not weakened by age or sickness (*v.* 23), *being wholly at ease and quiet,* under no apprehension at all of the approach of death, nor in any fear of it; but, on the contrary, because *his breasts are full of milk and his bones moistened with marrow* (*v.* 24), that is, he is healthful and vigorous, and of a good constitution, he counts upon nothing but to live many years in mirth and pleasure. Yet he is cut off in a moment by the stroke of death. Another dies slowly, and with a great deal of previous pain and misery (*v.* 23), *in the bitterness of his soul,* such as poor Job was himself now in, *and never eats with pleasure,* through sickness, or age, or sorrow of mind.

Verses 27-34

I. Job opposes the opinion of his friends, that the wicked are sure to fall into such visible ruin as Job had now fallen into, upon which principle they condemned Job as a wicked man. "*I know your thoughts,*" says Job (*v.* 27), "*and the devices which you wrongfully imagine against* my comfort and honour: and how can such men be convinced?" Job's friends were ready to say, "*Where is the house of the prince? (v.* 28). Where is Job's house, or the house of his eldest son, in which his children were feasting? Enquire into the circumstances of Job's house and family, and then ask, *Where are the dwelling-places of the wicked?* and you will soon see that Job's house is in the same predicament with the houses of tyrants and oppressors."

II. He lays down his own judgment to the contrary. He is willing to refer the cause to the next man that comes by (*v.* 29): "*Have you not asked those that go by the way.* Turn to which you will, and you will find them all of my mind, that the punishment of sinners is designed more for the other world than for this. *Do you not know the tokens* of this truth?"

1. What is it that Job here asserts? Two things:— (1) That impenitent sinners will certainly be punished in the other world. (2) That therefore we are not to think it strange if they prosper greatly in this world. *Therefore* they are spared now, because they are to be punished then. The sinner is here supposed to be the terror of the wise and good, whom he keeps in such awe that none dares *declare his way to his face, v.* 31. None will take the liberty to reprove him. And, if none dares declare his way to his face, much less dare any repay him what he has done and make him refund what he has obtained by injustice. But there is a day coming when those shall be told of their faults. and those who would not repay the wrongs they had done shall have them repaid to them. He must die; but everything you can think of shall be done to take off the reproach of death. He shall have a splendid funeral—a poor thing for any man to be proud of the prospect of; yet with some it passes for a mighty thing. Well, *he shall be brought to the grave* in state. He shall have a stately monument erected over him. *He shall remain in the tomb* with a *Hic jacet—Here lies,* over him, and a large encomium. *The clods of the valley shall be sweet to him;* there shall be as much done as can be to take off the noisomeness of the grave. But it is all a jest; what is the light, or what the perfume, to a man that is dead? It shall be alleged, for the lessening of the disgrace of death, that it is the common lot: He has only yielded to fate, *and every man shall draw after him, as there are innumerable before him.*

2. From all this Job infers the impertinency of their discourses, *v.* 34. They went upon a wrong hypothesis: "*In your answers there remains falsehood.*" "*You comfort me in vain.*" Where there is not truth there is little comfort to be expected.

CHAPTER 22

Eliphaz here leads on a third attack upon poor Job, in which Bildad followed him, but Zophar drew back, and quitted the field. In this chapter, I. Eliphaz checks him for his complaints of God, and of his dealings with him, as if he thought God had done him wrong, ver. 2-4. II. He charges him with many high crimes and misdemeanours, for which he supposes God was now punishing him. 1. Oppression and injustice, ver. 5-11. 2. Atheism and infidelity, ver. 12-14. III. He compares his case to that of the old world, ver. 15-20. IV. He gives him very good counsel, assuring him that, if he could take it, God would return in mercy to him and he should return to his former prosperity, ver. 21-30.

Verses 1-4

What Eliphaz says here is unjustly applied to Job, but in itself it is very true and good,

I. That when God does us good it is not because he is indebted to us. Eliphaz here shows that the righteousness and perfection of the best man in the world are no real benefit or advantage to God, and therefore cannot be thought to merit anything from him. The gains of religion are infinitely greater than the losses of it, and so it will appear when they are balanced. But can a man be thus profitable to God? No, for such is the perfection of God that he cannot receive any benefit or advantage by men; what can be added to that which is infinite? *Is it any gain to him,* any real addition to his glory or wealth, *if we make our way perfect?* God has indeed expressed himself in his word well pleased with the righteous; his countenance beholds them and his delight is in them and their prayers; but all that adds nothing to the infinite satisfaction which the Eternal Mind has in itself.

II. That when God restrains or rebukes us it is not because he is in danger from us, or jealous of us (*v.* 4): "*Will he reprove thee for fear of thee.*" Satan indeed suggested to our first parents that God forbade them the tree of knowledge, for fear of them, lest they should be as gods, and so become rivals with him; but it was a base insinuation. God rebukes the good because he loves them, but he never rebukes the great because he fears them.

Verses 5–14

Eliphaz and his companions had condemned Job, in general, as a wicked man and a hypocrite. Eliphaz here positively and expressly charges him with many high crimes and misdemeanours. "Come," says Eliphaz, "we have been too long beating about the bush, too tender of Job. It is high time to deal plainly with him. We must plainly tell him, *Thou art the man,* the tyrant, the oppressor, the atheist, we have been speaking of all this while. *Is not thy wickedness great?* Certainly it is, or else thy troubles would not be so great." For aught I know, Eliphaz, in accusing Job falsely, as he does here, was guilty of as great a sin and as great a wrong to Job as the Sabeans and Chaldeans that robbed him; for a man's good name is more precious and valuable than his wealth. Eliphaz could produce no instances of Job's guilt in any of the particulars that follow here, but seems resolved to calumniate boldly, and throw all the reproach he could on Job, not doubting but that some would cleave to him. Job, whom God himself praised as the best man in the world, is here represented by one of his friends, and he a wise and good man too, as one of the greatest villains in nature.

I. He charges him with oppression and injustice, that, when he was in prosperity, he not only did no good with his wealth and power, but did a great deal of hurt with them. This was utterly false, as appears by the account Job gives of himself (*ch.* xxix. 12, &c.) and the character God gave of him, *ch.* i. He tells him he had been cruel and unmerciful to the poor. *Thou hast taken a pledge from thy brother for nought,* or, as the LXX. read it, *Thou hast taken thy brethren for pledges,* and that for nought, imprisoned them, enslaved them, because they had nothing to pay,— that he had taken the very clothes of his insolvent tenants and debtors, so that he had *stripped them naked.* He had not been charitable to the poor: "*Thou hast not given* so much as a cup of cold *water to the weary to drink,* nay, *thou hast withholden bread from the hungry* in their extremity. Poor widows thou hast sent away empty from thy doors with a sad heart, *v.* 9. Those who came to thee for justice, thou didst send away unheard, unhelped; and, worst of all, *the arms of the fatherless have been broken*; those that could help themselves but little thou hast quite disabled to help themselves." This, which is the blackest part of the charge, is but insinuated: *The arms of the fatherless have been broken.* "They have been broken by those under thee, and thou hast connived at it, which brings thee under the guilt." He had been partial to the rich and great (*v.* 8): "The poor were not fed at thy door, while the rich were feasted at thy table." He attributes all his present troubles to these supposed sins (*v.* 10, 11). "*Snares are round about thee,* and others are as hard upon thee as thou hast been upon the poor. No sin makes a louder cry there than unmercifulness; and, accordingly, *sudden fear troubles thee.*" Those that have not shown mercy may justly be denied the comfortable hope that they shall find mercy; and then what can they expect but snares, and darkness, and continual fear?

II. He charges him with atheism, infidelity, and gross impiety; he that did not fear God did not regard men. He would have it thought that Job was an Epicurean, who did indeed own the being of God, but denied his providence.

1. Eliphaz referred to an important truth, which he thought, if Job had duly considered it, would have prevented him from being so passionate in his complaints and bold in justifying himself (*v.* 12): *Is not God in the height of heaven?* There he is pleased to manifest himself in a way peculiar to the upper world, and thence he is pleased to manifest himself in a way suited to this lower world. When we *behold the height of the stars, how high they are,* we should, at the same time, also consider the transcendant majesty of God, who is above the stars, and how high he is.

2. He charged it upon Job that he made a bad use of this doctrine, which he might have made so good a use of, *v.* 13. "This is *holding the truth in unrighteousness*; thou art willing to own that *God is in the height of heaven* but thence thou inferrest, *How doth God know?*" Eliphaz suspected that Job had such a notion of God as this, that, because he is in the height of heaven, it is therefore impossible for him to see and hear what is done at so great a distance as this earth, especially since there is a *dark cloud* (*v.* 13), many *thick clouds* (*v.* 14), that come between him and us, and *are a covering to him*; so as if God had *eyes of flesh, ch.* x. 4. Distance of place creates no difficulty to him who fills immensity, any more than distance of time to him who is eternal. Or, *He walks in the circuit of heaven,* and has enough to do to enjoy himself and his own perfections and glory in that bright and quiet world; why should he trouble himself about us? This is gross absurdity, as well as gross impiety, which Eliphaz here fathers upon Job; for it supposes that the administration of government is a burden and disparagement to the supreme governor and that the acts of justice and mercy are a toil to a mind infinitely wise, holy, and good. If the sun, a creature, and inanimate, can with the light and influence reach this earth, and every part of it (Ps. xix. 6), even from that vast height of the visible heavens in which he is, and in the circuit of which he walks, and that through many a thick and dark cloud, shall we question it concerning the Creator?

Verses 15–20

Eliphaz, having endeavoured to convict Job, here endeavours to awaken him to a sense of his danger by reason of sin; and this he does by comparing his case with that of the sinners of the old world, who *were overflown with a flood* (v. 16), and the *remnant of whom the fire consumed* (v. 20), namely, the Sodomites, who, in comparison of the old world, were but a remnant. Eliphaz would have Job to *mark the old way which wicked men have trodden* (v. 15). They said to God, *Depart from us;* and then *what could the Almighty do with them but cut them off?* Those who will not submit to God's golden sceptre must expect to be broken to pieces with his iron rod. Others make it to denote: "What has he done to oblige us? What can he do in a way of wrath to make us miserable, or in a way of favour to make us happy?" *The Lord will not do good, neither will he do evil.*

Eliphaz shows the absurdity of this in one word, and that is, calling God *the Almighty*; for, if he be so, what cannot he do? *Yet he had filled their houses with good things*, v. 18. Many have their houses full of goods but their hearts empty of grace, and thereby are marked for ruin. *But the counsel of the wicked is far from me.* Job had said so (ch. xxi. 16) and Eliphaz will not be behind with him. If they cannot agree in their own principles concerning God, yet they agree in renouncing the principles of those that live without God in the world. They take occasion thence to expose the folly of sinners and show how ridiculous their principles are. "*Our substance is not cut down*, as theirs was, and as thine is; we continue to prosper, which is a sign that we are the favourites of Heaven, and in the right." The same rule that served him to condemn Job by served him to magnify himself and his companions by. *His* substance is cut down; therefore he is a wicked man; *ours* is not; therefore we are righteous.

Verses 21–30

Eliphaz had laid before Job the miserable condition of a wicked man, that he might frighten him into repentance. Here, on the other hand, he shows him the happiness which those may be sure of that do repent, that he might allure and encourage him to it. Ministers must try both ways in dealing with people, must speak to them from Mount Sinai by the terrors of the law, and from Mount Sion by the comforts of the gospel, must set before them both life and death, good and evil, the blessing and the curse.

I. The good counsel which Eliphaz gives to Job; it was built upon a false supposition that he was a wicked man. 1. *Acquaint now thyself with God:* be not such a stranger to him as thou hast made thyself by casting off the fear of him and restraining prayer before him. It is our honour that we are made capable of this acquaintance, our misery that by sin we have lost it, our privilege that through Christ we are invited to return to it. 2. "*Be at peace*, at peace with thyself. Be at peace with thy God; be reconciled to him." 3. *Receive the law from his mouth*, v. 22. "Having made thy peace with God, submit to his government, and resolve to be ruled by him, that thou mayest keep thyself in his love." 4. *Lay up his word in thy heart.* It is not enough to receive it, but we must retain it, Prov. iii. 18. 5. *Return to the Almighty*, v. 23. "Do not only turn from sin, but turn to God and thy duty. Do not only turn towards the Almighty in some good inclinations and good beginnings, but *return to him*; return home to him, quite to him." 6. *Put away iniquity far from thy tabernacle.* This was the advice Zophar gave him, ch. xi. 14. "*Let not wickedness dwell in thy tabernacle.* Put iniquity far off, the further the better, not only from thy heart and hand, but from thy house."

II. The encouragement which Eliphaz gives Job, that he shall be very happy, if he will but take this good counsel. In general, "*Thereby good shall come unto thee* (v. 21). Thou art now ruined and brought down, but, if thou return to God, *thou shalt be built up* again, and thy present ruins shall be repaired. Thy family shall be built up in children, thy estate in wealth, and thy soul in holiness and comfort."

1. Temporal blessings should be bestowed abundantly on him. It is promised, He shall be very rich (v. 23): "*Thou shalt lay up gold as dust*, in such great abundance, and *shalt have plenty of silver* (v. 25), whereas now thou art poor and stripped of all." *Thou shalt have silver of strength* (for so the word is), which, being honestly got, will wear well—silver like steel. Wealth is a blessing indeed when we are not ensnared with the love of it. Thou shalt *lay up gold as dust*, and *as the stones of the brooks.* So little shalt thou value it or expect from it that thou shalt lay

it at thy feet (Acts iv. 35), not in thy bosom. Yet he shall be very safe; for *the Almighty shall be thy defender*; nay, he shall be *thy defence*, v. 25. He *shall be thy gold*; so it is in the margin, and it is the same word that is used (v. 24) for gold, but it signifies also a strong-hold, because *money is a defence*, Eccles. vii. 12. Worldlings make gold their god, saints make God their gold; and those that are enriched with his favour and grace may truly be said *to have abundance of the best gold*, and best laid up.

2. He should be enriched with spiritual blessings: "*For then shalt thou have thy delight in the Almighty;* and *thus* the Almighty comes to be thy gold by thy delighting in him, as worldly people delight in their money." Then *shalt* thou *lift up thy face to God* with boldness, and not be afraid, as thou now art, to draw near to him. "Thou shalt by prayer send letters to God: *Thou shalt make thy prayer*" (the word is, Thou shalt *multiply* thy prayers) "unto him, and he will not think thy letters troublesome, though many and long. *He shall hear thee*, and make it to appear he does so by what he does for thee and in thee." He should have inward satisfaction in the management of all his outward affairs (v. 28): "*Thou shalt decree a thing and it shall be established unto thee*," that is, "Thou shalt frame all thy projects and purposes with so much wisdom, and grace, and resignation to the will of God, that the issue of them shall be to thy heart's content. Thou shalt *commit thy works unto the Lord* by faith and prayer, and then *thy thoughts shall be established*; thou shalt be easy and pleased, whatever occurs, Prov. xvi. 3. "Whereas now thou complainest of darkness round about thee, then *the light shall shine on thy ways;*" that is, "God shall guide and direct thee." Even in times of common calamity and danger he should have abundance of joy and hope (v. 29): "*When men are cast down round about thee*, desponding, *then shalt thou say, There is lifting up.*"

3. He should be a blessing to his country and an instrument of good to many (v. 30): *God shall*, in answer to thy prayers, *deliver the island of the innocent*, and have a regard therein to *the pureness of thy hands. He shall deliver those that are not innocent, and they are delivered by the pureness of thy hands;* so it may be read, and most probably. Note, A good man is a public good. Sinners fare the better for saints, whether they are aware of it or no. Eliphaz and his three friends were delivered by the *pureness of Job's hands*, ch. xlii. 8.

CHAPTER 23

This chapter begins Job's reply to Eliphaz. In this reply he appeals to God, begs to have his cause heard, and doubts not but to make it good, having the testimony of his own conscience concerning his integrity. Here seems to be a struggle between flesh and spirit, fear and faith, throughout this chapter. I. He complains of his calamitous condition and especially of God's withdrawings from him, so that he could not get his appeal heard (ver. 2–5), nor discern the meaning of God's dealings with him (ver. 8, 9), nor gain any hope of relief, ver. 13, 14. But, II. In the midst of these complaints he comforts himself with the assurance of God's clemency (ver. 6, 7) and his own integrity, which God himself was a witness to, ver. 10–12.

Verses 1–7

Job, ill as he is, will not give up the cause.

I. He justifies his own resentments and representations of his trouble (v. 2): "*Even today, I own, my complaint is bitter. Even today is my complaint* counted *rebellion.* But," says he, "I do not complain more than there is cause; *for my stroke is heavier than my groaning.* The pains of my body and the wounds of my spirit are such that I have reason enough for my complaints."

II. He appeals from the censures of his friends to the just judgment of God; and this he thought was an evidence for him that he was not a hypocrite, for then he durst not have made such an appeal as this.

1. He is so sure of the equity of God's tribunal that he longs to appear before it (*v.* 3): *O that I knew where I might find him!* This may properly express the pious breathings of a soul convinced that it has by sin lost God and is undone for ever if it recover not its interest in his favour.

2. He is so sure of the goodness of his own cause that he longs to be opening it at God's bar (*v.* 4): "*I would order my cause before him,* and set it in a true light." We may apply this to the duty of prayer, in which we have *boldness to enter into the holiest* and to come even to the footstool of the throne of grace. We have not only liberty of access, but liberty of speech. We have leave *to order our cause before God.* We durst not be so free with earthly princes as a humble holy soul may be with God. We are allowed, not only to pray, but to plead, not only to ask, but to argue; nay, to *fill our mouths with arguments,* not to move God (he is perfectly apprized of the merits of the cause without our showing), but to move ourselves, to excite our fervency and encourage our faith in prayer.

3. He is so sure of a sentence in favour of him that he even longed to hear it (*v.* 5): "*I would know the words which he would answer me.*" This becomes us, in all controversies; let the word of God determine them; let us know what he answers, and understand what he says.

III. He comforts himself with the hope that God would deal favourably with him in this matter, *v.* 6, 7. The same power that is engaged against proud sinners is engaged for humble saints, who prevail with God by strength derived from him, as Jacob did, Hos. xii. 3. See Ps. lxviii. 35. There in the court of heaven, when the final sentence is to be given, *the righteous might dispute with him* and come off in his righteousness. Now, even the upright are often *chastened of the Lord,* and they cannot dispute against it; integrity itself is no fence either against calamity or calumny. *Then you shall discern between the righteous and the wicked,* whereas now we can scarcely distinguish them, so little is the difference between them as to their outward condition. Then "*I shall be delivered for ever from my Judge.*" Those that are delivered up to God as their owner and ruler shall be for ever delivered from him as their judge and avenger; and there is no flying from his justice but by flying to his mercy.

Verses 8–12

I. Job complains that he cannot understand the meaning of God's providence concerning him (*v.* 8, 9): *I go forward, but he is not there,* &c. He had a great desire to appear before God, and get a hearing of his case, but the Judge was not to be found. Job, no doubt, believed that God is everywhere present, but by reason of the disorder and tumult his spirit was in, he could not fasten upon that which he knew to be in God. He could not perceive wherein he had sinned more than others, nor could he discern what other end God should aim at in afflicting him thus. He was quite at a loss to know what God designed to do with him.

II. He satisfies himself with this, that God himself was a witness to his integrity, and therefore did not doubt but the issue would be good.

1. After Job had almost lost himself in the labyrinth, how contentedly does he sit down with this thought: "Though *I* know not the way that he takes yet *he knows the way that I take,*" *v.* 10. It is a great comfort to those who mean honestly that God understands their meaning, though men do not, cannot, or will not. "He knows that, however I may sometimes have *taken a false step,* yet I have still *taken a good way,* have *chosen the way of truth,*" that is, he accepts it, and is well pleased with it, as he is said to know

the way of the righteous, Ps. i. 6. Job infers, *When he hath tried me I shall come forth as gold.* The trial will have an end. *God will not contend for ever.* They shall come forth as gold approved and improved, found to be good and made to be better.

2. Now that which encouraged Job to hope that his present troubles would thus end well was the testimony of his conscience. God's way was the way he walked in (*v.* 11): "*My foot hath held his steps,*" that is, "held to them, adhered closely to them; the steps he takes." God's word was the rule he walked by, *v.* 12. He governed himself by *the commandment of God's lips.* Job kept closely to the law of God. *I have esteemed the words of his mouth more than my necessary food;* that is, he could as well have lived without his daily bread as without the word of God. *I have laid it up* (so the word is), as those that lay up provision for a siege, or as Joseph laid up corn before the famine. The word of God is to our souls what our necessary food is to our bodies; it sustains the spiritual life and strengthens us for the actions of life.

Verses 13–17

Job reasons himself into a sort of *patience per force,* which he cannot do without reflecting upon God as dealing hardly with him; the worst he says is that God deals unaccountably with him.

I. He lays down good truths, *v.* 13, 14. 1. That God's counsels are immutable: *He is in one mind, and who can turn him? He is one* (so some read it) or *in one*; he has no counsellors by whose interest he might be prevailed with to alter his purpose. Prayer has prevailed to change God's way and his providence, but never was his will or purpose changed; for *known unto God are all his works.* 2. That his power is irresistible: *What his soul desires* or designs *even that he does. None can stay his hand. Whatever the Lord pleased that did he* (Ps. cxxxv. 6), and always will, for it is always best. *He performs the thing that is appointed for me. Many such things are with him,* that is, He does many things in the course of his providence which we can give no account of, but must resolve into his absolute sovereignty.

II. He makes but a bad use of these good truths. He said, *Therefore am I troubled at his presence, v.* 15. What confusion poor Job was now in, for he contradicted himself: just now he was troubled for God's absence (*v.* 8, 9); now he is troubled at his presence. *When I consider, I am afraid of him. The Almighty troubled him,* and so *made his heart soft,* a grievous softness, which apprehends everything that is present to be pressing and everything future to be threatening. He quarrels with God. *Because I was not cut off before the darkness, v.* 17.

Chapter 24

Job now applies himself to a further discussion of the doctrinal controversy between him and his friends concerning the prosperity of wicked people. That many live at ease who yet are ungodly and profane, and despise all the exercises of devotion, he had shown, ch. xxi. Now here he goes further, and shows that many who are mischievous to mankind, and live in open defiance to all the laws of justice and common honesty, yet thrive and succeed in their unrighteous practices in this world. What he had said before (ch. xii. 6), "The tabernacles of robbers prosper," he here enlarges upon. I. Those that openly do wrong to their poor neighbours are not reckoned with, nor the injured righted (ver. 2–12), though the former are very barbarous, ver. 21, 22. II. Those that secretly practise mischief often go undiscovered and unpunished, ver. 13–17. III. That God punishes such by secret judgments and reserves them for future judgments (ver. 18–20, and ver. 23–25), so that, upon the whole matter, we cannot say that all who are in trouble are wicked; for it is certain that all who are in prosperity are not righteous.

Verses 1–12

Job's friends had been very positive in it that they should soon see the fall of wicked people, how much soever they might prosper for a while. By no means, says Job; *though times are not hidden from the Almighty*, yet *those that know him do not presently see his day*, v. 1. God governs the world. Bad times are not hidden from him, though the bad men that make the times bad say one to another, He has *forsaken the earth*, Ps. xciv. 6, 7. Before Job will enquire into the reasons of the prosperity of wicked men he asserts God's omniscience. He yet asserts that those who know him (that is, wise and good people who are acquainted with him, and with whom his secret is) *do not see his day*,—the day of his judging for them. We shall shortly know why the judgment is deferred; even the wisest, and those who know God best, do not yet see it. God will exercise their faith and patience, and excite their prayers for the coming of his kingdom, for which they are to *cry day and night to him*, Luke xviii. 7. Job specifies two sorts of unrighteous ones, whom all the world saw thriving in their iniquity:—

I. Tyrants, and those that do wrong under pretence of law and authority. They *remove the land-marks*, under pretence that they were misplaced (v. 2), and so they think they effectually secure that to their posterity which they have got wrongfully. This was forbidden by the law of Moses (Deut. xix. 14), under a curse, Deut. xxvii. 17. *They violently take away flocks*, pretending they are forfeited, *and feed thereof*. If a poor fatherless child has but an ass of his own to get a little money with, they find some colour or other to take it away. It is all one if a widow has but an ox for what little husbandry she has; under pretence of distraining for some small debt, or arrears of rent, this ox shall be taken for a pledge, though perhaps it is the widow's all. God has taken it among the titles of his honour to be a *Father of the fatherless and a judge of the widows*; and therefore those will not be reckoned his friends that do not to their utmost protect them; but those he will certainly reckon with as his enemies that vex and oppress them. They love in their hearts to triumph over poor people, whom they turn out of the way of getting relief, threaten to punish them as vagabonds, and so force them to abscond. *They pluck the fatherless from the breast;* that is, having made poor infants fatherless, they make them motherless too; having taken away the father's life, they break the mother's heart, and so starve the children and leave them to perish. Those who show no mercy to such as lie at their mercy shall themselves have judgment without mercy. They squeeze them so with their extortion that they *cause them to go naked without clothing* (v. 10). They are very oppressive to the labourers they employ in their service. *Those that carry their sheaves are hungry;* so some read it (v. 10), and it agrees with v. 11, that those who *make oil within their walls*, and with a great deal of toil labour at the wine-presses, yet suffer thirst. In the cities also, we see the tears of the oppressed (v. 12): *Men groan from out of the city*, where the rich merchants and traders are as cruel with their poor debtors as the landlords in the country are with their poor tenants.

II. He speaks of robbers, and those that do wrong by downright force, as the bands of the Sabeans and Chaldeans, which had lately plundered him. Their character is that they are *as wild asses in the desert*, untamed, untractable, unreasonable. They choose the deserts for their dwelling. The desert is indeed the fittest place for such wild people, *ch.* xxxix. 6. But no desert can set men out of the reach of God's eye and hand. Their trade is to steal, and to make a prey of all about them. They are diligent and take pains at it: They *rise betimes for a prey*. They not only rob travellers, but they make incursions upon their neighbours, and *reap every one his corn in the field* (v. 6), that is, they enter upon other people's ground, cut their corn, and carry it away as freely as if it were their own. *They cause the naked*, whom they have stripped, not leaving them the clothes to their backs, *to lodge*, in the cold nights, *without clothing*, so that *they are wet with the showers of the mountains, and, for want of a* better *shelter, embrace the rock*, and are glad of a cave or den in it to preserve them from the injuries of the weather. The impunity of these oppressors and spoilers is expressed in one word (v. 12): *Yet God layeth not folly to them*, that is, he does not prosecute them with his judgments until he saith, *Thou fool, this night thy soul shall be required of thee*, Luke xii. 20.

Verses 13–17

Another sort of sinners who go unpunished, because they go undiscovered. *They rebel against the light*, v. 13. Some understand it figuratively. Of their own consciences they profess to know God, but they rebel against the knowledge they have of him. Others understand it literally: they have the daylight, and choose the night as the most advantageous season for their wickedness. In this paragraph Job specifies three sorts of sinners that shun the light:—1. Murderers, v. 14. 2. Adulterers. 3. Housebreakers, v. 16.

And, *lastly*, Job observes that they are in a continual terror for fear of being discovered (v. 17): *The morning is to them even as the shadow of death.* The light of the day, which is welcome to honest people, is a terror to bad people. They curse the sun because it discovers them.

Verses 18–25

Job in the conclusion of his discourse,

I. Gives some further instances of the wickedness of these cruel bloody men. 1. Some are pirates and robbers at sea. To this many interpreters apply those difficult expressions (v. 18), *He is swift upon the waters*. Their *portion is cursed in the earth*, and they *behold not the way of the vineyards*, that is, they despise the employment of those who till the ground and plant vineyards as poor and unprofitable. But others make this a further description of the conduct of those sinners that are afraid of the light: if they be discovered, they get away as fast as they can, and choose to lurk, not in the vineyards, for fear of being discovered, but in some cursed portion, a lonely and desolate place, which nobody looks after. 2. Some are abusive to those that are in trouble, and add affliction to the afflicted. Barrenness was looked upon as a great reproach, and those that fall under that affliction they upbraid with it. This is *evil entreating the barren that beareth not* (v. 21), or those that are childless. 3. There are those who, by inuring themselves to cruelty, come at last to be *the terror of the mighty in the land of the living* (v. 22): *He draws the mighty* into a snare with his power; *he rises up* in his passion, and lays about him with so much fury that *no man is sure of his life*.

II. Shows that these daring sinners prosper, and are at ease for a while, nay, and often end their days in peace. It is *given them to be in safety*, v. 23. *They are exalted for a while*. At length, they are carried out of the world very silently and gently. "They go down to the grave as easily as snow-water sinks into the dry ground when it is melted by the sun;" so Bishop Patrick explains v. 19. He paraphrases, v. 20, *The womb shall forget him*, &c. "God sets no such mark of his displeasure upon him but that his mother may soon forget him. Neither he nor his wickedness is any more remembered than a tree which is broken to shivers." And v. 24, *They are taken out of the way as all others*, that is, "they are shut up in their graves like all other men; nay, they die as easily as an ear of corn is cropped with your hand."

III. Foresees their fall however. God's *eyes are upon their ways*, v. 23. Though he keep silence yet he will make it to appear shortly that their most secret sins, which they thought *no eye should see* (v. 15), were under his eye and will be called over again. The *grave shall consume those that have sinned*; that land of darkness will be the lot of those that *love darkness rather than light*. Their pride shall be brought down and laid in the dust (v. 24). Job owns that wicked people will be miserable on the other side death, but utterly denies what his friends asserted, that ordinarily they are miserable in this life.

IV. Concludes with a bold challenge to all that were present to disprove what he had said (v. 25): "*If it be not so now*, as I have declared, and if it do not thence follow that I am unjustly condemned and censured, let those that can undertake to prove me a liar."

CHAPTER 25

Bildad makes a short reply to Job's last discourse. He drops the main question concerning the prosperity of wicked men, but, because he thought Job had made too bold with the divine majesty in his appeals to the divine tribunal (ch. xxiii), he in a few words shows the infinite distance there is between God and man, teaching us, I. To think highly and honourably of God, ver. 2, 3, 5. II. To think meanly of ourselves, ver. 4, 6. These, however misapplied to Job, are two good lessons for us all to learn.

Verses 1-6

Bildad is to be commended, 1. For speaking no more on the subject about which Job and he differed. 2. For speaking so well on the matter about which Job and he were agreed.

Two ways Bildad takes here to exalt God and abase man:

I. He shows how glorious God is, and thence infers how guilty and impure man is before him, v. 2-4. God is the sovereign Lord of all, and *with him is terrible majesty*. *Dominion and fear are with him*, v. 2. He that gave being has an incontestable authority to give laws, and can enforce the laws he gives. His having dominion (or being *Dominus—Lord*) bespeaks him both owner and ruler of all the creatures. They are all his, and they are all under his direction and at his disposal. *He maketh peace in his high places*. The holy angels never quarrel with him, nor with one another, but acquiesce in his will, and execute it without murmuring or disquieting. The high places are *his* high places; for *the heaven, even the heavens, are the Lord's* (Ps. cxv. 16). Peace is God's work; where it is made it is he that makes it, Isa. lvii. 19. In heaven there is perfect peace; for there is perfect holiness, and there is God, who is love. He is a God of irresistible power: *Is there any number of his armies?* v. 3. His providence extends itself to all: *Upon whom does not his light arise? How then can man be justified with God? Or how can he be clean?* Man is not only mean, but vile, not only earthy, but filthy; he cannot be justified, he cannot be clean, (1) In comparison with God. (2) In debate with God. (3) In the sight of God. If God is so great and glorious, how can man, who is guilty and impure, appear before him?

II. He shows how dark and defective even the heavenly bodies are in the sight of God, and in comparison with him, and thence infers how little, and mean, and worthless, man is. The lights of heaven have no glory by reason of the glory which excelleth, as a candle, though it burn, yet does not shine when it is set in the clear light of the sun. *The moon shall be confounded, and the sun ashamed, when the Lord of hosts shall reign in Mount Sion*. How durst Job then so confidently appeal to God, who would discover that amiss in him which he was not aware of in himself? The children of men, though noble creatures, are before God but as worms of the earth (v. 6): *How much less does man shine in honour,*

how much less is he pure in righteousness *that is a worm*. What little reason has man to be proud, and what great reason to be humble! Shall man be such a fool as to contend with his Maker.

CHAPTER 26

Job's short reply to Bildad's short discourse, in which he confirms what he had said, and out-does him in magnifying God to show what reason he had still to say, as he did (ch. xiii. 2), "What you know, the same do I know also." I. He shows that Bildad's discourse was very true and good, yet not to the purpose, ver. 2–4. II. That it was needless, for he knew it, and believed it, and could speak of it as well as he (ver. 5–13), concluding that all came short of the merit of the subject, ver. 14.

Verses 1-4

Bildad thought that he had made a fine speech, but Job peevishly enough shows that his performance was not so valuable as he thought it.

I. There was no great matter to be found in it (v. 3): *How hast thou plentifully declared the thing as it is?* This is spoken ironically, upbraiding Bildad. 1. He thought he had spoken very clearly, had *declared the thing as it is*. 2. He thought he had spoken very fully. It was but poorly and scantily that he declared it, in comparison with the vast compass of the subject.

II. There was no great use to be made of it. *Cui bono—What good hast thou done* by all that thou hast said? *How hast thou*, with all this mighty flourish, *helped him that is without power?* v. 2. Job would convince him, 1. That he had done God no service by it. 2. That he had done his cause no service by it. 3. That he had done him no service by it. He pretended to convince, instruct, and comfort, Job; but, alas! what he had said was little to the purpose. "*To whom hast thou uttered words? v. 4*. Was it to me that thou didst direct thy discourse? And dost thou take me for such a child as to need these instructions?" Everything that is true and good is not suitable and seasonable. To one that was humbled, and broken, as Job was, he ought to have preached of the grace and mercy of God, rather than of his greatness and majesty. Job asks him, *Whose spirit came from thee?* that is, "What troubled soul would ever been revived, and relieved, and brought to itself, by such discourses as these?"

Verses 5-14

Now they are upon a subject in which they were all agreed, the infinite glory and power of God.

I. Many instances are here given of the wisdom and power of God in the creation and preservation of the world.

1. If we look about us, to the earth and waters here below, we shall see striking instances of omnipotence, which we may gather out of these verses. (1) *He hangs the earth upon nothing*, v. 7. The art of man could not hang a feather upon nothing, yet the divine wisdom hangs the whole earth so. (2) He *sets bounds to the waters of the sea*, and compasses them in (v. 10), that they may not *return to cover the earth*. (3) He *forms dead things under the waters*. *Rephaim—giants, are formed under the waters*, that is, vast creatures, of prodigious bulk, as whales. (4) By mighty storms and tempests he shakes the mountains, which are here called *the pillars of heaven* (v. 11), and even *divides the sea, and smites through its proud waves*, v. 12.

2. By *hell and destruction* (v. 6) we may understand the grave, and those who are buried in it, that they are under the eye of God, though laid out of our sight, which may strengthen our belief of the resurrection of the dead. We may also consider them as referring to the place of the damned.

3. If we look up to heaven above, we shall see instances of God's sovereignty and power. *He stretches out the north over the empty place*, v. 7. So he did

at first, when *he stretched out the heavens like a curtain* (Ps. civ. 2). *He binds up the waters in his thick clouds,* as if they were tied closely in a bag, and, notwithstanding the vast weight of water so raised and laid up, yet *the cloud is not rent under them,* but they distil through the cloud, and so come drop by drop, in mercy to the earth, in small rain, or great rain, as he pleases. *He holds back the face of his throne,* that light in which he dwells, *and spreads a cloud upon it,* through which *he judges,* ch. xxii. 13. *By his Spirit,* the eternal Spirit that moved upon the face of the waters, *he has garnished the heavens,* not only made them, but beautified them, has curiously bespangled them with stars by night and painted them with the light of the sun by day. "If the pavement be so richly inlaid, what must the palace be! If the visible heavens be so glorious, what are those that are out of sight!" What is meant here by *the crooked serpent* which his hands have formed is not certain. Some make it part of the garnishing of the heavens, the milky-way, say some; some particular constellation, so called, say others. It is the same word that is used for leviathan (Isa. xxvii. 1), and probably may be meant of the whale or crocodile, in which appears much of the power of the Creator; and why may not Job conclude with that inference, when God himself does so? *ch.* xli.

II. He concludes (*v.* 14): *Lo, these are parts of his ways,* by which he makes himself known to the children of men. Here he acknowledges, with adoration, the discoveries that were made of God. These things which he himself had said, and which Bildad had said, are his ways, and this is something of God. He admires the depth of that which is undiscovered. What we know of God is nothing in comparison with what is in God and what God is. He is infinite and incomprehensible; our understandings and capacities are weak and shallow, and the full discoveries of the divine glory are reserved for the future state.

CHAPTER 27

Job had sometimes complained of his friends that would scarcely let him put in a word. But now they left him room to say what he would. What Job had said (ch. xxvi) was a sufficient answer to Bildad's discourse; and Job himself went on, and said all he desired to say in this matter. I. He begins with a solemn protestation of his integrity and of his resolution to hold it fast, ver. 2–6. II. He expresses the dread he had of that hypocrisy which they charged him with, ver. 7–10. III. He shows the miserable end of wicked people, notwithstanding their long prosperity, and the curse that attends them and is entailed upon their families, ver. 11–23.

Verses 1–6

Job's discourse here is called a *parable* (*mashal*), the title of Solomon's proverbs, because it was very instructive, and he spoke as one having authority. It comes from a word that signifies *to rule,* or *have dominion;* and some think it intimates that Job now triumphed over his opponents. We say of an excellent preacher that he knows how *to command his hearers.* Job here backs all he had said in maintainance of his own integrity with a solemn oath, to silence contradiction, and take the blame entirely upon himself if he prevaricated.

I. The form of his oath (*v.* 2): *As God liveth, who hath taken away my judgment.* He speaks highly of God, in calling him *the living God* (which means *ever-living,* the eternal God, that has life in himself). Yet he speaks hardly of him, and unbecomingly, in saying that he had taken away his judgment (that is, refused to do him justice in this controversy and to appear in defence of him), and that by continuing his troubles, on which his friends grounded their censures of him, he had taken from him the opportunity he hoped ere now to have of clearing himself. He also charges it upon God that he had *vexed his soul* by laying such grievous afflictions upon him. Yet see Job's confidence in the goodness both of his cause and of his God, that though God seemed to be angry with him, and to act against him for the present, yet he could cheerfully commit his cause to him.

II. The matter of his oath, *v.* 3, 4. 1. That he would not *speak wickedness, nor utter deceit*—that, as in this debate he had all along spoken as he thought so he would never wrong his conscience by speaking otherwise; he would never maintain any doctrine, nor assert any matter of fact, but what he believed to be true; nor would he deny the truth, how much soever it might make against him. He would not be brought by their unjust censures, falsely to accuse himself. 2. That he would adhere to this resolution as long as he lived (*v.* 3): *All the while my breath is in me.* In things doubtful and indifferent, it is not safe to be thus peremptory. We know not what reason we may see to change our mind. But in so plain a thing as this we cannot be too positive that we will never speak wickedness.

III. The explication of his oath (*v.* 5, 6): "*God forbid that I should justify you* in your uncharitable censures of me, by owning myself a hypocrite: no, *until I die I will not remove my integrity from me; my righteousness I hold fast, and I will not let it go.*" Job complained much of the reproaches of his friends; but (says he) *my heart shall not reproach me,* that is, "I will never give my heart cause to reproach me, but will keep a conscience void of offence; and, while I do so, I will not give my heart leave to reproach me."

Verses 7–10

Job here expresses the dread he had of being found a hypocrite.

I. He looked upon the condition of a hypocrite to be certainly the most miserable condition that any man could be in (*v.* 7): *Let my enemy be as the wicked,* a proverbial expression. If he might wish the greatest evil to the worst enemy he had, he would wish him the portion of a wicked man, knowing that worse he could not wish him.

II. The reasons of it.

1. Because the hypocrite's hopes will not be crowned (*v.* 8): *For what is the hope of the hypocrite?* Job's friends would persuade him that all his hope was but the hope of the hypocrite, *ch.* iv. 6. "Nay," says he, "I would not, for all the world, be so foolish as to build upon such a rotten foundation; for *what is the hope of the hypocrite?*" It is certain that a formal hypocrite, with all his gains and all his hopes, will be miserable in a dying hour.

2. Because the hypocrite's prayer will not be heard (*v.* 9): *Will God hear his cry when trouble comes upon him?* If true repentance come upon him, God will hear his cry and accept him (Isa. i. 18); but if he continue impenitent and unchanged, let him not think to find favour with God.

3. Because the hypocrite's religion is neither comfortable nor constant (*v.* 10): *Will he delight himself in the Almighty? Will he always call upon God?* No, in prosperity he will not call upon God, but slight him; in adversity he will not call upon God but curse him. The reason why hypocrites do not persevere in religion is because they have no pleasure in it.

Verses 11–23

Now that the heat of the battle was nearly over Job was willing to own how far he agreed with his friends, and where the difference between his opinion and theirs lay. 1. He agreed with them that wicked people are miserable people, that God will surely reckon with cruel oppressors, make reprisals upon them for all the affronts they have put upon God and all the wrongs they have done to their neighbours.

This truth is abundantly confirmed by the entire concurrence even of these angry disputants in it. But, 2. In *this* they differed—they held that these deserved judgments are presently and visibly brought upon wicked oppressors. Now Job held that, in many cases, judgments do not fall upon them quickly, but are deferred for some time.

I. Job here undertakes to set this matter in a true light (v. 11, 12): *I will teach you.* 1. What he would teach them: *"That which is with the Almighty,"* that is, "the counsels and purposes of God concerning wicked people." This, says Job, *will I not conceal. Things revealed belong to us and our children.* 2. How he would teach them: *By the hand of God.* Those whom God teaches with a strong hand are best able to teach others, Isa. viii. 11. 3. What reason they had to learn those things which he was about to teach them (v. 12), *"You yourselves have seen it. Why then are you thus altogether vain,* to condemn me for a wicked man because I am afflicted?" He offers now to lay before them *the portion of a wicked man with God,* particularly of *oppressors,* v. 13. Compare ch. xx. 29. Their portion in the world may be wealth and preferment, but their portion with God is ruin and misery.

II. He does it, by showing that wicked people may, in some instances, prosper, but that ruin follows them and that is their portion.

1. They may prosper in their children, but ruin attends them. *His children* perhaps *are multiplied* (v. 14) or *magnified* (so some); they are very numerous and are raised to honour and great estates. (1) Some of them shall die by the sword, the sword of war, by the sword of justice for their crimes, or the sword of the murderer for their estates. (2) Others of them shall die by famine (v. 14): *His offspring shall not be satisfied with bread.* (3) Those that *remain shall be buried in death,* that is, shall die of the plague, which is called *death* (Rev. vi. 8), and be buried privately and in haste, without any solemnity, *buried with the burial of an ass*; and even their *widows shall not weep.*

2. They may prosper in their estates, but ruin attends *them* too, v. 16–18. *They heap up silver* in abundance *as the dust,* and *prepare raiment as the clay*; they have heaps of clothes about them, as plentiful as heaps of clay. But what comes of it? God will so order it that *the just shall wear his raiment and the innocent shall divide his silver.* Good men shall come honestly by that wealth which the wicked man came dishonestly by. They shall do good with it. The innocent shall not hoard the silver, but shall divide it to the poor. Money is like manure, good for nothing if it be not spread. Suppose them to have built themselves strong and stately houses; but they are like the house which the moth makes for herself in an old garment, out of which she will soon be shaken, v. 18. He is very secure in it, as a moth, and has no apprehension of danger; but it will prove of as short continuance as *a booth which the keeper makes,* which will quickly be taken down.

3. Destruction attends their persons, though they lived long in health and at ease (v. 19): *The rich man shall lie down* to sleep, *but he shall not be gathered,* that is, he shall not have his mind composed, and gathered in, to enjoy his wealth. He does not sleep so contentedly as people think he does. *His abundance will not suffer him to sleep* so sweetly as the *labouring man,* Eccles. v. 12. His cares increase his fears, and both together make him uneasy. He is miserable in death. It is to him the king of terrors, v. 20, 21. *Terrors take hold of him as waters,* as if he were surrounded by the flowing tides. He trembles to think of leaving this world, and much more of removing to another. The tempest of death, may be said *to steal him away in the night.* He is said *to be carried away,* and hurled out of his place as with a storm,

and with an east wind, violent, and noisy, and very dreadful. Death, to a godly man, is like a fair gale of wind to convey him to the heavenly country. But the wicked man is miserable after death. His soul falls under the just indignation of God. *For God shall cast upon him and not spare.* Those who will not be persuaded now to fly to the arms of divine grace, which are stretched out to receive them, will not be able to flee from the arms of divine wrath. *Men shall clap their hands at him,* that is, they shall be well pleased in his fall.

CHAPTER 28

Job forgets his sores, and all his sorrows, and talks like a philosopher. The knowledge of the reasons in God's government of the world is kept from us, and we must neither pretend to it nor reach after it. Zophar had wished that God would show Job the "secrets of wisdom", ch. xi. 6. No, says Job, "secret things belong not to us, but things revealed," Deut. xxix. 29. And here he shows, I. Concerning worldly wealth, how industriously that is sought for by the children of men, and what hazards they run to get it, ver. 1–11. II. Concerning wisdom, ver. 12. In general, the price of it is very great; it is of inestimable value, ver. 15–19. The place of it is very secret, ver. 14, 20, 22. In particular, there is a wisdom which is hidden in God (ver. 23–27) and there is a wisdom which is revealed to the children of men, ver. 28. Our enquiries into the former must be checked, into the latter quickened.

Verses 1–11

Here Job shows, 1. What a great way the wit of man may go in diving into the depths of nature and seizing the riches of it. But does it therefore follow that men may, by their wit, comprehend the reasons why some wicked people prosper and others are punished. By no means. The caverns of the earth may be discovered, but not the counsels of heaven. 2. What a great deal of pains worldly men take to get riches. He shows whence that silver came and how it was obtained, to show what little reason wicked rich men have to be proud of their wealth and pomp.

I. The wealth of this world is hidden in the earth. Thence the silver and the gold, which afterwards they refine, are fetched, v. 1. Iron and less costly but more serviceable metals, are *taken out of the earth* (v. 2), and are there found in great abundance, which abates their price indeed, but is a great kindness to man, who could much better be without gold than without iron. Nay, *out of the earth comes bread,* that is, bread-corn, the necessary support of life, v. 5. Thence man's maintenance is fetched, to remind him of his own original; he is of the earth. *Under it is turned up as it were fire,* precious stones, that sparkle as fire—coal, that is proper to feed fire. The wisdom of the Creator has placed these things, 1. Out of our sight, to teach us not to set our eyes upon them, Prov. xxiii. 5. 2. Under our feet, to teach us to trample upon them with a holy contempt.

II. The wealth that is hidden in the earth cannot be obtained but with a great deal of difficulty. 1. It is hard to be found out: there is but here and there *a vein for the silver,* v. 1. 2. When found out it is hard to be fetched out. If one method fail, they must try another, till they have *searched out all perfection,* and turned every stone to effect it, v. 3. They must grapple with subterraneous waters (v. 4, 10, 11), and force their way through rocks which are, as it were, the roots of the mountains, v. 9. Now God has made the getting of gold, and silver, and precious stones, so difficult, (1) For the engaging of industry. If valuable things were too easily obtained men would never learn to take pains. (2) For the checking and restraining of pomp and luxury. What is for necessity is had with a little labour from the surface of the earth; but what is for ornament must be dug with a great deal of pains out of the bowels of it. To be fed is cheap, but to be fine is chargeable.

III. Though the subterraneous wealth is thus hard to obtain, yet men will have it. They *search out all perfection,* v. 3. They have arts and engines to dry up the waters, and carry them off, when they break in upon them in their mines and threaten to drown the work, *v.* 4. They have pumps and pipes, and canals, to clear their way, and, obstacles being removed, they tread *the path which no fowl knoweth* (*v.* 7, 8), unseen by the vulture's eye, which is piercing and quick-sighted, and untrodden by the lion's whelps, which traverse all the paths of the wilderness. They work their way through the rocks and undermine the moun-trains, *v.* 10. Those that dig in the mines have their lives in their hands; for they are obliged to *bind the floods from overflowing* (*v.* 11), and are continually in danger of being suffocated by damps or crushed or buried alive by the fall of the earth upon them. *Their eye sees every precious thing, v.* 10. In the prospect of laying hold of them, they make nothing of all these difficulties. Go to the miner's then, thou sluggard in religion; consider their ways, and be wise. Let their courage, diligence, and constancy in seeking the wealth that perisheth shame us out of slothfulness and faint-heartedness in labouring for the true riches.

Verses 14–19

Job here comes to speak of another more valuable jewel, and that is, *wisdom and understanding,* the knowing and enjoying of God and ourselves. There is more true knowledge, satisfaction, and happiness, in sound divinity, which shows us the way to the joys of heaven, than in natural philosophy or mathematics, which help us to find a way into the bowels of the earth. Two things cannot be found out concerning this wisdom:—

I. The price of it, for that is inestimable; its worth is infinitely more than all the riches in this world: *Man knows not the price thereof* (*v.* 13). Few put a due value upon it. The cock in the fable knew not the value of the precious stone he found in the dung-hill, and therefore would rather have lighted on a barley-corn. Men know not the worth of grace, and therefore will take no pains to get it. None can possibly give valuable consideration for it. This Job enlarges upon *v.* 15, &c., where he makes an inventory of the *bona notabilia—the most valuable treasures* of this world. There is no purchasing wisdom with these. It is a gift of *the Holy Ghost,* which *cannot be bought with money,* Acts viii. 20. Spiritual gifts are conferred without money and without price, because no money can be a price for them. It is *better to get wisdom than gold.* Gold is another's, wisdom our own; gold is for the body and time, wisdom for the soul and eternity.

II. The place of it, for that is undiscoverable. *Where shall wisdom be found? v.* 12. This is a question we should all put. While the most of men are asking, "Where shall money be found?" we should ask, *Where may wisdom be found?* not vain philosophy, or carnal policy, but true religion; for that is the only true wisdom, *It is not found in* this *land of the living, v.* 13. We cannot attain to a right understanding of God and his will, of ourselves and our duty and inter-est, by reading any books or men, but by reading God's book and the men of God. Such is the degen-eracy of human nature that there is no true wisdom to be found with any but those who are born again, and who, through grace, partake of the divine nature. Ask the miners, and by them *the depth will say, It is not in me, v.* 14. Ask the mariners, and by them *the sea will say, It is not in me.* It can never be got either by trading on the waters or diving into them, can never be *sucked from the abundance of the seas or the treasures hidden in the sand.*

Verses 20–28

There is a twofold wisdom, one *hidden in God,* which is secret and *belongs not to us,* the other made known by him and revealed to man, which *belongs to us and to our children.*

I. The knowledge of God's secret will, the will of his providence, is out of our reach. It *belongs to the Lord our God.* To know what God will do hereafter, and the reasons of what he is doing now, is the knowledge Job first speaks of.

1. This knowledge is hidden from us. It is high, we cannot attain unto it (*v.* 21, 22): *It is hid from the eyes of all living,* even of philosophers, politicians, and saints; it is *kept close from the fowls of the air;* though their eyes behold afar off (*ch.* 29). Even those who, in their speculations, soar highest above the heads of other people, cannot pretend to this know-ledge. "What fools are we" (says Job) "to fight in the dark thus, to dispute about that which we do not understand!" The line and plummet of human reason can never fathom the abyss of the divine counsels. Yet there is a world on the other side death and the grave, and there we shall see clearly what we are now in the dark about. When *the mystery of God shall be finished* it will be laid open, and we shall know as we are known: when the veil of flesh is rent, and the interposing clouds are scattered, we shall know what God does, though we know not now, John xiii. 7.

2. This knowledge is hidden in God, as the apostle speaks, Eph. iii. 9. Men sometimes do that which they cannot give a good reason for, but in every will of God there is a counsel: he knows both what he does and why he does it. Two reasons why God must needs understand his own way, and he only:—

(1) Because all events are now directed by an all-seeing and almighty Providence, *v.* 24, 25. He that governs the world is Omniscient. One day's events, and one man's affairs, have such a reference to, and such a dependence upon, another's, that he only to whom all events and all affairs are naked and open, and who sees the whole at one entire and certain view, is a competent Judge of every part. He is omnipotent. For proof of this Job mentions the winds and waters, *v.* 25. What is lighter than the wind? Yet God hath ways of poising it. The waters of the sea, and the rainwaters, he both weighs and measures, allotting the proportion of every tide and every shower. A great and constant communication there is between clouds and seas, the waters above the firmament and those under it. Vapours go up, rains come down, air is condensed into water, water rarefied into air; but the great God keeps an exact account of all the stock with which this trade is carried on for the public benefit. Now, if in these things, Providence be so exact, much more in dispensing frowns and favours, rewards and punishments, to the children of men, according to the rules of equity.

(2) Because all events were from eternity designed and determined by an infallible prescience and im-mutable decree, *v.* 26, 27. He settled the course of nature. Job mentions particularly *a decree for the rain* and *a way for the thunder and lightning.* The general method, and the particular uses of these strange performances, both their causes and their effects, were appointed by the divine purpose. Some make Job to speak of wisdom here as a person, and trans-late it, *Then he saw her and showed her,* &c.

II. The knowledge of God's revealed will is within our reach; it is level to our capacity, and will do us good (*v.* 28): *Unto man he said, Behold, the fear of the Lord that is wisdom.* Let it not be said that when God concealed his counsels from man, it was because he grudged him anything that would contribute to his real bliss and satisfaction. He let him know as much as is needful and fit for a subject, but he must not think himself fit to be a privy-counsellor. No less wisdom (says Archbishop Tillotson) than that which made the world can thoroughly understand the philosophy of it. But let him look upon this as his wisdom, to fear the Lord and to depart from evil.

When God forbade man the tree of knowledge he allowed him the tree of life. We cannot attain true wisdom but by divine revelation. *The fear of the Lord, that is the wisdom.* Pure religion, and undefiled, is to *fear the Lord and depart from evil*, which agrees with God's character of Job, *ch.* i. 1. The *fear of the Lord* is the spring and summary of all religion. There is a slavish fear of God, springing from hard thoughts of him, which is contrary to religion, Matt. xxv. 24. There is a selfish fear of God springing from dreadful thoughts of him, which may be a good step towards religion, Acts ix. 5. But there is a filial fear of God, springing from great and high thoughts of him, which is the life and soul of all religion. And, wherever this reigns in the heart, it will appear by a constant care to *depart from evil*, Prov. xvi. 6. This is essential to religion.

CHAPTER 29

I. He describes the height of the prosperity from which he had fallen. And, II. The depth of the adversity into which he had fallen; and this he does to move the pity of his friends, and to justify his own complaints. But then, III. To obviate his friends' censures of him, he makes a protestation of his own integrity. In this chapter he looks back to the days of his prosperity, and shows, 1. What comfort he had in his house and family, ver. 1–6. 2. What honour he had in his country, ver. 7–10. 3. What abundance of good he did as a magistrate, ver. 11–17. 4. What prospect he had of the continuance of his comfort at home (ver. 18–20) and of his interest abroad, ver. 21–25.

Verses 1–6

Job begins here with a wish (*v.* 2): *O that I were as in months past!* so he brings in this account of his prosperity. "O that I might be restored to my prosperity, and then the censures and reproaches of my friends would be effectually silenced, even upon their own principles, and for ever rolled away!" He wishes he now had his spirit as much encouraged in the service of God as he had then, and that he had as much freedom and fellowship with him. This was *in the days of his youth* (*v.* 4), when he was in the prime. Two things made the months past pleasant to Job:—

I. That he had comfort in his God. This was the chief thing he rejoiced in, in his prosperity, as the spring of it and the sweetness of it, that he had the favour of God and the tokens of that favour. They were *the days when God preserved me*, *v.* 2. *God's candle shone upon his head*, that is, God lifted up the light of his countenance upon him. That guided him in his doubts, comforted him in his griefs, bore him up under his burdens, and helped him through all his difficulties. *The secret of God was upon my tabernacle*, that is, God conversed freely with him, as one bosom-friend with another. He knew God's mind, and was not in the dark about it, as, of late, he had been. *The Almighty was yet with me.* Now he thought God had departed from him, but in those days he was *with him*, and that was all in all to him. God's presence with a man in his house, though it be but a cottage, makes it both a castle and a palace.

II. That he had comfort in his family. Everything was agreeable there: he had both mouths for his meat and meat for his mouths; the want of either is a great affliction. Job speaks very feelingly of this comfort now that he was deprived of it. Yet we reckon amiss if, when we have lost our children, we cannot comfort ourselves with this, that we have not lost our God. He had a plentiful estate for the support of this numerous family, *v.* 6. His dairy abounded to such a degree that he might, if he pleased, *wash his steps with butter*; and his olive-yards were so fruitful that it seemed as if the *rock poured him out rivers of oil*. He reckons his wealth, not by his silver and gold, which were for hoarding, but by his butter and oil, which were for use; for what is an estate good for unless we take the good of it ourselves and do good with it to others?

Verses 7–17

Job in a post of honour and power. Judgment was administered in the gate, in the street, in the places of concourse, to which every man might have a free access, that every one who would might be a witness to all that was said and done. Job being a magistrate, we are here told,

I. What a profound respect was paid to him, not only for the dignity of his place, but for his personal merit. The people honoured him and stood in awe of him, *v.* 8. *The young men*, who, it may be, were conscious of something amiss, *hid themselves*, and got out of his way; *and the aged*, though they kept their ground, yet would not keep their seats: they *arose and stood up* to do homage to him. The princes and nobles paid great deference to him, *v.* 9, 10. When he came into court *the princes refrained talking, the nobles held their peace*, that they might the more diligently hearken to what he said.

II. What a great deal of good he did in his place. Job valued himself, not by the honour of his family, the great estate he had, and the court that was made to him, but by his usefulness. All that heard what he said, and saw how he laid out himself for the public good with all the authority and tender affection of a father to his country, blessed him, and gave witness to him, *v.* 11. Such was the blessing of him who was ready to perish (*v.* 13) and who by Job's means was rescued from perishing. If the poor were injured or oppressed, they might cry to Job, and, if he found the allegations of their petitions true he *delivered the poor that cried* (*v.* 12) and would not suffer them to be trampled upon. He was *a father to the poor*, not only a judge to protect them and to see that they were not wronged, but a father to provide for them and to see that they did not want, to counsel and direct them. Those that were ready to perish he saved from perishing, taking care of those that were sick, that were outcasts, that were falsely accused, or in danger of being turned out of their estates. The widows that were sighing for grief, and trembling for fear, he made to sing for joy. Those that were upon any account at a loss Job gave suitable and seasonable relief to (*v.* 15): *I was eyes to the blind*, and *feet to the lame.* He devoted himself to the administration of justice (*v.* 14): *I put on righteousness and it clothed me*, that is, he had an habitual disposition to execute justice. He always appeared in it, as in his clothing, and never without it. *My judgment was as a robe and a diadem.* If a magistrate do the duty of his place, that is an honour to him far beyond his gold or purple. If he do not make conscience of his duty, his robe and diadem, his gown and cap, are but a reproach. As clothes on a dead man will never make him warm, so robes on a base man will never make him honourable. *The cause which I knew not I searched out.* He diligently enquired into the matters of fact, patiently and impartially heard both sides. He valued himself by the check he gave to the violence of proud and evil men (*v.* 17): *I broke the jaws of the wicked.* He does not say that he broke their necks. He did not take away their lives, but he broke their jaws, he took away their power of doing mischief. Good magistrates must thus be a terror and restraint to evil-doers and a protection to the innocent. A judge upon the bench has as much need to be bold and brave as a commander in the field.

Verses 18–25

I. Job's thoughts in his prosperity (*v.* 18): *Then I said, I shall die in my nest.* He saw no storm arising to shake down his nest; and therefore concluded, *Tomorrow shall be as this day.* In the midst of his prosperity he thought of dying. Yet he flattered himself he should *multiply his days as the sand.* He means as the sand on the sea-shore; whereas we should rather reckon our days by the sand in the hour-glass, which will have run out in a little time.

II. The ground of these thoughts. He found no bodily distemper growing upon him; his estate did not lie under any incumbrance; nor was he sensible of any worm at the root of it. He was like a tree whose root is not only spread out, which fixes it and keep it firm, so that it is in no danger of being over-turned, but *spread out by the waters*, which feed it. Blessed with the fatness of the earth, so also with the kind influences of heaven too; for the *dew lay all night upon his branch. His bow* also *was renewed in his hand*, that is, his power to protect himself, so that he had little reason to fear the insults of the Sabeans and Chaldeans. Neither had he any reason to distrust the fidelity of his friends. Nothing surely could be done against him when really nothing was done without him. He was consulted as an oracle, *v.* 21. When others could not be heard all men *gave ear* to him, *and kept silence at his counsel*, knowing that, as nothing could be said against it, so nothing needed to be added to it. And therefore, *after his words, they spoke not again, v.* 22. He had the hearts and affections of all his neighbours. Those were thought happy to whom he spoke. His speech dropped upon them, and they waited for it as for the rain (*v.* 22, 23). "*If I laughed on them*, designing thereby to show myself pleased in them, or pleasant with them, it was such a favour that *they believed it not for joy*," or because it was so rare a thing to see this grave man smile. He *chose out their way*, sat at the helm, and steered for them. He *dwelt as a king in the army*, giving orders which were not to be disputed. Everyone that has the spirit of wisdom has not the spirit of government, but Job had both. Yet he had the tenderness of a comforter. Our Lord Jesus is such a King as Job was, the poor man's King.

CHAPTER 30

It is a melancholy "But now" which this chapter begins with. I. He had lived in great honour, but now he had fallen into disgrace, and was as much vilified, even by the meanest, as ever he had been magnified by the greatest, ver. 1–14. II. He had had much inward comfort, but now he was a burden to himself (ver. 15, 16), and overwhelmed with sorrow, ver. 28–31. III. He had long enjoyed good health, but now he was sick and in pain, ver. 17–19, 29, 30. IV. Time was when the secret of God was with him, but now his communication with heaven was cut off, ver. 20–22. V. He had promised himself a long life, but now he saw death at the door, ver. 23. But two things gave him some relief:—1. That his troubles would not follow him to the grave, ver. 24. 2. That his conscience witnessed for him that, in his prosperity, he had sympathised with those that were in misery, ver. 25.

Verses 1–14

Here Job makes complaint of the great disgrace he had fallen into, from the height of honour and reputation. Two things he insists upon as greatly aggravating his affliction:

I. The meanness of the persons that affronted him. He was spurned by the meanest and most contemptible of mankind. They were young, younger than he (*v.* 1), *the youth* (*v.* 12), who ought to have behaved themselves respectfully towards him for his age and gravity. Their fathers were so very despicable that such a man as Job would have disdained to take them into the lowest service about his house, as that of tending the sheep and attending the shepherds with the dogs of his flock, *v.* 1. Job himself, with all his prudence and patience, could make nothing of them, *v.* 2. The young were not fit for labour, they were so lazy. *Whereto might the strength of their hands profit me?* The old were not to be advised with in the smallest matters, for their *old age was perished*, they were twice children. Being brought into straits by their own slothfulness and wasteful-ness, nobody was forward to relieve them. Hence they were forced to flee into the deserts both for

shelter and sustenance, and were put to sorry shifts indeed, when they *cut up mallows by the bushes*, and were glad to eat them, for want of food that was fit for them, *v.* 4. This beggarly world is full of the devil's poor. *They were driven forth from among men, v.* 5. An idle fellow is a public nuisance; but it is better to drive such into a workhouse than, as here, into a wilderness, which will punish them indeed, but never reform them. They were forced to dwell in *caves of the earth*, and *they brayed* like asses *among the bushes, v.* 6, 7. *They groan among the trees* (so Broughton) *and smart among the nettles*; they are stung and scratched there, where they hoped to be sheltered and protected. But such as these were abusive to Job because when he was in prosperity and power, like a good magistrate, he put in execution the laws which were in force against vagabonds, and rogues, and sturdy beggars, which these base people now remembered against him. They thought he had now become like one of them.

II. The greatness of the affronts that were given him. *I am their song and their byword.* They shunned him as a loathsome spectacle, abhorred him, fled far from him (*v.* 10), as an ugly monster or as one infected. They tripped up his heels, pushed away his feet (*v.* 12), kicked him, either in wrath or in sport. *They raise up against me the ways of their destruction;* or (as some read it), *They cast upon me the cause of their woe;* that is, "They lay the blame of their being driven out upon me;" and it is common for criminals to hate the judges and laws by which they are punished. They misrepresented his former con-versation, which is here called *marring his path.* They reflected upon him as a tyrant because he had done justice upon them; and perhaps Job's friends grounded their uncharitable censures of him (ch. xxii. 6, &c.) upon the clamours of these sorry people. They are fools in other things, but wise enough to do mischief, and need no help in inventing that. Some read it thus, *They hold my heaviness a profit, though they be never the better. They came upon me as a wide breaking in of waters*, when the dam is broken; or, "They came as soldiers into a broad breach which they have made in the wall of a besieged city, pouring in upon me with the utmost fury." *They rolled themselves in the desolation* with all the weight of their malice.

III. All this contempt put upon him was caused by the troubles he was in (*v.* 11): "*Because he has loosed my cord*, has taken away the honour and power with which I was girded (ch. xii. 18), because he has afflicted me, therefore *they have let loose the bridle before me*," that is, "have given themselves a liberty to say and do what they please against me." "Be-cause he hath loosed *his* cord," that is, "because he has taken off his bridle of restraint from off their malice, they cast away the bridle from me," that is, "they make no account of my authority, nor stand in any awe of me." Those that today cry *Hosannah* may tomorrow cry *Crucify.* But there is an honour which comes from God, which if we secure, we shall find it not thus changeable and losable.

Verses 15–31

This second part of Job's complaint is very bitter.

I. Affliction seized him, and surprised him. *The days of affliction have taken hold upon me, have caught me* (so some); *they have arrested me*, as the bailiff arrests the debtor. It surprised him (*v.* 27): "*The days of affliction prevented me*," that is, "they came upon me without giving me any previous warning. I did not make any provision for such an evil day." He was in great sorrow by reason of it. His *bowels boiled* with grief, *and rested not, v.* 27. The sense of his calamities was continually preying upon his spirits without any intermission. He *went mourning* from day to day, and such a cloud was constantly upon his

mind that he went, in effect, *without the sun*, *v.* 28.
Thus he was *a brother to dragons and owls* (*v.* 29),
both in choosing solitude and retirement, as they do
(Isa. xxxiv. 13), and in making a fearful hideous
noise as they do. The terror and trouble that seized
his soul were the sorest part of his calamity, *v.* 15, 16.
He complained, at first, of the *terrors of God setting
themselves in array against him*, ch. vi. 4. And still,
which way soever he looked, they turned upon him;
which way soever he fled, they pursued him. The
soul is the principal part of the man and therefore
that which pursues the soul, and threatens, should be
most dreaded. *My welfare* and prosperity *pass away*,
as suddenly, swiftly, and irrecoverably, *as a cloud*.
If he looked within, he found his spirit not only
wounded, but *poured out upon him*, *v.* 16. His bodily
diseases went to the bone, *v.* 17. It was a *sword in
his bones*, which *pierced him in the night season*. His
sinews took no rest. By reason of his pain, sleep departed from his eyes. *His bones were burnt with heat*,
v. 30. He was in a constant fever. He was full of
sores. His *skin was black upon him*, *v.* 30. Some think
that Job was ill of a quinsy and that it was this
which bound him like a collar. Thus was he *cast into
the mire* (*v.* 19), *compared to mire* (so some); his body
looked more like a heap of dirt than anything else.
That which afflicted him most of all was that God
seemed to be his enemy and to fight against him.
"*I cry unto thee*, as one in earnest, *I stand up* and cry,
as one waiting for an answer, but thou hearest not,
thou regardest not, for anything I can perceive."
That which he here says of God is one of the worst
words that ever Job spoke (*v.* 21): *Thou hast become
cruel to me*. Job was unjust and ungrateful when he
said so of him. He thought God fought against him
and stirred up his whole strength to ruin him: *With
thy strong hand thou opposest thyself*, or art an adversary against me. He thought he insulted over him
(*v.* 22): *Thou liftest me up to the wind*, as a feather or
the chaff which the wind plays with. He expected
now that God would shortly make an end of him:
"*I know that thou wilt bring me*, with so much the
more terror, *to death*, though I might have been
brought thither without all this ado, for it is *the house
appointed for all living*," *v.* 23. "*When I looked for
good*, for more good, or at least for the continuance
of what I had, *then evil came*"—such uncertain things
are all our worldly enjoyments. "*My harp is turned
to mourning, and my organ into the voice of those
that weep*." Job, in his prosperity, had taken *the
timbrel and harp*, and rejoiced at the sound of the
organ, ch. xxi. 12.

II. Something in the midst of all with which he
comforts himself. He foresees that death will be the
period of all his calamities (*v.* 24): Though God now
opposed himself against him, "yet," says he, "*he
will not stretch out his hand to the grave*." He reflects
with comfort upon the concern he always had for
the calamities of others when he was himself at ease
(*v.* 25): *Did not I weep for him that was in trouble?*
His conscience witnessed for him that he had always
sympathised with persons in misery and done what
he could to help them, and therefore he had reason
to expect that, at length, both God and his friends
would pity him. *Did not my soul burn for the poor?*
so some read it, comparing it with that of St. Paul,
2 Cor. xi. 29, *Who is offended, and I burn not?*

CHAPTER 31

Job protested his integrity to clear himself from those crimes with
which his friends had falsely charged him. Job's friends had been
particular in their articles of impeachment against him, and therefore he is so in his protestation, which seems to refer especially
to what Eliphaz had accused him of, ch. xxii. 6, &c. I. The sins
from which he here acquits himself are, 1. Wantonness and uncleanness of heart, ver. 1–4. 2. Fraud and injustice in commerce,
ver. 4–8. 3. Adultery, ver. 9–12. 4. Haughtiness and severity

towards his servants, ver. 13–15. 5. Unmercifulness to the poor,
the widows, and the fatherless, ver. 16–23. 6. Confidence in his
worldly wealth, ver. 24, 25. 7. Idolatry, ver. 26–28. 8. Revenge,
ver. 29–31. 9. Neglect of poor strangers, ver. 32. 10. Hypocrisy
in concealing his own sins and cowardice in conniving at the sins
of others, ver. 33, 34. 11. Oppression, and the violent invasion of
other people's rights, ver. 38–40. And, towards the close, he
appeals to God's judgment concerning his integrity, ver. 35–37.
Now, II. In all this we may see, 1. The sense of the patriarchal
age concerning good and evil and what was so long ago condemned as sinful. 2. A noble pattern of piety and virtue proposed
to us for our imitation.

Verses 1–8

The lusts of the flesh, and the love of the world,
are the two fatal rocks on which multitudes split;
against these Job protests he was always careful to
stand upon his guard.

I. Against the lusts of the flesh. He not only kept
himself clear from adultery, from defiling his neighbours' wives (*v.* 9), but from all lewdness with any
woman whatsoever. *I made a covenant with my eyes*,
that is, "I watched against the occasions of the sin;
why then should I think upon a maid?" that is, "by
that means, through the grace of God, I kept myself
from the very first step towards it." He would not
so much as admit a wanton look. Those that would
keep their hearts pure must guard their eyes, which
are both the outlets and inlets of uncleanness. He
would not so much as allow a wanton thought. It was
not for fear of reproach among men, though that is
to be considered (Prov. vi. 33), but for fear of the
wrath and curse of God. Uncleanness is a sin that
forfeits all good, and shuts us out from the hope of
it (*v.* 2): *What portion of God is there from above?
Is not destruction*, a swift and sure destruction, *to
those wicked people, and a strange punishment to
the workers of* this *iniquity? Is there not alienation*
(so some read it) *to the workers of iniquity?* This is
the sinfulness of the sin that it alienates the mind
from God (Eph. iv. 18, 19). *Doth not he see my ways?
O God! thou hast searched me and known me.* God
sees what rule we walk by, what company we walk
with, what end we walk towards, and therefore what
ways we walk in. He *counts all my steps*, all my false
steps in the way of duty, all my by-steps into the way
of sin. God takes a more exact notice of us than
we do of ourselves; for who ever counted his own
steps? yet God counts them.

II. He stood upon his guard against the love of the
world, and carefully avoided all sinful means of getting
wealth. He dreaded all forbidden profit as much as
all forbidden pleasure. He never *walked with vanity*
(*v.* 5), that is, he never durst tell a lie to get a good
bargain. He never *hasted to deceit*. He never made
haste to be rich by deceit, but always acted cautiously,
lest, through inconsideration, he should do an unjust
thing. His *steps never turned out of the way*, the way
of justice and fair dealing; from that he never deviated, *v.* 7. His heart did not *walk after his eyes*,
that is, he did not covet what he saw that was another's
nor wish it his own. Covetousness is called the *lust
of the eye*, 1 John ii. 16. *No blot had cleaved to his
hands*, that is, he was not chargeable with getting
anything dishonestly, or keeping that which was
another's. Injustice is a blot, a blot to the estate, a blot
to the owner; it spoils the beauty of both. Job ratifies
his protestation. He is willing to have his goods
searched (*v.* 6): *Let me be weighed in an even balance*,
that is, "Let what I have got be enquired into and it
will be found to weigh well." He is willing to forfeit
the whole cargo if there be found any prohibited or
contraband goods, anything but what he came honestly by (*v.* 8): "*Let me sow, and let another eat*,"
which was already agreed to be the doom of oppressors
(ch. v. 5), "and *let my offspring*, all the trees that I
have planted, *be rooted out*." He knew himself
innocent and would venture all the poor remains of
his estate upon the issue of the trial.

Verses 9–15

Two more instances of Job's integrity:

I. He had a very great abhorrence of the sin of adultery. He was careful not to offer any injury to his neighbour's marriage bed. He did not so much as covet his neighbour's wife; for even *his heart was not deceived by a woman.* He never *laid wait at his neighbour's door,* to get an opportunity to debauch his wife in his absence. He owns that, if he were guilty: *Let my wife grind to another.* Let her be a *slave* (so some), a *harlot,* so others. God often punishes the sins of one with the sin of another, the adultery of the husband with the adultery of the wife. Those who are not just and faithful to their relations must not think it strange if their relations be unjust and unfaithful to them. *For it is an iniquity to be punished by the judges.* Adultery is a crime which the civil magistrate ought to take cognizance of and punish. *It is a fire.* Lust is a fire in the soul: those that indulge it are said to burn.

II. He had a very great tenderness for his servants and ruled them with a gentle hand. He did not *despise the cause of his man-servant,* no, nor of his *maid-servant, when they contended with him.* If they had offended him, or were accused to him, if they complained of any hardship he put upon them, he gave them leave to tell their story, and redressed their grievances as far as it appeared they had right on their side. He considered, "If I should be imperious and severe with my servants, *what then shall I do when God riseth up?*" When he was tempted to be harsh with his servants this thought came very seasonably into his mind, "*Did not he that made me in the womb make him?* I am a creature as well as he, and my being is derived and depending as well as his. He partakes of the same nature that I do and is the work of the same hand.

Verses 16–23

Eliphaz had particularly charged Job with unmercifulness to the poor (*ch.* xxii. 6, &c.). It appears, by Job's protestation, that it was utterly false and groundless.

I. He was always compassionate to the poor, and careful of them, especially the widows and fatherless, always ready to grant their desires and answer their expectations, *v.* 16. If he could but perceive by the widow's look that she expected an alms from him, he had compassion enough to give it, and *never caused the eyes of the widow to fail.* He was a father to the fatherless, took care of orphans. He provided food convenient for them; they ate of the same morsels that he did (*v.* 17), did not eat after him, of the crumbs that fell from his table, but with him, of the best dish upon his table. He took particular care to clothe those that were without covering, which would be more expensive to him than feeding them, *v.* 19. If Job knew of any that were in this distress he had good warm strong clothes made on purpose for them of *the fleece of his sheep* (*v.* 20). He never so much as *lifted up his hand against the fatherless* (*v.* 21). He never used his power to crush those that stood in his way, though he *saw his help in the gate,* that is, though he had interest enough, both in the people and in the judges, both to enable him to do it and to bear him out when he had done it.

II. The imprecation with which he confirms this protestation (*v.* 22): "If I have been oppressive to the poor, *let my arm fall from my shoulder-blade and my arm be broken from the bone,*" that is, "let the flesh rot off from the bone and one bone be disjoined and broken off from another."

III. The principles by which Job was restrained from all uncharitableness and unmercifulness. "*Destruction from God was a terror to me,* whenever I was tempted to this sin, and *by reason of his highness*

I could not endure the thought of making him my enemy." He thought of the infinite distance between him and God. Those who oppress the poor, and pervert judgment and justice, forget that *he who is higher than the highest regards,* and *there is a higher than they,* who is able to deal with them (Eccles. v. 8); but Job considered this.

Verses 24–32

Four articles more of Job's protestation not only assure us what he was and did, but teach us what we should be and do:

I. He protests that he never set his heart upon the wealth of this world. His *wealth was great,* and he *had gotten much.* Job put no great confidence in it: he did not *make gold his hope, v.* 24. It is hard to have riches and not to trust in riches; and it is this which makes it so difficult for *a rich man to enter into the kingdom of God,* Matt. xix. 23; Mark x. 24.

II. He protests that he never gave the worship and glory to the creature which are due to God only; he was never guilty of idolatry, *v.* 26–28. He not only never bowed the knee to Baal (which, some think, was designed to represent the sun), never fell down and worshipped the sun, but he kept his eye, his heart, and his lips, clean from this sin. This was his covenant, that, whenever he looked at the lights of heaven, he should by faith look through them, and beyond them, to the Father of lights. He did not perform the least and lowest act of adoration: *His mouth did not kiss his hand,* which, it is likely, was a ceremony then commonly used even by some that yet would not be thought idolaters. In giving divine honours to the sun and moon, they could not reach to kiss them, but to show their goodwill, they kissed their hand, reverencing those as their masters which God has made servants to this lower world, to hold the candle for us. He looked upon it as an affront to the civil magistrate: It *were an iniquity to be punished by the judge,* as a public nuisance. He looked upon it as a much greater affront to the God of heaven, and no less than high treason against his crown and dignity. Idolatry is in effect atheism.

III. He protests that he was so far from doing or designing mischief to any that he neither desired nor delighted in the hurt of the worst enemy he had. He did not so much as rejoice when any mischief befell them, *v.* 29. He did not so much as wish in his own mind that evil might befall them, *v.* 30. He was violently urged to revenge, and yet he kept himself thus clear from it (*v.* 31): *The men of his tabernacle,* his domestics, his servants, and those about him, were enraged at Job's enemy who hated him. "*O that we had of his flesh!* Our master is satisfied to forgive him, but *we cannot be so satisfied.*"

IV. He protests that he had never been unkind or inhospitable to strangers (*v.* 32). *The stranger lodged not in the street. He opened his door to the road* (so it may be read); he kept the street-door open, that he might see who passed by and invite them in, as Abraham, Gen. xviii. 1.

Verses 33–40

Job's protestation against three more sins.

I. Of dissimulation and hypocrisy. The general crime of which his friends accused him was that really he was as bad as other people, but had the art of concealing it. Zophar insinuated (*ch.* xx. 12) that he *hid his iniquity under his tongue.* "No," says Job, "I never did (*v.* 33), *I never covered my transgression as Adam,* never palliated a sin with frivolous excuses, nor ever *hid my iniquity in my bosom.*"

II. His courage in that which is good he produces as an evidence of his sincerity in it (*v.* 34): *Did I fear a great multitude, that I kept silence?* No, all that knew Job knew him to be a man of undaunted resolution in a good cause, and did not fear the face of man, but set his face as a flint. He did not, he durst not, keep silence when he had a call to speak in an honest cause, or keep within doors when he had a call to go abroad to do good. He valued not the clamours of the mob, feared not a great multitude, nor did he value the menaces of the mighty: *The contempt of families never terrified him.*

III. The charge of oppression and violence, and doing wrong to his poor neighbours. The estate he had he both got and used honestly, so that his *land could not cry out against him nor the furrows thereof complain* (v. 38), as they do against those who get the possession of them by fraud and extortion, Hab. ii. 9–11. Two things he could say safely concerning his estate:—1. That he *never ate the fruits of it without money*, v. 39. What he purchased he paid for. The labourers that he employed had their wages duly paid them. 2. That he never caused the owners thereof to lose their life, never got an estate, as Ahab got Naboth's vineyard, by killing the heir and seizing the inheritance, never starved those that held lands of him nor killed them with hard bargains and hard usage. "If I have got my estate unjustly, *let thistles grow instead of wheat*, the worst of weeds instead of the best of grains." Job, towards the close of his protestation, appeals to the judgment-seat of God concerning the truth of it (v. 35–37): *O that I would hear me*, even *that the Almighty would answer me!* An upright heart does not dread a scrutiny. He that means honestly wishes he had a window in his breast, that all men might see the intents of his heart. But an upright heart does particularly desire to be determined in everything by the judgment of God which we are sure is according to truth. "*O that my adversary had written a book*—that my friends, who charge me with hypocrisy, would draw up their charge in writing, that it might be reduced to a certainty, and that we might the better join issue upon it." If it discovered to him any sin he had been guilty of, which he did not yet see, he should be glad to know it, that he might repent of it and get it pardoned. If it charged him with what was false, he doubted not but to disprove the allegations. The defendant is ready to make his appearance and to give his accusers all the fair play they can desire. He will *declare unto them the number of his steps*, v. 37. He will let them into the history of his own life. So confident he is of his integrity that as a prince to be crowned, rather than as a prisoner to be tried, he would *go near to him*, both to his accuser to hear his charge and to his judge to hear his doom. He has now said all he would say in answer to his friends: he afterwards said something in a way of self-reproach and condemnation (ch. xl. 4, 5; xlii. 2, &c.), but here ends what he had to say in a way of self-defence and vindication.

CHAPTER 32

The stage is clear, it is therefore seasonable for a moderator to interpose, and Elihu is the man. I. Some account of him, his parentage, his presence at this dispute, and his sentiments concerning it, ver. 1–5. II. The apology he made for his bold undertaking to speak to a question which had been so largely and learnedly argued by his seniors. He pleads, 1. That, though he had not the experience of an old man, yet he had the understanding of a man, ver. 6–10. 2. That he had patiently heard all they had to say, ver. 11–13. 3. That he had something new to offer, ver. 14–17. 4. That his mind was full of this matter, and it would be a refreshment to him to give it vent, ver. 18–20. 5. That he was resolved to speak impartially, ver. 21, 22. And he did speak so well that Job made no reply to him, and God gave him no rebuke.

Verses 1–5

When old men were the disputants, as a rebuke to them for their unbecoming heat, a young man is raised up to be the moderator.

I. The reason why Job's three friends were now silent. They *ceased to answer him*, and let him have

his saying, *because he was righteous in his own eyes*. It was to no purpose to argue with a man that was so opinionative, v. 1. But they did not judge fairly concerning Job: he was really righteous before God, and not righteous in his own eyes only.

II. The reasons why Elihu, the fourth, now spoke. His name *Elihu* signifies *My God is he.* He is said to be a *Buzite*, from Buz, Nahor's second son (Gen. xxii. 21), and *of the kindred of Ram*, that is, *Aram* (so some), whence the Syrians or Aramites descended and were denominated, Gen. xxii. 21. *Of the kindred of Abram;* so the Chaldee-paraphrase, supposing him to be first called *Ram—high*, then *Abram—a high father*, and lastly *Abraham—the high father of a multitude.*

1. Elihu spoke because he was angry and thought he had good cause to be so. He was angry at Job, because he thought he did not speak so reverently of God as he ought to have done; and that was too true (v. 2): *He justified himself more than God*, that is, took more care and pains to clear himself from the imputation of unrighteousness in being thus afflicted than to clear God from the imputation of unrighteousness in afflicting him. Elihu owned Job to be a good man. He was angry at his friends because he thought they had not conducted themselves so charitably towards Job as they ought to have done (v. 3): *They had found no answer, and yet had condemned Job.* Seldom is a quarrel carried on to the length that this was, in which there is not a fault on both sides. Elihu, as became a moderator, took part with neither.

2. Elihu had waited on Job's speeches, had patiently heard him out, until the words of Job were ended.

Verses 6–14

Elihu appears to have been,

I. A man of great modesty and humility. "*I am young, and therefore I was afraid, and durst not show you my opinion*, for fear I should either prove mistaken or do that which was unbecoming me." It becomes us to be swift to hear the sentiments of others and slow to speak our own, especially when we go contrary to the judgment of those for whom, upon the score of their learning and piety, we justly have a veneration. *I said, Days should speak.* Age and experience give a man great advantage in judging of things, both as they furnish a man with so much the more matter for his thoughts to work upon and as they ripen and improve the faculties. It is good *lodging with an old disciple*, Acts xxi. 16; Titus ii. 4. Elihu's modesty appeared in the patient attention he gave to what his seniors said, v. 11, 12. He attended to them with diligence and care. Though they had often seek for matter and words, paused and hesitated, yet he *gave ear to their reasons*. We must often be willing to hear what we do not like, else we cannot prove all things. Those that have heard may speak, and those that have learned may teach.

II. A man of great sense and courage, and one that knew as well when and how to speak as when and how to keep silence. Though he had so much respect to his friends as not to interrupt them with his speaking, yet he had so much regard to truth and justice (his better friends) as not to betray them by his silence.

1. Man is a rational creature, and therefore has for himself a judgment of discretion and ought to be allowed a liberty of speech in his turn. He means the same that Job did (ch. xii. 3, *But I have understanding as well as you*) when he says (v. 8), *But there is a spirit in man;* only he expresses it a little more modestly, that one man has understanding as well as another, and no man can pretend to have the monopoly of reason. *Therefore hearken to me.* The soul is a spirit, neither material itself nor dependent upon matter. It is an understanding spirit. It is able

to discover and receive truth, to discourse and reason upon it, and to direct and rule accordingly. This understanding spirit is in every man; it is the light *that lighteth every man*, John i. 9. It is the inspiration of the Almighty that gives us this understanding spirit.

2. Those who are advanced above others in grandeur and gravity do not always proportionally go beyond them in knowledge and wisdom (*v.* 9): *Great men are not always wise;* it is a pity but they were, for then they would never do hurt with their greatness and would do so much the more good with their wisdom. The aged do not always understand judgment; even *they* may be mistaken, and they must not take it as an affront to be contradicted, but rather take it as a kindness to be instructed, by their juniors: *Therefore I said, hearken to me, v.* 10. He that has a good eye can see further upon level ground than he that is purblind can from the top of the highest mountain. *Better is a poor and wise child than an old and foolish king*, Eccles. iv. 13.

3. It was requisite for something to be said, for the setting of this controversy in a true light. "I must speak, *lest you should say, We have found out wisdom*, lest you should think your argument against Job conclusive and that he cannot be convinced and humbled by any other argument than this of yours, *that God casteth him down and not man*, that it appears by his extraordinary afflictions that God is his enemy, and therefore he is certainly a wicked man. I must show you that this is a false hypothesis and that Job may be convinced without maintaining it."

4. He had something new to offer. He will not reply to Job's protestations of his integrity, but allows the truth of them, and therefore does not interpose as his enemy: "*He hath not directed his words against me.*" He will not repeat their arguments, nor go upon their principles: "*Neither will I answer him with your speeches*—not with the same matter, for should I only say what has been said I might justly be silenced as impertinent,—nor in the same manner; I will not be guilty of that peevishness towards him myself which I dislike in you."

Verses 15–22

Three things here apologize for Elihu's interposing as he does in this controversy which had already been canvassed by such learned disputants:—

1. The stage was clear, and he did not break in upon any of the managers on either side: *They were amazed* (*v.* 15); *they stood still, and answered no more, v.* 16. The judgment is the Lord's, and by him it must be determined who is in the right and who is in the wrong; but, since you have each of you shown your opinion, I also will show mine, and let it take its fate with the rest.

2. He was uneasy, and even in pain, to be delivered of his thoughts upon this matter. "*I am full of matter*, having carefully attended to all that has hitherto been said, and made my own reflections upon it. *The spirit within me* not only instructs me what to say, but puts me on to say it; so that if I have not vent I shall *burst like bottles of new wine* when it is working," *v.* 19. *I will speak, that I may be refreshed*, not only that I may be eased of the pain of stifling my thoughts, but that I may have the pleasure of endeavouring, according to my place and capacity, to do good.

3. That he was resolved to speak, with sincerity, what he thought was true, not what he thought would please (*v.* 21, 22): "*Let me not accept any man's person*, as partial judges do, that aim to enrich themselves, not to do justice. I am resolved to flatter no man." He that made us hates all dissimulation and flattery, and will soon *put lying lips to silence* and *cut off flattering lips*, Ps. xii. 3.

CHAPTER 33

Elihu's discourse here does not disappoint the expectations which his preface had raised. It is substantial, and lively, and very much to the purpose. I. He bespeaks Job's favourable acceptance of what he should say, ver. 1–7. II. He does, in God's name, bring an action against him, for words which he had spoken, in the heat of disputation, reflecting upon God as dealing hardly with him, ver. 8–11. III. He endeavours to convince him of his fault and folly herein, by showing him, 1. God's sovereign dominion over man, ver. 12, 13. 2. The care God takes of man when he lays bodily afflictions upon him, ver. 14. (1) Job had sometimes complained of unquiet dreams, ch. vii. 14. "Why," says Elihu, "God sometimes speaks conviction and instruction to men by such dreams," ver. 15–18. (2) Job had especially complained of his sicknesses and pains; and, as to these, he shows largely that they were so far from being tokens of God's wrath, as Job took them, or evidences of Job's hypocrisy, as his friends took them, that they were really wise and gracious methods, which divine grace took for the increase of his acquaintance with God, to work patience, experience, and hope, ver. 19–30. And, lastly, he concludes with a request to Job, either to answer him or give him leave to go on, ver. 31–33.

Verses 1–7

Elihu does not join with his three friends against him. He has, in the foregoing chapter, declared his dislike of their proceedings, disclaimed their hypothesis, and quite set aside the method they took of healing Job. "*Wherefore, Job, I pray thee, hear my speech, v.* 1. I am trying a new way, *therefore hearken to all my words.*" He *opened his mouth* (*v.* 2), with deliberation and design. "*My words shall be of the uprightness of my heart*, the genuine product of my convictions and sentiments." What he said should be easy, and not dark and hard to be understood: *My lips shall utter knowledge clearly.* He owns himself unfit to enter into the lists with his seniors, yet he desires they will not despise his youth. He would be very willing to hear what Job could object against what he had to say (*v.* 5): "*If thou canst, answer me.*" He had often wished for one that would appear for God, with whom he might freely expostulate, and to whom, as arbitrator, he might refer the matter, and such a one Elihu would be (*v.* 6): *I am, according to thy wish, in God's stead.* "*I also am formed out of the clay.* I also as well as thou." Job had urged this with God as a reason why he should not bear hard upon him (*ch.* x. 9), *Remember that thou hast made me as the clay.* "I," says Elihu, "am *formed out of the clay* as well as thou," *formed of the same clay*, so some read it. "*My terror shall not make thee afraid.*" If we would rightly convince men, it must be by reason, not by terror, by fair arguing, not by a heavy hand.

Verses 8–13

I. Elihu particularly charges Job with some expressions that had dropped from him, reflecting upon the justice and goodness of God in his dealings with him. "*Thou hast spoken it in my hearing*, and in the hearing of all this company." When we hear anything said that tends to God's dishonour we ought publicly to bear our testimony against it. What is said amiss in our hearing we are concerned to reprove; for *you are my witnesses, saith the Lord*, to confront the accuser. Job had represented himself as innocent (*v.* 9): *I am clean without transgression.* Job had not said this *in so many words*; he had owned himself to have sinned and to be impure before God; but he had indeed said, *Thou knowest that I am not wicked, my righteousness I hold fast.* Elihu did not deal fairly in charging Job with saying that he was clean and innocent from all transgression, when he only pleaded that he was upright and innocent from the great transgression. He had represented God as severe in marking what he did amiss (*v.* 10, 11), as if he sought opportunity to pick quarrels with him. *He findeth occasions against me.*

II. He endeavours to convince him that he had spoken amiss in speaking thus, and that he ought to humble himself before God for it, and by repentance to unsay it (*v.* 12): *Behold, in this thou art not just.* See the difference between the charge which Elihu exhibited against Job and that which was preferred against him by his other friends; they would not own that he was just at all, but Elihu only says, "In this, in saying this, thou art not just." Job himself said a great deal, and admirably well, concerning the greatness of God, his irresistible power and incontestable sovereignty, his terrible majesty and unsearchable immensity. "Now," said Elihu, "do but consider what thou thyself hast said concerning the greatness of God, and apply it to thyself; if he is greater than man, he is greater than thou, and thou wilt see reason enough to repent of these ill-natured reflections upon him, and tremble to think of thy own presumption." There is enough in this one plain truth, *That God is greater than man,* to put to silence all our complaints of his providence and our exceptions against his dealings with us. He is not only more wise and powerful than we are, but more holy, just, and good, for these are the transcendent glories and excellencies of the divine nature; in these God is greater than man, and therefore it is absurd and unreasonable to find fault with him. God is not accountable to us (*v.* 13): *Why dost thou strive against him?* It is an unreasonable thing for us, weak, foolish, sinful, creatures, to strive with a God of infinite wisdom, power, and goodness. *He gives not account of all his matters* (so some read it); he reveals as much as it is fit for us to know, as follows here (*v.* 14).

Verses 14–18

Job had complained that God kept him wholly in the dark concerning the meaning of his dealings with him, and therefore concluded he dealt with him as his enemy. "No," says Elihu, "he speaks to you, but you do not perceive him; so that the fault is yours, not his; and he is designing your real good even in those dispensations which you put this harsh construction upon." 1. What a friend God is to our welfare: *He speaketh to us once, yea, twice, v.* 14. When one warning is neglected he gives another. 2. What enemies we are to our own welfare: *Man perceives it not,* is not aware that it is the voice of God. He stops his ear, stands in his own light, rejects the counsel of God against himself. God teaches and admonishes the children of men by their own consciences.

I. The proper season and opportunity for these admonitions (*v.* 15): *In a dream, in slumberings upon the bed,* when men are retired from the world and the business and conversation of it. Thus he made his mind known to the prophets by visions and dreams (Num. xii. 6). When he stirred up conscience, that ordinary deputy of his, in the soul, to do its office, he took that opportunity, either when deep sleep fell on men (for, though dreams mostly come from fancy, some may come from conscience) or in slumberings, when men are between sleeping and waking, reflecting at night upon the business of the foregoing day or projecting in the morning the business of the ensuing day; then is a proper time for their hearts to reproach them for what they have done ill and to admonish them what they should do.

II. The power and force with which those admonitions come, *v.* 16. *Then he opens the ears of men,* which were before shut. He opens the heart, as he opened Lydia's, and so opens the ears. *He sealeth their instruction,* that is, the instruction that is designed for them and is suited to them; this he makes their souls to receive the deep and lasting impression of, as the wax of the seal.

III. The end and design of these admonitions that are sent. 1. To keep men from sin, and particularly the sin of pride (*v.* 17). *That he may withdraw man*

from his purpose, that is, from his evil purposes. Many a man has been stopped in the full career of a sinful pursuit by the seasonable checks of his own conscience, saying, *Do not this abominable thing which the Lord hates.* Particularly, God does, by this means, *hide pride from man.* That he may *take away pride from man* (so some read it), that he may pluck up that root of bitterness which is the cause of so much sin. 2. To keep men from ruin, *v.* 18. God, by the admonitions of conscience, withdraws them from sin, he thereby *keeps back* their souls *from the pit.* What a mercy it is to be under the restraints of an awakened conscience. Faithful are the wounds, and kind are the bonds, of that friend.

Verses 19–28

God speaks a second time, and tries another way to convince and reclaim sinners, and that is by providences, afflictive and merciful (in which he speaks twice). Job complained much of his diseases and judged by them that God was angry with him; but Elihu shows that God often afflicts the body in love, and with gracious designs of good to the soul. This part of Elihu's discourse will be of great use to us for the due improvement of sickness, by which God speaks to men.

I. See what work sickness makes (*v.* 19, &c.) when God sends it with commission. 1. The sick man is full of pain all over him (*v.* 19): *He is chastened with pain upon his bed.* Pain and sickness will turn a bed of down into a bed of thorns. Frequently the stronger the patient the stronger the pain. It is not the smarting of the flesh that is complained of, but the aching of the bones. It is an inward rooted pain; and not only the bones of one limb, but *the multitude of the bones,* are thus chastened. By the grace of God, the pain of the body is often made a means of good to the soul. 2. He has quite lost his appetite, the common effect of sickness (*v.* 20): *His life abhorreth bread,* the most necessary food. 3. He has become a perfect skeleton, nothing but skin and bones, *v.* 21. 4. *His soul draws near to the grave,* and in the apprehension of all about him, as well as in his own, he is a dying man. The pangs of death, here called *the destroyers,* are ready to seize him.

II. The provision made for his instruction, that, when God in that way speaks to man, he may be heard and understood, *v.* 23. He is happy *if there be a messenger with him an interpreter* to expound the providence and give him to understand the meaning of it, *a man of wisdom* that knows the voice of the rod and its interpretation. The advice and help of a good minister are as needful and seasonable, and should be as acceptable, in sickness, as of a good physician, especially if he be well skilled in the art of explaining and improving providences. His business at such a time is *to show his uprightness,* that is, God's uprightness, that in faithfulness he afflicts him. If it appear that the sick person is truly pious, the interpreter will not do as Job's friends had done, make it his business to prove him a hypocrite because he is afflicted, but will show him his uprightness, notwithstanding his afflictions, that he may be easy.

III. God's gracious acceptance of him, upon his repentance, *v.* 24. Wherever God finds a gracious heart he will be found a gracious God; and, 1. He will give a gracious order for his discharge. He says, *Deliver him* (that is, let him be delivered) *from going down to the pit,* from that death which is the wages of sin. 2. He will give a gracious reason for this order: *I have found a ransom,* or propitiation; Jesus Christ is that ransom, so Elihu calls him, as Job had called him his Redeemer, for he is both the purchaser and the price, the priest and the sacrifice. God glories in the invention here, εὑρηκα, εὑρηκα—"I have found, I have found, the ransom; I, even I, am he that has done it."

IV. The recovery of the sick man hereupon. When the patient becomes a penitent see what a blessed change follows. 1. His body recovers its health, *v.* 25. This is not always the consequence of a sick man's repentance and return to God, but sometimes it is; and recovery from sickness is a mercy indeed when it arises from the remission of sin. Interest him in the ransom, and then *his flesh shall be fresher than a child's* and there shall be no remains of his distemper, but *he shall return to the days of his youth*, to the beauty and strength which he had then. 2. His soul recovers its peace, *v.* 26. (1) The patient, being a penitent, is a supplicant, and has learned to pray. (2) His prayers are accepted. All true penitents rejoice more in the returns of God's favour than in any instance whatsoever of prosperity or pleasure, Ps. iv. 6, 7.

V. The general rule which God will go by in dealing with the children of men inferred from this instance, *v.* 27, 28. As sick people, upon their submission, are restored so all others that truly repent of their sins shall find mercy with God. Would we know the nature of sin and the malignity of it? It is the perverting of that which is right; it is a most unjust unreasonable thing; it is the rebellion of the creature against the Creator, the usurped dominion of the flesh over the spirit. Would we know what is to be got by sin? *It profiteth us not*. What reason we have to repent. We must confess the fault of sin, the iniquity, the dishonesty of it (*I have perverted that which was right*); we must confess the folly of sin— "so foolish have I been and ignorant, for *it profited me not*." God looked upon sinners with an eye of compassion, desiring to hear this from them; for he has no pleasure in their ruin. He shall be happy in everlasting life and joy: *His life shall see the light*, that is, all good, in the vision and fruition of God.

Verses 29–33

Elihu briefly sums up what he had said, showing that God's great and gracious design, in all the dispensations of his providence towards the children of men, is to save them from being for ever miserable and bring them to be for ever happy, *v.* 29, 30. He deals with them by conscience, by providences, by ministers, by mercies, by afflictions. He makes them sick, and makes them well again. All providences are to be looked upon as God's workings with man, his strivings with him. Why does he take all this pains with man? It is *to bring back his soul from the pit*, *v.* 30. Job is welcome to make what objections he can (*v.* 32): *If thou hast anything to say* for thyself, in thy own vindication, *answer me. Speak, for I desire to justify thee*. Elihu lets him know that he has something more to say, which he desires him patiently to attend to (*v.* 33): *Hold thy peace, and I will teach thee wisdom*.

Chapter 34

Elihu, it is likely, paused awhile, to see if Job had anything to say; but he sitting silent, Elihu proceeds. I. He bespeaks not only the audience, but the assistance of the company, ver. 2–4. II. He charges Job with some more expressions that had dropped from him, ver. 5–9. III. He undertakes to convince him that he had spoken amiss, by showing very fully, 1. God's incontestable justice, ver. 10–12, 17, 19, 23. 2. His sovereign dominion, ver. 13–15. 3. His almighty power, ver. 20, 24. 4. His omniscience, ver. 21, 22, 25. 5. His severity against sinners, ver. 26–28. 6. His overruling providence, ver. 29, 30. IV. He teaches him what he should say, ver. 31, 32. And then, lastly, he leaves the matter to Job's own conscience, and concludes with a sharp reproof for his discontent, ver. 33–37. All this Job not only bore patiently, but took kindly, because, whereas his other friends had accused him of that from which his own conscience acquitted him, Elihu charged him with that only for which, it is probable, his own heart, now upon the reflection, began to smite him.

Verses 1–9

I. Elihu addresses himself to the auditors, and endeavours to gain their goodwill and attention.

1. He calls them *wise men*, and men that *had knowledge*, *v.* 2. It is comfortable dealing with such as understand sense. Elihu differed in opinion from them, and yet he calls them wise and knowing men. 2. He appeals to their judgment, and therefore submits to their trial, *v.* 3. *The ear* of the judicious *tries words*, whether what is said to be true or false, right or wrong, and he that speaks must stand the test of the intelligent. 3. He takes them into partnership with him in the examination and discussion of this matter, *v.* 4. He does not pretend to be sole dictator. "Let us agree to lay aside all animosities and prejudices and *let us choose to ourselves judgment*; and *let us know among ourselves*, by comparing notes and communicating our reasons, *what is good* and what is otherwise."

II. He warmly accuses Job for some passionate words which he had spoken, that reflected on the divine government.

1. He recites the words which Job had spoken, as nearly as he can remember. Job hath said, *I am righteous* (*v.* 5), and, when urged to confess his guilt, had stiffly maintained his plea of, *Not guilty: Should I lie against my right? v.* 6. *My wound is incurable*, and likely to be mortal, and yet *without transgression*; *not for any injustice in my hand*, ch. xvi. 16, 17. He had, in effect, said that there is nothing to be got in the service of God and that no man will be the better at last for his religion (*v.* 9). This Elihu gathers as Job's opinion, by an innuendo from what he said (*ch.* ix. 22), *He destroys the perfect and the wicked*, which has a truth in it (for all things come alike to all), but it was ill expressed. Job sat down silently under it and attempted not his own vindication, whence Mr. Caryl well observes that good men sometimes speak worse than they mean, and that a good man will rather bear more blame than he deserves than stand to excuse himself when he has deserved any blame.

2. He charges Job: *What man is like Job? v.* 7. Did you ever know such a man as Job, or ever hear a man talk at such an extravagant rate? "He *drinketh up scorning like water*." By these foolish expressions of his he makes himself the object of scorn, lays himself very open to reproach, and gives occasion to others to laugh at him. He *goes in company with the workers of iniquity* (*v.* 8), not that in his conversation he did associate with them, but in his opinion he did favour and countenance them, and strengthen their hands.

Verses 10–15

The scope of Elihu's discourse is to reconcile Job to his afflictions. God meant him no hurt in afflicting him, but intended it for his spiritual benefit. In these verses he directs his discourse to all the company: "*Hearken to me, you men of understanding*" (*v.* 10). The righteous God never did, nor ever will do, any wrong to any of his creatures, but his ways are equal, ours are unequal.

I. This truth is laid down, both negatively and positively. *God cannot do wickedness, nor the Almighty commit iniquity*, *v.* 10. It is inconsistent with the perfection of his nature, and so it is also with the purity of his will (*v.* 12): *God will not do wickedly, neither will the Almighty pervert judgment*. He will never either do any man wrong or deny any man right, but *the heavens will shortly declare his righteousness*. Though he be Almighty, yet he never uses his power for the support of injustice. He is *Shaddai*— God *all-sufficient*, and therefore he cannot be *tempted with evil* (James i. 13). He ministers justice to all (*v.* 11): *The work of a man shall he render unto him*.

II. How warmly it is asserted, 1. With an assurance of the truth of it: *Yea, surely*, *v.* 12. 2. With an abhorrence of the very thought of the contrary

(v. 10): *Far be it from God that he should do wickedness*, and from us that we should imagine such a thing.

III. How evidently it is proved by two arguments:

1. His independent absolute sovereignty and dominion (v. 13): *Who has given him a charge over the earth?* He has the sole administration of the kingdoms of men, and has it of himself.

2. His irresistible power (v. 14): *If he set his heart upon man*, to contend with him, much more *if* (as some read it) *he set his heart against man*, to ruin him, if he should deal with man either by *summa potestas— mere sovereignty*, or by *summum jus—strict justice*, there were no standing before him; man's spirit and breath would soon be gone and *all flesh would perish together, v.* 15.

Verses 16–30

Elihu here addresses himself more directly to Job.

I. God is not to be quarrelled with for anything that he does. *Shall even he that hates right govern? v.* 17. The righteous Lord so loves righteousness that, in comparison with him, even Job himself, though a perfect and upright man, might be said to hate right; and shall he govern? Shall he pretend to direct God or correct what he does? *Wilt thou condemn him that is righteous in all his ways*, and cannot but he so? *He regardeth not the rich more than the poor*, and therefore it is fit he should rule, and it is not fit we should find fault with him, *v.* 19. A great man shall fare never the better, nor find any favour, for his wealth and greatness; nor shall a poor man fare ever the worse for his poverty, nor an honest cause be starved.

II. God is to be acknowledged and submitted to in all that he does. Divers considerations Elihu here suggests to Job, to beget in him great and high thoughts of God, and so to persuade him to submit and proceed no further in his quarrel with him.

1. God is almighty, and able to deal with the strongest of men when he enters into judgment with them (v. 20); even *the people*, the body of a nation, though ever so numerous, *shall be troubled*, unhinged, and put into disorder, when God pleases; even *the mighty* man, the prince, *shall*, if God speak the word, *be taken away* out of his throne. Nor is it one single mighty man only that he can thus overpower, but even hosts of them (v. 24).

2. God is omniscient, and can discover that which is most secret. As the strongest cannot oppose his arm, so the most subtle cannot escape his eye; and therefore, if some are punished either more or less than we think they should be, instead of quarrelling with God, it becomes us to ascribe it to some secret cause known to God only. Everything is open before him (v. 21): *His eyes are upon the ways of man. There is no darkness nor shadow of death* so close, so remote from light or sight as that in it *the workers of iniquity may hide themselves* from the discovering eye of the righteous God. The workers of iniquity may find ways and means to hide themselves from men, but not from God: *He knows their works* (v. 25), both what they do and what they design.

3. God is righteous. *He will not lay upon man more than right, v.* 23. As he will not punish the innocent, so he will not exact of those that are guilty more than their iniquities deserve; and of the proportion between the sin and the punishment Infinite Wisdom shall be the judge. Therefore Job was to be blamed for his complaints of God. These unjust judges were rebels to God: They *turned back from him*, cast off the fear of him, and abandoned the very thoughts of him; for *they would not consider any of his ways*, took no heed either to his precepts or to his providences, but lived without God in the world. They were tyrants to all mankind, *v.* 28.

4. God has an uncontrollable dominion in all the affairs of the children of men, and so guides and governs whatever concerns both communities and particular persons, that, as what he designs cannot be defeated, so what he does cannot be changed, *v.* 29. The frowns of all the world cannot trouble those whom God quiets with his smiles. *When he gives quietness who then can make trouble? v.* 29. If God give outward peace to a nation, he can secure what he gives. If God give inward peace to a man only, neither the accusations of Satan nor the afflictions of this present time, no, nor the arrests of death itself, can give trouble. See Phil. iv. 7. If God in displeasure, *hide his face*, and withhold the comfort of his favour, *who then can behold him?*

5. God is wise, and careful of the public welfare, and therefore provides *that the hypocrite reign not, lest the people be ensnared, v.* 30. The pride of hypocrites. They aim to reign; the praise of men, and power in the world, are their reward. The policy of tyrants. When they aim to set up themselves they sometimes make use of religion as a cloak and cover for their ambition. The danger the people are in when hypocrites reign. They are likely to be ensnared in sin, or trouble, or both.

Verses 31–37

I. Elihu instructs Job what he should say under his affliction, *v.* 31, 32. In general, he would have him repent of his expressions, under his affliction. Job's other friends would have had him own himself a wicked man, and by overdoing they undid. Elihu will oblige him only to own that he had, in the management of this controversy, *spoken unadvisedly with his lips.* He directs Job, 1. To humble himself before God for his sins, and to accept the punishment of them: "*I have borne chastisement.*" Many are chastised that do not bear chastisement, do not bear it well, and so, in effect, do not bear it at all. Penitents, if sincere, will take all well that God does, and will bear chastisement as a medicinal operation intended for good. 2. To pray to God to discover his sins to him (v. 32). 3. To promise reformation (v. 31): *I will not offend any more.* "*If I have done iniquity* (or *seeing I have*), *I will do so no more;* whatever thou shalt discover to me to have been amiss, by thy grace I will amend it for the future."

II. He reasons with him concerning his discontent and uneasiness under his affliction, *v.* 33. We are ready to think every thing that concerns us should be just as we would have it; but Elihu here shows it is absurd and unreasonable to expect this: "*Should it be according to thy mind?* No, what reason for that?"

III. He appeals to all intelligent indifferent persons whether there was not sin and folly in that which Job said. "*My desire is that Job may be tried unto the end.* Let the trial be continued till the end be obtained." He appeals both to God and man, and desires the judgment of both upon it. Some read *v.* 36 as an appeal to God: *O my Father! let Job be tried.* So the margin of our Bibles, for the same word signifies *my desire* and *my father*; and some suppose that he lifted up his eyes when he said this, meaning, "*O my Father who art in heaven! let Job be tried till he be subdued.*"

CHAPTER 35

Job, being still silent, Elihu a third time, undertakes to show him that he had spoken amiss, and ought to recant. I. He had represented religion as an indifferent unprofitable thing; Elihu evinces the contrary, ver. 1–8. II. He had complained of God as deaf to the cries of the oppressed, ver. 9–13. III. He had despaired of the return of God's favour to him, because it was so long deferred, but Elihu shows him the true cause of the delay, ver. 14–16.

Verses 1–8

I. The bad words which Elihu charges upon Job, *v.* 2, 3. It intimates his good opinion of Job, that he thought better than he spoke, and that, when he perceived his mistake, he would not stand to it. "Thou hast, in effect, said, *My righteousness is more than God's.*" Job did in effect say, *My righteousness is more than God's* (v. 2); for if he got nothing by his religion, God was more beholden to him than he was to God. But, though there might be some colour for it, yet it was not fair to charge these words upon Job, when he himself had made them the wicked words of prospering sinners (ch. xxi. 15, *What profit shall we have if we pray to him?*).

II. The good answer which Elihu gives to this (v. 4): "*I will* undertake to *answer thee, and thy companions with thee,*" that is, all those that approve thy sayings. To do this he has recourse to his old maxim (ch. xxxiii. 12), *that God is greater than man.* Elihu needs not prove that God is above man; it is agreed by all; but he endeavours to affect Job and us with it, by an ocular demonstration of the height of the heavens and the clouds, v. 5. They are far above us, and God is far above them; how much then is he set out of the reach either of our sins or of our services! *Look unto the heavens, and behold the clouds.* He utterly denies that God can be either prejudiced or advantaged by what any, even the greatest men of the earth, do, or can do. Sin is said to *be against God* because so the sinner intends it and so God takes it, and it is an injury to his honour; yet it cannot *do anything against him.* Job therefore spoke amiss in saying *What profit is it that I am cleansed from my sin?* God was no gainer by his reformation; and who then would gain if he himself did not? The services of the best saints are no profit to him (v. 7): *If thou be righteous, what givest thou to him?*

Verses 9–13

Elihu returns an answer to another word that Job had said, which, he thought, reflected upon the justice and goodness of God.

I. Job complained that God did not regard the cries of the oppressed against their oppressors (v. 9): "*By reason of the multitude of oppressions they make the oppressed to cry;* but it is to no purpose: God does not appear to right them." This seems to refer to those words of Job (ch. xxiv. 12), *Men groan from out of the city, and the soul of the wounded cries out against the oppressors, yet God lays not folly to them. Is there a righteous God, and can it be that he should so slowly hear, so slowly see?*

II. How Elihu solves the difficulty. If the cries of the oppressed be not heard, the fault is in themselves; they *ask and have not,* but it is *because they ask amiss,* James iv. 3. *They cry out by reason of the arm of the mighty,* but it is not a penitent praying cry, the cry of nature and passion, not of grace.

1. They do not enquire after God, nor seek to acquaint themselves with him, under their affliction (v. 10): *But none saith, Where is God my Maker?* God is our Maker, the author of our being. It is our duty therefore to enquire after him. Where is he, that we may pay our homage to him? All are asking, Where is mirth? Where is wealth? Where is a good bargain? But none ask, *Where is God my Maker?*

2. They do not take notice of the mercies they enjoy in their afflictions. He provides for our inward comfort and joy under our outward troubles. He *gives songs in the night,* that is, when our condition is ever so dark, and sad, and melancholy, there is that in God, in his providence and promise. He preserves to us the use of our reason and understanding (v. 11): *Who teaches us more than the beasts of the earth,* that is, who has endued us with more noble powers and faculties than they are endued with and has made us capable of more excellent pleasures and employments here and for ever. Now this fur-

nishes us with matter for thanksgiving, even under the heaviest burden of affliction. Whatever we are deprived of, we have our immortal souls continued to us; even those that kill the body cannot hurt *them.* This is the greatest excellency of reason, that it makes us capable of religion, and it is in that especially that we are *taught more than the beasts and the fowls.* They have wonderful instincts and sagacities in seeking out their food, their physic, their shelter; but none of them are capable of enquiring, *Where is God my Maker?* Something like logic, and philosophy, and politics, has been observed among the brute-creatures, but never anything of divinity or religion; these are peculiar to man. If therefore the oppressed only *cry by reason of the arm of the mighty,* and do not look up to God, they do no more than the brutes (who complain when they are hurt). God relieves the brute-creatures because they cry to him according to the best of their capacity, ch. xxxviii. 41; Ps. civ. 21. But what reason have men to expect relief, who are capable of enquiring after God as their Maker and yet cry to him no otherwise than as brutes do? *There they cry but none gives answer.* God does not work deliverance for them, *because of the pride of evil men;* they *regard iniquity in their hearts,* and therefore God will not hear their prayers, Ps. lxvi. 18; Isa. i. 15. The case is plain then, If we cry to God for the removal of the oppression and affliction we are under, and it is not removed, the reason is not because the Lord's hand is shortened or his ear heavy, but because the affliction has not done its work; we are not sufficiently humbled, and therefore must thank ourselves that it is continued.

Verses 14–16

I. Another improper word for which Elihu reproves Job (v. 14): *Thou sayest thou shalt not see him;* that is, 1. "Thou complainest that thou dost not understand the meaning of his severe dealings with thee." As, when we are in prosperity, we are ready to think our mountain will never be brought low, so when we are in adversity we are ready to think our valley will never be filled, but, in both, to conclude that *to-morrow must be as this day,* which is as absurd as to think, when the weather is either fair or foul, that it will be always so, that the flowing tide will always flow, or the ebbing tide will always ebb.

II. The answer which Elihu gives is this, 1. That, when he looked up to God, he had no just reason to speak thus despairingly: *Judgment is before him,* that is, "He knows what he has to do, and will do all in infinite wisdom and justice; he has the entire plan and model of providence before him. *Therefore trust in him,* depend upon him, wait for him, and believe that the issue will be good at last." He is a God of judgment (Isa. xxx. 18), we shall see no reason to despair of relief from him, but all the reason in the world to hope in him. "*Because it is not so,* because thou dost not thus trust in him, therefore the affliction which came at first from love has now displeasure mixed with it. Now God *has visited thee in his anger.*" Elihu concludes therefore that *Job opens his mouth in vain* (v. 16), because he does not trust in God and wait for him. Let not that man who distrusts God *think that he shall receive anything from him,* James i. 7. He did not, as his other friends, condemn him for a hypocrite, but charged him only with Moses's sin, *speaking unadvisedly with his lips* when his spirit was provoked.

CHAPTER 36

Elihu, having largely reproved Job for some of his unadvised speeches, urges many reasons, taken from the wisdom and righteousness of God, his care of his people, and especially his greatness and almighty power, with which he persuades him to submit to the hand of God. I. His preface, ver. 2–4. II. The account he gives of the methods of God's providence towards the children of men, according as they conduct themselves, ver. 5–15. III. The fair warning and good counsel he gives to Job thereupon, ver. 16–21. IV. His demonstration of God's sovereignty and omnipotence, which is a reason why we should all submit to him in his dealings with us, ver. 22–23.

Verses 1–4

Once more Elihu begs the patience of the auditory, and Job's particularly. To gain this he pleads, 1. That he had a good cause, and a noble and very fruitful subject: *I have yet to speak on God's behalf.* 2. That he had something to offer: *I will fetch my knowledge from afar* (v. 3), that is, we will have recourse to our first principles. It is worth while to go far for this knowledge of God, to dig for it, to travel for it; it will recompense our pains, and, though far-fetched, is not dear-bought. *"My words shall not be false.* He who is perfect or upright in knowledge is now reasoning with thee; and therefore let him not only have a fair hearing, but let what he says be taken in good part, as meant well."

Verses 5–14

Elihu, being to speak on God's behalf, shows that the disposals of divine Providence are all according to the eternal rules of equity. God acts as a righteous governor, for,

I. He does not think it below him to take notice of the meanest of his subjects, but *God is mighty,* infinitely so, and yet he *despises not any,* v. 5. Job thought himself and his cause slighted because God did not immediately appear for him. "No," says Elihu, *God despises not any,* which is a good reason why we should honour all men.

II. He gives no countenance to the greatest, if they be bad (v. 6): *He preserves not the life of the wicked.* Though their life may be prolonged, yet not under any special care of the divine Providence, but only its common protection.

III. He is always ready to right those that are any way injured, and to plead, their cause (v. 6). If men will not right the injured poor, God will.

IV. He takes a particular care for the protection of his good subjects, v. 7. He not only looks on them, but he never looks off them: *He withdraws not his eyes from the righteous.* Though they may seem sometimes neglected and forgotten, yet the tender careful eye of their heavenly Father never withdraws from them.

1. Sometimes he prefers good people to places of trust and honour (v. 7): *With kings are they on the throne,* and every sheaf is made to bow to theirs. When righteous persons are advanced to places of honour and power, it is in mercy to them. It is also in mercy to those over whom they are set: *When the righteous bear rule the city rejoices.*

2. If at any time he bring them into affliction, it is for the good of their souls, v. 8–10. *If they be bound in fetters,* laid in prison as Joseph was, or *holden in the cords of* any other *affliction,* confined by pain and sickness, hampered by poverty, it is for the benefit of their souls, the consideration of which should reconcile us to affliction. Three things God intends when he afflicts us:—(1) To discover past sins to us. *He shows them their work.* Sin is our own work. (2) To dispose our hearts to receive present instructions: Then *he opens their ear to discipline,* v. 10. Whom God chastens *he teaches* (Ps. xciv. 12), and the affliction makes people willing to learn, softens the wax, that it may receive the impression of the seal; yet it does not do this of itself, but the grace of God working with and by it. (3) To deter and draw us off from iniquity for the future.

3. If the affliction do its work, and accomplish that for which it is sent, he will comfort them again, according to the time that he has afflicted them (v. 11). If we faithfully serve God, (1) We have the promise of outward prosperity, the promise of the life that now is, and the comforts of it, as far as is for God's glory and our good; and who would desire them any further? (2) We have the possession of inward pleasures, the comfort of communion with God and a good conscience, and that great peace which those have that love God's law.

4. If the affliction do not do its work, let them expect the consuming fire will prevail if the refining fire do not; for when God judges he will overcome.

V. He brings ruin upon hypocrites, the secret enemies of his kingdom (such as Elihu described, v. 12). *They cry not when he binds them,* that is, when they are in affliction, bound with the cords of trouble, their hearts are hardened, they are stubborn and unhumbled, and will not cry to God nor make their application to him. *They die in youth, and their life is among the unclean,* v. 14.

Verses 15–23

Elihu here comes more closely to Job; and,

I. He tells him what God would have done for him before this if he had been duly humbled under his affliction (v. 15). "The poor in spirit, those that are of a broken and contrite heart, he looks upon with tenderness, and, when they are in affliction, is ready to help them. He *opens their ears,* and makes them to hear joy and gladness, even *in* their *oppressions.* If thou hadst accommodated thyself to the will of God, thy liberty and plenty would have been restored to thee with advantage." 1. "Thou wouldst have been enlarged, and not confined thus by thy sickness and disgrace: *He would have removed thee into a broad place where is no straitness,* and thou wouldst no longer have been cramped thus and have had all thy measures broken." 2. "Thou wouldst have been enriched, and wouldst not have been left in this poor condition; thou wouldst have had thy table richly spread, not only with food convenient, but with the finest of the wheat."

II. He charges him with standing in his own light, and makes him the cause of the continuance of his own trouble (v. 17): *"But thou hast fulfilled the judgment of the wicked,"* that is, "Whatever thou art really, in this thing thou hast conducted thyself like a wicked man, and *therefore* judgment and justice take hold on thee as a wicked man."

III. He cautions him not to persist in his frowardness. *"Because there is wrath"* (that is, "because God is a righteous governor, because thou hast reason to fear that thou art under God's displeasure) therefore *beware lest he take thee away* suddenly *with his stroke,* and be so wise as to make thy peace with him quickly and get his anger turned away from thee." This was a friendly caution to Job, and necessary. There is no escaping by money, no purchasing a pardon with silver, or gold, and such corruptible things: "Even *a great ransom cannot deliver thee* when God enters into judgment with thee. If *all the forces of strength* were at thy command, if thou couldst muster ever so many servants and vassals to appear for thee it were all in vain. There is *none that can deliver out of his hand.*" There is no escaping by absconding (v. 20): *"Desire not the night,* which often favours the retreat of a conquered army and covers it; think not that thou canst so escape the righteous judgment of God, for the *darkness hideth not from him,"* Ps. cxxxix. 11, 12. *"Take heed,* look well to thy own spirit, and *regard not iniquity,* return not to it (so some), for it is at thy peril if thou do." Let him not dare to prescribe to God, nor give him his measures (v. 22, 23): *"Behold, God exalteth by his power,"* that is, "He does, may, and can set up and pull down whom he pleases, and therefore it is not for thee nor me to contend with him." He is an incomparable teacher: *Who teaches like him?* It is absurd for us to teach him who is himself the fountain of light, truth, knowledge, and instruction. *He that teaches man knowledge*, and so as none else can, *shall not he know?* Shall we light a candle to the sun? When Elihu would give glory to God as a ruler he praises him as a teacher, for rulers must teach. He teaches by the Bible, and that is the best book, teaches by his Son, and he is the best Master.

Verses 24–33

Elihu is here endeavouring to give Job great and high thoughts of God, and so to persuade him into a cheerful submission to his providence.

I. He represents the work of God, in general, *v.* 24. God does nothing mean. His visible works, those of nature, are such as we admire and commend, and in which we observe the Creator's wisdom, power, and goodness; shall we then find fault with his dispensations concerning us. Look which way we will, we see: "This is *the work of God*," the finger of God; it is the Lord's doing. Every man may see, afar off, the heaven and all its lights, the earth and all its fruits, to be the work of Omnipotence. Look at the minutest works of nature through a microscope; do they not appear curious? The eternal power and godhead of the Creator are *clearly seen and understood* by the *things that are made*, Rom. i. 20. It ought to be marvellous in our eyes. The beauty and excellency of the work of God, and the agreement of all the parts of it, are what we must remember to magnify and highly to extol.

II. He represents God, the author of them, as infinite and unsearchable, *v.* 26. The streams of being, power, and perfection should lead us to the fountain. *God is great*, infinitely so, and therefore greatly to be praised,—great, and therefore *we know him not*. We know that he is, but not what he is. We know what he is not, but not what he is. We know in part, but not in perfection. *The number of his years cannot* possibly *be searched out*, for he is eternal; there is no number of them. He is a Being without beginning, succession, or period, who ever was, and ever will be, and ever the same, the great *I AM*. This is a good reason why we should not prescribe to him, nor quarrel with him.

III. He gives some instances of God's wisdom, power, and sovereign dominion, beginning in this chapter with the clouds and the rain that descends from them. We need not be critical in examining either the phrase or the philosophy of this noble discourse. The general scope of it is to show that God is infinitely great, and the Lord of all, the first cause and supreme director of all the creatures, and *has all power in heaven and earth* (whom therefore we ought, with all humility and reverence, to adore, to speak well of, and to give honour to), and that it is presumption for us to prescribe to him the rules and methods of his special providence towards the children of men. Elihu, to affect Job with God's sublimity and sovereignty, had directed him (*ch.* xxxv. 5) to look unto the clouds. Consider the clouds,

1. As springs to this lower world, the source and treasure of its moisture. The clouds above distil upon the earth below. If the heavens become brass, the earth becomes iron; therefore thus the promise of plenty runs, *I will hear the heavens and they shall hear the earth*. Every good gift is from above, from him who is both Father of lights and Father of the rain. They are here said to *distil upon man* (*v.* 28); for, though indeed God *causes it to rain in the wilderness where no man is* (*ch.* xxxviii. 26; Ps. civ. 11), yet special respect is had to man herein, to whom the inferior creatures are all made serviceable. Among men, he *causes his rain to fall upon the just and upon the unjust*, Matt. v. 45. They are said to distil the water in *small drops*, not in spouts, as when the

windows of heaven were opened, Gen. vii. 11. God waters the earth with that with which he once drowned it. Though it comes down in drops, yet it distils upon man *abundantly* (*v.* 28), and therefore is called *the river of God which is full of water*, Ps. lxv. 9. The clouds *pour down according to the vapour* that they draw up, *v.* 27. So just the heavens are to the earth, but the earth is not so in the return it makes.

2. As shadows to the upper world (*v.* 29): *Can any understand the spreading of the clouds?* Shall we then pretend to understand the reasons and methods of God's judicial proceedings with the children of men whose characters and cases are so various. By the interposition of the clouds between us and the sun, we are favoured; for they serve as an umbrella to shelter us from the violent heat of the sun. A *cloud of dew in the heat of harvest* is spoken of as a very great refreshment, Isa. xviii. 4. Sometimes we are by them frowned upon; for they darken the earth at noon-day and eclipse the light of the sun. Sin is compared to a cloud (Isa. xliv. 22), because it comes between us and the light of God's countenance and obstructs the shining of it. But though the clouds darken the sun for a time, and pour down rain, yet after he has wearied the cloud, *he spreads his light upon it*, *v.* 30. There is a *clear shining after rain*, 2 Sam. xxiii. 4.

Chapter 37

Elihu here goes on to extol the wonderful power of God in the meteors and all the changes of the weather: if, in those changes, we submit to the will of God, take the weather as it is and make the best of it, why should we not do so in other changes of our condition? Here he observes the hand of God, I. In the thunder and lightning, ver. 1–5. II. In the frost and snow, the rains and wind, ver. 6–13. III. He applies it to Job, and challenges him to solve the phenomena of these works of nature, that, confessing his ignorance in them, he might own himself as incompetent judge in the proceedings of divine Providence, ver. 14–22. And then, IV. Concludes with his principle, God is great and greatly to be feared, ver. 23, 24.

Verses 1–5

Thunder and lightning are sensible indications of the glory and majesty of Almighty God. In these God leaves not himself without witness of his greatness, as, in the rain from heaven and fruitful seasons, he leaves not himself without witness of his goodness (Acts xiv. 17). It is very probable that at this time, when Elihu was speaking, it thundered and lightened, for he speaks of the phenomena as present; and, God being about to speak (*ch.* xxxviii. 1), these were, as on Mount Sinai, the proper prefaces to command attention and awe. Elihu was himself affected, and desired to affect Job, with the appearance of God's glory in the thunder and lightning (*v.* 1, 2): "For my part," says Elihu, "*my heart trembles* at it; it is still terrible to me, and makes my heart beat as if it would move *out of its place*." He also calls upon Job to attend to it (*v.* 2): *Hear attentively the noise of his voice*. To apprehend and understand the instructions God thereby gives us, we have need to hear with great attention and application of mind. God directs the thunder, and the lightning is his, *v.* 3. Their production and motion are not from chance, though to us they seem accidental and ungovernable. The claps of thunder roll *under the whole heaven*, and are heard far and near; so are the lightnings darted to *the ends of the earth*. The lightning is first directed, and *after it a voice roars*, *v.* 4. The thunder is here called *the voice of God's excellency*, because by it he proclaims his transcendent power and greatness. He will not stay the rains and showers that usually follow upon the thunder, but will pour them out upon the earth *when his voice is heard*. Does God thunder thus marvellously with his voice? From this one instance we may argue to all, that, in the dispensations of his providence, there is that which is too great, too strong, for us to oppose or strive against.

Verses 6–13

The changes and extremities of the weather, wet or dry, hot or cold, are the subject of a great deal of our common talk, but how seldom do we think and speak of these things, as Elihu does here, with regard to God. We must take notice of the glory of God, not only in the thunder and lightning, but in the more common revolutions of the weather.

I. In the snow and rain, *v.* 6. Then *he saith to the snow, Be thou on the earth.* He speaks, and it is done: as in the creation of the world, *Let there be light,* so in the words of common providence, *Snow, be thou on the earth.* Saying and doing are not two things with God, though they are with us. When he speaks the word *the small rain* distils and *the great rain pours down* as he pleases—*the winter-rain.* The providence of God is to be acknowledged, both by husbandmen in the fields and travellers upon the road, in every shower of rain, whether it does them a kindness or a diskindness. It is sin and folly to contend with God's providence in the weather. The effect of the extremity of the winter-weather obliges both men and beasts to retire. *He seals up the hand of every man.* In frost and snow, husbandmen cannot follow their business, nor some tradesmen, nor travellers. The plough is laid by, the shipping laid up. Men, being taken off from their own work, *may know his work,* and contemplate that, and give him the glory. When we are confined to our houses we should thereby be driven to our Bibles and ours knees. *The beasts* also *retire to* their *dens and remain in their close places, v.* 8. The wild beasts must seek a shelter for themselves, to which by instinct they are directed, while the tame beasts, which are serviceable to man, are housed and protected by his care.

II. In the winds, which blow from different quarters and produce different effects (*v.* 9): *Out of the hidden place* (so it may be read) *comes the whirlwind;* it turns round, and so it is hard to say from which point it comes but it comes from *the secret chamber,* as the word signifies, which I am not so willing to understand of the *south,* because he says here (*v.* 17) that the wind out of the south is so far from being a whirlwind that it is a warming, quieting, wind.

III. In the frost, *v.* 10. See the cause of it: It *is given by the breath of God,* that is, by the word of his power and the command of his will; or, as some understand it, by the wind, which is the breath of God, as the thunder is his voice; it is caused by the cold freezing wind out of the north. See the effect of it: *The breadth of the waters is straightened,* that is, the waters are congealed, benumbed, arrested, bound up in crystal fetters. This is such an instance of the power of God as, if it were not common, would be next to a miracle.

IV. In the clouds. Three sorts of clouds he here speaks of: 1. Close, black, thick clouds, pregnant with showers; and these with watering *he wearies* (*v.* 11), that is, they spend themselves, and are exhausted by the rain into which they melt and are dissolved, pouring out water till they are weary and can pour out no more. The clouds water the earth till they are weary; they spend and are spent for our benefit. 2. Bright thin clouds, clouds without water; and these *he scattereth;* they are dispersed of themselves. 3. Flying clouds, which do not dissolve, as the thick cloud, into a close rain, but are carried upon the wings of the wind from place to place, dropping showers as they go; and these are said to be *turned round about* by his counsels, *v.* 12.

Verses 14–20

Elihu here addresses himself closely to Job, desiring him to apply what he had hitherto said to himself. He begs that he would hearken to this discourse (*v.* 14), that he would pause awhile: *Stand still, and consider the wondrous works of God.* Elihu, for the humbling of Job, shows him,

I. That he had no insight into natural causes, could neither see the springs of them nor foresee the effects of them (*v.* 15–17): *Dost thou know* this and know that which are the *wondrous works of him who is perfect in knowledge?* We are here taught, 1. The perfection of God's knowledge. It is one of the most glorious perfections of God that he is perfect in knowledge; he is omniscient. His knowledge is intuitive: he *sees.* It is intimate and entire. To his knowledge there is nothing distant, but all near—nothing future, but all present—nothing hid, but all open. 2. The imperfection of our knowledge. The greatest philosophers are much in the dark concerning the powers and works of nature. We are a paradox to ourselves, and about us is a mystery. It is good for us to be made sensible of our own ignorance. Some have confessed their ignorance, and those that would not do this have betrayed it. But what incompetent judges we are of the divine politics, when we understand so little even of the divine mechanics. If we foresee the change of weather a few hours before, by vulgar observation, or when second causes have begun to work by the weather-glass, yet how little do these show us of the purposes of God by these changes! We know not how the clouds are poised in the air, the *balancing* of them, which is one of the wondrous works of God, so balanced that they do not fall at once, nor burst into cataracts or waterspouts. *He quiets the earth by the south wind,* when the spring comes. As he has a blustering freezing north wind, so he has a thawing, composing, south wind; the Spirit is compared to both, because he both convinces and comforts, Cant. iv. 16.

II. That he had no share at all in the first making of the world (*v.* 18): *Hast thou with him spread out the sky?* It *is strong,* and has its name from its stability. It still is what it was, and suffers no decay, nor shall the ordinances of heaven be altered till the lease expires with time. It is a *molten looking-glass,* smooth and polished, and without the least flaw or crack. In this, as in a looking-glass, we may *behold the glory of God* and the wisdom of *his handiwork,* Ps. xix. 1.

III. That neither he nor they were able to speak of the glory of God in any proportion to the merit of the subject, *v.* 19, 20. He challenges Job ironically: "*Teach us,* if thou canst, *what we shall say unto him, v.* 19. Thou hast a mind to reason with God, and wouldst have us to contend with him on thy behalf; teach us then what we shall say." He owns his own insufficiency: *We cannot order our speech by reason of darkness.* Those that through grace know much of God, yet know little in comparison with what is to be known, and what will be known, when that which is perfect shall come and the veil shall be rent. He is even ashamed of what he has said, not of the cause, but of his own management of it: "*Shall it be told him that I speak? v.* 20. By no means; let it never be spoken of," for he fears that the subject has suffered by his undertaking it, as a fine face is wronged by a bad painter.

Verses 21–24

Elihu here concludes his discourse with some short but great sayings concerning the glory of God, who has said that he will *dwell in the thick darkness* and *make that his pavilion* (2 Chron. vi. 1; Ps. xviii. 11). He saw the cloud, with a whirlwind in the bosom of it, coming out of the south; but now it hung so thick, so black, over their heads, that they could none of them *see the bright light which* just before *was in the clouds.* Yet he looks to the north, and sees it clear that way, which gives him hope that the clouds are not gathering for a deluge; they are covered, but not surrounded, with them. He expects that *the wind will pass* (so it may be read) *and cleanse them*, and then *fair weather will come out of the north* (v. 22) and all will be well. God will not always frown, nor contend for ever. He hastens to conclude, now that God is about to speak. He observes, (1) That *with God is terrible majesty*. He is a God of glory and transcendent perfection. (2) That when we speak *touching the Almighty* we must own that *we cannot find him out*; our finite understandings cannot comprehend his infinite perfections, v. 23. Can we put the sea into an egg-shell? (3) That *he is excellent in power*. (4) That he is no less excellent in wisdom and righteousness, *in judgment and plenty of justice*, else there would be little excellency in his power. (5) That *he will not afflict*, that is, that he will not afflict willingly; it is no pleasure to him to grieve the children of men, much less his own children. Some read it thus: "*The Almighty, whom we cannot find out, is great in power, but he will not afflict in judgment, and with him is plenty of justice*, nor is he extreme to mark what we do amiss." (6) He values not the censures of those who are wise in their own conceit: *He respecteth them not*, v. 24.

CHAPTER 38

In most disputes the strife is who shall have the last word. Job's friends had in this controversy, tamely yielded it to Job, and then he to Elihu. But, after all the wranglings of the counsel at bar, the judge upon the bench must have the last word; so God had here, and so he will have in every controversy. Job had often appealed to God, and had talked boldly, but, when God took the throne, Job had nothing to say in his own defence, but was silent, before him. Job's friends had sometimes appealed to God too: "O that God would speak!" ch. xi. 5. And now, at length, God does speak, when Job, by Elihu's clear and close arguings, was mollified a little, and mortified. It is the office of ministers to prepare the way of the Lord. That which the great God designs in this discourse is to humble Job, and bring him to repent of, and to recant, his passionate indecent expressions concerning God's providential dealings and this he does by calling upon Job to compare God's eternity with his own time, God's omniscience with his own ignorance, and God's omnipotence with his own impotency. I. He begins with an awakening challenge and demand in general, ver. 2, 3. II. He proceeds in divers particular instances and proofs of Job's utter inability to contend with God: for, 1. He knew nothing of the founding of the earth, ver. 4–7. 2. Nothing of the limiting of the sea, ver. 8–11. 3. Nothing of the morning-light, ver. 12–15. 4. Nothing of the dark recesses of the sea and earth, ver. 16–21. 5. Nothing of the springs in the clouds (ver. 22–27), nor the secret counsels by which they are directed. 6. He could do nothing towards the production of the rain, or frost, or lightning (ver. 28–30, 34, 35, 37, 38), nothing towards the directing of the stars and their influences (ver. 31–33), nothing towards the making of his own soul, ver. 36. And, lastly, he could not provide for the lions and the ravens, ver. 39–41. If, in these ordinary works of nature, Job was puzzled, how durst he pretend to dive into the counsels of God's government and to judge of them?

Verses 1–3

1. Who speaks—*The Lord*, Jehovah, not a created angel, but the eternal Word himself, the second person in the blessed Trinity, for it is he by whom the worlds were made, and that was no other than the Son of God. He begins with the creation of the world. Elihu had said, *God speaks to men and they do not perceive it* (ch. xxxiii. 14); but this they could not but perceive. 2. When he spoke—*Then*. When they had all had their saying, then it was time for God to interpose, whose judgment is according to truth. Job had silenced his three friends, and yet could not convince them of his integrity in the main. Elihu had silenced Job, and yet could not bring him to acknowledge his mismanagement of this dispute. But now God comes, and does both, convinces Job first of his unadvised speaking and makes him cry, *Peccavi—I have done wrong;* and, having humbled him, he puts honour upon him, by convincing his three friends that they had done him wrong. 3. How he spoke—*Out of the whirlwind*, the rolling and involving cloud. A whirlwind prefaced Ezekiel's vision (Ezek. i. 4), and Elijah's, 1 Kings xix. 11. God is said to have *his way in the whirlwind* (Nah. i. 3), and, to show that even the stormy wind fulfils his word, here it was made the

vehicle of it. 4. To whom he spoke: He *answered Job*, directed his speech to him, to convince him of what was amiss, before he cleared him from the unjust aspersions cast upon him. 5. What he said. The preface is very searching. (1) God charges him with ignorance and presumption in what he had said (v. 2): "*Who is this* that talks at this rate? Is it Job? What! my servant Job, a perfect and an upright man? Can he so far forget himself, and act unlike himself? Who, where is he *that darkens counsel thus by words without knowledge?* Let him show his face if he dare and stand to what he has said." A humble faith and sincere obedience shall see further and better into the secret of the Lord than all the philosophy of the schools, and the searches of science. This first word which God spoke is the more observable because Job, in his repentance, fastens upon it as that which silenced and humbled him, ch. xlii. 3. This he repeated and echoed as the arrow that stuck fast in him: "I am the fool that has darkened counsel." (2) He challenges him to give such proofs of his knowledge as would serve to justify his enquiries into the divine counsels (v. 3): "*Gird up now thy loins like a* stout *man; I will demand of thee*, will put some questions to thee, *and answer me* if thou canst, before I answer thine."

Verses 4–11

For the humbling of Job, God here shows him his ignorance even concerning the earth and the sea. I. Concerning the founding of the earth. 1. Let him tell where he was when this lower world was made (v. 4): "*Where wast thou when I laid the foundations of the earth?* Wast thou present when the world was made?" See here, (1) The greatness and glory of God: *I laid the foundations of the earth.* (2) The meanness of man: *Where wast thou* then? So far were we from having any hand in the creation of the world, which might entitle us to a dominion in it, or so much as being witnesses of it, by which we might have gained an insight into it, that we were not then in being. The first man was not, much less were we. It is the honour of Christ that he was present when this was done (Prov. viii. 22, &c.; John i. 1, 2); but *we are of yesterday and know nothing*. Let us not therefore find fault with the works of God.

2. Let him describe how this world was made, "*Declare, if thou hast* so much *understanding*, what were the advances of that work. Stand forth, and *tell who laid the measures thereof* and *stretched out the line upon it*. Wast thou the architect that formed the model and then drew the dimensions by rule according to it?" The vast bulk of the earth is moulded as regularly as if it had been done by line and measure; but who can describe how it was cast into this figure? How it came to be so firmly fixed. Though it is hung upon nothing, yet it is established, but who can tell *upon what the foundations of it are fastened*, that it may not sink with its own weight, or *who laid the corner-stone thereof*, that the parts of it may not fall asunder? v. 6.

3. Let him repeat if he can, the songs of praise which were sung at that solemnity (v. 7), *when the morning-stars sang together*, the blessed angels, who, in the morning of time, shone as brightly as the morning star, going immediately before the light which God commanded to shine out of darkness upon the earth, which was without form and void. They were *the sons of God*, who *shouted for joy* when they saw the foundations of the earth laid. The angels are called *the sons of God* because they bear much of his image, are with him in his house above, and serve him as a son does his father.

II. Concerning the limiting of the sea to the place appointed for it, v. 8, &c. This refers to the third day's work, when God said (Gen. i. 9), *Let the waters under the heaven be gathered together unto one place, and it was so.* 1. Out of the great deep or chaos, in which earth and water were intermixed, in obedience to the divine command the waters *broke forth like a child out of the* teeming *womb, v.* 8. 2. This new-born babe is clothed and swaddled, *v.* 9. *The cloud* is made *the garment thereof,* with which it is covered, and *thick darkness* (that is, shores vastly remote and distant from one another and quite in the dark one to another) *is a swaddling-band for it.* It is not said, He made *rocks and mountains* its swaddling bands, but *clouds and darkness,* something that we are not aware of and should think least likely for such a purpose. 3. There is a cradle too provided for this babe: *I broke up for it my decreed place, v.* 10. Valleys were sunk for it in the earth, capacious enough to receive it, and there it is laid to sleep; and, if it be sometimes tossed with winds, that (as Bishop Patrick observes) is but the rocking of the cradle, which makes it sleep the faster. As for the sea, so for every one of us, there is a decreed place; for he that determined the times before appointed determined also the bounds of our habitation. 4. This babe being made unruly and dangerous by the sin of man, which was the original of all unquietness and danger in this lower world, there is also a prison provided for it; *bars and doors are set, v.* 10. And it is said to it, by way of check to its insolence, *Hitherto shalt thou come, but no further.* The sea is God's, for he made it, he restrains it; he says to it, *Here shall thy proud waves be stayed, v.* 11. This may be considered as an act of God's power over the sea. Though it is so vast a body, and though its motion is sometimes extremely violent, yet God has it under check. Its waves rise no higher, its tides roll no further, than God permits; and this is mentioned as a reason why we should stand in awe of God (Jer. v. 22), and yet why we should encourage ourselves in him, for he that stops the noise of the sea, even the noise of her waves, can, when he pleases, still the tumult of the people, Ps. lxv. 7.

Verses 12-24

The Lord here proceeds to ask Job many puzzling questions, to convince him of his ignorance, and so to shame him for his folly in prescribing to God. Job is here challenged to give an account of six things :—

I. Of the springs of the morning, the dayspring from on high, *v.* 12-15. It was not we, it was not any man, that commanded the morning-light at first, or appointed the place of its springing up and shining forth, or the time of it. The constant and regular succession of day and night was no contrivance of ours; it is the glory of God that it shows, and his handy work, not ours, Ps. xix. 1, 2. It is quite out of our power to alter this course: "*Hast thou countermanded the morning since thy days?* No, never. Why then wilt thou pretend to direct the divine counsels, or expect to have the methods of Providence altered in favour of thee?" It is God that has appointed the day-spring to visit the earth, and diffuses the morning light through the air, which receives it as readily as the clay does the seal (*v.* 14), immediately admitting the impressions of it, so as of a sudden to be all over enlightened by it, as the seal stamps its image on the wax; *and they stand as a garment,* or as if they were clothed with a garment. The earth puts on a new face every morning, and dresses itself as we do, puts on light as a garment, and is then to be seen. This is made a terror to evil-doers. God makes the light a minister of his justice as well as of his mercy. It is designed *to shake the wicked out of the earth,* and for that purpose *it takes hold of the ends of it,* as we take hold of the ends of a garment to shake the dust and moths out of it. Job had observed what a terror the

morning light is to criminals, because it discovers them (*ch.* xxiv. 13, &c.), and God here asks him whether the world was indebted to him for that kindness? No, the great Judge of the world sends forth the beams of the morning light as his messengers to detect criminals (*v.* 15), that their light may be *withholden* from them (that is, that they may lose their comfort, their confidence, their liberties, their lives) and that their *high arm,* which they have listed up against God and man, may be *broken,* and they deprived of their power to do mischief. Here we are reminded of the *Benedictus* (Luke i. 78, By the *tender mercy of our God the day-spring from on high has visited us, to give light to those that sit in darkness,* 2 Cor. iv. 6), and the *Magnificat* (Luke i. 51), showing that God, in his gospel, has *shown strength with his arm, scattered the proud, and put down the mighty,* by that light by which he designed to shake the wicked, to shake wickedness itself out of the earth, and break its high arm.

II. Of the springs of the sea (*v.* 16): "*Hast thou entered into* them, or *hast thou walked in the search of the depth?* God's way in the government of the world is said to be *in the sea,* and *in the great waters* (Ps. lxxvii. 19), intimating that it is hidden from us and not to be pried into by us.

III. Of the gates of death: *Have* these *been open to thee? v.* 16. Death is a grand secret. *Man knows not his time.* We cannot describe what death is. Let us make sure that the gates of heaven shall be opened to us on the other side death, and then we need not fear the opening of the gates of death, though it is a way we are to go but once. While we are here, in a world of sense, we speak of the world of spirits as blind men do of colours.

IV. Of the breadth of the earth (*v.* 18): *Hast thou perceived* that? The knowledge of this might seem most level to him and within his reach; yet he is challenged to declare this if he can. It is but a point to the universe yet, small as it is, we cannot be exact in declaring the dimensions of it. Job had never sailed round the world, nor any before him; so little did men know the breadth of the earth that it was but a few ages ago that the vast continent of America was discovered, which had, time out of mind, lain hidden. It is presumption for us, who perceive not the breadth of the earth, to dive into the depth of God's counsels.

V. Of the place and way of light and darkness. Of the day-spring he had spoken before (*v.* 12) and he returns to speak of it again (*v.* 19): *Where is the way where light dwells?* And again (*v.* 24): *By what way is the light parted?* When God, in the beginning, first spread darkness upon the face of the deep, and afterwards commanded the light to shine out of darkness, by that mighty word, *Let there be light,* was Job a witness to the order, to the operation? Though we long ever so much either for the shining forth of the morning or the shadows of the evening, we know not whither to send, or go, to fetch them, nor can tell *the paths to the house thereof, v.* 20. We were not then born, nor is the number of our days so great that we can describe the birth of that first-born of the visible creation, *v.* 21. Shall we then undertake to discourse of God's counsels, which were from eternity, or to find out the paths to the house thereof, to solicit for the alteration of them? It is no order of ours, that is executed by the outgoings of the morning light and the darkness of the night. We cannot so much as tell whence they come nor whither they go (*v.* 24): *By what way is the light parted* in the morning, when, in an instant, it shoots itself into all the parts of the air above the horizon. It is a marvellous change that passes over us every morning by the return of the light and every evening by the return of the darkness; but we expect them, and so they are no surprise nor uneasiness to us. If we would, in like manner, reckon upon changes in our outward condition, we should neither in the brightest noon expect perpetual day nor in the darkest midnight despair of the return of the morning. God has set the one over against the other, like the day and night; and so must we, Eccles. vii. 14.

VI. Of the *treasures of the snow and hail* (v. 22, 23): "*Hast thou entered* into these and taken a view of them?" In the clouds the snow and hail are generated, and thence they come in such abundance that one would think there were treasures of them laid up in store there, whereas indeed they are produced *for the occasion.* What folly it is to strive against God, who is thus prepared for battle and war, and how much it is our interest to make our peace with him and to keep ourselves in his love.

Verses 25–41

Hitherto God had put questions to Job to convince him of his ignorance. Now he comes, in the same manner, to show his weakness. It is but little that he knows, and therefore he ought not to arraign the divine counsels. It is but little that he can do, and therefore he ought not to oppose the proceedings of Providence. Let him consider what great things God does, and try whether he can do the like.

I. God has thunder, and lightning, and rain, and frost, at command, but Job has not, and therefore let him not dare to compare himself with God, or to contend with him. He has a sovereign dominion over the waters, even when they seem to overflow and to be from under his check, v. 25. He has *divided a watercourse.* Thus the hearts of kings are said to be in *God's hand*; and as the rains, those rivers of God, he turns them whithersoever he will. The lightning or the thunder, are not blind bullets, but go the way that God himself, who means no hurt to them, directs.

In directing the course of the rain he does not neglect the wilderness, the desert land (v. 26, 27), *where no man is.* God's providence reaches further than man's industry. If he had not more kindness for many of the inferior creatures than man has, it would go ill with them. When *there was not a man to till the ground*, yet there went up a mist and watered it. But we cannot make it fruitful without God; it is he that gives the increase. God has enough for all, and wonderfully provides even for those creatures that man neither has service from nor makes provision for. He is, in a sense, *the Father of the rain*, v. 28. Even the small drops of the dew he distils upon the earth, as the God of nature; and, as the God of grace, he rains righteousness upon us and is himself as the dew unto Israel. See Hos. xiv. 5, 6; Micah v. 7. The ice and the frost, by which the waters are congealed are produced by his providence, v. 29, 30. These are very common things, which lessens the strangeness of them. But, considering what a vast change is made by them in a very little time, we may well ask, "*Out of whose womb came the ice?* What created power could produce such a wonderful work?" No power but that of the Creator himself. Job cannot command one shower of rain: "*Canst thou lift up thy voice to the clouds*, those bottles of heaven, *that abundance of waters may cover thee*, to water thy fields when they are dry and parched? *Canst thou send lightnings, that they may go* on thy errand. Will they come at thy call, and say unto thee, *Here we are?*" No, the ministers of God's wrath will not be ministers of ours.

II. God has the stars of heaven under his command and cognizance. God mentions particularly the fixed stars. It is supposed that they have an influence upon this earth, notwithstanding their vast distance, not upon the minds of men or the events of providence (men's fate is not determined by their stars), but upon the ordinary course of nature. And if the stars have such a dominion over this earth (v. 33), though they are but mere matter, much more has he who is their Maker and ours, and who is an Eternal Mind. *Canst thou bind the sweet influences of Pleiades? Canst thou loose the bands of Orion?* Both summer and winter will have their course. God can change them when he pleases, can make the spring cold, and so bind the sweet influences of Pleiades, and the winter warm, and so loose the bands of Orion; but we cannot. God, who *calls the stars by their names* (Ps. cxlvii. 4), calls them forth in their respective seasons, appointing them the time of their rising and setting. But this is not our province; we cannot *bring forth Mazzaroth*—the stars in the southern signs, nor *guide Arcturus*—those in the northern, v. 32. We *know not the ordinances of heaven*, v. 33. So far are we from being able to change them that we can give no account of them; they are a secret to us. Shall we then pretend to know God's counsels. Shall we then teach God how to govern the world?

III. God is the author and giver, the father and fountain of all wisdom and understanding, v. 36. The souls of men are nobler and more excellent beings than the stars of heaven and shine more brightly. The powers and faculties of reason with which man is endued bring him into some alliance to the blessed angels; and whence comes this light, but from the Father of lights? *Who* else *has put wisdom into the inner parts* of man, and *given understanding to the heart?* The rational soul itself, and its capacities, come from him as the God of nature; for he forms the spirit of man within him. We did not make our own souls, nor can we describe how they act, nor how they are united to our bodies. He only that made them knows them. Shall we pretend to be wiser than God, when we have all our wisdom from him?

IV. God has the clouds under his cognizance and government, v. 37. Can any man, with all his wisdom, undertake to *number the clouds.* And when the clouds have poured down rain in abundance, so that *the dust grows into* solid mire and *the clods cleave fast together* (v. 38), *who can stay the bottles of heaven?* As we cannot command a shower of rain, so we cannot command a fair day, without God.

V. God provides food for the inferior creatures. The following chapter is wholly taken up with the instances of God's power and goodness about animals, and therefore some transfer to it the last three verses of this chapter, which speak of the provision made, v. 39, 40. "Let us try that then: *Wilt thou hunt the prey for the lion?* Thou valuest thyself upon thy possessions of cattle which thou wast once owner of, the oxen, and asses, and camels, that were fed at thy crib; but wilt thou undertake the maintenance of the lions, and *the young lions, when they couch in their dens*, waiting for a prey? No, they can shift for themselves without thee: But I do it." The all-sufficiency of the divine providence has wherewithal to satisfy the desire of every living thing. See the bounty of the divine Providence, that, wherever it has given life, it will give livelihood. The young ravens, v. 41, ravenous birds, are fed by the divine Providence. *Who* but God *provides for the raven his food?* They *cry* and this is interpreted a crying to God. It being the cry of nature, it is looked upon as directed to the God of nature. Some way or other he provides for them, so that they grow up, and come to maturity. And he that takes this care of the young ravens certainly will not be wanting to his people.

CHAPTER 39

God proceeds here to show Job what little reason he had to charge him with unkindness who was so compassionate to the inferior creatures and took such a tender care of them. He shows him also what reason he had to be humble who knew so little of the nature of the creatures about him and had so little influence upon them, and to submit to that God on whom they all depend. I. Concerning the wild goats and the hinds, ver. 1–4. II. Concerning the wild ass, ver. 5–8. III. Concerning the unicorn, ver. 9–12. IV. Concerning the peacock, ver. 13. V. Concerning the ostrich, ver. 13–18. VI. Concerning the horse, ver. 19–25. VII. Concerning the hawk and the eagle, ver. 26–30.

Verses 1–12

God here shows Job what little acquaintance he had with the untamed creatures that run wild in the deserts, but are the care of the divine Providence.

I. The *wild goats* and the *hinds.* Though they bring forth their young with a great deal of difficulty and sorrow, and have no assistance from man, yet, by the good providence of God, their young ones are safely produced, *v.* 3. Concerning the growth of their young (*v.* 4): *They are in good liking;* after their dams have suckled them awhile they shift for themselves in the cornfields, and are no more burdensome to them, which is an example to children, when they have grown up, not to be always hanging upon their parents.

II. The *wild ass,* a creature we frequently read of in Scripture, some say untameable. *Who* but God *has sent out the wild ass free?* He has given a disposition to it, and therefore a dispensation for it. Freedom from service, and liberty to range at pleasure, are but the privileges of a wild ass. It is a pity that any of the children of men should covet such a liberty. It is better to labour and be good for something than ramble and be good for nothing (v. 6). *Whose house I have made the wilderness,* where he has room enough to traverse his ways. The tame ass, that labours, and is serviceable to man, has his master's crib to go to both for shelter and food, and lives in a fruitful land: but the wild ass, that will have his liberty, must have it in a barren land. He has no owner, nor will he be in subjection: *He scorns the multitude of the city,* and *the crying of the driver* is nothing to him. The *range of the mountains is his pasture,* and a bare pasture it is; there he *searches after here and there a green thing,* as he can find it and pick it up; whereas the labouring asses have green things in plenty, without their searching for them. From the untamableness of this and other creatures we may infer how unfit we are to give law to Providence, who cannot give law even to a wild ass's colt.

III. The unicorn—*rhem,* a strong creature (Num. xxiii. 22), a stately proud creature, Ps. xcii. 10. He is able to serve, but not willing; and God here challenges Job to force him to it. "Since thou dost pretend" (says God) "to bring everything beneath thy sway, begin with the unicorn, and try thy skill upon him. Now that thy oxen and asses are all gone, try whether he will be willing to serve thee in their stead (*v.* 9) and whether he will be content with the provision thou usedst to make for them: *Will he abide by thy crib?* No; Thou canst not tame him, nor *bind him with his band,* nor set him to *draw the harrow,*" *v.* 10. Though the wild bull (which some think is meant here by the unicorn) will not serve him, nor submit to his band in the furrows, yet there are tame bullocks that will. "Thou darest not trust him; though *his strength is great,* yet thou wilt not leave thy labour to him, as thou dost with thy asses or oxen. Thou wilt never depend upon the wild bull, as likely to come to thy harvest-work, much less to go through it, to *bring home thy seed and gather it into thy barn,*" *v.* 11, 12.

Verses 13–18

The ostrich is a very large bird, but it never flies. Some have called it *a winged camel.*

I. Something that it has in common with the peacock, that is, beautiful feathers (*v.* 13): *Gavest thou proud wings unto the peacocks?* Fine feathers make proud birds. The peacock is an emblem of pride; proud birds. The peacock is an emblem of pride; the ostrich too has goodly feathers, and yet is a foolish bird. God gives his gifts variously, and those gifts are not always the most valuable that make the finest show. Who would not rather have the voice of the nightingale than the tail of the peacock, the eye of the eagle and her soaring wing, and the natural affection of the stork, than the beautiful wings and feathers of the ostrich, which can never rise above the earth, and is without natural affection?

II. Something that is peculiar to itself. Most birds, as well as other animals, are strangely guided by natural instinct in providing for the preservation of their young. But the ostrich is a monster, for she drops her eggs anywhere upon the ground and takes no care to hatch them. If the sand and the sun will hatch them, well and good; for she will not warm them, *v.* 14. *The foot* of the traveller *may crush them,* and *the wild beast break them, v.* 15. *She is hardened against her young ones.* Her labour in laying her eggs is in vain, because she has not that tender concern for them that she should have. *God has deprived her of wisdom.* This intimates that the art which other animals have to nourish and preserve their young is God's gift, and that, where it exists not, God denies it, that by the folly of the ostrich, as well as by the wisdom of the ant, we may learn to be wise. So careless are many parents of their children; some of their bodies, not providing for their own house, and therefore as bad as the ostrich; but many more are thus careless of their children's souls, take no care of their education, send them abroad into the world untaught, unarmed, forgetting what corruption there is in the world through lust. She leaves her eggs in danger, but, if she herself be in danger, she lifts up her wings, and, with the help of them, runs so fast that a horseman at full speed cannot overtake her: *She scorneth the horse and his rider.* Those that are least under the law of natural affection often contend most for the law of self-preservation.

Verses 19–25

God, having displayed his power in those creatures that despise man, here shows it in one serviceable to man, and that is the horse, especially *the horse that is prepared against the day of battle.* It seems, there was, in Job's country, a noble breed of horses. The great horse has a great deal of strength and spirit (*v.* 19): *Hast thou given the horse strength?* He uses his strength for man, but God gave it to him, who is the fountain of all the powers of nature. It is a mercy to man to have such a servant, which, though very strong, submits to the management of a child, and rebels not against his owner. His neck is *clothed with thunder,* with a large and flowing mane. *The glory of his nostrils,* when he snorts, flings up his head, and throws foam about, *is terrible, v.* 20. How frolicsome he is (*v.* 21): *He paws in the valley. He goes on to meet the armed men,* animated only by *the sound of the trumpet, the thunder of the captains, and the shouting* of the soldiers, *v.* 25. How fearless he is (*v.* 22): *He mocks at fear,* and makes a jest of it. High mettle is the praise of a horse rather than of a man, whom fierceness and rage ill become. This description of the war-horse will help to explain that character which is given of presumptuous sinners, Jer. viii. 6.

Verses 26–30

The birds of the air are proofs of the wonderful power and providence of God. 1. The *hawk,* a noble bird of great strength and sagacity, and yet a bird of prey, *v.* 26. This bird is here taken notice of for her flight, which is swift and strong, and especially for the course she steers *towards the south,* whither she follows the sun in winter. This is her wisdom, and it was God that gave her this wisdom, not man. 2. The *eagle,* a royal bird is here taken notice of.

(1) For the height of her flight. No bird soars so high, has so strong a wing, nor can so well bear the light of the sun. Now, "*Doth she mount at thy command? v.* 27. No; it is by the natural power and instinct God has given her." (2) For the strength of her nest. Her house is her castle and stronghold; she makes it *on high* and *on the rock, the crag of the rock* (*v.* 28), which sets her and her young out of the reach of danger. (3) For her quicksightedness (*v.* 29): *Her eyes behold afar off,* not upwards, but downwards, in quest of her prey. In this she is an emblem of a hypocrite, who, while, in the profession of religion, he seems to rise towards heaven, keeps his eye and heart upon the prey on earth, some temporal advantage, some widow's house or other that he hopes to devour, under pretence of devotion. (4) For the way she has of maintaining herself and her young. She preys upon living animals, which she seizes and tears to pieces, and then carries to her young ones, which are taught to *suck up blood;* they do it by instinct, and know no better. Our Saviour refers to this instinct of the eagle, Matt. xxiv. 28. *Wheresoever the carcase is, there will the eagles be gathered together.*

CHAPTER 40

Many humbling questions God had put to Job, now, in this chapter, I. He demands an answer to them, ver. 1, 2. II. Job submits in a humble silence, ver. 3–5. III. God proceeds to reason with him, for his conviction, concerning the infinite distance and disproportion between him and God, showing that he was by no means an equal match for God. He challenges him (ver. 6, 7) to vie with him, if he durst, for justice (ver. 8), power (ver. 9), majesty (ver. 10), and dominion over the proud (ver. 11–14), and he gives an instance of his power in one particular animal, here called "Behemoth," ver. 15–24.

Verses 1–5

I. A humbling challenge which God gave to Job. Job remained silent, and therefore God put him upon replying, *v.* 1, 2. Some think God said it in a still small voice, which wrought more upon Job than the whirlwind did, as upon Elijah, 1 Kings xix. 12, 13. 1. God puts a convincing question to him: "*Shall he that contendeth with the Almighty instruct him?*" Those who quarrel with God do, in effect, go about to teach him how to mend his work. Some read it, *Is it any wisdom to contend with the Almighty?* 2. He demands a speedy reply to it: "*He that reproaches God let him answer* this question to his own conscience, and answer it thus, *Far be it from me to contend with the Almighty* or to *instruct him.*"

II. Job's humble submission. Now Job came to himself, and began to melt into godly sorrow. When his friends reasoned with him he did not yield. They had condemned him for a wicked man; Elihu himself had been very sharp upon him (*ch.* xxxiv. 7, 8, 37); but God had not given him such hard words. We may expect better treatment from God than we meet with from our friends. This the good man is here overcome by, and yields himself a conquered captive to the grace of God. 1. He owns himself an offender (*v.* 4): "*Behold, I am vile,* and abominable in my own eyes." Repentance changes men's opinion of themselves. When God talked with him, he had nothing to say. *What shall I answer thee?* Here he gives the reason of his silence; it was not because he was sullen, but because he was convinced he had been in the wrong. 2. He promises not to offend any more. He enjoins himself silence (*v.* 4): "*I will lay my hand upon my mouth,* will keep that as with a bridle, to suppress all passionate thoughts which may arise in my mind, and keep them from breaking out in intemperate speeches." Job had suffered his evil thoughts to vent themselves: "*Once have I spoken* amiss, *yea, twice,*" that is, "divers times, in one discourse and in another; but I have done: *I will not answer;* I will not stand to what I have said, nor say it again; *I will proceed no further.*"

Verses 6–14

Job was greatly humbled for what God had already said, but not sufficiently; God here proceeds to reason with him as before, *v.* 6. God begins with a challenge (*v.* 7): "*Gird up thy loins now like a man; if* thou hast the courage and confidence thou hast pretended to, show them now."

I. We cannot vie with God for justice, the Lord is righteous and holy in his dealings with us, but we are unrighteous and unholy in our conduct towards him; we have a great deal to blame ourselves for, but nothing to blame him for (*v.* 8): "*Wilt thou disannul my judgment?*" "*Wilt thou,*" says God, "*condemn me, that thou mayest be righteous?* Must my honour suffer for the support of thy reputation?"

II. We cannot vie with God for power; and therefore, as it is great impiety, so it is great impudence to contest with him: "*Hast thou an arm like God,* equal to his in length and strength? *Or canst thou thunder with a voice like him,* as he did (*ch.* xxxvii. 1, 2), or does man out of the whirlwind?" Man cannot speak so convincingly, so powerfully, nor with such a commanding conquering force as God can, who *speaks, and it is done.* His creating voice is called his *thunder* (Ps. civ. 7), so is that voice of his with which he terrifies and discomfits his enemies, 1 Sam. ii. 10. *Out of heaven shall he thunder upon them.*

III. We cannot vie with God for beauty and majesty, *v.* 10. "If thou wilt enter into a comparison with him, and appear more amiable, put on thy best attire: *Deck thyself now with majesty and excellency.* Appear in all the martial pomp, in all the royal pageantry that thou hast; make the best of everything that will set thee off: *Array thyself with glory and beauty,* such as may awe thy enemies and charm thy friends; but what is it all to the divine majesty and beauty? No more than the light of a glow-worm to that of the sun when he goes forth in his strength."

IV. We cannot vie with God for dominion over the proud, *v.* 11–14. If Job can humble and abase proud tyrants and oppressors as easily and effectually as God can, it shall be acknowledged that he has some colour to compete with God.

1. The justice Job is here challenged to do is to bring the proud low with a look.

(1) It is here supposed that God can do it and will do it himself, else he would not have put it thus upon Job. By this God proves himself to be God, that he resists the proud, sits Judge upon them, and is able to bring them to ruin. Proud people are wicked people, and pride is at the bottom of a great deal of the wickedness that is in this world. Proud people will certainly be abased and brought low; for *pride goes before destruction.* The wrath of God, scattered among the proud, will humble them, and break them, and bring them down. *Who knows the power of his anger?* God can and does easily abase proud tyrants; he can *look upon them, and bring them low,* by one angry look, as he can, by a gracious look, revive the hearts of the contrite ones. He can not only bring them to the dust, from which they might hope to arise, but *hide them in the dust,* like the proud Egyptian whom Moses slew and *hid in the sand* (Exod. ii. 12). They were proud of the figure they made, but they shall be buried in oblivion and be no more remembered than those that are hidden in the dust. They were linked in leagues and confederacies to do mischief, and are now bound in bundles. They are hidden *together, ch.* xvii. 16. He *binds their faces in secret* or as dead men. Thus complete will be the victory that God will gain, at last, over proud sinners that set themselves in opposition to him.

(2) It is here proposed to Job to do it. He had been passionately quarrelling with God and his providence. "Come," says God, "try thy hand first upon proud men, and thou wilt soon see how little they value the

rage of thy wrath; and shall I then regard it, or be moved by it?" If God, and he only, has power enough to humble and bring down proud men, no doubt he has wisdom enough to know when and how to do it, and it is not for us to prescribe to him or to teach him how to govern the world.

2. The justice which is here promised to be done him if he can perform such mighty works as these (v. 14): "*Then I will also confess unto thee that thy right hand* is sufficient to save thee, though, after all, it would be too weak to contend with me."

Verses 15-24

God, for the further proving of his own power, concludes his discourse with the description of two mighty animals, far exceeding man in bulk and strength, one he calls *behemoth*, the other *leviathan*. In these verses we have the former described. "*Behold now behemoth*, and consider whether thou art able to contend with him who made that beast and gave him all the power he has, and whether it is not his wisdom rather to submit to him and make thy peace with him." *Behemoth* signifies *beasts* in general, but must here be meant of some one particular species. Some understand it of the *bull*; others of an amphibious animal called the *river-horse* (*hippopotamus*), living in the river Nile.

I. The description here given of the behemoth.

1. His body is very strong and well built. *His strength is in his loins, v. 16. His bones*, compared with those of other creatures, *are like bars of iron, v. 18.* His back-bone is so strong that, though his tail be not large, yet he moves it like a cedar, with a commanding force, *v. 17*.

2. He feeds on the productions of the earth and does not prey upon other animals: He *eats grass as an ox* (*v. 15*), the *mountains bring him forth food* (*v. 20*), and the beasts of the field do not tremble before him nor flee from him, as from a lion, but they play about him, knowing they are in no danger from him.

3. He *lodges under the shady trees* (*v. 21*), which *cover him with their shadow* (*v. 22*), where he has a free and open air to breathe in, while lions, which live by prey, when they would repose themselves, are obliged to retire into a close and dark den, to live therein, and to abide in the covert of that, *ch.* xxxviii. 40. Those who are a terror to others cannot but be sometimes a terror to themselves too; but those will be easy who will let others be easy about them; and the reed and fens, and the willows of the brook, though a very weak and slender fortification, yet are sufficient for the defence and security of those who *therefore* dread no harm, because they design none.

4. He is a very great and greedy drinker. His size is prodigious, and therefore he must have supply accordingly, *v. 23*. His eye anticipates more than he can take; for, when he is very thirsty *he trusts that he can drink up Jordan in his mouth*, and even *takes it with his eyes, v. 24*. His nose has in it strength for, when he goes greedily to drink with it, he *pierces through snares* or nets.

II. This description of this mountain of a beast is an argument with us to humble ourselves before the great God. He made this vast animal; it is *behemoth which I made, v. 15.* This beast is here called the *chief*, in its kind, *of the ways of God* (*v. 19*), an eminent instance of the Creator's power and wisdom. "It is *behemoth, which I made with thee*; I made that beast as well as thee, and he does not quarrel with me; why then dost thou? *He that made him can make his sword to approach to him* (*v. 19*), that is, the same hand that made him, notwithstanding his great bulk and strength can unmake him again at pleasure and kill an elephant as easily as a worm or a fly, without any difficulty. God that gave to all the creatures their being may take away the being he gave; for may he not do what

he will with his own? The *behemoth* perhaps is here intended (as well as the *leviathan* afterwards) to represent those proud tyrants and oppressors whom God had just now challenged Job to abase and bring down. He that framed the engine, and put the parts of it together, knows how to take it in pieces.

Chapter 41

The description here given of the leviathan, a very large, strong, formidable fish, or water-animal, is designed yet further to convince Job of his own impotency, and of God's omnipotence. I. To convince Job of his own weakness he is here challenged to subdue and take this leviathan (ver. 1–9). II. To convince Job of God's power and terrible majesty several particular instances are here given of the strength and terror of the leviathan, which is no more than what God has given him, nor more than he has under his check, ver. 11, 12. The face of the leviathan is here described to be terrible (ver. 13, 14), his scales close (ver. 15–17), his breath and neesings sparkling (ver. 18–21), his flesh firm (ver. 22–24), his strength and spirit, when he is attacked, insuperable (ver. 25–30), his motions turbulent (ver. 31, 32), so that, upon the whole, he is a very terrible creature, and man is no match for him, ver. 33, 34.

Verses 1-10

Whether this leviathan be a whale or a crocodile is a great dispute among the learned. The whale is much larger and a nobler animal and the creation of whales was generally looked upon as a most illustrious proof of the eternal power of the Creator.

I. How unable Job was to master the leviathan. 1. He could not catch him with angling, *v. 1*, 2. He had no bait wherewith to deceive him, no hook wherewith to catch him, no fish-line wherewith to draw him out of the water, nor a thorn to run through his gills, on which to carry him home. 2. He could not force him to cry for quarter, *v. 3, 4*. "He knows his own strength too well to *make many supplications to thee*, and to *make a covenant with thee* to be thy servant on condition thou wilt save his life." 3. He could not entice him into a cage, and keep him there as a bird for the children to play with, *v. 5*. 4. He could not have him served up to his table; he and his companions could not make a banquet of him. 5. They could not enrich themselves with the spoil of him: *Shall they part him among the merchants*, the bones to one, the oil to another? If they can catch him, they will; but the art of fishing for whales was not brought to perfection then, as it has been since. 6. They could not destroy him, could not *fill his head with fish-spears, v. 7.* 7. It was to no purpose to attempt it: *The hope of* taking *him is in vain, v. 9. Shall not one be cast down even at the sight of him?* "Touch him if thou dare; *remember the battle*, how unable thou art to encounter such a force." Job is hereby admonished not to proceed in his controversy with God, but to make his peace with him.

II. Thence he infers how unable he was to contend with the Almighty. *None is so fierce*, none so foolhardy, *that he dares* to stir up the leviathan (*v. 10*), and *who then is able to stand before God*.

Verses 11-34

I. God's sovereign dominion and independency laid down, *v. 11*. 1. That he is indebted to none of his creatures. "*Who has prevented me?*" that is, "who has laid any obligations upon me by any services he has done me?" 2. That he is the rightful Lord and owner of all the creatures: "*Whatsoever is under the whole heaven*, animate or inanimate, is *mine*."

II. The proof and illustration of it, from the wonderful structure of the leviathan, *v. 12*.

1. The parts of his body, the power he exerts, are what God will not conceal. Though he is a creature of monstrous bulk, yet there is in him a *comely proportion*. (1) The leviathan, *at first sight*, appears formidable and inaccessible, *v. 13, 14*. Who dares come so near him while he is alive as to take a distinct

view of *the face of the garment*, the skin with which
he is clothed, so near him as to bridle him, or to be
within reach of his jaws, which are like *a double
bridle*? Who will venture to look into his mouth,
as we do into a horse's mouth? He that *opens the
doors of his face* will see *his teeth terrible round about*.
(2) *His scales are* his beauty and strength, and therefore *his pride, v.* 15–17. The crocodile is indeed
remarkable for his scales; if we understand it of the
whale, we must understand by these *shields* (for so
the word is) the several coats of his skin. (3) He scatters terror with his very breath; if he spout up water,
it is like a light shining, either with the froth or the
light of the sun shining through it, *v.* 18. The eyes
of the whale are reported to shine in the night-time
like the eye-lids of the morning; the same they say
of the crocodile. Probably these hyperbolical expressions (*v.* 19–21) are used concerning the leviathan
to intimate the terror of the wrath of God. (4) He
is of invincible strength so that he frightens all that
come in his way, but is not himself frightened by
any. Take a view of his neck, and there remains
strength, *v.* 22. *Sorrow rejoices* (or *rides in triumph*)
before him, for he makes terrible work wherever he
comes. *His flesh is of brass*, which Job had complained
his was not, *ch.* vi. 12. *His heart is as firm as a stone,
v.* 24. He has spirit equal to his bodily strength.
When he raises up himself like a moving mountain
in the great waters even *the mighty are afraid* lest he
should overturn their ships. (5) All the instruments
of slaughter that are used against him do him no hurt
and therefore are no terror to him, *v.* 26–29. (6) His
very motion in the water troubles it and puts it into
a ferment, *v.* 31, 32.

2. He concludes with four things in general concerning this animal:—(1) *Upon earth there is not his
like, v.* 33. No creature in this world is comparable
to him for strength. It is well for man that he is
confined to the waters and there has *a watch set
upon him* (*ch.* vii. 12). (2) He *is made without fear*.
(3) He is himself very proud; though lodged in the
deep, yet *he beholds all high things, v.* 34. (4) *He is
a king over all the children of pride*. Whatever bodily
accomplishments men are proud of, and puffed up
with, the leviathan excels them and is a *king over
them*. Some read it so as to understand it of God:
*He that beholds all high things, even he, is King over
all the children of pride;* he can tame the behemoth
(*ch.* xl. 15) and the leviathan. This discourse concerning those two animals was brought in to prove
that it is God only who can *look upon proud men
and abase them* (*ch.* xl. 11–13). He is *King over all
the children of pride*, whether brutal or rational, and
can make them all either bend or break before him,
Isa. ii. 11.

CHAPTER 42

Solomon says, "Better is the end of a thing than the beginning
thereof," Eccles. vii. 8. It was so here in the story of Job; at
evening-time it was light. Three things we have met with in this
book which, I confess, have troubled me very much; but we find
all the three grievances redressed, in this chapter, every thing
set to rights. I. It has been a great trouble to us to see such a
holy man as Job so fretful, and especially to hear him quarrel
with God. Here he recovers his temper, is sorry for what he
has said amiss, unsays it, and humbles himself before God, ver.
1–6. II. It has been likewise a great trouble to us to see Job and
his friends so much at variance, though they were all very wise
and good men; but here we have this grievance redressed likewise,
the differences between them happily adjusted, and all joining in
sacrifices and prayers, mutually accepted of God, ver. 7–9.
III. It has troubled us to see a man of such eminent piety and usefulness as Job so grievously afflicted, so poor, so slighted, and made
the very centre of all the calamities of human life; but here we
have this grievance redressed too, Job healed of all his ailments,
more honoured and beloved than ever, enriched with an estate
double to what he had before, surrounded with all the comforts
of life, and as great an instance of prosperity as ever he had been
of affliction and patience, ver. 10–17. All this is written, that we,
under these and the like discouragements that we meet, through
patience and comfort of this scripture may have hope.

Verses 1–6

The words of Job justifying himself were ended,
ch. xxxi. 40. The words of Job judging and condemning himself began, *ch.* xl. 4, 5. Here he goes on
with words to the same purport. Though his patience
had not its perfect work, his repentance for his impatience had. He is here thoroughly humbled for
his folly and unadvised speaking, and it was forgiven
him. When God had said all that to him concerning
his own greatness and power appearing in the creatures
then Job answered the Lord (*v.* 1), by way of submission.

I. He subscribes to the truth of God's unlimited
power, knowledge, and dominion, to prove which
was the scope of God's discourse out of the whirlwind, *v.* 2. 1. He owns that God can do everything.
What can be too hard for him that made behemoth
and leviathan, and manages both as he pleases?
He knew this before, and had himself discoursed very
well upon the subject, but now he knew it with application. "*Thou canst do everything*, and therefore canst
raise me out of this low condition, which I have so
often foolishly despaired of as impossible: I now
believe thou art able to do this." 2. *No thought can
be withholden from him*. Not a fretful, discontented,
unbelieving thought is in our minds at any time but
God is a witness to it. *Whatever the Lord pleased,
that did he*. Job had said this passionately, complaining of it (*ch.* xxiii. 13), *What his soul desireth
even that he doeth;* now he says, with pleasure and
satisfaction, that *God's counsels shall stand*. If God's
thoughts concerning us be *thoughts of good*, *to give
us an unexpected end*, he cannot be withheld from
accomplishing his gracious purposes.

II. He owns himself to be guilty of that which God
had charged him with in the beginning of his discourse, *v.* 3. "Lord, the first word thou saidst was,
*Who is this that darkens counsel by words without
knowledge?* That word convinced me. I own *I am
the man* that has been so foolish. That word reached
my conscience, and set my sin in order before me.
I have ignorantly overlooked the counsels and designs
of God in afflicting me, and therefore have quarrelled
with God, and insisted too much upon my own
justification: *Therefore I uttered that which I understood not*," that is, "I have passed a judgment upon
the dispensations of Providence, though I was utterly
a stranger to the reasons of them." He owns himself
ignorant of the divine counsels; and so we are all.
We see what God does, but we neither know why he
does it nor what he will bring it to. The reason why
we quarrel with Providence is because we do not
understand it. He owns himself presumptuous in
undertaking to discourse of that which he did not
understand and to arraign that which he could not
judge of. *He that answereth a matter before he heareth
it, it is folly and shame to him*.

III. He will not answer, but he will *make supplication to his Judge*, as he had said, *ch.* ix. 15. "*Hear,
I beseech thee, and I will speak* (*v.* 4), not speak either
as plaintiff or defendant (*ch.* xiii. 22), but as a humble
petitioner."

IV. He puts himself into the posture of a penitent.
In true repentance there must be not only conviction
of sin, but contrition and godly sorrow for it, sorrow
according to God, 2 Cor. vii. 9.

1. "*I have heard of thee by the hearing of the ear*.
I have known something of thy greatness, and power,
and sovereign dominion. But *now* thou hast by immediate revelation discovered thyself to me in thy
glorious majesty; *now my eyes see thee*; and therefore
now I repent, and unsay what I have foolishly said."
It is a great mercy to have a good education, and to
know the things of God by the instructions of his
word and ministers. When the understanding is
enlightened by the Spirit of grace our knowledge of

divine things as far exceeds what we had before as that by ocular demonstration exceeds that by report and common fame. By the teachings of men God reveals his Son to us; but by the teachings of his Spirit he reveals his Son in us (Gal. i. 16), and so *changes us into the same image*, 2 Cor. iii. 18. God is pleased sometimes to manifest himself most fully to his people by the rebukes of his word and providence. *Blessed is the man whom thou chastenest and teachest.*

2. Job thought hardly of himself (*v.* 6): *Wherefore I abhor myself, and repent in dust and ashes.* Even good people, that have no gross enormities to repent of, must be greatly afflicted in soul for the workings and breakings out of pride, passion, peevishness, and discontent, and all their hasty unadvised speeches. The more we see of the glory and majesty of God, and the more we see of the vileness and odiousness of sin and of ourselves because of sin, the more we shall abase and abhor ourselves for it. Let us leave it to God to govern the world, and make it our care, in the strength of his grace, to govern ourselves and our own hearts well.

Verses 7–9

While God was catechising Job out of the whirlwind one would have thought that he only was in the wrong, and that the cause would certainly go against him; but here we find the sentence given in Job's favour. Wherefore judge nothing before the time. Those who are truly righteous before God may have their righteousness clouded and eclipsed by great and uncommon affections, by the severe censures of men, by the sharp reproofs of conscience, and yet, in due time, these clouds shall all blow over, and God will *bring forth their righteousness as the light and their judgment as the noon-day*, Ps. xxxvii. 6.

I. Judgment given against Job's three friends, upon the controversy between them and Job. Elihu is not censured here, for he acted, not as a party, but as a moderator. Job is magnified and his three friends are mortified. Something of truth we thought they both had on their side, but it is well that the judgment is the Lord's and by it we will abide.

1. Job is greatly magnified and comes off with honour. When God appeared for him he had brought him to repentance for what he had said amiss, then he owned him in what he had said well. True penitents shall find favour with God, and what they have said and done amiss shall no more be mentioned against them. God calls him again and again *his servant Job,* four times in two verses, and he seems to take a pleasure in calling him so, as before his troubles (*ch.* i. 8), "*Hast thou considered my servant Job?* Though he is poor and despised, he is my servant notwithstanding, and as dear to me as when he was in prosperity. Though he has his faults, and has appeared to be a man subject to like passions as others, though he has contended with me, has gone about to disannul my judgment, and has darkened counsel by words without knowledge, yet he sees his error and retracts it, and therefore he is my servant Job still." If God says, *Well done, good and faithful servant,* it is of little consequence who says otherwise. He owns that he had *spoken of him the thing that was right,* beyond what his antagonists had done. Job had given a much better and truer account of the divine Providence than they had done. They had wronged God by making prosperity a mark of the true church and affliction a certain indication of God's wrath. Job had referred things to the future judgment, and the future state, more than his friends had done, and therefore he spoke of God that which was right, better than his friends had done. Though he had spoken some things amiss, even concerning God, yet he is commended for what he spoke that was right.

Job was in the right, and his friends were in the wrong, and yet he was in pain and they were at ease—a plain evidence that we cannot judge of men by looking in their faces or purses. He only can do it infallibly who sees men's hearts. Notwithstanding all the wrong his friends had done him, he is so good a man, and of such a humble, tender, forgiving spirit, that he will very readily pray for them. *My servant Job will pray for you.* True penitents shall not only find favour as petitioners for themselves, but be accepted as intercessors for others also. And, as Job prayed and offered sacrifice for those that had grieved and wounded his spirit, so Christ prayed and died for his persecutors, and ever lives *making intercession for the transgressors.*

2. Job's friends are greatly mortified, and come off with disgrace. They were good men and belonged to God, and therefore he would not let them lie still in their mistake any more than Job, but, having humbled them by a discourse out of the whirlwind, he takes another course to humble them. In most disputes and controversies there is something amiss on both sides, either in the merits of the cause or in the management, if not in both; and it is fit that both sides should be told of it, and made to see their errors. God tells them plainly that they had *not spoken of him the thing that was right, like Job,* that is, they had censured and condemned Job upon a false hypothesis, had represented God fighting against Job as an enemy when really he was only trying him as a friend. Those do not say well of God who represent his fatherly chastisements of his own children as judicial punishments. It is a dangerous thing to judge uncharitably of the spiritual and eternal state of others, for in so doing we may perhaps condemn those whom God has accepted. *My wrath is kindled against thee and thy two friends.* He requires from them a sacrifice, to make atonement for what they had said amiss. They must bring each of them *seven bullocks, and* each of them *seven rams,* to be offered up to God for a *burnt-offering.* He orders them to go to Job, and beg of him to offer their sacrifices, and pray for them, otherwise they should not be accepted. They thought that they only were the favourites of Heaven, and that Job had no interest there; but God gives them to understand that he had a better interest there than they had. Job and his friends had differed in their opinion about many things, but now they were to be made friends. They must agree in a sacrifice and a prayer, and that must reconcile them. Those who differ in judgment about minor things are yet one in Christ the great sacrifice, and meet at the same throne of grace, and therefore ought to love and bear with one another. Our quarrels with God always begin on our part, but the reconciliation begins on his.

II. The acquiescence of Job's friends in this judgment given, *v.* 9. They were good men, and, as soon as they understood what the mind of the Lord was, they did as he commanded them. Peace with God is to be had only in his own way and upon his own terms, and they will never seem hard to those who know how to value the privilege. Job's friends had all joined in accusing Job, and now they join in begging his pardon. Those that have sinned together should repent together.

Verses 10–17

You have heard of the patience of Job (says the apostle, James v. 11) *and have seen the end of the Lord,* that is, what end the Lord, at length, put to his troubles. In the beginning of this book we had Job's patience under his troubles, for an example; here, in the close, for our encouragement to follow that example, we have the happy issue of his troubles and the prosperous condition to which he was restored.

Perhaps, too, the extraordinary prosperity which Job was crowned with after his afflictions was intended to be to us Christians a type and figure of the glory and happiness of heaven, which the afflictions of this present time are working for us. He that rightly endures temptation, when he is tried, shall receive a *crown of life* (James i. 12).

I. God returned in ways of mercy to him. This put a new face upon his affairs immediately, and everything now looked as pleasing and promising as before it had looked gloomy and frightful. God *turned his captivity*, that is, he redressed his grievances and took away all the causes of his complaints; he loosed him from the bond with whicn Satan had now, for a great while, bound him. What was more, he felt a very great alteration in his mind; the tumult was all over, and the consolations of God were now as much the delight of his soul as his terrors had been its burden. The tide thus turned, his troubles began to ebb as fast as they had flowed, just then *when he was praying for his friends*. We are really doing our business when we are praying for our friends, if we pray in a right manner, for in those prayers there is not only faith, but love. Christ has taught us to pray with and for others in teaching us to say, *Our Father*; and, in seeking mercy for others, we may find mercy ourselves. God doubled his possessions: *Also the Lord gave Job twice as much as he had before.* He suffered for the glory of God, and therefore God made it up to him with advantage, and allowed him more than interest upon interest. God will take care that none shall lose by him. Job's friends had often said, *If thou wert pure and upright, surely now he would awake for thee*, ch. viii. 6. But he does not awake for thee; therefore thou art not upright. "Well," says God, "though your argument be not conclusive, I will even by that demonstrate the integrity of my servant Job; his latter end shall greatly increase."

II. His old acquaintance, neighbours, and relations, were very kind to him, *v.* 11. They wept for his griefs, and rejoiced in his joys, and proved not such miserable comforters as his three friends, that, at first, were so forward and officious to attend him. These were not such great men nor such learned and eloquent men as those, but they proved much more skilful and kind in comforting Job. They made a collection among them for the repair of his losses and the setting of him up again. *Every one gave him a piece of money and everyone an ear-ring of gold*, which would be as good as money to him. When God was friendly to him they were all willing to be friendly too, Ps. cxix. 74, 79. Others of them, it may be, withdrew because he was poor, and sore, and a rueful spectacle, but now that he began to recover they were willing to renew their acquaintance with him. Swallow-friends,

that are gone in winter, will return in the spring, though their friendship is of little value. Job *prayed for his friends*, and then they flocked about him, overcome by his kindness, and everyone desiring an interest in his prayers.

III. His estate strangely increased, by the blessing of God upon the little that his friends gave him. He thankfully received their courtesy, and did not think it below him to have his estate repaired by contributions. God gave him that which was far better than their money and ear-rings, and that was his blessing, *v.* 12. The Lord comforted him now according to the days wherein he had afflicted him, and *blessed his latter end more than his beginning*. The last days of a good man sometimes prove his best days, his last works his best works, his last comforts his best comforts; for his path, like that of the morning light, shines more and more to the perfect day. We know not what good times we may yet be reserved for in our latter end.

IV. His family was built up again, and he had great comfort in his children, *v.* 13-15. The number of his children was the same as before, *seven sons and three daughters*. Some give this reason why they were not doubled as his cattle were, because his children that were dead were not lost, but gone before to a better world; and therefore he has two fleeces of children (as I may say) *mahanaim—two hosts*, one in heaven, the other on earth. The names of his daughters are here registered (*v.* 14), because, in the significations of them, they seemed designed to perpetuate the remembrance of God's great goodness to him in the surprising change of his condition. He called the first *Jemima—The day*, because of the shining forth of his prosperity after a dark night of affliction. The next *Kezia*, a spice of a very fragrant smell. The third *Keren-happuch* (that is, *Plenty restored*, or *A horn of paint*), because (says he) God had wiped away the tears which fouled his face, ch. xvi. 16. Concerning these daughters, God adorned them with great beauty, *no women so fair as the daughters of Job*, *v.* 15. He made them co-heirs with their brethren.

V. His life was long. He lived to have much of the comfort of this life, for he saw his posterity to the fourth generation, *v.* 16. Though his children were not doubled to him, yet in his children's children (and those are the crown of old men) they were more than doubled. God has ways to repair the losses and balance the griefs of those who are written childless, as Job was when he had buried all his children. He died full of days, satisfied with living in this world, and willing to leave it; not peevishly so, as in the days of his affliction, but piously so, and thus, as Eliphaz had encouraged him to hope, he *came to his grave like a shock of corn in his season.*

AN EXPOSITION, WITH PRACTICAL OBSERVATIONS, OF

THE BOOK OF PSALMS

The History of Israel led us to camps and council-boards, and there instructed us in the knowledge of God. The book of Job brought us into the schools, and treated us with disputations concerning God and his providence. But this book brings us into the sanctuary, draws us off from converse with the politicians, philosophers, or disputers of this world, and directs us into communion with God, lifting up and letting out our hearts towards him. Thus may we be in the mount with God.

I. The title of this book. It is called, 1. The *Psalms*; under that title is it referred to, Luke xxiv. 44. The Hebrew calls it *Tehillim*, which properly signifies *Psalms of praise*, because many of them are such; but *Psalms* is a more general word, meaning all metrical compositions fitted to be sung, which may as well be historical, doctrinal, or supplicatory, as laudatory. Though singing be properly the voice of joy, yet the intention of songs is to assist the memory, and to express and excite all the other affections as well as this of joy. The priests had a mournful muse as well as joyful ones; and the divine institution of singing psalms is thus largely intended; for we are directed not only to praise God, but to teach and admonish ourselves and one another *in psalms, and hymns, and spiritual songs*, Col. iii. 16. 2. It is called the *Book of Psalms*: so it is quoted by St. Peter, Acts i. 20. It is a collection of psalms, of all the psalms that were divinely inspired.

II. The author of this book. It is, no doubt, derived originally from the blessed Spirit. They are spiritual songs, words which the Holy Ghost taught. The penman of most of them was David the son of Jesse, who is therefore called the *sweet psalmist of Israel*, 2 Sam. xxiii. 1. Some that have not his name in their titles yet are expressly ascribed to him elsewhere, as Ps. ii. (Acts iv. 25) and Ps. xcvi. and cv. (1 Chron. xvi.). One psalm is expressly said to be *the prayer of Moses* (Ps. xc.); and that some of the psalms were penned by Asaph is intimated, 2 Chron. xxix. 30, where they are said to *praise the Lord in the words of David and Asaph*, who is there called a *seer* or *prophet*. Some of the psalms seem to have been penned long after, as Ps. cxxxvii, at the time of the captivity in Babylon; but the far greater part of them were certainly penned by David himself.

III. The scope of it. It is manifestly intended, 1. To assist the exercises of natural religion, and to kindle in the souls of men those devout affections which we owe to God as our Creator, owner, ruler, and benefactor. The book of Job helps to prove our first principles of the divine perfections and providence; but this helps to improve them in prayers and praises, and professions of dependence on him. Other parts of scripture show that God is infinitely above man, and his sovereign Lord; but this shows us that there are ways in which we may keep up communion with him in all the various conditions of human life. 2. To advance the excellencies of revealed religion, and in the most pleasing powerful manner to recommend it to the world. There is indeed little or nothing of the ceremonial law in the book of *Psalms*. Though sacrifice and offering were yet to continue many ages, yet they are here represented as things which God did not desire (Ps. xl. 6, li. 16), as things comparatively little, and which in time were to vanish away. But the word and law of God, those parts of it which are moral and of perpetual obligation, are here magnified and made honourable. And Christ, the crown and centre of revealed religion, the foundation, corner, and top-stone, of that blessed building, is here clearly spoken of in type and prophecy, his sufferings and the glory that should follow, and the kingdom that he should set up in the world.

IV. The use of it. All scripture is profitable to convey divine light into our understandings; but this book is of singular use to convey divine life and power, and a holy warmth, into our affections. 1. It is of use to be sung. What the rules of the Hebrew metre were even the learned are not certain. But these psalms ought to be rendered according to the metre of every language, at least so that they may be sung for the edification of the church. So rich, so well made, are these divine poems, that they can never be exhausted, can never be worn thread-bare. 2. It is of use to be read by the ministers of Christ, as containing excellent truths, and rules concerning good and evil. 3. It is of use to be read and meditated upon by all good people. The Psalmist's experiences are of great use for our direction, caution, and encouragement. In telling us, as he often does, what passed between God and his soul, he lets us know what we may expect from God, and what he will expect, and require, and graciously accept from us. Even the Psalmist's expressions too are of great use; and by them the Spirit helps our praying infirmities. If we make David's psalms familiar to us, whatever errand we have at the throne of grace, we may there find apt words wherewith to clothe it, sound speech which cannot be condemned. We may take sometimes one choice psalm and sometimes another, and pray it over, that is, enlarge upon each verse in our own thoughts, and offer up our meditations to God as they arise from the expressions we find there. Nor is it only our devotion that the book of Psalms assists, teaching us how to offer praise so as to glorify God, but it is also a directory to the actions of our lives and teaches us how to *order our conversation aright, so as that*, in the end, *we may see the salvation of God*, Ps. l. 23. The Psalms were thus serviceable to the Old Testament church, but to us Christians they may be of more use than they could be to those who lived before the coming of Christ; for, as Moses's sacrifices, so David's songs, are expounded and made more intelligible by the gospel of Christ, which lets us within the veil; so that if to David's prayers and praises we add St. Paul's prayers in his epistles, and the new songs in the Revelation, we shall be thoroughly furnished for this good work.

The seven penitential Psalms have been in a particular manner singled out by the devotions of many. They are reckoned to be Ps. vi., xxxii., xxxviii., li., cii., cxxx., and cxliii. The Psalms were divided into five books, each concluding with *Amen, Amen*, or *Hallelujah*; the first ending with Ps. xli., the second with Ps. lxxii., the third with Ps. lxxxix., the fourth with Ps. cvi., the fifth with Ps. cl. Let good Christians divide them for themselves, so as may best increase their acquaintance with them, that they may have them at hand upon all occasions and may sing them in the spirit and with the understanding.

PSALM 1

This is a psalm of instruction concerning good and evil, setting before us life and death, the blessing and the curse, that we may take the right way which leads to happiness and avoid that which will certainly end in our misery and ruin. This psalm shows us, I. The holiness and happiness of a godly man, ver. 1–3. II. The sinfulness and misery of a wicked man, ver. 4, 5. III. The ground and reason of both, ver. 6.

Verses 1–3

The psalmist begins with the character and condition of a godly man.

I. The Lord knows those that are his by name, but we must know them by their character. The character of a good man is here given by the rules he chooses to walk by.

1. A godly man (*v.* 1) *walks not in the council of the ungodly*, &c. This part of his character is put first, because departing from evil is that in which wisdom begins. (1) He sees evil-doers round about him; the the world is full of them. They are here described by three characters, *ungoldly*, *sinners*, and *scornful*. They are *ungodly* first, casting off the fear of God. When the services of religion are laid aside, they come to be *sinners*, that is, they break out into open rebellion against God. Omissions make way for commissions, and by these the heart is so hardened that at length they come to be *scorners*, that is, they openly defy all that is sacred, scoff at religion, and make a jest of sin. The word which we translate *ungodly* signifies such as are unsettled, aim at no certain end and walk by no certain rule, but are at the command of every lust and at the beck of every temptation. These the good man sees with a sad heart. He does not do as they do. He does *not walk in the counsel of the ungodly*. He does not take his measures from their principles, nor act according to the advice which they give and take. He *stands not in the way of sinners*; he avoids doing as they do; their way shall not be his way. He *sits not in the seat of the scornful*. He does not associate with those that sit in close cabal to find out ways and means for the support and advancement of the devil's kingdom.

2. A godly man, that he may do that which is good and cleave to it, submits to the guidance of the word of God and makes that familiar to him, *v.* 2. All who are well pleased that there is a God must be well pleased that there is a Bible, a revelation of God, of his will, and of the only way to happiness in him. *In that law doth he meditate day and night*. To meditate in God's word is to discourse with ourselves concerning the great things contained in it, with a close application of mind, a fixedness of thought, till we be suitably affected with those things and experience the savour and power of them in our hearts.

II. An assurance given of the godly man's happiness. God blesses him, and that blessing will make him happy. Goodness and holiness are not only the way to happiness (Rev. xxii. 14) but happiness itself; supposing there were not another life after this, yet that man is a happy man that keeps in the way of his duty. *He shall be like a tree*, fruitful and flourishing. The divine blessing produces real effects. A good man is planted by the grace of God. These trees were by nature wild olives, and will continue so till they are grafted anew, and so planted by a power from above. Never any good tree grew of itself; it is *the planting of the Lord*, and therefore he must in it be glorified. Isa. lxi. 3. He is placed by the means of grace, here called *the rivers of water*; from these a good man receives supplies of strength and vigour, but in secret undiscerned ways. It is expected from those who enjoy the mercies of grace that, both in the temper of their minds and in the tenor of their lives, they comply with the intentions of that grace, and bring forth fruit. *His leaf also shall not wither.*

As to those who bring forth only the leaves of profession, without any good fruit, even their leaf will wither; but, if the word of God rule in the heart, that will keep the profession green; the laurels thus won shall never wither.

Verses 4–6

I. The description of the ungodly given, *v.* 5. 1. In general, they are the reverse of the righteous, both in character and condition: they bring forth no fruit but grapes of Sodom; they cumber the ground. In particular, whereas the righteous are like valuable, useful, fruitful trees, *they are like the chaff which the wind drives away*, the very lightest of the chaff, the dust which the owner of the floor desires to have driven away, as not capable of being put to any use.

II. The doom of the ungodly, *v.* 5. *They shall not stand in the judgment*, that is, they shall be found guilty. They shall not stand *in the congregation of the righteous*. The wicked shall not have a place in that congregation. Into the new Jerusalem none unclean nor unsanctified shall enter. Hypocrites in this world, under the disguise of a plausible profession, may thrust themselves into the congregation of the righteous and remain undisturbed and undiscovered there; but Christ cannot be imposed upon, though his ministers may.

III. The reason rendered of this different state of the godly and wicked, *v.* 6. The Lord approves and is well pleased with the way of the righteous, and therefore, under the influence of his gracious smiles, it shall prosper and end well; but he is angry at the way of the wicked, all they do is offensive to him, and therefore it shall perish, and they in it.

In singing these verses, and praying over them, let us possess ourselves with a holy dread of the wicked man's portion, and with a holy care to approve ourselves to God in everything, entreating his favour with our whole hearts.

PSALM 2

As the foregoing psalm was moral, and showed us our duty, so this is evangelical, and shows us our Saviour. Under the type of David's kingdom (which was of divine appointment, met with much opposition, but prevailed at last) the kingdom of the Messiah, the Son of David, is prophesied. It is interpreted of Christ, Acts iv. 27; xiii. 33; Heb. i. 5. The Holy Ghost here foretells, I. The opposition that should be given to the kingdom of the Messiah, ver. 1–3. II. The baffling and chastising of that opposition, ver. 4, 5. III. The setting up of the kingdom of Christ, notwithstanding that opposition, ver. 6. IV. The confirmation and establishment of it, ver. 7. V. A promise of the enlargement and success of it, ver. 8, 9. VI. A call and exhortation to kings and princes to yield themselves the willing subjects of this kingdom, ver. 10–12. Or thus: We have here, I. Threatenings denounced against the adversaries of Christ's kingdom, ver 1–6. II. Promises made to Christ himself, the head of this kingdom, ver. 7–9. III. Counsel given to all to espouse the interests of this kingdom, ver. 10–12.

Verses 1–6

We have here a very great struggle about the kingdom of Christ, hell and heaven contesting it; the seat of the war is this earth.

I. The mighty opposition that would be given to the Messiah and his kingdom, *v.* 1–3. One would have expected that so great a blessing to this world would be universally welcomed and embraced. Never were the notions of any sect of philosophers, nor the powers of any prince, opposed with so much violence as the doctrine and government of Christ. Princes and people, court and country, have sometimes separate interests, but here they are united against Christ. Though his kingdom is not of this world, nor in the least calculated to weaken their interests, yet the kings of the earth and rulers are up in arms immediately. As the Philistines and their lords, Saul and his courtiers, the disaffected party and their ringleaders, opposed David's coming to the crown, so Herod and Pilate, the Gentiles and the Jews, did their utmost against Christ and his interest in men, Acts iv. 27.

They quarrel *against the Lord and against his anointed*, that is, against all religion in general and the Christian religion in particular. The great author of our holy religion is here called *the Lord's anointed*, or *Messiah*, or *Christ*, in allusion to the anointing of David to be king. It is a most spiteful and malicious opposition. They *rage* and fret; they gnash their teeth for vexation at the setting up of Christ's kingdom. It is a deliberate and politic opposition. They *imagine*, that is, they contrive means to suppress the rising interests of Christ's kingdom. It is a resolute and obstinate opposition. They *set themselves* in defiance of reason. It is a combined and confederate opposition. They *take counsel together*, to assist and animate one another. They will be content to entertain such notions of the kingdom of God and the Messiah as will serve to support their own dominion. If the Lord and his anointed will make them rich and great in the world, they will bid them welcome; but if they will restrain their corrupt appetites and passions, *they will not have this man to reign over them*, Luke xix. 14. Christ has *bands and cords* for us; but they are *cords of a man*, agreeable to right reason, and *bands of love*, conductive to our true interest. Why do men oppose religion but because they are impatient of its restraints and obligations? They would break asunder the bands of conscience they are under and the cords of God's commandments. They are here reasoned with concerning it, *v.* 1. Why do they do this? They can show no good cause for opposing so just, holy, and gracious a government. They can hope for no good success in opposing so powerful a kingdom. It is *a vain thing*; when they have done their worst Christ will have a church in the world glorious and triumphant. It is *built upon a rock, and the gates of hell shall not prevail against it*.

II. The mighty conquest gained over all this threatening opposition. The perfect repose of the Eternal Mind may be our comfort under all the disquietments of our mind. We are tossed on earth, and in the sea, but he sits in the heavens, where he has prepared his throne for judgment.

1. The attempts of Christ's enemies are easily ridiculed. God *laughs at* them as a company of fools.

2. They are justly punished, *v.* 5. Though God despises them as impotent, yet he is justly displeased with them. The enemies rage, but cannot vex God. His setting up this kingdom of his Son, in spite of them, is the greatest vexation to them that can be.

3. They are certainly defeated, and all their counsels turned headlong (*v.* 6): *Yet have I set my king upon my holy hill of Zion.* Jesus Christ is a King, and God is pleased to call him *his* King, because he is appointed by him, and entrusted by him with the sole administration of government and judgment. He is his King, for he is dear to the Father, and one in whom he is well pleased. Christ took not this honour to himself, but was called to it. Being called to this honour, he was confirmed in it: "*I have set him*, I have settled him."

We are to sing these verses with a holy exultation, triumphing in Jesus Christ as the great trustee of power; and we are to pray, in firm belief of the assurance here given, "Father in heaven, *Thy kingdom come*; let thy Son's kingdom come."

Verses 7–9

Let us now hear what the Messiah himself has to say for his kingdom.

I. The kingdom of the Messiah is founded upon a decree, an eternal decree, of God the Father. It was not a sudden resolve, it was not the trial of an experiment, but the result of the counsels of the divine wisdom.

II. There is a declaration of that decree, as far as is necessary for the satisfaction of all those who are called and commanded to yield themselves subjects to this king, and to leave those inexcusable who will not have him to reign over them. Christ here makes a twofold title to his kingdom:—1. A title by inheritance (*v.* 7): *Thou art my Son, this day have I begotten thee.* This scripture the apostle quotes (Heb. i. 5) to prove that Christ has a more excellent name than the angels, but that he *obtained it by inheritance*, *v.* 4. He is the Son of God, and therefore of the same nature with the Father, has in him all the fulness of the godhead, infinite wisdom, power, and holiness. Upon this account we are to receive him as a King; for because *the Father loveth the Son he hath given all things into his hand*, John iii. 35 v. 20. Being a Son, he is heir of all things, and the Father having made the worlds by him, it is easy to infer thence that by him also he governs them; for he is the eternal Wisdom and the eternal Word. Immediately after his resurrection he entered upon the administration of his mediatorial kingdom; it was then that he said, *All power is given unto me.* 2. A title by agreement, *v.* 8, 9. The agreement is, in short, this: the Son must undertake the office of an intercessor, and, upon that condition, he shall have the honour and power of a universal monarch. The Father will grant more than the half of the kingdom, even the kingdom itself. It is here promised him, he shall have *the heathen* for his inheritance, not the Jews only, but the Gentiles also. A great part of the Gentile world received the gospel when it was first preached, and it is to be yet further accomplished when *the kingdoms of this world shall become the kingdoms of the Lord and of his Christ*, Rev. xi. 15. It shall be victorious: *Thou shalt break them* (those of them that oppose thy kingdom) *with a rod of iron*, *v.* 9. This was in part fulfilled when the nation of the Jews, those that persisted in unbelief and enmity to Christ's gospel, were destroyed by the Roman power. It had a further accomplishment in the destruction of the pagan powers, when the Christian religion came to be established; but it will not be completely fulfilled till all opposing rule, principality, and power, shall be finally put down, 1 Cor. xv. 24. See cx. 5, 6.

In singing this, and praying it over, we must give glory to Christ as the eternal Son of God and our rightful Lord, and must take comfort from this promise, and plead it with God, that the kingdom of Christ shall be enlarged and established and shall triumph over all opposition.

Verses 10–12

The practical application of this gospel doctrine concerning the kingdom of the Messiah, by way of exhortation to the kings and judges of the earth. They hear that it is in vain to oppose Christ's government; let them therefore be so wise for themselves as to submit to it. He that has power to destroy them shows that he has no pleasure in their destruction, for he puts them into a way to make themselves happy, *v.* 10. What is said to them is said to all. We are exhorted,

I. To reverence God and to stand in awe of him, *v.* 11. This is the great duty of natural religion. We must serve God in all ordinances of worship, with a holy fear. We must rejoice in God, but still with a holy trembling. Our salvation must be wrought out *with fear and trembling*, Phil. ii. 12.

II. To welcome Jesus Christ and to submit to him, *v.* 12. This is the great duty of the Christian religion.

1. The command given to this purport: *Kiss the Son.* Christ is called the *Son* because so he was declared (*v.* 7), *Thou art my Son.* He is the Son of God by eternal generation, and, upon that account, he is to be adored by us. Our duty to Christ is here expressed figuratively: *Kiss the Son*, not with a betraying kiss, as Judas kissed him, but with a believing kiss.

With a kiss of affection and sincere love: "*Kiss the Son;* enter into a covenant of friendship with him, and let him be very dear and precious to you; love him above all, love him in sincerity, love him much, as she did to whom much was forgiven, and, in token of it, kissed his feet," Luke vii. 38. With a kiss of allegiance and loyalty, submit to his government, take his yoke upon you.

2. The reasons to enforce this command;

(1) The certain ruin we run upon if we refuse and reject Christ: "*Kiss the Son;* for it is at your peril if you do not." Do it, *lest he be angry.*

(2) The happiness we are sure of if we yield ourselves to Christ. Blessed will those be in the day of wrath, who, by trusting in Christ, have made him their refuge and patron; when the hearts of others fail them for fear they shall lift up their heads with joy.

In singing this, and praying it over, we should have our hearts filled with a holy awe of God, but at the same time borne up with a cheerful confidence in Christ, in whose mediation we may comfort and encourage ourselves and one another.

PSALM 3

As the foregoing psalm, in the type of David in preferment, showed us the royal dignity of the Redeemer, so this, by the example of David in distress, shows us the peace and holy security of the redeemed under the divine protection. David, being now driven out from his palace, from the royal city, from the holy city, by his rebellious son Absalom, I. Complains to God of his enemies, ver. 1, 2. II. Confides in God, and encourages himself in him as his God, notwithstanding, ver. 3. III. Recollects the satisfaction he had in the gracious answers God gave to his prayers, and his experience of his goodness to him, ver. 4, 5. IV. Triumphs over his fears (ver. 6) and over his enemies, ver. 7. V. Gives God the glory and takes to himself the comfort of the divine blessing and salvation which are sure to all the people of God, ver. 8.

A psalm of David, when he fled from Absalom his son.

Verses 1-3

The title of this psalm and many others is as a key hung ready at the door, to open it. When we know upon what occasion a psalm was penned we know the better how to expound it. 1. David was in great grief; when, in his flight, he went up the Mount of Olives, he wept greatly, with his head covered, and marching bare-foot; yet *then* he composed this comfortable psalm. He wept and prayed, wept and sung, wept and believed. Is any afflicted with undutiful disobedient children? David was; and yet that did not hinder his joy in God, nor put him out of tune for holy songs. 2. He was in great danger; the plot against him was laid deep, the party that sought his ruin was very formidable, and his own son at the head of them, so that his affairs seemed to be at the last extremity; yet *then* he kept hold of his interest in God and improved that. Perils and frights should drive us to God, not drive us from him. 3. He had now a great deal of provocation given him by those from whom he had reason to expect better things, from his son, whom he had been indulgent of, from his subjects, whom he had been so great a blessing to. 4. He was suffering for his sin in the matter of Uriah; this was the evil which, for that sin, God threatened to *raise up against him out of his own house* (2 Sam. xii. 11). Yet he did not *therefore* cast away his confidence in the divine power and goodness, nor despair of succour. Even our sorrow for sin must not hinder either our joy in God or our hope in God. 5. He seemed cowardly in fleeing from Absalom, and quitting his royal city, before he had had one struggle for it; and yet, by this psalm, it appears he was full of true courage arising from his faith in God.

In these three verses he applies to God. Whither else should we go but to him when anything grieves us or frightens us?

I. With a representation of his distress, *v.* 1, 2. He looks round, and as it were takes a view of his enemies' number. David had had the hearts of his subjects as much as ever any king had, and yet now, of a sudden, he had lost them. They rose up against him; they aimed to trouble him; but that was not all: they said of his soul, *There is no help for him in God.* They put a spiteful and invidious construction upon his troubles, as Job's friends did upon his, concluding that, because his servants and subjects forsook him thus and did not help him, God had deserted him and abandoned his cause, and he was therefore to be looked *on,* or rather to be looked *off,* as a hypocrite and a wicked man. They endeavoured to shake his confidence in God and drive him to despair of relief from him: "They have said it *to* my soul"; so it may be read; compare xi. 1; xlii. 10. David comes to God, and tells him what his enemies said of him. "They say, *There is no help for me in thee;* but, Lord, if it be so, I am undone. They say to my soul, *There is no salvation*" (for so the word is) "*for him in God;* but, Lord, do thou say unto my soul, *I am thy salvation* (xxxv. 3) and that shall satisfy me, and in due time silence them." To this complaint he adds *Selah.* Some refer it to the music with which, in David's time, the psalms were sung; others to the sense, and that it is a note commanding a solemn pause. *Selah—Mark that,* or, "*Stop there,* and consider a little." As here, they say, *There is no help for him in God, Selah.*

II. With a profession of his dependence upon God, *v.* 3. David here, when his enemies said, *There is no help for him in God,* cries out with so much the more assurance, "*But thou, O Lord! art a shield for me. Thou art a shield for me,* a shield *about* me" (so some), "to secure me on all sides, since my enemies surrounded me." *Thou art my glory Thou art the lifter up of my head.* If, in the worst of times, God's people can lift up their heads with joy, knowing that all shall work for good to them, they will own it is God that is the lifter up of their head, that gives them both cause to rejoice and hearts to rejoice.

Verse 4-8

David, having stirred up himself by the irritations of his enemies to take hold on God as his God, and so gained comfort in looking upward when, if he looked round about him, nothing appeared but what was discouraging, here looks back with pleasing reflections and looks forward with pleasing expectations of a happy issue to which the dark dispensation he was now under would shortly be brought.

I. David had been exercised with many difficulties, often oppressed and brought very low; but still he had found God all-sufficient.

1. His troubles had always brought him to his knees, and, in all his difficulties and dangers, he had been enabled to acknowledge God and to lift up his heart to him, and his voice too: *I cried unto God with my voice.*

2. He had always found God ready to answer his prayers: *He heard me out of his holy hill,* from heaven, the high and holy place, from the ark on Mount Sion, whence he used to give answers to those that sought to him. Christ was *set King upon the holy hill of Zion* (ii. 6), and it is through him, whom the Father hears always, that our prayers are heard.

3. He had always been very safe and very easy under the divine protection (*v.* 5): "*I laid myself down and slept,* composed and quiet; *and awaked refreshed, for the Lord sustained me.*" (1) This is applicable to the common mercies of every night, which we ought to give thanks for alone, and with our families, every morning. (2) It seems here to be meant of the wonderful quietness and calmness of

David's spirit, in the midst of his dangers. Having by prayer committed himself and his cause to God, and being sure of his protection, his heart was fixed, and he was easy.

4. God had often broken the power and restrained the malice of his enemies, had *smitten them upon the cheek-bone* (v. 7), had silenced them and spoiled their speaking.

II. See with what confidence he looks forward to the dangers he had yet in prospect. 1. His *fears were all stilled and silenced*, v. 6. "*I will not be afraid of ten thousands of people*, that either in a foreign invasion or an intestine rebellion *set themselves*, or encamp, *against me round about*." When David, in his flight from Absalom, bade Zadok carry back the ark, he spoke doubtfully of the issue of his present troubles, and concluded, like a humble penitent, *Here I am; let him do to me what seemeth to him good*, 2 Sam. xv. 26. But now, like a strong believer, he speaks confidently, and has no fear concerning the event. 2. His prayers were quickened and encouraged, v. 7. He believed God was his Saviour, and yet prays: nay, he *therefore* prays, *Arise, O Lord! save me, O my God!* 3. His faith became triumphant. He began the psalm with complaints of the strength and malice of his enemies, but concludes it with exultation in the power and grace of his God, and now sees more with him than against him, v. 8. Two great truths he here builds his confidence upon. (1) That *salvation belongeth unto the Lord*; he has power to save, be the danger ever so great. (2) That his blessing is upon his people; he not only has power to save them, but he has assured them of his gracious intentions. He has, in his word, pronounced a blessing upon his people; and we are bound to believe that that blessing does accordingly rest upon them, though there be not the visible effects of it.

PSALM 4

David was a preacher and many of his psalms are doctrinal and practical as well as devotional. The greatest part of this psalm is so. Here, I. David begins with a short prayer (ver. 1) and that prayer preaches. II. He directs his speech to the children of men, and, 1. In God's name reproves them for the dishonour they do to God and the damage they do their own souls, ver. 2. 2. He sets before them the happiness of godly people, for their encouragement to be religious, ver. 3. 3. He calls upon them to consider their ways, ver. 4. III. He exhorts them to serve God and trust in him, ver. 5. IV. He gives an account of his own experiences of the grace of God working in him.

To the chief musician on Neginoth. A psalm of David.

Verses 1–5

The title of the psalm acquaints us that David, having penned it by divine inspiration for the use of the church, delivered it to the chief musician. We have a particular account of the constitution, the modelling of the several classes of singers, each with a chief, and the share each bore in the work, 1 Chron. xxv.

I. David addresses himself to God, v. 1. All the notice God is pleased to take of our prayers, and all the returns he is pleased to make to them, must be ascribed, not to our merit, but purely to his mercy. "Hear me for thy mercy-sake" is our best plea. Two things David here pleads further:—1. "Thou art *the God of my righteousness*; not only a righteous God thyself, but the author of my righteous dispositions, who hast by thy grace wrought that good that is in me, hast made me a righteous man; therefore *hear me*." 2. "*Thou hast* formerly *enlarged me when I was in distress*, enlarged me in holy joy and comfort under my distresses, enlarged my condition by bringing me out of my distresses; therefore *now, Lord*, have mercy upon me, and hear me." "*Thou hast; wilt thou not?* For thou art God, and changest not; thy work is perfect."

II. He addresses himself to the children of men, for the conviction and conversion of those that are yet strangers to God, and that will not have the Messiah, the Son of David, to reign over them.

1. He endeavours to convince them of the folly of their impiety (v. 2). "You debase yourselves, for you are *sons of men*" (the word signifies man as a noble creature); "consider the dignity of your nature, and do not act thus irrationally and unbecoming yourselves." "You dishonour your Maker, and *turn his glory into shame*." Those that profane God's holy name, that ridicule his word and ordinances, and, while they profess to know him, in works deny him, do what in them lies to *turn his glory into shame*. "You set your hearts upon that which will prove, at last, but vanity and a lie." Those that love the world, and seek the things that are beneath, love vanity, and seek lies.

2. He shows them the peculiar favour which God has for good people, the special protection they are under, and the singular privileges to which they are entitled, v. 3. It is at their peril if they *offend one of these little ones*, whom God has *set apart for himself*, Matt. xviii. 6. God reckons that those who touch them touch the apple of his eye; and he will make their persecutors to know it, sooner or later. *They shall be mine, saith the Lord, in that day when I make up my jewels. Know this;* let godly people know it, and let wicked people know it, and take heed how they hurt those whom God protects.

3. He warns them against sin, and exhorts them both to frighten and to reason themselves out of it (v. 4): "*Stand in awe and sin not*" (*be angry and sin not*, so the LXX). One good means of preventing sin, and preserving a holy awe, is to be frequent and serious in *communing with our own hearts*: "*Talk with your hearts;* you have a great deal to say to them; they may be spoken with at any time; let it not be unsaid." A thinking man is in a fair way to be a wise and a good man. "Choose a solitary time; do it when you lie awake *upon your beds*. Before you turn yourself to go to sleep at night" (as some of the heathen moralists have directed) "examine your consciences with respect to what you have done that day, particularly what you have done amiss, that you may repent of it. When you awake in the night meditate upon God, and the things that belong to your peace."

4. He counsels them to make conscience of their duty (v. 5): *Offer to God the sacrifice of righteousness*. We must not only cease to do evil, but learn to do well. "*Offer sacrifices to him*, your own selves first, and your best sacrifices." "Let all your devotions come from an upright heart; let all your alms be sacrifices of righteousness." Honour him, by trusting in him only, and not in your wealth nor in an arm of flesh; trust in his providence, and lean not to your own understanding; trust in his grace, and go not about to establish your own righteousness or sufficiency.

Verses 6–8

I. The foolish wish of worldly people: *There be many that say, Who will show us any good? Who will make us to see good?* What good they meant is intimated, v. 7. It was the increase of their corn and wine; all they desired was plenty of the wealth of this world, that they might enjoy abundance of the delights of sense. They enquire for good that may be seen, and they show no concern for the good things that are out of sight and are the objects of faith only. As we must be taught to worship an unseen God, so to seek an unseen good, 2 Cor. iv. 18. We look with an eye of faith further than we can see with an eye of sense. All they want is outward good, present good, partial good, good meat, good drink, a good trade, and a good estate; and what are all these worth without a good God and a good heart? Any good will serve the turn of most men, but a gracious soul will not be put off so.

II. The wise choice which godly people make. David, and the pious few that adhered to him, joined in this prayer, *Lord lift thou up the light of thy countenance upon us.* He and his friends agree in their choice of God's favour as their felicity; it is this which in their account is better than life and all the comforts of life. Though David speaks of himself only in the 7th and 8th verses, he speaks, in this prayer, for others also,—"*upon us,*" as Christ taught us to pray, "*Our Father.*" All the saints come to the throne of grace on the same errand, and in this they are one, they all desire God's favour as their chief good. We should beg it for others as well as for ourselves, for in God's favour there is enough for us all and we shall have never the less for others sharing in what we have. This is what, above anything, they rejoice in (*v.* 7): "*Thou hast hereby often put gladness into my heart.*" When God puts grace in the heart he *puts gladness in the heart*; inward, solid, substantial joy. "*I will lay myself down* (having the assurance of thy favour) *in peace, for thou only makest me to dwell in safety.*" When he comes to sleep the sleep of death, he will then, with good old Simeon, *depart in peace* (Luke ii. 29), being assured that God will receive his soul. He commits all his affairs to God, and contentedly leaves the issue of them with him.

PSALM 5

This psalm is a prayer, a solemn address to God, at a time when the psalmist was brought into distress by the malice of his enemies. I. David settles a correspondence between his soul and God, promising to pray, and promising himself that God would certainly hear him, ver. 1-3. II. He gives to God the glory, and takes to himself the comfort, of God's holiness, ver. 4-6. III. He declares his resolution to keep close to the public worship of God, ver. 7. IV. He prayed, 1. For himself, that God would guide him, ver. 8. 2. Against his enemies, that God would destroy them, ver. 9, 10. 3. For all the people of God, that God would give them joy, and keep them safe, ver. 11, 12.

To the chief musician upon Nehiloth. A psalm of David.

Verses 1-6

In these verses David prays to God,

I. As a prayer-hearing God; such he has always been ever since men began to call upon the name of the Lord, and yet is still as ready to hear prayer as ever. David here styles him: *O Lord* (*v.* 1, 3), *Jehovah,* a self-existent, self-sufficient, Being, whom we are bound to adore, and, "*my King and my God* (*v.* 2), to whom I have sworn allegiance, and under whose protection I have put myself as my King." We believe that the God we pray to is a King and a God. The most powerful plea in prayer, is to look upon him as *our* King and *our* God.

1. What David here prays for, which may encourage our faith and hopes in all our addresses to God. *Give ear to my words, O Lord!* Men perhaps will not or cannot hear us; our enemies are so haughty that they will not, our friends at such a distance that they cannot; but God, though high, though in heaven, can, and will. *Consider my meditation.* David's prayers were not his words only, but his meditations. Meditation and prayer should go together, xix. 14.

2. Four things David here promises, and so must we:—(1) That he will pray, that he will make conscience of praying. The assurances God has given us of his readiness to hear prayer should confirm our resolution to live and die praying. (2) That he will pray *in the morning.* Morning prayer is our duty; we are the fittest for prayer when we are in the most fresh, and lively, and composed frame, got clear of the slumbers of the night, revived by them, and not

yet filled with the business of the day. We have then most need of prayer. (3) That he will have his eye single: *I will direct my prayer,* as a marksman directs his arrow to the white; with such a fixedness and steadiness of mind should we address ourselves to God. Let our first petition be, *Hallowed,* glorified, *be thy name,* and then we may be sure of the same gracious answer to it that was given to Christ himself: *I have glorified it, and I will glorify it yet again.* (4) That he will patiently wait for an answer of peace: "I *will look up,* will look after my prayers, and *hear what God the Lord will speak* (lxxxv. 8; Hab. ii. 1), that, if he grant what I asked, I may be thankful—if he deny, I may be patient—if he defer, I may continue to pray and wait and may not faint."

II. As a sin-hating God, *v.* 4-6. David takes notice of this. As the God with whom we have to do is gracious and merciful, so he is pure and holy; though he is ready to hear prayer, yet, if we regard iniquity in our heart, he will not hear our prayers, lxvi. 18. God has no pleasure in wickedness, though covered with a cloak of religion. Let those therefore who delight in sin know that God has no delight in them. Those whom thou hatest thou shalt destroy; particularly two sorts of sinners, who are here marked for destruction: Those that are fools, that speak leasing or lying, and that are deceitful. Those that are cruel: *Thou wilt abhor the bloody man;* for inhumanity is no less contrary, no less hateful, to the God of mercy, whom mercy pleases.

Verses 7-12

In these verses David gives three characters—of himself, of his enemies, and of all the people of God, and subjoins a prayer to each of them.

I. He gives an account of himself and prays for himself, *v.* 7, 8.

1. He is steadfastly resolved to keep closely to God and to his worship. (1) To worship God, to pay his homage to him, and give unto God the glory due unto his name. (2) To worship him publicly: "*I will come into thy house,* the courts of thy house, to worship there with other faithful worshippers." David was much in secret worship, prayed often alone (*v.* 2, 3), and yet was very constant and devout in his attendance on the sanctuary. (3) To worship him reverently and with a due sense of the infinite distance there is between God and man. (4) To take his encouragement in worship, from God himself only. The mercy of God should ever be both the foundation of our hopes and the fountain of our joy in everything wherein we have to do with him.

2. He earnestly prays that God by his grace, would guide and preserve him always in the way of his duty (*v.* 8): *Lead me in thy righteousness, because of my enemies*—Heb. "*Because of those who observe me,* who watch for my halting and seek occasion against me."

II. He gives an account of his enemies, and prays against them, *v.* 9, 10. He had spoken (*v.* 6) of God's hating the bloody and deceitful man. "Now, Lord," says he, "that is the character of my enemies: they are deceitful; there is no trusting them, for there is no faithfulness in their mouth." "They have by their sins deserved destruction; there is enough to justify God in their utter rejection: *Cast them out in the multitude of their transgressions,* by which they have filled up the measure of their iniquity and have become ripe for ruin." He pleads, "*They have rebelled against thee.* Had they been only my enemies, I could safely have forgiven them; but they are rebels against God, his crown and dignity; they oppose his government, and will not repent, to give him glory, and therefore I plainly foresee their ruin." His prayer for their destruction comes not from a spirit of revenge, but from a spirit of prophecy, by which he foretold that all who rebel against God will certainly be destroyed by their own counsels.

III. He gives an account of the people of God, and prays for them, concluding with an assurance of their bliss. They are the righteous (*v.* 12); for they *put their trust in God*, are well assured of his power and all-sufficiency, venture their all upon his promise, and are confident of his protection. *Let them rejoice;* let them have cause to rejoice and hearts to rejoice; fill them with joy, with great joy and unspeakable. Let all that are entitled to God's promises have a share in our prayers; grace be with all that love Christ in sincerity. "They are safe under the protection of thy favour; with that thou wilt *crown* him." A shield, in war, guards only one side, but the favour of God is to the saints a defence on every side; like the hedge about Job, round about, so that, while they keep themselves under the divine protection, they are entirely safe and ought to be entirely satisfied.

PSALM 6

David was a weeping prophet as well as Jeremiah, and this psalm is one of his lamentations: it was penned at a time of great trouble, both outward and inward. Is any afflicted? Is any sick? Let him sing this psalm. He begins with doleful complaints, but ends with joyful praises. Three things the psalmist is here complaining of:—1. Sickness of body. 2. Trouble of mind. 3. The insults of his enemies upon occasion of both. Now here, I. He pours out his complaints before God, deprecates his wrath, and begs earnestly for the return of his favour, ver. 1-7. II. He assures himself of an answer of peace, shortly, to his full satisfaction, ver. 8-10. This psalm is like the book of Job.

To the chief musician on Neginoth upon Sheminith. A psalm of David.

Verses 1-7

These verses speak the language of a heart truly humbled under humbling providences, of a broken and contrite spirit under great afflictions.

I. The representation he makes to God of his grievances. He pours out his complaint before him. Whither else should a child go with his complaints, but to his father? He complains of bodily pain and sickness (*v.* 2): *My bones are vexed.* His bones and his flesh, like Job's, were touched. He complains of inward trouble: *My soul is also sorely vexed;* and that is much more grievous than the vexation of the bones. It is a sad thing for a man to have his bones and his soul vexed at the same time. *Thou, O Lord! how long?* To the living God we must, at such a time, address ourselves, who is the only physician both of body and mind, and not to the Assyrians, not to the god of Ekron.

II. The impression which his troubles made upon him. They lay very heavily; he *groaned till he was weary.* David had more courage and consideration than to mourn thus for any outward affliction; but, when sin sat heavily upon his conscience then he thus grieved and mourned in secret, and even his soul refused to be comforted. True penitents weep in their retirements. David mourned in the night upon the bed where he lay communing with his own heart, and no eye was a witness to his grief, but the eye of him who is all eye. Peter went out, covered his face, and wept. David's eye waxed old because of his enemies, who rejoiced in his afflictions and put bad constructions upon his tears.

III. The petitions which he offers up to God in this sorrowful and distressed state. That which he dreads as the greatest evil is the anger of God. Therefore he prays (*v.* 1), *O Lord! rebuke me not in thy anger,* though I have deserved it, *neither chasten me in thy hot displeasure.* He can bear the rebuke and chastening well enough if God, at the same time, lift up the light of his countenance upon him and by his Spirit make him to hear the joy and gladness of his loving-kindness; the affliction of his body will be tolerable if he have but comfort in his soul. That

which he desires as the greatest good, and which would be to him the restoration of all good, is the favour and friendship of God. He prays, That God would pity him and look upon him with compassion. That God would pardon his sins. That God would put forth his power for his relief: *Lord, heal me* (*v.* 2), *save me* (*v.* 4). That he would be at peace with him: *Return, O Lord!* receive me into thy favour again, and be reconciled to me. That he would especially preserve the inward man and the interests of that, whatever might become of the body: "*O Lord! deliver my soul.*"

IV. The pleas with which he enforces his petitions, not to move God but to move himself. He pleads his own misery. He pleads God's mercy. He pleads God's glory (*v.* 5): "*For in death there is no remembrance of thee.*"

Verses 8-10

What a sudden change is here for the better! He that was groaning, and weeping, and giving up all for gone (*v.* 6, 7), here looks and speaks very pleasantly.

I. He distinguishes himself from the wicked and ungodly, and fortifies himself against their insults (*v.* 8): *Depart from me, all you workers of iniquity.* The workers of iniquity that had teased him, and taunted him, and asked him, "Where is thy God?" triumphing in his despondency and despair; but now he had wherewith to answer those that reproached him, for God had now comforted his spirit and would shortly complete his deliverance. But now, "*depart from me:* I will never lend an ear to your counsel; you would have had me to curse God and die, but I will bless him and live." When God has done great things for us, this would put us upon studying what we shall do for him.

II. He assures himself that God was, and would be, propitious to him, notwithstanding the present intimations of wrath which he was under. He is confident of a gracious answer to this prayer which he is now making. While he is yet speaking, he is aware that God hears and therefore speaks of it with an air of triumph, "*The Lord hath heard.*" (*v.* 8), and again (*v.* 9), "*The Lord hath heard.*" Thence he infers the like favourable audience of all his other prayers: "He *has heard the voice of my supplication,* and therefore he *will receive my prayer.*"

III. He either prays for the conversion or predicts the destruction of his enemies and persecutors, *v.* 10. 1. It may very well be taken as a prayer for their conversion: "Let them all be ashamed of the censures they have passed upon me. Let them be (as all true penitents are) vexed at themselves for their own folly; let them return to a better temper and disposition of mind." 2. If they be not converted, it is a prediction of their confusion and ruin. *They shall be ashamed and sorely vexed* (so it may be read), and that justly. They rejoiced that David was vexed (*v.* 2, 3), and therefore, as usually happens, the evil returns upon themselves; they also shall be sorely vexed.

PSALM 7

It appears by the title that this psalm was penned with a particular reference to the malicious imputations that David was unjustly laid under by some of his enemies. Being thus wronged, I. He applies to God for favour, ver. 1, 2. II. He appeals to God concerning his innocency, ver. 3-5. III. He prays to God to plead his cause and judge for him against his persecutors, ver. 6-9. IV. He expresses his confidence in God that he would do so, ver. 10-16. V. He promises to give God the glory of his deliverance, ver. 17.

Shiggaion of David, which he sang unto the Lord concerning the words of Cush the Benjamite.

Verses 1-9

Shiggaion is a *song* or *psalm* (the word is used so only here and Hab. iii. 1)—a *wandering* song (so some), the matter and composition of the several parts being different, but artificially put together— a *charming* song (so others), very delightful. David not only penned it, but sang it himself in a devout religious manner unto the Lord, *concerning the words* or affairs *of Cush the Benjamite*, that is, of some kinsman of Saul named *Cush*, who was an inveterate enemy to David, and made mischief between him and Saul. David, thus basely abused, has recourse to the Lord. His spirit was not ruffled by it, and it did not occasion one jarring string in his harp. Thus let the injuries we receive from men, instead of provoking our passions, kindle and excite our devotions.

I. He puts himself under God's protection (*v.* 1): "*Lord, save me, and deliver me* from the power and malice of *all those that persecute me*, that they may not have their will against me." He pleads, 1. His relation to God. "Thou art *my God*, and therefore whither else should I go but to thee?" 2. His confidence in God: "Lord, save me, for I depend upon thee: *In thee do I put my trust*, and not in any arm of flesh." 3. The rage and malice of his enemies, and the imminent danger he was in of being swallowed up by them: "Lord, save me, or I am gone; he will *tear my soul like a lion* tearing his prey." 4. The failure of all other helpers: "*Lord*, be thou pleased to deliver me, for otherwise *there is none to deliver*," *v.* 2.

II. He makes a solemn protestation of his innocence as to those things whereof he was accused, and by a dreadful imprecation appeals to God, the searcher of hearts, concerning it, *v.* 3–5. David had no court on earth to appeal to. But he had the court of heaven, and a righteous Judge there, whom he could call *his God*. He was charged with a traitorous design against Saul's crown and life. This he utterly denies. *I have delivered him that without cause is my enemy, v.* 4. David had no design against Saul's life—Providence so ordered it that Saul lay at his mercy, and there were those about him that would soon have dispatched him, but David prevented it, when he cut off his skirt (1 Sam. xxiv. 4) and afterwards when he took away his spear (1 Sam. xxvi. 12), to attest for him what he could have done. If he were guilty (*v.* 5): *Let the enemy persecute my soul* to the death, and my good name when I am gone: let him *lay my honour in the dust*. With such an oath, or imprecation, David here ratifies the protestation of his innocency.

III. Having this testimony of his conscience concerning his innocency, he humbly prays to God to appear for him against his persecutors, and backs every petition with a proper plea.

1. He prays that God would manifest his wrath against his enemies. "Lord, they are unjustly angry at me, be thou justly angry with them and let them know that thou art so, *v.* 6. *In thy anger lift up thyself* to the seat of judgment, *because of the rage of my enemies.*"

2. He prays that God would plead his cause. *Awake for me to judgment* (that is, let my cause have a hearing), to *the judgment which thou hast commanded;* He prays (*v.* 7), "*Return thou on high* that it may be universally acknowledged that heaven itself owns and pleads David's cause." He prays again (*v.* 8), "*Judge me*, judge for me, give sentence on my side" *The Lord shall judge the people, v.* 8. It is his place; it is his promise. *God is the judge;* "Therefore, Lord, judge me." It would be much for the glory of God and the edification and comfort of his people if God would appear for him: "*So shall the congregation of the people compass thee about;* therefore do it for their sakes, that they may attend thee with their praises and services in the courts of thy house."

3. He prays, in general, for the conversion of sinners and the establishment of saints (*v.* 9): "*O let the wickedness*, not only of my wicked enemies, but *of all the wicked, come to an end! but establish the just.*" Here are two things which every one of us must desire and may hope for:— (1) The destruction of sin, that it may be brought to an end in ourselves and others. And this is that which all that love God, and for his sake hate evil, desire and pray for. (2) The perpetuity of righteousness: *But establish the just.* As we pray that the bad may be made good, so we pray that the good may be made better.

Verses 10–17

David having lodged his appeal with God by prayer and a solemn profession of his integrity, does, as it were, take out judgment upon the appeal, by faith in the word of God, and the assurance it gives of the happiness and safety of the righteous and the certain destruction of wicked people that continue impenitent.

I. David is confident that he shall find God his powerful protector and Saviour, and the patron of his oppressed innocency (*v.* 10): "*My defence is of God. My shield is upon God* (so some read it); there is that in God which gives an assurance of protection to all that are his. Two things David builds this confidence upon:—1. The particular favour God has for all that are sincere: *He saves the upright in heart*, and therefore will *preserve them to his heavenly kingdom*; he saves them out of their present troubles, as far as is good for them. 2. The general respect he has for justice and equity: *God judgeth the righteous;* he owns every righteous cause, and will maintain it in every righteous man, and will protect him. *God is a righteous Judge* (so some read it), who not only doeth righteousness himself, but will take care that righteousness be done by the children of men and will avenge and punish all unrighteousness.

II. He is no less confident of the destruction of all his persecutors, even as many of them as would not *repent, to give glory to God*. He reads their doom here, for their good, if possible, that they might cease from their enmity, or, however, for his own comfort, that he might not be afraid of them nor aggrieved at their prosperity and success for a time. God is angry with the wicked even in the merriest and most prosperous of their days. The destruction of sinners may be prevented by their conversion, for it is threatened with that proviso: *If he turn not* from his evil way, if he do not let fall his enmity against the people of God, then let him expect it will be his ruin; but, if he turn, it is implied that his sin shall be pardoned and all shall be well. Thus even the threatenings of wrath are introduced with a gracious implication of mercy. While God is preparing his instruments of death, he gives the sinners timely warning of their danger, and space to repent and prevent it. He is slow to punish, and *longsuffering to us-ward, not willing that any should perish*. Of all sinners persecutors are set up as the fairest marks of divine wrath; against them, more than any other, God has ordained his arrows. They set God at defiance, but cannot set themselves out of the reach of his judgments. They will destroy themselves, *v.* 14–16. The sinner is here described as taking a great deal of pains to ruin himself. The sinner's head with its politics *conceives mischief*, contrives it with a great deal of art, lays the plot deep, and keeps it close; the sinner's heart with its passions *travails with iniquity*, and is in pain to be delivered of the malicious projects it is hatching against the people of God. But what does it come to when it comes to the birth? It is falsehood; it is a cheat upon himself; it is a lie in his right hand. A labouring man works hard to dig a pit, and then falls into it and perishes in it. This is true, in a sense, of all sinners. They prepare destruction for themselves by preparing themselves for destruction.

PSALM 8

This psalm is a solemn meditation on the glory and greatness of God. It begins and ends with the same acknowledgment of the transcendent excellency of God's name. For the proof of God's glory the psalmist gives instances of his goodness to man; for God's goodness is his glory. God is to be glorified, I. For making known himself and his great name to us, ver. 1. II. For making use of the weakest of the children of men, by them to serve his own purposes, ver. 2. III. For making even the heavenly bodies useful to man, ver. 3, 4. IV. For making him to have dominion over the creatures in this lower world, and thereby placing him but little lower than the angels, ver. 5–8. This psalm is, in the New Testament, applied to Christ and the work of our redemption which he wrought out; the honour given by the children of men to him (ver. 2, compared with Matt. xxi. 16) and the honour put upon the children of men by him, both in his humiliation, when he was made a little lower than the angels, and in his exaltation, when he was crowned with glory and honour. Compare ver. 5, 6, with Heb. ii. 6–8, 1 Cor. xv. 27.

To the chief musician upon Gittith, A psalm of David.

Verses 1–2

The psalmist here sets himself to give to God the glory due to his name. Two things David here admires:—

I. How plainly God displays his glory himself, *v.* 1. He addresses himself to God with all humility and reverence, as the Lord and his people's Lord: *O Lord our Lord!* If we believe that God is the Lord, we must avouch and acknowledge him to be ours. 1. How brightly God's glory shines even in this lower world: *How excellent is thy name in all the earth!* The works of creation and Providence evince and proclaim to all the world that there is an infinite Being. There is no speech or language but the voice of God's name either is heard in it or may be. 2. How much more brightly it shines in the upper world: *Who hast set thy glory above the heavens.* (1) God is infinitely more glorious and excellent than the noblest of creatures and those that shine most brightly. (2) Whereas we, on this earth, only hear God's excellent name, and praise that, the angels and blessed spirits above see his glory, and praise that, and yet he is exalted far above even their blessing and praise. (3) In the exaltation of the Lord Jesus to the right hand of God, who is the brightness of his Father's glory and the express image of his person, God set his glory above the heavens, far above all principalities and powers.

II. How powerfully he proclaims it by the weakest of his creatures (*v.* 2): *Out of the mouth of babes and sucklings hast thou ordained strength*, or perfected praise, the praise of thy strength, Matt. xxi. 16. This intimates the glory of God, 1. In the kingdom of nature. The care God takes of little children (when they first come into the world the most helpless of all animals), the special protection they are under, and the provision nature has made for them, ought to be acknowledged by every one of us, to the glory of God, as a great instance of his power and goodness, and the more because we have all had the benefit of it. 2. In the kingdom of Providence. In the government of this lower world he makes use of the children of men. 3. In the kingdom of grace, the kingdom of the Messiah. It is here foretold that by the apostles, who were looked upon but as babes, *unlearned and ignorant men* (Acts iv. 13), mean and despicable, and *by the foolishness of their preaching*, the devil's kingdom should be thrown down, as Jericho's walls were by the sound of rams' horns. The gospel is called *the arm of the Lord* and *the rod of his strength*; this was ordained to work wonders, not out of the mouth of philosophers or orators, politicians or statesmen, but of a company of poor fishermen. We hear children crying, *Hosanna to the Son of David*, when the chief priests and Pharisees owned him not. Sometimes the grace of God appears wonderfully in young children, and he *teaches* those *knowledge* and makes those *to understand doctrine, who are* but *newly weaned from the milk and drawn from the breasts*, Isa. xxviii. 9. Sometimes the power of God brings to pass great things in his church by very weak and unlikely instruments.

Verses 3–9

David here goes on to magnify the honour of God by recounting the honours he has put upon man, especially the man Christ Jesus. The condescensions of the divine grace call for our praises as much as the elevations of the divine glory. See here,

I. What it is that leads him to admire the condescending favour of God to man; it is his consideration of the lustre and influence of the heavenly bodies, which are within the view of sense (*v.* 3): *I consider thy heavens*, and there, particularly, *the moon and the stars.* It is our duty to consider the heavens. We see them, we cannot but see them. By this, among other things, man is distinguished from the beasts, that, while *they* are so framed as to look downwards to the earth, man is made erect to look upwards towards heaven. *The heavens, even the heavens, are the Lord's* (cxv. 16), because they are the work of his fingers. He made them; he made them easily. The stretching out of the heavens needed not any outstretched arm; it was done with a word; it was but *the work of his fingers.* Even the inferior lights, the moon and stars, show the glory and power of the Father of lights, and furnish us with matter for praise. God not only made them, but *ordained* them, and the ordinances of heaven can never be altered. When we consider how the glory of God shines in the upper world we may well wonder that he should take cognizance of such a mean creature as man. When we consider of what great use the heavens are to men on earth, we may well say, "*Lord, what is man* that thou shouldst settle the ordinances of heaven with an eye to him and to his benefit, and that his comfort and convenience should be so consulted in the making of the lights of heaven and directing their motions!"

II. How he expresses this admiration (*v.* 4): "*Lord, what is man* (*enosh*, sinful, weak, miserable man, a creature so forgetful of thee and his duty to thee) *that thou art* thus *mindful of him*, that thou takest cognizance of him and of his actions and affairs, that in the making of the world thou hadst a respect to him! What is the *son of man, that thou visitest him* as one friend visits another, art pleased to converse with him and concern thyself for him!"

1. To mankind in general. Though man is a worm (Job xxv. 6), yet God puts a respect upon him, and shows him abundance of kindness; man is, above all the creatures in this lower world, the favourite and darling of Providence. We may be sure he takes precedence of all the inhabitants of this lower world, for he is made but a *little lower than the angels* (*v.* 5), lower indeed, because by his body he is allied to the earth and to the beasts that perish, and yet by his soul, which is spiritual and immortal, he is so near akin to the holy angels that he may be truly said to be but *a little lower than they*, and is, in order, next to them. He is but for a little while lower than the angels, while his great soul is cooped up in a house of clay, but the children of the resurrection shall be *ἰσάγγελοι*—angels' peers (Luke xx. 36) and no longer lower than they. He is endued with noble faculties and capacities: *Thou hast crowned him with glory and honour.* Man's reason is his crown of glory; let him not profane that crown by disturbing the use of it nor forfeit that crown by acting contrary to its dictates. God has put all things under man's feet, that he might serve himself, not only of the labour, but of the productions and lives of the inferior creatures; they are all delivered into his hand, nay,

they are all *put under his feet.* He specifies some of the inferior animals (*v.* 7, 8), not only *sheep and oxen,* which man takes care of and provides for, but *the beasts of the field,* as well as those of the flood, yea, and those creatures which are most at a distance from man, as *the fowl of the air,* yea, *and the fish of the sea,* which live in another element and pass unseen through the paths of the seas. Man has arts to take these; though many of them are much stronger and many of them much swifter than he.

2. But this refers, in a particular manner, to Jesus Christ. Of him we are taught to expound it, Heb. ii. 6–8, where the apostle, to prove the sovereign dominion of Christ both in heaven and in earth, shows that he is that man, that son of man, here spoken of, whom God *has crowned with glory and honour* and made to *have dominion over the works of his hands.* We have reason humbly to value ourselves by it and thankfully to admire the grace of God in it, (1) That Jesus Christ assumed the nature of man, and, in that nature, humbled himself. He was, *for a little while* (so the apostle interprets it), made lower than the angels, when he took upon him the form of a servant and made himself of no reputation. (2) That, in that nature, he is exalted to be Lord of all. God the Father exalted him, because he had humbled himself, *crowned him with glory and honour,* the glory which he had with him before the worlds were. All the creatures are put under his feet; and, even in the days of his flesh, he gave some specimens of his power over them, as when he commanded the winds and the seas.

Psalm 9

In this psalm, I. David praises God for pleading his cause, and giving him victory over the enemies of his country (ver. 1–6), and calls upon others to join with him in his songs of praise, ver. 11, 12. II. He prays to God that he might have still further occasion to praise him, ver. 13, 14, 19, 20. III. He triumphs in the assurance he had of God's judging the world (ver. 7, 8), protecting his oppressed people (ver. 9, 10, 18), and bringing his and their implacable enemies to ruin, ver. 15–17.

To the chief musician upon Muth-labben. A psalm of David.

Verses 1–10

The title of this psalm gives a very uncertain sound concerning the occasion of penning it. It is upon *Muth-labben,* which some make to refer to the death of Goliath, others of Nabel, others of Absolom; but I incline to think it signifies only some tune, or some musical instrument, to which this psalm was intended to be sung; and that the enemies are the Philistines, and other neighbouring nations, 2 Sam. v. 8.

I. David praises God for his mercies and the great things he had of late done for him and his government, *v.* 1, 2. Holy joy is the life of thankful praise, as thankful praise is the language of holy joy: *I will be glad and rejoice in thee.* The triumphs of the Redeemer ought to be the triumphs of the redeemed; see Rev. xii. 10; xix. 5; xv. 3, 4.

II. He acknowledges the almighty power of God as that which the strongest and stoutest of his enemies were no way able to contest with or stand before, *v.* 3. They are forced to turn back. When once they turn back, they fall and perish; even their retreat will be their ruin, and they will save themselves no more by flying than by fighting. The presence of the Lord and the glory of his power, are sufficient for the destruction of his and his people's enemies. This was fulfilled when our Lord Jesus, with one word, *I am he,* made his enemies to *fall back at his presence* (John xviii. 6).

III. He gives to God the glory of his righteousness, in his appearing on his behalf (*v.* 4): "*Thou hast maintained my right and my cause,* that is, my righteous cause; when that came on, *thou satest in the throne, judging right.*"

IV. He records, with joy, the triumphs of the God of heaven over all the powers of hell and attends those triumphs with his praises, *v.* 5. "*Thou hast rebuked the heathen,* hast given them real proofs of thy displeasure against them." *Thou hast destroyed the wicked.* He had buried them in oblivion.

V. He exults over the enemy whom God thus appears against (*v.* 6): *Thou hast destroyed cities.* Either, "Thou, O enemy! hast destroyed our cities, at least in intention and imagination," or "Thou, O God! hast destroyed their cities by the desolation brought upon their country." It may be taken either way.

VI. He comforts himself and others in God, and pleases himself with the thoughts of him. 1. With the thoughts of his eternity. On this earth we see nothing durable, even strong cities are buried in rubbish and forgotten; *but the Lord shall endure for ever,* v. 7. 2. With the thoughts of his sovereignty both in government and judgment: *He has prepared his throne,* has fixed it by his infinite wisdom, has fixed it by his immutable counsel. 3. With the thoughts of his justice and righteousness in all the administrations of his government. *He shall judge the world,* all persons and all controversies, *shall minister judgment* to the people (shall determine their lot both in this and in the future state) in righteousness and *in uprightness,* so that there shall not be the least colour of exception against it. 4. With the thoughts of that peculiar favour which God bears to his own people and the special protection which he takes them under. *He will be a refuge for the oppressed,* a high place, a strong place, for the oppressed, *in times of trouble.* 5. With the thoughts of that sweet satisfaction and repose of mind which those have that make God their refuge (*v.* 10): "*Those that know thy name will put their trust in thee,* as I have done, and then they will find, as I have found, that thou dost not forsake those that seek thee." The better God is known the more he is trusted. Those who know him to be a God of infinite wisdom will trust him *further than they can see him* (Job xxxv. 14); those who know him to be a God of almighty power will trust him when creature-confidences fail and they have nothing else to trust to (2 Chron. xx. 12); and those who know him to be a God of infinite grace and goodness will trust him *though he slay them,* Job xiii. 15. Those who know him to be a God of inviolable truth and faithfulness will rejoice in his word of promise, and rest upon that. Those who know him to be the Father of spirits, and an everlasting Father, will trust him with their souls even to the end.

Verses 11–20

I. David, having praised God himself, calls upon and invites others to praise him likewise, *v.* 11. *Sing praises to the Lord who dwelleth in Zion.* As the special residence of his glory is in heaven, so the special residence of his grace is in his church, of which Zion was a type. Let them particularly take notice of the justice of God in avenging the blood of his people Israel on the Philistines and their other wicked neighbours, who had, in making war upon them, used them barbarously and given them no quarter, *v.* 12.

II. David, having praised God for former mercies and deliverances, earnestly prays that God would still appear for him; for he sees not yet all things put under him. "*Have mercy upon me,* who, having misery only, and no merit, to speak for me, must depend upon mere mercy for relief. *Lord, consider my trouble,* and do for me as thou thinkest fit." The experience he had had of divine succours and the expectation he now had of the continuance of them: "*O thou that liftest me up,* that canst do it, that hast done it, that wilt do it, whose prerogative it is to lift up thy people *from the gates of death!*" We are never brought so low, so near to death, but God can raise us up. If he has saved us from spiritual and eternal death, we may thence take encouragement to hope that in all our distresses he will be a very present help to us. His sincere purpose to praise God when his victories should be completed (*v.* 14).

III. David by faith foresees and foretells the certain ruin of all wicked people, both in this world and in that to come. God executes judgment upon them when the measure of their iniquities is full, for they sink into the pit which they themselves digged (vii. 15). Drunkards kill themselves; prodigals beggar themselves, the contentious bring mischief upon themselves. In these judgments the wrath of God is revealed from heaven against all ungodliness and unrighteousness of men. *The wicked shall be turned into hell,* as captives into the prison-house, even *all the nations that forget God.* Forgetfulness of God is the cause of all the wickedness of the wicked.

IV. David encourages the people of God to wait for his salvation, though it should be long deferred, *v.* 18. The needy may think themselves, and others may think them, forgotten for a while, and their expectation of help from God may seem to have perished. But he that believes does not make haste; the vision is for an appointed time, and at the end it shall speak. We may build upon it as undoubtedly true that God's people shall not always be forgotten, nor shall they be disappointed of their hopes from the promise.

V. He concludes with prayer that God would humble the pride, break the power, and blast the projects, of all the wicked enemies of his church: "*Arise, O Lord!* (*v.* 19), stir up thyself, exert thy power, take thy seat, and deal with all these proud and daring enemies of thy name, and cause, and people. *Let not man prevail;* consult thy own honour, and let not weak and mortal men prevail against the kingdom and interest of the almighty and immortal God. *Shall mortal man be too hard for God, too strong for his Maker?*" It is a very desirable thing, much for the glory of God and the peace and welfare of the universe, that men should know and consider themselves to be but men, depending creatures, mutable, mortal, and accountable.

PSALM 10

The Septuagint translation joins this psalm with the ninth, and makes them but one; but the Hebrew makes it a distinct psalm, and the scope and style are certainly different. In this psalm, I. David complains of the wickedness of the wicked, and notices the delay of God's appearing against them, ver. 1–11. II. He prays to God to appear against them for the relief of his people and comforts himself with hopes that he would do so in due time, ver. 12–18.

Verses 1–11

David, in these verses, discovers,

I. A very great affection to God and his favour; for, in the time of trouble, that which he complains of most feelingly is God's withdrawing his gracious presence (*v.* 1): "*Why standest thou afar off,* as one unconcerned in the indignities done to thy name and the injuries done to the people?" It is because we judge by outward appearance; we stand afar off from God by our unbelief, and then we complain that God stands afar off from us.

II. A very great indignation against sin. He beholds the transgressors and is grieved, is amazed, and brings to his heavenly Father their evil report. Passionate and satirical invectives against bad men do more hurt than good; if we will speak of their badness, let it be to God in prayer, for he alone can make them better. This long representation of the wickedness of the wicked is here summed up in the first words of it (*v.* 2), *The wicked in his pride doth persecute the poor,* where two things are laid to their charge, pride and persecution, the former the cause

of the latter. Tyranny, both in state and church, owes its origin to pride. The psalmist, having begun this description, presently inserts a short prayer, a prayer in a parenthesis. *Let them be taken,* as proud people often are, *in the devices that they have imagined, v.* 2. The sinner proudly glories in his power and success. He *boasts of his heart's desire,* boasts that he can do what he pleases. He proudly contradicts the judgment of God, which, we are sure, is according to truth; for he *blesses the covetous, whom the Lord abhors.* See how God and men differ in their sentiments of persons: God abhors covetous worldlings who make money their God and idolise it; he looks upon them as his enemies, and will have no communion with them. *The friendship of the world is enmity to God.* But proud persecutors bless them, and approve their sayings, xlix. 13. He proudly casts off the thoughts of God (*v.* 4). *God is not in all his thoughts,* not in any of them. *All his thoughts are that there is no God.* The cause of this impiety and irreligion is pride. Men will not seek after God because they think they have no need of him, their own hands are sufficient for them. He proudly makes light of God's commandments and judgments (*v.* 5): *His ways are always grievous.* Tell him of God's judgments which will be executed upon those that go on still in their trespasses, and he will not be convinced that there is any reality in them; they are *far above out of his sight,* and therefore he thinks they are mere bugbears. He proudly sets trouble at defiance and is confident of the continuance of his own prosperity (*v.* 6): *He hath said in his heart,* and pleased himself with the thought, *I shall not be moved, my goods are laid up for many years,* and *I shall never be in adversity*: like Babylon, that said, *I shall be a lady for ever,* Isa. xlvii. 7; Rev. xviii. 7. Those are nearest ruin who thus set it furthest from them. For the gratifying of their pride and covetousness, and in opposition to God and religion, they are very oppressive to all within their reach. They are very bitter and malicious (*v.* 7): *His mouth is full of cursing.* They are very false and treacherous. Like Esau, that cunning hunter, *he sits in the lurking places, in the secret places,* and *his eyes are privily set* to do mischief (*v.* 8), not because he is ashamed of what he does (if he blushed, there were some hopes he would repent), nor because he is afraid of the wrath of God, for he imagines God will never call him to an account (*v.* 11), but because he is afraid lest the discovery of his designs should be the breaking of them. Those that have power ought to protect the innocent and provide for the poor; yet these will be the destroyers of those whose guardians they ought to be. And what do they aim at? It is to *catch the poor,* and *draw them into their net,* that is, get them into their power, not to strip them only, but to *murder them.* They hunt for the precious life. It is God's poor people that they are persecuting, against whom they bear a mortal hatred for his sake whose they are and whose image they bear. *He lies in wait as a lion* that thirsts after blood, and feeds with pleasure upon the prey. *He crouches and humbles himself,* as beasts of prey do, that they may get their prey within their reach. This intimates that the sordid spirits of persecutors and oppressors will stoop to anything, though ever so mean, for the compassing of their wicked designs. They could not thus break through all the laws of justice and goodness towards man if they had not first shaken off all sense of religion, and risen up in rebellion against the light of its most sacred and self-evident principles: *He hath said in his heart, God has forgotten.*

Verses 12–18

David, upon the foregoing representation of the inhumanity and impiety of the oppressors, grounds an address to God.

I. What he prays for. 1. That God would himself appear (*v.* 12): "*Arise, O Lord! O God! lift up thy hand*, manifest thy presence and providence in the affairs of this lower world. *Arise, O Lord!* to the confusion of those who say that thou hidest thy face." 2. That he could appear for his people: "*Forget not the humble, the afflicted*, that are poor, that are made poorer, and are poor in spirit. Their oppressors, in their presumption, say that thou hast forgotten them; and they, in their despair, are ready to say the same. Lord, make it to appear that they are both mistaken." 3. That he would appear against their persecutors, *v.* 15. *Break thou the arm of the wicked*, take away his power, *that the hypocrite reign not, lest the people be ensnared*, Job xxxiv. 30.

II. What he pleads for the encouraging of his own faith in these petitions.

1. He pleads the great affronts which these proud oppressors put upon God himself (*v.* 13): "*Wherefore do the wicked contemn God?*" He does so; for he says, "*Thou wilt not require it;* thou wilt never call us to an account for what we do," than which they could not put a greater indignity upon the righteous God. *Wherefore do the wicked thus contemn God?* It is because they do not know him. Why are they suffered thus to contemn God? It is because the day of reckoning is yet to come.

2. He pleads the notice God took of the impiety and iniquity of these oppressors (*v.* 14).

3. He pleads the dependence which the oppressed had upon him: "*The poor commits himself unto thee*, each of them does so, I among the rest. *They leave themselves with thee*" (so some read it), "not prescribing, but subscribing, to thy wisdom and will. They are thy willing subjects, and put themselves under thy protection; therefore protect them."

4. He pleads the relation in which God is pleased to stand to us, (1) As a great God. He *is King for ever and ever, v.* 16. "Lord, let all that pay homage and tribute to thee as their King have the benefit of thy government and find thee their refuge." (2) As a good God. He is the helper of the fatherless (*v.* 14), of those who have no one else to help them and have many to injure them.

5. He pleads the experience which God's church and people had had of God's readiness to appear for them. "*The heathen have perished out of this land;* the remainders of the Canaanites, the seven devoted nations, which have long been as thorns in the eyes and goads in the sides of Israel, are now, at length, utterly rooted out; and this is an encouragement to us to hope that God will, in like manner, break the arm of the oppressive Israelites, who were, in some respects, worse than heathens." He had heard and answered their prayers (*v.* 17): "Lord, thou hast many a time *heard the desire of the humble*, and never saidst to a distressed suppliant, *Seek in vain*. Why may not we hope for the continuance and repetition of the wonders, the favours, which our father told us of?" Thou art the same, and thy power, and promise, and relation to thy people are the same, and the work and workings of grace are the same in them; why therefore may not we hope that he who has been will still be, will ever be, a God hearing prayer? He prepares the heart for prayer by kindling holy desires, and strengthening our most holy faith, fixing the thoughts and raising the affections and then he graciously accepts the prayer. He will plead the cause of the persecuted, will judge the fatherless and oppressed, clear up their innocency, restore their comforts, and recompense them for all the loss and damage. He will put an end to the fury of the persecutors. See how light the psalmist now makes of the power of that proud persecutor whom he had been describing in this psalm. He is but *a man of the earth*, a man *out of* the earth (so the word is), sprung out of the earth, and therefore mean, and weak. He is but *man that shall die, a son of man that shall be as grass?* Isa. li. 12. He that protects us is the Lord of heaven; he that persecutes us is but a man of the earth.

PSALM 11

In this psalm we have David's struggle with and triumph over a strong temptation to distrust God. It is supposed to have been penned when he began to feel the resentments of Saul's envy, and had had the javelin thrown at him once and again. He was then advised to run his country. "No," says he, "I trust in God, and therefore will keep my ground." Observe, I. How he represents the temptation, and perhaps parleys with it, ver. 1–2. II. How he answers it, and puts it to silence with the consideration of God's dominion and providence (ver. 4), his favour to the righteous, and the wrath which the wicked are reserved for, ver. 5–7. In times of public fear, when the insults of the church's enemies are daring and threatening, it will be profitable to meditate on this psalm.

To the chief musician. A psalm of David.

Verses 1–3

I. David's fixed resolution to make God his confidence: *In the Lord put I my trust, v.* 1. The psalmist before he gives an account of the temptation he was in to distrust God, records his resolution to trust in him, as that which he was resolved to live and die by.

II. His resentment of a temptation to the contrary: "*How say you to my soul, Flee as a bird to your mountain*, to be safe there out of the reach of the fowler?" This may be taken either,

1. As the serious advice of his timorous friends: some that were hearty wellwishers to David, when they saw how Saul maliciously sought his life, pressed him by all means to flee. (1) Because he could not be safe where he was, *v.* 2. "Observe," say they, "how *the wicked bend their bow*; Saul and his instruments aim at thy life, and the uprightness of thy heart will not be thy security." (2) Because he could be no longer useful where he was. "For," say they, "*if the foundations be destroyed*" (as they were by Saul's mal-administration), "if the civil state and government be unhinged and all out of course" (lxxv. 3; lxxxii. 5), "what canst thou do with thy righteousness to redress the grievances?"

2. It may be taken as a taunt wherewith his enemies bantered him, upbraiding him with the professions he used to make of confidence in God, and scornfully bidding him try what stead that would stand him in now. "You say, God is your mountain; flee to him now, and see what the better you will be." Taking it thus, the two following verses are David's answer to this sarcasm, in which, (1) He complains of the malice of those who did thus abuse him (*v.* 2): *They bend their bow and make ready their arrows;* and we are told (lxiv. 3) what their arrows are, even bitter words, by which they endeavour to discourage hope in God. (2) He resists the temptation with a gracious abhorrence, *v.* 3. The principles of religion are the foundations on which the faith and hope of the righteous are built.

Verses 4–7

The shaking of a tree (they say) makes it take the deeper and faster root. The attempt of David's enemies to discourage his confidence in God engages him to cleave so much the more closely to his first principles. That which was shocking to his faith, and has been so to the faith of many, was the prosperity of wicked people in their wicked ways, and the straits and distresses which the best men are sometimes reduced to: hence an evil thought was apt to arise, *Surely it is vain to serve God*. But, in order to stifle and shame all such thoughts, consider,

I. That there is a God in heaven: *The Lord is in his holy Temple* above, where, though he is out of our sight, we are not out of his. Or, He is in his holy temple, that is, in his church; he is a God in covenant and communion with his people.

II. That this God governs the world. The Lord has not only his residence, but his throne, in heaven, and he has *set the dominion thereof in the earth* (Job xxxviii. 33). Let us by faith see God on his throne, on his throne of glory—on his throne of government, giving law, giving motion, and giving aim, to all the creatures—on his throne of judgment—and on his throne of grace, to which his people may come boldly for mercy and grace; we shall then see no reason to be discouraged by the pride and power of oppressors, or any of the afflictions that attend the righteous.

III. That this God perfectly knows every man's true character: *His eyes behold, his eyelids try, the children of men;* he not only sees them, but he sees through them, not only knows all they say and do, but knows what they think, what they design, whatever they pretend.

IV. That, if he afflict good people, it is for their trial and therefore for their good, *v.* 5. The Lord tries all the children of men that he may *do them good in their latter end,* Deut. viii. 16.

V. That, however persecutors and oppressors may prosper and prevail awhile, they now lie under, and will for ever perish under, the wrath of God. *The wicked and him that loveth violence, his soul hateth.* Their prosperity is so far from being an evidence of God's love that their abuse of it does certainly make them the objects of his hatred. He that hates nothing that he has made, yet hates those who have thus ill-made themselves. *Upon the wicked he shall rain snares.* Here is a double metaphor, to denote the unavoidableness of the punishment of wicked men. It shall surprise them as a sudden shower sometimes surprises the traveller in a summer's day. It shall be as snares upon them, to hold them fast, and keep them prisoners, till the day of reckoning comes. It is *fire, and brimstone, and a horrible tempest,* which plainly alludes to the destruction of Sodom and Gomorrah.

VI. That, though honest good people may be run down, yet God does and will own them, and favour them, and that is the reason why God will severely reckon with persecutors and oppressors, because those whom they oppress and persecute are dear to him; so that *whosoever toucheth them toucheth the apple of his eye, v.* 7. He looks graciously upon them: *His countenance doth behold the upright.* He, like a tender father, looks upon them with pleasure, and they, like dutiful children, are pleased and abundantly satisfied with his smiles. They walk in the light of the Lord.

PSALM 12

It is supposed that David penned this psalm in Saul's reign, when there was a general decay of piety, which he here complains of to God, and very feelingly, for he himself suffered by the treachery of his false friends and his sworn enemies. I. He begs help of God, because there were none among men whom he durst trust, ver. 1, 2. II. He foretells the destruction of his proud and threatening enemies, ver. 3, 4. III. He assures himself and others that, how ill soever things went now (ver. 8), God would preserve and secure to himself his own people (ver. 5, 7), and would certainly make good his promises to them, ver. 6.

To the chief musician upon Sheminith. A psalm of David.

Verses 1-8

This psalm furnishes us with good thoughts for bad times.

I. Let us see here what it is that makes the times bad, and when they may be said to be so. Scarcity of money, decay of trade, and the desolations of war, make the times bad. But the scripture lays the badness of the times upon causes of another nature. 2 Tim. iii. 1, *Perilous times shall come,* for iniquity shall abound; and that is the thing David here complains of. The times are bad:—

1. When there is a general decay of piety and honesty among men the times are then truly bad (*v.* 1): *When the godly man ceases and the faithful fail.* Observe how these two characters are here put together, the godly and the faithful. As there is no true policy, so there is no true piety, without honesty. Godly men are faithful men, *fast* men, so they have sometimes been called; they make conscience of being true both to God and man. They are here said to cease and fail. Those that were godly and faithful were taken away, and those that were left had sadly degenerated and were not what they had been.

2. When men are so spiteful as to design against their neighbours the worst of mischiefs, and yet so base as to cover the design with plausible professions of friendship. Thus *they speak vanity* (that is, false-hood and a lie) *everyone to his neighbour, with flat-tering lips and a double heart.* They will kiss and kill. This is the devil's image complete, a complication of malice and falsehood. The times are bad indeed when there is no such thing as sincerity to be met with.

3. The times are very bad, when proud sinners have arrived at such a pitch of impiety as to say, "*With our tongue will we prevail* against the cause of virtue; *our lips are our own* and we may say what we will; *who is lord over us,* either to restrain us or to call us to an account?" *v.* 4. *Our lips are our own* (an unjust pretension, for who made man's mouth, in whose hand is his breath, and whose is the air he breathes in?) and as if he had no authority either to command them or to judge them: *Who is Lord over us?* Like Pharaoh, Exod. v. 2.

4. When the poor and needy are oppressed, and abused, and puffed at, then the times are very bad. This is implied (*v.* 5) where God himself takes notice of *the oppression of the poor* and *the sighing of the needy.*

5. When wickedness abounds, and goes barefaced under the protection and countenance of those in authority, then the times are very bad, *v.* 8. *When the vilest men are exalted* to places of trust and power then *the wicked walk on every side. When the wicked bear rule the people mourn.*

II. When times are thus bad it is comfortable to think,

1. That we have a God to go to, from whom we may ask and expect the redress of all our grievances. This he begins with (*v.* 1): "*Help, Lord, for the godly man ceaseth. It is time for thee, Lord, to work.*"

2. That God will certainly reckon with false and proud men, and will punish and restrain their insolence. Men cannot discover the falsehood of flatterers, nor humble the haughtiness of those that speak proud things; but the righteous God will *cut off all flattering lips* (*v.* 3). Some translate it as a prayer, "May God cut off those false and spiteful lips."

3. That God will, in due time, work deliverance for his oppressed people, and shelter them from the malicious designs of their persecutors (*v.* 5): *Now, will I arise, saith the Lord.* When the oppressors are in the height of their pride and insolence—when they say, *Who is lord over us?*—then is God's time to let them know, to their cost, that he is above them. When the oppressed are in the depth of their distress and despondency, then is God's time to appear for them, as for Israel when they were most dejected and Pharaoh was most elevated. *Now will I arise. I will set him in safety,* or in salvation, not only protect him, but restore him to his former prosperity, will *bring him out into a wealthy place* (lxvi. 12), so that, upon the whole, he shall lose nothing by his sufferings.

4. That, though men are false, God is faithful; *the words of the Lord are pure words* (*v.* 6), not only all true, but all pure, like silver tried in a furnace of earth or a crucible.

5. That God will secure his chosen remnant to himself, how bad soever the times are (*v.* 7): *Thou shalt preserve them from this generation for ever.* In times of general apostasy the Lord knows those those that are his, and they shall be enabled to keep their integrity.

PSALM 13

This psalm is the deserted soul's case and cure. Whether it was penned upon any particular occasion does not appear, but in general, I. David sadly complains that God had long withdrawn from him and delayed to relieve him, ver. 1, 2. II. He earnestly prays to God to consider his case and comfort him, ver. 3, 4. III. He assures himself of an answer of peace, and therefore concludes the psalm with joy and triumph, because he concludes his deliverance to be as good as wrought, ver. 5, 6.

To the chief musician. A psalm of David.

Verses 1-6

David, in affliction, is here pouring out his soul before God.

I. It is some ease to a troubled spirit to give vent to its griefs, especially to give vent to them at the throne of grace, where we are sure to find one who is afflicted in the afflictions of his people. Thither we have boldness of access by faith, and there we have παρρησία—*freedom of speech.* David thought God had forgotten him. Not that any good man can doubt the omniscience, goodness, and faithfulness of God; but it is a peevish expression of prevailing fear, which yet, when it arises from a high esteem and earnest desire of God's favour, though it be indecent and culpable, shall be passed by and pardoned, for the second thought will retract it and repent of it. He was racked with care, which filled his head: *I take counsel in my soul;* "I am at a loss, and am *without a friend* that I can put any confidence in. *I have sorrow in my heart daily.*" The bread of sorrow is sometimes the saint's daily bread. Our Master himself was a man of sorrows. His enemies' insolence added to his grief. He expostulates with God "*How long* shall it be thus?" And, "Shall it be thus *for ever?*" It is a common temptation, when trouble lasts long, to think it will last always; despondency then turns into despair, and those that have long been without joy begin, at last, to be without hope.

II. His complaints stir up his prayers, *v.* 3, 4. We should never allow ourselves to make any complaints but what are fit to be offered up to God and what drive us to our knees. "*Consider* my case, *hear* my complaints and *enlighten my eyes.* Strengthen my faith"; for faith is the eye of the soul, with which it sees above, and sees through, the things of sense. "Lord, enable me to look beyond my present troubles and to foresee a happy issue of them." If his eyes were not enlightened quickly he must perish: "I shall *sleep the sleep of death*; I cannot live under the weight of all this care and grief." It would gratify the pride of his enemy: He will say, "*I have prevailed,* I have gotten the day, and been too hard for him and his God."

III. His prayers are soon turned into praises (*v.* 5, 6): But *my heart shall rejoice and I will sing to the Lord.* What a surprising change is here in a few lines! In the beginning of the psalm we have him drooping, trembling, and ready to sink into melancholy and despair; but, in the close of it, rejoicing in God, and elevated and enlarged in his praises. See the power of faith, the power of prayer, and how good it is to draw near to God. "In former distresses *I have trusted in the mercy of God,* and I never found that it failed me. Even in the depth of this distress, when God hid his face from me, when without were fightings and within were fears, yet *I trusted in the mercy of God* and that was as an anchor in a storm, by the help of which, though I was tossed, I was not overset." And still *I do trust in thy mercy*; so some

read it. His faith in God's mercy filled his heart with *joy in his salvation*; for joy and peace come *by believing,* Rom. xv. 13. *Believing, you rejoice,* 1 Pet. i. 8. "*I will sing unto the Lord,* sing in remembrance of what he has done formerly; though I should never recover the peace I have had, I will die blessing God that ever I had it. He has dealt bountifully with me formerly, and he shall have the glory of that, however he is pleased to deal with me now. I will sing in hope of what he will do for me at last, being confident that all will end well, will end everlastingly well."

PSALM 14

It does not appear upon what occasion this psalm was penned. Some say David penned it when Saul persecuted him; others, when Absalom rebelled against him. But they are mere conjectures, which have not certainty enough to warrant us to expound the psalm by them. The apostle, in quoting part of this psalm (Rom. iii. 10, &c.) to prove that Jews and Gentiles are all under sin (ver. 9) and that all the world is guilty before God (ver. 19), leads us to understand it, in general, as a description of the depravity of human nature. In all the psalms from the 3rd to this (except the 8th) David had been complaining of those that hated and persecuted him, insulted him and abused him; now here he traces all those bitter streams to the fountain, the general corruption of nature, and sees that not his enemies only, but all the children of men, were thus corrupted. Here is, I. A charge exhibited against a wicked world, ver. 1. II. The proof of the charge, ver. 2, 3. III. A serious expostulation with sinners, especially with persecutors, upon it, ver. 4-6. IV. A believing prayer for the salvation of Israel and a joyful expectation of it, ver. 7.

To the chief musician. A psalm of David.

Verses 1-3

Sin is the disease of mankind, and it appears here to be malignant and epidemic.

1. See how malignant it is (*v.* 1) in two things:—

(1) The contempt it puts upon the honour of God: for there is something of practical atheism at the bottom of all sin. *The fool hath said in his heart, There is no God.* We are sometimes tempted to think, "Surely there never was so much atheism and profaneness as there is in our days"; but we see the former days were no better. The sinner is one that *saith in his heart, There is no God*; he is an atheist. He cannot be sure there is one, and therefore he is willing to think there is none. He is a fool; he is simple and unwise, and this is an evidence of it; he is wicked and profane, and this is the cause of it.

(2) The disgrace and debasement it puts upon the nature of man. Sinners are corrupt, quite degenerated from what man was in his innocent estate: *They have become filthy* (*v.* 3), putrid. *They are corrupt* indeed; for they do God no service, bring him no honour, nor do themselves any real kindness. They do a great deal of hurt. *They have done abominable works,* for such all sinful works are. This follows upon their saying, *There is no God;* for those that *profess they know God, but in works deny him, are abominable, and to every good work reprobate,* Titus. i. 16.

2. See how epidemic this disease is; it has infected the whole race of mankind. God himself is here brought in for a witness, *v.* 2, 3. *The Lord looked down from heaven,* he took a view of all *the children of men,* and the question was, *Whether there were any* among them *that did understand* themselves aright, their duty and interests, and did seek God and set him before them. The result of this enquiry, *v.* 3. Upon his search, it appeared, *They have all gone aside,* the apostasy is universal, *there is none that doeth good, no, not one,* till the free and mighty grace of God has wrought a change. When God had made the world he looked upon his own work, and *all was very good* (Gen. i. 31); but, some time after, he looked upon man's work, and, behold, all was very bad (Gen. vi. 5).

Verses 4–7

In these verses the psalmist endeavours,

I. To convince sinners of the evil and danger of the way they are in, how secure soever they are in that way. Three things he shows them, which, it may be, they are not very willing to see—their wickedness, their folly, and their danger.

1. Their wickedness. This is described in four instances:—(1) They are themselves *workers of iniquity*; and take as much pleasure in it as ever any man did in his business. (2) They *eat up God's people* with as much greediness *as they eat bread* because they really hate God, whose people they are. It is meat and drink to persecutors to be doing mischief. (3) They *call not upon the Lord.* What good can be expected from those that live without prayer? (4) They *shame the counsel of the poor*, and upbraid them with making God their refuge, as David's enemies upbraided him, *xi.* 1.

2. Their folly: *They have no knowledge.*

3. Their danger (*v.* 5): *There were they in great fear.* Many instances there have been of proud and cruel persecutors who have been made *terrors to themselves* and all about them.

II. He endeavours to comfort the people of God. They have God's presence (*v.* 5): He *is in the generation of the righteous.* They have his protection (*v.* 6): *The Lord is their refuge.* When David was driven out by Absalom and his rebellious accomplices, he comforted himself with an assurance that God would in due time *turn again his captivity.* But surely this pleasing prospect looks further. He had, in the beginning of the psalm, lamented the general corruption of mankind; and, in the melancholy view of that, wishes for the salvation which in the fulness of time was to come out of Zion—salvation from sin, that great salvation which should be wrought out by the Redeemer, who was expected *to come to Zion*, to *turn away ungodliness from Jacob*, Rom. xi. 26.

PSALM 15

The scope of this short but excellent psalm is to show us the way to heaven, and to convince us that, if we would be happy, we must be holy and honest, and that Christ, who is himself the way, and in whom we must walk as our way, has also shown us the same way that is here prescribed, Matt. xix. 17. "If thou wilt enter into life, keep the commandments." In this psalm, I. By the question (ver. 1) we are directed and excited to enquire for the way. II. By the answer to that question, in the rest of the psalm, we are directed to walk in that way, ver. 2–5. III. By the assurance given in the close of the psalm of the safety and happiness of those who answer these characters we are encouraged to walk in that way, ver. 5.

A psalm of David.

Verses 1–5

I. A very serious and weighty question concerning the character of a citizen of Zion (*v.* 1): "*Lord, who shall abide in thy tabernacle? Let me know who shall go to heaven.*" Not, who by name (in this way the *Lord* only knows those that are his), but who by description: "What kind of people are those whom thou wilt own and crown with distinguishing and everlasting favours?" It concerns us all to put this question to ourselves, Lord, *what shall I be, and do, that I may abide in thy tabernacle?* Luke xviii. 18; Acts xvi. 30. 1. Observe to whom this enquiry is addressed—to God himself. 2. How it is expressed in Old Testament language. (1) By the *tabernacle* we may understand the church militant, typified by Moses's tabernacle, fitted to a wilderness-state, mean and movable. There God manifests himself, and there he meets his people, as of old in the tabernacle of the testimony, the tabernacle of meeting. (2) By the *holy hill* we may understand the church triumphant, alluding to Mount Zion, on which the temple was to be built by Solomon. It concerns us to know who shall dwell there, that we may make it sure to ourselves that we shall have a place among them.

II. A very plain and particular answer to this question of the particular character of a citizen of Zion.

1. He is one that is sincere and entire in his religion: He *walketh uprightly*, according to the condition of the covenant (Gen. xvii. 1), "*Walk before me, and be thou perfect*" (it is the same word that is here used) "and then thou shalt find me a God all-sufficient." He is really what he professes to be, is sound at heart, and can approve himself to God, in his integrity, in all he does. His eye perhaps is weak, but it is single; he has his spots indeed, but he does not paint; he is an *Israelite indeed in whom is no guile*, John i. 47; 2 Cor. i. 12. I know no religion but sincerity.

2. He is one that is conscientiously honest and just in all his dealings, faithful and fair to all with whom he has to do: He *worketh righteousness.* He reckons that that cannot be a good bargain, nor a saving one, which is made with a lie, and that he who wrongs his neighbour, though ever so plausibly, will prove, in the end, to have done the greatest injury to himself.

3. He is one that contrives to do all the good he can to his neighbours, but is very careful to do hurt to no man, and is, in a particular manner, tender of his neighbour's reputation, *v.* 3. He makes the best of everybody, and the worst of nobody. If an ill-natured character of his neighbour be given him, or an ill-natured story be told him, he will disprove it if he can; if not, it shall die with him and go no further. His *charity will cover a multitude of sins.*

4. He is one that values men by their virtue and piety, and not by the figure they make in the world, *v.* 5. He thinks the worse of no man's piety for his poverty and meanness, *but he knows those that fear the Lord.* He reckons that serious piety, wherever it is found, puts an honour upon a man, and makes his face to shine, more than wealth, or wit, or a great name among men, does or can. He honours such.

5. He is one that always prefers a good conscience before any secular interest or advantage whatsoever; for, if he has promised upon oath to do anything, though afterwards it appear much to his damage and prejudice in his worldly estate, yet he adheres to it and *changes not, v.* 4.

6. He is one that will not increase his estate by any unjust practices, *v.* 5. *He putteth not out his money to usury*, that he may live at ease upon the labours of others. Not that it is any breach of the law of justice or charity for the lender to share in the profit which the borrower makes of his money, any more than for the owner of the land to demand rent from the occupant, money being, by art and labour, as improvable as land. But a citizen of Zion will freely lend to the poor, according to his ability, and not be rigorous and severe in recovering his right from those that are reduced by Providence. He will not *take a reward against the innocent*; if he be any way employed in the administration of public justice, he will not, for any gain, or hope of it, to himself, do anything to the prejudice of a righteous cause.

III. The psalm concludes with a ratification of this character of the citizen of Zion. He is like Zion-hill itself, which cannot be moved. Every true living member of the church, like the church itself, is built upon a rock, which the gates of hell cannot prevail against: *He that doeth these things shall never be moved.*

PSALM 16

This psalm has something of David in it, but much more of Christ. It begins with such expressions of devotion as may be applied to Christ; but concludes with such confidence of a resurrection as must be applied to Christ, to him only, and cannot be understood of David, as both St. Peter and St. Paul have observed, Acts ii.

24; xiii. 36. I David speaks the language of all good Christians, professing his confidence in God (ver. 1), his consent to him (ver. 2), his affection to the people of God (ver. 3), his adherence to the true worship of God. II. He speaks of himself as a type of Christ, and so he speaks the language of Christ himself, to whom all the rest of the psalm is expressly and at large applied, Acts ii. 25, &c. He spoke, 1. Of the special presence of God with the Redeemer in his services and sufferings, ver. 8. 2. Of the prospect which the Redeemer has of his own resurrection and the glory that should follow, which carried him cheerfully through his undertaking, ver. 9–11.

Michtam of David.

Verses 1–7

This psalm is entitled *Michtam*, which some translate *a golden* psalm, more to be valued than much fine gold, because it speaks so plainly of Christ and his resurrection, who is the true treasure hidden in the field of the Old Testament.

I. David here flies to God's protection: "*Preserve me, O God!* from the deaths, and especially from the sins, to which I am continually exposed: *for in thee,* and in thee only, *do I put my trust.*" This is applicable to Christ, who prayed, *Father, save me from this hour,* and trusted in God that he would deliver him.

II. He recognises his solemn dedication of himself to God as his God (v. 2): "*O my soul! thou hast said unto the Lord, Thou art my Lord,* and therefore thou mayest venture to trust him." *Adonai* signifies *My stayer,* the strength of my heart.

III. He devotes himself to the honour of God in the service of the saints (v. 2, 3): *My goodness extends not to thee, but to the saints.* If God be ours, we must, for his sake, extend our goodness to those that are his, to the saints in the earth; for what is done to them he is pleased to take as done to himself, having constituted them his receivers. Those that are renewed by the grace of God, and devoted to the glory of God, are saints on earth. Christ delights even in the saints on earth, notwithstanding their weaknesses and manifold infirmities, which is a good reason why we should (John xvii. 19).

IV. He disclaims the worship of all false gods and all communion with their worshippers, v. 4. He reads the doom of idolaters. *Their sorrows shall be multiplied,* both by the judgments they bring upon themselves from the true God whom they forsake and by the disappointment they will meet with in the false gods they embrace. "*Their drink-offerings of blood will I not offer,* not only because the gods they are offered to are a lie, but because the offerings themselves are barbarous." At God's altar, because the blood made atonement, the drinking of it was most strictly prohibited, and the drink-offerings were of wine; but the devil prescribed to his worshippers to drink of the blood of the sacrifices, to teach them cruelty. Some make this also applicable to Christ and his undertaking, showing the nature of the sacrifice he offered (it was not the blood of bulls and goats, which was offered according to the law; that was never named, nor did he ever make any mention of it, but his own blood).

V. He repeats the solemn choice he had made of God for his portion and happiness (v. 5), takes to himself the comfort of the choice (v. 6), and gives God the glory of it, v. 7. Heaven is an inheritance. We must take that for our home, our rest, our everlasting good, and look upon this world to be no more ours than the country through which our road lies when we are on a journey. Confiding in him for the securing of this portion: "*Thou maintainest my lot.* Thou that hast by promise made over thyself to me, wilt graciously make good what thou hast promised. *The lines have fallen to me in pleasant places.* Those have reason to say so that have God for their portion. What can they desire more? *Return unto thy rest, O my soul!* and look no further. Those whose lot is cast, as David's was, in a land of light, in a valley of vision,

where God is known and worshipped, have, upon that account, reason to say, *The lines have fallen to me in pleasant places;* much more those who have not only Immanuel's land, but Immanuel's love.

"*I will bless the Lord who has given me counsel,* this counsel, to take him for my portion and happiness." If we have the pleasure of it, let God have the praise of it. God having given him counsel by his word and Spirit, his own *reins* also (his own thoughts) instructed him in the night-season; when he was silent and solitary, and retired from the world, then his own conscience (which is called the reins, Jer. xvii. 10) not only reflected with comfort upon the choice he had made, but instructed or admonished him concerning the duties arising out of this choice.

All this may be applied to Christ, who made the Lord his portion and was pleased with that portion, made his Father's glory his highest end. We may also apply it to ourselves, in singing it, renewing our choice of God as ours, with a holy complacency and satisfaction.

Verses 8–11

All these verses are quoted by St. Peter in his first sermon, after the pouring out of the Spirit on the day of Pentecost (Acts ii. 25–28); and he tells us expressly that David in them speaks concerning Christ and particularly of his resurrection. Something we may allow here of the workings of David's own pious and devout affections towards God, but in these holy elevations towards God and heaven he was carried by the spirit of prophecy quite beyond the consideration of himself and his own case, to foretell the glory of the Messiah. The New Testament furnishes us with a key to let us into the mystery of these lines.

I. These verses must certainly be applied to Christ; of him speaks the prophet this, as did many of the Old Testament prophets, who *testified beforehand the sufferings of Christ and the glory that should follow* (1 Pet. i. 11), and that is the subject of this prophecy here.

1. That he should suffer and die. When he says, "*My flesh shall rest,*" it is implied that he must put off the body, that he should not only die, but be buried, and abide for some time under the power of death.

2. That he should be wonderfully borne up by the divine power in suffering and dying. That he should not be moved till he could say, *It is finished.* That his heart should rejoice and his glory be glad, that he should go on with his undertaking, not only resolutely, but cheerfully. By his glory is meant his *tongue,* as appears, Acts ii. 26. Now there were three things which carried him on thus cheerfully:—(1) The respect he had to his Father's will and glory in what he did: *I have set the Lord always before me.* (2) The assurance he had of his Father's presence with him in his sufferings: *He is at my right hand,* a present help to me, nigh at hand in the time of need. (3) The prospect he had of a glorious issue of his sufferings. It was *for the joy set before him* that *he endured the cross,* Heb. xii. 2. He rested in hope, and that made his rest glorious, Isa. xi. 10. See John xiii. 31, 32.

3. That he should be brought through his sufferings, and brought from under the power of death by a glorious resurrection.

4. That he should be abundantly recompensed for his sufferings, with the joy set before him, v. 11. "*Thou wilt show me the path of life,* and lead me to that life through this darksome valley." In confidence of this, when he gave up the ghost, he said, *Father, into thy hands I commit my spirit;* and, a little before, *Father, glorify me with thy own self.*

II. Christ being the Head of the body, the church, these verses may, for the most part, be applied to all good Christians, who are guided and animated by the Spirit of Christ; and, in singing them, when we have first given glory to Christ, we may then encourage and edify ourselves and one another with them. Dying Christians, as well as a dying Christ, may cheerfully put off the body, in a believing expectation of a joyful resurrection: *My flesh also shall rest in hope.*

PSALM 17

David, being in great distress and danger by the malice of his enemies, does, in this psalm, by prayer address himself to God, his tried refuge, and seeks shelter in him. I. He appeals to God concerning his integrity, ver. 1–4. II. He prays to God still to be upheld in his integrity and preserved from the malice of his enemies, ver. 5–8, 13. III. He gives a character of his enemies, using that as a plea with God for his preservation, ver. 9–12, 14. IV. He comforts himself with the hopes of his future happiness, ver. 15.

A prayer of David.

Verses 1–7

This psalm is a prayer. A time for praise and a time for prayer. David was now persecuted, probably by Saul. He addresses himself to God in these verses both by way of appeal (*Hear the right, O Lord!* let my righteous cause have a hearing before his tribunal, and give judgment upon it) and by way of petition (*Give ear unto my prayer, v.* 1, and again (*v.* 6), *Incline thy ear unto me and hear my speech*). He was sincere, and did not dissemble with God in his prayer: *It goeth not out of feigned lips.* Feigned prayers are fruitless. "*I have called upon thee* formerly (*v.* 6); therefore, Lord, hear me now." It will be a great comfort to us if trouble, when it comes, find the wheels of prayer a-going, for then we may come with the more boldness to the throne of grace. He was encouraged by his faith to expect God would take notice of his prayers: "*I know thou wilt hear me,* and therefore, O God, *incline thy ear to me.*"

I. He makes his appeal to the court of heaven. "Lord, do thou hear the right, for Saul is so passionate, so prejudiced, that he will not hear it. Lord, *let my sentence come forth from thy presence, v.* 2. Men sentence me to be pursued and cut off as an evil-doer. Lord, I appeal from them to thee." Sincerity dreads no scrutiny, no, not that of God himself, according to the tenor of the covenant of grace: *Let thy eyes behold the things that are equal. Thou hast proved my heart.* He knew God had tried him, by his own conscience, which is God's deputy in the soul. *The spirit of a man is the candle of the Lord,* with this God had searched him, and *visited him in the night,* when he *communed with his own heart upon his bed.* God had tried him by the fair opportunity he had, once and again, to kill Saul. He had a fixed resolution against all sins of the tongue: "*I have purposed* and fully determined, in the strength of God's grace, *that my mouth shall not transgress.*" He had been as careful to refrain from sinful actions as from sinful words (*v.* 4): "*Concerning the* common *works of men,* the actions and affairs of human life, *I have,* by the direction of thy word, *kept myself from the paths of the destroyer.*" Some understand it particularly, that he had not been himself a destroyer of Saul, when it lay in his power. But it may be taken more generally; he kept himself from all evil works, and endeavoured, according to the duty of his place, to keep others from them too.

II. His petition is that he might experience the good work of God in him, as an evidence of and qualification for the goodwill of God towards him: this is grace and peace from God the Father. 1. He prays for the work of God's grace in him (*v.* 5): "*Hold up my goings in thy paths.* Lord, I have, by thy grace, kept myself from the paths of the destroyer; by the same grace let me be kept in thy paths. 2. He prays for the tokens of God's favour to him, *v.* 7. *O thou that savest by thy right hand* (by thy own power,

and needest not the agency of any other) *those who put their trust in thee from those that rise up against them.* Those that trust in God have many enemies, but they have one friend that is able to deal with them all. The margin reads it, *O thou that savest those who trust in thee from those that rise up against thy right hand.* Those that are enemies to the saints are rebels against God and his right hand. *Show thy marvellous loving-kindness.* "Set apart thy loving-kindnesses for me; put me not off with common mercies, but be gracious to me, *as thou usest to do to those who love thy name.*"

Verses 8–15

I. What David prays for. This prayer is both a prediction of the preservation of Christ through all the hardships and difficulties of his humiliation, and a pattern to Christians to commit the keeping of their souls to God, trusting him to *preserve them to his heavenly kingdom.* He prays,

1. That he himself might be protected (*v.* 8): "Keep me safe, hide me close, where I may not be found, where I may not be come at. Deliver my soul, not only my mortal life from death, but my immortal spirit from sin." He prays that God would keep him as a man keeps the apple of his eye, which nature has wonderfully fenced and teaches us to guard. If we keep God's law as the *apple of our eye* (Prov. vii. 2), we may expect that God will so keep us; for it is said concerning his people that whoso *touches them touches the apple of his eye,* Zech. ii. 8. He prays that God would keep him with as much tenderness as the hen gathers her young ones under her wings. Christ uses the similitude, Matt. xxiii. 37. "*Hide me under the shadow of thy wings,* where I may be both safe and warm." Or, perhaps, it rather alludes to the wings of the cherubim shadowing the mercy-seat: "Let me be taken under the protection of that glorious grace which is peculiar to God's Israel." David further prays, "Lord, keep me from the wicked, from men of the world."

2. That all the designs of his enemies to bring him either into sin or into trouble might be defeated (*v.* 13): "*Arise, O Lord!* appear for me, disappoint him, and cast him down in his own eyes by the disappointment." While Saul persecuted David, how often did he miss his prey, when he thought he had him sure! And how were Christ's enemies disappointed by his resurrection, who thought they had gained their point when they had put him to death!

II. For the encouraging of his own faith in these petitions, he pleads,

1. The malice and wickedness of his enemies: They are *my deadly enemies, enemies against the soul,* so the word is. They are sensual, insolent and haughty (*v.* 10): *They are enclosed in their own fat,* wrap themselves, hug themselves, in their own honour, and power, and plenty, and then make light of God, and set his judgments at defiance, lxxiii. 7; Job xv. 27. They *compass me about, v.* 9. "They are watchful and intent upon it, to do us a mischief; they are down-looked, and never let slip any opportunity of compassing their design." "The ringleader of them (that was Saul) is in a special manner bloody and barbarous (*v.* 12), *like a lion* that lives by prey and is therefore greedy of it." This is fitly applied to Saul, who sought David *on the rocks of the wild goats* (1 Sam. xxiv. 2) and in *the wilderness of Ziph* (ch. xxvi. 2), where lions used to lurk for their prey.

2. The power God had over them, to control and restrain them. Lord, they are *thy sword*—God's sword, which he can manage as he pleases, which cannot move without him, and which he will sheathe when he has done his work with it. "They are *thy hand,* by which thou dost chastise thy people and make them feel thy displeasure."

3. Their outward prosperity (*v.* 14). They are *men of the world*, actuated by the spirit of the world, in love with the wealth and pleasure of this world. They *have their portion in this life*. They have abundance of the world. *Their bellies thou fillest with thy hidden treasures*. The things of this world are called *treasures*, because they are so accounted; otherwise, to a soul, and in comparison with eternal blessings, they are but trash. Those that fare deliciously every day have their *bellies filled with these hidden treasures*; and they will but *fill the belly* (1 Cor. vi. 13); they will not fill the soul. They have numerous families, and a great deal to leave to them: *They are full of children*, and they have enough for them all, and *leave the rest of their substance to their babes*, to their grand-children.

4. He pleads his own dependence upon God as his portion and happiness. "They have their portion in this life, but as for me (*v.* 15) I am none of them, I have but little of the world." When the soul awakes, at death, out of its slumber in the body, and when the body awakes, at the resurrection, out of its slumber in the grave blessedness will consist in three things:— (1) The immediate vision of God and his glory: *I shall behold thy face*, not, as in this world, through a glass darkly. (2) The participation of his likeness. *When he shall appear we shall be like him, for we shall see him as he is.* (3) A complete and full satisfaction resulting from all this: *I shall be satisfied*, abundantly satisfied with it.

PSALM 18

This psalm we met with before, in the history of David's life, 2 Sam. xxii. That was the first edition of it; here we have it revived, altered a little, and fitted for the service of the church. It is David's thanksgiving for the many deliverances God had wrought for him. The poetry is very fine, the images are bold, the expressions lofty, and every word is proper and significant; but the piety far exceeds the poetry. Holy faith, and love, and joy, and praise, and hope, are here lively, active, and upon the wing. I. He triumphs in God, ver. 1–3. II. He magnifies the deliverances God had wrought for him, ver. 4–19. III. He takes the comfort of his integrity, which God had thereby cleared up, ver. 20–28. IV. He gives to God the glory of all his achievements, ver. 29–42. V. He encourages himself with the expectation of what God would further do for him and his, ver. 43–50.

To the chief musician, *A psalm* of David, the servant of the Lord, who spoke unto the Lord the words of this song, in the day *that* the Lord delivered him from the hand of all his enemies, and from the hand of Saul.

Verses 1–19

This psalm we had before (2 Sam. xxii. 1), only here we are told that the psalm was delivered *to the chief musician*, or precentor, in the temple-songs. David is here called *the servant of the Lord*, as Moses was. It was more his honour that he was a servant of the Lord than that he was king of a great kingdom; and so he himself accounted it (cxvi. 16): *O Lord! truly I am thy servant*.

I. He triumphs in God and his relation to him. The first words of the psalm, *I will love thee, O Lord! my strength*, are here prefixed as the scope and contents of the whole. An interest in the person loved is the lover's delight; this string therefore he touches, and on this he harps with much pleasure (*v.* 2): "*The Lord* Jehovah *is my* God; and then he is my *rock, my fortress*, all that I need and can desire in my present distress."

II. He sets himself to magnify the deliverances God had wrought for him, that he might be the more affected in his returns of praise.

1. The more imminent and threatening the danger was out of which we were delivered the greater is the mercy of the deliverance. David now remembered how the forces of his enemies poured in upon him, which he calls *the floods of Belial*.

2. The more earnest we have been with God for deliverance, and the more direct answer it is to our prayers, the more we are obliged to be thankful. David's deliverances were so, *v.* 6. David was found a praying man, and God was found a prayer-hearing God.

3. The more wonderful God's appearances are in any deliverance the greater it is: such were the deliverances wrought for David, in which God's manifestation of his presence and glorious attributes is most magnificently described, *v.* 7, &c. Little appeared of man, but much of God, in these deliverances. He moved even the *foundations of the hills* (*v.* 7), as of old at Mount Sinai. He showed his anger and displeasure against the enemies and persecutors of his people: *He was wroth, v.* 7. His wrath smoked (*v.* 8), and *coals were kindled by it.* He showed his readiness to plead his people's cause and work deliverance for them; for he rode upon a cherub and did fly, for the maintaining of right and the relieving of his distressed servants, *v.* 10. No opposition, no obstruction, can be given to him *who rides upon the wings of the wind, who rides on the heavens, for the help of his people, and, in his excellency, on the skies.* He showed his condescension, in taking cognizance of David's case: *He bowed the heavens and came down* (*v.* 9), did not send an angel, but came himself, as one afflicted in the afflictions of his people. He wrapped himself in darkness, and yet commanded light to shine out of darkness for his people, Isa. xlv. 15. He *made darkness his pavilion, v.* 11. His glory is invisible; we know not the way that he takes, even when he is coming towards us in ways of mercy; but, when his designs are secret, they are kind; for, though he hide himself, he is the God of Israel, the Saviour. And, *at his brightness, the thick clouds pass* (*v.* 12).

4. The greater the difficulties are that lie in the way of deliverance the more glorious the deliverance is. For the rescuing of David, the waters were to be divided till the very channels were seen; the earth was to be cloven till the very foundations of it were discovered, *v.* 15. There were waters deep and many, waters out of which he was to be drawn (*v.* 16), as Moses, who had his name from being drawn out of the water literally, as David was figuratively. His enemies were too quick for him; for they *prevented him* in the day of his calamity, *v.* 18. But, in the midst of his troubles, the Lord was his stay, so that he did not sink. Note, God will not only deliver his people out of their troubles in due time, but he will sustain them and bear them up under their troubles in the mean time.

5. That which especially magnified the deliverance was that his comfort was the fruit of it. "He brought me forth also out of my straits into a large place, where I had room, not only to turn, but to thrive in." "*He delivered me because he delighted in me*, not for my merit, but for his own grace and goodwill."

In singing this we may apply it to Christ the Son of David. The sorrows of death surrounded him; in his distress he prayed (Heb. v. 7); God made the earth to shake and tremble, and the rocks to cleave, and brought him out, in his resurrection, into a large place, because he delighted in him and in his undertaking.

Verses 20–28

I. David reflects with comfort upon his own integrity, and rejoices in the testimony of his conscience that he had had his conversation in godly sincerity and not with fleshly wisdom, 2 Cor. i. 12. His deliverances were an evidence of this, and this was the great comfort of his deliverances. His deliverances cleared his innocency before men, and acquitted him from those crimes which he was falsely accused of.

This he calls *rewarding him according to his righte-ousness* (v. 20, 24). They confirmed the testimony of his own conscience for him, which he here reviews with a great deal of pleasure, v. 21–23. Though we are conscious of many a stumble, and many a false step taken, yet if we recover ourselves by repentance, and go on in the way of our duty, it shall not be construed into a departure, for it is not a wicked departure, from our God. He had kept his eye upon the rule of God's commands (v. 22): *All his judgments were before me.*

II. He takes occasion thence to lay down the rules of God's government and judgment, that we may know not only what God expects from us, but what we may expect from him, v. 25, 26. Those that show mercy to others shall find mercy with God, Matt. v. 7. Wherever God finds an upright man, he will be found an upright God.

III. Hence he speaks comfort to the humble "*Thou wilt save the afflicted people*, that are wronged and bear it patiently", terror to the proud "Thou *wilt bring down high looks*, that aim high, and expect great things for themselves, and look with scorn and disdain upon the poor and pious", and encouragement to himself—"*Thou wilt light my candle*, that is, thou wilt revive and comfort my sorrowful spirit, and not leave me melancholy. Thou wilt light my candle to work by, and give me an opportunity of serving thee and the interests of thy kingdom among men."

Verses 29–50

I. David looks back, with thankfulness, upon the great things which God had done for him. When we set ourselves to praise God for one mercy we must be led by that to observe the many more with which we have been compassed about, and followed, all our days. Many things had contributed to David's advancement, and he owns the hand of God in them all, to teach us to do likewise. 1. God had given him all his skill and understanding in military affairs, which he was not bred up to nor designed for, his genius leading him more to music, and poetry, and a contemplative life: *He teaches my hands to war*, v. 34. 2. God had given him bodily strength to go through the business and fatigue of war: God *girded him with strength* (v. 32, 39) to such a degree that he could break even a bow of steel, v. 34. What service God designs men for he will be sure to fit them for. 3. God had likewise given him great swiftness, not to flee from the enemies but to fly upon them (v. 33): *He makes my feet like hinds' feet*, v. 36. "*Thou hast enlarged my steps under me;* but" (whereas those that take large steps are apt to tread awry) "my feet did not slip." 4. God had made him very bold. If a troop stood in his way, he made nothing of running through them; if a wall, he made nothing of leaping over it (v. 29); if ramparts and bulwarks, he soon mounted them, and by divine assistance set his feet upon the high places of the enemy, v. 33. 5. God had protected him, and kept him safe, in the midst of the greatest perils. "*Thou hast given me the shield of thy salvation* (v. 35), and that has compassed me on every side. By that I have been delivered from the strivings of the people who aimed at my destruction (v. 43), particularly from the violent man" (v. 48), that is, Saul, who more than once threw a javelin at him. 6. God had prospered him in his designs; he it was that made his way perfect (v. 32) and it was his right hand that held him up, v. 35. 7. Those whom God has abandoned are easily vanquished: *Then did I beat them small as the dust*, v. 42. But those whose cause is just he avenges (v. 47), and those whom he favours will certainly be *lifted up above those that rise up against them*, v. 48. 8. God had raised him to the throne, and not only delivered

him and kept him alive but dignified him and made him great (v. 35): *Thy gentleness has increased me—thy discipline* and *instruction;* so some. The good lessons David learned in his affliction prepared him for the dignity and power that were intended him; and the lessening of him helped very much to increase his greatness.

II. David looks up with humble and reverent adorations of the divine glory and perfection. He endeavours, with his praises, to magnify God, to bless him and exalt him, v. 46. He gives honour to him, 1. As a living God: *The Lord liveth*, v. 46. The gods of the heathen were dead gods. But God lives, lives for ever, and will not fail those that trust in him, but, because he lives, they shall live also; for he is their life. 2. As a finishing God: *As for God*, he is not only perfect himself, but *his way is perfect*, v. 30. What God begins to build he is able to finish. 3. As a faithful God: *The word of the Lord is tried.* "I have tried it" (says David), "and it has not failed me." David, in God's providences concerning him, takes notice of the performance of his promises to him, which, as it puts sweetness into the providence, so it puts honour upon the promise. 4. As the protector and defender of his people. David had found him so to him: "*He is the God of my salvation* (v. 46), by whose power and grace I am and hope to be saved; but not of mine only: he is *a buckler to all those that trust in him* (v. 30); he shelters and protects them all, is both able and ready to do so."

III. David looks forward, with a believing hope that God would still do him good. He promises himself his enemies should be completely subdued, and that his government should be extensive, so that even a people whom he had not known should serve him (v. 43). *As soon as they hear of me they shall obey me*, v. 44. His seed should be for ever continued in the Messiah, who, he foresaw, should come from his loins, v. 50. He *shows mercy to his anointed*, his Messiah, *to David* himself, the anointed of the God of Jacob in the type, *and to his seed for evermore.*

PSALM 19

There are two excellent books which the great God has published for the instruction and edification of the children of men; this psalm treats of them both, and recommends them both to our diligent study. I. The book of the creatures, in which we may easily read the power and godhead of the Creator, ver. 1–6. II. The book of the scriptures, which makes known to us the will of God concerning our duty. He shows the excellency and usefulness of that book (ver. 7–11) and then teaches us how to improve it, ver. 12–14.

To the chief musician. A psalm of David.

Verses 1–6

From the things that are seen every day by all the world the psalmist, in these verses, leads us to the consideration of the invisible things of God, whose glory shines transcendently bright in the visible heavens, the structure and beauty of them, and the order and influence of the heavenly bodies. This instance of the divine power serves not only to show the folly of atheists, who see there is a heaven and yet say, "There is no God," who see the effect and yet say, "There is no cause," but to show the folly of idolaters also, and the vanity of their imagination, who, though the heavens declare the glory of God, yet gave that glory to the lights of heaven which those very lights directed them to give to God only, the Father of lights.

1. What that is which the creatures notify to us. They are in many ways useful and serviceable to us, but in nothing so much as in this, that they declare the glory of God, by showing his handiworks, v. 1. They plainly speak themselves to be God's handiworks; all succession and motion must have had a

beginning; they could not make themselves, that is a contradiction; they could not be produced by a casual hit of atoms, that is an absurdity, fit rather to be bantered than reasoned with: therefore they must have a Creator, who can be no other than an eternal mind, infinitely wise, powerful, and good. From the excellency of the work we may easily infer the infinite perfection of its great author. From the brightness of the heavens we may collect that the Creator is light; their vastness of extent bespeaks his immensity, their height his transcendency and sovereignty, their influence upon this earth his dominion, and providence, and universal beneficence: and all declare his almighty power.

II. What are some of those things which notify this? 1. The heavens and the firmament—the vast expanse of air and ether, and the spheres of the planets and fixed stars. Man has this advantage above the beasts, in the structure of his body, that whereas they are made to look downwards, as their spirits must go, he is made erect, to look upwards, because upwards his spirit must shortly go and his thoughts should now rise. 2. The constant and regular succession of day and night (*v.* 2): *Day unto day, and night unto night*, speak the glory of that God who first divided between the light and the darkness. He not only glorifies himself, but gratifies us, by his constant revolution; for, as the light of the morning befriends the business of the day, so the shadows of the evening befriend the repose of the night; every day and every night speak the goodness of God, and, when they have finished their testimony, leave it to the next day, to the next night, to say the same. 3. The light and influence of the sun do, in a special manner, declare the glory of God; for of all the heavenly bodies that is the most conspicuous in itself and most useful to this lower world, which would be all dungeon, and all desert, without it. In the heavens God has *set a tabernacle for the sun*. The heavenly bodies are called *hosts of heaven*, and therefore are fitly said to *dwell in tents*, as soldiers in their encampments. That glorious creature was not made to be idle, but *his going forth* (at least as it appears to our eye) *is from one point of the heavens, and his circuit* thence to the opposite point, and thence (to complete his diurnal revolution) to the same point again; and this with such steadiness and constancy that we can certainly foretell the hour and the minute at which the sun will rise at such a place, any day to come. The brightness wherein he appears. He is *as a bridegroom coming out of his chamber*, richly dressed and adorned, as fine as hands can make him, looking pleasantly himself and making all about him pleasant. The cheerfulness wherewith he makes his tour. For the service of man he *rejoices as a strong man to run a race*.

III. To whom this declaration is made of the glory of God. It is made to all parts of the world (*v.* 3, 4): *There is no speech nor language where their voice is not heard. Their line has gone through all the earth* (the equinoctial line suppose) *and* with it *their words to the end of the world*, proclaiming the eternal power of the God of nature, *v.* 4. *They have no speech or language* (so some read it) *and yet their voice is heard*. All people may hear these natural immortal preachers speak to them in their own tongue the wonderful works of God.

Verses 7–14

God's glory (that is, his goodness to man) appears much in the works of creation, but much more in and by divine revelation. The holy scripture, as it is a rule both of our duty to God and of our expectation from him, is of much greater use and benefit to us than day or night, than the air we breathe in, or the light of the sun.

I. The psalmist gives an account of the excellent properties and uses of the word of God, in six sentences (*v.* 7–9), in each of which the name *Jehovah* is repeated. Here are six several titles of the word of God, to take in the whole of divine revelation, precepts, and promises, and especially the gospel. 1. *The law of the Lord is perfect.* It is perfectly free from all corruption, perfectly filled with all good, and perfectly fitted for the end for which it is designed, 2 Tim. iii. 17. Nothing is to be added to it nor taken from it. It is of use to *convert the soul*, to bring us back to ourselves, to our God, to our duty. 2. *The testimony of the Lord is sure.* It is a sure fountain of living comforts and a sure foundation of lasting hopes. It will make even *the simple* wise for their souls and eternity. Those that are humbly simple, sensible of their own folly and willing to be taught, shall be made wise by the word of God, xxv. 9. 3. *The statutes of the Lord are right*, exactly agreeing with the eternal rules and principles of good and evil. Because they are right, they *rejoice the heart*. The law, as we see it in the hands of Christ, gives cause for joy; and, when it is written in our hearts, it lays a foundation for lasting joy, by restoring us to our right mind. 4. *The commandment of the Lord is pure.* It is the ordinary means which the Spirit uses in *enlightening the eyes*; it brings us to a sight and sense of our sin and misery, and directs us in the way of duty. 5. *The fear of the Lord* will cleanse our way, cxix. 9. And it *endureth for ever.* The ceremonial law is long since done away, but the law concerning the fear of God is ever the same. Time will not alter the nature of moral good and evil. 6. *The judgments of the Lord* (all his precepts, which are framed in infinite wisdom) *are true altogether.* They are all of a piece.

II. He expresses the great value he had for the word of God, and the great advantage he had, and hoped to have, from it, *v.* 10, 11. He prized the commandments of God before all the wealth of the world. Gold is of the earth, earthly; but grace is the image of the heavenly. Gold is only for the body and the concerns of time; but grace is for the soul and the concerns of eternity. The word of God, received by faith, is sweet to the soul, *sweeter than honey and the honeycomb.* The pleasures of sense are deceitful, will soon surfeit, and yet never satisfiy; but those of religion are substantial and satisfying, and there is no danger of exceeding in them. The word of God is a word of warning to the children of men; it warns us of the duty we are to do, the dangers we are to avoid. There is a reward, not only after keeping, but in keeping, God's commandments, a present great reward of obedience in obedience.

III. The excellency of the word of God.

1. He takes occasion to make a penitent reflection upon his sins; for *by the law is the knowledge of sin.* "Is the commandment thus holy, just, and good? Then *who can understand his errors*? I cannot, whoever can." From the rectitude of the divine law he learns to call his sins his *errors.* Every transgression of the commandment is an error, a deviation from the rule we are to work by. God knows a great deal more evil of us than we do of ourselves.

2. He takes occasion hence to pray against sin. Finding himself unable to specify all the particulars of his transgressions, he cries out, *Lord, cleanse me from my secret faults*; not secret to God, so none are, nor only such as were secret to the world, but such as were hidden from his own observation of himself. Having prayed that his sins of infirmity might be pardoned, he prays that presumptuous sins might be prevented, *v.* 13. His plea: "*So shall I be upright; and I shall be innocent from the great transgression*"; so he calls a presumptuous sin, because no sacrifice was accepted for it, Num. xv. 28–30.

3. He takes occasion humbly to beg the divine acceptance of his thoughts and affections, *v.* 14, and then begs he would accept his performances. His services were—the *words of his mouth and the meditations of his heart*, his holy affections offered up to God. His care that they might be acceptable with God; for, if our services be not acceptable to God, what do they avail us?

PSALM 20

This psalm is a prayer, and the next a thanksgiving, for the king. In this psalm we may observe, I. What it is they beg of God for the king, ver. 1–4. II. With what assurance they beg it. The people triumph (ver. 5), the prince (ver. 6), both together (ver. 7, 8), and so he concludes with a prayer to God for audience, ver. 9.

To the chief musician. A psalm of David.

Verses 1–5

This prayer for David is entitled *a psalm of David*. It is very proper for those who desire the prayers of their friends to tell them particularly what they would have to be asked of God for them. Paul often begged of his friends to pray for him.

I. What it is that they are taught to ask of God for the king. *The Lord hear thee in the day of trouble* (*v.* 1), and *the Lord fulfil all thy petitions, v.* 5. It was often a day of trouble with David himself, of disappointment and distress, of treading down and of perplexity. Neither the crown on his head nor the grace in his heart would exempt him from trouble. The prayers of others for us must be desired, not to supersede, but to second, our own for ourselves. "*The name of the God of Jacob defend thee,* and set thee out of the reach of thy enemies." Mercies out of the sanctuary are the sweetest mercies, *v.* 2. *The Lord remember all thy offerings and accept thy burnt-sacrifices* (*v.* 3) or *turn them to ashes*; that is, "The Lord give thee the victory and success which thou didst by prayer with sacrifices ask of him, and thereby give as full proof of his acceptance of the sacrifice as ever he did by kindling it with fire from heaven." By this we may now know that God accepts our spiritual sacrifices, if by his Spirit he kindles in our souls a holy fire of pious and divine affection, and with that makes our hearts burn within us. *The Lord grant thee according to thy own heart.* This they might in faith pray for, because they knew David was a man after God's own heart, and would design nothing but what was pleasing to him.

II. What confidence they had of an answer of peace to these petitions for themselves and their good king (*v.* 5): "*We will rejoice in thy salvation.* We that are subjects will rejoice in the preservation and prosperity of our prince." *In the name of our God will we set up our banners.* These prayers for David are prophecies concerning Christ the Son of David, and in him they were abundantly answered; he undertook the work of our redemption, and made war upon the powers of darkness. In the day of trouble, when his soul was exceedingly sorrowful, the Lord heard him, heard him in that he feared (Heb. v. 7), *sent him help out of the sanctuary.*

Verses 6–9

I. Holy David himself triumphs in the interest he had in the prayers of good people (*v.* 6): "*Now know I that the Lord saveth his anointed,* because he hath stirred up the hearts of the seed of Jacob to pray for him." *He will hear him from his holy heaven,* of which the sanctuary was a type (Heb. ix. 23), from the throne he hath prepared in heaven, of which the mercy-seat was a type. He will hear him *with the saving strength of his right hand*; not by letter, nor by word of mouth, but by his right hand, by the saving strength of his right hand. He will make it

to appear that he hears him by what he does for him.

II. His people triumph in God and their relation to him, and his revelation of himself to them. The children of this world trust in second causes, and think all is well if those do but smile upon them; they trust *in chariots and in horses,* and the more of them they can bring into the field the more sure they are of success in their wars. "But," say the Israelites, "we neither have chariots and horses to trust to nor do we want them, nor, if we had them, would we build our hopes of success upon that; *but we will remember,* and rely upon, *the name of the Lord our God.* Those that trusted in their chariots and horses are brought down and fallen, and their chariots and horses were so far from saving them that they helped to sink them, and made them the easier and the richer prey to the conqueror, 2 Sam. viii. 4. But we that trust in the name of the Lord our God not only stand upright, and keep our ground, but have risen, and have got ground against the enemy, and have triumphed over them.

III. They conclude their prayer for the king with a *Hosanna,* "*Save now, we beseech thee,* O Lord!" *v.* 9. As we read this verse, it may be taken as a prayer that God would not only bless the king, "Save, Lord, give him success," but that he would make him a blessing to them, "*Let the king hear us* when we call to him for justice and mercy." Those that would have good of their magistrates must thus pray for them, for they, as all other creatures, are that to us (and no more) which God makes them to be.

PSALM 21

As the foregoing psalm was a prayer for the king that God would protect and prosper him, so this is a thanksgiving for the success God had blessed him with. They are here taught, I. To congratulate him on his victories, and the honour he had achieved, ver. 1–6. II. To confide in the power of God for the completing of the ruin of the enemies of his kingdom, ver. 7–13.

To the chief musician. A psalm of David.

Verses 1–6

David here speaks professing that his joy was in God's strength and in his salvation, and not in the strength or success of his armies. He also directs his subjects herein to rejoice with him, and to give God all the glory of the victories he had obtained. They congratulate the king on his joys: "*The king rejoices,* and so do we." They give God all the praise of those things which were the matter of their king's rejoicing. *Thou hast given him his heart's desire. Thou preventest him with the blessings of goodness.* The psalmist here reckons that these blessings were given in a preventing way. When God's blessings come sooner and prove richer than we imagine, when they are given before we prayed for them, before we were ready for them, nay, when we feared the contrary, then it may be truly said that he prevented us with them. "*Thou hast set a crown of pure gold upon his head* and kept it there, when his enemies attempted to throw it off." When he went forth upon a perilous expedition *he asked* his *life of thee, and thou* not only *gavest him that,* but withal gavest him *length of days for ever and ever,* didst not only prolong his life far beyond his expectation, but didst assure him of a blessed immortality in a future state and of the continuance of his kingdom in the Messiah that should come of his loins. "*His glory is great,* far transcending that of all the neighbouring princes, in the salvation thou hast wrought for him and by him." The glory which every good man is ambitious of is to see the salvation of the Lord. God had given him the satisfaction of being the channel of all bliss to mankind (*v.* 6): "*Thou hast set him to be blessings for ever*" (so the margin reads it), "thou has made him to be a universal everlasting blessing to the world, in whom the families of the earth are, and shall be, blessed." See how the spirit of prophecy gradually rises here to that which is peculiar to Christ, for none besides is blessed for ever, much less a blessing for ever.

Verses 7–13

The psalmist, having taught his people to look back with joy and praise on what God had done for him and them, here teaches them to look forward with faith, and hope, and prayer, upon what God would further do for them: *The king rejoices in God* (v. 1), and therefore we will be thankful; *the king trusteth in God* (v. 7), therefore will we be encouraged. The joy and confidence of Christ our King is the ground of all our joy and confidence.

I. They are confident of the stability of David's kingdom. *Through the mercy of the Most High*, and not through his own merit or strength, *he shall not be moved*.

II. They are confident of the destruction of all the impenitent implacable enemies of David's kingdom. The success with which God had blessed David's arms hitherto was an earnest of the rest which God would give him from all his enemies round about. They hated David because God had set him apart for himself, hated Christ because they hated the light; but both were hated without any just cause, and in both God was hated, John xv. 23, 25. *They intended evil against thee, and imagined a mischievous device;* they pretended to fight against David only, but their enmity was against God himself. Those that aimed to un-king David aimed, in effect, to un-God Jehovah. "They devise what they are *not able to perform*," v. 11. Their malice is impotent, and they *imagine a vain thing*, ii. 1. The discovery of them (v. 8): "*Thy hand shall find them out.* Though ever so artfully disguised by the pretences and professions of friendship, though mingled with the faithful subjects of this kingdom and hardly to be distinguished from them, though flying from justice and absconding in their close places, yet thy hand shall find them out wherever they are." *Their fruit and their seed shall be destroyed*, v. 10.

III. In this confidence they beg of God that he would still appear for his anointed (v. 13), that he would act for him in his own strength, by the immediate operations of his power as Lord of hosts and Father of spirits.

PSALM 22

The Spirit of Christ, which was in the prophets, testifies in this psalm, as clearly and fully as any where in all the Old Testament, "the sufferings of Christ and the glory that should follow" (1 Pet. i. 11); of him, no doubt, David here speaks, and not of himself, or any other man. Much of it is expressly applied to Christ in the New Testament, all of it may be applied to him, and some of it must be understood of him only. I. Of the humiliation of Christ (ver. 1–21), 1. He complains, and mixes comforts with his complaints; he complains (ver. 1, 2), but comforts himself (ver. 3–5), complains again (ver. 6–8), but comforts himself again, ver. 9, 10. 2. He complains, and mixes prayers with his complaints; he complains of the power and rage of his enemies (ver. 12, 13, 16, 18), of his bodily weakness and decay (ver. 14, 15, 17); but prays that God would not be far from him, (ver. 11, 19), that he would save and deliver him, ver. 19–21. II. Of the exaltation of Christ, that his undertaking should be for the glory of God (ver. 22–25), for the salvation and joy of his people (ver. 26–29), and for the perpetuating of his own kingdom, ver. 30, 31. In singing this psalm we must keep our thoughts fixed upon Christ.

To the chief musician upon Aijeleth Shahar. A psalm of David.

Verses 1–10

I. A sad complaint of God's withdrawings, v. 1, 2.

1. This may be applied to David, or any other child of God, apprehending himself forsaken of God, unhelped, unheard, yet calling him, again and again, "*My God*," and continuing to cry day and night

earnestly desiring his gracious return. Spiritual desertions are the saints' sorest afflictions. To cry out, "My God, why am I sick? Why am I poor?" would give cause to suspect discontent and worldliness. But, *Why hast thou forsaken me?* is the language of a heart binding up its happiness in God's favour. When we want the faith of assurance we must live by a faith of adherence. "However it be, yet God is good, and he is mine; *though he slay me, yet will I trust in him*."

2. But it must be applied to Christ; for, in the first words of this complaint, he poured out his soul before God when he was upon the cross (Matt. xxvii. 46); and, some think, repeated the whole psalm, if not aloud yet to himself. Christ, in his sufferings, cried earnestly to his Father *in the daytime*, upon the cross, *and in the night season*, when he was in his agony in the garden. But, Christ having made himself sin for us, in conformity thereunto the Father laid him under the present impressions of his wrath and displeasure against sin. *It pleased the Lord to bruise him and put him to grief*, Isa. liii. 10.

II. Encouragement taken, in reference hereunto, v. 3–5. "*But thou art holy*, not unjust, untrue, nor unkind, in any of thy dispensations. Though thou dost not immediately come in to the relief of thy afflicted people, yet thou lovest them, art true to thy covenant with them, and dost not countenance the iniquity of their persecutors, Hab. i. 13. *Thou inhabitest the praises of Israel;* thou art pleased to manifest thy glory, and grace, and special presence with thy people, in the sanctuary, where they attend thee with their praises. There thou art always ready to receive their homage, and of the tabernacle of meeting thou hast said, *This is my rest for ever*." Though God seem, for a while, to turn a deaf ear yet he is so well pleased with his people's praises that he will, in due time, give them cause to change their note: *Hope in God, for I shall yet praise him*. He will take comfort from the experiences which the saints in former ages had of the benefit of faith and prayer (v. 4, 5):. "*Our fathers trusted in thee, cried unto thee, and thou didst deliver them*; therefore thou wilt, in due time, deliver me, for never any that hoped in thee were made ashamed of their hope, never any that sought thee sought thee in vain. And thou art still the same in thyself."

III. The complaint renewed of another grievance, and that is the contempt and reproach of men. This complaint is by no means so bitter as that before of God's withdrawings; but, as that touches a gracious soul, so this a generous soul, in a very tender part, v. 6–8. Man, at the best, is a worm; but he became *a worm, and no man*. If he had not made himself a worm, he could not have been trampled upon as he was. He was reproached as a bad man, as a blasphemer, a sabbath-breaker, a wine-bibber, a false prophet, an enemy to Caesar, a confederate with the prince of the devils. He was despised of the people as a mean contemptible man, not worth taking notice of, his country in no repute, his relations poor mechanics, his followers none of the rulers, or the Pharisees, but the mob. He was ridiculed as a foolish man, and one that not only deceived others, but himself too. David was sometimes taunted for his confidence in God; but in the sufferings of Christ this was literally and exactly fulfilled. *He trusted in God; let him deliver him*.

IV. Encouragement taken as to this also (v. 9, 10): Men despise me, *but thou art he that took me out of the womb*. David and other good men have often, for direction to us, encouraged themselves with this, that God was not only the *God of their fathers*, as before (v. 4) but the God of their infancy, who began betimes to take care of them, as soon as they had a being, and therefore, they hope, will never cast them off. He that did so well for us in that helpless useless state will not leave us when he has reared us and nursed us up into some capacity of serving him. See the early instances of God's providential care for us: *He took us also out of the womb*, else we had died there, or been stifled in the birth. *"Then didst thou make me hope";* that is, "thou didst that for me, in providing sustenance for me and protecting me from the dangers to which I was exposed, which encourages me to hope in thee all my days." The blessings of the breasts, as they crown the blessings of the womb, so they are earnests of the blessings of our whole lives; surely he that fed us then will never starve us, Job iii. 12. *I was cast upon thee from the womb*, which perhaps refers to his circumcision on the eighth day; he was then by his parents committed and given up to God as his God in covenant; for circumcision was a seal of the covenant; and this encouraged him to trust in God. In the experience we have had of God's goodness to us all along ever since, drawn out in a constant uninterrupted series of preservations and supplies: *Thou art my God*, providing for me and watching over me for good, *from my mother's belly*, that is, from my coming into the world unto this day. This is applicable to our Lord Jesus, over whose incarnation and birth the divine Providence watched with a peculiar care, when he was born in a stable, laid in a manger, and immediately exposed to the malice of Herod, and forced to flee into Egypt.

Verses 11–21

1. Here is Christ suffering. David indeed was often in trouble, and beset with enemies; but many of the particulars here specified are such as were never true of David, and therefore must be appropriated to Christ in the depth of his humiliation.

1. He is here deserted by his friends: *Trouble* and distress are *near*, and *there is none to help*, none to uphold, *v.* 11. He trod the wine-press alone; for all his disciples forsook him and fled.

2. He is here insulted and surrounded by his enemies, who, for their strength and fury, are compared to bulls, *strong bulls of Bashan (v.* 12), such were the chief priests and elders that persecuted Christ; and others who are compared to dogs *(v.* 16), filthy and greedy, and unwearied in running him down. There was an assembly of the wicked plotting against him *(v.* 16); for the chief priests sat in council, to consult of ways and means to take Christ. They have enclosed me, *v.* 16. They are formidable and threatening *(v.* 13): *They gaped upon me with their mouths*, to show me that they would swallow me up.

3. He is here crucified. The very manner of his death is described, though never in use among the Jews: *They pierced my hands and my feet (v.* 16), which were nailed to the accursed tree.

4. He is here dying *(v.* 14, 15), dying in pain and anguish, because he was to satisfy for sin. *I am poured out like water. My heart is like wax. My strength is dried up. My tongue cleaveth to my jaws.* "Thou *hast brought me to the dust of death;* I am just ready to drop into the grave"; for nothing less would satisfy divine justice. The life of the sinner was forfeited, and therefore the life of the sacrifice must be the ransom for it. The sentence of death passed upon Adam was thus expressed: *Unto dust thou shalt return.* And therefore Christ, in his obedience to death, here uses a similar expression: *Thou hast brought me to the dust of death.*

5. He was stripped. The shame of nakedness was the immediate consequence of sin; and therefore our Lord Jesus was stripped of his clothes, when he was crucified, that he might clothe us with the robe of his righteousness, and that the shame of our nakedness might not appear. Now here we are told, (1) How

his body looked when it was thus stripped: *I may tell all my bones, v.* 17. *They look and stare upon me,* "the standers by, the passers by, are amazed to see my bones start out thus; and, instead of pitying me, are pleased even with such a rueful spectacle." (2) What they did with his clothes, which they took from him (*v.* 18): *They part my garments among them,* to every soldier a part, and *upon my vesture,* the seamless coat, *do they cast lots.* This very circumstance was exactly fulfilled, John xix. 23, 24. And, though it was no great instance of Christ's suffering, yet it is a great instance of the fulfilling of the scripture in him. *Thus it was written, and* therefore *thus it behoved Christ to suffer.*

II. Christ, in his agony, prayed that the cup might pass from him. And of that David's praying here was a type. He calls God his *strength, v.* 19. He prays, *Be thou not far from me (v.* 11), and again, *v.* 19. "Whoever stands aloof from my sore, Lord, do not thou." And the Father *heard him in that he feared* (Heb. v. 7) and enabled him to go through with his work. The psalmist here calls his soul his *darling,* his *only one* (so the word is): *"My soul is my only one.* I have but one soul to take care of, and therefore the greater is my shame if I neglect it." He prays to be delivered, *from the sword,* the flaming sword of divine wrath, which turns every way. "O deliver my soul from that. Lord, though I lose my life, let me not lose thy love. Save me from *the power of the dog,* and *from the lion's mouth."* This seems to be meant of Satan, that old enemy. "Lord, save me from being overpowered by his terrors." He pleads, "Thou hast formerly *heard me from the horns of the unicorn,"* that is, "saved me from him in answer to my prayer." Has God delivered us *from the horns of the unicorn,* that we be not tossed? Let that encourage us to hope that we shall be delivered from the lion's mouth, that we be not torn. This prayer of Christ was answered, for the Father suffered him not to see corruption, but, the third day, raised him out of the dust of death, which was a greater instance of God's favour to him than if he had helped him down from the cross; for that would have hindered his undertaking, whereas his resurrection crowned it.

Verses 22–30

As the first words of the complaint were used by Christ himself upon the cross, so the first words of the triumph are expressly applied to him (Heb. ii. 12) and are made his own words: *I will declare thy name unto my brethren, in the midst of the church will I sing praise unto thee.*

Five things are here spoken of the satisfaction and triumph of Christ in his sufferings:—

I. That he should have a church in the world. This is implied here; that he should *see his seed,* Isa. liii. 10. By the declaring of God's name, by the preaching of the everlasting gospel in its plainness and purity, many should be effectually called to him and to God by him. Those who are thus called in should be brought into a very near and dear relation to him as his brethren; not the believing Jews only, but those of the Gentiles also who became fellow-heirs and of the same body, Heb. ii. 11. These his brethren should be incorporated into a great congregation; such is the universal church, the whole family that is named from him, into which all the *children of God that were scattered abroad are collected,* and in which they are united (John xi. 52, Eph. i. 10), and that they should also be incorporated into smaller societies, members of that great body. These should be accounted the seed of Jacob and Israel *(v.* 23), that on them, though Gentiles, the blessing of Abraham might come (Gal. iii. 14). The gospel church is called *the Israel of God,* Gal. vi. 16.

II. That God should be greatly honoured and glorified in him by that church. He foresees with pleasure, 1. That God would be glorified by the church that should be gathered to him. All that fear the Lord will praise him (*v.* 23), even every Israelite indeed. See cxviii. 2–4; cxxxv. 19, 20. 2. That God would be glorified in the Redeemer and in his undertaking. *Therefore* Christ is said to *praise God in the church.* All our praises must centre in the work of redemption.

III. That all humble gracious souls should have a full satisfaction and happiness in him, *v.* 26. Those that are much in praying shall be much in thanksgiving: *Those shall praise the Lord that seek him,* because through Christ they are sure of finding him, in the hopes of which they have reason to praise him even while they are seeking him. The souls that are devoted to him shall be for ever happy with him: "*Your heart shall live for ever.*"

IV. That the church of Christ, and with it the kingdom of God among men, should extend itself to all corners of the earth (*v.* 27, 28). Whereas the Jews had long been the only professing people of God, now all the ends of the world should come into the church, and, the partition-wall being taken down, the Gentiles should be taken in. It is here prophesied, they should be converted: They *shall remember, and turn to the Lord.* Serious reflection is the first step, and a good step it is, towards true conversion. We must consider and turn. The prodigal came first to himself, and then to his father. Then they should be admitted into communion with God and with the assemblies that serve him: *They shall worship before thee,* for *in every place incense shall be offered to God,* Mal. i. 11; Isa. lxvi. 23. For (*v.* 28) *the kingdom is the Lord's.* 1. The kingdom of nature is the Lord Jehovah's, and his providence rules among the nations. 2. The kingdom of grace is the Lord Christ's, and he, as Mediator, is appointed governor among the nations, head over all things to his church. High and low, rich and poor, bond and free, meet in Christ. Christ shall have the homage of many of the great ones. *Those that are fat upon the earth,* that *shall eat and worship.* The poor also shall receive his gospel: *Those that go down to the dust,* that sit in the dust (cxiii. 7), that can scarcely keep life and soul together, *shall bow before him,* before the Lord Jesus, who reckons it his honour to be the poor man's King (lxxii. 12). Seeing we cannot keep alive our own souls, it is our wisdom, by an obedient faith, to commit our souls to Jesus Christ, who is able to save them and keep them alive for ever.

V. That the church of Christ, and with it the kingdom of God among men, should continue through all the ages of time. *A seed shall serve him;* there shall be a remnant, enough to preserve the entail. *They shall be accounted to him for a generation;* he will be the same to them that he was to those who went before them. *They shall come,* shall rise up in their day, not only to keep up the virtue of the generation that is past, but to serve the welfare of souls in the generations to come; they shall transmit to them the gospel of Christ.

In singing this we must triumph in the name of Christ, rejoice in the honours others do him, and in the assurance we have that there shall be a people praising him on earth when we are praising him in heaven.

PSALM 23

A psalm which has been sung by good Christians, and will be while the world stands, with a great deal of pleasure and satisfaction. I. The psalmist here claims relation to God, as his shepherd, ver. 1. II. He recounts his experience of the kind things God had done for him as his shepherd, ver. 2, 3, 5. III. Hence he infers that he should want no good (ver. 1), that he needed to fear no evil (ver. 4), that God would never leave nor forsake him in a way of mercy; and therefore he resolves never to leave nor forsake God in a way of duty, ver. 6. And, as in the foregoing psalm he represented Christ dying for his sheep, so here he represents Christians receiving the benefit of all the care and tenderness of that great and good shepherd.

A psalm of David.

Verses 1–6

I. From God's being his shepherd he infers that he shall not want anything that is good for him, *v.* 1. Time was when David was himself a shepherd; he was taken from following the ewes great with young (lxxviii. 70, 71), and so he knew by experience the cares and tender affections of a good shepherd towards his flock. He remembered what need they had of a shepherd, and he once ventured his life to rescue a lamb. By this therefore he illustrates God's care of his people; and to this our Saviour seems to refer when he says, *I am the shepherd of the sheep; the good shepherd,* John x. 11. He takes them into his fold, and provides for them. We must know the shepherd's voice, and follow him. When David considers that God is his shepherd, he can boldly say, *I shall not want.* More is implied than is expressed, not only, *I shall not want,* but, "I shall be supplied with whatever I need; and, if I have not everything I desire, I may conclude it is either not fit for me or not good for me, or I shall have it in due time."

II. From his performing the office of a good shepherd to him he infers that he needs not fear any evil in the greatest dangers and difficulties he could be in, *v.* 2–4. See the happiness of the saints as the sheep of God's pasture. (1) They are well placed, well laid: *He maketh me to lie down in green pastures.* We have the comforts of this life from God's good hand, our daily bread from him as our Father. The greatest abundance is but a dry pasture to a wicked man, who relishes that only in it which pleases the senses; but to a godly man, who tastes the goodness of God in all his enjoyments, though he has but little of the world, it is a green pasture, xxxvii. 16; Prov. xv. 16, 17. God makes his saints to lie down; he gives them quiet and contentment in their own minds, whatever their lot is; their souls dwell at ease in him, and that makes every pasture green. (2) They are well guided, well led. *He leadeth me beside the still waters.* Those that feed on God's goodness must follow his direction; he directs their eye, their way, and their heart, into his love. God provides for his people not only food and rest, but refreshment also and pleasure. God leads his people, not to the standing waters which corrupt and gather filth, nor to the troubled sea, nor to the rapid rolling floods, but to the silent purling waters; for the still but running waters agree best with those spirits that flow out towards God and yet do it silently. *He leadeth me in the paths of righteousness,* in the way of my duty; in that he instructs me by his word and directs me by conscience and providence. The way of duty is the truly pleasant way. In these paths we cannot walk unless God both lead us into them and lead us in them. (3) They are well helped when anything ails them: *He restoreth my soul.* When, after one sin, David's heart smote him, and, after another, Nathan was sent to tell him, *Thou art the man,* God restored his soul. Though God may suffer his people to fall into sin, he will not suffer them to lie still in it. "Having had such experience of God's goodness to me all my days, yet in six troubles and in seven, I will never distrust him, no, not in the last extremity." "*Though I walk through the valley of the shadow of death,* that is, though I am in peril of death, though in the midst of dangers, deep as a valley, yet I am easy." But, even in the supposition of the distress, there are four words which lessen the terror. It is but the *shadow* of death; there is no substantial evil in it; the shadow of a serpent will not sting nor the shadow of a sword kill. It is the *valley* of the shadow, deep indeed, and dark, and dirty; but the valleys are fruitful, and so is death itself fruitful of comforts to God's people. It is but a *walk* in this valley, a gentle pleasant walk. It is a walk *through* it; they shall not be lost in this valley, but get safely to the mountain of spices on the other side of it. There is no evil in it to a child of God; death cannot separate us from the love of God; it kills the body, but cannot touch the soul. The good shepherd will not only conduct, but convoy, his sheep through this valley. His presence shall comfort them: *Thou art with me.* His word and Spirit shall comfort them—*his rod and staff*, alluding to the shepherd's crook, or the rod under which the sheep passed when they were counted (Lev. xxvii. 32), or the staff with which the shepherds drove away the dogs that would worry the sheep.

III. From the good gifts of God's bounty to him now he infers the constancy and perpetuity of his mercy, *v.* 5, 6. "*Thou preparest a table before me;* thou hast provided for me all things requisite both for body and soul, for time and eternity": food convenient, a table spread, a cup filled, meat for his hunger, drink for his thirst. "*My cup runs over*, enough for myself and my friends too." *Thou anointest my head with oil.* He had said (*v.* 1), *I shall not want;* but now he speaks more positively, *Surely goodness and mercy shall follow me all the days of my life.* His hope rises, and his faith is strengthened, by being exercised. It shall *follow* me, as the water out of the rock followed the camp of Israel through the wilderness. It shall follow me *all my life long*, even to the last; for whom God loves he loves to the end. *Surely* it shall. "Goodness and mercy having followed me all the days of my life on this earth, when that is ended I shall remove to a better world, to *dwell in the house of the Lord for ever*, in our Father's house above, where there are many mansions."

PSALM 24

This psalm is concerning the kingdom of Jesus Christ, I. His providential kingdom, by which he rules the world, ver. 1, 2. II. The kingdom of his grace, by which he rules in his church. 1. Concerning the subjects of that kingdom; their character (ver. 4, 6), their charter, ver. 5. 2. Concerning the King of that kingdom; and a summons to all to give him admission, ver. 7–10.

A psalm of David.

Verses 1–2

I. We are not to think that the heavens, even the heavens only, are the Lord's, and that this earth, being so small and inconsiderable a part of the creation, is neglected, and that he claims no interest in it. No, even the earth is his. 1. When God gave the earth to the children of men he still reserved to himself the property, and only let it out to them as tenants: *The earth is the Lord's and the fulness thereof.* The mines, the fruits it produces, all the beasts of the forest and the cattle upon a thousand hills, our lands and houses, and all the improvements that are made of this earth by the skill and industry of man, are all his. These indeed, in the kingdom of grace, are justly looked upon as emptiness; for they are vanity of vanities, nothing to a soul; but, in the kingdom of providence, they are fulness. *The earth is full of God's riches, so is the great and wide sea also.* 2. The habitable part of this earth (Prov. viii. 31) is his in a special manner—*the world and those that dwell therein.* We ourselves are not our own, our bodies, our souls, are not.

II. The earth is his by an indisputable title, *for he hath founded it upon the seas* and *established it upon the floods, v.* 2. He made it and fitted it for the use of man. The matter is his, for he made it out of nothing; the form is his, for he made it according to the eternal counsels and ideas of his own mind. He continues it, he has *established* it, fixed it, so that, though one generation passes and another comes, the earth abides, Eccles. i. 4. And his providence is a continued creation, cxix. 90.

Verses 3–6

From this world, and the fulness thereof, the psalmist's meditations rise, of a sudden, to the great things of another world, the foundation of which is not on the seas, nor on the floods.

I. This earth is God's footstool; we must be here but a while, must shortly go hence, and *Who then shall ascend into the hill of the Lord?* Who shall go to heaven hereafter, and, as an earnest of that, have communion with God in holy ordinances now? A soul that knows and considers its own nature, origin, and immortality, when it has viewed the earth and the fulness thereof, will sit down unsatisfied; "What shall I do to rise to that high place, that hill, where the Lord dwells, that I may abide in that happy holy place where he meets his people?"

II. An answer to this enquiry. The properties of God's peculiar people, who shall have communion with him in grace and glory. They are such as keep themselves from all the gross acts of sin. They have *clean hands.* The hands lifted up in prayer must be pure hands, no blot of unjust gain cleaving to them, nor anything else that defiles the man and is offensive to the holy God. They are such as make conscience of being inwardly good as they seem to be outwardly. They have *pure hearts.* That is a pure heart which is sincere, purified by faith, and conformed to the image and will of God; see Matt. v. 8. They are such as do not set their affections upon the things of this world, do not *lift up their souls unto vanity.* They are such as deal honestly both with God and man. They are a praying people (*v.* 6): *This is the generation of those that seek him.* In every age there is a remnant of such as these, men of this character, who are accounted to the Lord for a generation, xxii. 30. It is to the hill of the Lord that we must ascend, and, the way being up-hill, we have need to put forth ourselves to the utmost, as those that seek diligently. They join themselves to the people of God, to seek God with them. They seek God's face, as Jacob, who was *therefore* surnamed *Israel*, because he wrestled with God and prevailed, sought him and found him. As soon as ever Paul was converted he *joined himself to the disciples*, Acts ix. 26. *Thy face, O God of Jacob!* so our margin supplies it, and makes it easy. They shall be made truly and for ever happy. They shall be justified and sanctified. These are the spiritual blessings in heavenly things which they shall receive, even righteousness, the very thing they hunger and thirst after, Matt. v. 6. They shall be saved; for God himself will be the God of their salvation.

Verses 7–10

What is spoken once is spoken a second time; such repetitions are usual in songs. Entrance once and again demanded for the King of glory; the doors and gates are to be thrown open. *Who is this King of glory? It is the Lord, strong and mighty, the Lord, mighty in battle, the Lord of hosts, v.* 8, 10.

I. This splendid entry here described probably refers to the solemn bringing in of the ark into the tent David pitched for it or the temple Solomon built for it; for, when David prepared materials for the building of it, it was proper for him to prepare a psalm for the dedication of it. The doors are called *everlasting doors*, because much more durable than the door of the tabernacle, which was but a curtain. God, in his word and ordinances, is thus to be welcomed by us. The doors and gates must be thrown open to him.

II. Doubtless it points at Christ, of whom the ark, with the mercy-seat, was a type. We may apply it to the ascension of Christ into heaven and the welcome given to him there. The gates of heaven must then be opened to him, those doors that may be truly called *everlasting*. Our Redeemer found them shut, but, having by his blood made atonement for sin and gained a title to *enter into the holy place* (Heb. ix. 12), as one having authority, he demanded entrance, not for himself only, but for us; for, as the fore-runner, he has for us entered and *opened the kingdom of heaven to all believers*. We may apply it to Christ's entrance into the souls of men by his word and Spirit, that they may be his temples. Christ's presence in them is like that of the ark in the temple; it sancti-fies them. *Behold, he stands at the door and knocks*, Rev. iii. 20. It is required that the gates and doors of the heart be opened to him, not only as admission is given to a guest, but as possession is delivered to the rightful owner. This is the gospel call and de-mand, that we let Jesus Christ, the King of glory, come into our souls, and welcome him with hosannas, *Blessed is he that cometh*.

PSALM 25

This psalm is full of devout affection to God, the out-goings of holy desires towards his favour and grace and the lively actings of faith in his promises. We may learn out of it, I. What it is to pray, ver. 1, 15. II. What we must pray for, the pardon of sin (ver. 6, 7, 18), direction in the way of duty (ver. 4, 5), the favour of God (ver. 16), deliverance out of our troubles (ver. 17, 18), preservation from our enemies (ver. 20, 21), and the salvation of the church of God, ver. 22. III. What we may plead in prayer, our confidence in God (ver. 2, 3, 5, 20, 21), our distress and the malice of our enemies (ver. 17, 19), our sincerity, ver. 21. IV. What precious promises we have to encourage us in prayer, of guidance and instruction (ver. 8, 9, 12), the benefit of the covenant (ver. 10), and the pleasure of communion with God, ver. 13, 14.

A psalm of David.

Verses 1–7

David's professions of desire towards God and dependence on him. He often begins his psalms with such professions, not to move God, but to move himself.

I. He professes his desire towards God: *Unto thee, O Lord! do I lift up my soul*, v. 1. In worshipping God we must lift up our souls to him. Prayer is the ascent of the soul to God. *Sursum corda—Up with your hearts*, was anciently used as a call to devotion.

II. He professes his dependence upon God (v. 2): *O my God! I trust in thee*. His conscience witnessed for him that he had no confidence in himself nor in any creature. He pleases himself with this pro-fession of faith in God. "*Let me not be ashamed* of my confidence in thee; let me not be shaken from it by any prevailing fears, and let me not be, in the issue, disappointed of what I depend upon thee for; but, Lord, *keep what I have committed unto thee*." *Let those be ashamed that transgress without cause*, or *vainly*, as the word is. The weaker the temptation is by which men are drawn to sin the stronger the cor-ruption is by which they are driven to it. Those are the worst transgressors that sin for sinning-sake.

III. He begs direction from God in the way of his duty, v. 4, 5. Once and again he here prays to God to teach him. "*Teach me*, not fine words or fine notions, but *thy ways, thy paths, thy truth*, the ways in which thou walkest towards me, which are *all mercy and truth* (v. 10), and the ways in which thou wouldst have me to walk towards thee. *Show me thy way*, and so *teach me*." In doubtful cases we should pray earnestly that God would make it plain to us what he would have us to do. "*Lead me*, and so teach me." *Thou art the God of my salvation*. If God save us, he will teach us and lead us. He that gives salvation will give instruction. *On thee do I wait all the day*. Whence should a servant expect direction but from his own master, on whom he waits all the day?

IV. He appeals to God's infinite mercy, not pre-tending to any merit of his own (v. 6): "*Remember, O Lord! thy tender mercies*, and, for the sake of those mercies, lead me, and teach me; for they *have been ever of old*."

V. He is earnest for the pardon of his sins (v. 7): "*O remember not the sins of my youth*. Lord, remem-ber thy mercies (v. 6), which speak for me, and not my sins, which speak against me." When God par-dons sin he is said to *remember it no more*, which denotes a plenary remission; he forgives and forgets.

Verses 8–14

God's promises are here mixed with David's prayers. Many petitions there were in the former part of the psalm, and many we shall find in the latter; and here, in the middle of the psalm, he meditates upon the promises. The promises of God are not only the best foundation of prayer, telling us what to pray for, but they are a present answer to prayer. Let the prayer be made according to the promise, and then the promise may be read as a return to the prayer; and we are to believe the prayer is heard because the promise will be performed. But, in the midst of the promises, we find one petition which seems to come in somewhat abruptly, and should have followed upon v. 7. It is (v. 11), *Pardon my iniquity*. He enforces this petition with a double plea. "*For thy name's sake pardon my iniquity. Pardon my iniquity, for it is great*, and therefore I am undone, if infinite mercy do not interpose for the pardon of it."

Let us now view the great and precious promises which we have in these verses,

I. These promises are sure to those who, though they have been sinners, yet now keep God's word. Though, through the infirmity of the flesh, they sometimes break the command, yet by a sincere repentance when at any time they do amiss, and a constant adherence by faith to God as their God, they keep the covenant and do not break that. Such as fear him (v. 12 and again v. 14), such as stand in awe of his majesty and worship him with reverence, submit to his authority and obey him with cheerfulness.

II. Two things which ratify and confirm all the promises:—1. The perfections of God's nature. We value the promise by the character of him that makes it. We may therefore depend upon God's promises; for *good and upright is the Lord*, and there-fore he will be as good as his word. 2. The agreeable-ness of all he says and does with the perfections of his nature (v. 10): *All the paths of the Lord* (that is, all his promises and all his providences) *are mercy and truth*; they are, like himself, good and upright.

III. What these promises are.

1. That God will instruct and direct them in the way of their duty. This is most insisted upon, because it is an answer to David's prayers (v. 4, 5), *Show me thy ways and lead me*. We should fix our thoughts on those promises which suit our present case. (1) He will *teach sinners in the way*, because they are sinners, and therefore need teaching. When they desire teaching, then he will teach them the way of recon-ciliation to God, the way to a well-grounded peace of conscience, and the way to eternal life. (2) *The meek will he guide*, that is, those that are humble, distrustful of themselves, desirous to be taught, and honestly resolved to follow the divine guidance. These he will guide *in judgment*, that is, by the rule of the written word. (3) *Him that feareth the Lord he will teach in the way that he shall choose*, either in the way that God shall choose or that the good man shall choose. It comes all to one, for he that fears the Lord chooses the things that please him.

2. That God will make them easy (v. 13): *His soul shall dwell at ease, shall lodge in goodness*, marg.

Those that devote themselves to the fear of God, and give up themselves to be taught of God, will be easy.

3. That he will give to them and theirs as much of this world as is good for them: *His seed shall inherit the earth.* Their children shall fare the better for their prayers when they are gone.

4. That God will admit them into the secret of communion with himself (v. 14): *The secret of the Lord is with those that fear him.* They understand his word; for, *if any man do his will, he shall know of the doctrine whether it be of God,* John vii. 17.

Verses 15-22

David, encouraged by the promises he had been meditating upon, concludes the psalm, as he began, with professions of dependence upon God and desires towards him.

I. He lays open before God the calamitous condition he was in. His feet were in the net, held fast and entangled, so that he could not extricate himself out of his difficulties, v. 15. He was *desolate and afflicted,* v. 16. David calls himself *desolate and solitary* because he depended not upon his servants and soldiers, but relied as entirely upon God as if he had no prospect at all of help and succour from any creature. *The troubles of his heart were enlarged* (v. 17), he grew more and more melancholy and troubled in mind.

II. He expresses the dependence he had upon God in these distresses (v. 15): *My eyes are ever towards the Lord.* Those that have their eye ever towards God shall not have their feet long in the net. He repeats his profession of dependence upon God (v. 20)—*Let me not be ashamed, for I put my trust in thee;* and of expectation from him—*I wait on thee,* v. 21.

III. He prays earnestly to God for relief and succour, *Forgive all my sins,* Lord, *forgive all, take away all iniquity.* It is observable that, as to his affliction, he asks for no more than God's regard to it: "*Look upon my affliction and my pain,* and do with it as thou pleasest." But, as to his sin, he asks for no less than a full pardon: *Forgive all my sins. Turn thou unto me.* His condition was troubled, and, in reference to that, he prays, "*O bring thou me out of my distresses.* I see no way of deliverance open; but thou canst either find one or make one." He pleads God's mercy: *Have mercy upon me.* Men of the greatest merits would be undone if they had not to do with a God of infinite mercies. He pleads his own misery, which made him the proper object of divine mercy. He pleads the iniquity of his enemies: "*Lord,* consider them, how cruel they are, and deliver me out of their hands." He pleads his own integrity, v. 21. Though he had owned himself guilty before God, yet, as to his enemies, he had the testimony of his conscience that he had done them no wrong. Sincerity will be our best security in the worst of times. *Redeem Israel, O God! out of all his troubles.* David's troubles were enlarged, and very earnest he was with God to deliver him, yet he forgets not the distresses of God's church.

PSALM 26

David is in this psalm putting himself upon a solemn trial by God and his own conscience, to both which he appeals touching his integrity (ver. 1, 2), for the proof of which he alleges, I. His constant regard to God and his grace, ver. 3. II. His rooted antipathy to sin and sinners, ver. 4, 5. III. His sincere affection to the ordinances of God, and his care about them, ver. 6-8. Having thus proved his integrity, 1. He deprecates the doom of the wicked, ver. 9, 10. 2. He casts himself upon the mercy and grace of God, with a resolution to hold fast his integrity, and his hope in God, ver. 11, 12.

A psalm of David.

Verses 1-5

It is probable that David penned this psalm when he was persecuted by Saul, who represented him as a very bad man, and falsely accused him of many crimes. Herein he was a type of Christ, who was made a reproach of men. Now see what David does in this case.

I. He appeals to God's righteous sentence (v. 1): "*Judge me, O God!* be thou Judge between me and my accusers." He cannot justify himself against the charge of sin; he owns his iniquity is great and he is undone if God, in his infinite mercy, do not forgive him; but he can justify himself against the charge of hypocrisy. It is a comfort to all who are sincere in religion that God himself is a witness to their sincerity.

II. He submits to his unerring search (v. 2): *Examine me, O Lord! and prove me,* as gold is proved, whether it be standard. So sincere was he in his devotion to his God that he wished he had a window in his bosom, that whoever would might look into his heart.

III. He solemnly protests his sincerity (v. 1): "*I have walked in my integrity;* my conversation has agreed with my profession, and one part of it has been of a piece with another." Proofs of his integrity encouraged him to trust in the Lord as his righteous Judge, *therefore I shall not slide.* Those that are sincere in religion may trust in God that they shall not slide, that is, that they shall not apostatize from their religion.

1. He had a constant regard to God and to his grace, v. 3. *Thy loving-kindness is before my eyes.* He governed himself by the word of God as his rule: "*I have walked in thy truth,* that is, according to thy law, for thy law is truth."

2. He had no fellowship with the unfruitful works of darkness, nor with the workers of those works, v. 4, 5. Great care to avoid bad company is both a good evidence of our integrity and a good means to preserve us in it. "*I have not sat with them,* and I *will not go in with them.*" The company of dissemblers is as dangerous company as any, and as much to be shunned. Evil-doers pretend friendship to those whom they would decoy into their snares, but they dissemble. *When they speak fair, believe them not.* Though sometimes he could not avoid being in the company of bad people, yet he would not *go in with them,* he would not choose such for his companions. I have hated *ecclesiam malignantium* —*the church of the malignant;* so the Latin reads it. As good men, in concert, make one another better, and are enabled to do so much the more good, so bad men, in combination, make one another worse, and do so much the more mischief.

Verses 6-12

I. David mentions, as a further evidence of his integrity, the sincere affection he had to the ordinances of God.

1. He was very careful and conscientious in his preparation for holy ordinances: *I will wash my hands in innocency.* In our preparations for solemn ordinances we must not only be able to clear ourselves from the charge of hypocrisy, and to protest our innocency of that (which was signified by *washing the hands,* Deut. xxi. 6), but we must take pains to cleanse ourselves by renewing our repentance.

2. He was very diligent and serious in his attendance upon them: *I will compass thy altar,* alluding to the custom of the priests, who, while the sacrifice was in offering, walked round the altar, and probably the offerers likewise did so at some distance, denoting a diligent regard to what was done and a dutiful attendance in the service.

3. In all his attendance on God's ordinances he aimed at the glory of God.

4. He did this with delight. "*Lord,* thou knowest how dearly *I have loved the habitation of thy house*

(v. 8), the tabernacle where thou art pleased to manifest thy residénce among thy people and receive their homage, *the place where thy honour dwells*."

II. David, having given proofs of his integrity, earnestly prays that he might not fall under the doom of the wicked (v. 9, 10). *Gather not my soul with sinners*. "They are *bloody men*, that thirst after blood and lie under a great deal of the guilt of blood. They do mischief, and mischief is always in their hands. Though they get by their wickedness (for *their right hand is full of bribes* which they have taken to pervert justice), yet that will make their case never the better; for *what is a man profited if he gain the world and lose his soul?*" He dreads having his lot with them.

III. David, with a holy humble confidence, commits himself to the grace of God, v. 11, 12. "*As for me*, whatever others do, *I will walk in my integrity*." He prays for the divine grace both to enable him to do so and to give him the comfort of it: "*Redeem me out of the hands of bribes*, *and be merciful to me*, living and dying." He pleases himself with his steadiness: "*My foot stands in an even place*, where I shall not stumble and whence I shall not fall." He promises himself that though he was now perhaps banished from public ordinances, yet he should again have an opportunity of blessing God in the congregation of his people.

PSALM 27

Some think David penned this psalm before his coming to the throne, when he was in the midst of his troubles, and perhaps upon occasion of the death of his parents; but the Jews think he penned it when he was old, upon occasion of the wonderful deliverance he had from the sword of the giant, when Abishai succoured him (2 Sam. xxi. 16, 17). Perhaps it was not penned upon any particular occasion; but it is very expressive of the pious and devout affections with which gracious souls are carried out towards God at all times, especially in times of trouble. I. The courage and holy bravery of his faith, ver. 1–3. II. The complacency he took in communion with God and the benefit he experienced by it, ver. 4–6. III. His desire towards God, and his favour and grace, ver. 7–9, 11, 12. IV. His expectations from God, and the encouragement he gives to others to hope in him, ver. 10, 13, 14.

A psalm of David.

Verses 1–6

I. With what a lively faith David triumphs in God, glories in his holy name. 1. *The Lord is my light*. David's subjects called him *the light of Israel*, 2 Sam. xxi. 17. And he was indeed a burning and a shining light: but he owns that he shone, as the moon does, with a borrowed light; what light God darted upon him reflected upon them: *The Lord is my light*. 2. "He is *my salvation*, in whom I am safe and by whom I shall be saved." 3. "He is *the strength of my life*, not only the protector of my exposed life, but the strength of my frail weak life."

II. With what an undaunted courage he triumphs over his enemies; no fortitude like that of faith. If God be for him, who can be against him? *Whom shall I fear? Of whom shall I be afraid?* His enemies came upon him, *to eat up his flesh*, aiming at no less and assured of that, but they fell; not, "He smote them and they fell," but, "They *stumbled and fell*"; they were so confounded and weakened that they could not go on with their enterprise. "Though they be numerous, *a host* of them, though they *encamp against me*, an army against one man, yet *my heart shall not fear*." Hosts cannot hurt us if the Lord of hosts protect us. Nay, in this assurance that God is for me *I will be confident*. "He shall *hide me*, not in the strongholds of En-gedi (1 Sam. xxiii. 29), but *in the secret of his tabernacle*. Now shall my head be lifted up above my enemies, not only so as that they cannot reach it with their darts, but so as that I shall be exalted to bear rule over them."

III. With what a gracious earnestness he prays for a constant communion with God in holy ordinances, v. 4.

1. What it is he desires—*to dwell in the house of the Lord*. In the courts of God's house the priests had their lodgings, and David wished he had been one of them. All God's children desire to dwell in God's house; where should they dwell else? Do we hope that praising God will be the blessedness of our eternity? Surely then we ought to make it the business of our time.

2. How earnestly he covets this: "This is the *one thing I have desired of the Lord* and which I will seek after." If he were to ask but one thing of God, this should be it; for this he had at heart more than anything. He would dwell in God's house *to behold the beauty of the Lord and to enquire in his temple*. He knew something of the beauty of the Lord; his holiness is his beauty (cx. 3); his goodness is his beauty, Zech. ix. 17. The harmony of all his attributes is the beauty of his nature. In God's house troubles would not find him. Joash, one of David's seed, was hidden in the house of the Lord six years, and there not only preserved from the sword, but reserved to the crown, 2 Kings xi. 3. The temple was thought a safe place for Nehemiah to abscond in, Neh. vi. 10. The safety of believers however is not in the walls of the temple, but in the God of the temple and their comfort in communion with him.

Verses 7–14

David in these verses expresses,

I. His desire towards God, in many petitions. If he cannot now go up to the house of the Lord, yet, wherever he is, he can find a way to the throne of grace by prayer. "*Hear, O Lord, when I cry*, not only with my heart, but, as one in earnest, *with my voice* too." If we pray and believe, God will graciously hear and answer. David fastens, in his thoughts, upon the call God had given him to the throne of his grace. *My heart said unto thee* (so it begins in the original) or *of* thee, *Seek you my face*; he first revolved that, and preached that over again to himself (and that is the best preaching; it is hearing twice what God speaks once)—*Thou saidst Seek you my face;* and then he returns what he had so meditated upon, in this pious resolution, *Thy face, Lord, will I seek*. The opening of his hand will satisfy the desire of living things (cxlv. 16), but it is only the shining of his face that will satisfy the desire of a living soul, iv. 6, 7. He owns he had deserved God's displeasure, but begs that, however God might correct him, he would not cast him away from his presence. "*O leave me not, neither forsake me;* withdraw not the operations of thy power from me, for then I am helpless; withdraw not the tokens of thy goodwill to me, for then I am comfortless." "*Teach me thy way, O Lord!* give me to understand the meaning of thy providences towards me that I may not mistake it, but may walk rightly, and that I may not do it with hesitation, but may walk surely." He begs to be guided in *a plain path, because of his enemies*, or (as the margin reads it) his *observers*. "*Deliver me not over to the will of my enemies*. Lord, let them not gain their point, for it aims at my life, and I have no fence against them, but thy power over their consciences; for *false witnesses have risen up against me*, that aim further than to take away my reputation, for they *breathe out cruelty*; it is the blood they thirst after."

II. He expresses his dependence upon God: "*When my father and my mother forsake me*, the nearest and dearest friends I have in the world, from whom I may expect most relief and with most reason, when they die, or are at a distance from me, or are disabled to help me in the time of need, or are unkind to me or unmindful of me, and will not help me, when I am as helpless as ever poor orphan was that was left fatherless and motherless, then I know *the Lord* will take me up." He believed he should *see the goodness of the Lord in the land of the living*; and, if he had not done so, he would *have fainted* under his afflictions. Those that walk by faith in the goodness of the Lord shall in due time walk in the sight of that goodness. It is his comfort, not so much that he shall see the land of the living as that he shall see the goodness of God in it; for that is the comfort of all creature-comforts to a gracious soul. In heaven is that land that may truly be called *the land of the living*. This earth is the land of the dying. There is nothing like the believing hope of eternal life to keep us from fainting under all the calamities of this present time. In the meantime he says to himself, or to his friends, *He shall strengthen thy heart*, shall sustain the spirit. In that strength, *Wait on the Lord* by faith, and prayer, and a humble resignation to his will; *wait, I say, on the Lord*; whatever you do, grow not remiss in your attendance upon God. Those that wait upon the Lord have reason to be of good courage.

PSALM 28

The former part of this psalm is the prayer of a saint militant and now in distress (ver. 1–3), to which is added the doom of God's implacable enemies, ver. 4, 5. The latter part of the psalm is the thanksgiving of a saint triumphant, and delivered out of his distresses (ver. 6–8), to which is added a prophetical prayer for all God's faithful loyal subjects, ver. 9.

A psalm of David.

Verses 1–5

David is very earnest in prayer.

I. He prays that God would graciously hear and answer him, now that, in his distress, he called upon him, v. 1, 2. "*O Lord, my rock* (denoting his belief of God's power), *to thee will I cry*, as one in earnest, being ready to sink, unless thou come in with seasonable succour. *If thou be silent to me*, and I have not the tokens of thy favour, I am *like those that go down into the pit* (that is, I am a dead man, lost and undone); if God be not my friend my hope and my help will have perished." *I lift up my hands towards thy holy oracle*, thence to receive an answer of peace. The most holy place within the veil is here, as elsewhere, called the *oracle*; there the ark and the mercy-seat were, there God was said to *dwell between the cherubim*, and thence he spoke to his people, Num. vii. 89. That was a type of Christ, and it is to him that we must lift up our eyes and hands, for through him all good comes from God to us.

II. He deprecates the doom of wicked people. "Lord, I attend thy holy oracle, *draw me not away* from that *with the wicked, and with the workers of iniquity*," v. 3. "Lord, never leave me to myself, to use such arts of deceit and treachery for my safety as they use for my ruin."

III. He imprecates the just judgments of God upon the workers of iniquity (v. 4): *Give them according to their deeds*. This is not the language of passion or revenge, nor is it inconsistent with the duty of praying for our enemies. But he would show how far he was from complying with the workers of iniquity. If what has been done amiss be not undone by repentance, there will certainly come a reckoning day, when God will render to every man who persists in his evil deeds according to them. It is a prophecy particularly of the destruction of destroyers : "*They speak peace to their neighbours, but mischief is in their hearts;* Lord, *give them according to their deeds*."

IV. He foretells their destruction for their contempt of God and his hand (v. 5): "*Because they regard not the works of the Lord and the operations of his hands*, by which he manifests himself and speaks to the children of men, *he will destroy them* in this world and in the other, *and not build them up*." Why do men question the being or attributes of God, but because they do not duly regard his handiworks, which declare his glory, and in which the invisible things of him are clearly seen?

Verses 6–9

I. David gives God thanks. It was in faith that David prayed (v. 2), *Hear the voice of my supplications;* and by the same faith he gives thanks (v. 6) that *God has heard the voice of his supplications*. Those that pray in faith may rejoice in hope. What we win by prayer we must wear with praise.

II. He encourages himself to hope in God for the perfecting of everything that concerned him. This is the method of attaining peace: let us begin with praise that it is attainable. His experience of the benefit of that dependence: "*My heart trusted in him*, and in his power and promise; and it has not been in vain to do so, for *I am helped*, I have been often helped; not only God has given to me, in his due time, the help I trusted to him for, but my very trusting in him has helped me, in the mean time, and kept me from fainting," xxvii. 13. *Therefore my heart greatly rejoices*.

III. He pleases himself with the interest which all good people, through Christ, have in God (v. 8): "*The Lord is their strength;* not mine only, but the strength of every believer." This is our communion with all saints, that God is their strength and ours, Christ their Lord and ours, 1 Cor. i. 2.

IV. He concludes with a short but comprehensive prayer for the church of God, v. 9. He prays for Israel, not as his people ("save my people, and bless my inheritance"), though they were so, but, "*thine*." *The Lord's portion is his people*. That which he begs of God for them is, 1. That he would save them from their enemies. 2. That he would bless them with all good. 3. That he would *feed them*. "Direct their counsels and actions aright, and overrule their affairs for good. Feed them, and rule them; set pastors, set rulers, over them, that shall do their office with wisdom and understanding." 4. That he would *lift them up for ever*, lift them up out of their troubles and distresses, and do this, not only for those of that age, but for his people in every age to come, even to the end.

PSALM 29

It is the probable conjecture that David penned this psalm at the time of a great storm of thunder, lightning, and rain, as the eighth psalm was his meditation in a moonlight night and the nineteenth in a sunny morning. I. He calls upon the great ones of the world to give glory to God, ver. 1, 2. II. To convince them of the goodness of that God whom they were to adore, he takes notice of his power in the thunder, and lightning, and thunder-showers (ver. 3–9), his sovereign dominion over the world (ver. 10), and his special favour to his church, ver. 11.

A psalm of David.

Verses 1–11

I. A demand of the homage of the great men of the earth to be paid to the great God. Every clap of thunder David interpreted as a call to himself and other princes to give glory to the great God. "*O you mighty* (v. 1), you sons of the mighty, who have power, *give unto the Lord*, and again, and a third time, *Give unto the Lord* the recognition of his glory, and of his dominion over us. *Give unto the Lord* your ownselves, in the first place, and then your services. *Give unto the Lord glory and strength;* acknowledge his glory and strength, and whatever glory or strength he has entrusted you with offer it to him, to be used for his honour, in his service. Give him your crowns; let them be laid at his feet; give him your sceptres, your swords, your keys; put all into his hand, that you, in the use of them, may be to him for a name and a praise." What is here said to the mighty is said to all: *Worship God;* it is the sum and substance of the everlasting gospel,

Rev. xiv. 6, 7. Religious worship is *giving to the Lord the glory due to his name, v.* 2. *Worship the Lord in the beauty of holiness.* Adore him, not only as infinitely awful and therefore to be feared above all, but as infinitely amiable and therefore to be loved and delighted in above all; especially we must have an eye to the beauty of his holiness. There is a beauty in holiness, and it is that which puts an acceptable beauty upon all the acts of worship.

II. Good reason given for this demand.

1. His sufficiency in himself, intimated in his name *Jehovah—I am that I am,* which is repeated here no fewer than eighteen times in this short psalm, twice in every verse but three, and once in two of those three.

2. His sovereignty over all things. The psalmist here sets forth God's dominion,

(1) In the kingdom of nature. In the wonderful effects of natural causes, and the operations of the powers of nature. It is the God of glory that thunders, *v.* 3. Every one that hears the thunder will own that *the voice of the Lord is full of majesty* (xxix. 4). For if his voice be so terrible, what is his arm? *The voice of the Lord,* in the thunder, often *broke the cedars,* even those of Lebanon, the strongest, the stateliest. Some understand it of the violent winds which shook the cedars, and tore off their tops. Earthquakes also shook the ground itself on which the trees grew, and made *Lebanon and Sirion* to dance; *the wilderness of Kadesh* also was in like manner shaken (*v.* 8), the trees by winds, the ground by earthquakes. Dr. Hammond understands it of the conquest of the neighbouring kingdoms that warred with Israel and opposed David, as the Syrians, whose country lay near the forest of Lebanon, the Amorites that bordered on Mount Hermon, and the Moabites and Ammonites that lay about the wilderness of Kadesh. Fires have been kindled by lightnings, accordingly the voice of the Lord, in the thunder, is here said to *divide the flames of fire* (*v.* 7). The terror of thunder makes the hinds to calve sooner, and some think more easily, than otherwise they would. The thunder is said here to *discover the forest,* that is, it so terrifies the wild beasts of the forest that they quit the dens and thickets in which they hid themselves and so are discovered.

(2) In the kingdom of providence, *v.* 10. God is to be praised as the governor of the world of mankind. He *sits upon the flood; he sits King for ever.* The ebbings and flowings of this lower world, and the agitations and revolutions of the affairs in it, give not the least shake to the repose nor to the counsels of the Eternal Mind. *He sits King for ever;* no period can, or shall, be put to his government. The administration of his kingdom is consonant to his counsels from eternity and pursuant to his designs for eternity.

(3) In the kingdom of grace. Here his glory shines most brightly. *In his temples,* where his people attend his discoveries of himself and his mind and attend him with their praises *everyone speaks of his glory. All his works do praise him,* but his saints only do bless him, and speak of his glory in his works, cxlv. 10. *He will give strength to his people,* to fortify them against every evil work and to furnish them for every good work. *He will bless his people with peace.* Peace is a blessing of inestimable value, which God designs for all his people.

PSALM 30

This is a psalm of thanksgiving for the great deliverances which God had wrought for David, penned upon occasion of the dedicating of his house of cedar. I. He here praises God for the deliverances he had wrought for him, ver. 1–3. II. He calls upon others to praise him too, ver. 4, 5. III. He blames himself for his former security, ver. 6, 7. IV. He recollects the prayers and complaints he had made in his distress, ver. 8–10. With them he stirs up himself to be very thankful to God for the present change, ver. 11, 12.

A psalm *and* song *at* the dedication of the house of David.

Verses 1–5

It was the laudable practice of the pious Jews, and, though not expressly appointed, yet allowed and accepted, when they had built a new house, to *dedicate it to God,* Deut. xx. 5. David did so when his house was built, and he took possession of it (2 Sam. v. 11). The houses we dwell in should, at our first entrance upon them, be dedicated to God, as little sanctuaries. We must solemnly commit ourselves, our families, and all our family affairs, to God's guidance and pray for his presence and blessing.

I. David does himself give God thanks for the great deliverances he had wrought for him (*v.* 1): "*I will extol thee, O Lord!* I will exalt thy name, will praise thee as one high and lifted up. *I cried to thee, and thou hast* not only heard me, but *healed me,* healed the distempered body, healed the disturbed and disquieted mind, healed the disordered distracted affairs of the kingdom." He was brought to the last extremity, dropping into the grave, and ready *to go down into the pit,* and yet rescued and kept alive, *v.* 3. A life from the dead ought to be spent in extolling the God of our life.

II. He calls upon others to join with him in praise. *Sing unto the Lord, O you saints of his!* "Let them give thanks at the remembrance of his holiness; let them praise his holy name, for holiness is his memorial throughout all generations." It is a good sign that we are in some measure partakers of his holiness if we can heartily rejoice and give thanks at the remembrance of it. We have found his frowns very short. Though we have deserved that they should be everlasting, and that he should be angry with us till he had consumed us, and should never be reconciled, yet *his anger endureth but for a moment, v.* 5. If *weeping endureth for a night,* yet, as sure as the light of the morning returns, so sure will joy and comfort return in a short time to the people of God; for the covenant of grace is as firm as the covenant of the day. *In his favour is life,* that is, all good. It is the life of the soul, it is spiritual life, the earnest of life eternal.

Verses 6–12

An account of three several states that David was in successively, and of the workings of his heart towards God in each of those states.

I. "*In my prosperity,* when I was in health of body and God had *given me rest from all my enemies, I said I shall never be moved;* I never had any apprehensions of danger upon any account." He thought his prosperity fixed like a mountain; *Thou, through thy favour, hast made my mountain to stand strong, v.* 7. He does not look upon it as his *heaven* (as worldly people do, who make their prosperity their felicity), only his *mountain;* it is earth still, only raised a little higher than the common level.

II. On a sudden he fell into trouble, and then he prayed to God, and pleaded earnestly for relief and succour. His mountain was shaken and he with it; it proved, when he grew secure, that he was least safe: "*Thou didst hide thy face and I was troubled,* in mind, body, or estate." If God hide his face, a good man is certainly troubled, though no other calamity befall him; when the sun sets night certainly follows, and the moon and all the stars cannot make day. When his mountain was shaken he lifted up his eyes above the hills. Is any troubled? *Let him pray. I cried to thee, O Lord!* It seems God's withdrawings made his prayers the more vehement. *What profit is there in my blood?* implying that he would willingly die if he could thereby do any real service to God or his country (Phil. ii. 17), but he saw not what good could be done by his dying in the bed of sickness, as might be if he had died in the bed of honour. *Shall the dust praise thee?* The sanctified spirit, which returns to God shall be still praising him; but the dust, which returns to the earth, shall not praise him, nor declare his truth.

III. In due time God delivered him out of his troubles and restored him to his former prosperity. His prayers were answered and his *mourning was turned into dancing, v.* 11. But what temper of mind was he in upon this happy change of the face of his affairs? What does he say now? He tells us, *v.* 12. His complaints were turned into praises. *I will give thanks unto thee for ever.* Thus must we learn to accommodate ourselves to the various providences of God.

PSALM 31

It is probable that David penned this psalm when he was persecuted by Saul; some passages in it agree particularly to the narrow escapes he had, at Keilah (1 Sam. xxiii. 13), then in the wilderness of Maon, when Saul marched on one side of the hill and he on the other, and, soon after, in the cave in the wilderness of Engedi. It is a mixture of prayers, and praises, and professions of confidence in God. I. David professes his cheerful confidence in God, and, in that confidence, prays for deliverance out of his present troubles, ver. 1–8. II. He complains of the deplorable condition he was in, and still prays that God would graciously appear for him against his persecutors, ver. 9–18. III. He concludes the psalm with praise and triumph, giving glory to God, and encouraging himself and others to trust in him, ver. 19–24.

To the chief musician. A psalm of David.

Verses 1–8

Faith and prayer must go together.

I. David, in distress, is very earnest with God in prayer for succour and relief. He prays that God, not only in mercy, but in righteousness, would deliver him, as a righteous Judge betwixt him and his unrighteous persecutors. The psalmist prays also that he would deliver him speedily, lest, if the deliverance were long deferred, his faith should fail. "*Be thou my strong rock,* immovable, impregnable, as a fastness framed by nature, and my *house of defence,* a fortress framed by art, and all *to save me. Lord, lead me and guide me*" (*v.* 3). Those that resolve to follow God's direction may in faith pray for it.

II. In this prayer he gives glory to God by a repeated profession of his confidence in him and dependence on him. "*In thee, O Lord! do I put my trust,* and not in myself, or any sufficiency of my own, or in any creature; *let me never be ashamed,* let me not be disappointed of any of that good which thou hast promised me. *Thou art my rock and my fortress,* by thy covenant with me and my believing consent to that covenant; therefore *be my strong rock,*" *v.* 2. If God be our strength, we may hope that he will both put his strength in us and put forth his strength for us. *Into thy hands I commit my spirit* (*v.* 5). David is here to be looked upon as a man in distress and trouble. His great care is about his soul, his spirit, his better part. Our outward afflictions should increase our concern for our souls. Many think that while they are perplexed about their worldly affairs, they may be excused if they neglect their souls; whereas the greater hazard our lives and secular interests lie at the more we are concerned to look to our souls, that we may keep possession of our souls when we can keep possession of nothing else, Luke xxi. 19. He thinks the best he can do for his soul is to commit it into the hand of God. He had prayed (*v.* 4) to be plucked out of the net of outward trouble, but, as not insisting upon that (God's will be done), he immediately lets fall that petition, and commits the spirit, the inward man, into God's hand. "Lord, however it goes with me, as to my body, let it go well with my soul."

III. He disclaimed all confederacy with those that made an arm of flesh their confidence (*v.* 6): *I have hated those that regard lying vanities*—idolaters (so some), who expect aid from false gods, which are vanity and a lie—astrologers, and those that give heed to them, so others.

IV. He comforted himself with his hope in God, and made himself, not only easy, but cheerful, with it, *v.* 7.

V. He encouraged himself in this hope with the experiences he had had of late. "*Thou hast considered my trouble,* with wisdom to suit relief to it, with condescension and compassion regarding the low estate of thy servant. *Thou hast known my soul in adversities,* with a tender concern and care for it. *Thou hast not shut me up into the hand of the enemy,* but set me at liberty, in *a large room,* where I may shift for my own safety," *v.* 8.

Verses 9–18

In the foregoing verses David had appealed to God's righteousness; here he appeals to his mercy, and pleads the greatness of his own misery, which made his case the proper object of that mercy.

I. The complaint he makes of his trouble and distress (*v.* 9): "*Have mercy upon me, O Lord! for I am in trouble,* and need thy mercy." His troubles had made him a man of sorrows. We may guess by David's complexion, which was ruddy and sanguine, by his genius for music, and by his daring enterprises in his early days, that his natural disposition was both cheerful and firm, that he was apt to be cheerful, and not to lay trouble to his heart; yet here we see he has almost wept out his eyes, and sighed away his breath. His body was affected with the sorrows of his mind (*v.* 10): *My strength fails, my bones are consumed,* and all *because of my iniquity.* His friends were unkind and became shy of him. He was *a fear to his acquaintance,* when they saw him they *fled from him, v.* 11. He was forgotten by them, *as a dead man out of mind* (*v.* 12), and looked upon with contempt *as a broken vessel.* Such swallow-friends the world is full of, that are gone in winter. His enemies were unjust in their censures of him. He was a *reproach among all his enemies,* but especially among his neighbours, *v.* 11. Thus he *heard the slander of many*; everyone had a stone to throw at him, because *fear was on every side.*

II. His confidence in God in the midst of these troubles. Everything looked black and dismal round about him, and threatened to drive him to despair: "*But I trusted in thee, O Lord!* (*v.* 14) and was thereby kept from sinking." His enemies robbed him of his reputation among men, but they could not rob him of his comfort in God, because they could not drive him from his confidence in God. "*Thou art my God;* I have chosen thee for mine, and thou hast promised to be mine." *My times are in thy hand.* Join this with the former and it makes the comfort complete. If God have our times in his hand, he can help us; and, if he be our God, he will help us; and then what can discourage us?

III. His petitions to God, in this faith and confidence. Our opportunities are in God's hand (so some read it), and therefore he knows how to choose the best and fittest time for our deliverance, and we must be willing to wait that time. When David had Saul at his mercy in the cave those about him said, "*This is the time* in which God will deliver thee," 1 Sam. xxiv. 4. "No," says David, "the time has not come for my deliverance till it can be wrought without sin; and I will wait for that time; for it is God's time, and that is the best time." Particularly, he prays for the silencing of those that reproach and calumniate the people of God (*v.* 18): *Let lying lips be put to silence, that speak grievous things proudly and contemptuously against the righteous.* One would think they thought it no sin to tell a deliberate lie if it might but serve to expose a good man either to hatred or contempt. *Hear, O our God! for we are despised.*

Verses 19–24

I. The acknowledgment which David makes of God's goodness to his people in general, *v.* 19, 20. God is good to all, but he is, in a special manner, good to Israel. Those who are interested in this goodness are described to be such as fear God and trust in him, as stand in awe of his greatness and rely on his grace. This goodness is said to be *laid up for them* and *wrought for them.* There is enough in bank and enough in hand. This goodness is wrought, in the actual performance of the promise, for those that trust in him. If what is laid up for us in the treasures of the everlasting covenant be not wrought for us, it is our own fault, because we do not believe. God is, in a special manner, the protector of his own people (*v.* 20): *Thou shalt hide them.* The saints are God's hidden ones. See the defence they are under: *Thou shalt hide them in the secret of thy presence, in a pavilion.* God's providence shall keep them safe from the malice of their enemies. He has many ways of sheltering them. When Baruch and Jeremiah were sought for *the Lord hid them*, Jer. xxxvi. 26.

II. The thankful returns which David makes for God's goodness to him in particular, *v.* 21, 22. "*He has shown me his marvellous loving-kindness,* beyond what I could have expected." Special preservations call for particular thanksgiving. Within were fears; but God was better to him than his fears, *v.* 22. Though his faith failed, God's promise did not: *Thou heardest the voice of my supplication,* for all this. He mentions his own unbelief as a foil to God's fidelity, serving to make his loving-kindness the more marvellous, the more illustrious.

III. The exhortation and encouragement which he hereupon gives to all the saints, *v.* 23, 24. *O love the Lord! all you his saints.* It is the character of the saints that they do love God; and yet they must be still called upon to love him, to love him more and love him better, and give proofs of their love. He would have them set their hope in God (*v.* 24): "*Be of good courage;* have a good heart on it; whatever difficulties or dangers you may meet with, the God you trust in shall by that trust strengthen your heart."

PSALM 32

This psalm, though it speaks not of Christ, has yet a great deal of gospel in it. We have here a summary, I. Of gospel grace in the pardon of sin (ver. 1, 2), in divine protection (ver. 7), and divine guidance, ver. 8. II. Of gospel duty. To confess sin (ver. 3–5), to pray (ver. 6), to govern ourselves well (ver. 9, 10), and to rejoice in God, ver. 11. Grotius thinks it was designed to be sung on the day of atonement.

A psalm of David, Maschil.

Verses 1–6

This psalm is entitled *Maschil*, which some take to be only the name of the tune to which it was set and was to be sung. But others think it is significant; our margin reads it, *A psalm of David giving instruction*, and there is nothing in which we have more need of instruction than in the nature of true blessedness—what we must do that we may be happy. In general our happiness consists in the favour of God, and not in the wealth of this world—in spiritual blessings. When it is here said, *Blessed is the man whose iniquity is forgiven*, the meaning is, "This is the ground of his blessedness: this is that fundamental privilege from which all the other ingredients of his blessedness flow."

I. Concerning the nature of the pardon of sin. 1. It is the forgiving of transgression. *Sin is the transgression of the law.* Upon our repentance, the transgression is forgiven; that is, the obligation to punishment which we lay under is cancelled: it is *lifted off* (so some read it), that by the pardon of it we may be eased of a burden, a heavy burden. 2. It is the covering of sin, as nakedness is covered, that it may

not appear to our shame, Rev. iii. 18. When sin is pardoned, it is covered with the robe of Christ's righteousness. 3. It is the not imputing of iniquity, not laying it to the sinner's charge. The righteousness of Christ being imputed to us, and we being made *the righteousness of God in him*, our iniquity is not imputed, God having *laid upon him the iniquity of us all* and made him *sin for us.*

II. Concerning the character of those whose sins are pardoned: *in whose spirit there is no guile.* He does not say, "There is no *guilt*" (for who is there that lives and sins not?), but no *guile*; the pardoned sinner is one that does not dissemble with God in his professions of repentance and faith. *While I kept silence my bones waxed old.* Those may be said to keep silence who stifle their convictions, who, when they cannot but see the evil of sin and their danger by reason of it, ease themselves by not thinking of it and diverting their minds to something else, who will not unburden their consciences by a penitent confession, and who choose rather to pine away in their iniquities than to take the method which God has appointed of finding rest for their souls.

III. Concerning the true and only way to peace of conscience. We are here taught to confess our sins, that they may be forgiven, to declare them, that we may be justified. This course David took: *I acknowledged my sin unto thee*, and no longer *hid my iniquity*, *v.* 5.

IV. Concerning God's readiness to pardon sin to those who truly repent of it: "*I said, I will confess* and immediately *thou forgavest the iniquity of my sin*, and gavest me the comfort of the pardon in my own conscience; immediately I found rest to my soul." Thus the father of the prodigal saw his returning son *when he was yet afar off*, and ran to meet him with the kiss that sealed his pardon. *For this shall every one that is godly pray unto thee.* All godly people are praying people. As soon as ever Paul was converted, *Behold, he prays,* Acts ix. 11. Those that are sincere and abundant in prayer will find the benefit of it when they are in trouble: *Surely in the floods of great waters*, which are very threatening, *they shall not come nigh them.*

Verses 7–11

I. David speaks to God, and professes his confidence in him and expectation from him, *v.* 7. "*Thou art my hiding-place;* when by faith I have recourse to thee I shall see all the reason in the world to be easy, and to think myself out of the reach of any real evil. *Thou shalt preserve me from trouble*, from the sting of it, and from the strokes of it as far as is good for me. *Thou shalt preserve me from* such trouble as I was in *while I kept silence*," *v.* 3. When God has pardoned our sins, if he leaves us to ourselves, we shall soon run as far in debt again as ever, and therefore, when we have received the comfort of our remission, we must fly to the grace of God to be preserved from returning to folly again. "Thou shalt not only deliver me, but *compass me about with songs of deliverance.* As *everyone that is godly shall pray with me*, so they shall give thanks with me."

II. He turns his speech to the children of men. Being himself converted, he does what he can to *strengthen his brethren* (Luke xxii. 32): *I will instruct thee*, whoever thou art that desirest instruction, *and teach thee in the way which thou shalt go*, *v.* 8. When Solomon became a penitent he immediately became a preacher, Eccles. i. 1. *I will guide thee with my eye.* Some apply this to God's conduct and direction. But it is rather to be taken as David's promise to those who sat under his instruction, his own children and family especially: "*I will counsel thee; my eye shall be upon thee*" (so the margin reads it); "I will give thee the best counsel I can and then observe whether thou takest it or no." Spiritual guides must be overseers. Here is a word of caution to sinners, not to be unruly and ungovernable: *Be you not as the horse and the mule, which have no understanding, v. 9.* It is our honour and happiness that we have understanding, that we are capable of being governed by reason and of reasoning with ourselves. Where there is renewing grace there is no need of the bit and bridle of restraining grace. The reason for this caution is because the way of sin will certainly end in sorrow (*v.* 10). Here is a word of comfort to saints. They are assured that if they will but trust in the Lord, and keep closely to him, *mercy shall compass them about* on every side (*v.* 10).

PSALM 33

This is a psalm of praise. The psalmist, I. Calls upon the righteous to praise God, ver. 1–3. II. Furnishes us with matter for praise. 1. For his justice, goodness, and truth, appearing in his word, and in all his works, ver. 4, 5. 2. For his power appearing in the work of creation, ver. 6–9. 3. For the sovereignty of his providence in the government of the world, ver. 10, 11, and again ver. 13–17. 4. For the peculiar favour which he bears to his own chosen people, ver. 12 and again ver. 18–22.

Verses 1–11

I. The great desire that God might be praised. Holy joy is the heart and soul of praise (*v.* 1): *Rejoice in the Lord, you righteous;* so the foregoing psalm concluded and so this begins. Thankful praise is holy joy (*v.* 2): *"Praise the Lord;* speak well of him, and give him the glory due to his name." Religious songs are the proper expressions of thankful praise (*v.* 3): *"Sing unto him a new song*, the best you have." Music was then used with the temple-songs (*v.* 2): *Sing unto him with the psaltery.* A good rule for this duty: "Do it *skilfully*, and *with a loud noise;* let it have the best both of head and heart; let it be done intelligently and with a clear head, affectionately and with a warm heart." A good reason for this duty: *For praise is comely for the upright.*

II. The high thoughts he had of God, and of his infinite perfections, *v.* 4, 5. God makes himself known to us, 1. In his *word,* here put for all divine revelation, all that which God at sundry times and in divers manners spoke to the children of men. 2. In his *works,* and those are all *done in truth.* The copy in all God's works agrees exactly with the great original, the plan laid in the Eternal Mind, and varies not in the least jot. God has made it to appear in his works that he is a God of inflexible justice: *He loveth righteousness and judgment.* He is a God of inexhaustible bounty: *The earth is full of his goodness,* that is, of the proofs and instances of it. The benign influences which the earth receives from above, and the fruits it is thereby enabled to produce, the provision that is made both for man and beast, and the common blessings with which all the nations of the earth are blessed, plainly declare that *the earth is full of his goodness*—the darkest, the coldest, the hottest, and the most dry and desert part of it not excepted. What a pity it is that this earth, which is so full of God's goodness, should be so empty of his praises, and that of the multitudes that live upon his bounty there are so few that live to his glory!

III. The conviction he was under of the almighty power of God, evidenced in the creation of the world. We "believe in God," and therefore we praise him as "the Father Almighty, maker of heaven and earth", so we are here taught to praise him.

1. God made the world, and brought all things into being. (1) How easily: All things were made *by the word of the Lord and by the breath of his mouth.* Christ is the Word, the Spirit is the breath, so that God the Father made the world, as he rules it and redeems it, by his Son and Spirit. *He spoke,* and he commanded (*v.* 9), and that was enough; there needed no more. With men saying and doing

are two things, but it is not so with God. (2) How effectually it was done: *And it stood fast.* What God does he does to purpose; he does it and it stands fast.

2. What he made. He made all things, but notice is here taken, (1) Of *the heavens, and the host of them, v.* 6. The visible heavens, and the sun, moon, and stars, their hosts—the highest heavens, and the angels, their hosts. (2) Of the waters, and the treasures of them, *v.* 7. The earth was at first covered with the water, and *he gathered the waters together on a heap,* that the dry land might appear, yet left them not to continue on a heap, but *laid up the depth in storehouses.*

3. What use is to be made of this (*v.* 8): *Let all the earth fear the Lord,* and *stand in awe of him;* that is, let all the children of men worship him and give glory to him, xcv. 5, 6.

IV. The satisfaction he had of God's sovereignty and dominion, *v.* 10, 11. Come and see with an eye of faith God in the throne, 1. Frustrating the devices of his enemies: *He bringeth the counsel of the heathen to nought.* 2. Fulfilling his own decrees: *The counsel of the Lord standeth for ever.* Through all the revolutions of time God never changed his measures, but in every event, even that which to us is most surprising, the eternal counsel of God is fulfilled.

Verses 12–22

Give to God the glory,

I. Of his common providence towards all the children of men. 1. The children of men are all under his eye, even their hearts are so; and all the motions and operations of their souls, which none know but they themselves, he knows better than they themselves, *v.* 13, 14. He not only beholds them, but he *looks upon them;* he looks narrowly upon them (so the word here used is sometimes rendered). 2. *He fashions their hearts.* He formed the spirit of each man within him. Hence he is called *the Father of spirits.* The artist that made the clock, can account for the motions of every wheel. David uses this argument with application to himself, cxxxix. 1, 14. *He fashions them together* (so some read it); as the wheels of a watch, though of different shapes, sizes, and motions, are yet all put together, to serve one and the same purpose, so the hearts of men and their dispositions, however varying from each other and seeming to contradict one another, are yet all overruled to serve the divine purpose, which is one. All the powers of the creature have a dependence upon him, and are of no account, of no avail at all, without him, *v.* 16, 17. The strength of an army is nothing without God. *The multitude of a host* cannot secure those under whose command they act, unless God make them a security to them. The strength of a giant is nothing without God. *A mighty man,* such as Goliath was, *is not delivered by* his *much strength,* when his day comes to fall. *Let not the strong man* then *glory in his strength,* but let us all strengthen ourselves in the Lord our God. The strength of a horse is nothing without God (*v.* 17): *A horse is a vain thing for safety.* In war horses were then so highly accounted of, and so much depended on, that God forbade the kings of Israel to *multiply horses* (Deut. xvii. 16), lest they should be tempted to trust to them and their confidence should thereby be taken off from God. David houghed the horses of the Syrians (2 Sam. viii. 4); here he houghs all the horses in the world, by pronouncing a horse a vain thing for safety in the day of battle.

II. We are to give God the glory of his special grace. *Blessed is the nation whose God is the Lord.* It is their wisdom that they take the Lord for their God. It is their happiness that they are the people whom God has chosen for his own inheritance, whom he protects and cultivates and improves as a man does his inheritance, Deut. xxxii. 9. God beholds all the sons of men with an eye of observation, but his eye of favour and complacency is upon those that fear him. While those that depend on arms and armies, on chariots and horses, perish in the disappointment of their expectations, God's people, under his protection, are safe, for he shall deliver their soul from death when there seems to be but a step between them and it. If he do not deliver the body from temporal death, yet he will deliver the soul from spiritual and eternal death. Their souls, whatever happens, shall live and praise him, either in this world or in a better. He shall *keep them alive in famine*. When visible means fail, God will find out some way or other to supply them. We must attend the motions of his providence, and accommodate ourselves to them. Our souls must wait for him, *v*. 20. We must rely on God, *hope in his mercy*. This is *trusting in his holy name* (*v*. 21). We must rejoice in God, *v*. 21. Our expectations from God are not to supersede, but to quicken and encourage, our applications to him; and therefore the psalm concludes with a short but comprehensive prayer, "*Let thy mercy, O Lord! be upon us;* let us always have the comfort and benefit of it, not according as we merit from thee, but *according as we hope in thee*, that is, according to the promise which thou hast in thy word given to us and according to the faith which thou hast by thy Spirit and grace wrought in us."

PSALM 34

This psalm was penned upon a particular occasion, as appears by the title. I. He praises God for the experience which he and others had had of his goodness, ver. 1–6. II. He encourages all good people to trust in God, ver. 7–10. III. He gives good counsel to us all, to make conscience of our duty both to God and man, ver. 11–14. IV. To enforce this good counsel he sets before us good and evil, the blessing and the curse, ver. 15–22.

A psalm of David when he changed his behaviour before Abimelech, who drove him away, and he departed.

Verses 1–10

David, being forced to flee from his country, which was made too hot for him by the rage of Saul, sought shelter as near it as he could, in the land of the Philistines. There it was soon discovered who he was, and he was brought before the king, here *Abimelech* (his title); and lest he should be treated as a spy, he feigned himself to be a madman that Achish might dismiss him as a contemptible man, rather than take cognizance of him as a dangerous man. And by this stratagem he escaped the hand that otherwise would have handled him roughly. Even when he was in danger his heart was so fixed, trusting in God, that he penned this excellent psalm, which has as much in it of the marks of a calm sedate spirit as any psalm in all the book; and there is something curious too in the composition, for it is what is called an alphabetical psalm, that is, a psalm in which every verse begins with each letter in its order as it stands in the Hebrew alphabet.

I. David engages and excites himself to praise God. "*I will bless the Lord at all times*, upon all occasions. *His praise shall continually be in my mouth*." He will praise him heartily: "*My soul shall make her boast in the Lord*, in my relation to him, my interest in him, and expectations from him."

II. He calls upon others to join with him herein. He expects they will (*v*. 2): "*The humble shall hear thereof*, both of my deliverance and of my thankfulness, *and be glad*." We cannot make God greater or higher than he is; but if we adore him as infinitely great, and higher than the highest, he is pleased to reckon this magnifying and exalting him. This we must do together. God's praises sound best in concert. David has found him a prayer-hearing God (*v*. 4): "*I sought the Lord*, in my distress, entreated

his favour, begged his help, *and he heard me*, answered my request immediately, *and delivered me from all my fears*, both from the death I feared and from the disquietude and disturbance produced by my fear of it." The former he does by his providence working for us, the latter by his grace working in us, to silence our fears and still the tumult of the spirits. Many besides him have *looked unto God* by faith and prayer, *and have been lightened by it*, *v*. 5. It has wonderfully revived and comforted them; witness Hannah, who, when she had prayed, *went her way, and did eat, and her countenance was no more sad*. These here spoken of had their expectations raised. *Their faces were not ashamed* of their confidence. *This poor man cried*, a single person, mean and inconsiderable, whom no man looked upon with any respect or looked after with any concern; yet he was as welcome to the throne of grace as David or any of his worthies: *The Lord heard him*, took cognizance of his case and of his prayers, *and saved him out of all his troubles*, *v*. 6. *The angel of the Lord*, a guard of angels (so some), *encamps round about those that fear God*, as the life-guard about the prince, *and delivers them*. David would have us to join with him in kind and good thoughts of God (*v*. 8): *O taste and see that the Lord is good!* The goodness of God includes both the beauty and amiableness of his being and the bounty and beneficence of his providence and grace. He would have us join with him in a resolution to seek God and serve him, and continue in his fear (*v*. 9): *O fear the Lord! you his saints. Fear the Lord;* that is, worship him, and make conscience of your duty to him in everything, not fear him and shun him, but fear him and seek him (*v*. 10). To encourage us to fear God and seek him, it is here promised that those that do so, even in this wanting world, *shall want no good thing*. They shall have grace sufficient for the support of the spiritual life (2 Cor. xii. 9; Ps. lxxxiv. 11); and, as to this life, they shall have what is necessary to the support of it from the hand of God: as a Father, he will feed them with food convenient. What further comforts they desire they shall have, as far as Infinite Wisdom sees good, and what they want in one thing shall be made up in another. What God denies them he will give them grace to be content without and then they do not want it, Deut. iii. 26. Paul had all and abounded, because he was content, Phil. iv. 11, 18.

Verses 11–22

David, in this latter part of the psalm, undertakes to teach children. It does not appear that he had now any children of his own, he instructs the children of his people, and therefore calls together a congregation of them (*v*. 11): "*Come, you children, hearken unto me*, leave your play, lay by your toys, and hear what I have to say to you; not only give me the hearing, but observe and obey me." He undertakes to teach them—*the fear of the Lord*, inclusive of all the duties of religion.

I. He supposes that we all aim to be happy (*v*. 12): *What man is he that desireth life?*

II. He prescribes the true and only way to happiness both in this world and that to come, *v*. 13, 14. 1. We must learn to bridle our tongues, and be careful what we say, that we never speak amiss, to God's dishonour or our neighbour's prejudice: *Keep thy tongue from evil speaking, lying, and slandering*. 2. We must be upright and sincere in everything we say, and not double-tongued. 3. We must *depart from evil*, from evil works and evil workers. 4. It is not enough not to do hurt in the world, but we must study to be useful, and live to some purpose. 5. We must *seek peace and pursue it; follow peace with all men*, willing to deny ourselves a great deal, both in honour and interest, for peace' sake.

III. Here are life and death, good and evil, the blessing and the curse, plainly stated before us, that we may choose life and live. See Isa. iii. 10, 11.

1. *Woe to the wicked, it shall be ill with them,* however they may bless themselves in their own way. *The face of the Lord is against those that do evil, v.* 16. *Evil shall slay the wicked, v.* 21. Their death shall be miserable; and so it will certainly be, though they die on a bed of down or on the bed of honour. The *evil* here, which slays the wicked, is the same word, in the singular number, that is used (*v.* 19) for the afflictions of the righteous, to intimate that godly people have many troubles, and yet they do them no hurt, for God will deliver them out of them all; whereas wicked people have fewer troubles, perhaps but one, and yet that one may prove their utter ruin. One trouble with a curse in it kills, but many, with a blessing in them, are harmless, nay, gainful.

2. Yet *say to the righteous, It shall be well with them.* All good people are under God's special favour and protection. *The eyes of the Lord are upon the righteous* (*v.* 15), to direct and guide them, to protect and keep them. Parents that are very fond of a child will not let it be out of their sight; none of God's children are ever from under his eye. They *cry, and the Lord hears them,* and hears them as the tender mother the cry of her sucking child, which another would take no notice of. He not only takes notice of what we say, but is ready to us for our relief (*v.* 18): *He is nigh to those that are of a broken heart, and saves them.* He is near them to good purpose. *He keepeth all his bones;* not only his soul, but his body; not only his body in general, but every bone in it: *Not one of them is broken.* He that has a broken heart shall not have a broken bone; for David himself had found that, when he had a contrite heart, the *broken bones were made to rejoice,* li. 8, 17. *Many are the afflictions of the righteous,* witness David and his afflictions, cxxxii. 1. God has engaged for their deliverance and salvation: *He delivers them out of all their troubles* (*v.* 17, 19); he saves them (*v.* 18), so that, though they may fall into trouble, it shall not be their ruin.

PSALM 35

David, in this psalm, appeals to the righteous Judge of heaven and earth against his enemies that hated and persecuted him. It is supposed that Saul and his party are the persons he means, for with them he had the greatest struggles. I. He complains to God of the injuries they did him. II. He pleads his own innocency, that he never gave them any provocation (ver. 7, 19), but, on the contrary, had studied to oblige them, ver. 12-14. III. He prays to God to protect and deliver him. IV. He prophesies the destruction of his persecutors, ver. 4-6, 8. V. He promises himself that he shall yet see better days (ver. 9, 10), and promises God that he will then attend him with his praises, ver. 18, 28.

A psalm of David.

Verses 1-10

I. David's representation of his case to God, setting forth the restless rage and malice of his persecutors. They persecuted him with an unwearied enmity, *sought after his soul* (*v.* 4), that is, his life, no less would satisfy their bloody minds.

II. His appeal to God concerning his integrity and the justice of his cause. If a fellow-subject had wronged him, he might have appealed to his prince, as St. Paul did to Caesar; but, when his prince wronged him, he appealed to his God, who is prince and Judge of the kings of the earth: *Plead my cause, O Lord! v.* 1.

III. His prayer to God to manifest himself both for him and to him, in this trial. He prays that God would *fight against* his enemies, so as to disable them to hurt him, and defeat their designs against him. If God be our friend, no matter who is our enemy.

IV. His prospect of the destruction of his enemies, which he prays for, not in malice or revenge. In

v. 4-6 Dr. Hammond reads, *They shall be confounded, they shall be turned back.* This may be taken as a prayer for their repentance, for all penitents are put to shame for their sins and turned back from them. *They shall be as chaff before the wind,* so unable will wicked men be to stand before the judgments of God. Their way shall be *dark and slippery, darkness and slipperiness* (so the margin reads it).

V. His prospect of his own deliverance, which, having committed his cause to God, he did not doubt of, *v.* 9, 10. 1. He hoped that he should have the comfort of it: "*My soul shall be joyful,* not in my own ease and safety, but *in the Lord* and in his favour, in his promise and *in his salvation* according to the promise." He promised that then God should have the glory of it (*v.* 10): *All my bones shall say, Lord, who is like unto thee?*

Verses 11-16

Two very wicked things David here lays to the charge of his enemies—perjury and ingratitude.

I. Perjury, *v.* 11. When Saul would have David attainted of treason, in order to his being outlawed, *False witnesses did rise up,* who would swear anything; *they laid to my charge things that I knew not.* This instance of the wrong done to David was typical, and had its accomplishment in the Son of David, against whom false witnesses did arise, Matt. xxvi. 60.

II. Ingratitude. Call a man ungrateful and you can call him no worse. This was the character of David's enemies (*v.* 12): *They rewarded me evil for good.* He had deserved well not only of the public in general, but of those particular persons that were now most bitter against him. Probably it was then well known whom he meant; it may be Saul himself.

1. How tenderly, and with what a cordial affection, he had behaved towards them in their afflictions (*v.* 13, 14). He prayed for them. With his prayers he joined humiliation and self-affliction, both in his diet (he fasted, at least from pleasant bread) and in his dress; he clothed himself with sackcloth, thus expressing his grief, not only for their affliction, but for their sin; for this was the guise and practice of a penitent. His fasting also put an edge upon his praying. He was so intent in his devotions that he had no appetite to meat, nor would allow himself time for eating: *My prayer returned into my own bosom.*

2. How basely and insolently and with what a brutish enmity, and worse than brutish, they had behaved towards him (*v.* 15, 16): *In my adversity they rejoiced. They gnashed upon him with their teeth.* David was the fool in the play, and his disappointment all the table-talk of the hypocritical mockers at feasts; it was the song of the drunkards. Such has often been the hard fate of the best of men. The apostles were made a spectacle to the world.

Verses 17-28

I. David describes the great injustice, malice, and insolence, of his persecutors, pleading this with God as a reason why he should protect him from them. *They hated him without a cause;* nay, for that for which they ought rather to have loved and honoured him. This is quoted, with application to Christ, and is said to be fulfilled in him. John xv. 25, *They hated me without cause. They speak not peace;* if they met him, they had not the good manners to give him the time of the day; like Joseph's brethren, that could not *speak peaceably to him,* Gen. xxxvii. 4. *They opened their mouth wide against me.* They set themselves against all the sober good people that adhered to David (*v.* 20): *They devised deceitful matters,* to trepan and ruin *those that were quiet in the land.* He appeals to God against them, the *God to whom vengeance belongs,* appeals to his knowledge (*v.* 22): *This thou hast seen.* He appeals to God's justice: *Awake to my judgment, even to my cause,* and let it have a hearing at thy bar, *v.* 23. "*Judge me, O Lord my God!* pass sentence upon this appeal, *according to the righteousness* of thy nature and government," *v.* 24.

II. He prays earnestly to God to appear graciously for him and his friends, that God would act for him, and not stand by as a spectator (*v.* 17): "*Lord, how long wilt thou look on? Rescue my soul from the destructions* they are plotting against it; rescue *my darling,* my only one, *from the lions.* My soul is my only one, and therefore the greater is the shame if I neglect it and the greater the loss if I lose it: it is my only one, and therefore ought to be my darling, ought to be carefully protected and provided for. It is my soul that is in danger; Lord, rescue it. He desires that his innocency might be so cleared that they might be ashamed of the calumnies with which they had loaded him, that his interest might be so confirmed that they might be ashamed of their designs against him and their expectations of his ruin, that they might either be brought to that shame which would be a step towards their reformation or that that might be their portion which would be their everlasting misery. Notwithstanding the arts that were used to blacken David, and make him odious, and to frighten people from owning him, there were some that favoured his righteous cause, and he prays for them. *Let them say continually, The Lord be magnified,* by us and others, *who hath pleasure in the prosperity of his servant.*

III. The mercy he hoped to win by prayer he promises to wear with praise: "*I will give thee thanks,* as the author of my deliverance (*v.* 18), *and my tongue shall speak of thy righteousness,* the justice of thy judgments and the equity of all thy dispensations."

PSALM 36

I. The sinfulness of sin, and how mischievous it is, ver. 1–4. II. The goodness of God, and how gracious he is, 1. To all his creatures in general, ver. 5, 6. 2. To his own people in a special manner, ver. 7–9. By this the psalmist is encouraged to pray for all the saints (ver. 10), for himself in particular and his own preservation (ver. 11), and to triumph in the certain fall of his enemies, ver. 12. If, in singing this psalm, our hearts be duly affected with the hatred of sin and satisfaction in God's loving-kindness, we sing it with grace and understanding.

To the chief musician. A psalm of David the servant of the Lord.

Verses 1–4

David, in the title of this psalm, is styled *the servant of the Lord*; why in this, and not in any other, except in xviii (*title*), no reason can be given; but so he was, not only as every good man is God's servant, but as a king, as a prophet.

David, in these verses, describes the wickedness of the wicked, sin in its causes and sin in its colours, in its root and in its branches.

I. Here is the root of bitterness, from which all the wickedness of the wicked comes. "*The transgression of the wicked* (as it is described afterwards, *v.* 3, 4) *saith within my heart* (makes me to conclude within myself) *that there is no fear of God before his eyes:* for, if there were, he would not break the laws of God, and violate his covenants with him, if he had any awe of his majesty or dread of his wrath." *He flattereth himself in his own eyes;* that is, while he goes on in sin he thinks he does wisely and well for himself, and either does not see or will not own the evil and danger of his wicked practices; he calls evil good and good evil; his licentiousness he pretends to be but his just liberty, his fraud passes for his prudence and policy, and his persecuting the people of God, he suggests to himself, is a piece of necessary justice. But the day is coming when the sinner will be undeceived, when *his iniquity shall be found to be hateful.*

II. Here are the cursed branches which spring from this root of bitterness. The sinner defies God. *The words of his mouth are iniquity and deceit,* contrived to do wrong, and yet to cover it with specious and plausible pretences. The sparks of virtue are extinguished, their convictions baffled, their good beginnings come to nothing: They have *left off to be wise and to do good. He devises mischief upon his bed.* Those that leave off to do good begin to do evil. Doing evil themselves, they have no dislike at all of it in others: *He abhors not evil,* but, on the contrary, takes pleasure in it, and is glad to see others as bad as himself.

Verses 5–12

David, having looked round with grief upon the wickedness of the wicked, here looks up with comfort upon the goodness of God.

I. His meditations upon the grace of God.

1. The transcendent perfections of the divine nature. *Thy mercy, O Lord! is in the heavens.* How bad soever the world is, let us never think the worse of God nor of his government; but, let us take occasion, instead of reflecting upon God's purity, as if he countenanced sin, to admire his patience, that he bears so much with those that so impudently provoke him, nay, and causes his sun to shine and his rain to fall upon them. He is a God of inviolable truth: *Thy faithfulness reaches unto the clouds.* God's faithfulness reaches so high that it does not change with the weather, as men's does, for it reaches to the *skies* (so it should be read, as some think), above the clouds, and all the changes of the lower region. He is a God of incontestable justice and equity: *Thy righteousness is like the great mountains,* immovable and inflexible. He is a God of unsearchable wisdom and design: "*Thy judgments are a great deep,* not to be fathomed with the line and plummet of any finite understanding."

2. The extensive care and beneficence of the divine Providence: "*Thou preservest man and beast,* not only protectest them from mischief, but suppliest them with that which is needful for the support of life."

3. The peculiar favour of God to the saints.

(1) Their character, *v.* 7. They are such as are allured by the *excellency of God's loving-kindness to put their trust under the shadow of his wings.*

(2) Their privilege. *They shall be abundantly satisfied with the fatness of thy house,* their wants supplied, their cravings gratified, and their capacities filled. In God all-sufficient they shall have enough, all that which an enlightened enlarged soul can desire or receive. A gracious soul, though still desiring more of God, never desires more than God. *I have all, and abound,* Phil. iv. 18. Their joys shall be constant: *Thou shalt make them drink of the river of thy pleasures.* There are pleasures that are truly divine. "They are *thy pleasures,* not only which come from thee as the giver of them, but which terminate in thee as the matter and centre of them." There is a river of these pleasures, always full, always fresh, always flowing. The pleasures of sense are putrid puddle-water; those of faith are pure and pleasant, *clear as crystal,* Rev. xxii. 1. Having God himself for their felicity they have a fountain of life, from which those rivers of pleasure flow, *v.* 8. In him they have light in perfection, wisdom, knowledge, and joy, all included in this light: *In thy light we shall see light.* "In the knowledge of thee in grace, and the vision of thee in glory, we shall have that which will abundantly suit and satisfy our understandings." That divine light which shines in the scripture, and especially in the face of Christ, the light of the world, has all truth in it. "In communion with thee

now; by the communications of thy grace to us and the return of our devout affections to thee, we have all the good we can desire."

II. We have here David's prayers, intercessions, and holy triumphs, grounded upon these meditations.

1. He intercedes for all saints, *v.* 10. (1) The persons he prays for are those that know God—the upright in heart, that are sincere in their profession of religion, and faithful both to God and man. (2) The blessing he begs for them is God's loving-kindness (that is, the tokens of his favour towards them) and his righteousness (that is, the workings of his grace in them).

2. He prays for himself, that he might be preserved in his integrity and comfort (*v.* 11): "*Let not the foot of pride come against me*, to trip up my heels, and trample upon me; *and let not the hand of the wicked*, which is stretched out against me, prevail to *remove me*, either from my purity and integrity, by any temptation, or from my peace and comfort, by any trouble."

PSALM 37

This psalm is a sermon, and an excellent useful sermon it is, calculated not (as most of the psalms) for our devotion, but for our conversation; there is nothing in it of prayer or praise, but it is all instruction; it is "Maschil—a teaching psalm"; it is an exposition of some of the hardest chapters in the book of Providence, the advancement of the wicked and the disgrace of the righteous. The scope of the prophet in this psalm, I. He forbids us to fret at the prosperity of the wicked in their wicked ways, ver. 1, 7, 8. II. He gives very good reasons why we should not fret at it. 1. Because of the scandalous character of the wicked, ver. 12, 14, 21, 32) notwithstanding their prosperity, and the honourable character of the righteous, ver. 21, 26, 30, 31. 2. Because of the destruction and ruin which the wicked are nigh to (ver. 2, 9, 10, 20, 35, 36, 38) and the salvation and protection which the righteous are sure of from all the malicious designs of the wicked, ver. 13, 15, 17, 28, 33, 39, 40. 3. Because of the particular mercy God has in store for all good people and the favour he shows them, ver. 11, 16, 18, 19, 22–25, 28, 29, 37. III. He prescribes very good remedies against this sin of envying the prosperity of the wicked, and great encouragement to use those remedies, ver. 3–6, 27, 34.

A psalm of David.

Verses 1-6

I. We are here cautioned against discontent at the prosperity and success of evildoers (*v.* 1, 2): *Fret not thyself, neither be thou envious.* We may suppose that David speaks this to himself first. That is preached best, and with most probability of success, to others, which is first preached to ourselves. When we look abroad we see the world full of evildoers and workers of iniquity, that flourish and prosper. When we look within we find ourselves tempted to fret at this, and to be envious. We are apt to fret at God, as if he were unkind to the world and unkind to his church in permitting such men to live, and prosper, and prevail, as they do. We are apt to envy them the liberty they take in getting wealth, and perhaps by unlawful means, and in the indulgence of their lusts, and to wish that we should shake off the restraints of conscience and do so too. When we look forward with an eye of faith we shall see no reason to envy wicked people their prosperity, for their ruin is at the door and they are ripening apace for it, *v.* 2. They flourish, but as the grass, and as the green herb, which nobody envies nor frets at. They will soon wither of themselves. Outward prosperity is a fading thing, and so is the life itself to which it is confined.

II. We are here counselled to live a life of confidence in God, and that will keep us from fretting at the prosperity of evil-doers; if we do well for our own souls, we shall see little reason to envy those that do so ill for theirs. Here are three excellent precepts, and three precious promises,

1. We must make God our hope in the way of duty and then we shall have a comfortable subsistence in this world, *v.* 3. It is required that we *trust in the Lord and do good.* We must not think to trust in God and then live as we list. It is promised that we shall be well provided for in this world: *So shalt thou dwell in the land, and verily thou shalt be fed.* "Thou shalt have a settlement, a quiet settlement, and a maintenance, a comfortable maintenance: *Verily thou shalt be fed.*" Some read it, *Thou shalt be fed by faith,* as the just are said to live by faith, and it is good living, good feeding, upon the promises.

2. We must make God our heart's delight and then we shall have our heart's desire, *v.* 4. We were commanded (*v.* 3) to do good, and then follows this command to delight in God, which is as much a privilege as a duty. And this pleasant duty has a promise annexed to it, *He shall give thee the desires of thy heart.* He has not promised to gratify all the appetites of the body, but to grant all the desires of the heart, all the cravings of the soul. What is the desire of the heart of a good man? It is this, to know, and love, and live to God, to please him and to be pleased in him.

3. We must make God our guide, and submit in everything to his guidance, and then all our affairs, even those that seem most intricate and perplexed, shall be made to issue well, *v.* 5, 6. The duty is very easy; and, if we do it aright, it will make us easy: *Commit thy way unto the Lord; roll thy way upon the Lord* (so the margin reads it), Prov. xvi. 3; Ps. lv. 22. *Cast thy burden upon the Lord,* the burden of thy care, 1 Pet. v. 7. *Reveal thy way unto the Lord* (so the LXX), that is, "By prayer spread thy case, and all thy cares about it, before the Lord, and then trust in him to bring it to a good issue, with a full satisfaction that all is well that God does." We must follow Providence, and not force it, subscribe to Infinite Wisdom and not prescribe. The promise is very sweet. "*He shall bring that to pass,* whatever it is, which thou hast committed to him, if not to thy contrivance, yet to thy content. He will find means to extricate thee out of thy straits, to prevent thy fears, and bring about thy purposes, to thy satisfaction." *He shall bring forth thy righteousness as the light and thy judgment as the noon-day*" (*v.* 6), that is, "he shall make it to appear that thou art an honest man, and that is honour enough." If we take care to keep a good conscience, we may leave it to God to take care of our good name.

Verses 7-20

I. The foregoing precepts inculcated. 1. Let us compose ourselves by believing in God: "*Rest in the Lord, and wait patiently for him*" (*v.* 7), that is, be well reconciled to all he does and acquiesce in it, and be well satisfied that he will still make all to work for good to us, though we know not how or which way. *Be silent to the Lord* (so the word is), not with a sullen, but a submissive silence. 2. Let us not discompose ourselves at what we see in this world: "*Fret not thyself, because of him who prospers in his wicked way,* who, though he is a bad man, yet thrives and grows rich and great in the world. If thy heart begins to rise at it, stroke down thy folly, and *cease from anger* (*v.* 8). *Fret not thyself in any wise to do evil;* do not envy them their prosperity, lest thou be tempted to fall in with them and to take the same evil course that they take to enrich and advance themselves or some desperate course to avoid them and their power."

II. The foregoing reasons repeated.

1. Good people have no reason to envy the worldly prosperity of wicked people. *Evil-doers shall be cut off* by some sudden stroke of divine justice in the midst of their prosperity. The condition of the righteous, even in this life, is every way better and more desirable than that of the wicked, *v.* 16. A godly man's little is really better than a wicked man's much, see Prov. xv. 16, 17; xiv 8; xxviii. 6. It comes from

a better hand, from a hand of special love and not merely from a hand of common providence. *Those that wait upon the Lord*, as dependents on him, expectants from him, and suppliants to him, *shall inherit the earth*, as a token of his present favour to them and an earnest of better things intended for them in the other world. *The meek shall inherit the earth.* Our Saviour has made this a gospel promise, and a confirmation of the blessing he pronounced on the meek, Matt. v. 5. They *shall delight themselves in the abundance of peace*, v. 11. That peace which the world cannot give (John xiv. 27), they shall delight themselves in. God *knows their days*, v. 18. He takes particular notice of them, of all they do and of all that happens to them. He keeps account of the days of their service, and not one day's work shall go unrewarded. *Their inheritance shall be for ever.* Their time on earth is reckoned by days, which will soon be numbered. God takes cognizance of them, and gives them the blessings of every day in its day; but it was never intended that their inheritance should be confined within the limits of those days. No, that must be the portion of an immortal soul, and therefore must last as long as that lasts, and will run parallel with the longest line of eternity itself: *Their inheritance shall be for ever;* not their inheritance in the earth, but that incorruptible indefeasible one which is laid up for them in heaven.

2. Good people have no reason to fret at the occasional success of the designs of the wicked against the just.

(1) Their plots will be their shame, v. 12, 13. It is true *the wicked plotteth against the just.* They are proud and insolent, but God despises all their attempts as vain and ineffectual. Men have their day now. God's day will give a decisive judgment.

(2) Their attempts will be their destruction, v. 14, 15. They *have drawn the sword, and bent the bow;* and all these military preparations are made against the helpless, *the poor and needy* and against the guiltless, *such as are of upright conversation.* How justly their malice recoils upon themselves: *Their sword shall turn into their own heart.*

(3) Those that are not suddenly cut off shall yet be so disabled for doing any further mischief: *Their bows shall be broken* (v. 15); the instruments of their cruelty shall fail them and *their arms shall be broken*, so that they shall not be able to go on with their enterprises, v. 17.

Verses 21–33

I. What is required of us as the way to our happiness. If we would be blessed of God, 1. We must make conscience of giving everybody his own; for *the wicked borrows and pays not again*, v. 21. It is the first thing which the Lord our God requires of us, that we do justly, and render to all their due. 2. We must be ready to all acts of charity and beneficence; for, as it is an instance of God's goodness to the righteous that he puts it into the power of his hand to be kind and to do good, so it is an instance of the goodness of the righteous man that he has a heart proportionable to his estate: *He shows mercy, and gives*, v. 21. *He is ever merciful and lends*, and sometimes there is as true charity in lending as in giving. 3. We must leave our sins, and engage in the practice of serious godliness (v. 27): *Depart from evil and do good.* 4. We must abound in good discourse, and with our tongues must glorify God and edify others. It is part of the character of a righteous man (v. 30) that his *mouth speaketh wisdom.* Out of the abundance of a good heart will the mouth speak that which is good and to the use of edifying. 5. We must have our wills brought into an entire subjection to the will and word of God (v. 31): *The law of God*, of his God, *is in his heart*; and in vain do we pretend that God is

our God if we do not receive his law into our hearts and resign ourselves to the government of it.

II. What is assured to us, as instances of our happiness and comfort, upon these conditions.

1. That we shall have the blessing of God, and that blessing shall be the spring, and sweetness, and security of all our temporal comforts and enjoyments (v. 22): *Such as are blessed of God*, as all the righteous are, with a Father's blessing, by virtue of that *shall inherit the earth*, or *the land* (for so the same word is translated, v. 29), the land of Canaan, that glory of all lands.

2. That God will direct and dispose of our actions and affairs so as may be most for his glory (v. 23): *The steps of a good man are ordered by the Lord.* God orders the steps of a good man; not only his way in general, by his written word, but his particular steps, by the whispers of conscience, saying, *This is the way, walk in it.* He does not always show him his way at a distance, but leads him step by step, as children are led, and so keeps him in a continual dependence upon his guidance.

3. That God will keep us from being ruined by our falls either into sin or into trouble (v. 24): *Though he fall, he shall not be utterly cast down.* A good man may be overtaken in a fault, but the grace of God shall recover him to repentance, so that he shall not be utterly cast down. Though he may, for a time, lose the joys of God's salvation, yet they shall be restored to him; for God shall uphold him with his hand, uphold him with his free Spirit. The root shall be kept alive, though the leaf wither; and there will come a spring after the winter.

4. That we shall not want the necessary supports of this life (v. 25): "*I have been young and now am old*, and, among all the changes I have seen in men's outward condition and the observations I have made upon them, *I never saw the righteous forsaken* of God and man." There are very few instances of good men, or their families, that are reduced to such extreme poverty as many wicked people bring themselves to by their wickedness. Some make this promise relate especially to those that are charitable and liberal to the poor, and to intimate that David never observed any that brought themselves to poverty by their charity.

5. That God will not desert us, but graciously protect us in our difficulties and straits (v. 28): *The Lord loves judgment;* he delights in doing justice himself and he delights in those that do justice.

6. That we shall have a comfortable settlement in this world, and in a better when we leave this. That we shall *dwell for evermore* (v. 27), and not be *cut off* as the *seed of the wicked*, v. 28. That we *shall inherit the land* which the Lord our God gives us *and dwell therein for ever*, v. 29. But on this earth there is no dwelling for ever, no continuing city; it is in heaven only, that city which has foundations, that the righteous shall dwell for ever; that will be their everlasting habitation.

7. That we shall not become a prey to our adversaries who seek our ruin, v. 32, 33.

Verses 34–40

The psalmist's conclusion of this sermon.

I. The duty here pressed upon us is still the same (v. 34): *Wait on the Lord and keep his way.* If we make conscience of *keeping God's way*, we may with cheerfulness wait on him and commit to him our way; and we shall find him a good Master both to his working servants and to his waiting servants.

II. The reasons to enforce this duty are much the same too, taken from the certain destruction of the wicked and the certain salvation of the righteous.

1. The misery of the wicked at last, however they may prosper awhile: *The end of the wicked shall be*

cut off (v. 38); and that cannot be well that will undoubtedly end so ill. *The transgressors shall be destroyed together*, v. 38. In this world God singles out here one sinner and there another, out of many, to be made an example *in terrorem*—as a warning; but in the day of judgment there will be a general destruction of all the transgressors, and not one shall escape.

2. The blessedness of the righteous, at last. Those that keep God's way may be assured that in due time he will *exalt them to inherit the land* (v. 34); he will advance them to a place in the heavenly mansions, to dignity, and honour, and true wealth, in the New Jerusalem, to inherit that good land, that land of promise, of which Canaan was a type; he will exalt them above all contempt and danger. Let all people *mark the perfect man, and behold the upright*; take notice of him to observe what comes of him, and you will find that *the end of that man is peace. The salvation of the righteous is of the Lord;* it will be the Lord's doing. He shall *save them*, not only keep them safe, but make them happy, *because they trust in him.*

PSALM 38

This is one of the penitential psalms; it is full of grief and complaint, from the beginning to the end. David's sins and his afflictions are the cause of his grief and the matter of his complaints. He complains, I. Of God's displeasure, and of his own sin which provoked God against him, ver. 1–5. II. Of his bodily sickness, ver. 6–10. III. Of the unkindness of his friends, ver. 11. IV. Of the injuries which his enemies did him, pleading his good conduct towards them, yet confessing his sins against God, ver. 12–20. Lastly, he concludes the psalm with earnest prayers to God for his gracious presence and help, ver. 21, 22.

A psalm of David to bring to remembrance.

Verses 1–11

The title of this psalm is a psalm *to bring to remembrance;* the 70th psalm, which was likewise penned in a day of affliction, is so entitled.

I. He deprecates the wrath of God and his displeasure in his affliction (v. 1): *O Lord! rebuke me not in thy wrath.* However God rebukes and chastens us, it may not be in wrath and displeasure, for that will be wormwood and gall in the affliction and misery. Those that would escape the wrath of God must pray against that more than any outward affliction, and be content to bear any outward affliction while it comes from, and consists with, the love of God.

II. He bitterly laments the impressions of God's displeasure upon his soul (v. 2): *Thy arrows stick fast in me.* He complains of God's wrath as that which inflicted the bodily distemper he was under (v. 3): *There is no soundness in my flesh because of thy anger.* The bitterness of it, infused in his mind, affected his body; but that was not the worst: it caused the disquietude of his heart, by reason of which he forgot the courage of a soldier, the dignity of a prince, and all the cheerfulness of the sweet psalmist of Israel, and roared terribly, v. 8.

III. He acknowledges his sin to be the cause of all his troubles, and groans more under the load of guilt than any other load, v. 3. He complains that his flesh had no soundness. "It is *because of thy anger;* that kindles the fire which burns so fiercely"; but, in the next words, he justifies God herein, and takes all the blame upon himself: "It is *because of my sin.* I have deserved it, and so have brought it upon myself. My own iniquities do correct me." It is sin therefore that this good man complains most of, a burden, a heavy burden (v. 4): "*My iniquities have gone over my head*, as proud waters over a man that is sinking and drowning, or as a heavy burden upon my head, pressing me down more than I am able to bear or to bear up under." It keeps men from soaring upward and pressing forward. "My

wounds stink and are corrupt (as wounds in the body rankle, and fester, and grow foul, for want of being dressed and looked after), and it is through my own *foolishness.*" Sins are wounds (Gen. iv. 23), painful mortal wounds. A slight sore, neglected, may prove of fatal consequence, and so may a slight sin slighted and left unrepented of.

IV. He bemoans himself because of his afflictions, and gives ease to his grief by giving vent to it and pouring out his complaint before the Lord.

1. He was troubled in mind, his conscience was pained, and he had no rest in his own spirit; and a wounded spirit who can bear? He was *troubled*, or distorted, *bowed down greatly*, and went *mourning all the day long*, v. 6.

2. He was sick and weak in body; his loins were filled with a loathsome disease, some swelling, or ulcer, or inflammation (some think a plague-sore, such as Hezekiah's boil), and there was *no soundness in his flesh*, but, like Job, he was all over distempered. Sickness will tame the strongest body and the stoutest spirit. David was famed for his courage and great exploits; and yet, when God contended with him by bodily sickness and the impressions of his wrath upon his mind, his heart fails him, and he becomes weak as water.

3. His friends were unkind to him (v. 11): *My lovers* (such as had been merry with him in the day of his mirth) now *stand aloof from my sore.* Even *his kinsmen*, that were bound to him by blood and alliance, *stood afar off.*

V. In the midst of his complaints, he comforts himself with the cognizance God graciously took both of his griefs and of his prayers (v. 9): "*Lord, all my desire is before thee.* Thou knowest what I want and what I would have: *My groaning is not hidden from thee.* Thou knowest the burdens I groan under and the blessings I groan after."

Verses 12–22

I. David complains of the power and malice of his enemies, who, it should seem, not only took occasion from the weakness of his body and the trouble of his mind to insult over him, but took advantage thence to do him a mischief. He has a great deal to say against them, which he humbly offers as a reason why God should appear for him, as xxv. 19, *Consider my enemies.* "They are very subtle and politic. They *lay snares*, they *imagine deceits*, and herein they are restless and unwearied: they do it *all the day long.* They are very insolent and abusive: *When my foot slips*, when I make any mistake, or take a false step, they magnify themselves against me; they are pleased with it. They are not only unjust, but very ungrateful: They *hate me wrongfully*, v. 19. I never did them any ill turn; *they render evil for good*, v. 20. Many a kindness I have done them, for which I might have expected a return of kindness; but *for my love they are my adversaries*, cix. 4. "*They are my adversaries* merely *because I follow the thing that" good is.* They hated him, not only for his kindness to them, but for his devotion and obedience to God; they hated him because they hated God and all that bear his image.

II. He reflects, with comfort, upon his own peaceable and pious behaviour under all the injuries and indignities that were done him. If still we hold fast our integrity and our peace, who can hurt us? This David did here. He kept his temper, and was not ruffled nor discomposed by any of the mischievous things that were said or done against him (v. 13, 14): *I, as a deaf man, heard not.* Herein David was a type of Christ, who was as a sheep dumb before the shearer, and, when he was reviled, reviled not again; and both are examples to us not to render railing for railing. He kept close to his God by faith and prayer.

His friends, that should have owned him, and stood by him, and appeared as witnesses for him, withdrew from him, *v.* 10. But God is a friend that will never fail us if we hope in him. *Thou shalt answer, Lord, for me.*

III. He here bewails his own follies and infirmities. *I am ready to halt, v.* 17. This will best be explained by a reflection like this which the psalmist made upon himself in a similar case (lxxiii. 2): *My feet were almost gone, when I saw the prosperity of the wicked.* So here: *I was ready to halt*, ready to say, *I have cleansed my hands in vain.* Good men, by setting their sorrow continually before them, have been ready to halt, who, by setting God always before them, have kept their standing. Though before men he could justify himself, before God he will judge and condemn himself (*v.* 18): "*I will declare my iniquity*, and not cover it; *I will be sorry for my sin*, and not make a light matter of it"; and this helped to make him silent under the rebukes of Providence and the reproaches of men.

IV. He concludes with very earnest prayers to God for his gracious presence (*v.* 21, 22): "*Forsake me not, O Lord!* though my friends forsake me, and though I deserve to be forsaken by thee. Be not far from me, as my unbelieving heart is ready to fear thou art."

PSALM 39

David seems to have been in a great strait when he penned this psalm, for it is with some difficulty that he composes his spirit himself to take that good counsel which he had given to others (xxxvii) to rest in the Lord, and wait patiently for him, without fretting. I. He relates the struggle that was in his breast between grace and corruption, between passion and patience, ver. 1–3. II. He meditates upon the doctrine of man's frailty and mortality, and prays to God to instruct him in it, ver. 4–6. III. He applies to God for the pardon of his sins, the removal of his afflictions, and the lengthening out of his life till he was ready for death, ver. 7–13.

To the chief musician, *even* to Jeduthun. A psalm of David.

Verses 1–6

David here recollects, and leaves upon record, the workings of his heart under his afflictions.

I. He remembered the covenants he had made with God. When at any time we are tempted to sin we must call to mind the solemn vows we have made against the particular sin we are upon the brink of.

1. He remembers that he had resolved to be circumspect in his walking (*v.* 1): *I said, I will take heed to my ways.* Having resolved to take heed to our ways, we must, upon all occasions, remind ourselves of that resolution.

2. He remembers that he had in particular covenanted against tongue-sins. It is not so easy as we could wish not to sin in thought; but, if an evil thought should arise in his mind, he would lay his hand upon his mouth, and suppress it, that it should go no further. "*I will keep a bridle*, or muzzle, *upon my mouth.*" Watchfulness in the habit is the bridle upon the head; watchfulness in the act and exercise is the hand upon the bridle. He would keep a muzzle upon it, as upon an unruly dog that is fierce and does mischief; by particular steadfast resolution corruption is restrained from breaking out at the lips, and so is muzzled. When he was in company with the wicked he would take heed of saying any thing that might harden them or give occasion to them to blaspheme.

II. Pursuant to these covenants he made a shift with much ado to bridle his tongue (*v.* 2): *I was dumb with silence; I held my peace even from good.* But what shall we say of his keeping silence *even from good*? I rather think it was his weakness; because he might not say anything, he would say nothing, but ran into an extreme.

III. The less he spoke the more he thought and the more warmly. Binding the distempered part did but draw the humour to it: *My sorrow was stirred, my heart was hot within me, v.* 3. He could bridle his tongue but he could not keep his passion under. Note, Those that are of a fretful discontented spirit ought not to pore much, for, while they suffer their thoughts to dwell upon the causes of the calamity, the fire of their discontent is fed with fuel and burns the more furiously. If therefore we would prevent the mischief of ungoverned passions, we must redress the grievance of ungoverned thoughts.

IV. When he did speak, at last, it was to the purpose: *At the last I spoke with my tongue.* I rather take it to be, not the breach of his good purpose, but the reformation of his mistake in carrying it too far; he had kept silence from good, but now he would so keep silence no longer.

1. He prays to God to make him sensible of the shortness and uncertainty of life and the near approach of death (*v.* 4): *Lord, make me to know my end and the measure of my days.* He does not mean, "Lord, let me know how long I shall live and when I shall die." But, *Lord, make me to know my end*, means, "Lord, give me wisdom and grace to consider it (Deut. xxxii. 29) and to improve what I know concerning it. Lord, make me to consider the end of my life." It is a final period to our state of probation. To the wicked man it is the end of all joys; to a godly man it is the end of all griefs. When we look upon death as a thing at a distance we are tempted to adjourn the necessary preparations for it; but, when we consider how short life is, we shall see ourselves concerned to do what our hand finds to do, not only with all our might, but with all possible expedition.

2. He meditates upon the brevity and vanity of life, pleading them with God for relief under the burdens of life and pleading them with himself for his quickening to the business of life. *Behold, thou hast made my days as a hand-breadth*, the breadth of four fingers, a certain dimension, a small one, and the measure whereof we have always about us, always before our eyes. We need no skill in arithmetic wherewith to compute the number of them. No; we have the standard of them at our fingers' end, and it is but one hand-breadth in all. Our time is short, and God has made it so; for *the number of our months is with him.* It is short, and he knows it to be so: It *is as nothing before thee.* All time is nothing to God's eternity, much less our share of time. Men's life on earth is vain, and therefore it is wisdom to make sure of a better life. *All man is all vanity* (so it may be read); everything about him is uncertain; nothing is substantial and durable but what relates to the new man. *Selah* is annexed, as a note commanding observation. "Stop here, and pause awhile, that you may take time to consider and apply this truth, that every man is vanity." For the proof of the vanity of man, as mortal, he here mentions three things, *v.* 6, *First*, The vanity of our joys and honours: *Surely every man walks* (even when he walks in state, when he walks in pleasure) in a shadow, in an image, *in a vain show. Secondly*, The vanity of our griefs and fears. *Surely they are disquieted in vain.* The occasions of our trouble are often the creatures of our own fancy and they are always fruitless. *Thirdly*, The vanity of our cares and toils. Man takes a great deal of pains to *heap up riches*, and they are but like heaps of manure in the furrows of the field, good for nothing unless they be spread.

Verses 7–13

The psalmist, in these verses, turns his eyes and heart heaven-ward. When there is no solid satisfaction to be had in the creature it is to be found in God, and in communion with him; and to him we should be driven by our disappointments in the world.

I. His dependence on God, *v.* 7. He despairs of a happiness in the things of the world, and disclaims all expectations from it: "*Now, Lord, what wait I for?* Even nothing from the things of sense and time; I have nothing to wish for, nothing to hope for, from this earth." We cannot reckon upon constant health and prosperity, nor upon comfort in any relation; for it is all as uncertain as our continuance here. He takes hold of happiness and satisfaction in God: *My hope is in thee.*

II. His submission to God, and his cheerful acquiescence in his holy will, *v.* 9. "*Because thou didst it;* it did not come to pass by chance, but according to thy appointment." Of every event we may say, "This is the finger of God; it is the Lord's doing," whoever were the instruments.

III. His desire towards God, and the prayers he puts up to him.

1. For the pardoning of his sin and the preventing of his shame, *v.* 8. Before he prays (*v.* 10), *Remove thy stroke from me*, he prays (*v.* 8), "*Deliver me from all my offences*, from the guilt I have contracted, the punishment I have deserved." He pleads, *Make me not a reproach to the foolish.* Wicked people are foolish people; and they then show their folly most when they think to show their wit, by scoffing at God's people.

2. For the removal of his affliction, that he might speedily be eased of his present burdens (*v.* 10): *Remove thy stroke away from me. I am consumed by the blow of thy hand.* His sickness prevailed to such a degree that his spirits failed, his strength was wasted, and his body emaciated. Our ways and our doings procure the trouble to ourselves, and we are beaten with a rod of our own making. It is the yoke of our transgressions, though it be *bound with his hand*, Lam. i. 14. God's rebukes make man's *beauty to consume away like a moth.* Some make the moth to represent man, who is as easily crushed as a moth with the touch of a finger, Job iv. 19. Others make it to represent the divine rebukes, which silently and insensibly waste and consume us, as the moth does the garment. He pleads the good impressions made upon him by his affliction. He hoped that the end was accomplished for which it was sent, and that therefore it would be removed in mercy. It had set him a-weeping, and he hoped God would take notice of that. *Lord, hold not thy peace at my tears, v.* 12. He that does not willingly afflict and grieve the children of men, much less his own children, will not hold his peace at their tears, but will either speak deliverance for them or in the meantime speak comfort to them. It had set him a-praying; and afflictions are sent to stir up prayer. It had helped to wean him from the world and to take his affections off from it. Now he began, more than ever, to look upon himself as *a stranger and sojourner* here, like all his fathers, not at home in this world, but travelling through it to another, to a better, and would never reckon himself at home till he came to heaven.

3. He prays for a reprieve yet a little longer (*v.* 13): "*O spare me*, ease me, raise me up from this illness, that I may recover strength both in body and mind, that I may get into a more calm and composed frame of spirit, and may be better prepared for another world, *before I go hence* by death, *and* shall *be no more* in this world." *Let my soul live, and it shall praise thee.*

PSALM 40

It should seem David penned this psalm upon occasion of his deliverance, by the power and goodness of God, from some great and pressing trouble, by which he was in danger of being overwhelmed; probably it was some trouble of mind arising from a sense of sin and of God's displeasure against him for it. In this psalm, I. David records God's favour to him in delivering him out of his deep distress, with thankfulness to his praise, ver. 1-5.

II. Thence he takes occasion to speak of the work of our redemption by Christ, ver. 6-10. III. That gives him encouragement to pray to God for mercy and grace both for himself and for his friends, ver. 11-17.

To the chief musician. A psalm of David.

Verses 1-5

I. The great distress and trouble that the psalmist had been in.

II. His humble attendance upon God and his believing expectations from him in those depths: *I waited patiently for the Lord, v.* 1. *Waiting, I waited.* He expected relief from no other than from God; the same hand that tears must heal, that smites must bind up (Hos. vi. 1), or it will never be done. But he waited patiently, which intimates that the relief did not come quickly; yet he doubted not but it would come, and resolved to continue believing, and hoping, and praying, till it did come. Now this is very applicable to Christ. His agony, both in the garden and on the cross, was the same continued, and it was a horrible pit and miry clay. Then was his soul troubled and exceedingly sorrowful; but then he prayed, *Father, glorify thy name; Father, save me;* then he kept hold of his relation to his Father, "My God, my God," and thus waited patiently for him.

III. His comfortable experience of God's goodness to him in his distress, which he records for the honour of God and his own and others' encouragement. *He inclined unto me and heard my cry.* Those that have been under the prevalency of a religious melancholy, and by the grace of God have been relieved, may apply this very feelingly to themselves; they are brought up out of a horrible pit. The mercy is completed by the setting of their feet upon a rock, where they find firm footing, are as much elevated with the hopes of heaven as they were before cast down with the fears of hell. "*He has put a new song in my mouth;* he has given me cause to rejoice and a heart to rejoice." He was brought, as it were, into a new world, and that filled his mouth with a new song, *even praise to our God.*

IV. David's experience would be an encouragement to many to hope in God, and, for that end, he leaves it here upon record: *Many shall see, and fear, and trust in the Lord.* There is a holy reverent fear of God, which is not only consistent with, but the foundation of our hope in him. They shall not fear him and shun him, but fear him and trust in him in their greatest straits, not doubting but to find him as able and ready to help as David did in his distress. The psalmist invites others to make God their hope, as he did, by pronouncing those happy that do so (*v.* 4): "*Blessed is the man that makes the Lord his trust, and respects not the proud*, does not do as those that trust in themselves, nor depends upon those who proudly encourage others to trust in them; for both the one and the other turn aside to lies, as indeed all those do that turn aside from God." This is applicable, particularly, to our faith in Christ. Blessed are those that trust in him, and in his righteousness alone. The joyful sense he had of this mercy led him to observe, with thankfulness, the many other favours he had received from God, *v.* 5. "*Many, O Lord my God, are thy wonderful works which thou hast done*, both for me and others; this is but one of many." All his wonderful works are the product of his thoughts to us-ward. They are the projects of infinite wisdom, the designs of everlasting love (1 Cor. ii. 7, Jer. xxxi. 3), *thoughts of good and not of evil*, Jer. xxix. 11. How the links of the golden chain are joined, is a mystery to us, and what we shall not be able to account for till the veil be rent and the mystery of God finished. When we have said the most we can of the wonders of divine love to us we must conclude with an *et cetera*—and such like, and adore the depth, despairing to find the bottom.

Verses 6–10

The psalmist, being struck with amazement at the wonderful works that God had done for his people, is strangely carried out here to foretell that work of wonder which excels all the rest and is the foundation and fountain of all, that of our redemption by our Lord Jesus Christ. This paragraph is quoted by the apostle (Heb. x. 5, &c.) and applied to Christ and his undertaking for us.

I. The utter insufficiency of the legal sacrifices to atone for sin in order to our peace with God and our happiness in him: *Sacrifice and offering thou didst not desire;* thou wouldst not have the Redeemer to offer them. Something he must have to offer, but not these (Heb. viii. 3). Even while the law concerning them was in full force it might be said, God did not desire them, nor accept them, for their own sake. They could not take away the guilt of sin by satisfying God's justice. The life of a sheep, which is so much inferior in value to that of a man (Matt. xii. 12), could not pretend to be an equivalent, much less an expedient to preserve the honour of God's government and laws and repair the injury done to that honour by the sin of man. They could not take away the terror of sin by pacifying the conscience, nor the power of sin by sanctifying the nature; it was impossible, Heb. ix. 9; x. 1–4. What there was in them that was valuable resulted from their reference to Jesus Christ, of whom they were types—shadows indeed, but shadows of good things to come, and trials of the faith and obedience of God's people, of their obedience to the law and their faith in the gospel. But the substance must come, which is Christ, who must bring that glory to God and that grace to man which it was impossible those sacrifices should ever do.

II. The designation of our Lord Jesus to the work and office of Mediator: *My ears hast thou opened.* God the Father disposed him to the undertaking (Isa. l. 5, 6) and then obliged him to go through with it. *My ear hast thou digged.* It is supposed to allude to the law and custom of binding servants to serve for ever by boring their ear to the doorpost; see Exod. xxi. 6.

III. His own voluntary consent to this undertaking: "*Then said I, Lo, I come;* then, when sacrifice and offering would not do, rather than the work should be undone, I said, Lo, I come, to enter the lists with the powers of darkness, and to advance the interests of God's glory and kingdom." He freely offered himself to this service. He firmly obliged himself to it: "I come; I promise to come in the fulness of time." He frankly owned himself engaged: He said, *Lo, I come,* said it all along to the Old Testament saints, who therefore knew him by the title of ὁ ἐρχόμενος—*He that should come.*

IV. The reason why he came, in pursuance of his undertaking—because *in the volume of the book it was written of him,* 1. In the close rolls of the divine decree and counsel; there it was written that his ear was opened, and he said, *Lo, I come;* there the covenant of redemption was recorded.

V. The pleasure he took in his undertaking. Having freely offered himself to it, he did not fail, nor was discouraged, but proceeded with all possible satisfaction to himself (*v.* 8, 9): *I delight to do thy will, O my God!*

VI. The publication of the gospel to the children of men, even *in the great congregation, v.* 9, 10. The same that as a priest wrought out redemption for us, as a prophet, by his own preaching first, then by his apostles, and still by his word and Spirit, makes it known to us. The *great salvation began to be spoken by the Lord,* Heb. ii. 3. What is preached is *righteousness* (*v.* 9), God's righteousness (*v.* 10), God's *faithfulness* to his promise, God's *loving-kindness* and his *truth,* his mercy according to his word. It is

preached—*to the congregation, v.* 9, and again *v.* 10. The gospel was preached both to Jews and Gentiles, to great congregations of both. It is preached—freely and openly: *I have not refrained my lips; I have not hid it; I have not concealed it.*

Verses 11–17

The psalmist, having meditated upon the work of redemption, and spoken of it in the person of the Messiah, now speaks in his own person.

I. This may encourage us to pray for the mercy of God, and to put ourselves under the protection of that mercy, *v.* 11. "Lord, thou hast not spared thy Son, nor withheld him; *withhold not thou thy tender mercies* then, which thou hast laid up for us in him; for wilt thou not *with him also freely give us all things?* Rom. viii. 32. *Let thy lovingkindness and thy truth continually preserve me.*"

II. This may encourage us in reference to the guilt of sin, that Jesus Christ has done that towards our discharge from it which sacrifice and offering could not do. The psalmist saw his iniquities to be evils, the worst of evils; he saw that they *compassed him about more than the hairs of his head.* The sight of sin so oppressed him that he could not hold up his head—*I am not able to look up;* much less could he keep up his heart—*therefore my heart fails me.* With what a holy passion does he cry out, "*Be pleased, O Lord! to deliver me* (*v.* 13). In a case of this nature, where the bliss of an immortal soul is concerned, delays are dangerous; therefore, *O Lord! make haste to help me.*"

III. This may encourage us to hope for victory over our spiritual enemies that seek after our souls to destroy them (*v.* 14). If Christ has triumphed over them, we, through him, shall be more than conquerors. In the belief of this we may pray, with humble boldness, *Let them be ashamed and confounded together,* and *driven backward, v.* 14. *Let them be desolate, v.* 15. When a child of God is brought into that horrible pit, and the miry clay, Satan cries *Aha! aha!* thinking he has gained his point; but he shall rage when he sees the brand plucked out of the fire, and shall be *desolate, for a reward of his shame.*

IV. This may encourage all that seek God, and love his salvation, to rejoice in him and to praise him, *v.* 16.

V. This may encourage the saints, in distress and affliction, to trust in God and comfort themselves in him, *v.* 17. David himself was one of these: *I am poor and needy, yet the Lord thinketh upon me* in and through the Mediator, by whom we are made accepted.

PSALM 41

God's kindness and truth have often been the support and comfort of the saints when they have had experience of men's unkindness and treachery. David found his enemies very barbarous, but his God very gracious. I. He here comforts himself in his communion with God under his sickness, by faith receiving and laying hold of God's promises (ver. 1–3) and lifting up his heart in prayer, ver. 4. II. He represents the malice of his enemies against him, ver. 5–9. III. He leaves his case with God (ver. 10–12), and so the psalm concludes with a doxology, ver. 13. Is any afflicted with sickness? let him sing the beginning of this psalm. Is any persecuted by enemies? let him sing the latter end of it.

To the chief musician. A psalm of David.

Verses 1–4

I. God's promises of succour and comfort to those that consider the poor;

1. David makes mention of these with application either, (1) To his friends, who were kind to him, *Blessed is he that considers* poor David. The provocations which his enemies gave him did but endear his friends so much the more to him. Or, (2) To himself. He had considered the poor and had provided for their relief, and therefore was sure God

would, according to his promise, strengthen and comfort him in his sickness.

2. We must regard them more generally with application to ourselves. *Blessed are the merciful, for they shall obtain mercy.* The mercy which is required of us is to consider the poor or afflicted, whether in mind, body, or estate. We must take notice of their affliction and enquire into their state, must sympathise with them and judge charitably concerning them. He that considers the poor *shall be blessed upon the earth.* This branch of godliness, as much as any, has the promise of the life that now is and is usually recompensed with temporal blessings. Those who thus distinguish themselves from those that have hard hearts God will distinguish from those that have hard usage. *"They shall be preserved and kept alive,"* when the arrows of death fly thickly round about them." The goodwill of a God that loves us is sufficient to secure us from the ill-will of all that hate us, men and devils; and that goodwill we may promise ourselves if we have considered the poor and helped to relieve and rescue them. In sickness (*v.* 3): *The Lord will strengthen him,* both in body and mind, *upon the bed of languishing,* on which he had lain sick, and *he will make all his bed*—a very condescending expression, alluding to the care of those that nurse and tend sick people, especially of mothers for their children when they are sick, which is to make their beds easy for them. He will make all his bed from head to foot, so that no part shall be uneasy; he will *turn* his bed (so the word is), to shake it up and make it very easy; or he will turn it into a bed of health. He has not promised that they shall never be sick, nor that their sickness shall not be unto death; but he has promised to enable them to bear their affliction with patience, and cheerfully to wait the issue. The soul shall by his grace be made to dwell at ease when the body lies in pain.

II. David's prayer, directed and encouraged by these promises (*v.* 4): *I said, Heal my soul.* Sin is the sickness of the soul; pardoning mercy heals it; renewing grace heals it; and this spiritual healing we should be more earnest for than for bodily health.

Verses 5–13

David often complains of the insolent conduct of his enemies towards him when he was sick. *My enemies speak evil of me,* designing thereby to grieve his spirit, to ruin his reputation.

I. His enemies longed for his death: *When shall he die, and his name perish* with him? They envied him his name, and the honour he had won, and doubted not but, if he were dead, that would be laid in the dust with him; but his name lives and flourishes to this day in the sacred writings, and will to the end of time; for *the memory of the just is,* and shall be, *blessed.* They picked up everything they could to reproach him with (*v.* 6): *"If he come to see me"* (as it has always been reckoned a piece of neighbourly kindness to visit the sick) *"he speaks vanity;* that is, he pretends friendship, but it is all flattery and falsehood." We complain, and justly, of the want of sincerity in our days, and that there is scarcely any true friendship to be found among men; but it seems, by this, that the former days were no better than these. They make invidious remarks upon everything he said or did: *His heart gathereth iniquity to itself,* puts ill constructions upon everything. If he prayed, or gave them good counsel, they would banter it, and call it *canting;* if he kept silence from good, when the wicked were before him, they would say that he had forgotten his religion now that he was sick. They *whispered together against him* (*v.* 7), speaking that secretly in one another's ears which they could not for shame speak out, and which, if they did, they knew would be confuted. Whisperers and backbiters

are put together among the worst of sinners, Rom. i. 29, 30. "The disease he is now under will certainly make an end of him; for it is the punishment of some great enormous crime, which he will not be brought to repent of, and proves him, however he has appeared, a son of Belial." There was one particularly in whom he had reposed a great deal of confidence, that took part with his enemies (*v.* 9): *My own familiar friend;* probably he means Ahithophel, who had been his bosom-friend and prime-minister of state, in whom he trusted, and who *did eat of his bread,* that is, with whom he had been very intimate. Yet this base and treacherous confidant of David's forgot all the eaten bread, and *lifted up his heel against him* that had lifted up his head. Let us not think it strange if we receive abuses from such: David did, and the Son of David; our Saviour himself so expounds this, and *therefore* gave Judas the sop, that the scripture might be fulfilled, *He that eats bread with me has lifted up his heel against me,* John xiii. 18, 26. Nay, have not we ourselves behaved thus perfidiously and disingenuously towards God? We *eat of his bread* daily, and yet *lift up the heel against him.*

II. How did David bear this insolent ill-natured conduct of his enemies towards him. He said nothing to them, but turned himself to God: *"O Lord! be thou merciful to me,* for they are unmerciful, *v.* 10. Raise me up *that I may requite them,* that I may render them good for evil" (so some), for that was David's practice, vii. 4; xxxv. 13. They hoped for his death, but he found himself, through mercy, recovering, and this would add to the comfort of his recovery. "Because thou dost, by thy grace, uphold me in my integrity, I know that thou wilt, in thy glory, set me for ever before thy face." The best man in the world holds his integrity no longer than God upholds him in it; for by his grace we are what we are; if we be left to ourselves, we shall not only fall, but fall away. The psalm concludes with a solemn doxology, or adoration of God as *the Lord God of Israel, v.* 13. It is not certain whether this verse pertains to this particular psalm or whether it was added as the conclusion of the first book of *Psalms,* which is reckoned to end here (the like being subjoined to lxxii, lxxxix, cvi), and then it teaches us to make God the Omega who is the Alpha, to make him the end who is the beginning of every good work.

PSALM 42

If the book of Psalms be, as some have styled it, a mirror or looking-glass of pious and devout affections, this psalm in particular deserves to be so entitled. Gracious desires are here strong and fervent; gracious hopes and fears, joys and sorrows, are here struggling, but the pleasing passion comes off a conqueror. Or we may take it for a conflict between sense and faith, sense objecting and faith answering. I. Faith begins with holy desires towards God and communion with him, ver. 1, 2. II. Sense complains of the darkness and cloudiness of the present condition, aggravated by the remembrance of the former enjoyments, ver. 3, 4. III. Faith silences the complaint with the assurance of a good issue at last, ver. 5. IV. Sense renews its complaints of the present dark and melancholy state, ver. 6, 7. V. Faith holds up the heart, notwithstanding, with hope that the day will dawn, ver. 9. VI. Sense repeats its lamentations (ver. 9, 10) and sighs out the same remonstrance it had before made of its grievances. VII. Faith gets the last word (ver. 11), for the silencing of the complaints of sense. The title does not tell us who was the penman of this psalm, but most probably it was David, and we may conjecture that it was penned by him at a time when, either by Saul's persecution or Absalom's rebellion, he was driven from the sanctuary and cut off from the privilege of waiting upon God in public ordinances.

To the chief musician, Maschil, for the sons of Korah.

Verses 1–5

Holy love to God is the very life and soul of religion. Here we have some of the expressions of that love.

I. Holy love thirsting, love upon the wing, soaring upwards in holy desires towards the Lord and towards the remembrance of his name (v. 1, 2): "*My soul panteth, thirsteth, for God,* for nothing more than God, but still for more and more of him."

1. David thus expressed his vehement desire towards God, when he was debarred from his outward opportunities of waiting on God, when he was banished to the land of Jordan, a great way off from the courts of God's house. Note, Sometimes God teaches us effectually to know the worth of mercies by the want of them, and whets our appetite for the means of grace by cutting us short in those means. He now went mourning, but he went on panting.

2. What is the object of his desire and what it is he thus thirsts after. He pants after God, he thirsts for God, not the ordinances themselves, but the God of the ordinances. Living souls can never take up their rest anywhere short of a living God. He longs to *come and appear before God,*—to make himself known to him, as being conscious to himself of his own sincerity,—to attend on him, as a servant appears before his master. To appear before God is as much the desire of the upright as it is the dread of the hypocrite.

3. What is the degree of this desire. His longing for the water of the well of Bethlehem was nothing to this. He compares it to the *panting of a hart,* or deer, which is naturally hot and dry, especially of a hunted buck, *after the water-brooks.* Thus earnestly does a gracious soul desire communion with God.

II. Holy love mourning for God's present withdrawings (v. 3): "*My tears have been my meat day and night* during this forced absence from God's house." Even the royal prophet was a weeping prophet when he wanted the comforts of God's house. His tears were mingled with his meat; nay, they were *his meat day and night*; he fed, he feasted, upon his own tears. His enemies teased him: *They continually say unto me, Where is thy God?* Because he was absent from the ark, the token of God's presence, they concluded he had lost his God. Those are mistaken who think that when they have robbed us of our Bibles, and our ministers, and our solemn assemblies, they have robbed us of our God; for, though God has tied us to them when they are to be had, he has not tied himself to them. We know where our God is, and where to find him, when we know not where his ark is, nor where to find that. Wherever we are there is a way open heaven-ward. Because God did not immediately appear for his deliverance they concluded that he had abandoned him; but herein also they were deceived: it does not follow that the saints have lost their God because they have lost all their other friends. However, by this base reflection on God and his people, they added affliction to the afflicted, and that was what they aimed at. Nothing is more grievous to a gracious soul than that which is intended to shake its hope and confidence in God. David remembered the *days of old,* and then *his soul was poured out in him*; he melted away, and the thought almost broke his heart. He poured out his soul within him in sorrow, and then poured out his soul before God in prayer. It was not the remembrance of the pleasures at court, or the entertainments of his own house, from which he was now banished, that afflicted him, but the remembrance of the free access he had formerly had to God's house. He *went to the house of God,* though in his time it was but a tent; at the time of his being persecuted by Saul, the ark was in a private house, 2 Sam. vi. 3. But the meanness of the place did not lessen his esteem of that sacred symbol of the divine presence. He *went with the multitude,* and thought it no disparagement to his dignity to be at the head of a crowd in attending upon God. Nay, this added to the pleasure of it, that he was accompanied with a multitude, and therefore it is twice mentioned, as that which he greatly lamented the want of now. He went *with the voice of joy and praise,* not only with joy and praise in his heart, but with the outward expressions of it. He went to keep holy-days, not to keep them in vain mirth and recreation, but in religious exercises.

III. Holy love hoping (v. 5): *Why art thou cast down, O my soul?* His sorrow was upon a very good account, and yet it must not exceed its due limits, nor prevail to depress his spirits; he therefore communes with his own heart, for his relief. "Thou art disquieted, in confusion and disorder; now why art thou so?" Our disquietudes would in many cases vanish before a strict scrutiny into the grounds and reasons of them. "*Why am I cast down?* Is there a cause, a real cause? Have not others more cause, that do not make so much ado? Have not we, at the same time, cause to be encouraged?" A believing confidence in God is a sovereign antidote against prevailing despondency and disquietude of spirit. And therefore, when we chide ourselves for our dejections, we must charge ourselves to hope in God; when the soul embraces itself it sinks; if it catch hold on the power and promise of God, it keeps the head above water. *Hope thou in God for I shall yet praise him;* I shall experience such a change in my spirit that I shall not want a heart for praise. We shall praise him *for the help of his countenance,* for his favour, the support we have by it and the satisfaction we have in it.

Verses 6–11

Complaints and comforts here take their turn, like day and night in the course of nature.

I. He complains of the dejections of his spirit, but comforts himself with the thoughts of God, v. 6. His soul was dejected, and he goes to God and tells him so: *O my God! my soul is cast down within me.* He had often remembered God and was comforted, and therefore had recourse to that expedient now. He was now driven to the utmost borders of the land of Canaan, to shelter himself there from the rage of his persecutors—sometimes to *the country about Jordan,* and, when discovered there, to *the land of the Hermonites,* or to a hill called *Mizar,* or *the little hill.* Wherever he went he took his religion along with him. In all these places, he remembered God, and lifted up his heart to him, and kept his secret communion with him. Distance and time could not make him forget that which his heart was so much upon and which lay so near it.

II. He complains of the tokens of God's displeasure against him, but comforts himself with the hopes of the return of his favour in due time.

1. He saw his troubles coming from God's wrath, and that discouraged him (v. 7): "*Deep calls unto deep,* one affliction comes upon the neck of another, as if it were called to hasten after it; and thy water-spouts give the signal and sound the alarm of war." The waves and billows are under a divine check. Let not good men think it strange if they be exercised with many and various trials, and if they come thickly upon them; God knows what he does, and so shall they shortly.

2. He expected his deliverance to come from God's favour (v. 8): *Yet the Lord will command his loving-kindness.* After the storm there will come a calm, and the prospect of this supported him when deep called unto deep. He eyes the favour of God as the fountain of all the good he looked for. God's conferring his favour is called his *commanding* it. This intimates the freeness of it; we cannot pretend to merit it, but it is bestowed in a way of sovereignty,

he gives like a king. By commanding his loving-kindness, he commands down the waves and the billows, and they shall obey him. This he will do *in the daytime,* for God's lovingkindness will make day in the soul at any time. If God command his lovingkindness for him, he will meet it, and bid it welcome, with his best affections and devotions. He will rejoice in God: *In the night his song shall be with me. My prayer shall be to the God of my life.* God is the God of our life, in whom we live and move, the author and giver of all our comforts; and there-fore to whom should we apply by prayer, but to him?

III. He complains of the insolence of his enemies, and yet comforts himself in God as his friend, *v.* 9–11. He did not break out into indecent passions, but silently wept out his grief and for this we cannot blame him: it must needs grieve a man that truly loves his country, to see himself persecuted, as if he were an enemy to it. Yet David ought not hence to have concluded that God had forgotten him and cast him off. *Why go I mourning?* and *why hast thou forgotten me?* We may complain to God, but we are not allowed thus to complain of him. *They say daily unto me, Where is thy God?*—a reproach which was intended to discourage his hope in God. His com-fort is that God is his rock (*v.* 9)—a rock to build upon, a rock to take shelter in. To God his rock he might say what he had to say, and be sure of a gracious audience. He therefore repeats what he had before said (*v.* 5), and concludes with it (*v.* 11): *Why art thou cast down, O my soul?* But here, at length, his faith came off a conqueror and forced the enemies to quit the field. And he gains this victory, (1) By repeating what he had before said, chiding himself, as before, for his dejections and disquietudes, and encouraging himself to trust in the name of the Lord and to stay himself upon his God. It may be of great use to us to think our good thoughts over again, and, if we do not gain our point with them at first, perhaps we may the second time.

PSALM 43

This psalm, it is likely, was penned upon the same occasion with the former, and, having no title, may be looked upon as an appendix to it; the malady presently returning, he had immediate recourse to the same remedy, because he had entered it in his book, with a "probatum est—it has been proved", upon it. Christ himself, when there was occasion, prayed a second and third time "saying the same words", Matt. xxvi. 44. In this psalm, I. David appeals to God concerning the injuries that were done him by his enemies, ver. 1, 2. II. He prays to God to restore to him the free enjoyment of public ordinances again, and prom-ises to make a good improvement of them, ver. 3, 4. III. He endeavours to still the tumult of his own spirit with a lively hope and confidence in God (ver. 5).

Verses 1–5

David here makes application to God, by faith and prayer, as his judge, his strength, his guide, his joy, his hope.

I. As his Judge (*v.* 1): *Judge me, O God! and plead my cause.* There were those that impeached him; against them he is defendant. Here a sinful body of men, whom he calls an *ungodly* or *unmerciful nation.* And here was one bad man the head of them, a deceitful and unjust man, most probably Saul, who not only showed no kindness to David, but dealt most perfidiously and dishonestly with him. If Absalom was the man he meant, his character was no better. As to the quarrel God had with him for sin, he prays, *"Enter not into judgment with me,* for then I shall be condemned"; but, as to the quarrel his enemies had with him he prays, "Lord, *judge me,* for I know that I shall be justified; *plead my cause against them,* take my part, and in thy providence appear on my behalf."

II. As his strength, his all-sufficient strength; so he eyes God (*v.* 2): *"Thou art the God of my strength, my God, my strength,* from whom all my strength is

derived, in whom I strengthen myself, who hast often strengthened me, and without whom I am weak as water and utterly unable either to do or suffer any-thing for thee." David now went mourning, destitute of spiritual joys, yet he found God to be the God of his strength. If we cannot comfort ourselves in God, we may stay ourselves upon him, and may have spiritual supports when we want spritual de-lights. "Thou art the God on whom I depend as my strength; why then dost thou cast me off?" This was a mistake; for God never cast off any that trusted in him, whatever melancholy apprehensions they may have had of their own state.

III. As his guide, his faithful guide (*v.* 3): *Lead me, bring me to thy holy hill.* His heart is upon *the holy hill and the tabernacles,* not upon his family-comforts, his court-preferments, or his diversions; but he is impatient to see God's tabernacles again. In order to this he prays, *"Send out thy light and thy truth;* let me have this as a fruit of thy favour, which is light, and the performance of thy promise, which is truth." We are still to pray for God's light and truth, the Spirit of light and truth, who supplies the want of Christ's bodily presence, to lead us into the mystery of godliness and to guide us in the way to heaven.

IV. As his joy, his exceeding joy. If God guide him to his tabernacles, if he restore him to his former liberties, he knows very well what he has to do: *Then will I go unto the altar of God, v.* 4. He will get as near as he can unto God, his exceeding joy. Those that come unto God must come to him as their exceeding joy, not only as their future bliss, but as their present joy, and that not a common, but an exceeding joy, far exceeding all the joys of sense and time. The phrase, in the original, is very em-phatic—*unto God the gladness of my joy,* or of my triumph.

V. As his hope, his never-failing hope, *v.* 5. Here, as before, David quarrels with himself for his de-jections and despondencies: *Why art thou cast down O my soul?* He then quiets himself in the believing expectation he had of giving glory to God (*Hope in God, for I shall yet praise him*) and of enjoying glory with God; (*He is the health of my countenance and my God.*)

PSALM 44

We are not told who was the penman of this psalm or when and upon what occasion it was penned. It is a psalm calculated for a day of fasting and humiliation upon occasion of some public calamity, either pressing or threatening. In it the church is taught, I. To own with thankfulness, to the glory of God, the great things God has done for their fathers, ver. 1–8. II. To exhibit a memorial of their present calamitous estate, ver. 9–16. III. To file a protestation of their integrity and adherence to God notwithstanding, ver. 17–22. IV. To lodge a petition at the throne of grace for succour and relief, ver. 22–26.

To the chief musician for the sons of Korah, Maschil.

Verses 1–8

In these verses the church, though now trampled upon, calls to remembrance the days of her triumph. This is mentioned here, 1. As an aggravation of the present distress. The yoke of servitude cannot but lie very heavily on the necks of those that used to wear the crown of victory; and the tokens of God's displeasure must needs be most grievous to those that have been long accustomed to the tokens of his favour. 2. As an encouragement to hope that God would yet turn again their captivity; accordingly he mixes prayers and comfortable expectations with his record of former mercies.

I. Their commemoration of the great things God had formerly done for them. *Our fathers have told us what work thou didst in their days.* "They have told us the *work* which thou didst"; for there is a wonderful harmony and uniformity in all that God does, and the many wheels make but one wheel (Ezek. x. 13), many works make but one work. It is a debt which every age owes to posterity to keep an account of God's works of wonder, and to transmit the knowledge of them to the next generation. Children must attend to what their parents tell them of the wonderful works of God. How wonderfully God planted Israel in Canaan at first, v. 2, 3. This was not owing to their own merit, but to God's favour and free grace: It was *through the light of thy countenance, because thou hadst a favour to them.* It was not by their own sword that they got the land in possession, though they had great numbers of mighty men; nor did their own arm save them from being driven back by the Canaanites and put to shame. It was God that planted Israel in that good land, as the careful husbandman plants a tree, from which he promises himself fruit. This is applicable to the planting of the Christian church in the world, by the preaching of the gospel. Paganism was driven out, as the Canaanites, not all at once, but by little and little, not by any human policy or power (for God chose to do it by the weak and foolish things of the world), but by the wisdom and power of God—Christ by his Spirit went forth conquering and to conquer; and the remembrance of that is a great support and comfort to those that groan under the yoke of antichristian tyranny. *Thou hast,* many a time, *saved us from our enemies,* and hast put to flight, and so put to shame, *those that hated us,* witness the successes of the judges against the nations that oppressed Israel. Many a time have the persecutors of the Christian church, and those that hate it, been put to shame by the power of truth, Acts vi. 10.

II. The good use they make of this record of the great things God had done for their fathers of old. They had taken God for their sovereign Lord (v. 4): *Thou art my King, O God!* The psalmist speaks for himself here: "Lord, *Thou art my King;* whither shall I go with my petitions, but to thee? The favour I ask is not for myself, but for thy church." They had always applied to him by prayer for deliverance when at any time they were in distress: *Command deliverances for Jacob.* "Command it, as one having authority, whose command will be obeyed." As they owned it was not their own sword and bow that had saved them (v. 3), so neither did they trust to their own sword or bow to save them for the future (v. 6): "*I will not trust in my bow,* nor in any of my military preparations, as if those would stand me in stead without God. *Through thy name* (by virtue of thy wisdom directing us, thy power strengthening us and working for us, and thy promise securing success to us) we shall, we *will, tread those under that rise up against us. In God we have boasted;* in him we do and will boast, every day, and all the day long."

Verses 9–15

The people of God here complain to him of the low and afflicted condition that they were now in, under the prevailing power of their enemies and oppressors.

I. They wanted the usual tokens of God's favour to them and presence with them (v. 9): "*Thou hast cast off;* thou seemest to have cast us off and our cause, and so hast put us to shame." God's people, when they are cast down, are tempted to think themselves cast off and forsaken of God; but it is a mistake.

II. They were put to the worst before their enemies in the field of battle (v. 10): *Thou makest us to turn back from the enemy,* as Joshua complained when they met with a repulse at Ai (Joshua vii. 8): "We are

dispirited. Attempts to shake off the Babylonish yoke have been ineffectual, and we have rather lost ground by them."

III. They were doomed to the sword and to captivity (v. 11): "*Thou hast given us like sheep appointed for meat.* They make no more scruple of killing an Israelite than of killing a sheep." They looked upon themselves as bought and sold, and charged it upon God, *Thou sellest thy people,* when they should have charged it upon their own sin. *Thou dost not increase thy wealth by their price,* intimating that they could have suffered this contentedly if they had been sure that it would redound to the glory of God.

IV. They were loaded with contempt, and all possible ignominy was put upon them. In this also they acknowledge God: "*Thou makest us a reproach.*" The heathen, the people that were strangers to the commonwealth of Israel and aliens to the covenants of promise, made them a by-word. The reproach was constant and incessant (v. 15): *My confusion is continually before me. The shame of my face has covered me.* It reflected upon God himself; the reproach which the enemy and the avenger cast upon them was downright blasphemy against God, v. 16, and 2 Kings xix. 3.

Verses 17–26

The people of God, being greatly afflicted and oppressed, here apply to him.

I. By way of appeal, concerning their integrity, though they suffered these hard things, yet they kept close to God and to their duty (v. 17): "*All this has come upon us, and it is as bad perhaps as bad can be, yet have we not forgotten thee,* neither cast off the thoughts of thee nor deserted the worship of thee; for, though we cannot deny but that we have dealt foolishly, yet we have not *dealt falsely in thy covenant,* so as to cast thee off and take to other gods. Though idolaters were our conquerors, yet we have not therefore forsaken thee." The trouble they had been long in was very great: "We have been *sorely broken in the place of dragons,* among men as fierce, and furious, and cruel, as dragons. We have been *covered with the shadow of death,* that is, we have been under deep melancholy and apprehensive of nothing short of death. Though thou hast slain us, we have continued to trust in thee: *Our heart has not turned back;* we have not secretly withdrawn our affections from thee, neither have our steps *declined from thy way* (v. 18), the way which thou hast appointed us to walk in." While our troubles do not drive us from our duty to God we should not suffer them to drive us from our comfort in God; for he will not leave us if we do not leave him. "*If we have forgotten the name of our God,* under pretence that he had forgotten us, or in our distress have *stretched out our hands to a strange god,* as more likely to help us, *shall not God search this out?* Shall he not judge it, and call us to an account for it?" They suffered these hard things because they kept close to God and to their duty (v. 22): "It is *for thy sake that we are killed all the day long,* because we stand related to thee, are called by thy name, call upon thy name, and will not worship other gods."

II. By way of petition, with reference to their present distress, that God would work deliverance for them. *Awake, arise, v. 23. Arise for our help; redeem us* (v. 26). They had complained (v. 12) that God had sold them; here they pray (v. 26) that God would redeem them; for there is no appealing from God, but by appealing to him. They had complained (v. 9), *Thou hast cast us off;* but here they pray (v. 23), "*Cast us not off for ever;* let us not be finally forsaken of God." The expostulations are very moving: *Why sleepest thou? v. 23.* The expression is figurative (as lxxviii. 65, *Then the Lord awaked as one out of sleep*); but it was applicable to Christ in the letter (Matt. viii. 24); he was asleep when his disciples were in a storm, and they awoke him, saying, *Lord, save us, we perish.* They plead the poor sinner's pleas. *"Our soul is bowed down to the dust* under prevailing grief and fear. We have become as creeping things, the most despicable animals: *Our belly cleaves unto the earth;* we cannot lift up ourselves, neither revive our own drooping spirits nor recover ourselves out of our low and sad condition, and we lie exposed to be trodden on by every insulting foe. *O redeem us for thy mercies' sake."*

PSALM 45

This psalm is an illustrious prophecy of Messiah the Prince: it is all over gospel, and points at him only, as a bridegroom espousing the church to himself and as a king ruling in it and ruling for it. It is probable that our Saviour has reference to this psalm when he compares the kingdom of heaven, more than once, to a nuptial solemnity, the solemnity of a royal nuptial, Matt. xxii. 2; xxv. 1. The preface speaks the excellency of the song, ver. 1. The psalm speaks, I. Of the royal bridegroom, who is Christ. 1. The transcendent excellency of his person, ver. 2. 2. The glory of his victories, ver. 3–5. 3. The righteousness of his government, ver. 6, 7. 4. The splendour of his court, ver. 8, 9. II. Of the royal bride, which is the church. 1. Her consent gained, ver. 10, 11. 2. The nuptials solemnised, ver. 12–15. 3. The issue of this marriage ver. 16, 17.

To the chief musician upon Shoshannim, for the sons of Korah, Maschil. A song of loves.

Verses 1–5

Some make *Shoshannim,* in the title, to signify an instrument of six strings; others take it in its primitive signification for lilies or roses, which probably were strewed, with other flowers, at nuptial solemnities. It is *a song of loves,* concerning the holy love that is between Christ and his church. It is *a song of the well-beloved,* the virgins, the companions of the bride (*v.* 14), prepared to be sung by them.

I. The preface (*v.* 1) speaks, 1. The dignity of the subject. It is *a good matter.* It is *touching the King,* King Jesus, and his kingdom and government. 2. The excellency of the management. This song was a confession with the mouth of faith in the heart concerning Christ and his church. *My heart is inditing it.* We speak best of Christ and divine things when we speak from the heart that which has warmed and affected us. It was well expressed: *I will speak of the things which I have made.* Not, "I will speak the things I have heard from others," that is speaking by rote; but, "the things which I have myself studied. *My tongue is* as *the pen of a ready writer,* guided by my heart in every word as the pen is by the hand." We call the prophets the *penmen* of scripture, whereas really they were but the pen. The tongue of the most subtle disputant, and the most eloquent orator, is but the pen with which God writes what he pleases.

II. In these verses the Lord Jesus is represented,

1. As most beautiful and amiable in himself. It is a marriage-song; and therefore the transcendent excellencies of Christ are represented by the beauty of the royal bridegroom (*v.* 2): *Thou art fairer than the children of men,* than any of them. He proposed (*v.* 1) to speak of the King, but immediately directs his speech to him. Those that have an admiration and affection for Christ love to go to him and tell him so. *Thou art fair,* thou art *fairer than the children of men.*

2. As the great favourite of heaven. He is *fairer than the children of men.* He has grace, and he has it for us: *Grace is poured into thy lips.* By his word, his promise, his gospel, the goodwill of God is made known to us and the good work of God is begun and carried on in us. The gospel of grace is poured into his lips; for it *began to be spoken by the Lord,* and from him we receive it. He has the words of eternal life. *The spirit of prophecy is put into thy lips;* so the

Chaldee. "Therefore, because thou art the great trustee of divine grace for the use and benefit of the children of men, *therefore God has blessed thee for ever,* has made thee an everlasting blessing, so that in thee all the nations of the earth shall be blessed."

3. As victorious over all his enemies. The royal bridegroom is to rescue his spouse by dint of sword out of her captivity, to conquer her, and to conquer for her, and then to marry her.

(1) His preparations for war (*v.* 3): *Gird thy sword upon thy thigh, O Most Mighty!* The word of God is the sword of the Spirit. By the promises of that word, and the grace contained in those promises, souls are made willing to submit to Jesus Christ and become his loyal subjects. By the gospel of Christ many Jews and Gentiles were converted.

(2) His expedition to this holy war: He goes forth *with his glory and his majesty,* as a great king takes the field with abundance of pomp and magnificence— his sword, his glory, and majesty. In his gospel he appears transcendently great and excellent, bright and blessed, in the honour and majesty which the Father has laid upon him. Christ, both in his person and in his gospel, had nothing of external glory or majesty, nothing to charm men (for he had no form nor comeliness), nothing to awe men, for he *took upon him the form of a servant;* it was all spiritual glory, spiritual majesty. *In thy majesty ride prosperously, v.* 4. *"Thy kingdom come;* Go on and prosper."

(3) The glorious cause in which he is engaged— *because of truth, and meekness, and righteousness,* which were, in a manner, sunk and lost among men, and which Christ came to retrieve and rescue. The gospel itself is *truth, meekness, and righteousness;* it commands by the power of truth and righteousness; for Christianity has these, incontestably, on its side, and yet it is to be promoted by meekness and gentleness, 1 Cor. iv. 12, 13; 2 Tim. ii. 25. Christ appears in it in his *truth, meekness,* and *righteousness,* and these are his glory and majesty, and because of these he shall prosper. Men are brought to believe on him because he is true, to learn of him because he is meek, Matt. xi. 29 (the gentleness of Christ is of mighty force, 2 Cor. x. 1), and to submit to him because he is righteous and rules with equity.

(4) The success of his expedition: *"Thy right hand shall teach thee terrible things."* In order to the conversion and reduction of souls to him, there are terrible things to be done; the heart must be pricked, conscience must be startled, and the terrors of the Lord must make way for his consolations. The next verse describes these terrible things (*v.* 5): *Thy arrows are sharp in the heart of the king's enemies.* Those that were by nature enemies are thus wounded, in order to their being subdued and reconciled. Convictions are like the arrows of the bow, which are sharp in the heart on which they fasten, and bring people to fall under Christ, in subjection to his laws and government.

Verses 6–9

We have here the royal bridegroom filling his throne with judgment and keeping his court with splendour.

I. He here fills his throne with judgment. It is God the Father that says to the Son here, *Thy throne, O God! is for ever and ever,* as appears Heb. i. 8, 9, where this is quoted to prove that he is God and and has a *more excellent name than the angels.* Concerning his government observe, 1. The eternity of it; it is *for ever and ever.* It shall continue on earth throughout all the ages of time. Even when the kingdom shall be *delivered up to God even the Father* (1 Cor. xv. 24) the throne of the Redeemer will continue. 2. The equity of it: *The sceptre of thy kingdom,* the administration of thy government, *is right*, exactly according to the eternal counsel and will of God, which is the eternal rule and reason of good and evil. 3. The establishment and elevation of it: *Therefore God, even thy God* (Christ, as Mediator, called God *his God*, John xx. 17, as commissioned by him, and the head of those that are taken into covenant with him), *has anointed thee with the oil of gladness.* "In recompence of what thou hast done and suffered for the advancement of righteousness and the destruction of sin God has anointed thee with the oil of gladness, has brought thee to all the honours and all the joys of thy exalted state." *Because he humbled himself, God has highly exalted him*, Phil. ii. 8, 9. His anointing him denotes the power and glory to which he is exalted; he is invested in all the dignities and authorities of the Messiah.

II. He keeps his court with splendour and magnificence. 1. His robes of state, wherein he appears, are taken notice of, not for their pomp, which might strike an awe upon the spectator, but their pleasantness and the gratefulness of the odours with which they were perfumed (*v*. 8): *They smell of myrrh, aloes, and cassia* (the *oil of gladness* with which he and his garments were anointed); these were some of the ingredients of the holy anointing oil which God appointed, the like to which was not to be made up for any common use (Exod. xxx. 23, 24), which was typical of the unction of the Spirit which Christ, the great high priest of our profession, received, and to which therefore there seems here to be a reference. 2. His royal palaces are said to be *ivory* ones, such as were then reckoned most magnificent. The mansions of light above are the *ivory palaces*, whence all the joys both of Christ and believers come, and where they will be for ever in perfection. *Kings' daughters are among thy honourable women.* All true believers are born from above; they are the children of the King of kings. The church is here compared to the queen herself—the queen-consort, whom, by an everlasting covenant, he hath betrothed to himself. She stands *at his right hand in gold of Ophir.* This is *the bride, the Lamb's wife*, whose graces, which are her ornaments, are compared to *fine linen, clean and white* (Rev. xix. 8), for their purity, here to *gold of Ophir*, for their costliness; for, as we owe our redemption, so we owe our adorning, not to corruptible things, but to *the precious blood of the Son of God.*

Verses 10–17

This latter part of the psalm is addressed to the royal bride, standing on the right hand of the royal bridegroom. God, who said to the Son, *Thy throne is for ever and ever*, says this to the church.

I. He tells her of the duties expected from her, which ought to be considered by all those that come into relation to the Lord Jesus: "*Hearken*, therefore, *and consider* this, *and incline thy ear*, that is, submit to those conditions of thy espousals, and bring thy will to comply with them."

1. She must renounce all others. "*Forget thy own people and thy father's house*, according to the law of marriage." This shows, (1) How necessary it was for those who were converted from Judaism or paganism to the faith of Christ wholly to cast out the old leaven, and not to bring into their Christian profession either the Jewish ceremonies or the heathen idolatries, for these would make such a mongrel religion in Christianity as the Samaritans had. (2) How necessary it is for us all, when we give up our names to Jesus Christ, to hate father and mother, and all that is dear to us in this world, in comparison, that is, to love them less than Christ. *So shall the king greatly desire thy beauty*, which intimates that the mixing of her old rites and customs, whether Jewish or Gentile, with her religion, would blemish

her beauty. The beauty of holiness, both on the church and on particular believers, is in the sight of Christ of great price.

2. She must reverence him, must love, honour, and obey him: *He is thy Lord, and worship thou him.* We must worship him as God, and our Lord; for this is the will of God, that *all men should honour the Son even as they honour the Father.*

II. He tells her of the honours designed for her.

1. Great court should be made to her, and rich presents brought her (*v*. 12): "*The daughter of Tyre*," a rich and splendid city, "the *daughter of the King of Tyre* shall be *there with a gift*; every royal family round about shall send a branch, as a representative of the whole, to seek thy favour and to make an interest in thee; *even the rich among the people shall entreat thy favour*, for his sake to whom thou art espoused, that by thee they may make him their friend."

2. She shall be very splendid, and highly esteemed in the eyes of all (*v*. 13): *The king's daughter is all glorious within.* The glory of the church is spiritual glory, and that is indeed all glory; it is the glory of the soul, and that is the man; it is glory in God's sight, and it is an earnest of eternal glory. Though all her glory is within yet *her clothing* also *is of wrought gold*; the conversation of Christians, in which they appear in the world, must be enriched with good works, like wrought gold, which is worked with a great deal of care and caution.

3. Her nuptials shall be celebrated with a great deal of honour and joy (*v*. 14, 15): *She shall be brought to the king.* None are brought to Christ but whom the Father brings, and he has undertaken to do it; none besides are so brought *to the king* (*v*. 14) as to *enter into the king's palace, v*. 15.

4. The progeny of this marriage shall be illustrious (*v*. 16): *Instead of thy fathers shall be thy children.* Instead of the Old Testament church, the economy of which had waxed old, and ready to *vanish away* (Heb. viii. 13), as the fathers that are going off, there shall be a New Testament church, drafted into the same olive.

5. The praise of this marriage shall be perpetual in the praises of the royal bridegroom (*v*. 17): *I will make thy name to be remembered.* His Father has given him *a name above every name*, and here promises to make it perpetual, by keeping up a succession of ministers and Christians in every age, that shall bear up his name, which shall thus *endure for ever* (lxxii. 17).

PSALM 46

This psalm encourages us, I. To take comfort in God when things look very black and threatening, ver. 1–5. II. To mention, to his praise, the great things he has wrought for his church against its enemies, ver. 6–9. III. To assure ourselves that God who has glorified his own name will glorify it yet again, ver. 10, 11. We may, in singing it, apply it either to our spiritual enemies, and the encouragement we have to hope that through Christ we shall be more than conquerors over them, or to the public enemies of Christ's kingdom in the world. It is said of Luther that, when he heard any discouraging news, he would say, Come let us sing the forty-sixth psalm.

To the chief musician for the sons of Korah.
A song upon Alamoth.

Verses 1–5

The psalmist teaches us by his own example.

I. To triumph in God, and his presence with us, especially when we have had some fresh experiences of his appearing in our behalf (*v*. 1): *God is our refuge and strength.* Are we in distress? He is a help, *a present help, a help found* (so the word is), one whom we have found to be so, a help on which we may write *Probatum est—It is tried*, as Christ is called a *tried stone*, Isa. xxviii. 16.

II. To triumph over the greatest dangers: *God is our strength and our help*, a God all-sufficient to us;

therefore will not we fear. It is our duty, it is our privilege, to be thus fearless; it is an evidence of a clear conscience, of an honest heart, and of a lively faith in God and his providence and promise. We will suppose the earth to be removed, and thrown into the sea, even the mountains, the strongest and firmest parts of the earth, to lie buried in the unfathomed ocean; we will suppose the sea to roar and rage, even to *shake the mountains, v.* 3. Though kingdoms and states be in confusion, embroiled in wars, tossed with tumults—though their powers combine against the church and people of God—yet will not we fear, knowing that all these troubles will end well for the church. It is not any private particular concern of our own that we are in pain about; it is the city of God, *the holy place of the tabernacles of the Most High*; it is the ark of God for which our hearts tremble. But, when we consider what God has provided for the comfort and safety of his church, we shall see reason to have our hearts fixed, and set above the fear of evil tidings. *There is a river the streams whereof shall make* it glad, even then when the waters of the sea roar and threaten it. The covenant of grace is the river, the promises of which are the streams; or the Spirit of grace is the river (John vii. 38, 39), the comforts of which are *the streams, that make glad the city of our God.* Though heaven and earth are shaken, yet *God is in the midst of her, she shall not be moved, v.* 5. The church shall survive the world, and be in bliss when that is in ruins. God shall help her out of her troubles, *and that right early*—when the morning appears; that is, very speedily, for he is *a present help* (*v.* 1), and very seasonably, when things are brought to the last extremity and when the relief will be most welcome.

Verses 6–11

These verses give glory to God both as King of nations and as King of saints.

I. As King of nations. He checks the rage and breaks the power of the nations that oppose him and his interests in the world (*v.* 6): *The heathen raged* at David's coming to the throne, and at the setting up of the kingdom of the Son of David; compare ii. 1, 2. *The kingdoms were moved* with indignation, and rose in a tumultuous furious manner to oppose it; but God *uttered his voice, spoke to them in his wrath*, and they were moved in another sense, they were struck into confusion and consternation. Such a melting of the spirits of the enemies is described, Judges v. 4, 5; and see Luke xxi. 25, 26. When he pleases he can make great havoc among the nations and lay all waste (*v.* 8): *Come, behold the works of the Lord*; they are to be observed (lxvi. 5), and to be sought out, cxi. 2. War is a tragedy which commonly destroys the stage it is acted on; David carried the war into the enemies' country; and O what desolations did it make there! Stand in awe of God; say, *How terrible art thou in thy works!* lxvi. 3. When he pleases to sheathe his sword, he puts an end to the wars of the nations and crowns them with peace, *v.* 9. *He makes wars to cease unto the end of the earth,* sometimes in pity to the nations, that they may have a breathing-time, when, by long wars with each other, they have run themselves out of breath. The total destruction of Gog and Magog is prophetically described by the burning of their weapons of war (Ezek. xxxix. 9, 10), which intimates likewise the church's perfect security and assurance of lasting peace, which made it needless to lay up those weapons of war for their own service. The bringing of a long war to a good issue is a work of the Lord, which we ought to behold with wonder and thankfulness.

II. As King of saints, and as such we must own that *great and marvellous are his works,* Rev. xv. 3. He does and will do great things. Let his enemies be

still, and threaten no more, but know that he is God, one infinitely above them; let them rage no more, for it is all in vain: *he that sits in heaven, laughs at them*; and, in spite of all their impotent malice, he will be exalted in the earth and not merely in the church. Men will set up themselves, but let them know that God will be exalted, will glorify his own name, and *wherein they deal proudly he will be above them,* and make them know that he is so. Let his own people be still and tremble no more, but know, to their comfort, that the Lord is God. When we pray, *Father, glorify thy name,* we ought to exercise faith upon the answer given to that prayer when Christ himself prayed it, *I have both glorified it and I will glorify it yet again.* Amen. Lord, so be it. Let all believers triumph in this. 1. They have the presence of a God of power, of all power: *The Lord of hosts is with is.* This sovereign Lord is with us, sides with us, acts with us, and has promised he will never leave us. Hosts may be against us, but we need not fear them if the Lord of hosts be with us. 2. They are under the protection of a God in covenant, who not only is able to help them, but is engaged in honour and faithfulness to help them. He is the God of Jacob, not only Jacob the person, but Jacob the people.

PSALM 47

The scope of this psalm is to stir us up to praise God, and, I. We are directed in what manner to do it, publicly, cheerfully, and intelligently, ver. 1, 6, 7. II. We are furnished with matter for praise. 1. God's majesty, ver. 2. 2. His sovereign and universal dominion, ver. 2, 7–9. 3. The great things he had done, and will do, for his people, ver. 3–5. Many suppose that this psalm was penned upon occasion of the bringing up of the ark to Mount Zion, which ver. 5 seems to refer to ("God has gone up with a shout");—but it looks further, to the ascension of Christ into the heavenly Zion, after he had finished his undertaking on earth, and to the setting up of his kingdom in the world.

To the chief musician. A psalm for the sons of Korah.

Verses 1–4

The psalmist, his own heart filled with great and good thoughts of God, endeavours to engage all about him in the blessed work of praise.

I. Who are called upon to praise God: "*All you people*, all you people of Israel"; so it may be taken as a prophecy of the conversion of the Gentiles and the bringing of them into the church; see Rom. xv. 11.

II. What they are called upon to do: "*Clap your hands,* as men that cannot contain themselves; *shout unto God,* not to make him hear, but to make all about you hear. Shout *with the voice of triumph* in him, and in his power and goodness, that others may join with you in the triumph."

III. What is suggested to us as matter for our praise. *The Lord most high is terrible, a King over all the earth;* and he takes a particular care of his people and their concerns, has done so and ever will. This God had done for them, witness the planting of them in Canaan, and their continuance there unto this day. The kingdom of the Messiah was to be set over all the earth, and not confined to the Jewish nation. Jesus Christ shall subdue the Gentiles; he shall bring *them in as sheep into the fold* (so the word signifies), not for slaughter, but for preservation. *He shall choose our inheritance for us.* He had chosen the land of Canaan to be an inheritance for Israel; it was the land which the Lord their God spied out for them; see Deut. xxxii. 8. And the setting up of God's sanctuary in it made it *the excellency,* the honour, *of Jacob* (Amos vi. 8). Apply this spiritually, 1. The happiness of the saints, that God himself has chosen their inheritance for them, and has laid up for them in the other world an inheritance incorruptible, 1 Pet. i. 4. 2. The faith and submission of the saints to God. This is the language of every gracious soul, "God shall choose my inheritance for me. He knows what is good for me better than I do for myself, and therefore I will have no will of my own but what is resolved into his."

Verses 5–9

Should not subjects praise their king? God is our God, our King, and therefore we must praise him. But here is a needful rule subjoined (v. 7): *Sing you praises with understanding*, with *Maschil*. 1. "Intelligently; as those that do yourselves understand why and for what reasons you praise God and what is the meaning of the service." This is the gospel-rule (1 Cor. xiv. 15). 2. "Instructively, as those that desire to make others understand God's glorious perfections, and to teach them to praise him."

I. We must praise God going up (v. 5): *God has gone up with a shout*, which may refer, 1. To the carrying up of the ark to the hill of Zion. The ark being the instituted token of God's special presence with them, when that was brought up by warrant from him he might be said to *go up*. 2. To the ascension of our Lord Jesus into heaven, when he had finished his work on earth, Acts i. 9. Then *God went up with a shout*, the shout of a King, of a conqueror.

II. We must praise God reigning, v. 7, 8. *He sits upon the throne of his holiness*, which he has prepared in the heavens, and there he rules over all. See here the extent of God's government; all are born within his allegiance; even the heathen that serve other gods are ruled by the true God, our God, whether they will or no. See the equity of his government; it is a throne of holiness, on which he sits, whence he gives warrants, orders, and judgment, in which we are sure there is no iniquity. Jesus Christ, who is God, and whose *throne is for ever and ever, reigns over the heathen*; not only is he entrusted with the administration of the providential kingdom, but he shall set up the kingdom of his grace in the Gentile world, and rule in the hearts of multitudes that were bred up in heathenism, Eph. ii. 12, 13.

III. We must praise God as attended and honoured by *the princes of the people*, v. 9. It was the honour of Israel that they were *the people of the God of Abraham*. 1. It was their happiness that they had a settled government, *princes of their people*, who were the *shields of their land*. Magistracy is the shield of a nation, it is likewise the honour of God that, in another sense, the *shields of the earth do belong to him*; magistracy is his institution, and he serves his own purposes by it in the government of the world. The unanimous agreement of the great ones of a nation in the things that belong to its peace is a very happy omen, which promises abundance of blessings. 2. It may be applied to the calling of the Gentiles into the church of Christ, and taken as a prophecy that in the days of the Messiah the kings of the earth and their people should join themselves to the church. When the *shields of the earth*, the ensigns of royal dignity (1 Kings xiv. 27, 28), are surrendered to the Lord Jesus, as the keys of a city are presented to the conqueror or sovereign, when princes use their power for the advancement of the interests of religion, then Christ is greatly exalted.

PSALM 48

This psalm, as the two former, is a triumphant song; some think it was penned on occasion of Jehoshaphat's victory (2 Chron. xx), others of Sennacherib's defeat, when his army laid siege to Jerusalem in Hezekiah's time. Jerusalem is here praised, I. For its relation to God, ver. 1, 2. II. For God's care of it, ver. 3. III. For the terror it strikes upon its enemies, ver. 4–7. IV. For the pleasure it gives to its friends, who delight to think, 1. Of what God has done, does, and will do for it, ver. 8. 2. Of the gracious discoveries he makes of himself in and for that holy city, ver. 9, 10. 3. Of the effectual provision which is made for its safety, ver. 11–13. 4. Of the assurance we have of the perpetuity of God's covenant with the children of Zion, ver. 14.

A song *and* psalm for the sons of Korah.

Verses 1–7

What is here said to the honour of Jerusalem is,

I. Of Zion he said kinder things than ever he said of any place upon earth. *This is my rest for ever; here will I dwell, for I have desired it*, cxxxii. 13, 14. It is *the city of the great King* (v. 2), the King of all the earth, who is pleased to declare himself in a special manner present there. *In Judah God is known, and his name is great*. In Jerusalem *God is great* (v. 1). It is therefore called *the mountain of his holiness*, for *holiness to the Lord* is written upon it and all the furniture of it, Zech. xiv. 20, 21. God was known, not only in the streets, but even in the palaces of Jerusalem, for a refuge. Upon all these accounts, Jerusalem, and especially Mount Zion, on which the temple was built, were universally beloved and admired—*beautiful for situation*, and *the joy of the whole earth*, v. 2. The situation must needs be every way agreeable, when Infinite Wisdom chose it for the place of the sanctuary; and that which made it beautiful was that it was the mountain of holiness, for there is a beauty in holiness. Mount Zion was on the north side of Jerusalem and so was a shelter to the city from the cold and bleak winds that blew from that quarter.

II. That the kings of the earth were afraid of it. They had had but too much occasion to fear their enemies; for *the kings were assembled*, v. 4. They passed, advanced, and marched on together, not doubting but they should soon make themselves masters of that city which should have been the joy, but was the envy of the whole earth. The very sight of Jerusalem struck them into a consternation and gave check to their fury, as the sight of the tents of Jacob frightened Balaam from his purpose to curse Israel (Num. xxiv. 2): *They saw it and marvelled, and hasted away*, v. 5. Not that there was anything to be seen in Jerusalem that was so very formidable; but the sight of it brought to mind what they had heard concerning the special presence of God in that city and the divine protection it was under. They knew themselves an unequal match for Omnipotence, and therefore *fear came upon them, and pain*, v. 6. The fright they were in upon the sight of Jerusalem is here compared to the throes of a woman in travail. The defeat hereby given to their designs upon Jerusalem is compared to the dreadful work made with a fleet of ships by a violent storm, when some are split, others shattered, all dispersed (v. 7).

Verses 8–14

I. Let our faith in the word of God be hereby confirmed. "As we have heard done in former providences, in the days of old, so have we seen done in our own days. We have heard that God is the Lord of hosts, and that Jerusalem is the city of our God, is dear to him, in his particular care; and now we have seen it; we have seen the power of our God; we have seen his goodness; we have seen his care and concern for us, that he is a *wall of fire round about Jerusalem and the glory in the midst of her*."

II. Let our hope of the stability and perpetuity of the church be hereby encouraged. "From what we have seen, compared with what we have heard, in the city of our God, we may conclude that God will establish it for ever." This was not fulfilled in Jerusalem (that city was long since destroyed, and all its glory laid in the dust), but has its accomplishment in the gospel church.

III. Let our minds be hereby filled with good thoughts of God. "From what we have heard, and seen, and hope for, we may take occasion to think much of God's lovingkindness, whenever we meet *in the midst of his temple*," v. 9.

IV. Let us give to God the glory of the great things which he has done for us, and mention them to his honour (*v.* 10): "*According to thy name, O God! so is thy praise*, not only in Jerusalem, but to the ends of the earth." As far as his name goes his praise will go, at least it should go, and, at length, it shall go, when all the ends of the world shall praise him, xxii. 27; Rev. xi. 15. Some, by his *name*, understand especially that glorious name of his, *the Lord of hosts*; according to that name, so is his praise; for all the creatures, even to the ends of the earth, are under his command.

V. Let all the members of the church in particular take to themselves the comfort of what God does for his church in general (*v.* 11): "*Let Mount Zion rejoice*, the priests and Levites that attend the sanctuary, and then *let all the daughters of Judah*, the country towns, and the inhabitants of them, be glad: let the women in their songs and dances, as usual on occasion of public joys, celebrate with thankfulness the great salvation which God has wrought for us."

VI. Let us diligently observe the instances and evidences of the church's beauty, strength, and safety, and faithfully transmit our observations to those that shall come after us (*v.* 12, 13): *Walk about Zion.* Some think this refers to the ceremony of the triumph; let those who are employed in that solemnity walk round the walls (as they did, Neh. xii. 31), singing and praising God. In doing this let *them tell the towers and mark well the bulwarks*, magnify the late wonderful deliverance God had wrought for them. Let them observe, with wonder, that the towers and bulwarks are all in their full strength and none of them damaged by the kings that were assembled. *Tell this to the generation following*, as a wonderful instance of God's care of his holy city. *Set your heart to her bulwarks.* This intimates that the principal bulwarks of Zion were not the objects of sense, which they might set their eye upon, but the objects of faith, which they must set their hearts upon. Calvin observes here that when they are directed to transmit to posterity a particular account of the towers, and bulwarks, and palaces of Jerusalem, it is intimated that in process of time they would all be destroyed and remain no longer to be seen; for, otherwise, what need was there to preserve the description and history of them? When the disciples were admiring the buildings of the temple their Master told them that in a little time one stone of it should not be *left upon another*, Matt. xxiv. 1, 2. This must certainly be applied to the gospel church. See it founded on Christ, the rock fortified by the divine power, guarded by him that neither slumbers nor sleeps.

VII. Let us triumph in God, and in the assurances we have of his everlasting loving-kindness, *v.* 14. Tell this to the generation following: That *this God*, who has now done such great things for us, *is our God for ever and ever.* If he be our God, *he will be our guide*, our faithful constant guide. He will be our guide *above* death (so some); he will so guide us as to set us above the reach of death. He will be our guide *beyond* death (so others); he will conduct us safely to a happiness on the other side death, to a life in which there shall be no more death.

PSALM 49

himself and other good people, (1) Against the fear of death, ver. 15. (2) Against the fear of the prospering power of wicked people, ver. 16–20.

To the chief musician. A psalm for the sons of Korah.

Verses 1–5

This is the psalmist's preface to his discourse concerning the vanity of the world and its insufficiency to make us happy.

I. He demands attention (*v.* 1, 2): *Hear, all you people, and give ear, all you inhabitants of the world;* for this doctrine is not peculiar to those that are blessed with divine revelation, but even the light of nature witnesses to it. All men may know, and therefore let all men consider, that their riches will not profit them in the day of death. Poor people are as much in danger from an inordinate desire towards the wealth of the world as rich people from an inordinate delight in it. *My mouth shall speak of wisdom;* what he had to say is wisdom and understanding; it will make those wise and intelligent that receive it. It was what he had himself well digested.

II. He engages his own attention (*v.* 4): *I will incline my ear to a parable.* It is called a *parable*, not because it is figurative and obscure, but because it is a wise discourse and very instructive. It is the same word that is used concerning Solomon's proverbs. Those that undertake to teach others must first learn themselves.

III. He promises to make the matter as plain and as affecting as he could: *I will open my dark saying upon the harp.* Some understood it not, it was a riddle to them; tell them of the vanity of the things that are seen, and of the reality and weight of invisible things, and they say, *Ah Lord God! doth he not speak parables?* Others understood it well enough, but they were not moved by it, it never affected them, and for their sake he would open it upon the harp, and try that expedient to work upon them, to win upon them. *A verse may find him whom a sermon flies.* Herbert.

IV. He begins with the application of it to himself. *Wherefore should I fear?* he means, *Wherefore should I fear their fear* (Isa. viii. 12), the fears of worldly people. "Wherefore should I fear in the days of trouble and persecution, *when the iniquity of my heels*, or of my supplanters that endeavour to trip up my heels, *shall compass me about*, and they shall surround me with their mischievous attempts? Why should I be afraid of those whose power lies in their wealth? I will not fear their power, for it cannot enable them to ruin me." *The iniquity of our heels* (or of our steps, our past sins) will compass us about, will be set in order before us. In these days worldly wicked people will be afraid; nothing more dreadful to those that have set their hearts upon the world than to think of leaving it; but wherefore should a good man fear death, who has God with him? (xxiii. 4).

Verses 6–14

I. A description of the spirit and way of worldly people, whose portion is in this life, xvii. 14. A man may have abundance of the wealth of this world and be made better by it, may thereby have his heart enlarged in love, and thankfulness, and obedience, and may do that good with it which will be fruit abounding to his account; and therefore it is not men's having riches that denominates them worldly, but their setting their hearts upon them as the best things; and so these worldly people are here described. *They trust in their wealth* (*v.* 6); they depend upon it as their portion and happiness. Their gold is their hope (Job xxxi. 24), and so it becomes their God. Thus our Saviour explains the difficulty of the salvation of rich people (Mark x. 24): *How hard is it for those that trust in riches to enter into the kingdom of God!* See 1 Tim. vi. 17. *They call their lands after their own names,* hoping thereby to perpetuate their memory, and, if their lands do retain the names by which they called them, it is but a poor honour; but they often change their names when they change their owners. *Their inward thought is that their houses shall continue for ever,* and with this thought they please themselves.

II. A demonstration of their folly herein. In general (v. 13), *This their way is their folly.* God himself pronounced him *a fool* who thought his goods were laid up for many years, and that they would be a portion for his soul, Luke xii. 19, 20. The love of the world is a disease that runs in the blood; men have it by kind, till the grace of God cures it. With all their wealth they cannot save the life of the dearest friend they have in the world, nor purchase a reprieve for him when he is under the arrest of death (v. 7–9). Everlasting life is a jewel of too great a value to be purchased by the wealth of this world. We are *not redeemed with corruptible things, such as silver and gold,* 1 Pet. i. 18, 19. Christ did that for us which all the riches of the world could not do; well therefore may he be dearer to us than any worldly things. Christ did that for us which a brother, a friend, could not do for us, no, not one of the best estate or interest; and therefore those that *love father or brother more than him are not worthy of him.* Some rich people are wise, they are politicians, but they cannot out-wit death, nor evade his stroke, with all their art and management; others are fools and brutish. These, though they do no good, yet perhaps do no great hurt in the world: but that shall not excuse them; they shall perish, and be taken away by death, as well as the wise that did mischief with their craft. As their wealth will stand them in no stead in a dying hour, so neither will their honour (v. 12): *Man, being in honour, abides not.* We will suppose a man advanced to the highest pinnacle of preferment, as great and happy as the world can make him, man in splendour, yet then he abides not. His honour does not continue; that is a fleeting shadow. Their condition on the other side death will be very miser-able. While a saint can ask proud Death, *Where is thy sting?* Death will ask the proud sinner, *Where is thy wealth, thy pomp?* The beauty of holiness is that which the grave, that consumes all other beauty, cannot touch, or do any damage to.

Verses 15–20

Good reason is here given to good people,

I. Why they should not be afraid of death. There is no cause for that fear if they have such a com-fortable prospect as David here has of a happy state on the other side death, v. 15. The believing hopes of the soul's redemption from the grave, and reception to glory, are the great support and joy of the children of God in a dying hour. They hope,

1. That God will redeem their souls from the power of the grave, which includes, (1) The preserving of the soul from going to the grave with the body. The grave has a power over the body, by virtue of the sentence (Gen. iii. 19), and it is cruel enough in executing that power (Cant. viii. 6); but it has no such power over the soul. It has power to silence, and imprison, and consume the body; but the soul then moves, and acts, and converses, more freely than ever (Rev. vi. 9, 10); it is immaterial and immortal. When death breaks the dark lantern, yet it does not extinguish the candle that was pent up in it. (2) The reuniting of the soul and body at the resurrection. "*God shall redeem my soul from the sheol of hell*" (v. 15), and therefore the first death has no sting and the grave no victory.

2. That he will receive them to himself. He redeems their souls, that he may receive them. Ps. xxxi. 5, *Into thy hands I commit my spirit, for thou hast redeemed it.* He will receive them into his favour, will admit them into his kingdom, into the mansions that are prepared for them (John xiv. 2, 3), those everlasting habitations, Luke xvi. 9.

II. Why they should not be afraid of the prosperity and power of wicked people in this world.

1. He supposes the temptation very strong to envy the prosperity of sinners, for he supposes, they are made rich, and so are enabled to give law to all about them and have everything at command. They are very easy and secure in themselves and in their own minds (v. 18): *In his life-time he blessed his soul;* that is, he thought himself a very happy man because he prospered in the world. Believers *bless themselves in the God of truth* (Isa. lxv. 16), and think themselves happy if he be theirs; carnal people bless themselves in the wealth of the world, and think themselves happy if they have abundance of that. They applaud that in themselves which God condemns, and speak peace to themselves when God denounces war against them. "The worldling magnified himself; but thou that dost not, like him, speak well of thyself, but do well for thyself, in securing thy eternal welfare, thou shalt be praised, if not of men, yet of God, which will be thy everlasting honour."

2. He suggests that which is sufficient to take off the strength of the temptation, by directing us to look forward to the end of prosperous sinners (lxxiii. 17). *When he dies* it is taken for granted that he goes into another world himself, but *he shall carry nothing away with him* of all that which he has been so long heaping up. Grace is glory that will ascend with us, but no earthly glory will descend after us. *The soul shall go to the generation of his fathers,* his worldly wicked fathers, whose sayings he approved and whose steps he trod in, his fathers who would not hearken to the word of God, Zech. i. 4. A fool, a wicked man, in honour, is really as despicable an animal as any under the sun; he is *like the beasts that perish* (v. 20); nay, it is better to be a beast than to be a man that makes himself like a beast.

PSALM 50

This psalm, as the former, is a psalm of instruction, not of prayer or praise. God by his prophet deals in this psalm with those that were in profession, the church's children, to convince them of their sin and folly in placing their religion in ritual services, while they neglected practical godliness. 1. As a proof to the carnal Jews, both those that rested in the external performances of their religion, and were remiss in the more excellent duties of prayer and praise, and those that expounded the law to others, but lived wicked lives themselves. 2. As a prediction of the abolishing of the ceremonial law, and of the introducing of a spiritual way of worship, in and by the kingdom of the Messiah, John iv. 23, 24. 3. As a representation of the day of judgment, in which God will call men to an account concerning their observance of those things which they have thus been taught; men shall be judged "according to what is written in the books"; and therefore Christ is fitly represented speaking as a Judge, and when he speaks as a Lawgiver. Here is, I. The glorious appearance of the Prince that gives law and judgment, ver. 1–6. II. Instruction given to his worshippers, to turn their sacrifices into prayers, ver. 7–15. III. A rebuke to those that pretend to worship God, but live in disobedience to his commands (ver. 16–20), their doom read (ver. 21, 22), and warning given to all to look to their conversation as well as to their devotions, ver. 23.

A psalm of Asaph.

Verses 1–6

It is probable that Asaph was not only the chief musician, who put a tune to this psalm, but that he was himself the penman of it; in Hezekiah's time they praised God *in the words of David and Asaph the seer,* 2 Chron. xxix. 30.

I. The court called, in the name of the King of kings (v. 1): *The mighty God, even the Lord, hath spoken*—El, Elohim, Jehovah, the God of infinite power, justice, and mercy, Father, Son, and Holy

Ghost. God is the Judge, the Son of God came for judgment into the world, and the Holy Ghost is the Spirit of judgment. All the earth is called to attend.

II. The judgment set, and the Judge taking his seat. As, when God gave the law to Israel in the wilderness, it is said, *He came from Sinai, and rose up from Seir, and shone forth from Mount Paran, and then from his right hand went a fiery law* (Deut. xxxiii. 2), so when God comes to reprove them for their hypocrisy, and to send forth his gospel to supersede the legal institutions, it is said here, 1. That *he shall shine out of Zion*, as then from the top of Sinai, *v.* 2. Because in Zion his oracle was now fixed, thence his judgments upon that provoking people were denounced, and God, who always dwells in Zion, may be said to *shine out of Zion*. The gospel, which set up spiritual worship, was to *go forth from Mount Zion* (Isa. ii. 3, Mic. iv. 2), and the preachers of it were to *begin at Jerusalem* (Luke xxiv. 47). Zion is here called *the perfection of beauty*, because it was the holy hill; and holiness is indeed the perfection of beauty. 2. That he *shall come, and not keep silence*, but shall show his displeasure at them, and the partition-wall of the ceremonial law should be taken down; this shall now no longer be concealed. In the great day *our God shall come and shall not keep silence*, but shall make those to hear his judgment that would not hearken to his law. 3. That his appearance should be majestic and terrible: *A fire shall devour before him.* The fire of his judgments shall make way for the rebukes of his word, that the sinners in Zion might be startled out of their sins. When his gospel kingdom was to be set up Christ *came to send fire on the earth*, Luke xii. 49. The Spirit was given in cloven tongues as of fire, introduced by a rushing mighty wind, which was very tempestuous, Acts ii. 2, 3. And in the last judgment Christ shall come in flaming fire, 2 Thess. i. 8. 4. That as on Mount Sinai he came with *ten thousands of his saints*, so he shall now *call to the heavens from above*, to take notice of this solemn process (*v.* 4).

III. The parties summoned (*v.* 5): *Gather my saints together unto me.* This may be understood either, 1. Of saints indeed. When God will reject the services of those that only offered sacrifice, resting in the outside of the performance, he will graciously accept those who, in sacrificing, *make a covenant with him*, and so attend to and answer the end of the institution of sacrifices. It is only by sacrifice, by Christ the great sacrifice (from whom all the legal sacrifices derived what value they had), that we poor sinners can covenant with God so as to be accepted of him. Or, 2. It may be understood of saints in profession, such as the people of Israel were, who are called *a kingdom of priests* and *a holy nation*, Exod. xix. 6.

IV. The issue of this solemn trial foretold (*v.* 6): *The heavens shall declare his righteousness*, those heavens that were called to be witnesses to the trial (*v.* 4); the *people in heaven shall say, Hallelujah. As the heavens declare the glory*, the wisdom and power, of God the *Creator* (xix. 1), so they shall no less openly declare the glory, the justice and righteousness, of God the *Judge*; and so loudly do they proclaim both that *there is no speech nor language where their voice is not heard*, as it follows there, *v.* 3.

Verses 7–15

God is here dealing with those that placed all their religion in the observances of the ceremonial law, and thought those sufficient.

I. He lays down the original contract between him and Israel.

II. He puts a slight upon the legal sacrifices, *v.* 8.

1. This may be considered as looking back to the use of these under the law. God had a controversy with the Jews; but what was the ground of the controversy? They thought God was mightily beholden to them for the many sacrifices they had brought to his altar; but God here shows them he did not need their sacrifices. What occasion had he for their bullocks and goats who has the command of all *the beasts of the forest*, and the *cattle upon a thousand hills* (*v.* 9, 10). God's infinite self-sufficiency proves our utter insufficiency to add anything to him. He could not be benefited by their sacrifices. *Will I eat the flesh of bulls?* It is as absurd to think that their sacrifices could, of themselves, and by virtue of any innate excellency in them, add any pleasure or praise to God, as it would be to imagine that an infinite Spirit could be supported by meat and drink, as our bodies are. No; *to obey is better than sacrifice*, and to love God and our neighbour *better than all burnt-offerings.*

2. This may be considered as looking forward to the abolishing of these by the gospel of Christ. When God shall set up the kingdom of the Messiah he shall abolish the old way of worship by sacrifice and offerings; he will no more have those to be *continually before him* (*v.* 8); he will no more require of his worshippers to bring him their bullocks and their goats, to be burnt upon his altar, *v.* 9.

III. He directs to the best sacrifices of prayer and praise as those which, under the law, were preferred before all burnt-offerings and sacrifices, and on which then the greatest stress was laid, and which now, under the gospel, come in the room of those carnal ordinances which were imposed until the times of reformation. He shows us here (*v.* 14, 15) what is good, and what the Lord our God requires of us, and will accept, when sacrifices are slighted and superseded. 1. We must make a penitent acknowledgment of our sins: *Offer to God confession. A broken and contrite heart* is the sacrifice which *God will not despise*, li. 17. If the sin was not abandoned the sin-offering was not accepted. 2. We must give God thanks for his mercies to us: *Offer to God thanksgiving*, every day, often every day (*seven times a day will I praise thee*): and *this shall please the Lord*, if it come from a humble thankful heart, *better than an ox or bullock that has horns and hoofs*, lxix. 30, 31. 3. We must make conscience of performing our covenants with him: *Pay thy vows to the Most High*, forsake thy sins, and do thy duty better. Dr. Hammond applies this to the great gospel ordinance of the eucharist, in which we are to give thanks to God for his great love in sending his Son to save us. Instead of all the Old Testament types of a Christ to come, we have that blessed memorial of a Christ already come. 4. In the day of distress we must address ourselves to God by faithful and fervent prayer (*v.* 15): *Call upon me in the day of trouble.*

Verses 16–23

God, by the psalmist, having instructed his people in the right way of worshipping him, here directs his speech to the wicked.

I. The charge drawn up against them. 1. They are charged with invading and usurping the honours and privileges of religion (*v.* 16): *What hast thou to do*, O wicked man! *to declare my statutes?* This is a challenge to those that are really profane, but seemingly godly, to show what title they have to the cloak of religion. Some think it points prophetically at the scribes and Pharisees that were the teachers and leaders of the Jewish church at the time when the kingdom of the Messiah, and that evangelical way of worship spoken of in the foregoing verses, were to be set up. They violently opposed that great revolution, and used all the power and interest which they had by sitting in Moses's seat to hinder it; but the account which our blessed Saviour gives of them

(Matt. xxiii), and St. Paul (Rom. ii. 21, 22), makes this expostulation here agree very well to them. They took on them to declare God's statutes, but they hated Christ's instruction; and therefore what had they to do to expound the law, when they rejected the gospel? But it is applicable to all those that are practisers of iniquity, and yet professors of piety, especially if withal they be preachers of it. 2. They are charged with transgressing and violating the laws and precepts of religion. *Thou hatest instruction.* They loved to give instruction, and to tell others what they should do, for this fed their pride; but they hated to receive instruction from God himself, for that would be a mortification to them. *Thou castest my words behind thee.* 1, A close confederacy with the worst of sinners (*v.* 18): "*When thou sawest a thief,* instead of reproving him, *thou consentedst with him,* didst approve of his practices, and desire to share in the profits of his cursed trade; *and thou hast been partaker with adulterers.*" 2. A constant persisting in the worst of tongue-sins (*v.* 19): "*Thou givest thy mouth to evil,* not only allowest thyself in, but addictest thyself wholly to, all manner of evil-speaking." Lying: *Thy tongue frames deceit.* Slandering (*v.* 20): "*Thou sittest, and speakest against thy brother,* dost basely abuse and misrepresent him; *thou sittest* and doest this, as a judge upon the bench, with authority; thou sittest in the seat of the scornful, to deride and backbite those whom thou oughtest to respect and be kind to."

II. The proof of this charge (*v.* 21): "*These things thou hast done;* the fact is too plain to be denied, the fault too bad to be excused; these things God knows, and thy own heart knows, thou hast done."

III. The Judge's patience, and the sinner's abuse of that patience: *I kept silence,* did not give thee any disturbance in thy sinful way, but let thee alone to take thy course; sentence against thy evil works was respited, and not executed speedily." His patience is the more wonderful because the sinner makes such an ill use of it. Sinners take God's silence for consent and his patience for connivance; and therefore the longer they are reprieved the more are their hearts hardened.

IV. The fair warning given of the dreadful doom of hypocrites (*v.* 22): "*Now consider this, you that forget God,* consider that God knows and keeps account of all your sins, patience abused will turn into the greater wrath, for if these things be not considered, and the consideration of them improved, he will *tear you in pieces, and there will be none to deliver.*"

V. Full instructions given to us all how to prevent this fearful doom. 1. Man's chief end is to glorify God, and we are here told that *whoso offers praise glorifies him;* whether he be Jew or Gentile, those spiritual sacrifices shall be accepted from him. We must praise God, direct it to God, as every sacrifice was directed; see that it be made by fire, sacred fire, that it be kindled with the flame of holy and devout affection. 2. Man's chief end, in conjunction with this, is to enjoy God; and we are here told that those who *order their conversation aright shall see his salvation.* Thanksgiving is good, but thanks-living is better.

PSALM 51

This psalm is the most eminent of the penitential psalms, and most expressive of the cares and desires of a repenting sinner. In this psalm, I. David confesses his sin, ver. 3–6. II. He prays earnestly for the pardon of his sin, ver. 1, 2, 7, 9. III. For peace of conscience, ver. 8, 12. IV. For grace to go and sin no more, ver. 10, 11, 14. V. For liberty of access to God, ver. 15. VI. He promises to do what he could for the good of the souls of others (ver. 13) and for the glory of God, ver. 16, 17, 19. And, lastly, concludes with a prayer for Zion and Jerusalem, ver. 18. Those whose consciences charge them with any gross sin should, with a believing regard to Jesus Christ, the Mediator, again and again pray over this psalm.

To the chief musician. A psalm of David, when Nathan the prophet came unto him, after he had gone in to Bathsheba.

Verses 1–6

The title has reference to a very sad story, that of David's fall. 1. The sin which, in this psalm, he laments, was the folly and wickedness he committed with his neighbour's wife. This sin of David's is recorded for warning to all, that he who thinks he stands may take heed lest he fall. 2. The repentance which, in this psalm, he expresses, was brought through the ministry of Nathan, who was sent of God to convince him of his sin. But those that have been overtaken in any fault ought to reckon a faithful reproof the greatest kindness that can be done them and a wise reprover their best friend. *Let the righteous smite me, and it shall be excellent oil.* 3. David, being convinced of his sin, poured out his soul to God in prayer for mercy and grace. 4. He drew up, by divine inspiration, the workings of his heart towards God, upon this occasion, into a psalm.

In these words we have,

I. David's humble petition, *v.* 1, 2. His prayer is much the same with that which our Saviour puts into the mouth of his penitent publican in the parable: *God be merciful to me a sinner!* Luke xviii. 13. David does not balance his evil deeds with his good deeds, nor can he think that his services will atone for his offences; but he flies to God's infinite mercy, and depends upon that only for pardon and peace: *Have mercy upon me, O God!*

1. What his plea is for this mercy: "*Have mercy upon me, O God!* Have mercy upon me for mercy's sake. I have nothing to plead with thee but," (1) "The freeness of thy mercy, according to thy loving-kindness, thy clemency, the goodness of thy nature, which inclines thee to pity the miserable." (2) "The fulness of thy mercy."

2. What is the particular mercy that he begs—the pardon of sin. *Blot out my transgressions,* as a debt is blotted or crossed out of the book, when either the debtor has paid it or the creditor has remitted it. "*Wash me thoroughly from my iniquity. Cleanse me from my sin.*" Nathan had assured David, upon his first profession of repentance, that his sin was pardoned. *The Lord has taken away thy sin; thou shalt not die,* 2 Sam. xii. 13. Yet he prays, *Wash me, cleanse me, blot out my transgressions.* God had forgiven him, but he could not forgive himself; and therefore he is thus importunate for pardon.

II. David's penitential confessions, *v.* 3–5.

1. He was very free to own his guilt before God: *I acknowledge my transgressions;* this he had formerly found the only way of easing his conscience, xxxii. 4, 5. Nathan said, *Thou art the man. I am,* says David; *I have sinned.*

2. He had such a deep sense of it that he was continually thinking of it with sorrow and shame. "*My sin is ever before me. It is ever against me.*"

(1) He confesses his actual transgressions (*v.* 4): *Against thee, thee only, have I sinned.* The best men, if they sin, should give the best example of repentance. David published his confession of sin that when hereafter he should come into trouble none might say God had done him any wrong; for he owns the Lord is righteous: thus will all true penitents justify God by condemning themselves. *Thou art just in all that is brought upon us.*

(2) He confesses his original corruption (*v.* 5): *Behold, I was shapen in iniquity.* David elsewhere speaks of the admirable structure of his body (cxxxix. 14, 15); it was *curiously wrought;* and yet here he says it was *shapen in inquity,* sin was twisted in with it; not as it came out of God's hands. It is to be sadly lamented by everyone of us that we brought

into the world with us a corrupt nature, wretchedly degenerated from its primitive purity and rectitude. This is what we call *original sin*, because it is as ancient as our original, and because it is the original of all our actual transgressions. It is a bent to backslide from God.

III. David's acknowledgment of the grace of God (v. 6), both his goodwill towards us (*thou desirest truth in the inward parts*, thou wouldst have us all honest and sincere, and true to our profession") and his good work in us—"*In the hidden part thou hast made*," or shalt make, "*me to know wisdom*." Truth and wisdom will go very far towards making a man a good man. What God requires of us he himself works in us, and he works it in the regular way, enlightening the mind, and so gaining the will. David was conscious of the uprightness of his heart towards God in his repentance, and therefore doubted not but God would accept him. He hoped that God would enable him to make good his resolutions, that in the hidden part, in the new man, which is called the *hidden man of the heart* (1 Pet. iii. 4), he would make him to know wisdom so as to discern and avoid the designs of the tempter another time.

Verses 7–13

I. See here what David prays for. Many petitions he here puts up, to which if we do but add, "for Christ's sake," they are as evangelical as any other.

1. He prays that God would cleanse him from his sins and the defilement he had contracted by them (v. 7): *Purge me with hyssop*. The expression here alludes to a ceremonial distinction, that of cleansing the leper, or those that were unclean by the touch of a body by sprinkling water, or blood, or both upon them with a bunch of hyssop, by which they were, at length, discharged from the restraints they were laid under by their pollution. "Lord, let me be as well assured of my restoration to thy favour, and to the privilege of communion with thee, as they were thereby assured of their re-admission to their former privileges." But it is founded upon gospel-grace: *Purge me with hyssop*, that is, with the blood of Christ applied to my soul by a lively faith, as water of purification was sprinkled with a bunch of hyssop. It is the blood of Christ (which is therefore called *the blood of sprinkling*, Heb. xii. 24), that purges the conscience from dead works, from that guilt of sin and dread of God which shut us out of communion with him, as the touch of a dead body, under the law, shut a man out from the courts of God's house.

2. He prays that, his sins being pardoned, he might have the comfort of that pardon. He asks not to be comforted till first he is cleansed; but if sin, the bitter root of sorrow, be taken away, he can pray in faith, "*Make me to hear joy and gladness* (v. 8), that is, let me have a well-grounded peace, of thy creating, thy speaking." The pain of a heart truly broken for sin may well be compared to that of a broken bone; and it is the same Spirit who as a Spirit of bondage smites and wounds and as a Spirit of adoption heals and binds up.

3. He prays for a complete and effectual pardon. This is that which he is most earnest for as the foundation of his comfort (v. 9): "*Hide thy face from my sins*, that is, be not provoked by them to deal with me as I deserve; they are ever before me, let them be cast behind thy back. *Blot out all my iniquities* out of the book of thy account; blot them out, as a cloud is blotted out and dispelled by the beams of the sun," Isa. xliv. 22.

4. He prays for sanctifying grace. His great concern is to get his corrupt nature changed, and therefore he prays, *Create in me a clean heart, O God!* "Lord, *renew a right spirit within me*"; repair the decays of spiritual strength. Renew a *constant* spirit within me, so some. He had, in this matter, discovered much inconstancy and inconsistency with himself, and therefore he prays, "Lord, fix me for the time to come, that I may never in like manner depart from thee."

5. He prays for the continuance of God's goodwill towards him and the progress of his good work in him, v. 11. "*Cast me not away from thy presence*, as one whom thou abhorrest and canst not endure to look upon." *Take not thy Holy Spirit from me.* We are undone if God take his Holy Spirit from us. Saul was a sad instance of this. How exceedingly sinful, how exceedingly miserable, was he, when the Spirit of the Lord had departed from him! David knew it, and therefore begs thus earnestly: "Lord, whatever thou take from me, my children, my crown, my life, yet *take not thy Holy Spirit from me*."

6. He prays for the restoration of divine comforts and the perpetual communications of divine grace, v. 12. *Restore unto me the joy of thy salvation.* A child of God knows no true nor solid joy but the joy of God's salvation, joy in God his Saviour and in the hope of eternal life. "*Uphold me with thy free Spirit:* I am ready to fall, either into sin or into despair; Lord, sustain me; my own spirit is not sufficient; if I be left to myself, I shall certainly sink."

II. David here promises, v. 13, *I will teach transgressors thy ways.* He had been himself a transgressor, and therefore could speak experimentally to transgressors, and having found mercy with God in the way of repentance, could teach others God's ways. Penitents should be preachers. *Sinners shall be converted unto thee.*

Verses 14–19

I. David prays against the guilt of sin, and prays for the grace of God, enforcing both petitions from a plea taken from the glory of God, which he promises with thankfulness to show forth. The particular sin he prays against is blood-guiltiness, the sin he had now been guilty of, having slain Uriah with the sword of the children of Ammon. He promises that, if God would deliver him, *his tongue should sing aloud of his righteousness;* God should have the glory both of pardoning mercy and of preventing grace. He prays for the grace of God and promises to improve that grace to his glory (v. 15): "*O Lord! open thou my lips*, not only that I may teach and instruct sinners, but *that my mouth shall show forth thy praise*, that I may have a heart enlarged in praise." Guilt had closed his lips, and therefore he had little confidence towards God. To those that are tongue-tied by reason of guilt the assurance of the forgiveness of their sins says effectually, *Ephphatha—Be opened*; and, when the lips are opened, what should they speak but the praises of God.

II. David offers the sacrifice of a penitent contrite heart. He knew that the sacrificing of beasts was in itself of no account with God (v. 16). As they cannot make satisfaction for sin, so God cannot take any sactisfaction in them, any otherwise than as the offering of them is expressive of love and duty to him. He knew also how acceptable true repentance is to God (v. 17): *The sacrifices of God are a broken spirit.* It is a sharp work wrought there, no less than the breaking of the heart; not in despair but in necessary humiliation and sorrow for sin. It is a heart pliable to the word of God, a heart subdued and brought into obedience; it is a heart that is tender, like Josiah's, and trembles at God's word. The breaking of Christ's body for sin is the only sacrifice of atonement, for no sacrifice but that could take away sin; but the breaking of our hearts for sin is a sacrifice of acknowledgment.

III. David intercedes for Zion and Jerusalem.

1. For the good of the church of God (*v.* 18): *Do good in thy good pleasure unto Zion*, that is, "To all the particular worshippers in Zion, to all that love and fear thy name; keep them from falling into such wounding wasting sins as these of mine; defend and succour all that fear thy name." Those that have been in spiritual troubles themselves know how to pity and pray for those that are in like manner afflicted. We must not forget to pray for the church of God; nay, our Master has taught us in our daily prayers to begin with that, *Hallowed be thy name, Thy kingdom come.*

2. For the honour of the churches of God, *v.* 19. They will come to his tabernacle with whole burnt-offerings, which were intended purely for the glory of God, and they shall offer, not lambs and rams only, but bullocks, the costliest sacrifices, upon his altar. "*Thou shalt be pleased with them*, that is, we shall have reason to hope so when we perceive the sin taken away which threatened to hinder thy acceptance." It is a great comfort to think of the communion that is between God and his people in their public assemblies, how he is honoured by their humble attendance on him and they are happy in his gracious acceptance of it.

PSALM 52

David was in very great grief when he said to Abiathar (1 Sam. xxii. 22), "I have occasioned the death of all the persons of thy father's house", who were put to death upon Doeg's malicious information; and to gain some relief to his mind he penned this psalm. I. He arraigns Doeg for what he had done, ver. 1. II. He accuses him, ver. 2–4. III. He passes sentence upon him, ver. 5. IV. He foretells the triumphs of the righteous in the execution of the sentence, ver. 6, 7. V. He comforts himself in the mercy of God, ver. 8, 9.

To the chief musician, Maschil. *A psalm* of David, when Doeg the Edomite came and told Saul, and said unto him, David has come to the house of Ahimelech.

Verses 1–5

The title is a brief account of the story to which the psalm refers, 1 Sam. xxii. 1–23.

I. David argues the case fairly with this proud and mighty man, *v.* 1. Doeg was, by his office, a *mighty man*, for he was set over the servants of Saul, chamberlain of the household. This was he that boasted himself, not only in the power he had to do mischief, but in the mischief he did. It is uncertain how the following words come in: *The goodness of God endures continually.* The patience and forbearance of God are abused by sinners to the hardening of their hearts in their wicked ways. Because God is continually doing them good, therefore they boast in mischief. But it is rather to be taken to show the sinfulness of his sin: "God is continually doing good, and those that therein are like him have reason to glory in their being so; but thou art continually doing mischief, and therein art utterly unlike him, and contrary to him, and yet gloriest in being so."

II. He draws up a high charge against him in the court of heaven, *v.* 2–4. He accuses him of the wickedness of his tongue and the wickedness of his heart. Four things he charges him with:—1. Malice. His tongue does *mischief*, not only pricking like a needle, but cutting *like a sharp razor.* 2. Falsehood. It was a *deceitful tongue* that he did this mischief with (*v.* 4); he loved lying (*v.* 3), and this sharp razor did *work deceitfully* (*v.* 2). He told the truth, but not all the truth. It will not save us from the guilt of lying to be able to say, "There was some truth in what we said," if we pervert it, and make it to appear otherwise than it was. 3. Subtlety in sin: "*Thy tongue devises mischiefs;* that is, it speaks the mischief which thy heart devises." 4. Affection to sin: "*Thou*

lovest evil more than good; that is, thou lovest evil. Thou wouldst rather please Saul by telling a lie than please God by speaking truth." Those are of Doeg's spirit who, instead of being pleased with an opportunity of doing a man a kindness, are glad when they have a fair occasion to do a man a mischief.

III. He reads his doom and denounces the judgments of God against him for his wickedness (*v.* 5): "Thou hast destroyed the priests of the Lord and cut them off, and therefore *God shall likewise destroy thee for ever.*" Doeg is here condemned, 1. To be driven out of the church: *He shall pluck thee out of the tabernacle*, not thy dwelling-place, but God's." Justly was he deprived of all the privileges of God's house who had been so mischievous to his servants. 2. To be driven out of the world: "*He shall root thee out of the land of the living*, in which thou thoughtest thyself so deeply rooted."

Verses 6–9

David was at this time in great distress; the mischief Doeg had done him was but the beginning of his sorrows; and yet here we have him triumphing in tribulation.

I. In the fall of Doeg. They shall observe God's judgments on Doeg, and speak of them, 1. To the glory of God: *They shall see and fear* (*v.* 6); that is, they shall reverence the justice of God. 2. To the shame of Doeg. They shall laugh at him, not with a ludicrous, but a rational serious laughter, as *he that sits in heaven shall laugh at him*, ii. 4. He shall appear ridiculous, and worthy to be laughed at. *Lo, this is the man that made not God his strength.* Now that which ruined Doeg's prosperity was, (1) That he did not build it upon a rock: *He made not God his strength.* Those wretchedly deceive themselves that think to support themselves in their power and wealth without God and religion. (2) That he did build it upon the sand. He thought his wealth would support itself: *He trusted in the abundance of his riches*, which, he imagined, were *laid up for many years.*

II. In his own stability, *v.* 8, 9. "This mighty man is plucked up by the roots; *but I am like a green olive-tree*, planted and rooted, fixed and flourishing; he is turned out of God's dwelling-place, but I am established in it." Now what must we do that we may be as green olive-trees? 1. We must live a life of faith and holy confidence in God and his grace: *I trust in the mercy of God for ever and ever.* 2. We must live a life of thankfulness and holy joy in God (*v.* 9): "*I will praise thee for ever, because thou hast done it*, hast performed thy promise to me." 3. We must live a life of expectation and humble dependence upon God: "*I will wait on thy name;* I will attend upon thee in all those ways wherein thou hast made thyself known, hoping for the discoveries of thy favour to me and willing to tarry till the time appointed for them; *for it is good before thy saints.*"

PSALM 53

God, in this psalm, speaks twice, for this is the same almost verbatim with the fourteenth psalm. The scope of it is to convince us of our sins. The word, as a convincing word, is compared to a hammer, the strokes whereof must be frequently repeated. God, by the psalmist here, I. Shows us how bad we are, ver. 1. II. Proves it upon us by his own certain knowledge, ver. 2, 3. III. He speaks terror to persecutors, the worst of sinners, ver. 4, 5. IV. He speaks encouragement to God's persecuted people, ver. 6.

To the chief musician upon Mahalath, Maschil. *A psalm* of David.

Verses 1–6

1. The fact of sin. Is that proved? Yes, God is a witness to it. All the sinfulness of their hearts and lives is naked and open before him. 2. The fault of

sin. It is that which makes this world such an evil world as it is; it is going back from God, *v.* 3. 3. The fountain of sin. How comes it that men are so bad? Surely it is because *there is no fear of God before their eyes.* Men's bad practices flow from their bad principles. 4. The folly of sin. He is a fool that harbours corrupt thoughts. Atheists, whether in opinion or practice, are the greatest fools in the world. Those that do not seek God do not understand; they are like brute-beasts, for man is distinguished from the brutes, not so much by the powers of reason as by a capacity for religion. *The workers of iniquity* may truly be said to know nothing that do not know God, *v.* 4. 5. The filthiness of sin. Sinners are corrupt (*v.* 1); their nature is vitiated and spoiled, and the more noble the nature is the more vile it is when it is depraved. 6. The fruit of sin. See to what a degree of barbarity it brings men at last; when men's hearts are hardened through the deceitfulness of sin see their cruelty to their brethren, that are bone of their bone—because they will not *run with them to the same excess of riot*, they *eat them up as they eat bread*; as if they had not only become beasts, but beasts of prey. 7. The fear and shame that attend sin (*v.* 5): *There were those in great fear* who had made God their enemy. *The wicked flees when none pursues.* See the ground of this fear; it is because God has formerly *scattered the bones of those that encamped against* his people, not only broken their power and dispersed their forces, but slain them. 8. The faith of the saints, and their hope and power touching the cure of this great evil, *v.* 6. There will come a Saviour, a great salvation, a salvation from sin.

PSALM 54

The key of this psalm hangs at the door, for the title tells us upon what occasion it was penned—when the inhabitants of Ziph, men of Judah (types of Judas the traitor), betrayed David to Saul, by informing him where he was and putting him in a way how to seize him. This they did twice (1 Sam. xxiii. 19; xxvi. 1), and it is upon record to their everlasting infamy. The psalm is sweet; the former part of it, perhaps, was meditated when he was in his distress and put into writing when the danger was over, with the addition of the last two verses, which express his thankfulness for the deliverance, which yet might be written in faith, even when he was in the midst of his fright. Here, I. He complains to God of the malice of his enemies, and prays for help against them, ver. 1–3. II. He comforts himself with an assurance of the divine favour and protection, and that, in due time, his enemies should be confounded and he delivered, ver. 4–7.

To the chief musician on Neginoth, Maschil. *A psalm* of David, when the Ziphim came and said to Saul, Doth not David hide himself with us?

Verses 1-3

1. The great distress that David was now in. The Ziphim came of their own accord, and informed Saul where David was, with a promise to deliver him into his hand. Never let a good man expect to be safe and easy till he comes to heaven. How treacherous, how officious, were these Ziphim! 2. His prayer to God for succour and deliverance, *v.* 1, 2. David has no other plea to depend upon than God's name, no other power to depend upon than God's strength, and those he makes his refuge and confidence. Even in his flight, when he had not opportunity for solemn address to God, he was ever and anon lifting up to heaven: *Hear my prayer*, which comes from my heart, and *give ear to the words of my mouth.* 3. His plea which is taken from the character of his enemies, *v.* 3. They are *strangers*; such were the Ziphites, unworthy the name of Israelites. "They have used me more basely and barbarously than the Philistines themselves would have done." They are *oppressors*; such was Saul, who, as a king, should have used his power for the protection of all his good subjects, but abused it for their destruction. They were very

formidable and threatening; they not only hated him and wished him ill, but they rose up against him in a body, joining their power to do him a mischief. They were very spiteful and malicious: *They seek after my soul. They have not set God before them*, that is, they have quite cast off the thoughts of God; they do not consider that in fighting against his people, they fight against him.

Verses 4-7

David's faith in his prayer.

I. He was sure that he had God on his side, *Behold, God is my helper.* Though men and devils aim to be our destroyers, they shall not prevail while God is our helper: *The Lord is with those that uphold my soul.* Compare cxviii. 7, *"The Lord taketh my part with those that help me."*

II. God taking part with him, he doubted not but his enemies should fall before him (*v.* 5): "*He shall reward evil unto my enemies that observe me.* The evil they designed against me the righteous God will return upon their own heads." David would not render evil to them, but he knew God would: *I as a deaf man heard not, for thou wilt hear.* We must not avenge ourselves, because God has said, *Vengeance is mine.* But he prays, *Cut them off in thy truth.* This is not a prayer of malice, but a prayer of faith; for it has an eye to the word of God, and only desires the performance of that.

III. He promises to give thanks to God for all the experiences he had had of his goodness to him (*v.* 6): *I will sacrifice unto thee. I will praise thy name.* A thankful heart, and our lips giving thanks to his name, are the sacrifices God will accept.

IV. He speaks of his deliverance as a thing done (*v.* 7): I will praise thy name, and say, "*He has delivered me*; this shall be my song then." *My eye has seen its desire upon my enemies*, not seen them cut off and ruined, but forced to retreat, tidings being brought to Saul that the Philistines were upon him, 1 Sam. xxiii. 27, 28. All David desired was to be himself safe; when he saw Saul draw off his forces he saw his desire. This may perhaps point at Christ, of whom David was a type; God would deliver him out of all the troubles of his state of humiliation, and he was perfectly sure of it; and all things are said to be put under his feet; for, though we see not yet all things put under him, yet we are sure he shall reign till all his enemies be made his footstool, and he shall see his desire upon them.

PSALM 55

It is the conjecture of many expositors that David penned this psalm upon occasion of Absalom's rebellion, and that the particular enemy he here speaks of, that dealt treacherously with him, was Ahithophel; and some will therefore make David's troubles here typical of Christ's sufferings, and Ahithophel's treachery a figure of Judas's, because they both hanged themselves. But there is nothing in it that is particularly applied to Christ in the New Testament. David was in great distress when he penned this psalm. I. He prays that God would manifest his favour to him, and pleads his own sorrow and fear, ver. 1–8. II. He prays that God would manifest his displeasure against his enemies, and pleads their great wickedness and treachery, ver. 9–15 and again, ver. 20, 21. III. He assures himself that God would, in due time, appear for him against his enemies, comforts himself with the hopes of it, and encourages others to trust in God, ver. 16–19 and again ver. 22, 23.

To the chief musician on Neginoth, Maschil. *A psalm* of David.

Verses 1-8

I. David praying. Prayer is a salve for every sore and a relief to the spirit under every burden: *Give ear to my prayer, O God! v.* 1. *Hide not thyself from my supplication.* If we, in our prayers, sincerely lay open ourselves, our case, our hearts to God, we have reason to hope that he will not hide himself, his favours, his comforts, from us.

II. David weeping; for in this he was a type of Christ that he was a man of sorrows and often in tears (v. 2): "*I mourn in my complaint*" (or in my *meditation*, my *melancholy musings*), "and I make a noise; I cannot forbear such sighs and groans, and other expressions of grief, as discover it to those about me." It is *because of the voice of the enemy*, the menaces and insults of Absalom's party, that swelled, and hectored, and stirred up the people to cry out against David, and shout him out of his palace and capital city, as afterwards the chief priests stirred up the mob to cry out against the Son of David, *Away with him—Crucify him. They cast iniquity upon me.* They hated him themselves, and therefore they studied to make him odious, that others also might hate him. This made him mourn, and the more because he could remember the time when he was the darling of the people, and answered to his name, *David—a beloved one.*

III. David trembling, and in great consternation. We may well suppose him to be so upon the breaking out of Absalom's conspiracy and the general defection of the people. David was a man of great boldness, and in some very eminent instances had signalized his courage, and yet, when the danger was surprising and imminent, his heart failed him. Now David's *heart is sorely pained within him*; *the terrors of death have fallen upon him, v.* 4. Fearfulness of mind and trembling of body came upon him, and horror covered and overwhelmed him, *v.* 5. Sometimes David's faith made him, in a manner, fearless, and he could boldly say, when surrounded with enemies, *I will not be afraid what man can do unto me.* But at other times his fears prevail and tyrannize; for the best men are not always alike strong in faith. How desirous he was, in this fright, to retire into a desert, anywhere to be far enough from hearing the voice of the enemy and seeing their oppressions. He said (v. 6), to God in prayer, to himself in meditation, to his friends in complaint, *O that I had wings like a dove!* He was so surrounded with enemies that he saw not how he could escape but upon the wing, and therefore he wishes, *O that I had wings!* not like a hawk that flies strongly, but *like a dove* that flies swiftly; he wishes for wings, not to fly upon the prey, but to fly from the birds of prey, for such his enemies were. The dove flies low, and takes shelter as soon as she can, and thus would David fly. He would make his escape —*from the wind, storm, and tempest*, the tumult and ferment that the city was now in, and the danger to which he was exposed. "*I would fly away and be at rest, v.* 6. I would fly anywhere, if it were to a barren frightful wilderness, ever so far off, so I might be quiet," *v.* 7.

Verses 9–15

David here complains of his enemies, whose wicked plots had brought him, though not to his faith's end, yet to his wits' end.

I. The character he gives of the enemies. They were of the worst sort of men, and his description of them agrees very well with Absalom and his accomplices. He complains of the city of Jerusalem, which strangely fell in with Absalom and fell off from David: *How has that faithful city become a harlot!* David did himself see nothing but *violence and strife in the city* (v. 9). He saw that violence and strife went about it day and night, and mounted its guards, *v.* 10. *Wickedness*, all manner of wickedness, *is in the midst thereof.* Deceit and guile, and all manner of treacherous dealing, *departed not from her streets, v.* 11. Is Jerusalem, the headquarters of God's priests, so ill taught? Can Jerusalem be ungrateful to David himself, its own illustrious founder, and be made too hot for him, so that he cannot reside in it? He complains of one of the ringleaders of the conspiracy,

that had been very industrious to foment jealousies, to misrepresent him and his government, and to incense the city against him. Who was most active in it? "Not a sworn enemy, not Shimei, nor any of the nonjurors; then I could have borne it, for I should not have expected better from them." *But it was thou, a man, my equal, v.* 13. The Chaldee-paraphrase names Ahithophel as the person here meant. "*We took counsel together*, spent many an hour together, with a great deal of pleasure, in religious discourse," or, as Dr. Hammond reads it, "*We joined ourselves together to the assembly;* I gave him the right hand of fellowship in holy ordinances, and then *we walked to the house of God in company*, to attend the public service." There always has been, and always will be, a mixture of good and bad, sound and unsound, in the visible church. We must not wonder if we be sadly deceived in some that have made great pretensions to those two sacred things, religion and friendship; David himself, though a very wise man, was thus imposed upon, which may make similar disappointments the more tolerable. to us

II. His prayers against them. He prays, 1. That God would disperse them, as he did the Babel-builders (v. 9): "*Destroy, O Lord! and divide their tongues*; by making them to disagree among themselves, and clash with one another." God often destroys the church's enemies by dividing them; nor is there a surer way to the destruction of any people than their division. 2. That God would destroy them, as he did Dathan and Abiram, Num. xvi. 30. "*Let death seize upon them* by divine warrant, and *let them go down quickly into hell*; let them be dead, and buried, and so utterly destroyed, in a moment; for wickedness is wherever they are; it is in the midst of them."

Verses 16–23

In these verses,

I. David perseveres in his resolution to call upon God, being well assured that he should not seek him in vain (v. 16): "*As for me*, let them take what course they please to secure themselves, let violence and strife be their guards, prayer shall be mine; this I have found comfort in, and therefore this will I abide by: *I will call upon God*, and commit myself to him, and *the Lord shall save me*." "*I will pray and cry aloud. I will meditate*" (so the former word signifies). He will pray frequently, every day, and three times a day—*evening, and morning, and at noon*. Those that think three meals a day little enough for the body ought much more to think three solemn prayers a day little enough for the soul, and to count it a pleasure, not a task. It was Daniel's practice to pray three times a day (Dan. vi. 10), and noon was one of Peter's hours of prayer, Acts x. 9.

II. He assures himself that God would in due time give an answer of peace to his prayers.

1. That he himself should be delivered and his fears prevented. He begins to rejoice in hope (v. 18): *God has delivered my soul in peace*, that is, he will deliver it; David is as sure of the deliverance as if it were already wrought. With an eye of faith he now sees himself surrounded, as Elisha was, with chariots of fire and horses of fire, and therefore triumphs thus, *There are many with me*, more *with me than against me*, 2 Kings vi. 16, 17.

2. That his enemies should be reckoned with, and brought down.

(1) David here gives their character as the reason why he expected God would bring them down. They stand in no awe of God (v. 19): "*Because they have no changes* (no afflictions, no interruption to the constant course of their prosperity, no crosses to empty them from vessel to vessel) *therefore they fear*

not God." They are treacherous and false, and will not be held by the most sacred and solemn engagements (*v.* 20). They are base and hypocritical, pretending friendship while they design mischief (*v.* 21): "*The words of his mouth*" (probably, he means Ahithophel particularly) "*were smoother than butter and softer than oil*, yet, at the same time, *war was in his heart*, and those very words had such a mischievous design in them that they were as *drawn swords* designed to stab."

(2) David here foretells their ruin. *God shall hear and afflict them.* God shall *bring them down.* They were bloody men, and cut others off, and therefore God will justly cut them off: they were deceitful men, and defrauded others of the one-half perhaps of what was their due, and now God will cut them short.

III. He encourages himself and all good people to commit themselves to God, with confidence in him. "*I will trust in thee,* in thy providence, and power, and mercy, and not in my own prudence, strength, or merit; when bloody and deceitful men are cut off in the midst of their days I shall still live by faith in thee." And this he will have others to do (*v.* 22): "*Cast thy burden upon the Lord,* whoever thou art that art burdened, and whatever the burden is." *Cast thy care upon the Lord,* so the LXX, to which the apostle refers, 1 Pet. v. 7. Care is a burden; it makes the heart stoop (Prov. xii. 25). To cast our burden upon God is to stay ourselves on his providence and promise. If we do so, it is promised, 1. That he will sustain us. He has not promised to free us immediately from that trouble which gives rise to our cares and fears; but he will provide that we be not tempted above what we are able. 2. That he will never suffer the righteous to be moved, to be so shaken by any troubles as to quit either their duty to God, or their comfort in him.

PSALM 56

It seems by this, and many other psalms, that even in times of the greatest trouble and distress David never hung his harp upon the willow-trees, but that when his dangers and fears were greatest he was still in tune for singing God's praises. He was in imminent peril when he penned this psalm. I. He complains of the malice of his enemies, and begs mercy for himself and justice against them, ver. 1, 2, 5–7. II. He confides in God, being assured that he took his part and that while he lived he should praise God, ver. 3, 4, 8–13.

To the chief musician, upon Jonath-elem-rechokim, Michtam of David, when the Philistines took him to Gath.

Verses 1–7

David, in this psalm, by his faith throws himself into the hands of God, even when he had by his fear and folly thrown himself into the hands of the Philistines. 1 Sam. xxi. 10, 11. This is called *Michtam —a golden psalm.* So some other psalms are entitled, but this has something peculiar in the title; it is upon *Jonath-elem-rechokim,* which signifies *the silent dove afar off.* Some apply this to David himself, who wished for the wings of a dove on which to fly away. He was forced to wander afar off, to seek for shelter in distant countries; there he was like the doves of the valleys, mourning and melancholy; but silent, neither murmuring against God nor railing at the instruments of his trouble.

I. He complains to God the malice of his enemies, to show what reason he had to fear them (*v.* 1): *Be merciful unto me, O God!* That petition includes all the good we come to the throne of grace for. He prays that he might find mercy with God, for with men he could find no mercy. When he fled from the cruel hands of Saul he fell into the cruel hands of the Philistines. "Lord" (says he), "be thou merciful to me now, or I am undone." "*They*

are many that fight against me, and think to overpower me with numbers; take notice of this, *O thou Most High!* and make it to appear that wherein they deal proudly thou art above them." They were very barbarous: they would *swallow him up, v.* 1 and again *v.* 2. They were very unanimous (*v.* 6): *They gather themselves together;* though they were many, and of different interests among themselves, yet they united and combined against David, as Herod and Pilate against the Son of David. They were very powerful, quite too hard for him if God did not help him: "*They fight against me* (*v.* 2); *they oppress me, v.* 1. I am almost overcome and borne down by them, and reduced to the last extremity." They were very subtle and crafty (*v.* 6): "*They hide themselves;* they cover their designs, that they may the more effectually prosecute and pursue them. They hide themselves as a lion in his den, that they may mark my steps"; that is, "they observe everything I say and do with a critical eye, that they may have something to accuse me of." They were very spiteful and malicious. "*They wrest my words,* put them upon the rack, to extort that out of them which was never in them." They were very restless and unwearied. They continually waited for his soul; it was the life, the precious life, they hunted for; it was his death they longed for, *v.* 6.

II. He encourages himself in God, and in his promises, power, and providence, *v.* 3, 4. "*What time I am afraid,* in the day of my fear, when I am most terrified from without and most timorous within, then *I will trust in thee,* and thereby my fears shall be silenced." He resolves to make God's promises the matter of his praises, *In God I will praise,* not only his work which he has done, but *his* word which he has spoken. Some understand by *his word* his providences, every event that he orders and appoints: "When I speak well of God I will with him speak well of everything that he does." Thus supported, he will bid defiance to all adverse powers: "*When in God I have put my trust,* I am safe, I am easy, and *I will not fear what flesh can do unto me.*" As we must not trust to an arm of flesh when it is engaged for us, so we must not be afraid of an arm of flesh when it is stretched out against us.

III. He foresees and foretells the fall of those that fought against him (*v.* 7): *Shall they escape by iniquity?* They hope to escape God's judgments, as they escape men's, by violence and fraud, and the arts of injustice and treachery; but shall they escape? No, certainly they shall not. The sin of sinners will never be their security.

Verses 8–13

Several things David here comforts himself with in the day of his distress and fear.

I. That God took particular notice of all his grievances and all his griefs, *v.* 8. *Thou tellest my wanderings,* my *flittings,* so the old translation. David was now but a young man (under thirty) and yet he had had many removes, from his father's house to the court, thence to the camp, and now he was hunted like a partridge upon the mountains; but this comforted him, that God kept a particular account of all his motions, and numbered all the weary steps he took, by night or by day. When he was wandering he was often weeping, and therefore prays, "*Put thou my tears into thy bottle,* to be preserved and looked upon: nay, I know they are *in thy book,* the book of thy remembrance." God has a bottle and a book for his people's tears, both those for their sins and those for their afflictions. He observes them with compassion and tender concern; he is afflicted in their afflictions, and knows their souls in adversity. Paul was mindful of Timothy's tears (2 Tim. i. 4), and God will not forget the sorrows of his people. God will comfort his people according to the time wherein he has afflicted them, and give to those to reap in joy who sowed in tears. What was sown a tear will come up a pearl.

II. That his prayers would be powerful for the defeat and discomfiture of his enemies, as well as for his own support and encouragement (v. 9): "*When I cry unto thee, then shall my enemies turn back;* I need no other weapons than prayers and tears; *this I know, for God is for me,* to plead my cause, to protect and deliver me; and, if God be for me, who can be against me so as to prevail?" We fight best upon our knees, Eph. vi. 18.

III. That his faith in God would set him above the fear of man, v. 10, 11. Here he repeats, with a strong pathos, what he had said (v. 4), "*In God will I praise his word;* that is, I will firmly depend upon the promise for the sake of him that made it." *In God have I put my trust,* and in him only, and therefore "*I will not be afraid what man can do unto me* (v. 11), though I know very well what he would do if he could," v. 1, 2.

IV. That he was in bonds to God (v. 12): "*Thy vows are upon me, O God!*—not upon me as a burden which I am loaded with, but as a badge which I glory in. It ought to be the matter of our consideration and joy that *the vows of God are upon us*—our baptismal vows renewed at the Lord's table, our occasional vows under convictions, under corrections, by these we are bound to live to God.

V. That he should still have more and more occasion to praise him: *I will render praises unto thee.* This is part of the performance of his vows; for vows of thankfulness properly accompany prayers for mercy, and, when the mercy is received must be made good. "*Thou hast delivered my soul,* my life, *from death,* which was just ready to seize me." If God have delivered us from sin, either from the commission of it by preventing grace or from the punishment of it by pardoning mercy, we have reason to own that he has thereby delivered our souls from death, which is the wages of sin. "*Thou* wilt *deliver my feet from falling;* thou hast done the greater, and therefore thou wilt do the less; thou hast begun a good work, and therefore thou wilt carry it on and perfect it." Those that think they stand must take heed lest they fall, because the best stand no longer than God is pleased to uphold them. God never brought his people out of Egypt to slay them in the wilderness. He that in conversion delivers the soul from so great a death as sin is will not fail *to preserve it to his heavenly kingdom.*

PSALM 57

This psalm is very much like that which goes next before it; it was penned upon a like occasion, when David was both in danger of trouble and in temptation to sin; it begins as that did, "Be merciful to me"; the method also is the same. I. He begins with prayer and complaint, yet not without some assurance of speeding in his request, ver. 1–6. II. He concludes with joy and praise, ver. 7–11.

To the chief musician, Al-taschith, Michtam of David, when he fled from Saul in the cave.

Verses 1–6

The title of this psalm has one word new in it, *Al-taschith—Destroy not.* Some make it to be only some known tune to which this psalm was set; others apply it to the occasion and matter of the psalm. *Destroy not;* that is, David would not let Saul be destroyed, when now in the cave there was a fair opportunity of killing him, and his servants would fain have done so. No, says David, *destroy him not,* 1 Sam. xxiv. 4, 6. Or, rather, God would not let David be destroyed by Saul; he suffered him to persecute David, but still under his limitation, *Destroy him not.*

I. He supports himself with faith and hope in God, and prayer to him, v. 1, 2. *Be merciful to me, O Lord!* It was the publican's prayer, Luke xviii. 13. To recommend himself to God's mercy, he here professes,

1. That all his dependence is upon God: *My soul trusteth in thee,* v. 1. At the footstool of the throne of his grace, he humbly professes his confidence in him: *In the shadow of thy wings will I make my refuge,* as the chickens take shelter under the wings of the hen when the birds of prey are ready to strike at them, *until these calamities be over-past.* He was confident his troubles would end well, in due time; *these calamities will be over-past.* He comforted himself in the goodness of God's nature, by which he is inclined to succour and protect his people, as the hen is by instinct to shelter her young ones.

2. That all his desire is towards God (v. 2): "*I will cry unto God most high,* for succour and relief; to him that is most high will I lift up my soul, and pray earnestly, even *unto God that performs all things for me.*"

3. That all his expectation is from God (v. 3): *He shall send from heaven, and save me.* Those that make God their only refuge, and fly to him by faith and prayer, may be sure of salvation, in his way and time. Look which way he will, on this earth, refuge fails, no help appears; but he looks for it from heaven. Those that lift up their hearts to things above may thence expect all good. *God shall send forth his mercy and truth.* We need no more to make us happy than to have the benefit of the mercy and truth of God, xxv. 10.

II. He represents the power and malice of his enemies (v. 4): *My soul is among lions.* He describes their malicious projects against him (v. 6) and shows the issue of them: "*They have prepared a net for my steps,* in which to take me, and I might not again escape out of their hands; *they have digged a pit before me,* that I might, ere I am aware, run headlong into it." But let us see what comes of it. 1. It is indeed some disturbance to David: *My soul is bowed down.* But, 2. It was destruction to themselves; they dug a pit for David, *into the midst whereof they have fallen.*

III. He prays to God to glorify himself and his own great name (v. 5): "Whatever becomes of me and my interest, *be thou exalted, O God! above the heavens, and let thy glory be above* or over *all the earth;* let all the inhabitants of this earth be brought to know and praise thee." Thus God's glory should lie nearer our hearts, and we should be more concerned for it, than for any particular interests of our own. When David was in the greatest distress and disgrace he did not pray, *Lord, exalt me,* but, *Lord, exalt thy own name.* Thus the Son of David, when his soul was troubled, and he prayed, *Father, save me from this hour,* immediately withdrew that petition, and presented this in the room of it, *For this cause came I to this hour; Father, glorify thy name,* John xii. 27, 28.

Verses 7–11

How strangely is the tune altered here! David's prayer and complaints, by the lively actings of faith, are here, all of a sudden, turned into praises and thanksgivings. Observe,

I. How he prepares himself for the duty of praise (v. 7): *My heart is fixed, O God! my heart is fixed.* My heart is *erect,* or *lifted up* (so some), which was bowed down, v. 6. *My heart is fixed,* it is prepared for every event, being *stayed upon God,* cxii. 7; Isa. xxvi. 3. *My heart is fixed* to *sing and give praise, attending on the Lord without distraction.*

II. How he excites himself to the duty of praise (v. 8): *Awake up my glory,* that is, my tongue (our tongue is our glory, and never more so than when it is employed in praising God), or my soul, that must be first awakened; dull and sleepy devotions will never be acceptable to God.

III. How he pleases himself, and even prides himself, in the work of praise. He resolves to *praise him among the people* and to *sing unto him among the nations, v.* 9. This intimates, 1. That he would even make the earth ring with his sacred songs, that all might take notice how much he thought himself indebted to the goodness of God. 2. That he desires to bring others in to join with him in praising God. He will publish God's praises *among the people.* David, in his psalms, which fill the universal church, and will to the end of time, may be said to be still *praising God among the people* and *singing to him among the nations;* for all good people make use of his words in praising God.

IV. How he furnishes himself with matter for praise, *v.* 10. *Thy mercy is great unto the heavens,* great beyond conception and expression; and *thy truth unto the clouds,* great beyond discovery, for what eye can reach that which is wrapped up in the clouds?

V. How he leaves it at last to God to glorify his own name (*v.* 11): *Be thou exalted, O God!*

Psalm 58

It is the probable conjecture of some that before Saul began to persecute David by force of arms, he formed a process against him by course of law, upon which he was condemned unheard, and attainted as a traitor, by the great council, and then proclaimed "an outlawed wolf", whom any man might kill and no man might protect. The elders, in order to curry favour with Saul, having passed this bill of attainder, it is supposed that David penned this psalm on the occasion. I. He describes their sin, ver. 1–5. II. He imprecates and foretells their ruin (ver. 6–9), which would redound, 1. To the comfort of the saints, ver. 10. 2. To the glory of God, ver. 11.

To the chief musician, Al-taschith, Michtam of David.

Verses 1–5

We have reason to think that this psalm refers to the malice of Saul against David.

In these verses David, not as a king, for he had not yet come to the throne, but as a prophet, in God's name arraigns and convicts his judges. Two things he charges them with:—

I. The corruption of their government. They were a congregation, a bench of justices. One would not have thought a congregation of such could be bribed and biassed with pensions, and yet, it seems, they were, because the son of Kish could do that for them which the son of Jesse could not, 1 Sam. xxii. 7. The judges would not do right, would not protect or vindicate oppressed innocency (*v.* 1): *"Do you indeed speak righteousness, or judge uprightly?* No; your own consciences cannot but tell you that you do not discharge the trust reposed in you as magistrates, by which you are bound to be *a terror to evildoers and a praise to those that do well.* Remember you are sons of men; mortal and dying, and that you stand upon the same level before God with the meanest of those you trample upon, and must yourselves be called to an account and judged. *In heart you work wickedness.* The more there is of the heart in any act of wickedness the worse it is, Eccles. viii. 11. And what was their wickedness? *"You weigh the violence of your hands in the earth"* (or *in the land*), "the peace of which you are appointed to be the conservators of." They did all the violence and injury they could, either to enrich or avenge themselves, and they weighed it. They did it with a great deal of craft and caution: *"You frame it by rule and lines"* (so the word signifies). They did it under colour of justice.

II. The corruption of their nature. This was the root of bitterness from which that gall and wormwood sprang (*v.* 3): *The wicked,* who in heart work wickedness, *are estranged from the womb,* estranged from God and all good, *alienated from the divine life,* and its principles, powers, and pleasures, Eph. iv. 18. They are called, and not miscalled, *transgressors from the womb;* one can therefore expect no other than that they will *deal very treacherously;* see Isa. xlviii. 8. They go astray from God and their duty as soon as they are born (that is, as soon as possibly they can); the foolishness that is bound up in their hearts appears with the first operations of reason. Three instances are here given of the corruption of nature:—1. Falsehood. They soon learn to speak lies, and *bend their tongues, like their bows,* for that purpose, Jer. ix. 3. 2. Malice. *Their poison* (that is, their ill-will, and the spite they bore to goodness and all good men, particularly to David) was *like the poison of a serpent,* innate, venomous, and very mischievous, and that which they can never be cured of. 3. Untractableness. They are malicious, and nothing will work upon them, no reason, no kindness, to mollify them, and bring them to a better temper. *They are like the deaf adder that stops her ear, v.* 4, 5. David compares them to the deaf adder or viper, concerning which there was then this tradition, that whereas, by music or some other art, they had a way of charming serpents, to destroy them or at least disable them to do mischief, this deaf adder would lay one ear to the ground and stop the other with her tail, so that she could not hear the voice of the enchantment, and so defeated the intention of it and secured herself.

Verses 6–11

In these verses we have,

I. David's prayers against his enemies, and all the enemies of God's church and people. 1. He prays that they might be disabled to do any further mischief (*v.* 6): *Break their teeth, O God!* Not so much that they might not feed themselves as that they might not be able to make prey of others, iii. 7. He does not say, "Break their necks" (no; let them live to repent, *slay them not, lest my people forget*), but, "Break their teeth, for they are lions, they are young lions, that live by rapine." 2. That they might be disappointed in the plots they had already laid, and might not gain their point: *"When he bends his bow,* and takes aim *to shoot his arrows* at the upright in heart, *let them be as cut in pieces, v.* 7. Let them fall at his feet, and never come near the mark." 3. That they and their interest might waste and come to nothing, that they might *melt away as waters that run continually;* that is, as *water spilt upon the ground, which cannot be gathered up again,* but gradually dries away and disappears. He prays (*v.* 8) that they might *melt as a snail,* which wastes by its own motion, in every stretch it makes leaving some of its moisture behind, which, by degrees, must needs consume it, though it makes a path to shine after it. And he prays that they might be *like the untimely birth of a woman,* which dies as soon as it begins to live and never *sees the sun.*

II. His prediction of their ruin (*v.* 9): *"Before your pots can feel the heat of a fire of thorns* made under them." 1. The proverbial expressions are somewhat difficult, but the sense is plain, that the judgments of God often surprise wicked people in the midst of their jollity, and hurry them away of a sudden. 2. There are two things which the psalmist promises himself as the effects of sinners' destruction: (1) That saints would be encouraged and comforted by it (*v.* 10): *The righteous shall rejoice when he sees the vengeance.* The prosperity and success of the wicked are a discouragement to the righteous; they sadden their hearts, and are sometimes a strong temptation to them to question their foundations, lxxiii. 2, 13. But when they see the judgments of God they rejoice in the confirmation thereby given to their faith in the providence of God and his justice and righteousness in governing the world. (2) That sinners would be convinced and converted by it, *v.* 11. The vengeance God sometimes takes on the wicked in this world will bring men to say, *Verily, there is a reward for the righteous*. Some shall have their minds so changed that they shall willingly own it, and see with satisfaction, That God is, and, [1] That he is the bountiful rewarder of his saints and servants: *Verily* (however it be, so it may be read) *there is a fruit to the righteous*. Even in this world there is a reward for the righteous. [2] That he is the righteous governor of the world, and will surely reckon with the enemies of his kingdom. *He is a God* (so we read it), not a weak man, not an angel, not a mere name, not (as the atheists suggest) a creature of men's fear and fancy, not a deified hero, not the sun and moon, as idolaters imagined, but a God, a self-existent perfect Being; he it is that judges the earth.

PSALM 59

This psalm is of the same nature and scope with six or seven foregoing psalms; they are all filled with David's complaints of the malice of his enemies and of their cursed and cruel designs against him, his prayers and prophecies against them, and his comfort and confidence in God as his God. The first is the language of nature, and may be allowed; the second of a prophetical spirit, looking forward to Christ and the enemies of his kingdom, and therefore not to be drawn into a precedent; the third of grace and a most holy faith, which ought to be imitated by every one of us. In this psalm, I. He prays to God to defend and deliver him from his enemies, ver. 1–7. II. He foresees and foretells the destruction of his enemies, ver. 8–17.

To the chief musician, Al-taschith, Michtam of David, when Saul sent and they watched the house to kill him.

Verses 1–7

Saul sent a party of his guards to beset David's house in the night, that they might seize him and kill him; we have the story 1 Sam. xix. 11. It was when his hostilities against David were newly begun, and he had but just before narrowly escaped Saul's javelin. These first eruptions of Saul's malice could not but put David into disorder and be both grievous and terrifying, and yet he kept up his communion with God, and such a composure of mind as that he was never out of frame for prayer and praises.

I. David prays to be delivered out of the hands of his enemies, "*Deliver me from my enemies, O my God!* thou art *God*, and canst deliver me, *my* God, under whose protection I have put myself. Set me on high out of the reach of the power and malice of those that rise up against me. O deliver me! and save me." He prays (*v.* 4), "*Awake to help me*, take cognizance of my case, behold that with an eye of pity, and exert thy power for my relief." Thus the disciples, in the storm, awoke Christ, saying, *Master, save us, we perish*. And thus earnestly should we pray daily to be defended and delivered from our spiritual enemies, the temptations of Satan, and the corruptions of our own hearts, which war against our spiritual life.

II. He pleads for deliverance. Our God gives us leave to plead, not to move him, but to move ourselves. David does so here.

1. He pleads the bad character of his enemies. They are *workers of iniquity*, and therefore not only his enemies, but God's enemies; they are *bloody men*, and therefore not only his enemies, but enemies to all mankind.

2. He pleads their malice against him, and the imminent danger he was in from them, *v.* 3. "*They lie in wait*, taking an opportunity to do me a mischief. They are united by league, and actually *gathered together against me*. They are very ingenious in their

contrivances and (*v.* 4): *They run and prepare themselves*, with the utmost speed and fury, to do me a mischief." He takes particular notice of the brutish conduct of the messengers that Saul sent to take him (*v.* 6): "*They return at evening* from the posts assigned them in the day, to apply themselves to their works of darkness, and then *they make a noise like a hound* in pursuit of the hare." They belch out with their *mouth* the malice that boils in their hearts, *v.* 7. *Swords are in their lips;* that is, reproaches that wound my heart with grief (xlii. 10), and slanders that stab and wound my reputation.

3. He pleads his own innocency, not as to God (he was never backward to own himself guilty before him), but as to his persecutors, "*Not for my transgression, nor for my sin, O Lord!* thou knowest, who knowest all things." And again (*v.* 4), *without my fault*. The innocency of the godly will not secure them from the malignity of the wicked. Though our innocency will not secure us from troubles, yet it will greatly support and comfort us under our troubles. If we are conscious to ourselves of our innocency, we may with humble confidence appeal to God and beg of him to plead our injured cause.

4. He pleads that his enemies were profane and atheistical, and bolstered themselves up in their enmity to David, with the contempt of God: *For who*, say they, *doth hear? v.* 7. Not God himself, x. 11; xciv. 7.

III. He refers himself and his cause to the just judgment of God, *v.* 5. *Be not merciful to any wicked transgressors. Selah—Mark that*. Though he had transgressed, he was a penitent transgressor, and did not obstinately persist in what he had done amiss. Therefore he could appeal to God in this way.

Verses 8–17

David here encourages himself, in reference to the threatening power of his enemies, with a pious resolution to wait upon God.

I. He resolves to wait upon God (*v.* 9): "*Because of his strength*." It is our wisdom and duty, in times of danger and difficulty, to wait upon God; for he is our defence. He hopes God will be to him a God of mercy (*v.* 10): "*The God of my mercy shall prevent me* with the blessings of his goodness and the gifts of his mercy, and be better to me than my own expectations." Whatever mercy there is in God, it is laid up for us; and is ready to be laid out upon us. Here are several things which he foretells concerning his enemies. He foresees that God would expose them to scorn, as they had indeed made themselves ridiculous, *v.* 8. "They think *God does not hear them, but thou, O Lord! shalt laugh at them* for their folly, to think that he who planted the ear shall not hear, and *thou shalt have* all such other heathenish people that live without God in the world, *in derision*." God would make them standing monuments of his justice (*v.* 11): *Slay them not;* let them not be killed outright, *lest my people forget*. Thus Cain himself, though a murderer, was not slain, lest the vengeance should be forgotten, but was sentenced to be *a fugitive and a vagabond*. "So scatter them that they may never again unite to do mischief, *bring them down, O Lord, our shield!*" *For the sin of their mouth, even for the words of their lips, let them* for this be *taken in their pride*, even for their cursing others and themselves (as sin Saul was subject to, 1 Sam. xiv. 28, 44), and lying. Saul and his party think to rule and carry all before them, but they shall be made to know that there is a higher than they, that there is one who does and will overrule them. He *rules in Jacob*; for there he keeps his court; there he is known, and his name is great. But he *rules to the end of the earth*; for all nations are within the territories of his kingdom. Their sin was their hunting for

David to make a prey of him; their punishment should be that they should be reduced to such extreme poverty that they should hunt about for meat to satisfy their hunger. Thus they should be, not cut off at once, but scattered (*v.* 11). He foretells that they should be forced to beg their bread from door to door. *They shall make a noise like a dog.* When they were in quest of David they made a noise like an angry dog snarling and barking; now, when they are in quest of meat, they shall make a noise like a hungry dog howling and wailing. Those that repent of their sins *mourn,* when in trouble, *like doves;* those whose hearts are hardened make a noise, when in trouble, like dogs, *like a wild bull in a net, full of the fury of the Lord. If they be not satisfied, they will tarry all night,* so that what people do give them is not with goodwill, but only to get rid of them, lest by their continual coming they weary them. It is not poverty, but discontent, that makes a man unhappy.

II. He expects to praise God, that God's providence would find him matter for praise and that God's grace would work in him a heart for praise, *v.* 16, 17.

1. He would praise his power and his mercy; both should be the subject-matter of his song. Power, without mercy, is to be dreaded; mercy, without power, is not what a man can expect much benefit from; but God's power by which he is able to help us, and his mercy by which he is inclined to help us, will justly be the everlasting praise of all the saints. He would praise him because he had, many a time, found him his defence and his refuge in the day of trouble.

2. He would *sing aloud,* as one much affected with the glory of God, that was not ashamed to own it, and that desired to affect others with it.

PSALM 60

After many psalms which David penned in a day of distress this was calculated for a day of triumph; it was penned after he was settled in the throne, upon occasion of an illustrious victory which God blessed his forces with over the Syrians and Edomites; it was when David was in the zenith of his prosperity, and the affairs of his kingdom seem to have been in a better posture than ever they were either before or after. See 2 Sam. viii. 3, 13; 1 Chron. xviii. 3, 12. David, in prosperity, was as devout as David in adversity. In this psalm, I. He reflects upon the bad state of the public interests, for many years, ver. 1-3. II. He takes notice of the happy turn lately given to their affairs, ver. 4. III. He prays for the deliverance of God's Israel from their enemies, ver. 5. IV. He triumphs in hope of their victories, ver. 6-12.

To the chief musician, upon Shushan-eduth, Michtam of David, to teach, when he strove with Aram-naharaim, and with Aramzobah, when Joab returned and smote of Edom in the valley of salt 12,000.

Verses 1-5

The general design of the psalm. It is *Michtam—David's jewel,* and it is *to teach.* The Levites must teach it to the people, and by it teach them both to trust in God and to triumph in him. He was at war with the Syrians, and still had a conflict with them, both those of Mesopotamia and those of Zobah. He had gained a great victory over the Edomites, by his forces, under the command of Joab, who had left 12,000 of the enemy dead upon the spot. He is in care about his strife with the Assyrians, and in reference to that he prays.

In these verses, which begin the psalm, we have,

I. A melancholy memorial of the many disgraces and disappointments which God had, for some years past, put the people under. 1. He complains of *hard things* which they had seen (that is, which they had suffered), while the Philistines and other ill-disposed neighbours took all advantages against them, *v.* 3. 2. He owns God's displeasure to be the cause of all the hardships they had undergone: "*Thou hast been displeased* by us, displeased against us (*v.* 1), and in thy displeasure hast cast us off and scattered us, else

our enemies could not have prevailed thus against us." 3. He laments the ill effects and consequences of the miscarriages of the late years. The whole nation was in a convulsion: *Thou hast made the earth* (or *the land*) *to tremble, v.* 2. The good people themselves were in a consternation: "*Thou hast made us to drink the wine of astonishment* (*v.* 3); we were like men intoxicated, and at our wits' end, not knowing how to reconcile these dispensations with God's promises; we can do nothing, nor know we what to do." When God is turning his hand in our favour, it is good to remember our former calamities. Our calamities serve as foils to our joys.

II. A thankful notice of the encouragement God had given them to hope that, though things had been long bad, they would now begin to mend (*v.* 4): "*Thou hast given a banner to those that fear thee* (for, as bad as the times are, there is a remnant among us that desire to fear thy name, for whom thou hast a tender concern), *that it may be displayed* by thee, *because of the truth* of thy promise which thou wilt perform, and to be displayed by them, in defence of truth and equity," xlv. 4. This banner was David's government, the establishment and enlargement of it over all Israel. It united them, as soldiers are gathered together to their colours. It animated them, and put life and courage into them. It struck a terror upon their enemies, to whom they could now hang out a flag of defiance. Christ, the Son of David, is given *for an ensign of the people* (Isa. xi. 10), for a banner to those that fear God; in him, as the centre of their unity, they glory and take courage. His love is the banner over them; in his name and strength they wage war with the powers of darkness, and under him the church becomes terrible as an army with banners.

III. A humble petition for seasonable mercy. *O turn thyself to us again!* (*v.* 1); smile upon us, be at peace with us, and in that peace we shall have peace. "*Heal the breaches of our land* (*v.* 2), not only the breaches made upon us by our enemies, but the breaches made among ourselves by our unhappy divisions." Thus they might be preserved out of the hands of their enemies (*v.* 5): "*That thy beloved may be delivered, save with thy right hand,* and by such instruments as thou art pleased to make the men of thy right hand, *and hear me.*" God's praying people may take the general deliverances of the church as answers to their prayers in particular.

Verses 6-12

David is here rejoicing in hope and praying in hope (*v.* 6): "*God has spoken in his holiness* (that is, he has given me his word of promise, has *sworn by his holiness, and he will not lie unto David,* lxxxix. 35), therefore *I will rejoice* with the hopes of the performance of the promise, which was intended for more than a pleasing promise."

I. David here rejoices in prospect of two things:—

1. The perfecting of this revolution in his own kingdom. God having *spoken in his holiness* that David shall be king, he doubts not but the kingdom is all his own, as sure as if it were already in his hand: *I will divide Shechem* (a pleasant city in Mount Ephraim) *and mete out the valley of Succoth,* as my own. *Gilead is mine, and Manasseh is mine,* and both are entirely reduced, *v.* 7. Ephraim would furnish him with soldiers for his lifeguards and his standing forces; Judah would furnish him with able judges for his courts of justice; and thus Ephraim would be *the strength of his head* and Judah *his lawgiver.* Thus may an active believer triumph in the promises, for they are all yea and amen in Christ. "*God has spoken in his holiness,* and then pardon is mine, peace mine, grace mine, Christ mine, heaven mine, God himself mine." *All is yours, for you are Christ's,* 1 Cor. iii. 22, 23.

2. The conquering of the neighbouring nations, which had been vexatious to Israel, and which were still dangerous, and opposed to David, *v.* 8. Moab shall be enslaved, and put to the meanest drudgery. *The Moabites became David's servants,* 2 Sam. viii. 2. Edom shall be made a dunghill to throw old shoes upon; at least David shall take possession of it as his own, which was signified by *drawing off his shoe* over, it, Ruth iv. 7. As for the Philistines, let them, if they dare, triumph over him as they had done; he will soon force them to change their note. But the war is not yet brought to an end; there is a *strong city,* Rabbah (perhaps) of the children of Ammon, which yet holds out; Edom is not yet subdued. Now David is here enquiring for help to carry on the war: "*Who will bring me into the strong city? Wilt not thou, O God?* For thou hast *spoken in thy holiness*; and wilt not thou be as good as thy word?" He takes notice of the frowns of Providence they had been under: *Thou hadst,* in appearance, *cast us off; thou didst not go forth with our armies.* At the same time that they own God's justice in what was past they hope in his mercy for what was to come.

II. He prays in hope. His prayer is, *Give us help from trouble, v.* 11. Even in the day of their triumph they see themselves in trouble, because still in war, which is troublesome even to the prevailing side. Though now they were conquerors yet (so uncertain are the issues of war), unless God gave them help in the next engagement, they might be defeated; therefore, *Lord, send us help from the sanctuary. Help from trouble* is rest from war, which they prayed for, as those that contended for equity, not for victory. "*Through God we shall do valiantly,* and so we shall do victoriously; for *he it is,* and he only, *that shall tread down our enemies,* and shall have the praise of doing it." Though *it is God that performs all things for us,* yet there is something to be done by us. Hope in God is the best principle of true courage. Those that do their duty under his conduct may afford to do it valiantly; for what need those fear who have God on their side?

PSALM 61

David, in this psalm, as in many others, begins with prayers and tears, but ends with songs of praise. Thus the soul, by being lifted up to God, returns to the enjoyment of itself. It should seem David was driven out and banished when he penned this psalm, whether by Saul or Absalom is uncertain. I. He will call upon God because God had protected him, ver. 1-3. II. He will call upon God because God had provided well for him, ver. 4, 5. III. He will praise God because he had an assurance of the continuance of God's favour to him, ver. 6-8.

To the chief musician upon Neginah. *A psalm of David.*

Verses 1-4

I. David's close adherence and application to God by prayer in the day of his distress and trouble: "Whatever comes, *I will cry unto thee (v.* 2), as one that will not let thee go except thou bless me." This he will do, "*From the end of the earth,* or of *the land,* from the most remote and obscure corner of the country, *will I cry unto thee.* Though *my heart is overwhelmed,* it is not so sunk, so burdened, but that it may be lifted up to God in prayer. Nay, because my heart is ready to be overwhelmed, therefore *I will cry unto thee,* for by that means it will be supported and relieved." Weeping must quicken praying, and not deaden it.

II. The particular petition he put up to God when his heart was overwhelmed and he was ready to sink: *Lead me to the rock that is higher than I;* that is, "To the rock which is too high for me to get up to unless thou help me to it. To the rock on the top of which I shall be set further out of the reach of my troubles, and nearer the serene and quiet region,

than I can be by any power or wisdom of my own." This rock is Christ; those are safe that are in him.

III. His desire and expectation of an answer of peace. He begs in faith *(v.* 1): "*Hear my cry, O God! attend unto my prayer;* that is, let me have the present comfort of knowing that I am heard (xx. 6), and in due time let me have that which I pray for."

IV. The ground of this expectation, and the plea he uses to enforce his petition *(v.* 3): "*Thou hast been a shelter for me;* I have found in thee a rock higher than I: therefore I trust thou wilt still lead me to that rock."

V. His resolution to continue in the way of duty to God and dependence on him, *v.* 4. David was now banished from the tabernacle, which was his greatest grievance, but he is assured that God by his providence would bring him back. He speaks of abiding in it *for ever* because that tabernacle was a type and figure of heaven, Heb. ix. 8, 9, 24. Those that dwell in God's tabernacle, as it is a house of duty, during their short *ever* on earth, shall dwell in that tabernacle which is the house of glory during an endless *ever. I will make my refuge in the covert of his wings,* as the chickens seek both warmth and safety under the wings of the hen.

Verses 5-8

I. With what pleasure David looks back upon what God had done for him formerly *(v.* 5): *Thou, O God! hast heard my vows.* God is a witness to all our vows, all our good purposes, and all our solemn promises of new obedience. "The prayers thou hast graciously heard and answered," encouraged him now to pray, *O God! hear my cry.* "Thou hast heard my vows, and given a real answer to them; for *thou hast given me a heritage of those that fear thy name.*" We need desire no better heritage than that of those who fear God.

II. With what assurance he looks forward to the continuance of his life *(v.* 6): *Thou shalt prolong the king's life.* His resolution was to abide in God's tabernacle for ever *(v.* 4), in a way of duty; and now his hope is that he shall abide before God for ever, in a way of comfort.

III. With what importunity he begs of God to take him and keep him always under his protection: *O prepare mercy and truth which may preserve him!* David is sure that God will prolong his life, and therefore prays that he would preserve it, not that he would prepare him a strong lifeguard, or a well-fortified castle, but that he would prepare mercy and truth for his preservation. We need not desire to be better secured than under the protection of God's mercy and truth.

IV. With what cheerfulness he vows the grateful returns of duty to God *(v.* 8): *So will I sing praise unto thy name for ever. That I may daily perform my vows.* His praising God was itself the performance of his vows.

PSALM 62

This psalm has nothing in it directly either of prayer or praise, nor does it appear upon what occasion it was penned, nor whether upon any particular occasion, whether mournful or joyful. But in it, I. David with a great deal of pleasure professes his own confidence in God and dependence upon him, ver. 1-7. II. With a great deal of earnestness he excites and encourages others to trust in God likewise, and not in any creature, ver. 8-12.

To the chief musician, to Jeduthun. A psalm of David.

Verses 1-7

I. David's profession of dependence upon God, and upon him only, for all good *(v.* 1): *Truly my soul waiteth upon God. Nevertheless* (so some) or "*However it be,* whatever difficulties or dangers I may meet with, though God frown upon me and I meet with discouragements in my attendance on him, yet still my soul waits upon God" (or *is silent to God*, as the word is), "says nothing against what he does, but quietly expects what he will do." "From him I know it will come, and therefore on him will I patiently wait till it does come, for his time is the best time."

II. The ground and reason of this dependence (*v.* 2): *He only is my rock and my salvation; he is my defence.* Creatures are insufficient; they are nothing without him, and therefore I will look above them to him.

III. The improvement he makes of his confidence in God. "If God is my strength and mighty deliverer, *I shall not be greatly moved* (that is, I shall not be undone and ruined); I may be shocked, but I shall not be sunk." His enemies are slighted, and all their attempts against him looked upon by him with contempt, *v.* 3, 4. "*How long will you* do it? Will you never be convinced of your error? Will your malice never have spent itself?" Envy was at the bottom of their malice; they were grieved at David's advancement, and therefore plotted, by diminishing his character, to hinder his preferment. *They delight in lies. They bless with their mouth* (they compliment David to his face), *but they curse inwardly;* in their hearts they wish him all mischief, and privately they are carrying on some evil design or other, by which they hope to ruin him. It is dangerous putting our trust in men who are thus false; but God is faithful. *You shall be slain all of you*, by the righteous judgments of God. Saul and his servants were slain by the Philistines on Mount Gilboa, according to this prediction. God's church is built upon a rock which will stand, but those that fight against it shall be *as a bowing wall and a tottering fence*, which, having a rotten foundation, falls of a sudden, and buries those in the ruins of it that put themselves under the shadow and shelter of it. David is himself encouraged to continue waiting upon God (*v.* 5–7). "If God will save my soul, as to everything else let him do what he pleases with me, and I will acquiesce in his disposals, knowing they shall *all turn to my salvation*," Phil. i. 19. He repeats (*v.* 6) what he had said concerning God (*v.* 2), as one that dwelt much upon it in his thoughts: *He only is my rock and my salvation; he is my defence*, I know he is; but there he adds, *I shall not be greatly moved*, here, *I shall not be moved at all.* And, as David's faith in God advances to an unshaken stayedness, so his joy in God improves itself into a holy triumph (*v.* 7): *In God is my salvation and my glory.*

Verses 8–12

Here we have David's exhortation to others to trust in God and wait upon him.

I. He counsels all to wait upon God, as he did, *v.* 8. *You people* (that is, all people); all shall be welcome to trust in God, for he is *the confidence of all the ends of the earth*, lxv. 5. "*Trust in him;* depend upon him to perform all things for you, upon his wisdom and goodness, his power and promise, his providence and grace. Do this *at all times.*" *Pour out your heart before him.* The expression seems to allude to the pouring out of the drink-offerings before the Lord. When we make a penitent confession of sin our hearts are therein *poured out before God*, 1 Sam. vii. 6. But here it is meant of prayer, which, if it be as it should be, is the pouring out of the heart before God. We must lay our grievances before him, offer up our desires to him with all humble freedom, patiently submitting our wills to his: this is pouring out our hearts. *God is a refuge for us*, not only my refuge (*v.* 7), but a refuge for us all, even as many as will flee to him and take shelter in him.

II. He cautions us to take heed of misplacing our confidence. Let us not trust in the men of this world, for they are broken reeds (*v.* 9): *Surely men of low degree are vanity*, utterly unable to help us, and *men of high degree are a lie*, that will deceive us if we trust to them. But lay them *in the balance*, the balance of the scripture, or rather make trial of them, see how they will prove, whether they will answer your expectations from them or no, and you will write *Tekel* upon them; they are alike *lighter than vanity*. Let us not trust in the wealth of this world, let not that be made our strong city (*v.* 10): *Trust not in oppression;* that is, in riches got by fraud and violence. Nay, because it is hard to have riches and not to trust in them, if they increase, though by lawful and honest means, we must take heed lest we let out our affections inordinately towards them: "*Set not your heart upon them;* be not eager for them." This we are most in danger of doing when riches increase.

III. He gives a very good reason why we should make God our confidence, because he is a God of infinite power, mercy, and righteousness, *v.* 11, 12. "God has spoken it, and I have heard it, once, yea, twice. He has spoken it, and I have heard once, yea, twice (that is, many a time), by the events that have concerned me in particular. He has spoken it and I have heard it by the light of revelation, by dreams and visions (Job iv. 15), by the glorious manifestation of himself upon Mount Sinai" (to which, some think, it does especially refer), "and by the written word." To some God speaks twice and they will not hear once; but to others he speaks but once, and they hear twice. Compare Job xxxiii. 14. Now what is it which is thus spoken and thus heard? *Power belongs to God;* he is almighty, and can do everything; with him nothing is impossible. He is a God of infinite goodness. Here the psalmist turns his speech to God himself, as being desirous to give him the glory of his goodness, which is his glory: *Also unto thee, O Lord! belongeth mercy.* He is merciful in a way peculiar to himself; he is the *Father of mercies*, 2 Cor. i. 3. He never did, nor ever will do, any wrong to any of his creatures: *For thou renderest to every man according to his work.*

PSALM 63

This psalm has in it as much of warmth and lively devotion as any of David's psalms in so little a compass. As the sweetest of Paul's epistles were those that bore date out of a prison, so some of the sweetest of David's psalms were those that were penned, as this was, in a wilderness. I. His desire towards God, ver. 1, 2. II. His esteem of God, ver. 3, 4. III. His satisfaction in God, ver. 5. IV. His secret communion with God, ver. 6. V. His joyful dependence upon God, ver. 7, 8. VI. His holy triumph in God over his enemies and in the assurance of his own safety, ver. 9–11.

A psalm of David, when he was in the wilderness of Judah.

Verses 1–2

The title tells us when the psalm was penned, when David was *in the wilderness of Judah*; that is, *in the forest of Hareth* (1 Sam. xxii. 5) or in *the wilderness of Ziph*, 1 Sam. xxiii. 15. Even in Canaan, though a fruitful land and the people numerous, yet there were wildernesses, places less fruitful and less inhabited than other places. It will be so in the world, in the church, but not in heaven; there *the wilderness shall blossom as the rose*. The best and dearest of God's saints and servants may sometimes have their lot cast in a wilderness. There are psalms proper for a wilderness, and we have reason to thank God that it is the wilderness of Judah we are in, not the wilderness of Sin.

David, in these verses, *stirs up himself to take hold on God*,

I. By a lively active faith: *O God! thou art my God.* We must acknowledge that God is, that we speak to one that really exists and is present with us, when we say, *O God!* which is a serious word; pity it should ever be used as a by-word.

II. By pious and devout affections,

1. He resolves to seek God, and his favour and grace: *Thou art my God*, and therefore *I will seek*

thee; for *should not a people seek unto their God?* Isa. viii. 19. *Early will I seek thee.* "*My soul thirsteth for thee* and *my flesh longeth for thee* (that is, my whole man is affected with this pursuit) here *in a dry and thirsty land.*"

2. He longs to enjoy God. What is it that he does so passionately wish for? What is his petition and what is his request? It is this (*v.* 2), *To see thy power and thy glory, so as I have seen thee in the sanctuary.* That is, "To see it here in this wilderness as I have seen it in the tabernacle, to see it in secret as I have seen it in the solemn assembly." He longs to be brought out of the wilderness, not that he might see his friends again and be restored to the pleasures and gaieties of the court, but that he might have access to the sanctuary, not to see the priests there, and the ceremony of the worship, but *to see thy power and glory.* He does not say, as I have seen them, but "as I have seen *thee.*" We cannot see the essence of God, but we see him in seeing by faith his attributes and perfections. Those were precious minutes which he spent in communion with God; he loved to think them over again.

Verses 3–6

How soon are David's complaints and prayers turned into praises and thanksgivings! David was now in a wilderness, and yet had his heart much enlarged in blessing God.

I. What David will praise God for (*v.* 3): *Because thy loving kindness is better than life.* It is our spiritual life, and that is better than temporal life, xxx. 5. We have better provisions and better possessions than the wealth of this world can afford us, and in the service of God, and in communion with him, we have better employments and better enjoyments than we can have in the business and converse of this world.

II. How he will praise God, and how long, *v.* 4. "*Thus will I bless thee,* thus as I have now begun; the present devout affections shall not pass away, like the morning cloud, but shine more and more, like the morning sun." *I will bless thee while I live.* Praising God must be the work of our whole lives. *I will lift up my hands in thy name.* In all our prayers and praises we are taught to begin with,—*Hallowed be thy name,* and to conclude with,—*Thine is the glory.*

III. With what pleasure and delight he would praise God, *v.* 5. *My soul shall be satisfied as with marrow and fatness,* not only as with bread, which is nourishing, but as with marrow, which is pleasant and delicious, Isa. xxv. 6. There is that in a gracious God, and in communion with him, which gives abundant satisfaction to a gracious soul, xxxvi. 8; lxv. 4. And there is that in a gracious soul which takes abundant satisfaction in God and communion with him. He will praise God *with joyful lips.* When with the heart man believes and is thankful with the mouth confession must be made of both, to the glory of God; not that the performances of the mouth are accepted without the heart (Matt. xv. 8), but out of the abundance of the heart the mouth must speak (xlv. 1). Praising lips must be joyful lips.

IV. How he would entertain himself with thoughts of God when he was most retired (*v.* 6): I will praise thee *when I remember thee upon my bed.* God was in all his thoughts, which is the reverse of the wicked man's character, x. 4. The thoughts of God were ready to him: "*I remember thee;* that is, when I go to think, I find thee at my right hand, present to my mind." And they were fixed in him: "*I meditate on thee.*" Thoughts of God must not be transient thoughts, passing through the mind, but abiding thoughts, dwelling in the mind. David was now wandering and unsettled, but, wherever he came,

he brought his religion along with him. When sleep departs from our eyes (through pain, or sickness of body, or any disturbance in the mind) our souls, by remembering God, may be at ease, and repose themselves. Perhaps an hour's pious meditation will do us more good than an hour's sleep would have done. See xvi. 7; xvii. 3; iv. 4; cxix. 62.

Verses 7–11

David here expresses his confidence in God and his joyful expectations from him (*v.* 7): *In the shadow of thy wings I will rejoice,* alluding either to the wings of the cherubim stretched out over the ark of the covenant, between which God is said to dwell, or to the wings of a fowl, under which the helpless young ones have shelter, as the eagle's young ones (Exod. xix. 4; Deut. xxxii. 11), which speaks the divine power, and the young ones of the common hen (Matt. xxiii. 37), which speaks more of divine tenderness. It is a phrase often used in the psalms (xvii. 8; xxxvi. 7; lvii. 1; lxi. 4; xci. 4), and nowhere else in this sense, except Ruth ii. 12, where Ruth, when she became a proselyte, is said to *trust under the wings of the God of Israel.* It is our duty to *rejoice in the shadow of God's wings,* which denotes our recourse to him by faith and prayer, as naturally as the chickens, when they are cold or frightened, run by instinct under the wings of the hen.

I. What were the supports and encouragements of David's confidence in God.

1. His former experiences of God's power in relieving him: "*Because thou hast been my help* when other helps and helpers failed me, therefore I will still rejoice in thy salvation, will trust in thee for the future, and will do it with delight and holy joy."

2. The present sense he had of God's grace carrying him on in these pursuits (*v.* 8): *My soul follows hard after thee,* which speaks a very earnest desire and a serious vigorous endeavour to keep up communion with God. David owns, to the glory of God, *Thy right hand upholds me.*

II. David triumphed in the hope,

1. That his enemies should be ruined, *v.* 9, 10. There were those that *sought his soul to destroy it,* not only his life (which they struck at, both to prevent his coming to the crown and because they envied and hated him for his wisdom, piety, and usefulness), but his soul, which they sought to destroy by banishing him from God's ordinances. But they shall *go into the lower parts of the earth,* to the grave, to hell; their enmity to David would be their death. *They shall be a portion for foxes;* either their dead bodies shall be a prey to ravenous beasts or their houses and estates shall be a habitation for wild beasts, Isa. xxxiv. 14.

2. That he himself should gain his point at last (*v.* 11), that he should be advanced to the throne to which he had been anointed: *The king shall rejoice in God.* David's advancement would be the consolation of his friends. *Every one that swears to him* (that is, to David), that comes into his interest and takes an oath of allegiance to him, *shall glory* in his success. *Those that fear thee will be glad when they see me.* Those that heartily espouse the cause of Christ shall glory in its victory at last. *If we suffer with him, we shall reign with him.* It would be the confutation of his enemies: *The mouth of those that speak lies,* of Saul, and Doeg, and others that misrepresented David, *shall be* quite *stopped.*

PSALM 64

This whole psalm has reference to David's enemies, persecutors, and slanders. I. He prays to God to preserve him from their malicious designs against him, ver. 1, 2. II. He gives a very bad character of them, ver. 3–6. III. By the spirit of prophecy he foretells their destruction.

To the chief musician. A psalm of David.

Verses 1-6

David, in these verses, puts in before God a representation of his own danger and of his enemies' character.

I. He earnestly begs of God to preserve him (v. 1, 2): *Hear my voice, O God! in my prayer;* that is, grant me the thing I pray for, and this is it, *Lord, preserve my life from fear of the enemy.* He prays, "*Hide me from the secret counsel of the wicked,* from the mischief which they secretly consult among themselves to do against me, and *from the insurrection of the workers of iniquity,* who join forces, as they join counsels, to do me a mischief."

II. He complains of the great malice and wickedness of his enemies.

1. They are very spiteful in their calumnies and reproaches, v. 3, 4. They are described as military men, with their sword and bow, archers that take aim exactly, secretly, and suddenly, and shoot at the harmless bird that apprehends not herself in any danger. Their tongues are their swords. The tongue is a little member, but, like the sword, it is a dangerous weapon. *Bitter words* are *their arrows*—scurrilous reflections, opprobrious nicknames, false representations, slanders, and calumnies. The upright man is their mark. The better any man is the more he is envied by those that are themselves bad, and the more ill is said of him. They *shoot in secret,* that those they shoot at may not discover them and avoid the danger, for *in vain is the net spread in the sight of any bird.* And *suddenly do they shoot,* without giving a man lawful warning or any opportunity to defend himself. Herein *they fear not,* that is, they are confident of their success.

2. They are very close and very resolute in their malicious projects, v. 5. They consult with themselves and one another how to do the most mischief and most effectually: *They commune of laying snares privily.* All their communion is in sin and all their communication is how to sin securely. *They say, Who shall see them?* A practical disbelief of God's omniscience is at the bottom of all the wickedness of the wicked.

3. They are very industrious in putting their projects in execution (v. 6): "*They search out iniquity;* they take a great deal of pains to find out some iniquity or other to lay to my charge; they dig deep, and look far back, and put things to the utmost stretch, that they may have something to accuse me of." Half the pains that many take to damn their souls would serve to save them.

Verses 7-10

I. The judgments of God upon these malicious persecutors of David. The punishments answer the sin. 1. They shot at David secretly and suddenly, to wound him; but God shall shoot at them, for he *ordains his arrows against the persecutors* (vii. 13), against the face of them, xxi. 12. And God's arrows will hit surer, and fly swifter, and pierce deeper, than theirs do or can. 2. Their tongues fell upon him, but God shall *make their tongues to fall upon themselves.* Those that love cursing, it shall come unto them. Sometimes men's secret wickedness is brought to light by their own confession, and then their own tongue falls upon them.

II. The influence which these judgments should have upon others.

1. Their neighbours shall shun them and shift for their own safety. They *shall flee away,* for fear of being involved in their ruin.

2. Spectators shall reverence the providence of God therein, v. 9. *They shall wisely consider his doing.* They shall be affected with a holy awe of God

upon the consideration of it. They shall speak to one another and to all about them of the justice of God in punishing persecutors. *This is the finger of God.*

3. Good people shall in a special manner take notice of it, v. 10. *The righteous shall be glad in the Lord,* not glad of the misery and ruin of their fellow-creatures, but glad that God is glorified, and his word fulfilled, and the cause of injured innocency pleaded effectually. It shall encourage their faith.

PSALM 65

In this psalm we are directed to give to God the glory of his power and goodness, which appear, I. In the kingdom of grace (ver. 1), hearing prayer (ver. 2), pardoning sin (ver. 3), satisfying the souls of the people (ver. 4), protecting and supporting them, ver. 5. II. In the kingdom of Providence, fixing the mountains (ver. 6), calming the sea (ver. 7), preserving the regular succession of day and night (ver. 8), and making the earth fruitful, ver. 9-13.

To the chief musician. A psalm *and* song of David.

Verses 1-5

The psalmist here has no particular concern of his own at the throne of grace, but begins with an address to God, as the mouth of a congregation.

I. How he gives glory to God, v. 1. 1. By humble thankfulness: *Praise waiteth for thee, O God! in Zion,* waits in expectation of the mercy desired, waits till it arrives, that it may be received with thankfulness at its first approach. "Praise waits, with an entire satisfaction in thy holy will and dependence on thy mercy." *Praise is silent unto thee* (so the word is), as wanting words to express the great goodness of God. As there are holy *groanings which cannot be uttered,* so there are holy adorings which cannot be uttered. 2. By sincere faithfulness: *Unto thee shall the vow be performed,* that is, the sacrifice shall be offered up which was vowed. Better it is not to vow than to vow and not to pay.

II. What he gives him glory for.

1. For hearing prayer (v. 2): *Praise waits for thee;* and why is it so ready? (1) "Because thou art ready to grant our petitions. *O thou that hearest prayer!* thou canst answer every prayer, for thou art able to do for us more than we are able to ask or think (Eph. iii. 20), and thou wilt answer every prayer of faith, either in kind or kindness." (2) Because, for that reason, we are ready to run to him when we are in our straits. "*Therefore,* because thou art a God hearing prayer, *unto thee shall all flesh come.*"

2. For pardoning sin. In this *who is a God like unto him?* Micah vii. 18. "Our sins reach to the heavens, *iniquities prevail against us,* our own consciences accuse us and we have no reply to make; and yet, *as for our transgressions, thou shalt purge them away,* so that we shall not come into condemnation for them."

3. For the kind entertainment he gives to those that attend upon him and the comfort they have in communion with him. Iniquity must first be purged away (v. 3) and then we are welcome to compass God's altars, v. 4.

(1) They are blessed. Not only blessed is the nation (xxxiii. 12), but *blessed is the man,* the particular person, how mean soever, *whom thou choosest, and causest to approach unto thee, that he may dwell in thy courts.* To come into communion with God is to converse with him as one we love and value. It is to dwell in his courts, as the priests and Levites did, that were at home in God's house; it is to be constant in the exercises of religion. We come into communion with God, not recommended by any merit of our own, but by God's free choice: "*Blessed is the man whom thou choosest,* and so distinguishest from others who are left to themselves."

(2) They shall be satisfied. Here the psalmist changes the person, not, *He* shall be satisfied (the

man whom thou choosest), but, *We* shall, which teaches us to apply the promises to ourselves: *We shall be satisfied with the goodness of thy house, even of thy holy temple.* God keeps a good house. There is abundance of goodness in his house, righteousness, grace, and all the comforts of the everlasting covenant; there is enough for all, enough for each; it is ready, always ready; and all on free cost, without money and without price.

4. For the operations of his power on their behalf (*v.* 5): *By terrible things in righteousness wilt thou answer us, O God of our salvation!* This may be understood of the rebukes which God in his providence sometimes gives to his own people; he often answers them by terrible things, for the awakening and quickening of them, but always in righteousness; he neither does them any wrong nor means them any hurt, for even then he is the God of their salvation. See Isa. xlv. 15.

5. For the care he takes of all his people. He is *the confidence of all the ends of the earth* that is, of all the saints all the world over, and not theirs only that were of the seed of Israel; for he is the God of the Gentiles as well as of the Jews.

Verses 6–13

His power and sovereignty as the God of nature.

I. He establishes the earth and it abides, cxix. 90. *By his* own *strength* he *setteth fast the mountains* (*v.* 6). Hence they are called *everlasting mountains*, Hab. iii. 6. Yet God's covenant with his people is said to stand more firmly than they, Isa. liv. 10.

II. He stills the sea, and it is quiet, *v.* 7. The sea in a storm makes a great noise, but, when God pleases, he commands silence among the waves and billows, and lays them to sleep, turns the storm into a calm quickly, cvii. 29. And by the sea, as well as by the unchangeableness of the earth, it appears that he whose the sea and the dry land are is girded with power. And by this our Lord Jesus gave a proof of his divine power, that he *commanded the winds and waves, and they obeyed him.* To this quieting of the sea he adds, as a thing much of the same nature, that he stills *the tumult of the people.*

III. He renews the morning and evening, *v.* 8. This regular succession of day and night may be considered, 1. As an instance of God's great power, and so it strikes an awe upon all: *Those that dwell in the uttermost parts of the earth are afraid at thy* signs or *tokens*; they are by them convinced that there is a supreme deity, a sovereign monarch, before whom they ought to fear and tremble. 2. As an instance of God's great goodness, and so it brings comfort to all: *Thou makest the outgoings of the morning,* before the sun rises, *and of the evening,* before the sun sets, *to rejoice.* As it is God that scatters the light of the morning and draws the curtains of the evening, so he gives occasion to us to rejoice in both. We are to look upon our daily worship, alone and with our families to be both the most needful of our daily occupations and the most delightful of our daily comforts.

IV. He waters the earth and makes it fruitful. How much the fruitfulness of this lower part of the creation depends upon the influence of the upper is easy to observe; if the heavens be as brass, the earth is as iron, which is a sensible intimation to a stupid world that every good and perfect gift is from above. All God's blessings, even spiritual ones, are expressed by his raining righteousness upon us. The common blessing of rain from heaven and fruitful seasons is here described.

1. How much there is in it of the power and goodness of God. God that made the earth hereby visits it, sends to it, gives proof of his care of it, *v.* 9. God that made it dry land, hereby waters it, in order to its fruitfulness. Though the productions of the

earth flourished before God had caused it to rain, yet even then there was a mist which answered the intention, and *watered the whole face of the ground,* Gen. ii. 5, 6. Our hearts are dry and barren unless God himself be as the dew to us and water us; and the plants of his own planting he will water and make them to increase. Rain is *the river of God, which is full of water.* This river of God enriches the earth, which without it would quickly be a poor thing. The riches of the earth are abundantly more useful to man than those which are hidden in its bowels; we might live well enough without silver and gold, but not without corn and grass.

2. How much benefit is derived from it to the earth and to man upon it. (1) To the earth itself. The rain in season gives it a new face. Even *the ridges* of the earth, off which the rain seems to slide, are watered *abundantly*, for they drink in the rain which comes often upon them; *the furrows* of it, which are turned up by the plough, are settled by the rain and made fit to receive the seed (*v.* 10); they are settled by being made soft. That which makes the soil of the heart tender settles it; for the heart is established with that grace. Thus the spring is an earnest of a blessing upon the whole year, which God is therefore said to *crown with his goodness* (*v.* 11). And his paths are said to *drop fatness.* These communications of God's goodness to this lower world are very extensive (*v.* 12): *They drop upon the pastures of the wilderness,* and not merely upon the pastures of the inhabited land. The deserts, which man takes no care of and receives no profit from, are under the care of the divine Providence, and we ought to be thankful not only for that which serves us, but for that which serves any part of the creation. So extensive are the gifts of God's bounty that in them the hills, *the little hills, rejoice on every side,* even the north side, that lies most from the sun. Hills are not above the need of God's providence; little hills are not below the cognizance of it. (2) To man upon the earth. *As for the earth, out of it comes bread* (Job xxviii. 5), for out of it comes corn; but every grain of corn that comes out of it God himself prepared; and therefore he provides rain for the earth, that thereby he may prepare corn for man, under whose feet he has put the rest of the creatures and for whose use he has fitted them. The yearly produce of the corn is not only an operation of the same power that raises the dead, but an instance of that power not much unlike it (as appears by that of our Saviour, John xii. 24), and the constant benefit we have from it is an instance of that goodness which endures for ever. Corn and cattle are the two staple commodities, and both are owing to the divine goodness in watering the earth, *v.* 13. The valleys are so fruitful that they seem to be *covered over with corn,* in the time of harvest. The lowest parts of the earth are commonly the most fruitful, and one acre of the humble valleys is worth five of the lofty mountains. But both corn-ground and pasture-ground, answering the end of their creation, are said to *shout for joy and sing,* because they are serviceable to the honour of God and the comfort of man.

PSALM 66

This is a thanksgiving psalm. All people are here called upon to praise God, I. For the general instances of his sovereign power in the whole creation, ver. 1–7. II. For the special tokens of his favour to the church, his peculiar people, ver. 8–12. And then, III. The psalmist praises God for his own experiences of his goodness to him in particular, especially in answering his prayers, ver. 13–20.

To the chief musician. A song *or* psalm.

Verses 1–7

I. In these verses the psalmist calls upon all people to praise God, *all lands, all the earth, v.* 1. This speaks the glory of God for he is good to all. 2. The duty of man, that all are obliged to praise God; it is part of the law of creation, and therefore is required of every creature. 3. A prediction of the conversion of the Gentiles to the faith of Christ; the time should come when all lands should praise God. 4. The psalmist will abound in it himself, and wishes that God might have his tribute paid him by all the nations of the earth and not by the land of Israel only. We must be hearty and zealous, open and public, as those that are not ashamed of our Master. And both these are implied in making a noise, a joyful noise. In praising God we must do it so as to glorify him. *Reckon it your greatest glory to praise God*, so some.

II. He had called upon all lands to praise God (v. 1), and he foretells (v. 4) that they shall do so: *All the earth shall worship thee.* They shall *sing to God*, that is, *sing to his name*, for it is only to his declarative glory, that by which he has made himself known, not to his essential glory, that we can contribute anything by our praises.

III. We are here called upon *to come and see the works of God*; for *his own works praise him*, whether we do or no; and the reason why we do not praise him more and better is because we do not duly and attentively observe them. Let us therefore see God's works (v. 5), and then speak of them, and speak of them to him (v. 3): *Say unto God, How terrible art thou in thy works, terrible in thy doings!* 1. God's works are wonderful in themselves. God *is terrible* (that is, admirable) in his works. In all his doings towards the children of men he is terrible, and to be eyed with a holy awe. Much of religion lies in a reverence for the divine Providence. 2. They are formidable to his enemies, and have many a time forced and frightened them into a feigned submission (v. 3): *Through the greatness of thy power*, before which none can stand, *shall thy enemies submit themselves unto thee*; *they shall lie unto thee* (so the word is), that is, they shall be compelled, sorely against their wills, to make their peace with thee upon any terms. 3. They are comfortable and beneficial to his people, v. 6. When Israel came out of Egypt, *he turned the sea into dry land before them*, which encouraged them to follow God's guidance through the wilderness; and, when they were to enter Canaan, for their encouragement in their wars Jordan was divided before them, and *they went through that flood on foot.* The joys of our fathers were our joys, and we ought to look upon ourselves as sharers in them. 4. They are commanding to all. God by his works keeps up his dominion in the world (v. 7): *He rules by his power for ever; his eyes behold the nations.* He has a commanding arm. *Strong is his hand, and high is his right hand.* Hence he infers, *Let not the rebellious exalt themselves;* let not those that have revolting and rebellious hearts dare to rise up in any acts of rebellion against God.

Verses 8–12

Two things we have reason to bless God for:—

I. Common protection (v. 9): *He holdeth our soul in life. He puts our soul in life*, so the word is. He that gave us our being, by a constant renewed act upholds us in our being, and his providence is a continued creation. *It is not existence, but happiness, that deserves the name of life.* He *suffers not our feet to be moved*, preventing many unforeseen evils.

II. Special deliverance from great distress.

1. How grievous the distress and danger were, v. 11, 12. What particular trouble of the church this refers to does not appear; it might be the trouble of some private persons or families only. But, whatever it was, they were pressed down with it, and kept under as with a load *upon their loins*, v. 11. Is anything more dangerous than fire and water? *We went through both*, that is, afflictions of different kinds. When men rose up against us, that was fire and water. That was the case here: "*Thou hast caused men to ride over our heads*, to trample upon us and insult over us, to hector and abuse us, nay, and to make perfect slaves of us; they have said to our souls, *Bow down, that we may go over*," Isa. li. 23.

2. How gracious God's design was in bringing them into this distress and danger. See what the meaning of it is (v. 10): *Thou, O God! hast proved us, and tried us.* By afflictions we are proved as silver in the fire. Our graces, by being exercised, may be made more strong and active, and so we may be improved, as silver when it is refined by the fire and made more clear from its dross; and this will be to our unspeakable advantage, for thus we are made partakers of God's holiness, Heb. xii. 10.

3. How glorious the issue was at last. The troubles of the church will certainly end well. They are in fire and water, but they get through them: "*We went through fire and water*, and did not perish in the flames or floods." Whatever the troubles of the saints are, blessed be God, there is a way through them. *Thou broughtest us out into a wealthy place* into a well-watered place (so the word is), *like the gardens of the Lord*, and therefore fruitful.

Verses 13–20

The psalmist, having before stirred up all people to bless the Lord, here stirs up himself.

I. In his devotions to his God, v. 13–15. 1. By costly sacrifices (v. 13): *I will go into thy house with burnt-offerings.* His sacrifices should be public, in the place which God had chosen: "I will go into thy house with them." Christ is our temple, to whom we must bring our spiritual gifts, and by whom they are sanctified. They should be the best of the kind—*burnt-sacrifices*, which were wholly consumed upon the altar. He will *offer bullocks with goats with the incense of rams. Or rams with incense.* The incense typifies Christ's intercession, without which the fattest of our sacrifices will not be accepted. 2. By a conscientious performance of his vows. This was the psalmist's resolution (v. 13, 14), *I will pay thee my vows, which my lips have uttered when I was in trouble.*

II. In his declarations to his friends, v. 16. He calls together a congregation of good people to hear his thankful narrative of God's favours to him: "*Come and hear, all you that fear God.*" God's people should communicate their experiences to each other. We should take all occasions to tell one another of the great things which God has done for our souls, the spiritual blessings with which he has blessed us. Now what was it that God had done for his soul? (1) He had wrought in him a love to the duty of prayer, and had by his grace enlarged his heart in that duty (v. 17): *I cried unto him with my mouth.* God has given us leave to pray, a command to pray, encouragements to pray, and (to crown all) a heart to pray. By crying to him we do indeed extol him. He is pleased to reckon himself honoured by the humble believing prayers of the upright. In seeking our own welfare, we seek his glory. *His exaltation was under my tongue* (so it may be read); that is, I was considering in my mind how I might exalt and magnify his name. When prayers are in our mouths praises must be in our hearts. (2) He had wrought in him a dread of sin as an enemy to prayer (v. 18): *If I regard iniquity in my heart, I know very well the Lord will not hear me.* The sense of this place is plain: *If I regard iniquity in my heart*, that is, "If I have favourable thoughts of it, if I love it, indulge it, and allow myself in it, God will not hear my prayer, nor can I expect an answer of peace to it." (3) He had graciously granted him an answer of peace to his prayers (*v.* 19). This God did for his soul, by answering his prayer, he gave him a token of his favour. And therefore he concludes (*v.* 20), *Blessed be God.* What we win by prayer we must wear with praise. Lest it should be thought that the deliverance was granted for the sake of some worthiness in his prayer, he ascribes it to God's mercy. "It was not my prayer that fetched the deliverance, but his mercy that sent it."

PSALM 67

Here is, I. A prayer for the prosperity of the church of Israel, ver. 1. II. A prayer for the conversion of the Gentiles and the bringing of them into the church, ver. 2-5. III. A prospect of happy and glorious times when God shall do this, ver. 6, 7.

To the chief musician on Negonoth. A psalm *or* song.

Verses 1–7

The psalmist was elevated to receive the spirit of prophecy concerning the enlargement of God's kingdom.

I. He begins with a prayer for the welfare and prosperity of the church then in being, *v.* 1. Our Saviour, in teaching us to say, *Our Father,* has intimated that we ought to pray with and for others; so the psalmist here prays not, *God be merciful to me, and bless me,* but to *us,* and bless *us.* We are here taught, 1. That all our happiness comes from God's mercy and takes rise in that; and therefore the first thing prayed for is, *God be merciful to us,* to us sinners. 2. *God bless us;* that is, give us an interest in his promises, and confer upon us all the good contained in them. *God bless us* is a comprehensive prayer. 3. *God cause his face to shine upon us*; that is, God by his grace qualify us for his favour and then give us the tokens of his favour. *To shine with us* (so the margin reads it); *with us* doing our endeavour, and let it crown that endeavour with success.

II. He passes from this to a prayer for the conversion of the Gentiles (*v.* 2): *That thy way may be known upon earth.* Thus public-spirited must we be in our prayers. *Father in heaven, hallowed be thy name, thy kingdom come.*

1. These verses, which point at the conversion of the Gentiles, may be taken, (1) As a prayer; and so it speaks the desire of the Old Testament saints. They desired nothing more than the throwing down of the enclosure and the laying open of the advantages. See then how the spirit of the Jews, in the days of Christ and his apostles, differed from the spirit of their fathers. The Israelites indeed that were of old desired that God's name might be known among the Gentiles; those counterfeit Jews were enraged at the preaching of the gospel to the Gentiles. (2) As a prophecy that it shall be as he here prays.

2. Three things are here prayed for, with reference to the Gentiles:—

(1) That divine revelation might be sent among them, *v.* 2. "Let them all know, as well as we do, *what is good and what the Lord our God requires of them;* let them be blessed and honoured with the same righteous statutes and judgments which are so much the praise of our nation and the envy of all its neighbours," Deut. iv. 8. If God make known his way to us, and we walk in it, he will show us his saving health, l. 23. Those that have themselves experimentally known the pleasantness of God's ways, and the comforts of his salvation, cannot but desire and pray that they may be known to others, even among all nations.

(2) That divine worship may be set up among them, as it will be where divine revelation is received and embraced (*v.* 3): "*Let the people praise thee, O God!* let them have matter for praise, let them have hearts for praise; yea, let not only some, but *all the people, praise thee.*" It is a prayer, [1] That the gospel might be preached to them, and then they would have cause enough to praise God, as for the day-spring after a long and dark night. [2] That they might be converted and brought into the church, and then they would have a disposition to praise God. [3] That they might be incorporated into solemn assemblies, that they might all together praise him with one mind and one mouth.

(3) That the divine government may be acknowledged (*v.* 4): *O let the nations be glad, and sing for joy!* The joy he wishes to the nations is holy joy; for it is joy that *God has taken to himself his great power and has reigned.* Let them be glad that *thou shalt judge the people righteously.* Let us all be glad that we are not to be one another's judges, but that he that judges us is the Lord, whose judgment we are sure is according to truth.

III. He concludes with a joyful prospect of all good when God shall do this, when the nations shall be converted and brought to praise God.

1. The lower world shall smile upon them, and they shall have the fruits of that (*v.* 6): *Then shall the earth yield her increase.* Not but that God gave rain from heaven and fruitful seasons to the nations when they *sat in darkness* (Acts xiv. 17); but when they were converted the earth yielded its increase to God; and then it was fruitful to some good purpose. Then it yielded its increase more than before to the comfort of men, who through Christ acquired a covenant-title to the fruits of it and had a sanctified use of it.

2. The upper world shall smile upon them, and they shall have the favours of that, which is much better: *God, even our own God, shall bless us, v.* 6. And again (*v.* 7), *God shall bless us.* We receive the increase of the earth as a mercy indeed when with it God, even our own God, gives us his blessing.

3. All the world shall hereby be brought to do like them: *The ends of the earth shall fear him,* that is, worship him, which is to be done with a godly fear.

PSALM 68

It does not appear upon what occasion David penned this psalm; but probably it was when he brought the ark from the house of Obed-edom to the tent he had pitched for it in Zion; for the first words are the prayer which Moses used at the removing of the ark, Num. x. 35. I. He begins with prayer, both against God's enemies (ver. 1, 2) and for his people, ver. 3. II. He proceeds to praise, which takes up the rest of the psalm. 1. The greatness and goodness of God, ver. 4-6. 2. The wonderful works God had wrought for his people formerly, bringing them through the wilderness (ver. 7, 8), settling them in Canaan (ver. 9, 10), giving them victory over their enemies (ver. 11, 12), and delivering them out of the hands of their oppressors, ver. 13, 14. 3. The special presence of God in his church, ver. 15-17. 4. The ascension of Christ (ver. 18) and the salvation of his people by him, ver. 19, 20. 5. The victories which Christ would obtain over his enemies, and the favours he would bestow upon his church, ver. 21-28. 6. The enlargement of the church by the accession of the Gentiles to it ver. 29-31. And so he concludes the psalm with an awful acknowledgment of the glory and grace of God, ver. 32-35.

To the chief musician. A psalm *or* song of David.

Verses 1–6

I. David prays that God would appear in his glory,

1. For the confusion of his enemies (*v.* 1, 2): "*Let God arise,* as a judge to pass sentence upon them, as a general to take the field and do execution upon them; *and let them be scattered.* Let God arise, as the sun when he goes forth in his strength; and the children of darkness shall be scattered, as the shadows of the evening flee before the rising sun." Thus does David comment upon Moses' prayer, and not only repeats it with application to himself and his own times, but enlarges upon it, to direct us how to make use of scripture-prayers. Though we are to pray for our enemies as such, yet we are to pray against

God's enemies as such, against their enmity to him and all their attempts upon his kingdom.

2. For the comfort and joy of his own people (v. 3): "*Let the righteous be glad, that are now in sorrow; let them rejoice before God, let them rejoice with gladness.*"

II. He praises God for his glorious appearances,

1. As a great God, infinitely great (v. 4): He *rides upon the heavens, by his name JAH.* He is the spring of all the motions of the heavenly bodies, as he that rides in the chariot sets it a-going, has a supreme command of the influences of heaven. He rules these by his name, *Jah*, or *Jehovah*, a self-existent self-sufficient being, the fountain of all being, power, motion, and perfection; this is his name for ever.

2. As a gracious God, a God of mercy and tender compassion. He is great, but being a God of great power, he uses his power for the relief of those that are distressed, v. 5, 6. The fatherless, the widows, the solitary, find him a God all-sufficient to them. He that *rides on the heavens* glories that he is *a Father of the fatherless. Though God be high, yet has he respect unto the lowly.* He is a *Father of the fatherless,* to pity them, to bless them, to teach them, to provide for them, to portion them. They have liberty to call him Father, and to plead their relation to him as their guardian, cxlvi. 9; x. 14, 18. He is a patron of the widows, to give them counsel and to redress their grievances, to own them and plead their cause, Prov. xxii. 23. He has an ear open to all their complaints and a hand open to all their wants. He is so *in his holy habitation;* let them go to his holy habitation, to his word and ordinances; there they may find him and find comfort in him. When families are to be built up he is the founder of them: *God sets the solitary in families,* brings those into comfortable relations that were lonely, he *makes those dwell at home that were* forced to *seek* for relief *abroad* (so Dr. Hammond), putting those that were destitute into a way of getting their livelihood.

3. As a righteous God, (1) In relieving the oppressed. He *brings out those that are bound with chains,* and sets those at liberty who were unjustly imprisoned and brought into servitude. No chains can detain those whom God will make free. (2) In reckoning with the oppressors: *The rebellious dwell in a dry land* and have no comfort in that which they have got by fraud and injury.

Verses 7–14

Fresh mercies should put us in mind of former mercies and revive our grateful sense of them. Let it never be forgotten.

I. That God himself was the guide of Israel through the wilderness, v. 7. It was not a journey, but a march, for they went as soldiers, as an army with banners.

II. That he manifested his glorious presence with them at Mount Sinai, v. 8. Never did any people see the glory of God, nor hear his voice, as Israel did, Deut. iv. 32, 33. Never had any people such an excellent law given them, so expounded, so enforced. *Sinai itself,* that vast mountain, that long ridge of mountains, *was moved at the presence of God;* see Judges v. 4, 5; Deut. xxxiii. 2; Hab. iii. 3. It would encourage their faith in him and dependence upon him. Whatever mountains of difficulty lay in the way of their happy settlement, he that could move Sinai itself could remove them.

III. That he provided very comfortably for them both in the wilderness and in Canaan (v. 9, 10): *Thou didst send a plentiful rain and hast prepared of thy goodness for the poor.* This may refer, 1. To the victualling of their camp with manna in the wilderness, which was rained upon them, as were also the quails (lxxviii. 24, 27). Or, 2. To the seasonable

supplies granted them in Canaan, that land *flowing with milk and honey,* which is said to *drink water of the rain of heaven,* Deut. xi. 11. This looks further to the spiritual provision made for God's Israel; the Spirit of grace and the gospel of grace are the plentiful rain with which God confirms his inheritance, and from which their fruit is found, Isa. xlv. 8.

IV. That he often gave them victory over their enemies. *The Lord gave the word,* as general of their armies. He raised up judges for them, gave them their commissions and instructions, and assured them of success. God gave them his word (*the word of the Lord* came unto them) and then *great was the company of the preachers*—prophets and *prophetesses,* for the word is feminine. *Kings of armies did flee,* retired without striking a stroke; they fled apace, fled and never rallied again. *She that tarried at home divided the spoil.* Not only the men, the soldiers that abode by the stuff, who were to share the prey (1 Sam. xxx. 24), but even the women that tarried at home had a share, which intimates the abundance of spoil that should be taken. *When the Almighty scattered kings for her* (for the church) *she was white as snow in Salmon,* purified and refined by the mercies of God; *when the host went forth against the enemy they kept themselves from every wicked thing,* and so the host returned victorious, and Israel by the victory were confirmed in their purity and piety. By the resurrection of Christ our spiritual enemies were made to flee, they were for ever disabled to hurt any of God's people.

V. That from a low and despised condition they had been advanced to splendour and prosperity. When they were bond-slaves in Egypt, and afterwards when they were oppressed sometimes by one potent neighbour and sometimes by another, they did, as it were, *lie among the pots* or rubbish, as despised broken vessels. But God, at length, *delivered them from the pots* (lxxxi. 6), and in David's time they were in a fair way to be one of the most prosperous kingdoms in the world, *like the wings of a dove covered with silver,* v. 13. "And so," says Dr. Hammond, "under Christ's kingdom, the heathen idolaters worshipping wood and stone, and given up to the vilest lusts, should from that detestable condition be advanced to the service of Christ, and the practice of all Christian virtues, the greatest inward beauties in the world."

Verses 15–21

David here comes to give him praise as Zion's God in a special manner; compare ix. 11. *Sing praises to the Lord who dwelleth in Zion,* for which reason Zion is called *the hill of God.*

I. He compares it with the hill of Bashan and other high and fruitful hills, and prefers it before them, v. 15, 16. It is true, Zion was but little and low in comparison with them, yet it has the pre-eminence above them all, that it is *the hill of God.* "Why do you insult over poor Zion, and boast of your own height? This is the hill which God has chosen." Zion was especially honourable because it was a type of the gospel church, which is therefore called Mount Zion (Heb. xii. 22), and this is intimated here, when he said, *The Lord will dwell in it for ever.*

II. He compares it with Mount Sinai, of which he had spoken (v. 8), and shows that it has the Shechinah or divine presence in it as really, though not as sensibly, as Sinai itself had, v. 17. Angels are *the chariots of God.* They are vastly numerous: *Twenty thousands,* even thousands multiplied. There is an *innumerable company of angels* in the heavenly Jerusalem, Heb. xii. 22. Some read the last words of the verse, *Sinai is in the sanctuary;* that is, the sanctuary was to Israel instead of Mount Sinai, whence they received divine oracles.

III. The glory of Mount Zion was the King whom God *set on that holy hill* (ii. 6). Of his ascension the psalmist here speaks, and to it his language is expressly applied (Eph. iv. 8): *Thou hast ascended on high* (v. 18); compare xlvii. 5, 6. Christ's ascending on high is spoken of to his honour. He then triumphed over the gates of hell. He led *captivity captive;* that is, he led his captives in triumph, as great conquerors used to do, Col. ii. 15. He led those captive who had led us captive, and who, if he had not interposed, would have held us captive for ever. Nay, he *led captivity itself captive,* having quite broken the power of sin and Satan. This intimates the complete victory which Jesus Christ obtained over our spiritual enemies; it was such that through him *we also are more than conquerors,* that is, triumphers, Rom. viii. 37. He then opened the gates of heaven to all believers: *Thou hast received gifts for men.* He *gave gifts to men,* so the apostle reads it, Eph. iv. 8. And he gave what he had received; having received power to give eternal life, he bestows it upon *as many as were given him,* John xvii. 2. *Thou hast received gifts in man* (so the margin), that is, in the human nature which Christ was pleased to clothe himself with, that he might be a *merciful and faithful high priest in things pertaining to God.* To magnify the kindness and love of Christ to us in receiving these gifts for us, he received them for the *rebellious also,* for those that had been rebellious. Perhaps it is especially meant of the Gentiles, that had been *enemies in their minds by wicked works,* Col. i. 21. This magnifies the grace of Christ exceedingly that through him rebels are, upon their submission, not only pardoned, but preferred. Christ came to a rebellious world, not to condemn it, but that through him it might be saved. He *received gifts for the rebellious,* that *the Lord God might dwell among them,* that he might set up a church in a rebellious world.

IV. The glory of Zion's King is that he is a Saviour and benefactor to all his willing people and a consuming fire to all those that persist in rebellion against him, v. 19-21. We have here good and evil, life and death, the blessing and the curse, set before us (Mark xvi. 16), So many, so weighty, are the gifts of God's bounty to us that he may be truly said to *load us* with them; he *pours out blessings till there is no room to receive them,* Mal. iii. 10. *He is our God,* and therefore he will be the God of eternal salvation to us; for that only will answer the vast extent of his covenant-relation to us as our God. Those that persist in their enmity to him will certainly be ruined (v. 21): *God shall wound the head of his enemies,*—of Satan the old serpent (of whom it was by the first promise foretold that *the seed of the woman should break his head,* Gen. iii. 15). He will *wound the hairy scalp of such a one as goeth on still in his trespasses.* In calling the head *the hairy scalp* perhaps there is an allusion to Absalom, whose bushy hair was his halter. Or it denotes the most fierce and barbarous of his enemies, who let their hair grow, to make themselves look the more frightful.

Verses 22-31

In these verses we have three things:—

I. The gracious promise which God makes of the redemption of his people, and their victory over his and their enemies (v. 22, 23): *The Lord said,* "I will do great things for my people, as the God of their salvation," v. 20. "I will *again bring them from the depths of the sea,*" as he did Israel when he brought them out of the slavery of Egypt into the ease and liberty of the wilderness; "and *I will again bring them from Bashan,*" as he did Israel when he brought them from their wants and wanderings in the wilderness into the fulness and settlement of the land of Canaan; for the land of Bashan was on the other side Jordan,

where they had wars with Sihon and Og, and whence their next removal was into Canaan. But this is not all. He will make them victorious over their enemies (v. 23): *That thy feet may be dipped,* as thou passest along, *in the blood of thy enemies,* and the *tongue of thy dogs* may lap *in the same.* Dogs licked the blood of Ahab; and, in the destruction of the anti-christian generation, we read of blood up *to the horses' bridles,* Rev. xiv. 20.

II. The welcome which God's own people shall give to these glorious discoveries of his grace. "*They have seen,* thy people have seen, *thy goings, O God!* While others regard not the work of the Lord, they have seen *the goings of my God, my King, in the sanctuary.*" An active faith appropriates God; he is God and King; but that is not all, he is *my* God and *my* King. God's most remarkable outgoings are, even in the sanctuary, in and by his word and ordinances, and among his people in the gospel church especially. When we see *his goings in his sanctuary,* those that are immediately employed in the service of the temple praise him, v. 25. It was expected that the Levites should lead in his praises. And, it being a day of extraordinary triumph, *among them were damsels playing with timbrels.* "Thus (says Dr. Hammond) when Christ has gone up to heaven the apostles shall celebrate and publish it to all the world, and even the women that were witnesses of it shall affectionately join with them in divulging it." Let all the people of Israel in their solemn religious assembly give glory to God: *Bless God,* not only in temples, but in the synagogues, or schools of the prophets, or wherever there is a congregation of those that *come forth from the fountain of Israel.* Public mercies, which we jointly share in, call for public thanksgivings, which all should join in. Let those among them who are the most eminent go before the rest in praising God, v. 27. There was *little Benjamin* (that was the royal tribe in Saul's time) *with their rulers, the princes of Judah* (that was the royal tribe in David's time), and *their council,* their captains or leaders. We depend upon him, for the perfecting of what he has begun, v. 28. In the former part of the verse the psalmist speaks to Israel: "*Thy God has commanded thy strength;* that is, whatever is done for thee, or whatever strength thou hast to help thyself, it comes from God, his power and grace, and the word which he has commanded." In the latter part he speaks to God, encouraged by his experiences: "*Strengthen, O God! that which thou hast wrought for us.* Lord, confirm what thou hast commanded, perform what thou hast promised, and bring to a happy end that good work which thou hast so gloriously begun."

III. The powerful invitation and inducement which would hereby be given to those that are without to come in and join themselves to the church, v. 29-31. This was in part fulfilled by the accession of many proselytes to the Jewish religion in the days of David and Solomon; but it was to have its full accomplishment in the conversion of the Gentile nations to the faith of Christ, Eph. iii. 6. Some shall submit for fear (v. 30): "*The company of spearmen,* that stand it out against Christ and his gospel, that are furious and outrageous as a multitude of bulls, fat and wanton as the calves of the people" (which is a description of those Jews and Gentiles that opposed the gospel of Christ and did what they could to prevent the setting up of his kingdom in the world), "Lord, rebuke them, abate their pride and confound their devices, till, conquered by the convictions of their consciences, they be every one of them brought, to *submit themselves with pieces of silver,* as being glad to make their peace with the church upon any terms." Many, by being rebuked, have been happily saved from being ruined. But as for those that will not submit, he prays for their dispersion, which amounts to a prophecy of it: *Scatter thou the people that delight in war.* This may refer to the unbelieving Jews, who delighted in making war upon the holy seed, and would not submit themselves, and were therefore scattered over the face of the earth. David had himself been a man of war, but could appeal to God that he never delighted in war and bloodshed for its own sake. Others shall submit willingly (v. 29, 31): *Because of thy temple at Jerusalem* (this David speaks of in faith, for the temple of Jerusalem was not built in his time, only the materials and model were prepared) *kings shall bring presents unto thee.* He mentions *Egypt* and *Ethiopia*, two countries out of which subjects and suppliants were least to be expected (v. 31): *Princes shall come out of Egypt* as ambassadors to seek God's favour and submit to him; and they shall be accepted, for the *Lord of hosts shall* thereupon *bless them, saying, Blessed be Egypt my people,* Isa. xix. 25. Even Ethiopia, that had stretched out her hands against God's Israel (2 Chron. xiv. 9), should now *stretch out her hands unto God,* in prayer, in presents, and to take hold on him, and that soon.

Verses 32–35

The psalmist, having prayed for the Gentiles, here invites them to come in and join with the devout Israelites in praising God, intimating that their accession to the church would be the matter of their joy and praise (v. 32): Let the *kingdoms of the earth sing praises to the Lord.*

I. Because of his supreme and sovereign dominion: *He rides upon the heavens of heavens which were of old* (v. 33); compare v. 4. He has from the beginning, nay, from before all time, prepared his throne; he sits on the circuit of heaven, and dispenses the influences of his power and goodness to this lower world.

II. Because of his awful and terrible majesty: *He sends out his voice, and that a mighty voice.* This may refer either generally to the thunder, which is called *the voice of the Lord* and is said to be *powerful and full of majesty* (xxix. 3, 4), or in particular to that thunder in which God spoke to Israel at Mount Sinai.

III. Because of his mighty power: *Ascribe you strength unto God* (v. 34). *Thine is the kingdom and power,* and therefore *thine is the glory.* We must acknowledge his power. In the kingdom of grace: *His excellency is over Israel;* he shows his sovereign care in protecting and governing his church. In the kingdom of providence: *His strength is in the clouds,* whence comes the thunder of his power, the *small rain, and the great rain of his strength.*

IV. Because of the glory of his sanctuary and the wonders wrought there (v. 35): *O God! thou art terrible out of thy holy places.* God is to be admired and adored with reverence and godly fear by all those that attend him in his holy places, that receive his oracles. Nor is any attribute of God more dreadful to sinners than his holiness.

V. Because of the grace bestowed upon his people: *The God of Israel is he that gives strength and power unto his people,* which the gods of the nations, that were vanity and a lie, could not give to their worshippers; how should they help them, when they could not help themselves? If it be the God of Israel that gives strength and power unto his people, they ought to say, *Blessed be God.* If all be from him, let all be to him.

PSALM 69

David penned this psalm when he was in affliction. I. He complains of the great distress and trouble he was in and earnestly begs of God to relieve and succour him, ver. 1–21. II. He imprecates the judgments of God upon his persecutors, ver. 22–29. III. He concludes with the voice of joy and praise, in an assurance that God would help and succour him, and would do well

for the church, ver. 30–36. Now divers passages in this psalm are applied to Christ in the New Testament and are said to have their accomplishment in him (ver. 4, 9, 21), and ver. 22 refers to the enemies of Christ. So that (like the twenty-second psalm) it begins with the humiliation and ends with the exaltation of Christ.

To the chief musician upon Shoshannim. *A psalm of David.*

Verses 1–12

In these verses David complains of his troubles.

I. His complaints are very sad, and he pours them out before the Lord, as one that hoped thus to ease himself of a burden that lay very heavy upon him.

1. He complains of the deep impressions that his troubles made upon his spirit (v. 1, 2): "The *waters of affliction,* those bitter waters, *have come unto my soul,* not only threaten my life, but disquiet my mind, so that I cannot enjoy God and myself as I used to do." The *spirit of a man will sustain his infirmity;* but what shall we do when the spirit is wounded? That was David's case here. This points at Christ's sufferings in his soul, and the inward agony he was in when he said, *Now is my soul troubled;* and, *My soul is exceedingly sorrowful;* for it was his soul that he made an offering for sin.

2. He complains of the long continuance of his troubles (v. 3): *I am weary of my crying.* He cried to his God, and the more death was in his view the more life was in his prayers; yet he had not immediately an answer of peace given. *My eyes fail while I wait for my God.* Yet his pleading this with God is an indication that he is resolved not to give up believing and praying. His throat is dried, but his heart is not; his eyes fail, but his faith does not. Thus our Lord Jesus, on the cross, cried out, *Why hast thou forsaken me?* yet, at the same time, he kept hold of his relation to him: *My God, my God.*

3. He complains of the malice and multitude of his enemies, their injustice and cruelty, and the hardships they put upon him, v. 4. "*They hate me without a cause;* I never did them the least injury, that they should bear me such ill-will." Our Saviour applies this to himself (John xv. 25): *They hated me without a cause.* These enemies were not to be despised, but were very formidable both for their number —*They are more than the hairs of my head*—and for their strength—They *are mighty* in authority and power. *Then I restored that which I took not away.* Applying this to David, it was what his enemies compelled him to, and it was what he consented to, that, if possible, he might pacify them and make them to be at peace with him. But, applying it to Christ, it is an observable description of the satisfaction which he made to God for our sin by his blood: *Then he restored that which he took not away;* he underwent the punishment that was due to us, paid our debt, suffered for our offence. God's glory, in some instances of it, was taken away by the sin of man; man's honour, and peace, and happiness, were taken away; it was not he that took them away, and yet by the merit of his death he restored them.

4. He complains of the unkindness of his friends and relations (v. 8): "*I have become a stranger to my brethren;* they make themselves strange to me and are shy of conversing with me and ashamed to own me." This was fulfilled in Christ, whose *brethren did not believe on him* (John vii. 5), who *came to his own and his own received him not* (John i. 11), and who was forsaken by his disciples.

5. He complains of the contempt that was put upon him and the reproach with which he was continually loaded. And in this especially his complaint points at Christ, who for our sakes submitted to the greatest disgrace and made himself of no reputation. David here takes notice of aggravations of the indignities done him. They ridiculed him for that by which he both humbled himself and honoured

God. When David, purely in devotion to God and to testify his respect to him, *wept, and chastened his soul with fasting*, and *made sackcloth his garment*, as humble penitents used to do, instead of commending his devotion, they did all they could to prevent others from following his good example; for *that was to his reproach*. They laughed at him as a fool for mortifying himself thus; and even for this he *became a proverb to them*. Even the gravest and the most honourable, from whom better was expected: *Those that sit in the gate speak against me*. He was the song of the drunkards; they made themselves and their companions merry with him. See what is commonly the lot of the best of men: those that are the praise of the wise are the song of fools. But it is easy to those that rightly judge of things to despise being thus despised.

II. His confessions of sin are very serious (v. 5): "*O God! thou knowest my foolishness*, both what is and what is not; and therefore thou knowest how innocent I am of those crimes which they charge upon me." This is the genuine confession of a penitent, who knows that he cannot prosper in covering his sin, and that *therefore* it is his wisdom to acknowledge it, because it is naked and open before God. He knows the corruption of our nature: *Thou knowest the foolishness* that is bound up in my heart. He knows the transgressions of our lives, even those that are committed most secretly. They are all done in his sight, and are never cast behind his back till they are repented of and pardoned.

III. His supplications are very earnest. "*Save me, O God!* save me from sinking, from despairing." *Let not those that wait on thee, O Lord God of hosts! and that seek thee, O God of Israel! be ashamed and confounded for my sake*. This intimates his fear that if God did not appear for him it would be a discouragement to all other good people and would give their enemies occasion to triumph over them. If Jesus Christ had not been owned and accepted of his Father in his sufferings, all that seek God, and wait for him, would have been ashamed and confounded; but they have confidence towards God, and in his name come boldly to the throne [of grace.

IV. His plea is very powerful, v. 7, 9. "Lord, roll away the reproach, and plead my cause. *For thy sake I have borne reproach*." Those that are evil spoken of for well-doing may with a humble confidence leave it to God to *bring forth their righteousness as the light. The zeal of thy house has eaten me up*. Those that hate thee and thy house for that reason hate me, because they know how zealously affected I am to it. It is this that has eaten up all the love and respect I had among them. Or it may be construed as an instance of David's zeal for God's house, that he resented all the indignities done to God's name as if they had been done to his own name. He laid to heart all the contempt cast upon religion. Both the parts of this verse are applied to Christ. 1. It was an instance of his love to his Father that *the zeal of his house did even eat him up* when he whipped the buyers and sellers out of the temple, which reminded his disciples of this text, John ii. 17. 2. It was an instance of his self-denial, and that he pleased not himself, that the *reproaches of those that reproached God fell upon him* (Rom. xv. 3), and therein he set us an example.

Verses 13–21

They spoke ill of him for his fasting and praying, and for that he was made the song of the drunkards; but, notwithstanding that, he resolves to continue praying. Though we may be jeered for well-doing, we must never be jeered out of it. *As for me, my prayer is unto thee, O Lord!*

I. What his requests are. *Hear me* (v. 13), and again, *Hear me, O Lord!* (v. 16), *Hear me speedily* (v. 17), not only hear what I say, but grant what I ask. *Deliver me out of the mire;* let me not stick in it, so some, but help me out, and *set my feet on a rock*, xl. 2. "*Let me be delivered from those that hate me*, as a lamb from the paw of a lion, v. 14. Though I have come into deep waters (v. 2), let not the waterflood overflow me, v. 15. Let me not fall into the gulf of despair; let not that deep swallow me up; let not that pit shut her mouth upon me, for then I am undone." He prayed that God would turn to him (v. 16), that he would smile upon him, and not hide his face from him, v. 17.

II. What his pleas are to enforce these petitions. 1. He pleads God's mercy and truth (v. 13): *In the multitude of thy mercy hear me*. He repeats his argument taken from the mercy of God: "*Hear me*, for *thy lovingkindness is good*. It is so in itself; it is rich and plentiful and abundant. Turn to me, *according to the multitude of thy tender mercies*," v. 16. 2. He pleads his own distress and affliction: "*Hide not thy face* from me, *for I am in trouble* (v. 17), and therefore need thy favour; therefore it will come seasonably, and therefore I shall know how to value it." *Thou hast known my reproach, my shame, and my dishonour*. The psalmist speaks the language of an ingenuous nature when he says (v. 20): *Reproach has broken my heart; I am full of heaviness;* for it bears hard upon one that knows the worth of a good name to be put under a bad character; but when we consider what an honour it is to be dishonoured for God, and to be counted worthy to suffer shame for his name (as they deemed it, Acts v. 41), we shall see there is no reason at all why it should be any heart-breaking to us. 3. He pleads the insolence and cruelty of his enemies (v. 18): "*My adversaries are all before thee* (v. 19); thou knowest what danger I am in from them, what enemies they are to thee, in what they do and design against me." One instance of their barbarity is given (v. 21): *They gave me gall for my meat* (the word signifies a bitter herb, and is often joined with wormwood) *and in my thirst they gave me vinegar to drink*. 4. He pleads the unkindness of his friends and his disappointment in them (v. 20): *I looked for some to take pity, but there was none;* they all failed him like the brooks in summer. This was fulfilled in Christ, for in his sufferings all his disciples forsook him and fled.

Verses 22–29

These imprecations are not David's prayers against his enemies, but prophecies of the destruction of Christ's persecutors, especially the Jewish nation, which our Lord himself foretold with tears, and which was accomplished about forty years after the death of Christ. The first two verses of this paragraph are expressly applied to the judgments of God upon the unbelieving Jews by the apostle (Rom. xi. 9, 10), and therefore the whole must look that way.

I. The judgments which should come upon the crucifiers of Christ; not upon all of them, for there were those who had a hand in his death and yet repented and found mercy (Acts ii. 23; iii. 14, 15), but upon those of them and their successors who justified it by an obstinate infidelity and rejection of his gospel, and by an inveterate enmity to his disciples and followers. See 1 Thess. ii. 15, 16. It is here foretold,

1. That their sacrifices and offerings should be a mischief and prejudice to them (v. 22): *Let their table become a snare*. This may be understood of the altar of the Lord, which is called *his table and theirs*, because in feasting upon the sacrifices they were partakers of the altar. Or it may be understood of their common creature-comforts, even their necessary

food; they had given Christ gall and vinegar, and therefore justly shall their meat and drink be made gall and vinegar to them.

2. That they should never have the comfort either of that knowledge or of that peace which believers are blessed with in the gospel of Christ (v. 23). _Let their eyes be darkened_, that they see not the glory of God in the face of Christ. Their sin was that they would not see, but shut their eyes against the light. "Let them be driven to despair, and filled with constant confusion." This was fulfilled in the desperate counsels of the Jews when the Romans came upon them.

3. That they should fall and lie under God's anger and fiery indignation (v. 24): _Pour out thy indignation upon them._

4. That their place and nation should be utterly taken away, the very thing they were afraid of, and to prevent which, as they pretended, they persecuted Christ (John xi. 48): _Let their habitation be desolate_ (v. 25), which was fulfilled when their country was laid waste by the Romans, and _Zion, for their sakes, was ploughed as a field_, Mic. iii. 12. The temple was the house which they were in a particular manner proud of, but this was _left unto them desolate_, Matt. xxiii. 38. _Let none dwell in their tents_, which was remarkably fulfilled in Judah and Jerusalem, for after the destruction of the Jews it was long ere the country was inhabited to any purpose.

5. That their way to ruin should be downhill, and nothing should stop them (v. 27): "Lord, leave them to themselves, to _add iniquity to iniquity._" _Let them not come into thy righteousness._ Not that God shuts out any from that righteousness, for the gospel excludes none that do not by their unbelief exclude themselves.

6. That they should be cut off from all hopes of happiness (v. 28): _Let them be blotted out of the book of the living;_ let them not be suffered to live any longer, since, the longer they live, the more mischief they do. Multitudes of the unbelieving Jews fell by sword and famine. The nation, as a nation, was blotted out, and became not a people.

II. What the sin is for which these dreadful judgments should be brought upon them (v. 26): _They persecute him whom thou hast smitten, and talk to the grief of thy wounded._ Christ was he whom God had smitten, for _it pleased the Lord to bruise him_, and he was esteemed _stricken, smitten of God, and afflicted_, and therefore men _hid their faces from him_, Isa. liii. 3, 4, 10. They persecuted him with a rage reaching up to heaven; they cried, _Crucify him, crucify him._

III. What the psalmist thinks of himself in the midst of all (v. 29): "_But I am poor and sorrowful;_ that is the worst of my case, under outward afflictions, yet _written among the righteous_, and not under God's indignation as they are."

Verses 30–36

The psalmist here, both as a type of Christ and as an example to Christians, concludes a psalm with holy joy and praise which he began with complaints and remonstrances of his griefs.

I. He resolves to praise God himself (v. 30, 31): "_I will praise the name of God_, not only with my heart, but with my song, and _magnify him with thanksgiving._" And _this shall please the Lord_, through Christ the Mediator of our praises as well as of our prayers, better than the most valuable of the legal sacrifices (v. 31), _an ox or bullock_. This is a plain intimation that in the days of the Messiah an end should be put, not only to the sacrifices of atonement, but to those of praise and acknowledgment which were instituted by the ceremonial law; and, instead of them, spiritual sacrifices of praise and thanksgiving are accepted.

It is a great comfort to us that humble and thankful praises are more pleasing to God than the most costly pompous sacrifices are or ever were.

II. He encourages other good people to rejoice in God and continue seeking him (v. 32, 33): _The humble shall see this and be glad._ They shall see 1. How ready God is to hear the poor when they cry to him, and to give them that which they call upon him for. 2. The exaltation of the Saviour, for of him the psalmist had been speaking, and of himself as a type of him.

III. He calls upon all the creatures to praise God, the heaven, and earth, and sea, and the inhabitants of each, v. 34. The praises of the world must be offered for God's favours to his church, v. 35, 36. for God will save Zion, the holy mountain, where his service was kept up. _The cities of Judah shall be built_, particular churches shall be formed and incorporated according to the gospel model, that there may be a remnant to _dwell there_ and to _have it in possession_. Those that love his name, that have a kindness for religion in general, shall embrace the Christian religion, and take their place in the Christian church; they shall dwell therein, as citizens, and of the household of God. David shall never want a man to stand before him. The Redeemer shall see his seed, and prolong his days in them, till the mystery of God shall be finished and the mystical body completed.

PSALM 70

This psalm is adapted to a state of affliction; it is copied almost word for word from the fortieth, and, some think for that reason, is entitled, "a psalm to bring to remembrance". David here prays that God would send, I. Help to himself, ver. 1, 5. II. Shame to his enemies, ver. 2, 3. III. Joy to his friends, ver. 4. These five verses were the last five verses of Ps. xl.

To the chief musician. _A psalm_ of David, to bring to remembrance.

Verses 1–5

The title tells us that this psalm was designed to bring to remembrance; that is, to put God in remembrance of his mercy and promises. We may in prayer use the words we have often used before: our Saviour in his agony prayed thrice, saying the same words; so David here uses the words he had used before.

I. David here prays that God would make haste to relieve and succour him (v. 1, 5): _I am poor and needy_, in want and distress, and much at a loss within myself. "_Make haste unto me_, for the longing desire of my soul is towards thee; I shall perish if I be not speedily helped. I have no other to expect relief from: _Thou art my help and my deliverer_. Thou hast engaged to be so to all that seek thee; I depend upon thee to be so to me; I have often found thee so; and thou art sufficient, all-sufficient, to be so; therefore make haste to me."

II. He prays that God would fill the faces of his enemies with shame, v. 2, 3. "_Let them be ashamed;_ let them be brought to repentance, so filled with shame as that they may seek thy name (lxxxiii. 16); let them see their folly in fighting against those whom thou dost protect. However, let their designs against me be frustrated and then they will be ashamed and confounded, and _much cast down in their own eyes_," Neh. vi. 16.

III. He prays that God would fill the hearts of his friends with joy (v. 4). Let us make the service of God our great business and the favour of God our great delight and pleasure, for that is seeking him and loving his salvation. Let us then be assured that, if it be not our own fault, the joy of the Lord shall fill our minds and the high praises of the Lord shall fill our mouths. All who wish well to the comfort of the saints, and to the glory of God, cannot but say a hearty _amen_ to this prayer, that those who love God's salvation may say continually, _Let God be magnified._

PSALM 71

David penned this psalm in his old age. But he is not over-particular in representing his case, because he intended it for the general use of God's people in their afflictions, especially those they meet with in their declining years; for this psalm, above any other, is fitted for the use of the old disciples of Jesus Christ. I. He begins the psalm with believing prayers, with prayers that God would deliver him and save him (ver. 2, 4) and not cast him off (ver. 9) or be far from him (ver. 12), and that his enemies might be put to shame, ver. 13. He pleads his confidence in God (ver. 1, 3, 5, 7), the experience he had had of help from God (ver. 6), and the malice of his enemies against him, ver. 10, 11. II. He concludes the psalm with believing praises, ver. 14, &c. Never was his hope more established, ver. 16, 18, 20, 21. Never were his joys and thanksgivings more enlarged, ver. 15, 19, 22–24. He is in an ecstasy of joyful praise.

Verses 1–13

I. He prays that he might never be made ashamed of his dependence upon God nor disappointed in his believing expectations from him. With this petition every true believer may come boldly to the throne of grace.

1. David professes his confidence in God, and repeats his profession of that confidence, still presenting the profession of it to God and pleading it with him. We praise God by telling him (if it be indeed true) what an entire confidence we have in him (v. 1): "*In thee, O Lord! and in thee only, do I put my trust.* Whatever others do, I choose the God of Jacob for my help." *Thou art my rock and my fortress* (v. 3); and again, "*Thou art my refuge, my strong refuge*" (v. 7); that is, "I fly to thee, and am sure to be safe in thee, and under thy protection. If thou secure me, none can hurt me. *Thou art my hope and my trust*" (v. 5); that is, "thou hast proposed thyself to me in thy word as the proper object of my hope and trust; I have hoped in thee, and never found it in vain to do so."

2. His confidence in God is supported and encouraged by his experiences (v. 5, 6): "*Thou hast been my trust from my youth;* ever since I was capable of discerning between my right hand and my left, I stayed myself upon thee, for *by thee have I been holden up from the womb.*" He that was our help from our birth ought to be our hope from our youth. If we received so much mercy from God before we were capable of doing him any service, we should lose no time when we are capable. "Thou art he that took me into the arms of thy grace, under the shadow of thy wings, into the bond of thy covenant. I have reason to hope that thou wilt protect me; thou that hast held me up hitherto wilt not let me fall now; thou that helpedst me when I could not help myself wilt not abandon me now that I am as helpless as I was then. *My praise shall therefore be continually of thee.*"

3. His requests to God are,

(1) That he might *never be put to confusion* (v. 1), that he might not be disappointed of the mercy he expected and so made ashamed of his expectation.

(2) That he might be delivered out of the hand of his enemies (v. 2): "*Deliver me in thy righteousness.* As thou art the righteous Judge of the world, pleading the cause of the injured, cause me in some way or other to escape. *Incline thy ear unto my prayers,* and, answer to them, save me out of my troubles," v. 4. *Thou hast given commandment to save me* (v. 3); that is, thou hast promised to do it, and such efficacy is there in God's promises that they are often spoken of as commands, like that. The many eyes that were upon him (v. 7): "*I am as a wonder unto many;* everyone waits to see what will be the issue of such extraordinary troubles as I have fallen into and such extraordinary confidence as I profess to have in God." Or, "I am looked upon as a monster, whom everybody shuns, and therefore am undone if the Lord be not my refuge. Men abandon me, but God will not."

(3) That he might always find rest and safety in God (v. 3): *Be thou my strong habitation;* be thou to me *a rock of repose, whereto I may continually resort.* Those that are at home in God, that live a life of communion with him and confidence in him, that continually resort unto him by faith and prayer, may promise themselves a strong habitation, such as will never fall of itself nor can ever be broken through by any invading power. "*Let my mouth be filled with thy praise,* as now it is with my complaints, and then I shall not be ashamed of my hope, but my enemies will be ashamed of their insolence."

(4) That he might not be neglected now in his declining years (v. 9): *Cast me not off* now *in the time of* my *old age; forsake me not when my strength fails.* Observe here. The infirmities of age: *My strength fails.* Where there was strength of body and vigour of mind, strong sight, a strong voice, strong limbs, alas! in old age they fail. 2. God's presence with him under these infirmities: *Lord, cast me not off; do not then forsake me.* To be cast off and forsaken of God is a thing to be dreaded at any time, especially in the time of old age and when our strength fails us; for it is God that is the strength of our heart. But that the faithful servants of God may be comfortably assured that he will not cast them off in old age, nor forsake them when their strength fails them. He is a Master that is not wont to cast off old servants. In this confidence David here prays again (v. 12): "*O God! be not far from me; O my God! make haste for my help,* lest I perish before help come."

II. He prays that his enemies might be made ashamed of their designs against him. *They lay wait for my soul* (v. 10), and are adversaries to that, v. 13. *They take counsel together.* They say, *God has forsaken him; persecute and take him.* Here their premises are utterly false. All are not forsaken of God who think themselves so or whom others think to be so. And, as their premises were false, so their inference was barbarous. But *rejoice not against me, O my enemy! though I fall, I shall rise.* He that seems to forsake for a small moment will gather with everlasting kindness. "*Let them be confounded and consumed that are adversaries to my soul.* If they will not be confounded by repentance, and so saved, let them be confounded with everlasting dishonour, and so ruined."

Verses 14–24

David is here in a holy transport of joy and praise, arising from his faith and hope in God; we have both together, v. 14, where there is a sudden and remarkable change of his voice; his fears are all silenced, his hopes raised, and his prayers turned into thanksgivings. "Let my enemies say what they will, to drive me to despair, *I will hope continually,* hope in all conditions, in the most cloudy and dark day; I will live upon hope and will hope to the end."

I. His heart is established in faith and hope. "*I will go in the strength of the Lord God,* not sit down in despair, but stir up myself, will go forth and go on, not in any strength of my own, but in God's strength, and in the strength of his grace. *I will make mention of thy righteousness,* that is, thy faithfulness to every word which thou hast spoken, the equity of thy disposals, and thy kindness to thy people that trust in thee. This I will make mention of as my plea in prayer for thy mercy." He hopes that God will not leave him in his old age, but will be the same to him to the end that he had been all along, v. 17, 18. *Thou hast taught me from my youth.* The good education and good instructions which his parents gave him when he was young he owns himself obliged to give God thanks for as a great favour. When he was middle-aged he had *declared all God's wondrous works.* Those that have got good when they are young must be doing good when they are grown up, and must continue to communicate what they have received. *Now that I am old and grey-headed,* dying to this world and hastening to another, *O God! forsake me not.* Those that have been taught of God from their youth, and have made it the business of their lives to honour him, may be sure that he will not leave them when they are old and grey-headed, but will make the evil days of old age their best days. "I will not only *show thy strength,* by my own experience of it, *to this generation,* but I will leave my observations upon record for the benefit of posterity, and so show it *to everyone that is to come.*" It is a debt which the old disciples of Christ owe to the succeeding generations to leave behind them a solemn testimony to the power, pleasure, and advantage of religion, and the truth of God's promises. He hopes that God would revive him and raise him up out of his present low and disconsolate condition (*v.* 20): *Thou who hast made me to see and feel great and sore troubles,* above most men, *shalt quicken me again.* He does not say, "Thou hast burdened me with those troubles," but "shown them to me," as the tender father shows the child. If we have a due regard to the hand of God in our troubles, we may promise ourselves, in due time, a deliverance out of them. "Thou shalt not only restore me to *my greatness* again, but shalt *increase* it, and give me a better interest, after this shock, than before; thou shalt not only comfort me, but *comfort me on every side,* so that I shall see nothing black or threatening on any side." Sometimes God makes his people's troubles contribute to the increase of their greatness, and their sun shines the brighter for having been under a cloud. He hopes that all his enemies would be put to confusion, *v.* 24. *They are confounded, they are brought to shame, that seek my hurt.*

II. Let us now see how his heart is enlarged in joy and praises, how he rejoices in hope, and sings in hope; for we are saved by hope. *My mouth shall show forth thy righteousness and thy salvation;* and again (*v.* 24), *My tongue shall talk of thy righteousness,* and this *all the day.* God's righteousness, which David seems here to be in a particular manner affected with, includes a great deal: the rectitude of his nature, the equity of his providential disposals, the righteous laws he has given us to be ruled by, the righteous promises he has given us to depend upon, and the everlasting righteousness which his Son has brought in for our justification. God's righteousness and his salvation are here joined together. "*I know not the numbers thereof* (*v.* 15). Though I cannot give a particular account of thy favours to me, they are so many, yet, knowing them to be numberless, I will be still speaking of them, for in them I shall find new matter," *v.* 19. This is praising God, acknowledging his perfections and performances to be so high that we cannot apprehend them, so great that we cannot comprehend them. *O God! who is like unto thee?* None in heaven, none on earth, no angel, no king. God is a non-such; we do not rightly praise him if we do not own him to be so. *I will praise thee, even thy truth.* God is made known by his word; if we praise that, and the truth of that, we praise him. It is God's honour that he is a Holy One; it is his people's honour that he is the Holy One of Israel. He will express his joy and exultation in sacred music—*with the psaltery, with the harp;* at these David excelled, and the best of his skill shall be employed in setting forth God's praises to such advantage as might affect others. "*Unto thee will I sing,* to thy honour, and with a desire to be accepted of thee. *My lips shall greatly rejoice when I sing unto thee,* knowing they cannot be better employed. *My soul* shall rejoice *which thou hast redeemed.*" We do not make melody to the Lord,

in singing his praises, if we do not do it with our hearts. My lips shall rejoice, but that is nothing; lip-labour, though ever so well laboured, if that be all, is but lost labour in serving God; the soul must be at work, and with all that is within us we must bless his holy name.

PSALM 72

The foregoing psalm was penned by David when he was old, and, it should seem, so was this too; for Solomon was now standing fair for the crown; that was his prayer for himself, this for his son and successor, and with these two the prayers of David the son of Jesse are ended, as we find in the close of this psalm. This is entitled "a psalm for Solomon": it is probable that David dictated it, or, rather, that it was by the blessed Spirit dictated to him, when, a little before he died, by divine direction he settled the succession, and gave orders to proclaim Solomon king, 1 Kings i. 30, &c. But, though Solomon's name is here made use of, Christ's kingdom is here prophesied of under the type and figure of Solomon's. David, in spirit, I. Begins with a short prayer for his successor, ver. 1. II. He passes immediately into a long prediction of the glories of his reign, ver. 2–17. And, III. He concludes with praise to the God of Israel, ver. 18–20.

A psalm for Solomon.

Verse 1

This verse is a prayer for the king, even the king's son.

I. We may apply it to Solomon: *Give him thy judgments, O God! and thy righteousness;* make him a man, a king; make him a good man, a good king. 1. It is the prayer of a father for his child, a dying blessing, such as the patriarchs bequeathed to their children. Solomon learned to pray for himself as his father had prayed for him, not that God would give him riches and honour, but a wise and understanding heart. Parents cannot give grace to their children, but may by prayer bring them to the God of grace. 2. It is the prayer of a king for his successor. David had executed judgment and justice during his reign, and now he prays that his son might do so too. Such a concern as this we should have for posterity. 3. It is the prayer of subjects for their king. It should seem, David penned this psalm for the use of the people, that they, in singing, might pray for Solomon. Those who would live quiet and peaceable lives must pray for kings and all in authority, that God would give them his judgments and righteousness.

II. We may apply it to Christ; not that he who intercedes for us needs us to intercede for him; but, 1. It is a prayer of the Old Testament church for sending the Messiah. 2. It is an expression of the satisfaction which all true believers take in the authority which the Lord Jesus has received from the Father: "Let him have all power both in heaven and earth, and be the Lord our righteousness; let him be the great trustee of divine grace for all that are his."

Verses 2–17

This is a prophecy of the prosperity and perpetuity of the kingdom of Christ under the shadow of the reign of Solomon. 1. As a plea to enforce the prayer: "Lord, give him thy judgments and thy righteousness" (*v.* 1). 2. As an answer of peace to the prayer. That this prophecy must refer to the kingdom of the Messiah is plain, because there are many passages in it which cannot be applied to the reign of Solomon. The kingdom here spoken of is to last as long as the sun, but Solomon's was soon extinct. Therefore even the Jewish expositors understand it of the kingdom of the Messiah.

I. That it should be a *righteous government* (*v.* 2): *He shall judge thy people with righteousness.* Compare Isa. xi. 4. All the laws of Christ's kingdom are consonant to the eternal rules of equity. The peace of his kingdom shall be supported by righteousness (*v.* 3).

II. That it should be a peaceable government: *The mountains shall bring peace, and the little hills* (v. 3); that is (says Dr. Hammond), both the superior and the inferior courts of judicature in Solomon's kingdom. There shall be *abundance of peace*, v. 7. Solomon's name signifies *peaceable*, and such was his reign. But peace is, in a special manner, the glory of Christ's kingdom; for, as far as it prevails, it reconciles men to God, to themselves, and to one another, and slays all enmities; for he is our peace.

III. That the poor and needy should be, in a particular manner, taken under the protection of this government: *He shall judge thy poor*, v. 2. *The poor of the people*, and *the children of the needy*, he will be sure so to judge as to save, v. 4. This is insisted upon again (v. 12, 13), intimating that Christ will be sure to carry his cause on behalf of his injured poor. *He will deliver the needy* that lie at the mercy of their oppressors. *He will spare the needy* that throw themselves on his mercy, he will *save their souls*, and that is all they desire. *Blessed are the poor in spirit, for theirs is the kingdom of heaven.* Christ is the poor man's King.

IV. That proud oppressors shall be reckoned with: *He shall break them in pieces* (v. 4). The devil is the great oppressor, whom Christ will break in pieces and of whose kingdom he will be the destruction. So *precious shall their blood be unto him* that not a drop of it shall be shed, by the deceit or violence of Satan or his instruments, without being reckoned for. Christ is a King, who, though he calls his subjects sometimes to resist unto blood for him, yet is not prodigal of their blood.

V. That religion shall flourish under Christ's government (v. 5): *They shall fear thee as long as the sun and moon endure.* Solomon indeed built the temple, but it did not last long; this therefore must point at Christ's kingdom. Faith in Christ will set up, and keep up, the fear of God; and therefore this is the everlasting gospel that is preached. And, as Christ's government promotes devotion towards God, so it promotes both justice and charity among men (v. 7): *In his days shall the righteous flourish.* The law of Christ, written in the heart, disposes men to be honest and just, and to render to all their due; it likewise disposes men to live in love, and so it produces abundance of peace and beats swords into ploughshares. Both holiness and love shall be perpetual in Christ's kingdom, and shall never go to decay, for the subjects of it shall *fear God as long as the sun and moon endure*; Christianity, having got footing in the world, shall keep its ground till the end of time, and having got footing in the heart, it will continue there till, by death, the sun, and the moon, and the stars (that is, the bodily senses) are darkened.

VI. That Christ's government shall be very comfortable to all his faithful loving subjects (v. 6): *He shall*, by the graces and comforts of his Spirit, *come down like rain upon the mown grass*; not on that which is cut down, but that which is left growing, that it may spring again, though it was beheaded.

VII. That Christ's kingdom shall be greatly enlarged.

1. The extent of his territories (v. 8): *He shall have dominion from sea to sea* (from the South Sea to the North, or from the Red Sea to the Mediterranean) *and from the river* Euphrates, or Nile, *to the ends of the earth.* Solomon's dominion was very large (1 Kings iv. 21), according to the promise, Gen. xv. 18. But no sea, no river, is named, that it might, by these proverbial expressions, intimate the universal monarchy of the Lord Jesus. His gospel has been, or shall be, preached *to all nations* (Matt. xxiv. 14). His territories shall be extended to those countries, (1) That were strangers to him: *Those that dwell in the wilderness*, that seldom hear news, shall hear the glad tidings of the Redeemer, *shall bow before him*, shall believe in him, worship him, and take his yoke upon them. (2) That were enemies to him, and had fought against him: *They shall lick the dust.*

2. The dignity of his tributaries. He shall not only reign over those that dwell in the wilderness, the peasants and cottagers, but over those that dwell in the palaces (v. 10): *The kings of Tarshish, and of the isles*, that lie most remote from Israel and are *the isles of the Gentiles* (Gen. x. 5), *shall bring presents* to him as their sovereign Lord. This was literally fulfilled in Solomon (for *all the kings of the earth sought the wisdom of Solomon, and brought every man his present*, 2 Chron. ix. 23, 24), and in Christ too, when the wise men of the east came to worship him and *brought him presents*, Matt. ii. 11.

VIII. That he shall be honoured and beloved by all his subjects (v. 15): *He shall live;* his subjects shall desire his life (*O king! live for ever*) and with good reason; for he has said, *Because I live, you shall live also.* Presents shall be made to him. Though he shall be able to live without them, for he needs neither the gifts nor the services of any, yet to him *shall be given of the gold of Sheba.* He that is best must be served with the best. Prayers shall be made for him, and that continually. The people prayed for Solomon, and that helped to make him and his reign so great a blessing to them. But how is this applied to Christ? He needs not our prayers, nor can have any benefit by them. But the Old Testament saints prayed for his coming, prayed continually for it; for they called him, *He that should come.* And now that he has come we must pray for the success of his gospel and the advancement of his kingdom, which he calls praying for him. Praises shall be made of him. *Daily shall he be praised.*

IX. That under his government there shall be a wonderful increase both of meat and mouths. The country shall grow rich. Sow but a *handful of corn on the top of the mountains*, whence one would expect but little, and yet *the fruit of it shall shake like Lebanon*; it shall come up like a wood, so thick, and tall, and strong, like the cedars of Lebanon. This is applicable to the wonderful productions of the seed of the gospel in the days of the Messiah. A handful of that seed, sown in the mountainous and barren soil of the Gentile world, produced a wonderful harvest gathered in to Christ. The fields were *white unto harvest*, John iv. 35; Matt. ix. 37. The towns shall grow populous: *Those of the city shall flourish like grass*, for number, for verdure.

X. That his government shall be perpetual, both to his honour and to the happiness of his subjects. The Lord Jesus shall reign for ever, and of him only this must be understood, and not at all of Solomon. It is Christ only that shall *be feared throughout all generations* (v. 5) and *as long as the sun and moon endure*, v. 7. 1. The honour of the prince is immortal and shall never be sullied (v. 17): *His name shall endure for ever.* As the names of earthly princes are continued in their posterity, so Christ's in himself. 2. The happiness of the people is universal, too; *Men shall be blessed*, truly and for ever blessed, *in him.*

Verses 18–20

I. The psalmist is here enlarged in thanksgivings for the prophecy and promise, v. 18, 19. So sure is every word of God that we have reason enough to give thanks for what he has said, though it be not yet done. We must own that for all the great things he has done for the world God is worthy to be praised; *Blessed be the Lord*, that is, *blessed be his glorious name.* We are here taught to bless the name of Christ, and to bless God in Christ. 1. As the Lord God, as a self-existent self-sufficient Being, and our sovereign Lord. 2. As the God of Israel, in covenant with that people and worshipped by them. 3. As the God *who only does wondrous things*, in creation and providence, and especially this work of redemption, which excels them all.

II. He is earnest in prayer for the accomplishment of this prophecy and promise: *Let the whole earth be filled with his glory.* David shuts up the prayer with a double seal: "*Amen and amen.*" He even shuts up his life with this prayer, *v.* 20. This was the last psalm that ever he penned, though not placed last in this collection. With this he breathes his last: "Let God be glorified, let the kingdom of the Messiah be set up, and I desire no more. With this let *the prayers of David the son of Jesse* be *ended.* Even so, come, Lord Jesus, come quickly."

PSALM 73

This psalm, and the ten that next follow it, carry the name of Asaph in the titles of them. If he was the penman of them (as many think), we rightly call them psalms of Asaph. If he was only the chief musician, to whom they were delivered, our marginal reading is right, which calls them psalms for Asaph. Though the Spirit of prophecy by sacred songs descended chiefly on David, who is therefore styled "the sweet psalmist of Israel", yet God put some of that Spirit upon those about him. This psalm gives us an account of the conflict which the psalmist had with a strong temptation to envy the prosperity of wicked people. He begins his account with sacred principle, by the help of which he kept his ground, ver. 1. He then tells us, I. How he got into the temptation, ver. 2–14. II. How he got out of the temptation, ver. 15–20. III. How he gained by the temptation and was the better for it, ver. 21–28.

A psalm of Asaph.

Verses 1–14

This psalm begins somewhat abruptly: *Yet God is good to Israel* (so the margin reads it). Though wicked people receive many of the gifts of his providential bounty, yet we must own that he is, in a peculiar manner, good to Israel.

The psalmist designs an account of a temptation to envy the prosperity of the wicked.

I. He lays down, in the first place, that great principle which he is resolved to abide by while he was parleying with this temptation, *v.* 1. Job, when he was entering into such a temptation, fixed for his principle the omniscience of God: *Times are not hidden from the Almighty*, Job xxiv. 1. Jeremiah's principle is the justice of God: *Righteous art thou, O God! when I plead with thee*, Jer. xii. 1. Habakkuk's principle is the holiness of God: *Thou art of purer eyes than to behold iniquity*, Hab. i. 13. The psalmist's, here, is the goodness of God. He had had many thoughts in his mind concerning the providences of God, but this word, at last, settled him: "For all this, God is good, *good to Israel, even to those that are of a clean heart.*" Those are the Israel of God that are of a clean heart. God, who is good to all, is in a special manner good to his church and people, as he was to Israel of old.

II. He comes now to relate the shock that was given to his faith in God's distinguishing goodness to Israel, by a strong temptation to think that the Israel of God are no happier than other people and that God is no kinder to them than to others.

1. He speaks of it as a very narrow escape that he had not been overthrown by this temptation (*v.* 2): "*But as for me*, though I was so well satisfied in the goodness of God to Israel, yet *my feet were almost gone* (the tempter had almost tripped up my heels), *my steps had well-nigh slipped, for I was envious at the foolish.*" There are storms that will try the firmest anchors. Many a precious soul, that shall live for ever, had once a very narrow turn for its life.

2. The psalmist's temptation. He *saw*, with grief, *the prosperity of the wicked, v.* 3. They seem to have the least share of the troubles and calamities of this

life (*v.* 5): *They are not in the troubles of other men*, even of wise and good men, *neither are they plagued like other men*, but seem as if by some special privilege they were exempted from the common lot of sorrows. They seem to have the greatest share of the comforts of this life. They live at ease so that *their eyes stand out with fatness*, *v.* 7. There are many who have a great deal of this life in their hands, but nothing of the other life in their hearts. They are ungodly, and yet they prosper and *increase in riches*, *v.* 12. *They are the prosperous of the age*, so some read it. Their end seems to be peace. This is mentioned first, as the most strange of all (*v.* 4): *There are no bands in their death.* They are not taken off by a violent death. Nay, they are not bound by the terrors of conscience in their dying moments. We cannot judge of men's state on the other side death. Men may die like lambs, and yet have their place with the goats. They made a very bad use of their outward prosperity and were hardened by it in their wickedness. It made them very proud and haughty. Because they live at ease, *pride compasses them as a chain*, *v.* 6. *Pride ties on their chain*, or necklace; so Dr. Hammond reads it. It is no harm to wear a chain or necklace; but when it is worn to gratify a vain mind, it ceases to be an ornament. And, as the pride of sinners appears in their dress, so it does in their talk: *They speak loftily* (*v.* 8); they affect *great swelling words of vanity* (2 Pet. ii. 18). It made them oppressive to their poor neighbours (*v.* 6): *Violence covers them as a garment. They speak wickedly concerning oppression;* they oppress, and justify themselves in it. *They are corrupt*, that is, dissolved in pleasures and everything that is luxurious (so some). It made them very insolent in their demeanour towards both God and man (*v.* 9): *They set their mouth against the heavens*, putting contempt upon God himself. They cannot reach the heavens with their hands, to shake God's throne, but they show their ill-will by setting their mouth against the heavens. *Their tongue* also *walks through the earth*, and they take liberty to abuse all that come in their way. They could not have been thus wicked if they had not learned to say (*v.* 11), *How doth God know? And is there knowledge in the Most High?* What an affront is it to the God of infinite knowledge, from whom all knowledge is, to ask, *Is there knowledge in him?* Well may he say (*v.* 12), *Behold, these are the ungodly.* He observed that while wicked men thus prospered in their impiety, good people were in great affliction, and he himself in particular. He looked abroad and saw many of God's people greatly at a loss (*v.* 10): "Because the wicked are so very daring *therefore his people return hither;* they know not what to say to it any more than I do, and the rather because *waters of a full cup are wrung out to them*; they are not only made to drink of the bitter cup of affliction, but to drink all. Care is taken that they lose not a drop of that unpleasant potion; the waters are wrung out unto them, that they may have the dregs of the cup." These are the waters wrung out to them: "For my part," says he, "*all the day long have I been plagued* with one affliction or another, *and chastened every morning*, as duly as the morning comes." From all this arose a very strong temptation to cast off his religion. There are those, even among God's professing people, that say, "*How does God know?* Surely all things are left to blind fortune, and not disposed of by an all-seeing God." Though the psalmist's feet were not so far gone as to question God's omniscience, yet he was tempted to question the benefit of religion, and to say (*v.* 13), *Verily, I have cleansed my heart in vain*, and have, to no purpose, *washed my hands in innocency.* But when the pure in heart, those blessed ones, shall see God (Matt. v. 8), they will not say that they cleansed their hearts in vain.

Verses 15–20

How he kept his footing and got the victory.

I. He kept up a respect for God's people, and restrained himself from speaking what he had thought amiss, *v.* 15. He got the victory by degrees, and this was the first point he gained; he was ready to say, *Verily, I have cleansed my heart in vain,* but he kept his mouth with this consideration, "*If I say, I will speak thus, behold, I should* give the greatest offence imaginable to *the generation of thy children.*" Though he thought amiss, he took care not to utter that evil thought which he had conceived. If therefore thou hast been so foolish as to think evil, *lay thy hand upon thy mouth,* and let it go no further, Prov. xxx. 32. We must think twice before we speak once, both because some things may be thought which may not be spoken and because the second thoughts may correct the mistakes of the first. There is nothing that can give more general offence to the generation of God's children than to say that *we have cleansed our heart in vain* or that it is vain to serve God.

II. He foresaw the ruin of wicked people. "I endeavoured to understand the meaning of this unaccountable dispensation of Providence; but *it was too painful for me.* I could not conquer it by the strength of my own reasoning." If there were not another life after this, we could not fully reconcile the prosperity of the wicked with the justice of God. But (*v.* 17) *he went into the sanctuary of God;* he consulted the scriptures, and he prayed to God to make this matter plain to him, and, at length, he understood wicked people were rather to be pitied than envied, for they were but ripening for ruin. The sanctuary must be the resort of a tempted soul. All is well that ends well, everlastingly well; but nothing well that ends ill, everlastingly ill. The prosperity of the wicked is short and uncertain. The high places in which Providence sets them are *slippery places* (*v.* 18). Their destruction is sure, and sudden, and very great. They flourish for a time, but are undone for ever. He speaks of it as God's doing, and therefore it cannot be resisted: *Thou castest them down.* It is swift; for *how are they brought into desolation as in a moment! v.* 19. It is a total and final ruin: *They are utterly consumed with terrors.* Their prosperity is therefore not to be envied at all, but despised. *As a dream when one awaketh, so, O Lord! when thou awakest,* or when they awake (as some read it), *thou shalt despise their image,* their shadow, *and make it to vanish. In the day of the great judgment* (so the Chaldee paraphrase reads it), *they shall rise to shame and everlasting contempt.* They shall be made to awake out of the sleep of their carnal security, and then God shall despise their image. How did God despise that rich man's image when he said, *Thou fool, this night thy soul shall be required of thee!* Luke xii. 19, 20.

Verses 21–28

An account of the good improvement which the psalmist made of that sore temptation with which he had been assaulted and by which he was almost overcome.

I. He learned to think very humbly of himself and to abase and accuse himself before God (*v.* 21, 22); *My heart was grieved, and I was pricked in my reins;* temptation was to Paul as a thorn in the flesh, 2 Cor. xii. 7. The working of envy and discontent is as painful as any. The psalmist owns it was his ignorance to vex himself at this: "So ignorant was I of that which I might have known. *I was as a beast (Behemoth—a great beast) before thee.* Beasts mind present things only, and never look before at what is to come; and so did I. To be ready to wish myself one of them, and to think of changing conditions with them! *So foolish was I.*"

II. He took occasion hence to own his dependence on the grace of God (*v.* 23): "*Nevertheless,* foolish as I am, *I am continually with thee* and in thy favour; *thou hast holden me by my right hand.*" He had said, in the hour of temptation (*v.* 14), *All the day long have I been plagued;* but here he corrects himself for that passionate complaint: "Though God has chastened me, he has not cast me off; notwithstanding all the crosses of my life, *I have been continually* with thee. Though God has sometimes written bitter things against me, yet he has still *holden me by my right hand* to prevent my losing my way in the wildernesses through which I have walked." If he has thus maintained the spiritual life, the earnest of eternal life, we ought not to complain. "*My feet were almost gone,* and they would have quite gone, past recovery, but that thou hast holden me by my right hand and so kept me from falling."

III. He encouraged himself to hope that the same God who had delivered him from this evil work would *preserve him to his heavenly kingdom,* as St. Paul does (2 Tim. iv. 18): "I am now upheld by thee, therefore *thou shalt guide me with thy counsel,* leading me, as thou hast done hitherto, and thou *shalt afterwards receive me to glory,*" *v.* 24. The psalmist had like to have paid dearly for following his own counsels in this temptation and therefore resolves for the future to take God's advice. If God direct us in the way of our duty, he will afterwards reconcile us to all the dark providences that now puzzle and perplex us, and ease us of the pain we have been put into by some threatening temptations.

IV. He was hereby quickened to cleave the more closely to God, and very much confirmed and comforted in the choice he had made of him, *v.* 25, 26. He had complained of his afflictions (*v.* 14); but this makes them very light and easy, *All is well if God be mine.* We have here the breathings of a sanctified soul towards God, and its repose in him. *Whom have I in heaven but thee?* There is scarcely a verse in all the psalms more expressive than this of the pious and devout affections of a soul to God. God alone, that made the soul, can make it happy. If God be our felicity we must have him (*Whom have I but thee?*), we must choose him. Our desires must not only be offered up to God, but they must all terminate in him, desiring nothing more than God, but still more and more of him. "*There is none in heaven but thee. I desire none on earth besides thee;* not only none in heaven, which we have but little acquaintance with, but none on earth, where we have many friends and where much of our present interest and concern lie." *My flesh and my heart fail,* Others have experienced and we must expect, the failing both of flesh and heart. The body will fail by sickness, age, and death. *But God is the strength of my heart and my portion for ever.* He speaks as one careless of the body (let that fail, there is no remedy), but as one concerned about the soul, to be *strengthened in the inner man.*

V. He was fully convinced of the miserable condition of all wicked people. This he learned in the sanctuary upon this occasion, and he would never forget it (*v.* 27): *Lo, those that are far from thee,* in a state of distance and estrangement, that desire the Almighty to depart from them, *shall* certainly *perish.*

VI. He was greatly encouraged to cleave to God and to confide in him, *v.* 28. Our drawing near to God takes rise from his drawing near to us, and it is the happy meeting that makes the bliss. Here is a great truth laid down, That it is good to draw near to God; but the life of it lies in the application, "It is good for *me.*" If wicked men, notwithstanding all their prosperity, shall perish and be destroyed, then let us trust in the Lord God, in him, not in them (see cxlvi. 3–5), in him, and not in our worldly prosperity; let us trust in God, and neither fret at them nor be afraid of them.

Psalm 74

This psalm does so particularly describe the destruction of Jerusalem and the temple by Nebuchadnezzar that interpreters incline to think that either it was penned by David, or Asaph in David's time, or that it was penned by another Asaph, who lived at the time of the captivity, or by Jeremiah, and, after the return out of captivity, was delivered to the sons of Asaph, who were called by his name, for the public service of the church. That was the most eminent family of the singers in Ezra's time. See Ezra ii. 41; iii. 10; Neh. xi. 17, 22; xii. 35, 46. The deplorable case of the people of God at that time is here spread before the Lord, and left with him. The prophet, in the name of the church, I. Puts in complaining pleas of the miseries they suffered, for the quickening of their desires in prayer, ver. 1–11. II. He puts in comfortable pleas for the encouraging of their faith in prayer, ver. 12–17. III. He concludes with divers petitions to God for deliverance, ver. 18–23.

Maschil of Asaph.

Verses 1–11

This psalm is entitled *Maschil—a psalm to give instruction*, for it was penned in a day of affliction, which is intended for instruction.

I. The displeasure of God against the people of God was the cause and bitterness of all their calamities. They expostulate with God (*v.* 1). Christ himself, upon the cross, cried out, *My God, my God, why hast thou forsaken me?* So the church here, *O God! why hast thou forsaken us for ever?* Here they speak according to their present dark and melancholy apprehensions. The people of God must not think that because they are cast down they are therefore cast off, that because men cast them off therefore God does. This expostulation intimates that they dreaded God's casting them off more than anything. *Why does thy anger smoke?* that is, why does it rise up to such a degree that all about us take notice of it. They plead their relation to him: "We are *the sheep of thy pasture.* That the wolves worry the sheep is not strange; but was ever any shepherd thus displeased at his own sheep? *Remember,* we are *thy congregation* (*v.* 2), and devoted to thy praise; we are *the rod*, or tribe, *of thy inheritance*, from whom thou hast received praise and worship more than from the neighbouring nations. We are pleading for *Mount Zion, wherein thou hast dwelt*, which has been the place of thy peculiar delight and residence, thy demesne and mansion. It is *thy congregation*, which thou hast *purchased of old* by many miracles of mercy when they were first formed into a people; it is *thy inheritance, which thou hast redeemed* when they were sold into servitude. Now, Lord, wilt thou now abandon a people that cost thee so dear, and has been so dear to thee?" Much more reason have we to hope that God will not cast off any whom Christ has redeemed with his own blood. *"Lift up thy feet;* that is, come with speed to repair the desolations that are made in thy sanctuary, which otherwise will be perpetual and irreparable."

II. They complain of the outrage and cruelty of their enemies, but only what they had done against the sanctuary and the synagogue. The temple at Jerusalem was the *dwelling-place of God's name*, and therefore the *sanctuary*, or *holy place, v.* 7. In this the enemies did wickedly (*v.* 3), for they destroyed it in downright contempt of God and affront to him. They *roared in the midst of God's congregations, v.* 4, where God's faithful people attended on him with a humble reverent silence. *They set up their ensigns for signs.* The banners of their army they set up in the temple. This daring defiance of God and his power touched his people in a tender part. Men took a pride in destroying *the carved work* of the temple, *v.* 5, 6. Some read it thus: *They show themselves, as one that lifts up axes on high in a thicket of trees*, for so do

they break down the carved work of the temple; they make no more scruple of breaking down the rich wainscot of the temple than woodcutters do of hewing trees in the forest. They set fire to it, and so violated or *destroyed it to the ground, v.* 7. The Chaldeans burnt the house of God, 2 Chron. xxxvi. 19. And the Romans *left not there one stone upon another* (Matt. xxiv. 2), till Zion, the holy mountain, was by Titus Vespasian ploughed as a field. He complains of the desolations of the synagogues, or schools of the prophets. *Let us destroy them together;* not only the temple, but all the places of religious worship and the worshippers with them. They *burnt up all the synagogues of God in the land* and laid them all waste.

III. The great aggravation of all these calamities was that they had no prospect at all of relief, nor could they foresee an end of them (*v.* 9): "We see our enemy's sign set up in the sanctuary, but *we see not our signs. There is no more any prophet* to tell us how long the trouble will last and when things concerning us shall have an end, that hope may support us under our troubles." *How long shall the adversary reproach and blaspheme thy name?* Not "How long shall we be troubled?" but "How long shall God be blasphemed? *Why withdrawest thou thy hand*, and dost not stretch it out, to deliver thy people and destroy thy enemies?"

Verses 12–17

Two things quiet the minds of those that are here sorrowing for the solemn assembly:—

I. That God is the God of Israel, a God in covenant with his people (*v.* 12): *God is my King of old*. This comes in both as a plea in prayer to God and as a prop to their own faith and hope, to encourage themselves to expect deliverance, considering the *days of old*, lxxvii. 5. Several things are here mentioned which God had done for his people as their King of old, which encouraged them to commit themselves to him and depend upon him.

1. He had divided the sea before them when they came out of Egypt, not by the strength of Moses or his rod, but by his own strength; and he that could do that could do anything.

2. He had destroyed Pharaoh and the Egyptians. Pharaoh was the *leviathan*; the Egyptians were *the dragons*, fierce, and cruel. God crushed their powers, though complicated, and at last drowned them all in the Red Sea. This was typical of Christ's victory over Satan and his kingdom, pursuant to the first promise, that the seed of the woman should break the serpent's head. This providence was meat to their faith and hope, to encourage them in the other difficulties they were likely to meet in the wilderness.

3. God had both ways altered the course of nature, both in fetching streams out of the rock and turning streams into rock, *v.* 15. He had dissolved the rock into waters: *Thou didst bring out the fountain and the flood* out of the rock, out of the flinty rock. Let this never be forgotten, but let it especially be remembered that the rock was Christ, and the waters out of it were spiritual drink. He had congealed the waters into rock: *Thou driedst up mighty rapid rivers*, Jordan particularly at the time when it overflowed all its banks. He that did these things could now deliver his oppressed people.

II. That the God of Israel is the God of nature, *v.* 16, 17. It is he that orders the regular successions and revolutions, day and night. He is the Lord of all time. It is he that opens the eyelids of the morning light, and draws the curtains of the evening shadow. *He has prepared the moon and the sun.* "Thou hast *appointed all the bounds of the earth*, and the different climates of its several regions, for *thou hast made summer and winter*, the frigid and the torrid zones;

or, rather, the constant revolutions of the year and its several seasons." He that had power at first to settle, and still to preserve, this course of nature by the diurnal and annual motions of the heavenly bodies, has certainly all power both to save and to destroy. He that is faithful to his covenant with the day and with the night, will certainly make good his promise to his people. His covenant with Abraham and his seed is as firm as that with Noah and his sons, Gen. viii. 21.

Verses 18–23

The psalmist here, in the name of the church, most earnestly begs that God would appear for them against their enemies, and put an end to their present troubles. *Arise, O God! plead thy own cause.*

I. The persecutors are God's sworn enemies: "Lord, they have not only abused us, they have directly and immediately reproached thee, and *blasphemed thy name,*" *v.* 18. The psalmist insists much upon this: "We dare not answer their reproaches; Lord, do thou answer them. Remember that the *foolish people have blasphemed thy name* (v. 18) and that still *the foolish man reproaches thee daily.*" Those that reproach God are foolish. As atheism is folly (xiv. 1), profaneness and blasphemy are no less so. Perhaps those are cried up as the wits of the age that ridicule religion and sacred things; but really they are the greatest fools. They do not hide their blasphemous thoughts in their own bosoms, but proclaim them with a loud voice (*forget not the voice of thy enemies, v.* 23). God needs not to be put in remembrance by us of what he has to do, but thus we must show our concern for his honour and believe that he will vindicate us.

II. The persecuted are his covenant-people. They have fallen into the hands of *the multitude of the wicked, v.* 19. *The dark places of the earth are full of the habitations of cruelty.* The land of the Chaldeans where there was none of the light of the knowledge of the true God (though otherwise it was famed for learning and arts), was indeed a dark place; the inhabitants of it were *alienated from the life of God through the ignorance that was in them,* and therefore they were cruel: where there was no true divinity there was scarcely to be found common humanity. The psalmist pleads with God: "It is *thy turtle-dove* that is ready to be swallowed up by the multitude of the wicked," *v.* 19. The church is a dove for harmlessness and mildness, a dove for mournfulness in a day of distress, a turtle-dove for fidelity and the constancy of love. "Shall thy turtle-dove, that is true to thee and devoted to thy honour, be delivered into the *hand of the multitude of the wicked?* Lord, it will be thy honour to help the weak, especially thy own. Wilt thou not perform the promises thou hast, in thy covenant, made to them? Appear, Lord, for those that will praise thy name, against those that blaspheme it."

PSALM 75

Though this psalm is attributed to Asaph in the title, yet it does so exactly agree with David's circumstances, at his coming to the crown after the death of Saul, that most interpreters apply it to that juncture, and suppose that either Asaph penned it, in the person of David, as his poet-laureate, or that David penned it, and delivered it to Asaph as precentor of the temple. In this psalm, I. David returns God thanks for bringing him to the throne, ver. 1, 9. II. He promises to lay out himself for the public good, in the use of the power God had given him, ver. 2, 3, 10. III. He checks the insolence of those that opposed his coming to the throne, ver. 4, 5. IV. He fetches a reason for all this from God's sovereign dominion in the affairs of the children of men, ver. 6–8.

To the chief musician, Al-taschith. A psalm *or* song of Asaph.

Verses 1–5

I. The psalmist gives to God the praise of the great things he had done for him and for his people Israel (*v.* 1): *Unto thee, O God! do we give thanks.* Not only *I* do give thanks, but *we* do, I and all my friends. There are many works which God does for his people that may truly be called *wondrous works,* out of the common course of providence. These wondrous works declare the nearness of his name.

II. He lays himself under an obligation to use his power well (*v.* 2): *When I shall receive the congregation I will judge uprightly.* Here he takes it for granted that God would, in due time, perfect that which concerned him. "When I am a judge I will judge, and *judge uprightly;* not as those that went before me, who either neglected judgment or perverted it." Public trusts are to be managed with great integrity; those that judge must judge uprightly, according to the rules of justice, without respect of persons.

III. He promises himself that his government would be a public blessing to Israel, *v.* 3. The present state of the kingdom was very bad: *The earth and all the inhabitants thereof are dissolved;* and no marvel, when the former reign was so dissolute that all went to rack and ruin. They were all to pieces, two against three and three against two, crumbled into factions and parties, which was likely to issue in their ruin; but *I bear up the pillars of it.* The fabric would have sunk if David had not held up the pillars of it. This may well be applied to Christ and his government.

IV. He checks those that opposed his government, that were against his accession to it and obstructed the administration of it. *I said unto the fools, Deal not foolishly.* As soon as he came to the crown he issued a proclamation against vice and profaneness, and here we have the contents of it. 1. To the simple sneaking sinners, the fools in Israel, that corrupted themselves, he said, "*Deal not foolishly;* do not act so directly contrary both to your reason and to your interest." 2. To the proud daring sinners, the wicked, that set God himself at defiance, he says, "*Lift not up the horn;* boast not of your power and prerogatives; *lift not up your horn on high,* as though you could have what you will and do what you will; *speak not with a stiff neck,* in which is an iron sinew, that will never bend to the will of God in the government; for those that will not bend shall break."

Verses 6–10

I. Here are two great truths laid down concerning God's government of the world.

1. That from God alone kings receive their power (*v.* 6, 7), and therefore to God alone David would give the praise of his advancement. We see strange revolutions in states and kingdoms, and are surprised at the sudden disgrace of some and elevation of others. *Promotion comes not from the east, nor from the west, nor from the desert.* Men cannot gain promotion either by the wisdom or wealth of the children of the east, nor by the numerous forces of the isles of the Gentiles, that lay westward, nor those of Egypt or Arabia, that lay south; no concurring smiles of second causes will raise men to preferment without the first cause. The learned Bishop Lloyd (*Serm. in loc.*) gives this gloss upon it: "All men took the original of power to be from heaven, but from whom there many knew not; the eastern nations, who were generally given to astrology, took it to come from their stars, especially the sun, their god. No, says David, it comes neither from the east nor from the west, neither from the rising nor from the setting of such a planet, or such a constellation, nor from the south, nor from the exaltation of the sun or any star in the mid-heaven." He mentions not the north because the same word that signifies the north signifies the secret place, and from the secret of God's counsel it does come, or from the oracle in Zion, which lay on the north side of Jerusalem. *God is the judge,*

the governor or umpire. When parties contend for the prize, he *puts down one and sets up another* as he sees fit, so as to serve his own purposes and bring to pass his own counsels. He, who is infinitely wise, holy, and good, has power to set up and put down whom, and when, and how he pleases.

2. That from God alone all must receive their doom (*v.* 8): *In the hand of the Lord there is a cup*, which he puts into the hands of the children of men, a cup of providence, mixed up of many ingredients. The sufferings of Christ are called a *cup*, Matt. xx. 22; John xviii. 11. *The wine is red*, denoting the wrath of God, which is infused into the judgments executed on sinners. It is red as fire for it burns. It is *full of mixture*. There are mixtures of mercy and grace in the cup of affliction when it is put into the hands of God's own people, mixtures of the curse when it is put into the hands of the wicked; it is wine mingled with gall. Some drops of this wrath may light on good people; they have their share in common calamities; but the dregs of the cup are reserved for the wicked. The calamity itself is but the vehicle into which the curse is infused, the top of which has little of the infusion; but the sediment is pure wrath, and that shall fall to the share of sinners. They shall *wring them out*, that not a drop of the wrath may be left behind.

II. Here are two practical inferences. 1. He will praise God, and give him glory, for the power to which he has advanced him (*v.* 9): *I will declare for ever* that which *thy wondrous works declare*, *v.* 1. He will give glory to God, as the God of Jacob, knowing it was for Jacob his servant's sake, and because he loved his people Israel, that he made him king over them. 2. He will use the power with which he is entrusted for the great ends for which it was put into his hands, *v.* 10, as before, *v.* 2, 4. "Though not all the heads, yet *all the horns, of the wicked will I cut off*, with which they push their poor neighbours; I will disable them to do mischief."

PSALM 76

This psalm seems to have been penned upon occasion of some great victory. The LXX call it, "A song upon the Assyrians", whence many good interpreters conjecture that it was penned when Sennacherib's army, then besieging Jerusalem, was entirely cut off by a destroying angel in Hezekiah's time. Or it might be penned by Asaph who lived in David's time, upon occasion of the many triumphs with which God delighted to honour that reign. I. The psalmist congratulates the happiness of the church in having God so nigh, ver. 1–3. II. He celebrates the glory of God's power, ver. 4–6. III. He infers hence what reason all have to fear before him, ver. 7–9. And, IV. What reason his people have to trust in him and to pay their vows to him, ver. 10–12. It is a psalm proper for a thanksgiving day.

To the chief musician on Neginoth. A psalm *or* song of Asaph.

Verses 1-6

The psalmist triumphs here in God, the centre of all our triumphs.

I. In the revelation God had made of himself to them, *v.* 1. It is the honour and privilege of Judah and Israel that among them *God is known*, and where he is known *his name* will be *great*.

II. In the tokens of God's special presence with them in his ordinances, *v.* 2. In the whole land of Judah and Israel God was known, but *in Salem, in Zion*, were *his tabernacle* and *his dwelling-place*. There he kept court; there he received the homage of his people by their sacrifices; thither they came to address themselves to him, and of that place he said, *Here will I dwell, for I have desired it.*

III. In the victories they had obtained over their enemies (*v.* 3): *There broke he the arrows of the bow*.

1. Here are bow and arrows, shield and sword, and all for battle; but all are broken and rendered useless. In the tabernacle and dwelling-place in Zion, there he broke the arrows of the bow; it was done in the field

of battle, and yet it is said to be done in the sanctuary, because done in answer to the prayers which God's people there made to him. Public successes are owing as much to what is done in the church as to what is done in the camp. Now,

2. This victory redounded very much to the immortal honour of Israel's God (*v.* 4): "*Thou art*, and hast manifested thyself to be, *more glorious and excellent than the mountains of prey*. Than the great and mighty ones who think themselves firmly fixed like mountains, but are really mountains of prey, oppressive to all about them. It is their glory to destroy; it is thine to deliver." *The stouthearted have despoiled and disarmed themselves* (so some read it); when God pleases he can make his enemies to weaken and destroy themselves. *They have slept*, not the sleep of the righteous, but *their sleep*, the sleep of sinners, that shall awake to everlasting shame. The men of might can no more *find their hands* than the stout-hearted can their spirit. As the bold men are cowed, so the strong men are lamed, and cannot so much as find their hands, to save their own heads, much less to hurt their enemies.

Verses 7-12

This victory is here made to speak three things:—

I. Terror to God's enemies (*v.* 7-9): *Thou, even thou, art to be feared*. Let all the world learn by this event to stand in awe of the great God. *Who may stand in thy sight from the minute that thou art angry?* God's people are the *meek of the earth* (Zeph. ii, 3) that can bear any wrong, but do none. Though the meek of the earth are by their meekness exposed to injury, yet God will, sooner or later, appear for their salvation. When God comes to save *all the meek of the earth*, he will *cause judgment to be heard from heaven*. The righteous God long seems to keep silence, yet, sooner or later he will make judgment to be heard. When God is speaking judgment from heaven it is time for the earth to compose itself into an awful and reverent silence: *The earth feared and was still.*

II. Comfort to God's people, *v.* 10. *Surely the wrath of man shall praise thee*, not only by the checks given to it, when it shall be forced to confess its own impotency, but even by the liberty given to it for a time. The more *the heathen rage* and plot *against the Lord and his anointed* the more will God be praised for setting *his King upon his holy hill of Zion* in spite of them, ii. 1, 6. What will not turn to his praise shall not be suffered to break out: *The remainder of wrath shalt thou restrain.*

III. Duty to all, *v.* 11, 12. Let all submit themselves to this great God and become his loyal subjects. We are commanded to do homage to the King of kings: *Vow and pay;* that is, take an oath of allegiance to him and make conscience of keeping it. And, having taken him for our King, let us bring presents to him. Not that God needs any present we can bring, but prayers and praises, and especially our hearts, are the presents we should bring to the Lord our God. He ought to be feared: *He is the fear* (so the word is); his name is glorious and with him is terrible majesty. He shall *cut off the spirit of princes;* he shall slip it off as easily as we slip off a flower from the stalk or a bunch of grapes from the vine; so the word signifies.

PSALM 77

This psalm begins with sorrowful complaints but ends with comfortable encouragements. The complaints seem to be of personal grievances, but the encouragements relate to the public concerns of the church. One of the rabbin says, This psalm is spoken in the dialect of the captives; and therefore some think it was penned in the captivity in Babylon. I. The psalmist complains here of the deep impressions which his troubles made upon his spirits, ver. 1–10. II. He encourages himself to hope that it would be well at last, by the remembrance of God's former appearances for the help of his people, ver. 11–20.

To the chief musician, to Jeduthun. A psalm of Asaph.

Verses 1–10

We have here the lively protraiture of a good man under prevailing melancholy. Drooping saints, that are of a sorrowful spirit, may here as in a glass see their own faces. The griefs and fears seem to have been over when he penned this record, for he says (*v.* 1), *I cried unto God, and he gave ear unto me.* He inserts it in the beginning of his narrative as an intimation that his trouble did not end in despair.

I. His melancholy prayers. *My voice was unto God, and I cried, even with my voice unto God.* Thus he gave vent to his grief and gained some ease; and thus he took the right way in order to relief (*v.* 2): *In the day of my trouble I sought the Lord.* Those that are under trouble of mind must not think to drink it away, or laugh it away, but must pray it away.

II. His melancholy grief. *My sore,* or wound, *ran in the night,* and bled inwardly, and it ceased not, no, not in the time appointed for rest and sleep. *My soul refused to be comforted;* he had no mind to hearken to those that would be his comforters. Those that are in sorrow affront God, if they refuse to be comforted.

III. His melancholy musings. When he remembered God his thoughts fastened only upon his justice, and wrath, and dreadful majesty, and thus God himself became a terror to him. He could not enjoy sleep, which, if it be quiet and refreshing, is a parenthesis to our griefs and cares: *"Thou holdest my eyes waking* with thy terrors, which make me full of *tossings to and fro until the dawning of the day."* He was so troubled that he could not speak and refresh himself. Grief never preys so much upon the spirits as when it is thus smothered and pent up.

IV. His melancholy reflections (*v.* 5, 6): *"I have considered the days of old,* and compared them with the present days; and our former prosperity does but aggravate our present calamities: for we see not the wonders that our fathers told us of." But *say not thou* that *the former days were better than these.* Neither let the remembrance of the comforts we have lost make us unthankful for those that are left. Particularly he *called to remembrance his song in the night,* but he was out of tune, and the remembrance did but *pour out his soul in him,* xlii. 4. See Job xxxv. 10.

V. His melancholy fears and apprehensions: *"I communed with my own heart, v.* 6. Come, my soul, what will be the issue of these things? And thus I began to reason, *Will the Lord cast off for ever,* as he does for the present? His *tender mercies* have been withheld, but *are they shut up,* shut up *in anger?"* (*v.* 7–9). This is the language of a disconsolate deserted soul, not uncommon even with those that *fear the Lord,* Isa. l. 10. Spiritual trouble is of all trouble most grievous to a gracious soul; nothing wounds and pierces it like the apprehensions of God's being angry. God's own people, in a cloudy and dark day, may be tempted to make desperate conclusions about their own spiritual state and the condition of God's church and kingdom in the world, and, as to both, to give up all for gone. But we must not give way to such suggestions as these. Let faith answer them from the Scripture: *Will the Lord cast off for ever?* God forbid, Rom. xi. 1. *Is his mercy clean gone for ever?* No; his *mercy endures for ever,* ciii. 17. *Doth his promise fail for evermore?* No; *it is impossible for God to lie,* Heb. vi. 18. *Has he in anger shut up his tender mercies?* No; they are *new every morning* (Lam. iii. 23); and therefore, *How shall I give thee up, Ephraim?* Hos. xi. 8, 9. On a sudden, he checked himself with that word, *Selah,* "Stop there; go no further," and he then chid himself (*v.* 10): *I said,*

This is my infirmity. He is soon aware that it is not well said, and therefore, "*Why art thou cast down, O my soul? I said, This is my affliction;* everyone has his affliction, his trouble in the flesh; and this is mine, the cross I must take up." Despondency of spirit, and distrust of God, under affliction, are too often the infirmities of good people. When at any time it is working in us we must thus suppress the rising of it. We must argue down the insurrections of unbelief, *But I will remember the years of the right hand of the Most High.* He had been considering the *years of ancient times* (*v.* 5), the blessings formerly enjoyed, but now he considered them as *the years of the right hand of the Most High,* that those blessings of ancient times came from the sovereign disposal of his right hand who is *over all, God blessed for ever,* and this satisfied him.

Verses 11–20

The psalmist here recovers himself. He tried again, and, upon this second trial, found it not in vain. "*I will remember, surely I will,* what God has done for his people of old, till I can thence infer a happy issue of the present dark dispensations," *v.* 11, 12. The due remembrance of the works of God will be a powerful antidote against distrust of his promise, for he is God and changes not.

Two things, in general, satisfied him:

I. That *God's way is in the sanctuary, v.* 13. It is *in holiness,* so some. He has holy ends in all he does. His way is according to his promise, which he has made known in the sanctuary. All he does is intended for the good of his church.

II. That *God's way is in the sea.* Though God is holy, just, and good, yet we cannot give an account of the reasons of his proceedings. *His path is in the great waters and his footsteps are not known, v.* 19. God's ways are like the deep waters which cannot be fathomed (xxxvi. 6), like the way of a ship in the sea, which cannot be tracked, Prov. xxx. 18, 19. *Who is so great a God as our God?* Let us first give to God the glory of the great things he has done for his people, and acknowledge him, herein, great above all comparison. "*Thou art the God that* alone *doest wonders,* above the power of any creature; *thou hast* visibly, and beyond any contradiction, *declared thy strength among the people."* God brought Israel out of Egypt, *v.* 15. This was the beginning of mercy to them. Though they were delivered by power, yet they are said to be redeemed, as if it had been done by price, because it was typical of the great redemption, which was to be wrought out, in the fulness of time, both by price and power. He divided the Red Sea before them (*v.* 16): *The waters* gave way, and a lane was made through. Not only the surface of the waters, but *the depths, were troubled,* and opened to the right and to the left. He destroyed the Egyptians (*v.* 17): *The skies sent out a sound; thy arrows also went abroad,* which is explained (*v.* 18): *The voice of thy thunder was heard in the heaven* (that was the sound which the skies sent forth); *the lightnings lightened the world*—those were the arrows which went abroad, by which the host of the Egyptians was discomfited, and yet when the waters returned to their place *his footsteps were not known* (*v.* 19); there was no mark set upon the place. He took his people Israel under his own guidance and protection (*v.* 20): *Thou leddest thy people like a flock.* God went before them with all the care and tenderness of a shepherd. Moses and Aaron led them; they could not do it without God, but God did it with and by them. Moses was their governor, Aaron their high priest. The two great ordinances of magistracy and ministry is, though not so great a miracle, yet as great a mercy to any people as the pillar of cloud and fire was to Israel in the wilderness.

Psalm 78

This psalm is historical. Here is, I. The preface to this church history, recommending it to the study of the generations to come, ver. 1–8. II. The history itself from Moses to David; it is put into a psalm or song that the singing of it might affect them with the things here related, more than they would be with a bare narrative of them. The general scope of this psalm we have ver. 9–11. As to the particulars, we are here told, 1. What wonderful works God had wrought for them. 2. How ungrateful they were to God for his favours. How they murmured against God and distrusted him, and did but counterfeit repentance and submission when he punished them. How they affronted God with their idolatries after they came to Canaan. 3. How God had justly punished them for their sins in the wilderness, and now, of late, when the ark was taken by the Philistines, ver. 59–64. 4. How graciously God had spared them and returned in mercy to them, notwithstanding their provocations, and brought them under a happy establishment both in church and state, ver. 65–72. "These things happened unto them for ensamples," 1 Cor. x. 11; Heb. iv. 11.

Maschil of Asaph.

Verses 1–8

These verses contain the preface to this history. It is indeed *Maschil—a psalm to give instruction.*

I. The psalmist demands attention (v. 1): *Give ear, O my people! to my law.* Some make these the psalmist's words. He calls his instructions his *law* or *edict*; such was their commanding force in themselves. David was a king, and he would interpose his royal power for the edification of his people. Or the psalmist, being a prophet, speaks as God's mouth, and so calls them *his people*, and demands subjection to what was said as to a law.

II. Several reasons are given why we should diligently attend. 1. The things here discoursed of are weighty (v. 2): *I will open my mouth in a parable, I will utter dark sayings*, which challenge your most serious regard. These are called *dark sayings*, not because they are hard to be understood, but because they are carefully to be looked into. 2. They are the monuments of antiquity—*dark sayings of old which our fathers have told us*, v. 3. They are things of undoubted certainty. The honour we owe to our parents and ancestors obliges us to attend to that which our fathers have told us. 3. They are to be transmitted to posterity, and it lies as a charge upon us carefully to hand them down (v. 4); because our fathers told them to us *we will not hide them from their children.* Our care must be for posterity in general. That which we are to transmit to our children is not only the knowledge of languages, arts and sciences, liberty and property, but especially the praises of the Lord, and the wonderful works he has done. Our great care must be to lodge our religion, that great deposit, pure and entire in the hands of those that succeed us. (1) The law of God was given with a particular charge to teach it diligently to their children (v. 5): *He established a testimony* or covenant, and enacted a law, in Jacob and Israel, which he *commanded them to make known to their children*, Deut. vi. 7, 20. The church of God, as the historian says of the Roman commonwealth, was not to be *a thing of one age*, but was to be kept up from one generation to another. (2) The providences of God concerning them. God gave order that his laws should be made known to posterity. It is requisite that with them his works also should be made known. Let these be told to our children and our children's children, *that, not forgetting the works of God* wrought in former days, *they* might *set their hope in God and keep his commandments.* Those only may with confidence hope for God's salvation that make conscience of doing his commandments. They may take warning (v. 8): *That they might not be as their fathers, a stubborn and rebellious generation.* Though they were the seed of Abraham, taken into covenant with God, their *spirit was not steadfast with him*, but upon every occasion they flew off from him.

Verses 9–39

In these verses,

I. The psalmist observes the rebukes that the people of Israel had brought upon themselves by their dealing treacherously with God, v. 9–11. *The children of Ephraim*, in which tribe Shiloh was, though they were well armed and shot with bows, yet *turned back in the day of battle.* This seems to refer to that shameful defeat which the Philistines gave them in Eli's time, when they took the ark prisoner, 1 Sam. iv. 10, 11. Well might that event be thus fresh in mind in David's time, above forty years after, for the ark, which in that memorable battle was seized by the Philistines, though it was quickly brought out of captivity, was never brought out of obscurity till David fetched it from Kirjath-jearim to his own city. Note: the shameful cowardice of the children of Ephraim. Sin dispirits men and takes away the heart. They were basely treacherous and perfidious, for *they kept not the covenant of God.* They *forgot his works and his wonders.* Our forgetfulness of God's works is at the bottom of our disobedience to his laws.

II. He takes occasion hence to consult precedents. The narrative in these verses is very remarkable, for it relates a kind of struggle between God's goodness and man's badness, and mercy, at length, rejoices against judgment.

1. God did great things for his people Israel when he first incorporated them and formed them into a people: *Marvellous things did he in the sight of their fathers.* He made a lane for them through the Red Sea, and caused them, gave them courage, to pass through, though the waters stood over their heads as a heap, v. 13. He provided a guide for them through the untrodden paths of the wilderness (v. 14); he led them step by step, *in the day time by a cloud*, which also sheltered them from the heat, and *all the night with a light of fire*, which made the darkness of night less frightful, and perhaps kept off wild beasts, Zech. ii. 5. He furnished their camp with fresh water in a dry and thirsty land by broaching a rock (v. 15, 16): *He clave the rocks in the wilderness.* Out of the dry and hard rock he gave them drink, not distilled as out of an alembic, drop by drop, but in streams *running down like rivers*, and as out of the great depths. God gives abundantly, and is rich in mercy.

2. When God began thus to bless them they began to affront him (v. 17): *They sinned yet more against him.* They bore the miseries of their servitude better than the difficulties of their deliverance, and never murmured at their taskmasters so much as they did at Moses and Aaron. *They provoked the Most High.* In the wilderness they said and did that which they knew would provoke him: *They tempted God in their heart*, v. 18. (1) By desiring, or rather demanding, that which he had not thought fit to give them: *They asked meat for their lust.* God had given them the manna, wholesome pleasant food and in abundance. But this would not serve; they must have meat for their lust, dainties and varieties. (2) By distrusting his power to give them what they desired. They challenged him to give them flesh; and, if he did not, they would say it was because he could not (v. 19): *They spoke against God.* It was as injurious a reflection as could be cast upon God to say, *Can God furnish a table in the wilderness?* What an unreasonable insatiable thing is luxury! Such a mighty thing did these epicures think a table well furnished to be that they thought it was more than God himself could give them in that wilderness. And which is easier, to furnish a table in the wilderness, which a rich man can do, or to fetch water out of a rock, which the greatest potentate on the earth cannot do? Be it ever so great a thing that we ask, it becomes us to own, *Lord, if thou wilt, thou canst.*

3. God justly resented the provocation and was much displeased with them (*v.* 21): *The Lord heard this, and was wroth.* God thus resented the provocation (*v.* 22): *Because* by this it appeared that *they believed not in God. They trusted not in the salvation* he had begun to work for them; for then they would not thus have questioned its progress. He *commanded the clouds from above.* Usually by their showers they contribute to the earth's producing corn; but now, when God so commanded them, they showered down corn themselves, which is therefore called here *the corn of heaven.* Everyone, even the least child in Israel, did *eat the bread of the mighty* (so the margin reads it); and yet it was strong meat for strong men. They were not stinted, for *he sent them meat to the full.* The daily provision God makes for us has no less of mercy. He expressed his resentment of the provocation, not in denying them what they so inordinately lusted after, but in granting it to them. *He caused an east wind to blow and a south wind,* either a south-east wind, or an east wind first to bring in the quails from that quarter and then a south wind to bring in more from that quarter; so that *he rained flesh upon them*; an abundance of it, *as dust, as the sand of the sea* (*v.* 27), so that the meanest Israelite might have sufficient; and it cost them nothing, no, not the pains of fetching it from the mountains, for *he let it fall in the midst of their camp, round about their habitation, v.* 28. We have the account, Num. xi. 31, 32. He made them pay dearly for their quails; for, though he *gave them their own desire, they were not estranged from their lust* (*v.* 29, 30); their appetite was insatiable; they were well filled and yet they were not satisfied. Such is the nature of lust; the more it is humoured the more humoursome it grows. There were some contented Israelites, that did eat moderately of the quails and were never the worse; for it was not the meat that poisoned them, but their own lust.

4. The judgments of God upon them did not reform them any more than his mercies (*v.* 32): *For all this, they sinned still;* they murmured and quarrelled with God and Moses as much as ever. Those hearts are hard indeed that will neither be melted by the mercies of God nor broken by his judgments.

5. They persisting in their sins, God proceeded in his judgments, but they were judgments of another nature, which wrought not suddenly, but slowly. *Therefore their days did he consume in vanity* in the wilderness *and their years in trouble.* They were condemned to wear out thirty-eight tedious years in the wilderness, which indeed were consumed in vanity; for in all those years there was not a step taken nearer Canaan, but they were turned back again, and wandered to and fro as in a labyrinth. Those that sin still must expect to be in trouble still. And the reason why we spend our days in so much vanity and trouble, why we live with so little comfort and to so little purpose, is because we do not live by faith.

6. Under these rebukes they professed repentance, but they were not sincere in this profession. Their profession was plausible enough (*v.* 34, 35): *When he slew them,* or condemned them to be slain, *then they sought him.* In a fright they cried to God for mercy, and promised they would reform and be very good; then *they returned to God, and enquired early after him.* They were not sincere in this profession (*v.* 36, 37): *They did but flatter him with their mouth,* as if they thought by fair speeches to prevail with him to revoke the sentence. They thawed in the sun, but froze in the shade. They did but *lie to God wtih their tongues, for their heart was not with him.*

7. God hereupon, in pity to them, put a stop to the judgments which were threatened and in part executed (*v.* 38, 39): *But he, being full of compassion, forgave their iniquity.* He spared their lives till they had reared another generation which should enter into the promised land. Because he was *full of compassion,* he said, *How shall I give thee up, Ephraim? How shall I deliver thee, Israel?* Hos. xi. 8. Though they did not rightly remember that he was their rock, he *remembered that they were but flesh.* He considered what an easy thing it would be to crush them: *They are as a wind that passeth away and cometh not again.* It were easy to argue they may justly be cut off, but God argues, on the contrary, therefore he will not destroy them; for the true reason is, *He is full of compassion.*

Verses 40-72

The matter and scope of this paragraph are the same with the former, showing what great mercies God had bestowed upon Israel, how provoking they had been, what judgments he had brought upon them for their sins, and yet how, in judgment, he remembered mercy at last.

I. The sins of Israel in the wilderness again reflected on (*v.* 40, 41): *How often did they provoke him in the wilderness!* God kept an account, Num. xiv. 22, *They have tempted me these ten times.* By provoking him they did not so much anger him as grieve him, for he looked upon them as his children (*Israel is my son, my first-born*). They grieved him because they put him under a necessity of afflicting them, which he did not willingly. After they had humbled themselves before him they *turned back and tempted God,* prescribing to him what proofs he should give of his power and presence with them and what methods he should take in leading them and providing for them. It is presumption for us to limit *the Holy One of Israel*; for, being *the Holy One of Israel,* he will do what is most for our good. That which occasioned their limiting God was their forgetting his former favours (*v.* 42). There are some days made remarkable by signal deliverances, which ought never to be forgotten.

II. The mercies of God to Israel, and this catalogue of the works of wonder which God wrought for them begins higher, and is carried down further, than that before, *v.* 12, &c.

1. This begins with their deliverance out of Egypt, and the plagues with which God compelled the Egyptians to let them go. Several of the plagues of Egypt are here specified, which speak aloud the power of God and his favour to Israel. The turning of the waters into blood; they had made themselves drunk with the blood of God's people, even the infants, and now God gave them blood to drink, *for they were worthy, v.* 44. The flies and frogs infested them, *v.* 45. The plague of locusts, which devoured their increase, and that for which they had laboured, *v.* 46. The *hail,* which *destroyed* their trees, especially *their vines,* the weakest of trees (*v.* 47), and *their cattle,* especially *their flocks* of sheep, the weakest of their cattle (*v.* 48), and the *frost,* or congealed rain (as the word signifies), was so violent that it destroyed even the *sycamore-trees.* The death of the first-born was the last and sorest of the plagues of Egypt, and that which perfected the deliverance of Israel; it was first in intention (Exod. iv. 23), but last in execution; for, if gentler methods would have done the work, this would have been prevented. Pharaoh's heart having been often hardened after less judgments had softened it, God now *stirred up all his wrath. He made a way,* or (as the word is) *he weighed a path, to his anger.* He did not cast it upon them uncertainly, but by weight. His anger was weighed with the greatest exactness in the balances of justice; for, in his greatest displeasure, he never did, nor ever will do, any wrong to any of his creatures: the path of his anger is always weighed. *He sent evil angels among them,* not evil in their own nature, but in

respect to the errand upon which they were sent; they were destroying angels, or angels of punishment. The execution itself was very severe. *He smote all the first-born in Egypt* (v. 51) *the chief of their strength,* the hopes of their respective families. God made a way for *his own people to go forth like sheep,* not knowing whither they went, and *guided them in the wilderness,* as a shepherd guides his flock, with all possible care and tenderness, v. 52. *He led them on safely,* though in dangerous paths, so that *they feared not,* that is, they needed not to fear. *But the sea overwhelmed their enemies* that ventured to pursue them into it, v. 53. It was a lane to them, but a grave to their persecutors.

2. It is carried down as far as their settlement in Canaan (v. 54): *He brought them to the border of his sanctuary,* to that land in the midst of which he set up his sanctuary. That is a happy land which is the border of God's sanctuary. The whole land in general, and Zion in particular, was *the mountain which his right hand had purchased.* He *made them to ride on the high places of the earth,* Isa. lviii. 14; Deut. xxxii. 13. They found the Canaanites in the full possession of that land, but God made his people *Israel tread upon their high places, dividing* each tribe *an inheritance by line.*

III. The sins of Israel after they were settled in Canaan, v. 56–58. The children were *like their fathers,* and brought their old corruptions into their new habitations. They seemed sometimes devoted to God, but they presently *turned aside,* and *provoked him to anger with their high places and their graven images.* Idolatry was the sin that did most easily beset them, and which, though they often professed their repentance for, they as often relapsed into.

IV. The judgments God brought upon them for these sins. Idolatry is winked at among the Gentiles, but not in Israel (v. 59): *When God heard this,* when he heard the cry of their iniquity, which came up before him, *he was wroth.* He deserted his tabernacle among them, and removed the defence which was upon that glory, v. 60. God never leaves us till we leave him. The *tabernacle at Shiloh* was *the tent God had placed among men,* in which God would *in very deed dwell with men upon the earth*; but, when his people treacherously forsook it, he justly forsook it, and then all its glory departed. He gave up all into the hands of the enemy. Those whom God forsakes become an easy prey to the destroyer. God permits them to take the ark prisoner, and carry it off as a trophy of their victory, to show that he had not only forsaken the tabernacle, but even the ark itself (v. 61): *He delivered his strength into captivity,* as if it had been weakened and overcome, *and his glory* fell under the disgrace of being abandoned *into the enemy's hand.* We have the story, 1 Sam. iv. 11. He suffers the armies of Israel to be routed by the Philistines (v. 62, 63): *He gave his people over unto the sword,* for he *was wroth with his inheritance*; and that wrath of his was the *fire which consumed their young men,* in the prime of their time, and made such a devastation of them that *their maidens were not praised,* that is, *were not given in marriage* because there were no young men for them to be given to. Even *their priests,* who attended the ark, *fell by the sword,* Hophni and Phinehas. Justly they fell, for they made themselves vile, and were sinners before the Lord. When the priests fell *their widows made no lamentation,* v. 64. The widow of Phinehas, instead of lamenting her husband's death, died herself, when she had called her son *Ichabod,* 1 Sam. iv. 19, &c.

V. God's return, in mercy, to them, and his gracious appearances for them after this. God was *grieved for the miseries of Israel* (Judges x. 16). And therefore *then the Lord awaked as one out of sleep* (v. 65), *and like a mighty man that shouteth by reason of wine,*

like one that is refreshed with sleep, and whose heart is made glad by the sober and moderate use of wine, and is therefore the more vigorous.

1. He plagued the Philistines who held the ark in captivity, v. 66. He smote them with emerods, *in the hinder parts.* Sooner or later God will glorify himself by putting disgrace upon his enemies, even when they are most elevated with their successes.

2. He provided a new settlement for his ark after it had been some months in captivity and some years in obscurity. He did indeed *refuse the tabernacle of Joseph*; he never sent it back to Shiloh, in the tribe of Ephraim, v. 67. The ruins of that place were standing monuments of divine justice. *Go, see what I did to Shiloh,* Jer. vii. 12. The moving of the ark is not the removing of it. Shiloh has lost it, but Israel has not. God will have a church in the world, and a kingdom among men, though this or that place may have its candlestick removed. When God *chose not the tribe of Ephraim,* of which tribe Joshua was, he *chose the tribe of Judah* (v. 68), because of that tribe Jesus was to be, who is greater than Joshua. Kirjath-jearim, the place to which the ark was brought after its rescue out of the hands of the Philistines, was in the tribe of Judah. Thence it was removed to Zion, *that Mount Zion which he loved* (v. 68), which *was beautiful for situation, the joy of the whole earth;* there it was that he *built his sanctuary like high palaces* and *like the earth,* v. 69. David indeed erected only a tent for the ark, but a temple was then designed and prepared for, and finished by his son. Solomon built it, and yet here it is said *God built it,* for his father had taught him, perhaps with reference to this undertaking, that *except the Lord build the house those labour in vain* that build it, cxxvii. 1. It was not finally destroyed till the gospel temple was erected, which is to continue *as long as the sun and moon endure* (lxxxix. 36, 37) and against which the *gates of hell shall not prevail.*

3. He set a good government over them, a monarchy, and a monarch after his own heart: *He chose David his servant* out of all the thousands of Israel, and put the sceptre into his hand, from whom Christ was to come, and who was to be a type of him, v. 70. Concerning David, he descended from the prince of the tribe of Judah, but his education was poor. He was bred not a scholar, not a soldier, but a shepherd. He was *taken from the sheepfolds,* as Moses was; for God delights to put honour upon the humble and diligent, and sometimes he finds those most fit for public action that have spent the beginning of their time in solitude and contemplation. The son of David was upbraided with the obscurity of his original: *Is not this the carpenter?* David was taken, he does not say from leading the rams, but *from following the ewes,* especially those *great with young,* which intimated that of all the good properties of a shepherd he was most remarkable for his tenderness and compassion to those of his flock that most needed his care. It was a great honour that God put upon him, in advancing him to be a king, especially to be king over Jacob and Israel, God's peculiar people, near and dear to him; but withal it was a great trust. David, having so great a trust put into his hands, obtained mercy of the Lord to be found both skilful and faithful in the discharge of it (v. 72): *So he fed them;* he ruled them and taught them, guided and protected them, *according to the integrity of his heart,* aiming at nothing but the glory of God and the good of the people committed to his charge. He was not only very sincere in what he designed, but very prudent in what he did. Happy the people that are under such a government! With good reason does the psalmist make this the finishing crowning instance of God's favour to Israel, for David was a type of Christ the great and good Shepherd.

PSALM 79

This psalm is with most probability made to refer to the destruction of Jerusalem and the temple. It is set to the same tune as the Lamentations of Jeremiah, and that weeping prophet borrows two verses out of it (ver. 6, 7) and makes use of them in his prayer, Jer. x. 25. Some think it was penned long before by the spirit of prophecy, prepared for the use of the church in that cloudy and dark day. Whatever the particular occasion was, we have here, I. A representation of the very deplorable condition that the people of God were in at this time, ver. 1–5. II. A petition to God for succour and relief (ver. 6, 7, 10, 12), that their sins might be pardoned (ver. 8, 9), and that they might be delivered, ver. 11. III. A plea taken from the readiness of his people to praise him, ver. 13.

A psalm of Asaph.

Verses 1–5

We have here a sad complaint exhibited in the court of heaven.

I. They complain here of the outrageous fury of the oppressor, exerted against places, *v.* 1. They did all the mischief they could to the holy land; they invaded that, and made inroads into it: *"The heathen have come into thy inheritance,* to plunder that, and lay it waste." Canaan was dearer to the pious Israelites as God's inheritance than as their own. Injuries done to religion should grieve us more than even those done to common right, nay, to our own right. This psalmist had mentioned it in the foregoing psalm as an instance of God's great favour to Israel that he had *cast out the heathen before them,* lxxviii. 55. But see what a change sin made; now the heathen are suffered to pour in upon them. *They have laid Jerusalem on heaps.* The inhabitants were buried in the ruins of their own houses. That sanctuary which God had built and which was thought to be established as the earth, was now laid level with the ground: *Thy holy temple have they defiled,* by entering into it and laying it waste. God's own people had defiled it by their sins, and therefore God suffered their enemies to defile it by their insolence. They were prodigal of blood, and killed God's people without mercy; nor did they give any quarter (*v.* 3): *Their blood have they shed like water,* wherever they met with them, *round about Jerusalem,* in all the avenues of the city; whoever *went out or came in* was *waited for of the sword.* Even the *dead bodies of God's servants, the flesh of his saints,* whose names and memories they had a particular spite at, they dug up again, and *gave them to be meat to the fowls of the heaven and to the beasts of the earth;* they hung them in chains, which was grievous to the Jews, because God had given them an express law against this, as a barbarous thing, Deut. xxi. 23. *"We that survive have become a reproach to our neighbours;* they all study to abuse us and load us with contempt, so that we have become *a scorn and derision to those that are round about us."* If God's professing people degenerate from what themselves and their fathers were, they must expect to be told of it.

II. They wonder more at God's anger, *v.* 5. This they discern in the anger of their neighbours. *How long, Lord, wilt thou be angry?* Shall it be *for ever?* This intimates that they desired no more than that God would be reconciled to them, and then the remainder of men's wrath would be restrained.

Verses 6–13

The petitions here put up to God are very suitable to the present distresses of the church.

I. They pray that God would so turn away his anger from them as to turn it upon those that persecuted and abused them (*v.* 6). This prayer is in effect a prophecy, in which the *wrath of God is revealed from heaven against all ungodliness and unrighteousness of men.* The reason why men do not call upon God is because they do not know him, how

able and willing he is to help them. Those that persist in ignorance of God, and neglect of prayer, are the ungodly, who live *without God in the world. They have devoured Jacob, v.* 7. They have not only disturbed, but devoured, Jacob, not only encroached upon his dwelling-place, the land of Canaan, but laid it waste by plundering and depopulating it. *"Pour out thy wrath* upon them; not only restrain them from doing further mischief, but reckon with them for the mischief they have done."

II. They pray for the pardon of sin, which they own to be the cause of all their calamities. "Remember not against us our first sins," which some make to look as far back as the golden calf. If the children by repentance cut off the entail of the parents' sin, they may in faith pray that God will not *remember them against them.* When God pardons sin he blots it out and remembers it no more. *Deliver us, and purge away our sins, v.* 9. Then deliverances from trouble are granted in love, and are mercies indeed.

III. They pray that God would bring their troubles to a good end and that speedily: *Let thy tender mercies speedily prevent us, v.* 8. Unless divine mercy did speedily interpose to prevent their ruin, they were undone. This whets their importunity: *"Lord, help us; Lord, deliver us;* help us under our troubles, that we may bear them well. Deliver us from sin, from sinking. *We are brought very low,* and, being low, shall be lost if thou help us not." Those who make God the God of their salvation shall find him so. They plead no merit of theirs; they pretend to none; but, *"Help us for the glory of thy name;* pardon us for thy name's sake. Wherefore should the heathen say, Where is their God?* He has forsaken them, and forgotten them; and this they get by worshipping a God whom they cannot see." "Lord," say they, "make it to appear that thou art by making it to appear that thou art with us, and for us, that when we are asked, *Where is your God?* we may be able to say, He is nigh unto us and you see he is so by what he does for us."

IV. They pray that God would avenge them on their adversaries. "Let the avenging of our blood" (according to the ancient law, Gen. ix. 6) "be known among the heathen; and by this means *let God be known among the heathen as the God to whom vengeance belongs* (xciv. 1) and the God that espouses his people's cause." The reproach wherewith they have blasphemed God himself we may in faith pray that God would render seven-fold into their bosoms, to humble them, and bring them to repentance.

V. They pray that God would find out a way for the rescue of his poor prisoners, *v.* 11. Their brethren who had fallen into the hands of the enemy, were kept close prisoners, and, because they durst not be heard to bemoan themselves, they vented their griefs in deep and silent sighs. "*Let their sighs come up before thee,* and be thou pleased to take cognizance of their moans." They promise the returns of praise for the answers of prayer (*v.* 13): *So we will give thee thanks for ever.* They oblige themselves not only to give God thanks at present, but to *show forth his praise unto all generations.*

PSALM 80

This psalm is much to the same purport with the foregoing. Some think it was penned upon occasion of the desolation and captivity of the ten tribes. But many were the distresses of the Israel of God, many perhaps which are not recorded in the sacred history, some whereof might give occasion for the drawing up of this psalm. The psalmist here, I. Begs for the tokens of God's presence with them and favour to them, ver. 1–3. II. He complains of the present rebukes they were under, ver. 4–7. III. He illustrates the present desolations of the church, by the comparison of a vine and a vineyard, which had flourished, but was now destroyed, ver. 8–16. IV. He concludes with prayer to God for the preparing of mercy for them and the preparing of them for mercy, ver. 17–19.

To the chief musician upon Shoshannim, Eduth.
A psalm of Asaph.

Verses 1–7

The psalmist here applies to God by prayer, with reference to the present afflicted state of Israel.

I. He entreats God's favour for them (*v.* 1, 2), as the Shepherd of Israel, under whose guidance and care Israel was. He *leads Joseph like a flock*, to the best pastures and out of the way of danger. He *dwells between the cherubim*, where he is ready to receive petitions and to give directions. The mercy-seat was between the cherubim; and it is very comfortable in prayer to look up to God as sitting on a throne of grace. He desires from God, that he would give ear to the cry of their miseries and of their prayers, that he would *stir up his strength*. It had seemed to slumber: "Lord, awaken it. Lord, be to thy people a powerful help and a present help; Lord, do this *before Ephraim, Benjamin and Manasseh*." Perhaps these three tribes are named because they were the tribes which formed that squadron of the camp of Israel that in their march through the wilderness followed next after the tabernacle; so that before them the ark of God's strength rose to scatter their enemies.

II. He complains of God's displeasure. God was angry, and he dreads that more than anything, *v.* 4. He apprehended that God was *angry against the prayers of his people.* That God should be angry at the sins of his people and at the prayers of his enemies is not strange; but that he should be angry at the prayers of his people is strange indeed. If he be really angry at the prayers of his people, we may be sure it is because they ask amiss, James iv. 3. But perhaps it is only in their own apprehension; he seems angry with their prayers when really he is not; for thus he will try their perseverance in prayer, as Christ tried the woman of Canaan when he said: *It is not meet to take the children's bread and cast it to dogs.* Now the tokens of God's displeasure which they had been long under were both their sorrow and shame. *Thou feedest them with the bread of tears;* they eat their meat from day to day in tears; this is the vinegar in which they *dipped their morsel*, xlii. 3. Many that spend their time in sorrow shall spend their eternity in joy. It is to their shame, *v.* 6. Their enemies laughed among themselves to see the frights they were in, and the disappointments they met with.

III. He prays earnestly for converting grace in order to their salvation: *Turn us again, O God! v.* 3. *Turn us again, O God of hosts!* (*v.* 7) and then *cause thy face to shine and we shall be saved.* It is the burden of the song, for we have it again, *v.* 19. "Lord, turn us to thee in a way of repentance and reformation, and then, no doubt, thou wilt return to us in a way of mercy and deliverance." Observe, 1. No salvation but from God's favour. 2. No obtaining favour with God unless we be converted to him. 3. No conversion to God but by his own grace. *Turn thou me, and I shall be turned.* The prayer here is for a national conversion. National holiness would secure national happiness.

Verses 8–19

The psalmist is here presenting his suit for the Israel of God, and pressing it home at the throne of grace. The church is here represented as a vine (*v.* 8, 14) and a vineyard, *v.* 15. The root of this vine is Christ, Rom. xi. 18. The branches are believers, John xv. 5. The church is like a vine, weak and needing support, unsightly and having an unpromising outside, but spreading and fruitful, and its fruit most excellent. The church is a choice and noble vine; we have reason to acknowledge the goodness of God that he has planted such a vine in the wilderness of this world, and preserved it to this day.

I. How the vine of the Old Testament church was planted at first. It was *brought out of Egypt* with a high hand; *the heathen were cast out* of Canaan to make room for it, seven nations to make room for that one.

II. How it spread and flourished. 1. The land of Canaan itself was fully peopled. At first they were not so numerous as to replenish it, Exod. xxiii. 29. But in Solomon's time *Judah and Israel were many as the sand of the sea.* Israel not only had abundance of men, but those mighty men of valour. 2. They extended their conquests and dominion to the neighbouring countries (*v.* 11): *She sent out her boughs to the sea*, the great sea westward, and *her branches to the river*, to the river of Egypt southward, the river of Damascus northward, or rather the river Euphrates eastward, Gen. xv. 18. But it is observable here concerning this vine that it is praised for its *shadow*, its *boughs*, and its *branches*, but not a word of its fruit, for *Israel was an empty vine*, Hos. x. 1. God came looking for grapes, but, behold, wild grapes, Isa. v. 2. And, if a vine do not bring forth fruit, no tree so useless, so worthless, Ezek. xv. 2, 6.

III. How it was wasted and ruined: "Lord, thou hast done great things for this vine, and why shall it be all undone again? Will God desert and abandon that which he himself gave being to?" *v.* 12. *Why hast thou then broken down her hedges?* There was a good reason. This noble vine had become *the degenerate plant of a strange vine* (Jer. ii. 21). As soon as ever God *broke down their hedges* and left them exposed troops of enemies presently broke in. Those that passed by the way plucked at them; the *boar out of the wood* and the *wild beast of the field* were ready to ravage it, *v.* 13. But till God had *broken down their hedges* they could not pluck a leaf of this vine. The deplorable state of Israel is described (*v.* 16): *It is burnt with fire; it is cut down;* the people are treated like thorns and briers, that are nigh unto cursing and whose end is to be burned, and no longer like vines that are protected and cherished.

IV. Their requests to God hereupon. 1. That God would help the vine (*v.* 14, 15). "*Look down from heaven*, that place of prospect, that place of power, whence thou canst send effectual relief—thence make a gracious visit, to this vine. Lord, it is formed by thyself and for thyself, and therefore it may with a humble confidence be committed to thyself and to thy own care." What we read the *branch*, in the Hebrew is the *son* (*Ben*), whom in thy counsel thou hast made strong for thyself. That branch was to come out of the stock of Israel (*my servant the branch*, Zech. iii. 8), and therefore, till he should come, Israel in general, and the house of David in particular, must be preserved. *He is the true vine*, John xv. i; Isa. xi. 1. "*Let thy hand be upon the man of thy right hand*," that king (whoever it was) of the house of David that was now to go in and out before them; "let thy hand be upon him, not only to protect and cover him, but to own him, and strengthen him, and give him success." *So will not we go back from thee.* Adding also this prayer, "*Quicken us*, put life into us, and then *we will call upon thy name*." We cannot call upon God's name in a right manner unless he quicken us. But many interpreters, both Jewish and Christian, apply this to the Messiah, the Son of David, the protector and Saviour of the church and the keeper of the vineyard. He is the man of God's right hand, to whom he has *sworn by his right hand* (so the Chaldee), whom he has exalted to his right hand, and who is indeed his right hand, the arm of the Lord, for all power is given to him. The stability and constancy of believers are entirely owing to the grace and strength which are laid up for us in Jesus Christ, lxviii. 28.

PSALM 81

This psalm was penned, as is supposed, for the solemnity of a particular ordinance, either that of the new-moon in general or that of the feast of trumpets into the new moon of the seventh month, Lev. xxiii. 24; Num. xxix. 1. When David, by the Spirit, introduced the singing of psalms into the temple-service, this psalm was intended for that day. The two great intentions of our religious assemblies are answered in this psalm, which are, to give glory to God and to receive instruction from God to "behold the beauty of the Lord and to enquire in his temple": accordingly by this psalm we are assisted on our solemn feastdays, I. In praising God for what he is to his people (ver. 1-3), and has done for them, ver. 4-7. II. In teaching and admonishing one another concerning the obligations we lie under to God (ver. 8-10), the danger of revolting from him (ver. 11, 12), and the happiness we should have if we would but keep close to him, ver. 13-16.

To the chief musician upon Gittith. *A psalm of Asaph.*

Verses 1-7

When the people of God were gathered together in *the solemn day, the day of the feast of the Lord,* they must be told that they had business to do, for we do not go to church to sleep nor to be idle.

I. The worshippers of God are excited to their work, and are taught, by singing this psalm, to stir up both themselves and one another, to it *v.* 1-3. In doing this we must eye God as *our strength,* and as *the God of Jacob, v.* 1. To him, as our strength, we must pray, and we must sing praise to him as the God of all the wrestling seed of Jacob, with whom we have a spiritual communion. We must do this by all the expressions of holy joy and triumph. It was then to be done by musical instruments, the *timbrel, harp, and psaltery*; and by blowing *the trumpet,* some think in remembrance of the sound of the trumpet on Mount Sinai, which waxed louder and louder. Singing aloud intimates that we must be warm and affectionate in praising God. No time is amiss for praising God, but some are times appointed, not for God to meet us (he is always ready), but for us to meet one another, that we may join together in praising God.

II. They are here directed in their work. *This was a statute for Israel,* for the keeping up of a face of religion among them; it was *a law of the God of Jacob,* which all the seed of Jacob are bound by, and must be subject to. This solemn service was *ordained for a testimony* (*v.* 5), a standing traditional evidence, that they might know and remember what God had done for their fathers. When God went out against the land of Egypt, that he might force Pharaoh to let Israel go, then he ordained solemn feast-days to be observed by a statute for ever in their generations, as a memorial of it, particularly the passover, which perhaps is meant by the *solemn-feast-day* (*v.* 3). Here he changes the person, *v.* 6. God speaks by him, saying, *I removed the shoulder from the burden.* Let him remember this on the feast-day, God had brought them out of the house of bondage, had removed their shoulder from the burden of oppression under which they were ready to sink, *had delivered their hands from the pots,* or panniers, or baskets, in which they carried clay or bricks. God had delivered them at the Red Sea. He answered them with a real answer, out of *the secret place of thunder.* It may be meant of the giving of the law at Mount Sinai, which was the secret place, for it was death to gaze (Exod. xix. 21), and it was in thunder that God then spoke. God had borne their manners in the wilderness: "*I proved thee at the waters of Meribah;* thou didst there show thy temper, what an unbelieving murmuring people thou wast, and yet I continued my favour to thee." Now if they, on their solemn feast-days, were thus to call to mind their redemption out of Egypt, much more ought we, on the Christian sabbath, to call to mind a more glorious redemption wrought out for us by Jesus Christ from worse than Egyptian bondage.

Verses 8-16

God, by the psalmist, here speaks to Israel, and in them to us.

I. He demands their diligent and serious attention to what he was about to say (*v.* 8): "*Hear, O my people!* Hear what is said with the greatest solemnity, for it is what *I will testify unto thee.* Do not only give me the hearing, but *hearken unto me,* that is, be advised by me, be ruled by me."

II. He puts them in mind of their obligation to him as the Lord their God and Redeemer (*v.* 10): *I am the Lord thy God, who brought thee out of the land of Egypt;* this is the preface to the ten commandments, and a powerful reason for the keeping of them.

III. He gives them an abstract both of the precepts and of the promises which he gave them, as the Lord and their God, upon their coming out of Egypt. The great command was that they should have no other gods before him (*v.* 9): *There shall no strange god be in thee,* none besides thy own God. The great promise was that God himself, as a God all-sufficient, would be nigh unto them (Deut. iv. 7), that, if they would adhere to him as their powerful protector and ruler, they should always find him their bountiful benefactor: "*Open thy mouth wide and I will fill it,* as the young ravens that cry open their mouths wide and the old ones fill them." We cannot look for too little from the creature nor too much from the Creator. The pleasures of sense will surfeit and never satisfy (Isa. lv. 2); divine pleasures will satisfy and never surfeit.

IV. He charges them with a high contempt of his authority, *v.* 11. He had done much for them, and designed to do more; but all in vain: "*My people would not hearken to my voice,* but turned a deaf ear to all I said." *They would none of me. They acquiesced not in my word* (so the Chaldee); God was willing to be to them a God, but they were not willing to be to him a people. "Israel, the seed of Jacob my friend, set me at nought, and *would* have *none of me.*" All the wickedness of the wicked world is owing to the wilfulness of the wicked will.

V. He justifies himself with this in the spiritual judgments he had brought upon them (*v.* 12): *So I gave them up unto their own hearts' lusts,* which would be more dangerous enemies and more mischievous oppressors to them than any of the neighbouring nations ever were. God withdrew his Spirit from them, took off the bridle of restraining grace, left them to themselves. *Ephraim is joined to idols; let him alone.* Let them take their course. And see what follows: *They walked in their own counsels.* "I left them to do as they would, and then they did all that was ill."

VI. He testifies his goodwill to them. He saw how sad their case was, and how sure their ruin, when they were delivered up to their own lusts. Now here God looks upon them with pity, and shows that it was with reluctance that he thus abandoned them to their folly and fate. *O that my people had hearkened!* See Isa. xlviii. 18. Thus Christ lamented the obstinacy of Jerusalem, *If thou hadst known,* Luke xix. 42. The expressions here are very affecting (*v.* 13-16), designed to show how unwilling God is that any should perish and desirous that all should come to repentance.

1. The great mercy God had in store for his people, and which he would have wrought for them if they had been obedient. *I should have subdued their enemies;* and it is God only that is to be depended on for the subduing of our enemies. He would *soon* have done it. If he but turn his hand, the *haters of the Lord will submit themselves to him* (*v.* 15). In spite of all the attempts of their enemies against them, *their time should have endured for ever,* and they should never have been disturbed in the possession of the

good land God had given them. He would have given them great plenty of all good things (*v.* 16): *He should have fed them with the finest of the wheat,* with the best grain and the best of the kind. Wheat was the staple commodity of Canaan. He would not only have provided for them the best sort of bread, but *with honey out of the rock would he have satisfied them.* In short, God designed to make them every way easy and happy.

2. The duty God required from them as the condition of all this mercy. He expected no more than that they should *hearken to him,* as a scholar to his teacher, to receive his instructions—as a servant to his master, to receive his commands; and that they should *walk in his ways.*

3. Observe how the reason of the withholding of the mercy is laid in their neglect of the duty: If they had *hearkened to me, I would soon have subdued their enemies.* National sin or disobedience is the great and only thing that retards and obstructs national deliverance. It is sin that makes our troubles long and salvation slow.

Psalm 82

This psalm is calculated for princes' courts and courts of justice, not in Israel only, but in other nations, "to instruct the judges of the earth" (as ii. and x.), to tell them their duty (as 2 Sam. xxiii. 3), and to tell them of their faults, as lviii. 1. We have here, I. The dignity of magistracy and its dependence upon God, ver. 1. II. The duty of magistrates, ver. 3, 4. III. The degeneracy of bad magistrates and the mischief they do, ver. 2, 5. IV. Their doom read, ver. 6, 7. V. The desire and prayer of all good people that the kingdom of God may be set up more and more, ver. 8.

A psalm of Asaph.

Verses 1-5

I. God's supreme presidency and power in all councils and courts (*v.* 1): *God stands,* as chief director, *in the congregation of the mighty,* the mighty One, *in the councils of the prince,* the supreme magistrate, and *he judges among the gods,* the inferior magistrates; both the legislative and the executive power of princes is under his eye and his hand. The magistrates are the *mighty.* They are so in authority, for the public good. They are, in the Hebrew dialect, called *gods;* the same word is used for these subordinate governors that is used for the sovereign ruler of the world. They are *elohim.* Angels are so called because God is pleased to make use of their service in the government of this lower world; and magistrates in an inferior capacity are likewise the ministers for the keeping of order and peace, and particularly of his justice in punishing evil-doers and protecting those that do well. Good magistrates are God's vicegerents, and great blessings to any people. In a mixed monarchy, the sovereign, and his congregation, his privy-council, his parliament, his bench of judges. *God stands,* he *judges among them;* they have their power from him and are accountable to him. *By him kings reign.* God has their hearts in his hands, and his counsels shall stand, whatever devices are in men's hearts. Let magistrates consider this and be awed by it; God is with them in the judgment, 2 Chron. xix. 6; Deut. i. 17. Let subjects consider this and be comforted with it; for good princes and good judges are under a divine direction, and bad ones are under a divine restraint.

II. A charge given to all magistrates to do good with their power, as they will answer it to him by whom they are entrusted with it, *v.* 3, 4. *Defend the poor,* who have no money wherewith to fee counsel, *and the fatherless,* who, while they are young and unable to help themselves, have lost those who would have been the guides of their youth. Magistrates must be fathers to their country in general. They are to administer justice impartially, and do *right to the afflicted and needy.* They are to rescue those who have already fallen into the hands of oppressors (*v.* 4): *Rid them out of the hand of the wicked.* These are clients whom there is nothing to be got by, yet these are those whose cause they must espouse.

III. A charge drawn up against bad magistrates, *v.* 2, 5. They *judge unjustly,* contrary to the rules of equity and the dictates of their consciences. To do unjustly is bad, but to judge unjustly is much worse, because it is doing wrong under colour of right. They were told plainly enough that it was their office and duty to protect and deliver the poor; yet they judge unjustly, for *they know not, neither will they understand.* They have baffled their own consciences, and so they walk on in darkness. What were the consequences of this sin: *All the foundations of the earth* (or *of the land*) *are out of course.* The miscarriages of public persons are public mischiefs.

Verses 6-8

The dignity of their character is acknowledged (*v.* 6): *I have said, You are gods.* He called them *gods* because they had a commission from God, and were delegated and appointed by him to be the conservators of the public peace. God has put some of his honour upon them, and employs them in his providential government of the world. It is a hard thing for men to have so much honour put upon them by the hand of God, and so much honour paid them, as ought to be by the children of men, and not to be proud of it and puffed up with it. But here follows a mortifying consideration: *You shall die like men.* This may be taken either, 1. As the punishment of bad magistrates, such as judged unjustly, and by their misrule put the *foundations of the earth out of course.* They shall die like other wicked men, *and fall like one of the* heathen *princes.* Or, 2. As the period of the glory of all magistrates in this world. "You are called gods, but you have no patent for immortality; *you shall die like men,* like common men; *and like one of them, you, O princes! shall fall.*" *Death mingles sceptres with spades.*

The God of heaven exalted, *v.* 8. The psalmist finds it to little purpose to reason with these proud oppressors; and therefore he looks up to God and begs of him *to take unto himself his great power; Arise, O God! judge the earth; Thou shalt inherit all nations.* In this faith we must pray, "*Arise, O God! judge the earth,* appear against those that judge unjustly, and set shepherds over thy people after thy own heart." It is a prayer that Christ would come, who is to judge the earth, and that God shall *give him the heathen for his inheritance.*

Psalm 83

This psalm is the last of those that go under the name of Asaph. Some think it was penned upon occasion of the threatening descent which was made upon the land of Judah in Jehoshaphat's time by the Moabites and Ammonites, those children of Lot here spoken of (ver. 8), who were at the head of the alliance, 2 Chron. xx. 1. Others think it was penned with reference to all the confederacies of the neighbouring nations against Israel, from first to last. The psalmist here makes an appeal, I. To God's knowledge, by a representation of their designs and endeavours to destroy Israel, ver. 1-8. II. To God's justice by an earnest prayer for the defeat of their attempt, ver. 9-18.

A song *or* psalm of Asaph.

Verses 1-8

The Israel of God were in danger and great distress.

I. The psalmist here begs of God to appear on the behalf of his threatened people (*v.* 1): "*Keep not thou silence, O God!* but give judgment for us against those that do us an apparent wrong." Sometimes God holds his peace, as if he would observe an exact neutrality, and let them fight it out. Then he gives us leave to call upon him, as here, "*Keep not thou silence, O God!* Lord, speak to us by the prophets for our encouragement against our fears. Lord, speak for us by thy providence and speak against our enemies; speak deliverance to us and disappointment to them."

II. An account of the grand alliance of the neighbouring nations against Israel, which he begs of God to break.

This confederacy is formed against the Israel of God, and so, in effect, against the God of Israel. They hated the religious worshippers of God, because they hated God's holy religion and the worship of him. *They are confederate against thee*, v. 5. "Lord," says the psalmist, "they are thy enemies, for they consult against thy hidden ones." God's people are his hidden ones. Their life is *hid with Christ in God*. God takes them under his special protection, hides them in the hollow of his hand. They resolve to destroy those whom God resolves to preserve. *Thy enemies make a tumult*, v. 2. They are noisy in their clamours. This comes in as a reason why God should not keep silence: "The enemies talk big and talk much; Lord, let them not talk all, but do thou *speak to them in thy wrath*," ii. 5. *They have lifted up the head*. In confidence of their success, they are so elevated as if they could overpower the Almighty. They have *taken crafty counsel*, v. 3. Whatever separate clashing interest they have among themselves, against the people of God they *consult with one consent* (v. 5). It is no less than the utter ruin and extirpation of Israel that they design (v. 4): "*Come, let us cut them off from being a nation, that the name of Israel may be no more in remembrance*, no, not in history." It is the secret wish of many wicked men that the church of God might not have a being in the world, that there might be no such thing as religion among mankind. Having banished the sense of it out of their own hearts, they would gladly see the whole earth rid of it. But *he that sits in heaven shall laugh at them*. The nations that entered into this alliance are here mentioned (v. 6–8); the Edomites and Ishmaelites, both descendants from Abraham, lead the van. These were allied to Israel in blood and yet in alliance against Israel. There are no bonds of nature so strong but the spirit of persecution has broken through them. *The brother shall betray the brother to death*. The Philistines were long a thorn in Israel's side, and very vexatious. *Assur* (that is, the Assyrian) *also is joined with them*.

Verses 9–18

The psalmist prays for the destruction of those confederate forces, and, in God's name, foretells it. This prophecy reaches to all the enemies of the gospel-church.

I. The defeat and discomfiture of former combinations may be pleaded in prayer to God, because God is the same still to his people and the same against his and their enemies; with him is no variableness. *Do to them as to the Midianites;* let them be routed by their own fears, for so the Midianites were, more than by Gideon's 300 men. Do to them as to the army under the command of Sisera (who was general under Jabin king of Canaan) which God discomfited (Judges iv. 15). *They became as dung on the earth;* their dead bodies were thrown like dung laid in heaps by Barak's small but victorious army. *So let all thy enemies perish, O Lord!* that is, So they shall perish. He prays that their leaders might be destroyed as they had been formerly, v. 11, 12. They said, *Let us take to ourselves the houses of God in possession* (v. 12), the *pleasant places* of God (so the word is), by which we may understand the land of Canaan, which was a pleasant land and was Immanuel's land, or the temple, which was indeed God's pleasant place (Isa. lxiv. 11), or (as Dr. Hammond suggests) the pleasant pastures, which these Arabians, who traded in cattle, did in a particular

manner seek after. They shall be made *like Oreb and Zeeb* (Judges vii. 25), and *like Zeba and Zalmunna* (Judges viii. 21).

II. He prays that God would *make them like a wheel* (v. 13), that they might be in continual motion, unsettled and giddy in all their counsels, that they might roll down easily and speedily to their own ruin. Or, as some think, that they might be broken by the judgments of God, as the corn is broken, or beaten out, by the wheel which was then used in threshing. "The wheel, though it continually turn round, is fixed on its own axis; but let them have no more fixation than the light stubble has, which the wind hurried away." When the stubble is driven by the wind it will rest, at last, under some hedge, in some ditch or other; but he prays that they might not only be driven away as stubble, but burnt up as stubble. The application of these comparisons we have (v. 15): *So persecute them with thy tempest*, persecute them to their utter ruin, and make *them afraid with thy storm*.

III. He illustrates it by the good consequences of their confusion, v. 16–18. They did what they could to put God's people to shame, but the shame will at length return upon themselves. The beginning of this shame might be a means of their conversion: "Let them be broken and baffled in their attempts, *that they may seek thy name, O Lord!*" That which we should earnestly desire and beg of God for our enemies and persecutors is that God would bring them to repentance, and we should desire no other confusion to them than what may be a step towards their conversion. If they will not be ashamed and repent, let them be put to shame, that other men may know and own, if they themselves will not, *that thou, whose name alone is JEHOVAH* (that incommunicable, though not ineffable name) *art the Most High over all the earth*.

PSALM 84

It is supposed that David penned this psalm when he was forced by Absalom's rebellion to quit his city, which he lamented his absence from, because it was the holy city. This psalm contains the pious breathings of a gracious soul after God and communion with him. Though it be not entitled, yet it may fitly be looked upon as a psalm or song for the sabbath day. The psalmist here with great devotion expresses his affection, I. To the ordinances of God (ver. 1), his desire towards them (ver. 2, 3), his conviction of the happiness of those that did enjoy them (ver. 4–7), and his enjoyment of them, ver. 10. II. To the God of the ordinances; his desire towards him (ver. 8, 9), his faith in him (ver. 11), and the happiness of those that put their confidence in him, ver. 12.

To the chief musician upon Gittith. A psalm for the sons of Korah.

Verses 1–7

The psalmist here, being by force restrained from waiting upon God in public ordinances, is brought under a more sensible conviction than ever of the worth of them.

I. The wonderful beauty he saw in holy institutions (v. 1): *How amiable are thy tabernacles. O Lord of hosts!* The tabernacle is spoken of as more than one (*thy tabernacles*) because there were several courts in which the people attended, and because the tabernacle itself consisted of a holy place and a most holy. How lovely is the sanctuary in the eyes of all that are truly sanctified! Gracious souls see a wonderful, an inexpressible, beauty in holiness, and in holy work. A tabernacle was a mean habitation, but the beauty of holiness is spiritual, and the glory is within.

II. The longing desire he had to return to the enjoyment of public ordinances, or rather of God in them, v. 2. It was an entire desire; body, soul, and spirit. It was an intense desire. He longed, he fainted, he cried out. Yet it was not so much the courts of the Lord that he coveted, but he cried out, in prayer, for the living God himself. Ordinances are empty things if we meet not with God in the ordinances.

III. His grudging the happiness of the little birds that made their nests in the buildings that were adjoining to God's altars, v. 3. *The sparrow has found a house and the swallow a nest for herself.* These little birds, by the instinct and direction of nature, provide habitations for themselves in houses, as other birds do in the woods: some such David supposes there were in the buildings about the courts of God's house, and wishes himself with them. He would rather live in a bird's nest nigh God's altars than in a palace at a distance from them. He sometimes wished for *the wings of a dove*, on which to *fly into the wilderness* (v. 6); here for the wings of a sparrow, that he might fly undiscovered into God's courts. The word for a sparrow signifies any little bird, and (if I may offer a conjecture) perhaps when, in David's time, music was introduced so much into the sacred service, to complete the harmony they had singing-birds in cages hung about the courts of the tabernacle (for we find the singing of birds taken notice of to the glory of God, civ. 12), and David envies the happiness of these, and would gladly change places with them. David envies the happiness not of those birds that flew over the altars, but of those that had nests for themselves there. David will not think it enough to sojourn in God's house *as a wayfaring man to tarry for a night*; but let this be his rest, his home; here he will dwell. And he takes notice that these birds not only have nests for themselves there, but that there they lay their young; for those who have a place in God's courts themselves cannot but desire that their children also may have in God's house, a place and a name. Observe how he eyes God in this address: Thou art the *Lord of hosts, my King and my God.* Where should a poor, distressed subject seek for protection but with his king? *And should not a people seek unto their God?* My King, my God, is Lord of hosts; by him and his altars let me live and die.

IV. His acknowledgment of the happiness both of the ministers and of the people that had liberty of attendance on God's altars. Blessed are the ministers, the priests and Levites, who have their residence about the tabernacle and are in their courses employed in the service of it (v. 4). *They will be still praising thee;* and, if there be a heaven upon earth, it is in praising God, in continually praising him. Apply this to his house above; blessed are those that dwell there, angels and glorified saints, for they *rest not day nor night from praising God.* Blessed are the people, the inhabitants of the country, who, though they do not constantly dwell in God's house as the priests do, yet have liberty of access to it, v. 5–7. *Blessed is the man whose strength is in thee,* who makes thee his strength and strongly stays himself upon thee. They are such as have a love for holy ordinances: *In whose heart are the ways of them,* that is, who, having placed their happiness in God as their end, rejoice in all the ways that lead to him. They are such as will break through difficulties and discouragements in waiting upon God in holy ordinances, v. 6. When they come up out of the country to worship at the feasts their way lies through many a dry and sandy valley (so some), in which they are ready to perish for thirst; but they dig little pits to receive and keep the rain-water for their refreshments. Their way lay through many a weeping valley, so Baca signifies, that is (as others understand it), many watery valleys, which in wet weather, when *the rain filled the pools*, were impassable; but, by draining and trenching them, they made a road through them for the benefit of those who went up to Jerusalem. Care should be taken to keep those roads in repair that lead to church, as well as those that lead to market.

But all this is intended to show they had a good will to the journey. Our way to heaven lies through a valley of Baca, but even that may be made a well if we make a due improvement of the comforts God has provided for the pilgrims to the heavenly city. They are such as are still pressing forward till they come to their journey's end at length (v. 7): *They go from strength to strength.* Instead of being fatigued with the tediousness of their journey and the difficulties they met with, the nearer they came to Jerusalem the more lively and cheerful they were. Those that press forward in their Christian course shall find God adding grace to their graces, John i. 16.

Verses 8-12

I. The psalmist prays for audience and acceptance with God. He prays (v. 8, 9), only that God would hear his prayer and give ear. He calls himself (as many think) *God's anointed*, for David was anointed by him and anointed for him. He has an eye to God under several of his glorious titles—as *the Lord God of hosts*, who has all the creatures at his command, as the *God of Jacob*, a God in covenant with his own people, and as *God our shield*, who takes his people under his special protection.

II. He pleads his love to God's ordinances and his dependence upon God himself.

1. God's courts were his choice, v. 10. *A day spent in thy courts*, in attending on the services of religion, wholly abstracted from all secular affairs, *is better than a thousand*, anywhere else in this world. *I would rather be a doorkeeper*, rather be in the meanest place and office, *in the house of my God, than dwell* in state, as Master, *in the tents of wickedness.* I would rather be a porter in God's house than a prince in those tents where wickedness reigns, rather lie at the threshold (so the word is); that was the beggar's place (Acts iii. 2): "no matter" (says David), "let that be my place rather than none."

2. God himself was his hope, and joy, and all. *The Lord God is a sun and shield.* We are here in darkness, but, if God be our God, he will be to us a sun, to enlighten and enliven us, to guide and direct us. We are here in danger, but he will be to us a shield to secure us. *The Lord will give grace and glory.* Grace signifies both the goodwill of God towards us and the good work of God in us; glory signifies both the honour which he now puts upon us, in giving us the adoption of sons, and that which he has prepared for us in the inheritance of sons. God will give them grace in this world as a preparation for glory, and glory in the other world as the perfection of grace; both are God's gift, his free gift. *No good thing will be withheld from those that walk uprightly.* This is a comprehensive promise, and is such an assurance of the present comfort of the saints that, whatever they desire, and think they need, they may be sure that either Infinite Wisdom sees it is not good for them or Infinite Goodness will give it to them in due time. Those are blessed who have the privileges of God's house. If we cannot go to the house of the Lord, we may go by faith to the Lord of the house, and in him we shall be happy and may be easy.

PSALM 85

Interpreters are generally of opinion that this psalm was penned after the return of the Jews out of their captivity in Babylon, when they still remained under some tokens of God's displeasure. The church was here in a deluge; above were clouds, below were waves; everything was dark and dismal. The church is like Noah in the ark, between life and death, between hope and fear; being so, I. Here is the dove sent forth in prayer. The petitions are against sin and wrath (ver. 4) and for mercy and grace, ver. 7. II. Here is the dove returning with an olive branch of peace and good tidings; the psalmist expects her return (ver. 8) and then recounts the favours to God's Israel which by the spirit of prophecy he gave assurance of to others, and by the spirit of faith he took the assurance of to himself, ver. 9–13.

To the chief musician. A psalm for the sons of
Korah.

Verses 1–7

The people of God, in a very low and weak condition, are here taught how to address themselves
to God.

I. They are to acknowledge with thankfulness the
great things God had done for them (*v.* 1–3). God
had shown himself propitious to their land, and
had smiled upon it as his own: "*Thou hast been
favourable to thy land*, as thine, with distinguishing
favours." He had not dealt with them according to
the desert of their provocations (*v.* 2): "*Thou hast
forgiven the iniquity of thy people*, and not punished
them as in justice thou mightest. *Thou hast covered
all their sin*." The bringing back of their captivity
was *then* an instance of God's favour to them, when
it was accompanied with the pardon of their iniquity.
"Having *covered all their sin*, thou hast *taken away
all thy wrath*"; for when sin is set aside God's anger
ceases; God is pacified if we are purified.

II. They are taught to pray to God for grace and
mercy, in reference to their present distress; this is
inferred from the former: "Thou hast done well
for our fathers; do well for us, for we are the children
of the same covenant." 1. They pray for converting
grace: "*Turn us, O God of our salvation!*" 2. They
pray for the removal of the tokens of God's displeasure: "*Cause thine anger towards us to cease.*"
Observe the method, "First turn us to thee, and then
cause thy anger to turn from us." 3. They pray for
the manifestation of God's goodwill to them (*v.* 7):
"*Show us thy mercy, O Lord!* let us know that thou
hast mercy on us and mercy in store for us." 4. They
pray that God would appear on their behalf: "*Grant
us thy salvation;* grant it by thy promise, and then,
no doubt, thou wilt work by it thy providence."

III. They are taught humbly to expostulate with
God concerning their present troubles, *v.* 5, 6. "*Wilt
thou be angry with us for ever? Wilt thou draw out
thy anger unto all generations?* Thou wast not angry
with our fathers for ever, but didst soon turn thyself
from the fierceness of thy wrath; why then wilt thou
be angry with us for ever? *Wilt thou not revive us
again* (*v.* 6), revive us with deliverances wrought for
us?" God had granted to the children of the captivity
some reviving in their bondage, Ezra ix. 8. Their return out of Babylon was as *life from the dead*, Ezek.
xxxvii. 11, 12. Now, Lord (say they), *wilt thou not
revive us again*, and *put thy hand again the second
time* to gather us in? Isa. xi. 11; Ps. cxxvi. 1, 4.
Revive thy work in the midst of the years, Hab. iii. 2.
"Revive us again." If God be the fountain of all
our mercies, he must be the centre of all our joys.

Verses 8–13

We have here an answer to the prayers and expostulations.

I. In general, it is an answer of peace. The psalmist
(*v.* 8), *stands upon his watch-tower* to *hear what God
will say unto him.* "Compose thyself, O my soul!
in a humble silence to attend upon God and wait his
motions. I have spoken enough; now I will hear
what God will speak, and welcome his holy will.
What saith my Lord unto his servant?" *He will speak
peace to his people, and to his saints.* Sooner or later,
God will speak peace to them; if he do not command
outward peace, yet he will suggest inward peace,
speaking that to their hearts by his Spirit which he
has spoken to their ears by his word and ministers
and making them to hear joy and gladness. He takes
the comfort of it; and so must we: "*I will hear what
God the Lord will speak*, hear the assurances he gives
of peace, in answer to prayer." *But let them not turn
again to folly;* for it is on these terms, and no other,
that peace is to be expected.

II. Here are the particulars of this answer of peace.
He gives us the pleasing prospect of the flourishing
estate of the church in the last five verses of the
psalm, which describe the peace and prosperity
God blessed the children of the captivity with, when
at length they gained a settlement in their own land.
But it may be taken both as a promise also to all who
fear God and work righteousness, that they shall be
easy and happy, and as a prophecy of the kingdom,
of the Messiah and the blessings with which that
kingdom should be enriched.

1. Help at hand (*v.* 9): "*Surely his salvation is nigh.*"
When the tale of bricks is doubled, then Moses comes.
When trouble is nigh salvation is nigh, for God is a
very present help in time of trouble to all who are his.

2. Honour secured: "*That glory may dwell in our
land*, that we may have the worship of God settled
and established among us; for that is the glory of a
land. When that goes, *Ichabod—the glory has departed*; when that stays glory dwells."

3. Graces meeting, and happily embracing (*v.*
10, 11): *Mercy and truth, righteousness and peace,
kiss each other.* This may be understood, (1) Of the
reformation of the people and of the government.
When in every congress mercy and truth meet, in
every embrace righteousness and peace kiss, and
common honesty is indeed common, then glory
dwells in a land. (2) Of the return of God's favour.
When a people return to God he will return to them
and abide with them in a way of mercy. So some
understand this, man's truth and God's mercy, man's
righteousness and God's peace, meet together. If
truth spring out of the earth, that is (as Dr. Hammond
expounds it), out of the hearts of men, the proper soil
for it to grow in, righteousness (that is, God's mercy)
shall look down from heaven, as the sun does upon
the world when it sheds its influences on the productions of the earth and cherishes them. (3) Of the
harmony of the divine attributes in the Messiah's
undertaking. Our salvation is so well contrived, so
well concerted, that God may have mercy upon poor
sinners, and be at peace with them, without any
wrong to his truth and righteousness.

4. Great plenty of everything desirable (*v.* 12):
The Lord shall give that which is good, everything that
he sees to be good for us. When the glory of the gospel
dwells in our land, then it shall yield its increase.

5. A sure guidance in the good way (*v.* 13): *The
righteousness* of his promise assuring us of happiness,
and the righteousness of sanctification, shall go before
him to prepare his way; and these shall be our guide
to *set us in the way of his steps*, that we may go forth
to meet him when he is coming towards us in ways
of mercy.

PSALM 86

This psalm is entitled "a prayer of David"; probably it was a
prayer he often used himself, and recommended to others for
their use, especially in a day of affliction. David, in this prayer,
I. Gives glory to God, ver. 8–10, 12, 13. II. Seeks for grace that
God would hear his prayers (ver. 1, 6, 7), preserve and save him,
and be merciful to him (ver. 2, 3, 16), that he would give him
joy, and grace, and strength, and put honour upon him, ver. 4,
11, 17. He pleads God's goodness (ver. 5, 15) and the malice of
his enemies, ver. 14.

A prayer of David.

Verses 1–7

This psalm was published under the title of *a prayer
of David*.

I. The petitions he puts up to God. *Unto thee,
O Lord! do I lift up my soul*, as he had said xxv. 1.
In all the parts of prayer the soul must ascend upon
the wings of faith and holy desire. 1. He begs that
God would give a gracious audience to his prayers
(*v.* 1): *Bow down thy ear, O Lord! hear me.* When God
hears our prayers it is fitly said that he *bows down his
ear* to them, for it is admirable condescension in God
that he is pleased to take notice of such mean creatures

as we are and such defective prayers as ours are. 2. He begs that God would take him under his special protection (v. 2): *Preserve my soul; save thy servant.* "Preserve my soul from that one evil and dangerous thing to souls, even from sin; preserve my soul, and so save me." All those whom God will save he preserves, and will preserve them to his heavenly kingdom. 3. He begs that God would look upon him with an eye of pity and compassion (v. 3): *Be merciful to me, O Lord!* "Men show no mercy; we ourselves deserve no mercy; but, Lord, for mercy-sake, be *merciful unto me.*" 4. He begs that God would fill him with inward comfort (v. 4): *Rejoice the soul of thy servant.* It is God only that can *put gladness into the heart and make the soul to rejoice,* and, as it is the duty of those who are God's servants to *serve him with gladness,* so it is their privilege to be *filled with joy and peace in believing,* and in faith to pray. Prayer is the nurse of spiritual joy.

II. The pleas with which he enforces these petitions. 1. He pleads his relation to God: "Thou art my God, to whom I have devoted myself, and on whom I depend, and I am thy servant (v. 2)." 2. He pleads his distress: "*Hear me, for I am poor and needy.*" 3. He pleads God's goodwill towards all that seek him (v. 5): "To thee do I *lift up my soul* in desire and expectation; *for thou, Lord, art good.*" 4. He pleads God's good work in himself, by which he had qualified him for the tokens of his favour. *I am holy,* therefore preserve my soul. He does not say this in pride and vain glory, but with humble thankfulness to God. *I am one whom thou favourest* (so the margin reads it), whom thou hast *set apart for thyself. I am holy* (v. 2), and yet needy, *poor in the world, but rich in faith. I cry unto thee daily, and all the day,* v. 3. It is comfortable if an affliction finds the wheels of prayer a-going, and that they are not then to be set a-going. "*In the day of my trouble,* whatever others do, *I will call upon thee,* and commit my case to thee, for thou wilt hear and answer me.

Verses 8–17

David is here going on in his prayer.

I. He gives glory to God. *Among the gods,* the false gods, whom the heathens worshipped, the angels, the kings of the earth, among them all, *there is none like unto thee, O Lord!* none so wise, so mighty, so good; *neither are there any works like unto thy works,* which is an undeniable proof that there is none like him. As the fountain of all being and the centre of all praise (v. 9): "*Thou hast made all nations,* made them all of one blood; they all derive their being from thee, and have a constant dependence on thee, and therefore *they shall come and worship before thee and glorify thy name.*" This was to have its full accomplishment in the days of the Messiah. "Therefore all nations shall worship before thee, because as King of nations *thou art great,* thy sovereignty absolute, and, for the proof of this, *thou doest wondrous things,* thou art God alone, not only none like thee, but none besides thee." Man is bad, very wicked and vile (v. 14); no mercy is to be expected from him; *but thou, O Lord! art a God full of compassion, and gracious,* v. 15. Men are barbarous, but God is gracious; men are false, but God is faithful. God is not only compassionate, but full of compassion, and in him *mercy rejoiceth against judgment.* It is some satisfaction to a good man to think that others shall praise and glorify God, but it is his greatest care and pleasure to do it himself. "Whatever others do" (says David), "*I will praise thee, O Lord my God!* not only as the Lord, but as my God. I will do it as long as I live, and hope to be doing it to eternity." With good reason does he resolve to be thus praising God: *For great is thy mercy towards me. Thou hast delivered my soul from the lowest hell.*

II. He prays earnestly for mercy and grace from God. He complains of the restless and implacable malice of his enemies against him (v. 14): "They were *proud men, violent men.* They *rise up against me* in open rebellion; and the design is not only to depose me, but to destroy me. Lord, appear against them, for they are thy enemies as well as mine." His petitions are,

1. For the operations of God's grace in him, v. 11. "*Teach my thy way, O Lord!* the way that thou hast appointed me to walk in; when I am in doubt concerning it, make it plain to me what I should do; let me hear the voice saying, *This is the way.*" *Teach me thy way; I will walk in thy truth.* One would think it should be, *Teach me thy truth, and I will walk in thy way;* but it comes all to one; it is the way of truth that God teaches and that we must choose and walk in, Ps. cxix. 30. Christ is the way and the truth, and we must both learn Christ and walk in him. "*Unite my heart to fear thy name.* Make me sincere in religion. A hypocrite has a double heart; let mine be single and entire for God, not divided between him and the world, not straggling from him."

2. For the tokens of God's favour to him, v. 16, 17. Three things he here prays for:—(1) That God would speak peace and comfort to him: "*O turn unto me,* as to one thou lovest.*" (2) That God would work deliverance for him, and set him in safety: "Give me *thy strength;* put strength into me, that I may help myself, and put forth thy strength for me, that I may be saved out of the hands of those that seek my ruin." (3) That God would put a reputation on him: "*Show me a token for good.* Let me have some instances of thy favour to me, *that those who hate me may see it, and be ashamed* of their enmity to me, as they will have reason to be when they perceive that *thou, Lord, hast helped me and comforted me.*"

PSALM 87

The foregoing psalm was very plain, but in this are things dark and hard to be understood. It is an encomium of Zion, as a type and figure of the gospel-church. Zion, for the temple's sake, is here preferred, I. Before the rest of the land of Canaan, as being crowned with special tokens of God's favour, ver. 1–3. II. Before any other place or country whatsoever, as being replenished with more eminent men and with a greater plenty of divine blessings, ver. 4–7. Some think it was penned to express the joy of God's people when Zion was in a flourishing state; others think it was penned to encourage their faith and hope when Zion was in ruins and was to be rebuilt after the captivity.

A psalm *or* song for the sons of Korah.

Verses 1–3

Some make the first words of the psalm to be part of the title; it is a psalm or song whose subject is the holy mountains—the temple built in Zion upon Mount Moriah. Three things are here observed, in praise of the temple:—1. That it was founded on the holy mountains, v. 1. It is built high; the *mountain of the Lord's house is established upon the top of the mountains,* Isa. ii. 2. It is built firmly upon the everlasting mountains and the perpetual hills; for sooner shall the mountains depart, and the hills be removed, than the covenant of God's peace shall be disannulled, and on that the church is built, Isa. liv. 10. Holiness is the strength and stability of the church: it is this that will support it and keep it from sinking; not so much that it is built upon mountains as that it is built upon holy mountains—upon the promise of God. 2. That God had expressed a particular affection for it (v. 2): *The Lord loveth the gates of Zion,* of the temple, of *the houses of doctrine* (so the Chaldee), *more than all the dwellings of Jacob,* whether in Jerusalem or anywhere else in the country. 3. That there was much said concerning it in the word of God (v. 3): *Glorious things are spoken of thee, O city of God!* God said of the temple, *My eyes and my heart shall* be there perpetually; I have sanctified this house, that my name may be there for ever, 2 Chron. vii. 16. Yet more glorious things are spoken of the gospel-church. It is the spouse of Christ, the purchase of his blood; it is a *peculiar people, a holy nation, a royal priesthood*, and the *gates of hell shall not prevail against it*.

Verses 4–7

Zion is here compared with other places, and preferred before them; the church of Christ is more glorious and excellent than the nations of the earth. 1. It is owned that other places have their glories (v. 4): "*I will make mention of Rahab*" (that is, *Egypt*) "*and Babylon, to those that know me; behold Philistia and Tyre, with Ethiopia*, we will observe that *this man was born there*; here and there one famous man, eminent for knowledge and virtue, may be produced, that was a native of these countries; here and there one that becomes a proselyte and a worshipper of the true God." But some give another sense of it, supposing that it is a prophecy. God says, "*I will reckon Egypt and Babylon with those that know me*. I will reckon them my people as much as Israel when they shall receive the gospel of Christ, and own them as born in Zion, born again there, and admitted to the privileges of Zion as freely as a true-born Israelite." Those that were strangers and foreigners became *fellow-citizens with the saints*, Eph. ii. 19. 2. It is proved that the glory of Zion outshines them all, upon many accounts; for, (1) Zion shall produce many great and good men, many prophets and kings, who should be greater favourites of heaven and greater blessings to the earth, than ever were bred in Egypt or Babylon. *A man, a man was born in her*, by which some understand Christ, born at Bethlehem near Zion. The greatest honour that ever was put upon the Jewish nation was, that of them, *as concerning the flesh, Christ came*, Rom. xi. 5. (2) Zion's interest shall be strengthened and settled by an almighty power. *The Highest himself shall* undertake to *establish her* upon an everlasting foundation, whatever convulsions and revolutions there are of states and kingdoms, and however heaven and earth may be shaken, these are things which cannot be shaken, but must remain. (3) Zion's sons shall be registered with honour (v. 6): *The Lord shall count, when he writes up the people*, and takes a catalogue of his subjects, *that this man was born there*, and so is a subject by birth, by the first birth, being born in his house—by the second birth, being born again of his Spirit. (4) Zion's songs shall be sung with joy and triumph: *As well the singers as the players on instruments shall be there* to praise God, v. 7. It was much to the honour of Zion, and is to the honour of the gospel-church, that there God is served and worshipped with rejoicing: his work is done, and done cheerfully; see lxviii. 25. *All my springs are in thee*, O Zion!

PSALM 88

This psalm is a lamentation and it does not conclude, as usually the melancholy psalms do, with the least intimation of comfort or joy, but, from first to last, it is mourning and woe. It is upon a personal account, especially trouble of mind. It is reckoned among the penitential psalms. I. The great pressure of spirit that the psalmist was under, ver. 3–6. II. The wrath of God, which was the cause of that pressure, ver. 7, 15–17. III. The wickedness of his friends, ver. 8, 18. IV. The application he made to God by prayer, ver. 1, 2, 9, 12. V. His humble expostulations and pleadings with God, ver. 10, 12, 14.

A song *or* psalm for the sons of Korah, to the chief musician upon Mahalath Leannoth, Maschil of Heman the Ezrahite.

Verses 1–9

The very first words are the only words of comfort in all the psalm. But, before he begins his complaint,

the psalmist calls God *the God of his salvation*, which intimates that, bad as things were, he looked up to God for salvation and depended upon him to be the author of it.

I. A man of prayer. It is his comfort that he had prayed; it is his complaint that, notwithstanding his prayer, he was still in affliction. "*I have cried unto thee* (v. 1), and have *stretched out my hands unto thee* (v. 9), as one that would take hold on thee, and even catch at the mercy, with a holy fear of coming short and missing of it." He was very frequent and constant in prayer: *I have called upon thee daily* (v. 9), nay, *day and night*, v. 1. He directed his prayer to God, and from him expected and desired an answer (v. 2): "*Let my prayer come before thee*, to be accepted of thee."

II. He was a man of sorrows, and therefore some make him, in this psalm, a type of Christ. He cries out (v. 3): *My soul is full of troubles;* so Christ said, *Now is my soul troubled;* and, in his agony, *My soul is exceedingly sorrowful even unto death*, like the psalmist's here, for he says, *My life draws nigh unto the grave*.

III. He looked upon himself as a dying man, whose heart was ready to break with sorrow (v. 5): *Free among the dead like the slain that lie in the grave*, whom thou rememberest no more, to protect or provide for the dead bodies. "*Thou hast laid me in the lowest pit*, as low as possible, my condition low, my spirits low, *in darkness, in the deep* (v. 6)." Thus greatly may good men be afflicted through the power of melancholy and the weakness of faith.

IV. He complained most of God's displeasure against him (v. 7): *Thy wrath lies hard upon me*. Could he have discerned the favour and love of God in his affliction, it would have lain light upon him; but it lay hard, very hard, upon him, so that he was ready to sink and faint under it.

V. It added to his affliction that his friends deserted him. When we are in trouble it is some comfort to have those about us that love us, and sympathize with us; but this good man had none such (v. 8): *Thou hast put away my acquaintance far from me*. "*Thou hast made me an abomination to them;* they are not only shy of me, but sick of me, and I am looked upon by them, not only with contempt, but with abhorrence."

VI. He looked upon his case as helpless and deplorable: "*I am shut up, and I cannot come forth*, a prisoner, and no way open of escape." Thus he bemoans himself (v. 9): *My eye mourneth by reason of affliction*. Yet weeping must not hinder praying; we must sow in tears: *My eye mourns*, but *I cry unto thee daily*.

Verses 10–18

I. The psalmist expostulates with God concerning the present deplorable condition he was in (v. 10–12): "*Wilt thou do a miraculous work to the dead*, and raise them to life again? Shall those that are dead and buried *rise up to praise thee*? Departed souls may indeed know God's wonders and declare his faithfulness, justice, and lovingkindness; but deceased bodies cannot; they can neither receive God's favours in comfort nor return them in praise." But he thus pleads with God for speedy relief: "Lord, thou art good, thou art faithful, thou art righteous; these attributes of thine will be made known in my deliverance, but, if it be not hastened, it will come too late."

II. He resolves to continue instant in prayer, because the deliverance was deferred (v. 13): "*Unto thee have I cried* many a time, and found comfort in so doing, and therefore I will continue to do so; *in the morning shall my prayer prevent thee*." How could he say, *My prayer shall prevent thee?* It intimates that he would be up earlier than ordinary to pray, would *prevent* (that is, go before) his usual hour of prayer. "My prayer shall not stay for the encouragement of the beginning of mercy, but reach towards it with faith and expectation even before the day dawns."

III. He sets down what he will say to God in prayer. He will humbly reason (v. 14): "*Lord, why castest thou off my soul?* What is it that provokes thee to treat me as one abandoned? *Show me wherefore thou contendest with me.*" Nothing grieves a child of God so much as God's hiding his face from him, nor is there anything he so much dreads as God's casting off his soul. If the sun be clouded, that darkens the earth; but if the sun should abandon the earth, and quite cast it off, what a dungeon would it be! *I suffer thy terrors*, v. 15. The psalmist here explains himself, and tells us what he means by God's terrors, even his *fierce wrath.* "*I am so afflicted* with them that I am *ready to die*, and" (as the word is) "*to give up the ghost. Thy terrors have cut me off,*" v. 16. They had almost taken away the use of his reason: *When I suffer thy terrors I am distracted.* This had continued long: *From my youth up I suffer thy terrors.* He had been from his childhood afflicted with melancholy. Sometimes those whom God designs for eminent services are prepared for them by exercises of this kind. No friend was a comfort to him (v. 18): *Lover and friend hast thou put far from me.* Next to the comforts of religion are those of friendship and society; therefore to be friendless is (as to this life) almost to be comfortless.

PSALM 89

Many psalms that begin with complaint and prayer end with joy and praise, but this begins with joy and praise and ends with sad complaints and petitions. It is uncertain when it was penned; only, in general, that it was at a time when the house of David was woefully eclipsed. I. The psalmist, in the joyful pleasant part of the psalm, gives glory to God, mentioning God's mercy and truth (ver. 1) and his covenant (ver. 2–4), but more largely in the following verses, wherein, 1. He adores the glory and perfection of God, ver. 5–14. 2. He pleases himself in the happiness of those that are admitted into communion with him, ver. 15–18. 3. He builds all his hope upon God's covenant with David, as a type of Christ, ver. 19–37. II. In the melancholy part of the psalm he laments the present calamitous state of the prince and royal family (ver. 38–45), expostulates with God upon it (ver. 46–49), and then concludes with prayer for redress, ver. 50, 51.

Maschil of Ethan the Ezrahite.

Verses 1–4

The psalmist has a very sad complaint to make of the deplorable condition of the family of David at this time, and yet he begins the psalm with songs of praise. Let our complaints be turned into thanksgivings. 1. However it be, the everlasting God is good and true, v. 1. God's mercies are inexhaustible and his truth is inviolable; and these must be the matter of our joy and praise: "*I will sing of the mercies of the Lord for ever*, sing a praising song to God's honour, a pleasant song for my own solace, an instructive song, for the edification of others." 2. However it be, the everlasting covenant is firm and sure, v. 2–4. "Things now look black, and threaten the utter extirpation of the house of David; but *I have said*, and I have warrant from the word of God to say it, that *mercy shall be built up for ever.*" If mercy shall be built for ever, then the *tabernacle of David, which has fallen down*, shall *be raised out of its ruins*, and *built up as in the days of old*, Amos ix. 11. An abstract of the covenant upon which this faith and hope are built: *I have said it*, says the psalmist, for *God hath sworn it.* He brings in God speaking (v. 3), owning, to the comfort of his people, "*I have made a covenant*, and therefore will make it good." The covenant is made with David, representing the covenant of grace made with Christ as head of the church and with all believers as his spiritual seed. It was promised that his family should continue—*Thy*

seed will I establish for ever. I will build up thy throne to all generations. This has its accomplishment only in Christ, of the seed of David, who lives for ever.

Verses 5–14

These verses are full of the praises of God. I. Where, and by whom, God is to be praised. *The heavens shall praise thy wonders, O Lord!* v. 5. The works of God are wonders even to those that are best acquainted and most intimately conversant with them; the more God's works are known the more they are admired and praised. God is praised by the assemblies of his saints on earth. "Thy faithfulness and the truth of thy promise, that rock on which the church is built, shall be praised in the congregation of the saints, who owe their all to that faithfulness, and whose constant comfort it is that there is a promise, and that he is faithful who has promised." In religious assemblies God has promised the presence of his grace, but we must also, in them, have an eye to his glorious presence, that the familiarity we are admitted to may not breed the least contempt. A holy awe of God must fall upon us, and fill us, in all our approaches to God, even in secret. II. What it is to praise God; it is to acknowledge that there is none like him, v. 6. *To whom will you liken me, or shall I be equal? saith the Holy One*, Isa. xl. 25. This is insisted on again (v. 8): *Who is a strong Lord like unto thee?* Among men it is too often found that those who are most able to break their word are least careful to keep it; but God is both strong and faithful; he can do everything, and yet will never do an unjust thing. III. What we ought, in our praises, to give God the glory of. 1. The command God has of the most ungovernable creatures (v. 9) *Thou rulest the raging of the sea.* This coming in here as an act of omnipotence, what manner of man then was the Lord Jesus, whom the *winds and seas obeyed?* 2. The victories God has obtained over the enemies of his church. *Thou hast broken Rahab*, many a *proud enemy* (so it signifies), Egypt in particular, which is sometimes called *Rahab*, broken it in pieces, as one that is slain and utterly unable to make head again. The remembrance of the breaking of Egypt in pieces is a comfort to the church, in reference to the present power of Babylon; for God is still the same. 3. The incontestable property he has (v. 11, 12): "Men are honoured for their large possessions; but *the heavens are thine, O Lord! the earth also is thine. The world and the fulness thereof*, all the riches contained in it, all the inhabitants of it, both the tenements and the tenants, are all thine; for *thou hast founded them*," He specifies (1) The remotest parts of the world: "*Thou hast created them*, and therefore knowest them, takest care of them, and hast tributes of praise from them." The north is said to be *hung over the empty place*; yet what fulness there is there God is the owner of it. (2) The highest parts of the world. He mentions the two highest hills in Canaan—"*Tabor and Hermon*, these shall rejoice in thy name, and they produce offerings for thy altar." Tabor is commonly supposed to be that high mountain in Galilee on the top of which Christ was transfigured. 4. The power and justice, the mercy and truth, with which he governs the world and rules in the affairs of the children of men, v. 13, 14. God is able to do everything; for he is the Lord God Almighty. He never did, nor ever will do, anything that is either unjust or unwise; for *righteousness and judgment are the habitation of his throne.* He always does that which is kind to his people and consonant to the word which he has spoken: "*Mercy and truth shall go before thy face*, truth in being as good as thy word, mercy in being better."

Verses 15–18

The psalmist, having largely shown the blessed-ness of the God of Israel, here shows the blessedness of the Israel of God. As *there is none like unto the God of Jeshurun, so, happy art thou, O Israel! there is none like unto thee, O people!* especially as a type of the gospel-Israel, consisting of all true believers, whose happiness is here described.

I. Glorious discoveries are made to them, and glad tidings of good brought to them; they hear, *they know the joyful sound, v.* 15. This may allude 1. To the shout of a victorious army. Israel have the tokens of God's presence with them in their wars. Or, 2. To the sound that was made over the sacrifices and on the solemn feastdays, lxxxi. 1–3. This was the happiness of Israel, that they had among them the free and open profession of God's holy religion. Or, 3. To the sound of the jubilee-trumpet; a joyful sound it was to servants and debtors, to whom it proclaimed release. The gospel is indeed a joyful sound, a sound of victory, of liberty, of communion with God; blessed are the people that hear it, and know it, and bid it welcome.

II. Special tokens of God's favour are granted them: "*They shall walk, O Lord! in the light of thy countenance;* they shall govern themselves by thy directions, shall be guided by thy eye; and they shall delight themselves in thy consolations."

III. They never want matter for joy. Those that rejoice in Christ Jesus have enough to counterbalance their grievances and silence their griefs; and therefore their joy is full (1 John i. 4).

IV. Their relation to God is their honour and dignity. "In *thy righteousness shall they be exalted,* and not in any righteousness of their own. In thy favour, which through Christ we hope for, *our horn shall be exalted.* The horn denotes beauty, plenty, and power."

V. Their relation to God is their protection and safety (*v.* 18): "*For our shield is of the Lord*" (so the margin), "and *our king is from the Holy One of Israel.* If God be our ruler, he will be our defender; and who is he then that can harm us?"

Verses 19–37

The covenant God made with David and his seed was mentioned before (*v.* 3, 4); but in these verses it is enlarged upon. Certainly it looks at Christ, and has its accomplishment in him much more than in David. The comforts of our redemption flow from the covenant of redemption; all our springs are in that, Isa. lv. 3. *I will make an everlasting covenant with you, even the sure mercies of David,* Acts xiii. 34.

I. What assurance we have of the truth of the promise, which may encourage us to build upon it. *Thou didst speak in vision to thy Holy One.* God's promise to David, which is especially referred to here, was spoken in vision to Nathan the prophet, 2 Sam. vii. 12–17. *Then,* when the *Holy One of Israel was their king* (*v.* 18), he appointed David to be his viceroy. How it was sworn to and ratified (*v.* 35): *Once have I sworn by my holiness.* His swearing once is enough; he needs not swear again, as David did (1 Sam. xx. 17); for his word and oath are two immutable things.

II. The choice made of the person to whom the promise is given, *v.* 19, 20. David was a king of God's own choosing, so is Christ, and therefore both are called *God's kings,* Ps. ii. 6. David was mighty, a man chosen out of the people. God exalted him, and ordered Samuel to anoint him. But this is to be applied to Christ. 1. He is mighty, *able to save to the uttermost,* for he is the Son of God—mighty in love. 2. He is *chosen out of the people,* one of us, bone of our bone, that takes part with us of flesh and blood. 3. God has found him. He is a

Saviour of God's own providing. 4. God has *laid help upon him.* He has exalted him, by constituting him the prophet, priest, and king of his church, clothing him with power, raising him from the dead, and setting him at his own right hand. He is called *Messiah,* or *Christ,* the *Anointed.*

III. The promises made to this chosen one, to David in the type and the Son of David in the antitype.

1. With reference to himself, as king and God's servant, it is here promised, (1) That God would stand by him and strengthen him in his undertaking (*v.* 21): "*With him my hand* not only shall be, but *shall be established,* by promise. My arm also shall *strengthen him* to break through and bear up under all his difficulties." (2) That he should be victorious over his enemies, that they should not encroach upon him (*v.* 22): *The son of wickedness shall not exact upon him,* nor afflict him. Christ became a surety for our debt, and thereby Satan and death thought to gain advantage against him; but he satisfied the demands of God's justice, and then they could not exact upon him. *The prince of this world cometh, but he has nothing in me,* John xiv. 30. *I will beat down his foes before his face;* the prince of this world shall be cast out, principalities and powers spoiled, and he shall be the death of death itself, and the destruction of the grave, Hos. xiii. 14. (3) *My faithfulness and my mercy shall be with him.* They were with David; God continued merciful to him, and so approved himself faithful. They were with Christ; God made good all his promises to him. But that is not all; God's mercy to us, and his faithfulness to us, are with Christ; and it is in him that all the promises of God are yea and amen. So that if any poor sinners hope for benefit by the faithfulness and mercy of God, let them know it is with Christ, and to him they must apply for it (*v.* 28): *My mercy will I keep for him, for evermore;* in the channel of Christ's mediation all the streams of divine goodness will for ever run. And, as the mercy of God flows to us through him, so the promise of God is, through him, firm to us: *My covenant shall stand fast with him,* both the covenant of redemption made with him and the covenant of grace made with us in him. (4) That his kingdom should be greatly enlarged (*v.* 25): *I will set his hand in the sea* (he shall have the dominion of the seas, and the isles of the sea), and *his right hand in the rivers,* the inland countries that are watered with rivers. David's kingdom extended itself to the Great Sea, and the Red Sea, to the river of Egypt and the river Euphrates. But it is in the kingdom of the Messiah that this has its full accomplishment, and shall have more and more, when *the kingdoms of this world shall become the kingdoms of the Lord and of his Christ* (Rev. xi. 15). (5) That he should own God as his Father, and God would own him as his Son, his firstborn, *v.* 26, 27. This is a comment upon these words in Nathan's message concerning Solomon (for he also was a type of Christ as well as David), *I will be his Father and he shall be my Son* (2 Sam. vii. 14), and the relation shall be owned on both sides. *He shall cry unto me, Thou art my Father.* Christ did so, in the days of his flesh, when he offered up strong cries to God, and taught us to address ourselves to him as *our Father in heaven. I will make him my firstborn.* It is Christ's prerogative to be *the firstborn of every creature,* and, as such, the *heir of all things,* Col. i. 15; Heb. i, 2, 6.

2. With reference to his seed. God's covenants always took in the seed of the covenanters (*v.* 29, 36): *His seed shall endure for ever,* and with it his throne. Now this will be differently understood according as we apply it to Christ or David.

(1) If we apply it to David, by his seed we are to understand his successors, Solomon and the following kings of Judah. It is supposed that they might

degenerate; in such a case they must expect to come under divine rebukes. But though they were corrected, they should not be disinherited. This refers to that part of Nathan's message (2 Sam. vii. 14, 15), *If he commit iniquity, I will chasten him,* but *my mercy shall not depart from him.* Thus far David's seed and throne did endure. The family of David continued a family of distinction till that Son of David came whose throne should endure for ever; see Luke i. 27, 32; ii. 4, 11.

(2) If we apply it to Christ, by his seed we are to understand his subjects, all believers, his spiritual seed, the children which God has given him, Heb. ii. 13. This is that seed which shall be made to endure for ever, and his throne in the midst of them, in the church in the heart, *as the days of heaven.* To the end Christ shall have a people in the world to serve and honour him. *He shall see his seed; he shall prolong his days.* Thus Christ's throne and kingdom shall be perpetuated: the kingdom of his grace shall continue through all the ages of time and the kingdom of his glory to the endless ages of eternity. It is here supposed that there will be much amiss in the subjects of Christ's kingdom. His children may *forsake God's law* (v. 30) by omissions, and *break his statutes* (v. 31) by commissions. Many corruptions there are in the church, as well as in the hearts of those who are the members of it. They are here told that they must smart for it (v. 32): *I will visit their transgressions with a rod.* Their being related to Christ shall not excuse them from being called to an account. But observe what affliction is to God's people. 1. It is but a rod, not an axe, not a sword; it is for correction, not for destruction. 2. It is a rod in the hand of God (*I will visit them*). *If they break my law, then I will visit their transgression with the rod,* but not else. The continuance of Christ's kingdom is made certain by the inviolable promise and oath of God, notwithstanding all this (v. 23): *Nevertheless, my kindness will I not* totally and finally *take from him.* Afflictions are not only consistent with covenant-love, but to the people of God they flow from it. For Christ's sake, in him the mercy is laid up for us, and God says, *I will not take it from him* (v. 33), *I will not lie unto David,* v. 35. *My faithfulness shall not fail, my covenant will I not break.* That which is said and sworn is that God will have a church in the world as long as sun and moon endure, v. 36, 37. The *seed of Christ shall be established for ever,* as *lights of the world* while the world stands, to shine in it, and, when it is at an end, they shall be established lights shining in the firmament of the Father.

Verses 38–52

I. A very melancholy complaint of the present deplorable state of David's family, which the psalmist thinks hard to be reconciled to the covenant God made with David. "Thou saidst thou wouldst not *take away thy lovingkindness, but thou hast cast off.*" Sometimes, it is no easy thing to reconcile God's providences with his promises, and yet God's works fulfil his word and never contradict it. 1. David's house seemed to have lost its interest in God. God had been pleased with his anointed, but now he was *wroth with him* (v. 38). 2. The honour of the house of David was lost and laid in the dust: *Thou hast profaned his crown* (which was always looked upon as sacred) by *casting it to the ground,* to be trampled on, v. 39. 3. It was exposed and made a prey to all the neighbours (v. 40): *Thou hast broken down all his hedges* (all those things that were a defence to them, and particularly that hedge of protection which they thought God's covenant and promise had made about them) and thou *hast made even his strongholds a ruin. He is a reproach to his neighbours,* who triumph in his fall from so great a degree of honour. Everyone helps

forward the calamity (v. 42): "*Thou hast set up the right hand of his adversaries,* not only given them power, but inclined them to turn their power this way." 4. It was disabled to help itself (v. 43): "*Thou hast turned the edge of his sword,* and made it blunt, that it cannot do execution as it has done; and (which is worse) thou hast turned the edge of his spirit, and taken off his courage, *and hast not made him to stand* as he used to do *in the battle.*" 5. It was upon the brink of an inglorious exit (v. 45): *The days of his youth hast thou shortened.* This seems to intimate that the psalm was penned in Rehoboam's time, when the house of David was but in the days of its youth, and yet waxed old and began to decay already. When posterity degenerates, it falls into disgrace, and iniquity stains their glory. How apt we are to place the happiness of the church in something external, and to think the promise fails. Our Master has so expressly told us that his kingdom is not of this world.

II. A very pathetic expostulation with God upon this. *How long, O Lord! wilt thou hide thyself? For ever?* That which grieved them most was that God himself had kept them long in the dark. It seemed an eternal night, when God had withdrawn: *Thou hidest thyself for ever.* He pleads the shortness and vanity of life (v. 47): *Remember how short my time is, how transitory I am* (say some), therefore unable to bear the power of thy wrath, and therefore a proper object of thy pity. *Wherefore hast thou made all men in vain?* or, *Unto what vanity hast thou created all the sons of Adam!* If the ancient lovingkindnesses spoken of (v. 49) be forgotten (those relating to another life), man is indeed made in vain. Considering man as mortal, if there were not a future state on the other side of death, we might be ready to think that man was made in vain. If we think that God has made men in vain because so many have short lives, it is true that God has made them so, but it is not true that *therefore* they are made in vain. For those whose days are few may yet glorify God and do some good, may keep their communion with God and get to heaven. If we think that God has made men in vain because most men neither serve him nor enjoy him, it is true that, as to themselves, they were made in vain, but it was not owing to God that they were made in vain; it was owing to themselves. He pleads the universality of death (v. 48): "*What man*" (what *strong man,* so the word is), "*is he that liveth and shall not see death?*" The king himself is not exempted. Lord, since he is under a fatal necessity of dying, let not his whole life be made miserable. Let him not therefore be delivered into the hand of the grave by the miseries of a dying life, till his time shall come." It concerns us therefore to make sure of happiness on the other side of death, that, *when we fail, we may be received into everlasting habitations.* The next plea is taken from the kindness God had for his servant David (v. 49): *Lord, where are thy former lovingkindnesses,* which thou showedst, nay, *which thou swaredst,* to *David in thy truth?* Wilt thou fail of doing what thou hast promised? God's unchangeableness and faithfulness assure us that God will not cast off those whom he has chosen and covenanted with. The last plea is taken from the indignity done to God's anointed (v. 50, 51). "They are thy enemies who do thus reproach us; and wilt thou not appear against them as such? *They have reproached the footsteps of thy anointed.*" They reflected upon all the steps which the king had taken in the course of his administration, tracked him in all his motions. Or, if we apply it to Christ, the Lord's Messiah, they reproached the Jews with the slowness of his coming. They called him, *He that should come;* but, because he had not yet come, they told them he would never come, they must give over looking for him.

III. The psalm concludes with praise, even after this sad complaint (*v.* 52): *Blessed be the Lord for evermore, Amen, and amen.* Thus he confronts the reproaches of his enemies. The more others blaspheme God the more we should bless him. Thus he corrects his own complaints. He began the psalm with thanksgiving, before he made his complaint (*v.* 1); and now he concludes it with a doxology.

PSALM 90

This psalm was penned by Moses (as appears by the title), the most ancient penman of sacred writ. We have upon record a praising song of his (Exod. xv, which is alluded to in Rev. xv. 3), and an instructing song of his, Deut. xxxii. But this is called a prayer. It is supposed that this psalm was penned upon occasion of the sentence passed upon Israel, in the wilderness for their unbelief, murmuring, and rebellion, that their carcases should fall in the wilderness, that they should be wasted away by a series of miseries for thirty-eight years together, and that none of them that were then of age should enter Canaan. We have the story to which this psalm seems to refer, Num. xiv. Probably Moses penned this prayer to be daily used by the people in their tents, or by the priests in the tabernacle-service in the wilderness. In it, I. Moses comforts himself and his people with the eternity of God and their interest in him, ver. 1, 2. II. He humbles himself and his people with the consideration of the frailty of man, ver. 3–6. III. He submits himself and his people to the righteous sentence of God passed upon them, ver. 7–11. IV. He commits himself and his people to God, by prayer for divine mercy and grace, and the return of God's favour, ver. 12–17. It is very applicable to the frailty of human life in general, and, in singing it, we may apply it to the years of our passage through the wilderness of this world, and it furnishes us with meditations and prayers very suitable to the solemnity of a funeral.

A prayer of Moses the man of God.

Verses 1–6

This psalm is entitled *a prayer of Moses*. Moses taught the people of Israel to pray, and put words into their mouths which they might make use of in turning to the Lord. In these verses we are taught,

I. To give God the praise of his care concerning his people at all times (*v.* 1): *Lord, thou hast been to us a habitation,* or *dwelling-place, a refuge* or *help, in all generations.* They plead his former kindnesses to their ancestors. Canaan was a land of pilgrimage to their fathers the patriarchs, who dwelt there in tabernacles; but then God was their habitation, and, wherever they went, they were at home, at rest, in him. Egypt had been a land of bondage for many years, but even then God was their refuge.

II. To give God the glory of his eternity (*v.* 2): *Before the mountains were brought forth, before he made the highest part of the dust of the world* (as it is expressed, Prov. viii. 26), *before the earth fell in travail,* or, as we may read it, *before thou hadst formed the earth and the world* (that is, before the beginning of time) thou hadst a being; *even from everlasting to everlasting thou art God.* Again at all the grievances that arise from our own mortality, we may take comfort from God's immortality.

III. To own God's absolute sovereign dominion over man, and his power to dispose of him as he pleases (*v.* 3): *Thou turnest man to destruction,* to the destruction of the body, of the earthly house; *and thou sayest, Return, you children of men.* He does thereby call men to repent of their sins and live a new life. Sometimes he wonderfully restores them, and says, as the old translation reads it, *Again thou sayest, Return* to life and health again. Though God turns all men to destruction, yet he will again say, *Return, you children of men,* at the general resurrection, when, though a man dies, yet he shall live again.

IV. To acknowledge the infinite disproportion there is between God and men, *v.* 4. "A thousand years, to us, are a long period, which we cannot expect to survive; but it is, *in thy sight, as yesterday,* as one day; nay, it is but as a *watch of the night,*" which was but three hours. Betwixt a minute and a million of years there is some proportion, but betwixt time and

eternity there is none. But it might be objected against the doctrine of the resurrection that it is a long time since it was expected and it has not yet come. Let that be no difficulty, for a thousand years, in God's sight, are but as one day.

V. To see the frailty of man, and his vanity even at his best estate (*v.* 5, 6); look upon all the children of men, and we shall see their life is a dying life: *Thou carriest them away as with a flood.* As soon as we are born we begin to die, and every day of our life carries us so much nearer death. Men are carried away as with a flood and yet *they are as a sleep.* They consider not their own frailty. Like men asleep, they imagine great things to themselves, till death wakes them. Time passes unobserved by us, as it does with men asleep. It is a short and transient life, like that of the grass which grows up and flourishes, in the morning looks green and pleasant, but in the evening the mower cuts it down, and it withers and loses all its beauty. Death will change us shortly, perhaps suddenly; and it is a great change that death will make with us in a little time. Man, in his prime, does but flourish as the grass.

Verses 7–11

Moses had, in the foregoing verses, lamented the frailty of human life in general. But here he teaches the people of Israel to confess before God that righteous sentence of death which by their sins they had brought upon themselves.

I. They are here taught to acknowledge the wrath of God to be the cause of all their miseries. *We are consumed, we are troubled,* and it is *by thy anger,* by *thy wrath* (*v.* 7); *our days have passed away in thy wrath, v.* 9. We are too apt to look upon death as no more than a debt owing to nature; whereas it is not so; if the nature of man had continued in its primitive purity, there would have been no such debt owing to it. It is a debt to the justice of God, a debt to the law. *Sin entered into the world, and death by sin.*

II. They are taught to confess their sins (*v.* 8): *Thou hast set our iniquities before thee, even our secret sins.* God had herein an eye to their unbelief and murmuring, their distrusting his power and their despising the pleasant land. "*Thou hast set our secret sins* (those which go no further than the heart, and which are at the bottom of all the overt acts) *in the light of thy countenance*; that is, thou hast discovered these, and brought these also to the account, and made us to see them, who before overlooked them."

III. They are taught to look upon themselves as dying and passing away, and not to think either of a long life or of a pleasant one (*v.* 9). Though we are not quite deprived of the residue of our years, yet we are likely to *spend* them *as a tale that is told.* The thirty-eight years they wore away in the wilderness, for little or nothing is recorded of that which happened to them from the second years to the fortieth. Their joyful prospect of a prosperous glorious life in Canaan was turned into the melancholy prospect of a tedious death in the wilderness. That is applicable to the state of every one of us in the wilderness of this world: *We spend our years, we bring them to an end,* each year, and all at last, *as a tale that is told.* Some of our years are as a pleasant story, others as a tragical one, most mixed, but all short and transient: that which was long in the doing may be told in a short time. Every year passed *as a tale that is told*; but what was the number of them? As they were vain, so they were few (*v.* 10), seventy or eighty at most, which may be understood either 1. Of the lives of the Israelites in the wilderness; all those that were numbered when they came out of Egypt, above twenty years old, were to die within thirty-eight years; they numbered those only that *were* *able to go forth to war,* most of whom, we may suppose, were between twenty and forty, who therefore must have all died before eighty years old, and many before sixty. See what work sin made. Or, 2. Of the lives of men in general, ever since the days of Moses. It may be taken thus: *Our years are seventy, and the years of some, by reason of strength, are eighty; but the breadth of our years* (for so the latter word signifies, rather than strength), *the whole extent of them, from infancy to old age, is but labour and sorrow.* In the sweat of our face we must eat bread.

IV. They are taught by all this to stand in awe of the wrath of God (*v.* 11): *Who knows the power of thy anger?* The psalmist speaks as one afraid of God's anger, and amazed at the greatness of the power of it. *Who knows it,* so as to improve the knowledge of it? Those who make a mock at sin, and make light of Christ, surely do not know the power of God's anger.

Verses 12–17

These are the petitions of this prayer, grounded upon the foregoing meditations and acknowledgments. Four things they are here directed to pray for:—

I. For a sanctified use of the sad dispensation they were now under. "*Lord, teach us to number our days* (*v.* 12); Lord, give us grace duly to consider how few they are, and how little a while we have to live in this world." We must so number our days as to compare our work with them, and mind it accordingly with a double diligence, as those that have no time to trifle. Those that would learn this arithmetic must pray for divine instruction.

II. For the turning away of God's anger from them, "*Yet return, O Lord!* be thou reconciled to us, and *let it repent thee concerning thy servants* (*v.* 13); send us tidings of peace to comfort us again after these heavy tidings. *We are thy servants, thy people* (Isa. lxiv. 9); when wilt thou change thy way towards us?" In answer to this prayer, and upon their profession of repentance (Num. xiv. 39, 40), God, in the next chapter, proceeded with the laws concerning sacrifices (Num. xv. 1, &c.), which was a token that it repented him concerning his servants; for, *if the Lord had been pleased to kill them, he would not have shown them such things as these.*

III. For comfort and joy in the returns of God's favour to them, *v.* 14, 15. They pray for the mercy of God; for they pretend not to plead any merit of their own. *Have mercy upon us, O God! Early in the morning* of our days, when we are young and flourishing, *v.* 6. "*O satisfy us with thy mercy,* not only that we may be easy and at rest within ourselves, which we can never be while we lie under thy wrath, but that we *may rejoice and be glad,* not only for a time, upon the first indications of thy favour, but *all our days,* though we are to spend them in the wilderness. *Make us glad according to the days wherein thou hast afflicted us;* let the days of our joy in thy favour be as many as the days of our pain for thy displeasure have been and as pleasant as those have been gloomy. Now put into our hands the cup of salvation."

IV. For the progress of the work of God among them notwithstanding, *v.* 16, 17. "*Let thy work appear upon thy servants;* let it appear that thou hast wrought upon us, to bring us home to thyself and to fit us for thyself. Let thy work appear, and in it thy glory will appear to us and those that shall come after us." Perhaps, in this prayer, they distinguish between themselves and their children, for so God distinguished in his late message to them (Num. xiv. 31, *Your carcases shall fall in this wilderness, but your little ones will I bring into Canaan*): "Lord," say they, "let *thy work appear upon us,* to

reform us, and bring us to a better temper, and then *let thy glory appear to our children,* in performing the promise to them which we have forfeited." *Let the beauty of the Lord our God be upon us;* let it appear that God favours us. Let the grace of God in us, and the light of our good works, make our faces to shine, and let divine consolations put gladness into our hearts, and a lustre upon our countenances, and that also will be the beauty of the Lord upon us. *Establish thou the work of our hands upon us.* God's working upon us (*v.* 16) does not discharge us from using our utmost endeavours in serving him and working out our salvation. But, when we have done all, we must wait upon God for the success.

PSALM 91

It is probable that this psalm was penned by David; it is a writ of protection for all true believers, not in the name of king David, but in the name of the King of kings, and under the broad seal of Heaven. I. The psalmist's own resolution to take God for his keeper (ver. 1), from which he gives both direction and encouragement to others, ver. 9. II. The promises which are here made, in God's name, to all those that do so in sincerity. 1. They shall be taken under the peculiar care of Heaven, ver. 1, 4. 2. They shall be delivered from the malice of the powers of darkness (ver. 3, 5, 6), and that by a distinguishing preservation, ver. 7, 8. 3. They shall be the charge of the holy angels, ver. 10–12. 4. They shall triumph over their enemies, ver. 13. 5. They shall be the special favourites of God himself, ver. 14–15.

Verses 1–8

I. A great truth laid down in general, That all those who live a life of communion with God are constantly safe under his protection, and may therefore preserve a holy serenity of mind at all times (*v.* 1). It is the character of a true believer that he *dwells in the secret place of the Most High*; he is at home in God, returns to God, and reposes in him as his rest; he acquaints himself with inward religion, and makes heart-work of the service of God, worships within the veil. It is the privilege and comfort of those that do so that they *abide under the shadow of the Almighty*; he shelters them. They shall have a residence, under God's protection.

II. The psalmist's comfortable application of this to himself (*v.* 2): *I will say of the Lord,* whatever others say of him, *He is my refuge.* Idolaters called their idols *Mahuzzim,* their *most stronghold* (Dan. xi. 39), but therein they deceived themselves; those only secure themselves that make the Lord their God, their fortress. There being no reason to question his sufficiency, fitly does it follow, *In him will I trust.*

III. The great encouragement he gives to others to do likewise, not only from his own experience but from the truth of God's promise (*v.* 3, 4, &c.): *Surely he shall deliver thee.* Now here it is promised,

1. That believers shall be kept from imminent danger which would be fatal to them (*v.* 3). This promise protects, (1) The natural life, and is often fulfilled in our preservation from these dangers which are very threatening and very near. (2) The spiritual life, which is protected by divine grace from the temptations of Satan.

2. That God himself will be their protector. *He shall cover thee with his feathers, under his wings,* which alludes to the hen *gathering her chickens under her wings,* Matt. xxiii. 37. By natural instinct she not only protects them, but calls them under that protection when she sees them in danger, not only keeps them safe, but cherishes them and keeps them warm. To this the great God is pleased to compare his care of his people. Wings and feathers, though spread with the greatest tenderness, are yet weak, and easily broken through, and therefore it is added, *His truth shall be thy shield and buckler,* a strong defence. God is as willing to guard his people as the hen is to guard the chickens, and as able as a man of war in armour.

3. That he will not only keep them from evil, but from the fear of evil, *v.* 5, 6. God by his grace will keep thee from disquieting distrustful fear (that fear which hath torment) in the midst of the greatest dangers. Wisdom shall keep thee from being causelessly afraid, and faith shall keep thee from being inordinately afraid. Thou shalt not be afraid of the arrow, as knowing that though it may hit thee it cannot hurt thee; if it take away the natural life, yet it shall be so far from doing any prejudice to the spiritual life that it shall be its perfection.

4. That they shall be preserved in common calamities, in a distinguishing way (*v.* 7): "When *thousands and ten thousands* fall, fall by sickness, or fall by the sword in battle, *fall at thy side, at thy right hand, yet it shall not come nigh thee*, the fear of death shall not." When multitudes die round about us, though thereby we must be awakened to prepare for our own death, yet we must not be *afraid with any amazement*, nor make ourselves subject to bondage, as many do all their life-time, *through fear of death*, Heb. ii. 15. *Only with thy eyes shalt thou behold and see the just reward of the wicked*, which perhaps refers to the destruction of the first-born of Egypt by the pestilence.

Verses 9–16

More promises to the same purport with those in the foregoing verses.

I. The psalmist assures believers of divine protection, from his own experience. The character of those who shall have the benefit and comfort of these promises. They are such as make *the Most High their habitation* (*v.* 9), as dwell in love and so dwell in God. It is our duty to be at home in God, to make our choice of him, and then to live our life in him as our habitation. We shall be welcome to him as a man to his own habitation. To encourage us to make the Lord our habitation, and to hope for safety and satisfaction in him, the psalmist intimates the comfort he had had in doing so: "He whom thou makest thy *habitation is my refuge*; and I have found him firm and faithful, and in him there is room enough, and shelter enough, both for thee and me." The promises are sure to all those who have thus made *the Most High* their *habitation*. Whatever happens to them, nothing shall hurt them (*v.* 10). Though trouble or affliction befall thee, yet there shall be no real evil in it, for it shall come from the love of God and shall be sanctified; it shall come, not for thy hurt, but for thy good; and though, for *the present, it be not joyous but grievous* yet, in the end, it shall yield so well that thou thyself shalt own *no evil befell thee*. He who is the Lord of the angels, who gave them their being and gives laws to them, whose they are and whom they were made to serve, *he shall give his angels a charge over thee*, not only over the church in general, but over every particular believer. The charge is *to keep thee in all thy ways*; here is a limitation of the promise: They *shall keep thee in thy ways*. Wherever the saints go the angels are charged with them, as the servants are with the children. *Thou shalt tread upon the lion and adder*. The devil is called *a roaring lion, the old serpent, the red dragon*; so that to this promise the apostle seems to refer (Rom. xvi. 20), *The God of peace shall tread Satan under your feet*. Christ has broken the serpent's head, spoiled our spiritual enemies (Col. ii. 15). It may be applied to that care of the divine Providence by which we are preserved from ravenous noxious creatures (*the wild beasts of the field shall be at peace with thee*, Job v. 23); yea, and have ways and means of taming them, James iii. 7.

II. He brings in God himself speaking words of comfort to the saints, and declaring the mercy he had in store for them, *v.* 14–16. Observe,

1. To whom these promises do belong; they are described by three characters:—(1) They are such as

know God's name. His nature we cannot fully know; but by his name he has made himself known. (1) They are such as have set their love upon him; those who rightly know him will love him. (3) They are such as by prayer keep up a constant correspondence with him.

2. What the promises are which God makes to the saints. (1) That he will, in due time, deliver them out of trouble: *I will deliver him* (*v.* 14 and again *v.* 15), denoting a double deliverance, living and dying, a deliverance in trouble and a deliverance out of trouble. (2) That he will, in the mean time, *be with them in trouble, v.* 15. If he does not immediately put a period to their afflictions, yet they shall have his gracious presence with them in their troubles. (3) That herein he will answer their prayers: *He shall call upon me;* I will pour upon him the spirit of prayer, *and then I will answer*, by providences, and answer by graces, *strengthening them with strength in their souls* (cxxxviii. 3); thus he answered Paul with *grace sufficient*, 2 Cor. xii. 9. (4) That he will exalt and dignify them: *I will set him on high*, out of the reach of trouble, above the stormy region, on a rock *above the waves*, Isa. xxxiii. 16. They shall be enabled, by the grace of God, to look down upon the things of this world with a holy contempt and indifference, to look up to the things of the other world with a holy ambition and concern. (5) That they shall have a sufficiency of life in this world (*v.* 16). *With length of days will I satisfy him.* They shall live long enough: they shall be continued in this world till they have done the work they were sent into this world for and are ready for heaven, and that is long enough. A man may die young, and yet die full of days, *satur dierum—satisfied with living*. (6) That they shall have an eternal life in the other world. This crowns the blessedness: *I will show him my salvation.* It is probable that the word refers to the better country, that is, the heavenly.

PSALM 92

It is probable that it was penned by David. I. Praise, the business of the sabbath, is here recommended, ver. 1–3. II. God's works, which gave occasion for the sabbath, are here celebrated as great and unsearchable in general, ver. 4–6. In particular, with reference to the works both of providence and redemption, the psalmist sings unto God both of mercy and judgment, three times counterchanged. 1. The wicked shall perish (ver. 7), but God is eternal, ver. 8. 2. God's enemies shall be cut off, but David shall be exalted, ver. 9, 10. 3. David's enemies shall be confounded (ver. 11), but all the righteous shall be fruitful and flourishing, ver. 12–15.

A psalm or song for the sabbath day.

Verses 1–6

This psalm was appointed to be sung, at least it usually was sung, in the house of the sanctuary on the sabbath day. The sabbath day must be a day, not only of holy rest, but of holy work. The proper work of the sabbath is praising God; every sabbath day must be a thanksgiving day. One of the Jewish writers refers it to the kingdom of the Messiah, and calls it, *A psalm or song for the age to come*, which shall be all sabbath.

I. We are called upon and encouraged to praise God (*v.* 1–3): *It is a good thing to give thanks unto the Lord.* Praising God is good work: it is good in itself and good for us. 1. How we must praise God. We must do it by *showing forth his lovingkindness and his faithfulness*. We must show forth, not only his greatness and majesty, his holiness and justice, which magnify him and strike an awe upon us, but his lovingkindness and his faithfulness; for his goodness is his glory (Exod. xxxiii. 18, 19), and by these he proclaims his name. His mercy and truth are the great supports of our faith and hope, and the great encouragements of our love and obedience. This was then done, not only by singing, but by music joined with it, *upon an instrument of ten strings* (v. 3). 2. When we must praise God—*in the morning and every night*, not only on sabbath days, but every day; not only in public assemblies, but in secret, and in our families. We must begin and end every day with praising God.

II. We have an example set before us in the psalmist himself (v. 4): *Thou, Lord, hast made me glad through thy work. I will triumph in the works of thy hands.* From a joyful remembrance of what God has done for us we may raise a joyful prospect of what he will do. We cannot comprehend the greatness of God's works, and therefore must reverently and awfully wonder at them. "Men's works are little and trifling, for their thoughts are shallow; but, Lord, *thy works are great* and such as cannot be measured; for *thy thoughts are very deep* and such as cannot be fathomed." The greatness of God's works shall lead us to consider the depth of his thoughts.

III. We are admonished not to neglect the works of God, by the character of those who do so, v. 6. Those are fools who will not acquaint themselves with them, nor give him the glory of them.

Verses 7–15

The psalmist had said (v. 4) that from the works of God he would take occasion to triumph; and here he does so.

I. He triumphs over God's enemies (v. 7, 9, 11). When they are flourishing (v. 7) as *the grass* in spring (so thickly sown, so green, and growing so fast), *and all the workers of iniquity do flourish* in pomp, and power, one would think that it was a certain evidence of God's favour; but it is quite otherwise. The very *prosperity of fools shall slay them*, Prov. i. 32. Though they are daring, v. 9. They are thy enemies, and they fight against God. They shall perish: for *who ever hardened his heart against God and prospered*? Though they had a particular malice against the psalmist, yet he triumphs over them (v. 11): "*My eye shall see my desire on my enemies that rise up against me;* I shall see them not only disabled from doing me any further mischief, but reckoned with for the mischief they have done me, and brought either to repentance or ruin."

II. He triumphs in God, and his glory and grace. 1. In the glory of God (v. 8). 2. In the grace of God, his favour and the fruits of it (v. 10). *My horn shall thou exalt*, when *thy enemies perish;* for *then shall the righteous shine forth as the sun*, when the wicked shall be doomed to *shame and everlasting contempt*. He adds, *I shall be anointed with fresh oil*, which denotes a fresh confirmation in his office to which he had been anointed, or abundance of plenty, so that he should have fresh oil as often as he pleased, or renewed comforts to revive him when his spirits drooped. Grace is the anointing of the Spirit. The saints are here represented as *trees of righteousness*, Isa. lxi. 3; Ps. i. 3. They are *planted in the house of the Lord*, v. 13. The trees of righteousness do not grow of themselves; they are *planted*, not in common soil, but *in the house of the Lord*. Trees are not usually planted in a house; but God's trees are said to be planted in his house because it is from his grace, by his word and Spirit, that they receive all the sap and virtue that keep them alive and make them fruitful. It is here promised that they shall grow, v. 12. Where God gives true grace he will give more grace. God's trees shall grow higher, like the tall cedars in Lebanon; they shall grow nearer heaven; they shall grow stronger, like the cedars, and fitter for use. They shall be cheerful and respected by all about them. *They shall flourish like the palm-tree*, which has a stately body and large boughs. Dates, the fruit of it, are very pleasant, and it is ever green. The wicked flourish as the grass (v. 7), which is soon withered, but the righteous as the palm-tree, which is long-lived and which the winter does not change. It has been said of the palm-tree, *Sub pondere crescit—The more it is pressed down the more it grows;* so the righteous flourish under their burdens. They shall be fruitful. The products of sanctification, all the instances of a lively devotion, good works, by which God is glorified and others are edified, these are the fruits of righteousness, in which it is the privilege of the righteous to abound. It is promised that they shall bring forth fruit in old age. Other trees, when they are old, leave off bearing, but in God's trees the strength of grace does not fail with the strength of nature. The last days of the saints are sometimes their best days, and their last work is their best work. As it is by the promises that believers first partake of a divine nature, so it is by the promises that that divine nature is preserved and kept up. All that ever trusted in God found him faithful and all-sufficient, and none ever made ashamed of their hope in him.

PSALM 93

This short psalm sets forth the honour of the kingdom of God among men. It relates to the kingdom of his providence, by which he governs the world, and to the kingdom of his grace, by which he secures the church. The administration of both these kingdoms is put into the hands of the Messiah, and to him, doubtless, the prophet here bears witness, and to his kingdom. Concerning God's kingdom glorious things are here spoken. I. Have other kings their royal robes? So has he, ver. 1. II. Have they their thrones? So has he, ver. 2. III. Have they their enemies whom they subdue and triumph over? So has he, ver. 3, 4. IV. Is it their honour to be faithful and holy? So is it his, ver. 5.

Verses 1–5

The Lord reigns. It is the song of the gospel church, of the glorified church (Rev. xix. 6), *Hallelujah;* the Lord *God omnipotent reigns.* Here we are told how he reigns.

I. The Lord reigns gloriously: *He is clothed with majesty*.

II. He reigns powerfully. He is not only clothed with majesty, as a prince in his court, but he is *clothed with strength*, as a general in the camp. He has wherewithal to support his greatness and to make it truly formidable. See him not only clad in robes, but clad in armour. With this power *he has girded himself;* it is not derived from any other, nor does the executing of it depend upon any other. The world is established by the creating power of God, when he founded it upon the seas; it is so still, by that providence which upholds all things and is a continued creation. Though God clothes himself with majesty, yet he condescends to take care of this lower world and to settle its affairs; and, if he established the world, much more will he establish his church, that it cannot be moved.

III. He reigns eternally (v. 2): *Thy throne is established of old.* The whole administration of his government was settled in his eternal counsels before all worlds. Because God himself was from everlasting, his throne and all the determinations of it were so too; for in an eternal mind there could not but be eternal thoughts.

IV. He reigns triumphantly, v. 3, 4. *The floods have lifted up, O Lord!* (to God himself the remonstrance is made) *the floods have lifted up their voice*, which speaks terror. It alludes to a tempestuous sea. The church is said to *be tossed with tempests* (Isa. liv. 11). We may apply it to the tumults that are sometimes in our own bosoms, but, if the Lord reign there, even the winds and seas shall obey him. An immovable anchor is cast in this storm (v. 4): *The Lord himself is mightier.* The power of the church's enemies is but *as the noise of many waters;* there is more of sound than substance in it. *Pharaoh king of Egypt is but a noise*, Jer. xlvi. 17. The unlimited sovereignty and irresistible power of the great Jehovah are very encouraging to the people of God, in reference to all the noises and hurries they meet with in this world, Ps. xlvi. 1, 2.

V. He reigns in truth and holiness, v. 5. All his promises are inviolably faithful: *Thy testimonies are very sure.* As God is able to protect his church, so he is true to the promises he has made of its safety and victory. God's church is his house. The holiness of it is its beauty. and it is its strength and safety; it is the holiness of God's house that secures it against the many waters and their noise. Where there is purity there shall be peace.

PSALM 94

This psalm was penned when the church of God was under hatches, oppressed and persecuted; and it is an appeal to God, for his people against his and their enemies. Two things this psalm speaks:—I. Conviction and terror to the persecutors (ver. 1–11), showing them their danger and folly, and arguing with them. II. Comfort and peace to the persecuted (ver. 12–23), assuring them, both from God's promise and from the psalmist's own experience, that their troubles would end well.

Verses 1–11

I. A solemn appeal to God against the cruel oppressors of his people, v. 1, 2.

1. The titles they give to God for the encouraging of their faith in this appeal: *O God! to whom vengeance belongeth;* and *thou Judge of the earth.* He is judge, supreme judge, judge alone, from whom every man's judgments proceeds. He that gives law gives sentence upon every man according to his works, by the rule of that law. His throne is the last refuge (the *dernier ressort,* as the law speaks) of oppressed innocence. He is *judge of the earth,* of the whole earth. As he has authority to avenge wrong, so it is his nature, and property. *O God! to whom vengeance belongs,* who wilt not suffer might always to prevail against right. This is a good reason why we must not avenge ourselves, because God has said, *Vengeance is mine;* and it is daring presumption to usurp his prerogative and step into his throne, Rom. xii. 19.

2. What is it they ask of God. "Lord," say they, "show thyself; make them know that thou art and that thou art ready to *show thyself strong on the behalf of those whose hearts are upright with thee.*" The enemies thought God was conquered because his people were. *Render a reward to the proud;* that is, "Reckon with them for all their insolence, and the injuries they have done to thy people."

II. A humble complaint to God of the pride and cruelty of the oppressors, v. 3. They are wicked; they are *workers of iniquity*; and therefore they hate and persecute those whose goodness shames and condemns them. They are insolent, and take a pleasure in magnifying themselves. Those that speak highly of themselves, that triumph and boast, are apt to speak hardly of others. "*They break in pieces thy people, O Lord!* and do all they can to afflict thy heritage, to grieve them, to crush them, to run them down, to root them out." God's people are his heritage. They are inhuman, and take a pleasure in wronging those that are least able to help themselves (v. 6). "Lord, *how long* shall they do thus?"

III. A charge of atheism exhibited against the persecutors. Their atheistical thoughts are here discovered (v. 7): *They say, The Lord shall not see.* They have the confidence to say, "The Lord shall not *see;* he will not only wink at small faults, but shut his eyes at great ones too." He that says either that Jehovah the living God shall not see or that the God of Jacob shall not regard the injuries done to his people, *Nabal* is his name and folly is with him (v. 8): "*Understand, you brutish among the people,* and let reason guide you." God sees and regards all you say and do. None are so bad but means are to be

used for the reclaiming and reforming of them, none so brutish, so foolish, but it should be tried whether they may not yet be made wise; while there is life there is hope. The works of creation (v. 9), the formation of human bodies, prove that there is a God, prove also that God has infinitely and transcendently in himself all those perfections that are in any creature. *He that planted the ear shall he not hear? He that formed the eye shall he not see?* Could he give, would he give, that perfection to a creature which he has not in himself? By the knowledge of ourselves we may be led a great way towards the knowledge of God—if by the knowledge of our own bodies, and the organs of sense, so as to conclude that if we can see and hear much more can God, then certainly by the knowledge of our own souls. The gods of the heathen had eyes and saw not, ears and heard not; our God has no eyes nor ears, as we have, and yet we must conclude he both sees and hears, because we have our sight and hearing from him. *He that chastises the heathen* for their polytheism and idolatry, *shall not he* much more *correct* his own people for their atheism and profaneness? Dr. Hammond gives another very probable sense of this: "*He that instructs the nations* (that is, gives them his law), *shall not he correct,* that is, shall not he judge them according to that law, and call them to an account for their violations of it?" The same word signifies to chastise and to instruct, because chastisement is intended for instruction and instruction should go along with chastisement. *He that teaches man knowledge, shall he not know?* He not only, as the God of nature, has given the light of reason, but, as the God of grace, has given the light of revelation, has shown man what is true wisdom and understanding; and he that does this, shall he not know? Job xxviii. 23, 28. God will take cognizance even of what we think (v. 11): *The Lord knows the thoughts of man, that they are vanity.* Even in good thoughts there is a fickleness and inconstancy which may well be called *vanity.* Thoughts are words to God, and vain thoughts are provocations.

Verses 12–23

The psalmist speaks comfort to suffering saints from God's promises and his own experience.

I. From God's promises, which are such as not only save them from being miserable, but secure a happiness to them (v. 12): *Blessed is the man whom thou chastenest.* Here he looks above the instruments of trouble, and eyes the hand of God, which puts quite another colour upon it. The enemies break in pieces God's people (v. 5); but God by them chastens his people, as the father the son in whom he delights, and the persecutors are only the rod he makes use of. Now it is here promised,

1. That God's people shall get good by their sufferings. When he chastens them he will teach them, and blessed is the man who is thus taken under a divine discipline, for *none teaches like God.* When we are chastened we must pray to be taught, and look into the law as the best expositor of Providence. It is not the chastening itself that does good, but the teaching that goes along with it and is the exposition of it.

2. That they shall see through their sufferings (v. 13): *That thou mayest give him rest from the days of adversity.* The days of their adversity shall not last always. God *therefore* teaches his people by their troubles, that he may prepare them for deliverance, and so give them rest from their troubles, that the affliction, having done its work, may be removed.

3. That they shall see the ruin of those that are the instruments of their sufferings.

4. That, though they may be cast down, yet certainly they shall not be cast off, v. 14. Whatever their

friends do, God will not cast them off, nor throw them out of his covenant or out of his care. St. Paul comforted himself with this, Rom. xi. 1.

5. That, bad as things are, they shall mend (*v.* 15): *Judgment shall return unto righteousness;* the seeming disorders of Providence (for real ones there never were) shall be rectified. Then *all the upright in heart shall be after it;* they shall return to a prosperous and flourishing condition, and shine forth out of obscurity; they shall accommodate themselves to the dispensations of divine Providence with suitable affections. Dr. Hammond thinks this was most eminently fulfilled in the destruction of Jerusalem first, and afterwards of heathen Rome, the crucifiers of Christ and persecutors of Christians, and the rest which the churches had thereby.

II. From his own experiences and observations.

1. He and his friends had been oppressed by cruel and imperious men, that had power in their hands and abused it by abusing all good people with it. They were *evil-doers* and *workers of iniquity* (*v.* 16); they abandoned themselves to all manner of impiety and immorality, and then their throne was a *throne of iniquity, v.* 20. Iniquity is daring enough even when human laws are against it, which often prove too weak to give an effectual check to it; but how insolent, how mischievous, is it when it is backed by a law! These workers of iniquity *condemn the innocent blood* for violating their decrees. See an instance in Daniel's enemies; they *framed mischief by a law* when they obtained an impious edict against prayer (Dan. vi. 7), and, when Daniel would not obey it, *condemned his innocent blood* to the lions. The best benefactors of mankind have often been thus treated, under colour of law and justice, as the worst of malefactors.

2. The oppression they were under bore very hard upon them. The psalmist *had almost dwelt in silence* (*v.* 17); he was at his wits' end, and knew not what to say or do; he was ready to drop into the grave, that land of silence. (St. Paul, in a like case, *received a sentence of death within himself,* 2 Cor. i. 8, 9). He said, "*My foot slippeth* (*v.* 18); I must *fall. I shall one day perish by the hand of Saul.* My hope fails me; I do not find such firm footing for my faith as I have sometimes found." See Ps. lxxiii. 2. He had a multitude of perplexed entangled thoughts within him concerning the course he should take and what was likely to be the issue of it.

3. In this distress they sought for help, and succour, and some relief (*v,* 16): "*Who will rise up for me against the evil-doers?* Have I any friend who, in love to me will appear for me?" He looked, but there was none to save, there was none to uphold. When St. Paul was brought before Nero's throne of iniquity *no man stood by him,* 2 Tim. iv. 16. They cried out: "Lord, *shall the throne of iniquity have fellowship with thee?* Wilt thou countenance and support these tyrants in their wickedness? We know thou wilt not." A throne has fellowship with God when it is a throne of justice and answers the end of the erecting of it; but, when it becomes a *throne of iniquity,* it has no longer fellowship with God.

4. They found succour and relief in God, and in him only. *Unless I had* made him *my help,* by putting my trust in him and expecting relief from him, I could never have kept possession of my own soul; but living by faith in him has kept my head above water, has given me breath, and something to say. We are beholden not only to God's power, but to his pity, for spiritual supports: *Thy mercy,* the gifts of thy mercy and my hope in thy mercy, *held me up.* "*In the multitude of my thoughts within me,* crowding and jostling one another like a multitude, *thy comforts delight my soul*; silence my unquiet thoughts and keep my mind easy." God's comforts will reach

the soul, and not the fancy only, and will bring with them that peace and that pleasure which the smiles of the world cannot give and which the frowns of the world cannot take away.

5. God is, and will be, as a righteous Judge, the protector of right and the punisher of wrong; this the psalmist had both the assurance of and the experience of. "When none else will, nor can, nor dare, shelter me, *the Lord is my defence,* to preserve me from the evil of my troubles, from sinking under them and being ruined by them; and he is *the rock of my refuge,* in the clefts of which I may take shelter, and on the top of which I may set my feet, to be out of the reach of danger."

PSALM 95

For the expounding of this psalm we may borrow a great deal of light from Heb. iii and iv, where it appears both to have been penned by David and to have been calculated for the days of the Messiah; for it is there said expressly (Heb. iv. 7) that the day here spoken of (ver. 7) is to be understood of the gospel day, in which God speaks to us by his Son and proposes to us a rest besides that of Canaan. In singing psalms it is intended, I. That we should "make melody unto the Lord" (ver. 1, 2) as a great God (ver. 3-5) and as our gracious benefactor, ver. 6, 7. II. That we should teach and admonish ourselves and one another; and we are here taught and warned to hear God's voice (ver. 7), and not to harden our hearts, as the Israelites in the wilderness did (ver. 8, 9), lest we fall under God's wrath and fall short of his rest, as they did, ver. 10, 11.

Verses 1-7

The psalmist here, as often elsewhere, stirs up himself and others to praise God.

I. How God is to be praised. The praising song must be *a joyful noise, v.* 1 and again *v.* 2. Spiritual joy is the heart and soul of thankful praise. *Rejoice in him* as our Father and King, and a God in covenant with us. With humble reverence, and holy awe (*v.* 6): "*Let us worship, and bow down, and kneel before him,* as becomes those who know what an infinite distance there is between us and God, how much we are in danger of his wrath and in need of his mercy." We must speak forth, sing forth, his praises out of the abundance of a heart filled with love, and joy, and thankfulness—*Sing to the Lord; make a noise, a joyful noise to him, with psalms.* We must praise God in concert, in the solemn assemblies: "*Come, let us sing;* let us join in singing to the Lord. *Let us come* together *before his presence,* where his people are wont to expect his manifestations of himself."

II. Why God is to be praised.

1. Because he is *a great God,* and sovereign Lord of all, *v.* 3. (1) He has great power: *He is a great King above all gods,* above all deputed deities, all magistrates, to whom he said, *You are gods* above all counterfeit deities. (2) He has great possessions. This lower world is here particularly specified. How great is that God whose *the whole earth is, and the fulness thereof,* in whose hand it is, as he has the actual directing and disposing of all (*v.* 4); even *the deep places of the earth are in his hand;* and *the height of the hills,* whatever grows or feeds upon them, *is his also.* Whatever strength is in any creature it is derived from God and employed for him (*v.* 5): *The sea is his* for *he made it,* gathered its waters and fixed its shores; *the dry land is his,* for *his hands formed it,* when his word made *the dry land* appear. His being the Creator of all makes him, without dispute, the owner of all. This being a gospel psalm, we may very well suppose that it is the Lord Jesus whom we are here taught to praise. As Mediator, he is *a great King above all gods; by him,* as the eternal Word, *all things were made* (John i. 3), and it was fit he should be the restorer and reconciler of all who was the Creator of all, Col. i. 16, 20.

2. Because he is our God, not only has he dominion over us, as he has over all the creatures, but stands in special relation to us (*v.* 7): *He is our God.* He is

our Creator; we must *kneel before the Lord our Maker*, v. 6. Idolaters kneel before gods which they themselves made; we kneel before a God who made us. He is our Saviour, and the author of our blessedness. He is here called *the rock of our salvation* (v. 1). We are therefore his, under all possible obligations: *We are the people of his pasture and the sheep of his hand.* We must praise him, because he preserves and maintains us. All the church's children are in a special manner so; Israel *are the people of his pasture and the sheep of his hand*; and therefore he demands their homage in a special manner. The gospel church is his flock. Christ is the great and good Shepherd of it, and therefore to him must be *glory in the churches throughout all ages*, Eph. iii. 21.

Verses 7-11

The latter part of this psalm is an exhortation to those who sing gospel psalms to live gospel lives.

I. The duty required of all those that *are the people of* Christ's *pasture and the sheep of his hand*. He expects that they *hear his voice*, for he has said, *My sheep hear my voice*, John x. 27. If you call him *Master*, or *Lord*, then *do the things which he says*, and be his willing obedient people. Hearing the voice of Christ is the same with believing.

II. The sin they are warned against is hardness of heart. *If you will hear his voice*, and profit by what you hear, then do *not harden your hearts*; for the seed sown on the rock never brought any fruit to perfection.

III. The example of the Israelites in the wilderness.

1. "Take heed of sinning as they did, lest you be shut out of the everlasting rest as they were out of Canaan." So often did they provoke God by their distrusts and murmurings that the whole time of their continuance in the wilderness might be called a *day of temptation*, or *Massah*, the other name given to that place (Exod. xvii. 7), because they tempted the Lord, saying, *Is the Lord among us or is he not?* The more experience we have had of the power and goodness of God the greater is our sin if we distrust him.

2. The charge drawn up, in God's name, against the unbelieving Israelites, v. 9, 10. Their sin was unbelief: they *tempted* God and *proved* him, Num. xiv. 3, 4. This is called *rebellion*, Deut. i. 26, 32. The aggravation of this sin was that they *saw God's work*; they saw what he had done for them in bringing them out of Egypt, what he was now doing for them every day in the bread he rained from heaven, and the water out of the rock, than which they could not have more unquestionable evidences of God's presence with them. *It is a people that do err in their hearts, and they have not known my ways.* Men's unbelief and distrust of God, their murmurings and quarrels with him, are the effect of their ignorance. They saw his work (v. 9) and he *made known his acts to them* (ciii. 7); and yet they *did not know* the ways of his providence, or the ways of his commandments. The reason why people slight and forsake the ways of God is because they do not know them. *They do err in their heart;* they wander out of the way; in heart they turn back. The sins of God's professing people do not only anger him, but grieve him, especially their distrust of him. See the patience of God towards provoking sinners; he was grieved with them forty years, and yet those years ended in a triumphant entrance into Canaan made by the next generation. The sentence passed upon them for their sin (v. 11). He *swore solemnly in his wrath*, his just and holy wrath. God is not subject to such passions as we are; but he is said to be angry at sin and sinners, to show the malignity of sin and the justice of God's government. *That they should not enter into his rest*, the rest which he had prepared for them, a settlement for them and theirs.

Now this case of Israel may be applied to those of their posterity that lived in David's time, when this psalm was penned. But it must be applied to us Christians, because so the apostle applies it. There is a spiritual and eternal rest set before us, and promised to us, of which Canaan was a·type. Those that, like Israel, distrust God, will justly be shut out from his rest: they themselves have decided it, Heb. iv. 1.

PSALM 96

This psalm was sung at the translation of the ark. It looks further, to the kingdom of Christ, and is designed to celebrate the glories of that kingdom, especially the accession of the Gentiles to it. Here is, I. A call given to all people to praise God, to worship him as a great and glorious God, ver. 1-9. II. Notice given to all people of God's universal government and judgment, which ought to be the matter of universal joy, ver. 10-13.

Verses 1-9

The call here given us to praise God is very lively.

I. We are here required to honour God,

1. With songs, v. 1, 2. Three times we are here called to *sing unto the Lord*; that is, "Bless his name, speak well of him, that you may bring others to think well of him." *Sing a new song*, the product of new affections. A new song is a song for new favours. A new song is a New Testament song, a song of praise for the new covenant and the precious privileges of that covenant. A new song is a song that shall be ever new. This is a prophecy of the calling of the Gentiles; all the earth shall have this *new song put into their mouths*. Let the subject-matter of this song be *his salvation*, the great salvation which was to be wrought out by the Lord Jesus.

2. With sermons (v. 3): *Declare his glory among the heathen*, even *his wonders among all people*. Salvation by Christ is here spoken of as a work of wonder. This salvation was, in the Old Testament times, as heaven's happiness is now, *a glory to be revealed*.

3. With religious services, v. 7-9. Hitherto, though in every nation those that feared God and wrought righteousness were accepted of him, yet instituted ordinances were the peculiarities of the Jewish religion. All the earth is here summoned to fear before the Lord, to worship him. The acts of devotion to God are here described. We must *give unto the Lord*. It is what must be paid, and, if not, will be recovered, and yet, if it come from holy love, God is pleased to accept it as a gift. We must *give unto the Lord the glory due unto his name*. We must *bring an offering into his courts*. We must bring ourselves in the first place, the *offering up of the Gentiles*, Rom. xv. 16. We must *worship him in the beauty of holiness*, with holy hearts, sanctified by the grace of God, devoted to the glory of God. All the acts of worship must be performed with a holy awe and reverence.

II. Glorious things are here said of him; *The Lord is great*, and therefore *greatly to be praised* (v. 4) and *to be feared*. Even the new song proclaims God great as well as good. He is great in his sovereignty over all that pretend to be deities; *feared above all gods*—all princes, who were often deified after their deaths. He is great in his right, even to the noblest part of the creation; for it is his own work and derives its being from him. *Splendour and majesty are before him*, in his immediate presence above, where the angels cover their faces, as unable to bear the dazzling lustre of his glory. *Strength and beauty are in his sanctuary*, both that above and this below. If we attend him in his sanctuary, we shall behold his beauty, for *God is love*, and experience his strength for *he is our rock*.

Verses 10-13

Instructions given to those who were to preach the gospel to the nations.

I. Let it be told *that the Lord reigns*, the Lord Christ reigns, that King whom God determined to set upon his holy hill of Zion. See how this was first said *among the heathen* by Peter, Acts x. 42. Some of the ancients added a gloss to this, which by degrees crept into the text, *The Lord reigneth from the tree* (so Justin Martyr, Austin, and others, quote it), meaning the cross, when he had this title written over him, *The King of the Jews*.

II. Let it be told that Christ's government will be the world's happy settlement: *The world also shall be established, that it shall not be moved*. Sin had given it a shock, and still threatens it; but Christ, as Redeemer, upholds all things, and preserves the course of nature. The Christian religion, as far as it is embraced, shall establish states and kingdoms, and preserve good order among men.

III. Let them be told that Christ's government will be just and righteous, *v.* 13. He says' himself, *For judgment have I come into this world* (John ix. 39, xii. 31), and declares that *all judgment was committed to him*, John v. 22, 27. He shall rule in the hearts and consciences of men by the commanding power of truth and the Spirit of righteousness and sanctification. When Pilate asked our Saviour, *Art thou a king?* he answered, *For this cause came I into the world, that I should bear witness unto the truth* (John xviii. 37).

IV. Let them be told that his coming draws nigh, that this King, this Judge, standeth before the door. Between this and his first coming the revolutions of many ages intervened, and yet he came at the set time, and so sure will his second coming be.

V. Let them be called upon to rejoice in the Messiah, and this great trust that is to be lodged in his hand (*v.* 11, 12): *Let heaven and earth rejoice, the sea, the field, and all the trees of the wood*. The meaning is, 1. That the days of the Messiah will be joyful days. When Samaria received the gospel *there was great joy in that city* (Acts viii. 8), and, when the eunuch was baptized, *he went on his way rejoicing, v.* 39. 2. That it is the duty of every one of us to bid Christ and his kingdom welcome; for, though he comes conquering and to conquer, yet he comes peaceably. 3. That the whole creation will have reason to rejoice in the setting up of Christ's kingdom, even *the sea* and *the field*. There will, in the first place, be *joy in heaven, joy in the presence of the angels of God*.

PSALM 97

This psalm is set to the same tune with the foregoing psalm. Christ is the Alpha and the Omega of both. He it is that reigns, to the joy of all mankind (ver. 1); and his government speaks, I. Terror to his enemies; for he is a prince of inflexible justice and irresistible power, ver. 2–7. II. Comfort to his friends and loyal subjects, arising from his sovereign dominion, the care he takes of his people, and the provision he makes for them, ver. 8–12.

Verses 1–7

What was to be said among the heathen in the foregoing psalm (*v.* 10) is here said again (*v.* 1) and is made the subject of this psalm, and of psalm xcix. *The Lord reigns;* that is the great truth here laid down. The Lord Jesus reigns.

I. *Let the earth rejoice*, for hereby it is *established* (xcvi. 10). Not only let the people of Israel rejoice in him as King of the Jews, and the daughter of Zion as her King, but let all the earth rejoice. *Let the multitude of isles*, the many or great isles, *be glad thereof*. All have reason to rejoice in Christ's government. Sometimes indeed *clouds and darkness are round about him*; his dispensations are altogether unaccountable; *his way is in the sea and his path in the great waters*. There is a depth in his counsels, which we must not pretend to fathom. But still *righteousness and judgment are the habitation of his*

throne; a golden thread of justice runs through the whole web of his administration. In this he resides, for it is his habitation. In this he rules, for it is *the habitation of his throne. His commandments are*, and will be, *all righteous*. Who can contradict or dispute what the *heavens declare? All the people see his glory*, or may see it. The glory of God, in the face of Christ, was made to shine in distant countries. *Worship him, all you gods*. The words in Heb. i. 6, "*Let all the angels of God worship him*," are a key to this whole psalm, and show us that it must be applied to the exalted Redeemer. All power is given him both in heaven and earth, *angels, authorities, and powers, being made subject unto him*, 1 Pet. iii. 22.

II. Christ's government, though it may be matter of joy to all, will yet be matter of terror to some, and it is their own fault that it is so, *v.* 3–5, 7. He that reigns, to the *joy of the whole earth*, yet, as he has his subjects, so he has *his enemies* (*v.* 3). These enemies are here called *hills* (*v.* 5), for their height, and strength, and immovable obstinacy. Their persecuting the apostles, and *forbidding them to speak to the Gentiles*, filled up their sin, and brought *wrath upon them to the uttermost*, 1 Thess. ii. 15, 16. That wrath is here compared to consuming fire, which will not only burn the rubbish upon the hills, but will even *melt the hills* themselves *like wax, v.* 5. The most resolute and daring opposition will be baffled *at the presence of the Lord. The earth saw and trembled*, and the ears of all that heard were made to tingle. This was fulfilled in the destruction of Jerusalem and the Jewish nation by the Romans, about forty years after Christ's resurrection, which, like fire, and like lightning, astonished all their neighbours (Deut. xxix. 24). Idolaters also would be put to confusion by the setting up of Christ's kingdom (*v.* 7): *Confounded be all those who serve graven images*, the Gentile world, who *did service to those that by nature are no gods* (Gal. iv. 8). This is a prayer for the conversion of the Gentiles, that those who have been so long serving dumb idols may be convinced of their error, ashamed of their folly, and may, by the power of Christ's gospel, be brought to serve the only living and true God. The destruction of Paganism in the Roman empire was fulfilled about 300 years after Christ.

Verses 8–12

I. The reasons that are given for Zion's joy in the government of the Redeemer. God is glorified, and whatever redounds to his honour is his people's pleasure. *Thou, Lord, art high above all the earth* (*v.* 9). The exaltation of Christ, and the advancement of God's glory among men thereby, are the rejoicing of all the saints. *He preserves the souls of the saints;* he preserves their lives as long as he has any work for them to do. But something more is meant than their lives; for those that will be his disciples must be willing to lay down their lives. It is the *immortal soul* that Christ preserves, the *inward man*, which may be renewed more and more when the *outward man* decays. *Light is sown for the righteous*, that is, gladness *for the upright in heart*. The subjects of Christ's kingdom are told to expect tribulation in the world, yet let them know, to their comfort, that *light is sown* for them. What is sown will come up again in due time; though, like winter seed, it may lie long under the clods, yet it will return in a rich and plentiful increase. Christ told his disciples, at parting (John xvi. 20), *You shall be sorrowful, but your sorrow shall be turned into joy*.

II. The rules that are given for Zion's joy. Let it be a pure and holy joy. You that love the Lord Jesus, that *love his appearing* and kingdom, that love his word and his exaltation, see that you hate evil. A true love to God will show itself in a real hatred of all sin, as that abominable thing which he hates. Let the joy terminate in God (*v.* 12): *Rejoice in the Lord, you righteous.* All the lines of joy must meet in him as in the centre. See Phil. iii. 3; iv. 4. Let it express itself in praise and thanksgiving: *Give thanks at the remembrance of his holiness.*

PSALM 98

This psalm is to the same purport with the two foregoing psalms; it is a prophecy of the kingdom of the Messiah, the setting of it up in the world, and the bringing of the Gentiles into it. The Chaldee entitles it a prophetic psalm. It sets forth, I. The glory of the Redeemer, ver. 1–3. II. The joy of the redeemed, ver. 4–9.

A psalm

Verses 1–3

A song of praise for redeeming love is a *new song.* Converts sing a *new song;* they change their wonder and change their joy, and therefore change their note.

I. The wonders he has wrought: *He has done marvellous things, v.* 1. The work of our salvation by Christ is a work of wonder. The more it is known the more it will be admired.

II. The conquests he has won: *His right hand and his holy arm have gotten him the victory.* Our Redeemer has surmounted all the difficulties that lay in the way of our redemption. He got his victory by his own power.

III. The discoveries he has made to the world of the work of redemption. What he has wrought for us he has revealed to us, and both by his Son; the gospel-revelation is that on which the gospel-kingdom is founded—*the word which God sent,* Acts x. 36.

IV. The accomplishment of the prophecies and promises of the Old Testament. God is said, in sending Christ, to *perform the mercy promised to our fathers, and to remember the holy covenant,* Luke i. 72. It was in consideration of that, and not of their merit.

Verses 4–9

The setting up of the kingdom of Christ is here represented as a matter of joy and praise.

I. Let all the children of men rejoice in it, for they all have, or may have, benefit by it. Again and again we are here called upon by all ways and means possible to express our joy in it and give God praise for it. Let sacred songs attend the new King. Let these be music, not only with the soft and gentle melody of *the harp,* but since it is a victorious King whose glory is to be celebrated, let him be proclaimed with the martial sound of the *trumpet* and *cornet, v.* 6.

II. Let the inferior creatures rejoice in it, *v.* 7–9. This is to the same purport with what we had before (xcvi. 11–13): *Let the sea roar,* and let that be called, not as it used to be, a *dreadful noise,* but a *joyful noise;* for the coming of Christ, and the salvation wrought out by him, have quite altered the property of the troubles and terrors of this world, so that when the floods *lift up their voice, lift up their waves,* we must not construe that to be the sea roaring against us, but rather rejoicing with us. One would think that Virgil had these psalms in his eye, as well as the oracles of the Cumean Sibyl, in his fourth eclogue, where he either ignorantly or basely applies to Asinius Pollio the ancient prophecies, which at that time were expected to be fulfilled; for he lived in the reign of Augustus Caesar, a little before our Saviour's birth. He owns they looked for the birth of a child from heaven that should be a great blessing to the world, and restore the golden age:—

A new race descends from the lofty sky;
Thy influence shall efface every stain of corruption,
And free the world from alarm.

Many other things he says of this long-looked-for child, which Ludovicus Vives thinks applicable to

Christ; and he concludes, as the psalmist here, with a prospect of the rejoicing of the whole creation herein:

See how this promis'd age makes all rejoice.

And, if all rejoice, why should not we?

PSALM 99

This psalm seems to dwell more upon the Old Testament dispensation and the manifestation of God's glory and grace in that. To Israel indeed pertained the promises, which they were bound to believe; but to them pertained also the giving of the law, and the service of God, which they were also bound dutifully and conscientiously to attend to, Rom. ix. 4. And this they are called to do in this psalm, where yet there is much of Christ, for the government of the church was in the hands of the eternal Word before he was incarnate; and, besides, the ceremonial services were types and figures of evangelical worship. The people of Israel are here required to praise and exalt God, and to worship before him, in consideration of these two things:— I. The happy constitution of the government they were under, both in sacred and civil things, ver. 1–5. II. Some instances of the happy administration of it, ver. 6–9.

Verses 1–5

The foundation of all religion is laid in this truth, That *the Lord reigns.* God governs the world by his providence, governs the church by his grace, and both by his Son. We are to believe not only that *the Lord lives,* but that *the Lord reigns.* This is the triumph of the Christian church, and here it was the triumph of the Jewish church, that Jehovah was their King; and hence it is inferred, *Let the people tremble.* The Old Testament dispensation had much of terror in it. But we are not now come to *that mount that burned with fire,* Heb. xii. 18. Now that *the Lord reigns let the earth rejoice.* Then he ruled more by the power of holy fear; now he rules by the power of holy love. *The Lord reigns, let the earth be moved.* Those that submit to him shall be established, and not *moved* (xcvi. 10); but those that oppose him will be moved. The kingdom of Christ cannot be moved; the *things which cannot be shaken shall remain,* Heb. xii. 27. *In these is continuance,* Isa. lxiv. 5.

God's kingdom, set up in Israel, is here the subject of the psalmist's praise.

I. Two things the psalmist affirms:—1. God presided in the affairs of religion: *He sitteth between the cherubim* (*v.* 1), to give law by the oracles thence delivered. This was the honour of Israel, that they had among them the Shechinah, or special presence of God. *The Lord is great in Zion* (*v.* 2); there he is known and praised (lxxvi. 1, 2). *He is high* there *above all people;* so in Zion the perfections of the divine nature appear more illustrious than anywhere else. Therefore *let those* that dwell in Zion, and worship there, *praise thy great and terrible name, for it is holy.* 2. He was all in all in their civil government, *v.* 4. As in Jerusalem was the testimony of Israel, so *there were set thrones of judgment,* cxxii. 4, 5. Their government was a theocracy. God raised up David to rule over them, and he is *the king* whose *strength loves judgment.* He is strong; all his strength he has from God. The people of Israel had a good king; but they are here taught to look up to God as he by whom their king reigns: *Thou dost establish equity* (that is, God gave them those excellent laws by which they were governed), and *thou executest judgment and righteousness in Jacob.*

II. Putting these two things together, we see what was the happiness of Israel above any other people (*v.* 5): *"Exalt you the Lord our God, and worship at his footstool;* give him the glory of the good government you are under, as it is now established, both in church and state."*

Verses 6–9

The happiness of Israel in God's government is here further made out by some particular instances of his administration, especially with reference to those that were the most useful governors of that people—Moses, Aaron, and Samuel, in the two former of whom the theocracy or divine government began, and in the last of whom that form of government, in a great measure, ended.

I. The intimate communion they had with God. None of all the nations of the earth could produce three such men as these, that had such an intercourse with Heaven, and whom God *knew by name,* Exod. xxxiii. 17. Samuel, though not among his priests, yet was *among those that called on his name;* and for *this* they were all famous, *They called upon the Lord.* By their obedience: *They kept his testimonies, and the ordinances that he gave them;* they made conscience of their duty. Moses did all according to the pattern shown him; it is often repeated, *According to all that God commanded Moses, so did he.* Aaron and Samuel did likewise. They all wonderfully prevailed with God in prayer; miracles were wrought at their special instance and request. He communed with them as one friend familiarly converses with another (v. 7).

II. The good offices they did to Israel. They interceded for the people, and for them also they obtained many an answer of peace. *Moses stood in the gap,* and *Aaron between the living and the dead;* and, when Israel was in distress, Samuel cried unto the Lord for them, 1 Sam. vii. 9. This is here referred to (v. 8): "*Thou answeredst them, O Lord our God! thou wast a God that forgavest*" the people they prayed for. The people are again called upon to praise God (v. 9): "*Exalt the Lord our God,* on account of what he has done for us formerly, as well as of late, *and worship at his holy hill* of Zion."

PSALM 100

It is with good reason that many sing this psalm very frequently in their religious assemblies. The Jews say it was penned to be sung with their thank-offerings; but we say that as there is nothing in it peculiar to their economy so its beginning with a call to all lands to praise God plainly extends it to the gospel-church. Here, I. We are called upon to praise God and rejoice in him, ver. 1, 2, 4. II. We are furnished with matter for praise; considering his being and relation to us (ver. 3) and his mercy and truth, ver. 5.

A psalm of praise.

Verses 1-5

The psalm does indeed answer to the title, *A psalm of praise.* If we take the foregoing psalm to be a call to the Jewish church to rejoice in the administration of God's kingdom, which they were under (as the four psalms before it were calculated for the days of the Messiah), this psalm, perhaps, was intended for proselytes, that came over out of all lands to the Jews' religion.

I. A strong invitation to worship God. In all acts of religious worship, whether in secret or in our families, we come into God's presence, and serve him; but it is in public worship especially that we *enter into his gates and into his courts. Serve the Lord with gladness.* By holy joy we do really serve God. Gospel-worshippers should be joyful worshippers. We must *come before his presence with singing,* not only songs of joy, but songs of praise. *Enter into his gates with thanksgiving,* v. 4. We must take it as a favour to be admitted into his service, and that we have ordinances instituted and opportunity continued of waiting upon God in those ordinances.

II. The matter of praise, and motives to it, are very important, v. 3, 5. Know you what God is in himself and what he is to you. Knowledge is the mother of devotion and of all obedience: blind sacrifices will never please a seeing God. Let us know then these six things concerning the Lord Jehovah:—
1. *That the Lord he is God,* the only living and true God—that he is a Being infinitely perfect, self-existent, and self-sufficient, and the fountain of all

being. He is an eternal Spirit, incomprehensible and independent, the first cause and last end. 2. That he is our Creator: *It is he that has made us, and not we ourselves.* He gave us being, he gave us this being; he is both the former of our bodies and the Father of our spirits. We did not, we could not, make ourselves. 3. That therefore he is our rightful owner. The Masorites, by altering one letter in the Hebrew, read it, *He made us, and his we are,* or *to him we belong.* Put both the readings together, and we learn that because God *made us, and not we ourselves,* therefore we are not our own, but his. 4. That he is our sovereign ruler: *We are his people.* 5. That he is our bountiful benefactor. We are *the sheep of his pasture,* whom he takes care of; the *flock of his feeding* (so it may be read). 6. That he is a God of infinite mercy and goodness (v. 5).

PSALM 101

David was certainly the penman of this psalm; it is a solemn vow which he made to God when he took upon him the charge of a family and of the kingdom. Whether it was penned when he entered upon the government, immediately after the death of Saul (as some think), or when he began to reign over all Israel, and brought up the ark to the city of David (as others think), is not material; it is an excellent plan or model for the good government of a court, or the keeping up of virtue and piety, and, by that means, good order, in it: but it is applicable to private families; it is the householder's psalm. I. The general scope of David's vow, ver. 1, 2. II. The particulars of it (ver. 3-5, 7, 8), and that he would favour and encourage such as were virtuous, ver. 6.

A psalm of David.

Verses 1-8

David here cuts out to himself and others a pattern both of a good magistrate and a good master of a family.

I. The chosen subject of the psalm (v. 1): *I will sing of mercy and judgment,* that is, David since he was first anointed to be king, had met with many a rebuke and much hardship on the one hand, and yet, on the other hand, had had many wonderful deliverances wrought for him and favours bestowed upon him; of these he will sing unto God. God's providences concerning his people are commonly mixed —*mercy and judgment;* God has set the one over-against the other, and appointed them April-days, showers and sunshine. Whatever our outward condition neither the laughter of a prosperous condition nor the tears of an afflicted condition must put us out of tune for sacred songs. It may be understood of David's mercy and judgment; he would, in this psalm, promise to be merciful, and just. Family-mercies and family-afflictions are both of them calls to family-religion.

II. The general resolution David took up to conduct himself carefully and conscientiously in his court, v. 2. We have here,

1. A good purpose concerning his conversation; he would live by rule. In his family particularly, he would *walk within his house,* where he was more out of the eye of the world, but where he still saw himself under the eye of God. He resolves to *walk in a perfect way,* in the way of God's commandments. *I will behave myself wisely.*

2. A good prayer: *O when wilt thou come unto me?* It is a desirable thing, when a man has a house of his own, to have God come to him and dwell with him in it. David, as he purposed, *behaved himself wisely in all his ways; and,* as he prayed, *the Lord was with him.*

III. His particular resolution to practise no evil himself (v. 3): "*I will set no wicked thing before my eyes;* I will not design nor aim at anything but what is for the glory of God and the public welfare."

IV. His further resolution not to keep bad servants, nor to employ those about him that were vicious. He will have nothing to do with spiteful malicious people, who care not what mischief they do to those they have a pique against (v. 4): "*A froward heart* (one that delights to be cross and perverse) *shall depart from me*, as not fit for society, the bond of which is love, *I will not know*." "*Whoso privily slanders his neighbour*, either raises or spreads false stories, to the prejudice of his good name, *him will I cut off* from my family and court." David will prevent the preferment of those that hope to curry favour with him. "Therefore him *that has a high look and a proud heart will I not suffer*; I will have no patience with those that are still grasping at all preferments, for it is certain that they do not aim at doing good, but only at aggrandizing themselves and their families." God resists the proud, and so will David. "*He that worketh deceit*, though he may insinuate himself into my family, yet, as soon as he is discovered, *shall not dwell within my house*." David will make use of no such persons as agents for him.

V. His resolution to put those in trust under him that were honest and good (v. 6): *My eyes shall be upon the faithful in the land.* The kingdom must be searched for honest men to make courtiers of; and, if any man is better than another, he must be preferred. Saul chose servants for their goodliness (1 Sam. viii. 16), but David for their goodness.

VI. His resolution to extend his zeal to the reformation of the city and country, as well as of the court (v. 8). He would be forward and zealous in promoting the reformation of manners and suppression of vice. That which he aimed at was not only the securing of his own government and the peace of the country, but the honour of God in the purity of his church, *That I may cut off all wicked doers from the city of the Lord.*

PSALM 102

Some think that David penned this psalm at the time of Absalom's rebellion; others that Daniel, Nehemiah, or some other prophet, penned it for the use of the church, when it was in captivity in Babylon. But it is clear, from the application of ver. 25, 26, to Christ (Heb. i. 10–12), that the psalm has reference to the days of the Messiah, and speaks either of his affliction or of the afflictions of his church for his sake. In the psalm we have, I. A sorrowful complaint which the psalmist makes, either for himself or in the name of the church, of great afflictions, ver. 1–11. II. Seasonable comfort, 1. From the eternity of God, ver. 12, 24, 27. 2. From a believing prospect of the deliverance which God would, in due time, work for his afflicted church (ver. 13–22) and the continuance of it in the world, ver. 28.

A prayer of the afflicted, when he is overwhelmed, and poureth out his complaint before the Lord.

Verses 1–11

The title of this psalm is *a prayer of the afflicted.* Here is a prayer put into the hands of the afflicted: let them set, not their hands, but their hearts to it, and present it to God. When our state and our spirits are overwhelmed, it is our duty by prayer to *pour out our complaints before the Lord*, which intimates the leave God gives us to be free with him and the liberty of speech we have before him. It intimates also what an ease it is to an afflicted spirit to unburden itself by a humble representation of its grievances and griefs.

I. The psalmist humbly begs of God to take notice of his affliction, and of his prayer in his affliction, v. 1, 2. Let us *lift up the prayer*, and our souls with it. If we put up a *prayer in faith*, we may in faith say, *Hear my prayer, O Lord!* "Manifest thyself for me; not only hear me, but answer me; grant me the deliverance I am in want of and in pursuit of; answer me speedily, even *in the day when I call.*"

II. He makes a lamentable complaint of the low condition to which he was reduced by his afflictions. His body was emaciated. As prosperity and joy are represented by *making fat the bones*, so great trouble and grief are here represented by the contrary: *My bones are burnt as a hearth* (v. 3); they *cleave to my skin* (v. 5); nay, *my heart is smitten, and withered like grass* (v. 4). *I am withered like grass* (v. 11), scorched with the burning heat of my troubles. He was so taken up with the thoughts of his troubles that he *forgot to eat his bread* (v. 4); he had no appetite. He affected solitude, as melancholy people do. His friends deserted him and were shy of him (v. 6, 7): "*I am like a pelican of the wilderness*, or a *bittern* (so some) that makes a doleful noise; *I am like an owl*, that affects to lodge in deserted ruined buildings; *I watch, and am as a sparrow upon the house-top.* I live in a garret, and there spend my hours in poring on my troubles and bemoaning myself." When his friends went off from him his foes set themselves against him (v. 8). When they could not otherwise reach him they shot arrows at him, even *bitter words*. He fasted and wept under the tokens of God's displeasure (v. 9, 10). It was not so much the trouble itself that troubled him as the wrath of God which he was under the apprehensions of as the cause of the trouble. *My days are consumed like smoke* (v. 3), which vanishes away quickly. They are *like a shadow that declines* (v. 11), like the evening-shadow. Now all this is properly a prayer for a particular person afflicted, yet is supposed to be a description of the afflictions of the church of God, with which the psalmist sympathizes, making public grievances his own.

Verses 12–22

Many exceedingly great and precious comforts are here to balance the foregoing complaints; for *unto the upright there arises light in the darkness.*

I. We are dying creatures, and our interests and comforts are dying, but God is an everliving everlasting God (v. 12): "*My days are like a shadow;* there is no remedy; night is coming upon me; but, *thou, O Lord! shalt endure for ever.*" God *endures for ever*, his church's faithful protector; and we may be confident that they shall not be neglected.

II. Poor Zion is now in distress, but there will come a time for her relief and succour (v. 13). The hope of deliverance is built upon the goodness of God and upon the power of God. There is a time set for the deliverance of the church, which will come at the time which Infinite Wisdom has appointed (and therefore it is the best time) and which Eternal Truth has fixed it to, and therefore it is a certain time, and shall not be forgotten nor further adjourned. Zion was now in ruins, that is, the temple that was built in the city of David: the favouring of Zion is the building of the temple up again, as it is explained, v. 16. *Thy servants take pleasure* even in *the stones* of the temple, though they were thrown down and scattered, and *favour the dust*, the very rubbish and ruins of it, v. 14. When the temple was ruined, yet the stones of it were to be had for a new building, and there were those who encouraged themselves with that. *The heathen shall fear the name of the Lord*, shall have better thoughts of the church of God than they have had, when God by his providence thus puts an honour upon it. They shall say, We will go with you, for we have *seen that God is with you*, Zech. viii. 23. All that have made his glory their highest end desire it and pray for it.

III. The prayers of God's people now seem to be slighted and no notice taken of them, but they will be reviewed and greatly encouraged (v. 17): *He will regard the prayer of the destitute.* They are the *destitute.* It is an elegant word that is here used, which signifies the heath in the wilderness, a low shrub, or bush, like the hyssop of the wall. They are in a low and broken state, enriched with spiritual blessings, but destitute of temporal good things. When we consider our own meanness, our darkness and deadness, and the manifold defects in our prayers, we have cause to suspect that our prayers will be received with disdain in heaven; but we are here assured of the contrary, for we have an advocate with the Father, and are under grace, not under the law. *This shall be written for the generation to come, that none may despair,* though they be destitute, nor think their prayers forgotten because they have not an answer to them immediately. Many that are now unborn, shall, by reading the history of the church, praise the Lord for his answers to prayer.

IV. The prisoners under condemnation unjustly seem as sheep appointed for the slaughter, but care shall be taken for their discharge (v. 19, 20): God has *looked down from the height of his sanctuary, from heaven, to do acts of grace, to hear the groaning of the prisoners, to loose those that are appointed to death.* God takes notice not only of the prayers of his afflicted people, which are the language of grace, but even of their groans, which are the language of nature. We have an instance in Peter, Acts xii. 6. If God by his providences declare his name, we must by our acknowledgments of them declare his praise, which ought to be the echo of his name. God will discharge his people that were prisoners and captives in Babylon, *that they may declare his name in Zion,* the place he has chosen to put his name, *and his praise in Jerusalem,* at their return thither. They will help to draw in others to the worship of God (v. 22): *When the people of God are gathered together* at Jerusalem (as they were after their return out of Babylon) many out of the kingdoms joined with them *to serve the Lord* (Ezra vi. 21). But look further, at the conversion of the Gentiles to the faith of Christ in the latter days. Christ has proclaimed *liberty to the captives,* and *the opening of the prison to those that were bound,* that they may declare the name of the Lord in the gospelchurch, in which Jews and Gentiles shall unite.

Verses 23–28

I. The imminent danger that the Jewish church was in of being quite extirpated and cut off by the captivity in Babylon (v. 23): *He weakened my strength in the way.* This the psalmist speaks of as in his own person, and it is very applicable to common afflictions. Bodily distempers soon *weaken our strength in the way.* When in the midst of our days our strength is weakened, what can we expect but that the *number of our months should be cut off in the midst?* It has often been the lot of those that have used their strength well to have it weakened, and of those that could very ill be spared to have their days shortened.

II. A prayer for continuance (v. 24): *"O my God! take me not away in the midst of my days."* This is a prayer for the afflicted, that God would not *take us away in the midst of our days,* but that, if it be his will, he would spare us to do him further service and to be made riper for heaven.

III. A plea to enforce this prayer taken from the eternity of the Messiah promised, v. 25–27. The apostle quotes these verses (Heb. i. 10–12). It is very comfortable, in reference to all the changes and all the dangers that *Jesus Christ is the same yesterday, to-day, and for ever. Thy years are throughout all generations,* and cannot be shortened. It is comfortable in reference to the death of our own bodies, and the removal of our friends from us, that God is an ever living God, and that therefore, if he be ours, in him we may have everlasting consolation. Earth and heaven, the universe and its fulness, derive their being from God by his Son (v. 25): *"Of old hast thou laid the foundation of the earth,* which is founded *on the seas* and *on the floods* and yet *it abides";* much more shall the church, which is *built upon a rock."* God

will unmake the world again (v. 26, 27): *They shall perish,* for *thou shalt change them* by the same almighty power that made them, and *thou shalt endure; thou art the same.* God and the world, Christ and the creature, are rivals for the innermost and uppermost place in the soul of man, the immortal soul. 1. A portion in the creature is fading and dying: *They shall perish;* they will not last so long as we shall last. Heaven and earth shall *wax old as a garment. As a vesture shalt thou change them, and they shall be changed,* altered, so that they shall be *new heavens and a new earth.* See God's sovereign dominion over heaven and earth. He can change them as he pleases and when he pleases; and the revolutions of day and night, summer and winter, are earnests of their last and final change, when *the heavens* and *time* (which is measured by them) *shall be no more.* 2. A portion in God is perpetual and everlasting: *Thou art the same,* subject to no change; and *thy years have no end, v.* 27. Christ will be the same in the performance that he was in the promise, the same to his church in captivity that he was to his church at liberty. Let not the church fear the weakening of her strength, or the shortening of her days, while Christ himself is both her strength and her life; he is the same, and has said, *Because I live you shall live also.*

IV. A comfortable assurance of an answer to this prayer (v. 28): *The children of thy servants shall continue;* since Christ is the same, the church shall continue from one generation to another; from the eternity of the head we may infer the perpetuity of the body, though often weak and distempered, and even at death's door. Those that hope to *wear out the saints of the Most High* will be mistaken.

PSALM 103

This psalm calls more for devotion than exposition. The psalmist, I. Stirs up himself and his own soul to praise God (ver. 1, 2) for his favour to him in particular (ver. 3–5), to the church in general, and to all good men, to whom he is, and will be, just, and kind, and constant (ver. 6–18), and for his government of the world, ver. 19. II. He desires the assistance of the holy angels, and all the works of God, in praising him, ver. 20–22.

A psalm of David.

Verses 1–5

David is here communing with his own heart, and he is no fool that thus talks to himself.

I. How he stirs up himself to the duty of praise, v. 1, 2. It is the Lord that is to be blessed. It is the soul that is to be employed in blessing God, *and all that is within* us. The work requires the inward man, the whole man, and all little enough.

II. How he furnishes himself with abundant matter for praise: "Come, my soul, consider what God has done for thee." 1. "He has pardoned thy sins (v. 3); he has forgiven, and *does forgive, all thy iniquities.*" This is mentioned first because by the pardon of sin that is taken away which kept good things from us, and we are restored to the favour of God, which bestows good things on us. He is still forgiving, as we are still sinning and repenting. 2. "He has cured thy sickness." Our crimes were capital, but God saves our lives by pardoning them; our diseases were mortal, but God saves our lives by healing them. These two go together; for, as for God, his work is perfect and not done by halves; if God take away the guilt of sin by pardoning mercy, he will break the power of it by renewing grace. 3. "He has rescued thee from danger." *The redemption of the soul is precious;* we cannot compass it, and therefore are the more indebted to divine grace that has wrought it out, to him who has *obtained eternal redemption for us.* See Job xxxiii. 24, 28. 4. "He has not only saved thee from death and ruin, but has made thee truly and completely happy, with honour, pleasure, and long life." *He crowns thee with his lovingkindness and tender mercies,* and what greater dignity is a poor soul capable of than to be advanced into the love and favour of God? " He has given thee a prospect and pledge of long life: *Thy youth is renewed like the eagle's.*" The eagle is long-lived, and, as naturalists say, when she is old, casts all her feathers (as indeed she changes them every year at moulting time), and fresh ones come, so that she becomes young again. When God, by the graces and comforts of his Spirit, recovers his people from their decays, and fills them with new life and joy, an earnest of eternal life and joy, then they may be said to *return to the days of their youth,* Job xxxiii. 25.

Verses 6–18

I. Truly God is good to all (*v.* 6): He *executes righteousness and judgment for all that are oppressed.*

II. He is in a special manner good to Israel.

1. He has revealed himself and his grace to us (*v.* 7): *He made known his ways unto Moses,* and by him *his acts to the children of Israel.* Divine revelation is one of the greatest of divine favours, for God restores us to himself by revealing himself to us, and gives us all good by giving us knowledge.

2. He has never been rigorous and severe with us, but always tender, full of compassion, and ready to forgive.

(1) It is in his nature to be so (*v.* 8): *The Lord is merciful and gracious.* He is not soon angry, *v.* 8. He is *slow to anger,* bears long with those that are very provoking, defers punishing, that he may give space to repent, and does not speedily execute the sentence of his law. Though he signify his displeasure against us for our sins by the rebukes of Providence, and the reproaches of our own consciences, yet he will not always keep us in pain and terror, but, after the spirit of bondage, will give the spirit of adoption.

(2) We have found him so; *he has not dealt with us after our sins,* v. 10. He has not inflicted the judgments which we have merited; *God's patience should lead us to repentance,* Rom. ii. 4.

3. He has pardoned our sins, not only my *iniquity* (*v.* 3), but *our transgressions,* v. 12. *As the heaven is high above the earth* (*v.* 11) (so high that the earth is but a point to the vast expanse), so God's mercy is above the merits of those that fear him most, so much above and beyond them that there is no proportion at all between them. The fulness of his pardons, an evidence of the riches of his mercy (*v.* 12): *As far as the east is from the west so far has he removed our transgressions from us,* so that they shall never be laid to our charge, nor rise up in judgment against us. If we thoroughly forsake them, God will thoroughly forgive them.

4. He has pitied our sorrows, *v.* 13, 14. God is a Father to those that fear him and owns them for his children, and he is tender of them as a father. The father pities his children that are weak in knowledge and instructs them, pities them when they are froward and bears with them, pities them when they are sick and comforts them (Isa. lxvi. 13), pities them when they have fallen and helps them up again, pities them when they have offended, and, upon their submission, forgives them, pities them when they are wronged and gives them redress; thus *the Lord pities those that fear him.* He has reason to know our frame, for he framed us; and, having himself made man of the dust, *he remembers that he is dust.*

5. He has perpetuated his covenant-mercy and thereby provided relief for our frailty, *v.* 15–18. *As for man, his days are as grass,* which grows out of the earth, rises but a little way above it, and soon withers. Man, in his best estate, is but *like a flower of the field,* which, though distinguished a little from the grass, will wither with it. The flower of the garden is commonly more choice and valuable, and, though in its own nature withering, will last the longer for its being sheltered by the garden wall and the gardener's care; but the flower of the field (to which life is here compared) is not only withering in itself, but exposed to the cold blasts, and liable to be cropped and trodden on by the beasts of the field. Man's life is not only wasting of itself, but its period may be anticipated by a thousand accidents. God considers this, and pities him; let him consider it himself, and be humble. How long and lasting God's mercy is to his people (*v.* 17, 18): it will continue longer than their lives, and will survive their present state. Those only shall have the benefit of God's promises that make conscience of his precepts. The continuance of the mercy which belongs to such as these; it will last them longer than their lives on earth, and therefore they need not be troubled though their lives be short, since death itself will be no abridgement, no infringement, of their bliss. God's mercy is better than life, for it will out-live it.

Verses 19–22

I. The doctrine of universal providence laid down, *v.* 19. He has secured the happiness of his peculiar people by promise and covenant, but the order of mankind, and the world in general, he secures by common providence. *The Lord has a throne* of his own, a throne of glory, a throne of government. But though God's throne is in heaven, and there he keeps his court, and thither we are to direct to him (*Our Father who art in heaven*), yet *his kingdom rules over all.* He takes cognizance of all the inhabitants, and all the affairs, of this lower world. *His kingdom rules over all.*

II. The duty of universal praise inferred from it: if all are under God's dominion, all must do him homage.

1. Let the holy angels praise him (*v.* 20, 21): not as if they needed any excitement of ours to praise God, they do it continually; but thus David expresses his high thoughts of God as worthy of the adorations of the holy angels.

2. Let *all his works* praise him (*v.* 22), that is, all the children of men, in all parts of the world, let them all praise God; yea, and the inferior creatures too, which are God's works also; let them praise him objectively, though they cannot praise him actually, cxlv. 10. He began with *Bless the Lord, O my soul!* and, when he had penned and sung this excellent hymn to his honour, David does not say, Now, O my soul! thou hast blessed the Lord, sit down, and rest thee, but, *Bless the Lord, O my soul!* yet more and more.

PSALM 104

It is very probable that this psalm was penned by the same hand, and at the same time as the former; for as that ended this begins, with "Bless the Lord, O my soul!" and concludes with it too. The style indeed is somewhat different, because the matter is so: the scope of the foregoing psalm was to celebrate the goodness of God and his tender mercy and compassion, to which a soft and sweet style was most agreeable; the scope of this is to celebrate his greatness, and majesty, and sovereign dominion, which ought to be done in the most stately lofty strains of poetry. God is there praised as the God of grace, here as the God of nature. This noble poem is thought by very competent judges greatly to excel, not only for piety and devotion (that is past dispute), but for flight of fancy, and all the beauties and ornaments of expression, the Greek and Latin poets upon any subject of this nature. Many great things the psalmist here gives God the glory of. I. The splendour of his majesty in the upper world, ver. 1–4. II. The creation of the sea and the dry land, ver. 5–9. III. The provision he makes for the maintenance of all the creatures according to their nature, ver. 10–18 and again ver. 27, 28. IV. The regular course of the sun and moon, ver. 19–24. V. The furniture of the sea, ver. 25, 26. VI. God's sovereign power over all the creatures, ver. 29–32. And, lastly, he concludes with a pleasant and firm resolution to continue praising God (ver. 33–35).

Verses 1–9

When we are addressing ourselves to any religious service we must *stir up ourselves to take hold on God* in it (Isa. lxiv. 7); so David does here.

I. The psalmist looks up to the divine glory shining in the upper world, of which, though it is one of the things not seen, faith is the evidence. With what reverence and holy awe does he begin his meditation: *O Lord my God! thou art very great!* Princes appear great, 1. In their robes; and what are God's robes? *Thou art clothed with honour and majesty, v.* 1. Thou *coverest thyself with light as with a garment, v.* 2. God *dwells in light* (1 Tim. vi. 16); he clothes himself with it. 2. In their palaces or pavilions; and what is God's palace and his pavilion? He *stretches out the heavens like a curtain, v.* 2. So he did at first, when he made the firmament, which in the Hebrew has its name from its being expanded, or *stretched out,* Gen. i. 7. God *covers himself with light,* yet, in compassion to us, *he makes darkness his pavilion. Thick clouds are a covering to him.* The vastness of this pavilion may lead us to consider how great, how very great, he is that *fills heaven and earth.* Though air and water are fluid bodies, yet, by the divine power, they are kept as tight and as firm in the place assigned them as a chamber is with beams and rafters. How great a God is he whose presence-chamber is thus reared, thus fixed! 3. In their coaches of state, with their stately horses, which add much to the magnificence of their entries; but God *makes the clouds his chariots.* He descended in a cloud, as in a chariot, to Mount Sinai, to give the law, and to Mount Tabor, to proclaim the gospel (Matt. xvii. 5), and he *walks* (a gentle pace indeed, yet stately) *upon the wings of the wind.* 4. In their retinue or train of attendants; and here also God is very great, for (*v.* 4) he *makes his angels spirits.*

II. He looks down, and looks about, to the power of God shining in this lower world.

1. He has founded the earth, *v.* 5. Though he has *hung it upon nothing* (Job xxvi. 2), yet it is as immovable as if it had been laid upon the surest foundations. Though it has received a dangerous shock by the sin of man, and the malice of hell strikes at it, yet *it shall not be removed for ever,* that is, not till the end of time, when it must give way to the new earth.

2. He has set bounds to the sea; for that also is his. (1) He brought it within bounds in the creation. God said, *Let the waters under the heaven be gathered to one place, and let the dry land appear,* Gen. i. 9. This command of God is here called his *rebuke,* as if he gave it because he was displeased that the earth was not fit for man to dwell on. Power went along with this word, and therefore it is also called here *the voice of his thunder, v.* 7. *At thy rebuke,* as if they were made sensible that they were out of their place, *they fled.* As it is said on another occasion (lxxvii. 16), *The waters saw thee, O God! the waters saw thee; they were afraid.* So here; God rebuked the waters for man's sake, to prepare room for him. (2) He keeps it within bounds, *v.* 9. The waters are forbidden to pass over the limits set them; they may not, and therefore they do not, *turn again to cover the earth.*

Verses 10–18

I. He provides fresh water: *He sends the springs into the valleys, v.* 10. It is God that *sends the springs into the brooks, which* walk by easy steps between *the hills,* and receive increase from the rain-water that descends from them. These *give drink,* not only to man, and those creatures that are immediately useful to him, but *to every beast of the field* (*v.* 11); for where God has given life he provides a livelihood.

II. He provides food convenient for them, both for man and beast: *He waters the hills from his chambers* (*v.* 13), from those chambers spoken of (*v.* 3), *the beams of which he lays in the waters,* those store-chambers, the clouds that distil fruitful showers. It is a satisfaction to the earth to bear the fruit of God's works for the benefit of man, for thus it answers the end of its creation.

1. For the cattle there is grass, and the beasts of prey, that live not on grass, feed on those that do; for man there is herb, *wine, and oil, and bread, v.* 15. We have a necessary dependence upon God for all the supports of this life. Let us also consider that we are in this respect fellow-commoners with the beasts; the same earth, the same spot of ground, that brings grass for the cattle, brings corn for man.

2. The divine providence not only furnishes animals with their proper food, but vegetables also with theirs (*v.* 16): *The trees of the Lord are full of sap,* not only men's trees, which they take care of and have an eye to, in their orchards, and parks, and other enclosures, but God's trees, which grow in the wildernesses, and are taken care of only by his providence: they *are full of sap* and want no nourishment. Even *the cedars of Lebanon* have enough from the earth; they are trees *which he has planted,* and which therefore he will protect and provide for. We may apply this to the trees of righteousness, which are the planting of the Lord, planted in his vineyard; these *are full of sap,* for what God plants he will water, and those that *are planted in the house of the Lord shall flourish in the courts of our God,* xcii. 13.

III. He takes care that they shall have suitable habitations to dwell in. To men God has given discretion to build for themselves and for the cattle that are serviceable to them; but there are some creatures which God more immediately provides a settlement for. 1. The birds. Some birds, by instinct, make their nests in the bushes near rivers (*v.* 12): *By the springs* that *run among the hills* some of the *fowls of heaven have their habitation, which sing among the branches.* They sing, according to their capacity, to the honour of their Creator and benefactor, and their singing may shame our silence. Our *heavenly Father feeds them* (Matt. vi. 26). Those that fly heavenward shall not want resting-places. *The stork* is particularly mentioned; *the fir-trees,* which are very high, *are her house,* her castle. 2. The smaller sorts of beasts (*v.* 18): *The wild goats* are guided by instinct to *the high hills,* which are a refuge to them; and *the rabbits,* which are also helpless animals, find shelter in *the rocks,* where they can set the beasts of prey at defiance. Does God provide thus for the inferior creatures; and will he not himself be a refuge and dwelling-place to his own people?

Verses 19–30

We are here taught to praise and magnify God,

I. For the constant revolutions and succession of day and night, and the dominion of sun and moon over them. The heathen worshipped them as deities; and therefore the scripture takes all occasions to show that the gods they worshipped are the creatures and servants of the true God (*v.* 19). 1. The shadows of the evening befriend the repose of the night (*v.* 20): *Thou makest darkness and it is night,* which, though black, contributes to the beauty of nature, and is as a foil to the light of the day; and under the protection of the night *all the beasts of the forest creep forth* to feed, which they are afraid to do in the day. 2. The light of the morning befriends the business of the day (*v.* 22, 23): *The sun arises* (for, as he *knows his going down,* so, thanks be to God, he knows his rising again), and then the wild beasts betake themselves to their rest. The beasts of prey creep forth with fear; man goes forth with boldness, as one that has dominion.

II. For the replenishing of the ocean (*v.* 25, 26): As *the earth is full of God's riches, so is this great and wide sea.* God has appointed it its place and made it serviceable to man both for navigation, and also to be his storehouse for fish. God made not the sea in vain, any more than the earth.

III. For the seasonable and plentiful provision which is made for all the creatures, *v.* 27, 28. God is a bountiful benefactor to them: He *gives them their meat*; he *opens his hand and they are filled with good.* Even the meanest creatures are not below his cognizance. They *all wait upon him.* They seek their food, according to the natural instinct God has put into them and in the proper season for it.

IV. For the absolute power and sovereign dominion which he has over all the creatures, by which every species is still continued, though the individuals of each are daily dying and dropping off. *Thou takest away their breath*, which is in thy hand, and then, and not till then, *they die and return to their dust*, to their first principles. The *spirit of the beast, which goes downward*, is at God's command, as well as *the spirit of a man, which goes upward.* Though one generation of them passes away, another comes, and from time to time they are created; new ones rise up instead of the old ones, and this is a continual creation. Thus the *face of the earth is renewed* from day to day by the light of the sun (which beautifies it anew every morning), from year to year by the products of it, which enrich it anew every spring and put quite another face upon it from what it had all winter.

In the midst of this discourse the psalmist breaks out into wonder at the works of God (*v.* 24): *O Lord! how manifold are thy works! in wisdom hast thou made them all.*

Verses 31–35

The psalmist concludes this meditation with:

I. Praise to God: *The glory of the Lord shall endure for ever, v.* 31. It shall endure to the end of time in his works of creation and providence; it shall endure to eternity in the felicity and adorations of saints and angels. Man's glory is fading; God's glory is everlasting. *The Lord shall rejoice in his works.* We often do that which, upon review, we cannot rejoice in, but are displeased at, and wish undone again. But God always *rejoices in his works*, because they are all done in wisdom. As a God of almighty power (*v.* 32): *He looks on the earth, and it trembles*, as unable to bear his frowns—trembles, as Sinai did, *at the presence of the Lord. He touches the hills, and they smoke.* The volcanoes, or burning mountains, such as Etna, are emblems of the power of God's wrath, fastening upon proud unhumbled sinners. *Who knows the power of his anger?* Who then dares set it at defiance? Because we have our being from God, and depend upon him for the support and continuance of it, as long as we live and have our being we must continue to praise God; and when we have no life, no being, on earth, we hope to have a better life and better being in a better world and there to be doing this work in a better manner and in better company.

II. Joy to himself (*v.* 34): *My meditation of him shall be sweet;* it shall be fixed and close; it shall be affecting and influencing; and therefore it shall be sweet. "*I will be glad in the Lord;* it shall be a pleasure to me to praise him; I will be glad of all opportunities to set forth his glory; and I will *rejoice in the Lord always* and in him only."

III. Terror to the wicked (*v.* 35): *Let the sinners be consumed out of the earth; and let the wicked be no more.* None can prosper that harden themselves against the Almighty. When *the wicked are no more* I hope to be praising God world without end; and therefore, *Praise you the Lord*; let all about me join with me in praising God. *Hallelujah;* sing praise to Jehovah. This is the first time that we meet with *Hallelujah.*

PSALM 105

This is a long psalm; the general scope is the same with most of the psalms, to set forth the glory of God, but the subject-matter is particular. Every time we come to the throne of grace we may, if we please, furnish ourselves out of the word of God with new songs. In the foregoing psalm we are taught to praise God for his wondrous works of common providence with reference to the world in general. In this we are directed to praise him for his special favours to his church. We find the first eleven verses of this psalm in the beginning of that psalm which David delivered to Asaph to be used (as it should seem) in the daily service of the sanctuary when the ark was fixed in the place he had prepared for it, 1 Chron. xvi. 7. David by it designed to instruct his people in the obligations they lay under to adhere faithfully to their holy religion. Here is the preface (ver. 1–7) and the history itself in several articles. I. God's covenant with the patriarchs, ver. 8–11. II. His care of them while they were strangers, ver. 12–15. III. His raising up Joseph to be the shepherd and stone of Israel, ver. 16–22. IV. The increase of Israel in Egypt and their deliverance out of Egypt, ver. 23–38. V. The care he took of them in the wilderness and their settlement in Canaan, ver. 39–45.

Verses 1–7

I. Give unto God the glory due unto his name. 1. We must *give thanks to him*, as one who has always been our bountiful benefactor. 2. *Call upon his name*, as one whom you depend upon for further favours. Praying for further mercies is an acknowledgement of former mercies. 3. *Make known his deeds* (*v.* 1), that others may join with you in praising him. *Talk of all his wondrous works* (*v.* 2), as we talk of things that we are full of. We should talk of them *as we sit in the house and as we go by the way* (Deut. vi. 7). 4. *Sing psalms to* God's honour, as those that rejoice in him, and desire to testify that joy and to transmit it to posterity, as memorable things anciently were handed down by songs, when writing was scarce. 5. *Glory in his holy name;* glory not of their own achievements, but of their acquaintance with God and their relation to him, Jer. ix. 23, 24. 6. *Seek him;* place your happiness in him, and then pursue that happiness. *Seek his strength*, that is, his grace, the strength of his Spirit to work in you that which is good, which we cannot do but by strength derived from him. "*Seek his face evermore.* Seek it while you live in this world, and you shall have it while you live in the other world, and even there shall be for ever seeking it in an infinite progression, and be ever satisfied." 7. *Let the hearts of those rejoice that do seek him* (*v.* 3); for they have chosen well. If those have reason to rejoice that *seek the Lord*, much more those that have *found him.*

II. Some arguments to quicken us to these duties. 1. "Consider both what he has said and what he has done to engage us for ever to him. Remember the wonders of his providence which he has *wrought for you* and those who are gone before you—the wonders of his law, which he has written to you, and entrusted you with, *the judgments of his mouth*, as well as the judgments of his hand," *v.* 5. 2. "Consider the relation you stand in to him (*v.* 6): *You are the seed of Abraham his servant; the children of Jacob his chosen, chosen* and *beloved* for the fathers' sake, and therefore ought to tread in the steps of those whose honours you inherit. You are the children of godly parents; do not degenerate. You are God's church upon earth, and, if you do not praise him, who should?"

Verses 8–24

We are here taught, in praising God, to look a great way back, and to give him the glory of what he did for his church in former ages, especially when it was in the founding and forming. We may fetch proper matter for praise from the histories of the gospels and the acts of the apostles, which relate the birth of the Christian church, as the psalmist here does from the histories of Genesis and Exodus, which relate the birth of the Jewish church.

I. God's promise to the patriarchs, that he would give to their seed the land of Canaan for an inheritance, was a type of the promise of eternal life made in Christ to all believers. In all the marvellous works which God did for Israel *he remembered his covenant* (v. 8) and he will remember it *for ever.* In the parallel place it is expressed as our duty (1 Chron. xvi. 15), *Be you mindful always of his covenant.* The promise is here called a *covenant,* because there was something required on man's part as the condition of the promise. See to whom God *swore by himself,* Heb. vi. 13, 14. The covenant itself: *Unto thee will I give the land of Canaan, v.* 11. The patriarchs had a right to it, not by providence, but by promise; and their seed should be put in possession of it, as *the lot of their inheritance,* a sure title, by virtue of their birth; it shall come to them by the favour of God, and not any merit of their own. Heaven is the inheritance we have obtained, Eph. i. 11. And *this is the promise which God has promised us* (as Canaan was the promise he promised them), *even eternal life,* 1 John ii. 25; Tit. i. 2.

II. His providences concerning the patriarchs while they were waiting for the accomplishment of this promise, which represent to us the care God takes of his people in this world, while they are yet on this side the heavenly Canaan; for these things *happened unto them for examples* and encouragements to all the heirs of promise, that live by faith as they did.

1. They were wonderfully protected and sheltered, and (as the Jewish masters express it) *gathered under the wings of the divine Majesty.* This is accounted for, *v.* 12–15. They were exposed to injuries from men. To the three renowned patriarchs, Abraham, and Isaac, and Jacob, God's promises were very rich; again and again he told them he would be their God. Even in this world he was not wanting to them, but that he might appear, to do uncommon things for them, he exercised them with uncommon trials. (1) They were few, very few. Abraham was called alone (Isa. li. 2). (2) They were strangers, and therefore were the most likely to be abused. Their religion made them to be looked upon as strangers (1 Pet. iv. 4) and to be hooted at as *speckled birds,* Jer. xii. 9. (3) They were unsettled (v. 13): *They went from one nation to another,* from one part of that land to another, *from one kingdom to another people,* from Canaan to Egypt, from Egypt to the land of the Philistines, forced to it by famine. They were guarded by the special providence of God, *v.* 14, 15. They were not able to help themselves and yet, (4) No men were suffered to wrong them, but even those that hated them, had their hands tied, and could not do what they would. This may refer to Gen. xxxv. 5, where we find that *the terror of God was upon the cities that were round about them,* so that, though provoked, *they did not pursue after the sons of Jacob.* (5) Even crowned heads, that did offer to wrong them, were controlled and baffled. *He reproved kings for their sakes* in dreams and visions, saying, "*Touch not my anointed; do my prophets no harm.*" Pharaoh king of Egypt was plagued (Gen. xii. 17) and Abimelech king of Gerar was sharply rebuked (Gen. xx. 6) for doing wrong to Abraham.

2. They were wonderfully provided for and supplied. To try the faith of the patriarchs, God *broke the whole staff of bread,* even in that good land. God graciously took care for their relief. It was in obedience to his precept, and in dependence upon his promise, that they were now sojourners in Canaan, and therefore he could not in honour suffer any good thing to be wanting to them. As he restrained one Pharaoh from doing them wrong, so he raised up another to do them a kindness, by preferring and entrusting Joseph, of whose story we have here an abstract. Many years before the famine began, he

was sent before them, to nourish them in the famine. He went not so much as a factor or commissary; but *he was sold* thither *for a servant,* a slave for term of life, without any prospect of being ever set at liberty. And yet he was brought lower; he was made a prisoner (v. 18): *His feet they hurt with fetters.* Being unjustly charged with a rape upon his mistress, *the iron entered into his soul,* that is, was very painful to him; yet all this was the way to his preferment. He continued a prisoner, neither tried nor bailed, *until the time* appointed of God for his release (v. 19), when *his word came,* that is, his interpretations of dreams came to pass, and the report thereof came to Pharaoh's ears by the chief butler. And then *the word of the Lord cleared him*; that is, the power God gave him to foretell things to come rolled away the reproach his mistress had loaded him with; for it could not be thought that God would give such a power to so bad a man as he was represented to be. *God's word tried him,* tried his faith and patience, and then it came in power to give command for his release. There is a time set when God's word will come for the comfort of all that trust in it, Hab. ii. 3. *At the end it shall speak, and not lie.* God gave the word, and then *the king sent and loosed him.* Pharaoh, finding him to be a favourite of Heaven, *let him go free.* He advanced him to the highest posts of honour, *v.* 21, 22, lord high chamberlain of his household. He made him prime minister of state. In all this Joseph was designed to save the house of Israel from perishing by the famine. Joseph being thus sent before, and put into a capacity of maintaining all his father's house, *Israel also came into Egypt* (v. 23), where he and all his were comfortably provided for many years.

3. They were wonderfully multiplied, according to the promise made to Abraham that his seed should be as the sand of the sea for multitude, *v.* 24.

Verses 25–45

After the history of the patriarchs follows the history of the people of Israel, when they grew into a nation.

I. Their affliction in Egypt (v. 25): *He turned* the *heart* of the Egyptians, who had protected them, *to hate* them and *deal subtilely* with them. God's goodness to his people exasperated the Egyptians against them. They *dealt subtilely* with them, to find out ways and means to weaken them and prevent their growth; they made their burdens heavy and their lives bitter, and slew their male children as soon as they were born.

II. Their deliverance out of Egypt, that it might never be forgotten, is put into the preface to the ten commandments.

1. The instruments employed in that deliverance (v. 26): *He sent Moses his servant* on this errand and joined Aaron in commission with him. Moses was designed to be their lawgiver and chief magistrate, Aaron to be their chief priest.

2. The means of accomplishing that deliverance; these were the plagues of Egypt. *They showed the words of his signs* (so it is in the original), for every plague had an exposition going along with it; they spoke loud. They are all or most of them here specified, though not in the order in which they were inflicted. (1) The plague of darkness, *v.* 28. This was one of the last, though here mentioned first. *They were not obedient to his word,* which may be applied to Pharaoh and the Egyptians, who, notwithstanding the terror of this plague, *would not let the people go.* (2) The turning of the river Nilus (which they idolized) *into blood,* which *slew their fish* (v. 29), Num. xi. 5. (3) The frogs, shoals of which their land brought forth. (4) Flies of divers sorts swarmed in their air, and lice in their clothes, *v.* 31; Exod. viii.

17, 24. (5) Hail-stones shattered their trees, even the strongest timber-trees in *their coasts*, and killed their vines, and their other fruit-trees, *v.* 32, 33; Exod. ix. 23. (6) *Locusts and caterpillars* destroyed *all the* herbs which were made for the service of man and ate the bread out of their mouths, *v.* 34, 35. (7) Having mentioned all the plagues but those of the murrain and boils, he concludes with that which gave the conquering stroke, and that was the death of *the first-born, v.* 36.

3. The mercies that accompanied this deliverance. They had been impoverished, and yet they came out rich and wealthy. God not only brought them forth, but he *brought them forth with silver and gold, v.* 37. Their lives had been made bitter to them, and their bodies and spirits broken by their bondage; and yet, when God brought them forth, *there was not one feeble person*, none sick, none so much as sickly, *among their tribes*. They had been trampled upon and insulted over; and yet they were brought out with honour (*v.* 38). They had spent their days in sorrow and in sighing, by reason of their bondage; but now he brought them forth *with joy and gladness, v.* 43.

4. The special care God took of them in the wilderness. He *spread a cloud for a covering* (*v.* 39), which was to them not only a screen and umbrella, but a cloth of state. A cloud was often God's pavilion (xviii. 11) and now it was Israel's. He appointed a pillar of *fire to give light in the night*. He fed them both with necessaries and dainties (*v.* 40). *He opened the rock, and the waters gushed out, v.* 41.

5. Their entrance, at length, into Canaan (*v.* 44): *He gave them the lands of the heathen.*

6. The reasons why God did all this for them. (1) Because he would himself perform the promises of the world, *v.* 42. *Because he remembered the word of his holiness* (that is, his covenant) *with Abraham his servant*, he would not suffer one iota or tittle of that to fall to the ground. See Deut. vii. 8. (2) Because he would have them to perform the precepts of the word, to bind them to which was the greatest kindness he could put upon them. God having thus done them good, they might the more cheerfully receive his law, designed for their good, and might be sensible of their obligations in gratitude to live in obedience to him. We are *therefore* made, maintained, and redeemed, that we may live in obedience to the will of God; and the hallelujah with which the psalm concludes may be taken as a thankful acknowledgment of God's favours.

PSALM 106

We must give glory to God by making confession, not only of his goodness but our own badness. The foregoing psalm was a history of God's goodness to Israel; this is a history of their rebellions and provocations, and yet it begins and ends with Hallelujah; for even sorrow for sin must not put us out of tune for praising God. In this psalm we have, I. The preface to the narrative, speaking honour to God (ver. 1, 2), comfort to the saints (ver. 3), and the desire of the faithful towards God's favour, ver. 4, 5. II. The narrative itself of the sins of Israel, aggravated by the great things God did for them, an account of which is intermixed. Their provocations at the Red Sea (ver. 6–12), lusting (ver. 13–15), mutinying (ver. 16–18), worshipping the golden calf (ver. 19–23), murmuring (ver. 24–27), joining themselves to Baal-peor (ver. 28–31), quarrelling with Moses (ver. 32, 33), incorporating themselves with the nations of Canaan, ver. 34–39. To this is added an account how God had rebuked them for their sins, and yet saved them from ruin, ver. 40–46. III. The conclusion of the psalm with prayer and praise, ver. 47, 48.

Verses 1–5

I. Bless God (*v.* 1, 2). Give him thanks for his goodness. Give him the glory of his greatness, his *mighty acts*. When we have said the most we can of the mighty acts of the Lord, the one half is not told.

II. Bless the people of God, account them happy (*v.* 3). God's people are those whose principles are sound—*They keep judgment; they do righteousness,*

are just to God and to all men, and herein they are steady and constant.

III. Bless ourselves in the favour of God, place our happiness in it, and seek it, accordingly, with all seriousness, *v.* 4, 5.   As there are a people in the world who are in a peculiar manner God's people, so there is a peculiar favour which God bears to that people, which all gracious souls desire an interest in. *O visit me with thy salvation*. That salvation be my portion for ever (*v.* 5): "*That I may see the good of thy chosen* and be as happy as the saints are; and happier I do not desire to be."

Verses 6–12

A penitential confession of sin, which was in a special manner seasonable now that the church was in distress; thus we must justify God in all that he brings upon us, acknowledging that *therefore* he has done right, because *we have done wickedly*.

I. God's afflicted people here own themselves guilty before God (*v.* 6): "*We have sinned with our fathers. We have committed iniquity*, that which is in its own nature sinful, and we have sinned with a high hand presumptuously."

II. They bewail the sins of their fathers when they were first formed into a people.

1. The strange stupidity of Israel in the midst of the favours God bestowed upon them (*v.* 7): *They understood not thy wonders in Egypt*. They thought the plagues of Egypt were intended for their deliverance, whereas they were intended also for their instruction and conviction, not only to force them out of their Egyptian slavery, but to cure them of their inclination to Egyptian idolatry. We lose the benefit of providences for want of understanding them. And, as their understandings were dull, so their memories were treacherous; *they remembered not the multitude of* God's *mercies* in them.

2. Their perverseness arising from this stupidity: *They provoked him at the sea, even at the Red Sea*. The provocation was, despair of deliverance and wishing they had been left in Egypt still, Exod. xiv. 11, 12. They reproach him, as if all that power had no mercy in it, but he had brought them out of Egypt on purpose to *kill them in the wilderness*.

3. The great salvation God wrought for them notwithstanding their provocations, *v.* 8–11. He forced a passage for them through the sea. He interposed between them and their pursuers, and prevented them from cutting them off, as they designed. The Red Sea, which was a lane to them, was a grave to the Egyptians (*v.* 11) (Exod. xiv. 30). Though they did not deserve this favour, he designed it; and their undeservings should not alter his designs, nor make him withdraw his promise, or fail in the performance of it. Moses prays (Num. xiv. 17, 19), *Let the power of my Lord be great and pardon the iniquity of this people*. The power of the God of grace in pardoning sin and sparing sinners is as much to be admired as the power of the God of nature in dividing the waters.

4. The good impression this made upon them for the present (*v.* 12): *Then believed they his words*, and acknowledged that God was with them of a truth, and had, in mercy to them, brought them out of Egypt, and not with any design to slay them in the wilderness. Then *they sang his praise*, in that song of Moses penned on this great occasion, Exod. xv. 1.

Verses 13–33

This is an abridgment of the history of Israel's provocations in the wilderness, and this abridgment is abridged by the apostle, with application to us Christians (1 Cor. x. 5, &c.).

I. The cause of their sin was disregard to the works and word of God, *v.* 13. 1. They minded not what he had done for them: *They soon forgot his works. They made haste;* their expectations anticipated God's promises; they expected to be in Canaan shortly, and because they were not they questioned whether they should ever be there. Again (*v.* 21, 22): *They forgot God their Saviour.* Those that forget the works of God forget God himself, who makes himself known by his works. 2. They minded not what God had said to them nor would they depend upon it: *They waited not for his counsel.* They had not patience to tarry God's time. The difficulties were looked upon as insuperable.

II. Many of their sins are here mentioned, together with the tokens of God's displeasure which they fell under for those sins.

1. They would have flesh, and yet would not believe that God would give it to them (*v.* 14). They were also, in all probability, within a step of Canaan, yet had not patience to stay for dainties till they came thither. Now how did God show his displeasure against them for this. We are told how (*v.* 15): *He gave them their request,* but gave it them in anger, and with a curse, for he *sent leanness into their soul*; he filled them with uneasiness of mind, and terror of conscience, and a self-reproach. Or this is put for that great plague with which the Lord smote them, *while the flesh was yet between their teeth,* as we read, Num. xi. 33.

2. They quarrelled with the government which God had set over them both in church and state (*v.* 16): *They envied Moses* his authority *in the camp,* as generalissimo and chief justice; they envied *Aaron* his power, as *saint of the Lord,* consecrated to the office of high priest, and Korah would needs put in for the pontificate, while Dathan and Abiram, as princes of the tribe of Reuben, Jacob's eldest son, would claim to be chief magistrates. How did God show his displeasure for this? We are told how (*v.* 17, 18); we have the story, Num. xvi. 32, 35. Those that flew in the face of the civil authority were punished by *the earth,* which *opened and swallowed them up.* Those that would usurp the ecclesiastical authority in things pertaining to God suffered the vengeance of heaven, and the pretending sacrificers were themselves sacrificed to divine justice.

3. They made and worshipped the golden calf, and this in Horeb, where the law was given, and where God had expressly said, *Thou shalt* neither *make any graven image* nor *bow down* to it; they did both: *They made a calf and worshipped it, v.* 19. Herein they put an affront upon the two great lights which God has made to rule the moral world: That of human reason; for *they changed their glory,* their God, *into the similitude* of Apis, one of the Egyptian idols, *an ox that eateth grass,* than which nothing could be more grossly and scandalously absurd, *v.* 20. That of divine revelation, which was afforded to them, not only in the words God spoke to them, but in the works he wrought for them, *v.* 21, 22. For this God showed his displeasure by declaring the decree that he would cut them off from being a people, as they had, as far as lay in their power, in effect cut him off from being a God; he *spoke of destroying them* (*v.* 23), and certainly he would have done it if *Moses, his chosen, had not stood before him in the breach* (*v.* 23). See the power of prayer, and the interest which God's chosen have in heaven. See a type of Christ, God's *chosen,* his elect, *in whom his soul delights,* who *stood before him in the breach* to *turn away* his wrath from a provoking world, and ever lives, for this end, making intercession.

4. They gave credit to the report of the evil spies concerning the land of Canaan, in contradiction to the promise of God (*v.* 24), and therefore were for making a captain and returning to Egypt again, basely charging God with a design upon them in bringing them thither that they might become a prey to the Canaanites, Num. xiv. 2, 3. And, when they were reminded of God's power and promise, they were so far from hearkening to that voice of the Lord that they attempted to stone those who spoke to them, Num. xiv. 10. This also was displeasing to God, for he swore in his wrath that they should not enter into his rest (xcv. 11; Num. xiv. 28); and he threatened that their children also should be *overthrown and scattered* (*v.* 26, 27), and the whole nation dispersed; but Moses prevailed for mercy for their seed, that they might enter Canaan.

5. They were guilty of a great sin in the matter of Peor; and this was the sin of the new generation, when they were within a step of Canaan (*v.* 28): *They joined themselves to Baal-peor,* and so were entangled both in idolatry and in adultery, in corporeal and in spiritual whoredom, Num. xxv. 1–3. Those that did often partake of the altar of the living God now *ate the sacrifices of the dead,* of the idols of Moab (that were dead images, or dead men canonized or deified), or sacrifices to the infernal deities on the behalf of their dead friends. *Thus they provoked God to anger with their inventions* (*v.* 29). A plague among them, in a little time swept away 24,000 of those impudent sinners. God stirred up Phinehas to use his power as a magistrate for the suppressing of the sin and checking the contagion of it. He stood up in his zeal for the Lord of hosts, and executed judgment upon Zimri and Cozbi, a service so pleasing to God that upon it *the plague was stayed, v.* 30. But, Phinehas herein signalizing himself, a special mark of honour was put upon him, for what he did was *counted to him for righteousness to all generations* (*v.* 31).

6. Their continued murmurings to the very last of their wanderings; for in the fortieth year they *angered God at the waters of strife* (*v.* 32), which refers to that story, Num. xx. 3–5. *It went ill with Moses for their sakes;* for, though he was the meekest of all the men in the earth, yet their clamours at that time were so peevish and provoking that they put him into a passion, and, having now grown very old and off his guard, *he spoke unadvisedly with his lips* (*v.* 33). For he said in a heat, *Hear now, you rebels, must we fetch water out of this rock for you?* God shows his displeasure against this sin of theirs by shutting Moses and Aaron out of Canaan for their misconduct upon this occasion. If he deals thus severely with Moses for one unadvised word, what does their sin deserve who have spoken so many presumptuous wicked words? God deprived them of the blessing of Moses's guidance and government at a time when they most needed it, so that his death was more a punishment to them than to himself.

Verses 34–48

I. The narrative concludes with an account of Israel's conduct in Canaan, which was of a piece with that in the wilderness, and God's dealings with them, wherein, as all along, both justice and mercy appeared.

1. They were very provoking to God. By the time they were just settled in Canaan they corrupted themselves, and forsook God. They spared the nations which God had doomed to destruction (*v.* 34). They promised themselves that, notwithstanding this, they would not join in any dangerous affinity with them. The next news we hear is, They were *mingled among the heathen,* made leagues with them and contracted an intimacy with them, so that they *learned their works, v.* 35. They thought they would never join with them in their worship; but by degrees they learned that too (*v.* 36). That sin drew on many more, and brought the judgments of God upon them. When

they joined with them in some of their idolatrous services, they little thought that ever they should be guilty of that barbarous and inhuman piece of idolatry the sacrificing of their living children to their dead gods; but they came to that at last (*v.* 37, 38). *They sacrificed their sons and daughters*, pieces of themselves, to devils, and added the most unnatural murder to their idolatry. They *shed innocent blood*, the most innocent, for it was infant-blood, nay, it was the *blood of their sons and daughters*. Their sin was, in part, their own punishment; for by it *The land was polluted with blood*, *v.* 38. They wronged their consciences (*v.* 39), and so debauched their own minds, and were rendered odious in the eyes of the holy God.

2. God brought his judgments upon them; and what else could be expected? He was angry with them, for from them he took it as more ungrateful than from the heathen that never knew him. *He abhorred his own inheritance.* This is the worst thing in sin, that it makes us loathsome to God; and the nearer any are to God in profession the more loathsome are they if they rebel against him, like a dunghill at our door. Their enemies then fell upon them, and their defence having departed, made an easy prey of them (*v.* 41, 42): *He gave them into the hands of the heathen.* The punishment answered to the sin. They *mingled with the heathen and learned their works;* and therefore God justly made use of them as the instruments of their correction. The heathen hated them. Apostates lose all the love on God's side, and get none on Satan's; and when those that *hated them ruled over them,* no marvel that they oppressed them. When God granted them some relief, yet they went on in their sins, and their troubles also were continued, *v.* 43. This refers to the days of the Judges, when God often raised up deliverers and wrought deliverances for them, and yet they relapsed to idolatry. Those that will not by repentance humble themselves, are justly debased. At length they cried unto God, and God returned in favour to them, *v.* 44–46. They were chastened for their sins, but not destroyed, cast down, but not cast off. God *heard their cry* with tender compassion (Exod. iii. 7) and overlooked their provocations. Though he is not a *man that he should repent,* so as to change his mind, yet he is a gracious God, who pities us, and changes his way. Bad as they were, he would not break with them, because he would not break his own promise. He not only restrained the remainder of their enemies' wrath, but he infused compassion even into their stony hearts, and made them relent, which was more than any art of man could have done.

II. The psalm concludes with prayer and praise. 1. Prayer for the completing of his people's deliverance. Many who were forced into foreign countries, in the times of the Judges (as Naomi was, Ruth i. 1), had not returned in the beginning of David's reign, and therefore it was seasonable to pray, Lord, gather the dispersed Israelites *from among the heathen, to give thanks to thy holy name,* in the Lord's house, from which they were now banished. 2. Praise for the beginning and progress of it (*v.* 48): *Blessed be the Lord God of Israel from everlasting to everlasting.* Let the priests say this, and then *let all the people say, Amen, Hallelujah.*

Psalm 107

The psalmist here observes some of the instances of his providential care of the children of men in general, especially in their distresses; for he is the God of the whole earth, and a common Father to all mankind. There were those who pertained not to the commonwealth of Israel and yet were worshippers of the true God; and even those who worshipped images had some knowledge of a supreme "Numen", to whom, when they were in earnest, they looked above all their false gods. And of these, when they prayed in their distresses, God took a particular care. I. The psalmist specifies some of the most common calamities of human life, and shows how God succours those that labour under them, in

answer to their prayers. 1. Banishment and dispersion, ver. 2–9. 2. Captivity and imprisonment, ver. 10–16. 3. Sickness and distemper of body, ver. 17–22. 4. Danger and distress at sea, ver. 23–32. II. He specifies events concerning nations and families, in which God's hand is to be eyed by his own people, with joyful acknowledgments of his goodness, ver. 33–43.

Verses 1–9

I. A general call to all to give thanks to God, *v.* 1.

II. A particular demand hereof from *the redeemed of the Lord,* which may well be applied spiritually to the *children of God that were scattered abroad,* whom Christ died to *gather together in one,* out of all lands, John xi. 52; Matt. xxiv. 31. But it seems here to be meant of a temporal deliverance, wrought for them when *they cried unto the Lord, v.* 6. 1. They were in an enemy's country, but God wrought out their rescue: *He redeemed them from the hand of the enemy* (*v.* 2), it may be *by the Spirit of God* working on the spirits of men. 2. They were dispersed as outcasts, but God gathered them out of all the countries whither they were scattered, *v.* 3. God knows those that are his, and where to find them. 3. They were bewildered, had no road to travel in, no dwelling place to rest in, *v.* 4. *They wandered in the wilderness.* But *God led them forth by the right way* (*v.* 7), directed them *that they might go to a city of habitation,* which they themselves should inhabit. This may refer to poor travellers in general, those particularly whose way lay through the wilds of Arabia, where they were often at a loss. Or it has an eye to the wanderings of the children of Israel in the wilderness for forty years. 4. They were ready to perish for hunger (*v.* 5). Israel's wants were seasonably supplied. The same God that has led us has fed us all our life long unto this day. Now for all this those who receive mercy are called upon to return thanks (*v.* 8): *Oh that men* (it is meant especially of those men whom God has graciously relieved) *would praise the Lord for his goodness* to them in particular, *and for his wonderful works to* others of *the children of men!*

Verses 10–16

The goodness of God towards prisoners and captives. Prisoners are said to *sit in darkness* (*v.* 10), desolate and disconsolate; they sit *in the shadow of death,* which intimates great danger. They are *bound in affliction, and* many times *in iron, because they rebelled against the words of God. They contemned the counsel of the Most High,* and thought they neither needed it nor could be the better for it; and those that will not be counselled cannot be helped. For this they are bound in affliction. The design of this affliction is to bring *down their heart* (*v.* 12), to humble them for sin. The duty of this afflicted state is to pray (*v.* 13). Prisoners have time to pray, who, when they were at liberty, could not find time; they see they have need of God's help, though formerly they thought they could do well enough without him. *They cried unto the Lord, and he saved them, v.* 13. *He brought them out of darkness into light,* and their liberty was to them life from the dead, *v.* 14. Were they *fettered?* He broke their bands asunder. Were they imprisoned in strong castles? *He broke the gates of brass* and the *bars of iron* wherewith those gates were made fast; he did not put back, but *cut in sunder.*

Verses 17–22

Bodily sickness is another of the calamities of this life which gives us an opportunity of experiencing the goodness of God.

I. If we knew no sin, we should know no sickness. Sinners are fools; they wrong themselves, and all against their own interest, not only their spiritual, but their secular interest. They prejudice their bodily health by intemperance and endanger their lives by indulging their appetites. Those that dote most on the meat that perishes, when they come to be sick are sick of it, and the dainties they love are loathed. And when the appetite is gone the life is as good as gone: *Then they cry unto the Lord*, v. 19. Is any sick? Let him pray; let him be prayed for. Prayer is a salve for every sore.

II. It is by the power and mercy of God that we are recovered from sickness, and then it is our duty to be thankful. *He sent his word and healed them*, v. 20. This may be applied to the miraculous cures which Christ wrought when he was upon earth; he said, *Be clean, Be whole*, and the work was done. It may also be applied to the spiritual cures which the Spirit of grace works in regeneration; he sends his word, and heals souls. In the common instances of recovery from sickness God in his providence does but speak, and it is done. When those that have been sick are restored they must return to God an answer of praise (v. 21, 22): *Let all men praise the Lord for his goodness*, and let those, particularly, to whom God has thus granted a new life, spend it in his service; *let them sacrifice with thanksgiving*, not only bring a thank-offering to the altar, but a thankful heart to God.

Verses 23–32

The psalmist here calls upon those to give glory to God who are delivered from dangers at sea. Though the Israelites dealt not much in merchandise, yet their neighbours the Tyrians and Zidonians did, and for them perhaps this part of the psalm was especially calculated.

I. The power of God appears at all times in the sea, v. 23, 24. It appears to those *that go down to the sea in ships*, as mariners, merchants, fishermen, or passengers, *that do business in great waters. These see the works of the Lord, and his wonders*. The deep itself is a wonder, its vastness, its saltness, its ebbing and flowing. The great variety of living creatures in the sea is wonderful. Let those that go to sea be led, by all the wonders they observe there, to consider and adore the infinite perfections of that God whose the sea is, for he made it and manages it.

II. It especially appears in storms at sea. *Then* wonders begin to appear in the deep, when God *commands and raises the* strong *wind*, which *fulfils his word*, cxlviii. 8. A stranger, who had never seen it, would not think it possible for a ship to live at sea, as it will in a storm, and ride it out, and yet God taught man to make ships that should so strangely keep above water. When the storm is very high, even those that are used to the sea can neither shake off nor dissemble their fears, but are quite *at their wits' end* (v. 27), not knowing what to do more for their preservation. Those that go to sea must expect such perils and the best preparation for them is liberty of access to God by prayer. We have a saying, "Let those that would learn to pray go to sea"; I say, Let those that will go to sea learn to pray. Those that have the Lord for their God have a present help in every time of need, so that when they are at their wits' end they are not at their faith's end. God sometimes appears for those that are in distress at sea, in answer to their prayers: *He brings them out* of the danger. *He makes the storm a calm*, v. 29. The seamen are made easy. The voyage becomes prosperous and successful: *So he brings them to their desired haven*, v. 30. Thus he carries his people safely through all the storms and tempests that they meet with in their voyage heaven-ward, and lands them, at length, in the desired harbour.

Verses 33–43

The psalmist, having given God the glory of the providential reliefs granted to persons in distress, here gives him the glory of the revolutions of providence, and the surprising changes it sometimes makes in the affairs of the children of men.

I. He gives some instances of these revolutions.

1. Fruitful countries are made barren and barren countries are made fruitful. Much of the comfort of this life depends upon the soil in which our lot is cast. The sin of man has often marred the fruitfulness of the soil, v. 33, 34. The goodness of God has often mended the barrenness of the soil, and turned a *wilderness*, a land of drought, *into water-springs*, v. 35.

2. Necessitous families are raised and enriched, while prosperous families are impoverished and go to decay. We see many greatly increasing whose beginning was small, v. 36–38. Those that were *hungry* are made to *dwell* in fruitful lands; there they take root, and gain a settlement. Providence puts good land under their hands, and they build upon it. But lodgings, though ever so convenient, will not serve without lands, and therefore they must *sow the fields, and plant vineyards* (v. 37). Man's industry must attend God's blessing, and then God's blessing will crown man's industry. The fruitfulness of the soil should engage, for it does encourage, diligence; and, ordinarily, *the hand of the diligent*, by the blessing of God, *makes rich*, v. 38. We see many that have suddenly risen as suddenly sunk and brought to nothing (v. 39) by adverse providences, and end their days as low as they began them; or their families after them lose as fast as they got, and scatter what they heaped together. Those that were high and great in the world are abased, and those that were mean and despicable are advanced to honour, v. 40, 41. Those that exalt themselves God will abase. He makes *them to wander in the wilderness, where there is no way*. Those that were afflicted and trampled on are not only delivered, but set on high out of the reach of their troubles. God is to be acknowledged both in setting up families and in building them up. Let not princes be envied, nor the poor despised, for God has many ways of changing the condition of both.

II. Such surprising turns as these are of use, 1. For the solacing of saints. They observe these dispensations with pleasure (v. 42). It is a great comfort to a good man to see how God manages the children of men, as the potter does the clay, to see despised virtue advanced and impious pride brought low, to see it evinced that *verily there is a God that judges in the earth*. 2. For the silencing of sinners. When sinners see how their punishment answers to their sin, and how justly God deals with them in taking away from them those gifts of his which they had abused, they shall not have one word to say for themselves. 3. For the satisfying of all concerning the divine goodness (v. 43): *Whoso is wise, and will observe these things*, these various dispensations of divine providence, *even they shall understand the lovingkindness of the Lord*. A prudent observance of the providences of God will contribute very much to the accomplishing of a good Christian.

PSALM 108

This psalm begins with praise and concludes with prayer, and faith is at work in both. I. David here gives thanks to God for mercies to himself, ver. 1–5. II. He prays to God for mercies for the land, ver. 6–13. The former part is taken out of Ps. lvii. 7, &c., the latter out of Ps. lx. 5, &c. It intimates likewise that it is not only allowable, but sometimes convenient, to gather some verses out of one psalm and some out of another, and to put them together, to be sung to the glory of God.

A song or psalm of David.

Verses 1–5

We may here learn how to praise God from the example of one who was master of the art. 1. We must praise God with fixedness of heart. Wandering straggling thoughts must be gathered in, and kept close to the business. 2. We must praise God with freeness of expression: I will praise him *with my glory*, that is, with my tongue. Our tongue is our glory, and never more so than when it is employed in praising God. David's skill in music was his glory, it made him famous, and this should be consecrated to the praise of God. Whatever gift we excel in we must praise God with. 3. We must praise God with affection, and must stir up ourselves that it may be done in a lively manner and not carelessly (v. 2): *Awake, psaltery and harp;* let it not be done with a dull and sleepy tune, but let the airs be all lively. Warm devotions honour God. 4. We must praise God publicly, as those that are not ashamed to own our obligations to him. 5. We must, in our praises, magnify the mercy and truth of God (v. 4). We cannot see further than the heavens and clouds; whatever we see of God's mercy and truth there is still more to be seen, more reserved to be seen, in the other world.

Verses 6–13

We must be public-spirited in prayer, and bear upon our hearts the concerns of the church of God, v. 6. It is God's *beloved*, and therefore must be ours; and therefore we must pray for its deliverance. An active faith can rejoice in what God has said, though it be not yet done; for with him saying and doing are not two things, whatever they are with us. God had promised David to give him the hearts of his subjects; and therefore he surveys the several parts of the country as his own already: "*Shechem* and *Succoth, Gilead* and *Manassah, Ephraim* and *Judah*, are all my own," v. 8. He will, without fail, give him the heathen for his *inheritance and the utmost parts of the earth for his possessions*. David looks upon *Moab*, and *Edom*, and *Philistia*, as his own already (v. 9). We must take encouragement from the beginnings of mercy to pray and hope for the perfecting of it (v. 10, 11): "*Who will bring me into the strong cities that are yet unconquered? Who will make me master of the country of Edom, which is yet unsubdued?*" The question was probably to be debated in a council of war, what methods they should take to subdue the Edomites; but he brings it into his prayers, *Wilt not thou, O God?* We must not be discouraged in prayer, nor beaten off from our hold of God, though Providence has in some instances frowned upon us. We must seek help from God, renouncing all confidence in the creature (v. 12). *Vain is the help of man.* "It is really so, and therefore we are undone if thou do not help us; we apprehend it to be so, and therefore depend upon thee for help and have the more reason to expect it." We must do our part, but we can do nothing of ourselves; it is only *through God that we shall do valiantly*.

Psalm 109

Whether David penned this psalm when he was persecuted by Saul, or when his son Absalom rebelled against him, or upon occasion of some other trouble is uncertain; but the imprecation (ver. 8) is applied to Judas, Acts i. 20. The rest of the prayers here against his enemies were the expressions, not of passion, but of the Spirit of prophecy. I. He lodges a complaint of the malice of his enemies and with it an appeal to the righteous God, ver. 1–5. II. He prays against his enemies, ver. 6–20. III. He prays for himself, that God would help him in his low condition, ver. 21–29. IV. He concludes with a joyful expectation that God would appear for him, ver. 30, 31.

To the chief Musician. A psalm of David.

Verses 1–5

It is the unspeakable comfort of all good people that, whoever is against them, God is for them.

I. David refers himself to God's judgment (v. 1): "*Hold not thy peace,* but *let my sentence come forth from thy presence,* xvii. 2. Delay not to give judgment upon the appeal made to thee." The title he gives to

God is: "*O God of my praise!* the God in whom *I glory,* and not in any wisdom or strength of my own."

II. He complains of his enemies. They are *wicked*; they delight in doing mischief (v. 2); their words are *words of hatred*, v. 3. "They are *deceitful* in their protestations and professions of kindness, while at the same time they speak against me behind my back, *with a lying tongue.*" They were restless in their designs. They were unjust; their accusations of him, and sentence against him, were all groundless: "*They have fought against me without a cause;* I never gave them any provocation." They were very ungrateful, and *rewarded him evil for good,* v. 5. *For my love they are my adversaries.* The more he endeavoured to gratify them the more they hated him.

III. He resolves to keep close to his duty and take the comfort of that: *But I give myself unto prayer* (v. 4). When David's enemies falsely accused him, and misrepresented him, he applied to God and by prayer committed his cause to him. Though they were his adversaries for his love, yet he continued to pray for them; if others are abusive and injurious to us, yet let not us fail to do our duty to them, nor *sin against the Lord in ceasing to pray for them,* 1 Sam. xii. 23. Now herein David was a type of Christ, who was compassed about with *words of hatred,* and yet *gave himself to prayer*, to pray for them. *Father, forgive them.*

Verses 6–20

David here fastens upon one particular person worse than the rest of his enemies, and in a holy zeal for God and against sin and the enemies of Christ, particularly Judas who betrayed him, he imprecates and predicts his destruction, and such a one as our Saviour calls him, *A son of perdition.* Calvin speaks of it as a detestable piece of sacrilege, common in his time among Franciscan friars and other monks, that if anyone had malice against a neighbour he might hire some of them to curse him every day, which he would do in the words of these verses. Greater impiety can scarcely be imagined than to vent a devilish passion in the language of sacred writ.

I. The imprecations here are very terrible in full force against the implacable enemies and persecutors of God's church and people, that *will not repent, to give him glory.* It is here foretold concerning this bad man,

1. That he should be sentenced as a criminal (v. 6, 7): *Set thou a wicked man over him,* to be as cruel and oppressive to him as he has been to others. Set his own wicked heart over him, set his own conscience against him; let that fly in his face.

2. That, being condemned, he should be executed as a most notorious malefactor. He should lose his life, and the number of his months be cut off in the midst, by the sword of justice. Such bloody and *deceitful men shall not live out half their days*. Consequently all his places should be disposed of to others. His family should be beheaded and beggared, *his wife* should be made *a widow* and *his children fatherless*, by his untimely death, v. 9. They shall be *vagabonds and shall beg*, because they are conscious to themselves that all mankind have reason to hate them for their father's sake. His estate should be ruined, as the estates of malefactors are confiscated (v. 11). This wicked man having never shown mercy there shall *be none to extend mercy to him,* by *favouring his fatherless children* when he is gone, v. 12. The children of wicked parents often fare the worse for their parents' wickedness in this way that the bowels of men's compassion are shut up from them, which yet ought not to be, for why should children suffer for that which was not their fault, but their infelicity?

What hurries some to shameful deaths, and brings the families and estates of others to ruin, makes them and theirs despicable and odious, and entails poverty, and shame, and misery, upon their posterity. It is sin, that mischievous destructive thing.

II. The ground of these imprecations bespeaks them just, though they sound very severe. 1. To justify the imprecations of vengeance upon the sinner's posterity, the sin of his ancestors is here brought into the account (v. 14, 15), *the iniquity of his fathers* and *the sin of his mother*. All the innocent blood that had been shed upon the earth, from that of righteous Abel, was required from that persecuting generation, who, by putting Christ to death, *filled up the measure of their fathers*. 2. To justify the imprecations of vengeance upon the sinner himself, his own sin is here charged upon him, which called aloud for it. He had loved cruelty, persecuted the poor, whom he should have protected and relieved, and *slew the broken in heart*, whom he should have comforted and healed. Here is a barbarous man indeed, not fit to live. He had loved cursing, and therefore let the curse come upon his head, v. 17–19. Let God's cursing him be his shame, as his cursing his neighbour was his pride. This points at the utter ruin of Judas, and the spiritual judgments which fell on the Jews for crucifying Christ. The psalmist concludes his imprecations with a terrible *Amen*.

Verses 21–31

David takes God's comforts to himself, but in a very humble manner.

I. "*I am poor and needy*, and one that needs and craves thy help." He was troubled in mind (v. 22): *My heart is wounded within me*, not only broken with outward troubles, but wounded with a sense of guilt; and *a wounded spirit who can bear*? He was unsettled, *tossed up and down like the locust*, his mind unsteady, hunted like a partridge on the mountains. His body was wasted, and almost worn away (v. 24): *My knees are weak through fasting*, either forced fasting or voluntary fasting, when he chastened his soul. But it is better to have this leanness in the body, while the soul prospers and is in health, than, like Israel, to have leanness sent into the soul, while the body is feasted. In all this David was a type of Christ, who in his humiliation was thus weakened, thus reproached.

II. He prays for mercy for himself. "Lord, do for me what seems good in thy eyes. Do that which thou knowest will be for me, really for me, in the issue for me, though for the present it may seem to make against me." More particularly, he prays (v. 26): "*Help me, O Lord my God! O save me!* Save me from sin, help me to do my duty." He prays (v. 28), Though they *curse, bless thou*. If God bless us, we need not care who curses us.

III. He prays that his enemies might *be ashamed* (v. 28), *clothed with shame* (v. 29), that they might *cover themselves with their own confusion*, that they might be left to themselves, to do that which would expose them and *manifest their folly before all men*. In this he prays that they might be brought to repentance which is the chief thing we should beg of God for our enemies.

IV. He pleads God's glory, the honour of his name. "*Deliver me, because thy mercy is good;* let that be the measure, of my salvation." He concludes the psalm with joy, the joy of faith. He promises God that he will praise him (v. 30). He promises himself that he shall have cause to praise God (v. 31). God was David's protector in his sufferings, and was present also with the Lord Jesus in his, saved his soul from those that pretended to be the judges of it, and received it into his own hands.

PSALM 110

This psalm is pure gospel; concerning Christ, the Messiah promised to the fathers and expected by them. It is plain that the Jews of old, even the worst of them, so understood it; for when the Lord Jesus proposed a question to the Pharisees upon the first words of this psalm, where he takes it for granted that David, in spirit, calls Christ his Lord though he was his Son, they chose rather to say nothing, than to make it a question whether David does indeed speak of the Messiah or no; for they freely yield so plain a truth, though they foresee it will turn to their own disgrace, Matt. xxii. 41, &c. Christ, as our Redeemer, executes the office of a prophet, of a priest, and of a king, with reference both to his humiliation and his exaltation; and of each of these we have here an account. I. His prophetical office, ver. 2. II. His priestly office, ver. 4. III. His kingly office, ver. 1, 3, 5, 6. IV. His estates of humiliation and exaltation, ver. 7.

A psalm of David.

Verses 1–4

Some have called this psalm *David's creed*, almost all the articles of the Christian faith being found in it, the title calls it *David's psalm*, for in the believing foresight of the Messiah he both praised God and solaced himself. Much more may we, in singing it, to whom that is fulfilled, which is here foretold. Glorious things are here spoken of Christ.

I. He is David's Lord. We must take special notice of this because he himself does. Matt. xxii. 43, *David, in spirit, calls him Lord*.

II. He is constituted a sovereign Lord by the counsel and decree of God himself: *The Lord*, Jehovah, *said unto him, Sit* as a king. He *receives of the Father* this honour and glory (2 Pet. i. 17).

III. He was to be advanced to the highest honour, and entrusted with absolute sovereign power. *Sit thou at my right hand*. Sitting is a resting posture; after his services and sufferings, he entered into rest. It is a ruling posture; he sits to give law, to give judgment.

IV. All his enemies were in due time to be made his footstool. Even Christ himself has enemies that fight against his kingdom. There are those that will not have him to reign over them, and thereby they join themselves to Satan, who will not have him to reign at all. These enemies will *be made his footstool*. It will not be done immediately. This the apostle observes. Heb. ii. 8, *We see not yet all things put under him*. Christ himself shall wait till it is done.

V. He should have a kingdom set up in the world, beginning at Jerusalem (v. 2). The kingdom of Christ took rise from Zion, the city of David, for he was the Son of David, and was to have *the throne of his father David*. By the rod of his strength, or his strong rod, is meant his everlasting gospel, and the power of the Holy Ghost. This strong rod God sent forth; he poured out the Spirit, and gave both commissions and qualifications to those that preached the word, and *ministered the Spirit*, Gal. iii. 5. It was sent out of Zion, for there the Spirit was given, and there the preaching of the gospel among all nations must begin, at Jerusalem.

VI. That his kingdom, being set up, should be maintained and kept up in the world, in spite of all the opposition of the power of darkness. He shall rule *in the midst of his enemies*. He sits in heaven in the midst of his friends; he rules on earth in the midst of his enemies.

VII. He should have a great number of subjects, who should be to him for a name and a praise, v. 3.

1. They are given to him by the Father. *Thine they were and thou gavest them me*, John xvii. 6. They are redeemed by him, Tit. ii. 14. They are his by right, antecedent to their consent.

2. They should be *a willing people*, servants that choose their service, soldiers that are volunteers and not pressed men.

3. That they should be so *in the day of his power, in the day of thy muster. In the day of thy armies* (so some); "when the first preachers of the gospel shall be sent forth, as Christ's armies, then all that are *thy people shall be willing*; that will be thy time of setting up thy kingdom."

4. They should be so *in the beauty of holiness*; they shall be charmed into a subjection to Christ by the

sight given them of his beauty, who is the holy Jesus. They shall be admitted by him into the beauty of holiness, as spiritual priests, to minister in his sanctuary in the beautiful attire or ornaments of grace and sanctification. Holiness is the livery of Christ's family and that which *becomes his house for ever.* Christ's soldiers are all thus clothed; these are the colours they wear.

5. He should have great numbers of people devoted to him. In the early days of the gospel, in the morning of the New Testament, the youth of the church, great numbers flocked to Christ, and there were *multitudes that believed,* a *remnant of Jacob,* that was as a *dew from the Lord,* Mic. v. 7; Isa. lxiv. 4, 8. *The dew of the youth* is a numerous, illustrious, hopeful show of young people flocking to Christ, which would be to the world as dew to the ground, to make it fruitful.

6. He should be not only a king, but a priest, *v.* 4. Our Lord Jesus Christ is God's minister to us, and our advocate with God, and so is a Mediator between us and God. He is said to be *a priest for ever,* not only because we are never to expect any other dispensation of grace than this by the priesthood of Christ, but because the blessed fruits and consequences of it will remain to eternity. He is a priest, not of the order of Aaron, but of that of Melchizedek, which, as it was prior, so it was upon many accounts superior. The apostle comments largely upon these words (Heb. vii) and builds on them his discourse of Christ's priestly office, which he shows was no new notion, but built upon this most sure word of prophecy. For, as the New Testament explains the Old, so the Old Testament confirms the New, and Jesus Christ is the Alpha and Omega of both.

Verses 5–7

Here we have our great Redeemer.

I. Conquering his enemies (*v.* 5, 6): Our Lord Jesus will certainly bring to nought all the opposition made to his kingdom.

1. The conqueror: *The Lord—Adonai,* the Lord Jesus, he to whom all judgment is committed, he shall make his own part good against his enemies. Christ's sitting at the right hand of God speaks as much terror to his enemies as happiness to his people.

2. The time fixed for this victory: *In the day of his wrath,* that is, the time appointed for it, when the measure of their iniquities is full and they are ripe for ruin.

3. The extent of this victory. He *shall strike through kings.* Satan is the prince of this world, Death the king of terrors, and we read of kings that make war with the Lamb; but they shall all be brought down and broken. The trophies of Christ's victories will be set up *among the heathen,* and in many countries, wherever any of his enemies are.

4. The equity of this victory: *He shall judge among them.* It is not a military execution, which is done in fury, but a judicial one.

5. The effect of this victory; it shall be the complete and utter ruin of all his enemies. He shall *wound the heads,* which seems to refer to the first promise of the Messiah (Gen. iii. 15), that he should *bruise the serpent's head.* He shall *fill the places with the dead bodies.* The slain of the Lord shall be many.

II. We have here the Redeemer saving his friends and comforting them (*v.* 7). 1. He shall be humbled: *He shall drink of the brook in the way,* that bitter cup which the Father put into his hand. Christ drank of this brook when he was made a curse for us, and therefore, when he entered upon his suffering, he *went over the brook Kidron,* John xviii. 1. 2. He shall be exalted: *Therefore shall he lift up the head.* When he died he *bowed the head* (John xix. 30), but he soon lifted up the head by his own power in

his resurrection. He lifted up the head as a conqueror. Because he drank of the brook in the way therefore he lifted up his own head, and so lifted up the heads of all his faithful followers, who, *if they suffer with him, shall also reign with him.*

PSALM 111

This and divers of the psalms that follow it seem to have been penned by David for the service of the church in their solemn feasts. This is a psalm of praise. The title of it is "Hallelujah—Praise you the Lord", intimating that we must address ourselves to the use of this psalm with hearts disposed to praise God. It is composed alphabetically, each sentence beginning with a several letter of the Hebrew alphabet, in order exactly, two sentences to each verse, and three a piece to the last two. The psalmist, exhorting to praise God, I. Sets himself for an example, ver. 1. II. Furnishes us with matter for praise from the works of God. III. Recommends the holy fear of God, and a conscientious obedience to his commands, as the most acceptable way of praising God, ver. 10.

Verses 1–5

The title of the psalm being *Hallelujah,* the psalmist keeps to his text.

I. He resolves to praise God himself, *v.* 1. We must praise God both in private and in public, in less and greater assemblies, in our own families and in the courts of the Lord's house.

II. He recommends to us the *works of the Lord* as the proper subject of our meditations when we are praising him—the dispensations of his providence towards the world, towards the church, and towards particular persons. 1. God's works are great like himself; there is nothing in them that is mean or trifling: they are the products of infinite wisdom and power. 2. They are entertaining and exercising to the inquisitive—*sought out of all those that have pleasure therein.* Those that have pleasure in the works of God will not take up with a superficial transient view of them, but will diligently search into them and observe them. In studying both natural and political history we discover the greatness and glory of God's works. 3. They are all just and holy: *His righteousness endures for ever.* 4. They are memorable, fit to be registered and kept on record. Much that we do is so trifling that the greatest kindness is to forget it. But notice is to be taken of God's works, and an account to be kept of them (*v.* 4). *He has made his wonderful works to be remembered.* 5. In them the Lord shows that he is *gracious and full of compassion. He will be ever mindful of his covenant;* so that they can taste covenant-love even in common mercies. Some refer this to the manna with which God fed his people Israel in the wilderness.

Verses 6–10

Glory to God,

I. For the great things he has done for his people, for his people Israel, of old and of late: *He has shown his people the power of his works* (*v.* 6). 1. The possession God gave to Israel in the land of Canaan. This he did in Joshua's time, when the seven nations were subdued, and in Davids' time, when the neighbouring nations became tributaries to David. 2. The many deliverances which he wrought for his people when by their iniquities they had sold themselves into the hand of their enemies (*v.* 9). These redemptions were typical of the great redemption which in the fulness of time was to be wrought out by the Lord Jesus.

II. For the stability both of his word and of his works, which assure us of the great things he will do for them. 1. What God has done shall never be undone. He will not undo it himself, and men and devils cannot (*v.* 7): *The works of his hand are verity and judgment* (*v.* 8), that is, they *are done in truth and uprightness.* Upon the beginning of his works we may depend for the perfecting of them. 2. What

God has said shall never be unsaid: *All his commandments are sure,* all straight and therefore all steady.

III. For the setting up and establishing of religion among men. Because the discoveries of religion tend so much to his honour. Review what he has made known of himself in his word and in his works, and you will see, and say, that God is great. Because the dictates of religion tend so much to man's happiness. Reverence of him and obedience to him are as much our interest as they are our duty. Men can never begin to be wise till they begin to fear God; all true wisdom takes its rise from true religion, and has its foundation in it. *A good understanding have all those that do his commandments.* Where the fear of the Lord rules in the heart there will be a constant conscientious care to keep his commandments, not to talk of them, but to do them; and such have a good understanding. Their obedience is a plain indication of their mind that they do indeed fear God. We have reason to praise God, to praise him for ever, for putting man into such a fair way to happiness.

PSALM 112

This psalm is composed alphabetically, as the former is, and is (like the former) entitled "Hallelujah", though it treats of the happiness of the saints, because it redounds to the glory of God. It is a comment upon the last verse of the foregoing psalm, and shows how much it is our wisdom to fear God and do his commandments. I. The character of the righteous, ver. 1. II. The blessedness of the righteous. III. The misery of the wicked, ver. 10. So then good and evil are set before us, the blessing and the curse.

Verses 1–5

The psalmist begins with a call to us to praise God, but immediately applies himself to praise the people of God. We have reason to praise the Lord that there are a people in the world who fear him and serve him, and that they are a happy people, both which are owing entirely to the grace of God.

I. A description of those who are here pronounced blessed, and to whom these promises are made.

1. They are well-principled, well affected to his government, such as stand in awe of God and have a constant reverence for his majesty and deference to his will. He *that fears the Lord,* as a Father, with the disposition of a child, not of a slave, *delights greatly in his commandments.* They are written in his heart and he calls them an easy, a pleasant, yoke. He delights not only in God's promises, but in his precepts.

2. They are honest and sincere in their professions and intentions. They are called *the upright* (v. 2, 4), who are really as good as they seem to be, and deal faithfully both with God and man. There is no true religion without sincerity; that is gospel-perfection.

3. They are both just and kind in all their dealings. One instance is given of his beneficence (v. 5): He *shows favour and lends.* Sometimes there is as much charity in lending as in giving, as it obliges the borrower both to industry and honesty.

II. The blessedness that is here entailed upon those that answer to these characters. Happiness, all happiness, to *the man that feareth the Lord.*

1. The posterity of good men shall fare the better for his goodness (v. 2): *His seed shall be mighty on earth.* Religion has been the raising of many a family, if not so as to advance it high, yet so as to fix it firmly. When good men themselves are happy in heaven their seed perhaps are considerable on earth, and will themselves own that it is by virtue of a blessing descending from them. *The generation of the upright shall be blessed;* if they tread in their steps, they shall be the more blessed for their relation to them.

2. They shall prosper in the world, and especially their souls shall prosper, v. 3. They shall be blessed with outward prosperity as far as is good for them. But, which is much better, is that they shall be blessed with spiritual blessings, which are the true riches. Grace is better than gold, for it will outlast it. He shall have wealth and riches, and yet shall keep up his religion. When this endures in the family, and the heirs of the father's estate inherit his virtues too, that is a happy family indeed.

3. They shall have comfort in affliction (v. 4): *Unto the upright there arises light in the darkness.* They shall have their share in the common calamities of human life; but, *when they sit in darkness, the Lord shall be a light to them,* Mic. vii. 8.

4. They shall have wisdom for the management of all their concerns, v. 5. It is part of the character of a good man that he will use his discretion in managing his affairs, in getting and saving, that he may have to give.

Verses 6–10

I. The satisfaction of saints, and their stability. It is the happiness of a good man that *he shall not be moved for ever,* v. 6.

1. A good man will have a settled reputation. A good name with God and good people: *The righteous shall be in everlasting remembrance* (v. 6). There are those that do all they can to sully his reputation and to load him with reproach; but his integrity shall survive him. Some that have been eminently righteous are *had in a lasting remembrance* on earth; but in heaven their remembrance shall be truly everlasting. Those that are forgotten on earth, and despised, are remembered there, and honoured, and *their righteousness found unto praise, and honour, and glory* (1 Pet. i. 7). That which shall especially turn to the honour of good men is their liberality to the poor: *He has dispersed, he has given to the poor;* he has not suffered his charity to run all in one channel, or directed it to some few objects that he had a particular kindness for, but he has dispersed it.

2. A good man shall have a settled spirit, for *he shall not be afraid; his heart is established,* v. 7, 8. It is their endeavour to keep their minds stayed upon God, and so to keep them calm and God has promised them both cause to do so and grace to do so. The fixedness of the heart is a sovereign remedy against the disquieting fear of evil tidings. Trusting in the Lord is the best and surest way of fixing and establishing the heart. *He shall not be afraid, till he see his desire upon his enemies,* that is, till he come to heaven, where he shall see Satan, and all his spiritual enemies, trodden under his feet. *Till he look upon his oppressors,* look boldly in their faces, as being now no longer under their power.

II. The vexation of sinners, v. 10. Two things shall fret them:—1. The felicity of the righteous. It will vex them to see those whom they hated and despised, and whose ruin they sought and hoped to see, the favourites of Heaven, and advanced to have *dominion over them* (xlix. 14).

PSALM 113

This psalm begins and ends with "Hallelujah"; for, as many others, it is designed to promote the great and good work of praising God. I. We are urged to praise God, ver. 1–3. II. We are furnished with matter for praise. The elevations of his glory and greatness, ver. 4, 5. The condescensions of his grace and goodness (ver. 6–9), very much illustrate one another.

Verses 1–9

I. Glory to God,

1. The invitation is very pressing: *Praise you the Lord,* and again and again, *Praise him, praise him; blessed be his name,* for it is to be praised, v. 1–3.

2. The invitation is very extensive. God has praise —from his own people. They have most reason to praise him. The angels are the servants of the Lord; they praise God, and praise him better than we can.

Let God be praised through all the generations of time. *Blessed be his name now and always. From the rising of the sun to the going down of the same,* that is, throughout the habitable world. It ought to be praised by all nations; for in every place, from east to west, there appear the manifest proofs and products of his wisdom, power, and goodness.

II. We are here directed what to give him the glory of. Let us look up with an eye of faith, and see how high his glory is in the upper world, and mention that to his praise, *v.* 4, 5. Put all the nations together, and he is above them all; they are before him as the *drop of the bucket and the small dust of the balance,* Isa. xl. 15, 17. The throne of his glory is in the highest heavens. *His glory is above the heavens,* that is, above the angels; he is above what they are—above what they do, for they are under his command—and above what even they can speak him to be. He is a God *who exalts himself to dwell, who humbles himself, in heaven, and in earth.* God is said to *exalt himself* and to *humble himself,* both are his own act and deed. God's condescending goodness appears in the cognizance he takes of the world below him. His glory is *above the nations* and *above the heavens,* and yet neither is neglected by him. *God is great,* yet *he despises not any,* Job xxxvi. 5. *He humbles himself to behold* all his creatures. Considering the infinite perfection, sufficiency, and felicity of the divine nature, it must be acknowledged as an act of wonderful condescension that God is pleased to take into the thoughts of his eternal counsel, and into the hand of his universal Providence, both the armies of heaven and the inhabitants of the earth (Dan. iv. 35); even in this dominion he humbles himself. If it be such condescension for God to behold things in heaven and earth, what an amazing condescension was it for the Son of God to come from heaven to earth and take our nature upon him, that he might *seek and save those that were lost*! He not only beholds the great things in the earth, but the meanest, and does wonders for them, out of the common road of providence and chain of causes, which shows that the world is governed, not by a course of nature, for that would always run in the same channel, but by a God of nature, who delights in doing things we looked not for. Sometimes, on a sudden (*v.* 7, 8): *He raises up the poor out of the dust, that he may set him with princes.* Gideon is fetched from threshing, Saul from seeking the asses, and David from keeping the sheep; the apostles are sent from fishing to be *fishers of men.* The treasure of the gospel is put into earthen vessels, and the weak and foolish ones of the world are pitched upon to be preachers of it, to confound the *wise and mighty* (1 Cor. i. 27, 28), that the excellency of the power may be of God. When Joseph's virtue was tried and manifested he was raised from the prison-dust and *set with princes.* Those that have been long barren are sometimes, on a sudden, made fruitful, *v.* 9. This may look back to Sarah and Rebecca, Rachel, Hannah, and Samson's mother, or forward to Elizabeth; and many such instances there have been, in which God has looked on the affliction of his handmaids and taken away their reproach. *He makes the barren woman to keep house,* not only builds up the family, but thereby finds the heads of the family something to do.

PSALM 114

The deliverance of Israel out of Egypt gave birth to their church and nation. In this psalm it is celebrated in lively strains of praise; it was fitly therefore made a part of the great Hallelujah, or song of praise, which the Jews were wont to sing at the close of the passover-supper. It must never be forgotten, I. That they were brought out of slavery, ver. 1. II. That God set up his tabernacle among them, ver. 2. III. That the sea and Jordan were divided before them, ver. 3, 5. IV. That the earth shook at the giving of the law, when God came down on Mount Sinai, ver. 4, 6, 7. V. That God gave them water out of the rock, ver. 8.

Verses 1–8

The psalmist is here remembering *the days of old,* and the wonders which their fathers told them of (Judges vi. 13), for time, as it does not wear out the guilt of sin, so it should not wear out the sense of mercy.

I. God brought Israel out of the house of bondage with a high hand and a stretched-out arm: *Israel went out of Egypt, v.* 1. They did not steal out clandestinely, but marched out with all the marks of honour.

II. God himself framed their civil and sacred constitution (*v.* 2): *Judah and Israel were his sanctuary, his dominion.* When he delivered them out of the hand of their oppressors it was *that they might serve him* in the duties of religious worship and in obedience to the moral law. He set up his sanctuary among them, in which he gave them the special tokens of his presence with them and promised to receive their homage and tribute. He was himself their lawgiver and their judge, and their government was a theocracy: *The Lord was their King.*

III. The Red Sea was divided before them at their coming out of Egypt, both for their rescue and the ruin of their enemies; and the river Jordan, when they entered into Canaan (*v.* 3). The psalmist asks, in a poetical strain (*v.* 5), *What ailed thee, O thou sea! that thou fleddest?* And furnishes the sea with an answer (*v.* 7); it was *at the presence of the Lord.* This is designed to express that it was not from any natural cause, but it was *at the presence of the Lord,* who gave the word. Israel are taught to triumph over the sea, and Jordan. There is no sea, no Jordan, so deep, so broad, but, when God's time shall come for the redemption of his people, it shall be divided and driven back if it stand in their way. Apply this, (1) To the planting of the Christian church in the world. What ailed Satan and the powers of darkness, that they trembled and truckled as they did? Mark i. 34. What ailed the heathen oracles, that they were silenced, struck dead? What ailed their idolatries, and witchcrafts, that they died away before the gospel. What ailed the persecutors and opposers of the gospel, that they gave up their cause, and called to rocks and mountains for shelter? It was *at the presence of the Lord,* and that power which went along with the gospel. (2.) To the work of grace in the heart. What turns the stream in a regenerate soul? What ails the lusts and corruptions, that they fly back, that the prejudices are removed and the whole man has become new? It is at the presence of God's Spirit that imaginations are *cast down,* 2 Cor. x. 5.

IV. The earth shook and trembled when God came down on Mount Sinai to give the law (*v.* 4): *The mountains skipped like rams, and* then *the little hills* might well be excused if they skipped *like lambs,* either when they are frightened or when they sport themselves.

V. God supplied them with water out of the rock, which followed them through the dry and sandy deserts. The same almighty power that turned waters into a rock to be a wall to Israel (Exod. xiv. 22) turned the rock into waters to be a well to Israel: as they were protected, so they were provided for, by miracles; for such was the standing water, that fountain of waters into which the rock, the flinty rock, was turned, *and that rock was Christ,* 1 Cor. x. 4.

PSALM 115

Many ancient translations join this psalm to that which goes next before it, the Septuagint particularly, and the vulgar Latin; but it is, in the Hebrew, a distinct psalm. In it we are taught to give glory, I. To God, and not to ourselves, ver. 1. II. To God, and not to idols, ver. 2–8. We must give glory to God, 1. By trusting in him, and in his promise and blessing, ver. 9–15. 2. By blessing him, ver. 16–18.

Verses 1–8

I. Boasting is here for ever excluded, *v.* 1. Let no opinion of our own merits have any room either in our prayers or in our praises, but let both centre in God's glory. All the good we do is done by the power of his grace, and all the good we have is the gift of his mere mercy, and therefore he must have all the praise. All our songs must be sung to this humble tune, *Not unto us, O Lord!* and again, *Not unto us, but to thy name,* let all the glory be given. This must be our highest and ultimate end in our prayers, and therefore it is made the first petition in the Lord's prayer, as that which guides all the rest, *Hallowed be thy name;* and, in order to that, *Give us our daily bread,* &c.

II. The reproach of the heathen is here for ever silenced.

1. The psalmist complains of the reproach of the heathen (*v.* 2): *Wherefore should they say, Where is now their God?* Do they not know that our God is everywhere by his providence and always nigh to us by his promise and grace?

2. He gives a direct answer to their question, *v.* 3. "Do they ask where is our God? *Our God is in the heavens,* where the gods of the heathen never were, *in the heavens,* and therefore out of sight; but, though his majesty be unapproachable, it does not therefore follow that his being is questionable. In the lower world are the products of his power. Do you ask where he is? He is at the beginning and end of everything, *and not far from any of us.*

3. He returns their question upon themselves. He does in effect ask, What are the gods of the heathen? He shows that their gods, though they are not shapeless things, are senseless things. Idolaters, at first, worshipped the sun and moon (Job xxxi. 26), which was bad enough, but not so bad as that which they were now come to, which was the worshipping of images, *v.* 4. The matter of them was *silver and gold,* dug out of the earth (*man found them poor and dirty in a mine*), proper things to make money of, but not to make gods of. The make of them was from the artificer; they are creatures of men's vain imaginations and *the works of men's hands,* and therefore can have no divinity in them. *The workmen made it, therefore it is not God,* Hos. viii. 6. These idols are represented here as the most ridiculous things, a mere jest, fitter for a toy-shop than a temple, for children to play with than for men to pray to. The painter, the carver, the statuary, did their part well enough; they made them with *mouths* and *eyes, ears* and *noses, hands* and *feet,* but they could put no life into them and therefore no sense. They had better have worshipped a dead carcase (for that had life in it once) than a dead image, which neither has life nor can have. *They speak not,* in answer to those that consult them; the crafty priest must speak for them. In Baal's image there was *no voice, neither any that answered. They see not* the prostrations of their worshippers before them, much less their burdens and wants. *They hear not* their prayers, though ever so loud; *they smell not* their incense, though ever so strong, ever so sweet; *they handle not* the gifts presented to them, much less have they any gifts to bestow on their worshippers; they cannot *stretch forth their hands to the needy. They walk not,* they cannot stir a step for the relief of those that apply to them. Nay, they do not so much as *breathe through their throat;* they have not the least sign or symptom of life. He thence infers the sottishness of their worshippers (*v.* 8): *Those that make them* images show their ingenuity, and doubtless are sensible men; *but those that make them* gods show their stupidity and folly. *They see not* the invisible things of the true and living God in the works of creation; *they hear not* the voice of the day and the night, which in every speech and language declare

his glory, xix. 2, 3. By worshipping these foolish puppets, they make themselves more and more foolish like them, and set themselves at a greater distance from everything that is spiritual, sinking themselves deeper into the mire of sense.

Verses 9–18

I. We are earnestly exhorted, all of us, to repose our confidence in God, and not suffer our confidence in him to be shaken by the heathens' insulting over us upon the account of our present distresses. It is folly to trust in dead images, but it is wisdom to trust in the living God, for he is a *help and a shield* to those that do *trust in them.* Therefore, let Israel trust in the Lord; the body of the people, as to their public interests, and every particular Israelite, as to his own private concerns. Let the priests, the Lord's ministers, and all the families of the *house of Aaron, trust in the Lord* (*v.* 10). They ought to be examples to others of a cheerful confidence in God in the worst of times. Let the proselytes, who are not of the seed of Israel, but *fear the Lord,* who worship him and make conscience of their duty to him, let them *trust in him,* for he will not fail nor forsake them, *v.* 11.

II. We are greatly encouraged to trust in God. *The Lord has been mindful of us.* All our comforts are derived from God's *thoughts to us-ward; he has been mindful of us,* though we have forgotten him. From what he has done for us we may infer, *He will bless us;* he that has been our *help and our shield* will be so; so that we have reason to hope that he who has delivered, and does, will yet deliver. *He will bless us;* he has promised that he will. God's blessing us is not only speaking good to us, but doing well for us. Nay (*v.* 13), *he will bless those that fear the Lord,* though they be not of the house of Israel or the house of Aaron; for it was a truth, before Peter perceived it, *That in every nation he that fears God is accepted of him,* and blessed, Acts x. 34, 35. Both the weak in grace and the strong shall be blessed of God, the lambs and the sheep of his flock. It is promised (*v.* 14), *The Lord shall increase you,* especially increase in spiritual blessings, with the increasings of God. He will bless you with the increase of knowledge and wisdom, of grace, holiness and joy. "*He shall increase you more and more;* so that, as long as you live, you shall be still increasing, till you come to perfection, as the shining light," Prov. iv. 18. "*You and your children;* you in your children." For (*v.* 15), *You are blessed of the Lord,* you and your children are so; *all that see them shall acknowledge them, that they are the seed which the Lord has blessed,* Isa. lxi. 9.

III. We are stirred up to praise God by the psalmist's example, who concludes with a resolution to persevere in his praises. God is to be praised, *v.* 16. See how stately his palace is, and the throne he has prepared in the heavens: *The heaven, even the heavens are the Lord's. The earth he has given to the children of men,* having designed it, when he made it, for their use, to find them meat, drink, and lodging. The dead are not capable of praising him (*v.* 17), nor *any that go into silence.* The soul indeed lives in a state of separation from the body and is capable of praising God; and *the souls of the faithful, after they are delivered from the burdens of the flesh,* do praise God, are still praising him; for they go up to the land of perfect light and constant business. Therefore it concerns us to praise him (*v.* 18): *But we,* we that are alive, *will bless the Lord from this time forth* and to eternity. *Hallelujah.*

PSALM 116

This is a thanksgiving psalm. I. The great distress and danger that the psalmist was in, which almost drove him to despair, ver. 3, 10, 11. II. The application he made to God in that distress, ver. 4. III. The experience he had of God's goodness to him, in answer to prayer; God heard him (ver. 1, 2), pitied him (ver. 5, 6), delivered him, ver. 8. IV. His care respecting the acknowledgments he should make of the goodness of God to him, ver. 12. 1. He will love God, ver. 1. 2. He will continue to call upon him, ver. 2, 13, 17. 3. He will rest in him, ver. 7. 4. He will walk before him, ver. 9. 5. He will pay his vows of thanksgiving, in which he will own the tender regard God had to him, and this publicly, ver. 13–15, 17–19. Lastly, He will continue God's faithful servant to his life's end, ver. 16. These are such breathings of a holy soul as bespeak it very happy.

Verses 1–9

I. A general account of David's experience, and his pious resolutions (*v.* 1, 2), which are as the contents of the whole psalm, and give an idea of it. He had experienced God's goodness to him in answer to prayer. *He has inclined his ear to me.* It is wonderful condescension in God to hear prayer; it is bowing his ear. He begins the psalm somewhat abruptly with a profession of that which his heart was full of: *I love the Lord* (as xviii. 1); and fitly does he begin with this, in compliance with the first and great commandment. *Therefore I will call upon him.* Why should we glean in any other field when we have been so well treated in this? Nay, *I will call upon him as long as I live* (Heb., *In my days*), every day, to the last day.

II. A more particular narrative of God's gracious dealings with him. Let us review David's experiences. He was in great distress and trouble (*v.* 3): *The sorrows of death compassed me,* that is, such sorrows as were likely to be his death. Perhaps the extremity of bodily pain, or trouble of mind, is called here *the pains of hell.* In his trouble he had recourse to God by faithful and fervent prayer, *v.* 4. He tells us that he prayed: *Then called I upon the name of the Lord.* He tells us what his prayer was; it was short, but to the purpose: "*O Lord! I beseech thee, deliver my soul;* save me from death, and save me from sin, for that is it that is killing to the soul." He found by experience that God is gracious and merciful, and in his compassion *preserves the simple, v.* 6. Because they are simple (that is, sincere, and upright, and without guile) therefore God preserves them, as he preserved Paul, who had his conversation in the world *not with fleshly wisdom, but in simplicity and godly sincerity.* Let David speak his own experience. "*I was brought low,* was plunged into the depth of misery, and then *he helped me,* helped me both to bear the worst and to hope the best, helped me to pray, else desire had failed, helped me to wait, else faith had failed. I was one of the simple ones whom God preserved, the poor man who *cried and the Lord heard him*", xxxiv. 6. God graciously delivered, *First,* His *soul from death.* It is God's great mercy to us that we are alive; and the mercy is the more sensible if we have been at death's door and yet have been spared and raised up. The deliverance of the soul from spiritual death is especially to be acknowledged by all those who are now sanctified and shall be shortly glorified. *Secondly,* His *eyes from tears,* that is, his heart from inordinate grief. *Thirdly,* His *feet from falling,* from falling into sin and so into misery. God had done all this for him, and therefore he will live a life of delight in God (*v.* 7): *Return unto thy rest, O my soul!* God has dealt kindly with thee, and therefore thou needest not fear that ever he will deal hardly with thee. God is the soul's rest; in him only it can *dwell at ease;* to him therefore it must retire, and rejoice in him. Return to that rest which Christ gives to *the weary and heavy-laden,* Matt. xi. 28. He will live a life of devotedness to God (*v.* 9): *I will walk before the Lord in the land of the living,* that is, in this world, as long as I continue to live in it. The *land of the living* is a land of mercy, which we ought to be thankful for; it is a land of opportunity, which we should improve.

Verses 10–19

The Septuagint and some other ancient versions make these verses a distinct psalm separate from the former; and some have called it the *Martyr's psalm,* for the sake of *v.* 15. Three things David here makes confession of:—

I. His faith (*v.* 10): *I believed, therefore have I spoken.* This is quoted by the apostle (2 Cor. iv. 13) with application to himself and his fellow-ministers, who, though they suffered for Christ, were not ashamed to own him. David believed the being, providence, and promise of God, particularly the assurance God had given him by Samuel that he should exchange his crook for a sceptre: a great deal of hardship he went through in the belief of this, and therefore he spoke, spoke to God by prayer (*v.* 4), by praise, *v.* 12.

II. His fear (*v.* 11): *I was greatly afflicted,* and then *I said in my haste*—in my *amazement* (so some)—*in my flight* (so others), when Saul was in pursuit of me, *All men are liars,* all with whom he had to do, Saul and all his courtiers; his friends, who he thought would stand by him, deserted him and disowned him when he fell into disgrace at court. What we speak amiss, in haste, we must by repentance unsay again (as David, xxxi. 22), and then it shall not be laid to our charge.

III. His gratitude, *v.* 12, &c. God had been better to him than his fears, and had graciously delivered him out of his distresses. *What shall I render unto the Lord for all his benefits towards me?* Here he speaks, sensible of many mercies received from God—*all his benefits.* Not as if he thought he could render anything proportionable, for what he had received; but he desired to render something acceptable, as the acknowledgment of a grateful mind. He will in the most devout and solemn manner offer up his praises and prayers to God, *v.* 13, 17. "*I will take the cup of salvation,* that is, I will offer the drink-offerings appointed by the law, in token of my thankfulness to God, and rejoice with my friends in God's goodness to me"; this is called *the cup of deliverance* because drunk in memory of the deliverance. "God, having bestowed so many benefits upon me, whatever cup he shall put into my hands I will readily take it, and not dispute it; but welcome his holy will." David spoke the language of the Son of David. John xviii. 11, *The cup that my Father has given me, shall I not* take it and *drink it?* We must first *give our own selves* to God as *living sacrifices* (Rom. xii. 1, 2 Cor. viii. 5), and then lay out of what we have for his honour in works of piety and charity. Why should we offer that to God which costs us nothing? He will always entertain thoughts of God, as very tender of the lives and comforts of his people (*v.* 15): *Precious in the sight of the Lord is the death of his saints,* so precious that he will not gratify any of David's enemies, with his death. This truth David had comforted himself with in the depth of his distress and danger; and, the event having confirmed it, he comforts others with it. Having asked, *What shall I render?* here he surrenders himself, which was *more than all burnt-offerings and sacrifices* (*v.* 16): *O Lord! truly I am thy servant.* I choose to be so; I resolve to be so; I will live and die in thy service. He had called God's people, who are dear to him, *his saints;* but, when he comes to apply it to himself, he does not say, *Truly I am thy saint,* but, *I am thy servant.* David was a king, and yet he glories in this, that he was God's servant. Two ways men came to be servants:—*First,* By birth. "Lord, I was born in thy house; I am *the son of thy handmaid,* and therefore thine." It is a great mercy to be the children of godly parents, as it obliges us to duty and is pleadable with God for mercy. *Secondly,* By redemption. He that procured the release of a captive took him for his servant. *"Lord, thou hast loosed my bonds; and therefore I am thy servant*, and entitled to thy protection as well as obliged to thy work." *The very bonds which thou hast loosed shall tie me faster unto thee.* He will make conscience of paying his vows and making good what he had promised. Vows are debts that must be paid, for it is better not to vow than to vow and not pay. He will pay his vows in the courts of the tabernacle, *in the midst of Jerusalem* that he might bring devotion into more reputation.

PSALM 117

This psalm is short and sweet; I doubt the reason why we sing it so often as we do is for the shortness of it; but, if we rightly understood and considered it, we should sing it oftener for the sweetness of it. Here is, I. A solemn call to all nations to praise God, ver. 1. II. Proper matter for that praise suggested, ver. 2.

Verses 1-2

There is a great deal of gospel in this psalm. The apostle has furnished us with a key to it (Rom. xv. 11), where he quotes it as a proof that the gospel was to be preached to the Gentile nations, which yet was so great a stumbling-block to the Jews. Why should that offend them when it is said, and they themselves had often sung it, *Praise the Lord, all you Gentiles, and laud him, all you people.* Some of the Jewish writers confess that this psalm refers to the kingdom of the Messiah; nay, one of them has a fancy that it consists of two verses to signify that in the days of the Messiah God should be glorified by two sorts of people, by the Jews, according to the law of Moses, and by the Gentiles, according to the seven precepts of the sons of Noah, which yet should make one church, as these two verses make one psalm.

I. The vast extent of the gospel church, *v.* 1. Here *all nations* are called to praise the Lord, which could not be applied to the Old Testament times, because, unless the people of the land became Jews and were circumcised, they were not admitted to praise God with them. But the gospel of Christ is ordered to be preached to all nations, and by him the partition-wall is taken down, and those that were *afar off* are *made nigh.* Who should be admitted into the church? *All nations* and *all people.* The original words are the same that are used for the *heathen that rage* and *the people that imagine* against Christ (ii. 1); those that had been enemies to his kingdom should become his willing subjects. The gospel of the kingdom was to be preached *to all the world, for a witness to all nations*, Matt. xxiv. 14; Mark xvi. 15. The tidings of the gospel, being sent to all nations, should give them cause to praise God; the institution of gospel-ordinances would give them opportunity to praise God; and the power of gospel-grace would give them hearts to praise him.

II. The unsearchable riches of gospel-grace, which are to be the matter of our praise, *v.* 2. In the gospel those celebrated attributes of God, his mercy and his truth, shine most brightly in themselves and most comfortably to us. Things for which the Gentiles should glorify God (Rom. xv. 8, 9), for *the truth of God* and for *his mercy.* God's mercy is the fountain of all our comforts and his truth the foundation of all our hopes, and therefore for both we must praise the Lord.

PSALM 118

It is probable that David penned this psalm when he had, after many a storm, weathered his point at last, and gained a full possession of the kingdom to which he had been anointed. He then invites his friends to join with him in a believing expectation of the promised Messiah, of whose kingdom and his exaltation to it his were typical. To him, it is certain, the prophet here bears witness, in the latter part of the psalm. Christ himself applies it to himself (Matt. xxi. 42), and the former part of the psalm may fairly, and without forcing, be accommodated to him and his undertaking. Some think it was first calculated for the solemnity of the bringing of the ark to the city of David, and was afterwards sung at the feast of tabernacles. In it, I. David calls upon all about him to give to God the glory of his goodness, ver. 1-4. II. He encourages himself and others to trust in God, from the experience he had had of God's power and pity, ver. 5-18. III. He gives thanks for his advancement to the throne, as it was a figure of the exaltation of Christ, ver. 19-23. IV. The people, the priests, and the psalmist himself, triumph in the prospect of the Redeemer's kingdom, ver. 24-29.

Verses 1-18

It appears here, as often elsewhere, that David had his heart full of the goodness of God.

I. He celebrates God's mercy in general, and calls upon others to acknowledge it, from their own experience of it (*v.* 1). Priests and people, Jews and proselytes, must all own God's goodness, and all join in the same thankful song; if they can say no more, let them say this for him, that *his mercy endures for ever*, that they have had experience of it all their days.

II. He preserves an account of God's gracious dealings with him in particular. David had, in his time, waded through a great deal of difficulty, which gave him great experience of God's goodness. There are many who, when they are lifted up, care not for speaking of their former depressions; but David takes all occasions to remember his own low estate. He was *in distress* (*v.* 5), there were many that *hated him* (*v.* 7), and this could not but be a great grief to one of an ingenuous spirit, that strove to gain the good affections of all. *All nations compassed me about, v.* 10. All the nations adjacent to Israel set themselves to give disturbance to David, when he had newly come to the throne, Philistines, Moabites, Syrians, Ammonites, &c. They were confederate against him. They were virulent and violent, and, for a time, prevalent, in their attempts against him. *They compassed me about like bees*, came upon him in swarms, set upon him with their malignant stings; but it was to their own destruction, as the bee, they say, loses her life with her sting. Two ways David was brought into trouble:—(1) By the injuries that men did him (*v.* 13): *Thou* (O enemy!) *hast thrust sore at me. Thrusting thou hast thrust at me* (so the word is), so that I was *ready to fall.* (2) By the afflictions which God laid upon him (*v.* 18): *The Lord has chastened me sore.* Men thrust at him for his destruction; God chastened him for his instruction. They thrust at him with the malice of enemies; God chastened him with the love and tenderness of a Father. God heard his prayer (*v.* 5): "*He answered me* with enlargements; he did more for me than I was able to ask; he enlarged my heart in prayer and yet gave more largely than I desired." God baffled the designs of his enemies against him: They are *quenched as the fire of thorns* (*v.* 12), which burns furiously for a while, makes a great noise and a great blaze, but is presently out, and cannot do the mischief that it threatened. God preserved his life when there was but a step between him and death (*v.* 18): "He has *chastened me*, but he has not *given me over unto death*, for he has not given me over to the will of my enemies." From his own experience he can say, *It is better*, there is more reason *to trust in the Lord, than to put confidence in man*, yea, though it be *in princes*, *v.* 8, 9. It enabled him to triumph in that trust. *The Lord is on my side.* If we are on God's side, he is on ours; if we be for him and with him, he will be for us and with us (*v.* 7): "*The Lord takes my part, and stands up for me, with those that help me.* If God be our strength, he must be our song; if he work all our works in us, he must have all praise and glory from us. If he be our strength and our song, he has become not only our Saviour, but our salvation.

He triumphs in an assurance of the continuance of his comfort, his victory, and his life. *First,* Of his comfort (*v.* 15): *The voice of rejoicing and salvation is in the tabernacles of the righteous,* and in mine particularly, in my family. The dwellings of the righteous in this world are but tabernacles, mean and movable; here we have no city, *no continuing city.* But these tabernacles are more comfortable to them than the palaces of the wicked are to them; for in the house where religion rules, 1. There is salvation. 2. Where there is salvation there is cause for rejoicing, for continual joy in God. 3. Where there is rejoicing there ought to be *the voice* of rejoicing, that is, praise and thanksgiving. *Secondly,* Of his victory: *The right hand of the Lord does valiantly* (*v.* 15) and *is exalted;* for (as some read it) *it has exalted me.* *Thirdly,* Of his life (*v.* 17): "*I shall not die* by the hands of my enemies that seek my life, *but live and declare the works of the Lord;* I shall live a monument of God's mercy and power; his works shall be declared in me, and I will make it the business of my life to praise and magnify God, looking upon that as the end of my preservation."

Verses 19–29

An illustrious prophecy of the humiliation and exaltation of our Lord Jesus, his sufferings, and the glory that should follow. Peter thus applies it directly to the chief priests and scribes, and none of them could charge him with misapplying it, Acts iv. 11.

I. The preface with which this precious prophecy is introduced, *v.* 19–21. 1. The psalmist desires admission into the sanctuary of God, there to celebrate the glory of him *that cometh in the name of the Lord: Open to me the gates of righteousness.* So the temple gates are called. And when the gates of righteousness are opened to us we must *go into them,* must enter into the holiest, as far as we have leave, *and praise the Lord* (*v.* 20): *This is the gate of the Lord,* the gate of his appointing, *into which the righteous shall enter.* Some by this gate understand Christ, by whom we are taken into fellowship with God and our praises are accepted; he is *the way;* there is no coming to the Father but by him (John xiv. 6). The psalmist triumphs in the discovery that the gate of righteousness, which had been so long shut, and so long knocked at, was now at length opened. 3. He promises to give thanks to God for this favour (*v.* 21): *I will praise thee.* Those that saw Christ's day at so great a distance saw cause to praise God for the prospect; for in him they saw that God had heard them, had heard the prayers of the Old Testament saints for the coming of the Messiah, and would be their salvation.

II. The prophecy itself, *v.* 22, 23. This may have some reference to David's preferment; he was the stone which Saul and his courtiers rejected, but was by the wonderful providence of God advanced to be the headstone of the building. But its principal reference is to Christ; and here we have, 1. His humiliation. He is *the stone which the builders refused;* he is the *stone cut out of the mountain without hands,* Dan. ii. 34. This stone was *rejected by the builders,* by the rulers and people of the Jews (Acts iv. 8, 10, 11); they refused to own him as the Messiah. They *denied him in the presence of Pilate* (Acts iii. 13) when they said, *We have no king but Cæsar.* 2. His exaltation. He *has become the headstone of the corner;* he is advanced to the highest degree both of honour and usefulness, to be above all, and all in all. He is the chief-corner-stone in the foundation, in whom Jew and Gentile are united, that they may be built up one holy house. He is the chief top-stone in the corner, in whom the building is completed, and who must in all things have the pre-eminence, as the *author and finisher of our faith.* 3. The hand of

God in all this: His hand went with him throughout his whole undertaking, and from first to last he did his Father's will; and this ought to be *marvellous in our eyes.* Christ's name is *Wonderful;* and the redemption he wrought out is the most amazing of all God's works of wonder.

III. The joy wherewith it is entertained and the acclamations which attend this prediction.

1. Let the day be solemnized to the honour of God with great joy (*v.* 24): *This is the day the Lord has made.* Or it may very fitly be understood of the Christian sabbath, which we sanctify in remembrance of Christ's resurrection, when the rejected stone began to be exalted. Here is the doctrine of the Christian sabbath: *It is the day which the Lord has made,* has made remarkable, made holy, has distinguished from other days; he has made it for man. *We will rejoice and be glad in it,* not only in the institution of the day, but in the occasion of it, Christ's becoming the *head of the corner.* Sabbath days must be rejoicing days.

2. Let the exalted Redeemer be met, and attended, with joyful hosannas, *v.* 25, 26. This is like *Vivat rex —Long live the king,* and expresses a hearty joy for his accession to the crown. *Hosanna* signifies, *Save now, I beseech thee.* "Lord, save me, I beseech thee; let this Saviour be my Saviour, and, in order to that, my ruler; let me be taken under his protection and owned as one of his willing subjects. Let me have victory over those lusts *that war against my soul,* and let divine grace go on in my heart *conquering and to conquer.*" "Lord, preserve even the Saviour himself. Let his name be sanctified, his *kingdom come,* his *will be done.*" Thus *let prayer be made for him continually,* lxxii. 15. On the Lord's day, when we rejoice in his kingdom, we must pray for the advancement of it more and more. Let the priests, the Lord's ministers, do their part in this great solemnity, *v.* 26. Let them bless the prince with their praises: *Blessed is he that cometh in the name of the Lord.* We must bid him welcome into our hearts, saying, "Come in, thou blessed of the Lord; come in by thy grace and Spirit, and take possession of me for thy own." We must pray for the enlargement and edification of his church, for the ripening of things for his second coming and then that he who has said, *Surely I come quickly,* would *even so come.* Christ's ministers are not only warranted, but appointed to pronounce a blessing, in his name, upon all his loyal subjects that love him, and his government in sincerity, Eph. vi. 24.

3. Let sacrifices of thanksgiving be offered to his honour who offered for us the great atoning sacrifice, *v.* 27. *He has shown us light,* that is, he has given us the knowledge of himself and his will. He *has shined upon us* (so some); he has given us occasion for joy and rejoicing, which is light to the soul, by giving us a prospect of everlasting light in heaven. The duty which this privilege calls for: *Bind the sacrifice with cords,* that, being killed, the blood of it may be sprinkled *upon the horns of the altar,* according to the law. Or this may have a peculiar significancy here; the sacrifice we are to offer to God, in gratitude for redeeming love, is ourselves, not to be slain upon the altar, but *living sacrifices* (Rom. xii. 1), to be bound to the altar, spiritual sacrifices of prayer and praise.

4. The psalmist concludes with his own thankful acknowledgments of divine grace, in which he calls upon others to join with him, *v.* 28, 29. He will have all about him to give thanks to God for these glad tidings of great joy to all people, that there is a Redeemer, even Christ the Lord. In him it is that God *is good* to man and that *his mercy endures for ever.* He concludes this psalm as he began it (*v.* 1), for God's glory must be the Alpha and Omega, the beginning and the end, of all our addresses to him.

PSALM 119

This is a psalm by itself, like none of the rest; it excels them all. It seems to me to be a collection of David's pious and devout ejaculations, the short and sudden breathings and elevations of his soul to God, which he wrote down as they occurred. There is seldom any coherence between the verses, but, like Solomon's proverbs, it is a chest of gold rings, not a chain of gold links. And we may learn, by the psalmist's example, to accustom ourselves to such pious ejaculations, which are an excellent means of maintaining constant communion with God. What some have said of this psalm is true, "He that shall read it considerately, it will either warm him or shame him." The composition of it is singular and very exact. It is divided into twenty-two parts, according to the number of the letters of the Hebrew alphabet, and each part consists of eight verses, all the verses of the first part beginning with Aleph, all the verses of the second with Beth, and so on, without any flaw throughout the whole psalm. Some have called it the saints' alphabet. However, it would be of use to the learners, a help to them both in committing it to memory and in calling it to mind upon occasion; by the letter the first word would be got, and that would bring in the whole verse; thus young people would the more easily learn it by heart and retain it the better even in old age.

II. The general scope and design of it is to magnify the law, and make it honourable; to set forth the excellency and usefulness of divine revelation, and to recommend it to us for the government of ourselves, by the psalmist's own example, who speaks by experience of the benefit of it, and earnestly prays, from first to last, for the continuance of God's grace with him. There are ten different words by which divine revelation is called in this psalm, each of them expressive of the whole compass of it and of the system of religion which is founded upon it and guided by it. The things contained in the scripture, and drawn from it, are here called, 1. God's law, because they are enacted by him as our Sovereign. 2. His way, because they are the rule both of his providence and of our obedience. 3. His testimonies, because they are solemnly declared to the world. 4. His commandments, because given with authority, and lodged with us as a trust. 5. His precepts, because prescribed to us. 6. His word, or saying, because it is the declaration of his mind, and Christ, the essential eternal Word, is all in all in it. 7. His judgments, because by them we must both judge and be judged. 8. His righteousness, because it is all holy, just, and good, and the rule and standard of righteousness. 9. His statutes, because they are fixed, and of perpetual obligation. 10. His truth, or faithfulness, because the principles upon which the divine law is built are eternal truths. And I think there is but one verse (it is ver. 122) in all this long psalm in which there is not one or other of these ten words only in three or four they are used concerning God's providence or David's practice (as ver. 75, 84, 121), and ver. 132 they are called God's name. The great esteem and affection David had for the word of God, is the more admirable considering how little he had of it, in comparison with what we have, no more perhaps in writing than the first books of Moses, which were but the dawning of this day, which may shame us who enjoy the full discoveries of divine revelation and yet are so cold towards it. Many are the instructions which we here find about a religious life. Many are the sweet experiences of one that lived such a life. Here is something or other to suit the case of every Christian.

1. ALEPH

Verses 1–3

The psalmist here shows that godly people are happy people. What we must do and be that we may attain to it, we are here told. Those are happy, 1. Who make the will of God the rule of all their actions, *v.* 1. God's word is a law to them. They walk in the paths of that law. This is *walking in God's ways* (*v.* 3), the ways which he has marked out to us. 2. Who are upright and honest in their religion —*undefiled in the way*, not only who keep themselves *unspotted from the world*, but who are habitually sincere in their intentions, *in whose spirit there is no guile*, who are really as good as they seem to be and row the same way as they look. 3. Who are true to the trust reposed in them as God's professing people. Those who would *walk in the law of the Lord* must *keep his testimonies*, that is, his truths. Or *his testimonies* may denote his covenant; the ark of the covenant is called *the ark of the testimony*. Those do not keep covenant with God who do not keep the commandments of God. 4. Who have a single eye to God as their chief good and highest end in all they do in religion (*v.* 2): They *seek him with their whole heart*. 5. Who carefully avoid all sin (*v.* 3): *They do no iniquity*. They are conscious of much that clogs them in the ways of God, but not of that iniquity which draws them out of those ways.

Verses 4–6

We must own ourselves under the highest obligations to walk in God's law (*v.* 4): *Thou hast commanded us to keep thy precepts*, to make religion our rule, and look up to God for wisdom and grace to do so (*v.* 5). "Thou wouldest have me keep thy precepts, and, Lord, I fain would keep them." *This is the will of God, even our sanctification;* and it shall be our will. Every good man has a *respect to all* God's *commandments*, those that concern both the inward and the outward man, both the head and the heart. Those who have a sincere *respect to all* God's *commandments shall not be ashamed.* They shall have clearness and courage in their own souls.

Verses 7–8

I. David's endeavour to perfect himself in his religion. He hopes to *learn* God's *righteous judgments.* He knew much, but he was still pressing forward and desired to know more. As long as we live we must be scholars in Christ's school, and sit at his feet.

II. The use he would make of his divine learning. *I will praise thee when I have learned thy judgments*, intimating that he could not learn unless God taught him, and that divine instructions are special blessings. Those have well learned God's statutes who have come up to a full resolution, in the strength of his grace, to keep them.

III. His prayer to God not to leave him. Good men see themselves undone if God forsakes them; for then the tempter will be too hard for them.

2. BETH

Verse 9

1. A weighty question asked. By what means may the next generation be made better than this? *Wherewithal shall a young man cleanse his way?* 2. A satisfactory answer given to this question. Young men may effectually *cleanse their way by taking heed thereto according to* the *word* of God. Young men must make the word of God their rule; that will do more towards the cleansing of young men than the laws of princes or the morals of philosophers. They must carefully apply that rule as a standard, and steer by that chart and compass.

Verse 10

David's experience: "*I have sought thee*. If I have not yet found thee, *I have sought thee*, and thou never saidst, Seek in vain, nor wilt say so to me, for *I have sought thee with my whole heart.* Thou that hast inclined me to seek thy precepts, never suffer me to wander from them."

Verse 11

The close application which David made of the word of God to himself: *He hid it in his heart* that it might be ready to him whenever he had occasion to use it. God's word is a treasure worth laying up, and there is no laying it up safely but in our hearts; if we have it only in our heads, our memories may fail us: but if our hearts be delivered into the mould of it, and the impressions of it remain on our souls, it is safe.

Verse 12

David gives glory to God: "*Blessed art thou, O Lord!* He asks grace from God: *Teach me thy statutes;* give me to know and do my duty in everything."

Verses 13–16

I. David had edified others with what he had been taught out of the word of God (*v.* 13). This he did, not only as a king in making orders, and giving judgment, according to the word of God, nor only as a prophet, by his psalms, but in his common discourse.

II. He looks forward with a holy resolution never to cool in his affection to the word of God; (*v.* 15): *I will meditate in thy precepts.* He not only discoursed of them to others but he communed with his own heart about them. David took more delight in God's statutes than in the pleasures of his court or the honours of his camp, more than in his sword or in his harp. When the law is written in the heart duty becomes a delight.

3. GIMEL

Verse 17

David prays, *Deal bountifully with* me, *that I may live.* It was God's bounty that gave us life, that gave us this life; and the same bounty that gave it continues it, and gives all the supports and comforts of it. Therefore we ought to spend our lives in God's service.

Verse 18

There are *wondrous things* in God's *law*, not only strange things, which are unexpected, but excellent things, which are to be valued, and things which were long *hidden from the wise and prudent*, but are now *revealed unto babes.* If there were wonders in the law, much more in the gospel. We are by nature blind to the things of God, till his grace cause the scales to fall from our eyes. And the more God opens our eyes the more wonders we see in the word of God.

Verse 19

The acknowledgment which David makes of his own condition: *I am a stranger in the earth.* All good people confess themselves to be so; for heaven is their home, and the world is but their inn, the land of their pilgrimage. David was a man that knew as much of the world, and was as well known in it, as most men. He had a name like the names of the great men, and yet he calls himself a stranger. "Lord, show thy commandments to me; as long as I live, give me to be growing in my acquaintance with it. *I am a stranger*, and therefore stand in need of a guide, a guard, a companion, a comforter; let me have thy commandments always in view, for they will be all this to me, all that a poor stranger can desire."

Verse 20

David had prayed that God would open his eyes (*v.* 18) and open the law (*v.* 19); now here he pleads the earnestness of his desire for knowledge and grace.

Verse 21

The wretched character of wicked people. The temper of their minds is bad. They are *proud*; they magnify themselves above others. And yet that is not all: they magnify themselves against God, and set up their wills in opposition to the will of God. There is something of pride at the bottom of every wilful sin. They *do err from thy commandments*, and embrace principles contrary to thy commandments, and then no wonder that they err in practice. They are certainly cursed, for *God resists the proud*; and those that throw off the commands of the law lay themselves under its curse (Gal. iii. 10).

Verse 22

David prays against the reproach and contempt of men, that they might be *removed*, or (as the word is) *rolled, from off him.* This intimates that they lay upon him, and that neither his greatness nor his goodness could secure him from being libelled and lampooned. He was not jeered out of well-doing: "Lord, remove it from me, *for I have kept thy testimonies* notwithstanding." If in a day of trial we still retain our integrity, we may be sure it will end well.

Verse 23

David was abused even by great men, who should have known better his character and his case. Herein David was a type of Christ, for they were the princes of this world that vilified and *crucified the Lord of glory*, 1 Cor. ii. 8. Under these abuses: he *meditated in God's statutes*, went on in his duty, and did not regard them. When they spoke against him, he found that in the word of God which spoke for him, and spoke comfort to him, and then none of these things moved him.

Verse 24

Here David explains his meditating in God's statutes (*v.* 23), which was of such use to him when princes sat and spoke against him. God's statutes were *his counsellors*, and they counselled him to bear it patiently and commit his cause to God.

4. DALETH

Verse 25

I. David's complaint. *My soul cleaves to the dust*, which is a complaint either, 1. Of his corruptions, his inclination to the world, and a deadness to holy duties. David's complaint here is like St. Paul's of a body of death that he carried about with him. Or, 2. Of his afflictions, either trouble of mind or outward trouble, and both together brought him even to the *dust of death.*

II. His petition for relief: "*Quicken thou me according to thy word.* By thy providence put life into my affairs, by thy grace put life into my affections; cure me of my spiritual deadness and make me lively in my devotion."

Verses 26–27

David had opened his case, opened his very heart to God: "*I have declared my ways*, and acknowledged thee in them all, have taken thee along with me in all my designs and enterprises." It is an unspeakable comfort to a gracious soul to think with what tenderness all its complaints are received by a gracious God, 1 John v. 14, 15. "Let me have a good understanding of *the way of thy precepts*; *so shall I talk* with the more assurance *of thy wondrous works.*"

Verses 28–29

1. David's representation of his own griefs: *My soul melteth for heaviness*, which is to the same purport with *v.* 25, *My soul cleaveth to the dust.* Heaviness in the heart of man makes it to melt, to drop away like a candle that wastes. 2. His request for God's grace: "*Strengthen thou me* with strength in my soul, *according to thy word.* (Deut. xxxiii. 25): *Remove from me the way of lying.* David had, in a strait, cheated Ahimelech (1 Sam. xxi. 2), and Achish, *v.* 13 and *ch.* xxvii. 10. Great difficulties are great temptations to palliate a lie with the colour of a pious fraud and a necessary self-defence; therefore David prays that God would prevent him from falling into this sin any more. *Grant me thy law graciously;* grant me that to keep me from the *way of lying.* David had the law written with his own hand, for the king was obliged to transcribe a copy of it for his own use (Deut. xvii. 18); but he prays that he might have it written in his heart. "Grant it me *graciously*"; he begs it as a special token of God's favour.

Verses 30–32

Those who will make anything to purpose of their religion must first make it their deliberate choice; so David did: *I have chosen the way of truth. Thy judgments have I laid before me*, as he who learns to write lays his copy before him, that he may write according to it, as the workman lays his model and platform before him, that he may do his work exactly. We must have the word in our heart by an habitual conformity to it, that we may walk by rule. Those who make religion their choice and rule are likely to adhere to it faithfully. The choosing Christian is likely to be the steady Christian; while those that are Christians by chance tack about if the wind turn. *"Lord, put me not to shame; do not reject my services, which will put me to the greatest confusion."* The more comfort God gives us the more duty he expects from us, *v.* 32. God by his Spirit, enlarges the hearts of his people when he gives them wisdom (for that is called *largeness of heart,* 1 Kings iv. 29), when he *sheds abroad the love of God* in the heart, and puts gladness there. The joy of our Lord should be wheels to our obedience.

5. HE

Verses 33-34
I. David begs to be taught of God, as knowing that *none teaches like him,* Job xxxvi. 22. Teach me the way of my duty in such a way as no man could teach: *Lord, give me understanding.*
II. He promises faithfully that he would be a good scholar. If God would teach him, he was sure he should learn to good purpose: *"I shall keep the law,* which I shall never do unless I be taught of God."

Verses 35-36
He had before prayed to God to enlighten his understanding, that he might know his duty; here he prays to God to bow his will, and quicken the active powers of his soul, that he might do his duty; for *it is God that works in us both to will and to do,* as well as to understand, what is good, Phil. ii. 13. *"Make me to do;* strengthen me for every good work." *Incline my heart to thy testimonies,* to those things which thy testimonies prescribe; not only make me willing to do my duty, as that which I must do, but make me desirous to do my duty. Duty is done with delight when the heart is inclined to it: it is God's grace that inclines us. "Restrain and mortify the inclination there is in me to *covetousness."* That is a sin which stands opposed to all God's testimonies. Those that would have the love of God rooted in them must get the love of the world rooted out of them.

Verse 37
David prays for restraining grace: *Turn away my eyes from beholding vanity.* The honours, pleasures, and profits of the world are the vanities, the prospect of which draw multitudes away from the paths of religion and godliness. The eye, when fastened on these, infects the heart with the love of them, and so it is alienated from God and divine things; so we ought to pray that God by his providence would keep vanity out of our sight and that by his grace he would keep us from being enamoured with the sight of it.

Verse 38
A good man is *God's servant,* subject to his law and employed in his work, that is, *devoted to his fear,* given up to his direction and disposal, and taken up with high thoughts of him and all those acts of devotion which have a tendency to his glory. Those that are God's servants may, in faith and with humble boldness, pray that God would *establish his word to them,* that is, that he would fulfil his promises to them in due time. What God has promised we must pray for; we need not be so aspiring as to ask more; we need not be so modest as to ask less.

Verse 39
David prays against *reproach,* as before, *v.* 22. He had done that which might give *occasion to the* enemies of the Lord to blaspheme; now he prays that God, who has all men's hearts and tongues in his hands, would be pleased to prevent this, to *deliver him from all his transgressions,* that he *might not be the reproach of the foolish,* which he feared (xxxix. 8). "Lord, thou sittest in the throne, and *thy judgments are right* and *good,* just and kind, to those that are wronged, and therefore to thee I appeal from the unjust and unkind censures of men."

Verse 40
David professes the ardent affection he had to the word of God: *"I have longed after thy precepts,* not only loved them, but I have earnestly desired to know them more. Thou hast wrought in me this languishing desire, put life into me, that I may prosecute it; *quicken me in thy righteousness,* in thy righteous ways, according to thy righteous promise."

6. VAU

Verses 41-42
1. David's prayer for the salvation of the Lord. "Lord, thou art my Saviour; I am miserable in myself, and thou only canst make me happy; *let thy salvation come to me.* Hasten temporal salvation to me from my present distresses, and hasten me to the eternal salvation, by giving me the necessary qualifications for it." Dependence upon the grace and promise of God for that salvation are the two pillars on which our hope is built, and they will not fail us.

Verses 43-44
David's humble petition for the tongue of the learned, that he might know how to *speak a word in season* for the glory of God: *Take not the word of truth utterly out of my mouth.* He means, "Lord, let the word of truth be always in my mouth; let me have the wisdom and courage which are necessary to enable me both to use my knowledge for the instruction of others, and to make profession of my faith whenever I am called to it." He professes his resolution to adhere to his duty in the strength of God's grace: *"So I shall keep thy law continually.* If I have thy word not only in my heart, but in my mouth, I shall do all I should do, stand complete in thy whole will."

Verses 45-48
What David experienced of an affection to the law of God: *"I seek thy precepts, v.* 45. I do all I can to *understand what the will of the Lord is* and to discover his mind. *I seek thy precepts,* for *I have loved them, v.* 47, 48. I not only give consent to them as good, but as good for me." Five things he promises himself in the strength of God's grace:—(1) That he should be free and easy in his duty: *"I will walk at liberty,* freed from that which is evil, and free to that which is good, doing it not by constraint but willingly." (2) That he should be bold and courageous in his duty: *I will speak of thy testimonies also before kings.* We must never be afraid to our own religion, though it should expose us to the wrath of kings, but speak of it as that which we will live and die by, like the three children before Nebuchadnezzar, Dan. iii. 16; Acts iv. 20. (3) That he should be cheerful and pleasant in his duty (*v.* 47): *"I will delight myself in thy commandments,* in conversing with them, in conforming to them. I will never be so well pleased with myself as when I do that which is pleasing to God." (4) That he should be diligent and vigorous in his duty: *I will lift up my hands to thy commandments.* "I will lay my hands to the command, not only to praise it, but practise it; nay, I will lift up my hands to it, that is I will put forth all the strength I have to do it." (5) That he should be thoughtful and considerate in his duty (*v.* 48): *"I will meditate in thy statutes."*

7. Zain

Verse 49

David here pleads with God in prayer for that mercy and grace which he hoped for. God had given him the promise on which he hoped: "Lord, I desire no more than that thou wouldst *remember thy word unto thy servant*, and *do as thou hast said*"; see 1 Chron. xvii. 23. Thou art faithful, and therefore wilt perform what thou hast promised, and not break thy word. He that did by his Spirit work faith in us, will, according to our faith, work for us, and will not disappoint us.

Verse 50

David's experience of benefit by the word. *"Thy word has quickened me.* It made me alive when I was dead in sin; it has many a time made me lively when I was dead in duty; it has quickened me to that which is good when I was backward and averse to it, and it has quickened me in that which is good when I was cold and indifferent."

Verse 51

David had been jeered for his religion. Though he had done eminent services to his country, yet, because he was a devout conscientious man, *the proud had him greatly in derision*; they laughed at him for his praying, and called it *cant*, for his seriousness, and called it *mopishness*, for his strictness, and called it *needless preciseness*. Yet he had not been jeered out of his religion. The traveller goes on his way though the dogs bark at him. Those can bear but little for Christ that cannot bear a hard word for him.

Verse 52

When David was derided for his godliness he not only held fast his integrity, but comforted himself. He not only bore reproach, but bore it cheerfully. It was a comfort to him to think that it was for God's sake that he bore reproach. Those that are derided for their adherence to God's law may comfort themselves with this, that *the reproach of Christ* will prove, in the end, *greater riches* to them *than the treasures of Egypt.*

Verse 53

Those that are openly and grossly wicked: *They forsake thy law.* The impression which the wickedness of the wicked made upon David: it frightened him. He trembled to think of the dishonour done to God, the gratification given to Satan, and the mischiefs done to the souls of men. He dreaded the consequences of it both to the sinners themselves and to the interests of God's kingdom among men.

Verse 54

This world is the house of our pilgrimage, the house in which we are pilgrims. We must confess ourselves *strangers and pilgrims upon earth*, who are not at home here, nor must be here long. Even David's palace is but the house of his pilgrimage. *"Thy statutes have been my songs*, with which I here entertain myself," as travellers are wont to divert the thoughts of their weariness, and take off something of the tediousness of their journey, by singing a pleasant song now and then. David was the sweet singer of Israel, and here we are told whence he fetched his songs; they were all borrowed from the word of God.

Verses 55–56

When others were sleeping David was remembering God's name, and, by repeating that lesson, increasing his acquaintance with it; in the night of affliction this he called to mind. *I remembered thy*

name in the night, and therefore was careful to *keep thy law* all day. "I had the comfort of keeping thy law because I kept it." God's work is its own wages. A heart to obey the will of God is a most valuable reward of obedience.

8. Cheth

Verse 57

David can appeal to God in this matter: "Lord, thou knowest that I have chosen thee for my portion, and depend upon thee to make me happy." He makes the law of God his rule: *I have said that I would keep thy words;* and what I have said by thy grace I will do, and will abide by it to the end." Those that take God for their portion must take him for their prince.

Verse 58

David, having in the foregoing verse reflected upon his covenants with God, here reflects upon his prayers to God, and renews his petition. He prays, *"Be merciful to me*, in the forgiveness of what I have done amiss, and in giving me grace to do better for the future." He prayed—*with his whole heart.*

Verses 59–60

He *thought on his ways.* The word signifies a fixed abiding thought. Some make it an allusion to those who work embroidery, who are very exact and careful to cover the least flaw, or to those who cast up their accounts, who reckon with themselves, What do I owe? What am I worth? He *turned his feet to God's testimonies.* He determined to make the word of God his rule, and to walk by that rule. He did this immediately and without demur (*v.* 60): *I made haste and delayed not.* Now this account which David here gives of himself may refer either to his constant practice every day, or it may refer to his first acquaintance with God and religion, when he began to throw off the vanity of childhood and youth, and to remember his Creator.

Verse 61

David's enemies were wicked men, who hated him for his godliness and tried to take away his good name. But here are the testimonies of David's conscience for him that he had held fast his religion when he was stripped of everything else, as Job did when the bands of the Chaldeans and Sabeans had robbed him: *But I have not forgotten thy law.*

Verse 62

Though David is, in this psalm, much in prayer, yet he did not neglect the duty of thanksgiving; for those that pray much will have much to give thanks for. He does not say, "*I will give thanks* because of thy favours to me," but, "*Because of thy righteous judgments*, all the disposals of thy providence in wisdom and equity." David's heart was set upon his thanksgivings. He would *rise at midnight to give thanks* to God. Public worship will not excuse us from secret worship. He did not lie still and give thanks, but rose out of his bed, perhaps in the cold and in the dark, to do it the more solemnly.

Verse 63

David had often expressed the great love he had to God; here he expresses the great love he had to the people of God. He loved them; not so much because they were his best friends, and most forward to serve him, but because they were such as *feared God* and *kept his precepts.* He was *a companion of them.* He joined with them in holy ordinances in the courts of the Lord, where rich and poor, prince and peasant, meet together. He sympathized with them in their joys and sorrows (Heb. x. 33).

Verse 64

David pleads that God is good to all the creatures according to their necessities and capacities; as the heaven is full of God's glory, so *the earth is full of his mercy*. Not only the children of men upon the earth, but even the inferior creatures, taste of God's goodness. He therefore prays that God would be good to him according to his necessity and capacity.

9. TETH

Verses 65–66

David makes a thankful acknowledgment of God's gracious dealings with him all along: *Thou hast dealt well with thy servant*. However God has dealt with us, we must own he has dealt *well* with us, better than we deserve, and all in love and with design to work for our good. Upon these experiences he grounds a petition for divine instruction: "*Teach me good judgment and knowledge*." Teach me *a good taste* (so the word signifies), a good relish, to discern things that differ, to distinguish between truth and falsehood, good and evil; for *the ear tries words, as the mouth tastes meat*. Many have knowledge who have little judgment. Where God has given a good heart a good head too may in faith be prayed for.

Verse 67

David tells: 1. Of the temptations of a prosperous condition: "*Before I was afflicted*, while I lived in peace and plenty, and knew no sorrow, *I went astray* from God and my duty." Prosperity is the unhappy occasion of much iniquity; it makes people conceited of themselves, indulgent of the flesh, forgetful of God, in love with the world, and deaf to the reproofs of the word. See xxx. 6. 2. Of the benefit of an afflicted state: "*Now have I kept thy word*, and so have been recovered from my wanderings." God often makes use of afflictions as a means to reduce those to himself who have wandered from him. The prodigal's distress brought him to himself first and then to his father.

Verse 68

David praises God's goodness and gives him the glory of it: *Thou art good and doest good*. "Lord, thou doest good to all, art the bountiful benefactor of all the creatures; this is the good I beg thou wilt do to me,—Instruct me in my duty, incline me to it, and enable me to do it.

Verses 69–70

Those that were proud envied David's reputation, because it eclipsed them, and therefore did all they could to blemish him. They therefore persuaded themselves it was no sin to tell a deliberate lie if it might but expose him to contempt. David bore it patiently; he kept that precept which forbade him to render railing for railing. He did not envy their prosperity. *Their heart is as fat as grease*. The proud are *at ease* (cxxiii. 4); they are full of the world, and the wealth and pleasures of it; and this makes them secure, and stupid; they are past feeling. They roll themselves in the pleasures of sense. I would not change conditions with them. *I delight in thy law;* I build my security upon the promises of God's word. The children of God, who are acquainted with spiritual pleasures, need not envy the children of this world their carnal pleasures.

Verse 71

The proud and the wicked lived in pomp and pleasure, while David, though he kept close to God and his duty, was still in affliction. David could speak experimentally: *It was good for me;* many a good lesson he had learnt by his afflictions. The afflictions had contributed to the improvement of his knowledge and grace. He that chastened him taught him.

Verse 72

God's *law*, which he got acquaintance with by his affliction, was *better* to him than all the *gold and silver* which he lost by his affliction. David had but a little of the word of God in comparison with what we have, yet see how highly he valued it. We have both the Old and New Testament complete. He valued the law, because it is *the law of God's mouth*, the revelation of his will. His riches increased, and yet he did not set his heart upon them, but upon the word of God.

10. JOD

Verse 73

David adores God as the author of his being, Job x. 8. Every man is as truly the work of God's hands as the first man was, Ps. cxxxix. 15, 16. "*Thy hands have* not only *made me*, but *fashioned me*, and given me this being, this noble and excellent being, endued with these powers and faculties." He addresses himself to God as the God of grace, and begs he will be the author of his new and better being. "Lord, make me anew by thy grace, that I may answer the ends of my creation and live to some purpose: *Give me understanding, that I may learn thy commandments*."

Verse 74

The confidence of this good man in the hope of God's salvation: "*I have hoped in thy word*. It is a hope that *maketh not ashamed*; but is present satisfaction, and fruition at last." The comforts which some of God's children have in God, and the favours they have received from him, should be matter of joy to others of them.

Verse 75

Still David is in affliction, and owns his sin was justly corrected: *I know, O Lord! that thy judgments are right*, arc righteousness itself. We know that God is holy in his nature and wise and just in all the acts of his government, and therefore we cannot but know, in the general, that his *judgments are right*, though, in some particular instances, there may be difficulties which we cannot easily resolve. Afflictions are in the covenant, and therefore they are not meant for our hurt, but are intended for our good.

Verses 76–77

An earnest petition to God for his favour. Those that own the justice of God in their afflictions (as David had done, v. 75) may, in faith, and with humble boldness, be earnest for the mercy of God, and the tokens and fruits of that mercy, in their affliction. He prays for God's *merciful kindness* (v. 76), his *tender mercies*, v. 77. "Let these *come to me*," that is, "the evidence of them and the effects of them; let them work my relief and deliverance. That will comfort me when nothing else will; that will comfort me whatever grieves me."

Verses 78–79

There were those that dealt perversely with him and misconstrued all he said and did, but David regarded it not. He knew it was *without cause*. The causeless reproach, like the curse causeless, does not hurt us, and therefore should not move us. He could pray, in faith: "*Let* them *be ashamed*, that is, let them be brought either to repentance or to ruin." He valued the goodwill of saints. *Let those that fear thee turn to me*. Good men desire the friendship and society of those that are good. Some think it intimates that when David had been guilty of that foul sin in the murder of Uriah, those that feared God turned from him, for they were ashamed of him; this troubled him, and therefore he prays, Lord, let them *turn to me* again.

Verse 80

David's prayer for sincerity. His dread of the consequences of hypocrisy: "*Let my heart be sound, that I may come boldly to the throne of grace*, and may lift up my face without spot at the great day."

11. Caph

Verses 81–82

He longs *for the salvation of the Lord* and *for his word*, that is, salvation according to the word. He is eager for the objects of faith, salvation from the present calamities and doubts and fears. It may be understood of the coming of the Messiah; the souls of the faithful even *fainted to see* that salvation of which the prophets testified. (1 Pet. i. 10); their eyes failed for it. Abraham saw it at a distance, and so did others, but at such a distance that they could not steadfastly see it. David cried out, "*When wilt thou comfort me?*" When the *eyes fail* yet the faith must not; for *the vision is for an appointed time, and at the end it shall speak and shall not lie.*

Verse 83

David begs God would make haste to comfort him, *for I have become like a bottle in the smoke*, a leathern bottle, which, if it hung any while in the smoke, was not only blackened with soot, but dried, and parched, and shrivelled up. David was thus wasted by age, and sickness, and sorrow. David had been of a ruddy countenance, but now he is withered, his colour is gone, his cheeks are furrowed. A bottle, when it is thus wrinkled with the smoke, is thrown by, and there is no more use of it. Thus was David, in his low estate, looked upon *as a despised broken vessel*. Though his affliction was great, yet it had not driven him from his duty, and therefore he was within the reach of God's promise: *Yet do I not forget thy statutes.*

Verse 84

David prays against the instruments of his troubles. He prays not for power to avenge himself (he bore no malice to any), but that God would take to himself the vengeance that belonged to him. "*The days of my affliction are many;* thou seest, Lord, how many they be; when wilt thou return in mercy to me? O let the days of my trouble be shortened."

Verses 85–87

David's state was *herein* a type and figure of the state both of Christ and Christians grievously persecuted. His persecutors were *proud*. They were unjust. *They dug pits for him*, which intimates that they were deliberate in their designs against him. They herein showed their enmity to God himself. The pits they *dug for him* were *not after God's law*; he means they were very much against his law, which forbids to *devise evil to our neighbour*. The law appointed that, if a man dug a pit which occasioned any mischief, he should answer for the mischief (Exod. xxi. 33, 34), much more when it was dug with a mischievous design. He begs that God would stand by him, and succour him: "*They persecute me; help thou me;* help me under my troubles, that I may bear them patiently, and in due time help me out of my troubles." *God help me* is an excellent comprehensive prayer; it is a pity that it should ever be used lightly and as a by-word.

Verse 88

David at prayer for divine grace: "*Quicken me after thy lovingkindness; so shall I keep thy testimonies.*" He had prayed before, *Quicken me in thy righteousness* (v. 40); but here, *Quicken me after thy lovingkindness*. The surest token of God's goodwill toward us is his good work in us.

12. Lamed

Verses 89–91

The psalmist acknowledges the unchangeableness of the word of God and of all his counsels: "*For ever, O Lord! thy word is settled. Thou art for ever thyself* (so some read it); thou art the same, and with thee there is no variableness and this is a proof of it. *Thy word*, by which the heavens were made, *is settled* there in the abiding products of it." *Thy faithfulness is unto all generations.* He produces, for proof of it, the constancy of the course of nature: *Thou hast established the earth for ever and it abides.* It is by virtue of God's promise to Noah (Gen. viii. 22) that *day and night, summer and winter*, observe a steady course. All the creatures are, in their places, and according to their capacities, serviceable to their Creator, and answer the ends of their creation; and shall man be the only rebel, the only revolter from his allegiance, and the only unprofitable burden of the earth?

Verse 92

David was in affliction, and ready to *perish in his affliction*, not likely to die, so much as likely to despair; he therefore admires the goodness of God to him, that he had kept the possession of his own soul, was enabled to keep close to his God and was not driven from his religion. God's law was his delight in his affliction; it afforded him abundant matter of comfort. His meditations on it, were his delightful entertainment in solitude and sorrow. A Bible is a pleasant companion at any time.

Verse 93

The best evidence of our love to the word of God is never to forget it. See here what is the best help for bad memories, namely, good affections.

Verse 94

David claims relation to God: "*I am thine*, devoted to thee and owned by thee, thine in covenant." He proves his claim: "*I have sought thy precepts.*" This will be the best evidence that we belong to God.

Verse 95

David complains of the malice of his enemies. He comforts himself in the word of God as his protection: "While they are contriving my destruction, *I consider thy testimonies*, which secure to me my salvation."

Verse 96

David's testimony: *I have seen an end of all perfection.* Poor perfection which one sees an end of! Yet such are all those things in this world which pass for perfections. David, in his time, had seen Goliath, the strongest, overcome, Asahel, the swiftest, overtaken, Ahithophel, the wisest, befooled, Absalom, the fairest, deformed; and, in short, he had *seen an end of perfection*, of *all perfection*. The glory of man is but as the flower of the grass. *But thy commandment is broad, exceedingly broad.* The word of God reaches to all cases, to all times.

13. Mem

Verse 97

David's inexpressible love to the word of God: *O how love I thy law!* He not only loved the promises, but loved the law, and delighted in it after the inner man. What we love we love to think of; by *this* it appeared that David loved the word of God that it was his *meditation*.

Verses 98–100

An account of David's learning. In his youth he minded business in the country as a shepherd; from his youth he minded business in the court and camp. Which way then could he get any great stock of learning? He had it from God as the author: *Thou hast made me wise.* He had it by the word of God as the means, by *his commandments* and *his testimonies.* A good man, wherever he goes, carries his Bible along with him, if not in his hands, yet in his head and in his heart. The best way to improve in knowledge is to abide and abound in all the instances of serious godliness; for, *if any man do his will, he shall know of the doctrine* of Christ, shall know more and more of it, John vii. 17. The love of the truth prepares for the light of it; the *pure in heart shall see God* here. He outwitted his enemies; God, by these means, made him wiser to baffle and defeat their designs. He outstripped his *teachers,* and had more understanding than all of them. He may mean those who had been his teachers when he was young; he built so well upon the foundation which they had laid that, with the help of his Bible, he became able to teach them. It is no reflection upon our teachers, but rather an honour to them, to improve so as to excel them. He outdid *the ancients, either those of his day* or those of former days. In short, the written word is a surer guide to heaven than all the doctors and fathers, the teachers and ancients, of the church; and the sacred writings kept, and kept to, will teach us more wisdom than all their writings.

Verse 101

David's care to avoid the ways of sin: "*I have refrained my feet from the evil ways* they were ready to step aside into. I checked myself and drew back as soon as I was aware that I was entering into temptation." His abstaining from sin was evidence that he did conscientiously aim to keep God's word and had made that his rule.

Verse 102

David's constancy in his religion. He had *not departed from God's judgments*; he had not chosen any other rule than the word of God, nor had he wilfully deviated from that rule. "It was divine grace in my heart that enabled me to receive those instructions."

Verses 103–104

The pleasure and delight which David took in the word of God; it was *sweet to his taste, sweeter than honey.* There is such a thing as a spiritual taste, an inward savour and relish of divine things. The word of God helped him to a good head: "*Through thy precepts I get understanding* to discern between truth and falsehood, good, and evil, so as not to mistake either in the conduct of my own life or in advising others." It helped him to a good heart: "*Therefore,* because I have got understanding of the truth, *I hate every false way,* and am steadfastly resolved not to turn aside into it."

14. NUN

Verse 105

The nature of the word of God, and the great intention of giving it to the world; it is a *lamp and a light.* It discovers to us, concerning God and ourselves, that which otherwise we could not have known. The commandment is a lamp kept burning with the oil of the Spirit; it is like the lamps in the sanctuary, and the pillar of fire to Israel. It must be not only a *light to our eyes,* to gratify them, but a *light to our feet* and *to our path,* to direct us in the choice of our way in general and in the particular steps we take in that way.

Verse 106

The notion David had of religion; it is *keeping God's righteous judgments.* God's commands are his judgments. It is good for us to bind ourselves with a solemn oath to be religious. We must swear to the Lord as subjects swear allegiance to their sovereign, promising fealty, appealing to God concerning our sincerity in this promise.

Verse 107

David laboured under many discouragements. The recourse he has to God in this condition; he prays for his grace: "*Quicken me, O Lord!* make me lively, make me cheerful; quicken me by afflictions to greater diligence in my work."

Verse 108

What David here earnestly prays for are the acceptance of the *free-will-offerings,* not of his purse, but of his *mouth,* his prayers and praises. They must be *free-will-offerings,* for we must offer them abundantly and cheerfully, and it is this willing mind that is accepted.

Verses 109–110

David in danger of losing his life. There is but a step between him and death, for the *wicked have laid a snare* for him; Saul did so many a time, because he hated him for his piety. What they could not effect by open force they hoped to compass by treachery, which made him say, *My soul is continually in my hand.* In the multitude of his cares for his own safety he finds room in his head and heart for the word of God, and has that in his mind as fresh as ever; and where that dwells richly it will be a *well of living water.*

Verses 111–112

The psalmist resolves to stick to the word of God and to live and die by it. "*Thy testimonies* (the truths, the promises, of thy word) *have I taken as a heritage for ever, for they are the rejoicing of my heart.*" He expected an eternal happiness in God's testimonies. The covenant God had made with him was an everlasting covenant, and therefore he took it as *a heritage for ever.* He resolves to govern himself by it: *I have inclined my heart to do thy statutes.* Those that would have the blessings of God's testimonies must come under the bonds of his statutes.

15. SAMECH

Verse 113

David's dread of the risings of sin, and the first beginnings of it: *I hate* vain *thoughts.* Though David could not say that he was free from vain thoughts, yet he could say that he hated them; he did not countenance them, nor give them any entertainment, but did what he could to keep them out, at least to keep them under. *But thy law do I love,* which forbids those vain thoughts, and threatens them. The more we love the law of God the more we shall get the mastery of our vain thoughts, the more hateful they will be to us.

Verse 114

David, when Saul pursued him, often betook himself to close places for shelter; in war he guarded himself with his shield. Now God was both these to him, a hiding-place to preserve him from danger and a shield to preserve him in danger, his life from death and his soul from sin.

Verse 115

I will keep the commandments of my God. Bravely resolved! like a saint, like a soldier; for true courage consists in a steady resolution against all sin and for all duty. Those that resolve to keep the commandments of God must have no society with evil-doers; for bad company is a great hindrance to a holy life.

We must not choose wicked people for our companions, Ps. i. 1; Eph. v. 11.

Verses 116–117

David prays for sustaining grace; for this grace sufficient he besought the Lord twice: *Uphold me;* and again, *Hold thou me up.* He sees himself not only unable to go on in his duty by any strength of his own, but in danger of falling into sin unless he was prevented by divine grace. We stand no longer than God holds us and go no further than he carries us. Those that hope in God's word may be sure that the word will not fail them, and therefore their hope will not make them ashamed.

Verses 118–120

God's judgment on wicked people, on those that *wander from his statutes*, that will not have God to reign over them. Now see how God deals with them, that you may neither fear them nor envy them. He *puts them all away like dross.* Wicked people are as dross, which, though it be mingled with the good metal in the ore, and seems to be of the same substance with it, must be separated from it. God casts them off because they *err from his statutes* and because *their deceit is falsehood*, that is, because they deceive themselves by setting up false rules, in opposition to God's statutes, and because they go about to deceive others with their hypocritical pretences. David's fear of the wrath of God: *My flesh trembles for fear of thee.* Instead of insulting over those who fell under God's displeasure, he humbled himself.

16. Ain

Verses 121–122

David had not done wrong; he could truly say, "*I have done judgment and justice*, I have made conscience of rendering to all their due, and have not by force or fraud hindered any of their right." He is sensible that he cannot make his part good himself, and therefore begs that God would appear for him. Christ is our surety with God; and, if he be so, Providence shall be our surety against all the world.

Verse 123

David, being oppressed, is here waiting and wishing for the salvation of the Lord. He cannot but think that it comes slowly. He was sometimes ready to despair and to think that, because the salvation did not come when he looked for it, it would never come. Though our eyes fail, yet God's word does not, and therefore those that build upon it, though now discouraged, shall in due time see his salvation.

Verses 124–125

David's petition for divine instruction: "*Teach me thy statutes*; give me to know all my duty." In difficult times we should desire more to be told what we must do than what we may expect, and should pray more to be led into the knowledge of scripture-precepts than of scripture-prophecies. He pleads his relation to God: "*I am thy servant*, and have work to do for thee; therefore *teach me* to do it and to do it well."

Verse 126

A complaint of the daring impiety of the wicked. A desire that God would appear, for the vindication of his own honour: "*It is time for thee, Lord, to work*, to do something for the effectual confutation of atheists and infidels, and the silencing of those that set their mouth against the heavens." Some read it, and the original will bear it, *It is time to work for thee, O Lord!* it is time for everyone in his place to appear on the Lord's side—against the threatening growth of profaneness and immorality.

Verses 127–128

David here, as often in this psalm, professes the great love he had to the word and law of God. David saw that the word of God answers all purposes better than money does, for it enriches the soul towards God; and therefore he loved it better than gold, for it had done that for him which gold could not do, and would stand him in stead when the wealth of the world would fail him.

17. Pe

Verse 129

The word of God gives us admirable discoveries of God, and Christ, and another world; admirable proofs of divine love and grace. The majesty of the style, the purity of the matter, the harmony of the parts, are all wonderful. Its effects upon the consciences of men, both for conviction and comfort, are wonderful.

Verse 130

The great use for which the word of God was intended, to give light, that is, to give understanding. Even *the entrance of God's word gives light.* If we begin at the beginning, and take it before us, we shall find that the very first verses of the Bible give us surprising and yet satisfying discoveries of the origin of the universe. We find we begin to see when we begin to study the word of God. Some understand it of the New Testament, which is the opening or unfolding of the Old, which would give light concerning life and immortality. It shows us a way to heaven so plain that the *wayfaring men, though fools, shall not err therein.*

Verse 131

When Christ is formed in the soul there are gracious longings. *I opened my mouth and panted*, as one overcome with heat, or almost stifled, pants for a mouthful of fresh air.

Verse 132

David's request for God's favour to himself: "*Look* graciously *upon me; and be merciful to me.*" How humble his petition is! He asks not for the operations of God's hand, only for the smiles of his face; and for that he does not plead merit, but implores mercy. "Lord, I am one of *those that love thy name*, love thee and thy word, and thou usest to be kind to those that do so." The dealings of God with those that love him are such that a man needs not desire to be any better dealt with, 1 Cor. x. 13.

Verse 133

David is, in this verse, as earnest for the good work of God in him, as in the verse before, for the goodwill of God towards him. "*Order my steps in thy word;* having led me into the right way, let every step I take in that way be under the guidance of thy grace." "*Let no iniquity have dominion over me* that I should be led captive by it."

Verse 134

David prays that he might live a quiet and peaceable life, and might not be harassed and discomposed by those that studied to be vexatious. "Let me be delivered out of the hands of my enemies, so shall I keep thy precepts more cheerfully."

Verse 135

David here, as often elsewhere, writes himself God's servant, a title he gloried in, though he was a king. He is very ambitious of his Master's favour, accounting that his happiness and chief good. "*Make thy face to shine upon thy servant;* let me be accepted of thee, and let me know that I am so. If the world frown upon me, yet do thou smile."

Verse 136

David in sorrow, to such a degree that he weeps *rivers of tears*. David had prayed for comfort in God's favour (*v.* 135); now he pleads that he was qualified for that comfort, and had need of it, for he was one of those that mourned in Zion, Isa. lxi. 3. He wept not for his troubles, though they were many, but for the dishonour done to God: *Because they keep not thy law*, that is, those about me, *v.* 139.

18. TZADDI

Verses 137–138

The righteousness of God. He rules the world by his providence, according to the principles of justice and never did, nor ever can do, any wrong to any of his creatures. As he acts like himself, so his law requires that we act like ourselves and like him, that we be just to ourselves and to all we deal with, true to all the engagements we lay ourselves under both to God and man.

Verse 139

The great contempt which wicked men put upon religion: *My enemies have forgotten thy words*. David reckoned those his enemies who forgot the words of God because they were enemies to religion, therefore his *zeal consumed him*, when he observed their impieties. Zeal against sin should constrain us to do what we can against it in our places, at least to do so much the more in religion ourselves.

Verse 140

Every good man, being a servant of God, loves the word of God, because it lets him know his Master's will and directs him in his Master's work.

Verse 141

God has chosen the foolish things of the world, and it has been the common lot of his people to be a despised people. David poor and yet pious, would not throw off his religion, though it exposed him to contempt, for he knew that was designed to try his constancy.

Verse 142

God's word is a law, and that law is truth. We are reasonable creatures, and as such we must be ruled by truth. If the principles be true, the practices must be agreeable to them, else we do not act rationally. We are creatures, and therefore subjects, and must be ruled by our Creator; and whatever he commands we are bound to obey as a law. Here is truth brought to the understanding, there to sit chief, and direct the motions of the whole man; but, lest the authority of that should become weak through the flesh, here is a law to bind the will and bring that into subjection.

Verses 143–144

David finds himself not only mean, but miserable, as far as this world could make him so: *Trouble and anguish have taken hold on me*—trouble without, anguish within. *Yet thy commandments are my delights*. There are delights, variety of delights, in the word of God, which the saints have often the sweetest enjoyment of when they are in trouble and anguish, 2 Cor. i. 5. He does not say, "Give me a further revelation," but, *Give me a further understanding*.

19. KOPH

Verses 145–146

David's good prayers. He *cried with his whole heart*; we are likely to speed when we thus strive and wrestle in prayer. He cried unto God. Whither should the child go but to his father when anything ails him? The great thing he prayed for was salvation: *Save me*. We need desire no more than God's salvation (l. 23) and the *things that accompany it*, Heb. vi. 9.

Verses 147–148

Hope in God's word encouraged him to continue instant in prayer, though the answer did not come immediately: "*I hoped in thy word*, which I knew would not fail me." The more intimately we converse with the word of God, and the more we dwell upon it in our thoughts, the better able we shall be to speak to God. Reading the word will not serve, but we must meditate in it. David began the day with God. The first thing he did in the morning, before he admitted any business, was to pray. If our first thoughts in the morning be of God they will help to keep us in his fear all the day long. Even in *the night-watches*, when he awaked from his first sleep, he would rather meditate and pray than turn himself and go to sleep again.

Verse 149

David applies to God for grace and comfort with much solemnity. "*Lord, quicken me;* stir me up to that which is good, and make me vigorous, and lively, and cheerful in it. Let habits of grace be drawn out into act."

Verses 150–151

David was in danger from his enemies. They followed him closely and he was just ready to fall into their hands: *They draw nigh*. They were at his heels. God sometimes suffers persecutors to prevail very far against his people, so that, as David said (1 Sam. xx. 3), *There is but a step between them and death*. It is the happiness of the saints that, when trouble is near, God is near, and no trouble can separate between them and him. He is never far to seek, but he is within our call, Deut. iv. 7.

Verse 152

This confirms the foregoing verse, *All thy commandments are truth;* he means the covenant, the word which God has commanded to a thousand generations. The promises are *founded for ever*, so that when heaven and earth shall have passed away every iota and tittle of the promise shall stand firm, 2 Cor. i. 20. David *knew of old*, from the days of his youth, ever since he began to look towards God, that the word of God is what one may venture one's all upon.

20. RESH

Verses 153–154

David has an eye to God's pity, and prays, "*Consider my affliction*." He has an eye to God's power and prays, "*Deliver me;*" and again, "*Deliver me*." He has an eye to God's righteousness, and prays, "*Plead my cause;* and take me for thy client." He has an eye to God's grace, and prays, "*Quicken me*. Lord, Revive and comfort me, till the deliverance is wrought!"

Verse 155

How can those expect to seek God's favour with success, when they are in adversity, who never sought his statutes when they were in prosperity? But eternal salvation is certainly far from them. They thrust it from them by thrusting the Saviour from them; it is so far from them that they cannot reach it, and the longer they persist in sin the further it is.

Verse 156

David had spoken of the misery of the wicked (*v.* 155); but God is good notwithstanding; there were tender mercies sufficient in God to have saved them, if they had not *despised the riches of those mercies*.

Verse 157

David, being a public person, had many enemies, but withal he had many friends, who loved him and wished him well; let him set the one over-against the other. In this David was a type both of Christ and his church. The enemies, the persecutors, of both, are many. A man who is steady in the way of his duty, though he may have many enemies, needs fear none.

Verse 158

David *beheld the transgressors*, and it *grieved* him to see them dishonour God, serve Satan, debauch the world, and ruin their own souls.

Verse 159

David does not say, "Consider how I fulfil thy precepts"; he was conscious to himself that in many things he came short; but, "Consider how I love them." Our obedience is pleasing to God, and pleasant to ourselves, only when it comes from a principle of love.

Verse 160

David here comforts himself with the faithfulness of God's word. *It is true from the beginning.* Ever since God began to reveal himself to the children of men all he said was true and to be trusted. The church, from its beginning, was built upon this rock. It has not gained its validity by lapse of time. But the *beginning of God's word was true* (so some read it); his government was laid on a sure foundation. It will be found faithful to the end.

21. Schin

Verse 161

It has been the common lot of the best men to be persecuted; and the case is the worse if princes be the persecutors, for they have not only the sword in their hand, but they have the law on their side, and can do it with reputation and a colour of justice. It is sad that the power which magistrates have from God, and should use for him, should ever be employed against him. David never gave them provocation. "They would make me stand in awe of them and their word, and do as they bid me; but *my heart stands in awe of thy word*, and I am resolved to please God, and keep in with him, whoever is displeased and falls out with me."

Verse 162

He had just now said that his heart stood in awe of his word, and yet here he declares that he rejoiced in it. The more reverence we have for the word of God the more joy we shall find in it.

Verse 163

Love and hatred are the leading affections of the soul; if those be fixed aright, the rest move accordingly. Here we have them fixed aright in David. 1. He had a rooted antipathy to sin; he could not endure to think of it: *I hate and abhor lying*, which may be taken for all sin. Hypocrisy is lying; false doctrine is lying; breach of faith is lying. Lying, in commerce or conversation, is a sin which every good man hates. 2. He had a rooted affection to the word of God: *Thy law do I love*. And the reason why he loved the law of God was because of the truth of it.

Verse 164

Many think that once a week will serve, or once or twice a day, but David would praise God seven times a day at least. We must praise God at every meal, in everything give thanks. We must praise

God for his precepts, for his promises, even for our afflictions, if through grace we get good by them.

Verse 165

Good men, who are governed by a principle of love to the word of God are easy, and have a holy serenity; none enjoy themselves more than they do. They may be in great troubles without and yet enjoy great peace within, *sat lucis intus—abundance of internal light*. They will make the best of that which is, and not quarrel with anything that God does.

Verse 166

Here is the whole duty of man; to keep our eye upon God's favour as our end: "*Lord, I have hoped for thy salvation.*" To keep our eye upon God's word as our rule: *I have done thy commandments*. God has joined these two together, and let no man put them asunder. We cannot, upon good grounds, hope for God's salvation, unless we set ourselves to do his commandments, Rev. xxii. 14.

Verses 167–168

Our love to the word of God must be a superlative love, and it must be a victorious love, such as will subdue and mortify our lusts. Bodily exercise profits little in religion; we must make heart-work of it or we make nothing of it.

22. Tau

Verses 169–170

We must come to God as beggars come to our doors for an alms. He is concerned that his prayer might come before God, might come near before him, that is, that he might have grace and strength by faith and fervency to lift up his prayers, that no guilt might interpose to shut out his prayers and to separate between him and God, and that God would graciously receive his prayers and take notice of them.

Verse 171

A great favour which David expects from God, that he will teach him his *statutes*. This he had often prayed for in this psalm, and now that he is drawing towards the close of the psalm he speaks of it as taken for granted. *My lips shall utter praise when thou hast taught me.* Then he shall have cause to praise God. Then he shall know how to praise God, and have a heart to do it.

Verse 172

The more we see of God's commandments the more industrious we should be to bring others acquainted with them. We should always make the word of God the governor of our discourse, so as never to transgress it by sinful speaking or sinful silence; and we should often make it the subject-matter of our discourse, that it may feed many and *minister grace to the hearers*.

Verses 173–174

David prays that divine grace would work for him: *Let thy hand help me*. He looks up to God in hopes that the hand that had made him would help him; for, if the Lord do not help us, whence can any creature help us? Three things he pleads:—(1) That he had made religion his serious and deliberate choice: "*I have chosen thy precepts.*" (2) That his heart was upon heaven: "*I have longed for thy salvation.*" (3) That he took pleasure in doing his duty: "*Thy law is my delight.*"

Verse 175

"Let me live that, in doing this, I may praise God here in this world of conflict and opposition." *Let my soul live,* that is, let me be sanctified and comforted, for sanctification and comfort are the life of the soul, *and then it shall praise thee.*

Verse 176

As unconverted sinners are like lost sheep (Luke xv. 4), so weak unsteady saints are like lost sheep, Matt. xviii. 12, 13. We are apt to wander like the sheep, and very unapt, when we have gone astray, to find the way again. "Lord, seek me, as I used to seek my sheep when they went astray"; for David had been himself a tender shepherd. "Lord, own me for one of thine; for, though I am a stray sheep, I have thy mark." Thus he concludes the psalm with a penitent sense of his own sin and a believing dependence on God's grace.

PSALM 120

This psalm is the first of those fifteen which are here put together under the title of "songs of degrees". Some think they were sung on the fifteen steps or stairs, by which they went up from the outward court of the temple to the inner, others at so many stages of the people's journey, when they returned out of captivity. This psalm is supposed to have been penned by David upon occasion of Doeg's accusing him and the priests to Saul, because it is like lii., which was penned on that occasion, and because the psalmist complains of his being driven out of the congregation of the Lord and his being forced among barbarous people. I. He prays to God to deliver him from the mischief designed him by false and malicious tongues, ver. 1, 2. II. He threatens the judgments of God against such, ver. 3, 4. III. He complains of his wicked neighbours that were quarrelsome and vexatious, ver. 5-7.

A song of degrees.
Verses 1-4

David brought into distress by *lying lips and a deceitful tongue.* There were those that sought his ruin, and had almost effected it. They flattered him that they might without suspicion carry on their designs against him. They smiled in his face and kissed him, even when they were aiming to smite him under the fifth rib. David was herein a type of Christ, who was distressed by lying lips and deceitful tongues. Having no fence against false tongues, he appealed to him who has all men's hearts in his hand, and can, when he pleases, bridle their tongues. His prayer was, *"Deliver my soul, O Lord! from lying lips."* He obtained a gracious answer to this prayer. Let liars consider what shall be given to them: *God shall shoot at them with an arrow; suddenly shall they be wounded.* They set God at a distance from them, but from afar his arrows can reach them. They will strike deep into the hardest heart. His wrath is compared to burning coals of juniper, which do not flame or crackle, like thorns under a pot, but have a vehement heat, and keep fire very long even when they seem to be gone out.

Verses 5-7

The psalmist here complains of the bad neighbourhood into which he was driven; and some apply the two foregoing verses to this: "What shall the deceitful tongue do to those that lie open to it? What shall a man get by living among such malicious deceitful men? Nothing but *sharp arrows and coals of juniper." Woe is me,* says David, *that I sojourn in Mesech and Kedar.* Not that David dwelt in the country of Mesech or Kedar; but he dwelt among rude and barbarous people, like the inhabitants of Mesech and Kedar. While he was in banishment, he looked upon himself as a sojourner, never at home. A good man cannot think himself at home while he is banished from God's ordinances. It is a great grief to all that love God to be without the means of grace and of communion with God. He *dwelt in the tents of Kedar,* where the shepherds were probably in an ill name for being litigious, like the herdsmen

of Abraham and Lot. Those that David dwelt with were such as not only hated him, but hated peace. Perhaps Saul's court was the Mesech and Kedar in which David dwelt, and Saul was the man he meant that hated peace. *I peace* (so it is in the original); "I love peace and pursue peace; *I am for peace,* and have made it to appear that I am so."

PSALM 121

Some call this the soldier's psalm, and think it was penned in the camp, when David was hazarding his life in the high places of the field. Others call it the traveller's psalm (for there is nothing in it of military dangers) and think David penned it for a good man's convoy and companion in a journey or voyage. But wherever we are, at home or abroad, we are exposed to danger more than we are aware of: and this psalm directs and encourages us to repose ourselves and our confidence in God.

A song of degrees.
Verses 1-8

This psalm teaches us to stay ourselves upon God as a God all-sufficient for us. *"Shall I lift up my eyes to the hills?"*—so some read it. "Does my help come thence? Shall I depend upon the powers of the earth, upon the strength of princes, who hold up their heads towards heaven? No; I never expect help to come from them; my confidence is in God only." *We must lift up our eyes above the hills* (so some read it); we must look beyond instruments to God, who makes them that to us which they are. *"My help comes from the Lord;* in his own way and time." We must encourage our confidence in God with this that he *made heaven and earth,* and he who did that can do anything. God himself has undertaken to be our protector: *The Lord is thy keeper, v.* 5. The same that is the protector of the church in general is engaged for the preservation of every particular believer, the same wisdom, the same power, the same promises. *He that keepeth Israel* (v. 4) *is thy keeper, v.* 5. The shepherd of the flock is the shepherd of every sheep, and will take care that not one, even of the little ones, shall perish. He is a wakeful watchful keeper: *"He that keepeth Israel,* that keepeth thee, O Israelite! *shall neither slumber nor sleep."* He not only protects those whom he is the keeper of, but he refreshes them: He *is their shade.* He is always near to his people for their protection and refreshment, and never at a distance; he *is* their *keeper* and *shade on their right hand;* so that he is never far to seek. The right hand is the working hand; let them but turn themselves dexterously to their duty, and they shall find God ready to them, to assist them and give them success, Ps. xvi. 8. *The sun shall not smite thee* with his heat *by day nor the moon* with her cold and moisture *by night.* He will keep them *night and day* (Isa. xxvii. 3). It may be understood figuratively: "Thou shalt not be hurt either by the open assaults of thy enemies, which are as visible as the scorching beams of the sun, or by their secret treacherous attempts, which are like the insensible insinuations of the cold by night." *"The Lord shall preserve thee from all evil,* the evil of sin and the evil of trouble. Even that which kills shall not hurt." It is the spiritual life, especially, that God will take under his protection: *He shall preserve thy soul.* He will keep us in all our ways: *"He shall preserve thy going out and thy coming in.* Thou shalt be under his protection in all thy journeys and voyages, outward-bound or homeward-bound. He will keep thee in life and death, thy going out and going on while thou livest and thy coming in when thou diest, going out to thy labour in the morning of thy days and coming home to thy rest when the evening of old age calls thee in," civ. 23. He will continue his care over us *from this time forth and even for evermore.*

PSALM 122

This psalm seems to have been penned by David for the use of the people of Israel, when they came up to Jerusalem to worship at the three solemn feasts. It was in David's time that Jerusalem was first chosen to be the city where God would record his name. I. The joy with which they were to go up to Jerusalem, ver. 1, 2. II. The great esteem they were to have of Jerusalem, ver. 3–5. III. The great concern they were to have for Jerusalem, and the prayers they were to put up for its welfare, ver. 6–9.

A song of degrees of David.

Verses 1–5

We ought to worship God in our own houses, but that is not enough; we must *go into the house of the Lord*, to pay our homage to him there, and *not forsake the assembling of ourselves together*. Those that rejoice in God will rejoice in calls and opportunities to wait upon him. We should desire our Christian friends, when they have any good work in hand, to call for us and take us along with them. Those that came out of the country, when they found the journey tedious, comforted themselves with this, that they should be in Jerusalem shortly, and that would make amends for all the fatigues of their journey. It is the beautiful city, not only for situation, but for building. It is built uniform, *compact together*, the houses strengthening and supporting one another. It was a type of the gospel-church, which is compact together in holy love and Christian communion, so that it is all as one city. It is the holy city, *v.* 4, the place where all Israel meet one another: *Thither the tribes go up*, from all parts of the country, to their general rendezvous; and they come together to hear what God has to say to them. It is the royal city (*v.* 5): *There are set thrones of judgment. Therefore* the people had reason to be in love with Jerusalem, because justice was administered there by a man after God's own heart.

Verses 6–9

David calls upon others to wish well to Jerusalem, *v.* 6, 7. *Pray for the peace of Jerusalem*, for the welfare of it, for all good to it, particularly for the uniting of the inhabitants among themselves. The peace and welfare of the gospel church, particularly in our land, is to be earnestly desired and prayed for by every one of us. Words are put into our mouths (*v.* 7): *Peace be within thy walls*, for all the inhabitants in general, all within the walls, from the least to the greatest. Peace be in thy fortifications; let them never be attacked, or, if they be, let them never be taken, but be an effectual security to the city. Let *prosperity* be *in the palaces* of the great men that sit at the helm and have the direction of public affairs. He resolved that whatever others do he will say, *Peace be within thee.* He did not say, "Let others pray for the public peace, the priests and the prophets, whose business it is, and the people, that have nothing else to do, and I will fight for it and rule for it." No; " I will pray for it too." It is *for my brethren and companions' sakes*, that is, for the sake of all true-hearted Israelites, whom I look upon as my brethren (so he calls them, 1 Chron. xxviii. 2) and who have often been my companions in the worship of God, which has knit my heart to them. Our concern for the public welfare is right when it is the effect of a sincere love to God's institutions and his faithful worshippers.

PSALM 123

This psalm was penned at a time when the church of God was brought low; some think it was when the Jews were captives in Babylon. The psalmist begins as if he spoke for himself only (ver. 1), but presently speaks in the name of the church. I. Their expectation of mercy from God, ver. 1, 2. II. Their plea for mercy with God, ver. 3, 4.

Verses 1–4

The title here given to God: *O thou that dwellest in the heavens.* Our Lord Jesus has taught us, in prayer, to have an eye to God as *our Father in heaven.* Heaven is a place of prospect and a place of power; he that dwells there beholds thence all the calamities of his people and thence can send to save them. In every prayer we lift up our soul, the eye of our soul, to God, especially in trouble, which was the case here. Our eyes must wait upon God as *the Lord,* and *our God, until that he have mercy upon us.* This is illustrated (*v.* 2) by a similitude: Our eyes are to God as *the eyes of a servant,* and *handmaid, to the hand of their master and mistress.* The eyes of a servant are to his master's directing hand, expecting that he will appoint him his work. Servants look to their master, or their mistress, for their portion of meat in due season, Prov. xxxi. 15. And to God must we look for daily bread, for grace sufficient. If the servant meet with opposition in his work, if he be questioned for what he does, who should bear him out and right him, but his master that set him on work? The people of God, when they are persecuted, may appeal to their Master, *We are thine; save us.* The people of God were now under his rebukes; and whither should they turn but to him that smote them? Isa. ix. 13. They submit themselves to and humble themselves under God's mighty hand. The servant expects his wages, his *well-done,* from his master. Hypocrites have their eye to the world's hand; thence *they have their reward* (Matt. vi. 2); but true Christians have their eye to God as their rewarder. The humble address which God's people present to him in their calamitous condition (*v.* 3, 4): *Have mercy upon us, O Lord! have mercy upon us.* They set forth their grievances: *We are exceedingly filled with contempt.* Reproach is the wound. Some translate the words which we render, *those that are at ease,* and *the proud,* so as to signify the persons that are scorned and contemned. "Our soul is troubled to see how those that are at peace, and the excellent ones, are scorned and despised." Taking the words as we read them, they were the epicures who lived at ease, carnal sensual people, Job xii. 5. They trampled on God's people, thinking they magnified themselves by vilifying them.

PSALM 124

David penned this psalm (we suppose) upon occasion of some great deliverance which God wrought for him and his people. Whatever it was he seems to have been himself much affected, and very desirous to affect others, with the goodness of God, in making a way for them to escape. I. He here magnifies the greatness of the danger they were in, ver. 1–5. II. He gives God the glory of their escape, ver. 6, 7, compared with ver. 1, 2. III. He takes encouragement thence to trust in God, ver. 8.

A song of degrees of David.

Verses 1–5

The people of God were reduced to the very brink of ruin. The more desperate the disease appears to have been the more does the skill of the Physician appear in the cure. *Men rose up against us,* creatures of our own kind, and yet bent upon our ruin. No less would serve than the destruction of those they had conceived a displeasure against. "God was on our side; he took our part, espoused our cause, and appeared for us. That God was Jehovah; there the emphasis lies. If it had not been Jehovah himself, a God of infinite power and perfection, that had undertaken our deliverance, our enemies would have overpowered us." Happy the people, therefore, whose God is all-sufficient.

Verses 6–8

The psalmist further magnifies the great deliverance God had lately wrought for them. They were delivered like a lamb out of the very jaws of a beast of prey. They were rescued like *a bird*, a little bird (the word signifies a sparrow), *out of the snare of the fowler*. God's people are taken in the snare, and are as unable to help themselves out as any weak and silly bird is; and *then* God breaks the snare, and turns the counsel of the enemies into foolishness. *Our help is in the name of the Lord*. David had directed us (cxxi. 2) to depend upon God for help as to our personal concerns—here as to the concerns of the public. It is a comfort that Israel's God is the same that made the world, and therefore will have a church in the world, and can secure that church in times of the greatest danger and distress.

PSALM 125

This short psalm may be summed up in those words of the prophet (Isa. iii. 10, 11), "Say you to the righteous, It shall be well with him. Woe to the wicked, it shall be ill with him." I. It is certainly well with the people of God; for, 1. They have the promises of a good God that they shall be fixed (ver. 1), and safe (ver. 2), and not always under the hatches, ver. 3. 2. They have the prayers of a good man, which shall be heard for them, ver. 4. II. It is certainly ill with the wicked, and particularly with the apostates, ver. 5.

A song of degrees.
Verses 1-3
Three very precious promises made to the people of God.

I. The character of God's people, to whom these promises belong. 1. Who are *righteous* (*v.* 3), righteous before God, righteous to God, and righteous to all men. 2. Who *trust in the Lord*, who depend upon his care and devote themselves to his honour. The closer our expectations are confined to God the higher our expectations may be raised from him.

II. The promises themselves.

1. That their hearts shall be established by faith: those minds shall be truly stayed that are stayed on God. Their faith shall be their fixation, Isa. vii. 9. *They shall be as Mount Zion*, which is firm as it is a mountain supported by providence, much more as a holy mountain supported by promise.

2. That, committing themselves to God, they shall be safe, under his protection, from all the insults of their enemies, as Jerusalem had a natural fastness and fortification in the *mountains* that *were round about* it, *v.* 2.

3. That their troubles shall last no longer than their strength will serve to bear them up under them, *v.* 3. It is promised that, though it may come upon their lot, it shall not rest there; it shall not continue so long as the enemies design, and as the people of God fear, but God will cut the work short in righteousness, so short that even *with the temptation he will make a way for them to escape*.

Verses 4-5
The prayer the psalmist puts up for the happiness of those that are sincere and constant (*v.* 4): *Do good, O Lord! unto those that are good.* He does not say, Do good, O Lord! to those that are perfect, that are sinless and spotless, but to those that are sincere and honest. God's promises should quicken our prayers. The prospect he has of the ruin of hypocrites and deserters; he does not pray for it but he predicts it. The last words, *Peace upon Israel*, may be taken as a prayer: "God preserve his Israel in peace, when his judgments are abroad reckoning with evil-doers." We read them as a promise: *Peace shall be upon Israel.*

PSALM 126

It was with reference to some great and surprising deliverance of the people of God out of bondage and distress that this psalm was penned, most likely their return out of Babylon in Ezra's time. Though Babylon be not mentioned here (as it is, Ps. cxxxvii.) yet their captivity was most remarkable both in itself and as their return was typical of our redemption by Christ.

Probably this psalm was penned by Ezra, or some of the prophets that came up with the first. I. Those that had returned out of captivity are here called upon to be thankful, ver. 1-3. II. Those that were yet remaining in captivity are here prayed for (ver. 4) and encouraged, ver. 5, 6.

A song of degrees.
Verses 1-3
While the people of Israel were captives in Babylon their harps were hung upon the willow-trees, but now that their captivity is turned they resume their harps; Providence pipes to them, and they dance. The long want of mercies greatly sweetens their return. Cyrus, for reasons of state, proclaimed liberty to God's captives, and yet it was *the Lord's doing*, according to his word many years before. God sent them into captivity, not as dross is put into the fire to be consumed, but as gold to be refined. It came so suddenly that at first they were in confusion, not knowing what to make of it, nor what it was tending to: "We thought ourselves *like men that dream*; we thought it too good news to be true." The surprise of it put them into such an ecstasy and transport of joy that they could scarcely contain themselves within the bounds of decency in the expressions of it: *Our mouth was filled with laughter and our tongue with singing.* The notice which their neighbours took: *They said among the heathen*, Jehovah, the God of Israel, *has done great things* for that people, such as our gods cannot do for us. The heathen were but spectators, and spoke of it only as matter of news; they had no part nor lot in the matter; but the people of God spoke of it as sharers in it. Thus it is comfortable speaking of the redemption Christ has wrought out as wrought out for us. *Who loved me, and gave himself for me.*

Verses 4-6
These verses look forward to the mercies that were yet wanted. Those that had come out of captivity were still in distress, even in their own land (Neh. i. 3) and many yet remained in Babylon. "*Turn again our captivity.* Let those that have returned to their own land be eased of the burdens which they are yet groaning under. Let those that remain in Babylon have their hearts stirred up, as ours were, to take the benefit of the liberty granted." The beginnings of mercy are encouragements to us to pray for the completing of it. All the saints may comfort themselves with this confidence, that their tears will certainly end in a harvest of joy at last, *v.* 5, 6. Weeping must not hinder sowing; when we suffer ill we must be doing well. Yea, as the ground is by the rain prepared for the seed. There are tears which are themselves the seed that we must sow, tears of sorrow for sin, our own and others, tears of sympathy with the afflicted church, and tears of tenderness in prayer and under the word. Job, and Joseph, and David, and many others, had harvests of joy after sorrow. Those that sow in the tears of godly sorrow shall reap in the joy of a sealed pardon and a settled peace.

PSALM 127

This is a family-psalm, as divers before were state-poems and church-poems. It is entitled (as we read it) "for Solomon", dedicated to him by his father. He having a house to build, a city to keep, and seed to raise up to his father, David directs him to look up to God, and to depend upon his providence, without which all his wisdom, care, and industry, would not serve. Some take it to have been penned by Solomon himself, and they compare it with the Ecclesiastes, the scope of both being the same, to show the vanity of worldly care and how necessary it is that we keep in favour with God. On him we must depend, I. For wealth, ver. 1, 2. II. For heirs to leave it to, ver. 3-5.

A song of degrees for Solomon.
Verses 1-5
Solomon would be apt to lean to his own understanding and forecast, and therefore his father teaches

him to look higher, and to take God along with him in his undertakings. We must depend upon God's blessing and not our own contrivance, 1. For the raising of a family: *Except the Lord build the house, by his providence and blessing, those labour in vain, though ever so ingenious, that build it.* We may understand it of the material house: except the Lord bless the building it is to no purpose for men to build. If the model and design be laid in pride and vanity, or if the foundations be laid in oppression and injustice (Hab. ii. 11, 12), God certainly does not build there; nay, if God be not acknowledged, we have no reason to expect his blessing, and without his blessing all is nothing. Or it is to be understood of the making of a family considerable that was mean: men labour to do this by advantageous matches, offices, employments, purchases; but all in vain, unless God build up the family. If the guards of the city cannot secure it without God, much less can the good man of the house save his house from being broken up. 2. For the enriching of a family; this is a work of time and thought, but cannot be effected without the favour of Providence. "*It is vain for you to rise up early and sit up late,* and so to deny yourselves your bodily refreshments, in the eager pursuit of the wealth of the world." All this is to get money, and all in vain except God prosper them, for *riches are* not always *to men of understanding,* Eccles. ix. 11. Those that love God, and are beloved of him, have their minds easy and live very comfortably without this ado. God gives us sleep as he gives it to his beloved when with it he gives us grace to lie down in his fear (our souls returning to him and reposing in him as our rest), and when we awake to be still with him and to use the refreshment we have by sleep in his service. *He gives his beloved sleep,* that is, quietness and contentment of mind, a comfortable enjoyment of what is present and a comfortable expectation of what is to come. Children are *God's gift, v.* 3, and they are to us what he makes them, comforts or crosses. *Children are a heritage,* and a *reward,* and are so to be accounted, blessings and not burdens; for he that sends mouths will send meat if we trust in him. Children are a heritage for the Lord, as well as from him. The family that has a large stock of children is like a quiver full of arrows, of different sizes we may suppose, but all of use one time or other; children of different capacities and inclinations.

PSALM 128

This, as the former, is a psalm for families. In that we were taught that the prosperity of our families depends upon the blessing of God; in this we are taught that the only way to obtain that blessing which will make our families comfortable is to live in the fear of God and in obedience to him. Those that do so, in general, shall be blessed, ver. 1, 2, 4. In particular, I. They shall be prosperous and successful in their employments, ver. 2. II. Their relations shall be agreeable, ver. 3. III. They shall live to see their families brought up, ver. 6. IV. They shall have the satisfaction of seeing the church of God in a flourishing condition, ver. 5, 6.

A song of degrees.
Verse 1–6

Godliness has the promise of the life that now is and of that which is to come. In every nation he that fears God and works righteousness is accepted of him, and therefore is blessed whether he be high or low, rich or poor, in the world; if religion rule him, it will protect him and enrich him. "*Happy shalt thou be;* if thou *fear God and walk in his ways. It shall be well with thee;* whatever befalls thee, good shall be brought out of it; it shall be well with thee while thou livest, better when thou diest, and best of all to eternity." *Thou shalt eat the labour of thy hands.* Here is a double promise, (1) That they shall have something to do (for an idle life is a miserable uncomfortable life) and shall have capacity to do it,

and shall not be forced to be beholden to others for necessary food, and to live upon the labours of other people. (2) That they shall succeed in their employments, and they and theirs shall enjoy what they get. As the sleep, so the food, of a labouring man is sweet. They shall have comfort in their family-relations. As a wife and children are very much a man's care, so, if by the grace of God they are such as they should be, they are very much a man's delight. The *wife* shall be *as a vine by the sides of the house*, not only as a spreading vine which serves for an ornament, but as a fruitful vine, and with the fruit whereof both God and man are honoured, Judges ix. 13. The vine is a weak and tender plant, and needs to be supported and cherished, but it is a very valuable plant. The wife's place is the husband's house; there her business lies, and that is her castle. *Where is Sarah thy wife? Behold, in the tent;* where should she be else? Her place is *by the sides of the house,* not under-foot to be trampled on, nor yet upon the house-top to domineer. The *children* shall be *as olive plants,* likely in time to be olive-trees. It is pleasant to parents who have a table spread, though but with ordinary fare, to see their children round about it, and not scattered, or the parents forced from them. Parents love to have their children at table, to keep up the pleasantness of the table-talk, to have them in health, craving food and not physic, to have them like *olive-plants,* straight and green, sucking in the sap of their good education. "Thy family shall be built up and continued, and thou shalt have the pleasure of seeing it." *Children's children,* if they be good children, *are the crown of old men* (Prov. xvii. 6), who are apt to be fond of their grandchildren. "Thou shalt *see the good of Jerusalem* as long as thou shalt live, though thou shouldest live long, and shalt not have thy private comforts allayed and embittered by public troubles."

PSALM 129

This psalm relates to the public concerns of God's Israel. It was penned, probably when they were in captivity in Babylon, or about the time of their return. I. They look back with thankfulness for the former deliverances, ver. 1–4. II. They look forward with a believing prayer for the destruction of all the enemies of Zion, ver. 5–8.

A song of degrees.
Verses 1–4

The church of God here speaks, as one single person, now old and grey-headed, but calling to remembrance the former days. 1. The church has been often greatly distressed by its enemies on earth. God's people have always had many enemies, and the state of the church, from its infancy, has frequently been an afflicted state. *The ploughers ploughed upon my back, v.* 3. The enemies of God's people have all along used them very barbarously. They tore them, as the husbandman tears the ground with his plough-share. When God permitted them to plough thus he intended it for his people's good, that, their fallow ground being thus broken up, he might sow the seeds of his grace upon them, and reap a harvest of good fruit from them: howbeit, the enemies meant not so; *they made long their furrows,* never knew when to have done, aiming at the destruction of the church. Many by the *furrows* they made on the backs of God's people understand the stripes they gave them. *The cutters cut upon my back,* so they read it. The saints have often *had trials of cruel scourgings,* and so it was fulfilled in Christ, who *gave his back to the smiters,* Isa. l. 6. 2. The church has been always graciously delivered by her friend in heaven. The enemies' projects have been defeated. Christ has built his church upon a rock, and the gates of hell have not prevailed against it, nor ever shall. God *has cut asunder the cords of the wicked,* has cut their gears, their traces, and so spoiled their ploughing, has cut their scourges, and so spoiled their lashing, has cut the bands of captivity in which they held God's people.

Verses 5-8

The psalmist concludes his psalm as Deborah did her song, *So let all thy enemies perish, O Lord!* Judges v. 31. The confusion predicted is illustrated by a similitude; while God's people shall flourish as the loaded palm-tree, or the green and fruitful olive, their enemies shall *wither as the grass upon the house-top.* As they are enemies to Zion they are so certainly marked for ruin that they may be looked upon as the grass on the house-tops, which is little, and short, and sour, and good for nothing. It *withers before it grows up* to any maturity, having no root; and the higher its place is, which perhaps is its pride, the more it is exposed to the scorching heat of the sun, and consequently the sooner does it wither. Mowing the grass on the house-top would be a jest, and therefore those that have a reverence for the name of God will not prostitute to it the usual forms of salutation, which savoured of devotion.

PSALM 130

This psalm is wholly taken up with the affairs of the soul. It is reckoned one of the seven penitential psalms, which have sometimes been made use of by penitents, upon their admission into the church; and, in singing it, we are all concerned to apply it to ourselves. The psalmist here expresses, I. His desire towards God, ver. 1, 2. II. His repentance before God, ver. 3, 4. III. His attendance upon God, ver. 5, 6. IV. His expectation from God, ver. 7, 8.

A song of degrees.

Verses 1-4

The best men may sometimes be in *the depths*, in great trouble and affliction. But, in the greatest depths, it is our privilege that we may cry unto God and be heard. To cry unto God is the likeliest way both to prevent our sinking lower and to recover us out of the *horrible pit and miry clay*, xl. 1, 2. *If thou, Lord, shouldst mark iniquities, O Lord! who shall stand?* His calling God *Lord* twice, in so few words, *Jah* and *Adonai*, is very emphatic, and intimates a very awful sense of God's glorious majesty and a dread of his wrath. We cannot justify ourselves before God, or plead Not guilty. If God deal with us in strict justice, we are undone. *It is of his mercy that we are not consumed* by his wrath. It is our unspeakable comfort, in all our approaches to God, that there is forgiveness with him, for that is what we need. He has promised to forgive the sins of those that do repent. *There is a propitiation with thee*, so some read it. Jesus Christ is the great propitiation, and through him we hope to obtain forgiveness. But this encourages us to come into his service that we shall not be turned off for every misdemeanour; no, nor for any, if we truly repent.

Verses 5-8

"*I wait for the Lord;* from him I expect relief and comfort, believing it will come, longing till it does come, but patiently bearing the delay of it, and resolving to look for it from no other hand. *My soul doth wait. In his word do I hope.*" We must hope for that only which he has promised in his word, and not for the creatures of our own fancy and imagination. "Well-assured that the morning will come; so am I that God will return in mercy to me, for God's covenant is more firm than the ordinances of day and night, for they shall come to an end, but that is everlasting." Those that watch with sick people, and travellers that are abroad upon their journey, long before they wish to see the dawning of the day; but more earnestly does this good man long for the tokens of God's favour and the visits of his grace. *Mercy is with* him in all his works, in all his counsels. Jesus

Christ *saves his people from their sins* (Matt. i. 21), *redeems them from all iniquity* (Tit. ii. 14), and *turns away ungodliness from Jacob*, Rom. xi. 26. Redemption from sin includes redemption from all other evils, and therefore is a plenteous redemption.

PSALM 131

This psalm is David's profession of humility, with thankfulness to God for his grace. It is probable enough that David made this protestation in answer to Saul who represented David as an ambitious aspiring man, who, under pretence of a divine appointment, sought the kingdom, in the pride of his heart. But he appeals to God, that, on the contrary, I. He aimed at nothing high nor great, ver. 1. II. He was very easy in every condition which God allotted him (ver. 2); and therefore, III. He encourages all good people to trust in God as he did, ver. 3.

A song of degrees of David.

Verses 1-3

This was David's rejoicing, that his heart could witness for him that he had walked humbly with his God. He aimed not at a high condition, but, if God had so ordered, could have been well content to spend all his days in the sheepfolds. His own brother, in a passion, charged him with pride (1 Sam. xvii. 28), but the charge was groundless and unjust. He had neither a scornful nor an aspiring look: "*My eyes are not lofty*, either to look with envy upon those that are above me or to look with disdain upon those that are below me." As he had not proudly aimed at the kingdom, so, since God had appointed him to it, he had been as humble as a little child. Our Saviour has taught us humility by this comparison (Matt. xviii. 3); we must *become as little children.* Our hearts are naturally as desirous of worldly things as the babe of the breast. But, by the grace of God, a soul that is sanctified, is weaned from those things. Thus does a gracious soul quiet itself under the loss of that which it loved, and lives comfortably, upon God and the covenant-grace.

PSALM 132

It is probable that this psalm was penned by Solomon, to be sung at the dedication of the temple which he built according to the charge his father gave him, 1 Chron. xxviii. 2, &c. Having fulfilled his trust, he begs of God to own what he had done. I. He had built this house for the honour and service of God; and when he brings the ark into it, the token of God's presence, he desires that God himself would come and take possession of it, ver. 8-10. With these words Solomon concluded his prayer, 2 Chron. vi. 41, 42. In this psalm, I. He pleads David's piety towards God, ver. 1-7. 2. He pleads God's promise to David, ver. 11-18.

A song of degrees.

Verses 1-10

Solomon's address to God for his favour to him, and his acceptance of his building a house to God's name. What he had done was in pursuance of the pious vow which his father David had made to build a house for God. Solomon pleads not any merit of his own: "I am not worthy, for whom thou shouldst do this; but, *Lord, remember David*, with whom thou madest the covenant." He especially pleads the solemn vow that David had made as soon as ever he was settled in his government, and before he was well settled in a house of his own, that he would build a house for God. He had observed in the law frequent mention of the *place that God would choose to put his name there*, to which all the tribes should resort. When he came to the crown there was no such place; Shiloh was deserted, and no other place was pitched upon, for want of which the feasts of the Lord were not kept with due solemnity. "Well," says David, "I will find out such a place for the general rendezvous of all the tribes, a place of *habitation for the Mighty One of Jacob*, a place for the ark, where there shall be room both for the priests and people to attend upon it." The thing had been long talked of, and nothing done, till at last David when he went out one morning about public business, made a vow that before night he would determine the place either where the tent should be pitched for the reception of the ark, at the beginning of his reign, or rather where Solomon should build the temple, which was not fixed till the latter end of his reign. *Then David said, This is the house of the Lord.* It is good in the morning to cut out work for the day, binding ourselves that we will do it before we sleep, only with submission to Providence. The people of Israel, *v.* 6, 7, were inquisitive after the ark; for they lamented its obscurity, 1 Sam. vii. 2. They *heard of it at Ephratah* (that is, at Shiloh, in the tribe of Ephraim); there they were told it had been, but it was gone. They *found it*, at last, *in the fields of the wood*, that is, in Kirjath-jearim, which signifies *the city of woods.* Thence all Israel fetched it, with great solemnity, in the beginning of David's reign (1 Chron. xiii. 6), so that in building this house for the ark Solomon had gratified all Israel. They were resolved to attend it: "Let us but have a convenient place, and *we will go into his tabernacle*, to pay our homage there; *we will worship at his footstool* as subjects and suppliants, which we neglected to do, for want of such a place, *in the days of Saul*," 1 Chron. xiii. 3. He prays, *v.* 8–10. God would vouchsafe, not only to take possession of, but to take up his residence in, this temple which he had built. *Let thy priests be clothed with righteousness.* "They are *thy priests*, and will therefore discredit their relation to thee if they *be not clothed with righteousness.*" Let the people of God have the comfort of the due administration of holy ordinances among them. "*Turn not away the face of thy anointed*, that is, deny me not the things I have asked of thee, send me not away ashamed."

Verses 11–18

These promises relate to the establishment both in church and state, both to the throne of the house of David and to the testimony of Israel fixed on Mount Zion. The promises concerning Zion's hill are as applicable to the gospel-church as these concerning David's seed are to Christ, and therefore both pleadable by us and very comfortable to us.

I. The choice God made of David's house and Zion hill. Both were of divine appointment.

1. God chose David's family for the royal family and confirmed his choice by an oath, *v.* 11, 12. A long succession of kings should descend from his loins: *Of the fruit of thy body will I set upon thy throne*, which was fulfilled in Solomon; David himself lived to see it with great satisfaction, 1 Kings i. 48. The crown was also entailed conditionally upon his heirs for ever: *If thy children*, in following ages, *will keep my covenant and my testimony that I shall teach them.* The issue of this was that they did not keep God's covenant, and so the entail was at length cut off, and *the sceptre departed from Judah* by degrees. An everlasting successor, a king, should descend from his loins of *the increase of whose government and peace there shall be no end.* St. Peter applies this to Christ, nay, he tells us that David himself so understood it (Acts ii. 30).

2. God chose Zion hill for the holy hill, and confirmed his choice by the delight he took in it, *v.* 13, 14. God said, *Here will I dwell*, and therefore David said, *Here will I dwell*, for here he adhered to his principle, *It is good for me to be near to God.* Zion must be here looked upon as a type of the gospel-church, which is called *Mount Zion* (Heb. xii. 22), and in it what is here said of Zion has its full accomplishment. Zion was long since ploughed as a field, but the church of Christ *is the house of the living God* (1 Tim. iii. 15), and it is his *rest for ever*, and shall be blessed with his presence always, even to the end of the world.

II. The blessings God has in store for David's house and Zion hill. Whom God chooses he will bless.

1. The blessings of the life that now is; for godliness has the promise of them, *v.* 15. The earth shall yield her increase; where religion is set up there shall be provision. God's people have a special blessing upon common enjoyments, and that blessing puts a peculiar sweetness into them. The promise goes further: *I will satisfy her poor with bread.* They shall have provision enough. If there be scarcity, the poor are the first that feel it, so that it is a sure sign of plenty if they have sufficient. And this may be understood spiritually of the provision that is made for the soul in the word and ordinances; God will abundantly bless that for the nourishment of the new man, and satisfy the poor in spirit with the bread of life. The blessings of the life that is to come, things pertaining to godliness (*v.* 16), which is an answer to the prayer, *v.* 9. It was desired that the priests might be *clothed with righteousness*; it is here promised that God will clothe them with salvation. They shall both *save themselves and those that hear them*, and *add those to the church that shall be saved.*

2. God, having chosen David's family, here promises to bless that also with suitable blessings. *There*, in Zion, *will I make the horn of David to bud, v.* 17. The royal dignity shall increase more and more, and constant additions be made to the lustre of it. Christ is the *horn of salvation* which God has raised up, and made to bud, *in the house of his servant David. I have ordained a lamp for my anointed.* Thou wilt *light my candle*, xviii. 28. That lamp is likely to burn brightly which God ordains. A lamp is a successor, for, when a lamp is almost out, another may be lighted by it; it is a succession, for by this means David shall not want a man to stand before God. Christ is the lamp and the light of the world. "*His enemies*, who have formed designs against him, *will I clothe with shame*, when they shall see their designs baffled." *Upon himself shall his crown flourish*, that is, his government shall be more and more his honour. The crowns of earthly princes *endure not to all generations* (Prov. xxvii. 24), but Christ's crown shall endure to all eternity and the crowns reserved for his faithful subjects are such as *fade not away.*

PSALM 133

This psalm is a brief encomium on unity and brotherly love. Some conjecture that David penned this psalm upon occasion of the union between the tribes when they all met unanimously to make him king. I. The doctrine laid down of the happiness of brotherly love, ver. 1. II. The illustration of that doctrine, in two similitudes, ver. 2. 3. III. The proof of it, in a good reason given for it (ver. 3).

A song of degrees of David.

Verses 1–3

Sometimes it is chosen, as the best expedient for preserving peace, that brethren should live asunder and at a distance from each other; that indeed may prevent enmity and strife (Gen. xiii. 9), but the goodness and pleasantness are *for brethren to dwell together* and so *to dwell in unity*, to dwell even as one (so some read it), as having one heart, one soul, one interest.

The tribes of Israel had long had separate interests during the government of the Judges; but now they were united under one common head, now the ark was fixed, and with it the place of their rendezvous for public worship and the centre of their unity. Now let them live in love. It is a rare thing, and therefore admirable. It is fragrant as the holy anointing oil, which was strongly perfumed, and diffused its odours, when it was poured upon the head of Aaron, or his successor the high priest, so plentifully that it ran down the face, even to the collar or binding of the garment, *v.* 2. So must our brotherly love be, with a pure heart, devoted to God. Holy love, is in the sight of God, of great price. Christ's love to mankind was part of that *oil of gladness* with which he was *anointed above his fellows*. Aaron and his sons were not admitted to minister unto the Lord till they were anointed with this ointment, nor are our services acceptable to God without this holy love; if we have it not we are nothing, 1 Cor. xiii. 1, 2. It is profitable as well as pleasing; it is *as the dew*; it brings abundance of blessings along with it, as numerous as the drops of dew. It cools the scorching heat of men's passions, as the evening dews cool the air and refresh the earth. It moistens the heart, and makes it tender and fit to receive the good seed of the word. It is *as the dew of Hermon*, a common hill (for brotherly love is the beauty and benefit of civil societies), *and as the dew that descended upon the mountains of Zion*, a holy hill, for it contributes greatly to the fruitfulness of sacred societies. Loving people are blessed people. They are blessed of God, and therefore blessed indeed. The blessing which God commands on those that dwell in love is *life for evermore*; that is the blessing of blessings. Those that dwell in love not only dwell in God, but do already dwell in heaven.

PSALM 134

This is the last of the fifteen songs of degrees; and, if they were at any time sung all together in the temple-service, it is fitly made the conclusion of them, for the design of it is to stir up the ministers to go on with their work in the night, when the solemnities of the day were over. Some make this psalm to be a dialogue. I. In the first two verses, the priests or Levites who sat up all night to keep the watch of the house of the Lord are called upon to spend their time while they were upon the guard, not in idle talk, but in the acts of devotion. II. In the last verse those who were thus called upon to praise God pray for him that gave them the exhortation, either the high priest or the captain of the guard.

A song of degrees.

Verses 1-3

I. Our blessing God, that is, speaking well of him, which here we are taught to do, *v.* 1, 2. 1. It is a call to the *Levites* to do it. Some of them did *by night stand in the house of the Lord*, to guard the holy things of the temple, that they might not be profaned, and the rich things of the temple, that they might not be plundered. While the ark was in curtains there was the more need of guards upon it. They attended likewise to see that neither the fire on the altar nor the lamps in the candlestick went out. Probably it was usual for some devout and pious Israelites to sit up with them; we read of one that *departed not from the temple night or day*, Luke ii. 37. Now these are here called upon to *bless the Lord*. 2. It is a call to us to do it, who, as Christians, are made priests to our God, and Levites, Isa. lxvi. 21. We are the *servants of the Lord*; we have a place and a name in his house, in his sanctuary; we stand before him to minister to him. Let us therefore *bless the Lord*. Let us *lift up* our *hands* in prayer, in praise, in vows; let us do our work with diligence and cheerfulness, and an elevation of mind.

II. God's blessing us, and that is doing well for us, which we are here taught to desire, *v.* 3. We need desire no more to make us happy than to be blessed of the Lord, for those whom he blesses are blessed indeed.

PSALM 135

This is one of the Hallelujah-psalms; that is the title of it, and that is the Amen of it, both its Alpha and its Omega. I. It begins with a call to praise God, ver. 1-3. II. It goes on to furnish us with matter for praise. God is to be praised, 1. As the God of Jacob, ver. 4. 2. As the God of gods, ver. 5. 3. As the God of the whole world, ver. 6, 7. 4. As a terrible God to the enemies of Israel, ver. 8-11. 5. As a gracious God to Israel, ver. 12-14, 6. As the only living God, all other gods being vanity and a lie. ver. 15-18. III. It concludes with another exhortation to all persons concerned to praise God, ver. 19-21.

Verses 1-4

1. The duty we are called to—to *praise the Lord*, to *praise his name*; *praise him*, and again *praise him*. We must not only thank him for what he has done for us, but praise him for what he is in himself and has done for others. 2. The persons that are called upon to do this—the *servants of the Lord*, the priests and Levites *that stand in his house*, and all the devout and pious Israelites that stand *in the courts of his house* to worship there, *v.* 2. Who should praise him if they do not? 3. The reasons why we should praise God. He is good to all. His goodness is his glory, and we must make mention of it to his glory. The work is its own wages.

Verses 5-14

The psalmist had suggested to us the goodness of God, as the proper nature of our cheerful praises; here he suggests to us the greatness of God as the proper matter of our praises.

I. He asserts the doctrine of God's greatness (*v.* 5): *The Lord is great*, great indeed, who knows no limits of time or place.

II. He proves him to be a great God by the greatness of his power, *v.* 6. He has an absolute power, and may do what he will. This absolute almighty power is of universal extent; he does what he will *in heaven, in earth, in the seas*, and in *all the deep places* that are in the bottom of the sea or the bowels of the earth.

III. He gives instances of his great power,

1. In the kingdom of nature, *v.* 7. All the powers of nature prove the greatness of the God of nature, from whom they are derived and on whom they depend. The chain of natural causes was not only framed by him at first, but is preserved by him. It is by his power that exhalations are drawn up from the terraqueous globe. The heat of the sun raises them, but it has that power from God. It is he who, out of those vapours so raised, forms the rain. They are returned with advantage in fruitful showers. He *makes lightnings for the rain*; by them he shakes the clouds, that they may water the earth. Here are fire and water thoroughly reconciled by divine omnipotence. Winds blow where they list, from what point of the compass they will, and we are so far from directing them that we cannot tell whence they come nor whither they go, but God *brings them out of his treasuries* with exactness and design.

2. In the kingdoms of men. Observe God's sovereign dominion and irresistible power, (1) In bringing Israel out of Egypt, humbling Pharaoh by many plagues, and so forcing him to let them go. (2) In destroying the kingdoms of Canaan before them, *v.* 10. No power of hell or earth can prevent the accomplishment of the promise of God when the time, the set time, for it has come. (3) In settling them in the land of promise. He that gives kingdoms to whomsoever he pleases gave Canaan to be a heritage to Israel his people.

IV. He triumphs in the perpetuity of God's glory and grace. *Thy name, O God! endures for ever*. This seems to refer to Exod. iii. 15, where, when God had called himself *the God of Abraham, Isaac, and Jacob*, he adds, *This is my name for ever and this is my memorial unto all generations*. He will be kind to his people. He will plead their cause against others that contend with them. *He will judge his people*, that is, he will judge for them, and will not suffer them to be run down.

Verses 15-21

These verses design:—

I. To arm the people of God against idolatry and all false worships, by showing what sort of gods they were that the heathen worshipped, as we had it before, cxv. 4, &c. They were gods of their own making; being so, they could have no power but what their makers gave them. They had the shape of animals, but could not perform the least act, no, not of the *animal* life. Their worshippers were therefore as stupid and senseless as they were, both those that made them to be worshipped and those that trusted in them when they were made, v. 18.

II. To stir up the people of God to true devotion in the worship of the true God, v. 19-21. In the parallel place (cxv. 9-11), by way of inference from the impotency of idols, the duty thus pressed upon us is to *trust in the Lord*; here to bless him; by putting our trust in God we give glory to him.

PSALM 136

The scope of this psalm is the same with that of the foregoing psalm, but the latter half of each verse is the same, repeated throughout the psalm, "for his mercy endureth for ever". It is allowed that such burdens, or "keepings", as we call them, add very much to the beauty of a song, and help to make it moving and affecting. The repetition of it here twenty-six times intimates, 1. That God's mercies to his people are thus repeated and drawn, as it were, with a continuando from the beginning to the end. 2. That in every particular favour we ought to take notice of the mercy of God. 3. That the everlasting continuance of the mercy of God is very much his honour. This most excellent sentence that God's mercy endureth for ever, is magnified above all the truths concerning God, not only by the repetition of it here, but by the signal tokens of divine acceptance with which God owned the singing of it (2 Chron. v. 13; xx. 21, 22). We must praise God, I. As great and good in himself, ver. 1-3. II. As the Creator of the world, ver. 5-9. III. As Israel's God and Saviour, ver. 10-22. IV. As our Redeemer, ver. 23, 24. V. As the great benefactor of the whole creation, and God over all, blessed for evermore, ver. 25, 26.

Verses 1-9

The duty we are here again and again called to is to *give thanks*, to *offer the sacrifice of praise continually*, not the fruits of our ground or cattle, but *the fruits of our lips, giving thanks to his name*, Heb. xiii. 15. We must give thanks *to the Lord*, Jehovah, Israel's God (v. 1), *the God of gods*, the God whom angels adore, from whom magistrates derive their power (v. 2), *to the Lord of lords*, the Sovereign of all sovereigns, v. 3. We must give thanks to God for his goodness and mercy (v. 1): *Give thanks to the Lord*, not only because he does good, but because he is good. Not only for that mercy which is now handed out to us here on earth, but for that which shall endure for ever in the glories and joys of heaven. We must give God thanks for the instances of his power and wisdom. He made the heavens, and stretched them out, and in them we not only see his wisdom and power, but we taste his mercy in their benign influences; as long as the heavens endure the mercy of God endures in them, v. 5. *The earth hath he given to the children of men*, and all its products. The sun, moon, and stars, he placed in the firmament of heaven, to shed their light and influences upon this earth, v. 7-9.

Verses 10-22

The great things God did for Israel, when he formed them into a people, and set up his kingdom among them, are here mentioned, as often elsewhere in the psalms, as instances both of the power of God and of the particular kindness he had for Israel. He brought them out of Egypt, v. 10-12. He forced them a way through the Red Sea, which obstructed them at their first setting out. He not only divided the sea, but gave his people courage to go through it when it was divided, which was an instance of God's power over men's hearts, as the former of his power over the waters. He conducted them through a vast howling wilderness (v. 16); there he led them and fed them. He destroyed kings before them, to make room for them (v. 17, 18). It is good to enter into the detail of God's favours and not to view them in the

gross, and in each instance to observe, and own, that God's *mercy endureth for ever*. He put them in possession of a good land, v. 21, 22. As he said to the Egyptians, *Let my people go*, so to the Canaanites, *Let my people in*, that they may serve me. In this God's *mercy* to them *endureth for ever*, because it was a figure of the heavenly Canaan, the *mercy of our Lord Jesus Christ unto eternal life*.

Verses 23-26

God's everlasting mercy is here celebrated in the redemption of his church, v. 23, 24. In the many redemptions wrought for the Jewish church out of the hands of their oppressors (when, in the years of their servitude, their estate was very low, God remembered them, and raised them up saviours, the judges, and David), but especially in the great redemption of the universal church, of which these were types, we have a great deal of reason to say, "*He remembered us in our low estate*, in our lost estate, *for his mercy endureth for ever*; he sent his Son to redeem us from sin, and death, and hell, and all our spiritual enemies, *for his mercy endureth for ever*." It is an instance of the mercy of God's providence that wherever he has given life he gives food agreeable and sufficient; and he is a good housekeeper that provides for so large a family. In all his glories, and all his gifts (v. 26): *Give thanks to the God of heaven*. This and that particular mercy may perhaps endure but a while, but the mercy that is in God *endures for ever*; it is an inexhaustible fountain.

PSALM 137

There are divers psalms which are thought to have been penned in the latter days of the Jewish church, when prophecy was near expiring and the canon of the Old Testament ready to be closed up, but none of them appears so plainly to be of a late date as this, which was penned when the people of God were captives in Babylon; probably it was towards the latter end of their captivity; for now they saw the destruction of Babylon hastening on apace (ver. 8), which would be their discharge. It is a mournful psalm, a lamentation. I. The melancholy captives cannot enjoy themselves, ver. 1, 2. II. They cannot humour their proud oppressors, ver. 3, 4. III. They cannot forget Jerusalem, ver. 5, 6. IV. They cannot forgive Edom and Babylon, ver. 7-9.

Verses 1-6

I. The people of God in tears, but sowing in tears. They were posted *by the rivers of Babylon*, in a strange land, a great way from their own country, whence they were brought as prisoners of war. The land of Babylon was now a house of bondage to that people, as Egypt had been in their beginning. Their conquerors quartered them *by the rivers*, with design to employ them there. We find some of them by the river *Chebar* (Ezek. i. 3). There they *sat down* to indulge their grief by poring on their miseries. Thoughts of Zion drew tears from their eyes; but they were deliberate tears (we *sat down and wept*), tears with consideration—*we wept when we remembered Zion*, the holy hill on which the temple was built. Their affection to God's house swallowed up their concern for their own houses. They laid by their instruments of music (v. 2): *We hung our harps upon the willows*. They did not hide their harps in the bushes, or the hollows of the rocks; but hung them up in view, that the sight of them might affect them with this deplorable change. Yet perhaps they were faulty in doing this; for praising God is never out of season.

II. The abuses which their enemies put upon them when they were in this melancholy condition, v. 3. They had *carried them away captive* from their own land and then *wasted them* in the land of their captivity. To complete their woes they insulted over them: They *required of us mirth and a song*. It argues a base and sordid spirit to upbraid those that are in distress either with their former joys or with their present griefs, or to challenge those to be merry who, we know, are out of tune for it. No songs would serve them but the *songs of Zion*, with which God had been honoured; so that in this demand they reflected upon God himself as Belshazzar, when he drank wine in temple-bowls.

III. The patience wherewith they bore these abuses, *v.* 4. They had laid by their harps, and would not resume them. Profane scoffers are not to be humoured. The reason they gave is very mild and pious: *How shall we sing the Lord's song in a strange land?* "It is the *Lord's song*; it is a sacred thing; it is peculiar to the temple-service, and therefore we dare not sing it in the land of a stranger, among idolaters."

IV. The constant affection they retained for Jerusalem, the city of their solemnities, even now that they were in Babylon. It was always in their minds; they remembered it; many of them had never seen it. In their daily prayers they opened their windows towards Jerusalem; and how then could they forget it. *"Let my right hand forget her art"* (which the hand of an expert musician never can, unless it be withered), "nay, *let my tongue cleave to the roof of my mouth*, if I have not a good word to say for Jerusalem wherever I am."

Verses 7-9

The pious Jews in Babylon, having afflicted themselves with the thoughts of the ruins of Jerusalem, here please themselves with the prospect of the ruin of her impenitent implacable enemies; but this not from a spirit of revenge, but from a holy zeal for the glory of God and the honour of his kingdom. And all this was a fruit of the old enmity of Esau against Jacob, because he got the birthright and the blessing. *Lord, remember* them, says the psalmist, which is an appeal to his justice against them. Far be it from us to avenge ourselves, if ever it should be in our power, but we will leave it to him who has said, *Vengeance is mine. O daughter of Babylon!* proud and secure as thou art, we know well thou *art to be destroyed*, or (as Dr. Hammond reads it) *who art the destroyer*. The destroyers shall be destroyed. "Thou shalt be served *as thou hast served us*, as barbarously used by the destroyers as we have been by thee." Let not those expect to find mercy who, when they had power, did not show mercy. None escape if the little ones perish. Those are the seed of another generation; so that, if they be cut off, the ruin will be not only total, as Jerusalem's was, but final.

Psalm 138

It does not appear upon what occasion David penned this psalm; but in it, I. He looks back with thankfulness upon the experiences he had had of God's goodness to him, ver. 1-3. II. He looks forward with comfort, in hopes, 1. That others would go on to praise God like him, ver. 4, 5. 2. That God would go on to do good to him, ver. 6-8.

A psalm of David.

Verses 1-5

I. He would praise God with sincerity and zeal— *"With my heart, with my whole heart*, with that which is within me and with all that is within me, inward impressions agreeing with outward expressions." *Before the gods will I sing praise unto thee*, before the princes, and judges, and great men. *I will worship towards thy holy temple*. The priests alone went into the temple; the people, at the nearest, did but worship towards it, and that they might do at a distance. Christ is our temple, and towards him we must look as Mediator between us and God, in all our praises of him. Heaven is God's holy temple, and thitherward we must lift up our eyes in all our addresses to God. *Our Father in heaven.*

II. He would praise God for the fountain of his comforts—*for thy lovingkindness and for thy truth.*

For thou hast magnified thy word (thy promise, which is truth) *above all thy name*. God has made himself known to us in many ways in creation and providence, but most clearly by his word. Some good interpreters understand it of Christ, the essential Word, and of his gospel, which are magnified above all the discoveries God had before made of himself to the fathers. He had been in affliction, and he remembers. *Thou strengthenedst me with strength in my soul.* If God give us strength in our souls to bear the burdens, resist the temptations, and do the duties of an afflicted state, if he strengthen us to keep hold of himself by faith, to maintain the peace of our own minds and to wait with patience for the issue, we must own that he has answered us, and we are bound to be thankful.

III. David was himself a king, and therefore he hoped that kings would be wrought upon by his experiences, and his example, to embrace religion. This may have reference to the kings that were neighbours to David, as Hiram and others. "They shall all praise thee." When they visited David, and, after his death, Solomon (as *all the kings of the earth* are expressly said to have done, 2 Chron. ix. 23), they readily joined in the worship of the God of Israel. It may look further, to the calling of the Gentiles and the discipling of all nations by the gospel of Christ, of whom it is said that *all kings shall fall down before him*, Ps. lxxii. 11. They shall *sing in the ways of the Lord*, in the ways of his providence and grace towards them.

Verses 6-8

David here comforts himself with three things:—

I. The favour God bears to his humble people (*v.* 6): *Though the Lord be high, yet has he respect unto the lowly*, smiles upon them as well pleased with them, and, sooner or later, he will put honour upon them, while *he knows the proud afar off*, knows them, but disowns them.

II. The care God takes of his afflicted oppressed people, *v.* 7. David, though a great and good man, expects to *walk in the midst of trouble*, but encourages himself with hope. "When my spirit is ready to sink and fail, *thou* shalt *revive me*, and make me easy and cheerful under my troubles." He would protect him: *"Thou shalt stretch forth thy hand*, though not against my enemies to destroy them, yet *against the wrath of my enemies*, to restrain that and set bounds to it." He would in due time work deliverance for him: *Thy right hand shall save me.* Christ is the right hand of the Lord, that shall save all those who serve him.

III. Whatever good work God has begun for his people he will perform it (*v.* 8): *The Lord will perfect that which concerns me*, which is most needful for me. Every good man is most concerned about his duty to God and his happiness in God, that the former may be faithfully done and the latter effectually secured; and if indeed these are the things that our hearts are most upon, there is a good work begun in us, and he that has begun it will perfect it, Phil. i. 6. Our hopes that we shall persevere must be founded, not upon our own strength, for that will fail us, but upon the mercy of God, for that will not fail. It is well pleaded, *"Lord, thy mercy endures for ever;* let me be for ever a monument of it." He turns his expectation into a petition: *"Forsake not*, do not let go, *the work of thy own hands*. Lord, I am the work of thy own hands, my soul is so, do not forsake me."

Psalm 139

Some of the Jewish doctors are of opinion that this is the most excellent of all the psalms of David; and a very pious devout meditation it is upon the doctrine of God's omniscience. I. This doctrine is here asserted, ver. 1-6. II. It is confirmed by two arguments:—1. God is everywhere present; therefore he knows all, ver. 7–12. 2. He made us, therefore he knows us, ver. 13–16. III. Some inferences are drawn from this doctrine. I. It may fill us with pleasing admiration of God, ver. 17, 18. 2. With a holy detestation of sin and sinners, ver. 19–22. 3. With a holy satisfaction in our own integrity, ver. 23, 24.

To the chief musician. A psalm of David.

Verses 1–6

God with whom we have to do has a perfect knowledge of us, and all the motions and actions both of our inward and of our outward man are open before him.

I. David lays down this doctrine of address to God; acknowledging it to him, and giving him the glory. When we speak to God of himself we shall find ourselves concerned to speak with the utmost degree both of sincerity and reverence.

II. He lays it down in a way of application to himself, not "Thou hast known *all*," but, "Thou hast known *me*." So here, "*Thou hast searched me, and known me*." David was a king, and *the hearts of kings are unsearchable* to their subjects (Prov. xxv. 3), but they are not so to their Sovereign.

III. He descends to particulars: "Thou knowest me wherever I am and whatever I am doing, me and all that belongs to me. *Thou knowest* me and all my motions, *my down-sitting* to rest, *my up-rising* to work. Thou knowest me when I come home, how I walk before my house, and when I go abroad, on what errands I go. Thou knowest all my imaginations. It is often unobserved by ourselves, and yet *thou understandest my thoughts afar off*." Or, "*Thou understandest them afar off*, even before I think them, and long after I have thought them and have myself forgotten them." Or "*Thou understandest them from afar;* from the height of heaven thou seest into the depths of the heart," xxxiii. 14. "*Thou compassest* every particular *path*, so as thoroughly to distinguish between the good and evil of what I do. "*Thou knowest* me in all my retirements; thou knowest *my lying down*; when I am reflecting upon what has passed all day, thou knowest what I have in my heart and with what thoughts I go to bed." *There is not a word in my tongue*, not a vain word, nor a good word, *but thou knowest it altogether. When there is not a word in my tongue, O Lord! thou knowest all* (so some read it); for thoughts are words to God. *Thou hast beset me behind and before.* Wherever we are we are under the eye and hand of God. God knows us as we know not only what we see, but what we feel.

IV. He speaks of it with admiration (*v.* 6): *It is too wonderful for me; it is high.* We cannot by searching find out how God searches and finds out us; nor do we know how we are known.

Verses 7–16

David is sure that God perfectly knows him and all his ways,

I. Because he is always under his eye. If God is omnipresent, he must needs be omniscient. Heaven and earth include the whole creation, and the Creator fills both (Jer. xxiii. 24); he not only knows both, and governs both, but he fills both. Every part of the creation is under God's influence. No flight can remove us out of God's presence: "*Whither shall I go from thy Spirit, from thy presence*, that is, from thy spiritual presence, from thyself, who art a Spirit?" *God is a Spirit*, and therefore it is folly to think that because we cannot see him he cannot see us: *Whither shall I flee from thy presence? (Quocunque te flexeris, ibi Deum videbis occurrentem tibi—Whithersoever thou turnest thyself, thou wilt see God meeting thee*, said Seneca.) David specifies the most remote and distant places, and counts upon meeting God in them. (1) In heaven: "*If I ascend* thither, as I hope to do shortly, *thou art there*, and it will be my eternal bliss

to be with thee there." (2) *In hell*—in *Sheol*, which may be understood of the depth of the earth, the very centre of it. Should we dig as deep as we can underground, and think to hide ourselves there, we should be mistaken. Or it may be understood of the state of the dead. When we are removed out of the sight of all living, we are not out of sight of the living God; from his eye we cannot hide ourselves. Or it may be understood of the place of the damned: *If I make my bed in hell* (an uncomfortable place to make a bed in) *behold, thou art there*, in thy power and justice. In the remotest corners of this world: "*If I take the wings of the morning*, the rays of the morning-light (called the wings of the sun, Mal. iv. 2), than which nothing more swift, and flee upon them to *the uttermost parts of the sea*, or of the earth, should I flee to the most distant and obscure islands (the *ultima Thule*, the *Terra incognita*), I should find thee there; *there shall thy hand lead me*, as far as I go, *and thy right hand shall hold me*, that I can go no further, that I cannot go out of thy reach."

2. No veil can hide us from God's eye, *v.* 11, 12. "*If I say*, Yet *the darkness shall cover me*, when nothing else will, I find myself deceived; the curtains of the evening will stand me in no more stead than the wings of the morning; *even the night shall be light about me*." No hypocritical mask or disguise, how specious soever, can save any person or action from appearing in a true light before God.

II. Because he is the work of his hands. He that framed the engine knows all the motions of it. God made us, and therefore he knows us. "*Thou hast possessed my reins*. The possession thou hast of my reins is a rightful possession, *for thou coveredst me in my mother's womb*, that is, thou madest me (Job x. 11), thou madest me in secret." The soul is concealed from all about us. It was God himself that thus covered us, and therefore he can, when he pleases, discover us. "*I will praise thee*, the author of my being; my parents were only the instruments of it." We were his work, according to the divine model: *In thy book all my members were written.* Eternal wisdom formed the plan. We are *fearfully and wonderfully made*; we may justly be astonished at these living temples, the composition of every part, and the harmony of all together. As a great mercy all our members *in continuance were fashioned*, according as they were written in the book of God's wise counsel, *when as yet there was none of them.*

Verses 17–24

Here the psalmist makes application of the doctrine of God's omniscience,

I. He acknowledges, with wonder and thankfulness, the care God had taken of him all his days, *v.* 17, 18. God, who knew him, thought of him, and his thoughts towards him were thoughts of love. God's omniscience has watched over us to do us good, Jer. xxxi. 28. Providence has had a vast reach in its dispensations concerning us, and has brought things about for our good quite beyond our contrivance and foresight. We cannot conceive the multitude of God's compassions, which are all new every morning. "*When I awake*, every morning, *I am still with thee*, under thy eye and care, safe and easy under thy protection."

II. He concludes from this doctrine that ruin will certainly be the end of sinners. God knows all the wickedness of the wicked, and therefore he will reckon for it. God will punish them, because they set him at defiance (*v.* 20): *They speak against thee wickedly.* They are his *enemies*, and declare their enmity by *taking his name in vain.* Some make it to be a description of hypocrites: "They speak of thee for mischief; they talk of God, pretending to piety, and, being enemies to God, while they pretend friendship, they *take* his *name in vain*; they swear falsely." 1. He defies them: "*Depart from me, you bloody men;* you shall not debauch me, for I will not admit your friendship nor have fellowship with you; and you cannot destroy me. David detests them *v.* 21, 22: "Lord, thou knowest the heart, and canst witness for me; *do not I hate those that hate thee,* because they hate thee? I hate them because I love thee, and hate to see such indignities put upon thy blessed name. *Am not I grieved with those that rise up against thee,* grieved to see their rebellion and to foresee their ruin, which it will certainly end in?" Sin is hatred, and sinners are lamented, by all that fear God. "*I hate them*" (that is, *I hate the work of them that turn aside,* ci. 3).

III. He appeals to God concerning his sincerity, *v.* 23, 24. "Lord, I hope I am not in a wicked way, but *see if there be any wicked way in me,* any corrupt inclination remaining; let me see it; and root it out of me, for I do not allow it." *Lead me in the way everlasting.*

PSALM 140

This and the four following psalms are much of a piece, and the scope of them the same with many that we met with in the beginning and middle of the book of Psalms. They were penned by David (as it should seem) when he was persecuted by Saul. In this psalm, I. David complains of the malice of his enemies, and prays to God to preserve him from them, ver. 1-5. II. He encourages himself in God as his God, ver. 6, 7. III. He prays for, and prophesies, the destruction of his persecutors, ver. 8-11. IV. He assures all God's afflicted people that their troubles would in due time end well (ver. 12, 13).

To the chief musician. A psalm of David.

Verses 1-7

In *this*, as in other things, David was a type of Christ, that he suffered before he reigned, was humbled before he was exalted, and that as there were many who loved and valued him, and sought to do him honour, so there were many who hated and envied him, and sought to do him mischief.

I. He gives a character of his enemies. There was one that seems to have been the ring-leader of them, whom he calls *the evil man* and *the man of violences* (*v.* 1, 4), probably he means Saul. But there were many besides this one who were confederate against David. They are very subtle (*v.* 2), have laid the scheme with all the cunning imaginable. *They have,* like mighty hunters, *hidden a snare,* and *spread a net,* and *set gins* (*v.* 5), that he might fall into their hands ere he was aware. Great persecutors have often been great politicians, which has indeed made them the more formidable; but *the Lord preserves the simple. They have sharpened their tongues like a serpent,* that infuses his venom with his tongue; and there is so much malignity in all they say that one would think there was nothing *under their lips* but *adders' poison, v.* 3. They are all *gathered together* against me *for war, v.* 2. Those who can agree in nothing else can agree to persecute a good man. Herod and Pilate will unite in this, and in this they resemble Satan, who is not divided against himself, all the devils agreeing in Beelzebub. The pride of persecutors may be the encouragement of the persecuted, for the more haughty they are the faster are they ripening for ruin.

II. He prays: "Lord, *deliver me, preserve me, keep me* (*v.* 1, 4); let them not prevail to take away my life, my reputation, my interest, my comfort, and to prevent my coming to the throne. *Keep me* from doing as they do, or as they promise themselves I shall do."

III. He triumphs in God, and thereby, in effect, he triumphs over his persecutors, *v.* 6, 7. "*I said, Thou art my God;* and, if my God, then my shield and mighty protector." In his access to God, it comforted him, that he was not only taken into covenant with God, but into communion with him. He had help from God and happiness in him: "*O God the Lord—Jehovah Adonai!* as *Jehovah* thou art self-existent and self-sufficient, an infinitely perfect being; as *Adonai* thou art my stay and support, my ruler and governor, and therefore *the strength of my salvation,* my strong Saviour. *Thou hast covered my head in the day of battle.*"

Verses 8-13

David prays: "*Grant not, O Lord!* the desires of the wicked, but frustrate them; *hear the voice of my supplications.*" He prays: "*O further not his wicked device;* let not Providence favour any of his designs, but cross them; suffer *not his wicked device* to proceed, but chain his wheels, and stop him in the career of his pursuits." He foretells the ruin of his enemies: "*The mischief of their own lips* shall *cover* their heads (*v.* 9); the evil they have wished to me shall come upon themselves, their curses shall be blown back into their own faces, and the very designs which they have laid against me shall turn to their own ruin," vii. 15, 16. The judgments of God shall *fall upon them,* compared here to *burning coals,* in allusion to the destruction of Sodom. Evil speakers must expect to be shaken, for they shall never *be established in the earth.* What is got by fraud and falsehood, by calumny and unjust accusation, will not prosper. "*I know that the Lord will maintain the* just and injured *cause of* his *afflicted* people, and will not suffer might always to prevail against right, though it be but *the right of the poor.*" The closing words, *The upright shall dwell in thy presence,* denote both God's favour to them ("Thou shalt admit them to dwell in thy presence in grace here, in glory hereafter, and it shall be their safety and happiness") and their duty to God.

PSALM 141

David was in distress when he penned this psalm. I. He prays for God's favourable acceptance, ver. 1, 2. II. For his powerful assistance, ver. 3, 4. III. That others might be instrumental of good to his soul, as he hoped to be to the souls of others, ver. 5, 6. IV. That he and his friends being now brought to the last extremity God would graciously appear for their relief and rescue, ver. 7-10.

A psalm of David.

Verses 1-4

I. David loved prayer, and he begs of God that his prayers might be heard and answered, *v.* 1, 2. *David cried unto God.* His crying denotes fervency in prayer. "*Give ear to my voice;* let me have a gracious audience." Those that cry in prayer may hope to be heard in prayer, not for their loudness, but their liveliness. *Make haste unto me.* He that believes does not make haste, but he that prays may be earnest with God to make haste. His *praying* and the *lifting up of his hands in prayer* denotes both the elevation of his desire and the out-goings of his hope and expectation, the lifting up of the hand signifying the lifting up of the heart, and being used instead of lifting up the sacrifices which were heaved and waved before the Lord. Prayer is a spiritual sacrifice; it is the offering up of the soul, and its best affections, to God. Prayer is of a sweet-smelling savour to God, as incense, which yet has no savour without fire; nor has prayer without the fire of holy love and fervour.

II. David begs that he might be kept from sin, knowing that his prayers would not be accepted unless he took care to watch against sin. We must be as earnest for God's grace in us as for his favour towards us. "*Set a watch, O Lord! before my mouth,* and, nature having made my lips to be a door to my words, let grace keep that door, that no word may be suffered to go out which may in any way tend to the dishonour of God or the hurt of others. *Incline not my heart to any evil thing;* whatever inclination there is in me to sin, let it be not only restrained, but mortified, by divine grace." While we live in such an evil world, and carry about with us such evil hearts, we have need to pray that we may neither be drawn in by any allurement nor driven on by any provocation. "*Let me not eat of their dainties.* Let me not join with them, lest thereby I be inveigled into their sins." Good men will pray even against the sweets of sin.

Verses 5-10

I. David desires to be told of his faults. *Let the righteous smite me; it shall be a kindness.* We are here taught how to receive the reproofs of the righteous and wise. If my own heart does not *smite me*, as it ought, let my friend do it; let me never fall under that dreadful judgment of being let alone in sin. We must account it a piece of friendship. We must not only bear it patiently, but take it as a kindness. Though reproofs cut, it is in order to a cure, and therefore they are much more desirable than the kisses of an enemy (Prov. xxvii. 6) or the song of fools, Eccles. vii. 5. It *shall be as an excellent oil* to a wound, to mollify it and close it up; *it shall not break my head*, as some reckon it to do, who could as well bear to have their heads broken as to be told of their faults; but, says David, "I am not of that mind; it is my sin that has broken my head, that has broken my bones, Ps. li. 8. The reproof is an excellent oil, to cure the bruises sin has given me. It shall not *break my head*, if it may but help to break my heart."

II. David hopes his persecutors will, some time or other, bear to be told of their faults, as he was willing to be told of his (*v.* 6). Some think this refers to the relentings that were in Saul's breast when he said, with tears, *Is this thy voice, my son David?* 1 Sam. xxiv. 16; xxvi. 21.

III. David complains of the great extremity to which he and his friends were reduced (*v.* 7): *Our bones are scattered at the grave's mouth*, out of which they are thrown up, so long have we been dead; and they are as little regarded as chips among the hewers of wood, which are thrown in neglected heaps.

IV. David casts himself upon God, and depends upon him for deliverance: "*But my eyes are unto thee* (*v.* 8). From thee I expect relief, bad as things are, and in *thee is my trust.*"

PSALM 142

This psalm is a prayer, the substance of which David offered up to God when he was forced by Saul to take shelter in a cave, and which he afterwards penned in this form. Here is, I. The complaint he makes to God (ver. 1, 2) of the subtlety, strength, and malice, of his enemies (ver. 3, 6), and the coldness and indifference of his friends, ver. 4. II. The comfort he takes in God that he knew his case (ver. 3) and was his refuge, ver. 5. III. His expectation from God that he would hear and deliver him, ver. 6, 7. IV. His expectation from the righteous that they would join with him in praises, ver. 7.

Maschil of David. A prayer when he was in the cave.

Verses 1-3

Whether it was in the cave of *Adullam*, or that of *Engedi*, that David prayed this prayer, is not material; it is plain that he was in distress. When he durst not stretch forth his hands against his prince, he lifted them up to his God. There is no cave so deep, so dark, but we may out of it send up our souls in prayer, to God. He calls this prayer *Maschil—a psalm of instruction*, because of the good lessons he had himself learnt in the cave on his knees.

I. How David complained to God, *v.* 1, 2. When the danger was over he was not ashamed to own (as great spirits sometimes are) the fright he had been in. Let not men think it any disparagement to them, when they are in affliction, to cry to God, and to cry

like children to their parents when anything frightens them. *He cried unto the Lord with his voice*, with the voice of his mind (so some think), for, being hidden in the cave, he durst not speak with an audible voice, lest that should betray him; but mental prayer is vocal to God, and he hears the groanings which cannot, or dare not, be uttered, Rom. viii. 26. *I showed before him my trouble.* As one that put a confidence in God he unbosomed himself to him and then cheerfully left it with him. We are apt to show our trouble too much to ourselves, aggravating it, and poring upon it, whereas by showing it to God we might cast the care upon him who careth for us.

II. What he complained of: "*In the way wherein I walked*, suspecting no danger, *have they privily laid a snare for me*, to entrap me." Saul gave Michal his daughter to David on purpose that she might be *a snare to him*, 1 Sam. xviii. 21.

III. What comforted him in the midst of these complaints (*v.* 3): "*When my spirit was overwhelmed within me*, and ready to sink under the burden of grief and fear, *then thou knewest my path*, that is, then it was a pleasure to me to think that thou knewest it. Thou knewest it, that is, thou didst protect, preserve, and secure it," Ps. xxi. 7; Deut. ii. 7.

Verses 4-7

He was disowned and deserted by his friends, *v.* 4. When he was made an outlaw, then *no man would know him*, but everybody was shy of him. He looked *on his right hand* for an advocate (cix. 31), but, since Jonathan's appearing for him had like to have cost him his life, nobody was willing to venture in defence of his innocence. How many good men have been deceived by such swallow-friends, who are gone when winter comes! Herein he was a type of Christ, who was forsaken of all men, even of his own disciples, and trod the wine-press alone. David tells us what he said to God in the cave: "*Thou art my refuge and my portion in the land of the living.* The cave I am in is but a poor refuge. Lord, *thy name* is the *strong tower* that *I run into*. Thou art *my refuge*, in whom alone I shall think myself safe." Those who in sincerity take the Lord for their God shall find him all-sufficient and they may humbly claim their interest: "*Lord, thou art my refuge in the land of the living*, that is, while I live and have my being, whether in this world or in a better." He addressed himself to God (*v.* 6, 7): "Lord, *deliver me from my persecutors*, either tie their hands or turn their hearts, break their power or blast their projects, restrain them or rescue me, *for they are stronger than I*. Lord, *bring my soul out of prison*, not only bring me safe out of this cave, but bring me out of all my perplexities."

PSALM 143

This psalm, as those before, is a prayer of David, and full of complaints of the great distress and danger he was in. In this psalm, I. He complains of his troubles (ver. 3) and the weakness of his spirit, ver. 4, 5. II. He prays, and prays earnestly (ver. 6), 1. That God would hear him, ver. 1-7. 2. That he would not deal with him according to his sins, ver. 2. 3. That he would not hide his face from him (ver. 7), but manifest his favour to him, ver. 8. 4. That he would guide and direct him in the way of his duty (ver. 8, 10) and quicken him in it, ver. 11. 5. That he would deliver him out of his troubles, ver. 9, 11. 6. That he would in due time reckon with his persecutors, ver. 12.

A psalm of David.

Verses 1-6

I. David is a suppliant to his God, an appellant against his persecutors, and he begs that God will give judgment upon it, in his faithfulness as the Judge of right and wrong. We have no righteousness of our own to plead, and therefore must plead God's righteousness, the word of promise which he has freely given us and caused us to hope in.

II. He humbly begs not to be proceeded against in strict justice, *v.* 2. He seems here, if not to correct, yet to explain, his plea (*v.* 1), Deliver me *in thy righteousness*; "I mean," he says, "the righteous promises of the gospel, not the righteous threatenings of the law." His petition is, "*Enter not into judgment with thy servant;* do not deal with me in strict justice, as I deserve to be dealt with." David, before he prays for the removal of his trouble, prays for the pardon of his sin, and depends upon mere mercy for it.

III. He complains of his enemies (*v.* 3): "Saul, that great enemy, *has persecuted my soul,* sought my life, with a restless malice. He has forced me to *dwell in darkness,* not only in dark caves, but in dark thoughts and apprehensions, in the clouds of melancholy, *as* helpless, and hopeless as *those that have been long dead.* Lord, let me find mercy with thee, for I find no mercy with men."

IV. He bemoans the oppression of his mind, occasioned by his outward troubles (*v.* 4): *Therefore is my spirit* overpowered and *overwhelmed within me.*

V. He applies himself to the use of proper means for the relief of his troubled spirit. If he can keep possession of nothing else, he will do what he can to keep possession of his own soul and to preserve his inward peace. He looks back, and *remembers the days of old* (*v.* 5), God's former appearances for his afflicted people and for him in particular. He looks round, and takes notice of the works of God in the visible creation, and the providential government of the world: *I meditate on all thy works. I muse on,* or (as some read it) *I discourse of, the operation of thy hands,* how great, how good, it is! The more we consider the power of God the less we shall fear the face or force of man, Isa. li, 12, 13. He looks up with earnest desires towards God and his favour (*v.* 6): *I stretch forth my hands unto thee. My soul thirsteth after thee; it is to thee* (so the word is), entire for thee, intent on thee; it is *as a thirsty land,* which, being parched with excessive heat, gapes for rain.

Verses 7–12

Three things David here prays for:—

I. The manifestations of God's favour towards him. He dreads God's frowns: "Lord, *hide not thy face from me.*" Disconsolate saints have sometimes cried out of the wrath of God, as if they had been damned sinners, Job vi. 4; Ps. lxxxviii. 6. He entreats God's favour (*v.* 8): *Cause me to hear thy lovingkindness in the morning.* God speaks to us by his word and by his providence, and in both we should desire and endeavour to *hear his lovingkindness* (cvii. 43).

II. The operations of God's grace in him. *Cause me to know the way wherein I should walk.* A good man does not ask what is the way in which he must walk, or in which is the most pleasant walking, but what is the right way, the way in which he should walk. He pleads, "*I lift up my soul unto thee,* to be moulded and fashioned according to thy will." "*Teach me to do thy will,* not only show me what thy will is, but teach me how to do it." *Lead me into the land of uprightness,* into a settled course of holy living, which will lead to heaven. We cannot find the way that will bring us to that land unless God show us, nor go in that way unless he take us by the hand and lead us, as we lead those that are weak, or lame, or timorous, or dim-sighted. The plea is, "*Thy Spirit is good,* and able to make me good," good and willing to help those that are at a loss. *Let thy good Spirit lead me,* so some read it. He prays that he might be enlivened to do his will (*v.* 11): "*Quicken me, O Lord!* quicken my graces, that they may be active—quicken my devotions, that they may be lively."

III. The appearance of God's providence for him (*v.* 9): "*Deliver me, O Lord! from my enemies,* that they may not have their will against me; *for I flee unto thee to hide me.*" He prays: "Deliver me from my outward trouble, from the trouble of my soul, the trouble that threatens to overwhelm my spirit."

Psalm 144

The four preceding psalms seem to have been penned by David before his accession to the crown, when he was persecuted by Saul; this seems to have been penned afterwards. In this psalm, I. He acknowledges with triumph and thankfulness, the great goodness of God to him in advancing him to the government, ver. 1–4. II. He prays to God to help him against the enemies who threatened him, ver. 5–8, and again, ver. 11. III. He rejoices in the assurance of victory over them, ver. 9, 10. IV. He prays for the prosperity of his own kingdom, ver. 12–15.

A psalm of David.

Verses 1–8

I. David acknowledges his dependence upon God and his obligations to him, *v.* 1, 2. *Blessed be the Lord my rock* (*v.* 1), *my goodness my fortress.* He multiplies words to express the satisfaction he had in God. "He is *my strength,* on whom I stay. *My goodness,* not only good to me, but the author of all the goodness that is in me, and *from whom comes every good and perfect gift.*" David had formerly sheltered himself in strongholds at En-gedi (1 Sam. xxiii. 29), which perhaps were natural fastnesses. He had lately made himself master of the stronghold of Zion, which was fortified by art, and he *dwelt in the fort* (2 Sam. v. 7, 9), but he depends not on these. "Lord," says he, "thou art *my fortress* and *my high tower. My shield,* not only *my fortress* at home, but *my shield* abroad in the field of battle." Wherever a believer goes he carries his protection along with him. He was bred a shepherd, and seems not to have been designed by his parents or himself for anything more. But God had made him a soldier. His hands had been used to the crook and his fingers to the harp, but God *taught his hands to war and his fingers to fight,* because he designed him for Israel's champion. God had made him a sovereign prince, had taught him to wield the sceptre as well as the sword. He *subdueth my people under me.*

II. He admires God's condescension to man and to himself in particular (*v.* 3, 4): "*Lord, what is man,* what a poor little thing is he, *that thou takest knowledge of him, that thou makest account of him.*" The meanness and mortality of man, notwithstanding the dignity put upon him (*v.* 4): *Man is like to vanity;* so frail is he, so weak, so helpless, compassed about with so many infirmities, and his continuance here so very short and uncertain, that he is as like as may be to vanity itself.

III. He begs of God to give him success against the enemies that invaded him, *v.* 5–8. He does not specify who they were that he was in fear of, but says, *Scatter them, destroy them.* But afterwards he describes them (*v.* 7, 8): "They are *strange children,* Philistines, bad neighbours to Israel. One cannot take their word, for their *mouth speaketh vanity;* nay, if they give their hand upon it, or offer their hand to help you, there is no trusting them; for *their right hand is a right hand of falsehood.*" David prays that God would appear. "*Bow thy heavens, O Lord!* and make it evident that they are indeed thine, and that thou art the Lord of them, Isa. lxiv. 1. *Touch the mountains,* our strong and stately enemies, *and* let them *smoke.* Show thyself as thou didst upon Mount Sinai."

Verses 9–15

In this latter part of the psalm as in the former; David first gives glory to God and then begs mercy from him.

I. He praises God for the experiences he had had of his goodness to him, *v.* 9, 10. In the midst of his complaints concerning the power and treachery of his enemies, here is a holy exultation in his God: *I will sing a new song to thee, O God!* a song of praise for new mercies. He tells us what this new song shall be (*v.* 10): *It is he that giveth salvation unto kings.* Kings are the protectors of their people, but it is God that is *their* protector. How much service do they owe him then with their power who gives them all their salvations! He has engaged to give salvation to those kings that are his subjects and rule for him; witness the great things he had done for *David his servant.* This may refer to Christ the Son of David, and then it is a new song indeed, a New Testament song.

II. He prays for the continuance of God's favour.

1. That he might be delivered from the public enemies, *v.* 11. Here he repeats his prayer and plea, *v.* 7, 8.

2. That he might see the public peace and prosperity: "Lord, let us have victory, that we may have quietness, which we shall never have while our enemies have it in their power to do us mischief." David desired for his people (*v.* 12): "*That our sons and our daughters may be* in all respects such as we could wish." It is desirable to see *our daughters as cornerstones,* or corner-pillars, *polished after the similitude of a palace,* or temple. By daughters families are united and connected, to their mutual strength, as the parts of a building are by the cornerstones; and when they are graceful and beautiful both in body and mind they are then polished after the similitude of a nice structure. When we see our daughters well-established and stayed with wisdom and discretion—when we see them by faith united to Christ—when we see them purified and consecrated to God as living temples, we think ourselves happy in them. He prays for a growing estate with a growing family. *First,* That their storehouses might be well-replenished with the fruits and products of the earth: that, having abundance, we may be thankful to God, generous to our friends, and charitable to the poor. *Secondly,* That their flocks might greatly increase: *That our sheep may bring forth thousands, and ten thousands, in our* folds. Much of the wealth of their country consisted in their flocks. *Thirdly,* That their beasts designed for service might be fit for it: *That our oxen may be strong to labour* in the plough. "Let not our enemies break in upon us; let us not have occasion to march out against them." War brings with it abundance of mischiefs, whether it be offensive or defensive. Let there be no oppression nor faction—*no complaining in our streets,* that the people may have no cause to complain either of their government or of one another. It is desirable thus to dwell in quiet habitations. His reflection upon this description of the prosperity of the nation, which he so much desired (*v.* 15): *Happy are the people that are in such a case* (but it is seldom so, and never long so), *yea, happy are the people whose God is the Lord.*

PSALM 145

The five foregoing psalms were all of a piece, all full of prayers; this, and the five that follow it to the end of the book, are all of a piece too, all full of praises. And it is observable, 1. That after five psalms of prayer follow six psalms of praise; for those that are much in prayer shall not want matter for praise, and those that have sped in prayer must abound in praise. Our thanksgivings for mercy, when we have received it, should even exceed our supplications for it when we were in pursuit of it. 2. That the book of Psalms concludes with psalms of praise, all praise, for praise is the conclusion of the whole matter; it is that in which all the psalms centre. And it intimates that God's people, towards the end of their life, should abound much in praise, and the rather because, at the end of their life, they hope to remove to the world of everlasting praise, and the nearer they come to heaven the more they should accustom themselves to the work of

heaven. This is one of those psalms which are composed alphabetically (as Ps. xxv and xxxiv, &c), that it might be the more easily committed to memory, and kept in mind. The Jewish writers justly extol this psalm as a star of the first magnitude in this bright constellation; and some of them have an extravagant saying concerning it, not much unlike some of the popish superstitions, That whosoever will sing this psalm constantly three times a day shall certainly be happy in the world to come. In this psalm, I. David engages himself and others to praise God, ver. 1, 2, 4–7, 10–12. II. He fastens upon those things that are proper matter for praise, God's greatness (ver. 3), his goodness (ver. 8, 9), the proofs of both in the administration of his kingdom (ver. 13), the kingdom of providence (ver. 14–16), the kingdom of grace (ver. 17–20), and then he concludes with a resolution to continue praising God (ver. 21).

David's *psalm* of praise.

Verses 1–9

The entitling of this *David's psalm of praise* may intimate that he took a particular pleasure in it and sung it often; it was his companion wherever he went. In this former part of the psalm God's glorious attributes are praised as, in the latter part of the psalm, his kingdom and the administration of it.

I. Who shall be employed in giving glory to God. Whatever others do, the psalmist will himself be much in praising God. It was his duty; it was his delight. He would give glory to God, not only in his solemn devotions, but in his common conversation. He will be constant to this work: *Every day will I bless thee.* No day must pass, though ever so busy a day, though ever so sorrowful a day, without praising God. God is every day blessing us, doing well for us; there is therefore reason that we should be every day blessing him, speaking well of him. He doubts not but others also would be forward to this work. David's zeal would provoke many, and it has done so. They shall keep it up in an uninterrupted succession (*v.* 4): "*One generation shall praise thy works to another.*"

II. What we must give to God the glory of: his greatness and his great works. We must declare, *Great is the Lord, and,* if great, then *greatly to be praised,* with all that is within us, to the utmost of our power. His greatness indeed cannot be comprehended. When we cannot, by searching, find the bottom, we must sit down at the brink, and adore the depth, Rom. xi. 33. We must see God acting and working in all the affairs of this lower world.

His goodness is his glory, Exod. xxxiii. 19. *They shall abundantly utter the memory of thy great goodness,* v. 7. It can never be exhausted, for he ever will be as rich in mercy as he ever was. But, whenever we utter God's great goodness, we must not forget, at the same time, to *sing of his righteousness*; for, as he is gracious in rewarding those that serve him faithfully, so he is righteous in punishing those that rebel against him. There is a fountain of goodness in God's nature (*v.* 8): *The Lord is gracious* to those that serve him; he is *full of compassion* to those that need him, *slow to anger* to those that have offended him, *and of great mercy* to all that seek him and sue to him. He is ready to give, and ready to forgive.

Verse 10–21

The greatness and goodness of God were celebrated in the former part of the psalm; in these verses we are taught to give him *the glory of his kingdom*, in the administration of which his greatness and goodness shine so clearly, so very brightly. Praise is expected (*v.* 10): *All God's works shall praise* him. All God's works do praise him, as the beautiful building praises the builder or the well-drawn picture praises the painter; but the saints bless him as the children of prudent tender parents rise up and call them blessed. *They shall speak of thy kingdom.* His kingdom is great indeed, for all the kings and kingdoms of the earth are under his control. The courts of Solomon and Ahasuerus were magnificent; but, compared with the glorious majesty of God's kingdom, they were but as glow-worms to the sun. When *they speak of the glory of* God's *kingdom* they must *talk of* his *power* (v. 11); and, as a proof of it, let them *make known his mighty acts* (v. 12). Note the perpetuity of it, v. 13. The thrones of princes totter, and the flowers of their crowns wither, monarchies come to an end; but, Lord, *thy kingdom is an everlasting kingdom.* His royal style and title are, *The Lord God, gracious and merciful;* and his government answers to his title. The goodness of God appears in what he does, for all the creatures in general (v. 15, 16): He *provides food for all flesh.* All the creatures live upon God, and, as they had their being from him at first, so on him they depend for the continuance of it. The inferior creatures indeed have not the knowledge of God, nor are capable of it, and yet they are said to *wait upon God,* because they seek their food according to the instinct which the God of nature has put into them. *Thou givest them their meat in due season.* The children of men, in particular, he governs as reasonable creatures. In all the acts of government he is just, injurious to none, but administering justice to all. *The ways of the Lord are equal,* though ours are unequal. He supports those that are sinking, and it is his honour to help the weak, v. 14. He *upholds all that fall,* in that, though they fall, they are not utterly cast down. If those who were *bowed down* by oppression and affliction are *raised up,* it was God that raised them. And, with respect to all those *that are heavy-laden* under the burden of sin, if they come to Christ by faith, he will ease them, he will raise them. He is very ready to hear and answer the prayers of his people, v. 18, 19. In this appears the grace of his kingdom, that his subjects have not only liberty, of petitioning but all the encouragement that can be to petition. It was said (v. 16) that he *satisfies the desire of every living thing,* much more *will he fulfil the desire of those that fear him;* for he that feeds his birds will not starve his babes. *He will hear their call and will save them;* that is hearing them to purpose, as he heard David (that is, saved him) *from the horn of the unicorn,* xxii. 21. He will hear and help us if we worship and serve him with a holy awe of him. In all devotions inward impressions must be answerable to the outward expressions, else they are not performed in truth. He takes those under his special protection who have confidence in him (v. 20): *The Lord preserves all those that love him.* The psalmist concludes (v. 21): *My mouth shall speak the praise of the Lord.* When we have said what we can, in praising God, still there is more to be said. As the end of one mercy is the beginning of another, so should the end of one thanksgiving be. While I have breath to draw, my mouth shall still speak God's praises. *Let all flesh, all mankind, bless his holy name for ever and ever.*

PSALM 146

This and the rest of the psalms that follow begin and end with Hallelujah, a word which puts much of God's praise into a little compass; in it we praise him by his name Jah, the contraction of Jehovah. I. The psalmist engages himself to praise God, ver. 1, 2. II. He engages others to trust in God, which is one way of praising him. 1. He shows why we should not trust in men, ver. 3, 4. 2. Why we should trust in God (ver. 5), because of his power in the kingdom of nature (ver. 6), his dominion in the kingdom of providence (ver. 7), and his grace in the kingdom of the Messiah (ver. 8, 9), that everlasting kingdom (ver. 10), to which many of the Jewish writers refer this psalm.

Verses 1–4

David, himself a prince, considered his dignity as so far from excusing him from praise that it rather obliged him to lead in it; therefore he stirred up himself to it: *Praise the Lord, O my soul!* and he resolved to abide by it: "*I* will praise him with my heart, *I will sing praises* to him as *the Lord,* infinitely blessed and glorious in himself, and as *my God,* in covenant with me." It might be thought that he himself, having been so great a blessing to his country, should be adored, according to the usage of the heathen nations, who deified their heroes, that they should all come and *trust in his shadow.* "No," says David, "*Put not your trust in princes* (v. 3), not in me, not in any other; do not repose your confidence in them. Be not too sure of their constancy and fidelity; it is possible they may both change their minds and break their words." We cannot be sure of their continuance. Suppose he has it in his power to help us while he lives, yet he may be suddenly taken off when we expect most from him (v. 4). Princes are mortal, as well as other men, and therefore we cannot have that assurance of help from them which we may have from that Potentate who hath immortality.

Verses 5–10

The psalmist encourages us to put our confidence in God: *Happy is he that has the God of Jacob for his help, whose hope is in the Lord his God.* Those shall have God for their help who take him for their God, and serve and worship him, have their hope in him, and live a life of dependence upon him. Every believer may look upon him as the God of Jacob, of the church in general, and therefore may expect relief from him, in reference to public distresses, and as his God in particular, and therefore may depend upon him in all personal wants and straits. Dr. Hammond quotes one of the rabbis, who says of v. 10 that it belongs to the days of the Messiah. And that it does so he thinks will appear by comparing v. 7, 8, with the characters Christ gives of the Messiah (Matt. xi. 5, 6), *The blind receive their sight, the lame walk;* and the closing words there, *Blessed is he whosoever shall not be offended in me,* he thinks may very well be supposed to refer to v. 5. *The Lord our God* is the *Maker of the world,* and therefore has all power in himself, and the command of the powers of all the creatures (v. 6). It is very applicable to Christ, by whom God made the world, and *without whom was not anything made that was made.* It is a great support to faith that the Redeemer of the world is the same that was the Creator of it, and therefore has a goodwill to it. He is a God of inviolable fidelity. Our Lord Jesus is the Amen, *the faithful witness,* as well as *the beginning,* the author and principle, *of the creation of God,* Rev. iii. 14. He is the patron of injured innocency: *He pleads the cause of the oppressed,* and (as we read it) he *executes judgment* for them. The Messiah came to rescue the children of men out of the hands of Satan the great oppressor, and, all judgment being committed to him, the executing of judgment upon persecutors is so among the rest, Jude 15. He is a bountiful benefactor to the necessitous: *He gives food to the hungry;* so God does in an ordinary way for the answering of the cravings of nature; so he has done sometimes in an extraordinary way, as when ravens fed Elijah; so Christ did more than once when he fed thousands miraculously. This encourages us to hope in him as the nourisher of our souls with the bread of life. He is the author of liberty to those that were bound: *The Lord looseth the prisoners.* He brought Israel out of the house of bondage in Egypt and afterwards in Babylon. The miracles Christ wrought, in making the dumb to speak and the deaf to hear with that one word, *Ephphatha—Be opened,* his cleansing lepers, and so discharging them from their confinement, and his raising the dead out of their graves, may all be included in this one of *loosing the prisoners*; and we may take encouragement from those to hope in him for that spiritual liberty which he came to proclaim, Isa. lxi. 1, 2. He gives sight to those that have been long deprived of it: *The Lord can open the eyes of the blind*, and has often given to his afflicted people to see that comfort which before they were not aware of; witness Gen. xxi. 19, and the prophet's servant, 2 Kings vi. 17. But this has special reference to Christ; for *since the world began was it not heard that any man opened the eyes of one that was born blind* till Christ did it (John ix. 32) and thereby encouraged us to hope in him for spiritual illumination. He *raises those that are bowed down* by supporting them under their burdens, and, in due time, removing their burdens. This was literally performed by Christ when he made a poor woman straight that had been *bowed together, and could in no wise lift up herself* (Luke xiii. 12); and he still does it by his grace, giving rest to those that were weary and heavily laden, and raising up with his comforts those that were humbled and cast down. *The Lord loveth the righteous.* He has a tender concern for those that stand in special need of his care: *The Lord preserves the strangers.* It is the glory of the Messiah that he will subvert all the counsels of hell and earth that militate against his church. His kingdom shall continue through all the revolutions of time, to the utmost ages of eternity, *v.* 10. Let *this* encourage us to trust in God at all times that *the Lord shall reign for ever*, in spite of all the malignity of the powers of darkness, *even thy God, O Zion! unto all generations*.

PSALM 147

This is another psalm of praise. Some think it was penned after the return of the Jews from their captivity; but what is said ver. 2, 13, may well enough be applied to the first building and fortifying of Jerusalem, and the gathering in of those that had been outcasts in Saul's time. The Septuagint divides it into two; but both of the same import. I. We are called upon to praise God, ver. 1, 7, 12. II. We are furnished with matter for praise, for God is to be glorified, 1. As the God of nature, ver. 4, 5, 8, 9, 15–18. 2. As the God of grace, ver. 3, 6, 10, 11. 3. As the God of Israel, Jerusalem, and Zion, settling their civil state (ver. 2, 13, 14), and especially settling religion among them, ver. 19, 20.

Verses 1–11

I. The duty of praise is recommended to us. We are called to it again and again: *Praise you the Lord* (*v.* 1), and again (*v.* 7), *Sing unto the Lord with thanksgiving, sing praise upon the harp to our God* (let all our praises be directed to him and centre in him), *for it is good* to do so; it is our duty, and therefore good in itself. In giving honour to God we really do ourselves a great deal of honour.

II. God is the proper object of our praises. Is Jerusalem to be raised out of small beginnings? Is it to be recovered out of its ruins? In both cases, *The Lord builds up Jerusalem.* The gospel-church, the Jerusalem that is from above, is of his building. Are any of his people outcasts? Have they made themselves so by their own folly? He gathers them by giving them repentance and bringing them again into the communion of saints. They are *broken in heart*, humbled, and troubled, for sin, inwardly pained at the remembrance of it. Their very hearts are rent, under the sense of the dishonour they have done to God and the injury they have done to themselves by sin. To those whom God heals with the consolations of his Spirit he speaks peace. The stars are innumerable, but *he calleth them all by their names*. They are his servants, he musters them; they come and go at his bidding, and all their motions are under his direction. He mentions this as one instance of many, to show that *great is our Lord and of great power* (he can do what he pleases), and of *his understanding there is no computation.* Man's knowledge is soon drained. But God's knowledge is a depth that can never be fathomed. *The Lord lifts up the meek*, who abase themselves before him, and whom men trample on; but *the wicked*, who conduct themselves insolently towards God and scornfully

towards all mankind, who lift themselves in pride and folly, he *casteth down to the ground.* Though he is so great as to command the stars, he is so good as not to forget even the fowls *v.* 8, 9. *He covereth the heaven with clouds.* Clouds look melancholy, and yet without them we could have no rain and consequently no fruit. Thus afflictions, for the present, look black, and dark, and unpleasant, but from these clouds of affliction come those showers that make the harvest to *yield the peaceable fruits of righteousness* (Heb. xii. 11). By the rain which distils on the earth he *makes grass to grow upon the mountains*, even the high mountains, which man neither takes care of nor reaps the benefit of. This grass he *gives to the beast* for *his food*, the beast of the mountains which runs wild, which man makes no provision for. And even the *young ravens*, which, being forsaken by their old ones, *cry*, are heard by him, and ways are found to feed them. God will delight to honour, not the strength of armies, but the strength of grace. *He delighteth not in the strength of the horse*, the warhorse, nor in infantry, for he *taketh no pleasure in the legs of a man.* If one king, making war with another king, goes to God to pray for success, it will not avail him to plead, "Lord, I have a gallant army, the horse and foot in good order." But God is pleased to own the strength of grace. The Lord accepts and *takes pleasure* in those that *fear him and that hope in his mercy.* Our fear must save our hope from swelling into presumption, and our hope must save our fear from sinking into despair.

Verses 12–20

Jerusalem, and Zion, the holy city, the holy hill, are here called upon to *praise God, v.* 12. Jerusalem and Zion must praise God, 1. For their common safety. They had gates, and kept their gates barred in times of danger; but that would not have been an effectual security to them if God had not *strengthened the bars of their gates* and fortified their fortifications. 2. For the increase of their people. This strengthens the bars of the gates as much as anything. 3. For the public tranquillity, that they were delivered from the terrors and desolations of war: *He makes peace in thy borders*, by putting an end to the wars that were, and preventing the wars that were threatened and feared. 4. For great plenty, the common effect of peace: *He filleth thee with the finest of the wheat.* Canaan abounded with the best wheat (Deut. xxxii. 14) and exported it to the countries abroad, as appears, Ezek. xxvii. 17. The land of Israel was not enriched with precious stones nor spices, but with *the finest of the wheat*, with bread, which strengthens man's heart. He that protects Zion and Jerusalem is that God of power from whom all the powers of nature are derived and on whom they depend. As the world was at first made, so it is still upheld and governed, by a word of almighty power. *God speaks and it is done.* With him are the *treasures of the snow and the hail* (Job xxxviii. 22, 23), and out of these treasures he draws as he pleases. It falls silently, and makes no more noise than the fall of a lock of wool; it covers the earth, and keeps it warm like a fleece of wool, and so promotes its fruitfulness. God can work by contraries, and bring meat out of the eater, can warm the earth with cold snow. When he pleases (*v.* 18) *he sends out his word and melts them;* the frost, the snow, the ice, are all dissolved quickly, in order to which he *causes the wind*, the *south wind*, to blow, and *the waters*, which were frozen, *flow* again as they did before. This thawing word may represent the gospel of Christ, and this thawing wind the Spirit of Christ (for the Spirit is compared to the wind, John iii. 8); both are sent for the melting of frozen souls. Converting grace, like the thaw, softens the heart that was hard, moistens it, and melts it into tears of repentance; it warms good affections, and makes them to flow, which, before, were chilled and stopped up. It is very evident, and yet how it is done is unaccountable: such is the change wrought in the conversion of a soul, when God's word and Spirit are sent to melt it and restore it to itself. Jacob and Israel had God's statutes and judgments among them. They were under his peculiar government; the municipal laws of their nation were of his framing and enacting, and their constitution was a theocracy. They had the benefit of divine revelation; the great things of God's law were written to them. They did not find out God's statutes and judgments of themselves, but *God showed his word unto Jacob*, and by that word he made known to them his *statutes and judgments*. Other nations had plenty of outward good things; some nations were very rich, others had pompous powerful princes and polite literature, but none were blessed with God's statutes and judgments as Israel were. Let *Israel* therefore *praise the Lord* in the observance of these statutes.

PSALM 148

This psalm is a most solemn and earnest call to all creatures, according to their capacity, to praise their Creator, and to show forth his eternal power and Godhead, the invisible things of which are manifested in the things that are seen. Thereby the psalmist is very desirous that he may be more praised, and therefore does all he can to engage all about him, and all who shall come after him, whose hearts must be very dead and cold if they be not raised, in praising God, by the lofty flights of divine poetry which we find in this psalm. I. He calls upon the creatures that are placed in the upper world, to praise the Lord, both those that are intellectual beings, and are capable of doing it actively (ver. 1, 2), and those that are not, and are therefore capable of doing it only objectively, ver. 3–6. II. He calls upon the creatures of this lower world, both those that can only minister matter of praise (ver. 7–10), and those that, being endued with reason, are capable of offering up this sacrifice (ver. 11–13), especially his own people, who have more cause to do it than any other, ver. 14.

Verses 1–6

We, in this dark and depressed world, know but little of the world of light and exaltation. But this we know,

I. That there is above us a world of blessed angels by whom God is praised, an innumerable company of them. The psalmist has an eye here, *v.* 1, 2, to *the heavens*, to *the heights*. The heavens are the heights, and therefore we must lift up our souls above the world unto God in *the heavens*, and *on things above* we must *set our affections*. It is his delight to think that God is praised *in the heights*. When, in singing this psalm, we call upon the angels to praise God (as we did, ciii. 20), we mean that we desire God may be praised by the ablest hands and in the best manner, that we have a spiritual communion with those that dwell in his house above, and that we have come by faith, and hope, and holy love, to the *innumerable company of angels*, Heb. xii. 22.

II. That there is above us not only an assembly of blessed spirits, but a system of vast bodies too, and those bright ones, in which God is praised. There are the *sun, moon*, and *stars*, which continually, either day or night, present themselves to our view, as looking-glasses, in which we may see a faint shadow (for so I must call it, not a resemblance) of the glory of him that is *the Father of lights, v.* 3. *The heavens of heavens are the Lord's* (cxv. 16) and yet *they cannot contain him*, 1 Kings viii. 27. The Chaldee paraphrase reads it, *Praise him, you heavens of heavens, and you waters that depend on the word of him who is above the heavens. Let them praise the name of the Lord*, that is, let us praise the name of the Lord for them, and observe what constant and fresh matter for praise may be fetched from them. *He commanded* them (great as they are) out of nothing, *and they were created* at a word's speaking.

He still upholds and preserves them (*v.* 6): *He hath established them for ever and ever*, that is, to the end of time, a short ever, but it is their ever; they shall last as long as there is occasion for them.

Verses 7–14

Even in this world God is praised: *Praise you the Lord from the earth, v.* 7.

I. Even those creatures that are not dignified with the powers of reason are summoned into this concert, because God may be glorified in them, *v.* 7–10. Let the *dragons* or *whales*, that sport themselves in the mighty waters (civ. 26), dance before the Lord, to his glory. *All deeps*, and their inhabitants, praise God. *Out of the depths* God may be praised. There are fiery meteors; lightning is fire. There are watery meteors, *hail*, and *snow*, and the *vapours* of which they are gendered. There are *stormy winds*; be they ever so strong, so stormy, they *fulfil God's word*; and by *this* Christ showed himself to have a divine power, that he *commanded even the winds and the seas*, and *they obeyed him*. There are *mountains and all hills*, from which we may fetch matter for praise; there are plants, some exalted by their usefulness, as the *fruitful trees*, for the fruits of which God is to be praised, others by their stateliness, as *all cedars*, those *trees of the Lord*, civ. 16. In the animal kingdom we find God glorified, even by the *beasts* that run wild, *and all cattle* that are tame and in the service of man, *v.* 10. Even the *creeping things* have not sunk so low, nor do the *flying fowl* soar so high, as not to be called upon to *praise the Lord*. Much of the wisdom, power, and goodness of the Creator appears in the several capacities and instincts of the creatures, in the provision made for them and the use made of them. Surely we cannot but acknowledge God with wonder and thankfulness.

II. Much more those creatures that are dignified with the powers of reason ought to employ them in praising God: *Kings of the earth and all people, v.* 11, 12. God is to be praised in the order and constitution of kingdoms, the *pars imperans—the part that commands*, and the *pars subdita—the part that is subject: Kings of the earth and all people*. God is to be praised also in the constitution of families, for he is the founder of them; and for all the comfort of relations, the comfort that parents and children, brothers and sisters, have in each other, God is to be praised. Let all manner of persons praise God. Those on whom God has put honour must honour him with it, and the power they are entrusted with puts them in a capacity of bringing more glory to God and doing him more service than others. Yet the praises of the people are expected also. Christ despised not the hosannas of the multitude. *Young men and maidens*, let them turn their mirth into this channel. *Old men* must not think that either the gravity or the infirmity of their age will excuse them from it; *and children* too must begin betimes to praise God. *His glory is above* both *the earth and the heaven*, and let all the inhabitants both of earth and heaven praise him and yet acknowledge his name to be exalted *far above all blessing and praise*.

III. Most of all his own people, who are dignified with peculiar privileges, must in a peculiar manner give glory to him, *v.* 14. They had him *nigh to them in all that which they called upon him for*. This blessing has now come upon the Gentiles, through Christ, for those that *were afar off are* by *his blood made nigh*, Eph. ii 13. Let those whom God honours honour him.

PSALM 149

The foregoing psalm was a hymn of praise to the Creator; this is a hymn of praise to the Redeemer. It is a psalm of triumph in the God of Israel, and over the enemies of Israel. Some conjecture that it was penned when David had taken the stronghold of Zion, and settled his government there. But it looks further, to the kingdom of the Messiah, who goes forth conquering and to conquer. I. Abundance of joy to all the people of God, ver. 1–5. II. Abundance of terror to the proudest of their enemies, ver. 6–9.

Verses 1–5

I. The calls given to God's Israel to praise. *All his works* were, in the foregoing psalm, excited to *praise him*; but here his saints in a particular manner are required to bless him. *Israel* in general, the body of the church (*v.* 2), *the children of Zion* particularly, the inhabitants of that holy hill, who are nearer to God than other Israelites; those that have the word and ordinances of God near to them, are justly expected to do more in praising God than others. All true Christians may call themselves *the children of Zion*, for in faith and hope *we have come unto Mount Zion*, Heb. xii. 22. *Let Israel rejoice*, and *the children of Zion be joyful*, and *the saints be joyful in glory*. Much of the power of godliness in the heart consists in making God our chief joy and solacing ourselves in him; and our faith in Christ is described by our rejoicing in him. We must sing a *new song*, sing with new affections, which make the song new, though the words have been used before. The gospel-canon for psalmody is to *sing with the spirit* and with *the understanding*. We must praise God in public, in the *solemn assembly* (*v.* 1), *in the congregation of saints*. Thus God's name must be owned before the world. We must praise him in private. *Let the saints* be so transported with their joy in God as to *sing aloud upon their beds*, when they awake in the night, full of the praises of God, as David, cxix. 62.

II. The cause given to God's Israel for praise. He gave us our being as men, and we have reason to praise him for that, for it is a noble and excellent being. He gave Israel their being as a people, as a church. If he made them, he is their King; he that gave being no doubt may give law. He is a king that rules by love, and therefore to be praised; for *the Lord takes pleasure in his people*, in their services, in their prosperity, in communion with them, and in the communications of his favour to them. He has prepared for their future glory: *He will beautify the meek*, the lowly, and contrite in heart, that are patient under their afflictions and *show all meekness towards all men*. They shall appear comely, before all the world, with the comeliness that he puts upon them. The righteous shall be beautified in that day when they *shine forth as the sun*. In the hopes of this, let them now, in the darkest day, *sing a new song*.

Verses 6–9

The Israel of God are here represented triumphing over their enemies, which is both the matter of their praise (let them give to God the glory of those triumphs) and the recompence of their praise; those that are truly thankful to God for their tranquillity shall be blessed with victory. The many victories over the nations of Canaan and other nations that were devoted to destruction began in Moses and Joshua, who, when they taught Israel *the high praises of the Lord*, did withal put a *two-edged sword in their hand*; David did so too, for he was the captain of their hosts, and taught the children of Judah the use of the bow (2 Sam. i. 18). They *executed vengeance upon the heathen* (the Philistines, Moabites, Ammonites, and others, 2 Sam. viii. 1, &c.) *and punishments upon the people*, for all the wrong they had done to God's people, *v.* 7. Their kings and nobles were taken prisoners (*v.* 8). Some apply it to the time of the Maccabees, when the Jews sometimes gained great advantages against their oppressors. And if it seem strange that the meek should, notwithstanding that character, be thus severe, they do not do it from any personal malice and revenge, or any bloody politics that they govern

themselves by, but by commission from God, according to his direction, and in obedience to his command. But, since now no such special commissions can be produced, this will by no means justify the violence either of subjects against their princes or of princes against their subjects, or both against their neighbours, under pretence of religion; for Christ never intended that his gospel should be propagated by fire and sword or his righteousness wrought by the wrath of man. When the high praises of God are in our mouth with them we should have an olive-branch of peace in our hands. Christ's victories are by the power of his gospel and grace over spiritual enemies, in which all believers are more than conquerors. The word of God is the *two-edged sword* (Heb. iv. 12), the *sword of the Spirit* (Eph. vi. 17). With this two-edged sword the first preachers of the gospel obtained a glorious victory over the powers of darkness; vengeance was executed upon the gods of the heathen, by the conviction and conversion of those that had been long their worshippers. The strongholds of Satan were cast down (2 Cor. x. 4, 5); great men were made to tremble at the word, as Felix; Satan, the god of this world, was cast out, according to the judgment given against him. With this two-edged sword believers fight against their own corruptions, and, through the grace of God, subdue and mortify them; self, that once sat king, is bound with chains and brought into subjection to the yoke of Christ. *This honour have all the saints.*

PSALM 150

The first and last of the psalms are both short and very memorable. But the scope of them is very different: the first psalm is an elaborate instruction in our duty, to prepare us for the comforts of our devotion; this is all rapture and transport, and perhaps was penned on purpose to be the conclusion of these sacred songs. The psalmist had been himself full of the praises of God, and here he would fain fill all the world with them: again and again he calls, "Praise the Lord, praise him, praise him," no less than thirteen times in these six short verses. He shows, I. For what God is to be praised, ver. 1, 2. II. How God is to be praised, ver. 3–5. III. Who must praise the Lord; it is everyone's business, ver. 6.

Verses 1–6

If, as some suppose, this psalm was primarily intended for the Levites, to stir them up in the house of the Lord, as singers and players on instruments, yet we must take it as speaking to us, who are made to our God spiritual priests.

I. This tribute of praise comes, 1. From *his sanctuary*; praise him there. Let his priests, let his people, attend there with their praises. Where should he be praised, but there where he does, in a special manner, both manifest his glory and communicate his grace? 2. From *the firmament of his power*. *Praise him* because of his power and glory which appear in the firmament, its vastness, its brightness, and because of the powerful influences it has upon this earth.

II. Upon what account this tribute of praise is due, 1. The works of his power (*v.* 2): *Praise him for his mighty acts;* for *his mightinesses* (so the word is), for all the instances of his might, the power of his providence, the power of his grace, what he has done in the creation, government, and redemption of the world, for the children of men in general, for his own church and children in particular. 2. The glory and majesty of his being: *Praise him according to his excellent greatness*. Not that our praises can bear any proportion to God's greatness, for it is infinite. Be not afraid of saying too much in the praises of God, all the danger is of saying too little.

III. In what manner this tribute must be paid, with all the kinds of musical instruments that were then used in the temple-service, *v.* 3–5. In serving God we should spare no cost nor pains. The best music in God's ears is devout and pious affections, *not a melodious string, but a melodious heart.* Praise God with a strong faith; praise him with holy love and delight; praise him with an entire confidence in Christ; praise him with a believing triumph over the powers of darkness; praise him by a universal respect to all his commands; praise him by promoting the interests of the kingdom of his grace; praise him by a lively hope and expectation of the kingdom of his glory. Various instruments being used in praising God, it should yet be done with perfect harmony; they must not hinder, but help one another. The New Testament concert, is *with one mind and one mouth to glorify God*, Rom. xv. 6.

IV. Who must pay this tribute (*v.* 6): *Let everything that has breath praise the Lord.* He began with a call to those that had a place in his sanctuary and were employed in the temple-service; but he concludes with a call to all the children of men, in prospect of the time when the Gentiles should be taken into the church, and *in every place*, as acceptably as at Jerusalem, *this incense should be offered*, Mal. i. 11. The singing of birds is a sort of praising God. The brutes do in effect say to man, "We would praise God if we could; do you do it for us." Now that the gospel is ordered to be preached *to every creature*, to every human creature, it is required that every human creature praise the Lord. Prayers are called *our breathings*, Lam. iii. 56. Let everyone that breathes towards God in prayer, breathe forth his praises too. While we have breath let us praise the Lord, and when death runs us out of breath, we shall remove to a better state to breathe God's praises in a freer better air.

The first three of the five books of psalms (according to the Hebrew division) concluded with *Amen and Amen*, the fourth with *Amen, Hallelujah*, but the last, and in it the whole book, concludes with only *Hallelujah*, because the last six psalms are wholly taken up in praising God and there is not a word of complaint or petition in them. Let us often take a pleasure in thinking what glorified saints are doing in heaven, what those are doing whom we have been acquainted with on earth, but who have gone before us thither; and let it quicken us to do this part of the will of God on earth as those do it that are in heaven. *Hallelujah* is the word there; let us echo to it now, *Hallelujah, praise you the Lord.*

AN EXPOSITION, WITH PRACTICAL OBSERVATIONS, OF

THE PROVERBS

I. A new author, made use of by the Holy Ghost for making known the mind of God to us, is Solomon; through his hand came this book of Scripture and the two that follow it, Ecclesiastes and Canticles, a sermon and a song. Some think he wrote Canticles when he was very young, Proverbs in the midst of his days, and Ecclesiastes when he was old. 1. He was a king, and a king's son. The penmen of scripture, hitherto, were most of them men of rank in the world, as Moses and Joshua, Samuel and David, and now Solomon; but, after him, the inspired writers were generally poor prophets, men of no figure in the world, because that dispensation was approaching in which God would choose the *weak and foolish things of the world to confound the wise and mighty* and the poor should be employed to evangelize. Solomon was a very rich king, and his dominions were very large, and yet he was a prophet and a prophet's son. 2. He was one whom God endued with extraordinary measures of wisdom and knowledge, in answer to his prayers at his accession to the throne. His prayer was exemplary: *Give me a wise and an understanding heart;* the answer to it was encouraging: he had what he desired and *all other things were added to him.* 3. He was one who had his faults, and in his latter end turned aside from those good ways of God. But let those who are most eminently useful take warning by this not to be proud or secure; and let us all learn not to think the worse of good instructions though we have them from those who do not themselves altogether live up to them.

II. A new way of writing, in which divine wisdom is taught us by Proverbs, or short sentences, which contain their whole design within themselves and are not connected with one another. We have had divine *laws, histories,* and *songs,* and now divine *proverbs;* such various methods has Infinite Wisdom used for our instruction. Teaching by proverbs was, 1. An ancient way of teaching. It was the most ancient way among the Greeks; each of the seven wise men of Greece had some one saying that he valued himself upon, and that made him famous. These sentences were inscribed on pillars, and had in great veneration. 2. It was a plain and easy way of teaching. A proverb, which carries both its sense and its evidence in a little compass, is quickly apprehended and easily retained. 3. It was a very profitable way of teaching, and served admirably well to answer the end. The world is governed by proverbs. *As saith the proverb of the ancients* (1 Sam. xxiv. 13), or (as we commonly express it), *As the old saying is,* goes very far with most men in forming their notions and fixing their resolves. Some think we may judge of the temper and character of a nation by the complexion of its vulgar proverbs. Yet there are many corrupt proverbs, which tend to debauch men's minds and harden them in sin. The devil has his proverbs, and the world and the flesh have their proverbs, which reflect reproach on God and religion (as Ezek. xii. 22; xviii. 2). These proverbs of Solomon were not merely a collection of the wise sayings that had been formerly delivered, as some have imagined, but were the dictates of the Spirit of God in Solomon. The very first of them (*ch.* i. 7) agrees with what God said to man in the beginning (Job xxviii. 28, *Behold, the fear of the Lord, that is wisdom*); so that though Solomon was great, and his name may serve as much as any man's to recommend his writings, yet, behold, *a greater than Solomon is here.* It is God, by Solomon, that here speaks to us. The first nine chapters of this book are reckoned as a preface, by way of exhortation to the study and practice of wisdom's rules. We have then the first volume of Solomon's proverbs (*ch.* x—xxiv); after that a second volume (*ch.* xxv—xxix); and then Agur's prophecy (*ch.* xxx) and Lemuel's, *ch.* xxxi.

CHAPTER 1

Those who read David's psalms, especially those towards the latter end, would be tempted to think that religion is all rapture and consists in nothing but the ecstasies and transports of devotion; and doubtless there is a time for them; but, while we are on earth we have a life to live in the flesh, must have a conversation in the world, and into that we must now be taught to carry our religion, which is a rational thing, and very serviceable to the government of human life, to make the face shine before men, in a prudent, honest, useful conversation, and to make the heart burn towards God in holy and pious affections. In this chapter we have, I. The title of the book, showing the general scope and design of it, ver. 1–6. II. The first principle of it recommended to our serious consideration, ver. 7–9. III. A necessary caution against bad company, ver. 10–19. IV. A faithful and lively representation of wisdom's reasonings with the children of men, and the certain ruin of those who turn a deaf ear to those reasonings, ver. 20–33.

Verses 1–6

An introduction to this book, which some think was prefixed by the collector Ezra; but it is rather supposed to have been penned by Solomon himself, who, in the beginning of his book, proposes his end in writing it.

I. Who wrote these wise sayings, *v.* 1. They are *the proverbs of Solomon.* His name signifies *peaceable,* and the character both of his spirit and of his reign were peaceable. David, whose life was full of troubles, wrote a book of devotion; for *is any afflicted? let him pray.* Solomon, who lived quietly, wrote a book of instruction; for when the *churches had rest they were edified.* In times of peace we should learn ourselves, and teach others, that which in troublous times we must practise. He was *the son of David.* He had been blessed with a good education, and many a prayer had been put up for him (Ps. lxxii. 1), the effect of both appeared in his wisdom and usefulness. He was *king of Israel.* All the earth sought to Solomon *to hear his wisdom* (1 Kings iv. 30; x. 24). His servants had collected 3000 proverbs of his, but these, of his own writing, do not amount to a thousand. In these he was divinely inspired.

II. They were written (*v.* 2–4) for the use and benefit of all. This book will help us, 1. To form right notions of things, and to possess our minds with clear and distinct ideas, that we may know both how to speak and act wisely. 2. To distinguish between truth and falsehood, good and evil—*to perceive the words of understanding.* 3. To order our conversation aright, *v.* 3. This book will give that knowledge which will dispose us to render to all their due, to God the things that are God's, in all the exercises of religion, and to all men what is due to them.

III. They are of use to all, but are designed especially, 1. For *the simple, to give subtlety to them.* The instructions here given are plain, and those are likely to receive benefit by them who are sensible of their own ignorance and their need to be taught, and those who receive these instructions, though they be simple, will hereby be made subtle, to know the sin they should avoid and the duty they should do. 2. For young people, to give them *knowledge and discretion.* Youth is the learning age, receives impressions, and retains what is then received. Youth is rash, and heady, and inconsiderate; *man is born like the wild ass's colt,* and therefore needs to be broken by the restraints and managed by the rules we find here. Solomon had an eye to posterity in writing this book, hoping by it to season the minds of the rising generation with the generous principles of wisdom and virtue. Those who are young and simple may by them be made wise, and are not excluded from Solomon's school, as they were from Plato's, *v.* 5, 6. Even wise men must hear, and not think themselves too wise to learn. A wise man, by increasing in learning, is profitable to others, 1. As a counsellor. *A man of understanding* in these precepts of wisdom, *shall* by degrees *attain unto wise counsels;* he shall come to *sit at the helm,* so the word signifies. Those whom God has blessed with wisdom must study to do good with it. It is more dignity indeed to be counsellor to the prince, but it is more charity to be counsellor to the poor. 2. As an interpreter (*v.* 6)—*to understand a proverb.* Solomon was himself famous for expounding riddles and resolving hard questions, which was of old the celebrated entertainment of the eastern princes. Here he undertakes to furnish his readers with that talent. "They shall *understand a proverb,* even *the interpretation,* without which the proverb is a nut uncracked; when they hear a wise saying, though it be figurative, they shall take the sense of it, and know how to make use of it."

Verses 7–9

Solomon, having undertaken to *teach a young man knowledge and discretion,* here lays down two general rules, to fear God and honour his parents.

I. Let them have regard to God as their supreme.

1. He lays down this truth, that *the fear of the Lord is the beginning of knowledge* (*v.* 7); it is *the principal part of knowledge* (so the margin). We are not qualified to profit by the instructions that are given us unless our minds be possessed with a holy reverence of God, and every thought within us be brought into obedience to him.

2. To confirm this truth, he observes, *Fools* (atheists, who have no regard to God) *despise wisdom and instruction.* Those are fools who do not fear God and value the scriptures; and though they may pretend to be admirers of wit they are really strangers and enemies to wisdom.

II. Let them have regard to their parents (*v.* 8, 9): *My son, hear the instruction of thy father.* He means, not only that he would have his own children to be observant of him, nor only that he would have his pupils to look upon him as their father and attend to his precepts, but that he would have all children to be dutiful and respectful to their parents.

1. He takes it for granted that parents will, with all the wisdom they have, instruct their children, and, with all the authority they have, give law to them for their good. They are reasonable creatures, and when we tell them what they must do we must tell them why. But they are wilful, and therefore with the instruction there is need of a law.

2. He charges children both to receive and to retain the good lessons and laws their parents give them. "*Hear the instruction of thy father,* and be thankful for it, and subscribe to it. *Forsake not their law;* think not that when thou art grown up, and no longer under tutors and governors, thou mayest live at large; no, *the law of thy mother* was according to the law of thy God, and therefore it must never be forsaken." Some observe that whereas the laws of the Persians

and Romans, provided only that children should pay respect to their father, the divine law secures the honour of the mother also. "The instructions and laws of thy parents, carefully observed, *shall be an ornament of grace unto thy head* (*v.* 9), and shall make thee look as those that wear gold *chains about their necks.*"

Verses 10–19

Here Solomon gives another general rule to young people to take heed of the snare of bad company (*v.* 10): "*My son,* whom I love, and have a tender concern for, *if sinners entice thee, consent thou not.*" Sinners love company in sin; the angels that fell were tempters almost as soon as they were sinners. They do not threaten or argue, but entice with flattery and fair speech. "*Consent thou not;* and then, though they entice thee, they cannot force thee. Have no fellowship with them." To enforce this caution,

I. He represents the fallacious reasonings which sinners use in their enticements, for the beguiling of unstable souls. He specifies highwaymen, who do what they can to draw others into their gang, *v.* 11–14. "*Come with us* (*v.* 11); let us have thy company." At first they pretend to ask no more; but the courtship rises higher (*v.* 14): "*Cast in thy lot among us;* let us resolve to live and die together: and *let us all have one purse,* that what we get together we may spend merrily together." They thirst after blood, and hate those that are innocent, because by their honesty and industry they shame and condemn them: "*Let us* therefore *lay wait for* their *blood,* and *lurk privily* for them; they travel unarmed; therefore we shall make easy prey of them. And, O how sweet it will be to *swallow them up alive!*" (*v.* 12). They hope to get a good booty by it (*v.* 13): "We shall *find all precious substance* by following this trade. What though we venture our necks by it? we shall *fill our houses with spoil.*" They call it *precious substance;* whereas it is neither substance nor precious; it is a shadow; it is vanity, especially that which is got by robbery, Ps. lxii. 10.

II. He shows the perniciousness of these ways (*v.* 15): "*My son, walk not thou in the way with them; refrain thy foot from their path;* do not take example by them, nor do as they do." Consider their way (*v.* 16): *Their feet run to evil,* to that which is displeasing to God and hurtful to mankind, for they *make haste to shed blood.* The way of sin is down-hill; men not only cannot stop themselves, but, the longer they continue in it, the faster they run, and make haste in it. They are plainly told that this wicked way will certainly end in their own destruction, and yet they persist in it. They are like the silly bird, that sees the net spread to take her, and yet she is decoyed into it by the bait, and does not take the warning which her own eyes give her, *v.* 17. Their greediness of gain hurries them upon those practices which will not suffer them to live out half their days.

Now, though Solomon specifies only the temptation to rob on the highway, yet he intends hereby to warn us against all other evils which sinners entice men to. Such are the ways of the drunkards and unclean.

Verses 20–33

Solomon, having shown how dangerous it is to hearken to the temptations of Satan, here shows how dangerous it is not to hearken to the calls of God.

I. By whom God calls to us—by *wisdom.* It is *wisdom* that *crieth without.* The word is plural—*wisdoms,* for, as there is infinite wisdom in God, so there is the *manifold wisdom of God,* Eph. iii. 10. God speaks to the children of men by all the kinds of wisdom. 1. Human understanding is wisdom, the light and law of nature, the powers and faculties of reason, and the office of conscience, Job xxxviii. 36. 2. Civil government is wisdom; magistrates are his vicegerents. 3. Divine revelation is wisdom; all its dictates, all its laws, are wise as wisdom itself. God does, by the written word, by his servants the prophets, and all the ministers of this word, declare his mind to sinners. 4. Christ himself is Wisdom, is Wisdoms, for *in him are hidden all the treasures of wisdom and knowledge*, and he is the centre of all divine revelation, not only the *essential Wisdom*, but the *eternal Word*, by whom God speaks to us and to whom he has *committed all judgment*. He calls himself *Wisdom*, Luke vii. 35.

II. He calls to us, 1. Very publicly, that whosoever hath ears to hear may hear. The rules of wisdom are published *without in the streets*, not in the schools only, or in the palaces of princes, but among the common people that pass and repass *in the opening of the gates* and *in the city*. 2. Very pathetically; she *cries*, she *utters her words* with all possible clearness and affection. God is desirous to be heard and heeded.

III. What the call of God and Christ is.

1. He reproves sinners for their folly and their obstinately persisting in it, *v.* 22. In general, they are such as are *simple. Simple ones love simplicity*. They do foolishly, and are in their element, sporting themselves in their own deceivings and flattering themselves in their wickedness. *Scorners delight in scorning*, and make a jest of everything that comes in their way. Scoffers at religion are especially meant. *Fools hate knowledge*. Those are enemies to religion that do not understand it aright. And those are the worst of fools that hate to be instructed. The God of heaven desires the conversion and reformation of sinners and not their ruin, is much displeased with their dilatoriness, he waits to be gracious, and is willing to reason the case with them, *v.* 22.

2. He invites them to repent and become wise, *v.* 23. *Turn you at my reproof*, that is, return to your right mind, turn to God, turn to your duty, turn and live. Those that love simplicity find themselves under a moral impotency to change their own mind and way; they cannot turn by any power of their own. To this God answers, "*Behold, I will pour out my Spirit unto you;* set yourselves to do what you can, and the grace of God shall work in you both to will and to do that good which, without that grace, you could not do." *I will pour out my Spirit unto you*. The means of this grace is the word. It is therefore promised, "*I will make known my words unto you*, not only speak them to you, but give you to understand them."

3. He reads the doom of those that continue obstinate against all these means and methods of grace, *v.* 24–32. The crime is, in short, rejecting Christ and the offers of his grace, and refusing to submit to the terms of his gospel, which would have saved them both from the curse of the *law of God* and from the dominion of the *law of sin.* Christ *stretched out his hand* to offer them mercy, but they *refused* and *no man regarded.* Christ not only reproved them for what they did amiss, but counselled them to do better (those are *reproofs of instruction* and evidences of love and goodwill), but they *set at nought all his counsel* as not worth heeding, and *would none of his reproof, v.* 25. This is repeated (*v.* 30): "They *would none of my counsel*, but rejected it with disdain, *they despised all my reproof*, as if it were all a jest, and not worth taking notice of." They were exhorted to submit to the government of right reason and religion, but they rebelled against both. Reason should not rule them, for *they hated knowledge* (*v.* 29), because it discovered to them the evil of their deeds.

Religion could not rule them, for they *did not choose the fear of the Lord*, but chose to walk in the way of *their heart and in the sight of their eyes.* They would not take the benefit of God's mercy when it was offered them, and therefore justly fall as victims to his justice, *ch.* xxix. 1. Their *calamity will come* (*v.* 26); troubles will come, in mind, in estate, which will convince them of their folly in setting God at a distance. Their *fear shall come* (the thing they were afraid of shall befall them); it shall *come as desolation*, as a mighty deluge bearing down all before it; and it shall come *as a whirlwind*, which suddenly and forcibly drives away all the chaff. *Distress and anguish shall come upon them*, for they shall see no way to escape, *v.* 27. Now God pities their folly, but he will then *laugh at their calamity* (*v.* 26). Those that ridicule religion will thereby but make themselves ridiculous before all the world. Now God is ready to hear their prayers and to meet them with mercy, if they would but seek to him for it; but then the door will be shut, and they shall cry in vain (*v.* 28): "*Then shall they call upon me* when it is too late, *Lord, Lord, open to us*, but *I will not answer*, because, when I called, they would not answer." But, ordinarily, while there is life there is room for prayer and hope of speeding, and therefore this must refer to the inexorable justice of the last judgment. They shall *eat the fruit of their own way*; their wages shall be according to their work. Now they value themselves upon their worldly prosperity; but then that shall help to aggravate their ruin, *v.* 32. They are now proud of their own security and sensuality; but *the ease of the simple* (so the margin reads it) *shall slay them*; the more secure they are the more certain and the more dreadful will their destruction be, *and the prosperity of fools shall* help to *destroy them*, by puffing them up with pride, glueing their hearts to the world, furnishing them with fuel for their lusts, and hardening their hearts in their evil ways.

4. He concludes with an assurance of safety and happiness to all those that submit to the instructions of wisdom (*v.* 33): "*Whoso hearkeneth unto me*, and will be ruled by me, he *shall dwell* under the special protection of Heaven, so that nothing shall do him any real hurt. He shall have no disquieting apprehensions of danger; he shall not only be safe from evil, but *quiet from the fear of* it."

CHAPTER 2

Solomon, in this chapter, applies himself to those who are willing to be taught; and, I. He shows them that, if they would use the means of knowledge and grace, they should obtain of God the knowledge and grace which they seek, ver. 1–9. II. He shows them what advantage it would be to them. 1. It would preserve them from the snares of evil men (ver. 10–15) and of evil women, ver. 16–19. 2. It would direct them into, and keep them in, the way of good men, ver. 20–22.

Verses 1–9

Solomon tells us where we may find wisdom, and how we may get it.

I. What means we must use that we may obtain wisdom.

1. We must closely attend to the word of God, for that is the word of wisdom, *which is able to make us wise unto salvation, v.* 1, 2. The words of God are the fountain and standard of wisdom and understanding. Many wise things may be found in human compositions, but divine revelation, and true religion built upon it, are all wisdom.

2. We must be much in prayer, *v.* 3. We must *cry after knowledge*. We must *lift our voice for understanding*, lift it up to heaven; thence these good and perfect gifts must be expected. We must *give our voice to understanding* (so the word is), speak for it, vote for it, submit the tongue to the command of wisdom.

3. We must be willing to take pains (*v.* 4); we must *seek it as silver*, preferring it far before all the wealth of this world, and labouring in search of it as those who dig in the mines.

II. What success we may hope' for in the use of these means. Our labour shall not be in vain; for, "*Thou shalt understand the fear of the Lord* (*v.* 5). that is, thou shalt know how to worship him aright." *Thou shalt find the knowledge of God*, which is necessary to our fearing him aright. We shall know how to conduct ourselves aright towards all men (*v.* 9): "*Thou shalt understand*, by the word of God, *righteousness, and judgment, and equity*, shalt learn those principles of justice, and charity, and fair dealing, which shall make thee fit for every relation, and faithful to every trust. It shall give thee not only a right notion of justice, but a disposition to practise it, and to render to all their due."

III. What ground we have to hope for this success in our pursuits of wisdom; we must take our encouragement herein from God only, *v.* 6–8.

1. God has wisdom to bestow, *v.* 6. *The Lord* not only is wise himself, but he *gives wisdom*.

2. He has blessed the world with a revelation of his will. *Out of his mouth*, by the law and the prophets, by the written word and by his ministers, *come knowledge and understanding*, such a discovery of truth and good as will make us truly knowing and intelligent.

3. He has particularly provided that good men, who are sincerely disposed to do his will, shall have that *knowledge and* that *understanding*, *v.* 7, 8. *The righteous*, and those who *walk uprightly*, are *his saints*, devoted to his honour, and set apart for his service. The means of wisdom are given to all, but wisdom itself, *sound wisdom*, is laid *up for the righteous*, laid up in Christ their head. The same that is the Spirit of revelation in the word is a Spirit of wisdom in the souls of those that are sanctified. Some read it, He *lays up substance for the righteous*, not only substantial knowledge, but substantial happiness and comfort, Prov. viii. 21. Even those who *walk uprightly* may be brought into danger for the trial of their faith, but God is *a buckler to them*, so that nothing that happens to them shall do them any real hurt. If we depend upon God, and seek to him for wisdom, he will uphold us in our integrity, will enable us to *keep the paths of judgment*; for he *preserves the way of his saints*. *Work out your salvation*, for *God works in you*.

Verses 10–22

True wisdom will keep us from the paths of sin, and do us a greater kindness than if it enriched us with all the wealth of the world.

I. Our preservation from the evil of sin, and, consequently, from trouble that attends it. "When wisdom has entire possession of thee, it will *keep thee*." When it *enters into the heart* as the leaven into the dough, then it is likely to do us good. "When thou callest the practice of virtue, not a slavery and a task, but *liberty* and *pleasure*, then thou wilt find the benefit of it." More particularly, wisdom will preserve us from men of corrupt principles, atheistical profane men, who make it their business to debauch young men's judgments, and instil into their minds prejudices against religion and arguments for vice: "It will *deliver thee from the way of the evil man* (*v.* 12), *from the way* in which he walks, and in which he would persuade thee to walk." They *speak froward things*; they say all they can against religion. They *leave the paths of uprightness*, which they were trained up in, *to walk in the ways of darkness*, which hate the light, in which men are led blindfold by ignorance and error, and which lead men into utter darkness. They take a pleasure in sin, both in committing it

themselves and in seeing others commit it (*v.* 14). They *rejoice* in an opportunity *to do evil*. It is sport to fools to do mischief; to see those that are hopeful drawn into the ways of sin, and then to see them hardened and confirmed in those ways. Their *ways are crooked*, a great many windings and turnings to escape the pursuit of their convictions. Women of corrupt practices lead to *fleshly lusts*, which defile the body, that living temple, but withal *war against the soul*. The adulteress is here called *the strange woman*, to be shunned by every Israelite as if she were a heathen, and a stranger to that sacred commonwealth. She is false to him whom she entices. She speaks fair, tells him how much she admires him above any man, but she *flatters with her words*; she has no true affection for him, nor any desire of his welfare, any more than Delilah had of Samson's. All she designs is to pick his pocket and gratify a base lust of her own. She is false to her husband, and violates the sacred obligation she lies under to him. She is false to God himself: She *forgets the covenant of her God*, the marriage-covenant (*v.* 17), to which God is not only a witness, but a party, for, he having instituted the ordinance, both sides vow to him to be true to each other. Take heed of the sin of whoredom. It is a sin that has a direct tendency to the killing of the soul, the extinguishing of all good affections and dispositions in it. Let discretion preserve every man, not only from the evil woman, but from the evil house, for the *house inclines to death*; *and her paths unto Rephaim*, to the *giants* (so some read it), the sinners of the old world, who, living in luxury and excess of riot, were cut down out of time, and their foundation was overthrown with a flood. *None*, or next to none, *that go unto her, return again*. It is very rare that any who are caught in this snare of the devil recover themselves, so much is the heart hardened, and the mind blinded, by the deceitfulness of this sin. Many interpreters think that this caution against the *strange woman*, besides the literal sense, is to be understood figuratively, as a caution against idolatry, which is spiritual whoredom. Wisdom will keep thee from all familiarity with the worshippers of images. Wisdom will keep thee from being captivated by the carnal mind, and from subjecting the spirit to the dominion of the flesh.

II. This wisdom will be of use to guide and direct us in that which is good (*v.* 20): *That thou mayest walk in the way of good men*. It will be our wisdom to walk in that way, to ask for the good old way and walk therein, Jer. vi. 16; Heb. vi. 12; xii. 1. *The paths of the righteous* are the paths of life. "That thou mayest imitate those excellent persons, the patriarchs and prophets, and be preserved in *the paths of those righteous* men who followed after them." *The upright shall dwell in the land*, peaceably and quietly, as long as they live.

CHAPTER 3

This chapter is one of the most excellent in all this book, both for argument to persuade us to be religious and for directions therein. I. We must be constant to our duty because that is the way to be happy, ver. 1–4. II. We must live a life of dependence upon God because that is the way to be safe, ver. 5. III. We must keep up the fear of God because that is the way to be healthful, ver. 7, 8. IV. We must serve God with our estates because that is the way to be rich, ver. 9, 10. V. We must bear afflictions well because that is the way to get good by them, ver. 11, 12. VI. We must take pains to obtain wisdom because that is the way to gain her, ver. 13–20. VII. We must govern ourselves by the rules of wisdom, of right reason and religion, because that is the way to be easy, ver. 21–26. VIII. We must do all the good we can, and no hurt, to our neighbours, ver. 27–35.

Verses 1–6

A life of communion with God will be of unspeakable advantage.

I. We must have a continual regard to God's precepts, *v.* 1, 2. Fix God's law, and his commandments, as our rule. Not only our heads, but our hearts, must *keep God's commandments*. To encourage us to submit ourselves to all the restraints and injunctions of the divine law, we are assured (*v.* 2) that it is the certain way to long life and prosperity. Even the days of old age shall not be evil days, but days in which thou shalt have pleasure: *Peace shall they* be continually *adding to thee. Great* and growing *peace have those that love the law.*

II. We must have a continual regard to God's promises, which go along with his precepts (*v.* 3): "*Let not mercy and truth forsake thee*, God's mercy in promising, and his truth in performing. *Bind them about thy neck*, as the most graceful ornament." It is the greatest honour we are capable of in this world to have an interest in the mercy and truth of God. "*Write them upon the table of thy heart*, as dear to thee; take a pleasure in applying them and thinking them over." To encourage us to do this we are assured (*v.* 4) that this is the way to recommend ourselves both to our Creator and fellow-creatures: *So shalt thou find favour and good understanding*. A good man seeks the favour of God in the first place. He shall be owned as one of Wisdom's children, and shall have praise with God. He wishes to have favour with men also, to be *accepted of the multitude of his brethren* (Esther x. 3); they shall understand him aright.

III. We must have a continual regard to God's providence, must depend upon it in all our affairs, both by faith and prayer. We must therefore *trust in the Lord with all our hearts* (*v.* 5); we must believe that he is able to do what he will, wise to do what is best, and good, according to his promise, to do what is best for us, if we love him, and serve him. By prayer (*v.* 6): *In all thy ways acknowledge God*. We must ask his leave, and not design anything but what we are sure is lawful. We must ask his advice and beg direction from him. We must ask success of him, as those who know *the race is not to the swift*. For our encouragement to do this, it is promised, "*He shall direct thy paths*, so that thy way shall be safe and good and the issue happy at last."

Verses 7–12

Three exhortations, each enforced with a good reason:—

I. We must live in a humble and dutiful subjection to God and his government (*v.* 7): "*Fear the Lord*, as your sovereign Lord and Master; be ruled in everything by your religion and subject to the divine will." *Be not wise in thy own eyes*. There is not a greater enemy to the power of religion, and the fear of God in the heart, than conceitedness of our own wisdom. *Fear the Lord, and depart from evil;* take heed of doing anything to offend him and to forfeit his care. For our encouragement thus to live in the fear of God it is here promised (*v.* 8) that it shall be as serviceable even to the outward man as our necessary food. *It shall be health to thy navel.* It will be strengthening: It shall be *marrow to thy bones.* The prudence, temperance, and sobriety, the calmness and composure of mind, and the good government of the appetites and passions, which religion teaches, tend very much not only to the health of the soul, but to a good habit of body.

II. We must make a good use of our estates, and that is the way to increase them, *v.* 9, 10. *Honour the Lord with thy substance*. Worldly wealth is but poor substance, yet, such as it is, we must honour God with it, and then, if ever, it becomes substantial. We must honour God *with our increase*. It is meant of the increase of the earth, for we live upon annual products, to keep us in constant dependence on God. God, who is the first and best, must have the first and best of everything. *So shall thy barns be filled with plenty*. "God shall bless thee with an increase of that which is for use, not for show or ornament— for spending and laying out, not for hoarding and laying up." What we gave we have.

III. We must conduct ourselves aright under our afflictions, *v.* 11, 12. We must not despise an affliction, be it ever so light and short, as if it were not worth taking notice of, or as if it were not sent on an errand and therefore required no answer. We must not be stocks, and stones, and stoics, under our afflictions, hardening ourselves under them, and concluding we can easily get through them without God. We must not be weary of an affliction, not be dispirited, dispossessed of our own souls, or driven to despair. A divine correction is *the chastening of the Lord*. It is from God, and therefore we must not be weary of it, for he knows our frame, both what we need and what we can bear. A fatherly correction comes not from his vindictive justice as a Judge, but his wise affection as a Father. The father corrects *the son whom he* loves, nay, and because he loves him and desires he may be wise and good.

Verses 13–20

Happy is the man that findeth wisdom, that true wisdom which consists in the knowledge and love of God, and an entire conformity to all his truths, providences, and laws.

I. What it is to find wisdom so as to be made happy by it. He is the happy man who, having found it, makes it his own, who *draws out understanding* (so the word is). Having it not in himself, he draws it with the bucket of prayer from the fountain of all wisdom, *who gives liberally*. He takes pains for it, as he does who draws ore out of the mine. That is well got, and to good purpose, that is thus used to good purpose. We read here of the merchandise of wisdom, which intimates, we must make it our business, and not a by-business, as the merchant bestows the main of his thoughts and time upon his merchandise. This is that pearl of great price which, when we have found it, we must willingly sell all for the purchase of, Matt. xiii. 45, 46. *Buy the truth* (Prov. xxiii. 23); he does not say at what rate, because we must buy it at any rate rather than miss it. It is not enough to lay hold of wisdom, but we must keep our hold, hold it fast, with a resolution never to let it go, but to persevere in the ways of wisdom to the end.

II. The happiness of those who find it is a transcendent happiness, more than can be found in the wealth of this world, if we had ever so much of it, *v.* 14, 15. All would not purchase heavenly wisdom; it *cannot be gotten for gold*, Job xxviii. 15, &c. All would not countervail the want of heavenly wisdom nor be the ransom of a soul lost by its own folly. All would not make a man half so happy as those are who have true wisdom, though they have none of all these things. True happiness is inclusive of all those things which are supposed to make men happy, *v.* 16, 17. Wisdom is here represented as a bright and bountiful queen, reaching forth gifts to her faithful and loving subjects. She offers life *in her right hand*. Religion puts us into the best methods of prolonging life, and, though our days on earth should be no more than our neighbour's, yet it will secure to us everlasting life in a better world. Riches and honour she reaches out with *her left hand*. True piety has in it the greatest true pleasure. *Her ways are ways of pleasantness*. All the enjoyments and entertainments of sense are not comparable to the pleasure which gracious souls have in communion with God and doing good. The way of religion, as it is the right way, so it is a pleasant way; it is smooth and clean, and strewed with roses: *All her paths are peace*. There is not only peace in the end, but peace in the way. It is the happiness of paradise (v. 18): *She is a tree of life.* True grace is that to the soul which the tree of life would have been, from which our first parents were shut out for eating of the forbidden tree. Those that feed on this heavenly wisdom shall find an antidote against age and death; they shall *eat and live for ever.* It is a participation of the happiness of God himself, for wisdom is his everlasting glory and blessedness, v. 19, 20. *Happy is the man that finds wisdom,* for he will thereby be *thoroughly furnished for every good word and work.* He has wherewithal to make good all the foregoing promises of long life, riches, and honour; for all the wealth of heaven, earth, and seas, is his.

Verses 21–26

I. The exhortation is, to have religion's rules always in view and always at heart, v. 21. "*My son, let them not depart from thy eyes;* let not thy eyes ever depart from them to wander after vanity. Have them always in mind, and as long as thou livest, keep up and cultivate thy acquaintance with them." Have them always at heart; for it is in that treasury, the hidden man of the heart, that we must *keep sound wisdom and discretion.*

II. The argument to enforce this exhortation is taken from the unspeakable advantage which wisdom, thus kept, will be of to us. "It will be *life to thy soul* (v. 22); it will quicken thee to thy duty; it will revive thee under thy troubles when thou beginnest to droop and despond. It will be thy spiritual life, an earnest of life eternal." It shall be *grace to thy neck,* as a chain of gold, or a jewel. *Grace to thy jaws* (so the word is), grateful to thy *taste and relish* (so some); it shall infuse *grace into all thou sayest* (so others), shall furnish thee with acceptable words, which shall gain thee credit. Good people are taken under God's special protection, and are safe and may be easy, v. 23. If our religion be our companion, it will be our convoy: "*Then shalt thou walk in thy way safely.* The natural life, and all that belongs to it, shall be under the protection of God's providence; the spiritual life, and all its interests, are under the protection of his grace; so that thou shalt be kept from falling into sin or trouble." The way of duty is the way of safety. "We are in danger of falling, but wisdom will keep thee, that *thy foot shall not stumble* at those things which overthrow many, but which thou shalt know how to get over." By night, v. 24, we lie exposed and are most subject to frights. "But keep up communion with God, and keep a good conscience, and then *when thou liest down thou shalt not be afraid* of fire, or thieves, or spectres, or any of the terrors of darkness, knowing that when we, and all our friends, are asleep, yet *he that keeps Israel neither slumbers nor sleeps.*" The way to have a good night is to keep a good conscience; and the sleep, as of the labouring man, so of the wise and godly man, is sweet. Integrity and uprightness will preserve us, so that we need *not be afraid of sudden fear,* v. 25. But let not the wise and good man fear the *desolation of the wicked, when it comes,* that is, the desolation which the wicked ones make of religion and the religious.

Verses 27–35

Precepts of wisdom which relate to our neighbour.
I. We must render to all their due, both in justice and charity, and not delay to do it (v. 27, 28): "*Withhold not good from those to whom it is due, when it is in the power of thy hand to do it,* but it was thy great fault if thou didst, by thy extravagances, disable thyself to do justly and show mercy. If thou hast it by thee today, say not to thy neighbour, *Go thy way for this time,* and come at a more convenient season, and I will then see what will be done; *tomorrow I will give;*

whereas thou art not sure that thou shalt live till tomorrow, or that tomorrow thou shalt *have it by thee.* Make not excuses to shift off a duty that must be done, nor delight to keep thy neighbour in pain and in suspense, nor to show the authority which the giver has over the beggar; but readily and cheerfully, and from a principle of conscience towards God, give good to *those to whom it is due,*" to the *lords and owners of it* (so the word is), to those who upon any account are entitled to it. This requires us, 1. To pay our just debts without fraud or delay. 2. To give wages to those who have earned them. 3. To provide for our relations, and those that have dependence on us, for to them it is due. 4. To render dues both to church and state, magistrates and ministers. 5. To be ready to all acts of friendship and humanity, and in everything to be neighbourly; for these are things that are due by the law of doing as we would be done by. 6. To be charitable to the poor and necessitous.

II. We must never design any hurt or harm to anybody (v. 29): "*Devise not evil against thy neighbour;* and the rather because *he dwells securely by thee,* and entertains no jealousy or suspicion of thee, and therefore is off his guard."

III. We must not be quarrelsome and litigious (v. 30): "Do not *strive with a man without cause;* contend not for that which thou hast no title to; resent not that as a provocation which peradventure was but an oversight. Never trouble thy neighbour with frivolous complaints and accusations, or vexatious law-suits, when thou mightest right thyself in a friendly way." Law must be the last refuge.

IV. We must not envy the prosperity of evil-doers, v. 31. "*Envy not the oppressor;* though he be rich and great. *Choose none of his ways;* do not imitate him. Never think of doing as he does, though thou wert sure to get by it all that he has, for it would be dearly bought." Now, to show what little reason saints have to envy sinners, Solomon here, in the last four verses of the chapter, compares the condition of sinners and saints together. Saints are beloved, v. 32. The froward sinners, whose lives are a perverse contradiction to his will, are *abomination to the Lord.* He that hates nothing that he has made yet abhors those who have thus marred themselves. The righteous therefore have no reason to envy them, for he communicates to them the secret tokens of his love; they know his mind, and the meanings and intentions of his providence, better than others can. Saints are under his blessing, they and their habitation, v. 33. The just have a habitation, a poor cottage (the word is used for sheep-cotes), a very mean dwelling; but God blesses it from the beginning of the year to the end of it. Those who exalt themselves shall certainly be abased: *Surely he scorns the scorners.* Those who scorn to submit to the discipline of religion, who scoff at godliness and godly people, God will lay them open to scorn before all the world. Those who humble themselves shall be exalted, for *he gives grace to the lowly;* he works that in them which puts honour upon them and for which they are *accepted of God and approved of men.* The end of sinners will be everlasting shame, the end of saints endless honour, v. 35.

CHAPTER 4

Solomon, in this chapter, with a great variety of expression, inculcates the same things that he had pressed upon us in the foregoing chapters. I. An earnest exhortation to the study of wisdom, that is, of true religion and godliness, borrowed from the good instructions which his father gave him, and enforced with many considerable arguments, ver. 1–13. II. A necessary caution against bad company, ver. 14–19. III. Particular directions for the attaining and preserving of wisdom, and bringing forth the fruits of it, ver. 20–27.

Verses 1–13

I. The invitation which Solomon gives to his children (v. 1, 2): *Hear, you children, the instruction of a father.* "Let my own children, in the first place, receive those instructions which I set down for the use of others also." Magistrates and ministers are concerned to take a more than ordinary care for the instruction of their own families. Let all young people, in the days of their childhood and youth, take pains to get knowledge and grace, for then their minds are formed and seasoned. He does not say, *My* children, but *You* children. Let all that would receive instruction come with the disposition of children, though they be grown persons. Let all prejudices be laid aside, and the mind be as white paper. Let them be dutiful, tractable, and self-diffident, and take the word as the word of a father, which comes both with authority and with affection. We must see it coming from God as *our Father in heaven,* to whom we pray, from whom we expect blessings, the Father of our spirits. We must look upon our teachers as our fathers, who love us and seek our welfare. We are told (*v.* 1), not only that it is the *instruction of a father,* but that it is *understanding,* and therefore should be welcome to intelligent creatures. Religion has reason on its side, and we are taught it by fair reasoning. It is a law indeed (*v.* 2), but that law is founded upon unquestionable principles of truth, upon *good doctrine,* which is worthy of all acceptation. If we admit the doctrine, we cannot but submit to the law.

II. The instructions he gives them. He had them from his parents, and teaches his children the same that they taught him, *v.* 3, 4. His parents loved him, and therefore taught him: *I was my father's son.* David had many sons, but Solomon was his son *indeed,* as Isaac is called (Gen. xvii. 19) and for the same reason, because on him the covenant was entailed. He was *tender, and only beloved, in the sight of his mother.* Though he was a prince, and heir-apparent to the crown, yet they did not let him live at large; they tutored him. And perhaps David was the more strict with Solomon in his education because he had seen the ill effects of undue indulgence in Adonijah, whom he had not *crossed in anything* (1 Kings i. 6). What his parents taught him he teaches others. When Solomon was grown up he not only remembered, but took a pleasure in repeating, the good lessons his parents taught him when he was a child. Though Solomon was a wise man himself, and divinely inspired, yet, when he was to teach wisdom, he did not think it below him to quote his father. Those that would teach well, in religion, must not look with contempt upon the knowledge of their predecessors; if we must keep to the good old way, why should we scorn the good old words? Jer. vi. 16. Solomon enforces his exhortations with the authority of his father David, a man famous in his generation. These instructions were, *v.* 4–13, precept and exhortation. David, in teaching his son, expressed himself with great warmth and importunity, and inculcated the same thing again and again. He recommends to him his Bible, his father's *words* (*v.* 4), the *words of his mouth* (*v.* 5), his *sayings* (*v.* 10), all the good lessons he had taught him; and perhaps he means particularly the book of Psalms, many of which were *Maschils—psalms of instruction,* and two of them are expressly said to be *for Solomon.* He must *hear and receive them* (*v.* 10). He must *hold fast the form of sound words* which his father gave him (*v.* 4): *Let thy heart retain my words;* and except the word be hid in the heart, lodged in the will and affections, it will not be retained. He must govern himself by them: *Keep my commandments.* He must stick to them and abide by them: *"Decline not from the words of my mouth* (*v.* 5), as fearing they will be too great a check upon thee, but *take fast hold of instruction* (*v.* 13), as being resolved to keep thy hold and never let it go." A principle of religion in the

heart is the one thing needful; therefore, Get this *wisdom,* get this *understanding, v.* 5. And again, "*Get wisdom,* and, *with all thy getting, get understanding, v.* 7. Get wisdom by experience, get it *above all thy getting;* be more in care and take more pains to get this than to get the wealth of this world." True wisdom is God's gift. God gives it to those that labour for it. *Forget her not* (*v.* 5), *forsake her not* (*v.* 6), *let her not go* (*v.* 13) *but keep her. Love her* (*v.* 6), and *embrace her* (*v.* 8), as worldly men love their wealth and set their hearts upon it. If we cannot be great masters of wisdom, yet let us be true lovers of it; let us embrace it with a sincere affection, as those that admire its beauty. *Exalt her, v.* 8. Always keep up high thoughts of religion, and do all thou canst to maintain the credit of it among men. Let *Wisdom's* children not only justify her, but magnify her, honouring those that fear the Lord, though they are low in the world, and in regarding a *poor wise man,* we exalt wisdom. It is the main matter (*v.* 7): *Wisdom is the principal thing;* other things which are solicitous to get and keep are nothing to it. It is that which recommends us to God, which beautifies the soul, which enables us to live to some good purpose in the world, and to get to heaven at last; and therefore it is the principal thing. It has reason and equity on its side (*v.* 11): "*I have taught thee in the way of wisdom,* and so it will be found to be at last. *I have led thee in right paths,* agreeable to the eternal rules and reasons of good and evil." David not only taught his son by good instructions, but led him both by a good example and by applying general instructions to particular cases. *Keep my commandments and live, v.* 4. That of our Saviour agrees with this, *If thou wilt enter into life, keep the commandments,* Matt. xix. 17. "Receive wisdom's sayings, *and the years of thy life shall be many* (*v.* 10), as many in this world as Infinite Wisdom sees fit, and in the other world thou shalt live that life the years of which shall never be numbered. *Keep her* therefore, whatever it cost thee, *for she is thy life," v.* 13. "Love wisdom, and cleave to her, and she shall *preserve thee, she shall keep thee* (*v.* 6) from sin, the worst of evils; she shall keep thee from hurting thyself, and then none else can hurt thee." As we say, "Keep thy shop, and thy shop will keep thee"; so, "Keep thy wisdom, and thy wisdom will keep thee. It will be thy honour and reputation (*v.* 8): *Exalt* wisdom and though she needs not thy service she will abundantly recompence it, *she shall promote thee, she shall bring thee to honour.*" This he insists on (*v.* 9): "*She shall give to thy head an ornament of grace* in this world, and in the other world *a crown of glory shall she deliver to thee,* a crown that shall never wither."

Verses 14–19

Some make David's instructions to Solomon, which began *v.* 4, to continue to the end of the chapter; but it is more probable that Solomon begins here again. In these verses he cautions us against the path of the wicked.

I. The caution itself, *v.* 14, 15. We must take heed of falling in with sin and sinners; *Enter not into the paths of the wicked.* "If, ere thou wast aware, thou didst enter in at the gate, because it was wide, *go not* on *in the way of evil men.* As soon as thou art made sensible of thy mistake, retire immediately, take not a step more, stay not a minute longer, in the way that certainly leads to destruction." It intimates likewise at what a distance we should keep from sin and sinners; he does not say, Keep at a due distance, but at a great distance, the further the better; never think you can get far enough from it.

II. The reasons to enforce this caution. "Consider the character of the men whose way thou art warned to shun." They are mischievous men (*v.* 16, 17). They are continually endeavouring to *cause some to fall*, to ruin them body and soul. Mischief is rest and sleep to them. Mischief is meat and drink to them; they feed and feast upon it. *They eat the bread of wickedness and drink the wine of violence* (*v.* 17). All they eat and drink is got by rapine and oppression. "Shun those that delight to do mischief, for whatever friendship they may pretend, they will do thee mischief; thou wilt ruin thyself if thou dost concur with them (*ch.* i. 18) and they will ruin thee if thou dost not." The way of righteousness is light (*v.* 18): *The path of the just*, which they have chosen, and in which they walk, *is as light*; the *light shines on their ways* (Job xxii. 28). Christ is *their way* and he is *the light*. They are guided by the word of God and that is *a light to their feet*; they themselves are *light in the Lord* and they *walk in the light as he is in the light*. It is as the morning-light, which *shines out of obscurity* (Isa. lviii. 8, 10) and puts an end to the *works of darkness*. It is a growing light; it *shines more and more*, not like the light of a meteor, which soon disappears, or that of a candle, which burns dim and burns down, but like that of the rising sun, which mounts upward shining. It will arrive, in the end, at *the perfect day*. The *way of* sin *is as darkness, v.* 19. The works he had cautioned us not to have fellowship with are *works of darkness*. What true pleasure and satisfaction can those have who know no pleasure and satisfaction but what they have in doing mischief? *The way of the wicked is dark*, and therefore dangerous; for they stumble, and yet *know not at what they stumble*.

Verses 20–27

Solomon, having warned us not to do evil, here teaches us how to do well.

I. We must have a continual regard to the word of God.

1. The sayings of wisdom must be our principles by which we must govern ourselves, our monitors to warn us of duty and danger; therefore, "*Incline thy ear to them* (*v.* 20); humbly bow to them; diligently listen to them." We must retain them carefully (*v.* 21); we must lay them before us as our rule: "*Let them not depart from thy eyes;* view them, review them, and in everything aim to conform to them." We must lodge them within us, as a commanding principle: "*Keep them in the midst of thy heart*, as things dear to thee, and which thou art afraid of losing."

2. The reason why we must thus make much of the words of wisdom is because they will be both food and physic to us, like the *tree of life*, Rev. xxii. 2. (1) Food: *For they are life unto those that find them, v.* 22. As the spiritual life was begun by the word, so by the same word it is still nourished and maintained. (2) Physic. They are *health to all their flesh*, to the whole man, both body and soul; they help to keep both in good plight. They are *a medicine to all their flesh* (so the word is), to all their corruptions, for they are called flesh. There is in the word of God a proper remedy for all our spiritual maladies.

II. We must keep a watchful eye and a strict hand upon all the motions of our inward man, *v.* 23. *Keep thy heart with all diligence*. God, who gave us these souls, gave us a strict charge with them. We must set a strict guard, accordingly, upon all the avenues of the soul; keep our hearts from doing hurt and getting hurt, from being defiled by sin and disturbed by trouble; keep out bad thoughts; keep up good thoughts; keep the affections upon right objects and in due bounds. *Keep them with all keepings* (so the word is); there are many ways of keeping things—by care, by strength, by calling in help, and we must use them all in keeping our hearts. A good reason is

given for this care, because *out of it are the issues of life*. Out of a heart well kept will flow living issues, good products, to the glory of God and the edification of others.

III. We must set a *watch before the door of our lips*, that we offend not with our tongue (*v.* 24): *Put away from thee a froward mouth and perverse lips.* We must conceive a great detestation of all manner of evil words, cursing, swearing, lying, slandering, brawling, filthiness, and foolish talking, all which come from a *froward mouth and perverse lips*, that will not be governed either by reason or religion, but contradict both, and which are as unsightly and ill-favoured before God as a crooked distorted mouth drawn awry is before men.

IV. We must make a covenant with our eyes: "Let them *look right on and straight before thee*, (*v.* 25). Let the eye be fixed and not wandering; let it not rove after every thing that presents itself, for then it will be diverted from good and ensnared in evil. Let thy intentions be sincere and uniform, and look not asquint at any by-end." We must keep our eye upon our Master, and be careful to approve ourselves to him; keep our eye upon our rule, and conform to that; keep our eye upon our mark, the *prize of the high calling*, and direct all towards that. *Oculum in metam—The eye upon the goal.*

V. We must act considerately in all we do (*v.* 26): *Ponder the path of thy feet, weigh it* (so the word is); "put the word of God in one scale, and what thou hast done, or art about to do, in the other, and see how they agree. Do nothing rashly."

VI. We must act with steadiness, caution, and consistency: "*Let all thy ways be established* (*v.* 26) and be not unstable in them."

CHAPTER 5

The scope of this chapter is much the same with that of ch. ii. Here is, I. An exhortation to get acquaintance with and submit to the laws of wisdom in general, ver. 2. II. A particular caution against the sin of whoredom, ver. 3–14. III. Remedies prescribed against that sin. 1. Conjugal love, ver. 15–20. 2. A regard to God's omniscience, ver. 21. 3. A dread of the miserable end of wicked people, ver. 22, 23.

Verses 1–14

I. A solemn preface, to introduce the caution which follows, *v.* 1, 2. Solomon here addresses himself to his son, that is, to all young men, as unto his children. "It is *my wisdom, my understanding*; I undertake to teach thee wisdom, which is to be learned in my school." Solomon's lectures are not designed to fill our heads with matters of nice speculation, or doubtful disputation, but to guide us in the government of ourselves.

II. The caution itself is to abstain from fleshly lusts, from adultery, fornication, and all uncleanness. Some apply this figuratively, and by the adulterous woman here understand idolatry, or false doctrine, which tends to debauch men's minds and manners, but the primary scope of it is plainly to warn us against seventh-commandment sins. It is true *the lips of a strange woman drop as a honey-comb* (*v.* 3); the kisses of its mouth, the words of its mouth, are *smoother than oil*, that the poisonous pill may go down glibly and there may be no suspicion of harm in it. But consider: It *is bitter as wormwood, v.* 4. What was luscious in the mouth rises in the stomach and turns sour there. If some that have been guilty of this sin have repented and been saved, yet the direct tendency of the sin is to destruction of body and soul; the *feet* of it *go down to death, v.* 5. Consider how false the charms are. The adulteress flatters and speaks fair, her words are honey and oil, but she will deceive those that hearken to her: *Her ways are movable, that thou canst not know them.* Proteus-like, she puts on many shapes, that she may keep in with those whom she has a design upon. And what does she aim at with all this art and management? Nothing but to keep them from *pondering the path of life*, for she knows that, if they once come to do that, she shall certainly lose them. Those are *ignorant of Satan's devices* who do not understand that the great thing he drives at in all his temptations is to keep them from choosing the path of life, to prevent them from being religious. The caution itself is very pressing (v. 7, 8): "*Remove thy way far from her;* if thy way should happen to lie near her, change thy way, rather than expose thyself to danger; *come not nigh the door of her house;* go on the other side of the street, nay, go through some other street, though it be about." Such tinder there is in the corrupt nature that it is madness, upon any pretence whatsoever, to come near the sparks. This sin blasts the reputation. "Thou wilt *give thy honour unto others* (v. 9); thou wilt lose it thyself; thou wilt put into the hand of each of thy neighbours a stone to throw at thee, for they will cry shame on thee as a foolish man." It wastes the time, gives *the years*, the years of youth, the flower of men's time, *unto the cruel*. Those years that should be given to the honour of a gracious God are spent in the service of a cruel sin. It ruins the estate (v. 10): "*Strangers* will be *filled with thy wealth*, which thou art but entrusted with as a steward for thy family; and the fruit of *thy labours*, which should be provision for thy own house, will be in *the house of a stranger*, that neither has right to it nor will ever thank thee for it." It is destructive to the health, and shortens men's days: *Thy flesh and thy body* will be *consumed* by it, v. 11. The lusts of uncleanness not only *war against the soul*, which the sinner neglects and is in no care about, but they war against the body too, which he is so indulgent of and is in such care to pamper. "Though thou art merry now, *sporting thyself in thy own deceivings*, yet thou wilt certainly *mourn at the last*," v. 11. Solomon brings in the convinced sinner reproaching himself because he hated to be reformed and therefore hated to be informed, and could not endure either to be taught his duty or to be told of his faults—*My heart despised reproof*, v. 12. He cannot but own that parents and ministers had given him good counsel and fair warning (v. 13). He had not taken their counsel, had not *obeyed their voice*, for indeed he *never inclined his ear to those that instructed him*. By the frequent acts of sin the habits of it were so rooted and confirmed that his heart was fully set in him to commit it (v. 14): *I was almost in all evil in the midst of the congregation and assembly*.

Verses 15–23

Solomon, having shown the great evil that there is in adultery and fornication, prescribes remedies against them.

I. Enjoy with satisfaction the comforts of lawful marriage, which was ordained for the prevention of uncleanness. Let none complain that God has dealt unkindly with them in forbidding them those pleasures which they have a natural desire of, for he has graciously provided for the regular gratification of them. "Thou mayest not indeed eat of every tree of the garden, but choose thee out one, which thou pleasest, and of that thou mayest freely eat; nature will be content with that, but lust with nothing." Let young men marry, marry and not burn. Have a *cistern, a well of thy own* (v. 15), even the wife *of thy youth*, v. 18. *Wholly abstain, or wed.*—Herbert. Let him that is married take delight in his wife, and let him be very fond of her, not only because she is the wife that he himself has chosen and he ought to be pleased with his own choice, but because she is the wife that God in his providence appointed

for him. *Let thy fountain be blessed* (v. 18); think thyself very happy in her, look upon her as a blessed wife, let her have thy blessing, pray daily for her, and then *rejoice with her*. Mutual delight is the bond of mutual fidelity. Let him be fond of his wife and love her dearly (v. 19). If thou wilt suffer thy love to run into an excess, let it be only of thy own wife. Let him take delight in his children and look upon them with pleasure (v. 16, 17). Let him then scorn the offer of forbidden pleasures when he is *always ravished with the love* of a faithful virtuous wife; let him consider what an absurdity it will be for him to be *ravished with a strange woman* (v. 20). If the dictates of reason may be heard, the laws of virtue will be obeyed.

II. "See the eye of God always upon thee and let his fear rule in thy heart," v. 21. *The ways of man*, all his motions, all his actions, are *before the eyes of the Lord*. God sees it in a true light, and knows it with all its causes, circumstances, and consequences. He not only sees, but *ponders all his goings*, judges concerning them, as one that will shortly judge, the sinner for them.

III. "Foresee the certain ruin of those that go on still in their trespasses." Those that live in this sin promise themselves impunity, but they deceive themselves; their sin will find them out, v. 22, 23. As their own iniquities do arrest them in the reproaches of conscience and present rebukes (Jer. vii. 19), so their own iniquities shall arrest them and bind them over to the judgments of God. There needs no prison, no chains; they shall be *holden in the cords of their own sins*.

CHAPTER 6

In this chapter we have, I. A caution against rash suretiship, ver. 1–5. II. A rebuke to slothfulness, ver. 6–11. III. The character and fate of a malicious mischievous man, ver. 12–15. IV. An account of seven things which God hates, ver. 16–19. V. An exhortation to make the word of God familiar to us, ver. 20–23. VI. A repeated warning of the pernicious consequences of the sin of whoredom, ver. 24–35.

Verses 1–5

It is the excellency of the word of God that it teaches us not only divine wisdom for another world, but human prudence for this world, that we may order our affairs with discretion; and this is one good rule. To avoid suretiship, because by it poverty and ruin are often brought into families. 1. We must look upon suretiship as a snare and decline it accordingly, v. 1, 2. "It is dangerous enough for a man to be bound for his friend, though it be one whose circumstances he is well acquainted with, and well assured of his sufficiency, but much more to *strike the hands with a stranger*, to become surety for one whom thou dost not know to be either able or honest." If thou hast rashly entered into such engagements, either wheedled into them or in hopes to have the same kindness done for thee another time, know that *thou art snared with the words of thy mouth*. If we have been drawn into this snare, it will be our wisdom by all means, with all speed, to get out of it, v. 3–5. It sleeps for the present; we hear nothing of it. The debt is not demanded; the principal says, "Never fear, we will take care of it." But still the bond is in force, interest is running on, the creditor may come upon thee when he will and perhaps may be hasty and severe. Therefore *deliver thyself*; rest not till either the creditor give up the bond or the principal give thee counter-security. Leave no stone unturned till thou hast agreed with thy adversary and compromised the matter, so that thy bond may not come against thee or thine.

But how are we to understand this? We are not to think it is unlawful in any case to become surety, or bail, for another; it may be a piece of justice or charity. Paul became bound for Onesimus, Philem. 19. We may help a young man into business that we know to be honest, and gain him credit by passing our word for him, and so do him a great kindness without any detriment to ourselves. But, 1. It is every man's wisdom to keep out of debt as much as may be, for it is an incumbrance upon him, entangles him in the world, puts him in danger of doing wrong or suffering wrong. The *borrower is servant to the lender,* and makes himself very much a slave to the world. A man ought never to be bound as surety for more than he is both able and willing to pay, and can afford to pay without wronging his family.

Verses 6–11

Solomon addresses himself to the sluggard who loves his ease, lives in idleness, sticks to nothing, and in a particular manner is careless in the business of religion.

I. By way of instruction, *v.* 6–8, he sends him to school, for sluggards must be schooled. The sluggard is not willing to come to school to him (dreaming scholars will never love wakeful teachers) and therefore he has found him out another school, as low as he can desire. *Go to the ant, to the bee,* so the LXX. Man is taught more than the beasts of the earth, and made wiser than the fowls of heaven, and yet is so degenerated that he may learn wisdom from the meanest insects and be shamed by them. When we observe the wonderful sagacities of the inferior creatures we must receive instruction to ourselves; by spiritualizing common things, we may make the things of God ready to us, and converse with them daily. *Consider her ways.* The sluggard is so because he does not consider. In particular, learn to *provide meat in summer.* We must prepare for hereafter, and not eat up all, and lay up nothing, but in gathering time, treasure up for a spending time. Lay in for winter, for straits and wants that may happen, and for old age; much more in the affairs of our souls. In the enjoyment of the means of grace provide for the want of them, in life for death, in time for eternity. Even *in summer,* when the weather is hot, the ant is busy in *gathering food* and laying it up, and does not indulge her ease, nor take her pleasure, as the grasshopper, that sings and sports in the summer and then perishes in the winter. The ants help one another; if one have a grain of corn too big for her to carry home, her neighbours will come in to her assistance. It is our wisdom to improve the season while that favours us. *Walk while you have the light.* The ant has *no guides* and *rulers,* but does it of herself, following the instinct of nature. We have parents, masters, ministers, magistrates, to put us in mind of our duty, to direct us in it.

II. By way of reproof, *v.* 9–11.

1. He expostulates with the sluggard: *"How long wilt thou sleep, O sluggard? When wilt thou* think it time to *arise?"* Sluggards should be roused in the duties of their particular calling as men or their general calling as Christians. *"How long wilt thou* waste thy time, and *when wilt thou* be a better husband? *How long wilt thou* love thy ease, and *when wilt thou* learn to deny thyself, and to take pains? *How long wilt thou* delay, and put off, and trifle away thy opportunities; and *when wilt thou* stir up thyself to do what thou hast to do, which, if it be not done, will leave thee for ever undone?"

2. He exposes the frivolous excuses he makes for himself. When he is roused he stretches himself, and begs for more *sleep,* more *slumber;* he is well in his warm bed, and cannot endure to think of rising, especially of rising to work. He promises himself and his master that he will desire but *a little* more *sleep, a little* more *slumber,* and then he will get up and go to his business. But herein he deceives himself;

the more a slothful temper is indulged the more it prevails. Thus men's great work is left undone by being put off yet a little longer—*from day to day.* A little more sleep proves an everlasting sleep.

3. He gives him fair warning of the fatal consequences of his slothfulness, *v.* 11. *Poverty and want* will certainly come upon those that are slothful in their business. He that leaves his concerns at sixes and sevens will soon see them go to wreck and ruin, and bring his noble to nine-pence. Spiritual poverty comes upon those that are slothful in the service of God. *It will leave thee as naked as if thou wert stripped by a highwayman;* so Bishop Patrick.

Verses 12–19

I. If the slothful are to be condemned, that do nothing, much more those that do ill, and contrive to do all the ill they can. It is a *naughty person* that is here spoken of, Heb. *A man of Belial.* A man of Belial is here described. He is *a wicked man,* that makes a trade of doing evil, especially with his tongue, for he *walks* and works his designs *with a froward mouth* (*v.* 12), by lying and perverseness. He has the subtilty of the serpent, and carries on his projects with a great deal of craft (*v.* 13), *with his eyes, with his feet, with his fingers.* Those whom he makes use of as the tools of his wickedness, understand the ill meaning of a wink of his eye, a stamp of his feet, for the least motion of his fingers. He gives orders for evil-doing so that he may not be suspected. It is not so much ambition or covetousness that *is in his heart,* as downright *frowardness,* malice, and ill nature. He aims not so much to enrich and advance himself as to do an ill turn to those about him. *His calamity shall come* and *he shall be broken;* he that devised mischief shall fall into mischief. *Suddenly shall he be broken,* to punish him for all the wicked arts he had to surprise people into his snares.

II. A catalogue of those things which are in a special manner odious to God, all which are generally to be found in men of Belial. God hates every sin. But there are some sins which he does in a special manner hate; and all those here mentioned are such as are injurious to our neighbour. Those things which God hates we must hate in ourselves. 1. Haughtiness and contempt of others—*a proud look.* Pride is the first, because it is at the bottom of much sin. When the show of men's countenance witnesses against them that they overvalue themselves and undervalue all about them, this is in a special manner hateful to him. 2. Falsehood, and fraud, and dissimulation. Next to a *proud look,* nothing is more an abomination to God than *a lying tongue;* nothing more sacred than truth, nor more necessary to conversation than speaking truth. 3. Cruelty and blood-thirstiness. The devil was, from the beginning, a liar and a murderer (John viii. 44), so *hands that shed innocent blood* are hateful to God, because they have in them the devil's image and do him service. 4. Subtlety in the contrivance of sin, *a heart that* designs and a head that *devises wicked imaginations.* The more there is of craft and management in sin the more it is an abomination to God. 5. Vigour and diligence in the prosecution of sin—*feet that are swift in running to mischief.* The eagerness and industry of sinners, in their sinful pursuits, may shame us who go about that which is good so awkwardly and so coldly. 6. False-witness bearing: There cannot be a greater affront to God, nor a greater injury to our neighbour, than knowingly to give a false testimony. 7. Making mischief between relations and neighbours, and using all wicked means possible, not only to alienate their affections one from another, but to irritate their passions one against another. The God of love and peace hates *him that sows discord among brethren.*

Verses 20–35

I. A general exhortation faithfully to adhere to the word of God and to take it for our guide in all our actions.

1. We must look upon the word of God both as a light (*v.* 23) and as a law, *v.* 20, 23. It is a light, which our understandings must subscribe to; it *is a lamp* to our eyes for discovery, and so to our feet for direction. The word of God reveals to us truths of eternal certainty. Scripture-light is the sure light. It is a law, which our wills must submit to.

2. We must receive it as *our father's commandment* and *the law of our mother, v.* 20. It is God's commandment and his law. Our parents directed us to it, trained us up in the knowledge and observance of it. We believe indeed, not for their saying, for we have tried it ourselves and find it to be of God; but we were beholden to them for recommending it to us. The cautions, counsels, and commands which our parents gave us agree with the word of God, and therefore we must hold them fast.

3. We must retain the word of God and the good instructions which our parents gave us out of it. "*Keep thy father's commandment*, keep it still, and never forsake it." We must never lay them by (*v.* 21): *Bind them continually*, not only *upon thy hand* (as Moses had directed, Deut. vi. 8) but *upon thy heart*. Phylacteries upon the hand were of no value at all, any further than they occasioned pious thoughts and affections in the heart. *Tie them about thy neck*, as an ornament—*about thy throat* (so the word is); let them be a guard that no forbidden fruit may be suffered to go in nor any evil word suffered to go out through the throat. If we bind it continually upon our hearts, we must follow its direction. "*When thou goest, it shall lead thee* (*v.* 22); it shall lead thee in the good and right way. It will say unto thee, when thou art ready to turn aside, *This is the way; walk in it*. Let it be thy rule, and then thou shalt be led by the Spirit; he will be thy monitor and support." It will be our guard: "*When thou sleepest*, and liest exposed to the malignant powers of darkness, *it shall keep thee*; thou shalt be safe, and shalt think thyself so." It will be our companion: "*When thou awakest* in the night, and knowest not how to pass thy waking minutes, *it shall talk with thee*, with pleasant meditations in the night-watches; *when thou awakest* in the morning, and art contriving the work of the day, *it shall talk with thee* about it, and help thee to contrive for the best," Ps. i. 2.

II. A particular caution against the sin of uncleanness.

1. When we consider how much this iniquity abounds we shall not wonder that the cautions against it are so often repeated. "The reproofs of instruction are *the way of life* to thee, because they are designed *to keep thee from the evil woman*, who will be certain death to thee, from being enticed by *the flattery of the tongue of a strange woman*, who pretends to love thee, but intends to ruin thee." The greatest kindness we can do ourselves, is to keep at a distance from this sin (*v.* 25): "*Lust not after her beauty*, no, not *in thy heart*, for, if thou dost, thou hast *there* already committed adultery with her. Talk not of the charms in her face; *let her* not *take thee with her eye-lids*. Her looks are arrows and fiery darts; they call it a pleasing captivity, but it is a destroying one, it is worse than Egyptian slavery."

2. Divers arguments Solomon here urges to enforce this caution. It is a sin that impoverishes men, wastes their estates, and reduces them to beggary (*v.* 26): *By means of a whorish woman a man is brought to a piece of bread*. It threatens death; it kills men: *The adulteress will hunt for the precious life*, perhaps designedly, as Delilah for Samson's. It brings guilt upon the conscience. He that *touches his neighbour's*

wife, with an immodest touch, cannot be *innocent, v.* 29. The bold presumptuous sinner says, "I may sin and yet escape punishment." He might as well say, I will *take fire into my bosom and not burn my clothes*. It is a much more scandalous sin than stealing is, *v.* 30–33. When Nathan would convict David of the evil of his adultery he did it by a parable concerning the most aggravated theft, which, in David's judgment, deserved to be punished with death (2 Sam. xii. 5), and then showed him that his sin was *more exceedingly sinful* than that. It is a greater reproach to a man's reason, for he cannot excuse it, as a thief may, by saying that it was to satisfy his hunger. Therefore *whoso commits adultery with a woman lacks understanding*, and deserves to be stigmatized as an arrant fool. It will be *a wound* to his good name, a *dishonour* to his family, and, though the guilt of it may be done away by repentance, the *reproach* of it never will. David's sin in the matter of Uriah was not only a perpetual blemish upon his own character, but gave occasion to the enemies of the Lord to blaspheme his name too. He that touches his neighbour's wife, and is familiar with her, gives him occasion for jealousy, much more he that debauches her, which, if kept ever so secret, might then be *discovered by the waters of jealousy*, Num. v. 12, etc.

CHAPTER 7

The scope of this chapter is, as of several before, to warn young men against the lusts of the flesh. Solomon remembered of what ill consequence it was to his father, perhaps found himself, and perceived his son, addicted to it, and therefore he thought he could never say enough to dissuade men. In this chapter we have, I. A general exhortation to get our minds principled and governed by the word of God, as a sovereign antidote against this sin, ver. 1–5. II. A particular representation of the great danger, ver. 6–23. III. A serious caution to take heed of all approaches towards this sin, ver. 24–27. We should all pray, "Lord, lead us not into this temptation."

Verses 1–5

These verses are an introduction to his warning against fleshly lusts, much the same with that, *ch.* vi. 20, &c., and ending (*v.* 5) as that did (*v.* 24), *To keep thee from the strange woman*. He speaks in God's name; for it is God's *commandments* that we are to *keep*, his *words*, his *law*. We must keep it as our life: *Keep my commandments and live* (*v.* 2). Keep *my law as the apple of thy eye*. A little thing offends the eye, and therefore nature has so well guarded it. We pray, with David, that God would keep us as the apple of his eye (Ps. xvii. 8), that our lives and comforts may be precious in his sight; and they shall be so (Zech. ii. 8) if we be in like manner tender of his law and afraid of the least violation of it. "*Bind them upon thy fingers;* let them be precious to thee; look upon them as the *signet on thy right hand*; wear them continually as thy wedding-ring, the badge of thy espousals to God." Look upon the word of God as putting an honour upon thee, as an ensign of thy dignity. *Write them upon the table of thy heart*, as the names of the friends we dearly love, we say, are written in our hearts. "*Say unto wisdom, Thou art my sister*, whom I dearly love and take delight in; *and call understanding thy kinswoman*, to whom thou art nearly allied, and for whom thou hast a pure affection; call her thy friend, whom thou courtest." We must make the word of God familiar to us, for our defence and armour, to keep us *from the strange woman*, from sin, particularly from the sin of uncleanness, *v.* 5.

Verses 6–23

Solomon here, to enforce the caution he had given against the sin of whoredom, tells a story of a young man that was ruined to all intents and purposes by the enticements of an adulterous woman. Such a story as this would serve the lewd profane poets of our age to make a play of, and the harlot with them would be a heroine; nothing would be so entertaining to the audience, as her arts of beguiling the young gentleman. Her conquests would be celebrated as the triumphs of wit and love, and the comedy would conclude very pleasantly; and every young men that saw it acted would covet to be so picked up. Thus *fools make a mock at sin.* But Solomon here relates it, and all wise and good men read it, as a very melancholy story. The impudence of the adulterous woman is very justly looked upon with the highest indignation, and the easiness of the young man with the tenderest compassion. It is supposed to be a parable, or imagined case, but I doubt it was too true, and it is still too often true.

Solomon was a magistrate, and, as such, inspected the manners of his subjects. But here he writes as a minister, a prophet, who is by office a watchman, to give warning, that we may not be ignorant of Satan's devices, but may know where to double our guard.

I. The person tempted was a *young man*, v. 7. Fleshly lusts are called *youthful lusts* (2 Tim. ii. 22). Young people ought in a special manner to fortify their resolutions against this sin. He was a young man *void of understanding*, that went abroad into the world, not principled as he ought to have been with wisdom and the fear of God, and so ventured to sea without ballast, without pilot, cord, or compass. He kept bad company. He was sauntering, and had nothing to do, but *passed through the street* as one that knew not how to dispose of himself. One of the sins of filthy Sodom was *abundance of idleness*, Ezek. xvi. 49. He was a night-walker. Having fellowship with the unfruitful works of darkness, he begins to move *in the twilight in the evening*, v. 9. He steered his course towards the house of one that he thought would entertain him, and that he might be merry with; he went *near her corner*, the *way to her house* (v. 8), contrary to Solomon's advice (ch. v. 8), *Come not nigh the door of her house.*

II. The person tempting, not a common prostitute, was a married wife (v. 19), not suspected of any such wickedness, and yet, in the *twilight of the evening*, when her husband was abroad, abominably impudent. She had the *attire of a harlot* (v. 10), gaudy and flaunting. She is *subtle of heart*, mistress of all the arts of wheedling, and knowing how by all her caresses to serve her own base purposes. *She is loud and stubborn*, talkative and self-willed, noisy and troublesome, wilful and headstrong, and cannot bear to be counselled, much less reproved, by husband or parents, ministers or friends. She is a *daughter of Belial*, that will endure no yoke. She is all for gadding abroad, changing place and company. She is here, and there, and everywhere but where she should be. She *lies in wait at every corner*, to pick up such as she can make a prey of. Virtue is a penance to those to whom home is a prison.

III. She met the young spark. Perhaps she knew him; however she knew by his fashions that he was such a son as she wished for; so she *caught him about the neck and kissed* him, contrary to all the rules of modesty (v. 13), and *with an impudent face* invited him not only to *her house*, but to *her bed*. She courted him to sup with her (v. 14, 15): *I have peace-offerings with me.* Hereby she gives him to understand that she was compassed about with so many blessings that she had occasion to offer peace-offerings, in token of joy and thankfulness; so that he needed not fear having his pocket picked. She had been today at the temple, and was as well respected there as any that worshipped in the courts of the Lord. She had paid her vows, and, as she thought, made all even with God Almighty, and therefore might venture upon a new score of sins. It is sad that a show of

piety should become the shelter of iniquity. The Pharisees made long prayers, that they might the more plausibly carry on their covetous and mischievous designs. The greatest part of the flesh of the peace-offerings was by the law returned back to the offerers, to feast upon with their friends, Lev. vii. 15. "Come," says she, "come home with me, for I have good cheer enough, and only want good company to help me off with it." She pretends to have a very great affection for him above any man: "*Therefore*, because I have a good supper upon the table, *I came forth to meet thee*, for no friend in the world shall be so welcome to it as thou shalt," v. 15. They will sit down to eat and drink, and then play the wanton. The bed is *decked with coverings of tapestry* and *carved works.* The sheets are of *fine linen of Egypt*, v. 16. It is *perfumed* with the sweetest scents, v. 17. Come, therefore, and *let us take our fill of love*, v. 18. Of *love*, does she say? Of *lust* she means, but it is a pity that the name of love should be thus abused. True love is from heaven. "Never fear," says she, "the *good man is not at home*" (v. 19); she does not call him her *husband*, but "the *good man* of the house, of whom I am weary." But will he not return quickly? No: "he has *gone a long journey*, and cannot return on a sudden; he *appointed the day* of his return, and he never comes home sooner than he says he will. *He has taken a bag of money with him*—either to buy goods and he will not return till he has laid it all out, or to revel." Whether justly or not, she insinuates that he was a bad husband; so she would represent him, because she was resolved to be a bad wife, and must have that for an excuse; it is often groundlessly suggested, but is never a sufficient excuse.

IV. Promising the young man everything that was pleasant, and impunity in the enjoyment she gained her point, v. 21. It should seem, the youth, though very simple, had no ill design, else a word, a beck, a wink, would have served and there would have been no need of all this harangue; but though he did not intend any such thing, nay, had something in his conscience that opposed it, yet *with her much fair speech she caused him to yield.* His corruptions at length triumphed over his convictions. *With the flattery of her lips she forced him;* he could not stop his ear against such a charmer, but surrendered. With what pity does Solomon here look upon this foolish young man, when he sees him follow the adulterous woman! He gives him up for gone. Going without his breast-plate, he will receive his death's wound, v. 23. That which makes his case the more piteous is that he is not himself aware of his misery and danger; he goes laughing to his ruin.

Verses 24–27

We have here the application of the foregoing story: "*Hearken to me therefore*, and not to such seducers" (v. 24); give ear to a father, and not to an enemy." *Let not thy heart decline to her ways* (v. 25); never leave the paths of virtue. Do not only keep thy feet from those ways, but let not so much as thy heart incline to them. Let reason, and conscience, and the fear of God ruling in the heart, check the inclinations of the sensual appetite. Thousands have been undone by this sin; and those not only the weak and simple youths, such as he was of whom he had now spoken, but *many strong men have been slain by her*, v. 26. Therefore *stand in awe and sin not.*

CHAPTER 8

The word of God is wisdom. I. Divine revelation is the word and wisdom of God, and pure religion and undefiled is built upon it; and of that Solomon here speaks, ver. 1–21. God, by it, instructs, and governs, and blesses, the children of men. II. The Redeemer is the eternal Word and wisdom, the Logos. He is the Wisdom that speaks to the children of men in the former part of the chapter. All divine revelation passes through his hand, and centres in him; but of him as the personal Wisdom, the second person in the Godhead, Solomon here speaks, ver. 22–31. He concludes with a repeated charge to attend to the voice of God in his word, ver. 32–36.

Verses 1–11

I. The things revealed are easy to be known, for they *belong to us and to our children* (Deut. xxix. 29), for they are proclaimed in some measure by the works of the creation (Ps. xix. 1), more fully by the consciences of men and the eternal reasons and rules of good and evil, but most clearly by Moses and the prophets. The precepts of wisdom are proclaimed aloud (*v.* 1): *Does not Wisdom cry?* Yes, she cries aloud, and does not spare (Isa. lviii. 1). The curses and blessings were read with a loud voice by the Levites, Deut. xxvii. 14. And men's own hearts sometimes speak aloud to them; there are clamours of conscience, as well as whispers. They are proclaimed from on high (*v.* 2): *She stands in the top of high places;* it was from the top of Mount Sinai that the law was given, and Christ expounded it in a sermon upon the mount. Wisdom speaks openly; truth seeks no corners, but gladly appeals to the light, *in the places of concourse*, where multitudes are gathered together. Wisdom's discoveries and directions are given to all promiscuously. They are proclaimed where they are most needed, and therefore are published *in the places of the paths*, where many ways meet. The foolish man *knows not how to go to the city* (Eccles. x. 15), and therefore Wisdom stands ready to direct him, stands *at the gates, at the entry of the city*, ready to tell him where the seer's house is, 1 Sam. ix. 18. Nay, she follows men to their own houses, and cries to them *at the coming in at the doors*, saying, *Peace be to this house.* Wisdom speaks to us: *"Unto you, O men! I call* (*v.* 4), not to angels (they need not these instructions), not to devils (they are past them), not to the brute-creatures (they are not capable of them), but *to you, O men!"* They are designed to make them wise (*v.* 5); they are calculated not only for men that are capable of wisdom, but for sinful men, fallen men, foolish men, that need it, and are undone without it: *"O you simple ones! understand wisdom.* Though you are ever so simple, Wisdom will undertake to give you *an understanding heart."*

II. The things revealed are worthy of all acceptation. They are *excellent things* (*v.* 6), *princely things*, so the word is. Things which relate to an eternal God, an immortal soul, and an everlasting state, must needs be *excellent things.* They are *right things* (*v.* 6), *all in righteousness* (*v.* 8), and *nothing froward or perverse in them.* There is nothing in them that puts any hardship upon us, that lays us under any undue restraints, unbecoming the dignity and liberty of the human nature. They are of unquestionable truth. *My mouth shall speak truth* (*v.* 7). Every word of God is true. His word to us is *yea, and amen*; never then let ours be *yea and nay.* They are all *plain*, and not hard to be understood. If the book is sealed, it is to those who are willingly ignorant.

III. The right knowledge of those things is to be preferred before all the wealth of this world (*v.* 10, 11): *Receive my instruction, and not silver. Wisdom is* in itself, and therefore must be in our account, *better than rubies.* It will bring us in a better price, and it will be a better ornament than jewels.

Verses 12–21

Wisdom here is Christ, *in whom are hidden all the treasures of wisdom and knowledge*; it is Christ in the word and Christ in the heart, not only Christ revealed to us, but Christ revealed in us.

I. Divine wisdom gives men good heads (*v.* 12): *I Wisdom dwell with prudence*, not with carnal policy, for prudence is the product of religion and an ornament to religion; and there are more *witty inventions* found out with the help of the scripture, both for the right understanding of God's providences and for the doing of good in our generation, than were ever discovered by the learning of the philosophers or the politics of statesmen. We may apply it to Christ himself. We had found out many inventions for our ruin; he found out one for our recovery.

II. It gives men good hearts, *v.* 13. True religion, consisting in *the fear of the Lord*, teaches men, 1. To hate all sin, as displeasing to God and destructive to the soul: *The fear of the Lord is to hate evil, the evil way.* 2. Particularly to hate pride and passion, those two common and dangerous sins.

III. It has a great influence upon public affairs, *v.* 14. Christ, as God, has strength and wisdom: as Redeemer, he is *the wisdom of God and the power of God.* He is the wonderful counsellor and gives that grace which alone is *sound wisdom.* True religion gives men the best counsel in all difficult cases, and helps to make their way plain. And therefore Wisdom says, *By me kings reign* (*v.* 15, 16). They reign by him, and therefore ought to reign for him. Religion is very much the strength and support of the civil government; it teaches subjects their duty, and so *by it kings reign* over them the more easily; it teaches kings their duty, and so *by it kings reign* as they ought; they *decree justice*, while they *rule in the fear of God.* Those rule well whom religion rules.

IV. It will make all those happy that receive it. They shall be happy in the love of Christ; for he it is that says, *I love those that love me, v.* 17. *"Those that seek me early*, that is, seek me earnestly, seek me first before anything else, that begin betimes in the days of their youth to seek me, they shall find what they seek."* Christ shall be theirs, and they shall be his. They shall have as much riches and honour as Infinite Wisdom sees good for them (*v.* 18). They are *riches and righteousness*, riches honestly got, not by fraud and oppression, but in regular ways, and riches charitably used, for alms are called *righteousness.* Therefore they are *durable riches.* That which is well got will wear well and will be left to the children's children, and that which is well spent in works of piety and charity is put out to the best interest and so will be durable. They shall have that which is infinitely better, if they have not riches and honour in this world (*v.* 19): *"My fruit is better than gold*, and will turn to a better account, will be of more value in less compass, *and my revenue better than the choicest silver*, will serve a better trade."* They shall be happy in the grace of God now; that shall be their guide in the good way, *v.* 20. This is that fruit of wisdom which is *better than gold, than fine gold*, it *leads us in the way of righteousness*, shows us that way and goes before us in it, the way that God would have us walk in and which will certainly bring us to our desired end. They shall be happy in the glory of God hereafter, *v.* 21. It is a happiness which will subsist of itself, and stand alone, without the accidental supports of outward conveniences. Spiritual and eternal things are the only real and substantial things. Joy in God is substantial joy, solid and well-grounded. The promises are their bonds, Christ is their surety, and both substantial. It is satisfying; it will not only fill their hands, but *fill their treasures, v.* 21. The things of this world may fill men's bellies (Ps. xvii. 14), but not their treasures, for they cannot in them secure to themselves *goods for many years.*

Verses 22–31

Wisdom here has personal properties and actions; and that intelligent divine person can be no other than the Son of God himself, to whom the principal things here spoken of wisdom are attributed in other scriptures. The best exposition of these verses we have in the first four verses of St. John's gospel. *In the beginning was the Word*, &c. Concerning the Son of God observe,

I. His personality and distinct subsistence, one with the Father and of the same essence, and yet a person of himself, whom *the Lord possessed* (v. 22), *who was set up* (v. 23) *was brought forth* (v. 24, 25), *was by him* (v. 30), for he was *the express image of his person*, Heb. i. 3.

II. His eternity; he was begotten of the Father, for *the Lord possessed* him, as his own Son, his beloved Son, laid him in his bosom; he was *brought forth as the only-begotten of the Father*, and this *before all worlds*. The Word was eternal, and had a being before the world, before the beginning of time; and therefore it must follow that it was from eternity. *The Lord possessed him in the beginning of his way*, of his eternal counsels, for those were *before his works*. This way indeed had no beginning, for God's purposes in himself are eternal like himself, but God speaks to us in our own language. Wisdom explains herself (v. 23): *I was set up from everlasting, Before the earth was*, and before man was made. Before the sea was (v. 24), *when there were no depths* in which the waters were gathered together, *no fountains* from which those waters might arise, none of that deep on which the Spirit of God moved for the production of the visible creation, Gen. i. 2. Before the mountains were, v. 25, the eternal Word *brought forth*. Before the habitable parts of the world, which men cultivate (v. 26), *the fields* in the valleys, to which the mountains are as a wall, which are *the highest part of the dust of the world; the first part of the dust* (so some), the atoms which compose the several parts of the world; the *chief or principal part of the dust*, so it may be read, and understood of man, the principal part of the dust, dust enlivened, dust refined—the eternal Word had a being, *in him was the life of men*.

III. His agency in making the world. He not only had a being before the world, but he was present, not as a spectator, but as the architect, when the world was made. *By him God made the worlds*, Eph. iii. 9; Heb. i. 2; Col. i. 16. When, on the first day of the creation, God said, *Let there be light*, and with a word produced it, this eternal Wisdom was that almighty Word: Then *I was there, when he prepared the heavens*. He was no less active when, on the second day, he stretched out the firmament, the vast expanse, and *set* that as *a compass upon the face of the depth* (v. 27), surrounded it on all sides with that canopy, that curtain. He was also employed in the third day's work, when the *waters above the heavens* were gathered together by *establishing the clouds above*, and those under the heavens by *strengthening the fountains of the deep*, which send forth those waters (v. 28), and by preserving the bounds of the sea, which is the receptacle of those waters, v. 29.

IV. The infinite complacency which the Father had in him, and he in the Father (v. 30): *I was by him, as one brought up with him*. As by an eternal generation he was brought forth of the Father, so by an eternal counsel he was brought up with him. He did what he saw the Father do (John v. 19), pleased his Father, did according to the commandment he received from his Father, and all this *as one brought up with him*. He was *daily his Father's delight* (*my elect, in whom my soul delighteth*, says God, Isa. xlii. 1). This may be understood of the satisfaction they had in each other, with reference to the great work of man's redemption.

V. The gracious concern he had for mankind, v. 31. Wisdom *rejoiced*, not so much in the rich products of the earth, but in the redemption and salvation of man.

The application of Wisdom's discourse; the design and tendency of it is to bring us all into an entire subjection to the laws of religion, and to rectify what is amiss in our hearts and lives.

I. An exhortation to hear and obey the voice of Wisdom, to discern the voice of Christ, as the sheep know the shepherd's voice. *"Hearken unto me, O you children!"* v. 32. "Read the word written, sit under the word preached, bless God for both, and hear him in both speaking to you." Let Wisdom's children justify Wisdom by hearkening to her. Hear Wisdom's words with a willing heart (v. 33): *"Hear instruction, and refuse it not*, either as that which you need not or as that which you like not; it is offered you as a kindness, and it is at your peril if you refuse it." We must hear Wisdom so as to *watch daily at her gates*, as beggars to receive an alms, as clients and patients to receive advice, and as servants, with humility, and patience *at the posts of her doors*. We must watch and wait, as Christ's hearers, that *hanged on him* to hear him, as the word in the original is (Luke xix. 48 and *ch.* xxi. 38) *came early in the morning to hear him*.

II. An assurance of happiness to all those that do hearken to Wisdom. They shall find what they seek. But will it make them amends if they do find it? Yes (v. 35): *Whoso finds me finds life*, that is, all happiness, all that good which he needs or can desire. Christ is Wisdom, and he that finds Christ, *finds life*; for Christ is life to all believers.

III. The doom passed upon all those that reject Wisdom and her proposals, v. 26. They ruin themselves, and Wisdom will not hinder them, because they have set at nought all her counsel. They *sin against Christ*; they act in contempt of his authority, and in contradiction to all the purposes of his life and death. Those that offend Christ do the greatest wrong to themselves; they *wrong their own souls. O Israel! thou hast destroyed thyself*.

CHAPTER 9

Christ and sin are rivals for the soul of man. The design of this representation is to set before us life and death, good and evil; and there needs no more than a fair stating of the case to determine us which of those to choose. I. Christ, under the name of Wisdom, invites us to accept of his entertainment, and so to enter into communion with him, ver. 1–6. And having foretold the different success of his invitation (ver. 7–9) he shows, in short, what he requires from us (ver. 10) and what he designs for us (ver. 11), and then leaves it to our choice what we will do, ver. 12. II. Sin, under the character of a foolish woman, courts us to accept of her entertainment, and (ver. 13–16) pretends it is very charming, ver. 17. But Solomon tells us what the reckoning will be, ver. 18.

Verses 1–12

Wisdom is here introduced as a magnificent and munificent queen, great and generous; that Word of God is this Wisdom in which God makes known his goodwill towards men; God the Word is this Wisdom, to whom the Father has committed all judgment. The word is plural, *Wisdoms*; for in Christ are hid treasures of wisdom.

I. The rich provision which Wisdom has made for the reception of all those that will be her disciples. This is represented under the similitude of a sumptuous feast. 1. Here is a stately palace provided, v. 1. Wisdom, not finding a house capacious enough for all her guests, has built one on purpose, and, has *hewn out her seven pillars*. Heaven is the house which Wisdom has built to entertain all her guests that are called to the marriage-supper of the Lamb; that is her Father's house, where there are many mansions, and whither she has gone to prepare places for us. 2. Here is a splendid feast got ready (v. 2): *She has killed her beasts; she has mingled her wine*. She has *killed her sacrifice* (so the word is); it is a sumptuous but a sacred feast, a feast upon a sacrifice. *She has completely furnished her table* with all the satisfactions that a soul can desire—righteousness and grace, peace and joy, the assurances of God's love, the consolations of the Spirit, and all the pledges and earnests of eternal life.

II. The gracious invitation she has given, not to some particular friends, but to all in general. *She has sent forth her maidens, v.* 3. The ministers of the gospel are commissioned to give notice of the preparations which God has made, in the everlasting covenant, for all those that are willing to come up to the terms of it; and they, with maiden purity, not corrupting themselves or the word of God, and with an exact observance of their orders, are to call upon all they meet with, even in *the highways and hedges,* to come and feast with Wisdom, for *all things are now ready,* Luke xiv. 23. She herself *cries upon the highest places of the city,* as one earnestly desirous of the welfare of the children of men. The invitation is given: *Whoso is simple* and *wants understanding, v.* 4. Wisdom invites such, because what she has to give is what they must need. He that is simple is invited, that he may be made wise, and he that *wants a heart* (so the word is) let him come hither, and he shall have one. Her preparations are designed for the cure of the mind. We are invited to Wisdom's house: *Turn in hither.* I say *we* are, for which of us is there that must not own the character of the invited, that are *simple and want understanding?* We are invited to her table (*v.* 5): *Come, eat of my bread,* that is, taste of the true pleasures that are to be found in the knowledge and fear of God. By faith acting on the promises of the gospel we feed, we feast, upon the provisions Christ has made for poor souls. We must break off from all bad company: "*Forsake the foolish,* converse not with them." The first step towards virtue is to shun vice, and therefore to shun the vicious. "Live not a mere animal-life, but the life of men. *Live* and you *shall live;* live spiritually, and you shall live eternally," Eph. v. 14.

III. The instructions which Wisdom gives to the ministers and others, who in their places are endeavouring to serve her designs. Their work must be, not only to tell in general what preparation is made for souls, but they must address themselves to particular persons, tell them of their faults, *reprove, rebuke, v.* 7, 8. They must instruct them how to amend— *teach, v.* 9. The word of God is intended, and therefore so is the ministry of that word, *for reproof, for correction, and for instruction in righteousness.* They would meet with some *scorners* and *wicked men* who would mock the messengers of the Lord, and misuse them. And, though they are not forbidden to invite those simple ones to Wisdom's house, yet they are advised not to pursue the invitation by reproving and rebuking them. Thus Christ said of the Pharisees, *Let them alone,* Matt. xv. 14. They would meet with others, who are wise, and good, and just; thanks be to God, all are not scorners. We meet with some who are so wise as to be willing and glad to be taught. If there be occasion, we must reprove them; for wise men are not so perfectly wise but there is that in them which needs a reproof. The more wisdom a man has the more desirous he should be **to** have his weaknesses shown him. With our reproofs we must *give* them *instruction,* and must *teach* them, *v.* 9. It is as great an instance of wisdom to take a reproof well as to give it well. A *wise man* will be made wiser by the reproofs; he *will increase in learning,* will grow in knowledge, and so grow in grace.

IV. The instructions she gives to those that are invited, which her maidens must inculcate upon them.

1. Let them know wherein true wisdom consists, *v.* 10. The *fear of God is the beginning of wisdom.* A reverence of God's majesty, and a dread of his wrath, are the first steps towards true religion. *The knowledge of holy things* (the word is plural) *is understanding,* the things pertaining to the service of God (those are called *holy things*), that pertain to our own sanctification.

2. Let them know what will be the advantages of this wisdom (*v.* 11): "*By me thy days shall be multiplied.* It will contribute to the health of thy body, and so *the years of thy life* on earth *shall be increased.* It will bring thee to heaven, and there the *years of thy life shall be increased without end.*"

3. Let them know what will be the consequence of their choosing or refusing this fair offer, *v.* 12. "*If thou be wise, thou shalt be wise for thyself;* thou wilt be the gainer by it, not Wisdom. *If thou scornest* Wisdom's proffer, *thou alone shalt bear it.*"

Verses 13–18

How industrious the tempter is to seduce unwary souls into the paths of sin!

I. Who is the tempter—*a foolish woman,* Folly herself, in opposition to Wisdom. Carnal sensual pleasure I take to be especially meant by this *foolish woman* (*v.* 13); for that defiles the mind and stupefies conscience. This tempter is here described to be ignorant: *She is simple and knows nothing,* that is, she has no sufficient solid reason to offer. *Whoredom, and wine, and new wine, take away the heart;* they besot men, and make fools of them. The less she has to offer that is rational the more violent and pressing she is, and carries the day often by dint of impudence. She *is clamorous* and noisy (*v.* 13). *She sits at the door of her house* (*v.* 14), watching for a prey. *She sits on a seat* (*on a throne,* so the word signifies) *in the high places of the city,* as if she had authority, and perhaps she gains more by pretending to be fashionable than by pretending to be agreeable.

II. Who are the tempted—young people who have been well educated. They are *passengers that go right on their ways* (*v.* 15), that have been trained up in the paths of religion and virtue and set out very hopefully and well, and are not (as that young man, *ch.* vii. 8) *going the way to her house.* Such as these she lays snares for, and uses all her charms, to pervert them. She calls them *simple,* and *wanting understanding,* and therefore courts them to her school, that they may be cured of the restraints and formalities of their religion.

III. What the temptation is (*v.* 17): *Stolen waters are sweet.* It is to water and bread, whereas Wisdom invites to the beasts she has killed, and the wine she has mingled; however, bread and water are acceptable enough to those that are hungry and thirsty; and this is pretended to be more *sweet* and *pleasant* than common, for it is *stolen water and bread eaten in secret,* with a fear of being discovered. The pleasures of prohibited lusts are boasted of as more relishing than those of prescribed love; and dishonest gain is preferred to that which is justly gotten.

IV. An effectual antidote against the temptation, *v.* 18. He that so far wants understanding as to be drawn aside by these enticements is led on, ignorantly, to his own inevitable ruin: *He knows that the dead are there,* that those who live in pleasure are *dead while they live, dead in trespasses and sins. Her guests,* that are treated with these *stolen waters,* are led captive by Satan at his will.

CHAPTER 10

Hitherto we have been in the porch or preface to the proverbs; here they begin. They are short but weighty sentences; most of them are distichs, two sentences in one verse, illustrating each other; but it is seldom that there is any coherence between the verses, much less any thread of discourse, and therefore in these chapters we need not attempt to reduce the contents to their proper heads. The scope of them all is to set before us good and evil, the blessing and the curse. Many of the proverbs in this chapter relate to the good government of the tongue.

Verse 1

The comfort of parents, natural, political, and ecclesiastical, depends upon the good behaviour of those under their charge. Children should conduct themselves wisely, and live up to their good education, that they may gladden the hearts of their parents. It adds to the comfort of young people that thereby they do something towards recompensing their parents for all the care they have taken with them, and occasion pleasure to them in old age; and it is the duty of parents to rejoice in their children's wisdom and well-doing.

Verses 2–3

These two verses speak to the same purport. Wealth which men get unjustly will do them no good, because God will blast it: *Treasures of wickedness profit nothing*, v. 2. When profit and loss come to be balanced the profit gained by the treasures will by no means countervail the loss sustained by the wickedness, Matt. xvi. 26. They do not profit the soul. God *casts away the substance of the wicked* (v. 3). We often see that scattered by the justice of God which has been gathered together by the injustice of men. That which is honestly got will turn to a good account, for God will bless it. *Righteousness delivers from death*, that is, wealth gained, and kept, and used, in a right manner, answers the end of wealth, which is to keep us alive and be a defence to us.

Verse 4

Those are in a fair way to *become poor who deal with a slack hand*, who are careless and remiss in their business. Those *who deal with a deceitful hand* (so it may be read); who think to enrich themselves by fraud, will, in the end, impoverish themselves, not only by bringing the curse of God on what they have, but by forfeiting their reputation with men. Those who are diligent and honest, who are careful about their affairs, are likely to increase what they have. This is true in the affairs of our souls as well as in our worldly affairs; slothfulness and hypocrisy lead to spiritual poverty, but those who are *fervent in spirit, serving the Lord*, are likely to be *rich in faith* and *rich in good works*.

Verse 5

Those who improve their opportunities, who provide for hereafter while provision is to be made, *gather in summer*, which is gathering time. He who does so *is a wise son*. He acts wisely for his parents, whom, if there be occasion, he ought to maintain. *He who sleeps* idles away his time, and neglects his work, especially *who sleeps in harvest*, when he should be laying in for winter, *is a son that causes shame*; for he is a foolish son; he prepares shame for himself when winter comes. He who gets wisdom in the days of his youth *gathers in summer*, and he will have the credit of his industry; but he who idles away the days of his youth will bear the shame of his indolence when he is old.

Verse 6

Variety of blessings shall descend from above, and visibly abide on the head of good men. Blessings shall be on their head as a coronet to dignify them and as a helmet to protect them. *The mouth of the wicked is covered* with *violence*. Their mouths shall be stopped with shame for the violence which they have done.

Verse 7

Both the just and the wicked, when their days are fulfilled, must die. Between their bodies in the grave there is no visible difference; between the souls of the one and the other, in the world of spirits, there is a vast difference. Blessed men leave behind them blessed memories. Those that honour God he will thus honour, Ps. cxii. 3, 6, 9. It is part of the duty of the survivors: *Let the memory of the just be blessed*, so the Jews read it, and observe it as a precept, not naming an eminently just man that is dead without adding, *Let his memory be blessed*. Bad men are and shall be forgotten, or spoken of with contempt.

Verse 8

The obedient will take it as a privilege to be under government; and to be told their duty. And this is their wisdom; those are *wise in heart* who are tractable, and shall stand and be established. The disobedient, that will not be governed, nor endure any yoke, that will not be taught, nor take any advice, are fools, for they act against themselves and their own interest. They are commonly *prating fools*, full of talk, but full of nonsense, boasting of themselves.

Verse 9

Men's integrity will be their security: *He that walks uprightly* towards God and man, that is faithful to both and means as he says, *walks surely*; he is safe under a divine protection. He goes on his way with a humble boldness, being well armed against the temptations of Satan, the troubles of the world, and the reproaches of men. Men's dishonesty will be their shame: *He that perverts his way*, that dissembles with God and man, though he may for a time pass current, *shall be known* to be what he is.

Verse 10

Mischief is here said to attend designing, self-disguising sinners: *He that winks with the eye*, as if he took no notice of you, when he is watching an opportunity to do you an ill turn, that makes signs to his accomplices to assist him in executing his wicked projects, *causes sorrow* both to others and to himself. A *prating fool shall fall*, as was said before, v. 8. But his case is less dangerous of the two. He does not create so much sorrow to others as *he that winks with his eyes*. The dog that bites is not always the dog that barks.

Verse 11

How industrious a good man is, by communicating his goodness! *His mouth*, the outlet of his mind, *is a well of life*; it is a constant spring, whence issues good discourse for the edification of others. How industrious a bad man is, by concealing his badness: to do hurt with it: *The mouth of the wicked covers violence*, disguises the designed mischief with professions of friendship. *Violence covers the mouth of the wicked;* what he got by violence shall by violence be taken from him, Job v. 4, 5.

Verse 12

The great mischief-maker is malice. Even where there is no manifest occasion of strife, yet *hatred* seeks occasion and so *stirs it up*. Those are spiteful ill-natured people who take a pleasure in setting their neighbours by the ears, by tale-bearing, evil surmises, and misrepresentations, blowing up the sparks of contention into a flame, at which, with an unaccountable pleasure, they warm their hands. The great peace-maker, is *love*, which *covers all sins*, that is, the offences among relations which occasion discord. Love, instead of proclaiming and aggravating the offence, extenuates it as far as it is capable of being extenuated. Love will excuse the offence; when we are able to say that there was no ill intended, but it was an oversight, and we love our friend notwithstanding. It will also overlook the offence that is given us, and cover it, and by this means strife is prevented.

Verse 13

Wisdom and grace are the honour of good men. It is a man's honour to have wisdom, but much more to be instrumental to make others wise. Folly and sin are the shame of bad men: *A rod is for the back of him that is void of understanding—of him that wants a heart;* he exposes himself to the lashes of his own conscience, to the censures of the magistrate, and to the righteous judgments of God.

Verse 14

Observe, 1. It is the wisdom of the wise that they treasure up a stock of useful knowledge, which will be their preservation: *Wisdom is* therefore *found in their lips* (v. 13), because it is laid up in their hearts. 2. It is the folly of fools that they lay up mischief in their hearts. Their *mouth is near destruction,* having the *sharp arrows of bitter words* always at hand to throw about.

Verse 15

Rich people think themselves happy because they are rich; but it is their mistake: *The rich man's wealth is,* in his own conceit, *his strong city,* whereas the worst of evils it is utterly insufficient to protect them from. Poor people think themselves undone because they are poor; but it is their mistake. It sinks their spirits, whereas a man may live very comfortably, though he has but a little to live on, if he be but content, and keep a good conscience, and live by faith.

Verse 16

A righteous man eats only *the labour of his hands,* but that *labour tends to life;* he aims at nothing but to get an honest livelihood, to live and maintain his family. Nor does it tend only to his own life, but he would enable himself to do good to others; he labours *that he may have to gain* (Eph. iv. 28). A wicked man's wealth tends *to sin.* He makes it the food and fuel of his lusts, his pride and luxury; he does hurt with it and not good.

Verse 17

Those are in the right that do not only receive instruction, but retain it, keep it for their own use, that they may govern themselves by it, keep it for the benefit of others, that they may instruct them. Those are in the wrong that do not receive instruction, but wilfully and obstinately refuse it. They will not be taught their duty because it discovers their faults to them. The traveller that has missed his way, and cannot bear to be shown the right way, must needs err; he certainly misses *the way of life.*

Verse 18

Malice is folly and wickedness when it is concealed by flattery and dissimulation: He *is a fool,* though he may think himself a politician. *Lying lips* are bad enough of themselves, but have a peculiar malignity in them when they are made *a cloak of maliciousness. He that utters slander is a fool* too, for God will sooner or later bring forth that righteousness as the light which he endeavours to cloud.

Verse 19

Usually, those that speak much speak amiss, and among many words there cannot but be many idle words. Those that love to hear themselves talk do not consider what work they are making for repentance. It is therefore good to *keep our mouth as with a bridle: He that refrains his lips,* that often checks himself, is a wise man.

Verses 20–21

Value men, not by their wealth and preferment in the world, but by their virtue. Good men are good for something. As long as they have a mouth to speak, that will make them valuable and useful. *The tongue of the just is as choice silver;* they are sincere, freed from the dross of guile and evil design. They will enrich those that hear them with wisdom. It makes them useful: *The lips of the righteous feed many;* for they are full of the word of God, which is the bread of life, wherewith souls are nourished up. Bad men are good for nothing. *The heart of the wicked is little worth.* His principles, his notions, his thoughts, his purposes, and all the things that fill him, and affect him, are worldly and carnal, and therefore of no value. *He that is of the earth speaks of the earth,* and neither understands nor relishes the things of God, John iii. 31; 1 Cor. ii. 14.

Verse 22

Worldly wealth is that which most men have their hearts very much upon, but they generally mistake both the nature of the thing they desire and the way by which they hope to obtain it. Desirable wealth is to be expected, not by making ourselves drudges to the world (Ps. cxxvii. 2), but by *the blessing of God.* It is this that *makes rich and adds no sorrow;* what comes from the love of God has the sign of God, to preserve the soul from those turbulent lusts and passions of which the increase of riches is commonly the incentive.

Verse 23

It *is as laughter to a fool to do mischief.* He makes a laughing matter of sin. When he is warned not to sin, he makes a jest of the admonition. When he has sinned, he ridicules reproofs, and laughs away the convictions of his own conscience, ch. xiv. 9. Wisdom carries along with it the evidence of its own excellency. You need say no more in praise of *a man understanding* than this, "He is an *understanding man;* he *has wisdom."*

Verses 24–25

I. It shall be as ill with the wicked as they can fear, and as well with the righteous, as they can desire. The wicked, it is true, buoy themselves up sometimes in their wickedness with vain hopes which will deceive them, but at other times they cannot but be haunted with just fears, and those *fears shall come upon them.* The righteous it is true, sometimes have their fears, but their desire is towards the favour of God and a happiness in him, and that *desire shall be granted.* According to their faith, not according to their fear, it shall be *unto them,* Ps. xxxvii. 4.

II. The prosperity of the wicked shall quickly end, but the happiness of the righteous shall never end, v. 25.

Verse 26

Those that are of a slothful disposition are not fit to be sent on an errand. Such therefore are very unmeet to be ministers, Christ's messengers. A slothful servant is to his master as uneasy and troublesome as *vinegar to the teeth* and *smoke to the eyes;* he provokes his passion, as vinegar sets the teeth on edge, and occasions him grief to see his business neglected and undone, as smoke sets the eyes a-weeping.

Verses 27–28

Religion lengthens men's lives and crowns their hopes. *What man is he that would see good days?* Let him be religious, and then his days shall not only be many, but happy, for *the hope of the righteous shall be gladness.* Wickedness shortens men's lives, and frustrates their hopes.

Verses 29–30

Strength and stability are entailed upon integrity: *The way of the Lord is strength to the upright,* confirms him in his uprightness. All God's dealings with him, merciful and afflictive, serve to quicken him to his duty and animate him against his discouragements. A good conscience, kept pure from sin, gives a man boldness in a dangerous time. That *joy of the Lord* which is to be found only in the *way of the Lord* will be our strength (Neh. viii. 10), and therefore *the righteous shall never be removed*. Ruin and destruction are the certain consequences of wickedness. God's judgments will root them out.

Verses 31–32

It is both the proof and the praise of a man's wisdom and goodness that he speaks wisely and well. A good man, in his discourse, *brings forth wisdom* for the benefit of others. He *knows what is acceptable*, what discourse will be pleasing to God. It is the sin, and will be the ruin, of a wicked man, that he speaks wickedly.

Chapter 11

Verse 1

Nothing is more offensive to God than deceit in commerce. *A false balance* is here put for all manner of unjust and fraudulent practices in dealing with any person, which are all an *abomination to the Lord*. Men make light of such frauds, and think there is no sin in that which there is money to be got by. Nothing is more pleasing to God than fair and honest dealing, nor more necessary to make us and our devotions acceptable to him: *A just weight is his delight*.

Verse 2

Pride is a shame to a man who springs out of the earth, who lives upon alms, depends upon God, and has forfeited all he has, to be proud. He that is haughty makes himself contemptible; it is a sin for which God often brings men down, as he did Nebuchadnezzar and Herod, whose ignominy immediately attended their vain-glory. As with the proud there is folly, and will be shame, so *with the lowly there is wisdom*, and will be honour, for a man's wisdom gains him respect and makes his face to shine before men.

Verse 3

The integrity of an honest man will itself be his guide. His principles are fixed, his rule is certain, and therefore his way is plain; his sincerity keeps him steady, and he need not tack about every time the wind turns, having no other end to drive at than to keep a good conscience. The iniquity of a bad man will itself be his ruin. The perverseness of sinners will be their destruction, though they think themselves ever so well fortified.

Verse 4

Riches will stand men in no stead in that day. They will neither put by the stroke nor ease the pain, much less take out the sting; what profit will this world's birthrights be then? A good conscience will make death easy. It is the privilege of the righteous not to be hurt of the second death, and so not much hurt by the first.

Verses 5–6

These two verses are to the same purport with *v*. 3. The ways of religion are plain and safe, and in them we may enjoy a holy security. *The righteousness of the upright* shall be armour of proof to them, to deliver them from the allurements of the devil and the world, and from their menaces. The ways of wickedness are dangerous and destructive: *The wicked shall fall* into misery and ruin *by their own wickedness*. Their sin will be their punishment.

Verse 7

It will be the great aggravation of the misery of wicked people that their hopes will sink into despair just when they expect them to be crowned with fruition. When a godly man dies his expectations are outdone, and all his fears vanish; but when a wicked man dies his hopes vanish.

Verse 8

Good people are helped out of the distresses which they thought themselves lost in, and their feet are set in a large room, Ps. lxvi. 12; xxxiv. 19. God has found out a way to deliver his people even when they have despaired. The wicked have fallen into the distresses which they thought themselves far from. Mordecai is saved from the gallows, Daniel from the lion's den, and Peter from the prison; and their persecutors *come in their stead*. The Israelites are delivered out of the Red Sea and the Egyptians drowned in it.

Verse 9

It is not only the murderer with his sword, but the *hypocrite with his mouth*, that *destroys his neighbour*, decoying him into sin, or into mischief, by the specious pretences of kindness and goodwill. *Death and life are in the power of the tongue*, but no tongue more fatal than the flattering tongue.

Verses 10–11

Good men are generally well-beloved by their neighbours. *When it goes well with the righteous*, when they are advanced and put into a capacity of doing good according to their desire, it is so much the better for all about them, and *the city rejoices*. Wicked people may perhaps have here and there a well-wisher, but among the generality of their neighbours they get ill-will; they may be feared, but they are not loved, and therefore *when they perish there is shouting*. There is good reason for this, because those that are good do good. *Good men are public blessings. By the blessing of the upright*, the blessings with which they are blessed, which enlarge their sphere of usefulness,—by the blessings with which they bless their neighbours, their advice, their examples, their prayers,—by the blessings with which God blesses others for their sake,—by these *the city is exalted*. Wicked men are public nuisances.

Verses 12–13

Silence is recommended as an instance of true friendship. *A man of understanding*, that has rule over his own spirit, if he be provoked, *holds his peace*, that he may neither give vent to his passion nor kindle the passion of others by any opprobrious language or peevish reflections. *He that is void of wisdom* discovers his folly by this; he *despises his neighbour*, calls him *Raca*, and *Thou fool*, upon the least provocation. *A tale-bearer*, that carries all the stories he can pick up, true or false, from house to house, to make mischief and sow discord, *reveals secrets* which he has been entrusted with, and so breaks the laws, and forfeits all the privileges, of friendship and conversation.

Verse 14

Where no counsel is, no consultation, but everythi ng done rashly, only caballing for parties and divid ed interests, *the people fall*, crumble into factions, fall to pieces. Councils of war are necessary to the operations of war; two eyes see more than one; and mutual advice is mutual assistance. *In the multitude of counsellors*, that see their need one of another, and act in concert and with concern for the public welfare, *there is safety*.

Verse 15

Our estates are not our own; we are but stewards. There is a good husbandry which is good divinity, part of the character of a good man, Ps. cxii. 5. Every man must be just to his family, else he is not true to his stewardship. In particular, we must not enter rashly into suretiship. There is danger of bringing ourselves into trouble by it, and our families too when we are gone: *He that is surety for a stranger,* he *shall smart for it. He shall be sadly crushed and broken by it,* and perhaps become a bankrupt.

Verse 16

Strong men retain riches. Men of spirit and interest are able to make good against all who stand in their way, are likely to keep what they have and to get more. *A gracious woman* is as solicitous to preserve her reputation for wisdom and modesty, humility and courtesy, and all those other graces that are the true ornaments of her sex, as strong men are to secure their estates; and those women who are truly gracious will secure their honour by their good conduct.

Verse 17

A *merciful,* tender, good-humoured *man, does good to his own soul,* makes and keeps himself easy. He has the pleasure of doing his duty, and contributing to the comfort of those that are to him as *his own soul;* for *we are members one of another.* We may by the *soul* understand the *inward man,* as the apostle calls it, and then it teaches us that the first and great act of mercy is to provide well for our own souls the necessary supports of the spiritual life. A *cruel,* froward, ill-natured man, *troubles his own flesh,* and so his sin becomes his punishment.

Verse 18

The wicked works a deceitful work, builds himself a house upon the sand, which will deceive him when the storm comes. *Sin deceived me, and by it slew me.* He *that sows righteousness* shall have *a sure reward;* it is made as sure to him as eternal truth can make it.

Verse 19

True holiness is true happiness; it is a preparative for it, a pledge and earnest of it. *Righteousness* inclines, disposes, and leads, the soul *to life.* Those that indulge themselves in sin are fitting themselves for destruction.

Verse 20

It concerns us to know what God hates and what he loves, that we may govern ourselves accordingly. Nothing is more offensive to God than hypocrisy and double-dealing, for these are signified by the word which we translate *frowardness,* pretending justice, but intending wrong, walking in crooked ways, to avoid discovery. Nothing is more pleasing to God than sincerity and plain-dealing.

Verse 21

Confederacies in sin shall certainly be broken, and shall not avail to protect the sinners: *Though hand join in hand,* though there are many that concur by their practice to keep wickedness in countenance, though they are in league for the support and propagation of it, though wicked children tread in the steps of their wicked parents, they shall not be held guiltless; it will not excuse them to say that they did as the most did and as their company did. *The seed of the righteous,* that follow the steps of their righteousness, though they may fall into trouble, shall, in due time, *be delivered.*

Verse 22

By *discretion* here understand *religion* and *grace,* a true relish (so the word signifies) of the honours and pleasures that attend an unspotted virtue; so that *a woman without discretion* is a woman of a loose and dissolute conversation. Beauty or comeliness of body is *as a jewel of gold,* and, where there is wisdom and grace to guard against the temptations of it, it is a great ornament. A foolish wanton woman, of a light carriage, is fitly compared to a swine, though she be ever so handsome, wallowing in the mire of filthy lusts, with which the mind and conscience are defiled, and, though washed, returning to them. It is lamented that beauty should be so abused. It is quite misplaced, *as a jewel in a swine's snout,* with which he roots in the dunghill.

Verse 23

The righteous would have *good, only good;* all they desire is that it may go well with all about them; they wish no hurt to any, but happiness to all; as to themselves, their desire is to obtain the favour of a good God and to preserve the peace of a good conscience; and good they shall have, that good which they desire, Ps. xxxvii. 4. *The wicked* expect and desire mischief to others, but it shall return upon themselves; as they loved cursing, they shall have enough of it.

Verse 24

A man may grow rich by prudently spending what he has, may scatter in works of piety, charity, and generosity, and yet may increase; nay, by that means may increase, as the corn is increased by being sown. But it is especially to be ascribed to God; he blesses the giving hand, and so makes it a getting hand, 2 Cor. ix. 10. A man may grow poor by meanly sparing what he has, *withholding more than is meet,* not paying just debts, not relieving the poor, not providing what is convenient for the family. This *tends to poverty,* and forfeits the blessing of God.

Verse 25

The liberal soul that prays for the afflicted and provides for them, that scatters blessings with gracious lips and generous hands, that soul *shall be made fat* with true pleasure and enriched with more grace. *He that waters* others with the streams of his bounty *shall be also watered himself;* God will certainly return plentiful showers of his blessing. *He that waters, even he shall be as rain* (so some read it); he shall be recruited as the clouds are which return after the rain, and shall be further useful.

Verse 26

It is a sin, when corn is dear and scarce, to withhold it, in hopes that it will grow dearer, so to keep up and advance the market, when it is already so high that the poor suffer by it; and at such a time it is the duty of those that have stocks of corn by them to consider the poor, and to be willing to sell at the market-price, to be content with moderate profit.

Verse 27

He that rises early to that which is good (so the word is), that seeks opportunities of serving his friends and relieving the poor, and lays out himself therein, *procures favour.* All about him love him, and, which is better than life, he has God's loving-kindness. Those that are industrious to do mischief ruin themselves.

Verse 28

Our righteousness will stand us in stead when our riches fail us: *The righteous shall* then *flourish as a branch,* the branch of righteousness, like a tree whose leaf shall not wither, Ps. i. 3. When those that take root in the world wither those that are grafted into Christ shall be fruitful and flourishing.

Verse 29

Two extremes in the management of family-affairs are here condemned. 1. Carefulness and carnal policy, on the one hand. There are those that by their anxiety about their business and fretfulness about their losses, and their niggardliness towards their families, *trouble their own houses*; while others think, by supporting factions and feuds in their families, to serve some turn for themselves. But they will both be disappointed; they will *inherit the wind*. All they will get by these arts will be empty and worthless as the wind. 2. Carelessness and want of common prudence, on the other. He that is a fool in his business, that minds it not, that has no contrivance and consideration, not only loses his reputation, but becomes a *servant to the wise in heart*. He is impoverished, while those that manage wisely raise themselves, and come to have dominion over him.

Verse 30

The righteous are as *trees of life*; the fruits of their piety and charity, their instructions, reproofs, examples, and prayers, their interest in heaven, and their influence upon earth, are like the fruits of that tree, contributing to the nourishment of the spiritual life in many; they are the ornaments of paradise, God's church on earth. The wise are something more; they are as trees of knowledge, commanded to have knowledge. *He that is wise*, by communicating his wisdom, *wins souls*, wins them over into the interests of God's kingdom among men. Those that would win souls have need of wisdom to know how to deal with them.

Verse 31

This is the only one of Solomon's proverbs that has that note of attention prefixed to it, *Behold!* which intimates that it contains not only an evident truth, but an eminent truth. Some understand both parts of "recompence" as displeasure: *The righteous*, if they do amiss, shall be punished for their offences in this world; much more shall wicked people be punished for theirs, which are committed, not through infirmity, but with a high hand. Others understand it of a "recompence" of reward to the righteous and punishment to sinners. There are some recompences *in the earth*, in this world; but many sins go unpunished in the earth, and services unrewarded, which indicates that there is a judgment to come. Many times *the righteous* are *recompensed* for their righteousness here *in the earth*, though that is not the only reward intended for them, but whatever the word of God has promised them, or the wisdom of God sees good for them, they shall have *in the earth*. *The wicked* also, are sometimes remarkably punished in this life, nations, families, particular persons.

CHAPTER 12

Verse 1

Those that have grace will delight in all the instructions that are given them by the word or providence of God; they will value a good education, and think it not a hardship, but a happiness, to be under a strict and prudent discipline. Those show themselves not only void of grace, but void of common sense, that take it as an affront to be told of their faults, and an imposition upon their liberty to be put in mind of their duty. Those that desire to live in loose families and societies, where they may be under no check, are the *brutish*.

Verse 2

Our Father judges of his children very much by their conduct one to another; and therefore *a good man*, that is merciful, and charitable, and does good, *draws out favour from the Lord* by his prayers; but a malicious man, that devises wickedness against his neighbours, *he will condemn*, as unworthy of a place in his kingdom.

Verse 3

Though men may advance themselves by sinful arts, they cannot by such arts settle and secure themselves. *A man shall not be established by wickedness;* it may set him in high places, but they are slippery places, Ps. lxxiii. 18. Though good men may have but little of the world, yet what is honestly got will wear well.

Verse 4

He that is blessed with a good wife is as happy as if he were upon the throne, for she is no less than *a crown* to him. A virtuous woman is pious and prudent, active for the good of her family, makes conscience of her duty, a woman that can bear crosses without disturbance. She is faithful to him and by her example teaches his children and servants to be so too. A bad wife is no better than *rottenness in his bones*, an incurable disease, besides that *she makes him ashamed*. She that is silly and slothful, wasteful and wanton, passionate and ill-tongued, ruins both the credit and comfort of her husband.

Verse 5

We mistake if we imagine that thoughts are free; they are under the divine cognizance. A good man may have in his mind bad suggestions, but he does not indulge them and harbour them. It is a man's honour to mean honestly, though a word or action may be misplaced, or mistimed, or at least misinterpreted. But it is a man's shame to act with deceit, with trick and design, not only with a long reach, but with an overreach.

Verse 6

In the foregoing verse the *thoughts* of the wicked and righteous were compared. Wicked indeed those are whose *words* are to *lie in wait for blood*; their tongues are swords to those that stand in their way, to good men whom they hate and persecute. See an instance, Luke xx. 20, 21. Good men speak help to their neighbours: The *mouth of the upright* is ready to be opened in the cause of those that are oppressed (*ch.* xxxi. 8).

Verse 7

Turn the wicked, and they are not; they stand in such a slippery place that the least touch of trouble brings them down, like the apples of Sodom, which look fair, but touch them and they go to dust. The prosperity of the righteous will endure. Death will remove them, but their *house* shall *stand*, their families shall be kept up.

Verse 8

The best reputation is that which attends virtue and the prudent conduct of life: *A man shall be commended* not according to his riches or preferments, his craft and subtlely, but *according to his wisdom*, the honesty of his designs. The worst reproach is that which follows wickedness, that turns aside to crooked ways.

Verse 9

It is the folly of some that they covet to make a great figure abroad, and yet want necessaries at home, and, if their debts were paid, would not be worth a morsel of bread, nay, perhaps, pinch their bellies to put it on their backs, that they may appear very gay, because fine feathers make fine birds. The character of those is every way better who content themselves in a lower sphere, where they are despised for the plainness of their dress, that they may be able to afford themselves, not only necessaries, but conveniences, in their own houses, not only bread, but a servant.

Verse 10

A good man will be merciful. He regards even *the life of his beast*, not only because it is his servant, but because it is God's creature. The beasts that are under our care must be provided for, must have convenient food and rest. Balaam was checked for beating his ass. The law took care for oxen. A wicked man will be unmerciful; even his *tender mercies* are *cruel*; natural compassion is turned into hardheartedness.

Verse 11

It is men's wisdom to mind their business and follow an honest calling, for that is the way, by the blessing of God, to get a livelihood. Be busy, and that is the true way to be easy. Keep thy shop and thy shop will keep thee. It is men's folly to neglect their business, for then they come to want bread, and make themselves burdensome to others, eating the bread out of other people's mouths.

Verse 12

The care and aim of a wicked man. "Oh that I were but as cunning as such a man, that I had but his art of over-reaching, that I could but take my revenge on one I have spite to as effectually as he can!" A good man desires, to do good and to be fixed and confirmed in doing good. The wicked desires only a net wherewith to fish for himself; the righteous desires to yield fruit for the benefit of others and God's glory, Rom. xiv. 6.

Verse 13

Many a man has paid dearly in this world for the transgression of his lips, and has felt the lash on his back for want of a bridle upon his tongue, Ps. lxiv. 8. The righteous extricate themselves out of trouble by their own wisdom, when God in mercy comes in for their succour.

Verse 14

Even good words will turn to a good account (*v.* 14): *A man* shall gain present comfort, inward pleasure which is truly satisfying, by the good he does with his pious discourse and prudent advice. Good works: much more, will be abundantly rewarded.

Verse 15

A fool thinks he is in the right in everything he does, and *therefore* asks no advice. A wise man is willing to be advised, desires to have counsel given him, and *hearkens to counsel*, being diffident of his own judgment.

Verse 16

Passion is folly: a wise man may be angry when there is just cause for it, but then he has his anger under check, is *lord of his anger*, whereas a fool's anger lords it over him. Those that are soon angry, that are quickly put into a flame by the least spark, have not that rule which they ought to have over their own spirits. Meekness is wisdom: *A prudent man covers shame*. He covers the passion that is in his own breast; he keeps his mouth as with a bridle. It is a kindness to ourselves, and contributes to the repose of our own minds, to extenuate and excuse the injuries and affronts that we receive, instead of aggravating them and making the worst of them.

Verse 17

Here is, 1. A faithful witness representing everything fairly, to the best of his knowledge, whether in judgment or in common conversation, whether he be upon his oath or no, makes it to appear that he is governed and actuated by the principles and laws of righteousness, and he promotes justice by doing honour to it. 2. A false witness condemned for a cheat; he *shows forth deceit*, and is possessed by a lying spirit.

Verse 18

The tongue is death or life, poison or medicine, as it is used. Slanders, like a sword, wound the reputation of those of whom they are uttered. Whisperings and evil surmises, like a sword, divide and cut asunder the bonds of love and friendship, and separate those that have been dearest to each other. There are words that are curing and healing, closing up those wounds which the backbiting tongue had given, restoring peace, and persuading to reconciliation.

Verse 19

If truth be spoken, it will hold good. What is true will be always true; we may abide by it. A *lying tongue* will be disproved. The liar, when he comes to be examined, will be found not consistent with himself as he is that speaks truth. Truth may be eclipsed, but it will come to light.

Verse 20

Those that devise mischief deceive themselves. Let them imagine it ever so artfully, deceivers will be deceived. Those that study the things which make for peace and give peaceable advice, promote healing and further the public welfare, will have not only the credit, but the comfort of it. *Blessed are the peacemakers.*

Verse 21

If men be sincerely righteous, God has engaged that no evil shall happen to them. He will, by the power of his grace in them, keep them so that, though they be tempted, yet they shall not be overcome by the temptation, and though they come into trouble, yet those troubles shall have no evil in them (Ps. xci. 10), for they shall be overruled to work for their good. Those that live in contempt of God and man shall be made miserable with the mischiefs that shall come upon them. Those that delight in mischief shall have enough of it.

Verse 22

Lying is an abomination to the Lord, not only because it is a breach of his law, but because it is destructive to human society. Those that *deal truly* and sincerely in all their dealings are *his delight*, and he is well pleased with them.

Verse 23

He that is wise communicates his knowledge when it may turn to the edification of others, but he conceals it when the showing of it would only tend to his own commendation. Prudent men will carefully avoid everything that savours of ostentation. He that is foolish cannot avoid proclaiming his folly.

Verse 24

Industry is the way to preferment. Solomon advanced Jeroboam because he saw that he was an industrious young man, and minded his business, 1 Kings xi. 28. Those that are diligent when they are young will get that which will enable them to rule, and so to rest, when they are old. Knavery is the way to slavery. Those that, because they will not take pains in an honest calling, live by their shifts and arts of dishonesty, are paltry and beggarly, and will be kept under.

Verse 25

The cause and consequence of melancholy is *heaviness in the heart*; it is a load of care, and fear, and sorrow, upon the spirits; it makes them stoop, prostrates and sinks them. The cure of it: *A good word* from God, applied by faith, *makes it glad: Cast thy burden upon the Lord, and he shall sustain thee;* the good word of God, particularly the gospel, is designed to make the hearts glad that are weary and heavy laden, Matt. xi. 28.

Verse 26

The righteous is more abundant than his neighbour (so the margin); he is richer, though not in this world's goods, yet in the graces and comforts of the Spirit, which are the true riches. There is a true excellency in religion; it ennobles men, inspires them with generous principles. His neighbour may make a greater figure in the world, but the righteous man has the intrinsic worth. Wicked men walk in a way which *seduces them*. It seems to them to be a pleasant way, but it is all a cheat.

Verse 27

That which may make us hate slothfulness and deceit, for the word here signifies both: *The slothful deceitful man* has roast meat, but that which he roasts is not what he himself *took in hunting*. Or, if slothful deceitful men have taken anything by hunting, yet they do not roast it when they have taken it. The *substance of a diligent man*, though it be not great perhaps, *is* yet *precious*. It comes from the blessing of God; he has comfort in it; it does him good, and his family. It is his own daily bread, not bread out of other people's mouths.

Verse 28

Religion is a *pathway*, a way which God has cast up for us (Isa. xxxv. 8); it is a highway, the king's highway, the King of kings' highway, a way which is tracked before us by all the saints, the good old way, full of the footsteps of the flock. There is not only life at the end, but there is life in the way. In it *there is no death*, none of that sorrow of the world which works death.

CHAPTER 13

Verse 1

There is great hope of those that have a reverence for their parents, and are willing to be advised and admonished by them. There is little hope of those that will not so much as *hear rebuke*, but scorn to submit to government and scoff at those that deal faithfully with them. How can those mend a fault who will not be told of it.

Verse 2

Inward comfort and satisfaction will be daily bread. Violence done will recoil in the face of him that does it: *The soul of the transgressors* that plots mischief, and vents it by word and deed, *shall eat violence*; they shall have their belly full of it. Every man shall drink as he brews, eat as he speaks; for by our words we must be justified or condemned.

Verse 3

A guard upon the lips is a guard to the soul. He that is cautious, that thinks twice before he speaks once, *keeps his soul* from a great deal of guilt and

grief and saves himself the trouble of many bitter reflections. There is many a one ruined by an ungoverned tongue.

Verse 4

The slothful desire the gains which the diligent get, but they hate the pains which the diligent take; they covet everything that is to be coveted, but will do nothing that is to be done; and therefore it follows, They have nothing; for he that will not labour let him hunger, and let him not *eat*, 2 Thess. iii. 10. The happiness and honour of the diligent: they shall have abundance. This is especially true in spiritual affairs.

Verse 5

It is the undoubted character of every *righteous man* that he *hates lying* (that is, all sin, for every sin is a lie, and particularly all fraud and falsehood in commerce and conversation), not only that he will not tell a lie, but he abhors lying, from a rooted reigning principle of love to truth and justice, and conformity to God. If the wicked man's eyes were opened, and his conscience awakened, he would *abhor himself and repent in dust and ashes*.

Verse 6

Those that are *upright in their way* deal sincerely both with God and man, their integrity will keep them from the temptations of Satan, which shall not prevail over them. Those that are wicked, even their wickedness will be their overthrow at last, and they are held in the cords of it in the meantime.

Verse 7

The world is a great cheat. Some that are really poor would be thought to be rich and are thought to be so; they trade and spend as if they were rich, make a great show when perhaps, if all their debts were paid, they are not worth a groat. This is sin, and shame. Some that are really rich would be thought to be poor, because they sordidly and meanly live below what God has given them. In this there is an ingratitude to God, injustice to the family and neighbourhood, and uncharitableness to the poor. There are many presuming hypocrites, that are really poor and empty of grace and yet pretend themselves rich, and will not own their poverty. There are many timorous trembling Christians, that are spiritually rich, and full of grace, and yet think themselves poor, and by their doubts and fears, their complaints and griefs, *make themselves poor*.

Verse 8

We are apt to judge of men's blessedness, at least in this world, by their wealth, but Solomon shows what a gross mistake it is. Those that are rich, if by some they are respected for their riches, yet by others they are envied and brought in danger of their lives, which therefore they are forced to ransom with their riches. How little is a man beholden to his wealth when it only serves to redeem that life which otherwise would not have been exposed! Those that are poor, if by some, that should be their friends, they are despised and overlooked, yet are despised and overlooked by others that would be their enemies if they had anything to lose.

Verse 9

The light of the righteous rejoices, that is, it increases, and makes them glad. Even their outward prosperity is their joy, and much more those gifts, graces, and comforts, with which their souls are illuminated. *The lamp of the wicked* burns dimly and faint; it looks melancholy, like a taper in an urn and it will shortly *be put out*.

Verse 10

Foolish pride is the great make-bate. Would you know *whence come wars and fightings*? They come from this root of bitterness. Pride makes men impatient of contradiction, impatient of competition, impatient of contempt, or anything that looks like a slight, and hence arise quarrels among relations and neighbours, quarrels in states and kingdoms, in churches and Christian societies. Men will not forgive, because they are proud. Those that are humble and peaceable will ask and take advice, will consult their own consciences, their Bibles, their ministers, their friends, to preserve quietness and prevent quarrels.

Verse 11

That which is won ill will never wear well. That which is got by such employments as are not lawful, or not becoming Christians, that which is got by gaming, may as truly be said to be *gotten by vanity* as that which is got by fraud and lying, and *will be diminished*. That which is got by industry and honesty will grow more, instead of growing less; it will be a maintenance; it will be an inheritance; it will be an abundance.

Verse 12

Nothing is more grievous than the disappointment of a raised expectation, though not in the thing itself by a denial, yet in the time of it by a delay. Nothing is more grateful than to enjoy that, at last, which we have long wished and waited for: It puts men into a sort of paradise, a garden of pleasure, for *it is a tree of life*. It will make the happiness of heaven the more welcome to the saints that it is what they have earnestly longed for as the crown of their hopes.

Verse 13

Those that prefer the rules of carnal policy before divine precepts, and the allurements of the world and the flesh before God's promises and comforts, despise his word. *He that fears the commandment*, that stands in awe of God, has a reverence for his word, is afraid of displeasing God and incurring the penalties annexed to the commandment, *shall be rewarded* for his godly fear.

Verse 14

By *the law of the wise* we may understand the principles and rules by which they govern themselves: They will be constant springs of comfort, as *a fountain of life*; the closer we keep to those rules the more effectually we secure our own peace. Those that follow the dictates of this law will escape *the snares of death* which those run into that forsake *the law of the wise*.

Verse 15

Those that conduct themselves prudently, and *serve Christ*, are *accepted of God and approved of men*, Rom. xiv. 17, 19. The way of sinners is rough and uneasy. It is *hard*, hard upon others, who complain of it, hard to the sinner himself, who can have little enjoyment of himself while he is doing that which is disobliging to all mankind.

Verse 16

It is wisdom to be cautious: *Every prudent* discreet *man* acts with deliberation and is careful not to meddle with that which he has not some knowledge of. It is folly to be rash, as the *fool* is, who is forward to undertake that which he is no way fit for, and so makes himself ridiculous.

Verse 17

The ill consequences of betraying a trust. *A wicked messenger*, who, being sent to negotiate any business,

is false to him that employed him, will be discovered and punished. The happy effects of fidelity: An *ambassador* who *faithfully* discharges his trust, and serves the interests of those who employ him, is health to those by whom and for whom he is employed, heals differences between them; he is health to himself, for he secures his own interest. This is applicable to ministers, Christ's messengers.

Verse 18

He that is so proud that he scorns to be taught will certainly be abased. He that is so humble that he takes it well to be told of his faults shall certainly be exalted: *He that regards a reproof*, gains respect.

Verse 19

There are in man strong desires of happiness; God has provided for the accomplishment of those desires. *The desire* of good men towards the favour of God and spiritual blessings brings that which *is sweet to their souls*, Ps. iv. 6, 7. Yet evil men will not be happy; for *it is* an *abomination to* them *to depart from evil*, which is necessary to their being happy.

Verse 20

Those that would be good must keep good company, which is an evidence for them that they would be good (men's character is known by the company they choose). Multitudes are brought to ruin by bad company.

Verse 21

Whom God pursues he is sure to overtake. They may prosper for a while and grow very secure, but their damnation slumbers not, though they do. *The righteous* shall be abundantly recompensed for all the good they have done, and all the ill they have suffered, in this world.

Verse 22

A good man's estate lasts. It is part of his praise that he is thoughtful for posterity. He is careful, both by justice and charity, to obtain the blessing of God upon what he has, and to entail that blessing upon his children. If he should not leave them much of this world's goods, his prayers, his instructions, his good example, will be the best entail, and the promises of the covenant will be an inheritance to his *children's children*, Ps. ciii. 17. God, in his providence, often brings into their hands that which wicked people had laid up for themselves.

Verse 23

A small estate may be improved by industry, so that a man, by making the best of everything, may live comfortably upon it. The less compass the field is of the more let the skill and labour of the owner be employed about it, and it will turn to a very good account. Let him dig, and he need not beg. A great estate may be ruined by indiscretion. Men overbuild themselves or over-buy themselves, keep a better table, or more servants, than they can afford.

Verse 24

To the education of children in that which is good there is necessary a due correction for what is amiss. It is *his* rod that must be used, the rod of a parent, directed by wisdom and love, and designed for good, not the rod of a servant. It is good to begin the necessary restraints before vicious habits are confirmed. Those really hate their children, though they pretend to be fond of them, that do not keep them under a strict discipline.

Verse 25

It is the happiness of the righteous that they shall have enough and that they know when they have enough. Those that feed on the bread of life, eat, and are filled. It is the misery of the wicked that, through the insatiableness of their own desires, they are always needy; even their *belly shall want*; their sensual appetite is always craving.

Chapter 14

Verse 1

A good wife is a great blessing to a family. By a prudent wife, one that is pious, industrious, and considerate, the affairs of the family are made to prosper, debts are paid, the children well educated and the family has comfort within doors and credit without; thus is the house built. Many a family is brought to ruin by ill housewifery, as well as by ill husbandry. A *foolish* woman, that has no fear of God, that is wilful, and wasteful, and is all for jaunting and feasting, cards and the playhouse, will as certainly be the ruin of her house as if she *plucked it down with her hands.*

Verse 2

Grace reigning is a reverence of God, and gives honour to him. Sin reigning is no less than a contempt of God.

Verse 3

Where there is pride in the heart, and no wisdom in the head to suppress it, it commonly shows itself in the words: *In the mouth there is pride*, proud boasting, proud scorning; this is the *rod*, or branch, *of pride*; the word is used only here and Isa. xi. 1. It grows from that root of bitterness which is in the heart. The root must be plucked up, or we cannot conquer this branch. Or it is meant of a smiting beating rod, a *rod of pride* which strikes others. *The lips of the wise shall preserve them* from doing that mischief to others which proud men do with their tongues, and from bringing that mischief on themselves which haughty scorners are often involved in.

Verse 4

The neglect of husbandry is the way to poverty: *Where no oxen are*, to till the ground and tread out the corn, *the crib* is empty, *is clean*; there is no straw for the cattle, and consequently no bread for the service of man. *The crib* indeed *is clean* from dung, which pleases the neat and nice, that cannot endure husbandry because there is so much dirty work in it, and therefore will sell their oxen to keep the crib clean. This shows the folly of those who addict themselves to the pleasures of the country, but do not mind the business of it, who (as we say) keep more horses than kine, more dogs than swine; their families must needs suffer by it. Those who take pains about their ground are likely to reap the profit of it.

Verse 5

In the administration of justice much depends upon the witnesses, and therefore it is necessary to the common good that witnesses be principled. A witness that is conscientious will not dare to give in a testimony that is in the least untrue. But a witness that will be bribed, and biassed, and browbeaten, *will utter lies* with as much assurance as if what he said were all true.

Verse 6

The reason why some people seek wisdom, and do not find it, is because they do not seek it from a right principle. They are scorners, and it is in scorn that they ask instruction, that they may ridicule what is told them. He *that understands*, so as to *depart from evil* (for *that is understanding*), to quit his prejudices, to lay aside all corrupt dispositions

and affections, will easily apprehend instruction and receive the impressions of it.

Verse 7

A wicked man is *a foolish man*. We must decline such a one and depart from him. Sometimes the only way we have of reproving wicked discourse is by leaving the company and going out of the hearing of it.

Verse 8

It is not the wisdom of the learned, which consists only in speculation, that is here recommended, but *the wisdom of the prudent*, which is practical, and is of use to direct our actions. It *is to understand our own way*, not to be critics and busybodies in other men's matters, but to look well to ourselves and to understand the directions of our way. The bad conduct of a bad man; he puts a cheat upon himself. He does not rightly understand his way; he thinks he does, and so misses his way.

Verse 9

Wicked people are hardened in their wickedness: they *make a mock at sin*. They make a laughing matter of the sins of others, and they make a light matter of their own sins. Those that make light of sin make light of Christ. Good people, if they in anything offend, presently repent and obtain the favour of God. They have goodwill one to another; and, in their societies, there is mutual charity and compassion in cases of offences, and no mocking.

Verse 10

Every man feels his own burden, especially a burden upon the spirits. We must not censure the griefs of others, for we know not what they feel; their stroke perhaps is heavier than their groaning. Many enjoy divine consolations, which others are not aware of, much less are sharers in.

Verse 11

Sin is the ruin of great families. Righteousness is the rise and stability even of mean families: Even *the tabernacle of the upright*, though movable and despicable as a tent, *shall flourish*, if Infinite Wisdom see good.

Verse 12

The way of ignorance and carelessness, the way of sensuality and flesh-pleasing, seem right to those that walk in them, much more the way of hypocrisy in religion, external performances, partial reformations, and blind zeal; this they imagine will bring them to heaven. They will perish with a lie in their right hand. Self-deceivers will prove in the end self-destroyers.

Verse 13

Sometimes when sinners are under convictions, or some great trouble, they dissemble their grief by a forced mirth, because they will not seem to yield. When men really are merry, yet at the same time there is something that casts a damp upon it, their consciences tell them they have no reason to be merry (Hos. ix. 1); they cannot but see the vanity of it. Spiritual joy is seated in the soul; the joy of the hypocrite is but from the teeth outward. *The end of that mirth is heaviness.*

Verse 14

The *backslider in heart*, who for fear of suffering, or in hope of profit or pleasure, forsakes God and his duty, shall be *filled with his own ways*; God will give him enough of them. *He that is filthy shall be filthy still. A good man shall be* abundantly *satisfied from himself*, from what God has wrought in him. As sinners never think they have sin enough till it brings them to hell, so saints never think they have grace enough till it brings them to heaven.

Verse 15
It is folly to be credulous, to heed every flying report, to take things upon trust from common fame, and give credit to everyone that will promise payment. *The prudent man* will try before he trusts.

Verse 16
Holy fear is an excellent guard upon every holy thing, and against everything that is unholy. It is wisdom to depart *from evil*, to be afraid of coming near the borders of sin or dallying with the beginnings of it. Presumption is folly. He who, when he is warned of his danger, *rages and is confident*, furiously pushes on, persists in his rebellion, and plays upon the precipice, is a fool.

Verse 17
Men who are peevish and touchy, and are *soon angry*, say and do that which is ridiculous, and so expose themselves to contempt. *A man of wicked devices*, who stifles his resentments till he has an opportunity of being revenged, is hated by all mankind. An angry man through the surprise of a temptation disgraces himself, but it is soon over, and he is sorry for it. But that of a spiteful revengeful man is odious; there is no fence against him nor cure for him.

Verse 18
Sin is the shame of sinners: *The simple*, who love simplicity, get nothing by it; they *inherit folly*. What they value themselves upon is really foolish. They will for ever rue their own foolish choice. Wisdom is the honour of the wise: *The prudent crown* themselves *with knowledge*. Wise heads shall be respected as if they were crowned heads. Wisdom is not only justified, but glorified, of all her children.

Verse 19
The wicked are oftentimes impoverished and brought low, so that they are forced to beg, their wickedness having reduced them to straits; while good men, by the blessing of God, are enriched, and enabled to give, and do give, even to the evil; for where God grants life we must not deny a livelihood.

Verse 20
The poor, who should be pitied, and relieved, *is hated*, and kept at a distance, even *by his own neighbour*. Most are swallow-friends, that are gone in winter. It is good having God our friend, for he will not desert us when we are poor. *The rich have many friends* in hope to get something out of them.

Verse 21
Men's character and condition are measured by their conduct towards their poor neighbours. *He that despises his neighbour* because he is of a mean extraction, rustic education, and makes but a mean figure, that thinks it below him to take notice of him, *is a sinner*, and shall be dealt with as a sinner. *He that has mercy on the poor*, is ready to do all the good offices he can to him, and does that which is pleasing to God.

Verse 22
Those are that not only do evil, but devise it, think that by sinning with craft and carrying on their intrigues with more artifice than others, shall come off better. But they are mistaken. God's justice cannot be outwitted. Those that devise evil against their neighbours greatly err, for it will end in their own ruin. Those that are so liberal as to devise liberal things, that seek opportunities of doing good, and contrive how to make their charity most extensive and most acceptable to those that need it, *by liberal things they shall stand*, Isa. xxxii. 8.

Verse 23
Industrious people are generally thriving people. *The stirring hand gets a penny*. Those that love to boast of their business and make a noise about it, and that waste their time in tittle-tattle, waste what they have, and the course they take *tends to penury*. It is true in the affairs of our souls; those that take pains in the service of God, that strive earnestly in prayer, will find profit in it. But if men's religion runs all out in talk and noise, they will be spiritually poor, and come to nothing.

Verse 24
If men be wise and good, riches make them so much the more honourable and useful, and give them more influence. Those that have wealth, and wisdom to use it, will have a great opportunity of honouring God and doing good in the world. If men be wicked and corrupt, their wealth will but the more expose them.

Verse 25
A faithful witness *delivers the souls* of the innocent, who are falsely accused, and their good names, which are as dear to them as their lives. A false witness forges *lies*, and yet pours them out with the greatest assurance imaginable. It is the interest of a nation to detect and punish false-witness-bearing, for truth is the cement of society.

Verses 26–27
The *fear of the Lord* is here put for all gracious principles, producing gracious practices. Where this resigns it produces security and serenity of mind. It enables a man still to hold fast his peace, and gives him boldness before God and the world. It entails a blessing upon posterity. The children of religious parents often do the better for their parents' instructions and example and fare the better for their faith and prayers. "*Our fathers trusted in thee, therefore we will.*" It is an over-flowing ever-flowing spring of comfort and joy. It is a sovereign antidote against sin and temptation.

Verse 28
Here are two maxims in politics: 1. That it is much for the honour of a king to have a populous kingdom; it is a sign that he rules well, since strangers are hereby invited to come and settle under his protection and his own subjects live comfortably. It is therefore the wisdom of princes, by a mild and gentle government, by encouraging trade and husbandry, to promote the increase of their people. 2. That when the people are lessened the prince is weakened: *In the want of people is the leanness of the prince* (so some read it); trade lies dead, the ground lies untilled, the army wants to be recruited, the navy to be manned, and all because there are not hands sufficient.

Verse 29
Meekness is wisdom. *He* rightly understands himself, and the infirmities of human nature, who *is slow to anger*, and knows how to excuse the faults of others as well as his own, so as by no provocation to be put out of the possession of his own soul. Unbridled passion is folly proclaimed: *He that is hasty of spirit*, whose heart is tinder to every spark of provocation, that is all fire and tow, thinks to magnify himself, whereas really he *exalts his own folly*.

Verse 30

Our health depends on the government of our passions and the preserving of the temper of the mind. A healing spirit, made up of love and meekness, a hearty, friendly, cheerful disposition, is *the life of the flesh*; it contributes to a good constitution of body; people grow fat with good humour. A fretful, envious, discontented spirit, makes the countenance pale, and is the *rottenness of the bones*.

Verse 31

Whosoever he be that wrongs a poor man, let him know that he puts an affront upon his Maker. God made him, and gave him his being. We have all one Father, one Maker. He reckons himself honoured in the kindnesses that are done them; he takes them as done to himself, and will show himself accordingly pleased with them. *I was hungry, and you gave me meat*.

Verse 32

A wicked man cleaves so closely to the world that he cannot find in his heart to leave it, but is driven away out of it; his soul is required, is forced from him. He *is driven away in his wickedness*, dies in his sins. A godly man when he finishes his course, *has hope in his death* of a happiness on the other side death, of better things in another world than ever he had in this.

Verse 33

Modesty is the badge of wisdom. His *wisdom rests in his heart*; he digests what he knows, and has it ready to him, but does not make a noise with it. If fools have a little smattering of knowledge, they take all occasions to produce it.

Verse 34

Justice, reigning in a nation, puts an honour upon it. A righteous administration of the government, equity between man and man, public countenance given to religion, charity and compassion to strangers, uphold the throne, elevate the people's minds, and qualify a nation for the favour of God. Vice in a nation puts disgrace upon it: *Sin is a reproach to any* city or kingdom. The people of Israel were great when they were good, but when they forsook God all about them insulted them and trampled on them.

Verse 35

In a well-ordered court and government smiles and favours are dispensed among those in public trusts according to their merits. Those who behave themselves wisely shall be respected and preferred. No man's services shall be neglected to please a party or a favourite. Those who are selfish and false, who betray their country, oppress the poor, and sow discord, shall be displaced.

CHAPTER 15

Verse 1

Peace may be kept by soft words. If wrath be risen like a threatening cloud, pregnant with storms and thunder, *a soft answer* will disperse it and turn it away. Reason will be better spoken, and a righteous cause better pleaded, with meekness than with passion; hard arguments do best with soft words. Nothing stirs up anger, and sows discord, like *grievous words*, calling foul names, upbraiding men with their infirmities, or anything that lessens them and makes them mean.

Verse 2

He that has knowledge is not only to enjoy it, for his own entertainment, but use it aright, for the edification of others; and it is *the tongue* that must make use of it. A wicked heart by the tongue becomes very hurtful; for *the mouth of fools belches out foolishness*, whilst filthiness, and foolish talking, corrupt good manners.

Verse 3

The eyes of the Lord are in every place; for he not only sees all from on high (Ps. xxxiii. 13), but he is everywhere present. Secret sins, services, and sorrows, are under his eye. He is displeased with the evil and approves of the good. This speaks as much comfort to saints as terror to sinners.

Verse 4

A good tongue is healing to sin-sick souls by convincing them, and reconciling parties at variance; this is the healing of the tongue, which *is a tree of life*, the leaves of which have a sanative virtue, Rev. xxii. 2. He that knows how to discourse will make the place he lives in a paradise. An evil tongue is wounding.

Verse 5

Let superiors give instruction and reproof to those that are under their charge. They must not only instruct with the light of knowledge, but reprove with zeal; and both these must be done with the authority and affection of a father. It is indeed against the grain with good-humoured men to find fault, and make those about them uneasy; but better so than to suffer them to go on the way to ruin. He that slights his good education is a fool and is likely to live and die one.

Verse 6

Where righteousness is riches are, and the comforts of them. If there be not much of this world's goods, yet where there is grace there is true treasure; and those who have but little, if they have a heart to be therewith content, and to enjoy the comfort of that little, it is enough; it is all riches. Where wickedness is, though there may be riches, yet there is vexation of spirit.

Verse 7

We use knowledge aright when we disperse it, not confine it to a few of our intimates. We must take pains to spread and propagate useful knowledge, must teach some that they may teach others.

Verse 8

God has sacrifices brought him even by wicked men, but their sacrifices, though ever so costly, are not accepted of God, because not offered in sincerity nor from a good principle. God has such a love for upright good people that their *prayer is a delight* to him.

Verse 9

The sacrifices of the wicked are an abomination to God, not for want of some nice points of ceremony, but because the whole course and tenor of their conversation, is wicked.

Verse 10

This shows that those who cannot bear to be corrected must expect to be destroyed. Of all sinners, reproofs are worst resented by apostates.

Verse 11

This confirms what was said (*v.* 3) concerning God's omnipresence, in order to his judging of evil and good. God knows all things, even those things that are hidden from the eyes of all living. The word here used for *destruction* is *Abaddon*, which is one of the devil's names, Rev. ix. 11. That destroyer, though he deceives us, cannot evade or elude the divine cognizance. God sees through all his disguises, Job xxvi. 6. If he sees through the depths and wiles of Satan himself, *much more* can he search men's hearts. *God is greater than our hearts*, and knows them better than we know them ourselves, and therefore is an infallible Judge of every man's character, Heb. iv. 13.

Verse 12

A scorner is one that not only makes a jest of God and religion, but bids defiance to the methods employed for his conviction and reformation. He cannot endure to retire into his own heart and commune seriously, nor let his own heart smite him, if he can help it. That man's case is sad who is afraid of arguing with himself. He cannot endure the advice and admonitions of his friends.

Verse 13

Harmless mirth is recommended to us, as that which contributes to the health of the body, making men lively and fit for business, making the face to shine and rendering us pleasant one to another. A cheerful spirit under the government of wisdom and grace, is a great ornament to religion, puts a further lustre upon the beauty of holiness, and makes men the more capable of doing good. Hurtful melancholy is what we are cautioned against, as a great enemy to us, when it has dominion and plays the tyrant. *The spirit is broken*, and becomes unfit for the service of God.

Verse 14

Here are two things to be wondered at:—A wise man not satisfied with his wisdom, but still seeking the increase of it; the more he has the more he would have. A fool well satisfied with his folly and not seeking the cure of it.

Verse 15

Some are much in affliction, and of a sorrowful spirit, and all their days are evil days. Such are not to be censured or despised, but pitied and prayed for, succoured and comforted. Others are of a cheerful spirit; and they have not only good days, but have *a continual feast*; and if they serve God with gladness of heart, and it is oil to the wheels of their obedience (all this, and heaven too), then they serve a good Master.

Verses 16–17

Christian contentment, and joy in God, make life easy and pleasant. Cheerfulness of spirit will furnish a man with *a continual feast*, though he has but little in the world—holiness and love. A *little*, if we keep a good conscience, and serve God faithfully with the little we have, will be more comfortable, *than great treasure and trouble therewith*. Those that have *great treasure* have often great *trouble therewith*. If those that have great estates would do their duty with them, and then trust God with them, their treasure would not have so much trouble attending it. It is therefore far better to have but a little of the world, to keep up communion with God, and enjoy him in it, and live by faith, than to have the greatest plenty and live without God in the world. If *brethren dwell together in unity*, if they are friendly, and hearty, and pleasant, that will make *a dinner of herbs* a feast sufficient. Love will sweeten it and they may be as merry over it as if they had all dainties. If there be mutual enmity and strife, though there be a whole ox for dinner, a fat ox, there can be no comfort in it; the leaven of malice, of hating and being hated, is enough to sour it all.

Verse 18

Anger strikes the fire which sets cities and churches into a flame: *A wrathful man*, with his peevish passionate reflections, gives occasion to others to quarrel. *He that is slow to anger* not only *prevents* strife, but if it be already kindled, brings water to the flame, unites those again that have fallen out, and by gentle methods brings them to mutual concessions for peace-sake.

Verse 19

Those that have no heart to their work pretend that they cannot do their work without a great deal of hardship and danger; and therefore they go about it with as much reluctance as if they were to go barefoot through a thorny hedge. An honest desire and endeavour to do our duty will, by the grace of God, make it easy, and we shall find it strewed with roses.

Verse 20

Good children are the joy of their parents, who ought to have joy of them, having taken so much care and pains about them. And it adds much to the satisfaction of those that are good if they have reason to think that they have been a comfort to their parents in their declining years. Wicked children put contempt upon their parents, slight their authority, and make an ill requital for their kindness.

Verse 21

A wicked man sins, not only without regret, but with delight. A fool walks by no rule, acts with no sincerity or steadiness; *but a man of understanding*, the eyes of whose understanding are enlightened by the Spirit, *walks uprightly*, lives a regular life, and studies in everything to conform himself to the will of God.

Verse 22

If men will not take time and pains to deliberate with themselves, or are so confident of their own judgment that they scorn to consult with others, they are not likely to bring anything considerable to pass; circumstances defeat them which, with a little consultation, might have been foreseen and obviated.

Verse 23

We speak wisely when we speak seasonably: when it is needed, and, as we say, hits the joint. Many a good word comes short of doing the good it might have done, for want of being well-timed.

Verse 24

The way of wisdom and holiness is *the way of life*, the way that leads to eternal life. Be wise and live. It is the way to escape *from hell beneath*. A good man sets his *affections on things above*, and deals in those things. His *conversation is in heaven*; his way leads directly thither; there his treasure is, *above*, out of the reach of enemies, above the changes of this lower world.

Verse 25

The proud, that magnify themselves, and trample on all about them, are such as God *will destroy*, not them only, but *their houses*. Those that are dejected God delights to support. *He will establish the border* which the poor widow is not herself able to defend and make good.

Verse 26

The thoughts of wicked men, for the most part, are such as God hates, and are an offence to him, who not only knows the heart and all that passes and repasses there, but requires the innermost and uppermost place in it. The thoughts and *words of the pure* may be understood both of their devotions to God and of their discourses with men. Both are pleasant when they come from a pure, a purified, heart.

Verse 27

He that is greedy of gain, and makes himself a slave to the world, hurries, and puts himself and all about him upon the stretch, frets and vexes at every loss and disappointment, and quarrels with everybody that stands in the way of his profit—is a burden and vexation to his children and servants. Those that are generous entail a blessing upon their families; *He that* abhors all sinful indirect ways of getting money—that hates to be paltry and mercenary, and is willing, if there be occasion, to do good gratis—he shall have the comfort of life; his name and family shall live and continue.

Verse 28

It is the character of a righteous man that being convinced of the account he must give of his words, and of the good and bad influence of them upon others, he makes conscience of speaking truly (it is his *heart* that *answers*, he speaks as he thinks, Ps. xv. 2), and of speaking pertinently and profitably, and therefore he *studies to answer*, that his speech may be with grace, Neh. ii. 4; v. 7. A wicked man never heeds what he says, but his *mouth pours out evil things*, to the dishonour of God and religion.

Verse 29

God sets himself at a distance from those that set him at defiance. He will draw nigh to those in a way of mercy who draw nigh to him in a way of duty.

Verse 30

It is pleasant to have a good prospect, to see the light of the sun (Eccles. xi. 7) and by it to see the wonderful works of God, with which this lower world is beautiful and enriched. The consideration of this should make us thankful for our eyesight. It is also very comfortable to hear (as some understand it) *a good report* concerning others; a good man has no greater joy than to hear that his friends walk in the truth.

Verse 31

The ear that can take *the reproof* will love the reprover. Faithful friendly reproofs are here called *the reproofs of life* because they are means of spiritual life. Those that learn well, and obey well, are likely in time to teach well and rule well.

Verse 32

Those who *refuse correction* (margin) *despise their own souls*. The fundamental error of sinners is undervaluing their own souls; therefore they wrong the soul to please the body. *He that hears reproof*, and amends the faults, *gets understanding*, by which his soul is secured from bad ways and directed in good ways.

Verse 33

An awe of God upon our spirits will put us upon the wisest counsels and chastise us when we say or do unwisely. Where there is humility there is a happy presage of honour and preparative for it.

Chapter 16

Verse 1

In short, 1. *Man purposes*. He has a freedom of thought and a freedom of will permitted him; let him form his projects, and lay his schemes, as he thinks best: but, after all, 2. *God disposes*. Man cannot go on with his business without the assistance and blessing of God, who *made man's mouth* and teaches us what we shall say.

Verse 2

We are all apt to be partial in judging of ourselves. The judgment of God concerning us is according to truth: He *weighs the spirits* in a just and unerring balance, knows what is in us, and passes a judgment upon us accordingly, and by his judgment we must stand or fall.

Verse 3

The only way to have our *thoughts established* is to *commit our works to the Lord*. The great concerns of our souls must be committed to the grace of God. All our outward concerns must be committed to the providence of God, and to the sovereign, wise, and gracious disposal of that providence. *Roll thy works upon the Lord* (so the word is); roll the burden of thy care from thyself upon God.

Verse 4

God is the first cause. Even the wicked are his creatures, though they are rebels; he gave them those powers with which they fight against him. God is the last end. All is of him and from him, and therefore all is to him and for him.

Verse 5

The pride of sinners sets God against them. The power of sinners cannot secure them against God, though they strengthen themselves with both hands. Though they strengthen one another with their confederacies and combinations, joining forces against God, they shall not escape his righteous judgment.

Verse 6

The guilt of sin is taken away from us—by the *mercy and truth* of God, in Jesus Christ the Mediator, and not by the legal sacrifices, Mic. vi. 7, 8. The power of sin is broken in us. The corrupt inclinations are purged out. *By the fear of the Lord*, and the influence of that fear, *men depart from evil*; those will not dare to sin against God who keep up in their minds a holy dread and reverence of him.

Verse 7

God can turn foes into friends when he pleases. He that has all hearts in his hand can make *a man's enemies to be at peace with him*. He will do it for us when we please him. God made Esau to be at peace with Jacob, Abimelech with Isaac.

Verse 8

A small estate, honestly come by, which a man is content with, serves God with cheerfully, and puts to a right use, is much more valuable than a great estate ill-got, and then ill-kept or ill-spent. It carries with it more inward satisfaction, a better reputation with all that are wise and good; it will last longer, and will turn to a better account in the great day, when men will be judged, not according to what they had, but what they did.

Verse 9

Man is a reasonable creature, that has the faculty of contriving for himself. But as a depending creature, he is subject to the direction and dominion of his Maker. If men *devise their way*, so as to make God's glory their end and his will their rule, they may expect that he will *direct their steps* by his Spirit and grace, so that they shall not miss their way nor come short of their end. *Lord, direct my way*, 1 Thess. iii. 11.

Verse 10

It may be read as a precept to the kings and judges of the earth to be wise and instructed. Let them be just, and rule in the fear of God. It may be taken as a promise to all good kings, that if they sincerely aim at God's glory, and seek direction from him, he will qualify them with wisdom and grace above others, in proportion to the eminency of their station and the trusts lodged in their hands.

Verse 11

The administration of public justice by the magistrates is an ordinance of God; in it the scales are held, and ought to be held by a steady and impartial hand. The observance of justice in commerce between man and man is likewise a divine appointment.

Verse 12

A good king not only does justice, but it is *an abomination* to him to do otherwise. He hates the thought of doing wrong and perverting justice. He that makes conscience of using his power aright shall find that to be the best security of his government, and it will obtain the blessing of God, a basis to the throne and a strong guard about it.

Verse 13

Good kings hate parasites and those that flatter them. They not only do righteousness themselves, but take care to employ those under them that do righteousness too. A good king will therefore put those in power who are conscientious, and will say that which is righteous and discreet.

Verse 14–15

These two verses show the power of kings, which is everywhere great, but was especially so in those eastern countries, where they were absolute and arbitrary. We have reason to bless God for the happy constitution of the government we live under, which maintains the prerogative of the prince without any injury to the liberty of the subject. But here it is intimated. 1. How formidable *the wrath of a king is*: It is *as messengers of death*; the wrath of Ahasuerus was so to Haman. An angry word from an incensed prince has been to many a *messenger of death*. He must be a very *wise man* that knows how to *pacify* the wrath of a king with a world fitly spoken, as Jonathan once pacified his father's rage against David, 1 Sam. xix. 6. 2. How valuable and desirable the king's favour is to those that have incurred his displeasure; it is life from the dead if the king be reconciled to them. To others it is *as a cloud of the latter rain*, very refreshing to the ground. Those are fools who to escape the wrath, and obtain the favour, of an earthly prince, will throw themselves out of God's favour.

Verse 16

Heavenly wisdom is better than worldly wealth, and to be preferred before it. Grace is more valuable than gold. Grace is the gift of God's peculiar favour; gold only of common providence. Grace is for the soul and eternity; gold only for the body and time, Grace will stand us in stead in a dying hour, when gold will do us no good. There is vanity and vexation of spirit in getting wealth, but joy and satisfaction of Spirit in getting wisdom. *Great peace have those that love it.*

Verse 17

It is *the way of the upright* to avoid sin, and this is a highway marked out by authority, tracked by many that have gone before us. It is the care of the upright to preserve their souls. Those that adhere to their duty secure their felicity. Keep thy way and God will keep thee.

Verse 18

Pride will have a fall. It is the act of justice that those who have lifted up themselves should be laid low. Pharaoh, Sennacherib, Nebuchadnezzar, were instances of this. When proud men set God's judgments at defiance, it is a sign that they are at the door, witness the case of Benhadad and Herod. Therefore let us not fear the pride of others, but greatly fear pride in ourselves.

Verse 19

Those that are proud and will put forth themselves that thrust, and shove, and scramble, for preferment, are the men that commonly *divide the spoil* and share it among them. Humility, while it recommends us to the favour of God, qualifies us for his gracious visits, secures us from many temptations, and preserves the quiet and repose of our own souls, is much better than that high-spiritedness which, though it carry the honour and wealth of the world, makes God a man's enemy and the devil his master.

Verse 20

Prudence gains men respect and success: but it is piety only that will secure men's true happiness. Some read the former part of the verse as of piety, which is indeed true wisdom: *He that attends to the word* (the word of God, ch. xiii. 13) shall *find good* in it and good by it. And whoso *trusts in the Lord* is happy.

Verse 21

Those that have solid wisdom will have the credit of it; and a deference will be paid to their judgment. Those that with their wisdom deliver their sentiments easily and with a good grace, *increase learning*; they diffuse and propagate knowledge to others, and do good with it, and by that means increase their own stock. *To him that has, and uses what he has, more shall be given.*

Verse 22

There is always some good to be gotten by a wise and good man. His understanding is a *spring of life* to himself; within his own thoughts he entertains and edifies himself, if not others. There is nothing that is good to be gotten by a fool.

Verse 23

Solomon had commended eloquence, or *the sweetness of the lips* (v. 21), and seemed to prefer it before wisdom; but here he corrects himself, as it were, and shows that unless there be a good treasure within to support the eloquence it is worth little. Wisdom in *the heart* is the main matter. Quaint expressions please the ear, and humour the fancy, but it is learning that must convince the judgment and sway that, to which wisdom in the heart is necessary.

Verse 24

The *pleasant words* here commended must be those which *the heart of the wise teaches, and adds learning to* (v. 23), words of seasonable advice, instruction, and comfort, words taken from God's word, for that is it which Solomon had learned from his father to account *sweeter than honey and the honey-comb*, Ps. xix. 10. Many things are pleasant that are not profitable, but these *pleasant words are health to the bones*, to the inward man, as well as *sweet to the soul*.

Verse 25

This we had before (ch. xiv. 12), but here it is repeated, 1. By way of caution to us all to be impartial in self-examination. 2. By way of terror to those whose way is not right, however it may seem to themselves or others.

Verse 26

This is designed to engage us to diligence, and quicken us, both in our worldly business and in the work of religion; for in the original it is, *The soul that labours for itself*. It is heart-work which is here intended, the labour of the soul. If we make religion our business, God will make it our blessedness.

Verses 27–28

There are those that are not only vicious themselves, but spiteful and mischievous to others, and they are the worst of men. They *dig up evil*; they take a great deal of pains to find out something or other on which to ground a slander. If none appear above ground they will dig for it, by diving into what is secret, or looking a great way back, or by evil suspicions and surmises, and forced innuendos. In the lips of a slanderer and backbiter *there is as a fire*, to brand his neighbour's reputation. *A froward man*, that cannot find in his heart to love anybody but himself, is vexed to see others live in love, and therefore makes it his business to *sow strife*, by telling lies, and carrying ill-natured stories between *chief friends*, so as to *separate* them one from another. Those are bad men, and bad women, too, that do such ill offices; they are doing the devil's work.

Verse 29

Evil men described to us, that we may neither do like them nor have anything to do with them. They are *violent men*, that do all by rapine and oppression, that *shut their eyes*, meditating with the closest application *to devise froward things*, to contrive how they may do the greatest mischief to their neighbour. Then *moving their lips*, giving the word of command to their agents, they *bring the evil to pass*. Such do all they can to *entice* others to join in doing mischief, *leading them in a way that is not good*, but offensive to God.

Verse 31

Let old people be old disciples. If old people *be found in the way of righteousness*, their age will be their honour. Old age, as such, is honourable, and commands respect but, if it be found in the way of wickedness, its honour is forfeited, its crown laid in the dust, Isa. lxv. 20. Grace is the glory of old age.

Verse 32

The grace of meekness is to be *slow to anger*, not easily put into a passion, nor apt to resent provocation, so slow in our motions towards anger that we may be quickly stopped and pacified. It is to have the rule of our own spirits, particularly our passions. He that gets and keeps the mastery of his passions *is better than the mighty*. Behold, a greater than Alexander or Cæsar is here. The conquest of our own unruly passions, requires more true wisdom, and a more steady management, than the obtaining of a victory over an enemy. No lives or treasures are sacrificed to it. It is harder to quash an insurrection at home than to resist an invasion from abroad; such are the gains of meekness that by it *we are more than conquerors*.

Verse 33

Nothing comes to pass by chance, nor is an event determined by a blind fortune, but everything by the will and counsel of God. All the disposals of Providence concerning our affairs we must look upon to be the directing of our lot, the determining of what we referred to God, and we must be reconciled to them accordingly.

Chapter 17

Verse 1

These words recommend family-love and peace, as conducing very much to the comfort of human life. Those that live in unity and quietness, and that study to make themselves obliging to one another, live very comfortably, though they work hard and fare hard, though they have but each of them *a morsel*, and that *a dry morsel*. There may be peace and quietness where there are not three meals a day, provided there be a joint satisfaction in God's providence and a mutual satisfaction in each other's prudence. Holy love may be found in a cottage. Those that live in contention, that are always jarring and brawling, though they have plenty of dainties, live uncomfortably; they cannot expect the blessing of God upon them. Love will sweeten a *dry morsel*, but strife will sour and embitter *a house full of sacrifices*.

Verse 2

True merit does not go by dignity. Sometimes it so happens that the servant is wise, and a blessing and credit to the family, when the son is a fool, and a shame to the family. True dignity will go by merit. A prudent servant may perhaps come to have such an interest in his master as to be taken in for a child's share of the estate and to *have part of the inheritance among the brethren*.

Verse 3

As *the fining-pot is for silver*, both to prove it and to improve it, so *the Lord tries the hearts*; he searches whether they are standard or no, and those that are he refines and makes purer, Jer. xvii. 10. God tries the heart by affliction (Ps. lxvi. 10, 11), and often chooses his people in that furnace (Isa. xlviii. 10) and makes them choice. It is God only that *tries the hearts*. Men have no such way of trying one another's hearts.

Verse 4

Those that design to do ill support themselves by falsehood and lying: *A wicked doer gives ear*, with a great deal of pleasure, *to false lips*, that will justify him in the ill he does. Sinners will strengthen one another's hands.

Verse 5

Those who trample upon the poor, who ridicule their wants, *reproach their Maker*, who owns them, and takes care of them, and can, when he pleases, reduce us to that condition. *He that is glad at calamities*, that he may be built up upon the ruins of others, and regales himself with the judgments of God when they are abroad, let him know that he *shall not go unpunished*.

Verse 6

It is an honour to a man to live so long as to see his children's children (Ps. cxxviii. 6; Gen. l. 23), to see his house built up in them, and to see them likely to serve their generation according to the will of God. This crowns and completes their comfort in this world. It is an honour to children to have wise and godly parents, and to have them continued to them even after they have themselves grown up and settled in the world.

Verse 7

A fool, in Solomon's proverbs, signifies a wicked man, whom *excellent speech* does not become, because his conversation gives the lie to his excellent speech. If it is unbecoming a despicable man to presume to speak as a philosopher or politician, much more unbecoming is it for a prince, for a man of honour, to take advantage from the confidence that is put in him to lie, and dissemble, and make no conscience of breaking his word.

Verse 8

Rich men value a little money as if it were a *precious stone*, and value themselves on it as if it gave them not only ornament, but power, and every-one were bound to be at their beck, even justice itself. Whithersoever they turn this sparkling diamond they expect it should dazzle the eyes of all, and make them do just what they would have them do in hopes of it.

Verse 9

The way to preserve peace among relations and neighbours is to make the best of everything, not to tell others what has been said or done against them when it is not necessary to their safety, nor to take notice of what has been said or done against ourselves, but to excuse both, and put the best construction upon them. "It was an oversight; therefore overlook it. It was done through forgetfulness; therefore forget it."

Verse 10

A word is enough to the wise. Stripes are not enough for a fool, to make him sensible of his errors, that he may repent of them.

Verse 11

He is an evil man indeed that seeks all occasions to rebel against God, and the government God has set over him, and to contradict and quarrel with those about him. *A rebellious man seeks mischief* (so some read it), watches all opportunities to disturb the public peace. Because he will not be reclaimed by mild and gentle methods, *a cruel messenger shall be sent against him*, some dreadful judgment or other, as a messenger from God.

Verse 12

A passionate man is a brutish man in his passion ungoverned, and a *fool in his folly*. He is a dan-gerous man, falls foul of everyone that stands in his way, even the innocent. A bear robbed of her whelps sets upon the first man she meets as the robber. *Ira furor brevis est—Anger is temporary madness.* One may more easily guard against an enraged bear, than an outrageous angry man.

Verse 13

A malicious mischievous man is ungrateful to his friends. To render evil for evil is brutish, but to render evil for good is devilish. He is unkind to his family, for he entails a curse upon it.

Verse 14

The danger in *the beginning of strife*. One hot word begets another, and so on, till it proves like the cutting of a dam; when the water has got a little passage it does itself widen the breach, and there is then no stopping it. Take heed of the first spark of contention and put it out as soon as it appears.

Verse 15

When those that are entrusted with the adminis-tration of public justice, do either acquit the guilty or condemn those that are not guilty, this defeats the end of government, which is to protect the good and punish the bad.

Verse 16

God's great goodness to foolish men, in putting *a price into his hand to get wisdom*. We have rational souls, the means of grace, the strivings of the Spirit, access to God by prayer; we have time and oppor-tunity. Good parents, relations, ministers, friends, are helps to get wisdom. It is *a price*, therefore of value. We have reason to wonder that God should

entrust us with such advantages. Man's neglect of God's favour and his own interest, is absurd and un-accountable: *He has no part to it.*

Verse 17

Friends must be constant to each other *at all times.* That is not true friendship which is not constant. Swallow-friends fly to you in summer, but are gone in winter. But if I love my friend because he is wise, and good, though he fall into poverty and disgrace, still I shall love him. Christ is a friend that loves at all times (John xiii. 1) and we must so love him, Rom. viii. 35. Relations must in a special manner be tender of one another in affliction: *A brother is born* to succour a brother or sister in distress. Some take it thus: *A friend that loves at all times is born* (that is, becomes) a *brother in adversity*, and is so to be valued.

Verse 18

It is wisdom to keep out of debt as much as may be, especially to dread suretiship. Those that are *void of understanding* are commonly taken in this snare, to the prejudice of their families.

Verse 19

He that loves strife, that in his worldly business loves to go to law, in religion loves controversies, and in common conversation loves to fall out, *he loves transgression.* He pretends to stand up for truth, and for his right, but really he loves sin. Those that are ambitious expose themselves to trouble. *He that exalts his gate*, builds a stately house, at least a fine frontispiece, that he may outshine his neighbours, seeks his own destruction.

Verse 20

He that has a froward heart, that sows discord and is full of resentment, cannot take any rational satis-faction in it; he *finds no good. He that has a perverse tongue*, spiteful and abusive, scurrilous or backbiting, loses his friends, provokes his enemies, and pulls trouble upon his own head.

Verse 21

There was *joy when a man-child was born into the world*, and yet, if he prove vicious, his own father will wish he had never been born. The name of Ab-salom signifies his *father's peace*, but he was his greatest trouble. *The father of a fool* lays that so much to heart that he *has no joy* of anything else.

Verse 22

It is healthful to be cheerful. The Lord is for the body, and has provided for it, not only meat, but medicine, and has here told us that the best medicine is *a merry heart*, not a heart addicted to vain, carnal, sensual mirth. God gives us leave to be cheerful and cause to be cheerful, especially if by his grace he gives us hearts to be cheerful. This *does good to a medicine* (so some read it); it will make physic more efficient. Or *it does good as a medicine* to the body, making it easy and fit for business. The sorrows of the mind often contribute to the sickliness of the body: *A broken spirit*, sunk by the burden of afflictions, and especially a conscience wounded with the sense of guilt, *dries the bones.*

Verse 23

He is *a wicked man* that will *take a gift* to engage him to give a false testimony, verdict, or judgment; he is ashamed of it, for he takes it, with all the secrecy imaginable, *out of the bosom* where he knows it is laid ready for him; it is industriously concealed. The course of justice is not only obstructed but turned into injustice.

Verse 24

An intelligent man lays his *wisdom before him*, as his card and compass which he steers by, has his eye always upon it. He that has a roving rambling fancy, will never be fit for any solid business, and cannot fix his thoughts to one subject nor pursue any one purpose with steadiness.

Verse 25

Wicked children are an affliction to both their parents. They are an occasion of *anger* to the father (so the word signifies), because they contemn his authority, but of sorrow and *bitterness* to the mother, because they abuse her tenderness.

Verse 26

Let magistrates see to it that they never *punish the just*. When princes become tyrants and persecutors their thrones will be neither easy nor firm. Let subjects not find fault with the government for doing its duty, for it is a wicked thing *to strike princes for equity*, by defaming their administration.

Verse 27

A gracious spirit is a precious spirit, and renders a man amiable and *more excellent than his neighbour*. He is of a *cool spirit* (so some read it), not heated with passion. A cool head with a warm heart is an admirable composition. *He that has knowledge*, and aims to do good with it, is careful, when he does speak to speak to the purpose. He *spares his words*, because they are better spared than ill-spent.

CHAPTER 18

Verse 1

The original here is difficult. Some take it as a rebuke to an affected singularity. When men take a pride in *separating themselves* from the sentiments and society of others, in contradicting all that has been said and advancing new notions of their own, it is to gratify a desire of vain-glory, and they are seekers and meddlers and pretend to pass a judgment upon every man's matter. Our translation seems to take it as an excitement to diligence in the pursuit of wisdom. If we would get knowledge or grace, we must desire it, and must *separate ourselves* from all those things which would retard us in the pursuit, retire out of the noise of this world's vanities, and then *seek and intermeddle with all* the means and instructions of *wisdom*, and be acquainted with a variety of opinions, that we may prove all things and hold fast that which is good.

Verse 2

A fool may pretend to understanding but he has no true delight in it. He does not love his book, nor his business, nor his Bible, nor his prayers; he would rather be playing the fool with his sports. He has no good design in it, only *that his heart may discover itself*, that he may have something to make a show with, because he loves to hear himself talk.

Verse 3

This may include a double sense: 1. Wicked people are scornful people, and put *contempt* upon others. *When the wicked comes* into any company, into schools of wisdom or into assemblies for worship, *then comes contempt* of God, of his people and ministers, and of everything that is said and done. 2. Wicked people are shameful people, and bring *contempt* upon themselves, for God has said that those *who despise him shall be lightly esteemed*.

Verse 4

An intelligent man has in him a treasure of useful things, which furnishes him with something to say that is pertinent and profitable. This is as *deep waters*, which make no noise, but never run dry. The words of such *a man's mouth are as a flowing brook*. What he sees cause to speak flows naturally. It is clean and fresh.

Verse 5

This justly condemns those who, being employed in the administration of justice, pervert judgment, conniving at men's crimes because of their dignity or wealth. The merits of the cause must be regarded, not the person.

Verses 6–7

A fool's lips enter into contention by advancing foolish notions which others oppose, and so a quarrel is begun. Proud, and passionate men, and drunkards, are fools, whose lips *enter into contention*. The *fool's mouth* does, in effect, *call for strokes*; he has said that which deserves to be punished with strokes. They involve themselves in ruin: A *fool's mouth*, which has been, or would have been, the destruction of others, proves at length *his own destruction*.

Verse 8

Tale-bearers are those who secretly carry stories from house to house, told with design to blast reputation, to break friendship, to make mischief between relations. Now the words of such are here said to be, *Like as when men are wounded* (so the margin reads it); they pretend that it is with the greatest grief and reluctance that they speak of them. They look as if they themselves were wounded by it, whereas really they are fond of the story, and tell it with pride and pleasure. Thus their words seem; but they *go down as poison into the innermost parts of the belly*. The words of the tale-bearer wound him of whom they are spoken, his credit and interest, and him to whom they are spoken, his love and charity.

Verse 9

Those are justly branded as fools who are wasters of their estates, who live above what they have. Idleness is no better. He that is remiss in his work, whose *hands hang down* (so the word signifies), that stands, as we say, with his thumbs in his mouth, is own brother to him that is a prodigal. One scatters what he has, the other lets it run through his fingers.

Verse 10

Here is God's sufficiency for the saints: His *name is a strong tower* for them, in which they may take rest when they are weary and take sanctuary when they are pursued. The wealth laid up in this tower is enough to enrich them. The strength of this tower is enough to protect them.

Verse 11

The rich man has his portion and treasure in the things of this world. His wealth is as much his confidence, and he expects as much from it, as a godly man from his God. He makes his *wealth his city*, where he rules, with a great deal of self-complacency, and sets danger at defiance, as if nothing could hurt him. *His scales are his pride;* his wealth is his wall, and he thinks it a *high wall*, which cannot be scaled. Herein he cheats himself. It is a *strong city*, and a *high wall*, but it is so only *in his own conceit*.

Verse 12

Pride is the presage of ruin, and ruin will at last be the punishment of pride. Humility is the presage of honour, and honour shall at length be the reward of humility.

Verse 13

Some take a pride in being quick. They *answer a matter before they hear it.* When they have heard one side, they think the matter so plain that they need not trouble themselves to hear the other. Whereas, though a ready wit is an agreeable thing to play with, it is solid judgment and sound wisdom that do business. It is folly for a man to pass sentence upon a matter which he has not patience to make a strict enquiry into.

Verse 14

Many infirmities, many calamities, we are liable to in this world, in body, name, and estate, which a man may bear if he have but good courage, and act with reason and resolution, especially if he have a good conscience. If the *spirit of a man* will *sustain the infirmity*, much more will the spirit of a Christian, or rather the Spirit of God witnessing and working with our spirits in a day of trouble.

Verse 15

The more prudent a man is the more inquisitive will he be after knowledge, the knowledge of God and his duty, and the way to heaven, for that is the best knowledge. We must get knowledge, not only into our heads, but into our hearts.

Verse 16

A man's gift, if he be in prison, may procure his enlargement. Or, if a mean man know not how to get access to a great man, he may do it by a fee to his servants or a present to himself; those will make room for him. It will bring him to sit among *great men*, in honour and power. See how corrupt the world is when men's gifts will do that for them which their merits will not do, though ever so great.

Verse 17

This shows that one tale is good till another is told. He that speaks first will be sure to tell a story so that his cause shall appear good, whether it really be so or no. The defendant should be heard and perhaps may make the matter appear quite otherwise than it did. We must therefore remember that we have two ears, to hear both sides before we give judgment.

Verse 18

Contentions commonly happen among the mighty, that are confident of their being able to make their part good and therefore will hardly condescend to the necessary terms of an accommodation; whereas those that are poor are forced to be peaceable, and sit down losers. Even the contentions of the mighty may be ended by lot if they cannot otherwise be compromised.

Verse 19

Great care must be taken to prevent quarrels among relations, and those that are under special obligation to each other, because they are most unnatural and unbecoming. Great pains must be taken to compromise matters in variance between relations, with all speed, because it is a work of much difficulty.

Verse 20

Our comfort depends very much upon the testimony of our own consciences, for us or against us. The *belly* is here put for the conscience, as *ch.* xx. 27. The testimony of our consciences will be for us, or against us, according as we have or have not governed our tongues well. According as *the fruit of the mouth* is good or bad, so the character of the man is, and consequently the testimony of his conscience concerning him.

Verse 21

Many a one has been his own death by a foul tongue, or the death of others by a false tongue; and, on the contrary, many a one has saved his life by a prudent gentle tongue, and saved the lives of others by intercession for them.

Verse 22

A good wife is a great blessing to a man. He that *finds a wife* (that is, a wife indeed; a bad wife does not deserve to be called by a name of so much honour), that finds a help meet for him (that is a wife in the original acceptation of the word), has found that which will not only contribute more than anything to his comfort in this life, but will forward him in the way to heaven. God is to be acknowledged in it with thankfulness.

Verse 23

Poverty, though many inconveniences to the body attend it, has often a good effect upon the spirit, for it makes men humble. It teaches them to *use entreaties.* It tells them they must take what is given them and be thankful. At the throne of God's grace we are all poor, and must use entreaties. A prosperous condition, though it has many advantages, has often this mischief attending it, that it makes men proud, haughty and imperious. It is very foolish humour of some rich men, especially those who have risen from little, that they think it becomes them to answer roughly, whereas gentlemen ought to be gentle, James iii. 17.

Verse 24

Would we have friends and keep them, we must not only not affront them, but we must love them. We may promise ourselves a great deal of comfort in a true friend. Sometimes *there is a friend*, that is nothing akin to us, the bonds of whose esteem and love prove stronger than those of nature. Christ is a friend to all believers that *sticks closer than a brother*.

CHAPTER 19

Verse 1

1. The credit and comfort of a poor man: Let him be honest and *walk in integrity*, let him keep a good conscience, let him speak and act with sincerity when he is under the greatest temptations to break his word, and then let him value himself upon that, for all wise and good men will value him. 2. The shame of a rich man, notwithstanding all his pomp. If he have a shallow head and an evil tongue he *is a fool*.

Verse 2

To be without the knowledge of the soul is not good, so some read it. *He that hastes with his feet* (that does things inconsiderately and with precipitation, and will not take time to ponder the path of his feet) *sins.* As good not know as not consider.

Verse 3

The foolishness of man perverts his way. Men meet with crosses and disappointments in their affairs, and it is owing to themselves and their own folly; it is their own iniquity that corrects them. When they have done so they lay the blame upon God, and their hearts fret against him, as if he had done them wrong, whereas really they wrong themselves.

Verse 4

Wealth enables a man to send many presents, and do many good offices, and so gains him many friends, who flatter him, but really love what he has.

He, who while he prospered, was beloved and respected, if he fall into poverty is *separated from his neighbour*, is not owned nor looked upon, is bidden to keep his distance and told he is troublesome.

Verse 5
Men *teach their tongues to speak lies*, Jer. ix. 5. Those that will take a liberty to tell lies in discourse are in a fair way to be guilty of the greater wickedness of false-witness-bearing, whenever they are tempted to it, though they seemed to detest it. But it *shall not escape* the righteous judgment of God, who is jealous, and will not suffer his name to be profaned.

Verses 6–7
The prince that has power in his hand, and preferments at his disposal, has his antechamber thronged with petitioners, ready to adore him for what they can get. How earnest then should we be for the favour of God, which is far beyond that of any earthly prince. But, it should seem, liberality will go further than majesty itself to gain respect, for *every man is a friend to him that gives gifts*. Those that are accounted benefactors exercise an authority which may give them an opportunity of doing good, Luke xxii. 25. Those that are poor and low are slighted and despised. It should not be so; we must honour all men, even under their greatest abasements. *All the brethren of the poor do hate him;* even his own relations look upon him as a blemish to their family; and then others of his friends, that were nothing akin to him, *go far from him*, to get out of his way. *He pursues them with words*, hoping to prevail with them by his importunity to be kind to him, but all in vain; they have nothing for him. Let poor people therefore make God their friend, pursue him with their prayers, and he will not be wanting to them.

Verse 8
Get wisdom, get knowledge, and grace, and acquaintance with God; those that do so, show that they *love their own souls*, and will be found to have done themselves the greatest kindness imaginable. He that *keeps understanding* shall certainly *find good*, all good.

Verse 9
We have need to be again and again warned of the danger of the sin of lying and false-witness-bearing. His punishment shall be such as will be his destruction: he *shall perish*. It is a damning destroying sin.

Verse 10
Pleasure and liberty ill become a fool. A man that has not wisdom and grace has no right nor title to true joy, and therefore it is unseemly. Power and honour ill become a man of a servile spirit. None are so insolent and intolerable as a beggar on horseback, *a servant when he reigns*, ch. xxx. 22.

Verse 11
A wise man will observe these two rules about his anger: 1. Not to be over-hasty in his resentments: *Discretion* teaches us to *defer our anger* till we have thoroughly considered all the merits of the provocation, and then to defer the prosecution of it till there be no danger of running into any indecencies. Plato said to his servant, "I would beat thee, but that I am angry." 2. Not to be over-critical in his resentments. It is here made a man's *glory to pass over a transgression*, or, if he sees fit to take notice of it, yet to forgive it.

Verse 12
Kings are not common persons; their frowns are very terrible and their smiles very comfortable, and therefore it concerns them that they never frighten a good man from doing well with their frowns, nor ever give countenance to a wicked man in doing ill with their smiles, for then they abuse their influence, Rom. xiii. 3. To make subjects faithful and dutiful let them be encouraged in all good services to the public by the hopes of the favour of their prince.

Verse 13
A foolish son is a great affliction. A son that will apply himself to no study or business, that will take no advice, that lives a lewd, loose, rakish life, and spends what he has extravagantly, games it away, or that is proud, foppish, and conceited, such a one is the grief *of his father*. A cross peevish wife is as great an affliction: Her *contentions are continual*. Those that are accustomed to chide never want something or other to chide at; but it is *a continual dropping*, that is, a continual vexation, as it is to have a house so much out of repair that it rains in and a man cannot lie dry in it.

Verse 14
A discreet and virtuous wife is a choice gift of God's providence to a man—a wife that is *prudent*, in opposition, to one that is contentious, *v.* 13. *A prudent wife* makes the best of everything. If a man has such a wife let him ascribe it to the goodness of God, who made him a helpmeet for him, and perhaps by some hits and turns of providence that seemed casual brought her to him. A good estate may be *the inheritance of fathers*, which, by the common direction of Providence, comes in course to a man; but no man has a good wife by descent or entail.

Verse 15
A sluggish slothful disposition stupefies men, and makes them mindless of their own affairs, as if they were *cast into a deep sleep*, dreaming much, but doing nothing. Even their souls are idle and lulled asleep, their rational powers chilled and frozen. Those that will not labour cannot expect to eat, but must *suffer hunger*. One that is idle in the affairs of his soul, that takes no care or pains to work out his salvation, shall perish for want of that which is necessary to the life and happiness of the soul.

Verse 16
Those that make conscience of *keeping the commandment* in everything, that live by rule, *keep their own souls*; they secure their present peace and future bliss. If we keep God's word, God's word will keep us from everything really hurtful.

Verse 17
The duty of charity includes two things: 1. Compassion, which is the inward principle of charity in the heart; it is to *have pity on the poor*, 1 Cor. xiii. 3. 2. Bounty and liberality. We must not only pity the poor, but give, according to their necessity and our ability, James ii. 15, 16. It is charity to do for the poor, as well as to give. What is given to the poor, or done for them, God will place it to account as lent to him, *lent upon interest* (so the word signifies); he takes it kindly, as if it were done to himself. *He will pay him again*, in temporal, spiritual, and eternal blessings.

Verse 18
As soon as ever there appears a corrupt disposition in them check it immediately, before it is hardened into a habit. If the point can be gained without correction, well and good; but if you find that your forgiving them once, upon a dissembled repentance and promise of amendment, does but embolden them to offend again, put on resolution. It is better that

he should cry under thy rod than under the sword of the magistrate, or of divine vengeance.

Verse 19

Angry men never want woe. Those that are of headstrong passions, commonly bring themselves and their families into trouble by vexatious suits and quarrels. All which troubles to themselves and others would be prevented if they would get the rule of their own spirits. It may be read, *He that is of great wrath* (meaning the child that is to be corrected and is impatient of rebuke, cries and makes a noise) *deserves to be punished; for, if thou deliver him* for the sake of that, thou wilt be forced to punish him the more the next time.

Verse 20

It is well with those that are *wise in their latter end*, wise for their future state, wise for another world. Those that would *be wise in their latter end* must be willing to be taught, advised and reproved, when they are young.

Verse 21

God knows the *many devices that are in men's hearts* (as those, Ps. ii. 1–3, Micah iv. 11). His counsel often breaks men's measures and baffles their devices; but their devices cannot in the least alter his counsel, nor disturb the proceedings of it. Politic designing men think they can outwit all mankind, but there is a God in heaven that laughs at them! Ps. ii. 4. All God's purposes, which we are sure are right and good, shall be accomplished in due time!

Verse 22

It cannot but be *the desire of a man*, if he have any spark of virtue in him, to be kind. It is far better to have a heart to do good and want ability for it than to have ability for it and want a heart to it. *A poor man*, who wishes you well, but can promise you nothing, because he has nothing to be kind with, *is better than a liar*, who makes you believe he will do mighty things, but, when it comes to the setting, will do nothing.

Verse 23

Those that live in the fear of God *shall not be visited with evil*; they may be visited with afflictions, but there shall be nothing to hurt the soul, whereas all the satisfactions of sense are transient and soon gone. He shall have true and complete happiness. Serious godliness has a direct tendency *to life*, to all good, to eternal life.

Verse 24

A sluggard is here exposed as a fool. All his care is to save himself from labour and cold. He *hides his hand in his bosom*; his hands are cold, and he must warm them in his bosom. He is resolved against labour and hardship. He will not be at pains to feed himself, to take his hand out of his bosom, no, not to put meat into his own mouth.

Verse 25

The punishment of scorners will be a means of good to others. If it cure not the infected, it may prevent the spreading of the infection. The reproof of wise men will be a means of good to themselves. Do but *reprove one that has understanding and he will* so far understand himself, so kindly does he take reproof and so wisely improve it.

Verse 26

The sin of a prodigal son is injurious to his parents, and basely ungrateful to those that were the instruments of his being and have taken so much care about him: *He wastes his father*, wastes his estate which he should have to support him in his old age, and breaks his heart. He *chases away his mother*, makes her weary of the house, with his rudeness and insolence, and glad to retire for a little quietness; and, when he has spent all, he turns her out of doors.

Verse 27

There is that which seems designed for the instruction,˗ but really tends to the destruction of young men. The factors for vice will undertake to teach them how to palliate sins and stop the mouth of their own consciences, how to get clear of restraints. It is the wisdom of young men to turn a deaf ear to such instructions.

Verse 28

An ungodly witness is one that bears false witness against his neighbour, and will forswear himself to do another a mischief, in which there is great injustice, great impiety. Tell him of law and equity, that the scriptures and an oath are sacred things, that there will come a reckoning day; he laughs at it all. They are greedy, and glad of that which gives them an opportunity to sin.

Verse 29

Scorners are fools. Those that ridicule things sacred and serious do but make themselves ridiculous.

CHAPTER 20

Verse 1

Wine is a mocker; strong drink is raging. It smiles upon him at first, but *at the last it bites*. It rages in his conscience. It is raging in the body. *When the wine is in the wit is out*, and then the man, according as his natural temper is, either mocks like a fool or rages like a madman. Drunkenness, which pretends to be a sociable thing, renders men unfit for society. A drunkard is a fool, and a fool he is likely to be.

Verse 2

Those princes that rule by wisdom and love, rule like God himself, but those that rule merely by terror, and with a high hand, do but rule like a lion in the forest, with a brutal power. How unwise therefore those are that quarrel with them! They *sin against their own lives*. Much more do those do so that provoke the King of kings to anger.

Verse 3

He thinks himself a wise man that is quick in resenting affronts, that stands upon every nicety of honour and right, but he that thus meddles creates needless vexation to himself. Really *it is an honour for a man to cease from strife*, to drop a controversy, to forgive an injury, and to be friends.

Verse 4

Slothfulness keeps men from ploughing and sowing when the season is: some excuse or other he has to shift it off, but the true reason is that it is *cold* weather. Thus careless are many in the affairs of their souls. Those that *will not plough* in seedtime cannot expect to reap in harvest. They must beg their bread when the diligent are bringing home their sheaves with joy.

Verse 5

Though men's counsels and designs are carefully concealed by them, so that they are as *deep water* which one cannot fathom, yet there are those who by sly insinuations and questions will get out of them both what they have done and what they intend to do. Some are very able and fit to give counsel, but they are reserved; they have a great deal in them, but it is loth to come out. *A man of understanding will draw it out,* as wine out of a vessel.

Verse 6

Most men will talk a great deal of their charity, hospitality, and piety. But it is hard to find those that really are kind and liberal, that have done more than they care to hear spoken of, that will be true friends in a strait.

Verse 7

A good man keeps a good conscience, and has the comfort of it, for *it is his rejoicing.* He is not liable to those uneasinesses which those are liable to that walk in deceit. He does well for his family. God has mercy in store for the seed of the faithful.

Verse 8

He is *a king* that deserves to be called so who *sits in the throne,* not as a throne of honour, to take his ease and oblige men to keep their distance, but as a *throne of judgment,* that he may do justice, give redress to the injured. If he inspect his affairs himself, those that are employed will be restrained from doing wrong. If great men be good men, and will use their power as they may and ought, what good may they do and what evil may they prevent!

Verse 9

This question is not only a challenge to any man to prove himself sinless, but a lamentation of the corruption of mankind. Here, in this imperfect state, no person whatsoever can pretend to be without sin. Those that think themselves as good as they should be cannot, and those that are really good will not, dare not, say this.

Verse 10

In paying and receiving money, which was then commonly done by the scale, they had *divers weights,* an underweight for what they paid and an overweight for what they received; and *divers measures,* a scanty measure to sell by and a large measure to buy by. Under these is included all manner of fraud and deceit in commerce and trade. They are all *alike an abomination to the Lord.* He hates those that thus break the common faith by which justice is maintained.

Verse 11

The tree is known by its fruits, even a young tree, and *a child by his* childish things. Children will discover themselves. One may soon see what their temper is. Parents should observe their children, that they may discover their disposition and genius, and manage them accordingly, drive the nail that will go and draw out that which goes amiss.

Verse 12

God is the God of nature, and *formed the eye* and *planted the ear* (Ps. xciv. 9). Hearing and seeing are the learning senses, and we must particularly own God's goodness in them. It is he that gives the ear that hears God's voice, the eye that sees his beauty, for it is he that opens the understanding.

Verse 13

Though thou must sleep yet *love not sleep,* as those do that hate business. Love not sleep for its own sake, but only as it fits for further work. And, when thou art awake, look up, and do not let slip thy opportunities; apply thy mind closely to thy business.

Verse 14

What arts men use to get a good bargain and to buy cheap! They vilify and run down that which they know to be of value; they cry, "*It is naught, it is naught;* it has this and the other fault, and it is too dear; we can have better and cheaper elsewhere, or have bought better and cheaper." But the seller does as extravagantly commend his goods and justify the price he sets on them, and so there is a fault on both sides. When the buyer has beaten down the seller he goes his way, and boasts what excellent goods he has got at his own price.

Verse 15

The *lips of knowledge* (a good understanding to guide the lips and to diffuse the knowledge) are to be preferred before gold and rubies. They are more rare in themselves, more scarce and hard to be got. They make us rich towards God, rich in good works, 1 Tim. ii. 9, 10.

Verse 16

Those that will be bound for anybody that will ask them, in rash suretiship to oblige their idle companions, cannot hold out long. Those that are in league with abandoned women will be beggars in a little time; never give them credit without a good pledge.

Verse 17

All the pleasures and profits of sin are *bread of deceit.* They are stolen, for they are forbidden fruit; and they will deceive men, for they are not what they promise. For a time, however, they are *rolled under the tongue as a sweet morsel.* Afterwards the sinner's *mouth shall be filled with gravel.* Some nations have punished malefactors by mingling gravel with their bread.

Verse 18

Ask counsel of God, and beg direction from him. What is done hastily and with precipitation is repented of at leisure. It is especially our wisdom to be cautious in making war. Consider, and take advice, whether the war should be begun or no, and, when it is begun, consider how and by what arts it may be prosecuted, for management is as necessary as courage.

Verse 19

Tale-bearers are unprincipled people that go about carrying stories, make mischief among neighbours and relations, sow in the minds of people jealousies of their governors, of their ministers, and of one another, and reveal secrets. "Be not familiar with such; do not give them hearing for you may be sure that they will betray your secrets too and tell tales of you." Flatterers are commonly tale-bearers.

Verse 20

An undutiful child becomes very wicked by degrees. He began with despising his father and mother, but at length he arrives at such a pitch as to curse them, in defiance of God and his law, which has made this a capital crime (Exod. xxi. 17, Matt. xv. 4). An undutiful child becomes very miserable at last: *His lamp shall be put out in obscure darkness;* all his honour shall be laid in the dust.

Verse 21

There are those who will be rich, by right or wrong, who will cheat their own father, grudging themselves and their families food. An estate that is suddenly raised is often as suddenly ruined. It proves *soon ripe and soon rotten.*

Verse 22

We must not avenge ourselves. "*Say not thou I will recompense evil* for evil. Do not wish revenge.

Never say that thou wilt do a thing which thou canst not in faith pray to God to assist thee in, and *that* thou canst not do in meditating revenge." We must refer ourselves to God, and leave it to him to plead our cause, to maintain our right, and reckon with those that do us wrong in such a way and manner as he thinks fit and in his own due time.

Verse 23

This is to the same purport with what was said *v.* 10. It is here added, *A false balance is not good,* to intimate that it is not only abominable to God, but unprofitable to the sinner himself; there is really no good to be got by it, for a bargain made by fraud will prove a losing bargain in the end.

Verse 24

We have a constant dependence upon God. All our natural actions depend upon his providence, all our spiritual actions upon his grace. The best man is no better than God makes him. We have no foresight of future events, and therefore *How can a man understand his own way?* We so little understand own own way that we know not what is good for ourselves, and therefore we must commit our way unto the Lord.

Verse 25

Sacrilege, men's alienating holy things and converting them to their own use, is here called *devouring* them. What is devoted to the service of God ought to be conscientiously preserved to the purposes designed. Those that hurry over religious offices (their praying and preaching) may be said to *devour that which is holy. It is a snare to a man, after* he has made *vows* to God, *to enquire* how he may evade them or contrive excuses for the violating of them. If the matter of them was doubtful, and the expressions were ambiguous, that was his fault; he should have made them with more caution and consideration.

Verse 26

Magistrates must *scatter the wicked,* who are linked in confederacies, and there is no doing this but by *bringing the wheel over them,* that is, putting the laws in execution against them, crushing their power and quashing their projects.

Verse 27

The great soul of man is a divine light; it is the *candle of the Lord,* a candle of his lighting. Conscience, that noble faculty, is God's deputy in the soul; it is a candle not only lighted by him, but lighted for him. By the help of conscience we come to know ourselves. The spirit of a man has a self-consciousness (1 Cor. ii. 11); it searches into the dispositions and affections of the soul, praises what is good, condemns what is otherwise.

Verse 28

A good king must be strictly faithful to his word, must abhor all dissimulation, must support and countenance truth. He must likewise rule with clemency, and compassion. These virtues will make him easy and safe, beloved by his people.

Verse 29

Both young and old have their advantages and neither of them must despise nor envy the other. The young are strong and fit for action, able to break through difficulties. The old are grave, and fit for counsel, and, though they have not the strength that young men have, yet they have more wisdom and experience.

Verse 30

Many need severe rebukes. Some criminals must feel the rigour of the law and public justice; gentle methods will not work upon them; they must be beaten black and blue. Severe rebukes sometimes do a great deal of good, as corrosives contribute to the cure of a wound, eating out the proud flesh.

CHAPTER 21

Verse 1

Even the *hearts* of men are in God's hand. God can change men's minds, can turn them from that which they seemed most intent upon, as the husband-man, by canals and gutters, turns the water through his grounds, which does not alter the nature of the water, nor put any force upon it, any more than God's providence does upon the native freedom of man's will, but directs the course of it to serve his own purpose.

Verse 2

We are all apt to think too favourably of our own character. The proud heart is very ingenious in making that appear right to itself which is far from being so, to stop the mouth of conscience. God looks at the heart, and judges men according to their actions, their principles and intentions.

Verse 3

Many deceive themselves that, if they offer sacrifice, that will procure them a dispensation for unrighteousness. Living a good life (doing justly and loving mercy) is more pleasing to God than the most pompous devotion. Sacrifices were of divine institution, and were acceptable to God if they were offered in faith and with repentance, otherwise not, Isa. i. 11, &c. But even then moral duties were preferred before them (1 Sam. xv. 22).

Verse 4

He that carries himself insolently and scornfully towards both God and man, and that is always ploughing and plotting some mischief, is indeed a wicked man.

Verse 5

If we would live plentifully and comfortably we must be diligent in our business, and not shrink from the toil and trouble of it. Those that are rash and inconsiderate in their affairs, that are greedy of gain, by right or wrong, and make haste to be rich by unjust practices, are in the road to poverty.

Verse 6

Those that hope to enrich themselves by dishonest practices may perhaps heap up treasures, but will not meet with the satisfaction they expect. It is a *vanity tossed to and fro;* disappointment and vexation of spirit to them. They lay themselves open to the envy and ill-will of men and to the wrath of God.

Verse 7

Getting money by lying (*v.* 6) is no better than downright robbery. Cheating is stealing. Men *refuse to do judgment;* they will not render to all their due, but withhold it, and omissions make way for commissions; they come at length to robbery itself.

Verse 8

The froward man, the man of deceit, that acts by craft and trick, his way is strange, contrary to all the rules of honour and honesty. It is strange, for you know not when you have him. Men that are pure are proved to be such by their work, for it *is right,* it is just and regular; and they are accepted of God and approved of men.

Verse 9

What a great affliction it is to a man to have a brawling scolding woman for his wife, who is fretful to herself and furious to her children and servants. If a man has a wide house, spacious and pompous, this will embitter the comfort of it to him. He finds it his best way to retire *into a corner of the house-top*, and sit alone there, out of the hearing of her clamour.

Verse 10

A very wicked man desires that evil may be done and that he may have the pleasure of having a hand in it. *His neighbour*, his friend, his nearest relation, cannot gain from him the least kindness.

Verse 11

Let the law be executed upon a scorner, and even he that is simple will be awakened and alarmed by it, and will discern the evil of sin. *When the wise is instructed* by the preaching of the word *he* (not only the wise himself, but the simple that stands by) *receives knowledge*.

Verse 12

The righteous man (the judge or magistrate) *examines the house of the wicked*, searches it for arms or for stolen goods, makes a diligent enquiry concerning his family, that he may *overthrow the wicked for their wickedness* and prevent their doing any further mischief.

Verse 13

An uncharitable man *stops his ears at the cry of the poor*, turns them away from his door, and *shuts up the bowels of his compassion*, Acts vii. 57. He shall himself be reduced to straits, which will make him *cry*. Men will not hear him, but reward him as he has rewarded others. God will not hear him; for he that *showed no mercy shall have judgment without mercy* (James ii. 13).

Verse 14

A handsome present, prudently managed, will turn away some men's wrath when it seemed implacable. If it be a bribe to pervert justice, that is so scandalous that those who are fond of it are shamed of it.

Verse 15

It is a pleasure and satisfaction to good men to see justice administered by the government they live under, and also to practise it themselves. It is a terror to wicked men to see the laws put in execution against vice and profaneness.

Verse 16

The sinner *wanders out of the way of understanding*, and when once he has left that good way he wanders endlessly. The way of religion is *the way of understanding*; those that are not truly pious are not truly intelligent; and they go astray like lost sheep.

Verse 17

An epicure *loves pleasure*. God allows us to use the delights of sense soberly and temperately, *wine to make glad the heart*, and *oil to make the face to shine* and beautify the countenance; but he that sets his heart upon them is impatient of everything that crosses him in his pleasures. *He shall be a poor man* who once could not live without dainties and varieties. Many a beau becomes a beggar.

Verse 18

The wicked, that are the troublers of a land, ought to be punished, for the preventing of those national judgments which otherwise will be inflicted. God will rather leave many wicked people to be cut off than abandon his own people.

Verse 19

Unbridled passions embitter and spoil the comfort of all relations. Those cannot dwell in peace and happiness that cannot dwell in peace and love.

Verse 20

Those that are wise will increase what they have and live plentifully; their wisdom will teach them to proportion their expenses to their income and to lay up a good stock of all things convenient, particularly of *oil*, one of the staple commodities of Canaan. It is better to have an old-fashioned house, and have it well furnished, than a fine modern one, with sorry housekeeping.

Verse 21

We must do justly and love mercy, and, though we cannot attain to perfection, yet it will be a comfort to us if we aim at it. Those that do *follow after righteousness* shall *find righteousness*.

Verse 22

Those that have wisdom, though they are so modest as not to promise much, often perform great things, even against those that are so confident of their strength. A stratagem, well managed, may effectually *scale the city of the mighty and cast down the strength* it had such a confidence in. *A wise man* will gain upon the affections of people and conquer them by strength of reason, which is a more noble conquest than that obtained by strength of arms.

Verse 23

Those that would keep their souls must keep a watch before the door of their lips, must *keep the mouth* by temperance, that nothing be eaten or drunk to excess; they must *keep the tongue* also, that no forbidden word go out of the door of the lips, no corrupt communication. Keep thy heart, and that will keep thy tongue from sin; keep thy tongue, and that will keep thy heart from trouble.

Verse 24

Most of the wrath that inflames the spirits and societies of men is *proud wrath*. Men cannot bear the least slight, nor in anything to be crossed or contradicted, but they are in a heat, immediately. It makes them scornful when they are angry.

Verses 25–26

The slothful are as fit for labour as other men. They are enemies to themselves; for their slothfulness starves them, their desires at the same time stab them. Though their hands refuse to labour, their hearts cease not to covet riches, and pleasures, and honours. They expect everybody should do for them. Many that must have money with which to make provision for the flesh, and would not be at pains to get it honestly, have turned highwaymen, and that has killed them. The righteous and industrious have their desires satisfied, and enjoy not only that satisfaction, but the further satisfaction of doing good to others. The slothful are always gaping to receive, *but the righteous* are always contriving to give.

Verse 27

Sacrifices were of divine institution; and when they were offered in faith, and with repentance and reformation, God was well-pleased. They were an *abomination* when they were brought by wicked men, who did not repent of their sins, mortify their lusts, and amend their lives. *Much more when* they were brought with *wicked minds*, when their sacrifices were made serviceable to their wickedness. When men make a show of devotion, when holiness is pretended, but some wickedness intended, then the performance is an abomination, Isa. lxvi. 5.

Verse 28

A man may tell a lie perhaps in his haste; but he that gives in a false testimony does it with deliberation and solemnity, and it cannot but be a presumptuous sin. The vengeance he imprecated upon himself, when he took the false oath, will come upon him. He *who hears* (that is, obeys) the command of God, which is to *speak every man truth with his neighbour*, testifies nothing but what he knows to be true, *speaks constantly* (that is, consistently with himself).

Verse 29

A wicked man *hardens his face*—brazens it, that he may not blush—steels it, that he may not tremble when he commits the greatest crimes; he bids defiance to the terrors of the law and the checks of his own conscience. A good man does not say, What *would* I do? but, What *should* I do? And so he *directs his way* by a safe and certain rule.

Verse 30

There can be no success against God. Though men think they have *wisdom*, and *understanding*, and *counsel*, the best politics and politicians, on their side, yet if it be *against the Lord*, it cannot prosper long. There can be no success without God. Be the cause ever so good and the means of carrying it on ever so probable, still men must acknowledge God and take him along with them. Means indeed are to be used; *the horse* must be *prepared against the day of battle*, and the foot too. *But*, after all, *safety* and salvation *are of the Lord*; he can save without armies, but armies cannot save without him.

CHAPTER 22

Verse 1

We should be more careful to do that by which we may get and keep a good name than that by which we may raise and increase a great estate. By great riches we may relieve the bodily wants of others, but by a good name we may recommend religion to them. To be well beloved, to have an interest in the esteem and affections of all about us; this is better *than silver and gold*.

Verse 2

The greatest man in the world must acknowledge God to be his Maker, and is under the same obligations to be subject to him that the meanest is; and the poorest has the honour to be the work of God's hands as much as the greatest. *Rich and poor meet together* at the bar of God's justice, all guilty before God; and they meet at the throne of God's grace; the poor are as welcome there as the rich. There is the same Christ, the same scripture, the same Spirit, the same covenant of promises, for them both. There is the same heaven for poor saints that there is for rich.

Verse 3

A prudent man will *foresee an evil* before it comes and stand on his guard. When the clouds are gathering for a storm he takes the warning, and flies to the name of the Lord as his strong tower. *The simple*, who believe every word that flatters them, will believe none that warns them, and so they *pass on and are punished*. See an instance of both these, Exod. ix. 20, 21.

Verse 4

Religion does very much consist—in *humility and the fear of the Lord*; that is, walking humbly with God.

What is to be gotten by it—*riches, and honour*, and comfort, *and* long *life*, in this world, as far as God sees good, and the privileges of the covenant of grace, *and* eternal *life* at last.

Verse 5

In the way of the froward, that crooked way, *which* is contrary to the will and word of God, *thorns and snares are* found, thorns of grief for past sins and snares entangling them in further sin. *He that keeps his soul*, that watches carefully over his own heart and ways, is *far from* those *thorns and snares*, for his way is both plain and pleasant.

Verse 6

Train up children in that learning age. *Catechise* them; initiate them. *Train* them as soldiers, who are taught to handle their arms, keep rank, and observe the word of command. *Train* them up *in the way they should go*, the way in which, if you love them, you would have them go. *Train up a child according as he is capable* (so some take it), with a gentle hand, as nurses feed children, little and often, Deut. vi. 7. Good impressions made upon them then will abide upon them all their days.

Verse 7

The rich rule over the poor, and too often with pride and rigour, unlike to God, who, though he be great, yet despises not any. *The borrower is servant to the lender*, and must sometimes beg, *Have patience with me*. Some sell their liberty to gratify their luxury.

Verse 8

Ill-gotten gains will not prosper. *He that sows iniquity*, that does an unjust thing in hopes to get by it, *shall reap vanity*. If the rod of authority turn into a *rod of anger*, if men rule by passion instead of prudence, instead of the public welfare, their power shall not bear them out, Isa. x. 24, 25.

Verse 9

A charitable man has a *bountiful eye*, opposed to the evil eye (*ch. xxiii. 6*) and the same with the *single eye* (Matt. vi. 22),—an eye that seeks out objects of charity, that, upon the sight of one in want and misery, affects the heart with compassion,—an eye that with the alms gives a pleasant look, which makes the alms doubly acceptable. He has also a liberal hand: *He gives of his bread*, the bread appointed for his own eating. God himself will bless him.

Verse 10

The scorner sows discord. Much of the *strife and contention* which disturb the peace is owing to *the evil interpreter* (as some read it), that construes everything into the worst, and takes a pride in bantering all mankind. Those that would secure the peace must exclude the scorner.

Verse 11

A complete gentleman, fit to be employed in public business, must be an honest man, a man *that loves pureness of heart* and hates all impurity, free from all deceit, all selfishness and sinister designs, that is just and delights in keeping his own conscience clean. He must also speak with a good grace, not to daub and flatter, but to deliver his sentiments decently, in language as clean as his spirit. *The king*, if he be wise and good, and understand his own and his people's interest, *will be his friend*.

Verse 12

God takes special care to *preserve knowledge*, that is, to keep up religion in the world by keeping up among men the knowledge of himself and of good and evil. He preserves *men of knowledge*, wise and good men (2 Chron. xvi. 9), particularly faithful witnesses, who speak what they know. *He overthrows the words of the transgressor*, and *preserves knowledge* in spite of him.

Verse 13

Many frighten themselves from real duties by imaginary difficulties: *The slothful man* has work to do *without* in the fields, but he fancies *there is a lion* there. He talks of *a lion without*, but considers not his real danger from the devil, that *roaring lion*, which is in bed with him, and from his own slothfulness, which kills him.

Verse 14

This is designed to warn all young men against the lusts of uncleanness. As they regard the welfare of their souls, let them take heed of *the mouth of strange women*, of the kisses of their lips (*ch.* vii. 13), their charms and enticements. Dread them; have nothing to do with them. Those who abandon themselves to that sin are abandoned of God: who takes off the bridle of his restraining grace.

Verse 15

Sin is *foolishness*; it is contrary both to our reason and to our true interest. It *is in the heart*; there is an inward inclination to sin, to speak and act foolishly. It is not only *found* there, but it is *bound* there; it is annexed to the heart (so some); vicious dispositions cleave closely to the soul. Correction is necessary to the cure of it. There must be strictness and severity, which will cause grief. Children need to be corrected, and kept under discipline, by their parents; and we all need to be corrected by our heavenly Father (Heb. xii. 6, 7), and under the correction we must kiss the rod.

Verse 16

Rich men sometimes *oppress the poor and give to the rich*. They will not in charity relieve the poor, but they will make presents *to the rich*, and give them great entertainments, either in vain-glory, that they may look great, or in policy, that they may receive it again with advantage. Such *shall surely come to want*. Many have been beggared by a foolish generosity, but never any by a prudent charity. Christ bids us invite the poor, Luke xiv. 12, 13.

Verses 17–21

Solomon here changes his style. Since the beginning of *ch.* x, he had laid down doctrinal truths, leaving us to make the application as we went along; but here, to the end of *ch.* xxiv, he directs his speech to his son, his pupil, his reader, his hearer, speaking as to a particular person. Hitherto, for the most part, his sense was comprised in one verse, but here usually it is drawn out further. Here is,

I. An earnest exhortation to get wisdom and grace, by attending to *the words of the wise* men, both written and preached. To these *words*, to this *knowledge*, the ear must be *bowed down* and the *heart applied* by faith, and love, and close consideration. The ear will not serve without the heart.

II. Arguments to enforce this exhortation. Consider,

1. The worth and weight of the things themselves which Solomon in this book gives us. They are not trivial, jocular proverbs. They are *excellent things*, which concern the glory of God, the holiness and happiness of our souls, the welfare of mankind, *princely things* (so the word is), fit for kings to speak and senates to hear.

2. The clearness of these things and the directing of them to us in particular. The emphasis here is

that they are *made known to thee, even to thee*, and *written to thee*, as if it were a letter directed to thee by name. It is suited to thee and to thy case. If we make use of them in our discourse, they will be very becoming. *They shall be fitted in thy lips.*

3. The advantage designed us by them. The *excellent things* which God has *written to* us are not like the commands which the master gives his servant, which are all intended for the benefit of the master, but like those which the master gives his scholar, which are all intended for the benefit of the scholar. We cannot trust in God except in the way of duty; we are *therefore* taught our duty, that we may have reason to trust in God. It is a desirable thing to know, not only *the words of truth*, but *the certainty of* them, that our faith may be intelligent and rational, and may grow up to a full assurance. *If any man do his will, he shall know* for certain that the doctrine is of God, John vii. 17. Knowledge is given us to do good with, that others may light their candle at our lamp, and that we may in our place serve our generation according to the will of God.

Verses 22–23

After this solemn preface, one would have expected something new and surprising; but no; here is a plain but very needful caution against the inhuman practice of oppressing poor people. The sin itself is *robbing the poor* and making them poorer. It is bad to rob any man, but most absurd to rob the poor, whom we should relieve. To oppress *the afflicted*, and so to add affliction to them is not only a base and cowardly thing, to take advantage against a man because he is helpless, but it is unnatural, and proves men worse than beasts. He that robs and oppresses the poor does it at his peril. The oppressed will find God their powerful patron.

Verse 24

A good caution against being intimate with a passionate man. A man who is easily provoked, touchy, and apt to resent affronts, who, when he is in a passion, grows outrageous, is not fit to be made a friend, for he will be angry with us, and he will expect that we should, like him, be angry with others, and that will be our sin. It is dangerous conversing with those that throw about the sparks of their passion, "Lest thou imitate him, to humour him, and so contract an ill habit."

Verses 26–27

We must not cheat people of their money, by *striking hands* ourselves, or *becoming surety for others*, when we *have not to pay*. If a man is disabled to pay his debts, he ought to be pitied and helped; but he that takes up money or goods himself, or is bound for another, when he knows that he has not wherewithal to pay, does in effect pick his neighbour's pocket, and though, in all cases, compassion is to be used, yet he may thank himself if the law have its course and his *bed* be *taken from under him*, which might not be taken for a pledge to secure a debt, Exod. xxii. 26, 27. For, if a man appeared to be so poor that he had nothing else to give for security, he ought to be relieved, but, for the recovery of a debt, it seems it might be taken by the *strict operation of law*.

Verse 28

The land-marks, or meer-stones, are standing witnesses to every man's right; let not those be removed quite away, for thence come wars, and fightings, and endless disputes; let them not be removed so as to take from thy neighbour's lot to thy own, for that is downright robbing him and entailing the fraud upon posterity. Deference is to be paid, in all civil matters, to usages that have prevailed time out of mind.

Verse 29

A truly ingenious industrious man is here commended who lays out himself to get business, though it be but in a very low and narrow sphere. A man of despatch knows how to bring a deal of business into a little compass. Though now he *stands before mean men*, is employed by them, yet he will rise, and is likely enough to *stand before kings*, as an ambassador or prime-minister.

CHAPTER 23

Verses 1–3

We are in most danger of falling into this sin: "When thou hast great plenty before thee, varieties and dainties, such a table spread as thou hast seldom seen." The temptation may be stronger to one that is not used to such entertainments. We must alarm ourselves into temperance and moderation: "*Put a knife to thy throat*, that is, restrain thyself, as it were with a sword hanging over thy head. But that is not enough: lay the axe to the root; mortify that appetite which has such a power over thee."

Verses 4–5

Some are given to appetite (*v.* 2), others to covetousness. We must endeavour to live comfortably, and provide for our children and families, but we must not seek great things. Be not of those that will be rich, that design it as their highest end, 1 Tim. vi. 9. What thou hast, or doest, be master of it, and not a slave to it as those that *rise up early, sit up late*, and *eat the bread of carefulness*, and all to be rich. The things of this world are a show, a shadow, a sham upon the soul that trusts to them. Wilt thou do a thing so absurd in itself? What thou, a reasonable creature, wilt thou dote upon shadows? Riches are very uncertain things; *They make themselves wings, and fly away*. The wings they fly away upon are of their own making. They have in themselves the principles of their own corruption. They go irresistibly and irrecoverably, as *an eagle towards heaven*, that flies strongly, and flies out of sight and out of call (there is no bringing her back); thus do riches leave men in grief and vexation if they set their hearts upon them.

Verses 6–8

There are those that pretend to bid their friends welcome that are not hearty and sincere in it. They have a fair tongue, and know what they should say: *Eat and drink, saith he*, because it is expected that the master of the feast should so compliment his guests; but they have an *evil eye*, and grudge their guests every bit they eat. If a man be so mean that he cannot find in his heart to bid his friends welcome to what he has, he ought not to add to that the guilt of dissimulation by inviting them. "*Eat not thou the bread* of such a man; let him keep it to himself. Do not sponge upon those that are bountiful, but especially scorn to be beholden to those that are paltry and not sincere."

Verse 9

It is our duty to take all fit occasions to speak of divine things; but, some will make a jest of everything. A wise man is advised not to *speak in the ears* of such fools. If what a wise man says in his wisdom will not be heard, let him hold his peace, and try whether the wisdom of that will be regarded.

Verses 10–11

The fatherless are taken under God's special protection. He is *their Redeemer*, their *Goël*, their near kinsman, that will take their part and stand up for them. Every man therefore must be careful not to injure them in anything, or to invade their rights, either by a clandestine removal of the old landmarks or by a forcible entry into their fields.

Verses 12–16

A parent should persuade his child to attend to the words of knowledge so that he may learn what is his duty. A tender parent finds it hard to administer correction but, for his child's good, he beats *him with the rod*, gives him a gentle correction, the *stripes of the sons of men*, not such as we give to beasts. The rod will not kill him; it will prevent his killing himself by those vicious courses which the rod will restrain him from. It is to be hoped that those will do *right things* when they grow up who learn to *speak right things* when they are young. "Children, if you be wise and good, devout and conscientious, we shall think our labour in instructing you well bestowed. We shall rejoice in hope that you will be a credit and comfort to us, if we should live to be old, that you will bear up the name of Christ in your generation, that you will live comfortably in this world and happily in another."

Verses 17–18

"*Let not thy heart envy sinners;* do not grudge them either the liberty they take to sin or the success they have in sin; it will cost them dearly and they are to be pitied rather than envied." We must be in the fear of the Lord, taking a pleasure in contemplating God's glory and complying with his will. *There will be an end of the prosperity of the wicked*, therefore *do not envy them* (Ps. lxxiii. 17); there will be an end of thy afflictions, *perfect love will shortly cast out fear*, and *thy expectation* of the reward not only will be *not cut off*, or disappointed, but it will be infinitely outdone.

Verses 19–28

"*Hearken unto thy father who begat thee*, and who therefore has an authority over thee and an affection for thee, and can have no other design than thy own good." We ought to *give reverence to the fathers of our flesh*, who were the instruments of our being; much more ought we to obey and be in subjection to the *Father of our spirits*, who made us and is the author of our being. And since *the mother* also, from a sense of duty to God and from love to her child, gives him good instructions, let him not *despise her*, nor her advice, *when she is old. Buy the truth and sell it not* (*v.* 23). Truth is that by which the heart must be guided and governed, for without truth there is no goodness. We must buy it whatever it costs us, we shall not repent the bargain. Riches should be employed for the getting of knowledge, rather than knowledge for the getting of riches. When we are at pains in searching after truth, then we buy it. *Heaven concedes everything to the laborious*. We must not sell it. Do not part with it for pleasures, honours, riches, anything in this world. God, in this exhortation, speaks to us as unto children: "Son, Daughter, Give me thy heart." Thou shalt love the Lord thy God with all thy heart. To this call we must readily answer, "*My father, take my heart*, such as it is, and make it such as it should be; take possession of it, and set up thy throne in it." *Be not a wine-bibber. Be not an* excessive *eater of flesh*. Intemperance must be avoided in meat as well as drink. He fetches an argument against this sin from the expensiveness of it. *The drunkard and the glutton* hate to be reformed, though they are told they *shall come to poverty*. Drunkenness is the cause of *drowsiness*; it stupefies men, and makes them inattentive to business, and then all goes to wreck and ruin. Whoredom is a sin which bewitches men to their ruin: *The adulteress lies in wait as a robber*, pretending friendship, but designing to strip them both of their armour and of their ornaments. It is a sin that contributes more than any other to the spreading of vice and immorality in a kingdom. One adulteress may be the ruin of many a precious soul and may help to debauch a whole town. Houses of uncleanness are therefore such pest-houses as ought to be suppressed by those whose office it is to take care of the public welfare.

Verses 29–35

Solomon here gives fair warning against the sin of drunkenness, to confirm what he had said, *v.* 20. *Look not thou upon the wine when it is red.* Red wine was in Canaan looked upon as the best wine; it is therefore called *the blood of the grape.* Covet not that which pleases the eye, but let thy serious thoughts convince thee that that which seems delightful is really hurtful. The pernicious consequences of the sin of drunkenness: *At the last it bites, v.* 32. The drunkard is made sick by his surfeit, beggared and ruined in his estate, especially when his conscience is awakened and he cannot reflect upon it without horror and indignation at himself. It embroils men in quarrels. Many have woe and sorrow, and cannot help it; but drunkards wilfully create woe and sorrow to themselves. The wounds which men receive in defence of their country and its just rights are their honour; but *wounds without cause*, received in the service of their lusts, are marks of their infamy. Drunkenness makes men impure and insolent, *v.* 33. The *eyes* grow unruly and *behold strange women* to lust after them, and so let in adultery into the heart. The tongue also grows unruly and talks extravagantly; by it the *heart utters perverse things*, contrary to reason, religion, and common civility. What ridiculous incoherent nonsense men will talk when they are drunk! It stupefies and besots men, *v.* 34. Their judgments are clouded, and they have no more steadiness and consistency than he that sleeps *upon the top of a mast.* Set a drunkard in the stocks, and he is not sensible of the punishment. *"They have stricken me, and I was not sick; I felt it not."* Drunkenness turns men into stocks and stones; they are scarcely to be reckoned animals; they are dead while they live. *Look not upon the wine when it is red.*

CHAPTER 24

Verses 1–2

"Let not such a thought ever come into thy mind, O that I could shake off the restraints of religion and conscience, and take as great a liberty to indulge the sensual appetite, as I see such and such do! No; *desire not to be with them*, to do as they do and fare *as they fare*, and to *cast in thy lot among* them." Do not think with them, *for their heart studies destruction* to others, but it will prove destruction to themselves. It is therefore thy wisdom to have nothing to do with them. Nor hast thou any reason to look upon them with envy, but with pity rather, or a just indignation at their wicked practices.

Verses 3–6

A man, with prudent management, may raise his estate and family by lawful and honest means, with the blessing of God upon his industry; and, if the other be raised a little sooner, yet these will last a great deal longer. True wisdom will make men's outward affairs prosperous and successful. It will *build a house and establish it, v.* 3. Men may by unrighteous practices build their houses, but they cannot establish them, for the foundation is rotten (Hab. ii. 9, 10). It will enrich a house and furnish it, *v.* 4. *By knowledge the chambers* of the soul are filled with the graces and comforts of the Spirit, those *precious and pleasant riches.* It will fortify a house and turn it into a castle: *Wisdom is better than weapons of war*, offensive or defensive. The spirit is strengthened both for the spiritual work and the spiritual warfare by true wisdom. Wisdom will erect a college, or council of state. Wisdom will be of use, to make an advantageous peace.

Verses 7–9

It is no easy thing to get wisdom; those that have natural parts good enough, yet if they be foolish, that is, if they be slothful and will not take pains, if they be viciously inclined and keep bad company, it *is too high* for them; they are not likely to reach it. And, for want of it, they are unfit for the service of their country: They *open not their mouth in the gate*; they are not admitted into the council or magistracy, or, if they are, they are dumb statues, they say nothing, because they have nothing to say. This *devising evil* is *the thought of foolishness, v.* 9. It is bad to do evil, but it is worse to devise it; for that has in it the subtlety and poison of the old serpent. But it may be taken more generally. We contract guilt, not only by the act of foolishness, but by the thought of it, though it go no further; the first risings of sin in the heart are sin, offensive to God, and must be repented of or we are undone. *The scorner*, who takes a pleasure in affronting people and reflecting upon them, *is an abomination to men.*

Verse 10

In *the day of adversity* we are apt to *faint*, to droop and be discouraged, to desist from our work, and to despair of relief. "It is a sign that thou art not a man of any resolution, any firmness of thought, any consideration, any faith (for that is the strength of a soul), if thou canst not bear up under an afflictive change of thy condition." *Be of good courage* therefore, *and God shall strengthen thy heart.*

Verses 11–12

A great duty required of us is to appear for the relief of oppressed innocency. Though the persons be not such as we are under any particular obligation to, we must help them, out of a general zeal for justice. It is easy to make an excuse when we say, *We knew it not*, or, *We forgot.* It is not easy with such excuses to evade the judgment of God. God *ponders the heart and keeps the soul*; keeps an eye upon it. We should be tender of the lives of others, and do all we can to preserve them, because our lives have been precious in the sight of God and he has graciously kept them. He will *render to every man according to his works*, not only the commission of evil works, but the omission of good works.

Verse 13–14

The study of wisdom will be very pleasant. We *eat honey because it is sweet to the taste*, and upon that account we call it *good*, especially that which runs first from the *honeycomb.* Canaan was said to flow with milk and honey, and honey was the common food of the country (Luke xxiv. 41, 42), even for children, Isa. vii. 15. Thus should we feed upon wisdom, and relish the good instructions of it. Those that have experienced the power of truth and godliness are abundantly satisfied of the pleasure of both; they have tasted the sweetness of them, and all the atheists in the world with their sophistry, and the profane with their banter, cannot alter their sentiments.

Verses 15–16

The designs of the wicked against the righteous; the plot is laid deeply: They *lay wait against the dwelling of the righteous.* They doubt not but to *spoil his dwelling-place* because his condition is low and distressed, and he is almost down already. The righteous man, whose ruin was expected, recovers himself. The *just man falls*, sometimes *falls seven times* perhaps, sins of infirmity, through the surprise of temptation; but he *rises again* by repentance, finds mercy with God, and regains his peace. *The wicked man*, who expected to see his ruin and to help it forward, is undone.

Verses 17–18

If any have done us an ill turn, or if we bear them ill-will only because they stand in our way, when any damage comes to them (suppose they fall), our corrupt hearts are too apt to conceive a secret delight and satisfaction in it. "Men hope in the ruin of their enemies or rivals to wreak their revenge or to find their account; but be not thou so inhuman; *rejoice not when* the worst *enemy* thou hast *falls.*" The Lord will *see it*, though it be hidden in the heart only, *and it* will *displease him*, as it will displease a prudent father to see one child triumph in the correction of another, which he ought to take warning by, not knowing how soon it may be his own case, he having so often deserved it.

Verses 19–20

Even that which grieves us must not *fret* us; nor must our eye be evil against any because God is good. If wicked people prosper, we must not therefore incline to do as they do. Envy not their prosperity. There is no true happiness in it. *He has his reward*, Matt. vi. 2. Those are not to be envied that have their portion in this life and must out-live it, Ps. xvii. 14. Their *candle* shines brightly, but it shall presently *be put out*.

Verses 21–22

Religion and loyalty must go together. As men, it is our duty to honour our Creator, to worship and reverence him; as members of a community, incorporated for mutual benefit, it is our duty to be faithful and dutiful to the government God has set over us, Rom. xiii. 1, 2. Those are not truly loyal that are not religious. How should he be true to his prince that is false to his God? And, if they come in competition, it is an adjudged case, we must *obey God rather than men*. Those that are of restless, factious, turbulent spirits, commonly pull mischief upon their own heads ere they are aware: *Their calamity shall rise suddenly*.

Verses 23–26

As subjects must do their duty, and be obedient to magistrates, so magistrates must do their duty in administering justice to their subjects. They must always weigh the merits of a cause, and not be swayed by any regard, one way or other, to the parties concerned. A good judge will know the truth, not know faces, so as to countenance a friend and help him out in a bad cause, or so much as omit anything that can be said or done in favour of a righteous cause, when it is the cause of an enemy. They must discountenance and give check to all fraud, violence, injustice, and immorality. Let magistrates and ministers, and private persons too that are capable of doing it, rebuke the wicked, that they may bring them to repentance or put them to shame, and they shall have the comfort of it in their own bosoms: *To them shall be delight*, when their consciences witness for them that they have been witnesses for God. They must *give a right answer*, that is, give their opinion and pass sentence according to law and the true merits of the cause; and *everyone shall kiss his lips that* does so, that is, shall love and honour him with a kiss of allegiance. He that in common conversation speaks pertinently and with sincerity is beloved and respected by all.

Verse 27

This is a rule of prudence in the management of household affairs. We must prefer necessaries before conveniences, and not lay that out for show which should be expended for the support of the family. We must not think of building till we can afford it: "First apply thyself to *thy work without in the field*; look after thy husbandry, for it is that by which thou must get; and, when thou hast got well by that, then, and not till then, thou mayest think of rebuilding and beautifying *thy house.*"

Verses 28–29

As *a witness:* "Never bear a testimony against any man *without cause*, unless what thou sayest thou knowest to be punctually true and thou hast a clear call to testify it. Never bear a false testimony against anyone"; As a plaintiff or prosecutor: If there be occasion to bring an action or information against thy neighbour, let it not be from a spirit of revenge. Even a righteous cause becomes unrighteous when it is prosecuted with malice.

Verses 30–34

The view which Solomon took of *the field and vineyard of the slothful* man. He cast his eye upon a *field* and a *vineyard* unlike all the rest; for, though the soil was good, yet there was nothing growing in them but *thorns and nettles*; and, if there had been any fruit, it would have been eaten up by the beasts, for there was no fence. He paused a little *and considered it, looked* again *upon it, and received instruction*. He did not break out into any passionate censures of the owner, but he endeavoured himself to get good by the observation. Plutarch relates a saying of Cato Major, "That wise men profit more by fools than fools by wise men; for wise men will avoid the faults of fools, but fools will not imitate the virtues of wise men." What a scandalous thing slothfulness is, and how injurious to the family, and to the affairs of our souls! Our souls are our fields and vineyards, which we are every one of us to take care of, to dress, and to keep. They are capable of being improved with good husbandry. These fields and vineyards are often in a very bad state, not only no fruit brought forth, but all overgrown with *thorns* and *nettles* (scratching, stinging, inordinate lusts and passions, pride, covetousness, sensuality, malice, those are the thorns and nettles, the wild grapes, which the unsanctified heart produces), no guard kept against the enemy, but the *stone-wall broken down*. Where it is thus it is owing to the sinner's own slothfulness and folly.

CHAPTER 25

Verse 1

This verse is the title of this latter collection of Solomon's proverbs. The publishers were Hezekiah's servants, who, it is likely, herein acted as his servants, being appointed by him to do this good service to the church, among other good offices that he did *in the law and in the commandments*, 2 Chron. xxxi. 21. They copied out these proverbs from the records of Solomon's reign, and published them as an appendix to the former edition of this book. It may be a piece of very good service to the church to publish other men's works that have lain hidden in obscurity.

Verses 2–3

An instance given of the honour of God: *It is his glory to conceal a matter*. There is an unfathomable depth in his counsels, Rom. xi. 33. We see what he does, but we know not the reasons. It is God's glory that he needs not *search into a matter*, because he knows it without search; but it is the honour of kings to search out the matters that are brought before them, to take pains in examining offenders and not to give judgment hastily.

Verses 4–5

The vigorous endeavour of a prince to suppress vice, and reform the manners of his people, is the most effectual way to support his government. The duty of magistrates is to use their power for the terror of evil works and evil workers, not only to banish those that are vicious, but so to frighten them that they may not spread the infection of their wickedness among their subjects. This is called *taking away the dross from the silver*, which is done by the force of fire. The reformation of the court will promote the reformation of the kingdom, Ps. ci. 3, 8.

Verses 6–7

Religion is so far from destroying good manners that it teaches us to give place to those to whom it belongs. Religion teaches us humility and self-denial, which is a better lesson than that of good manners. This is really the way to advancement, as our Saviour shows in a parable that seems to be borrowed from this, Luke xiv. 9. It is better, more for a man's satisfaction and reputation, to be advanced above his pretensions and expectations, than to be thrust down below them.

Verses 8–10

"Be not hasty in bringing an action, before thou hast thyself considered it, and consulted with thy friends about it. Bring not an action before thou hast tried to end the matter amicably (*v.* 9): *Debate thy cause with thy neighbour* privately, and perhaps you will understand one another better and see that there is no occasion to go to law." *Reveal not the secret of another*, so some read it. "Do not, in revenge, to disgrace thy adversary, disclose that which should be kept private and which does not at all belong to the cause." Be thus cautious in going to law, otherwise the cause will be in danger of going against thee. It will turn very much to thy reproach if thou fall under the character of being litigious.

Verses 11–12

Instruction, advice, or comfort, given seasonably, and in apt expressions, adapted to the case of the person spoken to and agreeing with the character of the person speaking—*is like golden* balls resembling *apples*, brought to table in a silver network basket, or in a silver box of that which we call *philligree*-work, through which the golden apples might be seen. Doubtless it was some ornament of the table, then well known. A reproof with discretion, well given, by *a wise reprover*, and well taken, by an *obedient ear*, it is an *ear-ring of gold* and an *ornament of fine gold*, very graceful and well becoming both the reprover and the reproved.

Verse 13

A servant ought to be *faithful to him that sends him*, and to see to it that he does not, by mistake or with design, falsify his trust. This will be the satisfaction of the master; it will *refresh his soul* as much as ever the *cold of snow* (which in hot countries they preserve by art all the year round) refreshed the labourers in the harvest, that *bore the burden and heat of the day*.

Verse 14

Who pretends to have received or given that which he never had, which he never gave, makes a noise of his great accomplishments and his good services, but it is all false; he is not what he pretends to be. Such a one is like the morning-cloud, that passes away, and disappoints those who looked for rain from it to water the parched ground (Jude 12), *clouds without water*.

Verse 15

Two things recommended in dealing with others, 1. Patience, to bear a present heat without being put into a heat by it, and to wait for a fit opportunity to offer our reasons and to give persons time to consider them. By this means even a *prince* may be *persuaded*. 2. Mildness, to speak without passion or provocation: *A soft tongue breaks the bone;* it mollifies the roughest spirits and overcomes those that are most morose, like lightning, which, they say, has sometimes broken the bone, and yet not pierced the flesh.

Verse 16

"*Hast thou found honey?*" It is not forbidden fruit to thee, as it was to Jonathan; thou mayest eat of it with thanksgiving to God. *Eat as much as is sufficient,* and no more. We must use all pleasures as we do honey, with a check upon our appetite. The pleasures of sense lose their sweetness by the excessive use of them and become nauseous, as honey, which turns sour in the stomach.

Verse 17

It is a piece of civility to visit our neighbours sometimes. It is wisdom, as well as good manners, not to be troublesome to our friends in visiting them too often, nor stay too long, nor contrive to come at meal-time, nor make ourselves busy in the affairs of their families. *After the third day fish and company become distasteful.* Familiarity breeds contempt. How much better a friend then is God than any other friend; the oftener we come to him the better and the more welcome.

Verse 18

A false testimony is everything that is dangerous; it *is a maul* (or *club* to knock a man's brains out with), a flail, which there is no fence against; it is a *sword* to wound near at hand and a *sharp arrow* to wound at a distance; we have therefore need to pray, *Deliver my soul, O Lord! from lying lips*, Ps. cxx. 2.

Verse 19

Confidence in an unfaithful man (so we read it), in a man whom we thought trusty but who proves otherwise, proves not only unserviceable, but painful and vexatious, like a *broken tooth, or a foot out of joint*.

Verse 20

The absurdity here censured is *singing songs to a heavy heart*. Those that are in great sorrow are to be comforted by sympathizing with them, but we take a wrong course if we think to relieve them by being merry with them, and endeavouring to make them merry. *Taking away a garment* from a man in *cold weather*, makes him colder, and pouring *vinegar upon nitre* puts it into a ferment; so incongruous, is it to sing pleasant songs to one that is of a sorrowful spirit. Some read it in a contrary sense: *As he that puts on a garment in cold weather* warms the body, or as *vinegar upon nitre* dissolves it, so he that *sings songs* of comfort to a person in sorrow refreshes him and dispels his grief.

Verses 21–22

However the scribes and Pharisees had corrupted the law the commandment of loving our brethren, even that of loving our enemies, was not only a new, but also an old commandment, an Old Testament commandment, though our Saviour has given it to us with the new enforcement of his own great example in loving us when we were enemies. We shall mollify them as the refiner melts the metal in the crucible, not only by putting it over the fire, but by heaping coals of fire upon it. The way to turn an enemy into a friend is to act towards him in a friendly manner.

Verse 23

Slanders would not be so readily spoken as they are if they were not readily heard; but good manners would silence the slanderer if he saw that his tales displeased the company. If we cannot otherwise reprove, we may do it by our looks. Who knows but it may silence and drive away a *backbiting tongue*? Many abuse those they speak of only in hopes to curry favour with those they speak to.

Verse 24

This is the same with what he had said, *ch.* xxi. 9. Those are to be pitied that are unequally yoked, especially with such as are brawling and contentious, whether husband or wife; for it is equally true of both.

Verse 25

It is sometimes with impatience that we expect to hear from abroad; our souls thirst after it. How acceptable good news will be when it does come, as refreshing as cold water to one that is thirsty. Heaven is a country afar off; how refreshing is it to hear good news thence, both in the everlasting gospel, which signifies glad tidings, and in the witness of the Spirit with our spirits that we are God's children.

Verse 26

For the righteous to fall into sin in the sight of the wicked *troubles the fountains* by grieving some, and *corrupts the springs* by infecting others and emboldening them to do likewise. For the righteous to be oppressed and trampled upon, by the violence or subtlety of evil men, this is the troubling of the fountains of justice and corrupting the very springs of government, *ch.* xxviii. 12, 28; xxix. 2. For the righteous to be cowardly, to truckle to the wicked, this is a reflection upon religion, and so is like a *troubled fountain* and a *corrupt spring*.

Verse 27

It is true of all the delights of the children of men that they will surfeit, but never satisfy, and they are dangerous to those that allow themselves the liberal use of them. *For men to search their own glory,* to court applause is not their glory, but their shame; everyone will laugh at them for it. Some give another sense of this verse: *To eat much honey is not good,* but to search into glorious and excellent things is a great commendation, it is true glory; we cannot therein offend by excess.

Verse 28

A wise and virtuous man is one that has *rule over his own spirit.* A vicious man, who has not this rule over his own spirit, is *like a city that is broken down and without walls.* He lies exposed to all the temptations of Satan and becomes an easy prey.

CHAPTER 26

Verse 1

Bad men, who have neither wit nor grace, are sometimes preferred by princes, and applauded and cried up by the people. It is very absurd and unbecoming. It is as incongruous *as snow in summer,* as injurious *as rain in harvest,* which hinders the labourers and spoils the fruits of the earth when they are ready to be gathered.

Verse 2

He that is cursed without cause, whether by furious imprecations or solemn anathemas, the curse shall do him no more harm than the bird that flies over his head, than Goliath's curses did to David, 1 Sam. xvii. 43.

Verse 3

Wicked men are compared to *the horse* and *the ass,* so brutish are they, and not to be governed but by force or fear, so low has sin sunk men, so much below themselves. A *horse* unbroken needs *a whip* for correction, and an *ass a bridle* for direction and to check him when he would turn out of the way; so a vicious man, who will not be under the guidance and restraint of religion and reason, ought to be whipped and bridled, to be rebuked severely, and to be restrained from offending any more.

Verses 4–5

The scripture-style seems to contradict itself, but really does not. Wise men have need to be directed how to deal with fools; and they have need of wisdom in dealing with such, to know when to keep silence and when to speak, for there may be a time for both In some cases a wise man will not set his wit to that of a fool so far as to *answer him according to his folly.* "If he boast of himself, do not answer him by boasting of thyself. If he rail and talk passionately, do not thou rail and talk passionately too. If he tell one great lie, do not thou tell another to match it. If he banter, do not answer him in his own language, *lest thou be like him.*" Yet, in other cases, a wise man will use his wisdom for the conviction of a fool, when, by taking notice of what he says, there may be hopes of doing good. "If thou have reason to think that thy silence will be deemed an evidence of weakness, in such a case *answer him,* and let it be an answer *to the man,* beat him at his own weapons, and that will be an answer *to the point.* If he offer anything that looks like an argument, then give him an answer, *lest he be wise in his own conceit* and boast of a victory."

Verses 6–9

Solomon here shows that fools are fit for nothing; they are either sottish men, who will never think and design at all, or vicious men, who will never think and design well. They are not fit to be entrusted with any business, not fit to go on an errand (*v.* 6): *He that does but send a message by the hand of a fool,* of a careless heedless person, will find his message misunderstood, and so many blunders made that he might as well have *cut off his legs,* that is, never have sent him. He will *drink damage;* it will be very much to his prejudice to have employed such a one. People will be apt to judge of the master by his messenger. To *give honour to a fool* is to put a sword in a madman's hand, with which we know not what mischief he may do, even to those that put it into his hand. *A parable in the mouth of fools* ceases to be a parable, and becomes a jest. As *the legs of the lame are not equal,* by reason of which their going is unseemly, so unseemly is it for a fool to pretend to speak apophthegms, and give advice. His good words raise him up, but then his bad life takes him down, and so his *legs are not equal.* He does but do mischief with it to himself and others, as a drunkard does with a thorn, or any other sharp thing which he takes in his hand, with which he tears himself and those about him, because he knows not how to manage it.

Verse 10

Our translation gives this verse a different reading in the text and in the margin; and accordingly it expresses either, 1. The equity of a good God. *The* great God that formed all things at first, and still governs them in infinite wisdom, renders to every man according to his work. He *rewards the fool*, who sinned through ignorance, *with few stripes*; and he *rewards the transgressor*, who sinned presumptuously, *with many stripes*. Or, 2. The iniquity of a bad prince (so the margin reads it): *A great man grieves all, and he hires the fool; he hires also the transgressors*. When a wicked man gets power in his hand, by himself, and by the fools and knaves whom he employs under him, he grieves all who are under him and is vexatious to them.

Verse 11

What an abominable thing sin is! When his conscience is convinced, or he feels smart from his sin, he is sick of it, he seems then to detest it and to be willing to part with it. Sinners, who have been convinced only and not converted, return to sin again, forgetting how sick it made them.

Verse 12

A spiritual disease is self-conceit. Many a one, *wise in his own conceit*, has some little sense, but is proud of it, has such a conceit of his own abilities as makes him opinionative, dogmatical, and censorious. *There is more hope of a fool*, that knows and owns himself to be such, *than of* such a one.

Verse 13

The slothful man dreads *the way, the streets*, the place where work is to be done and a journey to be gone. He dreams of, and pretends to dread—*a lion in the way*. When he is pressed to be diligent, either in his worldly affairs or in religion, this is his excuse: *There is a lion in the way*, some insuperable difficulty or danger which he cannot pretend to grapple with. It is a foolish thing to frighten ourselves from real duties by fancied difficulties, Eccles. xi. 4.

Verse 14

Having seen the slothful man in fear of his work, here we find him in love with his ease; he lies in his bed on one side till he is weary of that, and then turns to the other, but still in his bed, when it is far in the day and work is to be done, as the door is moved, but not removed. The sluggard is one that does not care to get out of his bed, but seems to be hung upon it, *as the door upon the hinges*. He does not care to get forward with his business; in that he stirs to and fro a little, but to no purpose; he is where he was.

Verse 15

The sluggard has now, with much ado, got out of his bed, but he might as well have lain there still. He *hides his hand in his bosom* for fear of cold; next to his warm bed is his warm bosom. Or he pretends that he is lame, as some do that make a trade of begging; something ails his hand; he would have it thought that it is blistered with yesterday's hard work. He himself is the loser by it, for he starves himself: *It grieves him to bring his hand to his mouth*, that is, he cannot find in his heart to feed himself. It is an elegant hyperbole, aggravating his sin, that he cannot endure to take the least pains. Those that are slothful in religion will not be at pains to feed their own souls with the word of God, the bread of life, nor to fetch in promised blessings by prayer.

Verse 16

The sluggard thinks himself *wiser than seven men*, than seven wise men, for they are such as *can render a reason*. He that takes pains in religion can render a good reason for it; he knows that he is working

for a good Master and that *his labour shall not be in vain*. But *the sluggard* thinks himself *wiser than seven* such. It is *the sluggard*, above all men, that is thus self-conceited. His good opinion of himself is the cause of his slothfulness; he will not take pains to get wisdom because he thinks he is wise enough already. His slothfulness is the cause of his good opinion of himself. If he would but take pains to examine himself he would have other thoughts of himself.

Verse 17

That which is here condemned is *meddling with strife that belongs not to us*. If we can be instrumental to make peace between those that are at variance we must do it; but to make ourselves busy in other men's matters, and parties in other men's quarrels, is to court trouble. It is like taking a snarling cur *by the ears*, that will snap at you and bite you.

Verses 18–19

Those that make no scruple of *deceiving their neighbours* are *as madmen that cast firebrands, arrows, and death*. They value themselves as cunning men, but really they are *as madmen*. There is not a greater madness in the world than a wilful sin. The excuse which men commonly make for the mischief they do is that they did it in jest; *Am I not in sport?* But it will prove dangerous playing with fire and jesting with edge-tools. He that sins in jest must repent in earnest, or his sin will be his ruin. Truth is too valuable a thing to be sold for a jest, and so is the reputation of our neighbour.

Verses 20–22

Contention is as a fire; it heats the spirit, burns up all that is good, and puts families and societies into a flame. We must not give ear to *tale-bearers*, for they feed the fire of contention with fuel; nay, they spread it with combustible matter; the tales they carry are fireballs. Those who by insinuating base characters, revealing secrets, and misrepresenting words and actions, are to be banished, and then strife will as surely cease as the fire will go out when it has no fuel. Whisperers and backbiters are incendiaries not to be suffered. They wound love and charity and give a fatal stab to friendship and Christian fellowship. We must not associate with peevish passionate people. These are *contentious men* that *kindle strife*, v. 21. The less we have to do with such the better, for it will be very difficult to avoid quarrelling with those that are quarrelsome.

Verse 23

This may be meant either, 1. Of *a wicked heart* showing itself in *burning lips*, furious words, burning in malice; ill words and ill-will agree as well together as *a potsherd* and the *dross of silver*, which, now that the pot is broken and the dross separated from the silver, are fit to be thrown to the dunghill. Or 2. Of *a wicked heart* disguising itself with *burning lips*, burning with professions of love and friendship. This is *like a potsherd covered with* the scum or *dross of silver*, but a wise man is soon aware of the cheat.

Verses 24–26

The want of sincerity in men's profession of friendship, and the making of it subservient to the most malicious intentions is here spoken of as a common thing (v. 24): *He that hates* his neighbour, and is contriving to do him a mischief, yet *dissembles with his lips*, talks kindly with him, as Cain with Abel, this man *lays up deceit within him*, that is, he keeps in his mind the mischief he intends to do his neighbour. Remember to distrust when a man *speaks fair*; be not too forward to *believe him* unless you know him well, for it is possible there may be *seven abominations in his heart*. Though the fraud may be carried on plausibly awhile, it will be brought to light, *v.* 26. He *whose hatred is covered by deceit* will one time or other be discovered. Love (says one) is the best armour, but the worst cloak and will serve dissemblers as the disguise which Ahab put on and perished in.

Verse 27

What pains men take to do mischief to others, concealing their design with a profession of friendship! It is *digging a pit*, it is *rolling a stone*, hard work, and yet men will stick at it to gratify their passion and revenge. Their violent dealing will return upon their own heads; they shall themselves *fall into the pit they digged*, and the stone they rolled *will return upon them*, Ps. vii. 15, 16; ix. 15, 16.

Verse 28

There are two sorts of lies equally detestable: 1. A slandering lie: *A lying tongue hates those that are afflicted by it;* it afflicts them by calumnies and reproaches because it hates them. The mischief of this is obvious; it afflicts, it hates, and owns it, and everybody sees it. 2. A flattering lie secretly works ruin. It is little suspected, and men betray themselves by being credulous of the compliments that are passed upon them. A wise man therefore will be more afraid of a flatterer that kisses and kills than of a slanderer that proclaims war.

CHAPTER 27

Verse 1

Boast not thyself, no, not *of tomorrow*, much less of many days or years to come. This does not forbid preparing for tomorrow, but presuming upon tomorrow. We must not put off the great work of conversion, that one thing needful, till tomorrow, as if we were sure of it, *but today, while it is called today*, hear God's voice. *We know not what a day may bring forth*, what event may be in the teeming womb of time. God has wisely kept us in the dark concerning future events, that he may train us up in a dependence upon himself and a continued readiness for every event, Acts i. 7.

Verse 2

Let our own works be such as will praise us, even *in the gates*, Phil. iv. 8. When we have done it we must not commend ourselves, for that is an evidence of pride. There may be a just occasion for us to vindicate ourselves, but it does not become us to applaud ourselves.

Verses 3–4

The wrath of a fool, who when he is provoked cares not what he says and does, is more grievous than a great stone or a load of sand. Those who have no command of their passions sink under the load of them. The wrath of a fool lies heavily upon those he is enraged at. It is therefore our wisdom not to give provocation to a fool, but, if he be in a passion, to get out of his way. Rooted malice is much worse. *Wrath is cruel*, and does many a barbarous thing, but secret enmity of another, envy at his prosperity, and a desire of revenge for some affront, are much more mischievous. One may avoid a sudden heat, as David escaped Saul's javelin, but when it grows, as Saul's did, to a settled envy, there is no *standing before it.*

Verses 5–6

It is good for us to be reproved, and told of our faults, by our friends. *Faithful are the reproofs of a*

friend, though for the present they are painful as *wounds*. The physician's care is to cure the patient's disease, not to please his palate. It is dangerous to be caressed and flattered by *an enemy*, whose *kisses are deceitful*. Joab's kiss and Judas's were deceitful. Some read it: *The Lord deliver us from an enemy's kisses, from lying lips, and from a deceitful tongue.*

Verse 7

Solomon here, as often in this book, shows that the poor have in some respects the advantage of the rich; for, 1. They have a better relish of their enjoyments. Hunger is the best sauce. Coarse fare, with a good appetite to it, has a sensible pleasantness in it. Those that fare sumptuously every day nauseate even delicate food. Those that have no more than their necessary food, though it be such as *the full soul* would call *bitter*, to them it *is sweet*; they eat it with pleasure, digest it, and are refreshed by it. They are more thankful: *The hungry* will bless God for bread and water, while those that are *full* think the greatest dainties scarcely worth giving thanks for.

Verse 8

There are many that do not know when they are well off; they love to wander, they are glad of a pretence to go abroad, and do not care for staying long at a place. Those that thus desert the post assigned to them are like *a bird that wanders from her nest*. They are always wavering, like the wandering bird that hops from bough to bough and rests nowhere. When the bird wanders from her nest the eggs and young ones there are neglected. Those that love to be abroad leave their work at home undone.

Verses 9–10

A charge given to be faithful and constant to our friends, our old friends. It is good to have a bosom-friend, whom we can be free with. It is good also to have a special respect to those who have been friends to our family: *"Thy own friend*, especially if he have been *thy father's friend, forsake not*. He is a tried friend; he knows thy affairs; therefore be advised by him." It is a duty we owe to our parents, when they are gone, to love their friends. Solomon's son undid himself by forsaking the counsel of his father's friends. There is a great deal of *sweetness* in conversing with a cordial friend. It is like *ointment and perfume*, which exhilarate the spirits. It *rejoices the heart*; the burden of care is made lighter by unbosoming ourselves to our friend. *The sweetness of* friendship lies not in hearty mirth, but in *hearty counsel*, faithful advice, sincerely given and without flattery, *by counsel of the soul* (so the word is). We are here advised not to go into a *brother's house*, not to expect relief from a kinsman merely for kindred-sake, but rather to apply ourselves to our neighbours, who are at hand, and will be ready to help us at an exigence. It is wisdom to oblige them by being neighbourly.

Verse 11

Children may be a comfort to their parents and may *make their hearts glad*, even when *the evil days come*, and so recompense them for their care, *ch.* xxiii. 15. They may be a credit to them: *"That I may answer him that reproaches me* with having been over-strict and severe in bringing up my children." Those that have been blessed with a religious education should conduct themselves so as to silence those who say, *A young saint, an old devil;* and to prove the contrary, *A young saint, an old angel.*

Verse 12

Evil may be foreseen. Where there is temptation, it is easy to foresee that if we thrust ourselves into it there will be sin, and there will follow the evil of punishment; and, commonly, God warns before he wounds. The *prudent man, foreseeing the evil*, forecasts accordingly, *and hides himself, but the simple* is either so dull that he does not foresee it or so wilful and slothful that he will take no care to avoid it.

Verse 13

Those are hastening to poverty that have so little consideration as to be bound for everybody that will ask them and those that are given to women. Such as these will take up money as far as ever their credit will go, but they will certainly cheat their creditors at last, nay, they are cheating them all along.

Verse 14

It is our duty to give everyone his due praise, to applaud those who excel in knowledge, virtue, and usefulness, and to acknowledge the kindnesses we have received with thankfulness; but not to do this *with a loud voice, rising early in the morning*, to be always harping on this string, in all companies, even to our friend's face, to magnify the merits of our friend above measure. It is a greater folly to be fond of being ourselves extravagantly praised. Modest praises invite such as are present to add to the commendation, but immoderate praises tempt them to detract rather and to censure one that they hear over-commended. Over-praising a man makes him the object of envy. And the greatest danger of all is that it is a temptation to pride, 2. Cor. xii. 6.

Verses 15–16

Here, as before, Solomon laments the case of him that has a peevish passionate wife. It is a grievance that there is no avoiding, for it is like *a continual dropping in a very rainy day*. The contentions of a neighbour may be like a sharp shower, troublesome for the time, yet, while it lasts, one may take shelter; but *the contentions of a wife* are like a constant soaking rain, for which there is no remedy but patience. See *ch.* xix. 13. A wise man would hide it if he could, but he cannot, any more than he can conceal the noise of the wind when it blows or the smell of a strong perfume. Those that are froward and brawling will proclaim their own shame, even when their friends, in kindness to them, would cover it.

Verse 17

Wise and profitable discourse sharpens men's wits; and those that have ever so much knowledge may by conference have something added to them. Good men's graces are sharpened by converse with those that are good, and bad men's lusts and passions are sharpened by converse with those that are bad, as iron is sharpened by its like, especially by the file. Men are filed, made smooth, and bright, and fit for business (who were rough, and dull, and inactive), by conversation.

Verse 18

Though the calling be laborious and despicable, yet those who keep to it will find there is something to be got by it. Let not a poor gardener, who *keeps the fig-tree*, be discouraged; though it require constant care and attendance to nurse up fig-trees, and, when they have grown to maturity, to keep them in good order, and gather the figs in their season, yet he shall be paid for his pains: He *shall eat the fruit* of it, 1 Cor. ix. 7. A poor servant if he be diligent in *waiting on his master*, if *he keep his master* (so the word is), if he do all he can that his estate be not wasted, such a one *shall be honoured*, be preferred and rewarded. God is a Master who has engaged to put an honour on those that serve him faithfully, John xii. 26.

Verse 19

As the water is a looking-glass in which we may see our faces by reflection, so there are mirrors by which the *heart of a man* is discovered to *a man*, that is, to himself. Let a man examine his own conscience, his thoughts, affections, and intentions. Let him behold his *natural face in the glass* of the divine law (Jas. i. 23), and he may discern what kind of man he is and what is his true character, which it will be of great use to every man rightly to know. As there is a similitude between the face of a man and the reflection of it in the water, so there is between one man's heart and another's; for God has fashioned men's hearts alike.

Verse 20

Two things are insatiable, and near of kin—death and sin. Men labour for that which surfeits, but satisfies not. Those whose eyes are ever towards the Lord in him are satisfied, and shall for ever be so.

Verse 21

Silver and gold are tried by putting them into the furnace and fining-pot; so is a man tried by praising him. If a man be made, by the applause that is given him, proud and scornful,—if he take the glory to himself which he should transmit to God, thereby it will appear that he is a vain foolish man, and has nothing in him truly praise-worthy. If, on the contrary, a man is made by his praise more thankful to God, more respectful to his friends, more diligent to do good to others, by this it will appear that he is a wise and good man, 2 Cor. vi. 8.

Verse 22

Solomon had said (*ch.* xxii. 15), *The foolishness* which *is bound in the heart of a child may be driven out by the rod of correction*, for then the mind is to be moulded, the vicious habits not having taken root. Here he shows that, if it be not done then, it will be next to impossible to do it afterwards. Some are so bad that rough and severe methods must be used with them, after gentle means have been tried in vain; they must be *brayed in a mortar*. God will take this way with them by his judgments; the magistrates must take this way with them by the rigour of the law. Force must be used with those that will not be ruled by reason, and love, and their own interest.

Verses 23–27

A command given us to be diligent in our callings is directed to husbandmen and shepherds, but it is to be extended to all other lawful callings. We ought not to live in idleness. We ought to understand our business, and not meddle with that which we do not understand. We should, with our own eyes, inspect the *state of our flocks*; it is the master's eye that makes them fat. *Riches are not for ever*. "*Look well to thy flocks and herds*, thy estate in the country and the stock upon that, for these are staple commodities, which, in a succession, will be for ever, whereas riches in trade and merchandise will not be so; the *crown* itself may perhaps not be so sure to thy family as thy flocks and herds." *The hay appears*. In taking care of the *flocks and herds*, "There needs no great labour, no ploughing or sowing; the food for them is the spontaneous product of the ground; thou hast nothing to do but to turn them into it in the summer, *when the grass shows itself*, and to *gather the herbs of the mountains* for them against winter. God has done his part; thou art ungrateful to him, and unjustly refusest to serve his providence, if thou dost not do thine." Good husbandry is profitable in a family: "Keep thy sheep, and thy sheep will help to keep thee; thou shalt have food for thy children and servants, *goats' milk enough* (*v.* 27); and *enough is as good as a feast.* Thou shalt have raiment likewise: the *lambs' wool shall be for thy clothing.* Thou shalt have money to pay thy rent; the goats thou shalt have to sell shall be *the price of thy field*"; nay, as some understand it, "*Thou shalt become a purchaser*, and buy land to leave to thy children," *v.* 26. Plain food and plain clothing, if they be but competent, are all we should aim at. "Reckon thyself well done to if thou be clothed with home-spun cloth, with the fleece of thy own lambs, and fed with goats' milk; let that serve for thy food which serves for the *food of thy household and the maintenance of thy maidens.* Be not desirous of dainties, *far-fetched and dear-bought.*"

CHAPTER 28

Verse 1

Guilt in the conscience makes men a terror to themselves, so that they are ready *to flee when none pursues*; like one that absconds for debt, who thinks everyone he meets a bailiff. Sin makes men cowards. *The righteous are bold as a lion*, as a young lion; in the greatest dangers they have a God of almighty power to trust to. *Therefore will not we fear though the earth be removed.*

Verse 2

National sins bring national disorders. *For the transgression of a land*, and a general defection from God and religion to idolatry, profaneness, or immorality, *many are the princes thereof*, many at the same time pretending to the sovereignty, by which the people are crumbled into parties and factions, one cutting off another, or soon cut off by the hand of God or of a foreign enemy. The government sometimes suffers for the sins of the people. Wisdom will prevent or redress these grievances: *By a man* or by a people, *of understanding*, that come again to their right mind, things are kept in a good order. We cannot imagine what a great deal of service one wise man may do to a nation in a critical juncture.

Verse 3

Those who know by experience the miseries of poverty should be compassionate to those who suffer the like, but they are inexcusably barbarous if they be injurious to them. How imperious those commonly are who, being indigent and necessitous, get into power. If a prince promote a poor man, he forgets that ever he was poor, and none shall be so oppressive to the poor as he, nor squeeze them so cruelly. He *is like a sweeping rain*, which washes away the corn in the ground, and lays and beats out that which has grown, so that it *leaves no food.*

Verse 4

Those that *praise the wicked* make it to appear that they do themselves *forsake the law*, and go contrary to it, for that condemns the wicked. Wicked people will speak well of one another, and so strengthen one another's hands in their wicked ways, hoping thereby to silence the clamours of their own consciences and to serve the interests of the devil's kingdom. Those that do indeed make conscience of the law of God themselves will, in their places, vigorously oppose sin.

Verse 5

As the prevalency of men's lusts is owing to the darkness of their understandings, so the darkness of their understandings is very much owing to the dominion of their lusts. *Men understand not judgment*, because they are *evil men.* As men's *seeking the Lord* is a good sign that they do understand much, so it is

a good means of their understanding more, even of their understanding all things needful for them. If a man *do his will*, he shall *know his doctrine*, John vii. 17.

Verse 6

It is maintained as a paradox to a blind world that an honest, godly, poor man, is better than a wicked, ungodly, rich man, has a better character, is in a better condition, has more comfort in himself, is a greater blessing to the world, and is worthy of much more honour and respect. It is not only certain that his case will be better at death, but it is better in life.

Verse 7

Religion is true wisdom, and it makes men wise in every relation. Wickedness is not only a reproach to the sinner himself, but to all that are akin to him.

Verse 8

That which is ill-got, though it may increase much, will not last long. A man may perhaps raise a great estate, in a little time, by usury and fraud, but it will not continue; he gathers it for himself, but another man's shall be raised out of the ruins of it. Sometimes God in his providence so orders it that that which one got unjustly another uses charitably.

Verse 9

God speaks to us by his law, and expects we should hear him and heed him; *we* speak to him by prayer, to which we wait for an answer of peace.

Verse 10

The seducers, who attempt to draw good people into sin and mischief, shall not gain their point; they shall *fall themselves into their own pit*; and having been not only sinners, but tempters, their condemnation will be so much the greater, Matt. xxiii. 14, 15. The sincere shall not only be preserved from the evil way which the wicked would decoy them into, but they shall have the graces and comforts of God's Spirit.

Verse 11

Those that are rich are apt to think themselves wise, because, whatever else they are ignorant of, they know how to get and save; and expect that all they say should be regarded as an oracle and a law. A *poor man*, who has taken pains to get wisdom, having no other way (as the rich man has) to get a reputation, *searches him out*, and makes it to appear that he is not such a scholar, nor such a politician, as he is taken to be.

Verse 12

The comfort of the people of God is the honour of the nation in which they live. There is a *great glory* dwelling in the land when *the righteous do rejoice*, when they have their liberty, the free exercise of their religion, and are not persecuted. The advancement of the wicked is the eclipsing of the beauty of a nation: *When the wicked rise* and get head they make head against all that is sacred, and then *a man is hidden*, a good man is thrust into obscurity.

Verse 13

The folly of indulging sin, of palliating and excusing it, denying or extenuating it, diminishing it, dissembling it, or throwing the blame of it upon others: *He that* thus *covers his sins shall not prosper.* David owns himself to have been in a constant agitation while he *covered his sins*, Ps. xxxii. 3, 4. While the patient conceals his distemper he cannot expect a cure. *He that confesses* his guilt to God, and is careful not to return to sin again, shall *find mercy* with

God. His conscience shall be eased and his ruin prevented. See 1 John i. 9; Jer. iii. 12, 13.

Verse 14

Most people think that those are happy who never fear; but there is a fear which is so far from having torment in it that it has in it the greatest satisfaction. Happy is the man who always keeps up in his mind a holy awe and reverence of God, who is always afraid of incurring his displeasure, who keeps conscience tender and has a dread of the appearance of evil. *He that hardens his heart*, that mocks at fear, and sets God and his judgments at defiance, his presumption will be his ruin.

Verse 15

It is written indeed, *Thou shalt not speak evil of the ruler of thy people;* but if he be a wicked ruler, that oppresses the people, this scripture calls him *a roaring lion and a ranging bear.* He is brutish, barbarous, and blood-thirsty, to be put among the beasts of prey.

Verse 16

A ruler that is covetous will neither do justly nor love mercy, but the people under him shall be bought and sold. *He that hates covetousness shall prolong* his government and peace, shall be happy in the affections of his people and the blessing of his God.

Verse 17

This agrees with that ancient law, *Whoso sheddeth man's blood, by man shall his blood be shed* (Gen. ix. 6). He that has committed murder, though he flees for his life, shall be continually haunted with terrors, shall himself *flee to the pit*, betray himself, and torment himself like Cain. Those that acquit the murderer, or do anything to help him off, come in sharers in the guilt of blood.

Verse 18

Those that are honest are always safe. He that acts with sincerity, that speaks as he thinks, has a single eye to the glory of God and the good of his brethren, *shall be saved* hereafter. They shall be safe now. Integrity and unrightness will give them a holy security in the worst of times. They may be injured, but they cannot be hurt. Those that are false and dishonest are never safe.

Verse 19

He that *tills his land*, and tends his shop, and minds his business, whatever it is, he *shall have plenty of bread*, of that which is necessary for himself and his family and with which he may be charitable to the poor; he shall *eat the labour of his hands.* Those that are idle, and careless, and company-keepers, though they indulge themselves in living (as they think) easily and pleasantly, they take the way to live miserably.

Verse 20

We are directed in the true way to be happy, and that is to be holy and honest. He that is *faithful to* God and man shall be blessed of the Lord. Usefulness shall be the reward of faithfulness, and it is a good reward. We are cautioned against a false way to happiness, and that is, right or wrong, raising an estate suddenly. He shall not be accounted innocent by his neighbours, but shall have their ill will and ill word. He does not say that he *cannot be innocent*, but there is probability that he will not prove so: *He that hasteth with his feet sinneth*, stumbleth, falleth.

Verse 21

It is a fundamental error in the administration of justice to consider the parties concerned more than the merits of the cause, so as to favour one because he is a gentleman, my countryman, my own acquaintance, or is of my party and persuasion, and to bear hard on the other party because he is a stranger, a poor man, or has been my rival, or has voted against me. Those that are partial will be paltry. Those that have once broken through the bonds of equity, though, at first, it must be some great bribe, when they have debauched their consciences, they will, at length, be so sordid that *for a piece of bread* they will give judgment against their consciences.

Verse 22

Solomon shows the sin and folly of those that will *be rich;* they will be so with all speed. They *have an evil eye*, that is, they are always grieving at those that have more than they. *Poverty shall come upon* them.

Verse 23

Flatterers may please those for a time who, upon second thoughts, will detest and despise them. Reprovers may displease those at first who yet afterwards, when the passion is over and the bitter physic begins to work well, will love and respect them. He that cries out against his surgeon for hurting him when he is searching his wound will yet pay him well, and thank him too, when he has cured it.

Verse 24

As Christ shows the wickedness of those children who think it is no duty to maintain their parents (Matt. xv. 5), so Solomon here shows the wickedness of those who think it is no sin to rob their parents, either by force or by wheedling them or threatening them, or by running into debt and leaving them to pay it. He that does it *is the companion of a destroyer*, no better than a robber on the highway.

Verse 25

Those make themselves lean, and continually unquiet, that are haughty and quarrelsome, for they are opposed to those that *shall be made fat.* Those make themselves fat, and always easy, that live in a continual dependence upon God and his grace: *He who puts his trust in the Lord*, who, instead of struggling for himself, commits his cause to God, *shall be made fat.*

Verse 26

A fool *trusts to his own heart*, to his own wisdom, his own strength, his own merit and righteousness, and the good opinion he has of himself. He that *walks wisely*, that trusts not to his own heart, but is humble and self-diffident, and goes on in the strength of the Lord God, *he shall be delivered.*

Verse 27

He that gives to the poor shall himself be never the poorer for so doing; he *shall not lack. He that hides his eyes*, that he may not see the miseries of the poor lest his eye should affect his heart and extort some relief from him, he *shall have many a curse*, both from God and man.

Verse 28

This is to the same purport with what we had, *v.* 12. When power is put into the hands of the *wicked, men hide themselves;* wise men retire into privacy, and decline public business, not caring to be employed under them; rich men get out of the way, for fear of being squeezed for what they have; and good men abscond, despairing to do good and fearing to be ill-treated. When bad men are disgraced, and their power taken from them, then *the righteous increase;* for, *when they perish*, good men will be put in their room.

Chapter 29

Verse 1

The obstinacy of many wicked people is to be greatly lamented. They are *often reproved* by parents and friends, by magistrates and ministers, but they *harden their necks.* Perhaps they fling away, and will not so much as give the reproof a patient hearing. Those that go on in sin, in spite of admonition, *shall be destroyed;* if the rods answer not the end, expect the axes. They *shall be destroyed, and no healing,* so the word is.

Verse 2

This is what was said before, *ch.* xxviii. 12, 28. 1. *The people* will have cause to *rejoice* or *mourn* according as their rulers are *righteous* or *wicked;* for, if *the righteous* be in *authority,* sin will be punished and restrained; *but,* if *the wicked* get power, religion and religious people will be persecuted, and so the ends of government will be perverted. *The people* will actually *rejoice* or *mourn* according as their rulers are *righteous* or *wicked.*

Verse 3

A virtuous young man *loves wisdom,* he is *a philosopher (a lover of wisdom),* for religion is the best philosophy; he avoids bad company, and especially the company of lewd women. A vicious young man hates *wisdom; he keeps company with* scandalous women, who will be his ruin, both in soul and body.

Verse 4

A prince should *establish the land,* maintain its laws, settle the minds of his subjects, secure their liberties, and properties from hostilities and for posterity. This he must do *by judgment* and by the steady administration of justice, without respect of persons. *A man of oblations* (so it is in the margin) *overthrows the land;* a man that is either sacrilegious or superstitious, or a man that will, for a bribe, connive at the most guilty, and, in hope of one, persecute the innocent—such governors as these will ruin a country.

Verse 5

Those may be said to *flatter their neighbours* who applaud good in them, which really either is not or is not such as they represent it. These *spread a net for their* neighbours' feet. It has an ill effect on those who are flattered; it puffs them up with pride, and so proves a net that entangles them in sin. He that flatters others, in expectation that they will return his compliments and flatter him, does but make himself ridiculous and odious even to those he flatters.

Verse 6

One sin is a temptation to another, and there are troubles which, as *a snare,* come suddenly upon evil men in the midst of their transgressions. The snare that is *in the transgression of evil men* spoils all their mirth, *but righteous* men are kept from those snares, or delivered out of them; they walk at liberty, and therefore they *sing and rejoice.*

Verse 7

A *righteous* judge *considers the cause of the poor.* It is every man's duty to consider the poor (Ps. xli. 1), but the judgment of the poor is to be considered by those that sit in judgment. Sense of justice must make both judge and advocate as solicitous and industrious in the poor man's cause as if they hoped for the greatest advantage. A *wicked* man, because it is a poor man's cause, which there is nothing to be got by, *regards not to know it,* for he cares not which way it goes, right or wrong. See Job xxix. 16.

Verse 8

Scornful men employed in the business of the state do things with precipitation, because they scorn to deliberate. They scorn to be hampered by laws and constitutions; break their faith, because they scorn to be bound by their word. Thus they *bring a city into a snare* by their ill conduct, or (as the margin reads it) they *set a city on fire;* they sow discord among the citizens and run them into confusion. *Wise men* by promoting religion, which is true wisdom, *turn away the wrath* of God, and by prudent counsels, reconcile contending parties.

Verse 9

If a wise man contend with a wise man, he may hope to be understood, and, as far as he has reason and equity on his side, to carry his point and make it issue amicably; but, if he *contend with a foolish man, there is no rest;* he will see no end of it. Whether the foolish man take angrily or scornfully what is said to him, whether he rail at it or mock at it, there will be *no rest.* The wisest man must expect to be either scolded or ridiculed if he *contend with a fool.* Whether the wise man himself *rage or laugh,* whether he take the serious or the jocular way of dealing with the fool, no good is done.

Verse 10

Bad men hate their best friends: *The bloodthirsty,* all the seed of the old serpent, who *was a murderer from the beginning, hate the upright.* Bloody men do especially *hate upright* magistrates, who would restrain and reform them. *The just,* whom the bloody men hate, *seek their soul,* pray for their conversion, and would gladly do anything for their salvation. This Christ taught us. *Father, forgive them.*

Verse 11

He is *a fool* who *utters all his mind,* who, whatever is started in discourse, quickly shoots his bolt,— who, when he is provoked, will say anything that comes uppermost, whoever is reflected upon by it. *A wise man* will not *utter all his mind* at once, but will take time for a second thought, or reserve the present thought for a fitter time. He will not deliver himself in a continued speech, or starched discourse, but with pauses, that he may hear what is to be objected and answer it.

Verse 12

Lies will be told to those that will hearken to them; but the receiver, in this case, is as bad as the thief. Those that do so will have *all their servants wicked,* for they will have lies told of them; and they will be wicked, for they will tell lies to them.

Verse 13

This shows how wisely the great God serves the designs of his providence by persons of very different tempers. Some are *poor,* and honest, and laborious; others are rich, slothful, and *deceitful.* They *meet together* in the business of this world, and *the Lord enlightens both their eyes.* To some of both sorts he gives his grace. He enlightens the eyes of the poor by giving them patience, and of the deceitful by giving them repentance, as Zaccheus. *The poor and the deceitful* we are ready to look upon as blemishes of Providence, but God makes even them to display the beauty of Providence.

Verse 14

The rich will look to themselves, but *the poor* and needy the prince must *defend* (Ps. lxxxii. 3) and plead for, Prov. xxxi. 9. Those magistrates that do their duty *shall be established for ever.*

Verse 15

Parents must not only tell their children what is good and evil, but they must chide them, and correct them too, if need be. If a *reproof* will serve without *the rod*, it is well, but *the rod* must never be used without a rational and grave *reproof*; and then it will *give wisdom. A child* that is not restrained or reproved, but is *left to himself*, as Adonijah was, may do well if he will, but, if he take to ill courses, he proves a disgrace to his family, and *brings his mother to shame*.

Verse 16

The more sinners there are the more sin there is. In the old world, when *men began to multiply*, they began to degenerate and corrupt themselves and one another. The more sin there is the nearer is the ruin threatened. Let not *the righteous* have their faith and hope shocked by the increase of sin and sinners. Let them not say that *God has forsaken the earth*, but wait with patience; the transgressors shall fall into disgrace and destruction.

Verse 17

It is a pleasure to parents, which none know but those that are blessed with it, to see the happy fruit of the good education they have given their children, and to have a prospect of their well-doing for both worlds. Children must be trained and not suffered to do what they will and to go without rebuke when they do amiss.

Verse 18

Where there is no vision, no prophet to expound the law, no priest or Levite to teach the good knowledge of the Lord, no means of grace, the word of the Lord is scarce, there is *no open vision* (1 Sam. iii. 1), where it is so *the people perish*; the word has many significations. 1. *The people are made naked*, stripped of their ornaments and so exposed to shame, stripped of their armour and so exposed to danger. How bare does a place look without Bibles and ministers, and what an easy prey it is to the enemy of souls! 2. *The people rebel*, not only against God, but against their prince; good preaching would make people good subjects, but, for want of it, they are turbulent and factious. 3. *The people are idle*, or *they play*, as the scholars are apt to do when the master is absent. 4. *They are scattered as sheep having no shepherd*, for want of the masters of assemblies to call them and keep them together, Mark vi. 34. 5. *They perish;* they are *destroyed for lack of knowledge*, Hos. iv. 6.

Verse 19

Unprofitable, slothful, wicked servants serve not from conscience, or love, but purely from fear. No rational words will work upon them; they *will not be corrected* and reformed by fair means, no, nor by foul *words*. No rational words will be got from them. They are dogged and sullen; and, *though they understand* the questions you ask them, they *will not* give you an *answer*.

Verse 20

Seest thou a man that is hasty in his matters, that is of a light desultory wit, gallops over a book, but takes no time to digest it? *There is more hope of* making a scholar and a wise man of one that is dull and heavy, and slow in his studies, than of one that has such a mercurial genius and cannot fix. *Seest thou a man that is* forward to speak to every matter that is started, as if he were an oracle? *There is more hope of a* modest *fool*, who is sensible of his folly, than of such a self-conceited one.

Verse 21

It is an ungrateful thing in a servant to behave insolently because he has been used tenderly. The humble prodigal thinks himself unworthy *to be called a son*, and is content to be a servant; the pampered slave thinks himself too good to be called *a servant*, and will be *a son at the length*, will be on a par with his master, and perhaps pretend to the inheritance.

Verse 22

An angry, passionate, furious disposition makes men provoking to one another. It makes men provoking to God. Undue anger is a sin which is the cause of many sins.

Verse 23

Those that think to gain respect by lifting up themselves, talking big, appearing fine, and applauding themselves, will expose themselves to contempt, lose their reputation, and provoke God by humbling providences to bring them down and lay them *low*. Those who *humble themselves shall be exalted*, and shall be established in their dignity.

Verse 24

Those who are drawn away by the enticement of sinners incur guilt: *He* does so that goes *partner with* such as rob and defraud. The receiver is as bad as the thief; and, being drawn in to join with him in the commission of the sin, he cannot escape joining with him in the concealment of it, though it be with the most horrid perjuries and execrations. They even *hate their own souls*, for they wilfully do that which will be the inevitable destruction of them.

Verse 25

We are cautioned not to dread the power of man. Slavish fear *brings a snake*, that is, exposes men to many insults, or rather to many temptations. Abraham, for *fear of man*, denied his wife, and Peter his Master, and many a one his God and religion. *Whoso puts his trust in the Lord shall be* set on high, above the power of man and above the fear of that power.

Verse 26

Men, to advance and enrich themselves, *seek the ruler's favour*. Solomon was himself a *ruler*, and knew with what sedulity men made their application to him, some on one errand, others on another, but all for his *favour*. Haman had *the ruler's favour*, and yet it availed him nothing. Look up to God, and seek the favour of the Ruler of rulers; for *every man's judgment proceeds from the Lord*. It is not with us as the ruler pleases, it is as God pleases.

Verse 27

This expresses not only the innate contrariety that there is between virtue and vice, but the old enmity that has always been between the seed of the woman and the seed of the serpent, Gen. iii. 15. All that are sanctified have a rooted antipathy to wickedness and wicked people. They have a good will to the souls of all, but they hate the ways and practices of those that are impious. Thus *an unjust* man makes himself odious *to the just*, and it is one part of his present shame and punishment that good men cannot endure him. All that are unsanctified have a like rooted antipathy to godliness and godly people.

CHAPTER 30

This and the following chapter are an appendix to Solomon's proverbs; but they are both expressly called prophecies, by which it appears that the penmen were divinely inspired. This chapter was penned by one that bears the name of "Agur Ben Jakeh". We have here, I. His confession of faith, ver. 1–6. II. His prayer, ver. 7–9. III. A caution against wronging servants, ver. 10. IV. Four wicked generations, ver. 11–14. V. Four things insatiable (ver. 15, 16), to which is added fair warning to undutiful children, ver. 17. VI. Four things unsearchable, ver. 18–20. VII. Four things intolerable, ver. 21–23. VIII. Four things little and wise, ver. 24–28. IX. Four things stately, ver. 29 to the end.

Verses 1-6

Agur was a *collector* (so it signifies), a gatherer, one that collected the wise sayings and observations of others (v. 3), "*I have not learned wisdom* myself, but have been a scribe, or amanuensis, to other wise and learned men." *Ithiel* and *Ucal* are mentioned: 1. As the names of his pupils, whom he instructed. Probably they wrote what he dictated, as Baruch wrote from the mouth of Jeremiah. Or, 2. As the subject of his discourse. *Ithiel* signifies *God with me*, the application of *Immanuel, God with us. Ucal* signifies *the Mighty One*, for it is upon one that is mighty that help is laid for us.

Three things the prophet here aims at:—

I. To abase himself. Before he makes confession of his faith he makes confession of his folly and the weakness and deficiency of reason, which make it so necessary that we be guided and governed by faith. Agur, when he was applied to by others as wiser than most, acknowledged himself more foolish than any. Whatever high opinion others may have of us, it becomes us to have low thoughts of ourselves. He speaks of himself as wanting a revelation to guide him in the ways of truth and wisdom. The natural man, the natural powers, perceive not, nay, they *receive not, the things of the Spirit of God.*

II. To advance Jesus Christ, and the Father in him (v. 4): *Who hath ascended up into heaven*, &c. Some understand this of God and of his works, which are both incomparable and unsearchable. Others refer it to Christ, to Ithiel and Ucal, the Son of God, for it is the Son's name, as well as the Father's, that is here enquired after, and a challenge given to any to vie with him. What is *his Son's name*, by whom he does all these things? The Old Testament saints expected the Messiah to be the *Son of the Blessed*, and he is here spoken of as a person distinct from the Father, but his name as yet secret.

III. To assure us of the truth of the word of God, and to recommend it to us, v. 5, 6. Agur's pupils expect to be instructed by him in the things of God. "Alas!" says he, "I cannot undertake to instruct you; go to the word of God. *Every word of God is pure;* there is not the least mixture of falsehood and corruption in it." God in his word, God in his promise, is *a shield*, a sure protection, to all those that *put their trust in him.* It is sufficient, and therefore we must not add to it (v. 6). We must be content with what God has thought fit to make known to us of his mind, and not covet to be *wise above what is written.*

Verses 7-9

After Agur's confession and creed, here follows his litany,

I. The preface to his prayer: *Two things have I required* (that is, *requested*) of thee, O God! Before we go to pray it is good to consider what we need, and what the things are which we have to ask of God.

II. The prayer itself. The *two things* he requires are grace sufficient and food convenient. 1. Grace sufficient for his soul: *Remove from me vanity and lies.* Some understand it as a prayer for the pardon of sin, for, when God forgives sin, he removes it, he takes it away. 2. Food convenient for his body. "*Feed me with the bread of my allowance*, such bread as thou thinkest fit to allow me." Our Saviour seems to refer to this when he teaches us to pray, *Give us this day our daily bread.* He prays against the extremes of abundance and want: *Give me neither poverty nor riches.* He hereby intends to express the value which wise and good men have for a middle state of life, and, with submission to the will of God, desires that that might be his state, neither great honour nor great contempt. He gives a pious reason for his prayer, v. 9. "*Lest I be rich* and sin, or *poor* and sin." Sin is that which a good man is afraid of in every condition and under every event. Prosperity makes people proud and forgetful of God, as if they had no need of him. A good man also dreads the temptations of a poor condition: *Lest I be poor and steal.* Poverty is a strong temptation to dishonesty. Agur dreads this lest he should dishonour God by it.

Verses 10-14

I. A caution not to abuse other people's servants any more than our own, nor to make mischief between them and their masters. *Hurt not a servant with thy tongue* (so the margin reads it); for it argues a sordid disposition to smite anybody secretly with the scourge of the tongue, especially a servant, who is not a match for us.

II. An account of some wicked generations of men, that are justly abominable to all that are virtuous and good. 1. Such as are abusive to their parents. *There is a generation* of such; young men of that black character commonly herd together, and irritate one another against their parents, because they cannot endure the yoke. 2. Such as are conceited of themselves, and yet *are not cleansed from their filthiness*, the filthiness of their hearts, which they pretend to be the best part of them. 3. Such as are haughty and scornful to those about them, v. 13. There is a generation of such, on whom he that *resists the proud* will pour contempt. 4. Such as are cruel to the poor and barbarous to all that lie at their mercy (v. 14); their teeth are iron and steel, *swords and knives*, instruments of cruelty, with which they *devour the poor* with the greatest pleasure imaginable, and as greedily as hungry men cut their meat and eat it.

Verses 15-17

He had spoken before of those that devoured the poor (v. 14), now here he speaks of their insatiableness in doing this. Now those are *two daughters* of the *horse-leech*, its genuine offspring, that still cry, "*Give, give*, give more blood, give more money"; for the bloody are still blood-thirsty; being drunk with blood, they add thirst to their drunkenness, and will seek it yet again.

I. He specifies four other things which are insatiable, 1. The grave, into which multitudes fall, and yet still more will fall, and it swallows them all up, and returns none. 2. The *barren womb*, which is impatient of its affliction in being barren, and cries, as Rachel did, *Give me children*. 3. The *parched ground* in time of drought (especially in those hot countries), which still soaks in the rain that comes in abundance upon it and in a little time wants more. 4. The *fire*, which, when it has consumed abundance of fuel, yet still devours all the combustible matter that is thrown into it. So insatiable are the corrupt desires of sinners, and so little satisfaction have they even in the gratification of them.

II. He adds a terrible threatening to disobedient children (v. 17). Those that dishonour their parents shall be hanged in chains, as it were, for the birds of prey to pick out their eyes, those eyes with which they looked so scornfully on their good parents. The dead bodies of malefactors were not to hang all night, but before night the ravens would have picked out their eyes.

Verses 18-23

I. An account of four things that are *too wonderful* to be fully known,

1. The first three are natural things, and are only designed as comparisons for the illustration of the last. We cannot trace *An eagle in the air*. Which way she has flown cannot be discovered, nor can we account for the wonderful swiftness of her flight. *A serpent upon a rock*. The way of a serpent in the

sand we may find by the track, but not of a serpent upon the hard rock. *A ship in the midst of the sea* leaves no mark behind it. The kingdom of nature is full of wonders *past finding out.*

2. The fourth is a mystery of iniquity, more accountable than any of these; it belongs to the depths of Satan. The cursed arts which a vile adulterer has to debauch a maid, and to persuade her to yield to his wicked and abominable lust. The cursed arts which a vile adulteress has to conceal her wickedness; so close are her intrigues that it is as impossible to discover her as to track an *eagle in the air.* She eats the forbidden fruit, and then *wipes her mouth,* that it may not betray itself, and with a bold and impudent face says, *I have done no wickedness.* To her own conscience she denies the fault. Thus multitudes ruin their souls by calling evil good and out-facing their convictions with a self-justification.

II. An account of four things that are intolerable, that is, four sorts of persons that are very troublesome. 1. *A servant* when he is entrusted with power is most insolent and imperious. 2. *A fool,* a silly, rude, boisterous, vicious man, when he has grown rich, and is partaking of the pleasures of the table, will disturb all the company with his extravagant talk. 3. An ill-natured, cross-grained, *woman,* when she gets a husband, having made herself odious by her pride and sourness, so that one would not have thought anybody would ever love her, yet, if at last she be married, that honourable estate makes her more intolerably scornful and spiteful than ever. A gracious woman, when she is married, will be yet more obliging. 4. An old maid-servant that has prevailed with her mistress to leave her what she has will be intolerably proud and malicious, and think herself wronged if anything be left from her. Let those therefore whom Providence has advanced to honour from mean beginnings carefully watch against pride and haughtiness.

Verses 24–28

I. Agur, having specified four things that seem great and yet are really contemptible, here specifies four things that are little and yet are very admirable, great in miniature. They teach us, 1. Not to admire bodily bulk, or beauty, or strength, but to judge of men by their wisdom and conduct, their industry and application to business. 2. To admire the wisdom and power of the Creator in the smallest and most despicable animals, in an ant as much as in an elephant. 3. To blame ourselves who do not act so much for our own true interest as the meanest creatures do for theirs. 4. Not to despise the weak things of the world; there are those that are *little upon the earth,* and yet *are exceedingly wise.* Margin, *They are wise, made wise* by the special instinct of nature. All that are wise to salvation are made wise by the grace of God.

II. Those he specifies are, 1. The *ants,* minute and very weak, and yet are very industrious in gathering proper food in the summer, the proper time. This is so great a piece of wisdom that we may learn of them to be wise for futurity, *ch.* vi. 6. 2. The *conies,* the Arabian mice, weak creatures, and very timorous, have so much wisdom as to *make their houses in the rocks,* where they are well guarded. Sense of our own indigence and weakness should drive us to him that is a *rock higher than we* for shelter and support. 3. The *locusts* are little also, and *have no king,* as the bees have, but *they go forth all of them by bands,* like an army in battle-array (Joel ii. 25). *They go forth all of them gathered together* (so the margin); sense of weakness should engage us to keep together, that we may strengthen the hands of one another. 4. The *spider.* Spiders are very ingenious in weaving their webs with a fineness and exactness such as no

art can pretend to come near: They *take hold with their hands,* and spin a fine thread out of their own bowels, with a great art; and they are not only in poor men's cottages, but in *kings' palaces.*

Verses 29–33

I. An enumeration of four things which are majestic and stately in their going: 1. *A lion,* the king of beasts, because *strongest among beasts.* The lion *turns not away,* nor alters his pace, for fear of any pursuers. 2. *A greyhound* that is girt in the loins and fit for running; or (as the margin reads it) *a horse.* 3. *A he-goat,* the comeliness of whose going is when he goes first and leads the flock. It is the comeliness of a Christian's going to go first in a good work and to lead others in the right way. 4. *A king,* who, when he appears in his majesty, is looked upon with reverence and awe, and *there is no rising up against* him. And, if *there is no rising up* against an earthly prince, *woe to him* then *that strives with his Maker.* It is intended that we should learn courage and fortitude in all virtuous actions from the *lion* and *not to turn away for any* difficulty we meet with; from the *greyhound* we may learn quickness and despatch, from the *he-goat* the care of our family and those under our charge, and from *a king* to have our children in subjection with all gravity, and from them all to *go well,* so that we may not only be safe, but *comely, in going.*

II. A caution to us to keep our temper at all times and under all provocations. We must take shame to ourselves, whenever we are justly charged with a fault, and not insist upon our own innocency: If we have *lifted up ourselves* in peevish opposition, we have therein *done foolishly.* If we have but *thought evil,* if we are conscious to ourselves that we have harboured an ill design in our minds, we must *lay our hand upon our mouth,* that is humble ourselves for what we have done amiss. We must keep the evil thought we have conceived in our minds from breaking out in evil speeches. It is bad to think ill, but it is much worse to speak it, for that implies a consent to the evil thought. We must not irritate the passions of others. Some are so very provoking in their words and conduct that they even *force wrath,* and where that *is there is confusion and every evil work.* As the violent agitation of the cream fetches all the good out of the milk, and the hard *wringing of the nose* will extort blood from it, so this *forcing of wrath* wastes both the body and spirits of a man, and robs him of all the good that is in him. The spirit is heated by degrees with strong passions; one angry word begets another, and so it goes on till it ends in irreconcilable feuds.

CHAPTER 31

This chapter is added to Solomon's proverbs, some think because it is of the same author, supposing king Lemuel to be king Solomon; others only because it is of the same nature, though left in writing by another author, called Lemuel; however it be, it is a prophecy, given by inspiration and direction of God, which Lemuel was under in the writing of it, as his mother was in dictating to him the matter of it. I. An exhortation to Lemuel, a young prince, to take heed of the sins he would be tempted to and to do the duties of the place he was called, to ver. 1–9. II. The description of a virtuous woman, a wife and the mistress of a family, which Lemuel's mother drew up, either as an instruction to her daughters, as the foregoing verses were to her son, or as a direction to her son in the choice of a wife, ver. 10–31.

Verses 1–9

Most interpreters are of opinion that Lemuel is Solomon; the name signifies one that is *for God,* or *devoted to God.* Lemuel is supposed to be a fond, endearing name, by which his mother used to call him. One would the rather incline to think it is Solomon that here tells us what *his mother taught him* because he tells us (*ch.* iv. 4) what his father taught him. But some think that Lemuel was a prince of some neighbouring country, whose mother was a daughter of Israel. It is the duty of mothers, as well as fathers, to teach their children what is good, that they may do it, and what is evil, that they may avoid it; when they are young and tender they are most under the mother's eye, and she has then an opportunity of moulding their minds well.

I. Her expostulation with the young prince, by which she speaks as one considering what advice to give him: "Thou art descended from me; thou art *the son of my womb*, and therefore what I say comes from the authority and affection of a parent. Thou art a piece of myself. Be wise and good, and then I am well paid. Thou art *the son of my vows*, the son I prayed to God to give me and promised to give back to God." Our children that by baptism are dedicated to God, for whom and in whose name we covenanted with God, may well be called *the children of our vows*.

II. The caution she gives him against those two destroying sins of *uncleanness* and *drunkenness*: *Give not thy strength unto women*, unto strange women. He must not be soft and effeminate. It lessens the honour of kings and makes them mean. Are those fit to govern others that are themselves slaves to their own lusts? If they would preserve their people from the unclean spirit, they must themselves be patterns of purity. The king must not *drink wine* or *strong drink* to excess; *it is not for kings, to* allow themselves that liberty; it is a disparagement to their dignity, and profanes their crown, by confusing the head that wears it. All Christians are *made to our God kings and priests. It is not for* Christians *to drink* to excess; it ill becomes the heirs of the kingdom and the spiritual priests, Lev. x. 9. It is a sad complaint which is made of the priests and prophets (Isa. xxviii. 7), that *they have erred through wine, and through strong drink they are out of the way*; and tumble in judgment.

III. The counsel she gives him to do good with his wealth. "Thou hast wine or strong drink at command; instead of doing thyself hurt with it, do others good with it; let those have it that need it, through sickness or pain. We must deny ourselves in the gratifications of sense, that we may have to spare for the relief of the miseries of others. Wine is a cordial, and therefore to be used for want and not for wantonness, by those only that need cordials, as Timothy, who is advised to *drink a little wine*, only *for his stomach's sake and his often infirmities*, 1 Tim. v. 23. He must do good with his power, his knowledge, and must administer justice with care, courage, and compassion, *v. 8, 9*. He must *judge righteously*, and, without fear of the face of man, boldly pass sentence according to equity: *Open thy mouth*, which denotes the liberty of speech that princes and judges ought to use in passing sentence. He must especially look upon himself as obliged to be the patron of oppressed innocency, especially of those that were *dumb*, and knew not how to speak for themselves, either through fear, or being over-talked by the prosecutor or over-awed by the court.

Verses 10–31

This description of the *virtuous woman* is designed to show what wives the women should make and what wives the men should choose; it consists of twenty-two verses, each beginning with a letter of the Hebrew alphabet in order, which makes some think it was a poem by itself, written by some other hand, and perhaps commonly repeated for the ease of which it was made alphabetical. We have the abridgment of it in the New Testament (1 Tim. ii. 9, 10, 1 Pet. iii. 1–6), where the duty prescribed to wives agrees with this description of a good wife.

I. A general enquiry after such a one (*v. 10*). *A virtuous woman—a woman of strength* (so the word is), though the weaker vessel, yet made strong by wisdom and grace, and the fear of God: it is the same word that is used in the character of good judges (Exod. xviii. 21). *A virtuous woman* is a woman of spirit, who has the command of her own spirit and knows how to manage other people's. *A virtuous woman* is a woman of resolution, who, having espoused good principles, is firm and steady to them. *Who can find* her? Good women are very scarce. But he that designs to marry ought to take heed that he be not biassed by beauty or gaiety, wealth or parentage, dressing well or dancing well; for all these may be and yet the woman not be virtuous. The more rare good wives are the more they are to be valued.

II. A particular description of her and of her excellent qualifications.

1. She is very industrious to recommend herself to her husband's esteem and affection. She conducts herself so that he may repose an entire confidence in her. He trusts in her chastity. He trusts in her conduct, that she will act in all affairs with prudence and discretion. He trusts in her fidelity to his interests. When he goes abroad, to attend the concerns of the public, he can confide in her to order all his affairs at home. She contributes so much to his content *that he shall have no need of spoil*; he need not be griping and scraping abroad, as those must be whose wives are proud and wasteful at home. He thinks himself so happy in her that he envies not those who have most of the wealth of this world; he needs it not, he has enough, having such a wife. She shows her love to him, not by a foolish fondness, but by prudent endearments, giving him good words, and not bad ones, no, not when he is out of humour, studying to provide what is fit for him both in health and sickness. And this is her care *all the days of her life*; not at first only, or now and then, when she is in a good humour, but perpetually. If she survive him, still she is doing him good in her care of his children, his estate, and good name. She adds to his reputation in the world (*v. 23*): *Her husband is known in the gates*, known to have a good wife. By his cheerful countenance and pleasant humour it appears that he has an agreeable wife at home. One may know he has a good wife at home, that takes care of his clothes.

2. She is one that takes pains in the duty of her place and takes pleasure in it. She hates to sit still and do nothing: *She eats not the bread of idleness*, *v. 27*. She is careful to fill up time, that none of that be lost. When daylight is done her business lying within-doors, and her work worth candle-light, with that she lengthens out the day; and *her candle goes not out by night, v. 18. She rises* early, *while it is yet night* (*v. 15*), to give her servants their breakfast, that they may be ready to go cheerfully about their work. She is none of those who sit up playing cards, or dancing, till midnight, till morning, and then lie in bed till noon. She applies herself to the business that is proper for her. It is not in scholar's business, or statesman's business, or husbandman's business, that she employs herself, but in woman's business. *She seeks wool and flax*, where she may have the best of each, cheapest; she has a stock of both, and with this she does not only set the poor on work, which is a very good office, but does herself *work willingly with her hands. She lays her* own *hands to the spindle*, or spinning-wheel, *and her hands hold the distaff* (*v. 19*), and she does not reckon it an abridgment of her liberty. The spindle and the distaff are here mentioned as her honour, while the ornaments of the daughters of Zion are reckoned up to their reproach, Isa. iii. 18, &c. She does not employ herself in sitting work only, or in that which is only the nice performance of the fingers (there are works that are scarcely

one remove from doing nothing); but, if there be occasion, she will go through with work that requires all the strength she has, which she will use as one that knows it is the way to have more.

3. She is one that makes what she does to turn to a good account. She perceives that she can make things herself better and cheaper than she can buy them. She brings in provisions of all things necessary and convenient for her family, v. 14. She purchases lands, and enlarges the demesne of the family (v. 16): *She considers a field, and buys it.* She considers what an advantage it will be to the family. Though she have ever so much mind to it she will not buy it till she has first considered whether it be worth her money, whether the ground will answer the character given of it, and whether she has money at command to pay for it. *She* also *plants a vineyard,* but it is *with the fruit of her hands.* She furnishes her house well and has good clothing for herself and her family (v. 22): *She makes herself coverings of tapestry* to hang her rooms, and they are of her own making. *Her* own *clothing* is rich and fine: it is *silk and purple.* She has rich clothes and puts them on well. The senator's robes which her husband wears are of her own spinning, and they look better and wear better than any that are bought. She also gets good warm clothing for her children. She needs not fear the cold of the most pinching winter, for she and her family are well provided with clothes. *All her household are clothed in scarlet,* strong cloth and fit for winter, and yet making a good appearance. She makes more than she and her household have occasion for; and therefore, when she has sufficiently stocked her family, *she sells fine linen and girdles to the merchants* (v. 24), who carry them to Tyre, the mart of the nations, or some other trading city. She lays up for hereafter: *She shall rejoice in time to come,* having laid in a good stock for her family.

4. She takes care of her family and all the affairs of it, *gives meat to her household* (v. 15). *She looks well to the ways of her household* (v. 27).

5. She is charitable *to the poor, v.* 20. She is as intent upon giving as she is upon getting. *She reaches forth her hands to the needy* that are at a distance.

6. She is discreet, not talkative, censorious, nor peevish. When she does speak, it is with prudence and very much to the purpose. *In her tongue is the law of kindness.* The law of love and kindness is written in the heart, but it shows itself in the tongue. She is full of religious discourse, which shows how full her heart is of another world even when her hands are most busy about this world.

7. That which completes and crowns her character is that she *fears the Lord, v.* 30. With all those good qualities she lacks not that *one thing needful.* The fear of God reigning in the heart is the beauty of the soul; it recommends those that have it to the favour of God, and is, in his sight, of great price; it will last for ever, and bid defiance to death itself, which consumes the beauty of the body, but consummates the beauty of the soul.

III. The happiness of this virtuous woman.

1. She has the comfort and satisfaction of her virtue in her own mind (v. 25). She enjoys a firmness and constancy of mind, has spirit to bear up under many crosses and disappointments, and this is her clothing, for defence as well as decency. She deals honourably with all, *and shall rejoice in time to come;* she shall reflect upon it with comfort, when she comes to be old, that she was not idle or useless when she was young. Nay, *she shall rejoice* with *fulness of joy and pleasures for evermore.*

2. She is a great blessing to her relations, v. 28. *Her children* grow up in her place, *and they call her blessed. Her husband* thinks himself so happy in her that he takes all occasions to speak well of her.

3. She gets the good word of all her neighbours. A woman that fears the Lord, shall have praise *of God* (Rom. ii. 29). She shall be highly praised (v. 29): *Many have done virtuously, she excels them all.* Those ought to be praised the fruit of whose hands is praise-worthy. If her children be dutiful and respectful to her, they then *give her of the fruit of her hands;* she reaps the benefit of all the care she has taken of them. *Her own works* will *praise her;* if her relations and neighbours hold their peace, her good works will proclaim her praise. Thus is shut up this looking-glass for ladies, which they are desired to open and dress themselves by; and, if they do so, their adorning will be found to praise and honour, and glory, at the appearing of Jesus Christ.

Twenty chapters of the book of *Proverbs* (beginning with *ch.* x and ending with *ch.* xxix), consisting mostly of entire sentences in each verse, could not well be reduced to proper heads, and the contents of them gathered; I have therefore here put the contents of all these chapters together, which may be of some use to those who desire to see all that is said on any one head in these chapters.

1. Of the comfort, or grief, parents have in their children, according as they are wise or foolish, godly or ungodly, *ch.* x. 1; xv. 20; xvii. 21, 25; xix. 13, 26; xxiii. 15, 16, 24, 25; xxvii. 11; xxix. 3.

2. Of the world's insufficiency, and religion's sufficiency, to make us happy (*ch.* x. 2, 3; xi. 4) and the preference to be therefore given to the gains of virtue above those of this world, *ch.* xv. 16, 17; xvi. 8, 16; xvii. 1; xix. 1; xxviii. 6, 11.

3. Of slothfulness and diligence, *ch.* x. 4, 26; xii. 11, 24, 27; xiii. 4, 23; xv. 19; xvi. 26; xviii. 9; xix. 15, 24; xx. 4, 13; xxi. 5, 25, 26; xxii. 13, 29; xxiv. 30–34; xxvi. 13–16; xxvii. 18, 23; xxviii. 19; xxxi. 27. Particularly the improving or neglecting opportunities, *ch.* vi. 6; x. 5.

4. The happiness of the righteous, and the misery of the wicked, *ch.* x. 6, 9, 16, 24, 25, 27–30; xi. 3, 5–8, 18–21, 31; xii. 2, 3, 7, 13, 14, 21, 26, 28; xiii. 6, 9, 14, 15, 21, 22, 25; xiv. 11, 14,

19, 32; xv. 6, 8, 9, 24, 26, 29; xx. 7; xxi. 12, 15, 16, 18, 21; xxii. 12; xxviii. 10, 18; xxix. 6.

5. Of honour and dishonour, *ch.* x. 7; xii. 8, 9; xviii. 3; xxvi. 1; xxvii. 21. And of vain-glory, *ch.* xxv. 14, 27; xxvii. 2.

6. The wisdom of obedience, and folly of disobedience, *ch.* x. 8, 17; xii. 1, 15; xiii. 1, 13, 18; xv. 5, 10, 12, 31, 32; xix. 16; xxviii. 4, 7, 9.

7. Of mischievousness and usefulness, *ch.* x. 10, 23; xi. 9–11, 23, 27; xii. 5, 6, 12, 18, 20; xiii. 2; xiv. 22; xvi. 29, 30; xvii. 11; xxi. 10; xxiv. 8; xxvi. 23, 27.

8. The praise of wise and good discourse, and the hurt and shame of an ungoverned tongue, *ch.* x. 11, 12, 14, 20, 21, 31, 32; xi. 30; xiv. 3; xv. 2, 4, 7, 23, 28; xvi. 20, 23, 24; xvii. 7; xviii. 4, 7, 20, 21; xx. 15; xxi. 23; xxiii. 9; xxiv. 26; xxv. 11.

9. Of love and hatred, peaceableness and contention, *ch.* x. 12; xv. 17; xvii. 1, 9, 14, 19; xviii. 6, 17–19; xx. 3; xxv. 8; xxvi. 17, 21; xxix. 9.

10. Of the rich and poor, *ch*. x. 15, 22; xi. 28; xiii. 7, 8; xiv. 20, 24; xviii. 11, 23; xix. 1, 4, 7, 22; xxii. 2, 7; xxviii. 6, 11; xxix. 13.

11. Of lying, fraud, and dissimulation, and of truth and sincerity, *ch*. x. 18; xii. 17, 19, 22; xiii. 5; xvii. 4; xx. 14, 17; xxvi. 18, 19, 24–26, 28.

12. Of slandering, *ch*. x. 18; xvi. 27; xxv. 23.

13. Of talkativeness and silence, *ch*. x. 19; xi. 12; xii. 23; xiii. 3; xvii. 27, 28; xxix. 11, 20.

14. Of justice and injustice, *ch*. xi. 1; xvii. 26; xvi. 8, 11; xvii. 15, 26; xviii. 5; xx. 10, 23; xxii. 28; xxiii. 10, 11; xxix. 24.

15. Of pride and humility, *ch*. xi. 2; xiii. 10; xv. 25, 33; xvi. 5, 18, 19; xviii. 12; xxi. 4; xxv. 6, 7; xxviii. 26; xxix. 23.

16. Of despising and respecting others, *ch*. xi. 12; xiv. 21.

17. Of tale-bearing, *ch*. xi. 13; xvi. 28; xviii. 8; xx. 19; xxvi. 20, 22.

18. Of rashness and deliberation, *ch*. xi. 14; xv. 22; xviii. 13; xix. 2; xx. 5, 18; xxi. 29; xxii. 3; xxv. 8–10.

19. Of suretiship, *ch*. xi. 15; xvii. 18; xx. 16; xxii. 26, 27; xxvii. 13.

20. Of good and bad women, or wives, *ch*. xi. 16, 22; xii. 4; xiv. 1; xviii. 22; xix. 13, 14; xxi. 9, 19; xxv. 24; xxvii. 15, 16.

21. Of mercifulness and unmercifulness, *ch*. xi. 17; xii. 10; xiv. 21; xix. 17; xxi. 13.

22. Of charity to the poor and uncharitableness, *ch*. xi. 24–26; xiv. 31; xvii. 5; xxii. 9, 16, 22, 23; xxviii. 27; xxix. 7.

23. Of covetousness and contentment, *ch*. xi. 29; xv. 16, 17, 27, xxiii. 4, 5.

24. Of anger and meekness, *ch*. xii. 16; xiv. 17, 29; xv. 1, 18; xvi. 32; xvii. 12, 26; xix. 11, 19; xxii. 24, 25; xxv. 15, 28; xxvi. 21; xxix. 22.

25. Of melancholy and cheerfulness, *ch*. xii. 25; xiv. 10, 13; xv. 13, 15; xvii. 22; xviii. 14; xxv. 20, 25.

26. Of hope and expectation, *ch*. xiii. 12, 19.

27. Of prudence and foolishness, *ch*. xiii. 16; xiv. 8, 18, 33; xv. 13, 21; xvi. 21, 22; xvii. 24; xviii. 2, 15; xxiv. 3–7; vii. 27; xxvi. 6–11; xxviii. 5.

28. Of treachery and fidelity, *ch*. xiii. 17; xxv. 13, 19.

29. Of good and bad company, *ch*. xiii. 20; xiv. 7; xxviii. 7; xxix. 3.

30. Of the education of children, *ch*. xiii. 24; xix. 18; xx. 11; xxii. 6, 15; xxiii. 12; xxiv. 14; xxix. 15, 17.

31. Of the fear of the Lord, *ch*. xiv. 2, 26, 27; xv. 16, 33; xvi. 6; xix. 23; xxii. 4; xxiii. 17, 18.

32. Of true and false witness-bearing, *ch*. xiv. 5, 25; xix. 5, 9, 28; xxi. 28; xxiv. 28; xxv. 18.

33. Of scorners, *ch*. xiv. 6, 9; xxi. 24; xxii. 10; xxiv. 9; xxix. 8.

34. Of credulity and caution, *ch*. xiv. 15, 16; xxvii. 12.

35. Of kings and their subjects, *ch*. xiv. 28, 34, 35; xvi. 10, 12–15; xix. 6, 12; xx. 2, 8, 26, 28; xxii. 11; xxiv. 21; xxv. 2–5; xxviii. 2, 3, 15, 16; xxix. 4, 12, 14, 26.

36. Of envy, especially envying sinners, *ch*. xiv. 30; xxiii. 17, 18; xxiv. 1, 2, 19, 20; xxvii. 4.

37. Of God's omniscience and his universal providence, *ch*. xv. 3, 11; xvi. 1, 4, 9, 33; xvii. 3; xix. 21; xx. 12, 24; xxi. 1, 30, 31; xxix. 26.

38. Of a good and ill name, *ch*. xv. 30; xxii. 1.

39. Of men's good opinion of themselves, *ch*. xiv. 12; xvi. 2, 25; xx. 6; xxi. 2; xxvi. 12; xxviii. 26.

40. Of devotion towards God, and dependence on him, *ch*. xvi. 3; xviii. 10; xxiii. 26; xxvii. 1; xxviii. 25; xxix. 25.

41. Of the happiness of God's favour, *ch*. xvi. 7; xxix. 26.

42. Excitements to get wisdom, *ch*. xvi. 16; xviii. 1; xix. 8, 20; xxii. 17–21; xxiii. 15, 16, 22–25; xxiv. 13, 14; xxvii. 11.

43. Cautions against temptations, *ch*. xvi. 17; xxix. 27.

44. Of old age and youth, *ch*. xvi. 31; xvii. 6; xx. 29.

45. Of servants, xvii. 2; xix. 10; xxix. 19, 21.

46. Of bribery, *ch*. xvii. 8, 23; xviii. 16; xxi. 14; xxviii. 21.

47. Of reproof and correction, *ch*. xvii. 10; xix. 25, 29; xx. 30; xxi. 11; xxv. 12; xxvi. 3; xxvii. 5, 6, 22; xxviii. 23; xxix. 1.

48. Of ingratitude, *ch*. xvii. 13.

49. Of friendship, *ch*. xvii. 17; xviii. 24; xxvii. 9, 10, 14, 17.

50. Of sensual pleasures, *ch*. xxi. 17; xxiii. 1–3, 6–8, 19–21; xxvii. 7.

51. Of drunkenness, *ch*. xx. 1; xxiii. 20, 29–35.

52. Of the universal corruption of nature, *ch*. xx. 9.

53. Of flattery, *ch*. xx. 19; xxvi. 28; xxviii. 23; xxix. 5.

54. Of undutiful children, *ch*. xx. 20; xxviii. 24.

55. Of the short continuance of what is ill-gotten, *ch*. xx. 21; xxi. 6, 7; xxii. 8; xxviii. 8.

56. Of revenge, *ch*. xx. 22; xxiv. 17, 18, 29.

57. Of sacrilege, *ch*. xx. 25.

58. Of conscience, *ch*. xx. 27; xxvii. 19.

59. Of the preference of moral duties before ceremonial, *ch*. xv. 8; xxi. 3, 27.

60. Of prodigality and wastefulness, *ch*. xxi. 20.

61. The triumphs of wisdom and godliness, *ch*. xxi. 22; xxiv. 15, 16.

62. Of frowardness and tractableness, *ch*. xxii. 5.

63. Of uncleanness, *ch*. xxii. 14; xxiii. 27, 28.

64. Of fainting in affliction, *ch*. xxiv. 10.

65. Of helping the distressed, *ch*. xxiv. 11, 12.

66. Of loyalty to the government, *ch*. xxiv. 21, 22.

67. Of forgiving enemies, xxv. 21, 22.

68. Of causeless curse, *ch*. xxvi. 2.

69. Of answering fools, *ch*. xxvi. 4, 5.

70. Of unsettledness and unsatisfiedness, *ch*. xxvii. 8, 20.

71. Of cowardliness and courage, *ch*. xxviii. 1.

72. The people's interest in the character of their rulers, xi. 10, 11; *ch*. xxviii. 12, 28; xxix. 2, 16.

73. The benefit of repentance and holy fear, *ch*. xxviii. 13, 14.

74. The punishment of murder, *ch*. xxviii. 17.

75. Of hastening to be rich, *ch*. xxviii. 20, 22.

76. The enmity of the wicked against the godly, *ch*. xxix. 10, 27.

77. The necessity of the means of grace, *ch*. xxix. 18.

AN EXPOSITION, WITH PRACTICAL OBSERVATIONS, OF

THE BOOK
OF ECCLESIASTES

The account we have of Solomon's apostasy from God, in the latter end of his reign (1 Kings xi. 1), is the tragical part of his story; we may suppose that he spoke his *Proverbs* in the prime of his time, while he kept his integrity, but delivered his *Ecclesiastes* when he had grown old (for of the burdens and decays of age he speaks feelingly, *ch.* xii), and was, by the grace of God, recovered from his backslidings. There he dictated his observations; here he wrote his own experiences; this is what days speak and wisdom which the multitude of years teaches.

I. It is a sermon in print; the text is (*ch.* i. 2), *Vanity of vanities, all is vanity;* that is the doctrine too; it is proved at large by many arguments and divers objections are answered, and in the close we have the application, by way of exhortation, to *remember our Creator,* to *fear him,* and to *keep his commandments.* There are indeed many things in this book which are dark and hard to be understood, and some things which men *wrest to their own destruction,* for want of distinguishing between Solomon's arguments and the objections of atheists; but there is enough easy and plain to convince us of the vanity of the world, and its utter insufficiency to make us happy, the vileness of sin, and its certain tendency to make us miserable, and of the wisdom of being religious, and the solid comfort and satisfaction that are to be had in doing our duty both to God and man.

II. It is a penitential sermon; it is a recantation sermon, in which the preacher sadly laments his own folly in promising himself satisfaction in the things of this world, and even in the forbidden pleasures of sense, which now he finds more bitter than death. His fall is a proof of the weakness of man's nature: *Let not the wise man glory in his wisdom,* when Solomon himself, the wisest of men, played the fool so egregiously; nor *let the rich man glory in his riches,* since Solomon's wealth was so great a snare to him, and did him a great deal more hurt than Job's poverty did him. His recovery is a proof of the power of God's grace, in bringing one back to God that had gone so far from him.

III. It is a practical profitable sermon. Solomon, being brought to repentance, resolves, like his father, to *teach transgressors God's way* (Ps. li. 13). The fundamental error of the children of men is the same with that of our first parents, hoping to be *as gods* by entertaining themselves with that which seems *good for food, pleasant to the eyes,* and *desirable to make one wise.* Now the scope of this book is to show that this is a great mistake, that our happiness consists not in being as gods to ourselves to have what we will and do what we will, but in having him that made us to be a God to us. Solomon, in this book, assures us that *to fear God and to keep his commandments is the whole of man.* He shows the vanity of those things in which men commonly look for happiness, as human learning and policy, sensual delight, honour and power, riches and great possessions. He prescribes remedies. Though we cannot cure them of their vanity, we may prevent the trouble they give us, by sitting loose to them, but laying our expectations low from them, and acquiescing in the will of God, especially by remembering God in the days of our youth, and continuing in his fear and service all our days.

CHAPTER 1

In this chapter we have, I. The inscription, or title of the book, ver. 1. II. The general doctrine of the vanity of the creature laid down (ver. 2) and explained, ver. 3. III. The proof of this doctrine, taken, 1. From the shortness of human life, ver. 4. 2. From the inconstant nature of all the creatures, and the perpetual flux and reflux they are in, the sun, wind, and water, ver. 5–7. 3. From the abundant toil man has about them, ver. 8. 4. From the return of the same things again, which shows the end of all perfection, ver. 9, 10. 5. From the oblivion to which all things are condemned, ver. 11. IV. The first instance of the vanity of men's knowledge. 1. The trial Solomon made of these, ver. 12, 13, 16, 17. 2. His judgment of them, that all is vanity, ver. 14. There is no satisfaction in it, ver. 18. And, if this is vanity and vexation, all other things in this world, being much inferior to it in dignity and worth, must needs be so too.

Verses 1–3

I. An account of the penman of this book; it was Solomon, for no other son of David was king of Jerusalem; but he conceals his name *Solomon, peaceable,* because by his sin he had brought trouble upon himself and his kingdom, had broken his peace with God, and therefore was no more worthy of that name. Call me not *Solomon,* call me *Marah,* for, *behold, for peace I had great bitterness.* But he calls himself,

1. *The preacher,* which intimates his present character. He is *Koheleth,* which comes from a word which signifies *to gather.*

(1) Koheleth is a *penitent soul,* or one *gathered,* one that had gone astray like a lost sheep, but was

now gathered in from his wanderings. The spirit that was dissipated after a thousand vanities is now collected and made to centre in God. It is only the penitent soul that God will accept, the heart that is broken, not the head that is bowed down like a bulrush only for a day. And it is only the gathered soul that comes back from its by-paths.

(2) A *preaching soul* is one *gathering.* Being himself *gathered,* and being reconciled to the church, he endeavours to gather others to it that had gone astray like him. God by his Spirit made him a preacher, in token of his being reconciled to him; a commission is a tacit pardon. Christ sufficiently testifies his forgiving Peter by committing his lambs and sheep to his trust.

2. *The son of David.* He looked upon it as a great aggravation of his sin that he had such a father. His being the son of David encouraged him to repent and hope for mercy, for David had fallen into sin, but repented, and therein he took example from him and found mercy as he did.

3. *King of Jerusalem.* God had done much for him, in raising him to the throne, and yet he had so ill requited him. He thought it no disparagement to him, as a king, to be a preacher; but the people would regard him the more as a preacher because he was a king.

II. The general scope and design of the book is, for the making of us truly religious, to take down our esteem of and expectation from the things of this world. In order to this, he shows,

1. That they are *all vanity*, *v*. 2. It is *all vanity*, not only in the abuse of it, when it is perverted by the sin of man, but even in the use of it. It is expressed here very emphatically; not only, *All is vain*, but in the abstract, *All is vanity*; as if vanity were the *proprium quarto modo—property in the fourth mode*, of the things of this world, that which enters into the nature of them. They are not only *vanity*, but *vanity of vanities*, the vainest vanity, vanity in the highest degree. Many speak contemptuously of the world because they are hermits, and know it not, or beggars, and have it not; but Solomon knew it. He had dived into nature's depths (1 Kings iv. 33), and he had it, more of it perhaps than ever any man had. He spoke in God's name, and was divinely inspired to say it, deliberately, and laid it down as a fundamental principle, on which he grounded the necessity of being religious. One main thing he designed was to show that the everlasting throne and kingdom must be of another world; for all things in this world are subject to vanity, and therefore have not in them sufficient to answer the extent of that promise.

2. That they are insufficient to make us happy. *What profit has a man of all the pains he takes? v*. 3. The business of this world is *labour*; the word signifies both care and toil. It is work that wearies men. *What profit has a man of all that labour?* Solomon says (Prov. xiv. 23), *In all labour there is profit;* and yet here he denies that there is any profit. As to our present condition in the world, it is true that by labour we get that which we call *profit*; we *eat the labour of our hands*; but here he determines that it is not a real benefit. In short, the wealth and pleasure of this world, if we had ever so much of them, are not sufficient to make us happy. As goods are increased care about them is increased, and *those are increased that eat of them*, and a little thing will embitter all the comfort of them; and then *what profit has a man of all his labour?* As to the soul, and the life that is to come, we may much more truly say, *What profit has a man of all his labour?* All he gets by it will not supply the wants of the soul, will not atone for the sin of the soul, nor cure its diseases.

Verses 4–8

To prove the vanity of all things under the sun Solomon here shows the time of our enjoyment of these things is very short. We continue in the world but for one generation, which is continually passing away to make room for another, and we are passing with it. While the stream of mankind is continually flowing, how little enjoyment has one drop of that stream of the pleasant banks between which it glides! We may give God the glory of that constant succession of generations, but as to our own happiness, let us not expect it within such narrow limits, but in an eternal rest and consistency. It is well for mankind in general that the earth endures to the end of time, when it and all the works in it shall be burnt up; but what is that to particular persons, when they remove to the world of spirits? Man abides upon the earth but a little while. The sun sets indeed every night, yet it rises again in the morning, as bright and fresh as ever. *But man lies down and rises not*, Job xiv. 7, 12. All things in this world are movable and mutable, constant in nothing but inconstancy, still going, never resting. And can we expect rest in a world where all things are thus full of labour (*v*. 8), on a sea that is always ebbing and flowing, and her waves continually working and rolling? Man's mind is as restless in its pursuits as the sun, and wind, and rivers, but never satisfied, never contented; the more it has of the world the more it would have; and it would be no sooner filled with the streams of outward prosperity, than the sea is with *all the rivers that run into it*; it is still as it was, *a troubled sea that cannot rest*. The earth is where it was; the sun, and winds, and rivers, keep the same course. We must therefore look above the sun for satisfaction, and for a new world. Our senses are unsatisfied, and the objects of them unsatisfying. Curiosity is still inquisitive, because still unsatisfied, and the more it is humoured the more nice and peevish it grows, crying, *Give, give*.

Verses 9–11

How grateful it is to think that none ever made such advances in knowledge, and such discoveries by it, as we, that none ever made such improvements. We boast of new fashions, new hypotheses, new methods, new expressions, which jostle out the old, and put them down. But this is all a mistake. What is there in the kingdom of nature of which we may say, *This is new?* The powers of nature and the links of natural causes are still the same that ever they were. Men's hearts, and the corruptions of them, are still the same; their desires, and pursuits, and complaints, are still the same. Tatianus the Assyrian, showing the Grecians how all the arts which they valued themselves upon owed their original to those nations which they counted barbarous, thus reasons with them: "For shame, do not call those things εὑρήσεις—*inventions*, which are but μίμησεις—*imitations*." What reason have we to think that the world should be any kinder to us than it has been to those that have gone before us, since there is nothing in it that is new, and our predecessors have made as much of it as could be made? If we would be entertained with new things, we must acquaint ourselves with the things of God, get a new nature; then *old things pass away, and all things become new*, 2 Cor. v. 17. The gospel puts *a new song into our mouths*. Many think they have found satisfaction that their names shall be perpetuated, that posterity will celebrate the actions they have performed. How many *former things* and persons were there, which in their day looked very great and made a mighty figure, and yet *there is no remembrance* of them. Here and there one person or action that was remarkable met with a kind historian, and had the good hap to be recorded, when at the same time there were others, no less remarkable, that were dropped.

Verses 12–18

That which bids fairest to be the happiness of a reasonable creature is knowledge and learning; if this be vanity, everything else must needs be so. Now as to this,

I. Solomon tells us here what trial he had made of it, and that with such advantages that, if true satisfaction could have been found in it, he would have found it. He had his royal seat *in Jerusalem*, which then deserved, better than Athens ever did, to be called *the eye of the world*. Solomon's great wealth and honour put him into a capacity of making his court the centre of learning and the rendezvous of learned men. He made it his business to acquaint himself with *all the things that are done under the sun*, that are done by the providence of God or by the art and prudence of man. Though he was a prince, he made himself a drudge to learning, was not discouraged by its knots, nor took up short of its depths. And this he did not merely to gratify his own genius, but to qualify himself for the service of God and his generation, and to make an experiment how far the enlargement of the knowledge would go towards the settlement and repose of the mind. He *saw all the works that were done under the sun* (*v*. 14), works of nature in the upper and lower world, works of art, the product of men's wit, in a personal or social capacity. He had as much satisfaction in the success of his searches as ever any man had. Solomon must be acknowledged a competent judge of this matter, for he had not only got his head full of notions, but his *heart had great experience of wisdom and knowledge*, of the power and benefit of knowledge, as well as the entertainment of it; what he knew he had digested, and knew how to use. So industrious was Solomon to improve himself in knowledge that he gained instruction both by the wisdom of prudent men and by the madness of foolish men, by *the field of the slothful*, as well as of *the diligent*.

II. He tells us what was the result of this trial, to confirm what he had said, that *all is vanity*. He found that his searches after knowledge were very toilsome, and a weariness to the mind (v. 13). As bread for the body, so that for the soul, must be got and eaten *in the sweat of our face*. "*I have seen all the works* of a world full of business, have observed what the children of men are doing; *and behold*, whatever men think of their own words, I see *all is vanity and vexation of spirit*." The more we see of the world the more we see to make us uneasy, and, with Heraclitus, to look upon all with weeping eyes. Solomon especially perceived that the knowledge of *wisdom and folly* was *vexation of spirit*, v. 17. It vexed him to see many that had wisdom not use it, and many that had folly not strive against it. He found that when he had got some knowledge he could neither gain that satisfaction to himself, nor do that good to others with it which he expected, v. 15. The minds and manners of men are crooked and perverse. Solomon thought, with his wisdom and power together, thoroughly to reform his kingdom, but he was disappointed. All the philosophy and politics in the world will not restore the corrupt nature of man. Learning will not alter men's natural tempers, nor cure them of their sinful distempers. *That which is wanting* in our knowledge is so much that it *cannot be numbered*. The more we know the more we see of our own ignorance. Upon the whole, therefore, he concluded that great scholars do but make themselves great mourners; *for in much wisdom is much grief*, v. 18. Those *that increase knowledge* have so much the more quick and sensible perception of the calamities of this world. Let us not therefore be driven off from the pursuit of any useful knowledge, but put on patience to break through the sorrow of it; but let us despair of finding true happiness in this knowledge, and expect it only in the knowledge of God and the careful discharge of our duty to him.

CHAPTER 2

Solomon having pronounced all vanity goes on to show what reason he has to be tired of this world, and with what little reason most men are fond of it. I. He shows that there is no true happiness and satisfaction to be had in the delights of sense, ver. 1–11. II. He reconsiders wisdom, and allows it to be excellent and useful, and yet sees it insufficient to make a man happy, ver. 12–16. III. He enquires how far wealth will go towards making men happy, and concludes, from his own experience, that, to those who set their hearts upon it, "it is vanity and vexation of spirit" (ver. 17–23), and that, if there be any good in it, it is only to those that sit loose to it, ver. 24–26.

Verses 1–11

Solomon here, in pursuit of the *summum bonum—the felicity* of man, adjourns out of his study, where he had in vain sought for it, into the park and his garden; he exchanges the company of the philosophers and grave senators for that of the wits and gallants, to try if he could find true satisfaction and happiness among them. Here he takes a great step downward, from the noble pleasures of the intellect to the brutal ones of sense.

I. He resolved to try what mirth would do and the pleasures of wit. "*Enjoy pleasure*, and take thy fill of it; cast away care, and resolve to be merry." Many that are poor are very merry; beggars in a barn are so to a proverb. Mirth comes short of the solid delights of the rational powers, yet it is to be preferred before those that are merely carnal and sensual. Some distinguish man from the brutes, not only as *animal rationale—a rational animal*, but as *animal risibile—a laughing animal*. "Try therefore," says Solomon, "to laugh and be fat, to laugh and be happy." The judgment he passed upon this experiment: *I said of laughter, It is mad*, or, *Thou art mad, and of mirth, What doeth it?* Innocent mirth, soberly, seasonably, and moderately used, is a good thing, fits for business, and helps to soften the toils of human life; but, when it is excessive and immoderate, it is foolish and fruitless. It is but a palliative cure to the grievances of this present time.

II. Finding himself not happy in that which pleased his fancy, he resolved next to try that which would please the palate, v. 3. *I sought in my heart to give myself unto wine*, that is, to good meat and good drink. Solomon applied himself to it critically, and only to make an experiment. He sought *to lay hold on folly*, to see the utmost that that folly would do towards making men happy. He resolved that the folly should not take hold of him, not get the mastery of him. He took care at the same time to *acquaint* himself *with wisdom*, to manage himself wisely in the use of his pleasures, so that they should not do him any prejudice nor disfit him to be a competent judge of them. This Solomon proposed to himself, but he found it *vanity*. *Wine is a mocker;* and it will be impossible for any man to say that thus far he will give himself to it and no further. That which he aimed at was not to gratify his appetite, but to find out man's happiness. Observe the description he gives of man's happiness—it is *that good for the sons of men which they should do under the heaven all their days. Good Master, what good thing shall I do?* Our happiness consists not in being idle, but in doing aright, in being well employed. But that any man should give himself to wine, in hopes to find out in that the best way of living in this world, was an absurdity which Solomon here, in the reflection, condemns.

III. Perceiving quickly that it was folly to give himself to wine, he next tried the most costly entertainments and amusements.

1. He gave himself much to building, both in the city and in the country; and, having been at such vast expense in the beginning of his reign to build a house for God, he was the more excusable if afterwards he pleased his own fancy in building for himself. In building, he had the pleasure of employing the poor and doing good to posterity. We read of Solomon's buildings (1 Kings ix. 15–19), and they were all *great works*. See his mistake; he enquired after the *good* works he should do (v. 3), and, in pursuit of the enquiry, applied himself to *great* works. *Good* works indeed are truly great, but many are reputed great works which are far from being good.

2. He took to love a garden, which is to some as bewitching as building. He *planted himself vineyards*; he *made himself* fine *gardens and orchards* (v. 5). He had not only forests of timber-trees, but *trees of all kinds of fruit*, which he himself had planted.

3. He laid out a great deal of money in waterworks, ponds, and canals, not for sport and diversion, but for use, *to water the wood that brings forth trees* (v. 6); he not only planted, but watered, and then left it to God to give the increase.

4. When he proposed to himself to do *great works* he must employ many hands, and therefore procured *servants and maidens*, and of those he *had servants born in his house*, v. 7.

5. He *had large possessions of great and small cattle*, herds and flocks, as his father had before him (1 Chron. xxvii. 29, 31).

6. He grew very rich, and was not at all impoverished by his building and gardening.

7. He had all sorts of melody and music, vocal and instrumental. These are called *the delights of the sons of men.*

8. He enjoyed, more than ever any man did, a composition of rational and sensitive pleasures at the same time. In the midst of these entertainments *his wisdom remained with him, v.* 9. Yet his judgment and conscience gave no check to his pleasures, nor hindered him from extracting the very quintessence of the delights of sense, *v.* 10. He had as much pleasure in his business as ever any man had: *My heart rejoiced in all my labour.* It sweetened his business that he enjoyed the success of it, and it sweetened his enjoyments that they were the product of his business; so that, upon the whole, he was certainly as happy as the world could make him.

9. We have, at length, the judgment he deliberately gave of all this, *v.* 11. When Solomon reviewed *all his works that his hands had wrought* with the utmost cost and care, *and the labour that he had laboured to do* in order to make himself easy and happy, nothing answered his expectation; *behold, all was vanity and vexation of spirit; there was no profit under the sun,* neither by the employments nor by the enjoyments of this world.

Verses 12–16

Solomon having tried what satisfaction was to be had in learning, and in the pleasures of sense, here compares them and passes judgment upon them.

I. He sets himself to consider both wisdom and folly. He here turns himself again to behold them, to see if, upon a second view and second thoughts, he could gain more satisfaction. Let us acquiesce in Solomon's judgment of the things of this world, and not think of repeating the trial; for we can never have such advantages as he had to make the experiment nor be able to make it with equal application of mind.

II. He gives the preference to wisdom far before folly. I soon *saw* (says he) *that there is an excellency in wisdom more than in folly,* as much as there is in light above darkness. The pleasures of wisdom, though they suffice not to make men happy, yet vastly transcend the pleasures of wine. Wisdom enlightens the soul with surprising discoveries and necessary directions for the right government of itself; but sensuality clouds the mind, and is as darkness to it. *The wise man's eyes are in his head* (*v.* 14), where they should be, ready to discover both the dangers that are to be avoided and the advantages that are to be improved. *The fool walks in darkness,* and is ever and anon either at a loss, or at a plunge.

III. Yet he maintains that, in respect of lasting happiness and satisfaction, the wisdom of this world gives a man very little advantage. The same sickness, the same sword, devours wise men and fools. Solomon applies this mortifying observation to himself (*v.* 15). Why should I take so much pains to get wisdom, when, as to this life, it will stand me in so little stead? *Then I said in my heart that this also is vanity.* Wise men and fools are forgotten alike (*v.* 16): *There is no remembrance of the wise more than of the fool.* It is promised to the righteous that they *shall be had in everlasting remembrance,* and *their memory shall be blessed,* and they shall shortly *shine as the stars*; but there is no such promise made concerning the wisdom of this world, that that shall perpetuate men's names, for those names only are perpetuated that are *written in heaven.* Between the death of a godly and a wicked man there is a great difference, but not between the death of a wise man and a fool.

Verses 17–26

Solomon after a contemplative life and a voluptuous life, betook himself to an active life, and found no more satisfaction in it than in the other; still it is all *vanity and vexation of spirit.*

I. The business of which he made trial was business *under the sun* (*v.* 17–20), about the things of this world; it was the business of a king. It is *labour under the sun,* labour for the *meat that perishes* (John vi. 27; Isa. lv. 2), that Solomon here speaks of with so little satisfaction. It was the better sort of business *in wisdom, and knowledge, and equity, v.* 21. It was rational business, which related to the government of his kingdom. It was labour wherein he *showed himself wise* (*v.* 19), which many people have in their eye more than anything else in the prosecution of their worldly business.

II. He soon grew weary of it. He *hated all his labour.* After he had had his fine houses, and gardens, awhile, he began to look upon them with contempt. This expresses not a gracious hatred of these things, which is our duty, to love them less than God and religion (Luke xiv. 26), nor a sinful hatred of them, which is our folly, to be weary of the place God has assigned us and the work of it, but a natural hatred of them, arising from a surfeit and a sense of disappointment in them. Have we so often bored into this earth for some rich mine of satisfaction, and found not the least sign of it, but been always frustrated in the search, and shall we not at length despair of ever finding it? At length he *hated life itself* (*v.* 17), because it is subject to so many toils and troubles, and a constant series of disappointments.

III. Two things made him weary:

1. His business was so great a toil to himself: The *work that he had wrought under the sun was grievous unto him, v.* 17. A man of business is described to be uneasy both in his *going out* and his *coming in, v.* 23. He is deprived of his pleasure by day. He is disturbed in his repose *by night.* See what fools those are that make themselves drudges to the world, and do not make God their rest; night and day they cannot but be uneasy. So that, upon the whole matter, it is *all vanity, v.* 17.

2. The gains of his business must all be left to others. To a gracious soul this is no uneasiness at all; why should we not rather be pleased that, when we are gone, those that come after us shall fare the better for our wisdom and industry? He knows not what *he* will prove to whom he leaves it, whether *a wise man or a fool,* a wise man that will make it more or a fool that will bring it to nothing. It is probable that Solomon wrote this very feelingly, being afraid what Rehoboam would prove.

IV. The best use which is therefore to be made of the wealth of this world is to use it cheerfully and do good with it. With this he concludes the chapter, *v.* 24–26. That good which is here recommended to us is the utmost pleasure and profit we can expect or extract from the business of this world, and the furthest we can go to rescue it from its *vanity* and *vexation.* We must be more in care to use an estate well, for the ends for which we were entrusted with it, than how to increase it. He would not have us to give up business, and take our ease, that we may *eat and drink*; we must *enjoy good in our labour*; we must use these things, not to excuse us from, but to make us diligent and cheerful in, our worldly business. We must herein *acknowledge God*; we must see that *it is from the hand of God.* A heart to enjoy them is the gift of God's grace. Solomon himself, with all his possessions, could aim at no more and desire no better (*v.* 25). Yet Solomon could not obtain it by his own wisdom, without the special grace of God, and therefore directs us to expect it from the hand of God and pray to him for it. Riches are a blessing or a curse to a man according as he has or has not a heart to make good use of them. God makes them a reward to a good man, if with them he give him *wisdom, and knowledge, and joy,* to enjoy them cheerfully himself and to communicate them charitably to others. He makes them a punishment to a bad man if he denies him a heart to take the comfort of them, for they do but tantalize him and tyrannize over him. *Godliness, with contentment, is great gain.* Ungodliness is commonly punished with discontent and an insatiable covetousness, which are sins that are their own punishment.

CHAPTER 3

Solomon having shown the vanity of studies, pleasures, and business, and made it to appear that happiness is not to be found in the schools of the learned, nor in the gardens of Epicurus, nor upon the exchange, therefore we should cheerfully content ourselves with, and make use of, what God has given us, by showing, I. The mutability of all human affairs, ver. 1–10. II. The immutability of the divine counsels, ver. 11–15. III. The vanity of worldly honour and power, ver. 16. For a check to proud oppressors, and to show them their vanity, he reminds them, 1. That they will be called to account for it in the other world, ver. 17. 2. That their condition, in reference to this world, is no better than that of the brutes, ver. 18–21.

Verses 1–10

We live in a world of changes. The several events of time, and conditions of human life, are vastly different from one another, and we are continually passing and repassing between them. In the *wheel of nature* (James iii. 6) sometimes one spoke is uppermost and by and by the contrary; there is a constant ebbing and flowing, waxing and waning from one extreme to the other. When we are in prosperity, we should be easy, and yet not secure—not to be secure because we live in a world of changes, and yet to be easy, and, as he had advised (*ch.* ii. 24), *to enjoy the good of our labour*, in a humble dependence upon God, neither lifted up with hopes, nor cast down with fears, but with evenness of mind.

I. A general proposition is laid down: *To everything there is a season, v.* 1. Those things which seem most contrary the one to the other will, in the revolution of affairs, each take their turn and come into play. The day will give place to the night and the night again to the day. Is it summer? It will be winter. Is it winter? Stay a while, and it will be summer. Every purpose has its time.

II. Some of these changes are purely the act of God, others depend more upon the will of man. Everything *under heaven* is thus changeable, but in heaven there is an unchangeable state. 1. There is *a time to be born and a time to die.* But, as there is *a time to be born and a time to die*, so there will be a time to rise again. 2. There is *a time* for men *to plant,* a time of the year, a time of their lives; but, when *that which was planted* has grown fruitless and useless, it is *time to pluck it up.* 3. *A time to kill,* when the judgments of God are abroad in a land and lay all waste; but, when he returns in ways of mercy, then is *a time to heal* what *he has torn* (Hos. vi. 1, 2), to comfort a people after the time that he has *afflicted them*, Ps. xc. 15. 4. *A time to break down* a family, an estate, a kingdom, when it has ripened itself for destruction; but God will find *a time*, if they return and repent, to rebuild what he has broken down. 5. *A time* when God's providence calls *to weep and mourn*, but, on the other hand, there is a time when God calls to cheerfulness, *a time to laugh and dance*, and then he expects we should *serve him with joyfulness and gladness of heart.* 6. *A time to cast away stones*, by breaking down fortifications, when God gives peace in the borders, but there is *a time to gather stones together*, for the making of strongholds, *v.* 5. 7. *A time to embrace* a friend when we find him faithful, but *a time to refrain from embracing* when we

find he is unfair or unfaithful. It is commonly applied to conjugal embraces, and explained by 1 Cor. vii. 3–5; Joel ii. 16. 8. *A time to get* money, preferment, good bargains, when opportunity smiles, a time when a wise man will *seek* (so the word is); when he is setting out in the world and has a growing family, when he is in his prime, then it is time for him to be busy and make hay when the sun shines. There will come *a time to lose*, when what has been soon got will be soon scattered. 9. *A time to keep*, when we have use for what we have got, but there may come *a time to cast away*, when love to God may oblige us to cast away what we have, because we must deny Christ and wrong our consciences if we keep it (Matt. x. 37, 38). 10. *A time to rend* the garments, as upon occasion of some great grief, *and a time to sew* them again, in token that the grief is over. 11. *A time* when it is our duty *to keep silence*, when it is an *evil time* (Amos v. 13), or when we are in danger of speaking amiss (Ps. xxxix. 2); but there is also *a time to speak* for the glory of God when silence would be the betraying of a righteous cause. 12. *A time to love*, and to show ourselves friendly, to be free and cheerful, but there may come *a time to hate*, when we shall see cause to break off all familiarity with some that we have been fond of, and to be upon the reserve. 13. *A time of war*, when God draws the sword for judgment, when men draw the sword for justice, but we may hope for *a time of peace*, when the sword of the Lord shall be sheathed and he shall *make wars to cease* (Ps. xlvi. 9). War shall not last always, nor is there any peace to be called lasting on this side the everlasting peace.

III. If our present state be subject to such vicissitude, *What profit has he that works?* We must look upon ourselves as upon our probation in it. There is indeed no profit *in that wherein we labour*; the thing itself, when we have it, will do us little good; but, if we make a right use of the disposals of Providence about it, there will be profit in that (*v.* 10): *I have seen the travail which God has given to the sons of men*, not to make up a happiness by it, but *to be exercised in it*, to have various graces exercised by the variety of events, to have their dependence upon God tried by every change, and to be trained and taught. Every change cuts us out some new work, which we should be more solicitous about, than about the event.

Verses 11–15

Solomon shows the hand of God in all those changes.

I. We must make the best of *that which is*, and must believe it best for the present, and accommodate ourselves to it: *He has made everything beautiful in his time* (*v.* 11). Cold is as becoming in winter as heat in summer; and the night, in its turn, is a black beauty, as the day, in its turn, is a bright one. There is a wonderful harmony in the divine Providence and all its disposals, so that events considered in their relations and tendencies, together with the seasons of them, appear very beautiful, to the glory of God and the comfort of those that trust in him. Though we see not the complete beauty of Providence, yet we shall see it, and a glorious sight it will be, when the mystery of God shall be finished. Deut. xxxii. 4; Ezek. i. 18.

II. We must wait with patience for the full discovery of that which to us seems intricate and perplexed, acknowledging that we *cannot find out the work that God makes from the beginning to the end*, and therefore must judge nothing before the time. While the picture is in drawing, and the house in building, we see not the beauty of either; but when the artist has given them their finishing strokes, then all appears very good. We see but the middle of God's works, not from the beginning of them (then we should see how admirably the plan was laid in the divine counsels), nor to the end of them, which crowns the action (then we should see the product to be glorious); but we must wait till the veil be rent. Those words, *He has set the world in their hearts*, are differently understood. 1. Some make them to be a reason why we may know more of God's works than we do. If men did but give themselves to the exact observation of things, they might in most of them perceive an admirable order and contrivance. 2. Others make them to be a reason why we do not know so much of God's works as we might: "We have the world so much in our hearts, are so taken up with thoughts and cares of worldly things, that we have neither time nor spirit to eye God's hand in them."

III. *There is no* certain lasting, *good in* these things (*v.* 12, 13). All the *good* there is *in them* is *to do good* with them, to our families, to our neighbours, to the poor, to the public, to its civil and religious interests. What have we our beings, capacities, and estates for, but to be some way serviceable to our generation? It is *in this life*, where we are in a state of trial and probation for another life. Every man's life is his opportunity of doing that which will make for him in eternity. Let us make ourselves easy, *rejoice, and enjoy the good of our labour*, as *it is the gift of God*, and so enjoy God in it, and return him thanks.

IV. We must be satisfied in the disposals of divine Providence, both as to personal and public concerns. "Let it be as God wills", for, how cross soever it may be to our designs and interests, God's will is his wisdom. That counsel needs not to be altered. If we could see it altogether at one view, we should see it so perfect that *nothing can be put to it*, for there is no deficiency in it, *nor anything taken from it*, for there is nothing in it unnecessary, or that can be spared.

V. We must study to answer God's end in all his providences. Whatever changes we see or feel in this world, we must acknowledge the inviolable steadiness of God's government. With the events of Providence (*v.* 15): *That which has been is now*. The world, as it has been, is and will be constant in inconstancy; for *God requires that which is past*, that is, repeats what he has formerly done. There has no change befallen us, *but such as is common to men*.

Verses 16–22

Solomon is still showing that everything in this world, without piety and the fear of God, is vanity. In these verses he shows that power and life itself are nothing without the fear of God.

I. Here is the vanity of man, mighty upon the throne, man upon the judgment-seat, where, if he be governed by the laws of religion, he is God's vicegerent. But without the fear of God it *is vanity*, for, set that aside, and,

1. The judge will not judge aright. Solomon perceived that there was *wickedness in the place of judgment. Man being in honour, and not understanding* what he ought to do, *becomes like the beasts that perish*, like the beasts of prey. It would have been better for the people to have had no judges than to have had such. It would have been better for the judges to have had no power than to have used it to such ill purposes.

2. The judge will himself be judged for not judging aright. *I said in my heart* that this unrighteous judgment is not conclusive, for there will be a review of the judgment; *God shall judge* between *the righteous and the wicked*, shall judge for the righteous and plead their cause. It is an unspeakable comfort to the oppressed that their cause will be heard over again. Let them therefore wait with patience, for there is another *Judge* that *stands before the door. There is a*

time for the re-hearing of causes, redressing of grievances, and reversing of unjust decrees, though as yet we see it not here, Job xxiv. 1.

II. Here is the vanity of man as mortal. He now comes to speak more generally *concerning the estate of the sons of men* in this world, and shows that their reason, without religion and the fear of God, advances them but little above the beasts. Lay no blame on God; let them not say that he made this world to be man's prison and life to be his penance. God made man *little lower than the angels*; if he be mean and miserable, it is his own fault. It is no easy matter to convince proud men that *they are but men* (Ps. ix. 20), much more to convince bad men *that they are beasts*, being destitute of religion. A worldly, carnal, earthly-minded *man, has no pre-eminence above the beast, for all* that which he sets his heart upon *is vanity, v.* 19. *That which befalls the sons of men* is no other than that which *befalls beasts*; death makes much the same change with a beast that it does with a man. As to their bodies, the change is altogether the same, except the different respects that are paid to them by the survivors. Solomon here observes that *all go unto one place*; the dead bodies of men and beasts putrefy alike; *all turn to dust again* in their corruption. As to their spirits there is indeed a vast difference, but not a visible one, *v.* 21. It is certain that *the spirit of the sons of men at death goes upwards* to the Father of spirits, who made it; it dies not with the body, but *is redeemed from the power of the grave*, Ps. xlix. 15. The soul of a man is then like a candle taken out of a dark lantern, which leaves the lantern useless indeed, but does itself shine brighter. Those that live by sense, as all carnal sensualists do, that *walk in the sight of their eyes*, have no *pre-eminence above the beasts*. It is not strange that those live like beasts who think they shall die like beasts, but on such the noble faculties of reason are lost. An inference drawn from it (*v.* 22): *There is nothing better*, as to this world, *than that a man should rejoice in his own works*, that is, Keep a clear conscience, and never admit *iniquity* into *the place of righteousness*. Live a cheerful life. If God has prospered the work of our hands unto us, let us rejoice in it, and not make it a burden.

CHAPTER 4

Solomon shows, I. The temptation which the oppressed feel to discontent and impatience, ver. 1–3. II. The temptation which those that love their ease feel to take their ease, ver. 4–6. III. The folly of hoarding up abundance of worldly wealth, ver. 7, 8. IV. A remedy against that folly, in being made sensible of the benefit of mutual assistance, ver. 9–12. V. The mutability even of royal dignity, not only through the folly of the prince himself (ver. 13, 14), but through the fickleness of the people, ver. 15, 16.

Verses 1–3

Solomon had a large soul (1 Kings iv. 29) and it appeared by this, among other things, that he had a very tender concern for the miserable and the afflicted. He had taken the oppressors to task (*ch.* iii. 16, 17); now he observes the oppressed and here he does it as a preacher:

I. The troubles of their condition (*v.* 1) grieved him. Servants and labourers were oppressed by their masters, debtors by cruel creditors and creditors too by fraudulent debtors, tenants by hard landlords and orphans by treacherous guardians, and, worst of all, subjects oppressed by arbitrary princes and unjust judges. He *beheld the tears of such as were oppressed*, unable to help themselves: *On the side of their oppressors there was power*, when they had done wrong, to stand to it and make good what they had done, so that the poor were born down with a strong hand and had no way to obtain redress.

II. Being thus hardly used, they are tempted to envy those that are dead and in their graves, and to wish they had never been born (*v.* 2, 3); and Solomon is ready to agree with them. *"I praised the dead that are already dead* before they had well begun to live. I concluded that it is better with them than with *the living that are yet alive*, and that is all, dragging the long and heavy chain of life, and wearing out its tedious minutes." Better never to have been born than be born to *see the evil work that is done under the sun*, and not only to be in no capacity to mend the matter, but to suffer ill for doing well. A good man, how calamitous a condition soever he is in in this world, cannot have cause to wish he had never been born, since he is glorifying the Lord even in the fires.

Verses 4–6

I. If a man be acute, and dexterous, and successful in his business, he gets the ill-will of *his neighbours* (*v.* 4), and the more for the reputation he has got by his honesty. Cain envied Abel, Esau Jacob and Saul David, and all for their right works. This is downright diabolism. Those that excel in virtue will always be an eye-sore to those that exceed in vice, which should not discourage us from any right work, but drive us to expect the praise of it, not from men, but from God.

II. If a man be stupid and blundering in his business, he does ill for himself (*v.* 5): *The fool* that goes about his work as if *his hands* were muffled and *folded together*, that does everything awkwardly, *the sluggard* that loves his ease and *folds his hands together* to keep them warm, *eats his own flesh*, is a cannibal to himself, brings himself into such a poor condition that he has nothing to eat but his own flesh. The following words (*v.* 6), *Better is a handful with quietness than both the hands full with travail and vexation of spirit*, may be taken either, 1. As the sluggard's excuse of himself in his idleness, as if a little with idleness is better than abundance with honest labour. But, 2. I rather take it as Solomon's advice to keep the mean between *travail* and slothfulness. Let us by honest industry lay hold on the handful, that we may not want necessaries, but not grasp at both the hands full, which will but create us vexation of spirit. Moderate pains and moderate gains will do best.

Verses 7–12

Solomon fastens upon another instance of the vanity of this world, that frequently the more men have of it the more they would have; and on this they are so intent that they have no enjoyment of what they have.

I. Selfishness is the cause of this evil (*v.* 7, 8): *There is one alone*, that minds none but himself, cares for nobody; *there is not a second*, nor does he desire there should be: one mouth he thinks enough in a house. He makes himself a slave to his business. Though *he has neither child nor brother*, none to take care of but himself, nor dares he marry, for fear of the expense of a family, *yet is there no end to his labour*. He never thinks he has enough: *His eye is not satisfied with riches*. He has enough for his back, for his belly, for his calling, for his family, for his living decently in the world, but he has not enough for his eyes. He denies himself the comfort of what he has: He *bereaves his soul of good*. He has no excuse for doing this: *He has neither child nor brother*, none that are poor or dear to him. It is wisdom for those that take pains about this world to consider whom they take all this pains for, and whether it be really worth while. If men do not consider this, it *is vanity, and a sore travail*; they shame and vex themselves to no purpose.

II. Sociableness is the cure of this evil. Men are thus sordid because they are all for themselves. Solomon shows, by divers instances, that *it is not good*

for man to be alone (Gen. ii. 18); he designs to recommend to us both marriage and friendship. *Two are better than one*, and more happy jointly than either of them could be separately. *They have a good reward of their labour*. He that serves himself has himself only for his paymaster. But he that is kind to another has *a good reward*; the pleasure and advantage of holy love will be an abundant recompence for all the *work and labour of love*. He proves it by divers instances of the benefit of friendship and good conversation. It is good for two to travel together, *for if* one happen to *fall*, the other will be ready *to help him up*. If a man fall *into sin*, his friend will help to *restore him with the spirit of meekness*. Virtuous and gracious affections are excited by good society, and Christians warm one another by *provoking one another to love and to good works*. If an enemy find a man alone, he is likely to *prevail against him*; but, if he have a second, he may do well enough: *two shall withstand him*. As was said of the ancient Britons, when the Romans invaded them, *Dum singuli pugnant, universi vincuntur—While they fight in detached parties, they sacrifice the general cause*. In our spiritual warfare we may be helpful to one another as well as in our spiritual work; next to the comfort of communion with God, is that of the communion of saints. He concludes with this proverb, *A threefold cord is not easily broken*, any more than a bundle of arrows, though each single thread, and each single arrow, is. Two together he compares to *a threefold cord*; for where two are closely joined in holy love and fellowship, Christ will by his Spirit come to them, and make the third, as he joined himself to the two disciples going to Emmaus, and then there is *a threefold cord* that can never be *broken*.

Verses 13–16

I. A king is not happy unless he have wisdom, *v.* 13, 14. If he be *foolish* he will not suffer any counsel or admonition to be given him. Folly and wilfulness commonly go together, and those that most need admonition can worst bear it; but neither age nor titles will secure men respect if they have not true wisdom and virtue to recommend them; while wisdom and virtue will gain men honour even under the disadvantages of youth and poverty.

II. A king is not likely to continue if he have not a confirmed interest in the affections of the people. He that is king must have a successor, a *second*, a *child that shall stand up in his stead*, his own, spoken of, or perhaps that *poor and wise child* spoken of, *v.* 13. People are never long easy and satisfied: *There is no end*, no rest, *of all the people;* they are continually fond of changes, and know not what they would have. As it has been, so it is likely to be still: *Those that come after* will be of the same spirit, and *shall not long rejoice in him* whom at first they seemed extremely fond of. To-day, *Hosanna*—tomorrow, *Crucify. This is vanity and vexation of spirit.*

CHAPTER 5

Solomon, in this chapter, discourses, I. Concerning the worship of God, prescribing that as a remedy against all those vanities which he had already observed to be in wisdom, learning, pleasure, honour, power, and business. If our religion be a vain religion, how great is that vanity! Let us therefore take heed of vanity, 1. In hearing the word, and offering sacrifice, ver. 1. 2. In prayer, ver. 2, 3. 3. In making vows, ver. 4–6. 4. In pretending to divine dreams, ver. 7. II. Concerning the wealth of this world and the vanity and vexation that attend it. The fruits of the earth indeed are necessary to the support of life (ver. 9), but 1. Silver, and gold, and riches, are unsatisfying, ver. 10. 2. They are unprofitable, ver. 11. 3. They are disquieting, ver. 12. 4. They often prove hurtful and destroying, ver. 13. 5. They are perishing, ver. 14. 6. They must be left behind when we die, ver. 15, 16. 7. If we have not a heart to make use of them, they occasion a great deal of uneasiness, ver. 17. We can learn out of this chapter how to manage the business of religion, and the business of this world (which two take up most of our time), so that both may turn to a good account.

Verses 1–3

Solomon's design, in driving us off from the world, by showing us its vanity, is to drive us to God and to our duty.

I. He here sends us to *the house of God*, to the place of public worship. Let our disappointments in the creature turn our eyes to the Creator. In the word and prayer there is a balm for every wound.

II. He charges us to behave ourselves well there. Religious exercises are not vain things, but, if we mismanage them, they become vain to us. *"Keep thy foot*, not keep it back from the house of God (as Prov. xxv. 17), but *look well to thy goings, ponder the path of thy feet*, lest thou take a false step. Address thyself to the worship of God with a solemn pause, and take time to compose thyself, not going about it with precipitation, which is called *hasting with the feet*, Prov. xix. 2. Keep thy thoughts from roving and wandering; keep thy affections from running out towards wrong objects." Some think it alludes to the charge given to Moses and Joshua to *put off their shoes* (Exod. iii. 5, Joshua v. 15). We must take heed that the sacrifice we bring be not *the sacrifice of fools* —that we rest not in the sign and ceremony, and the outside of the performance, without regarding the sense and meaning of it, for that is the *sacrifice of fools*. Men may be doing evil even when they do not know it, when they do not consider it. Wicked minds cannot choose but sin, even in the acts of devotion. We must be *ready to hear*; must diligently *attend* to the word of God read and preached. *Hearing* is often put for *obeying*, and that is it that is *better than sacrifice*, 1 Sam. xv. 22; Isa. i. 15, 16. *Let the word of the Lord come* (said a good man), *and if I had* 600 *necks I would bow them all to the authority of it*. We must be very cautious in all approaches to God (*v.* 2): *Be not rash with thy mouth*, in making prayers, or protestations, or promises; *let not thy heart be hasty to utter anything before God*. If we come without an errand, we shall go away without any advantage. What we *utter before God* must come from *the heart*, and therefore we must never let our tongue outrun our thoughts in our devotions. Thoughts are words to God. It is not enough that what we say comes from the heart, but it must come from a composed heart, and not from a sudden heat or passion. *God is in heaven*, where he is *far exalted above all our blessing and praise. We are on earth*, the footstool of his throne, unworthy to have any communion with him. Therefore we must be grave, humble, serious, and reverent in speaking to him.

Verses 4–8

Four things we are exhorted to in these verses:

I. To be conscientious in paying our vows.

1. A vow is a bond upon the soul (Num. xxx. 2). When, under the sense of some affliction (Ps. lxvi. 14), or in the pursuit of some mercy (1 Sam. i. 11), thou hast vowed a vow *unto God*, know that *thou hast opened thy mouth unto the Lord and thou canst not go back*; therefore perform what thou hast promised. *Pay that which thou hast vowed;* pay it in full and *keep not back any part of the price*. Have we vowed to *give our own selves unto the Lord?* Let us then be as good as our word. *Defer not to pay it.*

2. Two reasons are here given why we should speedily and cheerfully pay our vows: (1) Because otherwise we affront God; we play the fool with him, as if we designed to put a trick upon him; and *God has no pleasure in fools*. (2) Because otherwise we wrong ourselves, we incur the penalty for the breach of it; so that it would have been better a great deal *not to have vowed*. Not to have *vowed* would have been but an omission, but to *vow and not pay* incurs the guilt of treachery, and perjury; it is *lying to God*, Acts v. 4.

II. To be cautious in making our vows. We must take heed that we never vow anything that is sinful, or that may be an occasion of sin, for such a vow is ill-made and must be broken. *Suffer not thy mouth*, by such a vow, *to cause thy flesh to sin*, as Herod's rash promise caused him to cut off the head of John the Baptist. "When thou hast made a *vow*, do not seek to evade it; *say not before the priest*, who is called the *angel or messenger of the Lord of hosts*, that, upon second thoughts, thou hast changed thy mind, and desirest to be absolved from the obligation of thy vow; but stick to it, and do not seek a hole to creep out at." If we treacherously cancel the words of our mouths, and revoke our vows, God will justly overthrow our projects.

III. To keep up the fear of God, *v.* 7. Many, of old, pretended to know the mind of God by *dreams*, and almost made God's people forget his name by their *dreams* (Jer. xxiii. 25, 26); and many now perplex themselves with their frightful or odd dreams, as if they foreboded disaster. Those that heed dreams shall have a multitude of them; but in them all *there are divers vanities*. Therefore never heed them; instead of repeating them lay no stress upon them, draw no disquieting conclusions from them, but *fear thou God*.

IV. Every good man that has a sense of justice and a concern for mankind, is angry to see *the oppression of the poor*, and the *violent perverting of judgment and justice in a province*, oppression under colour of law and backed with power. The kingdom in general may have a good government, and yet it may so happen that a particular province may be committed to a bad man. When things look thus dismal we may satisfy ourselves that, though oppressors be *high*, God is *higher than the highest* of creatures, than the highest of princes. God is the *Most High over all the earth*, and his *glory is above the heavens*. Though oppressors be secure, God has his eye upon them, and will reckon for all their violent perverting of judgment.

Verses 9–17

Solomon shows that there is as much vanity in great riches, and the *lust of the eye* about them, as there is in the *lusts of the flesh* and the *pride of life*, and a man can make himself no more happy by hoarding an estate than by spending it.

I. He grants that the products of the earth, for the support and comfort of human life, are valuable things (*v.* 9). There is *profit to be got out of the earth*, and it is *for all*; all need it; it is appointed for all; there is enough for all. The earth is our storehouse and the beasts are fellow-commoners with us. *The king himself is served of the field*, and would be starved, without its products. This puts a great honour upon the husbandman's calling, that it is the most necessary of all to the support of man's life.

II. He maintains that the riches that are more than these, that are for hoarding, not for use, are *vain things*, and will not make a man easy or happy. The more men have the more they would have, *v.* 10. Natural desires are at rest when that which is desired is obtained, but corrupt desires are insatiable. There are bodily desires which silver itself will not satisfy; if a man be hungry ingots of silver will do no more to satisfy his hunger than clods of clay. Much less will worldly abundance satisfy spiritual desires. *When goods increase, they are increased that eat them, v.* 11. *The more meat the more mouths*. Does the estate thrive? And does not the family at the same time grow more numerous and the children grow up to need more? The more men have the better house they must keep. The owner sees that as his own, which those about him enjoy as much of the real benefit of as he; only he has the satisfaction of doing good to others, which indeed is a satisfaction to one who believed what Christ said, that *it is more blessed to give than to receive*. The more men have the more care they have about it, which perplexes them and disturbs their repose, *v.* 12. Refreshing sleep is as much the support and comfort of this life as food is. Those commonly sleep best that work hard and have but what they work for: *The sleep of the labouring man is sweet*. Those that have everything else often fail to secure a good night's sleep. The more men have the more danger they are in both of doing mischief and of having mischief done them (*v.* 13): *There is an evil, a sore evil, riches kept for the owners thereof* (who have been industrious to hoard them and keep them safely) to *their hurt*; they would have been better without them. They *do hurt with their riches*, which not only put them into a capacity of gratifying their own lusts but give them an opportunity of oppressing others and dealing hardly with them. Often they sustain *hurt by their riches*. They would not be envied, would not be robbed, if they were not rich. Those riches that have been laid up with a great deal of pains *perish by evil travail*, by the very pains and care which they take to secure and increase them. Many a one has lost all by catching at all. How much soever men have when they die, they must leave it all behind them (*v.* 15, 16): *As he came forth of his mother's womb naked, so shall he return*. In respect of the body we must go as we came; the dust shall return to the earth as it was. But sad is our case if the soul return as it came, unsanctified. This is a *sore evil*; he thinks it so whose heart is glued to the world, that he *shall take nothing of his labour which he may carry away in his hand*; his riches will not go with him into another world nor stand him in any stead there. If we labour in religion, the grace and comfort we get by that labour we may carry away in our hearts, and shall be the better for it to eternity; that is meat that endures. Men will see that they have *laboured for the wind* when at death they find the profit of their labour is all gone, gone like the wind, they know not whither. Those that have much, if they set their hearts upon it, have not only uncomfortable deaths, but uncomfortable lives too, *v.* 17. This covetous worldling, that is so bent upon raising an estate, *all his days eats in darkness and much sorrow, and it is his sickness and wrath*; he has not only no pleasure of his estate, nor any enjoyment of it himself, for he *eats the bread of sorrow* (Ps. cxxvii. 2), but a great deal of vexation to see others eat of it.

Verse 18–20

Solomon, from the vanity of riches hoarded up, here infers that the best course we can take is to use well what we have, to serve God with it, to do good with it, and take the comfort of it to ourselves and our families; this he had pressed before, *ch.* ii. 24; iii. 22. Life is God's gift, and he has appointed us the *number of the days* of our life (Job xiv. 5); let us therefore spend those days in *serving the Lord our God with joyfulness and gladness of heart*. We must not do the business of our calling as a drudgery, and make ourselves slaves to it, but we must *rejoice in our labour*, not grasp at more business than we can go through without perplexity and disquiet. Those that cheerfully use what God has given them thereby honour the giver, answer the intention of the gift, act rationally and generously, do good in the world, and make what they have turn to the best account, and this is both their credit and their comfort; *it is good and comely*; there is duty and decency in it. A heart to do thus is such a gift of God's grace as crowns all the gifts of his providence. This is the way to relieve ourselves against the many toils and troubles which our lives on earth are incident to (*v.* 20): *He shall not much remember the*

days of his life, the days of his sorrow and sore travail, his working days, his weeping days. He shall either forget them or remember them as waters that pass away; he shall not much lay to heart his crosses, nor long retain the bitter relish of them, *because God answers him in the joy of his heart*, balances all the grievances of his labour with the joy of it and recompenses him for it by giving him to *eat the labour of his hands*.

CHAPTER 6

In this chapter, I. The royal preacher goes on further to show the vanity of worldly wealth. Riches, in the hands of a man that is wise and generous, are good for something, but in the hands of a sordid, sneaking, covetous miser, they are good for nothing. He takes an account of the possessions and enjoyments which such a man may have. He has wealth (ver. 2), he has children to inherit it (ver. 3), and lives long, ver. 3, 6. He describes his folly in not taking the comfort of it; he has no power to eat of it, lets strangers devour it, and at last has no burial, ver. 2, 3. He prefers the condition of a still-born child before the condition of such a one, ver. 3. The still-born child's infelicity is only negative (ver. 4, 5), but that of the covetous worldling is positive, ver. 6. He shows the vanity of riches as pertaining only to the body, and giving no satisfaction to the mind (ver. 7, 8), and of those boundless desires with which covetous people vex themselves (ver. 9), which, if they be gratified ever so fully, leave a man but a man still, ver. 10. II. He concludes this discourse of the vanity of the creature with this plain inference from the whole, That it is folly to think of making up a happiness for ourselves in the things of this world, ver. 11, 12. Our satisfaction must be in another life, not in this.

Verses 1–6

Solomon now shows the evil of having and not using. This *is an evil which* Solomon himself saw *under the sun, v.* 1. Solomon, as a king, took notice of this evil as a prejudice to the public, who are damaged not only by men's prodigality on the one hand, but by their penuriousness on the other. As it is with the blood in the natural body, so it is with the wealth of the body politic, if, instead of circulating, it stagnates, it will be of ill consequence. Solomon as a preacher observed the evils that were done that he might reprove them and warn people against them.

I. The abundant reason the miser has to serve God. *Riches* and *wealth* commonly gain people *honour* among men. *Riches, wealth, and honour*, are God's gifts, the gifts of his providence. Yet they are given to many that do not make a good use of them. *He wants nothing for his soul of all that he desires*. He does not desire grace for his soul, the better part; all he desires is enough to gratify the sensual appetite, and that he has. He is supposed to have a numerous family, to *beget a hundred children*, which are the stay and strength of his house and in whom he has the prospect of having his name built up. To complete his happiness, he is supposed to *live many years, a thousand years twice told*.

II. The little heart he has to use this which God gives him, for the ends and purposes for which it was given him. This is his fault. He cannot find in his heart to take the comfort of what he has himself. He has meat before him, but he has *not power to eat thereof*. His sordid niggardly temper will not suffer him to lay it out, no, not upon himself. Because he has not the will to serve God with it, God denies him the power to serve himself with it. God orders it so that *a stranger eats it*. This may be well called *vanity, and an evil disease*. Our worst diseases are those that arise from the corruption of our own hearts. He deprives himself of the good that he might have had of his worldly possessions. *His soul is not filled with good, v.* 3. *He has no burial*, none agreeable to his rank, no decent burial, but *the burial of an ass*.

III. *An untimely birth*, a child that is carried from the womb to the grave, *is better than he*. Solomon here pronounces *an untimely birth*, upon many accounts, to be very sad (*v.* 4, 5): *He comes in with vanity* and he *departs in darkness*; little or no notice is taken of him; being an abortive, he has no *name*, or, if he had, it would soon be forgotten and buried in oblivion; it would *be covered with darkness,* as the body is with the earth. Nay (*v.* 5), *he has not seen the sun,* but from the darkness of the womb he is hurried immediately to that of the grave, and, which is worse than not being known to any, he has not *known anything.*

Verses 7–10

The preacher here further shows the vanity and folly of heaping up worldly wealth and expecting happiness in it.

I. How much soever we toil about the world, and get out of it, we can have for ourselves no more than a maintenance (*v.* 7). A little will serve to sustain us comfortably and a great deal can do no more.

II. Those that have ever so much are still craving; let a man labour ever so much *for his mouth, yet the appetite is not filled.* The desires of the soul find nothing in the wealth of the world to give them any satisfaction. *The soul is not filled,* so the word is.

III. A fool may have as much worldly wealth, and may enjoy as much of the pleasure of it, as a wise man; nay, and perhaps not be so sensible of the vexation of it: *What has the wise more than the fool?* (*v.* 8). A fool can fare as well, can dress as well, and make as good a figure in any public appearance, as a wise man; so that if there were not pleasures and honour peculiar to the mind, which *the wise man has more than the fool,* as to this world they would be upon a level.

IV. Even a poor man, who has business, and is discreet, diligent, in the management of it, may get as comfortably through this world as he that is loaded with an overgrown estate. Why, he is better beloved and more respected among his neighbours, and has a better interest than many a rich man that is griping and haughty.

V. The enjoyment of what we have cannot but be acknowledged more rational than a greedy grasping at more (*v.* 9): *Better is the sight of the eyes,* making the best of that which is present, *than the wandering of the desire.* He is much happier that is always content, though he has ever so little, than he that is always coveting, though he has ever so much. We cannot say, *Better is the sight of the eyes than the* fixing *of the desire* upon God, and the resting of the soul in him.

VI. Whatever we attain to in this world, still we are but men, and the greatest possessions cannot set us above the common accidents of human life. That busy animal that makes such a stir and such a noise in the world, *is named already.* He that made him gave him his name, *and it is known that it is man;* and it is a humbling name, Gen. v. 2. He *called their name Adam;* and all theirs have the same character, *red earth.* It is good for rich and great men to know and consider that they are *but men,* Ps. ix. 20.

Verses 11–12

There be many things that increase vanity; even that which pretends to increase wealth and pleasure does but increase vanity and make it more vexatious. We do not know what to wish for, because that which we promise ourselves most satisfaction in often proves most vexatious to us. Thoughtful people are in care to do everything for the best, if they knew it; but it is an instance of the corruption of our hearts that we are apt to desire that as good for us which is really hurtful. Since everything is vanity, *Who can tell a man what shall be after him under the sun?* He can no more please himself with the hopes of *what shall be after him,* to his children and family, than with the relish of what is with him, since he can neither foresee himself, nor can anyone else foretell to him, *what shall be after him.*

Chapter 7

Solomon had given many proofs of the vanity of this world. In this chapter, I. He recommends to us some good means to be used for the redress of these grievances, that we may make the best of the bad, as, 1. Care of our reputation, ver. 1. 2. Seriousness, ver. 2–6. 3. Calmness of spirit, ver. 7–10. 4. Prudence in the management of all our affairs, ver. 11, 12. 5. Submission to the will of God in all events, ver. 13–15. 6. A conscientious avoiding of all dangerous extremes, ver. 16–18. 7. Mildness and tenderness towards those that have been injurious to us, ver. 19–22. In short, to keep our temper and to maintain a strict government of our passions. II. He laments his own iniquity, the having of many wives, by which he was drawn away from God and his duty, ver. 23–29.

Verses 1–6

In these verses Solomon lays down some great truths which seem paradoxes.

I. That the honour of virtue is really more valuable and desirable than all the wealth and pleasure in this world (*v.* 1): *A good name is before good ointment* (so it may be read). *Good ointment* is here put for all the profits of the earth (among the products of which oil was reckoned one of the most valuable), for all the delights of sense (it is called *the oil of gladness*), and for the highest titles of honour, for kings are anointed. *A good name is* better *than all riches* (Prov. xxii. 1). Christ paid Mary for her ointment with a *good name,* a name in the gospels (Matt. xxvi. 13).

II. If we have lived so as to merit a *good name, the day of our death,* which will put a period to our cares, and toils, and sorrows, and remove us to rest, and joy, and eternal satisfaction, *is better than the day of our birth.*

III. That it will do us more good to go to a funeral than to go to a festival (*v.* 2). We may possibly glorify God, and do good, and get good, in the house of feasting; but, considering how apt we are to be vain and frothy, proud and secure, and indulgent of the flesh, *it is better* for us *to go to the house of mourning,* not to see the pomp of the funeral, but to share in the sorrow of it. The uses to be gathered from *the house of mourning* are by way of information: *That is the end of all men.* By way of admonition: *The living will lay it to his heart.* Nothing is more easy and natural than by the death of others to be put in mind of our own. Some perhaps *will lay that to heart,* and *consider their latter end,* who would not lay a good sermon to heart. *The house of mourning* is the wise man's school, where he has learned many a good lesson. It is the character of a fool that his *heart is in the house of mirth.* If he be at any time in *the house of mourning,* he is under a restraint; his heart at the same time *is in the house of mirth.*

IV. The common proverb says, "An ounce of mirth is worth a pound of sorrow"; but the preacher teaches us a contrary lesson: *Sorrow is better than laughter. By the sadness* that appears in *the countenance, the heart* is often *made better.*

V. It is much better for us to have our corruptions mortified by the *rebuke of the wise* than to have them gratified by *the song of fools, v.* 5. And what an absurd thing it is for a man to dote so much upon such a transient pleasure as *the laughter of a fool,* which may fitly be compared to the burning *of thorns under a pot,* which makes a great noise and a great blaze, for a little while, but presently scatters its ashes, and contributes scarcely anything to the production of a boiling heat, for that requires a constant fire! *The laughter of a fool* is noisy and flashy, and is not an instance of true joy. *This is also vanity.*

Verses 7–10

Solomon had often complained before of *oppressions* which were a great discouragement to virtue and piety.

I. He grants the temptation to be strong (*v.* 7): *Surely* it is often too true that *oppression makes a wise man mad*. If a wise man be much and long oppressed, he is apt to speak and act unlike himself, to break out into indecent complaints against God and man. *It destroys the heart of a gift* (so the latter clause may be read); even the generous heart is destroyed by being oppressed. We should therefore make great allowances to those that are abused; we know not what we should do if it were our own case.

II. The character of oppressors is very bad, so some understand, *v.* 7. If he that had the reputation of *a wise man* becomes an *oppressor*, he becomes a *madman*; and *the gifts* he takes do but *destroy his heart* and extinguish the poor remains of sense and virtue in him, and he is rather to be pitied than envied; let him alone, and in a little time he will ruin himself. The issue, at length, will be good: *Better is the end of a thing than the beginning thereof*. *Better was the end of* Moses's treaty with Pharaoh, that proud oppressor, when Israel was brought forth with triumph, *than the beginning* of it, when the tale of bricks was doubled, and everything looked discouraging.

III. If we would not be driven mad by oppression, we must be clothed with humility; *for the proud in spirit* are those that grow outrageous when they are hardly bestead. We must put on patience, *bearing* patience, to submit to the will of God in the affliction, and *waiting* patience to expect the issue in God's due time. We must govern our passion with wisdom and grace (*v.* 9): *Be not hasty in thy spirit to be angry;* those that cannot brook delays are apt to be angry if they be not immediately gratified. "Be not long angry"; for though anger may come into the bosom of a wise man, and pass through it as a wayfaring man, it *rests* only *in the bosom of fools*. We must make the best of that which is (*v.* 10): "Take it not for granted *that the former days were better than these*, nor enquire *what is the cause* that they were so, for therein *thou does not enquire wisely*; thou art so much a stranger to the times past, and such an incompetent judge even of the present times, that thou canst not expect a satisfactory answer to the enquiry. It is folly to cry up the goodness of former times, so as to derogate from the mercy of God to us in our own times; as if God had been unjust and unkind to us in casting our lot in an iron age, compared with the golden ages that went before us; this arises from nothing but fretfulness and discontent, and an aptness to pick quarrels with God himself. We are not to think there is any universal decay in nature, or degeneracy in morals. God has been always good, and men always bad; and if, in some respects, the times are now worse than they have been, perhaps in other respects they are better.

Verses 11–22

I. The praises of wisdom. Wisdom is necessary to the managing and improving of our worldly possessions: *Wisdom is good with an inheritance*, that is, an inheritance is good for little without wisdom. Wisdom is not only good for the poor, but it is good for the rich too, good with riches to keep a man from getting hurt by them, and to enable a man to do good with them. *Wisdom is good* of itself, and makes a man useful; but, if he have a good estate with it, that will put him into a greater capacity of being useful, and with his wealth he may be more serviceable to his generation than he could have been without it. Wisdom contributes to our safety, and is a shelter to us from the storms of trouble and its scorching heat; it *is a shadow* (so the word is), *as the shadow of a great rock in a weary land*. *Wisdom is a defence, and money* (that is, as *money*) *is a defence*. As a rich man makes his wealth, so a wise man makes

his wisdom, a *strong city*. It is joy and true happiness to a man. This is *the excellency of knowledge*, divine knowledge, not only above money, but above wisdom too, human wisdom, *the wisdom of this world*, that it *gives life to those that have it*. *The fear of the Lord, that is wisdom*, and that is life; it prolongs life. It will put strength into a man, and be his stay and support (*v.* 19): *Wisdom strengthens the wise*, strengthens their spirits, and makes them bold and resolute, by keeping them always on sure grounds.

II. Some of the precepts of wisdom.

1. *Consider the work of God*. To silence our complaints concerning cross events, let us consider the hand of God in them and not open our mouths against that which is his doing. Consider that every work of God is wise, just, and good, and there is an admirable beauty and harmony in his works, and all will appear at last to have been for the best. *Who can make that straight which he has made crooked?* Who can change the nature of things from what is settled by the God of nature.

2. We must accommodate ourselves to the various dispensations of Providence that respect us, and do the work and duty of the day in its day, *v.* 14. Day and night, summer and winter, are set the one *over-against the other*, that in prosperity we may rejoice, *as though we rejoiced not*, and in adversity may weep *as though we wept not*, and it is *to the end that man may find nothing after him*, that he may live in a dependence upon Providence and be ready for whatever happens. Our religion, in general, must be the same in all conditions, but the particular instances and exercises of it must vary, as our outward condition does. *In a day of prosperity* we must *be joyful*, be doing good, and getting good, maintain a holy cheerfulness, *and serve the Lord with gladness of heart*. *In a day of adversity consider*. We cannot answer God's end in afflicting us unless we consider why and wherefore he contends with us.

3. We must not be offended at the greatest prosperity of wicked people, nor at the saddest calamities that may befall the godly in this life, *v.* 15. Wisdom will teach us how to construe those dark chapters of Providence so as to reconcile them with the wisdom, holiness, goodness, and faithfulness of God. *All things have I seen in the days of my vanity*. Though Solomon was so wise a man, he calls the days of his life *the days of his vanity*, for the best days on earth are so, in comparison with the days of eternity. The calamities of the righteous are preparing them for their future blessedness, and the wicked are but ripening for ruin. There is a judgment to come, which will rectify this seeming irregularity, and we must wait with patience till then.

4. Wisdom will be of use both for caution to saints in their way, and for a check to sinners in their way. *A just man may perish in his righteousness*, but let him not, by his own imprudence and rash zeal, pull trouble upon his own head, and then reflect upon Providence as dealing hardly with him. "*Be not righteous overmuch*," *v.* 16. Self-denial and mortification of the flesh are good; but if we prejudice our health by them, and unfit ourselves for the service of God, we are *righteous overmuch*. Be not opinionative, and conceited of thy own abilities. Set not up for a critic, to find fault with everything that is said and done. As to sinners: It is true *there is a wicked man that prolongs his life in his wickedness* (*v.* 15); but let none say that therefore they may safely be as wicked as they will; no, *be not overmuch wicked* (*v.* 17); "be not so foolish as to lay thyself open to the law, *why shouldst thou die before thy time?*"

5. Wisdom will direct us in the mean between two extremes, and keep us always in the way of our duty, which we shall find a plain and safe way (*v.* 18): "*It is good that thou shouldst take hold of this, this*

wisdom, this care, not to run thyself into snares. *Yea, also from this withdraw not thy hand.* Take hold of the bridle by which thy headstrong passions must be held in, as *the horse and mule that have no understanding;* and, having taken hold of it, keep thy hold. Be conscientious, and yet be cautious, and to this exercise thyself.

6. Wisdom will teach us how to conduct ourselves in reference to others. Wisdom teaches us not to expect that those we deal with should be faultless; we ourselves are not so, none are so. This *wisdom strengthens the wise* and arms them against provocation (*v.* 19), so that they are not put into any disorder by it. Those they have dealings with are not incarnate angels, but sinful sons and daughters of Adam: even the best are so, insomuch that *there is not a just man upon earth, that doeth good and sinneth not, v.* 20. Wisdom teaches us not to be quick-sighted in resenting affronts, but to wink at many of the injuries that are done us, and act as if we did not see them (*v.* 21): *"Take no heed to all words that are spoken; set not thy heart to them.* Be not solicitous or inquisitive to know what people say of thee. Approve thyself to God and thy own conscience, and then heed not what men say of thee. If thou heed every word that is spoken, perhaps *thou wilt hear thy own servant curse thee* when he thinks thou dost not hear him. It is easier to pass by twenty such affronts than to avenge one. Wisdom puts us in mind of our own faults (*v.* 22): *"Be not enraged at those that speak ill of thee, for oftentimes,* if thou retire into thyself, thy own conscience will tell thee *that thou thyself hast cursed others,* spoken ill of them, and thou art paid in thy own coin." If we be truly angry with ourselves, as we ought to be, for backbiting and censuring others, we shall be the less angry with others for backbiting and censuring us.

Verses 23–29

Solomon had hitherto been proving the vanity of the world and its utter insufficiency to make men happy; now here he comes to show the vileness of sin, and its certain tendency to make men miserable; and this, as the former, he proves from his own experience, and it was a dear-bought experience. He is here, more than anywhere in all this book, putting on the habit of a penitent.

I. He owns and laments the deficiencies of his wisdom.

1. His searches were industrious. God had given him a capacity for knowledge above any. He resolved, if it were possible, to gain his point: *I said, I will be wise.* He resolved to spare no pains (*v.* 25): *"I applied my heart* to know, and to search, and to seek out wisdom, to accomplish myself in all useful learning, philosophy, and divinity."

2. Yet his success was not answerable or satisfying: *"I said, I will be wise, but it was far from me;* I could not compass it. After all the more I know the more I see there is to be known, and the more sensible I am of my own ignorance. *That which is far off, and exceedingly deep, who can find it out?"* He means God himself, his counsels and his works; when he searched into these he presently found himself puzzled and run aground. Blessed be God, there is nothing which we have to do which is not plain and easy; *the word is nigh us* (Prov. viii. 9); but there is a great deal which we would wish to know which is *far off.*

II. He owns and laments the instances of his folly in which he had exceeded, as, in wisdom, he came short.

1. His enquiry concerning the evil of sin. He *applied his heart to know the wickedness of folly, even of foolishness and madness.* Sin has many disguises, as being loth to appear sin, and it is very hard to strip it of these and to see it in its true nature

and colours. It is necessary to our repentance for sin that we be acquainted with the evil of it, as it is necessary to the cure of a disease to know its nature, causes, and malignity. Solomon, who, in the days of his folly, had set his wits on work to invent pleasures and was ingenious in making provision for the flesh, now that God had opened his eyes is as industrious to find out the aggravations of sin and so to put an edge upon his repentance. Ingenious sinners should be ingenious penitents. Solomon lays the greatest stress upon *the wickedness of folly,* by which perhaps he means his own iniquity, the sin of uncleanness, for that was commonly called *folly in Israel,* Gen. xxxiv. 7; Deut. xxii. 21; Judges xx. 6; 2 Sam. xiii. 12. When he indulged himself in it, he made a light matter of it; but now he desires to see the *wickedness* of it. As there is a wickedness in folly, so there is a folly in wickedness, even foolishness and madness.

2. The result of this enquiry. He now discovered the evil of that great sin which he himself had been guilty of, the *loving of many strange women,* 1 Kings xi. 1. He found the remembrance of the sin very grievous. *I find it more bitter than death.* The heart of the adulterous woman is *snares and nets.* The unwary souls are enticed into them by the bait of pleasure. Her hands are as bands, with which, under colour of fond embraces, she holds those fast that she has seized. *He that pleases God shall escape from her.* He now endeavoured to find out the number of his actual transgressions (*v.* 27). He desired to find them out as a penitent, that he might the more particularly acknowledge them. He soon found himself at a loss, and perceived that they were innumerable (*v.* 28): *Which yet my soul seeks; I am still counting, but I cannot count them all.* I still make new discoveries of the wickedness that there is in my own heart, Jer. xvii. 9, 10. This he illustrates by comparing the corruption of his own heart and life with the corruption of the world, where he scarcely found one good man among a thousand. He found (*v.* 20) that he had sinned even in doing good. The source of all the folly and madness that are in the world is in man's apostasy from God and his degeneracy from his primitive rectitude (*v.* 29). Man, as he came out of God's hands, was (as we may say) a little picture of his Maker, who is *good and upright.* He was marred, and in effect unmade, by his own folly and badness: *They have sought out many inventions*—they, our first parents, or the whole race, all in general and every one in particular. Instead of being for God's institutions, he was for his own inventions.

CHAPTER 8

Solomon, in this chapter, comes to recommend wisdom to us as the most powerful antidote. I. The benefit and praise of wisdom, ver. 1. II. Some particular instances of wisdom prescribed to us. 1. We must keep in due subjection to the government God has set over us, ver. 2–5. 2. We must get ready for sudden evils, and especially for sudden death, ver. 6–8. 3. We must arm ourselves against the temptation of an oppressive government, ver. 9, 10. The impunity of oppressors makes them more daring (ver. 11), but in the issue it will be well with the righteous and ill with the wicked (ver. 12, 14). 4. We must cheerfully use the gifts of God's providence, ver. 15. 5. We must with an entire satisfaction acquiesce in the will of God. ver. 16, 17.

Verses 1–5

I. An encomium of *wisdom* (*v.* 1), that is, of true piety, guided in all its exercises by prudence and discreation. The wise man is the good man, that knows God and glorifies him. *Who is as the wise man?* Heavenly wisdom will make a man an incomparable man. No man without grace, though he be learned, or noble, or rich, is to be compared with a man that has true grace and is therefore accepted of God. It makes him useful among his neighbours: *Who but the wise man knows the interpretation of a thing,* that is, understands the times and events. *It makes his face to shine*, as Moses's did when he came down from the mount; it puts honour upon a man and a lustre on his whole conversation. *The strength of his face*, the sourness and severity of his *countenance* (so some understand the last clause), *shall be changed* by it into that which is sweet and obliging. Even those whose natural temper is rough and morose, by *wisdom* are strangely altered. It emboldens a man against his adversaries. *The boldness of his face shall be* doubled by wisdom; it will add to his courage when he not only has an honest cause to plead, but by his wisdom knows how to manage it.

II. A particular instance of wisdom is subjection to authority. We must be observant of the laws. In all those things wherein the civil power is to interpose, whether legislative or judicial, we ought to submit to its order. *I counsel thee; I charge thee*, not only as a prince but as a preacher: "I recommend it to thee as a piece of wisdom; I say, whatever those say that are given to change, *keep the king's commandment. Observe the mouth of a king*" (so the phrase is). Some understand the following clause as a limitation of this obedience: *Keep the king's commandment*, yet so as to have a *regard to the oath of God*, that is, so as to keep a good conscience and not to violate thy obligations to God, which are prior and superior to thy obligations to the king. We must not be forward to find fault with the public administration (*v.* 3): "*Be not hasty to go out of his sight*, when he is displeased at thee (*ch.* x. 4), or when thou art displeased at him; fly not off in a passion, nor forsake the kingdom." "*Stand not in an evil thing*; in any offence thou hast given to thy prince humble thyself, and do not justify thyself, for that will make the offence much more offensive." We must prudently accommodate ourselves to our opportunities, both for our own relief, if we think ourselves wronged, and for the redress of public grievances: *A wise man's heart discerns both time and judgment* (*v.* 5). We *must needs be subject, for conscience-sake*. "*Keep the king's commandments*, for he has sworn to rule thee in the fear of God, and thou hast sworn, in that fear, to be faithful to him." It is called *the oath of God* because he is a witness to it and will avenge the violation of it.

Verses 6–8
Solomon here shows that even the wisest may yet be surprised by a calamity which they had not any foresight of, and therefore it is our wisdom to expect and prepare for sudden changes. Man *knows not that which shall be* himself; and *who can tell him when* or how *it shall be?* (*v.* 7). The stars cannot foretell a man what shall be, or any of the arts of divination. God has, in wisdom, concealed from us the knowledge of future events, that we may be always ready for changes. *Because to every purpose there is* but one way, one method, one proper opportunity, *therefore the misery of man is great upon him.* Men are miserable because they are not sufficiently sagacious and attentive. Whatever other evils may be avoided, we are all under a fatal necessity of dying (*v.* 8). When the soul is required it must be resigned. *There is no man that has power over* his own *spirit, to retain it*, when it is summoned to return to God who gave it. Death is an enemy that we must all enter the lists with, sooner or later: *There is no discharge in that war.* Men's wickedness, by which they often evade or outface the justice of the prince, cannot secure them from the arrest of death, nor can the most obstinate sinner harden his heart against those terrors.

Verses 9–13
Solomon, in these verses, encourages us, in reference to the mischief of tyrannical and oppressive rulers. He had observed that many a time *one man*

rules over another to his hurt. It is sad with a people when those that should protect their religion and rights aim at the destruction of both. To the hurt of the rulers (so we render it), *to their own hurt. What hurt men do to others will return, in the end, to their own hurt.* He had observed them to prosper and flourish in the abuse of their power (*v.* 10): *I saw those wicked* rulers *come and go from the place of the holy*, go in state to and return in pomp from the place of judicature (which is called *the place of the Holy One* because *the judgment is the Lord's*, Deut. i. 17), and they continued all their days in office, were never reckoned with for their maladministration, but died in honour and were buried magnificently. *And they were forgotten in the city where they had so done;* their wicked practices were not remembered against them when they were gone. He had observed that their prosperity hardened them in their wickedness, *v.* 11. It is true of all sinners in general, and particularly of wicked rulers, that, *because sentence against their evil works is not executed speedily*, they think it will never be executed, and therefore they set the law at defiance and *their hearts are full in them to do evil*; they venture to do more mischief, and commit iniquity with a high hand. Sentence is passed against evil works and evil workers by the righteous Judge of heaven and earth, even against the evil works of princes and great men. The execution of this sentence is often delayed, and the sinner goes on, not only unpunished, but prosperous and successful. Sinners herein deceive themselves, for, though the *sentence* be *not executed speedily*, it will be executed the more severely at last. We should not be discouraged. "*It shall be well with those that fear God,* I say with all those, and those only, *who fear before him.*" When they lie at the mercy of proud oppressors they fear God more than they fear them. And therefore "*surely I know*, I know it by the promise of God, and the experience of all the saints, *that*, however it goes with others, *it shall go well with them.*" A good man's days have some substance in them; he lives to a good purpose. A wicked man's days are all *as a shadow*, empty and worthless. These days *shall not be prolonged* to what he promised himself. Though they may be *prolonged* (*v.* 12) beyond what others expected, yet his day shall come to fall. He shall fall short of everlasting life, and then his long life on earth will be worth little.

Verses 14–17
Wise and good men, have, of old, been perplexed with this difficulty, how the prosperity of the wicked and the troubles of the righteous can be reconciled with the holiness and goodness of the God that governs the world. Concerning this Solomon here gives us his advice.

I. He would not have us to be surprised at it, as though some strange thing happened, for he himself saw it in his days, *v.* 14. 1. He saw *just men to whom it happened according to the work of the wicked*, who, notwithstanding their righteousness, suffered very hard things. He saw *wicked men to whom it happened according to the work of the righteous*, who prospered as remarkably as if they had been rewarded for some good deed. We see the just troubled and perplexed in their own minds, the wicked easy, fearless, and secure.

II. He would have us not to charge God with iniquity, but to charge the world with vanity. No fault is to be found with God; but, as to the world, *This is vanity upon the earth*, and again, *This is also vanity*, that is, it is a certain evidence that the things of this world are not the best things nor were ever designed to make happiness for us, for, if they had, God would not have allotted so much of this world's wealth to his worst enemies and so much of its troubles to his best friends; there must therefore be another life after this the joys and griefs of which must be real and substantial.

III. He would have us not to fret ourselves about it, but cheerfully to enjoy what God has given us in the world, and make the best of it, though it be much better with others, and such as we think very unworthy (v. 15): *Then I commended joy*, a holy security and serenity of mind, arising from a confidence in God, and his power, and promise, *because a man has no better thing under the sun than to eat and drink*, that is, soberly and thankfully to make use of the things of this life, *and to be cheerful, whatever happens, for that shall abide with him of his labour*. Our present life is a life *under the sun*, but we look for *the life of the world to come*, which will commence and continue when *the sun shall be turned into darkness* and shine no more.

IV. He would not have us undertake to give a reason for that which God does, for *his way is in the sea and his path in the great waters*, past finding out, v. 16, 17. Both he himself and many others had very closely studied the point, and searched far into the reasons of the prosperity of the wicked and the afflictions of the righteous. It was all labour in vain, v. 17. When we look upon *all the works of God* and his providence, and compare one part with another, we *cannot find* that there is any certain method by which *the work that is done under the sun* is directed. God's ways are above ours, nor is he tied to his own former ways, but *his judgments are a great deep*.

CHAPTER 9

Solomon, for a further proof of the vanity of this world, gives us four observations. I. He observed that commonly, as to outward things, good and bad men fare much alike, ver. 1–3. II. That death puts a final period to all our employments and enjoyments in this world (ver. 4–6), whence he infers that it is our wisdom to enjoy the comforts of life and mind the business of life, while it lasts, ver. 7–10. III. That great calamities often surprise men ere they are aware, ver. 11, 12. IV. That wisdom often makes men very useful, and yet persons of great merit are slighted, ver. 13–18. And what is there then in this world that should make us fond of it?

Verses 1–3

It has been observed concerning those who have pretended to search for the philosophers' stone that, though they could never find what they sought for, yet in the search they have hit upon many other useful discoveries and experiments. Thus Solomon, when, in the close of the foregoing chapter, he *applied his heart to know the work of God*, he found out that which abundantly recompensed him for the search, and therefore *he considered all this in his heart*, and weighed it deliberately, that he might *declare* it for the good of others.

The great difficulty which Solomon met with in studying providence was the little difference that is made between good men and bad in the distribution of comforts and crosses. This has perplexed the minds of many wise men. Solomon says that which may prevent its being a stumbling-block to us.

I. Before he describes the temptation in its strength he lays down a great and unquestionable truth. Job lays down the doctrine of God's omniscience (Job xxiv. 1), Jeremiah the doctrine of his righteousness (Jer. xii. 1), another prophet that of his holiness (Hab. i. 13), the psalmist that of his goodness and peculiar favour to his own people (Ps. lxxiii. 1), and that is it which Solomon here resolves to abide by, that, though good and evil seem to be dispensed promiscuously, yet God has a particular care of and concern for his own people: *The righteous and the wise, and their works, are in the hand of God*, under his special protection and guidance; all their affairs are managed by him for their good; to be recompensed in the other world, though not in this. Whatever

happens all God's saints are in his hand, Deut. xxxiii. 3; John x. 29; Ps. xxxi. 15.

II. He lays this down for a rule, that the love and hatred of God are not to be measured and judged of by men's outward condition. *No man knows either love or hatred* by those things that are the objects of sense. These we may know by that which is within us if we love God with all our heart. These will be known by that which shall be hereafter, by men's everlasting state.

III. Having laid down these principles, he acknowledges that *all things come alike to all*. Some make this, and all that follows to v. 13, to be the perverse reasoning of the atheists against the doctrine of God's providence; but I rather take it to be Solomon's concession, when he had fixed those truths which are sufficient to guard against any ill use that may be made of what he grants.

1. The great difference that there is between the characters of the righteous and the wicked. (1) The righteous are *clean*, have *clean hands and pure hearts*; the wicked are *unclean*, under the dominion of unclean lusts. God will certainly put a difference *between the clean and the unclean* in the other world, though he does not seem to do so in this. (2) The righteous *sacrifice* both with inward and outward worship: the wicked *sacrifice not*, that is, they neglect God's worship and grudge to part with any thing for his honour. (3) The righteous do good in the world. (4) The wicked man *swears*, has no veneration for the name of God; but the righteous man *fears an oath* with great reverence.

2. The little difference there is between the conditions of the righteous and the wicked in this world: *There is one event to* both. Is David rich? So is Nabal. Is Ahab killed in a battle? So is Josiah. There is a vast difference between the nature of the same event to the one and to the other; the effects of it are likewise vastly different; the same providence to the one is *a savour of life unto life*, to the other of *death unto death*, though, to outward appearance, it is the same.

IV. He owns this to be a grievance to those that are wise and good: *"This is an evil*, the greatest perplexity, *among all things that are done under the sun"* (v. 3). It hardens atheists, and strengthens the hands of evildoers. When they see that *there is one event to the righteous and the wicked* they wickedly infer thence that it is all one to God whether they are righteous or wicked.

V. For the further clearing of this great difficulty he concludes with the doctrine of the misery of the wicked; however they may prosper, *madness is in their heart while they live, and after that they go to the dead*.

Verses 4–10

Solomon, in a fret, had *praised the dead more than the living* (ch. iv. 2); but here, considering the advantages of life to prepare for a better life, he seems to be of another mind

I. He shows the advantages which the living have above those that are dead, v. 4–6. If a man's condition be, upon any account, bad, *there is hope* it will be amended. If *the heart be full of evil, and madness be in it*, yet while there is life *there is hope* that by the grace of God there may be a blessed change wrought. *The living know they shall die;* it is a thing yet to come, and therefore provision may be made for it. *The dead know not anything. They have no more a reward* for their toils about the world, but all they got must be left to others; they have a reward for their holy actions, but not for their worldly ones. The things of this world will not be a portion for the soul. The world can only be an annuity for life, not a *portion for ever*. There is an end of their affections, their friendships and enmities: *Their love, and their hatred, and their envy have now perished.*

II. Hence he infers that it is our wisdom to make the best use of life while it does last. Solomon, having been ensnared by the abuse of delights, warns others of the danger, not by a total prohibition of them, but by directing to the moderate use of them. "Let thy spirit be easy and pleasant; then let there be *joy* and *a merry heart* within." We must enjoy ourselves, enjoy our friends, enjoy our God, and be careful to keep a good conscience. We must serve God with gladness, in the use of what he gives us, and be liberal in communicating it to others, and not suffer ourselves to be oppressed with inordinate care about the world. "Make use of the comforts and enjoyments which God has given thee. Evidence thy cheerfulness (*v.* 8): *Let thy garments be always white.* Be neat, wear clean linen, and be not slovenly." "Make thyself agreeable to thy relations: *Live joyfully with the wife whom thou lovest.* Do not engross thy delights, not caring what becomes of those about thee, but let them share with thee and make them easy too. Keep to thy wife, to one, and do not multiply wives. *Live joyfully with her,* and be most cheerful when thou art with her. Take pleasure in thy family, thy vine and thy olive plants." Those whose works God has accepted have reason to be cheerful and ought to be so. God loves to have his servants sing at their work. "Live joyfully. Let a gracious serenity of mind be a powerful antidote against the vanity of the world." *That is thy portion in* the things of *this life.* In God, and another life, thou shalt have a better portion. "Therefore *eat with joy* and *a merry heart* that thy soul may take the more pains and the joy of the Lord may be its strength and oil to its wheels," *v.* 10. This is the world of service; that to come is the world of recompence. This is the world of probation and preparation for eternity. Harvest-days are busy days; and we must make hay while the sun shines. Serving God and working out our salvation must be done with *all that is within us,* and all little enough.

Verses 11–12

The preacher had exhorted us (*v.* 10) to do what we have to do *with all our might;* but here he reminds us that, when we have done all, we must leave the issue with God.

I. We are often disappointed of the good we had great hopes of, *v.* 11. Events, both in public and private affairs, do not always agree even with the most rational prospects and probabilities. One would think that the lightest of foot should, in running, win the prize; and yet *the race is not* always *to the swift;* some accident happens to retard them, or they are too secure, and let those that are slower get the start of them. One would think that, in fighting, the most numerous and powerful army should be always victorious, and, in single combat, that the mighty champion should win; but *the battle is not* always *to the strong;* a host of Philistines was once put to flight by Jonathan and his man; the goodness of the cause has often carried the day against the most formidable power. One would think that men of sense should always be men of substance, and get great estates; and yet it does not always prove so; even *bread is not* always *to the wise,* much less *riches* always *to men of understanding.* One would think that those who understand men, and have the art of management, should always get preferment; but many ingenious men have spent their days in obscurity. All these disappointments to us seem casual, and we call them *chance,* but really they are according to the counsel of God, here called *time,* in the language of this book, *ch.* iii. 1; Ps. xxxi. 15. *Time and chance happen to them all.*

II. We are often surprised with evils (*v.* 12): *Man knows not his time,* the time of his calamity. It is *not for us to know the times,* no, not our own time, when or how we shall die. God has, in wisdom, kept us in the dark, that we may be always ready. We may meet with trouble in that very thing wherein we promise ourselves satisfaction, as the fishes and the birds are drawn into the snare and net by the bait. Men often find their bane where they sought their bliss. Let us be always ready for changes, that, though they may be sudden, they may be no terror to us.

Verses 13–18

Solomon still recommends wisdom to us as necessary to the preserving of our peace. This wisdom which enables a man to serve his country out of pure affection, when he himself gains no advantage by it, is the wisdom which, Solomon says, *seemed great unto him, v.* 13.

I. Solomon here gives an instance, probably a case in fact, of a *poor man* who with his wisdom did great service in a time of public distress and danger (*v.* 14): *There was a little city;* there were but *few men within it,* and ready to give up their city as not tenable. Against this little city a *great king* came with a numerous army, and besieged it. Did victory and success attend the *strong?* No; there was found in this little city, among the few men that were in it, *one poor wise man*—not preferred to any place of profit or power in the city. Being wise, he served the city, though he was poor. In their distress they found him out (Judges xi. 7) and begged his advice and assistance; and *he by his wisdom delivered the city,* either by prudent instructions given to the besieged, directing them to some unthought-of stratagem for their own security, or by a prudent treaty with the besiegers, as the woman at Abel, 2 Sam. xx. 16. *No man remembered that same poor man;* no recompence was made him, no marks of honour put upon him, but he lived in as much poverty and obscurity as he had done before.

II. From this instance he draws some useful inferences. He observes: *Wisdom is better than strength, v.* 16, *better than weapons of war,* offensive or defensive, *v.* 18. *The words of wise men are heard in quiet;* what they speak, being rational and to the purpose, spoken calmly and with deliberation, will gain respect, and sway with men more than the imperious clamour of him that *rules among fools,* who chose him to be their ruler, for his noise and blustering. A few close arguments are worth a great many big words. Wise and good men, notwithstanding this, must often content themselves with the satisfaction of having done good when they cannot have the praise they should have. Wisdom capacitates a man to serve his neighbours. Many a man is buried alive in poverty and obscurity who, if he had but fit encouragement given him, might be a great blessing to the world; many a pearl is lost in its shell. But there is a day coming when wisdom and goodness shall be in honour, and the *righteous shall shine forth.* From what he had observed of the great good which one wise and virtuous man may do he infers what a great deal of mischief one wicked man may do. A sinful condition is a wasteful condition. How many of the good gifts both of nature and Providence does one sinner destroy. One sinner, who makes its its his business to debauch others, may defeat and frustrate the intentions of a great many good laws.

CHAPTER 10

This chapter seems to be like Solomon's proverbs, a collection of wise sayings, but the preacher "set in order many proverbs", to be brought in in his preaching. The general scope is to recommend wisdom to us. I. He recommends wisdom to private persons in an inferior station. 1. It is our wisdom to preserve our reputation, in managing our affairs dexterously, ver. 1–3. 2. To be submissive to our superiors if at any time we have offended them, ver. 4. 3. To live quiet and peaceable lives, and not to meddle with those that are factious and seditious, ver. 8–11. 4. To govern our tongues, ver. 12–15. 5. To be diligent in our business and provide for our families, ver. 18, 19. 6. Not to speak ill of our rulers, ver. 20. II. He recommends wisdom to rulers; let them not think that, because their subjects must be quiet under them, therefore they may do what they please. 1. Let them be careful whom they prefer to places of trust and power, ver. 5–7. 2. Let them be generous and not childish, temperate and not luxurious, ver. 16, 17.

Verses 1–3

I. *A little folly* is a great blemish to him that *is in reputation for wisdom and honour*, and is as hurtful to his good name as *dead flies* are to a sweet perfume. True wisdom will gain a man a reputation, which is like a box of precious ointment. The reputation that is got by a great deal of wisdom, may be easily lost, by a *little folly*, because envy fastens upon eminency, and makes the worst of the mistakes of those who are cried up for wisdom.

II. *A wise man's heart is at his right hand*, so that he goes about his business with dexterity. But a *fool's heart is at his left hand*; it is always to seek when he has anything to do that is of importance, and therefore he goes awkwardly about it.

III. How apt fools are at every turn to proclaim their own folly, and expose themselves; he that is either silly or wicked *says to everyone he meets that he is a fool* (v. 3), that is, he discovers his folly as plainly as if he had told them so.

Verses 4–11

The scope of these verses is to keep subjects loyal and dutiful to the government.

I. Let not subjects carry on a quarrel with their prince upon any private personal disgust (v. 4): "*If the spirit of the ruler rise up against thee*, if he is displeased at thee, yet *leave not thy place*, forget not the duty of a subject, revolt not from thy allegiance, do not, in a passion, quit thy post in his service."

II. Let not subjects commence a quarrel with their prince. He grants *there is an evil often seen under the sun*, an evil which the king only can cure, for *it is an error which proceeds from the ruler* (v. 5); it is a mistake which rulers, consulting their personal affections, are too often guilty of, that men are not preferred according to their merit, but *folly is set in great dignity*. It is ill with a people when vicious men are advanced and men of worth are kept under hatches. This is illustrated v. 7. "*I have seen servants upon horses*, men not so much of mean extraction, but of sordid, servile, mercenary dispositions."

1. Let neither prince nor people violently attempt changes. Let not princes invade the rights and liberties of their subjects; let not subjects mutiny and rebel against their princes; for, (1) *He that digs a pit* for another, it is ten to one but he *falls into it* himself. If princes become tyrants, or subjects become rebels, all histories will tell both what is likely to be their fate. (2) *Whoso breaks a hedge*, an old hedge, that has long been a land-mark, let him expect that a *serpent*, or *adder*, such as harbour in rotten hedges, will *bite him*. (3) *Whoso removes stones*, to pull down a wall, or building, does but pluck them upon himself; he shall be *hurt therewith*. Those that go about to alter a well-modelled well-settled government, will quickly perceive that it is easier to find fault than to mend. (4) *He that cleaves the wood*, especially if, as it follows, he has sorry tools (v. 10), *shall be endangered thereby*; the chips, or his own axe-head, will fly in his face. If we meet with knotty pieces of timber, men of perverse and ungovernable spirits, and we think to master them by force and violence, the attempt may turn to our own damage.

2. Rather let both prince and people act towards each other with prudence, mildness, and good temper: *Wisdom is profitable to direct* the ruler how to manage a people that are inclined to be turbulent, so as neither, by a supine negligence to embolden them, nor by rigour and severity to provoke them to seditious practices. It is likewise profitable to direct the subjects how to act towards a prince that is inclined to bear hard upon them, so as not to alienate his affections, but to win upon him by humble remonstrances and peaceable expedients. Let wisdom direct to gentle methods and forbear violent ones. Wisdom will teach us to whet the tool we are to make use of, rather than, by leaving it blunt, oblige ourselves to exert so much the *more strength*, v. 10. Whet before we cut, that is, consider and premeditate what is fit to be said and done in every difficult case. The mower loses no time when he is whetting his scythe. Wisdom will teach us to enchant the serpent we are to contend with, rather than think to out-hiss it (v. 11): *The serpent will bite* if he be not by singing and music charmed. *A babbler is no better. He that is lord of the tongue* may say what he will, it is as dangerous dealing with him as with a serpent uncharmed. To those that may say anything it is wisdom to say nothing that is provoking.

Verses 12–15

Solomon here shows the mischief of folly.

I. Fools talk a great deal to no purpose, and they show their folly by the impertinence of their words: whereas *the words of a wise man's mouth are gracious*, and do good to all about him, *the lips of a fool* not only expose him to reproach, but *will swallow up himself* and bring him to ruin. A fool's talk takes rise from his own weakness and wickedness: *The beginning of the words of his mouth is foolishness*, the foolishness in his heart is the corrupt spring out of which all these polluted streams flow. *The end of his talk is madness. A fool also is full of words*, a passionate fool especially, that never knows when to leave off. He will have the last word, though it be but the same with that which was the first. Many who are empty of sense are *full of words*; and the least solid are the most noisy. He is *full of words*, for if he do but speak the most trite and common thing, *a man cannot tell what shall be*, because he loves to hear himself talk, he will say it again, *what shall be after him who can tell him*?

II. Fools toil a great deal to no purpose (v. 15); *The labour of the foolish*, to accomplish their designs, *wearies everyone of them*. All their labour is for the world and the body, and the meat that perishes. The foolish never bring anything to pass, *because they know not how to go to the city*, that is, because they have not capacity to apprehend the plainest thing, such as the entrance into a great city, where one would think it were impossible for a man to miss his road.

Verses 16–20

I. The happiness of a land depends upon the character of its rulers. 1. The people cannot be happy when their princes are childish and voluptuous (v. 16): *Woe unto thee, O land!* when *thy king is a child*, not so much in age as in understanding; when the prince is weak and foolish as a child, fickle, fretful and humoursome, it is ill with the people. Nor is it much better with a people when their princes *eat in the morning*, that is, make a god of their belly and make themselves slaves to their appetites. If the princes and privy-counsellors are wise the land may do the better; but if they addict themselves to their pleasures, before the despatch of the public business, by eating and drinking *in a morning*, when judges are epicures, and do not eat to live, but live to eat, what good can a nation expect! The people cannot but be happy when their rulers are generous and active, sober and temperate, and men of business, *v.* 17. Wisdom, virtue, and the fear of God, beneficence, and a readiness to do good to all mankind, these ennoble the royal blood. When the subordinate magistrates are more in care to discharge their trusts than to gratify their appetites; when they *eat in due season,* that is, when they have despatched their business, the land is blessed. Magistrates should *eat for strength,* that their bodies may be fitted to serve their souls in the service of God and their country. It is well with a people when their princes are examples of temperance, when those that have most to spend upon themselves know how to deny themselves.

II. Of what ill consequence slothfulness is both to private and public affairs (*v.* 18): *By much slothfulness and idleness of the hands,* the neglect of business, and the love of ease and pleasure, *the building decays, drops through* first, and by degrees drops down. If the king be a *child* and will take no care, if the *princes eat in the morning* and will take no pains, the affairs of the nation suffer loss, and all its foundations are out of course through the slothfulness and self-seeking of those that should be the *repairers of its breaches.*

III. How industrious generally all are, both princes and people, to get money, because that serves for all purposes, *v.* 19. He seems to prefer money before mirth: *A feast is made for laughter,* not the laughter of the fool, which is madness, but that of wise men, by which they fit themselves for business and severe studies. Money of itself answers nothing; it will neither feed nor clothe; but, as it is the instrument of commerce, it answers all the occasions of this present life. But it answers nothing to the soul; it will not procure the pardon of sin, the favour of God, the peace of conscience.

IV. How cautious subjects have need to be that they harbour not any disloyal purposes in their minds, nor keep up any factious cabals or consultations against the government. "*Curse not the king, no, not in thy thought,* do not wish ill to the government in thy mind." "*Curse not the rich,* the princes and governors, *in thy bedchamber,* in a conclave or club of persons disaffected to the government; associate not with such; *come not into their secret;* join not with them in plotting against it. Though the design be carried on ever so closely, *a bird of the air shall carry the voice* to the king, who has more spies about than thou art aware of, *and that which has wings shall tell the matter,* to thy confusion and ruin."

CHAPTER 11

I. A pressing exhortation to works of charity and bounty to the poor, ver. 1–6. II. A serious admonition to prepare for death and judgment, ver. 7–10.

Verses 1–6

Solomon presses rich people to abound in liberality to the poor.

I. The duty itself is recommended to us, *v.* 1. *Cast thy bread upon the waters, thy bread-corn upon the low places* (so some understand it), alluding to the husbandman, who *goes forth, bearing precious seed,* sparing bread-corn from his family for the seed, knowing that without that he can have no harvest another year; thus the charitable man takes from his bread-corn for seed-corn, to supply the poor, that he may *sow beside all waters* (Isa. xxxii. 20), because as he sows so he must *reap,* Gal. vi. 7. Give freely to the poor, though it may seem thrown away and lost, as that which is *cast upon the waters.* Send it a voyage, send it as a venture, as merchants that trade by sea. Trust it *upon the waters;* it shall not sink. "*Give a portion to seven and also to eight,* that is,

be free and liberal in works of charity." Give not a pittance, but *a portion,* a meal. Give to many, *to seven, and also to eight;* if thou meet with seven objects of charity, give to them all, and then, if thou meet with an eighth, give to that, and, if with eight more, give to them all too. God is rich in mercy to all, to us, though unworthy; he *gives liberally, and upbraids not* with former gifts.

II. The reasons with which it is pressed upon us. "Though thou *cast it upon the waters,* and it seem lost, yet *thou shalt find it after many days,* as the husbandman finds his seed again in a plentiful harvest. The return may be slow, but it is sure and will be so much the more plentiful." Wheat, the most valuable grain, lies longest in the ground. Our opportunity for well-doing is very uncertain: "*Thou knowest not what evil may be upon the earth,* which may deprive thee of thy estate, and put thee out of a capacity to do good. Many make use of this as an argument against giving to the poor, because they know not what hard times may come when they may want themselves; whereas we should therefore the rather be charitable, that, when *evil days come,* we may have the comfort of having done good while we were able.

III. The excuses of the uncharitable.

1. Some will say that what they have is their own, and will ask, Why should we *cast* it thus *upon the waters?* Look up, man, and consider how soon thou wouldest be starved in a barren ground, *if the clouds* over thy head should plead thus, that they have their waters for themselves. Are the heavens thus bountiful to the poor earth, that is so far below them, and wilt thou grudge thy bounty to thy poor brother, who is *bone of thy bone?*

2. Some will say that their sphere of usefulness is low and narrow; they cannot do the good that they see others can, who are in more public stations, and therefore they will sit still and do nothing. Nay, says he, *in the place where the tree falls,* or happens to be, *there it shall be,* for the benefit of those to whom it belongs; every man must labour to be a blessing to that place, whatever it is, where the providence of God casts him; wherever we are we may find good work to do if we have but hearts to do it.

3. Some will object to the many discouragements they have met with in their charity. They have been reproached for it as proud and pharisaical; they shall be despised if they do not give as others do; they have taxes to pay and they know not what use will be made of their charity; these, and a hundred such objections, he answers, in one word (*v.* 4): *He that observes the wind shall not sow,* which signifies doing good; *and he that regards the clouds shall not reap,* which signifies getting good. If we stand thus magnifying every little difficulty, starting objections and fancying hardship where there is none, we shall never go on with our work. If the husbandman should decline, or leave off, sowing for the sake of every flying cloud, and reaping for the sake of every blast of wind, he would make but an ill account of his husbandry at the year's end.

4. Some will say, "We do not see in which way what we expend in charity should ever be made up to us. To this he answers, "*Thou knowest not the work of God,* nor is it fit thou shouldst. Thou mayest be sure he will make good his word of promise, though he does not tell thee how." Our ignorance of the work of God shows, in two instances:—(1) We *know not what is the way of the Spirit,* of *the wind* (so some), we *know not whence it comes, or whither it goes,* or when it will turn; yet the seamen lie ready waiting for it, till it turns about in favour of them; so we must do our duty, in expectation of the time appointed for the blessing. Or it may be understood

of the human soul; we know that God made us, and gave us these souls, but how they entered into these bodies, animate them, and operate upon them, we know not; the soul is a mystery to itself, no marvel then that *the work of God* is so to us. (2) We know not *how the bones are fashioned in the womb of her that is with child*. We cannot describe the manner either of the formation of the body or of its information with a soul; both, we know, are *the work of God*, and we acquiesce in his work. Let him therefore that has done the greater for us be cheerfully depended upon to do the less.

5. Some say, "We have been charitable, and never yet saw any return for it; many days are past, and we have not *found it again*," to which he answers (v. 6), Yet go on, proceed and persevere in well-doing. *In the morning sow thy seed and in the evening do not withhold thy hand*. *In the morning* of youth lay out thyself to do good; give out of the little thou hast; *and in the evening* of old age yield not to the common temptation of old people to be penurious; even then *withhold not thy hand*, but do good to the last, *for thou knowest not* which work of charity *shall prosper*, both as to others and as to thyself, *this or that*, but hast reason to hope that *both shall be alike good*.

Verses 7–10

Having by many excellent precepts taught us how to live well, the preacher comes now to teach us how to die well.

I. He applies himself to the aged: *Truly the light is sweet;* the light of *the sun* is so; it is *a pleasant thing for the eyes to behold* it. It is pleasant to see the light; the heathen were so charmed with the pleasure of it that they worshipped the sun. It is pleasant by it to see other things. It cannot be denied that life is sweet. It is sweet to all men; nature says it is so; nor can death be desired for its own sake unless as a period to present evils or a passage to future good. *If a man live many years, yet let him remember the days of darkness* are coming. Here is, (1) A summer's day supposed to be enjoyed—that life may continue long, even many years, and that, by the goodness of God, it may be made comfortable and a man may *rejoice in them all*. However, some rejoice in their many years more than others; if these two things meet, a prosperous state and a cheerful spirit, these two indeed may do much towards enabling a man to *rejoice in them all*, and yet the most cheerful spirit has its damps; jovial sinners have their melancholy qualms, and cheerful saints have their gracious sorrows; so that it is but a supposition, not a case in fact, that a man should *live many years and rejoice in them all*. But, (2) Here is a winter's night to be expected after this summer's day: *Yet let* this hearty old man *remember the days of darkness, for they shall be many*. They are many, but they are not infinite. As the longest day will have its night, so the longest night will have its morning. *The days of darkness* will come with much the less terror if we have thought of them before.

II. He applies himself to the young to awaken them to think of death (v. 9, 10).

1. An ironical concession to the vanities and pleasures of youth: *Rejoice, O young man! in thy youth*. Solomon speaks thus ironically to the young man to expose his folly, and the absurdity of a voluptuous vicious course of life.

2. A powerful check given to these vanities and pleasures: *Know thou that for all these things God shall bring thee into judgment*.

3. A word of caution and exhortation inferred from all this, v. 10. Let young people look to themselves and manage well both their souls and their bodies. Let them take care that their minds be not lifted up with pride, nor disturbed with anger, or any sinful passion: *Remove sorrow*, or anger, *from thy heart;* the word signifies any disorder or perturbation of the mind. Young people are apt to be impatient of check and control, to fret at anything that is humbling, and their proud hearts rise against everything that crosses and contradicts them. Let them keep at a distance from everything which will be sorrow in the reflection. Let them take care that their bodies be not defiled by intemperance, uncleanness, or any fleshly lusts: *Put away evil from the flesh*, and let not the members of thy body be instruments of unrighteousness.

III. The preacher urges that which is the great argument of his discourse, the vanity of all present things, their uncertainty and insufficiency. 1. He reminds old people of this (v. 8): *All that comes is vanity;* yea, though *a man live many years and rejoice in them all*. 2. He reminds young people of this: *Childhood and youth are vanity*. The pleasures and advantages of childhood and youth are passing away; these flowers will wither, and these blossoms fall; let them therefore be knit into good fruit, which will continue and abound to a good account.

CHAPTER 12

The wise and penitent preacher is here closing his sermon; and he closes it with that which was likely to make the best impressions, powerful and lasting upon his hearers. Here is, I. An exhortation to young people to begin betimes to be religious and not to put it off to old age (ver. 1–7). II. A repetition of the great truth he had undertaken to prove in this discourse, the vanity of the world, ver. 8. III. A confirmation and recommendation of what he had written in this and his other books, as worthy to be duly weighed and considered, ver. 9–12. IV. The whole matter summed up and concluded, with a charge to all to be truly religious, ver. 13, 14.

Verses 1–7

I. A call to young people to think of God, and mind their duty to him, when they are young: *Remember now thy Creator in the days of thy youth*. "You that are young flatter yourselves with expectations of great things from the world, but it yields no solid satisfaction to a soul; therefore *remember your Creator*, and so guard yourselves against the mischiefs that arise from the vanity of the creature." It is the royal physician's antidote against the particular diseases of youth, the indulgence of sensual pleasures, the vanity which childhood and youth are subject to; to prevent and cure this, *remember thy Creator*. God is our Creator, he *made us and not we ourselves*, and is therefore our rightful Lord. We must pay him the honour and duty which we owe him as our Creator. *Remember thy Creators*; the word is plural, as it is Job xxxv. 10. For God said, *Let us make man*, us, Father, Son, and Holy Ghost. "Begin in the beginning of thy days to remember him from whom thou hadst thy being. Call him to mind through all the days of thy youth, and never forget him. Guard thus against the temptations of youth, and thus improve the advantages of it."

II. A reason to enforce this command: *While the evil days come not, and the years of which thou shalt say I have no pleasure in them*.

1. Do it quickly, "Before sickness and death come." Before old age comes, *years of which we shall say, We have no pleasure in them*,—when our *strength* shall be *labour and sorrow*,—when there will be *no pleasure* but in the reflection of a good life on earth and the expectation of a better life in heaven.

2. These two arguments he enlarges upon in the following verses, only inverting the order. It is the greatest absurdity and ingratitude imaginable to give the cream and flower of our days to the devil, and reserve the bran, and refuse, and dregs of them for God. If the calamities of age will be such as are here represented, we shall have need of something to support and comfort us then, and nothing will be

more effectual than the testimony of our consciences that we began betimes to remember our Creator. How can we expect God should help us when we are old, if we will not serve him when we are young? The infirmities of old age are here elegantly described in figurative expressions. Then *the sun* and *the light* of it, *the moon* and *the stars*, and the light which they borrow from it, will *be darkened*. They look dim to old people, in consequence of the decay of their sight; their intellectual powers and faculties, which are as lights in the soul, are weakened; their understanding and memory fail them. Then *the clouds return after the rain*; no sooner has one cloud blown over than another succeeds it, so it is with old people, when they have got free from one pain or ailment, they are seized with another. Then *the keepers of the house tremble*. The head, which is as the watch-tower, shakes, and the arms and hands, which are ready for the preservation of the body, shake too, and grow feeble. Then *the strong men shall bow themselves*; the legs cannot serve for travelling as they have done, but are soon tired. Then the *grinders cease because they are few*; the teeth cease to do their part, *because they are few. Those that look out of the windows are darkened*. Moses was a rare instance of one who, when 120 years old, had good eyesight. *The doors are shut in the streets*. Old people keep within doors, and care not for going abroad to entertainments. Old people *rise up at the voice of the bird*. They have no sound sleep as young people have, but a little thing disturbs them, even the chirping of a bird. With them *all the daughters of music* are *brought low*. Old people grow hard of hearing, and unapt to distinguish sounds and voices. They are *afraid of that which is high*, afraid to go to the top of any high place, either because, for want of breath, they cannot reach it, or, their heads being giddy, they dare not venture to it. *The almond-tree flourishes*. The old man's hair has grown white, so that his head looks like an almond-tree in the blossom. *The grasshopper is a burden and desire fails*. Old men can bear nothing; the lightest thing sits heavily upon them, both on their bodies and on their minds, a little thing sinks and breaks them. It is probable that Solomon wrote this when he was himself old, and could speak feelingly of the infirmities of age, which perhaps grew the faster upon him for the indulgence he had given himself in sensual pleasures. All this makes a good reason why we should *remember our Creator in the days of our youth*, that he may remember us when *evil days come*, and his comforts may delight our souls when the delights of sense are in a manner worn off. Death will fix us in an unchangeable state: *Man* shall then *go to his long home*. He has gone to his rest, to the place where he is to fix. He has gone *to his house of eternity*. This should make us willing to die, that, at death, we must *go home*; and why should we not long to go to our Father's house? Death will be an occasion of sorrow to our friends that love us. When *man goes to his long home the mourners go about the streets*—the real mourners, and the mourners for ceremony, that were hired to weep for the dead, both to express and to excite the real mourning. Death will dissolve the frame of nature and take down the earthly house of this tabernacle, which is elegantly described, *v*. 6. Then shall *the silver cord*, by which soul and body were wonderfully fastened together, *be loosed*, that sacred knot untied; *the golden bowl*, which held the waters of life for us, *be broken*; then shall *the pitcher* with which we used to fetch up water, for the constant support of life and the repair of its decays, *be broken*, even *at the fountain*, so that it can fetch up no more; and *the wheel* (all those organs that serve for the collecting and distributing of nourishment) shall be *broken*, and disabled to do their office any more. The body shall

become like a watch when the spring is broken, the motion of all the wheels is stopped and they all stand still. Death will resolve us into our first principles, *v*. 7. Man is a strange sort of creature, a ray of heaven united to a clod of earth; at death these are separated, and each goes to the place whence it came. The body, that clod of clay, *returns to* its own *earth*. The soul, that beam of light, *returns to* that *God* who, when he *made man of the dust of the ground, breathed into him the breath of life*, to make him *a living soul* (Gen. ii. 7). The soul does not die with the body; it is *redeemed from the power of the grave* (Ps. xlix. 15); it can subsist without it and will in a state of separation from it, as the candle burns, and burns brighter, when it is taken out of the dark lantern.

Verses 8–12

Solomon is here drawing towards a close. He repeats his text (*v*. 8). He recommends what he had written upon this subject by divine direction and inspiration to our serious consideration.

1. They are the words of one that was a convert, a penitent, that could speak by dear-bought experience of the vanity of the world and the folly of expecting great things from it. He was *Coheleth*, one gathered in from his wanderings. *Vanity of vanities, saith the* penitent.

2. They are the words of one that was wise, endued with extraordinary measures of wisdom, famous for it among his neighbours, who all sought unto him *to hear his wisdom*, and therefore a competent judge of this matter.

3. He was one that made it his business to do good, and to use wisdom aright.

4. He took a great deal of pains and care to do good, designing to *teach the people knowledge*. He chose the most profitable way of preaching, by proverbs or short sentences.

5. He put what he had to say in such a dress as he thought would be most pleasing: *He sought to find out acceptable words*, words of delight (*v*. 10); that good matter might not be spoiled by a bad style.

6. *That which was written was upright* and sincere, even *words of truth*. Most are for smooth things, that flatter them, rather than right things, that direct them (Isa. xxx. 10), but to those that understand themselves, and their own interest, *words of truth* will always be *acceptable words*.

7. That which he and other holy men wrote will be of great advantage to us, especially by the exposition of it, *v*. 11. The words are *as nails* to those that are wavering and inconstant, to fix them to that which is good. They are *as goads* to such as are dull and draw back, and *nails* to such as are desultory and draw aside, that what good there is in us may be *as a nail fastened in a sure place*, Ezra ix. 8. Solemn assemblies for religious worship are an ancient divine institution, intended for the honour of God and the edification of his church. There must be masters of these assemblies, who are Christ's ministers. Their business is to fasten the *words of the wise*, and drive them as *nails* to the head, in order to which the word of God is likewise as *a hammer*, Jer. xxiii. 29.

8. That which is written, and thus recommended to us, is of divine origin. Though it comes to us through various hands (many *wise men*, and many *masters of assemblies*), yet it is *given by one* and the same *shepherd*, the *shepherd of Israel, that leads Joseph like a flock*, Ps. lxxx. 1.

9. The sacred inspired writings, if we will but make use of them, are sufficient to guide us in the way to true happiness. "*And further*, nothing now remains but to tell thee that of *making many books there is no end*." Let men write ever so many books for the conduct of human life, write till they have tired

themselves with much study, they cannot give better instructions than those we have from the word of God.

Verses 13–14

The great enquiry which Solomon prosecutes in this book is, *What is that good which the sons of men should do? ch.* ii. 3. What is the true way to true happiness, the certain means to attain our great end? He had found it, by the help of that discovery which God anciently made to man (Job. xxviii. 28), that serious godliness is the only way to true happiness: *Let us hear the conclusion of the whole matter.*

I. The summary of religion. Setting aside all matters of doubtful disputation, to be religious is to *fear God and keep his commandments.* 1. The root of religion is the fear of God reigning in the heart, a reverence of his majesty, a deference to his authority, and a dread of his wrath. 2. The rule of religion is the law of God revealed in the scriptures. Our fear towards God must be taught by his commandments (Isa. xxix. 13), and those we must keep and carefully observe.

II. The vast importance of it: *This is the whole of man;* it is all his business and all his blessedness; our whole duty is summed up in this and our whole comfort is bound up in this.

III. A powerful inducement to this, *v.* 14. We shall see of what vast consequence it is to us that we be religious if we consider the account we must every one of us shortly give of himself to God. *God shall bring every work into judgment.* The great thing to be then judged concerning *every work* is whether it be good or evil. It highly concerns us now to be very strict in our walking with God, that we may *give up our account with joy.*

THE SONG OF SOLOMON

In our belief both of the divine extraction and of the spiritual exposition of this book we are confirmed by the concurring testimony both of the church of the Jews, and of the Christian church. This *Song of Solomon's* is very unlike the songs of his father David; there is not the name of God in it; it is never quoted in the New Testament; we find no expressions of natural religion or pious devotion, nor any of the marks of immediate revelation. It seems as hard as any part of scripture to be made *a savour of life unto life,* and to those who come to the reading of it with carnal minds and corrupt affections, it is in danger of being made a *savour of death unto death;* and therefore the Jewish doctors advised their young people not to read it till they were thirty years old, lest by the abuse of that which is most pure and sacred, the flames of lust should be kindled. But, on the other hand, with the help of the many faithful guides we have for the understanding of this book it appears to be a bright and powerful ray of heavenly light, admirably fitted to excite pious and devout affections in holy souls, and improve their acquaintance and communion with God. It is an allegory, the letter of which kills those who look no further, but the spirit of which gives life. It is a parable, which makes divine things more difficult to those who do not love them, but more plain and pleasant to those who do. Experienced Christians here find a counterpart of their experiences, and to them it is intelligible. It is an *Epithalamium,* or nuptial song, wherein, by the expressions of love between a bridegroom and his bride, are set forth and illustrated the mutual affections that pass between God and a remnant of mankind. It is a pastoral; the bride and bridegroom are brought in as a shepherd and his shepherdess. 1. This song might easily be taken in a spiritual sense by the Jewish church, for whose use it was first composed. God betrothed the people of Israel to himself; he entered into covenant with them, and it was a marriage-covenant. He had given abundant proofs of his love to them, and required of them that they should love him with all their heart and soul. Idolatry was often spoken of as spiritual adultery, to prevent which this song was penned. 2. It may be more easily taken in a spiritual sense by the Christian church, because the condescensions and communications of divine love appear more rich and free under the gospel than they did under the law, and the communion between heaven and earth more familiar. God sometimes spoke of himself as the husband of the Jewish church (Isa. liv. 5, Hos. ii. 16, 19), and rejoiced in it as his bride, Isa. lxii. 4, 5. But more frequently is Christ represented as the bridegroom of his church (Matt. xxv. 1, Rom. vii. 4, 2 Cor. xi. 2, Eph. v. 32), and the church as the bride, the Lamb's wife, Rev. xix. 7, xxi. 2, 9. The best key to this book is the 45th Psalm, which we find applied to Christ in the New Testament. It requires some pains to find out what is the meaning of the Holy Spirit in the several parts of this book; as David's songs are many of them level to the capacity of the meanest, and there are shallows in them in which a lamb may wade, so this of Solomon's will exercise the capacities of the most learned, and there are depths in it in which an elephant may swim.

CHAPTER 1

In this chapter, after the title of the book (ver. 1), we have Christ and his church, Christ and a believer, expressing their esteem for each other. I. The bride, the church, speaks to the bridegroom (ver. 2–4), to the daughters of Jerusalem (ver. 5, 6), and then to the bridegroom, ver. 7. II. Christ, the bridegroom, speaks in answer to the complaints and requests of his spouse, ver. 8–11. III. The church expresses the great value she has for Christ, and the delights she takes in communion with him, ver. 12–14. IV. Christ commends the church's beauty, ver. 15. V. The church returns the commendation, ver. 16, 17.

Verse 1

This book is a *song* to stir up the affections. It is evangelical; and gospel-times should be times of joy, for gospel-grace puts *a new song* into our mouths, Ps. xcviii. 1. The penman is Solomon. It is not the song of fools, as many of the songs of love are, but the song of the wisest of men; nor can any man give a better proof of his wisdom than to celebrate the love of God to mankind. Solomon's songs were a thousand and five (1 Kings iv. 32); those that were of other subjects are lost, but this of seraphic love remains. Solomon, like his father, was addicted to poetry, and, which way soever a man's genius lies, he should endeavour to honour God and edify the church with it. It is not certain when Solomon penned this sacred song. Some think that he penned it after he recovered himself by the grace of God from his backslidings. It is more probable that he penned it in the beginning of his time, while he kept close to God and kept up his communion with him. It is here fitly placed after *Ecclesiastes*; for when by that book we are thoroughly convinced of the vanity of the creature, and its insufficiency to satisfy us and make a happiness for us, we shall be quickened to seek for happiness in the love of Christ, and that trans-cendent pleasure which is to be found only in communion with God through him.

Verses 2–6

The spouse, in this dramatic poem, is here first introduced addressing herself to the bridegroom and then to the daughters of Jerusalem.

I. To the bridegroom, not giving him any name or title, but beginning abruptly: *Let him kiss me.* Two things the spouse desires,

1. The bridegroom's friendship (v. 2): "*Let him kiss me with the kisses of his mouth,* that is, be reconciled to me, and let me know that he is so; let me have the tokens of his favour." Thus the Old Testament church desired Christ's manifesting himself in the flesh. "Let him no longer send to me, but come himself, no longer speak by angels and prophets, but let me have the word of his own mouth, those *gracious words* (Luke iv. 22), which will be to me as the *kisses of his mouth,* sure tokens of reconciliation, as Esau's kissing Jacob was." All gospel-grace is summed up in his kissing us, as the father of the prodigal kissed him when he returned a penitent. It is a kiss of peace. She gives several reasons for this desire. (1) Because of the great esteem she has for his love: *Thy love is better than wine.* Gracious souls take more pleasure in loving Christ and being beloved of him, in the fruits and gifts of his love, than any man ever took in the most exquisite delights of sense. (2) Because of the fragrancy of his love and the fruits of it (v. 3): "*Because of the savour of thy good ointment* (the agreeableness and acceptableness of thy graces and comforts to all that rightly understand both them and themselves), *thy name is as ointment poured forth*; thy very name is precious to all the saints; it is an

ointment and perfume which rejoice the heart." (3) Because of the general affection that all holy souls have to him: *Therefore do the virgins love thee.* It is Christ's *love shed abroad in our hearts* that draws out all that are pure from the corruptions of sin. Those are the virgins that love Jesus Christ and *follow him whithersoever he goes,* Rev. xiv. 4. Christ is the darling of all the *pure in heart.*

2. The bridegroom's fellowship, *v.* 4.

(1) Her petition for divine grace: *Draw me.* "Draw me to thyself, draw me nearer, draw me home to thee." Christ has told us that none come to him but such as the Father draws, John vi. 44.

(2) Her promise to improve that grace: *Draw me,* and then *we will run after thee.* The flowing forth of the soul after Christ, and its ready compliance with him, are the effect of his grace; we could not run after him if he did not draw us, 2 Cor. iii. 5; Phil. iv. 13. When Christ pours out his Spirit upon the church in general, which is his bride, all the members of it do thence receive enlivening quickening influences.

(3) The immediate answer that was given to this prayer: *The King has* drawn me, has *brought me into his chambers.* It is not so much an answer fetched by faith from the word of Christ's grace as an answer fetched by experience from the workings of his grace. Those that are drawn to Christ are brought, not only into his courts, into his palaces (Ps. xlv. 15), but into his presence-chamber.

(4) Being *brought into the chamber,* "We have what we would have. Our desires are crowned with unspeakable delights; all our griefs vanish, and *we will be glad and rejoice.*" All our joy shall centre in God: "*We will rejoice,* not in the ointments, or the chambers, but *in thee.* It is God only that is our *exceeding joy,* Ps. xliii. 4. We have no joy but in Christ."

(5) The communion which a gracious soul has with all the saints in this communion with Christ. In the chambers to which we are brought we not only meet with him, but meet with one another. Whatever differences of apprehension and affection there may be among Christians in other things, this they are all agreed in, Jesus Christ is precious to them.

II. To *the daughters of Jerusalem, v.* 5, 6. The believer speaks to those that were in the church, but not of it, or to weak Christians, babes in Christ, willing to be taught in the things of God. She observed these by-standers look disdainfully upon her because of her blackness, in respect both of sins and sufferings, upon account of which they thought she had little reason to expect the kisses she wished for (*v.* 2) or to expect that they should join with her in her joys, *v.* 4. She owns she is *black.* Guilt blackens; the heresies, scandals, and offences, that happen in the church, make her *black*; and the best saints have their failings. Sorrow blackens; that seems to be especially meant; the church is often mean, and poor, and despicable, her beauty sullied with weeping. She asserts her own comeliness notwithstanding (*v.* 5): *I am black, but comely,* black *as the tents of Kedar,* in which the shepherds lived, which were very coarse, and never whitened, weatherbeaten and discoloured by long use, but comely *as the curtains of Solomon.* The church is sometimes *black* with persecution, *but comely* in patience, constancy, and consolation. True believers are *black* in themselves, *but comely* in Christ, with the comeliness that he puts upon them, *black* outwardly, for the *world knows them not,* but *all glorious within,* Ps. xlv. 13.

The blackness was not natural, but contracted, and was owing to the hard usage that had been given her: *Look not upon me* so scornfully *because I am black.*

(1) *I am black* by reason of my sufferings: *The sun has looked upon me.* She was fair and comely; white-

ness was her proper colour; but she got this blackness by *the burden and heat of the day,* which she was forced to bear. But what was the matter? She fell under the displeasure of those of her own house: *My mother's children were angry with me.* She was *in perils by false brethren.* The Samaritans, who claimed kindred to the Jews, were vexed at anything that tended to the prosperity of Jerusalem, Neh. ii. 10. They dealt very hardly with her: *They made me the keeper of the vineyards,* that is, "They seduced me to sin, drew me into false worships, to serve their gods, which was like dressing their vineyards." These are the grievances which good people complain most of in a time of persecution, that their consciences are forced. "They brought me into trouble, imposed that upon me which was toilsome, and very disgraceful." Keeping the vineyards was base servile work. Her mother's children made her the drudge of the family.

(2) "My sufferings are such as I have deserved; for *my own vineyard have I not kept.*"

Verses 7–11

I. The humble petition which the spouse presents to her beloved, the shepherdess to the shepherd, the church and every believer to Christ, for a more free and intimate communion with him. She turns from the *daughters of Jerusalem* and looks up to heaven for relief, *v.* 7. 1. The title she gives to Christ: *O thou whom my soul loveth.* 2. The opinion she has of him as the good shepherd of the sheep; she doubts not but he *feeds his flock* and *makes them rest at noon.* Jesus Christ graciously provides both repast and repose for his sheep. Is it with God's people a noon-time of outward troubles, inward conflicts? Christ has rest for them. 3. Her request to him that she might be admitted into his society: *Tell me, where thou feedest.* "Tell me where to find thee, where I may have conversation with thee, *where thou feedest* and tendest thy flock, that there I may have some of thy company." 4. The plea she uses for the enforcing of this request: "*For why should I be as one that turns aside by* (or after) *the flocks of thy companions,* that pretend to be so, but are really thy competitors, and rivals with thee." Turning aside from Christ after other lovers is that which gracious souls dread. Good Christians will be afraid of giving any occasion to those about them to question their faith in Christ and their love to him.

II. The gracious answer which the bridegroom gives to this request, *v.* 8. See how ready God is to answer prayer. How affectionately he speaks to her: *O thou fairest among women!* Believing souls are fair, in the eyes of the Lord Jesus, above any other. How mildly he checks her for her ignorance, in these words, *If thou know not.* What! dost thou not know where to find me and my flock? Compare Christ's answer to a like address of Philip's (John xiv. 9), *Have I been so long time with you, and yet hast thou not known me, Philip?* With what tenderness he acquaints her where she might find him. Follow the track, ask for the good old way, observe *the footsteps of the flock,* and *go forth by* them. Sit under the direction of good ministers: "*Feed thyself and thy kids beside the tents of the under-shepherds.* Bring thy charge with thee; they shall all be welcome; *the shepherds* will be helpers, therefore abide by their tents." Those that would have acquaintance and communion with Christ must adhere to holy ordinances, must join themselves to his people. Those that have the charge of families must bring them with them to religious assemblies; let their *kids,* their children, their servants, have the benefit of *the shepherds' tent.*

III. The high encomiums which the bridegroom gives of his spouse. 1. He calls her his *love* (*v.* 9); it is an endearing compellation often used in this book:

"My friend, my companion, my familiar." 2. He compares her to a set of strong and stately *horses in Pharaoh's chariots*. Egypt was famous for the best horses. The church had complained of her own weakness, and the danger of being made a prey by her enemies: "Fear not," says Christ; "*I have made thee like a company of horses;* I have put strength into thee, so that thou shalt *mock at fear. I have compared thee to my company of horses* which triumphed over *Pharaoh's chariots*, the holy angels, *horses of fire*." 3. He admires the beauty and ornaments of her countenance (*v.* 10): *Thy cheeks are comely with rows of jewels*, the attire of the head, curls of hair, or knots of ribbons; *thy neck also with chains*, such as persons of the first rank wear, *chains of gold*. The ordinances of Christ are the ornaments of the church. The graces, gifts, and comforts of the Spirit, are the adorning of every believing soul, and beautify it.

IV. His gracious purpose to add to her ornaments; for where God has given true grace he will give more grace. She shall be yet further beautified (*v.* 11): *We will make thee borders of gold*, inlaid, or enamelled, *with studs of silver*. The same that is the author will be the finisher of the good work; and it cannot miscarry.

Verses 12–17

Between Christ and his spouse endearments are exchanged.

I. Believers in communion with him.

1. The humble reverence believers have for Christ as their Sovereign, *v.* 12. He has fellowship with them and rejoices in them; he *sits at his table* to bid them welcome. When good Christians, in any religious duty, especially in the ordinance of the Lord's supper, where the King is pleased to *sit with us at his* own *table*, have their graces exercised, their hearts broken by repentance, healed by faith, and inflamed with holy love, then the *spikenard sends forth the smell thereof*.

2. The strong affection they have for Christ as their *beloved*, their *well-beloved*, *v.* 13. Christ is not only *beloved* by all believing souls, but is their *well-beloved*, their best-beloved, their only beloved. Christ is accounted *a bundle of myrrh* and *a cluster of camphire*, everything, that is pleasant and delightful. The doctrine of his gospel, and the comforts of his Spirit, are very refreshing to them, and they rest in his love. The word translated *camphire* is *copher*, the same word that signifies *atonement* or *propitiation*. Christ is *a cluster* of merit and righteousness to all believers; *he is the propitiation for their sins. He shall lie all night between my breasts*, near my heart. Christ lays the beloved disciples in his bosom; why then should not they lay their beloved Saviour in their bosoms?

II. Jesus Christ has a great love for his church and every true believer; they are amiable in his eyes (*v.* 15): *Behold, thou art fair, my love;* and again, *Behold, thou art fair*. He says this to show that there is a real beauty in holiness, that all who are sanctified are thereby beautified; they are truly fair. One instance of the beauty of the spouse is here mentioned, that she *has doves' eyes*, as *ch.* iv. 1. Those are fair, in Christ's account, who have, not the piercing eye of the eagle, but the pure and chaste eye of the *dove*, not like the hawk, who, when he soars upwards, still has his eye upon the prey on earth, but a humble modest eye, such an eye as discovers a simplicity and godly sincerity and a dove-like innocency, lightened and guided by the Holy Spirit.

III. The church expresses her value for Christ, and returns esteem for esteem (*v.* 16): *Behold, thou art fair*. Lord, saith the church, "Dost thou call me fair? I am fair no otherwise than as I have thy

image stamped upon me. Thou art *pleasant* to all that are thine." Having expressed her esteem of her husband's person, she next, like a loving spouse, applauds the accommodations he had for her entertainment, his *bed*, his *house*, his *rafters* or *galleries* (*v.* 16), which may fitly be applied to those holy ordinances in which believers have fellowship with Jesus Christ, receive the tokens of his love and return their devout affections to him. These she calls *ours*, Christ and believers having a joint-interest in them. They are his institutions and their privileges; in them Christ and believers meet. All is *ours* if we are Christ's. Does the colour of the bed, and the furniture belonging to it, help to set it off? *Our bed is green*, a colour which, in a pastoral, is preferred before any other, because it is the colour of the fields and groves. *The beams of our house are cedar* (*v.* 17), which probably refers to the temple Solomon had lately built for communion between God and Israel, which was of *cedar*, a strong sort of wood, sweet, durable, and which will never rot, typifying the firmness and continuance of the church. The galleries for walking are of *fir*, or *cypress*, wood that was pleasing both to the sight and to the smell, intimating the delight which the saints take in walking with Christ. Everything in the covenant of grace is very firm, very fine, and very fragrant.

CHAPTER 2

In this chapter, I. Christ speaks both concerning himself and concerning his church, ver. 1, 2. II. The church speaks, 1. Remembering the pleasure and satisfaction she had in communion with Christ, ver. 3, 4. 2. Entertaining herself with the present tokens of his favour, ver. 5–7. 3. Triumphing in his approaches towards her, ver, 8, 9. 4. Repeating the gracious calls he had given her to go along with him walking, invited by the pleasures of the returning spring (ver. 10–13), out of her obscurity (ver. 14), and the charge he had given to the servants to destroy that which would be hurtful to his vineyard, ver. 15. 5. Rejoicing in her interest in him, ver. 16. 6. Longing for his arrival, ver. 17. Those whose hearts are filled with love to Christ, and hope of heaven, know best what these things mean.

Verses 1–2

I. He that is the Son of the Highest calls and owns himself *the rose of Sharon, and the lily of the valleys*, to express his presence with his people in this world, the easiness of their access to him, and the beauty and sweetness which they find in him. *The rose*, for beauty and fragrancy, is the chief of flowers, and our Saviour prefers the clothing of *the lily* before that of *Solomon in all his glory*. Christ is *the rose of Sharon*, where the best roses grew, *the rose of the field* (so some), denoting that the gospel salvation lies open to all. He is not a rose locked up in a garden. He is a *lily* for whiteness, a *lily of the valleys* for sweetness. He is a *lily of the valleys*, or *low places*, in his humiliation. Humble souls see most beauty in him. To those that are in the *valleys* he is a *lily*.

II. His church is *as a lily*; he himself is *the lily* (*v.* 1). The beauty of believers consists in their resemblance to Jesus Christ. They are as lilies, for those are made like Christ in whose hearts his *love is shed abroad*. The church of Christ as far excels all other societies as a bed of roses excels a bush of thorns. *As a lily*, compassed with *thorns*. The wicked, *the daughters* of this world, such as have no love to Christ, are as *thorns*, worthless and useless, noxious and hurtful. God's people are *as lilies among* them, scratched and torn, shaded and obscured, by them; they are dear to Christ, and yet exposed to hardships and troubles.

Verses 3–7

I. The spouse commends her beloved and prefers him before all others: *As the apple-tree among the trees of the wood*, useful and serviceable to man, yielding pleasant and profitable fruit, while the other trees are of little use, no, not the cedars themselves, till they are cut down, *so is my beloved among the sons,*

II. She remembers the abundant comfort she has had in communion with him: She *sat down* by him *with great delight*, as shepherds sometimes repose themselves. A double advantage she found in sitting down so near the Lord Jesus:—1. A refreshing shade: *I sat down under his shadow*. Christ is to believers *as the shadow of a great tree*. Those that *are weary and heavily laden* may find *rest* in Christ. We must *sit down under this shadow with delight*, must put an entire confidence in the protection of it. 2. Pleasing nourishing food. This tree drops its fruits to those that *sit down under its shadow*, and they will find them *sweet unto their taste*. Promises are sweet to a believer. Pardons are sweet, and peace of conscience is sweet, assurances of God's love, joys of the Holy Ghost, the hopes of eternal life, and the present foretastes of it are sweet, all sweet to those that have their spiritual senses exercised.

III. She owns herself obliged to Jesus Christ for all the benefit and comfort she had in communion with him (*v.* 4): " *I sat down under* the apple-tree, but he admitted me to a more intimate communion with him." *He brought me to the house* of wine. One of the rabbin by *the banqueting-house* understands *the tabernacle of the congregation*; surely then we may apply it to Christian assemblies, where the gospel is preached and gospel-ordinances are administered, particularly the Lord's supper, that *banquet of wine*. We should never have come *into the banqueting-house*, never have been acquainted with spiritual pleasures, if Christ had not brought us. *His banner over me was love; he brought me* in with a banner displayed over my head. The gospel is compared to a *banner* or *ensign* (Isa. xi. 12), and that which is represented in this banner is *love, love*; and this is the entertainment in *the banqueting-house*.

IV. She professes her strong affection and most passionate love to Jesus Christ (*v.* 5): *I am sick of love*, overcome, overpowered, by it. She cries out: "Oh *stay me with flagons*, or *ointments*, or *flowers*, anything that is reviving; *comfort me with apples*, with the fruits of that *apple-tree*, Christ (*v.* 3), with the merit and mediation of Christ and the sense of his love to my soul."

V. She experiences the power and tenderness of divine grace, relieving her in her present faintings, *v.* 6. Though he seemed to have withdrawn, yet he was even then a very present help. "*His left hand is under my head*, to bear it up, nay, as a pillow to lay it easy. For, in the meantime, *his right hand embraces me*, and thereby gives me an unquestionable assurance of his love." Believers owe all their strength and comfort to the supporting left hand and embracing right hand of the Lord Jesus.

VI. Finding her beloved thus nigh unto her she is in great care that her communion with him be not interrupted (*v.* 7): *I charge you, O you daughters of Jerusalem*. She gives them this charge *by the roes and the hinds of the field*, that is, by everything that is amiable in their eyes, and dear to them, *as the loving hind and the pleasant roe*. Those that experience the sweetness of communion with Christ cannot but desire the continuance of these blessed visits.

Verses 8–13

The church is here pleasing herself with the thoughts of her further communion with Christ.

I. She rejoices in his approach, *v.* 8. She hears him speak: "It is *the voice of my beloved*, calling to me to tell me he is coming." She sees him come. This may very well be applied to the prospect which the Old Testament saints had of Christ's coming in the flesh. *Abraham saw his day* at a distance, *and was glad*. Those that waited for the consolation of Israel with an eye of faith saw him come, and triumphed in the sight. He comes cheerfully; he comes leaping and skipping *like a roe* and like *a young hart* (*v.* 9), as one pleased and that had his delights with the sons of men. He comes surmounting all the difficulties that lay in his way; he comes *leaping over the mountains, skipping over the hills*, making nothing of discouragements. The curse of the law, the death of the cross, must be undergone, all the powers of darkness must be grappled with, but, before the resolutions of his love, these great mountains become plains. Whatever opposition is given at any time to the deliverance of God's church, Christ will break through it. He comes speedily, *like a roe* or *a young hart*; they thought the time long, but really he hastened.

II. She pleases herself with the glimpses she has of him: "He *stands behind our wall*; I know he is there, for sometimes *he looks forth at the window*, and displays *himself through the lattice*." Such was the state of the Old Testament church while it was in expectation of the coming of the Messiah. They had him near them; they had him with them, though they could not see him clearly. They saw him looking through the windows of the ceremonial institutions and smiling through those lattices; in their sacrifices and purifications Christ discovered himself to them, and gave them intimations and earnests of his grace. In the sacraments Christ is near us, but it is *behind the wall* of external signs, through *those lattices* he manifests himself to us; but we shall shortly *see him as he is*.

III. She repeats the gracious invitation he had given her to come walking with him, *v.* 10–13.

1. He called her his love and his fair one. Those that take Christ for their beloved, he will own as his; never was any love lost that was bestowed upon Christ.

2. He called her to *rise and come away*, *v.* 10, and again, *v.* 13.

3. He gave for a reason the return of the spring, and the pleasantness of the weather. The season is elegantly described. *The winter is past*, the dark, cold, and barren winter; they do not endure always. And the spring would not be so pleasant as it is if it did not succeed the winter, which is a foil to its beauty, Eccles. vii. 14. *The rain is over and gone*, the winter-rain, the cold stormy rain; it is over now, and *the dew is as the dew of herbs. Thy flowers appear on the earth*. All winter they are dead and buried in their roots, and there is no sign of them; but in the spring they revive, and show themselves in a wonderful variety and verdure. *The time of the singing of birds has come*. The little birds, which all the winter lie hid in their retirements and scarcely live, when the spring returns forget all the calamities of the winter, and to the best of their capacity chant forth the praises of their Creator. Doubtless he who understands the birds that cry for want (Ps. cxlvii. 9) takes notice of those that *sing for joy*, Ps. civ. 12. *The voice of the turtle is heard in our land*, which is one of the season-birds mentioned Jer. viii. 7, that observe the time of their coming and the time of their singing, and so shame us who understand not the times, nor sing in singing time. *The fig-tree puts forth her green figs*, by which *we know that summer is nigh*. Now this description of the returning spring, as a reason for coming away with Christ, is applicable to the introducing of the gospel in the room of the Old Testament dispensation, during which it had been winter time with the church. Christ's gospel warms that which was cold, makes that fruitful which before was dead and barren; when it comes to any place it puts a beauty and glory upon that place (2 Cor. iii. 7, 8). Spring-time is pleasant time, and so is gospel-time. The delivering of the church from the power of persecuting enemies is like spring after a winter of suffering and restraint. When the storms of trouble are over and gone, when the *voice of the turtle*, the joyful sound

of the gospel of Christ, is again heard, and ordinances are enjoyed with freedom, then *arise and come away*, sing in the ways of the Lord. When the churches had rest, then were they edified, Acts ix. 31. The conversion of sinners from a state of nature to a state of grace is like the return of the spring, a universal change, a new creation; being born again. The soul that was hard, and cold, and frozen, and unprofitable, like the earth in winter, becomes fruitful, like the earth in spring, and by degrees, like it, brings its fruits to perfection. This blessed change is owing purely to the approaches and influences of the sun of righteousness. A child of God, under doubts and fears, is like the earth in winter, its nights long, its days dark. But comfort will return; the birds shall sing again, and the flowers appear. Arise therefore, poor drooping soul, and *come away*. The bones that lay in the grave, as the roots of plants in the ground during the winter, shall at the resurrection *flourish as a herb*, Isa. lxvi. 14; xxvi. 19. That will be an eternal farewell to winter and a joyful entrance upon an everlasting spring.

Verses 14–17

I. The invitation which Christ gives to the church, and every believing soul, to come into communion with him, v. 14.

1. David had called the church God's *turtle-dove* (Ps. lxxiv. 19), and so she is here called; a dove for beauty, for innocence and inoffensiveness; a gracious spirit is a dove-like spirit, loving quietness and cleanliness, and faithful to Christ, as the turtle to her mate. The Spirit descended *like a dove* on Christ, and so he does on all Christians, making them of a *meek and quiet spirit*.

2. This dove is *in the clefts of the rock and in the secret places of the stairs*. Christ is the rock, to whom she flies for shelter, as a dove in the hole of a rock, when struck at by the birds of prey, Jer. xlviii. 28. She retires *into the secret places of the stairs*, where she may be alone, and may the better commune with her own heart. Christ often withdrew to a mountain *himself alone, to pray*.

3. Christ calls her out of her retirements: Come, *let me see thy countenance, let me hear thy voice*.

4. For her encouragement, he tells her: *Sweet is thy voice;* thy praying voice is music in God's ears.

II. The charge which Christ gives to his servants to suppress that which is a terror to his church (v. 15): *Take us the foxes, the little foxes*, that creep in insensibly; for, though they are little, they *spoil the vines*, especially now when our vines have *tender grapes* that must be preserved, or the vintage will fail. Believers are as vines; their fruits are as *tender grapes* at first, which must have time to come to maturity. This charge to *take the foxes* is, 1. A charge to believers to mortify their own sinful appetites and passions, which are as *foxes, little foxes*, that destroy their graces, crush good beginnings, and prevent their coming to perfection. Seize the *little foxes*, the first risings of sin, those sins that seem little, for they often prove very dangerous. 2. A charge to all to oppose and prevent the spreading of such opinions and practices as tend to corrupt men's judgments, debauch their consciences, perplex their minds, and discourage their inclinations to virtue. Persecutors are foxes (Luke xiii. 32); false prophets are foxes, Ezek. xiii. 4. Those that sow the tares of heresy or schism, and obstruct the progress of the gospel, they are the *foxes, the little foxes*, which must be tamed, or restrained from doing mischief.

III. The profession which the church makes of her relation to Christ, and her interest in him and communion with him, v. 16. He had called her to *rise* and *come away* with him. Now this is her answer to that call:

1. She comforts herself with the thoughts of the relation between her and her beloved: *My beloved is mine;* this denotes propriety. Believers are partakers of Christ; they are taken not only into covenant, but into communion with him. All he has promised in the gospel, all he has prepared in heaven, all is yours.

2. She comforts herself with the thoughts of the communications of his grace to his people: *He feeds among the lilies*. He *feeds* among believers, that is, he takes pleasure in them and their assemblies.

IV. The church's hope and expectation of Christ's coming. 1. She doubts not but that the *day will break* and the *shadows* will *flee away*. The gospel-day will dawn, and the shadows of the ceremonial law will flee away. This was the comfort of the Old Testament church. Or it may refer to the second coming of Christ, and the eternal happiness of the saints. 2. She begs the presence of her beloved, in the meantime, to support and comfort her: "*Turn, my beloved*, come and visit me, *be with me always to the end of the age*. Come over even *the mountains of division*, with some gracious anticipations of that light and love."

CHAPTER 3

In this chapter, I. The church gives an account of a sore trial wherewith she was exercised through the withdrawing of her beloved from her, ver. 1–5. II. The daughters of Jerusalem admire the excellence of the church, ver. 6. III. The church admires Jesus Christ under the person of Solomon, his bed, and the life-guards about it (ver. 7, 8), his chariot, ver. 9, 10, 11.

Verses 1–5

It was hard to the Old Testament church to find Christ in the ceremonial law. Long was the consolation of Israel looked for before it came. At length Simeon had *him* in his arms *whom his soul loved*. It is applicable to the case of particular believers, who often walk in darkness, but those that seek Christ to the end shall find him at length.

I. How the spouse sought him in vain *upon her bed* (v. 1). She wanted the communion she used to have with him, as David when he *thirsted for God, for the living God*. She sought him, but she saw not her signs, and yet she sought them. She failed in her endeavour.

II. How she sought him in vain abroad, v. 2. And yet she is not driven off by the disappointment. She resolves, "*I will rise now;* I will not lie here if I cannot find my beloved here. *I will rise now* without delay, and seek him immediately, lest he withdraw further from me." Those that seek Christ must not startle at difficulties. "*I will rise, and go about the city*, the holy city, in the streets, and the broad-ways"; for she knew he was not to be found in any blind by-ways. We must seek in the city, in Jerusalem, which was a type of the gospel-church, in holy ordinances. She had a good purpose when she said, *I will arise now*, but the good performance was all in all. How heavy is the accent on this repeated complaint: *I sought him, but I found him not!*

III. How she enquired of the watchmen concerning him, v. 3. In the night the watchmen *go about the city*, for the preservation of its peace and safety; these met her in her walks, and she asked them if they could give her any tidings of her beloved. Gracious souls press through crowds of other delights in pursuit of Christ. *Saw you him whom my soul loveth?* We must search the scriptures, be much in prayer, keep close to ordinances, and all with this upon our heart, *Saw you him whom my soul loveth?* Those only who have seen Christ themselves are likely to direct others to a sight of him.

IV. How she found him at last, v. 4. She *passed from* the watchmen as soon as she perceived they could give her no tidings of her beloved. But soon after she parted from the watchmen she found him whom she sought. Those that continue seeking Christ shall find him at last, and when perhaps they were almost ready to despair of finding him. See Ps. xlii. 7, 8; lxxvii. 9, 10; Isa. liv. 7, 8.

V. How close she kept to him when she had found him. She is now as much in fear of losing him as before she was in care to find him. Those that hold Christ fast in the arms of faith and love shall *not let him go*; he will abide with them.

VI. How desirous she was to make others acquainted with him: "*I brought him to my mother's house*, that all my relations, all who are dear to me, might have the benefit of communion with him." Wherever we find Christ we must take him home with us to our houses, especially to our hearts. The church is our mother, and we should be concerned for her interests, that she may have Christ present with her.

VII. What care she was in that no disturbance might be given him (*v.* 5); she repeats the charge she had before given (*ch.* ii. 7) to the *daughters of Jerusalem* not to *stir up or awake her love*. Let all *clamour and bitterness be put* far *from you*, for that *grieves the Holy Spirit of God*, Eph. iv. 30, 31. Some make this to be Christ's charge not to disturb his church, nor trouble the minds of the disciples.

Verse 6

These are the words of the *daughters of Jerusalem*, to whom the charge was given, *v.* 5. They had looked shyly upon the bride because she was black (*ch.* i. 6); but now they admire her, and speak of her with great respect: *Who is this?* How beautiful she looks! Who would have expected such a person to *come out of the wilderness?* This is applicable to the Jewish church, when, after forty years' wandering in the wilderness, they came out of it, to take possession of the land of promise. Balaam said when he stood admiring them: *From the top of the rocks I see him. How goodly are thy tents, O Jacob!* Num. xxiii. 9; xxiv. 5. It is also applicable to the recovery of a gracious soul out of a state of desertion and despondency. She ascends *out of the wilderness*, the dry and barren land, *like pillars of smoke*, like a cloud of incense ascending from the altar. This intimates a fire of pious and devout affections in the soul. Christ's return to the soul gives life to its devotion, and its communion with God is most reviving when it ascends *out of a wilderness*. She is *perfumed with myrrh and frankincense*. She is replenished with the graces of God's Spirit, which are as sweet spices, or as the holy incense. *Who is this?* What a monument of mercy is this! The graces and comforts with which she is *perfumed* are called the *powders of the merchant*, for they are dear-bought, by our Lord Jesus, that blessed merchant, who took a long voyage, and was at vast expense, no less than that of his own blood, to purchase them for us.

Verses 7–11

The *daughters of Jerusalem* stood admiring the spouse and commending her, but she transfers all the glory to Christ, and directs them to look from her to him. Here he is three times called *Solomon*. It is Christ that is here meant, who is greater than Solomon, and of whom Solomon was an illustrious type for his wisdom and especially his building the temple.

Three things she admires:

I. The safety of his bed (*v.* 7): *Behold his bed*, even *Solomon's*, very rich and fine; for such *the curtains of Solomon* were. Christ's bed, though he had *not where to lay his head*, is better than Solomon's. The church is his bed, for he has said of it, *This is my rest for ever; here will I dwell*. The hearts of believers are his bed, for he lies all night between their breasts, Eph. iii. 17. That which she admires his bed for is the guard that surrounded it. Those that rest in Christ not only dwell at ease (many do so who yet are in the greatest danger) but they dwell in safety. This bed had *threescore valiant men about it*, as yeoman of the guard, well armed: *They all hold swords*, and know how to hold them; they are *expert in war*. They are in a posture of defence, *every man* with *his sword upon his thigh* and his hand upon his sword, ready to draw upon the first alarm, and this *because of fear in the night*, and the apprehension which the spouse may have of danger. These guards are set for her satisfaction, that she may be *quiet from the fear of evil*, which believers themselves are subject to, when they are under a cloud as to their spiritual state. Christ himself was under the special protection of his Father; he had legions of angels at his command. The church is well guarded; more are with her than against her. All the attributes of God are engaged for the safety of believers; his peace protects those in whom it rules (Phil. iv. 7). Our danger is from *the rulers of the darkness of this world*, but we are safe in the *armour of light*.

II. The splendour of his chariot, *v.* 9, 10. This chariot was of Solomon's own contriving and making, the materials very rich, *silver*, and *gold*, and *cedar*, and *purple*. Some by this *chariot* (the word is nowhere else used in scripture) understand the human nature of Christ, in which the divine nature rode as in an open chariot. It was a divine workmanship (*A body hast thou prepared me*); the structure was very fine, but that which was at the bottom of it was love, pure love to the children of men. Others make it to represent the everlasting gospel, in which, as in an open chariot, Christ shows himself. *The pillars* are of *silver*, for the words of the Lord are as *silver tried* (Ps. xii. 6). It is hung with *purple*, a princely colour; all the adornings of it are dyed in the precious blood of Christ. But that which completes the glory of it is *love*; *it is paved with love*, it is lined with love, *love of the daughters of Jerusalem*, a holy *love*. Silver is better than cedar, gold than silver, but love is better than gold, better than all, and it is put last, for nothing can be better than that. The gospel is all *love*.

III. The lustre of his royal person, when he appears in his greatest pomp, *v.* 11. The call that is given to the *daughters of Zion*: *Go forth, and behold* him. Christ, in his gospel, manifests himself. Let each of us add to the number of those that give honour to him. Look with pleasure upon Christ in his glory. Look upon him with an eye of faith, with a fixed eye. Take notice of his *crown*, either the crown of gold, adorned with jewels, which he wore on his coronation-day, or the garland or crown of flowers and green tied with ribbons which his mother made for him, to adorn the solemnity of his nuptials. Applying this to Christ: *Go forth*, and see king Jesus, *with the crown wherewith his* Father *crowned him*, when he declared him his *beloved Son, in whom* he was *well-pleased*, when he *set him as King upon his holy hill of Zion*. Some apply it to the *crown of thorns* with which *his mother*, the Jewish church, *crowned him* on the day of his death, which was *the day of his espousals* to his church, when he *loved it, and gave himself for it* (Eph. v. 25). It seems especially to mean the honour done him by his church, as his mother, and by all true believers. When believers accept of him as theirs, and join themselves to him in an everlasting covenant, it is his coronation-day in their souls. Before conversion they were crowning themselves, but then they begin to crown Christ, and continue to do so from that day forward. It is *the day of his espousals*, in which he betroths them to him for ever in lovingkindness and in mercies. It is *the day of the gladness of his heart*; he is pleased with the honour that his people do him.

CHAPTER 4

In this chapter, I. Jesus Christ, having espoused his church to himself (ch. iii. 11), highly commends her beauty, ver. 1–5, and again, ver. 7. II. He retires himself, and invites her with him, from the mountains of terror to those of delight, ver. 6, 8. III. He professes his love to her, ver. 9–14. IV. She ascribes all she had that was valuable in her to him, ver. 15, 16.

Verses 1–7

I. A particular account of the beauties of the church, and of gracious souls on whom the image of God is renewed, consisting *in the beauty of holiness*. Those that honour Christ he will honour, 1 Sam. ii. 30.

1. He does not flatter her, but encourages her under her present dejections. She was espoused to him, and that made her beautiful.

2. As to the representation here made of the beauty of the church, the images are certainly very bright, the shades strong, and the comparisons bold. Seven particulars are specified, a number of perfection, for the church is enriched with manifold graces by *the seven spirits* that *are before the throne*, Rev. i. 4; 1 Cor. i. 5, 7.

(1) Her *eyes*. A good eye contributes much to beauty: *Thou hast doves' eyes*, clear and chaste, and often cast up towards heaven. Wisdom and knowledge are the eyes of the new man; they must be clear, but not haughty, *not exercised in things too high for us*. When our aims and intentions are sincere and honest, then we have *doves' eyes*. The *doves' eyes* are *within the locks*, which are as a shade upon them. They cannot fully see. As long as we are here in this world we *know but in part*.

(2) Her *hair*; it is compared to *a flock of goats*, which looked white, and were, on the top of the mountains, like a fine head of hair. Some by the *hair* here understand the outward conversation of a believer, which ought to be comely, and decent, and agreeable to the holiness of the heart.

(3) Her *teeth*, v. 2. Ministers are the church's teeth; like nurses, they chew the meat for the babes of Christ. These are here compared to *a flock of sheep*. Christ called his disciples and ministers a *little flock*. It is the praise of teeth to be *even*, to be white, and kept clean, *like sheep from the washing*.

(4) Her *lips*; these are compared to *a thread of scarlet*, v. 3. Red lips are comely, and a sign of health, as the paleness of the lips is a sign of faintness and weakness. When we praise God with *our lips, and with the mouth make confession* of him *to salvation*, then they are as *a thread of scarlet*. All our good works and good words must be *washed in the blood of Christ*, dyed like the *scarlet thread*, and then they are acceptable to God.

(5) Her *temples*, or cheeks, which are here compared to *a piece of a pomegranate*, a fruit which, when cut in two, has rich veins or specks in it, like a blush in the face. Humility and modesty, blushing at the remembrance of sin and in a sense of our unworthiness of the honour put upon us, will beautify us very much in the eyes of Christ.

(6) Her *neck*; this is here compared to *the tower of David*, v. 4. This is generally applied to the grace of faith, by which we are united to Christ, as the body is united to the head by the neck; this *is like the tower of David*, furnishing us with weapons of war, especially *bucklers* and *shields*, as the soldiers were supplied with them out of that tower, for *faith is our shield* (Eph. vi. 16): those that have it never want a *buckler*, for God will compass them *with his favour as with a shield*.

(7) Her *breasts*; these *are like two young roes that are twins*, v. 5. The church's breasts are the *breasts of her consolation* (Isa. lxvi. 11). Some apply these to the two Testaments; others to the two sacraments, the seals of the covenant of grace; others to ministers,

who are to be spiritual nurses to the children of God and to give out to them the *sincere milk of the word, that they may grow thereby*, and, in order to that, are themselves to *feed among the lilies* where Christ feeds (*ch. ii. 16*).

II. The bridegroom's resolution hereupon to retire *to the mountain of myrrh* (v. 6) and there to make his residence. This *mountain of myrrh* is supposed to signify Mount Moriah, on which the temple was built, where incense was daily burnt to the honour of God. Christ's parting promise to his disciples, as the representatives of the church, answers to this: *Lo, I am with you always, even to the end of the world*. Where the ordinances of God are duly administered there Christ will be. The holy hill (as some observe) is here called both a *mountain of myrrh*, which is bitter, and a *hill of frankincense*, which is sweet, for there we have occasion both to mourn and rejoice; repentance is a bitter sweet. But in heaven it will be all frankincense, and no myrrh.

III. His repeated commendation of the beauty of his spouse (v. 7): *Thou art all fair, my love*. The particulars, as of those of the creation, he pronounces *all very good*. There is nothing amiss in thee, and thou hast all beauties in thee; thou art *sanctified wholly* in every part; *all things have become new* (2 Cor. v. 17); there is not only a new face and a new name, but a new man, a new nature.

Verses 8–14

These are still the words of Christ to his church, expressing his affection to her.

I. The endearing names and titles by which he calls her, to express his love to her, to assure her of it, and to engage and excite her love to him. Twice here he calls her *My spouse* (v. 8, 11) and three times *My sister, my spouse*, v. 9, 10, 12. Mention was made (*ch. iii. 11*) of *the day of his espousals*, and, after that, she is called his *spouse*, not before. There is a marriage-covenant between Christ and his church, between Christ and every true believer. Christ calls his church his *spouse*. Because no one relation among men is sufficient to set forth Christ's love to his church, and to show that all this must be understood spiritually, he owns her in two relations, *My sister, my spouse*. His calling her *sister* is grounded upon his taking our nature upon him in his incarnation.

II. The gracious call he gives her to come along with him as a faithful bride. 1. All that have by faith come to Christ must come with Christ, in holy obedience to him and compliance with him. Being joined to him, we must walk with him. This is his command to us daily: "*Come with me, my spouse;* come with me to God as a Father; come with me onward, heavenward; *come with me from Lebanon, from the top of Amana, from the lions' dens*." These mountains are to be considered, (1) As seemingly delightful places. Lebanon is called *that goodly mountain*, Deut. iii. 25. We read of the pleasant *dew of Hermon* (Ps. cxxxiii. 3) and the *joy of Hermon* (Ps. lxxxix. 12). This is Christ's call to his spouse to come off from the world, to sit loose to all the delights of sense. They must *come away* and live above the tops of the highest hills on earth, that they may have *their conversation in heaven. From the tops of Shenir and Hermon*, which were on the other side Jordan, as from Pisgah, they could see the land of Canaan; from this world we must look forward to the better country. (2) These hills indeed are pleasant enough, but there are in them *lions' dens*; they are *mountains of the leopards*, mountains of prey, though they seem glorious and excellent, Ps. lxxvi. 4. On the tops of these mountains there are many dangerous temptations. *Come with me from* the temples of idolaters, and the societies of wicked people; *come out from among them, and be you separate*. *Come from* under the dominion of your own lusts, which are as *lions* and *leopards*.

2. It may be taken as a promise: Thou shalt *come with me from Lebanon, from the lions' dens*; that is, "Many shall be brought home to me, as living members of the church, from every point, from Lebanon in the north, Amana in the west, Hermon in the east, Shenir in the south, from all parts, to *sit down with Abraham, Isaac and Jacob*, Matt. viii. 11. See Isa. xlix. 11, 12.

III. The great delight Christ takes in his church.

1. No expressions of love can be more passionate than these here, in which Christ manifests his affection to his church; and yet that great proof of his love, his dying for it, goes far beyond them all. A spouse so dearly bought and paid for could not but be dearly loved. *Thou hast ravished my heart;* the word is used only here. *Thou hast hearted me*, or *Thou hast unhearted me*. New words are coined to express the inexpressibleness of Christ's surprising love to his church. *Thou hast ravished my heart with one of thy eyes*, those *doves' eyes*, clear and chaste (which were commended, *v.* 1). The ornaments she has from him, that is, the obedience she yields to him, for that is the *chain of her neck*, the graces that enrich her soul. Having shaken off the *bands of our neck*, by which we were tied to this world (Isa. lii. 2), we are bound with the *cords of love*, as *chains of gold*, to Jesus Christ, and our necks are brought under his sweet and easy yoke. *How fair is thy love!* how beautiful is it! How well does it become a believer thus to love Christ. Nothing recommends us to Christ as this does. The ointments, the odours wherewith she is perfumed, that is to say, the gifts and graces of the Spirit, her good works, are *an odour of a sweet smell, a sacrifice acceptable, well-pleasing to God*, Phil. iv. 18. Love and obedience to God are more pleasing to Christ than sacrifice or incense. *The smell of her garments* too, the visible profession she makes of religion, and relation to Christ, is as *the smell of Lebanon*. Likewise, her words are sweet (*v.* 11): *Thy lips O my spouse! drop as the honeycomb*. If what God speaks to us be *sweeter* to us *than the honey and the honeycomb* (Ps. xix. 10), what we say to him in prayer and praise shall also be pleasing to him. In the word of God there is sweet and wholesome nourishment, milk for babies, honey for those that are grown up.

2. The church is fitly compared to a *garden*, to a garden which, as was usual, had *a fountain in it* (*v.* 12–14). This garden is *a garden enclosed*, a paradise separated from the common earth. It is appropriated to God; he has *set it apart for himself*; Israel is God's portion. It is enclosed for secrecy; the saints are God's hidden ones. Christ walks in his garden unseen. It is enclosed for safety; a hedge of protection is made about it, which all the powers of darkness cannot find. It has a spring in it, and a fountain, but it is *a spring shut up* and *a fountain sealed*, that it ✝may not by any injurious hand he muddied or polluted. The souls of believers are as *gardens enclosed*; grace in them is as *a spring shut up* there in *the hidden man of the heart*, where the water that Christ gives is *a well of living water*, John iv. 14; vii. 38. The Old Testament church was *a garden enclosed* by the partition wall of the ceremonial law. The Bible was then *a spring shut up* and *a fountain sealed*; it was confined to one nation; but now the wall of separation is removed, the gospel preached to every nation, and *in Jesus Christ there is neither Greek nor Jew. Thy plants*, or plantations, *are an orchard of pomegranates with pleasant fruits, v.* 13. Here are *fruits, pleasant fruits, all trees of frankincense*, and *all the chief spices, v.* 14. Here is great plenty of fruits, the best of the kind. Their *chief spices* were much more valuable than the choicest of our flowers. Saints in

the church, and graces in the saints, are very fitly compared to these *fruits* and *spices*; for *the trees of righteousness* are the *planting of the Lord* (Isa. lxi. 3). Saints are the blessings of this earth. They are permanent, and will be preserved to good purpose, when flowers are withered and good for nothing. Grace, ripened into glory, will last for ever.

Verses 15–16

These seem to be the words of the spouse, the church, in answer to the commendations which Christ, the bridegroom, had given of her as a pleasant fruitful garden.

I. She owns her dependence upon Christ himself to make this garden fruitful. To him she has an eye (*v.* 15) as the *fountain of gardens*. To him she gives all the glory of her fruitfulness, as being nothing without him. The church transmits the praise to Christ, and says to him, *All my springs are in thee;* thou art *the well of living waters* (Jer. ii. 13). Those that are gardens to Christ must acknowledge him a fountain to them, from whose fulness they receive and to whom it is owing that their souls are as *a watered garden*, Jer. xxxi. 12.

II. She implores the influences of the blessed Spirit to make this garden fragrant (*v.* 16): *Awake, O north wind! and come, thou south*. This is a prayer for the church in general, that there may be a plentiful effusion of the Spirit. This prayer was answered in the pouring out of the Spirit on *the day of pentecost* (Acts ii. 1), ushered in by a *mighty wind*; then the apostles, who were bound up before, flowed forth, and were *a sweet savour to God*, 2 Cor. ii. 15. Sanctified souls are as gardens, gardens of the Lord, enclosed for him. Graces in the soul are as spices in these gardens. The blessed Spirit, in his operations upon the soul, is as the *north and the south wind*. There is the north wind of convictions, and the south wind of comforts. The flowing forth of the spices of grace depends upon the gales of the Spirit.

III. She invites Christ to the best entertainment the garden affords: *Let my beloved* then *come into his garden and eat his pleasant fruits*; let him have the honour of all the products of the garden, and let me have the comfort of his acceptance of them. The believer can take little pleasure in his garden, unless Christ, the beloved of his soul, come to him, nor have any jot of the fruits of it, unless they redound some way or other to the glory of Christ.

CHAPTER 5

In this chapter we have, I. Christ's gracious acceptance of the invitation which his church had given him, ver. 1. II. The account which the spouse gives of her own folly, in putting a slight upon her beloved, and the distress she was in by reason of his withdrawings, ver. 2–8. III. The enquiry of the daughters of Jerusalem concerning the perfections of her beloved (ver. 9), and her particular answer to that enquiry, ver. 10–16. "Unto you that believe he is thus precious."

Verse 1

These words are Christ's answer to the church's prayer in the close of the foregoing chapter, *Let my beloved come into his garden;* here he has come. She called him *her beloved* because she loved him; in return he called her his *sister and spouse*. Those that make Christ their best beloved shall be owned by him in the nearest and dearest relations. She invited him to *come into his garden*, and he says, *I have come*. Those that throw open the door of their souls to Jesus Christ shall find him ready to come into them; and in every place where he records his name he will meet his people, and bless them, Exod. xx. 24. She only desired him to *eat the fruits* of the garden, but he brought along with him something more, *honey*, and *wine*, and *milk*, which yield substantial nourishment, and which were the products of Canaan,

Immanuel's land. The great work of man's redemption, and the riches of the covenant of grace, are a feast to the Lord Jesus and they ought to be so to us.

Verses 2-8

In this song of loves and joys we have here a melancholy scene; the spouse here speaks, not to her beloved, but of him, and it is a sad story she tells of her own folly and ill conduct.

I. Listlessness that had seized her. *She slept*, that is, pious affections cooled, she neglected her duty and grew remiss in it. True Christians are not always alike lively and vigorous in religion. But Grace was remaining, notwithstanding: "*My heart wakes; my own conscience reproaches me for it, and ceases not to rouse me out of my sluggishness. I sleep, but it is not a dead sleep; I strive against it; I cannot be easy under this indisposition.*" We ought to take notice of our own spiritual slumbers and distempers, and to reflect upon it with sorrow and shame that we have fallen asleep when Christ has been nigh us in his garden.

II. The call that Christ gave to her, when she was under this indisposition: *It is the voice of my beloved;* she knew it to be so, which was a sign that her heart was awake. Like the child Samuel, she heard at the first call, but did not, like him, mistake the person; she knew it to be the voice of Christ. He knocks, to awaken us to come and let him in, knocks by his word and Spirit, knocks by afflictions and by our own consciences. Those whom he loves he will not let alone in their carelessness, but will find some way or other to awaken them, to rebuke and chasten them. Observe how moving the call is: *Open to me, my sister, my love.* He sues for entrance who may demand it; he knocks who could easily knock the door down. He gives her all the most endearing titles imaginable: *My sister, my love, my dove, my undefiled;* he gives her no hard names. *His loving-kindness he will not utterly take away. Open to me.* Can we deny entrance to such a friend, to such a guest? He begs to be admitted *under the character of a poor traveller* that wants a lodging: "*My head is wet with the dew,* consider what hardships I have undergone, to merit thee, which surely may merit from thee so small a kindness as this." When Christ was crowned with thorns, then was his head *wet with the dew.* Do we thus requite him for his love?

III. The excuse she made to put off her compliance with this call (v. 3): *I have put off my coat; How shall I put it on again?* She is half asleep; she knows the voice of her beloved, but cannot find in her heart to open to him. She was undressed, she had *washed her feet,* and would not have occasion to wash them again. Frivolous excuses are the language of prevailing slothfulness in religion; Christ calls to us to open to him, but we pretend we have no mind, or we have no strength, or we have no time. Those put a great contempt upon Christ that cannot find in their hearts to bear a cold blast for him, or get out of a warm bed.

IV. The powerful influences of divine grace, by which she was made willing to rise and open to her beloved. When he could not prevail with her by persuasion he *put in his hand by the hole of the door,* to unbolt it, as one weary of waiting, v. 4. This intimates a work of the Spirit upon her soul. The conversion of Lydia is represented by the *opening of her heart* (Acts xvi. 14).

V. Her compliance with these methods of divine grace at last: *My bowels were moved for him.* She was moved with compassion to her beloved, because his *head was wet with the dew.* Did Christ redeem us in his pity? Let us in pity receive him, and for his sake, those that are his, when at any time they are in distress. He made her ashamed of her dullness and

slothfulness (v. 5, *I rose up, to open to my beloved*). It was her own act, and yet he wrought it in her. And now her *hands dropped with myrrh upon the handles of the lock.* Either, 1. She found it there when she applied her hand to the lock, to shoot it back; he that *put in his hand by the hole of the door* left it there as an evidence that he had been there. When Christ has wrought powerfully upon a soul he leaves a blessed sweetness in it. 2. She brought it thither. When she came to open to him she prepared to anoint his head, and so to refresh and comfort him; she was in such haste to meet him that she would not stay to make the usual preparation, but dipped her hand in her box of ointment, that she might readily anoint his head. Those that open the doors of their hearts to Christ, those *everlasting doors,* must meet him with the lively exercises of faith and other graces, and with these must anoint him.

VI. Her sad disappointment when she did open to her beloved. *I opened to my beloved,* as I intended, but, alas! *my beloved had withdrawn himself, and was gone. My beloved was gone, was gone,* so the word is. 1. She did not open to him at his first knock, and now she came too late. Christ will be sought while he may be found; if we slip our time, we may lose our passage. Christ justly rebukes our delays and suspends the communications of comfort from those that are remiss. 2. She still calls him her *beloved,* being resolved, how cloudy and dark soever the day be, she will not quit her relation to him. She now remembers the words he said to her when he called her: "*My soul failed when he spoke;* his words melted me when he said, *My head is wet with the dew;* and yet I lay still, and made excuses, and did not open to him." She went in pursuit of him: *I sought him; I called him. I could not find him; he gave me no answer.* There are those who have a true love for Christ, and yet have not immediate answers to their prayers for his smiles; but he gives them an equivalent if he strengthens them with strength in their souls to continue seeking him, Ps. cxxxviii. 3. St. Paul could not prevail for the removing of the *thorn in the flesh,* but was answered with grace sufficient for him. She was ill-treated by the watchmen: *They found me; they smote me; they wounded me,* v. 7. They took her for a lewd woman and beat her accordingly. Disconsolate saints are taken for sinners, and are censured and reproached as such. When she was disabled to prosecute her enquiry herself she gave charge to those about her to assist her (v. 8): *I charge you, O you daughters of Jerusalem!* all my friends and acquaintance, *if you find my beloved,* "Speak a good word for me; tell him that *I am sick of love.*" It is better to be sick of love to Christ than at ease in love to the world.

Verses 9-16

I. The daughters of Jerusalem answer to the charge she had given them, v. 9. Observe the respectful title they give to the spouse: *O thou fairest among women!* The church is the most excellent society in the world, and the beauty of the sanctuary a transcendent beauty. Holiness is the symmetry of the soul. Even those that have little acquaintance with Christ, as those daughters of Jerusalem, cannot but see beauty in those that bear his image. Their enquiry concerning her beloved: "*What is thy beloved more than another beloved?*" Some take it for a scornful question, blaming her for making such ado about him. Carnal hearts see nothing excellent or extraordinary in the Lord Jesus, in his person or offices, in his doctrine or in his favours. Others rather take it for a serious question, and suppose that those who put it intended to comfort the spouse, who, they knew would recover new spirits if she did but talk awhile of her beloved. They wondered what moved the spouse to charge them concerning her beloved with so much concern, and concluded there must be something more in him than in another. There begin to be hopes of people when they begin to enquire concerning Christ. And sometimes the extraordinary zeal of one, in enquiring after Christ, may be a means to provoke many (2 Cor. ix. 2).

II. The account which the spouse gives of her beloved in answer to this question. She assures them, in general, that he is one of incomparable perfections and unparalleled worth (v. 10). He has everything in him that is lovely: *My beloved is white and ruddy.* This points not at any extraordinary beauty of his body, when he should be incarnate, but at his divine glory, in the eyes of those that are enlightened to discern spiritual things. In him we may behold the *beauty of the Lord*; he was the *holy child Jesus*; that was his fairness. His love to us renders him lovely. He is *white* in the spotless innocency of his life, *ruddy* in the bloody sufferings he went through at his death,—*white*, in his glory, as God, *ruddy* in his assuming the nature of man, *Adam—red earth.* He has that loveliness in him which is not to be found in any other: He is *the chief among ten thousand.* She gives a particular detail of his accomplishments, conceals not his power or comely proportion. Ten instances she here gives of his beauty. The design, in general, is to show that he is every way qualified for his undertaking, and has all that in him which may recommend him to our esteem, love, and confidence. Christ's appearance to John (Rev. i. 13, &c.) may be compared with the description which the spouse gives of him here, the scope of both being to represent him transcendently glorious. (1) *His head is as the most fine gold. The head of Christ is God* (1 Cor. xi. 3). Christ's head bespeaks his sovereign dominion over all and his vital influence upon his church and all its members. (2) *His locks are bushy and black, black as a raven,* whose blackness is his beauty; *black and bushy,* denoting that he is ever young and that there is in him nothing that waxes old. (3) *His eyes are as the eyes of doves,* fair and clear, and chaste and kind (4) *His cheeks are as a bed of spices,* and *as sweet flowers,* or towers of sweetness. The half discoveries Christ makes of himself to the soul are reviving and refreshing, fragrant above the richest flowers and perfumes. (5) *His lips are like lilies,* sweet and pleasant. Such are *the words of his lips* to all that are sanctified; *grace is poured into his lips,* and those that heard him *wondered at the gracious words which proceeded out of his mouth.* (6) *His hands are as gold rings set with the beryl,* a noted precious stone, v. 14. Great men had their hands adorned with gold rings on their fingers, set with precious stones, but, in her eye, *his hands* themselves were *as gold rings*; all the instances of his power, the works of his hands, all the performances of his providence and grace, are all precious, as gold, *as the precious onyx and the sapphire,* all fitted to the purpose for which they were designed, and all beautiful, *as rings set with beryl.* (7) *His bowels are as bright ivory.* It denotes his tender compassion and affection for his spouse. This love of his is like *bright ivory,* finely polished, and richly *overlaid with sapphires.* The love itself is strong and firm, bright and sparkling. (8) *His legs are as pillars of marble,* v. 15. This bespeaks his stability and steadfastness; he is able to bear all the weight of the government that is upon his shoulders. (9) *His countenance* (his port and mien) *is as Lebanon,* that stately hill; his aspect beautiful and charming, *excellent as the cedars.* (10) *His mouth is most sweet;* it is *sweetness* (so the word is), v. 16. The words of his mouth are all sweet to a believer. The tokens of his love, have a transcendent sweetness in them, and

are most delightful to those who have their *spiritual senses exercised. To you that believe he is precious.* She concludes with a full assurance both of faith and hope, and so gets the mastery of her trouble. Here is a full assurance of faith concerning the complete beauty of the Lord Jesus: "*He is altogether lovely.*" Here is a full assurance of hope concerning her own interest in him: "*This is my beloved, and this is my friend;* and therefore wonder not that I thus long after him. He is mine, *my Lord and my God* (John xx. 28), mine according to the tenor of the gospel-covenant, mine in all relations, bestowed upon me, to be all that to me that my poor soul stands in need of." It is spoken of here with an air of triumph: "This is he whom I have chosen, and to whom I have given up myself. None but Christ, none but Christ. This is he on whom my heart is, for he is my best-beloved; this is he in whom I trust, and from whom I expect all good, for *this is my friend.*"

CHAPTER 6

In this chapter, I. The daughters of Jerusalem, moved with the description which the church had given of Christ, enquire after him, ver. 1. II. The church directs them where they may meet with him, ver. 2, 3. III. Christ is now found of those that sought him, and very highly applauds the beauty of his spouse (ver. 4–7), before all others (ver. 8, 9), recommending her to the love and esteem of all her neighbours (ver. 10), and expressing the great delight he took in her, ver. 11–13.

Verses 1–3

I. The enquiry which the daughters of Jerusalem made concerning Christ, v. 1. They still continue their high thoughts of the church, and call her, as before, the *fairest among women.* And now they raise their thoughts higher concerning Christ: *Whither has thy beloved gone, that we may seek him with thee?* This would be but an unacceptable compliment, if the song were not to be understood spiritually; for love is jealous of a rival; but those that truly love Christ are desirous that others should love him too. The spouse had described him and had expressed her own love to him, and that flame in her breast scattered sparks into theirs. As sinful lusts, when they break out, defile many, so the pious zeal of some may *provoke many,* 2 Cor. ix. 2.

II. The answer which the spouse gave to this enquiry, v. 2, 3. Now she knows very well where he is (v. 2): "*My beloved* is not to be found in the streets of the city, and the crowd and noise that are there, but he *has gone down to his garden,* a place of retirement." The more we withdraw from the hurry of the world the more likely we are to have acquaintance with Christ, who took his disciples into a garden, there to be witnesses of the agonies of his love. Christ's church is a garden enclosed, *his garden,* which he has planted. Those that would find Christ may expect to meet with him in *his garden* the church; they must attend upon him in the ordinances which he has instituted, the word, sacraments, and prayer, wherein he will be with us *always, even to the end of the world.* When Christ comes down to his church it is to feed his flock, which he feeds not, as other shepherds, in the open fields, but in his garden. He comes to feed his friends, and entertain them, *for the Lord takes pleasure in those that fear him.* He has many gardens, many particular churches of different sizes and shapes; but, while they are his, he manifests himself among them, and is well pleased with them. He picks the lilies one by one, and gathers them to himself; and there will be a general harvest of them at the great day. She had acted unkindly to her beloved, and he had justly withdrawn himself from her, and therefore there was occasion to take fresh hold of the covenant, which continues firm between Christ and believers, notwithstanding their failings and his frowns, Ps. lxxxix. 30–35. "I have been care-

less and wanting in my duty, and yet *I am my beloved's.*
He has justly hidden his face from me and yet *my
beloved is mine.*" When we have not a full assurance
of Christ's love we must live by a faithful adherence
to him. "Though I have not the sensible consolation
I used to have, yet I will cleave to this, *Christ is mine
and I am his.*"

Verses 4–10

Now we must suppose Christ graciously returned
to his spouse, having forgiven and forgotten all her
unkindness, for he speaks very tenderly and respectfully to her.

I. He pronounces her truly amiable (*v.* 4): *Thou
art beautiful, O my love! as Tirzah*, a city in the tribe
of Manasseh, whose name signifies *pleasant*, or
acceptable. Thou art comely as Jerusalem, a city
compact together (Ps. cxxii. 3), and which Solomon
had built and beautified. It was the holy city, and
that was the greatest beauty of it; and fitly is the
church compared to it. The gospel-church is *the
Jerusalem that is above* (Gal. iv. 26), *the heavenly
Jerusalem* (Heb. xii. 22); in it God has *his sanctuary*,
and is, in a special manner, present; therefore it is
comely as Jerusalem, and, being so, is *terrible as an
army with banners.*

II. He owns himself in love with her, *v.* 5, though,
for a small moment, he had hid his face from her.
Turn thy eyes towards me (so some read it), "turn
the eyes of faith and love towards me, *for they have
lifted me up*; look unto me, and be comforted."
When we are calling to God to turn the eye of his
favour towards us he is calling to us to turn the
eye of our obedience towards him.

III. He repeats, almost word for word, part of the
description, he had given of her beauty (*ch.* iv. 1–3),
her *hair*, her *teeth*, her *temples* (*v.* 5–7), to show that
he had still the same esteem for her that he had before.

IV. He sees all the beauties and perfections of others
meeting and centring in her (*v.* 8, 9): "*There are*, it
may be, *threescore queens*, who, like Esther, have by
their beauty attained to the royal state and dignity,
and fourscore concubines, virgins without number, but
my dove, my undefiled, is but one, a holy one." She
excels them all. Go through all the world, and view
the societies of men that reckon themselves wise
and happy, kingdoms, courts, senates, councils, they
are none of them to be compared with the church of
Christ. There are particular persons who are famed
for their accomplishments, the beauties of their
language, and performances, but the beauty of holiness is beyond all other beauty. "Though there are
many particular churches, some of greater dignity,
others of less, some of longer, others of shorter,
standing, and many particular believers, of different
gifts and attainments, yet they all constitute but one
catholic church, are all but parts of that whole, and
that is *my dove, my undefiled.*" Christ is the centre
of the church's unity.

V. He shows how much she was esteemed, not by
him only, but by all that had acquaintance with her.
As Solomon himself is said to have been *tender and
an only one in the sight of his mother* (Prov. iv. 3),
so was she *the only one of her mother*, as dear as if
she had been an only one, *the choice one of her that
bore her.* All the kingdoms of the world, and the
glory of them, are nothing, in Christ's account,
compared with the church. She was admired by all
her acquaintance, not only *the daughters*, her juniors,
but even *the queens and the concubines*, who might
have reason to be jealous of her as a rival; *they* all
blessed her, praised her, and spoke well of her. Those
that have any correct sense of things cannot but be
convinced in their consciences (whatever they say)
that godly people are excellent people; many will give
them their good word, and more their goodwill.

Jesus Christ is well pleased with those that honour
such as fear the Lord, and takes it ill of those that
offend any of his little ones.

VI. He produces the encomium that was given of
her, and makes it his own (*v.* 10): *Who is she that
looks forth as the morning?* This is applicable both
to the church in the world and to grace in the heart.
Christians are, or should be, the lights of the world.
The patriarchal church *looked forth as the morning*
when the promise of the Messiah was first made
known, and *the day-spring from on high visited* this
dark world. The Jewish church was *fair as the moon*;
the ceremonial law was an imperfect light; it shone
by reflection; did not make day, nor had *the sun
of righteousness yet risen*. But the Christian church
is *clear as the sun*, exhibits a great *light to those that
sat in darkness.* The beauty of the church and of
believers is *awful as an army with banners.* The
church, in this world, is *as an army*, as the camp of
Israel in the wilderness; its state is militant; it is in
the midst of enemies, and is engaged in a constant
conflict with them. Believers are soldiers in this
army. It has its *banners*; the gospel of Christ is an
ensign (Isa. xi. 12). It is marshalled, and kept in
order and under discipline. It is *terrible* to its enemies.
When the church preserves her purity she secures her
honour and victory; when she is *fair as the moon*,
and *clear as the sun*, she is truly great and formidable.

Verses 11–13

Christ having now returned to his spouse, and the
breach being entirely made up, here gives an account
of the distance and of the reconciliation.

I. When he had withdrawn from his church as his
spouse, yet even then he had his eye upon it as his
garden, which he took care of (*v.* 11): "*I went down
into the garden of nuts*, or nutmegs, *to see the fruits
of the valley*, with concern, to see them as my
own." When he was out of sight he was no further
off than the garden, observing *how the vine flourished*,
that he might do all which was necessary to promote
its flourishing. He went to see whether *the pomegranates budded.* Christ observes the first beginnings
of the good work of grace in the soul and the early
buddings of devout affections and inclinations there,
and is well pleased with them, as we are with the
blossoms of the spring.

II. Yet he could not long content himself with
this, but suddenly felt a powerful inclination to return
to his church, being moved with her lamentations
after him (*v.* 12): "*Or ever I was aware, my soul made
me like the chariots of Ammi-nadib;* I could not any
longer keep at a distance; and I presently resolved to
fly back to my love." And now the spouse perceives
that he *heard the voice of her supplications*, and became *like the chariots of Ammi-nadib*, which were
noted for their beauty and swiftness. Christ's people
ought to be a willing people. If they continue seeking
Christ and longing after him, even when he seems to
withdraw from them, he will return to them in due
time.

III. He, having returned to her, kindly courted her
return to him, notwithstanding the discouragements
she laboured under. Let her take the comfort of the
return of her beloved, *v.* 13. Here the church is called
the *Shulamite*, referring to *Salem*, the place of her
birth and residence, as the woman of *Shunem* is
called the *Shunamite.* Heaven is the Salem whence the
saints have their birth, and where they have their
citizenship. She is invited to return. As revolting
sinners have need to be called to again and again
(*Turn you, turn you, why will you die?*) so disquieted
saints have need to be called to again and again,
Turn you, turn you, why will you droop; *Why art thou
cast down, O my soul?* Having returned, she is desired
to show her face: *That we may look upon thee.* Go

no longer with thy face covered like a mourner. Christ is pleased with the cheerfulness and humble confidence of his people and would have them look pleasant. A short account is given of what is to be seen in her. The question is asked, *What will you see in the Shulamite?* And it is answered, *As it were the company of two armies.* (1) Some think she gives this account of herself. Alas! says she, *What will you see in the Shulamite?* nothing that is worth your looking upon, nothing but *as it were the company of two armies* actually engaged, where nothing is to be seen but blood and slaughter. The watchmen had wounded her, and she carried in her face the marks of those wounds, looked as if she had been fighting. She had said (*ch.* i. 6), *Look not upon me because I am black;* here she says, "Look not upon me because I am bloody." (2) Others think her beloved gives this account of her. "I will tell you what you shall *see in the Shulamite;* you shall see as noble a sight as that of two armies, or two parts of the same army, drawn out in rank and file; not only *as an army with banners,* but as *two armies,* with a majesty double to what was before. She is as *Mahanaim,* as the two hosts which Jacob saw (Gen. xxxii. 1, 2), a host of saints and a host of angels ministering to them; the church militant, the church triumphant."

CHAPTER 7

In this chapter, I. Christ, the royal bridegroom, goes on to describe the beauties of his spouse, the church, and to express his love to her, ver. 1–9. II. The spouse, the church, expresses her great delight in him, and the desire that she had of communion with him, ver. 10–13.

Verses 1–9

The title which Jesus Christ here gives to the church is new: *O prince's daughter!* agreeing with Ps. xlv. 13, where she is called *the king's daughter.* She is so in respect of her new birth, born from above, begotten of God, and his workmanship, bearing the image of the King of kings, and guided by his Spirit. She is so by marriage; Christ, by betrothing her to himself, though he found her mean and despicable, has made her a *prince's daughter.*

I. A copious description of the beauty of the spouse, which seems to be given by Christ himself, and to be designed to express his love to her as before, *ch.* iv. 1, &c., and *ch.* vi. 5, 6. The similitudes are here different from before, to show that the beauty of holiness is such as nothing in nature can reach. That commendation of the spouse, *ch.* iv, was immediately upon the espousals (*ch.* iii. 11), this upon her return from a by-path (*ch.* vi. 13); yet this exceeds that, to show the constancy of Christ's love to his people; *he loves them to the end.* The spouse had described the beauty of her beloved in ten particulars (*ch.* v. 11, &c.); and now he describes her in as many. The beauties of the church are reckoned from foot to head. 1. Her *feet* are here praised; the feet of Christ's ministers are beautiful in the eyes of the church (Isa. lii. 7), and her feet are here said to be beautiful in the eyes of Christ. *How beautiful are thy feet with shoes!* When believers, being made free from the captivity of sin (Acts xii. 8), have *their feet shod with the preparation of the gospel of peace,* and walk steadily according to the rule of the gospel, then their *feet are beautiful with shoes;* they tread firmly. 2. *The joints of the thighs are* here said to be *like jewels,* and those curiously wrought by *a cunning workman.* This is explained by Eph. iv. 16 and Col. ii. 19, where the mystical body of Christ is said to be held together by *joints and bands,* as the hips and knees (both which are *the joints of the thighs*) serve the natural body in its strength and motion. The church is *then* comely in Christ's eyes when those joints are kept firm by holy love and unity. 3. The *navel* is here

compared to a round cup or *goblet.* The fear of the Lord is said to be *health to the navel.* See Prov. iii. 8. 4. The *belly is like a heap of wheat* in the store-chamber, which perhaps was sometimes adorned with flowers. The *wheat* is useful, the *lilies* are beautiful; there is everything in the church which may be to the members of that body either for use or for ornament. All the body is nourished from the *belly;* it denotes the spiritual prosperity of a believer and the healthful constitution of the soul. 5. The *breasts are like two young roes that are twins,* v. 3. This comparison we had before, *ch.* iv. 5. 6. The *neck,* which before was compared to *the tower of David* (*ch.* iv. 4), is here compared to *a tower of ivory,* so white, so precious; such is the faith of the saints, by which they are joined to Christ their head. 7. The *eyes are* compared to *the fishpools in Heshbon,* or the artificial fish-ponds, *by a gate,* either of Jerusalem or of Heshbon, which is called *Bath-rabbim,* the daughter of a multitude, because a great thoroughfare. The understanding, the intentions of a believer, are clean and clear as these ponds. 8. The *nose* is like *the tower of Lebanon,* the forehead or face set *like a flint* (Isa. l. 7), undaunted as that tower was impregnable. So it denotes the magnanimity and holy bravery of the church, or (as others) a spiritual sagacity to discern things that differ, as animals strangely distinguish by the smell. This tower *looks towards Damascus,* the head city of Syria, denoting the boldness of the church in facing its enemies. 9. The *head like Carmel,* a very high hill near the sea, *v.* 5. The head of a believer is *lifted up above his enemies* (Ps. xxvii. 6), above the storms of the lower region, as the top of Carmel was, pointing heavenward. 10. *The hair of the head* is said to be *like purple.* This denotes the amiableness of a believer in the eyes of Christ, even to *the hair,* or (as some understand it) the pins with which *the hair* is dressed.

II. The church thus beautified and adorned is lovely indeed if she be so in his eyes. His love makes this comeliness truly valuable. 1. He delighted to look upon his church. *The king is held in the galleries,* and cannot leave them. And, if Christ has such delight *in the galleries* of communion with his people, much more reason have they to delight in them. 2. He was struck with admiration at the beauty of his church (*v.* 6): *How fair and how pleasant art thou, O love! How art thou made fair!* (so the word is), "not born so, but made so with the comeliness which I have put upon thee." 3. He determined to keep up communion with his church. He compares her *stature to a palm-tree* (*v.* 7), so straight, so strong, does she appear. The *palm-tree* is observed to flourish most when it is loaded; so the church, the more it has been afflicted, the more it has multiplied; and the branches of it are emblems of victory. Christ says, "*I will go up to the palm-tree,* to entertain myself with the shadow of it (*v.* 8) and *I will take hold of its boughs* and observe the beauty of them." He compares her *breasts* (her pious affections towards him) *to clusters of grapes,* a most pleasant fruit (*v.* 7), and he repeats it (*v.* 8): They *shall be* (that is, they shall be to me) *as clusters of the vine,* which *make glad the heart.* "Now that I come *up to the palm-tree* thy graces shall be exerted and excited." *The smell of* their nostrils is *like the smell of apples,* or oranges, which is pleasing and reviving. And, lastly, *the roof of her mouth is like the best wine* (*v.* 9); her spiritual taste and relish, of the words she speaks to God and man, which come from *the roof of the mouth,* these are pleasing to God. *The prayer of the upright is his delight.* It is like that wine which is palatable and grateful to the taste. It *goes down sweetly.* Nothing *goes down so sweetly* with a gracious soul as the wine of God's consolations. The presence of Christ by his Spirit with his people shall be reviving and refreshing to them, as that strong wine which makes *the lips* even *of those that are asleep* (that are ready to faint away in a delirium), *to speak.* Unconverted sinners are asleep; saints are often drowsy, and listless, and half asleep; but the word and Spirit of Christ will put life and vigour into the soul, and *out of the abundance of the heart* that is thus filled *the mouth* will *speak.*

Verses 10–13

These are the words of the spouse, the church, the believing soul.

I. She here triumphs in her relation to Christ. With what holy exultation does she say (*v.* 10), "*I am my beloved's,* not my own, but entirely devoted to him and owned by him." Glorying in this, that she is his, to serve him, she comforts herself with this, that his *desire is towards her.* Christ's desire was strongly towards his chosen remnant, when he came from heaven to earth to seek and save them. This is a comfort to believers that, whosoever slights them, Christ has a desire towards them, such a desire as will again bring him from heaven to earth to receive them to himself.

II. She humbly and earnestly desires communion with him (*v.* 11, 12): "*Come, my beloved,* let us take a walk together, that I may receive counsel, instruction, and comfort from thee, and may make known my wants and grievances to thee, with freedom, and without interruption." Thus Christ walked with the two disciples that were going to the village called *Emmaus,* and talked with them, till he made their *hearts burn within them.* She desires to go forth into the fields and villages to have this communion with him. Those that would converse with Christ must go forth from the world, must avoid everything that would divert the mind and be a hindrance to it when it should be wholly taken up with Christ. *Let us get up early to the vineyards.* It intimates her care to improve opportunities of conversing with her beloved. She will be content to take up her lodging in the villages. His presence will make them fine and pleasant. A gracious soul can reconcile itself to the poorest accommodations, if it may have communion with God in them.

III. She desires to be better acquainted with the state of her own soul and the present posture of its affairs (*v.* 12): *Let us see if the vine flourish.* Our own souls are our vineyards. We are made keepers of these vineyards, and therefore are concerned often to look into them, to examine the state of our own souls, to seek whether the *vine flourishes,* whether we be fruitful in the fruits of righteousness. And especially let us enquire whether *the tender grape appear* and whether *the pomegranates bud forth,* what good motions and dispositions there are in us that are yet but young and tender, that they may be protected and cherished with particular care, that they may bring forth fruit unto perfection. And, if we would be acquainted with ourselves, we must beg of him to search and try us, to help us in the search, and discover us to ourselves.

IV. She promises to her beloved the best entertainment she can give him; for he will come in to us, and sup with us, Rev. iii. 20. 1. She promises him her best affections. 2. She promises him her best provision, *v.* 13. "There we shall find pleasant odours, for *the mandrakes give a smell.* We shall also find that which is good for food, as well as pleasant to the eye: *At our gates are all manner of pleasant fruits.*" The fruits and exercises of grace are pleasant to the Lord Jesus. These must be carefully devoted to his service and honour, must be always ready, as that is which is laid up at our gates. There is a great variety of these pleasant fruits, with which our souls should be well stocked; we must have grace for all occasions. Those that truly love Christ will think all they have

even their most *pleasant fruits,* and what they have treasured up most carefully, too little to be bestowed upon him.

CHAPTER 8

The affections between Christ and his spouse are as strong in this closing chapter of the song, as ever. I. The spouse continues her importunity for a more intimate communion with him, ver. 1–3. II. She charges the daughters of Jerusalem not to interrupt her communion with her beloved (ver. 4); and they admire her dependence on him, ver. 5. III. She begs of her beloved, that he would by his grace confirm that blessed union with him to which she was admitted, ver. 6, 7. IV. She makes intercession for others also, that care might be taken of them (ver. 8, 9). V. She owns herself his tenant for a vineyard she held of him at Baal-hamon, ver. 11, 12. VI. The song concludes with an interchanging of parting requests. Christ charges his spouse that she should often let him hear from her (ver. 13), and she begs of him that he would hasten his return to her, ver. 14.

Verses 1–4

1. The spouse wishes for a constant intimacy and freedom with the Lord Jesus. She was obliged to be shy and to keep at some distance; she therefore wishes she may be taken for his sister, he having called her so (*ch.* v. 1), and that she might have the same chaste and innocent familiarity with him that a sister has with a brother. It is the wish of all believers for a more intimate communion with him, that they might *receive the Spirit of sanctification,* and so Christ might be as their brother, that is, that they might be as his brethren, which *then* they are when by grace they are made partakers of a divine nature, Heb. ii. 11, &c. 2. She promises herself then the satisfaction of making a more open profession of her relation to him than at present she could make: "*When I should find thee without,* anywhere, even before company, *I would kiss thee,* as a sister does her own brother." The church, since Christ's incarnation, can better own him than she could before, when she would have been laughed at for being so much in love with one that was not yet born. Christ has become as our brother; wherever we find him, therefore, let us be ready to own our relation to him and affection for him. 3. She promises to improve the opportunity she should then have for cultivating an acquaintance with him (*v.* 2): "*I would lead thee,* as my brother. I would bring *thee into my mother's house,* into the church, into the solemn assemblies (*ch.* iii. 4), and *there thou wouldst instruct me.*" It is the presence of Christ in and with his church that makes the word and ordinances instructive to her children, who shall all be taught of God. 4. She promises him to bid him welcome to the best she had; she would *cause him to drink of her spiced wine and the juice of her pomegranate.* The exercise of grace and the performance of duty are to the Lord Jesus, very acceptable to him, as expressive of a grateful sense of his favours. 5. She doubts not but to experience his tender care of her, that she should be supported by his power. (*His left hand shall be under my head*) and that she should be comforted with his love—*His right hand should embrace me.* While we are following hard after Christ his *right hand sustains* Ps. lxiii. 8. *Underneath are the everlasting arms.* 6. She charges those about her to take heed of doing anything to interrupt the pleasing communion she now had with her beloved (*v.* 4). The church, our common mother, charges all her children that they never do anything to provoke Christ to withdraw.

Verses 5–7

I. The spouse is much admired by those about her. It comes in in a parenthesis, but in it gospel-grace lies as plain, and as much above ground, as anywhere in this mystical song: *Who is this that comes up from the wilderness, leaning upon her beloved?* They are the words of the daughters of Jerusalem, to whom she spoke (*v.* 4); they see her, and bless her. The Jewish church came up from the wilderness supported by the divine power and favour, Deut. xxxii. 10, 11. The Christian church was raised up from a low and desolate condition by the grace of Christ relied on, Gal. iv. 27. Particular believers are admirable, and divine grace is to be admired in them, when by the power of that grace they are brought *up from the wilderness, leaning* with a holy confidence *upon* Jesus Christ *their beloved*. This bespeaks the beauty of a soul, and the wonders of divine grace.

II. She addresses herself to her beloved.

1. She puts him in mind of the former experience which she and others had had of comfort in applying to him. (1) For her own part: "*I raised thee up under the apple tree*, that is, I have many a time wrestled with thee by prayer and have prevailed. When I was alone in the acts of devotion, retired in the orchard, under *the apple-tree*, meditating and praying, then *I raised thee up*, to help me and comfort me," as the disciples raised him up in the storm, saying, *Master, carest thou not that we perish?* (Mark iv. 38). (2) Others also had had like experience of comfort in Christ. There *thy mother brought thee forth*, the universal church, or believing souls, in whom Christ was formed, Gal. iv. 15. Those that had *travailed* in convictions at last *brought forth* in consolations, and the *pain was forgotten* for joy of the Saviour's birth.

2. She begs of him that her union with him might be confirmed, and her communion with him continued and made more intimate (*v.* 6): *Set me as a seal upon thy heart, as a seal upon thy arm.* "Let me have a place in thy heart, an interest in thy love. Be thou my high priest; let my name be written on thy breast-plate, nearer thy heart. Let thy power be engaged for me, as an evidence of thy love to me; let me be not only a *seal upon thy heart*, but a *seal upon thy arm*; let me be ever borne up in thy arms, and know it to my comfort."

3. To enforce this petition, she pleads the power of love.

(1) Love is a vigorous passion. It is *strong as death*. Christ's love to us was *strong as death*, for it broke through death itself. *He loved us, and gave himself for us.* The love of true believers to Christ is *strong as death*, for it makes them dead to everything else. *Jealousy is cruel as the grave*, which swallows up and devours all; those that truly love Christ are jealous of everything that would draw them from him. *The coals thereof* burn with incredible fury and irresistible force, as the *coals of fire that have a most vehement flame*, a *flame of the Lord* (so some read it). Holy love is a fire that begets a vehement heat in the soul, and consumes the dross and chaff that are in it.

(2) Love is a valiant victorious passion. Holy love is so; the reigning love of God in the soul is constant and firm, and will not be drawn off from him by *life or death*, Rom. viii. 38. Death, and all its terrors, will not frighten a believer from loving Christ: *Many waters*, though they will quench fire, *cannot quench this love*, no, nor the *floods drown it, v.* 7. No waters could quench Christ's love to us, nor any floods drown it; he waded through the greatest difficulties, even seas of blood. Love sat king upon the floods; let nothing then abate our love to him. Life, and all its comforts, will not entice a believer from loving Christ. Love will enable us to repel and triumph over temptations from the smiles of the world, as much as from its frowns.

Verses 8–12

Christ and his spouse having sufficiently confirmed their love to each other, *strong as death* and inviolable, they are here, in these verses, consulting together about their affairs. Yoke-fellows, having laid their hearts together, lay their heads together.

I. They are here consulting about their sister, their little sister, and the disposing of her.

1. The spouse proposes her case with a compassionate concern (*v.* 8): *We have a little sister and she has no breasts* (she has not grown up to maturity); *what shall we do for* this *little sister* of *ours in the day that she shall be spoken for?* (1) This may be understood as spoken by the Jewish church concerning the Gentile world. God had espoused the church of the Jews, and she was richly endowed, but what shall become of the poor Gentiles. Their condition (say the pious Jews) is very forlorn; they are *sisters*, but they are *little*, because not dignified with the knowledge of God; they *have no breasts*, no divine revelation, no scriptures, no ministers, no breasts of consolation, being *strangers to the covenants of promise. What shall we do for* them? We can but pity them, and pray for them. Now the tables are turned; the Gentiles are betrothed to Christ, and ought to return the kindness by an equal concern for the bringing in of the Jews again, our eldest sister, that once had breasts, but now has none. Or, (2) It may be applied to any other that belong to the election of grace, but are yet uncalled. They are remotely related to Christ and his church, and sisters to them both, *other sheep that are not of this fold*, John x. 16; Acts xviii. 10. Those that through grace are brought to Christ themselves should contrive what they may do to help others to him, to carry on the great design of his gospel, which is to espouse souls to Christ, and convert sinners to him from whom they have departed.

2. Christ soon determines what to do in this case, and his spouse agrees with him in it (*v.* 9): "*If she be a wall*, if the good work be once begun with the Gentiles, with the souls that are to be called in, if the *little sister, when she shall be spoken for* by the gospel, will but receive the word, and build herself upon Christ the foundation, *we will build upon her a palace of silver*, we will carry on the good work that is begun, till the wall become a palace, the wall of stone a palace of silver." This *little sister*, when once she is joined to the Lord, shall be made to *grow into a holy temple, a habitation of God through the Spirit*, Eph. ii. 21, 22. *If she be a door*, when this palace comes to be finished, then *we will enclose her with boards of cedar*. Though the beginnings of grace be small, the latter end shall greatly increase. The church is in care concerning those that are yet uncalled. "Let me alone," says Christ; "I will do all that which is necessary to be done for them. Trust me with it."

3. The spouse takes this occasion to acknowledge with thankfulness his kindness to her, *v.* 10. She is very willing to trust him with her *little sister*, for she herself had had great experience of his grace, and, for her part, she owed her all to him: *I am a wall, and my breasts like towers. Then was I in his eyes as one that found favour*. With what joy and triumph we ought to speak of God's grace towards us, and with what satisfaction we should look back upon the special times and seasons when *we were in his eyes as those that find favour*; these were days never to be forgotten.

II. They are here consulting about *a vineyard* they had in the country, the church of Christ on earth considered under the notion of *a vineyard* (*v.* 11, 12): *Solomon had a vineyard at Baal-hamon*; his vineyard was a type of the church of Christ. Our Saviour has given us a key to these verses in the parable of the vineyard let out to unthankful husbandmen, Matt. xxi. 33. The bargain was that, every one of the tenants having so much of the vineyard assigned him as would contain 1000 vines, he was to pay the annual rent of 1000 *pieces of silver*; for we read (Isa. vii. 23) that in a fruitful soil there were 1000 *vines at* 1000 *silverlings*. 1. Christ's church is his vineyard, a pleasant place; he delights to walk in it, and is pleased with its fruits. 2. He has entrusted each of us with his vineyard, as *keepers* of it. The privileges of the church are that good thing which he has committed to us, to be kept as a sacred trust. The service of the church is to be our business. 3. He expects rent from those that are employed in his vineyard and entrusted with it. *He comes, seeking fruit,* and requires gospel-duty of all those that enjoy gospel-privileges. 4. Though Christ has *let out his vineyard to keepers,* yet still it is his, and he has his eye always upon it for good. Some take these for Christ's words (v. 12): *My vineyard, which is mine, is before me;* and they observe how he dwells upon his property in it: It is *my vineyard, which is mine;* so dear is his church to him, it is *his own in the world* (John xiii. 1), and therefore he will always have it under his protection. 5. The church, that enjoys the privileges of the vineyard, must have them always before her. The keeping of the vineyard requires constant care and diligence. They are rather the words of the spouse: *My vineyard, which is mine, is before me.* She had lamented her fault and folly in not keeping her *own vineyard* (*ch.* i. 6), but now she resolves to reform. Our hearts are our vineyards, which we must *keep with all diligence.* 6. Our great care must be to pay our rent for what we hold of Christ's vineyard. *Thou, O Solomon! must have* 1000, and shalt have. The main profits belong to Christ; to him all our fruits must be dedicated. 7. If we be careful to give Christ the praise of our church-privileges, we may then take to ourselves the comfort and benefit of them. If the owner of the vineyard have had his due, the keepers of it shall be well paid for their care and pains; they shall have 200, which sum, no doubt, was looked upon as good profit.

Verses 13-14

Christ and his spouse are here parting for a while; she must stay below *in the gardens* on earth, where she has work to do for him; he must remove to *the mountains of spices* in heaven, where he has business to attend for her, as *an advocate with the Father.*

I. He desires to hear often from her. "*Thou that,* for the present, *dwellest in the gardens,* dressing and keeping them till thou remove from the garden below to the paradise above—*thou,* O believer! *that dwellest in the gardens* of solemn ordinances, *in the gardens* of church-fellowship and communion, *the companions* are so happy as to hear *thy voice, cause me to hear it* too." *The communion of saints* is an article of our covenant, as well as an article of our creed, *to exhort one another daily. Hearken to the voice* of the church, as far as it agrees with the voice of Christ. In the midst of our communion with one another we must not neglect our communion with Christ; he here bespeaks it: "*The companions hearken to thy voice;* it is a pleasure to them; *cause me to hear it.* Pour out thy heart to me." We *cause him to hear* our prayers when we not only pray, but wrestle and strive in prayer.

II. She desires his speedy return to her (v. 14): *Make haste, my beloved,* to come again, and receive me to thyself; *be thou like a roe, or a young hart, upon the mountains of spices. Even so, come, Lord Jesus, come quickly.* True believers, as they are looking for, so they are hastening to, the coming of that *day of the Lord.* The spouse, after an endearing conference with her beloved, finding it must break off, concludes with this affectionate request for the perfecting and perpetuating of this happiness in the future state. It is good to conclude our devotions with a joyful expectation of the glory to be revealed, and holy humble breathings towards it. We should not part but with the prospect of meeting again. It is good to conclude every sabbath with thoughts of the everlasting sabbath, which shall have no night at the end of it, nor any week-day to come after it. It is good to conclude every sacrament with thoughts of the everlasting feast, when we shall sit down with Christ at his table in his kingdom, and to break up every religious assembly in hopes of *the general assembly of the church of the first-born,* when time and days shall be no more.

AN EXPOSITION, WITH PRACTICAL OBSERVATIONS, OF

THE BOOK OF
THE PROPHET ISAIAH

A prophet is one that has a great intimacy with Heaven and a great interest there, and consequently a commanding authority upon earth. Prophecy was most commonly by dreams, voices, or visions, communicated to prophets first, and by them to the children of men, Num. xii. 6. Before the sacred canon of the Old Testament began to be written there were prophets, who were instead of Bibles to the church. Our Saviour seems to reckon Abel among the prophets, Matt. xxiii. 31, 35. Enoch was a prophet; Noah was a preacher of righteousness. God said of Abraham, He *is a prophet*, Gen. xx. 7. Jacob foretold things to come, Gen. xlix. 1. Moses was, beyond all comparison, the most illustrious of all the Old Testament prophets, for with him the Lord spoke *face to face*, Deut. xxxiv. 10. But after the death of Moses, for some ages, the Spirit of the Lord appeared and acted in the church of Israel more as a martial spirit than as a spirit of prophecy, and inspired men more for acting than speaking in the time of the judges. We find the Spirit of the Lord coming upon Othniel, Gideon, Samson, and others, for the service of their country, with their swords, not with their pens. In all the book of Judges there is never once mention of a prophet, only Deborah is called a prophetess. Then the word of the Lord was precious; there was no open vision, 1 Sam. iii. 1. But in Samuel prophecy revived, and in him a famous period of the church began, a time of great light in a constant uninterrupted succession of prophets, till some time after the captivity, when the canon of the Old Testament was completed. Then prophecy ceased for nearly 400 years. We read of prophets raised up for special public services, among whom the most famous were Elijah and Elisha in the kingdom of Israel. There was nothing of their own writing but one epistle of Elijah's, 2 Chron. xxi. 12. But, towards the latter end of the kingdoms of Judah and Israel, it pleased God to direct his servants the prophets to write some of their sermons. The dates of many of their prophecies are uncertain, but the earliest of them was in the days of Uzziah king of Judah, and Jeroboam the second, his contemporary, king of Israel, about 200 years before the captivity. If they begin to murder the prophets, yet they shall not murder their prophecies; these shall remain as witnesses against them. Hosea was the first of the writing prophets; and Joel, Amos, and Obadiah, published their prophecies about the same time. Isaiah began some time after, but his prophecy is placed first, because it is the largest of them all, and has most in it of him to whom all the prophets bore witness; and indeed so much of Christ that he is justly styled the *Evangelical Prophet*, and, by some of the ancients, *a fifth Evangelist*.

I. Concerning the prophet himself. He was (if we may believe the tradition of the Jews) of the royal family, his father being (they say) brother to King Uzziah. He was certainly much at court, especially in Hezekiah's time. The Spirit of God sometimes served his own purpose by the particular genius of the prophet; for prophets were not speaking trumpets, *through* which the Spirit spoke, but speaking men, *by* whom the Spirit spoke, making use of their natural powers, in respect both of light and flame, and advancing them above themselves.

II. Concerning the prophecy. It is transcendently useful; serving for conviction of sin, direction in duty, and consolation in trouble. Two great distresses of the church are here referred to, Sennacherib's invasion, which happened in his own time, and the captivity in Babylon, which happened long after; and in encouragements laid up for these times of need we find abundance of the grace of the gospel. There are not so many quotations in the gospels out of any, perhaps not out of all, the prophecies of the Old Testament, as out of this; nor such express testimonies concerning Christ, witness that of his being born of a virgin (*ch.* vii) and that of his sufferings (*ch.* liii). The beginning of this book abounds most with reproofs for sin and threatenings of judgment; the latter end of it is full of good words and comfortable words. This method the Spirit of Christ took formerly in the prophets and does still, first to convince and then to comfort; and those that would be blessed with the comforts must submit to the convictions.

CHAPTER 1

The first verse of this chapter is intended for a title to the whole book. The sermon which is contained in this chapter has in it, I. A charge, in God's name, against the Jewish church and nation, 1. For their ingratitude, ver. 2, 3. 2. For their incorrigibleness, ver. 5. 3. For the universal corruption and degeneracy of the people, ver. 4, 6, 21, 22. 4. For the perversion of justice by their rulers, ver. 23. II. A sad complaint of the judgments of God, which they had brought upon themselves by their sins, and by which they were brought almost to utter ruin, ver. 7–9. III. A just rejection of those shadows of religion which they kept up among them, notwithstanding this general defection and apostasy, ver. 10–15. IV. An earnest call to repentance and reformation, setting before them life and death, ver. 16–20. V. A threatening of ruin to those that would not be reformed, ver. 24, 28–31. VI. A promise of a happy reformation at last, and a return to their primitive purity and prosperity, ver. 25–27.

Verse 1

I. The name of the prophet, *Isaiah*, which, in the New Testament, is read *Esaias*. His name signifies *the salvation of the Lord*—a proper name, especially for this prophet, who prophesies so much of Jesus

the Saviour and of the great salvation wrought out by him. He is said to be *the son of Amoz*, the brother, or son, of Amaziah king of Judah, a tradition uncertain as that rule, that, where a prophet's father is named, he also was himself a prophet.

II. The nature of the prophecy. It is a vision. The prophets were called *seers*, and therefore their prophecies are fitly called *visions*. It was what he saw with the eyes of his mind, and foresaw as clearly by divine revelation, as if he had seen it with his bodily eyes.

III. The subject of the prophecy. Some chapters there are in this book which relate to Babylon, Egypt, Tyre, and other neighbouring nations; but it takes its title from that which is the main substance of it, and is therefore said to be *concerning Judah and Jerusalem*. Isaiah brings to them in a special manner, 1. Instruction; for to them pertain the oracles of God. 2. Reproof and threatening; for if in Judah, if in Salem, iniquity be found, they, sooner than any other, shall be reckoned with for it. 3. Comfort and encouragement in evil times; for the children of Zion shall be joyful in their king.

IV. The date of the prophecy. Isaiah prophesied *in the days of Uzziah, Jotham, Ahaz, and Hezekiah.* By this it appears, 1. That he prophesied long, especially if (as the Jews say) he was at last put to death by Manasseh, being sawn asunder, to which some suppose the apostle refers, Heb. xi. 37. From the year that king Uzziah died (*ch.* vi. 1) to Hezekiah's sickness and recovery was forty-seven years; how much before, and after, he prophesied, is not certain. 2. That he passed through variety of times. Jotham was a good king, and Hezekiah a better, and no doubt took advice from this prophet; but between them, and when Isaiah was in the prime of his time, the reign of Ahaz was very profane and wicked.

Verses 2–9

I. The prophet, though he speaks in God's name, despairing to gain audience with the children of his people, addresses himself to the heavens and the earth (*v.* 2): *Hear, O heavens! and give ear, O earth!* Sooner will the inanimate creatures hear, who observe the law and answer the end of their creation, than this stupid senseless people. Let the lights of heaven shame their darkness, and the fruitfulness of the earth their barrenness, and the strictness of each to its time their irregularity. Moses begins thus in Deut. xxxii. 1.

II. He charges them with base ingratitude. Let heaven and earth hear and wonder at, 1. God's gracious dealings with such a peevish provoking people: "I have nourished and brought them up as children; they have been well fed and well taught" (Deut. xxxii. 6). 2. Their ill-natured conduct towards him, who was so tender of them: "*They have rebelled against me.*"

III. He attributes this to their ignorance and inconsideration (*v.* 3): *The ox knows, but Israel does not.* Observe, 1. The sagacity of the ox and the ass, creatures of the dullest sort; yet the ox has such a sense of duty as to know his owner and to serve him. The ass has such a sense of interest as to know his master's crib, where he is fed, and to abide by it. Man is shamed in knowledge by these silly animals, and is not only sent to school to them (Prov. vi. 6, 7), but set in a form below them (Jer. viii. 7). 2. The sottishness and stupidity of Israel. God is their owner and proprietor. He made us, and has provided well for us; yet many that are called the people of God ask, "*What is the Almighty, that we should serve him?*" They do not know, they do not consider. They know; but their knowledge does them no good, because they do not consider what they know; they do not apply it to their case, nor their minds to it. Inconsideration of what we do know is as great an enemy to us in religion as ignorance of what we should know. *Therefore* men revolt from God, and rebel against him.

IV. He laments the corruption of their church and kingdom. The disease of sin was epidemic, and all orders and degrees of men were infected with it: *Ah sinful nation! v.* 4. 1. The wickedness was universal. They were a sinful nation; the generality of the people were vicious and profane. Their wickedness was upon them as *a talent of lead,* Zech. v. 7, 8. They came of a bad stock, were a *seed of evil-doers.* Treachery ran in the blood. They were a race and family of rebels. They were not only corrupt children, but *children that were corrupters,* that propagated vice, and infected others with it. *They have provoked the Holy One of Israel unto anger* wilfully and designedly; they knew what would anger him, and that they did. 2. He illustrates it by a comparison taken from a

sick and diseased body, all overspread with leprosy, or, like Job's, with sore boils, *v.* 5, 6. The distemper has seized the vitals, and so threatens to be mortal. They had become corrupt in their judgment: the leprosy was in their head. It has overspread the whole body, and so becomes exceedingly noisome. There is *no soundness,* no good principles, no religion (for that is the health of the soul), nothing but *wounds and bruises,* guilt and corruption. No attempts were made for reformation, or, if they were, they proved ineffectual: The wounds *have not been closed, nor bound up, nor mollified with ointment.* While sin remains unrepented of, the wounds are not mollified or closed up, nor anything done towards the healing of them.

V. He sadly bewails the judgments of God which they had brought upon themselves. Their kingdom was almost ruined, *v.* 7. "Look and see how it is; *your country is desolate*; as for the fruits of your land, which should be food for your families, *strangers devour them before your eyes,* and you cannot prevent it; you starve while your enemies surfeit." Jerusalem, which was as the daughter of Zion (the temple built on Zion was a mother to Jerusalem), was now lost, deserted, and exposed *as a cottage in a vineyard,* which, when the vintage is over, nobody dwells in, and every person is afraid of coming near it as if it were *a besieged city, v.* 8. Probably this sermon was preached in the reign of Ahaz, when Judah was invaded by the kings of Syria and Israel, the Edomites and the Philistines, who slew many, and carried many away into captivity, 2 Chron. xxviii. 5, 17, 18. National impiety and immorality bring national desolation. Yet they were not at all reformed, and therefore God threatens to take another course with them (*v.* 5). God sometimes, in a way of righteous judgment, ceases to correct those who have been long incorrigible, and whom therefore he designs to destroy.

VI. He comforts himself with the consideration of a remnant that should be the monuments of divine grace and mercy, notwithstanding this general corruption and desolation, *v.* 9. *The Lord of hosts left unto them a very small remnant,* that were kept pure from the common apostasy and kept safe and alive from the common calamity. This is quoted by the apostle (Rom. ix. 27), and applied to those few of the Jewish nation who in his time embraced Christianity. This remnant is often a very small one. Multitude is no mark of the true church. Christ's is a little flock. It is good for a people that have been saved from utter ruin to look back and see how near they were to it, to see how much they owed to a few good men that stood in the gap, and that that was owing to a good God, who left them these good men.

Verses 10–15

I. God calls to them (but calls in vain) to hear his word, *v.* 10. 1. The title he gives them is very strange: *You rulers of Sodom,* and *people of Gomorrah.* This intimates what a righteous thing it would have been with God to make them like Sodom and Gomorrah (*v.* 9). The rulers are boldly attacked here by the prophet as rulers of Sodom; for he knew not how to give flattering titles. The tradition of the Jews is that for this he was long after put to death. His demand upon them is very reasonable: "*Hear the word of the Lord,* and *give ear to the law of our God; attend to that which God has to say to you,* and let his word be a law unto you."

II. He justly refuses to hear their prayers and accept their services, their sacrifices and burnt-offerings, the fat and blood of them (*v.* 11), their attendance in his courts (*v.* 12), their oblations, their incense, and their solemn assemblies (*v.* 13), their new moons and their appointed feasts (*v.* 14), their devoutest addresses (*v.* 15); they are all rejected, because their hands were full of blood.

1. There are many who are strangers, nay, enemies, to the power of religion, and yet seem very zealous for the show and shadow and form of it. This sinful nation brought to the altar of the God of Israel, sacrifices, peace-offerings and burnt-offerings, which were wholly consumed to the honour of God. They prayed, prayed often, made many prayers, thinking they should be heard for their much speaking. Their hearts were empty of true devotion. They came to *appear* before God (*v.* 12), *to be seen* before him (so the margin reads it). Their hands were full of blood. They were guilty of murder, rapine, and oppression, under colour of law and justice. Malice is heart-murder in the account of God; he that hates his brother in his heart has, in effect, his hands full of blood.

2. When sinners are under the judgments of God they will more easily be brought to fly to their devotions than to forsake their sins and reform their lives.

3. The most pompous and costly devotions of wicked people, without a thorough reformation of the heart and life, are so far from being acceptable to God that really they are an abomination to him. It is here shown in a great variety of expressions that *to obey is better than sacrifice*; nay, that sacrifice, without obedience, is a jest, an affront and provocation to God. Their sacrifices are here represented as fruitless and insignificant: *To what purpose is the multitude of your sacrifices? v.* 11. They are *vain oblations, v.* 13. Their attention to God's institutions was all lost labour, and served not to answer any good intention: *Who has required these things at your hands? v.* 12. They pray, but God will not hear, for, though they make many prayers, none of them come from an upright heart. "They are *your* sacrifices, they are none of mine; I am full of them, even surfeited with them." Their coming into his courts he calls *treading them*, or trampling upon them. Their incense, though ever so fragrant, was an abomination to him, for it was burnt in hypocrisy and with an ill design. Their solemn assemblies he could not *away with*, could not see with any patience. God is never weary of hearing the prayers of the upright, but soon weary of the costly sacrifices of the wicked. Sin is hateful to God, so hateful that it makes even men's prayers and their religious services hateful to him. Dissembled piety is double iniquity.

Verses 16–20

I. A call to repentance and reformation: "If you would have your sacrifices accepted, and your prayers answered, you must begin your work at the right end: *Be converted to my law* else expect not to be accepted in the acts of your devotion." As justice and charity will never atone for atheism and profaneness, so prayers and sacrifices will never atone for fraud and oppression.

1. They must *cease to do evil*, must do no more wrong, shed no more innocent blood. This is the meaning of washing themselves and *making themselves clean, v.* 16. We must put away not only the evil of our doings by refraining from the gross acts of sin, but the roots and habits of sin, that are in our hearts.

2. They must *learn to do well*. This was necessary to the completing of their repentance. We must be doing good, the good which the Lord our God requires. We must learn to do well; take pains to get the knowledge of our duty. He urges them particularly to second-table duties: "*Seek judgment;* enquire what is right, that you may do it. *Relieve the oppressed.* Avenge those that suffer wrong, the fatherless and the widow, whom, because they are weak and helpless, proud men trample upon and abuse. Speak for those that know not how to speak for themselves and that have not wherewithal to gratify you for your kindness."

II. A demonstration, at the bar of right reason, of the equity of God's proceedings with them: "*Come now, and let us reason together* (*v.* 18); while your hands are full of blood I will have nothing to do with you, though you bring me a multitude of sacrifices; but if you wash, and make yourselves clean, you are welcome to draw nigh to me; come now, and let us talk the matter over." Religion has reason on its side; there is all the reason in the world why we should do as God would have us do. The case needs only to be stated and it will determine itself.

1. They could not in reason expect any more than that, if they repented and reformed, they should be restored to God's favour, notwithstanding their former provocations. Here is no penance imposed, nor the yoke made heavier. He does not say, "If you be *perfectly* obedient", but, "If you be *willingly* so"; for, if there be a willing mind, it is accepted. All their sins should be pardoned, and should not be mentioned against them. Though our sins have been as scarlet and crimson, a deep dye, though we have been often dipped, by our many backslidings, into sin, and though we have lain long soaking in it, as the cloth does in the scarlet dye, yet pardoning mercy will thoroughly discharge the stain. If we make ourselves clean by repentance and reformation (*v.* 16), God will make us white by a full remission. "Be but willing and obedient, and *you shall eat the good of the land*, the land of promise." If sin be pardoned, creature-comforts become comforts indeed.

2. They could not in reason expect any other than that, if they continued obstinate in their disobedience, the sentence of the law should be executed upon them (*v.* 20).

Verses 21–30

I. The woeful degeneracy of Judah and Jerusalem is sadly lamented. The royal city had been a faithful city, faithful to God and the interests of his kingdom among men, faithful to the nation and its public interests. *It was full of judgment;* justice was duly administered. *Righteousness lodged in it.* That beauteous virtuous spouse was now become an adulteress; righteousness no longer dwelt in Jerusalem, even murderers lived undisturbed there; the princes themselves were so cruel and oppressive that they had become no better than murderers. The degeneracy of Jerusalem is illustrated (*v.* 22): *Thy silver has become dross.* This degeneracy of the magistrates is as great a reproach and injury to the kingdom as the debasing of their coin would be and the turning of their silver into dross. *Thy wine is mixed with water*, and so has become flat and sour. Dross may shine like silver, and the wine that is mixed with water may retain the colour of wine, but neither is worth anything. Thus they retained a show and pretence of virtue and justice, but had no true sense of either. "Thy princes, that should keep others in their allegiance to God and subjection to his law, are themselves rebellious, and set God and his law at defiance. Those that should restrain thieves, are themselves companions of thieves; they share with the thieves they protect in their unlawful gain. The profit of their places is all their aim, to make the best hand they can of them, right or wrong. They ought to protect those that are injured. But *they judge not the fatherless*, take no care to guard the orphans, *nor does the cause of the widow come unto them*, because the poor widow has no bribe to give, with which to bring her cause on."

II. A resolution is taken up to redress these grievances (*v.* 24): *Therefore saith the Lord, the Lord of hosts, the Mighty One of Israel*—who has power to make good what he says—*Ah! I will ease me of my adversaries.* God will find out a time and a way to ease himself of this burden. If God's professing people conform not to his image, as the Holy One of Israel (*v.* 4), they shall feel the weight of his hand as the Mighty One of Israel. Though the church has a great deal of dross in it, yet it shall not be thrown away, but refined (*v.* 25): "*I will purely purge away thy dross.* Vice shall be suppressed and oppressors deprived of their power to do mischief." The reformation of a people is God's own work: "*I will turn my hand upon thee;* I will do that for the reviving of religion which I did at first for the planting of it." He does it by blessing them with good magistrates and good ministers of state (*v.* 26): "*I will restore thy judges as at the first,* to put the laws in execution against evil-doers, *and thy counsellors,* to transact public affairs, *as at the beginning.*" He does it (*v.* 27), by planting in men's minds principles of justice and governing their lives by those principles. Men may do much by external restraints; but God does it effectually by the influences of *his Spirit.* All the redeemed of the Lord shall be converts, and their conversion is their redemption: "*Her converts,* or *those that return of her* (so the margin), shall be redeemed with righteousness." The reviving of a people's virtue is the restoring of their honour: *Afterwards thou shalt be called the city of righteousness, the faithful city.* Those that hate to be reformed shall be destroyed and not chastened only. The openly profane that have quite cast off all religion, and the hypocrites that live wicked lives under the cloak of a religious profession shall both be destroyed together. *And those that forsake the Lord,* to whom they had formerly joined themselves, *shall be consumed,* as the water in the conduit-pipe is soon consumed when it is cut off from the fountain. Their idols shall not be able to help them, *the oaks which they have desired, and the gardens which they have chosen;* that is, the images which they have worshipped in their groves and under the green trees, for which they forsook the true God, and which they worshipped privately in their own gardens. This was the practice of the transgressors and the sinners; but they shall be ashamed of it, not with a show of repentance, but of despair, *v.* 29. They shall be ashamed of their idols; for the idols themselves *shall go into captivity,* ch. xlvi. 1, 2. They shall not be able to help themselves (*v.* 31): "*Even the strong man shall be as tow,* not only soon broken and pulled to pieces, but easily catching fire; and *his work* (so the margin reads it), shall be as a spark to his own tow."

Now all this is applicable to, 1. The blessed work of reformation which was wrought in Hezekiah's time after the abominable corruptions of the reign of Ahaz. 2. To their return out of their captivity in Babylon. 3. To the gospel-kingdom and the pouring out of the Spirit, by which the New Testament church should be made a new Jerusalem, a city of righteousness. 4. To the second coming of Christ, when he shall thoroughly purge his floor.

CHAPTER 2

With this chapter begins a new sermon, which is continued in the two following chapters. The subject is Judah and Jerusalem, ver. 1. In this chapter the prophet speaks, I. Of the glory of the Christians, Jerusalem, the gospel-church in the latter days, in the accession of many to it (ver. 2, 3), and the great peace it should introduce into the world (ver. 4), whence he infers the duty of the house of Jacob, ver. 5. II. Of the shame of the Jews, Jerusalem, as it then was, and as it would be after its rejection of the gospel and being rejected of God. 1. Their sin was their shame, ver. 6–9. 2. God by his judgments would humble them and put them to shame, ver. 10–17. 3. They should themselves be ashamed of their confidence in their idols and in an arm of flesh, ver. 18–22.

Verses 1–5

The particular title of this sermon (*v.* 1) is the same with the general title of the book (*ch.* i. 1), only

that what is there called the *vision* is here called *the word which Isaiah saw.*

This sermon begins with the prophecy relating to the last days, the days of the Messiah, when his kingdom should be set up in the world, at the latter end of the Mosaic economy. In the last days of the earthly Jerusalem, just before the destruction of it, this heavenly Jerusalem should be erected, Heb. xii. 22; Gal. iv. 26. Gospel times are the last days. For, 1. They were a great while waited for by the Old Testament saints, and came at last. 2. We are not to look for any dispensation of divine grace but what we have in the gospel, Gal. i. 8, 9. 3. We are to look for the second coming of Jesus Christ at the end of time, 1 John ii. 18.

The prophet here foretells,

I. The planting of the Christian religion in the world. Christianity shall then be the mountain of the Lord's house. The gospel church shall then be the rendezvous of all the spiritual seed of Abraham. Now it is here promised, 1. That Christianity shall be openly preached and professed; it shall be *prepared* (so the margin reads it) in the top of the mountains, in the view and hearing of all. What the apostles did was not *done in a corner,* Acts xxvi. 26. It was the lighting of a beacon, the setting up of a standard. 2. That it shall be firmly fixed and rooted; it shall be established on the top of the everlasting mountains, built upon a *rock,* so that the *gates of hell shall not prevail against it,* unless they could pluck up mountains by the roots. 3. That it shall not only overcome all opposition, but overtop all competition; it shall be *exalted above the hills.* This *wisdom of God in a mystery* shall outshine all the wisdom of this world, all its philosophy and all its politics.

II. The bringing of the Gentiles into it. 1. The nations shall be admitted into it, even the uncircumcised, who were forbidden to come into the courts of the temple at Jerusalem. 2. *All nations shall flow into it;* having liberty of access, multitudes shall embrace the Christian faith.

III. The mutual assistance and encouragement which this confluence of converts shall give to one another. "*Come, and let us go up to the mountain of the Lord;* though it be uphill and against heart, yet it is *the mountain of the Lord,* who will assist the ascent of our souls towards him." The gospel church is here called, not only *the mountain of the Lord,* but *the house of the God of Jacob;* for in it God's covenant with Jacob and his praying seed is kept up and has its accomplishment. It is worth while to take pains to go up to his holy mountain to be taught his ways, and those who are willing to take that pains shall never find it labour in vain. "If he will *teach us his ways,* we will *walk in his paths;* if he will let us know our duty, we will by his grace make conscience of doing it."

IV. The means by which this shall be brought about: *Out of Zion shall go forth the law,* the New Testament law, the law of Christ, as of old the law of Moses from Mount Sinai, even *the word of the Lord from Jerusalem.* The gospel is a law, a law of faith; it is the *word of the Lord.* And in the temple on Mount Zion the disciples preached the gospel, Acts v. 20. And it was by this gospel, which took rise from Jerusalem, that the gospel church was *established on the top of the mountains.*

V. The erecting of the kingdom of the Redeemer in the world: *He shall judge among the nations.* By his Spirit working on men's consciences he shall judge, and try men and check them; his kingdom is spiritual, *and not of this world.*

VI. The great peace which should be the effect of the success of the gospel in the world (*v.* 4): *They shall beat their swords into ploughshares. Nation shall then not lift up sword against nation,* as now they do, *neither shall they learn war any more,* for they shall have no more occasion for it. The design and tendency of the gospel are to make peace and to slay all enmities. It has in it the most powerful obligations and inducements to peace. The gospel of Christ, as far as it prevails, disposes men to be peaceable, softens men's spirits, and sweetens them; and the love of Christ, shed abroad in the heart, constrains men to love one another. The primitive Christians were famous for brotherly love; their very adversaries took notice of it. Here is a practical inference drawn from all this (v. 5): *O house of Jacob! come you, and let us walk in the light of the Lord.* By the house of Jacob is meant either Israel according to the flesh, or spiritual Israel, all that are brought to the God of Jacob. Will God teach us his ways? Will he show us his glory in the face of Christ? Let us walk comfortably in the light of this peace. Shall there be no more war? Let us then go on our way rejoicing.

Verses 6–9

I. Israel's doom. This is set forth in two words, the first and the last of this paragraph; but they are two dreadful words. 1. Their case (v. 6): *Therefore thou hast forsaken thy people.* Miserable is the condition of that people whom God has forsaken. This was the deplorable case of the Jewish church after they had rejected Christ. *Your house is left unto you desolate,* Matt. xxiii. 38. 2. Their case desperate, wholly desperate (v. 9): *Therefore forgive them not.* This prophetical prayer amounts to a threatening that they should not be forgiven. This refers not to particular persons (many of them repented and were pardoned), but to the body of that nation.

II. Israel's doom, and the reasons upon which it is grounded. In general, it is sin that provokes God to forsake his people. The particular sins which the prophet specifies are such as abounded among them at that time. There was a partial and temporary rejection of them by the captivity in Babylon, which was a type of their final destruction by the Romans, and which the sins here mentioned brought upon them.

1. God set them apart for himself, as a peculiar people, dignified above all other people (Num. xxiii. 9); but they were *replenished from the east;* they *naturalized* foreigners, and encouraged them to settle among them, and mingled with them, Hos. vii. 8. Their country was peopled with Syrians and Chaldeans, Moabites and Ammonites, and with them they admitted the fashions and customs of those nations, and *pleased themselves in the children of strangers.* Thus did they profane their crown and their covenant.

2. God gave them his oracles, the scriptures and the seers, but they slighted these, and became soothsayers like the Philistines, introduced their arts of divination, and hearkened to those who by the stars, or the clouds, or the flight of birds, or the entrails of beasts, pretended to discover things secret or foretell things to come. The Philistines were noted diviners, 1 Sam. vi. 2.

3. God assured them that he would be their wealth and strength; but, distrusting his power and promise, they made gold their hope, and furnished themselves with horses and chariots, and relied upon them for their safety, v. 7. It is not having silver and gold, horses and chariots, that is a provocation to God, but desiring them insatiably.

4. God himself was their God, and instituted ordinances of worship for them; but they slighted both him and his institutions, v. 8. Their land was full of idols; every city had its god (Jer. xi. 13). Those that love idols will multiply them; so sottish were they that they *worshipped the work of their own hands.* God had enriched them with silver and gold, and yet of that silver and gold they made idols.

5. God had put honour upon them; but they basely diminished themselves (v. 9): *The mean man boweth down to his idol,* a thing below the meanest that has any spark of reason left. Nor is it only the illiterate that do this, but even the *great man* forgets his grandeur and humbles himself to worship idols, deifies men no better than himself, and consecrates stones so much baser than himself.

Verses 10–22

The prophet here goes on to show what a desolation would be brought upon their land when God should have forsaken them. This may refer particularly to their destruction by the Chaldeans first, and afterwards by the Romans.

I. To startle and awaken sinners, who bid defiance to God and his judgments (v. 10): "*Enter into the rock;* God will attack you with such terrible judgments that you shall be forced to *enter into the rock, and hide yourself in the dust, for fear of the Lord.* You shall lose all your courage, and tremble at the shaking of a leaf." To the same purport, v. 19. *They shall go into the holes of the rocks, and into the caves of the earth,* the darkest the deepest places. It was so particularly at the destruction of Jerusalem by the Romans (Luke xxiii. 30) and of the persecuting pagan powers, Rev. vi. 16. And all *for fear of the Lord, and of the glory of his majesty.* Those that will not fear God and flee to him will be forced to fear him and flee from him to a refuge of lies. It will be in vain to think of finding refuge in the caves of the earth when the earth itself is shaken; there will be no shelter then but in God and in things above.

II. To humble and abase proud sinners, v. 11: *The lofty looks of man shall be humbled.* It is repeated (v. 17), *The loftiness of man shall be bowed down.* Men's haughtiness will be brought down, either by the grace of God convincing them of the evil of their pride, and clothing them with humility, or by the providence of God depriving them of all those things they were proud of and laying them low. This shall be done: because the *Lord alone will be exalted.* This shall be done: by humbling judgments, that shall mortify men, and bring them down (v. 12): *The day of the Lord of hosts,* the day of his wrath and judgment, *shall be upon everyone that is proud.* This day of the Lord is here said to be upon *all the cedars of Lebanon, that are high and lifted up.* Here the day of the Lord is said to be *upon the cedars,* those of Lebanon, that were the straightest and stateliest,—upon the oaks, those of Bashan, that were the strongest and sturdiest, —upon the natural elevations, *the high mountains and the hills that are lifted up* (v. 14), that overtop the valleys and seem to push the skies,—and upon the artificial fastnesses, *every high tower and every fenced wall,* v. 15. Understand these, 1. As representing the proud people themselves, that are in their own apprehensions like the cedars and the oaks, firmly rooted, and not to be stirred by any storm, and looking on all around them as shrubs. *The highest hills are most exposed to lightning.* These vaunting men, who are as high towers in which the noisy bells are hung,—these fenced walls, that fortify themselves with their native hardiness, and intrench themselves in their fastnesses—shall be brought down. 2. As particularizing the things they are proud of, and of which they make their boast. He will *take from them all their armour wherein they trusted.* They were proud of their trade abroad; but the day of the Lord shall be *upon all the ships of Tarshish;* they shall founder at sea or be ship-wrecked in the harbour. The day of the Lord shall be *upon all pleasant pictures,* the curious painting they brought home in their ships from other countries.

III. To make idolaters ashamed of their idols, and of the respect they have paid to them (v. 18):

The idols he shall utterly abolish. When the Lord alone shall be exalted (*v.* 17) he will not only pour contempt upon proud men, but much more upon all pretended deities. Their friends shall desert them; their enemies shall destroy them. They cannot secure themselves, so far are they from being able to secure their worshippers. Their worshippers shall abandon them, either from a conviction of their falsehood or from a sad experience of their inability to help them, *v.* 20. When men are themselves frightened by the judgments of God into the holes of the rocks, they shall cast their idols, which they have made their gods and hoped to make their friends in the time of need, to the moles and to the bats. God can make men sick of those idols that they have been most fond of. Covetous men make silver and gold their idols, money their god; but the time may come when they may feel it as much their burden as ever they made it their confidence. There was a time when the mariners threw the wares, and even the *wheat, into the sea* (Jonah i. 5; Acts xxvii. 38). The darkest holes, where the moles and the bats lodge, are the fittest places for idols, that have eyes and see not. It is possible that sin may be both loathed and left and yet not truly repented of out of any love to God, but only from a slavish fear of his wrath.

IV. To make those that have trusted in an arm of flesh ashamed of their confidence (*v.* 22): "*Cease from man.* How weak man is: *His breath is in his nostrils,* puffed out every moment, soon gone for good and all. *Put not your trust in man.* Let not him be your fear, let not him be your hope; but look up to the power of God, to which all the powers of men are subject and subordinate; let your *hope be in the Lord your God.*"

CHAPTER 3

The prophet, in this chapter, goes on to foretell the desolations that were coming upon Judah and Jerusalem for their sins, both that by the Babylonians and that which completed their ruin by the Romans. God threatens, I. To deprive them of all the supports both of their life and of their government, ver. 1–3. II. To leave them to fall into confusion and disorder, ver. 4, 5, 12. III. To deny them the blessing of magistracy, ver. 6–8. IV. To strip the daughters of Zion of their ornaments, ver. 17–24. V. To lay all waste by the sword of war, ver. 25, 26. The sins that provoked God were, 1. Their defiance of God, ver. 8. 2. Their impudence, ver. 9. 3. The abuse of power to oppression and tyranny, ver. 12–15. 4. The pride of the daughters of Zion, ver. 16. In the midst of the chapter the prophet is directed (1) To assure good people that it should be well with them, ver. 10. (2) To assure wicked people that, however God might, in judgment, remember mercy, yet it should go ill with them, ver. 11.

Verses 1–8

God was now about to ruin all their creature-confidences, so that they should meet with nothing but disappointments in all their expectations from them (*v.* 1): *The stay and the staff* shall be taken away, all their supports. Their church and kingdom had now grown old and were going to decay, and they were (after the manner of aged men, Zech. viii. 4) leaning on a staff: now God threatens to take away their staff. St. Jerome refers this to the sensible decay of the Jewish nation after they had crucified our Saviour Rom. xi. 9, 10. I rather take it as a warning to all nations not to provoke God.

I. Bread is the staff of life: but God can *take away the whole stay of bread and the whole stay of water;* and it is just with him to do so when that which was given to be provision for the life is made provision for the lusts. He can take away the bread and the water by withholding the rain, Deut. xxviii. 23, 24. He can take away the stay of bread and the stay of water by withholding his blessing, by which man lives. Christ is the bread of life and the water of life; if he be our stay, we shall find that this is a good part not to be taken away, John iv. 14; vi. 27.

II. Their army—their generals, and commanders shall be taken away. *The mighty man, and the man of war,* and even the inferior officer, *the captain of fifty,* shall be removed. Let not the strong man therefore glory in his strength, nor any people trust too much to their mighty men.

III. Their ministers of state, their learned men, their politicians, their clergy, also should be taken away—*the judges, the prophets, the prudent,* who were assistants to the judges, *the diviners,* who used unlawful arts, *the ancients,* elders in age, in office. When the whole stay is to be broken, *the cunning artificer* too shall be taken away; and the last is *the eloquent orator,* the man skilful of speech, who in some cases may do good service. Moses cannot speak well, but Aaron can.

IV. It is the business of the sovereign to bear up the pillars of the land, Ps. lxxv. 3. But it is here threatened that this stay should fail them. When the mighty men and the prudent are removed *children shall be their princes*—children in age, who must be under tutors and governors, children in understanding and disposition, childish men, no more fit to rule than a child in the cradle. These shall rule over them, with all the folly, fickleness, and frowardness, of a child.

V. The union of the subjects among themselves, their good order and the good understanding is here threatened. God would send an evil spirit among them too (as Judges ix. 23), which would make them unneighbourly one towards another (*v.* 5): "*The people shall be oppressed every one by his neighbour,* and their princes, being children, will take no care to restrain the oppressors or relieve the oppressed." It is as ill an omen to a people as can be when the rising generation are untractable and ungovernable.

VI. The government shall go a-begging, *v.* 6. It is taken for granted that there is no way of redressing all these grievances, and bringing things into order again, but by good magistrates, who shall be invested with power by common consent, and shall exert that power for the good of the community. The case is represented as very deplorable, and things as having come to a sad pass; for children being their princes, every man will think himself fit to prescribe who shall be a magistrate. *A man shall take hold* by violence of one to make him a ruler; he shall urge it upon his brother. It will be looked upon as ground sufficient for the preferring of a man to be a ruler that he has clothing better than his neighbours. It would have been some sense to have said, "Thou hast wisdom, integrity, experience; be thou our ruler." But it was a jest to say, *Thou hast clothing; be thou our ruler.* Those who are thus pressed to come into office will swear themselves off, because they know themselves unable to bear the charges of the office (*v.* 7): *He shall swear* (shall lift up the hand, the ancient ceremony used in taking an oath) *I will not be a healer; make not me a ruler.* Rulers must be healers, and good rulers will be so; they must study to unite their subjects, and not widen the differences that are among them. But why will he not be a ruler? Because *in my house is neither bread nor clothing.* It was a sign that the case of the nation was very bad when nobody was willing to accept a place in the government of it. God brought things to this sad pass, not for want of goodwill to the country. *Jerusalem is ruined* and *Judah is fallen;* and they may thank themselves. They have brought their destruction upon their own heads, for *their tongue and their doings are against the Lord;* in word and action they broke the law of God. They provoked him to his face, as if the more they knew of his glory the greater pride they took in slighting it.

Verses 9–15

God proceeds in his controversy with his people. I. It was for sin that God contended with them; if they vex themselves they will see that they must *thank* themselves: *Woe unto their souls! For they have rewarded evil unto themselves. Alas for their souls!* (so it may be read, in a way of lamentation, *for they have procured evil to themselves, v. 9.* They had grown impudent, *v. 9.* This hardens men against repentance as much as anything. Those that are past shame (we say) are past grace, and then past hope (*v. 12*): "*Those who lead thee* (the princes, priests, and prophets) *mislead thee; they cause thee to err.*" Their judges, who should have patronised and protected the oppressed, were themselves the greatest oppressors, *v. 14, 15.* The elders of the people, and the princes *have eaten up the vineyard.* God's vineyard, which they were appointed to be the dressers and keepers of, they burnt (so the word signifies). God reasons with these great men (*v. 15*): "*What mean you, that you beat my people in pieces?* Do you think you had power given you for such a purpose as this?" *You grind the faces of the poor;* you put them to as much pain and terror as if they were ground in a mill.

II. In this controversy God himself is the prosecutor (*v. 13*): *The Lord stands up to plead,* and he *stands to judge the people,* for those that were oppressed; and he will *enter into judgment with the princes, v. 14.* The greatest of men cannot exempt themselves from the scrutiny and sentence of God's judgment. The indictment is proved: "Look upon the oppressors, and the *show of their countenance witnesses against them* (*v. 9*); look upon the oppressed, and you see how their faces are battered and abused," *v. 15.* To punish those that had abused their power God sets those over them that had not sense to use their power: *Children are their oppressors, and women rule over them* (*v. 12*), men that have as weak judgments and strong passions as women and children. Had they been righteous, it would have been well with them; but, if it be ill with them, it is because they are wicked and will be so (*v. 10, 11*). When the whole *stay of bread is taken away,* yet in the *day of famine the righteous shall be satisfied;* they *shall eat the fruit of their doings*—they shall have the testimony of their consciences that they kept themselves pure from iniquity, and therefore the common calamity is not to them what it is to others. There is a woe to wicked people, and it shall be ill with them.

Verses 16–26

The prophet's business was to show all sorts of people what they had contributed to the national guilt and what share they must expect in the national judgments that were coming. Here he reproves and warns the daughters of Zion.

I. The sin charged upon the daughters of Zion, *v. 16.* Two things they here stand indicted for—haughtiness and wantonness. They discovered the disposition of their mind by their gait and gesture. They are haughty, for they *walk with stretched-forth necks,* that they may seem tall. Their eyes are wanton, *deceiving* (so the word is). They affect a formal starched way of going, *mincing,* or nicely tripping. They make a *tinkling with their feet,* having, as some think, little bells upon their shoes. These were the daughters of Zion who should have behaved with the gravity that becomes women professing godliness.

II. The punishments threatened for this sin; and they answer the sin as face answers to face in a glass, *v. 17, 18.* 1. They *walked with stretched-forth necks,* but God will *smite with a scab the crown of their head,* which shall make them ashamed to show their heads, being obliged to cut off their hair. 2. They cared not what they laid out in great variety of fine clothes; but God will reduce them to such poverty and distress that they shall not have clothes sufficient to cover their nakedness. 3. They were extremely proud of their ornaments; but God will strip them of those

ornaments, when their houses shall be plundered, their treasures rifled, and they themselves led into captivity. It is not at all material to enquire what sort of ornaments these were. Fashions alter and so do the names of them. Many of these things, we may suppose, were ridiculous, and, if they had not been in fashion, would have been hooted at. Those things that were decent and convenient, as *the linen, the hoods, and the veils,* needed not to be provided in such abundance and variety.

III. They were very nice about their clothes; but God would make those bodies of theirs a reproach and burden to them (*v. 24*): *Instead of sweet smell* (those tablets, or boxes, of perfume, *houses of the soul* or *breath,* as they are called, *v. 20, margin*) *there shall be stink,* garments grown filthy with being long worn. *Instead of a* rich embroidered *girdle* used to make the clothes sit tight, there shall be *a rent*; old rotten clothes rent into rags. *Instead of well-set hair,* there shall be *baldness,* the hair being plucked off or shaven, as was usual in times of great affliction (*ch.* xv. 2; Jer. xvi. 6), or in great servitude, Ezek. xxix. 18. *Instead of a stomacher,* or sash, there shall be *a girding of sackcloth,* in token of deep humiliation; *and burning instead of beauty.* Those that had a good complexion when they are carried into captivity shall be tanned and sunburnt; the best faces are soonest injured by the weather. From all this let us learn not to affect that which is gay and costly. There shall be none to be charmed by them (*v. 25*): *Thy men shall fall by the sword, and thy mighty in the war.* And, when Zion's guards are cut off, no marvel that Zion's gates *lament and mourn* (*v. 26*). The city itself, being desolate, shall *sit upon the ground* like a disconsolate widow.

CHAPTER 4

In this chapter we have, I. A threatening of the paucity and scarceness of men (ver. 1). II. A promise of the restoration of Jerusalem's peace and purity, righteousness and safety, in the days of the Messiah, ver. 2–6. Thus, in wrath, mercy is remembered.

Verse 1

Here we have the effect and consequence of that great slaughter of men. Providence has so wisely ordered that, *on an average of years,* there is nearly an equal number of males and females born into the world, yet, through the devastations made by war, there should scarcely be one man in seven left alive. As there are deaths attending the bringing forth of children, which are peculiar to the woman, there are deaths peculiar to men, those by the sword perhaps devour more than child-bed does. It is foretold that there should be *seven women to one man.* By reason of the scarcity of men, whereas men ordinarily make their court to the women, the women should now take hold of the men. Seven should now, by consent, become the wives of one man,—and that whereas by the law the husband was obliged to provide food and raiment for his wife (Exod. xxi. 10), these women will be bound to support themselves; they will *eat bread of their own earning, and wear apparel of their own working,* and the man they court shall be at no expense, only they desire to be called his wives, to *take away the reproach* of a single life. They are willing to be wives upon any terms. All their care was to get husbands—modesty was forgotten, and with them the reproach of vice was nothing to the reproach of virginity.

Verses 2–6

By the foregoing threatenings everything looks melancholy. But here the sun breaks out from behind the cloud. Many exceedingly great and precious promises we have in these verses, giving assurance of comfort, and these certainly point at the kingdom of the Messiah, and the great redemption to be wrought out by him, under the figure of the restoration of Judah and Jerusalem by the reforming reign of Hezekiah after Ahaz and the return out of their captivity in Babylon; to both these events the passage may have some reference, but chiefly to Christ.

I. God will raise up a righteous branch, which shall produce fruits of righteousness (v. 2): *In that day*, when Jerusalem shall be destroyed, and the Jewish nation dispersed, the kingdom of the Messiah shall be set up.

1. Christ himself shall be exalted. He is the *branch of the Lord*; it is one of his prophetical names, *my servant the branch* (Zech. iii. 8; vi. 12), a *rod out of the stem of Jesse and a branch out of his roots* (ch. xi. 1). The ancient Chaldee paraphrase here reads, *The Christ, or Messiah, of the Lord*. He shall himself be advanced to the glory which he had with the Father before the world was.

2. His gospel shall be embraced. The success of the gospel is the fruit of the branch of the Lord; all the graces and comforts of the gospel spring from Christ. But it is called *the fruit of the earth* because it sprang up in this world. We may understand it of both the persons and the things that are the products of the gospel. If the branch of the Lord be beautiful and glorious in our eyes, even the fruit of the earth also will be excellent and comely, because then we may take it as the fruit of the promise, Ps. xxxvii. 16; 1 Tim. iv. 8.

II. God will reserve to himself a holy seed, v. 3. When the generality shall be cut off as withered branches, by their own unbelief, yet some shall be left. 1. This is a remnant such as are written among the living. Those that are kept alive in killing times were written for life in the book of divine Providence, *written in the Lamb's book of life*, Rev. xiii. 8. All that were *written among the living* shall be found among the living, every one; for of all that were given to Christ he will lose none. 2. It is a remnant *under the dominion of grace*; for everyone that is *written among the living* shall be called *holy*, and shall be accepted of God accordingly.

III. God will reform his church and will rectify and amend whatever is amiss in it, v. 4. Then the remnant shall be *called holy, when the Lord shall have washed away their filth*, washed it from among them by cutting off the wicked persons, washed it from within them by purging out the wicked thing. Jerusalem, though the holy city, needed reformation. By the daughters of Zion may be meant the country towns and villages, which were related to Jerusalem as the mother-city, and which needed reformation. The filth shall be washed away; for wickedness is filthiness, particularly blood-shed. *The Lord shall do it*. Reformation-work is God's work. But how? By the judgment of his providence the sinners were destroyed; but it is by the Spirit of his grace that they are reformed and converted. The Spirit herein acts, enlightening the mind, convincing the conscience, guiding us, separating between the precious and the vile, quickening and invigorating the affections, and making men zealous in good work.

IV. God will protect his church, and all that belong to it (v. 5, 6). Those that are sanctified are well fortified.

1. Their tabernacles shall be defended, v. 5, tabernacles of their rest, their houses, where they worship God with their families. God takes particular care of the dwelling-places of his people, the poorest cottage as well as the stateliest palace. Their assemblies or tabernacles of meeting for religious worship— all the congregations of Christians, though but two or three met together in Christ's name, shall be taken under the special protection of heaven. This writ

of protection is drawn up in a similitude taken from the safety of the camp of Israel when they marched through the wilderness. God will give to the Christian church as real proofs of his care of them, as he then gave to Israel. Though miracles have ceased, yet God is the same to the New Testament church that he was to Israel of old. A similitude is taken from the outside cover of rams' skins and badgers' skins that was upon the curtains of the tabernacle, as if every dwelling-place and every assembly were as dear to God as that tabernacle was: *Upon all the glory shall be a defence*, to save it from wind and weather. Gospel truths and ordinances, the scriptures and the ministry, are the church's glory; and upon all this glory there is a defence. If God himself be the glory in the midst of it, he will himself be a wall of fire round about it, impenetrable and impregnable. Grace in the soul is the glory of it, and those that have it are *kept by the power of God* as in a stronghold, 1 Pet. i. 5. The divine power and goodness shall be a tabernacle to all the saints. God himself will be their hiding-place (Ps. xxxii. 7); they shall be at home in him, Ps. xci. 9. God is a refuge to his people in all weathers.

CHAPTER 5

In this chapter the prophet, in God's name, shows the people of God their transgressions, and the judgments to be brought upon them for their sins. I. By a parable of an unfruitful vineyard, representing the favours God had bestowed, their disappointing his expectations from them, and the ruin they deserved, ver. 1–7. II. By an enumeration of the sins among them, with a threatening of punishments that should answer to the sins. 1. Covetousness, and greediness, which shall be punished with famine, ver. 8–10. 2. Rioting, revelling, and drunkenness (ver. 11, 12, 22, 23), which shall be punished with captivity, ver. 13–17. 3. Presumption and defying the justice of God, ver. 18, 19. 4. Confounding the distinctions between virtue and vice, and so undermining the principles of religion, ver. 20. 5. Self-conceit, ver. 21. 6. Perverting justice, for which great and general desolation is threatened (ver. 24, 25), which should be effected by a foreign invasion (ver. 26–30), referring perhaps to the havoc made not long after by Sennacherib's army.

Verses 1–7

God, to awaken sinners to repentance, speaks sometimes in plain terms and sometimes in parables, sometimes in prose and sometimes in verse, as here. God the Father dictates it to the honour of Christ his well beloved Son, whom he has constituted Lord of the vineyard. The prophet sings it to the honour of Christ. The Old Testament prophets were friends of the bridegroom. Christ is God's beloved Son and our beloved Saviour. This parable was put into a song that it might be the more moving and the more easily learned, remembered, and transmitted to posterity. It is an exposition of the song of Moses (Deut. xxxii), showing that what he then foretold was now fulfilled.

I. The great things which God had done for the Jewish church and nation. The soil they were planted in was *a very fruitful hill, the horn of the son of oil*: so it is in the margin. There was plenty, and there was dainty: they did there eat the fat and drink the sweet. Observe further what God did for this vineyard. 1. He fenced it. If they had not thrown down their fence, no inroad could have been made upon them, Ps. cxxv. 2; cxxi. 4. 2. He gathered the stones out of it. He proffered his grace to take away the stony heart. 3. He planted it with the choicest vine, set up a pure religion among them. 4. He built a tower in the midst of it for defence. The temple was this tower. 5. He made a wine-press therein, set up his altar, to which the sacrifices, as the fruits of the vineyard, should be brought.

II. The disappointment of his just expectations: *He looked that it should bring forth grapes*. God expects vineyard-fruit from those that enjoy vineyard-privileges. Good purposes and good beginnings are good things, but not enough; there must be fruit, a good heart and a good life, vineyard fruit, thoughts and affections, words and actions, agreeable to the Spirit. His expectations are frustrated: *It brought forth wild grapes.* 1. Wild grapes are the fruits of the corrupt nature. 2. Wild grapes are hypocritical performances in religion, that look like grapes.

III. An appeal to themselves whether God must not be justified and they condemned, *v.* 3, 4. *O inhabitants of Jerusalem, and men of Judah! judge, I pray you, betwixt me and my vineyard.* Here is a challenge to show wherein God had been wanting to them: *What could have been done more to my vineyard, that I have not done in it?* They had everything requisite. "Wherefore, what reason can be given why it should bring forth wild grapes, when I looked for grapes?"

IV. Their doom read, and sentence passed upon them (*v.* 5, 6): "*And now go to,* since nothing can be offered in excuse of the crime or arrest of the judgment, *I will tell you what I am now determined to do to my vineyard.* I will be troubled with it no more; in short, it shall cease to be a vineyard, and be turned into a wilderness: the church of the Jews shall be unchurched. *I will take away the hedge thereof,* and then it will become bare." God will remove all their defences and they will become an easy prey to their enemies. They shall no longer have the face of a vineyard, the form and shape of a church and commonwealth, but shall be levelled and laid waste. Those who would not bring forth good fruit should bring forth none. The curse of barrenness is the punishment of the sin of barrenness. This had its partial accomplishment in the destruction of Jerusalem by the Chaldeans, its full accomplishment in the final rejection of the Jews, and has its frequent accomplishment in the departure of God's Spirit from those who have long resisted him.

V. The explanation of this parable, or a key to it (*v.* 7). The vineyard is *the house of Israel,* the body of the people, incorporated in one church and commonwealth, and the vines are *the men of Judah*; these he had dealt graciously with, and from them he expected suitable returns. The grapes that were expected and the wild grapes that were produced: *He looked for judgment and righteousness,* that the people should be honest and the magistrates strictly administer justice. This might reasonably be expected; but the fact was quite otherwise; instead of judgment there was the cruelty of the oppressors, and instead of righteousness the cry of the oppressed.

Verses 8–17

Eagerness of the world, and indulgence of the flesh, are the two sins against which the prophet, in God's name, here denounces woes. These were sins which then abounded among the men of Judah, some of the wild grapes they brought forth (*v.* 4).

I. Here is a woe to those who set their hearts upon the wealth of the world (*v.* 8), who *join house to house and lay field to field, till there be no place,* no room for anybody to live by them. If they could succeed, they monopolize possessions and preferments. They are inordinate in their desires to enrich themselves. They are herein careless of others. They care not what hardships they put upon those that they have power over, nor what wicked arts they use to heap up treasure to themselves. The punishment of this sin is that neither the houses nor the fields should turn to any account, *v.* 9, 10. The houses they were so fond of should be untenanted, should stand long empty: *Many houses shall be desolate,* the people that should dwell in them, being cut off by sword, famine, or pestilence, or carried into captivity. We have a saying, That fools build houses for wise men to live in; but sometimes, as the event proves, they are built for no man to live in. The fields they were

so fond of should be unfruitful (*v.* 10): *Ten acres of vineyard shall yield* only such grapes as will make but *one bath* of wine (about eight gallons), *and the seed of a homer,* a bushel's sowing, shall yield but an ephah, the tenth part of a homer; so that they should not have more than a tenth part of their seed again.

II. Here is a woe to those that dote upon the pleasures of sense, *v.* 11, 12. Sensuality ruins men as certainly as worldliness and oppression. The sinners against whom this woe is denounced are such as are given to drink. They sit at their cups all day, *and continue till night, till wine inflame them*—inflame their lusts. They are such as never give their mind to anything that is serious: *They regard not the work of the Lord;* they observe not his power, wisdom, and goodness, in those creatures which they abuse, nor the bounty of his providence in giving them those good things which they make the food and fuel of their lusts. It is here foretold they should be dislodged; the land should spew out these drunkards (*v.* 13): *My people have therefore gone into captivity, because they have no knowledge*; how should they have knowledge when by their excessive drinking they make sots and fools of themselves? They should be impoverished, and come to want that which they had wasted and abused to excess: Even *their glory are men of famine,* subject to it and slain by it; and *their multitude are dried up with thirst.* Multitudes should be cut off by famine and sword (*v.* 14): *Therefore hell has enlarged herself.* Tophet, the common burying-place, proves too little; so many are there to be buried that they shall be forced to enlarge it. They should be humbled and abased, and all their honours laid in the dust. God shall be glorified, *v.* 16. He shall be exalted in the judgment and righteousness of these dispensations. Good people should be relieved and succoured (*v.* 17): *Then shall the lambs feed after their manner;* the meek ones of the earth, who followed the Lamb, who were persecuted and put into fear by those proud oppressors, shall feed quietly, and there shall be none to make them afraid. The country shall be laid waste, and become a prey to the neighbours: *The waste places of the fat ones,* the possessions of those rich men that lived at their ease, shall be eaten by strangers that were nothing akin to them.

Verses 18–30

I. Sins described which will bring judgments upon the men of Judah who lived at that time, and though it may relate primarily to them, is intended for warning to all people, in all ages. Those are here said to be in a woeful condition,

1. Who are violent in their sinful pursuits (*v.* 18), who *draw iniquity with cords of vanity,* who take as much pains to sin as the cattle do that draw in a team. They think themselves as sure of compassing their wicked project as if they were pulling it towards them with strong cart-ropes; but they will prove cords of vanity, which will break when they come to any stress. Those that sin through infirmity are drawn away by sin; those that sin presumptuously draw iniquity to them, in spite of the oppositions of Providence and the checks of conscience. Some by sin pull God's judgments upon their own heads, as it were, with cart-ropes.

2. Who set the justice of God at defiance, and challenge the Almighty to do his worst (*v.* 19): *They say, Let him make speed, and hasten his work.* They ridicule the prophets, and banter them. They will not believe the revelation of God's wrath from heaven unless they see it executed. If God should appear against them, as he has threatened, yet they think themselves able to make their part good with him. "We have heard his word, but it is all talk; let him hasten his work, we shall shift for ourselves well enough."

3. Who confound the distinctions between moral good and evil, *who call evil good and good evil* (v. 20). Those do a great deal of wrong to God, and religion, and conscience, to their own souls, and to the souls of others, who call drunkenness good fellowship, and covetousness good husbandry, and on the other hand, call seriousness ill-nature, and who say all manner of evil falsely concerning godliness.

4. Who though they are guilty of such gross mistakes have a great opinion of their own judgments (v. 21): They are *wise in their own eyes*; they think they can outwit Infinite Wisdom and countermine Providence itself.

5. Who glory that they are able to bear a great deal of strong liquor without being overcome by it (v. 22), *who are mighty to drink wine*, and use their strength in the service of their lusts. Drunkards ungratefully abuse their bodily strength, which God has given them for good purposes, and by degrees cannot but weaken it.

6. Who, as judges, pervert justice, v. 23. They *justify the wicked for reward*, and find some pretence or other to clear him from his guilt and shelter him from punishment; and they condemn the innocent, and *take away their righteousness from them*.

II. The judgments described, which these sins would bring upon them. The righteous God will take vengeance, v. 24–30. He had compared this people to a vine (v. 7), which, it was hoped, would be fruitful; but the grace of God was received in vain, and the root became rottenness, being dried up from beneath, and the blossom would blow off as dust. Sin weakens the strength, the root, of a people, so that they are easily rooted up; it defaces the beauty, the blossoms, of a people, and takes away the hopes of fruit. Sinners make themselves as stubble and chaff. *As the fire devours the stubble*, chaff is consumed, unhelped and unpitied. God does not reject men for every transgression of his law and word; but, when his word is despised and his law cast away, what can they expect but that God should utterly abandon them? The justice of God appoints it; for that is *the anger of the Lord* which is *kindled against his people*, his necessary vindication. *He has stretched forth his hand against them.* That hand which had many a time been stretched out for them against their enemies is now stretched out against them. When God comes forth in wrath against a people the hills tremble, fear seizes even their great men. What sight can be more frightful than the carcases of men thrown *as dung* (so the margin reads it) *in the midst of the streets*? This intimates that multitudes should be slain, not only soldiers in battle, but the inhabitants of their cities put to the sword in cold blood, and that the survivors should neither have hands nor hearts to bury them. This ruin should be done by a foreign enemy, that should lay all waste. Those who know him are not made use of to fulfil his counsel. If God set up his standard, he can incline men's hearts to enlist themselves under it, though perhaps they know not why or wherefore. *Behold, they shall come with speed swiftly.* This is described here in elegant and lofty expressions, v. 27–30. Though their marches be long, yet *none among them shall be weary*. Though the way be rough, yet none among them shall *stumble*. Though they be forced to keep constant watch, yet *none shall slumber nor sleep.* They shall not desire any rest or relaxation; they shall not put off their clothes, nor *loose the girdle of their loins*, but shall always have their belts on and swords by their sides. Not a *latchet of their shoes shall be broken* which they must stay to mend, as Joshua ix. 13. Their arms and ammunition shall all be fixed, and in good posture; *their arrows sharp, and all their bows bent*, none unstrung. Their horses and chariots of war shall all be fit for service; their horses so strong, that *their*

hoofs shall be like flint, and the wheels of their chariots not broken, or battered, but swift *like a whirlwind*. All the soldiers shall be bold and daring (v. 29): *Their roaring shall be like a lion*, who with his roaring animates himself, and terrifies all about him. *They shall roar like the roaring of the sea* in a storm. There shall not be the least prospect of relief or succour. If the light is darkened in the heavens, how great is that darkness! If God hide his face, no marvel the heavens hide theirs and appear gloomy, Job xxxiv. 29.

CHAPTER 6

Hitherto, Isaiah, having only a virtual and tacit commission, perhaps, having seen little success of his ministry, began to think of giving it up; and therefore God saw fit to renew his commission in such a manner as might encourage his zeal, though he seemed to labour in vain. In this chapter we have, I. A vision which Isaiah saw of the glory of God (ver. 1–4), the terror it put him into (ver. 5), and the relief given him against that terror by an assurance of the pardon of his sins, ver. 6, 7. II. A commission which Isaiah received to go as a prophet, in God's name (ver. 8), preaching to the impenitent (ver. 9–12), yet with a reservation of mercy for a remnant, ver. 13. And it was as to an evangelical prophet that these things were shown him and said to him.

Verses 1–4

The vision which Isaiah saw when he was, as is said of Samuel, *established to be a prophet of the Lord* (1 Sam. iii. 20), was intended to confirm his faith. Thus God appeared at first as a God of glory to Abraham (Acts vii. 2), and to Moses, Exod. iii. 2. Ezekiel's prophecies, and St. John's, begin with visions of the divine glory. Those who are to teach others the knowledge of God ought to be well acquainted with him themselves.

The vision was *in the year that king Uzziah died*, who had reigned as well as any of the kings of Judah, above fifty years. About the time that he died Isaiah saw this vision of God upon a throne. Israel's king dies, but Israel's God still lives. King Uzziah died a leper in an hospital, but the King of kings still sits upon his throne.

I. See God upon his throne, and that throne *high and lifted up*, not only above other thrones, as it transcends them, but over other thrones, as it rules them. Isaiah saw not *Jehovah*—the essence of God (no man has seen that, or can see it), but *Adonai*—his dominion. He saw the Lord Jesus; so this vision is explained John xii. 41, that Isaiah now saw Christ's glory. See the sovereignty of the Eternal Monarch: he sits *upon a throne*—a throne of glory, before which we must worship,—a throne of government, under which we must be subject,—and a throne of grace, to which we may come boldly.

II. See his temple, his church on earth, filled with the manifestations of his glory. His *train*, the skirts of his robes, *filled the temple*, the whole world (for it is all God's temple), or rather the Church, which is filled, enriched, and beautified with the tokens of God's special presence.

III. See the bright and blessed attendants on his throne (v. 2): *Above the throne the seraphim stood*, the holy angels, who are called *seraphim—burners*; for he *makes his ministers a flaming fire*, Ps. civ. 4. They burn in love to God, and zeal for his glory and against sin. It is the glory of the angels that they are seraphim, have heat proportionable to their light, have abundance, not only of divine knowledge, but of holy love. They had *each of them six wings*, not stretched upwards (as those whom Ezekiel saw, *ch.* i. 11), but, 1. Four were for covering; with the two upper wings they covered their faces, and with the two lowest wings they covered their feet. This bespeaks their great humility and reverence. They not only cover their feet, but even their faces. Two were made use of for flight; when they are sent on

God's errands they fly swiftly (Dan. ix. 21). This teaches us to do the work of God with cheerfulness and expedition.

IV. Hear the song of praise, which the angels sing to the honour of him that sits on the throne, *v.* 3. With zeal and fervency—*they cried* aloud; and with unanimity—*they cried one to another*, without the least jarring voice to interrupt the harmony. The song was the same which is sung by the four living creatures, Rev. iv. 8. The church above is the same in its praises; there is no change of times or notes there. Here is one of his most glorious titles praised: he is *the Lord of hosts*, of all hosts; and one of his most glorious attributes, his holiness. Power, without purity to guide it, would be a terror to mankind. God's power was spoken twice (Ps. lxii. 11), but his holiness thrice, *Holy, holy, holy*. It may refer to the three persons in the Godhead, Holy Father, Holy Son, and Holy Spirit (for it follows, *v.* 8, *Who will go for us?*) or perhaps to *that which was, and is, and is to come. The earth is full of his glory*, of the glory of his power and purity; for he is holy in all his works, Ps. cxlv. 17.

V. Observe the tokens of terror with which the temple was filled, upon this vision of the divine glory, *v.* 4. The house was *shaken*; even *the posts of the door*, which were firmly fixed, *moved at the voice of him that cried*, at the voice of God, who called to judgment (Ps. l. 4). The house was *darkened*; it was *filled with smoke*, which was as a *cloud spread* upon *the face of his throne* (Job xxvi. 9). In the temple above, everything will be seen clearly. There God dwells in light; here he *makes darkness his pavilion*, 2 Chron. vi. 1.

Verses 5–8

I. The consternation that the prophet was put into by the vision which he saw of the glory of God (*v.* 5): *Then said I, Woe is me!* One would think, he should have said, "Happy am I, nothing now shall trouble me"; but, on the contrary, he cries out, "*Woe is me! for I am undone*."

1. What the prophet reflected upon in himself which terrified him: "*I am undone because I am a man of unclean lips*." Some think he refers particularly to some rash word he had spoken, or to his sinful silence in not reproving sin with boldness. But it may be taken more generally: *I am a sinner;* particularly, *I have offended in word*. We all have reason to bewail it before the Lord, (1) That we are of unclean lips ourselves; our lips are not consecrated to God. We are unworthy to take God's name into our lips. The impurity of our lips ought to be the grief of our souls, for by our words we shall be justified or condemned. (2) That we dwell among those who are so too. The disease is hereditary and epidemic, which is so far from lessening our guilt that it should rather increase our grief, considering that we have not done what we might have done for the cleansing of the pollution of other people's lips; we have rather learned their way and spoken their language, as Joseph in Egypt learned the courtier's oath, Gen. xlii. 16.

2. What gave occasion for these sad reflections: *My eyes have seen the King, the Lord of hosts.* We are undone if there be not a Mediator between us and this holy God, 1 Sam. vi. 20. Isaiah was thus humbled, to prepare him for the honour he was now to be called to as a prophet.

II. The silencing of the prophet's fears by the comfortable words, with which the angel answered him, *v.* 6, 7. One of the seraphim immediately flew to him, to purify him. Those that are struck down with the visions of God's glory shall soon be raised up again with the visits of his grace. Here was one of the seraphim dismissed, for a time, from the throne of God's glory, to be a messenger of his grace to a

good man; and he came flying to him. To our Lord Jesus himself, in his agony, there *appeared an angel from heaven, strengthening him*, Luke xxii. 43. The seraph *brought a live coal from the altar*, and touched his lips with it to cleanse them. The blessed Spirit works as fire, Matt. iii. 11. The seraph put life into the prophet, for the way to purge the lips from the uncleanness of sin is to fire the soul with the love of God. "*Lo, this has touched thy lips*, to assure thee of this, that *thy iniquity is taken away and thy sin purged*. The guilt of thy sin is removed by pardoning mercy, the guilt of thy tongue-sins. Thy corrupt disposition to sin is removed by renewing grace; and therefore nothing can hinder thee from being accepted with God as a worshipper, or from being employed for God as a messenger to the children of men."

III. The renewing of the prophet's mission, *v.* 8. Here is a communication between God and Isaiah. How can we expect that God should speak by us if we never heard him speaking to us? God is here deliberating with himself: *Whom shall I send? And who will go for us?* Thus he would teach us that the sending forth of ministers is a work not to be done but upon mature deliberation. It puts an honour upon the ministry that, when God would send a prophet to speak in his name, he appeared in all the glories of the upper world. *Whom shall I send?* intimating that he would send them a *prophet from among their brethren*, Heb. ii. 17. God is pleased to send us his mind by men like ourselves, who are themselves concerned in the messages they bring. Those who are workers together with God are sinners and sufferers together with us. Who is sufficient? Such a degree of courage and concern for the souls of men, and withal such an insight into the mysteries of the kingdom of heaven, are seldom to be met with. None are allowed to go for God but those who are sent by him, Rom. x. 15. It is Christ's work to put men into the ministry, 1 Tim. i. 12. The office seemed to go a-begging, yet Isaiah offered himself: "I will go, and leave the success to God. Here am I; send me." What he says denotes readiness: "Here am I, a volunteer, not pressed into the service." *Behold me;* so the word is. "*Here I am*, ready to encounter the greatest difficulties. I have set my face as a flint."

Verses 9–13

God takes Isaiah at his word, and here sends him on a strange errand—to foretell the ruin of his people and even to ripen them for that ruin. And this was to be a type of the state of the Jewish church in the days of the Messiah, when they should obstinately reject the gospel, and should thereupon be rejected of God. These verses are quoted in part, or referred to, six times, in the New Testament. Isaiah is here given to understand these four things:

1. That the generality of the people to whom he was sent would turn a deaf ear to his preaching, and wilfully shut their eyes against all the discoveries of the mind and will of God which he had to make to them (*v.* 9).

2. That, as they would not be made better by his ministry, they should be made worse by it; those that were wilfully blind should be judicially blinded (*v.* 10): "They will not understand or perceive thee, and therefore thou shalt be instrumental to *make their heart fat*, senseless, and sensual, and so to *make their ears* yet more *heavy*, and to *shut their eyes* the closer; so that, at length, their recovery and repentance will become utterly impossible." Even the word of God oftentimes proves a means of hardening sinners.

3. That the consequence of this would be their *utter ruin, v.* 11, 12. The prophet asks, "*Lord, how long?*" (an abrupt question): "Shall it always be thus? Must I and other prophets always labour in vain

among them, and will things never be better?" In answer to this he is told that it should issue in the final destruction of the Jewish church and nation. "Their cities shall be uninhabited, and the land shall be untilled, *desolate with desolation* (as it is in the margin)." Spiritual judgments often bring temporal judgments upon persons and places. This was in part fulfilled in the destruction of Jerusalem by the Chaldeans, but, the foregoing predictions being so expressly applied in the New Testament to the Jews in our Saviour's time, doubtless this points at the final destruction of that people by the Romans.

4. That yet a remnant should be reserved to be the monuments of mercy, *v.* 13. *But in it shall be a tenth,* a certain number, but a very small number in comparison with the multitude that shall perish in their unbelief. Concerning this tithe, this saved remnant, we are here told, (1) That they shall return (*ch.* vi. 13; x. 21), shall return from sin to God and duty, shall return out of captivity to their own land. (2) That they shall be eaten, that is, shall be accepted of God as the tithe was, which was meat in God's house, Mal. iii. 10. (3) That they shall be like a timber-tree in winter, which has life, though it has no leaves: *As a teil-tree and as an oak, whose substance is in them even when they cast their leaves,* so this remnant, though they may be stripped of their outward prosperity, shall yet recover themselves, as a tree in the spring, and flourish again. (4) That this distinguished remnant shall be the stay and support of the public interests. *The holy seed* in the soul is the substance of the man; a principle of grace reigning in the heart will keep life there; he that is *born of God* has *his seed remaining in him,* 1 John iii. 9. As the trees that grow on either side of the causeway (the raised way, or terrace-walk, that leads from the king's palace to the temple (1 Kings x. 5), support the causeway by keeping up the earth, which would otherwise be crumbling away, so the small residue of religious, serious, praying people, are the support of the state, and help to keep things together and save them from going to decay.

Chapter 7

This chapter is an occasional sermon, in which the prophet sings both of mercy and judgment to those that did not perceive or understand either. Here is, I. The consternation that Ahaz was in upon an attempt of the confederate forces of Syria and Israel against Jerusalem, ver. 1, 2. II. The assurance which God, by the prophet, sent him for his encouragement, that the attempt should be defeated and Jerusalem should be preserved, ver. 3–9. III. The confirmation of this by a sign which God gave to Ahaz, ver. 10–16. IV. A threatening of the great desolation that God would bring upon Ahaz and his kingdom by the Assyrians, notwithstanding their escape from this present storm, because they went on still in their wickedness, ver. 17–25.

Verses 1–9

The prophet Isaiah had his commission renewed in the year that king Uzziah died, *ch.* vi. 1. Jotham his son reigned, and reigned well, sixteen years. All that time, no doubt, Isaiah prophesied as he was commanded, and yet we have not in this book any of his prophecies dated in the reign of Jotham; but this, which is put first, was in the days of Ahaz the son of Jotham.

I. A formidable design laid against Jerusalem by Rezin king of Syria and Pekah king of Israel, who had made descents upon Judah severally, 2 Kings xv. 37. But now, in the second or third year of the reign of Ahaz, they entered into an alliance against Judah. Because Ahaz, though he found the sword over his head, began his reign with idolatry, *God delivered him into the hand of the king of Syria and of the king of Israel* (2 Chron. xxviii. 5). Flushed with this victory, they went up towards Jerusalem to besiege it.

II. The great distress that Ahaz and his court were in when they received advice of this design: *It was told the house of David* that Syria and Ephraim had signed a league against Judah, *v.* 2. News being brought that the two armies of Syria and Israel had taken the field. *The heart of Ahaz was moved with fear,* and then no wonder that *the heart of his people was so, as the trees of the wood are moved with the wind.* Now that which caused this fright was the sense of guilt and the weakness of their faith. They had made God their enemy, and knew not how to make him their friend.

III. The orders given to Isaiah to encourage Ahaz in his distress, because he was a son of David and king of Judah. God had kindness for him for his father's sake, who must not be forgotten, and for his people's sake, who must not be abandoned. He ordered Isaiah to take his little son with him, because he carried a sermon in his name, *Shear-jashub—A remnant shall return.* This son was so called for the encouragement of those of God's people who were carried captive, assuring them that they should return. He directed him where he should find Ahaz, *at the end of the conduit of the upper pool,* where he was contriving how to order the water-works, so as to secure them to the city (*ch.* xxii. 9–11; 2 Chron. xxxii, 3, 4), or giving some necessary directions for the fortifying of the city. He put words in his mouth, else the prophet would not have known how to bring a message of good to such a bad man, but God intended it for the support of faithful Israelites. The prophet must rebuke their fears (*v.* 4): *Take heed, and be quiet.* Pluck up thy spirits and be courageous. He must teach them to despise their enemies, not in pride, or security, but in faith and dependence upon God. Ahaz's fear called them two powerful politic princes, for either of whom he was an unequal match. "No," says the prophet, "they are *two tails of smoking firebrands;* they are angry, they are fierce, as fireballs, and they make one another worse by being in a confederacy, as sticks of fire put together burn the more violently. But they are only smoking firebrands, *tails* of smoking firebrands, in a manner burnt out already; their force is spent; you may put your foot on them, and tread them out." He must assure them that the present design of these high allies (so they thought themselves) against Jerusalem should certainly be defeated and come to nothing, *v.* 5–7. Judah had done them no wrong; they had no pretence to quarrel with Ahaz; but, without any reason, they said, *Let us go up against Judah, and vex it.* They count upon dividing the kingdom into two parts, one for the king of Israel, the other for the king of Syria, who had agreed in one viceroy—*a king* to be *set in the midst of it, even the son of Tabeal,* some obscure person, it is uncertain whether a Syrian or an Israelite. So sure were they of gaining their point that they divided the prey before they had caught it. God himself gives them his word that the attempt should not take effect (*v.* 7): *Thus saith the Lord God, It shall not stand, neither shall it come to pass.* They should neither of them enlarge their dominions, nor push their conquests any further: *The head city of Syria is Damascus, and the head man of Damascus is Rezin;* this he glories in, and this let him be content with, *v.* 8. *The head city of Ephraim* has long been *Samaria, and the head man in Samaria is* now Pekah *the son of Remaliah.* These shall be made to know their own; their bounds are fixed, and they shall not pass them, to make themselves masters of the cities of Judah, much less to make Jerusalem their prey. Ephraim, which perhaps was the more malicious and forward enemy of the two, should shortly be quite rooted out, and should be so far from seizing other people's lands that they should not be able to hold their own. It was the greatest folly in the world for those to be ruining their neighbours who were themselves marked for ruin, and so near to it. He must urge them to mix faith with assurances (v. 9): "*If you will not believe* what is said to you, *surely you shall not be established*. The things told you are encouraging, yet they will not be so to you, unless you be willing to take God's word."

Verses 10–16

I. God, by the prophet, makes a gracious offer to Ahaz, to confirm the foregoing predictions by such sign or miracle as he should choose (v. 10, 11): *Ask thee a sign of the Lord thy God.* He considers our frame, and that, living in a world of sense, we are apt to require proofs, which he has favoured us with in sacramental signs and seals. See how gracious God is even to the evil and unthankful; Ahaz is bidden to choose his sign, as Gideon about the fleece (Judges vi. 37).

II. Ahaz rudely refuses this gracious offer (v. 12): *I will not ask.* The true reason why he would not ask for a sign was because, having a dependence upon the Assyrians, their forces, and their gods, for help, he would not thus far be beholden to the God of Israel. Yet he pretends a pious reason: *I will not tempt the Lord.*

III. The prophet reproves him and his court for their contempt of prophecy (v. 13): "*Is it a small thing for you to weary men* by your oppression and *will you weary my God also* with the affronts you put upon him? In affronting the prophets, you think you put a slight only upon men like yourselves, and consider not that you affront God himself, whose messengers they are."

IV. The prophet, in God's name, gives them a sign (v. 14), a sign in general of his goodwill to Israel and to the house of David. Of your nation, of your family, the Messiah is to be born, and you cannot be destroyed while that blessing is in you. You have been told that he should be born among you, I am now further to tell you that he shall be born of a virgin, which will signify both the divine power and the divine purity with which he shall be brought into the world. This, though it was to be accomplished above 500 years after, was a most encouraging sign to the house of David, and an assurance that God would not cast them off. The Messiah shall be introduced on a glorious errand, wrapped up in his glorious name: They *shall call his name Immanuel—God with us*, God in our nature, God at peace with us, in covenant with us. This was fulfilled in their calling him *Jesus—a Saviour* (Matt. i. 21–25), for, if he had not been *Immanuel—God with us*, he could not have been *Jesus—a Saviour*. The promised seed shall be Immanuel, *God with us*; let that word comfort you (ch. viii. 10), that *God is with us*, and (v. 8) that your land is Immanuel's land. Let not *the heart of the house of David* be moved thus (v. 2), nor let Judah fear the setting up of the son of Tabeal (v. 6), for nothing can cut off the entail on the Son of David that shall be Immanuel. The strongest consolations, in time of trouble, are those which are borrowed from Christ, our relation to him, our interest in him, and our expectations of him and from him. Of this child it is further foretold (v. 15), he shall be truly man, and shall be nursed and brought up like other children: *Butter and honey shall he eat.* Here is another sign in particular of the speedy destruction of these princes now a terror to Judah, v. 16. "Before *this* child (so it should be read), this child which I have now in my arms"—not Immanuel, but Shearjashub, his own son—v. 3, "*shall know how to refuse the evil and choose the good*, before this child be three or four years older, *the land that thou abhorrest*, these confederate forces of Israelites and Syrians *shall be forsaken of both their kings*, both Pekah and Rezin."

This was fully accomplished; for, within two or three years after this, Hoshea conspired against Pekah, and slew him (2 Kings xv. 30), and, before that, the king of Assyria took Damascus, and slew Rezin, 2 Kings xvi. 9. Nay, there was a present event, which happened immediately. *Shearjashub* signifies *The remnant shall return*, which doubtless points at the wonderful return of those 200,000 captives whom Pekah and Rezin had carried away, who were brought back, by the Spirit of the Lord of hosts. Read the story, 2 Chron. xxviii. 8–15. The prophetical naming of this child having thus had its accomplishment, no doubt this should have its accomplishment likewise. Syria and Israel should be deprived of both their kings.

Verses 17–25

After the comfortable promises made to Ahaz as a branch of the house of David, here follow terrible threatenings against him, as a degenerate branch of that house. His iniquity shall be *chastened with the rod.*

I. The judgment threatened is great, v. 17, brought upon the prince himself and upon the people, and upon the royal family, *upon* all *thy father's house.*

II. The enemy employed as the instrument of this judgment is the king of Assyria. Ahaz reposed great confidence in that prince for help against the confederate powers of Israel and Syria, 2 Kings xvi. 7, 8. Now God threatens that that king of Assyria whom he made his stay instead of God should become a scourge to him. Henceforward the kings of Assyria were, for a long time, grieving thorns to Judah. 1. Summons given to the invaders (v. 18): *The Lord shall whistle for the fly and the bee.* See ch. v. 26. Enemies that seem as contemptible as a fly or a bee and are as easily crushed, shall yet, when God pleases, do his work as effectually as lions and young lions. 2. Possession taken by them, v. 19. It should seem as if the country were in no condition to make resistance. They find no difficulties in forcing their way, but *come and rest all of them in the desolate valleys*, which the inhabitants had deserted upon the first alarm. They shall come and rest in the low grounds like swarms of flies and bees, and shall render themselves impregnable by taking shelter in the holes of the rocks, as bees often do, and show themselves formidable by appearing openly upon all thorns and all bushes; so generally shall the land be overspread with them. 3. Great desolations made, and the country generally depopulated (v. 20): *The Lord shall shave the hair of the head, and beard, and feet;* he shall sweep all away. God will make that to be an instrument of his destruction which he hired into his service. Many are beaten with that arm of flesh which they trusted to rather than to the arm of the Lord. 4. The consequences of this general depopulation: The flocks of cattle shall be all destroyed, so that a man shall with much ado save for his own use a young cow and two sheep—a poor stock (v. 21). The few cattle that are left shall have such a large compass of ground to feed in that *they shall give abundance of milk*, such as shall produce butter enough, v. 22. There shall also be such want of men that the milk of one cow and two sheep shall serve a whole family, which used to keep servants and consume a great deal. The country shall be so depopulated that there shall be butter and honey enough, for the few that are left in it. Good land, that used to be let well, shall be all overrun with briers and thorns (v. 23). The implements of husbandry shall be turned into instruments of war, v. 24, with arrows and bows, to hunt for wild beasts in the thickets, or to defend themselves from robbers. There shall be briers and thorns in abundance where they should not be, but none where they should be, *v.* 25. *The hills that shall be digged with the mattock*, for special use, from which the cattle used to be kept off with the fear of briers and thorns, shall now be thrown open, the *hedges broken down for the boar out of the wood* to waste it, Ps. lxxx. 12, 13.

CHAPTER 8

This chapter, and the four next that follow it (to chap. xiii) are all one continued discourse, the scope of which is to show the great destruction that should now shortly be brought upon the kingdom of Israel, but rich provision is made of comfort for those that feared God in those dark times. In this chapter we have, I. A prophecy of the destruction of the confederate kingdoms of Syria and Israel by the king of Assyria, ver. 1–4. II. Of the desolations that should be made by that proud victorious prince in the land of Israel and Judah, ver. 5–8. III. Great encouragement given to the people of God in the midst of those distractions; they are assured, 1. That the enemies shall not gain their point against them, ver. 9, 10. 2. That if they kept up the fear of God, and kept down the fear of man, they should find God their refuge (ver. 11–14), and while others fell into despair, they should be enabled to wait on God for better times, ver. 15–18. Lastly, He gives a necessary caution to all not to consult with familiar spirits, ver. 19–22.

Verses 1–8

In these verses we have a prophecy of the successes of the king of Assyria against Damascus, Samaria, and Judah, that the two former should be laid waste by him, and the last greatly frightened.

I. Orders given to the prophet to write this prophecy, to be read of all men, that when the thing came to pass they might know that God had sent him; for that was one end of prophecy, John xiv. 29. He must *take a great roll*, and he must write in it all that he had foretold concerning the king of Assyria's invading the country; he must *write it with a man's pen*, in the usual way. The prophet is directed to call his book *Maher-shalal-hash-baz—Make speed to the spoil, hasten to the prey*, intimating that the Assyrian army should come upon them with great speed and make great spoil.

II. The care of the prophet to get this record well attested (*v.* 2): *I took unto me faithful witnesses to record;* he wrote the prophecy in their presence that they might be ready to make oath of it, that the prophet had so long before foretold the descent which the Assyrians made upon that country. He names his witnesses. One was Uriah the priest; he is mentioned in the story of Ahaz (2 Kings xvi. 10, 11).

III. The making of the title of his book the name of his child. His wife (because the wife of a prophet) is called *the prophetess*; she *conceived and bore a son*, another son, who must carry a sermon in his name, as the former had done (*ch.* vii. 3), but with this difference, that spoke mercy, *Shearjashub—The remnant shall return;* but, that being slighted, this speaks judgment, *Maher-shalal-hash-baz—In making speed to the spoil he shall hasten*, or *he has hastened, to the prey*. Every time the child was called by his name, or any part of it, it would serve as a memorandum of the judgments approaching.

IV. The prophecy itself, which explains this mystical name.

1. That Syria and Israel, who were now in confederacy against Judah, should in a little time become an easy prey to the king of Assyria (*v.* 4): "*Before the child*, now newly born and named, shall have *knowledge to cry, My father, and, My mother*", that is, "in about a year or two, *the riches of Damascus, and the spoil of Samaria*, those cities that are now so secure, *shall be taken away before the king of Assyria*, who shall plunder both city and country as trophies of his victory."

2. That forasmuch as there were many in Judah that were secretly in the interests of Syria and Israel, and were disaffected to the house of David, God would chastise them also by the king of Assyria.

What was the sin of the discontented party in Judah (*v.* 6): *This people*, whom the prophet here speaks to, *refuse the waters of Shiloah that go softly*, despise their own country and love to run it down, because it does not make so great a noise in the world, as some other kings and kingdoms do. They refuse the comforts which God's prophets offer them from the word of God, but *they rejoice in Rezin and Remaliah's son*, who were the enemies of their country, and were now actually invading it. Such vipers does many a state foster in its bosom, that eat its bread, and yet adhere to its enemies, and are ready to quit its interests if they but seem to totter. The same king of Assyria that should lay Ephraim and Syria waste should be a scourge and terror to those of their party in Judah, *v.* 7, 8. Because they *refuse the waters of Shiloah the Lord brings upon them the waters of the river, strong and many*, the river Euphrates. They slighted the land of Judah, because it had no river to boast of comparable to that. "Well," says God, "if you be such admirers of Euphrates, you shall have enough of it; the king of Assyria, whose country lies upon that river, shall come with his great army. God shall bring that army upon you." Let us be best pleased with the waters of Shiloah, that go softly, for rapid streams are dangerous. It is threatened that the Assyrian army should break in upon them like a deluge, bearing down all before it. *He shall reach even to the neck*, that is, he shall advance so far as to lay siege to Jerusalem. In the greatest deluge of trouble God can and will keep the head of his people above water. Though the stretching out of the wings of the Assyrian, that bird of prey, though the right and left wing of his army, should fill the breadth of the land of Judah, yet still it is *thy land, O Immanuel!* It was to be Christ's land; for there he was to be born.

Verses 9–15

The prophet here returns to speak of the present distress that Ahaz and his court and kingdom were in upon account of the threatening confederacy of the ten tribes and the Syrians against them.

I. He triumphs over the invading enemies, and, in effect, bids them do their worst (*v.* 9, 10): "*O you people, you of far countries*, give ear to what the prophet says to you in God's name. We doubt not but you will now make your utmost efforts against Judah and Jerusalem. You *associate yourselves* in alliance. You *gird yourselves*, and again you *gird yourselves*. You *take counsel together*. *You speak the word;* you determine what to do, and are confident that the matter will be accomplished with a word's speaking. All your efforts will be ineffectual. *You shall be broken in pieces*. Not only shall your attempts be ruined, but your attempts shall be your ruin; you shall be broken by those designs you have formed against Jerusalem. *For God is with us:* he is on our side, to take our part and fight for us; and, *if God be for us, who can be against us?*"

II. He comforts and encourages the people of God with the same comforts and encouragements which he himself had received.

1. The prophet tells us how he was himself taught of God not to give way to such amazing fears (*v.* 11): "*The Lord spoke to me with a strong hand not to walk in the way of this people*, not to say as they say nor do as they do, not to approve of making peace upon any terms, or calling in the help of the Assyrians." God instructed the prophet not to go down the stream. There is a proneness in the best of men to be frightened at threatening clouds, especially when fears are epidemic.

2. Now what is it that he says to God's people?

(1) He cautions them against a sinful fear, *v.* 12. It seems it was the way of this people at this time, and fear is catching. He whose heart fails him makes

his brethren's heart to fail, like his heart (Deut. xx. 8); therefore *Say you not, A confederacy, to all those to whom this people shall say, A confederacy.* Do not join with those that are for making a league with the Assyrians, through unbelief, and distrust of God and their cause. Do not, when any little thing is amiss, cry out, There is a plot, a plot. When they talk what dismal news there is, *Syria is joined with Ephraim,* what will become of us? do not you fear their fear.

(2) He advises them to a gracious religious fear: *But sanctify the Lord of hosts himself, v.* 13. The believing fear of God is a special preservative against the disquieting fear of man; see 1 Pet. iii. 14, 15, where this is quoted, and applied to suffering Christians.

(3) He assures them of a holy security and serenity of mind in so doing (*v.* 14): *He shall be for a sanctuary;* make him your fear, and you shall find him your hope, your help, your defence, and your mighty deliverer. He will be your sanctuary, to which you may flee for safety, and where you shall not need to fear any evil.

III. He threatens the ruin of the ungodly and unbelieving, both in Judah and Israel. They have no part nor lot in the foregoing comforts. The prophet foresees that the greatest part of both the houses of Israel would not *sanctify the Lord of hosts.* What was a savour of life unto life to others would be a savour of death unto death to them. "So that *many among them shall stumble and fall.*"

Verses 16–22

I. The unspeakable privilege which the people of God enjoy in being entrusted with the sacred writings. That they may sanctify the Lord of hosts, may make him their fear and find him their sanctuary, *bind up the testimony, v.* 16. 1. It is a *testimony* and a *law;* God has attested it, and he has enjoined it. As a testimony it directs our faith; as a law it directs our practice; and we ought both to subscribe to the truths of it and to submit to the precepts of it. 2. This testimony and this law are bound up and sealed, for we are not to add to them nor diminish from them. 3. They are lodged as a sacred deposit in the hands of the disciples of *the children of the prophets and the covenant,* Acts iii. 25. This is the good thing which is committed to them, 2. Tim. i. 13, 14.

II. The good use which we ought to make of this privilege. This we are taught,

1. By the prophet's own practice and resolutions, *v.* 17, 18. He specifies two discouragements: (1) The frowns of God upon his people, whose interests lay very near his heart: "He *hides his face from the house of Jacob,* and seems at present to neglect them, and lay them under the tokens of his displeasure." (2) The contempt and reproaches of men, not only upon himself, but upon his disciples, among whom the law and the testimony were sealed: *I and the children whom the Lord has given me are for signs and wonders;* we are gazed at as outlandish people. Christ looks upon believers as his children, whom the Father gave him (John xvii. 6), and both he and they are for signs and wonders, spoken against (Luke ii. 34), everywhere spoken against, Acts xxviii. 22. He saw the hand of God in all that which was discouraging to him, and kept his eye upon that. He therefore resolved to wait upon the Lord and to look for him; to attend even while he hid his face, and to expect with a humble assurance his return in mercy.

2. By the counsel and advice which he gives to his disciples, to whom were committed the lively oracles. He supposes they would be tempted, in the day of their distress, to consult *those that had familiar spirits.* Thus Saul, when he was in straits, made his application to the witch of Endor (1 Sam. xxviii. 7, 15), and

Ahaziah to the god of Ekron, 2 Kings i. 2. These conjurors *peeped and muttered.* The words here may refer to their voice and manner of speaking. They spoke not with boldness and plainness, but as those who desire to amuse people rather than to instruct them. There were express laws against this wickedness (Lev. xix. 31; xx. 27), and yet it was found in Israel, is found even in Christian nations. Dread the use of spells and charms, and consulting those that by hidden arts pretend to tell fortunes, cure diseases. He furnishes them with an answer to this temptation, "If any go about thus to ensnare you, give them this reply: *Should not a people seek to their God?* What! *for the living to the dead!* Tell them that a people ought to seek unto their God; now Jehovah is our God, and therefore we ought to consult with him, and not with those that have familiar spirits, Mic. iv. 5. Should not a people under guilt, and in trouble, seek to their God for pardon and peace? Should not a people in doubt, in want, and in danger, seek to their God for direction, supply, and protection?" What can be more absurd than to expect that our friends that are dead should do that for us, when we deify them and pray to them, which our living friends cannot do? Necromancers consulted the dead, as the witch of Endor, and so proclaimed their own folly. He directs them to consult the oracles of God. If the prophets that were among them did not speak directly to every case, yet they had the written word, and to that they must have recourse. Those will never be drawn to consult wizards that know how to make a good use of their Bibles. Make God's statutes your counsellors, and you will be counselled aright. We must *speak according to that word,* that is, we must make this our standard (1 Tim. vi. 3). We must make this use of the law and the testimony because those that concur not with the word of God do thereby evince that *there is no light,* no morning light (so the word is) *in them.* Those that reject divine revelation have not human understanding; nor do those rightly admit the oracles of reason who will not admit the oracles of God. Some read it as a threatening: "If they speak not according to this word, there shall be no light to them, but they shall be driven to darkness and despair"; as it follows here, *v.* 21, 22. What light had Saul when he consulted the witch? 1 Sam. xxviii. 18, 20. He reads the doom of those that seek familiar spirits and regard not God's law and testimony; they may expect all horror and misery, *v.* 21, 22. They shall *pass through* the land, unfixed, unsettled; they shall be *hardly bestead* whither to go for the necessary supports of life. Those who used to be fed to the full shall be hungry. Those that go away from God go out of the way of all good. These people *when they shall be hungry shall fret themselves,* and shall be very provoking to all about them; they will forget all the rules of duty and decency, and will treasonably *curse their king* and blasphemously curse *their God.* When they have broken the bonds of their allegiance, no marvel if those of their religion do not hold them long: they next curse their God, curse him, and die. They shall look upward, but heaven shall frown upon them and look gloomy; and how can it be otherwise when they curse their God? They shall look to the earth, but what comfort can that yield to those with whom God is at war?

Chapter 9

The prophet in this chapter saith to the righteous, It shall be well with thee, but Woe to the wicked, it shall be ill with him. I. Gracious promises to those that adhere to the law and to the testimony; while those that seek familiar spirits shall be driven into darkness and dimness, they shall see a great light, relief in the midst of their distresses, typical of gospel grace. 1. In the doctrine of the Messiah, ver. 1–3. 2. His victories, ver. 4, 5. 3. His government and dominion as Immanuel, ver. 6, 7. II.

Dreadful threatenings against the people of Israel, who had revolted (ver. 8–10), their neighbours should make a prey of them (ver. 11, 12), for their impenitence and hypocrisy, all their ornaments and supports should be cut off (ver. 13–17), and by the wrath of God against them, and their wrath one against another, they should be brought to utter ruin, ver. 18–21.

Verses 1–7

The first words of this chapter plainly refer to the close of the foregoing chapter, where everything looked black and melancholy: *Behold, trouble, and darkness, and dimness*—but *to the upright there shall arise light in the darkness* (Ps. cxii. 4). *Nevertheless it shall not be such dimness* as sometimes there has been. In the worst of times God's people have a *nevertheless* to allay and balance their troubles; they are persecuted, but not forsaken (2 Cor. iv. 9), sorrowful yet always rejoicing, 2 Cor. vi. 10. And it is matter of comfort to us, when things are at the darkest, that he who *forms the light and creates the darkness* (ch. xlv. 7) has appointed to both their bounds and set the one over against the other, Gen. i. 4.

I. Three things are here promised, and they all point ultimately at the grace of the gospel, with which the saints were to comfort themselves in every cloudy and dark day.

1. A glorious light, which shall by degrees dispel the dimness, that it shall not be as it sometimes has been: *Not such as was in her vexation; when at first he lightly afflicted the land of Zebulun and Naphtali* (which lay remote and most exposed to the inroads of the neighbouring enemies, *and afterwards he more grievously afflicted the land by the way of the sea and beyond Jordan* (v. 1), 2 Kings x. 32. If a light affliction do not humble and reform us, we must expect to be afflicted more grievously. *Israel has been without the true God and a teaching priest, and in those times there was no peace.* But the dimness threatened (ch. viii. 22) shall not prevail to such a degree; for (v. 2) *the people that walked in darkness have seen a great light.* At this time when the prophet lived, there were many prophets in Judah and Israel, whose prophecies were a great light both for direction and comfort to the people of God, who adhered to the law and the testimony. This was to have its full accomplishment when our Lord Jesus began to appear as a prophet, and to preach the gospel in the land of Zebulun and Naphtali, and in Galilee of the Gentiles.

2. A glorious increase, and a universal joy arising from it (v. 3) "*Thou, O God! hast multiplied the nation*; it has been diminished by one sore judgment after another, yet now thou hast begun to multiply it again." Yet it follows, "*Thou hast not increased the joy*—the carnal joy and mirth. But, notwithstanding that, *they joy before thee*; there is a great deal of serious spiritual joy among them, joy in the presence of God." This is very applicable to the times of gospel light, spoken of v. 2. "And to him" (so the Masorites read it) "thou hast magnified the joy, to everyone that receives the light." The following words favour this reading: "*They joy before thee*; they come before thee in holy ordinances with great joy; their mirth is not like that of Israel under their vines and fig-trees (thou hast not increased that joy) but it is in the favour of God and in the tokens of his grace." It is holy joy: *They joy before thee*; they rejoice in spirit (as Christ did, Luke x. 21), and that is before God. It is a great joy; *according to the joy in harvest*, when those who have with patience waited for the precious fruits of the earth, reap in joy; and as in war men rejoice when, after a hazardous battle, *they divide the spoil*. The gospel brings with it plenty and victory.

3. A glorious liberty and enlargement (v. 4, 5): "They shall rejoice before thee, and with good reason, *for thou hast broken the yoke of his burden*, for he shall no longer be in servitude; and thou hast broken *the staff of his shoulder and the rod of his oppressor*, as the Midianites' yoke was broken from off the neck of Israel by the agency of Gideon." *Do unto them as to the Midianites.* What temporal deliverance this refers to is not clear, probably the preventing of Sennacherib from making himself master of Jerusalem, which was done, *as in the day of Midian*, by the immediate hand of God; done silently and without noise. But doubtless it looks further, to that great light which should visit those that sat in darkness; it would bring *deliverance to the captives*, Luke iv. 18. The design of the gospel is to break the yoke of sin and Satan, to remove the burden of guilt and corruption, that we might be brought into the glorious liberty of the children of God. Christ broke the yoke of the ceremonial law (Acts xv. 10; Gal. v. 1), and delivered us *out of the hand of our enemies*, that we might *serve him without fear*, Luke i. 74, 75. This is done by the Spirit working like fire (Matt. iii. 11), not as the battle of the warrior is fought, with confused noise; no, the weapons of our warfare are not carnal.

II. But who, where, is he that shall undertake and accomplish these great things for the church? The prophet tells us (v. 6, 7) they shall be done by the Messiah, *Immanuel* (ch. vii. 14), and now speaks of it, in the prophetic style, as a thing already done: *the child is born*, because the church before his incarnation reaped great benefit and advantage. As he was the Lamb slain, so he was the child born, *from the foundation of the world*, Rev. xiii. 8. All the great things that God did for the Old Testament church were done by him as the eternal Word, and for his sake as the Mediator. The Jewish nation, and particularly the house of David, were preserved many a time from imminent ruin only because that blessing was in them. The Chaldee paraphrast understands it of the man that shall endure for ever, even Christ.

1. See him in his humiliation. The same that is *the mighty God* is *a child born*; thus did he humble and empty himself, to exalt and fill us. He is born into our world. *The Word was made flesh, and dwelt among us.* God so loved the world that he gave him. He is born *to us*, he is given to us.

2. See him in his exaltation. This child, this Son of God, this Son of man, is invested with the highest honour and power so that we cannot but be happy if he be our friend. He shall be called *Wonderful, Counsellor, &c.* His people shall know him and worship him by these names. He is *wonderful, counsellor.* Justly is he called *wonderful*, for he is both God and man. He is the *counsellor*, for he was intimately acquainted with the counsels of God from eternity, and he gives counsel to the children of men. He is the wisdom of the Father, and is made of God to us wisdom. He is *the mighty God—God, the mighty One.* As he has wisdom, so he has strength. He is able to save to the utmost. He is *the everlasting Father*, or *the Father of eternity*; he is God, one with the Father, who is from everlasting to everlasting. He is the author of everlasting life and happiness to them, and so is to them the Father of a blessed eternity to them. He is *the prince of peace.* As a King, he preserves, commands, creates peace, in his kingdom. He is our peace. His throne is above every throne (v. 6): *The government shall be upon his shoulder* —his only. He shall not only wear the badge of it upon his shoulder (the *key of the house of David*, ch. xxii. 22), but he shall bear the burden of it. Glorious things are here spoken of Christ's government, v. 7. It shall be multiplied; the lustre of it shall increase, and it shall shine more and more brightly in the world. It shall be a peaceable government, agreeable to his character as the prince of peace. He shall rule by love, and as his government increases the peace shall increase. It shall be administered

with prudence and equity: *He shall order it, and settle it, with justice and judgment.* It shall be an everlasting kingdom: *There shall be no end of the increase of his government.* God himself has undertaken to bring all this about: *"The Lord of hosts*, who has all power in his hand and all creatures at his beck, *shall perform this."*

Verses 8–21

Here are terrible threatenings directed primarily against Israel, the kingdom of the ten tribes, Ephraim and Samaria, the ruin of which is here foretold, all which came to pass within a few years, but they look further and read the doom of all the nations that forget God, and will not have Christ to reign over them.

I. The preface to this prediction (*v.* 8): *The Lord sent a word into Jacob,* sent it by his servants the prophets. He warns before he wounds, but they took no care to turn away his wrath. It fell upon them as a storm of rain and hail from on high, which they could not avoid.

II. The sins charged upon the people of Israel, which provoked God to bring these judgments upon them. 1. Their insolent defiance of the justice of God, thinking themselves a match for him: "They *say, in the pride and stoutness of their heart,* Let God himself do his worst. If he ruin our houses, we will repair them, and make them stronger. If the houses that were built of bricks be demolished in the war, we will rebuild them with hewn stones. If the enemy cut down the sycamores, we will plant cedars." 2. Their incorrigibleness under all the rebukes of Providence hitherto (*v.* 13): *The people turn not unto him that smiteth them, neither do they seek the Lord of hosts;* either they are atheists, and have no religion, or idolators, and seek those gods that are the creatures of their own fancy and the works of their own hands. 3. Their general corruption of manners and abounding profaneness. Those that should have reformed them helped to debauch them (*v.* 16): *The leaders of this people* mislead them, and *cause them to err.* But it is ill with a people when their physicians are their worst disease. *"Those, that bless this people,* or *call them blessed* (so the margin reads it), that flatter them, and soothe them in their wickedness, and cry *Peace, peace, to them,* cause them to err." We have reason to be afraid of those that speak well of us when we do ill; see Prov. xxiv. 24; xxix. 5. Wickedness was universal, and all were infected with it (*v.* 17): *Every one is a hypocrite and an evil doer.* Everyone is profane towards God (so the word properly signifies) and an evil doer towards man. These two commonly go together: those that fear not God regard not men.

III. The judgments threatened against them for this wickedness of theirs.

1. In general, hereby they exposed themselves to the wrath of God. It should devour as fire (*v.* 18): *Wickedness shall burn as the fire.* The briers and thorns, when the fire consumes them, shall *mount up like the lifting up of smoke,* so that the whole land shall be darkened by it; they shall be in trouble, and see no way out (*v.* 19): *The people shall be as the fuel of the fire.*

2. God would arm the neighbouring powers against them, *v.* 11, 12. At this time Israel was in league with Syria against Judah; but the Assyrians, who were adversaries to the Syrians, when they had conquered them should invade Israel, and God would join the enemies of Israel together in alliance. Those that partake with each other in sin, as Syria and Israel in invading Judah, must expect to share in the punishment of sin. The Syrians themselves, whom they were now in league with, should be a scourge to them, they before and the Philistines behind. They should be surrounded with enemies on all sides, who should

devour them with open mouths, *v.* 12. The Philistines were not now looked upon as formidable enemies, and the Syrians were looked upon as firm friends; and yet these shall devour Israel.

3. God would take from the midst of them those they confided in, *v.* 14, 15. *The Lord will cut off head and tail, branch and rush,* which is explained in the next verse. (1) Their magistrates, who were honourable by birth and office were *the head,* these were the branch; but because these caused them to err they should be cut off. (2) Their false prophets, were *the tail* and the *rush,* the most despicable of all. A wicked minister is the worst of men. *Corruptio optimi est pessima—The best things become when corrupted the worst.*

4. The desolation should be as general as the corruption had been, and none should escape it, *v.* 17. *The Lord shall have no joy in their young men,* that were in the flower of their youth; nor will he say, *Deal gently with the young men for my sake.* He *shall not have mercy on their fatherless and widows,* though he is, in a particular manner, the patron and protector of such. They had corrupted their way like all the rest.

5. Every one should help forward the common ruin, *No man shall spare his brother.* Civil wars soon bring a kingdom to desolation. Such there were in Israel. In these broils, men *snatched on the right hand, and yet were hungry* still, and did eat the *flesh of their own arms,* preyed upon themselves for hunger, *v.* 20. This bespeaks famine and scarcity. These broils should be not only among particular persons and private families, but among the tribes (*v.* 21): *Manasseh shall devour Ephraim, and Ephraim Manasseh.* Those that could unite against Judah could not unite with one another. Mutual enmity and animosity among the tribes of God's Israel is a sin that ripens them for ruin, and a sad symptom of ruin hastening on apace.

6. Though they should be followed with all these judgments, yet God would not let fall his controversy with them. It is the burden of this song (*v.* 12, 21): *For all this his anger is not turned away, but his hand is stretched out still.* They do not repent and reform. His anger therefore continues to burn against them and *his hand is stretched out still. The people turn not to him that smites them,* and therefore he continues to smite them.

CHAPTER 10

The prophet, in this chapter, is dealing, I. With the proud oppressors of his people at home, that abused their power, ver. 1–4. II. With a threatening invader of his people from abroad, Sennacherib king of Assyria, concerning whom observe, 1. The commission given him to invade Judah, ver. 5, 6. 2. His pride and insolence in the execution of that commission, ver. 7–11, 13, 14. 3. A rebuke given to his haughtiness, and a threatening of his fall and ruin, when he had served the purposes for which God raised him up, ver. 12, 15–19. 4. A promise of grace to the people of God, to enable them to bear up under the affliction, ver. 20–23. 5. Great encouragement given to them not to fear this threatening storm, but to hope that it would end in the destruction of this formidable enemy, ver. 24–34.

Verses 1–4

Whether they were the princes and judges of Israel or Judah, or both, that the prophet denounced this woe against, is not certain. Here is,

I. The indictment drawn up against these oppressors, *v.* 1, 2. They are charged, 1. With making wicked laws and edicts: They *decree unrighteous decrees.* Woe to the superior powers that devise these decrees! And woe to the inferior officers that draw them up, and enter them upon record—*the writers that write the grievousness.* 2. With perverting justice in the execution of the laws that were made. 3. With enriching themselves by oppressing those that lay at their mercy. They *rob the fatherless* of the little that is left them, because they have no friend to appear for them.

II. A challenge given them with all their pride and power to outface the judgments of God (v. 3): "*What will you do? To whom will you flee?* You can trample upon the widows and fatherless; but *what will you do when God riseth up?*" Job xxxi. 14. "*Where will you leave your glory*, to find it again when the storm is over?" The wealth they had got was their glory, and they had no place of safety in which to deposit it.

III. Sentence passed upon them, by which they are doomed, some to imprisonment and captivity (*they shall bow down among the prisoners*, or *under them*) others to death. Those that had trampled upon the widows and fatherless shall themselves be trodden down, v. 4. "This it will come to," says God, "*without me*, that is, because you have deserted me and driven me away from you."

Verses 5–19

The destruction of the kingdom of Israel by Shalmaneser king of Assyria was foretold in the foregoing chapter, and it had its accomplishment in the sixth year of Hezekiah, 2 Kings xviii. 10. It was total and final, head and tail were all cut off. Now the correction of the kingdom of Judah by Sennacherib king of Assyria is foretold in this chapter; and this prediction was fulfilled in the fourteenth year of Hezekiah (2 Kings xviii. 13, 17). It ended in the confusion of the Assyrians and the great encouragement of Hezekiah and his people in their return to God.

I. God, in his sovereignty, deputed the king of Assyria to be his servant, and made use of him as a tool (v. 5, 6): "*O Assyrian!* know this, that thou art *the rod of my anger*; and I will send thee to be a scourge to *the people of my wrath.*" The Jews though they appeared very good, were *a hypocritical nation*, that made a profession of religion, and at this time particularly of reformation, but were not truly religious, not truly reformed. Hezekiah had in a great measure cured them of their idolatry, and now they ran into profaneness; hypocrisy is profaneness. Being a profane hypocritical nation, they are the people of God's wrath. See what a change sin made: those that had been God's chosen and hallowed people, had now become the *people of his wrath*, Amos iii. 2. The Assyrian, though he appeared very great, was but *the rod of God's anger*, an instrument God was pleased to make use of for the chastening of his people. *The staff in their hand*, wherewith they smite his people, *is his indignation*; it is his wrath that puts the staff into their hand. Sometimes God makes an idolatrous nation, that serves him not at all, a scourge to a hypocritical nation, that serves him not in sincerity and truth. The Assyrian is called the *rod of God's anger*. *I will send him; I will give him a charge.* The Assyrian is *to take the spoil and to take the prey*, not to shed any blood. He is to plunder the country, rifle the houses, drive away the cattle, strip the people of all their wealth and ornaments, and *tread them down like the mire of the streets*. But why must the Assyrian prevail thus against them? Not that they might be ruined, but that they might be reformed.

II. The king of Assyria, in his pride, pretended to be absolute and to act for his own honour. *God ordained him for judgment* to be an instrument of bringing his people to repentance, *howbeit he means not so, nor does his heart think so*, v. 7. He does not think that he is either God's servant or Israel's friend. God designs to correct his people, and to cure them of their hypocrisy, and bring them nearer to himself; but was that Sennacherib's design? He designs nothing but *to destroy and to cut off nations not a few*, and to make himself master of them. He designs to gratify his own covetousness and to set up for a universal monarch. By his general's letter to Hezekiah, written in his name, vainglory and arrogance seem to have entered into the spirit of the man. His haughtiness and presumption are here described, partly to represent him as ridiculous and partly to assure the people of God that he would be brought down. He boasts of the great things he had done to other nations. He had made their kings his courtiers (v. 8): "*My princes are altogether kings.* Those that are now my princes are such as have been kings." Or those that were absolute princes in their own dominions held their crowns under him, and did him homage. He had made himself master of cities. He names several (v. 9) that were all alike reduced by him. *Calno* soon yielded *as Carchemish* did, *Hamath* could not hold out any more than *Arpad*, and *Samaria* had become his as well as *Damascus*. He *found out the kingdoms of the idols* and found out ways to make them his own, v. 10. Sennacherib vainly imagined that every conquest of a kingdom was the conquest of a god. He had enlarged his own dominions, and *removed the bounds of the people* (v. 13), enclosing many large territories within the limits of his own kingdom. *I have robbed their treasures.* Great conquerors are often no better than great robbers. "*I have put down the inhabitants as a valiant man.* Those that sat high I have humbled." He boasts he had done all this by his own policy and power (v. 13): "*By the strength of my hand*, for I am valiant; *and by my wisdom, for I am prudent.*" He had done all this with ease, and had made but a diversion of it, as if he had been taking birds' nests (v. 14): *My hand has found as a nest the riches of the people.* "*As one gathers the eggs that are left* in the nest by the dam, so easily *have I gathered all the earth.*" Like Alexander, he thought he had conquered the world. He threatens what he will do to Jerusalem, which he was now about to lay siege to, v. 10, 11. He blasphemously calls the God of Israel an *idol*, and sets him on a level with the false gods of other nations, as if none were the true God but Mithras, the sun, whom he worshipped. He might have known that the worshippers of the God of Israel were expressly forbidden to make any graven images, and if any did it must be by stealth, and therefore they could not be so rich and pompous as those of other nations. If he means the ark and the mercy-seat, he speaks like himself, very foolishly. Those who make external pomp and splendour a mark of the true church go by the same rule. Because he had conquered Samaria he concluded Jerusalem would fall. But it did not follow; for Jerusalem adhered to her God, whereas Samaria had forsaken him.

III. God, in his justice, rebukes his pride and reads his doom.

1. He shows the vanity of his insolent and audacious boasts (v. 15): *Shall the axe boast itself against him that hews therewith? or shall the saw magnify itself against him that shaketh it?* "O what a dust do I make!" said the fly upon the cart-wheel in the fable. "What destruction do I make among the trees!" says the axe. Two ways the axe may be said to *boast itself against him that hews with it*: By way of resistance and opposition. Sennacherib blasphemed God, threatened to serve him as he had served the gods of the nations; now this was as if the axe should fly in the face of him that hews with it. The tool striving with the workman is no less absurd than the clay striving with the potter; and as it is a thing not to be justified that men should fight against God with the wit, and wealth, and power, which he gives them, so it is a thing not to be suffered. By way of competition. Shall the axe take to itself the praise of the work it is employed in? So absurd was it for Sennacherib to say, *By the strength of my hand I have done it, and by my wisdom*, v. 13. It is as if the rod, when it is shaken, should boast that it guides the hand which shakes it; whereas, *when the staff is lifted up, is it not wood still?*

2. He foretells his fall and ruin. When God had done his work by him he would then do his work upon him, *v.* 12. In reference to Sennacherib's invasion, God designed to do good to Zion and Jerusalem by this providence. When God brings his people into trouble it is to bring sin to their remembrance, and to awaken them to a sense of their duty, to teach them to pray and to love and help one another. When these points are, in some measure, gained by the affliction, it shall be removed, in mercy (Lev. xxvi. 41, 42). The rod shall *accomplish that for which God sends it.* When God had wrought this work of grace for his people he would work a work of wrath upon their invaders: *I will punish the fruit of the stout heart of the king of Assyria.* This attempt upon Zion and Jerusalem should certainly be baffled, and come to nothing, *v.* 16, 19. God himself will do it, as *the Lord of hosts,* and as *the light of Israel.* We are sure he can do it, for he is *the Lord of hosts,* of all the hosts of heaven and earth. We have reason to hope he will do it, for he is *the light of Israel, and his Holy One.* This destruction shall be as a consumption of the body by a disease: *The Lord shall send leanness among his fatnesses,* or *his fat ones.* His numerous army, that was like a body covered with fatness, shall be diminished, and waste away, and become like a skeleton. *Under his glory he will kindle a burning, as the burning of a fire,* which shall lay his army in ruins as suddenly as a raging fire lays a stately house in ashes. *The light of Israel shall be for a fire* to the Assyrians, as the same pillar of cloud was a light to the Israelites and a terror to the Egyptians in the Red Sea. *It shall burn and devour its thorns and briers,* his officers and soldiers, as thorns and briers. "Even *the glory of his forest* (*v.* 18), the choice troops of his army, that he valued as men do their timber-trees (the glory of their forest) or their fruit-trees (the glory of their Carmel), shall be put as briers and thorns before the fire." The prophet tells us the army would hereby be reduced to a very small number: *The rest of the trees of his forest shall be few.* Those few who remained should be quite dispirited: *They shall be as when a standard-bearer fainteth.*

Verses 20–23

The prophet had said (*v.* 12) that *the Lord would perform his whole work upon Mount Zion and upon Jerusalem,* by Sennacherib's invading the land.

I. The conversion of some, to whom this providence should yield the peaceable fruit of righteousness, though for the present it was not joyous, but grievous; these are but a remnant (*v.* 22), *the remnant of Israel* (*v.* 20), *the remnant of Jacob* (*v.* 21). This remnant of Israel are said to be *such as had escaped of the house of Jacob,* such as escaped the corruptions of the house of Jacob, and kept their integrity in times of common apostasy. "They *shall no more again stay upon him that smote them,* shall never depend upon the Assyrians for help against their other enemies, finding that they are themselves their worst enemies." "*The remnant shall return* (that was signified by the name of the prophet's son, *Shearjashub, ch.* vii. 3), *even the remnant of Jacob.* They shall return, after the raising of the siege of Jerusalem, not only to the quiet possession of their houses and lands, but to God and to their duty; they shall repent, and pray, and seek his face, and reform their lives." This promise of the conversion and salvation of a remnant of Israel is applied by the apostle (Rom. ix. 27) to the remnant of the Jews which at the first preaching of the gospel received and entertained it.

II. The consumption of others: *The Lord God of hosts shall make a consumption, v.* 23. This meant the consumption of the estates and families of many of the Jews by the Assyrian army. It is *determined,* not only that there shall be such a consumption, but it is *cut out* (so the word is); it is particularly appointed how far it shall extend and how long it shall continue. God will justly bring this consumption upon a provoking people, but he will wisely and graciously set bounds to it.

Verses 24–34

The prophet, in his preaching, distinguishes between the precious and the vile. He speaks terror, in Sennacherib's invasion, to the hypocrites, who were the *people of God's wrath, v.* 6. But here he speaks comfort to the sincere, who were the people of God's love.

I. An exhortation to God's people not to be frightened at this threatening calamity. *Let the sinners in Zion be afraid* (*ch.* xxxiii. 14); but *O my people, that dwellest in Zion, be not afraid of the Assyrian, v.* 24.

II. The silencing of their fear. The Assyrian shall do nothing against them but what God has appointed and determined. The storm shall soon blow over (*v.* 25): *Yet a very little while—a little, little while* (so the word is), *and the indignation shall cease, even my anger,* which is *the staff in their hand* (*v.* 5). The enemy that threatens them shall himself be reckoned with. He *lifted up his staff* against Zion, but God *shall stir up a scourge for him* (*v.* 26); he is a terror to God's people, but God will be a terror to him. The prophet, for the encouragement of God's people, quotes precedents. The destruction of the Assyrian shall be *According to the slaughter of Midian* (which was effected by an invisible power), and as, *at the rock of Oreb,* one of the princes of Midian, after the battle, was slain, so shall Sennacherib be after the defeat of his forces. *As his rod was upon the sea,* the Red Sea, to divide it for the escape of Israel and then to close it for the destruction of their pursuers so shall his rod now be *lifted up, after the manner of Egypt,* for the deliverance of Jerusalem and the destruction of the Assyrian. They shall be wholly delivered from the power of the Assyrian, and from the fear of it, *v.* 27. The yoke shall not only be taken away, but it *shall be destroyed, because of the anointing:* (1) For Hezekiah's sake, the anointed of the Lord, an active reformer, dear to God. (2) For David's sake. This is why God would defend Jerusalem from Sennacherib (*ch.* xxxvii. 35). (3) For his people Israel's sake, the good people among them. (4) For the sake of the Messiah, the Anointed of God.

III. The terror of the enemy and the terror with which many were struck, *v.* 28.

1. How formidable the Assyrians were! Here is a particular description of the march of Sennacherib, what swift advances he made: *He has come to Aiath,* &c. At Michmash he has laid up his carriages, as if he had no further occasion for his heavy artillery, so easily was every place reduced; or the store-cities of Judah, fortified, had now become his magazines. Some remarkable pass he had taken: *They have gone over the passage.*

2. How cowardly the men of Judah were, the degenerate seed of that lion's whelp. They *fled* upon the first alarm. And *poor Anathoth,* a priests' city, that should have been a pattern of courage, shrieks louder than any, *v.* 30. With respect to those that *gathered themselves* together, it was not to fight, but to flee by consent, *v* 31. This shows how fast the news of the enemy's progress flew through the kingdom: *He has come to Aiath,* says one, nay, says another, *He has passed to Migron,* &c.

3. How impotent his attempt upon Jerusalem shall be: *He shall remain at Nob,* whence he may see Mount Zion, and there *he shall shake his hand* against it, *v.* 32. He shall threaten it, and that shall be all.

4. How fatal it would prove to himself. When he *shakes his hand at Jerusalem, the Lord shall lop the bough with terror and cut down the thickets of the*

forest, v. 33, 34. The high and stately trees shall be hewn down; that is, the haughty shall be humbled. *The thickets of the forest he shall cut down.* The Assyrian soldiers under arms, their spears erect, looked like a forest, like Lebanon; but, when in one night they all became as dead, Lebanon was of a sudden cut down *by a mighty one*, by the destroying angel, and, if this be the exit of that proud invader, let not God's people be afraid of him.

CHAPTER 11

It is a very good transition in prophecy to pass from the prediction of the temporal deliverances of the church to that of the great salvation, which in the fulness of time should be wrought out by Jesus Christ, of which the other were types and figures. Upon the prophecy of the deliverance of Jerusalem from Sennacherib comes a prophecy concerning Messiah the Prince. I. His rise out of the house of David, ver. 1. II. His qualifications for his great undertaking, ver. 2, 3. III. The justice and equity of his government, ver. 3–5. IV. The peaceableness of his kingdom, ver. 6–9. V. The accession of the Gentiles to it (ver. 10), and with them the remnant of the Jews, that should be united with them in the Messiah's kingdom, ver. 11–16. God would shortly give them a type, and some dark representation, in the excellent government of Hezekiah, the great peace which the nation should enjoy under him, after the ruin of Sennacherib's design, and the return of many of the ten tribes out of their dispersion to their brethren of the land of Judah.

Verses 1–9

The prophet had before spoken of a child that should be born, on whose shoulders the government should be. He had said (*ch.* x. 27) that *the yoke should be destroyed because of the anointing*; now here he tells us on whom that anointing should rest.

I. The Messiah should, in due time, arise out of the house of David, as that *branch* of the Lord which he had said (*ch.* iv. 2) should be glorious. This branch should arise—from *Jesse*. He should be the son of David, with whom the covenant of royalty was made. David is often called *the son of Jesse*, and Christ is called so. He is called a *rod*, and a *branch*; both the words here used signify a small, tender product, a *twig* and a *sprig*, such as is easily broken off. The enemies of God's church were just before compared to stately boughs (*ch.* x. 33), but Christ to a tender branch (*ch.* liii. 2); yet he shall be victorious over them. He is said to come out of Jesse rather than David, because Jesse lived and died in meanness and obscurity; his family was of small account (1 Sam. xviii. 18). He comes forth out of the *stem*, or *stump*, of Jesse. The house of David was reduced and brought very low at the time of Christ's birth, witness the obscurity and poverty of Joseph and Mary. The Chaldee paraphrase reads this, *There shall come forth a King from the sons of Jesse, and the Messiah* (or Christ) *shall be anointed out of his sons' sons*.

II. He should be every way qualified for that great work to which he was designed. This tender branch should be so watered with the dews of heaven as to become a strong rod for a sceptre to rule, *v.* 2. *The Spirit of the Lord shall rest upon him.* He shall have the Spirit not by measure, but without measure, the fulness of the Godhead dwelling in him, Col. i. 19; ii. 9. He began his preaching with this (Luke iv. 18), *The Spirit of the Lord is upon me.* He shall have *the spirit of wisdom and understanding, of counsel and knowledge.* He shall know how to administer the affair of his spiritual kingdom to the glory of God and the welfare of men. He was famed for courage in his teaching the way of God in truth, and not caring for any man, Matt. xxii. 16.

III. He should be accurate, and exact in the administration of his government and the exercise of the power committed to him (*v.* 3): The Spirit wherewith he shall be clothed *shall make him of quick understanding in the fear of the Lord.* Jesus Christ had the spirit without measure, that he might perfectly understand his undertaking.

IV. He should be just and righteous in all the acts of his government. *He shall not judge after the sight of his eyes*, with respect of persons (Job xxxiv. 19), nor *reprove after the hearing of his ears*, by the representations of others, as men commonly do; nor by the fair words they speak, *calling him, Lord, Lord*; but he will judge by the hidden man of the heart, and the inward principles men are governed by, of which he is an infallible witness. He will judge righteous judgment (*v.* 5): *Righteousness shall be the girdle of his loins.* It shall constantly compass him and shall be his honour; he shall gird himself for every action, shall gird on his sword for war in righteousness. *With righteousness shall he judge the poor;* he shall judge in favour and defence of those that have right on their side, though they are poor in the world, and because they are poor in spirit. Christ is the poor man's King, Ps. lxxii. 2, 4. He shall *debate with evenness for the meek of the earth*, or of the land. Some read it, *He shall reprove or correct the meek of the earth with equity.* If his own people, the meek of the land, do amiss, he will *visit their transgression with the rod.* But he shall smite the earth, the man of the earth, that doth oppress (Ps. x. 18) *with the rod of his mouth*, the word of his mouth, speaking terror and ruin to them. *With the breath of his lips*, by the operation of his Spirit, according to his word, *he shall slay the wicked.*

V. That there should be great peace and tranquillity under his government (*ch.* ix. 6). Peace signifies two things:

1. Unity or concord, intimated in these figurative promises, that even *the wolf shall dwell* peaceably *with the lamb*; men of the most fierce and furious dispositions shall have their temper so strangely altered by the grace of Christ that they shall live in love even with the weakest and such as formerly were an easy prey. Christ, who is our peace, came to slay all enmities and to settle lasting friendships among his followers, particularly between Jews and Gentiles. *The leopard shall* not only not tear the kid, but shall *lie down with her*: even *their young ones shall lie down together*, and shall be trained up in blessed amity. *The lion* shall cease to be ravenous and *shall eat straw like the ox*, as some think all the beasts of prey did before the fall. *The asp* and *the cockatrice* shall cease to be venomous, so that parents shall let their children *play* with them. A generation of vipers shall become a seed of saints. This is fulfilled in the wonderful effect of the gospel upon the minds of those that sincerely embrace it; it changes the nature, and makes those that trampled on the meek of the earth, not only meek like them, but affectionate towards them. Some hope it shall yet have a further accomplishment in the latter days, when *swords shall be beaten into ploughshares.*

2. Safety or security. Christ, the great Shepherd, shall take such care of his flock that they shall not only not destroy one another, but no enemy from without shall be permitted to give them any molestation. God's people shall be delivered, not only from evil, but from the fear of it. The effect of it shall be tractableness, and a willingness to receive instruction: *A little child shall lead those* who formerly scorned to be controlled by the strongest man. The cause of it shall be the knowledge of God. The more there is of that the more there is of a disposition to peace. *The earth shall be full of the knowledge of the Lord*, which shall extinguish men's heats and animosities. There is much more of the knowledge of God to be got by the gospel of Christ than could be got by the law of Moses.

Verses 10–16

A further prophecy of the enlargement and advancement of the kingdom of the Messiah, under the figure of Judah in the latter end of Hezekiah's reign, after the defeat of Sennacherib.

I. This prediction was in part accomplished when the great things God did for Hezekiah and his people proved as an ensign, inviting the neighbouring nations to them *to enquire of the wonders done in the land*, on which errand the king of Babylon's ambassadors came. To them the Gentiles sought; and Jerusalem was then glorious, *v.* 10. Then many of the Israelites of the ten tribes, who were forced by the king of Assyria to flee for shelter into all the countries about, were encouraged to return to their own country and put themselves under the protection of the king of Judah. This is said to be a recovery of them *the second time* (*v.* 11), such an instance of the power of God as their first deliverance out of Egypt. Then the *outcasts of Israel* should be brought home, and those of Judah too. Then the old feud between Ephraim and Judah shall be forgotten, and they shall join against the Philistines and their other common enemies, *v,* 13, 14. When God's time has come for the deliverance of his people mountains of opposition shall become plain before him. Let us not despair therefore when the interests of the church seem to be brought very low; God can soon turn gloomy days into glorious ones.

II. It had a further reference to the days of the Messiah and the accession of the Gentiles to his kingdom; for to these the apostle applies *v.* 10, of which the following verses are a continuation. Rom. xv. 12, *There shall be a root of Jesse; and he that shall rise to reign over the Gentiles, in him shall the Gentiles trust.* That is a key to this prophecy, which speaks of Christ as the root of Jesse, or *a branch out of his roots* (*v.* 1), *a root out of a dry ground*, ch. liii. 2.

1. *He shall stand*, or be set up, *for an ensign of the people.* When he was crucified he was *lifted up from the earth*, that, as an ensign or beacon, he might *draw* the eyes and the hearts of *all men unto him*, John xii. 32. He is set up as an ensign in the preaching of the everlasting gospel, in which the ministers are as standard-bearers.

2. *To him shall the Gentiles seek.* We read of Greeks that did so (John xii. 21, *We would see Jesus*).

3. *His rest shall be glorious.* Some understand this of the death of Christ (the triumphs of the cross made even that glorious), others of his ascension, when he sat down to rest at the right hand of God. Or rather it is meant of the gospel church.

4. Both Jews and Gentiles shall be gathered to him, *v.* 11. A remnant of both, a little remnant in comparison, recovered with great difficulty. There shall be a remnant of the Jews gathered in: *The outcasts of Israel and the dispersed of Judah* (*v.* 12), many of whom, at the time of the bringing of them in to Christ, were *Jews of the dispersion*.

5. There shall be a happy accommodation between Judah and Ephraim, and both shall be safe from their adversaries and have dominion over them, *v.* 13, 14. The coalescence between Judah and Israel at that time was a type and figure of the uniting of Jews and Gentiles. *For they shall fly upon the shoulders of the Philistines*, as an eagle strikes at her prey, and shall extend their conquests eastward over the Edomites, Moabites, and Ammonites. Some of all nations shall become obedient to the faith.

6. Everything that might hinder the progress and success of the gospel shall be taken out of the way, so when Jews and Gentiles are to be brought together into the gospel church all obstructions shall be removed (*v.* 15, 16), difficulties that seemed insuperable shall be strangely got over, *the blind shall be led by a way that they knew not*. See *ch.* xlii. 15, 16; xliii. 19, 20. Converts shall be brought in chariots and in litters, *ch.* lxvi. 20.

CHAPTER 12

The salvation promised in the foregoing chapter was compared to that of Israel "in the day that he came up out of the land of Egypt". As Moses and the children of Israel then sang a song of praise to the glory of God (Exod. xv. 1) so shall the people of God do in that day when the root of Jesse shall stand for an ensign of the people and shall be the desire and joy of all nations. In that day, I. Every believer shall sing a song of praise (ver. 1, 3). "Thou shalt say, Lord, I will praise thee." II. Many shall join in praising God for the common benefit arising from this salvation (ver. 4–6).

Verses 1–3

This is the former part of the hymn of praise prepared for the use of the Jewish church when God would work great deliverances for them, and of the Christian church when the kingdom of the Messiah should be set up in the world. The scattered church, being united into one body, shall, as one man, thus praise God.

I. The promise is sure, and the blessings contained when they are bestowed, will furnish the church with abundant matter for thanksgiving.

II. *Thou shalt say*, that is, thou oughtest to say so. *In that day*, when many are brought home to Jesus Christ and flock to him as doves to their windows, *thou shalt say, O Lord! I will praise thee. O Lord! I will praise thee, though thou wast angry with me.* Even God's frowns must not put us out of tune for praising him. By Jesus Christ, the root of Jesse, God's anger against mankind was turned away; for *he is our peace*. Those whom God is reconciled to he comforts. God sometimes brings his people into a wilderness that there he may *speak comfortably to them*, Hosea ii. 14. They are taught to triumph in God (*v.* 2): "*Behold*, and wonder; *God is my salvation;* not only my Saviour, by whom I am saved, but my salvation, in whom I am safe." We have work to do and temptations to resist, and we may depend upon him to enable us for both. We have many troubles to undergo, and we may depend upon him to comfort us in all our tribulations, for he *giveth songs in the night.* Observe the title here given to God: *Jah, Jehovah.* Jah is the contraction of Jehovah, and both signify his eternity and unchangeableness, which are a great comfort to those that depend upon him as their strength and their song. "*Therefore*, because the Lord Jehovah is your strength and song and will be your salvation, *out of the wells of salvation* in God, who is the fountain of all good to his people, *you shall draw water with joy.* God's promises revealed, ratified, and given out to us, in his ordinances, are wells of salvation.

Verses 4–6

This is the second part of this evangelical song, and believers stir up themselves to praise God and here invite and encourage one another to do it.

I. *The inhabitants of Zion* and Jerusalem, whom God had protected from Sennacherib's violence, *v.* 6, ought to be most forward and zealous in praising him. *Thou inhabitress of Zion;* the word is feminine. Let women be strong in the Lord, and out of their mouth praise shall be perfected.

II. Praise the Lord by prayer: *Call upon his name.* We must not only speak to God, but speak to others concerning him, *proclaim his name. Declare his doings among the people*, among the heathen, that they may be brought into communion with Israel and the God of Israel. When the apostles preached the gospel to all nations, beginning at Jerusalem, then this scripture was fulfilled. "*Cry out and shout;* welcome the gospel to yourselves and publish it to others with huzzas and loud acclamations, as those that *shout for victory* (Exod. xxxii. 18) or for the coronation of a king," Num. xxiii. 21. *Great is the Holy One*, for he is glorious in holiness; *therefore* great, because holy. It is the happiness of Israel that the God who is in covenant with them, and in the midst of them, is infinitely great.

CHAPTER 13

Hitherto the prophecies of this book related only to Judah and Israel, and Jerusalem especially; but now the prophet begins to read the doom of the neighbouring states and kingdoms: for he that is King of saints is also King of nations. But the nations to whom these prophecies relate were all such as the people of God were in some way or other concerned with Deut. xxxii. 8, 9. The threatenings we find here against Babylon, Moab, Damascus, Egypt, Tyre, &c., were intended for comfort to those in Israel that feared God, but were terrified and oppressed by those potent neighbours, and for alarm to those among them that were wicked. This chapter and that which follows contain what God had to say to Babylon and Babylon's king, who would in process of time become a greater enemy to them than any other had been, for which God would at last reckon with them. In this chapter we have, I. A general rendezvous of the forces that were to be employed against Babylon, ver. 1–5. II. The bloody work that those forces should make in Babylon, ver. 6–18. III. The utter ruin and desolation of Babylon, ver. 19–22.

Verses 1–5

The general title of this book was, *The vision of Isaiah the son of Amoz, ch.* i. 1, but the particular inscription of this sermon is *the burden of Babylon.* It is a burden, a lesson they were to learn (so some understand it), but it would be a load which should lie heavily upon them. It is the burden of Babylon or Babel, which at this time was a dependent upon the Assyrian monarchy (the metropolis of which was Nineveh), but soon after revolted and became a monarchy of itself, a very potent one, in Nebuchadnezzar. This prophet afterwards foretold the captivity of the Jews in Babylon, *ch.* xxxix. 6. In these verses a summons is given to those powerful nations whom God would use as instruments for the destruction of Babylon; he names them (*v.* 17) the *Medes,* who, in conjunction with the Persians, under the command of Darius and Cyrus, were the ruin of the Babylonian monarchy.

I. Babylon is here called *the gates of the nobles* (*v.* 2), because of the abundance of noblemen's houses that were in it. But *the whole land* is doomed to destruction (*v.* 5); for, though the nobles were the leaders in persecuting, yet the whole land concurred with them in it.

II. The persons brought together to lay Babylon waste are here called God's *sanctified ones* (*v.* 3), designed for this service and set apart to it by the purpose and providence of God. It intimates that in God's intention, though not in theirs, it was a holy war; they designed the enlargement of their own empire, but God designed the release of his people. Cyrus, the person principally concerned, was justly called a *sanctified one,* for he was God's anointed (*ch.* xlv. 1) and a figure of him that was to come. They are called God's *mighty ones,* because they had their might from God and were now to use it for him. It is said of Cyrus that in this expedition *God held his right hand, ch.* xlv. 1. Though Cyrus did not know God, yet God used him as his servant (*ch.* xlv. 4, *I have surnamed thee* as my servant, though *thou hast not known me*). They are very numerous, *a multitude, a great people, kingdoms of nations* (*v.* 4), not rude and barbarous, but regular troops. *They come from a far country, from the end of* heaven. The vast country of Assyria lay between Babylon and Persia.

III. The summons given them is effectual, *A banner is lifted up upon the high mountain, v.* 2. It is the *Lord of hosts* that musters *the host of the battle, v.* 4.

Verses 6–18

We have here a description of the terrible desolation which should be made in Babylon by the Medes and Persians. Those that were now secure were bidden to *howl* and lament for,

I. *The day of the Lord is at hand* (*v.* 6), a little day of judgment, when God will act as a just avenger of his own and his people's injured cause. *The day of the Lord cometh, v.* 9. God will deal in severity with them for the severities they exercised upon God's people.

II. Their hearts shall fail them, and they shall have neither courage nor comfort left, *v.* 7, 8. Those that in the day of peace were *proud,* and *haughty,* and *terrible* (*v.* 11), shall, when trouble comes, be dispirited and at their wits' end: *All hands shall be faint,* and unable to hold a weapon, *and every man's heart shall melt, they shall be amazed one at another.* In frightening themselves, they shall frighten one another. *Their faces shall be as flames,* pale as flames, through fear, or red as flames, blushing at their cowardice.

III. All hope shall fail them (*v.* 10): *The stars of heaven shall not give their light,* but shall be clouded and *the sun shall be darkened in his going forth,* a certain sign of foul weather.

IV. God will visit them *for their iniquity,* particularly the sin of pride, *v.* 11. That pride must now have its fall: *The haughtiness of the terrible* must now be *laid low,* particularly of Nebuchadnezzar and his son Belshazzar, who had, in their pride, trampled upon the people of God.

V. So great a slaughter will produce a scarcity of men (*v.* 12): *I will make a man more precious than fine gold.* Populous countries are soon depopulated by war.

VI. Such a confusion of their affairs shall be like the *shaking of the heavens* with thunders and the *removing of the earth* by earthquakes. All shall go to rack and ruin *in the day of the wrath of the Lord of hosts, v.* 13. Babylon, which used to be like a roaring lion and a raging bear shall become *as a chased roe and as a sheep that no man takes up, v.* 14. The army consisting of troops of divers nations, shall be so dispirited and dispersed, that they shall *turn every man to his own people.*

VII. There shall be a scene of blood and horror, as is usual where the sword devours. The conqueror gives no quarter, but puts all to the sword. Those of other nations that come in to their assistance shall be cut off with them. Since the most sacred laws of nature, and of humanity itself are silenced by the fury of war, the conquerors shall, in the most barbarous manner, *dash the children to pieces, and ravish the wives, v.* 16.

VIII. The enemy shall be inexorable. These Medes, in conjunction with the Persians, shall take no bribes, *v.* 17. The Medes *shall not regard silver.* They shall show no pity (*v.* 18), not to *the young men* that are in the prime; nor to the age of innocency— *they shall have no pity on the fruit of the womb, nor spare little children.*

Verses 19–22

The great havoc and destruction which it was foretold should be made by the Medes and Persians in Babylon here end in final destruction. Babylon was a noble city. It was *the glory of kingdoms and the beauty of the Chaldees' excellency;* it was that *head of gold* (Dan. ii. 37, 38); it was called *the lady of kingdoms* (*ch.* xlvii. 5), *the praise of the whole earth* (Jer. li. 41), *like a pleasant roe* (so the word signifies); but it shall be as a *chased roe, v.* 14. It is foretold that it should be wholly destroyed, like Sodom and Gomorrah. Babylon was taken when Belshazzar was in his revels; and, though Cyrus and Darius did not demolish it, yet by degrees it went to ruin. It is foretold here (*v.* 20) *that it shall never be inhabited*: in Adrian's time nothing remained but the wall. And whereas it is prophesied concerning Nineveh, that when it should be deserted and left desolate yet flocks should lie down in the midst of it, it is here said concerning Babylon that *the Arabians, who were shepherds, should not make their folds there*; the country should be so barren that there would be no grazing for sheep. It shall be the receptacle of *wild beasts*, that affect solitude; the houses of Babylon *shall be full of doleful creatures, owls and satyrs*, that are themselves frightened thither, and by whom all others are frightened thence. Benjamin Bar-Jona, in his Itinerary, speaking of Babel, has these words: "This is that Babel which was thirty miles in breadth; it is now laid waste. There are the ruins of a palace of Nebuchadnezzar, but men dare not enter in, for fear of serpents and scorpions, which possess the place." It is intimated that this destruction should come shortly (*v.* 22): *Her time is near to come.* This prophecy of the destruction of Babylon was intended for the support and comfort of the people of God when they were captives there and grievously oppressed; and the accomplishment of the prophecy was nearly 200 years after the time when it was delivered.

CHAPTER 14

In this chapter, I. More weight is added to the burden of Babylon. 1. Israel's cause is pleaded in this quarrel with Babylon, ver. 1–3. 2. The king of Babylon shall be brought down, ver. 4–20. 3. The whole race of the Babylonians shall be cut off, ver. 21–23. II. A confirmation of the prophecy of the destruction of Babylon, which was a thing at a distance, is here given in the prophecy of the destruction of the Assyrian army that invaded the land, which happened not long after, ver. 24–27. III. The success of Hezekiah against the Philistines is here foretold, and the advantages which his people would gain thereby, ver. 28–32.

Verses 1–3

Babylon must be ruined, because God has mercy in store for his people. The injuries done to them must be revenged upon their persecutors. The yoke which Babylon had long laid on their necks must be broken and they must be set at liberty.

I. The ground of these favours to Jacob and Israel —the kindness God had for them and the choice he had made of them (*v.* 1): "*The Lord will have mercy on Jacob*, the seed of Jacob now captives in Babylon; and *will yet choose them*, though he has seemed for a time to refuse and reject them."

II. The particular favours he designed them. The *Lord will set them in their own land*, out of which they were driven—the holy land, the land of promise. *Strangers shall be joined with them*, saying, *We will go with you, for we have heard that God is with you*, Zech. viii. 23. These proselytes should be very helpful to them in their return home: *The people* among whom they live *shall take them*, take care of them, and *bring them to their place*—as friends—as servants, willing to do them all the good offices they could. In the return of the captives from Babylon, all that were about them, pursuant to Cyrus's proclamation, contributed to their removal (Ezra i. 4, 6), not as the Egyptians, because they were sick of them, but because they loved them. Many would of choice go with them. They *shall possess them in the land of the Lord for servants and handmaids.* The advantages of that land made it the paradise of those servants that had been strangers to the covenants of promise, for there was *one law to the stranger and to those that were born in the land.* They that would not be reconciled should be reduced and humbled by them: *They shall take those captives whose captives they were and shall rule over their oppressors*, righteously, but not revengefully. They should see a happy termination of all their grievances (*v.* 3): *The Lord shall give thee rest from thy sorrow and thy fear, and from thy hard bondage.* God himself undertakes to work a blessed change.

Verses 4–23

The kings of Babylon, successively, were oppressors of God's people. The Babylonian monarchy bade

fair to be an absolute, universal, and perpetual one, and, in these pretensions, vied with the Almighty; it is therefore very justly brought down and the last monarch, Belshazzar, *was slain on that night* that Babylon was taken (Dan. v. 30).

I. The fall of the king of Babylon: a most curious composition is here prepared. It gives us an account of the life and death of this mighty monarch, how he *went down slain to the pit*, though he had been *the terror of the mighty in the land of the living*, Ezek. xxxii. 27.

1. The prodigious height of wealth and power at which this monarch and monarchy arrived. Babylon was a *golden city, v.* 4. The king of Babylon, having so much wealth, by the help of that *ruled the nations* (*v.* 6), gave them law, and at his pleasure *weakened the nations* (*v.* 12), that they might not be able to make head against him. Such vast armies did he bring into the field, that he *made the earth to tremble, and shook kingdoms* (*v.* 16); all his neighbours were afraid of him, and were forced to submit to him.

2. The wretched abuse of all this wealth and power,

(1) Great oppression and cruelty. He is known by the name of the *oppressor* (*v.* 4); he has *the sceptre of the rulers* (*v.* 5), but it is *the staff of the wicked. He smote the people*, not in justice, for their correction and reformation, but *in wrath* (*v.* 6), *with a continual stroke.* He ruled them *in anger*, so that he who had the government of all about him had no government of himself. He *made the world as a wilderness, v.* 17. He was severe to his captives (*v.* 17). He *opened not the house of his prisoners*; he *did not let them loose homeward* (so the margin reads it); he kept them in close confinement, and never would suffer any to return to their own land. This refers especially to the people of the Jews. He was oppressive to his own subjects (*v.* 20): *Thou hast destroyed thy land, and slain thy people.*

(2) Great pride and haughtiness. Notice is here taken of his *pomp*, the extravagancy of his retinue, *v.* 11. But it was the temper of his mind that ripened him for ruin (*v.* 13, 14): *Thou hast said in thy heart*, like Lucifer, *I will ascend into heaven.* The king of Babylon here promises himself he shall surpass all his neighbours, and to be as far above those about him as the heaven is above the earth. He called for the vessels of the temple at Jerusalem, to profane them; see Dan. v. 2. In the same humour he here said, *I will sit upon the mount of the congregation in the sides of the north*; so Mount Zion is said to be situated, Ps. xlviii. 2. Perhaps Belshazzar was projecting an expedition to Jerusalem at the time when God cut him off. He would vie with the God of Israel, of whom he had heard that he had his residence *above the heights of the clouds.* "But thither," says he, "*will I ascend*, and be as great as he; I will be like him whom they call the *Most High.*" Some of the first founders of the Assyrian monarchy were deified and stars had their names from them. "But," says he, "*I will exalt my throne above them* all."

3. The utter ruin that should be brought upon him. It is foretold his wealth and power should be broken. He has been long an oppressor, but he shall cease to be so, *v.* 4. Those that will not cease to sin God will make to cease. *The Lord*, the righteous God, *has broken the staff of that wicked prince. He is persecuted* (*v.* 6); violent hands are laid upon him. It is the common fate of tyrants to be deserted by their flatterers. Tiberius and Nero thus saw themselves abandoned. He should be slain, and be *weak as the dead* are, and *like unto them, v.* 10. His *pomp is brought down to the grave* (*v.* 11), that is, it perishes with him. This mighty prince, that used to lie on a bed of down, now shall have the *worms spread under him and the worms covering him*, which, though he

fancied himself a god, proved him to be made of the same mould with other men. *The kings of the nations lie in glory* (v. 18), *everyone in his own house,* that is, his own burying-place. But this king of Babylon is *cast out* and has no grave (v. 19); his dead body is thrown, like that of a beast, into the ditch *like an abominable branch* of some noxious poisonous plant, which nobody will touch, or as the clothes of male-factors put to death and by the hand of justice *thrust through with a sword,* on whose dead bodies heaps of stones are raised. The king of Babylon's dead body shall be *trodden under feet* by the horses and soldiers and crushed to pieces. Thus he *shall not be joined with his ancestors in burial,* v. 20. Now that he is gone *the whole earth is at rest and is quiet,* for he was the great disturber of the peace; now they all *break forth into singing;* the fir-trees and cedars of Lebanon now think themselves safe; there is no danger now of their being cut down, to furnish him with timber. The neighbouring princes who are compared to fir-trees and cedars (Zech. xi. 2), may now be easy, and out of fear of being dispossessed of their rights. The dead will bid him welcome, especially those whom he had barbarously hastened thither (v. 9, 10): *Hell from beneath is moved for thee, to meet thee at thy coming. The chief ones of the earth,* who when they were alive were kept in awe by him shall scoffingly rise from their thrones and ask him if he will please to sit down in them, as he used to do in their thrones on earth? *"Hast thou also become weak as we?* Who would have thought it? Thou that didst rank thyself among the immortal gods, art thou come to take thy fate among us poor mortal men? *How hast thou fallen from heaven, O Lucifer! son of the morning!* v. 11, 12. Has such a star become a clod of clay? Did ever any man fall from such a height of honour and power into such an abyss of shame and misery?" *Those that see him shall narrowly look upon him, and consider him* (v. 15, 16). "Never was death so great a change to any man as it is to him. Is it possible that a man, who a few hours ago looked so great, should now look so ghastly, so despicable, and neglected? *Is this the man that made the earth to tremble and shook kingdoms?* Who could have thought he should ever come to this?" Ps. lxxxii. 7.

4. Here is an inference drawn from all this (v. 20): *The seed of evil-doers shall never be renowned.* The princes of the Babylonian monarchy were evildoers, and therefore they had this infamy entailed upon them. There is no credit in a sinful way.

II. The utter ruin of the royal family is here fore-told, together with the royal city.

1. The royal family is to be wholly extirpated. The Medes and Persians, that are to be employed in this destroying work, are ordered, when they have slain Belshazzar, to *prepare slaughter for his children* (v. 21). Nebuchadnezzar had slain Zedekiah's sons (Jer. lii. 10), and, for that iniquity of his, his seed are paid in the same coin, that they *may not rise up to possess the land* and do as much mischief in their day as their fathers had done in theirs. The providence of God consults the welfare of nations more than we are aware of by cutting off some who, if they had lived, would have done mischief.

2. The royal city is to be demolished and deserted, v. 23. It shall be a possession for solitary frightful birds, particularly *the bittern,* joined with the cor-morant and the owl, *ch.* xxxiv. 11.

Verses 24–32

It was almost 200 years from this prediction of Babylon's fall to the accomplishment of it. The people to whom Isaiah prophesied might ask, "What is this to us?" To the question he answers by a prediction of the ruin both of the Assyrians and of

the Philistines, shortly. These would be a pledge of future deliverance.

I. Assurance given of the destruction of the Assyrians (v. 25): *I will break the Assyrian in my land.* Sennacherib brought a formidable army into the land of Judah, but there God broke it. *"I will break the Assyrian;* let me alone to do it." The breaking of the power of the Assyrian would be the breaking of the yoke from off the neck of God's people: *His burden shall depart from off their shoulders,* the burden of quartering that vast army and paying contribution. This prophecy is here ratified and confirmed by an oath (v. 24): *The Lord of hosts hath sworn.* What is here said of this particular intention is true of all God's purposes. The breaking of the Assyrian power is made a specimen of what God would do with all the nations engaged against him and his church (v. 26), not only upon the Assyrian empire which was then reckoned to be all the world, as afterwards the Roman empire was (Luke ii. 1) for with it many nations fell that had dependence upon it. It is still true, and will ever be so. God will be an enemy to his people's enemies, Exod. xxiii. 22. All the powers on earth are defied to change God's plan (v. 27): *"The Lord of hosts has purposed* to break the Assyrian's yoke, *and who has power* enough *to turn it back* or to stay the course of his judgments?"

II. Assurance is likewise given of the destruction of the Philistines and their power. This came *in the year that king Ahaz died,* which was the first year of Hezekiah's reign, v. 28. The Philistines are rebuked for triumphing in the death of king Uzziah. He had been as a serpent to them (v. 29), had brought them very low, 2 Chron. xxvi. 6. He *warred against the Philistines, broke down their walls, and built cities among them.* But when Uzziah abdicated, it was told with joy in Gath and *published in the streets of Ash-kelon.* They made reprisals upon Ahaz, and took many cities of Judah (2 Chron. xxviii. 18), yet *out of the root* of Uzziah *should come a cockatrice,* a more formidable enemy than Uzziah, even Hezekiah, the fruit of whose government should be to them *a fiery flying serpent,* for he should fall upon them with incredible swiftness and fury. *He smote the Philistines even to Gaza* (2 Kings xviii. 8). "When the people of God, whom the Philistines had wasted, and distressed, and impoverished, shall enjoy plenty again, and *the first-born of their poor shall feed* (the poorest among them shall have food convenient), then, as for the Philistines, God will kill *their root with famine"* (v. 30). When the *needy* of God's people *shall lie down in safety,* delighting in the songs of peace, then every gate and every city of the Philistines shall be howling and crying (v. 31), and there shall be a total dissolution of their state; for from Judea, which lay north of the Philistines, *there shall come a smoke* (a vast army raising a great dust, the indication of a devouring fire at hand), *and none* of all that army *shall be alone in his appointed times;* none shall straggle or be missing when they are to engage.

III. The good use that should be made of all these events for the encouragement of the people of God (v. 32): *What shall one then answer the messengers of the nations?*

1. This implies that the great things God does for his people are noticed by their neighbours. Messengers will be sent to enquire concerning them. It concerns us always to be ready to give a reason of the hope that we have in the providence of God *with meek-ness and fear,* 1 Pet. iii. 15.

2. The answer which is to be given to the messen-gers: God is and will be a faithful friend to his church and people. Tell them that *the Lord has founded Zion.* God, in all the revolutions of states and kingdoms, is founding Zion; he is aiming at the advancement of his church's interests. The messengers of the nations,

when they sent to enquire concerning Hezekiah's successes against the Philistines, expected to learn of politics, and arts of war, but they are told that these successes were not owing to anything of that nature, but to the care God took of his church. *The poor of his people shall trust in it*, his poor people who have lately been brought very low. The *poor receive the gospel*, Matt. xi. 5. They shall trust to this, to this great truth, that the Lord has founded Zion; on this they shall build their hopes, and not on an arm of flesh. However it may go with particular parties, the church, having God himself for its founder and Christ the rock for its foundation, cannot but stand firm. They will not fear what man can do unto them.

CHAPTER 15

This chapter, and that which follows it, are the burden of Moab— a prophecy of some great desolation that was coming upon that country, which bordered upon this land of Israel, and had often been injurious and vexatious to it, though the Moabites were descended from Lot, Abraham's kinsman and companion, and though the Israelites, by the appointment of God, had spared them when they might both easily and justly have cut them off with their neighbours. In this chapter we have, I. Great lamentation made by the Moabites, and by the prophet himself for them, ver. 1–5. II. The great calamities which should occasion that lamentation and justify it, ver. 6–9.

Verses 1–5

The country of Moab was of small extent, but very fruitful. It bordered upon the lot of Reuben on the other side Jordan and upon the Dead Sea. Naomi went to sojourn there when there was a famine in Canaan. This is the country which (it is here foretold) should be wasted and grievously harassed. We find another prophecy of its ruin (Jer. xlviii), which was accomplished by Nebuchadnezzar. This prophecy here was to be fulfilled *within three years* (*ch.* xvi. 14), and therefore was fulfilled, either by the army of Shalmaneser, about the time of the taking of Samaria, in the fourth year of Hezekiah, or by the army of Sennacherib, which, ten years after, invaded Judah. The prophet delivered this prophecy to his own people to show them that there is a providence which governs the world and all the nations of it— and that to the God of Israel the worshippers of false gods were accountable. The accomplishment of this prophecy shortly (*within three years*) might be a confirmation of the prophet's mission and of the truth of all his other prophecies. Concerning Moab it is here foretold,

I. That their chief cities should be surprised and taken in a night by the enemy (*v.* 1): Therefore there shall be great grief, *because in the night Ar of Moab is laid waste and Kir of Moab*, the two principal cities of that kingdom. *In the night that they were taken*, or sacked, *Moab was cut off*. The seizing of them laid the whole country open, and made the wealth of it an easy prey. As the country feeds the cities, so the cities protect the country, and neither can say to the other, *I have no need of thee.*

II. That the Moabites should have recourse to their idols for relief (*v.* 2): *He* (that is, the king of Moab) *has gone up to Bajith* (or rather to the house or temple of Chemosh), *and Dibon*, the inhabitants of Dibon, *have gone up to the high places*, where they worshipped their idols, there to make their complaints.

III. That there should be universal grief all the country over. It is described here very affectingly. Moab shall be a vale of tears—a little map of this world, *v.* 2. The Moabites shall lament the loss of Nebo and Medeba, two considerable cities which, it is likely, were plundered and burnt. They shall tear their hair for grief to such a degree that *on all their heads shall be baldness, and they shall cut off their beards*, according to the customary expressions of mourning in those times and countries. In the

streets they shall gird themselves with sackcloth (*v.* 3). They shall go up to *the tops of their houses* which were flat-roofed, and there they shall *weep abundantly*, shall *howl*, crying to their gods. *They shall come down with weeping* (so the margin reads it) from the tops of their houses weeping as much as they did when they went up.

IV. That the courage of their militia should fail them. Though they were bred soldiers, they *shall cry out* and shriek for fear, and every one of them shall have *his life become grievous to him*, *v.* 4.

V. That the outcry for these calamities should propagate grief to all the adjacent parts, *v.* 5. The prophet himself has impressions made upon his spirit by the prediction of it: *My heart shall cry out for Moab;* though they are enemies to Israel, they are our fellow-creatures. It becomes God's ministers to be of a tender spirit, to be like their master, who wept over Jerusalem even when he gave her up to ruin, like their God, *who desires not the death of sinners.* All the neighbouring cities shall echo to the lamentations of Moab. *The fugitives*, who are making the best of their way to shift for their own safety, shall carry the cry *to Zoar*, the city to which their ancestor Lot fled for shelter from Sodom's flames and which was spared for his sake. They shall make as great a noise with their cry *as a heifer of three years old* does when she goes *lowing* for her calf, as 1 Sam. vi. 12. They shall go up the hill of *Luhith* (as David went up the ascent of Mount Olivet, many a weary step and all in tears, 2 Sam. xv. 30), and *in the way of Horonaim* (a dual termination), the way that leads to the two Beth-horons, the upper and the nether, which we read of, Joshua xvi. 3, 5.

Verses 6–9

"By this time *the cry has gone round about* all *the borders of Moab,*" *v.* 8. It has reached to *Eglaim*, a city at one end of the country, and to *Beer-elim*, a city as far the other way.

I. *The waters of Nimrim are desolate* (*v.* 6), that is, the country is plundered and impoverished. Famine is usually the sad effect of war. Look into the houses, and they are stripped too (*v.* 7): *The abundance* of wealth that *they had gotten* with a great deal of industry, and *that which they had laid up* with a great deal of care, *shall they carry away to the brook of the willows.* Either the owners shall carry it thither to hide it or the enemies shall pack it up and send it home, by water perhaps, to their own country.

II. *The waters of Dimon are turned into blood* (*v.* 9), that is, the inhabitants of the country are slain in great numbers. *Dimon* signifies *bloody*; the place shall answer to its name. *I will bring additions upon Dimon* (so the word is), additional plagues; I have yet more judgments in reserve for them. *For all this, God's anger is not turned away.* Some make their escape, others are overlooked, and are as a remnant of the land; but upon both God *will bring lions*, beasts of prey.

CHAPTER 16

This chapter continues and concludes the burden of Moab. In it, I. The prophet gives good counsel to the Moabites, to reform, and particularly to be kind to God's people, to prevent the judgments before threatened, ver. 1–5. II. Fearing they would not take this counsel, he goes on to foretell the devastation of their country within three years, ver. 6–14.

Verses 1–5

God has made it to appear that he delights not in the ruin of sinners by telling them what they may do to prevent the ruin; so he does here to Moab.

I. He advises them to be just to the house of David, and to pay the tribute they had formerly covenanted to pay (*v.* 1): *Send you the lamb to the ruler of the land.* David made the Moabites tributaries to him,

2 Sam. viii. 2. Afterwards they paid their tribute to the kings of Israel (2 Kings iii. 4), and paid it in lambs. Now the prophet requires them to pay it to Hezekiah. Let it be levied from all parts of the country, *from Selah*, a frontier city of Moab on the one side, *to the wilderness*, a boundary of the kingdom on the other side: and let it be sent *to the mount of the daughter of Zion*, the city of David. Some think it is spoken ironically. I rather take it as good advice seriously given, like that of Daniel to Nebuchadnezzar when he was reading him his doom, Dan. iv. 27. And it is applicable to the great gospel duty of submission to Christ, as the ruler of the land, and our ruler. When you come to God, the great ruler, come in the name of the Lamb, the Lamb of God. *The daughters of Moab* (the country villages, or the women of your country) shall flutter about the *fords of Arnon*, attempting that way to make their escape to some other land, *like a wandering bird thrown out of the nest* half-fledged.

II. He advises them to be *kind to the seed of Israel* (v. 3): Take counsel, reverse all the unrighteous decrees you have made, by which you have put hardships upon the people of God.

1. The prophet foresaw some storm coming upon the people of God, who, by the merciful providence of God, escaped the fury of the Assyrian army, but were put to the utmost extremity to shift for their own safety. The danger and trouble they were in were like the scorching heat at noon.

2. He bespeaks a shelter for them in the land of Moab, when their own land was made too hot for them. Thus kindly must they deal with the people of God. If they would continue in their habitations, let them now open their doors to the dispersed members of God's church, and be to them like a cool shade to those that *bear the burden and heat of the day*. "*Betray not him that wandereth*, nor deliver him up" (as the Edomites did, Obad. 13, 14), "but *hide the outcasts*." "Nay, do not only hide them for a time, but, if there be occasion, let them be naturalized: *Let my outcasts dwell with thee, Moab* (v. 4); find a lodging for them and *be thou a covert to them*." They are *outcasts*, but they are *my outcasts*. The Lord knows those that are his wherever he finds them, even where no one else knows them. He will himself be their dwelling-place if they have no other, and in him they shall be at home.

3. He assures them of the mercy God had in store for his people. They should not long need their kindness, or be troublesome to them: *For the extortioner is almost at an end* already, *and the spoiler ceases*. They should, ere long, be in a capacity to return their kindness (v. 5): "Though the throne of the ten tribes be overturned, yet *the throne of David shall be established in mercy*, and by the same methods may your throne be established if you please. Make Hezekiah your friend. He *shall sit upon the throne in truth*. Then he shall sit *judging*, and will then be a protector to those that have been a shelter to the people of God." And see in him the character of a good magistrate. He shall *seek judgment*; that is, he shall seek occasions of doing right to those that are wronged. He shall *hasten righteousness*, and not delay to do justice. Let the Moabites take example by this, and then assure themselves that their state shall be established.

Verses 6–14

I. The sins with which Moab is charged, v. 6. The prophet seems to check himself for going about to give good counsel to the Moabites. He would have healed them, but they would not be healed. Perhaps there are more precious souls ruined by pride than by any one lust whatsoever. The Moabites were notorious for this: "*We have heard* in both ears of *the pride of Moab*. They think themselves too wise to be advised; therefore they will not take example by Hezekiah to do justly and love mercy. We have heard of *his wrath* too (for those that are very proud are commonly very passionate), particularly his wrath against the people of God, whom he will rather persecute than protect. It is with *his lies* that he gains the gratifications of his pride and his passion; *but his lies shall not be so*; he shall not compass his proud and angry projects as he hoped he should."

II. The sorrows with which Moab is threatened (v. 7): *Therefore shall Moab howl for Moab. For the foundations of Kir-hareseth shall you mourn*. That great and strong city, which had held out against a mighty force (2 Kings iii. 25), should now be levelled with the ground. Moab was famous for its fields and vineyards; but those shall all be laid waste by the invading army, v. 8, 10. It was planted with choice and noble vines, with *principal plants*, which reached *even to Jazer*, and wound themselves along the ranges on which they were spread, even *through the wilderness* of Moab. There were vineyards there, *stretched out*, even to *the sea*, the Dead Sea. Many a time they had shouted *for their summer fruits, and for their harvest*. They had had *joy and gladness* in their fields and vineyards, *singing* and *shouting at the treading of their grapes*. Nothing is said of their praising God for their abundance, and giving him the glory of it. They made it the food and fuel of their lusts, therefore they should be stripped of all. "The fields shall *languish*. The soldiers, called here *the lords of the heathen*, shall break down all the plants, *principal plants*, the choicest that could be got. The joy of harvest has ceased; there is no more singing: the ruin of their country has marred their mirth." Destroy the vines and the fig-trees, and you make all the mirth of a carnal heart to cease, Hos. ii. 11, 12. But a gracious soul can rejoice in the Lord as the God of its salvation even when the fig-tree does not blossom and there is no fruit in the vine, Hab. iii. 17, 18. The concurrence of the prophet with them in this sorrow: "*I will with weeping bewail Jazer, and the vine of Sibmah*, and look with a compassionate concern upon the desolations of such a pleasant country. *I will water thee with my tears, O Heshbon!* and mingle them with thy tears;" nay (v. 11), it appears to be an inward grief: *My bowels shall sound like a harp for Moab*. The afflictions of the world, as well as those of the church, should be afflictions to us. See *ch.* xv. 5.

III. In the close of the chapter we see the insufficiency of the gods of Moab to help them, v. 12. "Moab shall be soon *weary of the high place*. He shall spend his spirits and strength in vain in praying to his idols; they cannot help him, and he shall be convinced that they cannot." But when he is weary of his high places, he will not go, as he should, to God's sanctuary, but to *his* sanctuary, to the temple of Chemosh, the principal idol of Moab (so it is generally understood); and he shall pray there to as little purpose. The thing itself was long since determined (v. 13): *This is the word*, this is the thing, *that the Lord has spoken concerning Moab, since the time* that he began to be so proud, and insolent, and abusive to God's people. The country was long ago doomed to ruin. Now it was made known when it should be done. *The Lord has spoken* that it shall be *within three years*, v. 14. God makes known his mind by degrees; the light of divine revelation shone more and more, and so does the light of divine grace in the heart. *The glory of Moab shall be contemned*, that is, it shall be contemptible, when all those things they have gloried in shall come to nothing. It was the glory of Moab that their country was very populous and their forces were courageous; but the little remnant that is left shall be *very small and feeble. Within three years, as the years of a hireling*, it shall be at the three years' end exactly, for a servant that is hired for a certain term keeps account to a day. Fair warning is given, and with it space to repent, which if they had improved, as Nineveh did, we have reason to think the judgments threatened would have been prevented.

CHAPTER 17

Syria and Ephraim were confederate against Judah (ch. vii. 1, 2), and, they being so closely linked together, this chapter, entitled "the burden of Damascus" (which was the head city of Syria), reads the doom of Israel too. 1. The destruction of the strong cities both of Syria and Israel is here foretold, ver. 1-5 and again ver. 9-11. II. In the midst of judgment mercy is remembered to Israel, and a gracious promise made that a remnant should be preserved from the calamities and should get good by them, ver. 6-8. III. The overthrow of the Assyrian army before Jerusalem is pointed at ver. 12-14. In order of time this chapter should be placed next after ch. ix, for the destruction of Damascus, here foretold, happened in the reign of Ahaz, 2 Kings xvi. 9.

Verses 1-5

We have here the burden of Damascus; the Chaldee paraphrase reads it, *The burden of the cup of the curse to drink to Damascus in;* and, the ten tribes being in alliance they must expect to pledge Damascus in this cup of trembling. 1. Damascus itself, the head city of Syria, must be destroyed; the houses will be burnt, the walls, and gates, and fortifications demolished, and the inhabitants carried away captive, so that it is *taken away from being a city*, and is reduced to *a ruinous heap*, v. 1. The country towns are abandoned by their inhabitants. *The cities of Aroer* (a province of Syria so called) *are forsaken* (v. 2); so that the places which should be for men to live in are for *flocks to lie down in.* Stately houses are converted into sheep-cotes. The strongholds of Israel, the kingdom of the ten tribes, will be brought to ruin: *The fortress shall cease from Ephraim* (v. 3). The Syrians were the ring-leaders in that confederacy against Judah, and therefore they are punished first and sorest; and, now that Israel is weakened, *The remnant of Syria shall be as the glory of the children of Israel;* those few that remain of the Syrians shall be in as mean and despicable a condition as the children of Israel are. The glory of Jacob is wasted like a man in a consumption, v. 4. *The glory of Jacob* was their numbers, but this glory *shall be made thin*, when many are cut off, and few left. Israel died of a lingering disease; the kingdom of the ten tribes wasted gradually. It is all gathered and carried away by the Assyrian army, v. 5. And the victorious army, like the careful husbandmen in the valley of Rephaim, where the corn was extraordinary, would not, if they could help it, leave an ear behind.

Verses 6-8

Mercy is here reserved, in a parenthesis in the midst of judgment, for a remnant that should escape the common ruin of the kingdom of the ten tribes. The meek of the earth were hidden in the day of the Lord's anger, and had their lives made comfortable to them by their retirement to the land of Judah. 1. They shall be but a small remnant, who shall be marked for preservation (v. 6): *Gleaning grapes shall be left in it.* The body of the people were carried into captivity. Those that are left are but like the poor remains of an olive tree when it has been carefully shaken: if there be *two or three berries in the top of the uppermost bough* (out of the reach of those that shook it), that is all. They shall be a sanctified remnant, v. 7, 8. These had repented of their sins and returned their lives, and therefore were snatched thus as brands out of the burning. They shall look up to their Creator, shall acknowledge his hand in all the events concerning them, merciful and afflictive, and shall submit to his hand. They shall look from their

idols, the creatures of their own fancy, shall no longer worship them, and expect relief from them. He that looks to his Maker must not *look to the altars, the work of his hands*, must not retain the least respect for *that which his fingers have made*, but break it to pieces.

Verses 9-11

Here the prophet returns to foretell the desolations that should be made in Israel by the army of the Assyrians. Even the strong cities, which should have protected the country, shall not be able to protect themselves: They *shall be as a forsaken bough and an uppermost branch* of an old tree, which has gone to decay, is bare, and dry, and dead. As the Canaanites fled before Israel, so Israel should now flee before the Assyrians. The country should be laid waste, v. 10, 11. "It is *because thou hast forgotten the God of thy salvation* and all the great salvations he has wrought for thee, and *hast not been mindful of the rock of thy strength*, who has been thy strength many a time, or thou wouldst have been broken long since." They had taken great care to improve their land and to make it more pleasant. It was like a garden and a vineyard; replenished with plants, the choicest of its own growth; and not content with them, they sent to all the neighbouring countries for strange slips. This instance seems to be put in general for their great industry in cultivating their ground; they doubt not but their plants will grow and flourish. But *the harvest shall be a heap*, all in confusion, *in the day of grief and of desperate sorrow*. The harvest had sometimes been a day of grief, if the crop was thin; and yet in that case there was hope that the next would be better. But this shall be desperate sorrow, for they shall see not only this year's products carried off, but the property of the ground altered and their conquerors lords of it.

Verses 12-14

These verses read the doom of those that rob the people of God. If the Assyrians and Israelites invade and plunder Judah, if the Assyrian army take God's people captive and lay their country waste, let them know that ruin will be their lot. The Assyrian army was made up out of divers nations: it was *the multitude of many people* (v. 12), by which weight they hoped to carry the cause. They were noisy, like the roaring of the seas, to frighten God's people from resisting them. Sennacherib and Rabshakeh, in their speeches and letters, made a mighty noise to strike terror upon Hezekiah and his people; the nations that followed them *made a rushing like the rushing of many waters.* They thought to carry their point by dint of noise; but (v. 12), he *shall rebuke them*, that is, God shall, *and then they shall flee afar off.* Sennacherib, and Rabshakeh, and the remains of their forces, shall be chased by their own terrors, *as the chaff of the mountains* which stand bleak *before the wind, and like a rolling thing before the whirlwind*, like thistledown (so the margin). God will make *them like a wheel* or rolling thing, and *make them afraid with his storm*, Ps. lxxxiii. 13, 15. This shall be done suddenly (v. 14): *At evening-tide* they are very troublesome, and threaten trouble to the people of God; but *before the morning they are not.* At sleeping time they are cast into a deep sleep, Ps. lxxvi. 5, 6. It was in the night that the angel routed the Assyrian army.

CHAPTER 18

Whatever country it is that is meant here by "the land shadowing with wings", God has, upon his people's account, a quarrel with it. I. They threaten God's people, ver. 1 2. II. All the neighbours are called to notice what will be the issue, ver. 3. III.

Though God seem unconcerned in the distress of his people for a time, he will at length appear against their enemies and cut them off, ver. 4–6.

Verses 1–7

Interpreters are very much at a loss where to find this land that lies beyond the rivers of Cush. Some take it to be Egypt, but against this it is objected that the next chapter is distinguished by the title of *the burden of Egypt*. Others take it to be Ethiopia, of which Tirhakah was king. He thought to protect the Jews, as it were, under *the shadow of his wings*, by giving a powerful diversion to the king of Assyria, when he was attacking Jerusalem, 2 Kings xix. 9. But though by his ambassadors he bade defiance to the king of Assyria, God will take another course to protect Jerusalem. But from a hint of Dr. Lightfoot's, in his Harmony of the Old Testament, I incline to understand this chapter as a prophecy against Assyria, and so a continuation of the last three verses of the foregoing chapter. That was against the army of the Assyrians which rushed in upon Judah; this is against the land of Assyria itself, which lay beyond the rivers Euphrates and Tigris.

I. The attempt made by this land (whatever it is) upon *a nation scattered and peeled, v.* 2. Whether this refer to the Ethiopians waging war with the Assyrians, or the Assyrians with Judah, it teaches us that a people which have been terrible from their beginning, and borne a mighty sway, may yet become scattered and peeled, and may be spoiled even by their own rivers, that should enrich both the husbandman and the merchant. "It is a nation that has been terrible, and is now a nation scattered and peeled, meted out and trodden down, and therefore an easy prey for us."

II. The alarm sounded to the nations about, by which they are summoned to take notice of what God is about to do, *v.* 3. *He lifts up an ensign upon the mountains, and blows a trumpet*, by which he proclaims war against the enemies of his church, and calls in all her friends. He is about to do some great work, as *Lord of hosts*.

III. The assurance God gives to his prophet, by him to be given to his people, that, though he might seem for a time to sit by as an unconcerned spectator, yet he would certainly appear for the comfort of his people and the confusion of his and their enemies (*v.* 4): *So the Lord said unto me*. He will take care of his people, and be a shelter to them. He will regard his *dwelling-place*; Zion is his rest for ever, and he will *look after it* (so some read it). He will be as a clear heat after rain (so the margin), like a dew and *a cloud in the heat of harvest*, which are very welcome, the dew to the ground and the cloud to the labourers. Great men have their winter-house and their summer-house (Amos iii. 15); but those that are at home with God have both in him. He will reckon with his and their enemies, *v.* 5, 6. When the Assyrian army promises itself a plentiful harvest in the taking of Jerusalem, God shall destroy that army as easily as the husbandman cuts off the sprigs of the vine with pruning hooks, or *takes away and cuts down the branches*. This seems to point at the dead bodies of the soldiers scattered like the branches of a wild vine, cut to pieces. *And they shall be left to the fowls of the earth*, to prey upon. *In that time*, when this shall be accomplished, *shall the present be brought unto the Lord of hosts*. Those that were *a people scattered and peeled, meted out, and trodden down* (*v.* 2), shall be a present to the Lord: and, though they seem useless and worthless, they shall be acceptable to him who judges men by the sincerity of their faith and love, not by the pomp and prosperity of their outward condition. It is prophesied (Ps. lxviii. 31) that *Ethiopia shall soon stretch out her hands unto God*. Others understand it of the spoil of Sennacherib's

army, out of which, presents were brought to *the Lord of hosts*.

CHAPTER 19

As Assyria was a rod to Judah, with which it was smitten, so Egypt was a broken reed, with which it was cheated; and therefore God had a quarrel with them both. Here we have the burden of Egypt, I. That it should be brought low, and should be as contemptible among the nations as now it was considerable, ver. 1–17. II. That at length God's holy religion should be brought into Egypt, in part by the Jews that should flee thither for refuge, but more fully by the preachers of the gospel of Christ, through whose ministry churches should be planted in Egypt in the days of the Messiah (ver. 18–25).

Verses 1–17

Though the land of Egypt had of old been a house of bondage to the people of God, the unbelieving Jews trusted to Egypt for help (*ch.* xxx. 2), and thither they fled, in disobedience to God's express command, when things were brought to the last extremity in their own country, Jer. xliii. 7. Rabshakeh upbraided Hezekiah with this, *ch.* xxxvi. 6. While they kept up an alliance with Egypt they stood not in awe of the judgments of God; they depended upon Egypt to protect them. To prevent all this mischief, Egypt must be mortified.

I. The gods of Egypt shall appear utterly unable to help them, *v.* 1. *"The Lord rides upon a cloud, a swift cloud, and shall come into Egypt.* As a judge goes in state to try and condemn the malefactors, so shall God come into Egypt with his judgments." In all this burden of Egypt there is no mention of any foreign enemy invading them; but God himself will come against them, and raise up the causes of their destruction from among themselves. When he comes *the idols of Egypt shall be moved.* Isis, Osiris, and Apis, idols of Egypt, being found unable to relieve their worshippers, shall be disowned and rejected by them. The Egyptians *shall seek to the idols*, when they are at their wits' end, and consult *the charmers and wizards* (*v.* 3); but all in vain.

II. The militia of Egypt, that had been famed for their valour, shall be disheartened. Their heroes, that used to be celebrated for courage, shall be posted for cowards: *The heart of Egypt shall melt in the midst of it*, like wax before the fire (*v.* 1); *the spirit of Egypt shall fail, v.* 3. They *shall be like women* (*v.* 16); they shall be frightened and put into confusion by the least alarm.

III. The Egyptians shall be embroiled in quarrels among themselves. There shall be no occasion to bring a foreign force upon them to destroy them; they shall destroy one another (*v.* 2): *I will set the Egyptians against the Egyptians; they shall fight everyone against his brother and neighbour, city against city, and kingdom against kingdom.* Egypt was then divided into twelve provinces, or dynasties; but Psammetichus, the governor of one of them, by setting them at variance with one another, at length made himself master of them all. A kingdom thus divided against itself would soon be brought to desolation.

IV. Their politics shall be turned into foolishness. When God will destroy the nation he will *destroy the counsel thereof* (*v.* 3). They make fools of one another, everyone betrays his own folly, and divine Providence makes fools of them all, *v.* 11. The nobles of Egypt boasted much of their antiquity, producing fabulous records of their succession for above 10,000 years. This humour prevailed much among them about this time, as appears by Herodotus, their common boast being that Egypt was some thousands of years more ancient than any other nation. "But *where are thy wise men? v.* 12. Let them with all their skill *know what the Lord of hosts has purposed upon Egypt*, and arm themselves accordingly. Nay, so far are they from doing this that they themselves are, in effect, contriving the ruin of Egypt, and, hastening it on, *v.* 13. *The princes of Noph are not only deceived themselves, but they have seduced Egypt.*" It is sad with a people when those that undertake for their safety are helping forward their destruction; so here (*v.* 14): *They have caused Egypt to err in every work thereof.*

V. The rod of government shall be turned into the serpent of tyranny and oppression (*v.* 4): "*The Egyptians will I give over into the hand of a cruel lord,* not a foreigner, but one that shall rule over them by an hereditary right, but shall be a fierce king and rule them with rigour."

VI. Egypt was famous for its river Nile, which was its wealth, and strength, and is here threatened that *the waters shall fail from the sea* and the river shall be *wasted and dried up, v.* 5. The fruitfulness of the country depended wholly upon the overflowing of the river; if that be dried up, their fruitful land will soon be turned into barrenness and their harvests cease: *Everything sown by the brooks will wither* of course, will *be driven away, and be no more, v.* 7. If the paper-reeds at the very mouth wither, much more the corn, which lies at a greater distance. The drying up of their rivers is the destruction of their fortifications, for they are *brooks of defence* (*v.* 6). But these *shall be emptied and dried up,* not by an enemy, as Sennacherib with the *sole of his foot dried up mighty rivers* (*ch.* xxxvii. 25), but by the providence of God, which sometimes *turns water-springs into dry ground,* Ps. cvii. 33. The drying up of the rivers will *kill the fish* (Ps. cv. 29), and will thereby ruin those who make it their business to catch fish, whether by angling or nets (*v.* 8); they shall *lament* and *languish,* for their trade is at an end. There were those that *made sluices and ponds for fish* (*v.* 10), but *they shall be broken in the purposes thereof;* their business will fail for want of water to fill their ponds. The loss of these advantages by the river is their own doing (*v.* 6): *They shall turn the rivers far away.* Their kings and great men will drain water from the main river to their own houses, preferring their private convenience before the public good. Herodotus tells us that Pharaoh-Necho, projecting to cut a free passage by water from Nilus into the Red Sea, employed a vast number of men to make a channel for that purpose, impaired the river, lost 120,000 of his people, and yet left the work unaccomplished.

VII. Egypt was famous for the linen manufacture; but that trade shall be ruined. Solomon's merchants traded with Egypt for linen-yarn, 1 Kings x. 28. Their country produced the best flax and the best hands to work it; but *those that work in fine flax shall be confounded* (*v.* 9). The trade of Egypt must needs sink, for (*v.* 15) *there shall not be any work for Egypt*; and where there is nothing to be done there is nothing to be got. There shall be *no work which either head or tail, branch or rush, may do;* nothing for high or low, weak or strong, to do.

VIII. A general consternation shall seize the Egyptians; they *shall be afraid and fear* (*v.* 16), an evidence of decay and of ruin. When they hear of the desolations made in Judah by the army of Sennacherib (*v.* 17), they will conclude it must be their turn next to become a prey to that victorious army. They shall *fear* (*v.* 16) *because of the shaking of the hand of the Lord of hosts,* and (*v.* 17) *because of the counsel of the Lord of hosts.* From the shaking of his hand they shall conclude *he has determined* against Egypt as well as Judah. For, if judgment begin at the house of God, where will it end?

Verses 18-25

Out of the threatening clouds of the prophecy the sun here breaks forth, and it is the sun of righteousness. Still God has mercy in store for Egypt, and he

will show it, by bringing the true religion among them, calling them to the worship of the one true God. The preaching (as is supposed) of Mark the Evangelist, led to the founding of Christian churches in Egypt. Many prophecies of this book point to the days of the Messiah; and why not this? It is no unusual thing to speak of gospel graces and ordinances in the language of the Old Testament institutions. And, in these prophecies, those words, *in that day,* perhaps have not always a reference to what goes immediately before, but have a peculiar significancy pointing at that day, when the day-spring from on high should visit this dark world. Yet it is not improbable that this prophecy was in part fulfilled when those Jews who fled from their own country to take shelter in Egypt, when Sennacherib invaded their land, brought their religion along with them. Josephus tells us that Onias the son of Onias the high priest, living an outlaw at Alexandria, obtained leave of Ptolemy Philometer, and Cleopatra his queen, to build a temple to the God of Israel, like that at Jerusalem, at Bubastis in Egypt, and pretended a warrant for doing it from this prophecy in Isaiah, that there shall be an *altar to the Lord in the land of Egypt.* The conversion of Egypt is here described.

I. They shall *speak the language of Canaan,* the holy language, the scripture language; they shall not only understand it, but use it (*v.* 18). *Five cities in Egypt* shall speak this language; so many Jews shall come to reside in Egypt, and shall soon replenish five cities, one of which shall be the city of Heliopolis, where the sun was worshipped, the most infamous of all the cities of Egypt for idolatry; even there shall be a wonderful reformation.

II. They shall swear to the Lord of hosts, not only swear by him, but shall by a solemn oath devote themselves to his honour and bind themselves to his service.

III. They shall set up the public worship of God in their land (*v.* 19): *There shall be an altar to the Lord* in the *midst of the land of Egypt,* an altar on which *they shall do sacrifice and oblation* (*v.* 21); this must be understood spiritually, for by the law of Moses there was to be no altar for sacrifice but that at Jerusalem. In Christ Jesus all distinction of nations is taken away; and a spiritual altar, a gospel church, in Egypt, is as acceptable to God as one in Israel.

IV. There shall be a face of religion upon the nation. Not only in the heart of the country, but even in *the borders* of it, *there shall be a pillar,* inscribed, *To Jehovah,* to his honour. Even in the land of Egypt he had some faithful worshippers, who made his name their strong tower.

V. Being in distress, they shall seek to God, and he shall be found of them; and this *shall be a sign and a witness for the Lord of hosts* that he is a *prayer-hearing God* to *all flesh* that *come to him, v.* 20, 22.

VI. They shall have an interest in the great Redeemer. Repenting Egyptians shall find the same favour with God that repenting Ninevites did. But all these deliverances wrought for them, as those for Israel, were but figures of gospel salvation.

VII. The knowledge of God shall prevail among them, *v.* 21. Perhaps this may in part refer to the translation of the Old Testament out of Hebrew into Greek by the LXX, which was done at Alexandria in Egypt. By the help of this (the Greeks having introduced their language into that country) *the Lord was known to Egypt.* It is promised that *the Egyptians shall know the Lord.*

VIII. They shall come into the communion of saints. Being joined to the Lord, they shall be added to the church. Enmities shall be slain. Mortal feuds there had been between Egypt and Assyria; but now *there shall be a highway between Egypt and Assyria* (*v.* 23); they shall trade with one another, and everything that passes between them shall be friendly. *The Egyptians shall serve with the Assyrians.* Those who have communion with the same God, meeting at the same throne of grace, and serving with each other should put an end to all heats and animosities, and knit our hearts to each other in holy love. The Gentile nations shall not only unite with each other in the gospel fold under Christ the great shepherd, but they shall all be united with the Jews. When Egypt and Assyria become partners in serving God *Israel* shall *make a third with* them (*v.* 24); they shall become a *three-fold cord, not easily broken.* Thus united, they shall be *a blessing in the midst of the land, whom the Lord of hosts shall bless,* v. 24, 25. They shall all be a blessing to the world. Though Egypt was formerly a house of bondage, and Assyria an unjust invader, all this shall now be forgiven and forgotten, and they shall be as welcome to God as Israel. They are all alike his people whom he takes under his protection.

Chapter 20

This chapter is a prediction of the carrying away of multitudes both of the Egyptians and the Ethiopians into captivity by the king of Assyria. Here is, I. The sign by which this was foretold, which was the prophet's going for some time barefoot and almost naked, like a poor captive, ver. 1–2. II. The explication of that sign, with application to Egypt and Ethiopia, ver. 3–5. III. The good use which the people of God should make of this, which is never to trust in an arm of flesh, because thus it will deceive them, ver. 6.

Verses 1–6

God here, as King of nations, brings a sore calamity upon Egypt and Ethiopia, but, as King of saints, brings good to his people out of it.

I. The date of this prophecy. It was in the year that Ashdod, a strong city of the Philistines, was besieged and taken by an army of the Assyrians. It is uncertain what year of Hezekiah that was. He that was now king of Assyria is called *Sargon.* Tartan, who was general, or commander-in-chief, in this expedition, was one of Sennacherib's officers, sent by him to bid defiance to Hezekiah, in concurrence with Rabshakeh, 2 Kings xviii. 17.

II. The making of Isaiah a sign, by his unusual dress. He had been a sign to his own people of the melancholy times that had come and were coming upon them, by the sackcloth which he had worn. Sackcloth he wore as a prophet, to show himself mortified to the world. Elijah wore hair-cloth (2 Kings i. 8), and John Baptist (Matt. iii. 4), but Isaiah has orders to *loose his sackcloth from his loins,* not to exchange it for better clothing, but for none at all, and he must *put off his shoes,* and go barefoot. This was a great hardship upon the prophet and would expose him to contempt and ridicule, but God bade him do it, that he might give a proof of his obedience to God, and so shame the disobedience of his people. When we are in the way of our duty we may trust God both with our credit and with our safety.

III. The exposition of this sign, *v.* 3, 4. It was intended to signify that the Egyptians and the Ethiopians should be led away captive by the king of Assyria, thus stripped, as Isaiah was. God calls him his *servant Isaiah,* because in this matter he had approved himself God's willing, obedient servant; and for this very thing, God gloried in him. Isaiah is said to have *walked naked and barefoot three years,* whenever in that time he appeared as a prophet. Three campaigns successively shall the Assyrian army make, in spoiling the Egyptians and Ethiopians, and carrying them away captive, now stripped, and scarcely having rags to cover their nakedness. It is particularly said to be *to the shame of Egypt* (*v.* 4), because the Egyptians were a proud people.

IV. The use and application of this, *v.* 5, 6. Those countries that were in danger of being overrun by the Assyrians expected that Tirhakah, king of Ethiopia, would put a stop to the progress of their victorious arms, and be a barrier to his neighbours; and that Egypt, a kingdom so famous for policy and prowess, would oblige them to raise the siege of Ashdod and retire. But, instead of this, by attempting to oppose the king of Assyria they did but make their country a prey to him. They were more afraid now than ever of the growing greatness of the king of Assyria, before whom Egypt and Ethiopia proved but as briers and thorns put to stop a consuming fire. The Jews in particular should be convinced of their folly in resting upon such broken reeds (*v.* 6): *The inhabitants of this isle* (the land of Judah, situated upon the sea, though not surrounded by it), everyone shall now have his eyes opened, and shall say, "*Behold, such is our expectation!* We have fled to the Egyptians and Ethiopians, and have hoped by them to be delivered from the king of Assyria; but, now that they are broken, how shall we escape, that are not able to bring such armies into the field as they did?"

Chapter 21

In this chapter we have a prophecy of sad times coming, and heavy burdens, I. Upon Babylon, here called "the desert of the sea", that it should be destroyed by the Medes and Persians, ver. 1–10. II. Upon Dumah, or Idumea, ver. 11, 12. III. Upon Arabia, or Kedar, ver. 13–17.

Verses 1–10

We had one burden of Babylon before (*ch.* xiii); here we have another prediction of its fall. Babylon sometimes pretended to be a friend to them (as *ch.* xxxix. 1), and God would hereby warn them not to trust to that friendship, and not to be afraid of their enmity. Babylon is marked for ruin; and all that believe God's prophets can see it tottering. Babylon is here called the *desert* or *plain of the sea;* for it was a flat country, and full of lakes, and was abundantly watered with the many streams of the river Euphrates. It did but lately begin to be famous, Nineveh having outshone it while the monarchy was in the Assyrian hands; but it became the lady of kingdoms; and, before Nebuchadnezzar's time, God by this prophet plainly foretold its fall, again and again, that his people might not be terrified at its rise, nor despair of relief when they were its prisoners, Job v. 3; Ps. xxxvii. 35, 36.

I. The powerful descent which the Medes and Persians should make upon Babylon (*v.* 1, 2): They will come *from the desert, from a terrible land.* The northern parts of Media and Persia were waste and mountainous, terrible to strangers. *Elam* (that is, Persia) is summoned to go up against Babylon, and, in conjunction with the forces of Media, to besiege it. These forces come *as whirlwinds from the south.* As is usual in such a case, some deserters will go over to them: *The treacherous dealers will deal treacherously.* Historians tell us of Gadatas and Gobryas, two great officers of the king of Babylon, that went over to Cyrus, and, being well acquainted with all the avenues of the city, led a party directly to the palace, where Belshazzar was slain. Thus with the help of the *treacherous dealers the spoilers spoiled.* The Persians shall pay the Babylonians in their own coin; those that by fraud, unrighteous wars and deceitful treaties, have made a prey of their neighbours, shall meet their match.

II. The different impressions made upon those in Babylon. To the poor captives it would be welcome news; for they had been told long ago that Babylon's destroyer would be their deliverer, and therefore, when they hear that Elam and Media are coming to besiege Babylon, *all their sighing will be made to cease.* To the proud oppressors it would be a grievous vision (*v.* 2), particularly to the king of Babylon, and it should seem that he it is who is here sadly lamenting his inevitable fate (*v.* 3, 4): *Therefore are my loins filled with pain; pangs have taken hold upon me, &c.,* which was literally fulfilled in Belshazzar, for that very night in which his city was taken, and himself slain, upon the sight of a hand writing mystic characters upon the wall *his countenance was changed and his thoughts troubled him, so that the joints of his loins were loosed and his knees smote one against another,* Dan. v. 6. He was slain on that night when he was in the height of his mirth and jollity, with his cups and concubines about him and a thousand of his lords revelling with him.

III. Babylon should be found all in festival gaiety (*v.* 5): "Prepare the table with all manner of dainties. Set the guards; let them watch in the watch-tower while we make merry; and, if any alarm should be given, the princes shall arise and anoint the shield, and be in readiness to give the enemy a warm reception."

IV. The alarm which should be given to Babylon upon its being forced by Cyrus and Darius. The Lord showed the prophet the watchman set in his watch-tower, and, according to the duty of a watchman, let *him declare what he sees, v.* 6. This watchman here discovered a chariot with a couple of horsemen, in which the commander-in-chief rides. He saw another chariot drawn by mules, much in use among the Persians, and a chariot drawn by camels, much in use among the Medes; so that these two chariots signify the two nations combined against Babylon. And (*v.* 8) *he cried, A lion;* this word, coming out of a watchman's mouth, no doubt everybody knew the meaning of it. Or *he cried as a lion,* very loud, the occasion being very urgent. "*I stand, my lord, continually upon the watch-tower,* and, till just now, all seemed safe and quiet." He shouts again (*v.* 9): *Here comes a chariot of men with a couple of horsemen.*

V. A certain account is at length given of the overthrow of Babylon. He in the chariot *answered and said* (when he heard the watchman speak), *Babylon has fallen, has fallen. All the graven images of her gods he has broken unto the ground.*

VI. Notice is given to the people of God, who were then captives in Babylon, that this prophecy of the downfall of Babylon was particularly intended for their encouragement, *v.* 10.

1. The title the prophet gives them in God's name: *O my threshing, and the corn of my floor!* The prophet calls them *his,* because they were his countrymen, but he speaks it as from God. The church is God's floor. True believers are the corn of God's floor. Hypocrites are but as the chaff and straw. The corn of God's floor must expect to be threshed by afflictions and persecutions. Even then God owns it for his threshing; it is his still.

2. The assurance he gives them which they might build their hopes upon: *That which I have heard of the Lord of hosts, the God of Israel, have I declared unto you.*

Verses 11–12

This prophecy concerning Dumah is very short, and hard to be understood. Some think that Dumah is a part of Arabia, and that the inhabitants descended from Dumah the sixth son of Ishmael. Others, because Mount Seir is here mentioned, by Dumah understand Idumea, the country of the Edomites. Some of Israel's neighbours are certainly meant, and their distress is foretold, not only for warning to them to prepare them for it, but for warning to Israel not to depend upon them, but upon God only. Someone *called out of*

Seir, as the man of Macedonia, in a vision, desired Paul to come over and help them (Acts xvi. 9). The question is serious: *What of the night?* It is put to a proper person, the *watchman.* He repeats the question as one in earnest. God's prophets and ministers are appointed to be watchmen. They are as watchmen in the city in a time of peace, to see that all be safe, to knock at every door by personal enquiries ("Is it locked? Is the fire safe?"). They are as watchmen in the camp in time of war, Ezek. xxxiii. 7. They are to take notice of the enemy and give warning. It is our duty to ask again and again, *What of the night?* "Watchman, what o'clock is it? After a long dark night is there any hope of the day dawning?" *What from the night?* (so some); "what vision has the prophet had tonight? We are ready to receive it." Or, "What occurs tonight? What weather is it? What news?" The watchman was neither asleep nor dumb, though it was a man of Mount Seir that called to him. "The morning comes," he answers. "There comes first a morning of light and peace and opportunity; you will enjoy one day of comfort more; but afterwards comes a night of trouble and calamity." Improve the present morning in preparation for the night that is coming after it. "*Enquire, return, come.* Be inquisitive, be penitent, and obedient."

Verses 13–17

Arabia was a large country, eastward and southward of Canaan. The *Dedanim* (*v.* 13), were descended from Dedan, Abraham's son by Keturah; the inhabitants of Tema and Kedar descended from Ishmael, Gen. xxv. 3, 13, 15. The Arabians lived in tents, kept cattle, a hardy people, inured to labour; the Jews depended upon them as a wall between them and the more warlike eastern nations; and therefore, to alarm them, they shall hear the *burden of Arabia.*

I. A destroying army shall be brought upon them, with a sword, with *a drawn sword,* with *a bow* ready *bent,* and with all the *grievousness of war, v.* 15. It is probable that the king of Assyria took Arabia in his way, and made an easy prey of them.

II. The poor country people will be forced to flee for shelter; so that *the travelling companies of Dedanim* shall be obliged to *lodge in the forest in Arabia* (*v.* 13).

III. They shall need refreshment in their flight from the invading army: "*O you inhabitants of the land of Tema!*" (who probably were next neighbours to the companies of Dedanim) "*bring you water*" (so the margin reads it) "*to him that is thirsty,* and *prevent with your bread those that flee,* for they are objects of your compassion; *they flee from the sword.*" Let us learn to look with compassion upon those that are in distress, and with all cheerfulness to relieve them. It is here remembered to the praise of the land of Tema that they relieved even those that were on the falling side.

IV. All the glory of Kedar shall vanish and fail. Their numerous herds and flocks shall all be driven away by the enemy. Their archers; and instead of foiling the enemy, shall fall themselves; and *the residue of their number shall be diminished* (*v.* 17); their able-bodied men shall become very few; for they were most exposed, and fell first by the enemies' sword.

V. All this shall be done in a little time: "*Within one year according to the years of a hireling* (within one year precisely reckoned) this judgment shall come upon Kedar.*" This fixing of the time might be of great use to the Arabians, to awaken them to repentance, that, like the men of Nineveh, they might prevent the judgment when they were thus told it was just at the door.

VI. It is all ratified by the truth of God (*v.* 16): "*Thus hath the Lord said to me.*" And again (*v.* 17): *The Lord God of Israel hath spoken it.*

CHAPTER 22

This chapter is "the burden of the valley of vision", Jerusalem; now let Jerusalem hear her own doom. This chapter concerns, I. The city of Jerusalem itself and the neighbourhood. 1. A prophecy of the grievous distress they should shortly be brought into by Sennacherib's invasion and siege, ver. 1–7. 2. A reproof given them for their misconduct in two things: (1) Not having an eye to God in the use of the means of their preservation, ver. 8–11. (2) Not humbling themselves under his mighty hand, ver. 12–14. II. The court of Hezekiah, and the officers of that court. 1. The displacing of Shebna, a bad man, and turning him out of the treasury, ver. 15–19, 25. 2. The preferring of Eliakim, who should do his country better service, ver. 20–24.

Verses 1–7

The title of this prophecy is *the burden of the valley of vision*, of Judah and Jerusalem. Jerusalem is called a valley, for the mountains were round about it, and the land of Judah abounded with valleys. It is called a *valley of vision* because there God was known and there the prophets were made acquainted with his mind by visions. Babylon, being a stranger to God, though rich and great, was called *the desert of the sea*; but Jerusalem, being trusted with his oracles, is *a valley of vision*.

Now the *burden of the valley of vision* here is that which will not quite ruin it, but only frighten it; for it refers not to the destruction of Jerusalem by Nebuchadnezzar, but to the attempt made upon it by Sennacherib, *ch.* x, and *ch.* xxxvi.

I. The consternation that the city should be in upon the approach of Sennacherib's army. It used to be a city of great trade, populous and noisy, a joyous revelling city. "But what ails thee now, that the shops are quitted, and *thou hast wholly gone up to the house-tops* (*v.* 1), to secure thyself from the enemy." But why is Jerusalem in such a fright? *Her slain men are not slain with the sword* (*v.* 2), but with famine (so some), or with fear. They were so disheartened that they seemed as effectually stabbed with fear as if they had been run through with a sword.

II. The inglorious flight of the rulers of Judah, who fled from all parts of the country, to Jerusalem (*v.* 3), and were found in Jerusalem, having left their respective cities to be a prey to the Assyrian army, which, meeting with no opposition, when it *came up against all the defenced cities of Judah* easily *took them, ch.* xxxvi. 1. These rulers *were bound from the bow* (so the word is); they not only quitted like cowards, but, when they came to Jerusalem, trembled, so that they could not draw a bow.

III. The great grief which this should occasion to all serious people, the prophet laying the thing to heart himself, *v.* 4, 5. He is not willing to proclaim his sorrow, and therefore bids those about him to look away from him; he will weep secretly. But what is the occasion of his grief? A poor prophet had little to lose, and had been inured to hardship, but it is for *the spoiling of the daughter of his people*. Our enemies tread us down, and our friends know not what course to take to do us a kindness. The enemies with their battering rams are breaking down the walls, and we are in vain crying to the mountains (to keep off the enemy, or to fall on us and cover us), or appealing to the mountains to hear our controversy (Mic. vi. 1) and to judge between us and our neighbours.

IV. The great strength of the enemy, that should besiege their city, *v.* 6, 7. Elam (that is, the Persians) come with their quiver full of arrows, and with chariots. Kir (that is, the Medes) get everything ready for battle, for the besieging of Jerusalem. Then the choice valleys about Jerusalem, that used to be clothed with flocks, shall be full of chariots of war, and at the gate of the city *the horsemen shall set themselves in array*, to cut off all provisions from going in.

Verses 8–14

What is meant by *the covering of Judah*, which in the beginning of this paragraph is said to be *discovered*, is not agreed. The fenced cities of Judah were a covering to the country; but these, being taken by the army of the Assyrians, ceased to be a shelter. The weakness of Judah now appeared; thus the covering of Judah was discovered. Its stores were now laid open for the public use. Dr. Lightfoot gives another sense of it, that by this distress into which Judah should be brought God would discover their covering (that is, unlock their hypocrisy), 2 Chron. xxxii. 31. Now they discovered both their carnal confidence (*v.* 9) and their carnal security, *v.* 13.

They were in a great fright, and in this fright they manifested:

I. A great contempt of God's goodness, and his power to help them. They made use of all the means they could think of for their own preservation; but, in doing this, they did not acknowledge God. When Sennacherib had made himself master of all the defenced cities of Judah it was resolved to stand upon their defence, and not tamely to surrender. They inspected the magazines and stores, to see if they were well stocked with arms: *They looked to the armour of the house of the forest*, which Solomon built in Jerusalem for an armoury (1 Kings x. 17). They viewed the fortifications, the *breaches of the city of David*; they walked round the walls, and observed where they had gone to decay for want of repairs. These breaches were many. By public distresses, we should be awakened by them to *repair our breaches*, and amend what is amiss. They made sure of water for the city: *You gathered together the water of the lower pool*. They *numbered the houses of Jerusalem*, that every house might send in its quota of men for the public service, or contribute in money, so much a house. Because private property ought to give way to the public safety, those houses in their way, when the wall was to be fortified, were broken down. They made a ditch between the outer and inner wall, for the greater security of the city; and they contrived to draw the water of the old pool to it, that they might have plenty of water themselves and might deprive the besiegers of it; lest the Assyrian army *should come and find much water* (2 Chron. xxxii. 4). How regardless they were of God in all these preparations: *But you have not looked unto the Maker thereof* (that is, of Jerusalem, the city you are so solicitous for the defence of) and of all the advantages which nature has furnished it with for its defence. It is God that made his Jerusalem, and fashioned it long ago, in his counsels. It is here charged upon them that they did not look to God. They fortified Jerusalem because it was a rich city and their own houses were in it, not because it was the holy city and God's house was in it. They did not depend upon him for a blessing upon their endeavours, but thought their own powers sufficient for them. Of Hezekiah himself it is said that *he trusted in God* (2 Kings xviii. 5), and particularly upon this occasion (2 Chron. xxxii. 8); but there were those about him, it seems, who were great statesmen and soldiers, but had little religion in them.

II. A great contempt of God's wrath and justice, *v.* 12–14. God's design in bringing this calamity upon them was to humble them, bring them to repentance. In that day of trouble the Lord did thereby *call to weeping and mourning*, and all the expressions of sorrow, even to *baldness and girding with sackcloth*; and this to lament their sins, to enforce their prayers, and to dispose themselves to a reformation of their lives. To this God called them by his prophet's explaining his providences. How contrary they walked to this design of God (*v.* 13). They were as secure and cheerful as if they had had no enemy or were in no danger. When they had taken precautions for their security, they set dangers at defiance, and resolved to be merry: *Let us eat and drink, for to-morrow we shall die.* This was the language of the profane scoffers who *mocked the messengers of the Lord and misused his prophets.* They made a jest of dying. They ridiculed the doctrine of a future state on the other side death. A practical disbelief of another life after this is at the bottom of the carnal security and brutish sensuality which are the sin, and shame, and ruin of so great a part of mankind. God signified his resentment of it to the prophet, *revealed it in his ears,* to be by him proclaimed upon the house-top: *Surely this iniquity shall not be purged from you till you die,* v. 14. Those that walk contrary to God shall find that he will walk contrary to them; with the froward he will show himself froward.

Verses 15–25

We have here a prophecy concerning the displacing of Shebna, a great officer at court, and the preferring of Eliakim to the post of honour and trust. By the accomplishment of what was foretold concerning these particular persons God designed to confirm his word in the mouth of Isaiah concerning other and greater events. It is probable that this prophecy was delivered at the same time with that in the former part of the chapter, and began to be fulfilled before Sennacherib's invasion; for now Shebna was *over the house,* but then Eliakim was (ch. xxxvi. 3); and Shebna, coming down gradually, was only scribe.

I. The prophecy of Shebna's disgrace. He is called *this treasurer,* being entrusted with the management of the revenue; and he is likewise said to be *over the house.* The Jews say, "He kept up a traitorous correspondence with the king of Assyria, and was in treaty with him to deliver the city into his hands." His pride, vanity, and security (v. 16): "*What hast thou here, and whom hast thou here?* What a mighty noise and bustle dost thou make! Art thou not mean and obscure that comest we know not whence? What is the meaning of this then, that thou hast built thyself a fine house, *hast graved thyself a habitation?*" It seemed engraven in a rock, so firmly was it founded and so impregnable was it. "Nay, *thou hast hewed thee out a sepulchre,*" as if he designed that his pomp should survive his funeral. A prophecy of his fall and the sullying of his glory (v. 19): *I will drive thee from thy station.* High places are slippery places; and those are justly deprived of their honour that are puffed up with it. To this v. 25 refers. "The nail that is *now fastened in the sure place* (that is, Shebna, who thinks himself immovably fixed in his office) *shall be removed, and cut down, and fall.*" After a while he should not only be driven from his station, but driven from his country: *The Lord will carry thee away with the captivity of a mighty man,* v. 17, 18. Some think the Assyrians seized him, and took him away, or perhaps Hezekiah, finding out his treachery, banished him. Grotius thinks he was stricken with a leprosy, which was a disease commonly supposed to come from God's displeasure, particularly for the punishment of the proud, and by reason of this disease he was *tossed like a ball* out of Jerusalem. Shebna thought his place too strait for him. God will therefore send him *into a large country,* where he shall have room to wander, but never find the way back again; *there the chariots* which had been the chariots of his glory, should but serve to upbraid him with his former grandeur, *to the shame of his lord's house,* of the court of Ahaz, who had advanced him.

II. The prophecy of Eliakim's advancement, v. 20, &c. He is God's servant, has approved himself faithfully so in other employments, and therefore God will call him to this high station. It is here foretold Eliakim should be put into Shebna's place of lord-chamberlain of the household, lord-treasurer, and prime-minister of state. The prophet must tell Shebna this, v. 21. "He shall have *thy robe,* the badge of honour, and *thy girdle,* the badge of power; for he shall have *thy government.*" *I will clothe him;* and then it follows, *I will strengthen him.* Those that are called to places of trust and power should seek unto God for grace to enable them to do the duty of their places. Eliakim's advancement is further described by the laying of the *key of the house of David upon his shoulders,* v. 22. He had access to *the house of the precious things, the silver, and the gold, and the spices;* and to the *house of the armour* and the *treasures* (ch. xxxix. 2), and disposed of the stores there as he thought fit for the public service. He should be fixed and confirmed in that office. He shall have it for life (v. 23): *I will fasten him as a nail in a sure place,* not to be removed or cut down. He shall be a blessing to his country (v. 21): *He shall be a father to the inhabitants of Jerusalem and to the house of Judah.* He shall take care not only of the affairs of the king's household, but of all the public interests in Jerusalem and Judah. It is happy with a people when the court, the city, and the country, have no separate interests, but the courtiers are true patriots, and whom the court blesses the country has reason to bless too. He shall be a blessing to his family (v. 23, 24): *He shall be for a glorious throne to his father's house.* Eliakim is *a nail in a sure place,* and all his family are said to have a dependence upon him, as in a house the vessels that have handles to them are hung up upon nails and pins. It intimates likewise that he shall generously take care of them all, and bear the weight of that care: *All the vessels,* not only *the flagons,* but *the cups, the vessels of small quantity,* the meanest that belong to his family, shall be provided for by him. Our Lord Jesus, having the key of the house of David, is as a *nail in a sure place,* and all *the glory of his father's house hangs* upon him. That soul cannot perish, nor that concern fall to the ground, though ever so weighty, that is by faith hung upon Christ.

CHAPTER 23

This chapter is concerning Tyre, an ancient wealthy city, situated upon the sea, celebrated for trade and merchandise. The lot of the tribe of Asher bordered upon it. See Joshua xix. 29, where it is called "the strong city Tyre". We seldom find it a dangerous enemy to Israel, but sometimes their faithful ally, as in the reigns of David and Solomon; for trading cities maintain their grandeur, not by the conquest of their neighbours, but by commerce with them. In this chapter is foretold, I. The lamentable desolation of Tyre, by Nebuchadnezzar and the Chaldean army, about the time they destroyed Jerusalem, ver. 1–14. II. The restoration of Tyre after seventy years, and the return of the Tyrians out of their captivity to their trade again, ver. 15–18.

Verses 1–14

Tyre being a sea-port town, this prophecy of its overthrow fitly begins and ends with, *Howl, you ships of Tarshish;* for all its business, wealth, and honour, depended upon its shipping; if that be ruined, they will be all undone.

I. Tyre flourishing. 1. *The merchants of Zidon,* who traded at sea, had at first *replenished her,* v. 2. Zidon was the more ancient city, situated upon the same sea-coast, a few leagues more to the north, and Tyre was at first only a colony of that; but the daughter had outgrown the mother. Egypt had helped very much to raise her, v. 3. Sihor was the river of Egypt: by that river, and the ocean into which it ran, the Egyptians traded with Tyre. Tyre became rich and great by industry, though she had no other ploughs going than those that plough the waters. She was a *joyous city,* noted for mirth and jollity, v. 7. This made them very loth to consider what warnings God gave them by his servants. Her *antiquity* likewise was *of ancient days*, and that helped to make her secure. She was *a crowning city* (v. 8), that crowned herself. *Her merchants are princes*, and *her traffickers*, whatever country they go to, *are the honourable of the earth*, respected by all.

II. Here is Tyre falling. It does not appear that she brought trouble upon herself by provoking her neighbours, but rather by tempting them with her wealth; but, if it was this that induced Nebuchadnezzar to fall upon Tyre, he was disappointed; for after it had stood out a siege of thirteen years, the inhabitants got away by sea, with their families and goods, and left Nebuchadnezzar nothing but the bare city. The destruction of Tyre is here foretold. The haven shall be spoiled, or at least neglected. There shall be no convenient harbour for the reception of the ships of Tarshish, but all *laid waste* (v. 1). Tyre is destroyed and laid waste; so that there is no more business there. The inhabitants are so overwhelmed with grief that they shall not be able to express it. The neighbours are amazed, and are in pain for them: *Zidon is ashamed* (v. 4), for the rolling waves of the sea brought to Zidon this news from Tyre; and there the *strength of the sea*, a high springtide, proclaimed saying, "*I travail not, nor bring forth children* now. I do not bring ship-loads of young people to Tyre, to be bred up there in trade and business," which was the thing that had made Tyre so rich and populous. Egypt indeed was a much larger and more considerable kingdom, and yet Tyre had so large a trade, that all the nations about shall be as much in pain, upon the report of the ruin of that one city, as they not long after were, upon the report of the ruin of all Egypt, v. 5. "*You* that have long been *inhabitants of this isle*, it is time to howl now, for you must pass over to Tarshish. The best course you can take is to make the best of your way to Tarshish, to the sea." Those that could not make their escape must expect no other than to be carried into captivity (v. 7): *Her own feet shall carry her afar off to sojourn;* they shall be hurried away on foot into captivity. Many of those that attempted to escape should fall into the hands of the enemy. Tyre shall *pass through her land as a river* (v. 10), running down into the abyss of misery. *There is no more strength;* they fall an easy prey into the hands of the enemy. And, as Tyre has no more strength, so her sister Zidon has no more comfort (v. 12): "*Thou shalt no more rejoice, O oppressed virgin, daughter of Zidon*, that art now ready to be overpowered by the victorious Chaldeans!" But whence shall all this trouble come? God will be the author of it; it is a *destruction from the Almighty*. It will be asked (v. 8): "*Who has taken this counsel against Tyre?*" God has designed it, who is infinitely wise and just. God did not bring those calamities upon Tyre to show an arbitrary power; but to punish the Tyrians for their pride. Many other sins, no doubt, reigned among them, but the sin of pride was the particular ground of God's controversy with Tyre. God tells the world what he meant. He designed to convince men of the vanity and uncertainty of all earthly glory, to show them what a withering thing it is even when it seems most substantial. Are men's learning and wealth, their pomp and power, their glory? Look upon the ruins of Tyre, and see all this glory stained, and sullied, and buried in the dust. *He stretched out his hand over the sea*. The Chaldeans shall be the instruments of it (v. 13): *Behold the land of the Chaldeans;* how easily they and their land were destroyed by the Assyrians. Though their own hands *founded it, set up the towers* of Babylon, and *raised up its palaces*, yet the Assyrians brought it to ruin, and so shall Tyre hereafter be brought to ruin by Nebuchadnezzar. If we looked more upon the falling of others,

we should not be so confident as we commonly are of the continuance of our own standing.

Verses 15–18

I. The time fixed for the continuance of the desolations of Tyre, which were not to be perpetual desolations: *Tyre shall be forgotten seventy years*, v. 15. It was destroyed by Nebuchadnezzar about the time that Jerusalem was, and lay as long in its ruins. He trampled on the pride of Tyre, and therein served God's purpose; but with greater pride, for which God soon after humbled him.

II. A prophecy of the restoration of Tyre to its glory again: *After the end of seventy years, according to the years of one king*, or one dynasty, that of Nebuchadnezzar. And we may presume that Cyrus at the same time when he released the Jews, and encouraged them to rebuild Jerusalem, released the Tyrians also, and encouraged them to rebuild Tyre. *The Lord will visit Tyre* in mercy; for he will not contend for ever. She shall use her best endeavours to recover her trade again. She shall sing as a harlot, that has been some time under correction for her lewdness; but, when she is set at liberty, she will use her old arts of temptation. The Tyrians having returned from their captivity, shall contrive how to force a trade, procure the best choice of goods, and be obliging to all customers; as a harlot that has been forgotten, when she comes to be spoken of again, recommends herself to company by singing and playing, *takes a harp, goes about the city*, serenading. Tyre shall by degrees come to be the mart of nations again; she shall *return to her hire*, to her traffic, *and shall commit fornication* (that is, she shall have dealings in trade, for the prophet carries on the similitude of a harlot) *with all the kingdoms of the world* that she had formerly traded with in her prosperity. The love of worldly wealth is a spiritual whoredom, and therefore covetous people are called *adulterers and adulteresses* (James iv. 4). Having recovered her trade again, she shall make a better use of it than formerly (v. 18): *Her merchandise, and her hire, shall be holiness to the Lord*. The trade of Tyre, and all the gains of her trade, shall be devoted to God, and employed in his service. It shall not be hoarded, but it shall be laid out in acts of piety and charity. What they can spare from the maintenance of themselves and their families *shall be for those that dwell before the Lord*, for the priests, the Lord's ministers. They and theirs may *eat sufficiently*, and may have *durable clothing*, strong and lasting. This supposes that religion should be set up in New Tyre, that they should come to the knowledge of the true God and into communion with the Israel of God. We find men of Tyre then dwelling in the land of Judah, Neh. xiii. 16. Tyre and Sidon were better disposed to religion in Christ's time than the cities of Israel; for, if Christ had gone among them, *they would have repented*, Matt. xi. 21. And we meet with Christians at Tyre (Acts xxi. 3, 4). Both the merchandise of the tradesmen and the hire of the day-labourers shall be devoted to God, must *be holiness to the Lord*, alluding to the motto engraven on the frontlet of the high priest (Exod. xxxix. 30), and to the separation of the tithe under the law, Lev. xxvii. 30. We must first give up ourselves to be holiness to the Lord before what we do, or have, or get, can be so. When we are liberal in relieving the poor, and supporting the ministry, and encouraging the gospel—then our merchandise and our hire are holiness to the Lord, if we sincerely look at his glory in them.

CHAPTER 24

Here begins a new sermon, which is continued to the end of chap. xxvii. And in it the prophet does, in many precious promises, "say to the righteous, It shall be well with them"; and, in many dreadful threatenings, he says, "Woe to the wicked, it shall be ill with them" (ch. iii. 10, 11); and these illustrate each other. This chapter is mostly threatening. It is not the burden of any particular city or kingdom, as those before, but the burden of the whole earth. 1. Some think that it is a prophecy of the great havoc that Sennacherib and his Assyrian army should now shortly make. 2. Others make it to point at like devastations which, about 100 years afterwards, Nebuchadnezzar and his armies should make in the same countries. The promises that are mixed with the threatenings are intended of the comfort of the people of God in those calamitous times. The prophet designs here to represent in general the calamitous state of mankind. Prophecies were written and preserved even for our learning, and therefore ought not to be looked upon as of private interpretation. In this chapter we have, I. A threatening of desolating judgments for sin (ver. 1–12), to which is added an assurance that in the midst of them good people should be comforted, ver. 13–15. II. A further threatening of the like desolations (ver. 16–22), to which is added an assurance that in the midst of all God should be glorified.

Verses 1–12

It is a very dark and melancholy scene that this prophecy presents to our view.

I. The earth is stripped; it is made *empty and waste* (v. 1), as if it were reduced to its first chaos, *Tohu* and *Bohu*, confusion and emptiness again (Gen. i. 2), *without form and void*. Earth sometimes signifies the *land*, and the same word *eretz* is here translated (v. 3): *The land shall be utterly emptied and utterly spoiled;* but it might be as v. 1, translated *the earth*. Many countries are empty of all solid comfort and satisfaction; a little thing makes them waste. We often see plentiful estates, utterly emptied and spoiled, by one judgment or other. Sin has turned the earth *upside down*; the earth has become quite a different thing to man from what it was when God made it to be his habitation. Sin has also *scattered abroad the inhabitants thereof*. The rebellion at Babel was the occasion of the dispersion there. To the same purport is v. 4: *The earth mourns, and fades away;* it disappoints those that placed their happiness in it. *The whole world languishes and fades away*. It is like a flower, which withers in the hands of those that please themselves too much with it. And, as the earth itself grows old, so those that dwell therein are desolate; men carry crazy sickly bodies along with them, are often solitary, and confined by affliction, v. 6. *The inhabitants of the earth are burned*, or consumed, some by one disease, others by another, and there are but *few men left*.

II. It is God that brings all these calamities upon the earth. *The Lord* that made the earth, and made it fruitful and beautiful, for the service and comfort of man, now *makes it empty and waste* (v. 1), for its Creator is and will be its Judge. It is *the Lord that has spoken this word*, and he will do the work (v. 3).

III. Persons of all ranks and conditions shall share in these calamities (v. 2): *It shall be as with the people, so with the priest*, &c. The dignity of magistrates and ministers shall not secure them. The priests had been as wicked as the people; and, if their character served not to restrain them from sin, how can they expect it should serve to secure them from judgments? *As with the servant, so with his master; as with the maid, so with her mistress*. Those that have money beforehand will fare no better than those that are impoverished.

IV. It is sin that brings these calamities upon the earth. The earth is made empty, and fades away, because it *is defiled under the inhabitants thereof* (v. 5); and therefore it is made desolate by the judgments of God. They have transgressed the laws of their creation, and their obligations to the God of nature. *They have changed the ordinances* of revealed religion, *neglected the ordinances* (so some read it), and made no conscience of observing them. They have passed over the laws, in the commission of sin, and have passed by the ordinance, in the omission of duty. Herein they have *broken the everlasting covenant*, which is a perpetual bond and will be to those that keep it a perpetual blessing.

V. These judgments shall humble men's pride (v. 4): *The haughty people of the earth do languish;* for they have lost that which supported their pride. It is a great damp to men's jollity. This is enlarged upon much (v. 7–9): *All the merry-hearted do sigh*. Such is the nature of carnal mirth, it is but *as the crackling of thorns under a pot*, Eccles. vii. 6. Carnal joy is a noisy thing; but the noise of it will soon be at an end, and the end of it is heaviness. Two things excite and express vain mirth. (1) Drinking: *The new wine mourns;* it has grown sour for want of drinking. *The vine languishes*, and gives little hopes of a vintage, and therefore *the merry-hearted do sigh*; for if you *destroy their vines and their fig-trees, you make all their mirth to cease*, Hosea ii. 11, 12. (2) Music: *The mirth of tabrets ceases, and the joy of the harp*, which used to be at their feasts, *ch*. v. 12. In short, *All joy is darkened;* there is not a pleasant look to be seen, nor has anyone power to force a smile.

VI. The cities will feel these desolations (v. 10): *The city of confusion is broken, is broken down* (so we read it); it lies exposed to invading powers. *Every house is shut up*, perhaps by reason of the plague, so that there are *few men left*, v. 6. *In the city*, in Jerusalem itself, there shall be left nothing but *desolation;* grass shall grow in the streets, and *the gate is smitten with destruction* (v. 12); all that used to pass and repass through the gate are smitten.

Verses 13–15

Here is mercy remembered in the midst of wrath. In Judah and Jerusalem, and the neighbouring countries, when they are overrun by the enemy, Sennacherib or Nebuchadnezzar, there shall be a remnant preserved from the general ruin.

I. The small number of this remnant, v. 13. When all goes to ruin *there shall be as the shaking of an olive tree, and the gleaning grapes*, here and there one who shall escape the common calamity. These few are dispersed like the gleanings of the olive-tree; and they are hid under the leaves. The Lord knows those that are his; the world does not.

II. The great devotion of this remnant, having so narrowly escaped this great destruction (v. 14): *They shall lift up their voice; they shall sing*. Those that rejoice in the Lord can rejoice in tribulation. They shall sing not only for the mercy but *for the majesty of the Lord*. Their dispersion shall help to spread the knowledge of God, and they shall make even remote shores to ring with his praises.

III. Their holy zeal to excite others to the same devotion (v. 15), *in the fires*, in the furnace of affliction, those fires by which the *inhabitants of the earth are burned*, v. 6. Those who are *in the isles of the sea*, whither they are banished, or are forced to flee for shelter, went *through fire and water* (Ps. lxvi. 12); yet in both let them glorify the Lord.

Verses 16–23

I. Comfort to saints. They may be driven, by common calamities, into *the uttermost parts of the earth*, or perhaps they are forced thither for their religion; but there they are singing, not sighing. And this is their song, *even glory to the righteous:* the word is singular, and may refer to *the righteous God*, or the meaning may be, "These songs redound to the glory or beauty of the righteous that sing them."

II. Terror to sinners. The prophet returns to lament the miseries he saw breaking in upon the earth: *"But I said, My leanness! my leanness! woe unto me!* The very thought of it frets me, and makes me lean," v. 16. He foresees that iniquity should abound (v. 16): *The treacherous dealers have dealt treacherously*. Men are false to one another; there is universal dishonesty. Truth, that sacred bond of society, has departed, and there is nothing but treachery in men's dealings. They are all false to their God, all treacherous dealers, and have dealt very treacherously with their God, in departing from their allegiance to him. The inhabitants of the earth will be pursued from place to place, by one mischief or other (*v.* 17, 18): *Fear, and the pit, and the snare* (fear of the pit and the snare) are upon them wherever they are. It is a common instance of the calamitous state of human life that when we seek to avoid one mischief we fall into a worse. The earth itself will be shaken to pieces. It will be literally so at last, when all *the works therein shall be burnt up*; and it is often figuratively so before that period. This is expressed (*v.* 19, 20): *The earth is utterly broken down; it is clean dissolved; it is moved exceedingly*, moved out of its place. Those who lay up their treasure in the things of the earth place their confidence in that which will shortly be *utterly broken down and dissolved. The earth shall reel to and fro like a drunkard*. Worldly men dwell in it as in a castle, an impregnable tower; but *it shall be removed like a cottage*, so easily, so suddenly, and with so little loss to the great landlord. It *shall fall, and not rise again*; but there shall be new heavens and a new earth, in which shall dwell nothing but righteousness. But what is it that shakes the earth thus and sinks it? It is the transgression that shall be heavy upon it. Sin is a burden to the whole creation. Sin is the ruin of states, and kingdoms, and families. God will have a particular controversy with the kings and great men of the earth (*v.* 21): *He will punish the host of the high ones*. The high ones, that think themselves out of the reach of any danger, God will visit upon them all their pride and cruelty, and it shall return upon their own heads. Let those that are trampled upon by the high ones of the earth comfort themselves with this, that though they cannot resist them, yet there is a God that will call them to account. It is particularly foretold (*v.* 22) that they shall be *gathered together as prisoners*, convicted condemned prisoners, *gathered in the pit*, or dungeon, and there they shall *be shut up* under close confinement. Let not the free man glory in his freedom, any more than the strong man in his strength, for he knows not what restraints he is reserved for. But *after many days they shall be visited*, either in wrath, or shall be reserved to the day of execution, *to the judgment of the great day*, Jude 6. Or they shall be visited in mercy, and be discharged from their imprisonment, and shall again obtain, if not their dignity, yet their liberty. Nebuchadnezzar made many kings and princes his captives, and kept them in the dungeon in Babylon, and, among the rest, Jehoiachin king of Judah; but after many days, when Nebuchadnezzar's head was laid, his son visited them, and with particular kindness to Jehoiachin *set his throne above the throne of the rest of the kings that were with him*, Jer. lii. 32. When the proud enemies of God's church are humbled it shall appear, beyond contradiction, that the Lord reigns. When the kings of the earth are punished for their tyranny, then it is proved to all the world that God is King of kings, that he reigns as *Lord of hosts*, of all hosts, of their hosts—that he reigns *in Mount Zion, and in Jerusalem*, in his church—that he reigns *before his ancients*. God's ancients, the old disciples, the experienced Christians, that have often, when they have been perplexed, gone into the sanctuary of God in Zion and Jerusalem, shall see more than others of God's dominion and sovereignty. Then it shall appear that he reigns *gloriously*, in such brightness and lustre that *the moon shall be confounded and the sun ashamed*, as the smaller lights are eclipsed and extinguished by the greater. The glory of the Creator infinitely outshines the glory of the brightest creatures.

CHAPTER 25

I. Thankful praises for what God had done, which the prophet offers to God, ver. 1–5. II. Precious promises of what God would yet further do for his church, especially in the grace of the gospel, ver. 6–8. III. The church's triumph in God over her enemies, ver. 9–12. This chapter looks as pleasantly upon the church as the former looked dreadfully upon the world.

Verses 1–5

I. The prophet determines to praise God himself (*v.* 1): "*O Lord! thou art my God*, a God in covenant with me." When God is punishing *the kings of the earth upon the earth*, a poor prophet can go to him, and, with a humble boldness, say, *O Lord! thou art my God*, and therefore *I will exalt thee, I will praise thy name*.

II. He pleases himself with the thought that others also shall be brought to praise God, *v.* 3. "*Therefore*, because of the *desolations thou hast made in the earth*, and the just vengeance thou hast taken, *shall the strong people glorify thee* in concert, *and the city* (the metropolis) *of the terrible nations shall fear thee*." This may be understood, 1. Of those that have been enemies to God's kingdom. They shall either be converted, and glorify God by joining with his people in his service, or at least convinced, so as to own themselves conquered. Or, 2. Of those that shall be now made strong and terrible for God and by him, though before they were weak. God shall so visibly appear for and with those that fear him and glorify him that all shall stand in awe of them.

III. He observes what ought to be, the matter of this praise. We must exalt God and praise him; for, 1. He has done wonders, according to the counsel of his own will, *v.* 1. These *wonderful things*, which are new and surprising to us, are according to his *counsels of old*. 2. He has in particular humbled the pride, and broken the power, of the mighty ones of the earth (*v.* 2): "*Thou hast made of a city a heap* of rubbish. Of many a defenced city, that thought itself well guarded by nature and art, thou hast made a ruin. Many a city so richly built that it might be called a *palace*, and so much visited by persons from all parts that it might be called a *palace of strangers*, is levelled with the ground, and shall never be built again." Cities that flourished once have gone to decay and are scarcely known (except by urns or coins digged up out of the earth). How many of the cities of Israel have long since been heaps and ruins! 3. He has relieved his necessitous people (*v.* 4): *Thou hast been a strength to the poor, a strength to the needy*. He strengthens the weak that are humble and stay themselves upon him. He not only makes them strong, but he is himself their strength. He is *a refuge from the storm* of rain or hail, and *a shadow from the* scorching *heat* of the sun in summer; *when the blast of the terrible ones is as a storm against the wall*, which makes a great noise, but cannot overthrow the wall. The enemies of God's poor are terrible ones. Their rage is like a blast of wind, loud, and blustering, and furious; but, like the wind, it is under a divine check; for God *holds the winds in his fist*. A storm beating on a ship tosses it, but that which beats on a wall never stirs it, Ps. lxxvi. 10; cxxxviii. 7. *Thou shalt*, or thou dost, *bring down the noise of strangers*; thou shalt abate and still it, as *the heat in a dry place* is abated and moderated *by the shadow of a cloud* interposing. The oppressors of God's people are called *strangers*; for they forget that those they oppress are of the same blood with them. They are called *terrible ones*; they would rather be feared than loved. The branches, even the top branches, of the terrible ones, will be broken off. If the labourers in God's vineyard be called to *bear the burden and heat of the day*, he will refresh them, as with the shadow of a cloud.

Verses 6–8

If we suppose (as many do) that this refers to the great joy which there should be in Zion and Jerusalem when the army of the Assyrians was routed by an angel, or when the Jews were released out of their captivity in Babylon, yet we cannot avoid making it to look further, to the grace of the gospel and the glory which is the crown and consummation of that grace. We have here a prophecy of the salvation and the grace brought unto us by Jesus Christ, into which *the prophets enquired and searched diligently*, 1 Pet. i. 10.

I. That the grace of the gospel should be a royal feast for all people; not like that of Ahasuerus, intended only to show the grandeur of the master of the feast (Esther i. 4); for this is intended to gratify the guests. 1. God himself is the Master of the feast. 2. The guests invited are *all people*, Gentiles as well as Jews. *Go preach the gospel to every creature*. 3. The place is *Mount Zion*; the preachers must begin at Jerusalem. The gospel church is the Jerusalem that is above. It is *a feast of fat things and full of marrow*; so nourishing are the comforts of the gospel to all those that feast upon them. It is a feast *of wines on the lees*, the strongest-bodied wines, that have been kept long upon the lees, and then are well refined.

II. That the world should be freed from that darkness of ignorance and mistake in the mists of which it had been so long lost and buried (*v.* 7): *He will destroy in this mountain the face of the covering* (the covering of the face). Their faces are covered as those of men condemned, or dead. There is a *veil spread over all nations*, for they all sit in darkness; the Jews themselves, among whom *God was known*, had a *veil upon their hearts*, 2 Cor. iii. 15. But this veil the Lord will destroy, by the light of his gospel shining in the world, and the power of his Spirit opening men's eyes to receive it.

III. That death should be conquered, the power of it broken: *He will swallow up death in victory*, *v.* 8. 1. Christ will himself, in his resurrection, triumph over death. The grave seemed to swallow him up, but really he swallowed it up. 2. The happiness of the saints shall be out of the reach of death. 3. Believers may triumph over death, as a conquered enemy: *O death! where is thy sting?* It is the last enemy.

IV. That grief shall be banished, and there shall be endless joy: *The Lord God will wipe away tears from off all faces*. In the covenant of grace there shall be that provided which is sufficient to counterbalance all the sorrows of this present time. God shall *wipe away all tears*, Rev. vii. 17; xxi. 4. And *there shall be no more sorrow*, because *there shall be no more death*. The hope of this should now wipe away all excessive tears, all the weeping that hinders sowing.

V. That all the reproach cast upon religion shall be for ever rolled away: *The rebuke of his people* the calumnies and misrepresentations by which they have been blackened, *shall be taken away*.

Verses 9–12

I. The welcome which the church shall give to these blessings (*v.* 9): *It shall be said in that day*, with humble exultation, *Lo, this is our God; we have waited for him!* With such a triumphant song as this will glorified saints *enter into the joy of their Lord*. It is an encouragement to hope for the perfection of this salvation: *We have waited for him, and he will save us*, will carry on what he has begun; for *as for God*, our God, *his work is perfect*.

II. A prospect of further blessings. *In this mountain shall the hand of the Lord rest, v.* 10. The church and people of God shall have continued proofs of God's presence among them. The power of their enemies shall be broken. *Moab* is here put for all the adversaries of God's people; they *shall* all *be trodden down* or threshed (for *then* they beat out the corn by treading it) and shall be thrown out as *straw to the dunghill,* being good for nothing else. God having *caused his hand to rest upon this mountain*, shall *spread forth his hands, in the midst* of his people, *like one that swims*, which intimates that he will employ and exert his power for them vigorously. On their behalf he will be continually active, for so the swimmer is. *He shall bring down the pride* of their enemies (and Moab was notoriously guilty of pride, *ch.* xvi. 6) by one humbling judgment after another. He shall bring down *the spoils of their hands*, shall take from them that which they have got by spoil and rapine. He shall ruin all their fortifications, *v.* 12. There is no fortress impregnable to Omnipotence. This destruction of Moab is typical of Christ's victory over death (spoken of *v.* 8), his spoiling principalities and powers in his cross (Col. ii. 15).

CHAPTER 26

This chapter is a song of holy joy and praise, in which the great things God had engaged to do for his people are celebrated: it is to be sung when that prophecy should be accomplished; for we must meet God with our thanksgivings when he is coming towards us with his mercies. Now the people of God are here taught, I. To triumph in the holy security of the church in general and of every member of it, under the divine protection, ver. 1–4. II. To triumph over all opposing powers, ver. 5, 6. III. To walk with God, and wait for him, in the darkest times, ver. 7–9. IV. To lament the stupidity of those who regarded not the providence of God, ver. 10, 11. V. To encourage themselves with hopes that God would still continue to do them good (ver. 13, 14), and engage themselves to continue in his service, ver. 13. VI. To recollect the kind providences of God towards them, ver. 15–18. VII. To rejoice in hope of a glorious deliverance, which should be as a resurrection to them (ver. 19), and to retire in the expectation of it, ver. 20, 21.

Verses 1–4

To the prophecies of gospel grace very fitly is a song annexed: *In that day this song shall be sung;* it shall be sung *in the land of Judah*, which was a figure of the gospel church; for the gospel covenant is said to be made *with the house of Judah*, Heb. viii. 8.

I. The church of God is strongly fortified against those that are bad (*v.* 1): *We have a strong city*. It is a city incorporated by the charter of the everlasting covenant, fitted for the reception of all that are made free by that charter; it is a strong city, as Jerusalem was, while it was a city compact together, and had God himself a wall of fire round about it. The church is a strong city, for it has *walls and bulwarks* of God's own appointing; for he has, in his promise, appointed salvation itself to be its defence.

II. The inhabitants of Jerusalem, if they are such as they should be, are its strength, Zech. xii. 5. The gates are here ordered to be opened, *that the righteous nation, which keeps the truth, may enter in, v.* 2. They had been banished and driven out by the iniquity of the former times, but now they have liberty to enter in again.

III. All who belong to it are safe and easy, and have a security and serenity of mind in the assurance of God's favour. *Thou wilt keep him in peace*, in *perfect peace*, inward peace, outward peace, peace with God, peace of conscience, peace under all events. Those that trust in God must have their minds stayed upon him, and such as do so God will keep in perpetual peace, and that peace shall keep them (Ps. cxii. 7). Trust in him for ever, at all times, when you have nothing else to trust to. Whatever we trust to the world for is confined within the limits of time. But what we trust in God for will last as long as we shall last. For in the *Lord Jehovah—Jah, Jehovah*, in him who was, and is, and is to come, there is a rock of ages, a firm and lasting foundation for faith to build upon; and the house built on that rock will stand in a storm.

Verses 5–11

The prophet encourages us to trust in the word, for,

I. He will make humble souls that trust in him to triumph over their proud enemies, *v.* 5, 6. Even the lofty city Babylon itself, or Nineveh, he lays it low, *ch.* xxv. 12. He does not say, Great armies shall tread them down; but, When God will have it done, even the feet of the poor shall do it, Mal. iv. 3. See Ps. cxlvii. 6; Rom. xvi. 20.

II. He takes cognizance of the way of his people and has delight in it (*v.* 7): *The way of the just is evenness* (so it may be read): it is their endeavour to walk with God in steady obedience. *Thou, most upright, dost level* (or *make even*) *the path of the just,* by removing those things that would be stumbling-blocks. God *weighs* it (so we read it); he considers it, and will give them grace sufficient to help them over all difficulties.

III. It is our duty to wait for God in the darkest and most discouraging times, *v.* 8, 9. This has always been the practice of God's people: "*In the way of thy judgments we* have still *waited for thee;* when thou hast corrected us we have looked to no other hand than thine to relieve us." Our troubles must never turn us away from God; but still *the desire of our soul must be to his name and to the remembrance of him.* Our great concern must be for God's name: "*Father, glorify thy name,* and we are satisfied." The remembrance of God must be our great support and pleasure. Our desires towards God must be inward, fervent, and sincere (Ps. xlii. 1).

IV. It is God's design, in his judgments, to bring *men to seek him*: *When thy judgments are upon the earth,* laying all waste, we have reason to expect that not only God's people, but even *the inhabitants of the world, will learn righteousness,* have their mistakes rectified and their lives reformed.

V. Those are wicked indeed that will not be wrought upon by the methods God takes to reform them; and it is necessary that God should deal with them in a severe way by his judgments. Sinners walk contrary to God, *v.* 10. *Favour is shown* to them. They receive many mercies from God, and the design of this is that they may be won to love and serve God; and yet it is all in vain: *they will not learn righteousness.* They live *in a land of uprightness,* in a land of *evenness,* where there are not so many stumbling-blocks as in other places —in a land of *correction,* where vice and profaneness are punished; yet there they will *deal unjustly,* and go on frowardly in their evil ways. Those that do wickedly deal unjustly and may expect the judgments of God upon them. They *will not behold the majesty of the Lord.* Even when we receive of the mercy of the Lord we must still behold the *majesty of the Lord and his goodness. They will not see,* and none so blind as those who will not see, who ascribe to chance, or common fate, a divine rebuke. *They will not see, but they shall see,* shall be made to see, whether they will or no, that God is angry with them. Atheists, scorners, and the secure, will shortly feel that *it is a fearful thing to fall into the hands of the living God.* They shall see that they have done God's people a great deal of wrong, and shall be ashamed of their enmity and ill usage of such as deserved better treatment. Their doom therefore is that, since they slighted the happiness of God's friends, *the fire of his enemies shall devour them.*

Verses 12–19

The prophet in these verses looks back and then looks forward.

I. His reviews and reflections are mixed. When he looks back upon the state of the church he finds God in many instances had done great things for them (*v.* 12): *Thou hast wrought all our works in us,* or *for* us. Whatever good work is done by us, it is owing to a good work wrought by the grace of God in us. In particular (*v.* 15): "*Thou hast increased the nation, O Lord!* so that a little one has become a thousand (in Egypt they multiplied exceedingly, and afterwards in Canaan, so that they filled the land); and in this *thou art glorified,* as faithful to the covenant with Abraham." The neighbouring nations had sometimes tyrannized over them (*v.* 13): "*O Lord our God!* thou who hast the sole right to rule us, whose subjects and servants we are, to thee we complain that *other lords besides thee have had dominion over us.*" When they had been careless in the service of God, God suffered their enemies to have dominion over them, that they might know the difference between his service *and the service of the kingdoms of the countries.* It may be understood as a confession of sin, their serving other gods, by which other lords (for they called their idols *baals, lords*) had dominion over them, besides God. But now they promise that it shall be so no more: "Henceforth *by thee only will we make mention of thy name*; we will worship thee only, and in that way only which thou hast instituted and appointed." The same may be our penitent reflection: *Other lords, besides God, have had dominion over us;* every lust has been our lord, and we have thus wronged both God and ourselves. They had sometimes been carried into captivity before their enemies (*v.* 15): "The nation which at first thou didst increase, thou hast now diminished, and *removed to all the ends of the earth, driven out to the utmost parts of heaven,*" as is threatened, Deut. xxx. 4; xxviii. 64. The prophet remembers that when they were thus oppressed and carried captive they cried unto God, which was evidence that they neither had quite forsaken him nor were quite forsaken of him, and that there were merciful intentions in the judgments they were under (*v.* 16): *Lord, in trouble have they visited thee.* Afflictions bring us to God, quicken us to our duty, and show us our dependence upon him. Afflictions bring us to secret prayer, in which we may be more free and particular in our addresses to him than we can be in public. He complains that their struggles for their liberty had been painful and perilous, but that they had not been successful, *v.* 17, 18. "We have been like a woman in labour, that cries out in her pangs; we have with a great deal of anxiety and toil endeavoured to help ourselves, and our troubles have been increased by those attempts." Whenever they came to *present themselves before the Lord* with their complaints and petitions they were in agonies like those of a woman in travail. "*We have been with child;* we have had great expectation of a happy deliverance. But, alas! *we have as it were brought forth wind*; it has proved a false conception; our expectations have been frustrated. All our efforts have proved abortive: *We have not wrought any deliverance in the earth,* for ourselves or for our friends, *neither have the inhabitants of the world fallen* before us, but they are still as high and arrogant as ever."

II. His prospects and hopes are very pleasant. In general, "*Thou wilt ordain peace for us*" (*v.* 12). What trouble soever may for a time be appointed to the people of God, peace will at length be ordained for them; for the *end of those men is peace.* "Thou hast heard the desire of the humble, and therefore we will give the glory of it to thee only, will depend upon thy grace only to enable us to do so." *They are dead,* those *other lords* that *have had dominion over us;* their power is broken. He has *made all their memory to perish.* Though the church rejoices not in the birth of the man-child, of which she travailed in pain, *but has as it were brought forth wind* (*v.* 18), yet *Thy dead men shall live.* A spirit of life from God shall enter into the slain witnesses, Rev. xi. 11. The *dry bones shall live,* and become an *exceedingly great army,* Ezek. xxxvii. 10. *Together with my dead body shall they arise.* When God's time shall have come, Jerusalem, the city of God, now lying like a dead body, shall arise, shall be rebuilt, and flourish again. And therefore let the poor, desolate, melancholy inhabitants, that dwell as in dust, *awake and sing.* The dew of God's favour shall be to it as the evening dew to the herbs that were parched with the heat of the sun all day, shall revive and refresh them. And as the spring-dews, that water the earth, and make the herbs that lay buried in it to put forth and bud, so shall they flourish again. "The Gentiles shall live; with my body shall they arise; that is, they shall be called in after Christ's resurrection, shall rise with him, and sit with him in heavenly places; nay, they shall arise my body (says Dr. Lightfoot); they shall become the mystical body of Christ, and shall arise as part of him."

Verses 20–21

These two verses are supposed not to belong to the song which takes up the rest of the chapter, but to begin a new matter, and to be rather an introduction to the following chapter than the conclusion of this.

I. God invites the people (*v.* 20): "*Come, my people,* come to me, come with me, let the storm that disperses others bring you nearer together. Come, and *enter into thy chambers*; stay not abroad, lest you be caught in the storm." We must by faith find a way into these chambers, and there hide ourselves; with serenity of mind, we must put ourselves under the divine protection. Come, as Noah into the ark, for he *shut the doors about him.* When dangers are threatening it is good to retire, and lie hid, as Elijah did by the brook Cherith. *Enter into thy chamber,* to examine thyself, and commune with thy own heart, to pray, and humble thyself before God.

II. He assures them that the trouble would be over in a very short time: "*Hide thyself for a moment,* the smallest part of time we can conceive. When it is over it will seem as nothing to you." When Athanasius was banished from Alexandria by an edict of Julian, and his friends greatly lamented it, he bade them be of good cheer. *Nubecula est quæ cito pertransibit—It is a little cloud, that will soon blow over.*

III. He assures them that their enemies should be reckoned with for all the mischief they had done them by the sword, *v.* 21. *The Lord comes out of his place, to punish the inhabitants of the earth for their iniquity.* God *comes out of his place to punish.* Some observe that God's place is the mercy-seat; there he delights to be; when he punishes he comes out of his place, for he has no pleasure in the death of sinners. The criminals shall be convicted: *The earth shall disclose her blood;* the innocent blood of the saints and martyrs, which has been shed shall now be brought to light, Gen. iv. 10, 11; Job xx. 27.

CHAPTER 27

In this chapter the prophet goes on to show, what great things God would do for his church and people in the deliverance of Jerusalem from Sennacherib and the destruction of the Assyrian army; but it is expressed generally, for the encouragement of the church in after ages. 1. That proud oppressors should be reckoned with, ver. 1. 2. That care should be taken of the church, as of God's vineyard, ver. 2, 3. 3. That God would let fall his controversy with the people, upon their return to him, ver. 4, 5. 4. That he would greatly multiply and increase them, ver. 6. 5. That, as to their afflictions, the property of them should be altered (ver. 7), they should be mitigated and moderated (ver. 8), and sanctified, ver. 9. 6. That though the church might be laid waste, and made desolate, for a time (ver. 10, 11), yet it should be restored, and the scattered members should be gathered together again, ver. 12, 13.

Verses 1–6

The prophet is here singing of judgment and mercy,

I. Of judgment upon the enemies of God's church (*v.* 1). When the Lord *comes out of his place, to punish the inhabitants of the earth* (ch. xxvi. 21), he will be sure to punish *leviathan,* the *dragon that is in the sea,* every proud oppressing tyrant, that is the terror of the mighty, and, like the leviathan, is *so fierce that none dares stir him up,* Job xli. 10, 24, 25. So Sennacherib was in his day, and Nebuchadnezzar in his, and Antiochus in his; so Pharaoh had been formerly, and is called *leviathan* and *the dragon, ch.* li. 9; Ps. lxxiv. 13, 14; Ezek. xxix. 3. The New Testament church has had its leviathans; we read of a great red dragon ready to devour it, Rev. xii. 3. Those malignant persecuting powers are here compared to the leviathan for bulk, and strength—to dragons for their rage and fury,—to serpents, *piercing serpents,* penetrating in their counsels,—to *crooked serpents,* subtle and insinuating, but perverse and mischievous. Great princes, if they oppose the people of God, are in God's account as dragons and serpents, the plagues of mankind. They are too big for men to deal with and call to an account, and therefore the great God will take the matter into his own hands. He has a *sore, and great, and strong sword,* when the *measure of their iniquity is full* and their *day has come to fall. In that day* he will punish, his day which is coming, Ps. xxxvii. 13. This is applicable to the spiritual victories obtained by our Lord Jesus over the powers of darkness. He not only disarmed the prince of this world, but with his strong sword, the virtue of his death and the preaching of his gospel, he does and will *destroy him that had the power of death, that is, the devil,* that great leviathan, that old serpent, the dragon (Rev. xx. 2, 3).

II. Of mercy to the church.

1. She is God's vineyard, and is under his particular care, *v.* 2, 3. She is, in God's eye, a *vineyard of red wine.* The world is as a worthless wilderness; but the church is enclosed as a vineyard, from which precious fruits are gathered, wherewith they honour God and man. It is a vineyard of *red wine,* yielding the best and choicest grapes, intimating the reformation of the church, whereas before it brought forth wild grapes, *ch.* v. 4. *I the Lord do keep it.* He has undertaken to be the keeper of Israel. Those that bring forth fruit to God are under his protection. God's vineyard in this world lies much exposed to injury; there are many that would hurt it (Ps. lxxx. 13); but God will suffer no real hurt to be done, but what he will bring good out of. God will keep it in the night of affliction and persecution, and in the day of peace and prosperity, the temptations of which are no less dangerous. This vineyard shall be well fenced. *I will water it every moment,* and yet it shall not be overwatered. The still and silent dews of God's grace and blessing shall continually descend upon it. God waters his vineyard by the ministry of the word by his servants the prophets. Paul plants, and Apollos waters, but God gives the increase.

2. Though sometimes he contends with his people, yet, upon their submission, he will be reconciled to them, *v.* 4, 5. *Fury is not in him* towards his vineyard. It is true if he find in it briers and thorns instead of vines, he will tread them down and burn them; but otherwise, "If I am angry with my people, let them humble themselves, and pray, and seek my face, and so *take hold of my strength* with a sincere desire to make their peace with me, and I will be reconciled to them, and all shall be well." Here is a quarrel supposed between God and man. It is an old quarrel, ever since sin first entered. Here is a gracious invitation given us to make up this quarrel. Pardoning mercy is called the power of our Lord; let him take

hold of that. Christ is the *arm of the Lord, ch.* liii. 1. Christ *crucified is the power of God* (1 Cor. i. 24); let him by a lively faith take hold of him. God is willing to be reconciled to us if we be but willing to be reconciled to him.

3. The church of God in the world shall be a growing body (*v.* 6): *In times to come* (so some read it), *in after-times,* when these calamities are overpast, or in the days of the gospel, *he shall cause Jacob to take root,* deeper root than ever. Many shall be brought into the church, proselytes shall be numerous, some out of all the nations about, and the converts shall be fruitful in the fruits of righteousness. The preaching of the gospel *brought forth fruit in all the world* (Col. i. 6), fruit that remains, John xv. 16.

Verses 7–13

Here is the prophet singing of mercy and judgment to the church, and mercy mixed with that judgment.

I. Here is judgment threatened even to Jacob and Israel. *They shall blossom and bud* (*v.* 6), but some shall be *smitten* and *slain* (*v.* 7). Judgment shall begin at the house of God. Jerusalem, their *defenced city, shall be desolate, v.* 10, 11. "God having tried methods with them for their reformation, which as to many, have proved ineffectual, he will for a time lay their country waste," which was accomplished when Jerusalem was destroyed by the Chaldeans; then that *habitation* was for a long time *forsaken.* Jerusalem had been a defenced city, not so much by art or nature as by grace and the divine protection; but, when God was provoked to withdraw, she was left like a wilderness. "And in the pleasant gardens of Jerusalem cattle shall feed, shall lie down there, and there shall be none to drive them away; and they shall eat the tender branches of the fruit-trees," which perhaps further signifies that the people should become an easy prey to their enemies. "*When the boughs thereof are withered* as they grow upon the tree, blasted by winds and frosts and not pruned, *they shall be broken off* for fuel, and *the women* and children shall *come and set them on fire.* There shall be a total destruction, for the very trees shall be destroyed." And this is a figure of the deplorable state of the vineyards. Our Saviour seems to refer to this when he says of the branches of the vine which *abide not in him* that they are *cast forth and withered, and men gather them, and cast them into the fire, and they are burned* (John xv. 6). *It is a people of no understanding,* that have no relish or savour of divine things, like a withered branch that has no sap in it; and this is at the bottom of all sins. Wicked people in their greatest concerns are of no understanding. *He that formed them* into a people, to show forth his praise, seeing they do not answer the end of their formation, but hate to be reformed, to be new-formed, will reject them, and *show them no favour.* If he that made us by his power do not make us happy in his favour, we had better never have been made.

II. Here is great mercy mixed with this judgment; for there are good people mixed with those that are corrupt and degenerate, on whom God will have mercy. Though they shall be smitten and slain, yet not to that degree, and in that manner, in which their enemies shall be smitten and slain, *v.* 7. God's people and God's enemies are here represented struggling with each other. In this contest there are slain on both sides. God makes use of wicked men to slay his people; for they are his sword, Ps. xvii. 13. But, when the cup of trembling comes to be put into their hand, it will be much worse with them than ever it was with God's people in their greatest straits. The seed of the woman has only his heel bruised, but the serpent has his head crushed and broken. There is really a vast difference between the afflictions and deaths of good people and the afflictions and deaths

of wicked people. The affliction shall be mitigated, moderated, and proportioned to their strength, not to their deserts, *v.* 8. Thus God orders the troubles of his people, not *suffering them to be tempted above what they are able,* 1 Cor. x. 13. He considers what we can bear when he begins to correct; and when it is the *day of his east-wind,* not only blustering and noisy, but blasting and noxious, he stays his rough wind, checks it, and sets bounds to it. When he is winnowing his corn, it is with a gentle gale, that shall only blow away the chaff, but not the good corn. Though God will afflict them, yet he will make their afflictions to work for the good of their souls, and correct them as the father does the child, to drive out the foolishness that is in their hearts (*v.* 9): *By this therefore shall the iniquity of Jacob be purged.* Therefore, because the affliction is moderated, and the rough wind stayed, we may conclude that he designs their reformation, not their destruction. The particular sin which the affliction was intended to cure was the sin of idolatry. But by the captivity in Babylon they were not only weaned from this sin, but set against it. *Ephraim shall say, What have I to do any more with idols?* Jacob has his sin taken away *when he makes all the stones of the altar,* of his idolatrous altar, the stones of which were precious and sacred to him, *as chalkstones that are beaten asunder;* he not only has them in contempt, and values them no more than chalkstones, but in a holy revenge, beats them asunder as easily as chalkstones are broken to pieces. *The groves and the images shall not* stand before this penitent, but they shall be thrown down too, never to be set up again. This was according to the law for the demolishing and destroying of all the monuments of idolatry (Deut. vii. 5); and since the captivity in Babylon, no people in the world have such a rooted aversion to idols and idolatry as the people of the Jews. Jerusalem shall be desolate and forsaken, for a time, yet there will come a day when its scattered friends shall resort to it again out of all the countries whither they were dispersed (*v.* 12, 13). These scattered Israelites shall be fetched: *The Lord shall beat them off* as fruit from the tree, or beat them out as corn out of the ear. He shall separate them from those among whom they dwelt, *from the channel of the river* Euphrates northeast, *unto* Nile, *the stream of Egypt,* which lay southwest—those that were driven into the land of Assyria, and were captives there in the land of their enemies, and those that were *outcasts in the land of Egypt,* whither many left behind, after the captivity in Babylon, went, contrary to God's express command (Jer. xliii. 6, 7), and there lived as outcasts: God has mercy in store for them all. Though they are cast out, they are not cast off. "*You shall be gathered one by one,* silently, and as it were by stealth, dropping in, first one, and then another." *The great trumpet shall be blown, and* then *they shall come.* Cyrus's proclamation of liberty to the captives is this great trumpet, which awakened the Jews that were asleep in their thraldom to bestir themselves. They shall be gathered together: *To worship the Lord in the holy mount at Jerusalem.* When the captives rallied again, and returned to their own land, the chief thing they applied themselves to, was the worship of God. The holy temple was in ruins, but they had the holy mount, *the place of the altar,* Gen. xiii. 4. Liberty to worship God is the most valuable and desirable liberty.

CHAPTER 28

In this chapter, I. The Ephraimites are reproved and threatened for their pride and sensuality, ver. 1–8. But, in the midst of this, here is a gracious promise of God's favour to the remnant of his people, ver. 5–6. II. They are likewise reproved and threatened for their dulness and stupidity, and unaptness to profit by the instructions which the prophets gave them in God's name, ver. 9–13. III. The rulers of Jerusalem are reproved and threatened for their insolent contempt of God's judgments, and setting them at defiance; and, after a gracious promise of Christ and his grace, they are made to know that the vain hopes of escaping the judgments of God with which they flattered themselves would certainly deceive them, ver. 14–22. IV. All this is confirmed by a comparison borrowed from the method which the husbandman takes with his ground and grain, according to which they must expect God would proceed with his people, whom he had lately called his threshing and the corn of his floor (ch. xxi. 10) ver. 23–29. This is written for our admonition, and is profitable for reproof and warning to us.

Verses 1–8

I. The prophet warns the ten tribes of the judgments coming for their sins when the king of Assyria laid their country waste, and carried the people into captivity. Ephraim had his name from *fruitfulness*, and had a great many *fat valleys* (v. 1, 4), and Samaria, which was situated on a hill, was *on the head of the fat valleys*. Their country was the glory of Canaan, their valleys were covered over with corn and vines.

1. What an ill use they made of their plenty! The goodness with which God crowned their years was to them a *crown of pride*. Pride was a sin that prevailed among them, and therefore the prophet boldly proclaims a *woe to the crown of pride*. They indulged themselves in sensuality. Ephraim was notorious for drunkenness, and Samaria, the head of the fat valleys, was full of those that were *overcome with wine*, were *broken with it*, so the margin. Drunkards make fools and brutes of themselves; the sin overcomes them, and *brings them into bondage* (2 Pet. ii. 19). Their constitution is broken by it, and their health ruined. They are brought to ruin by it. Their peace with God is broken and all this for the gratification of a base lust. Woe to these *drunkards of Ephraim*! There is a particular woe to the drunkards of Ephraim, for they are of God's professing people. Some make the *crown of pride* to belong to the drunkards, and to mean the garlands with which those were crowned that got the victory in their wicked drinking matches and drank down the rest of the company.

2. The justice of God in taking away their plenty from them, which they thus abused. Their *glorious beauty*, the plenty they were proud of, *is but a fading flower*. God can easily *take away their corn in the season thereof* (Hosea ii. 9), and recover those goods of his which they prepared for Baal. God has an officer ready to make a seizure for him, *a mighty and strong one*, even the king of Assyria, who *shall cast down to the earth with the hand* all that of which they are proud, *v.* 2. Then *the crown of pride*, and *the drunkards of Ephraim, shall be trodden under foot* (*v.* 3). Drunkards, in their folly, are apt to talk proudly; but they thereby render themselves ridiculous. The beauty of their valleys will wither of itself, and has in itself the principles of its own corruption. *The hasty fruit*, as soon as it is discovered, is plucked and eaten up; so the wealth of this world, besides that it is apt to decay of itself, is subject to be devoured by others as greedily as the first-ripe fruit.

II. He next turns to the kingdom of Judah, whom he calls the *residue of his people* (*v.* 5), for they were but two tribes to the other ten.

1. He promises them God's favours, and that they shall be taken under his guidance and protection when the beauty of Ephraim shall be left exposed to be trodden down and eaten up, *v.* 5, 6. *In that day,* when the Assyrian army is laying Israel waste, God will be to the residue of his people all they need and can desire; not only to the kingdom of Judah, but to those of Israel who had kept their integrity. When the Assyrian is in Israel as *a tempest of hail*, noisy and battering, as *a destroying storm*, and as *a flood of mighty waters overflowing* the country (*v.* 2), then *in that day will the Lord of hosts* distinguish by peculiar

favours his people who have distinguished themselves by a steady adherence to him. He will be to them *for a crown of glory and for a diadem of beauty*. He will so appear in them as to make it evident that they have his image renewed on them, and that shall be to them a diadem of beauty. He will give them all the wisdom and grace necessary. He will himself be *a spirit of judgment to those that sit in judgment*; the counsellors shall be guided by wisdom and discretion and the judges shall govern by justice and equity. He will give them all the courage requisite to carry them through difficulties. He will be *for strength to those that turn the battle to the gate*, to the gates of the cities they besiege, or to their own gates, when they sally out upon the enemies that besiege them. Where God gives these he is to that people a crown of glory. This may well be supposed to refer to Christ, and so the Chaldee understands it: *In that day shall the Messiah be a crown of glory.*

2. He complains of the many corrupt ones (*v.* 7): *But they also*, many of those of Judah, *have erred through wine*. There are drunkards of Jerusalem, as well as drunkards of Ephraim. Ephraim's sins are found in Judah, and yet not Ephraim's ruins. *They have erred through wine*. Their drinking to excess is itself a practical error; they ruin their judgment, and they think to preserve their health by it and help digestion, but they spoil their constitution and hasten diseases and deaths. Their understanding is clouded and their conscience debauched by it; and therefore they espouse corrupt notions, and form their minds in favour of their lusts. Three things are aggravations of this sin: (1) That those were guilty of it who ought to have set a better example: *The priest and the prophet are swallowed up of wine;* their office is drowned and lost in it. The priests, as sacrificers, were obliged by a particular law to be temperate (Lev. x. 9). The prophets were a kind of Nazarite (as appears by Amos ii. 11), and were concerned to keep at the utmost distance from the sins they reproved in others; yet there were many of them ensnared in this sin. (2) That the consequences of it were very pernicious, not only by the ill influence of their example, but the prophet, when he was drunk, *erred in vision*. The priest *stumbled in judgment and forgot the law* (Prov. xxxi. 5); he reeled and staggered as much in the operations of his mind as in the motions of his body. (3) That the disease was epidemic: *All tables are full of vomit, v.* 8. It is rude and ill-mannered enough to sicken the beholders, for the tables where they eat their meat are filthily stained.

Verses 9–13

The prophet here complains of the wretched stupidity of this people, that they were unteachable.

I. Their prophets and ministers designed to *teach knowledge*, the knowledge of God and his will, and to *make them understand doctrine, v.* 9. This is God's way of dealing with men, to enlighten men's minds first with the knowledge of his truth, and thus to gain their affections, and bring their wills into a compliance with his laws.

II. They left no means untried to do them good, but taught them as little children that are beginning to learn, that are taken from the breast to the book (*v.* 9), for among the Jews it was common for mothers to nurse their children till they were three years old, and almost ready for school. They teach them, as they are capable, the good knowledge of the Lord, and to instruct them even when they are but newly weaned from the milk. They have been taught, as children are taught to read, by *precept upon precept*, and taught to write by *line upon line, a little here* and *a little there*, a little of one thing and a little of another, that instructions might be pleasing—a little at one time and a little at another, that they might not have their memories overcharged—a little from one prophet and a little from another. It is requisite that we have precept upon precept and line upon line. The precept of justice must be upon the precept of piety, and the precept of charity upon that of justice. The same precept and the same line should be often repeated. Teachers should accommodate themselves to the capacity of the learners, give them what they most need, and a little at a time, Deut. vi. 6, 7. They courted and persuaded them to learn, *v.* 12. God, by his prophets, said to them, "*This way that we are directing you, is the rest, wherewith you may cause the weary to rest; and this will be the refreshing* of your own souls, and will bring rest to your country from the wars with which it has been long harassed."

III. They were as unapt to learn as young children (*v.* 9). They *would not hear* (*v.* 12) that which would be rest and refreshing to them. They kept up the old custom of attending upon the prophet's preaching and it was continually beating upon them, but it beat nothing into them.

IV. How severely God would reckon with them for this. He would deprive them of the privilege of plain preaching, and speak to them *with stammering lips and another tongue, v.* 11. Those that will not hear the comfortable voice of God's word shall be made to hear the dreadful voice of his rod. By their profane contempt of God and his word they are but hastening on their own ruin, and ripening themselves for it; it is *that they may go and fall backward,* and proceed from one sin to another, till they be quite *broken, and snared, and taken,* and ruined, *v.* 13.

Verses 14–22

The prophet, having reproved those that made a jest of the word of God, here goes on to reprove those that made a jest of the judgments of God. He addresses himself to *the scornful men who ruled in Jerusalem,* the magistrates of the city, *v.* 14.

I. These scornful men challenged God Almighty to do his worst (*v.* 15): *You have said, We have made a covenant with death and the grave.* They thought themselves sure of their lives, even when judgments were abroad, as if they had made a bargain with death not to take them away by violence but by old age. If we be at peace with God we have in effect made a covenant with death that, whenever it comes, it shall be no terror to us, nor do us any real damage (1 Cor. iii. 22, 23): but to think of making death our friend while by sin we are making God our enemy, is the greatest absurdity. It was a fond conceit which these scorners had, *When the overflowing scourge shall pass through* our country, and others shall fall under it, yet *it shall not come to us.* But what is the ground of their confidence? *We have made lies our refuge.* Those things which should be lies and falsehood to the enemy, who was *flagellum Dei—the scourge of God,* the overflowing scourge, would secure them by imposing upon the enemy their stratagems of war, or their feigned submissions in treaties of peace. The rulers of Jerusalem think themselves greater politicians than those of the country towns; they will compliment the king of Assyria with a promise to surrender their city, or to become tributaries to him, with a purpose to shake off his yoke as soon as the danger is over. Those that pursue their designs by trick and fraud may perhaps compass them, but cannot expect comfort in them.

II. God, by the prophet, shows them the folly of their security. He does not disturb their false confidences, till he has first shown them a firm bottom on which they may repose themselves (*v.* 16): *Behold,*

I lay in Zion for a foundation a stone. The foundation is made up of (*a*) The promises of God in general—his covenant with Abraham is a foundation of stone, firm and lasting, for faith to build upon; it is *a tried stone,* for all the saints have stayed themselves upon it and it never failed them. (*b*) The promise of Christ in particular; for to him this is expressly applied in the New Testament, 1 Pet. ii. 6–8. He is that stone which has become *the head of the corner.* Jesus Christ is a foundation of God's laying. He is a tried stone, a corner-stone, in whom the sides of the building are united, the *head-stone of the corner.* And *he that believes* these promises, and rests upon them, *shall not make haste,* but with a fixed heart shall quietly wait the event, saying, *Welcome the will of God.* The grounds which they now built on could not be safe (*v.* 17): *Judgment will I lay to the line, and righteousness to the plummet.* This denotes,

1 The building up of his church; having laid the foundation (*v.* 16), he will raise the structure, as builders do, by line and plummet, Zech. iv. 10. Righteousness shall be the line and judgment the plummet. The church, being founded on Christ, shall be formed and reformed by the scripture. Or,

2 The punishing of the church's enemies, against whom he will proceed by an exact rule. These scornful men will be made ashamed of the vain hopes with which they had deluded themselves. Those that make lies their refuge build upon the sand, and the building will fall when the storm comes, and bury the builder in the ruins of it. They fancied that when the overflowing scourge should pass through the land it should not come near them; but the prophet tells them (*v.* 19), that they shall be the first that shall fall by it: "*From the time it goes forth it shall take you,* as if it came on purpose to seize you. *Morning by morning shall it pass over;* you shall never be safe; there shall be a pestilence walking in darkness and a destruction wasting at noonday." The very report of it at a distance will be a terror to you. Evil tidings are a terror to scorners, but he whose heart is fixed, *trusting in God, is not afraid of them*; whereas, when the *overflowing scourge* comes, then all the comforts and confidences of scorners fail them, *v.* 20. *The bed is shorter than that a man can stretch himself upon it,* so that he is forced to cramp and contract himself. That in which they thought to shelter themselves proves insufficient: *The covering is narrower than that a man can wrap himself in.* When God comes to contend with these scorners, *He will do his work, and bring to pass his act,* as the righteous Judge of the earth. He will do it now against his people, as formerly he did it against their enemies; he will now *rise up against Jerusalem as,* in David's time, against the Philistines *in Mount Perazim* (2 Sam. v. 20), and as, in Joshua's time, against the Canaanites *in the valley of Gibeon.* If those that profess themselves members of God's church by their pride and scornfulness make themselves like Philistines and Canaanites, they must expect to be dealt with as such. This will be *his strange work, his strange act.* It is work that he is not used to as to his own people. It is a strange work indeed if he *turn to be their enemy and fight against them,* ch. lxiii. 10. The use and application of all this (*v.* 22): "*Therefore be you not mockers;* dare not to ridicule either the reproofs of God's word or his judgments. *Be you not mockers, lest your bands be made strong,* both the bands by which you are bound under the dominion of sin, and the bands by which you are bound over to the judgments of God." Let not these mockers make light of divine threatenings, for the prophet assures them that the Lord God of hosts has *determined a consumption upon the whole earth*; and can they think to escape?

Verses 23–29

This parable, which (like many of our Saviour's parables) is borrowed from the husbandman's calling, is ushered in with a solemn preface, *He that has ears to hear, let him hear*, v. 23.

I. The parable here is plain enough, that the husbandman applies himself to the business of his calling with pains and prudence, and observes a method and order in his work. 1. In his ploughing and sowing: *Does the ploughman plough all day to sow?* Yes, he *ploughs in hope* and *sows in hope*, 1 Cor. ix. 10. *Does he open and break the clods?* Yes, that the land may be fit to receive the seed. And *when he has thus made plain the face thereof* does he not sow seed suitable to the soil? For the husbandman knows what grain is fit for clay ground and what for sandy ground, and, accordingly, he sows each in its place— *wheat in the principal place* (so the margin reads it), for it was a staple commodity of Canaan (Ezek. xxvii. 17), *and barley in the appointed place*. 2. In his threshing, v. 27, 28. This also he proportions to the grain that is to be threshed out. *The fitches and the cummin*, being easily got out of their husk or ear, are only threshed with *a staff and a rod*; but *the bread-corn* requires more force, and therefore that must be bruised with *a threshing instrument*, a sledge shod with iron, that was drawn to and fro over it, to beat out the corn; and yet *he will not be ever threshing it*, nor any longer than is necessary to loosen the corn from the chaff; *he will not break it*, or crush it *with the wheel of his cart, nor bruise it* to pieces *with his horsemen*; the grinding of it is reserved for another operation. What pains are to be taken, not only for the earning, but for the preparing of our necessary food; and yet, after all, it is *meat that perishes*! Shall we then grudge to labour much more for the *meat which endures to everlasting life*? Bread-corn *is bruised*. Christ was so; *it pleased the Lord to bruise him*, that he might be the bread of life to us.

II. Most interpreters make the parable a further answer to those who set the judgments of God at defiance: "As the husbandman will not be always ploughing, but will at length sow his seed, so God will not be always threatening, but will at length bring upon sinners the judgments they have deserved; but in wisdom, that they may be reformed and brought to repentance." But we may give this parable a greater latitude. 1. It is God that *instructs the husbandman to discretion*, as *his God*, v. 26. Husbandmen have need of discretion wherewith to order their affairs. The advancing of the art of husbandry is a common service to mankind more than the cultivating of most other arts. The skill of the husbandman is from God. This takes off somewhat of the weight of the sentence passed on man for sin, that when God, in execution of it, sent man to till the ground, he taught him how to do it most to his advantage. It is he that gives men capacity for this business, an inclination to it, and a delight in it, and to him husbandmen must seek for direction for they, above other men, have an immediate dependence upon the divine Providence. As to the other instance of the husbandman's conduct in threshing his corn, it is said, *This also comes forth from the Lord of hosts*, v. 29. And, if it is from him that men do things wisely, we must needs acknowledge him to be *wise in counsel and excellent in working*. 2. God's church is his husbandry, 1 Cor. iii. 9. If Christ is the true vine, his Father is the husbandman (John xv. 1), and he is continually by his word and ordinances cultivating it. Does not God by his ministers break up the fallow ground? God sows his word by the hand of his ministers (Matt. xiii. 19). Whatever the soil of the heart is, there is some seed or other in the word proper for it. And, as the word of God, so the rod of God is thus wisely used. Afflictions are God's threshing-instruments, designed to

loosen us from the world, to separate between us and our chaff, but he will proportion them to our strength. If the rod and the staff will answer the end, he will not make use of his cart-wheel and his horsemen.

CHAPTER 29

This woe to Ariel, which we have in this chapter, is the same with the "burden of the valley of vision" (ch. xxii. 1), and (it is very probable) points at the same event—the besieging of Jerusalem by the Assyrian army, which was cut off there by an angel; yet it is applicable to the destruction of Jerusalem by the Chaldeans, and its last desolations by the Romans. I. The event foretold, that Jerusalem should be greatly distressed (ver. 1–4, 6), but that their enemies should be defeated, ver. 5, 7, 8. II. A reproof to three sorts of sinners: 1. Those that were regardless of warnings, ver. 9–12. 2. Those that were formal and hypocritical in their religious performances, ver. 13–14. 3. Those politicians that profanely despised God's providence, ver. 15, 16. III. Precious promises of grace and mercy to a remnant whom God would sanctify, ver. 17–24.

Verses 1–8

That it is Jerusalem which is here called *Ariel* is agreed, for that was the city where David dwelt; that part of it which was called *Zion* was in a particular manner the city of David, in which both the temple and the palace were. But why it is so called is uncertain. Cities, as well as persons, get surnames and nicknames. *Ariel* signifies *the lion of God*, or *the strong lion:* as the lion is king among beasts, so was Jerusalem among the cities. Jerusalem, while she was a righteous city, was bold as a lion. Some make *Ariel* to signify *the altar of burnt-offerings*, which devoured the beasts offered in sacrifice as the lion does his prey. I rather take it as a woe to Jerusalem, Jerusalem; it is repeated here, as it is Matt. xxiii. 37, that it might be the more awakening.

I. The distress of Jerusalem foretold. Though Jerusalem be a strong city, yet, if iniquity be found there, woe be to it. 1. Let Jerusalem know that her external performance of religious services will not serve as an exception from the judgments of God (v. 1): "*Add year to year;* go on in your annual feasts, let all your males appear there three times a year before the Lord, and none empty, and let them never miss any of these solemnities: *let them kill the sacrifices*, as they used to do; but, as long as their lives are unreformed and their hearts unhumbled, let them not think thus to pacify an offended God and to turn away his wrath." 2. Let her know that she shall be *visited of the Lord of hosts* (v. 6); her sins shall be punished with alarms like *thunder and earthquakes, storms and tempests, and devouring fire*. (1) Jerusalem shall be besieged. He does not say, *I will destroy Ariel*, but I will *distress Ariel*; and she is *therefore* brought into distress, that being awakened to repent, she may not be brought to destruction. *I will* (v. 3) *encamp against thee round about*. It was the enemy's army that encamped against it. When men fight against us we must, in them, see God contending with us. (2) She shall be in grief to see the country laid waste. "*There shall be heaviness and sorrow* (v. 2); they shall repent, and reform, and return to God, and then it shall be to me as Ariel. Jerusalem shall be like itself, shall become to me a Jerusalem again, a holy city," ch. i. 26. (3) She shall be humbled, and mortified (v. 4): "*Thou shalt be brought down* from the height of arrogancy, and now *thou shalt speak out of the ground, out of the dust, as one that has a familiar spirit, whispering out of the dust*. They should be faint and feeble, as those who are sick, their speech low and interrupted, being afraid lest their enemies should overhear them.

II. The destruction of Jerusalem's enemies is foretold (v. 5, 7): "*Thou shalt be brought down* (v. 4), *to speak out of the dust;* so low thou shalt be reduced. But*" (so it may be rendered) "*the multitude of thy strangers and the terrible ones*, the numerous armies of the enemy, *shall* themselves *be like small dust*, not able to speak at all, or so much as whisper, but *as chaff that passes away*. Thou shalt be abased, but they shall be quite dispersed and slain (*ch.* xxvii. 7). *Yea, it shall be in an instant, suddenly:* the enemy shall be surprised with the destruction, and you with the salvation." The army of the Assyrians was by an angel laid dead upon the spot, in an instant, suddenly. *The multitude of the nations that fight against Zion shall be as a hungry man who dreams that he eats*, but still is hungry. Whereas they hoped to make a prey of Jerusalem, and to enrich themselves with plunder, their hopes shall prove vain dreams. They themselves, and all their pomp, and power, and prosperity, shall vanish like a dream.

Verses 9–16

I. The prophet stands amazed at the stupidity of the greatest part of the Jewish nation. They had Levites, who taught *the good knowledge of the Lord*. They had prophets, who brought them messages immediately from God. *Surely this great nation, that has all the advantages of divine revelation, will be a wise and understanding people*, Deut. iv. 6. But, alas! it was quite otherwise, *v.* 9. The prophet addresses himself to the sober thinking part of them. "The rest sport themselves with their own deceivings; they riot and revel; but do you *cry out*, lament their folly, cry to God by prayer for them." They were drunk with the love of pleasures, with prejudices against religion, and with the corrupt principles they had imbibed. Like drunken men, they are not sensible of the divine rebukes they are under. *They have beaten me, and I felt it not*, says the drunkard, Prov. xxiii. 35. There is such a thing as spiritual drunkenness. God himself *poured out upon them a spirit of deep sleep, and closed their eyes* (*v.* 10) in righteous judgment, to punish them for their *loving darkness rather than light*, their loving sleep. They said, *Yet a little sleep, a little slumber;* and therefore he gave them up to strong delusions, and said, *Sleep on now*. This is applied to the unbelieving Jews, who rejected the gospel of Christ, and were justly hardened in their infidelity, till wrath came upon them to the uttermost. Rom. xi. 8, *God has given them the spirit of slumber*. This was fulfilled when, in the latter days of the Jewish church, the chief priests, and the scribes, and the elders of the people, were the great opposers of Christ and his gospel, and brought themselves under a judicial infatuation. Every vision, particularly that this prophet had seen, and published, had become unintelligible; they had it among them, but were never the wiser for it, any more than a man (though a good scholar) is for a book delivered to him sealed up. He sees it is a book, and that is all. So they knew that what Isaiah said was a vision and prophecy, but the meaning of it was hidden from them. But the same vision which to you is a *savour of death unto death* to others is and shall be a *savour of life unto life*. Knowledge is easy to him that understands.

II. The prophet, in God's name, threatens those that were formal and hypocritical in their devotion, *v.* 13, 14.

1. Their sin is dissembling with God in their religious performances, *v.* 13. He that knows the heart cannot be imposed upon with shows and pretences. If the heart be full of his love and fear, out of the abundance of that the mouth will speak. But there are many whose religion is lip-labour only. It is only from the teeth outward. They do not apply their minds to the service. They do not make the word of God the rule of their worship, nor his will their reason: *Their fear towards me is taught by the precept of men*. The tradition of the elders was of more value than the laws which God commanded Moses. This our Saviour applies to the Jews in his

time, who were formal in their devotions, Matt. xv. 8, 9.

2. It is a spiritual judgment with which God threatens to punish them for their spiritual wickedness (*v.* 14): *I will proceed to do a marvellous work*. They removed all sincerity from their hearts. Now God will remove all sagacity from their heads. *The wisdom of their wise men shall perish*. They played the hypocrite, and thought to put a cheat upon God, and now they are left to themselves to play the fool, to be easily cheated by all about them. This is a marvellous work; that wise men should of a sudden lose their wisdom and be given up to strong delusions.

III. He shows the folly of those that thought to act separately and secretly from God. Their politics described (*v.* 15): They *seek deep to hide their counsel from the Lord*, that he may not know either what they do or what they design. The absurdity of their politics demonstrated (*v.* 16): *Surely your turning of things upside down*—your inverting the order of things, and thinking to make God's providence give attendance to your projects, turning things upside down and beginning at the wrong end—*shall be esteemed as the potter's clay*. God will turn and manage you, and all your counsels, with as much ease as the potter fashions his clay.

Verses 17–24

God here tells them that he will turn things upside down. They disbelieve Providence: "Wait awhile," says God, "and you shall be convinced that there is a God who governs the world." The wonderful revolution here foretold may refer primarily to the happy settlement of the affairs of Judah and Jerusalem after the defeat of Sennacherib's attempt. But it may look further, to the rejection of the Jews at the first planting of the gospel.

I. A great change is here foretold, *v.* 17. *Lebanon, that was a forest, shall be turned into a fruitful field; and Carmel, that was a fruitful field shall become a forest*. It was a sign of the defeat of Sennacherib that the ground should be more than ordinarily fruitful (*ch.* xxxvii. 30): *You shall eat this year such as grows of itself;* food for man shall be (as food for beasts is) the spontaneous product of the soil. Then Lebanon became so fruitful that that which used to be reckoned a fruitful field in comparison with it was looked upon but as a forest. When a great harvest of souls was gathered in to Christ from among the Gentiles then the wilderness was turned into a fruitful field, *ch.* liv. 1.

II. Those that were ignorant shall become intelligent, *v.* 18. Those that understood not this prophecy shall, when it is accomplished, understand it, and shall acknowledge, not only the hand of God in the event, but the voice of God in the prediction of it: *The deaf shall then hear the words of the book*. The poor Gentiles shall then have divine revelation brought among them; and those that sat in darkness shall see a great light, for the gospel was sent to them to *open their eyes*, Acts xxvi. 18. Those that were erroneous shall become orthodox (*v.* 24): *Those that erred in spirit* shall come to a right understanding of things; the Spirit of truth shall lead them into all truth. Those that murmured at the truths of God as hard sayings, shall learn the true meaning and will be better reconciled to them. Those that erred concerning the providence of God and murmured shall see the issue of things and be aware of what God was designing in all, Hos. xiv. 9. Those that were melancholy shall become cheerful and pleasant (*v.* 19): *The meek also shall increase their joy in the Lord*. This intimates that even in their distress they kept up their joy in the Lord, but now they increased it. The grace of meekness will contribute very much to the increase of our holy joy. Sennacherib, that *terrible one*, and his great army, shall be *brought to nought* (*v.* 20). The power of Satan, that terrible one indeed, shall be broken by the prevalency of Christ's gospel, Heb. ii. 14. The persecutors shall be quieted. To complete the repose of God's people, the scorners at home shall be consumed and cut off by Hezekiah's reformation. They had been persecutors of God's people and prophets, probably of the prophet Isaiah. And this is very applicable to the chief priests and Pharisees, who persecuted Christ and his apostles, and for that sin were cut off and consumed. They lay in wait for an occasion against them. By their spies they *watch for iniquity*, to see if they can lay hold of anything that is said or done that may be called an iniquity. They *made a man*, though he were ever so wise and good, *an offender for a word*, a word mischosen or misplaced, when they could not but know that it was well meant, *v.* 21. Those that *reprove in the gates*, who were bound as prophets, as judges, and magistrates, to show people their transgressions, hated these and laid snares for them, as the Pharisees' emissaries, who were sent to watch our Saviour that they might *entangle him in his talk* (Matt. xxii. 15). *They turn aside the just for a thing of nought.* They run a man down, and misrepresent him, by all the little arts and tricks they can devise, as they did our Saviour.

Jacob made to blush by the reproaches of his enemies, shall now be relieved by the rolling away of those reproaches (*v.* 22): *Thus saith the Lord who redeemed Abraham* out of his troubles and will redeem all that are by faith his genuine seed out of theirs. He that began his care of his church in the redemption of Abraham will appear for the house of Jacob, and they shall not be ashamed, nor shall *their faces now wax pale*; but they shall gather courage. Jacob, who thought his family would be extinct, shall see his children, multitudes of believers and he *shall not be ashamed* (*v.* 22), but shall speak with his enemy in the gate, Ps. cxxvii. 5. It is some comfort to parents to think that their children are God's creatures, the work of the hands of his providence. But it will be much more a comfort to them to see their children his new creatures, the work of the hands of his grace.

CHAPTER 30

This chapter seems to relate to the approaching danger of Sennacherib's invasion. I. A just reproof to those who were all in a hurry to fetch succours from Egypt, ver. 1–7. II. A terrible threatening against those who slighted the good advice which God by his prophets gave them, ver. 8–17. III. A gracious promise to those who trusted in God, that they should see happy days, times of joy and reformation, outward good things and increasing joys and triumphs (ver. 18–26), and many of these promises are applicable to gospel grace. IV. A prophecy of the total rout of the Assyrian army, which should be an introduction to those happy times, ver. 27–33.

Verses 1–7

It was often the fault and folly of the people of the Jews that, when they were insulted by their neighbours on one side, they sought for succour from their neighbours on the other side, instead of looking up to God and putting their confidence in him. Against the Israelites they sought to the Syrians, 2 Chron. xvi. 2, 3. Against the Syrians they sought to the Assyrians, 2 Kings xvi. 7. Against the Assyrians they here sought to the Egyptians, 2 Kings xviii. 21.

I. This sin of theirs is described. They would not consult God. "They *take counsel* among themselves, and one from another; but they do not ask counsel, much less will they take counsel, of me. They *cover with a covering but not of my Spirit*, and therefore it will prove too short a covering, and a refuge of lies." They *strengthened themselves in the strength of Pharaoh. The shadow of Egypt* (and it was but a shadow) was the covering in which they wrapped themselves.

II. The evil of this sin. They were, in profession, God's children; but, not trusting in him, they were justly stigmatized as rebellious. They added sin to sin. They took so much pains to secure the Egyptians for their allies: *They walk to go down to Egypt*, travel up and down to find an advantageous road thither; but they *have not asked at my mouth*, never considered whether God would approve of it. They were at a vast expense to do it, *v.* 6. They load *the beasts of the south* (horses fetched from Egypt, which lay south from Judæa) with their riches, fancying, as is common with people in a fright, that they were safer anywhere than where they were. Or they sent their riches thither as bribes to Pharaoh's courtiers. God would have helped them *gratis*; but, if they will have help from the Egyptians, they must pay dearly for it. They carried their effects to Egypt through a land (so it may be read) of trouble and anguish, that vast howling wilderness, which lay between Canaan and Egypt, *whence come the lion and fiery serpent*, Deut. viii. 15.

III. The consequence of it. The Egyptians would receive their ambassadors, and be willing to treat with them (*v.* 4): *His princes were at Zoan*, and the king encouraged them to depend upon the succours he would send them. But they would not answer their expectation: They *could not profit them*, *v.* 5. God says, *They shall not profit them* (*v.* 6). The forces they were to furnish them with could not be raised in time; or the Egyptians would secretly incline to the Assyrians. *The Egyptians shall help in vain, and to no purpose*, *v.* 7. *The strength of Pharaoh*, which was your pride, *shall be your shame*; and you will upbraid yourselves, with your folly in trusting to it. And the *shadow of Egypt*, that *land shadowing with wings* (ch. xviii. 1), which was your confidence, shall be your confusion. The princes of Israel, who were so forward to court an alliance *shall all be ashamed of a people that could not be a help or profit to them*, but a *shame and reproach*, *v.* 5. Those that put confidence in any creature will sooner or later find it a reproach to them. The Creator is a rock of ages, the creature a broken reed. We cannot expect too little from man nor too much from God. *"Therefore have I cried concerning this* matter. *Their strength is to sit still*, in a humble dependence upon God and not to wander about to seek help from this and the other creature."

Verses 8–17

I. The preface is very awful. The prophet must write it (*v.* 8), *write it in a table, in a book*, to be preserved for posterity, *for a standing testimony* against this wicked generation. Let it be written to shame the men of the present age: their children may profit by it, though they will not. People will be tempted to think God was too hard upon them unless they know how bad they were, and what fair means God tried with them before he brought it to this extremity. It is designed for admonition to those of the remotest place and age.

II. The character given of the profane and wicked Jews. *This is a rebellious people*, *v.* 9. "They are *lying children*, that will not stand to what they say, that promise fair, but perform nothing." They rebelled against the divine authority: "They are *children that will not hear the law of the Lord*, nor heed it."

III. The sentence passed upon them is dreadful.

1. They forbade the prophets to speak to them in God's name. They did in effect *say to the seers, See not*. The prophets told them of their faults, and warned them of their danger by reason of sin, and they could not bear that. They must speak to them smooth things. Let a thing be ever so right and true, if it be not smooth, they will not hear it. Those

deserve to be deceived that desire to be so. The prophets stopped them in their sinful pursuits, and stood in their way like the angel in Balaam's road, with the sword of God's wrath drawn in their hand. When they went on frowardly in the way of their hearts they said to the prophets, "*Get you out of the way, turn aside out of the paths.*" The prophets were continually telling them of the Holy One of Israel, and how severely he will reckon with sinners; and this they could not endure. If the prophets will speak to them, they will make it their bargain that they shall not call God *the Holy One of Israel*; for God's holiness is that attribute which wicked people most of all dread. The doom passed upon them for this, *v.* 12, 13. *Thus saith the Holy One of Israel.* We must tell men that God is the *Holy One of Israel.* The ground of the judgment is: *Because they despise this word*—either, in general, every word that the prophets said to them, or this word in particular, which declares God to be the *Holy One of Israel.* They *trust in oppression and perverseness*, in the wealth they have got by fraud and violence, or in the sinful methods they have taken for their own security. On these they lean, and therefore it is just that they should fall. Judgment is passed upon them: "*This iniquity shall be to you as a breach ready to fall.* This confidence of yours will be like a house built upon the sand. Your contempt of that word of God which you might build upon will make everything else you trust to like a wall that bulges out, which, if any weight be laid upon it, often sinks with its own weight." *The breaking shall come suddenly, at an instant.* "You and all your confidences shall be not only weak as the potter's clay (*ch.* xxix. 16), but *broken to pieces as the potter's vessel.* But, when once it is broken so as to be unfit for use, let it be dashed, let it be crushed all to pieces, so that there may not remain one shred big enough to take up a little fire or water—two things we have daily need of, and which poor people commonly fetch in a piece of a broken pitcher.

2. They slighted the gracious directions God gave them; they would take their own way, *v.* 15-17. The God that knew them, and desired their welfare, gave them this prescription; and it is recommended to us all. Would we be saved from the evil of every calamity. It must be *in returning and rest*, in returning to God and reposing in him as our rest. Let us return from our evil ways, and settle in the way of God and duty, and that is the way to be saved. "Return from this project of going down to Egypt. *In returning* (in the thorough reformation of your hearts and lives) *and in rest* (in an entire submission of your souls to God) *you shall be saved.*" Would we be strengthened to do what is required of us? It must be *in quietness and in confidence.* We must rely upon God with a holy confidence that he can do what he will and will do what is best for his people. And this will be our strength. They would not take God's counsel, though it was so much for their own good. And justly will those die of their disease that will not take God for their physician. They would not so much as try the method prescribed: "*But you said, No* (*v.* 16), we will not compose ourselves, for *we will flee upon horses* and *we will ride upon the swift;* we will hurry hither and thither to fetch in foreign aids." When Sennacherib took all the fenced cities of Judah, those rebellious children would not be persuaded patiently to expect God's appearing for them, as he did wonderfully at last. Their sin shall be their punishment: "You will flee, and therefore *you shall flee;* you will be upon the full speed, and therefore so shall those be that pursue you." The dogs are most apt to run barking after him that rides fast. The conquerors protected those that sat still, but pursued those that made their escape. It is foretold,

v. 17, that they should be easily cut off; one of the enemy should defeat a thousand of them, and five put an army to flight. Only here and there one should escape alone in a solitary place, and be left *as a beacon upon the top of a mountain*, a warning to others.

Verses 18-26

The closing words of the foregoing paragraph (*You shall be left as a beacon upon a mountain*) some understand as a promise that a remnant of them should be reserved as monuments of mercy. The first words in this paragraph may be read by way of antithesis, *Notwithstanding this, yet will the Lord wait that he may be gracious.*

I. God will be gracious to them and will have mercy on them. "He will *wait to be gracious* (*v.* 18); he will wait till you return to him and seek his face, and then he will be ready to meet you with mercy. He will stir up himself to deliver you, will be exalted, will be *raised up out of his holy habitation* (Zech. ii. 13), *and thus he will be exalted*, that is, he will glorify his name." "*He will be gracious to thee, at the voice of thy cry*, the cry of thy necessity, when that is most urgent—the cry of thy prayer, when that is most fervent. *When he shall hear it*, there needs no more; at the first word *he will answer thee*, and say, *Here I am.*" Those who were disturbed in the possession of their estates shall again enjoy them quietly. When the danger is over *the people shall dwell in Zion, at Jerusalem*, as they used to do; they shall dwell safely, free from the fear of evil. Those who dwell in Zion, the holy city, will find enough there to wipe away tears from their eyes. This is grounded upon two great truths: (1) That *the Lord is a God of judgment;* he is both wise and just in all the disposals of his providence, true to his word and tender of his people. (2) That therefore all those are blessed who *wait for him*, who not only wait on him with their prayers, but wait for him with their hopes.

II. They shall not again know the want of the means of grace, *v.* 20, 21. It was promised (*v.* 19), that they should *weep no more* and that God would be *gracious to them;* and yet here it is taken for granted that God may give them the *bread of adversity and the water of affliction.* It is promised that their eyes should *see their teachers*, that is, that they should have faithful teachers among them, and should have hearts to regard them and not slight them as they had done; and then they might the better be reconciled to the bread of adversity and the water of affliction. It was a common saying among the old Puritans, *Brown bread and the gospel are good fare.* It seems that their teachers had been removed into corners. But God will find a time to call the teachers out of their corners again, and to replace them in their solemn assemblies. It is promised that they shall have the benefit, not only of the public ministry, but of private admonition and advice (*v.* 21): "*Thy ears shall hear a word behind thee*, calling after thee as a man calls after a traveller that he sees going out of his road." This word shall come—from *behind thee*, from someone whom thou dost not see, but who sees thee. "Thy eyes see thy teachers; but this is a teacher out of sight, it is thy own conscience, which shall now by the grace of God be awakened to do its office." The word shall be: *This is the way, walk you in it.* This word shall come *when you turn to the right hand or to the left.* There are right-hand and left-hand errors, extremes on each side virtue; the tempter is busy courting us into the by-paths. It is happy then if by the particular counsels of a faithful minister or friend, or the checks of conscience and the strivings of God's Spirit, we be set right and prevented from going wrong. "It shall not only be spoken, but thy ears shall hear it; whereas God has formerly *spoken once, yea, twice*, and thou *hast not perceived it* (Job xxxiii. 14), now thou shalt listen attentively to these secret whispers, and hear them with an obedient ear."

III. They shall be cured of their idolatry, shall fall out with their idols, and never be reconciled to them again, *v.* 22. They shall break off from their best-beloved sin. How mad they had formerly been in the day of their apostasy. They had *graven images of silver*, and *molten images of gold*, and, though gold needs no painting, they had coverings and ornaments on these; they spared no cost in doing honour to their idols. What a holy indignation they conceived against them in the day of their repentance. They not only degraded their images, but defaced them, in a pious fury threw away the gold and silver they were made of. Probably this was fulfilled in many persons, who, by the deliverance of Jerusalem from Sennacherib's army, were convinced of the folly of their idolatry and forsook it. It was fulfilled in the Jewish nation at their return from captivity in Babylon, for they abhorred idols ever after; and it is accomplished daily in the conversion of souls, by the power of divine grace, from spiritual idolatry to the fear and love of God.

IV. God will then give them plenty of all good things. When he gives them their teachers, and they give him their hearts, *then all other things shall be added to them*, Matt. vi. 33. And when the people are brought to praise God *then shall the earth yield her increase, and with it God, even our own God, shall bless us*, Ps. lxvii. 5, 6. So it follows here: "When you shall have abandoned your idols, *then shall God give the rain of your seed*," *v.* 23. God will give you rain to water the seed you sow. *Thou shalt sow the ground*, that is thy part, and then *God will give the rain of thy seed*, that is his part. It is so in spiritual fruit. The increase of the earth shall be *fat and fat, very fat and very good, fat and plenteous* (so we read it), good and enough of it. *The cattle shall feed in large pastures, shall eat clean provender*. The corn shall not be given them in the chaff to make it go the further, but they shall have good clean corn, *winnowed with the fan*. Even the tops of the mountains shall be so well watered with the rain that there shall be *rivers and streams* running down to the valleys (*v.* 25), and this *in the day of the great slaughter* made by the angel in the camp of the Assyrians, *when the towers* they had erected for the siege of Jerusalem, *should fall*.

V. The effect of all this should be comfort and joy to the people of God, *v.* 26. Light shall increase; that is, knowledge shall increase (when the prophecies are accomplished they shall be fully understood). *The light of the moon shall become as* bright and as strong as *that of the sun, and that of the sun* shall increase proportionably and be *as the light of seven days—when the Lord binds up the breach of his people*, heals the wounds that have been given them by this invasion and makes up all their losses. The light which the gospel brought into the world to those that sat in darkness as far exceeded the Old Testament light as that of the sun does that of the moon.

Verses 27–33

This terrible prediction of the ruin of the Assyrian army, is part of the promise to the Israel of God, that God would deter them from doing the like again.

I. God Almighty is here introduced in all the power and all the terror of his wrath, *v.* 27. *The name of Jehovah*, which the Assyrians disdain, *behold, it comes from far*. He is a messenger of wrath, *burning with his anger*. God's *lips are full of indignation* at the blasphemy of Rabshakeh, who compared the God of Israel with the gods of the heathen; *his tongue is as a devouring fire*. He does not stifle his resentments, but *shall cause his glorious voice to be heard*, *v.* 30. He shall display *the indignation of his anger* as the *flame of a devouring fire*, with *lightning* and with *tempest and hailstones*.

II. The execution done by this anger of the Lord. God will *show the lighting down of his arm*, *v.* 30. Those that *would not see the lifting up of his arm* (ch. xxvi. 11) shall feel the lighting down of it, and find to their cost, that the burden thereof is heavy (*v.* 27). Five things are here for the execution: 1. Here is *an overflowing stream, that shall reach to the midst of the neck*. The Assyrian army had been to Judah *as an overflowing stream, reaching even to the neck* (ch. viii. 7, 8), and now the breath of God's wrath will be so to it. 2. Here is *a sieve of vanity*, with which God would sift those nations of which the Assyrian army was composed, *v.* 28. He will sift them so as to shake them one against another, put them into great consternation, and shake them all away at last; for it is a sieve of vanity. 3. Here is *a bridle* to restrain them from doing mischief, and to force them to serve God's purposes against their own will, ch. x. 7. 4. Here is *a rod* and *a staff*, even *the voice of the Lord*, giving orders with which *the Assyrian shall be beaten down*, *v.* 31. There is no escaping it. In every place where an Assyrian is found, the Lord shall *lay it upon him*, and cause it to rest, *v.* 32. 5. Here is *Tophet ordained* and *prepared* for them, *v.* 33. The valley of the son of Hinnom, adjoining to Jerusalem, was called *Tophet*. In that valley, it is supposed, many of the Assyrian regiments lay encamped, and were there slain by the destroying angel.

III. The Assyrian's fall in Jerusalem's triumph (*v.* 29): *You shall have a song as in the night*, a psalm of praise such as those sing who *by night stand in the house of the Lord*, and sing to his glory who *gives songs in the night*.

CHAPTER 31

This chapter is an abridgment of the foregoing chapter. I. A woe to those who, when the Assyrian army invaded them, trusted to the Egyptians, and not to God, for succour, ver. 1–3. II. Assurance given of the care God would take of Jerusalem in that time of danger, ver. 4, 5. III. A call to repentance and reformation, ver. 6, 7. IV. A prediction of the fall of the Assyrian army, ver. 8, 9.

Verses 1–5

I. The sin here reproved, *v.* 1. They *go down to Egypt for help* in every exigence, as if the worshippers of false gods were more likely to have success on earth than the servants of the living and true God. The Egyptians had many chariots and horses and horsemen, and, if they could get forces thence into their service, they would think themselves able to deal with the king of Assyria. Slighting the God of Israel: *They look not to the Holy One of Israel*.

II. The absurdity of this sin. They do not seek the Lord, *yet he also is wise*, *v.* 2. Would not infinite wisdom, engaged on their side, stand them in more stead than all the policies of Egypt? They are at the pains of going down to Egypt, a tedious journey, when they might have had better help by looking up to heaven. But, if they will not court God's wisdom he *will arise against the house of the evil-doers*, this cabal of them that go down to Egypt. They trusted to those who were unable to help them and would soon appear to be so, *v.* 3. Let them know that *the Egyptians*, whom they depend so much upon, *are men and not God*. Everyone knows this, that the Egyptians are not God and their horses are not spirit; but those that seek to them for help do not consider it, else they would not put such confidence in them. The Egyptians were shortly to be reckoned with, as appears by the *burden of Egypt* (ch. xix), and then those who fled to them for shelter and succour should fall with them. They took God's work out of his hands. They pretended a great deal of care to preserve Jerusalem, in advising to an alliance with

Egypt. Now the prophet here tells them that Jerusalem should be preserved without aid from Egypt and that those who tarried there should be safe when those who fled to Egypt should be ruined. God would appear against Jerusalem's enemies with the boldness of a *lion over his prey, v.* 4. Wher. the lion comes out to seize his prey *a multitude of shepherds come out against him.* These shepherds dare not come near the lion; all they can do is to make a *noise,* and with that they think to frighten him. But does he regard it? *No; he will not be afraid of their voice.* Thus will *the Lord of hosts come down to fight for Mount Zion,* will as easily and irresistibly destroy the Assyrian army as a lion tears a lamb in pieces. Whoever appear against God, they are but like a multitude of poor simple shepherds shouting at a lion. God would appear for Jerusalem's friends with the tenderness of a bird over her young, *v.* 5. *As birds flying* to their nests with all possible speed, when they see them attacked, hovering over their young ones to protect them drive away the assailants, with such compassion and affection *will the Lord of hosts defend Jerusalem. Defending, he will deliver it. Passing over he will preserve it;* the word for passing over is used in this sense only here and Exod. xii. 12, 13, 27, concerning the destroying angel's passing over the houses of the Israelites when he slew all the first-born of the Egyptians. The Assyrian army was to be routed by a destroying angel who should pass over Jerusalem. They shall be slain by the pestilence, but none of the besieged shall take the infection. Thus he will again pass over the houses of his people and secure them.

Verses 6–9

I. Jerusalem, reformed, shall be delivered from her enemies, *v.* 6, 7. This was the Lord's voice crying in the city, and the voice of the prophets interpreting the judgment: *"Turn you* from your evil ways, *unto God,* return to your allegiance to him from whom you, *O children of Israel!* have revolted." He reminds them of their birth and parentage. They have been backsliding children, yet children; therefore let them return, and their backslidings shall be healed. A gracious promise (*v.* 7): *In that day every man shall cast away his idols,* in obedience to Hezekiah's orders, which, till they were alarmed by the Assyrian invasion, many refused to do. That is a happy fright which frightens us from our sins. It shall be a general reformation: every man shall cast away his own idols. It shall be a reformation upon a principle of piety, not of politics. They shall cast away their idols, because they have been unto them *for a sin,* an occasion of sin.

II. Jerusalem's besiegers shall be routed. When they have cast away their idols, *then shall the Assyrian fall, v.* 8, 9. 1. The army of the Assyrians shall be laid dead upon the spot, by the sword of the Lord in the hand of an angel. The king of Assyria shall flee from that invisible sword to some stronghold of his own. *His princes* that accompany him *shall be afraid of the ensign,* of every ensign they see, suspecting it is a party of the Jews pursuing them. But who will do this? It is *the Lord, whose fire is in Zion and his furnace in Jerusalem.* God there keeps house, as a man does where his fire and his oven are. Let not the Assyrians think to turn him out of the possession of his own house. He is himself *a wall of fire round about Jerusalem,* so that whoever assaults her does so at his peril.

CHAPTER 32

Here is, I. A prophecy of that good work of reformation with which Hezekiah should begin his reign, ver. 1–8. II. A prophecy of the great disturbance that would be given to the kingdom in the middle of his reign by the Assyrian invasion, ver. 9–14.

III. A promise of better times afterwards (ver. 15–20), which promise may be supposed to look as far forward as the days of the Messiah.

Verses 1–8

The description of a flourishing kingdom. It may be taken as a directory both to magistrates and subjects, what both ought to do, or as a panegyric to Hezekiah.

I. That magistrates should do their duty in their places, and the powers answer the great ends for which they were ordained, *v.* 1, 2. The princes must have a king, a monarch over them as supreme, in whom they may unite; and the king must have princes under him as officers, by whom he may act, 1 Pet. ii. 13, 14. They shall use their power according to law, and not against it. They shall reign in righteousness with wisdom and equity. Christ himself reigns by rule. Thus they shall be great blessings to the people (*v.* 2): *A man,* that king that reigns in righteousness, *shall be as a hiding-place.* When princes are as they should be people are as they would be. This good magistrate is a covert to the subject from the tempest of injury and violence; he *defends the poor and fatherless.* He is *as rivers of water in a dry place,* cooling the earth and making it fruitful, and *as the shadow of a great rock,* under which a poor traveller may shelter from the scorching heat. All this, and much more, the man Christ Jesus is to all the willing faithful subjects of his kingdom. In him we find rivers of water for those that hunger and thirst after righteousness, all the refreshment that a needy soul can desire, and the shadow of a rock, of a great rock, for the shelter of the traveller. As the covert, and the hiding-place, and the rock, do themselves receive the battering of the wind and storm, to save those that take shelter in them, so Christ bore the storm himself to keep it off from us.

II. That subjects should do their duty in their places. They shall be willing to be taught, and shall lay aside their prejudices against their rulers and teachers, and submit to the light and power of truth, *v.* 3. When this blessed work of reformation is set on foot, and men do their parts towards it, *the eyes of those that see,* of the prophets, the seers, *shall not be dim;* but God will bless them with visions, to be by them communicated to the people. Then *the ears of those that hear* the word preached *shall hearken.* There shall be a wonderful change wrought in them, *v.* 4. *The heart of those that were* hasty and *rash,* shall now be cured of their precipitation, and *shall understand knowledge;* for the Spirit of God will open their understanding. This blessed work Christ wrought in his disciples after his resurrection (Luke xxiv. 45, 1 John v. 20). *The tongue of the stammerers,* that used to blunder whenever they spoke of the things of God, *shall* now *be ready to speak plainly,* as those that understand, believe, and therefore speak. The differences between good and evil shall be no more confounded by those who put darkness for light and light for darkness (*v.* 5): *The vile shall no more be called liberal. Vile* persons, when they are advanced, are called *liberal* and *bountiful benefactors* (Luke xxii. 25): but when the world grows wiser, men shall be preferred according to their merit. Bad men shall be no more had in reputation among the people. In short, it is well with a people when men are valued by their virtue, and usefulness, and beneficence to mankind, and not by their wealth or titles of honour. To enforce this rule, here is a description both of the vile person and of the liberal. A vile person and a churl will do mischief the more if he have power in his hand; his honours will make him worse, *v.* 6, 7. These base ill-conditioned men are always plotting some unjust thing. There appears not in them the least spark of generosity. The more there is of plot and management in a sin the more there is of Satan in it. They *speak villainy*. When they are in a passion you will see what they are by the base ill language they give to those about them. They *utter error against the Lord*, and therein they practise profaneness; for so the word which we translate *hypocrisy* signifies. Nothing can be more impudently done against God than to use his name to patronise wickedness. Instead of supplying the wants of the poor, they impoverish them, they *make empty the souls of the hungry*; either taking away the food they have or denying the supply which they have to give. And they *cause the drink of the thirsty to fail*; they cut off the relief they used to have, though they need it as much as ever. These churls and vile persons have always bad instruments about them, that are ready to serve their villainous purposes: *All their servants are wicked.* One that is truly liberal, and deserves the honour of being called so, makes it his business to do good to everybody according as his sphere is, *v.* 8. He *devises liberal things.* Charity must be directed by wisdom, that it may not be charity misplaced. *By liberal things he shall stand.* The providence of God will reward him with a settled prosperity and an established reputation. The grace of God will give him peace in his own bosom.

Verses 9–20

In these verses we have God rising up to judgment against the vile persons, but returning in mercy to the liberal, to reward them for their liberality.

I. When there was so great a corruption of manners bad times might well be expected. The alarm is sounded to the *women that were at ease* (*v.* 9) and the *careless daughters*, to feed whose pride and luxury, their husbands and fathers were tempted to starve the poor. "*Rise up, and hear* with reverence and attention."

1. God was about to bring wasting desolating judgments upon the land in which they *lived in pleasure and were wanton*. This seems to refer primarily to the desolations made by Sennacherib's army when he seized all the fenced cities of Judah: but those words, *many days and years*, must be rendered (as the margin reads them) *days above a year*, that is, something above a year shall this havoc be in the making: so long it was from the first entrance of that army into the land of Judah to the overthrow of it. *You shall be troubled, you careless women.* The prophet here tells them the country whence they had their rents and dainties should shortly be laid waste: "*The vintage shall fail;* and then what will you do for wine to make merry with? *The gathering* of fruit *shall not come*, for there shall be none to be gathered, *v.* 10. You will want *the teats*, the good milk from the cows, *the pleasant fields* and their productions." The cities of Judah, where they lived at ease should be laid waste (*v.* 13, 14): *Briers and thorns*, the fruits of sin and the curse, *shall come up*, not only *upon the land of my people*, but upon *all the houses of joy in the joyous cities.* Then the stately houses *shall be for dens for ever*, which had been as forts and towers for strength and magnificence.

2. In the foresight of this let them *tremble* and *be troubled, strip themselves, and gird sackcloth upon their loins, v.* 11. This intimates not only that God's judgments would strip them, but that the best prevention of the trouble would be to repent and humble themselves before God in true remorse and godly sorrow. The best preparation for the trouble would be to deny themselves and to sit loose to all the delights of sense.

II. While there was still a remnant that kept their integrity they had reason to hope for good times at length. Such times they saw in the latter end of the reign of Hezekiah; but the prophecy may well be supposed to look further, to the days of the Messiah,

who is *King of righteousness* and *King of peace.* Those blessed times shall be introduced—by the *pouring out of the Spirit from on high* (*v.* 15), which speaks not only of the good-will of God towards us, but the good work of God in us. God's *giving his Holy Spirit to those that ask him* is in effect his giving them all good things, as appears by comparing Luke xi. 13 with Matt. vii. 11. This is the great thing that God's people comfort themselves with the hopes of, that *the Spirit shall be poured out upon them.* When God designs favours for his church he pours out his Spirit to qualify those whom he designs to employ as instruments of his favour. (The kingdom of the Messiah was brought in, and set up, by the pouring out of the Spirit (Acts ii), and so it will be to the end.) That which was *a wilderness*, dry and barren, *shall become a fruitful field. Then shall the earth yield her increase.* It is promised that in the days of the Messiah the *fruit of the earth shall shake like Lebanon*, Ps. lxxii. 16. Some apply this to the admission of the Gentiles into the gospel church. When the Spirit is poured out upon a land, *then judgment shall dwell in the wilderness* and turn it into a fruitful field, and *righteousness shall remain in the fruitful field* and make it yet more fruitful. Ministers shall expound the law and magistrates execute it, so judiciously and faithfully that the bad shall be made good and the good made better. Among all sorts of people, the poor and low and unlearned, that are neglected as the wilderness, and the rich and great and learned, that are valued as the fruitful field, there shall be right thoughts of things. Inward peace, *v.* 17, follows upon the indwelling of righteousness, *v.* 16. It is itself peace, and the effect of it is *quietness and assurance for ever*, that is, a holy serenity and security of mind. Those are the quiet and peaceable lives that are spent *in all godliness and honesty*, 1 Tim. ii. 2. Even *the work of righteousness shall be peace.* In the doing of our duty we shall find true pleasure. Though the work of righteousness may be toilsome and expose us to contempt, yet it is peace. *The effect of righteousness shall be quietness and assurance*, to the endless ages of eternity. When the terror of Sennacherib's invasion was over, the people were more sensible than ever of the mercy of a quiet habitation, not disturbed with the alarms of war. Let every family keep itself quiet from strifes and jars within the house, and put itself under God's protection. Jerusalem shall be a peaceable habitation; compare ch. xxxiii. 20. Even *when it shall hail*, and there shall be a violent battering storm *coming down on the forest* that lies bleak, then shall Jerusalem be *a quiet resting-place, for the city shall be low in a low place*, under the wind, not exposed to the fury of the storm, but sheltered by the *mountains that are round about Jerusalem*, Ps. cxxv. 2. There shall be good crops gathered in everywhere, and every year. God will give the increase, but the husbandman must be industrious, and sow beside all waters; and, if he do this, the corn shall come up so thick that he shall turn in his cattle, even the ox and the ass, to eat the tops of it and keep it under. Some think it points at the ministry of the apostles, who, as husbandmen, went forth to sow their seed (Matt. xiii. 3) beside all waters. When God sends these happy times blessed are those that improve them in doing good with what they have, that sow beside all waters.

CHAPTER 33

This chapter relates to the same events as the foregoing chapter, the distress of Judah and Jerusalem by Sennacherib's invasion and their deliverance by the destruction of the Assyrian army. I. The great distress that Judah and Jerusalem should then be brought into, ver. 7–9. II. The particular frights which the sinners in Zion should then be in, ver. 13, 14. III. The prayers of good people to God in this distress, ver. 2. IV. The holy security which they should enjoy in the midst of this trouble, ver. 15, 16. V. The destruction of the army of the Assyrians, ver. 1–3. VI. The enriching of the Jews with the spoil of the Assyrian camp, ver. 4, 23, 24. VII. The happy settlement of Jerusalem, and the Jewish state. Religion shall be uppermost, ver. 6, and their civil state shall flourish, ver. 17–22.

Verses 1–12

I. The proud and false Assyrian, for all his fraud and violence, laid under a woe, *v.* 1. He had spoiled the people of God, and broken his treaty of peace with them, and dealt treacherously. He spoiled those that had never done him any injury, and that he had no pretence to quarrel with, and dealt treacherously with those that had always dealt faithfully with him. He that spoiled the cities of Judah shall have his own army destroyed by an angel. The Chaldeans shall deal treacherously with the Assyrians and revolt from them. Two of Sennacherib's own sons shall deal treacherously with him and basely murder him at his devotions. When he shall have done his worst, when he shall have gone as far as God would permit him to go, then the cup of trembling shall be put into his hand.

II. The praying people of God, earnest at the throne of grace for mercy for the land now in its distress (*v.* 2): "*O Lord! be merciful to us.*" They prayed, 1. For those that were employed in military services for them: "*Be thou their arm every morning.* Hezekiah, and his princes, and all the men of war, need continual supplies of strength and courage from thee. Every morning, when they go forth and perhaps have new work to do and new difficulties to encounter, let them be invigorated, and, *as the day, so let the strength be.*" 2. For the body of the people: "*Be thou our salvation also in the time of trouble,* ours who sit still, and do not venture into the high places of the field." They depend upon God not only as their Saviour, to work deliverance for them, but as their salvation itself.

III. The Assyrian army ruined and their camp made a rich but easy prey to Judah and Jerusalem. No sooner is the prayer made (*v.* 2) than it is answered (*v.* 3), it is outdone. They prayed that God would save them from their enemies; but he did more than that; he gave them victory over their enemies. The strength of the Assyrian camp was broken (*v.* 3) when the destroying angel slew so many thousands of them: *At the noise of the tumult* the rest of *the people fled.* The spoil of the Assyrian camp is seized, by way of reprisal, for all the desolations of the defenced cities of Judah (*v.* 4): *Your spoil shall be gathered* by the inhabitants of Jerusalem, *like the gathering of the caterpillar,* and *as the running to and fro of locusts,* that is, the spoilers shall as easily and as quickly make themselves masters of the riches of the Assyrians as a host of caterpillars, or locusts make a field, or a tree, bare.

IV. The spoil of the enemy is thus gathered (*v.* 5): *The Lord is exalted.* His people will have the blessing of it. When God lifts up himself to scatter the nations in confederacy against Jerusalem (*v.* 3), *he has filled Zion with judgment and righteousness,* a sense of justice. It shall again be called, *The city of righteousness,* ch. i. 26. Hezekiah and his people are encouraged (*v.* 6) with an assurance that God would stand by them in their distress. *Wisdom and knowledge shall be the stability of thy times, and strength of salvation.* Here is a desirable end, that is *the stability of our times,* that things be not disturbed at home, and the *strength of salvation,* deliverance from enemies abroad. Here is also pious maxim of state for Hezekiah and his people to govern themselves by: *The fear of the Lord is his treasure.* True religion is the true treasure of any prince or people; it denominates them rich.

V. The great distress that Jerusalem was brought into described. It is here foretold, 1. That the enemy would be very insolent and there would be no dealing with him, either by treaties of peace (*for he has broken the covenant* as if it were below him to be a servant to his word), or by the preparations of war, for *he has despised the cities*; he scorns their petitions for mercy. He meets with so little resistance, that he despises them, and has no relentings when he puts all to the sword. He neither fears God nor regards man. 2. That therefore he would not be brought to any terms of reconciliation. *The ambassadors* sent by Hezekiah to treat *of peace,* finding him so unmanageable, *shall weep bitterly* for vexation like children, as despairing to find out any expedient to pacify him. 3. That the country should be made quite desolate for a time by his army. No man durst travel the roads; so that a stop was put to trade and commerce: *The highways lie waste. The traveller ceases.* No man had any profit from the grounds, *v.* 9. The desolation is universal. That part of the country which belonged to the ten tribes was already laid waste: "*Lebanon* famed for cedars, *Sharon* for roses, *Bashan* for cattle, *Carmel* for corn, all very fruitful, have now become like wildernesses, *are ashamed* to be called by their own names, they are so unlike what they were. They *shake off their fruits* before their time into the hand of the spoiler."

VI. God appearing, at length, against this proud invader, *v.* 10–12. He had seemed to sit by as an unconcerned spectator. He will not only demonstrate that there is a God that judges, but that he is God over all. When all other helpers fail, then is God's time to help. He will bring down the Assyrian. O Assyrians! *You shall conceive chaff, and bring forth stubble,* which is worthless and combustible, proper fuel for the fire, which it cannot escape, when *your own breath as fire shall devour you.* The threatenings and slaughter you breathe out against the people of God, this shall devour you. God would make their own breath to blow the fire that should consume them; and then no wonder that the people are *as the burnings of lime* in a lime-kiln, and *as thorns cut up,* which are withered, and therefore are soon burnt up. Such was the destruction of the Assyrian army.

Verses 13–24

What has God done in which we must acknowledge his might?

I. He has struck a terror upon the sinners in Zion (*v.* 14): *Fearfulness has surprised the hypocrites.* There are sinners that enjoy Zion's privileges and services, but their hearts are not right in the sight of God. Now those sinners in Zion, though always subject to secret rights and terrors, were struck with a more than ordinary consternation from the convictions of their own consciences. When they saw the Assyrian army besieging Jerusalem, and ready to set fire to it, they could not make their escape to Egypt, and distrusting the promises God had made by his prophets, they were at their wits' end, crying: "*Who among us shall dwell with devouring fire?* Let us therefore abandon the city, and shift for ourselves elsewhere." Or, it may mean that they saw the Assyrian army destroyed; for the destruction of that is the fire spoken of immediately before, *v.* 11, 12. When the sinners in Zion saw what dreadful execution the wrath of God made they were in a great fright, being conscious that they had provoked this God by secretly worshipping other gods.

II. He has graciously provided for the security of his people that trust in him: *Hear this, and acknowledge his* power in making those that *walk righteously,* and *speak uprightly,* to *dwell on high, v.* 15, 16. We have here,

1. The good man's character even in times of common iniquity: He walks righteously. He acts by rules of equity, rendering to all their due, to God his due, as well as to men theirs. He speaks uprightly,

uprightness (so the word is); he speaks with an honest intention. He thinks it a mean and sordid thing to enrich himself by any hardship put upon his neighbour. If he have a bribe at any time thrust into his hand, to prevent justice, *he shakes his hands from holding it*, taking it as an affront to have it offered him. *He stops his ears from hearing* anything that tends to cruelty, or any suggestions stirring him up to revenge, Job xxxi. 31. He *shuts his eyes from seeing evil*. He has such an abhorrence of sin that he cannot bear to see others commit it. Those that would preserve the purity of their souls must stop their ears to temptations, and turn away their eyes from beholding vanity.

2. The good man's comfort, which he may preserve even in times of common calamity, *v*. 16. He shall be safe; shall have communion with that God who is a devouring fire, but shall be to him a rejoicing light. And, as to present troubles, *he shall dwell on high*; he shall not be really harmed by them. *The floods of great waters shall not come nigh him;* or, if they should attack him, *his place of defence shall be the munitions of rocks*, fortified by nature as well as art. God, the rock of ages, will be his high tower. He shall want nothing that is necessary for him: *Bread shall be given him*, even when the siege is straitest; and *his waters shall be sure*. Those that fear the Lord shall not want anything that is good for them.

III. He will protect Jerusalem, and deliver it out of the hands of the invaders. Hezekiah shall put off his sackcloth and shall appear publicly in his beauty, in his royal robes (*v*. 17), to the great joy of all his loving subjects. Those that walk uprightly shall with an eye of faith see the King of kings in his beauty, the beauty of holiness, and that beauty shall be upon them. The siege being raised, they shall now be at liberty to go abroad without danger of falling into the enemies' hand: *They shall behold the land that is very far off;* they shall visit the utmost corners of the nation. Thus believers behold the heavenly Canaan, that land that is very far off, and comfort themselves with the prospect of it in evil times. The remembrance of the fright they were in shall add to the pleasure of their deliverance (*v*. 18): *Thy heart shall meditate terror* with pleasure when it is over. Thou shalt think thou still hearest the alarm in thy ears, "Arm, arm, arm! every man to his post. *Where is the scribe* or secretary of war? Let him appear to draw up the muster-roll. *Where is the receiver* and pay-master of the army? Let him see what he has in bank, to defray the charge of a defence. *Where is he that counted the towers?* That care may be taken to put a competent number of men in each." They shall no more be terrified with the sight of the Assyrians, who were a fierce people, and were of a strange language, that could understand neither their petitions nor their complaints, and therefore had a pretence for being deaf to them, nor could themselves be understood: They are *of a deeper speech than thou canst perceive*, *v*. 19. "*Look upon Zion, the city of our solemnities*, the city where our solemn sacred feasts are kept, where we used to meet to worship God in religious assemblies." The good people were most in pain for Zion upon this account, that the conquerors would burn their temple. Two things are here promised to Jerusalem: 1. A well-grounded security. It shall be *a quiet habitation* for the people of God; they shall not be disturbed, as they have been, by the alarms of war or persecution, *ch*. xxix. 20. "*Thou shalt see the good of Jerusalem, and peace upon Israel;* thou shalt live to see it and share in it." 2. An unmoved stability. Jerusalem, the city of our solemnities, is indeed but *a tabernacle*, in comparison with the New Jerusalem. The present manifestations of the divine glory and grace are nothing in comparison with those that are reserved for the future

state. But it is such a tabernacle as *shall not be taken down*. After this trouble is over Jerusalem shall long enjoy a confirmed peace; and her sacred privileges, which are the stakes and cords of her tabernacle, shall not be removed from her. God's church on earth is a tabernacle, which, though it may be shifted from one place to another, shall not be taken down while the world stands; for in every age Christ will have a seed to serve him. The promises of the covenant are its stakes, and the ordinances and institutions of the gospel are its cords, which shall never be broken. God himself will be their protector and Saviour, *v*. 21, 22. This is the principal ground of their confidence. God will be the Saviour of Jerusalem and her glorious Lord. He will be *a place of broad rivers and streams*. Jerusalem had no considerable river running by it, so wanted one of the best natural fortifications, as well as one of the greatest advantages for trade and commerce; but the presence and power of God are sufficient at any time to make up to us the deficiencies. If there be broad rivers and streams about Jerusalem, these are rivers and streams *in which shall go no galley with oars*. "*For the Lord is our Judge*, by whose judgment we abide. *He is our lawgiver;* and to him every thought is brought into obedience. *He is our King*, to whom we pay homage and therefore *he will save us*." The enemies shall be broken, like a ship at sea that cannot ride out the storm, but having her tackle torn, her masts split, and nothing wherewith to repair them, is given up for a wreck, *v*. 23. They thought themselves sure of Jerusalem; but when they were just entering the port as it were, and thought all was their own, they *could not spread their sail*. The wealth of their camp shall be a rich booty for the Jews: *Then is the prey of a great spoil divided*. They *left their tents as they were*, so that all the treasure in them fell into the hands of the besieged; and even *the lame take the prey*. Thus God brought good out of evil, and not only delivered Jerusalem, but enriched it. Both sickness and sin shall be taken away. *The inhabitant shall not say, I am sick. As the lame shall take the prey*, so shall the sick. There shall be such a universal transport of joy that even the sick shall forget their sickness and join in rejoicings; the deliverance of their city shall be their cure. Or those that are sick shall bear their sickness without complaining as long as they see it goes well with Jerusalem. *The people that dwell therein shall be forgiven their iniquity*. Sin is the sickness of the soul. When God pardons the sin he heals the disease.

CHAPTER 34

In this chapter we have the fatal doom of all the nations that are enemies to God's church and people. It is probable that this prophecy had its accomplishment in the great desolations made by the Assyrian army first, or rather by Nebuchadnezzar's army some time after, among those nations that were neighbours to Israel and had been in some way or other injurious to them. That mighty conqueror took a pride in shedding blood, and laying countries waste, and therein, quite beyond his design, he was fulfilling what God here threatened against his and his people's enemies. Here is, I. A demand of universal attention, ver. 1. II. A direful scene of blood and confusion presented, ver. 2–7. III. The reason given for these judgments, ver. 8. IV. The continuance of this desolation (ver. 9–15). V. The solemn ratification of all this, ver. 16, 17.

Verses 1–8

I. The war proclaimed, *v*. 1. All nations must hear and hearken because they are all concerned in it; God is angry with them; his indignation is upon all nations.

II. The manifesto published, setting forth,

1. Whom he makes war against (*v*. 2): *The indignation of the Lord is upon all nations;* they are all in confederacy against God and religion, all in the interests of the devil. As they have all had the benefit of his patience, so they must all expect now to feel his

resentments. *His fury is* in a special manner *upon all their armies.* With them they have done mischief to the people of God. With them they hope to make their part good against the justice and power of God; and therefore on them, in the first place, God's fury will come.

2. Whom he makes war for, and what are the grounds and reasons of the war (*v.* 8): *It is the day of the Lord's vengeance.* As there is a day of the Lord's patience, so there will be a day of his vengeance; for, though he bear long, he will not bear always. It is *the year of recompences for the controversy of Zion.* Zion is the holy city, a type and figure of the church of God in the world. Zion has a just quarrel with her neighbours for the wrongs they have done her. She has left it to God to plead her cause, and he will do so when the time shall have come.

III. The operations of the war. The sword of the Lord is *bathed in heaven, v.* 5. It may allude to some custom they had of bathing their swords in some liquor or other, to harden them or brighten them, Ezek. xxi. 9–11. God's sword is bathed in heaven, in his counsel and decree, in his justice and power. *It shall come down upon Idumea, the people of God's curse,* the people that lie under his curse. God's sword of war is always a sword of justice. Pursuant to the sentence, a terrible slaughter shall be made among them (*v.* 6). When the day of God's abused mercy and patience is over the sword of his justice gives no quarter. Men have by sin lost the honour of the human nature and made themselves like the beasts that perish; they are therefore killed as beasts, and no more is made of slaying an army of men than of butchering a flock of lambs or goats and feeding on the fat of the kidneys of rams. Nay, the sword of the Lord shall not only dispatch the lambs and goats, the poor common soldiers, but (*v.* 7) *the unicorns too shall* be made to *come down with them, and the bullocks with the bulls—the great men, and the mighty men, and the chief captains,* make as easy a prey as the lambs and the goats. The greatest of men are nothing before the wrath of the great God. Even *the mountains,* which are hard and rocky, *shall be melted with their blood, v.* 3. These expressions are hyperbolical and are made use of because they sound very dreadful to sense. This great slaughter will be a great sacrifice to the justice of God (*v.* 6). Sacrifices were intended for the honour of God, to make it appear that he hates sin and demands satisfaction for it, and that nothing but blood will make atonement. And thus would the whole earth have been soaked with the blood of sinners if Jesus Christ, the great propitiation, had not shed his blood for us. These slain shall be detestable to mankind (*v.* 3). The effect shall be universal confusion and desolation, as if the whole frame of nature were dissolved and melted down (*v.* 4). *The heavens* themselves *shall be rolled together as a scroll* of parchment when we have done with it, and when it is shrivelled up by the heat of the fire. The stars shall fall as the leaves in autumn; all the beauty, joy, and comfort, of the vanquished nation shall be lost and done away, magistracy and government shall be abolished.

Verses 9–17

This prophecy describes the melancholy changes that are often made by the divine Providence, in countries, cities, palaces, and families. Places that have flourished go to decay. We know not where to find the places where many great towns, celebrated in history, once stood. It describes the judgments which are the just punishment which God will inflict when *the year of the redeemed has come,* and *the year of recompences for the controversy of Zion.* Those that aim to ruin the church can never do that, but will infallibly ruin themselves.

I. The country shall become like the lake of Sodom, *v.* 9, 10. *The streams thereof,* that watered the land and refreshed the inhabitants, *shall now be turned into pitch,* shall be congealed. *The dust thereof shall be turned into brimstone;* so combustible has sin made their land that it shall take fire at the first spark of God's wrath. It shall burn continually, and *shall not be quenched night nor day.* The torment of those in hell, or that have a hell within them in their own consciences, is without interruption. As long as there are provoking sinners on earth, *from one generation to another,* it will be found, how light soever men make of it, that it is a *fearful thing to fall into the hands of the living God.*

II. The cities shall become like old decayed houses, deserted, being commonly possessed by beasts of prey or birds of ill omen. God shall mark them for ruin and destruction. *He shall stretch out upon Bozrah the line of confusion with the stones* or plummets *of emptiness, v.* 11. The confusion and emptiness that shall overspread the face of the whole country shall be like that of the whole earth when it was *Tohu and Bohu* (the very words here used)—*without form and void.* Gen. i. 2. Sin will soon turn a paradise into a chaos, and sully the beauty of the whole creation. When there is confusion there will soon be emptiness. Their great men shall be all cut off, and none of them shall dare to appear (*v.* 12): *They shall call the nobles of the kingdom* to take care of the arduous affairs which lie before them, but none shall be there.

III. Even the houses of state shall become as wildernesses (*v.* 13); *thorns shall come up, in her palaces, nettles and brambles in the fortresses thereof.*

IV. They shall become the residence and rendezvous of fearful beasts and birds. This desolation is much enlarged upon, *v.* 11. *The cormorant shall possess it,* or the pelican, which affects to be solitary (Ps. cii. 6); and *the bittern,* which makes a hideous noise, *the owl,* a melancholy bird, *the raven,* a bird of prey, invited by the dead carcases, shall dwell there, all the unclean birds, not for the service of man, *v.* 13. That which was a court for princes shall now be for owls or ostriches, *v.* 14. *The wild beasts of the desert shall meet with the wild beasts of the island,* the wet marshy country. *The satyr shall cry to his fellow* to go with him to this desert place. There shall *the screech-owl rest. The great owl shall there make her nest* (*v.* 15) *and lay and hatch. The vultures,* which feast on carcases, *shall be gathered there, every one with his mate.* What a dismal change sin makes; it turns a fruitful land into barrenness, a frequented city into a wilderness.

V. Here is an assurance given of the accomplishment of this prediction (*v.* 16, 17): *Seek you out of the book of the Lord and read.* What God's word has appointed his Spirit will effect and bring about, for no word of God shall fall to the ground. There is an exact order and proportion observed: *He has cast the lot* for these birds and beasts, so that each one shall know his place. *They shall not break their ranks, neither shall one thrust another.* Jerusalem of old recovered itself out of its ruins, till it gave place to the gospel Jerusalem, which may be brought low, but shall be rebuilt, and shall continue till it give place to the heavenly Jerusalem.

CHAPTER 35

As after a prediction of God's judgments upon the world (ch. xxiv) follows a promise of great mercy for his church (chap. xxv), so here after a black scene of confusion we have a bright and pleasant one, which, though it foretell the flourishing estate of Hezekiah's kingdom in the latter part of his reign, yet surely looks as far beyond that as the prophecy in the foregoing chapter does beyond the destruction of the Edomites; both were typical of the kingdom of Christ and the kingdom of heaven. The gospel church shall be set up and made to flourish. I. The Gentiles shall be brought into it, ver. 1, 2, 7. II. The wellwishers to it, who were weak and timorous, shall be encouraged, ver. 3, 4. III. Miracles shall be wrought both on the souls and on the bodies of men, ver. 5, 6. IV. The gospel church shall be conducted in the way of holiness, ver. 8, 9. V. It shall be brought at last to endless joys, ver. 10. Thus do we find more of Christ and heaven in this chapter than one would have expected in the Old Testament.

Verses 1–4

I. Here we have a wilderness turned into a good land. When the land of Judah was freed from the Assyrian army the country that had been made a wilderness began to recover and to blossom as the rose. When the Gentile nations, that had been long as a wilderness, bringing forth no fruit to God, received the gospel, joy came with it to them, Ps. lxvii. 3, 4; xcvi. 11, 12. When Christ was preached in Samaria there was *great joy in that city* (Acts viii. 8). Converting grace makes the soul that was *a wilderness to rejoice with joy and singing*, and to *blossom abundantly*. Whatever is valuable in any institution is brought into the gospel. All the beauty of the Jewish church was admitted into the Christian church as the apostle shows in his epistle to the Hebrews. Whatever was desirable in the Mosaic economy is translated into the evangelical institutes.

II. The glory of God shining forth: *They shall see the glory of the Lord.* God will manifest himself more than ever in his grace and love to mankind. This is that which will make the desert blossom. The more we see by faith of the glory of the Lord the more joyful and the more fruitful shall we be.

III. The feeble and faint-hearted encouraged, *v.* 3, 4. God's prophets and ministers are charged, by virtue of their office, to *strengthen the weak hands*, to comfort those who could not yet recover the fright they had been put into by the Assyrian army with an assurance that God would now return in mercy to them. This is the design of the gospel, 1. To strengthen those that are weak and to confirm them. Among true Christians there are many that have weak hands and feeble knees, that are yet but babes in Christ; but it is our duty (Luke xxii. 32), not only to bear with the weak, but to do what we can to confirm them, Rom. xv. 1; 1 Thess. v. 14. It is our duty also to strengthen ourselves (Heb. xii. 12), improving the strength God has given us. 2. To animate those that are timorous and discouraged: *Say to those that are of a fearful heart*, that are *hasty* (so the word is), that are for betaking themselves to flight upon the first alarm, that say, in their haste, "We are cut off and undone" (Ps. xxxi. 22), there is enough in the gospel to silence these fears. He that says to us *Be strong* has laid help for us upon one that is mighty.

IV. Assurance given of the approach of a Saviour: "*Your God will come with vengeance.* God will appear for you against your enemies, will recompense both their injuries and your losses." Those whose *hearts tremble for the ark of God*, and who are under a concern for his church in the world, may silence their fears with this, God will take the work into his own hands.

Verses 5–10

"*Then*, when your God shall come, even Christ, look for great things."

I. Wonders shall be wrought in the kingdoms both of nature and grace. 1. Wonders shall be wrought on men's bodies (*v.* 5, 6): *The eyes of the blind shall be opened;* this was often done by our Lord Jesus when he was here upon earth, Matt. ix. 27; xii. 22; xx. 30; John ix. 6. By his power the ears of the deaf also were unstopped, with one word, *Ephphatha—Be opened*, Mark vii. 34. Many that were lame had the use of their limbs restored, Acts iii. 8. The dumb also were enabled to speak, Matt. ix. 32, 33. These miracles Christ wrought to prove that he was sent of God (John iii. 2), nay, he was God, the same who at first made man's mouth, the hearing ear,

and the seeing eye. 2. Wonders, greater wonders, shall be wrought on men's souls. By the word and Spirit of Christ those that were spiritually blind were enlightened (Acts xxvi. 18), those that were deaf to the calls of God were made to hear them readily, as Lydia, whose heart *the Lord opened*, so *that she attended*, Acts xvi. 14. Those also that were dumb, and knew not how to speak of God or to God, having their understandings opened to know him, shall thereby have their lips opened to show forth his praise.

II. The Spirit shall be poured out from on high. There shall be *waters and streams* (*v.* 6), *in the wilderness*, where one would least expect it, *shall waters break out.* This was fulfilled when the *Holy Ghost fell upon the Gentiles* that *heard the word* (Acts x. 44). These waters are said to *break out*, a surprise to the Gentiles, such as brought them, as it were, into a new world. The blessed effect of this shall be that the *parched ground shall become a pool, v.* 7. In *the thirsty land*, where no water was, no ordinances (Ps. lxiii. 1), there shall be *springs of water*, a gospel ministry, *the river that makes glad the city of our God*, Ps. xlvi. 4. *In the habitation of dragons*, who chose to dwell in the parched scorched ground (*ch.* xxxiv. 9, 13), these waters shall flow, and dispossess them, so that, *where each lay shall be grass with reeds and rushes.* Thus it was when Christian churches were planted, and flourished greatly, in the cities of the Gentiles, which, for many ages, had been habitations of dragons, or devils rather, when they were converted to Christianity, then the habitations of dragons became fruitful fields.

III. The way of religion and godliness is here called *the way of holiness* (*v.* 8). "When our God shall come to save us he shall chalk out to us this way by his gospel, so as it had never been before described." It shall be an appointed way; *a highway.* It is the King's highway, the King of king's highway, in which, though we may be waylaid, we cannot be stopped. The *way of holiness* is the way of God's commandments; it is the *good old way*, Jer. vi. 16. *The unclean shall not pass over it*, either to defile it or to disturb those that walk in it. *It shall be for those* whom the Lord has *set apart for himself* (Ps. iv. 3), shall be reserved for them: *The redeemed shall walk there* out of the reach of molestation from an evil world. *The wayfaring men*, who choose to travel in it, *though fools*, of weak capacity in other things, shall have such plain directions from the word and Spirit of God in this way that they *shall not err therein*; they shall get well to their journey's end. Those that are in the narrow way, though some may fall into one path and others into another, not all equally right, yet all meet at last in the same end. The Spirit of truth shall lead them into all truth that is necessary for them. The way to heaven is a plain way, and easy to hit. It shall be a safe way: *No lion shall be there, nor any ravenous beast* (*v.* 9), none *to hurt or destroy.* Those that keep close to this way keep out of the reach of Satan the roaring lion. Those that walk in the way of holiness may proceed with serenity of mind, knowing that nothing can do them any real hurt. Those that walk in the *way of holiness* must separate themselves from the unclean and *save themselves from an untoward generation.* Let them walk *with the redeemed* who *shall walk there.*

IV. The end of this way shall be everlasting joy, *v.* 10. Here is good news for the citizens of Zion. *The ransomed of the Lord shall return and come to Zion.* God will open to them a door of escape out of their captivity. They shall join themselves to the gospel church, that *Mount Zion* that *city of the living God*, Heb. xii. 22. Those that by faith are made citizens of the gospel Zion may *go on their way rejoicing* (Acts viii. 39). They rejoice in Christ Jesus, and they that mourn are blessed, for they shall be comforted. When God's people returned out of Babylon to Zion they came *weeping* (Jer. l. 4); but they shall come to heaven singing a new song, which no man can learn, Rev. xiv. 3. Their joy shall be visible, and no longer a secret thing, as it is here in this world; it shall be proclaimed, to the glory of God. Our joyful hopes and prospects of eternal life should swallow up both all the sorrows and all the joys of this present time.

CHAPTER 36

The prophet Isaiah is, in this and the three following chapters, an historian. Many of the prophecies of the foregoing chapters had their accomplishment in Sennacherib's invading Judah and besieging Jerusalem, and the miraculous defeat he met with there; and therefore the story is here inserted for the confirmation of the prophecy. The key of prophecy is to be found in history; and here, that we might have the readier entrance, it is, as it were, hung at the door. The exact fulfilling of this prophecy might serve to confirm the faith of God's people in the other prophecies at a greater distance. Whether this story was taken from the book of the Kings and added here, or whether it was first written by Isaiah here and hence taken into the book of Kings, is not material. But the story is the same almost verbatim; 2 Kings xviii and xix, and here, and an abridgment of it likewise, 2 Chron. xxxii. In this chapter we have, I. The descent which the king of Assyria made upon Judah, ver. 1. II. The conference he desired to have with Hezekiah, ver. 2, 3. III. Rabshakeh's blasphemous speech, with which he designed to frighten Hezekiah into submission, ver. 4–10. IV. His appeal to the people, to desert Hezekiah, and so force him to surrender, ver. 11–20. V. The report of this made to Hezekiah by his agents, ver. 21, 22.

Verses 1–10

1. A people may be in the way of their duty and yet meet with trouble and distress. We must not wonder if, when we are doing well, God sends afflictions to quicken us to do better, to do our best, and to press forward towards perfection. The enemies of God's people endeavour to conquer them by frightening them, especially by frightening them from their confidence in God. Thus Rabshakeh here, with noise and banter, runs down Hezekiah as utterly unable to cope with his master. It concerns us therefore, that we may keep our ground against the enemies of our souls, to keep up our spirits by keeping up our hope in God. Those who forsake God's service forfeit his protection. It is an easy thing, and very common, for those that persecute the church and people of God to pretend a commission from him for so doing. Rabshakeh could say, *Have I now come up without the Lord?* when really he had come up *against* the Lord, ch. xxxvii. 28.

Verses 11–22

While princes and counsellors have public matters under debate, it is not fair to appeal to the people. It is therefore an unfair practice to incense subjects against their rulers by base insinuations. Proud scorners, the fairer they are spoken to, speak the fouler. Nothing could be said more mildly and respectfully than that which Hezekiah's agents said to Rabshakeh. *Speak, we pray thee;* but this made him the more spiteful and imperious. When Satan would tempt men from trusting in God, he does so by insinuating that in yielding to him they may better their condition. When the world and the flesh say to us, "*Make an agreement* with us *and come out to us*, submit to our dominion and come into our interests, and *you shall eat every one of his own vine*," they do but deceive us, promising liberty when they would lead us into the basest captivity and slavery. Therefore, *when they speak fair, believe them not.* Nothing can be more absurd in itself, nor a greater affront to the true and living God, than to compare him with the gods of the heathen. They are nothing; he is the great *I AM*: they are the creatures of men's fancy and the works of men's hands; he is the Creator of all things. Presumptuous sinners are ready to think that, because they have been too hard for their

fellow-creatures, they are therefore a match for their Creator. This and the other nation they have subdued, and therefore the Lord himself shall not deliver Jerusalem out of their hand. But, though the potsherds may strive with the potsherds of the earth, let them not strive with the potter. It is sometimes prudent not to *answer a fool according to his folly*. Hezekiah's command was, "*Answer him not;* leave it to God to stop his mouth, for you cannot." Though they *answered him not a word*, yet they rent their clothes, in zeal for the glory of God's name and indignation at the contempt put upon it.

CHAPTER 37

In this chapter we have a further repetition of the story which we had before in the book of Kings concerning Sennacherib. In the foregoing chapter we had him conquering and threatening to conquer. In this chapter we have him falling, and at last fallen, in answer to prayer, and in fulfilment of many of the prophecies which we have met with in the foregoing chapters. I. Hezekiah's pious reception of Rabshakeh's impious discourse, ver. 1. II. The gracious message he sent to Isaiah to desire his prayers, ver. 2–5. III. The encouraging answer which Isaiah sent to him from God, assuring him that God would plead his cause against the king of Assyria, ver. 6, 7. IV. An abusive letter which the king of Assyria sent to Hezekiah, to the same purport with Rabshakeh's speech, ver. 8–13. V. Hezekiah's humble prayer to God upon the receipt of this letter, ver. 14–20. VI. The answer which God sent him by Isaiah, promising him that his affairs should shortly take a happy turn, ver. 21–35. VII. The immediate accomplishment of this prophecy in the ruin of Sennacherib's army (ver. 36) and the murder of himself, ver. 37, 38 (2 Kings xix).

Verses 1–7

The best way to baffle the malicious designs of our enemies against us is to be driven by them to God and to our duty. Rabshakeh intended to frighten Hezekiah from the Lord, but it proves that he frightens him to the Lord. The wind, instead of forcing the traveller's coat from him, makes him wrap it the closer about him. The more Rabshakeh reproaches God the more Hezekiah studies to honour him. Hezekiah sent messengers to Isaiah, to desire his prayers, remembering how much his prophecies had looked towards the events of the present day. *This is a day of trouble*, therefore let it be a day of prayer. Now that the *children are brought to the birth*, but *there is not strength to bring forth*, now let prayer come. When pains are most strong let prayers be most lively. Prayer is the midwife of mercy, that helps to bring it forth. *It may be the Lord thy God will hear; who knows but he will return and repent?* Rabshakeh has blasphemed God, and therefore let not Hezekiah be afraid of him, *v.* 6. Judgment will certainly be given against him. Sinners' fears are but prefaces to their falls. He shall *hear the rumour* of the slaughter of his army, which shall oblige him to retire to his own land, and there he shall be slain, *v.* 7.

Verses 8–20

God, in his promise, may confirm us in our silently bearing reproaches. God answered Hezekiah, but it does not appear that he sent any answer to Rabshakeh; but quietly left the matter with him. *So Rabshakeh returned* to the king his master for fresh instructions. Sennacherib, without provocation given to him or warning given by him, went to war against Judah; and now with as little ceremony the king of Ethiopia goes to war against him, *v.* 9. Those that are quarrelsome may expect to be quarrelled with. It is bad to talk proudly and profanely, but it is worse to write so, for this argues more deliberation and design, and what is written spreads further, lasts longer, and does the more mischief. Great successes often harden sinners' hearts and make them the more daring. The kings of Assyria doubt not but to destroy God's land, because the idolatrous kings of Hamath and Arphad became an easy prey to them therefore the religious reforming king of Judah must needs be so too. Hezekiah took Sennacherib's letter, and spread it before the Lord, not designing to make any complaints against him but those grounded upon his own handwriting. Let the thing speak itself; here it is in black and white: *Open thy eyes, O Lord! and see.* He encouraged himself with this, that the God of Israel is *the Lord of hosts*, that he is God *alone*, the *God of all the kingdoms of the earth*, for he made heaven and earth, and therefore both can do anything and does everything. When we are afraid of men that are great destroyers we may with humble boldness appeal to God as the great Saviour.

Verses 21–38

Those who receive messages of terror from men with patience, and send messages of faith to God by prayer, may expect messages of grace and peace from God for their comfort. Isaiah sent a long answer to Hezekiah's prayer in God's name by way of return to his prayer: *"Whereas thou hast prayed to me,* know, for thy comfort, that thy prayer is heard." Those who abuse the people of God affront God himself. *Whom hast thou reproached?* Even *the Holy One of Israel.* And it aggravated the indignity Sennacherib did to God that he set his servants on to do the same: *By thy servants,* the abjects, *thou hast reproached me.* Those who boast of their own achievements reflect upon God and his providence: *"Thou hast said, I have digged, and drunk water;* and wilt not own that *I have done it,"* v. 24–26. The most active men are no more than God makes them: *"What I have formed of ancient times,* in an eternal counsel, *now have I brought to pass, that thou shouldst be to lay waste defenced cities;* it is therefore intolerable arrogance to make it thy own doing." Sennacherib was active and quick, here, and there, and everywhere, but God knew his going out and coming in, *v.* 28. And though he was very headstrong and unruly, he could and would *turn him back by the way which he came, v.* 29. *Hitherto he shall come and no further.* God had signed Sennacherib's commission against Judah (*ch.* x. 6); here he supersedes it. Jerusalem shall be defended (*v.* 35), the siegers shall not come into it, but thall be routed before they begin the siege, *v.* 33. But this is not all: God will return in mercy to his people. Their land shall be more than ordinarily fruitful, so that their losses shall be abundantly repaired. And let them not think that the desolations of their country would excuse them from observing the sabbatical year, though they had not now their usual stock beforehand for that year, yet they must religiously observe it, and depend upon God to provide for them. There is no standing before the judgments of God when they come with commission. One angel shall, in one night, lay a vast army of men dead upon the spot, when God commissions him so to do, *v.* 36. The greatest men cannot stand before them: *The great king, the king of Assyria,* looks very little when he is forced to return with terror and fear, lest the angel that had destroyed his army should destroy him; yet he is made to look less when his own sons, who should have guarded him, sacrificed him to his idol, whose protection he sought, *v.* 37, 38. He that has delivered does and will deliver.

Chapter 38

This chapter proceeds in the history of Hezekiah. I. His sickness, and the sentence of death he received within himself, ver. 1. II. His prayer in his sickness, ver. 2, 3. III. The answer of peace which God gave to that prayer, a sign to confirm his faith herein, the sun should go back ten degrees, ver. 4–8. And this we read before, 2 Kings xx 1 &c. But, IV. Here is Hezekiah's thanksgiving for his recovery, which we had not before, ver. 9–20. To which are added the means used, ver. 21, 22. This is a chapter which will encourage those that are confined by sickness.

Verses 1–8

Neither men's greatness nor their goodness will exempt them from the arrests of sickness and death. Hezekiah, a potentate on earth and a favourite of Heaven, is struck with a disease, which, without a miracle, will certainly be mortal; and this in the midst of his days and usefulness. This sickness seized him in the midst of his triumphs over the ruined army of the Assyrians. Our being ready for death will make it come never the sooner, but much the easier; and those that are fit to die are most fit to live. Is any afflicted with sickness? *Let him pray,* James v. 13. Prayer is a salve for every sore, personal or public. Afflictions bring us to our Bibles and to our knees. When Hezekiah was in health he *went up to the house of the Lord* to pray. When he was sick in bed *he turned his face towards the wall,* probably towards the temple. The testimony of our consciences that by the grace of God we have walked closely and humbly with God, will be a great comfort to us when we come to look death in the face. And though we may not depend upon it as our righteousness, by which to be justified before God, yet we may humbly plead it as an evidence of our interest in the righteousness of the Mediator. Hezekiah does not demand a reward from God for his good services, but modestly begs that God would remember how he had approved himself to God with a single eye and an honest heart: *I have walked before thee in truth* and sincerity, *and with a perfect,* that is, an upright, *heart;* for uprightness is our gospel perfection. The same prophet that was sent to Hezekiah with warning to prepare for death is sent to him with a promise that he shall not only recover, but be restored to a confirmed state of health and live fifteen years yet. When we pray in our sickness, though God send not to us such an answer, as he here sent to Hezekiah, yet, if by his Spirit he bids us be of good cheer, assures us that our sins are forgiven us, that his grace shall be sufficient for us, and that, whether we live or die, we shall be his, we have no reason to say that we pray in vain. God answers us if he *strengthens us with strength in our souls,* though not with bodily strength, Ps. cxxxviii. 3. God, knowing what lay near Hezekiah's heart, promised him not only that he should live, but that he should *see the good of Jerusalem all the days of his life* (Ps. cxxviii. 5). Jerusalem, now delivered, shall still be defended from the Assyrians. God had given Hezekiah repeated assurances of his favour; and yet, as if all were thought too little, a sign is given him. The sign was the going back of the shadow upon the sundial. The sun is a faithful measurer of time, and he that set that clock going can set it back when he pleases, for the Father of all lights is the director of them.

Verses 9–22

Hezekiah's thanksgiving-song, which he penned, by divine direction, after his recovery. He might have taken some of the psalms of his father David, but the occasion was extraordinary, and, his heart being full of devout affections, he would offer up his affections in his own words. It is good to write a memorial of the affliction, and of the frame of our hearts under it,—to keep a record of the thoughts we had of things when we were sick, a thanksgiving to God. It is an excellent writing which Hezekiah here left, upon his recovery; and yet we find (2 Chron. xxxii. 25) that *he rendered not again according to the benefit done to him.* The impressions, one would think, should never have worn off, and yet, it seems, they did. Thanksgiving is good, but thanksliving is better. Now in this writing, when his disease prevailed, and his despair of recovery, *v.* 10–13:

I. He tells us what his thoughts were of himself when he gave up himself for gone. We ought not to make the worst of our case, nor to think that every sick man must needs be a dead man presently. He that brings low can raise up. Thus David sometimes, when he was delivered out of trouble, reflected upon the black and melancholy conclusions he had made upon his own case when he was in trouble, and what he had then *said in his haste*, as Ps. xxxi. 22; lxxvii. 7–9. Hezekiah was now about thirty-nine years of age, with a fair prospect of many years and happy ones. This distemper that suddenly seized him he concluded would be the *cutting off of his days*, that he should now be *deprived of the residue of his years*, and with them he should be deprived not only of the comforts of life, but of all the opportunities he had of serving God and his generation. To the same purport (v. 12), "*My age has departed and gone*, and is removed from me as a shepherd's tent, out of which I am forcibly dislodged by the pulling of it down in an instant." Our present residence is but like that of a shepherd in his tent, a poor, mean, and cold lodging, which will easily be taken down. But it is only the removal of it to another world, where the tents of Kedar that are taken down, coarse, black, and weather-beaten, shall be set up again in the New Jerusalem, *comely as the curtains of Solomon*. He adds another similitude: *I have cut off, like a weaver, my life*. Not that he did by any act of his own cut off the thread of his life; but, being told that he must needs die, he was forced to cut off all his projects, his *purposes were broken off*, even the *thoughts of his heart*, as Job's were, *ch.* xvii. 11. Our days are compared to the weaver's shuttle (Job. vii. 6), passing and repassing very swiftly, every throw leaving a thread behind it; and, when they are finished, the thread is cut off, and the piece taken out of the loom, and shown to our Master, to be judged of whether it be well woven or no, that we may *receive according to the things done in the body*. But as the weaver, when he has cut off his threads, has done his work, so a good man, when his life is cut off, his cares are cut off with it, and he rests from his labours. "But did I say, *I have cut off my life*? No, my times are not in my own hand; they are in God's hand, and it is he that *will cut me off from the thrum* (so the margin reads it); he has appointed what shall be the length of the piece, and, when it comes to that length, he will cut it off." He reckoned that he should go to the gates of the grave—the gates of which are always open; for it is still crying, *Give, give*. He reckoned that he was deprived of worshipping God and doing good in the world (v. 11): "*I said, I shall not see the Lord*, as he manifests himself in his temple, *even the Lord* here *in the land of the living*." "*I shall see man no more*." He shall see his subjects no more, whom he may relieve, shall see his friends no more. He reckoned that the agonies of death would be very sharp and severe: "*He will cut me off with pining sickness*, which will waste me, and wear me off, quickly." He concluded that God, whose servants all diseases are, would by them, *as a lion, break all his bones* with grinding pain, v. 13. He thought that next morning was the utmost he could expect to live in such pain and misery. *From day even to night wilt thou make an end of me*. When we are sick we are very apt to be thus calculating our time, but after all, we are still at uncertainty. It should be more our care how we shall get safely to another world than how long we are likely to live in this world.

II. The complaints he made in this condition (v. 14): "*Like a crane, or swallow, so did I chatter;* I made a noise as those birds do when they are frightened." What a change sickness makes in a little time. Some think he refers to his praying in his affliction; it was so interrupted with groanings that it was more like the chattering of a crane or a swallow. Such mean thoughts had he of his own prayers, which yet were acceptable to God. He *mourned like a dove*, sadly, but silently and patiently. He had found God so ready to answer his prayers at other times, but now his *eyes failed*, and therefore he prays, "*I am oppressed*, and ready to sink; *Lord, undertake for me*. Come between me and the gates of the grave, to which I am ready to be hurried." When we receive the sentence of death within ourselves, we are undone if the divine grace do not undertake to carry us through the valley of the shadow of death, to the heavenly kingdom on the other side of it—if Christ do not do all we need, and cannot do for ourselves.

III. The grateful acknowledgment he makes of God's goodness to him in his recovery. "*What shall I say? He has spoken unto me;* he has sent his prophet to tell me that I shall recover and live fifteen years yet; *and he himself has done it:* it is as sure to be done as if it were done already, for no word of his shall fall to the ground." God having spoken it, he is sure of it (v. 16): *Thou wilt restore me, and make me to live. I will go softly all my years in the bitterness of my soul*, as one in sorrow for my murmurings under my affliction. When God has delivered me I will walk cheerfully with him, as having tasted that he is gracious. He will encourage himself and others with the experiences he had had of the goodness of God (v. 16): "*By these things* which thou hast done for me *they live*; by the same power and goodness that have restored me all men have their souls held in life. *In all these things is the life of my spirit*, maintained by what God has done for the preservation of my natural life." He was raised up from great extremity (v. 17): *Behold, for peace I had great bitterness*. Upon the defeat of Sennacherib, he was suddenly seized with sickness, which embittered him, and it seemed to be the bitterness of death itself—*bitterness, bitterness*, nothing but gall and wormwood. This was his condition when God sent him relief. It came from the love of God, from love to his soul. *He delivered me because he delighted in me* (Ps. xviii. 19); and the word here signifies a very affectionate love: *Thou hast loved my soul from the pit of corruption;* so it runs in the original. This is applicable to our redemption by Christ: *In his love and in his pity he redeemed us*. And the preservation of our bodies is doubly comfortable when it is in love to our souls—when God repairs the house because he has a kindness for the inhabitant. It was the effect of the pardon of sin: "*For thou hast cast all my sins behind thy back*, and thereby hast *delivered my soul from the pit of corruption*, in love to it." When we set them before our face in true repentance, as David did when his sin was ever before him, God casts them behind his back. If this sickness had been his death, it would have put a period to that course of service for the glory of God and the good of the church which he was now pursuing, v. 18. Having recovered from it, he resolves not only to proceed, but to abound, in praising and serving God (v. 19): *The living, the living, he shall praise thee*. We should not only praise him all the days of our life, but *the father to the children should make known his truth*, that the ages to come may give God the glory of his truth by trusting to it. Hezekiah, doubtless, did this himself, and yet Manasseh his son walked not in his steps. Parents may give their children many good things, good instructions, good examples, good books, but they cannot give them grace.

IV. In the last two verses of this chapter observe two lessons: 1. That God's promises are intended not to supersede, but to quicken and encourage, the use of means. Hezekiah is sure to recover, and yet he must *take a lump of figs and lay it on the boil*, v. 21. We must not put physicians, or physic, in the place of God, but make use of them in subordination to God and to his providence; help thyself and God will help thee. 2. That the chief end we should aim at, in desiring life and health, is that we may glorify God, and do good, and improve ourselves in knowledge and grace. Hezekiah, when he meant, *What is the sign that I shall recover?* asked, *What is the sign that I shall go up to the house of the Lord*, there to honour God? (*v.* 22).

CHAPTER 39

The story of this chapter likewise we had before, 2 Kings xx. 12, &c. It is here repeated, not only as a very memorable passage, but because it concludes with a prophecy of the captivity in Babylon; and as the former part of the prophecy of this book frequently referred to Sennacherib's invasion, so the latter part of this book speaks much of the Jews' captivity in Babylon and their deliverance. We have here, I. The pride and folly of Hezekiah, in showing his treasures to the king of Babylon's ambassadors that were sent to congratulate him on his recovery, ver. 1, 2. II. Isaiah's examination of him concerning it, and his confession, ver. 3, 4. III. The sentence passed upon him for it, that all his treasures should, in process of time, be carried to Babylon, ver. 5–7. IV. Hezekiah's penitent and patient submission to this sentence, ver. 8.

Verses 1–4

Humanity and common civility teach us to rejoice with our friends and neighbours when they rejoice, particularly on their recoveries from sickness. The king of Babylon, having heard that Hezekiah had recovered, sent to compliment him. The sun was the Babylonians' god; and when they understood that it was with a respect to Hezekiah that the sun went back ten degrees, on such a day, they thought themselves obliged to do Hezekiah all the honour they could. The king of Babylon made his court to Hezekiah, not because he was pious, but because he was prosperous, as the Philistines coveted an alliance with Isaac, Gen. xxvi. 28. The king of Babylon was an enemy to the king of Assyria, and therefore was fond of Hezekiah, because the Assyrians were so weakened by the power of his God. Hezekiah was a wise and good man, but, when one miracle after another was wrought in his favour, he found it hard to keep his heart from being lifted up into the snare of pride. What a poor thing it was for Hezekiah, whom God had so dignified, to be over proud of the respect paid him by a heathen prince as if that added anything to him! As far as we see cause to suspect that this sly and subtle sin of pride has insinuated itself into our breasts, let us be ashamed of it, as Hezekiah here.

Verses 5–8

If God love us, he will humble us. A mortifying message is sent to Hezekiah, that he might be humbled for the pride of his heart, and be convinced of the folly of it. When Hezekiah boasts of his treasures he is told that he acts like the foolish traveller who shows his money and gold to one that proves a thief and is thereby tempted to rob him. If Hezekiah had known that the successors of this king of Babylon would hereafter be the ruin of his family and kingdom, he would not have complimented his ambassadors as he did; and, when the prophet told him that it would be so, we may well imagine how he was vexed at himself for what he had done. Those that are fond of an alliance with irreligious men will have enough of it, and will have cause to repent it. Hezekiah thought himself very happy in the friendship of Babylon, though it was the mother of harlots and idolatries; but Babylon, who now courted Jerusalem, in process of time conquered her and carried her captive. Hezekiah reckoned *that* word of the Lord good which made him sensible that he had done amiss. When Hezekiah told of the punishment of his iniquity he said, *Good is the word of the Lord.*

CHAPTER 40

At this chapter begins the latter part of the prophecy of this book, which is not only divided from the former by the historical

chapters that come between, but distinguished from it in scope and style. This is all one continued discourse, and the prophet not so much as once named. That consisted of many burdens, many woes; this consists of many blessings. The distress which the people of God were in by the Assyrians is here spoken of as a thing past, ch. lii. 4.; and the captivity in Babylon, and their deliverance out of that, much greater events, are here largely foretold. Before God sent his people into captivity he furnished them with precious promises for their support in their trouble; and we may well imagine how much it helped to dry up their tears by the rivers of Babylon. But it looks further and to greater things; much of Christ and gospel grace. As if it were designed for a prophetic summary of the New Testament, it begins with that which begins the gospels, "The voice of one crying in the wilderness" (ch. xl. 3), and concludes with that which concludes the book of the Revelation, "The new heavens and the new earth", ch. lxvi. 22. While the prophet is speaking of redemption of the Jews he had in his thoughts a more glorious deliverance.

In this chapter we have, I. Orders given to preach and publish the glad tidings of redemption, ver. 1, 2. II. These glad tidings introduced by a voice in the wilderness, which gives assurance that all obstruction shall be removed (ver. 3–5), and that the word of God shall be established and accomplished, ver. 6–8. III. A joyful prospect given to the people of God of this redemption, ver. 9–11. IV. The sovereignty and power of God magnified, ver. 12–17. V. Idols therefore triumphed over and idolaters upbraided with their folly, ver. 18–26. VI. A reproof given to the people of God for their fears, ver. 27–31.

Verses 1–2

The commission and instructions given, not to this prophet only, but to all the Lord's prophets, and to all Christ's ministers, to proclaim comfort to God's people. Let them be sure that, notwithstanding all this, God had mercy in store for them. It was especially a direction to the prophets that should live in the time of the captivity, when Jerusalem was in ruins; they must encourage the captives to hope. Gospel ministers, being employed by the blessed Spirit as comforters, and as helpers of the joy of Christians, are here put in mind of their business.

I. Comfortable words directed to God's people in general, *v.* 1. The prophets have instructions from their God to comfort the people of God. There are a people in the world that are God's people. It is the will of God that his people should be a comforted people, even in the worst of times. Words of conviction, such as we had in the former part of this book, must be followed with words of comfort, such as we have here; for he that has torn will heal us.

II. Comfortable words directed to Jerusalem in particular: "*Speak to the heart of Jerusalem* (*v.* 2). Do not whisper it, but *cry unto her*: show saints their comforts as well as sinners their transgressions; make her hear it." *Her warfare is accomplished*, the set time of her servitude; the campaign is now at an end. Human life is a warfare (Job vii. 1); the Christian life much more. But the struggle will not last always; the warfare will be accomplished, and then the good soldiers shall not only enter into rest, but be sure of their pay. The cause of her trouble is removed, and, when that is taken away, the effect will cease. Tell her that *her iniquity is pardoned*, God is reconciled to her. Nothing can be spoken more comfortably than this, *Son, be of good cheer; thy sins are forgiven thee.* Troubles are *then* removed in love when sin is pardoned. *She has received of the Lord double for* the cure of *all her sins*, more than sufficient to separate between her and her idols, the worship of which was the great sin from which God designed to reclaim them by their captivity in Babylon. It begat in them a rooted antipathy to idolatry, and was physic doubly strong for the purging out of that iniquity. True penitents have indeed, in Christ and his sufferings, *received of the Lord's hand double for all their sins;* for the satisfaction Christ made by his death was of such an infinite value that it was more than double to the demerits of sin; *for God spared not his own Son.*

Verses 3–8

The time to favour Zion having come, the people of God must be prepared, by repentance and faith, for the favours designed them. We have here *the voice of one crying in the wilderness*, which *may* be applied to those prophets, with the captives who, when they saw the day of their deliverance dawn, called earnestly upon them to prepare for it. But it *must* be applied to John the Baptist; for, though God was the speaker, he was *the voice of one crying in the wilderness* to *prepare the way of the Lord*, to dispose men's minds for the reception of the gospel of Christ.

I. By repentance for sin; which John Baptist preached to all Judah and Jerusalem (Matt. iii. 2, 5), and thereby *made ready a people prepared for the Lord*, Luke i. 17. God is coming in a way of mercy, and we must prepare for him, *v.* 3–5. If we apply it to their captivity, it may be taken as a promise that, whatever difficulties lie in their way, when they return they shall be removed. This voice in the wilderness sets pioneers on work to level the roads. It is the same duty that we are called to, in preparation for Christ's entrance into our souls. We must get into such a frame of spirit as will dispose us to receive Christ and his gospel: "*Prepare you the way of the Lord;* and let all be suppressed which would be an obstruction to his entrance. Make room for Christ: *Make straight a highway for him.*" Those that are hindered from comfort in Christ by their dejections and despondencies are the valleys that must be exalted. Those that are hindered from comfort in Christ by a proud conceit are the mountains and hills that must be made low. Those that have entertained prejudices against the word and ways of God, that are untractable, are the crooked that must be made straight. When this is done *the glory of the Lord shall be revealed, v.* 5. When the captives are prepared for deliverance Cyrus shall proclaim it. When John Baptist has for some time preached repentance, and so made ready a people prepared for the Lord (Luke i. 17), then the Messiah himself shall be revealed in his glory, working miracles, and by his grace binding up and healing with consolations those whom John had wounded with convictions. And this revelation of divine glory shall be *a light to lighten the Gentiles. All flesh shall see it together*, and not the Jews only, as the return out of captivity was taken notice of by the neighbouring nations, Ps. cxxvi. 2.

II. By confidence in the word of the Lord, and not in any creature. By this accomplishment of the prophecies and promises of salvation, it appears that the word of the Lord is sure. The power of man, when it does appear against the deliverance, is not to be feared; for it shall be as grass before the word of the Lord: it shall wither and be trodden down. The insulting Babylonians are but as grass. The power of man, when it would appear for the deliverance, is not to be trusted, for it is but as grass. When God is about to work salvation for his people he will take them off from depending upon creatures, and looking for it from hills and mountains. The word of our God, that glory of the Lord which is now to be revealed, the gospel, and that grace which is brought with it to us and wrought by it in us, shall stand for ever. To prepare the way of the Lord we must be convinced that all flesh is grass, weak and withering. We ourselves therefore cannot save ourselves. All the beauty of the creature is but as the flower of grass. We must be convinced that the word of the Lord will furnish us with a happiness that will run parallel with the duration of our souls, which must live for ever.

Verses 9–11

It was promised (*v.* 5) *that the glory of the Lord shall be revealed.*

I. How it shall be revealed, *v.* 9. Notice shall be given of it to the remnant that are left in Zion and Jerusalem, the poor of the land, who were vine-dressers and husbandmen; it shall be told them that their brethren shall return to them. This shall be told also to the captives who belonged to Zion and Jerusalem. Zion is said to *dwell with the daughter of Babylon* (Zech ii. 7); and there she receives notice of Cyrus's gracious proclamation. It shall be published by Zion and Jerusalem (so the text reads it); those that remain there, or that have already returned, let them proclaim it as loudly as they can: let them *lift up their voice with strength.* Let them say to the cities of Judah, and all the inhabitants of the country, *Behold your God. This is our God, we have waited for him.* This may refer to the invitation which was sent forth from Jerusalem to the cities of Judah, as soon as they had set up an altar, immediately upon their return out of captivity, to come and join with them in their sacrifices, Ezra iii. 2–4. But this was to have its full accomplishment in the apostles' public and undaunted preaching of the gospel to all nations, beginning at Jerusalem.

II. What that glory is which shall be revealed. *He will come with strong hand*, too strong to be obstructed though it may be opposed. He shall recompense to all according to their works, as a righteous Judge: *His reward is with him. His work is before him. He himself knows what he will do.* God is the *Shepherd of Israel* (Ps. lxxx. 1); Christ is the good Shepherd, John x. 11. *He shall feed his flock like a shepherd.* His word is food for his flock to feed on; his ordinances are fields for them to feed in; his ministers are under-shepherds. He takes care of the lambs that are weak, and cannot help themselves and *those that are with young.* The good Shepherd has a tender care for children, for young converts, for weak believers, and those that are of a sorrowful spirit. These are the lambs of his flock. He will gather them in when they wander, gather them up when they fall, gather them together when they are dispersed, and gather them home to himself at last; and all this with his own arm, out of which none shall be able to pluck them, John x. 28. He will gently lead them.

Verses 12–17

These verses describe the greatness and glory of the Lord Jehovah, God of Israel, and were written to encourage his people that were captives in Babylon to hope, and depend upon him for deliverance, and to fill those who receive the glad tidings of redemption by Christ with a holy awe and reverence of God.

I. His power is unlimited, *v.* 12. 1. He has a vast reach. View the celestial globe, but the great God *metes the heavens with a span.* All the waters in the world he can *measure in the hollow of his hand*, and he *comprehends the dust of the earth in a measure*, or with his three fingers; it is no more to him that a *pugil*, or that which we take up between our thumb and two fingers. 2. He has a vast strength, and can as easily move mountains as the tradesman heaves his good into the scales; he poises them with his hand as exactly as if he weighed them in a pair of balances.

II. His wisdom is unsearchable, *v.* 13, 14. As none can do what God has done, so none can suggest anything to him which he thought not of. When the Lord made the world (Job xxvi. 13) there was none that gave him any advice. Nor does he need any counsellor to direct him in the government of the world.

III. The nations of the world are nothing in comparison, *v.* 15, 17. Take all the great and mighty nations, kings the most pompous, kingdoms the most populous; take the isles, the multitude of the isles of the Gentiles: *Before him* they are *as a drop of the bucket* compared with the vast ocean, or *the small dust of the balance* (which does not serve to turn it, and therefore is not regarded, it is so small) in comparison with all the dust of the earth. *He takes them* up as a very little thing. *They are counted by him,* and are to be counted by us *less than nothing, and vanity.* He can as easily bring them all into nothing as at first he brought them out of nothing. They are all *vanity;* the word used for the chaos (Gen. i. 2). This magnifies God's love to the world, that, though it is of such small account with him, yet, for the redemption of it, he *gave his only-begotten Son,* John iii. 16.

IV. The services of the church can make no addition to him (v. 16): *Lebanon is not sufficient to burn* for the fuel of the altar, nor the beasts of it for sacrifices, v. 16. He is exalted *far above all blessing and praise,* all burnt-offerings and sacrifices.

Verses 18–26

The prophet here reproves those, 1. Who made images and then said that they resembled God, and paid their homage to them. 2. Who put creatures in the place of God, who feared them more than God, or loved them more than God. Twice the challenge is here made, *To whom will you liken God? v.* 18, and again *v.* 25. *To whom will you liken me?* This shows the absurdity, (1) Of making visible images of him who is invisible, imagining the image to be animated by the deity. (2) Of making creatures equal with God in our affections. Proud people make themselves equal with God; covetous people make their money equal with God; and whatever we esteem or love, fear or hope in, more than God, that creature we equal with God, which is the highest affront imaginable. Now, to show the absurdity of this,

I. The prophet describes idols as worthy of the greatest contempt (v. 19, 20): "Look upon the better sort of them, made of some base metal, cast into what shape the founder pleases, and gilded, or overlaid with plates of gold, that it may pass for a golden image. It is a creature; for the workman made it; *therefore it is not God,* Hos. viii. 6. It is a cheat; for it is gold on the outside, but within it is lead or copper, in this representing the deities, that they were not what they seemed to be. *He that is so impoverished* that he has scarcely a sacrifice to offer to his god when he has made him, though he cannot procure one of brass or stone, he will have a wooden one rather than none, and *chooses a tree that will not soon rot,* and of that he will have his graven image made. The better sort have silver chains to fix theirs with; and, though it be but a wooden image, care is taken that it *shall not be moved.*" How these idolaters shame their own reason, in dreaming that gods of their own making (*Nehushtans,* pieces of brass or logs of wood) should be able to do them any kindness! See how these idolaters shame us, who worship the only living and true God. They spared no cost upon their idols; we grudge that as waste which is spent in the service of our God.

II. He describes God as infinitely great, and worthy of the highest veneration. To prove the greatness of God he appeals,

1. To what they had *heard of him by the hearing of the ear* (v. 21): "*Have you not known* by the very light of nature? *Has it not been told you by your fathers* and teachers, according to the constant tradition received from their ancestors and predecessors, even from the beginning? *Have you not understood* it as always acknowledged *from the foundation of the earth,* that God is a great God, and a great King above all gods?" The invisible things of God are *clearly seen from the creation of the world,* Rom. i. 20. Thou mayest not only ask thy father, and thy elders (Deut. xxxii. 7); but *ask those that go by the way* (Job xxi. 29), ask the first man you meet. God has the command of all the creatures. The heaven and the earth themselves are under his management: *He sits upon the circle,* or globe, *of the earth, v.* 22. He is still

stretching out the heavens, and will do so till the day comes that they shall be rolled together like a scroll. He spreads them out as easily as we draw a curtain, opening these curtains in the morning and drawing them close again at night. And the heaven is to this earth *as a tent to dwell in;* it is a canopy drawn over our heads. The numerous inhabitants of this earth are in his eye as grasshoppers in ours, so little and so easily crushed. If the spies thought themselves grasshoppers before the sons of Anak (Num. xiii. 33), what are we before the great God? Grasshoppers live but awhile, and live carelessly, not like the ant; so do the most of men. Those who act against him will certainly be brought down by the mighty hand of God, v. 23, 24. *They shall not be planted; they shall not be sown;* and those are the two ways of propagating plants, either by seed or slips. If they should so be planted or sown, yet *their stock shall not take root in the earth,* they shall not continue long in power.

2. He appeals to what *their eyes saw of him* (v. 26): "*Lift up your eyes on high;* be not always poring on this earth, but sometimes look up, behold the glorious lights of heaven, consider who has created them." What we see of the creature should lead us to the Creator. The idolaters, when they beheld the hosts of heaven, looked no further, but worshipped them, Deut. iv. 19. The Creator *brings out their host by number,* as a general draws out the squadrons and battalions of his army; *he calls them all by names* (Ps. cxlvii. 4); and *by the greatness of his might, not one of them fails,* but everyone does that to which he is appointed.

Verses 27–31

I. The prophet reproves the people of God, captives in Babylon for their unbelief and distrust of God (v. 27): "*Why sayest thou, O Jacob! to thyself and to those about thee, My way is hidden from the Lord?*" 1. The titles he here gives them were enough to shame them out of their distrusts: *O Jacob! O Israel!* They bore these names—as God's professing people, a people in covenant with him. 2. The way of reproving them is by reasoning with them. Many of our foolish fears would vanish before a strict enquiry into the causes of them. 3. They spoke of God, as if he had cast them off. 4. The ill word they said was a word of despair concerning their present condition. They were ready to conclude, (1) That God would not heed them: *My way is hidden from the Lord.* There are such difficulties in our case that even divine wisdom and power will be nonplussed. (2) That God could not help them: "*My judgment is passed over from my God;* my case is past relief, so far past it that God himself cannot redress the grievances of it."

II. He reminds them of that which was sufficient to silence all those fears and distrusts. For the conviction of idolaters (v. 21), he appeals to what they had known. Jacob and Israel were a knowing people and their knowledge came by hearing. Among other things, they had heard that *God had spoken once, twice,* yea, many a time they had *heard it, That power belongs unto God* (Ps. lxii. 11).

1. He is himself an almighty God. He must needs be so, for he is *the everlasting God,* and therefore with him there is no decay. He is without beginning or end and therefore with him there is no change. He is also *the Creator of the ends of the earth* and therefore is the rightful ruler of all, and is able to save his church as he was at first to make the world. *There is no searching out of his understanding,* so as to defeat its intentions. None can say, "Thus far God's wisdom can go, and no further." *He faints not, nor is weary;* he upholds the whole creation, and governs all the creatures, and has power to relieve his church, when it is brought low.

2. He gives strength to his people, and helps them to help themselves. He that is the strong God is the strength of Israel. (1) He can help the weak, *v.* 29. (2) He will help the willing, will help those who, in a humble dependence upon him, help themselves, and will do well for those who do their best, *v.* 30, 31. *The youths* and *the young men* are strong, but are apt to think themselves stronger than they are. And they *shall faint and be weary, shall utterly fail* in their conflicts, and under their burdens; they shall soon be made to see the folly of trusting to themselves. *But those that wait on the Lord,* and by faith rely upon him and commit themselves to his guidance, shall find that God will not fail them. They shall have grace sufficient for them: They *shall renew their strength.* God will be their *arm every morning, ch.* xxxiii. 2. They shall use this grace for the best purposes. They shall soar upward, upward towards God. Devout affections are the eagles' wings on which gracious souls mount up, Ps. xxv. 1. They shall press forward, forward towards heaven. They shall walk, they shall run, the way of God's commandments, cheerfully and with alacrity.

CHAPTER 41

This chapter is intended both for the conviction of idolaters and for the consolation of all God's faithful worshippers. And however this might be primarily intended for the conviction of Babylonians, and the comfort of Israelites, doubtless it was intended both for admonition and encouragement to us. I. God by the prophet shows the folly of those that worshipped idols, ver. 1–9. II. He encourages his faithful ones to trust in him, ver. 10–20. III. He challenges the idols, ver. 21–29. So that the chapter may be summed up in those words of Elijah, "If Jehovah be God, then follow him; but, if Baal be God, then follow him."

Verses 1–9

God's care for his people Israel in raising up Cyrus to be their deliverer is a proof of his sovereignty above all idols and of his power to protect his people.

I. A general challenge to the worshippers of idols, *v.* 1. It is renewed (*v.* 21): *Produce your cause.* The court is set, summonses are sent to the islands. Silence (as usual) is proclaimed while the cause is in trying: "*Keep silence before me,* and judge nothing before the time." The defenders of idolatry are called to say what they can in defence of it: "*Let them renew their strength,* in opposition to God. *Let them come near;* in vindication and honour of their idols, let *them speak* freely: *Let us come near together to judgment.*"

II. He particularly challenges the idols to do that for their worshippers, which he had done and would do for his worshippers.

1. That which is to be proved is, (1) That *the Lord is God* alone, *the first and with the last* (*v.* 4), that he is infinite, eternal, and unchangeable, that he governed the world from the beginning, and will to the end of time. (2) That *Israel* is *his servant* (*v.* 8), whom he protects, and employs, and in whom he is and will be glorified.

2. To prove this he shows,

(1) That it was he who called Abraham, the father of this despised nation, out of an idolatrous country. He is *the righteous man whom God raised up from the east.* Of him the Chaldee paraphrast expressly understands it: *Who brought Abraham publicly from the east?* To maintain the honour of the people of Israel, it was very proper to point to this great ancestor of theirs; and (*v.* 8) God calls Israel the *seed of Abraham my friend.* Also to put contempt upon the Chaldean idolatry, it was proper to show how Abraham was called from serving other gods (Joshua. xxiv. 2, 3, &c.). Also, to encourage the captives in Babylon to hope that God would find a way for their return to their own land, it was proper to remind them how he brought their father Abraham out of

the same country into this land, to give it to him for an inheritance, Gen. xv. 7. He was a *righteous man,* that *believed God, and it was counted to him for righteousness;* and so he became the father of all those who by faith in Christ are made the *righteousness of God through him,* Rom. iv. 3, 11; 2 Cor. v. 21; Gen. xviii. 19. God *raised him up from the east,* from Ur first and afterwards from Haran, which lay east from Canaan. He raised him out of iniquity and made him pious, out of obscurity and made him famous. He *called him to his foot,* to follow him with an implicit faith; for he *went out not knowing whither he went,* but whom he followed, Heb. xi. 8. We must all either come to his foot or be made his footstool. *He gave nations before him,* the nations of Canaan, and the Hittites acknowledged him a mighty prince, Gen. xxiii. 6. He *made him rule over* those *kings* whom he conquered for the rescue of his brother Lot, Gen. xiv. And when God *gave them as dust to his sword, and as driven stubble to his bow,* he then *pursued them, and passed safely,* or in peace, under the divine protection.

(2) That it is he who will, ere long, raise up Cyrus from the east. It is spoken of as a thing past, as if it were already done. *God will raise him up in righteousness* (so it may be read, *ch.* xlv. 13), *will call him to his foot,* make what use of him he pleases, and make him victorious over the nations that oppose his coming to the crown. He shall be a type of Christ, who is righteousness itself, whom God will, in the fulness of time, raise up and make victorious over the powers of darkness.

III. He exposes the folly of idolaters, who obstinately persisted in their idolatry (*v.* 5): *The isles of the Gentiles saw this,* not only what God did for Abraham himself, but what he did for his seed, how he brought them out of Egypt, and made them *rule over kings,* and *they feared,* Exod. xv. 14–16. They were afraid, *drew near, and came;* but, instead of helping to reason one another out of their sottish idolatries, they helped to confirm one another in them, *v.* 6, 7. They said one to another, *Be of good courage;* let us unanimously agree to keep up the reputation of our gods. One tradesman encourages another to come into a confederacy for the keeping up of the noble craft of god-making. They not only had recourse to their old gods for protection, but made *new ones,* Deut. xxxii. 17. *So the carpenter,* having done his part to the timber-work, *encouraged the goldsmith* to do his part in gilding or overlaying it; and, when it came into the goldsmith's hand, *he that smooths with the hammer,* that polishes it, or beats it thin, quickened *him that smote the anvil,* and told him it was *ready for the soldering,* which perhaps was the last operation about it, and then it is *fastened with nails,* and you have a god of it.

IV. He encourages his own people to trust in him (*v.* 8, 9): *But thou, Israel, art my servant.* "Idolaters put themselves under the protection of these impotent deities. *Those that make them are like unto them, and so is every one that trusts in them; but thou, O Israel!* art the servant of a better Master." They are God's servants. He has *chosen* them to be a peculiar people to himself. They were the seed of Abraham his friend. It was the honour of Abraham that he was *called the friend of God* (James ii. 23). And for the father's sake the people of Israel were beloved. He had not yet cast them away, though they had often provoked him, and therefore he would not now abandon them.

Verses 10–20

The scope of these verses is to silence the fears, and encourage the faith, of the servants of God in their distresses. Perhaps it is intended, in the first place, for the support of God's Israel, in captivity;

but all that faithfully serve God *through patience and comfort of this scripture may have hope.* A word of caution, counsel, and comfort, which is so often repeated, *Fear thou not;* and again (v. 13), *Fear not;* and (*v.* 14). It is against the mind of God that his people should be a timorous people.

I. They may depend upon his presence with them as their God. "*I will hold thy right hand,* go hand in hand with thee" (so some); as their guide. When we are weak he will hold us up, will encourage us, and so *hold us by the right hand,* Ps. lxxiii. 23. He will silence fears: *Saying unto thee, Fear not.* He has said it again and again in his word, but he will go further; he will by his Spirit say it to their hearts.

II. Though their enemies be now very formidable, yet the day is coming when God will reckon with them. There are those that are incensed against God's people, that *strive with them* (v. 11), that war against them (v. 12), that hate them. But let God's people wait God's time. They shall be convinced of the folly of striving with God's people. *They shall be ashamed and confounded,* which might bring them to repentance, but will rather fill them with rage. They shall be ruined and undone (v. 11): *They shall be as nothing* before the justice and power of God. This is repeated (*v.* 12).

III. They themselves should become a terror to those who were now a terror to them, and victory should turn on their side, *v.* 14–16. Jacob and Israel are reduced and brought very low. It is the *worm Jacob,* so little, so weak, and so defenceless, trampled on by everybody, forced to creep even into the earth for safety. Jacob's King calls himself *a worm and no man,* Ps. xxii. 6. God's people are sometimes as worms, but not vipers, as their enemies are, not of the serpent's seed. God regards Jacob's low estate, and says, "*Fear not, thou worm Jacob;* fear not that thou shalt be crushed; and *you men of Israel*" (*you few men,* so some read it, *you dead men,* so others), "do not give up yourselves for gone." *By whom shall Jacob arise, for he is small?* We are here told: *I will help thee, saith the Lord;* and it is the honour of God to help the weak. The Lord will help them by enabling them to help themselves and making Jacob to become *a threshing instrument.* Observe, He is but an instrument, a tool in God's hand. But, if God make him a threshing instrument, he will make him fit for use, *new* and *sharp,* and *having teeth,* or sharp spikes; and then, by divine direction and strength, *thou shalt thresh the mountains,* the highest, and strongest, and most stubborn of thy enemies. He pursues the metaphor, *v.* 16. Having threshed them, *thou shalt winnow them, and the wind shall scatter them.* This had its accomplishment, in part, in the victories of the Jews in the times of the Maccabees; but it seems designed to read the final doom of all the implacable enemies of the church of God in the triumphs of the cross of Christ over the powers of darkness, and *he that overcomes shall have power over the nations,* Rev. ii. 26.

IV. They shall have abundance of comfort in God, and God shall have abundance of honour from them: *Thou shalt rejoice in the Lord, v.* 16. "Thou shalt also *glory in the Holy One of Israel,* in what he has done for thee."

V. If there be occasion, God will again do for them as he did for Israel in their march from Egypt to Canaan, *v.* 17–19. When the captives, either in Babylon or in their return thence, want water or shelter, God will take care of them. Their return out of Babylon was typical of our redemption by Christ; and so these promises, 1. Were provided by the gospel of Christ. That glorious discovery of his love has given full assurance that God has provided sufficient for the supply of all their wants, and the answering of all their prayers. 2. They are applied by the grace

and Spirit of Christ to all believers, that they may have consolation in their way and a complete happiness in their end. It is here supposed that the people of God, in their passage through this world, are often in straits: *The poor and needy seek water, and there is none; the poor in spirit hunger and thirst after righteousness.* The soul of man seeks for satisfaction somewhere, but soon despairs of finding it in the world. It is here promised that their grievances shall be redressed: "*I the Lord will hear them,* will answer them, I will be with them as I have always been, in their distresses." While we are in the wilderness of this world this promise is to us what the pillar of cloud and fire was to Israel, an assurance of God's gracious presence. They shall have fresh water, as Israel had, even where one would least expect it (*v.* 18): *I will open rivers in high places,* rivers of grace, rivers of pleasure, *rivers of living water,* which he spoke of the Spirit (John vii. 38, 39). The preaching of the gospel to the world turned that wilderness into a pool of water. "*I will plant in the wilderness the cedar* (*v.* 19), so that they shall pass through with as much ease and delight as a man walks in his grove. These trees shall be to them what the pillar of cloud was to Israel, a shelter from the heat." Christ and his grace are so to believers. When God sets up his church in the Gentile wilderness there shall be as great a change in men's characters as if thorns and briers were turned into cedars. They shall see and acknowledge the hand of God in this, *v.* 20. *That they may see* this wonderful change is above the ordinary course of nature and therefore comes from a superior power.

Verses 21–29

The Lord, by the prophet, here repeats the challenge to idolaters: "*Produce your cause* (*v.* 21) and *bring forth the strongest reasons* you have to prove that your idols are gods, worthy of adoration."

I. The idols are here challenged to bring proofs of their knowledge and power. Understanding and active power are the accomplishments of a man. Whoever pretends to be a god must have these in perfection.

1. "They can tell us nothing that we did not know before, so ignorant are they. We challenge them to inform us," (1) "What has been formerly: *Let them show the former things.* What did they ever do that was worth taking notice of?" (2) What shall happen; to declare to us *things to come* (*v.* 22), and again (*v.* 23). No creature can foretell things to come, otherwise than by divine information, with any certainty.

2. "They can do nothing that we cannot do ourselves, so impotent are they." That which is charged upon these idols is that *they are of nothing, v.* 24. Some read it: "*The work they do is of nought,* and so is the ado that is made about them. Therefore *he that chooses you,* and gives you your deity, *is an abomination* to God." A servant is at liberty to choose his master, but a man is not at liberty to choose his God.

II. God here produces proofs that he is the true God, and that there is none besides him.

1. He has an irresistible power. This he will shortly make to appear in the raising up of Cyrus, a type of Christ (*v.* 25): *He will raise him up from the north* and *from the rising of the sun.* Cyrus by his father was a Mede, by his mother a Persian; and his army consisted of Medes, whose country lay north, and Persians, whose country lay east, from Babylon. God will raise him up to great power, and he shall come against Babylon with ends of his own to serve. But, (1) *He shall proclaim God's name;* so it may be read. So he did when, in his proclamation for the release of the Jews, he acknowledged that the Lord God of Israel was *the God.* (2) All opposition shall

fall before him: *He shall come upon the princes of Babylon* and trample upon them *as the potter treads clay.* Christ, as man, was raised up from the north, for Nazareth lay in the northern parts of Canaan; as the angel of the covenant, he ascends from the east. He maintained the honour of heaven (*he shall call upon my name*), and came upon the prince of darkness as mortar and trod him down.

2. He has an infallible foresight. Now the false gods not only could not do it, but they could not foresee it. (1) He challenges them to produce any of their pretended deities, or their diviners (v. 26). (2) He challenges to himself the sole honour of doing it and foretelling it (v. 27). I am he that *will give to Jerusalem one that brings good tidings.* This is applicable to the work of redemption, in which the Lord has given to us the glad tidings of reconciliation.

III. Judgment is here given upon this trial. 1. None of all the idols had foretold this work of wonder. Other nations besides the Jews were released out of captivity in Babylon by Cyrus, and yet none of them had any intelligence given them of it beforehand, by any of their gods or prophets. None of all the gods of the nations have shown their worshippers the way of salvation, which God will show by the Messiah. 2. None of those who pleaded for them could produce any instance of their knowledge or power that had in it any colour of proof that they were gods. Judgment must therefore be given against the defendant upon *Nihil dicit—He is mute.* 3. Sentence is therefore given according to the charge exhibited against them (v. 24).

CHAPTER 42

The prophet seems here to launch out yet further into the prophecy of the Messiah and his kingdom under the type of Cyrus. Here is, I. A prophecy of the Messiah's coming with meekness, and yet with power, ver. 1–4. II. His commission opened, which he received from the Father, ver. 5–9. III. The joy with which the glad tidings should be received, ver. 10–12. IV. The success of the gospel, for the overthrow of the devil's kingdom, ver. 13–17. V. The rejection of the Jews for their unbelief, ver. 18–25.

Verses 1–4

We are sure that these verses are to be understood of Christ, for the evangelist tells us expressly that in him this prophecy was fulfilled, Matt. xii. 17–21.

I. The Father's confidence in him. 1. God owns him: He is *my servant.* Though he was a Son, yet, as a Mediator, he *took upon him the form of a servant.* 2. As chosen by him: He is *my elect.* Infinite Wisdom made the choice and then avowed it. 3. As one he put confidence in: He is *my servant on whom I lean;* so some read it. 4. As one he took care of: He is *my servant whom I uphold;* so we read it. The Father stood by him and strengthened him. His delight was in him from eternity.

II. The qualification for his office: *I have put my Spirit upon him,* to enable him to go through his undertaking, *ch.* lxi. 1.

III. The work to which he is appointed: it is to *bring forth judgment to the Gentiles,* that is, to set up a religion in the world under the bonds of which the Gentiles should come and the blessings of which they should enjoy.

IV. The mildness and tenderness with which he should pursue this undertaking, v. 2, 3. He shall carry it on without noise. He shall have no trumpet sounded before him, nor any noisy retinue to follow him. The opposition he meets with he shall not strive against, but patiently *endure the contradiction of sinners against himself.* His kingdom is spiritual and therefore its weapons are not carnal, nor is its appearance pompous. Those that are wicked he will be patient with; when he has begun to crush them, so that they are as bruised reeds, he will give them space to repent; though they are very offensive, as smoking flax (*ch.* lxv. 5), yet he will bear with them,

as he did with Jerusalem. Those that are as a reed oppressed with doubts and fears, *as a bruised reed,* that are as *smoking flax,* as the wick of a candle newly lighted, which is ready to go out again, he will not despise. More is implied than is expressed. *He will not break the bruised reed,* but will strengthen it, that it may become as a cedar in the courts of our God. *He will not quench the smoking flax,* but blow it up into a flame.

V. The courage and constancy with which he should persevere (v. 4): Till he is able to say, *It is finished;* and he enables his apostles and ministers not to fail nor be discouraged, till they also have finished their testimony. He *sets judgment in the earth.* He erects his government in the world, a church for himself among men, reforms the world by the power of his gospel and grace.

Verses 5–12

I. The covenant God made with and the commission he gave to the Messiah, v. 5–7.

1. The royal titles by which the great God here makes himself known (v. 5): He is the fountain of all being and therefore the fountain of all power. In the upper world *he created the heavens and stretched them out* (*ch.* xl. 22). In the lower world *he spread forth the earth,* and made it a habitation, *and that which comes out of it* is produced by his power. In the world of mankind: *He gives breath to the people upon it;* he gives spirit, the powers and faculties of a rational soul. Now this is prefixed to God's covenant with the Messiah, and the commission given him to show that the work of redemption was to restore man to the allegiance he owes to God as his Maker.

2. The assurances which he gives to the Messiah of his presence with him, v. 6. The Messiah was called of God. He was no intruder (Heb. v. 4). When an angel was sent from heaven to strengthen him in his agonies, the Father himself was with him, and this promise was fulfilled.

3. The great intentions of this commission speak comfort to the children of men. God, in giving us Christ, has with him freely given us all the blessings of the new covenant. Two glorious blessings Christ, in his gospel, brings with him to the Gentile word—light and liberty. He is given *for a light to the Gentiles.* By his Spirit in the word he presents the object; by his Spirit in the heart he prepares the organ. He is sent to proclaim liberty to the captives, as Cyrus did, *to bring out the prisoners;* not only to open the prison doors, and give them leave to go out, which was all that Cyrus could do, but to bring them out, to enable them to make use of their liberty. This Christ does by his grace.

II. The ratification and confirmation of this grant. 1. The authority of him that makes the promise (v. 8): *I am the Lord, Jehovah, that is my name.* If he is the Lord that gives being and birth to all things, he will give being and birth to this promise. 2. The accomplishment of the promises he had formerly made concerning his church, are proofs of the kindness he bears to his people (v. 9): "*Behold, the former things have come to pass. And now new things do I declare.* Now I will make new promises, now I will bestow new favours. Old Testament blessings you have had abundantly; now I declare New Testament blessings, not a fruitful country and dominion over your neighbours, but *spiritual blessings in heavenly things. Before they spring forth* in the preaching of the gospel *I tell you of them,* under the type and figure of the former things."

III. The song of joy and praise which should be sung hereupon to the glory of God (v. 10): *Sing unto the Lord a new song,* a New Testament song. The giving of Christ for *a light to the Gentiles* (v. 6) was a new thing. The praises of God's grace shall be sung with joy and thankfulness, 1. By those that live in *the end of the earth*, in countries that lie most remote from Jerusalem. 2. By mariners and merchants, and those that *go down to the sea*. The Jews traded little at sea; if therefore God's praises be sung by those that go down to the sea, it must be by Gentiles. 3. By *the islands and the inhabitants thereof*, v. 10, and again, v. 12. 4. By *the wilderness and the cities thereof, and the villages of Kedar*. These lay east from Jerusalem, as the islands lay west. 5. By *the inhabitants of the rock*, and those that dwell *on the tops of the mountains*, by the inhabitants of the rock, the inhabitants of that part of Arabia which is called *Petræa—the rocky*.

Verses 13–17

These verses may be the song itself that is to be sung by the Gentile world or a prophecy of what God will do to make way for the singing of that song.

I. He will appear in his power and glory more than ever. So he did in the preaching of his gospel, and in the wonderful success it had in the *pulling down of Satan's strongholds*, v. 13, 14. *He had long held his peace*, but now *he shall go forth* to attack the devil's kingdom and give it a fatal blow. Christ, in it, went forth conquering and to conquer. The ministry of the apostles is called their *warfare*; and they were the soldiers of Jesus Christ. *He shall stir up jealousy*, shall appear more jealous than ever for his own name and against idolatry. *He shall cry*, in the preaching of his word, *cry like a travailing woman*; for the ministers of Christ preached as men that travailed in birth again till they saw Christ formed in the souls of the people, Gal. iv. 19. He shall conquer by the power of his Spirit. As a type and figure of this, to make way for the redemption of the Jews out of Babylon, God will break the power of their oppressors, and *will at once destroy and devour* the Babylonian monarchy. In accomplishing this destruction of Babylon by the Persian army under Cyrus, *he will make waste mountains and hills*, level the country, and *dry up all their herbs*. The army shall drain the fens and low grounds, to make way for the march of their army. Thus, when the gospel shall be preached, it shall have a free course.

II. He will manifest his favour and grace, and towards those who ask the way to Zion, he will show the way, and lead in it, v. 16. God will *lead by a way that they knew not*, will show them the way to life and happiness by Jesus Christ, who is the way. Thus, in the conversion of Paul, he was struck blind first, and then God revealed his Son, and made the scales to fall from his eyes. God will *make darkness light before them*. Insuperable difficulties are in the way of their obedience; but God will make *crooked things straight*; their way shall be plain. As a type of this, he will lead the Jews, when they return out of captivity, to their own land again.

III. He will put those to confusion who adhere to idols (v. 17). The Babylonians when they see how the Jews, who despise their images, are owned and delivered by the God they worship, shall be ashamed that ever they said to these molten images, *You are our gods*. In times of reformation sin becomes unfashionable.

Verses 18–25

The prophet, having spoken by way of encouragement to the believing Jews, here turns to those among them who were unbelieving. In them there was a type of the Jews who rejected Christ and were rejected by him.

I. The call that is given to this people (v. 18): "*Hear, you deaf*, and attend to the joyful sound, *and look you blind, that you may see* the joyful light." This call to the deaf to hear and the blind to see is like the command given to the man that had the withered

hand to stretch it forth; though he could not do this, because it was withered, yet, if he had not attempted to do it, he would not have been healed.

II. The character that is given of them (v. 19, 20): *Who is blind, but my servant, or deaf as my messenger?* The people of the Jews were in profession God's servants, and their priests and elders his messengers (Mal. ii. 7); but they were deaf and blind. He complains of their sottishness—they are blind; and of their stubbornness—they are deaf. They were even worse than the Gentiles themselves. Blindness and deafness in spiritual things are worse in those that profess themselves to be God's servants and messengers than in others. The prophet goes on (v. 20) to describe the blindness and obstinacy of the Jewish nation, just as our Saviour describes it in his time (Matt. xiii. 14, 15).

III. The care God will take of the honour of his own name, notwithstanding their blindness and deafness. The scripture was fulfilled in the casting off of the Jews as well as in the calling in of the Gentiles. *He will magnify the law* (divine revelation in all the parts of it) *and will make it honourable*. The law is truly honourable, and, if men will not magnify it by their obedience to it, God will magnify it by punishing them for their disobedience.

IV. The calamities God will bring upon the Jewish nation for their wilful blindness and deafness, v. 22. They are *robbed and spoiled*. Those that were impenitent and unreformed in Babylon were sentenced to perpetual captivity. It was for their sins that they were spoiled of all their possessions. They were some of them *snared in holes*, and others *hidden in prison-houses*. There they lie, and there they are likely to lie. This had its full acomplishment in the final destruction of the Jewish nation by the Romans.

V. The counsel given them in order to their relief; for, though their case be sad, it is not desperate. The generality of them are deaf; they will not harken to the voice of God's word. He will therefore try his rod, and see *who among them will give ear to that*, v. 23. If one method do not take effect, another may. We may all of us, if we will, hear the voice of God. In hearing the word we must hear for hereafter; we must especially hear for eternity. Acknowledge the hand of God in afflictions, and, whoever were the instruments, have an eye to him as the principal agent (v. 24): "*Who gave Jacob and Israel*, that people that used to have such an interest in heaven and such a dominion on earth, who gave them *for a spoil to the robbers*, as they are now to the Babylonians and to the Romans? *Did not the Lord?*" It is he *against whom we have sinned*; the prophet puts himself into the number of the sinners, as Dan. ix. 7, 8. See the mischief that sin makes; it provokes God to anger against a people, and so kindles a universal conflagration, sets all on fire.

CHAPTER 43

The contents of this chapter are much the same with those of the foregoing chapter. I. Precious promises made to God's people in their affliction, of his presence with them, for their support and their deliverance, ver. 1–7. II. A challenge to idols to vie with the omniscience and omnipotence of God, ver. 8–13. III. Encouragement given to the people of God to hope for their deliverance out of Babylon, ver. 14–21. IV. A method taken to prepare the people by putting them in mind of their sins, that they might repent and seek mercy, ver. 22–28.

Verses 1–7

This chapter has a plain connexion with the close of the foregoing chapter. It was there said that Jacob and Israel would not walk in God's ways, and now one would think it should have followed that God would abandon them; but no, the next words are, *But now, fear not, O Jacob! O Israel! I have redeemed thee, and thou art mine*. Though many among them were untractable, yet God would continue his love for his people, and the body of that nation should still be reserved for mercy. Now the sun, breaking out thus of a sudden from behind a thick and dark cloud, shines with a pleasing surprise. The expressions of God's goodwill to his people here speak abundance of comfort to all the spiritual seed of upright Jacob and praying Israel.

I. The grounds of God's care and concern for his people. Jacob and Israel, though in a sinful miserable condition, shall be looked after; for, 1. They are God's *workmanship, created by him unto good works*, Eph. ii. 10. He has created them, not only given them a being, but formed them into a people, constituted their government, and incorporated them by the charter of his covenant. 2. They are the people of his purchase: he has redeemed them. Out of the land of Egypt he first redeemed them, and out of many another bondage, *in his love, and in his pity* (*ch.* lxiii. 9); much more will he take care of those who are redeemed with the blood of his Son. 3. They are his peculiar people: he has called them by name. 4. He is their God in covenant (*v.* 3). Those that have God for them need not fear who or what can be against them.

II. The former instances of this care. 1. God had purchased them dearly: *I gave Egypt for thy ransom.* The Ethiopians had invaded them in Asa's time; but they shall be destroyed rather than Israel shall be disturbed. What are Ethiopia and Seba, all their lives and all their treasures, compared with the blood of Christ? 2. He had prized them accordingly, and they were very dear to him (*v.* 4).

III. The further instances God would yet give them of his care and kindness. 1. He would be present with them in their greatest difficulties and dangers (*v.* 2). 2. He would still, when there was occasion, make all the interests of the children of men give way to the interests of his own children. 3. Those of them that were scattered and dispersed in other nations should all be gathered in and share in the blessings of the public, *v.* 5–7. Some of the seed of Israel were dispersed into all countries, but those whose spirits God stirred up to go to Jerusalem should be fetched in from all parts. But who are the seed of Israel that shall be thus carefully gathered in? He tells us (*v.* 7) they are such as God has marked for mercy. They are called by his name. They are created for his glory. God is with the church, and therefore let her not fear; none that belong to her shall be lost.

Verses 8–13

God here challenges the worshippers of idols to produce proofs of the divinity of their false gods.

I. Their gods have *eyes and see not, ears and hear not,* and those that make them and trust in them are like unto them. They have the shape, capacities, and faculties, of men; but they are, in effect, destitute of reason and common sense, or they would never worship gods of their own making.

II. God's witnesses are summoned to appear, and give evidence for him (*v.* 10): "*You, O Israelites!* all you that are *called by my name,* you *are all my witnesses, and* so is *my servant whom I have chosen.*" It was Christ himself that was so described (*ch.* xlii. 1), *My servant and my elect.* 1. All the prophets that testified to Christ, and Christ himself, the great prophet, are here appealed to as God's witnesses. God's people are witnesses for him, and can attest, upon their own experience, concerning the power of his grace. But the Messiah especially is given to be a witness for him to the people; having lain in his bosom from eternity. 2. Let us see what the point is which these witnesses are called to prove (*v.* 12): *You are my witnesses, saith the Lord, that I am God.* I am a being self-existent and self-sufficient; I am he whom you are to fear, and worship, and trust in. Nay (*v.* 13), *before the day was* (before the first day of time, before the creation of the light, and, consequently, from eternity) *I am he.* The idols were gods formed (*dei facti—made gods,* or rather *fictitii—fictitious*); *by nature they were no gods,* Gal. iv. 8. But God had a being from eternity, before there were either idols or idolaters (truth is more ancient than error); and he will have a being to eternity. *I, even I, am the Lord,* the great Jehovah, who is, and was, and is to come; and *besides me there is no Saviour, v.* 11. God has an infinite and infallible knowledge, as is evident from *the predictions of his word* (*v.* 12): *I have declared and I have shown* that which has without fail come to pass. He has an infinite and irresistible power. He pleads not only, I have *shown,* but, I have *saved* (*v.* 13). The gods of the heathen cannot so much as inspire an historian, much less a prophet. They are challenged to join issue upon this: *Let them bring forth their witnesses,* to prove their omniscience and omnipotence.

Verses 14–21

I. God here takes to himself such titles as were very encouraging to his people. He is *the Lord their Redeemer,* the *Holy One of Israel* (*v.* 14), and again (*v.* 15), *their Holy One,* and therefore will make good every word he has spoken to them. He is *the Creator of Israel,* that made them a people out of nothing and he is their *King.*

II. He assures them he will break the power of their oppressors, *ch.* xiv. 17. God will take care to send a prince to Babylon, that shall *bring down all their nobles,* and all their people too, *even the Chaldeans, whose cry is in the ships,* or whose cry is *to the ships,* as their refuge when the city is taken, that they may escape by the river.

III. He reminds them of the great things he did for their fathers when he brought them out of the land of Egypt (*v.* 16, 17). He that did this can make a way for you in the sea when you return out of Babylon.

IV. He promises to do yet greater things for them than he had done in the days of old. They should see them repeated, nay, they should see them outdone (*v.* 18): "*Remember not the former things,* to undervalue the present things, as if *the former days were better than these. Behold, the Lord will do a new thing.*" The best exposition of this is, Jer. xvi. 14, 15; xxiii. 7, 8. Though former mercies must not be forgotten, fresh mercies must in a special manner be improved.

V. He promises not only to deliver them out of Babylon, but to conduct them safely and comfortably to their own land (*v.* 19, 20): *I will make a way in the wilderness and rivers in the desert.* The same power that made a *way in the sea* (*v.* 16) can make a *way in the wilderness.* And he can produce waters in the dryest land, in such abundance as not only to *give drink to his people, his chosen,* but to the *beasts of the field,* also *the dragons and the ostriches,* who are therefore said to honour God for it. This looks forward, not only to God's care of the Jewish church between their return from Babylon and the coming of Christ, but to the grace of the gospel, especially as it is manifested to the Gentile world. The sinners of the Gentiles, who had been as the beasts of the field, running wild, fierce as the dragons, stupid as the owls or ostriches, shall be brought to honour God for his grace.

VI. He traces up all these promised blessings to their great origin (*v.* 21): *This people have I formed for myself,* and therefore I do all this for them, that they may *show forth my praise.* The new heavens, the new earth, the new man, are the work of God's hand; they are fashioned according to his will. As he formed us, so he feeds us, and keeps us, and leads us.

Verses 22–28

This charge comes in here, 1. To clear God's justice in bringing them into captivity. They had neglected God and had cast him off, and therefore he justly rejected them and *gave them to the curse* (v. 28); and they must be brought to own this before they are prepared for deliverance.

I. The sins with which they are here charged.

1. Omissions of the good which God had commanded. Observe how it comes in with a *but*; compare *v.* 21, where God tells them what favours he had bestowed upon them and what his just expectations were from them. But they had made very ill returns to him for his favours. They had cast off prayer: *Thou hast not called upon me, O Jacob!* Jacob was a man famous for prayer (Hosea xii. 4). To boast of the name of Jacob, and yet live without prayer, is to mock God and deceive ourselves. They had grown weary of their religion. They grudged the expense of their devotion. They were for a cheap religion; and in those acts of devotion that were costly they desired to be excused. They had *not brought*, no, not their *small cattle*, the lambs and kids, which God required for *burnt-offerings* (v. 23), much less did they bring their greater cattle. *Sweet cane*, or *calamus*, was used for the holy oil, incense, and perfume; but they were not willing to be at the charge of that, *v.* 24. They were, in effect, as no sacrifices (*v.* 23): *Neither hast thou honoured me with thy sacrifices*. As God had appointed it, it was no burdensome thing; it was not a service that they had any reason at all to complain of: "*I have not caused thee to serve with an offering;* I have not made it a drudgery to you. I have *not wearied thee with incense*." They had many feasts and good days, but only one day in all the year in which they were to afflict their souls. The ordinances of the ceremonial law, though, in comparison with Christ's easy yoke, they are spoken of as heavy (Acts xv. 10), yet, in comparison with the service that idolaters did to their false gods, they were light. God did not require them to sacrifice their children, as Moloch did.

2. Commissions of the evil which God had forbidden. *Thou hast made me to serve with thy sins*. When we make God's gifts the food and fuel of our lusts, then we make God to serve with our sins. God had not made them to serve with their sacrifices, but they had made him to serve with their sins. The master had not tired the servants with his commands, but they had tired him with their disobedience.

II. What were the aggravations of their sin, *v.* 27.
1. That they were children of disobedience; for their *first father* (that is, their forefathers) *had sinned.*
2. That they were scholars of disobedience too; for *their teachers had transgressed against God*, were guilty of gross scandalous sins, and the people, no doubt, would learn to do as they did.

III. What were the tokens of God's displeasure against them for their sins, *v.* 28. *I have profaned the princes of the sanctuary*, that is, the priests and Levites who presided with great dignity in the temple-service; they profaned themselves, and made themselves vile, by their enormities, and then God profaned them and made them vile, by their calamities, Mal. ii. 9. The honour of their state was ruined likewise: "*I have given Jacob to the curse*, that is, to be cursed, and hated, and abused by all their neighbours, *and Israel to reproach*, to be insulted, ridiculed, and triumphed over by their enemies."

IV. What were the riches of God's mercy towards them notwithstanding (*v.* 25): *I, even I, am he who* notwithstanding all this *blotteth out thy transgressions*.
1. This gracious declaration of God's readiness to pardon sin comes in very strangely. The charge ran very high: *Thou hast wearied me with thy iniquities, v.* 24. Now one would think it should follow: "*I,*

even I, am he that will destroy thee, and burden myself no longer with care about thee." No, *I, even I, am he that will forgive thee;* as if the great God would teach us that forgiving injuries is the best way to keep ourselves from being wearied with them. Of the sins of every believing penitent, the pardon is expressed; he will *blot them out*, as a cloud is blotted out by the beams of the sun (*ch.* xliv. 22), as a debt is blotted out not to appear against the debtor (the book is crossed as if the debt were paid, because it is pardoned upon the payment which the surety has made). He *will not remember* the sin, which shall be no diminution to his love for the future. When God forgives he forgets. It is not for the sake of anything in us, but for his own sake, for his mercies' sake, and especially for his Son's sake.

2. Those words (*v.* 26), *Put me in remembrance*, may be understood either (1) As a rebuke to a proud Pharisee, that expects to find favour for his merits and not to be beholden to free grace: "If you have anything to offer for the sake of which you should be pardoned, put me in remembrance of it." Or, (2) As a direction and encouragement to a penitent publican. Put him in remembrance of the promises he has made to penitents, and the satisfaction his Son has made for them. This is the only way, and it is a sure way, to peace. *Only acknowledge thy transgression.*

CHAPTER 44

God, by the prophet, goes on in this chapter, as before, I. To encourage his people with the assurance of great blessings he had in store for them at their return out of captivity, and those typical of much greater in the days of the Messiah, ver. 1–8. II. To expose the folly of idol-makers and idol-worshippers, ver. 9–20. III. To confirm the assurances he had given to his people of those great blessings, and to raise their joyful expectations, ver. 21–28.

Verses 1–8

Two great truths in these verses:

I. That the people of God are a happy people, especially upon account of the covenant that is between them and God. Three things complete their happiness:

1. The covenant-relations wherein they stand to God, *v.* 1, 2. Israel is here called *Jeshurun—the upright one*; for those only, like Nathanael, are Israelites indeed, in whom is no guile. Jacob and Israel had been represented as very provoking and obnoxious to God's wrath, but mercy steps in with a *notwithstanding*: "*Yet now hear, O Jacob my servant!* thou and I will be friends again for all this." So and so I will do for them, says God (Heb. viii. 12), *for I will be merciful to their unrighteousness.* Now the relations wherein they stand to him are very encouraging. (1) They are his *servants*. (2) They are his *chosen*, and he will abide by his choice; those whom he has chosen he takes under special protection. (3) They are his creatures. He *made them*, and therefore he will help them over their difficulties and help them in their services.

2. The covenant-blessings which he has secured to them and theirs, *v.* 3, 4. (1) Those that are sensible of their spiritual wants, and the insufficiency of the creature to supply them, shall have abundant satisfaction in God: *I will pour water upon him that is thirsty.* (2) Those that are barren as the dry ground shall be watered with the grace of God. (3) The water God will pour out is *his Spirit* (John vii. 39). This is the great New Testament promise, that God, having sent his servant Christ, and upheld him, will send his Spirit to uphold us. To all who are thus made to partake of the privileges of adoption God will give the spirit of adoption. Hereby there shall be a great increase of the church. Thus it shall be spread to distant places, *v.* 4.

3. The consent they cheerfully give to their part of the covenant, *v.* 5. Many of those that were without

did at that time join themselves to them, invited by that glorious appearance of God for them, Zech. viii. 23. And doubtless it looks further yet, to the conversion of the Gentiles. These converts are *one and another*, very many, of different ranks and nations, and all welcome to God, Col. iii. 11. Everyone for himself shall say, "*I am the Lord's; living and dying I will be his.*" They shall *call themselves by the name of Jacob.* They shall love all God's people, and be willing to take their lot with them in all conditions. They shall do this very solemnly. Some of them shall *subscribe with their hand unto the Lord*, as a man sets his hand to it, and delivers it as his act and deed. The more express we are in our covenanting with God the better, Exod. xxiv. 7.

II. That, as the Israel of God are a happy people, so the God of Israel is a great God, and he is God alone. This speaks abundant satisfaction to all that trust in him, *v.* 6–8. The God we trust in is a God of incontestable sovereignty and irresistible power. He is *the Lord*, Jehovah, self-existent and self-sufficient; and he is *the Lord of hosts*, of all the hosts of heaven and earth, of angels and men. He is *the King of Israel and his Redeemer*; and those that take God for their King shall have him for their Redeemer. He is God from everlasting, before the world was, and will be so to everlasting. If there were not a God to create nothing would ever have been; and, if there were not a God to uphold, all would soon come to nothing again. He is God alone (*v.* 6): *Besides me there is no God.* There is no God besides Jehovah. He is all-sufficient, and therefore there needs no other. His people needed not to hope in any other God. Those on whom the sun shines need neither moon nor stars, nor the light of their own fire. They needed not to fear any other god. None besides could foretell these things to come, which God now by his prophet gave notice of to the world, above 200 years before they came to pass (*v.* 7).

Verses 9–20

This discourse is intended, 1. To arm the people of Israel against the strong temptation to worship idols when they were captives in Babylon, and to humour those who were now their lords and masters. 2. To cure them of their inclination to idolatry, which was the sin that did most easily beset them and to reform them from which they were sent into Babylon. As the rod of God is of use to enforce the word, so the word of God is of use to explain the rod. 3. To furnish them with something to say to their Chaldean task-masters. When they insulted over them, when they asked, *Where is your God?* they might hence ask them, *What are your gods?*

For the conviction of idolaters, we have,

I. A challenge given to them to clear themselves from the imputation of the most shameful folly imaginable, *v.* 9–11. They set their wits to contrive, and their hands to frame, graven images, and they call them *their delectable things.* We tell them that they deceive themselves and one another. *Their delectable things shall not profit* them, neither supply them with good nor protect them from evil. The *graven images* are *profitable for nothing* at all. *They are their own witnesses*, witnesses against themselves, if they would but give their own consciences leave to deal faithfully with them. *Who has formed a god?* Who but a madman, or one out of his wits, would think of forming a god, of making that which, if he make it a god, he must suppose to be his maker? *The workmen* that formed this god *are of men*, weak and impotent, and therefore cannot possibly make a being that shall be omnipotent.

II. A particular narrative of the whole proceeding in making a god.

1. The persons employed about it are handicraft tradesmen, the very same that you would employ in making the common utensils of your husbandry, a cart or a plough. You must have a *smith*, a blacksmith, who *with the tongs works in the coals*; and it is hard work. He cannot allow himself time to eat or drink, for *he drinks no water, and* therefore *is faint*, *v.* 12. The plates with which the smith was to cover the image, or whatever iron-work was to be done about it, *he fashioned with hammers*, and made it all very exact, according to the model given him. Then comes *the carpenter*, and he takes as much care and pains about the timber-work, *v.* 13. He brings his box of tools, for he has occasion for them all: *He stretches out his rule* upon the piece of wood, *marks it with a line*, where it must be sawed or cut off; *he fits it*, or polishes it, *with planes*, the greater first and then the less; *he marks out with the compasses* what must be the size and shape of it; and it is just what he pleases.

2. The form in which it is made is that of a man, a poor, weak, dying creature; but it is the noblest form and figure that he is acquainted with. He makes it *according to the beauty of a man*, but altogether unfit to represent the beauty of the Lord. God put a great honour upon man when, in respect of his soul, he made him after the image of God; but man does a great dishonour to God when he makes him, in respect of bodily parts, after the image of man. All the *beauty of the body of a man*, when pretended to be put upon him who is an infinite Spirit, is a deformity and diminution to him. And, when the goodly piece is finished, it must *remain in the house*, in the temple or shrine prepared for it.

3. The matter of which it is mostly made is sorry stuff to make a god of; it is the stock of a tree. (1) The tree itself was fetched out *of the forest*, where it grew among other trees, of no more virtue or value than its neighbours. It was a *cedar*, it may be, or a *cypress*, or an *oak*, *v.* 14. Perhaps he had an eye upon it some time before for this use, and *strengthened it for himself*, used some art or other to make it stronger and better-grown than other trees were. Or, it may be, it pleases his fancy better to take *an ash*, which is of a quicker growth, and which was of his own planting for this use, and which has been nourished with rain from heaven. What an affront he puts upon the God of heaven in setting up that as a rival which was nourished by his rain, that rain which falls upon the just and unjust.

(2) The boughs of this tree were good for nothing but for fuel; to that use were they put, and so were the chips that were cut off, *v.* 15, 16. To show that that tree has no innate virtue in it for its own protection, it is as capable of being burnt as any other tree; he who chose it had no more value for it than for any other tree, throwing part of it into the fire as common rubbish, asking no question for conscience' sake. It serves him for his parlour-fire: *He will take thereof and warm himself* (*v.* 15), and he finds the comfort of it, *Aha! I am warm; I have seen the fire;* and certainly that part of the tree which served him for fuel, the use for which God and nature designed it, does him a much greater kindness and yields him more satisfaction than ever that will of which he makes a god. It serves him for his kitchen-fire: he *roasteth roast, and is satisfied* that he has not done amiss to put it to this use. It serves him to heat the oven: *He kindles it and bakes bread* with the heat of it, and none charges him with doing wrong.

(3) The stock or body of the tree shall serve to make a god. It might as well have served to make a bench. When the besotted idolater has thus served the meanest purposes with part of his tree, and the rest has had time to season: He *makes it a graven image, and falls down thereto* (*v.* 15), that is (*v.* 17), *The*

residue thereof he makes a god, even his graven image; he *falls down to it, and worships it*; *he prays to it*, as having a dependence upon it, and great expectations from it: *he saith, Deliver me, for thou art my god.*

III. Here is judgment given upon this whole matter, *v.* 18–20. Man has become worse than the beasts that perish; for they act according to the dictates of sense, but man acts not according to the dictates of reason (*v.* 18). Men that act rationally in other things in this act most absurdly. They are rebels against the great law of consideration (*v.* 12) *None considers in his heart*, nor has so much application of mind as to reason thus with himself: "*I have burnt part of this tree in the fire*, for baking and roasting; *and* now *shall I make the residue thereof an abomination?* Shall I be such a fool as to fall down to the stock of a tree—a senseless, lifeless, helpless thing?" These idolaters put a cheat upon themselves (*v.* 20): *They feed on ashes;* they will be disappointed as much as a man that would expect nourishment by feeding on ashes. The apostasy of sinners from God is owing entirely to themselves and to the evil heart of unbelief that is in their own bosom. There is none of them that can be persuaded so far to suspect himself as to say, *Is there not a lie in my right hand?* and so to think of delivering his soul. Self-suspicion is the first step towards self-deliverance.

Verses 21–28

I. The duty which Jacob and Israel, now in captivity, were called to, that they might be qualified for deliverance. Our first care must be to get good by our afflictions, and then we may hope to get out of them. The duty is expressed in two words: *Remember* and *return*. 1. "*Remember these, O Jacob! Remember* the folly of idolatry, and that *thou art my servant*, and therefore must not serve other masters." 2. *Return unto me, v.* 22.

II. The favours of which Jacob and Israel, now in captivity, were assured; and what is here promised to them upon their remembering and returning to God is in a spiritual sense promised to all that in like manner return to God. When we begin to remember God he will begin to remember us; it is he that remembers us first.

1. The grounds upon which God's favourable intentions to his people were built. (1) They are his servants, and therefore he has a just quarrel with those that detain them. *Let my people go, that they may serve me.* (2) He formed them into a people, *v.* 24. From the first beginning of their increase into a nation they were under his particular care. (3) He has redeemed them formerly, and he is still the same. The *Lord has redeemed Jacob*; he is about to do it (*v.* 23); he has determined to do it; for he is the Lord their Redeemer, *v.* 24. (4) He has *glorified himself in them* (*v.* 23), and therefore will do so still, John xii. 28. (5) He has pardoned their sins, which were the only obstruction to their deliverance, *v.* 22. *Therefore* he will break the yoke of captivity because he has *blotted out, as a thick cloud, their transgressions.* Our transgressions and our sins as a cloud interpose between heaven and earth. When God pardons sin he blots out this cloud, this thick cloud, so that the intercourse with heaven is laid open again.

2. The universal joy which the deliverance of God's people should bring along with it (*v.* 23): *Sing, O you heavens!* The whole creation shall have cause for joy and rejoicing in the redemption of God's people; and it is assured that though now it groans, being burdened, it shall at last be delivered from the bondage of corruption. The greatest establishment of the world is the kingdom of God in it, Ps. xcvi. 11–13; xcviii. 7–9. The angels shall rejoice in it. The heavens shall sing, for the Lord has done it. And

there is joy in heaven when God and man are reconciled (Luke xv. 7). Even the inhabitants of the Gentile world, should join in these praises, as sharing in these joys.

3. The encouragement we have to hope that though great difficulties lie in the way of the church's deliverance, yet, when the time for it shall come, they shall all be got over with ease; for *thus saith Israel's Redeemer, I am the Lord that maketh all things*, did make them at first and am still making them; for providence is a continued creation.

4. The confusion which this would put upon the oracles of Babylon, by the confutation it would give them, *v.* 25. God, by delivering his people out of Babylon, would *frustrate the tokens of the liars*, of all the lying prophets, that said the Babylonian monarchy had many ages yet to live. Nor would it only baffle their pretended prophets, but their celebrated politicians too: He *turns the wise men backward.* Those that are made acquainted with Christ see all the knowledge they had before to be foolishness, and themselves *taken in their own craftiness*, 1 Cor. iii. 19.

5. The confirmation which this would give to the oracles of God, which the Jews had distrusted and their enemies despised: God *confirms the word of his servant* (*v.* 26); and *performs the counsel of the messengers* whom he hath many a time sent to his people.

6. The particular favours God designed for his people, that were now in captivity, *v.* 26–28. It is here supposed that Jerusalem, and the cities of Judah, should for a time lie in ruins, dispeopled and uninhabited; but it is promised that they shall be rebuilt and repeopled. God has said to Jerusalem, *Thou shalt be inhabited;* for, while the world stands, God will have a church in it. The cities of Judah too shall again be built. The Assyrian army under Sennacherib only took them, and then, upon the defeat of that army, they returned undamaged to the right owners; but the Chaldean army demolished them, and by carrying away the inhabitants left them to go to decay of themselves. Yet these desolations shall not be perpetual. God will *raise up the* wastes and *decayed places.* It is here supposed that the temple too should be destroyed, and lie for a time razed to the foundations; but it is promised that the foundation of it shall again be laid, and no doubt built upon. As the desolation of the sanctuary was to all the pious Jews the most mournful part of the destruction, so the restoration and re-establishment of it would be the most joyful part of the deliverance. It is here supposed that very great difficulties would lie in the way of this deliverance, but it is promised that by a divine power they shall all be removed (*v.* 27): *God saith to the deep, Be dry;* so he did when he brought Israel out of Egypt, and so he will again when he brings them out of Babylon. *Who art thou, O great deep?* Dost thou retard their passage and think to block it up? Thou shalt be dry. When Cyrus took Babylon by draining the river Euphrates into many channels, and so making it passable for his army, this was fulfilled. *God saith of Cyrus, He is my shepherd* (*v.* 28). Israel is his people, and the sheep of his pasture. These sheep are now in the midst of wolves; they are impounded for trespass. Now Cyrus shall be his shepherd, employed by him to release these sheep. It was more the praise of Cyrus to be God's shepherd than to be emperor of Persia. God makes what use he pleases of men; in those very things wherein they are serving themselves, and look no further than that, God is serving his own purposes by them.

CHAPTER 45

Cyrus was nominated in the foregoing chapter to be God's shepherd, he was to be a type of the Great Redeemer. We have here, I. The great things which God would do for Cyrus, that he might release God's people, ver. 1–4. II. The proof God would hereby give of his eternal power, ver. 5–7. III. A prayer for the hastening of this deliverance, ver. 8. IV. A check to the unbelieving Jews, ver. 9, 10. V. Encouragement given to the believing Jews, who trusted in God and continued instant in prayer, ver. 11–15. VI. A challenge given to the worshippers of idols and their doom read, and satisfaction given to the worshippers of the true God and their comfort secured, ver. 16–25.

Verses 1–4

Cyrus was a Mede, descended (as some say) from Astyages, king of Media. The pagan writers are not agreed in their accounts of his origin. Some tell us that in his infancy, he was an outcast, left exposed, and was saved from perishing by a herdsman's wife. However, it is agreed that Croesus king of Lydia made a descent upon his country, which he repulsed, prosecuting the advantages he had gained against Croesus with such vigour that in a little time he took Sardis and made himself master of the rich kingdom of Lydia and the many provinces that then belonged to it. This made him very great (for Croesus was rich to a proverb); but it was nearly ten years afterwards that, in conjunction with his uncle Darius and with the forces of Persia, he made his famous attack upon Babylon. Babylon had now grown rich and strong. Some say the walls were so thick that six chariots might drive abreast upon them. Cyrus had a great ambition to make himself master of this place, and at last he performed it. Here, years before it came to pass, we are told,

I. What great things God would do for him, that he might put it into his power to release his people. In order to this he shall be a mighty conqueror and a wealthy monarch, and nations shall become tributaries to him and help him both with men and money. Cyrus is here called God's *anointed*, because he was designed for this great service by God, and was to be herein a type of the Messiah. God engages to hold his right hand, as Elisha put his hands upon the king's hands when he was to shoot his arrow against Syria, 2 Kings xiii. 16. Being under such direction,

1. He shall extend his conquests very far and shall make nothing of the opposition that will be given him. Populous kingdoms shall yield to him. God will *subdue nations before him*; the battle is his, and therefore his is the victory. Potent kings shall fall before him: *I will loose the loins of kings*, and it was literally fulfilled in Belshazzar, for, when he was terrified by the handwriting on the wall, *the joints of his loins were loosed*, Dan. v. 6. Great cities shall surrender themselves into his hands. God will incline the keepers of the city to *open before him the two-leaved gates*, from a full conviction that it is to no purpose to contend with him. The longest and most dangerous marches shall be made easy and ready to him: *I will go before thee*, to clear the way, and to conduct thee in it, and then the *crooked places* shall be made *straight*; or, as some read it, the hilly places shall be levelled and made even. No opposition shall stand before him. He that gives him his commission *will break in pieces the gates of brass* that are shut against him, *and cut asunder the bars of iron* wherewith they are fastened. This was fulfilled if that be true which Herodotus reports, that the city of Babylon had 100 gates all of brass, with posts and hooks of the same metal.

2. He shall replenish his coffers (*v.* 3): *I will give thee the treasures of darkness*, treasures of gold and silver, that had been buried under ground by the inhabitants. Cyrus owned God's goodness to him, and in consideration of that, released the captives. Ezra i. 2, *God has given me all the kingdoms of the earth* and thereby has obliged *me to build him a house at Jerusalem*.

II. We are here told what God designed in doing all this for Cyrus.

1. *"That thou mayest know* by all this *that I the Lord am the God of Israel*; for I have *called thee by thy name* long before thou wast born."

2. It was that the Israel of God might be released, *v.* 4. Though he knew not God, God bespoke him for his shepherd. He called him by his name, *Cyrus*, and called him his *anointed*. And why did God do all this for Cyrus? Not for his own sake, whether he was a man of virtue or no is questioned. Xenophon indeed, when he would describe the heroic virtues of an excellent prince, made use of Cyrus's name, but other historians represent him as haughty, cruel, and bloodthirsty. The reason why God preferred him was *for Jacob his servant's sake*. Cyrus was a type of Christ, victorious over principalities and powers, and entrusted with unsearchable riches, for the use and benefit of God's servants. *When he ascended on high he led captivity captive*, took those captives that had taken others captives, and *opened the prison to those that were bound*.

Verses 5–10

God here asserts his sole dominion, manifest to the world in all the great things he did for Cyrus and by him. Observe,

I. This doctrine is here laid down in two things: 1. That there is no God besides him. This is a fundamental truth, which would abolish idolatry out of the world. With what an awful, commanding, air of majesty and authority does the great God here proclaim it to the world: *I am the Lord, I the Lord, Jehovah*, and *there is none else, there is no God besides me*, no other self-existent, self-sufficient, infinite and eternal. *I am the Lord, and there is none else*. This is here said to Cyrus, not only to cure him of the sin of his ancestors, which was the worshipping of idols, but to prevent his falling into the sin of some of his predecessors in victory and universal monarchy, which was the setting up of themselves for gods and being idolized. Let Cyrus remember that still he is but a man, and there is no God but one. 2. That he is Lord of all, and there is nothing done without him (*v.* 7): *I form the light, I create darkness, I make peace* (put here for all good) and *I create evil*, not the evil of sin (God is not the author of that), but the evil of punishment. Light and darkness are opposite to each other. In the revolution of every day each takes its turn. The self-same cause of both is he that is the first Cause of all. He who formed the natural light (Gen. i. 3) still forms the providential light. He who at first made peace among the jarring principles of nature makes peace in the affairs of men. He who allowed the natural darkness, which was a mere privation, creates the providential darkness.

II. How this doctrine is here proved and published. 1. It is proved by that which God did for Cyrus: *There is no God besides me*, for (*v.* 5) *I girded thee, though thou hast not known me*. By *this* it appears that the God of Israel makes what use he pleases even of those that are strangers to him and pay their homage to other gods. 2. It is published to all the world by the word of God, by his providence, and by the testimony of the suffering Jews in Babylon. The wonderful deliverance of the Israel of God proclaimed to all the world that *there is none like unto the God of Jeshurun, that rides on the heavens for their help*.

III. How this doctrine is here improved and applied.

1. For the comfort of those that quietly waited, for the redemption of Israel (*v.* 8): *Drop down, you heavens, from above*. Some take this as the saints' prayer for the deliverance. I rather take it as God's precept concerning it; for he is said to *command deliverances*, Ps. xliv. 4. All the creatures shall be made to contribute to the carrying on of this great

work. We must not expect salvation without righteousness, for they spring up together and together the Lord hath created them. Christ died to save us from our sins, not in our sins, and is made redemption to us by being made to us righteousness and sanctification. This great deliverance is from heaven, and, if our hearts be open to receive it, the product will be the fruits of righteousness and the great salvation.

2. For reproof to those of the church's enemies that opposed this salvation, or those of her friends that despaired of it (*v.* 9): *Woe unto him that strives with his Maker!* Woe to the insulting Babylonians that set God at defiance, and will not let his people go! Let not the oppressed, in dejection quarrel with God for the prolonging of their captivity. *Shall the clay say to him that forms it, "What makest thou?* Why dost thou make me of this shape and not that?" Shall we impeach God's wisdom, or question his power, who are ourselves so wonderfully made? Shall we say, *He has no hands,* whose hands made us and in whose hands we are? It is as unnatural as for the child to find fault with the parents, to say to the father, *What begettest thou?* or to the mother, "*What hast thou brought forth;* Why was I not begotten and born an angel, exempt from the infirmities of human nature and the calamities of human life?"

Verses 11–19

The people in captivity, who reconciled themselves to the will of God and were content to wait his time for their deliverance, are assured they should not wait in vain.

I. They are invited to enquire concerning the issue of their troubles, *v.* 11. "*Ask of me things to come;* have recourse to the prophets and see what they say. Ask the watchmen, What of the night? Ask them, How long?" We may not strive with our Maker by passionate complaints, but we may wrestle with him by faithful and fervent prayer. See the power of prayer and its prevalency with God: *Thou shalt cry, and he shall say, Here I am; what would you that I should do unto you?*

II. They are encouraged to depend upon the power of God when they are brought very low and are utterly incapable of helping themselves, *v.* 12. Their *help stands in the name of the Lord, who made heaven and earth.*

III. They are particularly told what God would do for them, and this shall lead them to expect a more glorious Redeemer of whom Cyrus was a type.

1. Liberty shall be proclaimed to them, *v.* 13. Cyrus is the man that shall proclaim it: *I have raised him up in righteousness,* that is, in pursuance of my promises. *I will direct all his ways.* Two things Cyrus must do for God: (1) Jerusalem is God's city, now in ruins, and he must rebuild it. (2) Israel is God's people, but they are now captives, and he must release them, not demanding any ransom. And Christ is anointed to do that for poor captive souls which Cyrus was to do for the captive Jews, to proclaim the *opening of the prison to those that were bound* (*ch.* lxi. 1), in a worse bondage than that in Babylon.

2. Provision shall be made for them. They went out poor, and unable to bear the expenses of their re-establishment; and therefore it is promised that the labour of Egypt and other nations should *come over to them and be theirs,* v. 14. They did not go out empty from Babylon any more than from Egypt. Those that are redeemed by Christ shall be enriched. Those whose spirits God stirs up to go to the heavenly Zion may depend upon him to bear their charges. The world is theirs as far as is good for them.

3. Proselytes shall be brought over to them: *Men of stature shall come after thee in chains; they shall fall down to thee, saying, Surely God is in thee.* This was in part fulfilled when many of the people of the land became Jews (Esther viii. 17), *and said, We will go with you, for we have heard that God is with you,* Zech. viii. 23. But this was to have its full accomplishment in the gospel church,—when the Gentiles shall become obedient by word and deed to the faith of Christ (Rom. xv. 18).

IV. They are taught to trust God further than they can see him. The prophet puts this word into their mouths (*v.* 15): *Verily, thou art a God that hidest thyself.* He hid himself when he was bringing them out of the trouble. The salvation of the church is carried on in a mysterious way, by the Spirit of the Lord of hosts working on men's spirits (Zech. iv. 6), by weak and unlikely instruments, small and accidental occurrences, but this is our comfort, though God hide himself, we are sure he is *the God of Israel,* the *Saviour.* See Job xxxv. 14.

V. They are instructed to triumph over idolaters and all the worshippers of other gods (*v.* 16).

VI. They are assured that those who trust in God shall never be made ashamed of their confidence in him, *v.* 17. They shall be saved in him; for his name shall be their strong tower. Beyond this temporal deliverance they must think of that salvation by the Messiah which is the salvation of the soul, a restoration to everlasting bliss. "You shall not only be delivered from the *everlasting shame and contempt* which will be the portion of idolaters (Dan. xii. 2), but you shall have everlasting honour and glory." Those who are confounded as penitents for their own sin shall not be confounded as believers in God's promise and power.

VII. They are engaged for ever to cleave to God, and never to desert him. That the Lord we serve and trust is God alone appears by the two great lights, that of nature and that of revelation.

1. It appears by the light of nature; for he made the world, and therefore may justly demand its homage (*v.* 18): "*Thus saith the Lord, that created the heavens and formed the earth, I am the Lord,* the sovereign Lord of all, *and there is none else.*" When he had made it he established it, *founded it on the seas* (Ps. xxiv. 2), *hung it on nothing* (Job xxvi. 7) as at first he made it of nothing. He fitted it for the service of man, to whom he designed to give it. He made nothing in vain, but intended everything for some end. If any man prove to have been made in vain, it is his own fault.

2. It appears by the light of revelation. As the works of God abundantly prove that he is God alone, so does his word, and the discovery he has made of himself and of his mind and will by it. All that God has said is plain: *I have not spoken in secret, in a dark place of the earth.* The Pagan deities delivered their oracles out of dens and caverns, with a low and hollow voice, and in ambiguous expressions; those that had familiar spirits whispered and muttered (*ch.* viii. 19); but God delivered his law from the top of Mount Sinai, distinct, audible, and intelligible. The vision is written, and made plain, so that he who runs may read it. If it be obscure to any, they may thank themselves. Christ pleaded in his own defence that what God says here, *In secret have I said nothing,* John xviii. 20. God has in his word invited men to seek him, so he never denied their believing prayers. If he did not think fit to give them the particular thing they prayed for, yet he gave them such grace, comfort and satisfaction of soul as were equivalent. What we say of winter is true of prayer, It never rots in the skies.

Verses 20–25

What is here said is intended,

I. For *idolaters,* to show them their folly in worshipping gods that cannot help them, and neglecting a God that can. Let all *that have escaped of the nations,* not only the Jews, but those of other nations that were by Cyrus released, hear what is to be said against the worshipping of idols. *They set up the wood of their graven image.* Though they overlay it with gold, deck it with ornaments, and make a god of it, yet still it is but wood. They *pray to a god that cannot save.* "Summon them all; tell them that the great cause shall again be tried between God and Baal. *There is no other God besides me.*" None besides is fit to rule. None besides is able to help. As he is a just god, so he is *the Saviour.*

II. For the comfort and encouragement of God's faithful worshippers, whoever they are, *v.* 22. God says it to all his people, though they seem to be lost and forgotten in their dispersion, "Let them but *look to me* by faith and prayer, look above second causes, look up to me, and they shall *be saved.*" When Christ is lifted up from the earth, as the brazen serpent upon the pole, he shall draw the eyes of all men to him. *I have sworn by myself* (and God can swear by no greater, Heb. vi. 13); *the word has gone out of my mouth*, that he who made all should be Lord of all, that, since all beings are derived from him, they should all be devoted to him. He has assured us that the kingdoms of the world shall become his kingdom. This is applied to the dominion of our Lord Jesus, Rom. xiv. 10, 11. *Unto him shall men of distant countries come*, to implore his favour. *All that are incensed against him shall be ashamed;* some shall be brought to a penitential shame for it, others to a remediless ruin. In the Lord the captive Jews had righteousness (that is, grace both to sanctify their afflictions and to qualify them for deliverance) and strength for their support and escape. In the Lord Jesus we have righteousness to recommend us to the goodwill of God towards us, and strength to begin and carry on the good work of God in us. The people of the Jews shall in the Lord be justified before men and openly glory in their God. All true Christians, that depend upon Christ for strength and righteousness, in him shall be justified and shall glory in that.

CHAPTER 46

God, by the prophet prepares them for deliverance by possessing them with a detestation of idols and with a believing confidence in God. I. Let them not be afraid of the idols of Babylon (ver. 1, 2); but let them trust in that God who had often delivered them, to do it now, ver. 3, 4. II. Let them not think to make idols of their own, ver. 5–7, but have an eye to God in his word, not in an image; let them depend upon the promises and God's power to accomplish them all, ver. 9–11. And let them know that the unbelief of man shall not make the word of God of no effect, ver. 12, 13.

Verses 1–4

I. The false gods will certainly fail their worshippers, *v.* 1, 2. Bel and Nebo were two celebrated idols of Babylon. As Bel was a deified prince, so (some think) Nebo was a deified prophet, for so Nebo signifies; so that Bel and Nebo were their Jupiter and Mercury or Apollo. God here tells them what shall become of these idols. When Cyrus takes Babylon, down go the idols. Bel and Nebo, that were set up on high, shall *stoop and bow down* at the feet of the soldiers that plunder their temples. And because there is a great deal of gold and silver upon them they carry them away with the rest of the spoil. The mules are laden with them and their other idols, to be sent among other lumber (for so it seems they accounted them rather than treasure) into Persia. *They stoop, they bow down together.* They are all alike, tottering things, and their day has come to fall.

II. The true God will never fail his worshippers. He formed them into a people and gave them their constitution. Every good man is what God makes him. You have been *borne by me from the belly*, and *carried from the womb.* And as God began early

to do them good he had constantly continued to do them good: he had carried them from the womb to this day. We have been carried in the arms of his power and in the bosom of his love and pity. Our spiritual life is sustained by his grace as necessarily and constantly as our natural life by his providence. "You have been *borne by me from the belly*, nursed when you were children; and *even to your old age I am he*, when, by reason of your infirmities, you will need help as much as in your infancy." Israel was now growing old. And they had hastened their old age, and the calamities of it, by their irregularities. But God is still their God, will still carry them in the same everlasting arms that were laid under them in Moses's time, Deut. xxxiii. 27. I will now bear them upon eagles' wings out of Babylon, as in their infancy I bore them out of Egypt. This promise to aged Israel is applicable to every aged Israelite. "*Even to your old age*, when you grow unfit for business, when you are compassed with infirmities, and perhaps your relations begin to grow weary of you, yet *I am he*, the very same by whom you have been borne from the belly and carried from the womb. You change, but I am the same. *I will carry you*, will bear you up and bear you out, and will carry you home at last."

Verses 5–13

The deliverance of Israel by the destruction of Babylon is again promised, for the conviction of idolaters and of oppressors.

I. For the conviction of those who made and worshipped idols, especially those of Israel who did so.

1. He challenges them either to frame an image that should be thought a resemblance of him (*v.* 5): *To whom will you liken me?* It is absurd to think of representing an infinite and eternal Spirit by the figure of any creature whatsoever. None ever saw any similitude of him, nor can see his face and live.

2. He exposes the folly of those who made idols and then prayed to them, *v.* 6, 7. *They lavish gold out of the bag*, though they pinch their families and weaken their estates by it. *They weigh silver in the balance*, either to be the matter of their idol, or to pay the workman's wages. They were in great care about their idols (*v.* 7): *They bear him upon their* own *shoulders*; they *carry him, and set him in his place*, more like a dead corpse than a living God. They set him on a pedestal, *and he stands.* They take pains to fasten him, and *from his place he shall not remove*, though they know he can neither move a hand nor stir a step to do them any kindness. When the goldsmith has made it that which they please to call a god *they fall down, yea, they worship it.* Now shall any that have some knowledge of the true and living God, thus make fools of themselves?

3. He puts it to their own reason, let that judge (*v.* 8): "*Remember this*, what senseless helpless things idols are, *and show yourselves men*—and not brutes, men and not babes. Act with reason and scorn to disparage your own judgment as you do when you worship idols."

4. He again produces incontestable proofs that he is God (*v.* 9): *I am God, and there is none like me.* "*Remember the former things of old*, what the God of Israel did for his people in their beginnings. Remember those things, and you will own that *I am God and there is none else.*" He is God alone, for it is he only that *declares the end from the beginning*, *v.* 10. Many scripture prophecies which are delivered long ago are not yet accomplished; but the accomplishment of some in the meantime is an earnest of the accomplishment of the rest in due time. The accomplishment of this particular prophecy, which relates to the elevation of Cyrus and his agency in the deliverance of God's people out of their captivity,

is mentioned for the confirmation of this truth. God by his counsel *calls a ravenous bird from the east,* a bird of prey, *Cyrus,* who (they say) had a nose like the beak of a hawk or eagle, to which some think this alludes, or (as others say) to the eagle which was his standard, as it was afterwards that of the Romans, to which there is supposed to be a reference, Matt. xxiv. 28. Cyrus came from the east at God's call. "*I have spoken it* by my servants the prophets, and what I have spoken is what *I have purposed.*" For, though God has many things in his purposes which are not in his prophecies, he had nothing in his prophecies but what are in his purposes.

II. For the conviction of those that opposed the counsels of God assurance is here given that they shall be accomplished very shortly, *v.* 12, 13.

1. This is addressed to the *stout-hearted,* that is, either, (1) The proud and obstinate Babylonians, *that are far from righteousness,* that say they will never let the oppressed go free, in spite of their petitions or God's predictions. Or, (2) The unhumbled Jews, that have been long in the furnace, but are not melted, that, like the unbelieving murmuring Israelites in the wilderness, keep good things from themselves, as their fathers, who could not enter into the land of promise because of unbelief. This is applicable to the Jewish nation when they rejected the gospel of Christ; though they *followed after the law of righteousness,* they *attained not to righteousness, because they sought it not by faith,* Rom. ix. 31, 32.

2. Now God says that, whatever they think, the one in presumption, the other in despair, (1) Salvation shall be certainly wrought for God's people. If men will not do them justice, God will. He *will place salvation in Zion,* that is, he will make Jerusalem a place of safety and defence to all those who will plant themselves there. (2) It shall be very shortly wrought.

CHAPTER 47

Infinite Wisdom could have ordered things so that Israel might have been released and yet Babylon unhurt; but if they will harden their hearts, and will not let the people go, they must thank themselves that their ruin is made to pave the way to Israel's release. That ruin is here to encourage Israel's faith and hope concerning deliverance, and to be a type of the downfall of that great enemy of the New Testament church which, in the Revelation, goes under the name of "Babylon". In this chapter we have, I. The ruin threatened, that Babylon should be brought down to the dust, ver. 1–5. II. The sins that provoked God to bring this ruin upon them. 1. Their cruelty to the people of God, ver. 6. 2. Their pride and carnal security, ver. 7–9. 3. Their contempt of God, ver. 10. 4. Their use of magic arts and their dependence upon enchantments and sorceries, ver. 11–15.

Verses 1–6

In these verses God by the prophet sends a messenger to Babylon, like that of Jonah to Nineveh: "The time is at hand when Babylon shall be destroyed." Fair warning is thus given her, that she may by repentance prevent the ruin and there may be a lengthening of her tranquillity.

I. God's controversy with Babylon. She has made God her enemy. Let her know that the righteous Judge, to whom vengeance belongs, has said (*v.* 3), *I will take vengeance.* He says, "*I will not meet thee as a man,* not with the strength of a man, which is easily resisted, but with the power of a God, which cannot be resisted. Not with the justice of a man, which may be bribed, but with the justice of a God, which can never be evaded."

II. The particular ground of this controversy. God will plead his people's cause against them. It is acknowledged.(*v.* 6) that God had delivered his people into the hands of the Babylonians, had made use of them for the correction of his children, and had by their means *polluted his inheritance.* But the Babylonians carried the matter too far, and, when they had them in their hands with a base and servile spirit

they trampled upon them, *and showed them no mercy.* They *laid the yoke on very heavily,* adding affliction to the afflicted, *on the ancient*—the elders in years, who were past their labour, and must sink under a yoke—the elders in office.

III. The terror of this controversy. She has reason to tremble when she is told who it is that has this quarrel with her (*v.* 4). "He is *the Lord of hosts,* that has all the creatures at his command, and therefore has *all power both in heaven and in earth.* He is the *Holy One of Israel,* a God in covenant with us." This may fitly be applied to Christ, our great Redeemer. He is both Lord of hosts and the Holy One of Israel.

IV. The consequences of it to Babylon. She was beautiful as a virgin, and courted by all about her; she had been called *tender and delicate* (*v.* 1), and *the lady of kingdoms* (*v.* 5); but now the case is altered. Her honour is gone, and she must bid farewell to all her dignity. Her power is gone, and she must bid farewell to all her dominion. *There is no throne,* none for thee, *O daughter of the Chaldeans!* Those that abuse their honour or power provoke God to deprive them of it, and to make them *come down and sit in the dust.* Her ease and pleasure are gone: "She shall *no more be called tender and delicate,* but shall be put to hard service and made to feel both want and pain. Her liberty is gone, and she is brought into a state of servitude and sore bondage." Even the great men of Babylon must now receive the same law from the conquerors that they used to give to the conquered: "*Take the millstones and grind meal* (*v.* 2), set to work, to hard labour which will make thee sweat so that thou must throw off all thy head-dresses, and *uncover thy locks.*" At the capricious humours of their masters, they must be forced to wade through the waters, to *make bare the leg* and *uncover the thigh,* that they might *pass over the rivers,* which would be a great mortification. All her glory, and all her glorying, are gone. Instead of glory, she has ignominy (*v.* 3). *Thy nakedness shall be uncovered and thy shame shall be seen,* according to the base and barbarous usage they commonly gave their captives. Instead of glorying she *sits silently, and gets into darkness* (*v.* 5), ashamed to show her face, for she *shall no more be called the lady of kingdoms.*

Verses 7–15

Babylon, now doomed to ruin, is here justly upbraided with her pride, in the day of her prosperity, and particularly in the prognostications and counsels of the astrologers.

I. The Babylonians are here upbraided with their pride and haughtiness; it was the language both of the government and of the body of the people: *Thou sayest in thy heart I am, and none else besides me, v.* 8 and 10. It is the very word that God has often said concerning himself, *I am, and none else besides me,* denoting his self-existence, his infinite and incomparable perfections, and his sole supremacy.

II. They are upbraided with their luxury and love of ease (*v.* 8): "*Thou that art given to pleasures* and *dwellest carelessly* and layest nothing to heart." Great wealth and plenty are great temptations to sensuality, and, where there is fulness of bread, there is commonly abundance of idleness.

III. They are upbraided with their carnal security and their vain confidence.

1. The cause of their security. They thought themselves safe. They lulled themselves asleep in ease and pleasure, and dreamt of nothing else but that *tomorrow should be as this day,* and *much more abundant.* They did not *remember the latter end of it*—the latter end of their prosperity, that it is a fading flower, and will wither—the latter end of their iniquity, that it will be bitterness. *She did not remember her latter end* (so some read it).

2. The ground of their security. They trusted in their wickedness and in their wisdom, v. 10. Their power and wealth, which they had gotten by fraud and oppression, were their confidence. They doubt not but they shall be too hard for all their enemies, because they dare lie, and kill, and forswear themselves, and do anything for their interest. Their policy and craft, which they called their *wisdom*, were their confidence. But their *wisdom and knowledge perverted them.*

3. The expressions of their security. Three things this proud and haughty monarchy said, in her security: (1) "*I shall be a lady for ever*," v. 7. Thus the New Testament Babylon says, *I sit as a queen, and shall see no sorrow*, Rev. xviii. 7. (2) "*I shall not sit as a widow*, in solitude and sorrow, shall never lose the power and wealth I am thus wedded to; the monarchy shall never want a monarch to espouse and protect it, and be a husband to the state; *nor shall I know the loss of children*," v. 8. (3) "*No one sees me* when I do amiss, and therefore there will be none to call me to an account," v. 10.

4. The punishment of their security. It shall be their ruin. "*These two things shall come upon thee* (the very two things that thou didst set at defiance), *loss of children and widowhood*, v. 9. Both thy princes and thy people shall be cut off, so that thou shalt be no more a government, no more a nation." It will be a sudden and surprising ruin. "*Evil shall come upon thee* (v. 11) and thou shalt have neither time nor way to prepare for it; for *thou shalt not know whence it rises*, and therefore shalt not know where to stand upon thy guard." Babylon pretended to great wisdom and knowledge (v. 10), but with all her knowledge she cannot foresee, nor with all her wisdom prevent, the ruin threatened. Fair warning was indeed given them, by Isaiah and other prophets of the Lord, of this desolation; but they slighted that notice, and would give no credit to it.

IV. They are upbraided with their divinations, their magical and astrological arts and sciences.

This is one of their provoking sins, v. 9. "These evils shall come upon thee to punish thee *for the multitude of thy sorceries, and the great abundance of thy enchantments*." Witchcraft is a sin in giving that honour to the devil which is due to God only, making God's enemy our guide. In Babylon it had the protection of the government. They are here upbraided with the mighty pains they had taken about their sorceries: Thou hast *laboured in them from thy youth*, v. 12. They had their *astrologers*, or viewers of the heavens, that under pretence of foretelling future events by them, viewed the heavens and forget him that made them. They had their *star-gazers*, who by the motions of the stars, their conjunctions and oppositions, read the doom of states and kingdoms. They are upbraided with the utter inability and insufficiency of all these pretenders in the day of their distress. This baffling of the diviners was literally fulfilled when, the night that Babylon was taken and Belshazzar slain, all his astrologers, soothsayers, and wise men, were quite nonplussed with the handwriting on the wall that pronounced the fatal sentence, Dan. v. 8. They are upbraided with the fall of the wise men themselves in the common ruin, v. 14. *They shall be as stubble* before a consuming fire. The Persians, to make room for their own wise men, will cut off those of Babylon; that *fire shall burn them*, and *they shall not deliver themselves from the power of the flame*. These astrologers, that dealt in the black art, were in effect their merchants; fortune-telling was one of the best trades in Babylon. Yet when some were devoured, others fled their country, *everyone to his quarter*, and there was none to save Babylon.

CHAPTER 48

God, having in the foregoing chapter reckoned with the Babylonians, comes, in this chapter, to show the house of Jacob their sins, but, withal, the mercy God had in store for them, that by their repentance and reformation they might be prepared for that mercy. I. He charges them with hypocrisy in that which is good and obstinacy in that which is evil, especially in their idolatry, ver. 1–8. II. He assures them that their deliverance would be wrought, not for any merit of theirs, ver. 9–11. III. He encourages them to depend purely upon God's power and promise for this deliverance, ver. 12–15. IV. He shows them that, as it was by their own sin that they brought themselves into captivity, so it would be only by the grace of God that they would obtain their enlargement, ver. 16–19. V. He proclaims their release, yet with a proviso that the wicked shall have no benefit by it, ver. 20–22.

Verses 1–8

I. The hypocritical profession which many of the Jews made of religion and relation to God.

1. How high their profession of religion soared, and what a good face they put upon a very bad heart. (1) They were the *house of Jacob*; they had a place and a name in the visible church. *Jacob have I loved.* (2) They were *called by the name of Israel*, an honourable name. *Israel* signifies *a prince with God;* and they prided themselves in being of that princely race. (3) *They came forth out of the waters of Judah*, and were of the royal tribe, the tribe that adhered to God when the rest revolted. (4) They *swore by the name of the Lord*, and thereby owned him to be the true God. (5) They *made mention of the God of Israel* in their prayers and praises. (6) They *called themselves of the holy city*. (7) They *stayed themselves upon the God of Israel*, and boasted of his promises and his covenant with them; they *leaned on the Lord*, Mic. iii. 11.

2. How low their profession of religion sunk, notwithstanding all this. It was all in vain. Their hearts were not true nor right in these professions.

II. The means God used to keep them close to himself, and to prevent their turning aside to idolatry. The many excellent laws he gave them would not serve to restrain them from sin, and therefore to those God added remarkable prophecies, and remarkable providences, which were all designed to convince them that it was their duty to adhere to him. 1. He favoured them with remarkable prophecies (v. 3): *I have declared the former things from the beginning.* Nothing material happened to their nation from its original which was not prophesied of before—their bondage in Egypt, their deliverance thence, the situation of their tribes in Canaan, &c. The very calamities they were now groaning under in Babylon God did from the beginning declare to them, Lev. xxvi. 31, &c.; Deut. xxviii. 26, &c.; xxix. 28. He also declared to them their return to God, and to their own land again, Deut. xxx. 4, &c.; Lev. xxvi. 44, 45. 2. He dignified them with remarkable providences (v. 6): *I have shown thee new things from this time.* He showed them new things by the prophets of their own day, and created them. They were *hidden things*, which they could not otherwise know, as the prophecy concerning Cyrus and the exact time of their release out of Babylon. These things God *created now*, v. 7. "Consider," says God, "how it was told you by the prophets, when it was the furthest thing from your thoughts, when you had not any reason to expect it (v. 7, 8), when the thing seemed utterly impossible." God had shown them hidden things, and done for them great things. "Now," says he (v. 6), "*thou hast heard; see all this.* Thou hast heard the prophecy; see the accomplishment of it. Will you not own that your God has been a good God to you? Declare this to his honour, and your own shame."

III. The reasons why God would take this method with them.

1. Because he would anticipate their boasting of themselves and their idols. "I spoke of it," says God, "*lest thou shouldst say, My idol has done it or has commanded it to be done*," *v.* 5. Those that were not so profane as to have ascribed the thing itself to an idol were yet so proud as to have pretended that by their own sagacity they foresaw it.

2. God took pains with them, because he knew they were obstinate, *v.* 4. *I knew that thou wast hard;* so the word is. "*Thy neck is an iron sinew*, unapt to submit to the yoke of God's commandments; not flexible to the will of God, nor manageable by his providence. *Thy brow is brass;* thou art impudent and canst not blush, but wilt thrust on in the way of thy heart." God sent his prophets to them, but they did not hear, they would not know. Thou *wast called* and not miscalled, *a transgressor from the womb.* They were prone to idolatry. They were murmurers as soon as ever they began their march to Canaan. Therefore *I knew that thou wouldst deal very treacherously.*

Verses 9–15

The deliverance of God's people out of their captivity in Babylon was so improbable that there was need of the encouragement of God's people concerning it. Two things were discouraging— their own unworthiness that God should do it for them and the many difficulties in the thing itself; now both these discouragements are removed,

I. A reason why God would do it for them, though they were unworthy, *v.* 9–11. 1. It is true they had been very provoking. Their captivity was the punishment of their iniquity. "But," says God, "*I will defer my anger*" (or, rather, *stifle and suppress it*). And why will God thus stay his hand? *For my name's sake;* because this people was called by his name, and, if they were cut off, the enemies would blaspheme his name. *It is for my praise;* because it would redound to the honour of his mercy. 2. It is true they were corrupt and ill-disposed, but God would make them fit for the mercy he intended for them: "*I have refined thee*, that thou mightest be made a vessel of honour." And this accounts for his bringing them into the trouble, and continuing them in it so long as he did. It was not to cut them off, but to do them good. He therefore takes them as they are, refined in part only, and not thoroughly. "*I have chosen thee in the furnace of affliction*, and then designed thee for great things." Many have been brought home to God as chosen vessels and a good work of grace has been begun in them in the furnace of affliction. God will do it, not because he owes them such a favour, but that they may not be polluted by the insolent triumphs of the heathen, who, in triumphing over Israel, thought they triumphed over the God of Israel. Moses pleaded this often with God: Lord, *what will the Egyptians say*?

II. Here is a proof that God could do it for them, though they were unable to help themselves and the thing seemed altogether impracticable. They are *called according to his purpose*, called by him out of Egypt. (Hos. xi. 1) and now out of Babylon. He will deliver them by his own strength. They need not fear then, for He is God alone, and the eternal God (*v.* 12): "*I am he* who can do what I will and will do what is best. *I am the first; I also am the last*." What room then is left to doubt of their deliverance when *he* undertakes it? He is the God that made the world, and he that did that can do anything, *v.* 13. *If the palm of his right hand* (so the margin reads it) has gone so far as to stretch out the heavens, what will he do with his outstretched arm? He has the command of all the hosts of earth and heaven. *They stand up together*, helping one another in the service of their Maker. If God therefore will deliver his people, he cannot be at a loss for instruments in effecting their

deliverance. "*All you* of the house of Jacob, *assemble yourselves, and hear* this for your comfort, *Which among them*, among the gods of the heathen, or their wise men, *has declared these things*, or could declare them?" (*v.* 14). None could out-see him, and therefore we may be sure that none could outdo him. Cyrus is the man who must do it. *The Lord has loved him* (*v.* 14); he has done him this honour, to make him an instrument in the redemption of his people and therein a type of the great Redeemer, God's beloved Son, *in whom he was well pleased. I have called him*, and therefore will bear him out. "*I have brought him from a far* country, brought him step by step, beyond his own intentions." Cyrus will *do God's pleasure on Babylon. His arm* (Cyrus's army, and in it God's arm) *shall* come, and *be upon the Chaldeans*, to bring them down (*v.* 14); for, if God call him, he will certainly *make his way prosperous, v.* 15.

Verses 16–22

Jacob and Israel are summoned to hearken to God speaking in and by the prophet. Those that draw nigh to God may depend upon this, that his secret shall be with them.

I. God refers them to what he had said to them and done for them formerly. He had always spoken plainly to them *from the beginning*, by Moses and all the prophets: *I have not spoken in secret*; he did not deliver his oracles obscurely and ambiguously, but so that they might be understood, Hab. ii. 2. "*From the time* that they were first formed into a *people there am I* (he sent them prophets, raised them up judges, and frequently appeared for them), and therefore there I will be still."

II. The prophet himself asserts his own commission: *Now the Lord God has by his Spirit sent me, v.* 16. Whom God sends, the Spirit sends.

III. God by the prophet sends them a gracious message. The preface to this message is both awful and encouraging (*v.* 17): *Thus saith Jehovah*, the eternal God, *thy Redeemer*, for he is *the Holy One*, that cannot deceive. The same words that introduce the law, and give authority to that, introduce the promise, and give validity to that.

1. Here is the good work which God undertakes to fulfil in them. He that is their Redeemer will be their instructor: "*I am thy God that teaches thee to profit*, that is, teaches thee such things that belong to thy peace." Whom God redeems he teaches; whom he designs to deliver out of their afflictions he first teaches to profit by their afflictions. *He leads them* to the way and *in the way by which they should go.* He not only enlightens their eyes, but directs their steps. By his grace he leads them in the way of duty, by his providence he leads them in the way of deliverance.

2. Here is the goodwill which God declares he had for them, *v.* 18, 19. (1) As when he gave them his law, he earnestly wished they might be obedient, Deut. v. 29. *O that thou hadst hearkened to my commandments; v.* 18. This confirms what God had said and sworn that he has *no pleasure in the death of sinners.* (2) He assures them that, if they had been obedient, that would not only have prevented their captivity, but would have advanced and perpetuated their prosperity. "*Thy peace should have been as a river;* thou shouldst have enjoyed a series of mercies, one continually following another, as the waters of a river, which always last." Their honour, and the justice of their cause, should in all cases have borne down opposition by their own strength, *as the waves of the sea.* Such should their righteousness have been that nothing should have stood before it; whereas, now they had been disobedient, the current of their prosperity was interrupted, and their righteousness overpowered. The

rising generation should have been numerous and prosperous; whereas they were now very few, as appears by the small number of the returning captives (Ezra ii. 64). The honour of Israel should still have been unstained, untouched: *His name should not have been cut off*, as now it is in the land of Israel, which is either desolate or inhabited by strangers; nor should it have *been destroyed from before God. This* should engage us (I might say, enrage us) against sin, that it has not only deprived us of the good things we have enjoyed, but prevented the good things God had in store for us. Nothing but a prerogative of mercy would have saved them.

3. Here is assurance given of the great work which God designed to work for them, even their salvation out of their captivity. God proclaimed, long before Cyrus did, that whoever would might return to his own land (*v.* 20). Send the tidings of it by word of mouth *to the ends of the earth*. This was a figure of the publishing of the gospel to all the world. Let them all know those whom God owns for his are such as he has dearly bought and paid for: *The Lord has redeemed his servant Jacob*. The bonds God had loosed tied them the faster to him. He that redeemed us has an unquestionable right to us. Those whom God designs to bring home to himself he will take care care of, that they want not for the necessary expenses of their journey. *Through the deserts*, they *thirsted not* (*v.* 21), for in all their removals the water out of the rock followed them. He can fetch in necessary supplies for his people in a way that they think the least likely. This refers to what he did for them when he brought them out of Egypt; when all this was literally true. But it should now be in effect done again, in their return out of Babylon. God does his work as effectually by marvellous providences as by miracles. This is applicable to those treasures of grace laid up for us in Jesus Christ, from which all good flows to us as the water did to Israel out of the rock, for that rock is Christ. But (*v.* 22), though God's thoughts were thoughts of peace, yet to those that were *wicked* and hated to be reformed *there is no peace*, no peace with God or their own consciences. What have those to do with peace who are enemies to God?

CHAPTER 49

Glorious things had been spoken in the previous chapters concerning the deliverance of the Jews out of Babylon; but the prophecy had a further intention, and was to have its full accomplishment in a redemption that should as far outdo these expressions as the other seemed to come short of them, even the redemption of the world by Jesus Christ. In this chapter we have, I. The designation of Christ, under the type of Isaiah, to his office as Mediator, ver. 1.–3 II. The assurance given him of the success of his undertaking among the Gentiles, ver. 4–8. III. The redemption that should be wrought by him, ver. 9–12. IV. The encouragement given hence to the afflicted church, ver. 13–17. V. The addition of many to it, and the setting up of a church among the Gentiles, ver. 18–23. VI. A ratification of the prophecy of the Jews' release out of Babylon, which was to be the figure and type of all these blessings, ver. 24–26. If this chapter be rightly understood, we shall see ourselves to be more concerned in the prophecies relating to the Jews' deliverance out of Babylon than we thought we were.

Verses 1–6

I. The foregoing chapter was directed to the house of Jacob and the people of Israel, *v.* 1, 12. But this is directed to the isles (that is, the Gentiles, for they are called *the isles of the Gentiles*, Gen. x. 5) and to *the people from far*, that were *strangers to the commonwealth of Israel*, and afar off. Let these listen. The tidings of a Redeemer are sent to the Gentiles, and they listened to the gospel when the Jews were deaf to it.

II. The great author of the redemption produces his authority from heaven. 1. God had appointed him; *The Lord has called me from the womb* to this office and *made mention of my name*, nominated me

to be the Saviour. By an angel he called him *Jesus— a Saviour*, who *should save his people from their sins*, Matt. i. 21. This was said of some of the prophets, as types of him, Jer. i. 5. Paul was separated to the apostleship from his mother's womb, Gal. i. 15. 2. God had fitted him for the service. He *made his mouth like a sharp sword*, and *made him* like *a polished shaft*, or a bright arrow, to fight God's battles against the powers of darkness, to conquer Satan, and bring back God's revolted subjects to their allegiance, by his word: that is the *two-edged sword* (Heb. iv. 12). 3. God had preferred him to the service for which he had reserved him: *He has hidden me in the shadow of his hand*, which denotes, (1) Concealment. The gospel of Christ, and the calling in of the Gentiles by it, were long hidden in the shadow of the ceremonial law and the Old Testament types. (2) Protection. The house of David was the particular care of the divine Providence, because that blessing was in it. Christ in his infancy was sheltered from the rage of Herod. God had owned him, had said unto him, *Thou art my servant*, thou art Israel, in effect, *the prince with God*. Some read the words in two clauses: *Thou art my servant* (so Christ is, *ch.* xlii. 1); *it is Israel in whom I will be glorified by thee;* it is the spiritual Israel, the elect, in the salvation of whom by Jesus Christ, God will be glorified.

III. He is assured of the good success of his undertaking.

1. The discouragement he had met with at his first setting out (*v.* 4): "Then I said, with a sad heart, *I have laboured in vain*; those that were careless, and strangers to God, are so still: *I have called, and they have refused;* I have *stretched out my hands to a gainsaying people*." This was Isaiah's complaint. The same was a temptation to Jeremiah to resolve he would labour no more, Jer. xx. 9. It is the complaint of many a faithful minister, that has not loitered, but laboured, not spared, but spent, his strength, and himself with it, and yet, as to many, it is all in vain: they will not repent and believe. But here it seems to point at the obstinacy of the Jews, among whom Christ went in person preaching the gospel of the kingdom, laboured and spent his strength, and yet the rulers and the body of the nation rejected him and his doctrine. Let not the ministers think it strange that they are slighted when the Master himself was.

2. He comforts himself under this discouragement with this consideration, that it was the cause of God in which he was engaged: *Yet surely my judgment is with the Lord*, who is the Judge of all, *and my work with my God*, whose servant I am. His comfort may be the comfort of all faithful ministers, when they see little success of their labours. They are with God, and for God; they are on his side, and workers together with him. "*He knows the way that I take; my judgment is with the Lord*, to determine whether I have not delivered my soul and left the blood of those that perish on their own heads." Though the labour be in vain as to those that are laboured with, yet not as to the labourer himself, if he be faithful: the Lord will justify him and bear him out, though men condemn him. The work is with the Lord, to give them success, according to his purpose, in his own way and time.

3. He receives from God a further answer, *v.* 5, 6. Those whom God designs to employ as his servants he is fashioning and preparing when perhaps neither themselves nor others are aware of it. Christ was to be *his servant, to bring Jacob again to him*, that had treacherously departed from him. The seed of Jacob therefore, according to the flesh, must first be dealt with, and means used to bring them back. Christ, and the word of salvation by him, are sent first *to the lost sheep of the house of Israel*. But what if Jacob will not be brought back to God and Israel

will not be gathered? In that case, (1) Christ will be glorious in the eyes of the Lord. Though few of the Jewish nation were converted by Christ's preaching and miracles, and many loaded him with ignominy, yet God made him glorious, at his baptism, and in his transfiguration, spoke to him from heaven, sent angels to minister to him, made even his shameful death glorious, much more his resurrection. In his sufferings God was his strength, so that though he met with all the discouragement imaginable, yet he *did not fail nor was discouraged.* An angel was sent from heaven to *strengthen* him, Luke xxii. 43. Faithful ministers, though they see not the fruit of their labours, shall yet be accepted of God, and in that they shall be truly glorious. (2) The gospel shall be glorious in the eyes of the world; it shall be entertained by the nations, *v.* 6. The Messiah seemed as if he had been primarily designed to *bring Jacob back, v.* 5. But it is comparatively but a small matter; a larger sphere of usefulness, is designed him: "And therefore *I will give thee for a light to the Gentiles, that thou mayest be my salvation to the end of the earth.*" Hence Simeon learned to call Christ *a light to lighten the Gentiles* (Luke ii. 32), and St. Paul's exposition serves for a key to the context, Acts xiii. 47. *Therefore,* says he, we turn to the Gentiles, to preach the gospel to them, *because so has the Lord commanded us, saying, I have set thee to be a light to the Gentiles.* In this the Redeemer was truly glorious, the setting up of his kingdom in the Gentile world was more his honour than if he had raised up all the tribes of Jacob. This promise is in part fulfilled already, and will have a further accomplishment.

Verses 7–12

I. The humiliation and exaltation of the Messiah (*v.* 7). He was one *whom man despised.* He is *despised and rejected of men, ch.* liii. 3. Man, whom he came to save and to put honour upon, yet despised him and put contempt upon him. They not only made him despicable, but odious. He was *one whom the nation abhorred*; they cried out, *Crucify him, crucify him.* He was *a servant of rulers,* trampled upon, abused, scourged, and crucified as a slave. Yet Herod the king stood in awe of him, saying, *It is John the Baptist;* noblemen, rulers, centurions came and kneeled to him. It is for the honour of his kingdom among men when the great ones of the earth appear for him and do homage to him. This shall be the accomplishment of God's promise, and he will give him the heathen for his inheritance.

II. The blessings he has in store for all those to whom he is made salvation. God will own and stand by him in his undertaking (*v.* 8). Violent attacks were made upon Lord Jesus by the powers of darkness, when it was their hour, to drive him off from his undertakings, but God promises to preserve him and would preserve his kingdom among men, though fought against on all sides.

1. He shall be guarantee of the treaty of peace between God and man: I will *give thee for a covenant of the people.* It was in him that God was *reconciling the world to himself*; and he that *spared not his own Son* will deny us nothing. He is given for a covenant, as he is the blessed *days-man who has laid his hand upon us both.*

2. He shall repair the decays of the church and build it upon a rock. He shall *cause the desolate heritages to be inherited*; so the cities of Judah were after the return out of captivity, and so the church, which in the last and degenerate ages of the Jewish nation had been as a country laid waste, was again replenished by the fruits of the preaching of the gospel.

3. He shall free the souls of men from the bondage of guilt and corruption and bring them into the glorious liberty of God's children. He shall *say to*

the prisoners that were bound under the power of Satan, *Go forth, v.* 9. Pardoning mercy is a release from the curse of the law, and renewing grace is a release from the dominion of sin. Both are from Christ. It is he that says, *Go forth;* it is the Son that makes us free, and then we are free indeed. He saith *to those that are in darkness, Show yourselves;* "not only *see,* but *be seen,* to the glory of God and your own comfort."

4. He shall provide for the comfortable passage of those whom he sets at liberty to the place of their happy settlement, *v.* 9-11. These verses refer to the provision made for the Jews' return, but they are applicable to that guidance of divine grace which all God's spiritual Israel are under. The world leads its followers to broken cisterns, or brooks that fail in summer; but God leads those that are his by springs of water. And those whom God guides shall find a ready road (*v.* 11): *I will make all my mountains a way.*

5. He shall bring them all together from all parts, that they may return in a body, that they may encourage one another. They were dispersed as their enemies pleased, to prevent any combination among themselves. But, when God's time shall come to bring them home together, one spirit shall animate them all, *v.* 12. Here shall a party *come from far,* some *from the north,* some *from the west,* some *from the land of Sinim,* a country belonging to one of the chief cities of Egypt, called *Sin,* of which we read, Ezek. xxx. 15, 16.

Verses 13–17

The return of the people of God, and the eternal redemption to be wrought out by Christ (of which that was a type), would be great occasions of joy and great proofs of the tender care God has of the church.

I. Nothing can furnish us with better matter for songs of praise and thanksgiving, *v.* 13. Let there be joy in heaven; let the earth and the mountains *be joyful,* and *break forth into singing* (Rom. viii. 19, 21), for *God has comforted his people* that were in sorrow.

II. Nothing can furnish us with more convincing arguments to prove the most tender concern God has for his church.

1. The troubles of the church have given some occasion to question God's care for it, *v.* 14. *Zion,* in distress, *said, The Lord has forsaken me,* and looks after me no more. Infidels, in their presumption, say *God has forsaken the earth* (Ezek. viii. 12). Weak believers, in their despondency, are ready to say, God has forsaken his church. But we have no more reason to question his promise and grace than we have to question his providence and justice.

2. The triumphs of the church, after her troubles, will put the matter out of question. What God will do for Zion we are told, *v.* 17. Her friends, who had deserted her, shall be gathered to her: *Thy children shall make haste.* Converts to the faith of Christ are the children of the church; they shall join themselves to her with great readiness. "*Thy builders shall make haste*" (so some read it), "who shall build up thy houses, thy walls, especially thy temple." Her enemies, who had threatened, shall be forced to withdraw from her. By Christ the prince of this world, the great destroyer, is cast out, and his attempts quite baffled. Zion's suggestions were altogether groundless. God had not forsaken her, nor forgotten her, nor ever will. "You think that I have forgotten you. *Can a woman forget her sucking child?*" A mother cannot but be concerned for her own child; for it is a piece of herself, and very lately one with her. It is possible that she may forget. But, says God, *I will not forget thee.* He has a constant care of his church and people (*v.* 16): *I have*

engraven thee upon the palms of my hands. This alludes to the custom of those who tie a string upon their hands or fingers to put them in mind of things which they are afraid they shall forget, or to the wearing of signet or locket-rings in remembrance of some dear friend. His setting them thus as a seal upon his arm denotes his setting them as a seal upon his heart, and his being ever mindful of them and their interests. He adds, *"Thy walls shall be continually before me;* thy ruined walls, though no pleasing spectacle, shall be in my thoughts of compassion. The plan and model of thy walls, that are to be rebuilt, is before me, and they shall certainly be built according to it."

Verses 18–23

Two things are promised to be in part accomplished in the reviving of the Jewish church after its return, but more fully in the planting of the Christian church by the preaching of the gospel of Christ:

I. The church shall be replenished with great numbers added to it. It was promised (*v.* 17) that *her children should make haste.*

1. Multitudes shall flock to the church from all parts. *Look round, and see how they gather themselves to thee* (*v.* 18), by a local accession to the Jewish church. They come to Jerusalem for that was then the centre of their unity; but, under the gospel, it is by a spiritual accession to the mystical body of Christ in faith and love.

2. Such as are added to the church shall not be a burden and blemish to her, but her strength and ornament. *As I live, saith the Lord, thou shalt surely clothe thyself with them all.* When those that are added to the church are serious, and holy, and exemplary in their conversation, they are an ornament to it.

3. The country which was waste and desolate, and *without inhabitant* (*ch.* v. 9; vi. 11), shall be again peopled, nay, it shall be over-peopled (*v.* 19): *"Thy waste and thy desolate places,* that have long lain so, *and the land of thy destruction,* that land of thine which was destroyed with thee, shall now be so full of people that there shall be no room for the inhabitants." Thus the *kingdom of God among men,* which had been impoverished and almost depopulated, was again peopled and enriched by the setting up of the Christian church.

4. The new converts shall strangely increase and multiply. Jerusalem, after she has lost abundance of her children by sword, famine, and captivity, shall have a new family growing up, children which she *shall have after she has lost the other* (*v.* 20), as Seth, who was *appointed another seed instead of Abel.* God will repair his church's losses and secure to himself a seed to serve him in it. The children shall complain for want of room: "Our numbers increase so fast that *the place is too strait for us";* as the sons of the prophets complained, 2 Kings vi. 1. But, strait as the place is, still more shall desire to be admitted, even when the *poor and the maimed, the halt and the blind,* are brought in, *yet still there is room,* room enough for those that are in and room for more, Luke xiv. 21, 22. The mother shall stand amazed at the increase of her family, *v.* 21. She shall say, *Who has begotten me these?* and, *Who has brought up these?* They come to her with all the affection of children; and yet she never bore any pain for them, but has them ready reared to her hand. The church is not perpetually visible, but there are times when it is desolate, and made few in number. Yet on the other hand its desolations shall not be perpetual. God will out of stones raise up children unto Abraham. Sometimes this is done in a very surprising way, as when a nation is born at once, *ch.* lxvi. 8.

5. This shall be done with the help of the Gentiles, *v.* 22. The Jews were cast off, among whom it was expected that the church should be built up. The Gentiles shall be called in. God will *lift up his hand to them,* to invite or beckon them, having all the day stretched it out in vain to the Jews, *ch.* lxv. 2. And he will *set up his standard to them,* the preaching of the everlasting gospel. *They shall bring thy sons in their arms.* They shall assist the sons of Zion, which are found among them, in their return to their own country. God can raise up friends for returning Israelites even among Gentiles. "Dost thou ask, *Who has begotten and brought up these?* Know that they were begotten and brought up among the Gentiles, but they are now brought into thy family."

II. The church shall have a prevailing interest in the nations, *v.* 22, 23. *Kings shall be thy nursing fathers,* to carry thy sons in their arms (as Moses, Num. xi. 12); and *their queens shall be thy nursing mothers.* This promise was in part fulfilled to the Jews, after their return out of captivity. Several of the kings of Persia countenanced and encouraged them, as Cyrus, Darius, and Artaxerxes; Esther the queen was a nursing mother to the Jews that remained in their captivity, putting her life in her hand to snatch the child out of the flames. The Christian church, after a long captivity, was happy in some such kings and queens as Constantine and his mother Helena, and afterwards Theodosius, and others, who nursed the church with all possible care and tenderness. The church in this world is in an infant state, and it is in the power of princes and magistrates to do it great service. Others who stand out against the church's interests, will be forced to yield. *They shall bow down to thee and lick the dust.* The promise to the church of Philadelphia seems to be borrowed from this (Rev. iii. 9): *I will make those of the synagogue of Satan to come and worship before thy feet.*

Verses 24–26

I. An objection against the promise of the Jews' release suggesting that it was not to be expected; for (*v.* 24) they were a prey in the hand of the mighty, and therefore it was not likely they should be rescued by force. They were lawful captives; by the law of God, having offended, they were justly delivered into captivity; and by the law of nations, being taken in war, they were justly detained in captivity till they should be ransomed or exchanged. Now this is spoken either by the enemies, as justifying themselves in their refusal to let them go, or by their friends, either in a way of distrust, or in a way of thankfulness. "Who would have thought that ever the prey should be *taken from the mighty?* Yet it is done." This is applicable to our redemption by Christ.

II. This objection answered by express promises. "*Even the captives of the mighty,* though they are mighty, shall be taken away; *and the prey of the terrible,* though they are terrible, shall be delivered; they cannot with all their impudence outface, the deliverance and the counsels of God concerning it" (*v.* 25). Here is a further promise God will bring judgments upon the oppressors, and so will work salvation for the oppressed: "*I will contend with him that contends with thee,* and thus *I will save thy children."* The captives shall be delivered by *leading captivity captive,* that is, sending those into captivity that had held God's people captive (*v.* 26): "*I will feed those that oppress thee with their own flesh,* and *they shall be drunken with their own blood.* The proud Babylonians shall become an easy prey to one another. Their ruin, which was begun by a foreign invasion, shall be completed by their intestine divisions. They shall *bite and devour one another,* till they are *consumed one of another."* See how cruel men sometimes are to themselves and to one another. They not only thirst after blood, but drink it with as much pleasure as if it were sweet wine.

III. The effect of Babylon's ruin: *All flesh shall know that I the Lord am thy Saviour.* God will make it to appear, to all the world, that, though Israel seem lost, they have a Redeemer.

CHAPTER 50

I. Those to whom God sends are justly charged with bringing all the troubles they were in upon themselves, it being made to appear that God was able and ready to help them if they had been fit for deliverance, ver. 1–3. II. He by whom God sends produces his commission (ver. 4), alleges his own readiness to submit to all the sufferings he was called to in the execution of it (ver. 5, 6), and assures himself that God, who sent him, would bear him out against all opposition, ver. 7–9. III. The message that is sent is life and death, comfort to desponding saints and terror to presuming sinners, ver. 10, 11. Now all this seems to have a double reference, 1. To the unbelieving Jews in Babylon, and to the prophet Isaiah. 2. To the unbelieving Jews in our Saviour's time, whose own fault it was that they were rejected, Christ having preached much to them, and suffered much from them. The prophet concludes with an exhortation to trust in God and not in ourselves.

Verses 1–3

Those who have professed to be the people of God, and yet seem to be dealt severely with, are apt to complain of God. But, in answer to their murmurings, we have,

I. A challenge given them to prove that the quarrel began on God's side, *v.* 1. He had been a husband to them; and husbands were then allowed a power to put away their wives upon any little disgust, Deut. xxiv. 1; Matt. xix. 7. But they could not say that God had dealt so with them. It is true they were now separated from him, and had abode many days without ephod, altar, or sacrifice; but whose fault was that? He had been a father to them; and fathers had then a power to sell their children for slaves to their creditors, in satisfaction for debts. Now it is true the Jews were sold to the Babylonians then, and afterwards to the Romans; but did God sell them for payment of his debts? No, he was not indebted to any of those to whom they were sold.

II. A charge, showing that they were themselves the authors of their own ruin: "*Behold, for your iniquities,* for the pleasure of them and the gratification of your own base lusts, *you have sold yourselves, for your iniquities you are sold.* You sold yourselves to work wickedness, and therefore God justly sold you into the hands of your enemies," 2 Chron. xii. 5, 8. The Jews were sent into Babylon for their idolatry, and were at last rejected for crucifying the Lord of glory; these were the iniquities for which they were sold and put away.

III. The confirmation of this challenge and this charge. God came and offered them his favour, offered them his helping hand, either to prevent their trouble or to deliver them out of it, but they slighted him and his grace. "Do you lay it upon me?" (says God); "tell me, then, wherefore, *when I came, was there no man to meet me, when I called, was there none to answer me?*" *v.* 2. God came to them by his servants the prophets, but *there was* no man that had any regard to the warnings which the prophets gave them. Because they *mocked the messengers of the Lord,* therefore *God brought upon them the king of the Chaldeans,* 2 Chron. xxxvi. 16, 17. Last of all *he sent unto them his Son.* He *came to his own,* but *his own received him not;* they knew not, because they would not know, the things that belonged to their peace, and for that transgression it was that they were put away and their house was left desolate, Matt. xxi. 41; xxiii. 37, 38; Luke xix. 41, 42. It is plain that it was not owing to a want of power in God, for he is almighty, and could have recovered them from so great a death; nor was it owing to a want of power in Christ, for he is *able to save to the uttermost. Can this man save us?* For *himself he cannot save.* "But" (says God) "*is my hand shortened at all,*

or is it weakened?" Can any limits be set to Omnipotence? Cannot he redeem who is the great Redeemer? The expression our Saviour sometimes used concerning the power of faith, that it will *remove mountains and plant sycamores in the sea,* is not unlike this; if their faith could do that, no doubt their faith would save them.

Verses 4–9

Our Lord Jesus, having proved himself able to save, here shows himself as willing as he is able. We suppose the prophet Isaiah to say something of himself in these verses, encouraging himself to go on in his work as a prophet, notwithstanding hardships, not doubting but that God would strengthen him; but, like David, he speaks of himself as a type of Christ.

I. As an acceptable preacher. Isaiah, as a prophet, was qualified for the work to which he was called, but Christ was anointed with the Spirit above his fellows. To make the man of God perfect, he has, 1. *The tongue of the learned,* to know how to give instruction, *how to speak a word in season to him that is weary, v.* 4. God gave to Christ the tongue of the learned, for the comfort of those that are weary and heavily laden under the burden of sin, Matt. xi. 28. See what is the best learning of a minister, to know how to comfort troubled consciences, and to speak properly, and plainly, to the various cases of poor souls. An ability to do this is God's gift. 2. The ear of the learned, to receive instruction. Prophets have as much need of this as of the tongue of the learned; for they must hear the word from God's mouth attentively, that they may speak it exactly, Ezek. iii. 17. None must undertake to be teachers who have not first been learners. Christ's apostles were first disciples. Those that would hear as the learned must be awake, for we are naturally drowsy and hear by halves and do not heed. We need to be awakened *morning by morning.* The morning, when our spirits are most lively, is a proper time for communion with God. The people came *early in the morning* to hear Christ in the temple (Luke xxi. 38), for, it seems, his were morning lectures.

II. As a patient sufferer, *v.* 5, 6. One who is commissioned to speak comfort to the weary has hard work to do and hard usage to undergo. *My ear hast thou opened; then said I, Lo, I come; I was not rebellious, neither turned away back.* Though he foresaw difficulty and discouragement, though he was to give constant attendance as a servant, though he was to humble himself to that which was very mean, yet he did not fly off, did not fail, nor was discouraged. In submission he resigned himself. *I gave my back to the smiters; I gave my cheeks to those that* not only smote them, but *plucked off the hair* of the beard, which was a greater degree both of pain and of ignominy. *I hid not my face from shame and spitting.* All this Christ underwent for us, and voluntarily, to convince us of his willingness to save us.

III. As a courageous champion, *v.* 7–9. The Redeemer is as famous for his boldness as for his humility and patience, and, though he yields, yet he is more than a conqueror. What was the prophet Isaiah's support was the support of Christ himself (*v.* 7): *The Lord God will help me;* and again, *v.* 9. God, having laid help upon his Son for us, gave help to him, and his hand was all along *with the man of his right hand. He is near that justifieth me.* Isaiah, no doubt, was loaded with reproach and calumny, as other prophets were; but he despised the reproach, knowing that God would roll it away and bring forth his righteousness as the light, perhaps in this world (Ps. xxxvii. 6), at furthest in the great day, when there will be a resurrection of names as well as bodies, and the righteous shall shine forth as the morning sun. "If God will help me, if he will justify me, will stand by me and bear me out, *I shall not be confounded. I know that I shall not be ashamed.*" In this confidence he bids defiance to all opposers and opposition: God will help me, and *therefore have I set my face like a flint.* The prophet was bold in reproving sin, in warning sinners (Ezek. iii. 8, 9), and in asserting the truth of his predictions. Christ went on in his work, as Mediator, with unshaken constancy and undaunted resolution. *Who will contend with me,* either in law or by the sword? *Let us stand together,* as combatants, or as the plaintiff and defendant. Many offered to dispute with Christ, but he put them to silence. The prophet speaks this in the name of all faithful ministers; those who keep close to the pure word of God, in delivering their message, need not fear contradiction. *Great is the truth and will prevail.* Christ speaks this in the name of all believers, speaks it as their champion. *Who is he that shall condemn me?* The prophet perhaps was condemned to die; Christ we are sure was; and yet both could say, *Who is he that shall condemn?* For there is no condemnation to those whom God justifies. The righteous cause of Christ and his prophets shall outlive all opposition. The *moth shall eat them up* silently and insensibly; a little thing will serve to destroy them.

Verses 10–11

The prophet, having the tongue of the learned, here makes use of it. It is the summary of the gospel. *He that believes shall be saved,* though for a while he walk in darkness, but *he that believes not,* though for a while he walk in the light of his own fire, yet he shall lie down in sorrow.

I. Comfort is here spoken to disconsolate saints, and they are encouraged to trust in God's grace, *v.* 10. A child of God is one that fears the Lord with a filial fear, that stands in awe of his majesty and is afraid of incurring his displeasure. He is one that obeys the voice of God's servant, is willing to be ruled by the Lord Jesus in the great work of man's redemption. Those that truly fear God will obey the voice of Christ. It is no new thing for the children and heirs of light sometimes to walk in darkness, and for a time not to have any glimpse or gleam of light. He that is thus in the dark, *Let him trust in the name of the Lord,* in the goodness of his nature, his wisdom, power, and goodness. *The name of the Lord is a strong tower.* If he walk before God, which a man may do though he walk in the dark, he shall find God all-sufficient to him. Let him keep hold of his covenant-relation to God, and call God *his God,* as Christ on the cross, *My God, My God.*

II. Presuming sinners are warned not to trust in themselves, *v.* 11. They *kindle a fire,* and *walk in the light of that fire.* They depend upon their own righteousness, and burn their incense, with that fire (as Nadab and Abihu) and not with the fire from heaven. They *compass themselves about with sparks of their own kindling.* As they trust in their own righteousness, and not in the righteousness of Christ, so they place their happiness in their worldly possessions and enjoyments, and not in the favour of God. Creature-comforts are as sparks, short-lived and soon gone. They are ironically told to *walk in the light of their own fire.* Those that make the world their comfort, and their own righteousness their confidence, will meet with bitterness in the end. A godly man's way may be melancholy, but his end shall be peace and everlasting light. A wicked man's way may be pleasant, but his end will be darkness.

CHAPTER 51

This chapter is designed for the encouragement of those that fear God and keep his commandments, even when they walk in darkness and have no light. Whenever the church of God is in distress her friends may comfort themselves and one another with these words, I. That God, who raised his church at first out of nothing, will take care that it shall not perish, ver. 1–3. II. That the righteousness and salvation he designs for his church are sure and near, ver. 4–6. III. That the persecutors of the church are weak creatures, ver. 7, 8. IV. That the same power which did wonders for the church formerly is now employed for her deliverance, ver. 9–11. V. That God himself, the Maker of the world, had undertaken to deliver his people out of their distress, and sent his prophet to assure them of it, ver. 12–16. VI. That, deplorable as the condition of the church now was (ver. 17–20), to the same woeful circumstances her persecutors and oppressors should shortly be reduced, ver. 21–23. The first three paragraphs of this chapter begin with, "Hearken unto me", and they are God's people that are all along called to hearken. The two other paragraphs of this chapter begin with "Awake, awake"; in the former (ver. 9) God's people call upon him to awake and help them; in the latter (ver. 17) God calls upon them to awake and help themselves.

Verses 1–3

The people of God are such as *follow after righteousness,* those *that seek the Lord,* for it is only in the way of righteousness that we can seek him with any hope of finding him. They are here directed to look back to their original, and the smallness of their beginning: "*Look unto the rock whence you were hewn*" (the idolatrous family in Ur of the Chaldees, out of which Abraham was taken, the generation of slaves which the heads and fathers of their tribes were in Egypt); "look unto *the hole of the pit out of which you were digged,* as clay, when God formed you into a people." How hard was that rock out of which we were hewn, unapt to receive impressions, and how miserable *the hole of that pit out of which we were digged!* The consideration of this should fill us with low thoughts of ourselves and high thoughts of divine grace. "*Look unto Abraham your father,* the father of all the faithful, of all that follow after the righteousness of faith as he did (Rom. iv. 11), *and unto Sarah that bore you,* and whose daughters you all are as long as you do well. Think how Abraham was *called alone,* and yet was *blessed* and *multiplied*; and let that encourage you to depend upon the promise of God. "Look unto Abraham, and see what he got by trusting in the promise of God, and take example by him to follow God with an implicit faith." They are here assured that their present tears should at length end in joys, *v.* 3. God will find out a time and way to *comfort Zion.* It is the greatest comfort of the church to be made serviceable to the glory of God, and to be as his garden in which he delights. He will make them cheerful, and give them hearts to rejoice. With the *fruits of righteousness, joy and gladness shall be found therein;* for the more holiness men have, and the more good they do, the more gladness they have.

Verses 4–8

The perpetuity of God's righteousness and his salvation.

I. This comfort belongs to "*My people,* and *my nation,* that I have set apart for myself, that own me and are owned by me." They are a people who *know righteousness,* and are able to form a right judgment of truth and falsehood, good and evil. And, as they have good heads, so they have good hearts, for they have the law of God in them. Even those who know righteousness, and have the law of God in their hearts, may yet be in great distress and loaded with reproach and contempt; but their God will comfort them.

II. The comfort that belongs to God's people. 1. The gospel of Christ shall be preached to the world: *A law shall proceed from me,* an evangelical law, the law of Christ, the law of faith, *ch.* ii. 3. This is that law of liberty by which the world shall be governed. It shall take deep root in the world, not only for the benefit of the Jews, but *for a light of the people* of other nations. 2. This law shall open a ready way to the children of men, that they may be justified and saved, *v. 5*. There is no salvation without righteousness; and, wherever there is the *righteousness of God*, there shall be his salvation. 3. This righteousness and salvation shall shortly appear: *My righteousness is near*. It is near in time and in place, Rom. x. 8. 4. This evangelical righteousness and salvation shall not be confined to the Jewish nation, but shall be extended to the Gentiles: *My arms shall judge the people*. Those that will not yield to the judgments of God's mouth shall be crushed by the judgments of his hand. Some shall thus be judged by the gospel, but others, and those of *the isles, shall wait upon him*, and bid his gospel, the commands as well as the comforts of it, welcome. It was a comfort to God's people, that multitudes should be added to them. It is added, *And on my arm shall they trust*, that *arm of the Lord* which is revealed in Christ, *ch. liii. 1.* 5. This righteousness and salvation *shall be for ever, v. 8*. As it shall spread through all the nations of the earth, so it shall last through all the ages of the world. The visible heavens above shall *vanish like smoke*; they shall be rolled like a scroll. The earth shall *wax old like a garment*. But when *heaven and earth pass away*, when all flesh and the glory of it wither as grass, the *word of the Lord endures for ever*. Those whose happiness is bound up in Christ's righteousness and salvation will have the comfort of it when time and days shall be no more.

III. If God's righteousness and salvation are near to them, then let them *not fear the reproach of men*, nor be *afraid of their revilings*, who bid you sing them the songs of Zion, or who ask you, in scorn, *Where is now your God?* Those can bear but little for Christ that cannot bear a hard word for him. Let us not fear the reproach of men. They will be quickly silenced (*v. 8*): *The moth shall eat them up like a garment, ch. l. 9. The worm shall eat them like wool*, or woollen cloth. The falsehood of their reproaches will be detected, but truth shall triumph. Clouds darken the sun, but give no obstruction to his progress.

Verses 9–16

I. A prayer that God would appear and act for the deliverance of his people. *Awake, awake! put on strength, O arm of the Lord! v. 9*. The arm of the Lord is Christ, or it is put for God himself, as Ps. xliv. 23. The arm of the Lord is said to awake when on his people's behalf it is stretched forth for action. God needs not to be reminded nor excited by us, but he gives us leave to be humbly earnest for such appearances of his power as will be for his own praise. The church sees her case bad, her enemies many and mighty, her friends few and feeble; and therefore she depends purely upon the strength of God's arm for her relief.

II. The pleas to enforce this prayer. 1. They plead precedents, their ancestors, and the great things God had done for them. "Let the arm of the Lord be made bare on our behalf. It did wonders against the Egyptians; it *cut Rahab* to pieces with one direful plague after another, *and wounded* Pharaoh, *the dragon*. It did wonders for Israel. *It dried up the sea*, to open *a way for the ransomed to pass over*," *v. 10*. Past experiences are good pleas in prayer. *Thou hast; wilt thou not?* Ps. lxxxv. 1–6. 2. They plead promises (*v. 11*): *And the redeemed of the Lord shall return*, that is (as it may be supplied), *thou hast said, They shall*, referring to *ch. xxxv. 10*. Sinners, when they are brought out of the slavery of sin into the glorious liberty of God's children, may come singing, as a bird got loose out of the cage. The souls of believers, when they are delivered out of the prison of the body, come to the heavenly Zion with singing. He that designs such joy for us at last will not work such deliverances for us in the meantime as our case requires?

III. The answer immediately given to this prayer (*v. 12*): *I, even I, am he that comforteth you*. They prayed for the appearances of his power; he answers them with the consolations of his grace, which may well be accepted as an equivalent. If God do not answer immediately *with the saving strength of his right hand*, we must be thankful if he answer us, as an angel himself was answered (Zech. i. 13) *with good words and comfortable words*. See how God resolves to comfort his people: He takes the work into his own hands: *I, even I*, will do it.

1. He comforts the timorous by chiding them: *Why art thou cast down, and why disquieted? v. 12, 13*.

(1) The absurdity of those fears. It is a disparagement to us to give way to them: *Who art thou, that thou shouldst be afraid?* It is absurd to be in such dread of a dying man. What! *afraid of a man that shall die, who shall be made as grass*, shall wither and be trodden down or eaten up? We ought to look upon every man as a man that shall die. Those we fear we must look upon as frail and mortal, and consider what a foolish thing it is for the servants of the living God to be afraid of dying men, that are here today and gone tomorrow. It is absurd to *fear continually every day* (*v. 13*). Now and then a danger may be imminent and threatening, and it may be prudent to fear it; but to be always in a toss, and to tremble at the shaking of every leaf, is to make ourselves all our lifetime *subject to bondage* (Heb. ii. 15). It is absurd to fear beyond what there is cause: "Thou art *afraid of the fury of the oppressor*. Where is the fury of the oppressor? It is gone in an instant, and the danger is over ere thou art aware." *Pharaoh king of Egypt is but a noise*, and the king of Babylon no more. What has become of all the furious oppressors of God's Israel, that were a terror to them? they passed away, and, lo, they were not; and so shall these.

(2) The impiety of those fears: "Thou art *afraid of a man that shall die, and forgettest the Lord thy Maker*, who is also the Maker of all the world." Our inordinate fear of man is a tacit forgetfulness of God. When we disquiet ourselves with the fear of man we forget that there is a God above him. We forget the experiences we have had of his care, and his interposition for our relief many a time, when we thought the oppressor ready to destroy; we forget our Jehovah-jirehs, monuments of mercy in the mount of the Lord.

2. He comforts those that were in bonds, *v. 14, 15*. *The captive exile hastens that he may be loosed* and may return to his own country, from which he is banished; his care is *that he may not die in the pit* (not die a prisoner), and that *his bread should not fail*. Now some understand this as his fault. He is impatient of delays, cannot wait God's time, but thinks he must die in the pit if he be not released immediately. Others take it to be his praise, that when the doors are thrown open he does not linger. And then it follows, *But I am the Lord thy God*, which intimates God will do for them that which they cannot do for themselves. He will find out a way to still the threatening storm, and bring them safely into the harbour. *The Lord of hosts is his name*, the name by which his people have long known him.

3. He comforts all his people who depended upon what the prophets said to them in the name of the Lord. When the deliverances which the prophets spoke of either did not come soon or did not come up to their expectation they began to be cast down; but are encouraged (*v. 16*) by what God says to his messenger, as he does here, *I have put my words in thy mouth, that by them I may plant the heavens*. God undertook to comfort his people (*v. 12*); but he does it by his prophets, by his gospel. He owns what they have said to be what he had enjoined them to say:

"*I have put my words in thy mouth*, and therefore he that receives thee and them receives me." God's Spirit revealed to them the words they should speak (2 Pet. i. 21; 1 Cor. ii. 13). I have *covered thee in the shadow of my hand* (as before, *ch.* xlix. 2) speaks the special protection not only of the prophets, but of their prophecies, not only of Christ, but of Christianity, of the gospel of Christ. "*I have put my words in thy mouth*, not that by the performance of them I may plant a nation, or found a city, but *that I may plant the heavens and lay the foundations of the earth,* which will be a new creation." This must look far forward to the great work done by the gospel of Christ and the setting up of his holy religion in the world. As God by Christ made the world at first (Heb. i. 2), so by him he will set up a new world, will again plant the heavens and found the earth. Sin having put the whole creation into disorder, Christ's taking away the sin of the world put all into order again.

Verses 17–23

A call to awake not so much out of the sleep of sin (though that also is necessary in order to their being ready for deliverance) as out of the stupor of despair. When the inhabitants of Jerusalem were in captivity they were so overwhelmed with the sense of their troubles that they had no heart to mind anything that tended to their comfort.

I. Jerusalem had long been in the depths of misery.

1. She had lain under the tokens of God's displeasure. He had put into her hand *the cup of his fury.* She had provoked him to anger and was made to taste the bitter fruits of it. The cup of God's fury is, and will be, a *cup of trembling* to all those that have it put into their hands. It is said (Ps. lxxv. 8) that *the dregs of the cup, all the wicked of the earth shall wring them out, and drink them.* Wherever there has been a cup of fornication, as there had been in Jerusalem's hand when she was idolatrous, sooner or later there will be a cup of fury.

2. Those that should have helped her in her distress failed her, *v.* 18. She staggers, and is very unsteady. She knows not what she says or does, much less what to say or do, and, in this unhappy condition, *of all the sons that she has brought forth* and brought up, *there is none to guide her,* none to lend either a hand to help her out of her trouble or a tongue to comfort her under it. *These two things have come unto thee* (*v.* 19), to complete thy desolation and destruction, even *the famine and the sword,* by which the city was wasted and by which the citizens perished. These two things that had come upon Jerusalem are the same with the two things that were afterwards to come upon Babylon (*ch.* xlvii. 9), *loss of children and widowhood*—piteous case that calls for comfort; and yet, when thou art froward under thy trouble, *by whom shall I comfort thee?* Those who should have been her comforters were their own tormenters (*v.* 20): *They have fainted,* driven to despair; they have no patience in which to keep possession of their own souls, nor any confidence in God's promise. They throw themselves upon the ground, in vexation at their troubles, and there *they lie at the head of all the streets.* There they lie like *a wild bull in a net,* fretting and raging, struggling to help themselves, but making their condition the worse by their own passions and discontents. Those that are of a froward peevish spirit never enquire wherefore he contends with them, and therefore nothing appears in them but anger at God.

II. It is promised that Jerusalem's troubles shall at length come to an end, and be transferred to her persecutors (*v.* 21): *Nevertheless hear this, thou afflicted:* "*Thus saith thy Lord, the Lord, and thy God*—the Lord, who is able to help thee—thy God, in covenant with thee, and who has undertaken to

make thee happy—he is the God *who pleads the cause of his people,* who takes what is done against them as done against himself." It is his own cause; he has espoused it, and therefore will plead it. "*I will take out of thy hand the cup of trembling,* that bitter cup; it shall pass from thee." It is promised, "*Thou shalt no more drink it again.*" Their persecutors and oppressors should be made to drink of the same bitter cup of which they had drunk so deeply, *v.* 23. Herein the New Testament Babylon treads in the steps of that old oppressor, tyrannizing over men's consciences, putting them upon the rack, and compelling them to sinful compliances. Babylon's case shall be as bad as ever Jerusalem's was. Daniel's persecutors shall be thrown into Daniel's den.

CHAPTER 52

The greater part of this chapter is on the same subject with the chapter before, but the last three verses are on the same subject with the following chapter, concerning the person of the Redeemer, his humiliation and exaltation. I. The encouragement that is given to the Jews in captivity to hope that God would deliver them in his own way and time, ver. 1–6. II. The great joy that shall be both with ministers and people upon that occasion, ver. 7–10. III. The call given to those that remained in captivity, when liberty was proclaimed, ver. 11, 12. IV. A short idea given here of the Messiah, which is enlarged in the next chapter, ver. 13–15.

Verses 1–6

I. God's people are stirred up to appear vigorous for their own deliverance, *v.* 1, 2. Let them awake from their despondency, and pluck up their spirits, encourage themselves and one another. Let them awake from their distrust, look above them, look about them, look into the promises, look into the providences of God that were working for them, and let them raise their expectations of great things from God. Let them awake from their dullness. God here gives them an assurance, 1. That they should be reformed by their captivity: *There shall no more come into thee the uncircumcised and the unclean* (*v.* 1); their idolatrous customs should be no more introduced, or at least not harboured. Thus the gospel Jerusalem is purified by the blood of Christ and the grace of God, and made indeed a holy city. 2. That they should be rescued out of their captivity, that they should not be any more invaded: *There shall no more come against thee* (so it may be read) *the uncircumcised and the unclean.* If they keep close to God, and keep in with him, God will keep off, will keep out the enemy; but, if they again corrupt themselves, Antiochus will profane their temple and the Romans will destroy it. However, for some time they shall have peace. Let them prepare for joy: "*Put on thy beautiful garments,* no longer appear in mourning weeds. Put on a new face, a smiling countenance, now that a new and pleasant scene begins to open." Let them prepare for liberty: "*Shake thyself from the dust* into which thy proud oppressors have trodden thee (*ch.* li. 23), or into which thou hast in thy sorrow rolled thyself." *Arise, and set up;* so it may be read. "O Jerusalem! get clear of all the marks of servitude: *Loose thyself from the bands of thy neck;* assert thy own liberty." The gospel proclaims liberty to those who were bound with fears and makes it their duty to take hold of their liberty. Let those who have been weary and heavily laden under the burden of sin, finding relief in Christ, loose themselves from those bands; for, *if the Son make them free, they shall be free indeed.*

II. God stirs up himself for the deliverance of his people.

1. The Chaldeans who oppressed them never acknowledged God any more than Sennacherib did, *ch.* x. 6, 7. "*You have sold yourselves for nought;* you got nothing by it, nor did I," *v.* 3. The Babylonians gave him no thanks for them, but rather reproached

and blasphemed his name upon that account. "And therefore they, having so long had you for nothing, shall at last restore you for nothing: *You shall be redeemed without price*," as was promised, *ch.* xlv. 13.

2. They had been often before in similar distress, and it was a pity that they should now be left in the hand of these oppressors (*v.* 4): "*My people went down into Egypt*, in an amicable way to settle there; but they enslaved them, and ruled them with rigour." And then they were delivered. Why may we not think God will deliver his people now? At other times *the Assyrian oppressed* the people of God *without cause*, as when the ten tribes were carried away captive by the king of Assyria; soon afterwards Sennacherib, another Assyrian, made himself master of all the defenced cities of Judah. The Babylonians might be called *Assyrians*, their monarchy being a branch of the Assyrians; and they now oppressed them without cause.

3. God's glory suffered by the injuries that were done to his people (*v.* 5): *What have I here*, what do I get by it, *that my people are taken away for nought?* The captives are so dispirited that they cannot praise him: *Those that rule over them make them to howl*, as the Egyptians of old made them to sigh, Exod. ii. 23. However God heard them, and came down to deliver them, as he did out of Egypt, Exod. iii. 7, 8. The natives, blaspheming, boasted that they were too hard for God because they were too hard for his people, and set him at defiance, as unable to deliver them. "Now," says God, "I will go down to deliver them; for their oppressors will neither praise God themselves nor let them do it."

4. His glory would be manifested by their deliverance (*v.* 6): "*Therefore*, because my name is thus blasphemed, I will arise, and *my people shall know my name*, my name Jehovah."

Verses 7–12

The removal of the Jews from Babylon, and the application of *v.* 7 to the preaching of the gospel (by the apostle, Rom. x. 15) plainly intimates that that deliverance was a type and figure of the redemption of mankind by Jesus Christ.

I. It is here spoken of as a great blessing, which ought to be welcomed with joy. 1. Those that bring the tidings of their release shall be very acceptable (*v.* 7), as they come over the mountains round about Jerusalem. It is meant of some of the Jews themselves, who immediately went themselves, or sent their own messengers, to Jerusalem itself, to tell the few who remained there that their brethren would be with them shortly; for it is published as a proof that Zion's God reigns, for they say unto Zion, *Thy God reigns*. This must be applied to the preaching of the gospel, which is a proclamation of peace and salvation; it is gospel indeed, good news of victory over our spiritual enemies and liberty from our spiritual bondage. The good news is that the Lord Jesus reigns. Christ himself brought these tidings first (Luke iv. 18, Heb. ii. 3), and of him the text speaks: *How beautiful are his feet!* his feet that were nailed to the cross, how beautiful upon Mount Calvary! 2. Zion's watchmen shall rejoice, *v.* 8. The watchmen (*ch.* lxii. 6) were such as God set on the walls of Jerusalem, to make mention of his name, and to continue instant in prayer to him, till he again *made Jerusalem a praise in the earth*. They stand upon their watch-tower, waiting for an answer to their prayers (Hab. ii. 1); and therefore when the good news comes they have it first. They shall *lift up the voice, with the voice together shall they sing*, to invite others to join with them in their praises. They shall see an exact agreement between the prophecy and the event, the promise and the performance; they shall see how they look one upon another

eye to eye, and be satisfied that the same God spoke the one and did the other. Applying this also, as the foregoing verse, to gospel times, it is a promise of the pouring out of the Spirit upon gospel ministers, as a spirit of wisdom and revelation, to lead them into all truth, so that they shall see eye to eye, and be unanimous in these great things concerning the common salvation. Zion's waste places shall then rejoice because they shall be surprisingly comforted (*v.* 9): *Break forth into joy, sing together, you waste places of Jerusalem*. The redemption of Jerusalem is the joy of all God's people, Luke ii. 38. God will have the glory of it, *v.* 10. He *has made bare his holy arm* (manifested and displayed his power) *in the eyes of all the nations*.

II. When the liberty is proclaimed, let the people of God hasten out of Babylon with all convenient speed: *Depart, depart* (*v.* 11), *go out from the midst of her*; be gone. Babylon is no place for Israelites, Ezra i. 5. And it is a call to all those who are yet in the bondage of sin and Satan to make use of the liberty which Christ has proclaimed to them. Let them take heed of carrying away with them any of the pollutions of Babylon: *Touch no unclean thing*. Let them depend upon the presence of God with them and his protection in their removal (*v.* 12): *You shall not go out with haste*. They were to go with a diligent haste, but not with a diffident distrustful haste, as if they were afraid of being pursued. Cyrus shall give them an honourable discharge, and they shall have an honourable return, and not steal away; *for the Lord will go before them*. God will both lead their van and bring up their rear.

Verses 13–15

This prophecy, which begins here and is continued to the end of the next chapter, points as plainly as can be at Jesus Christ; the ancient Jews understood it of the Messiah, though some will have it understood of Jeremiah. But Philip has put it past dispute that *of him speaks the prophet this*, of him and of no other man, Acts viii. 34, 35.

I. God owns Christ to be commissioned for his undertaking. He is appointed to it. "He is *my servant*, whom I employ and therefore will uphold." In his undertaking he does his Father's will, seeks his Father's honour, and serves the interests of his Father's kingdom. He *shall deal prudently*, for the *spirit of wisdom and understanding shall rest upon him, ch.* xi. 2.

II. He gives a short prospect both of his humiliation and his exaltation. *Many were astonished at him* by reason of his sorrows. *His visage was marred more than any man's* when he was buffeted, smitten on the cheek, and crowned with thorns, and *hid not his face from shame and spitting*. He was *a man of sorrows*. Never was sorrow like unto his sorrow. How highly God exalted him, and exalted him because he humbled himself! Three words are used for this (*v.* 13): *He shall be exalted and extolled and be very high*. God shall exalt him, men shall extol him, and with both he shall be higher than the highest, higher than the heavens. Many nations shall be the better for him, for *he shall sprinkle them*; the blood of sprinkling shall be applied to their consciences, to purify them, for in his death there was *a fountain opened*, Zech. xiii. 1. He shall do it by baptism. So that this promise had its accomplishment when Christ sent his apostles to disciple all nations, by baptizing or sprinkling them. *Kings shall shut their mouths at him*, that is, they shall not open their mouths against him, as they have done. They shall with great humility and reverence receive his oracles and laws. *That which had not been told them shall they see;* the gospel brings to light things which will awaken the reverence of kings and kingdoms. They shall see and consider the glory of God shining in the face of Christ, which before they had not been told of—*they had not heard.* Christ disappointed the expectations of those who looked for a Messiah according to their fancies, as the carnal Jews, but outdid theirs who looked for such a Messiah as was promised.

Chapter 53

The two great things which the Spirit of Christ in the Old Testament prophets testified beforehand were the sufferings of Christ and the glory that should follow, 1 Pet. i. 11. But nowhere in all the Old Testament are these two so plainly and fully prophesied of as here in this chapter. This chapter is so replenished with the unsearchable riches of Christ that it may be called rather the gospel of the evangelist Isaiah than the prophecy of the prophet Isaiah. I. The reproach of Christ's sufferings—the meanness of his appearance, the greatness of his grief, and the prejudices which many conceived in consequence against his doctrine, ver. 1–3. II. The rolling away of this reproach, and the stamping of immortal honour upon his sufferings, by four considerations: 1. That therein he did his Father's will, ver. 4, 6, 10. 2. That thereby he made atonement for the sin of man (ver. 4–6, 8, 11, 12), for it was not for any sin of his own that he suffered, ver. 9. 3. That he bore his sufferings with an invincible patience, ver. 7. 4. That he should prosper in his undertaking, and his sufferings should end in his immortal honour, ver. 10–12.

Verses 1–3

The prophet, in the close of the former chapter, had foreseen and foretold the kind reception which the gospel of Christ should find among the Gentiles. Now here he foretells, with wonder, the unbelief of the Jews, notwithstanding the previous notices they had of the coming of the Messiah.

I. The contempt they put upon the gospel of Christ, *v.* 1. And it is applied likewise to the little success which the apostles' preaching met with among Jews and Gentiles, Rom. x. 16. Few believed the prophets who spoke before of Christ; when he came himself none of the rulers nor of the Pharisees followed him, and but here and there one of the common people; and, when the apostles carried this report all the world over, some in every place believed, but comparatively very few. To this day, of the many that profess to believe this report, there are few that cordially embrace it and submit to the power of it. They do not discern that divine power which goes along with the word, that working of the Spirit which makes the word effectual. They believe not the gospel because, by rebelling against the light they had, they had forfeited the grace of God.

II. The contempt they put upon the person of Christ because of the meanness of his appearance, *v.* 2, 3.

1. The low condition he submitted to, and how he abased and emptied himself. The entry he made into the world, and the character he wore in it, were no way agreeable to the ideas which the Jews had formed of the Messiah. It was expected that his extraction would be very great and noble. He was to be the Son of David, but he sprang out of this royal and illustrious family when it was reduced and sunk, and Joseph was but a poor carpenter. This is here meant by his being *a root out of a dry ground*, his being born of a mean and despicable family, in the north, in Galilee, of a family out of which, like a dry and desert ground, nothing green, nothing great, was expected, in a country of such small repute that it was thought no good thing could come out of it. It was expected that he should make a public entry, and come ·in pomp and with observation; but, instead of that, he grew up before God, not before men. *He grew up as a tender plant*, silently and insensibly, as the corn grows up, *we know not how*, Mark iv. 27. It was expected that he should have some uncommon beauty in his face and person, which should charm the eye, attract the heart, and raise the expectations of all that saw him. But there was nothing of this kind in him; not that he was deformed or misshapen,

but *he had no form nor comeliness*, nothing extraordinary, which one might have thought to meet in an incarnate deity. Moses, when he was born, was exceedingly fair, to such a degree that it was looked upon as a happy presage, Acts, vii. 20; Heb. xi. 23. David, when he was anointed, was *of a beautiful countenance, and goodly to look to*, 1 Sam. xvi. 12. But the appearing of our Lord Jesus in the world had nothing in it of sensible glory. His gospel is preached, *not with the enticing words of man's wisdom*, but with all plainness. It was expected that he should live a pleasant life, which would have invited all sorts to him; but, on the contrary, he was *a man of sorrows and acquainted with grief*. His condition was, upon many accounts, sorrowful. He was unsettled, had not where to lay his head, lived upon alms, was opposed and menaced, and *endured the contradiction of sinners against himself*. His spirit was tender, and he admitted the impressions of sorrow. Grief was his intimate acquaintance; for he acquainted himself with the griefs of others, and sympathized with them.

2. The low opinion that men had of him, upon this account. There was in him the beauty of holiness and the beauty of goodness, enough to render him *the desire of all nations*; but the greater part of those among whom he lived, saw none of this beauty, for it was spiritually discerned. He was rejected as a bad man. *We hid as it were our faces from him.* It may be read, *He hid as it were his face from us*, concealed the glory of his majesty, and drew a veil over it, and therefore *he was despised and we esteemed him not*, because we could not see through that veil.

Verses 4–9

I. A further account of the sufferings of Christ. More is said here of the condition to which he humbled himself, to which he became obedient even to the death of the cross. 1. He had griefs and sorrows. He bore them, and blamed not his lot; he did neither shrink from them, nor sink under them, but persevered to the end, till he said, *It is finished.* 2. He had blows and bruises; he was *stricken, smitten, and afflicted*. All along he was smitten with the tongue, when he was contradicted, put under the worst of characters, and had all manner of evil said against him. At last he was smitten with the hand, with blow after blow. 3. He was scourged, not under the merciful restriction of the Jewish law, which allowed not above forty stripes to be given to the worst of malefactors, but according to the usage of the Romans. Pilate intended it as an equivalent for his crucifixion, and yet it proved a preface to it. He was wounded in his hands, and feet, and side. 4. He was wronged and abused (*v.* 7): *He was oppressed*, but our Lord Jesus kept possession of his own soul. 5. He was *taken from prison and judgment, v.* 8. He was proceeded against as a malefactor; he was apprehended and taken into custody, and made a prisoner; he was judged, accused, tried, and condemned. 6. He was *cut off* by an untimely death *from the land of the living.* He made his grave *with the wicked* (for he was crucified between two thieves, as if he had been the worst of the three) and yet *with the rich*, for he was buried in a sepulchre that belonged to Joseph, an honourable counsellor.

II. An account of the meaning of his sufferings. It is natural to ask with amazement, "How came it about? What evil had he done?" His enemies *esteemed him stricken, smitten of God, and afflicted, v.* 4. Because they hated him, and persecuted him, they thought that God did. It is true he was *smitten of God, v.* 10 (or, as some read it, *he was God's smitten and afflicted*, the Son of God, though smitten and afflicted), but not in the sense in which they meant it.

1. He never did anything in the least to deserve this hard usage. Whereas he was charged with perverting the nation, and sowing sedition, it was utterly false; he had *done no violence*, but went about doing good. And, whereas he was called *that deceiver, there was no deceit in his mouth* (v. 9), compare 1 Pet. ii. 22. He never offended either in word or deed. The judge that condemned him owned he found no fault in him, and the centurion that executed him professed that certainly he was a righteous man.

2. Though he was *oppressed and afflicted*, yet he *opened not his mouth* (v. 7), no, not so much as to plead his own innocency, but freely offered himself to suffer and die for us. This takes away the scandal of the cross, that he voluntarily submitted to it, for great and holy ends. By his wisdom he could have evaded the sentence, and by his power have resisted the execution; but *thus it was written, and thus it behoved him to suffer*. This commandment he received *from his Father*, and therefore he was led *as a lamb to the slaughter*. As *a sheep is dumb before the shearers*, nay, before the butchers, so he *opened not his mouth*, which denotes his cheerful compliance with his Father's will. By this will we are sanctified, his making his own soul, his own life, an offering for our sin.

3. It was for our good, and in our stead, that Jesus Christ suffered. This is asserted here plainly and fully.

(1) It is certain that we are all guilty before God. We have all sinned, and have come short of the glory of God (v. 6): *All we like sheep have gone astray*. Every particular person stands charged with many actual transgressions. We have gone astray like sheep, which are apt to wander, and are unapt to find the way home again. That is our true character; we are bent to backslide from God, but altogether unable of ourselves to return to him. We turn aside everyone to his own way, and thereby set up our own will, in competition with God and his will, which is the malignity of sin.

(2) Our sins are our sorrows and our griefs (v. 4), or, as it may be read, *our sicknesses and our wounds*.

(3) Our Lord Jesus was appointed and did undertake to make satisfaction for our sins. For *the Lord has laid on him the iniquity of us all*. The laying of our sins upon Christ implies the taking of them off from us; we shall not fall under the curse of the law if we submit to the grace of the gospel. They were laid upon Christ when he was *made sin* (that is, a sin-offering) *for us*. Thus he put himself into a capacity to make those easy that come to him heavily laden under the burden of sin. See Ps. xl. 6–12. None but God had power to lay our sins upon Christ, both because the sin was committed against him, and because Christ was his own Son, who himself knew no sin. It was *the iniquity of us all* that was laid on Christ; for in Christ there is a sufficiency of merit for the salvation of all, and a serious offer made of that salvation to all, which excludes none that do not exclude themselves. God laid upon him our iniquity; but did he consent to it? Yes, he did; for some think that the true reading of the next words (v. 7) is, *It was exacted, and he answered.*

(4) Having undertaken our debt, he underwent the penalty. *He bore our griefs and carried our sorrows*, v. 4. Christ bore our sins, and so *bore our griefs*, bore them off us, that we should never be pressed above measure. *He was wounded for our transgressions*. Our sins were the thorns in his head, the nails in his hands and feet, the spear in his side. *He was bruised*, or crushed, *for our iniquities;* they were the procuring cause of his death. To the same purport is v. 8, *for the transgression of my people was he smitten, the stroke* was *upon him* that should have been upon us.

(5) The consequence of this to us is our peace and healing, v. 5. *The chastisement of our peace was upon him. He is our peace*, Eph. ii. 14. Christ was in pain that we might be at ease, knowing that through him our sins are forgiven us. Hereby we have healing; for *by his stripes we are healed*. Sin is not only a crime, for which we were condemned to die, but it is a disease, which tends directly to the death of our souls and for which Christ provided the cure. By his stripes he purchased for us the Spirit and grace of God to mortify our corruptions, which are the distempers of our souls, and to put our souls in a good state of health, that they may be fit to serve God. The dominion of sin is broken in us and we are fortified against that which feeds the disease.

(6) The consequence of this to Christ was his resurrection, for, being *delivered for our offences*, he was *raised again for our justification*. He rose *to die no more; death had no more dominion over him*. He that *was dead is alive*, and *lives for evermore*.

Verses 10–12

In the foregoing verses the prophet had testified of the sufferings of Christ; here he foretells the glory that should follow.

I. The services and sufferings of Christ's state of humiliation. Come, and see how he loved us, see what he did for us.

1. He submitted to the frowns of Heaven (v. 10): *Yet it pleased the Lord to bruise him, to put him to grief*. Men esteemed him smitten of God for some very great sin of his own (v. 4); now it was true that he was smitten of God, but it was for our sin.

2. He substituted himself in the room of sinners, as a sacrifice. He *made his soul an offering for sin;* he himself explains this (Matt. xx. 28), that *he came to give his life a ransom for many*. We could not put him in our stead, but he put himself.

3. He subjected himself to that which to us is the wages of sin (v. 12): *He has poured out his soul unto death*, poured it out as water, so little account did he make of it, when the laying of it down was the appointed means of our redemption and salvation.

4. He suffered himself to be ranked with sinners, and yet offered himself to be an intercessor for sinners, v. 12. He was *numbered with transgressors*, not only condemned as a malefactor, but executed in company with two notorious malefactors, and he in the midst, as if he had been the worst of the three. In his whole life he was numbered among the transgressors; for he was called and accounted a sabbath-breaker, a drunkard, and a friend to publicans and sinners. In his sufferings he *made intercession for the transgressors*, for those that reviled and crucified him; for he prayed, *Father, forgive them*, thereby showing, not only that he forgave them, but that he was now doing that upon which their forgiveness, and the forgiveness of all other transgressors, were to be founded. That prayer was the language of his blood, crying, not for vengeance, but for mercy.

II. The graces and glories of his state of exaltation. It is promised,

1. That the Redeemer shall have a seed to serve him and to bear up his name, Ps. xxii. 30. True believers are the seed of Christ; the Father gave them to him to be so, John xvii. 6.

2. That he shall live to see his seed, and because he lives they shall live also, for he is their life.

3. That he shall himself continue to take care of the affairs of this family: *He shall prolong his days*. Christ will not commit the care of his family to any other. *Of the increase of his government and peace there shall be no end*, for he ever lives.

4. That his great undertaking shall answer expectation: *The pleasure of the Lord shall prosper in his*

hand. God's purposes shall take effect, and not one iota or tittle of them shall fail.

5. That he shall himself have abundant satisfaction in it (v. 11): *He shall see of the travail of his soul, and shall be satisfied.* He shall see it beforehand (so it may be understood); he shall with the prospect of his sufferings have a prospect of the fruit. He shall see it when it is accomplished in the conversion and salvation of poor sinners. Christ does and will see the blessed fruit of the travail of his soul in the founding and building up of his church and the eternal salvation of all that were given him.

Note, The great privilege that flows to us from the death of Christ is justification from sin, our being acquitted from that guilt which alone can ruin us, and accepted into God's favour, which alone can make us happy. Christ, who purchased our justification for us, applies it to us, by his intercession made for us, his gospel preached to us, and his Spirit witnessing in us. It is by faith that we are justified, by our consent to Christ and the covenant of grace; in this way we are saved. Faith is the knowledge of Christ, and without knowledge there can be no true faith. That knowledge of Christ, and that faith in him, by which we are justified, have reference to him both as a servant to God and as a surety for us. It is according to God's will that he does it. He is himself righteous, and of his righteousness have all we received. We must know him, and believe in him, as one that bore our iniquities—saved us from sinking under the load by taking it upon himself. The Father makes clear the victory of the Son. "I will set him among the great, highly exalt him, and give him a name above every name." Christ comes at his glory by conquest. He has vanquished principalities and powers, sin and Satan, death and hell, the world and the flesh; these are the strong that he has disarmed and taken the spoil of. The spoil which he has divided, consists in the vast multitudes of willing, faithful, loyal subjects, that shall be brought in to him; for so some read it: *I will give many to him, and he shall obtain many for a spoil.* God will *give him the heathen for his inheritance and the uttermost parts of the earth for his possession,* Ps. ii. 8. The spoil which God divided to Christ he divides (it is the same word), he distributes, among his followers; for, when he *led captivity captive,* he received gifts for men, that he might give gifts to men.

Chapter 54

The death of Christ is the life of the church and of all that truly belong to it; and therefore very fitly, after the prophet had foretold the sufferings of Christ, he foretells the flourishing of the church, which is a part of his glory, and that exaltation of him which was the reward of his humiliation: it was promised him that he should see his seed, and this chapter is an explication of that promise. It may easily be granted that it has a primary reference to the welfare and prosperity of the Jewish church after their return out of Babylon, which was typical of the glorious liberty of the children of God, which through Christ we are brought into; yet it cannot be denied but that it has a further reference to the gospel church, into which the Gentiles were to be admitted. And the first words being understood by the apostle Paul of the New Testament Jerusalem (Gal. iv. 26, 27) may serve as a key to the whole chapter and that which follows. It is here promised concerning the Christian church, I. That, though the beginnings of it were small, it should be greatly enlarged by the accession of many to it among the Gentiles, ver. 1–5. II. That though sometimes God might seem to withdraw from her, he would return in mercy, ver. 6–10. III. That, though for a while she was in sorrow and under oppression, she should at length be advanced to greater honour, ver. 11, 12. IV. That knowledge, righteousness, and peace, should flourish and prevail, ver. 13, 14. V. That all attempts against the church should be baffled, ver. 14–17.

Verses 1–5

If we apply this to the state of the Jews after their return out of captivity, it is a prophecy of the increase of their nation after they were settled in their own land. Jerusalem had been in the condition of a wife written childless, or a desolate solitary widow; but now it is promised that the city should be replenished and the country peopled again, that the ruins of Jerusalem should be repaired, and that those estates which had for many years been wrongfully held by the Babylonian Gentiles should now return to the right owners. God will again be a husband to them, and the reproach of their captivity, and the small number to which they were then reduced, shall be forgotten. But we must apply it to the church of God in general; I mean the kingdom of God among men, God's city in the world.

I. The low state of religion in the world long before Christianity was brought in. It was like one *barren, that did not bear,* or like one desolate, that had lost husband and children; the church lay in a little compass, and brought forth little fruit. The Gentiles had less religion among them than the Jews, and the children of God, like the children of a broken, reduced family, were *scattered abroad* (John xi. 52).

II. Its recovery from this low condition by the preaching of the gospel and the planting of the Christian church.

1. Multitudes were converted from idols to the living God. Those were the church's children that were born again, were partakers of a new and divine nature, by the word. There were more found in the Gentile church (when that was set up) than ever were found in the Jewish church. The increase of church is the joy of all its friends and strengthens their hands. Even in heaven, among the angels of God, there is an uncommon joy for a sinner that repents, much more for a nation that does so.

2. The bounds of the church were extended much further than ever before, v. 2, 3. (1) It is here supposed that the present state of the church is a tabernacle state; it dwells in tents, like the heirs of promise of old (Heb. xi. 9). The city, the continuing city, is reserved for hereafter. A tent is soon taken down and shifted, and, when God pleases, it is as soon fixed elsewhere. (2) Though it be a tabernacle state, it is sometimes very remarkably a growing state, no matter though it be in a tent. Thus it was in the first preaching of the gospel; it was the business of the apostles to disciple all nations, and so to lengthen the cords of this tabernacle, that more might be enclosed, which would make it necessary to strengthen the stakes, that they might bear the weight of the enlarged curtains. The more numerous the church grows the more cautious she must be to fortify herself against errors and corruptions, and to support her seven pillars, Prov. ix. 1. (3) It was a proof of divine power that in all places it *grew and prevailed mightily,* Acts xix. 20. The gospel spread itself into all parts of the world; there were eastern and western churches.

3. This was the comfort and honour of the church (v. 4): *Fear not, for thou shalt not be ashamed,* as formerly, of the straitness of thy borders, and the fewness of thy children.

4. This was owing to the relation in which God stood to his church, as her husband (v. 5): *Thy Maker is thy husband.* Jesus Christ is the church's Maker, by whom she is formed into a people—her Redeemer, by whom she is brought out of captivity, the bondage of sin, the worst of slaveries. This is he that espoused her to himself: He is *the Lord of hosts, the Holy One of Israel,* the same that presided in the affairs of the Old Testament church and was the Mediator of the covenant made with it.

Verses 6–10

The succour and relief which God sent to his captives in Babylon are here foretold, as a type of all those consolations of God treasured up for all believers in the covenant of grace.

I. Look back to former troubles, and God's favours to his people, *v.* 6–8. 1. How sorrowful the church's condition had been. She had been as a woman forsaken, though she was *a wife of youth*, or she had been as one rejected, and full of discontent. Even those that are espoused to God may yet seem to be forsaken. The similitude is explained (*v.* 7, 8). When God continues his people long in trouble he seems to forsake them; so their enemies construe it (Ps. lxxi. 11). It was in wrath that he forsook them and hid his face from them (*ch.* lvii. 17); yet it was but in a little wrath in comparison with what they had deserved, and what others justly suffer. It was but *for a moment*, a *small* moment. As he is slow to anger, so he is swift to show mercy. 2. How sweet the returns of mercy would be to them when God should come and comfort them. God's gathering his people takes rise from his mercy, not any merit of theirs; and it is with *great mercies* (*v.* 7), *with everlasting kindness, v.* 8.

II. Look forward to future dangers, and in defiance of them God's favours appear constant, and his kindness everlasting; for it is formed into a *covenant of peace.*

1. This is as firm *as the waters of Noah*, that is, as that promise which was made concerning the deluge that there should never be the like again, *v.* 9; see Gen. viii. 21, 22; ix. 11. And God has kept his word, though the world has been very provoking. And thus inviolable is the covenant of grace: *I have sworn that I would not be wroth with thee*, as I have been, *and rebuke thee*, as I have done.

2. It is more firm than the strongest parts of the visible creation (*v.* 10): The *mountains shall depart*, and *the hills be removed*, Hab. iii. 6. Mountains have sometimes been shaken by earthquakes, and removed; but the promises of God were never broken by the shock of any event. When our friends fail us our God does not, nor does his kindness depart? Do the kings of the earth, and the rulers, set themselves against the Lord? They shall depart and be removed. God's kindness shall never depart from his people, for whom he loves he loves to the end. *Therefore* the covenant is immovable and inviolable, because it is built not on our merit, but on God's mercy, which is from everlasting to everlasting.

Verses 11–17

Very precious promises that God would not only continue his love to his people under their troubles, but that he would raise them to greater prosperity than any they had yet enjoyed. In the foregoing chapter we had the humiliation and exaltation of Christ; here we have the humiliation and exaltation of the church; for, if we suffer with him, we shall reign with him.

I. The distressed state of the church (*v.* 11): "*O thou afflicted*, poor, and indigent society, that art *tossed with tempests*, like a ship ready to be swallowed up by the waves, not comforted by any prospect of deliverance." This was the condition of the Jews in Babylon, and afterwards, for a time, under Antiochus. It is often the condition of Christian churches and of believers, like the disciples in a storm, ready to perish; and where is their faith?

II. The glorious state the church is advanced to by the promise of God. Let the people of God, when they are afflicted and tossed, think they hear God speaking comfortably to them by these words. In all their afflictions he is afflicted, and encourages her with the assurance of the great things he would do for her.

1. God promises that which would be her beauty and honour.

(1) This is promised by a similitude taken from a city, for the church is the city of the living God, the heavenly Jerusalem. Whereas now Jerusalem lay in ruins, a heap of rubbish, it shall be beautified, and appear more splendid than ever; the stones shall be laid not only firm, but fine. The foundations shall be garnished with *sapphires*, for Christ, and the foundation of the apostles and prophets, are precious above anything else. The windows of this house, city, or temple, shall be made of *agates*, the gates of *carbuncles*, and all the *borders* (the walls that enclose the courts) shall be *of pleasant stones, v.* 12. God, having graciously undertaken to build his church, the glory of the New Testament church shall far exceed that of the Jewish church, in those gifts and graces of the Spirit which are infinitely valuable.

(2) Those things that shall be the beauty and honour of the church are knowledge, holiness, and love, the very image of God, in which man was created, renewed, and restored. And these are the sapphires and carbuncles, the precious and pleasant stones, with which the gospel temple shall be beautified; *built upon the foundation*, 1 Cor. iii. 12. Then the church is all glorious, [1] When it is full of the knowledge of God (*v.* 13): *All thy children shall be taught of the Lord.* They shall be taught by those whom God shall appoint and whose labours shall be under his direction and blessing. It is a promise of the Spirit of illumination. Our Saviour quotes it with application to gospel grace (John vi. 45). [2] When the members of it live in love and unity among themselves: *Great shall be the peace of thy children.* All that are taught of God are taught to *love one another* (1 Thess. iv. 9). [3] When holiness reigns; for that above anything is the beauty of the church (*v.* 14): *In righteousness shalt thou be established.* The reformation of manners, the restoration of purity, the due administration of public justice, and the prevailing of honesty and fair dealing among men, are the strength and stability of any church or state.

2. Whereas now she lay in danger, God promises her protection and security. There shall be no fears within (*v.* 14): "*Thou shalt be far from oppression*, not only from evil, but from the fear of evil." There shall be no fightings without. Though attempts should be made upon them they should none of them succeed, *v.* 15. It is granted, "*They shall surely gather together against thee;* thou must expect it." As long as there is a devil in hell, and a persecutor out of it, God's people must expect frequent alarms; but God will not own them. Their attempt will end in their own ruin: "*Whosoever shall gather together against thee*, they *shall fall for thy sake*, or they shall fall before thee." We may with the greatest assurance depend upon God for the safety of his church. The smith that makes weapons is God's creature, and he gave him his skill to work in iron and brass (Exod. xxxi. 3, 4) and to make proper instruments for warlike purposes. *The smith blows the coals in the fire*, to make his iron malleable, that it may be hardened into steel, and so *he may bring forth an instrument proper for the work of those that seek to destroy.* It is the iron age that is the age of war. But *God has created the smith*, and therefore can tie his hands, so that the project of the enemy shall miscarry. They must have soldiers, and it is *God that created the waster to destroy.* Military men value themselves upon their splendid titles, but God calls them *wasters made to destroy*, for wasting and destruction are their business. They think their own ingenuity, labour, and experience, made them soldiers; but it was God that created them, and he will serve his own purposes and designs by them. The promise of God concerns the church's safety as *the heritage of the servants of the Lord* (*v.* 17). "*No weapon that is formed against thee shall prosper;* it shall not prove strong enough to do any harm to the people of God; it shall recoil in the face of him that uses it against thee." When the weapons of war do not prosper there are tongues

that rise in judgment. They are such as misrepresent them, and falsely accuse them to make them odious to the people and obnoxious to the government. This the enemies of the Jews did, to incense the kings of Persia against them, Ezra iv. 12; Esther iii. 8. "But these insulting threatening tongues thou shalt put to silence *by well-doing* (1 Pet. ii. 15), by doing that which will make thee manifest in the consciences even of thy adversaries, that thou art not what thou art represented to be." *This is the heritage of the servants of the Lord.* God's servants are his sons. God's promises are their *heritage for ever* (Ps. cxix. 111).

CHAPTER 55

In this chapter we have much of the covenant of grace made with us in Christ. The "sure mercies of David", which are promised here (ver. 3) are applied by the apostle to the benefits which flow to us from the resurrection of Christ (Acts xiii. 34). Here is, I. A free and gracious invitation to all to come and take the benefit of gospel grace, ver. 1. II. Pressing arguments to enforce this invitation, ver. 2–4. III. A promise of the success of this invitation among the Gentiles, ver. 5. IV. An exhortation to repentance and reformation, ver. 6–9. V. The ratification of all this, with the certain efficacy of the word of God, ver. 10, 11. And a particular instance of the accomplishment of it in the return of the Jews out of their captivity, a sign of the accomplishment of all these other promises.

Verses 1–5

I. We are all invited to come and take that provision which the grace of God has made for poor souls in the new covenant.

1. Who are invited: *Ho, everyone.* Not the Jews only, but the Gentiles, the poor and the maimed, the halt and the blind, whoever can be picked up out of the highways and the hedges. Ministers are to make a general offer of life and in gospel times the invitation should be sent to the Gentiles. The gospel covenant excludes none that do not exclude themselves.

2. What is the qualification required—they must thirst. Those that are satisfied with the world and its enjoyments—those that depend upon the merit of their own works for a righteousness—these do not thirst; they have no sense of their need, are in no pain or uneasiness about their souls. But those that thirst are invited to the waters, as those that labour, and are heavy-laden, are invited to Christ for rest. Where God gives grace he first gives a thirsting after it; and, where he has given a thirsting after it, he will give it, Ps. lxxxi. 10.

3. Whither they are invited: *Come you to the waters.* Come to Christ; for he is the fountain opened; he is the rock smitten. Come to holy ordinances, to those streams that make glad the city of our God; to those who believe in Christ the things signified will be as wine and milk, abundantly refreshing. Come to the healing waters; come to the living waters. Our Saviour referred to it, John vii. 37. *If any man thirst, let him come to me and drink.*

4. What they are invited to do. (1) *Come and buy.* "Come and buy, stand not hesitating about the terms, nor deliberating whether you shall agree to them." (2) "*Come, and eat;* make it still more your own, as that which we eat is more our own than that which we only buy."

5. What is the provision they are invited to: "*Come, and buy wine and milk,* which will not only quench the thirst" (fair water would do that), "but nourish the body, and revive the spirits." Christ outdoes our expectations. We come to the waters, and would be glad of them, but we find there wine and milk, which were the staple commodities of the tribe of Judah. We must part with our puddle-water, nay, with our poison, that we may procure this wine and milk.

6. The free communication of this provision: *Buy it without money, and without price.* Our buying without money intimates, (1) That the gifts offered us are invaluable and such as no price can be set upon.

(2) That he who offers them has no need of us, nor of any returns we can make him. (3) That the things offered are already bought and paid for. Christ purchased them not with money, but with *his own blood,* 1 Pet. i. 19. (4) That we shall be welcome to the benefits of the promise, and we must own it, that, if Christ and heaven be ours, we may see ourselves for ever indebted to free grace.

II. We are earnestly pressed to accept this invitation.

1. We are persuaded to hearken to God and to his proposals: "*Hearken diligently unto me, v.* 2. Not only give me the hearing, but apply it to yourselves (*v.* 3): *Incline your ear,* as you do to that which you find yourselves pleased with; come up to my terms."

2. The arguments used to persuade us,

(1) The unspeakable wrong we do to ourselves if we refuse this invitation: "*Wherefore do you spend money for that which is not bread,* when with me you may have wine and milk without money? *Wherefore do you spend your labour and toil for that which will not be so much as dry bread to you, for it satisfies not?*" The things of this world are not bread, not proper food for a soul. *They satisfy not.* The children of this world spend their money and labour for these uncertain unsatisfying things.

(2) The kindness we do to ourselves if we accept this invitation and comply with it. "If you hearken to Christ, you *eat that which is good,* which is both wholesome and pleasant, good in itself and good for you." God's good word and promise, a good conscience, and the comforts of God's good Spirit, are a continual feast to those that hearken obediently to Christ. Hereby we secure to ourselves lasting happiness: *Hear, and your soul shall live.* The great God graciously secures all this to us; "Come to me, *and I will make an everlasting covenant with you,* and thereby settle upon you *the sure mercies of David.*" The benefits of this covenant are the mercies of David, such mercies as God promised to David (Ps. lxxxix. 28, 29, &c.), which are called *the mercies of David his servant,* and are appealed to by Solomon, 2 Chron. vi. 42. By David here we are to understand the Messiah. Covenant-mercies are all *his* mercies; they are purchased by him; and out of his hands they are dispensed to us. He is the Mediator and trustee of the covenant. They are sure mercies for in Christ the promises are all yea and amen.

III. Jesus Christ is promised for the making good of all the other promises which we are here invited to accept, *v.* 4. He is that David whose sure mercies all the blessings and benefits of the covenant are. There was nothing in us to merit such a favour, but Christ is the gift of God. We know not how to find the way to the waters where we are to be supplied, but Christ is given to be *a leader.* We know not what to do, but he is given for *a commander,* to show us what to do and enable us to do it. Christ is a commander by his precept and a leader by his example; our business is to obey him and follow him.

IV. The Master of the feast being fixed, it is next to be furnished with guests. The Gentiles shall be called to this feast: *Thou shalt call a nation that thou knowest not,* that is, that was not formerly called and owned as thy nation. They shall come at the call: *Nations that knew not thee shall run unto thee.* There shall be a concourse of believing Gentiles to Christ, who, being lifted up from the earth, will draw all men to him. The Gentiles will thus flock to Christ because he is the Son of God. God will bring them to him because he is the Holy One of Israel, true to his promises, and he has promised to glorify him by giving him the heathen for his inheritance.

Verses 6–13

A further account of that covenant of grace which is made with us in Jesus Christ. This gracious discovery of God's goodwill is not to be confined either to the Jew or to the Gentile, to the Old Testament or to the New, much less to the captives in Babylon. The precepts and the promises are here given to all, to *everyone that thirsts after happiness, v. 1.*

I. A gracious offer made of pardon, and peace, and all happiness, to poor sinners, upon gospel terms, *v.* 6, 7.

1. Let them pray, and their prayers shall be heard and answered (*v.* 6): "*Seek the Lord while he may be found. Call upon him now while he is near*, and within call. Pray to him, to be reconciled, and, being reconciled, pray to him for everything else you need." Now his patience is waiting on us, his word is calling to us, and his Spirit striving with us. Let us now improve our advantages and opportunities; for now is the accepted time.

2. Let them repent and reform, and their sins shall be pardoned, *v.* 7. Here is a call to the unconverted, to *the wicked and the unrighteous*—to the wicked, who live in known gross sins, to the unrighteous, who live in the neglect of plain duties: to them is the word of this salvation sent, and all possible assurance given that penitent sinners shall find God a pardoning God. There are two things involved in repentance: (1) It is to turn from sin; it is to forsake it. There must be a change of the mind; the unrighteous must *forsake his thoughts.* Repentance, if it be true, strikes at the root, and washes the heart from wickedness. We must alter our judgments concerning persons and things, dislodge the corrupt imaginations and quit the vain pretences under which an unsanctified heart shelters itself. (2) To repent is to *return to the Lord;* against whom we have rebelled; it is to return to the Lord as the fountain of life. If we do so God *will have mercy.* Misery is the object of mercy. With God there are tender mercies. *He will abundantly pardon. He will multiply to pardon* (so the word is), as we have multiplied to offend.

II. Encouragements given us to accept this offer and to venture our souls upon it.

1. If we look up to heaven, we find God's counsels there high and transcendent, his thoughts and ways infinitely above ours, *v.* 8, 9. The wicked are urged to forsake their evil ways and thoughts (*v.* 7) and to bring their ways and thoughts to comply with his; "for" (says he) "my thoughts and ways are not as yours. Yours are conversant only about things beneath; but mine are above, *as the heaven is high above the earth;* and, if you would approve yourselves true penitents, yours must be so too, and your affections must be set on things above." Sinners may be ready to fear that God will not be reconciled to them, because they could not find in their hearts to be reconciled to one who should have so basely and so frequently offended them. "But" (says God) "my thoughts in this matter are not as yours, but as far above them as heaven is above the earth." We think God apt to take offence and backward to forgive—that, if he forgives once, he will not forgive a second time. Peter thought it a great deal to *forgive seven times* (Matt. xviii. 21), but God meets returning sinners with pardoning mercy. We forgive and cannot forget; but, when God forgives sin, he remembers it no more.

2. If we look down to this earth, we find God's word there powerful and effectual, *v.* 10, 11. He saith to the snow, Be thou on the earth; he appoints when it shall come, to what degree, and how long it shall lie there; he saith so *to the small rain and the great rain of his strength,* Job. xxxvii. 6. It returns not *without having accomplished its end,* but waters the earth. And the watering of the earth is in order to its fruitfulness. Thus he makes it to *bring forth and bud;* and thus it gives not only *bread to the eater,* present maintenance to the owner and his family, but *seed likewise to the sower,* that he may have food

for another year. The husbandman must be a sower as well as an eater, else he will soon see the end of what he has. "*So shall my word be,* as powerful in the mouth of prophets as it is in the hand of providence; *it shall not return unto me void, it shall accomplish that which I please, and it shall prosper in the thing for which I sent it.*" These promises of mercy and grace shall have as real an effect upon the souls of believers, for their sanctification and comfort, as ever the rain had upon the earth, to make it fruitful. Christ's coming into the world, as the dew from heaven (Hos. xiv. 5), will not be in vain.

3. If we take a special view of the church, we shall find what great things God has done, and will do, for it (*v.* 12, 13): *You shall go out with joy, and be led forth with peace.* This refers, (1) To the deliverance and return of the Jews out of Babylon. They shall go out of their captivity, and be led forth towards their own land again. They shall go out *with joy* and *peace.* They shall have the goodwill and good wishes of all the countries they pass through. *The hills* and their inhabitants *shall break forth into singing.* And, when they come to their own land, it shall be ready to bid them welcome. (2) Without doubt to something more. This shall be *for an everlasting sign,* that is, [1] The redemption of the Jews out of Babylon shall be a ratification of those promises that relate to gospel times. [2] It shall be a representation of the blessings promised and a figure of them. Gospel grace will set those at liberty that were in bondage to sin and Satan. They *shall go out and be led forth. Jacob shall rejoice, and Israel shall be glad.* It will make a great change in men's characters. Those that were as thorns and briers, good for nothing but the fire, shall become graceful and useful as the fir-tree and the myrtle-tree. The raising of pleasant trees in the room of them signifies the removal of the curse of the law and the introduction of gospel blessings. The covenant of grace is an everlasting covenant; for the present blessings of it are signs of everlasting ones.

CHAPTER 56

I. A solemn charge given to us all to make conscience of our duty, ver. 1, 2. II. Great encouragement given to strangers that were willing to come under the bonds of the covenant, ver. 3–8. III. A high charge drawn up against the watchmen of Israel, that were careless in the discharge of their duty (ver. 9–12), which seems to be the beginning of a new sermon, by way of reproof, continued in the following chapters.

Verses 1–2

When God is coming towards us in mercy we must go to meet him in a way of duty.

I. God here tells us what are his intentions of mercy to us (*v.* 1): *My salvation is near to come*—the great salvation wrought out by Jesus Christ typified by the salvation of the Jews from Sennacherib or out of Babylon. 1. The gospel salvation is the salvation of the Lord. 2. In that salvation God's righteousness is revealed, which St. Paul makes the ground of his glorying in it (Rom. i. 17). The law revealed that righteousness of God by which all sinners stand condemned, but the gospel reveals that by which all believers stand acquitted. 3. The Old Testament saints saw this salvation coming long before it came; and they had notice by the prophets of its approach.

II. He tells us what are his expectations of duty from us. Say not, "We see the salvation near, and therefore we may live as we list, for there is no danger now of missing it or coming short of it"; that is turning the grace of God into wantonness. But, on the contrary, when the salvation is near double your guard against sin. That which is here required to qualify and prepare us for the approaching salvation is,

1. That we be honest and just in all our dealings: *Keep you judgment and do justice.* God is true to us; let us be so to one another.

2. That we religiously observe the sabbath day, *v. 2.* We are not just if we rob God of his time. Sabbath-sanctification is here put for all the duties of the first table, the fruits of our love to God, as justice and judgment are put for all those of the second table, the fruits of our love to our neighbour. They might distinguish themselves from the heathen by putting a difference between God's day and other days.

3. That we have nothing to do with sin: *Blessed is the man* that *keeps his hand from doing evil,* any wrong to his neighbour, in body, goods, or good name—or, more generally, anything that is displeasing to God and hurtful to his own soul. The best evidence of our having kept the sabbath well will be to keep a good conscience all the week. It will appear that we have been in the mount with God if our faces shine in a holy conversation before men.

Verses 3–8

The prophet is here, in God's name, encouraging those that were joining themselves to God, yet laboured under great discouragements. 1. Some were discouraged because they were not of the seed of Abraham. They had *joined themselves to the Lord,* but they questioned whether God would accept them, because they were of *the sons of the stranger, v. 3.* They were Gentiles, aliens from the covenants of promise, and therefore feared they had no part nor lot in the matter. They said, *"The Lord has utterly separated me from his people,* and will not own me as one of them, nor admit me to their privileges." 2. Others were discouraged because they were not fathers in Israel. The eunuch said, *Behold, I am a dry tree.* He was thought to be of no use because he had no children, nor was ever likely to have any. This was the more grievous because eunuchs were not admitted to be priests (Lev. xxi. 20), nor to *enter into the congregation* (Deut. xxiii. 1). Yet God would not have the eunuchs to think that they should be excluded from the gospel church, and from being spiritual priests. As the taking down of the partition wall, contained in ordinances, admitted the Gentiles, so it let in likewise those that had been kept out by ceremonial pollutions. Now encouragements are given

I. To those who have no children of their own, though they had the honour to be the children of the church and the covenant themselves.

1. What a good character they have! They *keep God's sabbaths* as he has appointed them to be kept. They *choose those things that please God.* They *take hold of his covenant.* The covenant of grace is proffered to us in the gospel; to take hold of it is to accept the offer deliberately and sincerely to take God to be to us a God and to give up ourselves to be to him a people. We take hold of it as a criminal took hold of the horns of the altar to which he fled for refuge.

2. If they answer to this character, though they are not built up into families (*v. 5*): *Unto them will I give a better place and name.* There is a place and a name, which we have from sons and daughters, but there is a better place, and a better name, which those have that are in covenant with God, and it is sufficient to counterbalance the want of the former. A place and a name denote rest and reputation. Though they have not children to be the music of their house, yet they *shall* have a place and a name. God will give it to them by promise; he will himself be both their place and their name. He will give it to them in his house, and within his walls; there they shall have a place. Our relation to God, our interest in Christ, and our hopes of eternal life, are things that give us in God's house a blessed place and a

blessed name. It shall be *an everlasting name, that shall never be cut off.*

II. To those that are themselves the children of strangers.

1. It is here promised that they shall now be welcome to the church, *v. 6, 7.* When God's Israel come out of Babylon, let them bring their neighbours along with them, and God will find room enough for them all in his house. Let them know that the sons of the strangers shall have a place and a name in God's house provided, [1] That they forsake other gods. [2] That they join themselves to him as subjects to their prince and soldiers to their general, by an oath of fidelity and obedience. [3] That they join themselves to him as friends to his honour, *to love the name of the Lord.* Serving him and loving him go together, and that obedience is most acceptable to him, which flows from a principle of love, for then *his commandments are not grievous,* 1 John v. 3. Three things are promised them, in their coming to God: Assistance: *"I will bring them to my holy mountain,* not only bid them welcome when they come, but incline them to come, will show them the way, and lead them in it." Acceptance: *"Their burnt-offerings and their sacrifices shall be accepted on my altar,* and be never the less acceptable for being theirs, though they are sons of the stranger." Comfort: They shall not only be accepted, but they themselves shall have the pleasure of it: *I will make them joyful in my house of prayer.* Many a sorrowful spirit has been made joyful in the house of prayer.

2. It is here promised that multitudes of the Gentiles shall come to the church. *My house shall be called a house of prayer for all people.* Now concerning this house it is promised, (1) That it shall not be a house of sacrifice, but a house of prayer. (2) That it shall be a house of prayer, not for the people of the Jews only, but for all people. This was fulfilled when Peter was made, not only to perceive it himself, but to tell it to the world, that *in every nation he that fears God and works righteousness is accepted of him,* Acts x. 35. It had been declared again and again that *the stranger that comes nigh shall be put to death,* but Gentiles shall now be looked upon no longer as strangers and foreigners, Eph. ii. 19. And it is intimated here (*v.* 8) that when the Gentiles are called in they shall be incorporated into one body with the Jews, that (as Christ says, John x. 16) there may be *one fold and one Shepherd.* There are still more and more to be brought in. The church is a growing body: we may still hope there shall be more, till the mystical body be completed. *Other sheep I have.*

Verses 9–12

From words of comfort the prophet here, by a very sudden change passes to words of reproof in the three following chapters; and therefore some here begin a new sermon. He had assured the people that in due time God would deliver them out of captivity. Now here he shows what their sins and provocations were.

I. Desolating judgments are here summoned, *v.* 9. The sheep of God's pasture are now to be made the sheep of his slaughter, to fall as victims to his justice, and therefore *the beasts of the field and the forest* are called to come and devour. If this refers primarily to the descent made upon them by the Babylonians, and their devouring them, yet it may look further, to the destruction of Jerusalem and the Jewish nation by the Romans. The Roman armies came upon them as beasts of the forest to devour them, and they quite *took away their place and nation.*

II. The reason of these judgments is here given. The shepherds, who should have been the watchmen of the flock, were treacherous and minded not the trust reposed in them, and so the sheep became an easy prey to the wild beasts. Now this may refer to the false prophets in Isaiah's, Jeremiah's, and Ezekiel's time, and to the priests that bore rule by their means. Or it may refer to the wicked princes, the sons of Josiah, that *did evil in the sight of the Lord,* and wicked magistrates under them, who betrayed their trust, and augmented the fierce anger of the Lord instead of doing anything to turn it away. Or it may refer to those who were the nation's watchmen in our Saviour's time, the chief priests and the scribes, who should have given notice to the people of the approach of the Messiah, but who, instead of that, opposed him. *Woe unto thee, O land!* when thy guides are such. 1. They were ignorant of their work, and unfit to teach, being so ill-taught themselves: *His watchmen are blind,* and unfit to be watchmen. Christ describes the Pharisees to be *blind leaders of the blind,* Matt. xv. 14. The beasts of the field come to devour, and the watchmen are blind, and are not aware of them. *They are all ignorant* (v. 10), *shepherds that cannot understand* (v. 11), that know not what is to be done about the sheep. 2. As they were blind watchmen, that could not discern the danger, so they were *dumb dogs,* that would not give warning of it. They barked at God's prophets, bit them and worried the sheep, but made no opposition to the wolf or thief. 3. They were lazy, and loved their ease, *loving to slumber.* 4. They were covetous—*greedy dogs that can never have enough.* All their enquiry is what they shall get, not what they shall do. They are everyone looking to his *own way,* minding his own private interests, and have no regard at all to the public welfare. Everyone is for propagating his own opinion, advancing his own party, while the common concerns of the pubiic are wretchedly neglected and postponed. 5. They were never so much in their element as in their drunken revels (v. 12): *Come* (say they), *I will fetch wine and we will fill ourselves,* or be drunk, *with strong drink.* They courted the people to sit and drink with them, and so confirmed those in their wicked ways, whom they should have reproved. How could they think it any harm to be drunk when the watchmen themselves joined with them and led them to it! 6. They were confident of the continuance of their prosperity and ease; they said, *"To-morrow shall be as this day and much more abundant;* we shall have as much to spend upon our lusts tomorrow as we have today."

Chapter 57

The prophet makes his observations, I. Upon the deaths of good men, ver. 1, 2. II. Upon the gross idolatries and spiritual whoredoms which the Jews were guilty of, and the judgments they were thereby bringing upon themselves, ver. 3–12. III. Upon the gracious returns of God to his people to put an end to their captivity and re-establish their prosperity, ver. 13–21.

Verses 1–2

The prophet had condemned the watchmen for their ignorance and sottishness; here he shows the general stupidity and senselessness of the people.

I. The providence of God removing good men out of this world. *The righteous,* as to this world, *perish;* Piety exempts none from death. Righteousness delivers from the sting of death, but not from the stroke of it. Those are often removed that could be worst spared; the fruitful trees are cut down by death and the barren left still to cumber the ground.

II. The careless world slighting these providences: *No man lays it to heart, none considers it.* There are very few that lament it as a public loss, very few that take notice of it as a public warning. Little children, when they are little, least lament the death of their parents, because they know not what a loss it is to them.

III. The happiness of the righteous in their removal. They *are taken away from the evil to come.* When the deluge is coming they are called into the ark. In wrath to the world those are taken away that stood in the gap to turn away the judgments of God. It is a sign that God intends war when he calls home his ambassadors. The righteous man, when he dies *enters into peace* and *rests in his bed.* Those that practised uprightness, and persevered in it to the end, shall find it well with them when they die. Their souls then enter into peace.

Verses 3–12

A high charge, but a just one, against that wicked generation out of which God's righteous ones were removed, because the world was not worthy of them.

I. The name and title by which they stand indicted, v. 3. They are arraigned as *sons of the sorceress,* or of a witch, *the seed of an adulterer and a whore.* Sin is sorcery and adultery, for it is departing from God and dealing with the devil. They were *children of disobedience.* "Come," says the prophet, "draw near hither, and I will read you your doom; you are *children of transgression, a seed of falsehood"* (v. 4).

II. The particular crimes laid to their charge.

1. Scoffing at God and his word. They were a generation of scorners (v. 4): "*Against whom do you sport yourselves?* You think it is only against the poor prophets, whom you trample upon, but really it is against God himself, whose message they deliver." They made wry mouths at the prophets, and drew out the tongue, contrary to all the laws of good breeding: nor did they treat God's prophets with common civility.

2. Idolatry. This was that sin which the people of the Jews were most notoriously guilty of before the captivity; but that affliction cured them of it. In Isaiah's time it abounded, witness the abominable idolatries of Ahaz (which some think are particularly referred to here) and of Manasseh. (1) They were dotingly fond of their idols, inflamed themselves with them by their violent passions in the worship of them, 1 Kings xviii. 26, 28. They worshipped their idols *under every green tree,* in the open air, and in the shade; the beauty of the green trees made them the more fond of their idols which they worshipped there. (2) They were barbarous and unnaturally cruel in the worship of their idols. They slew their children, and offered them in sacrifice to their idols, in valleys, and *under the cliffs of the rock,* in dark and solitary places, the fittest for such works of darkness. (3) They were insatiable in their idolatries. [1] They had gods of the valleys, which they worshipped by the water side (v. 6): *Among the smooth stones of the valley,* or brook, *is thy portion.* If they saw a smooth carved stone, they were ready to worship it. "*To them hast thou poured a drink-offering, and offered a meat-offering,* as if they had given thee thy meat and drink." Have we taken the true God for our portion? Let us then serve him with our meat and drink, not by depriving ourselves of the use of them, but by eating and drinking to his glory. Here, in a parenthesis, comes in an expression of God's just resentment of this wickedness of theirs: *Should I receive comfort in these*—in such a people as this, who thus serve Baal? *Should I have compassion on these?* (so some), or *should I repent me concerning these?* so others. [2] They had gods of the hills too (v. 7): "*Upon a lofty and high mountain hast thou set thy bed,* thy idol, thy idol's temple and altar, the bed of thy uncleanness, where thou committest spiritual whoredom. *Thither wentest thou up* readily enough, though it was uphill, *to offer sacrifice."* [3] As if these were not enough, they had household-gods too, their *lares* and *penates. Behind the doors and the posts* (v. 8), where the law of God should be written, they

set up the remembrance of their idols to show to others how mindful they were of them, and to put their children in mind of them. They were hardened in their wickedness; they went as publicly, and in as great crowds, to the idol-temples, as ever they had gone to God's house. This was like an impudent harlot, *discovering themselves to another than God.* They *enlarged their bed,* that is, their idol-temples, and (as the margin reads the following words) *thou hewedst it for thyself larger than theirs,* than theirs from whom thou copiedst it, 2 Kings xvi. 10. "*Thou hast made a covenant with them,* with the idols, with the idol-worshippers, to live and die together. *Thou lovedst their bed,* that is, the temple of an idol, wherever thou sawest it."

3. Another sin charged upon them is their trusting to foreign aids and contracting a communion with the Gentile powers (*v.* 9): *Thou wentest to the king* which some understand of *Moloch,* which signifies *a king.* Or it may be meant of the king of Assyria, whom Ahaz made his court to, or of the king of Babylon, whose ambassadors Hezekiah caressed, that they might strengthen themselves by an alliance with them. They went *with ointments and perfumes,* either to beautify their own faces and so make themselves worthy the friendship of the greatest king, or to be presented to those whose favour they desired. They hereby disparaged themselves and laid the honour of their crown and nation in the dust: *Thou didst debase thyself even unto hell.* They debased themselves by truckling to their heathen neighbours, and depending upon them, when they had a God to go to who is all-sufficient and in covenant with them.

III. The aggravations of their sin. 1. They had been tired with disappointments in their wicked courses, and yet they would not be convinced of the folly of them (*v.* 10): "*Thou art wearied in the greatness of thy way;* thou hast undertaken a mighty task, to find out true satisfaction and happiness in that which is vanity and a lie." *Thou art wearied in the multitude,* or *multiplicity, of thy ways* (so some read it): those that forsake the only right way wander endlessly in a thousand by-paths, and lose themselves in the many inventions which they have sought out. 2. Though they were convinced that the way they were in was a sinful way, yet, because they had found sensual pleasure and worldly profit by it, they could not persuade themselves to be sorry for it: "*Thou hast found the life of thy hand*" (or *the living of it*); thou art not grieved, any more than Ephraim when he said (Hos. xii. 8), "*I have become rich; I have found out substance.*" Prosperity in sin is a great bar to conversion from sin. 3. They had dealt very unworthily with God by their sin; for, they pretended that the reason why they left God was because he was too terrible a majesty for them; they must have gods that they could be more familiar with. "But," says God, "*of whom hast thou been afraid or feared, that thou hast lied?* What did I ever do to frighten thee from me?" However, it is certain that they had no true reverence of God. "Thou *hast not remembered me,* neither what I have said nor what I have done, thou hast *not laid them to thy heart,* as thou wouldst have done if thou hadst feared me." They were hardened in their sin by the patience and forbearance of God.

IV. Here is God's resolution to call them to an account (*v.* 12): "*I will declare thy righteousness,* which thou makest thy boast of, and let the world see, and thyself too, to thy confusion, that it is all a sham. I will declare *thy works, they shall not profit thee,* nor turn to any account."

Verses 13–16

I. God shows how insufficient idols and creatures were to succour those that worshipped them (*v.* 13): '*When thou criest* in thy distress and callest for help,

let thy companies deliver thee, thy idol-gods, the troops of the confederate forces which thou hast relied so much upon, let them deliver thee; expect no other relief than what they can give." *The wind shall carry them all away;* they have made themselves as chaff, and therefore the wind will of course hurry them away.

II. He shows that there was a sufficiency, an all-sufficiency, in him. "*He that puts his trust in me,* and in me only, he shall be happy, both for soul and body, for this world and the other." Those that trust in God's providence take the best course to secure their secular interests. They *shall possess the land,* as much of it as is good for them. Those that trust in God's grace take the best course to secure their sacred interests. They *shall inherit my holy mountain.* They shall enjoy the privileges of the church on earth, and be brought at length to the joys of heaven; and no wind shall carry them away. More particularly,

1. The captives, that trust in God, shall be released (*v.* 14): *They shall say* (that is, the messengers of his word, and all the ministers of his providence, in that great event shall say), *Cast you up, cast you up, prepare the way.* When God's time shall have come for their deliverance the way of bringing it about shall be made plain and obstacles shall be removed. This refers to the provision which the gospel, and the grace of it, have made for our ready passage through this world to a better. The way of religion is now cast up; it is a highway; ministers' business is to direct people in it.

2. The contrite, that trust in God, shall be *revived,* v. 15. God's glory appears here very bright, (1) In his greatness and majesty: He is *the high and lofty One that inhabits eternity.* He is *the high and lofty One,* and there is no creature like him, nor any to be compared with him. The language likewise intimates his sovereign dominion over all and the incontestable right he has to give both law and judgment to all. He is both immortal and immutable. There is an infinite rectitude in his nature. His name is *holy,* and all that desire to be acquainted with him must know him as a holy God. "*I dwell in the high and holy place,* and will have all the world to know it." Whoever have any business with God must direct to him as their Father in heaven, for there he dwells. Though he is thus high yet he has respect unto the lowly; he that rides on the heavens by his name JAH stoops to concern himself for poor *widows* and *fatherless,* Ps. lxviii. 4, 5. (2) In his grace and mercy. He has a tender pity for the humble and contrite. If they be his people, he will not overlook them though they are poor and despised and trampled upon by men; but he here refers to the temper of their mind; he will have a tender regard to those who, being in affliction, accommodate themselves to their affliction, and bring their mind to their condition. With these God will dwell. He will visit them graciously, will converse with them by his word and Spirit, as a man does with those of his own family. He that dwells in the highest heavens dwells in the lowest hearts and inhabits sincerity as surely as he inhabits eternity. In these he delights. He will revive their heart and spirit, will speak to them, and work in them by the word and Spirit of his grace.

3. Those with whom he contends, if they trust in him, shall be relieved, and received into favour, *v.* 16. He will *revive the heart of the contrite ones,* for he will not contend for ever. It is not promised that he will never be angry with his people, for their sins are displeasing to him, or that he will never contend with them, for they must expect the rod; but he *will not contend for ever.* As he is not soon angry, so he is not long angry. "If I should contend for ever, the *spirit would fail before me, even the souls which I have made.*" Though the Lord is for the body, yet

he concerns himself chiefly for the souls of his people, that the spirit does not fail, nor its graces and comforts.

Verses 17–21

The body of the people of Israel, in this account of God's dealings with them, is spoken of as a particular person (v. 17, 18), but divided into two sorts, differently dealt with—some who were sons of peace, to whom peace is spoken (v. 19), and others who were not, who have nothing to do with peace, v. 20, 21.

I. The just rebukes which that people were brought under for their sin: *For the iniquity of his covetousness I was wroth, and smote him.* Covetousness was a sin that abounded. Those that did not worship images were yet carried away by this spiritual idolatry: for such is covetousness; it is making money the god, Col. iii. 5. Yet, covetous as they were, in the service of their idols they were prodigal, v. 6. And it is hard to say whether their profuseness in that or their covetousness in everything else was more provoking. Covetousness is an iniquity that is very displeasing to the God of heaven. He smote him, reproved him for it by his prophets, corrected him by his providence, punished him in those very things he so doted upon and was covetous of. God hid himself from him when he was under these rebukes. When we are under the rod, if God manifest himself to us, we may bear it the better; but if he hide himself from us, send us no prophets, speak to us no comfortable word, we are very miserable.

II. Their obstinacy and incorrigibleness under these rebukes: *He went on frowardly in the way of his heart,* in his evil way. See also how insufficient afflictions of themselves are to reform men, unless God's grace work with them.

III. God's wonderful return in mercy to them.

1. The greater part of them went on frowardly, but there were some among them that were mourners for the obstinacy of the rest; and God determines not to contend for ever with them. Such are the riches of divine mercy and grace, and so do they rejoice against judgment, that it follows, *I have seen his ways and will heal him.* Where sin has abounded grace much more abounds. God will first give him grace, and then, and not till then, give him peace: "I have seen his way, that he will never turn to me of himself, and therefore I will turn him." (1) God will heal him of his corrupt and vicious disposition. There is no spiritual disease so inveterate but almighty grace can conquer it. (2) God *will lead him also.* He goes on frowardly, as Saul, yet breathing out threatenings and slaughter, but God will lead him into a better mind, a better path. And then, (3) He will restore those comforts which he had forfeited, and for the return of which he had thus prepared him. There was a wonderful reformation wrought upon the captives in Babylon, and then a wonderful redemption wrought for them.

2. Now, as when that people went into captivity some of them were good figs, others of them bad figs, and accordingly their captivity was to them for their good or for *their hurt* (Jer. xxiv. 8, 9), so, when they came out of captivity, still some of them were good, others bad, and the deliverance was to them accordingly.

(1) To those among them that were good their return out of captivity was peace, a type of the peace which should be preached by Jesus Christ (v. 19): *I create the fruit of the lips, peace.* Creation is out of nothing, and this is surely out of worse than nothing, when God creates matter of praise for those that went on frowardly. In order to this, peace shall be published: *Peace, peace to him that is afar off* as well as *to him that is near.* Peace of conscience, a holy security and serenity of mind, after the many reproaches of conscience and agitations of spirit they

had been under in their captivity. When he speaks peace to us, we must speak praises to him. This peace is itself of God's creating. It is the fruit of preaching lips and praying lips; it is the fruit of Christ's lips, Eph. ii. 17: *He came and preached peace to you who were afar off,* you Gentiles as well as to the Jews, who were nigh—to after-ages, who were afar off in time, as well as to those of the present age.

(2) To those among them that were wicked, though they might return with the rest, their return was no peace, v. 20. The wicked, wherever he is, in Babylon or in Jerusalem, carries about with him the principle of his own uneasiness. The wicked would not be healed by the grace of God and therefore shall not be healed by his comforts. They are always like the sea in a storm, for they carry about with them, [1] Unmortified corruptions. They are not cured and their ungoverned lusts and passions make them like the troubled sea. [2] Unpacified consciences. They are under a frightful apprehension of guilt and wrath, like Cain, who always dwelt in the land of shaking. It is a certain truth, what this prophet had said before (ch. xlviii. 22), and here repeats (v. 21), *There is no peace to the wicked,* no reconciliation to God, while they go on still in their trespasses.

CHAPTER 58

The prophet has his commission renewed to reprove the sinners in Zion, ver. 1. It is intended for admonition and warning to all hypocrites, and is not to be confined to those of any one age. Some refer it primarily to those at that time when Isaiah prophesied; see chap. xxxiii. 14; xxix. 13. Others to the captives in Babylon, the wicked among them. They thought to shelter themselves with their external performances, particularly their fastings, which they kept up in Babylon, and for some time after their return to their own land, Zech. vii. 3, &c. Others think it is principally intended against the hypocrisy of the Jews, especially the Pharisees before and in our Saviour's time: they boasted of their fastings, but Christ (as the prophet here) showed them their transgressions (Matt. xxiii). Observe, I. The plausible profession of religion which they made, ver. 2. II. The boasts they made of that profession, and the blame they laid upon God for taking no notice, ver. 3. III. The sins they are charged with, which spoiled the acceptableness of their fasts, ver. 4, 5. IV. Instructions given them how to keep fasts aright, ver. 6, 7. V. Precious promises made to those who do so keep fasts, ver. 8–12. VI. The like precious promises made to those that sanctify sabbaths aright, ver. 13, 14.

Verses 1–2

When our Lord Jesus promised to send the Comforter he added, *When he shall come he shall convince* (John xvi. 7, 8); for conviction must prepare for comfort. God had appointed this prophet to comfort his people (ch. xl. 1); here he appoints him to convince them, and show them their sins.

I. He must tell them how bad they really were, v. 1. 1. He must deal faithfully and plainly with them. Though they are called *the people of God* and *the house of Jacob,* do not flatter them, but show them their transgressions, what sins are committed by them which they do not acknowledge to be sins; though in some things they are reformed, in other things they are still as bad as ever. 2. He must *cry aloud, and not spare,* not spare them, though he get their ill-will by it and get himself an ill name, yet he must not spare.

II. He must acknowledge how good they seemed to be, notwithstanding (v. 2): *Yet they seek me daily.* They pleaded that they could see no transgressions for they were diligent and constant in attending on God's worship—and what more would he have of them? Now,

1. He owns the fact to be true. As far as hypocrites do that which is good, they shall not be denied the praise of it. It is owned that they have a form of godliness. (1) They go to church, and observe their hours of prayer: *They seek me daily.* (2) They love to hear good preaching: *They delight to know my ways,* as Herod, who heard John gladly. (3) They

seem to take pleasure in the exercises of religion. *They delight in approaching to God,* not for his sake to whom they approach, but for the sake of some pleasing circumstance, the company, or the festival. (4) They are inquisitive concerning their duty and seem desirous only to know it: *They ask of me the ordinances of justice,* the rules of piety in the worship of God, the rules of equity in their dealings with men, both which are ordinances of justice. (5) They appear to the eye of the world as if they made conscience of doing their duty: *They are as a nation that did righteousness and forsook not the ordinances of their God;* others took them for such, and they themselves pretended to be such. Men may go a great way towards heaven and yet come short; may go to hell with a good reputation. But,

2. He intimates that this was so far from being a cover for their sin that really it was an aggravation of it.

Verses 3–7

I. The pleasure which these hypocrites conceived against God (*v.* 3): *Wherefore have we fasted, say they, and thou seest not?* Thus they went in the way of Cain, who was angry at God, and resented it as a gross affront that his offering was not accepted. They magnify their own performances: "*We have fasted and afflicted our souls;* we have not only sought God daily (*v.* 2), but have kept certain times of more solemn devotion." Some think this refers to the yearly fast (which was called *the day of atonement*), others to occasional fasts. The Pharisee (Luke xviii. 12) said *I fast twice in the week.* They thought God should take great notice of them, for their services. They charge God with injustice and partiality, and seem resolved to throw up their religion, and justify themselves in doing so with this, that they had found no *profit in praying* to God, Job xxi. 14, 15; Mal. iii. 14.

II. The true reason why God did not accept their fastings, nor answer the prayers they made on their fast-days; it was because they did not fast aright. They fasted indeed, but they did not, as the Ninevites, turn everyone from his evil way; but *in the day of their fast,* they went on to *find pleasure,* that is, to do whatsoever seemed right in their own eyes, *making their inclinations their law.* 1. They were as covetous and unmerciful as ever: "*You exact all your labours* from your servants, and will neither release them according to the law nor relax the rigour of their servitude. *You exact all your dues,* your *debts*" (so some read it); you are as rigorous and severe in extorting what you demand from those that are poor as ever you were, though it was at the close of the yearly fast that the release was proclaimed. 2. They were contentious and spiteful (*v.* 4): *Behold, you fast for strife and debate.* When they proclaimed a fast they pretended to search for those sins which provoked God, and under that pretence perhaps particular persons were falsely accused, as Naboth in the day of Jezebel's fast, 1 Kings xxi. 12. Thus, instead of judging themselves, which is the proper work of a fast-day, they condemned one another. They *fasted for strife,* with emulation which should make the most plausible appearance on a fast-day. Now while they thus *continued in sin,* God would not allow them the use of such solemnities: "*You shall not fast* at all if you fast *as you do this day, causing your voice to be heard on high. Bring me no more* of these empty, noisy, vain oblations," ch. i. 13.

III. Plain instructions given concerning the true nature of a religious fast.

1. In general, a fast is intended, (1) For the honouring and pleasing of God. (2) For the humbling and abasing of ourselves. A fast is *a day to afflict the soul;* if it do not express a genuine sorrow for sin, and do not promote a real mortification of sin, it is not a fast.

2. It concerns us therefore to enquire, on a fast-day, what it is that will be acceptable to God, and afflictive to our corrupt nature.

(1) We are here told negatively what is not the fast that God has chosen. [1] It is not enough to put on a melancholy aspect, to bow down the head like a bulrush that is withered and broken: as the hypocrites, that were *of a sad countenance, and disfigured their faces, that they might appear unto men to fast,* Matt. vi. 16. The publican, whose heart was truly humbled, *would not so much as lift up his eyes to heaven* (Luke xviii. 13); but when it was only mimicked, as here, it was justly ridiculed: it is but *hanging down the head like a bulrush.* [2] It is not enough to do penance, to mortify the body a little, while the body of sin is untouched. *Wilt thou call this a fast?* No, it is but the shadow of a fast.

(2) We are here told positively what is the fast that God has chosen. It *is not afflicting the soul for a day* (as some read it, *v.* 5); it must be the business of our whole lives. It is here required, [1] That we be just to those with whom we have dealt hardly (*v.* 6): *To loose the bands of wickedness,* the bands which we have wickedly tied, and by which others are bound. "Let the prisoner for debt that has nothing to pay be discharged, let the vexatious action be quashed, let the servant that is forcibly detained beyond the time of his servitude be released, and thus *break every yoke;* not only let go those that are wrongfully kept under the yoke, but break the yoke of slavery itself." [2] That we be charitable to those that stand in need of charity, *v.* 7. Contribute to the rescue and ransom of those that are oppressed by others, to the release of captives and the payment of the debts of the poor. This then, is the fast that God has chosen. *First,* To provide food for those that want it. It is *to break thy bread to the hungry.* It must be *thy* bread, that which is honestly got, the bread of thy allowance. We must deny ourselves, that we may have to give to him that needeth. This is the true fast, to break thy bread to the hungry, to give them loaves and not to put them off with scraps. *Secondly,* To provide lodging for those that want it: It is *to take care of the poor that are cast out.* "If they suffer unjustly do not only pay for their lodging, but, which is a greater act of kindness, bring them to thy own house. Be not forgetful to entertain strangers: for thou mayest entertain Christ himself. *I was a stranger and you took me in.*" *Thirdly,* To provide clothing for those that want it: "*When thou seest the naked, that you cover him; hide not thyself from thy own flesh.*" Some understand it of a man's own relations. Others understand it more generally; all that partake of the human nature are to be looked upon as our own flesh, for have we not all one Father?

Verses 8–12

Precious promises for those to feast freely and cheerfully who keep the fast that God has chosen.

I. A further account of the duty to be done (*v.* 9, 10). 1. We must abstain from all acts of violence and fraud. "Those must be *taken away from the midst of thee,* from the midst of *thy person,* out of *thy heart*" (so some); "thou must not only refrain from the practice of injury, but mortify in thee all inclination towards it." Or *from the midst of thy people.* Those in authority must do all they can to prevent oppression in all within their jurisdiction. They must not only *break the yoke* (*v.* 6), but take away the yoke; they must likewise *forbear threatening* (Eph. vi. 9) and take away the *putting forth of the finger,* to point at those that are poor and in misery, and so to expose them to contempt. And let them not *speak vanity,* flattery to one another, but let all conversation be governed by sincerity. 2. We must abound in all acts of charity and beneficence. We must give freely and cheerfully, and from a principle of charity. We must *draw out our soul to the hungry* (v. 10), not only draw out the money, but do this from the heart with a tender affection to such as we see to be in misery. Let the heart go along with the gift; for God loves a cheerful giver, and so does a poor man too. When our Lord Jesus healed and fed the multitude it was as having compassion on them. We must give plentifully and largely, so as not to tantalize, but to *satisfy, the afflicted soul.*

II. A full account of the blessings and benefits which attend the performance of this duty. God will surprise them with the return of mercy after great affliction, which shall be as welcome as the light of the morning after a long and dark night (v. 8): *Then shall thy light break forth as the morning* and (v. 10) *thy light shall rise in obscurity.* Those that are cheerful in doing good God will make cheerful in enjoying good; and this also is a special *gift of God,* Eccles. ii. 24. Those that have helped others out of trouble will obtain help of God when it is their turn. Good works shall be recompensed with a good name; this is included in that *light which rises out of obscurity.* "*Thy righteousness shall go before* thee as thy vanguard, to secure thee from enemies that charge thee in the front, and *the glory of the Lord shall be thy rearward,* the gathering host, to bring up those of thee that are weary and are left behind, and to secure thee from the enemies, that, like Amalek, fall upon thy rear." Good people are safe on all sides. Their defence is their righteousness, and the glory of the Lord, that is, as some suppose, Christ. He it is that is our rearward, on whom alone we can depend for safety when our sins pursue us and are ready to take hold on us. "*Then shalt thou call,* on thy fast-days, which ought to be days of prayer, *and the Lord shall answer,* shall give thee the things thou callest to him for; *thou shalt cry* when thou art in any distress or sudden fright, *and he shall say, Here I am.*" Wherever they are praying, God says, "Here I am hearing: I am *in the midst of you.*" He is *nigh unto them in all things,* Deut. iv. 7. *The Lord shall guide thee continually.* While we are here, in the wilderness of this world, we have need of continual direction from heaven. To a good man God gives not only wisdom and knowledge, but joy; he is satisfied in himself with the testimony of his conscience and the assurances of God's favour. These will *satisfy thy soul,* will put gladness into thy heart, even *in the drought* of affliction; *these will make fat thy bones,* will give thee that pleasure which will be a support to thee as the bones to the body. "*Thou shalt be like a watered garden,* fruitful in graces *and like a spring of water, whose waters fail not* either in droughts or in frosts." As a spring of water, though it is continually sending forth its streams, is yet always full, so the charitable man abounds in good as he abounds in doing good, and is never the poorer for his liberality. "*Those that* hereafter *shall be of thee,* thy posterity, shall be serviceable to their generation, as thou art to thine." They *shall build the old waste places,* which had lain long desolate. This was fulfilled when the captives, after their return, repaired the cities of Judah, and many of those in Israel. They shall carry on and finish that good work which was begun long before. *They shall raise up* to the top that building *the foundation of* which was laid long since and has been for *many generations* in the rearing. This was fulfilled when the building of the temple was revived after it had stood still for many years, Ezra v. 2. They shall have the blessing and praise of all about them: "*Thou shalt be called the repairer of the breach.*" "Thou shalt be *the restorer of paths,* safe and quiet paths, not only to travel in, but *to dwell in,* so safe and quiet that people shall make no difficulty of building their houses by the roadside."

The sum is that, if they keep such feasts as God has chosen, he will settle them again in their former peace and prosperity, and there shall be none to make them afraid.

Verses 13–14

Great stress was always laid upon the due observance of the sabbath day, and it was particularly required from the Jews when they were captives in Babylon, because by keeping that day, in honour of the Creator, they distinguished themselves from the worshippers of the gods that have not made the heavens and the earth. See *ch.* lvi. 1, 2.

I. How the sabbath is to be sanctified (v. 13); this law of the sabbath is still binding to us on our Lord's day.

1. Nothing must be done that puts contempt upon the sabbath day. We must *turn away our foot from the sabbath,* from trampling upon it; we must turn away our foot *from doing our pleasure on that holy day,* that is, from living at large, and taking a liberty to do what we please on sabbath days, without the control and restraint of conscience. On sabbath days we must not walk in *our own ways* (that is, not follow our callings), not *find our own pleasure* (that is, not follow our sports and recreations); nay, we must not *speak our own words,* for we must make religion the business of the day. We must speak of divine things as we sit in the house and walk by the way. In all we say and do we must put a difference between this day and other days.

2. We must call it *a delight,* not a *task and a burden.* We must not only count it a delight, but call it so. We must call it so to God, in thanksgiving for it. We must call it so to others, to invite them to come and share in the pleasure of it; and we must call it so to ourselves, that we may not entertain the least thought of wishing the sabbath gone that we may sell corn.

II. The reward of sabbath-sanctification, *v.* 14.

1. We shall have the comfort of it; the work will be its own wages. *If we call the sabbath a delight, then shall we delight ourselves in the Lord;* he will more and more manifest himself to us. If we go about duty with cheerfulness, we shall go from it with satisfaction.

2. We shall have the honour of it: *I will cause thee to ride upon the high places of the earth,* which denotes not only a great security, but great dignity. Those that honour God and his sabbath he will thus honour. If God by his grace enable us to live above the world, and so to manage it as not to be hindered by it, then he makes us *to ride on the high places of the earth.*

3. We shall have the profit of it: I will *feed thee with the heritage of Jacob thy father,* that is, with all the blessings of the covenant and all the precious products of Canaan (which was a type of heaven), for these were the heritage of Jacob.

CHAPTER 59

In this chapter we have sin appearing exceedingly sinful, and grace appearing exceedingly gracious; and, as what is here said of the sinner's sin (ver. 7, 8) is applied to the general corruption of mankind (Rom. iii. 15), so what is here said of a Redeemer (ver. 20) is applied to Christ, Rom. xi. 26. I. This people had themselves stopped the current of God's favours to them, ver. 1–8. II. They are told what the judgments were which they had brought upon their own heads (ver. 9–11) and what the sins were which provoked God to send those judgments, ver. 12–15. III. It is here promised, that notwithstanding this, God would work deliverance for them (ver. 16–19), and would reserve mercy in store for them and entail it upon them, ver. 20, 21.

Verses 1–8

The mistake of those who had been quarrelling with God because they had not the deliverances wrought for which they had been fasting and praying, *ch.* lviii. 3.

I. It was not owing to God. He was still as able

to help as ever: *His hand is not shortened,* his power is not lessened. God can reach as far as ever and with as strong a hand as ever, that has not waxed weak nor is it at all shortened. *Has the Lord's hand waxed short?* (says God to Moses, Num. xi. 23). No, it has not; he will not have it thought so. Neither length of time nor strength of enemies, no, nor weakness of instruments, can shorten or straiten the power of God. He was still as ready and willing to help as ever in answer to prayer: *His ear is not heavy, that it cannot hear.* More is implied than is expressed; not only his ear is not heavy, but he is quick of hearing. *Even before they call he answers,* ch. lxv. 24. If your prayers be not answered it is not because God is weary of hearing prayer, but because we are weary of praying, not because his ear is heavy when we speak to him, but because our ears are heavy when he speaks to us.

II. They stood in their own light and put a bar in their own door. *Your iniquities have kept good things from you,* Jer. v. 25.

1. The mischief sin does. It hinders God's mercies; it is a partition wall between us and God. Sin *hides his face from us* (which denotes great displeasure, Deut. xxxi. 17). Sin in its consequences is exceedingly hurtful, separating us from God, and so separating us not only *from all good,* but *to all evil* (Deut. xxix. 21).

2. The prophet shows how many and great their iniquities were, according to the charge given him (ch. lviii. 1) *to show God's people their transgressions.* He must begin with their thoughts, for there all sin begins: *Their thoughts are thoughts of iniquity,* v. 7. Their imaginations are so (v. 4): *They conceive mischief* and then they *bring forth iniquity.* Though it is in pain perhaps that the iniquity is brought forth, through the oppositions of Providence and the checks of their own consciences, yet, when they have compassed their wicked purpose, they look upon it with as much pride as if it were a *man-child born into the world;* thus, *when lust has conceived, it bringeth forth sin,* James i. 15. This is called (v. 5) *hatching the cockatrice's egg and weaving the spider's web.* The spider's web is a weak insignificant thing, which the besom sweeps away in an instant: such are the thoughts which worldly men entertain, building castles in the air. They hatch the eggs of the cockatrice or adder, which are poisonous and produce venomous creatures; such are the thoughts of the wicked who delight in doing mischief. *He that eats of their eggs* (that is, has any dealings with them) *dies* (that is, he is in danger of having some mischief or other done him), *and that which is crushed,* or which begins to be hatched, *breaks out into a viper,* which you meddle with at your peril. Out of this abundance of wickedness in the heart their mouth speaks, and yet it does not always speak out, but for the more effectually compassing the mischievous design, it is covered *with much fair speech* (v. 3): *Your lips have spoken lies;* and again (v. 4), *They speak lies,* pretending kindness when they intend mischief. *Your tongue has muttered perverseness.* Backbiters are called *whisperers.* They were guilty of shedding innocent blood: *Your hands are defiled with blood* (v. 3); blood is defiling; it leaves an indelible stain of guilt upon the conscience, which nothing but the blood of Christ can cleanse. *Their feet ran to this evil. They made haste to shed innocent blood.* With other iniquities are their *fingers defiled* (v. 3); they make everything their own that they can lay their hands on. *They trust in vanity* (v. 4); they depend upon their arts to enrich themselves, and their deceiving others will but deceive themselves. *The act of violence is in their hands,* according to the arts of violence that are in their heads and the thoughts of violence in their hearts. No methods are taken to redress these grievances and reform these abuses (v. 4): *None calls for justice.* When justice is not done

there is blame to be laid not only upon the magistrates, but upon the people. Private persons ought to contribute to the public good by discovering secret wickedness. Truth is opposed, and there is not any that *pleads for it,* not any that has the courage to confront a prosperous fraud. *The way of peace* is as little regarded as the way of truth; they *know it not,* that is, they never study the things that make for peace. *There is no judgment in their goings;* they have not any sense of justice in their dealings. Those that practise iniquity *trust in vanity,* v. 4. *Their webs,* which they weave with so much art and industry, *shall not become garments, neither shall they cover themselves,* either for shelter or for ornament, *with their works,* v. 6. There is nothing to be got by sin, and so it will appear when profit and loss come to be compared. Those paths of iniquity are *crooked paths* (v. 8), which will perplex them, but will never bring them to their journey's end.

Verses 9–15

Sin is the great mischief-maker. *Here* it seems to be spoken by the people to God, as an acknowledgment of their humble submission to the justice of God's proceedings.

I. They acknowledge that God had contended with them, v. 9–11. 1. They were in distress, oppressed by their enemies, and God did not appear for them, to plead their just and injured cause: "*Judgment is far from us, neither does justice overtake us,* v. 9. Though, as to our persecutors, we are sure that we have right on our side, and they are the wrong-doers, yet we have not done justice to one another, and therefore God suffers our enemies to deal thus unjustly with us." 2. Their expectations were sadly disappointed: *We wait for light* as those that wait for the morning, *but behold obscurity; we look for judgment, but there is none* (v. 11); we look for salvation, because God (we think) has promised it, and we have prayed for it with fasting; but still *we walk in darkness.* 3. They were at their wits' end (v. 10): *We grope for the wall like the blind.* Those that love darkness rather than light shall have their doom accordingly. 4. They sunk into despair. *We are in desolate places as dead men.* The state of the Jews in Babylon is represented by *dead and dry bones* (Ezek. xxxvii. 12) and the explanation of the comparison there (v. 11) explains this text: *Our hope is lost; we are cut off for our parts. We roar like bears;* the sorrow of others was silent, and preyed more upon their spirits: *We mourn sore like doves,* like doves of the valleys.

II. They acknowledge that they had provoked God, v. 12–15. 1. They owned that they had sinned. We are witnesses against ourselves: *As for our iniquities, we know them,* though we may have foolishly endeavoured to cover them. 2. They owned the evil of sin; it is *transgressing and lying against the Lord,* v. 13. The sins of God's people are upon *this* account worse than the sins of others, that in transgressing they *lie against the Lord;* they misrepresent him, perfidiously break covenant with him, which is *lying against him.* 3. They owned that there was a general decay of moral honesty; and those who were false to their God were unfaithful to one another. They *spoke oppression,* though it was a revolt from truth. They *conceived and uttered words of falsehood.* Many a word of falsehood is uttered in haste, for want of consideration; but these were conceived and uttered, were uttered deliberately and of malice prepense. They were words of falsehood, and yet they are said to be uttered *from the heart,* because they agreed with the malice and wickedness of the heart, and were the natural language of that; it was a *double heart,* Ps. xii. 2. 4. They owned that that was not done which might have been done to reform the land and to amend what was amiss, v. 14. "*Judgment,* that should run in its course like a river, like a mighty stream, *is turned away backward,* a contrary course. The administration of justice has become but a cover to the greatest injustice. *Justice stands afar off,* even from our courts of judicature. *Truth is fallen in the street, yea, truth fails* in common conversation, so that one knows not whom to believe nor whom to trust." 5. They owned that there was a prevailing enmity to those that were good: *He that does evil goes unpunished,* but *he that departs from evil makes himself a prey.* It is crime with them for a man not to do as they do, and they treat *him* as an enemy who will not partake with them in their wickedness. *He that departs from evil is accounted mad;* so the margin reads. 6. They owned that all this could not but be displeasing to the God of heaven. Though it was done secretly, and gilded over with specious pretences, yet it could not be concealed from his all-seeing eye. Though the sin displeased him, he would soon have been reconciled to the sinners upon their returning from their evil way.

Verses 16–21

Sin abounded in the former part of the chapter; grace does much more abound in these verses.

I. Why God wrought salvation, notwithstanding their provocations. It was purely for his own name's sake.

1. He took notice of their weakness and wickedness: *He saw that there was no man* that would do anything for the support of religion and virtue among them. Most were wicked, and those that were not so were weak. *There was no intercessor,* none to intercede with God (*v.* 16), no advocate to speak a good word for those who were made a prey because they kept their integrity, *v.* 15. They complained that God did not appear for them (*ch.* lviii. 3); but God with much more reason complains that they did nothing for themselves.

2. He engaged his own strength and righteousness for them. They shall be saved. The work of reformation (that is the first and principle article of the salvation) shall be wrought by the immediate influences of the divine grace on men's consciences. When God stirred up the spirit of Cyrus, and brought his people out of Babylon, *not by might, nor by power, but by the Spirit of the Lord of hosts,* then his own arm, which is never shortened, brought salvation. Divine justice, which by their sins they had armed against them, through grace appears for them. Though they can expect no favour as due to them, yet he will, in righteousness, punish the enemies of his people; see Deut. ix. 5. *Not for thy righteousness, but for the wickedness of these nations* they are driven out. In our redemption by Christ, since we had no righteousness of our own to produce, he brought in a righteousness by the merit and mediation of his own Son (it is called *the righteousness which is of God by faith,* Phil. iii. 9). *He put on righteousness as a breastplate,* securing his own honour, as a breastplate does the vitals, and put *a helmet of salvation upon his head.* When righteousness is his coat of arms, salvation is his crest. In allusion to this, among the pieces of a Christian's armour we find *the breastplate of righteousness,* and for a helmet *the hope of salvation* (Eph. vi. 14–17; 1 Thess. v. 8), and it is called *the armour of God,* because he wore it first and so fitted it for us. Because they have no spirit or zeal to do anything for themselves, God will *put on the garments of vengeance for clothing, and clothe himself with zeal as a cloak;* he will make his justice upon the enemies of his church and people to appear evident.

II. The salvation that shall be wrought by the righteousness of God himself.

1. There shall be a present temporal salvation wrought for the Jews in Babylon, or elsewhere in distress and captivity. This is promised (*v.* 18, 19) as a type of something further. It is here promised, (1) That God will reckon with his enemies and will render to them according to their deeds, to the enemies of his people abroad, to the enemies of justice and truth at home, for they also are God's enemies; he will deal with both as they have deserved, *according to former retributions;* as he has rendered to his enemies formerly, *fury to his adversaries, recompense to his enemies;* his fury shall not exceed the rules of justice. Even *to the islands,* that lie most remote, if they have appeared against him, *he will repay recompense;* for *his hand shall find out all his enemies* (Ps. xxi. 8), and his arrows reach them. (2) That, whatever attempts the enemies of God's people may afterwards make to disturb their peace, they shall be brought to nought: *When the enemy shall come in like a flood,* then *the Spirit of the Lord shall lift up a standard against him,* and so (as the margin reads it) *put him to flight.* (3) That all this should redound to the glory of God and the advancement of religion in the world (*v.* 19). This had its full accomplishments in gospel times, when many came *from the east and west,* to fill up the places of *the children of the kingdom* that were *cast out,* when there were set up eastern and western churches, Matt. viii. 11.

2. There shall be a more glorious salvation wrought out by the Messiah in the fulness of time. The two great promises relating to that salvation:

(1) That the Son of God shall come to us to be our Redeemer (*v.* 20). The coming of Christ as the Redeemer is the summary of all the promises both of the Old and New Testament, and this was the redemption in Jerusalem which the believing Jews looked for, Luke ii. 38. Christ is our *Goël,* our next kinsman, that redeems both the person and the estate of the poor debtor. [1] The place where this Redeemer shall appear: He *shall come to Zion,* for there, on that holy hill, the Lord would set him up as his King, Ps. ii. 6. Zion was a type of the gospel church. [2] The persons that shall have the comfort of the Redeemer's coming, knowing that their redemption draws nigh. He shall come *to those that turn from ungodliness in Jacob,* but to those only that turn from transgression, that repent, and reform.

(2) That the Spirit of God shall come to us to be our sanctifier, *v.* 21. But the promise is made to a single person—*My Spirit that is upon thee,* being directed either, [1] To Christ as the head of the church, who received that he might give. Or, [2] To the church; and so it is a promise of the continuance and perpetuity of the church in the world to the end of time, parallel to those promises that the throne and seed of Christ shall endure for ever, Ps. lxxxix. 29, 36; xxii. 30. *Instead of the fathers shall be the children.* It shall be kept up—*henceforth and for ever,* even *unto the end of the world.* The Spirit that was upon Christ shall always continue in the hearts of the faithful; there shall be some in every age on whom he shall work, and in whom he shall dwell, and thus the Comforter shall abide with the church for ever, John xiv. 16. There shall be some in every age who, *believing with the heart* unto righteousness, shall *with the tongue make confession unto salvation.* On these foundations the church is built, stands firmly, and shall stand for ever, Christ himself being the chief corner-stone.

CHAPTER 60

This whole chapter is a part of God's covenant with his church. The long continuance of the church, even unto the utmost ages of time, was there promised, and here the large extent of the church, even unto the utmost regions of the earth. It is here promised, I. That the church shall be enlightened, ver. 1, 2. II. That it shall be enlarged, ver. 3–8. III. That the new converts shall be greatly serviceable to the church, ver. 9–13. IV. That the church shall be in great honour among men, ver. 14–16.

V. That it shall enjoy a profound peace and tranquillity, ver. 17, 18. VI. That, the members of it being all righteous, the glory and joy of it shall be everlasting, ver. 19–22. Now this has some reference to the peaceable and prosperous condition which the Jews were in after their return into their own land; but it looks further, and was to have its full accomplishment in the kingdom of the Messiah, the enlargement of that kingdom by the bringing in of the Gentiles into it, and the spiritual blessings in heavenly things by Christ Jesus with which it should be enriched.

Verses 1–8

It is here promised that the gospel temple shall be very light and very large.

I. It shall be very light: *Thy light has come.* When the Jews returned out of captivity they had *light and gladness, and joy and honour*; they then were made to *know the Lord* and to *rejoice in his great goodness*. 1. What this light is, and whence it springs: *The Lord shall arise upon thee* (v. 2), *the glory of the Lord* (v. 1) *shall be seen upon thee.* When God appears to us, then *the glory of the Lord rises upon us* as the morning light; when he appears for us, then his glory is seen upon us. When Christ arose as the sun of righteousness, and in him *the day-spring from on high visited us*, then *the glory of the Lord was* seen upon us, the glory *as of the first-begotten of the Father.* 2. What a foil there shall be to this light: *Darkness shall cover the earth;* but, though it be gross darkness, that shall overspread the people, yet the church shall have light at the same time. 3. What is the duty which the rising of this light calls for: "*Arise, shine;* not only receive this light, and" (as the margin reads it) "*be enlightened by it*, but reflect this light: *arise and shine* with rays borrowed from it."

II. It shall be very large. When the Jews were settled in their own land, after their captivity, many of the people of the land joined themselves to them; but we must look further, to the bringing of the Gentiles into the gospel church, not their flocking to one particular place. There is no place now that is the centre of the church's unity; but the promise respects their flocking to Christ, and coming by faith, and hope, and holy love, into that family which is named from him, Eph. iii. 15. *You have come unto Mount Zion, to the city of the living God, the heavenly Jerusalem*, which serves for a key to this prophecy, Eph. ii. 19. 1. What shall invite such multitudes to the church: "They shall *come to thy light and to the brightness of thy rising*," v. 3. This light which discovers so much of God and his goodwill to man, by which life and immortality are brought to light, this shall invite all the serious well-affected part of mankind to come and join themselves to the church. The purity and love of the primitive Christians, their heavenly-mindedness, and patient sufferings, which drew many into it. 2. What multitudes shall come to the church. Great numbers *shall come, Gentiles* (or *nations*) *of those that are saved. Nations* shall be *discipled* (Matt. xxviii. 19). They come from all parts (v. 4): *Lift up thy eyes round about, and see* them coming, *devout men out of every nation under heaven*, Acts ii. 5. Sons and daughters shall come in the most dutiful manner, as thy sons and thy daughters, resolved to be of thy family. Those that would enjoy the dignities and privileges of Christ's family must submit to the discipline of it. 3. What they shall bring with them and what advantage shall accrue to the church by their accession to it. The merchants shall write *holiness to the Lord* upon their merchandise and their hire, as *ch.* xxiii. 18. "*The abundance of the sea* (the fish, the pearls) or that which is imported by sea, *shall* all *be converted to thee* and to thy use." The wealth of the rich merchants shall be laid out in works of piety and charity. The mighty men of the nations shall employ their might in the service of the church: "*The forces of the Gentiles shall come unto thee*, to guard thy coasts, and fight thy battles." *The camels and dromedaries that bring gold and incense, those of Midian and Sheba*, shall bring the richest commodities of their country, not to trade with, but to honour God with. This was in part fulfilled when the *wise men of the east came* to Christ, and presented to him treasures of *gold, frankincense, and myrrh*, Matt. ii. 11. Great numbers of sacrifices shall be brought to God's altar, and, though brought by Gentiles, shall find acceptance, v. 7. *Kedar* was famous for flocks, and probably the fattest rams were those of *Nebaioth*; these shall come up with acceptance on God's altar. This was fulfilled when by the decree of Darius the governors beyond the rivers were ordered to furnish the temple at Jerusalem *with bullocks, rams, and lambs, for the burnt-offering of the God of heaven*, Ezra vi. 9.

4. How God shall be honoured by the increase of the church! When they bring their gold and incense it shall be to *show forth the praises of the Lord*, v. 6. The church is the house of God's glory, where he manifests his glory to his people and receives that homage by which they do honour to him. And it is for the glory of this house that the Gentiles shall bring their offerings to it (v. 7).

5. How the church shall herself be affected with this increase of her numbers, v. 5. "*Thou shalt see* and *flow together*" (or flow to and fro). There shall be a mixture of fear with this joy: "*Thy heart shall fear*, doubting whether it be lawful to *go in to the uncircumcised* and *eat with them*." Peter was so impressed with this fear that he needed a vision and voice from heaven to help him over it, Acts x. 28. "When this fear is conquered thy heart shall be so enlarged that thou shalt have room in it for all the Gentile converts." These converts flocking to the church shall be greatly admired (v. 8): *Who are these that fly as a cloud?* The conversion of souls is flying like a cloud in great multitudes, yet with great unanimity, as a cloud flying on the wings of the wind. They shall *fly as doves to their windows;* on the wings of the harmless dove, which flies low, denoting innocency and humility. They fly to Christ, to the church, as doves, by instinct, to their own windows, to their own home.

Verses 9–14

The promises made to the church are repeated for the encouragement of the Jews after their return out of captivity, but looking further, to the enlargement and advancement of the gospel church.

I. God will be very gracious and propitious to them. "All shall now make court to thee, *for in my wrath I smote thee*, while thou wast in captivity, but now *in my favour have I had mercy on thee*, and therefore have all this mercy in store for thee."

II. Many shall be brought into the church, even from far countries (v. 9): *Surely the isles shall wait for me*, shall welcome the gospel. *The ships of Tarshish*, transport-ships, shall carry the ministers of the church to remote parts, to preach the gospel. They live at such a distance that they cannot bring their flocks, so turned them into money to *bring their silver and gold with them.*

III. Those that come into the church shall be welcome. "*Therefore thy gates shall be open continually* (v. 11), not only because thou hast no reason to fear thy enemies, but because thou hast reason to expect thy friends." It is usual with us to leave our doors open, or leave someone ready to open them, all night, if we look for a child or a guest to come in late. The gate of mercy is always open, night and day, or shall soon be opened to those that knock.

IV. All that are about the church shall be made in some way or other serviceable to it. So here (v. 10), "Even *the sons of strangers*, that have neither knowledge of thee nor kindness for thee, *shall build *up thy wall, and their kings shall* in that and other things *minister unto thee.*" This was fulfilled when the king of Persia, and the governors of the provinces by his order, were aiding Nehemiah in building the wall about Jerusalem. Even those that do not belong to the church may be a protection to it, for (*v.* 12), *The nation and kingdom that will not serve thee shall perish.*

V. There shall be abundance of beauty added to the ordinances of divine worship (*v.* 13): *The glory of Lebanon*, the strong and stately cedars that grow there, *shall come unto thee*, as of old to Solomon, when he built the temple (2 Chron. ii. 16), and with them shall be brought other timber, proper for the carved work. The temple, the *place of God's sanctuary*, shall be not only rebuilt, but beautified. It was likewise *adorned with goodly stones and gifts* (Luke xxi. 5), yet so slightly did Christ speak of them there that we must suppose it to have its full accomplishment in the beauties of holiness.

VI. The church shall appear truly great and honourable, *v.* 14. The people of the Jews, after their return out of captivity, by degrees became more considerable. This prophecy is further fulfilled when those that have been enemies to the church are wrought upon by the grace of God to see their error: "*The sons of those that afflicted thee*, if not they themselves, yet their children, shall crouch to thee, shall beg pardon for their folly and beg an interest in thy favour and admission into thy family," 1 Sam. ii. 36. The poor oppressed ones of the church shall have an opportunity of doing good to those who have done evil to them and saving those alive who have afflicted and despised them. It is a pleasure to a good man, and he accounts it an honour, to show mercy to those with whom he has found no mercy.

Verses 15–22

The happy and glorious state of the church is further foretold, referring ultimately to the Christian church under the type of that little gleam of outward peace which the Jews sometimes enjoyed after their return out of captivity.

I. Compared with what it had been.

1. She had been despised, but now she should be honoured, *v.* 15, 16. Jerusalem had been forsaken and hated. But now it shall be *the joy* of good people for *many generations*. Yet considering how short Jerusalem's excellency was, and how short it came of the vast compass of this promise, we must look for the full accomplishment of it in the perpetual excellencies of the gospel church, and the glorious privileges and advantages of the Christian religion. She shall find herself countenanced by her neighbours. The nations, and their kings, that are brought to embrace Christianity, shall lay themselves out for the good of the church. "*Thou shalt suck the milk of the Gentiles*, not suck their blood (that is not the spirit of the gospel); thou *shalt suck the breast of kings*, who shall be to thee as nursing fathers." She shall find herself countenanced by her God: "*Thou shalt know that I the Lord am thy Saviour and thy Redeemer*, shalt know it by experience." They before knew the Lord to be their God; now they know him to be their Saviour, their Redeemer.

2. She had been impoverished, but now she shall be enriched, *v.* 17. Those, who were raised out of the dust, instead of brass money in their purses have gold, and instead of iron vessels in their houses have silver ones. So shall the spiritual glory of the New Testament church exceed the external pomp and splendour of the Jewish economy. When we had baptism in the room of circumcision, the Lord's supper in the room of the passover, and a gospel ministry in the room of a Levitical priesthood, we had gold instead of brass. Sin turned gold into brass when Rehoboam made brazen shields instead of the

golden ones he had pawned; but God's favour, when that returns, will turn brass again into gold.

3. She had been oppressed by her own princes (*ch.* lix. 14); but now all the grievances of that kind shall be redressed (*v.* 17): "*I will make thy officers peace.* They shall *be peace*, that is, they shall sincerely seek thy welfare and by their means thou shalt enjoy good."

4. She had been insulted by her neighbours, invaded, and plundered; but now it shall be so no more (*v.* 18): "*Violence shall no more be heard in thy land;* but every man shall peaceably enjoy his own. There shall be no *wasting nor destruction*, but *thy walls shall be called salvation and thy gates shall be praise.*"

II. Compared with what it would be.

In the close of this chapter we are directed to look further yet, as far forward as to the glory and happiness of heaven, under the type and figure of the flourishing state of the church on earth. As the prophets sometimes insensibly pass from the blessings of the Jewish church to the spiritual blessings of the Christian church, which are eternal, so sometimes they rise from the church militant to the church triumphant, where, and where only, all the promised peace, and joy, and honour will be in perfection.

1. God shall be all in all in the happiness here promised (*v.* 19): *The sun and the moon shall be no more thy light.* "Idolaters worshipped the sun and moon (which some have thought the most ancient and plausible idolatry); but these *shall be no more thy light*, shall no more be idolized, but the Lord shall be to thee a constant light in the night of adversity as well as in the day of prosperity." 2. The happiness here promised shall know no change (*v.* 20): "*Thy sun shall no more go down,* but it shall be eternal sunshine with thee; that shall not be thy sun which is sometimes eclipsed, often clouded, and will certainly set and leave thee in the dark, in the cold, but *he* shall be a sun, who is himself the *Father of all lights*, with whom there is *no variableness*, nor *shadow of turning,*" James i. 17. The comforts and joys that are in heaven, the glories provided for the soul, as the light of the sun, and those prepared for the glorified body too, as the light of the moon, shall never know the least cessation. *And the days of thy mourning shall be ended.* 3. Those that are entitled to this happiness shall never be put out of the possession of it (*v.* 21). And they shall be *all the righteous* together who shall replenish the New Jerusalem. And, because they are *all righteous*, therefore *they shall inherit the land for ever*, for nothing but sin can turn them out of it. 4. The glory of the church: "They shall appear to be the *branch of my planting, the work of my hands*, and I will own them as such." 5. They will appear the more glorious, and God will be the more glorified in them, if we compare what they are with what they were (*v.* 22): "*A little one shall become a thousand and a small one a strong nation.*" The captives that returned out of Babylon strangely multiplied, and became a strong nation. The Christian church was a little one, a very small one at first—the number of their names was once but 120; yet it became a thousand. When they come to heaven, and look back upon the smallness of their beginning, they will wonder how they got thither. It may seem to be delayed, but, as the Lord will do it, so he will *hasten it;* he will do it in the time appointed by his wisdom, though not in the time prescribed by our folly. And this is really hastening it; for, though it seem to tarry, it does not tarry if it come in God's time.

Chapter 61

I. We find the grace of Christ under the type and figure of Isaiah's province, which was to foretell the deliverance of the Jews out of Babylon, ver. 1–3. II. We think we find the glories of the church of Christ, its spiritual glories, described under the type of the Jews' prosperity after their return. It is promised 1. That the decays of the church shall be repaired, ver. 4. 2. That those from without shall be made serviceable to the church, ver. 5. 3. That the church shall be a royal priesthood, maintained by the riches of the Gentiles, ver. 6. 4. That she shall have honour and joy in lieu of all her shame and sorrow, ver. 7. 5. That her affairs shall prosper, ver. 8. 6. That posterity shall enjoy these blessings, ver. 9. 7. That righteousness and salvation shall be the eternal matter of the church's rejoicings and thanksgiving, ver. 10, 11.

Verses 1-3

He that is the best expositor of scripture has given us the best exposition of these verses, even our Lord Jesus himself, who read this in the synagogue at Nazareth (perhaps it was the lesson for the day) and applied it entirely to himself, saying, *This day is this scripture fulfilled in your ears* (Luke iv. 17, 18, 21). As Isaiah was directed to proclaim liberty to the Jews in Babylon, so was Christ, God's messenger, to publish a more joyful jubilee to a lost world.

I. How he was fitted and qualified for this work: *The Spirit of the Lord God is upon me, v.* 1. The prophets had the Spirit of God moving them at times, both instructing them what to say and exciting them to say it. Christ had the Spirit always resting on him without measure. When he entered upon the execution of his prophetical office the Spirit, as a dove, *descended upon him*, Matt. iii. 16. This Spirit he communicated to those whom he sent to proclaim the same glad tidings, saying to them, when he gave them their commission, *Receive you the Holy Ghost.*

II. How he was appointed and ordained to it: *The Spirit of God is upon me, because the Lord God has anointed me.* Hence the Redeemer was called the *Messiah*, the *Christ*, because he was *anointed with the oil of gladness above his fellows. He has sent me.*

III. What the work was to which he was appointed and ordained.

1. He was to be a preacher, was to execute the office of a prophet. He must preach *good tidings* (so *gospel* signifies) *to the meek*, to the penitent, and humble, and poor in spirit; to them the tidings of a Redeemer will be indeed good tidings.

2. He was to be a healer. He was sent to *bind up the broken-hearted*. Those whose hearts are broken for sin, who are truly humbled under the sense of guilt and dread of wrath, are furnished in the gospel of Christ with that which will make them easy and silence their fears.

3. He was to be a deliverer. He was sent as a prophet to preach, as a priest to heal, and as a king to issue out proclamations: (1) Proclamations of peace to his friends: He shall *proclaim liberty to the captives* (as Cyrus did to the Jews in captivity) and the *opening of the prison to those that were bound.* Whereas, by the guilt of sin, we are bound over to the justice of God, sold for sin, Christ lets us know that he has made satisfaction to divine justice for that debt, that his satisfaction is accepted, and if we will plead that, and make over ourselves and all we have to him, we may by faith sue out our pardon; there is, and shall be, *no condemnation to us.* And whereas, by the dominion of sin in us, we are bound under the power of Satan, Christ lets us know that he has conquered Satan, and provided for us grace sufficient to enable us to shake off the yoke of sin and to loose ourselves from *those bands of our neck. The son* is ready by his Spirit to *make us free.* This is the gospel proclamation, and it is like the blowing of the jubilee-trumpet, which proclaimed the great year of release (Lev. xxv. 9, 40), in allusion to which it is here called *the acceptable year of the Lord*, because it publishes his free grace, and an *acceptable year* because it brings glad tidings to us, and what cannot but be very acceptable to those who know the capacities and necessities of their own souls. (2) Proclamations of war against his enemies. Christ proclaims *the day of vengeance of our God*, [1] On

sin and Satan, death and hell, and all the powers of darkness, to be destroyed in order to our deliverance; these Christ triumphed over in his cross. [2] On those of the children of men that stand it out against those fair offers.

4. He was to be a comforter, and so he is a preacher, healer, and deliverer; he is sent to *comfort all who mourn*, and who, mourning, seek to him, and not to the world, for comfort. As *blessings out of Zion* are spiritual blessings, so *mourners in Zion* are holy mourners, such as carry their sorrows to the throne of grace. To such as these Christ has appointed by his gospel, and will give by his Spirit (*v.* 3), those consolations which will not only support them under their sorrows, but turn them into songs of praise. He will give them, (1) *Beauty for ashes.* Here is an elegant *paronomasia* in the original: He will give them *pheer—beauty*, for *epher—ashes*; he will turn their sorrow into joy as quickly and as easily as you can transpose a letter; for he speaks, and it is done. (2) *The oil of joy*, which *makes the face to shine*, instead of *mourning*, which *disfigures the countenance* and makes it unlovely. (3) *The garments of praise*, such beautiful garments as were worn on thanksgiving-days, instead of the *spirit of heaviness*, dimness, or *contraction*—open joys for secret mournings.

5. He was to be a planter; for the church is God's husbandry. All that Christ does for us is to make us God's people, and some way serviceable to him as living trees, *planted in the house of the Lord*, and *flourishing in the courts of our God*; that others also may take occasion from God's favour shining on his people, and his grace shining in them, to praise him, and that he may be for ever *glorified in his saints.*

Verses 4-9

Promises are here made to the Jews now returned out of captivity which are to be extended to the gospel church through grace delivered out of spiritual thraldom.

I. It is promised that their houses shall be rebuilt (*v.* 4), that their cities shall be raised out of the ruins. The setting up of Christianity in the world repaired the decays of natural religion and raised up those desolations both of piety and honesty which had been for many generations the reproach of mankind. An unsanctified soul is like a city that is broken down, but by the power of Christ's gospel and grace it is fitted to be a habitation of God through the Spirit.

II. Those that were servants, working for their oppressors, shall now have servants to do their work. *Strangers, and the sons of the alien, shall keep their sheep, till their ground, and dress their gardens. Strangers shall feed your flocks, v.* 5.

III. They shall be released and honourably employed (*v.* 6): "While the strangers are *keeping your flocks*, you shall be keeping *the charge of the sanctuary*; instead of being slaves to your task-masters, *you shall be named the priests of the Lord*, a high and holy calling." Those whom God sets at liberty he *delivers them out of the hands of their enemies* that they may *serve him*, Luke i. 74, 75; Ps. cxvi. 16. But his service is perfect freedom. And the gospel church is a *royal priesthood*, 1 Pet. ii. 9.

IV. The wealth and honour of the Gentile converts shall redound to the benefit and credit of the church, *v.* 6. Those that were strangers shall become *fellow-citizens with the saints.* 1. They shall *eat the riches of the Gentiles* honourably presented to them, as *gifts brought to the altar.* 2. They shall *boast themselves in their glory.* Whatever was the honour of the Gentile converts before their conversion, it shall turn to the reputation of the church to which they have joined themselves; and whatever is their glory after their conversion—their holy zeal, their patient suffering, and that blessed change which divine grace has made in them—shall be very much for the glory of God.

V. They shall have abundance of comfort, *v.* 7. The Jews were thus privileged after their return; they were in a new world, and now knew how to value their liberty. Much more do all those rejoice whom Christ has brought into the glorious liberty of God's children, especially when the privileges of their adoption shall be completed in the resurrection of the body. 1. *They shall rejoice in their portion.* Though the houses, as well as their temple, be much inferior, yet they shall be *in their land*, their own land, the holy land, Immanuel's land, and therefore they shall rejoice. 2. *Everlasting joy shall be unto them* which shall last much longer than the captivity had lasted. Yet we must look for the accomplishment of this promise in the spiritual joy which believers have in God and the eternal joy they hope for in heaven. 3. This shall be a double recompense to them, for all the reproach and vexation they have lain under in the land of their captivity: "*For your shame you shall have double* honour, and *in your land* you *shall possess double* wealth; the blessing of God upon it. You shall be owned not only as *God's sons*, but as his *first-born* (Exod. iv. 22), and therefore entitled to a double portion." As the miseries of their captivity were so great that in them they are said to have received *double for all their sins* (*ch.* xl. 2), so the joys of their return shall be so great that in them they shall receive *double for all their shame.* The former is applicable to the fulness of Christ's satisfaction, in which God received *double for all our sins*; the latter to the fulness of heaven's joys, in which we shall receive more than *double for all services* and sufferings. Job's case illustrates this: when God *turned again his captivity*, he gave him *twice as much as he had before.*

VI. God will be a God in covenant with them (*v.* 8): *I will direct their work in truth.* God by his providence will order their affairs for the best. As a reason both of this and of the foregoing promise, those words come in, in the former part of the verse, *I the Lord love judgment.* He loves that judgment should be done among men, both between magistrates and subjects and between neighbour and neighbour, and therefore he hates all injustice. If men do not do justice, he loves to do judgment himself in giving redress to those that suffer wrong and punishing those that do wrong. It is a truth that ritual services will never atone for the violation of moral precepts, nor will it justify any man's robbery to say, "It was for burnt-offerings," or *Corban—It is a gift.*

VII. God will entail a blessing upon their posterity (*v.* 9): *Their seed* (the children of those persons that are now the blessed of the Lord, or the church's seed) shall be *accounted to the Lord for a generation*, Ps. xxii. 30. 1. *They shall be known among the Gentiles*, shall distinguish themselves, especially by that brotherly love by which all men shall know them to be Christ's disciples. God shall dignify them, by making them the blessings of their age and instruments of his glory. 2. God shall have the glory of this, for all that see them shall see so much of the grace of God in them, that they shall *acknowledge them to be the seed which the Lord has blessed* and doth bless.

Verses 10–11

We are here taught to rejoice with holy joy, to God's honour, 1. In the beginning of this good work, the clothing of the church *with righteousness and salvation, v.* 10. Upon this account *I will greatly rejoice in the Lord.* The first gospel song begins like this, *My soul doth magnify the Lord, and my spirit hath rejoiced in God my Saviour*, Luke i. 46, 47. The salvation God wrought for the Jews, and that reformation which appeared among them, made them look as glorious as if they had been clothed in robes

of state. Christ has clothed his church with an eternal salvation by clothing it with the righteousness both of justification and sanctification. Observe how these two are put together; those, and those only, shall be clothed with the garments of salvation hereafter that are covered with the robe of righteousness now. Such is the beauty of God's grace in those that are clothed with the robe of righteousness. 2. In the progress and continuance of this good work, *v.* 11. It is not like a day of triumph, which is glorious for the present, but is soon over. The church rejoices to think that these inestimable blessings shall both spring for future ages and spread to distant regions. They shall spring forth for ages to come, as the fruits of the earth which are produced every year. *As the garden* enclosed *causes the things that are sown in it to spring forth* in their season, so constantly *will the Lord God cause righteousness and praise to spring forth*, by virtue of the covenant of grace. Though it may sometimes be winter with the church, when those blessings seem to wither and do not appear, yet the root of them is fixed, a spring-time will come, when they shall flourish again. They shall spread far, and *spring forth before all the nations.*

CHAPTER 62

The business of prophets was both to preach and pray. I. The prophet determines to apply constantly to this business, ver. 1. II. God appoints him and others of his prophets to continue for the encouragement of his people during the delays of their deliverance, ver. 6, 7. III. The promises of the great things God would do for the Jews after their return out of captivity and for the Christian church when it shall be set up in the world. 1. The church shall be made honourable in the eyes of the world, ver. 2. 2. It shall appear to be very dear to God, precious and honourable in his sight, ver. 3–5. 3. It shall enjoy great plenty, ver. 8, 9. 4. It shall be released out of captivity and grow up again into a considerable nation, particularly favoured by heaven, ver. 10–12.

Verses 1–5

I. What he will do for the church. A prophet, as he is a seer, so he is a spokesman. He *will not hold his peace*; he *will not rest.* 1. What the prophet's resolution is: *He will not hold his peace.* He will continue instant in preaching. And he will continue instant in prayer. 2. What is the principle of this resolution—*for Zion's sake, and for Jerusalem's*, not for the sake of any private interest of his own, but for the church's sake, because he has an affection and concern for Zion, and it lies near his heart. It is God's Zion and his Jerusalem, and it is *therefore* dear to him, because it is so to God. 3. He resolves to continue this importunity—till the promise of the church's righteousness and salvation, given in the foregoing chapter, be accomplished. His prophecies will continue speaking of these things, and there shall in every age be a remnant that shall continue to pray for them. Then the church's *righteousness* and *salvation* will *go forth as brightness*, and *as a lamp that burns*, a light not only to the eyes but to the feet, and to *the paths* of those who before *sat in darkness and in the shadow of death.*

II. What God will do for the church. 1. The church shall be greatly admired. When that righteousness which is her salvation, her praise, and her glory, shall be *brought forth*, the *Gentiles shall see* it. "Even kings shall see and be in love with the *glory of thy righteousness*" (*v.* 2). 2. She shall be truly admirable. God is the fountain of honour and from him the church's honour comes: "*Thou shalt be called by a new name*, and those about thee shall have new thoughts of thee." Two names God shall give her: (1) He shall call her his crown (*v.* 3): *Thou shalt be a crown of glory in the hand of the Lord*, not on his head (as adding any real honour or power to him, as crowns do to those that are crowned with them), but in his hand, as a glory and beauty to him. "*Thou shalt be a crown o glory* and a *royal diadem*, through the hand, the good hand, of thy God upon thee. (2) He shall call her his spouse, *v.* 4, 5. This is a yet greater honour, considering what a forlorn condition she had been in. She was called *forsaken* and her land *desolate* during the captivity, like a woman reproachfully divorced or left a disconsolate widow. Such was the state of religion in the world before the preaching of the gospel. Instead of those two names of reproach, she shall be called by two honourable names. She shall be called *Hephzi-bah*, which signifies, *My delight is in her*, a proper name for a wife. God by his grace has wrought that in his church which makes her his delight, she being refined, and re-formed, and brought home to him. She shall be called *Beulah*, which signifies *married*, whereas she had been desolate. *She shall be married.* Her sons shall heartily espouse the land of their nativity. *Thy sons shall marry thee*, that is, they shall live with thee and take delight in thee. When they were in Babylon, they seemed to have espoused that land, Jer. xxix. 5–7. But now they shall again marry their own land, *as a young man marries a virgin*. *Her God* will take pleasure in his church: *As the bridegroom rejoices over the bride, so shall thy God rejoice over thee.*

Verses 6–9

Two things are here promised to Jerusalem:

I. Plenty of the means of grace—abundance of good preaching and good praying (*v.* 6, 7). Provision is made,

1. That ministers may do their duty as watchmen. He would set *watchmen on their walls who should never hold their peace.* They must take all opportunities to give warning to sinners, in season, out of season, and must never betray the cause of Christ by a treacherous or cowardly silence. They must never hold their peace at the throne of grace; must *pray, and not faint.*

2. That people may do their duty. Let them not think it enough that their watchmen pray for them, but let them pray for themselves. God's professing people must be a praying people, must be public-spirited in prayer.

II. Plenty of all other good things, *v.* 8. Their corn had been meat for their enemies. Here was a double grievance, that they themselves wanted that which was necessary to the support of life, whilst their enemies were strengthened by it. God is said to give their corn to their enemies, as the just punishment of their abuse of plenty. The wine which they had laboured for, strangers drank to gratify their lusts. But see the great fulness and satisfaction they should now be restored to (*v.* 9): *Those that have gathered it shall eat it, and praise the Lord.* We must gather what God gives, with care and industry; we must eat it freely and cheerfully. We must serve him with our abundance, use it in works of piety and charity, eat it and *drink it in the courts of his holiness,* where the altar, the priest, and the poor must all have their share. *The Lord has sworn by his right hand, and by the arm of his strength,* that he will do this for his people. It is a great satisfaction to those who build their hopes on God's promise to be sure that *what he has promised he is able to perform,* Rom. iv. 21.

Verses 10–12

This, like passages before, refers to the deliverance of the Jews out of Babylon, and to the great redemption wrought out by Jesus Christ, and the proclaiming of gospel grace and liberty through him. 1. Way shall be made for this salvation, *v.* 10. The gates of Babylon shall be thrown open, the way from Babylon to the land of Israel shall be prepared; causeways shall be made and cast up through wet and miry places, and the stones gathered out from places rough and rocky. Thus John Baptist was sent to *prepare the way of the Lord,* Matt. iii. 3. 2. Notice shall be given of this salvation, *v.* 11, 12. It shall be proclaimed to the captives that they are set at liberty. Let it be said to Zion, for her comfort, *Behold, thy salvation comes* (that is, thy Saviour, who brings salvation). It follows, they shall be called, *The holy people,* and the *redeemed of the Lord. The work before him,* which shall be wrought in them and upon them, shall denominate them a holy people, cured of their inclination to idolatry and consecrated to God only; and the *reward with him,* the deliverance wrought for them, shall denominate them the *redeemed of the Lord.* Jerusalem shall then be called, *Sought out, a city not forsaken.* She shall be sought out, visited, as much as ever. When Jerusalem is called a *holy city,* then it is called *sought out;* for holiness draws respect. But this being proclaimed to the end of the world must have a reference to the gospel of Christ. It is published immediately to the church, but is echoed to every nation: *Behold, thy salvation cometh.* Christ is not only the Saviour, but the salvation itself. Christians shall be called *saints* (1 Cor. i. 2), *the holy people,* for they shall be called *the redeemed of the Lord.*

CHAPTER 63

I. God coming towards his people in ways of mercy and deliverance, and this is to be joined to the close of the foregoing chapter, where it was said to Zion, "Behold, thy salvation comes"; for here it is shown how it comes, ver. 1–6. II. God's people meeting him with their devotions; and this part of the chapter is carried on to the close of the next. 1. A thankful acknowledgment of the great favours God has bestowed upon them, ver. 7. 2. The magnifying of these favours (ver. 8), his compassionate concern for them (ver. 9), their unworthiness (ver. 10), and former mercies, ver. 11–14. 3. A very humble prayer to God to appear for them in their present distress, pleading God's mercy (ver. 15), their relation to him (ver. 16), their desire towards him (ver. 17), and the insolence of their enemies, ver. 18, 19.

Verses 1–6

A glorious victory is obtained by the providence of God over the enemies of Israel. The victory is obtained over the Edomites who had triumphed in the destruction of Jerusalem by the Chaldeans (Ps. cxxxvii. 7) who cut off those who, making their way as far as they could from the enemy, escaped to them (Obad. 12, 13), and who were therefore reckoned with when Babylon was. Yet this victory over Edom is put as an instance or specimen of the like victories obtained over other nations that had been enemies to Israel. But this is not all: It is a victory obtained by the grace of God in Christ over our spiritual enemies. We find the garments dipped in blood adorning him whose name is called *The Word of God,* Rev. xix. 13.

In this representation of the victory we have,

I. An admiring question put to the conqueror, *v.* 1, 2, by the church, or by the prophet in the name of the church. He sees a mighty hero returning in triumph from a bloody engagement, and makes bold to ask him two questions: 1. Who he is. He observes him to come from the country of Edom, in such apparel as was glorious to a soldier, besmeared with blood and dirt. He observes that he does not come as one either frightened or fatigued, but that he *travels in the greatness of his strength.* The question, *Who is this?* perhaps means: *Art thou for us or for our adversaries?* 2. The other question is, *"Wherefore art thou red in thy apparel?* What hard service hast thou been engaged in, that thou carriest with thee these marks of toil and danger?" Is it possible that one who has such majesty should be employed in the servile work of *treading the wine-press?*

II. An admirable answer returned by him.

1. He tells who he is: *I that speak in righteousness, mighty to save.* He is the Saviour. He speaks *in*

righteousness, and will therefore make good every word that he has spoken. He is *mighty to save*, able to bring about the promised redemption.

2. He tells how he came to appear in this hue (*v.* 3): *I have trodden the wine-press alone.*

(1) He gains the victory purely by his own strength, *v.* 3. But his people, for whom the salvation was to be wrought, were weak and helpless, desponding and listless, and had no heart to do anything (*v.* 5): "*I looked, and there was none to help, none to uphold,* none that had the courage to join with Cyrus against their oppressors; *therefore my arm brought* about *the salvation*; *not by* created *might or power*, but *by the Spirit of the Lord of hosts*, my own arm." God can help when all other helpers fail; that is his time to help. But this is most fully applicable to Christ's victories over our spiritual enemies, which he obtained by a single combat. He trod the wine-press alone, and triumphed over principalities and powers *in himself*, Col. ii. 15. When he entered the lists with the powers of darkness, *all his disciples forsook him and fled.*

(2) He undertakes the war purely out of his own zeal. God wrought salvation for the oppressed Jews because he was very angry with the oppressing Babylonians, angry at their idolatries, their pride and cruelty, and the injuries they did to his people. Our Lord Jesus wrought out our redemption in a holy zeal for the honour of his Father and the happiness of mankind, and a holy indignation at the daring attempts Satan had made upon both. He had a zeal against his and his people's enemies: *The day of vengeance is in my heart* (*v.* 4). He had a zeal for his people, and for all that he designed to make sharers in the intended salvation: "*The year of my redeemed has come*, the year appointed for their redemption." With what pleasure he speaks of his people; they are his *redeemed*; they are his own, dear to him. Though their redemption is not yet wrought out, yet he calls them *his redeemed*, because it shall as surely be done as if it were done already.

(3) He will obtain a complete victory over them all. Much is already done; for he now appears *red in his apparel*. In the destruction of the antichristian powers we meet with abundance of bloodshed (Rev. xiv. 20; xix. 13), which yet, according to the dialect of prophecy, may be understood spiritually, and doubtless so may this here.

Verses 7–14

The prophet is here making a thankful recognition of God's dealings with his church all along, before he comes, in the latter end of this chapter and in the next, as a watchman upon the walls, earnestly to pray to God for his compassion towards her in her present deplorable state.

I. Here is a general acknowledgment of God's goodness to them all along, *v.* 7. He mentions the *kindness of God*, his loving-kindness; so plenteous are the springs of divine mercy, that he speaks of it in the plural number—*his loving-kindnesses*. He mentions his *praises*, that is, the thankful acknowledgements of his loving-kindness. He speaks of the goodness that is from God, *all that the Lord has bestowed* on us, relating to life and godliness, in our personal and family capacity. We must bless God for the mercies enjoyed by others as well as for those enjoyed by ourselves. God does good because he is good; what he bestowed upon us must be traced up to the original; it is *according to his mercies* (not according to our merits) and *according to the multitude of his loving-kindnesses*.

II. The steps of God's mercy to Israel ever since it was formed into a nation. When he brought them out of Egypt and took them into covenant he said, "*Surely they are my people, children that will not lie*,"

that will not *dissemble with God* in their covenantings. *So he was their Saviour* out of the bondage of Egypt, and many a time since he had been their Saviour. The principle that moved him to work salvation for them was *in his love and in his pity*. This is strangely expressed here: *In all their affliction he was afflicted;* thus far he sympathizes with them, that he takes what injury is done to them as done to himself. Their cries move him (Exod. iii. 7), as if he were pained in their pain. *Saul, Saul, why persecutest thou me?* God is so far from *afflicting willingly* (Lam. iii. 33) that, if they humble themselves he is *afflicted in their affliction*, as tender parents are in the case of a sick child. There is another reading of these words in the original: *In all their affliction there was no affliction;* though they were in great affliction, yet it was so altered by the grace of God for their good, and it was so allayed and balanced with mercies, they were so wonderfully supported and it ended so well, that it was in effect no affliction. The troubles of the saints are not afflictions, but medicines; saints are enabled to call them *light*, and *but for a moment*, and, with an eye to heaven as all in all, to make nothing of them. The highest angel in heaven, even the angel of his presence, is not thought too great to be sent on this errand. Thus the little ones' angels are said to be those that *always behold the face of our Father*, Matt. xviii. 10. But this is rather to be understood of Jesus Christ, the eternal Word, that angel of whom God spoke to Moses (Exod. xxiii. 20, 21), whose *voice Israel was to obey*. He is the angel of the covenant, God's messenger to the world, Mal. iii. 1. He is the *angel of God's face*, for he is the *express image of his person*; and the glory of God shines in the face of Christ. He that was to work out the eternal salvation wrought out the temporal salvations. He not only redeemed them out of their bondage, but *he bore them and carried them all the days of old*; in the wars they made upon the nations he stood by them, and though they were peevish, he bore with them, Acts xiii. 18. *But they rebelled*. They revolted from their allegiance to God and took up arms against him: *They rebelled, and vexed his Holy Spirit* with their unbelief and murmuring. The ungrateful rebellions of God's children against him are a vexation to his Holy Spirit. Thereupon he justly withdrew his protection. He who had been so much their friend was *turned to be their enemy and fought against them*, by one judgment after another, both in the wilderness and after their settlement in Canaan. Sin makes God an enemy, and makes him angry who was all love and pity. Sinners wilfully lose him for a friend. This refers especially to those calamities that were brought upon them by their captivity in Babylon for their idolatries and other sins. *Then he remembered the days of old*, *v.* 11.

1. This may be understood either of the people or of God. (1) We may understand it of the people. Israel then (spoken of as a single person) *remembered the days of old*, and reasoned, *Where are all the wonders that our fathers told us of?* "*Where is he that brought them up* out of Egypt? Is he not as able to bring us up out of Babylon? *Where is the Lord God of Elijah? Where is the Lord God of our fathers?*" Their fathers were a provoking people and yet found him a pardoning God; and why may not they find him so if they return to him? They use it as a plea with God in prayer for the turning again of their captivity, like that *ch.* li. 9, 10. (2) We may understand it of God; he put himself in mind of the days of old, of his covenant with Abraham (Lev. xxvi. 42). "Why should not I appear for them now as I did for their fathers, who were as undeserving, as ill-deserving, as they are?" He might have said, "I have delivered them formerly, but they have again brought trouble upon themselves (Prov. xix. 19); therefore *I will*

deliver them no more," Judges x. 13. But mercy turns the argument the other way: "I have formerly delivered them and therefore will now."

2. Which way soever we take it, whether the people plead it with God or God with himself, these verses call to mind what God did by Moses for his people, especially in bringing them through the Red Sea. God *led them by the right hand of Moses* (v. 12) and the wonder-working rod was in his hand. It was not Moses that led, any more than it was Moses that fed them (John vi. 32), but God by Moses. God was the owner of the flock, but Moses was a shepherd under him, inured to labour and patience, and so fitted for this pastoral care, by his being trained up to *keep the flock of his father Jethro.* Herein he was a type of Christ the good shepherd, that *lays down his life for his sheep.* He *put his holy Spirit within him; the Spirit of God was among them*, and not only his providence, but his grace, did work for them. He carried them safely through the Red Sea. *He divided the water before them* (v. 12), so that it gave them not only passage, but protection, a wall on either side. *He led them through the deep as a horse in the wilderness*, or *in the plain* (v. 13). If God make us a way, he will make it plain and level. He brought them safely to a place of rest: *As a beast goes down into the valley*, carefully and gradually, so *the Spirit of the Lord caused him to rest.* Many a time in their march through the wilderness they had resting-places provided for them, v. 14. And at length they were made to rest finally in Canaan, and the Spirit of the Lord gave them that rest according to the promise. God did it with his glorious arm, *the arm of his gallantry*, or *bravery*; so the word signifies.

Verses 15–19

This prayer, continued to the end of the next chapter, is an affectionate, importunate, pleading prayer. It is calculated for the time of the captivity. As they had promises, so they had prayers, prepared for them against that time of need. Some good interpreters think this prayer looks further, and that it expresses the complaints of the Jews under their last rejection from God and destruction by the Romans.

I. The petitions they put up to God. *Look down from heaven, and behold*, v. 15. *Look down from the habitation of thy holiness and of thy glory.* God's holiness is his glory. Heaven is his habitation, the throne of his glory (v. 17): "*Return;* change thy way towards us, return in mercy, and let us have thy gracious presence with us." God's people dread nothing more than his departures from them and desire nothing more than his returns to them.

II. The complaints they made to God. 1. That they were given up to themselves, and God's grace did not recover them, v. 17. It is a strange expostulation, *Why hast thou made us to err from thy ways; thou hast hardened our heart from thy fear.* Some make it to be the language of those that were impious and profane; when the prophets reproved them for the *error of their ways*, they with a daring impudence charged their sin upon God, made him the author of it. But I rather take it to be the language of those that lamented the unbelief and impenitence of their people, not accusing God of being the author of their wickedness, but complaining of it to him. They owned that they had *erred from God's ways*, that their *hearts* had been *hardened from his fear*, and this was the cause of all their errors from his ways; or *from his fear* may mean from the true worship of God. Now this they complain of, as their great misery and burden, that God had for their sins permitted them to *err from his ways* and had justly withheld his grace, so that their *hearts were hardened from his fear.* When they ask, *Why hast thou done this?* it is not as charging

him with wrong, but lamenting it as a sore judgment. God had *caused them to err and hardened their hearts* (v. 10) by a judicial sentence. Their troubles had alienated many of them from God, and prejudiced them against his service; their afflictions were their temptations, and to many of them invincible ones. 2. That they were given up to their enemies (v. 18): *Our adversaries have trodden down thy sanctuary.* They complained not so much of the adversaries treading down their houses and cities as of their treading down God's sanctuary, because thereby God was immediately affronted, and they were robbed of the comforts they valued most.

III. The pleas for mercy and deliverance. 1. They pleaded the tender compassion God used to show to his people, v. 15. The most prevailing arguments in prayer are those that are taken *from God himself.* It cannot be that divine zeal, which is infinitely wise and just, should be cooled, that divine strength, which is infinite, should be weakened. Has God, who so often remembered to be gracious, now forgotten to be so? *Has he in anger shut up his tender mercies?* It can never be. 2. They pleaded God's relation to them as their Father (v. 16): Thy tender mercies are not restrained, for they are the tender mercies of a father. *However it be, yet God is good;* for he is our Father. When the father is dead *his sons come to honour and he knows it not*, Job xiv. 21. "But *thou, O Lord! art our Father still* (the fathers of our flesh may call themselves *ever-loving*; but they are not *ever-living*; it is God only that is the immortal Father, that always knows us, and is never at a distance from us), and therefore *our Redeemer from everlasting is thy name*, the name by which we will know and own thee. We are so degenerate and corrupt that Abraham and Israel would not own us for their children, yet we fly to thee as our Father. Abraham cast out his son Ishmael; Jacob disinherited his son Reuben and cursed Simeon and Levi; but our heavenly Father, in pardoning sin, is *God, and not man*," Hos. xi. 9. 3. They pleaded that he was their Lord: "We are thy servants; what service we can do thou art entitled to, and therefore we ought not to serve strange kings and strange gods: *Return for thy servants' sake.*" We are the *tribes of thy inheritance*, not only thy servants, but thy tenants. Wilt thou suffer thy own servants and tenants to be thus abused? 4. They pleaded that they had had but a short enjoyment of the land of promise and the privileges of the sanctuary (v. 18): *The people of thy holiness have possessed it but a little while.* From Abraham to David were but fourteen generations, and from David to the captivity but fourteen more (Matt. i. 17), and that was but a little while in comparison with the promise of the *land of Canaan for an everlasting possession* (Gen. xvii. 8). 5. They pleaded that those who had their land were such as were strangers to God. "*Thou never didst bear rule over them*, nor did they ever yield thee any obedience. Will God suffer those that do not stand in any relation to him to trample upon those that do?"

CHAPTER 64

This chapter goes on with that pathetic pleading prayer. I. They pray that God would appear in some remarkable manner for them against his and their enemies, ver. 1, 2. II. They plead what God had formerly done, and was always ready to do, for his people, ver. 3–5. III. They confess that they had deserved the judgments they were now under, ver. 6, 7. IV. They refer themselves to the mercy of God as a Father, and submit themselves to his sovereignty, ver. 8. V. They earnestly pray for the pardon of sin and the turning away of God's anger, ver. 9–12.

Verses 1–5

Here, I. The petition is that God would appear wonderfully for them now, v. 1, 2. When God works some extraordinary deliverance for his people he is said to *shine forth*, to show himself strong; so, here, they pray that he would *rend the heavens and come down*. This is applicable to the second coming of Christ, when *the Lord himself shall descend from heaven with a shout*. They desire that *the mountains might flow down at thy presence*, that the fire of thy wrath may even dissolve the rockiest mountains and melt them as metal in the furnace, which is made liquid; so *the melting fire burns*, v. 2. Let things be put into a ferment, in order to a glorious revolution in favour of the church: *As the fire causes the waters to boil*. They desire that this may tend to the glory of God, *may make his name known*, not only to his friends, but to his adversaries, that they may know it and *tremble at his presence*. God's name, if it be not a stronghold for us, into which we may run and be safe, will be a stronghold against us, out of the reach of which we cannot run and be safe.

II. The plea is that God had appeared wonderfully for his people formerly.

1. They plead what he had done for his people Israel when he brought them out of Egypt, v. 3. He then *did terrible things* in the plagues of Egypt, *which they looked not for*. Then he came down upon Mount Sinai in such terror as made that and the adjacent mountains to *flow down at his presence*, to *skip like rams* (Ps. cxiv. 4). Some refer this to the defeat of Sennacherib's powerful army, which was as surprising an instance of the divine power as the melting down of rocks and mountains would be.

2. They plead the provision he has made for the safety and happiness of his people.

(1) It is very rich, v. 4. Men have not heard nor seen what God has *prepared for those that wait for him*. It is all that goodness which God has *laid up for those that fear him, and wrought for those that trust in him*, Ps. xxxi. 19. Much of it was concealed in former ages; they knew it not, because the *unsearchable riches of Christ* were *hidden in God*, were *hidden from the wise and prudent*; but in latter ages they were revealed by the gospel; so the apostle applies this (1 Cor. ii. 9), for it follows (v. 10), *But God has revealed them unto us by his Spirit*. That which men had not heard *since the beginning of the world* they should hear before the end of it. It cannot be fully comprehended by the human understanding; it is spiritual, and will far outdo our expectations. Even the present peace of believers, much more their future bliss, surpasses all expression, Phil. iv. 7. We must infer from God's works of wondrous grace, as well as from his works of wondrous power, from the kind things, as well as from the great things, he does, that there is *no god like him*.

(2) It is very ready (v. 5): "*Thou meetest him that rejoices and works righteousness*, meetest him with that good which thou hast prepared for him (v. 4), and dost not forget *those that remember thee in thy ways*." What communion there is between a gracious God and a gracious soul! We must be cheerful in doing our duty, we must *rejoice and work righteousness*, must delight ourselves in God and sing at our work. This intimates the friendship, fellowship, and familiarity to which God admits his people. He will *anticipate them with the blessings of his goodness*, will *rejoice to do good* to those that *rejoice in working righteousness*, and wait to be gracious to those that *wait for him*. He meets his penitent people with a pardon, as the father of the prodigal met his returning son, Luke xv. 20. He meets his praying people with an answer of peace, while they are yet speaking, ch. lxv. 24.

3. They plead the unchangeableness of God's favour and the stability of his promise: "*Behold, thou hast* many a time *been wroth with us because we have sinned*, and we have been under the tokens of thy wrath; *but in those*, those ways of thine, the ways of

mercy in which we have *remembered thee, in those is continuance*," or *in those thou art ever*. And by this continuance of the covenant we hope to be saved, for its being an everlasting covenant is all our salvation.

Verses 6–12

The Lamentations of Isaiah—the destruction of Jerusalem by the Chaldeans and the sin of Israel that brought that destruction.

I. The people of God in their affliction confess and bewail their sins. Now that they were under divine rebukes for sin they had nothing to trust to but the mere mercy of God.

1. There was a general corruption of manners among them (v. 6): *We are all as an unclean thing*, or as an unclean *person*, as one overspread with a leprosy, who was to be shut out of the camp. *Even all our righteousnesses are as filthy rags*. "The best of our persons are so; we are all corrupt and polluted. The best of our performances are so. There is not only a general corruption of manners, but a general defection in the exercises of devotion."

2. There was a general coldness of devotion among them, v. 7. Prayer was in a manner neglected: "*There is none that calls on thy name*, none that seeks to thee for grace to reform us, or for mercy to relieve us and take away the judgments which our sins have brought upon us." If there was here and there one that called on God's name, it was with a great deal of indifferency: *There is none that stirs up himself to take hold of God*. To pray is to *take hold of God*, by faith to take hold of the promises God has made of his goodwill to us—to take hold of him as he that wrestles takes hold of him he wrestles with. But when we *take hold of God* it is as the boatman with his hook takes hold on the shore, as if he would pull the shore to him, but really it is to pull himself to the shore; so we pray, not to bring God to our mind, but to bring ourselves to his. Those that would take hold of God in prayer must stir up themselves to do it; all that is within us must be employed in the duty (and all little enough), our thoughts fixed and our affections flaming.

II. They acknowledge their afflictions to be the fruit and product of their own sins and God's wrath. "*We are all as an unclean thing, and* therefore *we do all fade away as a leaf* (v. 6), we not only wither and lose our beauty, but we fall and drop off" (so the word signifies) "as leaves in autumn; our profession of religion withers, and we grow dry and sapless; and then *our iniquities like the wind have taken us away* and hurried us into captivity, as the winds in autumn blow off, and then blow away, the faded withered leaves," Ps. i. 3, 4.

III. They claim relation to God as their God, and humbly plead it with him (v. 8): "*But now, O Lord! thou art our Father*. Foolish and careless as we are, poor and despised by our enemies, yet still *thou art our Father*; to thee therefore we return in our repentance." God is their Father, he gave them their being, formed them into a people, shaped them as he pleased: "*We are the clay and thou our potter*, therefore we will hope that you who madest us wilt new-make us, new-form us, though we have unmade and deformed ourselves: *We are all as an unclean thing*, but *we are all the work of thy hands*, therefore *forsake us not*," Ps. cxxxviii. 8. *We are thy people*; and *should not a people seek unto their God? ch.* viii. 19. *We are thine;* save us, Ps. cxix. 94.

IV. They are importunate with God for the turning away of his anger and the pardoning of their sins (v. 9). They pray that God would be reconciled to them, and then they can be easy whether the affliction be continued or removed: "*Be not wroth to extremity*, but let thy anger be mitigated by the clemency and compassion of a father."

V. The lamentable condition they were in. 1. Their own houses were in ruins, *v.* 10.. The cities of Judah were destroyed by the Chaldeans and the inhabitants of them were carried away. *Thy holy cities are a wilderness.* The cities of Judah are called *holy cities,* for the people were unto God a kingdom of priests, therefore they lamented the ruins of them. Even *"Zion is a wilderness; the city of David itself lies in ruins; Jerusalem,* that was *beautiful,* has become the scorn and scandal of the whole earth; that noble city is a heap of rubbish." 2. God's house was in ruins, *v.* 11. This they lament most of all, that *the temple was burnt with fire.* It was *their holy and beautiful house;* the holiness of it was in their eye the greatest beauty of it, and consequently the profanation of it was the saddest part of its desolation. It was the place *where their fathers praised God* with their sacrifices and songs; what a pity is it that that should lie in ashes which had been for so many ages the glory of their nation! *All their pleasant things were laid waste,* all those things which were employed by them in the service of God; not only the furniture of the temple, the altars and table, but the sabbaths, and all their religious feasts, which they used to keep with gladness.

VI. They conclude by humbly arguing with God concerning their present desolations (*v.* 12): *Wilt thou refrain thyself for these things?* When we are abused we hold our peace, because vengeance does not belong to us. When God is injured in his honour it may justly be expected that he should speak in the vindication of it; his people prescribe not what he shall say, but their prayer is (as here) Ps. lxxxiii. 1, *"Keep not thou silence, O God!* Speak for the conviction of thy enemies, speak for the comfort and relief of thy people; for *wilt thou afflict us for ever?"* God has said that he *will not contend for ever,* and therefore his people may depend upon it that their afflictions shall be neither to extremity nor to eternity, but *light* and *for a moment.*

Chapter 65

The conclusion of this evangelical prophecy, the last two chapters of which direct us to look as far forward as the new heavens and the new earth, the new world which the gospel dispensation should bring in. And why should it seem absurd that the prophet here should speak of that to which all the prophets bore witness? 1 Pet. i. 10, 11. The rejection of the Jews, and the calling in of the Gentiles, are often mentioned in the New Testament as that which was foreseen and foretold by the prophets, Acts x. 34; xiii. 40; Rom. xvi. 26. In this chapter we have, I. The anticipating of the Gentiles with the gospel call, ver. 1. II. The rejection of the Jews for their obstinacy and unbelief, ver. 2–7. III. The saving of a remnant by bringing them into the gospel church, ver. 8–10. IV. The judgments of God that should pursue the rejected Jews, ver. 11–16. V. The blessings reserved for the Christian church, ver. 17–25. But these things are here prophesied of under the figure of the difference God would make between some and others of the Jews after their captivity, between those that feared God and those that did not.

Verses 1–7

The apostle Paul has told us what was the event pointed at, namely, the calling in of the Gentiles and the rejection of the Jews, by the preaching of the gospel, Rom. x. 20, 21. And he observes that herein *Esaias is very bold* in foretelling it to the Jews, who would take it as a gross affront to their nation.

I. It is here foretold that the Gentiles, who had been afar off, should be made nigh, *v.* 1. Paul reads it thus: *I was found of those that sought me not; I was made manifest to those that asked not for me.* 1. Those who had long been without God in the world shall now be set seeking him; those who had not said, *Where is God my maker?* shall now begin to enquire after him. With what pleasure does the great God here speak of his being sought. For there is great joy in heaven over sinners who repent. 2. God shall anticipate their prayers with his blessings: *I*

am found of those that sought me not. This happy acquaintance and correspondence between God and the Gentile world began on his side. Though in after-communion God is found of those that seek him (Prov. viii. 17), yet in the first conversion he is found of those that seek him not; for *therefore we love him because he first loved us.* 3. God gave the advantages of a divine revelation to those who had never made a profession of religion: *I said, Behold me, behold me* to those who *were not called by my name,* as the Jews for many ages had been. Christ said, *Behold me, behold me* with an eye of faith: *look unto me, and be you saved.*

II. It is here foretold that the Jews, who had long been a people near to God, should be·cast off and set at a distance, *v.* 2. The apostle applies this to the Jews in his time, Rom. x. 21: *But to Israel he saith, All day long I have stretched forth my hands unto a disobedient and gainsaying people.*

1. How the Jews were courted by the divine grace. God himself, by his prophets, by his Son, by his apostles, *stretched forth his hands to them.* God *spread out his hands to them,* as one reasoning and expostulating with them. When Christ was crucified his hands were *spread out and stretched forth,* as if he were preparing to receive returning sinners. He waited to be gracious, and was not weary of waiting; even those that came in at the eleventh hour of the day were not rejected.

2. They contemned the invitation; they were invited to the wedding-supper, and would not come, but *rejected the counsel of God against themselves.* The world shall see that it was not for nothing that they were rejected of God. They were very wilful. Right or wrong they would do as they had a mind. God had told them his thoughts, what his mind and will were, but they would walk *after their own thoughts,* would do what they thought best. This was God's complaint of them all along—they grieved him, they *vexed his Holy Spirit,* as if they would contrive how to make him their enemy. The prophet speaks more particularly of *their iniquities and the iniquities of their fathers,* as the ground of God's casting them off, *v.* 7. The most provoking iniquity of their fathers was idolatry. This was the sin that brought them into captivity, and, though the captivity pretty well cured them of it, yet, when the final ruin of that nation came, that was again brought into the account against them. Perhaps there were many, long after the captivity, who, though they did not worship other gods, married strange wives. They forsook God's temple, and *sacrificed in gardens or groves,* doing it in their own way, for they liked not God's institutions. They forsook God's altar, and *burnt incense upon bricks,* altars of their own contriving in comparison with the golden altar which God appointed them. "They used necromancy, or consulting with the dead, and, in order to that, they *remained among the graves, and lodged in the monuments.*" They violated the laws of God about their meat, and broke through the distinction between clean and unclean before it was taken away by the gospel. They *ate swine's flesh. And the broth,* or *pieces,* of other forbidden meats, called here *abominable things,* was *in their vessels,* and was made use of for food. The forbidden meat is called *an abomination,* and those that meddle with it are said to *make themselves abominable,* Lev. xi. 42, 43. Perhaps this is here put figuratively for all forbidden pleasures. But those who thus take a pride in venturing upon the borders of sin are in danger of falling into the depths of it. The iniquity of the Jews in our Saviour's time was their pride and hypocrisy, that sin of the scribes and Pharisees against which Christ denounced so many woes, *v.* 5. They say, *"Stand by thyself,* keep to thy own companions, but *come not near to me,* lest thou pollute me; *touch*

me not, for I am holier than thou." These are a smoke in my nose, such a smoke as comes not from a quick fire, which soon becomes glowing and pleasant, but from a fire of wet wood, which *burns all the day,* and is nothing but smoke. The proof against them is plain: *Behold, it is written before me, v.* 6. The *iniquity of their fathers* shall come against them; not but that their own sin deserved whatever judgments God brought upon them, and much heavier; and this they owned, Ezra ix. 13. *Your iniquities and the iniquities of your fathers* together, the one aggravating the other, shall be *measured into their bosom.*

Verses 8–10

This is expounded by St. *Paul,* Rom. xi. 1–5, where, when, upon occasion of the rejection of the Jews, it is asked, *Hath God then cast away his people?* he answers, No; for *at this time there is a remnant according to the election of grace.* This prophecy has reference to that distinguished remnant. Some of the Jews shall be brought to embrace the Christian faith, shall be added to the church, and so be saved. And our Saviour has told us that *for the sake of these elect* the days of the destruction of the Jews should be shortened, and a stop put to the desolation, Matt. xxiv. 22.

I. This is illustrated here by a comparison, *v.* 8. When a vine is so withered that there seems to be no sap nor life in it, and the dresser of the vineyard is inclined to cut it down, yet, if ever so little of the juice of the grape be found, though but in one cluster, a stander-by interposes, and says, *Destroy it not, for a blessing is in it;* there is life in the root. Sometimes God spares whole cities and nations for the sake of a few.

II. Those that shall make up this saving remnant. 1. They are such as serve God. It is *for my servants' sake (v.* 8), and they are *my servants* that *shall dwell there, v.* 9. God's faithful servants *serve their generation.* 2. They are such as seek God, make it the business of their lives to call upon him.

III. An account of the mercy God has in store for them. The remnant shall have a happy settlement again in their own land, as *a seed out of Jacob;* and these typify the remnant of Jacob that shall be incorporated into the gospel church by faith. They shall inherit *my mountains,* the holy mountains on which Jerusalem and the temple were built. They shall have a green pasture for their flocks, *v.* 10. *Sharon and the valley of Achor* shall again be well replenished with cattle. They shall recover possession of the whole land. Gospel-ordinances are the fields and valleys where the sheep of Christ *shall go in and out and find pasture* (John x. 9), and where they are *made to lie down* (Ps. xxiii. 2), as Israel's herds in *the valley of Achor,* Hos. ii. 15.

Verses 11–16

The different states of the godly and wicked, of the Jews that believed and of those that still persisted in unbelief.

I. The fearful doom of those that persisted in their idolatry after the deliverance out of Babylon, and in infidelity after the preaching of the gospel of Christ. 1. The doom is here threatened: "*I will number you to the sword* as sheep for the slaughter, and there shall be no escaping; *you shall all bow down to it,*" *v.* 12. 2. The sins that number them to the sword. (1) Idolatry was the ancient sin (*v.* 11): "*You are those* who, instead of serving me as my people, *forsake the Lord,* and cast him off to embrace other gods, who *forget my holy mountain* to burn incense upon the mountains of your idols (*v.* 7), and have deserted the one only living and true God." They *prepared a table for that troop of* deities which the heathen worship and *poured out drink-offerings to that* numberless

number of them; for those that thought one God too little never thought scores and hundreds sufficient. (2) Infidelity was the sin of the later Jews (*v.* 12): *When I called, you did not answer,* which refers to the same that *v.* 2 did, and that is applied to those who rejected the gospel. Our Lord Jesus himself called (he *stood and cried,* John vii. 37), but they would not answer. It is not strange that those who will not be persuaded to choose that which is good persist in their choice of that which is evil.

II. The aggravation of this doom, from the consideration of the happy state of those that were brought to repentance and faith. The blessedness of those that serve God, and the woeful condition of those that rebel against him, are here set the *one over-against the other,* that they may serve as a foil to each other, *v.* 13–16. It will add to the grief of those that perish to see the happiness of God's servants and especially to think that they might have shared in their bliss if it had not been their own fault. The difference of their states lies in two things.

1. In point of comfort and satisfaction. God's servants shall want nothing that is good for them. But those who set their hearts upon the world, shall be hungry and thirsty, always empty, always craving; for it is not bread; it surfeits, but it satisfies not. God's servants *shall rejoice* and sing for joy of heart. Heaven will be a world of everlasting joy to all that are now sowing in tears. But, on the other hand, those that forsake the Lord shut themselves out from all true joy, for *they shall be ashamed* of their vain confidence, and their own righteousness, and the hopes they had built thereon.

2. In point of honour and reputation, *v.* 15, 16. *The memory of the just is,* and shall be, *blessed, but the name of the wicked shall rot.* The name of the idolaters shall be *for a curse to God's chosen,* that is, for a warning to them. The name of God's chosen shall become a blessing: *He shall call his servants by another name.* The children of the covenant shall be called *Christians;* and to them, under that name, all the promises and privileges of the new covenant shall be secured. This other name shall not be confined to one nation, but with it men shall *bless themselves in the earth,* all the world over. God shall have servants out of all nations. They shall bless themselves *in the God of truth.* They shall give honour to God both in their prayers and in their solemn oaths. This is a part of the homage we owe to God; we must bless ourselves in him, that is, we have enough to make us happy, and can desire no more, if we have him for our God. Worldly people bless themselves in the abundance they have of this world's goods (Ps. xlix. 18; Luke xii. 19); but God's servants bless themselves in him, as a God all-sufficient for them. They shall give honour to him as *the God of truth, the God of the Amen* (so the word is); some understand it of Christ, in whom all the promises are *yea and amen,* 2 Cor. i. 20. They shall give him honour as the author of this blessed change, who has made them to forget their former troubles, the remembrance of them being swallowed up in their present comforts.

Verses 17–25

If these promises were in part fulfilled when the Jews, after their return out of captivity, were settled in peace in their own land and brought as it were into a new world, yet they were to have their full accomplishment in the gospel church. In the graces and comforts which believers have in and from Christ we are to look for this new heaven and new earth. It is in the gospel that *old things have passed away and all things have become new,* and by it that those who are in Christ are *new creatures,* 2 Cor. v. 17. It was a mighty and happy change that was described *v.* 16, that *the former troubles were forgotten;* but here it rises much higher: even the *former world* shall be *forgotten* and *shall no more come into mind*. When God is reconciled to us, which gives us a new heaven, the creatures too are reconciled to us, which gives us a new earth.

I. There shall be new joys. All the church's friends, and all that belong to her, shall rejoice (*v.* 18): You shall *be glad and rejoice for ever in that which I create. I create Jerusalem a rejoicing and her people a joy.* The church shall not only rejoice but be rejoiced in. The prosperity of the church shall be a rejoicing to God himself, who has pleasure in the prosperity of his servants (*v.* 19): *I will rejoice in Jerusalem's joy, and will joy in my people;* for *in all their affliction he was afflicted.* There shall be no allay of this joy: *The voice of weeping shall be no more heard in her.* The former occasions of grief shall not return. But in heaven it shall have a full accomplishment; there *all tears shall be wiped away.*

II. There shall be new life, *v.* 20. Untimely deaths by the sword or sickness shall be no more known as they have been, *v.* 19. Believers through Christ shall be satisfied with life, though it be ever so short on earth. Even the child shall be reckoned to *die a hundred years old*, for he shall rise again at full age, shall rise to eternal life. And, as for old men, it is promised that *they shall fill their days* with the *fruits of righteousness*, which they shall *still bring forth in old age.* An old man who is wise, and good, and useful, may truly be said to have *filled his days.* Old men who have their hearts upon the world have never filled their days. Unbelievers shall be unsatisfied and unhappy in life, though it be ever so long. The sinner, though he live to be *a hundred years old, shall be accursed*, and his long life is but a long reprieve. So that the matter is not great whether our lives on earth be long or short, but whether we live the lives of saints or the lives of sinners.

III. There shall be a new enjoyment of the comforts of life. Whereas before it was very uncertain and precarious, now it shall be otherwise; they shall *build houses and inhabit them*, shall *plant vineyards* and *eat the fruit of them*, *v.* 21, 22. Strangers shall not break in upon them, to expel them, as sometimes they have done: *My elect shall wear out*, or *long enjoy, the work of their hands;* it is honestly got, and it will wear well; it is *the work of their hands*, which they themselves have laboured for, and not the *bread of idleness*, or *bread of deceit.* If we live to enjoy it long, it is the gift of God's providence, for that is here promised: *As the days of a tree are the days of my people;* as the *days of an oak* (*ch.* vi. 13), *whose substance is in it, though it cast its leaves;* though it be stripped every winter, it lasts many years; as the days of the *tree of life;* so the LXX.

IV. There shall be a new generation rising up in their stead to inherit and enjoy these blessings (*v.* 23): *They shall not labour in vain*, for they shall not only enjoy the work of their hands themselves, but they shall leave it with satisfaction to those that shall come after them. God will make their children that rise up comforts to them; they shall have the joy of seeing them *walk in the truth.* He will make the times that come after comfortable to their children.

V. There shall be a good correspondence between them and their God (*v.* 24): *Even before they call, I will answer.* God will anticipate their prayers with the blessings of his goodness. The father of the prodigal met him in his return. God's readiness to hear prayer appears much more in the grace of the gospel than it did under the law.

VI. There shall be a good correspondence between them and their neighbours (*v.* 25): *The wolf and the lamb shall feed together.* God's people, though they are as sheep in the midst of wolves, shall be unhurt; for God will not so much break the power of their

enemies as formerly, but he will turn their hearts, will alter their dispositions by his grace. When Paul, who had been a persecutor of the disciples (and who, being of the tribe of Benjamin, ravened *as a wolf*, Gen. xlix. 27) joined himself to them and became one of them, then *the wolf and the lamb fed together.* Men shall be changed: *The lion shall no more be a beast of prey*, but *shall eat straw like the bullock*, shall *know his owner*, and *his master's crib*, as *the ox* does. When those that lived by spoil and rapine to enrich themselves, right or wrong, are brought by the grace of God to live by honest labour—when those that stole steal no more, but work with their hands the thing that is good—then this is fulfilled, that *the lion shall eat straw like the bullock.* Satan shall be chained, the dragon bound; for *dust shall be the serpent's meat again.* That great enemy has glutted himself with the precious blood of saints, who by his instigation have been persecuted, and with the precious souls of sinners, who by his instigation have ruined themselves forever; but now he shall be confined to dust, according to the sentence, *On thy belly shalt thou go, and dust shalt thou eat*, Gen. iii. 14. Christ shall reign as Zion's King till all the enemies of his kingdom be made his footstool.

CHAPTER 66

The first verse of this chapter is applied by Stephen to the dismantling of the temple by the planting of the Christian church (Acts vii. 49, 50), which may serve as a key to the whole chapter. I. The contempt God puts upon ceremonial services in comparison with moral duties, ver. 1–4. II. The salvation God will in due time work for his people out of the hands of their oppressors (ver. 5), speaking terror to the persecutors (ver. 6) and to the persecuted, a speedy and complete deliverance (ver. 7–9), a joyful settlement (ver. 10, 11), the accession of the Gentiles to them, ver. 12–14. III. The terrible vengeance which God will bring upon the enemies of his church and people, ver. 15–18. IV. The happy establishment of the church upon large and sure foundations, ver. 19–24. And we may well expect that this evangelical prophet, in the close of his prophecy, should look as far forward as to the latter days, to the last day, to the days of eternity.

Verses 1–4

I. The temple is slighted in comparison with a gracious soul, *v.* 1, 2. The prophets and Christ foretold the ruin of the temple, that God would leave it and then it would soon be desolate. After it was destroyed by the Chaldeans it soon recovered itself and the ceremonial services were revived with it; but by the Romans it was made a perpetual desolation, and the ceremonial law was abolished with it. Heaven is the throne of God's glory and government. The earth is his footstool, on which he stands, overruling all the affairs of it according to his will. If God has so bright a throne, so large a footstool, *where then is the house they can build* unto God, that can be the residence of his glory, or *where is the place of his rest?* What satisfaction can the Eternal Mind take in a house made with men's hands? If he required a house for himself to dwell in, he would have made one himself when he made the world; he had no need of a temple made with hands. He would not heed it as he would a humble, penitent, gracious heart. He has a heaven and earth of his own making, and a temple of man's making; but he overlooks them all, that he may look with favour to him that is poor in spirit, humble and serious, self-abasing and self-denying, whose heart is truly contrite for sin, penitent for it, and in pain to get it pardoned. Such a heart is a living temple for God; he dwells there, and it is the place of his rest; it is like heaven and earth, his throne and his footstool.

II. Sacrifices are slighted when they come from ungracious hands. *The sacrifice of the wicked* is not only unacceptable, but it *is an abomination to the Lord* (Prov. xv. 8); this is largely shown here, *v.* 3, 4. The carnal Jews, after their return out of captivity, grew very loose in the service of God; they brought the *torn, and the lame, and the sick* for *sacrifice* (Mal. i. 8, 13), and this made their services abominable to God. *He that kills an ox* for his own table is welcome to do it; but he that now kills it for God's altar, *is as if he slew a man*; he that does it does in effect set aside Christ's sacrifice. *He that sacrifices a lamb,* if it be a corrupt thing, and not the best he has, affronts God, instead of pleasing him; it is *as if he cut off a dog's neck*, a creature in the eye of the law so vile that, whereas an ass might be redeemed, the price of a dog was never to be brought into the treasury, Deut. xxiii. 18. *He that offers an oblation,* a meat-offering or drink-offering, is as if he thought to make atonement with *swine's blood*, a creature that must not be eaten nor touched, the *broth of it* was abominable (*ch.* lxv. 4), much more the blood of it. *He that burns incense to God*, and so puts contempt upon the incense of Christ's intercession, is *as if he blessed an idol.* Their wickedness made their sacrifices detestable. *They had chosen their own ways*, the ways of their own wicked hearts, and *their souls delighted in their abominations.* They were vicious and immoral, chose the way of sin rather than the way of God's commandments, and this made their sacrifices offensive to God, *ch.* i. 11–15. They turned a deaf ear to all the warnings of divine justice and all the offers of divine grace. They *chose their own ways,* therefore, says God, I also will *choose their delusions. They have made their choice, and now I will make mine; they have taken what course they pleased with me, and I will take what course I please with them.* They shall be deceived by those vain confidences with which they have deceived themselves. God will make their sin their punishment; they shall be hurried into ruin by their own delusions.

Verses 5–14

The prophet, having denounced God's judgments against a hypocritical nation, that made a jest of God's word, here turns his speech to those that *trembled at his word*, to comfort and encourage them; they shall not be involved in the judgments that are coming upon their unbelieving nation. The word of God has comforts in store for those that by true humiliation for sin are prepared to receive them. There were those (*v.* 4) who, when *God spoke*, would *not hear*; but, if the heart *tremble at the word*, the ear will be open to it.

I. God will plead their just but injured cause against their persecutors (*v.* 5): *Your brethren that hated you said, Let the Lord be glorified. But he shall appear to your joy.* The apostles were Jews by birth, and yet even in the cities of the Gentiles the Jews they met were their most bitter and implacable enemies and *stirred up the Gentiles* against them. Their brethren, who should have loved them and encouraged them for their work's sake hated them, and cast them out of their synagogues. Our Saviour explains this, and seems to have reference to it, John xvi. 2. *They shall put you out of their synagogues,* and *whosoever kills you will think that he does God service.* They were encouraged under these persecutions: "Let your faith and patience hold out yet a little while; your enemies hate you and oppress you, your brethren hate you and cast you out, but your Father in heaven loves you, and will appear for you when no one else will or dare." This was fulfilled when, upon the signals given of Jerusalem's approaching ruin, the *Jews' hearts failed them for fear*; but the disciples of Christ, whom they had hated and persecuted, *lifted up their heads with joy, knowing that their redemption drew nigh*, Luke xxi. 26, 28.

II. God's appearances for them will be such as will make a great noise in the world (*v.* 6): There shall be *a voice of noise from the city, from the temple.* Some

make it the joyful and triumphant voice of the church's friends, others the lamenting voice of her enemies, fleeing in vain to the temple for shelter. These voices do but echo to the *voice of the Lord,* who is now rendering a *recompence to his enemies.* A confused noise was in the city and temple when Jerusalem, after a long siege, was at last taken by the Romans. Some think this prophecy was fulfilled in the prodigies that went before that destruction of Jerusalem, related by Josephus in his History of the Wars of the Jews (*lib.* 7. *cap.* 31), that the temple-doors flew open suddenly of their own accord, and the priests heard a noise of motion or shifting in the most holy place, and presently a voice, saying, *Let us depart hence.* And, some time after, one Jesus Bar-Annas went up and down the city, at the feast of tabernacles, continually crying, *A voice from the east, a voice from the west, a voice from the four winds, a voice against Jerusalem and the temple, a voice against all this people.*

III. God will set up a church for himself in the world (*v.* 7): *Before she travailed she brought forth.* This is to be applied to the deliverance of the Jews out of their captivity in Babylon, which was brought about very easily and silently, without any pain or struggle. The man-child of the deliverance is rejoiced in, and yet the mother was never in labour for it; *before her pain came she was delivered.* This altogether without precedent, unless in the story which the Egyptian midwives told of the Hebrew women (Exod. i. 19), that *they were lively and were delivered ere the midwives came in unto them.* But *shall the earth be made to bring forth her fruits in one day?* No, it is the work of some weeks in the spring to *renew the face of the earth. Shall a land be brought forth in one day*, or *shall a nation be born at once? God does nothing abruptly.* Yet, in this case, *as soon as Zion travailed she brought forth.* Cyrus's proclamation was no sooner issued than the captives were ready to make the best of their way to their own land. And the reason is given (*v.* 9), because *it is the Lord's doing.* If he *bring to the birth* in preparing his people for deliverance, he will *cause to bring forth* in the accomplishment of the deliverance. When everything is ready, shall not I then *give strength to bring forth.* Does God cause mankind, and all the species of living creatures, to propagate, and *replenish the earth*, and *will he restrain Zion?* Will he not make her fruitful in a blessed offspring to replenish the church? But this was a figure of the setting up of the Christian church in the world, and the replenishing of that family with children to be named from Jesus Christ. When the Spirit was poured out, multitudes were converted in a little time and with little pains. The success of the gospel was astonishing. The same day that the Spirit was poured out there were 3,000 souls added to the church, *so mightily grew the word of God and prevailed.*

IV. Their present sorrows shall shortly be turned into abundant joys, *v.* 10, 11. The church's friends are such as *love her, and mourn* with her and *for her.* Those that have a sincere affection for the church have a cordial sympathy with her. They are encouraged: *Rejoice with her*, and again and again *I say, Rejoice.* Jerusalem shall have cause to rejoice; the days of her mourning shall be at an end. "You that mourned for her in her sorrows cannot but from the same principle rejoice with her in her joys." We must *suck and be satisfied with the breasts of her consolations.* The word of God, the covenant of grace (especially the promises of that covenant), the ordinances of God, and all the opportunities of conversing with him, are the breasts, which the church calls and counts the *breasts of her consolations.* We must take pleasure in our relation to God and communion with him. Whatever is the glory of the church must be *our glory and joy*, particularly her purity, unity, and increase.

V. He who gives them this call to rejoice will give them cause to do so and hearts to do so, *v.* 12–14. *I will extend peace to her* (that is, all good to her) *like a river* that runs in a constant stream. The gospel brings with it, wherever it is received in its power, such peace as this, which shall go on *like a river*, supplying souls with all good and making them fruitful, as a river does the lands it passes through. *The glory of the Gentiles* shall come to them *like a flowing stream*. God shall be glorified in all, and that ought to be more the matter of our joy than anything else (*v.* 14): *The hand of the Lord shall be known towards his servants*, he will at the same time make known *his indignation towards his enemies*. God's mercy and justice shall both be manifested. God will not only give them cause to rejoice, but will speak comfort *to their hearts*. Their country shall be their tender nurse: You shall be *carried on her sides*, under her arms, as little children are, and shall be *dandled upon her knees*. The great Shepherd *gathers the lambs in his arms and carries them in his bosom*, and so must the under-shepherds, that they may not be discouraged. God will himself be their powerful comforter: *As one whom his mother comforts*, when he is sick or in sorrow, *so will I comfort you*; not only with the rational arguments which a prudent father uses, but with the tender affections and compassions of a loving mother. They shall feel the blessed effects of this comfort in their own souls (*v.* 13). This was fulfilled in the wonderful satisfaction which Christ's disciples had in the success of their ministry. Christ tells them (John xvi. 22), *Your heart shall rejoice and your joy no man taketh from you*. Then *your bones*, that were dried and withered, shall recover a youthful strength and vigour and *shall flourish like a herb*.

Verses 15–24

These verses have a dark side towards the enemies of God's kingdom, and a bright side towards his faithful loyal subjects. Probably they refer to the Jews in captivity in Babylon, of whom some hated to be reformed, and therefore should be ruined by the calamity (Jer. xxiv. 9); others were sent thither for their good, and should in due time get well through it. But doubtless the prophecy looks further, to the judgment for which Christ did come once, and will come again.

I. Christ will appear to the confusion of all those that stand out against him. Sometimes he will appear in temporal judgments. The Jews that persisted in infidelity were cut off *by fire* and *by his sword*. The Lord then *pleaded with all flesh*; and, it being his sword with which they are cut off, they are called *his slain*. Idolaters will especially be contended with in the day of wrath, *v.* 17. Perhaps some of those who returned out of Babylon had their *idols in their gardens*, and there *purified themselves* when they went about their idolatrous rites, *one after another*, or, as we read it, *behind one tree in the midst*, behind *Ahad* or *Ehad*, some idol in honour of which they *ate swine's flesh, and other abominations*, as the *mouse*, or some other like animal. But the prophecy may refer to all those judgments which God will bring upon sinners, who are devoted to the world and the flesh: They *shall be consumed together*. God knows both what men do and with what design they do it.

II. He will appear to the comfort and joy of all that are faithful to him in the setting up of the kingdom of grace, the first-fruits of the kingdom of glory. The time shall come that he will *gather all nations and tongues to himself*, that they may *come and see his glory* as it shines in the face of Jesus Christ, *v.* 18. This was fulfilled when all nations were to be discipled and the gift of tongues was bestowed in order

thereunto. The church had hitherto been confined to one nation and in one tongue only God was worshipped.

1. Some of the Jewish nation should, by the grace of God, be distinguished from the rest, and marked for salvation: I will not only set up a *gathering ensign* among them, but there shall be those among them on whom *I will set a differencing sign*. Though they are a corrupt degenerate nation, yet God will set apart a remnant of them, that shall be devoted to him, and a mark shall be set upon them, with such certainty will God own them, Ezek. ix. 4. Christ's sheep are marked.

2. Those who are themselves distinguished thus shall be commissioned to be *sent to the nations* to carry the gospel among them, and preach it to every creature. They shall be sent to *the nations*, several of which are here named, Tarshish and Pul, and Lud, &c. It is uncertain what countries are here intended. *Tarshish* signifies in general *the sea*, yet some take it for Tarsus in Cilicia. *Pul* is the name of one of the kings of Assyria; perhaps some part of that country might likewise bear that name. *Lud* is supposed to be Lydia, a warlike nation, famed for archers, Jer. xlvi. 9. *Tubal*, some think, is Italy or Spain; and *Javan* Greece, the Iones; and the *isles of the Gentiles*, peopled by the posterity of Japhet (Gen. x. 5), probably are the *isles afar off*. In Judah only was God known, and other countries sat in darkness, heard not the joyful sound, saw not the joyful light. It is a pity that any of the children of men should be at such a distance from their Maker as not to hear his name and see his glory. Those that are sent to the nations shall go upon God's errand, to *declare his glory among the Gentiles*. The Jews that shall be dispersed among the nations shall declare the glory of God's providence concerning their nation all along. Some out of the nations shall *take hold of the skirt of him that is a Jew*, entreating him to take notice of them, "for *we will go with you, having heard that God is with you*," Zech. viii. 23.

3. Many converts shall hereby be made, *v.* 20. *They shall bring all your brethren* (for proselytes ought to be owned and embraced as brethren) *for an offering unto the Lord*. Some shall come *upon horses*, because they came from far. Some shall come in *chariots*, and the aged, and sickly, and little children, shall be brought *in litters* or covered waggons, and the young men *on mules and swift beasts*. They shall spare no trouble nor charge to get to Jerusalem. They shall come, not as formerly they used to come to Jerusalem, to be offerers, but to be themselves an *offering unto the Lord*, which must be understood spiritually, or their being presented to God as *living sacrifices*, Rom. xii. 1. They shall be brought *as the children of Israel bring an offering in a clean vessel*, with great care that they be holy, purified from sin, and sanctified to God. It is said of the converted Gentiles (Acts xv. 9) that *their hearts were purified by faith*. The apostle says of all true Christians that they *have come to Mount Zion, and the heavenly Jerusalem* (Heb. xii. 22), which explains this passage, and shows that the meaning of all this parade is only that they shall be brought into the church by the grace of God, as carefully as if they were carried in chariots and litters.

4. A gospel ministry shall be set up in the church (*v.* 21): *I will take of them* (the Gentile converts) *for priests and for Levites*, to minister in holy things. Hitherto the priests and Levites were all taken from among the Jews and all of one tribe; but in gospel times God will take of the converted Gentiles to minister, to teach the people, to be the stewards of the mysteries of God as the priests and Levites were under the law, to be pastors and teachers (or bishops), to *give themselves to the word and prayer*, and deacons

to *serve tables*, and, as the Levites, to take care of the *outward business of the house of God*, Phil. i. 1; Acts vi. 2–4. The apostles were all Jews, and so were the seventy disciples; the great apostle of the Gentiles was himself *a Hebrew of the Hebrews*; but, when churches were planted among the Gentiles, they had ministers who were *of themselves, elders in every church* (Acts xiv. 23, Tit. i. 5). God says, *I will take of them*, some of them. It is God's work originally to choose ministers by qualifying them and inclining them to the service, as well as by giving them their commission.

5. The church and ministry, being thus settled, shall be kept up in a succession from one generation to another, *v.* 22. The kingdom of the Messiah shall be a new world, *ch.* lxv. 17. *Old things have passed away*, behold *all things have become new* (2 Cor. v. 17), the old covenant of peculiarity is set aside, and a new covenant, a covenant of grace, established, Heb. viii. 13. New commandments are given relating both to heaven and earth, and new promises relating to both, and both together make a New Testament. It will be an abiding change, a new world that will be always new. The gospel dispensation is to continue to the end of time. It will be maintained in a seed that shall serve Christ: *Your seed*, and in them *your name, shall remain*; as one generation passes away, another shall come. The gates of hell, though they fight against the church, shall not *prevail*, nor *wear out the saints of the Most High*.

6. The public worship of God in religious assemblies shall be attended by all that are thus brought *as an offering to the Lord, v.* 23. This is described in expressions suited to the Old Testament dispensation, to show that though the ceremonial law should be abolished, and the temple service should come to an end, yet God should be still as regularly worshipped as ever. Heretofore only Jews went up to appear before God, and they were bound to attend only three times a year, and the males only; but now all flesh, Gentiles as well as Jews, women as well as men, shall *come and worship before God*, in his presence, though not in his temple at Jerusalem, but in assemblies dispersed all the world over, which shall be to them as the tabernacle of meeting was to the Jews. God will in them record his name, and, though but two or three come together, he will be among them, and bless them. There is no necessity of one certain place, as the temple was of old. Christ is our temple, in whom by faith all believers meet. But it is fit that there should be a certain time appointed, that the service may be done frequently, and a token thereby given of the spiritual communion which all Christian assemblies have with each other by faith, hope, and holy love. Where the Lord's day is weekly sanctified, and the Lord's supper monthly celebrated, and both duly attended, there the Christian new moons and sabbaths are observed.

7. Their thankful sense of God's distinguishing favour to them should be increased by the consideration of the destruction of those that persist in their impiety, *v.* 24. The wicked are men that have *transgressed against God*, not only broken his laws, but broken covenant with him. It may be meant especially of the unbelieving Jews that rejected the gospel of Christ. Their misery is represented by the spectacle of a field of battle, covered with the *carcases* of the slain, so that they are an *abhorring to all flesh*, nobody cares to come near them. Now this is accomplished in the destruction of Jerusalem and the Jewish nation by the Romans. It may refer likewise to the spiritual judgments that came upon the unbelieving Jews, which St. Paul looks upon, and shows us, Rom. xi. 8, &c. It will illustrate the joys and glories of the blessed to see that they were themselves as brands plucked out of that burning.

AN EXPOSITION, WITH PRACTICAL OBSERVATIONS, OF

THE BOOK OF
THE PROPHET JEREMIAH

Concerning this prophet Jeremiah we may observe, I. That he began young, and therefore could say, from his own experience, that it is good for a man to *bear the yoke in his youth*, the yoke both of service and of affliction, Lam. iii. 27. Jerome observes that Isaiah, who had more years, had his tongue touched with a coal of fire, to purge away his iniquity (*ch*. vi. 7), but that when God touched Jeremiah's mouth, nothing was said of the purging of his iniquity (*ch*. i. 9), because of his tender years. II. That he continued long a prophet, some reckon fifty years, others above forty. He began in the thirteenth year of Josiah, that good king, but he continued through all the wicked reigns that followed. III. That he was a reproving prophet, sent in God's name to tell Jacob of their sins and to warn them of the judgments of God; and the critics observe that therefore his style is more plain and rough, and less polite, than that of Isaiah and some others of the prophets. Plain-dealing is best when we are dealing with sinners to bring them to repentance. IV. That he was a weeping prophet; so he is commonly called, not only because he penned the Lamentations, but because he was all along a mournful spectator of the sins of his people. V. That he was a suffering prophet. He was persecuted by his own people more than any of them, as we shall find in the story of this book; for he lived and preached just before the Jews' destruction by the Chaldeans, when their character seems to have been the same as it was just before their destruction by the Romans, when they *killed the Lord Jesus, and persecuted his disciples, pleased not God, and were contrary to all men, for wrath had come upon them to the uttermost,* 1 Thess. ii. 15, 16. The last account we have of him is that the remaining Jews forced him to go down with them into Egypt; whereas the current tradition is, among Jews and Christians, that he suffered martyrdom. Hottinger, out of Elmakin, an Arabic historian, relates that, continuing to prophesy in Egypt against the Egyptians and other nations, he was stoned to death; and that long after, when Alexander entered Egypt, he took up the bones of Jeremiah where they were buried in obscurity, and carried them to Alexandria, and buried them there. The prophecies of this book which we have in the first nineteen chapters seem to be the heads of the sermons he preached in a way of general reproof for sin; afterwards they are more particular, mixed with the history of his day, but not placed in due order of time. With the threatenings are intermixed many gracious promises of mercy to the penitent, of the deliverance of the Jews out of their captivity, and some that have a plain reference to the kingdom of the Messiah. Among the Apocryphal writings an epistle is extant said to be written by Jeremiah to the captives in Babylon, warning them against the worship of idols, by exposing the vanity of idols and the folly of idolaters. It is in Baruch, *ch*. vi. But it is supposed not to be authentic; nor has it, I think, anything like the life and spirit of Jeremiah's writings. It is also related concerning Jeremiah (2 Mac. ii. 4) that, when Jerusalem was destroyed by the Chaldeans, he, by direction from God, took the ark and the altar of incense, and, carrying them to Mount Nebo lodged them in a hollow cave there and stopped the door; but some that followed him, and thought that they had marked the place, could not find it. He blamed them for seeking it, telling them that the place should be unknown till the time that God should gather his people together again.

CHAPTER 1

I. The general title of this book, with the time of Jeremiah's public ministry, ver. 1–3. II. The call of Jeremiah to the prophetic office, his modest objection against it answered, and an ample commission given him, ver. 4–10. III. The visions of an almond-rod and a seething-pot, signifying the approaching ruin of Judah and Jerusalem by the Chaldeans, ver. 11–16. IV. Encouragement given to the prophet to go on undauntedly in his work, ver. 17–19.

Verses 1–3

The genealogy of this prophet and the chronology of this prophecy. He was *the son of Hilkiah*, one *of the priests that were in Anathoth*. Jeremiah signifies one *raised up by the Lord*. He was *of the priests*, and, as a priest, was authorized and appointed to teach the people; but to that appointment God added the extraordinary commission of a prophet. Ezekiel also was a priest. Thus God would support the honour of the priesthood at a time when, by their sins and God's judgments upon them, it was sadly eclipsed. He was of the priests in Anathoth, a city of priests, which lay about three miles from Jerusalem. Abiathar had his country house there, 1 Kings ii. 26. He began to prophesy in the thirteenth year of Josiah's reign, *v.* 2. Josiah, in the twelfth year of his reign, began a work of reformation, applied himself with all sincerity to purge Judah and Jerusalem from the *high places, and the groves, and the images,* 2 Chron. xxxiv. 3. And very seasonably was this young prophet raised up to assist the young king in that good work. Now, one would

have expected when these two joined forces, such a prince, and such a prophet (as in a like case, Ezra v. 1, 2), and both young, such a complete reformation would be brought about as would prevent the ruin of the church and state; but it proved quite otherwise. In the eighteenth year of Josiah there were a great many of the relics of idolatry that were not purged out; for what can the best princes and prophets do to prevent the ruin of a people that hate to be reformed? And therefore Jeremiah continued to foretell the judgments that were coming upon them. Josiah and Jeremiah would have healed them, but they would not be healed. He continued to prophesy through the reigns of Jehoiakim and Zedekiah, each of whom reigned eleven years. He prophesied *to the carrying away of Jerusalem captive* (*v.* 3). He continued to prophesy after that, *ch*. xl. 1. From the thirteenth of Josiah to the captivity was just forty years. God, in this prophet, suffered their manners, their ill manners, forty years, and at length swore in his wrath that they should not continue in his rest.

Verses 4–10

I. Jeremiah's early designation to the office of a prophet (*v.* 4, 5): *The word of the Lord came to him,* and God told him, 1. That he had *ordained him a prophet to the nations*, the nation of the Jews in the first place, but to the neighbouring nations, to whom he was to *send yokes* (*ch*. xxvii. 2, 3) and whom he must make to *drink of the cup* of the Lord's anger, *ch.* xxv. 17. He is still, in his writings, a prophet to the nations (to our nation among the rest), to tell them what the national judgments are which may be expected for national sins. 2. That even in his eternal counsel, he had designed him to be so. This commission was given him in pursuance of the purpose God had purposed in himself concerning him, before he was born: "*I knew thee, and I sanctified thee,*" that is, "I determined that thou shouldst be a prophet and set thee apart for the office." What God has designed men for he will call them to. *Original endowment, not education, makes a prophet.*

II. His modestly declining this honourable employment, *v.* 6. "*Ah, Lord God! behold, I cannot speak* to great men and multitudes, as prophets must; I cannot speak fluently; I cannot speak with any authority, *for I am a child* and my youth will be despised." It becomes us, when we have any service to do for God, to be afraid lest we mismanage it, and lest it suffer through our weakness.

III. The assurance God graciously gave him that he would stand by him and carry him on in his work.

1. He is a child; he shall be a prophet for all that (*v.* 7): "Thou hast God's precept, and let not thy being young hinder thee from obeying it. Go to all *to whom I shall send thee and speak whatsoever I command thee.*" God was angry with Moses even for his modest excuses, Exod. iv. 14. Samuel delivered a message from God to Eli, when he was a little child. God can, when he pleases, make children prophets, and *ordain strength out of the mouth of babes and sucklings.*

2. Let him not object that he shall meet with much opposition; God will be his protector (*v.* 8): "*Be not afraid of their faces;* though they look big, and so think to outface thee. Thou speakest in the name of the King of kings, and by authority from him, and with that thou mayest *face them down.*" Those that have messages to deliver from God must not be *afraid of the face of man,* Ezek. iii. 9.

3. God will enable him to speak as one that had acquaintance with God, *v.* 9. He having now a vision of the divine glory, the Lord *put forth his hand, touched his mouth,* and with that touch *opened his lips.* God not only put knowledge into his head, but *words into his mouth;* for there are *words which the Holy Ghost teaches,* 1 Cor. ii. 13. He must speak as one that had authority from God, *v.* 10. *See, I have this day set thee over the nations and over the kingdoms.* This sounds very great, and yet Jeremiah is a poor priest still; he is not set over the kingdoms as a prince to rule them by the sword, but as a prophet by the power of the word of God. Jeremiah was *set over the nations,* not to demand tribute from them, but to *root out, and pull down,* and yet withal *to build and plant.* He must attempt to reform the nations, to *root out, and destroy* idolatry and other wickednesses among them, vicious habits and customs which had long taken root, to *throw down* the kingdom of sin, that religion and virtue might be *planted* and *built* among them. He must set before them *life and death, good and evil, ch.* xviii. 7–10. He must assure those who persisted in their wickedness that they should be *rooted out and destroyed,* and those who repented that they should be *built and planted.*

Verses 11–19

I. God gives Jeremiah, in vision, a view of the principal errand he was to go upon, which was to foretell the destruction of Judah and Jerusalem by the Chaldeans, for their sins, especially their idolatry.

1. He intimates to him that the people were ripening apace for ruin and that ruin was hastening apace towards him. He asks him, "*Jeremiah, what seest thou?* Look about thee, and observe now." "*I see a rod,*" denoting affliction and chastisement, a correcting rod hanging over us; and it is a *rod of an almond-tree,* which is one of the forwardest trees in the spring, is in the bud and blossom quickly, when other trees are scarcely broken out." (In Hebrew it is called a *hasty* tree.) God explained it in the next words (*v.* 12): *Thou hast well seen.* God commended him that he was so observant as to be aware, though it was the first vision he ever saw, that it was a *rod of an almond-tree.* "Thou hast seen a *hasty tree,* which signifies that *I will hasten my word to perform it.*" Jeremiah shall prophesy that which he himself shall live to see accomplished.

2. He intimates to him whence the intended ruin should arise. Jeremiah is a second time asked: *What seest thou?* and he sees *a seething-pot* upon the fire (*v.* 13), representing Jerusalem and Judah in great commotion, like boiling water, by reason of the descent which the Chaldean army made upon them; as boiling water evaporating and growing less and less. Now the face of the furnace over which this pot boiled, was *towards the north,* for thence the fire and the fuel were to come that must *make the pot boil thus.* So the vision is explained (*v.* 14). It had been long designed by the justice of God, and long deserved by the sin of the people, and yet hitherto the divine patience had restrained it, the enemies had intended it, and God had checked them; but now all restraints shall be taken off, and the *evil shall break forth.* Look for this storm to arise *out of the north, whence fair weather usually comes,* Job. xxxvii. 22. Sometimes the fiercest tempests come whence we expected fair weather. This is further explained *v.* 15, *I will call all the families of the kingdoms of the north, saith the Lord.* All the northern crowns shall unite under Nebuchadnezzar, and join with him in this expedition. God's summons shall be obeyed; those whom he calls shall come. The commanders of the troops of the several nations shall take their post in carrying on the siege of Jerusalem and the other cities of Judah.

3. He tells him plainly what was the cause of all these judgments; it was the *sin of Jerusalem* and of the *cities of Judah* (*v.* 16): *I will pass sentence upon them* (so it may be read) *because of all their wickedness.* They *have forsaken God* and have *burnt incense to other gods,* new gods, strange gods, and all false gods. Jeremiah was young, and perhaps did not know what abominable idolatries the children of his people were guilty of; but God tells him that he might himself be satisfied in the equity of the sentence which in God's name he was to pass upon them.

II. God encourages Jeremiah. A great trust is committed to him. He is sent as a herald at arms; for God is pleased to give warning of his judgments beforehand, that sinners may be awakened to meet him by repentance, and so *turn away his wrath.* With this trust Jeremiah has a charge given him (*v.* 17). He must be quick: *Arise,* and lose no time. He must be busy: *Arise, and speak unto them* in season, out of season. He must be bold: *Be not dismayed at their faces,* as before, *v.* 8.

1. In two things he must be faithful: (1) He must speak all that he is charged with: *Speak all that I command thee.* He must conceal nothing for fear of offending; he must *declare the whole counsel of God.* (2) He must not whisper it in a corner to a few particular friends, but he must appear *against the kings of Judah,* if they be wicked kings. He must not spare *the priests thereof;* though he himself was a priest, and was concerned to maintain the dignity of his order. He must appear against the *people of the land,* though they were his own people, as far as they were against the Lord.

2. Two reasons are here given why he should do thus: (1) Because he had reason to fear the wrath of God if he should be false: "*Be not dismayed at their*

faces, so as to desert thy office, or shrink from the duty of it, *lest I confound and dismay thee before them.*" The fear of God is the best antidote against the fear of man. It is better to have all the men in the world our enemies than God our enemy. (2) Because he had no reason to fear the wrath of men if he were faithful, *v.* 18. This young stripling of a prophet is made by the power of God as an impregnable city, fortified with iron pillars and surrounded with walls of brass; he sallies out upon the enemy in reproofs and threatenings, and *keeps them in awe.* They set upon him on every side; the kings and princes batter him with their power, the priests thunder against him with their church-censures, and *the people of the land* shoot their arrows at him, even slanderous and bitter words; but he shall keep his ground and shall still be a curb upon them (*v.* 19): *They shall fight against thee, but they shall not prevail to destroy thee, for I am with thee to deliver thee.*

CHAPTER 2

It is probable that this chapter was Jeremiah's first sermon after his ordination; and a most likely pathetic sermon. Let him not say, "I cannot speak, for I am a child"; for, God having touched his mouth and put his words into it, none can speak better. The scope of the chapter is to show God's people their transgressions, by way of reproof and conviction, that they might be brought to repent. The sin which they are most particularly charged with is idolatry. They are told, I. That this was ungrateful to God, ver. 1–8. II. That it was without precedent, that a nation should change their god, ver. 9–13. III. That hereby they had ruined themselves, ver. 14–19. IV. That they had broken their covenants and degenerated from their good beginnings, ver. 20, 21. V. That their wickedness was too bad to be excused, ver. 22, 23, 35. VI. That they persisted wilfully and obstinately in it, ver. 23, 25, 33, 36. VII. That they shamed themselves by their idolatry and should shortly be made ashamed of it when they should find their idols unable to help them, ver. 26–29, 37. VIII. That they had not been convinced and reformed by the rebukes of Providence, ver. 30. IX. That they had put a great contempt upon God, ver. 31, 32. X. That with their idolatries they had mixed the most unnatural murders, shedding the blood of the poor innocents, ver. 34.

Verses 1–8

I. A command given to Jeremiah to carry a message from God to the inhabitants of Jerusalem. Let a minister carefully compare what he has to deliver with the word of God, and see that it agrees with it, that he may be able to say, not only, *The Lord sent me,* but, He sent me to *speak this.* He must go from Anathoth, where he lived in a pleasant retirement, and in the study of the law, and make his appearance at Jerusalem, that noisy city, and *cry in their ears*: "Cry aloud, that all may hear. Go close to them, and *cry in the ears* of those that have stopped their ears."

II. The message he was commanded to deliver. He must upbraid them with their horrid ingratitude in forsaking a God who had been of old so kind to them.

1. God here puts them in mind of the favours he had of old bestowed upon them, when they were first formed into a people (*v.* 2): "*I remember for thy sake,* and I would have thee to remember it, and improve the remembrance of it for thy good; I cannot forget *the kindness of thy youth and the love of thy espousals.*" This may be understood of the kindness they had for God; it was not such indeed as they had any reason to boast of, yet God is pleased to mention it, for, though it was but little love that they showed him, he took it kindly. When *they believed the Lord and his servant Moses,* when they *sang God's praise at the Red Sea,* when at the foot of Mount Sinai they promised, *All that the Lord shall say unto us we will do and will be obedient,* then was the *kindness of their youth and the love of their espousals.* When they seemed so forward for God he said, *Surely they are my people,* and will be faithful to me, *children that will not lie.* In two things appeared the *kindness of their youth*: (1) That they followed the direction of

the pillar of cloud and fire in the wilderness; and for forty years *went after God in the wilderness,* and trusted him to provide for them, though it was *a land that was not sown.* This God took kindly. Thus, though Christ often chid his disciples, yet he commended them, at parting, for continuing with him, Luke xxii. 28. (2) That they set up the tabernacle among them. Israel *was then holiness to the Lord.* Thus they began in the spirit, and God puts them in mind of it, that they might be ashamed of ending *in the flesh.*

Or it may be understood of God's kindness to them; of that he afterwards speaks largely. *When Israel was a child, then I loved him,* Hos. xi. 1. [1] God appropriated them to himself. They were the *first fruits of his increase,* the first constituted church he had in the world; but the full harvest was to be gathered from among the Gentiles. [2] Having espoused them, he espoused their cause, and became an *enemy to their enemies,* Exod. xxiii. 22. Whoever offered any injury to the people of God did so at their peril. He had in a special manner a controversy with those that attempted to debauch them and draw them off from being *holiness to the Lord*; witness his *quarrel with the Midianites about the matter of Peor,* Num. xxv. 17, 18. [3] He *brought them out of Egypt* with a high hand and great terror (Deut. iv. 34), and yet with a kind hand and great tenderness led them through a vast howling wilderness (*v.* 6). In that darksome valley they walked forty years; but *God was with them*; and even there God *prepared a table for them* (Ps. xxiii. 4, 5), gave them bread out of the clouds and drink out of the rocks. All God's spiritual Israel must own their obligations to him for a safe conduct through the wilderness of this world, no less dangerous to the soul than that was to the body. [4] At length he settled them in Canaan (*v.* 7): *I brought you into a plentiful country.* They did *eat the fruit thereof* and the *goodness thereof.* I brought you *into a land of Carmel* (so the word is); Carmel was a place of extraordinary fruitfulness, and Canaan was as one great fruitful field, Deut. viii. 7. [5] God gave them the means of knowledge and grace, and communion with him; this is implied, *v.* 8.

2. He upbraids them with their ingratitude (*v.* 4). (1) He challenges them to produce any instance of his being unjust and unkind to them. He puts it fairly to them to show cause for their deserting him (*v.* 5): "*What iniquity have your fathers found in me,* or you either? Have you found God a hard master? You that have forsaken the ordinances of God, can you say that it was because they were a wearisome service. The disappointments you have met with were owing to yourselves, not to God. The yoke of his commandments is easy, and in the *keeping of them there is great reward.*" Though he afflicts us, he does us no wrong; all the iniquity is in our ways. (2) He charges them with being unjust and unkind to him notwithstanding. "*They have gone from me,* nay, they have gone *far from me.*" *They have walked after vanity,* that is, idolatry. They had with idolatry introduced all manner of wickedness. When they entered into the good land which God gave them they defiled it (*v.* 7), by defiling themselves. It was God's land, a holy land, Immanuel's land; but they *made it an abomination.* Having forsaken God they had no thoughts of returning to him again. Neither the people nor the priests made any enquiry after him, nor expressed any desire to recover his favour. The *people* said not, *Where is the Lord?* (*v.* 6). The *priests* said not, *Where is the Lord?* (*v.* 8). Those who should have instructed the people in the knowledge of God took no care to get the knowledge of him themselves. The scribes, who *handled the law,* did not know God nor his will. The pastors, who should have kept the flock from transgressing, were themselves ring-leaders in transgression: *They have transgressed*

against me. The pretenders to prophecy prophesied by Baal, to confront the Lord's prophets.

Verses 9–13

The prophet shows their unparalleled fickleness and folly (v. 9): *I will yet plead with you.* Before God punishes sinners he pleads with them, to bring them to repentance. Now he pleads with those who persisted in that *vain conversation received by tradition from their fathers*, and *with their children's children*, that is, with all that in every age tread in their steps.

I. He shows that they acted contrary to the usage of all nations. Their neighbours were more firm and faithful to their false gods than they were to the true God. Let them survey the present state of the isles of Chittim, Greece, and the European islands, the countries that were more polite and learned, and of Kedar; and they should not find an instance of a nation that had *changed their gods.* Such a veneration had they for their gods, that, though they were gods of wood and stone they would not change them for gods of silver and gold, no, not for the living and true God. *We praise them not.* But it may well be urged, to the reproach of Israel, that they, who were the only people that had no cause to change their God, were yet the only people that had changed him. The zeal and constancy of idolaters should shame Christians out of their coldness and inconstancy.

II. He shows that they acted contrary to the dictates of common sense, but changed for the worse, and made a bad bargain for themselves. 1. They parted from a God who made them truly glorious, for his glory had often appeared on their tabernacle. 2. They closed with gods that could do them no good, gods that *do not profit* their worshippers. Heaven itself is here called upon to stand amazed at the sin and folly of these apostates from God (v. 12, 13): *Be astonished, O you heavens! at this.* The meaning is that the conduct of this people towards God was, (1) Such as we may well wonder at, that ever men, who pretend to reason, should do a thing so very absurd. (2) Such as we ought to have a holy indignation at as impious, and a high affront to our Maker. "*My people,* whom I have taught, *have committed two* great evils, ingratitude and folly; they have acted contrary both to their duty and to their interest. *They have forsaken me, the fountain of living waters,* in whom they have an abundant and constant supply." God is their *fountain of life,* Ps. xxxvi. 9. There is in him an all-sufficiency of grace and strength; all our springs are in him. He has been to us a *fountain of living-waters,* over-flowing, ever-flowing, in the gifts of his favour. They have cheated themselves. They forsook *their own mercies* for lying vanities. They took a great deal of pains to *hew themselves out cisterns,* but they proved *broken cisterns,* so that they could *hold no water.* When they came to quench their thirst there they found nothing but mud and mire, and the filthy sediments of a standing lake. Such idols were to their worshippers. If we make an idol of any creature—wealth, or pleasure, or honour—if we make it our joy and love, we shall find it a cistern, which we take a great deal of pains to hew out and fill, and at the best it will hold but a little water, and that dead and flat. It is a broken cistern, that cracks in hot weather, so that the water is lost when we have most need of it, Job vi. 15. Let us therefore cleave to the Lord, he has *the words of eternal life.*

Verses 14–19

The folly of forsaking God had already cost them dear, for to this were owing all the calamities their country was now groaning under.

I. Their neighbours, who were their professed enemies, prevailed against them. 1. They were enslaved and lost their liberty (v. 14): *Is Israel a servant?*

No; *Israel is my son, my first-born,* Exod. iv. 22. They are children; they are heirs, the seed of Abraham. They were designed for dominion, not for servitude. *Why then is he spoiled* of his liberty? Why is he used as a servant, as a *home-born slave?* Why does he *make himself a slave* to his lusts, to his idols, to that which does not profit? *v.* 11. What a thing is this, that such a birthright should be sold for a mess of pottage, such a crown profaned and laid in the dust! The princes made slaves of their subjects, and masters made slaves of their servants (*ch.* xxxiv. 11), and so made their country mean and miserable, which God had made happy and honourable. The neighbouring princes and powers broke in upon them, and made some of them slaves even in their own country, and perhaps sold others for slaves into foreign countries. For *their iniquities they sold themselves,* Isa. l. 1. We may apply this spiritually. Is the soul of man a *servant?* Is it a home-born slave? No, it is not. Why then is it spoiled? It is because it has sold its own liberty and enslaved itself to divers lusts and passions. 2. They were impoverished and had lost their wealth. God brought them into a plentiful country (v. 7), but all their neighbours made a prey of it (v. 15): *Young lions roar aloud over him and yell.* Sometimes one potent enemy, and sometimes another, and sometimes many in confederacy, fall upon him, and triumph over him. They carry off the fruits of his land, and make that *waste,* and *burn his cities.* 3. They were abused, and insulted over, and beaten by everybody (v. 16): "Even *the children of Noph and Tahapanes,* despicable people, not famed for military courage nor strength, *have broken the crown of thy head.*" How calamitous the condition of Judah had been of late in the reign of Manasseh we find, 2 Chron. xxxiii. 11. 4. All this was owing to their sin (v. 17): *Hast thou not procured this unto thyself?* By their sinful confederacies with the nations, and conformity to them in their idolatrous customs, they had made themselves contemptible. "*Thou hast forsaken thy God at the time that he was leading thee by the way*" (so it should be read).

II. Their neighbours, their pretended friends, helped them not, and this also was owing to their sin. 1. They did in vain seek to Egypt and Assyria for help (v. 18): "*What hast thou to do in the way of Egypt?* Thou art for *drinking the waters of Sihor,*" that is, Nilus. "Thou reliest upon the fair promises they make thee. At other times thou art *in the way of Assyria,* going with all speed to fetch recruits thence, and thinkest to satisfy thyself with the *waters of the river Euphrates;* what *hast thou to do* there? What wilt thou get by applying to them? They shall *help in vain,* and what thou thoughtest a river will be but a broken cistern." 2. This also was because of their sin, v. 19. "*Thy own wickedness shall correct thee,* and then it is impossible for them to save thee; *know and see that it is an evil thing that thou hast forsaken God,* for it is that which makes thy enemies enemies indeed, and thy friends friends in vain." Sin is *forsaking the Lord* as our God; it is the soul's alienation from him. The cause of sin is because *his fear is not in us.* Sin is an evil that has no good in it. It is *bitter;* the wages of it is death, and death is bitter. As it is in itself evil and bitter, so it has a direct tendency to make us miserable: "*Thy own wickedness shall correct thee, and thy backslidings shall reprove thee;* the punishment will so inevitably follow the sin that the sin shall itself be said to punish thee. Thy own wickedness shall convince thee and stop thy mouth for ever and thou shalt be forced to own that *the Lord is righteous.*"

Verses 20–28

I. The sin itself—idolatry. 1. They frequented the places of idol-worship (v. 20): "*Upon every high hill and under every green tree*, in the high places and the groves, *thou wanderest*, unsettled, and unsatisfied; but in all *playing the harlot*," spiritual whoredom, and commonly accompanied with corporal whoredom. 2. They made images for themselves, and gave divine honour to them (v. 26, 27); not only the common people, but even the kings and princes, the priests and prophets, were themselves so stupid as to *say to a stock*, "*Thou art my father* (that is, Thou art my god, the author of my being, to whom I owe duty and on whom I have a dependence)," and *to a stone*, to an idol made of stone, "*Thou hast* begotten me, or *brought me forth*; therefore protect me." What greater affront could men put upon God our Father that has made us? When these were first made the objects of worship they were supposed to be animated by some celestial power or spirit; but by degrees the thought of this was lost. *In their imagination* the very idol was supposed to be their father, and adored accordingly. 3. They multiplied these dunghill deities endlessly (v. 28): *According to the number of thy cities are thy gods, O Judah!* They could not agree in the same god. One city fancied one deity and another another.

II. The proof of this. They pretended that they would acquit themselves from this guilt, they *washed themselves with nitre*, and *took much soap, v. 22*. They pretended that they did not worship these as gods, but as demons, or that it was not divine honour that they gave them, but civil respect; thus they sought to evade the convictions of God's word. They said, *I am not polluted, I have not gone after Baalim, v. 23*. Because it was done secretly, and industriously concealed (Ezek. viii. 12), they thought it could never be proved upon them. "*How canst thou* deny the fact, and *say, I have not gone after Baalim?*" "It is *imprinted deeply* and *stained* before me"; so some read it. "Though thou endeavour to wash it out, as murderers to get the stain of the blood of the person slain out of their clothes, yet it will never be got out." *See thy way in the valley* (they had worshipped idols, not only on the high hills, but in the valleys, Isa. lvii. 5, 6), in the *valley over against Beth-peor* (so some), (Deut. xxiv. 6, Num. xxv. 3), but, if it mean any particular valley, surely it is the *valley of the son of Hinnom*, for that was the place where they sacrificed their children to Moloch and which therefore witnessed against them more than any other.

III. The aggravations of this sin with which they are charged.

1. God has done great things for them, and yet they revolted from him and rebelled against him (v. 20): *Of old time I have broken thy yoke and burst thy bonds*. These bonds of theirs which God had loosed should have bound them for ever to him.

2. They had promised fair, but had not made good their promise: "*Thou saidst, I will not transgress*."

3. They had wretchedly degenerated from what they were when God first formed them into a people (v. 21): *I had planted thee a noble vine. Israel served the Lord*, and kept close to him *all the days of Joshua, and the elders that out-lived Joshua*, Joshua xxiv. 31. The very next generation *knew not the Lord, nor the works which he had done* (Judges ii. 10), and so they were worse and worse till they became *the degenerate plants of a strange vine*.

4. They were violent and eager in the pursuit of their idolatries, and they would not be restrained either by the word of God or by his providence. They are compared to a *swift dromedary traversing her ways*, a female hunting (v. 23), and, to the same purport, *a wild ass used to the wilderness* (v. 24), not tamed by labour, and therefore very wanton, *snuffing up the wind at her pleasure*, on such an occasion *who can turn her away*? Who can hinder her from that which she lusts after? *Those that seek her* then *will not weary themselves for her*, but will have patience till she is big with young, and then *they shall find her*, and she cannot out-run them. Eager lust is a brutish thing, and those that will not be turned away are to be reckoned as brute-beasts. Let them not be looked upon as rational creatures. Idolatry is strangely intoxicating. *Ephraim is joined to idols; let him alone*. The time will come when the most fierce will be tamed; when distress and anguish come upon them, then their ears will be open to discipline.

5. They were obstinate in their sin, and, as they could not be restrained, so they would not be reformed, v. 25. He would certainly bring them into a miserable captivity, when they should be forced to travel barefoot, and when they would be denied fair water, so that their throat should be dried with thirst. Those that affect strange gods, and strange ways of worship, will justly be made prisoners to a strange king in a strange land. They said to those that would have persuaded them to repent and reform, *There is no hope; no*, never expect us to cast away our idols, for *we have loved strangers, and after them we will go*. But, as we must not despair of the mercy of God, but believe that sufficient for the pardon of our sins, though ever so heinous, if we repent and sue for that mercy, so neither must we despair of the grace of God, but believe that able to subdue our corruptions, though ever so strong, if we pray for and improve that grace. A man must never say *There is no hope*, as long as he is on this side hell.

6. They had shamed themselves by putting him away that would have helped them, v. 26–28. *As the thief is ashamed* when he is found, and brought to punishment, *so are the house of Israel ashamed*, not with a penitent shame for the sin they had been guilty of, but with a penal shame for the disappointment they met with in that sin. In their prosperity they had turned the back to God, but in the time of their trouble they will find no satisfaction but in applying to him; then *they will say, Arise, and save us*. To bring them to this shame, if so they might be brought to repentance, they are sent *to the gods whom they served*, Judges x. 14. They cried to God, *Arise, and save us*. God says of the idols, "*Let them arise, and save thee*, for thou hast no reason to expect that I should."

Verses 29–37

I. The truth of the charge was evident beyond contradiction (v. 29): "*Wherefore will you plead with me?* You know *you have all transgressed*, one as well as another; why then do you *quarrel with me* for contending with you?"

II. He heightens it from the consideration both of their incorrigibleness and of their ingratitude. They had been under divine rebukes of many kinds. God therein designed to bring them to repentance; but it was *in vain*. Their consciences were not awakened, nor their hearts softened. *They received no instruction* by the *correction*, were not made the better by it. They *did not receive* the correction, and so they were *smitten in vain*. They had not been wrought upon by the word of God which he had sent them in the mouth of his servants the prophets; they had killed the messengers for the sake of the message: "*Your own sword has devoured your prophets like a destroying lion*" (v. 31): "*O generation!*" (he speaks gently, O you men of this generation!) "*see the word of the Lord*, do not only hear it." As we are bidden to *hear the rod* (Micah vi. 9), for that has its voice, so we are bidden to *see the word*, for that has its visions, its views. It is written as with a sunbeam, so that he that runs may read it: *Have I been a wilderness to Israel, a land of darkness?* The service of God has not been either an unpleasant or an unprofitable service. God sometimes has led his people *through a wilderness* and a *land of darkness*, but he himself was then to them all that which they needed; he so fed them with manna, and led them by a pillar of fire, that it was to them a fruitful field and a land of light. They had grown intolerably insolent and imperious. They say, *We are lords; we will come no more unto thee.* It is absurd for us who are beggars to say, *We are lords*, that is, We are rich, and we will come no more to God.

III. He lays the blame of all their wickedness upon their forgetting God (*v.* 32): *They have forgotten me; they have avoided all those things that would put them in mind of God.* They had neglected him, *days without number*, time out of mind. How many days of our lives have passed without suitable remembrance of God! Who can number those empty days? They had not had such a regard to him as young ladies have to their fine clothes: *Can a maid forget her ornaments or a bride her attire?* No; they are ever and anon thinking and speaking of them.

IV. He shows them what a bad influence their sins had had upon others (*v.* 33): *Why trimmest thou thy way to seek love?* There is an allusion here to lewd women who recommend themselves by their ogling looks and gay dress, as Jezebel, who *painted her face and tired her head.* Thus they courted their neighbours into sinful confederacies with them and *taught the wicked ones their ways* of mixing God's institutions with their idolatrous customs. Those have a great deal to answer for who, by their fellowship with the unfruitful works of darkness, made wicked ones more wicked than otherwise they would be.

V. He charges them with the guilt of murder (*v.* 34): *Also in thy skirts is found the blood of the souls,* the life-blood *of the poor innocents.* The reference is to the children that were offered in sacrifice to Moloch; or it may be taken more generally for all the *innocent blood* which Manasseh shed, and with which he had *filled Jerusalem* (2 Kings xxi. 16). This blood was found *not by secret search,* not *by digging* (so the word is), but *upon all these*; it was above ground. This intimates that the guilt was avowed and barefaced.

VI. He overrules their plea of *Not guilty* (*v.* 35). *I will plead with thee,* and will convince thee of thy mistake. They conclude that God will immediately let fall his action and *his anger shall be turned from them.* This is very provoking, and God will convince them that his anger is just, and he will never cease his controversy till they, instead of justifying themselves, judge and condemn themselves.

VII. He upbraids them with the shameful disappointments they met with, in making creatures their confidence, while they made God their enemy, *v.* 36, 37. It was a piece of spiritual idolatry that they trusted in *an arm of flesh* and their hearts *departed from the Lord. Why gaddest thou about so much to change thy way?* Those that make God their hope, and walk in continual dependence upon him, need not *gad about to change their way*; for their souls may return to him, and repose in him, as their rest. They first trusted to Assyria, and, when that proved a broken reed, they depended upon Egypt, and that proved no better. *Thou shalt be ashamed of Egypt,* which thou now trustest in, as formerly *thou wast of Assyria, who distressed them and helped them not,* 2 Chron. xxviii. 20. Thy ambassadors or envoys shall return from Egypt *disappointed,* lamenting the desperate condition of their people. Or, *Thou shalt go forth hence,* that is, into captivity in a strange land, *with thy hands upon thy head.* "And Egypt, that thou reliest on, shall not be able to prevent it nor to rescue thee out of captivity." As *there is no counsel or wisdom* that can prevail

against the Lord, so there is none that can prevail without him.

CHAPTER 3

In this chapter gracious invitations are given to return and repent, notwithstanding the multitude of their provocations, which are here specified, to show that as sin abounded grace did much more abound. Here, I. It is further shown how bad they had been, and yet how ready God was to receive them into his favour upon their repentance, ver. 1–5. II. The impenitence of Judah, ver. 6–11. III. Great encouragements are given to these backsliders to return and repent, and promises are made of great mercy which God had in store for them, ver. 12–19. IV. The charge renewed against them for their apostasy from God, and the invitation repeated, to which are here added the words, which they should make use of in their return to God, ver. 20–25.

Verses 1–5

These verses open a door of hope. God wounds that he may heal.

I. How basely this people had forsaken God and gone a-whoring from him. To have admitted one strange God among them would have been bad enough, but they were insatiable in their lustings after false worships: *Thou hast played the harlot with many lovers, v.* 1. They had sought opportunity for their idolatries and had sent about to enquire for new gods: *In the high-ways hast thou sat for them. As the Arabian in the wilderness*—the Arabian *huckster* (so some), that courts customers, or the *Arabian thief* (so others), that watches for his prey. They not only polluted themselves, but *their land, with their whoredoms and with their wickedness* (*v.* 2); for it became a national sin. And yet (*v.* 3), "*Thou hadst a whore's forehead,* a brazen face of thy own." *Thou refusedst to be ashamed.* Blushing is the colour of virtue, or at least a relic of it; but those that are past shame (we say) are past hope.

II. How gently God had corrected them for their sins. He only *withheld the showers from them,* and that only one part of the year.

III. How justly God might have refused ever to receive them again; this would have been but according to the known rule of divorces, *v.* 1. *They say* (Deut. xxiv. 4), that if a woman be once put away, and be joined to *another man,* her first husband shall never take her again to be his wife; such playing fast and loose with the marriage-bond would be a horrid profanation of that ordinance and would *greatly pollute that land.*

IV. How graciously he invites them to return to him. "Though thou hast been bad, *yet return again to me," v.* 1. God has not tied himself by the laws which he made for us, nor has he the peevish resentment that men have; he will be more kind to Israel than ever any injured husband was to an adulterous wife. He kindly directs them what to say to him (*v.* 4): "*Wilt thou not from this time cry unto me?* Now that thou hast been made to see thy sins (*v.* 2) and to smart for them (*v.* 3), wilt thou not now forsake them and return to me, saying, *I will go and return to my first husband, for then it was better with me than now?*" (Hos. ii. 7). He expects that they will claim relation to God, as theirs: *Wilt thou not cry unto me, My father, thou art the guide of my youth?* They will surely come towards him as a father, to beg his pardon for their undutiful behaviour to him. Or it may be taken more generally: "As *my Father,* thou *art the guide of my youth.*" Youth needs a guide. In our return to God we must thankfully remember that he *was the guide of our youth* in the way of comfort; he shall be our guide henceforward in the way of duty.

Verses 6–11

The date of this sermon was *in the days of Josiah,* who set on foot a blessed work of reformation, in which he was hearty, but the people were not sincere.

The case of the two kingdoms of Israel and Judah is here compared, the *ten tribes* that revolted from the throne of David and the temple of Jerusalem and the *two tribes* that adhered to both.

I. A short account of Israel, the ten tribes. She is called *backsliding Israel* because that kingdom was first founded in an apostasy from the divine institutions, both in church and state. They had *played the harlot upon every high mountain and under every green tree* (v. 6), that is, they had worshipped other gods in their high places and groves. God by his prophets had invited and encouraged them to repent and reform (v. 7): "*After she had done all these things*, for which she might justly have been abandoned, yet *I said* unto her, *Turn thou unto me* and I will receive thee." God sent his prophets among them, to call them to *return to him*, to the worship of him only, not insisting so much upon their return to the house of David, but pressing their return to the house of Aaron. We read not that Elijah, that great reformer, ever mentioned their return to the house of David. Notwithstanding this, they had persisted in their idolatries: *But she returned not*, and God *saw it*, v. 7, 8. He had therefore given them into the hands of their enemies (v. 8): *When I saw* (so it may be read) *that for all the actions wherein she had committed adultery I must dismiss her, I gave her a bill of divorce.* He scattered all their synagogues and the schools of the prophets and excluded them from laying any further claim to the covenant made with their fathers.

II. The case of Judah, the kingdom of the two tribes. She is called *treacherous sister Judah*, a sister because descended from the same common stock, Abraham and Jacob; but, as Israel had the character of a *backslider*, so Judah is called *treacherous*, because, though she professed to keep close to God when Israel had backslidden (she adhered to the kings and priests that were of God's own appointing), yet she proved treacherous. Israel's captivity was intended for Judah's admonition; but it had not the designed effect. Judah thought herself safe because she had Levites to be her priests and sons of David to be her kings. She *defiled the land*, and made it an abomination to God; for she *committed adultery with stones and stocks*, with the basest idols, those made of *wood and stone*. In the reigns of Manasseh and Amon, all the country was corrupted. God tried whether they would be good in a good reign, but the evil disposition was still the same: *They returned not to me with their whole heart, but feignedly*, v. 10. Josiah went further in destroying idolatry than the best of his predecessors had done, and he *turned to the Lord with all his heart and with all his soul* (2 Kings xxiii. 25). The people were forced to an external compliance with him (2 Chron. xxxiv. 32, xxxv. 17); but they were not sincere in it, nor were their *hearts right with God.* For this reason God at that very time said, *I will remove Judah out of my sight, as I removed Israel* (2 Kings xxiii. 27). I know no religion without sincerity.

III. The case of these sister kingdoms is compared, and of the two Judah was the worse (v. 11). This comparative justification will stand Israel in little stead; what will it avail us to say, *We are not so bad as others*, when yet we are not really good ourselves? Judah was in two respects worse than Israel: 1. More was expected from Judah than from Israel; Judah vilified a more sacred profession, and falsified a more solemn promise, than Israel did. 2. Judah might have taken warning by the ruin of Israel and would not.

Verses 12–19

There is a great deal of gospel in these verses. The prophet is directed to *proclaim these words towards the north*, for they are a call to backsliding Israel, the ten tribes that were carried captive into Assyria, which lay north from Jerusalem. That way he must look to upbraid the men of Judah with their obstinacy in refusing to answer the calls given them. *Backsliding Israel* will sooner accept of mercy, and have the benefit of it, than *treacherous Judah.* And perhaps the proclaiming of these words towards the north looks as far forward as the *preaching of repentance and remission of sins unto all nations, beginning at Jerusalem*, Luke xxiv. 47.

I. Here is an invitation given to *backsliding Israel*, and in them to the backsliding Gentiles, to *return unto God*, the God from whom they had revolted (v. 12): *Return, thou backsliding Israel.* And again (v. 14): "*Turn, O backsliding children!* Come back to that good way, out of which you have turned aside." They are encouraged to return. "You have incurred God's displeasure, but return to me, and *I will not cause my anger to fall upon you.*" They are directed how to return (v. 13): "*Only acknowledge thy iniquity*, own thyself in a fault and thereby take shame to thyself and give glory to God." This will aggravate the condemnation of sinners, that the terms of pardon and peace were brought so low, and yet they would not come up to them. *If the prophet had told thee to do some great thing wouldst thou not have done it? How much more when he says, Only acknowledge thy iniquity?* (2 Kings v. 13). We must own our actual sins: "*That thou hast transgressed against the Lord thy God*, hast affronted him and offended him." We must own the multitude of our transgressions: "*That thou hast scattered thy ways to the strangers*, run hither and thither in pursuit of thy idols, *under every green tree.* "You have not obeyed my voice; acknowledge that, and let that humble you more than anything else."

II. Here are precious promises made to these backsliding children, if they do return, which were in part fulfilled in the return of the Jews out of their captivity, but the prophecy is to have its full accomplishment in the gospel church, and the gathering together of *the children of God that were scattered abroad*: "Return, for, though you are backsliders, yet you are children; though a treacherous wife, yet a wife, for *I am married to you* (v. 14) and will not disown the relation." Thus God remembers his covenant with their fathers, Lev. xxvi. 42.

1. He promises to gather them together from all places whither they are dispersed and scattered abroad, John xi. 52, *I will take you, one of a city, and two of a family*, or clan; *and I will bring you to Zion*, v. 14. Of the many that have backslidden from God there are but few that return to him—*one of a city and two of a country.* Of those few, though dispersed, yet not one shall be lost. Though there be but *one in a city*, God will find out that one. God's chosen, scattered all the world over, shall be brought to *the gospel church*, that Mount Zion, the heavenly Jerusalem, that holy hill on which Christ reigns.

2. He promises to set those over them that shall be every way blessings to them (v. 15): *I will give you pastors after my heart.* (1) When a church is gathered it must be governed. "*I will bring them to Zion* to be under discipline, not as wild beasts, but as sheep, under the direction of a shepherd. *I will give them pastors*, that is, both magistrates and ministers." (2) It is well with a people when their pastors are *after God's own heart*, who shall make his will their rule in all their administrations, who rule for him, and, as they are capable, rule like him. (3) Those are pastors after God's own heart who feed the flock, not *fleece the flocks*, but who *feed them with wisdom and understanding.* Those who are not only pastors, but teachers, must feed them with the word of God, which is able to make us wise to salvation.

3. He promises that there shall be no more occasion for the *ark of the covenant*, which had been the token of God's presence with them; that shall be set aside (v. 16): *When you shall be multiplied and increased in the land*, when the kingdom of the Messiah shall be set up, then *they shall say no more, The ark of the covenant of the Lord*, because they shall have a pure spiritual way of worship set up, in which the whole ceremonial law shall be set aside, for Christ, the truth of all those types, exhibited to us in the word and sacraments of the New Testament, will be to us instead of all. But in the gospel temple Christ *is the ark*; he is the mercy-seat; and it is the spiritual presence of God in his ordinances that we are now to expect. Many expressions are here used concerning the setting aside of the ark, that it shall not *come to mind*, that they *shall not remember it*, that they shall *not visit it*, that none of these things shall be *any more done*; for the *true worshippers shall worship the Father in spirit and in truth*, John iv. 24.

4. He promises that the gospel church, here called *Jerusalem*, shall become eminent, v. 17. Two things shall make it famous: (1) God's special residence and dominion in it. It shall be called, *The throne of the Lord*—of his glory, of *his government, and his grace*. (2) The accession of the Gentiles to it. *All the nations shall* become subjects to that *throne of the Lord* which is there set up.

5. He promises that there shall be a wonderful reformation wrought in the church: *They shall not walk any more after the imagination of their evil hearts*. They shall not live as they list, but live by rules, according to the will of God. See what leads in sin—*the imagination of our own evil hearts*; sin is *walking after* that imagination, being governed by fancy and humour; converting grace takes us off from walking after *our own inventions* and brings us to be governed by religion and right reason.

6. That Judah and Israel shall be happily united in one body, v. 18. They were so in their return out of captivity and their settlement again in Canaan. This happy coalescence between Israel and Judah in Canaan was a type of the uniting of Jews and Gentiles in the gospel church, when, all enmities being slain, they should become one *sheepfold under one shepherd*.

III. Difficulty in the way of all this mercy.

1. God asks, *How shall I do this for thee?* Not as if God showed favour with reluctancy, but we are utterly unworthy of his favours, there is nothing in us to deserve them. How should we who are so mean and weak, so worthless and unworthy, and so provoking, ever be *put among the children?* To those whom God puts among the children he will *give the pleasant land*, the land of Canaan. It was a type of heaven, where there are *pleasures for evermore*. Who could expect a place in that *pleasant land* that has so often *despised it* (Ps. cvi. 24) and is so unfit for it?

2. He does himself return answer to this question: *But I said, Thou shalt call me, My Father*. God does himself answer all the objections. That he may put returning penitents *among the children*, he will give them the *Spirit of adoption*, teaching them *to cry, Abba, Father* (Gal. iv. 6). "*Thou shalt call me, My Father;* thou shalt return to me, and resign thyself to me as a father, and that shall recommend thee to my favour." He will *put his fear in their hearts*, that they may never *turn from him*, but may persevere to the end.

Verses 20–25

I. The charge against Israel for their treacherous departures, v. 20. They were joined to God by a marriage-covenant, but they broke that covenant, they *dealt treacherously* with God.

II. Their confession of the truth of this charge, v. 21. When God ·reproved them for their apostasy,

there were some whose *voice was heard upon the high places weeping and praying*, humbling themselves before the God of their fathers, that *they have perverted their way and forgotten the Lord their God*. Sin is the turning aside to crooked ways. Forgetting the Lord our God is at the bottom of all sin. If men would remember God, they would not transgress.

III. The invitation God gives them to return to him (v. 22): *Return, you backsliding children*. He calls them *children* in tenderness and compassion to them, froward as children, yet *his sons*, whom though he corrects he will not disinherit. God bears with such children, and so must parents. When they are convinced of sin (v. 21), then they are *invited* to *return*, as Christ invites those to him that are *weary* and *heavy-laden*. The promise to those that return is, *I will heal your backslidings*. God will *heal our backslidings* by his pardoning mercy, his quieting peace, and his renewing grace.

IV. The ready consent they give to this invitation. This is an echo to God's call; as a voice returned from broken walls, so this from broken hearts. God says, *Return;* they answer, *Behold, we come*. It is an immediate answer. 1. They come devoting themselves to God as theirs: "*Thou art the Lord our God. It is our sin and folly that we have gone from thee.*" 2. They come claiming succour from God only: "*In vain is salvation hoped for from the hills and from the multitude of the mountains.*" They worshipped their idols upon hills and mountains (v. 6), but now they will have no more to do with them. Therefore, 3. They come depending upon God only as their God: *In the Lord our God is the salvation of Israel*. It is applicable to the great salvation from sin, which Jesus Christ wrought for us; that is the *salvation of the Lord*, his *great salvation*. 4. They come justifying God in their troubles and judging themselves for their sins, v. 24, 25. They impute all the calamities they had been under to their idols. *Shame* (the idol, that shameful thing) *has devoured the labour of our fathers*. True penitents have learned to call sin *shame*. True penitents have learned to call sin death and ruin. "It has *devoured* all those good things which our fathers *laboured for* and left to us; we have found *from our youth* that our idolatry has been the destruction of our prosperity." Of the labour of their fathers, which their idols had devoured, they mention particularly *their flocks and their herds, their sons and their daughters*. They take to themselves the shame of their sin and folly (v. 25): "*We lie down in our shame*, being unable to bear up under it; *our confusion covers us*, that is, both our penal and our penitential shame. We are sinners by descent: *We and our fathers have sinned*. We have sinned *from our youth*; we have continued in sin, have sinned *even unto this day*, though often called to repent and forsake our sins. *We have not obeyed the voice of the Lord our God*, commanding us, when we have sinned, to repent." All this seems to be the language of the penitents of *the house of Israel* (v. 20), of the ten tribes, either of those that were in captivity or those of them that remained in their own land. And the prophet takes notice of their repentance to provoke the men of Judah to a holy emulation.

CHAPTER 4

It should seem that the first two verses of this chapter might better have been joined to the foregoing chapter, for they are directed to Israel, the ten tribes, encouraging them to hold their resolution, ver. 1, 2. The rest of the chapter concerns Judah and Jerusalem. I. They are called to repent and reform, ver. 3, 4. II. They are warned of the advance of Nebuchadnezzar and his forces against them, ver. 5–18. III. To affect them the more, the prophet does himself bitterly lament and sympathizes with his people in the calamities it brought upon them, ver. 19–31.

Verses 1-2

When God called to backsliding Israel to return (*ch.* iii. 22) they immediately answered, *Lord, we return;* now God here takes notice of their answer.

I. "Dost thou say, *I will return?* Then thou must *return unto me;* make a thorough work of it. Return to the instituted worship of the God of Israel." Thou must utterly abandon all sin, and not retain any of the relics of idolatry: *Put away thy abominations out of my sight.* Their idolatries were not only obvious, but offensive, to the eye of God. They must be *put away out of his sight,* because they were a provocation to the pure eyes of God's glory. They must not return to sin again; so some understand that, *Thou shalt not remove,* reading it, *Thou shalt not,* or *must not wander.* They must give unto God the glory due unto his name (*v.* 2): "*Thou shalt swear, The Lord liveth.* His existence shall be with thee the most sacred fact."

II. He encourages them to keep their resolutions. "*If thou wilt return to me,* then *thou shalt return,* that is, thou shalt be brought back out of thy captivity into thy own land again, as was of old promised," Deut. iv. 29; xxx. 2. They shall be blessings to others; for their returning to God again will be a means of others turning to him who never knew him. See Isa. lxv. 16. They shall bless themselves *in the God of truth,* and not in false gods, and *in him shall they glory;* they shall make him their glory.

Verses 3-4

The prophet here turns his speech, in God's name, to the men of the place where he lived. We have heard what words he proclaimed *towards the north* (*ch.* iii. 12), for the comfort of those that were now in captivity; let us now see what he says to the *men of Judah and Jerusalem,* who were now in prosperity, for their conviction and awakening. In these two verses he exhorts them to repentance and reformation, to prevent the desolating judgments that were ready to break in upon them.

I. The duties required of them,

1. They must do by their hearts as they do by their ground that they expect any good of; they must plough it up (*v.* 3): "*Break up your fallow-ground. Plough to yourselves a ploughing* (or *plough up your plough land*), that you *sow not among thorns,* that you may not labour in vain as you have been doing a great while. Put yourselves into a frame fit to receive mercy from God, and put away all that which keeps it from you, and then you may expect to receive mercy and to prosper in your endeavours to help yourselves." An unconvinced unhumbled heart is like fallow-ground, untilled, unoccupied. It is ground capable of improvement; but it is unfenced, unfruitful, overgrown with thorns and weeds, which are the natural product of the corrupt heart; and, if it be not renewed with grace, rain and sunshine are lost upon it, Heb. vi. 7, 8. We are concerned to get this fallow-ground ploughed up. We must search into our own hearts, must pluck up by the roots those corruptions which, as thorns, choke our endeavours.

2. They must do that to their souls which was done to their bodies when they were taken into covenant with God (*v.* 4): "*Circumcise yourselves to the Lord, and take away the foreskins of your heart.* Mortify the flesh and the lusts of it. Boast not of the circumcision of the body, for that is but a sign, and will not serve without the thing signified. It is a dedicating sign. Do that in sincerity which was done in profession by your circumcision; devote and consecrate yourselves unto the Lord."

II. The danger threatened. Repent and reform, *lest my fury come forth like fire.* That which is to be dreaded by us more than anything else is the wrath

of God. It is the *evil of our doings* that kindles the fire of God's wrath against us. The consideration of the imminent danger should awaken us to *sanctify ourselves to God's glory* and to see to it that we be *sanctified by his grace.*

Verses 5-18

God's usual method is to warn before he wounds. In these verses God gives notice to the Jews of the general desolation that would shortly be brought upon them by a foreign invasion. This must be declared in all the cities of Judah and streets of Jerusalem, that all might hear and be either brought to repentance or left inexcusable.

I. The war proclaimed, and notice given of the advance of the enemy. It is published now, some years before, by the prophet, *v.* 5, 6. The *trumpet* must be *blown,* the *standard* must be *set up,* a summons must be issued to the people, to *gather together* and to draw *towards Zion,* either to guard it or expecting to be guarded by it. The militia must be raised and all the forces mustered. Those that are fit for service, must *go into the defenced cities,* to garrison them; those that are weak must *retire,* and *not stay.*

II. An express arrived with intelligence of the approach of the king of Babylon and his army. The enemy is here compared, 1. To *a lion that comes up from his thicket,* when he is hungry, to seek his prey, *v.* 7. The helpless beasts are terrified and so become an easy prey to him. Nebuchadnezzar is this roaring tearing lion, *the destroyer of the nations,* now *on his way* towards the land of Judah. The *destroyer of the Gentiles* shall be the *destroyer of the Jews* too, when they have by their idolatry made themselves like the Gentiles. He has *gone forth from his place,* from Babylon, against *this land;* the cities shall be *laid waste, without inhabitants,* shall be *overgrown with grass* as a field; so some read it. 2. To a *drying* blasting *wind* (*v.* 11), which spoils the fruits of the earth and withers them, such as comes *out of the north,* which *drives away rain* (Prov. xxv. 23). A *black* freezing wind. Wherever they go, it shall surround them. It is a *wind of the high places in the wilderness* that beats upon the tops of the hills or that carries all before it in the plain. It shall come in its full force *towards the daughters of my people,* that have been brought up so tenderly. Now this fierce wind shall come against them, *not to fan, nor cleanse* them, but a *full wind* (*v.* 12). This shall come *to me,* or rather *for me;* it shall come with commission from God and shall accomplish that for which he sends it. 3. To clouds and whirlwinds for swiftness, *v.* 13. The Chaldean army shall *come up as clouds* driven with the wind. The horses are *swifter than eagles* when they fly upon their prey. 4. To watchers and the keepers of a field, *v.* 15-17. *The voice declares from Dan,* furthest north of all the cities of Canaan. They received the news and transmitted it to Jerusalem. Now, what is the news? "*Tell the nations,* the cities of the ten tribes, that they may provide for their own safety; but publish it *against Jerusalem,* let them know that *watchers have come from a far country,* that is, soldiers, that will watch all opportunities to do mischief. They are coming in full career, and *give out their voice against the cities of Judah.* As *keepers of a field* surround it, to keep all out from it, so shall they surround the cities of Judah till they surrender. They are *against her round about, compassing her in on every side.*" See Luke xix. 43.

III. The lamentable cause of this judgment. 1. They sinned against God; it was all owing to themselves: *She has been rebellious against me, saith the Lord, v.* 17. The Chaldeans were breaking in upon them, and it was sin that opened the gap at which they entered: *Thy way and thy doings have procured these things unto thee* (*v.* 18). Sin is the cause of all our troubles. 2. God was angry with them for their sin. It is the *fierce anger of the Lord* that makes the army of the Chaldeans thus fierce, *v.* 8. 3. In his just anger he condemned them to this punishment: *Now also will I give sentence against them, v.* 12.

IV. The lamentable effects of this judgment. The people that should fight shall despair and shall not have a heart to make the least stand against the enemy (*v.* 8): "*For this gird yourself with sackcloth, lament and howl.*" Instead of girding on the sword, they will gird on the sackcloth. While the enemy is yet at a distance they will give up and cry, *Woe unto us! for we are spoiled, v.* 13. Judah and Jerusalem had been famed for valiant men; but see the effect of sin: by depriving men of their confidence towards God, it deprives them of their courage towards men. *At that day the heart of the king shall perish,* both his wisdom and his courage. His princes and privy-counsellors shall be as much in despair as he. The business of the priests was to encourage the people; they were to say, *Fear not, and let not your hearts faint,* Deut. xx. 2, 3. But now *the priests* themselves *shall be astonished,* and shall have no heart to put spirit into the people. Our Saviour foretells that at the last destruction of Jerusalem *men's hearts* should *fail them for fear,* Luke xxi. 26.

V. The prophet's complaint of the people's being deceived, *v.* 10. It is expressed strangely: *Ah! Lord God, surely thou hast greatly deceived this people, saying, You shall have peace.* We are sure that God deceives none. But, 1. The people deceived themselves with the promises that God had made, building upon them, though they took no care to perform the conditions on which those promises did depend. Thus they cheated themselves and then wickedly complained that God had cheated them. 2. The false prophets deceived them with promises of peace, which they made them in God's name, *ch.* xxiii. 17; xxvii. 9. 3. God had permitted the false prophets to deceive, and the people to be deceived by them, giving both up to *strong delusions,* to punish them *for not receiving the truth in the love of it.* 4. It may be read with an interrogation, "*Hast thou indeed thus deceived this people?* It is plain that they are greatly deceived, for they expect *peace,* whereas *the sword reaches unto the soul.*" Now, was it God that deceived them? No, he had often given them warning of judgments, but their own prophets deceive them, and cry peace to those to whom the God of heaven does not speak peace. It is a pitiable thing to see people flattered into their own ruin, and promising themselves peace when war is at the door.

VI. The prophet's endeavour to undeceive them. 1. He shows them their wound. They might discover their punishment in their sin (*v.* 18): "*This is thy wickedness, because it is bitter.*" It produces bitter grief that *reaches unto the heart*; the sword *reaches to the soul,*" *v.* 10. 2. He shows them the cure, *v.* 14. "*O Jerusalem! wash thy heart from wickedness, that thou mayest be saved.*" By Jerusalem he means each one of the inhabitants of Jerusalem; for every man has a heart of his own, and it is personal reformation that must help the public. Every one must return from *his own evil way* and cleanse *his own evil heart.* Reformation is absolutely necessary to salvation. No reformation is saving but that which reaches the heart. There will be no effectual reformation of manners without a reformation of the mind. In the latter part of the verse he reasons with them: *How long shall thy vain thoughts lodge within thee? Thoughts of iniquity* or *mischief,* these are the evil thoughts that are the spawn of the evil *heart,* from which all other wickedness is produced, Matt. xv. 19. Some by vain thoughts here understand all those frivolous excuses with which they turned off the reproofs and calls of the word, and bolstered themselves up in their wickedness.

Verses 19–31

The prophet is here in an agony, and cries out like one upon the rack of pain. The expressions are pathetic enough to melt a heart of stone. *My bowels! my bowels! I am pained at my very heart.* A good man, in such a bad world as this is, cannot but be a *man of sorrows. My heart makes a noise in me,* through the tumult of my spirits, and *I cannot hold my peace.* It is not for himself, or any affliction in his family that he grieves thus; but it is purely upon the public account, it is his people's case that he lays to heart thus.

I. They are very sinful and will not be reformed, *v.* 22. These are the words of God himself. God calls them his people, though they are foolish. They have cast him off, but he has not cast them off, Rom. xi. 1. They are *foolish,* for *they have not known me.* They are *wise to do evil,* to plot mischief against the quiet in the land, wise to contrive the gratification of their lusts, and then to conceal and palliate them. But *to do good they have no knowledge,* no application of mind.

II. They are very miserable, and cannot be relieved.

1. He cries out, *Because thou hast heard, O my soul! the sound of the trumpet,* and *seen the standard,* both giving *the alarm of war, v.* 19, 21. He does not say, *Thou hast heard, O my ear!* but, O my *soul!* because it is by the spirit of prophecy that he sees it. His *soul* heard it from the words of God, as if he had heard it with his bodily ears. Though he foretold this calamity he was far from *desiring the woeful day.* He strove to awaken them to a holy fear, and so to prevent judgment by a true and timely repentance.

2. The destruction here foretold:

(1) It is swift and *sudden. Destruction upon destruction is cried* (*v.* 20), *breach upon breach,* one sad calamity treading upon the heels of another. The death of Josiah plucks up the floodgates; within three months after that his son and successor Jehoahaz is deposed by the king of Egypt; within two or three years after Nebuchadnezzar besieged Jerusalem and took it, and thenceforward he was continually making descents upon the land of Judah, till he completed the ruin in the destruction of Jerusalem: but *suddenly were their tents spoiled and their curtains in a moment.* The country was laid waste at first. The shepherds and all that lived in tents were plundered immediately; therefore we find the Rechabites, who dwelt in tents, upon the first coming of the army of the Chaldees into the land retiring to Jerusalem, Jer. xxxv. 11.

(2) This war continued, for the people were obstinate, and would not submit to the king of Babylon, but took all opportunities to rebel against him. This is complained of (*v.* 21): *How long shall I see the standard?* Shall the sword devour for ever?

(3) *The whole land is spoiled,* or plundered (*v.* 20); so it was at first, and at length it became a perfect chaos. The earth is *without form, and void* (*v.* 23), as it was Gen. i. 2. It is *Tohu* and *Bohu,* the words there used, as far as the land of Judæa goes. The *heavens* too are *without light.* This alludes to the *darkness* that was *upon the face of the deep* (Gen. i. 2). It was not only the earth that failed them, but heaven frowned upon them; and with their trouble they had darkness, for they could not see through their troubles. The smoke of their houses and cities which the enemy burnt, darkened the sun, so that *the heavens had no light.* Or it may be taken figuratively: *The earth* (that is, the common people) was impoverished and in confusion; and the *heavens* (that is, the princes and rulers) *had no light,* no wisdom in themselves, nor were any comfort to the people, nor a guide to them. The *mountains trembled, and the hills moved lightly,*

v. 24. The *everlasting mountains* seemed to be *scattered,* Hab. iii. 6. The mountains on which they had worshipped their idols, the mountains trembled, as if they had been conscious of the people's guilt. The hills moved lightly, as being eased of the burden of a *sinful nation,* Isa. i. 24. *I beheld* the cities, *and, lo, there was no man to be seen;* even *the birds of the heavens,* that used to fly about and *sing among the branches,* were no more seen or heard. The *land of Judah* had now become like the *lake of Sodom,* see Deut. xxix. 23. *Lo, the fruitful place was a wilderness.* The *cities* also and their gates and walls are *broken down* and levelled. Those that look no further than second causes impute it to the policy and fury of the invaders; but the prophet, who looks to the first cause, says that it is *at the presence of the Lord.* The nation shall be entirely ruined, for *the whole land shall be desolate,* corn land and pasture land shall all be laid waste (*v.* 27). *The whole city shall flee for fear of the horsemen and bowmen.* Rather than lie exposed to their fury, they shall *go into the thickets,* and they shall *climb up upon the rocks,* for *every city shall be forsaken.* It is a dismal idea of the approaching desolation; but in the midst of all these threatenings comes one comfortable word (*v.* 27): *Yet will not I make a full end*—for God will reserve a remnant. Jerusalem shall again be built and the land inhabited. This comes for the comfort of those that *trembled at God's word.*

(4) Their case was helpless and without remedy. God would not help them; so he tells them plainly, *v.* 28. They would not repent and turn back from their sins (*ch.* ii. 25), and therefore God will not repent and turn back from his judgments. They could not help themselves, *v.* 30, 31. They flattered themselves with hopes that they should find some means. But the prophet tells them that, when it comes to the setting to, they will be quite at a loss: *When thou art spoiled, what wilt thou do?* They will be despised by their allies whom they depended upon. He compares Jerusalem to a harlot abandoned by all the lewd ones that used to make court to her. She does what she can to make herself appear considerable among the nations, and a valuable ally. She compliments them by her ambassadors. She *clothes herself with crimson,* as if she were rich, and *decks herself with ornaments of gold,* as if her treasuries were still full. She *rents her face with painting,* puts the best colours she can upon her present distresses. But this painting, though it beautifies the face for the present, really rends it; spoils the skin, cracks it, and makes it rough. "And, after all, *in vain shalt thou make thyself fair;* all thy neighbours are sensible how low thou art brought; the Chaldeans will strip thee of thy crimson and ornaments." Here seems to be an allusion to the story of Jezebel, who thought, by making herself look fair and fine, to outface her doom, but in vain, 2 Kings ix. 30, 33. They will find their troubles to be like the pains of a woman in travail, which she cannot escape: *I have heard the voices of the daughter of Zion,* her groans echoing to the triumphant shouts of the Chaldean army, *v.* 15. Zion, since her neighbours refuse to pity her, *bewails herself,* fetching *deep sighs* (so the word signifies), and she *spreads her hands,* reaching them forth for succour.

CHAPTER 5

Reproofs for sin and threatenings of judgment are intermixed in this chapter: judgments are threatened, that the reproofs of sin might be the more effectual to bring them to repentance. I. The sins they are charged with: Injustice (ver. 1), hypocrisy in religion (ver. 2), incorrigibleness (ver. 3), the corruption and debauchery of both poor and rich (ver. 4, 5), idolatry and adultery (ver. 7, 8), treacherous departures from God (ver. 11), defiance of him (ver. 12, 13), and at the bottom of all this, want of the fear of God, ver. 20–24. In the close of the chapter they are charged with violence and oppression (ver. 26–28), to debauch the nation, ver. 30, 31. II. The judgments threatened are very terrible. A foreign enemy shall be brought in upon them (ver. 15–17), shall carry them away into captivity (ver. 19), and keep all good things from them, ver. 25. But, III. Here is an intimation twice given that God would not utterly destroy them, ver. 10, 18. This was the scope and purport of Jeremiah's preaching in the latter end of Josiah's reign and the beginning of Jehoiakim's.

Verses 1–9

I. A challenge to produce any one right honest man in Jerusalem, *v.* 1. Jerusalem had become like the old world, in which *all flesh had corrupted their way.* "Look in *the streets,* and in *the broad places,* where they keep their markets; *see if you can find a man, a magistrate* (so some), *that executes judgment,* and administers justice impartially." *Truth has fallen in the street* (Isa. lix. 14). If there were but ten righteous men in Sodom, if but one of a thousand, of ten thousand, in Jerusalem, it should be spared. "What do you make of those in Jerusalem that continue to make profession of religion—men for whose sakes Jerusalem may be spared?" No, they are not sincere in their profession (*v.* 2): *They say, The Lord liveth,* and will swear by his name only, but they *swear falsely.*

II. A complaint which the prophet makes to God of the wilfulness of these people. God had appealed to their eyes (*v.* 1); but here the prophet appeals to his eyes (*v.* 3): "*Are not thy eyes upon the truth?* Dost thou not see every man's true character? *They have made their faces harder than a rock. Thou hast consumed them,* hast corrected them severely; *but they have refused to receive correction.* They would not receive instruction by the correction."

III. The trial made both of rich and poor, and the bad character given of both.

1. The poor were ignorant. He found many that *refused to return,* for whom he was willing to make excuse (*v.* 4): "*Surely, these are poor, they are foolish.* They never had the advantage of a good education, nor have they wherewithal to help themselves now with the means of instruction." Prevailing ignorance is the lamentable cause of abounding impiety and iniquity. There are the devil's poor as well as God's, who, notwithstanding their poverty, might *know the way of the Lord,* so as to walk in it and do their duty, without being book-learned; but they are willingly ignorant.

2. The rich were insolent and haughty (*v.* 5): "*I will get me to the great men,* and see if I can find them more pliable to the word and providence of God. But though *they know the way of the Lord and the judgment of their God,* yet they are too stiff to stoop to his government: *These have altogether broken the yoke and burst the bonds.* They think themselves too big to be corrected even by the sovereign Lord of all himself. The poor are weak, the rich are wilful, and so neither do their duty."

IV. Some particular sins specified, which they were guilty of. Their transgressions indeed *were many* and they added to the number and grew more impudent in them, *v.* 6. Their spiritual whoredom gave that honour to idols which is due to God only. *They have sworn to them* (so it may be read), have joined themselves to them and covenanted with them. Their corporal whoredom: they had forsaken God and served idols, and those that dishonoured him were left to dishonour themselves and their own families. They *committed adultery* without sense of shame or fear of punishment, for they *assembled themselves by troops in the harlots' houses* and did not blush to be seen by one another. So impudent was their lust that they became beasts (*v.* 8); like high-fed horses, they *neighed everyone after his neighbour's wife, v.* 8.

V. God's wrath against them for the universal debauchery of their land. A foreign enemy shall break in and their country shall be as if it were overrun and perfectly mastered by *a lion of the forest*, or by *a wolf of the evening*, which comes out at night, when he is hungry, and is very fierce and ravenous, or by *a leopard*, which is very swift and cruel. The enemy shall *watch over their cities* to put the inhabitants to this sad dilemma—if they stay in, they are starved; if they stir out, they are stabbed: *Everyone that goeth out thence shall be torn in pieces.* And all this bloody work is owing to the *multitude of their transgressions.* It is sin that makes the slaughter. "*Shall I not visit for these things?* Can you think that a God of infinite purity will connive at such abominable uncleanness?" *Shall not my soul be avenged on such a nation as this?* (v. 9). Not but that those who have been guilty of these sins have found mercy with God (Manasseh himself did), but nations, *as such*, being punishable only in this life, it would not be for the glory of God to let a nation pass without some manifest tokens of his displeasure.

Verses 10-19

I. The sin of this people dooms them to destruction, *v. 10*. *The house of Israel and the house of Judah*, though at variance with one another, both agreed to *deal very treacherously against God.* They forsook the worship of him, and played the hypocrite. They defied the judgments of God and his threatenings in the mouth of his prophets, *v. 12, 13.* Multitudes are ruined by being made to believe that God will not be strict: *Neither shall we see sword nor famine.* The prophets gave them fair warning, but they turned it off with a jest: "They do but talk so, because it is their trade. It is not the word of the Lord, but only the language of their melancholy fancy." They threaten the prophets: "*They shall become wind*, and *thus shall it be done unto them.* Do they frighten us with famine? Let them be *fed with the bread of affliction.*" "Do they tell us of the sword? Let them perish by the sword," *ch. ii. 30.*

II. The punishment of this people for their sin. God turns to the prophet Jeremiah, who had been thus bantered: *Behold, I will make my words in thy mouth fire. The word shall be fire and the people wood.* Sinners by sin make themselves fuel. The enemy shall be brought upon them. God gives them their commission (v. 10): "*Go you up upon her walls,* mount them, trample upon them, tread them down. Walls of stone, before the divine commission, shall be but mud walls. You may *take away her battlements,* and leave the fenced fortified cities to lie open; for her battlements *are not the Lord's*; he will not protect and fortify them." What dreadful work these invaders should make is here described (v. 15): *Lo, I will bring a nation upon you, O house of Israel!* This nation of the Chaldeans is here said to be a remote nation; it is *brought upon them from afar*, and will make the longer stay, that the soldiers may pay themselves well for so long a march. It is a *mighty nation*, an *ancient nation*, that value themselves upon their antiquity and will therefore be the more imperious. It is *a nation whose language thou knowest not*; they spoke the Syriac tongue. The difference of language would make it the more difficult to treat with them of peace. "They shall not store up, but *eat up thy harvest* in the field *and thy bread* in the house, *which thy sons and thy daughters should eat.*" *They shall eat up thy flocks and herds,* out of which thou hast taken sacrifices for thy idols; they shall not leave thee the fruits of *thy vines and fig-trees.* They *shall impoverish thy fenced cities*—those cities *wherein thou trustedst* to be a protection to the country."

III. An intimation of the tender compassion God has yet for them. The enemy is commissioned to destroy and lay waste, but must not *make a full end*, *v. 10.* "Even *in those days*, dismal as they are, *I*

will not make a full end with you"; and, if God will not, the enemy shall not.

IV. The justification of God in these proceedings. As he will appear to be gracious in not making a full end, so he will appear to be righteous in coming so near it, *v. 19.* The people *will say, Wherefore doth the Lord our God do all this unto us?* As if against such a sinful nation there did not appear cause enough of action. The prophet is instructed what answer to give them. He must tell them that God does this against them for what they have done against him, and that they may read their sin in their punishment. Have they forgotten how often they served *strange gods in their own land*, and therefore is it not just with God to make them *serve strangers* in a strange land, Deut. xxviii. 47, 48.

Verses 20-24

The prophet, having reproved them, is here sent to them again upon another errand, which he must *publish in Judah*; to persuade them to fear God.

I. He complains of the shameful stupidity of this people. They are a *foolish people and without understanding*; they apprehend not the mind of God, though ever so plainly declared to them by his prophets, and by his providence (v. 21): *They have eyes, but they see not, ears, but they hear not.* They had intellectual faculties, but they did not employ them as they ought. Their wills were stubborn and unapt to submit to the rules of the divine law (v. 23): *This people has a revolting and a rebellious heart.* It is the corrupt bias of the will that besots the understanding. The character of this people is the true character of all people till the grace of God has wrought a change. We are *foolish*, slow of understanding, and have *a revolting and a rebellious heart*, not only revolting from him by a rooted aversion to that which is good, but rebellious against him by a strong inclination to that which is evil.

II. He ascribed this to the want of the fear of God. When he observes them to be without understanding he asks, "*Fear you not me, saith the Lord, and will you not tremble at my presence?*" (v. 22). When he observes that they have revolted and gone he adds this, as the cause of their apostasy (v. 24), *Neither say they in their hearts, Let us now fear the Lord our God.* Therefore bad thoughts come into their mind, because they will not admit and entertain good thoughts.

III. He suggests some of those things to possess us with a holy fear of God.

1. We must fear the Lord and his greatness, *v. 22.* Here is one instance: he keeps the sea within compass. Though the tides flow with a mighty strength twice every day, and if they should flow on would drown the world, though in a storm the billows dash to the shore with incredible force, yet they return, and no harm is done. *This is the Lord's doing*, and if it were not common, it would be *marvellous in our eyes.* A wall of sand shall be as effectual as a wall of brass to check the flowing waves, to teach us that a *soft answer turns away wrath*, and quiets a foaming rage, when *grievous words*, like hard rocks, do but exasperate. This bound is placed *by a perpetual decree*, and it sends us back to the creation of the world, when God divided between the sea and the dry land, Gen. i. 9, 10, Ps. civ. 6, &c., and Job xxxviii. 8, &c. It is a *perpetual decree*; it has had its effect to this day and shall still continue till day and night come to an end. Now this is a good reason why we should fear God; for we see that he is a God of universal sovereignty.

2. We must fear the Lord and his goodness, Hos. iii. 5. We must *fear the Lord our God*, that is, we must worship him, because he is continually doing us good:

he gives us both *the former and the latter rain*, the former a little after seed-time, the latter a little before harvest, and by this means *he reserves to us the appointed weeks of harvest*. In harvest mercies therefore God is to be acknowledged, his power, and goodness, and faithfulness, for they all come from him. And it is a good reason why we should fear him, that we may keep ourselves in his love.

Verses 25–31

I. The prophet shows them what mischief their sins had done them: "It is *your sin* that *has withholden good from you*, when God was ready to bestow it upon you." It is that which makes the heavens as brass and the earth as iron.

II. He shows them how great their sins were. When they had forsaken the worship of the true God, even moral honesty was lost among them: *Among my people are found wicked men* (v. 26), and so much the worse they were for being found among God's people. They were *found* (that is, caught) in the very act of their wickedness. As hunters or fowlers lay snares for their game, so did they *lie in wait to catch men*, and made a sport of it. They contrived ways of doing mischief to good people (whom they hated for their goodness), especially to those that faithfully reproved them (Isa. xxix. 21), or to those whose estates they coveted; so Jezebel ensnared Naboth for his vineyard. They were false and treacherous (v. 27): *As a cage*, or *coop*, is *full of birds*, and of food for them to fatten them for the table, so are *their houses full of deceit*, of wealth obtained by fraudulent practices. Whoever deals with them, they will cheat him if they can. Herein *they overpass the deeds of the wicked*, v. 28. Those that act by deceit, with a colour of law and justice, do more mischief perhaps than those wicked men (v. 26) that carry all before them by open force and violence. They prosper in these wicked courses and therefore their hearts are hardened in them. *They have become great in the world; they have waxen rich*, and thrive upon it. They are sleek and smooth: *They shine;* they look fair and gay; everybody admires them. And they *pass by matters of evil* (so some read the following words); they *are not in trouble as other men*, much less as we might expect bad men. When they had got power in their hands they did not do good with it. *They judge not the cause, the cause of the fatherless, and the right of the needy* And yet *they prosper* still; *God layeth not folly to them.* Certainly then the things of this world are not the best things, for oftentimes the worst men have the most of them; yet we are not to think that God allows of their practices. No; *though sentence against their evil works be not executed speedily*, it will be executed. There was a general corruption (v. 30, 31): *A wonderful and horrible thing is committed in the land.* The degeneracy of such a people, so privileged and advanced, was a wonderful thing, a horrible thing, to be detested. The leaders misled the people: *The prophets prophesy falsely.* Religion is never more dangerously attacked than under colour and pretence of divine revelation. *The priests bear rule by their means;* in grandeur and wealth, laziness and luxury. The people were well enough pleased to be so misled: "They are *my people*," says God, "and should have borne their testimony against the wickedness of their priests and prophets; but they *love to have it so.*" They love to be ridden with a loose rein, and like those rulers very well that will not restrain their lusts.

III. He shows them how fatal the consequences of this would be. *Shall not I visit for these things?* Here, judgment is reasoning against mercy: *Shall I not visit?* We are sure that Infinite Wisdom knows how to accommodate the matter between them. *Shall not my soul be avenged?* Yes, without doubt, if the sinner repent not. *What will you do in the end thereof?*

Those that walk in bad ways would do well to consider the tendency of them both to greater sin and utter ruin.

Chapter 6

In this chapter, as before, we have, I. A prophecy of the invading of the land of Judah and the besieging of Jerusalem by the Chaldean army (ver. 1–6), the spoils they should make of the country (ver. 9), and the terror on that occasion, ver. 22–26. II. An account of those sins of Judah and Jerusalem which provoke God to bring this desolating judgment. Their oppression (ver. 7), their contempt of the word of God (ver. 10–12), their worldliness (ver. 13), the treachery of their prophets (ver. 14), their impudence in sin (ver. 15), their obstinacy against reproofs (ver. 18, 19), which made their sacrifices unacceptable to him (ver. 20), and for which he gave them up to ruin (ver. 21), but tried them first (ver. 27) and then rejected them as irreclaimable, ver. 28–30. III. Good counsel given them in the midst of all this, but in vain, ver. 8, 16, 17.

Verses 1–8

I. Judgment threatened against Judah and Jerusalem. The city saw no cloud gathering, but everything looked safe and serene: but the prophet tells them that they shall shortly be invaded by a foreign power *from the north*, which shall cause a general desolation. It is here foretold,

1. That the alarm should be loud and terrible. This is represented, *v.* 1. The children of Benjamin, in which tribe part of Jerusalem lay, are here called to shift for their own safety in the country; for the city (to which it was first thought advisible for them to flee, *ch.* iv. 5, 6) would soon be made too hot for them. They are told to send the alarm into the country, and to do what they can for their own safety: *Blow the trumpet in Tekoa*, a city which lay twelve miles north from Jerusalem. *Set up a sign of fire* (that is, light the beacons) *in Beth-haccerem*, the *house of the vineyard*, which lay on a hill between Jerusalem and Tekoa. This may be taken ironically: "When you have done your best, it will be a great destruction, for it is in vain to contend with God's judgments."

2. That the attempt upon them should be formidable. *The daughter of Zion*, on whom the assault is made, is compared *to a comely and delicate woman* (v. 2), and, not being accustomed to hardship, she will be the less able either to resist the enemy or to bear the destruction. The generals and their armies are compared to *shepherds* and *their flocks* (v. 3), in such numbers did they come, the soldiers following their leaders as sheep their shepherds. The shepherds easily make themselves masters of an open field, which lies common, owned by none, *pitch their tents* in it, and their flocks quickly eat it bare; so shall the Chaldean army easily break in upon the land of Judah, force for themselves a free quarter where they please, and in a little time devour all. God shall commission them to make this destruction. It is he that says (v. 4), *Prepare you war against her;* for he is the *Lord of hosts*, and he has said (v. 6), *Hew you down trees, and cast a mount against Jerusalem.* God has said, "*This is the city to be visited* by the divine justice, and this is the time of her visitation." They resolve to be very expeditious. *Arise, let us go up at noon*, though it be in the heat of the day; nay (v. 5), *Arise, let us go up by night*, though it be in the dark. "*Let us go up*, and let us destroy her palaces and make ourselves masters of the wealth that is in them."

II. The cause of this judgment is all for their wickedness; they have brought it upon themselves; they must bear the blame of it. They are thus oppressed because they have been oppressors; they have dealt hardly with one another, each in his turn, as they have had power and advantage, and now the enemy shall come and deal hardly with them all. Sin had become in a manner natural to them (v. 7): She *casts out wickedness*, in malice and mischievousness, *as a fountain casts out her waters*, plentifully and constantly. The cry of it had come up before God as that of Sodom: *Before me continually are grief and wounds*—the complaint of those that find themselves unjustly wounded in bodies or spirits, in estates or reputation. He that is the common Parent of mankind regards and resents, and sooner or later will revenge, the mischiefs and wrongs that men do to one another.

III. How to prevent this judgment. "*Be thou instructed, O Jerusalem! v.* 8. Receive the instruction given thee both by the law of God and by his prophets; be wise at length for thyself." *Lest my soul depart*, or *be disjoined, from thee.* This intimates what a tender affection and concern God had for them; his very soul had been joined to them, and nothing but sin could disjoin it. The God of mercy is loth to depart even from a provoking people, and is earnest with them by true repentance and reformation to prevent things coming to that extremity.

Verses 9–17

I. The ruin of Judah and Jerusalem is here threatened. We had before the haste which the Chaldean army made (*v.* 4, 5); now here we have the havoc. The enemy shall be insatiable in their thirst after treasure. *They shall thoroughly glean the remnant of Israel as a vine;* as the *grape-gatherer*, who is resolved to leave none behind, still *turns back his hand into the baskets*, to put more in. Perhaps the people, being *given to covetousness* (*v.* 13), had not observed that law of God which forbade them to *glean all their grapes* (Lev. xix. 10), and now they themselves shall be *thoroughly gleaned.* The children perish in the calamity which the fathers' sins have procured. The execution shall reach *the assembly of young men*, their merry meetings; they shall be *cut off together. Even the husband with the wife shall be taken and the old with the full of days*, whose deaths can contribute no more to their safety than their lives to their service. *Their houses shall then be turned to others* (*v.* 12). The prophet justifies himself in preaching thus terribly (*v.* 11): *I am full of the fury of the Lord.* He, took no delight in threatening, but he could not contain himself; he was *weary with holding in*, but he was so *full of power by the Spirit of the Lord of hosts* that he must speak. *The priest and the prophet* have *dealt falsely*, have not told the people their faults and the danger they were in; they should have been their physicians, but they murdered their patients by giving them everything they had a mind to, and flattering them that they were in no danger (*v.* 14): They have *healed the hurt of the daughter of my people slightly*, soothing people in their sins, and giving them opiates to make them easy, while the disease was preying upon the vitals. They said, "*Peace, peace*—all shall be well", when *there is no peace*, because they went on in their daring impieties. Those are to be reckoned our false friends (that is, our worst and most dangerous enemies) who flatter us in a sinful way.

II. The sin of Judah and Jerusalem which provoked God to bring this ruin. 1. They would by no means bear to be told of their danger. God bids the prophet give them warning of the judgment coming (*v.* 9); "but," says, he "*to whom shall I speak and give warning?* I cannot speak *that they may hear*, for *their ear is uncircumcised. The word of the Lord is unto them a reproach;* the reproofs and the threatenings are so." Those reproofs that are counted reproaches, will certainly be turned into woes. 2. They were set upon the world, and carried away by the love of it (*v.* 13): "*From the least of them even to the greatest, everyone is given to covetousness*, greedy of filthy lucre," and this made them oppressive and violent (*v.* 6, 7). This hardened their hearts against the word of God.and his prophets. 3. They were past

shame. Their hearts were so hardened that *they were not at all ashamed, neither could they blush*, they had so brazened their faces. They resolved to face it out against God himself. Those that will not submit to a penitential shame shall not escape utter ruin: *Therefore they shall fall among* those *that fall;* they shall be made to tremble, because they would not blush. Those that sin and cannot blush for it are in an evil case now, and it will be worse with them shortly. At first they hardened themselves and would not blush, afterwards they were so hardened that they could not. *They have lost the only good property which once blended itself with many bad ones, that is, shame for having done amiss.*

III. The good counsel often given them in vain. God used to say to them, *Stand in the ways and see.* He would have them do as travellers who are in care to find the right way which will bring them to their journey's end, and therefore enquire for it. O that men would be thus *wise for their souls.* "*Ask for the old paths, enquire of the former age* (Job viii. 8), *ask thy father, thy elders* (Deut. xxxii. 7), and thou wilt find that the way of godliness has always been the way which God has owned and blessed and in which men have prospered. Ask for the *old paths*, the paths that the patriarchs travelled, Abraham, and Isaac, and Jacob; and, as you hope to inherit the promises made to them, tread in their steps. *Ask for the old paths, Where is the good way?*" But there is an *old way which wicked men have trodden*, Job. xxii. 15. When we ask for the old paths, it is only to find out the *good way.* Note, The way of religion and godliness is a good old way, the way that all the saints in all ages have walked in. "When you have found out which is the good way, *walk therein*, and persevere in it." Some make this counsel to be given them with reference to the struggles between the true and false prophets. "*Stand in the way*," says God, "and enquire, which agrees with the written word and the usual methods of God's providence, which of these directs you to the good way, and do accordingly. *Walk in the good old way* and you will enjoy God and yourselves, and the way will lead you to true rest. You will find an abundant recompence at your journey's end." *But they said*, "*We will not walk therein*, we will not deny ourselves and our humours so far as to *walk in it.*" Because they would not be ruled by fair reasoning, God, by less judgments threatens greater, and sends his prophets to frighten them with an apprehension of the danger they were in (*v.* 17): *Also I set watchmen over you.* This was the burden of their song; *Hearken to the sound of the trumpet.* God, in his providence, sounds the trumpet (Zech. ix. 14); the watchmen hear it (Jer. iv. 19), and they call upon others to hearken to it too. *But they said*, "*We will not hearken;* we will not heed, the prophets may as well save themselves and us the trouble."

Verses 18–30

I. God appeals to the whole world concerning the equity of his proceedings against Judah and Jerusalem (*v.* 18, 19): "*Hear, you nations, and know* particularly, *O congregation* of the mighty, the great men of the nations. Observe now Judah and Jerusalem; you all wonder that *I* should *bring evil upon this people*, that are in covenant with me, *Wherefore has the Lord done thus to this land?* Know then the evil brought upon them is *the fruit of their thought.* They thought to strengthen themselves by their alliance with foreigners, and by that they weakened and exposed themselves. That is the just punishment of their disobedience and rebellion. It is because *they have not hearkened to my words nor to my law*, but rejected it all. Therefore you cannot say that they have any wrong done them."

II. God rejects their plea, by which they insisted upon their services as sufficient to atone for their sins. It is a frivolous plea (*v.* 20): "*To what purpose come there to me incense and sweet cane*, to be burnt for a perfume on the golden altar? What care I for *your burnt-offerings* and *your sacrifices?*" Sacrifice and incense were appointed to direct them to a Mediator, and assist their faith in him. Where this good use was made of them they were acceptable, God had respect to them and to those that offered them. But when they were offered with an opinion that they purchased a license to go on in sin, far from being pleasing to God, they were a provocation to him.

III. He foretells the desolation. God designs their ruin because they hate to be reformed (*v.* 21): *I will lay stumbling-blocks before this people*, occasions of falling not into sin, but into trouble. God retards all the methods they take for their own safety. The parties of the enemy, were stumbling-blocks to them. *The fathers and the sons together shall fall upon them;* neither the fathers with their wisdom, nor the sons with their strength shall escape them. He will make the Chaldeans instruments. Babylon a great way northward, and some of the countries that were subject to the king of Babylon, must be employed in this service, *v.* 22, 23. It is *a great nation*, a warlike people. *They lay hold on bow and spear*, know how to use them. *They ride upon horses*, and therefore move the more swiftly, and in battle press the harder. They *are cruel and have no mercy*, their voice *roars like the sea*. They are *set in array against thee, O daughter of Zion!*

IV. He describes the consternation which Judah and Jerusalem should be in upon the approach of this formidable enemy, *v.* 24–26. "When *we have but heard the fame thereof our hands wax feeble*, and we have no heart to make any resistance; *anguish has taken hold of us*, and we are like *a woman in travail*." Sense of guilt dispirits men, upon the approach of trouble. They confine themselves to their houses; they would rather die tamely there than by fight or flight, to help themselves. They say one to another, "*Go not forth into the field, nor walk by the way;* it is at your peril if you do, for the *sword of the enemy*, and the fear of it, are *on every side*." The prophet calls upon them to lament: "*O daughter of my people*, hear thy God calling thee to mourning: do not only put on sackcloth for a day; do not only put ashes on thy head, but *wallow thyself in ashes* as parents *mourn for an only son*."

V. He constitutes the prophet a judge over this people that now stand upon their trial: *I have set thee for a tower*, or as a sentinel upon a tower, *among my people, that thou mayest know, and try their way*, *v.* 27. Thus God appeals to the prophet himself, and his own observation, that he might be fully satisfied in the equity of God's proceedings against them. God set him for a tower, but made him a *fortress, a strong tower*, gave him courage to bear the shock of their displeasure. He will find (*v.* 28): *They are all grievous revolters, revolters of revolters* (so the word is), the worst of revolters. They *walk with slanders*, back-biting one another. They are *brass and iron*, base metals. They were as silver and gold, but they have degenerated. As *they are all revolters*, so *they are all corrupters*, industrious to debauch others. It was in vain to think of reforming them, for various methods had been tried all to no purpose, *v.* 29, 30. He compares them to ore that was supposed to have some good metal in it, and was therefore put into the furnace by the refiner, but it proved all dross. God by his prophets and by his providences had used means to refine this people, but it was all in vain. By a series of afflictions, they had been kept in a constant fire, but all to no purpose. *The bellows* have been kept so near the fire, to blow it, that they *are burnt*

with the heat of it. The *lead*, which was then used in refining silver, as quicksilver is now, *is consumed of the fire*, and has not done its work. *The founder melts in vain;* his labour is lost, *for the wicked are not plucked away*, no care is taken to cast out of communion those who, being corrupt, are in danger of infecting others. Doom is passed upon them (*v.* 30): *Reprobate silver shall they be called*, useless and worthless; they glitter as if they had some silver in them, but there is nothing of real goodness to be found among them; and *the Lord has rejected them*. God has *no pleasure in the death* and ruin of sinners. He did not reject them till he had used all proper means to reform them; nor abandon them as dross till it appeared that they were *reprobate silver*.

CHAPTER 7

The prophet having in God's name reproved the people for their sins, I. He shows them the invalidity of the plea that they had the temple of God among them and constantly attended the service, ver. 1–11. II. He reminds them of the desolations of Shiloh, and foretells that such should be the desolations of Jerusalem, ver. 12–16. III. He represents to the prophet their abominable idolatries, ver. 17–20. IV. He sets before the people that maxim that "to obey is better than sacrifice" (1 Sam. xv. 22), and that God would not accept the sacrifices of those that persisted in disobedience, ver. 21–28. V. He threatens to lay the land waste for their idolatry and impiety, ver. 29–34.

Verses 1–15

These verses begin another sermon, which is continued in the two following chapters, to reason them to repentance.

I. The orders given to the prophet: This was *a word* that *came to him from the Lord*, *v.* 1. 1. Where it must be preached—*in the gate of the Lord's house*, through which they entered into the outer court. It would affront the priests, and expose the prophets to their rage, but the prophet must not fear the face of man. 2. To whom it must be preached—to the men of *Judah, that enter in at these gates to worship the Lord;* probably it was at one of the three feasts, when all the males were to appear and not to *appear empty*.

II. The contents and scope of the sermon itself. It is delivered in the name of *the Lord of hosts, the God of Israel*, who commands the world, but covenants with his people. The prophet here tells them,

1. What were the true words of God. In short, if they would repent and return to God, he would restore their peace, redress their grievances, and return to them in mercy (*v.* 3): *Amend your ways and your doings*. God shows them where and how they must amend, and promises to accept them: "*I will cause you to dwell quietly* and peaceably *in this place*, and a stop shall be put to that which threatens your expulsion." They must *thoroughly amend*; it must be a universal, constant, persevering reformation, not wavering, but constant. They must be honest and just in all their dealings. Those that had power must *thoroughly execute judgment between a man and his neighbour*, without partiality. They must not *oppress the stranger, the fatherless, or the widow*, nor protect those that did oppress. They must *not shed innocent blood*, and with it defile *this place* and the land wherein they dwelt. They must keep closely to the worship of the true God only: *Neither walk after other gods;* do not hanker after them. "Set about such a work of reformation with all speed, *and I will cause you to dwell in this place*, this temple; it shall continue your refuge, the place of your meeting with God and one another; and you shall never be turned out either from God's house or from your own." They shall enjoy it by covenant not by providence, but by promise. They shall not be disturbed *for ever and ever*; nothing but sin could throw them

out. An everlasting inheritance in the heavenly Canaan is hereby secured to all that live in godliness and honesty.

2. What were the lying words of their own hearts, which they must not trust. He cautions them (*v.* 4): "*Trust not in lying words.* You are told in what way you may be safe, and happy; do not flatter yourselves that you may be so in any other way." *Behold,* it is plain that *you* do *trust in lying words,* notwithstanding what is said to you; you trust in *words that cannot profit.* Now these lying words were, "*The temple of the Lord, the temple of the Lord, the temple of the Lord are these.* Here he resides, here he is worshipped, here we meet three times a year to pay our homage to him as our King in his palace." This they thought was security enough. When the prophets told them how sinful they were, still they appealed to the temple. It was the cant of the times; it was in their mouths upon all occasions. The privileges of a *form of godliness* are often the pride and confidence of those that are strangers and enemies to the power of it. It is common for those that are furthest from God to boast themselves most of their being near to the church (Zeph. iii. 11). If they knew anything either of the *temple of the Lord* or of the *Lord of the temple,* they must think that to plead that in excuse of their sin was most unreasonable. God is a holy God; but this plea made him the patron of sin, *v.* 9, 10. "When you have done the worst you can against God, will you brazen your faces so far as to *stand before him in this house which is called by his name*—stand before him as suppliants expecting his favour? It is as if you should say, *We are delivered to do all these abominations.*" Some take it thus: "You present yourselves before God with your sacrifices and sin-offerings, and then say, *We are delivered,* we are discharged from our guilt, when all this is but to blind the world, that you may the more easily *do all these abominations. Has this house, which is called by my name* and is a sign of God's kingdom, set up in opposition to the kingdom of sin and Satan—*has this become a den of robbers in your eyes?* Do you think it was built to be a refuge to malefactors?" Though the horns of the altar were a sanctuary to him that slew a man unawares, they were not so to a wilful murderer, Exod. xxi. 14; 1 Kings ii. 29. *Behold, I have seen it, saith the Lord,* have seen the real iniquity through the counterfeit piety. He shows them the insufficiency of this plea in the case of Shiloh. It is certain that Shiloh was ruined, though it had God's sanctuary in it, when by its wickedness it profaned that sanctuary (*v.* 12): *Go you now to my place which was in Shiloh.* There God *set his name at the first,* there the tabernacle was set up (Joshua xviii. 1), but those that attended the service of the tabernacle there corrupted both themselves and others, and from them arose the *wickedness of his people Israel,* and what came of it? Was it protected by its having the tabernacle in it? God *forsook* it (Ps. lxxviii. 60), sent his ark into captivity, cut off the house of Eli that presided there. *Remember Lot's wife;* remember Shiloh and the seven churches of Asia; and know that the ark and candlestick are movable things, Rev. ii. 5; Matt. xxi. 43. Jerusalem was now as sinful as ever Shiloh was (*v.* 13): "*You have done all these works,* you cannot deny it." God spoke, but they *heard not,* they never minded; he *called them,* but they *answered not;* they would not come at his call. Jerusalem shall shortly be as miserable as ever Shiloh was: *Therefore I will do unto this house as I did to Shiloh,* ruin it, and lay it waste, *v.* 14. "This house" (says God) "is *called by my name,* and therefore you may think that I should protect it; but the men of Shiloh thus flattered themselves and did but deceive themselves." He quotes another precedent (*v.* 15), the ruin of the kingdom of the ten tribes, who were the seed of Abraham, and yet their idolatries threw them out and extirpated them.

Verses 16–20

The temple and the service of it should not avail to prevent the judgment threatened. But there was the prophet's intercession for them; his prayers would do them more good than their own pleas: now that support is taken from those who have lost their interest in the prayers of God's ministers and people.

I. God here forbids the prophet to pray for them (*v.* 16): "The decree has gone forth, *pray not thou for this people,* that is, pray not for the preventing of this judgment threatened; they have *sinned unto death,* and therefore pray not for their life, but for the life of their souls," 1 John v. 16. God's prophets are praying men; Jeremiah foretold the destruction of Judah and Jerusalem, and yet prayed for their preservation. Even when we threaten sinners with damnation we must pray for their salvation, that they may *turn and live.* Jeremiah was persecuted, and reproached, by his people, and yet he prayed for them. God's praying prophets have a great interest in heaven. Those that will not regard good ministers' preaching cannot expect any benefit by their praying. If you will not hear us when we speak from God to you, God will not hear us when we speak to him for you.

II. He gives him a reason for this prohibition.

1. They are resolved to persist in their rebellion against God (*v.* 17): *Seest thou not what they do* openly and publicly, without either shame or fear, *in the cities of Judah and in the streets of Jerusalem?* This intimates that the sin was evident and that the sinners committed their wickedness even in the prophet's presence. He saw what they did, and yet they did it, which was an affront to him whose officer he was. Their idolatrous respects are paid to the *queen of heaven,* the moon, either in an image or in the original, or both. They worshipped it probably under the name of *Ashtaroth, ch.* xliv. 17, 19. They worshipped the creatures instead of him that made them, and the gifts instead of him that gave them. *With the queen of heaven* they worshipped *other gods,* for those that forsake the true God wander endlessly after false ones. To these deities of their own making they offer *cakes* for meat-offerings, and *pour out drink-offerings. The children* were sent to *gather wood; the fathers kindled the fire* to heat the oven, *the women kneaded the dough* with their own hands. Let us be instructed even by this bad example, in the service of our God. (1) Let us *honour him with our substance,* as those that have our subsistence from him, and eat and drink to the glory of him from whom we have our meat and drink. (2) Let us not decline the hardest services by which God may be honoured; for none shall *kindle a fire on God's altar for nought.* (3) Let our children be employed in doing something towards the keeping up of religious exercises. What is the direct tendency of this idolatry: "It is *that they may provoke me to anger;* they cannot design anything else in it. Is it because I am easily provoked? It is their own doing; and they alone shall bear it." *Is it against God that they provoke him to wrath?* It is malice against God, but it is impotent malice; it cannot hurt him: it will hurt themselves.

2. God is resolved to proceed in his judgments against them, and will not be turned back by the prophet's prayers (*v.* 20): *Thus saith the Lord God, Behold, my anger and my fury shall be poured out upon this place.* It shall reach both *man and beast,* like the plagues of Egypt, and shall destroy the *trees of the field and the fruit of the ground,* which they had *prepared for Baal,* and *cakes to the queen of heaven.* There is no extinguishing it: *It shall burn and shall not be quenched;* prayers and tears shall then avail nothing.

Verses 21–28

God, having shown the people that the temple would not protect them while they polluted it with their wickedness. here shows them that their sacrifices would not atone while they went on in disobedience. He speaks of their ceremonial service (v. 21): "*Put your burnt-offerings to your sacrifices;* add one sort of sacrifice to another; turn your *burnt-offerings* into *peace-offerings*, that you may *eat flesh*, but expect not any other benefit by them. *Keep your sacrifices to yourselves*, let them be served up at your own table, for they are no way acceptable at God's altars."

I. He shows them that obedience was the only thing he required of them, v. 22, 23. He appeals to the original contract, by which they were first formed into a people, when they were brought out of Egypt. God made them a *kingdom of priests* to himself, not that he might be regaled with their sacrifices, as the devils, whom the heathen worshipped, Deut. xxxii. 38. *I spoke not to your fathers concerning burnt-offerings or sacrifices, at first.* The precepts of the moral law were given before the ceremonial institutions; and those came afterwards, as trials of their obedience. The Levitical law begins thus: *If any man of you will bring an offering*, he must do so and so (Lev. i. 2, ii. 1), as if it were intended rather to regulate sacrifice than to require it. The condition of their being God's peculiar people was this (Exod. xix. 5), *If you will obey my voice indeed,* "Make conscience of the duties of natural religion, observe positive institutions from a principle of obedience, and then *I will be your God and you shall be my people.*" "Let your conversation be regular; *walk* within the bounds I have set, and *in all the ways that I have commanded you*, and then *it shall be well with you.*" The demand here is very reasonable, that we should be directed by Infinite Wisdom, that he that made us should command us, and that he should give us law who gives us our being.

II. He shows them that disobedience was the only thing for which he had a quarrel with them. 1. They set up their own will in competition with the will of God: *They hearkened not* to God and to his law; they *inclined not their ear* to attend to it, much less their hearts to comply with it. *Their own counsels* were their guide. *The imagination of their evil heart*, the appetites and passions of it, shall be a law to them. 2. They *went backward*, when they talked of making a captain, and returning to Egypt again, and would not go forward under God's conduct. They promised fair: *All that the Lord shall say unto us we will do;* but they drew back into the way of sin, and were worse than ever. 3. When God sent to them by the prophets, still they were disobedient. God had servants of his among them in every age, to tell them of their faults, whom he *rose up early to send* (as before, v. 13), but they were as deaf to the prophets as they were to the law (v. 26). Their practice and character were still the same. They are worse, and not better, *than their fathers.* Jeremiah can himself witness against them (v. 27): "*Thou shalt speak all these words to them. They will not hearken to thee*, nor heed thee. They will either give thee no answer at all or not an obedient answer; they will not come at thy call." The prophet must go to them and tell them (v. 28): "*Say unto them, This is a nation that obeys not the voice of the Lord their God.* They are notorious for their obstinacy; they sacrifice to the Lord, but they will not be ruled by him; they will not receive either the instruction of his word or the correction of his rod; they will not be reclaimed or reformed by either. They are false both to God and man."

Verses 29–34

I. A loud call to weeping and mourning. Jerusalem, that had been a joyous city must now *take up a lamentation on high places* (v. 29), where they had served their idols. In token both of sorrow and slavery, Jerusalem must now *cut off her hair and cast it away*; the word is peculiar to the hair of the Nazarites, which was the badge and token of their dedication to God. Jerusalem had been a city which was a Nazarite to God. but now must *cut off her hair*, be degraded, and separated from God, as she had been separated to him. It is time for those that have lost their holiness to lay aside their joy.

II. Just cause given for this great lamentation.

1. The sin of Jerusalem appears here very heinous (v. 30): *The children of Judah have done evil in my sight;* they have affronted me to my face. Here are two things charged upon them: (1) That they were impudent towards God and set him at defiance: *They have set their abominations in the house that is called by my name*, in the very courts of the temple, *to pollute it*, as if they would reconcile heaven and hell, God and Baal. They have particularly *built the high places of Tophet*, where the image of Moloch was set up, *in the valley of the son of Hinnom*, adjoining Jerusalem; and there *they burnt their sons and their daughters in the fire*, burnt them alive, to honour or appease those idols that were devils and not gods. Surely it was righteous judgment, because they had changed the glory of God into the similitude of a beast, that God gave them up to such vile affections that changed them into worse than beasts. God says of this that it was *what he commanded them not.* It never came into his heart to have children offered to him, yet they had forsaken his service for the service of such gods as showed themselves to be indeed enemies to mankind.

2. The destruction of Jerusalem speaks misery in general (v. 29), *The Lord hath rejected and forsaken the generation of his wrath.* Sin makes those the generation of God's wrath that had been the generation of his love. And God will reject those who have by their impenitence made themselves *vessels of wrath fitted to destruction.* "Verily, I say unto you, I know you not." (1) Death shall triumph over them, v. 32, 33. *Tophet shall be called the valley of slaughter*, for there multitudes shall be slain, when, in their attempts to escape, they fall into the hands of the besiegers. This valley of Tophet was a place where they sacrificed some of their children, and dedicated others to Moloch, and there they should fall as victims to divine justice. Tophet had formerly been the burying place, or burning place, of the dead bodies of the besiegers, and God will now turn it into a burying place for the besieged. So great shall that slaughter be that even the spacious valley of Tophet shall not be able to contain the slain; and at length there shall not be enough left alive to bury the dead, so that *the carcases of the people shall be meat* for the birds and beasts of prey, that shall feed upon them like carrion. Joy shall depart from them (v. 34): *Then will I cause to cease the voice of mirth.* It is threatened here that there shall be nothing to rejoice in. There shall be none of the joy of weddings; no mirth, for there shall be no marriages. Nor shall there be any more of the joy of harvest, *for the land shall be desolate*, uncultivated and unimproved. Both *the cities of Judah and the streets of Jerusalem* shall look melancholy.

CHAPTER 8

The prophet proceeds, in this chapter, to justify the destruction that God was bringing upon this people. I. He represents the judgments as so terrible that death should be desired, ver. 1–3. II. The wretched stupidity and wilfulness of this people brought this ruin upon them, ver. 4–12. III. He describes the great confusion and consternation that the whole land should be in, ver. 13–17. IV. The prophet is himself deeply affected, ver. 18–22.

Verses 1–3

These verses give a further description of the dreadful desolation which the army of the Chaldeans should make in the land.

I. Death shall not now be, as it always used to be—the repose of the dead. The ashes of the dead, even of *kings* and *princes*, shall be disturbed, and their *bones scattered at the grave's mouth*, Ps. cxli. 7. It was threatened in the close of the former chapter that the slain should be unburied, but here we find the graves of those that were buried maliciously opened by the enemy, who for covetousness, hoping to find treasure in the graves, *brought out the bones of the kings of Judah and the princes*. The dignity of their sepulchres could not secure them. The bones of the priests and prophets too were digged up and thrown about. The barbarous nations were sometimes guilty of these absurd and inhuman triumphs over those they had conquered. The bones, being dug out of the graves, were spread abroad upon the face of the earth in contempt. *They shall be spread before the sun* and before *the moon and stars*, even *all the host of heaven*, whom they have made idols of, *v.* 2. Before these lights of heaven, which they had courted, shall their dead bodies be cast, and left to putrefy.

II. Death shall now be what it never used to be—the choice of the living, not because there appears in it anything delightsome; yet everything in this world shall become so irksome, and all the prospects so black that *death shall be chosen rather than life* (*v.* 3); not in a believing hope of happiness in the other life, but in an utter despair of any ease in this life. These *remain* alive (and that is all) in the many *places whither they were driven* by the judgments of God, some prisoners in the country of their enemies, others beggars in their neighbour's country, and others fugitives and vagabonds in their own country.

Verses 4–12

The prophet here is instructed to set before this people the folly of their impenitence. They are here represented as senseless people that would not be made wise by all the methods that Infinite Wisdom took to bring them to themselves.

I. They would not attend to the dictates of reason. They would not act in the affairs of their souls with the same common prudence with which they acted in other things. *Come, and let us reason together, saith the Lord* (*v.* 4, 5): *Shall men fall and not arise?* If men happen to fall to the ground, to fall into the dirt, will they not get up again as fast as they can? *Shall a man turn aside* out of the right way? The most careful traveller may miss his way; but then, as soon as he is aware of it, *will he not return?* Thus men do in other things. *Why then has this people of Jerusalem slidden back by a perpetual backsliding?* Why do not they, when they have fallen into sin, hasten to get up again by repentance? Why do not they, when they see they have missed their way, correct their error and reform? Sin is a *backsliding*, it is going back from the right way, not only into a by-path, but into a contrary path, back from the way that leads to life to that which leads to destruction. The sinner not only wanders endlessly, but proceeds end-ways towards ruin. The tempter brings men to sin, and holds them fast in it, and they contribute to their own captivity: *They hold fast deceit*. The excuses they make for their sins are deceits, yet they will not be undeceived, and therefore *they refuse to return*.

II. They would not attend to the dictates of conscience, which is our reason reflecting upon ourselves and our own actions, *v.* 6. The prophet listened to see what effect his preaching had upon them; God himself listened, as one that desires not the death of sinners, that would have been glad to hear anything

that promised repentance. These expectations were disappointed: *They spoke not aright*, as I thought they would have done. God did not find any repenting of the national wickedness, which might have helped to empty the measure of public guilt. They did not so much as take the first step towards repentance; they did not say, *What have I done?* They went on resolutely in their sins: *Everyone turned to his course, as the horse rushes into the battle*, scorning to be curbed.

III. They would not attend to the dictates of providence, nor understand the voice of God in them, *v.* 7. They apprehend not the meaning either of a mercy or an affliction. They know not how to improve the grace that God affords them when he sends them his prophets, nor how to make use of the rebukes when *his voice cries in the city*. There is sagacity in the inferior creatures. *The stork in the heaven knows her appointed times;* so do other season-birds, *the turtle, the crane, and the swallow*. These by a natural instinct change their quarters, as the temper of the air alters; they come when the spring comes, and go when the winter approaches, probably into warmer climates.

IV. They would not attend to the dictates of the written word. They say, *We are wise;* but *how* can they say so? (*v.* 8). They think they are wise because *the law of the Lord is with them*, the book of the law and the interpreters of it, Deut. iv. 6. But their pretensions are groundless for all this. They might as well have been without the law, unless they had made a better use of it. *The pen of the scribes*, of those that first wrote the law and of those that now write expositions of it, *is in vain*. But it might be said, They have some wise men among them. To this it is answered (*v.* 9): *The wise men are ashamed* that they have not made a better use of their wisdom, and lived more up to it. *They are confounded and taken;* all their wisdom has not served to keep them from those courses that tend to their ruin. They talk of their wisdom, but, *Lo, they have rejected the word of the Lord*. The pretenders to wisdom, who said, "*We are wise and the law of the Lord is with us*," were the priests and the false prophets; with them the prophet here deals plainly. Their families and estates shall be ruined (*v.* 10): *Their wives shall be given to others*, when they are taken captives, *and their fields* shall be taken from them by their victorious enemy and shall be given *to those that shall inherit them*. And (*v.* 12), notwithstanding all their pretensions to wisdom and sanctity, *they shall fall among those that fall. In the time of their visitation*, when the wickedness of the land comes to be enquired into, it will be found that they have contributed to it more than any. He gives a reason for these judgments (*v.* 10–12). They were greedy of the wealth of this world. The *priests teach for hire* and the *prophets divine for money*, Mic. iii. 11. *Everyone deals falsely*, looks one way and rows another. There is no such thing as sincerity among them. They flattered people in their sins, and pretended to be the physicians of the state, but knew not how to apply proper remedies; they *healed them slightly*, killed the patient with palliative cures, silencing their fears with, "*Peace, peace*, all is well, and there is no danger." *They could not blush*, so perfectly lost were they to all sense of virtue and honour.

Verses 13–22

I. God threatening the destruction of a sinful people. He has borne long with them, but they are still more and more provoking. They shall be stripped of all their comforts (*v.* 13): *There shall be no grapes on the vine*, nothing left them wherewith to *make glad their hearts*. It is expounded in the last clause: *The things that I have given them shall pass away from them.* Mercies abused are forfeited, and it is just with God to take the forfeiture. *I will send serpents among you,* the Chaldean army, fiery serpents. They *shall not be charmed* with music. These are serpents of another nature; they are as *the deaf adder, that stops her ear, and will not hear the voice of the charmer.*

II. The people sinking into despair under the pressure of those calamities. Those that were void of fear are void of hope now that it breaks in upon them, and have no heart either to make head against it or to bear up under it, *v.* 14. *Why do we sit still here?* Let us *assemble, and go* in a body *into the defenced cities.* Though they could expect no other than to be cut off there at last, yet not so soon as in the country, and therefore, "*Let us go, and be silent there;* let us attempt nothing, nor so much as make a complaint; for to what purpose?" It is a sullen silence.

1. They are sensible that God is angry with them: "*The Lord our God has put us to silence,* has struck us with astonishment, and *given us water of gall to drink. Thou hast made us to drink the wine of astonishment.* To what purpose is it to contend with our fate when God himself fights against us?" They seem to quarrel with God as if he had dealt hardly with them in not permitting them to speak for themselves. At length they begin to see the hand of God stretched out in the calamities, and to own that they have provoked him.

2. They are sensible that the enemy is likely to be too hard for them, *v.* 16. *The snorting of the horses was heard from Dan,* the report of the strength of their cavalry was soon carried all over and everybody *trembled at the sound of the neighing of his steeds. They have come,* and there is no opposing them; they *have devoured the land and all that is in the city.*

3. They are disappointed in their expectations of deliverance. *We looked for peace, but no good came,* no good news from abroad; we looked *for a time of health* and prosperity to our nation, but, *behold, trouble,* the alarms of war. Their false prophets had cried *Peace, peace,* to them. The deliverance did not come when they had long expected it (*v.* 20): *The harvest is past, the summer is ended;* that is, there is a great deal of time gone. Harvest and summer are parts of the year, so the meaning is, "One year passes after another, one campaign after another, and yet our affairs are as bad as ever; no relief comes. *We are not saved.*" The season of action is over the summer and harvest are gone, and a cold and melancholy winter succeeds. They stand in their own light, and put a bar in their own door, and are not saved because they are not ready for salvation.

4. They are deceived in those things which they thought would have secured their peace to them (*v.* 19): *The daughter of my people* cries, cries aloud, *because of those that dwell in a far country,* because of the foreign enemy that comes from a far country to take possession of ours. *Is not the Lord in Zion? Is not her king in her?* These were the two things that they had all along depended upon, (1) That they had among them the temple of God, and the tokens of his special presence with them. (2) That they had the throne of the house of David. *Is not Zion's king in her?* And will not Zion's God protect Zion's king and his kingdom? This outcry of theirs reflects upon God, and therefore he returns an answer immediately: *Why have they provoked me to anger with their graven images?*

III. More of the lamentations of Jeremiah. He was an eye-witness of the desolations of his country: "*My heart is faint in me* (*v.* 18). *When I would comfort myself against my sorrow* every attempt to alleviate the grief does but aggravate it." Sometimes sorrow

is such that the more it is repressed the more it recoils. This may be the case of very good men, as of the prophet here, whose soul refused to be comforted. He tells us (*v.* 21): "It is *for the hurt of the daughter of my people* that *I am* thus *hurt;* it is for their sin, and the miseries they have brought upon themselves that *I am black,* that I go in black as mourners do, and that *astonishment has taken hold on me,* so that I know not which way to turn." A gracious spirit will be a public spirit, a tender spirit, a mourning spirit. Jeremiah had prophesied the destruction of Jerusalem, and, though the truth of his prophecy was questioned, yet he did not rejoice in the proof of the truth of it, preferring the welfare of his country before his own reputation. How small his hopes were (*v.* 22): "*Is there no balm in Gilead*—no medicine proper for a sick and dying kingdom? *Is there no physician there*—no skilful faithful hand to apply the medicine?" This verse may be understood as laying all the blame of the incurableness of their disease upon themselves. The question must be answered affirmatively: *Is there no balm in Gilead—no physician there?* Yes, certainly there is; God is able to help and heal them. Gilead was a place in their own land, not far off. They had among themselves God's law and his prophets, with the help of which they might have been brought to repentance, and their ruin might have been prevented. They had princes and priests, whose business it was to reform the nation and redress their greivances. *Why then was not* their health restored? Certainly it was not for want of balm and a physician, but because they would not admit the application nor submit to the methods of cure. The physician and physic were both ready, but the patient was wilful and would not be tied to rules.

Chapter 9

In this chapter the prophet goes on faithfully to reprove sin and to threaten God's judgments for it, and yet bitterly to lament both. I. He expresses his great grief for the miseries of Judah and Jerusalem, and his detestation of their sin, ver. 1–11. II. He justifies God in the destruction brought upon them, ver. 9–16. III. He calls upon others to bewail the woeful case, ver. 17–22. IV. He shows them the folly and vanity of trusting in their own strength or wisdom, or anything but God only, ver. 23–26.

Verses 1–11

The prophet commissioned to foretell the destruction and to point out the sin. What he said of both came from the heart, and one would have thought it would reach to the heart.

I. He abandons himself to sorrow in consideration of the calamitous condition of his people.

1. He laments the bloodshed and the lives lost (*v.* 1): "*O that my head were waters,* that so *my eyes* might be *fountains of tears,* still sending forth floods of tears as there still occur fresh occasions for them!" The same word in Hebrew signifies both *the eye* and *a fountain,* as if in this land of sorrows our eyes were designed rather for weeping than seeing. While we find our hearts such fountains of sin, it is fit that our eyes should be fountains of tears. But Jeremiah's grief here is upon the public account: he would *weep day and night for the slain of the daughter of his people,* the multitudes of his countrymen that fell by the sword of war. When we hear of the numbers of slain in great battles we ought to be much affected, for whatever people they are of, they are of the same human nature with us, and there are so many precious lives lost, as dear to them as ours to us.

2. He laments the desolations of the country. "Not only for the towns and cities, but *for the mountains, will I take up a weeping and wailing*" (the fruitful hills with which Judea abounded), and for *the habitations of the wilderness,* or rather *the pastures*

of the plain, that used to be *clothed with flocks or covered with corn*, but now *they are burnt up* by the Chaldean army. Everything looks so melancholy for they *hear not the voice of the cattle*. The havoc war makes in a country cannot but be for a lamentation to all tender spirits, for it is a tragedy which destroys the stage it is acted on.

II. He abandons himself to solitude. While all his neighbours are fleeing to the defenced cities (*ch.* iv. 5, 6), he is contriving to retire into some desert, in detestation of his people's sin (*v.* 2): "*O that I had in the wilderness a lodging-place of wayfaring men*, such as they have in the deserts of Arabia, for travellers, *that I might leave my people and go from them!*" We must not *go out of the world*, bad as it is, before our time. If he could not do good to many, yet he might to some. But it made him weary of his life to see them dishonouring God and destroying themselves. Jeremiah, in the courts of God's house, wishes himself in a wilderness.

1. He would not think of leaving them because they were in distress, but because they were wicked. They were filthy: *They are all adulterers*, that is, the generality of them are, *ch.* v. 8. They were false. Those that had been unfaithful to their God were so to one another. Go to church, to court, or to the exchange—and they are *an assembly of treacherous men*. There they will cheat deliberately with a malicious design, for (*v.* 3) *they bend their tongues, like their bow, for lies*, with craft. Their tongue turns as naturally to a lie as the bow to the string. *But they are not valiant for the truth upon the earth*. They might do good service if they would use the art and resolution which they are so much masters of in the cause of truth; but they will not do so. Those that will be faithful to the truth must be valiant, and not daunted by opposition. We must answer, another day, not only for our enmity in opposing truth, but for our cowardice in defending it. They will cheat their own brethren (*every brother will utterly supplant*). Jacob had his name from *supplanting*; it is the word here used. Go into company and you will find there is nothing of sincerity or common honesty among them. No man thinks himself bound to be either grateful or sincere. *Every neighbour will walk with slander;* they care not what ill they say one of another, though ever so false; that way that the slander goes they will go; they will *walk with it. They have taught their tongue to speak lies. They weary themselves to commit iniquity*. They are wearied *with* their sinful pursuits and yet not weary of them. They grow worse and worse (*v.* 3): *They proceed from evil to evil*, from one degree of sin to another. *No one reaches the height of vice at once*. They began with equivocating, but at last came to downright lying.

2. The prophet shows what God had determined against them. God had marked their sin. He could tell the prophet what sort of people they were. So here (*v.* 6): "*Thy habitation is in the midst of deceit*, all about thee are addicted to it; therefore stand upon thy guard." This charge is enlarged upon, *v.* 8. Their tongue was a *bow bent* (*v.* 3), plotting and preparing mischief; here it is *an arrow shot out*. It is a *slaying arrow* (so some readings have it); their tongue has been to many an instrument of death. They *speak peaceably to their neighbours*, against whom they are at the same time *lying in wait*; as Joab kissed Abner when he was about to kill him. Fair words, when they are not attended with good intentions, are despicable, but, when they are intended as a cloak and cover for wicked intentions, they are abominable. Sinners might be taught the good knowledge of the Lord but they will not learn; and where no knowledge of God is, what good can be expected? Hos. iv. 1. God had marked them for ruin, *v.* 7, 9, 11. Those that will not know God as their lawgiver shall be

made to know him as their judge. Some shall be refined (*v.* 7): "Because they are thus corrupt, *behold, will melt them and try them*, and see whether the furnace of affliction will purify them from their dross, and whether, when they are melted, they will be new-cast in a better mould." They shall not be *rejected as reprobate silver* till *the founder has melted in vain*, *ch.* vi. 29, 30. He speaks as one that could not find in his heart to give them up to ruin till he had first tried all means likely to bring them to repentance. The rest shall be ruined (*v.* 9): *Shall I not visit for these things?* Fraud and falsehood are sins which God hates and which he will reckon for. The sentence is passed, the decree has gone forth (*v.* 11): *I will make Jerusalem heaps* of rubbish; it shall be fit for nothing but to be *a den of dragons*; and *the cities of Judah* shall be *a desolation*.

Verses 12–22

Two things the prophet designs, in these verses, with reference to the approaching destruction of Judah and Jerusalem: 1. To convince people of the justice of God in that they had by sin brought it upon themselves. 2. To affect people with the greatness of the desolation that by a terrible prospect of it they might be awakened to repentance and reformation.

I. He calls for the thinking men to show people the equity of God's proceedings, though they seemed harsh (*v.* 12): "*Who, where, is the wise men*, or the prophet, *to whom the mouth of the Lord hath spoken?* You boast of your wisdom, and of the prophets you have among you; produce one and he will soon understand that there is a just ground of God's controversy with this people." Do these wise men enquire, *For what does the land perish?* It used to be a land that God cared for, but it is now a land that he has forsaken. *Wherefore has the Lord done thus unto this land?* God here gives a full answer.

1. The indictment preferred against them, upon which they had been found guilty, *v.* 13, 14. (1) They have revolted from their allegiance to their rightful Sovereign. *Therefore* God has *forsaken their land*, because they have *forsaken his law*, and had not *obeyed his voice*, nor *walked in* the ways. (2) They have entered into the service of usurpers, have not only withdrawn themselves from their obedience to their prince, but have taken up arms against him. They have set up their own will, the wills of the flesh, and the carnal mind, in contradiction to the will of God: *They have walked after the imagination of their own hearts;* they would do as they pleased, whatever God and conscience said to the contrary. *They have walked after Baalim:* the word is plural; they had many Baals, Baal-peor and Baal-berith, the Baal of this place and the Baal of the other place; for they had *lords many*, which *their fathers taught them* to worship, but which the God of their fathers had again and again forbidden. This was why *the land perished*.

2. The sentence upon the convicted rebels must now be executed: *The Lord of hosts, the God of Israel, hath said it* (*v.* 15, 16), and who can reverse it? Their comforts at home shall be poisoned and embittered to them: *I will feed this people with wormwood* (or rather with *wolf's-bane*, some herb that is both nauseous and noxious), *and* I will *give them water of gall* (or *juice of hemlock* or some other herb that is poisonous) *to drink*. Everything about them shall be a terror to them. God will *curse their blessings*, Mal. ii. 2. Their dispersion abroad shall be their destruction (*v.* 16): *I will scatter them among the heathen*. They shall lose themselves, where they lost their virtue, *among the heathen*; they had violated that truth which is the bond and cement of society and commerce, and therefore are justly crumbled

to dust and *scattered among the heathen*. And now we see for what the land perishes; all this desolation is the desert of their deeds.

II. He calls for the mourning women to lament these sad calamities that had come or were coming upon them, that the nation might prepare for them: *The Lord of hosts* himself *says, Call for the mourning women, that they may come, v.* 17. Here is work for the counterfeit mourners: *Send for the cunning women*, that are made use of at funerals to supply the want of true mourners. Let these *take up a wailing* for us, *v.* 18. Or, rather, it intimates the extreme stupidity of the people, that laid not to heart the judgments. God sent his mourning prophets to them, to call them to mourning, but his word in their mouths did not work upon their faith; rather therefore than they shall go laughing to their ruin, let the mourning women come. Here is work for the real mourners. The present scene is very tragical (*v.* 19): *A voice of wailing is heard out of Zion*. Some make this to be the song of the mourning women: it is rather an echo to it, returned by those whose affections were moved by their wailings. In Zion the voice of joy and praise used to be heard, while the people kept closely to God. But sin has altered the note; it is now the *voice of lamentation. We are confounded* because *we have forsaken the land* (forced so to do by the enemy), not because we *have* forsaken the Lord, being drawn aside of *our own lust and enticed— because our dwellings have cast us out*, not because our God has cast us off. Thus unhumbled hearts lament their calamity, but not their iniquity, the cause of it. Those whose land has *spewed them out* (as it did their predecessors the Canaanites, and justly, because they trod in their steps, Lev. xviii. 28) complain that they are driven into the city, but, after a while, those of the city, and they with them, shall be forced thence too: *Yet hear the word of the Lord* (*v.* 20); let *the women* hear it, for the men will not heed it, will not give it a patient hearing. The prophets will be glad to preach to a congregation of women that *tremble at God's word*. Let the women *teach their daughters wailing*. Let *everyone teach her neighbour lamentation*; this intimates that the trouble shall spread far, shall go from house to house. The judgment here threatened is made to look terrible. Multitudes shall be slain, *v.* 21. Death shall ride in triumph, and there shall be no escaping his arrest. Nor does it attack the cottages only, but it has *entered into our palaces*. Those that are slain shall be left unburied (*v.* 22).

Verses 23–26

The prophet had been endeavouring to possess this people with a holy fear of God and his judgments, but still they had recourse to some sorry subterfuge or other with which to excuse themselves in their obstinacy. He therefore sets himself here to drive them from these refuges of lies.

I. When they were told how inevitable the judgment would be they pleaded the defence of their politics and powers, which, with their wealth and treasure, they thought made their city impregnable. In answer to this he shows them the folly of trusting to these stays, while they have not a God in covenant, *v.* 23, 24. *Let not the wise man glory in his wisdom* as if with the help of that he could find out some evasion or other. But, if a man's policies fail him, yet surely he may gain his point by might and dint of courage. No: *Let not the strong man glory in his strength*, for the battle is not always to the strong. David the stripling proves too hard for Goliath the giant. All human force is nothing without God, worse than nothing against him. But may not the *rich man's wealth* be *his strong city*? (money answers all things) No: *Let not the rich man glory in his riches*,

as if they could make their part good against the Chaldeans because they have wise men to advise concerning the war, mighty men to fight their battles, and rich men to bear the charges of the war. Our only comfort in trouble will be that we have done our duty. Those that *refused to know God* (*v.* 6) will boast in vain of their wisdom and wealth; but those that *know God*, intelligently, that *understand* aright *that he is the Lord*, may *glory in this*, it will be their rejoicing in the day of evil. Our only confidence in trouble will be that, having through grace in some measure done our duty, we shall find God a God all-sufficient to us. We may *glory in this*, that, wherever we are, we have acquaintance with a God that *exercises lovingkindness, and judgment, and righteousness in the earth*, that is just to all his creatures, kind to all his children and will protect them and provide for them. The God they thus faithfully conform to they may cheerfully confide in, in their greatest straits. But the prophet intimates that the generality of this people took no care about this.

II. When they were told how provoking their sins were to God they vainly pleaded the covenant of their circumcision. They were undoubtedly the people of God; they had the mark of his children in their flesh. To this the prophet answers, God would punish all wicked people, without making any distinction between the circumcised and uncircumcised, *v.* 25, 26. They had lived in common with the uncircumcised nations, and so had forfeited the benefit of that peculiarity. The Judge of all the earth is impartial, and none shall fare the better at his bar for any external advantages. The condemnation of impenitent sinners that are baptized will be as sure as that of impenitent sinners that are unbaptized. Those *in the utmost corners, that dwell in the wilderness*, are supposed to be the Kedarenes and those of the kingdoms of Hazor, as appears by comparing *ch.* xlix. 28–32. Some think they are so called because they dwelt as it were in a corner of the world, others because they had *the hair of their head polled into corners*. However that was, they were uncircumcised in flesh, and the Jews are ranked with them; for *all the house of Israel are uncircumcised in the heart*; they have the sign, but not the thing signified, *ch.* iv. 4.

CHAPTER 10

The prophecy of this chapter has a double reference: I. To those that were carried away into the land of the Chaldeans, notorious for idolatry and superstition; and they are here cautioned not to learn the way of the heathen (ver. 1, 2), for their astrology and idolatry are both foolish things (ver. 3–5), and the worshippers of idols brutish, ver. 8, 9. So it will appear in the day of their visitation, ver. 14, 15. They are likewise exhorted to adhere firmly to the God of Israel, for there is none like him, ver. 6, 7. He is the true God and has the government of the world (ver. 10–13), and his people are happy in him, ver. 16. II. To those that yet remained in their own land. They are cautioned against security (ver. 17, 18) and a foreign enemy, which God would bring upon them for their sin, ver. 20–22. This calamity the prophet laments (ver. 19) and prays for the mitigation of it, ver. 23–25.

Verses 1–16

The prophet Jeremiah here arms people against the idolatrous usages of the heathen, that being convinced and reclaimed, by the word of God, the rod might be prevented; and it is *written for our learning*.

I. A solemn charge given to the people of God not to conform themselves to the ways of the heathen. Let Israel hear this word from the God of Israel: "*Learn not the way of the heathen*, do not approve of it, nor think indifferently concerning it. Let not any of their customs steal in among you nor mingle themselves with your religion." It was the way of the heathen to worship the host of heaven, the sun, moon, and stars; to them they gave divine honours, and from them they expected divine favours. Now God would not have his people to be *dismayed at the signs of heaven*, to reverence the stars as deities, nor to frighten themselves with any prognostications grounded upon them. Let them fear the God of heaven, and then they need not be *dismayed at the signs of heaven*, for the *stars in their courses* fight not against any that are at peace with God.

II. Good reasons given to enforce this charge.

1. The way of the heathen is absurd, and is condemned by the dictates of right reason, v. 3. The statutes and ordinances of the heathen are vanity. The Chaldeans valued themselves upon their wisdom, in which they thought that they excelled all their neighbours; but the prophet here shows that they, and all others that worshipped idols and expected help from them, had not common sense. Consider what the idol is that is worshipped. It was a *tree cut out of the forest* originally. It was fitted up by *the hands of the workmen*, squared, and sawed, and worked into shape; see Isa. xliv. 12, &c. But, after all, it was but the stock of a tree, fitter to make a gate-post of than anything else. But, to hide the wood, *they deck it with silver and gold. They fasten it* to its place *with nails and hammers*, that it fall not, nor is stolen, v. 4. The image is made straight enough; the workman did his part; it *is upright as the palm-tree* (v. 5); it looks stately, and stands up as if it were going to speak to you, but it *cannot speak*; nor can it take one step towards your relief. If there be any occasion for it to shift its place, it must be carried in procession, for it *cannot go.* Be not afraid of incurring their displeasure, for *they can do no evil*; be not afraid of forfeiting their favour, for *neither is it in them to do good.* Idols of gold and silver are as unworthy to be worshipped as wooden gods. *The stock is a doctrine of vanities, v.* 8. It teaches lies, teaches lies concerning God. It is *an instruction of vanities; it is wood.* A great deal of art is used, and pains taken, about it. They are not ordinary mechanics that are employed about these as about the wooden gods, v. 3. These are cunning men; it is *the work of the workman*; the graver must do his part when it has passed through *the hands of the founder.* And, that these gods might be reverenced as kings, *blue and purple are their clothing*, the colour of royal robes (v. 9). For what is the idol when it is made and when they have made the best they can of it? (v. 14): *They are falsehood;* they are not what they pretend to be. They are worshipped as the gods that give us breath and life and sense, whereas they are lifeless senseless things themselves, and *there is no breath in them*; there is *no spirit in them*, they are not animated, as they are supposed to be, by any *divine spirit* or *numen—divinity.* They have not so much as the *spirit of a beast that goes downward. They are vanity, and the work of errors, v.* 15. They are the creatures of a deluded fancy. The idolaters that worship these idols (v. 8), *are altogether brutish and foolish.* Though in the works of creation they cannot but see the eternal power and godhead of the Creator, yet they have become *vain in their imaginations, not liking to retain God in their knowledge.* See Rom. i. 21, 28.

2. The God of Israel is the one only living and true God; to set up any other in competition with him is the greatest affront that can be done him. The prophet turns from speaking with the utmost disdain of the idols of the heathen to speak with the most profound and awful reverence of the God of Israel (v. 6, 7). What is the glory of a man that invented a useful art or founded a flourishing kingdom (and these were grounds sufficient among the heathen to entitle a man to an apotheosis) compared with the glory of him that is the Creator of the world

and that *forms the spirit of man within him*? What is the glory of the greatest prince or potentate, compared with the glory of him whose *kingdom rules over all*? He acknowledges (v. 6), O Lord! *thou art great*, infinite and immense, and *thy name is great in might.* It is not only the house of Israel that is bound to worship the great Jehovah as the *God of Israel*, but all the families of the earth are bound to worship him as *King of nations.* His verity is as evident as the idol's vanity, v. 10. They are the work of men's hands, and the God of truth is God in truth. He is *the living God.* He is life itself, has life in himself, and is the fountain of life to all the creatures. The gods of the heathen are dead things, but ours is a living God and hath immortality. He is *an everlasting king, a King of eternity.* Though the nations should join together they would be utterly unable to resist, or even *to abide his indignation.* He is the God of nature, the fountain of all being; and all the powers of nature are at his command, v. 12, 13. If we look back, we find that the whole world owed its origin to him as its first cause. It was a common saying even among the Greeks—*He that sets up to be another god ought first to make another world.* God made us and all things. The earth has valuable treasures in its bowels and more valuable fruit on its surface. It and them he has *made by his power*; and it is by no less than an infinite power that it *hangs upon nothing.* The habitable part of the earth is admirably fitted for the use and service of man, and *he hath established it* so *by his wisdom. The heavens* are wonderfully *stretched out by his discretion* and that the motions of the heavenly bodies are directed for the benefit of this lower world. These *declare his glory* (Ps. xix. 1), and oblige us to declare it, and not give that glory to the heavens which we see is due to him that made them. If we look up, we see his providence to be a continued creation (v. 13): *When he uttereth his voice there is a multitude of waters in the heavens*, which are poured out on the earth. *He causes the vapours to ascend from the ends of the earth.* All the earth pays the tribute of vapours, because all the earth receives the blessing of rain. And thus the moisture in the universe, like the money in a kingdom and the blood in the body, is continually circulating for the good of the whole. There is no sort of weather but what furnishes us with a proof and instance of the wisdom and power of the great Creator. This God is Israel's God in covenant. Therefore let the house of Israel cleave to him, and not forsake him to embrace idols; for (v. 16) *the portion of Jacob is not like them*; their rock is not as our rock (Deut. xxxii. 31), nor ours like their mole-hills. If we have satisfaction in God as our portion, he will have a gracious delight in us as his people, whom he owns as *the rod of his inheritance*, with whom he dwells and by whom he is served and honoured. It is the unspeakable comfort of all the Lord's people that he who is their God is *the former of all things.*

3. The prophet, having thus compared the gods of the heathen with the God of Israel, reads the doom of all those pretenders, and directs the Jews, in God's name, to read it to the worshippers of idols (v. 11): *Thus shall you say unto them, The gods which have not made the heavens and the earth shall perish.* The primitive Christians would say, when they were urged to worship such a god, *Let him make a world and he shall be my god.* When God comes to reckon with idolaters he will make them weary of their idols, and glad to be rid of them. They shall *cast them to the moles and to the bats*, Isa. ii. 20.

Verses 17–25

I. The prophet threatens, in God's name, the approaching ruin of Judah and Jerusalem, v. 17, 18.

The Jews that continued in their own land, after some were carried into captivity, were very secure; they thought themselves *inhabitants of a fortress;* their country was their stronghold, impregnable; but they must prepare to go after their brethren, and pack up their effects in expectation: "*Gather up thy wares out of the land;* contract your affairs, and bring them into as small a compass as you can." Let not what you have lie scattered, for the Chaldeans will be upon you again, to be the executioners of the sentence God has passed upon you (*v.* 18): "*Behold, I will sling out the inhabitants of the land at this once;* they have hitherto dropped out, by a few at a time, but they shall be slung out as a stone out of a sling. They shall be thrown out with violence a great distance off, in a little time." He adds, *And I will distress them, that they may find it so.* Whithersoever they go, they shall be continually perplexed and straitened, that they may feel that which they would not believe. They were told that their sin would be their ruin, but now *they shall find it so.*

II. He brings in the people sadly lamenting their calamities (*v.* 19): *Woe is me for my hurt!* Some make this the prophet's own lamentation, not for himself, but for the calamities and desolations of his country. But it may be taken as the language of the people, considered as a body, and therefore speaking as a single person. The prophet puts into their mouths the words they *should* say; whether they would say them or no, they should have cause to say them. "*Woe is me for my hurt,* not for what I fear, but for what I feel." Nor is it a slight hurt, but a *wound* that is *grievous.* To what purpose is it to complain? *This is a grief, and I must bear it* as well as I can. This is patience per force, not a patience by principle. To say, "This is an evil, *and I must bear it,* because I cannot help it," argues a want of those good thoughts of God which we should always have, even under our afflictions, saying, not only, God can and will do what he pleases, but, *Let him do what he pleases.* The country was wasted (*v.* 20): *My tabernacle is spoiled.* Jerusalem, though a strong city, now proves weak: their government is dissolved, and their state has fallen to pieces. Their church is ruined, and all the supports of it fail. It was a general destruction of church and state, city and country, and there were none to repair these desolations. "*My children have gone forth of me;* some have fled, others are slain, others carried into captivity, so that *they are not*; for *there is none to stretch forth my tent any more,* none of my children to do me any service." The rulers took no proper measures for the re-establishing of their ruined state (*v.* 21): *The pastors have become brutish.* When the tents, the shepherds' tents, were spoiled (*v.* 20), it concerned the shepherds to look after them; but they were foolish shepherds. Their kings and princes had no regard at all for the public welfare. The priests, the pastors of God's tabernacle, did a great deal towards the ruin of religion, but nothing towards the repair of it. They neither acknowledged the judgment, nor expected the deliverance, to come from his hand. *Therefore they shall not prosper;* none of their attempts for the public safety shall succeed. Those cannot expect to prosper who do not by faith and prayer take God along with them in all their ways. The report of the enemy's approach was dreadful (*v.* 22): *The noise of the bruit has come,* of the report which at first was but whispered abroad, as wanting confirmation. It now proves too true: *A great commotion* arises *out of the north country,* which threatens to make all *the cities of Judah desolate and a den of dragons;* for they must all expect to be sacrificed to the avarice and fury of the Chaldean army.

III. He turns to God, and addresses himself to him, finding it too little purpose to speak to the people.

1. The prophet here acknowledges the sovereignty and dominion of the divine Providence, *v.* 23. We are not at our own disposal, but under a divine direction; the event is often overruled so as to be quite contrary to our expectation. Some think that the way of the Chaldean army being not in themselves, they can do no more than God permits them; he can set bounds to these proud waves, and say, *Hitherto they shall come, and no further.*

2. He deprecates the divine wrath, that it might not fall upon God's Israel, *v.* 24. He speaks not for himself only, but on behalf of his people: *O Lord, correct me, but with judgment* (no more than is necessary for the driving out of the foolishness that is bound up in our hearts), *not in thy anger,* let it come from thy love, and be made to work for good, not to *bring us to nothing,* but to bring us home to thyself. Let it not be according to the desert of our sins, but according to the designs of thy grace. We cannot pray in faith that we may never be corrected, while we are conscious to ourselves that we need correction and deserve it, and know that as many as God loves he chastens.

3. He imprecates the divine wrath against the persecutors of Israel (*v.* 25): *Pour out thy fury upon the heathen that know thee not.* This prayer does not come from a spirit of malice or revenge. It is an appeal to his justice. As if he had said, "Lord, we are a provoking people; but are there not other nations that are more so? We are thy children, and may expect a fatherly correction; but they are thy enemies, and against them thy indignation should be, not against us." The heathen are strangers to God, and are content to be so. They *know him not,* nor desire to know him. They live without prayer, have nothing of religion among them; they *call not on God's name.* They are persecutors of the people of God. *They have eaten up Jacob* with as much greediness as those that are hungry eat their necessary food; they have *devoured him, and consumed him, and made his habitation desolate,* that is, the land in which he lives, or the temple of God, which is his habitation among them.

CHAPTER 11

I. God by the prophet puts the people in mind of the covenant he had made with their fathers, ver. 1–7. II. He charges it upon them that they had obstinately refused to obey him, ver. 8–10. III. He threatens to punish them with utter ruin for their disobedience (ver. 11, 13); he tells them that their idols should not save them (ver. 12), that their prophets should not pray for them (ver. 14); he justifies his proceedings, they having brought all this mischief upon themselves, ver. 15–17. IV. Here is an account of a conspiracy formed against Jeremiah by his fellow-citizens, the men of Anathoth; God's discovery of it to him (ver. 18, 19), his prayer against them (ver. 20), and a prediction of God's judgments upon them for it, ver. 21–23.

Verses 1–10

The prophet draws up an indictment against the Jews for wilful disobedience to the commands of their rightful Sovereign.

I. God commanded him to *speak it to the men of Judah, v.* 1, 2. In the original it is plural: *Speak you this.* For what he said to Jeremiah was the same that he gave in charge to all his servants the prophets. They none of them said any other than what Moses, in the law, had said; to that therefore they must direct the people: "*Hear the words of this covenant;* be judged by them." Jeremiah must now proclaim this in the cities *of Judah and the streets of Jerusalem,* that all may hear, for all are concerned. Then, by comparing yourselves with the covenant, you will soon be aware upon what terms you now stand with him.

II. He opens the charter upon which their state was founded and by which they held their privileges. They had forgotten the tenor of it, and lived as if they thought that they might do what they pleased and yet have what God had promised, or as if they thought that the keeping up of the ceremonial observances was all that God required of them. He therefore shows them that the thing God insisted upon was *obedience*, which was *better than sacrifice*. He said, *Obey my voice*, v. 4, and again v. 7. "Own God for your Master. *Do my commandments*, but *according to all which I command you*; make conscience of moral duties especially, and rest not in those that are merely ritual; hear the words of the covenant, and do them." This was the original contract between God and them, when he first formed them into a people. It was what he *commanded their fathers* when he first *brought them forth out of the land of Egypt*, v. 4 and again v. 7. He redeemed them out of the service of the Egyptians, which was perfect slavery, that he might take them into his own service, which is perfect freedom, Luke i. 74, 75. This was made the condition of the relation between them and God: "*So shall you be my people and I will be your God;* I will own you for mine, and you may call upon me as yours." It was upon these terms that the land of Canaan was given them for a possession: *Obey my voice, that I may perform the oath sworn to your fathers, to give them a land flowing with milk and honey*, v. 5. *Cursed be the man*, though it were but a single person, *that obeys not the words of this covenant*, much more when it is the body of the nation that rebels. Lest this covenant should be forgotten God had from time to time called to them to remember it by his servants the prophets. This covenant was consented to (v. 5): *Then answered I, and said, So be it, O Lord!* These are the words of the prophet, expressing either, his own consent to the covenant for himself, and his desire to have the benefit of it. Or, his good will that his people might have the benefit of it. Or, his people's consent to the covenant: "*Then answered I*, in the name of the people, *So be it.*"

III. He charges them with breach of covenant, such a breach as amounted to a forfeiture of their charter, v. 8. "*Obey my voice*, do as you are bidden, and all shall be well"; *yet they obeyed not. They walked everyone in the imagination of their evil heart*; every man did as his fancy and humour led him, right or wrong, lawful or unlawful, both in their devotions and in their conversations; see *ch.* vii. 24. What then could they expect, but to fall under the curse of the covenant? That which aggravated their defection from God was that it was general, and as it were *by consent*, v. 9, 10. Jeremiah himself saw that many lived in open disobedience to God, but the Lord told him that the matter was worse than he thought: *A conspiracy is found among them.* There is a combination against God and religion, a dangerous design formed to overthrow God's government and bring in the counterfeit deities. They designed to overthrow divine revelation, and persuade people not to hear, not to heed, the words of God. Human reason shall be their god, a light within their god, an infallible judge their god, saints and angels their gods, the god of this or the other nation shall be theirs; thus, under several disguises, they are in the same confederacy *against the Lord and against his anointed. The inhabitants of Jerusalem* are in conspiracy with *the men of Judah.* Those of this generation seem to be in conspiracy with those of the foregoing generation, to carry on the war from age to age against religion. Judah and Israel, the kingdom of the ten tribes and that of the two, that were often at daggers-drawing one with another, were yet *in a conspiracy* to *break the covenant God had made with their fathers*, even with the heads of all the twelve tribes. The house of Israel began the revolt, but the house of Judah soon came into the conspiracy.

Verses 11–17

This paragraph contains much of God's wrath. *Therefore I will bring evil upon them* (v. 11), the evil of punishment for the evil of sin.

I. They cannot help themselves. It is *evil which they shall not be able to escape*, or to *go forth out of*, by any evasion whatsoever.

II. Their God will not help them; *Though they shall cry unto me, I will not hearken unto them.* For he has plainly told us that he that *turns away his ears from hearing the law*, as they did, for they *inclined not their ear* (v. 8), even his prayer shall be an abomination to him.

III. Their idols shall not help them, v. 12. They shall *go, and cry to the gods to whom they* now *offer incense. They shall not save them at all.* It is God only that is a friend at need, *a present powerful help in time of trouble.* If the idols could have done any real kindness to their worshippers, they would have done it for this people, who had multiplied them *according to the number of their cities* (v. 13), nay, in Jerusalem, *according to the number of their streets.*

IV. Jeremiah's prayers shall not help them, v. 14. God would give no encouragement to the prophets to pray for them, not for the body of the people, but for the remnant among them, to pray for their eternal salvation, not for their deliverance from temporal judgments.

V. The profession they make of religion shall stand them in no stead, v. 15. Once they had a place in *God's house*; they partook of God's altar; they ate of the flesh of their peace-offerings, here called the *holy flesh.* What harm could come to those who were God's beloved, who were under the protection of his house? Even when they *did evil* yet *they rejoiced* and gloried in this, but their confidence would deceive them, they themselves having forfeited the privileges. They have *wrought lewdness with many*, have worshipped many idols; and therefore, God's temple will *yield them no protection.* God's altar will yield them no satisfaction: "*The holy flesh has passed from thee*, that is, an end will soon be put to thy sacrifices, when the temple shall be laid in ruins; and where then will the holy flesh be, that thou art so proud of?" A holy heart will be a comfort to us when the holy flesh has passed from us; an inward principle of grace will make up the want of the outward means of grace. But woe unto us if the departure of the holy flesh be accompanied with the departure of the Holy Spirit.

VI. God's former favours to them shall stand them in no stead, v. 16, 17. God had *called Israel's name a green olive-tree*, and had made them so, he had *planted* them (v. 17), had formed them into a people, with all the advantages they could have to make them a fruitful and flourishing people, so good was their law and so good was their land. He had planted them a green olive, a good olive, but they had degenerated into a *wild olive*, Rom. xi. 17. Both *the house of Israel* and the *house of Judah* had *done evil*, had *provoked God to anger in burning incense unto Baal*, setting up other mediators besides the promised Messiah. He that planted this green olive-tree, and expected fruit from it, finding it barren and grown wild, *has kindled fire upon it*, to burn it as it stands; for, being without fruit, it is *twice dead, plucked up by the roots* (Jude 12), it is *cut down and cast into the fire.* The *branches of it*, the *high and lofty boughs* (so the word signifies), are *broken down*, both princes and priests cut off. And thus it proves that the evil done against God is really done *against their own souls.*

Verses 18–23

The prophet Jeremiah has much in his writings concerning himself, the times he lived in being very troublesome. Here we have the beginning of his sorrows, which arose from the people of his own city, Anathoth, a priest's city.

I. Their plot against him, *v.* 19. They *devised devices against him*, laid their heads together to contrive how they might be the death of him. They said concerning Jeremiah, *Let us destroy the tree with the fruit thereof*—a proverbial expression, meaning, "Let us utterly destroy him root and branch." Or rather "both the prophet and the prophecy; let us kill the one and defeat the other. Let us sink his reputation, and so spoil the credit of his predictions." The persecutors of God's prophets *hunt for* no less than *the precious life*. They thought to put an end to his days, but he survived most of his enemies; they thought to blast his memory, but it lives to this day, and will while time lasts.

II. The information which God gave him of this conspiracy. He knew nothing of it himself, so artfully had they concealed it; he came to Anathoth fearing no harm, *like a lamb or an ox*, that thinks he is driven as usual to the field, *when he is brought to the slaughter*. There is but a step between Jeremiah and death; but then *the Lord gave him knowledge of it*, by dream or vision, or impression upon his spirit, that he might save himself, as the king of Israel did upon the notice Elisha gave him, 2 Kings vi. 10. Thus he came to *know it*. God *showed him their doings*. See what care God takes of his prophets: He *suffers no man to do them wrong*; all the rage of their enemies cannot prevail to take them off till they have finished their testimony.

III. His appeal to God hereupon, *v.* 20. When men deal unjustly with us we have a God to go to who will plead the cause of injured innocency and appear against the injurious. God's justice, which is a terror to the wicked, is a comfort to the godly. He knew the integrity that was in Jeremiah's heart, and knew the wickedness that was in their hearts, though ever so cunningly concealed. Now Jeremiah prays judgment against them: "*Let me see thy vengeance on them*, that is, do justice between me and them in such a way as thou pleasest." Some think there was something of human frailty in this prayer; at least Christ has taught us another lesson, both by precept and by pattern, which is to pray for our persecutors. He refers his cause entirely to the judgment of God: "*Unto thee have I revealed my cause;* not desiring nor expecting to interest any other in it." When we are wronged, we have a God to commit our cause to, with a resolution to acquiesce in his definitive sentence, to subscribe, and not prescribe, to him.

IV. Judgment given against his persecutors, *the men of Anathoth*. It was to no purpose for him to appeal to the courts at Jerusalem; the priests there would stand by the priests at Anathoth, but God will *therefore* take cognizance of the cause himself, and we are sure that *his judgment is according to truth*. They sought the prophet's life, for they forbad him to prophesy upon pain of death; they were resolved either to silence him or to slay him. The provocation he gave them was his prophesying *in the name of the Lord*, and not prophesying such smooth things as they always bespoke. It is as bad to God's faithful ministers to have their mouth stopped as to have their breath stopped. It used to be said that *a prophet could not perish but at Jerusalem*, for there the great council sat; but so bitter were the men of Anathoth against Jeremiah that they would undertake to be the death of him themselves. The sentence passed upon them for this crime, *v.* 22, 23: God says, *I will punish them; I will visit* this *upon them;* so the word is. *The sword* shall devour their *young men*, though they were young priests, and *famine* shall destroy the *sons and daughters*. They sought Jeremiah's life, they would destroy him *root and branch*, that *his name*

might be *no more remembered*, and therefore *there shall be no remnant of them left*.

CHAPTER 12

I. The success that wicked people had in their wicked practices (ver. 1, 2) and his appeal to God concerning his own integrity (ver. 3), with a prayer that God would bring the wickedness to an end, ver. 3, 4. II. God's rebuke to the prophet for his uneasiness at his present troubles, ver. 5, 6. III. A sad lamentation of the present deplorable state of the Israel of God, ver. 7–13. IV. An intimation of mercy to God's people, in a denunciation of wrath against their neighbours, but with a promise that if they would at last join themselves with the people of God they should come in sharers in their privileges, ver. 14–17.

Verses 1–6

The prophet doubts not but it would be of use to others to know what had passed between God and his soul, and therefore he here tells us,

I. What liberty he humbly took to reason with God concerning his judgments, *v.* 1. He is about to *plead* with God, not to find fault with his proceedings, but to enquire into the meaning of them. We may not *strive with our Maker*, but we may reason with him. When we are most in the dark concerning the meaning of God's dispensations we must still resolve to keep up right thoughts of God, that he never did, nor ever will do, the least wrong to any of his creatures. When we find it hard to understand particular providences we must have recourse to general truths as our first principles, and abide by them; however dark the providence may be, *the Lord is righteous;* see Ps. lxxiii. 1.

II. What it was in the dispensations of divine Providence that he stumbled at. The designs and projects of wicked people seem successful: *The way of the wicked prospers;* they compass their malicious designs. Hypocrites are chiefly meant (as appears, *v.* 2), who dissemble and depart from their good beginnings, deal treacherously, yet *they are happy*. The prophet shows (*v.* 2) God had been indulgent to them: "They are planted in a good land, a land flowing with milk and honey, and *thou hast planted them*! nay, thou didst cast out the heathen to plant them," Ps. xliv. 2; lxxx. 8. *They have taken root;* their prosperity seems to be confirmed and settled. God had favoured them, though they had dealt treacherously with him: *Thou art near in their mouth and far from their reins*. Though they cared not for thinking of God, nor had any sincere affection to him, yet they could easily persuade themselves to speak of him with an air of seriousness. Piety from the teeth outward is no difficult thing. Though they had the name of God ready in their mouth, and those forms of speech that savoured of piety, yet they could not keep the fear of God in their hearts.

III. What comfort he had in appealing to God concerning his own integrity (*v.* 3): *But thou, O Lord! knowest me*. God knew he was not a deceiver and false prophet; those that thus abused him did not know him, 1 Cor. ii. 8. We are as our hearts are, and our hearts are good or bad according as they are, or are not, towards God.

IV. He prays that God would turn his hand against these wicked people, and not suffer them to prosper always, though they had prospered long: "Let some judgment come to *pull them out* of this fat pasture *as sheep for the slaughter*, that it may appear their long prosperity was but like the feeding of lambs to *prepare them for the day of slaughter*," Hos. iv. 16. God suffered them to prosper that by their pride and luxury they might fill up the measure of their iniquity and so be ripened for destruction. "*How long shall the land mourn for the wickedness of those that dwell therein?* Lord, shall those prosper themselves that ruin all about them?" *The herbs of every field wither* (the grass is burnt up). The beasts are consumed.

This was the effect of a long drought which happened at the latter end of Josiah's reign and the beginning of Jehoiakim's; *ch.* iii. 3, viii. 13, ix. 10, 12; *ch.* xiv. Now why was it that this *fruitful land* was *turned into barrenness for the wickedness of those that dwelt therein?* Therefore the prophet prays that these wicked people might *die for their own sin*, and that the whole nation might not suffer for it. *They said, He shall not see our last end*, either, 1. God himself shall not. He knows not what way we take nor what it will end in. Or, 2. Jeremiah *shall not see our last end.* They look upon him as a false prophet.

V. He acquaints us with the answer God gave to those complaints of his, *v.* 5, 6. Ministers have lessons to learn as well as lessons to teach, and must themselves hear God's voice and preach to themselves. Jeremiah complained of the wickedness of the men of Anathoth, and that they prospered. Now this seems to be an answer to that complaint. 1. It is allowed that he had cause to complain (*v.* 6): "*Thy brethren*, the priests of Anathoth, of *the house of thy father, even they have dealt treacherously with thee*, and, under colour of friendship, have done thee all the mischief they could; they *have called a multitude after thee*, raised the mob upon thee, to whom they have endeavoured to render thee despicable. They are indeed such as thou canst *not believe, though they speak fair words to thee.* They seem to be thy friends, but are really thy enemies." 2. Yet he is told that he laid the unkindness of his countrymen too much to heart. *They wearied* him, because it was *in a land of peace wherein he trusted, v.* 5. It was very grievous to him to be thus hated and abused by his own kindred. He was disturbed in his mind by it. He was discouraged in his work by it, began to be weary of prophesying, and to think of giving it up. He did not see this was but the beginning of his sorrow, and that he had sorer trials yet before him; and, whereas he should, by a patient bearing of this trouble, prepare himself for greater, by his uneasiness he did but unfit himself for what lay before him: *If thou hast run with the footmen and they have wearied thee*, and run thee quite out of breath, *then how wilt thou contend with horses?* If the injuries done him by the men of Anathoth made such an impression upon him, what would he do when the princes and chief priests at Jerusalem should set upon him with their power, *ch.* xx. 2; xxxii. 2. If he was so soon tired *in a land of peace*, where there was little peril, *what would he do in the swellings of Jordan*, when that overflows all its banks and frightens even lions out of their thickets? (*ch.* xlix. 19). How shall we preserve our integrity and peace when we come to *the swellings of Jordan?* We must approve ourselves well in present smaller trials, keep up our spirits, keep hold of the promise, with our eye upon the prize, and so run that we may obtain it.

Verses 7–13

The people of the Jews are here marked for ruin.

I. It is a terrible word that God here says (*v.* 7): *I have forsaken my house*—the temple, his palace; they had polluted it, and so forced him out of it: *I have left my heritage*, and will look after it no more. If they would have conducted themselves with propriety, he would have made the best of them, for they were *the beloved of his soul*; but they had provoked him to *give them into the hand of their enemies.* They had degenerated, had become like *beasts of prey*, which nobody loves, but everybody avoids (*v.* 8): *My heritage is unto me as a lion in the forest.* They *cry out against* God in the threatenings they breathe against his prophets that speak to them in his name. They blaspheme his name, oppose his authority, and bid defiance to his justice, and so *cry out against him as a lion in the forest.* Those that were the *sheep of God's pasture* had become barbarous and ravenous, and as ungovernable as lions in the forest; *therefore he hated them;* for what delight could the God of love take in people that had become as roaring lions and raging beasts, a vexation to all about them? They had become like *birds of prey*, unworthy a place in God's house, where neither beasts nor birds of prey were admitted to be offered in sacrifice (*v.* 9): *My heritage is unto me as a bird with talons* (so some read it, and so the margin); they have by their unnatural contentions made their country a cock-pit. Or *as a speckled bird*, sprinkled, or bedewed with the blood of her prey. *The birds round about are against her.* Some made her a *speckled bird*, upon account of their mixing the superstitious usages of the heathen with divine institutions in the worship of God; they were fond of a party-coloured religion.

II. The enemies will fall upon them and lay them desolate. And some think it is upon this account that they are compared to a speckled bird, because fowls usually make a noise about a bird of an odd unusual colour. God's people are, among the children of this world, as *men wondered at*, as a *speckled bird*; but this people had by their own folly made themselves so. Let *all the birds round* be *against her*, for God has forsaken her. The utter desolation of the land by the Chaldean army is here spoken of as a thing done, so near was it. God speaks of it as a thing which he had no pleasure in, any more than in the death of other sinners.

1. See with what a tender affection he speaks of this land, notwithstanding the sinfulness of it, in remembrance of his covenant: It is *my vineyard, my portion, my pleasant portion, v.* 10. Note, God has a kindness and concern for his church, though there be much amiss in it.

2. See with what a tender compassion he speaks of the desolations of this land: *Many pastors* (the Chaldean generals that made themselves masters of the country and ate it up with their armies as easily as the Arabian shepherds with their flocks eat up the fruits of the ground that lies common) *have destroyed my vineyard.* That which was a pleasant land they have made *a desolate wilderness.* It is made so by the sword of war: *The spoilers*, the Chaldean soldiers, *have come through the plain upon all high places*; they have made themselves masters of all the fastnesses, *v.* 12. *The sword devours from one end of the land to the other;* the army of the invaders disperse into every corner, so that *no flesh shall have peace.*

3. See whence all this misery comes. It is *the sword of the Lord* that *devours, v.* 12. While God's people keep close to him the sword is the sword of the Lord, witness that of Gideon; but when they have forsaken him, then the sword of their destroyers becomes the *sword of the Lord*; witness this of the Chaldeans. It is *because of the fierce anger of the Lord* (*v.* 13). It is their sin that has made God their enemy (*v.* 11): The land *mourns unto me*; the country that lies desolate does, as it were, pour out its complaint, but the inhabitants are so senseless and stupid that *none of them lays it to heart*; they do not mourn to God while the very ground shames them.

4. "*They have sown wheat*, that is, they have taken pains for their own security, but it is all in vain; *they shall reap thorns*, that is, that which shall prove vexatious to them. *They shall be ashamed of your revenues*, ashamed that they have depended so much upon their preparations for war." Money constitutes the sinews of war; they thought they had enough of that, but shall be ashamed of it; for their silver and gold shall not profit them in the day of the Lord's anger.

Verses 14–17

Here is a message to all those who had in their turn been one way or other injurious to God's people.

I. What the quarrel was that God had with them. They were *his evil neighbours* (*v.* 14), evil neighbours to his church, and what they did against it he took as done against himself. These evil neighbours were the Moabites, Ammonites, Syrians, Edomites, Egyptians, that had been evil neighbours to Israel in helping to debauch them and draw them from God, and now they helped to make them desolate, and joined with the Chaldeans against them. That which God lays to their charge is: They have *meddled with the inheritance which I have caused my people Israel to inherit*. They sacrilegiously turned to their own use that which was given to God's peculiar people. He that said, *Touch not my anointed*, said also, "*Touch not their inheritance.*"

II. What course he would take with them. He would break the power they had got over his people. *I will pluck out the house of Judah from among them.* God's people had been taken captive by them, or, when they fled to them for shelter, had been made prisoners. God will pluck them out, will by his Spirit compel them to come out and compel their task-masters to let them go, as he plucked Israel out of Egypt. He would bring upon them the same calamities that they had been instrumental to bring upon his people: *I will pluck them out of their land.* Judgment began at the house of God, but it did not end there.

III. What mercy God had in store for such of them as would join themselves to him and become his people, *v.* 15, 16. They had drawn God's people to join with them in the service of idols. If now they would be drawn by a returning people to join with them in the service of the true and living God, they should be received to stand upon the same level with the Israel of God. This had its accomplishment in part when, after the return out of captivity, many of the people that had been evil neighbours to Israel became Jews; and it was to have its full accomplishment in the conversion of the Gentiles to the faith of Christ. *After that I have plucked them out*, in justice for their sins, *I will return and have compassion on them.*

1. God would show favour to them always provided *that they will diligently learn the ways of my people*. There are good ways that are peculiarly *the ways of God's people*. The ways of holiness and heavenly-mindedness, of love and peaceableness, the ways of prayer and sabbath-sanctification, and diligent attendance on ordinances—these, and the like, are *the ways of God's people*. They must learn to say, *The Lord liveth* (to own him, to adore him, and to abide by his judgment), *as they taught my people to swear by Baal*. We must not despair of the conversion of the worst; no, not of those who have been instrumental to pervert and debauch others; even they may be brought to repentance, and, if they be, shall find mercy. The conversion of the deceived may prove a happy occasion of the conversion even of the deceivers. Thus those who fall together into the ditch are sometimes plucked together out of it.

2. When they return to God and God to them (*v.* 15): *I will bring them again every man to his heritage.* They shall become entitled to the spiritual privileges of God's Israel: *Be built in the midst of my people.* They shall have a name and a place in the house of the Lord, where there was a court for the Gentiles, they shall be built among them. *If they will not obey*, if any continue to stand it out, *I will utterly pluck up and destroy that nation*, that family, that particular person, *saith the Lord*.

CHAPTER 13

Still the prophet is attempting to awaken this stubborn people to repentance. He is to tell them, I. By the sign of a girdle spoiled that their pride should be stained, ver. 1–11. II. By the sign of bottles filled with wine that their counsels should be blasted, ver. 12–14. III. In consideration hereof he is to call them to repent and humble themselves, ver. 15–21. IV. He is to convince them that it is for their obstinacy that the judgments of God are so prolonged, ver. 22–27.

Verses 1–11

I. A sign, the marring of a girdle, which the prophet had worn for some time, by hiding it in a hole of a rock near the river Euphrates. He was to wear a linen girdle for some time, *v.* 1, 2. Some think he wore it under his clothes, because it is said to *cleave to his loins, v.* 11. It should rather seem to be worn upon his clothes, and probably was a fine sash, such as officers wear. He must *not put it in water*, that it might be less likely to rot. The prophet, like John Baptist, was none of those that wore soft clothing, and therefore it would be the more strange to see him with a linen girdle. After he had worn this linen girdle for some time, he must go, and *hide it in a hole of a rock* (*v.* 4) by the water's side, where, when the water was high, it would be wet, and when it fell would grow dry again, and by that means would soon rot. After many days, he should find it spoiled, gone to rags and good for nothing, *v.* 7. It seems hard to imagine that the prophet should be sent on two such long journeys as to the river Euphrates. For this reason most incline to think the journey, at least, was only in vision, and the explanation of this sign given only to the prophet himself (*v.* 8), not to the people.

II. The thing signified by this sign, *v.* 9–11.

1. The people of Israel had been to God as this girdle in two respects: (1) He had taken them into covenant and communion with himself: *As the girdle cleaves* very closely *to the loins of a man* and surrounds him, *so have I caused to cleave to me the houses of Israel and Judah*. He *caused them to cleave* to him by the law he gave them, the prophets he sent among them, and the favours he showed them. (2) When he took them to be *to him for a people*, it was that they might be to him *for a name, and for a praise, and for a glory*, as a girdle is an ornament to a man, and particularly the *curious girdle of the ephod* was to the high-priest *for glory and for beauty*.

2. They had by their idolatries and other iniquities loosed themselves from him, buried themselves in the earth, and foreign earth too, mingled among the nations, and were so spoiled and corrupted that they were *good for nothing*. They would not *cleave to God*, but *walked after other gods*, *to serve them*, and *to worship them*; they doted upon the gods of the heathen nations that lay towards Euphrates, so that they were quite spoiled for the service of their own God, and were *as this girdle*, this rotten girdle.

3. God would by his judgments separate them from him, send them into captivity, deface all their beauty so that they should be like a fine girdle gone to rags, a worthless people. God will after this manner *mar the pride of Judah, and the great pride of Jerusalem*. He speaks of *the pride of Judah* (the country people were proud of their good land), but of *the great pride of Jerusalem*; there the temple was, and the royal palace, and therefore those citizens were more proud. Pride will have a fall, for God resists the proud. Even the temple, when it became Jerusalem's pride, was marred and laid in ashes.

Verses 12–21

I. A judgment threatened against this people (*v.* 12): *Thus saith the Lord God of Israel, every bottle shall be filled with wine;* that is, those that by their sins have made themselves *vessels of wrath fitted to destruction* shall be filled with the wrath of God as a bottle is with wine; and they shall be brittle as bottles; and, like old bottles into which new wine is put, they shall burst and be broken to pieces, Matt. ix. 17. Or, They shall have their heads as full of wine as bottles are; for so it is explained, v. 13, *They shall be filled with drunkenness;* compare Isa. li. 17. They, not being aware of the prophet's meaning in it, ridiculed him for it: "*Do we not certainly know that every bottle shall be filled with wine?*" Perhaps they were thus touchy with the prophet because they apprehended this to be a reflection upon them for their drunkenness, and probably it was in part so intended. They *loved flagons of wine*, Hos. iii. 1. "Well," says the prophet, "you shall have your *bottles full of wine*, but not such wine as you desire." What he meant was this,

1. That they should be as giddy as men in drink. A drunken man is fitly compared to a bottle or cask full of wine; for, when the wine is in, the wit, and wisdom, and virtue, and all that is good for anything, are out. Now God threatens (v. 13) that they shall all be *filled with drunkenness*; they shall be full of confusion in their counsels, shall falter and stagger. They shall expose themselves to the contempt of all about them. *All the inhabitants* both *of the land* and *of Jerusalem* were as far gone as they. Whom God will destroy he infatuates.

2. That being giddy, they shall do mischief to themselves and one another (v. 14): *I will dash a man against his brother.* Not only their drunken follies, but their drunken frays, shall help to ruin them. This decree against them having gone forth, God says, *I will not pity, nor spare, nor have mercy, but destroy them;* for they *will not pity, nor spare, nor have mercy,* but destroy one another; see Hab. ii. 15, 16.

II. Here is good counsel given, which, if taken, would prevent this desolation. It is, in short, to *humble themselves under the mighty hand of God.* This is that which God has to say to them, *Be not proud,* v. 15. This was one of the sins for which God had a controversy with them (v. 9). "*Be not proud;* when God speaks to you by his prophets do not think yourselves too good to be taught; be not scornful."

1. "*Give glory to the Lord your God,* and not to your idols. Give him glory by confessing your sins, and accepting the punishment of your iniquity, v. 16. Give him glory by a sincere repentance and reformation." Then, and not till then, we begin to live to some good purpose. "Do this quickly *before he cause darkness,* before he bring his judgments upon you, which you will see no way of escaping." Their attempts to escape shall hasten their ruin: *Their feet shall stumble* when they are making all the haste they can over *the dark mountains.* Note, Those that think to out-run the judgments of God will find their road impassable. Their hopes of a better state of things will be disappointed: *While you look for light,* for comfort and relief, he will *turn it into the shadow of death,* and make it *gross darkness,* like that of Egypt, when Pharaoh continued to harden his heart, which was darkness that might be felt.

2. They must abase themselves; the prerogative of the king and queen will not exempt them from this (v. 18): "*Say to the king and queen,* that, great as they are, they must *humble themselves* by true repentance, and so give both glory to God and a good example to their subjects." When you are led away captives, where will your principality and all the badges of it be then?

III. This counsel is enforced by some arguments.

1. It will be the prophet's unspeakable grief (v. 7): "*If you will not hear it,* will not submit to the word, but continue refractory, not only my eye, but *my soul shall weep in secret places.*" It would grieve him

to see their sins unrepented of: "*My soul shall weep for your pride,* your haughtiness, and stubbornness, and vain confidence." The sins of others should be matter of sorrow to us. We must mourn for that which we cannot mend, and mourn the more for it because we cannot mend it.

2. It will be their own inevitable ruin, v. 19–21. *The cities of the south shall be shut up.* Some understand it of the cities of Egypt, which was south from Judah; the places there whence they expected succours shall fail them, and they shall find no access to them. *Judah shall be carried away captive.* So it was in the last captivity under Zedekiah, because they repented not. The enemy was now at hand that should do this (v. 20): "*Lift up your eyes. Behold, those that come from the north,* from the land of the Chaldeans; see how fast they advance, how fierce they appear." Upon this he addresses himself to the king, or rather (because the pronouns are feminine) to the city or state. "What will you do now with the people who are committed to your charge, and whom you ought to protect? *Where is the flock that was given thee, thy beautiful flock?* How can they escape these ravening wolves?" Masters of families, who neglect their children and suffer them to perish for want of a good education, and ministers who neglect their people, should think they hear God putting this question to them: *Where is the flock that was given thee* to feed, *that beauteous flock? What wilt thou say when he shall visit upon thee* the former days? (v. 21). Thou canst say nothing, but that *God is just in all that is brought upon thee.* "How will you bear the trouble that is at the door? *Shall not sorrows take thee as a woman in travail?* Sorrows will be more grievous in that there is no manchild to be born."

Verses 22–27

I. Ruin threatened as before, that the Jews shall go into captivity, and fall under all the miseries of beggary and bondage, shall be stripped of their clothes, *their skirts discovered* for want of upper garments to cover them, and their *heels made bare* for want of shoes, v. 22. Thus they used to deal with prisoners taken in war, when they drove them into captivity, *naked and barefoot*, Isa. xx. 4. Carried off into a strange country, they shall be scattered *as the stubble that is blown away by the wind of the wilderness,* v. 24. They shall be stripped of all their ornaments, and exposed to shame, as harlots, v. 26.

II. An enquiry made by the people into the cause of this ruin, v. 22. Thou wilt *say in thy heart: Wherefore came these things upon me?* They could not see that they had done anything which might justly provoke God to be thus angry with them.

III. God will be justified when he speaks and will oblige us to justify him, and therefore will set the sin of sinners in order before them.

1. It is for the greatness of their iniquities, v. 22. God does not take advantage against them for small faults; the sins for which he now punishes them are very heinous in their nature—for *the multitude of thy iniquity* (so it may be read), sins of every kind and often repeated. Some think we are more in danger from the multitude of our smaller sins than from the heinousness of our greater sins.

2. It is for their obstinacy in sin (v. 23): *Can the Ethiopian change his skin,* that is by nature black, or the *leopard his spots,* that are even woven into the skin? It is morally impossible to reclaim and reform these people. They were taught to do evil; they had served an apprenticeship to it. Their prophets despaired of ever bringing them to do good. Those that have been long accustomed to sin have shaken off the restraints of fear and shame; their consciences are seared; the habits of sin are confirmed. Sin is the blackness of the soul, the deformity of it.

But there is an almighty grace that is able to change the Ethiopian's skin, and that grace shall not be wanting to those who in a sense of their need of it seek it earnestly.

3. It is for their treacherous departures from the God of truth (v. 25): *"This is thy lot*, to be driven away; this is *the portion of thy measures from me*, the punishment assigned thee as by measure; it is *because thou hast forgotten me*, the favours I have bestowed upon thee, thou hast no remembrance, of these." Forgetfulness of God is at the bottom of all sin, as the remembrance of our Creator betimes is the happy and hopeful beginning of a holy life.

4. It is for their idolatry, of all sins most provoking to the *jealous God*. They are exposed to a shameful calamity (v. 26) because they have been guilty of a shameful iniquity and yet are shameless in it (v. 27): *"I have seen thy adulteries* (thy inordinate fancy for strange gods), even the *lewdness of thy whoredoms*, thy eager worshipping of idols *on the hills in the fields*, upon the high places. This is that for which a *woe* is denounced against thee, *O Jerusalem!* "

IV. Here is an affectionate expostulation with them upon the whole matter. While there is life there is hope, and therefore still he reasons with them to bring them to repentance, v. 27. *Wilt thou not be made clean?* It is an instance of the wonderful grace of God that he desires the repentance and conversion of sinners, and thinks the time long till they are brought to relent; but it is an instance of the wonderful folly of sinners that they put that off from time to time which is of such absolute necessity. They do not say that they will never be cleansed, but not yet.

CHAPTER 14

This chapter was upon occasion of a great drought. This judgment began in the latter end of Josiah's reign, but continued in the beginning of Jehoiakim's. This calamity was mentioned several times before, but in this chapter, more fully. I. A melancholy description of it, ver. 1–6. II. A prayer to God to put an end to this calamity, ver. 7–9. III. A severe threatening that God would proceed in his controversy, because they proceeded in their iniquity, ver. 10–12. IV. The prophet's excusing the people, by laying the blame on their false prophets, ver. 13–16. V. Directions given to the prophet, instead of interceding for them, to lament them, ver. 17–22.

Verses 1–9

I. The language of nature lamenting the calamity. When the heavens were as brass, and distilled no dews, the earth was as iron, and produced no fruits; the grief and confusion were universal. The people of the land were all in tears. *Judah mourns* (v. 2), not for the sin, but for the withholding of the rain. *The gates thereof*, all that go in and out at their gates, *languish*, look pale, and grow feeble, for want of the necessary supports of life and for fear of further judgment. *The gates* now look melancholy; the inhabitants are departing through them to seek for bread in other countries. Even those that sit in the gates languish; *they are black unto the ground*, they go in black as mourners and sit on the ground, as beggars. They fall to the ground through weakness. *The cry of Jerusalem has gone up;* that is, of the citizens (for the city is *served by the field*), or of people from all parts of the country met at Jerusalem to pray for rain. But I fear it was rather the cry of their trouble, than the cry of their prayer. The great men of the land felt this judgment (v. 3): *The nobles sent their little ones to the water.* Or, their *meaner ones*, their servants, they sent to seek for water, but there was none to be found: They *returned with their vessels empty*; the springs were dried up when there was no rain to feed them; and then *they* (their masters) *were ashamed and confounded.* The husbandmen felt it most immediately (v. 4): *The ploughmen were ashamed*, for the ground was so parched and hard

that it would not admit the plough. They were ashamed to be idle. See what an immediate dependence husbandmen have upon the divine Providence, for they cannot plough nor sow in hope unless God *water their furrows*, Ps. lxv. 10. The case even of the wild beasts was pitiable, v. 5, 6. Judah and Jerusalem have sinned, but the hinds and the wild asses, what have they done? The hinds are particularly tender of their young; and yet contrary to their nature, they leave their young, even when they most need them, to seek for grass elsewhere; and, if they can find none, they *abandon* them, because not able to suckle them. It grieved not the hind so much that she had no grass for herself as that she had none for her young, which will shame those who spend that upon their lusts which they should preserve for their families. One would be sorry even for the *wild asses*, for the *barren land* is now made too hot for them, so hot that they get to the *highest places* they can reach, where the air is coolest, and *snuff up the wind like dragons*, creatures which are continually panting for breath. *Their eyes fail*, and so does their strength, *because there is no grass.*

II. Here is the language of grace, lamenting the iniquity, and complaining to God of the calamity. The people are not forward to pray, but the prophet here prays for them, and so excites them to pray for themselves, v. 7–9. In this prayer, 1. Sin is humbly confessed. If we quarrel with God as dealing unjustly or unkindly with us in afflicting us, our iniquities testify that we do him wrong; "for *our backslidings are many* and too heinous to be excused, for they are against thee." 2. Mercy is earnestly begged: *"Though our iniquities testify against us, yet do thou it."* As becomes penitents and beggars, they refer the matter to God: "Do with us as thou thinkest fit," Judges x. 15. We have nothing to plead in ourselves, but everything in thee. There is another petition in this prayer (v. 9): *"Leave us not*, withdraw not thy favour and presence." 3. Their relation to God and their expectations from him are most pathetically pleaded, v. 8, 9. They look upon him as one that they have reason to think should deliver them. In him mercy has often rejoiced against judgment. God has encouraged his people to hope in him; in calling himself so often the *God of Israel*, the *rock of Israel*, and the *Holy One of Israel*, he has made himself the *hope of Israel*. They plead, *"Thou art in the midst of us;* we have the special tokens of thy presence with us, thy temple, thy ark, thy oracles, and *we are called by thy name*, the *Israel* of God; and therefore we hope thou wilt not leave us; *we are thine, save us.*" It grieves them to think that he does not appear for their deliverance. *What will the Egyptians say?* They will say, "Israel's hope and Saviour does not mind them; he has become *as a stranger in the land*, that does not interest himself in its interests; his temple, which he called *his rest for ever*, is no more so, but he is in it *as a wayfaring man, that turns aside to tarry but for a night in an inn.*" The enemies once said, Because the Lord *was not able to bring* his people to Canaan, he let them *perish in the wilderness* (Num. xiv. 16); so now they will say, "Either his wisdom or his power fails him; either he is *as a man astonished* (who, though he has the reason of a man, yet is quite at his wits' end) or as a *mighty man*—a man, and therefore having his power limited." Either of these would be a most insufferable reproach to the divine perfections; and therefore, why has the God that we are sure *is in the midst of us* become *as a stranger?* Why does the almighty God seem as though he would, yet cannot save?

Verses 10–16

The dispute between God and his prophet, in this chapter, seems to be like that between the owner and the dresser of the vineyard concerning the barren fig-tree, Luke xiii. 7. The justice of the owner condemns it to be cut down; the clemency of the dresser intercedes for a reprieve.

I. God overrules the plea. Thus he says concerning *this people*, v. 10. He does not say, concerning *my people*, because they had broken covenant with him. It is true they were *called by his name*, but they had sinned, and provoked God to withdraw. God here tells him they were not qualified for a pardon. The prophet had owned that *their backslidings were many*; and yet there was hope for them if they returned. But *this people* show no disposition at all to return; *they have loved to wander;* their backslidings have been their pleasure, which should have been their shame. It is not through necessity that they wander; their wanderings forfeit God's favour. They have not taken warning and *refrained their feet*. This is that for which God is now reckoning with them. When he denies them rain from heaven he is *remembering their iniquity* and *visiting their sin*, for which their *fruitful land* is thus *turned into barrenness*. Though they betook themselves to fasting and prayer and burnt-offerings and sacrifice: *The Lord doth not accept them*, v. 10. *He takes no pleasure in them* (so the word is). "*When they fast* (v. 12), which is a proper expression of repentance and reformation,—*when they offer a burnt offering and an oblation*, which was designed to be an expression of faith in a Mediator,—though their prayers be offered up in those vehicles that used to be acceptable yet, because they do not proceed from humble, penitent, and renewed hearts, but still *love to wander*, therefore *I will not hear their cry, nor will I accept them*, neither their persons nor their performances." They had forfeited all benefit by the prophet's prayers for them because they had not regarded his preaching. This is the meaning of that repeated prohibition given to the prophet (v. 11): *Pray not thou for this people for their good*, as before, *ch.* vii. 16; xi. 14. This did not forbid him thus to express his *goodwill* to them, but it forbade them to expect any good effect from it as long as they *turned away their ear from hearing the law*. It therefore follows (v. 12), *I will consume them*.

II. The prophet offers another plea in excuse for the people's obstinacy. The prophets, who pretended a commission from heaven, imposed upon them, and flattered them with assurances of peace, v. 13. He speaks of it with lamentation: "*Ah! Lord God*, there are those who in thy name tell them that they *shall not see the sword nor famine*; and they say it as from thee: *I will* continue you *in this place*, and will *give you assured peace*. I tell them the contrary; but I am one against many; therefore, Lord, pity and spare them, for *their leaders cause them to err*." This excuse would have been of some weight if they had not had warning given them, before, of false prophets.

III. God not only overrules this plea, but condemns both the blind leaders and the blind followers to fall together into the ditch. He disowns the flatteries (v. 14): *They prophesy lies in my name*. They had no commission from God to prophesy at all: *I neither sent them, nor commanded them, nor spoke unto them*. Those that oppose their own thoughts to God's word (God indeed says so, but they think otherwise) walk in the *deceit of their heart*, and it will be their ruin. He passes sentence upon the flatterers, v. 15. As for the prophets, let them know that they shall have no peace themselves. They undertook to warrant people that *sword and famine should not be in the land*; but they themselves shall be cut off by sword and famine. The *people to whom they prophesy lies*, and who willingly suffer themselves to be thus imposed upon, *shall die by sword and famine*, v. 16. Their bodies shall be *cast out*, even *in the streets of Jerusalem*; there they shall lie unburied.

Thus will God *pour their wickedness upon them*, that is, the punishment of their wickedness.

Verses 17–22

The present deplorable state of Judah and Jerusalem is here made the matter of the prophet's lamentation (v. 17, 18) and of his prayer for them (v. 19), and the latter, as well as the former, was by divine direction, and these words (v. 17), *Thus shalt thou say unto them*, refer to the intercession as well as to the lamentation, and then it amounts to a revocation of the directions given to the prophet not to pray for them, v. 11.

I. The prophet stands weeping over the ruins of his country. Jeremiah must say it not only to himself, but to them too: *Let my eyes run down with tears*, v. 17. Thus he must signify to them that he foresaw *the sword* coming, and another sort of famine, that would be in the city through the straitness of the siege. The prophet speaks as if he already saw the miseries attending the descent which the Chaldeans made upon them: *The virgin daughter of my people is broken with a great breach, with a very grievous blow*, more grievous than any she has yet sustained; for (v. 18) *in the field* multitudes lie dead that were *slain by the sword*, and in the city multitudes lie dying for want of food. "*The prophets and the priests*, the false prophets that flattered them with their lies and the wicked priests that persecuted the true prophets, are expelled, and *go about* either captives, or as fugitives and vagabonds, wherever they can find shelter *in a land that they know not*." Some understand this of the true prophets, Ezekiel and Daniel, that were carried to Babylon with the rest. The prophet's eyes must run down *with tears day and night*, in prospect of this, that the people might be convinced, not only that this woeful day would infallibly come, but that he would gladly have brought them messages of peace, if he might have had warrant from heaven to do it.

II. He stands up to make intercession for them. There were some who would join with him in his devotions, and set the seal of their *Amen* to them.

1. He humbly expostulates with God concerning their case, v. 19. Their expectations from their God failed them; they thought he had avouched Judah to be his, but now, it seems, he has *utterly rejected* it. They thought Zion was beloved, but now *his soul* even *loathes Zion*, loathes even the services there performed. All their other expectations failed them: *They were smitten*, their wounds were multiplied, but there was *no healing* for them; they *looked for peace*, because after a storm there usually comes a calm. They looked for a *healing time*, but could not gain so much as a *breathing time*. "*Behold, trouble* at the door, by which we hoped peace would enter. But wilt thou not at length in wrath remember mercy?"

2. He makes a penitent confession of sin, which they all should have spoken, though but few did (v. 20): "*We acknowledge our wickedness*, the abounding wickedness of our land *and the iniquity of our fathers*, which we have imitated. *We know, we acknowledge*, that *we have sinned against thee*, and therefore thou art just in all that is brought upon us; but, because we confess our sins, we hope to find thee faithful and just in forgiving our sins."

3. He deprecates God's displeasure, and by faith appeals to his promise, v. 21. His petition is, "*Do not abhor us;* though thou afflict us, *do not abhor us;* though thy hand be turned *against* us, let not thy heart be so, nor let thy mind be alienated from us." They own God might justly abhor them, yet they pray: "*Do not abhor us, for thy name's sake*, that name of thine by which we are called and which we call upon." The honour of his sanctuary is pleaded: "Lord, do not abhor us, for that will *disgrace the throne of thy glory*." We deserve to have disgrace

put upon us, but let not the desolations of the temple give occasion to the heathen to reproach him that used to be worshipped there. We may be sure that God will not *disgrace the throne of his glory* on earth. They are humbly bold to put him in mind: *Remember thy covenant with us, and break not that covenant.*

4. He professes a dependence upon God for the mercy of rain, *v.* 22. They will never make application to the idols of the heathen. *Are there any among the vanities of the Gentiles that can cause rain?* In a time of great drought in Israel, Baal, though all Israel presented their prayers to him in the days of Ahab, could not relieve them; it was only that God who *answered by fire* that could answer *by water* too. *Can the heavens give showers?* Not without orders from the God of heaven; for it is he that has the key of the clouds, that *opens the bottles of heaven* and *waters the earth from his chambers.* All their expectation therefore is from him. *Art not thou he, O Lord our God!* from whom we may expect succour and to whom we must apply? Art thou not he that *causest rain* and *givest showers?* For *thou hast made all these things;* thou gavest them being, and therefore thou givest them law and hast them all at thy command. We will *ask of the Lord rain,* Zech. x. 1. We will trust in him to give it to us in due time.

CHAPTER 15

I. Notwithstanding the prophet's prayers, God here ratifies the sentence given against the people, ver. 1–9. II. The prophet himself, notwithstanding the satisfaction he had in communion with God, still finds himself uneasy and out of temper. 1. He complains to God of his continual struggle with his persecutors, ver. 10. 2. God assures him that he shall be taken under special protection, though there was a general desolation coming upon the land, ver. 11–14. 3. He appeals to God concerning his sincerity in the discharge of his prophetic office, ver. 15–18. 4. Fresh security is given him that, upon condition he continue faithful, God will continue his care of him and his favour to him, ver. 19–21.

Verses 1–9

There are scarcely anywhere more pathetic expressions of divine wrath against a provoking people than in these verses. The prophet had prayed earnestly for them, and found some to join with him; and yet no reprieve was gained, nor the least mitigation of the judgment.

I. What the sin was upon which this severe sentence was grounded. It is because of Manasseh, for that which he did in Jerusalem, *v.* 4. What that was we are told, and that it was for it that Jerusalem was destroyed, 2 Kings xxiv. 3, 4. It was for his idolatry, and *the innocent blood which he shed, which the Lord would not pardon.* It is in consideration of their present impenitence. Their sin is described (*v.* 6): *Thou hast forsaken me,* my service and thy duty to me; *thou hast gone backward* and art become the reverse of what thou shouldst have been. The impenitence is described (*v.* 7): *They return · not from their ways,* the ways of their own hearts, into the ways of God's commandments again. There is mercy for those who have turned aside if they will return; but what favour can those expect that persist in their apostasy?

II. What the sentence is. It is ruin.

1. God himself abandons them: *My mind cannot be towards them.* It is not in a passion, but with a just and holy indignation, that he says, "*Cast them out of my sight,* and let *them go forth,* for I will be troubled with them no more."

2. He will not admit any intercession to be made for them (*v.* 1): "*Though Moses and Samuel stood before me,* by prayer or sacrifice to reconcile me to them, yet I could not admit them into favour."

3. He condemns them all to one destroying judgment or other. When God casts them out of his presence, *whither shall they go forth?* (*v.* 2). Such as are

for death to death, or *for the sword to the sword.* It is a choice like that which David was put to, and was thereby put into a *great strait,* 2 Sam. xxiv. 14. *Captivity* is mentioned last, some think, because the sorest judgment of all, it being a continuance of miseries. That of *the sword* is again repeated (*v.* 3), and is made the first of another four set of destroyers. As those that escape *the sword* shall be cut off by pestilence, famine, or captivity, so those that fall by the sword shall be cut off by divine vengeance. There shall be *dogs to tear* in the city and *fowls of the air* and *wild beasts* in the field to devour. And, if there be any that think to outrun justice: *They shall be removed into all kingdoms of the earth* (*v.* 4), like Cain, who became a *fugitive and a vagabond* in the earth.

4. They shall fall without being relieved. God appears against them: *I will stretch out my hand against thee,* a deliberate stroke, which will wound deeply. *I am weary with repenting* (*v.* 6); by their treacherous professions of repentance, they had put even infinite patience to the stretch. Now he will grant no more reprieves. Their own country expels them, and is ready to *spew them out. I will fan them with a fan in the gates of the land,* in their own gates, or *into the gates of the land,* into the cities of all the nations about them, *v.* 7. *I will bereave them of children;* they shall have little hope that the next generation will retrieve their affairs, for *I will destroy my people.* Nebuchadnezzar is here called *a spoiler at noon-day,* not a thief in the night, afraid of being discovered, but one that without fear shall break through and destroy. *I have brought against the mother a young man, a spoiler* (so some read it); for Nebuchadnezzar, when he first invaded Judah, was but a *young man,* in the first year of his reign. We read it, *I have brought upon them,* even *against the mother of the young men, a spoiler,* that is, against Jerusalem, a mother city, that had a very numerous family of young men. God *caused him to fall upon it,* that is, upon the spoil delivered to him, *suddenly;* and then *terrors* came *upon the city. I will cause to fall suddenly upon her* (upon Jerusalem) *a watcher and terrors;* the word is used for a watcher (Dan. iv. 13, 23), and the Chaldean soldiers were called watchers, *ch.* iv. xvi. A dreadful slaughter is here described. The wives are deprived of their husbands: *Their widows are increased above the sand of the seas.* God says, *They are increased to me.* Though the husbands were cut off by the sword of his justice, their poor widows were gathered in the arms of his mercy, who has taken it among the titles of his honour to be *the God of the widows.* The parents are deprived of their children. When the children are slain the mother *gives up the ghost,* for her life was bound up in theirs: *Her sun has gone down while it was yet day.* Some understand, by this languishing mother, Jerusalem lamenting the death of her inhabitants as passionately as ever poor mother bewailed her children.

5. They shall fall without being pitied (*v.* 5): "*For who shall have pity on thee, O Jerusalem?* When thy God has *cast thee out of his sight,* neither thy enemies nor thy friends shall have any compassion for thee. *O Israel! thou hast destroyed thyself.*"

Verses 10–14

Jeremiah has now returned from his public work and retired into his closet; what passed between him and his God there we have an account of in these verses.

I. The complaint which the prophet makes to God of the many discouragements he met with in his work, *v.* 10.

1. He met with a great deal of contradiction and opposition. He was a *man of strife and contention.* Both city and country quarrelled with him, and did

all they could to thwart him. He was a peaceable man, and yet *a man of strife*, not a man striving, but a man striven with; he was for peace, but, when he spoke, they were for war. The real cause of their quarrels with him was his faithfulness to God and to their souls. He showed them their sins that were working their ruin, and put them into a way to prevent that ruin, and yet they were incensed against him. The gospel of peace brings division, Matt. x. 34, 35; Luke xii. 49, 51. Now this made Jeremiah very uneasy. He cried out, *Woe is me, my mother, that thou hast borne me;* he is angry that she had *borne him a man of strife.* It was intended for a pathetic lamentation of his case. Even those who are most peaceable are often made men of strife. Yet, if we cannot live peaceably with our neighbours, we must not be so disturbed as to lose the repose of our own minds and put ourselves upon the fret.

2. He met with a great deal of contumely, and reproach. They branded him as a factious man and a sower of discord and sedition. They ought to have blessed him, and to have blessed God for him; but they cursed his messenger and did all they could to make him odious. But one would be apt to suspect that surely Jeremiah had given them some provocation! *"I have neither lent* money *nor borrowed* money." It is implied here that those who deal much in the business of this world are often involved in strife and contention. It was an instance of Jeremiah's prudence that, being called to be a prophet, he *entangled not himself in the affairs of this life,* that he might not give the least shadow of suspicion that he aimed at secular advantages in it. He *put out* no money, for he was no usurer; he *took up* no money, for he was no merchant. We find (*ch.* xvi. 2) that he had neither wife nor children to keep. And yet he lay under a general odium, through the iniquity of the times.

II. The answer which God gave to this complaint. 1. God assures him that he should weather the storm and be made easy at last, *v.* 11. "*If I* take not care of thee, let me never be counted faithful; *verily it shall go well with thy remnant,* with the remainder of thy life" (for so the word signifies); "the residue of thy days shall be more comfortable to thee than those hitherto have been." *Thy end shall be good;* so the Chaldee reads it. It should seem that Jeremiah was uneasy at the apprehension of sharing in the public judgments which he foresaw coming. "If my friends are thus abusive to me, and what will my enemies be?" But he quiets his mind with this promise: "*Verily I will cause the enemy to entreat thee well in the time of evil,* when all about thee shall be laid waste." This promise was accomplished when Nebuchadnezzar, having taken the city, charged the captain of the guard to be kind to Jeremiah, and let him have everything he had a mind to, *ch.* xxxix. 11, 12. The following words, *Shall iron break the northern iron, and the steel,* or *brass?* (*v.* 12), being compared with the promise of God made to Jeremiah (*ch.* i. 18), that he would make him an *iron pillar* and *brazen walls,* seem intended for his comfort. They were continually clashing with him, and were rough and hard as iron; but Jeremiah, being armed with power and courage from on high, is as northern iron, which is naturally stronger, and as steel, which is hardened by art; and therefore they shall not prevail against him; compare this with Ezek. ii. 6; iii. 8, 9. 2. God assures him that his enemies and persecutors should be lost in the storm, *v.* 13, 14. God here turns his speech from the prophet to the people. To them also *v.* 12 may be applied: *Shall iron break the northern iron, and the steel?* Shall their courage and strength, and the most hardy and vigorous of their efforts, be able to contest either with the counsel of God or with the army of the Chaldeans, which are as inflexible, as invincible, as the northern iron and steel.

Let them therefore hear their doom: *Thy substance and thy treasure will I give to the spoil,* and that *without price.* The prophet was poor; he had nothing to lose, neither *substance* nor *treasure,* and therefore the enemy will treat him well. But the people that had great estates in money and land would be slain for what they had. All parts of the country, even those which lay most remote, had contributed to the national guilt, and all shall now be brought to account. "*I will make thee to pass with thy enemies,* who shall lead thee in triumph *into a land that thou knowest not,* and therefore canst expect to find no comfort in it."

Verses 15–21

I. The prophet's humble address to God, "*O Lord! thou knowest;* thou knowest my sincerity, which men are resolved they will not acknowledge; thou knowest my distress, which men disdain to take notice of."

1. The prophet prays, *v.* 15. (1) That God would consider his case and be mindful of him: "*O Lord! remember me;* think upon me for good." (2) That God would communicate strength and comfort to him: "*Visit me.*" (3) That he would appear for him: *Revenge me of my persecutors,* or rather, *Vindicate me from my persecutors.* Further than this a good man will not desire that God should avenge him. Let something be done to convince the world that Jeremiah is a righteous man and the God whom he serves is a righteous God. (4) That he would yet spare him: "*Take me not away* by a sudden stroke, but *in thy long-suffering* lengthen out my days." Though in a passion he complained of his birth (*v.* 10), yet he desires here that his death might not be hastened; for life is sweet to nature, and the life of a useful man is so to grace.

2. He pleads with God for mercy and relief against his enemies, persecutors, and slanderers.

(1) That God's honour was interested in this case: *Know,* and make it known, *that for thy sake I have suffered rebuke.* If it is for doing well that we suffer ill, and for righteousness' sake that we have all manner of evil said against us, we may hope that God will vindicate our honour with his own. To the same purport (*v.* 16), *I am called by thy name, O Lord of hosts!*

(2) That the word of God, which he was employed to preach to others, he had experienced in his own soul, and therefore had the graces of the Spirit to qualify him for the divine favour, as well as his gifts. Jeremiah could say (*v.* 16): "*Thy words were found,* found *by me,* found *for me, and I did* not only taste them, but *did eat them,* received them entirely: they were welcome to me, as food to one that is hungry. The prophet was told to *eat the roll,* Ezek. ii. 8; Rev. x. 9. *I did eat it*—that is, as it follows, it *was to me the joy and rejoicing of my heart,* nothing could be more agreeable. Understand it, [1] Of the message itself which he was to deliver. Though he was to foretell the ruin of his country, which was dear to him, and in the ruin of which he could not but have a deep share, yet all natural affections were swallowed up in zeal for God's glory, and even these messages of wrath, being divine messages, were a satisfaction to him. He also rejoiced, at first, in hope that the people would take warning and prevent the judgment. Or, [2] Of the commission he received to deliver this message. Though the work he was called to was not attended with any secular advantages, but, on the contrary, exposed him to contempt and persecution, yet it was his *meat and drink to do the will of him that sent him,* John iv. 34. Or, [3] Of the promise God gave him that he would assist and own him in his work (*ch.* i. 8).

(3) That he had applied himself to the duty of his office with gravity and self-denial, though he had had of late but little satisfaction in it, *v.* 17. He *sat alone,*

spent a great deal of time in his closet, *because of the hand* of the Lord that was strong upon him to carry him on in his work, Ezek. iii. 14. "*For thou hast filled me with indignation*, with such messages of wrath against this people as have made me always pensive." It is his complaint that he had had but little pleasure in his work. It was at first the rejoicing of his heart, but of late it had made him melancholy, so that he had no heart to *sit in the meeting of those that make merry*. He *sat alone*, fretting at the people's obstinacy and the little success of his labours among them.

(4) He throws himself upon God's pity and promise in a very passionate expostulation (*v.* 18): "*Why is my pain perpetual*, and nothing done to ease it? Will the God that has promised me his presence *be to me as a liar*, the God on whom I depend be to me *as waters that fail?*" No; I know thou wilt not. God is not a man that he should lie. The fountain of life will never be to his people as *waters that fail*.

II. God's gracious answer to this address, *v.* 19–21.

1. What God here requires of him. God will own him. But, (1) He must recover his temper, and be reconciled to his work. He must *return*, must shake off these distrustful discontented thoughts and passions, and not give way to them. (2) He must resolve to be faithful in his work. Though there was no cause at all to charge Jeremiah with unfaithfulness, and God knew his heart to be sincere, yet God saw fit to give him this caution. Thou must *take forth the precious from the vile*. The righteous are the precious be they ever so mean and poor; the wicked are the vile be they ever so rich and great. In our congregations these are mixed, wheat and chaff in the same floor; we cannot distinguish them by name, but we must by character, and must give to each a portion, comfort to precious saints and terror to vile sinners: *Let them return to thee, but return not thou to them*, that is, he must do the utmost he can, in his preaching, to bring people up to the mind of God. Those that had flown off from him, "*Let them return to thee*, and, upon second thoughts, come up to the terms; but do not thou *return to them*, do not compliment them, nor think to make the matter easier to them than the word of God has made it."

2. What God here promises. If he approve himself well, (1) God will tranquillize his mind and pacify the present tumult of his spirits: *If thou return, I will bring thee again*, will *restore thy soul*, as Ps. xxiii. 3. (2) God will employ him in his service as a prophet. "*Thou shalt stand before me*, to receive instructions from me, as a servant from his master; and *thou shalt be as my mouth* to deliver my messages to the people, as an ambassador is the mouth of the prince that sends him." (3) He shall have strength and courage to face the many difficulties he meets in his work, and his spirit shall not fail as now it does (*v.* 20): "*I will make thee unto this people as a fenced brazen wall*, which the storm batters and beats violently upon, but cannot shake. *Return not thou to them* by any sinful compliances, and then trust thy God to arm thee by his grace with holy resolutions. Be not cowardly, and God will make thee daring." He had complained that he was made a *man of strife*. Expect to be so (says God); they will *fight against thee, but they shall not prevail against thee*. (4) He shall have God for his mighty deliverer: *I am with thee to save thee*. Those that have God with them have a Saviour with them who has wisdom and strength enough to deal with the most formidable enemy (*v.* 21). There are many things that appear very frightful that yet do not prove at all hurtful to a good man.

CHAPTER 16

I. The greatness of the calamity that was coming upon the Jewish nation is illustrated by prohibitions given to the prophet neither to set up a house of his own (ver. 1–4) nor to go into the house of mourning (ver. 5–7) nor into the house of feasting, ver. 8, 9. II. God is justified in these severe proceedings against them by an account of their great wickedness, ver. 10–13. III. An intimation is given of mercy in reserve, ver. 14, 15. IV. Some hopes are given that the punishment of the sin should prove the reformation of the sinners, ver. 16–21.

Verses 1–9

The prophet is here for a sign to the people. They would not regard what he said; let it be tried whether they will regard what he *does*. He must conduct himself as became one that expected to see his country in ruins very shortly. This he foretold, but he is to show that he is himself fully satisfied in the truth of it, he is forbidden marriage, mourning for the dead, and mirth.

I. Jeremiah must not marry, nor think of having a family (*v.* 2). The Jews valued early marriages and numerous offspring. But Jeremiah must live a bachelor. By this it appears that it was advisable only in calamitous times and times of *present distress*, 1 Cor. vii. 26. That it is so is a part of the calamity. When we see such times at hand it is wisdom for all, especially for prophets, to keep themselves from being encumbered with that which, the dearer it is to them, the more it will be their care, and fear, and grief. The reason here given is because the *fathers* and *mothers, the sons and the daughters, shall die of grievous deaths, v.* 3, 4. Those that have wives and children will have such a clog upon them that they cannot flee from those deaths. The death of every child, and the circumstances of it, will be a new death to the parent. Better have no children than have them brought forth and bred up *for the murderer* (Hos. ix. 13, 14), than see them live and die in misery. Bewailing the dead and burying them are denied: *They shall not be lamented*, but shall be carried off, as if all the world were weary of them; nay, they *shall not be buried*, but left exposed. *They shall be as dung upon the face of the earth*, not only despicable, but detestable. Being *consumed*, some *by the sword* and some *by famine, their carcases shall be meat for the fowls of heaven and the beasts of the earth*.

II. Jeremiah must not go to the house of mourning upon the death of any of his neighbours or relations (*v.* 5). It was usual to condole with those whose relations were dead, to *bemoan them*, to *cut themselves*, and *make themselves bald*, which was an expression of mourning, though forbidden by the law, Deut. xiv. 1. Sometimes, in a passion of grief, they did *tear themselves for them* (*v.* 6, 7). They used to mourn *to comfort them for the dead*, as the Jews with Martha and Mary; and it was a friendly office to *give them a cup of consolation to drink*, to provide cordials for them for the support of their spirits. Though they have lost their parents, yet they have friends left that have a concern for them. It is a good work to *go to the house of mourning*. The prophet Jeremiah had been wont to abound in good offices of this kind. But now God bids him not lament the death of his friends. His sorrow for the destruction of his country in general must swallow up his sorrow for particular deaths. Men shall be in deaths so often that they shall have no time, no room, no heart, for the ceremonies that used to attend death. All shall be mourners then, and no comforters; everyone will find it enough to bear his own burden; for (*v.* 5), "*I have taken away my peace from this people*, put a full period to their prosperity, deprived them of health, and wealth, and quiet, and friends, and everything wherewith they might comfort themselves and one another." Whatever peace we enjoy, it is God's peace; it is his gift, and, *if he give quietness, who then can make trouble*? But, if we make not a good use of his peace, he can and will take it away. Then farewell all good. All is none when God takes away from us his lovingkindness and his mercies.

III. Jeremiah must not go to the house of mirth, any more than to the house of mourning, v. 8. God was coming against them in his judgments; and it was time for them to *humble themselves*. Ministers ought to be examples of self-denial. His friends wondered that he would not meet them, as he used to do, in the house of feasting. But he lets them know it was to intimate to them that all their feasting would be at an end shortly (v. 9): "*I will cause to cease the voice of mirth.* You shall have nothing to feast on, nothing to rejoice in, but be surrounded with calamities that shall mar your mirth and cast a damp upon it." God can find ways to tame the most jovial. "This shall be done *in this place,* in Jerusalem, that used to be the *joyous city* and thought her joys were all secure to her. It shall be done *in your eyes,* in your sight, to be a vexation to you, who now look so haughty and so merry." The voice of praise they had made to cease by their iniquities and idolatries, and therefore justly God made to cease among them *the voice of mirth and gladness.* The voice of God's prophets was not heard, was not heeded, among them, and therefore no longer shall *the voice of the bride-groom and of the bride,* of the songs that used to grace the nuptials, be heard among them. See *ch.* vii. 34.

Verses 10–13

1. The reasons why God would bring those judg-ments (v. 10). "*What is our iniquity? Or what is our sin?* What crime have we ever been guilty of, pro-portionable to such a sentence?" Instead of humbling and condemning themselves, they stand upon their own justification and insinuate that God did them wrong in pronouncing this evil against them. Do they ask the prophet why God is thus angry with them? The righteous God is never *angry without cause,* without good cause; but he must tell them particularly what is the cause, that they may be humbled, or at least that God may be justified. God visited upon them the iniquities of their fathers (v. 11): *Your fathers have forsaken me, and have not kept my law.* They shook off divine institutions, and *walked after other gods,* whose' worship was more gay and pom-pous; and, being fond of variety and novelty, they *served them and worshipped them*; and this was the sin which God had said, in the second commandment, he would *visit upon their children,* who kept up these idolatrous usages. Also God reckoned with them for their own iniquities (v. 12): "You have made your father's sin your own, and have become obnoxious to the punishment which in their days was deferred, for *you have done worse than your fathers.*" If they had made a good use of their fathers' reprieve, and been led by the patience of God to repentance, the judgment would have been prevented, the reprieve turned into a national pardon. They were more im-pudent and obstinate in sin than their fathers. They suffered their own passions to be noisy, that they might drown the voice of their consciences. No wonder that God had taken this resolution (v. 13): "*I will cast you out of this land,* this land of light, this valley of vision—into a far country, *a land that you know not, neither you nor your fathers.*" Two things would make their case there very miserable, and both of them relate to the soul. (1) "It is the happiness of the soul to be employed in the service of God; but *there shall you serve other gods day and night;* per-haps compelled to do it by your cruel task-masters; and, when you are forced to worship idols, you will be as sick of such worship as ever you were fond of it when it was forbidden you by your godly kings." (2) "It is the happiness of the soul to have some tokens of the lovingkindness of God, but you shall go to a strange land, *where I will not show you favour.*"

Verses 14–21

There is a mixture of mercy and judgment in these verses, and some seem to look as far forward as the times of the gospel..

I. God will certainly execute judgment upon them for their idolatries. The decree has gone forth. God sees all their sins (v. 17). As his omniscience convicts them, so his justice condemns them: *I will recompense their iniquity and their sin double,* not double to what it deserves, but double to what they expect. The sin for which God has a controversy with them is their having *defiled God's land* with their idolatries. Idols are *carcases of detestable things.* God hates them, and so should we. He will raise up instruments of his wrath, that shall *cast them out of their land,* according to the sentence passed (v. 16): *I will send for many fishers and many hunters*—the Chaldean army, that shall have ways of ensnaring them, by fraud as fishers, by force as hunters. They shall discover them wherever they are hid, in *hills* or *mountains,* or *holes of the rocks.* Their bondage in Babylon shall be more grievous than that in Egypt, their task-masters more cruel, and their lives more bitter. This is implied in the promise (v. 14, 15), that their deliverance out of Babylon shall be more welcome to them, than that out of Egypt. Their slavery in Egypt came upon them gradually; that in Babylon came upon them at once and with all the aggravating circumstances of terror. In Egypt they had a Goshen of their own, but none such in Babylon. In Egypt they were used as servants that were useful, in Babylon as captives that had been hateful. These judgments have a voice. When God chastens them he teaches them. By this rod God expostulates with them (v. 20): "*Shall a man make gods to himself?*" God will be known by the judg-ments which he executes. "For *this once,* and no more, *I will cause them to know my hand,* how far it can reach and how deeply it can wound."

II. Yet he has mercy in store for them. It was said, with an air of severity (v. 13), that God would banish them into a strange land; but there follow immediately words of comfort.

1. *The days will come,* the joyful days, when the same hand that dispersed them shall gather them again, v. 14, 15. They are cast out, but they are not cast off, they are not cast away. *I will bring them again into their own land,* and settle them there. And the following words (v. 16) may be understood as a promise; God will send for fishers and hunters, the Medes and Persians, that shall find them out in the countries where they are scattered, and send them back to their own land.

2. Their deliverance out of Babylon should be more memorable than their deliverance out of Egypt. The fresh mercy shall be so surprising, so welcome, that it shall even abolish the memory of the former. The bringing of Israel out of Egypt was done *by might and power,* this *by the Spirit of the Lord of hosts,* Zech. iv. 6. In this there was more of pardoning mercy for their captivity in Babylon had more in it of the punishment of sin than their bondage in Egypt.

3. Their deliverance out of captivity shall be accom-panied with a blessed reformation, and they shall return cured of their inclination to idolatry. They had defiled their own land with their *detestable things,* v. 13. But, when they have smarted for so doing, they shall come and humble themselves before God, v. 19–21. They shall be quickened to return to him by the conversion of the Gentiles: *The Gentiles shall come to thee from the ends of the earth;* and therefore shall not we come? The prophet comforts himself with the hope of this: "*O Lord! my strength and my fortress,* I am now easy, since thou hast given me a prospect of multitudes that shall *come to thee from the ends of the earth,* both of Jewish converts and of

Gentile proselytes." They were smarting for the sins of their ancestors: "*Surely our fathers have inherited lies, vanity, and things wherein there is no profit.* We are now sensible that they were cheated in their idolatrous worship; it did not prove what it promised, and therefore what have we to do any more with it?" They shall reason themselves out of their idolatry; and that reformation is likely to be durable which results from a rational conviction of the gross absurdity there is in sin, *v.* 20. They shall herein give honour to God, that they are brought to know his name by what they are made to know of his hand, *v.* 21. Nothing less than the mighty hand of divine grace, known experimentally, can make us know rightly the name of God as it is revealed to us.

4. Their deliverance out of captivity shall be a type and figure of the great salvation to be wrought out by the Messiah, who shall *gather together in one the children of God that were scattered abroad.*

CHAPTER 17

I. God convicts the Jews of the sin of idolatry and condemns them to captivity for it, ver. 1–4. II. He shows them the folly of all their carnal confidences, ver. 5–11. III. The prophet makes his appeal to God upon occasion of the malice of his enemies against him, committing himself to the divine protection, and begging God to appear for him, ver. 12–18. IV. God, by the prophet, warns the people to keep holy the sabbath day, assuring them that, if they did, it should be the lengthening out of their tranquillity, ver. 19–27.

Verses 1–4

The people had asked (*ch.* xvi. 10), *What is our iniquity, and what is our sin?*

I. The indictment is fully proved upon the prisoners, both the fact and the fault. They cannot plead *Not guilty*, for their sins are upon record in their own conscience; and they are obvious to the world, *v.* 1, 2. They are *written* before God in the most legible and indelible characters, Deut. xxxii. 34. They are written there with *a pen of iron and with the point of a diamond*; what is so written will not be worn out by time. The sin of sinners is never forgotten till it is forgiven. *It is graven upon the table of their heart.* What is *graven on the heart* cannot be erased. We need go no further, for proof of the charge, than *the horns of their altars*, on which the blood of their idolatrous sacrifices was sprinkled. Their neighbours will witness against them, and their own children shall *remember the altars and the groves* to which their parents took them when they were little, *v.* 2. The bias of their minds is still as strong as ever towards their idols, and they are not wrought upon either by the word or rod of God to abate their affection to them. It is written *upon the horns of their altars*, for they have given up their names to their idols and have bound themselves, as with cords.

II. The indictment being thus proved, the judgment is affirmed and the sentence ratified, *v.* 3, 4. Their treasures shall be given into the hands of strangers. Jerusalem is God's *mountain in the field*; it was built on a hill in the midst of a plain. *All the treasures* of that wealthy city will God *give to the spoil. My mountain* (so the whole land was, Ps. lxxviii. 54, Deut. xi. 11) you have turned into *your high places for sin*, have worshipped your idols upon *the high hills* (*v.* 2), and now they shall be *given for a spoil in all your borders.* They shall be made to part with their inheritance, and shall be carried captives into a strange land (*v.* 4). Sin works a discontinuance of our comforts and deprives us of the enjoyment of that which God has given us. But it is intimated that upon their repentance they shall recover possession again. For the present, *you have kindled a fire in my anger*, which burns so fiercely that it seems as if it would burn *for ever.*

Verses 5–11

The prophet's sermons were not all prophetical, but some of them practical.

I. Concerning the disappointment and vexation those will certainly meet with who depend upon creatures for success and relief when they are in trouble (*v.* 5, 6): *Cursed* (that is, miserable) *is the man* that does so, for he leans upon a broken reed. The sin here condemned is *making flesh the arm* we stay upon, the arm we work with and on which we depend for protection. God is his people's *arm*, Isa. xxxiii. 2. The great malignity there is in this sin; it is the *departure of the evil heart of unbelief from the living God.* Those that trust in man perhaps draw nigh to God with their mouth, but really *their heart departs from him.* Cleaving to the cistern is leaving the fountain, and is resented accordingly. He that puts a confidence in man puts a cheat upon himself; for (*v.* 6) *he shall be like the heath in the desert*, a sorry shrub, the product of barren ground, sapless, useless, and worthless; his comforts shall all fail him and he shall wither, be dejected and trampled on by all about him. *When good comes he shall not see* it, shall not share in it; when the times mend they shall not mend with him, but he shall *inhabit the parched places in the wilderness*; when others have a harvest he shall have none. Those that trust to their own righteousness and think they can do well enough without the grace of Christ, *make flesh their arm*, and their souls cannot prosper; they can neither produce the fruits of acceptable services to God nor reap the fruits of saving blessings from him; they *dwell in a dry land.*

II. Concerning the abundant satisfaction which those have who make God their confidence, who live by faith and repose themselves in him and his love in the most unquiet times, *v.* 7, 8. The duty required of us is to *make the Lord our hope*, his favour the good we hope for and his power the strength we hope in. He that does so shall be *as a tree planted by the waters*, a choice tree, about which great care has been taken to set it in the best soil. He shall be like a tree that *spreads out its roots*, and firmly fixed, spreads them out *by the rivers*, whence it draws abundance of sap. Those who make God their hope are easy, and enjoy a continual security and serenity of mind. A tree thus planted, thus watered, shall *not see when heat comes*, shall not sustain any damage from the most scorching heats of summer; it is so well moistened from its roots that it shall be sufficiently guarded against drought. They shall flourish like a tree that is *always green*, whose leaf does not wither; they shall be cheerful to themselves and beautiful in the eyes of others. They shall be fixed in an inward peace and satisfaction: They *shall not be careful in a year of drought*, when there is want of rain; for, as the tree has *seed in itself*, so it has *its moisture.* We need not be solicitous about the breaking of a cistern as long as we have the fountain. Those who trust in God, and by faith derive strength and grace from him, *shall not cease from yielding fruit.*

III. Concerning the sinfulness of man's heart, and the divine inspection it is always under, *v.* 9, 10. It is folly to trust in man, for he is not only frail, but false and deceitful. We think that we trust in God when really we do not, as appears by this, that our hopes and fears rise or fall according as second causes smile or frown. There is wickedness in our hearts which we ourselves are not aware of and do not suspect to be there. *The heart*, the conscience of man, in his corrupt and fallen state, *is deceitful above all things.* It calls evil good and good evil, puts false colours upon things. When men say in their hearts that there is no God, or he does not see; in these, and a thousand similar suggestions, the heart is deceitful. The case is bad indeed, if the conscience which should rectify the errors of the other faculties is itself a mother of falsehood and a ring-leader in the delusion. We cannot know our own hearts, nor what they will do in an hour of temptation (Hezekiah did not, Peter did not). Much less can we know the hearts of others, or have any dependence upon them. Whatever wickedness there is in the heart, God sees it: *I the Lord search the heart.* And this judgment which he makes of the heart is *to give to every man according to his ways, and according to the fruit of his doings.*

IV. Concerning the curse that attends wealth unjustly gotten (*v.* 11): *He that gets riches and not by right,* though he may make them his hope, shall never have joy of them. He who has got *treasures* by *vanity* and a *lying tongue* may hug himself in his success, and say, *I am rich,* but they shall be taken from him, or he from them. Those that get grace will be wise *in the latter end,* will have the comfort of it in death and to eternity (Prov. xix. 20); but those that place their happiness in the wealth of the world will rue the folly of it when it is too late. This is like *the partridge that sits on eggs and hatches them not,* but they are broken (as Job xxxix. 15), or stolen (as Isa. x. 14), or they become addled. The rich man takes a great deal of pains to get an estate together, and sits brooding upon it, but never has any comfort nor satisfaction in it.

Verses 12–18

The prophet retired for private meditation, *alone with God.*

I. He acknowledges the great favour of God to his people in setting up a revealed religion among them, and dignifying them with divine institutions (*v.* 12): *A glorious high throne from the beginning is the place of our sanctuary.* The temple at Jerusalem, where God manifested his special presence, where the people paid their homage to their Sovereign, and whither they fled for refuge in distress, was the *place of their sanctuary.* It was a throne of holiness, God's throne. Jerusalem is called *the city of the great King,* not only Israel's King, but the King of the whole earth, so that it might justly be deemed the royal city, of the world. It was *from the beginning,* 2 Chron. ii. 9. Jeremiah here mentions this either as a plea with God for mercy to their land, or as an aggravation of the sin of his people in forsaking God though his throne was among them.

II. He acknowledges the righteousness of God in abandoning those to ruin that revolted from their allegiance to him, *v.* 13. He speaks to God, as subscribing to the equity of it: *O Lord! the hope of* those in Israel that adhere to thee, *all that forsake thee shall be ashamed. Let them be ashamed* (so some read it); and so it is a petition for his grace, to make them penitently ashamed. *"Those that depart from me,* from the word of God which I have preached, do in effect depart from God"; as those that return to God are said to return to the prophet, ch. xv. 19. *Those that depart from thee* (so some read it) shall be *written in the earth.* They shall soon be blotted out, as that is which is written in the dust. They have *forsaken the Lord, the fountain of living waters* (that is, spring waters), for broken cisterns.

III. He prays to God for healing saving mercy for himself. Lord, *heal me,* and *save me, v.* 14. He was wounded in spirit upon many accounts. He was continually exposed to the malice of unreasonable men. To enforce this petition he pleads: *Heal thou me, and then I shall be healed.* If God hold us up, we shall live; if he protect us, we shall be safe. *Thou shalt be my praise* (so some read it); heal me, and save me, and thou shalt have the glory of it.

IV. He complains of the infidelity and daring impiety of the people to whom he preached. He had faithfully delivered God's message to them; and what answer has he to return to him that sent him? *Behold, they say unto me, Where is the word of the Lord? Let it come now, v.* 15; Isa. v. 19. They bantered the prophet. They denied the truth of what he said: "If that be the *word of the Lord* which thou speakest to us, *where is it*? Why is it not fulfilled?" They defied what he said. "Let God Almighty do his worst; let all he has said come to pass; we shall do well enough; the lion is not so fierce as he is painted," Amos v. 18.

V. He appeals to God concerning his faithful discharge of the duty to which he was called, *v.* 16. He continued constant to his work. His office, instead of being his protection, exposed him to contempt, and injury. "Yet," says he, "*I have not hastened from being a pastor after thee;* I have not left my work." Such a pastor Jeremiah was; and, though he met with as much difficulty and discouragement as ever any man did, yet he did not fly off as Jonah did, nor desire to be excused from going any more on God's errands. He kept up his affection to the people. Though they were very abusive to him, he was compassionate to them: *I have not desired the woeful day.* The day of the accomplishment of his prophecies would be a woeful day indeed to Jerusalem, and therefore he wished it might never come. God does not, and therefore ministers must not, desire the death of sinners, but rather that they may turn and live. He kept closely to his instructions. Though he might have curried favour with the people, if he had not been so sharp in his reproofs, yet he would deliver his message faithfully.

VI. He humbly begs God that he would own him, and protect him, and carry him on cheerfully in that work to which he had so plainly called him. Two things he here desires: 1. That he might have comfort in serving the God that sent him (*v.* 17): *Be not thou a terror to me.* He pleads, *"Thou art my hope;* and then nothing else is my fear. My dependence is upon thee; and therefore *be not a terror to me.*" 2. That he might have courage in dealing with the people to whom he was sent, *v.* 18. Those persecute him who should have entertained and encouraged him. "Lord," says he, "*let them be confounded* (let them be ashamed of their obstinacy, or else let the judgments threatened be at length executed upon them), *but let not me be confounded,* let not me be terrified by their menaces, so as to betray my trust." As to his persecutors, he prays, *Bring upon them the day of evil,* in hope that the bringing of it upon them might prevent the bringing of it upon the country.

Verses 19–27

These verses are a sermon concerning sabbath-sanctification. This message concerning the sabbath was probably sent in the days of Josiah, for the furtherance of that work of reformation which he set on foot. It must be proclaimed at the court-gate first, the gate *by which the kings of Judah come in and go out, v.* 19. Let them be told their duty first; for, if sabbaths be not sanctified *the rulers of Judah are to be contended with,* for they are certainly wanting in their duty. He must also preach it *in all the gates of Jerusalem.* It is a matter of great and general concern; therefore let all take notice of it.

I. How the sabbath is to be sanctified, and what is the law concerning it, *v.* 21, 22. They must rest from their worldly employment on the sabbath day. They must *bear no burden* into the city nor out of it; husbandmen's burdens of corn must not be carried in, nor manure carried out; nor tradesmen's burdens, nor merchandise. There must not a loaded horse, or cart, or waggon, be seen on the sabbath day in the streets or the roads; the porters must not ply on that day, nor must the servants be suffered to fetch in provisions or fuel. It is a day of rest, and must not be made a day of labour, unless in case of necessity.

"*Hallow you the sabbath*, that is, consecrate it to the honour of God and spend it in his service and worship." Worldly business must be laid aside, that we may be intent upon that work which requires and deserves the whole man. "*Take heed to yourselves*, for it is at your peril if you rob God of that part of your time which he has reserved to himself." Let not the soul be burdened with the cares of this world on sabbath days. "This is no new imposition upon you, but is what *I commanded your fathers*."

II. How the sabbath had been profaned (*v.* 23): "Your fathers were required to keep holy the sabbath day, *but they obeyed not*; they *hardened their necks* against this as well as other commands that were given them." Where sabbaths are neglected all religion sensibly goes to decay.

III. What blessings God had in store for them if they would make conscience of sabbath-sanctification, *v.* 24–26. The court shall flourish. *Kings* in succession, with the other *princes* that *sit upon the thrones* of judgment, shall ride in great pomp *through the gates of Jerusalem*. The city shall flourish. Jerusalem, *the holy city, shall remain for ever, shall for ever be inhabited*, shall not be destroyed and dispeopled, as is threatened. The country shall flourish: *The cities of Judah and the land of Benjamin* shall be replenished with vast numbers of inhabitants, abounding in plenty and living in peace. The church shall flourish: *Meat-offerings, and incense, and sacrifices of praise*, shall be brought *to the house of the Lord*. A people truly flourish when religion flourishes among them. And this is the effect of sabbath-sanctification; when that branch of religion is kept up other instances of it are kept up likewise; but, when that is lost, devotion is lost either in superstition or in profaneness. The streams of all religion run either deep or shallow according as the banks of the sabbath are kept up or neglected.

IV. What judgments they must expect would come upon them if they persisted in the profanation of the sabbath (*v.* 27): "*If you will not hearken to me* in this matter, to keep the gates shut on sabbath days, so that there may be no unnecessary *entering in*, or going out, on that day—if you will break through the enclosure of the divine law, and lay that day in common with other days—know that God will *kindle a fire in the gates of* your city." Justly shall those gates be fired that are not used as they ought to be to shut out sin and to keep people in to an attendance on their duty.

CHAPTER 18

I. God's ways in dealing with nations and kingdoms (ver. 1–6). If he threaten their ruin, yet upon their repentance he will return in mercy to them, and, when he is coming towards them in mercy, nothing but their sin will stop the progress of his favours, ver. 7–10. II. A particular demonstration of the folly of the men of Judah and Jerusalem in departing from their God to idols, ver. 11–17. III. The prophet's complaint to God of the base ingratitude and malice of his enemies, and his prayers against them, ver. 18–23.

Verses 1–10

The prophet is here sent to *the potter's house*, not to preach a sermon, but to prepare a sermon, or rather to receive it ready prepared. "*Go to the potter's house*, and observe how he manages his work, and there *I will cause thee*, by silent whispers, *to hear my words*. There thou shalt receive a message, to be delivered to the people." The prophet therefore went to the potter's house (*v.* 3) and took notice how he *wrought his work upon the wheels*. And (*v.* 4) when a lump of clay that he designed to form into one shape either proved too stiff, or had a stone in it, or came to be *marred in his hand*, he presently turned it into another shape; just *as seems good to the potter*. Ministers will make a good use of their converse

with the business and affairs of this life if they learn thereby to speak more plainly and familiarly to people about the things of God, and to expound scripture comparisons. While Jeremiah looks carefully upon the potter's work, God darts into his mind these two great truths, which he must preach to *the house of Israel*:

I. That God has both an incontestable authority and an irresistible ability to form and fashion kingdoms and nations as he pleases to serve his own purposes. *Cannot I do with you as this potter, saith the Lord? v.* 6. God has a clearer title to a dominion over us than the potter has over the clay; for the potter only gives it its form, whereas we have both matter and form from God. This intimates that God has an incontestable sovereignty over us, and that it would be as absurd for us to dispute this as for the clay to quarrel with the potter. It is a very easy thing with God to make what use he pleases of us. One turn of the hand, one turn of the wheel, quite alters the shape of the clay, makes it a vessel, unmakes it, new-makes it. Thus are our times in God's hand. It is spoken here of nations. See this explained by Job (*ch.* xii. 23), Ps. cvii. 33, &c., and compare Job xxxiv. 29. If the potter's vessel be marred for one use, it shall serve for another; those that will not be monuments of mercy shall be monuments of justice. God formed us out of the clay (Job xxxiii. 6), and we are still as clay in his hands (Isa. lxiv. 8).

II. That, in the exercise of this authority and ability, he goes by fixed rules of equity and goodness. He dispenses favours indeed in a way of sovereignty, but never punishes by arbitrary power. In ways of judgment we may be sure that it is for our sins—national repentance will stop the progress of the judgments (*v.* 7, 8): *If God speak concerning a nation to pluck up* its fences that secure it, its fruit-trees that enrich it, pull down its fortifications, and so *destroy it* as either a vineyard or a city is destroyed—in this case, if *that nation* repent of their sins and reform their lives, turn every one from his evil way and return to God, God will return in mercy to them. It is an undoubted truth that a sincere conversion from the evil of sin be an effectual prevention of the evil of punishment; and God can as easily raise up a penitent people from their ruins as the potter can make anew the vessel of clay when it was *marred in his hand*. When God is coming towards us in ways of mercy, if any stop be given to the progress of that mercy, it is nothing but sin that gives it (*v.* 9, 10). Sin is the great mischief-maker between God and a people; it forfeits the benefit of his promises and spoils the success of their prayers. It defeats his kind intentions concerning them (Hos. vii. 1).

Verses 11–17

The application of the general truths laid down in the foregoing part of the chapter to the Jews.

I. "*Go, and tell them*" (saith God), "*Behold, I frame evil against you and devise a device against you*. Providence in all its operations is plainly working towards your ruin."

II. He invites them by repentance and reformation to meet him and so to prevent his further proceedings against them: "*Return you now everyone from his evil ways*, that so God may turn from the evil he had purposed to do unto you, and that providence which seemed to be framed like a vessel on the wheel against you shall immediately be thrown into a new shape, and the issue shall be in favour of you."

III. He foresees their obstinacy, and their perverse refusal (*v.* 12): *They said*, "*There is no hope*. We may even despair of ever being delivered, for we are resolved that *we will walk after our own devices*. It is to no purpose for the prophets to say any more to us; *we will do everyone the imagination of his* own *evil heart*, and will not be under the restraint of the divine law." They call it liberty to live at large; whereas for a man to be a slave to his lusts is the worst of slaveries.

IV. He upbraids them with the monstrous folly of their obstinacy, and their hating to be reformed (v. 13): *Ask you among the heathen*, even those that had not the benefit of divine revelation, no oracles, no prophets. *Who hath heard such a thing?* The Ninevites, when thus warned, turned from their evil ways. But *the virgin of Israel* bids defiance to repentance, whatever conscience and Providence say to the contrary, and thus *has done a horrible thing*. She should have preserved herself pure and chaste for God, who had espoused her to himself; but she has alienated herself from him, and refuses to return to him. Wilful impenitence is the grossest self-murder; and that is *a horrible thing*.

V. He shows their folly in two things:

1. In the nature of the sin itself: they forsook God for idols (v. 14, 15): *Will a* thirsty traveller *leave the snow*, which, being melted, runs down from the mountains *of Lebanon*, and, passing over *the rock of the field*, flows in clear, clean, crystal streams? Will he pass these by, and think to better himself with some dirty puddle-water? *Or shall the cold flowing waters that come from any other place be forsaken* in the heat of summer? When men are parched with heat and drought, and meet with cooling refreshing streams, they will make use of them. The margin reads it, "*Will a man* that is travelling the road *leave my fields*, which are plain and level, *for a rock*, which is rough and hard, *or for the snow of Lebanon*, which, lying in great drifts, makes the road impassable? *Or shall the running waters be forsaken for the strange cold waters?* But *my people have forgotten me* (v. 15), have quitted *a fountain of living waters for broken cisterns. They have burnt incense to* idols that are not what they pretend to be nor can perform what is expected from them." They left *the ancient paths*, appointed by the divine law, walked in by all the saints, therefore the right way to their journey's end, a safe way. But, when they were advised to keep to the good old way, they positively said that they would not, *ch.* vi. 16. They chose by-paths; they walked *in a way not cast up*, not in the highway, the King's highway. Such was the way of idolatry.

2. In the mischievous consequences of it. The direct tendency of it was *to make their land desolate, and*, consequently, themselves miserable. *Everyone that passes by* their land shall make his remarks upon it, and *shall be astonished, and wag his head*, some wondering, others commiserating, others triumphing in the desolations of a country that had been *the glory of all lands. Their land* being made *desolate*, in pursuance of their destruction, it is threatened (v. 17), *I will scatter them as with an east wind*, fierce and violent. That which completes their misery is, *I will show them the back, and not the face, in the day of their calamity*. Our calamities may be easily borne if God look towards us, and smile upon us, but if he turn *the back* upon us, if he show himself displeased, if he leave us to ourselves, we are quite undone.

Verses 18-23

The prophet here brings in his own affairs, for instruction to us.

I. The common methods of the persecutors, Jeremiah's enemies, v. 18.

1. They laid their heads together to consult what they should do against him, both to be revenged on him for what he had said and to stop his mouth for the future: *They said, Come and let us devise devices against Jeremiah*, not only against his person, but against the word he delivered to them.

2. Herein they pretended a mighty zeal for the church, which, they suggested, was in danger if Jeremiah was tolerated to preach as he did: "*Come*," say they, "let us silence and crush him, *for the law shall not perish from the priest; the law of truth is in their mouths* (Mal. ii. 6) and there we will seek it; the administration of ordinances according to the law is in their hands, and neither the one nor the other shall be wrested from them." Two things they insinuated: (1) That Jeremiah could not be himself a true prophet, but was a pretender, because he neither was commissioned by the priests nor concurred with the other prophets. (2) That the matter of his prophecies could not be from God, because it reflected sometimes upon the prophets and priests (ch. v. 31), deceiving the people (ch. xiv. 14). He had foretold that their *heart should perish*, and *be astonished* (ch. iv. 9), that *the wise men should be dismayed* (ch. viii. 9, 10), that the priests and prophets should be intoxicated, ch. xiii. 13.

3. They agreed to do all they could to blast his reputation: *Come, let us smite him with the tongue.*

4. To set others an example, they resolved that they would not themselves regard anything he said. *Let us not give heed to any of his words;* for, right or wrong, they will look upon them to be *his words*, and not the words of God.

5. That they may effectually silence him, they resolve to be the death of him (v. 23): *All their counsel against me* is *to slay me*. They *hunt for the precious life*.

II. The common relief of the persecuted. This we may see in the course that Jeremiah took. He immediately applied to his God by prayer.

1. He referred himself and his cause to God's cognizance, v. 19. They would not regard a word he said, would not admit his complaints, nor take any notice of his grievances; but, Lord (says he), *do thou give heed to me*. Hear the voice of my contenders, how noisy and clamorous they are, how false and malicious all they say is, and let them be *judged out of their own mouth*; *cause their own tongues to fall upon them*."

2. He complains of their base ingratitude to him (v. 20): "*Shall evil be recompensed for good*, and shall it go unpunished? Wilt not thou recompense me good for that evil?" *They have dug a pit for my soul;* they aimed to take away his life in a base, cowardly, clandestine way: *they dug pits for* him, which there was no fence against, Ps. cxix. 85. But how great the good he had done for them: *Remember that I stood before thee to speak good for them;* he had been an intercessor with God for them. But it was not strange that those who had forgotten their God did not know their best friends. It was very grievous to him, as the like was to David. Ps. xxxv. 13; cix. 4, *For my love they are my adversaries*. Thus do sinners deal with the great intercessor, crucifying him afresh, and speaking against him on earth, while his blood is speaking for them in heaven. It was a comfort to the prophet that, when they were so spiteful against him, he had the testimony of his conscience that he had done his duty to them.

3. He imprecates the judgments of God upon them, not from a revengeful disposition, but in indignation against their wickedness, v. 21-23. He prays, (1) That their families might be starved for want of bread. (2) That they might be cut off *by the sword* of war. (3) That the terrors and desolations of war might seize them suddenly and by surprise, that thus their punishment might answer to their sin (v. 22). (4) That they might be dealt with according to the desert of this sin, which was without excuse. (5) That God's wrath against them might be their ruin: *Let them be overthrown before thee*. Now this is not written for our imitation. Jeremiah was a prophet, and by the

impulse of the spirit of prophecy, in the foresight of the ruin certainly coming upon his persecutors, might pray such prayers as we may not; our Master has taught us, by his precept and pattern, to *bless those that curse us and pray for those that despitefully use us.*

CHAPTER 19

The same melancholy theme is the subject of this chapter that was of those foregoing—the approaching ruin of Judah and Jerusalem for their sins. I. He must set their sins in order before them, ver. 4, 5. II. He must describe the particular judgments which were now coming apace upon them, ver. 6–9. III. He must do this in the valley of Tophet, with great solemnity, ver. 2, 3. IV. He must summon a company of the elders together to be witnesses of this, ver. 1. V. He must confirm this by a sign, which was the breaking of an earthen bottle, signifying that they should be dashed to pieces like a potter's vessel, ver. 10–13. VI. When he had done this in the valley of Tophet he ratified it in the court of the temple, ver. 14, 15.

Verses 1–9

The prophet is here sent with a message he had often delivered.

I. He must take of the elders and chief men, both in church and state, to be his auditors and witnesses to what he said—*the ancients of the people and the ancients of the priests.* Though the generality of the elders were disaffected to him, yet it is likely that there were some few who looked upon him as a prophet of the Lord, and would pay this respect to the heavenly vision.

II. He must *go to the valley of the son of Hinnom*, and deliver this message there; for *the word of the Lord* is not bound to any one place; as good a sermon may be preached in the valley of Tophet as in the gate of the temple. Christ preached on a mountain and out of a ship. This sermon must be preached in *the valley of the son of Hinnom*, 1. Because there they had been guilty of the vilest of their idolatries, the sacrificing of their children to Moloch. The sight of the place might serve to remind them. 2. Because there they should feel the sorest of their calamities; and, it being the common sink of the city, let them see what a miserable spectacle this magnificent city would be when it should be all like the valley of Tophet. God bids him *proclaim there the words that I shall tell thee*, when thou comest thither. God's messages were frequently not revealed to the prophets before they were to deliver them.

III. He must give general notice of a general ruin now shortly coming upon Judah and Jerusalem, *v.* 3. *Hear you the word of the Lord*, though it be a terrible word. Both rulers and ruled must attend to it; the *kings of Judah*, the king and his sons, the king and his privy-counsellors, must hear the word of the King of kings, for, high as they are, he is above them. The *inhabitants of Jerusalem* also must hear what God has to say to them. Both princes and people have contributed to the national guilt and must concur in the national repentance, or they will both share in the national ruin. The ruin of Eli's house is thus described (1 Sam. iii. 11), and of Jerusalem, 2 Kings xxi. 12.

IV. He must plainly tell them what their sins were, *v.* 4, 5. They are charged with apostasy from God (*They have forsaken me*) and abuse of the privileges of the visible church, with which they had been dignified—*They have estranged this place.* He charges them with an affection for and the adoration of false *gods*, such as *neither they nor their fathers have known.* They took them at a venture for their gods; being fond of change and novelty, they liked them the better and new fashions in religion were as grateful to their fancies as in other things. They also stand charged with murder, wilful murder, from malice prepense: *They have filled this place with the blood of innocents.* As if idolatry and murder, committed

separately, were not bad enough, they have consolidated them into one complicated crime, that of burning their children in the fire to Baal (*v.* 5).

V. He must endeavour to affect them with the greatness of the desolation that was coming upon them. He must tell them that this *valley of the son of Hinnom* shall acquire a new name, *the valley of slaughter* (*v.* 6), for (*v.* 7) multitudes shall *fall there by the sword*, when either they sally out upon the besiegers and are repulsed or attempt to make their escape and are seized. And as for those that remain within the city, and will not capitulate with the besiegers, they shall perish for want of food, when first they have eaten *the flesh of their sons and daughters* and dearest *friends*, through the *straitness wherewith their enemies shall straiten them*, *v.* 9. And, *lastly*, the whole *city* shall be *desolate*. That place which holiness had made *the joy of the whole earth* sin had made the reproach and shame of the whole earth.

VI. He must assure them that all their attempts to prevent and avoid this ruin, so long as they continued impenitent and unreformed, would be fruitless and vain (*v.* 7): *I will make void the counsel of Judah and Jerusalem in this place.* There is no fleeing from God's justice but by fleeing to his mercy.

Verses 10–15

The message delivered in the foregoing verses is here enforced.

I. By a visible sign. The prophet was to take along with him an *earthen bottle* (*v.* 1), and, when he had delivered his message, he was to *break the bottle* to pieces (*v.* 10). He had compared this people, in the chapter before, to the potter's clay, which is easily marred in the making. But some might say, "It is past that with us; we have been made and hardened long since." "And what though you be," says he, "the potter's vessel is as soon broken in the hand of any man as the vessel while it is soft clay is marred in the potter's hand, and its case is, in this respect, much worse, that the vessel while it is soft clay, though it be marred, may be moulded again, but, after it is hardened, when it is broken it can never be pieced again." Sacramental signs, and teaching by symbols was anciently used. 1. As the bottle was easily and irrecoverably broken, so shall *Judah and Jerusalem* be broken by the Chaldean army, *v.* 11. They depended much upon the firmness of their constitution, and the fixedness of their courage, which they thought hardened them like a vessel of brass; but the prophet shows that all that did but harden them like a vessel of earth, which, though hard, is brittle and sooner broken than that which is not so hard. It is God himself, who made them, that resolves to unmake them: *I will break this people and this city*, dash them in pieces like *a potter's vessel*; the doom of the heathen (Ps. ii. 9, Rev. ii. 27), but now Jerusalem's doom, Isa. xxx. 14. *A potter's vessel*, when once broken, *cannot be made whole again, cannot be cured.* Jerusalem shall be an utter ruin; no hand can repair it but his that broke it; and if they return to him, though he has torn, he will heal. 2. This was done in Tophet, to signify two things: (1) *They shall bury in Tophet till there be no place to bury* any more there. (2) *I will make this city as Tophet.* As they had filled the valley of Tophet with the slain they sacrificed to their idols, so God will fill the whole city with the slain that shall fall as sacrifices to the justice of God. Dead carcases, and other filth of the city, were carried thither, and a fire was continually kept there for the burning of it. So execrable a place was it looked upon to be that, in the language of our Saviour's time, hell was called, in allusion to it, *Gehenna, the valley of Hinnom.* Even *the houses of Jerusalem, and* those *of the kings of Judah, shall be defiled as the place of Tophet* (*v.*

13), because of the idolatries that have been committed there. The flat roofs of their houses were sometimes used by devout people as convenient places for prayer (Acts x. 9), and by idolaters they were used as high places, on which they sacrificed to strange gods, especially to *the host of heaven*, the sun, moon, and stars. We read of those that *worshipped the host of heaven upon the house-tops* (Zeph. i. 5). This sin upon the house-tops brought a curse into the house.

II. By a solemn recognition and ratification of what he had said *in the court of the Lord's house, v.* 14, 15. The prophet returned from Tophet to the temple, which stood upon the hill over that valley, and there confirmed what he had said in the valley of Tophet. 1. The accomplishment of the prophecies is here the judgment threatened. The people flattered themselves that the threatening was but to frighten them, but the prophet tells them that they deceive themselves: *For thus saith the Lord of hosts*, who is able to make his words good, *I will bring upon this city, and upon all her towns, all the evil that I have pronounced against it.* God will appear as terrible against sin and sinners as the scripture makes him. 2. The contempt of the prophecies is here the sin charged upon them. It is *because they have hardened their necks*, and would *not hear my words*.

CHAPTER 20

Such plain dealing, if it did not convince and humble men, would provoke and exasperate them. I. Jeremiah persecuted by Pashur for preaching that sermon, ver. 1, 2. II. Pashur threatened for so doing, and the word which Jeremiah had preached confirmed, ver. 3–6. III. Jeremiah complaining to God concerning it (ver. 7–10), encouraging himself in God, lodging his appeal with him, not doubting but that he shall yet praise him (ver. 11–13), and yet peevishly cursing the day of his birth (ver. 14–18), by which it appears that he was a man subject to like passions as we are.

Verses 1–6

I. Pashur's unjust displeasure against Jeremiah, and the fruits of that displeasure, *v.* 1, 2. Pashur was a priest, and therefore should have protected Jeremiah, who was a priest too, and the more because he was a prophet of the Lord, whose interests the priests ought to consult. But this priest was a persecutor. He was *the son of Immer;* that is, he was of the sixteenth course of the priests, of which Immer, when these courses were first settled by David, was father (1 Chron. xxiv. 14). Thus this Pashur is distinguished from another of the same name mentioned *ch.* xxi. 1, who was of the fifth course. This Pashur was *chief governor in the temple;* perhaps he was only so *pro tempore—for a short period,* the course he was head of being now in waiting. This was Jeremiah's great enemy. We cannot suppose that Pashur was one of those that went with Jeremiah to the valley of Tophet to hear him prophesy; but, when he came into the courts of the Lord's house (*v.* 1): *He heard that Jeremiah prophesied these things,* and could not bear that he should dare to preach in the courts of the Lord's house, where he was *chief governor,* without his leave. Being incensed at Jeremiah, 1. He *smote* him, struck him with his hand or staff of authority. Perhaps it was a blow intended only to disgrace him. The method of proceeding here was illegal; the high priest, and the rest of the priests, ought to have been consulted, and Jeremiah's credentials examined. But these rules are set aside as mere formalities; right or wrong, Jeremiah must be run down. 2. He *put him in the stocks.* He continued in it all night, and in a public place too, *in the high gate of Benjamin, which was* in, or *by, the house of the Lord,* probably a gate through which they passed between the city and the temple. Pashur intended thus to chastise him, to expose him to contempt, that he might not be regarded if he did prophesy.

II. God's just displeasure against Pashur. *On the morrow Pashur* gave Jeremiah his discharge, *brought him out of the stocks* (*v.* 3). And now Jeremiah has a message from God to him. When he brought him out of the stocks, then God put a word into the prophet's mouth, which would awaken his conscience, if he had any.

1. Did he aim to establish himself by silencing one that told him of his faults and would be likely to lessen his reputation with the people? He shall not gain this point; for, (1) Though the prophet should be silent, his own conscience shall make him always uneasy. To confirm this he shall have a name given him, *Magor-missabib—Terror round about,* or *Fear on every side.* It seems to be a proverbial expression, bespeaking a man in despair, in fear on every side. *The wicked flee when no man pursues,* are in *great fear where no fear is.* This shall be Pashur's case (*v.* 4): *"Behold, I will make thee a terror to thyself;* and thy own imagination shall create thee a constant uneasiness."* Those that will not hear of their faults from God's prophets, shall be made to hear of them from conscience, which is a reprover in their own bosoms. *"I will make thee a terror to all thy friends; thou shalt express thyself with so much horror that all thy friends shall choose to stand aloof from thy torment."* (2) His friends shall all fail him. God lets him live miserably, like Cain in the *land of shaking,* in such a continual consternation that wherever he goes it is asked, "What makes this man in such a continual terror?" It shall be answered, "It is God's hand upon him for putting Jeremiah in the stocks." His friends, who should encourage him, shall *fall by the sword of the enemy,* and *his eyes shall behold it.* (3) He shall find that divine vengeance is waiting for him (*v.* 6); he and his family shall *go into captivity,* even *to Babylon;* he shall die a captive, and shall be buried in his chains, he *and all his friends.* Thus far is the doom of Pashur.

2. Did he aim to keep the people easy, to prevent the destruction that Jeremiah prophesied, and by sinking his reputation make his words fall to the ground? It appears by *v.* 6 that he himself set up for a prophet, and told the people that they should have peace. He *prophesied lies to them;* and because Jeremiah's prophecy contradicted his, therefore he set himself against him. But could he gain his point? Jeremiah stands to what he has said against Judah and Jerusalem. (1) The country shall be ruined (*v.* 4): *I will give all Judah into the hand of the king of Babylon.* It had long been God's own land, but he will now transfer his title to it to Nebuchadnezzar, he shall be master of the country and dispose of the inhabitants as he pleases, but none shall escape him. (2) The city shall be ruined too, *v.* 5. The king of Babylon shall carry all that is valuable in it to Babylon. He shall seize their military stores (here called *the strength of the city*) and turn them against them. He shall carry off all their wares and merchandise, here called *their labours.* He shall plunder their fine houses, and take away their furniture, here called their *precious things.* He shall rifle the exchequer, and take away the jewels of the crown and *all the treasures of the kings of Judah.*

Verses 7–13

Jeremiah is here, through the infirmity of the flesh, strangely agitated within himself. In these verses it appears that, upon occasion of the great injury that Pashur did to Jeremiah, there was a struggle in his breast between his graces and his corruptions.

I. Here is a sad representation of the wrong that was done him. He complains,

1. That he was ridiculed and laughed at; they made a jest of everything he said and did (*v.* 7, 8): *I am in derision; I am mocked.* And what was it that thus

exposed him to contempt and scorn? It was nothing but his faithful and zealous discharge of the duty of his office, *v.* 8. They could find nothing for which to deride him but his preaching; it was *the word of the Lord* that *was made a reproach.* Two things they derided him for: (1) The manner of his preaching: *Since he spoke, he cried out.* He had always been a lively affectionate preacher, and since he began to speak in God's name he always spoke as a man in earnest; he *cried aloud and did not spare.* Lively preachers are the scorn of careless unbelieving hearers. (2) The matter of his preaching: He *cried violence and spoil.* He reproved them for violence and spoil towards one another; and he prophesied violence and spoil should be brought upon them as punishment; for the former they ridiculed him as overprecise, for the latter as over-credulous. This was bad enough, yet he complains further.

2. That he was plotted against and his ruin contrived; he was not only ridiculed as a weak man, but reproached and misrepresented as a bad man and dangerous to the government, *v.* 10. But there were those that acted with more subtlety. (1) They spoke ill of him behind his back. *I heard,* at second hand, *the defaming of many, fear on every side (of many Magor-missabibs,* so some read it), of many such men as Pashur was. They represented Jeremiah as a man that instilled fears and jealousies on every side into the minds of the people, and so made them uneasy under the government, and disposed them to a rebellion. See how Jeremiah's enemies contrived the matter: *Report, say they, and we will report it.* "Let some very bad thing be said of him, which may render him obnoxious to the government, and, though it be false, we will second it, and spread it, and add to it." (2) They flattered him to his face, that they might get something from him on which to ground an accusation, as the spies that came to Christ, Luke xx. 20; xi. 53, 54. "If we accost him kindly we shall wheedle him to speak some treasonable words; and then *we shall prevail against him,* and *take our revenge on him* for telling us of our faults and threatening us with the judgment of God."

II. Here is an account of the temptation he was in under this affliction. 1. He was tempted to quarrel with God for making him a prophet. This he begins with (*v.* 7): *O Lord! thou hast deceived me, and I was deceived.* This is the language of Jeremiah's folly and corruption. He knew how the prophets before him had been persecuted, and had no reason to expect better treatment. God had expressly told him that all the *princes, priests, and people of the land would fight against him* (*ch.* i. 18, 19). Christ thus told his disciples what opposition they should meet with, *that they might not be offended,* John xvi. 1, 2. But the words may very well be read thus: *Thou hast persuaded me, and I was persuaded.* And this agrees best with what follows. Jeremiah was very backward to undertake the prophetic office; he pleaded that he was under age and unfit for the service; but God overruled his pleas, and told him that *he must go, ch.* i. 6, 7. "Now, Lord," says he, "since thou hast put this office upon me, why dost thou not stand by me in it? Had I thrust myself upon it, I might justly have been in derision; but why am I so when thou didst thrust me into it?" 2. He was tempted to quit his work partly because he himself met with so much hardship in it and partly because those to whom he was sent, instead of being edified and made better, were exasperated and made worse (*v.* 9).

III. An account of his faithful adherence to his work and cheerful dependence on his God notwithstanding.

1. He found the grace of God mighty in him to keep him to his business, "*I said,* in my haste, *I will speak no more in his name*; what I have in my heart

to deliver I will stifle and suppress. But I soon found it was *in my heart as a burning fire shut up in my bones,* which glowed inwardly, and must have vent; it was impossible to smother it; while *I kept silence from good my heart was hot within me,* it was *pain and grief to me,* and I must speak, that I might be refreshed"; Ps. xxxix. 2, 3; Job xxxii. 20. Jeremiah was soon weary with forbearing to preach, and could not contain himself; nothing puts faithful ministers to pain so much as being silenced, nor to terror so much as silencing themselves. Their convictions will soon triumph, for *woe is unto me if I preach not the gospel,* whatever it cost me, 1 Cor. ix. 16.

2. He was assured of God's presence with him, which would be sufficient to baffle all the attempts of his enemies (*v.* 11): "They say, *We shall prevail against him.* But I am sure that *they shall not prevail, they shall not prosper.* I can set them at defiance, for *the Lord is with me,* to take my part against them (Rom. viii. 31). He is with me to bear me up under the burden. He is with me to make the word I preach answer the end he designs. He is with me to strike a terror upon them, and so to overcome them." The most formidable enemies that act against us appear despicable when we see the Lord for us as a *mighty terrible one,* Neh. iv. 14. Jeremiah speaks now with a good assurance: If *the Lord be with me, my persecutors shall stumble,* so that, when they pursue me, they shall not overtake me (Ps. xxvii. 2), and then *they shall be greatly ashamed* of their impotent malice and fruitless attempts.

3. He appeals to God against them as a righteous Judge, and prays judgment upon his cause, *v.* 12. He that tries the righteous tries the unrighteous too, for he *sees the reins and the heart,* and therefore can pass an unerring judgment on their words and actions. *Unto thee have I opened my cause.* Not but that God perfectly knew his cause, and all the merits of it, but the cause we commit to God we must spread before him. He knows it, but he will know it from us, and allows us to be particular in the opening of it, not to affect him, but to affect ourselves.

4. He greatly rejoices and praises God, in a full confidence that God would appear for his deliverance, *v.* 13. In a transport of joy he stirs up himself and others to give God the glory of it: *Sing unto the Lord, praise you the Lord.* Here appears a great change with him since he began this discourse; the clouds are blown over, his complaints all silenced and turned into thanksgiving. It was the lively exercise of faith that made this happy change, that turned his sighs into songs and his tremblings into triumphs. "He hath delivered me formerly when I was in distress, and now of late out of the hand of Pashur, and he will continue to deliver me, 2 Cor. i. 10. He will deliver my soul from the sin that I am in danger of falling into when I am thus persecuted."

Verses 14–18

What is the meaning of this? Does there *proceed out of the same mouth blessing and cursing?* Could he that said so cheerfully (*v.* 13), *Sing unto the Lord, praise you the Lord,* say so passionately (*v.* 14), *Cursed be the day wherein I was born?* It seems to be an account of the ferment he had been in while he was in the stocks, out of which by faith and hope he had recovered himself, rather than a new temptation. When grace has got the victory it is good to remember the struggles, that we may be ashamed of ourselves and our own folly, may admire the goodness of God in not taking us at our word.

I. The prophet's language in this temptation. 1. He fastened a brand of infamy upon his birthday, as Job did in a heat (*ch.* iii. 1). It is a wish that he had never been born. Judas in hell has reason to wish so (Matt. xxvi. 24), but no man on earth has reason to wish so, because he knows not but he may yet become a vessel of mercy, much less has any good man reason to wish so. 2. He wished ill to the messenger that brought his father the news of his birth, *v.* 15. He is very fierce in the curses he pronounces (*v.* 16): "*Let him be as the cities of Sodom and Gomorrah, which the Lord utterly overthrew, and repented not. Let him hear the cry* of the invading besieging enemy *in the morning,* as soon as he is stirring; and by noon let him hear their *shouting* for victory. And thus let him live in constant terror." 3. He is angry that he was not *slain from the womb,* that his first breath was not his last, and that he was not strangled as soon as he came into the world, *v.* 17. 4. He thinks his present calamities sufficient to justify these passionate wishes (*v.* 18): "*Wherefore came I forth out of the womb,* where I lay hid, was not hated, where I lay safely and knew no evil, to see all this *labour and sorrow,* to have my *days consumed with shame,* to be continually abused, to have my life wasted and worn away by trouble?"

II. What use we may make of this. It is not recorded for our imitation, and yet we may learn good lessons from it. 1. See the vanity of human life and the vexation of spirit that attends it. 2. See the folly and absurdity of sinful passion, how unreasonably it talks when it is suffered to ramble. What nonsense is it to curse a day—to curse a messenger for the sake of his message! When the heart is hot, let the tongue be bridled, Ps. xxxix. 1, 2.

Chapter 21

The prophecies of this book are not placed here in the same order in which they were preached; for there are chapters after this which concern Jehoahaz, Jehoiakim, and Jeconiah, who all reigned before Zedekiah, in whose reign the prophecy of this chapter bears date. Here is, I. The message which Zedekiah sent to the prophet, to desire him to enquire of the Lord for them, ver. 1, 2. II. The answer which Jeremiah, in God's name, sent to that message, in which, 1. He foretells the certain and inevitable ruin of the city, ver. 3–7. 2. He advises the people to go over to the king of Babylon, ver. 8–10. 3. He advises the king and his family to repent and reform (ver. 11–14).

Verses 1–7

I. A very humble message which king Zedekiah, when he was in distress, sent to Jeremiah the prophet. He humbled himself so far as to desire the prophet's assistance, but not so far as to take his advice, or to be ruled by him.

1. The distress which king Zedekiah was now in: *Nebuchadrezzar made war upon him,* invaded the land, besieged the city, and had now actually invested it.

2. The messengers he sent—*Pashur and Zephaniah.* It would have been better if he had desired a personal conference with the prophet, which he might have had if he would so far have humbled himself. These priests when they were commanded by the king, must carry a respectful message to the prophet, which was a mortification to them and an honour to Jeremiah.

3. The message itself: *Enquire, I pray thee, of the Lord for us, v.* 2. Now that the Chaldean army had got into their borders, they were convinced that Jeremiah was a true prophet, though loth to own it. Under this conviction they desire him to stand their friend with God. "*Enquire of the Lord for us;* ask him what course we shall take in our present strait, for the measures we have hitherto taken are all broken." Those that will not take the direction of God's grace how to get clear of their sins would yet be glad of the directions of his providence how to get clear of their troubles. "*Entreat the Lord for us;* be an intercessor for us with God." *It may be the Lord will deal with us* now *according to the wondrous works he wrought for our fathers,* that the enemy

may raise the siege and *go up from us.* All their care is to get rid of their trouble, not to make their peace with God and be reconciled to him—"That our enemy may *go up from us,*" not, "That our God may return to us." Thus Pharaoh (Exod. x. 17). All their hope is that God had done wondrous works in the deliverance of Jerusalem when Sennacherib besieged it, at the prayer of Isaiah (2 Chron. xxxii. 20, 21), and who can tell but he may destroy these besiegers at the prayer of Jeremiah? But they did not consider how different the character of Zedekiah and his people was from that of Hezekiah and his people: those were days of general reformation and piety, these of general corruption and apostasy.

II. A very startling cutting reply which God, by the prophet, sent to that message. God knows their hearts better than Jeremiah does, and sends them an answer which has scarcely one word of comfort in it. He sends it to them in the name of *the Lord God of Israel* (*v.* 3), to intimate to them that though God allowed himself to be called the *God of Israel,* and had done great things for Israel formerly, and had still great things in store for Israel, yet this should stand the present generation in no stead, who were Israelites in name only. It is here foretold,

1. That God will render all their endeavours for their own security fruitless and ineffectual (*v.* 4).

2. That the besiegers shall in a little time make themselves masters of Jerusalem, and of all its wealth and strength: *I will assemble* those *in the midst of this city* who are now surrounding it.

3. That God himself will be their enemy; and then I know not who can befriend them, no, not Jeremiah himself (*v.* 5). Those who rebel against God may justly expect that he will make war upon them.

4. That those who, for their own safety, decline sallying out upon the besiegers, and so avoid their sword, shall yet not escape the sword of God's justice (*v.* 6): *I will smite those that abide in the city, both man and beast; they shall die of a great pestilence.*

5. That the king himself, and all the people that escape the *sword, famine,* and *pestilence,* shall fall *into the hands* of the Chaldeans (*v.* 7): They *shall not spare them,* nor *have pity* on them.

Verses 8–14

By the civil message which the king sent to Jeremiah it appeared that both he and the people began to have a respect for him; but the reply which God obliges him to make is enough to crush the little respect they begin to have for him, and to exasperate them against him more than ever. Not only the predictions in the foregoing verses, but the prescriptions in these, were provoking.

I. He advises the people to surrender to the Chaldeans, as the only means left to save their lives, *v.* 8–10. This counsel was displeasing to those who were flattered by their false prophets into a desperate resolution to hold out to the last, trusting to the strength of their walls and the courage of their soldiery, or to their foreign aids to raise the siege. The prophet assures them, "*The city shall be given into the hand of the king of Babylon,* and he shall not only plunder it, but *burn it with fire,* for God himself hath *set his face against this city for evil and not for good*; and therefore, if you would make the best of bad, you must beg quarter of the Chaldeans, and surrender prisoners of war." It was the best course they could take now that God was against them. Both the law and the prophets had often set before them life and death in another sense—life if they obey the voice of God, death if they persist in disobedience, Deut. xxx. 19. The expression (*v.* 8): *Behold, I set before you the way of life and the way of death,* denotes not, as that, a fair proposal, but a melancholy dilemma, advising them of two evils to choose the less. *He that abides in the city* shall certainly die either by *the sword* without the walls or *famine* or *pestilence* within. But he that can quit his vain hopes, go out, and fall *to the Chaldeans, his life shall be given him for a prey*; he shall save his life, as a prey is taken from the mighty. They thought to make a prey of the camp of the Chaldeans, as their ancestors did that of the Assyrians (Isa. xxxiii. 23), but if by yielding at discretion they can but save their lives, that is all the prey they must promise themselves.

II. He advises the king and princes to reform. In the reply there was a particular word for *the house of the king* to give them wholesome counsel (*v.* 11, 12): "*Execute judgment in the morning;* do it carefully and diligently. Do it quickly, and do not delay to do justice upon appeals made to you. You would be delivered out of the hand of those that distress you, and expect that God should do you justice; see then that you do justice to those that apply to you, and *deliver them out of the hand of their oppressors, lest my fury go out like fire,* and you fare worst who think to escape best, *because of the evil of your doings.*" It was the *evil of their doings* that kindled the fire of God's wrath. Thus plainly does he deal even with the *house of the king*; for those that would have the benefit of a prophet's prayers must thankfully take a prophet's reproofs. The princes must begin, and set a good example, and then the people will be invited to reform. They must use their power for the punishment of wrong, and then the people will be obliged to reform. He reminds them that they are *the house of David,* and therefore should tread in his steps, who executed judgment and justice to his people.

III. He shows them the vanity of all their hopes so long as they continued unreformed, *v.* 13, 14. Jerusalem is an *inhabitant of the valley,* guarded with mountains on all sides, which were their natural fortifications, making it difficult for an army to approach them. It is a *rock of the plain,* which made it difficult for an enemy to undermine them. These advantages they trusted to more than to the power and promise of God; and, thinking their city impregnable, they set the judgments of God at defiance, saying, "*Who shall come down against us?*" God soon shows the vanity of that challenge, *Who shall come down against us?* when he says (*v.* 13), *Behold, I am against thee.* He comes against them as a judge that cannot be resisted; for he says (*v.* 14), *I will punish you,* by due course of law, *according to the fruit of your doings.*

CHAPTER 22

Sermons which Jeremiah preached at court, in some preceding reigns, that it might appear they had had fair warning. I. A message sent to the royal family, as it should seem in the reign of Jehoiakim, relating partly to Jehoahaz, who was carried away captive into Egypt, and partly to Jehoiakim, who succeeded him and was now upon the throne, ver. 1–9. Jehoahaz, called here Shallum, is lamented, ver. 10–12. Jehoiakim is reproved and threatened, ver. 13–19. II. Another message sent them in the reign of Jehoiachin (alias, Jeconiah) the son of Jehoiakim. He is charged with an obstinate refusal to hear, and it is foretold that in him Solomon's house should fail, ver. 20–30.

Verses 1–9

I. Orders given to Jeremiah to go and preach before the king (*v.* 2): *Hear the word of the Lord, O king of Judah!* The *king of Judah* is here spoken to *as sitting upon the throne of David,* who was a man after God's own heart, as holding his dignity and power by the covenant made with David; let him therefore conform to his example, that he may have the benefit of the promises made to him.

II. Instructions given him what to preach.

1. He must tell them what the Lord their God required of them, *v.* 3. They must take care, (1) That they do all the good they can with the power they have. They must do justice in defence of those

that were injured. (2) That they do no hurt with it. They must *do no wrong to the stranger, fatherless, and widow;* for these God does in a particular manner take under his tuition, Exod. xxii. 21, 22.

2. He must assure them that the faithful discharge of their duty would advance their prosperity, *v.* 4. There shall then be an uninterrupted succession, *upon the throne of David,* enjoying tranquillity, and living in dignity. The most effectual way to preserve the dignity of the government is to do the duty of it.

3. He must likewise assure them that the iniquity, if they persisted in it, would be the ruin of their family (*v.* 5). Sin has often been the ruin of royal palaces, though ever so stately, ever so strong. Sin will be the ruin of the houses of princes as well as of mean men.

4. He must show how fatal their wickedness would be to their kingdom as well as to themselves, to Jerusalem especially, the royal city, *v.* 6–9. Judah and Jerusalem had been valuable in God's eyes: *Thou art Gilead unto me and the head of Lebanon.* Their lot was cast in a place that was rich and pleasant as Gilead; Zion was a stronghold, as stately as Lebanon: this they trusted their security. But the country that is now fruitful as Gilead shall be made *a wilderness.* The cities that are now strong as Lebanon shall be cities *not inhabited.* There shall be those that shall do it effectually (*v.* 7): "*I will prepare destroyers against thee;* I will *sanctify* them" (so the word is). And who can contend with destroyers of God's preparing? There shall be those who shall be ready to justify God in the doing of it (*v.* 8, 9); persons of *many nations,* when they *pass by* the ruins of *this city* in their travels, will ask, "*Wherefore hath the Lord done thus unto this city?*" Ask the next man you meet, and he will tell you it was because they changed their gods. God never casts any off until they first cast him off.

Verses 10–19

1. Here is the doom of Shallum, who doubtless is the same with Jehoahaz, for he is that son of Josiah king of Judah who reigned *in the stead of Josiah his father* (*v.* 11), which Jehoahaz did by the act of the people, who made him king though he was not the eldest son, 2 Kings xxiii. 30; 2 Chron. xxxvi. 1. Perhaps the people preferred him before his elder brother because they thought him a more active young man, and fitter to rule; but God soon showed them the folly of their injustice, for within three months the king of Egypt came upon him, deposed him, and carried him away prisoner into Egypt, as God had threatened, Deut. xxviii. 68. It does not appear that any of the people were taken into captivity with him. We have the story 2 Kings xxiii. 34; 2 Chron. xxxvi. 4. Now here, 1. The people are directed to lament him rather than his father Josiah: "*Weep not for the dead,* weep not any more for Josiah." Jeremiah had been himself a true mourner for him (2 Chron. xxxv. 25): yet now he will have them to turn their tears into another channel. They must weep sorely for Jehoahaz, who had gone into Egypt. Josiah went to the grave in peace and honour. *Weep not for him,* but for his unhappy son, who is likely to live and die in disgrace and misery, a wretched captive. Dying saints may be justly envied, while living sinners are justly pitied. He shall never return out of captivity, as he and his people expected, but shall die there. They were loth to believe this, therefore it is repeated here again and again. This came of his forsaking the good example of his father, and usurping the right of his elder brother.

II. The doom of Jehoiakim, who succeeded him. He ruled no better, and fared no better at last.

1. His sins reproved. Jehoiakim is not here charged with idolatry, but the crimes for which he is here

reproved are pride, and affection and splendour; as if all the business of a king were to look great, and to do good were to be the least of his care. He must build himself a stately palace, a *wide house*, and *large chambers*, *v.* 14. He must have *windows cut out* after the newest fashion. The rooms must be *ceiled with cedar*, the richest sort of wood, painted with *minium*, or *vermilion*, or as some read it, with *indigo*. Those therefore that are enlarging their houses, and making them more sumptuous, have need to look well to the frame of their own spirits in the doing of it, and carefully to watch against vain-glory. He reigned his first three years by the permission of the king of Egypt, and all the rest by the permission of the king of Babylon; and yet he that was no better than a viceroy will covet to vie with the greatest monarchs. He thought he must reign without any disturbance or interruption because he had *enclosed himself in cedar* (*v.* 15). Some think he is here charged with sacrilege, and robbing the house of God to beautify and adorn his own house. He *cuts him out my windows* (so it is in the margin), which some understand as if he had taken windows out of the temple to put into his own palace and then *painted them with vermilion*, that it might not be discovered. He is here charged with extortion and oppression, violence and injustice. He *built his house by unrighteousness*, with money unjustly got and materials not honestly come by. God takes notice of the wrong done by the greatest of men to their poor servants and labourers, and will repay those, in justice, that will not in justice pay those whom they employ. That which was at the bottom of all was covetousness, that love of *money which is the root of all evil*. *Thy eyes and thy heart are not but for covetousness;* for that, and nothing else. In covetousness the heart walks after the eyes: it is therefore called *the lust of the eye*, 1 John ii. 16; Job xxxi. 7. That which aggravated all his sins was that he was the son of a good father, who had left him a good example, if he would but have followed it (*v.* 15, 16). Jeremiah tells him he was directed to do his duty by his father's practice: He *did judgment and justice*. He not only did not abuse his power for the support of wrong, but he used it for the maintaining of right. He *judged the cause of the poor and needy*. He was encouraged to do his duty by his father's prosperity. God accepted him: "*Was not this to know me, saith the Lord?*" He had the comfort of it *Did he not eat and drink* soberly and cheerfully, so as to fit himself for his business, *for strength and not for drunkenness?* Eccles. x. 17. God blessed him with plenty, and he had the comfortable enjoyment of it himself and was hospitable and very charitable. It was Jehoiakim's pride that he had built a fine house, but Josiah's true praise that he kept a good house. It is better to live with Josiah in an old-fashioned house, and do good, than live with Jehoiakim in a stately house, and leave debts unpaid.

2. Jehoiakim's doom faithfully read, *v.* 18, 19. We may suppose that it was in peril of his own life that Jeremiah here foretold the shameful death of Jehoiakim; but *thus saith the Lord concerning* him and therefore thus saith he. He shall die unlamented; he shall make himself so odious by his oppression and cruelty that none shall do him the honour of dropping one tear for him. His relations shall not *lament him*. His subjects shall not lament him, as they used to do at the graves of their princes. Jehoiakim shall be *buried with the burial of an ass*, that is, he shall have no burial at all, but his dead body shall be cast into a ditch or upon a dunghill; it shall be *drawn*, or dragged, ignominiously, and *cast forth beyond the gates of Jerusalem*. Josephus says that Nebuchadnezzar slew him at Jerusalem, and left his body thus exposed, somewhere at a great distance from the *gates of Jerusalem*.

Verses 20–30

This prophecy seems to have been calculated for the inglorious reign of Jeconiah, or Jehoiachin, the son of Jehoiakim, who reigned but three months, and was then carried captive to Babylon, where he lived many years, *ch.* lii. 31.

I. The desolations of the kingdom were now hastening on apace, *v.* 20–23. Jerusalem and Judah are here spoken to as a single person, "*I spoke unto thee in thy prosperity*, spoke by my servants the prophets, reproofs, admonitions, counsels, *but thou saidest, I will not hear*." It is common for those that live at ease to live in contempt of the word of God. *This has been thy manner from thy youth*. "When thou seest *all thy lovers destroyed*, when thou findest thy idols unable to help thee and thy foreign alliances failing thee, thou wilt cry, *Help, help, or we are lost;* thou wilt *lift up thy voice* in fearful shrieks upon *Lebanon* and *Bashan*. Thou wilt *cry from the passages*, from the roads. Thou wilt cry to all about thee; but in vain, for (*v.* 22) *the wind shall eat up all thy pastors*, that should provide for thy safety; they shall be blasted, and withered, as buds and blossoms are by a bleak or freezing wind. *Thy lovers*, that thou hast an affection for, shall *go into captivity*, and shall not be able to save themselves. When there appears no relief from any of thy confederates, *then shalt thou be ashamed and confounded for all thy wickedness*," *v.* 22. The Jewish state is here called *an inhabitant of Lebanon*, because that famous forest was within their border (*v.* 23), and all their country was well-guarded as with Lebanon's natural fastnesses; but so proud were they that they are said to *make their nest in the cedars*, out of the reach of all danger, whence they looked with contempt upon all about them. "But, *how gracious wilt thou be when pangs come upon thee!* Then thou wilt humble thyself before God and promise amendment." Some give another sense of it: "What will all thy pomp and wealth avail thee? No more than *a woman in travail*, full of pains and fears, can take comfort in her ornaments while she is in that condition."

II. Here is a prophecy of the disgrace of the king; his name was *Jeconiah*, but he is here once and again called *Coniah*, in contempt. He shall be carried away *into captivity* and shall spend and end his days in bondage. God will abandon him, *v.* 24. "*Though he were the signet upon my right hand I will pluck him thence*." The godly kings of Judah had been as signets on God's right hand, near and dear to him; he had gloried in them. The king of Babylon shall seize him. *Those* know not what mischiefs they lie exposed to who have thrown themselves out of God's protection, *v.* 25. The Chaldeans had a spite to *Coniah*; they *sought his life* (they are those *whose face thou fearest*). He and his family shall be carried to Babylon, where they shall wear out many tedious years in a miserable captivity—*he and his mother* (*v.* 26), *he and his seed* (*v.* 28), that is, he and all the royal family—shall all be cast out to another country, *a country where they were not born, a land which they know not*, in which they have no acquaintance from whom to expect any kindness. *To the land whereunto they desire to return, thither shall they not return, v.* 27. Jehoahaz was carried to Egypt, the land of the south, Jeconiah to Babylon, the land of the north, never to meet again, nor to breathe their native air. There is something very emphatic in that part of this threatening (*v.* 26), *In the country where you were not born, there shall you die*. This shall render him despicable in the eyes of all his neighbours. They shall be ready to say (*v.* 28), "*Is this Coniah a despised broken idol?*" Time was when he was dignified, nay, when he was almost deified. The people who had seen his father lately deposed were ready to adore him when they saw him upon the throne, but now *he is a despised broken idol.* He shall leave no posterity to inherit his honour. Let all the world notice these judgments of God upon a nation and a family that had been near and dear to him, and thence infer that God is impartial in the administration of justice. Now that which is here to be taken notice of is that Jeconiah is *written childless* (*v.* 30), that is, as it follows, *No man of his seed shall prosper, sitting upon the throne of David.* Some think that he had children born in Babylon (*v.* 28) and that they died before him. We read in the genealogy (1 Chron. iii. 17) of seven sons of Jeconiah Assir (that is, Jeconiah the captive) of whom Salathiel is the first. Some think that they were only his adopted sons, and that when it is said (Matt. i. 12), *Jeconiah begat Salathiel,* no more is meant than that he bequeathed to him what claims he had to the government, because Salathiel is called the *son of Neri* of *the house of Nathan,* Luke iii. 27, 31. Whether he had children begotten, or only adopted, none of his seed ruled as kings in Judah.

CHAPTER 23

The prophet, in God's name, is dealing his reproofs. I. Among the careless princes, or pastors of the people (ver. 1, 2), yet promising to take care of the flock, ver. 3–8. II. Among the wicked prophets and priests, imposing upon the people with their pretended inspirations, for which they must expect to be punished, ver. 9–32. III. Among the profane people, who ridiculed God's prophets, ver. 33–40.

Verses 1–8

I. A word of terror to the negligent shepherds. *Woe be to the pastors* (to the *rulers,* both in church and state) who should be pastors to lead them, feed them, protect them, and take care of them. They are not owners of the sheep. God here calls them *the sheep of my pasture,* whom I have provided good pasture for. Woe be to those therefore who are commanded to feed God's people, and pretend to do it, but who, instead of that, *scatter the flock* by their violence and oppression. In not visiting them they did in effect drive them away. The beasts of prey scattered them, and the shepherds are in the fault, who should have kept them together.

II. A word of comfort to the neglected sheep. Though the under-shepherds take no care of them, the chief Shepherd will look after them. God will perform his promise, though those he employs do not perform their duty.

1. The dispersed Jews shall at length return to their own land, and be happily settled there under a good government, *v.* 3, 4. Though there be but a remnant of God's flock left, he will gather that remnant wherever they are and bring them back out of all countries *whither he had driven them. They shall be brought* to their former habitations, as sheep to their folds, and there *they shall be fruitful, and increase* in numbers. Formerly they were continually disturbed, but now *they shall fear no more, nor be dismayed.* Such pastors as Zerubbabel and Nehemiah, though they lived not in the pomp that Jehoiakim and Jeconiah did, were as great blessings to the people as the others were plagues to them.

2. Messiah the Prince, that great and good Shepherd of the sheep, shall in the latter days be raised up to bless his church, and to be *the glory of his people Israel,* v. 5, 6. The house of David seemed to be ruined by that threatening against Jeconiah (*ch.* xxii. 30). But here is a promise which effectually secures the honour of the covenant made with David; for by it the house will be raised out of its ruins to a greater lustre than ever. We have not so many prophecies of Christ in this book as we had in that of the prophet Isaiah; but here we have a very illustrious one. The first words intimate that it would be long ere this promise should have its accomplishment: *The days come,* but they are not yet. *I shall see him, but not now.* Christ is here spoken of as a *branch from David,* his appearance mean, his beginnings small, like those of a bud, and his rise seemingly out of the earth, but growing to be loaded with fruits. A branch from David's family, when it seemed to be a *root in a dry ground,* buried, and not likely to revive. In him doth the *horn of David bud,* Ps. cxxxii. 17, 18. He is *a righteous branch,* for he is righteous himself, and through him many, even all that are his, are made righteous. As an advocate, he is *Jesus Christ the righteous.* He is here spoken of as his church's King. He shall set up a kingdom in the world that shall be victorious over all opposition. In the chariot of the everlasting gospel he shall go forth, he shall go on *conquering and to conquer.* Christ shall, by his gospel, break the usurped power of Satan, institute a perfect rule of holy living, and, as far as it prevails, make all the world righteous. The effect of this shall be a holy security and serenity of mind in all his faithful loyal subjects. *In his days,* under his dominion, *Judah shall be saved and Israel shall dwell safely.* See Luke i. 74, 75. In the days of Christ's government in the soul, when he is uppermost there, the soul *dwells at ease.* He is *the Lord of our righteousness.* As God, he is *Jehovah,* the incommunicable name of God, denoting his eternity and self-existence. As Mediator, he is *our righteousness.* By making satisfaction to the justice of God for the sin of man, he has brought in an everlasting righteousness, and so made it over to us in the covenant of grace that, upon our consent to that covenant, it becomes ours. He is a sovereign, all-sufficient, eternal righteousness. All our righteousness has its being from him, and by him it subsists. *This is the name whereby he shall be called,* not only he shall be so, but he shall be known to be so. That is our righteousness by which we are justified before God, acquitted from guilt, and accepted into favour; and nothing else have we to plead but this, "Christ has died, yea, rather has risen again"; and we have taken him for our Lord.

3. This great salvation, which will come to the Jews in the latter days, after their return out of Babylon, shall far outshine the deliverance of Israel out of Egypt (*v.* 7, 8): *They shall no more say, The Lord liveth that brought up Israel out of Egypt; but, The Lord liveth that brought them up out of the north.* After they came out of Babylon Messiah the Prince set up the gospel temple, the greatest glory of that nation that was so wonderfully brought out of Babylon.

Verses 9–32

A long lesson for the false prophets. The prophet had complained to God of those false prophets (*ch.* xiv. 13), and had often foretold that they should be involved in the common ruin; but here they have woes of their own.

I. He expresses what a trouble it was to him to see men who pretended to a divine commission and inspiration ruining themselves, and the people among whom they dwelt, by their falsehood and treachery (*v.* 9): *My heart within me is broken; I am like a drunken man.* Jeremiah was a man that laid things much to heart, and what was any way threatening to his country made a deep impression upon his spirits. He is here in trouble, 1. *Because of the prophets* and their sin, the false doctrine they preached, the wicked lives they lived, pretending to have their instructions from him. 2. *"Because of the Lord, and his judgments,* which by this means are brought in upon us like a deluge."* He trembled to think of the ruin and desolation which were coming *from the face of the Lord* (so the word is) *and from the face of the word of his holiness.*

II. He laments the abounding abominable wickedness of the land and the present tokens of God's displeasure they were under for it (*v.* 10): *The land is full of adulterers;* it is full both of spiritual and corporal whoredom. Their land mourned now under the judgment of famine; the *pleasant places,* or rather *the pastures,* are dried up for want of rain, and yet we see no signs of repentance. They have a great deal of resolution, but it is turned the wrong way; they are *zealously affected,* but not *in a good thing,* though they see God thus contending with them.

III. He charges it all upon the prophets and priests, especially the prophets. They are *both profane* (*v.* 11); the priests profane the ordinances of God they pretend to administer; the prophets profane the word of God they pretend to deliver. They both *play the hypocrite* (so some read it); under sacred pretensions they carry on the vilest designs; *in my house have I found their wickedness;* in the temple, where the priests ministered, where the prophets prophesied, there were they guilty both of idolatry and immorality. Two things are charged upon them: 1. That they taught people to sin by their examples. He compares them with the prophets of Samaria, the head city of the kingdom of the ten tribes, which had been long since laid waste. It was the folly of the prophets of Samaria that *they prophesied in Baal,* in Baal's name; and so *they caused my people Israel to err,* to forsake the service of the true God and to worship Baal, *v.* 13. Now the prophets of Jerusalem did not do so; they prophesied in the name of the true God, and valued themselves upon that, that they were not like the prophets of Samaria, who prophesied in Baal; but they debauched the nation as much by their im moralities as the other had done by their idolatries! They make use of the name and the holy God, and yet wallow in all manner of impurity. They make use of the name of the God of truth, and yet *walk in lies.* Thus they encourage sinners for everyone will say, "Surely we may do as the prophets do; who can expect that we should be better than our teachers?" By this means Judah and Jerusalem have become *as Sodom and Gomorrah,* and God looked upon them accordingly as fit for nothing but to be destroyed. 2. That they encouraged people in sin by their false prophecies. They made themselves believe that there was no harm, no danger in sin, and practised accord ingly (*v.* 16): *They speak a vision of their own heart;* it is *not out of the mouth of the Lord.* They tell sinners that it shall be well with them though they persist in their sins, *v.* 17. Those that are devoted to their pleas ures put contempt upon their God. These prophets flattered them: they should have been still saying, There is no peace to those that go on in their evil ways, but they still said, *You shall have peace; no evil shall come upon you;* and, which was worst of all, they told them, *God has said so.*

IV. God disowns all that these false prophets said to sooth people in their sins (*v.* 21): *I have not sent these prophets;* they never had any mission from God. Yet they were very forward—*they ran;* they were very bold—*they prophesied* without any of that difficulty with which the true prophets sometimes struggled. They said to sinners, *You shall have peace.* But (*v.* 18): "*Who hath stood in the counsel of the Lord?* You deliver this message with a great deal of assurance; but have you consulted God about it? You have not *perceived and heard his word,* you have not compared this with the scripture; if you had taken notice of the constant tenor of it, you would never have delivered such a message." That they did not *stand in God's counsel* nor *hear his word* is proved afterwards, *v.* 22. *If they had stood in my counsel,* as they pretended, 1. They would have made the scriptures their standard: *They would have caused my people to hear my words.* 2. They would have made the conversion of souls their business, and would have aimed at that in all their preaching. 3. They

would have had some seals of their ministry. *If they had stood in my counsel,* and the words they had preached had been *my words,* then they should have *turned from their evil way.*

V. God threatens to punish these prophets for their wickedness. They promised the people *peace;* and to show them the folly of that God tells them that they should have no peace themselves. Evil is coming upon themselves and they are not aware of it, *v.* 12. Because the prophets and priests are profane, *there fore their ways shall be unto them as slippery ways in the darkness.* They pretend to show others the way, but they shall themselves be in the dark, or in a mist. They pretend to give assurances to others, but they themselves shall find no firm footing. They pretend to make the people easy with their flatteries, but they shall themselves be uneasy: *They shall be driven,* making their escape, *they shall fall in the way.* They pretend to prevent the evil that threatens others, but God will *bring evil upon them, even the year of their visitation. The year of visitation* is the year of recompenses. It is further threatened (*v.* 15), *I will feed them with wormwood,* which is not only nauseous, but noxious, and *make them drink waters of gall,* or (as some read it) *juice of hemlock;* see *ch.* ix. 15.

VI. The people are here warned not to give any credit to these false prophets (*v.* 16): "Take notice of what God says, and *hearken not to the words of these prophets;* for you will find that God's word shall stand, and not theirs. They tell you, *No evil shall come upon you;* but hear what God says (*v.* 19), *Behold, a whirlwind of the Lord has gone forth in fury.* They tell you, All shall be calm and serene; but God tells you, There is a storm coming, a *whirl wind of the Lord,* there is no standing before it." This sentence is irreversible (*v.* 20): *The anger of the Lord shall not return.* God will not alter his mind, nor suffer his anger to be turned away, *till he have executed* the sentence and *performed the thoughts of his heart.* This they will not consider now; but *in the latter days you shall consider it perfectly,* consider it *with under standing* (so the word is) or *with consideration.*

VII. Several things are here offered to the con sideration of these false prophets that they might be brought to recant their error.

1. Let them consider that though they may impose upon men God is too wise to be imposed upon.

(1) God asserts his own omnipresence and omni science in general, *v.* 23, 24. Though God's throne is prepared in the heavens, and this earth seems to be at a distance from him, yet he is a God here in this lower world, *v.* 23. The eye of God is the same on earth that it is in heaven. The power of God is the same on earth among its inhabitants that it is in heaven. With us nearness and distance make a great difference both in our observations and in our operations, but it is not so with God; to him darkness and light, at hand and afar off, are both alike. Men's char acters and counsels cannot possibly be concealed from God's all-seeing eye (*v.* 24): "*Can any hide him self in the secret places?* Can any hide his projects and intentions in the secret places of the heart, that I shall not see them?" He is everywhere present; he does not only rule heaven and earth, but he *fills heaven and earth* by his essential presence, Ps. cxxxix. 7, 8, &c. No place can either include him or exclude him.

(2) He applies this to these prophets, who had a notable art of disguising themselves (*v.* 25, 26). God will make them know that he knows all the shame they have put upon the world, under colour of divine revelation. God discovered the fraud. *Is it in the hearts of those prophets* (so some read it) *to be ever prophesying lies and prophesying the deceits of their own hearts?*

2. Let them consider that their palming upon people counterfeit revelations, and fathering their own fancies upon divine inspiration, was the ready way to bring all religion into contempt and make men turn atheists and infidels. *Thus saith the Lord, They think to cause my people to forget my name by their dreams.* The great thing Satan aims at is to make people forget God, and all that whereby he has made himself known. Sometimes he does it by setting up false gods (bring men in love with Baal, and they soon forget the name of God), sometimes by misrepresenting the true God.

3. Let them consider what a vast difference there was between their prophecies and those that were delivered by the true prophets of the Lord (*v.* 28): *The prophet that has a dream, let him tell it as a dream.* "Let him lay no more stress upon it than men do upon their dreams, nor expect any more regard to be had to it. But let the true prophet, that *has my word, speak my word faithfully,* speak it *as a truth*" (so some read it): "let him keep closely to his instructions, and you will soon perceive a vast difference between the dreams that the false prophets tell and the divine dictates which the true prophets deliver. Those that have spiritual senses exercised will be able to distinguish; for *what is the chaff to the wheat?*" Men's fancies are light and worthless, as the chaff *which the wind drives away.* But the word of God has substance in it; it is of value, is food for the soul, the bread of life. *Is not my word like a fire, saith the Lord?* Is their word so? Has it the power and efficacy that the word of God has? Fire has different effects, according as the matter is on which it works; it hardens clay, but softens wax; it consumes the dross, but purifies the gold. So the word of God is to some *a savour of life unto life, to others of death unto death.* It is compared likewise to a *hammer breaking the rock in pieces.* The unhumbled heart of man is like a rock; if it will not be melted by the word of God as the fire, it will be broken to pieces by it as the hammer.

4. Let them consider that while they went on in this course God was against them. Three times they are told this, *v.* 30, 31, 32. They stand indicted here. *They steal my word everyone from his neighbour.* Those that were strangers to the spirit of the true prophets mimicked their language, picked up some good sayings of theirs, and delivered them to the people as if they had been their own, but with an ill grace. Others understand it of the word of God as it was received by some of the people; they stole it out of their hearts, as the wicked one in the parable is said to steal the good seed of the word, Matt. xiii. 19. By their insinuations they diminished the authority, and so weakened the efficacy, of the word of God upon the minds of those that seemed to be under convictions by it. God is against them (*v.* 31), because they *use their tongues* at their pleasure in their discourses to the people, and then father it upon God, and say, He saith it. Some read it, *They smooth their tongues;* they are very complaisant to the people, and say nothing but what is pleasing and plausible. They stand indicted as common cheats (*v.* 32): *I am against them,* for they *prophesy false dreams,* pretending that to be a divine inspiration which is but an invention of their own. It is the people's fault that they err, that they take things upon trust, but it is much more the prophets' fault that they cause God's people to *err by their lies and by their lightness.* God disowns their having any commission from him: *I sent them not, nor commanded them;* they are not God's messengers. *Therefore they shall not profit this people at all.*

Verses 33–40

The profaneness of the people, of the priests and prophets, is here reproved in a particular instance, which may seem of small moment, but profaneness in common discourse, and the debauching of the language of a nation, is a notorious evidence of the prevalency of wickedness in it.

I. The sin here charged upon them is bantering God's prophets and the dialect they used. They asked, *What is the burden of the Lord?* (*v.* 33 and *v.* 34). This was the word that gave great offence to God, that, whenever they spoke of *the word of the Lord,* they called it, in scorn and derision, *the burden of the Lord.* This was a word that the prophets much used, and used it seriously, to show what a weight the word of God was upon their spirits. Now the profane scoffers took this word, and made a jest of it. The mocking of God's messengers was the baffling of his messages. Some think that when the *word of the Lord* is called a *burden* it signifies some word of reproof and threatening. In using this word *the burden of the Lord* in a canting way they reflected upon God as always bearing hard upon them, always frightening them, and so making the word of God a perpetual uneasiness to them. Those that were guilty of this sin were some of the false prophets, some of the priests and some of the people, who had learned of the profane priests and prophets to play with the things of God.

II. When they are reproved for this profane way of speaking they are directed how to express themselves decently. We find it used long after this (Zech. ix. 1; Mal. i. 1; Nah. i. 1; Hab. i. 1). But here God will have the prophet keep to his rule (*ch.* xv. 19). Do not thou leave off using this word, but let them leave off abusing it. You *shall not mention the burden of the Lord any more* in this profane careless manner (*v.* 36). How then must they express themselves? He tells them (*v.* 37): *Thus shalt thou say to the prophet,* when thou art enquiring of him, *What hath the Lord answered thee? And what hath the Lord spoken?* And they must say thus when they enquire of *their neighbours, v.* 35.

III. They would still say, *The burden of the Lord,* though God had sent to them to forbid them, *v.* 38. Those shall be severely reckoned with that thus *pervert the words of God,* that put a wrong construction on them. It is a great provocation to God to mock his messengers *v.* 34. *Every man's word shall be his own burden;* that is, the guilt of this sin shall be heavy upon him. God will give them enough of their jest, so that it will be too heavy to make a jest of. Do they ask, *What is the burden of the Lord?* Let the prophet ask them, *What burden* do you mean? Is it this: *I will even forsake you? v.* 33. This is the burden that shall be laid and bound upon them (*v.* 39, 40): "*Behold I, even I, will utterly forget you, and I will forsake you.*" God's word will be magnified and made honourable when those that mock at it shall be vilified and made contemptible.

Chapter 24

In the close of the foregoing chapter we had a general prediction of the utter ruin of Jerusalem, which made the prophet himself melancholy. Now, in this chapter, God encourages him, by showing him that, though the desolation seemed to be universal, yet all were not equally involved in it, but God knew how to distinguish between the precious and the vile. Some had gone into captivity already with Jeconiah; but God tells him that it should turn to their good. Others remained hardened in their sins, but those, God tells him, should go into captivity. To inform the prophet of this, he had, I. A vision of two baskets of figs, one very good and the other very bad, ver. 1–3. II. The explication of this vision, applying the good figs to those that were already sent into captivity for their good (ver. 4–7), the bad figs to those that should hereafter be sent into captivity for their hurt, ver. 8–10.

Verses 1–10

This short chapter helps us to put a comfortable construction upon many long ones, by showing us that the same providence which to some is a *savour* of death unto death may by the grace of God be made to others a *savour of life unto life*; and that, though God's people share with others in the same calamity, yet it is designed for their good; it is a correcting rod in the hand of a tender Father.

I. The date of this sermon. It was a little after Jeconiah's captivity, *v.* 1. Jeconiah was himself a *despised broken vessel*, but with him were carried away some very valuable persons, Ezekiel for one (Ezek. i. 12); many of the *princes of Judah* went into captivity; of the people only *the carpenters and the smiths* were forced away, because the Chaldeans needed men of those trades (they had plenty of astrologers and stargazers, but a great scarcity of smiths and carpenters). There were many good people carried away in that captivity, which the prophet laid to heart, while there were those that triumphed in it, and insulted over those to whose lot it fell to go into captivity.

II. The vision by which this distinction of the captives was represented to the prophet's mind. He saw *two baskets of figs, set before the temple*, ready to be offered as first-fruits to the honour of God. The figs in one basket were extraordinarily good, those in the other basket extremely bad. The children of men are all as the fruits of the fig-tree, capable of being made serviceable to God and man (Judges ix. 11); but some are as good figs, than which nothing is more pleasant, others as damaged rotten figs, than which nothing is more nauseous. The good figs were like those that are first ripe, which are most acceptable (Mic. vii. 1) and most prized. The bad figs are such as could *not be eaten, they were so evil*; were neither pleasant nor good for food. If God has no honour from men, nor their generation any service, they are like the bad figs, that cannot be eaten, that will not answer any good purpose. Of the persons that are presented to the Lord at the door of his tabernacle, some are sincere, and they are very good; others dissemble with God, and they are very bad.

III. The exposition and application of this vision. God intended by it to raise the dejected spirit of those that had gone into captivity, by assuring them of a happy return, and to humble and awaken the proud spirits of those who continued yet in Jerusalem, by assuring them of a miserable captivity.

1. The moral of the good figs, the first ripe. These represented the pious captives, that seemed first ripe for ruin, for they went first into captivity, but should prove first ripe for mercy, and their captivity should help to ripen them; these are pleasing to God and shall be carefully preserved. When God's judgments are abroad those are not always the worst that are first seized by them. Early suffering sometimes proves for the best. The sooner the child is corrected the better effect the correction is likely to have. Those that went first into captivity were as the son whom the *father loves, and chastens betimes*, chastens while there is hope. But those that stayed behind were like a child long *left to himself*, who, when afterwards corrected, is stubborn, and made worse, Lam. iii. 27. God owns their captivity to be his doing (*v.* 5): *I have sent them out of this place into the land of the Chaldeans.* It is God that puts his gold into the furnace, to be tried; his hand is, in a special manner, in the afflictions of good people. The judge orders the malefactor into the hand of an executioner, but the father corrects the child with his own hand. It seemed to be every way for their hurt, not only as it was the ruin of their estates and liberties, but as it sunk their spirits, discouraged their faith, deprived them of the benefit of God's oracles and ordinances, and exposed them to temptations; and yet it was designed for their good, and proved so. By their afflictions they were convinced of sin, humbled under the hand of God, weaned from the world, taught to

pray, and turned from their iniquity. The scornful relations they left behind will scarcely own them, but God says, *I will acknowledge them.* Being sent into captivity *for their good*, they shall not be lost there; but it shall be with them as it is with gold which the refiner puts into the furnace. He has his eye upon it while it is there, and it is a careful eye, to see that it sustain no damage: "*I will set my eyes upon them for good.*" He will take it out of the furnace again as soon as the work designed is done: *I will bring them again to this land.* They were sent abroad for improvement under a severe discipline; but they shall be fetched back to their Father's house. He will fashion his gold when he has refined it, will make it a vessel of honour fit for his use; so, when God has brought them back from their trial, he *will build them* and make them a habitation for himself, will *plant them* and make them a vineyard for himself. Their captivity was to square the rough stones and make them fit for his building, to prune up the young trees and make them fit for his planting. He engages to prepare them for these temporal mercies which he designed for them by bestowing spiritual mercies upon them, *v.* 7. They should learn more of God by his providences in Babylon than they had learned by all his oracles and ordinances in Jerusalem. It is here promised, *I will give them*, not so much a head to know me, but *a heart to know me. They shall return to me with their whole heart.* God himself undertakes for them that they shall; and, if he turn us, we shall be turned. Thus they should be again taken into covenant with God: *They shall be my people, and I will be their God.* Those that have backslidden from God, if they do in sincerity return to him, are admitted as freely as any to all the privileges and comforts of the everlasting covenant.

2. The moral of the bad figs. *Zedekiah and his princes* and partisans *yet remain in the land*, proud and secure enough, Ezek. xi. 3. Many had fled into Egypt, for shelter, and their own safety, and boasted that though therein they had gone contrary to the command of God yet they had acted prudently for themselves. Now as to these, that looked so scornfully upon those that had gone into captivity, it is here threatened, (1) That, whereas those who were already carried away were settled in one country, where they had the comfort of one another's society, these should be dispersed *and removed into all the kingdoms of the earth.* (2) That, whereas those were carried captives for their good, these should be removed into all countries *for their hurt.* Their afflictions should harden them; not bring them nearer to God, but set them at a greater distance from him. (3) That, whereas those should have the honour of being owned of God in their troubles, these should have the shame of being abandoned by all mankind: *In all places whither I shall drive them they shall be a reproach and a proverb.* (4) That, whereas those should *return to their own land*, these should be *consumed from that land*, never to see it more. (5) That, whereas those were reserved for better times, these were reserved for worse; wherever they are removed *the sword, and famine, and pestilence*, shall be sent after them. It is probable that this has a typical reference to the last destruction of the Jews by the Romans, in which those that believed were taken care of, but those that continued obstinate in unbelief were driven into all countries for *a taunt and a curse.*

CHAPTER 25

The prophecy of this chapter bears date some time before the chapters next foregoing. This is dated in the first year of Nebuchadrezzar, that remarkable year when the sword of the Lord began to be drawn. I. A review of the prophecies that had been delivered to Judah and Jerusalem for many years past, by Jeremiah himself and other prophets, with the little regard given to them, ver. 1–7. II. A very express threatening of the destruction of Judah and Jerusalem, by the king of Babylon, for their continuance in sin (ver. 8–11), to which is annexed a promise of their deliverance out of their captivity in Babylon, after 70 years, ver. 12–14. III. A prediction of the devastation of divers other nations, by Nebuchadrezzar, represented by a "cup of fury" put into their hands (ver. 15–28), by a sword sent among them (ver. 29–33), and a desolation made among the shepherds and their flocks and pastures (ver. 34–38).

Verses 1–7

A message from God concerning all the people of Judah (*v.* 1), which Jeremiah delivered unto all the people of Judah, *v.* 2. Jeremiah is sent to *all the people*, probably when they had all come up to Jerusalem to worship at one of the solemn feasts.

This prophecy is dated in the fourth year of Jehoiakim and the first of Nebuchadrezzar. Now that that martial prince began to set up for the world's master, God, by his prophet, gives notice that he is his servant. Nebuchadrezzar should not bid so fair for universal monarchy (universal tyranny) but that God had purposes of his own to serve by them.

In this message observe the great pains that had been taken with the people to bring them to repentance, which they are here put in mind of, as a justification of God in his proceedings against them.

I. Jeremiah, for his part, had been a constant preacher among them twenty-three years. *These three years* (these three and twenty years) *have I come seeking fruit on this fig-tree.* All this while God had been constant in sending messages to them, as there was occasion: "From that time *to this very day the word of the Lord has come unto me,* for your use." Thus God's Spirit was striving with them, as with the old world, Gen. vi. 3. Jeremiah had been faithful and industrious in delivering those messages. *I have spoken to you, rising early and speaking.* He had declared to them *the whole counsel of God.*

II. Besides him, God had sent them other prophets, on the same errand, *v.* 4. There were many other of God's *servants the prophets* who preached awakening sermons, which were never published.

III. They all told them of their faults, *their evil way,* and the *evil of their doings.* Those were not of God's sending who flattered them as if there were nothing amiss. They all reproved them for their idolatry, their *going after other gods, to serve them and to worship them,* gods that were *the work of their own hands.* They all called on them to repent of their sins and to reform their lives. This was the burden of every song. Personal reformation must be insisted on as necessary to a national deliverance: *every one* must *turn from his* own *evil way.* The street will not be clean unless everyone sweep before his own door. The mercies they enjoyed should be continued to them: "*You shall dwell in the land,* dwell at ease, dwell in peace, in this good land, *which the Lord has given you and your fathers.* Nothing but sin will turn you out of it, and that shall not if you turn from it."

IV. Yet all was to no purpose. They were not wrought upon to take the right and only method to turn away the wrath of God. Jeremiah was a very lively affectionate preacher, yet *they hearkened not* to him, *v.* 3. The other prophets dealt faithfully with them, but neither did they *hearken to them,* nor *incline their ear, v.* 4.

Verses 8–14

Here is the sentence grounded upon the foregoing charge: "*Because you have not heard my words,* I must take another course with you," *v.* 8. The sinner must either be parted from his sin or perish in it.

I. The ruin of the land of Judah by the king of Babylon's armies is here decreed, *v.* 9. God sent to them *his servants the prophets,* and they were not heeded, and therefore God will send for *his servant the*

king of Babylon. The messengers of God's wrath will be sent against those that would not receive the messengers of his mercy. Nebuchadrezzar, though a stranger to the true God, was yet, in the descent he made upon this country, *God's servant,* an instrument in his hand for the correction of his people. He was really serving God's designs when he thought he was serving his own ends. The most potent and absolute monarchs are his servants. Nebuchadrezzar, who is an instrument of his wrath, is as truly his servant as Cyrus, who is an instrument of his mercy. The utter destruction of this and all the neighbouring lands is here described, *v.* 9–11. This desolation shall be the ruin of their credit among their neighbours; it shall *make them an astonishment and a hissing. I will take from them the voice of mirth;* they shall neither have cause for it nor hearts for it. *The sound of the mill-stones shall not be heard;* for, when the enemy has seized their stores, the sound of the grinding must needs be low. An end shall be put to all business; there shall not be seen *the light of a candle,* for there shall be no work to be done worth candle-light. And, *lastly,* they shall be deprived of their liberty: *Those nations shall serve the king of Babylon seventy years.* The fixing of the time during which the captivity should last would be of great use, not only for the confirmation of the prophecy, but for the comfort of the people of God in their calamity and the encouragement of faith and prayer. *Known unto God are all his works from the beginning of the world,* which appears by this, that, when he has thought fit, some of them have been made known to his servants the prophets and by them to his church.

II. The ruin of Babylon, at last, is here foretold, as it had been, long before, by Isaiah, *v.* 12–14. The destroyers must themselves be destroyed. This shall be done when *seventy years are accomplished.* It is doubtful when these *seventy years* commence; some date them from the captivity in the fourth year of Jehoiakim and first of Nebuchadrezzar, others from the captivity of Jehoiachin eight years after. When the set time to favour Zion has come, the king of Babylon must be visited, and all his tyranny reckoned for; then that nation shall be punished *for their iniquity.* That land must then be a *perpetual desolation,* such as they had made other lands. This destruction of Babylon was to be brought about by the Medes and Persians. God had said: *I will bring upon that land all my words.* The same Jeremiah that prophesied the destruction of other nations by the Chaldeans foretold also the destruction of the Chaldeans themselves, *v.* 13. *I will recompense them according to their deeds,* by which they transgressed the law of God, even then when they were made to serve his purposes. *Many nations and great kings,* in alliance with Cyrus king of Persia, shall *serve themselves of them* also, shall make themselves masters of their country, and make them the footstool by which to mount the throne of universal monarchy.

Verses 15–29

Under the similitude of a cup going round, is here represented the universal desolation that was now coming. The cup in the vision is to be a sword in the accomplishment of it: so it is explained, *v.* 16.

I. The circumstances of this judgment,

1. This destroying sword should come—*from the hand of God.* Wicked men are made use of as his sword, Ps. xvii. 13. It is *the wine-cup of his fury.* It is the just anger of God that sends this judgment. These are compared to some intoxicating liquor, which they shall be forced to drink of, as, formerly, condemned malefactors were sometimes executed by being compelled to drink poison. The wicked are said to *drink the wrath of the Almighty,* Job xxi. 20; Rev. xiv. 10.

2. It should be sent to them—by the hand of Jeremiah as the judge *set over the nations* (ch. i. 10), to pass sentence upon them, and by the hand of Nebuchadrezzar as the executioner. Jeremiah must *take the cup at God's hand*, and compel the nations to *drink it.*

3. It should be sent on all the nations within the lines of Israel's communication. Jeremiah took the cup, and *made all the nations to drink of it*, that is, he prophesied concerning each of the nations here mentioned that they should share in this great desolation. *Jerusalem and the cities of Judah* are put first (*v.* 18); for *judgment begins at the house of God* (1 Pet. iv. 17), at the sanctuary, Ezek. ix. 6. And this part of the prophecy was already begun to be accomplished; this is denoted by that parenthesis (*as it is this day*), for in the fourth year of Jehoiakim things had come into a very bad posture. *Pharaoh king of Egypt* comes next, because the Jews trusted to that broken reed (*v.* 19); the remains of them fled to Egypt, and there Jeremiah particularly foretold the destruction of that country, *ch.* xliii. 10, 11. All the other nations that bordered upon Canaan must pledge Jerusalem in this bitter cup. The *mingled people*, the Arabians, rovers of divers nations that lived by rapine; *the kings of the land of Uz*, joined to the country of the Edomites. The Philistines had been vexatious to Israel, but now their cities become a prey. Edom, Moab, Ammon, Tyre, and Zidon, are places well known to border upon Israel; the *Isles beyond*, or *beside, the sea*, are supposed to be those parts of Phoenicia and Syria that lay upon the coast of the Mediterranean Sea. Dedan and the other countries mentioned (*v.* 23, 24) seem to have lain upon the confines of Idumea and Arabia the desert. Those of Elam are the Persians. with whom the Medes are joined. The *kings of the north*, that lay nearer to Babylon will be seized by the victorious sword of Nebuchadrezzar. He shall push on his victories with such incredible fury that all the kingdoms of the world should become sacrifices to his ambition. Thus Alexander is said to have conquered *the world*, and the Roman empire is called *the world*, Luke ii. 1. Or it may be taken as reading the doom of *all the kingdoms* of the earth; one time or other, they shall feel the dreadful effects of war. The world has been, and will be, a great cockpit, while men's lusts war as they do *in their members*, Jas. iv. 1. The *king of Sheshach shall drink after them*, that is, the king of Babylon himself, who has given his neighbours all this trouble, shall at length have it return upon his own head. That by Sheshach is meant Babylon is plain from *ch.* li. 41. Babylon's ruin was foretold, *v.* 12, 13.

4. The desolations in all these kingdoms are represented by the consequences of excessive drinking (*v.* 16): *They shall drink, and be moved, and be mad. They shall be drunken, and spew, and fall and rise no more, v.* 27. Men in drink often *fall and rise no more*; it is a sin that is its own punishment. When God sends the sword upon a nation, with warrant to make it desolate, it soon becomes like a drunken man, filled with confusion; its counsellors *mad*, and at their wits' end, sick at heart with continual vexation, *falling* down before the enemy, and unable to do anything to help themselves.

5. They will *refuse to take the cup at thy hand*; they will not give credit to the prediction of so despicable a man as Jeremiah. But he must tell them that it is *the word of the Lord of hosts*, and it is vain for them to struggle with Omnipotence: *You shall certainly drink.* And he must give them this reason, It is a time of visitation, it is a reckoning day, and Jerusalem has been called to account already: *I begin to bring evil on the city that is called by my name; and should you be utterly unpunished?* If Jerusalem be punished for learning idolatry of the nations, shall not the nations

be punished, of whom they learned it? *I will call for a sword upon all the inhabitants of the earth*, for they have helped to debauch the inhabitants of Jerusalem.

II. There is a God that judges in the earth, to whom all the nations of the earth are accountable, and by whose judgment they must abide. Those who have been vexatious and mischievous to the people of God will be reckoned with for it at last. The year of the redeemer will come, even the *year of recompenses.* The *burden of the word of the Lord* will at last become the burden of his judgments. Isaiah had prophesied long since against most of these nations (*ch.* xiii. &c) and now all his prophecies will have their fulfilling. Nebuchadrezzar was so proud of his might that he had no sense of right. These are the men that turn the world upside down, and yet expect to be admired and adored. Alexander thought himself a great prince when others thought him no better than a great pirate.

Verses 30–38

A further description of those terrible desolations which the king of Babylon with his armies should make in all the countries round about Jerusalem.

They will soon be aware of Nebuchadrezzar's making war upon them; but the prophet is directed to tell them that it is God himself that makes war upon them (*v.* 30): *The Lord shall roar from on high. He shall mightily roar upon his habitation* on earth from that above. He *roars as a lion* that has *forsaken his covert* (*v.* 38), and is going abroad to seek his prey. *The Lord has a controversy with the nations.* His quarrel with them is for their wickedness, their contempt of his authority and kindness to them. *He will give those that are wicked to the sword.* They have provoked God to anger, and thence comes all this destruction. *A noise will come even to the ends of the earth. v.* 31. The alarm is not given by trumpet, or beat of drum, but by a *whirlwind, a great whirlwind, storm*, or *tempest*, which shall be *raised up from the coasts*, the remote coasts *of the earth, v.* 32. The Chaldean army shall be like a hurricane raised in the north, but thence carried on with swiftness, bearing down all before it. Now the shepherds shall *howl and cry*, the kings, and princes, and the great ones of the earth, the *principal of the flock.* They used to be the most courageous but now their hearts shall fail them; *they shall wallow themselves in the ashes, v.* 34. There shall be *a voice of the cry of the shepherds*, and a *howling of the principal of the flock shall be heard, v.* 36. Perhaps, carrying on the metaphor of a lion roaring, it alludes to the great fright that shepherds are in when they hear a roaring lion coming towards their flocks, and find they have *no way to flee* (*v.* 35) for their own safety, neither can the *principal of their flock escape.* When our neighbour's house is on fire it is time to be concerned for our own. When one nation is a seat of war every neighbouring nation should hear, and fear, and make its peace with God. Multitudes shall fall by the sword of the merciless Chaldeans so that *the slain of the Lord* shall be everywhere found. The slain for sin are the *slain of the Lord.* They shall have no friends left to bury them, and the enemies shall not have so much humanity in them as to do it. The effect of this war will be the *desolation of the whole land* that is the seat of it (*v.* 38), one land after another. But here are two expressions more that make the case piteous. (1) *You shall fall like a pleasant vessel, v.* 34. The most desirable persons among them, who were looked upon as *vessels of honour*, shall fall by the sword. You shall fall as a Venice glass or a China dish, which is soon broken all to pieces. (2) Even *the peaceable habitations are cut down.* Those who used to be quiet, and not molesting any of their neighbours, those who lived in peace, and gave no provocation to any, even those shall not escape. This is one of the direful effects of war. Blessed be God, there is a *peaceable habitation* above for all the sons of peace, which is out of the reach of fire and sword.

CHAPTER 26

As in the Acts of the Apostles their preaching and their suffering are interwoven, so it is in the account we have of the prophet Jeremiah. I. How faithfully he preached, ver. 1–6. II. How spitefully he was persecuted for so doing by the priests and the prophets, ver. 7–11. III. How bravely he stood to his doctrine, in the face of his persecutors, ver. 12–15. IV. How wonderfully he was protected and delivered by the prudence of the princes and elders, ver. 16–19. Though Urijah, another prophet, was about the same time put to death by Jehoiakim (ver. 20–23), yet Jeremiah met with those that sheltered him, ver. 24.

Verses 1–6

The sermon that Jeremiah preached, which gave such offence that he was in danger of losing his life for it. It is left upon record, by way of appeal to the judgment of impartial men in all ages.

I. God directed him where to preach this sermon, and when, and to what auditory, *v.* 2. God gave him orders to preach *in the court of the Lord's house*, which was within the peculiar jurisdiction of his sworn enemies the priests. He must preach this, at the time of one of the most solemn festivals, when persons had come from all the *cities of Judah* to *worship in the Lord's house*. These worshippers had a great veneration for their priests, and would strengthen their hands against Jeremiah. But none of these things must daunt him; he must preach this sermon, which, if it were not convincing, would be provoking. God charges him particularly *not to diminish a word*, but to speak *all the words*, that he had commanded him.

II. God directed him what to preach. He must assure them that if they would *repent of their sins*, and turn from them, though judgments were just at the door, yet a stop should be put to them, and God would proceed no further in his controversy with them, *v.* 3. This was the main thing God intended in sending him to them. God *waits to be gracious*, waits till we are duly qualified, till we are fit, and in the meantime tries a variety of methods. He must, on the other hand, assure them that if they continued obstinate to all the calls God gave them, it would certainly end in the ruin of their city and temple, *v.* 4–6. That which God required of them was that they should *walk in all his law which he set before them*, the law of Moses and the ordinances and commandments of it, and should *hearken to the words of his servants the prophets*. The law was what God himself set before them. The prophets were his own servants, and were sent by him to them. They had hitherto been deaf both to the law and to the prophets: *You have not hearkened*. All he expects now is that at length they should heed what he said, and make his word their rule. In case of refusal this city, and the temple in it, shall fare as their predecessors did, Shiloh and the tabernacle there, for a like refusal to hearken. This was not the first time he had given them warning to this effect; see *ch.* vii. 12–14.

Verses 7–15

The sermon instead of awakening their convictions, did but exasperate their corruptions.

I. Jeremiah is charged with a crime that he had preached such a sermon, and is apprehended for it as a criminal. The *priests*, and *false prophets*, and *people*, *heard him speak these words*, *v.* 7. This shall suffice to ground an indictment upon: He hath said, *This house shall be like Shiloh*, *v.* 9. See how unfair they are in representing his words. He had said, in God's name, *If you will not hearken to me, then will I make this house like Shiloh;* but they leave out God's hand and their own hand in not hearkening to the voice of God, and charge it upon him that he *blasphemed this holy place*, the crime charged both on our Lord Jesus and on Stephen: He said, *This house shall be like Shiloh*. When the accusation was so weakly grounded, no marvel that the sentence was unjust: *Thou shalt surely die*. What he had said agreed with what God had said (1 Kings ix. 6–8), *If you shall at all turn from following after me, then this house shall be* abandoned; and yet he is condemned to die for saying it. This outcry of the priests and prophets raised the mob, and *all the people were gathered together against Jeremiah* in a popular tumult, ready to pull him to pieces.

II. He is arraigned and indicted for it. The *princes of Judah* were his judges, *v.* 10. The elders of Israel, hearing of this tumult in the temple, *came up from the king's house of the Lord*, to enquire into this matter. They *sat down in the entry of the new gate of the Lord's house*, and held a court. The *priests and prophets* were his prosecutors and accusers, and were violently set against him. They appealed to *the princes*, and *to all the people*, whether *this man* were not *worthy to die*, *v.* 11. When Jeremiah prophesied in the house of the king concerning the fall of the royal family (*ch.* xxii. 1, &c.), the court, though very corrupt, bore it patiently, and we do not find that they persecuted him for it; but when he comes into the *house of the Lord*, and touches the copyhold of the priests, and contradicts the lies and flatteries of the false prophets, then he is adjudged *worthy to die*, *ch.* v. 31.

III. Jeremiah makes his defence before the princes and the people. He does not deny the words. What he has said he will stand to, though it cost him his life; he had prophesied against *this house* and *this city*, but, 1. He asserts that he did this by good authority, not maliciously nor seditiously, but, *The Lord sent me* to prophesy thus: so he begins his apology (*v.* 12), and so he concludes it (*v.* 15): *Of a truth the Lord hath sent me unto you, to speak all these words*. As long as ministers keep closely to the instructions they have from heaven they need not fear the opposition they may meet with from hell or earth. He is under the divine protection, and whatever affront they offer to the ambassador will be resented by the Prince that sent him. It was said, not by way of fatal sentence, but of fair warning, *v.* 13. "*As for me*, the matter is not great what becomes of me; *behold, I am in your hand*; I neither have any power, to oppose you, nor is it so much my concern to save my own life: *do with me as seems meet unto you*." But, for themselves, he tells them that it is at their peril if they put him to death: *You shall surely bring innocent blood upon yourselves*, *v.* 15.

Verses 16–24

I. The acquitting of Jeremiah. He had indeed spoken the words laid in the indictment, but they are not looked upon to be seditious or treasonable, and the court find him not guilty. The priests and prophets continued to demand judgment against him; but the princes, and all the people, are clear that *this man is not worthy to die* (*v.* 16); for (say they) *he hath spoken to us*, not of himself, but *in the name of the Lord our God*. And are they willing to own that he did indeed speak to them *in the name of the Lord* and that that Lord is their God? Why then did they not amend their ways and doings?

II. A precedent quoted to justify them in acquitting Jeremiah. Some of the *elders of the land*, or the more intelligent men of the people, stood up, and put the assembly in mind of a former case. The case referred to is that of Micah. 1. Was it thought strange that Jeremiah prophesied against this city and the temple? Micah did so before him, even in the reign of Hezekiah, that reign of reformation, *v.* 18. Micah said it as publicly as Jeremiah had now spoken, *Zion shall be ploughed like a field*, the building shall be all destroyed, so that nothing shall hinder but it may be ploughed; *Jerusalem shall become heaps* of ruins, and *the mountain of the house* on which the temple is built shall be *as the high places of the forest*, overrun with briers and thorns, Mic. iii. 12. By this it appears that a man may be, as Micah was, a true prophet of the Lord, and yet may prophesy the destruction of Zion and Jerusalem. 2. Was it thought fit by the princes to justify Jeremiah in what he had done? It was what Hezekiah did before them in a like case. Did Hezekiah, and the people of Judah put Micah to death? On the contrary, they took the warning he gave them. Hezekiah set a good example before his successors, for he *feared the Lord* (v. 19). Micah's preaching drove him to his knees; he *besought the Lord* to turn away the judgment threatened and to be reconciled to them, and he found it was not in vain for *the Lord repented him of the evil* and returned in mercy to them; he sent an angel, who routed the army of the Assyrians, that threatened to plough *Zion like a field*.

III. An instance of another prophet that was put to death by Jehoiakim for prophesying as Jeremiah had done, *v.* 12, &c. Some make this to be urged by the prosecutors, as a case that favoured the prosecution, a modern case, in which speaking such words as Jeremiah had spoken was adjudged treason. Others think that the elders, who were advocates for Jeremiah, alleged this to show that thus they might *procure great evil against their souls*, for it would be adding sin to sin. Jehoiakim, the present king, had slain one prophet already; let them not fill up the measure by slaying another. But some good interpreters take this narrative from the historian that penned the book, Jeremiah himself, or Baruch. Urijah's prophecy was *against this city, and this land, according to all the words of Jeremiah*. The prophets of the Lord agreed in their testimony, and one would have thought that out of the mouth of so many witnesses the word would be regarded. Jehoiakim and his courtiers were exasperated against him, and *sought to put him to death. When he heard* that the king sought his life, *he was afraid, and fled, and went into Egypt*. This was certainly an effect of the weakness of his faith, and it sped accordingly. He distrusted God, and his power to protect him and bear him out. It was especially unbecoming to flee *into Egypt*. There are many that have much grace, but they have little courage, that are very honest, but withal very timorous. Jehoiakim's malice, one would think, might have contented itself with his banishment. So implacable is his revenge that he sends soldiers into Egypt, and they bring him back by force of arms. They *brought him to Jehoiakim*, and he *slew him with the sword*. He loads the dead body with infamy, cast it into *the graves of the common people*, as if he had not been a prophet of the Lord. Thus Jehoiakim hoped both to ruin his reputation with the people, that no heed might be given to his predictions, and to deter others from prophesying in like manner; but in vain. Herod thought he had gained his point when he had cut off John Baptist's head, but found himself deceived when, soon after, he heard of Jesus Christ, and said, in a fright, *This is John the Baptist*.

IV. Jeremiah's deliverance. Urijah was lately put to death, yet God wonderfully preserved Jeremiah, though he did not flee, but stood his ground. He that had an extraordinary mission might expect an extraordinary protection. God raised up a friend for Jeremiah; he took him by the hand in a friendly way, and assisted him. It was *Ahikam the son of Shaphan*, one that was a minister of state in Josiah's time; we read of him, 2 Kings xxii. 12. He had great influence among the princes, and he used it in favour of Jeremiah.

CHAPTER 27

Jeremiah, the prophet, since he cannot persuade people to submit to God's precept, and so to prevent the destruction of their country, is here persuading them to submit to God's providence, by yielding tamely to the king of Babylon, and becoming tributaries to him, which was the wisest course they could now take, and would prevent the laying of their country waste by fire and sword. I. He gives this counsel, in God's name, to the kings of the neighbouring nations, assuring them that there was no remedy, but they must serve the king of Babylon; and yet there should be relief, for his dominion should last but 70 years, ver. 1–11. II. He gives this counsel to Zedekiah king of Judah particularly (ver. 12–15) and to the priests and people, assuring them that the king of Babylon should still proceed against them till things were brought to the last extremity, and a patient submission would be the only way to mitigate the calamity, ver. 16–22.

Verses 1–11

Some difficulty occurs in the date of this prophecy. Dr. Lightfoot solves it thus: In the beginning of Jehoiakim's reign Jeremiah is to make these bonds and yokes, and to put them upon his own neck, in token of Judah's subjection to the king of Babylon, which began at that time; but he is to send them to the neighbouring kings afterwards in the reign of Zedekiah, of whose succession to Jehoiakim, and the ambassadors sent to him, mention is made by way of prediction.

I. Jeremiah is to prepare a sign of the general reduction of all these countries into subjection to the king of Babylon (*v.* 2): *Make thee bonds and yokes*, yokes with bonds to fasten them, that the beast may not slip his neck out of the yoke. Into these the prophet must put his own neck for everyone would enquire, What is the meaning of Jeremiah's yokes? We find him with one on, *ch.* xxviii. 10. Hereby he intimated that he advised them to nothing but what he was resolved to do himself.

II. He is to send this, with a sermon annexed to it, to all the neighbouring princes; those are mentioned (*v.* 3) that lay next to the land of Canaan. It should seem, there was a treaty of alliance on foot between the king of Judah and all those other kings. Jerusalem was the place appointed for the treaty. Thither they all sent their plenipotentiaries; and it was agreed that they should bind themselves in a league offensive and defensive, in opposition to the threatening greatness of the king of Babylon. They had great confidence in their strength thus united; but, when the envoys were returning to their respective masters with the ratification of this treaty, Jeremiah gives each of them a yoke to carry to his master, to signify to him that he must become a servant to the king of Babylon. In the sermon, 1. God asserts his own indisputable right to dispose of kingdoms as he pleases, *v.* 5. He is the Creator of all things; he *made the earth* at first, established it, and it abides: it is still the same, though *one generation passes away and another comes*. He still by a continued creation produces *man and beast upon the ground*, and it is by his *great power* and *outstretched arm*. As he hath graciously *given the earth to the children of men* in general (Ps. cxv. 16), so he gives to each his share of it, be it more or less. 2. He publishes a grant of all these countries to Nebuchadnezzar. "This is to certify to all whom it may concern that I have *given all these lands*, with all the wealth of them, into *the hands of the king of Babylon*; even the beasts *of the field*, whether tame or wild, *have I given to him*, parks and pastures; they are all his own." Nebuchadnezzar was a proud wicked man, an idolater; and yet God, in his providence, gives him this large dominion, these vast possessions. Note, The things of this world are not the best things, for God often gives the largest share of them to bad men, that are rebels against him. Dominion is not founded in grace. Nebuchadnezzar is a bad man, and yet God calls him his servant, because he employed him as an instrument of his providence for the chastising of the nations. 3. He assures them that they should all be unavoidably brought under the dominion of the king of Babylon for a time (v. 7): *All nations*, all these nations and many others, shall serve *him, and his son, and his son's son.* His son was Evil-merodach, and his son's son Belshazzar, in whom his kingdom ceased: then the time of reckoning came, and *many nations and great kings*, incorporated into the empire of the Medes and Persians, *served themselves of him,* as before, ch. xxv. 14. 4. He threatens those that stood out and would not submit to the king of Babylon (v. 8): That nation that will not *put their neck under his yoke* I will *punish with sword and famine*, with one judgment after another, till it is *consumed by his hand.* 5. He shows them the vanity of all the hopes they fed themselves with, that they should preserve their liberties, v. 9, 10. These nations had their prophets too, that pretended to foretell future events by the stars, or by dreams, or enchantments; and they, to please their patrons, assured them that they *should not serve the king of Babylon.* Thus they designed to animate them to a vigorous resistance. But he tells them that it would prove to their destruction. Particular prophesies against these nations that bordered on Israel we shall meet with, ch. xlviii and xlix, and Ezek. xxv. 6. He puts them in a fair way to prevent their destruction by a quiet and easy submission, v. 11. The nations that will be content to *serve the king of Babylon*, and pay him tribute for seventy years (ten apprenticeships), *those will I let remain still in their own land. Serve the king of Babylon and you shall till the land* and *dwell therein.* Some would condemn this as the evidence of a mean spirit, but the prophet recommends it as that of a meek spirit, which yields to necessity, and by a quiet submission to the hardest turns of Providence makes the best of bad. Many might have prevented destroying providences by humbling themselves under humbling providences. It is better to take up a lighter cross in our way than to pull a heavier on our own head.

Verses 12–22

What was said to all the nations is here with a particular tenderness applied to the Jews, for whom Jeremiah was concerned. The case at present stood thus: Judah and Jerusalem had contested with the king of Babylon, and were worsted; many both of their valuable persons and goods were carried to Babylon already, and some of the *vessels of the Lord's house.* Now how this struggle would issue was the question. They had those at Jerusalem who pretended to be prophets, who bade them hold out and recover all that they had lost. Now Jeremiah is sent to bid them yield, for instead of recovering what they had lost, they would otherwise lose all that remained.

I. Jeremiah humbly addresses the king of Judah, to persuade him to surrender to the king of Babylon. His act would be the people's and therefore he speaks to him as to them all (v. 12): *Bring your necks under the yoke of the king of Babylon and live.* Is it their wisdom to submit to the heavy iron yoke of a cruel tyrant, that they may secure the lives of their bodies? And is it not much more our wisdom to submit to the sweet and easy yoke of our rightful Lord and Master Jesus Christ, that we may secure the lives of our souls? Bring down your spirits to repentance and faith, and that is the way to bring up your spirits to heaven and glory.

II. He addresses himself likewise to the priests and the people (v. 16), to persuade them to *serve the king of Babylon*, that they might *live*, and might prevent the desolation of the city (v. 17): "*Wherefore should it be laid waste*, as certainly it will be if you stand out?"

III. In both these addresses he warns them against giving credit to the false prophets that rocked them asleep in their security: "*Hearken not to the word of the prophets* (v. 14), *your prophets, v.* 16. They are not God's prophets; he never sent them; they are yours, for they say what you would have them say, and aim at nothing but to please you." Two things their prophets said: 1. That the power which the king of Babylon had gained over them should now shortly be broken. They said (v. 14), "*You shall not serve the king of Babylon;* you need not submit voluntarily, for you shall not be compelled to submit." This they prophesied *in the name of the Lord* (v. 15), as if God had sent them. But it was a lie: *I have not sent them, saith the Lord.* 2. They prophesied that the vessels of the temple, which the king of Babylon had already carried away, should now shortly be brought back (v. 16); knowing how acceptable it would be to the priests who loved the *gold of the temple* better than the *temple that sanctified the gold.* These vessels were taken away when Jeconiah was carried captive into Babylon, v. 20. We have the story, and it is a melancholy one, 2 Kings xxiv. 13, 15; 2 Chron. xxxvi. 10. The temple was their pride, and the stripping of that was too plain an indication of that which the true prophet told them, that their *God had departed from them.* Their false prophets therefore had no other way to make them easy than by telling them that the king of Babylon should be forced to restore them in a little while. Now here Jeremiah bids them think of preserving the vessels that remained by their prayers, rather than of bringing back those that were gone by their prophecies (v. 18): *If they be prophets*, as they pretend, and if *the word of the Lord be with them*—if they have any intercourse with heaven, let them stand *between the living and the dead*, between that which is carried away and that which remains, that *the plague may be stayed; let them make intercession with the Lord of hosts,* that the vessels which are left go not after the rest. Instead of prophesying, let them pray. He assures them that the brazen vessels should go after the golden ones, v. 19, 20. Nebuchadnezzar would be sure to come again and take all he could find, not only in *the house of the Lord*, but in the *king's house.* But he concludes with a gracious promise that the time should come when they should all be returned: *Until the day that I visit them in mercy*, and *then I will bring* those vessels *up again, and restore them to this place.* Surely they were under the protection of a special Providence, else they would have been melted down, but there was to be a second temple, for which they were to be reserved. We read particularly of the return of them, Ezra i. 8. Though the return of the church's prosperity do not come in our time, we must not therefore despair of it, for it will come in God's time.

CHAPTER 28

In the foregoing chapter Jeremiah had charged those prophets with lies who foretold the speedy breaking of the yoke of the king of Babylon and the return of the vessels of the sanctuary; now here we have his contest with a particular prophet. I. Hananiah, a pretender to prophecy, foretold the sinking of Nebuchadnezzar's power and the return both of the persons and of the vessels that were carried away (ver. 1–4), and, as a sign of this, he broke the yoke from the neck of Jeremiah, ver. 10, 11. II. Jeremiah wished his words might prove true, but appealed to the event, not doubting but that would disprove them, ver. 5–9. III. The doom both of the deceived and the deceiver is here read. The people should have their yoke of wood turned into a yoke of iron (ver. 12–14), and the prophet should be shortly cut off by death, ver. 15–17.

Verses 1–9

This struggle between a true prophet and a false one is said to have happened *in the beginning of the reign of Zedekiah*, and yet *in the fourth year*, for the the first four years of his reign might well be called *the beginning*, because during those years he reigned under the dominion of the king of Babylon and as a tributary to him; whereas the rest of his reign, which might well be called the *latter part* of it, in distinction from that *former part*, he reigned in rebellion against the king of Babylon. In this fourth year of his reign he went in person to Babylon (as we find, *ch.* li. 59). This gave the people some hope that in person he would put a good end to the war, in which hope the false prophets encouraged them, Hananiah particularly.

I. The prediction which Hananiah delivered solemnly, *in the house of the Lord*, and in the name of the Lord, *in the presence of the priests and of all the people*. In delivering this prophecy, he faced Jeremiah, he spoke it to him (*v.* 1), designing to contradict him, as much as to say, "Jeremiah, thou liest." Now this prediction is that the king of Babylon's power over Judah and Jerusalem should be speedily broken, that *within two full years* the vessels of the temple should be brought back, and Jeremiah, and all the captives carried away with him, should return; whereas Jeremiah had foretold that the yoke of the king of Babylon should be bound on yet faster, and that the vessels and captives should not return for 70 years, *v.* 2–4. Upon the reading of this sham prophecy, and comparing it with the messages that God sent by the true prophets, what a vast difference there is between them. Here is nothing of the spirit and life, the sublimity of expression, that appear in the discourses of God's prophets. But that which is especially wanting here is an air of piety; he speaks of the return of their prosperity, but not a word of good counsel given them to repent, and return to God, to pray, and seek his face. He promises them temporal mercies, in God's name, but makes no mention of those spiritual mercies which God always promised, *ch.* xxiv. 7: *I will give them a heart to know me.*

II. Jeremiah's reply to this pretended prophecy. 1. He heartily wishes it might prove true. Such an affection has he for his country, and so truly desirous is he that their ruin might be prevented. He said, *Amen; the Lord do so; the Lord perform thy words*, *v.* 5, 6. This was not the first time that Jeremiah had prayed for his people, though he had prophesied against them, as Christ prayed, *Father, if it be possible, let this cup pass from me*, when yet he knew it must not pass from him. God himself, though he has determined, does not desire, the death of sinners, but would *have all men to be saved*. 2. He appeals to the event, to prove it false, *v.* 7–9. The false prophets reflected upon Jeremiah, as Ahab upon Micaiah, because he never *prophesied good concerning them, but evil*. Prophets of old prophesied against *many countries and great kingdoms*, so bold were they in delivering the messages which God sent by them, and so far from fearing men, or seeking to please them, as Hananiah did. They made no difficulty, any more than Jeremiah did, of threatening war, famine, and pestilence, and what they said was regarded as coming from God; why then should Jeremiah be run down as *a pestilent fellow, and a sower of sedition*, when he preached no otherwise than God's prophets had always done before him? But the prophet that *prophesied of peace* and prosperity especially as Hananiah did, absolutely and unconditionally, without adding that necessary proviso, that they do not by wilful sin put a bar in their own door and stop the current of God's favours, will be proved a true prophet only by the accomplishment of his prediction; if it come to pass, then it shall be known that *the Lord has sent him*, but, if not, he will appear to be a cheat and an impostor.

Verses 10–17

I. The insolence of the false prophet. To complete the affront he designed Jeremiah. *he took the yoke*

from off his neck which he carried as a memorial of what he had prophesied concerning the enslaving of the nations of Nebuchadnezzar, and he broke it, that he might give a sign of the accomplishment of his prophecy, as Jeremiah had given of his, and might seem to have defeated the intention of his prophecy. The lying spirit, in the mouth of this false prophet, mimics the language of the Spirit of truth: *Thus saith the Lord, So will I break the yoke of the king of Babylon*, not only from the neck of this nation, but *from the neck of all nations, within two full years.*

II. The patience of the true prophet. Jeremiah quietly *went his way*, not because he had nothing to answer, but because he was willing to stay till God was pleased to furnish him with a direct answer, which as yet he had not received. He expected that God would send a special message to Hananiah. *I, as a deaf man, heard not, for thou wilt hear*, and *thou shalt answer, Lord, for me.*

III. The justice of God in giving judgment between Jeremiah and his adversary. Jeremiah went his way, as a man *in whose mouth there was no rebuke*, but God soon put a word into his mouth. Let not Jeremiah himself distrust the truth of what he had delivered in God's name because it met with such contradiction. If what we have spoken be the truth of God, we must not unsay it because men gainsay it; for *great is the truth and will prevail*. Hananiah has broken the *yokes of wood*, but Jeremiah must make for them *yokes of iron*, which cannot be broken (*v.* 13), for (says God), "*I have put a yoke of iron upon the neck of all these nations*, which shall lie heavier, and bind harder, upon them (*v.* 14), *that they may serve the king of Babylon.*" What was said before is repeated again: *I have given him the beasts of the field also*, as if there were something significant in that. Men had by their wickedness made themselves *like the beasts that perish*, and therefore deserved to be ruled as beasts are ruled, and such a power Nebuchadnezzar ruled with; for *whom he would he slew and whom he would he kept alive*. Hananiah is sentenced to die for contradicting it, and Jeremiah, when he has received commission from God, boldly tells him so to his face. The crimes of which Hananiah stands convicted are cheating the people and affronting God: *Thou makest this people to trust in a lie; thou hast taught rebellion against the Lord*. The judgment given against him is, "*I will cast thee off from the face of the earth. This year thou shalt die*, and die as a rebel against the Lord." This sentence was executed, *v.* 17. Hananiah died the same year, within two months.

CHAPTER 29

The contest between Jeremiah and the false prophets was carried on before by preaching, here by writing. I. A letter which Jeremiah wrote to the captives in Babylon, against their prophets that they had there (ver. 1–3), in which letter, 1. He endeavours to reconcile them to their captivity, ver. 4–7. 2. He cautions them not to give any credit to their false prophets, who fed them with hopes of a speedy release, ver. 8, 9. 3. He assures them that God would restore them in mercy to their own land again, at the end of 70 years, ver. 10–14. 4. He foretells the destruction of those who yet continued, ver. 15–19. 5. He prophesies the destruction of two of their false prophets in Babylon, that soothed them in their sins and set them bad examples (ver. 20–23). II. Here is a letter which Shemaiah, a false prophet in Babylon, wrote to the priests at Jerusalem, to stir them up to persecute Jeremiah (ver. 24–29), and a denunciation of God's wrath against him for writing such a letter, ver. 30–32.

Verses 1–7

I. Jeremiah wrote to the captives in Babylon, in the name of the Lord. Jeconiah had surrendered himself a prisoner, with the queen his mother, the chamberlains of his household, called there the *eunuchs*, and many of *the princes of Judah and Jerusalem. The carpenters and smiths* likewise were yielded up, that those who remained might not have any proper hands to fortify their city. By this tame submission it was hoped that Nebuchadnezzar would be pacified, but the imperious conqueror grows upon their concessions. And, not content with this, when these had *departed from Jerusalem* he comes again, and fetches away many more of *the elders, the priests, the prophets, and the people* (v. 1). The case of these captives was very melancholy, the rather because they looked as if they were greater sinners than all men who dwelt at Jerusalem. Jeremiah therefore writes a letter to them, to comfort them. This letter of Jeremiah's was sent to the captives in Babylon by the hands of the ambassadors whom king Zedekiah sent to Nebuchadnezzar, probably to pay him his tribute and renew his submission to him. By such messengers Jeremiah chose to send this message, because it was a message from God.

II. A copy of the letter at large follows here to v. 24.

1. He assures them that he wrote in the name of the *Lord of hosts, the God of Israel*; Jeremiah was but the scribe or amanuensis. It would be comfortable to them, in their captivity, to hear that God is *the Lord of hosts*, able to help and deliver them; and that he is the *God of Israel* still, in covenant with his people. This would be an admonition to stand upon their guard against all temptations to the idolatry of Babylon. God's sending to them in this letter might be an encouragement, as it was evidence that he had not cast them off, had not disinherited them, though he was displeased with them and corrected them.

2. God by him owns the hand he had in their captivity: *I have caused you to be carried away*, v. 4 and again, v. 7. If God caused them to be carried captives, they might be sure that he neither did them any wrong nor meant them any hurt.

3. He bids them think of nothing but settling there; and therefore let them resolve to make the best of it (v. 5, 6): *Build yourselves houses and dwell in them*, &c. They must not feed themselves with hopes of a speedy return out of their captivity. Let them therefore accommodate themselves to it as well as they can. Let them *build*, and *plant*, and *marry*, and dispose of their children there as if they were at home in their own land. If they live in the fear of God, what should hinder them but they may live comfortably in Babylon? They cannot but *weep* sometimes *when they remember Zion*. But let not weeping hinder sowing. In all conditions of life it is our wisdom and duty to make the best of that which is, and not to throw away the comfort of what we may have because we have not all we would have. We have a natural affection for our native country; if Providence remove us to some other country, we must resolve to live easy there. If the *earth be the Lord's*, then, wherever a child of God goes, he does not go off his Father's ground. They must not disquiet themselves with fears of intolerable hardships in their captivity.

4. He directs them to seek the good of the country where they were captives (v. 7), to pray for it, to endeavour to promote it. This forbids them to attempt anything against the public peace while they were subjects to the king of Babylon. They must live *quiet and peaceable lives* under him, *in all godliness and honesty*, not plotting to shake off his yoke, but patiently leaving it to God in due time to work deliverance for them. *For in the peace thereof you shall have peace.* Thus the primitive Christians, according to the temper of their holy religion, prayed for the powers that were, though they were persecuting powers. Every passenger is concerned in the safety of the ship.

Verses 8–14

I. God takes them from building upon the false foundation which their pretended prophets laid, v. 8, 9. They told them that their captivity should be short, and therefore that they must not think of taking root in Babylon. "Now herein *they deceive you*," says God; "they *prophesy a lie to you*, though they prophesy *in my name*. But *let them not deceive you*, suffer not yourselves to be deluded by them." *Hearken not to your dreams, which you cause to be dreamed.* He means either the dreams or fancies which the people pleased themselves with, or the dreams which the prophets dreamed and grounded their prophecies upon. They *caused them to be dreamed*; for they encouraged the prophets to put such deceits upon them, desiring them to prophesy nothing but *smooth things*, Isa. xxx. 10. They were dreams of their own bespeaking.

II. He gives them a good foundation to build their hopes upon. God here promises them that, though they should not return quickly, they should return at length, *after seventy years be accomplished*. He will put an end to *their captivity*. Though they are dispersed, some in one country and some in another, he will *gather them from all the places whither they are driven*, and incorporate them again in one body. They shall be brought again to their own land, *to the place whence* they were *carried captive*, v. 14. This shall be the performance of God's promise to them (v. 10): *I will perform my good word towards you.* This will make their return out of captivity very comfortable, that it will be the performance of God's good word to them, the product of a gracious promise. This shall be in pursuance of God's purposes concerning them (v. 11): *I know the thoughts that I think towards you.* His thoughts are all working towards the expected end, which he will give in due time. Let them have patience till the fruit is ripe, and then they shall have it. He will give them an *end, and expectation*, so it is in the original. When things are at the worst they will begin to mend; and he will give them to see the glorious perfection of their deliverance. He that in the beginning finished the *heavens and the earth*, and all the *hosts* of both, will finish all the blessings of both to his people. God does nothing by halves. He will give them to see the *expectation*, that *end* which they desire. He will give them not the expectations of their fears, nor the expectations of their fancies, but the expectations of their faith. This shall be in answer to their prayers (v. 12–14). *Then shall you call upon me*, and *you shall go, and pray unto me.* When deliverance is coming we must by prayer go forth to meet it. *I will hearken unto you*, and *I will be found of you.* God has said it, and we may depend upon it, *Seek and you shall find.* We have a general rule laid down (v. 13): *You shall find me when you shall search for me with all your heart.*

Verses 15–23

Jeremiah here turns to those who slighted the counsels and comforts that Jeremiah ministered and depended upon the false prophets. When this letter came from Jeremiah they would be ready to say, "Why should he make himself so busy, and take upon him to advise us? *The Lord has raised us up prophets in Babylon*, v. 15. We are satisfied with those prophets, and can depend upon them, and have no occasion to hear from any prophets in Jerusalem." These prophets of their own told them that no more should be carried captive, but that those who were in captivity should shortly return. In answer to this the prophet here foretells the utter destruction of those who remained still at Jerusalem: "As for the *king* and *people* that *dwell in the city*, who, you think, will be ready to bid you welcome when you return, you are deceived; they shall be followed with one judgment after another, *sword, famine*, and *pestilence*, which shall cut off multitudes; and the poor and miserable remains shall be *removed into all kingdoms of the earth*," v. 16, 18. And thus God *will make them*, or rather deal with them, *like vile figs*. This refers to the vision and the prophecy which we had *ch.* xxiv. And the reason given is the same (*v.* 19): *Because they have not hearkened to my words. I called, but they refused.* He calls upon all the children of the captivity, who boasted of them as prophets of God's raising up (*v.* 20): "Stand still, and hear the doom of the prophets you are so fond of." The two prophets are named here, *Ahab* and *Zedekiah*, *v.* 21. The crimes charged upon them—impiety and immorality: They *prophesied lies in God's name* (*v.* 21), and again (*v.* 23), They have *spoken lying words in my name.* Fathering their lies upon the God of truth was worst of all. Here it appears why they flattered others in their sins—because they could not reprove them without condemning themselves. *The king of Babylon shall slay them before your eyes;* nay, he shall put them to a miserable death, *roast them in the fire, v.* 22. We may suppose that it was not for their impiety and immorality that Nebuchadnezzar punished them thus severely, but for sedition, and some attempts of their turbulent spirits upon the public peace, and stirring up the people to revolt and rebel. Their names shall be a curse among the captives in Babylon, *v.* 22. When men would imprecate the greatest evil upon one they hated they could not load them with a heavier curse, in fewer words, than to say, *The Lord make thee like Zedekiah and like Ahab.*

Verses 24–32

The false prophets were enraged at the contents of Jeremiah's letter. One of them, Shemaiah, showed his malice against the prophet.

I. This busy fellow is called *Shemaiah the Nehelamite,* the *dreamer* (so the margin reads it), because all his prophecies he pretended to have received from God in a dream. He had got a copy of Jeremiah's letter to the captives, or information was given to him concerning it, and it nettled him exceedingly; he will answer it, yea, that he will. But how? He does not write to Jeremiah in justification of his own mission, but he writes to the priests, and instigates them to persecute Jeremiah. He writes in his own name as if he must be dictator to all mankind. But it is chiefly directed to Zephaniah, who was either the immediate son of Maaseiah, or of the 24th course of the priests, of which Maaseiah was the father and head. He was not the high priest, but suffragan to the high priest, or in some considerable post of command in the temple, as Pashur, *ch.* xx. 1. 1. He puts him and the other priests in mind of the duty of their place (*v.* 26): *The Lord hath made thee priest instead of Jehoiada the priest.* Some think that he refers to the famous Jehoiada, that great reformer in the days of Joash. Or, rather, it was some other Jehoiada, his immediate predecessor in this office, who perhaps was carried to Babylon among the priests, *v.* 1. Zephaniah is advanced, sooner than he expected, to this place of trust and power, and Shemaiah would have him think that Providence had preferred him that he might persecute God's prophets, that he had come to this government for such a time as this. These priests' business was to examine *every man that is mad and makes himself a prophet.* God's faithful prophets are here represented as prophets of their own making, usurpers of the office, and lay-intruders, as men that were mad, actuated by some demon, distracted men and men in a frenzy. 2. He informs them of the letter which Jeremiah had written to the captives (*v.* 28). The false prophets had formerly said that the captivity would never come, *ch.* xiv. 13. Jeremiah had said that it would come, and the event had already proved him in the right. 3. He demands judgment against him, taking it for granted that he is *mad,* and *makes himself a prophet.* He expects that they will order him to be put *in prison* and *in the*

stocks (*v.* 26), hoping that the captives in Babylon would not be influenced by him. He takes upon him to chide Zephaniah for his neglect (*v.* 27): *Why hast thou not rebuked and restrained Jeremiah of Anathoth?* God had confirmed his word in the mouth of Jeremiah; it had *taken hold* of them (Zech. i. 6); and yet, because he does not prophesy to them the smooth things they desired, they are resolved to look upon him as not duly called to the office of a prophet. They were now sent into a miserable thraldom for *mocking the messengers of the Lord* and *misusing his prophets.* Afflictions will not of themselves cure men of their sins, unless the grace of God work with them, but will rather exasperate the corruptions they are intended to mortify (Prov. xxvii. 22), *Though thou shouldst bray a fool in a mortar, yet will not his foolishness depart from him.*

II. *Zephaniah read this letter in the ears of Jeremiah.* He had a respect for Jeremiah (for we find him employed in messages to him as a *prophet, ch.* xxi. 1, xxxvii. 3), and therefore protected him. He made Jeremiah acquainted with the contents of the letter, that he might see what enemies he had even among the captives.

III. The sentence passed upon Shemaiah for writing this letter. God sent him an answer: it was ordered to be sent *to those of the captivity,* who encouraged and countenanced him as if he had been a prophet of God's raising up, *v.* 31, 32. Shemaiah had made fools of them. He promised them peace in God's name, but God did not send him; he forced a commission, and made the people *to trust in a lie,* and by preaching false comfort to them deprived them of true comfort. He had made traitors of them; he had *taught rebellion against the Lord,* as Hananiah had done, *ch.* xxviii. 16. At his end *he shall also be a fool* (as the expression is, *ch.* xvii. 11); his name and family shall be buried in oblivion: *He shall not have a man to dwell among this people;* and neither he nor any that come from him shall *behold the good that I will do for my people.*

CHAPTER 30

The sermon which we have in this and the following chapter is very different. Most hitherto was by way of reproof; but these two chapters are wholly taken up with precious promises of a return out of captivity, typical of the glorious things reserved for the church in the days of the Messiah. The prophet is told to write it, because it is intended for the comfort of the generation to come, ver. 1–3. It is here promised, I. That they should hereafter have a joyful restoration. 1. Though they were now in great terror, ver. 4–7. 2. Though their oppressors were strong, ver. 8–10. 3. Though they were not restored, ver. 11. 4. Though all means of their deliverance seemed to fail and be cut off, ver. 12–14. 5. Though God himself had sent them into captivity, ver. 15, 16. 6. Though all looked upon their case as desperate, ver. 17. II. That after their joyful restoration they should have a happy settlement, their city should be rebuilt (ver. 18), their numbers increased (ver. 19, 20), their government established (ver. 21), God's covenant with them renewed (ver. 22), and their enemies destroyed and cut off, ver. 23, 24.

Verses 1–9

I. Jeremiah is directed to *write* what God had spoken to him in hopes that those might take more notice of it when in reading it they had leisure for a more considerate review. He must collect them and put them together, and God will now add unto them many like words. He must write them for the generations to come, who should see them accomplished. He must write them not *in a letter,* but *in a book,* to be preserved in the archives. And this prophecy must be written, that it may be read so it may appear how exactly the accomplishment answers the prediction. It is intimated that they shall be *beloved for their fathers' sake* (Rom. xi. 28); for *therefore* God will bring them again to Canaan, because it was *the land that he gave to their fathers,* which therefore *they shall possess.*

II. He is directed what to write. The very words are such as the Holy Ghost teaches, *v.* 4. 1. He must write a description of the consternation which the people were now in, and were likely to be in upon every attack that the Chaldeans made upon them (*v.* 5): *We have heard a voice of trembling—*terror echoing to the alarms of danger. The false prophets told them that they should have *peace*, but *there is fear and not peace*, so the margin reads. Even the men of war shall be overwhelmed with the calamities of their nation, and shall look like *women in labour*, whose pains come upon them in great extremity and they know that they cannot escape them, *v.* 6. *Alas! for that day is great*, a day of judgment, which is called the *great day*, the *great and terrible day of the Lord* (Joel ii. 31, Jude 6), great, so that *there has been none like it*. The last destruction of Jerusalem is thus spoken of by our Saviour as unparalleled, Matt. xxiv. 21. *It is even the time of Jacob's trouble*, a sad time, when God's professing people shall be in distress above other people. The whole time of the captivity was a time of Jacob's trouble. 2. He must write the assurances which God had given that a happy end should at length be put to these calamities. (1) Jacob's troubles shall cease: *He shall be saved out of them.* (2) Jacob's troublers shall be disabled from doing him any further mischief, *v.* 8. "*I will break his yoke from off thy neck*, which has long lain so heavy, and has so sorely galled thee. *I will burst thy bonds* and restore thee to liberty and ease, they shall no more enrich themselves either by thy possessions or by thy labours." (3) That which crowns and completes the mercy is that they shall be restored to the free exercise of their religion again, *v.* 9. When the time shall come that they should be *saved out of their trouble*, God will prepare and qualify them for it by giving them a *heart to serve him*, and by giving them opportunity to serve him. *Therefore* we are *delivered out of the hands of our enemies*, that we may *serve God*, Luke i. 74, 75. They shall serve their own God, and neither be inclined, nor compelled, as they had been in the day of their captivity, to serve other gods. They shall serve *David their king*, such governors as God should from time to time set over them, of the line of David (as Zerubbabel). But this has a further meaning. The Chaldee paraphrase reads it, *They shall obey* (or *hearken to*) *the Messiah* (or *Christ*), the *Son of David, their king*. To him the Jewish interpreters apply it. That dispensation which commenced at their return out of captivity brought them to the Messiah. He is called *David their king* because he was the *Son of David* (Matt. xxii. 42) and he answered to the name, Matt. xx, 31, 32. God is often in the New Testament said to have *raised up Jesus*, raised him up as a King, Acts iii. 26; xiii. 23, 33. Those that serve the Lord as their God must give up themselves to Jesus Christ, to be ruled by him. For all men must *honour the Son as they honour the Father*, and come into the service and worship of God by him as Mediator. Those to whom he gives rest must take his yoke upon them.

Verses 10–17

The deplorable case of the Jews in captivity is set forth, but many precious promises are given them.

I. God himself appeared against them: he *scattered* them (*v.* 11); he did *all these things unto them*, *v.* 15. This was intended by him as a fatherly chastisement, and no other (*v.* 11): "*I will correct thee in measure*, or *according to judgment*, no more than thou deservest, no more than thou canst well bear." God hates sin most in those that are nearest to him. God here corrects his people *for the multitude of their iniquity*, and *because their sins were increased*, *v.* 14, 15. What God intended as a fatherly chastisement they and others interpreted as an act of hostility; they

looked upon him as having *wounded them with the wound of an enemy* and *with the chastisement of a cruel one* (*v.* 14). It did indeed seem as if God had dealt thus severely with them, as if he had fought against them, Isa. lxiii. 10. Job complains that God had become cruel to him and *multiplied his wounds*.

II. Their friends forsook them, *v.* 13. If we be reproached, we expect that our friends should appear in vindication of us. If we be sick, or sore, or wounded, we expect our friends should sympathise with us, and, if occasion be, lend a hand for the healing. Here there is none to do that, none to bind up thy wounds. *All thy lovers have forgotten thee.* When God is against a people who will be for them? Their case seemed desperate and past relief (*v.* 12): *Thy bruise is incurable, thy wound grievous*, and (*v.* 15) *thy sorrow is incurable.* Their sorrow would not admit of any alleviation, but they seemed to be hardened in it. In this deplorable condition they are looked upon with disdain (*v.* 17): *They called thee an outcast*, abandoned to ruin; they said, *This is Zion, whom no man seeks after.* Now all was in ruins. When they looked on the people that formerly dwelt in Zion, but were now in captivity, they called them outcasts; these are those who belong to Zion, but *no man seeks after* them, or enquires concerning them.

III. For all this God will work deliverance and salvation for them in due time. 1. Though he seemed to stand at a distance from them, yet he assures them of his presence with them, *I will save thee*, *v.* 10 *I am with thee, to save thee*, *v.* 11. 2. Though they were remote from their own land, *afar off in the land of their captivity*, yet there shall salvation find them out, thence shall it fetch them, and their *seed*, *v.* 10. 3. Though they were now full of fears, yet the time shall come when they *shall be in rest and quiet*, safe and easy, *and none shall make them afraid*, *v.* 10. 4. Though the nations into which they were dispersed should be brought to ruin, yet they should be preserved (*v.* 11): *Though I make a full end of the nations whither I have scattered thee, yet I will not make a full end of thee.* God's church may sometimes be brought very low, but he *will not make a full end of it*, *ch.* v. 10, 18. 5. Though God correct them, and justly, yet he will return in mercy to them, and even their sin shall not prevent their deliverance when God's time shall come. 6. Though their adversaries were mighty, God will break their power (*v.* 16): *All that devour thee shall be devoured.* "They *shall everyone of them*, without exception, go into captivity, and the day will come when *those that* now *spoil thee shall be a spoil*." 7. Though the wound seem incurable, God will make a cure of it (*v.* 17): *I will restore health unto thee.*

IV. They are cautioned against inordinate fear and grief, for in these precious promises there is enough to silence both. *Fear thou not, O my servant Jacob! neither be dismayed.* They must not sorrow as those that have no hope, *v.* 15. "*Why criest thou for thy affliction?* It is *for thy sin* (*v.* 14, 15), and therefore, instead of repining, thou shouldst be repenting."

Verses 18–24

Further intimations of the favour God had in reserve for them after the days of their calamity were over.

I. The city and temple should be rebuilt, *v.* 18. *Jacob's tents*, and *his dwelling-places*, felt the effects of *the captivity*, for they lay in ruins, but the habitations shall be repaired, and therein God will *have mercy upon their dwelling-places*, that had been monuments of his justice. Then *the city* of Jerusalem *shall be built upon her own heap*, her own hill, though now it be no better than a ruinous heap. He that can *make of a city a heap* (Isa. xxv. 2) can when he pleases *make of a heap a city* again. *The palace* (the temple, God's palace) *shall remain after the manner thereof;* it shall be built after the old model.

II. The sacred feasts should again be solemnized (v. 19): *Out of* the city, and the temple, and all the dwelling-places of Jacob, *shall proceed thanksgiving and the voice of those that make merry.*

III. The people should be multiplied, and increased: *They shall not be few, they shall not be small,* but shall make a figure among the nations: for *I will multiply them* and *I will glorify them.* It is for the honour of the church to have many added to it that shall be saved. There shall be a constant succession of faithful magistrates in the congregation of the elders, and of faithful worshippers in the congregation of the saints.

IV. They shall be blessed with a good government (v. 21): *Their nobles* and judges *shall be of themselves,* of their own nation, and they shall no longer be ruled by strangers and enemies; *their governor shall proceed from the midst of them,* shall be one that has been a sharer with them in the afflictions of their captive state; and this has reference to Christ our *governor, David our king* (v. 9); he is of ourselves, *in all things made like unto his brethren. And I will cause him to draw near;* this may be understood either, 1. Of the people, Jacob and Israel: "*I will cause* them *to draw near* to me in the temple service, as formerly, to come into covenant with me, as *my people*" (v. 22). 2. It may be understood of the governor; for it is a single person that is spoken of: *Their governor shall* be duly called to his office, shall *draw near* to God to consult him upon all occasions. But it looks further, to Christ, to him as Mediator. The proper work and office of Christ, as Mediator, is *to draw near and approach unto* God, for us, and in our name and stead, as the high priest of our profession. God the Father did *cause* Jesus Christ thus *to draw near and approach to* him as Mediator. He anointed him for this purpose, and declared himself well pleased in him. His own voluntary undertaking, in compliance with his Father's will and in compassion to fallen man, engaged him.

V. They shall be taken again into covenant with God, according to the covenant made with their fathers (v. 22): *You shall be my people;* and it is God's good work in us that makes us *to him a people, a people for his name,* Acts. xv. 14.

VI. Their enemies shall be reckoned with and brought down (v. 20): *I will punish all* those *that oppress them,* so that it shall appear to all a dangerous thing to *touch God's anointed,* Ps. cv. 15. These two verses (23–24) we had before (ch. xxiii. 19, 20); *there* they were a denunciation of God's wrath against the wicked hypocrites in Israel; *here* against the wicked oppressors of Israel. The wrath of God against the wicked is here represented to be like a whirlwind, irresistible. Whirlwinds are usually short, but this shall be *a continuing whirlwind.* It shall accomplish that for which it is sent: *The anger of the Lord shall not return till he have done it.* The purposes of his wrath, as well as the purposes of his love, will all be fulfilled; he will *perform the intents of his heart.*

CHAPTER 31

Good words and comfortable words for the encouragement of the captives, assuring them that God would in due time make them a great and happy nation again, especially by sending them the Messiah, in whose kingdom and grace many of these promises were to have their full accomplishment. I. They shall be restored to peace and joy, ver. 1–14. II. Their sorrow for the loss of their children shall be at an end, ver. 15–17. III. They shall repent of their sins, and God will graciously accept them, ver. 18–20. IV. They shall be increased, both their children and their cattle, ver. 21–30. V. God will renew his covenant with them, and enrich it with spiritual blessings, ver. 31–34. VI. These blessings shall be secured to theirs after them, ver. 25–37. VII. As an earnest of this the city of Jerusalem shall be rebuilt, ver. 38–40.

Verses 1–9

God assures his people,

I. That he will again take them into a covenant relation to himself. His own people shall be owned by him as the children of his love: *I will be the God* (that is, I will show myself to be the God) *of all the families of Israel* (v. 1)—not of the two tribes only, but of all the tribes; not only their state in general, but their particular families, and the interests of them, shall have a special relation to God. If we and our houses serve the Lord, we and our houses shall be protected and blessed by him, Prov. iii. 33.

II. That he will do for them, in bringing them out of Babylon, as he had done for their fathers when he delivered them out of Egypt. 1. He puts them in mind of what he did for their fathers when he brought them out of Egypt, v. 2. They were then, as these were, *a people left of the sword,* that sword of Pharaoh with which he cut off all the male children as soon as they were born. They were then *in the wilderness,* where they seemed to be lost and forgotten, as these were now in a strange land, and yet they found grace in God's sight, were owned and highly honoured by him, and he was at this time going *to cause them to rest* in Canaan. God is still the same. 2. They put him in mind of what God had done for their fathers, intimating that they now saw not such signs, and were ready to ask, as Gideon did, *Where are all the wonders that our fathers told us of?* The years of ancient times were glorious years; but now it is otherwise; what good will it do us that he *appeared of old* to us when now he is *a God that hides himself* from us? Isa. xlv. 15. 3. To this he answers with an assurance of the constancy of his love: *Yea, I have loved thee,* not only with an ancient love, but *with an everlasting love,* a love that shall never fail, however the comforts of it may for a time be suspended. Nothing can separate them from that love. Those whom God loves with this love he will draw into covenant and communion with himself, by the influences of his Spirit upon their souls.

III. That he will again form them into a people, and give them a very joyful settlement in their own land, v. 4, 5. They shall resume their harps which had been hung upon the willow-trees, shall tune them, and shall themselves be in tune to make use of them. Is the joy of the city maintained by the products of the country? It is so; and therefore it is promised (v. 5), *Thou shalt yet plant vines upon the mountains of Samaria,* which had been the head city of the kingdom of Israel, in opposition to that of Judah; but they shall now be united (Ezek. xxxvii. 22), and there shall be such perfect peace and security that men shall apply themselves wholly to the improvement of their ground: *The planters shall plant,* not fearing the soldiers' coming to eat the fruits of what they had planted, or to pluck it up; but they themselves *shall eat them* freely, as *common things,* not forbidden fruits.

IV. That they shall have liberty and opportunity to worship God in the ordinances of his own appointment (v. 6): *There shall be a day,* and a glorious day it will be, when the *watchmen upon Mount Ephraim,* that are set to stand sentinel there, to give notice of the approach of the enemy, finding that all is very quiet and that there is no appearance of danger, shall desire for a time to be discharged from their post, that they may *go up to Zion,* to praise God for the public peace. But that which is most observable here is *that the watchmen of Ephraim* are forward to promote the worship of God at Jerusalem, whereas formerly *the watchman of Ephraim was hatred against the house of his God* (Hos. ix. 8), and, instead of inviting people to Zion, laid snares for those that set their faces thitherward, Hos. v. 1.

V. That God shall have the glory and the church, the honour and comfort of this blessed change (*v.* 7): *Sing with gladness for Jacob,* that is, let all her friends and wellwishers rejoice with her, Deut. xxxii. 43. *Rejoice, you Gentiles with his people,* Rom. xv. 10. *Publish you, praise you.* In publishing these tidings, praise the God of Israel, praise the Israel of God, speak honourably of both.

VI. That, in order to a happy settlement in their own land, they shall have a joyful return out of the land of their captivity (*v.* 8, 9). 1. Though they are scattered to places far remote, yet they shall be brought together *from the north country, and from the coasts of the earth.* 2. Though many of them are very unfit for travel, yet that shall be no hindrance to them: *The blind and the lame* shall come; such a goodwill shall they have to their journey, and such a good heart upon it, that they shall not make their blindness and lameness an excuse for staying where they are. Their companions will be ready to help them, will be *eyes to the blind and legs to the lame,* as good Christians ought to be to one another in their travels heavenward, Job. xxix. 15. But, above all, their God will help them; and let none plead that he is blind who has God for his guide, or lame who has God for his strength. *The women with child* are heavy, and it is not fit that they should undertake such a journey, much less those *that travail with child;* and yet, when it is to return to Zion, neither the one nor the other shall make any difficulty of it. When God calls we must not plead any inability to come; for he that calls us will help us, will strengthen us. They shall weep with more bitterness and more tenderness for sin, when they are delivered out of their captivity, than ever they did when they were groaning under it. Prayers help to wipe away tears. *With favours will I lead them* (so the margin reads it). Is the country they pass through dry and thirsty? *I will cause them to walk by the rivers of waters,* not the waters of a landflood, which fail in summer. Is it a wilderness where there is no road, no track? *I will cause them to walk in a straight way,* which they shall not miss. Is it a rough and rocky country? Yet *they shall not stumble.* Whithersoever God gives his people a clear call he will either find them or make them a ready way. A reason given why God will take all this care of his people: *For I am a Father to Israel,* and therefore will maintain him (Ps. ciii. 13): *and Ephraim is my firstborn;* even *Ephraim,* who, having gone astray from God, was *no more worthy to be called a son,* shall yet be owned as a *first-born,* particularly dear, and heir of a double portion of blessings. The same reason that was given for their release out of Egypt is given for their release out of Babylon; they are free-born and therefore must not be enslaved, are born to God and therefore must not be the servants of men. Exod. iv. 22, 23, *Israel is my son, even my first-born; let my son go that he may serve me.*

Verses 10–17

The purposes of God's love concerning his people. This is a *word of the Lord* which the *nations* must *hear,* for it is a prophecy of a work of the Lord. It will be a piece of news that will spread all the world over.

It is foretold, 1. That those who are dispersed shall be brought together again from their dispersions: *He that scattereth Israel will gather him,* v. 10, and when he has gathered him into one body, one fold, he will *keep him, as a shepherd does his flock,* from being scattered again. 2. That those who are sold and alienated shall be redeemed and brought back, *v.* 11. Though the enemy that had got possession of him was *stronger than he,* yet *the Lord,* who is stronger than all, *has redeemed and ransomed him,* not by price, but by power. 3. That with their liberty they shall have plenty and joy, and God shall be honoured,

v. 12, 13. When they shall have returned to their own land *they shall come and sing in the high place of Zion;* on the top of that holy mountain they shall sing to the praise and glory of God. We read that they did so when the foundation of the temple was laid there, Ezra iii. 11. They *shall flow together to the goodness of the Lord;* that is, they shall flock in great numbers and with great cheerfulness, as streams of water, *to the goodness of the Lord,* to the temple where he causes his goodness to pass before his people. They shall come together in solemn assemblies, to *praise him for his goodness,* and to pray for the continuance of it; they shall come to bless him for his goodness, in giving them *wheat, and wine, and oil, and the young of the flock and of the herd.* Therefore they honour God with the first-fruits out of which they bring offerings to his altar. Our souls are as gardens when they are watered with the dews of God's Spirit and grace. It is a precious promise that *they shall not sorrow any more at all;* it is only in that new Jerusalem *that all tears shall be wiped away,* Rev. xxi. 4. However, the returned captives had not any more those causes for sorrow which they had formerly had; and therefore (*v.* 13) *young men and old shall rejoice together.* 4. That both the ministers and those they minister to shall have abundant satisfaction in what God gives them (*v.* 14): *I will satiate the soul of the priests with fatness;* there shall be such a plenty of sacrifices brought to the altar that those who *live upon the altar* shall live comfortably, they and their families shall be *satiated with fatness, and my people shall be satisfied with my goodness.* This is applicable to the spiritual blessings which the redeemed of the Lord enjoy by Jesus Christ, infinitely more valuable than corn, and wine, and oil. 5. That those particularly who had been in sorrow for the loss of their children who were carried into captivity should have that sorrow turned into joy upon their return, *v.* 15–17. *In Ramah was there a voice heard,* at the time when the general captivity was nothing but *lamentation, and bitter weeping,* more there than in other places, because there Nebuzaradan had the general rendezvous of his captives, as appears, *ch.* xl. 1, where we find him sending Jeremiah back from Ramah. *Rachel* is here said to *weep for her children.* The sepulchre of Rachel was between Ramah and Bethlehem. Benjamin, one of the two tribes, and Ephraim, head of the ten tribes, were both descendants from Rachel. She had but two sons, the elder of whom was one for whom his father grieved and *refused to be comforted* (Gen. xxxvii. 35); the other she herself called *Benoni—the son of my sorrow.* Now the inhabitants of Ramah did in like manner *grieve for their sons and their daughters* that were carried away (as 1 Sam. xxx. 6). The tender parents even *refused to be comforted for their children, because they were not,* were not with them, but were in the hands of their enemies; they were never likely to see them any more. This is applied by the evangelists to the great mourning that was at Bethlehem for the murder of the infants there by Herod (Matt. ii. 17–18), and this scripture is said to be then fulfilled. Though we mourn, we must not murmur. In order to repress inordinate grief, we must consider that *there is hope in our end,* hope that the trouble will not last always, that it will be a happy end—the end will be peace. Though one generation falls in the wilderness, the next shall enter Canaan. *Thy* suffering *work shall be rewarded.* God makes his people *glad according to the days wherein he has afflicted them,* and so there is a proportion between the joys and the sorrows, as between the reward and the work, Rom. viii. 18. There is hope concerning children removed by death that they shall *return to their own border,* to the happy lot assigned them in the resurrection, a lot in the heavenly Canaan, that border of his sanctuary.

Verses 18–26

I. Ephraim's repentance, and return to God. *Ephraim shall say, What have I to do any more with idols?* Ephraim, the people, shall be as one man in their repentance. Ephraim is here weeping for sin, perhaps because Ephraim, the person from whom that tribe had its denomination, was a man of a tender spirit, *mourned for his children many days* (1 Chron. vii. 21, 22), and sorrow for sin is compared to that *for an only son.* He charges upon himself, in the first place, impatience under correction: *"Thou hast chastised me;* I have been under the rod, and I needed it, I deserved it; I was justly chastised, chastised *as a bullock,* who would never have felt the goad if he had not first rebelled against the yoke." This is the sin he finds himself guilty of now; but (*v.* 19) he reflects upon his sins in the days of his youth; now he remembers *the reproach of his youth.* He is here angry, having a holy indignation at himself for his sin and folly: He *smote upon his thigh,* as the publican upon his breast. He was amazed at his own stupidity and frowardness: He *was ashamed, yea even confounded.* He finds he cannot by any power of his own keep himself close with God, much less, when he has revolted, bring himself back to God, and therefore he prays, *Turn thou me and I shall be turned.* See *ch.* xvii. 14, *Heal me and I shall be healed.* He is here rejoicing in the experience he had of the blessed effect of divine grace: *Surely after that I was turned I repented.* All the pious workings of our heart towards God are the consequence of the working of his grace in us. When sinners come to a right knowledge they will come to a right way. Ephraim was chastised, and that did not produce the desired effect, it went no further: *I was chastised,* and that was all. But, when the instructions of God's Spirit accompanied the corrections of his providence, then the work was done.

II. God's compassion on Ephraim and the kind reception he finds with God, *v.* 20. 1. God owns him for a child, though he has been an undutiful child and a prodigal: *Is Ephraim my dear son? Is he a pleasant child?* Or, as it is sometimes supplied, *Is not Ephraim my dear son? Is he not a pleasant child?* Yes, now he repents and returns. *I do earnestly remember him still,* my thoughts towards him are thoughts of peace. When God afflicts his people, he does not forget them; when he casts them out of their land, he does not cast them out of sight, nor out of mind. It was God's compassion that mitigated Ephraim's punishment. *My heart is turned within me* (Hos. xi. 8, 9); and now the same compassion accepted Ephraim's repentance. He resolves to do him good: *I will surely have mercy upon him, saith the Lord.*

III. Gracious encouragements given to the people of God in Babylon to prepare for their return to their own land. Let them not tremble and lose their spirits; let them not trifle and lose their time; but with a firm resolution and a close application address themselves to their journey, *v.* 21, 22. *"Turn again, O virgin of Israel!* a virgin to be again espoused to thy God; *turn again to these thy cities;* though they are laid waste and in ruins, they are *thy cities,* which thy God gave thee, and therefore *turn again* to them." They must return the same way that they went, that the remembrance of the sorrows which attended them, or which their fathers had told them of, might make them the more thankful for their deliverance. Those that departed into the bondage of sin must return to the duties they neglected, must *do their first works. Set thy heart towards the highway.* The way from Babylon to Zion, from the bondage of sin to the glorious liberty of God's children, is a highway; yet none are likely to walk in it, unless they *set their hearts towards it. Set thee up way-marks,* and *make thee high heaps* or *pillars;* send before to

have such set up in all places where there is any danger of missing the road. Let those that go first, and are best acquainted with the way, set up such directions for those that follow. *How long wilt thou go about, O backsliding daughter?* Let not their minds fluctuate, or be uncertain. Let them not distract themselves with care and fear, but let them cast themselves upon God, and then let their minds be fixed. They are encouraged to do this by an assurance God gives them that he would *create a new thing in the earth, a woman shall compass a man.* The church of God, that is weak and feeble as a woman, altogether unapt for military employments (Isa. liv. 6), shall besiege, and prevail against a mighty man. The church is compared to a woman, Rev. xii. 1. And, whereas we find *armies compassing the camp of the saints* (Rev. xx. 9), now the camp of the saints shall compass them. Many good interpreters understand this *new thing* to be the incarnation of Christ, which had sometimes been given them for a sign, Isa. vii. 14; ix. 6. *A woman,* the virgin Mary, enclosed in her womb *the Mighty One;* for so *Geber,* the word here used, signifies; and God is called *Gibbor, the Mighty God* (ch. xxxii. 18), as also is Christ in Isa. ix. 6. He is *El-Gibbor, the mighty God.*

IV. A prospect given them of a happy settlement in their own land again. All their neighbours will give them a good word and put up a good prayer for them (*v.* 23): *As yet,* or rather *yet again* (though Judah and Jerusalem have long been a hissing), *this speech shall be used,* as it was formerly, *concerning the land of Judah and the cities thereof, The Lord bless you, O habitation of justice and mountain of holiness!* This intimates that they shall return much reformed; and this reformation shall be so conspicuous that all about them shall take notice of it. The *cities,* that used to be nests of pirates, shall be *habitations of justice;* the *mountain of Israel,* and especially Mount Zion, shall be a *mountain of holiness.* There shall be great plenty among them (*v.* 24, 25): *There shall dwell in Judah itself,* though it has now long lain waste, both husbandmen and shepherds, the two ancient and honourable employments of Cain and Abel, Gen. iv. 2. "I have *satiated the weary and sorrowful soul";* those that have been long sorrowful in their captivity, shall now enjoy great plenty. This is applicable to the spiritual blessings God has in store for all true penitents.

V. The prophet tells us what pleasure the discovery of this brought, *v.* 26. *"Upon this I awaked,* overcome with joy, which burst the fetters of sleep; and I reflected upon my dream, and it was such as had made *my sleep sweet to me;* I was refreshed, as men are with quiet sleep."

Verses 27–34

It is here further promised,

I. The people of God shall become both numerous and prosperous. Israel and Judah shall be replenished both with men and cattle, *v.* 27. This should be a type of the wonderful increase of the gospel-church. God will build them, and plant them, *v.* 28. He *will watch over them* to do them good. Everything for a long time had turned so much against them, that it seemed as if God had *watched over them to pluck up and to throw down;* but now everything shall happily strengthen and advance their interests.

II. They shall be reckoned with no further for the sins of their fathers (*v.* 29, 30). Our Saviour tells the wicked Jews in his days that they should smart for their fathers' sins, because they persisted in them, Matt. xxiii. 35, 36. But it is here promised that God would proceed no further for their fathers' sins, but remember his covenant with their fathers and do them good according to that covenant: *They shall no more* complain, as they have done, that *the fathers* have eaten sour grapes and the children's teeth are set on edge, but *everyone shall die for his own iniquity* still; he will reckon with particular persons that provoke him.

III. God will renew his covenant with them, so that all these blessings they shall have, not by providence only, but by promise. But this covenant refers to gospel times, the latter days that *shall come*; for of gospel grace the apostle understands it (Heb. viii. 8, 9, &c.), where this whole passage is quoted as a summary of the covenant of grace made with believers in Jesus Christ. This covenant is made—*with the house of Israel and Judah*, with the gospel church, *the Israel of God* on which *peace shall be* (Gal. vi. 16), with the spiritual seed of believing Abraham and praying Jacob. Judah and Israel had been two separate kingdoms, but were united after their return, in the joint favours God bestowed upon them; so Jews and Gentiles were in the gospel church and covenant. It is a *new covenant* and *not according to the covenant made with them when they came out of Egypt*. The ordinances and promises are more spiritual and heavenly, and the discoveries much more clear. That covenant God made with them when he *took them by the hand*, as if they had been blind, or lame, or weak, *to lead them out of the land of Egypt, which covenant they broke*. It was God that made this covenant, but it was the people that broke it; for our salvation is of God, but our sin and ruin are of ourselves. The particular articles of his covenant all contain spiritual blessings; not, "I will give them the land of Canaan and a numerous issue," but, "I will give them pardon, and peace, and grace, good heads and good hearts." He promises he will incline them to their duty: *I will put my law in their inward part and write it in their heart*. He will take them into relation to himself: *I will be their God*, a God all-sufficient to them, *and they shall be my people*, a loyal obedient people to me. Those that rightly know God's name will seek him, and serve him, and put their trust in him (v. 34): *All shall know me;* all shall be welcome to the knowledge of God and shall have the means of that knowledge; *his ways shall be known upon earth*, whereas, for many ages, *in Judah only was God known*. The priests preached but now and then, and in the temple, and to a few in comparison; but now all shall or may know God by frequenting the assemblies of Christians, wherein, through all parts of the church, the good knowledge of God shall be taught. In short, the things of God shall by the gospel of Christ be brought to a clearer light than ever (2. Tim. i. 10), and the people of God shall by the grace of Christ be brought to a clearer sight of those things than ever, Eph. i. 17, 18. Sin shall be pardoned. This is made the reason of all the rest: *For I will forgive their iniquity, will forgive* and forget: *I will remember their sin no more*.

Verses 35–40

The great thing here secured to us is that while the world stands God will have a church in it, which, though sometimes it may be brought very low, shall yet be raised again, and its interests re-established; it is *built upon a rock, and the gates of hell shall not prevail against it*.

I. The building of the world, and the firmness of that building, are evidences of the power and faithfulness of God who has undertaken the establishment of his church. *He that built all things* at first *is God* (Heb. iii. 4). The constancy of the kingdom of nature may encourage us to depend upon the divine promise for the continuance of the glories of the kingdom of grace.

1. The glories of the kingdom of nature. *He gives the sun for a light by day* (v. 35), not only made it at first to be so, but still gives it to be so; for the light

and heat, and all the influences of the sun, continually depend upon its great Creator. He gives *the ordinances of the moon and stars for a light by night*; their motions are called *ordinances* because they are regular and under rule. See Job xxxviii. 31–33. Notice the government of the sea, and the check that is given to its proud billows: *The Lord of hosts divides the sea*, or (as some read it) *settles the sea, when the waves thereof roar*. Notice the vastness of the heavens and the unmeasurable extent of the firmament; the *heavens above cannot be measured* (v. 37), and yet God fills them. Notice the mysteriousness even of that part of the creation in which our lot is cast. Notice the immovable steadfastness of all these (v. 36): *These ordinances cannot depart from before God; for all are his servants*, Ps. cxix. 90, 91. The heavens are often clouded, and the sun and moon often eclipsed, the earth may quake and the sea be tossed, but they all keep their place, are moved, but not removed.

2. The securities of the kingdom of grace inferred hence: *the seed of Israel shall not cease from being a nation*, 1 Pet. ii. 9. When Israel according to the flesh is no longer a nation the *children of the promise are counted for the seed* (Rom. ix. 8) and God *will not cast off all the seed of Israel*, though they have done very wickedly, v. 37. The God that has undertaken the preservation of the church is a God of almighty power, who *upholds all things by his* almighty *word*. *Our help stands in his name who made heaven and earth*, and therefore can do anything. God would not take all this care of the world but that he designs glory; and how shall he have it but by securing to himself a church in it, a people that *shall be to him for a name and a praise?* If the order of the creation therefore continues firm because it was well-fixed at first, and is not altered because it needs no alteration, the method of grace shall for the same reason continue invariable, as it was at first well settled. He who has promised to preserve a church for himself has approved himself faithful to the word which he has spoken concerning the stability of the world.

II. The rebuilding of Jerusalem, now in ruins, shall be an earnest of these great things that God will do for the gospel church, the *heavenly Jerusalem*, v. 38–40. *The days will come*, though they may be long in coming, when Jerusalem shall be entirely built again, as large as ever it was. The wall which Nehemiah built, and which, the more punctually to fulfil the prophecy, began about the *tower of Hananeel*, here mentioned (Neh. iii. 1), enclosed as much ground as is here intended, though we cannot certainly determine the places here called *the gate of the corner*, *the hill Gareb*, &c. When built it shall be consecrated to God and to his service (v. 38), and even the suburbs and fields adjacent *shall be holy unto the Lord*. The whole city shall be as it were one temple, one holy place, as the new Jerusalem is, which *therefore* has no temple, because it is all temple. It shall continue very long, the time of the new city from the return to its last destruction being as long as that of the old from David to the captivity. But this promise was to have its full accomplishment in the gospel church, which is the spiritual Israel, and therefore God will not cast it off. It is the holy city, and therefore all the powers of men *shall not pluck it up, nor throw it down*.

CHAPTER 32

I. Jeremiah imprisoned for foretelling the destruction of Jerusalem and the captivity of king Zedekiah, ver. 1–5. II. We have him buying land, by divine appointment, as an assurance that in due time a happy end should be put to the present troubles, ver. 6–15. III. We have his prayer, which he offered up to God upon that occasion, ver. 16–25. IV. We have a message which God entrusted him to deliver to the people. 1. He must foretell the utter destruction of Judah and Jerusalem for their sins, ver. 26–35. But, 2. At the same time he must assure them that, though the destruction was total, it should not be final, ver. 36–44.

Verses 1–15

The desolations of Judah and Jerusalem by the Chaldeans came gradually upon them, but, they not meeting him by repentance in the way of his judgments, he proceeded till all was laid waste, which was in the eleventh year of Zedekiah; now what is here recorded happened in the tenth. The king of Babylon's army had now invested Jerusalem and was carrying on the siege with vigour.

I. Jeremiah prophesies that both the city and the court shall fall into the hands of the king of Babylon. He tells them that God, whose city it was, will give it into their hands and put it out of his protection (*v.* 3)—that, though Zedekiah attempt to make his escape, he shall be overtaken, and shall be delivered a prisoner into the hands of Nebuchadnezzar. He shall hear the king of Babylon pronounce his doom, and see with what fury and indignation he will look upon him (*His eyes shall behold his eyes, v.* 4)—that Zedekiah shall be carried to Babylon, and continue a miserable captive there, *until God visit him,* that is, till God put an end to his life by a natural death, as Nebuchadnezzar had long before put an end to his days by putting out his eyes.

II. For prophesying thus he is imprisoned, not in the common gaol, but *in the king of Judah's house,* and there not closely confined, but would be sheltered from the abuses of the mob. However, it was a prison, and Zedekiah shut him up in it for prophesying as he did, *v.* 2, 3. So far was he from *humbling himself before Jeremiah* (2 Chron. xxxvi. 12), that he *hardened himself* against him. Though he had formerly so far owned him a prophet as to desire him to *enquire of the Lord for them* (ch. xxi. 2), yet now he chides him for prophesying (*v.* 3), and shuts him up in prison, perhaps to restrain him from prophesying any further.

III. Being in prison, he purchases from a near relation of his a piece of ground that lay in Anathoth, *v.* 6, 7, &c. It was most strange that he should buy a *piece of land* when he himself knew that the whole land was now to be laid waste and fall into the hands of the Chaldeans. But it was the will of God that he should buy it, and he submitted, though the money seemed to be thrown away. His kinsman came to offer it to him; it was not of his own seeking; besides, the *right of redemption* belonged to him (*v.* 8), and if he refused it he would not do the kinsman's part. It was land that lay within the suburbs of a priests' city, and, if he should refuse it, there was danger lest, in these times of disorder, it might be sold to one of another tribe, which was contrary to the law. It would likewise be a kindness to his kinsman, who probably was at this time in great want of money. When Jeremiah knew by Hanameel's coming to him, as God had foretold he would, that *it was the word of the Lord,* that it was his mind that he should make this purchase, he made no more difficulty of it, but *bought the field.* He was very honest and exact in paying. He *weighed him the money,* did not press him to take it upon his report. It was *seventeen shekels of silver.* We shall not wonder at the smallness of the price if we consider what scarcity there was of money at this time and how little lands were counted upon. He was very prudent in preserving the writings. They were subscribed *before witnesses.* One copy was *sealed up,* the other was *open.* The deeds of purchase were lodged in the hands of Baruch, before witnesses, and he was ordered to lay them up in an *earthen vessel* that they might *continue many days,* for the use of Jeremiah's heirs. The design of having this bargain made was to signify that though Jerusalem was now besieged, and the whole country was likely to be laid waste, yet the time should come when *houses, and fields, and vineyards should be again possessed in this land, v.* 15. As God appointed Jeremiah to confirm his predictions of the approaching

destruction of Jerusalem by his own practice in living unmarried, so he now appointed him to confirm his predictions of the future restoration of Jerusalem by his own practice in purchasing this field. Lucius Florus relates it as a great instance of the bravery of the Roman citizens that in the time of the second Punic War, when Hannibal besieged Rome and was very near making himself master of it, a field on which part of his army lay, being offered to sale at that time, was immediately purchased, in a firm belief that the Roman valour would raise the siege, *lib.* ii. *cap.* 6. And have not we much more reason to venture our all upon the word of God.

Verses 16–25

Jeremiah's prayer to God upon occasion of the discoveries God had made to him of his purposes concerning this nation, to pull it down, and in time to build it up again, which puzzled the prophet, who, though he delivered his messages faithfully, yet, in reflecting upon them, was greatly at a loss how to reconcile them; in that perplexity he poured out his soul before God in prayer. Jeremiah was in prison, in distress, in the dark about the meaning of God's providences, and then he prays.

I. Jeremiah adores God and gives him the glory due to his name as the Creator, *v.* 17–19. When at any time we are perplexed about the particular dispensations of Providence it is good for us to satisfy ourselves with the general doctrines of God's wisdom, power, and goodness. Let us consider, as Jeremiah does here, 1. That God is the fountain of all being, power, life, motion, and perfection: He *made the heaven and the earth with his outstretched arm.* 2. That with him nothing is impossible: *Nothing is too hard for thee.* 3. That he is a God of boundless mercy: "Thou not only art kind, but thou *showest lovingkindness,* not to a few, to here and there one, but *to thousands,* thousands of persons, thousands of generations." 4. That he is a God of impartial and inflexible justice. 5. That he is a God of universal dominion and command: He is *the great God,* for he is *the mighty God.* He is *the Lord of hosts,* of all hosts, that *is his name.* 6. That he contrives everything for the best: He is *great in counsel,* so deep are the designs of his wisdom.

II. He acknowledges the universal cognizance God takes of all the actions of the children of men (*v.* 19): *Thy eyes are open upon all the sons of men,* wherever they are, beholding the evil and the good, and upon all *their ways,* not as an unconcerned spectator, but as an observing judge; for men shall find God as they are found of him.

III. He recounts the great things God had done for his people Israel formerly. 1. He brought them out of Egypt, that house of bondage, with *signs and wonders. Israel* were reminded of it every year by the ordinance of the passover. All the neighbouring nations spoke of it, as that which redounded exceedingly to the glory of the God of Israel, and made him *a name as at this day.* 2. He brought them into Canaan, that *land flowing with milk and honey.* He *swore to their fathers to give it them,* and he did give it to the children (*v.* 22) *and they came in and possessed it.* It is good for us often to reflect upon the great things God did for his church formerly, especially in the first erecting of it, that work of wonder.

IV. He bewails the rebellions they had been guilty of against God, and the judgments God had brought upon them for these rebellions. It is a sad account he here gives of the ungrateful conduct of that people towards God. He had done everything that he had promised to do, but they had *done nothing of all that he commanded them to do* (*v.* 23). 1. He compares the present state of Jerusalem with the divine predictions, and finds that what God *has spoken* has come to pass. God had given them fair warning of it before; and, if they had regarded this, the ruin would have been prevented. 2. He commits the present state of Jerusalem to the divine compassion (*v.* 24): *Behold the mounts,* or *ramparts,* or the *engines* which they make use of to batter the city. "*Behold thou seest it. Is this the city that thou hast chosen to put thy name there? And shall it be thus abandoned?*" He neither complains of God for what he had done nor prescribes to God what he should do, but desires he would behold their case. Whatever trouble we are in we may comfort ourselves with this, that God sees it and sees how to remedy it.

V. He seems desirous to be let further into the meaning of the order God had now given him to purchase his kinsman's field (*v.* 25): "*Though the city is given into the hands of the Chaldeans,* and no man is likely to enjoy what he has, yet *thou hast said unto me, Buy thou the field.*" As soon as he understood that it was the mind of God he did it; but, when he had done it, he desired better to understand why God had ordered him to do it. Though we are bound to follow God with an implicit obedience, yet we should endeavour that it may be more and more an intelligent obedience. We must never dispute God's statutes and judgments, but we may and must enquire, *What mean these statutes and judgments?* Deut. vi. 20.

Verses 26–44

God's answer to Jeremiah's prayer to quiet his mind. It is a full discovery of the purposes of God's wrath against the present generation and the purposes of his grace concerning the future generations. Jeremiah knew not how to *sing both of mercy and judgment,* but God here teaches to sing unto him of both. When Jeremiah was ordered to buy the field in Anathoth he hoped that God was about to order the Chaldeans to raise the siege. "No," says God, "the execution of the sentence shall go on; Jerusalem shall be laid in ruins." But, lest Jeremiah should think that his being ordered to buy this field intimated that all the mercy God had in store for his people, after their return, was only that they should have the possession of their own land again, he informs him that that was but a type of those spiritual blessings which should then be abundantly bestowed upon them, unspeakably more valuable than fields and vineyards; in this *word of the Lord* to Jeremiah, we have first as dreadful threatenings and then as precious promises as perhaps any we have in the Old Testament.

I. The ruin of Judah and Jerusalem is here pronounced. 1. God here asserts his own sovereignty and power (*v.* 27): *Behold, I am Jehovah,* a selfexistent self-sufficient being; *I am that I am; I am the God of all flesh,* that is, of all mankind. 2. He abides by what he had often said of the destruction of Jerusalem by the king of Babylon (*v.* 28): *I will give this city into his hand, and he shall take it, v.* 29. *The Chaldeans shall come and set fire to it,* shall burn it and all the *houses in it,* God's house not excepted, nor the king's either. 3. The reason for these severe proceedings against the city. It is sin that ruins it. They were impudent and daring in sin. They *offered incense to Baal,* not in corners, as men ashamed, but upon the *tops of their houses* (*v.* 29). They did it *to provoke me to anger, v.* 29. *They have only provoked me to anger with the works of their hands, v.* 30. And again (*v.* 32), *All the evil which they have done was to provoke me to anger.* They resolved to try his jealousy and dare him to his face. "Jerusalem has been *to me a provocation of my anger and fury," v.* 31. They had continued provoking God: "They have *done evil before me from their youth,* ever since they were first formed into a people (*v.* 30), witness their murmurings and rebellions in the wilderness." And as for Jerusalem, though it was the *holy city,* it has been *a provocation from the day that they built it, even to this day, v.* 31. All contributed to the common guilt, and therefore were justly involved in the common ruin. Not only the *children of Israel,* that had revolted from the temple, but the *children of Judah* too, that still adhered to it. God had again and again called them to repentance, but they rudely turned their back on him. "*I taught them* better manners, *rising up early, in teaching them,* studying to adapt the teaching to their capacities, but all in vain." There was in their idolatries an impious contempt of God; for (*v.* 34) *they set their abominations* (their idols) *in the house which is called by my name, to defile it.* They were guilty of the most unnatural cruelty to their own children; for *they sacrificed them to Moloch, v.* 35. They *caused Judah to sin, v.* 35. The whole country was infected with the contagious idolatries and iniquities of Jerusalem.

II. The restoration of Judah and Jerusalem is here promised, *v.* 36, &c. God will in judgment remember mercy, and there will a time come, a set time, to favour Zion. This people were now at length brought to despair. When the judgment was threatened at a distance they had no fear; when it attacked them they had no hope. They said concerning the city (*v.* 36), *It shall be delivered into the hand of the king of Babylon, by the sword, famine, and pestilence.* Concerning the country they said, with vexation (*v.* 43), *It is desolate, without man or beast;* there is no relief, there is no remedy. *It is given into the hand of the Chaldeans.* The hope that God gives them of mercy: Though their carcasses must fall in captivity, yet their children shall again see this good land and the goodness of God in it. They shall be brought up from their captivity and shall come and settle again in this land, *v.* 37. He had dispersed them, and *driven them into all countries.* Those that fled dispersed themselves; those that fell into the enemies' hands were dispersed by them, in policy, to prevent combinations among them. God's hand was in both. But now God will *gather them out of all the countries whither they were driven,* as he promised in the law (Deut. xxx. 3, 4). Being reformed, and having returned to God, neither their own consciences within nor their enemies without shall be a terror to them. He promises (*v.* 41): *I will plant them in this land assuredly;* they shall here enjoy a holy security and repose, and they shall take root here, shall be *planted in stability.* God will renew his covenant with them, a covenant of grace, the blessings of which are spiritual. It is called an *everlasting covenant* (*v.* 40), not only because God will be for ever faithful to it, but because the consequences of it will be everlasting. For, doubtless, here the promises look further than to Israel according to the flesh, and are sure to all believers. Good Christians may apply them to themselves and plead them with God. *They shall be my people.* He will make them his by working in them all the characters and dispositions of his people. "And, to make them truly, completely, and eternally happy, *I will be their God.*" God will give them a heart to fear him, *v.* 39. That which he requires of those whom he takes into covenant with him as his people is that they reverence his majesty, dread his wrath, stand in awe of his authority, pay homage to him, and give him the glory due unto his name. It is repeated (*v.* 40): *I will put my fear in their hearts,* that is, work in them gracious principles and dispositions, that shall influence and govern their whole conversation. Teachers may put good things into our heads, but it is God only that can put them into our hearts, that can work in us *both to will and to do.* He will effectually provide for their perseverance in grace and the perpetuating of the covenant between himself and them. God will never leave nor forsake them: *I will not turn away from them to do them good.* Earthly princes are fickle, but God's *mercy endures for ever.* God may seem to turn from this people (Isa. liv. 8), but even then he does not turn from doing and designing them good. We have no reason to distrust God's fidelity and constancy, but our own; and therefore it is here promised that God will *give them a heart to fear him for ever* (Prov. xxiii. 17). He will entail a blessing upon their seed, will give them grace to fear him, *for the good of them and of their children after them.* As their departures from God had been to the prejudice of their children, so their adherence to God should be to the advantage of their children. We cannot better consult the good of posterity than by setting up the fear and worship of God in our families. When he punishes them it is with reluctance. *How shall I give thee up, Ephraim?* But, when he restores them he rejoices in doing them good. He is himself a cheerful giver, and therefore loves a cheerful servant. All things shall appear at last so to have been working for the good of the church that it will be said, The governor of the world is entirely taken up with the care of his church. These promises shall as surely be performed as the foregoing threatenings were. *As I have brought all this great evil upon them,* pursuant to divine justice, *so I will bring upon them all this good,* pursuant to the promise, and for the glory of divine mercy. As an earnest of all this, houses and lands shall again fetch a good price in Judah and Jerusalem (v. 43, 44): *Fields shall be bought in this land;* here rather than anywhere else. In *the places about Jerusalem, in the cities of Judah* and of Israel, in all parts of the country, *men shall buy fields, and subscribe evidences.* Trade shall revive. Husbandry shall revive. Laws shall again have their due course, for they shall *subscribe evidences and seal them.* This is mentioned to reconcile Jeremiah to his new purchase. Though he had bought a piece of ground and could not go to see it, this was the pledge of many a purchase, and those but faint resemblances of the purchased possessions in the heavenly Canaan, reserved for all those who have God's fear in their hearts.

CHAPTER 33

This chapter is much the same—to confirm the promise of the restoration of the Jews, notwithstanding the present desolations of their country and dispersions of their people. And these promises have, in type, a reference as far forward as to the gospel church. It is here promised, I. That the city shall be rebuilt and re-established, ver. 1–6. II. That the captives, having their sins pardoned, shall be restored, ver. 7, 8. III. That this shall redound to the glory of God, ver. 9. IV. That the country shall have both joy and plenty, ver. 10–14. V. That way shall be made for the coming of the Messiah, ver. 15, 16. VI. That the house of David, the house of Levi, and the house of Israel, shall flourish again, and all three in the kingdom of Christ; a gospel ministry and the gospel church shall continue while the world stands, ver. 17–26.

Verses 1–9

I. The date of this comfortable prophecy was after that in the foregoing chapter, when things were still growing worse and worse; it was *the second time.* God speaketh once, yea, twice, for the encouragement of his people. We are not only so disobedient that we have need of *precept upon precept* to bring us to our duty, but so distrustful that we have need of promise upon promise to bring us to our comfort. This word, as the former, *came to Jeremiah* when *he was in prison.*

II. The prophecy itself.

1. Who it is that secures this comfort to them (v. 2): It is *the Lord, the maker thereof, the Lord that framed it.* He is the maker and former of heaven and earth. He is the maker and former of Jerusalem, of Zion, built them at first, and therefore can rebuild them—built them for his own praise, and therefore *will.* He is the maker and former of this promise; he has laid the scheme for Jerusalem's restoration, and he that has made the promise will make it good; for Jehovah *is his name,* a God giving being to his promises by the performance of them, known by that name (Exod. vi. 3), a perfecting God. When the heavens and the earth were finished, then, and not till then, the Creator is called *Jehovah,* Gen. ii. 4.

2. How this comfort must be obtained—by prayer (v. 3): *Call upon me, and I will answer thee.* Christ himself must *ask, and it shall be given him,* Ps. ii. 8. *I will show thee great and mighty things, hidden things, which,* though in part discovered already, yet *thou knowest not.* Promises are given, not to supersede, but to quicken and encourage prayer. See Ezek. xxxvi. 37.

3. The condition of Jerusalem made it necessary that such comforts as these should be provided for it (v. 4, 5): *The houses of this city,* not excepting those *of the kings of Judah, are thrown down by the mounts,* or engines of battery, *and by the sword,* or axes, or hammers. The strongest stateliest houses were levelled with the ground. Those that *came to fight with the Chaldeans* did more hurt than good, provoked the enemy to be more fierce and furious in their assaults, so that the houses in Jerusalem were filled *with the dead bodies of men.* God says that they were such as he had *slain in his anger,* for the enemies' sword was his sword. But, it seems, the men that were slain had distinguished themselves by their wickedness, the very men *for whose wickedness God did now hide himself from this city.*

4. The blessings which God has in store for Judah and Jerusalem, such as will redress all their grievances. God will provide for the healing, though the disease was thought mortal and incurable, ch. viii. 22. "*The whole head is sick, and the whole heart faint* (Isa. i. 5); but (v. 6) *I will bring it health and cure;* I will prevent the death, remove the sickness, and set all to rights again," ch. xxx. 17. The sin of Jerusalem was the sickness of it (Isa. i. 6); its reformation therefore will be its recovery. "*I will reveal unto them the abundance of peace and truth.*" *Peace* stands here for all good; peace and the true religion, peace and the true worship of God, in opposition to the many falsehoods and deceits by which they had been led away from God. We may apply it more generally. Peace and truth are the great subject-matter of divine revelation. These promises here lead us to the gospel of Christ, and in that God has revealed to us *peace and truth*—truth to direct us, peace to make us easy. *Grace and truth,* and abundance of both, *come by Jesus Christ.* Peace and truth are the life of the soul, and Christ *came that we might have* that *life, and might have it more abundantly.* Christ rules by the power of truth (John xviii. 37) and by it he gives *abundance of peace,* Ps. lxxii. 7; lxxxv. 10. The divine revelation of peace and truth brings health and cure to all those that by faith receive it. Are they scattered and enslaved, and is their nation laid in ruins? "*I will cause their captivity to return* (v. 7), both that of Israel and that of Judah." Is sin the procuring cause of all their troubles? That shall be pardoned and subdued, and so the root of the judgments shall be killed, v. 8. As those that were ceremonially unclean, and were therefore shut out from the tabernacle, when they were sprinkled with the *water of purification* had liberty of access to it again, so had they to their own land, and the privileges of it, when God had *cleansed them from their iniquities.* Have both their sins and their sufferings turned to the dishonour of God? Their reformation and restoration shall redound as much to his praise, v. 9. The neighbouring nations shall look upon the growing greatness of the Jewish nation as really formidable, and shall be afraid of making them their enemies. When the church is *fair as the moon,* and *clear as the sun,* she is *terrible as an army with banners.*

Verses 10–16

A further prediction of the happy state of Judah and Jerusalem after their glorious return out of captivity, issuing gloriously at length in the kingdom of the Messiah.

I. It is promised that the people who were long in sorrow shall again be filled with joy. Everyone concluded now that the country would lie for ever desolate, that *no beasts* would be found in the land of Judah, no inhabitant *in the streets of Jerusalem* (*v.* 10); but, though weeping may endure for a time, joy will return. There shall be common joy there, *the voice of the bridegroom and the voice of the bride;* marriages shall again be celebrated, as formerly, with songs. There shall be religious joy there; temple-songs shall be revived, *the Lord's songs,* which they could not *sing in a strange land.* They shall praise him both as *the Lord of hosts* and as the God who *is good* and whose *mercy endures for ever.* This, though a song of old, yet, being sung upon this fresh occasion, will be a new song. We find this literally fulfilled at their return out of Babylon, Ezra iii. 11. All the sacrifices were intended for the praise of God, but this seems to be meant of the spiritual sacrifices of humble adorations and joyful thanksgivings, *the calves of our lips* (Hos. xiv. 2), which *shall please the Lord better than an ox or bullock.*

II. It is promised that the country, which had lain long depopulated, shall be replenished and stocked again. *In all the cities of Judah and Benjamin there shall be a habitation of shepherds, v.* 12, 13. The country, after their return, shall not be a habitation of beggars, who have nothing, but of shepherds and husbandmen. The seed of Jacob, in their beginning, gloried in this, that they were shepherds (Gen. xlvii. 3), and so they shall now be again, giving themselves wholly to that innocent employment, *causing their flocks to lie down* (*v.* 12) and to *pass under the hands of him that telleth them* (*v.* 13); flocks to number them, that they may know if any be missing. Now because it seemed incredible that a people, reduced as now they were, should ever recover such a degree of peace and plenty as this, here is subjoined a general ratification of these promises (*v.* 14): *I will perform that good thing which I have promised.*

III. To crown all these blessings which God has in store for them, here is a promise of the Messiah, and of that everlasting righteousness which he should bring in (*v.* 15, 16), and probably this is *that good thing,* that great good thing, which in the latter days, days that were yet to come, God would perform, as he had promised to Judah and Israel, and to which their return out of captivity and their settlement again in their own land was preparatory. *From the captivity to Christ* is one of the famous periods, Matt. i. 17. This promise of the Messiah we had before (*ch.* xxiii. 5, 6), and there it came in as a confirmation of the promise of the shepherds whom God would set over them, which would make one think that the promise here concerning the shepherds and their flocks, which introduces it, is to be understood figuratively. Christ is here prophesied, 1. As a rightful King. He is a *branch of righteousness,* not a usurper, for he *grows up unto David.* 2. As a righteous king, righteous in enacting laws, waging wars, and giving judgment, righteous in vindicating those that suffer wrong and punishing those that do wrong: *He shall execute judgment and righteousness in the land.* 3. As a king that shall protect his subjects from all injury. By him *Judah shall be saved* from wrath and the curse, and, being so saved, *Jerusalem shall dwell safely,* quiet from the fear of evil, and enjoying serenity of mind, in dependence upon this prince of their peace. 4. As a king that shall be praised by his subjects: *"This is the name whereby they shall call him"* (so the Chaldee reads it, the Syriac, and vulgar Latin); *"this name of his they shall celebrate and triumph in, and by this name they shall call upon him."* The city is called *The Lord our righteousness,* because they glory in Jehovah as their righteousness. That which was before said to be the name of Christ is here made the name of Jerusalem, the city of the Messiah, the church of Christ. He it is that imparts righteousness to her, for he is *made of God to us righteousness,* and she, by bearing that name, professes to have her whole righteousness, not from herself, but from him.

Verses 17–26

Three of God's covenants, that of royalty with David and his seed, that of the priesthood with Aaron and his seed, and that with Abraham and his seed, seemed to be all broken and lost while the captivity lasted; but it is here promised that the true intents and meaning of them shall be abundantly answered in the New Testament blessings, typified by those conferred on the Jews after their return out of captivity.

I. The covenant of royalty shall have full accomplishment in the kingdom of Christ, the Son of David, *v.* 17. The throne of Israel was overturned in the captivity; there was not *a man to sit on the throne of Israel.* After their return the house of David made a figure again; but it is in the Messiah that this promise is performed that *David shall never want a man to sit on the throne of Israel.* For as long as Christ Jesus sits on the right hand of the throne of God, glorified head over all things, as long as he is *King upon the holy hill of Zion,* David does not want a successor, nor is the covenant with him broken. *The Lord God shall give him the throne of his father David and he shall reign over the house of Jacob for ever,* Luke i. 32, 33. It is promised that the covenant with David shall be as firm as the ordinances of heaven. There is a covenant of nature here called *a covenant of the day and the night* (*v.* 20, 25), because this is one of the articles of it, That there shall be *day and night in their season.* God divided between the light and the darkness, and established a government to each, that *the sun* should *rule by day* and *the moon and stars by night* (Gen. i. 4, 5, 16). The *morning and* the *evening* have both of them their regular *out-goings* (Ps. lxv. 8); the *day-spring knows its place, knows its time,* and keeps both, so do *the shadows of the evening;* and, while the world stands, this course shall not be altered, this covenant shall not be broken. Thus firm shall the covenant of redemption be with the Redeemer—God's servant, but David our King, *v.* 21. Christ shall have a church on earth to the world's end; till time and day shall be no more. Christ's *kingdom is an everlasting kingdom;* and when *the end cometh,* and not till then, it *shall be delivered up to God,* even *the Father.* But the condition of it in this world shall be intermixed, prosperity and adversity succeeding each other, as day and night. Though the sun will set to-night, it will rise again to-morrow morning, whether we live to see it or no, so sure we may be that, though the kingdom of the Redeemer in the world may for a time be clouded by corruptions and persecutions, yet it will shine forth again in the time appointed. *The seed of David* shall be as numerous *as the host of heaven,* that is, the spiritual seed of the Messiah, born to him by the efficacy of his gospel and his Spirit working with it. Christ's seed are not, as David's were, his successors, but his subjects; yet the day is coming when they also shall reign with him (*v.* 22).

II. The covenant of priesthood shall be secured, and the promises of that also shall have their full accomplishment. During the captivity there was no altar, no temple service, for the priests to attend upon; but this also shall revive. Immediately upon their coming back to Jerusalem there were priests and Levites ready to *offer burnt-offerings* and to *do sacrifice continually* (Ezra iii. 2, 3), as is here promised, *v.* 18. But that priesthood soon grew corrupt; *the covenant of Levi was profaned* (as appears Mal. ii. 8), and in the destruction of Jerusalem by the Romans it came to a final period. The priesthood of Christ supersedes that of Aaron, and is the substance of that shadow. While that great *high priest of our profession* is always appearing *in the presence of God for us*, it may truly be said that *the Levites do not want a man before God to offer continually*, Heb. vii. 3, 17. He is a priest for ever. While there are faithful ministers to preside in religious assemblies, and to offer up the spiritual sacrifices of prayer and praise, *the priests, the Levites*, do not want successors, and such as *have obtained a more excellent ministry*. The apostle makes those that preach the gospel to come in the room of those that served at the altar, 1 Cor. ix. 13, 14. All true believers are *a holy priesthood, a royal priesthood* (1 Pet. ii. 5, 9), who are *made to our God kings and priests* (Rev. i. 6); they *offer up spiritual sacrifices, acceptable to God*, and themselves, in the first place, *living sacrifices*. Of these Levites this promise must be understood (*v.* 22), that they shall be as numerous *as the sand of the sea*, for all God's spiritual Israel are spiritual priests, Rev. v. 9, 10; vii. 9, 15.

III. The covenant of peculiarity likewise shall be secured and the promises of that covenant shall have their full accomplishment in the gospel Israel. This covenant was looked upon as broken during the captivity, *v.* 24. Either the enemies of Israel, or the unbelieving Israelites themselves, have broken covenant with God, as if he had not dealt faithfully with them. "*Thus have they despised my people*, that is, despised the privilege of being my people as if it were a privilege of no value at all." The covenant stands notwithstanding, as firm as that with day and night; sooner will God suffer day and night to cease than he will *cast away the seed of Jacob*. This cannot refer to the seed of Jacob according to the flesh, for they are cast away, but to the Christian church, in which all these promises were to be lodged, as appears by the apostle's discourse, Rom. xi. 1, &c. Christianity shall continue in the dominion of Christ, and the subjection of Christians to him, till day and night come to an end. *I will cause their captivity to return;* and, having brought them back, *I will have mercy on them.* To whom this promise refers appears Gal. vi. 16, where all that *walk according to the gospel rule* are made to be the *Israel of God*, on whom *peace and mercy* shall be.

CHAPTER 34

Two messages which God sent by Jeremiah. I. One to foretell the fate of Zedekiah king of Judah, that he should fall into the hands of the king of Babylon, a captive, but should die in peace in his captivity, ver. 1–7. II. Another to read the doom both of prince and people for their treacherous dealings with God, in bringing back into bondage their servants whom they had released according to the law (ver. 8–11), and therefore God would bring the Chaldean army again when they began to hope that they had got clear of them, ver. 12–22.

Verses 1–7

This prophecy concerning Zedekiah was delivered to Jeremiah, and by him to the parties concerned, before he was shut up in the prison, *ch.* xxxii. 4.

I. This message was sent to Zedekiah *when the king of Babylon*, with all his forces, *fought against Jerusalem and the cities thereof* (*v.* 1), designing to destroy them. The cities that now remained, and yet held out, are named (*v.* 7), *Lachish and Azekah*. This intimates that things were now brought to the last extremity, and yet Zedekiah obstinately stood it out.

II. The message was sent to him. He is told that which he had been often told before, that the city

shall be taken by the Chaldeans *and burnt with fire* (*v.* 2), that he shall be made a prisoner, brought before Nebuchadnezzar, and be carried away captive into Babylon (*v.* 3); yet Ezekiel prophesied that he *should not see Babylon*; nor did he, for his eyes were put out, Ezek. xii. 13. He shall die a captive, but *not by the sword*; he *shall die in peace*, *v.* 5. What evil he had *done in the sight of the Lord* he repented of in his captivity, and, God being reconciled to him, he might truly be said to *die in peace*. A man may die in a prison and yet *die in peace*. His afflictions wrought such a change in him that his death was looked upon as a great loss. It is better to live and die penitent in a prison than to live and die impenitent in a palace. *They will lament thee, saying, Ah lord!* an honour which his brother Jehoiakim had not, *ch.* xxii. 18.

III. Jeremiah's faithfulness in delivering this message. Though he knew it might prove, as indeed it did, dangerous to himself (for he was imprisoned for it), yet he *spoke all these words to Zedekiah, v.* 6.

Verses 8–22

Another prophecy upon a particular occasion.

I. When Jerusalem was closely besieged by the Chaldean army the princes and people agreed upon a reformation concerning their servants. The law of God was very express, that those of their own nation should not be held in servitude above seven years, but, after they had served one apprenticeship, they should have their liberty; though they had sold themselves for the payment of their debts, or though they were *sold by the judges* for the punishment of their crimes. Those of other nations taken in war, or bought with money, might be held in perpetual slavery, but their brethren must serve but for seven years. This God calls the covenant that he had made with them when he *brought them out of the land of Egypt*, *v.* 13, 14. This was the first of the judicial laws which God gave them (Exod. xxi. 2). God had brought them out of slavery in Egypt, and he would have them thus to express their grateful sense of that favour, by letting those go to whom their houses were *houses of bondage*, as Egypt had been to their fore-fathers. God's compassions towards us should engage our compassions towards our brethren; we must release as we are released. This law they and their fathers had broken. Their worldly profit swayed more with them than God's covenant. When their servants had lived seven years with them they understood their business better than they did, and therefore they would by no means part with them. *Your fathers hearkened not to me* in this matter (*v.* 14), and they thought they might do it because their fathers did it. For this sin of theirs, and their fathers, God now brought them into servitude, and justly. When they were besieged by the Chaldeans they, being told of their fault in this matter, immediately reformed, and let go all their servants that were entitled to their freedom, as Pharaoh, when the plague was upon him, consented to *let the people go*. The prophets admonished them concerning their sin. From them they heard that they should let their Hebrew servants *go free*, *v.* 10. The *king*, and the *princes*, and *all the people*, agreed to *let go their servants*. The people could not for shame but follow. They bound themselves by a solemn oath and covenant that they would do this, whereby they engaged themselves to God and one another. This covenant was made in a sacred place, *made before me, in the house which is called by my name* (*v.* 15), in the presence of God. It was ratified by a significant sign; they *cut a calf in two, and passed between the parts thereof* (*v.* 18, 19) with this dreadful imprecation, "Let us be in like manner cut asunder if we do not perform what we now promise." They conformed themselves herein to the command of God and *let their servants go*, though the city was besieged and they could very ill spare them. Thus they did *right in God's sight, v.* 15.

II. When there was some hope that the siege was raised and the danger over they undid the good they had done, and forced the servants they had released into their services again. The *king of Babylon's army* had now *gone up from them, v.* 21. Pharaoh was bringing an army of Egyptians to oppose the progress of the king of Babylon's victories, and the Chaldeans raised the siege for a time, *ch.* xxxvii. 5. It was especially an affront to God; in doing this they *polluted his name, v.* 16.

III. For this treacherous dealing with God they are here severely threatened. *Be not deceived; God is not mocked.* Those that think to put a cheat upon God by a partial temporary reformation, will put the greatest cheat upon their own souls. Since they had not given liberty to their servants to go where they pleased, God would give all his judgments liberty to take their course (*v.* 17): *You have not proclaimed liberty to your servants.* "*Therefore I will proclaim a liberty for you;* I will discharge you from my service, and put you out of my protection, which those forfeit that withdraw from their allegiance. You shall have liberty to choose which of these judgments you will be cut off by, *sword, famine, or pestilence.*" Since they had brought their servants back into confinement in their houses, God would *make them to be removed into all the kingdoms of the earth,* where they should live in servitude. "*I will make the men which have transgressed my covenant as the calf which they cut in twain;* I will divide them asunder as they divided it asunder." They had all dealt treacherously with God, and therefore shall all be involved in the common ruin without exception, *v.* 19. Since they had emboldened themselves in returning to their sin, contrary to their covenant, by the retreat of the Chaldean army from them, God would therefore bring it upon them again: "They have now *gone up from you,* and your fright is over for the present, but I *will command them* to face about as they were; they shall *return to this city, and take it and burn it,*" *v.* 22. If we repent of the good we had purposed, God will repent of the good he had purposed. *With the froward thou wilt show thyself froward.*

Chapter 35

A variety of methods is tried to awaken the Jews to a sense of their sin and to bring them to repentance. The scope and tendency of many of the prophet's sermons was to frighten them out of their disobedience, by setting before them what would be the end thereof if they persisted in it. The scope of this sermon, in this chapter, is to shame them out of their disobedience if they had any sense of honour left in them. I. He sets before them the obedience of the family of the Rechabites to the commands which were left them by Jonadab their ancestor, ver. 1–11. II. The disobedience of the Jews to God and their contempt of his precepts, ver. 12–15. III. He foretells the judgments of God upon the Jews for their impious disobedience, ver. 16, 17. IV. He assures the Rechabites of the blessing of God upon them for their pious obedience, ver. 18, 19.

Verses 1–11

What is contained in this chapter was said and done *in the days of Jehoiakim* (*v.* 1); in the latter part of his reign, for it was after the king of Babylon with his army *came up into the land* (*v.* 11), which seems to refer to the invasion mentioned 2 Kings xxiv. 2, upon occasion of Jehoiakim's rebelling against Nebuchadnezzar. Jeremiah sets before the rebellious people the example of the Rechabites, a family that kept distinct by themselves. They were originally Kenites, as appears 1 Chron. ii. 55, *These are the Kenites that came out of Hemath, the father of the house of Rechab.* The Kenites, at least those of them that gained a settlement in the land of Israel, were of the posterity of Hobab, Moses's father-in-law, Judges i. 16; 1 Sam. xv. 6; Judges iv. 17. One family

of these Kenites had their name from Rechab. His son, or a lineal descendant from him, was Jonadab, a man famous in his time for wisdom and piety. He flourished in the days of Jehu, king of Israel, nearly 300 years before this (2 Kings x. 15, 16).

I. The rules of living which Jonadab charged his children, and his posterity religiously to observe; they were such as he himself had all his days observed.

1. They were comprised in two remarkable precepts: (1) He forbade them to *drink wine,* according to the law of the Nazarites. We are so apt to abuse it and get hurt by it that it is a commendable piece of self-denial either not to use it at all or very sparingly and medicinally, as Timothy used it, 1 Tim. v. 23. (2) He appointed them to *dwell in tents,* and not to build houses, nor purchase lands, nor rent or occupy either, *v.* 7. This was an instance of strictness and mortification. Tents were mean dwellings, so that this would teach them to be humble; they were cold dwellings, so that this would teach them to be hardy and not to indulge the body; they were movable dwellings, so that this would teach them not to think of settling or taking root anywhere in this world. They must dwell in tents *all their days.* They must thus accustom themselves to endure hardness.

2. Why did Jonadab prescribe these rules of living to his posterity? It was to show his wisdom, and the real concern he had for their welfare, not tying them by any oath or vow, but only advising them to conform to this discipline as far as they found it for edification, *v.* 11. His ancestors had addicted themselves to a pastoral life (Exod ii. 16), and he would have his posterity keep to it. Moses had put them in hopes that they should be naturalized (Num. x. 32); but they were still *strangers in the land* (*v.* 7), had no inheritance in it, and therefore must live by their employment and accustom themselves to hard fare and hard lodging. Humility and contentment in obscurity are often the best policy and men's surest protection. Jonadab saw a general corruption of manners; the drunkards of Ephraim abounded, and he was afraid lest his children should be debauched by them; and therefore he obliged them to live by themselves, retired in the country; and, that they might not run into any unlawful pleasures, to deny themselves the use even of lawful delights. Jonadab might foresee the destruction of a people so wretchedly degenerated, and he would have his family provide, that, even in the midst of the troubles, *they might have peace.* Let them sit loose to what they had, and then they might with less pain be stripped of it. They must learn to live by rule and under discipline. It is good for us all to do so, and to teach our children to do so.

II. How strictly his posterity observed these rules, *v.* 8–10. They had in their respective generations all of them *obeyed the voice of Jonadab their father,* had *done according to all that he commanded them.* They *drank no wine,* though they dwelt in a country where there was plenty of it. They built no houses, tilled no ground, but lived upon the products of their cattle. As to one of the particulars, in a case of necessity they dispensed with it (*v.* 11): *When the king of Babylon came into the land* with his army, though they had hitherto dwelt in tents, they now quitted their tents, and came and dwelt in Jerusalem, and in houses there. The rules of a strict discipline must not be made too strict, but so as to admit of a dispensation when the necessity of a case calls for it. These Rechabites would have tempted God, and not trusted him, if they had not used proper means for their own safety, notwithstanding the law and custom of their family. Jeremiah took them into the temple (*v.* 2), into a *prophet's chamber,* because he had a message from God. There he not only asked the Rechabites whether they would drink any wine, but he set *pots full of wine before them*, made the temptation as strong as possible, and said, "*Drink you wine*, you shall have it free. You have broken one of the rules of your order, in coming to live at Jerusalem; why may you not break this too, and when you are in the city do as they there do?" But they peremptorily refused. They all agreed in the refusal. "No, *we will drink no wine*; for with us it is against the law." The prophet saw they were steadfastly resolved.

Verses 12–19

The trial of the Rechabites' constancy was intended but for a sign; here we have the application of it.

I. The Rechabites' observance of their father's charge to them and the disobedience of the Jews to God. Let them see it and be ashamed. The prophet asks them, in God's name, "*Will you not* at length *receive instruction? v.* 13. Will nothing prevail to discover sin and duty to you? You see how obedient the Rechabites are to their father's commandment (*v.* 14); but *you have not inclined your ear to me*" (*v.* 15). The Rechabites were obedient to one who was but a man like themselves, but the Jews were disobedient to an infinite and eternal God, who had an absolute authority over them, as the Father of their spirits. The Rechabites were never put in mind of their obligations to their father; but God often sent his prophets to his people (*v.* 14). God had given his people a *good land*, and promised them that, if they would be obedient, they should still dwell in it, so that they were bound both in gratitude and interest to be obedient, and yet they would not *hearken*.

II. Judgments are threatened, as often before, against Judah and Jerusalem. The Rechabites shall rise up in judgment against them, for they *performed the commandment of their father*, and continued in their obedience to it (*v.* 16); but *this people*, this rebellious and gainsaying people, *have not hearkened unto me*. "*I will bring upon them*, by the Chaldean army, *all the evil pronounced against them* both in the law, and in the prophets, for *I have spoken to them, I have called to them*—spoken by my word, called by my providence, and yet they have not *heard* nor *answered*."

III. Mercy is here promised to the family of the Rechabites for their steady adherence to the laws of their house. Though it was only for the shaming of Israel that their constancy was tried, yet, being unshaken, it was *found unto praise, and honour, and glory* (*v.* 18, 19). The family shall *never want a man* to inherit what they had, though they had no inheritance to leave. Though they are neither priests nor Levites, nor appear to have had any post in the temple service, yet in a constant course of regular devotion, they stand before God, to minister to him.

Chapter 36

Another expedient tried to work upon this heedless and untoward people, but in vain. A roll of a book is provided, containing an abstract of all the sermons that Jeremiah had preached to them. I. The writing of this roll by Baruch, as Jeremiah dictated it, ver. 1–4. II. The reading of the roll by Baruch to all the people publicly on a fast-day (ver. 5–10), afterwards by Baruch to the princes privately (ver. 11–19), and lastly by Jehudi to the king, ver. 20, 21. III. The burning of the roll by the king, with orders to prosecute Jeremiah and Baruch, ver. 22–26. IV. The writing of another roll, with large additions, particularly of Jehoiakim's doom for burning the former, ver. 27–32.

Verses 1–8

In the beginning of Ezekiel's prophecy we meet with *a roll* written *in vision*, Ezek. ii. 9, 10; iii. 1. Here, in the latter end of Jeremiah's prophecy, we meet with *a roll* written *in fact*, for discovery of the things contained therein to the people.

I. The command which God gave to Jeremiah to write a summary of his sermons, ever since he first began to be a preacher, in the thirteenth year of Josiah, *to this day*, which was in the fourth year of Jehoiakim, *v.* 2, 3. What they had heard once must be recapitulated, and rehearsed to them again, that what was forgotten might be called to mind again and what made no impression upon them at the first hearing might take hold of them when they heard it the second time. The reason here given for the writing of this roll (*v.* 3): *It may be the house of Judah will hear*. What it is hoped they will thus hear: *All that evil which I purpose to do unto them*. What it is hoped will be produced thereby: *They will hear, that they may return every man from his evil way*. The conversion of sinners is that which ministers should aim at in preaching; and people hear the word in vain if that point be not gained with them. *That I may forgive their iniquity*. This plainly implies God's justice. It is not consistent that he should forgive the sin unless the sinner repent of it. It plainly expresses his mercy, that he is very ready to forgive sin and only waits till the sinner be qualified to receive forgiveness, and therefore uses various means to bring us to repentance, *that he may forgive*.

II. The instructions which Jeremiah gave to Baruch his scribe, pursuant to the command he had received from God, *v.* 4. God bade Jeremiah write, but, it should seem, he had not the *pen of a ready writer*, he could not write fast, or fair, as Baruch could, and therefore he made use of him as his amanuensis. St. Paul wrote but few of his epistles with his own hand, Gal. vi. 11; Rom. xvi. 22. God dispenses his gifts variously; some have a good faculty at speaking, others at writing, and neither can say to the other, We have *no need of you*, 1 Cor. xii. 21. The Spirit of God dictated to Jeremiah, and he to Baruch. If we may credit the apocryphal book that bears his name, he was afterwards himself a prophet to the captives in Babylon. Baruch wrote in a *roll of a book*, on pieces of parchment, or vellum, which were joined together, so making one long scroll, which was rolled perhaps upon a staff.

III. The orders which Jeremiah gave to Baruch to read what he had written to the people. Jeremiah, it seems, was *shut up*, and *could not go to the house of the Lord* himself, *v.* 5. Though he was not a close prisoner, for then there would have been no occasion to send officers to seize him (*v.* 26), yet he was forbidden by the king to appear in the temple. Thus St. Paul wrote epistles to the churches which he could not visit in person. When God ordered the reading of the roll he said, *It may be they will hear and return from their evil ways, v.* 3. When Jeremiah orders it, he says, *It may be they will pray* and will *return from their evil way*. Prayer to God for grace to turn us is necessary in order to our turning. According to these orders, Baruch did read *out of the book the words of the Lord*, whenever there was a *holy convocation, v.* 8.

Verses 9–19

It would seem that Baruch had been frequently reading the book, to all that would give him hearing, before the most solemn reading of it altogether; for the directions were given about it in the *fourth year of Jehoiakim*, whereas this was done *in the fifth year, v.* 9. But some think that the writing of the book took up so much time that it was another year ere it was perfected. 1. The government appointed a public fast to be religiously observed (*v.* 9), on account either of the distress brought by the army of the Chaldeans or of the want of rain (*ch.* xiv. 1): *They proclaimed a fast to the people*. Great shows of piety and devotion may be found even among those who, though they keep up these *forms of godliness*, are strangers and enemies to *the power* of it. But what will such hypocritical services avail? Fasting, without reforming and turning away from sin, will never turn away the judgments of God, Jonah iii. 10. 2. Baruch repeated Jeremiah's sermons publicly in the house of the Lord, on the fast-day. He stood in a chamber that belonged to Gemariah, and out of a window, or balcony, read to the people that were in the court, *v.* 10. 3. An account was brought to the princes that were now together in the secretary's office, here called *the scribe's chamber, v.* 12. It should seem, though the princes had called the people to meet in the house of God, to fast, and pray, and hear the word, they did not think fit to attend there themselves. Michaiah informed the princes of what Baruch had read; for his father Gemariah so far countenanced Baruch as to lend him his chamber. 4. Baruch is sent for, and is ordered to sit down among them and read it all over again to them (*v.* 14, 15), which he readily did. 5. The princes were for the present much affected with the word that was read to them, *v.* 16. And, *when they had heard all, they were afraid*, were all afraid, *one* as well as *another*; like Felix, who trembled at Paul's reasonings. The reproofs were just, and the predictions now in a fair way to be fulfilled; so that they were in a great consternation. We are not told what impressions this reading of the roll made upon the people (*v.* 10), but the princes were put into a fright by it, and (as some read it) *looked one upon another*, not knowing what to say. They agreed to *tell the king of all these words*; and, if he think fit to give credit to them, they will. At the same time they knew the king's mind so far that they advised Baruch and Jeremiah to hide themselves (*v.* 19) and to shift for their own safety, expecting that the king, instead of being convinced would be exasperated. 6. They asked Baruch a trifling question, *How he wrote all these words* (*v.* 17), as if they suspected there was something extraordinary in it; but Baruch gives them a plain answer—Jeremiah dictated, and he wrote, *v.* 18.

Verses 20–32

The roll and the king.

I. Upon notice given him concerning it, he sent for it, and ordered it to be read to him, *v.* 20, 21. He did not desire that Baruch would read it himself, who could read it more intelligently and with more authority and affection than anyone else; but Jehudi, one of his pages now in waiting, who was sent to fetch it, is bidden to read it. Those who thus despise the word of God will soon make it to appear, as this king did, that they hate it, and have not only low, but ill thoughts of it.

II. He had not patience to hear it read through as the princes had, but, when he had heard *three or four leaves* read, in a rage he *cut it with his penknife*, and threw it piece by piece *into the fire*, that he might be sure to see it *all consumed, v.* 22, 23. This was a most impudent affront to the God of heaven, whose message this was. Thus he showed his impatience of reproof. 2. Thus he showed his indignation at Baruch and Jeremiah; he would have cut them in pieces, and burnt them, if he had had them in his reach, when he was in this passion. 3. Thus he expressed an obstinate resolution never to comply with the intentions of the warnings given him. 4. Thus he foolishly hoped to defeat the threatenings denounced against him. He thought he had effectually provided that the things contained in this roll should spread no further.

III. Neither the king himself nor any of his princes were at all affected with the word: *They were not afraid* (*v.* 24), no, not those princes that *trembled at the word* when they heard it the first time, *v.* 16. They showed some concern till they saw how light the king made of it, and then they shook off all that concern.

IV. There were three of the princes who had so much sense and grace left as to interpose for the preventing of the burning of the roll, but in vain. *v.* 25.

V. Jehoiakim, when he had thus in effect burnt God's warrant by which he was arrested, in a way of revenge, now signed a warrant for the apprehending of Jeremiah and Baruch, God's ministers (*v.* 26): *But the Lord hid them.*

VI. Jeremiah had orders and instructions to write in another roll the same words that were written in the roll which Jehoiakim had burnt, *v.* 27, 28. Enemies may prevail to burn many a Bible, but they cannot abolish the word of God, nor defeat the accomplishment of it. Though the tables of the law were broken, they were renewed again; and so out of the ashes of the roll that was burnt arose another Phoenix. *The word of the Lord endures for ever.*

VII. The king of Judah, though a king, was severely reckoned with by the King of kings for this indignity done to the written word. Jehoiakim was angry because it was *written therein, saying,* Surely *the king of Babylon shall come and destroy this land, v.* 29. God and his prophets had *therefore become his enemies because they told him the truth*, told him of the desolation that was coming, but at the same time putting him in a fair way to prevent it. The wrath of God shall come upon him and his family, in the first place, by the hand of Nebuchadnezzar. He shall be cut off, and in a few weeks his son shall be dethroned, and exchange his royal robes for prison-garments, so that *he shall have none to sit upon the throne of David; his dead body* shall lie unburied, or *he shall be buried with the burial of an ass*, that is, thrown into the ditch. Even *his seed and his servants* shall fare the worse for their relation to him (*v.* 31), for they shall be punished, not for his iniquity, but so much the sooner for their own. All the evil pronounced against Judah and Jerusalem in that roll shall be brought upon them.

VIII. When the roll was written anew, *there were added* to the former *many like words* (*v.* 32), many more threatenings, for, since they will yet *walk contrary to God*, he will *heat the furnace seven times hotter.*

CHAPTER 37

This chapter brings us near the destruction of Jerusalem by the Chaldeans, for the story of it lies in the latter end of Zedekiah's reign. I. A general idea of the bad character of that reign, ver. 1, 2. II. The message which Zedekiah, notwithstanding, sent to Jeremiah to desire his prayers, ver. 3. III. The flattering hopes that the Chaldeans would quit the siege of Jerusalem, ver. 5. IV. The assurance God gave them by Jeremiah (who was now at liberty, ver. 4) that the Chaldean army should renew the siege and take the city, ver. 6–10. V. The imprisonment of Jeremiah, under pretence that he was a deserter, ver. 11–15. VI. The kindness which Zedekiah showed him when he was a prisoner, ver. 16–21.

Verses 1–10

1. Jeremiah's preaching slighted, *v.* 1, 2. Zedekiah succeeded Coniah, or Jeconiah, and, though he saw in his predecessor the fatal consequences of condemning the word of God, yet he did not take warning. *Neither he, nor his* courtiers, *nor the people of the land, hearkened unto the words of the Lord*, though they already began to be fulfilled. 2. Jeremiah's prayers desired. Zedekiah sent messengers to him, saying, *Pray now unto the Lord our God for us*. He did so before (*ch.* xxi. 1, 2), and one of the messengers, Zephaniah, is the same there and here. Zedekiah is to be commended for this, and it shows that he had some good in him, some sense of his need of God's favour. When we are in distress we ought to desire the prayers of our ministers and Christian friends, for thereby we put an honour upon prayer, and an esteem upon our brethren. Kings themselves should look upon their praying people as the strength of the nation, Zech. xii. 5, 10. And yet this does but help

to condemn Zedekiah out of his own mouth. If indeed he looked upon Jeremiah as a prophet, whose prayers might avail, why did he not *hearken to the words of the Lord* which he spoke by him? How can we expect that God should hear others speaking to him for us if we will not hear them speaking to us from him and for him? When Zedekiah sent to the prophet to pray for him, he had better have sent for the prophet to pray with him. 3. Jerusalem flattered by the retreat of the Chaldean army from it. Jeremiah was now at liberty (*v.* 4); Jerusalem also, for the present, was at liberty, *v.* 5. Zedekiah, though a tributary to the king of Babylon, had entered into a private league with Pharaoh king of Egypt (Ezek. xvii. 15), pursuant to which, when the king of Babylon came to chastise him for his treachery, the king of Egypt sent forces to relieve Jerusalem when it was besieged. The Chaldeans raised the siege, probably not for fear of them, but in policy, to fight them at a distance, before any of the Jewish forces could join them. From this they encouraged themselves to hope that Jerusalem was delivered for good. 4. Jerusalem threatened with the return of the Chaldean army. Zedekiah sent to Jeremiah to desire him to pray that the Chaldean army might not return; but Jeremiah sends him word back that the decree had gone forth, and that it was but a folly for them to expect peace. *Thus saith the Lord, Deceive not yourselves, v.* 9. Satan himself though he is the great deceiver, could not deceive us if we did not deceive ourselves. Jeremiah uses no dark metaphors, but tells them plainly, (1) That the Egyptians shall retreat into *their own land, v.* 7. (2) That the Chaldeans shall return, and shall renew the siege: *They shall not depart* for good and all (*v.* 9); *they shall come again* (*v.* 8); they shall *fight against the city.* (3) That Jerusalem shall certainly be delivered into the hand of the Chaldeans: *They shall take it, and burn it with fire, v* 8. "*Though you had smitten* their army, so that many were slain and all the rest wounded, yet those *wounded men should rise up and burn this city*," *v.* 10.

Verses 11–21

A further account concerning Jeremiah, who relates more passages concerning himself than any other of the prophets.

I. Jeremiah, when he had opportunity, attempted to retire out of Jerusalem into the country (*v.* 11, 12): *When the Chaldeans* had *broken up from Jerusalem* because *of Pharaoh's army,* Jeremiah determined *to go into the* country, and (as the margin reads it) *to slip away from Jerusalem in the midst of the people,* who, in that interval of the siege, went out into the country to look after their affairs. He endeavoured to steal away in the crowd; for, though he was a man of great eminence, he was content to be lost in the multitude and buried alive in a cottage. Jeremiah found he could do no good in Jerusalem; he laboured in vain among them, and therefore determined to leave them.

II. In this attempt he was seized as a deserter and committed to prison (*v.* 13–15): *He was in the gate of Benjamin,* when *a captain of the ward,* who probably had the charge of that gate, discovered him and *took him* into custody. He was the grandson of Hananiah, who, the Jews say, was Hananiah the false prophet, who contested with Jeremiah (*ch.* xxviii. 10), and they add that this young captain had a spite to Jeremiah upon that account. That which he charges upon him is, *Thou fallest away to the Chaldeans*—an unlikely story, for the Chaldeans had now gone. Jeremiah therefore with good reason, and with both the confidence and the mildness of an innocent man, denies the charge: "*It is false; I fall not away to the Chaldeans;* I am going upon my own lawful occasions." Jeremiah's protestation of his integrity, though he is a

prophet, and is ready to say it *on the word of a priest,* is not regarded; but is brought before the privy-council, who without examining him, but upon the base insinuation of the captain, fell into a passion with him: they *were wroth.* They beat him and then *put him in prison,* in the worst prison they had, that *in the house of Jonathan the scribe.* Into this prison Jeremiah was thrust, *into the dungeon,* which was dark and cold, damp and dirty. In the cells or *cabins,* there he must lodge. *There Jeremiah remained many days.*

III. Zedekiah at length sent for him, and showed him some favour; but probably not till the Chaldean army had returned and had laid fresh siege to the city. When their vain hopes had all vanished, then they were in a greater confusion and consternation than ever. "O then" (says Zedekiah), "send in all haste for the prophet; let me have some talk with him." 1. The king sent for him to give him private audience as an ambassador from God. He *asked him secretly in his house,* being ashamed to be seen in his company, "*Is there any word from the Lord? (v.* 17)— any word of comfort? Canst thou give us any hopes that the Chaldeans shall again retire?" Jeremiah's life and comfort are in Zedekiah's hand, and he has now a petition to present to him for his favour, and yet, having this opportunity, he tells him plainly that *there is a word from the Lord,* but no word of comfort for him or his people: *Thou shalt be delivered into the hand of the king of Babylon.* If Jeremiah had consulted with flesh and blood, he would have given him a plausible answer; he might have chosen whether he would tell him the worst at this time. But Jeremiah was one that had *obtained mercy of the Lord to be faithful,* and would not, to obtain mercy of man, be unfaithful either to God or to his prince; he therefore tells him the truth, the whole truth. Jeremiah takes this occasion to upbraid him and his people with the credit they gave to the false prophets, who told them that *the king of Babylon* should *not come* at all, or, when he had withdrawn, should *not come* again *against* them, *v.* 19. "*Where are now your prophets,* who told you that you should have peace?" 2. He improved this opportunity for the presenting of a private petition, as a poor prisoner, *v.* 18, 20. He humbly expostulates with the king: "*What have I offended against thee, or thy servants, or this people,* what law have I broken, *that you have put me in prison?*" He likewise earnestly begs, and very pathetically (*v.* 20), *Cause me not to return* to yonder noisome gaol, *to the house of Jonathan the scribe, lest I die there. Hear me, I pray thee, O my Lord the king! let my supplication, I pray thee, be accepted before thee.* Here is not a word of complaint of the princes that unjustly committed him, but a modest supplication to the king. A lion in God's cause must be a lamb in his own. (1) The king gave him his request, took care that he should not die in the dungeon, but ordered that he should have the liberty of the *court of the prison,* where he might breathe a free air. (2) He ordered him his *daily bread out of the* public stock, *till all the bread was spent.* Zedekiah ought to have released him, but he had not courage to do that; it was well he did as he did. God can make even confinement turn to advantage and the court of a prison to become as green pastures.

CHAPTER 38

Jeremiah greatly debased under the frowns of the princes, and yet greatly honoured by the favour of the king. They used him as a criminal; he used him as a privy-counsellor. I. Jeremiah for his faithfulness is put into the dungeon by the princes, ver. 1–6. II. At the intercession of Ebed-melech the Ethiopian, by special order from the king, he is taken up out of the dungeon and confined only to the court of the prison, ver. 7–13. III. He has a private conference with the king upon present affairs, ver. 14–23. IV. Care is taken to keep that conference private, ver. 24–28.

Verses 1–13

1. Jeremiah persists in his plain preaching (*v.* 3): *This city shall be given into the hand of the king of Babylon;* though it hold out long, it will be taken at last. Nor would he have so often repeated this unwelcome message but that he could put them in a certain way, though not to save the city, yet to save themselves, *v.* 2. Let him *go forth to the Chaldeans,* and throw himself upon their mercy, before things come to extremity, and then he *shall live;* they will give him quarter, and he shall escape *the famine and pestilence,* which will be the death of multitudes within the city. 2. The princes persist in their malice against Jeremiah. He was faithful to his country and to his trust as a prophet, and, though at this time he ate the king's bread, yet that did not stop his mouth. But his persecutors complained that he abused the liberty he had of walking in the court of the prison; for, though he could not go to the temple to preach, yet he said the same things in private conversation to those that came to visit him, and therefore (*v.* 4) they represented him to the king as a dangerous man, disaffected to the government he lived under: *He seeks not the welfare of this people, but the hurt*—yet no man had done more for the good of Jerusalem than he. They represent his preaching *as weakening their hands* and discouraging them. It is common for wicked people to look upon God's faithful ministers as their enemies, only because they show them what enemies they are to themselves while they continue impenitent. 3. Jeremiah hereupon, by the king's permission, is put into a dungeon, with a view to his destruction there. Zedekiah, though he felt a conviction that Jeremiah was a prophet, sent of God, had not courage to own it. *He is in your hand.* Those will have a great deal to answer for who, though they have a secret kindness for good people, dare not own it in a time of need. The princes, having this general warrant from the king, immediately put poor *Jeremiah into the dungeon of Malchiah, that was in the court of the prison* (*v.* 6), a deep dungeon, for they *let* him *down* into it *with cords,* and a dirty one, for *there was no water* in it, *but mire;* and he *sunk in the mire, up to his neck,* says Josephus. Those that put him here doubtless designed that he should die of hunger and cold, and so die obscurely, fearing, if they should put him to death openly, the people might be incensed against them. Many of God's faithful witnesses have thus been privately made away, and starved to death, in prisons, whose blood will be brought to account in the day of discovery. What Jeremiah did in this distress, he tells us himself (Lam. iii. 55, 57), *I called upon thy name, O Lord! out of the low dungeon, and thou drewest near, saying, Fear not.* 4. Application is made to the king by *Ebed-melech,* one of the gentlemen of the bed-chamber, in behalf of the poor sufferer. *Ebed-melech* was an Ethiopian a *stranger to the commonwealth of Israel,* and yet had in him more humanity and more divinity too, than Israelites had. Christ found more faith among Gentiles than among Jews. Ebed-melech lived in a wicked court and in a corrupt degenerate age, and yet had a great sense both of equity and piety. God has his remnant in all places. There were *saints* even *in Cæsar's household.* The king was now *sitting in the gate of Benjamin* to receive appeals and petitions. Thither Ebed-melech went immediately, for the case would not admit delay. He boldly asserts that Jeremiah had a deal of wrong done him, and is not afraid to tell the king so. He does not mince the matter; he tells the king faithfully, let him take it as he will, *These men have done ill in all that they have done to Jeremiah.* God can raise up friends for his people in distress where they little thought of them. 5. Orders are immediately given for his release, and Ebed-melech takes care to see them executed. The king had his heart wonderfully

changed on a sudden, and will now have Jeremiah released in defiance of the princes, for he orders no less than thirty men to be employed in fetching him out of the dungeon, lest the princes should raise a party to oppose it, *v.* 10. Ebed-melech gained his point, and soon brought Jeremiah the good news. Special notice is taken of his great tenderness in providing old soft rags for Jeremiah to put under his arm-holes, to keep the cords wherewith he was to be drawn up from hurting him, his arm-holes being probably galled by the cords wherewith he was let down. Nor did he throw the rags down to him, lest they should be lost in the mire, but carefully let them down, *v.* 11, 12. Jeremiah is brought up out of the dungeon, and is now where he was, *in the court of the prison, v.* 13.

Verses 14–28

The king in close conference with Jeremiah, though (*v.* 5) he had before given him up into the hands of his enemies.

I. The honour that Zedekiah did to the prophet. When he was newly fetched out of the dungeon he sent for him to advise with him privately. He met him in *the third entry,* or (as the margin reads it) *the principal entry,* that *is in,* or leads towards, *the house of the Lord, v.* 14. Perhaps he intended to show a respect for *the house of God,* now that he was desiring to hear *the word of God.* Zedekiah would ask *Jeremiah a thing;* it should rather be rendered, *a word.* "I am here asking thee for *a word of prediction,* of counsel, of comfort, *a word from the Lord,* ch. xxxvii. 17. Whatever word thou hast *hide it not from me;* let me know the worst." He hopes to get a more pleasing answer, as if God, who is *in one mind,* were such a one as himself, who was in many minds.

II. The bargain that Jeremiah made with him before he would give him his advice, *v.* 15. "And if I do," says Jeremiah, *"wilt thou not put me to death?* I am afraid *thou wilt"* (so some take it); "what else can I expect when thou art led blindfold by the princes?" Not that Jeremiah was backward to seal the doctrine he preached with his blood, but, in doing our duty, we ought to use all lawful means for our own preservation; even the apostles of Christ did so. He is willing to give him wholesome advice, and does not upbraid him with his unkindness in suffering him to be put into the dungeon. *"Wilt thou not hearken unto me?* Surely thou wilt; I am in hopes to find thee pliable at last, and now *in this thy day willing to know the things that belong to thy peace."* Some read it as spoken despairingly: "*If I give thee counsel, thou wilt not hearken unto me;* I have reason to fear thou wilt not, and then I might as well keep my counsel to myself." Zedekiah makes him no answer, will not promise to hearken to his advice. As to the prophet's safety, he promises him, upon the word of a king, *I will neither put thee to death nor deliver thee into the hands of those that will, v.* 16. Zedekiah's oath on this occasion is solemn: "*As the Lord liveth, who made us this soul,* who gave me my life and thee thine, I dare not take away thy life unjustly, knowing that then I should forfeit my own to him that is the Lord of life."

III. The good advice that Jeremiah gave him, with good reason why he should take it, not from any prudence or politics of his own, but in the *name of the Lord, the God of hosts* and *God of Israel.* Not as a statesman, but as a prophet, he advises him by all means to surrender himself and his city *to the king of Babylon's princes:* "*Go forth to them,* and make the best terms thou canst with them," *v.* 17. This was the advice he had given to the people (*v.* 2, and before, *ch.* xxi. 9), to submit to divine judgments. To persuade him to take this counsel, he sets before him good and evil, life and death. If he will yield he shall save his children from the sword and Jerusalem from the flames. If he will but acknowledge God's justice, he shall experience his mercy: *The city shall not be burnt*, and *thou shalt live and thy house*. But, if he will obstinately stand out, it will be the ruin both of his house and Jerusalem (*v.* 18). This is the case of sinners with God; let them humbly submit to his grace and government and they shall live.

IV. The objection which Zedekiah made against the prophet's advice, *v.* 19. If he had had a due regard to the divine authority, wisdom, and goodness, as soon as he understood what the mind of God was he would immediately have acquiesced, but he advances against it some prudential considerations of his own. All he suggests is, "*I am afraid*, not of the Chaldeans; their princes are men of honour, but of the Jews, that have already gone over to the Chaldeans; when they see *me* follow them, who had so much opposed their going, they will laugh at me, and say, *Hast thou also become weak as water?*" Isa. xiv. 10. Though it had been really the greatest personal mischief that he could imagine it to be, yet he ought to have ventured it, in obedience to God, and for the preservation of his family and city.

V. The pressing importunity with which Jeremiah followed the advice he had given the king. He assures him that, if he would comply with the will of God herein, the thing he feared should not come upon him (*v.* 20): *They shall not deliver thee up*, but treat thee as becomes thy character. *Obey, I beseech thee, the voice of the Lord*, because it is his voice, so it *shall be well unto thee*. But he tells him what would be the consequence if he would not obey. He himself would *fall into the hands of the Chaldeans*. "*Thou shalt not escape*, as thou hopest to do," *v.* 23. He would himself be chargeable with the destruction of Jerusalem: "*Thou shalt cause this city to be burnt with fire*, for by a little submission and self-denial thou mightest have prevented it." He should certainly fall under a just reproach for standing out, and that from women too, *v.* 22. Thus will Zedekiah be bantered by the women, when all his wives and children shall be made a prey to the conquerors, *v.* 23.

VI. The care which Zedekiah took to keep this conference private (*v.* 24): *Let no man know of these words*. He has nothing to object against Jeremiah's advice, and yet he will not follow it. Zedekiah is concerned to keep it private, not so much for Jeremiah's safety, but for his own reputation. He is instructed what to say to the princes if they should examine him about it. He must tell them that he was petitioning the king not to remand him back to *the house of Jonathan the scribe* (*v.* 25, 26), and he did tell them so (*v.* 27), and no doubt it was true.

CHAPTER 39

The prophet Jeremiah, after he had largely foretold the delivering of Jerusalem into the hands of the king of Babylon, gives a particular account of that sad event. That melancholy story we have in this chapter, which serves to confirm the word of God's messengers. I. Jerusalem, after eighteen months' siege, was taken by the Chaldean army, ver. 1–3. II. King Zedekiah, attempting to make his escape, was seized and made a miserable captive to the king of Babylon, ver. 4–7. III. Jerusalem was burnt to the ground, and the people were carried captive, except the poor, ver. 8–10. IV. The Chaldeans were very kind to Jeremiah, and took particular care of him, ver. 11–14. V. Ebed-melech too, for his kindness, had a protection from God himself in this day of desolation, ver. 15–18.

Verses 1–10

Jeremiah abode patiently in the court of the prison, until the day that Jerusalem was taken. He gave the princes no further disturbance by his prophesying, nor they him by their persecutions.

I. The city is at length taken by storm. Nebuchadnezzar's army sat down before it in the *ninth* year of Zedekiah, *in the tenth month* (*v.* 1). Nebuchadnezzar

left his generals to carry on the siege: they renewed it with redoubled vigour. At length, *in the eleventh year, in the fourth month*, they entered the city, the soldiers being so weakened by famine, that they were not able to make any resistance, *v.* 2. Sin had provoked God to withdraw his protection, and then, like Samson when his hair was cut, it was weak as other cities.

II. The princes of the king of Babylon take possession of the *middle gate*, *v.* 3. Some think that this was the *second gate* (Zeph. i. 10), in the middle wall that divided one part of the city from the other. Here they cautiously made a halt, and durst not go forward among men that perhaps would sell their lives as dearly as they could, until they searched all places, that they might not be surprised by any ambush. There, where *Eliakim* and *Hilkiah*, who bore the name of the God of Israel, used to sit, now sit *Nergal-sharezer*, and *Samgar-nebo*, &c., who bore the names of the heathen gods. *Sarsechim* was *Rab-saris*, that is, *captain of the guard*; and *Nergal-sharezer*, *camp-master*, or quarter-master. And now was fulfilled what Jeremiah prophesied (*ch.* i. 15), that the families of the kingdoms of the north should set everyone his throne at the entering of the gates of Jerusalem.

III. Zedekiah thought it high time to shift for his own safety, and, loaded with guilt and fear, he *went out of the city*, under protection of *the night* (*v.* 4). He was discovered, pursued, and overtaken *in the plains of Jericho*, *v.* 5. Thence he was brought prisoner to Riblah, where the king of Babylon passed sentence. He *slew his sons before his eyes*. Zedekiah himself was now but thirty-two years of age, and the death of these babes must needs be so many deaths to himself, especially when he considered that his own obstinacy was the cause of it. *They shall bring forth thy wives and children to the Chaldeans*, ch. xxxviii. 23. He *slew all the nobles of Judah* (*v.* 6). He ordered Zedekiah to have his eyes put out (*v.* 7), so condemning *him* to darkness for life who had shut his eyes against the clear light of God's word. He *bound him with two brazen chains or fetters* (so the margin reads it), to carry him away to Babylon, there to spend the rest of his days in misery.

IV. Some time afterwards the city was burnt, temple and palace, and the wall of it broken down, *v.* 8.

V. The people that were left were all *carried away captives to Babylon*, *v.* 9. They must be driven hundreds of miles, like beasts, before the conquerors, that were now their cruel masters; must lie at their mercy in a strange land. Some few, *the poor of the people*, never made any resistance, and were left to tarry at home. The *captain of the guard gave them vineyards and fields at the same time*, such as they were never masters of before, *v.* 10. The rich had been proud oppressors, and now they were justly punished for their injustice; the poor had been patient sufferers, and now they were graciously rewarded for their patience.

Verses 11–18

I. A gracious providence concerning Jeremiah. Nebuchadnezzar had given orders that care should be taken of him, and that he should be in all respects well used, *v.* 11, 12. Nebuzar-adan and the rest of the king of Babylon's princes discharged him out of prison, and did everything to make him easy, *v.* 13, 14. 1. A very generous act of Nebuchadnezzar, who took cognizance of this poor prophet. It was honourably done of the king to give this charge even before the city was taken, and of the captains to observe it even in the heat of action, and it is recorded for imitation. 2. A reproach to Zedekiah and the princes of Israel. They put him in prison, and the king of Babylon and his princes took him out. 3. The performance of God's promise to Jeremiah, in recompence for his services. *I will cause the enemy to treat thee well in the day of evil*, ch. xv. 11. Jeremiah had been fathful to his trust as a prophet, and now God approves himself faithful to him and the promise he had made him. The same that were the instruments of punishing the persecutors were the instruments of relieving the persecuted; and Jeremiah thought never the worse of his deliverance for its coming by the hand of the king of Babylon, but saw the more of the hand of God in it.

II. A gracious message to Ebed-melech, to assure him of a recompence for his kindness to Jeremiah. He relieved *a prophet in the name of a prophet*, and thus he had *a prophet's reward*. Jeremiah tells him that God would certainly bring upon Jerusalem the ruin that had been long threatened; and, for his further satisfaction in having been kind to Jeremiah he should see him abundantly proved a true prophet, *v.* 16. He shall be delivered from having a share in the common calamity: *I will deliver thee; I will surely deliver thee*. He had been instrumental to deliver God's prophet out of the dungeon, and now God promises to deliver him, *because thou hast put thy trust in me, saith the Lord.* Ebed-melech trusted in God that he would own him, and stand by him, and then he was not afraid of the face of man. And those who trust God, as this good man did, in the way of duty, will find that their hope shall not make them ashamed in times of the greatest danger.

CHAPTER 40

In this and the four following chapters the story of those few Jews that were left in the land after their brethren were carried away, is a very melancholy story; for they soon appeared as obstinate in sin as ever, unhumbled and unreformed. I. A more particular account of Jeremiah's discharge and his settlement with Gedaliah, ver. 1–6. II. The great resort of the Jews that remained scattered in the neighbouring countries to Gedaliah, who was made their governor under the king of Babylon; and the good posture they were in for a while under him, ver. 7–12. III. A treacherous design formed against Gedaliah, by Ishmael, ver. 13–16.

Verses 1–6

In these verses we have Jeremiah's adhering, by the advice of Nebuzar-adan, to Gedaliah. Jeremiah was very honourably fetched out of the court of the prison by the king of Babylon's princes (*ch.* xxxix. 13, 14), but afterwards being found among the people in the city, when orders were given to the inferior officers to bind all they found in order to their being carried captives to Babylon, he, through ignorance and mistake, was bound among the rest and hurried away. But when the captives were brought manacled to Ramah, Jeremiah was soon distinguished from the rest, and discharged. 1. The captain of the guard solemnly owns him to be a true prophet (*v.* 2, 3): "*The Lord thy God has* by thee *pronounced this evil upon this place*; they had fair warning given, but they would not take the warning, and *now the Lord hath brought it*, and, as by thy mouth he said it, so by my hand *he hath done what he said.*" He tells all the people that were now in chains before him, *It is because you have sinned against the Lord that this thing has come upon you.* The princes of Israel would never be brought to acknowledge this, but this heathen prince plainly sees it. 2. He gives the prophet leave to dispose of himself as he thought fit. He *loosed him from his chains* a second time (*v.* 4), invited him to come to Babylon as a friend, as a companion; and *I will set my eye upon thee* (so the word is), "I will show thee respect, and will see that thou be well provided for." If he was not disposed to go to Babylon, he might dwell where he pleased in his own country. 3. He advises him to go to Gedaliah and settle with him. This Gedaliah, *made governor of the* land under *the king of Babylon*, was an honest Jew

who (it is probable) went over to the Chaldeans, and approved himself so well that he had this great trust put into his hands, *v.* 5. *While* Jeremiah had *not yet gone back*, but stood considering what he should do, Nebuzar-adan bade him by all means *go to Gedaliah*. Nor does he only give him his liberty, and an approbation of the measures he shall take, but provides for his support: He *gave him victuals and a present*, either in clothes or money, *and* so *let him go*. Jeremiah accepted his kindness, took his advice, and went to Gedaliah, to Mizpah, *and dwelt with him, v.* 6. It did not prove at all to his comfort. However, we may commend his pious affection to the land of Israel, that he would not forsake it, but chose rather to dwell with the poor in the holy land than with princes in an unholy one.

Verses 7–16

I. A bright sky opening upon the remnant of the Jews that were left in their own land, and a prospect given them of peace and quietness after the many years of trouble and terror. Providence seemed to raise and encourage such an expectation, and it would be to that miserable people as life from the dead.

1. Gedaliah, one of themselves, is made *governor in the land*, by *the king of Babylon, v.* 7. He was *the son of Ahikam, the son of Shaphan*, one of the princes. His father (*ch.* xxvi. 24) took Jeremiah's part against the people. He seems to have been a man of great wisdom and a mild temper, and under whose government the few that were left might have been very happy.

2. All those that were now the Jews of the dispersion came and put themselves under his government and protection. The great men that had escaped the Chaldeans came and quietly submitted to Gedaliah. Several are here named, *v.* 8. *They came* with *their men*, their servants, their soldiers, and the king of Babylon had such a good opinion of Gedaliah that he was not jealous of the increase of their numbers, but rather pleased with it. The poor men that had escaped by flight into the neighbouring countries of Moab, Ammon, and Edom, were induced by the love they bore to their own land to return as soon as they heard that Gedaliah was in authority there, *v.* 11, 12. God remembered mercy, and admitted some of them upon a further trial of their obedience.

3. The model of this new government is drawn up and settled by an original contract (*v.* 9): "Come" (says Gedaliah), "*fear not to serve the Chaldeans.*" Though the divine law had forbidden them to make leagues with the heathen, yet the divine sentence had obliged them to yield to the king of Babylon. It is no disgrace to any to comply with him. Fear not the consequences of it. If you will but live peaceably, peaceably, you shall live; disturb not the government, and it will not disturb you. *Serve the king of Babylon and it shall be well with you.* Gedaliah, probably by instruction from the king of Babylon, undertakes upon all occasions to act for them (*v.* 10): "*As for me, behold, I will dwell at Mizpah, to serve the Chaldeans,* to do homage to them in the name of the whole body if there be occasion, to receive orders, and to pay them their tribute when they *come to us.*" Gedaliah gives them the assurance of an oath that he will protect them, but, being charitable, he did not require an oath from them that they would be faithful to him, else the following mischief might have been prevented. Though they own their lands to belong to the Chaldeans, yet, upon that condition, they shall have the free enjoyment of them and all the profits of them (*v.* 10): "*Gather you wine and summer fruits,* and take them for your own use; *put them in your vessels,* to be laid up for winter-store, as those do that live in a land of peace and hope to *eat the labour*

of your hand." And accordingly they *gathered wine and summer fruits very much*, for their corn-harvest was over some time before Jerusalem was taken. Gedaliah left them to enjoy the advantages of the public plenty, and, for aught that appears, demanded no tribute from them; for he sought not his own profit.

II. Here is a dark cloud gathering over this infant state, and threatening a dreadful storm. *Baalis the king of the Ammonites* hated Gedaliah, and was contriving to kill him, either out of malice to the Jews, or personal pique against Gedaliah, *v.* 14. Some make Baalis to signify the queen-mother of the king of the Ammonites, or queen-dowager. One would have thought this little remnant might be safe when the great king of Babylon protected it; and yet it is ruined by the artifices of this petty prince or princess. Happy are those that have the King of kings on their side, for the greatest earthly king cannot with all his power secure us against treachery. He employed *Ishmael, the son of Nethaniah*, as the instrument of his malice, instigated him to murder Gedaliah, and, that he might have a fair opportunity, directed him to enrol himself among his subjects and promise him fealty. Ishmael was of the seed royal, and would therefore be easily tempted to envy one that set up for a governor in Judah, who was not of David's line. Johanan, a brisk and active man, having got scent of this plot, informed Gedaliah of it: *Dost thou certainly know?* surely thou dost, *v.* 15. He proffered his service to prevent it: *I will slay* him. *Wherefore should he slay thee?* Gedaliah, being a man of sincerity himself, would by no means give credit to Ishmael's treachery. He said, *Thou speakest falsely of Ishmael.* Many have been ruined by being over-confident of the fidelity of those about them.

CHAPTER 41

It is a very tragical story that is related in this chapter, and shows that evil pursues sinners. The black cloud bursts in a dreadful storm. Those few Jews that escaped the captivity were proud to think that they were still in their own land, and secure under Gedaliah's protectorship. I. Gedaliah is barbarously slain by Ishmael, ver. 1, 2. II. All the Jews that were with him were slain likewise (ver. 3) and a pit filled with their dead bodies, ver. 9. III. Some devout men, to the number of fourscore, that were going towards Jerusalem, were drawn in by Ishmael, and murdered likewise, ver. 4–7. Only ten of them escaped, ver. 8. IV. Those that escaped the sword were taken prisoners by Ishmael, and carried off towards the country of the Ammonites, ver. 10. V. By the conduct and courage of Johanan, the prisoners are recovered, and he now becomes their commander-in-chief, ver. 11–16. VI. His project is to carry them into the land of Egypt (ver. 17, 18).

Verses 1–10

Such base, barbarous, bloody work is here done by men who by their birth should have been men of honour, by their religion just men, and this done upon those of their own nation, their own religion, and their brethren in affliction, upon no provocation— all done in cold blood.

I. Ishmael and his party treacherously killed Gedaliah himself in the first place. The king of Babylon had made him a great man, *governor of the land.* God had made him a good man and a great blessing to his country, and his agency for its welfare was as life from the dead. Ishmael was of *the seed royal* (*v.* 1) and therefore jealous of Gedaliah's growing greatness. He had *ten men* with him that were *princes of the king* too, guided by the same peevish resentments. These had put themselves under his protection (ch. xl. 8), and now came again, *and they did eat bread together in Mizpah.* He entertained them generously. They pretended friendship and gave him no warning to stand on his guard. But those that did *eat bread* with him *lifted up the heel* against him. They watched an opportunity, when they had him alone, and assassinated him, *v.* 2.

II. They likewise put all to the sword, both Jews and Chaldeans, all that were employed under Gedaliah, *v.* 3. The vine-dressers and the husbandmen were busy in the fields, and knew nothing of this bloody massacre; so artfully concealed.

III. Some good honest men, that were going to lament the desolations of Jerusalem, were murdered with the rest. They came (*v.* 5)—*from Shechem, Samaria,* and *Shiloh,* places that had been famous, but were now reduced. They were going—*to the house of the Lord,* the temple at Jerusalem, to pay their respects to its ashes. They took *offerings and incense in their hand,* that they might not be without something to offer. They showed their goodwill, though the altar was gone. These went with *their clothes rent* and *their heads shaven.* They were decoyed into a fatal snare by Ishmael's malice. These pilgrims towards Jerusalem he hated for the sake of their errand. Ishmael went out to meet them with crocodiles' tears, pretending to bewail the desolations of Jerusalem as much as they; and, to try how they stood to Gedaliah and his government, he courted them and found them to have a respect for him, which confirmed him in his resolution to murder them. *He said, Come to Gedaliah,* pretending he would have them come and live with him, when really he intended that they should come and die with him, *v.* 6. Ishmael, when he had them *in the midst of the* town, fell upon them and *slew them* (*v.* 7). The dead bodies of these and the rest that he had slain he tumbled into a great pit (*v.* 7), the same pit that Asa king of Judah had digged long before, to be a frontier-garrison against *Baasha king of Israel* and *for fear of* him, *v.* 9. Among these last that were doomed to the slaughter there were ten that obtained a pardon, by working on the covetousness of those that had them at their mercy, *v.* 8. They *said to Ishmael, Slay us not, for we have treasures in the field,* country treasures, large stocks upon the ground, *wheat and barley, and oil and honey.* This bait prevailed. Ishmael saved them, not for the love of mercy, but for the love of money.

IV. He carried off the people prisoners. *The king's daughters* and the poor of the land, the vine-dressers and husbandmen, that were committed to Gedaliah's charge, were all led away prisoners towards the country of *the Ammonites* (*v.* 10). These prisoners thought, *Surely the bitterness of death,* and of captivity, *is past;* and yet some died by the sword and others went into captivity. There is many a ship wrecked in the harbour. We can never be sure of peace on this side heaven.

Verses 11–18

It would have been well if Johanan, when he gave information to Gedaliah of Ishmael's treasonable design, had stayed with Gedaliah; for he, and his captains and their forces, might have been a life-guard to Gedaliah, but it seems they were out upon some expedition when they should have been upon the best service. Those that affect to ramble are many times out of their place when they are most needed. However, at length they *hear of all the evil that Ishmael had done* (*v.* 11). Johanan prevailed only to rescue the captives. Johanan gathered what forces he could *and went to fight with Ishmael* (*v.* 12). He pursued him, and overtook him by the great *pool of Gibeon,* which we read of, 2 Sam. ii. 13. And, upon his appearing with such a force, Ishmael's heart failed him, and he durst not stand his ground. The poor captives *were glad when they saw Johanan* and *the captains that were with him,* looking upon them as their deliverers (*v.* 13), and they found a way to wheel about and come over to them (*v.* 14), Ishmael not offering to detain them. Ishmael quitted his prey to save his life, and *escaped with eight men, v.* 15. It seems, two of his ten men, that were his banditti or assassins (spoken of v. 1), deserted him. He made his way to the Ammonites, and we hear no more of him. The resolution of Johanan and the captains was very rash; nothing would serve them but they would *go to enter into Egypt* (v. 17), and, in order to that, they encamped for a time *in the habitation of Chimham, by Bethlehem*, David's city. Here Johanan made his headquarters, steering his course towards Egypt, either from a personal affection to that country or an ancient confidence in the Egyptians. Some of the *mighty men of war*, it seems, had escaped; those he took with him, *and the women and children, whom he had recovered from Ishmael.*

CHAPTER 42

Johanan and the captains being bent upon going into Egypt, either their affections or politics advising them to take that course, they had a great desire that God should direct them to do so too like Balaam, who, when he was determined to go and curse Israel, asked God leave. I. The bargain that was made between Jeremiah and them about consulting God in this matter, ver. 1–6. II. The message which God sent them, in which, 1. They are commanded to continue in the land of Judah, and assured that if they did so it should be well with them, ver. 7–12. 2. They are forbidden to go to Egypt; if they did it would be their ruin, ver. 13–18. 3. They are charged with dissimulation in asking what God's will was, and disobedience when they were told what it was; and sentence is passed upon them, ver. 19–22.

Verses 1–6

Jeremiah the prophet escaped the sword of Ishmael; and it was not the first time that the Lord hid him. At length, to serve a turn, Jeremiah is sought out, and *all the captains, Johanan* himself not excepted, with *all the people from the least to the greatest*, make him a visit; they *came near* (v. 1). Hitherto they had kept at a distance from the prophet and had been shy of him.

I. They desire him by prayer to ask direction from God what they should do in the present critical juncture, v. 2, 3. They express themselves with great respect to the prophet. Though he was poor and low, yet they apply to him with humility as petitioners for his assistance: *Let, we beseech thee, our supplication be accepted before thee.* They compliment him thus to persuade him to say as they would have him say. "*Pray for us*, who know not how to pray for ourselves. *Pray to the Lord thy God*, for we are unworthy to call him ours, nor have we reason to expect any favour from him." They speak of themselves as objects of compassion: "*We are but a remnant, but a few of many*; how easily will such a remnant be swallowed up. *Thy eyes* see what distress we are in; if thou canst do anything, help us. Let *the Lord thy God* take this ruin into his thoughts, and *show us the way wherein we may walk* and may expect to have his presence with us, *and the thing that we may do*, the course we may take for our own safety."

II. Jeremiah faithfully promises to pray for direction for them, and, whatever message God should send to them by him, he would deliver it to them just as he received it, v. 4. Though they had slighted him, yet, like Samuel when he was slighted, he will not *sin against the Lord in ceasing to pray for* them, 1 Sam. xii. 23. He will *declare to them the whole counsel of God*, that they may approve themselves true to their trust.

III. They promise that they will be governed by the will of God, as soon as they know what it is (v. 5, 6). They now call God *their* God, for Jeremiah had encouraged them to call him so (v. 4): *I will pray to the Lord your God*. They promise to *obey his voice* because they sent the prophet to him to consult him. They will do what God appoints them to do, *whether it be good or whether it be evil*; "Though it may seem evil to us, yet we will believe that if God command it it is certainly good, and we must not dispute it, but do it. Whatever God commands, whether it

be easy or difficult, if it be our duty, we will do it."

Verses 7–22

The answer which Jeremiah was sent to deliver to those who employed him to ask counsel of God.

I. It did not come till *ten days after*, v. 7. They were thus long held in suspense, perhaps, to punish them for their hypocrisy or to show that Jeremiah did not speak of himself, but must wait for instructions. *The vision is for an appointed time, and at the end it shall speak.*

II. When it did come he delivered it publicly, both to the *captains* and to all the *people*, fully and faithfully as he received it. What he has to advise is what *the Lord the God of Israel saith*, to whom they had sent him.

1. It is the will of God that they should stay where they are, and his promise that, if they do so, it shall be *well with them*, v. 10. Their brethren were forced out of it into captivity; let those therefore count it a mercy that they may stay in it and a duty to stay in it. He expresses a very tender concern for them in their calamitous condition: *It repenteth me of the evil that I have done unto you.* Not that he changed his mind, but he was very ready to change his way and to return in mercy to them. He answers the argument they had against abiding in this land. *They feared the king of Babylon* (ch. xli. 18), lest he should come and avenge the death of Gedaliah upon them, though they were no way accessory to it. "*Be not afraid of the king of Babylon*, for that fear will bring a snare: fear not for *I am with you*; and, if God be for you to save you, who can be against you to hurt you?" He assures them that if they will still abide in this land they shall not only be safe from the king of Babylon, but be made happy by the King of kings: "*I will build you and plant you;* you shall take root again, and be the new foundation of another state, a phoenix-kingdom, rising out of the ashes of the last." God will show them mercy in this, that not only the king of Babylon shall not destroy them, but he shall *have mercy upon them* and help to settle them. God has made that our duty which is really our privilege, and our obedience will be its own recompence.

2. They must by no means think of going into Egypt of all places, not to that land out of which God had delivered their fathers and with which he had so often warned them not to make alliance. "You begin to say, *We will not dwell in this land* (v. 13); no, not though God himself undertake our protection. We will *go into the land of Egypt*, and *there will we dwell*, whether God give us leave and go along with us or no," v. 14. It is supposed that their hearts were upon it: "*If you wholly set your faces to enter into Egypt*, then take what follows." Now the reason for their resolution is that "*in Egypt we shall see no war, nor have hunger of bread*, as we have had for a long time in this land," v. 14. The sentence passed upon them for this sin, if they will persist in it is pronounced in God's name (v. 15): "*Hear the word of the Lord, you remnant of Judah*, who think that because you are a remnant you must be spared" (v. 2). Did the sword and famine frighten them? Those very judgments shall pursue them into Egypt and overcome them there (v. 16, 17): "You think, because war and famine have long been raging in this land, that they are entailed upon it; whereas, if you trust in God, he can make even this land a land of peace to you." The men that go to Egypt in contradiction to God's will, to escape *the sword and famine*, shall *die in Egypt by sword and famine.* Did the desolations of Jerusalem frighten them? Were they willing to get as far as they could from them? They shall meet with the second part of them too in Egypt (v. 18). When God's professing people

mingle with infidels, and make their court to them, they lose their dignity and make themselves a reproach.

3. God knew their hypocrisy in their enquiries of him, and that when they asked what he would have them to do they were resolved to take their own way; and therefore the sentence. The prophet solemnly protests that he had faithfully delivered his message, *v.* 19. The conclusion of the whole matter is, "*Go not down into Egypt;* you disobey the command of God if you do. I have plainly *admonished you*; you cannot now plead ignorance of the mind of God." He charges them with base dissimulation in the application they made to him for divine direction (*v.* 20) "*You dissembled in your hearts;* you professed one thing and intended another, promising what you never meant to perform." *You have used deceit against your souls* (so the margin reads it). *Know certainly that you shall die by the sword, v.* 22. God's threatenings may be vilified, but cannot be nullified, by the unbelief of man.

Chapter 43

Jeremiah had faithfully delivered his message from God. Here is, I. The people's contempt of this message; they denied it to be the word of God (ver. 1–3). Into Egypt they went, and took Jeremiah himself along with them, ver. 4–7. II. God's pursuit of them with another message, foretelling the king of Babylon's pursuit of them into Egypt, ver. 8–13.

Verses 1–7

What God said to the builders of Babel may be truly said of this people: *Now nothing will be restrained from them which they have imagined to do,* Gen. xi. 6. They have a fancy for Egypt, and to Egypt they will go, whatever God himself says. Jeremiah made them hear all he had to say; it was what the Lord their God had sent him to speak to them, and they shall have it all.

I. They deny it to be a message from God: *Johanan, and all the proud men, said to Jeremiah, Thou speakest falsely, v.* 2. The cause of their disobedience was pride. They were *proud men* that gave the lie to the prophet. They could not bear the control of their designs, no, not by the divine wisdom, by the divine will itself. Either they were not convinced that what was said came from God or though they were convinced of it they would not own it. Had they not consulted Jeremiah as a prophet? Had he not waited to receive instructions from God what to say to them? And had not God proved him a prophet indeed? They had some good thoughts of Jeremiah, but they suggest (*v.* 3), *Baruch sets thee on against us.* If Jeremiah and he had been so well affected to the Chaldeans they would have gone away with Nebuzaradan to Babylon, and not have stayed to take their lot with this despised ungrateful remnant. If Baruch had been so ill disposed, could they think Jeremiah would be so influenced by him as to make God's name an authority to patronise so villainous a purpose?

II. They determine to go to Egypt notwithstanding. They resolve not to *dwell in the land of Judah,* as God had ordered them (*v.* 4), but to go with one consent to Egypt. Those that came *from all the nations whither they had been driven, to dwell in the land of Judah,* out of a sincere affection to that land, they would not leave to their liberty, but forced them to go with them into Egypt (*v.* 5), *men, women, and children* (*v.* 6). These proud men compelled even Jeremiah the prophet and Baruch his scribe to go along with them to Egypt. They *came to Tahpanhes,* a famous city of Egypt (so called from a queen of that name, 1 Kings xi. 19). Pharaoh's house was there, *v.* 9. If they had had the spirit of Israelites, they would have chosen rather to dwell in the wilderness of Judah than in the most pompous populous cities of Egypt.

Verses 8–13

Here, as also in the next chapter, Jeremiah is prophesying in Egypt. Jeremiah was now in Tahpanhes, among idolatrous Egyptians and treacherous Israelites; but there he received *the word of the Lord;* it *came to him.* God can find his people, with the visits of his grace, wherever they are. The spirit of prophecy was not confined to the land of Israel. When Jeremiah went into Egypt by constraint, God withdrew not his wonted favour from him. What he received of the Lord he delivered to the people. These two messages Jeremiah was appointed and entrusted to deliver when he was in Egypt—one in this chapter, relating to Egypt, and foretelling its destruction, the other in the next chapter, relating to the Jews in Egypt. God had told them that if they went into Egypt the sword should follow them; here he tells them further that the sword of Nebuchadrezzar should follow them.

I. This is foretold by a sign. Jeremiah must take *great stones* and *lay them in the clay of the furnace, or brick-kiln,* which is in *the open way,* or *beside the way* that leads *to Pharaoh's house* (*v.* 9). Egypt was famous for brick-kilns (Exod. v. 7). The foundation of Egypt's desolation was laid in those brick-kilns, in *that clay.* This he must do in *the sight of the men of Judah* to whom he was sent, that, since he could not prevent their going into Egypt, he might bring them to repent of their going.

II. It is foretold, 1. That the present king of Babylon, Nebuchadrezzar, should come in person against the land of Egypt, and should *set his throne* in that very place where *these stones* were laid, *v.* 10. This circumstance is particularly foretold, that, when it was accomplished, they might be confirmed in their belief of the certainty of the divine prescience, to which the smallest events are evident. God calls Nebuchadnezzar his servant, because herein he executed God's will. 2. That he should destroy many of the Egyptians, and have them all at his mercy (*v.* 11): *He shall smite the land of Egypt;* whom he will he shall slay. And whom he will he shall save alive and carry into *captivity.* 3. That he shall destroy the idols of Egypt, the temples and the images of their gods (*v.* 12): *He shall burn the houses of the Gods of Egypt. Beth-shemesh,* or *the house of the sun,* was so called from a temple there built to the sun. The statues he shall *break in pieces* (*v.* 13) The king of Babylon was himself a great idolater and had his temples and images in honour of the sun. Yet he is employed to destroy the idols of Egypt. 4. That he shall make himself master of the land. *He shall array himself with the rich spoils of the land of Egypt.* He shall array himself with them as ornaments and as armour; and this, though it shall be a heavy booty, he shall slip on with as much ease *as a shepherd slips on his garment,* when he goes to turn out his sheep in a morning. He shall make no more of the spoils of the land of Egypt than of a shepherd's coat. He shall *go forth in peace,* without any molestation so effectually reduced shall the land of Egypt be. This destruction of Egypt by the king of Babylon is foretold, Ezek. xxix. 19 and xxx. 10.

Chapter 44

I. An awakening sermon which Jeremiah preaches to the Jews in Egypt, to reprove them for their idolatry, ver. 1–14. II. The contempt which the people put upon this admonition, and their resolution to persist in their idolatries in despite of God and Jeremiah, ver. 15–19. III. The sentence passed upon them that they should all be cut off and perish in Egypt except a very small number; and, as a sign or earnest of it, the king of Egypt should shortly fall into the hands of the king of Babylon and be unable any longer to protect them, ver. 20–30.

Verses 1–14

The Jews in Egypt were now dispersed into various parts of the country, into *Migdol, and Noph,* and other places, and Jeremiah was sent on an errand from God to them (*v.* 15).

I. God puts them in mind of the desolations of Judah and Jerusalem, which the fugitives in the cities of Egypt seem to have forgotten (*v.* 2): *You have seen what a deplorable condition Judah and Jerusalem are brought into;* now will you consider whence those desolations came? From the wrath of God; it was his anger which made Jerusalem and *the cities of Judah waste and desolate* (*v.* 6).

II. He puts them in mind of the sins that brought those desolations upon Judah and Jerusalem. It was for *their wickedness* (*v.* 3), giving honour to counterfeit deities, which should have been given to the true God only. They forsook the God who was known among them. *"Neither they nor you, nor your fathers,* could give any rational account why *the God of Israel* was exchanged for such impostors."

III. He puts them in mind of the frequent and fair warnings he had given them by his word not to serve other gods, *v.* 4. *The prophets* were sent with a great deal of care to call to them, saying, *Oh! do not this abominable thing that I hate.* It becomes us to give warning of the danger of sin: *"Oh! do not* do it. If you love God, do not, for it is provoking to him; if you love your own souls do not, for it is destructive to them."* If God hates it, thou shouldst hate it. But *"They hearkened not, nor inclined their ear* (*v.* 5). Now this was intended for warning to you, who have not only heard the judgments of God's mouth, as they did, but have likewise seen the judgments of his hand."

IV. He reproves them for their continued idolatries (*v.* 8): You *burn incense to other gods in the land of Egypt.* They went against God's mind into Egypt, and when we thrust ourselves into places of temptation, it is just with God to leave us to ourselves. They did a great deal of injury to themselves and their families: *"You commit this great evil against your souls"* (*v.* 7). "It is the ready way to *cut yourselves off* from all comfort and hope (*v.* 8), to cut off your name and honour; so that you will by your sin and by your misery, become *a curse and a reproach among all nations."* They filled up the iniquity of their fathers, and added to it (*v.* 9): *"Have you forgotten the wickedness* of those who are gone before you?" *Have you forgotten the punishments of your fathers?* so some read it. He reminds them of the sins and punishments *of the kings of Judah,* and *the wickedness of their wives,* who had seduced them to idolatry. In the original it is, *And of his wives,* which, Dr. Lightfoot thinks, tacitly reflects upon Solomon's wives, particularly his Egyptian wives. *Have you forgotten your own wickedness and the wickedness of your wives,* when you lived in prosperity in Jerusalem, and what ruin it brought upon you?

V. He threatens their utter ruin for their persisting in their idolatry now that they were in Egypt. They shall perish in Egypt. Those that think not only to affront, but to confront, God Almighty, will find themselves outfaced. They shall not be wasted by natural deaths, as Israel in the wilderness, but by sore judgments. None (except a very few that will narrowly escape) shall ever *return to the land of Judah* again, *v.* 14. Those that are fretful and discontented will be uneasy and fond of change wherever they are. The Israelites, when they were in the land of Judah, desired to go into Egypt (*ch.* xlii. 22), but when they were in Egypt they desired to *return to the land of Judah* again; they *lifted up their soul* to it (so it is in the margin), which denotes an earnest desire.

Verses 15–19

The people's obstinate refusal to submit to the power of the word of God in the mouth of Jeremiah.

I. The persons who thus set God and his judgments

at defiance were such as knew either themselves or their wives to be guilty of the idolatry Jeremiah had reproved, *v.* 15. The women had been more guilty of idolatry and superstition than the men, not because the men stuck closer to the true God, but because they were generally atheists, and were for no God and no religion at all, and therefore could easily allow their wives to be of a false religion. It was consciousness of guilt that made them impatient of reproof: *They knew that their wives had burnt incense to other gods,* and that they had countenanced them in it, *and the women that stood by* knew that they had joined with them in idolatrous usages; so that what Jeremiah said touched them in a sore place.

II. The reply which these persons made to Jeremiah, and in him to God himself.

1. They declare their resolution not to do as God commanded them, but what they themselves had a mind to do; that is, they would worship the moon, here called *the queen of heaven;* some understand it of the sun, which was much worshipped in Egypt (*ch.* xliii. 13) and had been so at Jerusalem (2 Kings xxiii. 11). And others understand it of all *the host of heaven,* or *the frame of heaven,* the whole machine, *ch.* vii. 18. These daring sinners do not now go about to make excuses for their refusal, nor suggest that Jeremiah spoke from himself and not from God (as before, *ch.* xliii. 2), but they tell him flatly, *"We will not hearken unto thee;* we will do that which is forbidden and run the hazard of that which is threatened." Those that live in disobedience to God commonly grow worse and worse, and the heart is more and more hardened by *the deceitfulness of sin.* What they said many think. It is that which the young man would be at *in the days of his youth;* he would have and do everything he has a mind to, Eccles. xi. 9.

2. They give some sort of reasons for their resolution. They plead antiquity: We are resolved *to burn incense to the queen of heaven,* for *our fathers* did so. They plead authority. Those that had power practised it themselves and prescribed it to others: *Our kings and our princes* did it, whom God set over us, and who were of the seed of David. They plead unity. We all with one consent, we that are a *great multitude* (*v.* 15), we did it. They plead universality. It was done *in the cities of Judah.* They plead visibility. It was not done in dark and shady groves only, but *in the streets,* openly. They plead that it was the practice of the mother-church; it had been done in *Jerusalem.* They plead prosperity: *Then had we plenty* of bread, *and* of all good things: we *were well and saw no evil.* But, supposing all to be true, yet this does not excuse them from idolatry; it is the law of God that we must be judged by, not the practice of men. They suggest that the judgments they had been under were brought upon them for *leaving off to burn incense to the queen of heaven, v.* 18. Thus, in the first ages of Christianity, when God chastised the nations by any public calamities for opposing the Christians and persecuting them, they put a contrary sense upon the calamities, as if they were sent to punish them for conniving at the Christians and tolerating them, and cried, *Christianos ad leones—Throw the Christians to the lions.* They plead that, though the women were most active in their idolatries, yet they did it with the approbation of their husbands; the women were busy to *make cakes* for meat-offerings *to the queen of heaven* and to prepare *and pour out the drink-offerings, v.* 19. Some understand this as spoken by the husbands (*v.* 15), who plead that they did not do it *without their men,* that is, without their elders and rulers, but, because the making of the *cakes* and the pouring out of *the drink-offerings* are expressly spoke of as the women's work (*ch.* vii. 18), it seems rather to be understood as their plea.

Verses 20-30

I. Jeremiah has something to say to them from himself. They said that these miseries came upon them because they had now *left off burning incense to the queen of heaven*. "No," says he, "it was because you had formerly done it, not because you had now left it off." The incense which they and their fathers had burnt to other gods did indeed go unpunished a great while, for God was long-suffering, and during the day of his patience it was perhaps, as they said, *well with them, and* they *saw no evil*; but at length they grew so provoking *that the Lord could no longer bear* (v. 22), whereupon some of them did a little reform. But their old corrupt inclinations being still the same, God remembered against them the idolatries of *their fathers, their kings, and their princes, in the streets of Jerusalem*, which they gloried in (v. 21). All the *abominations which they had committed* were brought to account; and *therefore is their land a desolation and a curse, as at this day* (v. 22); *therefore* for their old transgressions, has all *this evil happened to them, as at this day*, v. 23.

II. Jeremiah has something to say to them, *to the women* particularly, from *the Lord of hosts, the God of Israel*. They have given their answer; now let them hear God's reply, v. 24.

1. Since they were fully determined to persist in their idolatry, he would go on to punish them. God repeats what they had said (v. 25): "*You and your wives* are agreed in this obstinacy; *you have spoken with your mouths and fulfilled with your hands;* you have said, *We will surely perform our vows that we have vowed, to burn incense to the queen of heaven,*" as if, though it were a sin, yet their having vowed to do it were sufficient to justify them in the doing of it; whereas no man can by his vow make that lawful to himself, much less duty, which God has already made sin. He had sworn that what little remains of religion there were among them, should be lost, v. 26. Though they joined with the Egyptians in their idolatries, yet they continued to make mention of the name of Jehovah, particularly in their solemn oaths; they said, *Jehovah liveth*, he is *the living God*, so they owned 'him to be, though they worshipped dead idols; they swear, *The Lord liveth* (ch. v. 2). But God declares that his *name shall no more be* thus *named* by *any man of Judah in all the land of Egypt*. Those are very miserable whom God has so far left to themselves that they have quite forgotten their religion. To those whom God finds impenitent sinners he will be found an implacable Judge. They said that they should recover themselves when they returned to worship *the queen of heaven*; God said they should ruin themselves.

2. He tells them that few of them should *escape the sword*, and *return into the land of Judah, a small number* (v. 28), in comparison with the great numbers that should return out of the land of the Chaldeans.

3. He gives them a sign that all these threatenings shall be accomplished in Egypt. *Pharaoh-hophra*, the present *king of Egypt*, shall be delivered *into the hand of his enemies that seek his life—of his own rebellious subjects* (so some) under Amasis, who usurped his throne—*of Nebuchadnezzar king of Babylon* (so others), who invaded his kingdom; the former is related by Herodotus, the latter by Josephus. They expected more from him than from Zedekiah king of Judah; he was a more potent prince. "But," says God, "*I will give him into the hand of his enemies, as I gave Zedekiah*."

CHAPTER 45

The prophecy in this chapter concerns Baruch only. It is placed here after the story of the destruction of Jerusalem and the dispersion of the Jews, but was delivered long before, in the fourth year of Jehoiakim. I. How Baruch was terrified when he was brought into trouble for writing and reading Jeremiah's roll. ver. 1-3. II. How his fears were checked and silenced with a promise of special preservation, ver. 4, 5.

Verses 1-5

Baruch was employed in writing Jeremiah's prophecies, and reading them, *ch.* xxxvi, and was threatened for it by the king. He escaped under a divine protection to which story this chapter is a sequel.

I. The consternation that poor Baruch was in when he was sought for by the king's messengers, and the notice which God took of it. He was a young man willing to serve God and his prophet. But when he found it exposed him to contempt, he cried out, "I am undone; I shall fall into the pursuers' hands, and be imprisoned, and put to death, or banished: *The Lord has added grief to my sorrow*. After the grief of writing and reading the prophecies of my country's ruin, I have the sorrow of being treated as a criminal for so doing; it is a burden too heavy for me. *I fainted in my sighing and I find no rest*." Young beginners in religion are apt to be discouraged with the little difficulties which they meet at first in the service of God. They do but *run with the footmen*, and it *wearies them*; they *faint* upon the very dawning of *the day of adversity*, and it is an evidence that *their strength is small* (Prov. xxiv. 10), their faith weak. Baruch should have rejoiced that he was counted worthy to suffer in such a good cause and with such good company, but, instead of that, he reflects upon his god, as if he had dealt hardly with him.

II. Jeremiah was troubled to see him in such agitation, and knew not what to say to him. He was loth to chide him, and willing to comfort him, but God tells him what he *shall say to him*, v. 4. It is our over-fondness for the good things of this present time that makes us impatient under its evil things. Now God shows him that it was his fault and folly to desire an abundance of the wealth and honour of this world. The ship was sinking. Ruin was coming upon the Jewish nation: "*That which I have built*, to be a house for myself, *I am breaking down, and that which I have planted*, to be a vineyard for myself, *I am plucking up, even this whole land*, the Jewish church and state; and dost thou now *seek great things for thyself*? Dost thou expect to be rich and honourable and to make a figure now? Canst thou expect to be high when all are brought low?"

III. God gave him hope that though he should not be great, yet he should be safe: "*I will bring evil upon all flesh*, all nations, *but thy life will I give to thee for a prey*" (*thy soul*, so the word is) "*in all places whither thou goest*. Thou must be hurried from place to place, and in danger, but thou shalt escape, though often very narrowly, shalt have thy life, but it shall be as a prey, got with much difficulty and danger; thou shalt be saved as by fire."

CHAPTER 46

Judgment began at the house of God, but it did not end there. In this and the following chapters we have predictions of the desolations of the neighbouring nations, brought upon them mostly by the king of Babylon, till at length Babylon itself comes to be reckoned with. The prophecy against Egypt is put first. I. A prophecy of the defeat of Pharaoh-necho's army by the Chaldean forces at Carchemish, ver. 1-12. II. A prophecy of the descent which Nebuchadnezzar should make upon the land of Egypt, which was accomplished some years after the destruction of Jerusalem, ver. 13-26. III. A word of comfort to the Israel of God in the midst of those calamities, ver. 27, 28.

Verses 1-11

The first verse is the title of that part of this book which relates to the neighbouring nations. It is *the word of the Lord which came to Jeremiah against the Gentiles*. In the Old Testament we have *the word of the Lord* against *the Gentiles*; in the New Testament we have *the word of the Lord* for *the Gentiles*, that those who were *afar off are made nigh*.

He begins with Egypt, because they were of old Israel's oppressors and of late their deceivers. In these verses he foretells the overthrow of *the army of Pharaoh-necho*, by Nebuchadnezzar, *in the fourth year of Jehoakim*. This defeat (as we find, 2 Kings xxiv. 7), made him pay dearly for his expedition against the king of Assyria four years before, in which he slew Josiah, 2 Kings xxiii. 29. This event is here foretold in lofty expressions of triumph over Egypt thus foiled, which Jeremiah would speak of with pleasure, because the death of Josiah was now avenged on Pharaoh-necho.

I. The Egyptians are upbraided with the mighty preparations they made for this expedition, in which the prophet challenges them to do their utmost: "Come then, *order the buckler*, let the weapons of war be got ready," *v.* 3. Egypt was famous for *horses* —let them be *harnessed* and the cavalry well mounted: *Get up, you horsemen, and stand forth*, &c., *v.* 4. He compares this expedition to the rising of their river Nile (*v.* 7, 8): *Egypt* now *rises up like a flood*, threatening to overflow all the neighbouring lands. It is a very formidable army. The prophet summons them (*v.* 9): *Come up, you horses; rage, you chariots*. He challenges them to bring all their confederate troops together, *the Ethiopians*, who descended from the same stock as the Egyptians (Gen. x. 6), and were their neighbours and allies, *the Libyans and Lydians*, both in Africa, to the west of Egypt, from whom the Egyptians fetched their auxiliary forces. It shall be all in vain; they shall be shamefully defeated, for God will fight against them, Prov. xxi. 30, 31.

II. They are upbraided with the great expectations they had from this expedition. They knew their own thoughts, and God knew them, *but they knew not the thoughts of the Lord, for he gathers them as sheaves into the floor*, Mic. iv. 11, 12. Egypt saith (*v.* 8): *I will go up; I will cover the earth*, and none *shall hinder me*; *I will destroy the city*, whatever city it is that stands in my way. Like Pharaoh of old, *I will pursue, I will overtake*. But God saith that it shall be his day: *This is the day of the Lord God of hosts* (*v.* 10), in which he will be exalted in the overthrow of the Egyptians.

III. They are upbraided with their cowardice (*v.* 5, 6): "*Wherefore have I seen them*, notwithstanding all these mighty and vast preparations, when the Chaldean army faces them, *dismayed, turned back*, and no spirit left in them." Even *their mighty ones*, who, one would think, should have stood their ground, *flee a flight*, flee by consent, in confusion; they have neither time nor heart to *look back*, but *fear is round about* them. They cannot make their escape. *They shall stumble* in their flight, *and fall towards the north*, towards their enemies' country; for such confusion were they in that instead of making homeward, they made forward.

IV. They are upbraided with their inability ever to recover this blow, *v.* 11, 12. The damsel, *the daughter of Egypt*, that lived in great pomp and state, is sorely wounded by this defeat. Let her now seek for *balm in Gilead*; let her use all the medicines her wise men can prescribe for the repairing of the loss sustained by this defeat; but all in vain; *no cure shall be* to them; they shall never be able to bring such a powerful army into the field again. "*The nations* that rang of thy glory and strength *have* now *heard of thy shame*, how shamefully thou wast routed and how thou art weakened by it." *Thy cry hath filled the* country about; such confusion were they in.

Verses 12–28

I. Confusion and terror spoken to Egypt. The accomplishment of the prediction in the former part of the chapter disabled the Egyptians from making any attempts upon other nations. But still they remained strong at home, and none of their neighbours durst make any attempts upon them. The scope of the prophecy here is to show *how the king of Babylon should* shortly *come and smite the land of Egypt*, *v.* 13. This was fulfilled by the same hand with the former, even Nebuchadnezzar's, but many years after.

1. The alarm of war sounded in Egypt (*v.* 14). The enemy is approaching, *the sword is devouring round about* in the neighbouring countries, and it is time for the Egyptians to prepare to give the enemy a warm reception. This must be proclaimed in all parts of Egypt, particularly in Migdol, Noph, and Tahpanhes, because in these places the Jewish refugees had planted themselves, in contempt of God's command (*ch.* xliv. 1). Let them hear what a sorry shelter Egypt is likely to be to them.

2. The retreat of the forces of other nations which the Egyptians had in their pay is here foretold. Some were posted upon the frontiers to guard them, where they were beaten off by the invaders and put to flight. Then were the *valiant men swept away* (*v.* 15) as with *a sweeping rain* (it is the word that is used Prov. xxviii. 3); they can none of them stand their ground, *because the Lord drives them* from their posts; he drives them by enabling the Chaldeans to drive them. If God please, they shall be made to *fall upon one another*, *every man's sword against his fellow*. *Her hired men*, the troops Egypt has in her service, are indeed *in the midst of her like fatted bullocks*, lusty men, able bodied, who were likely to make good against the enemy: but *they are turned back*; and, instead of fighting, they have *fled away together*. They all made homeward towards their own country (*v.* 16): *They said, "Arise, and let us go again to our own people*, safe *from the oppressing sword of the* Chaldeans, that bears down all before it." In times of exigence little confidence is to be put in mercenary troops, that fight purely for pay. They exclaimed vehemently against Pharaoh, to whose bad management their defeat was owing. When he posted them there upon the borders of his country it is probable that he told them he would come himself with a gallant army to support them, but he failed them. No marvel that they deserted crying out, *Pharaoh king of Egypt is but a noise* (*v.* 17). *He has passed the time appointed;* he did not keep his word.

3. The formidable power of the Chaldean army is described as bearing down all before it. *The King* of kings, *whose name is the Lord of hosts*, hath said it, *As I live, saith* this *King, as Tabor* overtops *the mountains and Carmel* overlooks *the sea, so shall* the king of Babylon overpower all the force of Egypt, *v.* 18. He and his *army shall come against* Egypt *with axes, as hewers of wood* (*v.* 22), and the Egyptians shall be no more able to resist them than the tree is to resist the man that comes with an axe to *cut it down*.

4. The desolation of Egypt is foretold, and the waste that should be made of that rich country. *Egypt is* now *like a very fair heifer*, or calf (*v.* 20), fat and shining, and not *accustomed to the yoke* of subjection, wanton as a heifer that is well fed. Some think here is an allusion to Apis, the bull or calf which the Egyptians worshipped, from whom the children of Israel learned to worship the golden calf. Egypt is as fair as a goddess, *but destruction comes*; *cutting up comes* (so some read it); *it comes out of the north*; thence the Chaldean soldiers shall come to kill and cut up this *fair heifer*. *The daughters of Egypt shall be confounded* (*v.* 24), shall be filled with astonishment. *Their voice shall go like a serpent*, that is, it shall be very low and submissive. They shall not dare to make loud complaints of the cruelty of the conquerors, but vent their griefs in silent murmurs. They shall not now answer roughly, but, with *the poor, use entreaties* and beg for their lives. They shall

be carried away prisoners into their enemy's land (v. 19): "*O thou daughter! dwelling securely and delicately in Egypt, furnish thyself to go into captivity;* instead of rich clothes, which will but tempt the enemy to strip thee, get plain and warm clothes; and inure thyself to hardship, that thou mayest bear it the better." The Egyptians must prepare to flee; for their cities shall be evacuated. Noph particularly *shall be desolate, without an inhabitant. The multitude of No shall be punished:* it is called *populous No*, Nah. iii. 8. *Though hand join in hand*, they shall not escape; nor think to go off in the crowd. Pharaoh shall be brought down, and *all those that trust in him* (v. 25), particularly the Jews that came to sojourn in his country, trusting in him rather than in God. All these shall be *delivered into the hands of the northern nations* (v. 24).

5. An intimation is given that in process of time Egypt shall recover itself again (v. 26): *Afterwards it shall be inhabited.*

II. Comfort and peace are here spoken to the Israel of God, v. 27, 28. It may refer to the captives in Babylon, whom God had mercy in store for, or, more generally, to all the people of God, designed for their encouragement in the most difficult times, when the judgments of God are abroad among the nations. Let the wicked of the earth tremble, *but fear not thou, O my servant Jacob! and be not dismayed, O Israel!* and again, *Fear thou not, O Jacob!* God would not have his people to be a timorous people. God's people shall be found out and gathered though they be far off. The wicked *is like the troubled sea when it cannot rest;* they *flee when none pursues.* But Jacob, being at home in God, *shall be at rest and at ease, and none shall make him afraid;* for *what time he is afraid* he has a *God to trust to.* Nations have their periods, but the gospel church, God's spiritual Israel, still continues, and will to the end of time.

CHAPTER 47

This chapter reads the Philistines their doom, as the former read the Egyptians theirs and by the same hand, that of Nebuchadnezzar. It is short, but terrible; and Tyre and Zidon come in sharers with them in the destruction. I. It is foretold that forces should come from the north, ver. 1–5. II. That the war should continue long, and their endeavours to put an end to it should be in vain, ver. 6–7.

Verses 1–7

As the Egyptians had often proved false friends, so the Philistines had always been sworn enemies, to the Israel of God, and the more dangerous, for their being such near neighbours to them. They were humbled in David's time, but, it seems, they had got head again till Nebuchadnezzar cut them off with their neighbours, which is the event here foretold. The date of this prophecy was *before Pharaoh smote Gaza.* When this blow was given to Gaza by the king of Egypt is not certain, but this word of the Lord came to Jeremiah against the Philistines when they were in no peril from any adversary, yet then Jeremiah foretold their ruin. It is here foretold, 1. That a foreign enemy shall be brought upon them: *Waters rise up out of the north*, v. 2. Now a terrible storm comes out of that cold climate. The Chaldean army shall overflow the land like a deluge. 2. That they shall all be in a consternation upon it. The men shall have no heart to fight: *All the inhabitants of the land shall howl*, so that nothing but lamentation shall be heard in all places. Before it comes to killing and slaying, the very *stamping of the horses* and *rattling of the chariots*, shall strike terror to such a degree that parents in their fright shall seem void of natural affection, *for they shall not look back to their children*, to provide for their safety. 3. That the country of the Philistines

shall be spoiled and laid waste, v. 4. Tyre and Zidon were strong and wealthy cities, and they used to help the Philistines in a strait, but now they shall themselves be involved in the common ruin, and God will cut off from them every *helper that remains.* Who the *remnant of the country of Caphtor* were is uncertain, but the Caphtorim were near akin to the Philistines (Gen. x. 14), and probably when their own country was destroyed such as remained settled with their kinsmen the Philistines. Some particular places are here named, *Gaza, and Ashkelon*, v. 5. *Baldness has come upon them;* the invaders have stripped them of all their ornaments, and they are *cut off.* The prophet, with his usual tenderness, asks them first (v. 5), *How long will you cut yourselves*, as men in extreme sorrow and anguish do? But he turns from the effect to the cause: *They cut themselves*, for the sword of the Lord cuts them. *O thou sword of the Lord! how long will it be ere thou be quiet?* He begs it would *put up itself into the scabbard.* This expresses the prophet's earnest desire to see an end of the war, looking with compassion, even upon the Philistines themselves. Yet he stops the mouth of his own complaint (v. 7): *How can it be quiet, seeing the Lord hath given it a charge* against such and such places. When the sword is drawn we cannot expect it should be sheathed till it has fulfilled its charge. As the word of God, so his rod and his sword, shall accomplish that for which he sends them.

CHAPTER 48

Isaiah's predictions concerning Moab had had their accomplishment (we had the predictions Isa. xv and xvi and the like Amos ii. 1), and they were fulfilled when the Assyrians, under Salmanassar, invaded and distressed Moab. But this is a prophecy of the desolations of Moab by the Chaldeans, which were accomplished under Nebuzaradan, about five years after he had destroyed Jerusalem. I. The destruction foretold (ver. 1–6, 8, and again ver. 21–25, 34), that spoilers should come upon them and force some to flee (ver. 9), should carry many into captivity (ver. 12, 46), that the enemy should come shortly (ver. 16), come swiftly and surprise them (ver. 40, 41), that he should make thorough work (ver. 10) and lay the country waste (ver. 14, 15), that there should be no escaping them (ver. 42, 45), that this should force them to quit their idols (ver. 13, 35) and put an end to all their joy (ver. 33, 34), that their neighbours shall lament them (ver. 17–19) and the prophet himself does, ver. 31, 36, &c. II. The causes of this destruction assigned; it was their pride, and security, and carnal confidence (ver. 7, 11, 14, 29), and their contempt of God and his people, ver. 26, 27, 30. III. A promise of the restoration of Moab, ver. 47.

Verses 1–13

I. The author of Moab's destruction is *the Lord of hosts*, and *the God of Israel* (v. 1), who will herein plead the cause of his Israel against a people that have always been vexatious to them, and will punish them now for the injuries done to Israel of old.

II. The instruments of it: *Spoilers shall come* (v. 8), shall come with a sword, a sword that shall *pursue them*, v. 2. "*I will send unto him wanderers*, such as come from afar, as if they had missed their way, but they shall *cause him to wander.*" These destroyers *have devised evil against Heshbon*, one of the principal cities of Moab, and they aim at the ruin of the kingdom: *Come, and let us cut it off from being a nation* (v. 2). The prophet, in God's name, engages them to make thorough work of it (v. 10): *Cursed be he that does the work of the Lord deceitfully.* To this work is applied that general rule given to all that are employed in any service for God, *Cursed be he that does the work of the Lord deceitfully* or negligently.

III. The effects of this destruction. The cities shall be laid in ruins; they shall be *spoiled* (v. 1) and cut down (v. 2); they shall be *desolate* (v. 9), *without any to dwell therein.* The *country* also shall be wasted, the *valley shall perish*, and the *plain be destroyed*, v. 8. The corn and the flocks, which used to cover the plains and make the valleys rejoice, shall all be destroyed, eaten up, trodden down, or carried off. The *priests and princes shall go together into captivity.* Chemosh, the god they worship, shall share with them in the ruin; his temples shall be laid in ashes and his image carried away with the rest of the spoil. The consequence will be shame and confusion: *Kirjathaim is confounded*, and Misgah is so. *There shall be no more vaunting in Moab concerning Heshbon* (so it might be read, *v.* 2). Nor shall they any more boast of their gods (*v.* 13); they *shall be ashamed of Chemosh, as Israel was ashamed of Beth-el*, of the golden calf they had at Beth-el, for it was not able to save them from the Assyrians; nor shall Chemosh be able to save the Moabites from the Chaldeans. Go up to the hills, go down to the valleys, and you meet with *continual weeping* (*weeping with weeping*); all are in tears; you meet none with dry eyes. They will cry to one another: "Away, away! *flee, save your lives* (*v.* 6); shift for your own safety, though you escape as naked as the *heath*, or grig, or dry shrub, *in the wilderness.* Take shelter, though it be in a barren wilderness. The danger will come suddenly and swiftly; and therefore *give wings unto Moab* (*v.* 9)."

IV. God will now reckon with Moab because they have been secure, and have trusted in their wealth and strength, *in their works* and *in their treasures, v.* 7. They trusted *in the abundance of their riches and strengthened themselves in their wickedness,* Ps. lii. 7. They had been long undisturbed: *Moab has been at ease from his youth.* It was an ancient kingdom before Israel was, and had enjoyed great tranquillity, though a small country. He has not been unsettled, nor *gone into captivity,* and yet Moab is a wicked idolatrous nation, and one of the confederates against *God's hidden ones,* Ps. lxxxiii. 3, 6. They had been long corrupt and unreformed: He *has settled on his lees*; he has been secure and sensual in his prosperity. *His taste remained in him, and his scent is not changed;* he is still the same, as bad as ever he was.

Verses 14–47

The destruction is here further prophesied in moving language, designed not only to awaken them by a national repentance to prevent the trouble, or by a personal repentance to prepare for it, but to affect us with the calamitous state of human life, and with the power of God's anger with a provoking people.

I. It is a surprising destruction, and very sudden, that is here threatened. They thought themselves *strong for war* and able to deal with the most powerful enemy (*v.* 14), and yet the calamity is near, and he is not able to keep it off. As an eagle flies upon his prey, *he shall spread his wings,* the wings of his army, *over Moab*; that none may escape. *The strongholds of* Moab are taken by *surprise* (*v.* 41), so that all their strength stood them in no stead. It requires more than ordinary courage not to be *afraid of sudden fear.*

II. It lays Moab all in ruins: *Moab is spoiled* (*v.* 15), quite spoiled, is *confounded and broken down* (*v.* 20). The kingdom is deprived of its dignity and authority: *The horn of Moab is cut off,* the horn of its strength and power, both offensive and defensive; *his arm is broken,* that he can neither give a blow nor prevent a blow, *v.* 25. The youth of the kingdom went down to the battle promising themselves that they should return victorious; but God told them that they went *down to the slaughter.* Those that are enemies to God's people will soon be made no people.

III. It is a lamentable destruction and will turn joy into heaviness. The prophet does himself lament. His very *heart shall mourn for* them (*v.* 31); he will *weep for the vine of Sibmah* (*v.* 32); his heart *shall sound like pipes for Moab, v.* 36. The ruin of sinners is no pleasure to God, and therefore should be a pain to us. These passages, and many others in this

chapter, are much the same as Isaiah's in his prophecies against Moab (Isa. xv. 1); for, though there was a long distance of time between that prophecy and this, yet they were both dictated by one and the same Spirit. Moabites themselves shall lament. Those that sat in *glory,* in the midst of wealth, and mirth, shall *sit in thirst,* in a dry land, where no water, no comfort is, *v.* 18. The Moabites in the remote corners of the country, will ask everyone *that escapes, What is done? v.* 19. And when they are told that all is gone, they will *howl and cry,* in anguish of spirit (*v.* 20). They will *leave the cities and dwell in the rock,* where they may have their fill of melancholy; they shall no more be singing birds, but mourning birds, *like the dove* (*v.* 28), *the doves of the valley,* Ezek. vii. 16. That which Moab used to rejoice in was their pleasant fruits and the abundance of their rich wines. The delights of sense were all the matter of their joy. Take away these, destroy their gardens and vineyards, and you make *all their mirth to cease,* Hos. ii. 11, 12. *Take joy and gladness from the plentiful field, and* you take it *from the land of Moab, v.* 33. Those who make the delights of sense their chief joy, since these are things they may easily be deprived of in a little time, subject themselves to the tyranny of the greatest grief; whereas those who rejoice in God may do that even when *the fig-tree does not blossom and there is no fruit in the vine.* All their neighbours are called to mourn with them, and to condole with them on their ruin (*v.* 17): *All you that are about him bemoan him.* Let none be puffed up with or put confidence in their strength or beauty, for neither will be a security against the judgments of God.

IV. It is a shameful destruction and such as shall expose them to contempt: *Moab is made drunk* (*v.* 26).

V. It is the destruction of that which is dear to them, not only of their summer fruits and their vintage, but of their wealth (*v.* 36): *The riches that he has gotten have perished.* Riches, like dust, slip through our fingers even when we hold them fast. Yet this is not the worst; even those whose religion was false were fond of it above anything, and therefore, though it was really a promise, yet to them it was a threatening (*v.* 35), that God *will cause to cease him that offers in the high places,* for the high places shall be destroyed, and the fields of offerings shall be laid waste, and the priests themselves, *who burnt incense to their gods,* shall be slain or carried into captivity, *v.* 7.

VI. It is a just destruction which they have deserved and brought upon themselves by sin.

1. The sin which they had been most notoriously guilty of, was pride. It is mentioned six times, *v.* 29. *We have* all *heard of the pride of Moab.* It was charged upon them, Isa. xvi. 6, but here it is expressed more largely than there. Two instances are here given of the pride of Moab: (1) He had conducted himself insolently towards God. He must be brought down with shame (*v.* 26), for *he has magnified himself against the Lord.* The Moabites preferred Chemosh before Jehovah, and thought themselves a match for the God of Israel. (2) He had conducted himself scornfully towards Israel, in their late troubles; therefore Moab shall fall into the same troubles, and be a derision, for Israel was *a derision to him, v.* 26, 27. But the Moabites industriously proclaimed their joy, triumphing over every Israelite they met with in distress and laughing at him.

2. Besides this they had been guilty of malice against God's people, and treachery in their dealings with them, *v.* 30. The nation, whose fall they triumph in, shall recover itself. What was said of sinners in general (Isa. xxiv. 17, 18), that those who *flee from the fear shall fall into the pit* and those who come up out of the pit shall be taken in the snare, is here particularly foretold concerning the sinners of Moab

(*v.* 44). The figurative expressions used *v.* 44 are explained in one instance (*v.* 45): *Those that fled out of the villages for fear of the enemy's forces put themselves under the shadow of Heshbon*, stood there, and supposed they stood safely, as now armies sometimes retire under the cannon of a fortified city, but here they should be disappointed; for, when *they flee out of the pit, they fall into the snare;* Heshbon, which they thought would shelter them, devours them as Moses had foretold long since (Num. xxi. 28). The chapter concludes with a short promise of their return out of *captivity in the latter days*. God, who brings them into captivity, *will bring again* their *captivity, v.* 47. Thus tenderly does God deal with Moabites, much more with his own people! Even with Moabites he *will not contend for ever, nor be always wrath*. This prophecy concerning Moab is long, but here it ends; it ends comfortably: *Thus far is the judgment of Moab*.

CHAPTER 49

The cup of trembling still goes round, and the nations must all drink of it, ch. xxv. 15. This chapter puts it into the hands, I. Of the Ammonites, ver. 1–6. II. Of the Edomites, ver. 7–22. III. Of the Syrians, ver. 23–27. IV. Of the Kedarenes, and the kingdoms of Hazor, ver. 28–33. V. Of the Elamites, ver. 34–39.

Verses 1–6

The Ammonites were next, both in kindred and neighbourhood, to the Moabites. 1. An action is here brought, in God's name, against the Ammonites, for an illegal encroachment upon the rightful possessions of the tribe of Gad, that lay next them, *v.* 1. Those territories upon the carrying away of the Gileadites, by the king of Assyria (2 Kings xv. 29, 1 Chron. v. 26), were left almost dispeopled, and an easy prey to the next invader. "Are there no Gadites left, to whom the right of inheritance belongs? Or, if there were not, are there no Israelites, none left of Judah, that are nearer akin to them than you are?" *Why then does their king,* as if he were entitled to the forfeited estates, or Milcom, their idol, as if he had the right to dispose of it to his worshippers, *inherit Gad, and his people dwell in the cities* which fell by lot to that tribe of God's people? *They magnified themselves against their border* and boasted it was their own, Zeph. ii. 8. Those will find themselves mistaken who think everything their own which they can lay their hands on. As there is justice owing to owners, so also to their heirs, whom it is a great sin to defraud, though they either know not their right or know not how to come at it. 2. Judgment is here given against them for this violence. God *will cause an alarm of war to be heard,* even *in Rabbah,* their capital city and a very strong one, *v.* 2. Their cities shall be laid in ruins. Their country, which they were so proud of, shall be wasted (*v.* 4). They are charged with backsliding, for they were the posterity of righteous Lot. *They were untoward and refractory* (so some read it); and, when they had forsaken their God, *they gloried in their valleys*. These they had violently taken away from Israel. They gloried in the strength of their valleys, so surrounded with mountains that they were inaccessible, gloried in the products of them. They flattered themselves that they should never be disturbed in the enjoyment of them: *To-morrow shall be as this day;* therefore they set God and his judgments at defiance. *Their king and his princes,* and Milcom, their god, *and his priests, shall go into captivity* (*v.* 3), *and every man shall be driven out right forth,* shall make the best of it in his flight (*v.* 5). And, to complete their misery, *none shall gather up him that wanders,* none shall open their doors to them. Then the country of the Ammonites shall fall into the hands of the remaining Israelites (*v.* 2).

3. Yet there is a prospect given them of mercy hereafter (*v.* 6), as before to Moab.

Verses 7–22

The Edomites come next to receive their doom from God, by the mouth of Jeremiah: they also were old enemies to the Israel of God. Many of the expressions used in this prophecy *concerning Edom* are borrowed from the prophecy of Obadiah, which is *concerning Edom*; for, all the prophets are inspired by one and the same Spirit.

I. That the country of Edom should be all wasted and made desolate, that *the calamity of Esau* should be *brought upon him,* the calamity he has deserved, for his old sins, *v.* 8. The time is at hand when God *will visit him,* and call him to an account, and then they shall *flee* from the sword, *turn back* from the battle, and *dwell deep* in caverns, where they shall hide. All they have shall be carried off by the conqueror; those that destroy them shall never be satiated (*v.* 9, 10); they shall make *Esau* quite *bare,* shall strip the Edomites of all they have. *His brethren* the Moabites, *and his neighbours* the Philistines, whom he might have expected succours from, or at least shelter, are spoiled as well as he. The Chaldee makes these to be the words of God to his people, distinguishing them from the Edomites in this calamity; and they read it, "*But you, O house of Israel! you shall not leave your orphans; I will secure them, and let your widows rest on my word*. Whatever becomes of the widows and fatherless of the Edomites, I will take care of yours." They had made a mighty figure, but God will make *them small among the heathen;* and those that despised God's people shall themselves be *despised among men* (*v.* 15, Obad. 2). *Edom shall be* such *a desolation* that none shall care for coming near the ruins of it, *no man shall abide there* (*v.* 18).

II. That the instruments of this destruction should be very resolute and formidable. God has determined that Edom shall be laid waste, and then he that is to be employed in wasting it shall come swiftly and strongly. Nebuchadnezzar is he of whom it is here foretold. He *shall come up like a lion,* with fierceness and fury, like a lion enraged by *the swelling of Jordan* overflowing his banks, which forces him out of his covert by the water-side into the higher grounds, *v.* 19. *Even the least of the flock shall draw them out* (*v.* 20); the meanest servant in Nebuchadnezzar's retinue shall *draw them out* for the slaughter, shall force them to surrender. Nebuchadnezzar shall come, not only like a lion, the king of beasts, but like an eagle, the king of birds (*v.* 22): He *shall fly as the eagle* upon his prey, so swiftly, so strongly, and immediately *the hearts of the mighty men* shall fail them, for they shall see he is an enemy that it is in vain to struggle with.

III. That the Edomites' confidences should all fail them in the day of their distress. 1. They trusted to their wisdom, but that shall stand them in no stead. This is the first thing fastened upon in this prophecy against Edom, *v.* 7. That nation used to be famous for wisdom, and their statesmen were thought to excel in politics; and yet now they shall take such wrong measures, and be so baffled in all their designs, that people shall ask, with wonder, What is the matter with the Edomites? *Is wisdom no more in Teman?* It is so, when God is designing the ruin of a people; for whom he will destroy he infatuates. See Job xii. 20. *Has their wisdom vanished? Is it tired?* (so some); *is it worn out?* (so others); *has it become useless?* (so others). 2. They trusted to their strength, but neither shall that avail them, *v.* 16. They had been a terror to all their neighbours, because no neighbouring nation durst meddle with them, they thought no nation in the world durst. Their country was mountainous, having many passes, which they thought themselves able to make good against any invader. See Obad. 3, 4, 8.

IV. That their destruction should be inevitable. 1. God hath determined it (*v.* 12); (*v.* 13), he hath *sworn it*, that they shall *drink the cup of trembling*, which is put into the hands of all their neighbours. 2. All the world shall take notice of it (*v.* 21): The *earth is moved*, and all the nations are put into a concern, *at the noise of their fall*. *The noise of the outcry is heard to the Red Sea*, which flowed upon the coasts of Edom. It shall be heard among the ships that lie in the Red Sea to take in lading (1 Kings ix. 26).

Verses 23–27

The kingdom of Syria, north of Canaan, had been often vexatious to the Israel of God. Damascus was the metropolis of that kingdom. Hamath and Arpad, two other considerable cities, are named (*v.* 23), and *the palaces of Ben-hadad*, which he built, are particularly marked for ruin, *v.* 27; see also Amos i. 4. The judgment of Damascus begins with fright and faint-heartedness. They *hear evil tidings*, that the king of Babylon, with all his force, is coming against them, and *they are confounded*; their souls are melted, *they are faint-hearted*, they are like *the troubled sea, that cannot be quiet* (Isa. lvii. 20), or like men *in a storm* at sea (Ps. cvii. 26); or the sorrow that begins in the city shall go to the sea-coast, *v.* 23. *Damascus* now *waxes feeble* (*v.* 24), and owns it is to no more purpose to think of contending with her fate than for *a woman in* labour to contend with her pains, which she cannot escape. It was a *city of praise* (*v.* 25), not praise to God, but to herself, a city much admired by all strangers that visited it. It was a *city of joy*. But now it is all overwhelmed with fear and grief. It ends with a terrible fall and fire. The inhabitants are slain (*v.* 26): The *young men*, who should have defend the city, *shall fall by the sword in her streets; and all the men of war shall be cut off*. The city is laid in ashes (*v.* 27): The *fire* is *kindled* by the besiegers *in the wall*, but it shall devour *the palaces of Ben-hadad* particularly, where so much mischief had formerly been hatched against God's Israel.

Verses 28–33

These verses foretell the desolation that Nebuchadnezzar and his forces should make among the people of Kedar (who descended from Kedar the son of Ishmael, and inhabited a part of Arabia the Stony), and of Hazor, who perhaps were originally Canaanites, of the kingdom of Hazor, in the north of Canaan, which had Jabin for its king, but, being driven thence, settled in the deserts of Arabia. They dwelt in *tents* and had no walls, but *curtains* (*v.* 29), no fortified cities; they had *neither gates nor bars*, *v.* 31. They were shepherds, and had no treasures, no money, but flocks and camels. They had no soldiers among them, for they were in no fear of invaders for they *dwelt alone*, *v.* 31. Though they had no trade, no treasures, yet they are here said to be a *wealthy nation* (*v.* 31). Those are truly rich who have enough to supply their necessities, and know when they have enough. We need not go to the treasures of kings and provinces, or to the cash of merchants, to look for wealthy people; they may be found among shepherds *that dwell in tents*. The king of Babylon resolves it shall never be said that he, who had conquered so many strong cities, will leave those unconquered *that dwell in tents*. It was strange that that eagle should stoop to catch these flies. These people had lived inoffensively among their neighbours. God said (*v.* 28): *Arise, go up to Kedar, and spoil the men of the east*. God orders it for the correcting of an unthankful people. The amazement that this put them into, and the desolation hereby made among them: *They shall cry unto them;* those on the borders shall send the alarm into all parts of the country, which shall be put into the utmost confusion by it; they shall cry, "*Fear is on every side*—We are surrounded by the enemy." They shall none of them have any heart to make resistance. The enemy need not strike a stroke; they shall shout them out of their tents, *v.* 29. There are *fears on every side* when there are foes on every side. The Chaldeans shall *take to themselves their curtains and vessels*; though they are but plain and coarse, yet they shall spoil for spoiling sake. *They shall carry away their tents and their flocks*, *v.* 29. Their camels shall be a booty to those that came for nothing else, *v.* 32. It is not said that any of them shall be slain, for they attempt not to make any resistance and their tents and flocks are accepted as a ransom for their lives; but they shall be dislodged and dispersed. Their country shall lie uninhabited; remote and having neither cities nor lands inviting to strangers, none shall care to succeed them, so that *Hazor shall be a desolation for ever*, *v.* 33.

Verses 34–39

This prophecy is dated in the beginning of Zedekiah's reign. The Elamites were the Persians, descended from Elam the son of Shem (Gen. x. 22); yet some think it was only that part of Persia which lay nearest to the Jews which, say they, had acted against God's Israel, *bore the quiver* in an expedition against them (Isa. xxii. 6), and therefore must be reckoned with among the rest. It is here foretold, in general, that God will *bring evil upon them, even* his *fierce anger*, *v.* 37. Their forces shall be disabled. The Elamites were famous archers, but, *Behold, I will break the bow of Elam* (*v.* 35), will ruin their artillery, and then *the chief of their might* is gone. God often orders it so that that which we most trust to first fails us, and that which was *the chief of our might* proves the least of our help. Their people shall be dispersed. There shall come enemies against them from all parts and they shall all carry some of them away captive into their respective countries, *v.* 36. *The four winds* shall be brought upon them; the storm shall come sometimes from one point and sometimes from another. Their princes shall be destroyed and the government quite changed (*v.* 38): *I will set my throne in Elam*. The throne of Nebuchadnezzar shall be set there, or the throne of Cyrus, who began his conquests with Elymais. Or it may be meant of the throne on which God sits for judgment. The king of Elam was famous of old, Gen. xiv. 1. Chedorlaomer was king of Elam, and a mighty man he was in his day; his successors, we may suppose, made a great figure; but the king of Elam is no more to God than another man. Yet the destruction of Elam shall not be perpetual (*v.* 39): *In the latter days I will bring again the captivity of Elam*. When Cyrus had destroyed Babylon, brought the empire into the hands of the Persians, the Elamites no doubt returned in triumph, and settled again in their own country. But this promise was to have its full accomplishment in the days of the Messiah, when we find Elamites among those who, when the Holy Ghost was given, heard spoken *in their own tongues the wonderful works of God* (Acts ii. 9, 11), and that is the most desirable return of the captivity.

CHAPTER 50

In this chapter, and that which follows, we have the judgment of Babylon, which is put last of Jeremiah's prophecies against the Gentiles because it was last accomplished. Babylon was employed as the rod in God's hand for the chastising of all the other nations, and now at length that rod shall be thrown into the fire. The destruction of Babylon by Cyrus was foretold by Isaiah, and now again, when it has come to its height, by Jeremiah; for, though at this time he saw that kingdom flourishing "like a green bay-tree," yet at the same time he foresaw it withered and cut down. And as Isaiah's prophecies of the destruction of Babylon and the deliverance of Israel seem designed to typify the evangelical triumphs of all believers over the powers of darkness, and the great salvation wrought out by our Lord Jesus Christ, so Jeremiah's prophecies of the same events seem designed to point at the apocalyptic triumphs of the gospel church over the New Testament Babylon. The kingdom of Babylon being much larger and stronger than any other of the kingdoms here prophesied against, its fall was the more considerable in itself; and what was foretold in general often before (ch. xxv. 12 and xxvii. 7) is here more particularly described, and with a great deal of prophetic heat as well as light. Babylon was destroyed to make way for the turning again of the captivity of God's people. Here is, I. The ruin of Babylon, ver. 1–3, and again ver. 9–16, and again ver. 21–22, and again ver. 35–46. II. The redemption of God's people, ver. 4–8, and again ver. 17–20, and again ver. 33, 34.

Verses 1–8

I. Here is a word spoken against Babylon. The king of Babylon had been very kind to Jeremiah, and yet he must foretell the ruin of that kingdom; for God's prophets must not be governed by favour or affection. Whoever are our friends, if, notwithstanding, they are God's enemies, we dare not speak peace to them. 1. The destruction of Babylon is here spoken of as a thing done, v. 2. 2. It is spoken of as a thing done thoroughly. The very idols of Babylon, which the people would protect with all possible care, shall be destroyed. Bel and Merodach their two principal deities shall be *confounded*, and the images of them *broken to pieces*. The country shall be laid waste (v. 3) out *of the north*, from Media, which lay north of Babylon, and from Assyria, through which Cyrus made his descent upon Babylon; thence the nation shall come that shall make *her land desolate*.

II. Here is a word spoken for the people of God for, their comfort, both *the children of Israel* and *of Judah*.

1. It is promised that they shall return to their God first and then to their own land; and the promise of their conversion and reformation is that which makes way for all the other promises, v. 4, 5. They shall *lament after the Lord* as the whole house of Israel did in Samuel's time (1 Sam. vii. 2); they shall *go weeping*. These tears flow from godly sorrow; they are tears of repentance for sin, tears of joy for the goodness of God, in the dawning of the day of their deliverance. That prevails to *lead them to repentance* when captivity did not prevail to drive them to it. They shall *enquire after the Lord*; they shall not sink under their sorrows, but *shall go weeping to seek the Lord their God*. They shall *seek the Lord as their God*, and shall now have no more to do with idols. They shall think of returning to their own country again; they shall think of it not only as a mercy, but as a duty (v. 5): *They shall ask the way to Zion with their faces thitherward*. The journey is long and they know not the road, but they will *ask the way*. This represents the return of poor souls to God. In all true converts there are both a sincere desire to attain the end and a constant care to keep in the way. They shall renew their covenant to walk with God more closely for the future: *Come, and let us join ourselves to the Lord in a perpetual covenant*.

2. Their present case is lamented as very sad, and as having been long so: "*My people have been lost sheep* (v. 6); they have *gone from mountain to hill*, and could find no pasture; *they have forgotten their resting-place* in their own country and cannot find their way to it." They were *led astray by their own shepherds*, their own princes and priests; they turned them from their duty, and so provoked God to turn them out of their own land. It is with them as with wandering sheep, *all that found them have devoured them* and made a prey of them; they laughed at them, telling them it was what their own prophets had many a time told them they deserved. They had put a contempt upon the temple and upon the tradition of their ancestors, and therefore deserved to suffer these hard things.

3. They are called upon to hasten away, as soon as ever the door of liberty was opened to them (v. 8): "*Remove*, not only out of the borders, but *out of the midst of Babylon;* hasten to Zion, and *be as the he-goats before the flocks*; strive which shall be foremost, which shall lead in so good a work."

Verses 9–20

God is here by his prophet proceeding in his controversy with Babylon.

I. The commission and charge given to the instruments that were to be employed in destroying Babylon. The army that is to do it is called *an assembly of great nations* (v. 9), the Medes and Persians, and all their allies and auxiliaries. God will *raise them up* to do it, and fit them for this service, and then he will *cause them to come up*, to *put themselves in array against Babylon* (v. 14). God shall bid them *shoot at her and spare no arrows* (v. 14). When God gives commission he will give success. They are bidden not only to *shoot at her* (v. 14), but to *shout against her* (v. 15) with a triumphant shout, as those that are already sure of victory.

II. The desolation and destruction that shall be brought upon Babylon is set forth in a great variety of expressions. 1. The wealth of Babylon shall be a rich and easy prey to the conquerors (v. 10). 2. The country of Babylon shall be depopulated and lie uninhabited (v. 13). 3. Their ancestors shall be ashamed of their cowardice, in fleeing from the first onset (v. 12), or, *Your mother*, Babylon itself, the mother-city, *shall be confounded*, when she sees herself deserted. 4. The great admirers of Babylon shall see it rendered despicable: the very tail of the nations, *shall it be, a wilderness, a dry land, a desert*, v. 12. 5. The great city, the head of it, shall be quite ruined. It is the vengeance of the Lord, which nothing can contend with either in law or battle. 6. There shall not be left in Babylon so much as *the poor of the land, for vine-dressers and husbandmen* (v. 16). Harvest shall come, and there shall be no reapers; seed-time shall come, but there shall be no sower.

III. The cause of this destruction. It comes from God's displeasure; it is *because of the wrath of the Lord* that Babylon *shall be wholly desolate* (v. 13), and his wrath is righteous, for (v. 14) *she hath sinned against the Lord*, therefore *spare no arrows*. What they did against Jerusalem they did with pleasure (v. 11): *You were glad, you rejoiced*. When Titus Vespasian destroyed Jerusalem he wept over it, but these Chaldeans triumphed over it. The spoils of Jerusalem they made use of to feed their own luxury. Those that have thus swallowed riches must vomit them up again. Therefore they have *given their hand* (v. 15). They aimed at nothing less than the utter ruin of God's Israel: *Israel is a scattered sheep*, as before (v. 6), that is not only barked at and worried by dogs, but even lions have roared and *driven him away*, v. 17. One king of Assyria carried the ten tribes away and devoured them; another invaded Judah, and impoverished it, tore the fleece and flesh of this poor sheep; and now at last this Nebuchadnezzar has fallen upon him and *broken his bones*, and therefore the king of Babylon must be punished as the king of Assyria was, v. 18.

IV. The mercy promised to the Israel of God. They shall be released out of their bondage, and *brought again to their own habitation* as sheep that were scattered to their own fold, v. 19. He will restore their prosperity; they shall not only live, but live comfortably, in their own land again; they shall *feed upon Carmel and Bashan*, the richest and most fruitful parts of the country. They *enquired the way to Zion* (v. 5), where God was to be served and worshipped. This was what they chiefly aimed at in their return; but God will bring them to Carmel and

Bashan, where they shall abundantly feed themselves. God will pardon their iniquity; this is the root of all the rest (*v.* 20): *In these days the iniquity of Israel shall be sought for, and there shall be none.* Not only the punishments of their iniquity shall be taken off, but the offence which it gave to God shall be forgotten, and he will be reconciled to them. This denotes how fully God forgives sin; he *remembers it no more.* This may include also a thorough reformation of hearts and lives, as well as a full remission of sins. Those whose sins God pardons he reserves for something very great; for *whom he justifies, them he glorifies.*

Verses 21–32

1. The forces are mustered and commissioned to destroy Babylon. The forces of Cyrus are called to go up against Babylon (*v.* 21), to *come against her from the utmost border.* Let all come together, for there will be both work and pay enough for them all, *v.* 26. *The archers* particularly must be *called together against Babylon, v.* 29. Thus *the Lord hath opened his armoury* (*v.* 25), *his treasury* (so the word is), *and hath brought forth the weapons of his indignation.* Media and Persia are now God's armoury; thence he fetches the weapons of his wrath, Cyrus and his officers and armies. 2. Instructions are given them what to do, *v.* 21. They must *open her store-houses* (*v.* 26), rifle her treasures, *cast her up as heaps.* Their princes and great men shall fall by the sword, not as men of war in the field of battle, but as beasts (*v.* 27). 3. Assurances are given them of success. Let them do what God commands, and they shall accomplish what he threatens. Cyrus shall no doubt prevail, for he fights under God. 4. Reasons are given for these severe dealings with Babylon. (1) Babylon has been very troublesome, vexatious, and injurious, to all its neighbours; it has been *the hammer of the whole earth* (*v.* 23). He that is the God of nations will sooner or later assert the injured rights of nations against those that unjustly and violently invade them. (2) Babylon has bidden defiance to God himself: *Thou hast striven against the Lord* (*v.* 24), *hast joined issue with him* (so the word signifies) as in law or battle, hast openly opposed him, therefore *thou art* now *found, and caught,* as in a snare. (3) Babylon ruined Jerusalem, the holy city, and the holy house there, *v.* 28. The burning of the temple, and the carrying away of its vessels, were articles in the charge against Babylon on which greater stress was laid than upon its being *the hammer of the whole earth;* for Zion was *the joy* and glory *of the whole earth.* (4) Babylon has been haughty and insolent, and therefore must have a fall, Job. xl. 12. They shall fall not so much by others thrusting them down as by their own stumbling; for they hold their heads so high that they never look under their feet.

Verses 33–46

I. Israel's sufferings, and their deliverance out of those sufferings. *Israel and Judah were oppressed together, v.* 33. Those that remained of the captives of the ten tribes, upon the uniting of the kingdoms of Assyria and Chaldea, seem to have come and mingled with those of the two tribes, so that they were *oppressed together.* This is their comfort in distress, that, though they are weak, *their Redeemer is strong* (*v.* 34), *their Avenger* (so the word signifies). *The Lord of hosts is his name,* and he will answer to his name, and will be that to them for which they depend upon him. *He shall thoroughly plead their cause that he may give rest to the land,* to his people's land, rest from all their enemies round about. This is applicable to all believers, who complain of the dominion of sin and corruption, and of their own weakness. Let them know that *their Redeemer is strong;* he is able

to keep what they commit to him. Sin shall not have dominion over them; he will *make them free,* and they shall be *free indeed;* he will give them *rest,* that *rest which remains for the people of God.*

II. Babylon's sin, and their punishment for that sin.

1. The sins they are charged with are idolatry and persecution. (1) They oppressed the people of God; they *held them fast,* and would not let *them go.* They *opened not the house of his prisoners,* Isa. xiv. 17. (2) They wronged God himself, and robbed him, giving that glory to others which is due to him alone; for (*v.* 38) *it is the land of graven images.* The word here used for idols properly signifies *terrors—Enim,* the name given to giants that were formidable, because they made the images of their gods to look frightful, to strike terror upon fools and children. Babylon was *the mother of harlots* (Rev. xvii. 5), the source of idolatry.

2. The judgments of God upon them for these sins are such as will ruin them.

(1) All that should be their defence and support shall be cut off by the sword. The Chaldeans had long been God's sword, wherewith he had done execution upon the sinful nations round about: but now, they being as bad as any of them, or worse, *a sword* is brought upon them (*v.* 35), a sword of war; and in God's hand a sword of justice. It shall be *Upon their princes* and *their wise men.* Their philosophers, their statesmen, and privy-counsellors; their learning and policy shall neither secure them nor stand the public in any stead. Their soothsayers and astrologers, here called *the liars* (*v.* 36), for they cheated with their prognostications of peace and prosperity, shall talk like fools, and be as men that have lost all their wits. *Their mighty men shall be dismayed,* and shall be no longer *mighty men. The sword shall be upon their horses and chariots;* the invaders shall seize their horses and chariots. The troops of other nations that were in their service shall be disheartened: *The mingled people shall become as* weak and timorous as *women.* The *sword* shall be *upon her treasures,* which are the sinews of war, *and they shall be robbed,* and made use of by the enemy against them.

(2) The country shall be made desolate (*v.* 38): *The waters shall be dried up,* the water that secures the city. Cyrus drew the river Euphrates into so many channels as made it passable for his army, so that they got with ease to the walls of Babylon, which, it was thought, that river had rendered inaccessible. The water likewise that made the country fruitful shall *be dried up, v.* 39. This was foretold concerning Babylon, Isa. xiii. 19–22.

(3) The king and kingdom shall be put into the utmost confusion and consternation by the enemies' invading them, *v.* 41–43. Those who have dealt cruelly, and have shown no mercy, may expect to be cruelly dealt with, and to find no mercy.

(4) They shall be as much hurt as frightened, for the invader shall *come up like a lion* to tear and destroy (*v.* 44) and shall make them and their *habitation desolate* (*v.* 45), and the desolation shall be so astonishing that all the nations about shall be terrified by it, *v.* 46. These three verses we had before (*ch.* xlix. 19–21) in the prophecy of the destruction of Edom, which was accomplished by the Chaldeans, and they are here repeated in the prophecy of the destruction of Babylon, which was to be accomplished upon the Chaldeans.

CHAPTER 51

This prophet, in this chapter, goes on with the prediction of Babylon's fall, to which other prophets also bore witness. Here is, I. The record of Babylon's doom, with the particulars of many aggravations of her fall, and great encouragements given thence to the Israel of God, that suffered such hard things by her, ver. 1-58. II. The representation and ratification of this by the throwing of a copy of this prophecy into the river Euphrates, ver. 59-64.

Verses 1-58

I. An acknowledgment of the great pomp and power that Babylon had been in and the use that God in his providence had made of it (v. 7): *Babylon hath been a golden cup,* a rich and glorious empire, *a golden city* (Isa. xiv. 4), *a head of gold* (Dan. ii. 38), *a golden cup in the Lord's hand;* he had made the earth *drunk with this cup*; some were intoxicated with her pleasures, others intoxicated with her terrors and destroyed by her. In both senses the New Testament Babylon is said to have made the kings of the earth drunk, Rev. xvii. 2; xviii. 3. Babylon had also been God's *battle-axe*; it was so at this time, when Jeremiah prophesied, v. 20. The forces of Babylon were God's *weapons of war*, tools in his hand, with which he broke in pieces *nations* and *kingdoms,—horses* and *chariots*, which are so much the strength of kingdoms (v. 21),—*man and woman, young and old,* with which kingdoms are replenished (v. 22),—*the shepherd and his flock, the husbandman and his oxen,* with which kingdoms are maintained and supplied, v. 23. Such havoc as this the Chaldeans had made when God employed them as instruments of his wrath for the chastising of the nations; and yet now Babylon itself must fall.

II. A charge drawn up against her by the Israel of God. 1. She is complained of for her incorrigible wickedness (v. 9). The people of God that were captives among the Babylonians endeavoured (Jer. x. 11), to convince them of the folly of their idolatry, but they could not do it. Yet some understand this as spoken by the forces they had hired for their assistance, declaring that they had done their best to save her from ruin, but that it was all to no purpose, and therefore they might as well go home to their respective countries; "for *her judgment reaches unto heaven,* and it is in vain to withstand it or think to avert it." 2. She is complained of for her inveterate malice against Israel. Other nations had been hardly used by the Chaldeans, but Israel only complains to God of it, and with confidence appeals to him (v. 34, 35). *Zion and Jerusalem shall say,* "Let *the violence done to me and* my children, that are *my* own *flesh,* and pieces of myself, and all the blood of my people, which they have shed like water, *be upon* them; let the guilt of it lie upon them, and let it be required at their hands."

III. Judgment given upon this appeal by the righteous Judge of heaven and earth, on behalf of Israel against Babylon. He answers (v. 36): "*I will plead thy cause.* Leave it with me; I will in due time plead it effectually *and take vengeance for thee,* and every drop of Jerusalem's blood shall be accounted for with interest." God deals better with Israel than they deserve, and, notwithstanding their iniquities and his severities, *Israel is not forsaken.* God is his God still, and will act for him as the Lord of hosts, a God of power. *The Lord God of recompences,* the *God to whom vengeance belongs, will surely requite* (v. 56), will pay them home; he will *render unto Babylon all the evil they have done in Zion* (v. 24). Cyrus shall measure to the Chaldeans the same that they measured to the Jews. Zion's children shall triumph (v. 10): *The Lord has brought forth our righteousness;* he has appeared in our behalf against those that dealt unjustly with us, and has given us redress. Let it therefore be spoken of to his praise: *Come and let us declare in Zion the work of the Lord our God,* that others may be invited to join with us in praising him.

IV. A declaration of the sovereignty of God who espouses Zion's cause and undertakes to reckon with this proud and potent enemy, v. 14. He will fill Babylon with vast numbers of the enemy's forces, will *fill it with men as with caterpillars,* that shall overpower it. But who is he that can break so powerful a kingdom as Babylon? The prophet gives an account of him from the description he had formerly given (Jer. x. 12-16), and it is here repeated to show that God will convince those by his judgments who would not be convinced by his word that he is *God over all.* 1. He is the God that made the world (v. 15). 2. He has the command of all the creatures that he has made (v. 16); his providence is a continued creation. 3. The idols that oppose the accomplishment of his word are a mere sham and their worshippers brutish people, v. 17, 18. But between the God of Israel and these gods of the heathen there is no comparison (v. 19): *The portion of Jacob is not like them;* the God who speaks this and will do it is the *former of all things* and *the Lord of all hosts,* and there is a near relation between him and his people, for he is *their portion* and they are his.

V. A description of the instruments that are to be employed in this service. God has *raised up the spirit of the kings of the Medes* (v. 11), Darius and Cyrus, who come against Babylon by a divine instinct; for *God's device is against Babylon to destroy it.* Those whom God employs against Babylon are compared (v. 1) to a *destroying wind,* which either by its coldness blasts the fruits of the earth or by its fierceness blows down all before it. This wind is *brought out of God's treasuries* (v. 16), *raised up against those that dwell in the midst of the Chaldeans,* those of other nations that are incorporated with them. These enemies are compared to fanners (v. 2), who shall *drive them away as chaff* is driven away by the fan. The Chaldeans had been fanners to winnow God's people (ch. xv. 7).

VI. An ample commission given them to lay all waste. Let them *bend their bow* against the archers of the Chaldeans (v. 3). Let all necessary preparations be made. This they are called to, v. 27, 28. Let *a standard be set up,* under which to enlist soldiers, *let a trumpet be blown* to call men together to it, let the nations, out of which Cyrus's army is to be raised, prepare their recruits. Let the kingdoms of *Ararat,* and *Minni, and Ashkenaz,* of Armenia, both the higher and the lower, and of Ascania, about Phrygia and Bithynia, send in their quota of men for his service; let them lay the country waste, as *caterpillars* do (Joel i. 4).

VII. The weakness of the Chaldeans, and their inability to make head against this threatening force. They are called upon here to prepare for action, but it is ironical (v. 11): *Make bright the arrows,* which have grown rusty through disuse; *gather the shields,* which in a long time of peace and security have been scattered and thrown out of the way (v. 12); *set up the standard upon the walls of Babylon.* But they shall have no heart to come at the call, v. 29. *The mighty men of Babylon have forborne to fight,* v. 30. God having taken away their strength and spirit, they have *remained in their holds,* so that the enemy has, without any resistance, *burnt her dwelling-places* and *broken her bars.* It is to the same purport with v. 56-58. When the spoiler comes upon Babylon her mighty men are immediately taken, *everyone of their bows is broken.* Their politics fail them. Their princes and captains, who sit in council as men intoxicated through stupidity or despair. The *walls of their city* fail them, v. 58. When the enemy had found ways to ford Euphrates, which was thought impassable, yet surely, think they, the walls are impregnable, they are *the broad walls of Babylon.* Some say that there was a threefold wall about the inner city and the like about the outer, and yet these shall be *utterly broken,* and *the high gates and towers shall be burnt.*

VIII. It is a certain destruction; a divine power is engaged against it, which cannot be resisted (v. 8), though when Jeremiah prophesied this, and many a year after, it was in the height of its power and greatness. It is a righteous destruction. Babylon has made herself meet for it, and therefore cannot fail to meet with it. For (v. 25) *Babylon* has been a *destroying mountain, destroying all the earth*, as the stones that are tumbled from high mountains spoil the grounds about them; but now it shall itself be *rolled down from its rocks*. Again (v. 33), "*Babylon is like a threshing-floor*, in which the people of God have been long threshed; but now the time has come that she shall herself be threshed. Babylon seems to be well-fenced and fortified against it: *She dwells upon many waters* (v. 13); the march of an enemy into it is so embarrassed by rivers. *Babylon* is *abundant in treasures;* and yet "*thy end has come*, and neither thy waters nor thy wealth shall secure thee. *A rumour will come one year* that Cyrus is making vast preparations for war, *and after that, in another year, shall come a rumour* that his design is upon Babylon"; when he was a great way off they might have sent and desired conditions of peace; but they were too proud, and their hearts were hardened to their destruction. The king of Babylon was himself at such a distance from the place where the attack was made that it was a great while ere he had notice that the city was taken; so that those posted near the place sent one messenger after another, *v.* 31. They are to tell him that the enemy has *seized the passes* (v. 32), the forts or blockades upon the river, and that, having got over the river, he has set fire to the reeds on the river side, to alarm and terrify the city, so that all the men surrendered. The messengers come with these tidings, which are immediately confirmed by the enemies' being in the palace and slaying the king himself, Dan. v. 30. That profane feast which they were celebrating at the very time when the city was taken seems here to be referred to (v. 38, 39): *They shall roar together like lions*, as men in their revels do, when the wine has got into their heads. They have passed their cup round; now *the cup of the Lord's right hand shall be turned unto them* (Hab. ii. 15, 16); let them be as merry as they can with that bitter cup, for *on that night*, in the midst of the jollity, was *Belshazzar slain*. The strength of the enemy is here compared to an inundation of waters (v. 42): *The sea has come up upon Babylon*, which, when it has once broken through its bounds, there is no fence against, so that she is *covered with the multitude of its waves*, overpowered by a numerous army; her cities then become *a desolation*, an uninhabited uncultivated desert, *v.* 43. It is a destruction that shall reach the gods of Babylon, the idols and images. "In token that *the whole land shall be confounded* and all *her slain shall fall*, and that throughout all the country *the wounded shall groan, I will do judgment upon her graven images*," *v.* 47 and again *v.* 53. Though the invaders are themselves idolaters, yet they shall destroy the images and temples of the gods of Babylon. Bel was the principal idol that the Babylonians worshipped, and therefore that is by name here marked for destruction (v. 44): *I will punish Bel*, that image to which such abundance of sacrifices are offered. His altars shall be forsaken, none shall regard him any more, and so that idol shall fail them. *Babylon* shall *become heaps* (v. 37), no use shall be made even of the ruins (v. 26): *They shall not take of thee a stone for a corner, nor a stone for foundations*.

IX. Here is a call to God's people to go out of Babylon. It is their wisdom, when the ruin is approaching, to quit the city (v. 6): "*Flee out of the midst of Babylon*, that you may not be cut off in her iniquity." It is their wisdom to *get out of the midst of Babylon*, lest they be involved, if not in her ruins, yet in her fears (v. 45, 46). Those who have not grace enough to keep their temper in temptation should have wisdom

enough to keep out of the way of temptation. They are told, v. 50, 51: "*You* Israelites, *who have escaped the sword of the Chaldeans* your oppressors, and of the Persians their destroyers, *go away, stand not still*; hasten to your own country, for this is not your rest, but Canaan is." The returning captives (v. 51), being reminded of Jerusalem, cry out, "*We are confounded;* we cannot bear the thought of it; *shame covers our faces* at the mention of it, for *we have heard of the reproach of the sanctuary*, that is profaned and ruined by strangers; how can we think of it with any pleasure?" To this he answers (v. 52) that the God of Israel will now triumph over the gods of Babylon, and so that reproach will be for ever rolled away.

X. The diversified feeling excited by Babylon's fall. 1. Some shall lament the destruction of Babylon. There *is the sound of a cry* from Babylon (v. 54), lamenting this great destruction, *v.* 55. They shall say in their lamentations (v. 41): "*How is Sheshach taken*, and how are we mistaken concerning her! How is that city become an *astonishment among the nations* that was the glory, and admiration of the whole earth!" 2. Yet some shall rejoice in Babylon's fall, not as the misery of their fellow-creatures, but as the manifestation of the righteous judgment of God and as it opens the way for the release of God's captives (v. 48).

Verses 59–64

1. A copy is taken of this prophecy, it should seem by Jeremiah himself, for Baruch his scribe is not mentioned here (v. 60): *Jeremiah wrote in a book all these words that are here written against Babylon*. 2. It is sent to Babylon, to the captives there, by the hand of Seraiah, who went there attendant on king Zedekiah, *in the fourth year of his reign*, v. 59. He *went with Zedekiah*, or (as the margin reads it) *on the behalf of Zedekiah, into Babylon*. The character given of him is that *Seraiah was a quiet prince*, a prince of rest. He was in honour, but not hot and heady, heading factions. He was of a calm temper, and studied the things that made for peace. Jeremiah might safely entrust such a man with his errand. It is the real honour of great men to be quiet men. 3. Seraiah is desired to read it to his countrymen that had already gone into captivity: "*When thou shalt come to Babylon, and shalt see* what a magnificent place it is, how large a city, how rich, and how well fortified, and shalt be tempted to think, Surely, it will stand for ever, *then thou shalt read all these words* to thyself and thy friends, for their encouragement in captivity: let them with an eye of faith see the end of these threatening powers." 4. He is directed to make a solemn protestation of the divine authority and certainty of that which he had read (v. 63). Though Seraiah sees Babylon flourishing, having read this prophecy he must foresee Babylon falling. When we see what this world is, how glittering its shows are and how flattering its proposals, let us read in the book of the Lord that its *fashion passes away*, and we shall learn to look upon it with a holy contempt. 5. He must then tie a stone to the book and throw it into the midst of the river Euphrates, as a confirming sign of the things contained in it, saying, "*Thus shall Babylon sink, and not rise*," v. 53, 64. In the sign it was the stone that sunk the book. But in *the thing signified* it was rather the book that sunk the stone; it was the divine sentence passed upon Babylon in this prophecy that sunk that city, which seemed *as firm as a stone*. The last words of the chapter seal up the vision and prophecy of this book: *Thus far are the words of Jeremiah*. This prophecy was dated in the *fourth year* of Zedekiah (v. 59), long before he finished his testimony; but it was to be last accomplished of all his prophecies against the Gentiles, *ch.* xlvi. 1. And the chapter which remains is

purely historical, and, as some think, was added by some other hand.

CHAPTER 52

History is the best expositor of prophecy; and therefore, for the better understanding of the prophecies which relate to the destruction of Jerusalem and the kingdom of Judah, we are here furnished with an account. It is much the same with the history 2 Kings xxiv and xxv, but the matter is here repeated to give light to the book of the Lamentations. I. The bad reign of Zedekiah, ver. 1–3. II. The besieging and taking of Jerusalem by the Chaldeans, ver. 4–7. III. The severe usage which Zedekiah and the princes met with, ver. 8–11. IV. The destruction of the temple and the city, ver. 12–14. V. The captivity of the people (ver. 15, 16) and the numbers of those that were carried away into captivity, ver. 28–30. VI. The carrying off of the plunder of the temple, ver. 17–23. VII. The slaughter of the priests, and other great men, ver. 24–27. VIII. The better days which king Jehoiachin lived to see in the latter end of his time, after the death of Nebuchadnezzar, ver. 31–34.

Verses 1–11

This narrative begins in the beginning of the reign of Zedekiah, though there were two captivities before, one in the fourth year of Jehoiakim, the other in the first of Jeconiah. 1. God's just displeasure against Judah and Jerusalem for their sin, *v.* 3. He determined to *cast them out from his presence*. He expelled them from that good land that had such tokens of his presence in providential bounty and that holy city and temple that had such tokens of his presence in covenant-grace and love. 2. Zedekiah's bad conduct and management for which God punished him. Zedekiah had arrived at years of discretion when he came to the throne; he *was twenty-one years old* (*v.* 1); he was not the worst of the kings (we never read of his idolatries), yet he *did evil in the eyes of the Lord*, for he did not do the good he should have done. But that evil deed of his which did hasten his destruction was his *rebelling against the king of Babylon*, which was both his sin and his folly, and brought ruin upon his people. God was greatly displeased with him for his perfidious dealing with the king of Babylon (Ezek. xvii. 15, &c.). 3. The Chaldeans gained Jerusalem, after eighteen months' siege. In remembrance of two steps towards their ruin, while they were in captivity, they kept a *fast in the fourth month*, and a *fast in the tenth* (Zech. viii. 19): that in the *fifth month* was in remembrance of the burning of the temple, and that in the *seventh* of the murder of Gedaliah. For a year and a half the city was besieged. Supplies of food were cut off. In spite of constant attacks, the garrison refused to surrender, but soon there was *famine in the city* (*v.* 6); *no bread for the people of the land*, and then no wonder that *the city was broken up, v.* 7. Walls, in such a case, will not hold out long without men, any more than men without walls; nor will both together stand people in any stead without God and his protection. 4. The king and his mighty men got out of the city *by night* (*v.* 7); but the king was overtaken by pursuers in *the plains of Jericho*, his guards were dispersed, and all his army was *scattered from him, v.* 8. 5. The doom passed upon Zedekiah by the king of Babylon. He treated him as a rebel, *gave judgment upon him, v.* 9. *His sons were slain before his eyes*, and all *the princes of Judah* (*v.* 10); then *his eyes were put out*, and he was *bound in chains*, carried in triumph to Babylon. He was condemned to perpetual imprisonment, wearing out the remainder of his life (I cannot say his days, for he saw day no more) in darkness and misery. Jeremiah had often told him what it would come to, but he would not take warning when he might have prevented it.

Verses 12–23

An account of the woeful havoc that was made by the Chaldean army, a month after the city was taken, under the command of Nebuzaradan, who was *captain of the guard*. 1. He laid the temple in ashes,

having first plundered it of every thing that was valuable: He *burnt the house of the Lord*, that holy and beautiful house, where their *fathers praised him*, Isa. lxiv. 11. 2. He burnt the royal palace, probably that which Solomon built after he had built the temple, which was, ever since, *the king's house*. 3. He burnt *all the houses of Jerusalem*. 4. He *broke down all the walls of Jerusalem*, to be revenged upon them for standing in the way of his army so long. Thus, of a defenced city, it was made a ruin, Isa. xxv. 2. 5. He *carried away many into captivity* (*v.* 15); he took away *certain of the poor of the people*, that is, of the people in the city, for *the poor of the land* (the poor of the country) he left for *vine-dressers and husbandmen*. He also carried off *the residue of the people that remained in the city*, that had escaped the sword and famine, and the deserters. 6. The vessels which were still in the temple were looted. All that were of great value had been carried away before, *the vessels of silver and gold*, yet some remained, *v.* 19. But most of the temple-prey that was now seized was of brass, which being of less value, was carried off last. When the walls of the city were demolished, the pillars of the temple were pulled down, too, and both in token that God, who was the strength and stay both of their civil and their ecclesiastical government, had departed from them. No walls can protect those, nor pillars sustain those, from whom God withdraws. These pillars of the temple were for ornament. They were called *Jachin—He will establish;* and *Boaz—In him is strength;* so that the breaking of these signified that God would no longer establish his house nor be the strength of it. These pillars are here described (*v.* 21–23, from 1 Kings vii. 15). All the vessels that belonged to the brazen altar were carried away; for the iniquity of Jerusalem, like that of Eli's house, was not to be purged by sacrifice or offering, 1 Sam. iii. 14. It is said (*v.* 20), *The brass of all these vessels was without weight;* so it was in the making of them (1 Kings vii. 47), *the weight of the brass was not then found out* (2 Chron. iv. 18). Those that made spoil of them did not stand to weigh them, as purchasers do.

Verses 24–30

A very melancholy account, 1. Of the slaughter of some great men, in cold blood, at Riblah, seventy-two in number (according to the number of the elders of Israel, Num. xi. 24, 25), so they are computed, 2 Kings xxv. 18, 19. The account here agrees except that there it is said that there were five, here there were seven *near the king*. Dr. Lightfoot thinks that he took away seven of those near the king, but two of them were Jeremiah and Ebed-melech, who were both discharged, so that there were only five of them put to death. *Seraiah the chief priest* is put first. Seraiah the prince was *a quiet prince* (*ch.* li. 59), but perhaps Seraiah the priest was turbulent and had made himself obnoxious to the king of Babylon. The leaders of this people had caused them to err, and now they are objects of divine justice. 2. Of the captivity of the rest. *Judah was carried away captive out of his own land* (*v.* 27), Lev. xviii. 28. An account, (1) Of two captivities, one in the seventh year of Nebuchadnezzar (the same with that which is said to be in his eighth year, 2 Kings xxiv. 12), another in his eighteenth year, the same with that which is said (*v.* 12) to be in his nineteenth year. But the numbers here are small, in comparison with what we find expressed concerning the former (2 Kings xxiv. 14, 16), when there were 18,000 carried captive, whereas here they are said to be 3,023. When all the residue of the people were carried away (*v.* 15), one would think there should be more than 832 souls; therefore Dr. Lightfoot conjectures that, these accounts being joined to the story of the putting to death of the great men at Riblah, all that are here said to be carried away were *put to death* as rebels. (2) Of a third captivity, not mentioned before, which was in the twenty-third year of Nebuchadnezzar, four years after the destruction of Jerusalem (*v.* 30): Then *Nebuzaradan* came, and *carried away* 745 Jews; it is probable that this was done in revenge of the murder of Gedaliah, which was another rebellion against the king of Babylon, and that those who were now taken were put to death. If this be the sum total of the captives (*all the persons were* 4,600, *v.* 30), they were reduced from what they had been, but the Lord made them fruitful in the land of their affliction, and the more they were oppressed the more they multiplied.

Verses 31–34

This story concerning the reviving which king Jehoiachin had in his bondage we had before (2 Kings xxv. 27–30), only there it is said to be done on *the twenty-seventh day of the twelfth month,* here on *the twenty-fifth.* It is probable that the orders were given for his release on the twenty-fifth day, but that he was not presented to the king till the twenty-seventh. Nebuchadnezzar had long kept this unhappy prince in prison; and his son, though well-affected to the prisoner, could not procure him any favour; but, when the old man was dead, his son countenanced Jehoiachin and made him a favourite. Jehoiachin fell from a throne into a prison, but here he is advanced again to a throne of state (*v.* 32), though not to a throne of power. As, before, the robes were changed into prison-garments, so now they were converted into robes again. Though the night of affliction be very long, yet we must not despair. The day may dawn at last. Jehoiachin was thirty-seven years a prisoner, in confinement, in contempt, since he was eighteen years old. Let those whose afflictions have been lengthened out encourage themselves with this instance; the vision will at the end speak comfortably, and therefore wait for it. God can make his people find favour in the eyes of their oppressors, and turn their hearts to pity them (Ps. cvi. 46), *He made them to be pitied of all those that carried them captives.* It is not in vain to hope and quietly to *wait for the salvation of the Lord.* And now, comparing the prophecy and the history of this book, we may learn, (1) That it is no new thing for churches and persons highly dignified to degenerate, and become corrupt. (2) That iniquity tends to the ruin of those that harbour it; and, if it be not repented of and forsaken, will certainly end in ruin.

AN EXPOSITION, WITH PRACTICAL OBSERVATIONS, OF

THE LAMENTATIONS OF JEREMIAH

I. The title of this book; in the Hebrew it has none, but is called (as the books of Moses are) from the first word *Ecah—How;* but the Jewish commentators call it, as the Greeks do, and we from them, *Kinoth—Lamentations.* As we have sacred odes or songs of joy, so have we sacred elegies or songs of lamentation. II. The penman of this book is here Jeremiah the poet, therefore this book is fitly joined to the book of his prophecy, and is as an appendix to it. We have there the predictions of the desolations of Judah and Jerusalem, and then the history of them, to show how the predictions were accomplished, and here we have the expressions of his sorrow upon occasion of them. When he saw these calamities at a distance, he wished that his head *were waters and his eyes fountains of tears:* and, when they came, he wept and was far from being disaffected to his country. Though his country had been unkind to him, and though the ruin of it was a proof that he was a true prophet, yet he sadly lamented it. III. The occasion of these Lamentations was the destruction of Judah and Jerusalem by the Chaldean army and the dissolution of the Jewish state both civil and ecclesiastical. Some will have these to be the Lamentations which Jeremiah penned upon occasion of the death of Josiah, 2 Chron. xxxv. 25. But, they seem to be penned of those calamities when they had already come, and there is nothing of Josiah in them. No, it is Jerusalem's funeral that this is an elegy upon. IV. The composition of it is not only poetical, but alphabetical, all except the 5th chapter. Each verse begins with a letter in the order of the Hebrew alphabet, the first *aleph,* the second, *beth, &c.,* but the 3rd chapter is a triple alphabet, the first three beginning with *aleph,* the next three with *beth, &c.,* which was a help to memory and an elegance in writing. In the 2nd, 3rd, and 4th chapters the letter *pe* is put before *ajin,* which in all the Hebrew alphabets follows it. Dr. Lightfoot offers this conjecture, That the letter *ajin,* which is the numeral letter for LXX, by being displaced, put them in mind of the seventy years at the end of which God would turn again their captivity. V. The use of it to the pious Jews in their sufferings, furnishing them with spiritual language to express their natural grief, helping to preserve the remembrance of Zion among them, when they were in Babylon. They are here taught to mourn for sin and mourn to God.

CHAPTER 1

The first alphabet of this lamentation, twenty-two stanzas, in which the miseries of Jerusalem are bewailed and her present deplorable condition is aggravated by comparing it with her former prosperous state; sin is acknowledged as the cause of all these miseries; and God is appealed to for justice against their enemies and for compassion towards them. I. A complaint made to God of their calamities, ver. 1–11. II. The same complaint made to their friends, ver. 12–17. III. An appeal to God and his righteousness concerning it (ver. 18–22), in which he is humbly solicited.

Verses 1–11

I. The miseries of Jerusalem.

1. As to their civil state. (1) A city that was populous is now depopulated, *v.* 1. She was full of her own people that replenished her, and full of the people of other nations that resorted to her, with whom she had profitable commerce, but now her own people are carried into captivity, and she *sits solitary.* The *chief places of the city* are not now, as they used to be, *places of concourse. How has she become as a widow!* Her king that was as a husband to her is gone; her God has departed from her; she is emptied of her children, is solitary and sorrowful as a widow. (2) A city that had dominion is now in subjection. She had been *great among the nations,* greatly loved by some and greatly feared by others. Some made her presents, and others paid her taxes; so that she was really *princess among the provinces.* But now she has not only lost her friends and *sits solitary,* but has lost her freedom and sits *tributary;* she paid tribute to Egypt first and then to Babylon. Sin brings a people not only into solitude, but into slavery. (3) A city that used to be full of mirth has now become full of grief. Jerusalem had been a joyous city, whither the tribes went to rejoice before the Lord: she was *the joy of the whole earth,* but now *she weeps sorely,* she weeps *in the night,* in silence and solitude; *in the night,* when others rest, her thoughts are intent upon her troubles. Her head is—*as waters, and* her *eyes fountains of tears,* so that she *weeps day and night* (Jer.

ix. 1); *her tears are* continually *on her cheeks.* (4) Those that were separated from the heathen now *dwell among the heathen;* those that were a peculiar people are now a mingled people (*v.* 3): *Judah has gone into captivity,* out of her own land into the land of her enemies, among those that are aliens to God and the covenants of promise, with whom *she finds no rest.* "*Her children have gone into captivity before the enemy;* those that were to have been the seed of the next generation are carried off; so that the land is likely to be still desolate for want of heirs." Those that dwell among their own people, a free people, and in their own land, would be more thankful for mercies if they would but consider the miseries of those forced into strange countries. (5) Those that used to conquer are now conquered. *All her persecutors overlook her between the straits* (*v.* 3); so that her people unavoidably *fell into the hand of the enemy,* for there was no way to escape (*v.* 7). Everywhere *her adversaries are the chief and her enemies prosper* (*v.* 5). (6) Those that had been a dignified people, on whom God had put honour, and to whom their neighbours had paid respect, are now brought into contempt (*v.* 8): *All that honoured her before despise her.* They have vilified themselves by their sins: *The enemies magnify themselves* against them (*v.* 9). *Sin is the reproach of any people.* (7) Those that lived in a fruitful land were ready to perish for want of necessary food (*v.* 11): *All her people sigh* in despondency and despair. There was *no bread for the people of the land* (Jer. lii. 6), and in their captivity they had much ado to get bread, *ch.* v. 6. *They have given their pleasant things for meat to relieve the soul,* or (as the margin is) *to make the soul come again,* when they were ready to faint away.

2. An account of their miseries in their ecclesiastical state. (1) Their religious feasts were no more observed (*v.* 4): *The ways of Zion do mourn;* overgrown with weeds. *The solemn feasts* had been neglected

and profaned (Isa. i. 11, 12), and therefore justly is an end now put to them. And, as *the ways of Zion mourned*, so *the gates of Zion*, in which the faithful worshippers used to meet, *are desolate*. (2) *Her priests sigh* for the desolations of the temple; their songs are turned into sighs. In the day of Zion's prosperity, Ps. lxviii. 25, *Among them were the damsels playing with timbrels*, and notice is taken of the failing now. *Her virgins are afflicted*, and therefore *she is in bitterness*; that is, all the inhabitants of Zion are *sorrowful for the solemn assembly*, and to them *the reproach of it is a burden*, Zeph. iii. 18. (3) Their religious places were profaned (*v.* 10): *The heathen entered into her sanctuary*, into the temple itself, into which no Israelite was permitted to enter, though ever so reverently and devoutly, but the priests only. The heathen now crowd rudely in, not to worship, but to plunder. (4) All the rich things with which the temple was adorned, and which were made use of in the worship of God, were a prey to the enemy (*v.* 10): *The adversary has spread out his hand upon all her pleasant things*. What these pleasant things are we may learn from Isa. lxiv. 11, where, to the complaint of the burning of the temple, it is added, *All our pleasant things are laid waste;* the ark and the altar, and all the other tokens of God's presence with them, pleasant above any other things, were now broken to pieces and carried away. Thus from *the daughter of Zion all her beauty has departed, v.* 6. *The beauty of holiness* was the *beauty of the daughter of Zion;* when the temple, that holy and beautiful house, was destroyed, her beauty was gone. (5) Their religious days were made a jest of (*v.* 7): *The adversaries saw her, and did mock at her sabbaths*. They laughed at them for observing one day in seven as a day of rest. Juvenal ridicules the Jews for losing a seventh part of their time:

> ————cui septima quæque fuit lux
> Ignava et vitæ partem non attigit ullam—
> They keep their sabbaths to their cost,
> For thus one day in sev'n is lost;

whereas sabbaths, if they be sanctified as they ought to be, will turn to a better account than all the days of the week besides. And whereas the Jews professed that they did it in obedience to their God, their adversaries asked them, "What profit have you in keeping the ordinances of your God, who now deserts you in your distress?" (6) Her state at present was just the reverse of what it had been formerly, *v.* 7. Now, *in the days of affliction and misery*, when everything was black and dismal, *she remembers all her pleasant things that she had in the days of old*. God often makes us know the worth of mercies by the want of them.

II. The sins of Jerusalem are the cause of all these calamities. It is *the Lord* that *has afflicted her* (*v.* 5) and he had done it as a righteous Judge, for *she has sinned*. Are her troubles many? Her sins are many more. See Jer. xxx. 14. They are heinous (*v.* 8): *Jerusalem has grievously sinned*, has *sinned sin* (so the word is), sinned wilfully, deliberately. Jerusalem, that makes such a profession and enjoys such privileges, *sinned grievously* (*v.* 8), and therefore (*v.* 9) she *came down wonderfully*. They have been oppressive and therefore are justly oppressed (*v.* 3): *Judah has gone into captivity*, and it is *because of affliction and great servitude*, because the rich among them afflicted the poor, and particularly (as the Chaldee paraphrases it) because they had oppressed their Hebrew servants, which is charged upon them, Jer. xxxiv. 11. They all *despise her* (*v.* 8), for *her filthiness is in her skirts;* she has rolled them in the mire of sin.

III. Jerusalem's friends are here complained of as false and unkind: They *have all dealt treacherously*

with her (*v.* 2), so that, in effect, *they have become her enemies. Her princes are like harts*, that, upon the first alarm, betake themselves to flight. They *are like harts*, famished for want of *pasture*, and therefore *are gone without strength before the pursuer*. Her neighbours are unneighbourly. There is none *to help her* (*v.* 7). *She has no comforter*, none to sympathize, or alleviate her griefs, *v.* 7, 9.

IV. Jerusalem's God is here besought, and all is referred to his compassionate consideration (*v.* 9): "*O Lord! behold my affliction*," and (*v.* 11), "*See, O Lord! and consider*." The only way to make ourselves easy under our burdens is to cast them upon God first, and leave it to him to do with us as seemeth him good.

Verses 12–22

In these verses the prophet, in the name of the lamenting church, does more particularly acknowledge the hand of God in these calamities, and the righteousness of his hand.

I. The church in distress here magnifies her affliction. She appeals to all spectators: *See if there be any sorrow like unto my sorrow, v.* 12. This might perhaps be truly said of Jerusalem's griefs; but we are apt to apply it too sensibly to ourselves when we are in trouble. If our troubles were to be thrown into a common stock with those of others, and then an equal dividend made, share and share alike, we should each of us say, "Pray, give me my own again."

II. She here looks beyond the instruments to the author of her troubles: "*It is the Lord* that *has afflicted me*, and he has *afflicted me* because he is angry with me; it is *in the day of his fierce anger*," *v.* 12. She is as one in a fever: "*He has sent fire into my bones*" (*v.* 13). She is as one in a net, which the more he struggles to get out the more he is entangled. She is as one in a wilderness, whose way is solitary: "*He has turned me back*, that I cannot go on, *has made me desolate*, that I have nothing to support me with, but am *faint all the day*." She is as one in a yoke, not yoked for service, but for penance (*v.* 14): *The yoke of my transgressions is bound by his hand*. The yoke of Christ's commands is an *easy yoke* (Matt. xi. 30), but that of our own transgressions is a heavy one. When conscience, as his deputy, binds us over to his judgment, then *the yoke is bound* and *wreathed by the hand* of his justice, and nothing but the hand of his pardoning mercy will unbind it. He it is that has *trodden under foot all her mighty men, v.* 15. She is as one in a wine-press, and it is God that has thus *trodden the virgin, the daughter of Judah*. She is in the hand of her enemies, and it is the Lord that has delivered her *into their hands* (*v.* 14). He that has many a time *commanded deliverances for Jacob* (Ps. xliv. 4) now commands an invasion against Jacob, because Jacob has disobeyed the commands of his law.

III. She justly demands a share in the compassion of those that were the spectators of her misery (*v.* 12): "*Is it nothing to you, all you that pass by*? Can you look upon me without concern? Is it nothing to you that your neighbour's house is on fire?"

IV. She justifies her own grief (*v.* 16): "*For these things I weep*, I weep in the night (*v.* 2), when none sees; *my eye, my eye, runs down with water*." *Zion spreads forth her hands* (*v.* 17), which is here an expression rather of despair than of desire. Her God has withdrawn from her. It is no marvel that the souls of the saints faint away, when God, who is the only Comforter that can relieve them, keeps at a distance. Her children are removed from her, and are in no capacity to help her: they cannot help themselves, and how should they help her? Both the damsels and the youths, that were her joy and hope; *have gone into captivity, v.* 18. Her friends failed her, some would not and others could not give her any relief. She *spread forth her hands*, as begging relief, but *there is none to comfort her* (v. 17). Her idols were her lovers.　Egypt and Assyria were her confidants. But they deceived her. The *priests* and the *elders*, that should have appeared at the head of affairs, died for hunger (v. 19); or went begging for bread to keep them alive. *Abroad the sword bereaves* and slays all that comes in its way, and *at home* all provisions are cut off by the besiegers, so that *there is as death*, that is, famine. The enemies, that were the instruments of the calamity, were barbarous, so were those that were the standers by, the Edomites and Ammonites, that bore ill will to Israel: They have *heard of my trouble, and are glad that thou hast done it* (v. 21). It pleases them to find that God and his Israel have fallen out.

V. She justifies God, acknowledging that her sins had deserved these chastenings. The yoke that lies so heavily, and binds so hard, is *the yoke of her transgressions*, v. 14. It is with our own rod that we are beaten. She owns the equity of God's actions, by owning the iniquity of her own: *I have rebelled against his commandments* (v. 18); and again (v. 20), *I have grievously rebelled*. We cannot speak ill enough of sin, and we must always speak worst of our own sin, must call it *rebellion, grievous rebellion*. Sorrow for sin must be great sorrow and must affect the soul.

VI. She appeals both to the mercy and to the justice of God in her present case. *Behold, O Lord! for I am in distress*. She appeals to the justice of God concerning the injuries that her enemies did her (v. 21, 22): "*Thou wilt bring the day that thou hast called*, the day that is fixed in the counsels of God and published in the prophecies, when my enemies *shall be like unto me*, when the cup of trembling, now put into my hands, shall be put into theirs." It may be read as a prayer, "Let the day appointed come," and so it goes on, "*Let their wickedness come before thee;* hasten the time when thou wilt *do to them* for their transgressions *as thou hast done to me* for mine." This prayer amounts to a protestation against all thoughts of a coalition with them. Our prayers must agree with God's word; and though we are bound in charity to forgive our enemies, and to pray for them, yet we may in faith pray for the accomplishment of that which God has spoken against his and his church's enemies.

CHAPTER 2

The second alphabetical elegy is set to the same mournful tune and the substance of it is much the same; it begins with Ecah, as that did, "How sad is our case! Alas for us!" I. Here is the anger of Zion's God as the cause of her calamities, ver. 1-9. II. Here is the sorrow of Zion's children as the effect of her calamities, ver. 10-19. III. The matter referred to his compassionate consideration, ver. 20-22. The hand that wounded must make whole.

Verses 1-9

A very sad representation is here made of the state of God's church, of Jacob and Israel, of Zion and Jerusalem; but the emphasis in these verses seems to be laid all along upon the hand of God. The grief is that God appears angry with them; it is he that chastens them, and chastens them *in his displeasure*.

I. Time was when God's delight was in his church, and he appeared to her as a friend. But now he is angry with her, and appears against her as an enemy. To those who know how to value God's favour nothing appears more dreadful than his finger; corrections in love are easily borne, but rebukes in love wound deeply. It is God's wrath that *burns against Jacob like a flaming fire* (v. 3), but it was their sin that kindled this fire. God is such a tender Father to his children that we may be sure he is never angry with them but when they give him cause to be angry.

Now he is an enemy to them; at least he is *as an enemy*, v. 5. He has *bent his bow like an enemy*, v. 4. He stood *with his right hand* stretched out against them, and a sword drawn in it *as an adversary*. God is not really an enemy to his people, no, not when he is angry with them and corrects them in anger. But sometimes he is *as an enemy* to them, when all his providences concerning them seem in outward appearance to have a tendency to their ruin. But, blessed be God, Christ is *our peace*, our peacemaker, who has slain the enmity.

II. Time was when God's church appeared very bright, and considerable among the nations; but now *the Lord has covered the daughter of Zion with a cloud* (v. 1), a dark cloud, through which she cannot see his face; *a thick cloud* (so the word signifies), a *black cloud*, not such as that under which God conducted them through the wilderness, or that in which God took possession of the temple and filled it with his glory: no, that side of the cloud is now turned towards them which was turned towards the Egyptians in the Red Sea. He *turned back their right hand*, so that they were not able to ward off the blow which was given them. What can their right hand do against the enemy when God draws it back, and withers it, as he did Jeroboam's?

III. Time was when Jerusalem and the cities of Judah were strong and well fortified. But now the Lord has in anger *swallowed them up*. They are so totally ruined that they seem to have been *swallowed up*. He has *swallowed up all her palaces* (v. 5), though those were stately, and strong, rich and well guarded. He has destroyed not only their dwelling-places, but their *strongholds*. Thus has he *increased in the daughter of Judah mourning and lamentation*, when they saw all their defence departed from them. This is again insisted on, v. 7-9. He has *given up into the hand of the enemy the walls of her palaces*. The walls of palaces cannot protect them, unless God himself be a wall of fire round about them. Whatever desolations God makes in his church, they are all according to his counsels. But, when it is done, he has *stretched out a line*, a measuring line, to do it exactly and by measure: hitherto the destruction shall go, and no further.

IV. Time was when their government flourished, and the balance of power was on their side; but now it is otherwise: *He has polluted the kingdom and the princes thereof*, v. 2. They had first polluted themselves with their idolatries, and then God dealt with them as with polluted things. No marvel that the king and the priest, whose characters were always deemed venerable and inviolable, are despised by everybody, when God has, *in the indignation of his anger, despised the king and the priest*, v. 6. The crown has fallen from their heads, for *her king and her princes are among the Gentiles*, prisoners among them (v. 9), and treated as the basest, without any regard to their character. It is just with God to debase those by his judgments who have by sin debased themselves.

V. Time was when the ordinances of God were administered in their purity, and they had those tokens of God's presence with them; but now that part of the *beauty of Israel* was gone which was indeed their greatest beauty. The ark was God's footstool, under the mercy-seat, between the cherubim; this was of all others the most sacred symbol of God's presence (it is called his *footstool*, 1 Chron. xxviii. 2; Ps. xcix. 5; cxxxii. 7); there the Shechinah rested, but now he *remembered not his footstool*. The ark itself was suffered, as it should seem, to fall into the hands of the Chaldeans. Of what little value are the tokens of his presence when his presence is gone! God and his kingdom can stand without that footstool. Those that ministered in holy things had been *pleasant to the eye in the tabernacle of the daughter of Zion*

(v. 4); they had been *purer than snow, whiter than milk* (*ch.* iv. 7). But now these are slain, and their *blood is mingled with their sacrifices.* The temple was God's tabernacle (as the tabernacle, while that was in being, was called *his temple,* Ps. xxvii. 4) and this *he has violently taken away* (*v.* 6); he has plucked up the stakes of it and cut the cords; it shall be no more a tabernacle, much less his. When men profane God's tabernacle it is just with him to take it from them. He has now *abhorred his sanctuary* (*v.* 7); it has been defiled with sin, that only thing which he hates, and for the sake of that he abhors even his sanctuary, which he had delighted in and called *his rest for ever,* Ps. cxxxii. 14. Some, by the *places of the assembly* (*v.* 6), understand not only the temple, but the synagogues, and the schools of the prophets, which the enemy had *burnt up,* Ps. lxxiv. 8. The solemn feasts and the sabbaths had been carefully remembered, but now the Lord has *caused those to be forgotten* even in Zion itself. Now that Zion was in ruins no difference was made between sabbath time and other times; every day was a day of mourning, so that all the *solemn feasts were forgotten.* The altar that had sanctified their gifts is now cast off, for God will no more accept their gifts, nor be honoured by their sacrifices, *v.* 7. The altar was *the table of the Lord,* but God will no longer keep house among them; he will neither feast them nor feast with them. They had been blest with prophets and teachers of the law; but now *the law is no more* (*v.* 9); it is no more read by the people, no more expounded by the scribes; the tables of the law are gone with the ark; the book of the law is taken from them. *Her prophets also find no vision from the Lord.* They had persecuted God's prophets, and despised the visions they had from the Lord, and therefore it is just with God to say that they shall have no more prophets, no more visions.

Verses 10–22

Justly are these called *Lamentations,* the expressions of grief in perfection, like the contents of Ezekiel's roll, Ezek. ii. 10.

I. Copies of lamentations are here presented and they are painted to the life. 1. The judges and magistrates, who used to appear in robes of state, are stripped of them, and put on the habit of mourners (*v.* 10); the elders now sit no longer in the judgment-seats, the *thrones of the house of David,* but they *sit upon the ground.* They *keep silence,* overwhelmed with grief, and not knowing what to say. They have *cast dust upon their heads, and girded themselves with sackcloth.* 2. *The virgins of Jerusalem hang down their heads to the ground;* those know sorrow who were always disposed to be merry. 3. The prophet himself is a pattern to the mourners, *v.* 11. His *eyes do fail with tears;* he has wept till he can weep no more; wept himself blind. Jeremiah himself had better treatment than his neighbours, better than he had had before from his own countrymen; their destruction was his deliverance, and yet his private interests are swallowed up in a concern for the public, and he bewails the *destruction of the daughter of his people* as if he himself had been the greatest sufferer in that common calamity.

II. *The heart of the people cried unto the Lord, v.* 18. Some fear it was a cry of bitter complaint, but many of them did in sincerity cry unto God for mercy in their distress; and the prophet bids them go on to do so: "*O wall of the daughter of Zion!* either you that stand upon the wall, you *watchmen on the walls* (Isa. lxii. 6), or *because* of the *breaking down of the wall* (which was not done till about a month after the city was taken), let *the daughter of Zion lament* still." This was a thing which Nehemiah lamented long after, Neh. i. 3, 4. "*Let tears run down like a river day and night,* weep without intermission, give thyself no rest from weeping, *let not the apple of thy eye cease.*" The calamities would be continuing, and the causes of grief would recur, and fresh occasion be given them every day and every night to bemoan themselves. They would be apt, by degrees, to grow insensible, and would need to afflict their souls, till their proud and hard hearts were thoroughly humbled and softened.

III. Causes for lamentation are here assigned,

1. Multitudes perish by famine. God had corrected them by scarcity of provisions through want of rain some time before (Jer. xiv. 1), and now by the straitness of the siege God brought it upon them in extremity; for, The children died for hunger in their mothers' arms (*v.* 11). This is mentioned again (*v.* 19): *They faint for hunger in the top of every street.* There were little children that were slain by their mothers' hands and eaten, *v.* 20. The like was done in the siege of Samaria, 2 Kings vi. 29.

2. Multitudes fall by the sword, which devours one as well as another, especially when it is in the hand of such cruel enemies as the Chaldeans were. They spared no age, not those who, by reason of their tender or their decrepit age, were exempted from taking up the sword; for even they *perished by the sword.* They spared no sex: *My virgins and my young men have fallen by the sword.* This was the *Lord's doing.* But that which follows is very harsh: *Thou hast killed, and not pitied;* for his soul is *grieved for the misery of Israel.*

3. Their false prophets cheated them, *v.* 14. This was a thing which Jeremiah had lamented long before, and had observed with a great concern (Jer. xiv. 13): *Ah! Lord God, the prophets say unto them, You shall not see the sword;* and here he inserts it among his lamentations. Their visions were all their own fancies, and it is most likely that they themselves knew that the visions they pretended were counterfeit. The people set them up, told them what they should say, so that they were *prophets after their hearts.* Prophets should tell people of their faults, should show them their sins, that they may bring them to repentance, and so prevent their ruin; but these prophets knew that would lose them the people's affections and contributions. Therefore *they have not discovered thy iniquity*; though that might have been a means, by taking away their iniquity, to turn away their captivity.

4. Their neighbours laughed at them (*v.* 15): *All that pass by thee clap their hands at thee. Is this the city* (said they) *that men called the perfection of beauty?* (Ps. l. 2). How is it now the perfection of deformity! Where is all its beauty now?

5. Their enemies triumphed over them, *v.* 16. Those that wished ill to Jerusalem now *open their mouths,* nay, they widen them; they *hiss and gnash their teeth* in scorn and indignation. "*We have swallowed her up;* it is our doing, and it is our gain; it is all our own now. *Certainly this is the day that we have* long *looked for; we have found it; we have seen it; aha! so would we have it.*"

6. Their God, in all this, appeared against them (*v.* 17): *The Lord has done that which he had devised.* What God devises against his people is designed for them, and so it will be found in the issue. When he gave them his law by Moses he told them what judgments he would certainly inflict upon them if they transgressed that law; and now that they had been guilty of the transgression of this law he had executed the sentence of it, according to Lev. xxvi. 16, &c., Deut. xxviii. 15.

IV. Comforts for the cure of these lamentations are here sought for and prescribed. They are sought for, *v.* 13. The prophet seeks to find out some suitable acceptable words to say to her in this case:

Wherewith shall I comfort thee, O virgin! daughter of Zion? We endeavour to comfort our friends by telling them their case is not singular; there are many whose trouble is greater than theirs; but Jerusalem's case will not admit this argument: "*What thing shall I liken to thee*, or *what shall I equal to thee, that I may comfort thee?* What city, what country, is there, whose case is parallel to thine?" Alas! there is none, no sorrow like thine, because there is none whose honour was like thine. We tell them that their case is not desperate, but that it may easily be remedied; but neither will that be admitted here, upon a view of human probabilities; for *thy breach is great, like the sea*, like the breach which the sea sometimes makes upon the land, which cannot be repaired, but grows wider and wider. Thou art wounded, and *who shall heal thee?* No wisdom nor power of man can repair such a broken shattered state. It is to no purpose therefore to administer any of these common cordials. The method of cure prescribed is to address themselves to God, and by a penitent prayer to commit their case to him, and to be instant and constant in such prayers (*v.* 19): "*Arise* out of thy dust, out of thy despondency, *cry out in the night*, when others are asleep, be thou upon thy knees, importunate with God for mercy; *in the beginning of the watches*, of each of the four watches of the night, then *pour out thy heart like water before the Lord*, be free and full in prayer, be sincere and serious in prayer, open thy mind, spread thy case before the Lord; *lift up thy hands towards him* in holy desire and expectation; beg for *the life of thy young children*. These poor lambs, what have they done? Take with you words, take with you these words (*v.* 20), *Behold, O Lord! and consider to whom thou hast done this.* Are they not thy own, the seed of Abraham thy friend and of Jacob thy chosen? Lord, take their case into thy compassionate consideration!"

CHAPTER 3

The scope of this chapter is the same with that of the two foregoing chapters, but the composition is different; that was in long verse, this is in short, another kind of metre; that was in single alphabets, this is in a treble one. I. A sad complaint of God's displeasure and the fruits of it, ver. 1–20. II. Words of comfort to God's people, ver. 21–36. III. Duty prescribed in this afflicted state, ver. 37–41. IV. The complaint renewed, ver. 42–54. V. Encouragement taken to hope in God, ver. 55–66. Some make all this to be spoken by the prophet himself when he was imprisoned and persecuted; but it seems rather to be spoken in the person of the church now in captivity and desolate, and in the desolations of which the prophet did in a particular manner interest himself. But the complaints here are more general than those in the foregoing chapter, and intended for the use of the closet rather than of the solemn assembly. Some think Jeremiah makes these complaints, not only as an intercessor for Israel, but as a type of Christ.

Verses 1–20

The title of the 102nd Psalm might very fitly be prefixed to this chapter—*The prayer of the afflicted, when he is overwhelmed, and pours out his complaint before the Lord.* The prophet complains, 1. That God is angry. This gives both birth and bitterness to the affliction (*v.* 1): *I am the man that has seen affliction, and has felt it sensibly, by the rod of his wrath.* God is sometimes angry with his own people; yet it is not as a sword to cut off, but only as a rod to correct; it is to them *the rod of his wrath*, though grievous for the present, in the issue advantageous. By this rod we must expect to *see affliction*, and if we be made to see more than ordinary affliction, we must not quarrel, for we are sure that the anger is just and the affliction mixed with mercy. 2. That he is in the dark. Darkness is put for trouble and perplexity; this was the case of the complainant (*v.* 2): "*He has led me by* an unaccountable chain of events, *into darkness and not into light*, the darkness I feared and not into the light I hoped for." And (*v.* 6), *He has set me in dark places*, dark as the grave, *like those*

that are dead of old, that are quite forgotten. 3. That God appears against him as an enemy. "*Surely against me is he turned* (*v.* 3), as far as I can discern; for *his hand is turned against me all the day. I am chastened every morning*," Ps. lxxiii. 14. When God's hand is turned against us, we are tempted to think that his heart is turned against us too. "*He was unto me as a bear lying in wait*, surprising me with his judgments, *and as a lion in secret places*; so that which way soever I went I could never think myself safe." *He has bent his bow, v.* 12. *He has set me as a mark for his sorrow*, and *the arrows of his quiver enter into my veins*, give me an inward wound, *v.* 13. 4. That the Jewish state may be fitly compared to a man wrinkled with age (*v.* 4): "*My flesh and my skin has he made old;* they are wasted and withered, and *he has broken my bones, v.* 15. *He has filled me with bitterness*, a bitter sense of these calamities." *He has* mingled *gravel* with my bread, so that *my teeth* are *broken* with it (*v.* 16). *He has covered me with ashes*, as mourners used to be, or (as some read it) *he has fed me with ashes.* 5. That he is not able to discern any way of escape (*v.* 5): "*He has built against me*, as forts and batteries are built against a besieged city. Where there was a way open it is now quite made up: *He has compassed me* on every side *with gall and travail*; I vex and fret, and tire myself, to find a way of escape, but can find none, *v.* 7. *He has hedged me about, that I cannot get out.* I am chained; and as notorious malefactors are double-fettered, so he *has made my chain heavy. He has* also (*v.* 9) *enclosed my ways with hewn stone*, with a stone wall, which cannot be broken through, so that *my paths are made crooked*; I traverse to and fro, but am still turned back." So (*v.* 11), "*He has turned aside my ways*; ruined my projects. He has *pulled me in pieces*; and *made me desolate*, has deprived me of all comfort in my own soul." 6. That God turns a deaf ear to his prayers (*v.* 8): "*When I cry and shout*, as one in earnest, that would make him hear, yet he *shuts out my prayer.* Sometimes God seems to be angry even against *the prayers of his people* (Ps. lxxx. 4), and their case is deplorable indeed when they are denied the comfort of acceptance. 7. That his neighbours make a laughing matter of his troubles (*v.* 14): *I was a derision to all my people*, to all the wicked among them, who made one another merry with the public judgments, and particularly the prophet Jeremiah's griefs. 8. That he was ready to despair of deliverance: "Thou hast not only taken peace from me, but hast *removed my soul far off from peace* (*v.* 17). *I forget prosperity;* it is so long since I had it that I have lost the idea of it. I have been so inured to sorrow and servitude that I know not what joy and liberty mean. *My strength and my hope have perished from the Lord* (*v.* 18); I can no longer stay myself upon God as my support, even my God inexorable." 9. That grief returned upon every remembrance of his troubles, and his reflections were as melancholy as his prospects, *v.* 19, 20. *My affliction and my transgression* (so some read it), my trouble and my sin that brought it upon me; this was *the wormwood and the gall* in *the affliction and the misery.* It is sin that makes the cup of affliction a bitter cup. The captives in Babylon had all the miseries of the siege in their mind continually, and *wept when* they *remembered Zion;* nay, they could *never forget Jerusalem*, Ps. cxxxvii. 1, 5.

Verses 21–36

Here the clouds begin to disperse and the sky to clear up. Here the tune is altered and the mourners in Zion begin to look a little pleasant. But for hope, the heart would break. To save the heart from being quite broken, here is something *called to mind*, which gives ground for *hope* (*v.* 21). *I make to return to my heart* (so the margin words it); what we have had in our hearts is sometimes as if it were forgotten, till God by his grace make it return to our hearts. "*I recall it to mind; therefore have I hope*, and am kept from downright despair."

I. Bad as things are, it is owing to the mercy of God that they are not worse. We are *afflicted by the rod of his wrath*, but *it is of the Lord's mercies that we are not consumed, v.* 22. 1. The streams of mercy acknowledged: *We are not consumed*. The church of God is like Moses's bush, burning, yet *not consumed*. It is *persecuted* of men, *but not forsaken* of God, and therefore, though it is *cast down*, it is *not destroyed* (2 Cor. iv. 9), corrected, yet *not consumed*, refined in the furnace as silver, but *not consumed* as dross. These streams followed up to the fountain: *It is of the Lord's mercies*. God is an inexhaustible *fountain of mercy, the Father of mercies*. Had we been dealt with *according to our sins*, we should have been consumed long ago; but we have been dealt with *according to God's mercies*.

II. Even in the depth of their affliction they still have experience of the tenderness of the divine pity and the truth of the divine promise. They had several times complained that God had not pitied (*ch.* ii. 17, 21), but here they correct themselves, and own, 1. That *God's compassions fail not*; they do not really fail, no, not even when in anger he seems to have *shut up his tender mercies*. These rivers of mercy run fully and constantly, but never run dry. *They are new every morning;* every morning we have fresh instances of God's compassion towards us; *every morning does he bring his judgment to light*, Zeph. iii. 5. When our comforts fail, yet God's compassions do not. 2. That *great is his faithfulness*. Though Jerusalem be in ruins, *the truth of the Lord endures for ever*.

III. God is, and ever will be, the all-sufficient happiness of his people, and they depend upon him to be such (*v.* 24): *The Lord is my portion, saith my soul;* that is, 1. "When I have lost all I have in the world, liberty, and livelihood, and almost life itself, yet I have not lost my interest in God." 2. "While I have an interest in God, therein I have enough; I have that which is sufficient to counterbalance all my troubles and make up all my losses." 3. "This is that which I depend upon: *Therefore will I hope in him*. I will stay myself upon him, when all other supports fail me."

IV. Those who deal with God will find it is not in vain to trust in him, *v.* 25. While we *wait for him* by faith, we must *seek him* by prayer. Our seeking will help to keep up our waiting. *It is good* (it is our duty and will be our unspeakable comfort and satisfaction) *to hope and quietly to wait for the salvation of the Lord*, to hope that it will come, to wait till it does come, and while we wait to be quiet and silent, not quarrelling with God but acquiescing in the divine disposals. *Father, thy will be done.*

V. Afflictions are really good for us, and, if we bear them aright, will work for our good. It is not only good to wait for the salvation, but it is good to be under the trouble in the meantime (*v.* 27): *It is good for a man that he bear the yoke in his youth*. Many of the young men were carried into captivity. He tells them that it was good for them to *bear the yoke* of that captivity, and they would find it so if they would labour to answer God's ends in laying that heavy yoke upon them. Here it seems to be meant of the yoke of affliction. Many have found it good to bear this in youth; it has made those humble who otherwise would have been proud and unruly, and *as a bullock unaccustomed to the yoke*. But when do we *bear the yoke* so that it is really *good for us to bear it in our youth*? 1. When we are quiet under our afflictions, when we *sit alone and keep silence*, that we may converse with God and *commune with our own hearts*, silencing all discontented distrustful thoughts. 2. When we are humble and patient under our affliction. *He* gets good by the yoke who *puts his mouth in the dust*, not only *lays his hand upon his mouth*, in token of submission to the will of God, but *puts it in the dust*, in token of sorrow at the remembrance of sin. Those who are truly humbled for sin will be glad to obtain a good hope, through grace, though they *put their mouth in the dust* for it. 3. When we are meek towards those who are the instruments of our trouble, and are of a forgiving spirit, *v.* 30. Our Lord Jesus has left us an example of this, for he *gave his back to the smiter*, Isa. l. 6. He who can bear contempt and reproach, and not *render railing for railing* and bitterness for bitterness, shall find that *it is good to bear the yoke*, that it shall turn to his spiritual advantage.

VI. God will graciously return to his people with comforts *according to the time that he has afflicted them, v.* 31, 32. We may bear ourselves up with this, 1. That, when we are cast down, yet we are not cast off; the father's correcting his son is not a disinheriting of him. 2. That though we may seem to be cast off for a time, yet we are not really cast off. 3. That, whatever sorrow we are in, his hand is in it, and therefore we may be assured it is but *for a season*, 1. Pet. i. 6. 4. That God has compassions and comforts in store even for those whom he has himself grieved. He has torn, and he will heal us, Hos. vi. 1. 5. That, when God returns to deal graciously with us, it will not be according to our merits, but according to his mercies.

VII. When God does cause grief, it is for wise and holy ends, and he takes not delight in our calamities, *v.* 33. He does not do it *willingly*, not *from the heart*; so the word is. 1. He never afflicts us but when we give him cause to do it. If he show us kindness, it is because *so it seems good* unto him; but, if he write bitter things against us, it is because we both deserve them and need them. 2. He delights not in the death of sinners, or the disquiet of saints, but punishes with reluctance. He delights not in the misery of any of his creatures, he is so far from it that in all their afflictions he is afflicted and his soul is grieved for the misery of Israel. 3. He retains his kindness for his people even when he afflicts them. If he does not *willingly grieve the children of men*, much less his own children. They may by faith see love in his heart even when they see frowns in his face and a rod in his hand.

VIII. Though he makes use of men as his hand, or rather instruments in his hand, for the correcting of his people, yet he is far from being pleased with the injustice and the wrong they do them, *v.* 34–36. Two ways the people of God are oppressed by their enemies, and the prophet here assures us that God does not approve of either of them: 1. If men injure them by force of arms, God does not approve of that. He does not himself *crush under his feet the prisoners of the earth*, but he regards the cry of the prisoners; nor does he approve of men's doing it. It is barbarous to trample on those that are down. 2. If men injure them in the pretended administration of justice,—if they *turn aside the right of a man*, so that he cannot discover what his rights are,—if they *subvert a man in his cause*, and bring in a wrong verdict, or give a false judgment, let them know God sees them. It is *before the face of the Most High* (*v.* 35). God does not approve of them. More is implied than is expressed. The perverting of justice, and the subverting of the just, are a great affront to God; he will sooner or later severely reckon with those that do thus.

Verses 37–41

I. We must not quarrel with God for any affliction that he lays upon us at any time (*v.* 39): *Wherefore does a living man complain?* From the doctrine of God's sovereign and universal providence he draws this inference, *Wherefore does a living man complain?* The sufferers in the captivity must submit to the will of God in all their sufferings. Shall *a living man complain, a man for the punishment of his sins?* We are sinful men, and that which we complain of is the just *punishment of our sins*; it is far less than our iniquities have deserved. Then let us not complain; instead of repining, we must be repenting; and, as an evidence that God is reconciled to us, we must be endeavouring to reconcile ourselves to his holy will.

II. We must set ourselves to answer God's intention in afflicting us, which is to bring sin to our remembrance, and to bring us home to himself, *v.* 40. *Let us search and try our ways.* Let conscience be employed both to search and to try. *Let us try our ways*, that by them we may try ourselves, for we are to judge of our state not by our faint wishes, but by our step, not by one particular step, but by our ways, the ends we aim at, the rules we go by, and the tenor of our lives to those ends and those rules. When we are in affliction it is seasonable to *consider our ways* (Hag. i. 5), that what is amiss may be repented of and amended for the future, and so we may answer the intention of the affliction. We are apt, in times of public calamity, to reflect upon other people's ways, and lay blame upon them; whereas our business is to *search and try our* own ways. "Let us *turn again to the Lord.* We have been with him, and it has never been well with us since we forsook him; let us therefore now turn again to him." Our hearts must go along with our prayers. We must *lift up our hearts with our hands*, as we must pour out our souls with our words. Praying is lifting up the soul to God (Ps. xxv. 1) as to *our Father in heaven*; and the soul that hopes to be with God in heaven for ever will, by frequent acts of devotion, be still learning the way thither and pressing forward in that way.

Verses 42–54

The prophet had owned that a living man should not complain, yet here the clouds return.

I. They confess the righteousness of God in afflicting them (*v.* 42): *We have transgressed and have rebelled.* Call sin a transgression, call it a rebellion, and you do not miscall it.

II. They complain of the afflictions they are under, not without some reflections upon God.

1. They complain of the tokens of his displeasure (*v.* 42), *Thou hast not pardoned. Thou hast not pitied, v.* 43. They complain that there was a wall of partition between them and God. "*Thou hast covered us* up as men that are buried are covered up and forgotten." It hindered their prayers from coming up unto God (*v.* 44): *Thou hast covered thyself with a cloud* so thick *that our prayers* seem as if they were lost in it."

2. They complain of the contempt of their neighbours (*v.* 45): "*Thou hast made us as the off-scouring.*" If they had not made themselves vile, their enemies could not have made them so.

3. They complain of the destruction that their enemies made of them (*v.* 37): The *destruction of the daughter of my people* (*v.* 48), *of all the daughters of my city, v.* 51. Their enemies chased them till they had quite prevailed over them (*v.* 53): *They have cut off my life in the dungeon.* They are as it were thrown into the dungeon or grave and a *stone cast upon them*, such as used to be *rolled to the door of the sepulchres.* They look upon the Jewish nation as dead and buried. Their destruction is compared to the sinking of a living man into the water, *v.* 54.

4. They complain of their own excessive grief and fear (*v.* 48, 49). It is added (*v.* 51), "*My eye affects my heart.* The more I look upon the desolations of the city and country the more I am grieved."

5. In the midst of these sad complaints here is one word of comfort, *v.* 50. We continue weeping *till the Lord look down and behold from heaven.* Bad as the case is, one favourable look from heaven will set all to rights. While they continued weeping they continued waiting; nothing shall wipe tears from their eyes *till he look down.*

Verses 55–65

A struggle in the prophet's breast between faith, fear and hope. But faith gets the last word and comes off conqueror. In three things the prophet and his friends had found God good: 1. He had *heard their prayers*; though they had been ready to fear that the cloud of wrath was such as their *prayers could not pass through* (*v.* 44). When they were *in the low dungeon*, as *free among the dead*, they *called upon God's name* (*v.* 55). *Thou didst not hide thy ear at my breathing, at my cry.* Observe how he calls prayer *his breathing*; for in prayer we breathe towards God, we breathe after him. Prayer is the breath of the new man, sucking in the air of mercy in petitions and returning it in praises; it is both the evidence and the maintenance of the spiritual life. 2. He had silenced their fears (*v.* 57): "*Thou drewest near in the day that I called upon thee.*" When we draw nigh to God in a way of duty we may by faith see him drawing nigh to us in a way of mercy. *Thou saidst, Fear not.* 3. He had already begun to appear for them (*v.* 58): "*O Lord! thou hast pleaded the causes of my soul*" (that is, as it follows), "*thou hast redeemed my life.*" He comforts himself with an appeal to God's justice, and to his omniscience. "*O Lord! thou hast seen my wrong*, that I have done no wrong at all, but suffer a great deal." *Thou hast seen all their imaginations against me* (*v.* 60). They make themselves and one another merry with my miseries, as the Philistines made sport with Samson. Let them be dealt with as they have dealt with us; let thy hand be against them as their hand has been against us.

CHAPTER 4

This chapter is another single alphabet of Lamentations for the destruction of Jerusalem, like those in the first two chapters. I. The prophet here laments the indignities done to those to whom respect used to be shown, ver. 1, 2. II. He laments the effects of the famine, ver. 3–10. III. He laments the sacking of Jerusalem, ver. 11, 12. IV. He acknowledges that the sins of their leaders were the cause of all these calamities, ver. 13–16. V. He gives up all as doomed to ruin, ver. 17–20. VI. He foretells the destruction of the Edomites who triumphed in Jerusalem's fall, ver. 21. VII. He foretells the return of the captivity of Zion at last, ver. 22.

Verses 1–12

The elegy in this chapter begins with a lamentation of the sad change in Jerusalem. The city that was formerly as *the most fine gold* has lost its lustre; it has become dross.

I. The temple was laid waste, which was the glory of Jerusalem and its protection. And some understand the gold (*v.* 1) to be the *gold of the temple*, the find gold with which it was overlaid (1 Kings vi. 22); when the temple was burned the gold was sullied. *The stones of the sanctuary* were brought down by the fire, and thrown about *in the top of every street*; they lay mingled among the common ruins.

II. The princes and priests, who were in a special manner the *sons of Zion*, were abused, *v.* 2. Israel was more rich in them than in treasures of gold and silver. But now they are broken as *earthen pitchers*. They have grown poor, are brought into captivity, and rendered mean and despicable.

III. Little children were starved for want of bread and water, *v.* 3, 4.

IV. Persons of rank were reduced to poverty, *v.* 5. Those who were well-born and well bred, being stripped of all by the war, are *desolate in the streets*, have not a bed to lie on. As sometimes the *needy* are *raised out of the dunghill* (Ps. cxiii. 7), so there are instances of the *wealthy* being brought *to the dunghill*.

V. Persons who were eminent for dignity, perhaps for sanctity, shared with others in the common calamity, *v.* 7, 8. *Her Nazarites* are changed. These *Nazarites*, by reason of their temperate diet, especially the pleasure they had in devoting themselves to God, which made their faces to shine as *Moses's*, were *purer than snow* and *whiter than milk*; drinking no wine nor strong drink, they had a healthful complexion and cheerful countenance. But now *their visage is marred* (as is said of Christ, Isa. lii. 14); it is *blacker than a coal*; they look miserably, partly through hunger and partly through grief and perplexity. *They are not known in the streets;* those who respected them now take no notice of them.

VI. Jerusalem died a lingering death; for the famine contributed more to her destruction than any other judgment. Jerusalem dies by inches, dies so as to feel herself die. The iniquity of Jerusalem is more aggravated than that of Sodom, no wonder that the punishment of it is so. Sodom never had the means of grace that Jerusalem had. *The hands of the pitiful women have* slain and then *sodden their own children.* The case was sad enough that they had not wherewithal to feed their children and make meat for them (*v.* 4), but much worse that they could find in their hearts to feed upon their children and make meat of them. The destruction of Jerusalem is a complete destruction (*v.* 11), an amazing destruction, *v.* 12. It was a surprise to the kings of the earth, and to *all the inhabitants of the world* who knew Jerusalem. They knew that it was the *city of the great King*, and therefore they thought that it was so much under the divine protection that it would be in vain for any of its enemies to make an attack upon it.

Verses 13–20

I. The sins for which God brought this destruction upon them served to justify God in it (*v.* 13, 14): It is *for the sins of her prophets*, and the *iniquities of her priests.* The particular sin charged upon them is persecution; the false prophets and corrupt priests joined to *shed the blood of the just in the midst of her.* They not only shed the blood of their innocent children, whom they sacrificed to Moloch, but the blood of the righteous men among them, whom they sacrificed to that more cruel idol of enmity to the truth and true religion. There is nothing that will make prophets and priests to be abhorred so much as a spirit of persecution.

II. The testimony of their neighbours to convict them of sin and to show the equity of God's proceedings against them. They upbraided them with their pretended purity, while they lived in iniquity. *They cried to them, Depart you; it is unclean.* They all cried out shame on them, and could easily foresee that God would not long suffer so provoking a people to continue in so good a land. The land would spew them out, as it had done their predecessors, and, when they saw the dispersed of *Jacob fleeing and wandering*, they told them of it. They said, Now *the anger of the Lord has divided them.* They said, when they saw them expelled, *God will no more regard them*, and how then can they help themselves? Herein they were mistaken. God has not cast them off, for all this.

III. Their despair under their calamities. "*As for us*, we look upon our case to be in a manner helpless. *Our end is near* (*v.* 18), the end both of our church and of our state." The refuges they fled to disappointed them. They looked for help from this and

the other powerful ally, but to no purpose. Looking for that which never came (*v.* 17); they *watched in watching*; *for a nation* that frustrated their expectations. The persecutors overcame them (*v.* 18): *They hunt our steps, that we cannot go in our streets.* When the Chaldeans besieged the city they raised their batteries so high above the walls that they could shoot at people as they went along the streets. They *hunted them* with the arrows from place to place. Their *persecutors were swifter than the eagles of heaven, v.* 19.

Verses 21–22

David's psalms of lamentation commonly conclude with some word of comfort, which is as life from the dead and light shining out of darkness; so does this lamentation in this chapter. It is here foretold, for the encouragement of God's people,

I. That an end shall be put to Zion's troubles (*v.* 22). The troubles of God's people shall be continued no longer than till they have done their work for which they were sent.

II. That an end shall be put to Edom's triumphs. It is spoken ironically (*v.* 21): *Rejoice and be glad, O daughter of Edom! The cup* of trembling, which it is now Jerusalem's turn to drink deeply of, *shall pass through unto thee.* The destruction of the Edomites was foretold by this prophet (Jer. xlix. 7, &c.). "*The cup* that *shall pass unto thee* shall intoxicate thee. *Thou shalt be drunken*, and at thy wits' end, shalt stagger and stumble, and then, as Noah when he was drunk, *thou shalt make thyself naked* and expose thyself to contempt."

Chapter 5

This chapter, though it has the same number of verses with the 1st, 2nd, and 4th, is not alphabetical. I. A representation of the present calamitous state of God's people in their captivity, ver. 1–16. II. A protestation of their concern for God's sanctuary, ver. 17, 18. III. A humble supplication to God for the returns of mercy (ver. 19–22). Some ancient versions call this chapter, "The Prayer of Jeremiah."

Verses 1–16

The people of God, overwhelmed with grief, give vent to their sorrows at the throne of grace. *Remember what is* past, *consider and behold* what is present, and *let not all the trouble* we are in *seem little to thee*, and not worth taking notice of," Neh. ix. 32. The one word in which all their grievances are summed up is *reproach: Consider, and behold, our reproach.* As it was a reproach, it reflected upon the name and honour of that God who had owned them for his people.

I. They acknowledge the reproach of sin, *the reproach of their youth*, of the early days of their nation. It is a penitent confession of the sins of their ancestors, which they themselves had persisted in, for which they now justly suffered.

II. They represent the reproach they bear, in divers particulars, which tend to their disgrace.

1. They are robbed of that good land which God gave them, *v.* 2. "It is turned to strangers; they dwell in the houses that we built, and this is our reproach."

2. Their state and nation are like widows and orphans (*v.* 3): "*We are fatherless* (that is, helpless). Our king, who is the father of the country, is cut off; nay, God our Father seems to have forsaken us; *our mothers*, our cities, *are* now *as widows*, exposed to wrong and injury, and this is our reproach."

3. They are put hard to it to provide necessaries. Water used to be free but now (*v.* 4), *We have drunk our water for money.* Formerly they had fuel for the fetching; but now, "*Our wood is sold to us*, and we pay dearly for every faggot." But what must they do for bread? Some of them sold their liberty for it

(*v.* 6): "*We have given the hand to the Egyptians and to the Assyrians,* have made the best bargain we could, that we might *be satisfied with bread. We got our bread with the peril of our lives.*" They stole out of the city to fetch in some supply; they were in danger of being put to the sword, *the sword of the wilderness* it is called.

4. They are brought into slavery, and this is as much as anything their reproach (*v.* 5): *Our necks are under* the grievous yoke of *persecution.* The poor captives in Babylon *laboured and had no rest,* no night's rest, no sabbath-rest. They would not be ruled by their God, and by his servants the prophets, whose rule was gentle and gracious, and therefore justly are they ruled with rigour by their enemies and their servants.

5. Those who used to be feasted are now famished (*v.* 10): *Our skin was black like an oven,* dried and parched too, *because of the terrible famine,* the *storms of famine* (so the word is).

6. All sorts of people were abused and dishonoured. The *women* were *ravished,* even *the women in Zion,* that holy mountain, *v.* 11.

7. An end was put to all their gladness (*v.* 14): *The young men,* who used to be disposed to mirth, have ceased *from their music.* It was so with the body of the people (*v.* 15): *The joy of their heart ceased. Our dance is turned into mourning.* This may refer to the joy of their solemn feasts, and the dancing used in them (Judges xxi. 21), which was not only modest, but sacred dancing.

8. An end was put to all their glory. The public administration of justice was their glory, but that was gone (*v.* 14). The royal dignity was their glory, but that also was gone: *The crown has fallen from our head,* not only the *king* himself fallen into disgrace, but *the crown;* he has no successor. Earthly crowns are fading falling things; but, blessed be God, there is *a crown of glory that fades not away,* that never falls, *a kingdom that cannot be moved.*

Verses 17–22

I. The people of God express the deep concern they had for the ruins of the temple, more than for any other of their calamities (*v.* 17, 18). "The people have polluted the *mountain of Zion* with their sins, and God has justly made it *desolate; the foxes walk upon it* as freely and commonly as they do in the woods."

II. They comfort themselves with the doctrine of God's eternity (*v.* 19): But *thou, O Lord! remainest for ever.* What shakes the world gives no disturbance to him who made it; whatever revolutions there are on earth there is no change in the Eternal Mind; God is still the same, and *remains for ever* infinitely wise and holy, just and good.

III. They humbly expostulate with God concerning the frowns of heaven they were now under (*v.* 20): "*Wherefore dost thou forget us for ever,* as if we were quite cast out of mind? Thou art the same, and, though the throne of thy sanctuary is demolished, wilt thou not be the same to us?" Though we may not quarrel with God, yet we may plead with him (Jer. xii. 1).

IV. They earnestly pray to God for mercy and grace; "Lord, do not reject *us for ever,* but *turn thou us unto thee; renew our days,*" *v.* 21. Though these words are not put last, yet the Rabbin, because they would not have the book to conclude with those melancholy words (*v.* 22), repeat this prayer again, and so make these the last words both in writing and reading this chapter. This agrees with that repeated prayer (Ps. lxxx. 3, 7, 19), *Turn us again, and then cause thy face to shine. Turn us* from our idols to thyself, by a sincere repentance and reformation, *and* then *we shall be turned.* If God by his grace renew our hearts, he will by his favour *renew our days.*

AN EXPOSITION, WITH PRACTICAL OBSERVATIONS, OF

THE BOOK OF
THE PROPHET EZEKIEL

The writings of the prophets, which speak of the *things that should be hereafter,* seem to utter the same call that St. John had (Rev. iv. 1), *Come up hither; but* the prophecy of this book is as if the voice said, *Come up higher;* as we go forward in time (for Ezekiel prophesied in the captivity, as Jeremiah prophesied just before it), so we soar upward in discoveries yet more sublime of the divine glory. These waters of the sanctuary still grow deeper; so far are they from being fordable that in some places they are scarcely fathomable; yet, deep as they are, out of them flow streams which *make glad the city of our God.* I. The writer was Ezekiel; his name signifies, *The strength of God,* or one *girt* or *strengthened of God.* He girded up the loins of his mind to the service, and God put strength into him. *I have made thy face strong against their faces.* If we give credit to the tradition of the Jews, he was put to death by the captives in Babylon, for his boldness in reproving them; it is stated that his brains were dashed out. An Arabic historian says that he was put to death and was buried in the sepulchre of Shem the son of Noah. II. Concerning the date, the place, and the time. The scene is laid in Babylon, when it was a *house* of bondage to the *Israel of God;* there the prophecies of this book were written, when the prophet himself, and the people to whom he prophesied, were captives there. Ezekiel prophesied in the beginning of the captivity. It was an indication of God's goodwill and his gracious designs in their affliction, that he raised up prophets to convince them when, in the beginning of their troubles they were unhumbled, which was Ezekiel's business, and to comfort them when they were dejected and discouraged. III. Concerning the matter and scope of it. 1. There is much that is mysterious, dark, and hard to be understood, especially in the beginning and the latter end of it, therefore the Jews forbade the reading of it to their young men, till they came to be thirty years of age, lest by the difficulties they met they should be prejudiced against the scriptures; but if we read these difficult parts with humility and reverence, and search them diligently, though we may not be able to untie all the knots, any more than we can solve all the phenomena in the book of nature, yet we may from them, as from the book of nature, gather a great deal for the confirming of our faith and the encouraging of our hope in God. 2. Though the visions here be intricate, such as an elephant may swim in, yet the sermons are mostly plain, such as a lamb may wade in; and the chief design is to *show God's people their transgressions,* that in their captivity they might be repenting and not repining. As it was of great use to the oppressed captives themselves to have a prophet with them, so it was a testimony to their religion against their oppressors who ridiculed it and them. 3. Though the reproofs and the threatenings here are sharp and bold, yet towards the close of the book very comfortable assurances are given of great mercy God had in store for them; and there one finds some reference to gospel times, and its accomplishment in the kingdom of the Messiah. By opening the *terrors of the Lord* he prepares Christ's way. The visions were the prophet's credentials. In *ch.* i–iii, the reproofs and threatenings; *ch.* iv–xxiv, the comforts in the latter part of the book, and in between are messages sent to the nations that bordered upon the land of Israel, whose destruction is foretold (*ch.* xxv–xxxv), to make way for the restoration of God's Israel and the re-establishment of their city and temple, which are foretold, *ch.* xxxvi to the end.

CHAPTER 1

I. The circumstances of the prophecy now to be delivered, the time when it was delivered (ver. 1), the place where (ver. 2), and the person by whom, ver. 3. II. The introduction to it by a vision of the glory of God, 1. In the upper world, where his throne is surrounded with angels, here called "living creatures", ver. 4–14. 2. In his providences concerning the lower world, represented by the wheels and their motions, ver. 15–25. 3. In the face of Jesus Christ sitting upon the throne, ver. 26–28. And the more we are acquainted, and the more intimately we converse, with the glory of God in these three branches of it, the more commanding influence will divine revelation have upon us.

Verses 1–3

The circumstances of the vision which Ezekiel saw, and in which he received his commission, are here particularly set down, that the narrative may appear to be authentic. It may be of use to keep an account when and where God has been pleased to manifest himself to our souls in a peculiar manner.

I. The time when Ezekiel had this vision was *in the thirtieth year, v.* 1. Some make it the thirtieth year of the prophet's age; being a priest, he was at that age to enter upon the full execution of the priestly office. Others make it to be the thirtieth year from the beginning of the reign of Nabopolassar, the father of Nebuchadnezzar. But the Chaldee paraphrase fixes upon another era, and says that this was the thirtieth year after *Hilkiah the priest found the book of the law in the house of the sanctuary, at* midnight, *after the setting of the moon, in the days of Josiah the king.* It was in the *fourth month,* answering to our June, and in the *fifth day of the month,* that Ezekiel had this vision, *v.* 2. It is probable that it was on the sabbath day, because we read (*ch.* iii. 16) that *at the end of seven days,* the next sabbath, the word of the Lord came to him again.

II. The melancholy circumstances he was in when God honoured him. He was *among the captives, by the river of Chebar, and it was in the fifth year of king Jehoiachin's captivity.*

1. The people of God were now, some of them, *captives in the land of the Chaldeans.* The body of the Jewish nation yet remained in their own land, but these were the first-fruits of the captivity, and they were some of the best. The word of instruction and the rod of correction may be of great service to us, in concert and concurrence with each other, the word to explain the rod and the rod to enforce the word: both together give wisdom. In their captivity they were destitute of ordinary helps for their souls, and therefore God raised them up these extraordinary ones; for God's children, if they be hindered in their education one way, shall have it made up another way. The Jews that remained in their own land had Jeremiah with them, those that had gone into captivity had Ezekiel with them; for wherever the children of God are scattered abroad he will find out tutors for them.

2. The prophet was himself among the captives by *the river Chebar*. Interpreters agree not what river this of Chebar was. The best men, and those that are dearest to God, often share in the public and national judgments that are inflicted for sin; those feel the smart who contributed nothing to the guilt. The captives will be best instructed by one who is a captive among them and experimentally knows their sorrows. Wherever we are we may keep up our communion with God. When St. Paul was a prisoner the gospel had a free course. When St. John was banished into the Isle of Patmos Christ visited him there.

III. The discovery which God was pleased to make of himself to the prophet. He here tells us what he saw, what he heard, and what he felt. 1. He *saw visions of God, v.* 1. No man can *see God and live*; but many have seen visions of God, displays of the divine glory as have instructed them. Ezekiel was employed in turning the hearts of the people to the Lord their God, and therefore he must himself see the visions of God. It concerns those to be well acquainted with God themselves, and much affected with what they know of him, whose business it is to bring others to the knowledge and love of him. That he might see the *visions of God the heavens were opened*; the darkness and distance which hindered his visions were conquered. 2. He heard the voice of God (*v.* 3): *The word of the Lord came expressly* to him, and what he saw was designed to prepare him for what he was to hear. *The essential Word* (so we may take it), *the Word who is, who is what he is, came to Ezekiel*, to send him on his errand. 3. He felt the power of God opening his eyes to see the visions, opening his ear to hear the voice, and opening his heart to receive both.

Verses 4–14

The scope and intention of these visions, 1. To possess the prophet's mind with high, and honourable thoughts of God by whom he was commissioned. It is *the likeness of the glory of the Lord* that he sees (*v.* 28). So great a God as this must be served *with reverence and godly fear*. 2. To strike a terror upon the sinners who remained in Zion, and those who had already come to Babylon, who bade defiance to the threatenings of Jerusalem's ruin. That this vision had a reference to the destruction of Jerusalem seems plain from *ch.* xliii. 3. 3. To speak comfort to those that feared God, and humbled themselves under his mighty hand. "Let them know that, though they are captives in Babylon, yet they have God nigh unto them; though they have not *the place of the sanctuary* they have the God of the sanctuary. Now that the church is to be planted for a long time in another country, the Lord shows a glory in the midst of them, as he had done at their first constituting into a church in the wilderness." The first part of the vision represents God as attended and served by an innumerable company of angels, who are all his ministers, *doing his commandments* and *hearkening to the voice of his word*.

I. The introduction to this vision of the angels is magnificent and awakening, *v.* 4. The prophet, observing the heavens to open, *looked*, looked up. To clear the way, *behold, a whirlwind came out of the north*, which would drive away the interposing mists. God can by a whirlwind clear the sky and air, and produce that serenity of mind which is necessary to our communion with Heaven. This whirlwind came to Ezekiel (as that to Elijah, 1 Kings xix. 11), to *prepare the way of the Lord*.

II. The vision itself. God's pavilion in which he rests, his chariot in which he rides, is *darkness and thick clouds*, Ps. xviii. 11; civ. 3. The cloud is accompanied with *a fire*, as upon Mount Sinai, where God resided in a *thick cloud*; but *the sight of his glory was like devouring fire* (Exod. xxiv. 16, 17), and his first appearance to Moses was *in a flame of fire in the bush*; for *our God is a consuming fire*. The fire is surrounded with a glory: *A brightness was about it*. Though we cannot see into the fire, cannot by searching find out God to perfection, yet we see the brightness that is round about it. Moses might see God's back parts, but not his face. Nothing is more easy than to determine that God is, nothing more difficult than to describe what he is. The *living creatures* which he saw coming *out of the midst of the fire* were *seraphim—burners—*not the *living creatures* themselves (angels are spirits, and cannot be seen), but *the likeness* of them, such as God saw fit to use for the leading of the prophet. *The likeness of these living creatures came out of the midst of the fire*. The prophet himself explains this vision (*ch.* x. 20): *I knew that the living creatures were the cherubim*. They are living creatures; the creatures of God, the work of his hands. The sun (say some) is a flame of *fire enfolding itself*, but it is not a living creature. The prophet sees four of these living creatures to intimate that they are sent towards the four winds of heaven, Matt. xxiv. 31. Zechariah saw them as four chariots going forth east, west, north and south, Zech. vi. 1. God has messengers to send every way. *They had the likeness of a man;* they are reasonable, intelligent beings, who have that *spirit of a man* which is *the candle of the Lord*. The angels of God appear in *the likeness of man* because in *the fulness of time* the Son of God was not only to appear in that likeness, but to assume that nature. They *all four had the face of a man, v.* 5, but, besides that, they had *the face of a lion, an ox*, and *an eagle*, each masterly in its kind, *the lion* among *wild* beasts, *the ox* among *tame* ones, and *the eagle* among fowls, *v.* 10. The scattered perfections of the living creatures on earth meet in the angels of heaven. They have *the understanding of a man*, and such as far exceeds it; they also resemble man in tenderness and humanity. But a *lion* excels man in strength, and boldness, therefore the angels, who in this resemble them, put on the *face of a lion*. *An ox* excels man in diligence, and patience, in the work he has to do; therefore the angels, employed in the service of God and the church, put on *the face of an ox*. *An eagle* excels man in quickness and piercing sight, and in soaring high; and therefore the angels, who seek things above, and see far into divine mysteries, put on *the face of a flying eagle*. *Every one had four wings, v.* 6. Faith and hope are the soul's wings, upon which it soars upward; pious and devout affections are its wings on which it is carried forward. Their wings were joined (*v.* 9–11) in token of their perfect unity and unanimity. Two of their wings were made use of in covering their bodies, the spiritual bodies they assumed. Their feet were *straight feet* (*v.* 7); they stood straight, and firm, and steady. *Their feet were winged* (so the LXX); they went so swiftly that it was as if they flew. They had not only wings for motion, but hands for action (*v.* 8). They are *the hands of a man*, which are wonderfully made and fitted for service, guided by reason and understanding. Calves' feet denote the swiftness of their motion. The living creatures are active beings. Whatever service they went about *they went everyone straight forward* (*v.* 9, 12). If thus *our eye be single*, our *whole body will be full of light*. The singleness of the eye is the sincerity of the heart. *They went straight forward*, everyone about his own work; they did not thwart one another. *They turned not when they went, v.* 9, 12. They minded no diversions; as they turned not back, so they turned not aside. *They went whither the Spirit was to go* (*v.* 12). Whithersoever *the Spirit* of God would have them *go*, thither *they went*. The prophet saw these living creatures (*v.* 13), by their own light, for *their appearance was like burning coals of fire.* He saw them by the light of *lamps,* which *went up and down among* them, the shining whereof *was* very *bright.* The angels of light are in the light, but we see them and their works only by candle-light, by the dim light *of lamps* that go *up and down among* them; when *the day breaks, and the shadows flee away,* we shall see them clearly.

Verses 15–25

I. The vision of the *wheels, v.* 15–21. The glory of God appears not only in the splendour of the upper world, but in the steadiness of his government here in this lower world. *As he beheld the living creatures,* and was contemplating the glory this other vision presented itself to his view. 1. The dispensations of Providence are compared to *wheels,* the wheels of a chariot. *Wheels,* though they move not of themselves, as *the living creatures* do, are yet made movable. The wheel is said to be *by the living creatures.* Such a close connexion is there between *the living creatures* and the *wheels* that they moved and rested together. *When the living creatures went, the wheels went by them;* when God has work to do by the ministry of angels second causes are all found, or made, ready to concur in it. If *the living creatures were lifted up from the earth,* were elevated to any service above the common course of nature, the wheels move in concert with them, and *are lifted up over against them, v.* 19–21. The reason is because *the spirit of the living creatures was in the wheels;* the same wisdom, power, and holiness of God, that guides and governs the angels, orders all the motions of the ceatures in this lower world. God is the soul of the world, and animates the whole, both that above and that beneath, so that they move in perfect harmony, as the upper and lower parts of the natural body do, so that *whithersoever the Spirit is to go* (whatever God wills and purposes to be done) *thither their spirit is to go.* The wheel is said to have four *faces,* looking four several ways (*v.* 15), denoting that the providence of God exerts itself east, west, north, and south, and extends itself to the remotest corners. At first Ezekiel saw it as *one wheel* (*v.* 15), one sphere; but afterwards he saw it was four, but *they* four *had one likeness* (*v.* 16). Various events answer the same intention. *Their appearance and their work* are said to be *like the colour of a beryl* (*v.* 16), *the colour of Tarshish* (so the word is), that is, of the sea. The nature of things in this world is like that of the sea, in continual flux and yet there is a constant coherence. The sea ebbs and flows, so does Providence in its disposals. The sea looks blue, as the air does, because of the shortness of our sight, which can see but a little way of either. We cannot find out that which God does *from the beginning to the end,* Eccles. iii. 11. We see but *parts of his ways* (Job. xxvi. 14), and all beyond looks blue. It is *far above out of our sight. Their appearance and their work are as it were a wheel in the middle of a wheel.* We pretend not to give a mathematical description of it. The disposals of Providence seem to us intricate, perplexed, and unaccountable, and yet they will appear in the issue to have been all wisely ordered. The motion of these wheels was steady and constant: *They returned not when they went* (*v.* 17), because they never went amiss. God takes his work before him, and he will have it forward; and it is going on even when it seems to us to be going backward. *They went* as the Spirit directed them, and therefore *returned not.* We should not have occasion to return back as we have, and to undo that by repentance which we have done amiss, and to do it over again, if we were but *led by the Spirit* and followed his direction. *The Spirit of life* (so some

read it) *was in the wheels,* which carried them on with ease and evenness. They were *full of eyes round about,* plainly denoting that the motions of Providence are all directed by infinite wisdom. The issues of things are not determined by a blind fortune, but by those *eyes of the Lord* which *run to and fro through the earth,* and *are in every place, beholding the evil and the good.*

II. The notice he took of *the firmament* above *over the heads of the living creatures.* What is done on earth is done under the heaven, under its inspection and influence. He saw: *The firmament was as the colour of the terrible crystal;* the vastness and brightness of it struck him with an awful reverence. God is on high, *above the firmament;* the angels are *under the firmament,* which denotes their subjection to God's dominion. He heard the *noise of the angels' wings, v.* 24—to awaken the attention of the prophet to that which God was about to say to him from *the firmament, v.* 25. He heard a *voice from the firmament,* from him that sits upon the throne, *v.* 25. When the angels had roused a careless world, they stood still, and *let down their wings,* that there might be a profound silence, and so God's voice might be the better heard. The voice of Providence is designed to open men's ears to the voice of the word.

Verses 26–28

The other parts of this vision were but a preface. God in them had made himself known as Lord of angels and supreme director of all the affairs of this lower world. But now that a divine revelation is to be given to a prophet, we must look higher than the living creatures or the wheels, and must expect that from the eternal Word. Ezekiel, hearing a voice from the firmament, looked up, as John did, to *see the voice that spoke with him,* and he *saw one like unto the Son of man,* Rev. i. 12, 13. This glory of Christ that the prophet saw *was above the firmament* that was *over the heads* of the living creatures, *v.* 26. This dignity and dominion of the Redeemer before his incarnation magnify his condescension in his incarnation. The first thing he observed was a *throne;* for divine revelation comes backed with a royal authority. We must have an eye of faith to God and Christ as upon a throne. The first thing that John discovered in his visions was *a throne set in heaven* (Rev. iv. 2). It is a throne of glory, a throne of grace, a throne of triumph, a throne of government, a throne of judgment. On the throne he saw *the appearance of a man.* This is good news to the children of men, that the throne above the firmament is filled with one that is not ashamed to appear, even there, in the likeness of man. He saw him as a prince and judge upon this throne, in more than human glory, *v.* 27, for God dwells in light, and *covers himself with light as with a garment.* There was the *appearance of fire, round about within the amber;* it was inward and involved. That below was outward. Some make the former to signify Christ's divine nature, hidden within the *colour of amber;* it is what no man has seen nor can see. The latter they suppose to be his human nature, the glory of which there were those who saw; the glory as of *the only begotten of the Father, full of grace and truth,* John i. 14. The throne is surrounded with a rainbow, *v.* 28. It is so in St. John's vision, Rev. iv. 3. As it is a display of majesty, so it is a pledge of mercy, for it is a confirmation of the gracious promise God has made. Now that the fire of God's wrath was breaking out against Jerusalem, he would *look upon the bow and remember the covenant,* as he promised in such a case, Lev. xxvi. 42. The conclusion of this vision. *This was the appearance of the likeness of the glory of the Lord.* Here, as all along, the prophet is careful to guard against all gross corporeal thoughts of God. He does not say, *This was the Lord* (for he is invisible), but, *This was the glory of the Lord*, in which he was pleased to manifest himself a glorious being; yet it is not *the glory of the Lord*, but *the likeness of that glory*, some faint resemblance of it; nor is it any adequate likeness of that glory, but only *the appearance of that likeness*, a shadow of it, and not the very *image of the thing*, Heb. x. 1. *When I saw it, I fell upon my face*. He was overpowered by it. He fell upon his face in token of that holy awe and reverence with which his mind was possessed and filled. All he saw was only to prepare him for that which he was to hear; for *faith comes by hearing*. God delights to teach the humble.

CHAPTER 2

What our Lord Jesus said to St. Paul (Acts xxvi. 16) may fitly be applied to the prophet Ezekiel, "Rise and stand upon thy feet, for I have appeared unto thee for this purpose, to make thee a minister." We have here Ezekiel's ordination to his office. I. He is commissioned to go as a prophet to the house of Israel, now captive in Babylon, ver. 1–5. II. He is cautioned not to be afraid of them, ver. 6. III. He is instructed what to say to them, signified by the vision of a roll (ver. 7–10).

Verses 1–5

God calls him, *Son of man* (v. 1, 3), *Son of Adam, Son of the earth*. We may take it, 1. As a humble diminishing title. Lest Ezekiel should be lifted up with the abundance of the revelations, he is put in mind of this, that still he is a *son of man*. Or, 2. We may take it as an honourable title; for it is one of the titles of the Messiah in the Old Testament (Dan. vii. 13, *I saw one like the Son of man come with the clouds of heaven*).

I. Ezekiel is made to stand, that he might receive his commission, *v*. 1, 2.

1. By a divine command: *Son of man, stand upon thy feet*. His lying prostrate was a posture of greater reverence, but his standing up would be a posture of greater readiness.

2. By a divine power going along with that command, *v*. 2. God made him *stand up*; but, because he had not strength of his own to recover his feet nor courage to face the vision, *the Spirit entered into him* and *set him upon his feet*. The *Spirit set him upon his feet*, made him willing to do as he was bidden, and then he *heard him that spoke* to him.

II. Ezekiel is sent with a message to the children of Israel (*v*. 3): *I send thee to the children of Israel*. They were now sent into captivity, for abusing God's messengers, and yet even there God sends this prophet among them.

1. The rebellion of the people to whom this ambassador is sent. They are called *children of Israel*; they retain the name of their pious ancestors, but they have degenerated, they have become *Goim—nations*, the word commonly used for the Gentiles. They had been all along a rebellious generation and had persisted in their rebellion: *They and their fathers have transgressed against me*. They were now hardened, *impudent children*, brazen-faced, self-willed.

2. "*I do send thee unto them*, and therefore *thou shalt say* thus and thus unto them," *v*. 4. All he said to them must be spoken in God's name, enforced by his authority, and delivered as from him. The writings of the prophets are the word of God, and so are to be regarded. When men's hearts are made to burn under the word, and their wills to bow to it, then they know and bear the witness in themselves that it is not the *word of men, but of God*. If they turn a deaf ear to the word they shall be made to know that he whom they slighted is indeed a prophet, by the reproaches of their own consciences and the just judgments of God upon them for refusing him.

Verses 6–10

The prophet, having received his commission, here receives a charge. It is here required of him,

I. That he be bold. *Son of man, be not afraid of them*, *v*. 6. Those to whom he sent him are *briers and thorns*, vexing a man, which way soever he turns. Wicked men are as briers and thorns, which hinder God's husbandry. They are *scorpions*, venomous and malignant. The sting of a scorpion is a thousand times more hurtful than the scratch of a brier. Ezekiel had been in vision, conversing with angels, but when he comes down from this mount he finds he *dwells with scorpions*. They would hector him and threaten him, that they might drive him off from being a prophet, or at least from threatening them with the judgments of God.

II. It is required that he be faithful, *v*. 7. 1. He must be faithful to Christ who sent him. 2. He must be faithful to the souls of those to whom he was sent. "It is true they are *most rebellious*; but, *speak my words* to them, whether they are pleasing or unpleasing."

III. It is required that he be observant of,

1. The instructions that were given him in the book which was *spread before him, v*. 10. The roll was *written within and without*, on the inside and on the outside. One side contained their sins; the other side contained the judgments of God coming upon them for those sins. He was sent on a sad errand; the matter contained in the book was, *lamentations, and mourning, and woe*. What could be more lamentable, more mournful, more woeful, than to see a holy happy people sunk into such sin and misery!

2. An express charge is given to the prophet both in receiving his message and delivering it. He is to attend diligently to it: *Son of man, hear what I say unto thee, v*. 8. If ministers connive at sin and indulge sinners for fear of displeasing them, they hereby make themselves partakers of their guilt. "Do not only *hear what I say unto thee*, but *open thy mouth, and eat that which I give thee*. Eat it willingly and with an appetite." He that brought it to the prophet *spread it before him*, that he might fully understand the contents of it, and then receive it and make it his own.

CHAPTER 3

The further preparation of the prophet for the work to which God called him. I. His eating the roll that was presented to him, ver. 1–3. II. Further instructions and encouragements, ver. 4–11. III. The mighty impulse he was under, with which he was carried to those that were to be his hearers, ver. 12–15. IV. His office and business as a prophet, under the similitude of a watchman, ver. 16–21. V. The restraining and restoring of the prophet's liberty of speech, ver. 22–27.

Verses 1–15

These verses are fitly joined by some translators to the foregoing chapter, as being a continuation of the same vision.

I. How he must receive divine revelation himself, *v*. 1. "*Son of man, eat this roll*, imprint it in thy mind, let thy soul be nourished and strengthened by it; be full of it, as thou art of the meat thou hast eaten." Whatever we find to be the word of God, whatever is brought to us by him who is the Word of God, we must receive it without disputing. If he that *opens the roll*, and by his Spirit, spreads it before us, did not also *open our understanding*, and by his Spirit, give us the knowledge of it and *cause us to eat* it, we should be for ever strangers to it. Though the roll was *filled with lamentations, and mourning, and woe*, yet it was to the prophet *as honey for sweetness*.

II. He must deliver that divine revelation to others which he himself had received (*v*. 1): *Eat this roll, and then go, speak to the house of Israel*. He is not sent to the Chaldeans to reprove them for their sins, but *to the house of Israel* to reprove them for theirs; for the father corrects his own child if he do amiss, not the child of a stranger. He must remember that they are *the house of Israel* whom he is sent to speak to, God's house and his own. They were such as he had an intimate acquaintance with, being not only their countryman, but their *companion in tribulation*. He must remember what God had already told him of the character of those to whom he was sent, that, if he met with discouragement and disappointment he might not be offended. They *are impudent and hard-hearted* (v. 7), no convictions of sin would make them blush, no denunciations would make them tremble. They were obstinate against God himself: "They *will not hearken unto thee*, and no marvel, *for they will not hearken unto me*." They are prejudiced against the law of God, and for that reason turn a deaf ear to his prophets, whose business it is to enforce his law. God will enable him to put a good face on it: "*I have made thy face strong against their faces*, endued thee with all firmness and boldness." The more impudent wicked people are in their opposition to religion the more openly and resolutely should God's people appear in the practice and defence of it. When vice is daring let not virtue be sneaking. He is therefore commanded to have a good heart and to go on in his work, not valuing either the censures or the threats of his enemies. Let not the angry countenance that drives away a backbiting tongue give any check to a reproving tongue. He must *tell them* not only what the Lord said, but that the Lord said it: *Thus saith the Lord God; tell them* so, *whether they will hear or whether they will forbear*. Not that it may be indifferent to us what success our ministry has, but, whatever it be, we must go on with our work and leave the issue to God. He *heard a voice of a great rushing* (v. 12), as if the angels thronged and crowded to see the inauguration of a prophet. He *heard the noise of their wings that touched*, and *the noise of the wheels* of Providence moving *over against* the angels and in concert with them. But all this noise ended in the voice of praise. He heard them saying, *Blessed be the glory of the Lord from his place*. With reluctance of his own spirit, and yet with a mighty efficacy of *the Spirit of God*, the prophet was brought to the execution of his office. The Spirit led him with a strong hand. God bade him go, but he stirred not till *the Spirit took him up* (v. 14), *lifted him up, and took him away* to his work. Ezekiel would willingly have kept all he heard and saw to himself, but he was carried on by the prophetical impulse, so that he could not *but speak the things which he had heard and seen*, as the apostles, Acts iv. 20. He followed with a sad heart: *The Spirit took me away*, says he, *and* then *I went*, but it was *in bitterness, in the heat of my spirit*. He had perhaps seen what a hard task Jeremiah had at Jerusalem, what ill treatment he met with, and all to no purpose. "*I went*, not *disobedient to the heavenly vision*, or shrinking from the work, as Jonah, but *I went in bitterness*, not at all pleased with it." He *went in the heat of his spirit*, because of the discouragements he foresaw, *but the hand of the Lord was strong upon* him, to fit him and animate him against the difficulties he would meet and, when he found it so, he was reconciled to his business and applied himself to it: *Then he came to those of the captivity* (v. 15), *and sat where they sat*, and continued *among them seven days* to hear what they said and observe what they did; and all that time he was waiting for *the word of the Lord* to come to him. He was *there astonished*, overwhelmed with grief for the sins and miseries of his people and overpowered by the vision he had seen.

Verses 16–21

These further instructions God gave to the prophet *at the end of seven days*, that is, on the seventh day

after the vision he had; and it is probable that both that and this were on the sabbath day. *The word of the Lord* then and there *came to* him. He that had been musing and meditating on the things of God all the week, was fit to speak to the people in God's name on the sabbath day, and to hear God speak to him. He is plainly, and by a similitude, told his duty, which he is to communicate to the people.

I. The office to which the prophet is called: *Son of man, I have made thee a watchman to the house of Israel*, v. 17. He is *a watchman*, appointed to be as *a watchman* in the city, as *a watchman* over the flock, as *a watchman* in the camp, in an invaded country or a besieged town, to watch the motions of the enemy, and to sound an alarm upon the approach of danger. This supposes *the house of Israel* to be in a military state, and exposed to enemies, who are subtle. Watchmen are in peril of death from the enemy, who gain their point if they kill the sentinel; and yet they dare not quit their post upon pain of death from their general. Such a dilemma are the church's watchmen in; men will curse them if they be faithful, and God will curse them if they be false.

II. The work of a watchman is to take notice and to give notice.

1. The prophet, as a watchman, must take notice of what God said concerning this people. He must not, as other watchmen, look round to spy danger and gain intelligence, but he must look up to God, and further he need not look: *Hear the word at my mouth*, v. 17.

2. He must give notice of what he heard, not in his own name, or as from himself, but in God's name, and from him. God has said, and does say, to every wicked man, that if he go on still in his trespasses he *shall surely die*. *His iniquity* shall undoubtedly be his ruin. If a *wicked man turn from his wickedness*, and *from his wicked way, he shall live*, and the ruin he is threatened with shall be prevented; and, that he may do so, he is warned of the danger he is in. It is the duty of ministers both to warn sinners of the danger of sin and to assure them of the benefit of repentance. Those that are faithful shall have their reward, though they be not successful. Some of those Ezekiel had to deal with were *righteous*, and he must warn them not to *turn away from their righteousness*, v. 20, 21. One good means to keep us from falling is to keep up a holy fear of falling, Heb. iv. 1. When men *turn from their righteousness* they soon learn to commit iniquity. When they grow careless and remiss in the duties of God's worship, they become an easy prey to the tempter. The righteousness which men relinquish will stand them in no stead because not continued. We must not only not flatter the wicked, but not flatter even the righteous as if they were perfectly safe anywhere on this side heaven. Nothing is more beautiful than *a wise reprover upon an obedient ear*; the one *shall live because he is warned* and the other *has delivered his soul*.

Verses 22–27

After all this discovery which God had made of himself to the prophet, and the full instructions he had given him, his work, at first, seems not in proportion to his call. To encourage him against the difficulties he foresaw, God favours him with another vision of his glory. God calls him out *to the plain* (v. 22) to *talk with him*. See the condescension of God in conversing thus familiarly with a poor captive, nay, with a sinful man, who *went in bitterness of spirit*, and was at this time out of humour with his work. It is very comfortable to be alone with God, withdrawn from the world for converse with him, to speak to him; and a good man will say that he is never less alone than when thus alone. Ezekiel *went forth into the plain* more willingly than he went among those of the captivity (v. 15). He *went out into the plain*, and there saw the same vision that he had seen *by the river of Chebar*. God called him out to *talk with him*, but did more than that: he showed him his *glory*, v. 23. We are not now to expect such visions, but we must own that we have a favour done us if we so by faith *behold the glory of the Lord* as to be *changed into the same image, by the Spirit of the Lord*. One would have expected now that God would send him directly to the chief place of concourse, and make him and his message acceptable, that he would have a wider door of opportunity opened to him, but what is here said to him is the reverse of all this. Instead of sending him to a public assembly, he orders him to confine himself to his own lodgings: *Go, shut thyself within thy house*, v. 24. He was not willing to appear in public, and, when he did, the people did not regard him, and as a just rebuke both to him and them, to him for his shyness and to them for their coldness, God forbids him to appear in public. He must *shut himself within his house*, that he might receive further discoveries of the mind of God. *The elders of Judah* visited him and *sat before* him *in his house* (ch. viii. 1), to be witnesses of his ecstasies; but it was not till *ch.* xi. 25 that he *spoke to those of the captivity all the things that the Lord had shown him*. Instead of securing him the esteem and affections of those to whom he sent him God tells him that *they shall put bands upon him* and bind him (v. 25) in order to further punish him as a disturber of the peace. Though they were themselves sent into bondage in Babylon for persecuting the prophets, yet there they continue to persecute them. They would bind him, under pretence of his being mad. Instead of opening his lips that his mouth might show forth God's praise, God silenced him, so that he was dumb for a considerable time, v. 26. He that can speak best is forbidden to speak at all; and the reason given is because *they are a rebellious house* to whom he is sent, and they are not worthy to have him for *a reprover*. But when God *speaks with* him, and designs to speak by him, he *will open* his *mouth*, v. 27. Instead of giving him assurance of success when he should at any time speak to the people, he here leaves the matter doubtful, and Ezekiel must not perplex and disquiet himself about it, but let it be as it will.

CHAPTER 4

The captives in Babylon had Jerusalem still upon their hearts; the pious looked towards it with an eye of faith, the presumptuous looked towards it with an eye of pride, and flattered themselves with a conceit that they should shortly return. Those that remained corresponded with the captives, and buoyed them up with hopes that all would be well yet, as long as Jerusalem was standing in its strength. God gives the prophet, in this chapter, a very clear and affecting foresight of the besieging of Jerusalem by the Chaldean army and the calamities which would attend that siege. I. The fortifications that should be raised against the city (ver. 1–8). II. The famine that should rage within the city; signified by his eating coarse fare, ver. 9–17.

Verses 1–8

The prophet is here ordered to represent by signs *the siege of Jerusalem*; and this amounted to a prediction.

I. He was ordered to engrave a draught of Jerusalem upon a tile, v. 1. It was Jerusalem's honour that God had *graven her upon the palms of his hands* (Isa. xlix. 16), and the names of the tribes were engraven in precious stones on the breastplate of the high priest; but, now that *the faithful city has become a harlot*, a worthless brittle tile or brick is thought good enough to *portray it upon*.

II. He was ordered to build little forts against this portraiture of the city, resembling the batteries raised by the besiegers, v. 2. Between the city and the besieger he was to set up an *iron pan*, as an *iron wall*,

v. 3. This represented the inflexible resolution of both sides; the Chaldeans resolved they would never quit till they had conquered; the Jews resolved never to capitulate.

III. He was ordered to lie upon his side before it, as it were to surround it, representing the Chaldean army lying before it to block it up. He was to lie on his left side 390 *days* (v. 5); the siege of Jerusalem is to last eighteen months (Jer. lii. 4–6), but if we deduct from that five months' interval, when the besiegers withdrew upon the approach of Pharaoh's army (Jer. xxxvii. 5–8), the number of the days of the close siege will be 390. Yet that also had another signification. The 390 days signified 390 years; and, when the prophet lies so many days on his side, he bears the guilt of that iniquity which *the house of Israel*, the ten tribes, had borne 390 years, reckoning from their first apostasy under Jeroboam to the destruction of Jerusalem, which completed the ruin of those small remains of them that had incorporated with Judah. He is then to lie forty days *upon his right side*, and so long to bear *the iniquity of the house of Judah*, the kingdom of the two tribes, because their sins were those which they were guilty of during the last forty years before their captivity. Judah, that had Josiah and Jeremiah, fills the measure of its iniquity in less time than Israel does. The prophet lay every day at a certain time of the day. When he received visits he was found lying 390 *days on his left side* and *forty days on his right side* before his portraiture of Jerusalem, which all might understand to mean the besieging of that city.

IV. He was ordered to prosecute the siege with vigour (v. 7): *Thou shalt set thy face towards the siege of Jerusalem*, as wholly intent upon it; so the Chaldeans would be. Nebuchadnezzar's indignation at Zedekiah's treachery in breaking his league with him made him very furious in pushing on this siege, that he might chastise that faithless prince and people. They exerted themselves to the utmost in all the operations of the siege, which the prophet was to represent by the *uncovering of his arm*, the *stretching out* of his arm, as it were to deal blows. He is said to *make bare his arm*, Isa. lii. 10. In short, The Chaldeans will go about their business, and go on in it, as men in earnest, who resolve to go through with it. Now, 1. This is intended to be a *sign to the house of Israel* (v. 3), to those in Babylon, and to those who remained in their own land. The prophet was *dumb* and *could not speak* (ch. iii. 26); but God *left not himself without witness*, but ordered him to make signs, to *make known his mind* (that is, the mind of God) to the people, who through their stupidity and dullness must be taught as children are, by pictures. Or the prophet made use of signs for the same reason that Christ made use of parables. Thus the prophet *prophesies against Jerusalem* (v. 7); and there were those who were the more affected with it by its being so represented, for images to the eye make deeper impressions upon the mind than words can, and for this reason sacraments are instituted to represent divine things. The power of imagination, if it be rightly used, and kept under the direction and correction of reason and faith, may be of good use to kindle devout affections. Fancy is like fire, a *good servant, but a bad master*. This whole transaction seemed childish and tiresome, but our ease must be sacrificed to our duty, and we must never call God's service a hard service. It could not but be against the grain to appear thus against Jerusalem, the city of God; but he is a prophet, and must follow his instructions, not his affections, and must plainly preach the ruin of a sinful place, though its welfare is what he passionately desires. All this that the prophet sets before the children of his people concerning the destruction of Jerusalem is designed to bring them to repentance. But observe, It is a day of punishment for a year of sin: *I have appointed thee each day for a year.* The siege is a calamity of 390 days.

Verses 9–17

The best exposition of this part of Ezekiel's prediction of Jerusalem's desolation is Jeremiah's lamentation of it, Lam. iv. 3, 4, &c., and v. 10.

I. The prophet here, to affect the people with the foresight of it, must confine himself for 390 days to coarse fare and short commons, ill-dressed, for they should want both food and fuel.

1. His food was to be of the worst bread, made of but little wheat and barley, and the rest of beans, and lentiles, and millet, and fitches, such as we feed horses or hogs, mixed as that in the beggar's bag, that has a dish full of one sort of corn at one house and of another at another house, *v.* 9. The prophet must eat but twenty *shekels*' weight of bread a day (*v.* 10), that was about ten ounces; and he must drink but the *sixth part of a bin of water,* that was half a pint, about eight ounces, *v.* 11. The prophet in Babylon had bread enough and to spare, yet, that he might confirm his prediction and be a sign to the children of Israel, God obliges him to live thus sparingly. Nature is content with a little, grace with less, but lust with nothing. It is good to stint ourselves of choice, that we may the better bear it if ever we should come to be stinted by necessity. He must *bake it with man's dung* (*v.* 12); that must serve for fuel to heat his oven. The coarse bread, thus baked, he must *eat as barley-cakes.* This nauseous piece of cookery he must exercise publicly *in their sight,* that they might be the more affected with the calamity approaching. In the extremity of the famine they should not only have nothing that was dainty, but nothing that was cleanly, about them. This circumstance of the sign, the baking of his bread with man's dung, the prophet humbly desired might be dispensed with (*v.* 14); it seemed a ceremonial pollution, for there was a law that man's dung should *be covered with earth,* that God might *see no unclean thing in their camp,* Deut. xxiii. 13, 14. And must he go and gather a thing so offensive, and use it in the dressing of his meat in the sight of the people? "*Ah! Lord God,*" says he, "*behold, my soul has not been polluted,*" and I am afraid lest by this it be polluted." The pollution of the soul by sin is what good people dread, and yet sometimes tender consciences fear it without cause, with scruples about lawful things, as the prophet here, who had not yet learned that it is not that which *goes into the mouth that defiles the man,* Matt. xv. 11. Now, because Ezekiel with a manifest tenderness of conscience made this scruple, God dispensed with him in this matter. God allowed Ezekiel to use *cow's dung* instead of *man's dung, v.* 15.

II. This sign signified,

1. That those who remained in Jerusalem should be brought to extreme misery for want of necessary food. All supplies being cut off by the besiegers, *the staff of bread* would be *broken in Jerusalem, v.* 16. Multitudes of them shall die of famine, they shall die so as to *feel themselves die.* And it is sin that brings all this misery upon them: *They shall consume away in their iniquity* (so it may be read). It is a righteous thing with God to deprive us of those enjoyments which we have made the food and fuel of our lusts.

2. It signified that those who were carried into captivity should be forced to *eat their defiled bread among the Gentiles* (*v.* 13), to eat meat made up by Gentile hands otherwise than according to the law of the Jewish church, which they were always taught to call *defiled.* Or they should be forced to eat putrid meat, such as their oppressors would allow

them in their slavery, and such as formerly they would have scorned to touch.

Chapter 5

A further, and no less terrible, denunciation of the judgments of God, which were coming upon the Jewish nation. This destruction of Judah and Jerusalem is here, I. Represented by a sign the cutting, and burning, and scattering of hair, ver. 1–4. II. That sign is expounded, and applied to Jerusalem. 1. Sin is charged upon Jerusalem as the cause—contempt of God's law (ver. 5–7) and profanation of his sanctuary, ver. 11. 2. Wrath is threatened (ver. 8–10), a variety of miseries (ver. 12, 16, 17), such as should be their reproach and ruin, ver. 13–15.

Verses 1–4

The sign by which the utter destruction of Jerusalem is set forth; as before, the prophet is himself the sign, that the people might see how much he affected himself with the case of Jerusalem, and how near it lay to his heart.

I. He must *shave off the hair of his head and beard* (*v.* 1), which signified God's utter rejecting that people, as a worthless generation, such as could well be spared. Jerusalem had been the head, but, having degenerated, had become as the *hair,* which, when it grows thick and long, is but a burden. Ezekiel must not cut off that hair only which was superfluous but *cut it all off,* denoting the end that God would make of Jerusalem.

II. He must *weigh the hair* and *divide it into three parts.* Some make the shaving of the hair to denote the loss of their liberty and of their honour: it was looked upon as a mark of ignominy, as in the disgrace of Hanun put on David's ambassadors. It denotes also the loss of their joy, for they shaved their heads upon occasion of great mourning.

III. He must dispose of the hair so that it might all be destroyed, *v.* 2. 1. One *third part* must *be burnt in the midst of the city,* denoting the multitudes that should perish by famine and pestilence, and perhaps in the conflagration of the city, *when the days of the siege were fulfilled.* 2. Another third part was to be *cut in pieces with a knife,* representing the many who, during the siege, were slain by the sword. 3. Another third part was to be *scattered in the wind,* denoting the carrying away of some into the land of the conqueror and the flight of others into the neighbouring countries for shelter.

IV. He must preserve a small quantity of the third sort that were to be *scattered in the wind,* and *bind them in his skirts, v.* 3. This signified perhaps that little handful of people which were left under the government of Gedaliah, who, it was hoped, would keep possession of the land when the body of the people was carried into captivity. Thus God would have done well for them if they would have done well for themselves.

Verses 5–17

The explanation of the foregoing similitude: *This is Jerusalem.* The prophet's head, which was to be shaved, signified Jerusalem, which by the judgments of God was now to be stripped of its ornaments, to be emptied of its inhabitants, and to be set *naked and bare,* to be *shaved with a razor that is hired,* Isa. vii. 20. The head of one that was a priest, a prophet, a holy person, was fittest to represent Jerusalem, the holy city.

I. The privileges Jerusalem was honoured with (*v.* 5): *I have set it in the midst of the nations and countries that are round about her.* Jerusalem was situated in the midst of kingdoms that were populous, civilized, famed for learning, arts, and sciences. It was *set in the midst of* them as excelling them all— set in the midst of them as a candle upon a candlestick to spread the light of divine revelation to all the dark corners of the neighbouring nations, even to the ends of the earth. Jerusalem was to be as the heart in the body, to invigorate this dead world with a divine life. Had they preserved this reputation (1 Kings iv. 34), what a blessing would Jerusalem have been to all the nations about! But, failing to be so, the accomplishment of this intention was reserved for its latter days, *when out of Zion went forth the* gospel *law and the word of the Lord* Jesus *from Jerusalem.*

II. Jerusalem was guilty. A charge is here drawn up and proved beyond contradiction. 1. She had *not walked in God's statutes,* nor *kept his judgments* (*v.* 7); nay, the inhabitants of Jerusalem had *refused his judgments and his statutes* (*v.* 6). The people had not only broken God's laws, but had so perverted and abused them that they had made them the excuse and colour of their wickedness. They introduced the abominable customs and usages of the heathen, instead of God's institutions. *She has changed my judgments,* by idolatries and false worship, *more than the nations* (*v.* 6), and she has *multiplied* idols and altars, gods and temples, *more than the nations that were round about.* Israel's God is one, his name one, his altar one; but they multiplied their gods. They corrupted revealed religion more than the Gentiles had corrupted natural religion. Jerusalem profaned the holy things, which she had been both entrusted and honoured with (*v.* 11).

III. The punishments that Jerusalem should fall under.

1. God will take this work of punishing Jerusalem into his own hands. "You think it is only the Chaldean army that is against you, but they are God's hand, or rather the staff in his hand; it is *I, even I, that am against thee,* to speak against thee by prophets, to act against thee by providence." Those who will not observe the judgments of God's mouth shall not escape the judgments of his hand.

2. These punishments shall come from his displeasure. As to the body of the people, it shall not be a correction in love, but *in furious rebukes* (*v.* 15), strange expressions to come from a God who has said, *Fury is not in me,* and who has declared himself *gracious, and merciful,* and *slow to anger.* But they are designed to show the malignity of sin. As, when God is dishonoured by the sins of men, he is said to be *grieved* (Ps. xcv. 10), so when he is honoured by their destruction he is said to be *comforted.*

3. Punishments shall be public and open: *I will execute* these *judgments in the sight of the nations* (*v.* 8). Public sins call for public reproofs, so, if those prevail not, they call for public judgments. The nations will fear before the God of Israel, when they see how severely he punishes sin even in those that are nearest to him. *It shall be an instruction to the nations, v.* 15. Jerusalem should have taught her neighbours the fear of God by her piety and virtue, but, she not doing that, God will teach it to them by her ruin.

4. These punishments shall be such as have no precedent (*v.* 9): "*I will do in thee that which I have not done* in thee before, though thou hast long since deserved it." This is a rhetorical expression of the most grievous judgments, like that character of Hezekiah, that there was *none like him, before or after him.* The strongest bonds of natural affection will be broken which will be a just punishment for their wilfully breaking the bonds of duty to God (*v.* 10): *The fathers shall eat the sons, and the sons shall eat the fathers,* through the famine, or shall be compelled to do it by their barbarous conquerors. Some shall be taken away by the plague (*v.* 12); the *pestilence shall pass through thee* (*v.* 17), others *shall be consumed with famine* (*v.* 12). Others *shall fall by the sword round about* Jerusalem, *v.* 17. Others are devoured by *evil beasts,* which will make a prey of those that fly for shelter to the deserts and mountains. And, *lastly,* those who escape shall be *scattered into*

all parts of the world, *into all the winds* (so it is expressed, *v.* 10, 12).

5. These punishments will prove their ruin by degrees. They shall be *diminished* (*v.* 11); *bereaved* (*v.* 17), emptied of all that which was their joy and confidence. We may well suppose that it looks further, to the final destruction of that great city by the Romans.

6. All this is ratified by the divine authority and veracity, *v.* 17. *And they shall know that I the Lord have spoken it, v.* 13. There were those who thought it was only the prophet that spoke it in his delirium; but God's word will prove itself.

CHAPTER 6

I. A threatening of the destruction of Israel for their idolatry, and the destruction of their idols with them, ver. 1–7. II. A promise of the gracious return of a remnant of them to God, by true repentance and reformation, ver. 8–10. III. Directions given to the prophet, to lament the iniquities and the calamities of Israel, ver. 11–14.

Verses 1–7

I. The prophecy is directed to *the mountains of Israel* (*v.* 1, 2); the prophet must *set his face towards* them. If he could see so far as the land of Israel, *the mountains* would be first seen; towards them therefore he must look, steadfastly, as the judge looks at the prisoner, when he passes sentence upon him. Though *the mountains of Israel* be ever so strong, he must *set his face against* them, as having judgments to denounce that should shake their foundation. *The mountains of Israel* had been *holy mountains,* but now that they had polluted them with their high places God set his face against them and therefore the prophet must. But from *the mountains the word of the Lord* echoes *to the hills, to the rivers, and to the valleys;* for to them also *the Lord God* speaks.

II. That which is threatened is the utter destruction of the idols and the idolaters. God himself says, *Behold, I, even I, will bring a sword upon you* (*v.* 3); the sword of the Chaldeans is at God's command. The *high places,* which were on the tops of mountains (*v.* 3), shall be levelled *and made desolate* (*v.* 6). The *altars,* on which they offered sacrifice to strange gods, *shall be broken* to pieces and *laid waste;* the *images* and *idols* shall be defaced, *shall be broken and cease, v.* 4, 6. As *all their high places shall be laid waste,* so shall all *their dwelling-places* too, even *all their cities, v.* 6. It is added as a remarkable circumstance that they shall fall *before their idols* (*v.* 4), that their *dead carcases* should be *laid,* and their *bones scattered, about their altars, v.* 5. Thus the idols were upbraided with their inability to help their worshippers, and idolaters were upbraided with the folly of trusting in them.

Verses 8–10

Judgment had hitherto triumphed, but in these verses mercy rejoices against judgment. The ruin seems to be universal, and *yet will I leave a remnant,* a little remnant, and it is God that leaves them.

I. It is a preserved remnant, saved from the ruin (*v.* 8). None of those who were to *fall by the sword about* Jerusalem *shall escape;* for they trust to Jerusalem's walls for security. But some of them *shall escape the sword among the nations,* where, being deprived of all other steps, they stay themselves upon God only. They shall be the seed of another generation, out of which Jerusalem shall flourish again.

II. It is a penitent remnant (*v.* 9): *Those who escape of you shall remember me.* Where God designs grace to repent he allows space to repent; yet many who have the space want the grace, many who *escape the sword* do not forsake the sin.

1. The occasion of their repentance is a mixture of judgment and mercy—they were *carried captives,* but

they *escaped the sword* in the land of their captivity. True repentance shall be accepted of God, though we are brought to it by our troubles; nay, sanctified afflictions often prove means of conversion.

2. The root and principle of their repentance: *They shall remember me among the nations.* The prodigal son never bethought himself of his father's house till he was ready to perish for hunger in the far country. Their remembering God was the first step they took in returning to him. They *departed from* God, from his word, which they should have made their rule, from his work, which they should have made their business. *Their hearts departed from* him. *Their eyes* also *go after their idols.* The malignity of this sin is that it is spiritual whoredom; it is a *whorish heart* that *departs from* God. They remember what a grief this was to him and how he resented it. In the day of their repentance it shall humble them more than anything, not so much that their peace was broken, and their country broken, as *that God was broken* by their sin.

3. The evidence of their repentance: *They shall loathe themelves for the evils which they have committed in all their abominations.* True penitents see sin to be an abominable thing, that *abominable thing which the Lord hates* and which makes sinners, and even their services, odious to him, Jer. xliv. 4; Isa. i. 11. It defiles the sinner's own conscience, and makes him, unless he be past feeling, an abomination to himself.

4. The glory that will redound to God by their repentance (*v.* 10): "*They shall know that I am the Lord;* finding that what I have said is made good, and made to work for good, and to answer a good intention."

Verses 11–14

The same threatenings are repeated, with a direction to the prophet to lament them.

I. He must by his gestures in preaching express the sense he had of the iniquities and the calamities of the house of Israel (*v.* 11): *Smite with thy hand and stamp with thy foot.* Two things the prophet must thus lament: 1. National sins. *Alas! for all the evil abominations of the house of Israel.* The sins of sinners are the sorrows of God's faithful servants. 2. National judgments. It is our duty to be affected not only with our own sins and sufferings, but with the sins and sufferings of others; and to look with compassion upon the miseries that wicked people bring upon themselves; as Christ *beheld Jerusalem and wept over it.*

II. He must inculcate what he had said before concerning the destruction that was coming upon them. 1. They shall be run down and ruined by a variety of judgments which shall find them out and follow them wherever they are (*v.* 12). 2. They shall read their sin in their punishment, *v.* 5–7. Where they had prostrated themselves in honour of their idols, God will lay them dead, to their own reproach and the reproach of their idols. 3. The country shall be all laid waste, as, before, *the cities* (*v.* 6): *I will make the land desolate.*

CHAPTER 7

The prophet must tell them, I. That it will be a complete destruction, which will make a miserable end, ver. 1–6. II. That it is just at the door, ver. 7–10. III. That it is unavoidable, ver. 10–15. IV. That their strength and wealth should be no fence against it, ver. 16–19. V. That the temple shall itself be ruined, ver. 20–22. VI. That it shall be universal, the sin that brought it having been universal, ver. 23–27.

Verses 1–15

The prophet here proclaims, *An end! an end! it has come, it has come. He that hath ears to hear let him hear.*

I. The end which all the foregoing judgments had been working towards, as means to bring it about, was long in coming, but *now it has come.* This perhaps looks further, to the last destruction of that nation by the Romans. *The end of all things is at hand;* and Jerusalem's last end was a type of *the end of the world,* Matt. xxiv. 3.

II. *An evil, an only evil, behold, has come,* v. 5. Sin is *an evil, an only evil, an evil* that has no good in it; it is the worst of evils. But this is spoken of the evil of trouble. It is *an evil* without precedent or parallel, *an evil* that stands alone; you cannot produce such another instance. The wicked have *the dregs of that cup* to drink which to the righteous is full of *mixtures of mercy,* Ps. lxxv. 8.

III. *The time has come,* the set time, for to all God's purposes *there is a time,* a proper time. Though threatened judgments may be long deferred, yet they shall not be dropped. Though God's patience may put them off, nothing but man's sincere repentance and reformation will put them by.

IV. The whole body of the nation has become a *vessel of wrath, fitted for destruction.* Those shall *have judgment without mercy* who made light of mercy when it was offered them.

V. All this is the just punishment of their sins, and it is what they have by their own folly brought upon themselves. Two sins are particularly specified as provoking God to bring these judgments upon them—pride and oppression. 1. God will humble them by his judgments, for they have magnified themselves. *The rod* of affliction *has blossomed,* but it was *pride* that *budded,* v. 10. 2. Their enemies shall deal hardly with them, for they have dealt hardly with one another (*v.* 11).

VI. There is no escape from these judgments. Men shall be safe nowhere; for *he that is in the field shall die by the sword* (every field shall be to them a field of battle) *and he that is in the city,* though it be a holy city, yet it shall not be his *protection,* but *famine and pestilence shall devour him.* Sin had abounded both in city and country. Those that fall shall not be lamented (*v.* 11): *There shall be no wailing for them,* for there shall be none left to bewail them. *None ever hardened his heart against God and prospered.* Those that strengthen themselves in their wickedness will be found not only to weaken, but to ruin, themselves, Ps. lii. 7. *The multitude* cannot resist the torrent of these judgments, nor make head against them (*v.* 14): *They have blown the trumpet,* to call their soldiers, but all in vain. "*Let not the buyer rejoice that he is increasing his estate and has become a purchaser;* nor let *the seller mourn* that he is lessening his estate and has become a bankrupt," *v.* 12. See the vanity of the things of this world, and how worthless they are—in a time of trouble. It is added (*v.* 13), "*The seller shall not return,* at the year of jubilee, *to that which is sold,* according to the law, though he should escape the sword, and live till that year comes; for no inheritances shall be enjoyed here till the seventy years be accomplished, and then men shall return to their possessions, shall claim and have their own again."

Verses 16–22

Some of them *shall escape* (*v.* 16), but what the better? As good die once as, in a miserable life, die a thousand deaths, and escape only like Cain to be *fugitives and vagabonds,* and afraid of being slain by everyone they meet; so shall these be.

I. They shall have no comforter or satisfaction in their own minds, for, wherever they go, they carry about with them guilty consciences, which make them a burden to themselves. They shall be always solitary, alone *upon the mountains,* ashamed of the low circumstances to which they are reduced. They shall be always sorrowful. Those that once thought themselves as lions, now become as the *doves of the valleys*, so timid, and so dispirited, ready to *flee when none pursues* and to tremble at the shaking of a leaf. Sooner or later sin will have sorrow of one kind or other; and those that will not repent of their iniquity may justly be left to pine away in it. They shall be deprived of all their strength of body and mind (*v.* 17). They shall be deprived of all their hopes (*v.* 18).

II. They shall have no benefit from their wealth and riches, *v.* 19. They thought their wealth would be *their strong city*, that with it they could bribe enemies and buy friends, that it would be the ransom of their lives. It was no relief to them now in the day of their adversity; for *gold and silver* could not protect them from the judgments of God. Their *gold and silver* could not satisfy their hunger, nor serve to make one meal's meat for them. We could better be without mines of gold than fields of corn. Much less could they satisfy their souls, or yield them any inward comfort. Their *gold and silver shall be thrown into the streets*, because it would be an incumbrance to them and retard their flight, or because it would expose them and be a temptation to the enemy to cut their throats for their money.

III. God's temple shall stand them in no stead, *v.* 20–22. But here is the great dishonour they had done to God in profaning his sanctuary; they *made the images of their* counterfeit deities, and these they set up in God's temple, than which a greater affront could not be put upon him. And therefore, they shall be deprived of the temple, and it shall be no succour to them. Let the soldiers do as they will; let them *enter into the secret place*, into the holy of holies; its defence has departed.

Verses 23–27

I. The prisoner arraigned: *Make a chain*, in which to drag the criminal to the bar. The chain signified the siege of Jerusalem, or the slavery of those that were carried into captivity, or that they were all bound by the righteous judgment of God.

II. The indictment drawn up against the prisoner: *The land is full of bloody crimes*, full of *the judgments of blood* (so the word is). It is full of such crimes as by the law were to be punished with death, *the judgment of blood*. Idolatry, blasphemy, witchcraft, sodomy, and the like, were *bloody crimes*.

III. Judgment given upon this indictment. God will reckon with them not only for the profaning of his sanctuary, but for the perverting of justice between man and man. Since they had walked in the way of the heathen, and done worse than they, God would *bring the worst of the heathen upon them* to destroy them. Since they had filled their house with goods unjustly gotten, and used their power for oppressing the weak, God would give their houses to be possessed by strangers, and *make the pomp of the strong to cease*. Since they had set up the images of other gods in the temple, God would remove thence the tokens of the presence of their own God. Since they had followed one sin with another, God would pursue them with one judgment upon another— *mischief upon mischief*, and *rumour upon rumour* to frighten you, like the waves in a storm. They shall not have the direction in the trouble that they expect (*v.* 26): *They shall seek a vision of the prophet* to be assured of a happy issue. They did not desire a vision to reprove them for sin, nor to warn them of danger, but to promise them deliverance. They would not hear what God had to say to them by way of conviction, and therefore he has nothing to say to them by way of encouragement. *Counsel shall perish from the ancients;* the elders of the people, that should advise them what to do in this difficult

juncture, shall be at their wits' end. None of the men of might shall *find their hands*.

Chapter 8

God, having given the prophet a clear foresight of the people's miseries that were hastening on, here gives him a clear insight into the people's wickedness. Here God, in vision, brings him to Jerusalem, to show him the sins that were committed there (ver. 1–4), and there he sees, I. The image of jealousy set up at the gate of the altar, ver. 5, 6. II. The elders of Israel worshipping all manner of images in a secret chamber, ver. 7–12. III. The women weeping for Tammuz, ver. 13, 14. IV. The men worshipping the sun, ver. 15, 16. God then appeals to him whether such a provoking people should have any pity shown them, ver. 17, 18.

Verses 1–6

Ezekiel was now in Babylon; but the messages of wrath he had delivered in the foregoing chapters related to Jerusalem. Here he has a vision of what was done at Jerusalem, and this vision is continued to the close of the 11th chapter.

I. The date of this vision. The first vision he had was in *the fifth year of the captivity, in the fourth month* and *the fifth day of the month*, ch. i. 1, 2. This was just fourteen months after. Perhaps it was after he had lain 390 days on his left side, to bear the iniquity of Israel, and before he began the forty days on his right side, to bear the iniquity of Judah; for now he was sitting in the house, not lying.

II. The prophet was himself *sitting in his house* deep perhaps in contemplation. *The elders of Judah*, that were now in captivity with him, *sat before him*. Some think it was on some extraordinary occasion that they attended him, to enquire of the Lord, and *sat down* at his feet to *hear his word*. Now that the elders of Judah were in captivity they paid more respect to God's prophets, and his word in their mouth. A minister's house should be a church for all his neighbours. Paul preached in his own hired house at Rome, and God owned him there, and *no man forbad him*.

III. The divine influence that the prophet was now under: *The hand of the Lord fell there upon me*.

IV. The vision that the prophet saw, *v.* 2. He *beheld a likeness*, all *brightness* above and all *fire* below, fire and flame. This agreed with the description we had before, ch. i. 27.

V. The prophet's vision of Jerusalem. He was *lifted up between heaven and earth*, and then perhaps in a trance or ecstasy, he had the following visions, *whether in the body or out of the body*, we may suppose, he *could not tell*, any more than Paul in a like case, much less can we. Those are best prepared for communion with God and the communications of divine light that by divine grace are raised up above the earth and the things of it. He was carried in vision to Jerusalem, and to God's sanctuary there.

VI. The discoveries made to him.

1. He saw the glory of God (*v.* 4), the same appearance that he had seen, ch. i. Ezekiel has this repeated vision of the glory of God. But it seems to have a further intention here. The more glorious we see God to be, the more odious we shall see sin to be, especially idolatry.

2. There he saw the reproach of Israel—*the image of jealousy*, set *northward, at the gate of the altar*, *v.* 3, 5. This was probably an image of Baal, which Manasseh made and set in the temple (2 Kings xxi. 7, 2 Chron. xxxiii. 3), which Josiah removed, but his successors, it seems, replaced there, as probably they did the *chariots of the sun* which he found *at the entering in of the house of the Lord* (2 Kings xxiii. 11), here said to be *in the entry*. But the prophet tells us that it was *the image of jealousy*, to convince our consciences that, whatever image it was, it was in the highest degree offensive to God and *provoked him to jealousy*. And now God appeals to him whether

this was not sufficient ground for God to cast off this people. He will no more dignify and protect his sanctuary, but will give it up to reproach. *But turn thyself yet again.* Where there is one abomination it will be found that there are many more. Sins do not go alone.

Verses 7–12

A further discovery of the abominations committed at Jerusalem within the confines of the temple.

I. How this discovery is made. God, in vision, brought Ezekiel to the *door of the court*, the outer court, along the sides of which the priests' lodgings were. But, *behold, a hole in the wall* (v. 7), a spy-hole. This *hole in the wall* Ezekiel made wider, and *behold a door, v.* 8. This door he goes in by into *the treasury*, or some of the apartments of the priests, and sees *the wicked abominations that they do there, v.* 9.

II. What the discovery is. He sees a chamber set round with idolatrous pictures (v. 10). This was a sort of pantheon, a collection of all the idols together. Though the second commandment, in the letter of it, forbids any graven images, yet painted ones are as bad and as dangerous. He sees this chamber filled with idolatrous worshippers (v. 11): There were *seventy men of the elders of Israel* offering incense to these painted idols. They had *every man his censer in his hand.* They would all be their own priests. They think themselves out of God's sight: *They say, The Lord seeth us not.*

Verses 13–18

I. More abominations discovered to the prophet, v. 13–15. *Women weeping for Tammuz, v.* 14. Some think it was for Adonis, an idol among the Greeks, others for Osiris, an idol of the Egyptians, that they shed these tears. The image, they say, was made to weep, and then the worshippers wept with it. They bewailed the death of this Tammuz, and anon rejoiced in its returning to life again. These mourning women *sat at the door of the gate of the Lord's house,* and there shed their idolatrous tears, and some think, prostrating themselves also to corporeal whoredom. *Men worshipping the sun, v.* 16. And this was practised *in the inner court of the Lord's house at the door of the temple of the Lord, between the porch and the altar.* They turned *their backs towards the temple of the Lord,* and turned *their faces towards the east, and worshipped the sun,* the rising sun.

II. The inference drawn from these discoveries (v. 17): "*Hast thou seen this, O son of man!* and couldst thou have thought ever to see such things done in the temple of the Lord?" He appeals to the prophet himself. Is it an excusable thing in those that have God's oracles and ordinances *that they commit the abominations which they commit here?* Do not those deserve to suffer that thus sin? "They *return to provoke me* (they repeat the provocation, do it, and do it again), *and lo, they put the branch to their nose*"—a proverbial expression denoting perhaps their scoffing at God. Dr. Lightfoot says, *They put the branch to their wrath,* or *to his wrath,* as the Masorites read it; that is, they are still bringing more fuel to the fire of divine wrath, which they have already kindled. *Though they cry in my ears with a loud voice, yet will I not hear them;* for still their sins cry more loudly for vengeance than their prayers cry for mercy.

CHAPTER 9

I. Preparation made of instruments that were to be employed in the destruction of the city, ver. 1, 2. II. The removal of the Shechinah from the cherubim to the threshold of the temple, ver. 3. III. Orders given for the marking of a remnant to be preserved from the common destruction, ver. 3, 4. IV. The warrant signed and the execution begun, ver. 5–7. V. The prophet's intercession for the mitigation of the sentence, ver. 8–10.

VI. The report made by him that was to mark the pious remnant of what he had done in that matter, ver. 11.

Verses 1–4

I. The summons given to Jerusalem's destroyers. God's angels have received a charge now to lay that city waste, which they had long had a charge to protect and watch over. They are at hand, as destroying angels, as ministers of wrath, for *every man has his destroying weapon in his hand*, as the angel that kept the way of the tree of life with a flaming sword.

II. Their appearance, upon this summons, is recorded. Immediately *six men came* (v. 2), one for each of the principal gates of Jerusalem. The nations of which the king of Babylon's army was composed, which some reckon to be six, and the commanders of his army (of whom *six* are named as principal, Jer. xxxix. 3), may be called *the slaughter-weapons* in the hands of the angels. They came—*from the way of the higher gate, which lies towards the north* (v. 2), either because the Chaldeans came from the north (Jer. i. 14), or because the image of jealousy was set up *at the door of the inner gate that looks towards the north,* ch. viii. 3, 5.

III. The notice taken of one among the destroying angels. It should seem he was not one of the six, but *among them,* to see that mercy was mixed with judgment, v. 2. This *man was clothed with linen,* as the priests were, and he had *a writer's inkhorn* hanging at *his side,* as anciently attorneys had, which he was to make use of, as the other six were to make use of their *destroying weapons.* Here the honours of the pen exceeded those of the sword, for it is generally agreed that he represented Christ as Mediator saving those that are his from the flaming sword of divine justice. As high priest he wears fine *linen,* Rev. xix. 8. As a prophet he wears the *writer's inkhorn.* The book of life is the Lamb's book. The great things of the law and gospel which God has written to us are of his writing, and the Bible is *the revelation of Jesus Christ.* In the midst of the destroyers and the destructions that are abroad, there is a Mediator, a great high priest.

IV. The removal of the appearance of the divine glory from over the cherubim. Some think it was that display of the divine glory which the prophet now saw over the cherubim in vision. Ezekiel immediately observed that *the glory of the God of Israel had gone up from the cherub:* and what is a vision of angels if God be gone?

V. The charge given *to the man clothed in linen* to secure the pious remnant from the general desolation. We do not read that this Saviour was summoned and sent for, as the destroyers were; for he is always ready, *appearing in the presence of God for us.* This remnant that is to be saved are such as *sigh and cry,* sigh in themselves, as men in distress, cry to God in prayer. These pious few had witnessed against those abominations and had done what they could to suppress them. Orders are given to find those that are of such a pious public spirit: "*Go through the midst of the city* in quest of them, discover them, *and set a mark upon* their *foreheads.*" A work of grace in the soul is to God *a mark upon the forehead,* which he will acknowledge as his mark, and by which *he knows those that are his.* God will set a mark upon his mourners, will book their sighs and bottle their tears.

Verses 5–11

I. A command given to the destroyers to do execution according to their commission.

1. They are ordered to destroy all. This was fulfilled in the death of multitudes by famine and pestilence, especially by the sword of the Chaldeans, as far as the military execution went. But what an evil thing

is sin, then, which provokes the God of infinite mercy to such severity! *Let not your eye spare, neither have you pity* (v. 5). Those that live in sin, and hate to be reformed, will perish in sin; they might easily have prevented the ruin, and would not.

2. They are warned not to do the least hurt to those that were marked for salvation: *"Come not near any man upon whom is the mark;* do not so much as threaten or frighten any of them."* God had promised that *it should go well with his remnant* and they *should be well treated* (Jer. xv. 11); and we have reason to think that none of the mourning praying remnant fell by the sword of the Chaldeans. In the last destruction of Jerusalem by the Romans the Christians were all secured in a city called *Pella*, and none of them perished.

3. They are directed to *begin at the sanctuary* (v. 6). They must begin there because there the wickedness began which provoked God to send these judgments. God's temple is a sanctuary, a refuge and protection for penitent sinners, but not for any that *go on still in their trespasses*.

4. They are appointed to *go forth into the city*, v. 6, 7. Though *judgment begins at the house of God*, yet it shall not end there.

II. They observed their orders. *They began at the elders, the ancient men that were before the house*, either those seventy ancients who worshipped idols in their chambers (*ch.* viii. 12) or those twenty-five who *worshipped the sun between the porch and the altar*. They proceeded to the common people.

III. Here is the prophet's intercession for a mitigation of the judgment (v. 8): *While they were slaying them, and I was left, I fell upon my face*. He speaks as one that narrowly escaped the destruction, attributing it to God's goodness, not his own deserts. We must look upon it that we are spared, that we may do good in our places, may do good by our prayers.

IV. Here is God's denial of the prophet's request for a mitigation of the judgment, v. 9, 10. God was as willing to show mercy as the prophet could desire; he always is so. But here the case will not admit of it; it is such that mercy cannot be granted without wrong to justice. The sinners justify themselves with the same atheistical profane principle with which they flattered themselves in their idolatry, *ch.* viii. 12. *"The Lord has forsaken the earth*, and left it to us to do what we will in it; he will not intermeddle in the affairs of it; and, whatever wrong we do, he *sees not*."* Now how can those expect benefit by the mercy of God who thus bid defiance to his justice?

V. The writ of protection for the securing of those that mourned in Zion (v. 11): *The man clothed with linen reported the matter*, gave an account of what he had done: He had found out all that mourned in secret for the sins of the land, and cried out against them, and had marked them all in the forehead. Lord, *I have done as thou hast commanded me*.

CHAPTER 10

Again the prophet sees the vision of the glory of God as he saw it by the river Chebar. I. The scattering of the coals of fire upon the city, taken from between the cherubim, ver. 1–7. II. The removal of the glory of God from the temple, ver. 8–22.

Verses 1–7

I. The glorious appearance of divine majesty. Something of the invisible world is here made visible, faint representations of its brightness and beauty, shadows, but such as are no more to be compared with the truth and substance than a picture with the life. He is here *in the firmament above the head of the cherubim*, v. 1. It is *the firmament of his power* and of his prospect too; for thence *he beholds* all *the children of men*. He is here upon the throne. God's glory and government infinitely transcend all the

brightest ideas our minds can either form or receive. The appearance of his glory is veiled with a cloud, and yet out of that cloud darts forth a dazzling lustre; in *the house* and *inner court* there was *a cloud* and darkness, which filled them, and yet the outer court *was full of the brightness of the Lord's glory*, v. 3, 4. Thus (Hab. iii. 4) *he had rays coming out of his hand, and yet there was the hiding of his power*. Nothing is more clear than that God *is*, nothing more dark than *what* he is. God *covers himself with light*, and yet *makes darkness his pavilion*. (See also, comments on Ezekiel *ch.* i.)

II. Further orders are to be given for the destruction of Jerusalem. Here we have a command to lay the city in ashes, by *scattering coals of fire* upon it, which in the vision were fetched *from between the cherubim*. *The glory of the Lord* was lifted *up from the cherub and stood* upon *the threshold of the house*, in imitation of the courts of judgment, which they kept in the gates of their cities. He that sits on the throne calls *to the man clothed in linen* to go in between the wheels, and fill his hand with coals of fire *from between the cherubim, and scatter them over the city*. This intimates the burning of the city and temple by the Chaldeans. The fire on God's altar, where atonement was made, had been slighted. The prophet, when he first saw this vision, observed that there were *burning coals of fire*, and *lamps*, that *went up and down among the living creatures* (*ch.* i. 13); thence this fire was taken, v. 7. The *spirit of burning, the refiner's fire*, by which Christ purifies his church, is of a divine original.

Verses 8–22

A further account of the vision of God's glory which Ezekiel saw, here intended to introduce the departure of that glory from them.

I. Ezekiel sees the glory of God shining in the sanctuary, as he had seen it *by the river of Chebar*. Ezekiel here sees the operations of divine Providence in the government of the lower world. The agency of the angels in directing the affairs of this world is represented by the close communication that was between the *living creatures* and the *wheels*, the wheels being guided by them in all their motions, as the chariot is by him that drives it. But the same Spirit being both in the *living creatures* and in the *wheels* denotes that infinite wisdom which serves its own purposes by the ministration of angels and all the occurrences of this lower world. The prophet observes that this was *the same vision* with that he saw by the river of Chebar (v. 15, 22). This world is subject to changes and revolutions. The course of affairs in it is represented by *wheels* (v. 9). Their appearance is as if there were a *wheel in the midst of a wheel* (v. 10), which intimates the references of providences to each other, their dependence on each other, and the tendency of all to one common end, while their motions are intricate and seemingly contrary. There is an admirable harmony and uniformity in the various occurrences of providence (v. 13): *As for the wheels*, though they moved several ways, yet *it was cried to them, O wheel!* they were all as one, being guided by one Spirit to one end. The motions of Providence are steady and regular, and whatever the Lord pleases that he does. *The wheels turned not as they went* (v. 11), and the *living creatures went everyone straight forward*, v. 22. The Spirit of God directs all the creatures, both upper and lower, so as to make them serve the divine purpose. Events are not determined by the *wheel of fortune*, which is blind, but by the *wheels of Providence*, which are full of eyes.

II. Ezekiel sees the glory of God removing out of the sanctuary, the place where God's honour had long dwelt, and this sight is sad. The *glory of the Lord* stood over the threshold, *v. 4*. But now it *departed from off the threshold*, and it *stood over the cherubim*, those that Ezekiel now saw in vision, *v. 18*. And immediately *the cherubim lifted up their wings (v. 19)*, *mounted up from the earth*, and, *when they went out*, the wheels of this chariot were not drawn, but went *beside them*, by which it appeared that *the Spirit of the living creatures was in the wheels*. In the courts of the temple the people of Israel had dishonoured their God. The *cherubim, and the glory of God above them, stood at the door of the east gate of the Lord's house*, ready to depart and leave the house, *v. 19*. But with many stops and pauses God departs, as loth to go as if to see if there be any that will intercede with him to return. God removes by degrees from a provoking people; and, when he is ready to depart in displeasure, would return to them in mercy if they were but a repenting praying people.

Chapter 11

This chapter concludes the vision which Ezekiel saw. I. A message of wrath against those who continued still at Jerusalem, ver. 1–13. II. A message of comfort to those who were carried captives into Babylon and were there in the depth of despondency. And, as the former are assured that God has judgments in store for them, so the latter are assured that God has mercy in store for them notwithstanding their present distress, ver. 14–21. And so the glory of God removes further, ver. 22, 23. The vision disappears (ver. 24), and Ezekiel faithfully gives his hearers an account of it, ver. 25.

Verses 1–13

I. The security of the princes of Jerusalem. The prophet was brought, in vision, to the gate of the temple where these princes sat in council. *The Spirit lifted me up, and brought me to the east gate of the Lord's house, and behold twenty-five men were there.* They are charged, not with corruptions in worship, but with mal-administration in the government; two of them are named, *Pelatiah* and *Jaazaniah*, the *son of Azur*. Some tell us that Jerusalem was divided into twenty-four wards, and that these were the aldermen of those wards, with their mayor or president. *"These are the men that devise mischief;* under pretence of public safety they harden people in their sins, and take off their fear of God's judgments threatened by the prophets; they *give wicked counsel in this city*, counselling them to silence the prophets, to rebel against the king of Babylon, and to resolve upon holding out to the last extremity." They are indicted for words spoken at their council-board (*v. 3*); they said to this effect, *"It is not near;* the destruction of our city, so often threatened by the prophets." Where Satan cannot persuade men to look upon the judgment to come as a thing doubtful and uncertain, yet he gains his point by persuading them to look upon it as a thing at a distance. If the destruction is not near, they conclude, *Let us build houses;* let us count upon a continuance, for *this city is the cauldron and we are the flesh*. This seems to be a proverbial expression, signifying, "We are as safe in this city as flesh in a boiling pot; the walls of the city shall be to us as *walls of brass*, and shall receive no more damage from the besiegers about it than the *cauldron* does from *the fire under it*." Perhaps it has reference to *the flesh of the peace-offerings*, which it was so great an offence for the priests themselves to take out of *the cauldron* while it was in seething (as we find 1 Sam. ii. 13, 14), and then it intimates that they were the more secure because Jerusalem was the holy city, and they thought themselves a holy people in it, not to be meddled with.

II. The method taken to awaken them out of their security. To help them to understand, the word of God is sent to them to give them warning (*v. 4*): *Therefore prophesy against them*, and try to undeceive them; *prophesy, O son of man!* upon these dead and dry bones. *The Spirit of the Lord fell upon him*, to make him full of power and courage, and *said unto him, Speak*. Let them know that God takes notice (*v. 5*): *"I know the things which come into your minds every one of them*, what secret reasons you have for these resolutions, putting so good a face upon a matter you know to be bad." God knows not only the things that come out of our mouths, but the things that come into our minds, not only all we say, but all we think. Thus you, with your stubborn humour, have *filled the streets of Jerusalem with the slain*, *v. 6*. Now these slain are the only flesh that shall be left in this *cauldron, v. 7*. They had provoked God to forsake the city, and thought they should do well enough by their own policy and strength when he was gone; but God will make them know that there is no peace to those that have left their God. Let them know that all this is the due punishment of their sin, and *the revelation of the righteous judgment of God* against them: *You shall know that I am the Lord, v. 10* and again *v. 12*.

III. This awakening word is here immediately followed by an awakening providence, *v. 13*. *It came to pass, when I prophesied, that Pelatiah the son of Benaiah died*. It should seem, this was done in vision now, but it was an assurance that when this prophecy should be published it should be done in fact. The death of Pelatiah was an earnest of the complete accomplishment of this prophecy. Though the sudden death of Pelatiah was a confirmation of Ezekiel's prophecy, he was in deep concern about it, and laid it to heart as if he had been his relation or friend: *He fell on his face and cried with a loud voice, "Ah! Lord God, wilt thou make a full end of the remnant of Israel?* Shall the remnant which have escaped the sword die thus by the immediate hand of heaven?"

Verses 14–21

The prophet Ezekiel, having received instructions for the awakening of those that were *at ease in Zion*, is in these verses furnished with comfortable words for those that mourned in Babylon when they *remembered Zion*.

I. The pious captives were trampled upon and insulted by those who continued in Jerusalem, *v. 15*. They are *thy brethren* (says God to the prophet), they are *the men of thy kindred*. They are *the whole house of Israel*; God so accounts of them because they only have retained their integrity. They were not only of the same family and nation with Ezekiel, but of the same spirit. Those that were at ease scorned their brethren that were humbled. They cut them off from being members of their church. Because they had in compliance with the will of God surrendered themselves to the king of Babylon, they excommunicated them, and said, *"Get you far from the Lord;* we will have nothing to do with you. *Unto us is this land given in possession*, and you have forfeited your estates by surrendering to the king of Babylon, and we have thereby become entitled to them."

II. The gracious promises which God made to them. Those that hated them and cast them out said, *Let the Lord be glorified;* but *he shall appear to their joy*, Isa. lxvi. 5. God owns that his hand had gone out against them (*v. 16*): "It is true *I have cast them far off among the heathen* and *scattered them among the countries;* they look as if they were an abandoned people, but I have mercy in store for them." He will make up to them the want of the temple (*v. 16*): *I will be to them as a little sanctuary, in the countries where they shall come*. Those at Jerusalem have the temple, but without God; those in Babylon have God, though without the temple. God would in due time put an end to their afflictions, bring them out of the land of their captivity, and settle them again, them or their children, in their own land (*v*. 17). "*You shall have the title as the patriarchs had, and those that come after shall have the possession.*" Their captivity shall effectually cure them of their idolatry. God will plant good principles in them; he will make the tree good, *v*. 19. This is a gospel promise, and is made good to all those whom God designs for the heavenly Canaan. All that are sanctified have *a new spirit*; they act from new principles, walk by new rules, and aim at new ends. A new name, or a new face, will not serve without a new spirit. This is God's work, his gift by promise. Their practices shall be consonant to those principles: *That they may walk in my statutes* in their whole conversation *and keep my ordinances* in all acts of religious worship, *v*. 20. But, *as for those* that have no grace, what have they *to do with peace?* Their *heart walks after the heart of their detestable things.* They have a *heart after the heart of their idols.*

Verses 22–25

The departure of God's presence from the city and temple. When the message was committed to the prophet, and he was fully apprized of it, *then the cherubim lifted up their wings and the wheels beside them* (*v*. 22) as before, *ch*. x. 19. The glory of the Lord removed to *the mountain which is on the east side of the city* (*v*. 23); that was the *mount of Olives*. On this mountain they had set up their idols, to confront God in his temple (1 Kings xi. 7). From that mountain there was a full prospect of the city; thither God removed, to make good what he had said (Deut. xxxii. 20), *I will hide my face from them, I will see what their end shall be.* It was from this mountain that Christ *beheld the city and wept over it*, in the foresight of its last destruction by the Romans. *The glory of the Lord* removed thither, to be as it were yet within call, if *in this their day*, they would have *understood the things that belonged to their peace.* The departure of this vision from the prophet: it *went up from him* (*v*. 24); he saw it mount upwards, till it went out of sight, a confirmation to his faith that it was a heavenly vision. The same spirit that had carried him in a trance or ecstasy to Jerusalem brought him back to Chaldea; for that is the place of his service. He delivered his message very honestly: he *spoke all that*, and that only, which God *had shown* him. It is better to be in Babylon under the favour of God than in Jerusalem under his wrath and curse.

CHAPTER 12

Though the vision of God's glory had gone up from the prophet, yet his word comes to him still. I. The prophet, by removing his stuff, and quitting his lodgings, must be a sign to set forth Zedekiah's flight out of Jerusalem in the utmost confusion when the Chaldeans took the city, ver. 1–16. II. The prophet, by eating his meat with trembling, must be a sign to set forth the famine in the city during the siege, ver. 17–20. III. A message is sent from God to the people, to assure them that all these predictions should have their accomplishment very shortly, ver. 21–28.

Verses 1–16

Perhaps Ezekiel reflected upon the vision he had had of the glory of God, that often he was wishing it might come down to him again, but we do not find that he ever saw it any more, and yet *the word of the Lord comes to* him. We may keep up our communion with God without raptures and ecstasies. In these verses the prophet is directed,

I. By what signs and actions to express the approaching captivity of Zedekiah king of Judah; that was the thing to be foretold, and it is foretold to those that are already in captivity, because as long as Zedekiah was upon the throne they flattered themselves with hopes that he would rescue them shortly. It was therefore necessary to convince them that Zedekiah,

instead of being their deliverer, should very shortly be their fellow-sufferer. To prepare them he must first give them a sign, must speak to their eyes first and then to their ears. He must speak to them by signs, as deaf people are taught. He must furnish himself with all necessaries *for removing* (*v*. 3), provide for a journey clothes and money; he must *remove from one place to another*, as one unsettled and forced to shift; this he must do *by day, in the sight* of the people; he must bring out all his household goods, to be packed up and sent away (*v*. 4); and, because all the doors and gates were either locked up or guarded he must *dig through the wall*, and convey his goods away clandestinely through that breach in the wall, *v*. 5. He must carry his goods away himself upon his own shoulders, *in the twilight*, that he might not be discovered; must himself steal away *at evening in their sight*, with fear and trembling, and must go *as those that go forth into captivity* (*v*. 4); he must *cover* his *face* (*v*. 6) in token of very great sorrow and must go away as a poor broken man, who quits his country. Thus Ezekiel must be himself a sign to them. God says (*v*. 3) "*It may be they will consider*, and will by it be taken off from their vain confidences, *though they be a rebellious house*." Ezekiel's ready obedience to the orders God gave him (*v*. 7): *I did so as I was commanded.*

II. He is directed by what words to explain those signs and actions. The prophet must do a strange uncouth thing, that they might enquire what it meant. The prophet is to tell them (*v*. 10), *This burden concerns the prince in Jerusalem.* "But tell them," says God, "that in what thou hast done they may read the doom of their friends at Jerusalem. *Say, I am your sign*," *v*. 11. The people shall be led away into captivity (*v*. 11): As *I have done, so shall it be done unto them;* they shall be forced away from their own houses, no more to return to them. The prince shall in vain attempt to make his escape; for he also shall go into captivity. Ezekiel here foretells it to those who promised themselves relief through him. He shall himself carry away his own goods. God can turn a prince into a porter. He that was wont to have the regalia carried before him, shall now himself carry his goods on his back and steal away out of the city in the twilight. All the avenues to the palace being carefully watched by the enemy, *they shall dig through the wall to carry out thereby.* He shall attempt to escape in a disguise, with a mask which *shall cover his face*, so that he shall *not see the ground with his eyes.* He shall be made a prisoner and carried captive into Babylon (*v*. 13). Jeremiah had said that king Zedekiah should *see the king of Babylon* and that he should *go to Babylon;* Ezekiel says, He shall be *brought to Babylon*, yet he *shall not see it*, though *he shall die there.* One said, He shall *see the king of Babylon*, the other said, He shall *not see Babylon;* and yet both proved true: he did *see the king of Babylon* at Riblah, where he passed sentence upon him for his rebellion, but there he had his eyes put out, so that he did *not see Babylon* when he was brought thither. Little joy could they have in seeing him when he could not see them. All his guards should be dispersed (*v*. 14): *I will scatter all that are about him to help him*, so that he shall be left helpless; *and disperse them in the countries* (*v*. 15). Yet of Zedekiah's scattered troops some shall escape (*v*. 16): *That they may declare all their abominations among the heathen whither they come;* and then they will acknowledge the justice of God and will make confession of their sins; and by this it shall appear that they were spared in mercy.

Verses 17–20

Here again the prophet is made a sign to them of the desolations that were coming on Judah and

Jerusalem. He must himself eat and drink in care and fear, especially when he was in company, *v.* 17, 18, that he might express the calamitous condition of those that should be in Jerusalem during the siege. He must tell them that *the inhabitants of Jerusalem* should in like manner eat and drink with care and fear, *v.* 19, 20, either because they are afraid it will not hold out, or because they are continually expecting the alarms of the enemy. The decay of virtue in a nation brings on a decay of everything else; and when neighbours devour one another it is just with God to bring enemies upon them to devour them all.

Verses 21–28

Various methods had been used to awaken this secure and careless people, that they might be stirred up, by repentance and reformation. The prophecies of their ruin were confirmed by visions, and illustrated by signs, but here we are told how they evaded the conviction, by telling themselves, and one another, that though these judgments threatened should come at last yet they would not come for a long time.

I. One saying they had, which had become proverbial *in the land of Israel, v.* 22. They said, *"The days are prolonged;* because the destruction has not come yet it will never come; we will never trust a prophet again, for we have been more frightened than hurt." And another saying was, *"The vision is for* a great while *to come*; it refers to events at a vast distance, so that we need not trouble our heads about them" (*v.* 27). That forbearance of God which should have led them to repentance hardened them in sin.

II. They are assured that they do but deceive themselves: *Tell them, therefore, The days are at hand* (*v.* 23), and again, *There shall none of my words be prolonged any more, v.* 28. God will certainly silence the lying proverbs, and the lying prophecies, with which they buoyed up their vain hopes: *There shall be no more any vain vision, v.* 24. God will certainly, and very shortly, accomplish every word that he has spoken. With what majesty does he say it (*v.* 25): I *am the* LORD! *I am Jehovah!* Those that *see the visions of the Almighty* do not see *vain visions*; God *confirms the word of his servants* by performing it. *The days are at hand* when you shall see *the effect of every vision, v.* 23.

CHAPTER 13

God's faithful prophets are nowhere so sharp upon any sort of sinners as upon the false prophets, not because they were the most spiteful enemies to them, but because they put the highest affront upon God and did the greatest mischief to his people. The prophet here shows the sin and punishment, I. Of the false prophets, ver. 1–16. II. Of the false prophetesses, ver. 17–23. Both agreed to sooth men in their sins, and to flatter them with hopes that they should yet have peace; but the prophets shall be proved liars, their prophecies shams, and the expectations of the people illusions.

Verses 1–9

The false prophets were some of them at Jerusalem (Jer. xxiii. 14): *I have seen in the prophets at Jerusalem a horrible thing;* some of them among the captives in Babylon, for to them Jeremiah writes (Jer. xxix. 8), *Let not your diviners, that be in the midst of you, deceive you.* Ezekiel must prophesy against them, in hopes that the people might be cautioned not to hearken unto them.

Ezekiel had express orders to *prophesy against the prophets of Israel;* so they called themselves, as if none but they had been worthy of the name of Israel's prophets, who were indeed Israel's deceivers. Ezekiel is directed

I. To discover their sin to them. They are here called *foolish prophets* (*v.* 3). They thrust themselves into the prophetic office, without warrant from him who is *the Lord God* of the holy prophets, which was a foolish thing; for how could they expect that God should own them in a work to which he never called them? They are *prophets out of their own hearts* (so the margin reads it, *v.* 2), prophets of their own making, *v.* 6. They put a reproach upon divine revelation, lessen its credit, and weaken its credibility. When these pretenders are found to be deceivers, atheists and infidels will thence infer, They are all so. *The Lord has not sent them. They followed their own spirit* (*v.* 3); they delivered that as a message from God which was the product either of their subtle invention, or of their own crazed and heated imagination. For *they have seen nothing*, they have not really had any heavenly vision. *You have spoken vanity and seen lies;* what they saw and what they said was all alike, a mere sham. Again (*v.* 9), They *see vanity and divine lies*; they pretended to have had visions, as the true prophets had, but either it was the creature of their own fancy that was *seeing vanity*, or it was a fiction of their own politics, and they knew they had none, and then they *saw lies, and divined lies.* They are like *the foxes in the deserts*, seeming to be in a great hurry, but it was to get away and shift for their own safety, not to do any good. They should have made intercession to turn away the wrath of God; but they were not praying prophets. They should have made it their business by preaching and advice to bring people to repentance and reformation, and so have *made up the hedge*, but they contrived how to please people, not how to profit them.

II. He is directed to declare the judgments of God against them for these sins, from which their pretending to the character of prophets would not exempt them. They are sentenced to be excluded from all the privileges of the commonwealth of Israel, for they are adjudged to have forfeited them all (*v.* 9). *They shall not be in the secret of my people;* their folly shall be so clearly manifested that they shall never be consulted, nor their advice asked; they shall not be in the assembly of God's people for religious worship. They shall die in their captivity, and shall die childless.

Verses 10–16

I. How the people are deceived by the false prophets. Those flatterers seduce them, saying, *Peace, and there was no peace, v.* 10. They told the idolaters and other sinners that there was neither harm nor danger in the way they were in. Thus they *seduced God's people.* Now this is compared to the building of a slight rotten wall, or, according to our Saviour's similitude (Matt. vii. 26), the *building of a house upon the sand*, which seems to be a shelter and protection for a while, but will fall when a storm comes. One false prophet built the wall, set up the notion that God was not at all displeased with Jerusalem, but that the city should be victorious over the powers that now threatened it. This notion was very pleasing, and he that started it made himself very acceptable by it. They made the matter look yet more plausible and promising; they *daubed the wall*, which the first had built, but it was with *untempered mortar.* And the wall thus built, when it comes to any stress, much more to any distress, will bulge and totter, and come down by degrees.

II. How they will be soon undeceived by the judgment of God, which, we are sure, is according to truth. The descent which the Chaldean army shall make upon Judah, and the siege which they shall lay to Jerusalem, will be as *an overflowing shower.* The fury of Nebuchadnezzar and his princes, who highly resented Zedekiah's treachery, made the invasion very formidable, but that was nothing in comparison with God's displeasure. This storm shall overturn the wall: *it shall fall*, and the wind shall *rend it* (v. 11), the *hailstones shall consume it* (v. 13); I will *break it down* (v. 14) and *bring it to the ground*, so that the *foundation thereof shall be discovered*; it will appear how false, how rotten it was, to the prophetical reproach of the builders. Men's anger cannot shake that which God has built, but God's anger will overthrow that which men have built in opposition to him. The builders of the wall, and those that daubed it, will themselves be buried in the ruins of it: *It shall fall, and you shall* be *consumed in the midst thereof*, v. 14. Both the deceivers and the deceived, when they thus perish together, will justly be ridiculed (v. 12): *When the wall has fallen shall it not be said unto you*, by those that gave credit to the true prophets, and feared the word of the Lord, "Now *where is the daubing wherewith you have daubed the wall?* What has become of all the fair promises wherewith you flattered and all the assurances you gave that the troubles of the nation should soon be at an end?" They will say unto you (v. 15), "*The wall is no more, neither he that daubed it;* your hopes have vanished, and those that supported them, even *the prophets of Israel*," v. 16.

Verses 17–23

As God has promised that when he pours out his Spirit upon his people both *their sons and their daughters shall prophesy*, so the devil, when he acts as a spirit of lies and falsehood, is so in the mouth not only of false prophets, but of false prophetesses too. *Son of man, set thy face against the daughters of thy people*, v. 17. The women pretend to a spirit of prophecy, and are in the same song with the men. They *prophesy out of their own heart* too; they say what comes uppermost. The prophet must *set his face against them*.

I. The sin of these false prophetesses is described. They told deliberate lies to those who consulted them, and came to them to be advised, and to be told their fortune: You do mischief *by your lying to my people that hear your lies* (v. 19). *You pollute my name among my people*, and make use of that for the patronising of your lies. Yet this they did *for handfuls of barley and pieces of bread.* They would sell you a false prophecy that should please you for the beggar's dole, a *piece of bread* or *a handful of barley*; and yet that was more than it was worth. They kept people in awe, and terrified them with their pretensions: *You hunt the souls of my people* (v. 18), *hunt them to make them flee* (v. 20). Thus they beguiled unstable souls that had a concern about salvation. They discouraged those that were honest and good, and encouraged those that were wicked and profane, v. 19. "You have promised sinners life in their sinful ways, have told them that they shall have peace though they go on, by which their *hands have been strengthened* and their hearts hardened." They mimicked the true prophets, by giving signs illustrating their false predictions (as Hananiah did, Jer. xxviii. 10), signs agreeable to their sex; they *sewed little pillows to the people's arm-holes*, to signify that they might repose themselves, and not be disquieted with apprehensions of trouble. And they *made kerchiefs upon the head of every stature*, of persons of every age, young and old, distinguishable by their stature, v. 18. These kerchiefs were badges of liberty or triumph, intimating that they should be delivered from the Chaldeans. Some think these were superstitious rites which they used with those to whom they delivered their divinations, preparing them by putting enchanted pillows under their arms and handkerchiefs on their heads.

II. God declares himself against the methods they took to delude and deceive, v. 20. They shall be confounded in their attempts (v. 23). God's people shall be delivered out of their hands. The *pillows shall be torn from their arms*, and the *kerchiefs from their heads*; the fallacies shall be discovered, their frauds detected, and the people of God shall no more be in their hand, to be hunted as they had been.

CHAPTER 14

I. The elders of Israel come to hear the word, and enquire of the prophet, but, because they are not duly qualified, they meet with a rebuke instead of acceptance (ver. 1–5) and are called upon to repent of their sins and reform their lives, ver. 6–11. II. Noah, Daniel, and Job, are supposed to pray for this people, and yet their prayers shall not be answered, ver. 12–21. And yet it is promised, in the close, that a remnant shall escape, ver. 22, 23.

Verses 1–11

I. The address which some of the elders of Israel made to the prophet, as an oracle, to enquire of the Lord by him. They *came, and sat before him*, v. 1. By the severe answer given them one would suspect they had a design to ensnare the prophet.

II. God gives him their real character (v. 3); they were idolaters, and did only consult Ezekiel as they would any oracle of a pretended deity, to gratify their curiosity, and therefore God says: "*Should I be enquired of at all by them? They have set up their idols in their heart.*" It may be understood of spiritual idolatry; those whose affections are placed upon the wealth of the world and the pleasures of sense, whose god is their money, *whose god is their belly*, they *set up their idols in their heart*. It intimates that they are resolved to go on in sin, whatever comes of it. *I have loved strangers, and after them I will go;* that is the language of their hearts. Can those expect an answer of peace from God who thus continue their acts of hostility against him?

III. The answer which God orders Ezekiel to give them, v. 4. Let them know that it is a rule for *every man of the house of Israel*, that if he continue in love and league with his idols, and come to enquire of God, God will answer him according to his real iniquity, not according to his pretended piety. *I the Lord*, who *speak and it is done, I will answer him that cometh, according to the multitude of his idols.* He will give them up *to their own hearts' lust*, and leave them to themselves to be as bad as they have a mind to be, till they *have filled up the measure of their iniquity*. If God discover them, if he bind them over to his judgment, it is all by *their own hearts. O Israel!* thou hast destroyed thyself.

IV. This answer was for all *the house of Israel*, v. 7, 8. It concerns not only everyone of the house of Israel (as before, v. 4), but *the stranger that sojourns in Israel*. Even proselytes shall not be countenanced if they be not sincere. Hypocrites *separate themselves from* God by their fellowship with idols; they cut themselves off from their relation to God. He shall have his answer, not by the words of the prophet, but by the judgments of God. *And I will set my face against that man.* God will make him an example; for *thus shall it be done to the man that separates himself from* God, and yet pretends to *enquire concerning him.* The hypocrite thought to pass for one of God's people, but God *will cut him off from the midst of his people.*

V. The doom of those pretenders to prophecy who give countenance to these pretenders to piety, v. 9, 10. These hypocritical enquirers, though Ezekiel will not give them a comfortable answer, yet hope to meet with some other prophets that will; and if they do, as perhaps they may, let them know that God permits those lying prophets to deceive them in punishment. *I will stretch out my hand upon him and will destroy him.*

VI. The counsel that is given them for the preventing of this fearful doom (v. 6): "*Therefore repent, and* turn yourselves from your idols. Turn from them as from abominations that you are sick of; and then you will be welcome to enquire of the Lord."

VII. The pretending prophets, and the pretending saints, shall perish together, that, some being made examples, the body of the people may be reformed, *that the house of Israel may go no more astray from me, v.* 11.

Verses 12–23

I. National sins bring national judgments. *When the land sins against me,* when vice and wickedness become epidemical, when gross impieties and immoralities universally prevail, *then I will stretch forth my hand upon it,* for the punishment of it.

II. God has a variety of judgments wherewith to punish sinful nations. *Four sore judgments* are here specified: 1. *Famine, v.* 13. The denying and withholding of common mercies is itself judgment enough; he *cuts off man and beast* by cutting off the provisions which nature makes for both in the annual products of the earth. 2. Hurtful *beasts, noisome* and noxious. God can make these *to pass through the land (v.* 15), so *that no man may pass through because of the beasts.* When men revolt from their allegiance to God it is just that the inferior creatures should rise up in arms against man, Lev. xxvi. 22. 3. War. God often chastises sinful nations by bringing a sword upon them (*v.* 17): He says, *Sword, go through the land.* 4. *Pestilence (v.* 19), a dreadful disease, which has sometimes depopulated cities.

III. When God's professing people rebel against him, they may justly expect a complication of judgments to fall upon them.

IV. There commonly are some few very good men, even in those places that by sin are ripened for ruin. Even in a land that has *trespassed grievously,* there may be *three* such *men* as *Noah, Daniel,* and *Job.* Daniel was carried away into captivity, Dan. i. 6. Some of the better sort of people in Jerusalem might perhaps think that, if Daniel (of whose fame in the king of Babylon's court they had heard much) had but continued in Jerusalem, it would have been spared for his sake. "No," says God, "though you had him, who was as eminently good in bad times and places as Noah in the old world and Job in the land of Uz, yet a reprieve should not be obtained."

V. God often spares very wicked places for the sake of a few godly people in them. This is implied here as the expectation of Jerusalem's friends: "Surely God will stay his controversy with us; for are there not some among us that are emptying the measure of national guilt by their prayers, as others are filling it by their sins? And, rather than God will *destroy the righteous with the wicked,* he will preserve *the wicked with the righteous.*"

VI. Such men as Noah, Daniel, and Job, will prevail, if any can, to turn away the wrath of God from a sinful people. Noah kept his integrity, and, for his sake, his family, though one of them was wicked (Ham), was saved in the ark. Job was mighty in prayer for his children, for his friends; and God turned his captivity when he prayed. Daniel, their neighbour, and *companion in tribulation,* being a man of great humility, instant and constant in prayer, had as good an interest in heaven as Noah or Job. Why may not God raise up as great and good men now as he did formerly, and do as much for them?

VII. When the sin of a people has come to its height, and the decree has gone forth for their ruin, the piety and prayers of the best men shall not prevail to finish the controversy. *Though these three men were in* Jerusalem at this time, yet they should *deliver neither son nor daughter.*

VIII. Though pious praying men may not prevail to deliver others, yet *they shall deliver their own*

souls by their righteousness, so that, though they may suffer in the common calamity, yet it is not to them what it is to the wicked; it is sanctified, and does them good. If their bodies be not *delivered,* yet *their souls* are.

IX. Even when God makes the greatest desolations by his judgments, he reserves some to be monuments of his mercy, *v.* 22, 23. In Jerusalem itself, though marked for utter ruin, yet *there shall be left a remnant,* who shall be carried into captivity, both *sons and daughters,* the seed of a new generation. The young ones *shall be brought forth* by the victorious enemy, and *behold they shall come forth to you* that are in captivity, and shall come the more willingly to Babylon because so many of their friends have gone thither before them. And, when they come, *you shall see their ways and their doings;* you shall hear them make a free confession of sins and a humble profession of repentance with promises of reformation; and you shall see instances of their reformation, shall see what good their affliction has done them. *They shall comfort you when you see their ways.* "*You shall be comforted concerning all the evil that I have brought upon Jerusalem* when you better understand. *You shall know that I have not done without cause,* not without a just provocation, and yet not without a gracious design, *all that I have done in it.*"

Chapter 15

Ezekiel has again and again, in God's name, foretold the utter ruin of Jerusalem; but, it should seem, he finds it hard to reconcile himself to it. Here, in this short chapter, God shows him that it was as requisite Jerusalem should be destroyed as that the dead and withered branches of a vine should be cut off and thrown into the fire. I. The similitude is very elegant (ver. 1–5), but, II. The explanation of the similitude is very dreadful, ver. 6–8.

Verses 1–8

The prophet, we may suppose, was thinking what a glorious city Jerusalem was, and therefore what a pity it was that it should be destroyed. God here returns an answer to them by comparing Jerusalem to a vine. It is true, if a vine be fruitful, it is a most valuable tree. So Jerusalem was *planted a choice and noble vine, wholly a right seed* (Jer. ii. 21); and, if it had brought forth fruit suitable to its character as a holy city, it would have been the glory both of God and Israel. But, if it be not fruitful, it is as worthless as thorns and briers are. *What is the vine more than any tree if the branch of it be as the trees of the forest;* that is, if it bear no fruit, as forest-trees seldom do, being designed for timber-trees, not fruit-trees? Now there are some fruit-trees which, if they do not bear, are nevertheless of good use, as the wood of them may be made to turn to a good account; but the vine is not of this sort: if that do not answer its end as a fruit-tree, it is worth nothing as a timber-tree.

I. How this similitude is expressed here. The wild vine or the empty vine (which Israel is compared to, Hos. x. 1), is good for nothing. The *wood* of it is not *taken to do any work;* one cannot so much as make *a pin of it to hang a vessel upon, v.* 3. Among the plants, the roots of some, the seed or fruits of others, the leaves of others, and of some the stalks, are most serviceable to us; so, among trees, some are strong and not fruitful, as the oaks and cedars; others are weak but very fruitful, as the vine. The unfruitful tree *is not meet for any work, it is cast into the fire, v.* 4. When it is good for nothing else it is useful this way.

II. This similitude is applied to Jerusalem. 1. That holy city had become unprofitable and good for nothing. It had been as *the vine-tree among the trees of the* vineyard, abounding in the fruits of righteousness to the glory of God. When the pure worship of

God was kept up, many a joyful vintage was gathered from it; and, while it continued so, God made a hedge about it, it was his *pleasant plant* (Isa. v. 7); he *watered it every moment* and *kept it night and day* (Isa. xxvii. 3); but it had now become *the degenerate plant of a strange vine, a vine-tree among the trees of the forest*, which, being wild, *brings forth wild grapes* (Isa. v. 4), nauseous and noxious (Deut. xxxii. 32), *their grapes are grapes of gall, and their clusters are bitter*. It is explained (v. 8): "*They have trespassed a trespass*, treacherously prevaricated with God." The Jewish nation, being famous as a holy people, when they became wicked, were thenceforth *good for nothing*; they lost all their usefulness, and became the most base and despicable people under the sun, *trodden under foot of the Gentiles*. Those who are not fruitful to the glory of God's grace will be fuel to the fire of his wrath (v. 6). *The inhabitants of Jerusalem* were like a vinebranch, rotten and awkward; and therefore (v. 7), *I will set my face against them*, as they set their faces against God, to defeat all his designs. *I will make the land* quite *desolate*, and therefore, when they *go out from one fire, another fire shall devour them* (v. 7); they shall go from misery in their own country to misery in Babylon.

CHAPTER 16

God shows the prophet, and orders him to show the people, that he did but punish them as their sins deserved. In the foregoing chapter he had compared Jerusalem to an unfruitful vine; in this chapter he compafes it to an adulteress, that, in justice, ought to be abandoned. I. The despicable and deplorable beginnings of that church and nation, ver. 3–5. II. The many honours and favours God had bestowed upon them, ver. 6–14. III. Their ungrateful departures from him to the services of idols, ver. 15–34. IV. A threatening of judgments, which God would bring upon them for this sin, ver. 35–43. V. A comparison with Sodom and Samaria, ver. 44–59. VI. A promise of mercy which God would show to a penitent remnant, ver. 60–68.

Verses 1–5

Ezekiel is now among the captives in Babylon; but, as Jeremiah at Jerusalem wrote for the use of the captives (*ch. xxix*), so Ezekiel wrote for the use of Jerusalem. Jeremiah wrote to the captives for their consolation, Ezekiel is directed to write to the inhabitants of Jerusalem for their conviction and humiliation.

I. This is his commission (v. 2): "*Cause Jerusalem to know her abominations* (that is, her sins); set them in order before her." We should know our sins, that we may confess them.

II. That Jerusalem may be made *to know her abominations*, it was requisite that she should be put in mind of the great things God had done for her. She is in these verses made to know from what poor beginnings God raised her, and how unworthy she was of his favour. Jerusalem is here put for the Jewish church and nation, which is here compared to an outcast child, base-born and abandoned. 1. The extraction of the Jewish nation was mean: "*Thy birth is of the land of Canaan* (v. 3); thou hadst from the very first the spirit and disposition of a Canaanite." The patriarchs dwelt in Canaan, and they were there but *strangers and sojourners*, had not one foot of ground of their own but a buryingplace. Abraham and Sarah were indeed their *father and mother*, but they were only inmates with the Amorites and Hittites, who, having the dominion, seemed to be as parents to the seed of Abraham (Gen. xxiii. 4, 8); the dependence they had upon their neighbours the Canaanites, and the fear they were in of them, Gen. xiii. 7; xxxiv. 30. The patriarchs, at their first coming to Canaan, *went from one nation to another* (Ps. cv. 13), as tenants from one farm to another. Their fathers had *served other gods in Ur of the Chaldees* (Joshua xxiv. 2); even in Jacob's family there were *strange gods*, Gen. xxxv. 2. The

children of Israel, when they began to increase into a people were thrown out from the country intended for them; a famine drove them thence. Egypt was *the open field* into which they were cast; there they were ruled with rigour, and their lives embittered. The nation of Israel was doomed to destruction, like an infant newborn, not clothed, *not swaddled*, because not *pitied*, v. 4, 5. This infant is said to be *cast out, to the loathing of her person*. The Israelites were an abomination to the Egyptians, as we find Gen. xliii. 32; xlvi. 34. Moses tells them (v. 24), *You have been rebellious against the Lord from the day that I knew you*. They were not *suppled*, nor *washed*, nor *swaddled*; they were not at all tractable or manageable, nor cast into any good shape. God took them to be his people, not because he saw anything in them inviting or promising, but *so it seemed good in his sight*.

Verses 6–14

An account of the great things which God did for the Jewish nation in raising them up by degrees to be very considerable. 1. God saved them from the ruin they were upon the brink of in Egypt (v. 6). Those shall live to whom God commands life. God looked upon the world of mankind, designing it *life, and that more abundantly*. By converting grace, he says to the soul, *Live*. 2. He looked upon them with kindness and a tender affection, *set his love upon them*, though there was nothing lovely in them; but *I looked upon thee*, and, *behold, thy time was the time of love, v. 8*. It was *the kindness and love of God our Saviour* that sent Christ to redeem us, that sends the Spirit to sanctify us, that brought us out of a state of nature into a state of grace. 3. He took them under his protection. God took them into his care, as an *eagle bears her young ones upon her wings*, Deut. xxxii. 11, 12. When God sent Moses to Egypt to deliver them, then he *spread his skirt over them*. 4. He cleared them from the reproachful character which their bondage in Egypt laid them under (v. 9). All the disgrace of their slavery was rolled away when they were brought, *with a high hand and a stretched-out arm, into the glorious liberty of the children of God*. 5. He multiplied them and built them up into a people. This is here mentioned (v. 7) before his *spreading his skirt over them*, because their numbers increased exceedingly while they were yet bond-slaves in Egypt. 6. He admitted them into covenant with himself. This was done at Mount Sinai; "when the covenant between God and Israel was sealed and ratified then *thou becamest mine*." God called them his people, and himself the God of Israel. 7. He beautified and adorned them. This maid cannot forget her ornaments, and she is gratified with abundance of them, v. 10–13. We need not be particular in the application of these. Her wardrobe was well furnished with rich apparel. It may be taken figuratively for all those blessings of heaven which adorned both their church and state. In a little time they came to *excellent ornaments, v. 7*. The laws and ordinances which God gave them were to them as *ornaments of grace to the head and chains about the neck*, Prov. i. 9. God's sanctuary, which he set up among them, was *a beautiful crown upon their head*; it was the *beauty of holiness*. 8. He fed them with abundance, with plenty, with dainty. In Canaan they did eat bread to the full, the finest of the wheat, Deut. xxxii. 13, 14. 9. He gave them great reputation among their neighbours, and made them considerable. *Thou didst prosper into a kingdom* (v. 13), and, *Thy renown went forth among the heathen for thy beauty, v. 14*. Solomon's wisdom, and Solomon's temple, were very much *the renown* of that nation; and, if we put all the privileges of the Jewish church and kingdom together, we must own that it was the most accomplished beauty of all the nations of the earth.

We may apply this spiritually. Sanctified souls are truly beautiful; they are so in God's sight and they themselves may take the comfort of it.

Verses 15–34

An account of the great wickedness of the people of Israel, notwithstanding the great favours that God had conferred upon them. This wickedness of theirs is here represented by the lewd and scandalous conversation of that beautiful maid which was rescued from ruin. Their idolatry was the great provoking sin that they were guilty of; it began in the latter end of Solomon's time, and thenceforward continued till the captivity; and, though it now and then met with some check from the reforming kings, yet it was never totally suppressed.

This is that which is here represented under the similitude of whoredom and adultery, 1. Because it is the violation of a marriage-covenant with God. 2. Because it is the corrupting and defiling of the mind, and the enslaving of the spiritual part of the man. 3. Because it debauches the conscience.

I. The causes of this sin. 1. They grew proud (v. 15): "*Thou trustedst to thy beauty*, and didst expect that that should make thee an interest, and didst *play the harlot because of thy renown*." Solomon admitted idolatry, to gratify his wives and their relations. 2. They forgot their beginning (v. 22). 3. They were weak in understanding and in resolution (v. 30). The strength of men's lusts is an evidence of the weakness of their hearts.

II. The particulars of it. 1. They worshipped all the idols that came in their way, all that they were ever courted to the worship of; they were at the beck of all their neighbours (v. 15). 2. They adorned their idol-temples, and groves, and high places, with the fine rich clothing that God had given them (v. 16, 18). 3. They made images for worship of the jewels which God had given them (v. 17): *The jewels of my gold and my silver which I had given thee*. It is God that gives us our gold and silver. It is his still, so that we ought to serve and honour him with it, and are accountable to him for the disposal of it. Every penny has God's image upon it as well as Cæsar's. 4. They served their idols with the good things which God gave them (v. 18): "*Thou hast set my oil and my incense before them*, upon their altars; *my meat, and fine flour, and oil*, and that honey which Canaan flowed with, and *wherewith I fed thee*, thou hast regaled their hungry priests with, hast made an offering of it to them for *a sweet savour*. He that knows all things knows it." 5. They had sacrificed their children to their idols. *Thou hast taken thy sons and thy daughters*, and not only made them to pass through the fire, in token of their being dedicated to Moloch, but thou hast *sacrificed them to be devoured*, v. 20. It was an irreparable wrong to God himself. They are *my children* (v. 21), the *sons and daughters which thou hast borne unto me*, v. 20. He is the *Father of spirits*, and rational souls are in a particular manner his; and therefore the taking away of life, human life, unjustly, is a high affront to the *God of life*. How absurd was this, that the children which were born to God should be *sacrificed to devils*! The children of parents that are members of the visible church are to be looked upon as born unto God, and his children; as such, we are to love them, and pray for them, bring them up for him, and, if he calls for them, cheerfully part with them to him; for *may he not do what he will with his own*? 6. They built temples in honour of their idols. "*After all thy wickedness* of this kind committed in private, thou hast at length arrived at such a pitch of impudence as to proclaim it; now thou canst not blush," v. 23–25. *Thou hast built there an eminent place*, a *brothel-house* (so the margin reads it), and such their

idol temples were. *Thou hast made thy beauty to be abhorred*. The Jewish nation, by leaving their own God, and doting on the gods of the nations round about them, had made themselves despicable in the eyes even of their heathen neighbours.

III. The aggravations of this sin.

1. They were fond of the idols of those nations which had been their oppressors and persecutors. As, (1) The Egyptians, (2) The Assyrians.

2. They had been under the rebukes of Providence, and yet persisted (v. 27): *I have stretched out my hand over thee*, to threaten and frighten thee. So God did before he *laid his hand upon them* to destroy them; and that is his method, to try to bring men to repentance first by less judgments.

3. They were insatiable in their spiritual whoredom: Thou *couldst not be satisfied*, v. 28 and again v. 29.

4. They were at great expense with their idolatry, and laid out a great deal of wealth in images and altars, and hiring priests to attend upon them from other countries. This is much insisted on, v. 31–34.

And now is not Jerusalem in all this made to know her abominations? Here we see with wonder and horror what the corrupt nature of men is when God leaves them to themselves, yea, though they have the greatest advantages to be better and do better.

Verses 35–43

This notorious adulteress, being found guilty, has sentence passed upon her. It is ushered in with solemnity, v. 53. An apostate church is a harlot. Jerusalem is so if she become idolatrous. *How has the faithful city become a harlot!*

I. The crime is stated and the articles of the charge are summed up (v. 36 and 43). 1. The violation of the first two commandments of the first table by idolatry, her *whoredoms with her lovers*, that is, with *all the idols of her abominations*. 2. The violation of the first two commandments of the second table by the murder of their own innocent infants: *The blood of thy children which thou didst give unto them*. Their base ingratitude is another aggravation of their sins: "*Thou hast not remembered the days of thy youth*, and the kindness that was done thee then, when otherwise thou wouldst have perished," v. 43. "*Thou hast fretted me in all these things*, not only angered me, but grieved me."

II. The sentence is passed in general: *I will judge thee as women that break wedlock and shed blood are judged* (v. 38), and those two crimes were punished with an ignominious death. This criminal must be exposed to public shame, v. 37. The calamities of Jerusalem will be the grief of her friends and the joy of her foes. Those whom they have suffered to strip them of their virtue shall see them stripped. And *they shall stone thee with stones*, and *thrust thee through with their swords*. When the walls of Jerusalem were battered down with stones shot against them, and the inhabitants of Jerusalem were put to the sword, then this sentence was executed in the letter of it. *They shall throw down thy eminent place*, and (v. 41) they *shall burn thy houses*, as the habitations of bad women are destroyed. It was the complaint, in the best reigns of the kings of Judah, that *the high places were not taken away*; but now the army of the Chaldeans shall break them down. The captivity in Babylon made the people of Israel to cease for ever *from playing the harlot*; it effectually cured them of their inclination to idolatry. Then (v. 42) *my jealousy shall depart. I will be quiet, and no more angry*.

Verses 44–59

Now God by the prophet shows Jerusalem,

I. That she was as bad as *her mother*, that is, as the accursed Canaanites that were the possessors of this land before her. *As is the mother, so is her daughter*, v. 44. The character of the mother was that she *loathed her husband and her children*, she had all the marks of an adulteress; and that is the character of the daughter. When God brought Israel into Canaan he particularly warned them not to do according to the abominations of *the men of that land, who went before them* (for which *it had spewed them out*, Lev. xviii. 27, 28), but they learned their way, and trod in their steps. It might truly be said that *their mother* was a *Hittite* and their *father* an *Amorite* (v. 45), for they resembled them more than Abraham and Sarah.

II. That she was worse than her sisters Sodom and Samaria, that were adulteresses too, that were weary of the gods of their fathers, and were for introducing new gods, and new fashions in religion.

1. Jerusalem's sisters, v. 45. Samaria is called the *elder* sister, or rather the *greater*, because it was much larger, and more nearly allied to Israel. This city of Samaria, and its villages, had been *lately* destroyed for their *spiritual whoredom*. Sodom, and the adjacent towns and villages was her *less sister*, less than Jerusalem, less than Samaria, and these were of old destroyed for their corporeal whoredom, Jude 7.

2. Jerusalem's sins resembled her sisters', particularly Sodom's (v. 49): *This was the iniquity of Sodom, pride, fulness of bread, and abundance of idleness*. Their *going after strange flesh*, which was Sodom's most flagrant wickedness, is not mentioned, but those sins which opened the door to these more enormous crimes by their unnatural filthiness. Pride was the first sin that turned angels into devils, and the *garden of the Lord* into a *hell upon earth*. Gluttony is here called *fulness of bread*. Idleness, *abundance of idleness* was a dread of labour and a love of ease. Idleness is an inlet to much sin. The standing waters gather filth, and the sitting bird is the fowler's mark. Neither did she *strengthen the hands of the poor and needy*; probably it is implied that she weakened their hands and *broke* their arms.

3. The sins of Jerusalem exceeded those of Sodom and Samaria. The wickedness of the holy city, that was so dear to God, was more provoking to him than the wickedness of Sodom and Samaria, that had not Jerusalem's privileges and means of grace, v. 48. *Samaria has not committed half thy sins* (v. 51), has not worshipped half so many idols, nor slain half so many prophets. By this they *justified Sodom and Samaria*, v. 51. They pretended, in their haughtiness to *judge them*, and in the days of old, when they retained their integrity, they did judge them, v. 52. It will look like some extenuation of their sins that, bad as they were, Jerusalem was worse. For this they ought themselves to be greatly ashamed: "Thou who hast *judged thy sisters*, and cried out shame on them, now *bear thy own shame, for thy sins which thou hast committed* are *more abominable than theirs*," v. 52. There is nothing in sin which we have more reason to be ashamed of than that by our sin we have encouraged others in sin. They had looked with so much disdain upon their neighbours: *Thy sister Sodom was not mentioned by thee in the day of thy pride*, v. 56. If the Jews had but talked more frequently and seriously to one another, and to their children, concerning *the wrath of God revealed from heaven* against *Sodom's ungodliness and unrighteousness*, it might have prevented their treading in their steps.

4. What desolations God had brought and was bringing upon Jerusalem for these wickednesses, wherein they had exceeded Sodom and Samaria. (1) She has already long ago been disgraced, and has fallen into contempt, among her neighbours (v. 57). (2) She is now *in captivity*, or hastening into captivity, not only for her lewdness (v. 58), but for her perfidiousness and covenant-breaking (v. 59). Those that will not adhere to God as their God have no reason to expect that he should continue to own them as his people. (3) The captivity of the wicked Jews, and their ruin, shall be as irrevocable as that of Sodom and Samaria. In this sense, as a threatening, most interpreters take v. 53, 55. Sodom and Samaria were never brought back, nor ever returned to their former estate, and therefore let not Jerusalem expect it, that is, those who now remained there, whom God would *deliver to be removed into all the kingdoms of the earth for their hurt*, Jer. xxiv. 9, 10.

Verses 60–63

In the close of the chapter, after a most shameful conviction of sin and most dreadful judgments, mercy is remembered, for those who shall come after. As was when God swore in his wrath concerning those who came out of Egypt that they should not enter Canaan, "Yet" (says God) "your little ones shall"; so here. And some think that what is said of the return of Sodom and Samaria (v. 53, 55), and of Jerusalem with them, is a promise; it may be understood so, if by Sodom we understand the Moabites and Ammonites, the posterity of Lot, who once dwelt in Sodom (Jer. xlviii. 47; xlix. 6). But these closing verses are, without doubt, a precious promise, which was in part fulfilled at the return of the penitent and reformed Jews out of Babylon, but was to have its full accomplishment in gospel-times, and in that *repentance and* that *remission of sins preached to all nations, beginning at Jerusalem*.

I. This mercy should take rise—from *God himself*, and his *remembering his covenant* with them (v. 60): "*Nevertheless, I will remember my covenant with thee*, that covenant which I made with thee *in the days of thy youth*, and will revive it again. Though thou hast *broken the covenant* (v. 59), I will remember it, and it shall flourish again."

II. They should be prepared and qualified for this mercy (v. 61): "*Thou shalt remember thy ways*, thy evil ways; God will put thee in mind of them, will set them in order before thee, that thou mayest be *ashamed of them*."

III. The mercy that God has in reserve for them. 1. He will take them into covenant with himself (v. 60): *I will establish unto thee an everlasting covenant*; and again (v. 62), *I will establish*, re-establish, and establish more firmly than ever, *my covenant with thee*. 2. He will bring the Gentiles into church-communion with them (v. 61): "*Thou shalt receive thy sisters*, the Gentile nations that are round about thee, *thy elder and thy younger*, ancient nations and modern, and *I will give them unto thee for daughters*; they shall be nursed and educated, by that gospel which shall *go forth from* Zion and from *Jerusalem*; so that all the neighbours shall call Jerusalem *mother*. They shall be thy *daughters*, but *not by thy covenant*, not as being proselytes to the Jewish religion, but as being converts with thee to the Christian religion." Or *not by thy covenant* may mean, "not upon such terms as thou shalt think fit to impose upon them as conquered nations, to whom thou mayest give law at pleasure; they shall be thy *daughters by my covenant*, the covenant of grace made with thee and them. I will be a Father both to Jews and Gentiles, and so they shall become sisters to one another."

IV. What the fruit and effect of this will be. 1. God will hereby be glorified (v. 62): "*Thou shalt know that I am the Lord*. It shall hereby be known that the God of Israel is a God of power, faithful to his covenant." You shall know it to your comfort. 2. They shall hereby be more humbled for sin (v. 63): "*That thou mayest be* the more *confounded* at the *remembrance of all that thou hast done* amiss, and mayest never *open thy mouth any more* in contradiction to God, but mayest be for ever submissive *because of thy shame.*"

CHAPTER 17

God is reckoning with the king of Judah for his treachery in breaking covenant with the king of Babylon. Zedekiah was with the king of Egypt in a treacherous project he had formed to shake off the yoke of the king of Babylon, and violate the homage and fealty he had sworn to him. For this God by the prophet, I. Threatens the ruin of him and his kingdom, by a parable of two eagles and a vine (ver. 1–10), and the explanation of that parable, ver. 11–21. But, in the close, II. He promises hereafter to raise the royal family of Judah again, the house of David, in the Messiah and his kingdom, ver. 22–24.

Verses 1–21

1. The prophet is appointed to *put forth a riddle* to the *house of Israel* (*v.* 2), not to puzzle them for he is immediately to tell them the meaning of it. But he must deliver this message in a riddle or parable that they might the better remember it and tell it to others. Ministers should try various methods to do good; and should both bring that which is familiar into their preaching and their preaching too into their familiar discourse. 2. He is appointed to expound this riddle to *the rebellious house, v.* 12.

I. Nebuchadnezzar had some time ago carried off Jehoiachin, the same that was called *Jeconiah*, when he was but eighteen years of age and had reigned in Jerusalem but *three months*, him and his great men, and had brought them captives to Babylon, 2 Kings xxiv. 12. This in the parable is represented by an eagle's cropping the top and tender branch of *a cedar*, and carrying it into *a land of traffic*, a *city of merchants* (*v.* 3, 4), which is explained, *v.* 12. The *king of Babylon* took the *king of Jerusalem*, who was no more able to resist him than a young twig of a tree is to contend with the strongest bird of prey, that easily crops it off, perhaps towards the making of *her nest*. Nebuchadnezzar, in this parable, is the king of birds, a *great eagle*, that lives upon spoil. His dominion extends itself far and wide, like the great and long wings of an eagle; the people are numerous, for it is *full of feathers*; the court is splendid, for it has *divers colours*, which look like *embroidering*, as the word is. Jerusalem is Lebanon, a forest of houses. The royal family is *the cedar*; Jehoiachin is the *top branch*, the *top of the young twigs*. Babylon is the *land of traffic* and *city of merchants* where it is set.

II. When he carried him to Babylon he made his uncle Zedekiah king in his room, *v.* 5, 6. His name was *Mattaniah—the gift of the Lord*, which Nebuchadnezzar changed into *Zedekiah—the justice of the Lord*, to remind him to be just like the God he called his. This was *one of the seed of the land*, a native, not one of his Babylonian princes; he was *planted in a fruitful field*, for so Jerusalem as yet was; he *placed it by great waters*, like *a willow-tree*, which grows quickly, and grows best in moist ground, but is never expected to be a stately tree. He *set it with* care and *circumspection* (so some read it); that it might grow, but that it might not grow too big. *He took of the king's seed* (so it is explained, *v.* 13) and *made a covenant with him* that he should have the kingdom, and enjoy regal power, provided he held it as his vassal. He *took an oath of him*, made him swear allegiance by his own God, the God of Israel, that he would be a faithful tributary to him, 2 Chron. xxxvi. 13. He also *took away the mighty of the land*, the chief of the men of war, as hostages for the performance of the covenant, and that the king might be the less in temptation, to break his league. What he designed we are told (*v.* 14): *That the kingdom might be base*, might neither be a rival with its powerful neighbours, nor a terror to its feeble ones, that *it might not lift up itself* to vie with the kingdom of Babylon. But yet he designed that by *the keeping of this covenant it might stand*, and continue a kingdom. How sad a

change sin made with the royal family of Judah. Time was when all the nations about were tributaries.

III. Zedekiah, while he continued faithful to the king of Babylon, did very well, and, if he would but have reformed his kingdom, and returned to God and his duty, he might soon have recovered his former dignity, *v.* 6. This plant grew, and though it was *set as a willow-tree*, and little account was made of it, yet it became a *spreading vine of low stature*, a blessing to his own country, and his fruits *made glad their hearts*; and it is better to be a spreading vine of low stature than a lofty cedar of no use. Nebuchadnezzar was pleased, for *the branches turned towards him*, and rested on him as the vine on the wall, and he had his share of the fruits of this vine; *the roots thereof* too were *under him*, and at his disposal. The Jews had reason to be pleased, for they sat under their own vine, which *brought forth branches, and shot forth sprigs*. See how gradually the judgments of God came upon this provoking people, and so gave them space to repent. He made *their kingdom base*, to try if that would humble them.

IV. Zedekiah knew not when he was well off, but grew impatient of being a tributary to the king of Babylon, and entered into a private league with the king of Egypt. If he had dealt faithfully, he might have been a *goodly vine*. But there was *another great eagle* that he had an affection for, and put a confidence in, and that was the *king of Egypt, v.* 7. Those two great potentates, the kings of Babylon and Egypt, were two great eagles, *birds of prey*. This great eagle of Egypt is said to have *great wings*, but not to be *long-winged* as the king of Babylon, because it was not of such a vast extent as that of Babylon was. The great eagle is said to have *many feathers*, much wealth and many soldiers, but which really were no more than so *many feathers*. Zedekiah, promising himself liberty, made himself a vassal to the king of Egypt. Now *this vine* did secretly and under-hand *bend her roots towards* the king of Egypt, and after awhile did openly *shoot forth her branches towards him*, give him an intimation how much she coveted an alliance with him, *that he might water it by the furrows of her plantation*, whereas it was *planted by great waters*, and did not need any assistance from him. This is expounded, *v.* 15. Zedekiah rebelled against the king of Babylon in *sending his ambassadors into Egypt*, that they might *give him horses and much people*, to enable him to contend with the king of Babylon.

V. God here threatens Zedekiah with the utter destruction of him and his kingdom, for his treacherous revolt from the king of Babylon. This is represented in the parable (*v.* 9, 19) by the *plucking up of this vine by the roots, the cutting off of the fruit*, and *the withering of the leaves*. The project shall be blasted; it shall *utterly wither*. Shall he *break the covenant, and be delivered* from that vengeance which is the just punishment of his treachery?

1. His doom is ratified by the oath of God (*v.* 16): *As I live, saith the Lord God, he shall die* for it.

2. It is justified by the heinousness of the crime he had been guilty of. He had been very ungrateful to his benefactor, who had *made him king*, and had made him a prince when he might have as easily have made him a prisoner. He had been very false. He *despised the oath* and *broke it, v.* 15, 16, 18, 19. The oath by which he had bound himself to the king of Babylon was a solemn oath. An emphasis is laid upon this (*v.* 18): *When, lo, he had given his hand*, as a confederate with the king of Babylon, as his friend, the joining of hands being a token of the joining of hearts. God says (*v.* 19): It is *my oath* that he has despised and *my covenant that he has broken*. The oath of allegiance to a prince is particularly called *the oath of God* (Eccles. viii. 2). Now

Zedekiah's breaking this oath is the sin which God will *recompense upon his own head* (v. 19), the *trespass which he has trespassed against God, v.* 20. Though Nebuchadnezzar was a worshipper of false gods, yet the true God will avenge this quarrel when one of his worshippers breaks his league with him; for truth is a debt due to all men. Having *despised the oath*, and *broken the covenant*, he *shall not escape.*

3. The punishment is made to answer the sin. He had rebelled against the king of Babylon, and the king of Babylon should be his effectual conqueror, *v.* 16. God himself will now take part with the king of Babylon against him: *I will spread my net upon him, v.* 20. He had *relied upon the king of Egypt*, and the king of Egypt should be his ineffectual helper: *Pharaoh with his mighty army shall not make for him in the war* (v. 17). On the approach of the Egyptian army, the Chaldeans withdrew from the siege of Jerusalem, upon their retreat they returned to it again and took it. Yet Zedekiah had bands but those bands, though we may suppose they were the best soldiers his kingdom afforded, shall become *fugitives*, shall *fall by the sword* of the enemy, *v.* 21. This was fulfilled *when the city was broken up and all the men of war fled*, Jer. lii. 7.

Verses 22–24

The unbelief of man shall not invalidate the promise of God. He will find out another *seed of David* in which it shall be accomplished.

I. The house of David shall again be magnified, and out of its ashes another phœnix shall arise. The metaphor of a tree, which was made use of in the threatening, is here presented in the promise, *v.* 22, 23. This promise had its accomplishment in part when Zerubbabel, a branch of the house of David, was raised up to head the Jews in their return out of captivity, and to rebuild the city and temple and re-establish their church and state; but it was to have its full accomplishment in the kingdom of the Messiah, Luke i. 32. 1. God himself undertakes the restoring of the house of David. Nebuchadnezzar had attempted the re-establishing of the house of David in dependence upon him, *v.* 5. But his plantation withered and was plucked up. "Well," says God, "the next shall be of my planting: *I will also take of the highest branch of the high cedar and I will set it.*" 2. The house of David is revived in a *tender one cropped from the top of his young twigs.* Zerubbabel was so; that which was hopeful in him was but the *day of small things* (Zech. iv. 10), yet before him *great mountains* were *made plain.* Our Lord Jesus was *the highest branch of the high cedar*, the furthest of all from *the root*, but the nearest of all to heaven, for his kingdom was not of this world. He was *taken from the top of the young twigs, a tender* plant, and a *root out of a dry ground* (Isa. liii. 2), but a *branch of righteousness, the planting of the Lord.* 3. This branch is planted *in a high mountain* (v. 22), in the *mountain of the height of Israel, v.* 23. Thither he brought Zerubbabel in triumph; there he raised up Jesus, to gather the *lost sheep of the house of Israel* that were *scattered upon the mountains*, set him *his king* upon *his holy hill of Zion*, sent forth the gospel from *Mount Zion, the word of the Lord from Jerusalem*; there was the Christian church first planted. The churches of Judæa were the most primitive churches. 4. Thence it spreads far and wide. The Jewish state, though it began very low in Zerubbabel's time, was set as a tender branch, which might easily be plucked up, yet took root, spread and after some time those of other nations, *fowl of every wing*, put themselves under the protection of it. When the Gentiles flocked into the church then did the *fowl of every wing* come and *dwell under the shadow of this goodly cedar.* See Dan. iv. 21.

II. God himself will herein be glorified, *v.* 24. Never was there a more full conviction given of this truth, that all things are governed by an infinitely wise and mighty Providence, than that which was given by the exaltation of Christ and the establishment of his kingdom among men. *All the trees of the field shall know*, 1. That the tree which God will have to be *brought down*, and *dried up*, shall be so. 2. That the trees which God will have to be exalted, and to flourish, shall so be, though ever so low, and ever so dry. The house of Nebuchadnezzar, that now makes so great a figure, shall be extirpated, and the house of David that now makes so mean a figure, shall become famous again; and the Jewish nation, that is now despicable, shall be considerable. The kingdom of Satan, that has borne so long a sway, shall be broken, and the kingdom of Christ, that was looked upon with contempt, shall be established.

CHAPTER 18

This chapter appears to concern us all, for, without particular reference to Judah and Jerusalem, it lays down the rule of judgment according to which God will deal with the children of men. I. The corrupt proverb used by the profane Jews, which gave occasion to the message here sent them, ver. 1–3. The reply given to this proverb, in which God asserts sovereignty and justice, ver. 4. But say to the righteous, It shall be well with them, ver. 5–9. In particular, he assures us, 1. That it shall be ill with a wicked man, though he had a good father, ver. 10–13. 2. That it shall be well with a good man, though he had a wicked father, ver. 14–18. And therefore in this God is righteous, ver. 19, 20. 3. That it shall be well with penitents, though they began ever so ill, ver. 21–23, and again ver. 27, 28. That it shall be ill with apostates, though they began ever so well, ver. 24, 26.

Verses 1–9

Sometimes evil proverbs beget good prophecies.

I. An evil proverb commonly used by the Jews in their captivity. *This* charges God with injustice: "You use this proverb *concerning the land of Israel*, now that it is laid waste by the judgments of God, saying, *The fathers have eaten sour grapes and the children's teeth are set on edge;* we are punished for the sins of our ancestors, which is as absurd as if the children should have their teeth set on edge by the fathers' eating sour grapes, whereas, if men eat or drink anything amiss, they only themselves suffer by it." Now God had often said that he would *visit the iniquity of the fathers upon the children*, especially the sin of idolatry, intending thereby to express the evil of sin. He had often declared by his prophets that in bringing the present ruin upon Judah and Jerusalem he had an eye to the sins of Manasseh and other preceding kings. They intended it as a reflection upon God. It is true that those who are guilty of wilful sin *eat sour grapes;* they will set the sinner's teeth on edge. When conscience is awake it will spoil the relish. But they suggest it as unreasonable that the children should smart for the fathers' folly and feel the pain of that which they never tasted.

II. A just reply to this proverb: "Your own consciences shall tell you that you yourselves have eaten the same sour grapes that your fathers ate before you, or else your teeth would not have been set on edge." God does not punish the children for the fathers' sins unless they tread in their fathers' steps and *fill up the measure of their iniquity* (Matt. xxiii. 32). It is only in temporal calamities that children fare the worse for their parents' wickedness, and God can make them work for good to those that are visited with them; but as to spiritual and eternal misery (and that is the death here spoken of) the children shall by no means smart for the parents' sins. He asserts his own absolute sovereignty: *Behold, all souls are mine, v.* 4. He that is the Maker of *all things* is in a particular manner the *Father of spirits*, for his image is stamped on the souls of men; it was so in their creation; it is so in their renovation. He *forms the spirit of man within him.* God bears a goodwill both to father and son, and will put no hardship upon either. He has such a kindness for all souls that none die but through their own default. Sin is the act of the *soul* therefore the punishment of sin is the *tribulation and the anguish of the soul*, Rom. ii. 9. *If a man be just, do judgment and justice* (*v. 5*), *he shall surely live, saith the Lord God, v. 9.* A just man is careful to keep himself: 1. From sins against the second commandment. In the matters of God's worship he has not so much as *eaten upon the mountains*, that is, not had any communion with idolaters by *eating things sacrificed to idols*, 1 Cor. x. 20. 2. From sins against the seventh commandment. He will keep the appetites of the body always in subjection to reason and virtue. 3. From sins against the eighth commandment. He is a *just man*, who has not, by fraud, *oppressed any, spoiled any by violence, v. 7.* A just man will not take advantage of his neighbour's necessity, but is willing to share in loss as well as profit. This is his character towards his neighbours; to complete his character he must be so to his God likewise (*v. 9*). This is a just man, and *living he shall live*.

Verses 10–20

God, by the prophet, having laid down the general rule of judgment, comes, in these verses, to show that men's parentage shall not alter the case.

I. It often happens that godly parents have wicked children and wicked parents have godly children. 1. A wicked man shall perish in his iniquity, though he be the son of a pious father. He is here supposed to allow himself in all those enormities which his good father dreaded. This wicked man shall perish, notwithstanding his being the son of a good father. 2. A righteous man shall be happy, though he be the son of a wicked father. Though the father did eat the sour grapes, if the children do not meddle with them, they shall fare never the worse for that. The graceless father alone shall die in his iniquity, but his gracious son shall fare never the worse for it.

II. He appeals to themselves then whether they did not wrong God with their proverb. "Thus plain the case is, and *yet you say, Does not the son bear the iniquity of the father?* No, he does not; he shall not if he will himself *do that which is lawful and right*," *v.* 19. But this people that bore the iniquity of their fathers had not done that which is lawful and right, and therefore justly suffered for their own sin and had no reason to complain of God's proceedings against them as at all unjust, though they had reason to complain of the bad example their fathers had left them as very unkind. *Our fathers have sinned and are not, and we have borne their iniquity*, Lam. v. 7. It is true that there is a curse entailed upon wicked families, but it is as true that the entail may be cut off by repentance and reformation; let the impenitent and unreformed therefore thank themselves if they fall under it. The settled rule of judgment is therefore repeated (*v.* 20): *The soul that sins shall die*, and not another for it. What direction God has given to earthly judges (Deut. xxiv. 16) he will himself pursue: *The son shall not die*, not die eternally, *for the iniquity of the father*, if he do not tread in the steps of it, nor the father *for the iniquity of the son*, if he endeavour to do his duty for the preventing of it. In *the day of the revelation of the righteous judgment of God*, which is now clouded and eclipsed, *the righteousness of the righteous shall* appear before all the world to be *upon him*, to his everlasting comfort and honour, upon him as a robe, upon him as a crown; and *the wickedness of the wicked shall* be *upon him*, to his everlasting confusion, upon him as a chain, upon him as a load, as a mountain of lead to sink him to the bottomless pit.

Verses 21–29

Another rule of judgment by which is demonstrated the equity of God's government. Here he shows that he will reward or punish according to the change made in the person himself. While we are in this world we are in a state of probation; the time of trial lasts as long as the time of life.

I. The case fairly stated, much as it had been before (*ch.* iii. 18, &c.), and here it is laid down once (*v.* 21–24) and again (*v.* 26–28), because it is a matter of life and death.

1. A fair invitation given to wicked people, to turn from their wickedness. Assurance is given that, *if the wicked will turn*, he shall *surely live, v.* 21, 27. The first step towards conversion is consideration (*v.* 28): *Because he considers and turns*. This consideration must produce an aversion to sin. He must turn from *all* his sins without a reserve for any Delilah, any house of Rimmon. This must be accompanied with a conversion to God and duty. Those that do thus turn from sin to God shall *save their souls alive, v.* 27. A repenting returning sinner is conscious that his obedience for the future can never be compensation for his former disobedience; but God's nature and delight, is to have mercy and to forgive (*v.* 23).

2. A fair warning given to righteous people not to turn from their righteousness, *v.* 24–26.

II. An appeal to the consciences even of the house of Israel, though very corrupt, concerning God's equity in all these proceedings. The charge they drew up against God is blasphemous, *v.* 25, 29. God's reasonings with them are very gracious, for even these blasphemers God would rather have convinced and saved than condemned.

Verses 30–32

Behold, a miracle of mercy; the day of grace and divine patience is yet lengthened out; and therefore, though God will at last judge *everyone according to his ways*, yet he waits to be gracious, and closes with a call to repentance and a promise of pardon upon repentance.

CHAPTER 19

The scope of this chapter is much the same with that of the 17th to foretell and lament the ruin of the house of David, ver. 1. And he does it by similitudes. I. The kingdom of Judah and house of David are here compared to a lioness, and those princes to lions, that were fierce and ravenous, but were hunted down and taken in nets, ver. 2–9. II. That kingdom and that house are here compared to a vine, and these princes to branches, which had been strong and flourishing, but were now broken and burnt, ver. 10–14.

Verses 1–9

I. Orders given to the prophet to bewail the fall of the royal family. The kings of Judah are here called *princes of Israel*; for their glory was diminished.

II. The prophet must compare the kingdom of Judah to a *lioness, v.* 2. The royal family is as a mother to the kingdom, a *lioness*, fierce, and cruel, and ravenous. She *nourished her whelps among young lions*, taught the young princes the way of tyrants. If they had adhered to the divine law and promise, God would have preserved to them the might and majesty of a lion, and does it in Christ, the *Lion of the tribe of Judah*. But these *lions' whelps* were cruel and oppressive. Jehoahaz, one of the whelps *became a young lion* (*v.* 3); he was made king, and thought he was made so that he might do what he pleased. He did not prosper long in his tyranny: *The nations heard of him* (*v.* 4), *he was taken*, as a beast of prey, *in their pit*, and *brought in chains to the land of Egypt*. Jehoiakim, instead of taking warning by his brother's fate, trod in his brother's steps: *He went up and down among the lions, v.* 6. And he soon learned to *catch the prey*, and he *devoured men* (*v.* 6); he seized his subjects' estates, and swallowed up all that stood in his way. He had the art of discovering where the treasures were which they had hoarded up: he *knew their desolate places* (v. 7). By his oppression he *laid waste their cities*. It did but hasten his own ruin (v. 8). God brought against Jehoiakim bands of the Syrians, Moabites and Ammonites, with the Chaldees (2 Kings xxiv. 2), and he was *taken in their pit. Nebuchadnezzar bound him in fetters to carry him to Babylon*, 2 Chron. xxxvi. 6. There was an end of his tyranny: he was *buried with the burial of an ass* (Jer. xxii. 19).

Verses 10–14

Jerusalem, the mother-city, is here represented by another similitude; she is a vine, and the princes are her branches. This comparison we had before, *ch.* xv. Jerusalem is as *a vine*; the Jewish nation is so: *Like a vine in thy blood* (v. 10). Places of great wickedness may prosper for a while; and a vine set in blood may be full of branches. Jerusalem was full of able magistrates, that were *strong rods*, branches of uncommon strength, or poles for the support of this vine, for such magistrates are. The boughs had grown to such maturity that they were fit to make white staves for *the sceptres of those that bore rule*, v. 11. When the royal family of Judah was numerous, and the courts of justice were filled with men of sense and probity, then *Jerusalem's stature was exalted among thick branches*. When Zedekiah was quiet and easy under the king of Babylon's yoke his kingdom flourished thus. This vine is now destroyed. Nebuchadnezzar, provoked by Zedekiah's treachery, *plucked it up in fury* (v. 12), ruined the city, and cut off all the branches of the royal family. *The vine itself is planted in the wilderness*, v. 13. Babylon was as a wilderness to those of the people that were carried captives thither; the land of Judah was as a wilderness to Jerusalem. Those strong rods had been instruments of oppression, and now they are destroyed with him. Tyranny is the inlet to anarchy; and, when the rod of government is turned into the serpent of oppression, it is just with God to say, "There shall be no strong rod to be a sceptre to rule; but let men be as *are the fishes of the sea*, where the greater devour the less."

CHAPTER 20

Verses 1–4

Certain of the elders of Israel came to enquire of the Lord. Their enquiry was whether now that they were captives in Babylon, where they had no temple, no synagogue, for the worship of God, it was not lawful for them, to join in worship and do *as the families of these countries* do, that *serve wood and stone*. They must be made to know that God is justly angry with them (v. 4): "*Wilt thou judge them, son of man, wilt thou judge them? See, I have set thee over the nation;* wilt thou not declare to them the judgment of the Lord? Cause them therefore *to know the abominations of their fathers*."

Verses 5–9

I. The gracious purposes of God's law concerning Israel in Egypt, where they were bond-slaves to Pharaoh. 1. He chose Israel to be a peculiar people to himself, though their condition was bad and their character worse, that he might have the honour of mending both. 2. He *made himself known to them* by his name *Jehovah* (a new name, Exod. vi. 3), when by reason of their servitude they had almost lost the knowledge of that name by which he was known to their fathers, *God Almighty*. 3. He made over himself to them as their God in covenant: *I lifted up my hand unto them*, saying it, and confirming it with an oath, *I am the Lord your God*. 4. He promised to bring them out of Egypt; and made good what he promised. 5. He assured them that he would put them in possession of the land of Canaan. He *therefore* brought them out of Egypt, *that he might bring them into a land that he had spied out for them*, a second garden of Eden.

II. The reasonable commands he gave them: "*Cast you away every man* his images that he uses for worship, that should be the *abominations, of his eyes. Defile not yourselves with the idols of Egypt*."

III. Their unreasonable disobedience to these commands, for which God might justly have cut them off as soon as ever they were formed into a people (v. 8). It was strange that all the plagues of Egypt would not prevail to cure them of their affection to the *idols of Egypt*. Justly might he have said, "Let them die with the Egyptians."

IV. The wonderful deliverance which God wrought for them, notwithstanding. Though they forfeited the favour while it was in the bestowing, yet *mercy rejoiced against judgment*, and God did what he designed purely *for his own name's sake*, v. 9. When nothing in us will furnish him with a reason for his favours he furnishes himself with one.

Verses 10–26

The history of the struggle between the sins of Israel, by which they endeavoured to ruin themselves, and the mercies of God, by which he endeavoured to save them and make them happy, is here continued. The story of Israel in the wilderness is referred to in the New Testament (1 Cor. x and Heb. iii), as well as often in the Old, for warning to us Christians.

I. The great things God did for them, which he puts them in mind of, not as grudging them his favours, but to show how ungrateful they had been. God *brought them forth out of Egypt* (v. 10), though, as it follows, he *brought them into the wilderness* and not into Canaan immediately. It is better to be at liberty in a wilderness than bond-slaves in a land of plenty. But, when they met with the difficulties of a desert, some wished themselves in Egypt again. God *made them to know his judgments*, not only enacted laws for them, but showed them the reasonableness and equity of those laws. He revived the ancient institution of the sabbath day, which was lost and forgotten while they were bond-slaves in Egypt. Sabbaths are signs; it is a sign that men have a sense of religion. Sabbaths, if duly sanctified are the means of our sanctification.

II. Their disobedient undutiful conduct towards God, for which he might justly have thrown them out of covenant (v. 13): *They rebelled in the wilderness*. There where they received so much mercy from God, and were in their way to Canaan, they broke out in open rebellions against the God that led them and fed them.

III. God's determination to cut off that generation of them in the wilderness. That which was at the bottom of their disobedience to God, and their neglect of his institutions, was a secret affection to the gods of Egypt: *Their heart went after their idols*.

IV. When he looked upon them he had compassion on them, and did not *make an end of them*, but reprieved them till a new generation was reared.

V. The revolt of the next generation from God, by which they also made themselves obnoxious to the wrath of God (v. 21): *The children rebelled against me too*. They *polluted God's sabbaths*, as their fathers.

It is said of the children (v. 24) that *their eyes went after their fathers' idols*. If they must have gods, they would have such as they could see.

VI. The judgments of God upon them for their rebellion. God *gave them statutes and judgments* which *were not good*, and *by which they should not live*, v. 25. By this we may understand the several ways by which God punished them while they were in the wilderness—the plague that broke in upon them, the fiery serpent, and the like—which are called *judgments*, because inflicted by the justice of God, and *statutes*, because he commanded desolations as sometimes he had commanded deliverances. Spiritual judgments are the most dreadful. He made their sin to be their punishment, gave them up to a *reprobate mind*, as he did the Gentile idolaters (Rom. i. 24, 26). God sometimes makes sin to be its own punishment, and there needs no more to make men miserable than to give them up to their own vile appetites and passions.

Verses 27-32
The prophet goes on with the story of their rebellions.

I. They had persisted in them after they were settled in the land of Canaan, v. 27. They were often very near being cut off in the wilderness, and yet they came to Canaan at last. Even God's Israel get to heaven by hell-gates; so many are their transgressions, and so strong their corruptions, that it is a miracle of mercy they are happy at last; as hypocrites go to hell by heaven-gates. They obstinately persisted notwithstanding all the admonitions that were given them (v. 29).

II. They are persisting still. The prophet must *say to* the present *house of Israel*, some of whose elders were now sitting before him, "*Are you polluted after the manner of your fathers?*" These elders seem to have been projecting a coalition with the heathen. Now the prophet is here ordered to tell those who were for compounding between God and Baal, that they should have no comfort or benefit from either. There is nothing got by sinful compliances; and the carnal projects of hypocrites will stand them in no stead.

Verses 33-44
The design on foot among the elders was that the people of Israel should conform to those among whom they lived; but God had told them that the design should not take effect, v. 32. In these verses, he shows how it should be frustrated.

I. Babylon shall not protect them, nor any of the countries of the heathen; for God will cast them out of his protection and then what prince, what place, can be a sanctuary to them? They shall be brought *into the wilderness of the people* (v. 35), either into Babylon, which is called a *wilderness* (ch. xix. 13), or into some place which, though full of people, shall be a place where God will *plead with them face to face*, as he *pleaded with their fathers in the wilderness of Egypt* (v. 36)—where he will avenge the breach of his law with as much terror as that with which he gave it in the wilderness of Sinai.

II. Israel shall be no more able to protect them than Babylon could. There will come a distinguishing day, when God will separate between the precious and the vile; he will *cause them*, as the shepherd causes his sheep, to *pass under the rod*, when he tithes them (Lev. xxvii. 32), that he may mark which is for God. Or it may refer to those among them that repented and reformed; he will cause them to pass under the rod of affliction, and will bring them again *into the bond of the covenant*. The judgments of God shall find them out, and their naming the name of Israel shall be no shelter to them. It is promised that those who preserved their integrity, and would not serve idols, in other lands, shall return to their prosperity and shall serve the true God in their own land: *All of them in the land shall serve me*. He will give them true repentance for their sins, v. 43. He will give them the knowledge of himself: *They shall know* by experience that *he is the Lord*, kind to his people and faithful to his covenant with them.

Verses 45-48
A prophecy of wrath against Judah and Jerusalem, which would more fitly have begun the next chapter than conclude this. The beginning of the next chapter is the explication of it, when the people complained that this was a parable which they understood not. In this parable, 1. It is a forest that is prophesied against, *the forest of the south field*, Judah and Jerusalem. These lay south from Babylon, and therefore he is directed to *set his face towards the south* (v. 46), to intimate that God had set his face against them. But, though it be a message of wrath, he must deliver it with tenderness; he must *drop his word towards the south*; his doctrine must *distil as the rain* (Deut. xxxii. 2), that people's hearts might be softened by it. Judah and Jerusalem are called *forests* because they had been empty of fruit, for fruit-trees grow not in a forest. Those that should have been as the garden of the Lord had become like a forest, overgrown with *briers and thorns*. It is a fire kindled in his forest that is prophesied, v. 47. *I will kindle a fire in thee*. He that had been himself a protecting fire about Jerusalem is now a consuming fire in it. *All faces* (that is, all that covers the face of the earth) *from the south* of Canaan to the north, from Beersheba to Dan, shall be *burnt therein*. The people, on occasion of this discourse, said, *Does he not speak parables?*

CHAPTER 21

I. An explication of the prophecy in the close of the foregoing chapter concerning the fire in the forest (ver. 1-5), with directions to the prophet to show himself deeply affected with it, ver. 6, 7. II. A further prediction of the sword that was coming upon the land, ver. 8-17. III. A prospect given of the king of Babylon's approach to Jerusalem, ver. 18-24. IV. Sentence passed upon Zedekiah, king of Judah, ver. 25-27. V. The destruction of the Ammonites by the sword, foretold, ver. 28-32.

Verses 1-7
The prophet faithfully delivered the message in the terms wherein he received it, but the word of the Lord came to him again, and gave him a key to that figurative discourse. 1. The prophet is here directed against whom to level the arrow of this prophecy. He must *drop his word towards the holy places* (v. 2), towards Canaan the holy land, Jerusalem the holy city, the temple, the holy house. 2. The meaning of the fire that was to consume the forest of the south: it signified the sword of war which should make the land desolate (v. 3). Did the fire devour *every green tree* and *every dry tree*? The sword in like manner shall *cut off the righteous and the wicked*. The righteous were *cut off from the land of Israel* when they were sent captives in Babylon. In the beginning such excellent men as Daniel and his fellows, and Ezekiel, were cut off from it and conveyed to Babylon. But far be it from us to think that *the righteous are as the wicked*. God's graces and comforts make a great difference. The *good figs* are sent into Babylon *for their good*, Jer. xxiv. 5, 6. 3. The prophet is ordered, by expressions of his own grief and concern for these calamities that were coming on, to try to make impressions of the like upon the people. He must sigh as if his heart would burst, *sigh with bitterness*.

Verses 8-17
Another prophecy of the sword. The sword was unsheathed in the foregoing verses; here it is fitted

up to do execution, which the prophet is commanded to lament.

I. The sword is *sharpened*. It is *furbished*, that *it may glitter*, to the terror of those against whom it is drawn. This sword is *that rod of iron* which *contemns every tree* and will bear it down. Or, This sword is *the rod of my son*, a correcting rod, for the chastening of the transgression of God's people (2 Sam. vii. 14), not to cut them off from being a people. It is a sword to others, a rod to my son.

II. How the sword is here put into the hand of the executioners. *It is given into the hand*, not of the fencer to be played with, but *of the slayer* to do execution.

III. Against whom it is sent (*v.* 12): *It shall be upon my people;* they shall fall by this sword. *The sword* of the heathen shall be upon God's own people. But, if the sword be at any time upon God's people, have they not comfort within sufficient to arm them against everything that is frightful? They have, while they conduct themselves as becomes his people; but these had not done so, and therefore *terrors, by reason of the sword*, shall be upon those that call themselves *my people*. This sword is directed particularly *against the great men*, for they had been the greatest sinners among them. The sword, the *point of this sword*, is directed against *all their gates* (*v.* 15), against all those things with which they thought to keep it out. This sword is sent with a running warrant (*v.* 16): "*Go thee, one way or other*, which way thou wilt, turn *to the right hand or to the left*, thou wilt find those that are obnoxious, for there are none free from guilt."

IV. The nature of this sword, and the limitations of it as to the people of God, *v.* 13. It is a correction; it is designed to be so; the sword to others is a rod to them. This is a comfortable word which comes in in the midst of these terrible ones. Fears are silenced with an assurance that the sword shall not forget the errand on which it is sent: *It is a trial*, and it is *no more than a trial*. It is matter of comfort to the people of God, when his judgments are abroad that *when they are tried, they shall come forth as gold*, and the proving of their faith shall be the improving of it.

V. Here the prophet and the people must show themselves affected with these judgments threatened. The prophet must not study for fine words, *A sword! a sword!* and (*v.* 14), *Let the sword be doubled the third time* in thy preaching. Again (*v.* 14), *Prophesy, and smite thy hands together*, wring *thy hands*, as lamenting the desolation.

Verses 18–27

The prophet, in the verses before, had shown them the sword coming.

I. He must show the Chaldean army coming against Jerusalem. The prophet must *appoint him two ways*, two roads (*v.* 19), and must bring the king of Babylon's army to the place where the roads part, for there they will make a stand. One road leads to Rabbath, the head city of the Ammonites, and the other to Jerusalem. He is resolved to be the ruin of both, yet he is not determined which to attack first. Many of the inhabitants of Judah had now taken shelter in Jerusalem, and therefore it is called *Judah in Jerusalem the defenced*. The prophet must describe this dilemma (*v.* 21); for *the king of Babylon stood at the head of the two ways*. It seems, he knew neither his own interest nor his own mind. To come to a resolution he *used divination*. He *made his arrows bright*, to be drawn for the lots. Perhaps *Jerusalem* was written on one arrow and *Rabbath* on the other, and that which was first drawn out of the quiver he determined to attack first. Or he heard the observations which the augurs made upon the entrails of the sacrifices: *he looked in the liver*. Jerusalem being the mark set up (*v.* 22), the campaign is opened.

II. He must show the people and the prince that they bring this destruction upon themselves by their own sin.

1. The people do so, *v.* 23, 24. They slight the notices that are given them of the judgment coming. Ezekiel's prophecy is to them a *false divination*.

2. The prince likewise brings his ruin upon himself. Zedekiah was wicked, as he promoted sin among his people; he sinned, and *made Israel to sin*. He has forfeited his crown, and he shall no longer wear it; he has by his profaneness profaned his crown, and it shall be *cast to the ground* (*v.* 26): *Remove the diadem*. Crowns and diadems are losable things; it is only in the other world that there is a crown of glory that fades not away. Attempts to re-establish the government shall come to nothing. This monarchy shall never be restored till it is fixed for perpetuity in the hands of the Messiah.

Verses 28–32

The prediction of the destruction of the Ammonites, was effected by Nebuchadnezzar about five years after the destruction of Jerusalem.

I. The sin of the Ammonites is here intimated, *v.* 28. The reproach they put upon the Israel of God, when they triumphed in their afflictions, was inhuman. A conceit that they were a better people than Israel, being spared when they were cut off, made them so haughty that they did even *tread on the necks of the Israelites that were slain*.

II. The utter destruction of the Ammonites is threatened. God resents the indignities and injuries done to his people as done to himself (*v.* 31). "*I will judge thee where thou wast created*, where thou wast first formed into a people, and where thou hast been settled ever since, and therefore where thou seemest to have taken root; *the land of thy nativity* shall be the land of thy destruction."

CHAPTER 22

Three separate messages which God entrusts the prophet to deliver concerning Judah and Jerusalem, to show them their sins and the judgments that were coming. I. A catalogue of their sins, ver. 1–16. II. They are condemned as dross to the fire, ver. 17–22. III. All are found guilty, ver. 23–31.

Verses 1–16

The prophet is authorized to *judge the bloody city*, the *city of bloods*. Jerusalem is so called because her crimes in general were bloody crimes (*ch.* vii. 23), such as polluted her in her blood.

I. He is to find Jerusalem guilty of many heinous crimes. *The city sheds blood in the midst of it*, where the magistrates would, if anywhere, be vigilant. *She makes idols against herself to destroy herself*, *v.* 3. *In thee have* the children *set light by their father and mother*, mocked them, and despised them, *v.* 7. To enrich themselves they wronged the poor (*v.* 7). *Thou hast despised my holy things*, holy oracles, holy ordinances, *v.* 8. Jerusalem had been famous for its purity, but now *in the midst of thee they commit lewdness* (*v.* 9). Unmindfulness of God was at the bottom of all this wickedness (*v.* 12): "*Thou hast forgotten me*, else thou wouldst not have done thus."

II. He is to pass sentence upon Jerusalem for these crimes. Let her know that she has filled up the measure of her iniquity, and that her sins call for speedy vengeance. She has made her *time to come* (*v.* 3), *her days to draw near* for punishment (*v.* 4). God has justly exposed her to the contempt and scorn of all her neighbours (*v.* 4). Since she has walked in the way of the heathen, and learned their works, she shall have enough of them (*v.* 15): "*I will* not only send thee *among the heathen*, out of thy own land, but *I will scatter thee* among them and *disperse thee in the countries*."

Verses 17–22

I. The wretched degeneracy of the house of Israel is described. In David's and Solomon's time it had been *a head of gold*; when the kingdoms were divided it was as the *arms of silver*. It has degenerated into baser metal. *They are all brass, and tin, and iron, and lead,* which some make to signify divers sorts of sinners among them. The *house of Israel has become dross to me.* So she is in God's account. They were silver, but now they are *even the dross of silver;* the word signifies all the dirt, and rubbish, and worthless stuff, that are separated from the silver in the washing, melting, and refining of it.

II. The woeful destruction of this degenerate house of Israel is foretold. They are all gathered together in Jerusalem; thither people fled from all parts of the country as to a city of refuge. Now God tells them that their flocking into Jerusalem should be as the gathering of various sorts of metal into the furnace or crucible, to be melted down, and to have the dross separated from them.

Verses 23–31

I. A general idea given of the land of Israel, how well it deserved the judgments coming to destroy it and how much it needed these judgments to refine it. Let the prophet tell her plainly, *"Thou art the land that is not cleansed,* not refined as metal is, and therefore needest to be again put into the furnace."

II. They had all helped to fill the measure of the nation's guilt, but none had done anything towards the emptying of it. The *prophets,* who pretended to make known the mind of God to them, were not only *deceivers,* but *devourers* (v. 25). They devoured souls by flattering sinners into a false peace. The priests, who were teachers by office, violated the law of God, which they should have observed and taught others to observe. They did not *put a difference between the holy and profane, the clean and the unclean,* according to the directions of the law. They *hid their eyes from God's sabbaths* and looked another way when they should have inspected the behaviour of the people on sabbath days. The princes were as daring transgressors of the law as any (v. 27): *They are like wolves ravening the prey;* for such is power without justice and goodness to direct it. The prophets *daubed them with untempered mortar,* told them in God's name that there was no harm in what they did. Daubing prophets are the great supporters of ravening princes. The people that had any power in their hands learned of their princes to abuse it, *v.* 29. There is none that appears as an intercessor for them (v. 30): *I sought for a man among them that should stand in the gap, but I found none.* Sin makes a gap in the hedge of protection that is about a people at which good things run out from them and evil things pour in upon them. There is a way of standing in the gap, by repentance, and prayer, and reformation. Moses stood in the gap when he made intercession for Israel to *turn away the wrath of God,* Ps. cvi. 23.

Chapter 23

A history of the apostasies of God's people from him under the similitude of corporal whoredom and adultery. Here the kingdoms of Israel and Judah, the ten tribes and the two, with their capital cities, Samaria and Jerusalem, are considered distinctly. I. The apostasy of Israel and Samaria from God (ver. 1–8) and their ruin, ver. 9, 10. II. The apostasy of Judah and Jerusalem from God (ver. 11–21) and they shall in like manner be destroyed, ver. 22–35. III. The joint wickedness of them both (ver. 36–44) and the joint ruin of both, ver. 45–49.

Verses 1–10

The sinners that are here to be exposed are *two women,* two kingdoms, sister-kingdoms, Israel and Judah, *daughters of one mother,* having been for a long time but *one people.* 1. When they were one

(v. 3): *They committed whoredoms in Egypt,* for there they were guilty of idolatry, as we read before, *ch.* xx. 8. 2. Their names when they became two, *v.* 4. The kingdom of Israel is called the *elder sister,* because that first made the breach—the *greater sister* (so the word is), for ten tribes belonged to that kingdom and only two to the other. In this parable Samaria and the kingdom of Israel shall bear the name of *Aholah—her own tabernacle,* because the places of worship which that kingdom had were of their own devising, and the worship itself was their own invention. Jerusalem and the kingdom of Judah bear the name of *Aholibah—my tabernacle is in her,* because *their* temple was the place which God himself had *chosen to put his name there.* 3. The treacherous departure of the kingdom of Israel from God (v. 5). Though the ten tribes had deserted the house of David, yet God owned them for *his* still; as long as they worshipped the God of Israel only, though by images, he did not quite cast them off. But Aholah played the harlot, brought in the worship of Baal (1 Kings xvi. 31), in competition with Jehovah (1 Kings xviii. 21), as a vile adulteress *dotes on her lovers,* so she doted upon her neighbours, particularly the Assyrians. She admired their idols and worshipped them. The destruction of the kingdom of Israel for their apostasy from God (v. 9, 10): *I have delivered her into the hand of her lovers.* God first justly gave her up to her lust, and then gave her up to her lovers. We have the story at large 2 Kings xvii. 6, &c.

Verses 11–21

The prophet Hosea, in his time, observed that the two tribes retained their integrity, in a great measure, when the ten tribes had apostatized (Hos. xi. 12). By some unhappy matches made between the house of David and the house of Ahab the worship of Baal had been brought into the kingdom of Judah, but had been by the reforming kings worked out again. In the reign of Manasseh, soon after the kingdom of Judah had seen the destruction of the kingdom of Israel, they became more corrupt than Israel had been in their inordinate love of idols, *v.* 11.

I. Jerusalem, that had been a *faithful city, became a harlot,* Isa. i. 21. She also *doted upon the Assyrians* (v. 12), joined in league with them, joined in worship with them. And thus they grew to affect everything that was foreign and to despise their own nation; and even the religion of it was mean and homely. She doted upon the Babylonian captains (v. 15, 16), joined in alliance with that kingdom, and sent for patterns of their images, altars, and temples, and made use of them in their worship. And when she had had enough of the Chaldeans, she courted the *Egyptians* (v. 20), would come into an alliance with them, and would join in with them in their idolatries. Thus *she multiplied her whoredoms,* repeated her former whoredoms, and encouraged herself by calling *to remembrance the days of her youth.* Those who, instead of reflecting upon their former sins with sorrow and shame, reflect upon them with pleasure and pride, bid defiance to repentance. They called it *God's remembrance,* and provoked him to remember it against them.

II. God justly gives a bill of divorce to this now faithless city. Sin alienates God's mind from the sinner, and justly, for it is the alienation of the sinner's mind from God.

Verses 22–35

Jerusalem indicted by the name of *Aholibah,* as a false traitor to her sovereign Lord the God of heaven, not having his fear before her eyes, but moved by the instigation of the devil, had revolted from her allegiance to him.

I. Her old confederates must be her executioners (*v.* 22): "*I will raise up thy lovers against thee*, the Chaldeans, whom formerly thou didst admire and with whom thou hast perfidiously broken covenant."

II. The execution to be done upon her. Her enemies shall come against her *on every side* (*v.* 22). They shall come with military force (*v.* 24), a vast army, and well armed. They shall have justice on their side: "*I will set judgment before them.*" It being a war of revenge, *they shall deal with thee hatefully*, *v.* 29. The *clothes* and the *fair jewels*, with which she had endeavoured to recommend herself to her lovers, these she shall be stripped of, *v.* 26. Both city and country shall be impoverished and her children shall go into captivity. She shall be stigmatized and deformed: "They shall *take away thy nose and thy ears*, shall mark thee for a harlot, and render thee for ever odious," *v.* 25. Some will have this to be understood figuratively; and by the nose they think is meant the kingly dignity, and by the ears that of the priesthood. Because she had trod in the steps of Samaria's sins, she must expect no other than Samaria's fate, *v.* 31. They have been bad, very bad, and that justifies God in all that is brought upon them (*v.* 30): *I will do these things unto thee because thou hast gone a-whoring after the heathen*, and (*v.* 35) *because thou hast forgotten me and cast me behind thy back*. Forgetfulness of God is at the bottom of all our treacherous departures from him. This fire, though consuming to many, shall be refining to a remnant (*v.* 27). Before the captivity, no nation (all things considered) was more impetuously bent upon idols and idolatry than they were, after that captivity no nation was more vehemently set against idols and idolatry.

Verses 36–49

After the ten tribes were carried into captivity, the remains of it by degrees incorporated with the kingdom of Judah, and gained a settlement in Jerusalem; so that the *two sisters* had in effect become *one* again; and therefore, "Thou shalt now be employed, in God's name, to *judge them*, ch. xx. 4. The matter is rather worse than better since the union."

I. *Declare unto them* openly and boldly *their abominations*. They have been guilty of gross idolatry, here called *adultery* (*v.* 37), have broken their marriage-covenant with God. They have committed the most barbarous murders, in sacrificing their children to Moloch. They have profaned the sacred things with which God had dignified and distinguished them, *v.* 38. They *defiled the sanctuary* on *the same day* that they *profaned the sabbath*. They have courted foreign alliances. This also is represented by the sin of adultery, for it was a departure from God, *in* whom alone they ought to put their trust. Great preparation was made for the reception of these foreign ministers, for their public entry and public audience, which is compared to the pains that an adulteress takes to make herself look handsome, *v.* 40–42. The *men of the common sort* were there to increase the crowd; and *with them were brought Sabeans from the wilderness*. The margin reads it *drunkards from the wilderness*, that would drink healths to the prosperity of this grand alliance. But an alliance between the nation of the Jews and a heathen nation can never be for the advantage of either. They are *iron and clay*, that will not mix, nor will God bless such an alliance.

II. Let them be made to foresee the judgments that are coming upon them for these sins (*v.* 45). The prophets, whose office it was, in God's name, judge them and pass sentence upon them. This judgment being given by the righteous men, the righteous God will award execution, *v.* 46, 47. The same as before, *v.* 23, &c. The destruction of God's city,

like the death of God's saints, shall do that for them which ordinances and providences before could not do; so that Jerusalem shall rise out of its ashes a new lump, as gold comes out of the furnace purified from its dross.

Chapter 24

Two sermons in this chapter, preached on a particular occasion, and they are both from Mount Sinai, the mount of terror, both from Mount Ebal, the mount of curses; both speak the approaching fate of Jerusalem. The occasion of them was the king of Babylon's laying siege to Jerusalem. I. By the sign of flesh boiling in a pot over the fire are shown the miseries that Jerusalem should suffer during the siege, ver. 1–14. II. By the sign of Ezekiel's not mourning for the death of his wife is shown that the calamities coming upon Jerusalem were too great to be lamented, so great that they should sink down under them into a silent despair, ver. 15–27.

Verses 1–14

I. The notice God gives to Ezekiel in Babylon of Nebuchadnezzar's laying siege to Jerusalem (*v.* 2): "*Son of man*, take notice, *the king of Babylon*, who is now abroad with his army, thou knowest not where, *set himself against Jerusalem this same day.*" He tells the prophet, that the prophet might tell the people, that so when it proved to be punctually true, it might be a confirmation of the prophet's mission.

II. The notice which he orders him to take of it. He must enter it in his book, *memorandum*, that in the *ninth year* of Jehoiachin's captivity, in the tenth month, on the tenth day of the month, the king of Babylon laid siege to Jerusalem; and the date here agrees with the date in the history, 2 Kings xxv. 1.

III. The notice which he orders him to give to the people. A rebellious house will soon be a ruinous house.

1. He must show them this by a sign; that of a *boiling pot*. This agrees with Jeremiah's vision many years before (Jer. i. 13, *I see a seething pot, with the face towards the north;* and the explanation of it (*v.* 15) makes it to signify the besieging of Jerusalem by the *northern* nations); to confront the vain confidence of the princes of Jerusalem, who had said (ch. xi. 3), *This city is the cauldron and we are the flesh*, meaning, "We are as safe here as if we were surrounded with walls of brass." "Well," says God, "it shall be so; you shall be boiled in Jerusalem, as the *flesh in the cauldron.*" Those that from all parts of the country fled into Jerusalem for safety would be sadly disappointed; and yet there was no getting out of it, but they must be forced to abide by it, as the flesh in a boiling pot.

2. He must give them a comment upon this sign. It is to be construed as a *woe to the bloody city*, *v.* 6. Jerusalem, during the siege, is like a pot boiling over the fire. Care is taken to keep a good fire under the pot, which signifies the closeness of the siege. Commission is given to the Chaldeans (*v.* 10) to *heap on wood, and kindle the fire*. Here is no line, no lot of mercy, made use of; all goes to destruction. God would not take these severe methods with Jerusalem but that he is provoked to it (*v.* 7, 8). Jerusalem was to be made an example and therefore was made a spectacle, to the world. Because she is incurably wicked she is abandoned to ruin, without remedy. Methods and means of reformation had been tried in vain (*v.* 13). It is therefore resolved that no more such methods shall be used: *Thou shalt not be purged from thy filthiness any more*. The fire shall no longer be a refining fire, but a consuming fire.

Verses 15–27

These verses conclude Ezekiel's prophecies of the destruction of Jerusalem; for after this, though he prophesied much concerning other nations, he said no more concerning Jerusalem, till he heard of the destruction of it, almost three years after, *ch.* xxxiii. 21.

I. The sign by which this was represented to them.

1. He must lose a good wife, that should suddenly be taken from him by death. God gave him notice of it before (*v.* 16). A beloved wife is the *desire of the eyes*. When the desire of our eyes is taken away with a stroke we must see and own the hand of God in it: *I take away the desire of thy eyes*.

2. He must deny himself the satisfaction of mourning for his wife, which would have been both an honour to her and an ease to the oppression of his own spirit. But Ezekiel is not allowed to do this, though he would perhaps be ill thought of by the people if he did it not. He must not *eat the bread of men*, nor expect that his neighbours and friends should send him in provisions, as usually they did in such cases, presuming the mourners had no heart to provide meat for themselves; but, if it were sent, he must not eat of it. It could not but be greatly against the grain to flesh and blood not to lament the death of one he loved so dearly, but so God commands; and *I did in the morning as I was* commanded. He appeared in public without any signs of mourning. Here Ezekiel, to make himself a sign to the people, must exercise an extraordinary piece of self-denial.

II. The application of this sign. The people enquired the meaning of it (*v.* 19): *Wilt thou not tell us what these things are to us that thou doest so?* They knew that the death of his wife was a great affliction to him, and that he would not appear so unconcerned at it but for some good reason.

1. Let them know that if a faithful servant of God was thus afflicted only for his trial, shall such a generation of rebels against God go unpunished? That which was their public pride, the temple: *"I will profane my sanctuary*, by giving that into the enemy's hand, to be plundered and burnt." That which was their family-pleasure, which they looked upon with delight: *"Your sons and your daughters* (which are the dearer to you because they are but a few left of many, the rest having perished by famine and pestilence) shall *fall by the sword* of the Chaldeans." This was the punishment of sin.

2. Let them know that as Ezekiel wept not for his affliction so neither should they weep for theirs. He must say, *You shall do as I have done, v.* 22. *You shall not mourn nor weep, v.* 23. Their grief shall be so great that they shall be overwhelmed. Their calamities shall come so fast upon them, that by long custom they shall be *hardened in their sorrows* (Job. vi. 10) and stupefied. There shall be none of that sense of sorrow which would help to bring them to repentance, but that only which shall drive them to despair: *"You shall pine away for your iniquities*, with seared consciences and reprobate minds, and *you shall mourn*, not to God in prayer and confession of sin, but *one towards another,"* complaining of God.

III. *"When this comes*, as it is foretold, when Jerusalem, which is this day besieged, is quite destroyed, which now you cannot believe will ever be, *then you shall know that I am the Lord God*, who have given you this fair warning of it. Then you will remember that Ezekiel was to you a sign." *"He that escapes in that day* shall, by a special direction of Providence, *come to thee*, to bring thee intelligence of it," which we find was done, *ch.* xxxiii. 21. Whereas, from this time to that, Ezekiel was thus far dumb that he prophesied no more against the land of Israel, but against the neighbouring nations, as we shall find in the following chapters, then he shall have orders given him to *speak again to the children of his people* (ch. xxxiii. 2, 22). When God was speaking so loudly by the rod, there was the less need of speaking by the word.

CHAPTER 25

Ezekiel had finished his testimony which related to the destruction of Jerusalem. As to that he was ordered to say no more, but wait the issue; and yet he must not be silent; there are divers nations bordering upon the land of Israel, which he must prophesy against, as Isaiah and Jeremiah had done before. In this chapter we have his prophecy, I. Against the Ammonites, ver. 1–7. II. Against the Moabites, ver. 8–11. III. Against the Edomites, ver. 11–14. IV. Against the Philistines, ver. 15–17. That which is laid to the charge of each of them is their barbarous and insolent conduct towards God's Israel.

Verses 1–7

I. The prophet is ordered to address himself to the Ammonites, in the name of *the Lord Jehovah* the *God of Israel*, who is also the God of the whole earth. He is bidden to *set his face against the Ammonites*, for he is God's representative and thus he must signify that God *set his face against them*, for *the face of the Lord is against those that do evil*, Ps. xxxiv. 16. He must show that, though he had prophesied so long *against Israel*, yet still he was for Israel, and, while he witnessed against their corruptions, he gloried in God's covenant with them.

II. He is directed what to say to them. Ezekiel is now a captive in Babylon, and knows little of the nations that were about it; but God tells him what they were doing and what he was about to do with them.

1. He must upbraid the Ammonites with their insolent and barbarous triumphs over the people of Israel in their calamities, *v.* 3. The Ammonites, of all people, should not have rejoiced in Jerusalem's ruin, but should rather have trembled, because they themselves had such a narrow escape, *ch.* xxi. 20. And they had reason to think that the king of Babylon would set upon them next. It is a wicked thing to be glad at the calamities of any.

2. He must threaten the Ammonites with utter ruin for this insolence. He had before predicted the destruction of the Ammonites, *ch.* xxi. 28. Had they repented, that would have been revoked; but now it is ratified. The Chaldeans came from the north-east, and their army, under the command of Nebuchadnezzar, destroyed the country of the Ammonites, about five years after the destruction of Jerusalem, and then the Arabians, who were properly the *children of the east*, when the Chaldeans had made the country desolate, came and took possession of it for themselves. They made use even of the royal city for their cattle (*v.* 5): *I will make Rabbath*, that was a nice and splendid city, to be *a stable for camels*. Thus God will maintain his own honour, and will make it appear that he is the God of Israel, though he suffers them for a time to be captives in Babylon. Thus he will bring those that were strangers to him into an acquaintance with him.

Verses 8–17

Three more of Israel's ill-natured neighbours are here condemned to destruction, for contributing to and triumphing in Jerusalem's fall.

I. The Moabites. Seir, which was the seat of the Edomites, is joined with them (*v.* 8).

1. The Moabites said, *Behold, the house of Judah is like unto all the heathen*. They were pleased to see them forsake their God and worship idols. Let the Moabites know that, though there are those of the house of Judah who have made themselves *like the heathen*, yet there is a remnant that retain their integrity, the religion of the house of Judah shall recover itself. Their God is no more able to deliver them from this *overflowing scourge* of these parts of the world than the gods of the heathen are to deliver them. Those who judge only by outward appearance are ready to conclude that the people of God have lost all their privileges when they have lost their worldly prosperity.

2. The punishment of Moab for this sin; their country shall be in like manner overthrown with that of the Ammonites, who were guilty of the same sin (*v.* 9, 10). The frontier-towns, that were its strength, shall be demolished by the Chaldean forces, and laid open. *The men of the east,* when they come to take possession of the country of the Ammonites, shall seize that of the Moabites too. The Arabians, who are shepherds, and live quietly, plain men dwelling in tents, shall by an overruling Providence be put in possession of the land of the Moabites, who are soldiers, that live turbulently. The Chaldeans shall get it by war, and the Arabians shall enjoy it in peace.

II. The Edomites were the posterity of Esau, between whom and Jacob there had been an old enmity. They not only triumphed in the ruin of Judah and Jerusalem, as the Moabites and Ammonites had done, but they took advantage from the present distressed state to which the Jews were reduced to do them some real mischiefs, probably made inroads upon their frontiers and plundered their country, *v.* 12. Amaziah severely chastised them (2 Kings xiv. 7), and for this they *took vengeance.* Now they would pay off all the old scores. God will take them to task for it (*v.* 13): *I will stretch out my hand upon Edom.* Their country shall be desolate *from Teman* in the south, and *they shall fall by the sword unto Dedan,* which lay north. They suffered much by the Chaldeans, which seems to be referred to, Jer. xlix. 8. *Judas Maccabeus fought against the children of Esau in Idumea, gave them a great overthrow, abated their courage, and took their spoil* (1 Mac. v. 3), and Josephus says (*Antiq. lib.* 13, *cap.* 17), that Hircanus made the Edomites tributaries to Israel.

III. The Philistines. Their sin is much the same with that of the Edomites: They have *dealt by revenge* with the people of Israel, and have *taken vengeance with a despiteful heart,* to *destroy them,* for *the old hatred* (*v.* 15), the old grudge they bore them. Their punishment likewise is much the same, *v.* 16. Their country was wasted by the Chaldean army, not long after the destruction of Jerusalem, which is foretold, Jer. xlvii.

Chapter 26

The city of Tyre is next set to the bar; this, being a place of vast trade, was known all the world over; and therefore are three chapters, this and the two that follow, spent in the prediction of the destruction of Tyre. We have "the burden of Tyre," Isa. xxiii. It is but just mentioned in Jeremiah, ch. xxv. 22; xxvii. 3; xlvii. 4. But Ezekiel is ordered to be copious upon that head. In this chapter, I. The sin charged upon Tyre, which was triumphing in the destruction of Jerusalem, ver. 2. II. The destruction of Tyrus itself foretold. 1. The extremity of this destruction, ver. 4-6, 12-14. 2. The instruments of this destruction (ver. 3), and the king of Babylon with his vast victorious army, ver. 7-11. 3. The surprise of the neighbouring nations, ver. 15-21.

Verses 1–14

This prophecy is dated in the eleventh year, which was the year that Jerusalem was taken, and *in the first day of the month,* but it is not said what month.

I. The pleasure with which the Tyrians looked upon the ruins of Jerusalem (*v.* 2): "*Aha! she is broken,* broken to pieces, that was *the gates of the people!* all the wealth, power, and interest, which Jerusalem had, shall be turned to Tyre, and so *now that she is laid waste I shall be replenished.*" They were men of business, and therefore were not of a persecuting spirit. All their care was to get estates and enlarge their trade, and they looked upon Jerusalem not as an enemy, but as a rival. Tyre promised herself that the fall of Jerusalem would be an advantage to her in respect of trade and commerce, that now she shall have Jerusalem's customers, and thus the prosperity of Tyre will rise out of the ruins of Jerusalem. It is just with God to blast the designs and projects of those who thus contrive to raise themselves upon the ruins of others.

II. Tyrus was a pleasant and wealthy city, and might have continued so if she had sympathized with Jerusalem in her calamities. *Many nations shall come against thee,* an army made up of many nations, or one nation that shall be as strong as many. The person is named that shall bring this army upon them—*Nebuchadnezzar king of Babylon, a king of kings,* that had many kings tributaries to him, besides those that were his captives, Dan. ii. 37, 38. He shall come with a vast army, *horses and chariots,* &c. He shall (*v.* 8), *make a fort, and cast a mount,* and (*v.* 9) shall set *engines of war against the walls.* His troops shall raise a dust that shall cover the city, *v.* 10. The city held out a long siege, but it was taken at last. Not only the soldiers that are found in arms, but the burghers, shall be *put to the sword,* the king of Babylon being highly incensed against them for holding out so long. The wealth of the city shall all become a spoil to the conqueror (*v.* 12). All the *pleasant houses* shall be *destroyed* (*v.* 12). When Jerusalem was destroyed it was *ploughed like a field,* Mic. iii. 12. But the destruction of Tyre is carried further; the very soil of it shall be scraped away, and it shall be made *like the top of a rock* (*v.* 4, 14), that has no earth to cover it; it shall only be a place *for the spreading of nets* (*v.* 5, 14); it shall serve fishermen to dry their nets upon.

Verses 15–21

1. How high, how great, Tyre had been, how little likely ever to come to this! She was *inhabited of seas,* that is, of those that trade at sea, of those who from all parts came thither by sea. Everybody stood in awe of the Tyrians and was afraid of disobliging them.

2. How low, how little, Tyre is made, *v.* 19, 20. This *renowned city* is made a *desolate city,* a city overflowed by an inundation of waters, which *cover* it, and upon which the *deep* is *brought up.* The Tyrians shall be lost among the nations, so that people will look in vain for Tyre in Tyre: *Thou shalt be sought for, and never found again.*

3. What a distress the inhabitants of Tyre are in (*v.* 15): *There is a great slaughter made in the midst of thee.*

4. What a consternation all the neighbours are in upon the fall of Tyre. The *islands* shall *shake at the sound of thy fall* (*v.* 15). The *princes of the sea* shall be affected, who ruled in those islands. The rich merchants, who live like princes (Isa. xxiii. 8), and the masters of ships, who command like princes, these shall condole the fall of Tyre. When Jerusalem, the holy city, was destroyed, there were no such lamentations for it; it was *nothing* to *those that passed by* (Lam. i. 12); but when Tyre, the trading city, fell, it was universally bemoaned.

5. The irreparable ruin of Tyre is aggravated by the prospect of the restoration of Israel. Thus shall Tyre sink *when I shall set glory in the land of the living, v.* 20. None but holy souls are properly living souls.

Chapter 27

In this chapter we have, I. A large account of the dignity, wealth, and splendour of Tyre, while it was in its strength (ver. 1-25). II. A prediction of its fall and ruin, ver. 26-36. And this is intended to let us see the vanity and uncertainty of the riches, honours, and pleasures of the world.

Verses 1–25

I. The prophet is ordered to take up a lamentation for Tyrus, *v.* 2. It was yet in the height of its prosperity, and there appeared not the least symptom of its decay; yet the prophet must lament it, because its prosperity is its snare, which will make its fall the more grievous.

II. He is directed what to say, and to say it in the name of *the Lord Jehovah*.

1. He must upbraid Tyre with her pride: *O Tyrus! thou hast said, I am of perfect beauty* (v. 3), of *universal beauty* (so the word is), well-built and well-filled with money and trade.

2. He must upbraid Tyre with her prosperity, which was the matter of her pride. The city of Tyre stood at the east end of the Mediterranean, convenient for trade by land into all the Levant, so that she became a *merchant of the people for many isles*. Lying between Greece and Asia, it became the rendezvous of merchants from all parts: *Thy borders are in the heart of the seas*, v. 4. It has its haven replenished with abundance of *gallant ships*, Isa. xxxiii. 21. They made their *sails* of *fine linen* fetched from Egypt, and that *embroidered* too, v. 7. The word signifies a *banner* as well as a *sail*. They hung rooms on ship-board with *blue and purple*, the richest cloths and richest colours they could get. Tyre was itself famous for purple, which is therefore called the *Tyrian dye*. These gallant ships were well-manned. The pilots and masters of the ships were of their own city (v. 8): *Thy wise men, O Tyrus! that were in thee, were thy pilots. The inhabitants of Arvad and Zidon were thy mariners*. They sent to Gebal in Syria for *calkers*, or *strengtheners of the clefts* or *chinks*, to stop them when the ships come home, after long voyages, to be repaired. Their city was guarded by a military force that was considerable, v. 10, 11. The land of Israel (though it lay next them), furnished them with timber, but we do not find that it furnished them with men; that would have trenched upon the liberty and dignity of the Jewish nation, 2 Chron. ii. 17, 18. They had a vast trade and a correspondence with all parts of the known world. Ezekiel knew little, of his own knowledge, concerning the trade of Tyre. He was a priest, carried away captive far from Tyre, and there he had been eleven years. Yet he speaks of the particular merchandise of Tyre as nicely as if he had been comptroller of the custom-house there. The wisdom of God, and his goodness, as the common Father of mankind is seen in making one country to abound in one commodity and another in another, and all more or less serviceable. *One land does not supply all the varieties of produce*. Providence dispenses its gifts variously, some to each, and all to none, that there may be a mutual commerce among those whom God has *made of one blood*, though they are made *to dwell on all the face of the earth*, Acts xvii. 26. Let every nation therefore thank God for the productions of its country; though they be not so rich as those of others, yet there is use for them in the public service of the world. Judah and the *land of Israel* were merchants in Tyre. They traded mostly *in wheat*, a substantial commodity. Tyre was maintained by corn fetched from the land of Israel. Though Tyre got abundance by buying and selling, importing commodities from one place and exporting them, the *wares of their own making*, and a *multitude of such wares*, are here spoken of, v. 16, 18. It is the wisdom of a nation to encourage art and industry, for it contributes much to the wealth and honour of a nation to send abroad *wares of their own making*.

Verses 26–36

The destruction of Tyre was sudden. Her *sun went down at noon*. And all her wealth and grandeur, pomp and power, did but aggravate her ruin. She is as a great ship richly laden, that is sunk by the indiscretion of her steersmen: *Thy rowers have themselves brought thee into great* and dangerous *waters*; the governors of the city involved them in war with the Chaldeans which was the ruin of their state. By their insolence they provoked Nebuchadnezzar to make a descent upon them, and, by their obstinacy

enraged him to such a degree that he determined on the ruin of their state, and, *like an east wind, broke them in the midst of the seas*. All her wealth shall be buried with her, *her riches, her fairs, and her merchandise* (v. 27); all shall *fall with her into the midst of the seas, in the day of her ruin*. The pilots, her princes and governors, when they see how wretchedly they have mismanaged and how they have contributed to their own ruin, shall *cry out* so loud as to make even the *suburbs shake* (v. 28). Tyre should be upbraided with her former prosperity (v. 32, 33); she that was Tyrus the *renowned* shall now be called *Tyrus the destroyed* in the *midst of the sea*. Some shall be *sorely afraid*, and shall *be troubled* (v. 35). Others shall *hiss at her* (v. 36), shall ridicule her pride, and bad management, and think her ruin just.

CHAPTER 28

I. A prediction of the fall and ruin of the king of Tyre, who, in the destruction of that city, is particularly set up as a mark for God's arrows, ver. 1–10. II. A lamentation for the king of Tyre, though he falls by his own iniquity, ver. 11–19. III. A prophecy of the destruction of Zidon, which was in the neighbourhood of Tyre, ver. 20–23. IV. A promise of the restoration of the Israel of God, though in the day of their calamity they were insulted by their neighbours, ver. 24–26.

Verses 1–10

The prince of Tyrus is singled out from the rest. Here is a *message to him from God*, which the prophet must send him.

I. He must tell him of his pride. *His heart was lifted up*, v. 2. Out of the pride of his heart he said, *I am a god*. He thought that the city of Tyre had as necessary a dependence upon him as the world has upon the God that made it. "*I am the strong God*, and therefore will not be contradicted, because I cannot be controlled. *I sit in the seat of God;* I sit as safely as God, as safely *in the heart of the seas*, and as far out of the reach of danger, as he in the *height of heaven*." He shall be told, *Thou art a man, and not God*, a depending creature, a dying creature; thou art *flesh, and not spirit*, Isa. xxxi. 3. The king of Tyre, though he has such a mighty influence and though he is flattered by his courtiers and made a god of by his poets, yet he is *but a man*; he knows it; he fears it. He was proud of his wisdom. When the king of Tyre dreams himself to be a god he says, I am *wiser than Daniel. There is no secret that they can hide from thee*. He that was *wiser than Daniel* was prouder than Lucifer. As some of the kings of Judah *loved husbandry* (2 Chron. xxvi. 10), so the king of Tyre loved merchandise, and by it he *got riches, increased his riches, and filled his treasures with gold and silver*, v. 4, 5. He attributed the increase of his wealth, to himself and not to the providence of God, forgetting him who *gave him power to get wealth*, Deut. viii. 17, 18. He thought himself a wise man because he was a rich man; whereas a fool may have an estate (Eccles. ii. 19).

II. Since *pride goes before destruction, and a haughty spirit before a fall*, he must tell him of that destruction, of that fall. "*Because thou hast pretended to be a god* (v. 6), therefore thou shalt not be long a man,*" v. 7. *I will bring strangers upon thee*—the Chaldeans. They are people of a *strange language*. They are the *terrible of the nations*; it was an army made up of many nations, formidable both for strength and fury. *They shall draw their swords against the beauty of thy wisdom* (v. 7), against all those things which thou gloriest in as thy beauty and the product of thy wisdom. The king of Tyre's palace, his treasury, his city, his navy, his army, these he glories in as his brightness, these the victorious enemy shall defile, shall deface, shall deform. He shall be so vilified in his death that he may despair of being deified after his death. The sentence of death here passed upon the king of Tyre is ratified by a divine authority: *I have spoken it, saith the Lord God.* When the conqueror sets his sword to thy breast, and thou seest no way of escape, *wilt thou then say, I am God?* The fear of it will force thee to own that thou art not a god, but a weak, timorous, trembling, dying man.

Verses 11–19

After the ruin of the king of Tyre is foretold it is bewailed.

I. This is commonly understood of the prince who then reigned over Tyre, spoken to, *v.* 2. His name was *Ethbaal*, or *Ithobalus*, as Diodorus Siculus calls him that was king of Tyre when Nebuchadnezzar destroyed it. He was an accomplished man, but his iniquity was his ruin.

II. Some think that by *the king of Tyre* is meant the whole royal family. He is here spoken of as having lived in great splendour, *v.* 12–15. He was looked upon to be as wise as the reason of men could make him, and as happy as the wealth of this world and the enjoyment of it could make him. He seemed to be as wise and happy as Adam in innocency (*v.* 13): *"Thou hast been in Eden, even in the garden of God*; thou hast lived as it were in paradise all thy days, hast had dominion over all about thee, as Adam had."* His rooms were set round with jewels, so that he walked in the midst of them, and fancied himself as glorious as if, like God, he had been surrounded by so many angels, who are compared to a *flame of fire. Gold* is mentioned last, as far inferior in value to those precious stones; and he used to speak of it accordingly. Another thing that made him think his palace a paradise was the curious music he had, the *tabrets and pipes*, hand-instruments and wind-instruments. He appeared in as much splendour as the high priest when he was clothed with his garments for glory and beauty. *Thou wast perfect in thy ways;* thou didst prosper in all thy affairs and everything went well with thee; *from the day thou wast created, till iniquity was found in thee;* and that spoiled all (*v.* 15). And when iniquity was once *found in him* it increased; he grew worse and worse (*v.* 18). The king had so much to do with his merchandise, and was so wholly intent upon the gains of that, that he took no care to do justice, to give redress, to those that suffered wrong and to protect them from violence (*v.* 16). *"Thy heart was lifted up because of thy beauty;* thou wast in love with thyself, *v.* 17." He disgraces the crown he wears, and so has forfeited it, and shall be destroyed *from the midst of the stones of fire*, the precious stones with which his palace was garnished.

Verses 20–26

The destruction of Zidon, a city that lay near to Tyre, was more ancient, but not so considerable, had a dependence upon it and stood and fell with it. The Zidonians were more addicted to idolatry than the Tyrians, who, being men of business, were less under the power of bigotry and superstition. The Zidonians were noted for the worship of Ashtaroth. Jezebel was daughter to the king of Zidon, who brought the worship of Baal into Israel (1 Kings xvi. 31); so that God had been much dishonoured by the Zidonians. The judgments that shall be executed upon Zidon are war and pestilence, *v.* 23. Nor is it Tyre and Zidon only on which God would execute judgments, but on all those that despised his people Israel, and triumphed in their calamities; for this was now God's controversy with the nations that were *round about them, v.* 26. God will be glorified in the restoration of his people to their former prosperity. He had been dishonoured by the sins of his people, and their sufferings too had given occasion to the enemy to blaspheme (Isa. lii. 5); but God will now

both cure them of their sins and ease them of their troubles, and so *will be sanctified in them in the sight of the heathen, v.* 25. They shall enjoy great tranquillity there. When those that have been vexatious to them are taken off they shall live in quietness; there shall be no more *a pricking brier nor a grieving thorn, v.* 24. They shall have a happy settlement, for they shall *build houses*, and *plant vineyards*, and there shall be none to disquiet them or make them afraid, *v.* 26. But the full accomplishment of this promise is reserved for the heavenly Canaan, everything that offends shall be removed, and all griefs and fears for ever banished.

CHAPTER 29

Four chapters concerning Egypt and its king. Egypt had formerly been a house of bondage to God's people; of late they had depended too much upon it; and therefore, whether the prediction reached Egypt or no, it would be of use to Israel, to take them from their confidence in their alliance. In this chapter we have, I. The destruction of Pharaoh foretold, for his dealing deceitfully with Israel, ver. 1–7. II. The desolation of the land of Egypt foretold, ver. 8–12. III. A promise of the restoration thereof, in part, after forty years, ver. 13–16. IV. The possession that should be given to Nebuchadnezzar of the land of Egypt, ver. 17–20. V. A promise of mercy to Israel, ver. 21.

Verses 1–7

I. The date of this prophecy against Egypt. It was in the *tenth year of the captivity*. The first prophecy against Egypt was just at the time when the king of Egypt was coming to relieve Jerusalem and raise the siege (Jer. xxxvii. 5), but did not answer the expectations of the Jews.

II. This prophecy is directed against *Pharaoh king of Egypt, and against all Egypt, v.* 2. This begins with the prince, because it began to have its accomplishment in the rebellions of the people against the prince, not long after this.

III. The prophecy itself. Pharaoh Hophrah (for so was the reigning Pharaoh surnamed) is here represented by a *great dragon*, or crocodile, that *lies in the midst of his rivers* to *play therein, v.* 3. Nilus, the river of Egypt, was famed for crocodiles.

1. The pride and security of Pharaoh. He boasts that he is an absolute prince, a sole prince, and has neither partner in the government nor competitor. Pharaoh's reason for his pretensions is absurd: *My river is my own*, for *I have made it for myself*. Here he usurps two of the divine prerogatives, to be the author and the end of his own being and felicity. Self is the great idol that all the world worships, in contempt of God and his sovereignty.

2. The course God will take with this proud man, to humble him. He is a great dragon in the waters, and God will accordingly deal with him, *v.* 4, 5. Herodotus relates of this Pharaoh, who was now king of Egypt, that he had reigned in great prosperity for twenty-five years, and was so elevated with his successes that he said that *God himself could not cast him out of his kingdom. All his fish* shall be drawn out with him, his servants, his soldiers, and all that had a dependence on him. These shall *stick to his scales*, adhere to their king, resolving to live and die with him. But king and army, the dragon and all the fish that stick to his scales, shall perish together, as fish cast upon dry ground, *v.* 5. Now this is supposed to have had its accomplishment soon after, when this Pharaoh, in defence of Aricius king of Libya, who had been expelled his kingdom by the Cyrenians, levied a great army, and went out against the Cyrenians, to re-establish his friend, but was defeated in battle, which gave such disgust to his kingdom that they rose in rebellion against him. Thus was he left *thrown into the wilderness, he and all the fish of the river* with him.

3. The ground of the controversy God has with the Egyptians; it is because they have cheated his people.

They failed them (*v.* 6, 7). When any stress was laid upon them, they either could not or would not do that for them which was expected. The king of Egypt, it is probable, had encouraged Zedekiah to break his league with the king of Babylon, with a promise that he would stand by him, which he failed to do. God had told them, long since, that the Egyptians were broken reeds, Isa. xxx. 6, 7. And now they found it so.

Verses 8–16

I. A prophecy of the ruin of Egypt. The threatening is particular; and the sin is their pride, *v.* 9. God is against the king and against the people, *against thee and against thy rivers.* Waters signify *people and multitudes,* Rev. xvii. 15. Multitudes shall be cut off by war, the sword of civil war. The country shall be depopulated. The *land of Egypt shall be utterly waste* (*wastes of waste,* so the margin reads it), *and desolate* (*v.* 10); *neither men nor beasts shall pass through it, nor shall it be inhabited* (*v.* 11); it shall be *desolate in the midst of the countries that are so, v.* 12. This was the effect of the war which the king of Babylon made upon them. The people shall be dispersed and scattered among the nations (*v.* 12), so that those who thought the balance of power was in their hand should now become a contemptible people.

II. Of the restoration of Egypt after awhile, *v.* 13. Egypt shall lie *desolate forty years* (*v.* 12) and then *I will bring again the captivity of Egypt, v.* 14. The forty years end about the first year of Cyrus, when the seventy years' captivity of Judah ended, or soon after. God will gather the Egyptians, and make them to *return to the land of their habitation, v.* 14. They shall not make a figure as they have done. Egypt shall be *a kingdom* again, but it shall be the *basest of the kingdoms* (*v.* 15). For two reasons it shall be thus mortified: (1) That it may not domineer over its neighbours, but that it may know what it is to be low and despised. (2) That it may not deceive the people of God (*v.* 16): *It shall no more be the confidence of the house of Israel;* they shall no more trust in it as they have done.

Verses 17–21

The date of this prophecy is in the twenty-seventh year of Ezekiel's captivity, sixteen years after the prophecy in the former part of the chapter. After the destruction of Jerusalem Nebuchadnezzar spent two or three campaigns in the conquest of the Ammonites and Moabites. Then he spent thirteen years in the siege of Tyre. During all that time the Egyptians were embroiled in war with the Cyrenians, by which they were much weakened and impoverished; and at the end of the siege of Tyre God delivers this prophecy to Ezekiel, to signify to him that that utter destruction of Egypt which he had foretold fifteen or sixteen years before, should now be completed by Nebuchadnezzar. The prophecy which begins here, it should seem, is continued to the twentieth verse of the next chapter. It is the last prophecy we have of this prophet, but is laid here, that all the prophecies against Egypt might come together.

I. The success God would give to Nebuchadnezzar against Egypt, *v.* 19, 20. It was a cheap and easy prey. Jeremiah foretold that Nebuchadnezzar should *array himself with the land of Egypt as a shepherd puts on his coat,* which intimates what a rich and cheap prey it should be.

II. This success was a recompense for the hard service with which he had caused his army to serve against Tyre, *v.* 18, 20. 1. The taking of Tyre cost Nebuchadnezzar abundance of blood and treasure. In this siege *every head was made bald, and every shoulder peeled,* with carrying burdens and labouring in the water when they had a strong tide to contend

with. 2. In this service God owns that they *wrought for him, v.* 20. He set them at work, for the humbling of a proud city and its king, though *they meant not so, neither did their heart think so.* 3. For this service he had *no wages.* He was at vast expense to take Tyre; and he promised himself good plunder, but the Tyrians sent away by ship their best effects, and threw the rest into the sea, so that they had nothing but bare walls. 4. He shall have the spoil of Egypt to recompense him for his service against Tyre.

III. The mercy God had in store for the house of Israel. When the tide is at the highest it will turn, and so it will when it is at the lowest. Nebuchadnezzar was in the zenith of his glory when he had conquered Egypt, but within a year after he ran mad (Dan. iv). When he was at the highest Israel was at the lowest; but *in that day the horn of the house of Israel shall bud forth, v.* 21. Their princes are the *horns of the house of Israel,* the seat of their glory and power. These began to bud forth when Daniel and his fellows were highly preferred in Babylon (Dan. ii. 49). Within a year after the conquest of Egypt they were thus preferred; and, soon after, three of them were made famous by the honour God put upon them in bringing them alive out of the burning fiery furnace. And this promise had a further accomplishment in the elevation of Jehoiachin king of Judah, Jer. lii. 31, 32. God will honour their prophets: And *I will give thee the opening of the mouth.* Though none of Ezekiel's prophecies, after this, are recorded, yet we think he went on prophesying, and with more liberty, when Daniel and his fellows were in power, ready to protect him.

CHAPTER 30

I. A continuation of the prophecy against Egypt just before the desolation of that once flourishing kingdom was completed by Nebuchadnezzar, in which is foretold the destruction of all her allies and confederates, ver. 1–19. II. A repetition of a former prophecy against Egypt, just before the desolation of it begun by their own bad conduct, which gradually weakened them and prepared the way for the king of Babylon, ver. 20–26.

Verses 1–19

The prophecy of the destruction of Egypt is here very full.

I. It shall be a lamentable destruction, and such as shall occasion great sorrow (*v.* 2, 3). You have your day now, when you carry all before you, and trample on all about you, but God will have his day shortly. It will be *a cloudy day,* that is, dark and dismal, and it shall threaten a storm. *It shall be the time of the heathen,* of reckoning with the heathen for all their heathenish practices.

II. It shall be the destruction of Egypt, and of all the countries in confederacy with her. 1. Egypt herself shall fall (*v.* 4). 2. Her neighbours shall fall with her. When the slain fall so thickly in Egypt *great pain shall be in Ethiopia,* both in Africa, and in Asia. There were those of other countries who upon some account or other resided in Egypt, as did also *the men of the land that is in league,* some of the remains of the people of Israel and Judah, the *children of the covenant,* or league, as they are called (Acts iii. 25). These sojourned in Egypt contrary to God's command, and these shall *fall with them.*

III. All that pretend to support the sinking interests of Egypt shall come down with her (*v.* 6). Even *the multitude of Egypt shall be made to cease, v.* 10. That populous country shall be depopulated. Is the river Nile her support and are the several channels of it a defence to her? *I will make the rivers dry* (*v.* 12). Are her idols a support to her? They shall be destroyed. Is her royal family her support? *There shall be no more a prince in the land of Egypt;* the royal family shall be extirpated. Is her courage her support: *I will put a fear in the land of Egypt.* Is the rising generation her support? Alas! *the young men shall fall by the sword* (v. 17) and *the daughters shall go into captivity* (v. 18), and so she shall be robbed of all her hopes.

IV. God shall inflict these desolating judgments on Egypt (v. 8).

V. The king of Babylon and his army shall be employed as instruments of this destruction, v. 10. Those that undertook to protect Israel from the king of Babylon shall not be able to protect themselves.

VI. No place in the land of Egypt shall be exempted from the fury of the Chaldean army, not the strongest, not the remotest: *The sword shall go through the land.* Various places are here named: *Pathros, Zoan, and No* (v. 14), *Sin and Noph* (v. 15, 16), *Aven and Pi-beseth* (v. 17), and *Tehaphnehes*, v. 18. These shall be made desolate. The *pomp of their strength shall cease,* and *a cloud shall cover them.* And, *lastly,* the Ethiopians, who are at a distance from them, as well as those who are mingled with them, shall share in their pain and terror. The close of this prediction leaves, 1. The land of Egypt mortified: *Thus will I execute judgments on Egypt,* v. 19. 2. The God of Israel herein glorified: *They shall know that I am the Lord.*

Verses 20–26

This short prophecy of the weakening of the power of Egypt was delivered about the time that the army of the Egyptians, which attempted to raise the siege of Jerusalem, was frustrated and returned *without accomplishing their purpose.*

I. It is here foretold that the king of Egypt shall grow weaker and weaker. 1. This was in part done already (v. 21): *I have broken the arm of Pharaoh.* One arm of that kingdom might well be reckoned broken when the king of Babylon routed the forces of Pharaoh-Necho at Carchemish (Jer. xlvi. 2), and made himself master of *all that pertained to Egypt from the river of Egypt to Euphrates,* 2 Kings xxiv. 7. Before Egypt's heart and neck were broken its arm was. 2. This was to be done again. Now (v. 22), *I am against Pharaoh, and will break both his arms.* The king of Egypt shall be dispirited when he finds himself in danger of the king of Babylon's forces: he *shall groan before him with the groaning of a deadly wounded man.* The people of Egypt shall be dispersed (v. 23 and again v. 26): *I will scatter them among the nations.*

II. It is here foretold that the king of Babylon shall grow stronger and stronger, v. 24, 25.

CHAPTER 31

The prophecy of this chapter is against Egypt, and designed for the humbling of Pharaoh. Pharaoh stands indicted for his pride and haughtiness, and the injuries he had done to God's people; but he thinks himself so high as not to be accountable to any authority, so strong as not to be conquerable. The prophet is therefore directed to report to him the case of the king of Assyria, whose head city was Nineveh. I. He must show him how great a monarch the King of Assyria had been, what a vast empire he had, ver. 3–9. II. He must then show him how like he was to the king of Assyria in pride, ver. 10. III. He must next read him the history of the fall and ruin of the king of Assyria, ver. 11–17. IV. He must leave the king of Egypt to apply all this to himself to see his own face in the looking-glass of the king of Assyria's sin, and to foresee his own fall, ver. 18.

Verses 1–9

This prophecy bears date the month before Jerusalem was taken, as that in the close of the foregoing chapter about four months before. When God's people were in the depth of their distress, it would be some comfort to them to be told from heaven that the cup was going round, even the cup of trembling, that it would shortly be taken out of the hands of

God's people and put into the hands of those that hated them, Isa. li. 22, 23.

I. The prophet is directed to put Pharaoh searching for a case parallel to his own (v. 2). The falls of others, both into sin and ruin, are intended as admonitions to us not to be secure or *high-minded,* nor to think we stand out of danger.

II. He is directed to show him an instance of one whom he resembled in greatness (v. 3). Sennacherib was one of the mighty princes of that monarchy; but it sunk down soon after him, and the monarchy of Nebuchadnezzar was built upon its ruins. The king of Assyria is here compared to a stately cedar, v. 3. 1. The Assyrian monarch was a tall cedar, of a *high stature,* and *his top among the thick boughs.* He surpassed all the princes in his neighbourhood; they were all shrubs to him (v. 5): *His height was exalted above all the trees of the field;* he overtopped them all, v. 8. 2. He was a spreading cedar, denoting that his territories were large, and he extended his conquests far and his influences much further. His large dominions were well managed. His government was admirable in the eyes of all men. In all the surrounding nations there was no prince so much admired, so much courted, as the king of Assyria. 3. He was serviceable by his shadow (v. 6). The meaning is, *Under his shadow dwelt all great nations;* they all fled to him for safety, and were willing to swear allegiance to him if he would undertake to protect them. But the utmost security that any creature, even the king of Assyria himself, can give, is but like the shadow of a tree, which is but a scanty protection. God will take us *under the shadow of his wings,* where we shall be warmer and safer than under the shadow of the strongest and stateliest cedar, Ps. xvii. 8; xci. 4. 4. He seemed to be settled and established in his greatness and power. This cedar was not like the *heath in the desert, made to inhabit the parched places* (Jer. xvii. 6); it was not a *root in a dry ground,* Isa. liii. 2. He had abundance of wealth to support his power and grandeur (v. 4): *The waters made him great;* he had vast treasures, which were as *the deep that set him up on high, as rivers running round about his plants;* these enabled him to strengthen and secure his interests everywhere, for he *sent out his little rivers to all the trees of the field,* to water them; *their country was nourished by the king's country* (Acts xii. 20), and they would be serviceable and faithful to him.

Verses 10–18

The king of Egypt resembled the king of Assyria in pomp, and power, and prosperity.

I. He does likewise resemble him in his pride, v. 10. For the same temptation of a prosperous state by which some are overcome are fatal to many others too. "*Thou,* O king of Egypt! *hast lifted up thyself in height,* has been proud of thy wealth and power, *ch.* xxix. 3. And the king of Assyria *shot up his top among the thick boughs,* and grew insolent and imperious, set God himself at defiance, and trampled upon his people"; Isa. xxxvi. 4. How haughtily does he speak of his achievements!

II. How he shall therefore resemble him in his fall. 1. The fall of the king of Assyria. Cyaxares, king of the Medes, in conjunction with Nebuchadnezzar king of Babylon, destroyed Nineveh, and with it the Assyrian empire. Respecting the Assyrian three things are affirmed: (1) It is God himself that orders his ruin: *I have delivered him into the hand* of the executioner; *I have driven him out.* (2) It is his own sin that procures his ruin: *I have driven him out for his wickedness.* (3) It is a *mighty one of the heathen* that shall be the instrument of his ruin. In this history of the fall of the Assyrian there is still the similitude of the cedar. He grew very high, and extended his boughs very far; but his day comes to fall. This stately cedar was dropped: *The terrible of the nations cut him off.* They have lopped off his branches first, cities or countries broken off from the Assyrian monarchy. It was deserted: *All the people of the earth,* that had fled to him for shelter, have *gone down from his shadow and have left him. Upon his ruin shall all the fowls of the heaven remain,* to tread upon the broken branches of this cedar. *All the trees of Eden,* that had fallen before him, *all that drank water* of the rain of heaven, as the stump of the tree that is left in the *south* (Dan. iv. 23), *shall be comforted in the nether parts of the earth* when they see this proud cedar brought as low as themselves. But the trees of Lebanon, that are yet standing, *mourned for him,* because they could read their own destiny in his fall. By the cutting down of this cedar is signified the slaughter of this mighty monarch and all his supporters. God designed thereby, *First, To give an alarm* to the nations about (*v.* 16): *I made the nations to shake at the sound of his fall. Secondly,* To give an admonition to their kings (*v.* 14). It would have been well for Nebuchadnezzar, who was himself active in bringing down the Assyrian, if he had taken the admonition.

2. A prophecy of the fall of the king of Egypt in like manner, *v.* 18.

CHAPTER 32

The destruction of Pharaoh and Egypt enlarged upon. I. Perhaps it may look as far back as the book of Genesis (*ch.* xv. 14). II. Perhaps it may look as far forward as the book of the Revelation, where we find that the great enemy of the gospel-church is spiritually called Egypt, Rev. xi. 8. And, if so, between this prophecy of the ruin of Egypt and the prophecy of the destruction of the antichristian generation there is some analogy. We have two distinct prophecies in this chapter relating to Egypt, both in the same month. They are both lamentations to intimate how much the prophet himself should lament it, from a generous principle of love to mankind. The destruction is here represented under two similitudes: 1. The killing of some devouring creature, ver. 1-16. 2. The funeral of a great commander, ver. 17-32,

Verses 1-16

I. The prophet is ordered to *take up a lamentation for Pharaoh king of Egypt, v.* 2.

II. He is ordered to show cause for that lamentation.

1. Pharaoh has been a troubler of the nations, even of his own nation. He is *like a young lion of the nations* (*v.* 2), threatening as a lion when he roars. He is like *a whale,* like a crocodile (so some) *in the seas,* vexatious, as the *leviathan* that *makes the deep to boil like a pot,* Job. xli. 31. When Pharaoh engaged in an unnecessary war with the Cyrenians he *came forth with his rivers,* with his armies, *troubled the waters,* disturbed his own kingdom and the neighbouring nations.

2. He that has troubled others must expect to be himself troubled; for the Lord is righteous, Joshua vii. 25. This is set forth by a comparison. Is Pharaoh like a *great whale?* God has a net strong enough to secure him (*v.* 3): *I will spread my net over thee,* even the army of the Chaldeans, a *company of many people. The flesh* of this great whale shall be *laid upon the mountains* (*v.* 5) and the *valleys* shall be *filled with his height.* Such members of Pharaoh's soldiers shall be slain that the dead bodies shall be scattered upon the hills and piled up in the valleys. It is set forth by a prophecy of the deep impression which the destruction of Egypt should make upon the neighbouring nations. When Pharaoh, who had been like a blazing burning torch, is *put out* and *extinguished* it shall make all about him look black, *v.* 7. The *hearts of many people* will be *vexed* to see the word of the God of Israel fulfilled in the destruction of Egypt, and that all the *gods of Egypt* were not able to relieve it. It shall fill them with admiration (*v.* 10): They shall be *amazed at thee,* shall wonder to see such

great riches and power *come to nothing,* Rev. xviii. 17. It shall fill them with fear. When others are ruined by sin we have reason to quake for fear, as knowing ourselves guilty and obnoxious. It is the *sword of the king of Babylon* that shall *come upon thee* (*v.* 11), the *swords of the mighty,* even the *terrible of the nations, all of them* (*v.* 12). The multitude of Egypt shall be destroyed. The pomp of Egypt shall be spoiled. The cattle of Egypt, that used to feed by the rivers, shall be destroyed (*v.* 13), either by the sword or carried off for a prey. The *waters of Egypt,* that used to flow briskly, shall now grow slow, and heavy, and shall *run like oil* (*v.* 14), a figurative expression signifying that there should be such universal sadness and heaviness upon the whole nation that even the rivers should go softly and silently like mourners. The whole country of Egypt shall be stripped of its wealth (*v.* 15). *Then shall they know that I am the Lord.*

Verses 17-32

This prophecy completes the burden of Egypt.

I. The funeral of that once flourishing kingdom.

1. This dead kingdom is here brought to the grave. The prophet is ordered (*v.* 18), to foretell their destruction. Yet he must foretell it as one that had an affectionate concern for them; he must *wail for the multitude of Egypt,* even when he *casts them down.* When Egypt is slain, let her have an honourable funeral; let her be buried *with the daughters of the famous nations.*

2. This corpse of a kingdom is bid welcome to the grave, and Pharaoh is made free of the congregation of the dead, not without some pomp and ceremony. There lie the Assyrian empire, and all the princes and mighty men of that monarchy (*v.* 22). There lies the kingdom of Persia, which perhaps within the memory of man at that time had been wasted and brought down: *There is Elam and all her multitude,* the king of Elam and his numerous armies, *v.* 24, 25. There lies the Scythian power. *Meshech* and *Tubal,* those barbarous northern nations, had lately made a descent upon the Medes, and lived among them upon free quarter for some years, but at length Cyaxares, king of the Medes, obliged them to quit his country, *v.* 26. These Scythians are not buried with marks of honour. There lies the kingdom of Edom, which had flourished long, but before the destruction of Egypt, was made desolate, as was foretold, *ch.* xxv. 13. Among the sepulchres of the nations *there is Edom, v.* 29. There lie *the princes of the north, and all the Zidonians.* These were as well acquainted with maritime affairs as the Egyptians were, who relied much upon that part of their strength, but they have *gone down with the slain* (*v.* 30). All this is applied to Pharaoh and the Egyptians, who have no reason to flatter themselves with hopes of tranquillity when they see how the wisest, and wealthiest, and strongest of their neighbours have been laid waste (*v.* 28).

II. The view which this prophecy gives us of ruined states may show us something of this present world, and the empire of death in it. Men are ingenious at finding out ways to destroy one another. It is not only a great pit, but a great cockpit.

CHAPTER 33

The prophet now returns to the children of his people. I. He must let them know that he was a watchman, and had received a charge concerning them, ver. 1-9. The substance of this we had before, ch. iii. 17, &c. II. He must let them know upon what terms they stand with God, that they are upon their trial, ver. 10-20. III. A particular message sent to those who yet remained in the land of Israel, ver. 21-29. IV. A rebuke to those who personally attended Ezekiel's ministry, but were not sincere in their professions of devotion, ver. 30-33.

Verses 1–9

The prophet, now that Jerusalem is taken, is appointed again to direct his speech to them; and here his commission is renewed.

I. The office of a watchman laid down, the trust reposed in him, the charge given him, v. 2, 6. 1. It is supposed to be a public danger that gives occasion for the appointing of a watchman, v. 2. When a country is in fear of a foreign invasion, that they may not be surprised, but may have early notice of it, in order to give the invader a warm reception, they *set a man of their coast*, some likely person, that lives upon the borders of their country, and make him *their watchman.* One man may be of public service to a whole country. 2. It is supposed to be a public trust that is lodged in the watchman and that he is accountable to the public for the discharge of it. If he do his part, if he betimes give warning, he has discharged his trust, and not only *delivered his soul*, but earned his wages. If the people do not take warning it is their own fault; the blame is not to be laid upon the watchman. If the watchman did not do his duty, and *blew not the trumpet* to *warn the people*, so that some are surprised and cut off *in their iniquity* (v. 6), he shall be found guilty because he did not *give warning*. But if the watchman do his part, and the people do theirs, all is well.

II. The application of this to the prophet, v. 7, 9.

1. He is a *watchman to the house of Israel*. He had occasionally given warning to the nations about, but to the house of Israel he was a watchman by office. They did not *set him for a watchman*, but God did it for them; he appointed them a watchman.

2. His business as a watchman is to give warning to sinners of their danger by reason of sin. This is the word he must *hear from God's mouth* and *speak to them*. God has said, *The wicked man shall surely die*. Unless he repent, he shall be cut off from God. The wrath of God is revealed from heaven, not only against wicked nations, but against wicked persons. It is the will of God that the wicked man should be warned of this: *Warn them from me*. This intimates that there is a possibility of preventing it, else it were a jest to give warning of it; and that God is desirous it should be prevented. It is the work of ministers to say to the wicked, *It shall be ill with thee*, Isa. iii. 11. And he must say this, not in passion, to provoke the sinner, but in compassion, to *warn the wicked from his way*, warn him to *turn from it*, that he may live.

3. If souls perish through his neglect of his duty, he brings guilt upon himself.

4. If he do his duty, he may take the comfort of it, though he do not see the success of it (v. 9).

Verses 10–20

I. The cavils of the people against God's proceedings with them. God had *set life before them*, but they plead that he had set it out of their reach. The prophet had said (*ch.* xxiv. 23), *You shall pine away for your iniquities;* and this they now upbraided him with, as if it had been spoken to drive them to despair; whereas it was spoken conditionally, to bring them to repentance. They said, *The way of the Lord is not equal* (*ch.* xviii. 25), suggesting that God was partial in his proceedings, and that he was more severe against sin and sinners than there was cause.

II. A satisfactory answer given to both these cavils.

1. When they spoke of *pining away in their iniquity* God sent the prophet to them, with all speed, to tell them that there was yet *hope in Israel* (v. 11). God has no delight in the ruin of sinners, nor does he desire it. They questioned whether they should *live*, though they did repent and reform; yea, says God, as sure *as I live*, true penitents shall live also; for *their life is hid with Christ in God*. It is certain that,

if sinners perish in their impenitency, it is owing to themselves; they die because they will die.

2. The most plausible professors, if they apostatize, shall certainly perish for ever in their apostasy from God; and the most notorious sinners, if they repent, shall certainly be happy for ever in their return to God. These rules of judgment are so plainly just that they need no other confirmation of them than the repetition of them. If those that have made a great profession of religion throw off their profession, the profession they made shall stand them in no stead, v. 12, 13, 18. He that lives regularly shall live. Surely such a man as this cannot but be happy. Righteous men, who have very good hopes of themselves, are yet in danger of turning to iniquity by trusting to their righteousness. Or, he trusts to the strength of his own righteousness, and so by presuming on his own sufficiency he is brought to commit iniquity. If those that have lived a wicked life repent and reform, their sins shall be pardoned, and they shall be justified and saved. Thus even the threatenings of the word are to some, by the grace of God, a savour of life unto life, while even the promises of the word become to others, by their own corruption, a savour of death unto death. There is many a wicked man hastening to destruction who yet is wrought upon by the grace of God to return and repent. He *turns from his sin* (v. 14), and *restores the pledge* (v. 15) which he had taken uncharitably from the poor, *he gives again that which he had robbed* and taken unjustly from the rich. Nor does he only *cease to do evil*, but he *learns to do well*. And in this good way he perseveres *without committing iniquity*, though not free from infirmity, yet under the dominion of no iniquity. He *shall surely live; he shall not die*, v. 15. Again (v. 16), *He shall surely live*. Again (v. 19), *He has done that which is lawful and right*, and *he shall live thereby*. Now that there is a settled separation between him and sin there shall be no longer a separation between him and God. *None of the sins that he has committed shall be mentioned unto him* (v. 16), either as a clog to his pardon or as any diminution to the glory that is prepared for him. The conclusion of the whole matter is (v. 20): "*O you house of Israel, though you are all involved now in the common calamity, yet there shall be a distinction of persons made in the spiritual and eternal state, and I will judge you every one after his ways.*"

Verses 21–29

I. The tidings brought to Ezekiel of the burning of Jerusalem by the Chaldeans. The city was burnt in the eleventh year of the captivity and the fifth month, Jer. lii. 12, 13. Tidings were brought to the prophet by one that was an eye-witness of the destruction (v. 21), a year and almost five months after the thing was done. This was the first time he had an account of it from a refuge, from one who escaped.

II. The divine influences he was under, to prepare him for those heavy tidings (v. 22): *The hand of the Lord was upon me before he came, and had opened my mouth* to speak to the house of Israel. He prophesied now with more freedom and boldness. Now *the hand of the Lord came upon him*, renewed his commission, gave him fresh instructions, and *opened his mouth*, furnished him with power to speak to the people *as he ought to speak*.

III. The particular message he was entrusted with, relating to these Jews that yet remained in the *land of Israel*, and *inhabited the wastes* of that land, v. 24. Some few that had escaped the sword and captivity still continued there and began to think of re-settling. Though the providence of God concerning them had been very humbling, and still was very threatening, yet they were intolerably haughty. *They say,*

"*The land is given us for inheritance, v. 24.* Our partners being gone, it is now all our own; we shall have it all to ourselves." They think they can make out as good a title from God to this land as Abraham could: "If God *gave this land* to him, who was but one worshipper of him, as a reward of his service, much more will he give it to us, who are many worshippers of him, as the reward of our service." Since God's providences did neither humble them nor terrify them, he sends them a message sufficient to do both. He tells them of the wickedness they still persisted in, which rendered them utterly unworthy to possess this land. "You make no conscience of forbidden fruit, forbidden food: *You eat with the blood,*" Gen. ix. 4. "Idolatry is still the sin that most easily besets you. You are as fierce, and cruel, and barbarous as ever: *You shed blood,* innocent blood. You confide in your own strength, *You stand upon your sword (v. 26);* you think to carry all before you by force of arms. You are guilty of all manner of abominations, and, particularly, *you defile everyone his neighbour's wife, and shall you possess the land?*" To terrify them, he tells them of the further judgments God had in store for them. These that are in the cities, here called the *wastes,* shall *fall by the sword,* either by the sword of the Chaldeans, or by one another's swords. Those that are in the open field shall be *devoured by* wild *beasts.* Those that are *in the forts and in the caves,* that think themselves safe in artificial or natural fastnesses, shall *die of the pestilence.*

Verses 30–33

Those are reproved who were now in captivity in Babylon, under divine rebukes, and yet were not reformed by them. They made some show of religion and devotion; but their hearts were not right with God. The thing they are here accused of is *mocking the messengers of the Lord.* Two ways they mocked the prophet Ezekiel:

I. By invidious ill-natured reflections upon him, privately among themselves. The prophet did not know it. But God comes and tells him, *The children of thy people are still talking against thee (v.* 30). Those have arrived at a great pitch of profaneness who can make the preaching and hearing of the word of God a matter of sport and ridicule, though it be done in private conversation among themselves.

II. By dissembling with him in their attendance upon his ministry. Hypocrites mock God and mock his prophets.

1. The plausible profession which these people made. They are like those (Matt. xv. 8) who *draw nigh to God with their mouths and honour him with their lips, but their hearts are far from him.* They were diligent and constant in their attendance upon the means of grace: *They come unto thee as the people come.* In Babylon they had no temple or synagogue, but they went to the prophet's house (*ch.* viii. 1). Now these hypocrites came, *according to the coming of the people,* as duly and as early as any of the prophet's hearers. They behaved themselves very decently and reverently in the public assembly. They were very attentive to the word preached. They pretended to have a great kindness and respect for the prophet. Though, behind his back, they could not give him a good word, yet, to his face, *they showed much love* to him and his doctrine. They took a great deal of pleasure in the word. Ezekiel was to them as one *that had a pleasant voice* and could sing well, *or play well on an instrument.* Men may have their fancies pleased by the word, and yet not have their consciences touched nor their hearts changed, the itching ear gratified and yet not the corrupt nature sanctified.

2. The hypocrisy of these professions and pretensions. While they *show much love* it is only *with the* mouth, from the teeth outward, but *their heart goes after their covetousness;* they are as much set upon the world as ever. They *hear thy words,* but it is only a hearing that they *give thee,* for they *will not do them, v.* 31.

3. The end hereof: *Shall their unbelief* and carelessness *make the word of God of no effect?* God will confirm the prophet's word, though they make light of it, *v.* 33. When it comes to pass *they shall know,* shall know to their cost, that *a prophet has been among them,* though they made no more of him than as one that *had a pleasant voice.*

CHAPTER 34

In this chapter the shepherds of Israel, their rulers both in church and state, are called to account. I. A high charge exhibited against them for their negligence and unfaithfulness in the management of public affairs, ver. 1–6 and again ver. 8. II. Their discharge from their trust, ver. 7–10. III. A gracious promise that God would take care of his flock, though they did not, ver. 11–16. IV. Another charge against those of the flock that were strong, for the injuries they did to those that were weak, ver. 17–22. V. Another promise that God would in the fulness of time send the Messiah, to be the great and good Shepherd of the sheep, who should set everything to rights with the flock, ver. 23–31.

Verses 1–6

The prophecy of this chapter is not dated, nor any of those that follow it, till chap. xl.

I. The prophet is ordered to prophesy *against the shepherds of Israel*—the princes and magistrates, the priests and Levites, the kings especially, for there were two now captives in Babylon, who, as well as the people, must have their transgressions shown them, that they might repent. *Woe to the shepherds of Israel!* Though they are shepherds, and shepherds of Israel, yet he must not spare them.

II. Two things they are charged with: 1. That all their care was to advance and enrich themselves and to make themselves great. *Should not the shepherds feed the flocks?* They betray their trust if they do not. But *these* shepherds fed *themselves,* contrived everything to gratify and indulge their own appetite. They made sure of the fleece, and *clothed themselves with the wool.* 2. That they took no care for the benefit and welfare of those that were committed to their charge: *You feed not the flock.* The princes and judges took no care to right those that suffered wrong. They took no care of the poor. The priests took no care to instruct the ignorant. The ministers of state took no care to check the growing distempers of the kingdom. They did not do their duty to those of the flock that were driven away by enemies and forced to seek for shelter where they could find a place, or that *wandered* of choice upon *the mountains and hills (v.* 6). Thus were *they scattered because there was no shepherd, v.* 5. Christ complains that his flock were *as sheep having no shepherd,* when yet the scribes and Pharisees *sat in Moses' seat,* Matt. ix. 36.

Verses 7–16

I. How much displeased God is at the shepherds. Their crimes are repeated, *v.* 8. God's flock became a prey to the deceivers that drew them to idolatry, and to the destroyers that carried them into captivity; and these shepherds took no care to prevent either the one or the other. God is *against them,* and they shall know it. They shall be made to account for the manner in which they have discharged their trust: "*I will require my flock at their hands,* and charge it upon them that so many of them are missing." *They shall cease from feeding the flock,* that is, from pretending to feed it. "*Neither shall the shepherds feed themselves any more.*"

II. How much concerned God is for the flock; for *with him the fatherless finds mercy.* Precious promises, made here, were to have their accomplishment in the return of the Jews out of their captivity and their re-establishment in their own land. Let the shepherds *hear this word of the Lord*, and know that they have no part nor lot in the matter.

1. God will gather his sheep together that were scattered, and bring those back to the fold that had wandered from it. "*I will both search my sheep and find them out* (v. 11) as a *shepherd* does (v. 12), and bring them back as he does the stray-sheep, upon his shoulders, *from all the places where they have been scattered in the cloudy and dark day.*" God will both incline their hearts to come by his grace and will by his providence open a door for them and remove every difficulty that lies in the way. *I will seek that which was lost and bring again that which was driven away*, v. 16. This was done when so many thousand Jews returned triumphantly out of Babylon, under the conduct of Zerubbabel, Ezra, and others.

2. God will bring the returning captives safely to their own land (v. 13), *will feed them upon the mountains of Israel*, and that is a *good pasture*, and a *fat pasture* (v. 14); there shall their *feeding* be, and there shall be *their fold*; and it is a *good fold*. There God will *cause them to lie down* (v. 15), which denotes rest after their wanderings, and a continuing residence.

3. He will succour those that are hurt, will *bind up that which was broken and strengthen that which was sick*, will comfort those that *mourn in Zion* and with Zion.

Verses 17–31

The prophet has now a message to deliver to the flock. God had ordered him to speak tenderly to them, and to assure them of the mercy he had in store for them. But here he is ordered to make a difference between the precious and the vile and then to give them a promise of the Messiah.

I. Conviction spoken to those of the flock that were fat and strong, the *rams and the he-goats* (v. 17), those that, though they had not power, as shepherds and rulers, yet, being rich and wealthy, made use of the opportunity which this gave them to bear hard upon their poor neighbours. The *rams* and the *he-goats* not only kept all the good pasture to themselves, but they would not let the poor of the flock have any enjoyment of the little that was left them; they *trod down the residue of the pastures and fouled the residue of the waters*, v. 18, 19. They not only robbed the poor, to make them poorer, but were troublesome to the sick and weak of the flock (v. 21).

II. Comfort spoken to those of the flock that are poor and feeble, and that wait for the consolation of Israel (v. 22): "*I will save my flock*, and they shall no more be spoiled by the beasts of prey, by their own shepherds or by the rams and he-goats among themselves." Upon this occasion, as is usual in the prophets, comes in a prediction of the coming of the Messiah, and the setting up of his kingdom.

1. Concerning the Messiah himself. He shall have his commission from God: I will *set him up* (v. 23); *I will raise him up*, v. 29. He shall be the great *Shepherd* of the sheep, who shall do that for his flock which no one else could do. He is the *one Shepherd*, under whom Jews and Gentiles should be *one fold*. He is *God's servant* to re-establish his kingdom among men. He is David, one after God's own heart, set as his King upon the holy hill of Zion, made the head of the corner, with whom the covenant of royalty is made, and to whom God would *give the throne of his father David*. He is the *plant of renown*, because a *righteous branch* (Jer. xxiii. 5), *beautiful* and *glorious*, Isa. iv. 2. Some understand it of the church, the *planting of the Lord*, Isa. lxi. 3.

2. Concerning the great charter by which the kingdom of the Messiah should be founded (v. 25): *I*

will make with them a covenant of peace. The covenant of grace is a covenant of peace. The tenor of this covenant is: "*I the Lord will be their God*, a God all-sufficient to them (v. 24)." Those, and those only, that have the Lord Jesus for *their prince* have the Lord Jehovah for *their God*.

3. Concerning the privileges of those that are the faithful subjects of this kingdom of the Messiah. These are here set forth figuratively, as the blessings of the flock. But we have a key to it, v. 31. Those that belong to this flock, though they are spoken of as *sheep*, are really men.

(1) They shall enjoy a holy security under the divine protection. Christ, our good Shepherd, has *caused the evil beasts to cease out of the land* (v. 25), having vanquished all our spiritual enemies. Sin and Satan, death and hell, are conquered. And then *they shall dwell safely*, not only in the folds, but in the fields, *in the wilderness, in the woods*. Through Christ, God delivers his people not only from the things they have reason to fear, but from their fear even of death itself.

(2) They shall enjoy a spiritual plenty of all good things. *They shall no more be consumed with hunger in the land*, v. 29. *Showers of blessings* shall come upon them, v. 26, 27. The heavens shall yield their dews; the *trees of the field* also shall *yield their fruit*. All that are in the neighbourhood of Zion shall fare the better for it; and the nearer the church the nearer its God. The *effect of this plenty* is, *I will make them a blessing*. They shall be blessings to all about them. Those that are the *blessed of the Lord* must study to make themselves blessings to the world. He that is good, let him do *good*; he that has received the gift, the grace, let him minister the same.

CHAPTER 35

This chapter enlarges upon the promise concerning the destruction of the enemies of the church; the next chapter upon the promise, the replenishing of the church with blessings. Mount Seir (that is, Edom) is the enemy prophesied against in this chapter, but fitly put here, as in the prophecy of Obadiah, for all the enemies of the church. I. The sin charged upon the Edomites was their spite and malice to Israel, ver. 5, 10–13. II. God will be against them (ver. 2) and then their country shall be laid waste (ver. 4), and made desolate (ver. 6–9), and left so when other nations that had been wasted should recover themselves, ver. 14, 15.

Verses 1–9

Mount Seir was mentioned as partner with Moab in one of the threatenings we had before (ch. xxv. 8); but here it has woes of its own.

I. God espouses his people's cause, and takes what is done against them as done against himself; and it is upon their account that God now contends with the Edomites. 1. Because of the enmity they had against the people of God. "Thou hast had a *perpetual hatred* to them, to the very name of an Israelite." The Edomites kept up an *hereditary* malice against Israel, the same that Esau bore to Jacob. The posterity of Esau would never be reconciled to the seed of Jacob. It is strange how deeply-rooted national antipathies sometimes are, and how long they last. 2. Because of the injuries they had done to the people of God. They did not attack them as fair and open enemies, but laid wait for them, to *cut off* those of them that had escaped (Obad. 14).

II. What should be the effect and issue of that controversy. If God stretch out his hand against the country of Edom, he will *make it most desolate*, v. 3. *Thou hast not hated blood;* it implies, "Thou hast delighted in it and thirsted after it." Some read it, "*Unless thou hatest blood*" (that is, unless thou dost repent, and put off this bloody disposition) *blood shall pursue thee.*" Those that help forward the desolations of Israel may expect to be themselves made desolate. And that which completes the judgment is that Edom shall be made *perpetual desolations* (v. 9).

Verses 10-15

I. A further account of the sin of the Edomites, and their bad conduct towards the people of God. We find the church complaining of them for setting on the Babylonians, and irritating them against Jerusalem, saying, *Rase it, rase it* (Ps. cxxxvii. 7), inflaming a rage that needed no spur. They were glad when the Chaldeans did them a mischief. They pleased themselves with hopes that when the people of Israel were destroyed they should be let into the possession of their country. Those have the spirit of Edomites who desire the death of others, because they hope to get by it, or are pleased with their failing because they expect to come into their business. But in this case of the Edomites' coveting the land of Israel, and gaping for it, there was a particular affront to God. They expected possession upon a vacancy, because Israel was driven out, *whereas the Lord was* still *there*, v. 10. That was Immanuel's land (Isa. viii. 8); in that land he was to be born.

II. The notice God took of the barbarous insolence of the Edomites, and the doom passed upon them for it: *I have heard all thy blasphemies*, v. 12. And again (v. 13), *You have multiplied your words against me*, and *I have heard them*. God has heard the Edomites' blasphemy; let them therefore hear their doom, v. 14, 15. It was a national sin and therefore shall be punished with a national desolation. The punishment shall answer to the sin: "*As thou didst rejoice in the desolation of the house of Israel*, God will give thee enough of desolation; since thou art so fond of it, *thou shalt be desolate; I will make thee so*." Some read v. 14 so as to complete the resemblance between the sin and the punishment: *The whole earth shall rejoice when I make thee desolate, as thou didst rejoice when Israel* was made desolate.

CHAPTER 36

Two distinct prophecies in this chapter: I. The temporal estate of the Jews, wherein their present deplorable condition is described; but it is promised that their grievances shall be all redressed and that in due time they shall be settled again in their own land, in peace and plenty, ver. 1-15. II. Their spiritual estate, wherein they are reminded of their former sins, ver. 16-20. But it is promised, 1. That God would glorify himself in showing mercy to them, ver. 21-24. 2. That he would sanctify them, by giving them his grace and fitting them for his service in answer to their prayers, ver. 25-38.

Verses 1-15

Now God is returning in mercy the prophet must speak good words and comfortable words, v. 1 and again v. 4. *You mountains of Israel, hear the word of the Lord;* and what he says to them he says *to the hills, to the rivers, to the valleys, to the desolate wastes* in the country, and to the cities *that are forsaken*, v. 4. and again v. 6. The people were gone, but the places, the mountains and valleys; these the Chaldeans could not carry away with them. Now, to show the mercy God had in reserve for the people, he is to speak of him as having a dormant kindness for the place.

I. The compassionate notice God takes of the present deplorable condition of the land of Israel. It has become both a *prey* and a *derision to the heathen that are round about*, v. 4. 1. They are all enriched with the plunder of it. No one thought it any crime to strip an Israelite. It is the common cry, when a man is down, *Down with him*. 2. It has become a derision to them. *The enemy said, "Aha! even the ancient high places are ours in possession*," v. 2. God takes notice of it here as an aggravation of the present calamity of Israel: *You are taken up in the lips of talkers and are an infamy of the people*, v. 3.

II. The expressions of God's just displeasure against those who triumphed in the desolations of the land of Israel, and Idumea particularly. 1. They carved

out large possessions to themselves out of God's land; for so indeed it was: "*They have appointed my land into their possession* (v. 5), and so not only invaded their neighbour's property, but intrenched upon God's prerogative." Those that had not an opportunity of making a prey of God's people made a reproach of them; so that they were *the shame of the heathen*, v. 6. 2. God has determined to reckon with them for it, and this *in the fire of his jealousy*, both for his own honour and for the honour of his people, v. 5. They spoke in their malice against God's people, and God will speak *in his jealousy and in his fury*, v. 6. *Surely the heathen that are about you, they shall bear their shame*, v. 7.

III. The promises of God's favour to his Israel and assurances given of great mercy in store for them. The prophet must say to the *mountains of Israel*, now *desolate and despised*, that God is *for them* and will *turn to them*, v. 9. Their rightful owners should return to the possession of them: *My people Israel are at hand to come*, v. 8. Though they are dispersed in many countries, yet they shall *come again to their own border*, Jer. xxxi. 17. The time is at hand for their return. The mountains of Israel are now desolate; but God will *cause men to walk upon them* again, *even his people Israel*, not as travellers, but as inhabitants. It was a type of the heavenly Canaan, to which all God's children are heirs. When the land had *enjoyed her sabbaths* for so many years, it should be so much the more fruitful. *You shall be tilled and sown* (v. 9) and shall *yield your fruit to my people Israel*, v. 8. The people of Israel should have a comfortable settlement, in their own land: The *cities shall be inhabited; the wastes shall be builded*, v. 10. And *I will settle you after your old estates*, v. 11. *I will do better unto you* now *than at your beginnings*. God will bring back to it *all the house of Israel, even all of it* (observe what an emphasis is laid upon that, v. 10), all *whose spirits God stirred up* to return. God's kingdom in the world is a growing kingdom; and his church, though for a time it may be diminished, shall recover itself and be again replenished. The reproach long since cast upon the land of Israel by the evil spies, and of late revived, that *it was a land that ate up the inhabitants* of it by famine, sickness, and the sword, should be quite rolled away. *Thou shalt no more bereave them of men* (v. 12), shalt *devour men no more*, v. 14. When the nation is made to flourish in peace (v. 15), especially when it is reformed; when sin is taken away, then they *hear no more the reproach of the people*.

Verses 16-24

I. How God's name had suffered both by the sins and by the miseries of Israel. 1. God's glory had been injured by the sin of Israel when they were in their own land, v. 17. It was a good land, a land that had the eye of God upon it. *But they defiled it by their own way*. What was unclean might not be made use of. By the abuse of the gifts of God's bounty to us we forfeit the use of them; and, the mind and conscience being defiled with guilt, no comfort is allowed us, *nothing is pure* to us. They *shed blood and worshipped idols* (v. 18) and with those sins *defiled the land*. God was righteous for he *judged them according to their way and according to their doings*, v. 19. 2. When they *entered into the land of the heathen* God had no glory by them there; but, on the contrary, his holy name was profaned, v. 20. The enemies of God took occasion to reproach God, as unable to protect his own worshippers and to make good his own grants.

II. How God would retrieve his honour by working a great reformation upon them and then working a great salvation for them. "I *will gather you out of all countries and bring you into your own land*, v. 24.

Not for your sake, for you are most unworthy, but *for my holy name's sake* (v. 22), that *I may sanctify my great name*," v. 23.

Verses 25–38

The people of God might be discouraged in their hopes of a restoration by the sense of their unfitness, and that is answered in these verses, with a promise that God would by his grace prepare them for the mercy and then bestow it. And this was in part fulfilled in that wonderful effect which the captivity in Babylon had upon the Jews there, that it effectually cured them of their inclination to idolatry.

I. God here promises that he will work a good work in them, v. 25–27. 1. That God would cleanse them from the pollutions of sin (v. 25): *I will sprinkle clean water upon you*, which signifies both the blood of Christ sprinkled upon the conscience to purify that and to take away the sense of guilt, and the grace of the Spirit sprinkled on the whole soul to purify it from all corrupt inclinations, as Naaman was cleansed from his leprosy by dipping in Jordan. And (v. 29) *I will save you from all your uncleannesses*. 2. That God would give them a *new heart*, a disposition of mind vastly different from what it was before. 3. That, instead of a *heart of stone*, insensible and unapt to receive divine impressions and to return devout affections, God would give a *heart of flesh*, a soft and tender heart, that has spiritual senses exercised, complying in everything with the will of God. 4. That since, besides our inclination to sin, we complain of an inability to do our duty, God will *cause them to walk in his statutes* and thoroughly furnish them with wisdom and will, and active powers, for every good work.

II. God here promises that he will take them into covenant with himself. The sum of the covenant of grace we have, v. 28.

III. When they are thus prepared for mercy they shall return to their possessions and be settled again in them (v. 28): *You shall dwell in the land that I gave to your fathers*. This shall follow upon the blessed reformation God would work among them (v. 33): "*In the day that I shall have cleansed you from all your iniquities*, and so shall have made you meet for the inheritance, *I will cause you to dwell in the cities*, and so put you in possession of the inheritance." This is God's method of mercy indeed, first to part men from their sins, and then to restore them to their comforts. Then they shall enjoy a plenty of all good things. *I will call for the corn and will increase it*, v. 29. The land that had long *lain desolate in the sight of all that passed by*, who looked upon it, some with contempt and some with compassion, shall again *be tilled* (v. 34). And such a blessing will God command on the *hand of the diligent* that all who pass by shall take notice of it, with wonder, v. 35. Crowds are a lovely sight in God's temple.

IV. He shows what shall be *the happy effects of this blessed change*. It shall bring them to an ingenuous repentance for their sins (v. 31): *Then shall you remember your own evil ways and shall loathe yourselves*. It shall have a happy effect upon their neighbours, for it shall bring them to a more clear knowledge of God (v. 36).

V. He proposes these things to them, not as the *recompence* of their merits, but as the return of their prayers. They must own that the mercies they receive from God are not only not merited, but that they are a thousand times forfeited; they must be so far from boasting of their good works that they must be ashamed of their evil ways, and then they are best prepared for mercy. He requires that his people should *seek unto him*, when he is coming towards them in ways of mercy. They must pray for it, for by prayer God is sought.

CHAPTER 37

The promises of restoration and deliverance, which we have here in the latter part of the book, are for the encouraging of a humble faith. God had assured them that he would gather the house of Israel, even all of it, and return them to their own land; but there were two things that rendered this very unlikely: I. That they were so dispersed among their enemies, and so dispirited likewise in their own minds; they are here, in vision, compared to a valley full of the dry bones of dead men, which should be brought together and raised to life. The vision of this we have (ver. 1–10) and the explication of it, with its application to the present case, ver. 11–14. II. That they were so divided among themselves, too much of the old enmity between Judah and Ephraim remaining even in their captivity. But by a sign of two sticks made one in the hand of the prophet is foreshown the happy coalition that should be, at their return, between the two nations of Israel and Judah, ver. 15–22. In this there was a type of the uniting of Jews and Gentiles, Jews and Samaritans, in Christ and his church. And so the prophet slides into a prediction of the kingdom of Christ, ver. 23–28 .

Verses 1–14

I. The vision of a resurrection from death to life.

1. It is without doubt a most lively representation of a threefold resurrection. (1) The resurrection of souls from the death of sin to the life of righteousness, to a holy, heavenly, spiritual, and divine life, by the power of divine grace going along with the word of Christ, John v. 24, 25. (2) The resurrection of the gospel church, from an afflicted persecuted state, to liberty and peace. (3) The resurrection of the body at the great day, especially the bodies of believers that shall rise to life eternal.

2. The particulars of this vision.

(1) The deplorable condition of these dead bones. The prophet was in vision, carried out and set *in the midst of a valley*, probably that plain spoken of ch. iii. 22, where God then *talked with him*; and it was *full of bones*, of dead men's bones, scattered upon the face of the ground, as if some bloody battle had been fought there, and the slain left unburied, and nothing left but the bones, and those disjointed from one another and dispersed. *Lo, they were very dry*, having been long exposed to the sun and wind. The Jews in Babylon were like those dead and dry bones, unlikely ever to come together, less likely to be formed into a body, and least of all to be a living body. He was made to own their case deplorable, and not to be helped by any power less than that of God himself (v. 3): "Son of man, *can these bones live?* Can thy philosophy reach to put life into dry bones, or thy politics to restore a captive nation?" "Lord, thou knowest whether they can and whether they shall; if thou dost not put life into them, it is certain that they cannot live."

(2) The means used for the bringing of these dispersed bones together and these dead and dry bones to life. Ezekiel is ordered to *prophesy upon these bones* (v. 4 and again v. 9) to *prophesy to the wind*. So he *prophesied as he was commanded*, v. 7, 10. He must preach, and he did so; and the dead bones lived by a power that went along with the word of God which he preached. He must pray, and he did so; and the dead bones were made to live in answer to prayer; for a *spirit of life* entered into them. See the efficacy of the word and prayer, and the necessity of both, for the raising of dead souls. But we call in vain, still they are dead: still they are very dry; we must therefore be earnest with God in prayer for the working of the Spirit with the word: *Come, O breath!* and breathe upon them. God's grace can save souls without our preaching, but our preaching cannot save them without God's grace, and that grace must be sought by prayer.

(3) The wonderful effect of these means. Those that do as they are commanded, in the face of the greatest discouragements, need not doubt of success. Ezekiel looked down and prophesied upon the bones in the valley, and they became human bodies. *First,*

That which he had to *say to them* was that God would infallibly raise them to life, *v.* 5 and again *v.* 6. *Secondly,* That which was immediately done for them was that they were moulded anew into shape. Even dead and dry bones begin to move when they are called to hear the word of the Lord. This was fulfilled, when, upon Cyrus's proclamation of liberty, those whose spirits God had stirred up began to think of making use of that liberty, and getting ready to be gone. But this was not all: *The bones came together bone to his bone,* under a divine direction; and, though there is in man a multitude of bones, yet of all the bones of those numerous slain not one was missing, not one missed its way, not one missed its place, but each knew and found its fellow. The dispersed bones came together and the displaced bones were knit together. Thus it was in the return of the Jews; those that were scattered in several parts of the province of Babylon came to their respective families. By degrees *sinews* and *flesh* came upon these bones, and the *skin covered them, v.* 8. This was fulfilled when the captives got their effects about them, and the *men of their place helped them* with *silver,* and *gold,* and whatever they needed for their remove, Ezra i. 4. But still there was *no breath in them*; they wanted spirit and courage for such a difficult and hazardous enterprise as this was of returning to their own land. Ezekiel then looked up and prophesied to the *wind,* or *breath,* or *spirit,* and said, *Come, O breath! and breathe upon these slain.* In answer to this request, *the breath* immediately came *into them, v.* 10. The spirit of life is from God; he at first in the creation breathed into man the breath of life, and so he will at last in the resurrection. The dispirited captives were animated with resolution to break through all the discouragements that lay in the way of their return. And then they *stood upon their feet, an exceedingly great army*; not only living men, but effective men, fit for service and formidable.

II. The application of this vision to the present calamitous condition of the Jews in captivity: *These bones are the whole house of Israel,* both the ten tribes and the two.

1. The depth of despair to which they are now reduced, *v.* 11. When troubles continue long, hopes have been often frustrated, nothing but an active faith in the power, promise, and providence of God will keep them from quite dying away. "*Therefore,* because things have come thus to the last extremity, *prophesy to them,* and tell them, now is God's time to appear for them. *Jehovah-jireh—in the mount of the Lord it shall be seen,*" *v.* 12–14.

Verses 15–28

Precious promises made of the happy state of the Jews after their return to their own land; but they have a further reference to the kingdom of the Messiah and the glories of gospel-times.

I. It is here promised that Ephraim and Judah shall be happily united. Ever since the desertion of the ten tribes from the house of David under Jeroboam, there had been continual feuds and animosities between the two kingdoms of Israel and Judah, even in the land of their captivity. Now there should be a coalition between them. This is here illustrated by a sign. The prophet was to take *two sticks,* and write upon one, *For Judah* (including Benjamin, those of the *children of Israel* that were *his companions*), upon the other, *For Joseph,* including the rest of the tribes, *v.* 16. These two sticks must be so framed as to fall into *one in his hand, v.* 17. The meaning was that Judah and Israel should become *one in the hand of God, v.* 19. 1. They shall be one, one nation, *v.* 22. They shall have no separate interests, and, consequently, no divided affections. They had been two sticks crossing and thwarting

one another, beating and bruising one another; but now they shall become one, supporting and strengthening one another. 2. They shall be one in *God's hand*; by his power they shall be united. They shall be one in his hand, for his glory shall be the centre of their unity and his grace the cement of it. 3. They shall be one in their return out of captivity (*v.* 21). Their having been joint-sufferers will contribute to this blessed comprehension. Put many pieces of metal together into the furnace, and, when they are melted, they will run all together. God's loving them all was a good reason why they should love one another. 4. They shall all be the subjects of one king, and so they shall become one. The Jews, after their return, were under one government, and not divided as formerly. But this certainly looks further, to the kingdom of Christ; he is that one King in allegiance to whom all God's spiritual Israel shall cheerfully unite.

II. It is here promised that the Jews shall by their captivity be cured of their inclination to idolatry (*v.* 23). Two ways God will take to cure them of their idolatry: 1. By bringing them out of the way of temptation to it. 2. By changing the disposition of their mind: *I will cleanse them* (*v.* 23).

III. It is here promised that they shall be the people of God, and the subjects and sheep of Christ their King and Shepherd. These promises are here repeated (*v.* 23, 24) for the encouragement of the faith of Israel. *David, my servant, shall be king over them.* Christ is this David, Israel's King of old.

IV. It is here promised that they shall dwell comfortably, *v.* 25, 26. They shall dwell in the land of Israel. They shall have it by covenant; they shall come in again upon their old title, by virtue of the grant made unto *Jacob,* God's *servant.* They shall come to it by prescription. It was the inheritance of their ancestors, and therefore shall be theirs. They are *beloved for their fathers' sakes. They shall dwell therein* all their time, and shall leave it for an inheritance *to their children and their children's children for ever.* They shall live under a good government.

V. It is here promised that God will dwell among them: *I will set my sanctuary in the midst of them for evermore; my tabernacle also shall be with them, v.* 26, 27. They shall have opportunity of keeping up communion with him, which will be the comfort of their lives. They shall have the means of grace. By the oracles of God in his tabernacle they shall be made wiser and better, and all their children shall be taught of the Lord. Thus their covenant relation to God shall be improved and the bond of it strengthened.

VI. Both God and Israel shall have the honour of this among the heathen, *v.* 26. "The very heathen shall be made to know that *the Lord sanctifies* Israel, because his sanctuary is, and shall be, in the midst of them."

CHAPTER 38

This chapter, and that which follows it, are concerning Gog and Magog, a powerful enemy to the people of Israel, that should make a descent upon them, but their army should be routed and their design defeated; and this prophecy, it is most probable, had its accomplishment after the return of the people of Israel in the struggles they had with the kings of Syria, especially Antiochus Epiphanes, or in some other way. God had by the prophet assured his people of happy times after their return to their own land; but he here tells them, as Christ told his disciples, that in the world they shall have tribulation, but they may be of good cheer, for they shall be victorious at last. But the old Testament prophecies had their accomplishment in the Jewish church as the New Testament prophecies shall have when the time comes in the Christian church. I. The attempt that Gog and Magog should make upon the land of Israel, the vast army they should bring into the field, and their vast preparations (ver. 4–7), their project and design in it (ver. 8–13), God's hand in it, ver. 4. II. The great terror that this should strike upon the land of Israel, ver. 15, 16, 18–20. III. The divine protection that Israel should be under, ver. 2–4, and again ver. 14. IV. The defeat that should be given to those enemies by the immediate hand of God (ver. 21–23).

Verses 1–13

The critical expositors have enough to do here to enquire about Gog and Magog. Some think they find them afar off, in Scythia, Tartary, and Russia. Others think they find them nearer the land of Israel, in Syria, and Asia the Less. Ezekiel is appointed to prophesy against Gog, and to tell him that *God is against him, v.* 2, 3.

I. The confusion which God designed to put this enemy to. It is remarkable that this is put first in the prophecy; before it is foretold that God will *bring him forth* against Israel it is foretold that God will *put hooks into his jaws* and *turn him back* (v. 4).

II. The undertaking which he designed to engage him in, in order to this defeat. 1. The nations that shall be confederate in this enterprise against Israel are many, and great, and mighty (v. 5, 6), *Persia, Ethiopia,* &c. Antiochus had an army made up of all the nations here named. 2. They are well furnished with arms—*horses and horsemen* (v. 4) bravely equipped *with all sorts of armour, bucklers and shields* for defence, *and all handling swords* for offence. *"Be thou prepared, and do thou prepare"* (v. 7). This call to prepare seems to be ironical—*Do thy worst,* but I will *turn thee back;* like that Isa. viii. 9. 3. Their design is against *the mountains of Israel* (v. 8), against *the land that is brought back from the sword.* It is not long since it was harassed with the sword of war, and it has scarcely recovered any strength since it was brought down by war. It is a people that *dwell safely, all of them, in unwalled villages,* very secure, and *having neither bars nor gates, v.* 11. They intend no mischief to their neighbours, for they fear no mischief from them. 4. That which the enemy has in view, in forming this project, is to enrich himself and to make himself master, not of the country, but of the wealth of it. It came into Antiochus's mind what a singular people these religious Jews were, and how their worship condemned the idolatries of their neighbours, and therefore, in enmity to their religion, he would plague them. It came into his mind what a wealthy people they were, that they had *gotten cattle and goods in the midst of the land* (v. 12). He came to this resolve (v. 11, 12): *"I will go up to the land of unwalled villages;* yea, that I will; it will cost me nothing to make them all my own." These were the thoughts that came into the mind of this wicked prince, and God knew them. 5. According to the project thus formed he pours in all his forces upon the land of Israel, and finds those that are ready to come in to his assistance with the same prospects (v. 9).

Verses 14–23

This latter part of the chapter is a repetition of the former.

I. It is again foretold that this spiteful enemy should make a formidable descent upon the land of Israel (v. 15). Thou shalt soon find that there is *no enchantment against Jacob,* that *no weapon formed against them shall prosper;* thou shalt know to thy cost, shalt know to thy shame, that though they have no walls, nor bars, nor gates, they have God himself, a *wall of fire, round about them,* and that he who *touches them touches the apple of his eye;* whosoever meddles with them meddles to his own hurt. But God said: *I will bring thee against my land.* This is strange news, that God will not only permit his enemies to come against his own children, but will himself bring them. It is *"that the heathen may know me* to be the only living and true God *when I shall be sanctified in thee,* O Gog! that is, in thy defeat and destruction *before their eyes,* that all the nations may see, and say, *There is none like unto the God of Jeshurun, that rides on the heavens for the help of his people."*

II. Reference is herein had to the predictions of the former prophets (v. 17). Moses spoke in his prophecy of the latter days, Deut. xxxii. 43, and David, Ps. ix. 15, and often elsewhere in the Psalms. This is the leviathan of whom Isaiah spoke (Isa. xxvii. 1), that congress of the nations of which Joel spoke, Joel iii. 1.

III. It is here foretold that this furious formidable enemy should be utterly cut off in this attempt upon Israel. This is supposed by many to have its accomplishment in the many defeats given by the Maccabees to the forces of Antiochus. *When he comes up* in pride and anger *against the land of Israel,* then *God's fury shall come up in his face,* which is an allusion to men, whose colour rises in their faces when some high affront is offered them, v. 18. His forces shall be put into the greatest confusion and consternation imaginable (v. 19): *There shall be a great shaking of* them *in the land of Israel* (v. 20), such as shall affect the *fishes* and *fowls,* the *beasts* and *creeping things,* and much more *the men that are upon the face of the earth.* He shall be routed and utterly ruined; both earth and heaven shall be armed against him. The great men of Syria shall undermine and overthrow one another. The artillery of heaven shall also be drawn out against them: *I will rain upon him an overflowing rain, v.* 22. He comes like a storm upon Israel, v. 9. But God will come like a storm upon him.

CHAPTER 39

This chapter concludes the prophecy against Gog and Magog, in whose destruction God crowns his favour to his people Israel. I. An express prediction of the utter destruction of Gog and Magog, ver. 1–7. II. The vastness of that destruction: the burning of their weapons (ver. 8–10), the burying of their slain (ver. 11–16), and the feasting of the fowls with the dead bodies of those that were unburied, ver. 17–22. III. A declaration of God's gracious purposes concerning his people Israel, ver. 23–29.

Verses 1–7

This prophecy begins as that before (ch. xxxviii. 3, 4, *I am against thee, and I will turn thee back*). 1. His soldiers shall be disarmed and so disabled to carry on their enterprise, v. 3. 2. He and the greatest part of his army shall be slain in the field of battle (v. 4). Thou shalt *fall upon the open field* (v. 5). Even upon the mountains he shall not find a pass that he shall be able to maintain, and upon the open field he shall not find a road for his escape. Never was army so totally routed as this. And, for its greater infamy and reproach, their bodies shall be a feast to the birds of prey, v. 4. 3. His country also shall be made desolate: *I will send a fire on Magog* (v. 6) and *among those that dwell carelessly,* or confidently, *in the isles,* that is, the nations of the Gentiles. His people Israel shall hereby know more of God's name, of his power and goodness, his care of them, his faithfulness to them. And this is God's method of dealing with men, first to enlighten their understandings, and by that means to influence the whole man; he first makes us to know his holy name, and so keeps us from polluting it and engages us to honour it. The heathen those that never knew it, or would not own it, shall *know that I am the Lord, the Holy One in Israel.*

Verses 8–22

Though this prophecy was to have its accomplishment in the latter days, yet it is here spoken of as if it were already accomplished, because it is certain (v. 8). To represent the routing of the army of Gog as very great, here are three things specified as the consequences of it. It was God himself that gave the defeat; we do not find that the people of Israel drew a sword or struck a stroke: but,

I. They shall *burn their weapons,* their *bows and arrows,* which *fell out of their hands* (v. 3), everything that is combustible. They should have no occasion to *take wood out of the field or forests* for *seven years* together (*v.* 10), such vast quantities of weapons shall there be left upon the open field where the enemy fell.

II. They shall bury their dead. The slain lie dispersed on the mountains of Israel, and it is left to the house of Israel to bury them. A place shall be appointed for the burying of them, *the valley of the passengers, on the east of the sea,* either the salt sea or the sea of Tiberias. And it shall be called, *The valley of Hamon-gog,* that is, *of the multitude of Gog.* Acts of humanity add much to the renown of God's Israel; and a good work it is to bury the dead, though they be strangers and enemies to the commonwealth of Israel.

Verses 23–29

This has reference not only to the predictions concerning Gog and Magog, but to all the prophecies of this book concerning the captivity of the house of Israel, and their restoration and return out of their captivity.

I. God will let the heathen know the meaning of his people's troubles. Upon their reformation and return to him, he turned again their captivity, and brought them back to their own land, and wrought great salvations for them. Then it would be made to appear, even to the heathen, that there was no ground at all for their reflection, that Israel went into captivity because God could not protect them, but because they had by sin forfeited his favour and thrown themselves out of his protection (*v.* 23, 24). That was the true reason why God *hid his face from them* and *gave them into the hand of their enemies.* 1. God punishes sin even in his own people, because he hates it most in those that are nearest and dearest to him, Amos iii. 2. 2. When God gives up his people for a prey, it is to correct them and reform them, not to gratify their enemies, Isa. x. 7; xlii. 24. 3. No sooner do God's people humble themselves under the rod than he returns in mercy to them.

II. God will give his own people to know what favour he has in store for them (*v.* 25, 26).

1. Now God will *have mercy upon the whole house of Israel,* because they repent of their sins. God has justly brought them into a land of trouble, where everyone makes them afraid, because they had trespassed against him in a land of peace, where none made them afraid. And, when they thus humble themselves under humbling providences, God will bring again their captivity.

2. As God was reproached in the reproach they were under during their captivity, so he will be sanctified in their reformation and the making of them a holy people again, and will be glorified in their restoration and the making of them a happy glorious people again, *v.* 27. Then they shall have the benefit of it (*v.* 28): *They shall know that I am the Lord their God.*

CHAPTER 40

The waters of the sanctuary which this prophet saw in vision (ch. xlvii. 1) are a proper representation of this prophecy. Here is one continued vision, beginning at this chapter, to the end of the book, which is justly looked upon to be one of the most difficult portions of scripture. Many commentators, both ancient and modern, have owned themselves at a loss. But because it is hard to be understood we must humbly search it, get as far as we can into it and as much as we can out of it, and, when we despair of satisfaction in every difficulty, bless God that our salvation does not depend upon it, but that things necessary are plain enough. Here is the vision of a glorious temple (in this chapter and ch. xli and xlii), of God's taking possession of it (ch. xliii), orders concerning the priests that are to minister in this temple (ch. xliv), the division of the land, what portion should be allotted for the sanctuary, what for the city, and what for the prince (ch. xlv), and further instructions for him and the people, ch. xlvi. After the vision of the holy waters we have the borders of the holy land, and the portions assigned to the tribes, and the dimensions and gates of the holy city, ch. xlvii, xlviii. Some make this to represent what had been during the flourishing state

of the Jewish church, how glorious Solomon's temple was in its best days, that the captives might see what they had lost by sin. But that seems not probable. The general scope of it I take to be, 1. To assure the captives that they should not only return to their own land, and be settled there, but that they should be encouraged to build another temple, which God would own, and where he would meet them and bless them, that the ordinances of worship should be revived, and the sacred priesthood should there attend. 2. To direct them to look further than all this, and to expect the coming of the Messiah, who had before been prophesied of under the name of David. The dimensions of these visionary buildings being so large, plainly intimates, as Dr. Lightfoot observes, that these things cannot be literally, but must be spiritually, understood. And the gospel-temple, erected by Christ and his apostles, was so closely connected with the second material temple, was erected just at the time when that fell into decay, that it was proper enough that they should both be referred to in one and the same vision. Under the type and figure of a temple and altar, priests and sacrifices, is foreshown the spiritual worship that should be performed in gospel times, and perfected at last in the kingdom of glory, in which perhaps these visions will have their full accomplishment, and some think in some happy and glorious state of the gospel-church on this side heaven, in the latter days.

In this chapter we have, I. A general account of this vision of the temple and city, ver. 1–4. II. A particular account of it, and a description given, 1. Of the outside wall, ver. 5. 2. Of the east gate, ver. 6–19. 3. Of the north gate, ver. 20–23. 4. Of the south gate (ver. 24–31) and the chambers and other appurtenances be onging to these gates. 5. Of the inner court, both towards the east and towards the south, ver. 32–38. 6. Of the tables, ver. 39–43. 7. Of the lodgings for the singers and the priests, ver. 44–47 8. Of the porch of the house, ver. 48, 49.

Verses 1–4

1. The date of this vision. It was in the twenty-fifth year of Ezekiel's captivity (*v.* 1), which some compute to be the thirty-third year of the first captivity, and is here said to be the *fourteenth year after the city was smitten.* "Then *the hand of the Lord was upon me* and *brought me thither* to Jerusalem, now that it was in ruins, desolate and deserted"—a pitiable sight to the prophet. 2. The prophet was brought, *in the visions of God, to the land of Israel, v.* 2. Here he is carried thither to have a pleasing prospect of it in its glory. He was set *upon a very high mountain,* as Moses upon the top of Pisgah, to view this land, which was now a second time a *land of promise.* From the top of this mountain he saw this city was a temple as large as a city. It is a city for men to dwell in; it is a temple for God to dwell in; for in the church on earth God dwells with men, in that in heaven men dwell with God. 3. The particular discoveries of this city were made to him by *a man whose appearance was like the appearance of brass* (*v.* 3), Jesus Christ. It is through Christ that we have both acquaintance with and access to the benefits and privileges of God's house. His appearing like brass intimates both his brightness and his strength. 4. The dimensions of this city or temple were taken with a *line of flax* and a *measuring reed,* or *rod* (*v.* 3). 5. Directions are here given to the prophet to receive this revelation from the Lord and transmit it pure and entire to the church, *v.* 4.

Verses 5–26

The measuring-reed which was in the hand of the surveyor-general was mentioned before, *v.* 3. Here we are told (*v.* 5) what was the exact length of it. It was *six cubits long,* not the common cubit, but the *cubit of the sanctuary,* and that was a hand-breadth (that is, four inches) longer than the common cubit: the common cubit was eighteen inches, this twenty-two, see *ch.* xliii. 13. Some critics contend that this *measuring-reed* was but six common cubits in length, and one hand-breadth added to the whole. The former seems more probable. Here is an account,

I. Of the outer wall of the house, which encompassed it round, which denotes the separation between the church and the world.

II. Of the several gates with the chambers adjoining to them.

1. He begins with the *east gate,* because that was the usual way of entering into the lower end of the

temple, the holy of holies being at the west end. Now, in the account of this gate, observe, (1) That he went up to it by *stairs* (v. 6), for when we go to worship God we must ascend; so is the call, Rev. iv. 1. (2) That the chambers adjoining to the gates were but *little chambers*, about ten feet square, v. 7. These were for those to lodge in who attended the service of the house. (3) The chambers, as they were each of them four-square, so they were all of *one measure*, that there might be an equality among the attendants. (4) The chambers were very many; for in our Father's house there are *many mansions* (John xiv. 2), in his house above, and in that here on earth. Some make these chambers to represent the particular congregations of believers, which are parts of the great temple, the universal church. (5) It is said (v. 14), *He made also the posts.* (6) Here are posts of sixty cubits, which, some think, was literally fulfilled when Cyrus, in his edict for rebuilding the temple at Jerusalem, ordered that the height thereof should be sixty cubits, that is, thirty yards and more, Ezra vi. 3. (7) Here were windows to the little chambers, and windows to *the posts and arches* (that is, to the cloisters below), and *windows round about* (v. 16), to signify the light from heaven with which the church is illuminated. There were lights to the little chambers; even the least. But they are *narrow windows.* The discoveries made to the church on earth are but narrow compared with what shall be in the future state. (8) Divers courts are here spoken of, an outermost of all, then an outer court, then an inner, and then the innermost of all, into which the priests only entered. These courts had porches, or piazzas, round them, for the shelter of those that attended in them from wind and weather. (9) On the posts were palm-trees engraven (v. 16), to signify that *the righteous shall flourish like the palm-tree* in the courts of God's house, Ps. xcii. 12. The more they are depressed with the burden of affliction the more strongly do they grow, as they say of the palm-trees. (10) Notice is taken of the pavement of the court, v. 17, 18. The word intimates that the pavement was made of *porphyry-stone*, which was of the colour of *burning coals*; for the brightest glories of this world should be put under our feet when we draw near to God.

2. The gates that looked towards the north (v. 20) and towards the south (v. 24), are much the same with that towards the east, *after the measure of the first gate*, v. 21. This temple had not only a gate towards the east, to let into it the *children of the east*, that were famous for their wealth and wisdom, but it had a gate to the north, and another to the south, for the admission of the poorer and less civilised nations. The new Jerusalem has *twelve gates*, three towards each quarter of the world (Rev. xxi. 13); for many shall come from all parts to sit down there, Matt. viii. 11.

Verses 27–38

A delineation of the inner court. The survey of the inner court begins with the south side (v. 27), proceeds to the east (v. 32), and so to the north (v. 35). 1. These gates into the inner court were exactly uniform with those into the outer court. The work of grace is the same, for substance, in grown Christians that they are in young beginners. 2. The ascent into the outer court at each gate was by *seven steps*, but the ascent into the inner court at each gate was by *eight steps*. This is expressly taken notice of (v. 31, 34, 37), to signify that the nearer we approach to God the more we should rise above this world and the things of it. The people, who worshipped in the outer court, must rise seven steps above other people, but the priests, who attended in the inner court, must rise eight steps above them.

Verses 39–49

An account,

I. Of the tables that were in the porch of the gates of the inner court. Here were eight tables provided, whereon to *slay the sacrifices*, v. 41. They are to intimate the multitude of spiritual sacrifices that should be brought to God's house in gospel-times. Here were the shambles for the altar (v. 43), and there also they washed the burnt-offerings (v. 38), to intimate that before we draw near to God's altar we must wash our hands, our hearts, those spiritual sacrifices.

II. Of the use of the chambers. 1. Some were for the *singers*, v. 44. The singing of psalms should still continue a gospel-ordinance. Christians should be singers. 2. Others of them were for *the priests*, both those that kept *the charge of the house*, to cleanse it, and to keep it in good repair (v. 45), and those that *kept the charge of the altar* (v. 46).

III. Of the inner court, the court of the priests, which was fifty yards square, v. 47. The altar that *was before the house* was placed in the midst of this court. Christ is both our altar and our sacrifice, to whom we must look with faith in all our approaches to God.

IV. Of the porch of the house. There was a porch, to teach us not to rush hastily and inconsiderately into the presence of God, but gravely, and with solemnity, passing first through the outer court, then the inner, then the porch, ere we enter into the house.

CHAPTER 41

The temple itself, the description of which creates much difficulty to the critical expositors. It shall suffice us to observe, I. The dimensions, the posts (ver. 1), the door (ver. 2), the wall and the side-chambers (ver. 5, 6), the foundations and wall of the chambers, their doors (ver. 8–11), and the house itself, ver. 13. II. The dimensions of the most holy place, ver. 3, 4. III. An account of another building against the separate place, ver. 12–15. IV. The manner of the building of the house, ver. 7, 16, 17. V. The ornaments, ver. 18–20. VI. The altar of incense and the table, ver. 22. VII. The doors between the temple and the oracle, ver. 23–26. There is so much difference in the terms of architecture between one age and another, one place and another, that it ought not to be any stumbling-block that there is so much hard to be understood. To a common carpenter or mason among the Jews at that time we may suppose that all this, in the literal sense of it, was easy enough.

Verses 1–11

1. After the prophet had observed the courts he was at length *brought to the temple*, v. 1. If we diligently attend to the instructions given us in the plainer parts of religion, and profit by them, we shall be led further into an acquaintance with the mysteries of the kingdom of heaven. Those that are willing to dwell in God's courts shall at length be brought into his temple. 2. When our Lord Jesus spoke of the destroying of *this temple*, which his hearers understood of this second temple of Jerusalem, he spoke of the temple of his body (John ii. 19, 21); Ezekiel's vision had respect to them both, including also his mystical body the church, called the *house of God* (1 Tim. iii. 15), and all the members of that body, *living temples*, in which the Spirit dwells. 3. The very posts of this temple, the door-posts, were far one from the other, and consequently the door was wide. In comparison with what had been under the law we may say, *Wide is the gate* which leads into the church, the ceremonial law, that wall of partition which had so much straitened the gate, being taken down. 4. The most holy place was an exact square, v. 4. The new Jerusalem is exactly square (Rev. xxi. 16), denoting its stability. 5. The upper stories were larger than the lower, v. 7. Care was taken that the timber might have *fast hold* (though God builds high, he builds firmly). The higher we build up ourselves in our most holy faith the more should our hearts, those living temples, be enlarged.

Verses 12–26

1. An account of a building that was *before the separate place* (that is, before the temple), *at the end towards the west* (v. 12). This stood in a court by itself. Perhaps, in this vision, it signified the setting up of a church among the Gentiles not inferior to the Jewish temple, but of quite another nature. 2. A description of the ornaments of the temple, and the other building. The walls on the inside from top to bottom were adorned with *cherubim and palm-trees*, placed alternately. Each cherub is said to have two *faces*, the *face of a man* and the *face of a young lion*, v. 19. These seem to represent the angels, who have more than the wisdom of a man and the courage of a lion; the palms of victory are set before them. 3. A description of the posts of the doors both of the temple and of the sanctuary; they were *squared* (v. 21). In the tabernacle, and in Solomon's temple, the door of the sanctuary was narrower than that of the temple, but here it was as broad; for in gospel-times *the way into the holiest of all is made* more *manifest* than it was under the Old Testament (Heb. ix. 8). These doors are described, v. 23, 24. 4. The altar of incense, here said to be an *altar of wood*, v. 22. It would not bear the fire with which the incense was to be burned, unless it intimates that the incense to be offered in the gospel-temple shall be purely spiritual, and the fire spiritual. This altar is called a table. The great sacrifice being now offered, that which we have to do is to feast upon the sacrifice at the Lord's table.

CHAPTER 42

This chapter concludes the describing and measuring of this mystical temple. I. A description of the chambers that were about the courts (ver. 1–13), and the uses for which they were designed, ver. 13–14. II. A survey of the whole, and the courts belonging to it, ver. 15–20.

Verses 1–14

The prophet has taken a very exact view of the temple and is now brought again into the outer court.

I. A description of chambers which seems to us very intricate. We shall only observe, in general, 1. That about the temple, which was the place of public worship, there were private chambers. We must not only worship in the courts of God's house, but must, both before and after our attendance there, enter into our chambers, and read and meditate, and *pray to our Father in secret*. 2. That these chambers were many; there were *three stories* of them, v. 5, 6. There were many for such devout people as Anna the prophetess, who *departed not from the temple night or day*, Luke ii. 37. 3. That these chambers, though they were private, yet were near the temple, to prepare us for the exercises of devotion in public. 4. That before these chambers there were *walks of five yards broad* (v. 4), in which those that had lodgings in these chambers might meet and talk together, and share their experiences. Man is made for society, and Christians for the communion of saints.

II. The use of these chambers appointed, v. 13, 14. 1. They were *for the priests* that approach unto the Lord. *Therefore* they are called *holy chambers*, because they were for use of those that ministered in holy things during their ministration. 2. There the priests were to deposit *the most holy things*, those parts of the offerings which fell to their share. 3. There they were to lay their vestments, which God had appointed them to wear when they ministered at the altar. We read of the providing of priests garments after their return out of captivity, Neh. vii. 70, 72. When they had ended their service at the altar they must lay by those garments, but they must *put on other garments*, such as other people wear, when they approached to those things which were for the people, that is, to teach them the law and to answer their enquiries.

Verses 15–20

The measuring of this mystical temple to see how far the holy ground on which we tread extends. 1. It extended each way 500 reeds (v. 16–19), each reed above three yards and a half, so that it reached every way about an English measured mile. Thus large were the suburbs of this mystical temple, signifying the great extent of the gospel-times. Room should be made in God's courts for the numerous Gentiles, Isa. xlix. 18; lx. 4. 2. The dimensions were thus large to *make a separation*, by putting a distance *between the sanctuary* and *the profane place*. A difference is to be put between common and sacred things, between God's name and other names, between his day and other days, his book and other books.

CHAPTER 43

The prophet, having given us a view of the mystical temple, the gospel-church, as he received it from the Lord, comes to describe the worship that should be performed in it, but under the type of the Old Testament services. I. Possession taken of this temple, by the glory of God filling it, ver. 1–6. II. A promise given of the continuance of God's presence with his people upon condition of their return to the instituted way of worship, and their abandoning idolatry, ver. 7–12. III. A description of the altar of burnt-offerings, ver. 13–17. IV. Directions given for the consecration of that altar, ver. 18–27. Ezekiel seems there to stand between God and Israel, as Moses the servant of the Lord did when the sanctuary was first set up.

Verses 1–6

After Ezekiel has patiently surveyed the temple of God, the greatest glory of this earth, he is honoured with a sight of the glories of the upper world; *Come up hither*. He has seen the temple, spacious and splendid; but, till the glory of God comes into it, it is but like the dead bodies he had seen in vision (ch. xxxvii), that had *no breath* till the Spirit of life entered into them. Here therefore he sees the house filled with God's glory.

I. A vision of *the glory of God* (v. 2), *the glory of the God of Israel*, who is in covenant with Israel. The idols of the heathen have no glory but what they owe to the goldsmith or the painter. This glory came *from the way of the east*. Christ's *star was seen in the east*. For he is the morning star, he is the sun of righteousness. Two things in this appearance of the glory of God: 1. The power of his word which he heard: *His voice was like a noise of many waters*. Christ's gospel, in the glory of which he shines, was to be proclaimed aloud, the report of it to be heard far. 2. The brightness of his appearance which he saw: *The earth shone with his glory;* for God is light, and none can bear the lustre of his light, none *has seen* nor *can see it*. That glory of God which shines in the church shines on the world.

II. A vision of the entrance of this glory into the temple. When he saw this glory he *fell upon his face* (v. 3), in humble and reverent adoration. But the Spirit *took him up* (v. 5) when the *glory of the Lord* had *come into the house* (v. 4), that he might see how the house was filled with it. This was to have its accomplishment in that glory of the divine grace which shines so brightly in the gospel church, and fills it. Here is no mention of a cloud filling the house as formerly, for we now *with open face behold the glory of the Lord*, in the face of Christ, and not as of old through the cloud of types.

III. He receives instructions more immediately from the glory of the Lord, as Moses did when God had taken possession of the tabernacle (Lev. i. 1): *I heard him speaking to me out of the house*, v. 6.

Verses 7-12

God does here, in effect, renew his covenant with his people Israel, upon his retaking possession of the house.

I. God, by the prophet, puts them in mind of their former provocations. This is spoken to make way for the comforts designed them. They had formerly *defiled God's holy name*, v. 7. *They and their kings* had brought contempt on the religion they professed by setting up altars to their idols even in the courts of the temple, than which a more impudent affront could not be put upon the divine Majesty. Thus they set up a separation *wall between him and them*, which stopped the current of his favours to them. If often proves too true, *The nearer the church the further from God.*

II. He calls upon them to repent (v. 9): "*Now let them put away their whoredom*; and now that God is returning in mercy to them and setting up his sanctuary again in the midst of them, let them cast away their idols, those loathsome *carcases of their kings*." The prophet had the model or pattern of the temple to set before them. 1. If *they see that pattern*, they will surely be ashamed of their sins (v. 10). The goodness of God to us should lead us to repentance. Let *them measure the pattern* themselves, and see how much it exceeds the former pattern, and guess by that what great things God has in store for them. 2. If *they be ashamed* of their sins, they shall surely see more of the pattern, v. 11. "*Show them the form of the house*; and show them the ordinances and laws of it." With the privileges of God's house we must acquaint ourselves with the rules of it. *Show them* these ordinances, that they may *keep them* and *do them*.

III. He promises that they should be such as they should be, and then he will be to them such as they would have him to be, v. 7. Then *I will dwell in the midst of them for ever*; again v. 9.

IV. The general law of God's house is laid down (v. 12), That, whereas formerly only the chancel, or sanctuary, was *most holy*, now the whole *mountain of the house* shall be so. In gospel-times, 1. The whole church shall have the privilege of the *holy of holies*, that of a near access to God. All believers have now, under the gospel, *boldness to enter into the holiest* (Heb. x. 19), whereas the high priest entered in the virtue of the blood of bulls and goats, we enter in the virtue of the blood of Jesus, and, wherever we are, we have through him *access to the Father*.

Verses 13-27

This relates to the altar in this mystical temple, and that is mystical too; for Christ is our altar. The Jews, after their return out of captivity, had an altar long before they had a temple, Ezra iii. 3. But this was an altar in the temple.

I. The measures of the altar, v. 13. It was six yards square at the top and seven yards square at the bottom; it was four yards and a half high; it had a lower bench or shelf, here called a *settle*, a yard from the ground, on which some of the priests stood to minister, and another two yards above that, on which others of them stood. What was to be burnt on the altar was given up to those on the lower bench, and handed by them to those on the higher, and they laid it on the altar.

II. The ordinances of the altar. 1. *Seven days* were to be spent in the dedication of it, and every day sacrifices were to be offered (v. 25). Neither our persons nor our performances can be acceptable to God unless sin be taken away, and that cannot be taken away but by the blood of Christ, which both sanctifies the altar, and the gift upon the altar. The dedication of the altar is here called the *cleansing* and *purging* of it, v. 20, 26. All the sacrifices must be seasoned

with salt (v. 24). *Grace* is the *salt* with which all our religious performances must be seasoned, Col. iv. 6. 2. Concerning the constant use that should be made of the temple when it was dedicated (v. 27). It was *sanctified*, that it might *sanctify the gift* that was offered upon it. (1) Who were to serve at the altar: The *priests of the seed of Zadok*, v. 19. His name signifies *righteous*, for they are the righteous seed that are priests to God, through Christ *the Lord our righteousness*. (2) How they should prepare for this service (v. 26). Before we minister to the Lord in holy things we must consecrate ourselves.

CHAPTER 44

I. The appropriating of the east gate of the temple to the prince, ver. 1–3. II. A reproof sent to the house of Israel for their former profanations of God's sanctuary, ver. 4–9. III. The degrading of those Levites that had formerly been guilty of idolatry and the establishing of the priesthood in the family of Zadok, which had kept their integrity, ver. 10–16. IV. Divers laws and ordinances concerning the priests, ver. 17–31.

Verses 1-3

The prophet is brought a third time to the east gate, and finds it shut, which intimates that the rest of the gates were open at all times to the worshippers. But such an account is given of this gate's being shut as puts honour, 1. Upon the God of Israel. It is for the honour of him that the gate of the inner court, at which his glory entered when he took possession of the house, was ever after kept shut, v. 2. 2. Upon the prince of Israel, v. 3. (1) He shall *sit in this gate* to *eat* his share of the peace-offerings *before the Lord*. (2) He shall *enter by the way of the porch of that gate*, by some little door or wicket. Some by the prince here understand the high priest, and that he only was allowed to enter by this gate, for he was God's representative. Christ is the high priest of our profession, who entered himself into the holy place, and *opened the kingdom of heaven to all believers*.

Verses 4-9

The prophet must look again upon what he had before seen, and must be told again what he had before heard. Here, as before, he sees the house *filled with the glory of the Lord*, which strikes an awe upon him: *I fell upon my face*, v. 4.

I. God charges the prophet to take notice of all he saw, and all that was said to him (v. 5). 1. "*Behold with thy eyes* what is *shown* thee, particularly the *entering in of the house* and *every going forth* of it, all the inlets and all the outlets of the sanctuary." 2. *Hear with thy ears all that I say unto thee* about *the laws* and *ordinances* of *the house*, to instruct the people.

II. He sends him upon an errand to the people, *to the rebellious, even to the house of Israel*, v. 6.

1. He must show the house of Jacob their sins. They had admitted those to the privileges of the sanctuary that were not entitled to them (v. 7). Yet if these strangers had been devout, though they were not circumcised, the crime would not have been so great; but they were *uncircumcised in heart* too, strangers indeed to God and all goodness. They had employed those in the service of the sanctuary who were not fit for it. "*You have set keepers of my charge in my sanctuary for yourselves*, such as you had some favour or affection for; *thus you have not kept the charge of my holy things*."

2. He must tell them their duty (v. 9): "*No stranger shall enter into my sanctuary* till he has first submitted to the laws of it."

Verses 10-16

The Master of the house, being about to set up house again, takes account of his servants the priests, and sees who are fit to be kept.

I. Those who have been treacherous are degraded and put lower. Those Levites—or priests who were carried down the stream of the apostasy of Israel formerly (*v.* 10), who had complied with the idolatrous kings of Israel or Judah, who *ministered to them before their idols* (*v.* 12)—were justly put under the mark of God's displeasure. They are sentenced to be deprived in part, of their office, and from the dignity of priests are put down into the condition of ordinary Levites. Yet there is a mixture of mercy in this sentence. God mitigates the sentence, *v.* 11, 14. They shall help to *slay the sacrifice*, not at the altar, but *at the tables*, ch. xl. 39. They shall be porters *at the gates of the house*.

II. Those who have been faithful are honoured and established, *v.* 15, 16. "*But the sons of Zadok*, who kept their integrity in a time of general apostasy, who *went not astray* when others did, *they shall come near to me, shall come near to my table.*"

Verses 17–31

God's priests must be *regulars*, not *seculars*; and therefore here are rules laid down for them.

I. Concerning their clothes; they must wear *linen garments* when they *went in to minister*, and nothing that was *woollen*, because it would *cause sweat*, *v.* 17, 18. When they had finished their service they must change their clothes again, and lay up their linen garments in the chambers appointed for that purpose, *v.* 19, as before, *ch.* xlii. 14.

II. Concerning their hair; in that they must avoid extremes on both hands (*v.* 20); *They must not shave their heads*, in imitation of the Gentile priests; nor, on the other hand, must they *suffer their locks to grow long*, that they might be thought Nazarites, when really they were not; but they must be grave and modest, must *poll their heads* and keep their hair short.

III. Concerning their diet; they must be sure to *drink no wine* when they went in to minister, lest they should drink to excess, should drink and forget the law, *v.* 21.

IV. Concerning their marriages, *v.* 22. Here they must consult the credit of their office, and not marry one that had been *divorced*, that was under the suspicion of immodesty, nor a *widow*, unless she were a priest's widow, accustomed to the usages of the priests' families.

V. Concerning their preaching and church-government. It was part of their business to teach the people; and herein they must approve themselves both skilful and faithful (*v.* 23). It was part of their business to judge upon appeals made to them (Deut. xvii. 8, 9), and *in controversy they shall stand in judgment*, *v.* 24. They shall have the honesty to stand up for what is right, and, when they have passed a right judgment, shall have the courage to stand by it. Another part of their work, as church governors, is to *hallow God's sabbaths*, and to see that God's people also sanctify that day and do nothing to pollute it.

VI. Concerning their mourning for dead relations; the rule here agrees with the law of Moses, Lev. xxi. 1, 11. A priest shall not come near any *dead body* (for they must be purified *from dead works*) except of his next relations, *v.* 25.

VII. Concerning their maintenance; they must live upon the altar at which they served (*v.* 28). Some land was allowed them (*ch.* xlviii. 10), but their principal subsistence was by their office.

1. What the priests were to have from the people, for their maintenance and encouragement. They must have the flesh of many of the offerings. They must have every dedicated thing in Israel, which was in many cases to be turned into money and given to the priest. This is explained, *v.* 30. They were to have *the first of the dough* when it was going to the oven, as well as the first of their fruits when they were going to the barn. The priests being so well provided for, it would be inexcusable in them if they should *eat that which is torn or which died of itself*, *v.* 31.

2. What the people might expect from the priest for their recompence. Those that are kind to a prophet, to a priest, shall have a prophet's, a priest's reward (*v.* 30). It was part of the priest's work to *bless the people in the name of the Lord*, not only their congregations, but their families.

CHAPTER 45

In this chapter is further represented to the prophet, in vision, I. The division of the holy land, so much for the temple, and the priests that attended the service of it (ver. 1–4), so much for the Levites (ver. 5), so much for the city (ver. 6), so much for the prince, and the residue of the people, ver. 7, 8. II. The ordinances of justice that were given both to prince and people, ver. 9–12. III. The oblations they were to offer, ver. 13–17. Particularly in the beginning of the year (ver. 18–20) and in the passover, and the feast of tabernacles, ver. 21–25.

Verses 1–8

Directions are here given for the dividing of the land after their return to it. 1. Here is the portion of land assigned to *the sanctuary*, in the midst of which the temple was to be built (*v.* 1), *an oblation to the Lord;* for what is given for the maintenance of the worship of God and the advancement of religion, God accepts as given to him. This *holy portion of the land* was to be measured, and the borders of it fixed. The priests and Levites that were to come near to minister were to have their dwellings in this *portion of the land* that was round about the sanctuary. 2. Next to the lands of the sanctuary the city-lands are assigned, in which the holy city was to be built, and with the issues and profits of which the citizens were to be maintained (*v.* 6). 3. The next allotment after the church-lands and the city-lands is of the crown-lands, *v.* 7, 8. They are said to lie *on the one side and on the other side* of the church-lands and city-lands, to intimate that the prince with his wealth and power was to be a protection to both. *My princes shall no more oppress my people;* for God will make the *officers peace* and the *exactors righteousness.* Nehemiah was one that did not do as the *former governors*, Neh. v. 15, 18. 4. The rest of the lands were to be distributed to the people *according to their tribes.*

Verses 9–12

Some general rules of justice laid down both for prince and people. 1. That *princes do not oppress their subjects*, but duly and faithfully administer justice among them (*v.* 9). Let them *take away their exactions*, ease their subjects of those taxes which they find lie heavily upon them, and let them *execute judgment and justice* according to law. 2. That one neighbour do not cheat another in commerce (*v.* 10): *You shall have just balances.* It concerns God's Israel to be honest and just in all their dealings, punctual and exact in rendering to all their due, because otherwise they spoil the acceptableness of their profession with God and the reputation of it before men.

Verses 13–25

Having laid down the rules of righteousness towards men, he comes next to give some directions for their religion towards God.

I. It is required that they offer an oblation to the Lord (*v.* 13): *All the people of the land* must give an oblation, *v.* 16. They had offered an oblation out of their real estates (*v.* 1), a *holy portion of their land*; now they are directed to offer an oblation out of their goods and chattels.

II. The proportion of this oblation is here determined, which was not done by the law of Moses. 1. Out of their corn they were to offer a sixtieth part, v. 13. 2. Out of their oil they were to offer a hundredth part, v. 14. 3. Out of their flocks they were to give *one lamb* out of 200, v. 15. But it must be *out of the fat pastures of Israel.* They must offer to God the fattest and best they had, for *burnt-offerings* and *peace-offerings.* These sacrifices were to *make reconciliations* for them. Christ is our sacrifice of atonement, by whom reconciliation is made.

III. This oblation must be given *for the prince in Israel,* v. 16. Some read it *to* the prince, and understand it of Christ, to whom we must offer our oblations, to be presented to the Father. Or, They shall give it *with* the prince (v. 17). The people were to bring their oblations to him, and he was to bring them to the sanctuary, and to make up what fell short out of his own.

IV. Some particular solemnities are here appointed. 1. In the beginning of the year is the annual solemnity of cleansing the sanctuary. (1) *On the first day of the first month* they were to offer a sacrifice for the *cleansing of the sanctuary* (v. 18), and to implore grace for the better performance of the service of the sanctuary the ensuing year. By it atonement was intended to be made for the sins of all the servants that attended that house, priests, Levites, and people, even the sins that were found in all their services. They were here appointed to *cleanse the sanctuary* upon the first day of the month, because on the fourteenth day of the month they were to eat the *passover,* an ordinance which, of all Old Testament institutions, had most in it of Christ and gospel grace. (2) This sacrifice was to be repeated on *the seventh day of the first month,* v. 20. And then it was intended to make atonement *for everyone that errs, and for him that is simple.* It is spoken of those sins which are committed through ignorance, mistake, or inadvertency.

2. The passover was to be religiously observed at the time appointed, v. 21. Christ is *our passover,* that is *sacrificed for us.* We celebrate the memorial of that sacrifice in the Lord's supper, which is our passover-feast.

3. The feast of tabernacles; that is spoken of next (v. 25), and there is no mention of the feast of pentecost, which came between that of the passover and that of tabernacles. See the deficiency of the legal sacrifices for sin; they were therefore often repeated, not only every year, but every feast, every day of the feast. See the necessity of our frequently repeating the same religious exercises. Though the sacrifice of atonement is offered *once for all,* yet the sacrifices of acknowledgment, that of a broken heart, that of a thankful heart, those spiritual sacrifices which are acceptable to God through Christ Jesus, must be every day offered.

CHAPTER 46

I. Some further rules given both to the priests and to the people, relating to their worship, ver 1–15. II. A law concerning the prince's disposal of his inheritance, ver. 16–18. III. A description of the places provided for the boiling of the sacrifices and the baking of the meat-offerings, ver. 19–24.

Verses 1–15

We do not find in the history of that latter part of the Jewish church that they governed themselves by these ordinances, but only by the law of Moses, looking upon this *then* in the next age after as mystical, and not literal.

I. The place of worship was fixed, and rules given to prince and people.

1. The east gate, kept shut at other times, was to be opened on the sabbath days, on the new moons (v. 1), and whenever the prince offered a voluntary offering, v. 12. Some think he went in with the priests and Levites into the *inner court,* and they observe that magistrates and ministers should go hand in hand, in promoting the service of God. But it should rather seem that he went *by the way of the porch of the gate,* stood *at the post of the gate,* and *worshipped at the threshold of the gate* (v. 2), where he had a full view of the priests' performances at the altar, and the people stood behind him *at the door of that gate,* v. 3.

2. As to the north gate and south gate, by which they entered into the *court of the people*—whoever came in at the *north gate* should go out at the *south gate,* and whoever came in at the *south gate* should go out at the *north gate,* v. 9. Some think this was to prevent jostling.

3. *The people shall worship at the door of the east gate,* where the prince does, both *on the sabbath and on the new moons* (v. 3).

II. The ordinances of worship were fixed. 1. Every morning they must offer *a lamb* for a *burnt-offering,* v. 13. 2. On the sabbath days, whereas by the law of Moses two lambs were to be offered (Num. xxviii. 9) there shall be six lambs offered. 3. On the new moons, in the beginning of their months, there was the additional offering of a young bullock, v. 6. 4. All the sacrifices were to be *without blemish;* so Christ, the great sacrifice, was (1 Pet. i. 19), and so Christians, who present themselves to God as living sacrifices, should be—*blameless, and harmless, and without rebuke.* 5. All the sacrifices were to have their meat-offerings annexed to them, to show that we ought to honour him with the fruit of our ground as well as with the fruit of our cattle, Deut. xxviii. 4. The meat-offerings here are much larger in proportion than they were by the law of Moses, which intimates that under the gospel, the great atoning sacrifice having been offered, these unbloody sacrifices shall be more.

Verses 16–18

A law for the limiting of the power of the prince in disposing of the crown-lands. 1. If he have a *son* that has merited well, he may, in recompence for his services, settle some parts of his lands upon him (v. 16). 2. Yet, if he have a servant that is a favourite, he may not settle lands upon him, v. 17. But he may give him lands to the year of jubilee, and then they must return to the family again, v. 17. 3. What estates he gives his children must be of his own (v. 18): He *shall not take of the people's inheritance.* It is the interest of princes to rule in the hearts of their subjects. It is better to gain their affections by protecting their rights than to gain their estates by invading them.

Verses 19–24

Places in which to boil the flesh of the offerings, v. 20. There were some at the entry into the inner court (v. 19) and others in the four corners of the outer court, v. 21–23. In those places they were to *boil the trespass-offering and the sin-offering,* those parts of them which were allotted to the priests. There also they were to *bake the meat-offering,* v. 20.

CHAPTER 47

I. The vision of the holy waters, their rise, extent, depth, and healing virtue, the fish in them, and an account of the trees growing on the banks, ver. 1–12. II. An appointment of the borders of the land of Canaan, which was to be divided by lot to the tribes of Israel and the strangers that sojourned among them, ver. 13–23.

Verses 1–12

This part of Ezekiel's vision must necessarily have a mystical and spiritual meaning. The prophecy, Zech. xiv. 8, may explain it, of *living waters* that shall go out from Jerusalem, *half of them towards the former sea and half of them towards the hinder sea.* And there is plainly a reference to this in St. John's vision of *a pure river of water of life,* Rev. xxii. 1. That seems to represent the glory and joy which are grace perfected. This seems to represent the grace and joy which are glory begun. Most interpreters agree that these waters signify the gospel of Christ, which went forth from Jerusalem, and spread itself into the countries about, and the gifts and powers of the Holy Ghost which accompanied it, by virtue of which it spread far and produced blessed effects.

I. The rise of these waters (*v.* 1). *Waters issued out from the threshold of the house eastward,* and from *under the right side of the house,* that is, the south side of *the altar.* And again (*v.* 2), *There ran out waters on the right side,* signifying that *from Zion should go forth the law and the word of the Lord from Jerusalem,* Isa. ii. 3. There it was that the Spirit was poured out upon the apostles, and endued them with the gift of tongues, that they might carry these waters to all nations. In the temple first they were to stand and *preach the words of this life,* Acts v. 20. They must preach the gospel to all nations, but must *begin at Jerusalem,* Luke xxiv. 47. Christ is the temple; he is the door; from him those living waters flow, out of his pierced side. It is by believing in him that we receive from him *rivers of living water*; and *this spoke he of the Spirit,* John vii. 38, 39. The original of these waters was not above-ground, but they sprang up from under the threshold; for the fountain of a believer's life is a mystery; it is *hid with Christ in God,* Col. iii. 3.

II. The progress and increase of these waters: They *went forth eastward* (*v.* 3), *towards the east country* (*v.* 8). The prophet and his guide followed the stream as it ran down from the holy mountains, and when they had followed it about *a thousand cubits* they went across, to try the depth, and it was *to the ankles, v.* 3. Then they walked along on the bank of the river on the other side, a thousand cubits more, and then, to try the depth, they waded through it the second time, and it was up to *their knees, v.* 4. They walked along by it a thousand cubits more, and then forded it the third time, and then it was up to their middle—*the waters were to the loins.* They then walked a thousand cubits further, and attempted to repass it the fourth time, but found it impracticable: *The waters had risen,* so that they were *waters to swim in, a river that could not be passed over, v.* 5. Note, 1. The waters of the sanctuary are running waters, as those of a river, not standing waters, as those of a pond. Grace in the soul is still pressing forward; *onward still,* till it comes to perfection. 2. They are increasing waters. This river runs constantly, the further it goes the fuller it grows. The gospel-church was very small in its beginnings, like a little purling brook; but by degrees it came *to the ankles, to the knees*: many were added to it daily. The gifts of the Spirit increase by being exercised, and grace is growing, like the light of the morning, which *shines more and more to the perfect day.* 3. It is good for us to follow these waters. Observe the progress of the gospel in the world; observe the process of the work of grace in the heart; attend the motions of the blessed Spirit, as Ezekiel here did. If we search into the things of God, we shall find some very plain and easy to be understood, as the waters that were but to the ankles, others more difficult, as the water to the knees, and some quite beyond our reach, which we cannot penetrate, but, despairing to find the bottom, must, as St. Paul, sit down at the brink, and adore the *depth,* Rom. xi. 33.

III. The extent of this river: *It issues towards the east country,* but *goes down into the desert,* and so *goes into the sea,* either into the *dead sea,* which lay

south-east, or the sea of Tiberias, which lay *north-east,* or the great sea, which lay *west, v.* 8. This was accomplished when the gospel was preached throughout all the regions of Judæa and Samaria (Acts viii. 1), and afterwards the nations about, and even in the isles of the sea, were enlightened.

IV. The healing virtue of this river. Being *brought forth into the sea,* the sulphurous lake of Sodom, even those *waters shall be healed* (*v.* 8), shall become sweet, and healthful. This intimates the blessed change that the gospel would make, as great a change, as the turning of the dead sea into a fountain of gardens. The gospel was as that salt which Elisha cast, 2 Kings ii. 20, 21. Christ, coming into the world to be its physician, sent his gospel as the great medicine. Wherever these rivers come, they *make things to live* (*v.* 9); they are *the water of life,* Rev. xxii. 1, 17. Christ came, *that we might have life,* and for that end he sends his gospel. The grace of God makes dead sinners alive and living saints lively; everything is made fruitful and flourishing by it. But its effect is according as it is received, and as the mind is prepared and disposed to receive it.

V. The great plenty of fish that should be in this river. *Every living moving thing shall be found here,* shall *live here* (*v.* 9).

VI. The trees that were on the banks of this river— *many trees on the one side and on the other* (*v.* 7); they *are trees for meat,* and the *fruit* of them *shall not be consumed,* for it shall produce fresh fruit *every month* (*v.* 12). The *leaf* shall be *for medicine,* and it *shall not fade.* This part of the vision compares with St. John's vision (Rev. xxii. 2), where, on either side of the river, is said to grow the *tree of life,* which *yielded her fruit every month,* and *the leaves* were *for the healing of the nations.* The very leaves of these trees *are for medicine,* for *bruises* and sores, *margin.* Good Christians do good to those about them; they *strengthen the weak,* and bind up the broken-hearted. Their cheerfulness *does good like a medicine.* Their *leaf shall not fade,* having not only life in their root, but sap in all their branches. Each one of them shall bring forth fruit monthly, which denotes an abundant disposition to fruit-bearing (they shall never be weary of well-doing). And the reason of this extraordinary fruitfulness is *because their waters issued out of the sanctuary*; it is to be ascribed to the continual supplies of divine grace.

Verses 13–22

The affairs of the state. The land of Canaan is here secured to them for an inheritance (*v.* 14): *I lifted up my hand to give it unto your fathers.* God had not forgotten his oath which he swore to their fathers. *I lifted up my hand to give it,* and therefore it shall without fail *fall to you for an inheritance.* The bounds are fixed. It is God that *appoints the bounds of our habitation.* It is here ordered to be divided among the tribes of Israel, reckoning Joseph for two tribes, to make up the number of twelve, when Levi was taken out to attend the sanctuary, and had his lot adjoining to that (*v.* 13, 21): *You shall inherit it, one as well as another, v.* 14. The strangers who sojourn among them, *who shall beget children* and be built up into families, and so help to people their country, *shall have inheritance among the tribes,* as if they had been native Israelites (*v.* 22, 23). It certainly looks at gospel-times, when the partition-wall between Jew and Gentile was taken down, and both were put upon a level before God, both made one in Christ, in whom *there is no difference,* Rom. x. 12.

CHAPTER 48

Particular directions given for the distribution of the land. I. The portions of the twelve tribes, seven to the north of the sanctuary (ver. 1–7) and five to the south, ver. 23–29. II. The allotment of land for the sanctuary, and the priests (ver. 8–11), for the Levites (ver. 12–14), for the city (ver. 15–20), and for the prince, ver. 21, 22. III. A plan of the city, its gates, and the new name given to it (ver. 30–35), which concludes the vision and prophecy of this book.

Verses 1–30

A short way taken for the dividing of the land among the twelve tribes. In this distribution of the land we may observe, 1. That it differs very much from the division of it in Joshua's time. It is not so much to be understood literally as spiritually, though the mystery of it is very much hidden from us. The Israel of God is cast into a new method. 2. That the tribe of Dan, which was last provided for in the first division of Canaan (Joshua xix. 40), is first provided for here, *v.* 1. God, in the dispensation of his grace, does not follow the same method that he does in the disposals of his providence. 3. That all the ten tribes that were carried away by the king of Assyria, as well as the two tribes that were long afterwards carried to Babylon, have their allotment in this visionary land. We believe it has its designed accomplishment in the establishment and enlargement of the gospel church, and in the sure and sweet enjoyment of the privileges of the new covenant, in which there is enough for all and enough for each. 4. That every tribe in this visionary distribution had its particular lot assigned it by a divine appointment. We must not only acknowledge, but acquiesce, in the hand of God appointing us our lot, and be well pleased with it, believing it fittest for us. *He shall choose our inheritance for us*, Ps. xlvii. 4. 5. That the tribes lay contiguous. By *the border* of one tribe was *the portion* of another. It was a figure of the communion of churches and saints under the gospel-government; thus, though they are many, yet they are one, and should hold together in holy love and mutual assistance. 6. That the lot of Reuben, which before lay at a distance beyond Jordan, now lies next to Judah, and next but one to the sanctuary; for the scandal he lay under, for which he was told *he should not excel*, began by this time to wear off. 7. That the sanctuary was *in the midst* of them. There were seven tribes to the north of it, and the Levites, the princes, and the city's portion, with that of five tribes more, to the south of it; so that it was, as it ought to be, *in the heart of the kingdom*. 8. That where the sanctuary was the priests were: *For them, even for the priests, shall this holy oblation be*, *v.* 10. 9. Those priests had the priests' share of these lands that had approved themselves faithful to God in times of trial (*v.* 11): *It shall be for the sons of Zadok*, who, it seems, had signalized themselves in some critical juncture, and *went not astray* when the *children of Israel*, and the other *Levites, went astray*. 10. The land which was appropriated to the ministers of the sanctuary might by no means be alienated. They might not *sell it nor exchange it*, *v.* 14. It is sacrilege to convert that to other uses which is dedicated to

God. 11. The land allotted for the city and its suburbs is called a *profane place* (*v.* 15), or *common*. In comparison with the sanctuary, it was a profane place. 12. The city is made to be exactly square, and the suburbs extending themselves equally on all sides, as the Levites' cities did in the first division of the land (*v.* 16, 17), which, never being literally fulfilled in any city, intimates that it is to be understood spiritually of the beauty and stability of the gospel church, that *city of the living God*. 13. Whereas, before, the inhabitants of Jerusalem were principally of Judah and Benjamin, in whose tribe it lay, now *those that serve the city*, and bear office in it, *shall serve it out of all the tribes of Israel*, *v.* 19. 14. Those who applied themselves to public business in the city, as well as in the sanctuary, should have an honourable comfortable maintenance; lands are appointed, *the increase* whereof *shall be food unto those that serve the city*, *v.* 18. 15. The prince had a lot for himself, suited to the dignity of his high station (*v.* 21). 16. As Judah had his lot next the sanctuary on one side, so Benjamin had, of all the tribes, his lot nearest to it on the other side, which honour was reserved for those who adhered to the house of David and the temple at Jerusalem when the other ten tribes went astray from both.

Verses 31–35

A further account of the city that should be built for those who should come to worship in the sanctuary adjoining. It is nowhere called Jerusalem, nor is the land called Canaan; *old things are done away, behold all things have become new*. Concerning this city, 1. The measures of its out-lets and the grounds, *v.* 35. But what these measures were is uncertain. These things are to be understood spiritually. 2. The number of its gates. It had twelve gates in all, three on each side, inscribed to the twelve tribes. In St. John's vision, the new Jerusalem has *twelve gates*, three on a side, and on them are written *the names of the twelve tribes of the children of Israel*, Rev. xxi. 12, 13. Into the church of Christ, there is a free access by faith for all that come of every tribe, from every quarter. Christ has *opened the kingdom of heaven for all believers*. 3. The name given to this city: it shall be, not, as before, *Jerusalem—The vision of peace*, but, which is the original of that, *Jehovah Shammah—The Lord is there*, *v.* 35. This intimated, (1) That the captives, after their return, should have manifest tokens of God's presence with them and his residence among them. (2) That the gospel-church should likewise have the presence of God in it, though not in the *Shechinah*, as of old, yet in a token of it no less sure, that of his Spirit. *Lo, I am with you always even unto the end of the world*. Whatever soul has in it a living principle of grace, it may be truly said, *The Lord is there*. (3) That the glory and happiness of heaven should consist chiefly in this, that *the Lord is there*.

AN EXPOSITION, WITH PRACTICAL OBSERVATIONS, OF

THE BOOK OF
THE PROPHET DANIEL

The book of Ezekiel left Jerusalem all in ruins, but with a joyful prospect of all in glory again. This of Daniel fitly follows. Ezekiel told us what was seen, and what was foreseen, by him in the former years of the captivity: Daniel tells us what was seen, and foreseen, in the latter years of the captivity. And it was a comfort to the captives that they had first one prophet and then another, to show them that God had not quite cast them off. I. Concerning this prophet. His Hebrew name was *Daniel*, which signifies the *judgment of God*; his Chaldean name was *Belteshazzar*. He was of the tribe of Judah, and of the royal family, eminent for wisdom and piety. Ezekiel, his senior, speaks of him as an oracle when he upbraids the king of Tyre with his conceit: *Thou art wiser than Daniel*, Ezek. xxviii. 3. Noah, Daniel, and Job are reckoned as three men that had the greatest interest in heaven, Ezek. xiv. 14. Some of the Jewish rabbin rank his book among the *Hagiographa*, not among the prophecies. One reason is because he did not live such a mortified life as Jeremiah and other prophets, but lived like a prince, and was a prime-minister; whereas we find him persecuted as other prophets (*ch.* vi), and mortifying himself as other prophets did, when he *ate no pleasant bread* (*ch.* x. 3), and fainting and sick when he was under the power of the Spirit of prophecy, *ch.* viii. 27. Another reason they suggest is because he wrote his book in a heathen country, and *there* had his visions, and not in the land of Israel; but, for the same reason, Ezekiel also would be expunged out of the roll of prophets. But the true reason is that he speaks so plainly of the time of the Messiah's coming that the Jews do not care to hear of it. Josephus calls him one of the *greatest* of *the prophets*. He lived an active life in the courts and councils of some of the greatest monarchs, Nebuchadnezzar, Cyrus, Darius. The Spirit, as the wind, blows where it lists. And, if those that have much to do in the world plead that as an excuse for the slightness of their converse with God, Daniel will condemn them. II. Concerning this book. The first six chapters of it are historical, and are plain and easy; the last six are prophetical, and in them are many things hard to be understood, which would be more intelligible if we had a more complete history of the Jewish nation, from Daniel's time to the coming of the Messiah. The first chapter, and the first three verses of the second chapter, are in Hebrew; thence to the eighth chapter is in the Chaldee dialect; and thence to the end is in Hebrew. Mr. Broughton observes that, as the Chaldeans were kind to Daniel, and gave cups of cold water to him when he requested it, rather than the king's wine, God would not have them lose their reward, but made that language to have honour in his writings. Daniel, according to his computation, continues the holy story from the first surprising of Jerusalem by the Chaldean Babel, when he himself was carried away captive, until the last destruction of it by Rome, the mystical Babel, *ch.* ix. 27. The fables of Susannah, and of Bel and the Dragon are apocryphal stories being found only in the Greek, nor ever admitted by the Jewish church. There are some of the histories and prophecies of this book that bear date in the latter end of the Chaldean monarchy, and others that are dated in the beginning of the Persian monarchy. But both Nebuchadnezzar's dream, which Daniel interpreted, and his own visions, point at the Grecian and Roman monarchies, and particularly at the Jews' troubles under Antiochus.

CHAPTER 1

The beginning of Daniel's life. Daniel began with the study of human learning, and afterwards came divine visions. I. Jehoiakim's first captivity (ver. 1, 2), in which Daniel, with others of the seed-royal, was carried to Babylon. II. The choice made of Daniel, and some other young men, to be brought up in the Chaldean literature, that they might be fitted to serve the government, ver. 3–7. III. Their pious refusal to eat the king's meat, and their determining to live upon pulse and water, which the master of the eunuchs allowed them to do, finding that it agreed very well with them, ver 8–16. IV. Their wonderful improvement, above all their fellows, in wisdom and knowledge, ver. 17–21.

Verses 1–7

I. The first descent which Nebuchadnezzar, king of Babylon, in the first year of his reign, made upon Judah and Jerusalem, in the third year of the reign of Jehoiakim (*v.* 1, 2): He *besieged Jerusalem*, made himself master of it, seized the king, took whom he pleased and what he pleased, and then left Jehoiakim to reign as tributary to him.

II. He did not destroy the city or kingdom, but accomplished the first threatening of mischief by Babylon made when Hezekiah showed his treasures to the king of Babylon's ambassadors (Isa. xxxix. 6, 7). The vessels of the sanctuary were carried away, *v.* 2. Many of the holy vessels were taken away by the king of Babylon and brought to the *house of his god*, to whom, with a blind devotion, he gave the praise of his success. See the righteousness of God; his people had brought the images of other gods into his temple, and now he suffers the vessels of the temple to be carried into the treasuries of those other gods. It was only *part of them* that went now; some were left, to see if they would take the right course to prevent the carrying away of the remainder. See Jer. xxvii. 18. The children and young men, especially such as were of noble or royal extraction, sightly and promising, were carried away. These were taken away by Nebuchadnezzar as hostages for the fidelity of their parents in their own land. He took them away to train them up for employment and preferment. The directions which the king of Babylon gave for the choice of these youths, *v.* 4. They must not choose such as were deformed in body, but comely and well-favoured, *skilful in all wisdom*, and *cunning*, or *well-seen in knowledge*, and *understanding science*. He chose such as were young, because they would be tractable, would forget their own people and become Chaldeans. They must be such as had ability to *stand in the king's palace*, and to preside in his affairs. The care which he took concerning their education. They should be taught *the learning and tongue of the Chaldeans*. They must be trained in such learning as might qualify them to serve their generation. They had *daily provision of the king's meat, and of the wine which he drank*, *v.* 5. This was an instance of his generosity and humanity. With a liberal education there should be a liberal maintenance.

III. Daniel and his fellows were of the *children of Judah*, the royal tribe, and probably of the house of David. The *prince of the eunuchs* changed the names of Daniel and his fellows, in token of their being naturalized and made Chaldeans. Their Hebrew names, which they received at their circumcision, had something of God, or Jah, in them: *Daniel—God is my Judge; Hananiah—The grace of the Lord; Mishael—He that is the strong God; Azariah—The Lord is a help.* To make them forget the God of their fathers, the guide of their youth, they give them names that savour of the Chaldean idolatry. *Belteshazzar* signifies the *keeper of the hidden treasures of Bel; Shadrach—The inspiration of the sun*, which the Chaldeans worshipped; *Meshach—Of the goddess Shach*, under which name Venus was worshipped; *Abed-nego*, The *servant of the shining fire*, which they worshipped also.

Verses 8–16

I. Daniel was a favourite with the *prince of the eunuchs* (v. 9), as Joseph was with the keeper of the prison.

II. Daniel was still firm to his religion. They had changed his name, but they could not change his nature. Whatever they pleased to call him, he still retained the spirit of an Israelite indeed. He was resolved that *he would not defile himself with the portion of the king's meat*, he would not meddle with it, nor *with the wine which he drank*, v. 8. His fellows concurred in the same resolution, v. 11. This was from a principle of conscience. It was not in itself unlawful for them to *eat of the king's meat* or to *drink of his wine*. But, 1. They were scrupulous concerning the meat, lest it should be sinful. Sometimes such meat would be set before them as was forbidden by their law, as swine's flesh; or they were afraid lest it should have been offered in sacrifice to an idol, or blessed in the name of an idol. The Jews were distinguished from other nations very much by their meats (Lev. xi. 45, 46). If the command be against it, they must abide by that. 2. They were jealous lest, though it should not be sinful in itself, it should be an *occasion of sin* to them. 3. Jerusalem was in distress, and they themselves were in captivity. They had no heart *to drink wine in bowls*, so much were they *grieved for the affliction of Joseph*.

III. When Daniel requested that he might have none of the king's meat or wine, the prince of the eunuchs objected that, if he and his fellows were not in as good case as their companions, he would be in danger of losing his head, v. 10. Daniel desires the matter might be put to a trial. He applies to the under-officer, Melzar: "*Prove us for ten days;* let us have nothing but *pulse to eat*, nothing but herbs and fruits, parched peas or lentils, and nothing but *water to drink*, and see how we can live upon that," v. 13. Trial was accordingly made. Daniel and his fellows lived for ten days upon *pulse and water*. At the end of *the ten days* they were found *fairer and fatter in flesh* than *all those who did eat the portion of the king's meat*, v. 15. This was in part a natural effect of their temperance, but it must be ascribed to the special blessing of God, which will make a little to go a great way.

IV. The steward did not force them to eat against their consciences, but, as they desired, *gave them pulse and water* (v. 16). This abstemiousness fitted them for their eminent services. Hereby they kept their minds clear and unclouded. Those that had thus inured themselves to hardship, and lived a life of self-denial, could the more easily venture upon the fiery furnace and the den of lions.

Verses 17–21

The great learning which God gave Daniel and his fellows was, 1. A balance for their losses. They had,

for the iniquity of their fathers, been deprived of honours and pleasures, but to make them amends for that, God, in giving them learning, gave them better honours and pleasures. 2. A recompence for their integrity. They kept to their religion, even in the minutest instances. God rewarded them. To Daniel he gave a double portion; he had *understanding in visions and dreams* by a divine sagacity and wisdom which God gave him. After *three years* spent in their education they were presented to the king, v. 18. And the king examined them and *communed with them* himself, v. 19. The king examined them *in all matters of wisdom and understanding*, and found that they had *more understanding than the ancients*. He freely owned that, upon trial, he found those poor young captive Jews wiser and *better than all the magicians that were in all his realm*, v. 20. These four young students were *ten times* better than all the old practitioners. This judgment being given, they *stood before the king* (v. 19).

CHAPTER 2

This chapter is the history of a prophecy, by a dream and the interpretation of it. Nebuchadnezzar's dream, and Daniel's interpretation, look to the four monarchies, and the concerns of Israel in them, and the kingdom of the Messiah, which should be set up in the world upon the ruins of them. I. The great perplexity that Nebuchadnezzar was put into by a dream, and his command to the magicians to tell him what it was, ver. 1–11. II. Orders given for the destroying of all the wise men of Babylon, and of Daniel among the rest, with his fellows, ver. 12–15. III. The discovery of this secret to him, in answer to prayer, and the thanksgiving he offered up to God, ver. 16–23. IV. His admission to the king, and the discovery he made to him both of his dream and of the interpretation, ver. 24–45. V. The great honour which Nebuchadnezzar put upon Daniel, in recompence for this service, and the preferment of his companions with him, ver. 46–49.

Verses 1–13

There is difficulty in the date of this story; it is said to be in the second year of the reign of Nebuchadnezzar, v. 1. Now Daniel was carried to Babylon in his first year, and, it should seem, he was three years under tutors before he was presented to the king, *ch. i. 5.* How then could this happen in *the second year*? Perhaps Daniel had been but one year at school. Some make it to be the second year after he began to reign alone, but the fifth or sixth year since he began to reign in partnership with his *father*. Some read it, *and in the second year* (the second after Daniel and his fellows stood before the king), *in the kingdom of Nebuchadnezzar*, or *in his reign*, this happened. It appears in Ezekiel, that Daniel was soon famous both for wisdom and prevalence in prayer. He came to be eminent for both these early in Nebuchadnezzar's reign.

I. The perplexity that Nebuchadnezzar was in by reason of a dream which he had forgotten (v. 1). There was something in the impression it made upon him which was evidence of its divine origin and its prophetic significance. Nebuchadnezzar was a troubler of God's Israel, but God here troubled him. All the treasures and delights which this mighty monarch had could not procure him a little repose, when by reason of the trouble of his mind his *sleep broke from him*.

II. The trial that he made of his magicians and astrologers. They were immediately sent for, to *show the king his dreams*, v. 2. His dream had slipped out of his mind, and he could not possibly recollect it. The magicians were proud of being sent for into the king's bed-chamber. He tells them that he had *dreamed a dream*, v. 3. They desired him to tell his dream, and undertook with all possible assurance to interpret it, v. 4. But the king insisted that they must tell him the dream. And, if they could not do this, they should all be put to death as deceivers (v. 5), themselves *cut to pieces* and *their houses made a dunghill*. If they could, they should be rewarded, *v.* 6. The magicians insist that the king must tell them the dream, and then, if they do not tell him the interpretation of it, it is their fault, *v.* 7. But arbitrary power is deaf to reason. The king falls into a passion, gives them hard words, and charges them with trying to affront him: *You have prepared lying and corrupt words to speak before me.* He tells them that they did but dally with him, to gain time (*v.* 8), *till the time be changed* (*v.* 9), either till the king's desire to know his dream be over, or till they may hope he has so perfectly forgotten his dream that they may tell him what they please. And therefore, without delay, they must tell him the dream. In vain do they plead, 1. That there is *no man on earth* that can retrieve the king's dream, *v.* 10. They acknowledge that the gods may indeed *declare unto man what is his thought* (Amos iv. 13). But those who can do this are gods (*v.* 11), and it is they alone that can do this. See here an instance of the ignorance of these magicians, that they speak of many gods, whereas there is but one and can be but one infinite; yet see their knowledge that there is a God, who is a Spirit, and perfectly knows the spirits of men and all their thoughts. 2. That there is no king on earth that would expect or require such a thing, *v.* 10.

III. The doom passed upon all the magicians of Babylon. There is but *one decree for them all* (*v.* 9). They must every man of them be slain (*v.* 13), Daniel and his fellows (though they knew nothing of the matter) not excepted. Nebuchadnezzar is here a tyrant in true colours, speaking death when he cannot speak sense.

Verses 14–23

When the king sent for his wise men to tell them his dream (*v.* 2), Daniel was not summoned to appear. How miserable is the case of those who live under an arbitrary government, as this of Nebuchadnezzar's! Daniel was famous both for prudence and prayer; as a prince he had power with God and man; by prayer he had power with God, by prudence he had power with man, and in both he prevailed. In these verses we have a remarkable instance of both.

I. Daniel by prudence knew how to deal with men. When *Arioch, the captain of the guard*, appointed to slay all the wise men of Babylon, seized Daniel, he *answered with counsel and wisdom* (*v.* 14); he did not fall into a passion, but mildly asked, *Why is the decree so hasty?* *v.* 15. Daniel undertakes, if he may but have a little time to give the king all the satisfaction he desired, *v.* 16.

II. Daniel knew how by prayer to converse with God.

1. His humble petition that God would discover to him what was the king's dream, and the interpretation of it. He *went to his house* to be alone with his God, for from him alone, the Father of lights, he expected this great gift. He engaged his companions to pray for it too, *v.* 17, 18. St. Paul often entreats his friends to pray for him. Thus we must show that we put a value upon our friends, upon their prayers. He was particular in this prayer: *That they would desire mercies of the God of heaven concerning this secret*, *v.* 18. Whatever is the matter of our care must be the matter of our prayer; we must desire mercy of God concerning this thing and the other thing that occasions us trouble and fear. God gives us leave to be humbly free with him. We may in faith pray to him who has all hearts in his hand, and who in his providence does wonders, for the discovery of that which is out of our view and the obtaining of that which is out of our reach. The mercy which Daniel and his fellows prayed for was bestowed. The *secret* was *revealed unto Daniel* in

a *night-vision*, *v.* 19. Some think he dreamed the same dream, when he was asleep, that Nebuchadnezzar had dreamed.

2. His grateful thanksgiving for this mercy, *v.* 19. As he had prayed in a full assurance that God would do this for him, so he gave thanks in a full assurance that he had done it. *Blessed be the name of God for ever and ever.* There is that *for ever* in God which is to be blessed and praised; it is unchangeably and eternally in him. His companions were present with Daniel when the discovery was made, or as soon as he knew it he told them that those who had assisted him with their prayers might assist him in their praises; his joining them with him is an instance of his humility. Thus St. Paul sometimes joins Sylvanus, Timotheus, or some other minister, with himself in the inscriptions to many of his epistles.

Verses 24–30

The introduction to Daniel's declaring the dream, and the interpretation of it.

I. He immediately bespoke the reversing of the sentence against the wise men of Babylon, *v.* 24. He went with all speed to Arioch: *Destroy not the wise men of Babylon.*

II. He offered his service, with great assurance, to go to the king, and tell him his dream and the interpretation of it, *v.* 24, 25.

III. He contrived to give honour to God, upon this occasion. The king owned that it was a bold undertaking (*v.* 26): *Art thou able to make known unto me the dream?* The less likely it appeared to the king that Daniel should do this the more God was glorified in enabling him to do it. Daniel puts the king out of conceit with his soothsayers (*v.* 27): *"This secret they cannot show to the king.* Therefore let not the king be angry with them for not doing that which they cannot do; but rather cast them off, because they cannot do it. Though they cannot find out the secret, let not the king despair of having it found out, for *there is a God in heaven that reveals secrets,"* *v.* 28.

IV. He confirmed the king in his opinion that the dream was of great value. It was a divine discovery, a ray of light darted into his mind from the upper world, relating to the great affairs of this lower world. God in it *made known to the king what should be in the latter days* (*v.* 28). Some think that the *thoughts* which are said to have *come into the king's mind upon his bed, what should come to pass hereafter*, were his own thoughts when he was awake. Just before he fell asleep he was musing what would be the issue of his growing greatness, what his kingdom would herafter come to; and so the dream was an answer to those thoughts.

V. He solemnly professes that he could not pretend to have merited from God the favour of this discovery (*v.* 30): *"But, as for me, this secret is not found out by me, but is revealed to me, and that not for any wisdom that I have* to qualify me for the receiving of such a discovery." The secret was made known to him for the sake of his people, his brethren and companions in tribulation. God revealed this thing to Daniel that he might make it known to the king. Prophets receive that they may give, that the discoveries made to them may be communicated to the persons that are concerned.

Verses 31–45

Daniel here gives full satisfaction to Nebuchadnezzar concerning his dream and the interpretation. And now the king is abundantly repaid, and for receiving this prophet, though not in the name of a prophet, he had a prophet's reward.

I. The dream itself, *v.* 31, 45. Nebuchadnezzar was a worshipper of images, and now behold a *great image* is set before him in a dream. This was the image of a man erect: *It stood before him*, as a living man; and, because those monarchies represented by it were admirable in the eyes of their friends, the *brightness* of this image *was excellent*; and because they were formidable to their enemies, the *form* of this image is said to be *terrible*; both the features of the face and the postures of the body made it so. But that which was most remarkable was the different metals of which it was composed—the *head of gold* (the richest and most durable metal), the *breast and arms of silver* (the next to it in worth), the *belly and sides* (or *thighs*) *of brass*, the *legs and feet of iron* (still baser metals), and lastly the feet *part of iron and part of clay*. See what the things of this world are; the further we go in them the less valuable they appear. Some observe that in Daniel's visions the monarchies were represented by four beasts (*ch.* vii), for he looked upon that wisdom from beneath, to be earthly, and a tyrannical power, to have more in it of the beast than of the man. But to Nebuchadnezzar, a heathen prince, they were represented by a gay and pompous image of a man, for he was an admirer of the *kingdoms of this world and the glory of them*. But what became of this image? The next part of the dream shows it calcined, and brought to nothing. He saw a stone cut out of the quarry by an unseen power, and this stone fell upon the *feet of the image*, that were of *iron and clay*, and *broke them to pieces*; and then the image must fall and the gold, and silver, and brass, and iron, were all broken to pieces, beaten so small that they became like the *chaff of the summer threshing-floors*: but the stone *cut out of the mountain* became itself a *great mountain, and filled the earth*.

II. The interpretation of this dream.

1. This image represented the kingdoms of the earth that should successively bear rule among the nations and have influence on the affairs of the Jewish church. The four monarchies were not represented by four distinct statues, but by one image, because they were all of one and the same spirit, and all more or less against the church. It was the same power, only lodged in four different nations. (1) The *head of gold* signified the Chaldean monarchy, which was now in being (*v.* 37, 38): Thou art the *highest of kings* on earth at this time. It is *the God of heaven* that has *given thee a kingdom, power, and strength, and glory*, a kingdom that exercises great authority, stands firmly. The extent of his dominion is set forth (*v.* 38), that *wheresoever the children of men dwell* in all the nations of that part of the world, he was *ruler over them all*. Thus "*thou art the head of gold*; thou, and thy son, and thy son's son, for seventy years." Compare this with Jer. xxv. 9, 11, especially Jer. xxvii. 5–7. There were other powerful kingdoms in the world at this time, as that of the Scythians; but it was the kingdom of Babylon that reigned over the Jews. It is called a *head*, for its wisdom, and absolute power, a head of *gold* for its wealth (Isa. xiv. 4). Some make this monarchy to begin in Nimrod, and so bring into it all the Assyrian kings. But it had not been so long a monarchy of such vast extent, therefore others make only Nebuchadnezzar, Evil-merodach, and Belshazzar, to belong to this *head of gold*. (2) The *breast and arms of silver* signified the monarchy of the Medes and Persians. *There shall arise another kingdom inferior to thee* (*v.* 39), not so rich, powerful, or victorious. This kingdom was founded by Darius the Mede and Cyrus the Persian, in alliance and therefore represented by two arms. Cyrus was himself a Persian by his father, a Mede by his mother. (3) The *belly and thighs of brass* signified the monarchy of the Grecians, founded by Alexander, who conquered Darius, the last of the Persian emperors. This is the *third kingdom, of brass*, inferior in wealth and extent to the Persian monarchy, but in Alexander himself it shall by the power of the sword *bear rule over all*

the earth; for Alexander boasted that he had conquered the world. (4) The *legs and feet of iron* signified the Roman monarchy. It was in the time of that monarchy, when it was at its height, that the kingdom of Christ was set up in the world by the preaching of the everlasting gospel. The Roman kingdom strong as iron (*v.* 40), *broke in pieces* the Grecian empire and afterwards destroyed the nation of the Jews. Towards the latter end of the Roman monarchy it grew weak, and branched into ten kingdoms, which were as the toes of these feet. Some of these were weak as clay, others strong as iron, *v.* 42. They shall not cleave one to another, *v.* 43. This empire divided the government for a long time between the senate and the people, the nobles and the commons, but they did not coalesce. There were civil wars between Marius and Sulla, Caesar and Pompey, whose parties were as iron and clay.

2. The stone *cut out without hands* represented the kingdom of Jesus Christ, for it should be neither raised nor supported by human power or policy. (1) The gospel-church is a kingdom *not of this world*, and yet set up in it; it is the kingdom of God among men. (2) The *God of heaven* was to set up this kingdom, to give authority to Christ, to set him as *King upon his holy hill of Zion*. It is often in the *New Testament* called the *kingdom of heaven*, for its origin is from above and its tendency is upwards. (3) It was to be set up *in the days of these kings*, the kings of the fourth monarchy, of which particular notice is taken (Luke ii. 1). When these kings are contesting with each other, God will do his own work and fulfil his own counsels. (4) It is a kingdom that knows no decay, and will not admit any succession or revolution. As Christ is a monarch that has no successor (for he himself shall reign for ever), so his kingdom is a monarchy that has no revolution. The kingdom of God was indeed taken from the Jews and given to the Gentiles (Matt. xxi. 43), but still it was Christianity that ruled, the kingdom of the Messiah. (5) It is a kingdom that shall be victorious. It shall *break in pieces and consume all those kingdoms*, as the *stone cut out of the mountain without hands* broke in pieces the image, *v.* 44, 45. And in the kingdoms that submit to the kingdom of Christ tyranny, and idolatry, and everything that is their reproach, shall, as far as the gospel of Christ gets ground, be broken. Our Saviour seems to refer to this (Matt. xxi. 44) when he says, *On whomsoever this stone shall fall, it will grind him to powder*. (6) It shall be an everlasting kingdom. *The Lord shall reign for ever*, not only to the end of time, but when time and days shall be no more, and *God shall be all in all* to eternity.

III. Daniel having thus interpreted the dream, to the satisfaction of Nebuchadnezzar, closes with a solemn assertion, 1. Of the divine origin of this dream: *The great God has made known to the king what shall come to pass hereafter*, which the gods of the magicians could not do. 2. Of the undoubted certainty of the things foretold by this dream. Whatever God has made known we may depend upon.

Verses 46–49

Instead of resenting it as an affront, the king received it as an oracle, and here we are told what the expressions were of the impressions it made upon him. 1. He was ready to look upon Daniel as a little god. He concluded that he had certainly a divinity lodged in him, worthy his adoration; and therefore he *fell upon his face and worshipped Daniel*, *v.* 46. Thus did God magnify divine revelation *and make it honourable*. And that Daniel did say something to him which turned his eyes and thoughts another way is intimated in what follows (*v.* 47), *The king answered Daniel*. 2. He readily acknowledged the God of

Daniel to be the great God. If Daniel will not suffer himself to be worshipped, he will *worship God*, by confessing (v. 47), *Of a truth your God is a God of gods*, over all gods in dominion. 3. He preferred Daniel, made him a great man, *v.* 48. The king *gave him many great gifts.* He made him *ruler over the whole province of Babylon*, he made him chancellor of the university, *chief of the governors over all the wise men of Babylon.* 4. He preferred his companions for his sake, and upon his request, *v.* 49. Daniel himself *sat in the gate of the king*, and procured places in the government for Shadrach, Meshach, and Abednego. And these pious Jews, being thus preferred in Babylon, had opportunity of serving their brethren in captivity.

CHAPTER 3

Here we have those same three men as much under the king's displeasure as then they were in his favour, and yet more highly honoured by their God than there they were honoured by their prince, by the grace wherewith he enabled them rather to suffer than to sin. It is a memorable story and a great encouragement to the constancy of his people in trying times. The apostle mentions, among the believing heroes, those who by faith "quenched the violence of fire", Heb. xi. 34. I. Nebuchadnezzar's erecting a golden image, and his requiring all his subjects to fall down and worship it, and the general compliance of his people with that command, ver. 1–7. II. Information given against the Jewish princes for refusing to worship this golden image, ver. 8–12. III. Their constant persisting in that refusal, notwithstanding his menaces, ver. 13–18. IV. The casting of them into the fiery furnace for their refusal, ver. 19–23. V. Their miraculous preservation by the power of God, and their invitation out of the fire by the king, who was by this miracle convinced of his error in casting them in, ver. 24–27. VI. The honour which the king gave to God hereupon, and the favour he showed to those faithful men, ver. 28–30.

Verses 1–7

I. A *golden image set up* to be worshipped. Babylon was full of idols, but those who have forsaken the one only living God, and begin to set up many gods, will find the gods they set up so unsatisfying, that they will multiply them without measure. It was *an image of gold.* It was *threescore cubits high and six cubits broad*, as if its being monstrous would make amends for its being lifeless. Perhaps he set it up as an image of himself, and designed to be himself worshipped in it. The good impressions made upon him were quite lost, and quickly. He had acknowledged that the God of Israel is a *God of gods* and a *Lord of kings*; yet now, in defiance of the express law of that God, he sets up an image to be worshipped. The very dream and the interpretation of it, which made such good impressions upon him, now had a quite contrary effect. Now it made him set up for a bold competitor with God.

II. The states summoned to attend the dedication of this image, *v.* 2, 3. Long journeys many took upon a foolish errand; but, as the idols are senseless things, such are the worshippers.

III. A proclamation made, commanding all persons present to fall down and worship the image.

IV. The general compliance of the assembly with this command, *v.* 7. It was proclaimed, That whosoever would not *worship this golden image* should be immediately thrown *into the midst of a burning fiery furnace*, ready prepared for that purpose, *v.* 6.

Verses 8–18

It was strange that Shadrach, Meshach, and Abednego, would be present at this assembly. Surely because they would obey the king's orders and be ready to bear a public testimony against this gross idolatry.

I. Information is brought to the king by *certain Chaldeans* against these three, *v.* 8. Perhaps these that accused them were some of those *magicians or astrologers* that were particularly called *Chaldeans* (*ch.* ii. 2, 4). Perhaps they were such of the Chaldeans

as envied them their preferments; *and who can stand before envy?* They appeal to the king, 1. To put him in mind of the law he had lately made, That all manner of persons, without exception of nation or language, should *fall down and worship this golden image*, *v.* 10, 11. 2. To inform him that these three men, Shadrach, Meshach, and Abednego, had not conformed to this edict, *v.* 12. To incense the king the more against them, (1) They put him in mind of the dignity to which the criminals had been preferred. It was therefore an insufferable piece of insolence, for them to disobey the king's command. The high station they were in would make their refusal the more scandalous. (2) They suggest that it was done in contempt of him and his authority.

II. These three pious Jews are brought before the king, and examined upon this information. Nebuchadnezzar fell into a great passion, and *in his rage and fury commanded* them to be seized, *v.* 13.

III. The king asked them whether it was true that they had not worshipped the golden image when others did, *v.* 14. It may be, upon second thoughts, they will change their minds. The king is willing that if they will *worship the golden image*, well and good; their former omission shall be pardoned. The king is resolved, if they persist in their refusal, that they shall immediately be *cast into the fiery furnace. Turn, or burn;* and, because he knew they buoyed themselves up in their refusal with a confidence in their God, he set him at defiance: *"And who is that God that shall deliver you out of my hands?* Let him, if he can."

IV. They answer that they still adhere to their resolution not to worship the golden image, *v.* 16–18. We call these the *three children* (they were indeed *young men*), but we should rather call them the three champions, the *first three* of the *worthies* of God's *kingdom among men.* They did not go out of their way to court martyrdom; but, when they were duly called to the fiery trial, they acquitted themselves bravely.

1. Their contempt of death, and the noble negligence with which they look upon the dilemma: *O Nebuchadnezzar! we are not careful to answer thee in this matter.* They do not in sullenness deny him an answer, but they tell him that they are in no care about it. They needed no time to deliberate concerning their answer; for they did not hesitate whether they should comply or no. But the sin and duty in the case were determined by the letter of the second commandment, and no room was left to question what was right. They were not contriving an evasive answer, when a direct answer was expected from them.

2. Their confidence in God and their dependence upon him, *v.* 17. They trusted in the living God, and by that faith chose rather to suffer than to sin. "If we must be thrown into the fiery furnace unless we serve thy gods, know then, though we worship not *thy gods* yet we are not atheists; there is a God whom we call ours. We serve this God. We are well assured that this God is *able to deliver us from the burning fiery furnace.* If he do not deliver us from the fiery furnace, he will *deliver us out of thy hand.*" Nebuchadnezzar can but torment and kill the body, and, after that, there is no more than he can do. God will deliver us either from death or in death.

3. Their firm resolution to adhere to their principles, whatever might be the consequence (*v.* 18). They were not required to abjure their own God, or to renounce his worship. It was but one single act that was required of them, which would be done in a minute, and they might afterwards declare their sorrow for it. They might be excused if they should go down the stream, when it is so strong. Did not all the ten tribes, for many ages, worship gods of gold at Dan

and Bethel? If they should comply, they would save their lives and so be in a capacity to do a great deal of service to their brethren. But there is enough in that one word of God wherewith to answer and silence these and many more such like carnal reasonings: *Thou shalt not bow down thyself to any images, nor worship them.* They must rather suffer than sin, and must not do evil that good may come. And truly, the saving of them from this sinful compliance was as great a miracle as the saving of them out of the fiery furnace.

Verses 19–27

I. The casting of these three faithful servants of God into the fiery furnace. Nebuchadnezzar, instead of being convinced by what they said, was exasperated, and made more outrageous, v. 19. It made him *full of fury*, and the *form of his visage was changed* against these men. Nebuchadnezzar, in this heat, exchanged the awful majesty of a prince for the frightful fury of a *wild bull in a net*. Instead of mitigating their punishment, he ordered it to be heightened, that they should *heat the furnace seven times more than it was wont to be heated* for other malefactors. He ordered them to be bound in their clothes, and cast into the midst of the burning fiery furnace, which was done accordingly, v. 20, 21. God's providence ordered it for the increase of the miracle, in that their clothes were not so much as singed. The men that bound them, and threw them into the furnace, were themselves consumed or suffocated by the flame, v. 22. But these men were only the instruments of cruelty; he that bade them do it had the greater sin. Nebuchadnezzar himself was reserved for a further reckoning.

II. The deliverance of these three faithful servants of God out of the furnace.

1. Nebuchadnezzar finds them walking in the fire. *He was astonished, and rose up in haste*, v. 24. In his astonishment he calls his counsellors. *Did we not cast three men bound into the fire?* "*True, O king!*" say they. "But now," says the king, "I have been looking into the furnace, and *I see four men, loose, walking in the midst of the fire,*" v. 25. They were loosed from their bonds. The fire that did not so much as singe their clothes burnt the cords wherewith they were bound, and set them at liberty. They *walked in the midst of the fire*. The furnace was large, so that they had room to walk; they were unhurt, so that they were able to walk; their minds were easy, so that they were disposed to walk, as in a paradise or garden of pleasure. There was a fourth seen with them in the fire, whose form, in Nebuchadnezzar's judgment, was *like the Son of God*; he appeared as a divine person, a messenger from heaven, not as a servant, but as a son. In the apocryphal narrative of this story it is said, *The angel of the Lord came down into the furnace;* and Nebuchadnezzar here says (v. 28), God *sent his angel and delivered them*; and it was an angel that shut the lions' mouths when Daniel was in the den, *ch.* vi. 22. But some think it was the eternal Son of God. Those that suffer for Christ have his gracious presence with them in their sufferings, even in the fiery furnace, even in the valley of the shadow of death, and therefore even there they need *fear no evil*.

2. Nebuchadnezzar calls them out of the furnace (v. 26): He *comes near to the mouth of the burning fiery furnace*, and bids them *come forth and come hither*. He is convinced by their miraculous preservation that he did evil in casting them into the furnace. The *fourth*, whose *form was like the Son of God*, withdrew, but the other three *came forth out of the midst of the fire*, as brands out of the burning. They had not received the least damage by the fire, v. 27. There was not so much as *a hair of their head singed*. Their clothes did not change colour, nor smell of fire,

much less were their bodies scorched or blistered; no, *the fire had no power on them*. The Chaldeans worshipped the fire, as a sort of image of the sun, so that, in restraining the fire now, God put contempt, not only upon their king, but upon their god too.

Verses 28–30

The effect it had upon Nebuchadnezzar.

I. He gives glory to the God of Israel as a God able and ready to protect his worshippers (v. 28): *Blessed be the God of Shadrach, Meshach, and Abednego.* God can extort confessions of his blessedness even from those that have been ready to curse him to his face. 1. He gives him the glory of his power: *There is no other God that can deliver after this sort* (v. 29). If God can work such deliverance as no other can, he may demand such obedience as no other may. 2. He gives him the glory that he was ready to do it (v. 28): *He has sent his angel and delivered his servants.* Bel could not save his worshippers from being burnt at the mouth of the furnace, but the God of Israel saved his from being burnt when they were cast into the midst of the furnace because they refused to *worship any other god*.

II. He applauds the constancy of these three men in their religion, and describes it to their honour, v. 28. They *yielded their* own *bodies* to be cast into the fiery furnace rather than forsake their God. They *changed the king's word*, that is, they went contrary to it, and thereby made him repent. They did it with confidence in their God. They *trusted* that he would either bring them out of the fiery furnace on earth or lead them through the fiery furnace forward to their place in heaven; and in this confidence they became regardless of their own lives.

III. He issues a royal edict, strictly forbidding any to speak evil of the God of Israel, v. 29. The miracle now wrought by the power of this God in defence of his worshippers, publicly in the sight of the thousands of Babylon, was a sufficient justification of this edict. It is a great mercy to the church when its enemies, though they have not their hearts turned, yet have their mouths stopped and their tongues tied.

IV. He not only reverses the attainder of these three men, but restores them to their places in the government (*makes them to prosper*, so the word is).

CHAPTER 4

The story here recorded concerning Nebuchadnezzar is given us in his own words. I. The preface to his narrative, wherein he acknowledges God's dominion over him, ver. 1–3. II. The narrative itself, wherein he relates, 1. His dream, ver. 1–18. 2. The interpretation of his dream by Daniel, who showed him his own fall, advising him to repent and reform, ver. 19–27. 3. The accomplishment of it in his running stark mad for seven years, and then recovering the use of his reason again, ver. 28–36. 4. The conclusion of the narrative, with a humble acknowledgment and adoration of God as Lord of all, ver. 37.

Verses 1–3

I. The form, which was usual in proclamations issued by the king, v. 1. The royal style is short, and unaffected—*Nebuchadnezzar the king.* The declaration is directed *to all people, nations, and languages, that dwell in all the earth.* He salutes those to whom he writes, in the usual form, *Peace be multiplied unto you.*

II. He writes this, 1. To acquaint others with the providences of God that had related to him (v. 2): *I thought it good to show the signs and wonders that the high God* (so he calls the true God) *has wrought towards me.* It was a debt he owed to God and the world, now that he had recovered from his distraction, to relate how justly God had humbled him and how graciously he had at length restored him. We ought to give glory to God, not only by praising him for his mercies, but by confessing our sins, accepting the punishment of our iniquity. 2. To show how much he was himself convinced by them, v. 2. He admires God's doings. Nebuchadnezzar was now old, had reigned above forty years, and had seen much of the world and revolutions, yet never till now was he brought to admire God's signs and his wonders. Now, *How great, how mighty*, are they! He thence infers God's dominion. *His kingdom is an everlasting kingdom;* and not like his own kingdom, which he saw, in a dream, hastening towards a period. Other reigns are confined to one generation, and other dynasties to a few generations, but God's *dominion is from generation to generation.*

Verses 4–18

Nebuchadnezzar, before he relates the judgments of God wrought upon him for his pride, gives an account of the fair warning he had of them before they came.

I. This alarm was given to him (v. 4), when he was *at rest in his house, and flourishing in his palace*. He had lately conquered Egypt, and with it completed his victories, and ended his wars, about the thirty-fourth or thirty-fifth year of his reign, Ezek. xxix. 17. Then he had this dream, which was accomplished about a year after. Seven years of his distraction continued, upon his recovery from which he penned this declaration, lived about two years after, and died in his forty-fifth year.

II. The impression it made upon him (v. 5): *I saw a dream which made me afraid.* His *thoughts upon his bed* made him uneasy, and the *visions of his head*, the creatures of his own imagination, *troubled him*.

III. His consulting, in vain, with the magicians and astrologers. He had not now forgotten the dream, as before, *ch.* ii. He wanted to know the interpretation of it, v. 6. Orders are immediately given to summon *all the wise men of Babylon* to see if any could interpret the king's dream. His expectation from them was disappointed: He *told them the dream* (v. 7), but they *could not tell him the interpretation of it*, though they had boasted, with great assurance (*ch.* ii. 4, 7). Now was fulfilled what Isaiah foretold (*ch.* xlvii. 12, 13), that when the ruin of Babylon was drawing on her *enchantments* and *sorceries*, her *astrologers* and *star-gazers*, should not be able to do her any service.

IV. *At the last Daniel came in*, v. 8. Many make God's word their last refuge, and never have recourse to it till they are driven off from all other succours. He compliments Daniel very highly. He applauds his rare endowments: He has *the spirit of the holy gods*, so he tells him to his face (v. 9). Here is a strange medley in Nebuchadnezzar, but such as is common in those that side with their corruptions against their convictions. 1. He is an idolater, and his speech betrayeth him. He speaks of many gods. And some think, when he speaks of *the spirit of the holy gods*, that he supposes there are some evil malignant deities, and some who are good beneficent deities, and that by the spirit of the latter Daniel was animated. He also applauds Daniel, not as *a servant of God*, but as *master of the magicians* (v. 9). How loose his convictions sat, and how easily he had dropped them! He once called the God of Israel a *God of gods*, *ch.* ii. 47. Now he sets him upon a level with the rest of those whom he calls the *holy gods*. Nebuchadnezzar, not going forward with acknowledgments of the sovereignty of the true God, soon *went backwards*, yet professes a great opinion of Daniel, whom he knows to be a servant of the true God.

V. The account he gives him of his dream.

1. He saw a stately flourishing tree *planted in the midst of the earth* (v. 10), fitly representing him who reigned in Babylon, the midst of the then known world. His dignity was signified by the height of this tree, which was *exceedingly great*; it *reached unto heaven*. He over-topped those about him, and aimed to have divine honours given him. This tree had everything in it that was pleasant to the eye and good for food (v. 12): *The leaves thereof were fair*, denoting the pomp and splendour of Nebuchadnezzar's court. This tree was, (1) For protection; the boughs of it were for shelter. Princes should be a screen to their subjects *from the heat* and *from the storm*. (2) For provision. The Assyrian was compared to a *cedar* (Ezek. xxxi. 6), which affords shadow only; but this tree here had much fruit—in it was *meat for all* and *all flesh was fed of it*. This mighty monarch, it should seem by this, not only was great, but did good.

2. He heard the doom of this tree read. The sentence was passed upon it by an angel, whom he saw *come down from heaven*, and heard proclaim this sentence aloud. This angel is here called a *watcher*, or *watchman*. This angel was a *messenger*, or *ambassador* (so some read it), and *a holy one*.

(1) Orders are given that it be cut down (v. 14).

(2) Care is taken that the root be preserved (v. 15): "*Leave the stump of it in the earth*, exposed to all weathers. Let it be hooped round with *a band of iron and brass*, to keep it firm." God in judgment remembers mercy; and may yet have good things in store for those whose condition seems most forlorn. There is *hope of a tree, if it be cut down, that it will sprout again, that through the scent of water it will bud*, Job xiv. 7–9.

(3) The meaning of this is explained by the angel himself to Nebuchadnezzar, v. 16. Whoever is the person signified by this tree he is sentenced to be deposed from the dignity of a man, to be deprived of his reason, and to live like a brute, till *seven times pass over him. Let a beast's heart be given unto him*. This is surely the saddest and sorest of all temporal judgments. Those proud tyrants who *set their heart as the heart of God* (Ezek. xxviii. 2) may justly be deprived of the heart of man, and have a beast's heart given them.

(4) The truth of it is confirmed (v. 17). The angels of heaven have subscribed to it. It is by *the decree of the watchers*. Such was Nebuchadnezzar's doom; it was by the *decree of the watchers*. The saints on earth petitioned for it, as well as the angels in heaven: *The demand is by the word of the holy ones*. God's suffering people, that had long groaned under the heavy yoke of Nebuchadnezzar's tyranny, made the demand, and God gave this answer to it.

(5) The design of it is declared. Orders are given for the cutting down of this tree, *to the intent that the living may know that the Most High rules.*

Thus has Nebuchadnezzar fully and faithfully related his dream, what he saw and what he heard, and now demands of Daniel the interpretation of it (v. 18).

Verses 19–27

The interpretation of Nebuchadnezzar's dream; and when once it is declared that he is the tree in the dream, when once it is said, *Thou art the man*, there needs little more to be said for the explication of the dream. The thing was so plain that Daniel, upon hearing the dream, was *astonished for one hour*, v. 19. He was struck with amazement and terror at so great a judgment coming upon so great a prince. He was likewise struck with confusion when he found himself the man that must bring to the king *these heavy tidings*.

I. The king observed him stand as one astonished, and thinking he was loth to speak out for fear of offending him, encouraged him to deal plainly with him: *Let not the dream, nor the interpretation thereof, trouble thee*. This he speaks either, 1. As one that sincerely desired to know the truth. Or, 2. As one that despised the truth, and set it at defiance. Daniel is concerned for him, and therefore wishes, *"The dream be to those that hate thee.* Let the ill it bodes light on the head of thy enemies, not on thy head." Though Nebuchadnezzar was an oppressor of the people of God, yet he was, at present, Daniel's prince.

II. The interpretation itself is only a repetition of the dream, with application to the king. "As for *the tree* which thou sawest *flourishing* (v. 20, 21), *it is thou, O king!"* v. 22. He shows the king his present prosperous state in the glass of his own dream, *ch.* ii. 37, 38. "As for the doom passed upon the tree (v. 23), it is *the decree of the Most High, which comes upon my lord the king,"* v. 24. He must be deposed from his throne, *driven from men,* and being deprived of his reason, and having a beast's heart given him, his dwelling shall be *with the beasts of the field;* he shall *eat grass as oxen,* and, like them, lie out all weathers, till *seven times* pass over him, that is, *seven years;* and then he shall know that the *Most High rules,* and when he is brought to know and own this he shall be restored to his dominion again (v. 26). God is here called *the heavens,* and the influence which the visible heavens have upon this earth is intended as a faint representation of the dominion the God of heaven has over this lower world; we are said to *sin against heaven,* Luke xv. 18.

III. The close of the interpretation which Daniel, as a prophet, gave the king, v. 27. 1. How humbly he gives his advice, and with what tenderness and respect: *"O king! let my counsel be acceptable unto thee."* 2. He does not counsel him to enter into a course of physic, for the preventing of the distemper, but to break off a course of sin. He wronged his own subjects, and dealt unfairly with his allies. He had been cruel to the poor. 3. The motive with which he backs this advice: *If it may be a lengthening of thy tranquillity.*

Verses 28–33

Nebuchadnezzar's dream accomplished, and Daniel's application of it to him justified and confirmed.

I. God's patience with him: *All this came upon him,* but not till *twelve months after* (v. 29), so long there was a *lengthening of his tranquillity,* though it does not appear that he *broke off his sins,* or showed any *mercy to the poor* captives. God gave him space to repent; he *let him alone this year also,* this *one* year more.

II. His pride, and haughtiness, and abuse of that patience. He walked *in the palace of the kingdom of Babylon,* in pomp and pride. Everything in Babylon he thinks looks great; "and this *great Babylon I have built."* Babylon was built many ages before he was born, but he boasts that he has built it, as Augustus Caesar boasted concerning Rome, *I found it brick, but I left it marble.* He boasts that he built it *for the house of the kingdom,* the metropolis of his empire.

III. His punishment. The powerful word came from heaven, by which he was immediately deprived, 1. Of his honour as a king: *The kingdom has departed from thee.* 2. He is deprived of his honour as a man. He loses his reason, and by that means loses his dominion: *They shall drive thee from men,* v. 32. And it was fulfilled (v. 33): he was *driven from men the same hour.* On a sudden he fell stark mad. His understanding and memory were gone, and all the faculties of a rational soul broken. He went naked, and on all fours, like a brute, and ran wild into the fields and woods.- He was made to *eat grass as oxen.* Nebuchadnezzar would be more than a man, and therefore God justly makes him less than a man, and puts him upon a level with the beasts who set up for a rival with his Maker. See Job xl. 11–13.

Verses 34–37

We have here Nebuchadnezzar's recovery from his distraction, and his return to his right mind, *at the end of the days,* that is, of the seven years. *At the end of the days* (says he), *I lifted up my eyes unto heaven* (v. 34), looked no longer down towards the earth as a beast, but began to look up as a man. But there was more in it than this; he looked up as a penitent, as a humble petitioner for mercy.

I. He has the use of his reason so far restored to him that with it he glorifies God, and humbles himself. Men never rightly use their reason till they begin to be religious, nor live as men till they live to the glory of God. His folly was the means whereby he became wise. To bring him to himself, he must first be *beside himself.* His flatterers often complimented him with, *O king! live for ever.* But he is now convinced that no king lives for ever, but the God of Israel only. God's kingdom is like himself, *everlasting,* and his *dominion from generation to generation;* there is no succession, no revolution, in his kingdom. *All nations* before him are *as nothing.* His power is irresistible, for he *does according to his will.* Everything which God does is well done: His *works are truth,* for they all agree with his word. *His ways are judgment,* both wise and righteous, consonant to the rules of prudence and equity. *Those that walk in pride he is able to abase* (v. 37).

II. He has the use of his reason restored to him (v. 36). He is now established in his kingdom as firmly as if there had been no interruption. Afflictions shall last no longer than till they have done the work for which they were sent. When Nebuchadnezzar is restored to his kingdom he *praises, and extols, and honours the King of heaven* (v. 37).

It was not long after this that Nebuchadnezzar ended his life and reign. Abydenus, quoted by Eusebius (*Praep. Evang.* i. 9), reports that upon his death-bed he foretold the taking of Babylon by Cyrus. Whether he continued in the same good mind that here he seems to have been in we are not told. If our charity may reach so far as to hope he did, we must admire free grace, by which he lost his wits for a while, that he might save his soul for ever.

CHAPTER 5

Belshazzar now reigned in Babylon; some compute he had reigned seventeen years, others but three. About two years before this Cyrus king of Persia, a growing monarch, came against Babylon with a great army; Belshazzar met him, fought him, and was routed by him in a pitched battle. He and his scattered forces retired into the city, where Cyrus besieged them. They were very secure, because the river Euphrates was their bulwark, and they had twenty years' provision in the city; but in the second year of the siege he took it. I. The riotous, idolatrous, sacrilegious feast which Belshazzar made, ver. 1–4. II. The alarm given him by a hand writing on the wall, which none of his wise men could read, ver. 5–9. III. The interpretation of the mystical characters by Daniel, who dealt plainly with him, and showed him his doom written, ver. 10–28. IV. The immediate accomplishment of the interpretation in the slaying of the king and seizing of the kingdom, ver. 30, 31.

Verses 1–9

Belshazzar the king very gay, but all of a sudden very gloomy. He affronts God, and God affrights him.

I. He *made a great feast,* or *banquet of wine;* probably it was some anniversary. Historians say that Cyrus, who was now besieging Babylon, knew of this feast, and presuming that they then would be off their guard, *buried in sleep and wine,* took that opportunity to attack the city, and so made himself master of it. Belshazzar invited *a thousand of his lords to come and drink with him.* In this sumptuous feast, 1. He bade defiance to God's judgments. His city was now besieged; his life and kingdom lay at stake. He should therefore have proclaimed a fast; but, as one resolved to walk contrary to God, he proclaims a feast. 2. He put an affront upon the temple of God, *v. 2. While he tasted the wine, he commanded to bring the vessels* of the temple, that they might drink in them. 3. He put an affront upon God himself, and bade defiance to his deity; for *they drank wine, and praised the gods of gold and silver, v. 4.*

II. How God affrighted the king, and struck a terror upon him. Belshazzar and his lords are in the midst of their revels, but the hour had come when that must be fulfilled which had been long ago said of the king of Babylon, Isa. xxi. 2–4. *The night of my pleasures has he turned into fear to me.* 1. There appear the *fingers of a man's hand writing on the plaster of the wall,* before the king's face (*v.* 5). Here was no destroying angel with his sword drawn—only a pen in the hand, writing upon the wall, *over-against the candlestick,* where they might all see it by the light of their own candle. The king saw *the part of the hand that wrote,* but saw not the person whose hand it was. What we see of God, the part of the hand that writes in the book of the scriptures, may serve to possess us with awful thoughts concerning that of God which we do not see. If this be *the finger of God,* what is his arm made bare? 2. The king is immediately seized with a panic (*v.* 6): *His countenance was changed* (his colour went and came); *the joints of his loins were loosed, his knees smote one against another.* Why is he in such a fright? *His thoughts troubled him;* his own guilty conscience told him that he had no reason to expect any good news from Heaven. God can soon make the heart of the stoutest sinner to tremble; and there needs no more than to let loose his own thoughts upon him. 3. The wise men of Babylon are called in, to see what they can make of this writing upon the wall, *v.* 7. Whoever will may read the mind of God in the scriptures. The king promised that whoever would give him a satisfactory account of this writing should be dignified with the highest honours. 4. The king is disappointed; they can none of them *read the writing,* much less interpret it (*v.* 8), which increases the king's confusion, *v.* 9.

Verses 10–29

I. The information given to the king, by the queen-mother, concerning Daniel, how fit he was to be consulted in this difficult case. It is supposed that this queen was the widow of Evil-Merodach, that famous Nitocris whom Herodotus mentions as a woman of extraordinary prudence. Tidings being brought to her apartment, she came herself to the banqueting-house, to recommend to the king a physician for his melancholy. She could not read the writing herself, but directed him to one that could; let *Daniel be called* now, who should have been called first. He is a *man in whom is the spirit of the holy gods,* who has something in him more than human. She speaks honourably of him as a man that had *light, and understanding, and wisdom.* It was evident he was divinely inspired; he had *knowledge* and *understanding* beyond all the other wise men for *interpreting dreams.* He had an admirably good heart: *An excellent spirit was found in him.* "The king thy father," that is, thy grandfather, "*made him master of the magicians.*" He *named him Belteshazzar,* according to the name of his god, thinking thereby to put honour upon him. *Let Daniel be called, and he will show the interpretation.*

II. Daniel was *brought in before the king, v.* 13. The king asks, with an air of haughtiness: *Art thou that Daniel who art of the children of the captivity?* He acknowledges that all the wise men of Babylon were baffled; they could not *read this writing,* nor *show the interpretation, v.* 16. But he promises him the same rewards that he had promised them if he would do it, *v.* 16.

III. The interpretation which Daniel gave of these mystic characters, was far from easing the king of his fears. Daniel was now in years, and Belshazzar was young; and therefore he seems to take a greater liberty of dealing plainly and roundly with him than he had done upon the like occasions with Nebuchadnezzar.

1. He undertakes to read the writing which gave them this alarm, and to show them the interpretation of it, *v.* 17. He slights the offer of rewards, for he is not one of those that *divine for money. Let thy gifts be to thyself,* for they will not be long thine, and *give thy fee to another.* Let us do our duty in the world, read God's writing and make known the interpretation of it.

2. He recounts to the king God's dealings with his father Nebuchadnezzar, *v.* 18, 21. He describes the great dignity and power to which the divine Providence had advanced Nebuchadnezzar, *v.* 18, 19. His ability was so strong that it was irresistible. His authority was so absolute that it was uncontrollable. *Whom he would he slew, and whom he would he saved alive,* though both were equally innocent or equally guilty. *Whom he would he set up, and whom he would he put down.* He sets before him the sins which Nebuchadnezzar had been guilty of, whereby he had provoked God against him. The description given of his power intimates his abuse of his power. He behaved insolently towards the God above him, and grew proud and haughty (*v.* 20). He reminds him of the judgments of God that were brought upon him for his pride and obstinacy, how he was deprived of his reason, and so *deposed from his kingly throne* (*v.* 20), *driven from among men, to dwell with the wild asses, v.* 21.

3. In God's name, he exhibits articles of impeachment against Belshazzar. Before he reads him his doom, from the hand-writing on the wall, he shows him his crime. He had not taken warning by the judgments of God upon his father (*v.* 22): *Thou his son, O Belshazzar! hast not humbled thy heart, though thou knewest all this.* He had affronted God more impudently than Nebuchadnezzar himself had done, witness the revels of this very night (*v.* 23): *"Thou hast lifted up thyself against the Lord of heaven,* thou hast profaned the *vessels of his house,* and made the utensils of his sanctuary instruments of thy iniquity, and hast *praised the gods of silver and gold, which see not, nor hear, nor know* anything, as if they were to be preferred before the God that sees, and hears, and knows everything." He had not answered the end of his creation and maintenance: *The God in whose hand thy breath is, and whose are all thy ways, hast thou not glorified.* This is a general charge, which stands good against us all. Our dependence upon God as our Creator, preserver, benefactor, owner, and ruler; not only from his hand our breath was at first, but *in his hand our breath is* still; it is he that *holds our souls in life,* and, if he *take away our breath, we die.* We ought to glorify him, to devote ourselves to his honour and employ ourselves in his service. We have *all sinned, and have come short of the glory of God.* This is the indictment against Belshazzar.

4. He now proceeds to read the sentence, as he found it *written upon the wall:* "Then" (says Daniel) "when thou hast come to such a height of impiety as thus to trample upon the most sacred things, *then* when thou wast in the midst of thy sacrilegious idolatrous feast, then was *the part of the hand,* the writing fingers, sent *from him,* from God; he *sent them,* and *this writing,* thou now seest, *was written, v.* 24. Now the writing was, *Mene, Mene, Tekel, Upharsin, v.* 25. The signification of them is, *He has numbered, he has weighed, and they divide.* (1) *Mene;* repeated, for the thing is certain—*Mene, mene;* that signifies, both in Hebrew and Chaldee, *He has*

numbered and finished, which Daniel explains thus (v. 26): "*God has numbered thy kingdom*. Here is an end of thy kingdom." (2) *Tekel;* signifies, in Chaldee, *Thou art weighed*, and, in Hebrew, *Thou art too light*. God does not give judgment against him till he has first pondered his actions, and considered the merits of his case. (3) *Upharsin* (v. 28): "*Thy kingdom is divided*, is rent from thee, and *given to the Medes and Persians*, as a prey to be divided among them." Belshazzar was so far convicted by his own conscience of the reasonableness of all he said that he gave Daniel the reward he promised him, put on him the *scarlet gown* and the *gold chain*, and proclaimed him the *third ruler in the kingdom* (v. 29).

Verses 30–31

1. The death of the king. Heathen writers speak of Cyrus's taking Babylon by surprise, with the assistance of two deserters that showed him the best way into the city. 2. The transferring of the kingdom into other hands. From the head of gold we now descend to the breast and arms of silver. *Darius the Mede took the kingdom* in partnership with, and by the consent of Cyrus, who had conquered it, v. 31.

Chapter 6

Daniel selects such particular passages of story as serve for the confirming of our faith in God. Daniel by faith "stopped the mouths of lions," and so "obtained a good report," Heb. xi. 33. The three children were cast into the fiery furnace for not committing a known sin, Daniel was cast into the lion's den for not omitting a known duty. I. Daniel's preferment in the court of Darius, ver. 1–3. II. The envy and malice of his enemies against him, ver. 4, 5. III. The decree they obtained against prayer for thirty days, ver. 6–9. IV. Daniel's continuance and constancy in prayer, notwithstanding that decree, ver. 10. V. Information given against him for it, and the casting of him into the den of lions, ver. 11–17. VI. His miraculous preservation and deliverance, ver. 18–23. VII. The casting of his accusers into the den, and their destruction, ver. 24. VIII. The decree which Darius made upon this occasion, in honour of the God of Daniel, and the prosperity of Daniel afterwards, ver. 25–28.

Verses 1–5

Concerning Daniel,

I. What a *great man* he was. When Darius, upon his accession to the crown of Babylon by conquest, new-modelled the government, he made Daniel prime-minister of state. Darius *set over the kingdom* 120 *princes* (v. 1), and appointed them their districts. Over these princes there was a *triumvirate*, or *three presidents*, who were to take and state the public accounts *that the king should have no damage* (v. 2), that he should not sustain loss in his revenue. Of these three Daniel was the chief, *preferred above the presidents and princes* (v. 3). Daniel had been a great man in the kingdom that was conquered, and for that reason, one would think, should have been imprisoned or banished. He was a native of a foreign kingdom, and a ruined one, and might have been despised as a stranger and captive. But Darius was soon aware that Daniel had something extraordinary in him, and therefore, finding Daniel excel in prudence and virtue, and probably having heard of his being divinely inspired, he made him his right hand. Though Daniel was now very old yet he was as able as ever for business, and won respect from all by being an oak, not by being a willow, by a constancy in virtue, not by a pliableness to vice.

II. *An excellent spirit was in him, v. 3.* There was *no error*, or *fault, to be found in him, v. 4.*

III. The presidents and princes envied him because he was advanced above them. 1. The cause of envy is everything that is good. The better a man is the worse he is thought of by his rivals. 2. The effect of envy is everything that is bad. Those that envied Daniel sought no less than his ruin. His enemies set spies upon him; they *sought to find occasion against*

him. They concluded, at length, that they should not find any occasion against him except *concerning the law of his God, v. 5.* It seems then that Daniel kept up the profession of his religion, and there was no law that required him to be of the king's religion, or incapacitated him to bear office in the state unless he were. He was at the king's service *usque ad aras— as far as the altars;* but there he left him. In this matter therefore his enemies hoped to ensnare him.

Verses 6–10

Daniel's adversaries contrive a new law, by which they hope to ensnare him, and such was his fidelity to his God that they gained their point.

I. Darius's impious law—*Darius's*, because he gave the royal assent to it. The presidents and princes framed the edict. They intimate to the king that it was carried *unanimously*: "*All the presidents* are of this mind"; and yet we are sure that Daniel, the chief of the three presidents. did not agree to it. These designing men, under colour of doing honour to the king, press him to pass this into a law, and make it a royal statute, that *whosoever shall ask a petition of any god or man for thirty days, save of the king, shall be cast into the den of lions, v. 7.* All men must be made to believe that the king is so ready to all petitioners, that none in any distress need to apply either to God or man for relief, but to him only. And for thirty days together he will be ready to give audience to all that have any petition to present to him. There is a great deal in it that is apparently evil. Must not a beggar ask an alms, or one neighbour beg a kindness of another? If the child want bread, must he not ask it of his parents, or be cast into the den of lions if he do? But it was an impudent affront to all religion, to forbid asking a petition *of any god.* To interdict prayer for thirty days is to rob God of all the tribute he has from man and to rob man of all the comfort he has in God. Does not every man's heart direct him, when he is in want or distress, to call upon God, and must this be made high treason? Had they proposed only to prohibit the Jews from praying to their God, Daniel would have been as effectually ensnared; but they knew the king would not pass such a law, and therefore made it general.

II. Daniel's pious disobedience to this law, *v.* 10. He did not retire into the country, but stood his ground, knowing that he had now a fair opportunity of honouring God before men.

1. Daniel *prayed in his house*, sometimes himself alone and sometimes with his family about him, and made a solemn business of it. Every house not only may be, but ought to be, a house of prayer; where we have a tent God must have an altar, and on it we must offer spiritual sacrifices. In every prayer he gave thanks. When he prayed and gave thanks he *kneeled upon his knees.* Kneeling is a begging posture, and we come to God as beggars, beggars for our lives. He *opened the windows of his chamber*, that the sight of the visible heavens might affect his heart with awe. He *opened them towards Jerusalem*, the holy city, though now in ruins, to signify the affection he had for its very stones and dust (Ps. cii. 14). He did this *three times a day.* It is good to have our hours of prayer, not to bind, but to remind conscience; and, if we think our bodies require refreshment by food thrice a day, can we think seldomer will serve our souls? All who knew him knew it to be his practice; and he was not ashamed of it.

2. Daniel's constant adherence to this practice, even when it was made by the law a capital crime. When he knew that *the writing was signed* he continued to do as *he did aforetime.* Many a man, yea, and many a good man, would have thought it prudence to omit it for these thirty days, when he could not do it without hazard of his life; but Daniel, who had so

many eyes upon him, must act with courage. And we must take heed lest, under pretence of discretion, we be found guilty of cowardice in the cause of God.

Verses 11–17

Proof made of Daniel's praying to his God, notwithstanding the late edict to the contrary (v. 11): *These men assembled; they came tumultuously together*, so the word is, the same that was used v. 6. They came together to visit Daniel, perhaps under pretence of business, at that time which they knew to be his usual hour of devotion; and they *found him on his knees praying* and *making supplication before his God*. They lost no time, but applied to the king (v. 12), and proceeded to accuse Daniel, v. 13. They so describe him as to exasperate the king and incense him the more against him: "He is *of the children of the captivity of Judah*; and a captive in a despicable state, that can call nothing his own but what he has by the king's favour, and yet *he regards not thee, O king! nor the decree that thou hast signed.*" They do not say, He makes his petition to his God, lest Darius should take notice of that to his praise, but only, *He makes his petition*, which is the thing the law forbids. The king now perceived that, whatever they pretended, it was not to honour him, but to spite Daniel, v. 14. Now the king *sets his heart to deliver Daniel*; both by argument and by authority he labours *till the going down of the sun to deliver him*, that is, to persuade his accusers not to insist upon his prosecution. The prosecutors demanded judgment, v. 15. We are not told what Daniel said; the king himself is his advocate. But the prosecutors insist upon it that the law must have its course. The Persians magnified the wisdom of their king, by supposing that whatever law he solemnly ratified it was so well made that there could be no occasion to alter it. The king himself, with the utmost reluctance, and against his conscience, signs the warrant for his execution; and Daniel, that venerable grave man, who carried such a mixture of majesty and sweetness in his countenance, is purely for worshipping his God, *thrown into the den of lions*, to be devoured by them, v. 16. To make sure work, the stone *laid upon the mouth of the den* is *sealed* (v. 17). The encouragement which Darius gave to Daniel to trust in God: *Thy God whom thou servest continually, he will deliver thee*, v. 16. He justifies Daniel from guilt, owning all his crime to be serving his God continually. He leaves it to God to free him: *He will deliver thee*.

Verses 18–24

I. The melancholy night which the king had, upon Daniel's account, v. 18. He could not forgive himself for throwing him into the danger. He *passed the night fasting*. He forbade the music.

II. The early enquiry he made concerning Daniel the next morning, v. 19, 20. He *went in haste to the den of lions*. When he comes to the den, he cries, *with a lamentable voice, O Daniel! servant of the living God*, has *thy God whom thou servest* made it to appear that he is *able to deliver thee from the lions?*

III. Daniel is alive, is safe, and well, and unhurt in the lions' den, v. 21, 22. Daniel knew the king's voice: *O king! live for ever*. He does not reproach him, but has heartily forgiven him. The account Daniel gives the king is triumphant. 1. God has preserved his life by a miracle. He is *my God*, whom I own, and who owns me, for *he has sent his angel*. The same that was seen in *the form of the Son of God* with the three children in the fiery furnace had visited Daniel, and had *shut the lions' mouths*. See the care God takes of his faithful worshippers. He does in effect *stop the lions' mouths*, that they cannot hurt them. 2. Daniel was represented to the king as

disaffected to him and his government. We do not find that he said anything in his own vindication, but left it to God to establish his integrity, and he did it effectually, by working a miracle for his preservation.

IV. The discharge of Daniel from his confinement. His prosecutors cannot but own that the law is satisfied, though they are not. No cause can be shown why Daniel should not be fetched out of the den (v. 23).

V. The committing of his prosecutors to the same prison, v. 24. Darius is animated by this miracle wrought for Daniel, and now begins to take courage and act like himself. Daniel's accusers, now that his innocency is cleared, have the same punishment inflicted upon them which they designed against him.

Verses 25–28

Darius here studies to make amends for the dishonour he had done both to God and Daniel.

I. He gives honour to God by a decree published to all nations, by which they are required to fear before him. He sends this decree—*to all people, nations, and languages, that dwell in all the earth*, v. 25. The decree is—that *men tremble and fear before the God of Daniel*. This goes further than Nebuchadnezzar's decree, for that only restrained people from *speaking amiss* of this God, but this requires them to *fear before him*. But, though this decree goes far, it does not go far enough; had he come up to his present convictions, he would have commanded all men not only to fear before this God, but to love him and trust in him, to forsake the service of their idols, and to worship him only. There is good reason why all men should fear before this God, for, 1. His being is transcendent. 2. His government is incontestable. 3. Both his being and his government are unchangeable. 4. He has ability sufficient to support such an authority, v. 27. He delivers his faithful servants from trouble and rescues them out of trouble. 5. He has given a fresh proof of all this in *delivering* his servant *Daniel from the power of the lions*.

II. He puts honour upon Daniel (v. 28): *So this Daniel prospered*.

CHAPTER 7

The six former chapters of this book were historical; we now enter with fear and trembling upon the six latter, which are prophetical, wherein are many things dark and hard to be understood, which we dare not positively determine, and yet many things plain and profitable. I. Daniel's vision of the four beasts, ver. 1–8. II. His vision of God's throne of government and judgment, ver. 9–14. III. The interpretation of these visions, ver. 15–28. Whether those visions look as far forward as the end of time, or whether they were to have a speedy accomplishment, is hard to say, nor are the most judicious interpreters agreed concerning it.

Verses 1–8

The date of this chapter places it before *ch. v*, which was in the last year of Belshazzar, and *ch. vi*, which was in the first of Darius. Belshazzar's name here is, in the original, spelt *Bel-eshe-zar*—*Bel is on fire by the enemy*. Bel the god of the Chaldeans had prospered, but is now to be consumed.

Daniel's vision of the four monarchies that were oppressive to the Jews.

I. The circumstances of this vision (v. 1): He *had visions of his head upon his bed*, when he was asleep; so God sometimes revealed his mind to men, when deep sleep fell upon them (Job xxxiii. 15). When he was awake he *wrote the dream*, and *told the sum of the matters* to his brethren, and gave it to them in writing, that it might be preserved for their children, who shall see these things accomplished. The Jews, misunderstanding Jeremiah and Ezekiel, flattered themselves that, after their return, they should enjoy uninterrupted tranquillity. God by this prophet lets them know that they shall have tribulation.

II. The vision itself: 1. He observed the *four winds to strive upon the great sea*, v. 2. They strove which should blow strongest, and, at length, blow alone. This represents the contests among princes for empire. The four winds strive for mastery! That is what the kings of the nations are contending for in their wars, which are as noisy and violent as the battle of the winds. 2. He saw *four great beasts come up from the sea*, from the *troubled waters*. The monarchs and monarchies are represented by *beasts*. These beasts were *diverse one from another* (v. 3), to denote the different genius of the nations. *The first beast was like a lion*, v. 4. This was the Chaldean monarchy, fierce and strong, and the kings absolute. This lion had *eagle's wings*, denoting the speed that Nebuchadnezzar made in his conquest of kingdoms. But Daniel soon sees the *wings plucked*. Divers countries that had been tributaries revolt; so that this winged lion is made to *stand upon the feet as a man, and a man's heart is given to it*. It has lost the heart of a lion (one of our English kings was called *Coeur de Lion*—*Lion-heart*), has become feeble, dreading everything and daring nothing. The *second* beast was *like a bear*, v. 5. This was the Persian monarchy, less strong and generous, but no less ravenous. This bear *raised up itself on one side* against the lion, and soon mastered it. It *raised up one dominion*; so some read it. Persia and Media now set up a joint government. This bear had *three ribs in the mouth of it between the teeth*, the remains of those nations it had devoured; some ribs still stuck in the teeth of it, which it could not conquer. Whereupon it was said, "*Arise, devour much flesh;* set upon that which will be an easier prey." The princes will push on their conquests, and let nothing stand before them. The *third* beast was *like a leopard*, v. 6. This was the Grecian monarchy, founded by *Alexander the Great*, active, crafty, and cruel, like a *leopard*. He had *four wings of a fowl*; for though Nebuchadnezzar made great despatch in his conquests Alexander made much greater. In six years' time he gained the whole empire of Persia, a great part of Asia, made himself master of Syria, Egypt, India, and other nations. This beast had *four heads*; upon Alexander's death his conquests were divided among his four chief captains; Seleucus Nicanor had Asia the Great; Perdiccas, and after him Antigonus, had Asia the Less; Cassander had Macedonia; and Ptolemeus had Egypt. The *fourth* beast was more fierce and formidable than any of them. v. 7. The learned are not agreed concerning this anonymous beast; some make it to be the Roman empire, which comprehended ten kingdoms, Italy, France, Spain, Germany, Britain, Sarmatia, Pannonia, Asia, Greece, and Egypt; and then the little horn which rose by the fall of three of the other horns (v. 8) they make to be the Turkish empire, which rose in the room of Asia, Greece, and Egypt. Others make this fourth beast to be the kingdom of Syria, the family of the Seleucidae, which was very cruel to the Jews, as we find in Josephus and the history of the Maccabees. Their armies were the *great iron teeth* with which they *devoured and broke in pieces* the people of God, and *trampled upon the residue* of them. The *ten horns* are then supposed to be ten kings that reigned successively in Syria; and then the *little horn* is Antiochus Epiphanes, the last of the ten, who undermined three of the kings, and got the government. He was a man of great ingenuity, and therefore is said to have eyes *like the eyes of a man*.

Verses 9–14

Whether we understand the fourth beast to signify the Syrian empire, or the Roman, it is plain that these verses are intended for the comfort of the people of God in the persecutions they were likely to sustain. Three things are here discovered that are encouraging:

I. That there is a judgment to come, and God is the Judge. Now men have their day. *I beheld* (v. 9) *till the thrones were cast down*, not only the thrones of these beasts, but *all rule, authority, and power*, that are set up in opposition to the kingdom of God among men (1 Cor. xv. 24): such are the thrones of the kingdoms of the world, in comparison with God's kingdom. *I beheld till thrones were set up* (so it may as well be read), Christ's throne and the throne of his Father. It is the *judgment* that is here *set*, v. 10. This is intended to proclaim God's wise and righteous government of the world by his providence. Perhaps it points at the destruction brought upon Syria, or Rome, for their tyrannizing over the people of God. It seems principally designed to describe the last judgment. Many of the New Testament predictions of the judgment to come have a plain allusion to this vision, especially St. John's vision of it, Rev. xx. 11, 12. The Judge is *the Ancient of days* himself, *God the Father*. He is called *the Ancient of days*, because he is God *from everlasting to everlasting*. The glory of the Judge is set forth by his garment, *white as snow*, denoting his splendour and purity; and the *hair of his head as the pure wool*, white and venerable. The throne is *like the fiery flame*, dreadful to the wicked. The *wheels* thereof are *as burning fire*, to devour the adversaries. This is enlarged upon, v. 10. The attendants are numerous. The Shechinah is always attended with angels; it is so here (v. 10): *Thousand thousands minister to him*, and *ten thousand times ten thousand stand before him*. The judgment is set, publicly, and *the books are opened*.

II. That the cruel enemies of the church of God will be brought down in due time, v. 11, 12. This is here represented, 1. In the destroying of the fourth beast. God's quarrel with this beast is *because of the voice of the great words which the horn spoke*, bidding defiance to Heaven. The Syrian empire, after Antiochus, was destroyed. He himself died of a miserable disease, his family was rooted out, the kingdom wasted by the Parthians and Armenians, and at length made a province of the Roman empire by Pompey. And the Roman empire itself (if we take that for the fourth beast), after it began to persecute Christianity, declined and wasted away, and was destroyed. 2. In the weakening of the other three beasts (v. 12): They had *their dominion taken away*, and so were disabled from doing mischiefs to the people of God; but *a prolonging in life was given them, for a time and a season*. The power of the foregoing kingdoms was broken, but the people still remained in a mean, weak condition. And thus God deals with his church's enemies; sometimes he crushes the persecution, but reprieves the persecutors, that they may have space to repent.

III. That the kingdom of the Messiah shall be set up in the world, in spite of all the opposition of the powers of darkness. Daniel sees this in vision, and comforts his friends. 1. The Messiah is here called the Son of man—*one like unto the Son of man;* for he was *made in the likeness of sinful flesh*, was *found in fashion as a man*. *I saw one like unto the Son of man*. Our Saviour seems plainly to refer to this vision when he says (John v. 27) that the *Father has therefore given him authority to execute judgment* because he is *the Son of man*. 2. He is said to *come with the clouds of heaven*. Some refer this to his incarnation. I think it is rather to be referred to his ascension, Acts i. 9. When the cloud received him out of the sight of his disciples, it is worth while to enquire whither it carried him; and here we are told he ascended to *his Father and our Father*, to *his God and our God* (John xx. 17). He was *brought near*, as our high priest, who for us enters within the veil, and as our forerunner. He is represented as having a mighty influence upon this earth, *v.* 14. When he went to be glorified with his Father he had a *power given him over all flesh*, John xvii. 2, 5. With the prospect of this Daniel and his friends are comforted, that not only the dominion of the church's enemies shall be taken away (*v.* 12), but the church's head shall have *the dominion given him*; to him *every knee shall bow* and *every tongue confess*, Phil. ii. 9, 10. His *dominion* shall not *pass away*. The church shall continue militant to the end of time, and triumphant to the endless ages of eternity.

Verses 15–28

I. The deep impressions which these visions made upon the prophet (*v.* 15): *I Daniel was grieved in my spirit, in the midst of my body*. The word here used for the *body* properly signifies a *sheath* or *scabbard*, for the body is no more to the soul. The *visions of my head troubled me*, and again (*v.* 28), *my cogitations much troubled me*. The manner in which these things were discovered to him quite overwhelmed him.

II. His earnest desire to understand the meaning (*v.* 16).

III. The key that was given him.

1. *The great beasts* are great *kings* and their kingdoms, *which shall arise out of the earth*, as those beasts did *out of the sea*, *v.* 17.

2. Daniel understands the first three beasts, but concerning the fourth he desires to be better informed, *v.* 19. But especially he desired to know what the *little horn* was, that *had eyes*, and a *mouth that spoke very great things*, *v.* 20. It was this horn that *made war with the saints, and prevailed against them*, *v.* 21. It is time to ask, "What is the meaning of this? What is this same horn that shall prevail so far against the saints?" To this his interpreter answers (*v.* 23–25) that this *fourth beast* is a *fourth kingdom*, that *shall devour the whole earth*, or (as it may be read) *the whole land*. That the *ten horns are ten kings*, and the *little horn* is another king that shall subdue three kings, and shall be very abusive to God and his people. He shall *wear out the saints of the Most High*. He shall *think to change times and laws*, to abolish all the ordinances and institutions of religion. And in these daring attempts he shall for a time prosper and have success; they shall be given into his hand *until time, times, and half a time* (that is, for three years and a half). But at the end of that time the *judgment shall sit and take away his dominion* (*v.* 26), which he expounds (*v.* 11) of the beast being *slain and his body destroyed*. And (as Mr. Mede reads *v.* 12) *as to the rest of the beast*, the ten horns, especially the little *ruffling* horn, they had their dominion taken away. Now the question is, Who is this enemy? Interpreters are not agreed. Some will have the fourth kingdom to be that of the Seleucidae, and the little horn to be Antiochus, and show the accomplishment of all this in the history of the Maccabees; but others will have the fourth kingdom to be that of the Romans, and the *little horn* to be Julius Caesar, and the succeeding emperors (says Calvin), the antichrist, the papal kingdom. Others make the *little horn* to be the *Turkish empire*; so Luther, Vatablus, and others. Since prophecies sometimes have many fulfillings, I am willing to allow that they are both in the right, and that this prophecy has primary reference to the Syrian empire, and was intended for the encouragement of the Jews who suffered under Antiochus. But yet it has a further reference, and foretells the persecuting power in Rome, against the Christian religion. And St. John in his visions, which point primarily at Rome, has reference to these visions of Daniel.

3. He has a joyful prospect given him of God's kingdom among men, and its victory over all opposition at last. This is brought in abruptly (*v.* 18 and again *v.* 22), before it comes, in the course of the vision, to be interpreted, *v.* 26, 27. And this also refers, (1) To the prosperous days of the Jewish church, after it had weathered the storm under Antiochus. (2) To the setting up of the kingdom of the Messiah in the world by the preaching of his gospel. (3) To the second coming of Jesus Christ. *The Ancient of days shall come*, *v.* 22. God shall judge the world by his Son, to whom he has *committed all judgments. The judgment shall sit*, *v.* 26. God *judges in the earth*, both in wisdom and in equity. The *dominion* of the enemy shall be *taken away*, *v.* 26. All Christ's enemies shall be made his footstool. *Judgment is given to the saints of the Most High*. The apostles are entrusted with the preaching of a gospel by which the *world shall be judged*. That which is most insisted upon is that *the saints of the Most High shall take the kingdom, and possess the kingdom for ever*, *v.* 18. And again (*v.* 22), The *time came that the saints possessed the kingdom*. And again (*v.* 27), The *kingdom and dominion, and the greatness of the kingdom under the whole heavens, shall be given to the people of the saints of the Most High*. This intimates the spiritual dominion of the saints over their own lusts and corruptions, their victories over Satan and his temptations, and the triumphs of the martyrs over death and its terrors. It likewise promises that the gospel kingdom shall be set up, a kingdom of light, holiness, and love. The saints shall possess the kingdom for *ever, even for ever and ever*; and the reason is because he whose saints they are is the *Most High* and *his kingdom is an everlasting kingdom*, *v.* 27. *Because I live, you shall live also*, John xiv. 19. His kingdom is theirs.

Daniel, in the close, tells us what impressions this vision made upon him; it overwhelmed his spirits to such a degree that his *countenance* was *changed*, but he *kept the matter in his heart*. Daniel kept *the matter in his heart*, with a design, not to keep it from the church, but to keep it for the church.

CHAPTER 8

This chapter is written not in Chaldee, as the six foregoing chapters were, for the benefit of the Chaldeans, but in Hebrew, and so are the rest of the chapters to the end of the book, for the service of the Jews. I. The vision itself of the ram, and the he-goat, and the little horn that should fight and prevail against the people of God, for a limited time, ver. 1–14. II. The interpretation of this vision by an angel, showing that the ram signified the Persian empire, the he-goat the Grecian, and the little horn a king of the Grecian monarchy, that should set himself against the Jews, which was Antiochus Epiphanes, ver. 15–27. The Jewish church had been all along blessed with prophets, and men divinely inspired to explain God's mind to them, but, soon after Ezra's time, divine inspiration ceased, and there was no more any prophet till the gospel day dawned. And therefore the events of that time were here foretold by Daniel, and left upon record.

Verses 1–14

I. The date of this vision, *v.* 1. It was *in the third year of the reign of Belshazzar*, his last year, as many reckon; so that this chapter should be before the fifth. That Daniel might not be surprised at the destruction of Babylon, now at hand, God gives him a foresight of the destruction of other kingdoms hereafter. And this vision puts him in mind of a former vision which *appeared to him at the first*, and is an explication and confirmation of it, and points at many of the same events.

II. The scene of this vision. The place where that was laid was in *Shushan the palace*, situated in the province of Elam, that part of Persia next to Babylon. Daniel was not there in person, for he was now in Babylon, a captive. But he was there in vision; as Ezekiel, when a captive in Babylon, was often brought, in the spirit, to the land of Israel. The soul may be at liberty when the body is in captivity; for, when we are bound, the Spirit of the Lord is not bound.

III. The vision itself.

1. He saw a *ram* with *two horns, v.* 3. This was the second monarchy, of which the kingdoms of Media and Persia were the two horns. The horns were *very high*; but that which came up last was the higher. The kingdom of Persia, which rose last, in Cyrus, became more eminent than that of the Medes.

2. He saw this *ram pushing* all about him with his horns (*v.* 4), *westward* (towards Babylon, Syria, Greece, and Asia the less), *northward* (towards the Lydians, Armenians, and Scythians), and *southward* (towards Arabia, Ethiopia, and Egypt), for all these nations did the Persian empire make attempts upon for the enlarging of their dominion. And at last he became so powerful that *no beasts might stand before him.* The kings of Persia did according *to their will,* and *became great.*

3. He was considering the *ram* and, *behold, a he-goat came, v.* 5. This was Alexander the Great, the son of Philip king of Macedonia. He *came from the west,* from Greece. He did in effect conquer the world. He *touched not the ground,* so lightly did he move; that is, he met with little or no opposition. This *he-goat,* or buck, had a *notable horn between his eyes.* He had strength, and knew his own strength. Alexander pushed his conquests on so fast, and with so much fury, that none had courage to make a stand. This *he-goat* came to the *ram that had two horns, v.* 6. Alexander with his victorious army attacked the kingdom of Persia, an army consisting of no more than 30,000 foot and 5,000 horse. Alexander with his army came up with Darius Codomannus, then emperor of Persia, being *moved with choler against him, v.* 7. Alexander was too hard for him whenever he engaged him, *smote him, cast him down to the ground,* and *stamped upon him,* which three expressions some think, refer to the three famous victories that Alexander obtained over Darius, at Granicus, at Issus, and at Arbela, by which he was at length totally routed, having, in the last battle, had 600,000 men killed, so that Alexander became absolute master of all the Persian empire, *broke his two horns,* the kingdoms of Media and Persia.

4. He saw the he-goat made very considerable; but the *great horn,* that had done all this execution, *was broken, v.* 8. Alexander was twenty years old when he began his wars. When he was twenty-six he conquered Darius, and became master of the whole Persian empire; but when he was thirty-two *years of age,* in his full strength, he was *broken.* He died of a drunken surfeit, or, as some suspect, by poison, and left no child living.

5. He saw this kingdom divided into four parts, and instead of one great horn there came up *four notable ones,* Alexander's four captains. These *four notable horns* were towards the *four winds of heaven,* the kingdoms of Syria and Egypt, Asia and Greece.

6. He saw a *little horn* which became a great persecutor of the church and people of God; *ch.* xi. 30, &c. All agree that this was *Antiochus Epiphanes.* He is called here (as before. *ch.* vii. 8) a *little horn,* because he was in origin contemptible; there were others between him and the kingdom, and he had been a hostage and prisoner at Rome, whence he made his escape, and got the kingdom. He seized Egypt, and invaded Persia and Armenia. But that which is here noted is the mischief that he did to the Jews. (1) He set himself against *the pleasant land,* the land of Israel. Mount Zion was *beautiful for situation,* and the *joy of the whole earth,* Ps. xlviii. 2. We reckon that a pleasant place which is a holy place, in which God dwells, and where we may have opportunity of communing with him. (2) He fought against the *host of*

heaven, that is, the people of God, the church-militant here on earth. (3) He *cast down some of the host to the ground, and stamped upon them.* Some of those most eminent in church and state, burning and shining lights in their generation, he either forced to comply with his idolatries or put them to death, as good old Eleazar, and the *seven brethren,* whom he put to death with cruel tortures, because they would not eat swine's flesh, 2 Mac. vi. 7. (4) He *magnified himself even to the prince of the host.* He set himself against the high priest, Onias, or against God himself. (5) He *took away the daily sacrifice.* The morning and evening lamb, which God appointed to be offered upon his altar, Antiochus forbade. (6) He *cast down the place of his sanctuary.* He did not burn the temple, but made it the temple of Jupiter Olympus, and set up his image in it. He also *cast down the truth to the ground,* trampled upon the book of the law, and burnt it. God would not have permitted it if his people had not provoked him to do so. It is *by reason of transgression,* the transgression of Israel, that Antiochus is employed to give them all this trouble. The great transgression of the Jews after the captivity was a contempt and profanation of the holy things, *snuffing* at the service of God, *bringing the torn and the lame for sacrifice,* as if the *table of the Lord* were a *contemptible* thing (Mal. i. 7, 8, &c.), and therefore God sent Antiochus to *take away the daily sacrifice* and *cast down the place of his sanctuary.*

7. He heard the time of this calamity limited, *how long it should last,* that, when they had no more any *prophets to tell them how long,* they might have this prophecy to give them a prospect of deliverance. The question was asked: "*How long shall be the vision concerning the daily sacrifice?* How long shall the prohibition of it continue?" The answer was given to Daniel, because for his sake the question was asked: He *said unto me, v.* 14. Christ assures him that the trouble shall end; it shall continue 2,300 *days and no longer,* so many *evenings and mornings.* Understand them of so many natural days; 2,300 days make *six years* and *three months,* and about eighteen days; and just so long they reckon from the defection of the people, procured by Menelaus the high priest in the 142nd year of the kingdom of the Seleucidae, the sixth month of that year, and the 6th day of the month (so Josephus dates it), to the cleansing of the sanctuary, and the re-establishment of religion among them, which was in the 148th year, the 9th month, and the 25th *day of the month,* 1 Mac. iv. 52.

Verses 15–27

I. Daniel's earnest desire to have this vision explained to him (*v.* 15): *I sought the meaning.*

II. One *in the appearance of a man* (who, some think, was Christ himself), orders Gabriel to *make Daniel understand this vision.*

III. The consternation that Daniel was in upon the approach of his instructor (*v.* 17): *When he came near I was afraid.* Prostrate upon the ground, he *fell into a deep sleep* (*v.* 18).

IV. The relief which the angel gave to Daniel. 1. He *touched him,* and *set him upon his feet, v.* 18. He promised to inform him: "*Understand, O son of man! v.* 17. Thou shalt understand, if thou wilt but apply thy mind to understand." He assures him that he shall be made to know *what shall be in the last end of the indignation, v.* 19. Let it be a comfort to those who live to see these calamitous times that there shall be an end of them; *the indignation shall cease* (Isa. x. 25); it *shall be overpast,* Isa. xxvi. 20. Good will be brought out of it. He tells him (*v.* 17), "*At the time of the end shall be the vision;* when the last end of the indignation comes, when the course of this providence is completed, then the vision shall be made plain and intelligible by the event."

V. The exposition which he gave him of the vision.
1. Concerning the two monarchies of Persia and Greece, *v.* 20–22. The *ram* signified the succession of the kings of Media and Persia; the *rough goat* signified the kings of Greece; the *great horn* was Alexander; the *four horns* that rose in his room were the four kingdoms of which we read, *v.* 8. Josephus relates that when Alexander had taken Tyre, and was upon his march to Jerusalem Jaddas, then high priest, fearing his rage, had recourse to God by prayer, and was warned in a dream that upon Alexander's approach he should open the gates of the city, and that he and the rest of the priests should go forth to meet him in their habits, and all the people in white. Alexander, seeing this company at a distance, went alone to the high priest, and, having prostrated himself, saluted him; and, being asked by one of his own captains why he did so, he said that while he was yet in Macedon, musing on the conquest of Asia, there appeared to him a man thus attired, who invited him into Asia, and assured him of success in the conquest of it. The priests led him to the temple, where he offered sacrifice to the God of Israel as they directed him; and they showed him this book of the prophet Daniel, where it was foretold that a Grecian should destroy the Persians, which cheered him in the expedition against Darius. Hereupon he took the Jews and their religion under his protection, promised to be kind to those of their religion in Babylon and Media, whither he was now marching. *Joseph. lib.* 11.

2. Concerning Antiochus, and his oppression of the Jews. This is said to be in the *latter time of the* kingdom of the Greeks, *when the transgressors are come to the full* (*v.* 23), He shall be a *king of fierce countenance*, neither fearing God nor regarding man, *understanding dark sentences*, or (rather) *versed in dark practices*, the *hidden things of dishonesty*. He shall make havoc of the nations; *His power shall be mighty*, bearing down all before it (*v.* 24), by the assistance of his allies Eumenes and Attalus, partly by the baseness and treachery of many of the Jews. The princes of Egypt cannot stand before him with all their forces. He destroys the *holy people*, or *the people of the holy ones*; their sacred character does not deter him. He will gain this success by *craft* (*v.* 25), by deceit, and serpentine subtlety: He shall *cause craft to prosper*; he shall gain his point by the art of wheedling. *By peace he shall destroy many*, as others do by war; under the pretence of treaties, leagues, and alliances, he shall trick them into subjection to him. Sometimes what a nation truly brave has gained in a righteous war a nation truly base has regained in a treacherous peace. *He shall magnify himself in his heart*, so that he shall *stand up against the Prince of princes*, that is, against God himself. He will profane his temple and altar, and persecute his worshippers. The ruin that he shall be brought to at last: *He shall be broken without hand*. He shall not be slain in war, nor shall he be assassinated, but he shall fall into the hand of the living God and die. He, hearing that the Jews had cast the image of Jupiter Olympius out of the temple, where he had placed it, was so enraged that he vowed he would make Jerusalem *a common burial-place*, but no sooner had he spoken these proud words than he was struck with an incurable plague. He continued in this misery. At first he persisted in his menaces against the Jews; but at length, despairing of his recovery, he acknowledged the injuries he had done to the Jews and his profaning the temple at Jerusalem. Then he wrote courteous letters, and vowed that if he recovered he would let them have the free exercise of their religion. But, finding his disease grow upon him, he said, *It is meet to submit to God, and for man who is mortal not to set himself in competition with*

God, and so died in a strange land, on the mountains of Pacata near Babylon.

VI. Here is the conclusion of this vision, and the charge given to Daniel to keep it private for the present: *Shut thou up the vision; for it shall be for many days.* Let it be kept for the generations that should live about the time of the accomplishment of it, for to them it would be most serviceable.

Chapter 9

I. Daniel's prayer for the restoration of the Jews in captivity, ver. 1–19. II. An immediate answer to his prayer, in which, 1. He is assured of the speedy release of the Jews out of their captivity, ver. 20–23. And, 2. He is informed concerning the redemption of the world by Jesus Christ, ver. 24–27. And it is the clearest prophecy of the Messiah, in all the Old Testament.

Verses 1–3

Daniel here employed in better business than any the king had for him, speaking to God and hearing from him, not for himself only, but for the church. Daniel had this communion with God (*v.* 1), *in the first year of Darius the Mede*, who was newly made king of the Chaldeans, Babylon being conquered by him and his nephew, or grandson, Cyrus. In this year the seventy years of the Jews' captivity ended. He *understood by books* that seventy years was the time fixed for the continuance of *the desolations of Jerusalem, v.* 2. The *book* by which he understood this was the book of Jeremiah, in which he found it expressly foretold (Jer. xxix. 10), *After seventy years be accomplished in Babylon I will visit you, and perform my good word towards you*. It was likewise said (Jer. xxv. 11). *This whole land shall be seventy years a desolation* (*chorbath*), the same word that Daniel here uses for the *desolations of Jerusalem*, which shows that he had that prophecy before him when he wrote this. Now *Daniel sought by prayer and supplications* that the people might be prepared by the grace of God for the deliverance that God was about to work out for them. This prayer: *I set my face unto the Lord God to seek him*, denotes the fixedness of his thoughts, the firmness of his faith, in the duty. Probably, in token of his setting his face towards God, he set his face towards Jerusalem. In token of his deep humiliation before God for his own sins, and the sins of his people, when he prayed he *fasted* and put on *sackcloth* and *ashes*.

Verses 4–19

Daniel's prayer to God as his God, and the confession which he joined with that prayer: I *prayed, and made my confession*. In every prayer we must make confession, not only of our sins, but of our faith in God.

I. His humble, reverent address in which he gives glory to God, 1. As a God to be feared: "*O Lord! the great and dreadful God*, that art able to deal with the greatest and most terrible of the church's enemies." 2. As a God to be trusted: *Keeping the covenant and mercy to those that love him*, and, as a proof of their love to him, *keep his commandments*. He will be better than his word, for he keeps mercy to them, something more than was in the covenant. It was proper for Daniel to think of God's mercy now that he was to lay before him the miseries of his people, and to sue for the performance of a promise.

II. Here is a penitent confession of sin, *v.* 5, 6. When we seek for national mercies we ought to humble ourselves for national sins. Two things aggravated their sins: 1. That they had violated the laws God had given them by Moses. 2. That they had slighted the fair warnings God had given them by the prophets (*v.* 6): "*We have not hearkened to thy servants the prophets*, who have put us in mind of thy laws."

III. Here is a self-abasing acknowledgment of the righteousness of God in all the judgments brought upon them. He acknowledges that it was sin that plunged them in all these troubles. Israel is *dispersed* through *all the countries* about, and so weakened, impoverished, and exposed. It is *because of their trespass that they have trespassed* (v. 7); they mingled themselves with the nations that they might be debauched by them, and now God mingles them with the nations that they might be stripped by them. He takes notice of the fulfilling of the scripture in what was brought upon them. *The curse is poured upon us and the oath*, that is, the curse that was ratified by an oath in the law of Moses, v. 11. God did but inflict the penalty of the law. "It is not some of the common troubles of life that we are complaining of, but that which has in it special marks of divine displeasure; for *under the whole heaven has not been done as has been done upon Jerusalem*," v. 12. It is Jeremiah's lamentation in the name of the church, *Was ever sorrow like unto my sorrow?* which must suppose another similar question, *Was ever sin like unto my sin?* He puts shame upon the whole nation, from the highest to the lowest. If Israel had continued a holy people, they would have been *high above all nations in praise, and name, and honour* (Deut. xxvi. 19); but now that they have *sinned and done wickedly* confusion and disgrace belong to them, to *the men of Judah and the inhabitants of Jerusalem*, to *all Israel*, both to the two tribes, *that are near*, by the rivers of Babylon, and to the ten tribes, *that are afar off*, in the land of Assyria. He imputes the continuance of the judgment to their incorrigibleness (v. 13, 14). *We have not entreated the face of the Lord our God* (so the word is); "we have taken no care to make our peace with God and reconcile ourselves to him." If men were brought rightly to *understand God's truth*, and to submit to the power and authority of it, they would turn from the error of their ways. Now the first step towards this is to *make our prayer before the Lord our God*, that the affliction may be sanctified before it is removed.

IV. Here is a believing appeal to the mercy of God. 1. God has been always ready to pardon sin (v. 9). He is a *God of pardons* (Neh. ix. 17, marg.); he *multiplies to pardon*, Isa. lv. 7. 2. Daniel looks back for the encouragement of his faith (v. 15): "*Thou hast formerly brought thy people out of Egypt with a mighty hand*, and wilt thou not now with the same mighty hand bring them out of Babylon? And has not God said that their deliverance out of Babylon shall outshine even that out of Egypt?" Jer. xvi. 14, 15.

V. Here is a pathetic complaint of the reproach that God's people lay under, and the ruins that God's sanctuary lay in. Their neighbours laugh them to scorn, and triumph in their disgrace. God's holy place was desolate. Jerusalem, the holy city, was a reproach (v. 16), the holy house was desolate (v. 17), the altars were demolished, and all the buildings laid in ashes.

VI. Here is an importunate request to God for the restoring of the captive Jews. "*O Lord! I beseech thee, v. 16. Now therefore, O our God! hear the prayer of thy servant and his supplication (v. 17).*" Now what are his petitions? What are his requests? 1. That God would turn away his wrath from them; that is it which all the saints dread and deprecate more than any thing: O let *thy anger be turned away from thy Jerusalem, thy holy mountain!* (v. 16). He does not pray for the turning again of their captivity (let the Lord do with them as seems good in his eyes), but he prays first for the *turning away of God's wrath*. Take away the cause, and the effect will cease. 2. That he would lift up the light of his countenance upon them (v. 17): *Cause thy face to shine upon thy sanctuary that is desolate*. The shining of God's face upon the desolations of the sanctuary is all in all towards the repair of it; and upon that foundation it must be

rebuilt. If therefore its friends would begin their work at the right end, they must first be earnest with God in prayer for his favour.

VII. Here are several pleas and arguments to enforce the petitions. God gives us leave not only to pray, but to plead, not to move him (he himself knows what he will do), but to move ourselves, and encourage our faith. 1. They disdain a dependence upon any righteousness of their own; they pretend not to merit anything at God's hand but wrath and the curse (v. 18). Moses had told Israel that, whatever God did for them, it was *not for their righteousness*, Deut. ix. 4, 5. 2. They take their encouragement in prayer from God only, as knowing they are suing for grace and mercy from him. (1) "Do it *for thy own sake* (v. 19), for the accomplishment of thy own counsel, the performance of thy own promise." (2) "Do it for the Lord's sake." Christ is *the Lord*; he is Lord of all. It is for his sake that God causes his face to shine upon sinners when they repent and turn to him, because of the satisfaction he has made. (3) "Do it *according to all thy righteousness* (v. 16), that is, plead for us against our persecutors and oppressors *according to thy righteousness*." (4) "Do it *for thy great mercies* (v. 18), to make it to appear that thou art a merciful God." (5) "Do it for the sake of the relation we stand in to thee. The sanctuary that is desolate is thy sanctuary (v. 17). Jerusalem is *thy city* and *thy holy mountain* (v. 16); it is *the city which is called by thy name*," v. 18. "The people that have *become a reproach* are *thy people*, they are *called by thy name* (v. 19). They are *thine, save them*," Ps. cxix. 94.

Verses 20–27

The answer that was immediately sent to Daniel's prayer, contains the most illustrious prediction of Christ and gospel-grace that is extant in all the *Old Testament*.

I. The time when this answer was given.

1. It was while Daniel was at prayer. This he observed and laid a strong emphasis upon: *While I was speaking in prayer* (v. 21), before he rose from his knees, and while there was yet more which he intended to say. He was confessing sin and lamenting *my sin and the sin of my people Israel*. Now was fulfilled what God had spoken Isa. lxv. 24, *While they are yet speaking, I will hear*. Daniel grew very fervent in prayer, v. 18, 19. And, *while he was speaking* the angel came to him with a gracious answer. We cannot now expect that God should send us answers to our prayer by angels, but, if we pray with fervency for that which God has promised, we may by faith take the promise as an immediate answer to the prayer: for *he is faithful that has promised*. He had a discovery made to him of a far greater and more glorious redemption which God would work out for his church in the latter days.

2. It was *about the time of the evening oblation*, v. 21. The altar was in ruins, and there was no oblation offered upon it, but the pious Jews in their captivity were daily thoughtful of the time when it should have been offered, and hoped that their prayer should be *set forth before God as incense*, and the *lifting up of their hands*, and their hearts with their hands, should be acceptable in his sight *as the evening-sacrifice*, Ps. cxli. 2. The evening oblation was a type of the great sacrifice which Christ was to offer in the evening of the world, and it was in the virtue of that sacrifice that Daniel's prayer was accepted when he prayed *for the Lord's sake*.

II. The messenger by whom this answer was sent. It was not given him in a dream, nor by a voice from heaven, but an angel was sent on purpose, appearing in a human shape, to give this answer to Daniel. Gabriel is the only created angel that is named in scripture. It was he *whom I had seen in the vision at the beginning.* Daniel heard him called by his name, and thence learned it (Dan. viii. 16). This angel said to *Zacharias, I am Gabriel* (Luke i. 19). Note instructions received from the Father of lights to whom Daniel prayed (*v.* 23): *At the beginning of thy supplications* the word, *the commandment, came forth* from God. Perhaps it was *at the beginning of Daniel's supplications* that *Cyrus's word*, or *commandment, went forth to restore and to build Jerusalem, v.* 25. "The thing was done *this very day*; the proclamation of liberty to the Jews was signed this morning, just when thou wast praying for it." He *touched him* (*v.* 21) to give him a hint to break off his prayer. He *talked with him* (*v.* 22), familiarly, that *his terror might not make him afraid.* "*I have come to show thee*" (*v.* 23). He had shown him the troubles of the church under Antiochus, and the period of those troubles (*ch.* viii. 19); but now he has greater things to show him. "Nay, *I have now come forth to give thee skill and understanding* (*v.* 22), not only to show thee these things, but to *make thee understand* them." He assured him that he was a favourite of Heaven. *I have come to show thee, for thou art greatly beloved.* Those may reckon themselves greatly beloved of God to whom, and in whom, he *reveals his Son.*

III. The message itself was recorded with great exactness; but in it there are things dark and hard to be understood. Daniel, who understood by the prophet Jeremiah the expiration of the seventy years of the captivity, is now employed to make known to the church another more glorious release, at the end of seventy, not years, but weeks of years.

1. The times here determined are somewhat hard to be understood. In general, it is *seventy weeks*, that is, *seventy times seven years*, which makes just 490 years. The great affairs that are yet to come concerning the people of Israel, and the city of Jerusalem, will lie within the compass of these years. The land had *enjoyed its sabbaths*, in a melancholy sense, seventy years, Lev. xxvi. 34. But now the people of the Lord shall enjoy their sabbaths seven times seventy years, and in them seventy sabbatical years, which makes ten jubilees. Difficulties arise about these seventy weeks concerning the time when they commence and whence they are to be reckoned. They are here dated *from that going forth of the commandment to restore and to build Jerusalem, v.* 25. I should most incline to understand this of the edict of Cyrus mentioned Ezra i. 1. And it looks as though the seventy weeks should begin immediately upon the expiration of the seventy years, but by this reckoning the *Persian monarchy*, from the taking of Babylon by Cyrus to Alexander's conquest of Darius, lasted but 130 years; whereas, by the particular account given of the reigns of the Persian emperors, it is computed that it continued 230 years. So Thucydides, Xenophon, and others reckon. Mr. Poole, in his Latin Synopsis, has a vast and most elaborate collection of what has been said, *pro* and *con*, concerning the different beginnings of these weeks. Concerning the termination of them, interpreters are not agreed. Some make them to end at the death of Christ. But others think, because it is said that *in the midst of the weeks* (that is, the last of the seventy weeks) he *shall cause the sacrifice and the oblation to cease*, they end *three years and a half* after the death of Christ. Concerning the division of them into seven weeks, and sixty-two weeks, and one week, the reason is as hard to account for as anything else. In the first seven weeks, or forty-nine years, the temple and city were built: and in the last single week Christ preached his gospel, by which the foundations were laid of the gospel city and temple. But, whatever uncertainty we may labour under concerning the exact fixing of these times, there is enough certain to answer the two great ends.

(1) It did serve them to raise and support the expectations of believers. By the light of this prophecy they were directed about what time to expect him. (2) It does serve still to refute and silence the expectations of unbelievers, who will not own that Jesus is he who *should come*, but still *look for another*. Reckon these seventy weeks from which of the commandments to build Jerusalem we please, it is certain that they have expired above 1,500 years ago. We are confirmed in our belief of the Messiah's being come, and that our Jesus is he.

2. The events here foretold are more easy to be understood.

(1) Concerning the return of the Jews now speedily to their own land, and their settlement again there: Let this be a comfort to the pious Jews, that a *commandment* shall *go forth to restore and to build Jerusalem, v.* 25. God will carry on his own work, will build up his Jerusalem, will beautify it, will fortify it, *even in troublous times.*

(2) Concerning the Messiah. The carnal Jews looked for a Messiah that should deliver them from the Roman yoke and give them temporal power and wealth, whereas they were here told that the Messiah should come upon another errand, purely spiritual. Christ came to *take away sin*. Sin had made a quarrel between God and man, had alienated man from God and provoked God against man; it was this that brought misery upon mankind. Christ undertakes to *destroy the works of the devil*. He does not say to *finish your* transgressions and your sins, but *transgression* and *sin* in general, for he is the propitiation *for the sins of the whole world*. He came, First, To *finish transgression*, to *restrain* it (so some), to break the power of it, and to set up a kingdom of holiness and love in the hearts of men. *Secondly*, To *make an end of sin*, to abolish it, to *seal up sins* (so the margin reads it), that they may not break out against us. *Thirdly*, To *make reconciliation for iniquity*, as by a sacrifice, to *make peace* and bring God and man together. He is not only the *peace-maker*, but the *peace*. He is the *atonement*. God might justly have made an end of the sin by making an end of the sinner; but Christ found out another way, and so made an end of sin as to save the sinner, by providing a righteousness for him. The merit of his sacrifice is *our righteousness*. By faith we apply this to ourselves and plead it with God, and our *faith is imputed to us for righteousness*, Rom. iv. 3, 5. He came to *seal up the vision and prophecy*, all the prophetical visions of the Old Testament, which had reference to the Messiah. He *sealed them up*, that is, he accomplished them. He is called *Messiah* (*v.* 25, 26), which signifies *Christ—Anointed* (John i. 41), because he received the unction both for himself and for all that are his. When Paul preaches the death of Christ, he says that he preached nothing but *what the prophet said should come*, Acts xxvi. 22, 23. And *thus it behoved Christ to suffer.* He must be *cut off, but not for himself.* It was to atone for our sins, and to purchase life for us, that he was *cut off.* He must *cause the sacrifice and oblation to cease.* By offering himself a sacrifice once for all he shall put an end to all the Levitical sacrifices.

(3) Concerning the final destruction of Jerusalem, and of the Jewish church and nation; this follows immediately upon the cutting off of the Messiah, because it was the *just punishment* of those that put him to death. He died to take away the ceremonial law, to abolish *that law of commandments.* But the Jews would not be persuaded to quit it; they stoned Stephen for saying that Jesus should *change the customs which Moses delivered them* (Acts vi. 14). It is here foretold that *the people of the prince that shall come* shall be the instruments of this destruction, that is, the Roman armies, belonging to a monarchy

yet to come. The *city* and *sanctuary* shall in a particular manner be *destroyed* and laid waste. Titus the Roman general would fain have saved the temple, but his soldiers were so enraged against the Jews that he could not restrain them from burning it to the ground. The *sacrifice and oblation* shall be *made to cease*. There shall be *an overspreading of abominations*, to be understood of the armies of the Romans. These are the words which Christ refers to, Matt. xxiv. 15, *When you shall see the abomination of desolation, spoken of by Daniel, stand in the holy place, then let those who shall be in Judæa flee*, which is explained Luke xxi. 20.

CHAPTER 10

This chapter and the two next make up one entire vision and prophecy, communicated to Daniel for the use of the church, not by signs and figures, as before (*ch.* vii and viii), but by express words. Daniel prayed daily, but had a vision only now and then. In this chapter we have things introductory to the prophecy, in the eleventh chapter particular predictions, and *ch.* xii the conclusion of it. This chapter shows us, I. Daniel's solemn fasting and humiliation, before he had this vision, ver. 1–3. II. A glorious appearance of the Son of God to him, ver. 4–9. III. The encouragement given him to expect such a discovery of future events as should be useful to others and to himself, and that he should be enabled to understand the meaning of this discovery, ver. 10–21.

Verses 1–9

This vision is dated in the *third year of Cyrus*, that is, of his reign after the conquest of Babylon, his third year since Daniel became acquainted with him.

I. A general idea of this prophecy (*v.* 1): *The thing was true. But the time appointed was long;* to the end of the reign of Antiochus was 300 years. This prophecy looks in type as far forward as the end of the world and the resurrection of the dead; and then he might well say, *The time appointed was long.*

II. An account of Daniel's mortification of himself before he had this vision. He *was mourning full three weeks* (*v.* 2), for his own sins and the sins of his people, and their sorrows. Some think that the occasion of his mourning was the slothfulness of many of the Jews, who, though they had liberty to return to their own land, continued still in the land of their captivity. Others think that it was because he heard of the obstruction given to the building of the temple by the enemies of the Jews, who *hired counsellors against them, to frustrate their purpose* (Ezra iv. 4, 5), *all the days of Cyrus. Daniel ate no flesh, drank no wine, nor anointed himself*, for these three weeks' time, *v.* 3.

III. A description of that glorious person whom Daniel saw in vision, which, it is generally agreed, could be no other than Christ himself, the eternal Word. He was by the side of the river Hiddekel (*v.* 4), probably walking in contemplation, as Isaac walked in the field, to meditate. There he *looked up* and saw even *the man Christ Jesus* (*v.* 5–6). His attendants *saw not the vision*. Paul's companions were aware of the *light*, but *saw no man*, Acts ix. 7; xxii. 9. But, though they saw not the vision, *a great quaking fell upon them, so that they fled to hide themselves*, probably among the willows that grew by the river's side. Daniel saw it alone, but he was not able to bear the sight of it. It overwhelmed his spirit, so that *there remained no strength in him, v.* 8. But, though Daniel was thus dispirited with the vision of Christ, yet he *heard the voice of his words* and knew what he said. When the vision of Christ terrified Daniel the voice of his words composed him, and laid him to sleep in a holy security and serenity of mind: *When I heard the voice of his words I fell into a slumber*, a sweet slumber, *on my face*, and *my face towards the ground*.

Verses 10–21

Daniel is by degrees brought to himself.

I. The hand that *touched him* set him at first *upon his knees and the palms of his hands, v.* 10. Afterwards he is helped up, but he *stands trembling* (*v.* 11), for fear lest he fall again. Before God *gives strength and power unto his people* he makes them sensible of their own weakness. At length he recovered, not only the use of his feet, but the use of his tongue; and, when he *opened his mouth* (*v.* 16), that which he had to say was to excuse his having been so long silent. "*My sorrows are turned upon me.*" And again (*v.* 17), half dead with fright, "As for me, *straightway there remained no strength in me* to receive these displays of the divine glory and these discoveries of the divine will; nay, *there is no breath left in me.*"

II. The angel that was employed by Christ to converse with him gave him all the encouragement and comfort that could be. Christ himself comforted John when he in a like case *fell at his feet as dead* (Rev. i. 17); but here he did it *by the angel*.

1. He lent him his hand to help him (*v.* 10), else he would still have lain grovelling, *touched his lips* (*v.* 16), else he would have been still dumb; again he *touched him* (*v.* 18), and put strength into him. One touch from heaven brings us to our knees, sets us on our feet, opens our lips, and strengthens us; for it is God that works on us, and *works in us, both to will and to do* that which is good.

2. He assured him of the favour God had for him: Thou art *a man greatly beloved* (*v.* 11); and again (*v.* 19), *O man greatly beloved!* Those are greatly beloved indeed whom God loves; and it is comfort enough to know it.

3. He silenced his fears, and encouraged his hopes, with good words and comfortable words. *Fear not, Daniel* (*v.* 12); and again (*v.* 19), *O man greatly beloved! fear not; peace be unto thee; be strong, yea, be strong.* And now that Daniel has experienced the efficacy of God's strengthening word and grace, he is ready for anything.

4. He assured him that his fastings and prayers had come up for a memorial before God, *Fear not, Daniel, v.* 12. From the first day that we begin to look towards God in a way of duty he is ready to meet us in a way of mercy.

5. On what errand did this angel come to Daniel? He tells him (*v.* 14): *I have come to make thee understand what shall befall thy people in the latter days.* That which the angel is entrusted to communicate to Daniel, and which Daniel is encouraged to expect from him, is not speculation, though he is an angel, but what he has *received from the Lord*. It was the *revelation of Jesus Christ* that the angel gave to St. John to be *delivered to the churches*, Rev. i. 1. So here (*v.* 21): *I will show thee what is written in the scriptures of truth*. The *decree of God* is a thing written, it is a *scripture* which remains and cannot be altered.

6. He gave him a general account of the adversaries of the church's cause. (1) The *kings of the earth* are and will be its adversaries, Ps. ii. 2. The angel told Daniel that the *prince of the kingdom of Persia withstood him one and twenty days*, just the three weeks that Daniel had been fasting and praying. This new king of Persia, by hindering the temple, had hindered those good tidings which otherwise he should have brought him. "When *I have gone forth* from the kings of Persia, when their monarchy is brought down for their unkindness to the Jews, then *the prince of Grecia shall come,*" *v.* 20. The Grecian monarchy, though favourable to the Jews at first, as the Persian was, will yet come to be vexatious to them. (2) The *God of heaven* is, and will be, its protector. Gabriel resolves, when he has despatched this errand to Daniel, that he will return *to fight with the prince of Persia*, and will at length bring down that proud monarchy (*v.* 20). Here is Michael our prince, the great protector of the church: *The first of the chief princes, v.* 13. Some understand it of a created angel. Others think

that *Michael the archangel* is no other than Christ himself, *v.* 5. He *came to help me* (*v.* 13); and there is *none but he that holds with me in these things, v.* 21. Christ is the church's prince; angels are not, Heb. ii. 5.

CHAPTER 11

The angel Gabriel performs his promise made to Daniel in the foregoing chapter, that he would "show him what should befall his people in the latter days," according to that which was "written in the scriptures of truth." I. A brief prediction of the setting up of the Grecian monarchy upon the ruins of the Persian monarchy, ver. 1–4. II. A prediction of the affairs of the two kingdoms of Egypt and Syria, with reference to each other, ver. 5–20. III. Of the rise of Antiochus Epiphanes, and his actions and successes, ver. 21–29. IV. Of the great mischief that he should do to the Jewish nation and religion, and his contempt of all religion, ver. 30–39. V. Of his fall and ruin at last, ver. 40–45.

Verses 1–4

1. The angel Gabriel lets Daniel know the good service he has done to the Jewish nation (*v.* 1). Thus by the angel, and at the request of *the watcher*, the golden head was broken, and the axe laid to the root of the tree. God's care of his church formerly encourages us to depend upon him in further straits and difficulties. 2. He foretells the reign of four Persian kings (*v.* 2). (1) There shall stand up *three kings in Persia*, besides Darius, in whose reign this prophecy is dated, *ch.* ix. 1. Mr. Broughton makes these three to be Cyrus, Artaxasta or Artaxerxes, called by the Greeks *Cambyses*, and Ahasuerus that married Esther, called *Darius son of Hystaspes*. To these three the Persians gave these attributes—Cyrus was a father, Cambyses a master, and Darius a hoarder up. So Herodotus. (2) There shall be a fourth, *far richer than them all*, that is, Xerxes, of whose wealth the Greek authors take notice. By *his strength* (his vast army, consisting of 800,000 men at least) and *his riches* he *stirred up all* against the *realm of Greece*. Xerxes's expedition against Greece ended in shameful defeat. About thirty years after the first return from captivity, Darius, a young king, revived the building of the temple, owning the hand of God against his predecessors for hindering it, Ezra vi. 7. 3. He foretells Alexander's conquests and the partition of his kingdom, *v.* 3. He is that *mighty king* that shall *stand up* against the kings of Persia, shall *rule with great dominion*, and with despotic power, for he shall *do according to his will*. But (*v.* 4) his *kingdom* shall soon be *broken*, and *divided* into four parts, *but not to his posterity*. His *kingdom was plucked up for others besides those* of his own family. Arideus, his brother, was made king in Macedonia; Olympias, Alexander's mother, killed him, and poisoned Alexander's two sons, Hercules and Alexander. Thus was his family rooted out by its own hands.

Verses 5–20

I. The rise and power of two great kingdoms out of the remains of Alexander's conquests, *v.* 5. 1. Egypt was made considerable by Ptolemaeus Lagus, one of Alexander's captains. He is called the king of the *south*, that is, Egypt, *v.* 8, 42, 43. The countries that at first belonged to Ptolemy are Egypt, Phoenicia, Arabia, Libya, Ethiopia, &c. 2. The kingdom of Syria was set up by Seleucus Nicanor, or the *conqueror*; he was one of Alexander's princes, and the most powerful of all Alexander's successors. Ptolemy invaded Judæa, and took Jerusalem *on a sabbath*, pretending a friendly visit. Seleucus also gave disturbance to Judæa.

II. The fruitless attempt to unite these two kingdoms as iron and clay in Nebuchadnezzar's image (*v.* 6): "*At the end of certain years*, about seventy after Alexander's death, the Lagidae and the Seleucidae shall associate, but not in sincerity. Ptolemy Philadelphus, king of Egypt, shall marry his daughter Berenice to Antiochus Theos, king of Syria," who had already a wife called *Laodice*. "Berenice shall come to the *king of the north*, to make an agreement, but *she shall not retain the power of the arm*; neither she nor her posterity shall establish themselves in the kingdom of the north, but *she shall be given up and those that brought her.*" Antiochus divorced Berenice, took his former wife Laodice again, who poisoned him, procured Berenice and her son to be murdered, and set up her own son by Antiochus to be king, who was called *Seleucus Callinicus*.

III. A war between the two kingdoms, *v.* 7, 8. A branch from the same root with Berenice *shall stand up in his estate*. Ptolemaeus Euergetes, the son of Ptolemaeus Philadelphus, shall come against Seleucus Callinicus, king of Syria, to avenge his sister's quarrel, and shall prevail; and shall carry away rich booty into Egypt, and shall *continue more years than the king of the north*. But (*v.* 9) he shall be forced to *come into his kingdom* and *return into his own land*, to keep peace there.

IV. The long reign of *Antiochus the Great*, king of Syria. Seleucus Callinicus, that king of the north that was overcome (*v.* 7) and died miserably, left two sons, Seleucus and Antiochus; these are the sons of the *king of the north, that shall be stirred up, and shall assemble a multitude of great forces*, to recover what their father had lost, *v.* 10. But Seleucus the elder was poisoned, and reigned only two years; and his brother Antiochus succeeded him, who reigned thirty-seven years, and was called *the Great*. 1. The *king of the south*, in this war, shall at first have great success. Ptolemaeus Philopater, moved with indignation at the indignities done by *Antiochus the Great*, shall *come forth, and fight with him*, and shall bring a vast army. And the *other multitude*, the army of Antiochus, shall *be given into his hand*. Ptolemaeus Philopater, having gained this victory, *his heart was lifted up*; he went into the temple at Jerusalem, and entered the most holy place. 2. The *king of the north, Antiochus the Great*, shall *return* with a *greater army* than *the former*; and, at the *end of times* (*that is, years*) he shall *come with a mighty army, and great riches*, against the *king of the south*, that is, Ptolemaeus Epiphanes, who succeeded Ptolemaeus Philopater his father. In this expedition he had powerful allies (*v.* 14): Philip of Macedon was confederate with Antiochus against the king of Egypt. Antiochus routed him, destroyed a great part of his army; whereupon the Jews joined with him, helped him to besiege Ptolemaeus's garrisons. Then *the robbers of thy people shall exalt themselves to establish the vision*, but *they shall fall, and shall come to nothing, v.* 14. Hereupon (*v.* 15) the *king of the north*, this same Antiochus, shall carry on his design against the king of the south another way. (1) He shall surprise his strongholds; all that he has got in Syria and Samaria, and the king of Egypt, shall not be able to withstand him. (2) He shall make himself master of the land of Judæa (*v.* 16): *He that comes against him* (that is, the king of the north) shall carry all before him; so the land of Israel was wasted and consumed. The land of Judæa lay between these two potent kingdoms of Egypt and Syria, so that in all the struggles between them that was sure to suffer. (3) He shall still push on his war against the king of Egypt, and *set his face to enter with the strength of his whole kingdom*, taking advantage of the infancy of Ptolemy Epiphanes, *v.* 17. (4) His war with the Romans (*v.* 18): He shall *turn his face to the isles* (*v.* 18), Greece and Italy. He took many of the isles about the Hellespont, but a *prince*, or *state* (so some), shall *return his reproach upon himself*. This was fulfilled when the two Scipios were sent with an army against Antiochus, and gave him a total defeat. Thus he caused the *reproach offered by him to cease*.

(5) His fall. When he was routed by the Romans, and was forced to abandon to them all he had in Europe, he *turned to his own land*, and, to raise money to pay his tribute, he plundered a temple of Jupiter, which so incensed his own subjects against him that they killed him; so he *fell*, and *was no more found*, *v.* 19. (6) His next successor, *v.* 20. There rose up one in his place, a *raiser of taxes*, a *sender forth of the extortioner*. Seleucus Philopater, the elder son of Antiochus the Great, was a great oppressor of his subjects, and exacted abundance of money from them. He likewise attempted to rob the temple at Jerusalem. But *within a few days he shall be destroyed, neither in anger nor in battle*, but poisoned by Heliodorus, one of his own servants.

V. From all this let us learn, 1. That God in his providence sets up one, and pulls down another, as he pleases. Some have called great men the *foot-balls of fortune*; or, rather, they are the *tools of Providence*. 2. This world is full of *wars and fightings*, which come *from men's lusts*.

Verses 21–45

All this is a prophecy of the reign of Antiochus Epiphanes, the *little horn* (*ch.* viii. 9); a sworn enemy to the Jewish religion, and a bitter persecutor. Some things in this prediction concerning Antiochus are alluded to in the New Testament predictions of the antichrist, especially *v.* 36, 37.

I. His character: He called himself *Epiphanes—the illustrious*. The heathen writers describe him as an *odd-humoured* man, boisterous, base and sordid. He would sometimes steal out of the court into the city, and herd with any infamous company *in disguise*; some took him to be silly, others to be mad. He is called a *vile person*, for he had been a hostage at Rome for the fidelity of his father when the Romans had subdued him.

II. His accession to the crown. By a trick he got his elder brother's son, Demetrius, to be sent a hostage to Rome, in exchange for him, and his elder brother being killed by Heliodorus (*v.* 20), he took the kingdom. The states of Syria did not *give it to him* (*v.* 21), but he *came in peaceably*, pretending to reign for his brother's son, Demetrius, then a hostage at Rome. But *by flatteries he obtained the kingdom*, crushed Heliodorus; even to *the prince of the covenant*, his nephew, the rightful heir, he pretended to covenant that he would resign whenever he should return, *v.* 22. But (*v.* 23) *after the league made with him he shall work deceitfully*, as one whose avowed maxim it is that princes ought not to be bound by their word any longer than it is for their interest. And *with a small people*, that at first cleave to him, he shall *become strong*, and (*v.* 24) *he shall enter peaceably upon the fattest places* of the kingdom of Syria, shall *scatter* among the people the *prey, and the spoil, and riches*, to insinuate himself into their affections; but, at the same time, he shall *forecast his devices against the strongholds*, to make himself master of them. When he has got the garrisons into his hands he will scatter his spoil no more, but rule by force.

III. His war with Egypt, his second expedition thither, is described, *v.* 25, 27. Antiochus shall *stir up his power and courage* against Ptolemaeus Philometer king of Egypt. Ptolemy, thereupon, shall *be stirred up to battle* against him. Antiochus's army shall *overthrow* the Egyptian army. The king of Egypt shall be betrayed by his own counsellors. After the battle, a treaty of peace shall be set on foot, and these two kings shall meet but they shall neither of them be sincere in it. And then no marvel that *it shall not prosper*. The peace shall not last.

IV. Another expedition against Egypt. From the former he *returned with great riches* (*v.* 28), and therefore took the first occasion to invade Egypt again,

two years after, *v.* 29. But this attempt shall not succeed, for (*v.* 30) *the ships of Chittim shall come against him*, that is, the navy of the Romans, or ambassadors from the Roman senate, who came in ships. Ptolemaeus Philometer, king of Egypt, being now in a strict alliance with the Romans, craved their aid against Antiochus, who had besieged him and his mother Cleopatra in the city of Alexandria. The Roman senate thereupon sent an embassy to Antiochus, to command him to raise the siege, and, fearing the Roman power, he was forced to give orders for the raising of the siege and the retreat of his army out of Egypt. So Livy and others relate the story.

V. In his return from his expedition into Egypt, *v.* 28, he *did exploits* against the Jews; then he spoiled the city and temple. But the most terrible storm was in his return from Egypt, two years after, *v.* 30. Then he took Judæa in his way home; and, because he could not gain his point in Egypt by reason of the Romans interposing, he wreaked his revenge upon the Jews.

1. He had a rooted antipathy to the Jews' religion: *His heart* was *against the holy covenant*, *v.* 28. And (*v.* 30) *he had indignation against the holy covenant*. He hated the law of Moses and the worship of the true God, and was vexed at the privileges of the Jewish nation and the promises made to them.

2. He carried on his malicious designs against the Jews by the assistance of some apostate Jews. He kept up *intelligence with those that forsook the holy covenant* (*v.* 30). We read much in the book of the Maccabees of the mischief done to the Jews by these treacherous men of their own nation, Jason and Menelaus, and their party. "*Such as do wickedly against the covenant*, he shall *corrupt with flatteries*, to make use of them as decoys to draw in others," *v.* 32.

3. He profaned the temple. *Arms stand on his part* (*v.* 31), not only his own army, but deserters from the Jewish religion, and they *polluted the sanctuary of strength*. The story of this we have, 1 Mac. i. 21, &c. And (2 Mac. v. 15, &c.) *Antiochus went into the most holy temple, Menelaus, that traitor to the laws and to his own country, being his guide*. Antiochus *took away the daily sacrifice*, *v.* 31. Then he *set up the abomination of desolation upon the altar* (1 Mac. i. 54), even an *idol altar* (*v.* 59), and called the temple the temple of *Jupiter Olympius*, 2 Mac. vi. 2.

4. He persecuted those who retained their integrity. Though there are many who *forsake the covenant*, yet there is a people who do *know their God*, and *they shall be strong and do exploits*, *v.* 32. Good old Eleazar, one of the *principal scribes*, when he had swine's flesh thrust into his mouth, did bravely spit it out again, though he knew he must be tormented to death for so doing, 2 Mac. vi. 19. The mother and her seven sons were put to death for adhering to their religion, 2 Mac. vii. This might well be called *doing exploits*; for to choose suffering rather than sin is a great exploit. The right knowledge of God is the strength of the soul, and, in the strength of that, gracious souls do exploits. Concerning this people that knew their God, we are here told *they shall instruct many*, *v.* 33. They shall show others what they have learned of the difference between truth and falsehood, good and evil. Some understand this of a society newly erected for the propagating of divine knowledge, called *Assideans, pietists* (so the name signifies). *They shall fall* by the cruelty of Antiochus, shall be put to death by his rage. Their sufferings *for righteousness' sake* would try and purge the nation of the Jews. *When they shall fall* they shall not be utterly cast down, but *they shall be holpen with a little help*, *v.* 34. It is likewise foretold that *many shall cleave to them with flatteries*; when they see the Maccabees prosper some Jews shall join with them, but will only pretend friendship either with design

to *betray them* or in hope to *rise with them*; but the *fiery trial* (v. 35) will separate between the *precious and the vile*. Though these troubles may continue long, yet they will have *an end*.

5. He grew insolent, and profane, and, being puffed up with his conquests, bade defiance to Heaven, and trampled upon everything that was sacred, v. 36. He shall impiously dishonour the God of Israel, called here the *God of gods*. He shall, in defiance of him, *do according to his will* against his people and his holy religion. This was fulfilled when Antiochus forbade *sacrifices* to be *offered* in God's temple, and ordered the *sabbaths* to be *profaned*, the *sanctuary* and the *holy people* to be *polluted*, &c., to *the end that they might forget the law and change all the ordinances*, and this upon pain of death, 1 Mac. i. 45. Antiochus did not *regard any god*, but *magnified himself above all*, v. 37. Thus he carried all before him, *till the indignation was accomplished* (v. 36). Antiochus shall not *regard the god of his fathers*; he made laws to abolish the religion of his country, and to bring in the idols of the Greeks. He shall set up an unknown god, a new god, v. 38. *In his estate* he shall *honour the god of forces*, a supposed deity of power, a *god whom his fathers knew not*, nor worshipped. This seems to be Jupiter Olympius, but never introduced among the Syrians till Antiochus introduced it. Thus shall he do *in the most strongholds*, in the temple of Jerusalem, which is called *the sanctuary of strength* (v. 31), and here the *fortresses of munitions*; *there* he shall set up the image of this *strange god*. Some by the *Mahuzzim*, or *god of forces*, that Antiochus shall worship, understand *money*, which is said to *answer all things*.

VI. Here seems to be another expedition into Egypt. Ptolemy, *king of the south, pushes at him* (v. 40), makes an attempt upon some of his territories, whereupon Antiochus, the *king of the north, comes against him like a whirlwind*, with incredible swiftness and fury, *with chariots, and horses, and many ships*, a great force. He shall *come through countries, and shall overflow and pass over*. In this flying march *many countries shall be overthrown by him*; and he shall enter into *the glorious land*, the land of Israel. Some shall escape his fury, particularly Edom and Moab, and *the chief of the children of Ammon*, v. 41. But the land of Egypt *shall not escape. He shall have power over the treasures of gold and silver, and all the precious things of Egypt*, v. 43.

VII. Here is a prediction of the fall and ruin of Antiochus, as before (*ch.* viii. 25), when he is in the height of his honour, tidings *out of the east* and *out of the north* shall trouble him, v. 44. This obliged him to drop the enterprises he had in hand, and to go against the Persians and Parthians. Now comes the last effort of his rage against the Jews. When he finds himself perplexed and embarrassed in his affairs he shall *go forth with great fury to destroy and utterly to make away many*, v. 44. When impiety grows very impudent we may see its ruin near. *He shall come to his end and none shall help him*. This is the same with that which was foretold *ch.* viii. 25 (*He shall be broken without hand*).

CHAPTER 12

After the prediction of the troubles of the Jews under Antiochus, prefiguring the troubles of the Christian church under the antichristian power, we have here, I. Comforts for the support of God's people in those times of trouble, ver. 1-4. II. A conference between Christ and an angel concerning the time of these events, ver. 5-7. III. Daniel's enquiry for his own satisfaction, ver. 8. And the answer he received to that enquiry, ver. 9-13.

Verses 1-4

I. Jesus Christ shall appear his church's patron and protector: *At that time*, when the persecution is at the hottest, *Michael shall stand up, v.* 1. Christ is

that great prince. At that time Michael shall stand up for the working out of our eternal salvation; the Son of God shall be incarnate, shall be *manifested to destroy the works of the devil*. Christ *stood for the children of our people* when he was made sin and a curse for them, stood in their stead as a sacrifice, bore the curse for them, to bear it from them.

II. When Christ appears he will recompense tribulation to those that trouble his people. There shall *be a time of trouble*, threatening to all. This is applicable, 1. To the destruction of Jerusalem, which Christ calls such a *great tribulation as was not since the beginning of the world to this time*, Matt. xxiv. 21. Or, 2. To the judgment of the great day, that will be such a *day of trouble* as never was to all those whom Michael our prince stands against.

III. He will work salvation for his people: "*At that time thy people shall be delivered* from the mischief and ruin designed them by Antiochus."

IV. There shall be a resurrection of those that *sleep in the dust*, v. 2. 1. When God works deliverance for his people from persecution it is a kind of resurrection; so the Jews' release out of Babylon was represented in vision (Ezek. xxxvii) and so the deliverance of the Jews from Antiochus, they were as *life from the dead*. 2. When, upon the appearing of Michael our prince, his gospel is preached, many of those who *sleep in the dust*, both Jews and Gentiles, shall be awakened by it to take upon them a profession of religion. But, 3. It must be meant of the general resurrection at the last day: *The multitude of those that sleep in the dust shall awake*.

V. There shall be glorious reward conferred on those who, in the day of trouble and distress, being themselves *wise*, did *instruct many*. They should do eminent service, and yet should *fall by the sword and by flame*; now, if there were not another life after this, they would be *of all men most miserable*, and therefore we are here assured that they shall be recompensed *in the resurrection of the just* (v. 3). Those that turn *men to righteousness*, that *turn sinners from the errors of their ways* and help to *save their souls from death* (Jas. v. 20), will share in the glory of those they have helped to heaven, which will be a great addition to their own glory.

VI. This prophecy of those times, though sealed up now, would be of great use to those that should live then, v. 4. Daniel must now *shut up the words and seal the book* because the *time would be long* ere these things would be accomplished. He must keep it safely, as a treasure of great value, laid up for the ages to come. Those things of God which are now dark and obscure will hereafter be made clear, and easy to be understood. *Truth is the daughter of time*. Scripture prophecies will be expounded by the accomplishment of them.

Verses 5-13

Daniel had been made to foresee the amazing revolutions of states and kingdoms, as far as the Israel of God was concerned in them; in them he foresaw troublous times to the church. *When* shall the *end be?* And, *What* shall the *end be?*

I. The question, *When shall the end be?* is asked by an angel, v. 5, 6. Daniel had had discourse with the angel Gabriel, and now he *looks*, and *behold other two* (v. 5), two angels that he had not seen before, *one upon the bank of the river on one side and the other on the other side*. Christ stood *on the waters of the river* (v. 6), *between the banks of Ulai*. Daniel had not seen them before, but now, when they began to speak, he looked up, and saw them. The question was put, to the *man clothed in linen*, of whom we read before (*ch.* x. 5), to Christ our great high priest, *who was upon the waters of the river*. The angel asked as one concerned, *How long shall it be?* What is the time for the *end of these wonders*, these suffering trying times, that are to pass over the people of God? Here is a general account given to the angel that made the enquiry (*v.* 7). They shall continue *for a time, times, and a half*, that is, a year, two years, and half a year, as was before intimated (*ch.* vii. 25). Some understand it indefinitely, a certain time for an uncertain; it shall be *for a time* (a considerable time), for *times* (a longer time yet), and yet but *half a time*; when it is over it shall seem not half so much as was feared. But it is rather to be taken for a certain time; we meet with it in the Revelation, sometimes of three days and a half, put for three years and a half, sometimes forty-two months, sometimes 1,260 days. This Mighty One that Daniel saw stood with *both feet* on the water, and swore with *both hands* lifted up. God's time to succour and relieve his people is when their affairs are brought to the last extremity; *in the mount of the Lord it shall be seen* that Isaac is saved just when he lies ready to be sacrificed. Now the event answered the prediction; Josephus says that Antiochus surprised Jerusalem *and held it three years and six months*, and was then *cast out of the country* by the Maccabees. Christ's public ministry continued *three years and a half*, during which time he endured the contradiction of sinners against himself, and lived in poverty and disgrace; and then, when at his death, his enemies triumphed over him, he obtained the most glorious victory and said, *It is finished.* Here is something added more particularly concerning the time of the continuance of those troubles, in what is said to Daniel, *v.* 11, 12. The time of the trouble is to be dated, from the *taking away of the daily sacrifice* by Antiochus, and the *setting up* of the image of Jupiter upon the altar, which was the *abomination of desolation.* Their trouble shall last 1,290 days, *three years* and *seven months*, or (as some reckon) *three years, six months*, and *fifteen days*; and then it is probable, the daily sacrifice was restored, and the abomination of desolation taken away. It appears that the beginning of the trouble was in the 145th year of the Seleucidae, and the end of it in the 148th year. Thus we may learn, *First*, That there is a time fixed for the termination of the church's troubles, and the bringing about of her deliverance. *Secondly*, That this time must be waited for with faith and patience. *Thirdly*, That, when it comes, it will abundantly recompense us for our long expectation.

II. The question, *What shall the end be?* is asked by Daniel. Daniel asked this question because,

though he *heard what was said* to the angel, yet he did not *understand* it, *v.* 8. He directs his enquiry not to the angel that talked with him, but immediately to Christ. When we take a view of the affairs of this world, and of the church of God in it, we see things move as if they would end in the utter ruin of God's kingdom among men. When we see vice and impiety, the decay of religion, the sufferings of the righteous, and the triumphs of the ungodly, we may well ask, *O my Lord! what will be the end of these things?* Daniel must content himself with the discoveries that had been made to him: "*Go thy way, Daniel. Go thy way, and record what thou hast seen* and heard, for the benefit of posterity, and covet not to see and hear more at present." He must not expect that what had been said to him would be fully understood till it was accomplished. As long as the world stands, there will still be in it a mixture of good and bad; *bad men will do bad things; and a corrupt tree* will *never bring forth good fruit.* Wicked practices are the natural products of wicked principles and dispositions. We are told, before, that the *wicked will do wickedly.* They *will not understand*; they shut their eyes against the light, and none so blind as those that will not see. Wilful sin is the effect of wilful ignorance; they *will not understand* because *they are wicked*; they *hate the light*, and come not to the light, *because their deeds are evil*, John iii. 19. Yet, bad as the world is, God will secure to himself a remnant of good people in it. There shall be many, to whom the providences and ordinances of God shall be *a savour of life unto life. Many shall be purified, and made white, and tried*, by their troubles (compare *ch.* xi. 35). The word of God shall do them good. When the *wicked understand not*, but stumble at the word, the *wise shall understand.* Those who are governed by the divine law and love shall be illuminated with a divine light. For if any man will *do his will* he shall *know the truth*, John vii. 17. Time and days will have an end; not only our time and days will end very shortly, but all times and days will have an end at length; yet a little while, and time shall be no more, but all its revolutions will be numbered and finished. It was a comfort to Daniel, it is a comfort to all the saints, that, whatever their lot is in the days of time, they shall have a happy lot in *the end of the days.* A believing hope and prospect of a blessed lot in the heavenly Canaan, at the end of the days, will furnish us with living comforts in dying moments.

AN EXPOSITION, WITH PRACTICAL OBSERVATIONS, OF

THE BOOK OF
THE PROPHET HOSEA

I. The twelve minor prophets were sometimes grouped together as *one book*. They are called the minor prophets, not because their writings are of less authority than those of the greater prophets, but only because they are shorter. These prophets preached as much as the others, but did not write so much. These twelve, Josephus says, were put into one volume by the *men of the great synagogue* in Ezra's time. These are the fragments of prophecy carefully gathered up by the divine Providence and the care of the church. Nine of these prophets prophesied before the captivity, and the last three after the return of the Jews to their own land. Some difference there is in the order of these books. We place them as the ancient Hebrew did; and all agree to put Hosea first; but the ancient Septuagint places the first six in this order—Hosea, Amos, Micah, Joel, Obadiah, and Jonah. The thing is not material.

II. The prophecy of Hosea, who was the first of all the writing prophets. The ancients say, He was of Bethshemesh, and of the tribe of Issachar. He continued very long a prophet; so that, as Jerome observes, he prophesied of the destruction of the kingdom of the ten tribes, and lived himself to see and lament it. The scope of his prophecy is to discover sin, and to denounce the judgments of God against a people that would not be reformed. The style is concise and in some places it seems like the book of Proverbs, without connexion, and rather to be called Hosea's *sayings* than Hosea's *sermons*.

CHAPTER 1

The mind of God is revealed to this prophet, and by him to the people, in the first three chapters, by signs and types, but afterwards only by discourse. In this chapter we have, I. The title ver. 1. II. Some particular instructions which he was ordered to give to the people of God. 1. He must convince them of their sin in going a-whoring from God, ver. 2, 3. 2. He must foretell the ruin coming upon them for their sin, in the names of his sons, ver. 4–6, 8, 9. 3. He must speak comfortably to the kingdom of Judah, which still retained the pure worship of God, ver. 7. 4. The great mercy God had in store for Israel and Judah, in the latter days (ver. 10, 11).

Verse 1

1. The prophet's name, which he prefixes to his prophecy. His name, *Hosea*, or *Hoshea* (the same as Joshua's original name), signifies a *saviour*. His surname was *Ben-Beeri*, or *the son of Beeri*. *Beeri* signifies a *well*, which may put us in mind of living waters from which prophets must be continually drawing. 2. His authority and commission: *The word of the Lord came to him.* What he said and wrote was by divine inspiration. Therefore this book was received among the canonical books of the Old Testament, which is confirmed by what is quoted out of it in the New Testament, Matt. ii. 15; ix. 13; xii. 7; Rom. ix. 25, 26; 1 Pet. ii. 10. 3. Here is a particular account of the times in which he prophesied—*in the days of Uzziah, Jotham, Ahaz, and Hezekiah, kings of Judah, and in the days of Jeroboam the son of Joash, king of Israel.* Now by this account given of the reigns in which Hosea prophesied it appears that he prophesied a long time, that he began when he was young, and that he continued till he was very old. And yet the longer they enjoyed him the less they regarded him; they despised his youth first, and afterwards his age. Some of these kings were good, and encouraged him; others were bad, and frowned upon him and discouraged him; and yet he was still the same. He began to prophesy in Israel at a time when their kingdom was in a prosperous condition, as in the reign of Jeroboam the second, 2 Kings xiv. 25, yet then Hosea boldly tells them of their sins and foretells their destruction.

Verses 2–7

The beginning of the word of the Lord by Hosea, may refer either, 1. To that glorious set of prophets which was raised up. About this time there lived and prophesied Joel, Amos, Micah, Jonah, Obadiah, and Isaiah; but Hosea was the first of them that foretold the destruction of Israel. Or, rather, 2. To Hosea's own prophecies. This was the first message God sent him upon to this people, to tell them that they were *an evil and an adulterous generation.* He might have desired to be excused till he had gained authority and some interest in their affections. No; he must *begin with this,* that they might know what to expect from a prophet of the Lord.

I. The prophet must, as it were in a looking-glass, show them *their sin.* The prophet is ordered to *take unto him a wife of whoredoms and children of whoredoms, v.* 2. And he did so, *v.* 3. He married a woman of ill fame, *Gomer the daughter of Diblaim,* one that had lived scandalously in the single state. To marry such a one was not prudent, and therefore forbidden to the priests, and would be an affliction to the prophet, but not a sin. But most commentators think that it was done *in vision,* or that it is no more than a parable. He must take *a wife of whoredoms,* and have such children by her as everyone would suspect, though born in wedlock, to be *children of whoredoms.* "Now" (saith God) "Hosea, this people is to me such a dishonour, and such a grief and vexation, as a *wife of whoredoms* and *children of whoredoms* would be to thee. *For the land has committed great whoredoms.*" Their idolatry especially is the whoredom they are here charged with. *Idolatry* is *great whoredom,* worse than any other; it is departing from *the Lord. The land has committed whoredom;* the whole land is polluted with it. Is it not offensive to the *holy God* to have such a people as this to be called by his name and have a place in his house? It was as if he should have married Gomer the daughter of Diblaim, a noted harlot. The land of Israel was like Gomer the daughter of Diblaim. *Gomer* signifies *corruption; Diblaim* signifies *two cakes,* or *lumps of figs;* this denotes that Israel was near to ruin, and that their luxury and sensuality were the cause of it. It intimates sin to be the daughter of plenty and destruction the daughter of the abuse of plenty.

II. The prophet must, as it were through a perspective glass, show them their ruin; and this he does in the names given to the children born of this adulteress.

1. He foretells the fall of the royal family in the name he is appointed to give to his first child, which was a son: *Call his name Jezreel, v.* 4. Jezreel signifies *the seed of God*, but it signifies also the *scattered of God. Call them not Israel*, which signifies *dominion*, but call them Jezreel, which signified *dispersion. I will revenge the blood of Jezreel upon the house of Jehu*, the blood which Jehu shed when he destroyed the house of Ahab, with all the worshippers of Baal. God approved of what he did (2 Kings x. 30). Yet here God will avenge that *blood upon the house of Jehu*, when the time has expired during which it was promised that his family should reign. It was the execution of a righteous sentence passed upon the house of Ahab, and, as such, it was rewarded; but Jehu did it not in a right manner. He did it with a malice against the sinners, but not with any antipathy to the sin; for he kept up the worship of the golden calves, 2 Kings x. 31. And therefore when God came to reckon with them, the first article in the account is for the blood of the house of Ahab, here called the *blood of Jezreel*. Some make those words, *I will visit, or appoint, the blood of Jezreel upon the house of Jehu*, to signify, not the revenging of that bloodshed, but the repeating of that bloodshed: "I will punish the house of Jehu, as I punished the house of Ahab." After the death of Zechariah, the last of the house of Jehu, the kingdom of the ten tribes went to decay. And, in order to the ruin of it, it is threatened (*v.* 5), *I will break the bow of Israel in the valley of Jezreel*. The *breaking of the bow* intimates a sinking ruined power.

2. He foretells God's abandoning the whole nation in the name he gives to the second child. Call the name of this daughter *Lo-ruhamah—not beloved*, Rom. ix. 25, or *not having obtained mercy*, 1 Pet. ii. 10. This intimates that God had shown them great mercy, but they had abused his favours, and forfeited them. Though God has borne long, he will not bear always, with a people that hate to be reformed.

III. He must show them what mercy God had in store for the house of Judah, at the same time that he was thus contending with the house of Israel (*v.* 7): *But I will have mercy upon the house of Judah.* When the Assyrian armies had destroyed Samaria, and carried the ten tribes away into captivity, they proceeded to besiege Jerusalem; but God had mercy on the house of Judah, and saved them by the vast slaughter which an angel made, in one night, in the camp of the Assyrians; then they were *saved by the Lord their God*, and not by sword or bow. This may refer also to the salvation of Judah from idolatry, which qualified and prepared them for their other salvations. Just at the time that the kingdom of Israel was *utterly taken away*, under Hoshea, the kingdom of Judah was gloriously reformed, under Hezekiah; and in Babylon God saved them from their idolatry first, and then from their captivity. Some make this promise to look forward to the great salvation which, in the fulness of time, was to be wrought out *by the Lord our God*, Jesus Christ.

Verses 8–11

I. The rejection of Israel for a time is signified by the name of another child that Hosea had by his adulterous spouse, *v.* 8, 9. *When she had weaned her daughter, she conceived and bore a son.* Some think that her bearing another son signifies that people's persisting in their wickedness; lust still *conceived* and *brought forth sin*. The name given him: *Call him Lo-ammi—Not my people.* When they were told that God would *no more have mercy on them* they regarded it not, but buoyed up themselves with this conceit, that they were God's people, whom he

could not but have mercy on. And therefore he plucks that staff from under them, and disowns all relation to them: *You are not my people*, and *I will not be your God*. This was fulfilled in Israel when they were *utterly taken away* into the *land of Assyria*. They were no longer *God's people*; no prophets were sent to them, no promises made to them, as were to the two tribes in their captivity.

II. Of the reduction and restoration of Israel in the fulness of time. Here, as before, mercy is remembered in the midst of wrath; the rejection, as it shall not be total, so it shall not be final (*v.* 10, 11).

1. Some think that these promises had their accomplishment in the return of the Jews out of their captivity in Babylon, when many of the ten tribes joined themselves to Judah, and came out of the countries into which they were dispersed, to their own land, appointed Zerubbabel, their head, and coalesced into one people. And in their own land God would by his prophets own them as his children.

2. Some think that these promises will not have their accomplishment in full, till the general conversion of the Jews in the latter days.

3. This promise had its accomplishment in the setting up of the kingdom of Christ, and the bringing in both of Jews and Gentiles (Rom. ix. 25, 26 and 1 Pet. ii. 10). This Israel shall greatly multiply. Though Israel according to the flesh be diminished, the spiritual Israel shall be innumerable. In the multitudes that by the preaching of the gospel have been brought to Christ, in the first ages of Christianity and ever since, this promise is fulfilled, Rev. vii. 4, 9; Gal. iv. 27. God will renew his covenant with the gospel-Israel, and will incorporate it a church by as full a charter as that whereby the Old Testament church was incorporated. The *abandoned Gentiles* in their respective places, and the *rejected Jews* in theirs, shall be blessed. There, where the fathers were cast off for their unbelief, the children, upon their believing, shall be taken in. The privilege is enlarged; now it is not only, *You are my people*, as formerly, but *You are the sons of the living God*, whether by birth you were Jews or Gentiles. They were as children *under age*; now, under the gospel, they have grown up to greater understanding and greater liberty, Gal. iv. 1, 2. The sonship of believers shall be acknowledged; *You are the sons of the living God.* It will add to their honour, when they are dignified with the tokens of God's favour in that very place where they had long lain under the tokens of his displeasure. Those who had been at variance should be happily brought together (*v.* 11): *Then shall the children of Judah and the children of Israel be gathered together.* This uniting of Judah and Israel is mentioned only as a specimen, or one instance, of the happy effect of the setting up of Christ's kingdom in the world. The first disciples were partly Jews and partly Galileans. When the Samaritans believed, though between them and the Jews there was a much greater enmity, yet in Christ there was a perfect unanimity, Acts viii. 14. By the death of Christ, the partition-wall of the ceremonial law was taken down. See Eph. ii. 14–16. Jesus Christ should be the centre of unity to all God's spiritual Israel. To believe in Christ is to appoint him our head, that is, to consent to God's appointment, and willingly commit ourselves to his guidance and government; all good Christians that make him their head, though they are many, yet in him they are one, and so become one with each other. Having appointed Christ for their head, *they shall come up out of the land*; they shall come, some of all sorts, from all parts. It denotes not a local remove (for they are said to be in the same place, *v.* 10), but a change of their mind, a spiritual ascent to Christ. When all this comes to pass, *great shall be the day of Jezreel.* Israel is here called *Jezreel*, the

seed of God. This seed is now sown in the earth, and buried; but great shall be its day when the harvest comes.

CHAPTER 2

I. God, by the prophet, discovers to them the sin of their idolatry, their spiritual whoredom, ver. 1, 2, 5, 8. II. He threatens to take away from them all good things with which they had served their idols, ver. 3, 4, 6, 7, 9–13. III. Yet he promises at last to return in ways of mercy to them (ver. 14), to restore them to their former plenty (ver. 15), to cure them of their inclination to idolatry (ver. 16, 17), to renew his covenant with them (ver. 18–20), and to bless them with all good things, ver. 21–23.

Verses 1–5

The first words of this chapter some make the close of the foregoing chapter. When they shall have appointed Christ their head, "say to them, *Ammi*, and *Ruhamah*; call them so again, for they shall no longer lie under the reproach and doom of *Lo-ammi* and *Lo-ruhamah*; they shall now be *my people* again, and shall *obtain mercy*." The *mother* (*v.* 2) seems to be the same with the *brethren* and *sisters* (*v.* 1), the church of the ten tribes, and in a special manner the heads and leaders, who were as the mother by whom the rest were brought up and nursed. But who are the children that must *plead with their mother* thus? Either, 1. The godly that were among them, that witnessed against the iniquities of the times: let those that had not bowed the knee to Baal reason the case with those that had. Or, 2. The sufferers among them, that shared in the calamities of the times: let them not complain of God, nor lay the blame on him, as if he had dealt hardly with them, and not like a tender father. No; let them *plead with their mother*, and lay the fault on her, where it ought to be laid; compare Isa. l. 1.

I. They must put her in mind of the relation wherein she had stood to God, the kindness he had had for her. Let them tell their *brethren* and *sisters* that they had been *Ammi* and *Ruhamah*, God's people and vessels of his mercy.

II. They must charge her with the violation of the marriage-covenant between her and God. Tell her (*v.* 2) that *she is not my wife, neither am I her husband*, that by her spiritual whoredom she has forfeited her relation to God. They must charge this home upon her (*v.* 5): *Their mother has played the harlot; their congregation has run after idols*, wherein they were encouraged by their false prophets.

III. They must upbraid her with her ingratitude to God her benefactor, in ascribing to her idols the glory of the gifts he had given her, *v.* 5. *She said*, Whatever is offered to the contrary, *I will go after my lovers*, or *those that cause me to love them*. The Chaldee understands it of the nations whose alliance Israel courted, who supplied them with what they needed. "I will go after my lovers, because they give me my *bread and my water*, which are necessary to sustain the body, *my wool and my flax*, which are necessary to clothe the body, and pleasant things, *my oil*, and *my drink*, my liquors" (so the word is), "wine and strong drink." The idolaters made Ceres the goddess of their corn, Bacchus the god of their wine, &c., and then foolishly fancied they had their corn and wine from these, forgetting the Lord their God, who both gave them that good land and *gave them power to get wealth* out of it.

IV. God will disown her if she persist in her whoredoms, *v.* 2. Let her be convinced that it is possible for her to reform. True penitents will forsake both open sins and secret sins. They will both avoid the outward occasions of sin and mortify the inward disposition to it.

V. They must show her the utter ruin that will certainly be the consequence of her sin if she do not repent and reform (*v.* 3). She shall be starved, shall be deprived of her honours, her comforts and necessary supports. She shall be famished, shall be made *as a wilderness* and *a dry land*, and *slain with thirst*. Some understand it thus: *I will make her as* she was in the *wilderness*, and set her as she was *in the desert land*, where she was sometimes ready to perish *for thirst*. I will set her *as in the day that she was born*; for it was in the vast howling wilderness that Israel was first formed into a people.

Verses 6–13

I. They shall be perplexed and embarrassed in their counsels, and disappointed in their expectations. This is threatened, *v.* 6, 7. But to the threatening is annexed a promise that this shall be a means to convince them of their folly, and bring them home to their duty.

1. God will raise up difficulties and troubles: *I will hedge up thy way with thorns*. She said, "I will go after my lovers; I will pursue my leagues and alliances with foreign powers, and depend upon them." But God says, "She shall be frustrated in these projects, and not be able to proceed in them." She shall be as a traveller that finds no way at all to go forward. And then *she shall follow after her lovers, but shall not overtake them;* she shall endeavour to make an interest in the Assyrians and Egyptians, and to have them for her protectors, but she shall not gain her point. This is such a mercy, as Balaam met when the angel stood in his way, to hinder his going forward to *curse Israel*, Num. xxii. 22. Crosses and obstacles in an evil course are great blessings. They are God's hedges to restrain us from wandering, and to make the way of sin difficult.

2. These difficulties that God raises up in their way shall raise up in their minds thoughts of turning back. Two things are here extorted from this degenerate apostate people: (1) A just acknowledgment of the folly of their apostasy. (2) A good purpose, to come back again to their duty: *I will go, and return to my first husband;* and she knows so much of his goodness and readiness to forgive that she speaks without any doubt of his receiving her again.

II. The necessary supports and comforts of life shall be taken from them, because they had dishonoured God with them, *v.* 8, 9.

1. How graciously their plenty was given to them. God gave them not only corn but he *multiplied their silver and gold*, wherewith to traffic with other nations. He gave them *wool* and *flax* too, to *cover their nakedness*, Ezek. xvi. 10.

2. How basely their plenty was abused by them. (1) They robbed God of the honour of his gifts: *She did not know that I gave her corn and wine;* she did not remember it. (2) They served and honoured his enemies with them: *They prepared them for Baal;* they adorned their images with *gold and silver* (Jer. x. 4), and adorned themselves for the worship of their images, *v.* 13.

3. How justly their plenty should be taken from them: "*Therefore will I return;* I will alter my dealings with them, will take another course, *and will take away my corn* and other good things that I gave her." Those that abuse the mercies God gives them, to his dishonour, cannot expect to enjoy them long.

III. They shall lose *all their honour*, and be exposed to contempt (*v.* 10): "*I will discover her lewdness*, will bring to light her secret wickedness, to her shame. And this *in the sight of her lovers*, in the sight of the neighbouring nations, with whom she courted an alliance, and on whom she had a dependence; they shall not think her any longer worthy of their friendship." Those who will not deliver themselves into the hand of God's mercy cannot be delivered out of the hand of his justice.

IV. They shall lose all their pleasure, and shall be left melancholy (*v.* 11): *I will cause her mirth to cease.*

1. God will take away the occasions of their sacred mirth—*their feast-days, their new moons, their sabbaths, and all their solemn feasts.* These God instituted to be observed in a religious manner, and they were to be observed with rejoicing. They kept up the observance of these, not at God's temple at Jerusalem, for they had long since forsaken that, but probably at Dan and Bethel, where the calves were. Thus, when they had lost the power of godliness, yet, for the pleasing of a carnal mind, they kept up the form of it; and by this means their new-moons and their sabbaths became an iniquity which God *could not away with,* Isa. i. 13.

2. God will take away their provisions for these solemnities (*v.* 12): *I will destroy her vines and her fig-trees.* He will wither them with a blast, or bring in a foreign enemy that shall lay the country waste, so that their vineyards shall become *a forest;* the enclosures shall be thrown down, so that the *beasts of the field* shall eat their grapes and their figs. This shall be the ruin of their mirth: God will *cause all her mirth to cease.* "I will *destroy her vines and her fig-trees,* will take away her sensual pleasures, and then she will think herself undone indeed." This shall be the punishment of her idolatry (*v.* 13): "*I will visit upon her the days of Baalim.*" The *days of Baalim* are the solemn festival days which they kept in honour of their idols. These were the days wherein she *burnt incense* to idols, and *decked herself with her ear-rings and her jewels,* that the honour she did to Baal might be thought the greater.

Verses 14–23

The state of Israel, restrained by the divine grace, looks bright and pleasant here, and the more surprisingly so as the promises follow thus close upon the threatenings. When it was said, *She forgot me,* one would think it should have followed, "Therefore I will abandon her, I will never look after her more." No, *Therefore I will allure her.* God's thoughts and ways of mercy are infinitely above ours, Isa. lvii. 17, 18. Because she will not be restrained by the denunciations of wrath, God will try whether she will be wrought upon by the offers of mercy. Some think it may be translated, *Afterwards,* or *nevertheless,* I will allure her. It comes all to one; the design is plainly to magnify free grace to those on whom God will have mercy purely for mercy's sake.

I. Though now Israel was ready to despair it should again be revived with comforts and hopes, *v.* 14, 15. This is expressed here with an allusion to God's dealings with that people when he brought them out of Egypt, through the wilderness to Canaan, *in the day that they were born, v.* 3. They shall be new-formed by such miracles of love and mercy as they were first-formed by. He will *bring them into the wilderness,* as he did when he brought them out of Egypt. The land of their captivity shall be to them now, as that wilderness was then, the *furnace of affliction,* in which God will *choose them.* When God delivered Israel out of Egypt he led them into the wilderness, to *humble them and prove them, that he might do them good* (Deut. viii. 2, 3, 15, 16), and so he will do again. Those whom God has mercy in store for he first *brings into a wilderness*—into solitude and retirement, that they may the more freely converse with him out of the noise of this world, and sometimes into outward distress and trouble, thereby to open the ear to discipline. He will then *allure them and speak comfortably to them,* will *persuade them* and *speak to their hearts,* that is, he will by his word and Spirit incline their hearts to return to him, and encourage them to do so. *By the hand of my servants the prophets I will speak comfort to her heart;* so the Chaldee.

This refers to the offers of divine grace in the gospel, by which we are allured to forsake our sins and to turn to God. By the promise of rest in Christ we are invited to take his yoke upon us; and the work of conversion may be forwarded by comforts as well as by convictions. From that time and from that place where he has afflicted her, and brought her to see her folly, thenceforward he will *do her good.* He had *destroyed her vines* (*v.* 12), but now he will give her whole *vineyards,* and so she will be repaid; she shall not only have corn for necessity, but vineyards for delight. These denote the privileges and comforts of the gospel, which are prepared for those that *come up out of the wilderness leaning upon* Christ as *their beloved,* Cant. viii. 5. He will give her *the valley of Achor for a door of hope. The valley of Achor* was that in which Achan was stoned; it signifies *the valley of trouble,* because he troubled Israel, and there God troubled him. So when God returns to his people in mercy, and they to him in duty, it will be to them as happy an omen as anything. If they put away the accursed thing from among them, if by mortifying sin they stone the Achan that has troubled their camp, their subduing that enemy within themselves is an earnest to them of victory over all the kings of Canaan. *She shall sing there as in the days of her youth.* This plainly refers to that triumphant and prophetic song which Moses and the children of Israel sang at the *Red Sea,* Exod. xv. 1. When they are delivered out of captivity they shall repeat that song, and to them it shall be a new song.

II. Though they had been much addicted to the worship of Baal, they should now abandon all appearances of idolatry, and cleave to God only, *v.* 16, 17. The very *names of Baalim* shall be *taken out of their mouths.* Thus the apostle expresses the abhorrence we ought to have of all fleshly lusts: *Let them not be once named among you,* Eph. v. 3. God's grace in the heart will change the language by making that iniquity to be loathed which was beloved. The very word Baal shall be laid aside, even in its innocent signification. God says, *Thou shalt call me Ishi, and call me no more Baali;* both signify *my husband,* and both had been made use of concerning God. Isa. liv. 5, *Thy Maker is thy husband,* thy *Baal* (so the word is), thy patron, and protector.

III. Though they had been in continual troubles, as if the whole creation had been at war with them, now they shall enjoy perfect peace and tranquillity, as if they were in a league of friendship with the whole creation (*v.* 18). The inferior creatures shall do them no harm, as they had done when the *beasts of the field* ate up their vineyards (*v.* 12). God can make *the beasts of the field* to *honour* him (so he has promised, Isa. xliii. 20) and to contribute to his people's comfort. And it is our part of the covenant not to abuse them. But this is not all; men are more in danger from one another than from the brute beast, and therefore it is further promised that God will *make wars to cease,* will disarm the enemy: *I will break the bow, and sword, and battle.* He will do it for those whose *ways please him,* for he *makes even their enemies to be at peace with them,* Prov. xvi. 7. This agrees with the promise that in gospel-times *swords shall be beaten into ploughshares,* Isa. ii. 4.

IV. Though God had given them a bill of divorce for their whoredoms, yet, upon their repentance, he would again take them into a marriage-covenant, *v.* 19, 20. *I will betroth thee unto me;* and again, and a third time, *I will betroth thee.* All that are sincerely devoted to God are betrothed to him; God will love them, protect them, and provide for them. The covenant itself shall be inviolable; God will not break it on his part, and you shall not on yours; and the blessings of it shall be everlasting. "And," says God, "I will renew the covenant *in righteousness.*" Will it not reflect upon his wisdom? "No," says God; "I will do it *in judgment.*" *In loving kindness and in mercies*—God will deal tenderly and graciously in covenanting with them. It shall be a covenant of grace, made in a compassionate consideration of their infirmities. *Thou shalt know the Lord.* This is not only a promise that God will reveal himself to them more fully than ever, but that he will give them *a heart to know him*; they shall know him in another manner. They shall all be *taught of God* to know him.

V. Though the heavens had been to them as brass, and the earth as iron, now the heavens shall yield their dews, and by that means the earth its fruits, *v.* 21, 22. This promise of *corn and wine* is to be taken also in a spiritual sense: it is an effusion of those blessings and graces which relate to the soul that is here promised under the metaphor of temporal blessings, the dew of heaven, as well as the fatness of the earth, and that put first, as in the blessing of Jacob, Gen. xxvii. 28. "But," say the heavens, "we have no rain to give unless he who has the key of the clouds unlock them, and open these bottles; so that, *if the Lord do not help you*, we cannot." God will graciously take notice of their addresses to him. And then *I will hear the heavens*; I will *answer them* (so it may be read); and then they shall *hear and answer the earth*, and pour down seasonable rain upon it. See here the coherence of second causes with one another, as links in a chain, and the necessary dependence they all have upon God, the first Cause.

VI. That whereas they were now divided and scattered all the world over, God will turn this curse into a blessing: "I will not only water the earth for her, but will *sow her unto me in the earth*; like that of the seed in the field, wherever they are scattered they shall *take root downward and bear fruit upward. The good seed are the children of the kingdom. I will sow her unto me.*" When in all parts of the world Christianity got footing, then this promise was fulfilled.

VII. That, whereas they had been *Lo-ammi—not a people*, and *Lo-ruhamah—not finding mercy* with God, now they shall be restored to his favour (*v.* 23). God had mercy on those who *had not obtained mercy*. God's mercy must not be despaired of anywhere on this side hell. He says to them, "*Thou art my people*, whom I will own and bless," and they shall say, "*Thou art my God*, whom I will serve and worship, and to whose honour I will be for ever devoted."

CHAPTER 3

God is still by the prophet inculcating the same thing upon this careless people by a sign, that of the dealings of a husband with an adulterous wife. I. The bad character which the people of Israel now had, ver. 1. II. The low condition which they should be reduced to by their captivity, ver. 2-4. III. The blessed reformation that should be wrought upon them in the latter days, ver. 5.

Verses 1-5

Some think that this chapter refers to Judah, the two tribes, as the adulteress the prophet married (*ch.* i. 3) represented the *ten tribes.* But the *children of Israel* were the ten tribes, and therefore it is more probable that of them this parable is to be understood.

I. In this parable we may observe, God's goodness and Israel's badness serving for a foil to each other, *v.* 1. Israel is as a woman *beloved of her friend*, and *yet an adulteress*; such is the case between God and Israel. If they were restrained from bowing the knee to idols, yet they had *eyes full of that* spiritual *adultery.* And they loved *flagons of wine*; they joined with idolaters because they lived merrily and drank hard. Idolatry and sensuality commonly go together. Their badness had not put an end to God's goodness. Such is my *love to the children of Israel*; it is love to

the loveless, to the unlovely, to those that have a thousand times forfeited it. God humbles them (*v.* 2): *I bought her to me for fifteen pieces of silver, and a homer and a half of barley*, that is, I courted her to return to her first husband, as *ch.* ii. 14. But the present which the prophet brought her for the purchasing of her favour is a very small one; and in it she is reduced to a short allowance, and, to punish her for her pride, is made to look very mean. The prophet here visited his wife with *fifteen pieces of silver*, a small sum, till her husband thought fit to restore her to her first estate. She shall also have *a homer and a half of barley*, for bread-corn, and that is all she must expect till she be sufficiently humbled. God had given Egypt for Israel's ransom once, Isa. xliii. 3, 4. But now that they have gone a-whoring from him he will give but fifteen pieces of silver for them, so much have they lost in their value by their iniquity. Now see the new terms upon which God is willing to come (*v.* 3). They must be to him a people, and he will be to them a God. They must take to themselves the shame of their apostasy from him: *Thou shalt abide for me many days* in *solitude* and *silence*, as a widow that is *desolate* and in sorrow; they must *lay aside their ornaments*, and wait with patience and submission to know what God will do with them. It is not enough to take shame to ourselves for the sins we have committed, and to justify God in correcting us for them, but we must resolve, in the strength of God's grace, that we will not offend any more. In the land of their captivity they would be courted to worship the idols of the country; that would be a trial for them, a *long* trial, many days: "But if thou keep thy ground, and hold fast thy integrity, if, when *all this comes upon thee*, thou dost not *stretch out thy hand to a strange god*, thou wilt be qualified for the returns of God's favour."

II. In the last two verses we have the interpretation of the parable and the application of it to Israel. *They shall abide many days without a king, and without a prince;* and a nation in this condition may well be called *a widow. They shall* abide *without a sacrifice*, and *without an image* (or a *statue*, or *pillar;* the word is used concerning the pillars Jacob erected, Gen. xxviii. 18; xxxi. 45; xxxv. 20), and *without an ephod and teraphim.* The meaning is that in their captivity they should have no face of a nation upon them, no face of a church. They shall have *no ephod*, nor *teraphim*, no legal priesthood. This was the case of the Jews in their captivity; and it is so far the case of the scattered Jews at this day that, though they have their synagogues, they have no temple-service. They shall at length be received again as a wife (*v.* 5): *Afterwards*, in process of time, when they have gone through this discipline, *they shall return.* The Chaldee reads it, They shall *seek the service of the Lord their God*, and *shall obey Messiah, the Son of David their king.* Compare this with Jer. xxx. 9; Ezek. xxxiv. 23; xxxvii. 25. *They shall fear the Lord and his goodness.* Some by his *goodness* here understand the temple, towards which they shall look, in worshipping God. The Jews say, There were three things—which Israel cast off in the days of Rehoboam—the *kingdom of heaven*, the *family of David*, and the *house of the sanctuary.* But it is rather to be taken for that attribute of God which he showed as his glory, and by which he proclaimed his name. It is not only the Lord and his greatness that we are to fear, but the Lord and his goodness, not only his majesty, but his mercy.

CHAPTER 4

Prophets were sent to tell people of their faults, and to warn them of the judgments of God, so the prophet is employed in this and the following chapters as counsel for the King of kings, opening an indictment against the people of Israel. I. God's controversy with them, a general prevalency of vice and profaneness (ver. 1, 2), ignorance and forgetfulness of God (ver. 6, 7), the worldly-mindedness of the priests (ver. 8), drunkenness and uncleanness (ver. 11), divination and witchcraft (ver. 12), sacrifice in the high places (ver. 13), whoredoms (ver. 14, 18), and bribery among magistrates, ver. 18. II. He shows them what would be the consequences. God would punish them for these things, ver. 9. The whole land should be laid waste (ver. 3), all sorts of people cut off (ver. 5), their honour lost (ver. 7), their creature-comforts (ver. 10), and themselves made ashamed, ver. 19. And the sorest judgment of all, they should be let alone in their sins (ver. 17), they shall not reprove one another (ver. 4), God will not punish them (ver. 14), nay, he will let them prosper, ver. 16. III. He gives warning to Judah not to tread in the steps of Israel, ver. 15.

Verses 1–5

I. The court set, and attention demanded: "*Hear the word of the Lord, you children of Israel.*" They will be ready enough to hear when God speaks comfortably to them; but are they willing to hear when he has a controversy with them?

II. The indictment read, by which the whole nation stands charged with crimes by which God is highly provoked. 1. They are charged with national omissions of the most important duties. The people seemed to have no sense at all of honesty. Much less had they any sense of mercy, or any obligation they were under to pity and help the poor. What good can be expected where there is no knowledge of God? Hence follow national commissions of enormous sins against both the first and second table. *Swearing*, and *lying*, and *killing*, and *stealing*, and *committing adultery*, against the third, ninth, sixth, eighth, and seventh commandments, were to be found in all corners of the land, v. 2. They *break out*, that is, they transgress all bounds of reason and conscience, and the divine law. When they break out thus *blood touches blood*, murders are committed in all parts of the country. It was about this time that there was so much blood shed in grasping at the crown.

III. Sentence passed upon this guilty land, v. 3. It shall be utterly laid waste. The valleys are said to *mourn* when by war and famine they are made desolate. The destruction of the fruits of the earth shall be so great that there shall not be picking for the *fowls of the air.*

IV. The order (v. 4): *Yet let no man strive nor reprove another*, intimates that as long as there is any hope we ought to reprove sinners for their sins. Yet sometimes they are so hardened in sin that it will be to little purpose either to deal with them or to deal with God for them. *Thy people are as those that strive with the priests.* Those who rebel against ministerial reproof, which is an ordinance of God for their reformation, have forfeited the benefit of brotherly reproof too. Perhaps this may refer to the late wickedness of Joash king of Judah, and his people, who stoned Zechariah, 2 Chron. xxiv. 21. "*Therefore*, because thou wilt take no reproof, *thou shalt* stumble and *fall in the day*, and *the prophet*, the false prophet that flattered thee, shall *fall with thee in the night*; the darkness of the night shall not help to cover thee from trouble nor the light of the day help thee to flee from it." And did the children think that when they were in danger of falling their mother would help them? It shall be in vain to expect it, for *I will destroy thy mother*, Samaria, the mother-city, which is as a mother to every part. It shall all be *made silent*.

Verses 6–11

I. The people *strove with the priests*; justly therefore were they *destroyed for lack of knowledge*, v. 6. Those that rebel against the light can expect no other than to perish in the dark. Or it is a charge upon the priests, who should have been still *teaching the people knowledge* (Eccles. xii. 9), but they did not.

II. Both priests and people rejected knowledge; and justly therefore will God *reject them*. The reason why the people did not learn, and the priests did not teach, was not because they had not the light, but because they hated it.

III. They *forgot the law of God*, nor desired to transmit the remembrance of it to their posterity, and therefore will God *forget them* and *their children*, the people's children. Or it may be meant of the priests' children; they shall not succeed them in the priests' office, 1 Sam. ii. 20.

IV. They dishonoured God, v. 7. It was their honour that they were increased in number, wealth, power, and dignity. The beginning of their nation was small, but it *greatly increased*. But, *as they were increased, so they sinned* against God. Their wealth, honour, and power, did but make them the more daring in sin. Therefore, says God, *will I change their glory into shame.*

V. The priests ate up the sin of God's people, and therefore *they shall eat and not have enough*. They abused the maintenance that was allowed to the priests (v. 8). They *set their hearts* upon the people's *iniquities*; they *lifted up their soul* to them, that is, they were glad when people did commit iniquity, that they might be obliged to bring an offering to make atonement for it, of which they should have their share. God will therefore deny them his blessing upon their maintenance (v. 10): *They shall eat and not have enough*. Though they have great plenty by the abundance of offerings, yet they shall have no satisfaction in it.

VI. The more they increased the more they sinned (v. 7), and therefore though they *commit whoredom*, though they take the most wicked methods to multiply their people, yet *they shall not increase.*

VII. The people and the priests did harden one another in sin; and therefore justly shall they be sharers in the punishment (v. 9): *There shall be, like people, like priest.*

VIII. They indulged themselves in the delights of sense, to hold up their hearts; but they shall find that they *take away their hearts* (v. 11): *Whoredom, and wine, and new wine take away the heart.*

Verses 12–19

I. The sins charged upon the people of Israel. 1. Spiritual whoredom, or idolatry. They have in them a *spirit of whoredoms*, a strong inclination to that sin. So (v. 15) Israel has *played the harlot*; their conduct in the worship of their idols was like that of a harlot, wanton and impudent. And (v. 16), *Israel slideth back as a backsliding heifer*, as an *untamed* heifer (so some), or as a *perverse* or *refractory* one (so others), as a heifer that is turned loose runs madly about the pasture, or, if put under the yoke (which seems rather to be alluded to here), will draw back instead of going forward, will struggle to get her neck out of the yoke and her feet out of the furrow. Thus unruly, ungovernable, untractable, were the people of Israel. *My people ask counsel at their stocks*, their wooden gods. They *say to a stock, Thou art my father* (Jer. ii. 27). (It is probable that this refers to wicked methods of divination by a *piece of wood*, or by *a staff*, like Nebuchadnezzar's divining by *his arrows*, Ezek. xxi. 21.) They offered sacrifice to them as gods (v. 13): to atone and pacify them, and *burn incense* to them, to please and gratify them. They chose places, *upon the tops of the mountains* and *upon the hills*, foolishly imagining that the height of the ground gave them some advantage in their approaches towards heaven; places, *under oaks, and poplars, and elms*, because the shadow thereof is pleasant to them, and they fancied that a thick shade possesses the mind with something of awe, and therefore is proper for devotion.

2. Corporal whoredom is another crime here charged upon them: *They have committed whoredom continually*, v. 18. They drove a trade of uncleanness. Their false gods drew them to it; for the devil whom they worshipped, though a spirit, is an unclean spirit. To punish them for that God gave up their wives and daughters to the like vile affections.

3. The perverting of justice, v. 18. *Their rulers do love, Give ye*, that is, they love bribes, and have it continually in their mouths. Justice, duly administered, is refreshing, like drink to the thirsty, but when it is perverted, and rulers take rewards either to acquit the guilty or to condemn the innocent, the *drink is sour*.

II. The tokens of God's wrath against them for their sins. *I will not punish your daughters;* and, not being punished for their sin, they would go on in it. The impunity of one sinner is sometimes made the punishment of another. They themselves should prosper for a while, but their prosperity should help to destroy them (v. 16): *The Lord will feed them as a lamb in a large place;* but it shall be only to prepare them for the slaughter, as a lamb is that is so fed. But others make them feed as *a lamb on the common,* a large place indeed, but where it has short grass and lies exposed. The Shepherd of Israel will turn them both out of his pastures and out of his protection. *"Ephraim is joined to idols,* is in love with them and addicted to them, and therefore *let him alone,* as v. 4 and v. 17, *Let no man reprove* him." The father corrects not the rebellious son any more when he determines to disinherit him. Those that are not disturbed in their sin will be destroyed for their sin. They should be hurried away with a swift and shameful destruction (v. 19).

III. The warning given to Judah not to sin after the similitude of Israel's transgression. *Though thou, Israel, play the harlot, yet let not Judah offend.* This was a very needful caution. The men of Israel were near neighbours, more numerous, and prosperous. Judah has greater means of knowledge than Israel, has the temple and priesthood, and a king of the house of David; from Judah Shiloh is to come; therefore *let not Judah offend,* for more is expected from them than from Israel, and from them God will take it more unkindly. If *Israel play the harlot,* let not Judah do so too, for then God will have no professing people in the world. *Come not you unto Gilgal,* where *all their wickedness was* (ch. ix. 15; xii. 11); there they *multiplied transgression* (Amos iv. 4). And for the same reason they must *not go up to Bethel,* here called the *house of vanity,* for so *Bethaven* signifies, not the *house of God,* as *Bethel* signifies.

CHAPTER 5

I. They are called to hearken to the charge, ver. 1, 8. II. They are accused of many sins, which are here aggravated. 1. Persecution, ver. 1, 2. 2. Spiritual whoredom, ver. 3, 4. 3. Pride, ver. 5. 4. Apostasy from God, ver. 7. 5. The tyranny of the princes, and the tameness of the people in submitting to it, ver. 10, 11. III. They are threatened with God's displeasure for their sins (ver. 3) and he makes known his wrath against them for it, ver. 9. 1. They shall fall in their iniquity, ver. 5. 2. God will forsake them, ver. 6. 3. Their portions shall be devoured, ver. 7. 4. God will rebuke them, ver. 9, 10. 5. They shall be oppressed, ver. 11. 6. God will be as a moth to them in secret judgments (ver. 12) and as a lion in public judgments, ver. 14. IV. They are blamed for the wrong course they took under their afflictions, ver. 13. V. It is intimated that they shall at length take a right course, ver. 15.

Verses 1–7

I. All orders and degrees of men are cited (v. 1): *Hear you this, O priests!* "Hearken, *you house of Israel,* the common people, and *give ear, O house of the king!"* Let them all take notice, for they have all contributed to the national guilt, and shall share in the national judgments.

II. Witness is produced against them; it is God's omniscience (v. 3): *I know Ephraim, and Israel is not hidden from me.* They have *not known the Lord* (v. 4), but the Lord has known them.

III. They had been industrious to draw people either into sin or into trouble: You have been *a snare on Mizpah, and a net spread upon Tabor* (v. 1). They had been both crafty and cruel in carrying on their designs (v. 2): *The revolters are profaned to make slaughter.* They had *committed whoredom,* defiled their own bodies with fleshly lusts, defiled their own souls with the worship of idols, v. 3. They had no disposition at all to come into acquaintance and communion with God. The *spirit of whoredoms,* having *caused them to err* from him, keeps them wandering endlessly, v. 4. It is true we cannot by our own power, without the special grace of God, turn to him; but we may by the due improvement of our own faculties, and the common aids of his Spirit, *frame our doings* to turn to him. They were guilty of notorious arrogance, and insolence in sin (v. 5): *The pride of Israel doth testify to his face* in the gaiety and gaudiness of their worship, as a harlot is known by her attire, Prov. vii. 10. They departed from God to idols, and bred up their children in idolatry (v. 7). Those deal treacherously with God indeed who not only turn from following him themselves but train up their children in wicked ways.

IV. *"Judgment is towards you.* God is coming forth to contend with you, and to testify his displeasure against you for your sins." They shall *fall in their iniquity.* This follows upon their *pride testifying to their face* (v. 5). *Therefore shall Israel and Ephraim fall in their iniquity.* They shall fall short of God's favour when they profess to seek it (v. 6): *They shall go with their flocks and with their herds to seek the Lord,* but in vain; *they shall not find him.* This seems to be spoken principally of Judah. They went as usual, at the solemn feasts, *with their flocks and herds* to *seek the Lord;* but their hearts were not *entire for him.* Those that go *with their flocks and their herds* only to seek the Lord, and not with their hearts and souls, cannot expect to find him, for his favour is not to be purchased with *thousands of rams.* They and their portions shall all be swallowed up. They have *dealt treacherously against the Lord,* but *now shall a month devour them with their portions.* By their *portions* is meant their idols, whom they chose for their portion instead of God. A *month* shall *devour* them. The judgments of God sometimes make quick work with a sinful people. A month devours more, and more portions, than many years can repair.

Verses 8–15

I. A loud alarm sounded, giving notice of judgments coming (v. 8): *Blow you the cornet in Gibeah* and *in Ramah,* two cities in the confines of the two kingdoms of Judah and Israel, Gibeah a frontier-town of the kingdom of Judah, Ramah of Israel; so that the warning is hereby sent into both kingdoms. *"Cry aloud at Beth-aven,* or Bethel." He had before spoken of the judgments as certain; here he speaks of them as near. The blowing of this cornet is explained, v. 9. *Among the tribes of Israel have I made known that which shall surely be,* that which is *true* or *certain,* so the word is.

II. The ground of God's controversy. He has a quarrel with *the princes of Judah,* because they were daring leaders in sin, v. 10. They have encroached even upon God's rights, have trampled upon the distinctions between good and evil. Some have observed that the princes of Judah were more absolute, and assumed a more arbitrary power, than the princes of Israel did; now, for this, God has a controversy with them: *I will pour out my wrath upon them like water.* He has a quarrel with the *people of Ephraim*, because they were sneaking followers in sin (v. 11): *He willingly walked after the commandment*, that is, the commandment of Jeroboam and the succeeding kings of Israel, who obliged all their subjects by a law to worship the calves at Dan and Bethel, and never to go up to Jerusalem to worship. It is for this that *Ephraim is oppressed and broken in judgment*, has his civil rights and liberties broken. Nothing gives greater advantage to a mastiff-like tyranny, that is fierce and furious, than a spaniel-like submission, that is fawning and flattering.

III. The different methods that God would take both with Judah and Ephraim.

1. He would begin with less judgments, which should sometimes work silently and insensibly (v. 12): *I will be unto Ephraim as a moth;* they *are unto Ephraim as a moth*, for it is such a *sickness* as Ephraim now sees, v. 13. The judgments of God are sometimes to a sinful people *as a moth*, and *as rottenness*, or as *a worm*. Silently, so as they themselves shall not be sensible of it; they shall think themselves safe and thriving, but shall find themselves wasting and decaying. Slowly, and with long delays and intervals, that he may give them *space to repent*.

2. When it appeared that those had not done their work he would come upon them with greater (v. 14): *I will be unto Ephraim as a lion, and to the house of Judah as a young lion.* If less judgments prevail not to do their work, it may be expected that God will send greater. There is a more immediate work of God in some judgments than in others. *I will tear, and go away.*

IV. The different effects of those different methods. When God contended with them by less judgments they sought to creatures for relief, but sought in vain, v. 13. Then they sent *to the Assyrian*, to come to their assistance, made their court to king Jareb, which, some think, was one of the names of Tiglathpileser, king of Assyria, to whom both Israel and Judah applied for relief in their distress, hoping by an alliance to re-establish their declining interests. Carnal hearts, in time of trouble, see their sickness, but do not see the sin that is the cause of it. Instead of going the next way to the Creator, who could relieve them, they go to creatures, who can do them no service. The kings of Assyria, whom Judah and Israel sought unto, *distressed them* and *helped them not*, 2 Chron. xxviii. 16, 28. They had sent him *a present* (ch. x. 6), and, having so retained him, they doubted not of his fidelity to them; but he deceived them, Jer. xvii. 5, 6. When God brought greater judgments upon them, then they would at length be forced to apply to him, v. 15. *I will go and return to my place*, to heaven, or to the mercy-seat, the throne of grace. When God punishes sinners he *comes out of his place* (Isa. xxvi. 21); but, when he designs them favour, he *returns to his place*, where he *waits to be gracious*. He will bring them home to himself, by their afflictions, no longer withdraw from them. Two things are instances of their return: 1. Their penitent confession of sin: *Till they acknowledge their offence;* marg. *Till they be guilty*, that is, till they be sensible of their guilt, and humble themselves before God for it. When men begin to complain more of their sins than of their afflictions then there begins to be some hope of them. 2.Their humble petition for the favour of God: *Till they seek my face.* If they seek him thus, though it might be called seeking him late, yet it is not too late.

CHAPTER 6

The closing words of the foregoing chapter gave us some hopes that God and his Israel, notwithstanding their sins and his wrath, might yet be happily brought together again. Now this chapter carries that matter further. Some did repent and reform. I. Their resolution to return to God, and the comforts wherewith they

encourage themselves in their return, ver. 1–3. II. The instability of many of them in their promises of repentance, and the course which God therefore took with them, ver. 4, 5. III. The covenant God made with them, and his expectations from them (ver. 6); their violation of that covenant, ver. 7–11.

Verses 1–3

These may be taken either as the words of the prophet to the people, calling them to repentance, or as the words of the people to one another.

I. Let us go no more to the Assyrian, nor send to king Jareb; let us *return to the Lord*, return to the worship of him, and to our hope in him.

II. "Let us return to him, for *he has torn, he has smitten. Therefore* let us return to him, because it is for our revolts from him that he has smitten us, and we cannot expect that he should be reconciled to us till we return to him. He that has torn will *heal us*, he that has smitten will *bind us up*," as the skilful surgeon with a tender hand binds up the broken bone or bleeding wound. Of his mercy he will do it; nay, *therefore* he has torn that he may heal. Some think this points particularly to the return of the Jews out of Babylon. They promise themselves that their deliverance out of their troubles shall be to them as *life from the dead* (v. 2): "*After two days he will revive us* (that is, in a short time, in a day or two), *and the third day*, when it is expected that the dead body should be buried *out of our sight*, then will he *raise us up*, and *we shall live in his sight*, and it shall be reviving to us. Though he *forsake* for *a small moment*, he will *gather* with *everlasting kindness*." But this seems to have a further reference to the resurrection of Jesus Christ; and the time may be a figure of Christ's rising the *third day*, for all the prophets testified of *the sufferings of Christ and the glory that should follow.* Though they might not be aware of this mystery in the words, yet now that they are fulfilled to the letter in the resurrection of Christ it is a confirmation that *this is he that should come*, and we are to *look for no other.* And it is suitable that a prophecy of Christ's rising should be thus expressed, "He will raise *us* up, and *we* shall live," for Christ rose as the first-fruits, and we revive with him, we live through him. *Then shall we know, if we follow on to know, the Lord*, v. 3. When God returns in mercy to his people, he will give them more knowledge of himself; the earth shall be *full of that knowledge*, Isa. xi. 9. It may be taken as the fruit of Christ's resurrection, and the life we live by him, that we shall have not only greater means of knowledge, but grace to improve in knowledge. Our knowledge shall be perfected, and yet be eternally increasing. *His going forth is prepared as the morning*, that is, the returns of his favour, which he had withdrawn from us when he *returned to his place. He shall come to us*, and be welcome to us, *as the rain, as the latter and former rain unto the earth*, which refreshes it and makes it fruitful. Now this looks further than their deliverance out of captivity, and was to have its full accomplishment in Christ, and the grace of the gospel. *His going forth was prepared as the morning*, for he came in the fulness of time; *John Baptist* was himself the *bright and morning star. He shall come down as the rain upon the mown grass*, Ps. lxxii. 6. The grace of God in Christ is both the *latter and the former rain*, for by it the good work of our fruit-bearing is both begun and carried on.

Verses 4–11

Two evil things, both Judah and Ephraim are here charged with,

I. That they were unsteady, *unstable as water*, v. 4, 5. *O Ephraim! what shall I do unto thee? O Judah! what shall I do unto thee?* God speaks after the manner of men, to show how absurd and unreasonable they were. God would have done them good, but they were not qualified for it: "*What shall I do unto thee? What else can I do but cast thee off, when I cannot in honour save thee?*" See here their conduct towards God: *Their goodness*, or *kindness*, was *as the morning cloud.* What good appeared in them sometimes soon vanished *as the morning cloud and the early dew.* Shall he accept their goodness? No, for it *passes away.* That goodness will never be either pleasing to God or profitable to ourselves which is as the morning cloud and the early dew. When men promise fair and do not perform, when they are unsteady, uneven, and inconstant, then is their *goodness as the morning cloud and the early dew.* "*Therefore*, because they were so, *I have hewn them by the prophets*, as timber or stone is hewn for use; *I have slain them by the words of my mouth.*" They were ready to say that the prophets killed them, when they dealt faithfully with them. They were uneven in religion (*v.* 4), therefore God hewed them. The hearts of sinners are as rough stone, which requires a great deal of pains to bring it into shape, or as knotty timber, that is not squared without a great deal of difficulty. And there are those whom ministers must rebuke sharply; every word should cut, though the reproved fly in the face of the reprover and reckon him an enemy because he tells the truth.

God accomplished that which was foretold: "*I have slain them* by my judgments, according to the words of my mouth." The word of God will be the death either of the sin or of the sinner. His prophets had taken great pains with them, but the means used had not the desired effect. Now they cannot charge God with severity if he bring upon them the miseries threatened. The prophet acknowledges, *Thy judgments are as the light that goes forth*, evidently just and righteous.

II. That they were not faithful to God's covenant with them, *v.* 6, 7.

1. The covenant that God made with them (*v.* 6): *I desired mercy and not sacrifice*, and insisted upon *the knowledge of God more than* upon *burnt-offerings. Mercy* here is the same word which in *v.* 4 is rendered *goodness—chesed—piety, sanctity*; it is put for all practical religion; it is the same with *charity* in the New Testament, the reigning love of God and our neighbour. This is fully explained, Jer. vii. 22, 23. Perhaps this is mentioned here to show a difference between the God whom they deserted and the gods to whom they went. The *power of godliness* is the main thing God looks at and requires, and without it the *form of godliness* is of no avail.

2. How little they had regarded this covenant! There were *good things committed* to them to keep, the jewels of mercy and piety, and the knowledge of God, in the cabinet of sacrifice and burnt-offering, but they betrayed their trust, kept the cabinet, but pawned the jewels for the gratification of a base lust, and this is that for which God has justly a quarrel with them (*v.* 7). *They, like Adam, have transgressed the covenant* (so it might very well be read); as he transgressed the covenant of innocency, so they transgressed the covenant of grace. Dealing treacherously with God is here called dealing treacherously against him, for it is both an affront and an opposition. Look on the other side Jordan, to the country most exposed to neighbouring nations, and where therefore the people were concerned to keep themselves under the divine protection, and there you will find the most daring provocations of the divine Majesty, *v.* 8. Gilead, which lay in the lot of Gad and the half tribe of Manasseh, was *a city of the workers of iniquity.* Ramoth Gilead is one of the three cities of refuge on the other side Jordan, and a Levites' city; the inhabitants, though of the sacred tribe, were *workers of iniquity.* They would, for a bribe, protect those that were guilty of wilful murder. Those whose business it

was to minister in holy things were as bad as the worst (*v.* 9). The *companies of priests* were cruel and bloodthirsty. They were cunning. *They murder in the way to Shechem* (so the margin reads it, as a proper name) such as were going to Jerusalem (for that way Shechem lay) to worship. Or *in the way to Shechem* (some think) means in the same manner that their father Levi, with Simeon his brother, murdered the Shechemites (Gen. xxxiv), by fraud and deceit. *There is the whoredom of Ephraim*, both corporal and spiritual whoredom; too plain to be denied. Look into Judah, and you find them sharing with Israel (*v.* 11): *Also, O Judah! he has set a harvest for thee;* thou that hast *ploughed iniquity*, and *sown wickedness*, shalt *reap the same.*

CHAPTER 7

I. A general charge drawn up against Israel for those high crimes and misdemeanours by which they had obstructed the course of God's favours to them, ver. 1, 2. II. A particular accusation, 1. Of the court—the king, princes, and judges, ver. 3–7. 2. Of the country. Ephraim is here charged with conforming to the nations (ver. 8), senselessness and stupidity under the judgments of God (ver. 9–11), ingratitude to God for his mercies (ver. 13), incorrigibleness under his judgments (ver. 14), contempt of God (ver. 15), and hypocrisy in their pretences to return to him, ver. 16. They are also threatened with a severe chastisement, which shall humble them (ver. 12), and, if that prevail not, then with an utter destruction (ver. 13), particularly their princes, ver. 16.

Verses 1–7

I. A general idea given of the present state of Israel, *v.* 1, 2.

1. God graciously designed to do well for them: *I would have healed Israel.* He would have reformed them, would have purged out the corruptions that were among them. He would have delivered them out of their troubles, and restored to them their peace and prosperity. Their own folly put them back again.

2. They stood in their own light and put a bar in their own door. When God *would have healed them* that wickedness which had been concealed was *found out.* When endeavours were used to reform them vice grew more outrageous. They dissemble with God in their professions of repentance.

3. A practical disbelief of God's omniscience and government was at the bottom of all their wickedness (*v.* 2): "*They consider not in their hearts*, they never say it to their own hearts, never think of this, *that I remember all their wickedness.*" This is the sinner's atheism; as good say that there is *no God* as say that he is either ignorant or forgetful. But the time will come when those who thus deceive themselves shall be undeceived: *Now their own doings have beset them about.*

4. God had begun his judgments: *The thief comes in, and the troop of robbers spoils without.* Some take this as an instance of their wickedness, that they robbed and spoiled one another. It seems rather to be a punishment of their sin; they were infested with secret thieves among themselves, and *troops of robbers*, foreign invaders, that with open violence *spoiled abroad.*

II. A particular account of the sins of the court, of the king and princes, who were pleased with the wickedness of their subjects (*v.* 3): *They make the king and princes glad with their wickedness.* Drunkenness and revelling abound much at the court, *v.* 5. The *day of our king* was a merry day with them, and they *made him sick with bottles of wine.* When he was thus intoxicated, he *stretched out his hand with scorners*; then he that was entrusted with the government of a kingdom lost the government of himself. Adultery and uncleanness prevailed much among the courtiers. This is spoken of *v.* 4, 6, 7, and the charge of drunkenness comes in in the midst of this article; for wine is oil to the fire of lust, Prov. xxiii.

33. *Adulterers* (v. 4) are here again and again compared to an oven heated by the baker (v. 4): *They have made ready their heart like an oven* (v. 6); *they are all hot as an oven*, v. 7. An unclean heart is like an oven heated. The baker kindled a fire in his oven and laid sufficient fuel to it. In the morning he finds his oven well heated, and ready for his purpose. So these wicked people, when they have formed a design for the gratifying of some covetous or unclean lusts, have their hearts so fully set in them to do evil that, though they may stifle them for a while, yet the fire is still glowing within, and, as soon as there is an opportunity for it, their purposes break out into overt acts, as a fire flames out when it has vent given it. *They have devoured their judges*, those few good judges that were among them, that would have put out these fires with which they were heated. *All their kings* have *fallen* one after another, and their families with them, which could not but put the kingdom into confusion. There are heart-burnings; they are *hot as an oven* with rage and malice at one another, and this occasions the *devouring of their judges*, the *falling* of their *kings*. But in the midst of all this disorder *there is none among them that calls unto God.*

Verses 8–16

The *iniquity of Ephraim is discovered*, as well as *the sin of Samaria*, of the people as well as the princes.

I. They did not distinguish themselves from the heathen, as God had distinguished them: *Ephraim, he has mingled himself among the people*, has associated with them, and conformed himself to them, and lost his character among them. They went up and down among the heathen, to beg help of one of them against another. They were not entirely devoted to God: *Ephraim is a cake not turned*, and so is burnt on one side and dough on the other side, but good for nothing on either side.

II. They were strangely insensible of the judgments of God, v. 9. They were slowly drawing towards the ruin of their state partly by the encroachments of foreigners: *Strangers have devoured his strength*, and eaten him up. Some devoured them by open wars (as 2 Kings xiii. 7, when the king of Syria made them *like the dust by threshing*), others by pretending treaties of peace, in which they made them pay dearly for that which did them no good, as 2 Kings xvi. 9. They were reduced partly by their own maladministrations: *Yea, gray hairs are here and there upon him*, that is, the sad symptoms of a decaying declining state, which is *waxing old* and *ready to vanish away.*

III. They went on in their wicked ways (v. 10): *The pride of Israel* still *testifies to his face*, as it had done before (ch. v. 5); their hearts were still unhumbled; they *do not return to the Lord their God*, though they suffer for going astray, yet they think not of applying to God.

IV. They took wrong methods when they were in distress (v. 11, 12): *Ephraim is like a silly dove without heart.* To be harmless as a dove is commendable; but to be sottish as a dove is shame. This dove laments not the loss of her young that are taken from her, but will make her nest again in the same place; so they have their people carried away by the enemy, but continue their dealings with those that deal barbarously with them. She is easily enticed into the net, and has *no heart*, no understanding, to discern her danger. So they were drawn into leagues with neighbouring nations that were their ruin. When she is frightened, she has not courage to stay where she is safe, under the careful protection of her owner, but hovers, seeking shelter first in one place, then in another, and exposes herself the more. So this people in distress did not fly *like the doves to their windows*, where they might have been secured

from the birds of prey, but threw themselves out of God's protection, and *called to Egypt* to help them, and went *to Assyria*, to seek that aid which they might, by repentance, and prayer, have found in their God. They are ensnared: "*I will spread my net upon them*, bring them into straits, that they may see their folly and think of returning." They soar upward, proud of their foreign alliances; but *I will bring them down. I will chastise them as their congregation has heard;* they have been many a time told that *vain is the help of man*, that *in the son of man there is no help;* they have heard both from the law and from the prophets, and *as they have heard* now *they shall see*, they shall feel.

V. They revolted from God notwithstanding the methods he took to retain them, v. 13–15. God, as a gracious sovereign towards a people dear unto him, had *redeemed them* (v. 13), and delivered them out of many a distress. He had *bound and strengthened their arms*, v. 15. When their power was weakened, like an arm broken, God set it again. He had given Israel victories over the Syrians (2 Kings xiii. 16, 17), had *restored their coast* (2 Kings xiv. 25, 26), had *girded them with strength for battle.* He had taken them into covenant but *they fled from him*, as if he had been their dangerous enemy. He had given them his laws, which were all holy, just, and good, by which he designed to keep them in the right way; but they *transgressed against him.* They rejected his messages sent them by his prophets. In their hypocritical professions of religion, and promises of amendment, they lied to the Lord. He designed well for them, but they *imagined mischief against him*, v. 15. Sin is a mischievous thing; it is mischief against God, it is treason. They shall be punished for this (v. 13): *Woe unto them! for they have fled from me.*

VI. Their shows of devotion were but shows, v. 14. When they were under personal troubles, and called upon God, they were not sincere. They used many good words, but they did not *cry with their heart*, and therefore God reckons it as no crying to him. Moses is said to *cry unto God* when he spoke not a word, only his heart prayed with faith, Exod. xiv. 15. These made a great noise, and yet did not *cry to God*, because their hearts were not *right with him.* God is so far from approving their prayer and accepting it that he calls it *howling.* Some think it intimates the *noisiness* of their prayers as they used to cry to Baal. They did not pray for the grace of God or that God would pardon their sins, but only that he would not take away from them *their corn and wine.* Carnal hearts covet temporal mercies only, and dread no other but temporal judgments. They pretended reformation, but neither was that sincere, v. 16. *They return*, that is, they make as if they would return; whereas God says (Jer. iv. 1), *If thou wilt return, O Israel! return to me;* do not only *turn towards me*, but *return to me.* This dissimulation of theirs makes them like a *deceitful bow*, which is bent and drawn, but when strength comes to be laid to it, either the bow or the string breaks. The sin of the princes of Israel is *the rage of their tongue*, quarrelling with God and with all about them. The princes shall *fall by the sword* either of their enemies or of their own people, and *this shall be their derision*, v. 16.

CHAPTER 8

This chapter, as that before, divides itself into the sins and punishments of Israel. I. The sin of Israel is set forth, 1. In many general expressions, ver. 1, 3, 12, 14. 2. In many particular instances; setting up kings without God (ver. 4), setting up idols against God (ver. 4–6, 11), and courting alliances with the neighbouring nations, ver. 8–10. 3. They still kept up a profession of religion and relation to God, ver. 2, 13, 14. II. The punishment of Israel is set forth answering to the sin. God would bring an enemy upon them, ver. 1, 3. All their projects should be blasted, ver. 7. Their confidence in their idols and in their foreign alliances should disappoint them, ver. 6, 8, 10. Their strength at home should fail them, ver. 14.

Verses 1–7

The prophet must sound an alarm. An enemy is coming to seize their land.

I. The people have *transgressed my covenant*, v. 1. They have not only done foolishly, but have dealt deceitfully. They have *trespassed against my law*. They have cast off *the thing that is good*; the service and worship of God, which is, in effect, *casting God off*.

II. *The enemy shall come as an eagle against the house of the Lord*, and (v. 3) *shall pursue him*. If by *the house of the Lord* we understand the temple at Jerusalem, by the eagle we must suppose to be meant either Sennacherib, or Nebuchadnezzar, who burnt the temple. But, if we make it to point at the destruction of the kingdom of the ten tribes by the king of Assyria, we must reckon it is the body of that people which, as Israelites, is here called the *house of the Lord*. Those who break their covenant of friendship with God make themselves a cheap and easy prey.

III. The people's hypocritical claim of relation to God (v. 2): *Israel shall cry unto me;* and in their distress will pretend to that knowledge of God's ways which in their prosperity they *desired not*, but *despised*. But what stead will it stand a man in to be able to say, *My God, I know thee*, when he cannot say, "My God, I love thee"?

IV. The prophet's expostulation (v. 5): *How long will it be ere they attain to innocency?* It is not meant of absolute innocency, but how long will it be ere they become innocent and free from the sin of idolatry? In trouble they cry, *How long* will it be ere God return to us in a way of mercy? but they do not hear him ask, *How long* will it be ere they return to God in a way of duty?

V. Some particular sins.

1. In their civil affairs. They *set up kings without God*, v. 4. So they did when they rejected Samuel and chose Saul. So they did when they set up Jeroboam. So they did now about the time when Hosea prophesied, when it seems to have grown fashionable to *set up kings*, and depose them again, 2 Kings xv. 8, &c.

2. In their religious matters they did much worse; for they *set up calves against God*. They called them *gods* (1 Kings xii. 28, *Behold thy gods, O Israel!*) but God calls them *idols*; the word signifies *griefs*, or *troubles*, because they are offensive to God and will be ruining to those that worship them. Trace them to their original, and they will be found the creatures of their fancies and the work of their hands, v. 6. The calf they worshipped is here called *the calf of Samaria*, because it is probable that when Samaria, in Ahab's time, became the metropolis of the kingdom, a calf was set up there to be near the court. It was a device of their own (some think), not borrowed from the Egyptians, for, though they worshipped Apis in a living cow, they never worshipped a *golden calf*. The gold and silver of which it was made were collected from the people of Israel: it was a poor god that was framed by contribution. *The workmen made it, therefore it is not God*, v. 6. A made god is no God. If they are not gods, they will not last. They have made to themselves idols, *that they may be cut off* (v. 4) from God, from their own land, from the land of the living. Those that suffer themselves to be deceived into any idolatries will certainly find themselves deceived in them. Their disappointment in their idols is illustrated (v. 7) by a similitude: *They have sown the wind*. They have put themselves to a great deal of trouble and expense to make and worship their idols, as the husbandman does by sowing his corn, in expectation of reaping advantage from it.

They did it to be as prosperous as the neighbouring nations were, that worshipped idols. But it is like *sowing the wind*, which can yield no increase. They shall *reap the whirlwind*, a *great whirlwind*. They have not their false gods for them, but they set the true God against them. The service of idols is an unprofitable service, and the works of darkness are unfruitful; Rom. vi. 21, *The end of those things is death*.

Verses 8–14

I. They multiplied their alliances (v. 9): *They have hired lovers*. They were at great expense to purchase the friendship of the nations about them. Those surely have behaved ill among their neighbours who have no lovers, but what they hire. *Israel is swallowed up*, devoured by strangers, their land eaten up (v. 7), and being impoverished, they have lost their reputation, like a merchant that has become a bankrupt. Israel made court to the nations notwithstanding (v. 9): They have *gone to Assyria* to help them; and herein they are as a *wild ass alone by himself*, headstrong, and unruly. *Though they have hired among the nations*, what they provided for their own safety shall but make them easier prey to their enemies. The king of Assyria, whose friendship they courted, laid *burdens* upon Israel, levied taxes upon them, 2 Kings xv. 19, 20. And for these *they shall sorrow a little*. *They have begun to be diminished* (so some read it), *by the burden of the king of princes* (see Isa. x. 8).

II. They multiplied their altars and temples. They denied *the power of godliness* (v. 12): *I have written to him the great things of my law*. The things of God's law are *magnalia Dei—the great things of God*. They are things that proclaim the greatness of the Law-maker, things of great importance to us; they are our life, and our eternal welfare depends upon our observance of them and obedience to them. It is a great privilege to have the things of God's law written. Moses and the prophets were his amanuenses, and holy men wrote as they were moved by the Holy Ghost. And, if those were happy who had the *great things of God's law* written to them, how much happier are we who have the much greater things of his gospel written to us! But these great things of the law were *counted as a strange thing*, as unintelligible and unreasonable. *We desire not the knowledge of thy ways*. They kept up the form of godliness notwithstanding to little purpose. They multiplied their altars (v. 11): *Ephraim made many altars to sin*. Their multiplying of altars dedicated to the God of Israel would introduce altars dedicated to other gods. They multiplied their sacrifices, v. 13. Their altars were smoking altars: They *sacrificed flesh for the sacrifices of God's offerings*, as if they hoped by their observing a ceremonial law of their own to excuse themselves from the obligation of all God's moral precepts. *The Lord accepts them not*. How should he, when they only sacrificed flesh, but not the spiritual sacrifice of a penitent believing heart? A petition for leave to sin amounts to an imprecation of the curse for sin, and so it shall be answered, *according to the multitude of the idols*. *Israel has forgotten his Maker*, v. 14, *and builds temples*. Some by temples here understand *palaces*, which defy God's judgments. Judah is likewise charged with *multiplying fenced cities*, and trusting in them for safety, when the judgments of God were abroad.

CHAPTER 9

I. God threatens to deprive this degenerate seed of Israel of all their worldly enjoyments, ver. 1–5. II. He dooms them to ruin, for their own sins and the sins of their prophets, ver. 6–8. III. He upbraids them with the wickedness of their fathers whose steps they trod in, ver. 9, 10. IV. He threatens them with the rooting out of their posterity, ver. 11–17.

Verses 1-6

I. The people of Israel are charged with spiritual adultery: *O Israel! thou hast gone a whoring from thy God, v.* 1. When they set up idols and worshipped them, they *went a whoring from God* as their God, and honoured the pretenders with the affection, adoration, and confidence, which were due to God only. *They loved a reward upon every corn-floor,* to give to their idols the offerings and first-fruits. Or, they loved to receive rewards from their idols; and such they reckoned the fruits of the earth to be.

II. They are forbidden to rejoice: "*Rejoice not, O Israel! for joy. What peace,* what joy, what hast thou to do with either, while thy whoredoms and witchcrafts are so many?" (2 Kings ix. 19-22). Some think that they had at this time particular occasions for joy, probably upon the account of some league made with a potent ally.

III. They are threatened with judgments for their spiritual whoredoms. Their land shall not yield its wonted increase. Canaan, that *fruitful land,* shall be *turned into barrenness for the wickedness of those that dwell therein* (*v.* 2). *The floor and the winepress shall not feed them,* much less feast them. Their land shall not only cease to feed them, but cease to be a habitation for them; it shall *spue them out,* as it had done the Canaanites before them (*v.* 3). It was a sad and sore judgment to be driven out from such a land as this; it was like driving our first parents out of the garden of Eden. Note, Those cannot expect to dwell in the Lord's land that will not be subject to the Lord's laws. They shall have no rest nor satisfaction in any other land. Some shall *return into Egypt,* the old house of bondage; thither they shall flee from the Assyrian (*ch.* viii. 13). Others shall be carried captives to Assyria and there shall be forced to *eat unclean things*—things not fit for Jews to eat, being prohibited by their law. In the land of their enemies they shall have no opportunity either of giving honour to God or obtaining favour with God, by offering any acceptable sacrifice to him. They shall have no sacrifices to offer, nor any altar. They shall not so much as *offer drink-offerings* to the Lord, much less any other sacrifices. Instead of sacrifices of joy they shall *eat the bread of mourners.* Their *bread for their soul,* the bread which they shall have for the support of their lives, *shall not come into the house of the Lord.* The return of the days of their sacred feasts would therefore be uncomfortable to them (*v.* 5). They should perish in the land of their dispersion (*v.* 6): *For, lo, they have gone* out of the Lord's land, *gone because of destruction,* gone to Egypt because of the destruction of their own country by the Assyrians, flattering themselves that they shall return when the storm is over; but they shall find there are *graves in Egypt,* as their murmuring ancestors said (Exod. xiv. 11). As for *their tabernacles,* where they formerly dwelt and kept their stores, *the pleasant places for their silver,* they shall be laid in ruins, be overgrown with *nettles.*

Verses 7-10

I. The destruction spoken of shall come speedily. It is at the door (*v.* 7): *The days of visitation have come, the days of recompence have come,* and the time of the divine patience has expired.

II. Hereby they shall be made ashamed of their sentiments concerning their prophets. 1. They shall know then that the pretenders to prophecy, who flattered them in their sins, and rocked them asleep in their security (as Ahab's prophets did, 1 Kings xxii. 24), were *fools* and *madmen.* 2. They shall know then the *true prophets,* God's faithful ambassadors to them. Mocking the messengers of the Lord was the sin for which they were punished.

III. The wickedness of the false prophets themselves shall be manifested to their shame (*v.* 8). "The *watchman of Ephraim* pretends to have been *with my God,* and prefaces his lies with, *Thus saith the Lord;* but he is *a snare of a fowler in all his ways. The best things, when corrupted, become the worst.*

IV. God will now reckon with them for the sins of their fathers, *v.* 9, 10. They were as bad as their fathers: *They have deeply corrupted themselves;* they are far gone in the *depths of Satan* (Isa. xxxi. 6). Lewdness and wickedness were as impudent and daring now as in the days of Gibeah; and therefore what can be expected but such a vengeance as was then taken on Gibeah? Hence God takes occasion to upbraid them with the degeneracy of their ancestors, *v.* 10. God first formed them into a people: *I found Israel like grapes in the wilderness.* He took as much delight in them as a poor traveller would if he found grapes in a wilderness. God set them apart for himself as a peculiar people, but they went to Baal-peor, joined with the Moabites in sacrificing to that dirty dunghill deity (Num. xxv. 2, 3), and they *separated themselves unto that shame,* that shameful idol. This was the way of their fathers; God had done well for them, but they had acted ungratefully towards him, and in the same manner had the present generation *deeply corrupted themselves.*

Verses 11-17

I. The sin of Ephraim. Their worship was corrupt (*v.* 15): *All their wickedness is in Gilgal,* a place infamous for idolatry, as appears, *ch.* iv. 15; xii. 11; Amos iv. 4; v. 5. That place had been famous in other ages for solemn transactions between God and Israel, as Joshua v. 2, 10; 1 Sam. x. 8; xi. 15. Grotius conjectures that there is a mystical sense here. Golgotha in Syriac is the same with Gilgal in Hebrew, and therefore he thinks this may have reference to the putting of Christ to death at Golgotha, which was the greatest sin of the Jewish nation, and of which it might truly be said, *All their wickedness* was summed up in that.

II. The displeasure of God against Ephraim. He *departs from them, v.* 12. He hates them. *In Gilgal,* where *all their wickedness is, there I hated them.* There, where the abominations of sin are committed, there God abominates the sinners. *For the wickedness of their doings, I will drive them out of my house.* They shall be *castaways.*

III. The fruits of this displeasure comes in the cutting off and abandoning of their posterity. The name *Ephraim* is derived from *fruitfulness,* Gen. xli. 52. Moses's blessing foretold the *ten thousands of Ephraim,* Deut. xxxiii. 17. This was his glory, *v.* 11. Ephraim is as strong and rich as ever Tyre was, and as proud and secure. *Their glory shall fly away like a bird* (*v.* 11); their children shall be taken away and the hopes of their families cut off. *Ephraim is smitten; their root is dried up; they shall bear no fruit, v.* 16. They shall perish of themselves (*v.* 11): They shall *fly away from the birth, and from the womb, and from the conception.* They shall perish by the hand of their enemies; they shall die violent deaths (*v.* 12). Again (*v.* 13), *Ephraim shall bring forth his children to the murderer.* The mothers shall travail with pain to bear their children, and a cruel enemy comes and puts all to the sword. The Chaldee-paraphrase, and many of the rabbin, by the *murderers* to whom the children were brought forth, understand those that sacrificed their children to Moloch. Those few that escape shall be dispersed (*v.* 17): They shall be *wanderers among the nations.* The prophet's prayer relating to it (*v.* 14): *Give them, O Lord! what wilt thou give?* Rather let them have no children than have them to be made miserable. Christ said, *Blessed is the womb that never bore and the paps that never gave* suck, Luke xxiii. 29. "Give therefore *a miscarrying womb and dry breasts*; for it is better to fall into the hands of the Lord, whose mercies are great, than into the hands of man."

CHAPTER 10

I. The people of Israel are charged with gross corruptions in the worship of God, ver. 1, 2, 5, 6, 8. II. They are charged with corruptions in the administration of the civil government, ver. 3, 4, 7. III. They are charged with imitating the sins of their fathers, and their own sins, ver. 9–11. IV. They are earnestly invited to repent and reform, ver. 12–15.

Verses 1–8

I. National sins bring down national judgment.

1. They were not fruitful in the fruits of righteousness. Here all their wickedness began (v. 1): *Israel is an empty vine*. A vine is of all trees least serviceable if it do not bear fruit. It is thenceforth good for nothing, Ezek. xv. 3, 5.

2. They multiplied their altars and images, and the more bountiful God's providence was to them the more prodigal they were in serving their idols.

3. Their hearts were divided, v. 2. They were at variance about their idols, at variance about their kings, and alienated one from another, and there was no such thing as friendship among them. They *halted between God and Baal*, that was the dividing of their heart.

4. They made no conscience of what they said and what they did in the most solemn manner, v. 4. They *swore falsely in making a covenant*; subjects violated their oaths of allegiance and kings their coronation-oaths; they broke their leagues with the nations. God is greatly offended with corruptions, not only in his own worship, but in the administration of justice between man and man.

II. They shall have no joy of their kings and of their government. *Now they shall say, "We have no king*, that is, we are as if we had none, none to preserve the public peace nor to fight our battles; and justly has this come to us." Those that keep themselves in the fear and favour of God may say, "What can the greatest of men do against us?" But those that throw themselves out of his protection must say, with despair, "What can the greatest of men do for us?" Their civil government shall not only be weakened, but quite destroyed (v. 7): *As for Samaria, the royal city, her king is cut off as the foam from the water*. The foam makes a great show upon the face of the water, yet it is but a heap of bubbles. Such were the kings of Israel, after their revolt from the house of David, a mere scum; their government had no foundation. He *shall break down their altars*. God shall do it by the hand of the Assyrians: the Assyrians shall do it by order from God. He *shall spoil their images*, v. 2. If the grace of God prevail not to destroy the love of sin in us, it is just that the providence of God should destroy the food and fuel of sin about us. *The thorn and the thistle* shall *come up on their altars*, that is, they shall lie in ruins. Thus idolaters are brought in trembling when God arises to *shake terribly the earth*, Isa. ii. 21. And here (v. 8), *They shall say to the mountains, Cover us; and to the hills, Fall on us*.

Verses 9–15

I. They are put in mind of the sins of their fathers. It was told them (ch. ix. 9) that they had *corrupted themselves, as in the days of Gibeah*, and here (v. 9), *O Israel! thou hast sinned from the days of Gibeah*. The wickedness that was committed in that age is revived in this, and reacted. It has been continued in a constant series and succession through all the intervening ages. The case was bad then, for *there they stood*; and *the battle in Gibeah against the*

children of iniquity did not overtake them till the third engagement, and then did not overtake them all, for 600 made their escape. But thy sin is worse than theirs.

II. They have warning given them of the judgments of God that were coming upon them, v. 10. God had hitherto pitied and spared them. Because God does not desire the death and ruin of sinners, therefore he does desire their chastisement. "Because they receive not chastisement from me by my prophets, who in my name rebuke them, I will chastise them by the hands of the people who shall be *gathered against them, when they shall bind themselves in their two furrows*," that is, within a double entrenchment. Or, *When I shall bind them for their two transgressions* (so the margin reads it), meaning their corporal and spiritual whoredom. Or, *When I shall bind them to their two furrows*, that is, bring them into servitude to the Assyrians, as oxen in the plough, who are bound to the two furrows up the field and down it. Thus those that would not be God's freemen shall be their enemies' slaves.

III. Ephraim is *as a heifer that is taught to tread out the corn, and loves* that work, because, not muzzled, she has liberty to eat at pleasure, v. 11. "But," says God, "I have a yoke to put upon her fair neck. I will make Ephraim to ride*, I will cause them to be ridden by the Assyrians and other conquerors that shall rule them with rigour, as men do the beasts they ride upon (Ps. lxvi. 12); and *Judah shall be made to plough, and Jacob to break the clods*," that is, they shall be used hardly, but not so hardly as Ephraim. Dr. Pocock inclines to another sense of these words, as intimating the gentle methods God took with this people, to bring them into obedience to his law; he had managed them as the husbandman does his cattle that he trains up for service. Ephraim a docile heifer, fit to be employed, God took hold of her fair neck, to accustom her to the hand, *harnessed her*, or put the yoke of his commandment upon her, gave his people Israel a law, that they might not be tempted by the usages of the heathen. He had used all fair and likely means with them to keep them in their obedience, had set *Judah to plough* and *Jacob to break the clods*, and yet they would not be retained in their obedience, but started aside.

IV. They are invited and encouraged to return to God by prayer, repentance, and reformation, v. 12, 13. They are *God's husbandry* (1 Cor. iii. 9), and the duties are expressed in language borrowed from the husbandman's calling. Let them *break up the fallow ground*; let them cleanse their hearts from all corrupt affections and lusts, which are as weeds and thorns, and let them be of a broken and contrite spirit; let them prepare to receive the divine precepts, as the ground that is ploughed is to receive the seed, that it may take root. See Jer. iv. 3. Let them *sow to themselves in righteousness*; let them return to the practice of good works, and let them *sow to the Spirit*, as the apostle speaks, Gal. vi. 7, 8. Let them *seek the Lord*; let them look up to him for his grace, and beg of him to bless the *seed sown*. It is time to do it; it is *high time*. If we *sow to ourselves in righteousness* —if we be careful and diligent to do our duty, in a dependence upon his grace—he will shower down his grace upon us, will *rain righteousness*, the very thing that those need most who are to sow *in righteousness*. We have *ploughed wickedness and reaped iniquity*; and the time *past of our life may suffice* that we have done so, v. 13. "You have taken a great deal of pains in the service of sin, and will you grudge to bear the burden and heat of the day in God's service? You have done much to damn your souls; will you not undo it again, and do something to save them?" *"Thou didst trust in thy ways, in the multitude of thy mighty men;* thou hast stayed thyself upon creatures,* thy own power and policy, and thy hopes have deceived thee; come therefore, and seek the Lord, and thy hope in him shall not deceive thee."

V. They are threatened with utter destruction, both for their carnal practices and for their carnal confidences, *v.* 14, 15. *Therefore, a tumult shall arise among thy people,* either by insurrections at home or invasions from abroad. The *fortresses* which they confided in, shall be seized and rifled, as *Shalman spoiled Beth-arbel in the day of battle.* This refers to some event that had lately happened, and probably Shalman is the same with Shalmaneser king of Assyria, who had lately sacked some town, or castle (*Beth-arbel is the house of Arbel*), to terrify other garrisons into a speedy surrender. God tells them that thus Samaria should be *spoiled.* The inhabitants shall be put to the *sword,* as it was at *Beth-arbel. In a morning shall the king of Israel utterly be cut off, v.* 15. Hoshea was the last king of Israel; in him the whole kingdom was *cut off*; it may refer to him or to some of his predecessors that were cut off by treachery. It shall be done *in a morning,* as suddenly as the dawning of the morning. What is the spring of this bloodshed? He tells us (*v.* 15): *So shall Bethel do unto you.* Bethel was the place where one of the calves was; Gilgal, where *all their wickedness* is said to have been, was hard by; there was their *great wickedness,* the *evil of their evil* (so the word is), the sum and quintessence of their sin. He does not say, "So shall the *king of Assyria* do to you"; but, "So shall *Bethel* do to you." Whatever mischief is done to us it is sin that does it.

CHAPTER 11

I. The great goodness of God towards his people Israel, ver. 1, 3, 4. II. Their ungrateful conduct towards him, ver. 2–4, 7, 12. III. Threatenings of wrath against them for their treachery, ver. 5, 6. IV. Mercy remembered in the midst of wrath, ver. 8, 9. V. Promises of what God would yet do for them, ver. 10, 11. VI. An honourable character given of Judah, ver. 12.

Verses 1–7

I. God very gracious to Israel. 1. He had a kindness for them when they were young (*v.* 1): *When Israel was a child then I loved him;* when they first began to multiply into a nation in Egypt God then *set his love upon them,* and *chose them because he loved them,* Deut. vii. 7, 8. When they were helpless as children, foolish as children, when they were outcasts, and children exposed, then God *loved them.* Those that have grown up, nay, those that have grown old, ought often to reflect upon the goodness of God to them in their childhood. 2. He delivered them out of the house of bondage: *I called my son out of Egypt,* because a beloved son. These words are said to have been fulfilled in Christ, when, upon the death of Herod, he and his parents were *called out of Egypt* (Matt. ii. 15). The calling of Christ out of Egypt was a figure of the calling of all that are his, through him, out of spiritual slavery. *I taught Ephraim also to go,* as a child in leading-strings is taught. *He taught them to go* in the way of his commandments, by the institutions of the ceremonial law, which were as tutors. When anything was amiss with them he was their physician: *I healed them.* He brought them into his service by mild and gentle methods (*v.* 4): *I drew them with cords of a man, with bands of love.* He draws, (1) *With the cords of a man,* with such cords as men draw with that have a principle of humanity. (2) *With bands of love,* or *cart-ropes* of love. This word signifies stronger cords than the former. He eased them of burdens: *I was to them as those that take off the yoke on their jaws,* alluding to the care of the good husbandman, who is merciful to his beast, and will not tire him with hard and constant labour. In Egypt they fared hard, but, when

God brought them out, he *laid meat unto them,* as the husbandman, when he has unyoked his cattle, fodders them. God rained manna about their camp, bread from heaven, angels' food.

II. Israel ungrateful to God. They were deaf and disobedient to his voice. They were fond of idols, and worshipped them. Idolatry was the sin which from the beginning, and all along, had most easily beset them. They were regardless of God, and of his favours to them: *They knew not that I healed them.* Ignorance is at the bottom of ingratitude, *ch.* ii. 8. They were strongly inclined to apostasy. This is the blackest article in the charge (*v.* 7): *My people are bent to backsliding from me.* They are *bent to back-slide;* they are ready to sin. It also intimates that they are resolute in sin; their hearts are *fully set in them to do evil.* They were strangely averse to repentance and reformation. *They refused to return, v.* 5. God's prophets and ministers called them to return to the God from whom they had revolted, to the most high God, from whom they had sunk into this wretched degeneracy; but they called in vain.

III. God had brought them out of Egypt to take them for a people to himself but they would not be faithful to him (*v.* 5): "*Therefore Israel shall not return into the land of Egypt,* though that was a house of bondage grievous enough; but he shall go into a harder service, for *the Assyrian shall be his king,* who will use him worse than ever Pharaoh did." God, who gave them Canaan, shall bring his judgments upon them there (*v.* 6): *The sword* shall come upon them, the sword of a foreign enemy, triumphing over them. They continued their rebellions against God, and therefore God continued his judgments on them.

Verses 8–12

I. God's debate within himself concerning Israel's case, a debate between justice and mercy, in which victory plainly inclines to mercy's side. Not that there are such struggles in God as there are in us, but they are expressions after the manner of men, to show what severity the sin of Israel had deserved, and yet how divine grace would spare them notwithstanding. *How shall I give thee up?* 1. The proposals that justice makes concerning Israel. Let Ephraim be given up, as an incorrigible son. Let Israel be delivered into the enemy's hand, as a lamb to the lion to be torn in pieces; let them be made as Admah and set as Zeboim, the two cities that with Sodom and Gomorrah were destroyed. Ephraim and Israel deserve to be thus abandoned, and God will do them no wrong if he deal thus with them. 2. The opposition that mercy makes to these proposals: *How shall I do it?* As the tender father reasons with himself, "How can I cast off my untoward son? for he is my son. I cannot do it. They have been a people near unto me; there are yet some good among them; it may be they will yet repent and reform; and therefore how can I do it?" God speaks as if he were conscious to himself of a strange striving of affections in compassion to Israel: *My repentings are kindled together.* After a long contest mercy rejoices against judgment, and carries the day, *v.* 9. It is decreed that the reprieve shall be lengthened out yet longer, and *I will not* now *execute the fierceness of my anger.* They shall be corrected, but not consumed. The reason for this determination: *For I am God and not man, the Holy One of Israel.* He is *Lord of his anger,* whereas men's anger commonly lords it over them. It is a great encouragement to our hope in God's mercies to remember that he is *God, and not man.*

II. He will qualify them to receive the good he designs for them (*v.* 10, 11): *They shall walk after the Lord.* It is spoken of the ten tribes, and had its accomplishment, in part, in the return of some of them with those of the two tribes in Ezra's time; but it had its more full accomplishment in God's spiritual Israel, the gospel-church, brought together by the gospel of Christ. They were to be called and brought together. This call should make such an impression as the roaring of a lion makes upon all the beasts of the forest: *When he shall roar then the children shall tremble.* When those whose hearts the gospel reached trembled, and cried out, *What shall we do?*—when they were working out their salvation, and worshipping God with fear and trembling, then this promise was fulfilled. *The children shall tremble from the west.* This seems to have reference to the calling of the Gentiles that lay westward from Canaan, for that way especially the gospel spread. The apostle speaks of *mighty signs and wonders* that were wrought by the preaching of the gospel from *Jerusalem round about to Illyricum*, Rom. xv. 19. Then the children trembled from the west. And, whereas Israel after the flesh was dispersed in Egypt and Assyria, it is promised that they shall be effectually summoned thence (*v.* 11): *They shall tremble;* they shall come with all haste, *as a bird* upon the wing, *out of Egypt,* and *as a dove out of the land of Assyria.* Those that lay most remote from each other shall meet in Christ, and be incorporated in the church. Our holy trembling at the word of Christ will draw us to him, not drive us from him. When he *roars like a lion* the slaves tremble and flee from him, the children tremble and flee to him. At their return (*v.* 11): *I will place them in their houses;* all those that come at the gospel-call shall have a place and a name in the gospel-church. They shall dwell in God, and be at home in him as a man in his own house; they shall have mansions, for there are many in *our Father's house.*

III. The treachery of Ephraim and Israel may be an intimation that it is not Israel after the flesh, but the spiritual Israel, to whom the foregoing promises belong, for as for this Ephraim, this Israel, they *compass God about with lies and deceit.*

IV. A pleasant commendation of the integrity of the two tribes comes as an aggravation of the perfidiousness of the ten tribes, and a reason why God had that mercy in store for Judah which he had not for Israel (*ch.* i. 6, 7). *Judah rules with God,* that is, he serves God, and the service of God is dignity and dominion. They *walk in the way of good men;* and those that do so *rule with God,* they have a mighty interest in Heaven.

Chapter 12

I. A high charge drawn up against both Israel and Judah for their sins, ver. 1, 2. Particularly the sin of fraud and injustice, which Ephraim is charged with (ver. 7), and justifies himself in, ver. 8. And the sin of idolatry (ver. 11), by which God is provoked to contend with them, ver. 14. II. The aggravations of these sins they are charged with, taken from the honour God put upon their father Jacob (ver. 3–5), the advancement of them into a people from low and mean beginnings (ver. 12, 13), and the provision he had made them of helps for their souls by the prophets he sent them, ver. 10. III. A call to the unconverted to turn to God, ver. 6. IV. An intimation of mercy that God had in store for them, ver. 9.

Verses 1–6

I. Ephraim is convicted of folly, in staying himself upon Egypt and Assyria, when he was in straits (*v.* 1): *Ephraim feeds on wind.* The men of Ephraim thought to secure the Assyrians in their interests by a *solemn league*: *They make a covenant with the Assyrians,* but they will find that potent prince will be a slave to his word no longer than he pleases. They thought to secure the Egyptians for their confederates by a rich present: *Oil is carried into Egypt.* But the Egyptians, when they had got the bribe, dropped the cause.

II. *The Lord has also a controversy with Judah;* for though he had awhile ago *ruled with God,* and

been *faithful with the saints,* yet now he begins to degenerate.

III. Both Ephraim and Judah are put in mind of their father Jacob, that they might be encouraged to return to God. He had called this people Jacob (*v.* 2), threatening to punish them; but *how shall I give them up?* How shall that dear name be forgotten? From what passed between God and Jacob we may learn that *Jehovah, the Lord God of hosts,* is *the God of Israel;* he was the God of Jacob, and this is *his memorial* throughout all the generations of the seed of Jacob (*v.* 5). Here are two memorials by which he is distinguished from all others, and is to be acknowledged by us. The first denotes his *existence of himself.* He is Jehovah, much the same with *I AM,* the same that *was, and is, and is to come,* infinite, eternal, and unchangeable. Jehovah is *his memorial,* his peculiar name. The second denotes his dominion over all: He is the *God of hosts,* that has all the hosts of heaven and earth at his command. God's names, titles, and attributes, are the memorials of him; there is no need for images to be such. *"Therefore turn thou to thy God.* He that was the God of Jacob is the God of Israel, is *thy God;* from him thou hast revolted; therefore turn thou to him by repentance and faith, turn to him as thine, to love him, obey him, and depend upon him. *Keep mercy and judgment,* mercy in relieving and succouring the poor and distressed, judgment in rendering to all their due; be kind to all."

Verses 7–14

I. Reproofs for sin. Ephraim is charged with turning from his God by idolatry, and breaking the laws of justice and judgment.

1. *He is a merchant.* The margin reads it as a proper name, *He is Canaan,* or a Canaanite, unworthy to be dominated from Jacob and Israel. See Amos ix. 7. But Canaan sometimes signifies *a merchant,* and here Ephraim is charged with deceit in trade. Though God had given his people a land flowing with milk and honey, yet he did not forbid them to enrich themselves by merchandise. And, if they had been fair merchants, it would have been no reproach at all. But he is such a merchant as the Canaanites were, who cheated all they dealt with. Ephraim deceives and thereby oppresses. With a great deal of art and cunning: *The balances of deceit are in his hand.*

2. He justifies himself in this sin, *v.* 8. Ephraim stands indicted for a common cheat. He does not deny the charge, but insists upon his own justification. Suppose he did use balances of deceit, yet he had got a good estate. Let the prophet say what he pleased of his deceit, he could not be convinced there was any harm in it: *"Yet I have become rich, I have found me out substance."* Carnal hearts are often confirmed in their evil ways by their worldly prosperity and success in those ways. But it is a great mistake. Every word in what Ephraim says here proclaims his folly. It is folly to call the riches of this world substance, for they are things that are not, Prov. xxiii. 5. It is folly to think that what we have is for ourselves. *I have found me out substance,* as if we had it for our own use, whereas we hold it in trust, only as stewards. It is folly to think that growing rich in a sinful way makes us innocent, or will make us safe. See Isa. xlvii. 10; Prov. i. 32. He pleads that he had kept a good reputation. Carnal hearts are apt to build a good opinion of themselves upon the fair character they have among their neighbours. He excused the fraud, so that none condemned it: *"They shall find no iniquity in me that were sin,* nothing very bad, nothing but what is very excusable." It is a fashionable iniquity; it is customary; it is what everybody does; nobody will think the worse of them for it. But

God sees not as man sees; he judges not as man judges. He is also charged with idolatry, with the making and worshipping of images, which are vanities (v. 11): *Surely they are vanity; they do not profit, but deceive.* The prophet mentions two places notorious for idolatry: (1) Gilead on the other side Jordan, which had been branded for it before (*ch.* vi. 8): *Is there iniquity in Gilead?* It is a thing to be wondered at; it is a thing to be sadly lamented. (2) And in Gilgal too; there they *sacrifice bullocks* (*ch.* ix. 15), and there *their altars* are as thick *as heaps* of manure *in the furrows of the field* that is to be sown, *ch.* viii. 11.

II. Threatenings of wrath for sin. Some make that to be so (v. 9), *I will make thee to dwell in tabernacles as in the days of the appointed time,* as did the Israelites when they dwelt in tents and wandered for forty years; that was the *time appointed in the wilderness.* Ephraim thought that there was no iniquity in him that deserved to be called sin (v. 8); but God told him that there was that in him which was sin, and would be found so if he did not repent and reform. *Ephraim provoked him to anger most bitterly.* He shall take away his forfeited life: *He shall leave his blood upon him,* that is, he shall not hold him guiltless. *His blood shall be upon his own head* (2 Sam. i. 16). *His reproach shall his Lord return upon him.*

III. Here are memorials of former mercy, which come in to convict them of base ingratitude.

1. That God had raised them from meanness. When Ephraim had become rich he forgot that which God obliged them every year to acknowledge (Deut. xxvi. 5), *A Syrian ready to perish was my father.* But God here puts them in mind of it, v. 12. Let them remember, not only the honours of their father Jacob, v. 3, but what a poor servant he was to Laban. *Jacob fled into Syria* from a malicious brother, and there served a covetous uncle *for a wife* and *for a wife he kept sheep,* because he had no estate. He was a plain man, dwelling in tents, and keeping sheep; therefore *balances of deceit* ill became them. God wonderfully preserved him, which magnifies the goodness of God both to him and them and leaves them under the stain of base ingratitude to God who was their founder and benefactor.

2. That God had rescued them from misery, raised them out of poverty and slavery (v. 13). God *brought Israel out of Egypt by a prophet,* Moses, who, though he is called *king in Jeshurun* (Deut. xxxiii. 5), yet did what he did for Israel *as a prophet,* by direction from God and by the power of his word. This shows how ungrateful this people were in rejecting their God. They should have loved and valued his prophets and have studied to answer God's end in sending them, for the sake of that prophet by whom God had brought them out of Egypt.

3. That God had taken care of their education as they grew up. This instance of God's goodness we have, v. 10. As by a prophet he delivered them, so *by prophets* he still continued to speak to them.

IV. Here are intimations of further mercy in the midst of sin and wrath (as some understand v. 9): "*I that am the Lord thy God from the land of Egypt,* who then and there took thee to be my people, and have approved myself thy God ever since, in a constant series of merciful providences, have yet a kindness for thee, bad as thou art; and I will *make thee to dwell in tabernacles,* not as in the wilderness, but *as in the days of the solemn feast,*" the feast of tabernacles, which was celebrated with great joy, Lev. xxiii. 40.

CHAPTER 13

I. The people of Israel are reproved and threatened for their idolatry, ver. 1–4. II. They are reproved and threatened for their wantonness, pride, and luxury, and other abuses of their wealth and prosperity, ver. 5–8. III. The ruin coming upon them is foretold, ver. 12, 13, 15, 16. IV. Those among them that yet retain a respect for their God are here encouraged to hope that he will yet appear for their relief, ver. 9–11, 14.

Verses 1–4

Idolatry was the sin that did most easily beset the Jewish nation till after the captivity; the ten tribes from the first were guilty of it, but especially after the days of Ahab.

I. The provision that God made to prevent their falling into idolatry. This we have, v. 4. He made himself known to them as *the Lord their God.* He told them so from heaven at Mount Sinai. This he continued to prove to them by his prophets and by his providences. He gave them a law forbidding them to worship any other: "*Thou shalt know no God but me.*" He gave them a good reason for it: *There is no saviour besides me.*

II. The honour that Ephraim had, while he kept himself clear from idolatry (v. 1): *While Ephraim spoke trembling,* or *with trembling,* so long *he exalted himself in Israel.* Those that humble themselves, especially that humble themselves before God, *shall be exalted.*

III. The lamentable growth of idolatry among them (v. 2): *Now they sin more and more.* They made themselves *molten images.* They made them of *their silver.* They made them *according to their own understanding,* according to their own fancy. Or *according to their own likeness,* in the form of a man. Though they were thus the work of their hands, yet they were the beloved of their souls; for they say of them, *Let the men that sacrifice kiss the calves.*

IV. Threatenings of wrath for their idolatry. Because they are so fond of kissing their calves, therefore God will give them sensible convictions of their folly, v. 3. God tells them that they shall be disappointed, and *driven away in their wickedness.* They shall be like the *morning cloud* or the *early dew.* Both *pass away,* and the day proves as dry and hot as ever; so their prosperity should be, and so their expectations from their idols. They are *as the chaff,* light and worthless. They are *as the smoke,* noisome and offensive (see Isa. lxv. 5), and they shall be driven away *as the smoke out of the chimneys.*

Verses 5–8

1. The plentiful provision God had made for Israel (v. 5): "*I did know thee in the wilderness,* made provision for thee, even in *a land of great drought,* when no relief was to be had in an ordinary way." The God that knew them and fed them there, was a *friend indeed.* 2. Their unworthy ungrateful abuse of God's favour to them. God not only took care of them in the wilderness, but put them in possession of Canaan (v. 6), *according to their pasture so were they filled.* When they came into Canaan they fed themselves *to the full.* It would have promised better, if they had been more moderate in the use of their plenty. *They were filled, and their heart was exalted.* Their luxury and sensuality made them proud, insolent, and secure. The best comment upon this is that of Moses, Deut. xxxii. 13–15. But *Jeshurun waxed fat and kicked.* They began to think they had no further need of God: *Their heart was exalted, therefore have they forgotten me.* We ought to know that we live upon God when we live upon common providence, though we do not, as Israel in the wilderness, live upon miracles. 3. God's just resentment of their base ingratitude, v. 7, 8. *I will be unto them as a lion* and *as a leopard.* Some read it (and the original will bear it), *I will be as a leopard in the way of Assyria.* The judgments of God shall surprise them just when they are going to the Assyrians to seek for protection and help from them. He will *rend the caul of their heart.* The lion is observed to

aim at the heart of the beasts he preys upon, and thus will God *devour them like a lion.* The judgments of God against impenitent sinners will be terrible. They will *rend the caul of the heart,* will fill the soul with confusion.

Verses 9–16

The first of these verses is the summary, or contents, of all the rest (*v.* 9). 1. All the blame of Israel's ruin laid upon themselves: *O Israel! thy perdition is thence;* it is of and from thyself; or, "*It has destroyed thee, O Israel!*" 2. All the glory of Israel's relief ascribed to God: *But in me is thy help.* It may be: "Thy case is bad, but it is not desperate. *Thou hast destroyed thyself;* but come to me, and I will help thee."

I. Israel destroyed themselves. It is said (*v.* 16), They *rebelled against God.*

1. They treasure up wrath against the day of wrath, and so they destroy themselves. Their former sins contributed to their present destruction; for they were *laid up in store with God,* Deut. xxxii. 34, 35; Job xiv. 17. The sin of sinners is not forgotten till it is pardoned.

2. They are their own ruin because they will not do what they should do towards their own salvation, *v.* 13. They shall be thrown into pangs and agonies, very sharp and severe, and yet, like the pains of a woman in labour, in order to deliverance; and by these, though God corrects them, yet he designs their good. They are chastened, that they may not be destroyed. But they do not repent and so cannot expect the joy of deliverance, *v.* 13. Those are in danger of miscarrying in conversion who delay it. Here is a sad description of the desolation they are doomed to, *v.* 15, 16. It is taken for granted that *Ephraim* is *fruitful among his children;* but sin turns this fruitful tribe into barrenness. The instrument is an *east wind,* representing a foreign enemy that should invade it. It is called the *wind of the Lord.* Was it a rich tribe? The foreign enemy shall make it poor enough and shall exhaust the sources of its wealth. Was it a populous tribe, and numerous? The enemy shall depopulate it and make its men few: *Samaria shall become desolate,* without inhabitants.

II. How God was the help of this self-destroying people, their only help (*v.* 10): *I will be thy King,* to rule and save thee. Though they had rebelled against him, yet he would still be their King. Our case would be sad indeed if God were not better to us than we are to ourselves.

1. God will be their King when they have no other king. "*Where is the king that may save thee in all thy cities? Where are thy judges,* who by administering public justice should preserve the public peace?" They rejected Samuel when they said, *Give us a king* like the nations, whereas the *Lord was their King.* The ten tribes desired a kingly government different from that of the house of David, because they thought that bore too hard upon them, and they hoped to better themselves by setting up Jeroboam. Providence gave them Saul first, and afterwards Jeroboam. And what better were they for them? Saul was *given in anger* (given in *thunder,* 1 Sam. xii. 18, 19) and soon after was *taken away in wrath,* upon Mount Gilboa. The kingly government of the ten tribes was given in anger against the ten tribes, for their disaffection to the house of David; and God was now about to take that away in wrath by the power of the king of Assyria.

2. God will do that for them which no other king could do if they had one (*v.* 14): *I will ransom them from the power of the grave.* Their deliverance shall be by ransom; and we know who it was that paid their ransom, and what the ransom was, for it was the Son of man that *gave his life a ransom for many,* Matt. xx. 28. Christ has abolished death, has broken the power of it and altered the property of it, and so

enabled us to triumph over it. Thanks be to God therefore who gives us the victory.

CHAPTER 14

This chapter is a lesson for penitents; and some such there were in Israel. I. Direction in repenting, ver. 1–3. II. Encouragements to repent, taken from God's readiness to receive returning sinners (ver. 4, 8) and the comforts he has for them, ver. 5–7. III. A solemn recommendation of these things, ver. 9.

Verses 1–3

I. A kind invitation given to sinners to repent, *v.* 1. It is directed to Israel, God's professing people. They are called to *return.* Conversion must be preached even to those that are within the pale of the church as well as to heathen. "*Thou hast fallen by thy iniquity.*" *Thou hast stumbled;* so some read it. Their idols were their *stumbling-blocks.* Sin is a fall; and it concerns those that have fallen by sin to get up again by repentance. "*Return to the Lord thy God;* return to him as *the Lord* whom thou hast a dependance upon, *as thy God.*" Return *even to the Lord,* or *quite home* to the Lord. The ancient Jews had a saying, grounded on this, *Repentance is a great thing, for it brings men quite up to the throne of glory.*

II. How to repent. 1. They must bethink themselves what to say to God when they come to him: *Take with you words.* They are required to bring, not sacrifices and offerings, but penitential prayers, the *fruit* not of the lips only, but of the heart. The heart must dictate to the tongue. 2. They must bethink themselves what to do. They must not only take with them words, but must *turn to the Lord;* inwardly in their hearts, outwardly in their lives.

III. For their assistance and encouragement, God is pleased to put words into their mouths, to teach them what they shall say. They are,

1. Petitioning words. Two things we are here directed to petition for: (1) To be acquitted from guilt. When we return to the Lord we must say to him, "Lord, *take away all iniquity.* Lift it off as a *burden* or as the stumbling-block which we have often fallen over. Take it all away by a free and full remission, for we cannot strike it off by a satisfaction of our own." (2) To be accepted as righteous in God's sight: "*Receive us graciously.* Let us have thy favour and love. Receive our prayer graciously; be well pleased with that good which by thy grace we are enabled to do." *Take good* (so the word is); take it to bestow upon us, so the margin reads it—*Give good.* This follows upon the petition for the taking away of iniquity; for, till iniquity is taken away, we have no reason to expect any good from God. *Give good,* that good which will make us good and keep us from returning to iniquity again.

2. Promising words. These also are put into their mouths, not to move God, but to move themselves. Two things they are to promise and vow: (1) Thanksgiving. "Pardon our sins, and accept of us, so *will we render the calves of our lips,*" The *fruit of our lips* (so the LXX), a word they used for *burnt-offerings,* and so it agrees with the Hebrew. The apostle quotes this phrase (Heb. xiii. 15). (2) Amendment of life. They are taught to promise, not only verbal acknowledgments, but a real reformation. They will not trust to their alliances abroad: *Asshur* (that is, Assyria) *shall not save us.* "We will not court the help of the Assyrians when we are in distress, as we have done (*ch.* v. 13; vii. 11; viii. 9); we will scorn to be beholden to the Assyrians for help. *We will not ride upon horses,* that is, we will not make court to Egypt," for thence they fetched their horses, Deut. xvii. 16; Isa. xxx. 16; xxxi. 1, 3. We must promise that we will not set our hearts upon the gains of this world, nor pride ourselves in our external performances in religion, for that is, in effect, to say to the work of our hands, *You are our gods.*

3. Pleading words are here put into their mouths: For *in thee the fatherless find mercy.* Those may expect to find help in God that are truly sensible of their helplessness in themselves and are willing to acknowledge it. They plead God's wonted lovingkindness to such as were in that condition: *With thee the fatherless* not only may find, but *does find*, and shall find, *mercy.*

Verses 4–7

An answer of peace to the prayers of returning Israel. They seek God's face, and they shall not *seek in vain.*

I. Do they dread and deprecate God's displeasure, and therefore return to him? He assures them that, upon their submission, his *anger is turned away from them.* This is laid as the ground of all the other favours here promised.

II. Do they pray for the *taking away of iniquity*? He assures them that he will *heal their backslidings*; so he promised, Jer. iii. 22. He will heal the guilt of their backslidings by pardoning mercy and their *bent to backslide* by renewing grace.

III. Do they pray that God will receive them graciously? In answer to that, behold, it is promised, *I will love them freely.*

IV. Do they pray that God will *give good*, will make them good? In answer to that, behold, it is promised, *I will be as the dew unto Israel, v.* 5. This ensures *spiritual blessings in heavenly things*; and it follows upon the healing of their backslidings, for pardoning mercy is always accompanied with renewing grace. The bad being by the grace of God made good, they shall by the same grace be made better; for grace, wherever it is true, is growing. They *shall grow as the lily.* The growth of the lily is very speedy. The root of the lily seems lost in the ground all winter, but, when it is refreshed with the dews of the spring, it starts up in a little time; so the grace of God improves young converts sometimes very fast. They shall grow downwards, and be more firm. The lily indeed grows fast, and grows fine, but it soon fades and is easily plucked up; and therefore it is here promised to Israel that with the flower of the lily he shall have the root of the cedar: He shall *cast forth his roots as Lebanon*, as the *trees of Lebanon*, which, having taken deep root, cannot be plucked up, Amos ix. 15. Spiritual growth consists most in the growth of the root, which is out of sight. The more we depend upon Christ and draw sap and virtue from him, the more we act in religion from a principle and the more steadfast and resolved we are in it, the more we *cast forth our roots.* They shall grow round about (*v.* 6): *His branches shall spread* on all sides. And (*v.* 7) he shall *grow as the vine*, whose branches extend furthest of any tree. They shall be graceful and acceptable both to God and man. They are here compared to such trees as are pleasant, 1. To the sight: *His beauty shall be as the*

olive-tree, which is always green, Jer. xi. 16. Ordinances are the beauty of the church. Holiness is the beauty of a soul. 2. To the smell: *His smell* shall be *as Lebanon* (*v.* 6) and his *scent* as *the wine of Lebanon, v.* 7. The church is compared to a *garden of spices* (Cant. iv. 12, 14). Grace is the perfume of the soul, Eccles. vii. 1. *The memorial thereof shall be as the wine of Lebanon* (so the margin reads it), their surviving honours when they are gone, shall be as *the wine of Lebanon*, that has a delicate flavour. The church is compared here to the vine and the olive, which bring forth useful fruits, to the honour of God and man.

Verses 8–9

I. Concerning Ephraim, *v.* 8.

1. His repentance and reformation: *Ephraim shall say, What have I to do any more with idols?* As some read it, God here reasons and argues with him, why he should renounce idolatry: "*O Ephraim! what to me and idols? What concord* or agreement can there be *between me and idols?*" As we read it, God promises to bring Ephraim and keep him to this: *Ephraim shall say, What have I to do any more with idols?* He had promised (*v.* 3) not to *say any more to the works of his hands, You are my gods.* Ephraim had been *joined to idols* (ch. iv. 17), and yet God will work such a change in him that he shall loathe them as much as ever he loved them.

2. The gracious notice God is pleased to take of it: *I have heard him, and observed him. I have heard, and will look upon him;* so some read it. God *observed* Ephraim, to see whether he would bring forth fruits meet for this profession of repentance.

3. Before, Israel was compared to a tree, now God compares himself to one. "*I am like a green fir-tree*, and will be so to thee." He will be either *a sun and a shield* or a *shade and a shield*, according as their case requires. As the root of a tree: *From me is thy fruit found*—from him we receive grace and strength to enable us to do our duty. Whatever fruits of righteousness we bring forth, all the praise of them is due to God.

II. Concerning everyone that reads the words of the prophecy of this book (*v.* 9): *Who is wise? and he shall understand these things.* Those that are wise in the doing of their duty, that are prudent in practical religion, are most likely to know and understand the truths and providences of God, which are a mystery to others, John vii. 17. The right ways of God to those that are good are, and will be, a savour of life unto life: *The just shall walk in them. The transgressors shall fall* not only in their own wrong ways, but even *in the right ways of the Lord. Recipitur ad modum recipientis—What is received influences according to the qualities of the receiver.* The same sun softens wax and hardens clay. But of all transgressors those certainly have the most dangerous fatal falls that fall *in the ways of God.*

THE BOOK OF
THE PROPHET JOEL

We are uncertain concerning the time when this prophet prophesied; it is probable that it was about the same time that Amos prophesied. Hosea and Obadiah prophesied about the same time; and it appears that Amos prophesied in the days of Jeroboam II, king of Israel, Amos vii. 10. God sent a variety of prophets, that they might strengthen the hands one of another. In this prophecy, I. The desolations made by hosts of noxious insects is described, *ch.* i and part of *ch.* ii. II. The people are called to repentance, *ch.* ii. III. Promises are made of the return of mercy upon their repentance (*ch.* ii), and promises of the pouring out of the Spirit in the latter days. IV. The cause of God's people is pleaded against their enemies, whom God would in due time reckon with (*ch.* iii); and glorious things are spoken of the gospel-Jerusalem and of the prosperity and perpetuity of it.

CHAPTER 1

This chapter is the description of a lamentable devastation made of the country of Judah by locusts and caterpillars. Some think that the prophet speaks of it as a thing to come and gives warning of it beforehand, as usually the prophets did of judgments coming. Others think that it was now present, and that his business was to affect the people with it and awaken them by it to repentance. I. It is spoken of as a judgment, ver. 1–7. II. All sorts of people sharing in the calamity are called upon to lament it, ver. 8–13. III. They are directed to look up to God in their lamentations, and to humble themselves before him, ver. 14–20.

Verses 1–7

Joel here speaks of a sore judgment which was now brought, or to be brought, upon Judah, for their sins.

I. The judgment was such as could not be paralleled in the ages that were past, or in the memory of any living, *v.* 2. Those that outdo their predecessors in sin may expect to fall under greater judgments than any of their predecessors knew. It was such as would not be forgotten in the ages to come (*v.* 3): *"Tell you your children of it;* that they may take warning, and learn obedience by the things which you have suffered. Yea, let *your children tell their children, and their children another generation;* let them tell it to *teach their children* to stand in awe of God and of his judgments, and to tremble before him."

II. The judgment is an invasion of the country of Judea by a great army. Many interpreters both ancient and modern understand it of armies of men, the forces of the Assyrians, which, under Sennacherib, *took all the defended cities of Judah,* and made havoc of the country. Some make the four sorts of animals here named (*v.* 4) to signify the four monarchies which, in their turns, were oppressive to the Jews, one destroying what had escaped the fury of the other. But it seems much rather to be understood literally of armies of insects coming upon the land and eating up the fruits of it. The plague of locusts in Egypt lasted but for a few days; this seems to have continued for four years successively (as some think), because here are four sorts of insects mentioned (*v.* 4), but others think they came all in one year. Though a devastation by these insects is primarily intended here, yet it is expressed in language applicable to the destruction of the country by a foreign enemy. If this nation of worms do not subdue them, another nation shall come to ruin them. These animals are *locusts* and *caterpillars, palmer-worms* and *canker-worms, v.* 4. They were all little insects, but when they came in vast swarms they were formidable and ate up all before them. The weaker the instrument is that God employs the more is his power magnified.

They are here called a *nation* (*v.* 6), because they act as it were with a common design; for, though *the locusts have no king, yet go they forth all of them by bands* (Prov. xxx. 27). They are said to have the *teeth of a lion* because of the great and terrible execution they do. Locusts become as lions when they come armed with a divine commission. They destroy not only the grass and corn, but the trees (*v.* 7): The *vine is laid waste.* These vermin eat the leaves which should be a shelter to the fruit while it ripens. They eat the very bark of the fig-tree, and so kill it. Thus the *fig-tree does not blossom,* nor is there *fruit in the vine.*

III. A call to the drunkards to lament this judgment (*v.* 5): *Awake and weep, all you drinkers of wine.* It should touch them in a tender part; the *new wine* which they loved so well should be *cut off from their mouth.* The more men place their happiness in the gratifications of sense the more pressing temporal afflictions are upon them. The drinkers of water needed not to care when the vine was laid waste; they could live as well without it as they had done.

Verses 8–13

They are called to lament (*v.* 8), as a virgin laments the death of her lover to whom she was espoused, or as a young woman lately married, from whom the *husband of her youth,* or the husband to whom she was married when she was young, is suddenly taken away by death.

I. Let the husbandmen and vine-dressers lament, *v.* 11. They shall see the fruit of their labour eaten up before their eyes, and shall not be able to save any of it. *The field is laid waste* (*v.* 10); all is consumed that it produced; *the land mourns;* the ground has a melancholy aspect. They are justly brought to lament the loss and want of the *wheat and barley.* The trees are destroyed, not only the *vine and the fig-tree* (as before, *v.* 7), but the *pomegranate, palm-tree,* and *apple-tree,* all the *trees of the field,* as well as those of the orchard, timber-trees as well as fruit-trees. See what need we have to live in a continual dependence upon God and his providence, for our own hands are not sufficient for us.

II. Let the priests, the Lord's ministers, lament, for they share deeply in the calamity: *Gird yourselves with sackcloth* (*v.* 13). The ministers of the altar must *lament and howl.* "He is your God in a particular manner, and therefore it is expected that you should be more concerned than others for that which is a hindrance to the service of his sanctuary." As far as any public trouble is an obstruction to the course of religion it is to be upon that account, more than any other, sadly lamented, especially by the priests, the Lord's ministers.

Verses 14–20

Abundance of tears were shed for the destruction of the fruits of the earth by the locusts; now those tears must be turned into the right channel, that of repentance and humiliation before God.

I. A proclamation issued for a general fast. The priests are ordered to appoint one. Under public judgments there ought to be public humiliations. 1. A day is to be appointed for this purpose, a *day of restraint* (so the margin reads it), a day in which people must be restrained from their ordinary business. 2. It must be a *fast*, a religious abstaining from meat and drink, further than is of absolute necessity. Hereby we own ourselves unworthy of our necessary food, and that we have forfeited it. We punish ourselves and mortify the body. 3. There must be a solemn assembly. All had contributed to the national guilt, all shared in the national calamity, and therefore they must all join in the professions of repentance. 4. They must come together in the temple, *the house of the Lord* their *God*, because that was the house of prayer, and there they might hope to meet with God because it was the place which he had *chosen to put his name there.* 5. They must *sanctify* this fast, must observe it with sincere devotion.

II. Some considerations suggested to induce them to proclaim this fast and to observe it strictly. 1. God was beginning a controversy with them. It is time to *cry unto the Lord*, for *the day of the Lord is at hand*, v. 15. "The day of his judgment is very near, it is *at hand*; it *will not slumber*, and therefore you should not." It will be terrible. There is no fleeing from him but by fleeing to him. 2. They saw themselves already under the tokens of his displeasure. It is time to fast and pray, for their distress is very great, v. 16. Let them look into God's house, and see the effects of the judgment there; joy and gladness were *cut off from the house of God.* 3. The prophet returns to describe the grievousness of the calamity, in some particulars. Corn and cattle are the husbandman's staple commodities; now here he is deprived of both these. (1) The caterpillars have devoured the corn, v. 17. *The seed is rotten under the clods*, either through too much rain or for want of rain, or perhaps some insects underground ate it up. (2) The cattle perish too for want of grass (v. 18): *How do the beasts groan!* Even *the flocks of sheep*, which will live upon very short grass, *are made desolate.*

III. The prophet stirs them up to cry to God. 1. His own example (v. 19): *O Lord! to thee will I cry.* That which engaged him to *cry to God* was, not so much any personal affliction, as the national calamity: The *fire has devoured the pastures of the wilderness*, which seems to be meant of some parching scorching heat of the sun, which consumed them all. 2. The example of the inferior creatures: *"The beasts of the field* do not only *groan*, but *cry unto thee*, v. 20."* The complaints of the brute-creatures here are for want of water, and for want of grass.

CHAPTER 2

I. A further description of that terrible desolation which should be made in the land of Judah by the locusts and caterpillars, ver. 1–11. II. A call to the people to return and repent, to fast and pray, and to seek unto God for mercy, with directions how to do this aright, ver. 12–17. III. A promise that, upon their repentance, God would remove the judgment, and restore unto them plenty of all good things, ver. 18–27. IV. A prediction of the setting up of the kingdom of the Messiah in the world, by the pouring out of the Spirit in the latter days, ver. 28–32. Thus the beginning of this chapter is made terrible with the tokens of God's wrath, but the latter end of it made comfortable with the assurances of his favour, so that, though it is only the last paragraph of the chapter that points directly at gospel-times, yet the whole may be improved as a type and figure, representing the curses of the law and the comforts of the gospel flowing upon repentance.

Verses 1–11

God contending with his own professing people for their sins and executing upon them the judgment written in the law (Deut. xxviii. 42), *The fruit of thy land shall the locust consume*, v. 60.

I. The war proclaimed (v. 1): *Blow the trumpet in Zion* to give notice to Judah and Jerusalem of the approach of the judgment, that they might *prepare to meet their God* by prayers and tears. It was the priests' business to sound the trumpet (Num. x. 8), both as an appeal to God in the day of their distress, and a summons to the people to come together to seek his face. It is the work of ministers to give warning from the word of God of the fatal consequences of sin.

II. A general idea given of the day of battle which is *nigh at hand*. It is the *day of the Lord*, the day of his judgment, *a day of darkness and gloominess* (v. 2), literally so, the swarms of locusts and caterpillars being so large and so thick as to darken the sky (Exod. x. 15). The darkness of this day will come as suddenly as the morning light, as irresistibly.

III. The army drawn up in array (v. 2): They are a *great people, and a strong.* The army is here described to be daring: They *are as horses*, as war-horses, and *as horsemen*, carried on with martial fire and fury, *so they shall run*, v. 4. Some of the ancients have observed that the head of a locust is very like, in shape, to the head of a horse. They are loud and noisy— *like the noise of chariots* when driven furiously over rough ground, *on the tops of the mountains*, v. 5. The noise is like the *noise of a flame* that *devours the stubble.* When God's judgments are abroad they make a great noise. They are very regular, and keep ranks *as a strong people set in battle array* (v. 5). *They shall not break their ranks, nor one thrust another*, v. 7, 8.

IV. The terrible execution done by this formidable army, 1. In the country, v. 3. Look upon the fields that they have eaten up and they are *as a desolate wilderness.* 2. In the city. They shall *climb the wall* (v. 7), they shall *run upon the houses*, and *enter in at the windows like a thief* (v. 9).

V. The impressions upon the people. These enemies are invulnerable and therefore irresistible, v. 8. "One is in pain for his field, another for his vineyard, *and all faces gather blackness.*" When God frowns upon men the lights of heaven will be small joy to them.

VI. The commander-in-chief of this formidable army is God himself, v. 11. And this makes the *great day* of the Lord *very terrible.*

Verses 12–17

God brings us into straits, that he may bring us to repentance and so bring us to himself. Here is a gracious invitation.

I. To a personal repentance, exercised in the soul. Everyone must mend one and mourn for one, and then we should all be mended.

1. What it is to repent, for it is the same that the Lord our God still requires of us. (1) We must be truly humbled for our sins, must be sorry we have by sin offended God, and ashamed we have by sin wronged ourselves. There must be outward expressions of sorrow and shame, *fasting*, and *weeping*, and *mourning.* But the outward expressions of sorrow must spring from within. And therefore it follows, *Rend your heart, and not your garments.* Rending the heart is that which God looks for and requires; that is the *broken and contrite heart* which he *will not despise*, Ps. li. 17. (2) We must be thoroughly converted to our God, and come home to him when we fall out

with sin. *Turn you even to me, saith the Lord* (v. 12), and again (v. 13), *Turn unto the Lord your God.*

2. Arguments used to persuade this people thus to turn to the Lord *with all their hearts*. We are sure that he is a good God. We must *turn to the Lord our God*, not only because he has been just and righteous in punishing us for our sins, but because he is *gracious and merciful*, in receiving us upon our repentance. *He repents him of the evil*, not that he changes his mind, but, when the sinner's mind is changed, God's way towards him is changed; the sentence is reversed, and the curse of the law is taken off. There is no question at all but that if we truly repent of our sins God will forgive them, and be reconciled to us; but whether he will remove this or the other affliction which we are under may well be questioned, and yet the probability of it should encourage us to repent.

II. They are here called to a public national repentance, as a national act, for the glory of God, and that the neighbouring nations might know what it was that qualified them for God's gracious returns in mercy to them. The congregation must be called together, v. 15, 16. The trumpet was blown (v. 1), to sound an *alarm of war*; but now it must be blown in order to a treaty of peace. What was said *ch.* i. 14 is here repeated: "*Call a solemn assembly; gather the people; sanctify the congregation;* appoint a time for solemn preparation beforehand and put them in mind to prepare themselves. Let not the greatest be excused, but *assemble the elders*, the judges and magistrates. Let not the meanest be passed by, but *gather the children, and those that suck the breasts.*" Private joys must give way to public sorrows, both those for affliction and those for sin. The priests, *the Lord's ministers*, must preside in the congregation, and be God's mouth to the people, and theirs to God. They must officiate *between the porch and the altar*. There the people must see them weeping and wrestling, like their father Jacob, and be helped into the same devout frame. Their petition must be, *Spare thy people, O Lord!* "Let not the heathen make them *a proverb*, or a *by-word*" (so some read it); "let it never be said, *As poor and beggarly as an Israelite.*"

Verses 18–27

They prayed that God would *spare them*, and see here with what *good words and comfortable words* he answered them; for God's promises are real answers to the prayers of faith.

I. Whence this mercy promised shall take rise (v. 18): God will be *jealous for his land* and *pity his people*. He will restore them their forfeited comforts.

II. Instances of his mercy: 1. The destroying army shall be dispersed and defeated (v. 20): "*I will remove far off from you the northern army*, that army of locusts and caterpillars that invaded you from the north. Nothing shall remain of these swarms of insects but the ill savour of them. "Many interpreters, by this northern army, understand that of Sennacherib, which was dispersed when God by it had *accomplished his whole work upon Mount Zion and upon Jerusalem*, Isa. x. 12. It is promised (v. 22) that *the pastures of the wilderness*, the pastures which the locusts had left as bare as the wilderness, shall again *spring* and the *trees shall again bear their fruit*, particularly the *fig-tree and the vine*. It shall be, for (v. 23) *the Lord has given* and will give you *the former rain and the latter rain*, and will give them moderately, and in due season, the *latter rain in the first month*, when it was wanted and expected. All their losses shall be repaired (v. 25): "*I will restore to you the years that the locust has eaten;* you shall be comforted according to the time that you have been afflicted, and shall have years of plenty to balance the years of famine." Look into the stores and you shall find *the floors full*

of wheat, and the vats overflowing with wine and oil* (v. 24), whereas, in the day of their distress, the *wine and oil languished* and *the barns were broken down*, *ch.* i. 10, 17. Some expositors understand these promises figuratively, as pointing at gospel-grace. When God sends us his promises to be the matter of our comfort, his graces to be the grounds of it, and his Spirit to be the author of it, he has sent us (according to his promise here, v. 19) *corn, and wine, and oil*, or that which is unspeakably better.

III. What use shall be made of these returns of God's mercy.

1. God shall have the glory for they shall *rejoice in the Lord their God* (v. 23), and not praise their idols, nor call their corn and wine the *rewards that their lovers had given them.*

2. They shall have the comfort, and spiritual benefit, thereof. Their reputation shall be retrieved (v. 19): "*I will no more make you a reproach among the heathen*, that triumphed in your calamities and insulted over you; and v. 26, 27. Their joys shall be revived (v. 23). They shall *rejoice in the Lord their God*, not so much in the good things themselves that are given them as in the good hand that gives them. The *joy of harvest* and the joy of a feast must both terminate in God, whose love we should taste in all the gifts of his bounty, that we may make him our chief joy, as he is our chief good, and the fountain of all good to us. Their faith in God shall be confirmed and increased. This is promised here (v. 27): *You shall know that I am in the midst of Israel*, the *Holy One in the midst of thee* (Hos. xi. 9), *and that I am the Lord your God, and none else*. We should labour to grow in our acquaintance with God by all providences, both merciful and afflictive.

Verses 28–32

The promises of corn, and wine, and oil, would be acceptable to a wasted country; but we must not rest in those things. These verses have reference to better things, both the kingdom of grace and the kingdom of glory.

I. How the kingdom of grace shall be introduced by a plentiful *effusion of the Spirit*, v. 28, 29. The apostle Peter has given us an assurance that when the Spirit was poured out upon the apostles, on the day of Pentecost (Acts ii. 1, &c.), that was the very thing *which was spoken of here by the prophet Joel*, v. 16, 17. We often read in the Old Testament of the Spirit of the Lord coming by drops, as it were, upon the judges and prophets whom God raised up for extraordinary services; but now the Spirit shall be poured out plentifully in a full stream, as was promised, Isa. xliv. 3. The time fixed for this is *afterwards*; after the fulfilling of the foregoing promises this shall be fulfilled. The Spirit shall be *poured out upon all flesh*, not as hitherto upon Jews only, but upon Gentiles also; for in Christ there is no distinction between Jew and Greek, Rom. x. 11, 12. The Jews understand it of all flesh in the land of Israel, and Peter himself did not fully understand it as speaking of the Gentiles till he saw it accomplished in the descent of the Holy Ghost upon Cornelius and his friends, who were Gentiles (Acts x. 44, 45), which was but a continuation of the same gift which was bestowed on the day of Pentecost. "*Your old men*, who are past their vigour and whose spirits begin to decay, *your young men*, who have yet but little experience of divine things, shall yet *dream dreams* and *see visions*; God will reveal himself by dreams and visions both to young and old. *They shall prophesy;* they shall receive new discoveries of divine things, and that not for their own use only, but for the benefit of the church. They shall interpret scripture, and speak of things distant, and future. By these extraordinary gifts the Christian church was first founded and set up, and the scriptures were written, and the ministry settled.

II. How the kingdom of glory shall be introduced by the change of nature, v. 30, 31. The pouring out of the Spirit will be very comfortable to the righteous; but let the unrighteous hear this and tremble. There is a great and terrible day of the Lord coming. It will be accomplished in full at the end of time. It was accomplished in part in the death of Christ (which is called the *judgment of this world*, when the earth quaked and the sun was darkened), and in the destruction of Jerusalem, which was a figure of the general judgment. The judgments of God upon a sinful world, and the frequent destruction of wicked kingdoms by fire and sword, are presages of the judgment of the world in the last day.

III. The safety and happiness of all true believers both in the first and second coming of Jesus Christ, v. 32. This speaks of particular persons, for to them the New Testament has more respect, and less to kingdoms and nations, than the Old. Though the day of the Lord will be great and terrible, yet *in Mount Zion and in Jerusalem there shall be deliverance* from the terror of it. Christ is himself not only the *Saviour*, but *the salvation*; he is so *to the ends of the earth*. This deliverance, laid up for us in the covenant of grace, is in performance of the promises made to the fathers. See Luke i. 72. There is a remnant interested in this salvation, and for whom the deliverance is wrought. *Christ in you, the hope of glory.* Those that sincerely call upon God: *Whosoever shall call on the name of the Lord*, whether Jew or Gentile, Rom. x. 13, *shall be delivered*. This calling on God supposes knowledge of him, faith in him, desire towards him, dependence on him, and a conscientious obedience to him; for, without that, crying *Lord, Lord*, will not stand us in any stead.

CHAPTER 3

In the close of the foregoing chapter we had a gracious promise of deliverance in Mount Zion and Jerusalem; now this whole chapter is a comment upon that promise, showing what that deliverance shall be, how it shall be wrought by the destruction of the church's enemies, and how it shall be perfected in the everlasting rest and joy of the church. This was in part accomplished in the deliverance of Jerusalem from the attempt that Sennacherib made upon it in Hezekiah's time, and afterwards in the return of the Jews out of their captivity in Babylon, and other deliverances wrought for the Jewish church between that and Christ's coming. But it has a further reference, to the great redemption wrought out for us by Jesus Christ, and the destruction of our spiritual enemies and all their agents. Here is a prediction, I. Of God's reckoning with the enemies of his people, ver. 1–8. II. Of God's judging all nations when the measure of their iniquity is full, ver. 9–17. III. Of the provision God has made for the refreshment of his people, ver. 18–21. Those promises were written for our learning, "that we, through patience and comfort of this scripture, might have hope."

Verses 1–8

The *year of the redeemed*, and the *year of recompences for the controversy of Zion*. A prophecy of what shall be done whenever it comes, for it comes often, and at the end of time it will come once for all.

I. It shall be the *year of the redeemed*, for God will *bring again the captivity of Judah and Jerusalem, v. 1*. Though the bondage of God's people may be grievous and long, yet it shall not be everlasting. That in Egypt ended at length. *Let my son go, that he may serve me.* That in Babylon shall likewise end well. And the Lord Jesus will provide for the effectual redemption of enslaved souls from under the dominion of sin and Satan, and will proclaim that *acceptable year*, and the *opening of the prison to those that were bound*.

II. It shall be the *year of recompences for the controversy of Zion*. God will lead captivity captive (Ps. lxviii. 18), will lead those captive that led his people captive, Rev. xiii. 10. All nations had made themselves liable to the judgment of God for wrong done

to his people. Whatsoever nation injured God's nation, they should not go unpunished; for he that touches the Israel of God shall be made to know that he touches the apple of his eye. But the neighbouring nations shall be particularly reckoned with— *Tyre, and Sidon, and all the coasts of Palestine*, or the Philistines, who have been troublesome neighbours to the Israel of God, *v. 4*. They shall all be *gathered (v. 2)*. They shall be *brought down into the valley of Jehoshaphat*, which lay near Jerusalem, and there *God will plead with them*. It was in this valley of Jehoshaphat (as Dr. Lightfoot suggests) that Sennacherib's army, or part of it, lay, when it was destroyed by an angel. This prosecution is set on foot *for my people*, and *for my heritage Israel*. Many affronts they had put upon God by their idolatries, but that for which God has a quarrel with them is the affront they have put upon his people and upon the vessels of his sanctuary. They had been abusive to the people of Israel, had *scattered them among the nations*. They *parted their land*, and have *cast lots for my people*, and *sold them*. When they had taken them prisoners they did *not increase their wealth by their price*, but sold them for pleasure rather than profit; they *gave a boy* taken in war for the *hire of a harlot*, and *a girl* for so many bottles of wine as would serve them for one sitting, a *goodly price* for a son and daughter of Israel to be a slave and a drudge in a tavern or a brothel. That which is got by one sin is commonly spent upon another. The Tyrians and Philistines, when they seized any of the children of Judah and Jerusalem, sold them to the Grecians, that they *might remove them far from their* own *border, v. 6*. They had unjustly seized *God's silver and gold (v. 5)*, by which some understand the wealth of Israel. But it seems rather to be meant of the *vessels* and *treasures of the temple*, which God here calls his *goodly pleasant things*. These they *carried into their temples* as trophies of their victory over God's Israel, thinking that therein they triumphed over Israel's God, and that their idols triumphed over him. Thus the ark was put in Dagon's temple. Can they pretend that either God or his people have done them any injury, for which they may justify themselves in doing them these mischiefs? Those that contend with God will find themselves unable to make their part good with him. He will recompense them *suddenly*. They shall not gain their end in the mischief they designed against God's people. They thought to *remove them so far from their border* that they should never return to it again, *v. 6*. But (says God) "*I will raise them out of the place whither you have sold them*, and they shall not, as you intended, be buried alive there." The sellers shall be paid in their own coin. They shall justly be *sold to the Sabeans*, to a *people far off*. This (some think) had its accomplishment in the victories obtained by the Maccabees over the enemies of the Jews; others think it looks as far forward as the last day.

Verses 9–17

The notice of God's judging the nations may have reference to the destruction of Sennacherib, Nebuchadnezzar, Antiochus, and to the Antichrist especially, and all the proud enemies of the Christian church; but some of the best interpreters, ancient and modern, think the scope of these verses is to set forth the day of the last judgment.

I. A challenge given to all the enemies of God's kingdom, v. 9–11. It seems to be here spoken ironically: "*Proclaim you this among the Gentiles;* let all the forces of the nations be summoned to join in confederacy against God and his people." Thus does a God of almighty power bid defiance to all the opposition of the powers of darkness. The heathen must *come up to the valley of Jehoshaphat*, to receive their doom (*v.* 12). Jehoshaphat signifies *the judgment of the Lord.* Let them come to the place of God's judgment, which perhaps is the chief reason for the using of this name. The challenge (*v.* 9) is turned into a summons, *v.* 12.

II. A charge given to the ministers of God's justice to appear and act against these enemies of his kingdom among men: And therefore *cause thy mighty ones to come down, O Lord! v.* 11. Some think the words (*v.* 9, 10), *Prepare war, wake up the mighty men,* are not a challenge to the enemies' hosts, but a charge to God's hosts. However, it is plain that to them the charge is given (*v.* 13), *Put you in the sickle, for the harvest is ripe;* that is, *their wickedness is great,* they are ripe for ruin.

III. The vast appearance that shall be in that solemn day (*v.* 14): *Multitudes, multitudes, in the valley of decision,* the same which before was called the *valley of Jehoshaphat.* The day of judgment will be the *day of decision. The valley of the distribution of judgment* (so the Chaldee), when *every man shall receive according to the things done in the body. The valley of threshing* (so the margin), carrying on the metaphor of the *harvest, v.* 13. The proud enemies of God's people will then be made as the *dust of the summer threshing-floors.*

IV. The amazing change that shall then be made in the kingdom of nature (*v.* 15): *The sun and moon shall be darkened,* as before, *ch.* ii. 31. Their glory and lustre shall be eclipsed by the far greater brightness of that glory in which the Judge shall then appear.

V. The different impressions which that day will make. 1. To the wicked it will be a terrible day. *The Lord* shall then speak *from Zion and Jerusalem,* from the throne of his glory. His speaking will be to the wicked, terrible as the roaring of a lion (for so the word signifies). 2. To the righteous it will be a joyful day. Their longings shall be satisfied: *The Lord will be the hope of his people.* He will be the *harbour* of his people (so the word is), their home. Their happiness shall be confirmed. Their holiness shall be completed (*v.* 17): *Then shall Jerusalem be holy,* the *holy city* indeed. The gospel-church is a holy society, even in its militant state, but will never be holiness itself till it comes to be triumphant. There shall not enter into the New Jerusalem anything that defiles or works iniquity. *So shall you know that I am the Lord your God.* It is an experimental knowledge. They shall find him their *hope and strength* in the worst of times, and so they shall *know that he is the Lord their God.*

Verses 18–21

These promises have their accomplishment in part in the kingdom of grace, but will have their full accomplishment in the kingdom of glory.

I. It is promised that the enemies of the church shall be vanquished and brought down, *v.* 19. Egypt, that old enemy of Israel, and Edom, which had an inveterate enmity to Israel, these *shall be a desolation,* no more to be inhabited. The quarrel God has with these kingdoms is for their *violence against the children of Judah;* see Ezek. xxv. 3, 8, 12, 15; xxvi. 2.

II. It is promised that the church shall be very happy in spiritual privileges, even during its militant state, but much more when it comes to be triumphant. Three things are promised:

1. Purity. This is put last here, as a reason for the rest (*v.* 21); but we may consider it first, as the ground and foundation of the rest: *I will cleanse their blood that I have not cleansed.* That shall be cleansed by the blood of Christ which could not be cleansed by the sacrifices and purifications of the ceremonial law. Though the refining and reforming of the church is work that goes on slowly, and still there is something that is *not cleansed,* yet there is a day coming when everything that is amiss shall be amended.

2. Plenty, *v.* 18. It intimates the abundance of vineyards, and of cattle in the pastures. And, to make the corn-land fruitful, the *rivers of Judah shall flow with water,* so that the country shall be like the garden of Eden, Ps. lxv. 9. But this seems to be meant spiritually; the graces and comforts of the new covenant are compared to *wine and milk* (Isa. lv. 1), and the Spirit to *rivers of living water,* John vii. 38. And these gifts abound much more under the New Testament than they did under the Old. The fountain of this plenty is in the *house of God,* whence the streams take their rise, as those *waters of the sanctuary* (Ezek. xlvii. 1) from *under the threshold of the house.* Christ himself is this fountain; his merit and grace cleanse and refresh us. This is said to water *the valley of Shittim,* which lay on the other side of Jordan, a barren valley, which intimates that gospel-grace, flowing from Christ, shall reach far, even to the Gentile world.

3. Perpetuity. This crowns all the rest (*v.* 20): *Judah shall dwell for ever,* and Jerusalem shall continue *from generation to generation.* The church of Christ shall continue in the world to the end of time.

THE PROPHECY OF AMOS

Amos was a country-farmer. Amos signifies a *burden*, whence the Jews have a tradition that he spoke with stammering lips; we may rather say that his speech was *weighty* and his word the *burden of the Lord*. He was (as most think) of Judah, yet prophesied chiefly against Israel, and at Bethel, *ch.* vii. 13. Some think his style is plain and rustic. It appears by his contest with Amaziah the priest of Bethel that he met with opposition, but was faithful and bold in reproving sin, and pressing in his exhortations to repentance and reformation. He begins with threatenings against the neighbouring nations that were enemies to Israel, *ch.* i and ii. He then calls Israel to account, and judges them for their idolatry, and their incorrigibleness under God's judgments, *ch.* iii and iv. He calls them to repentance (*ch.* v), foretells the desolations that were coming upon them not withstanding their security (*ch.* vi), some particular judgments (*ch.* vii), particularly on Amaziah; and, after other reproofs and threatenings (*ch.* viii and ix), concludes with a promise of the setting up of the Messiah's kingdom and the happiness of God's spiritual Israel.

CHAPTER 1

I. The general title of this prophecy (ver. 1), with the general scope of it, ver. 2. II. God's particular controversy with Syria (ver. 3–5), with Palestine (ver. 6–8), with Tyre (ver. 9, 10), with Edom (ver. 11, 12), and with Ammon (ver. 13–15), for their cruelty to his people. This explains God's pleading with the nations, Joel iii. 2.

Verses 1–2

I. The general character of this prophecy. It consists of *the words which the prophet saw*. The prophet saw these words, that is they were revealed to him in a *vision*, as John is said to see *the voice* that spoke to him, Rev. i. 12.

II. The person by whom this prophecy was sent— *Amos, who was among the herdmen of Tekoa*, and was one of them. Some think he was a rich dealer in cattle. Others think he was a poor keeper of cattle, for we find (*ch.* vii. 14, 15) that he was withal a *gatherer of wild figs*, by which we may suppose he could but just get his bread. When God would send a prophet to reprove and warn his people, he employed a shepherd.

III. The persons concerned in the prophecy of this book; the *ten tribes*, who were now ripening apace for ruin. God had raised them up prophets among themselves (*ch.* ii. 11), but they regarded them not; therefore God sends them one from Tekoa, in the land of Judah.

IV. The book is dated by the reigns of the kings under whom the prophet prophesied. It was in the days of *Uzziah king of Judah*, when the affairs of that kingdom went very well, and of Jeroboam II, king of Israel, when the affairs of that kingdom went pretty well; yet then they must both be told of their sins and of the judgments that were coming upon them, that they might not with the present gleam of prosperity flatter themselves into a confidence of their perpetual security. It was *two years before the earthquake*, that earthquake which is mentioned to have been *in the days of Uzziah* (Zech. xiv. 5).

V. The introduction to these prophecies, containing the general scope of them (*v.* 2): *The Lord will roar from Zion*. His threatenings by his prophets will be as terrible as the roaring of a lion is to the shepherds and their flocks. See Hosea (*ch.* xi. 10) and Joel, *ch.* iii. 16.

Verses 3–15

What the Lord says here may be explained by what he says Jer. xii. 14. Damascus was a near neighbour to Israel on the north, Tyre and Gaza on the west, Edom on the south, Ammon and Moab on the east; and all had been evil neighbours.

I. Though those nations will not worship him as their God, yet they shall be made to know that they are accountable to him as their Judge.

1. The indictment drawn up against them all is thus far the same, (1) That they are charged in general with *three transgressions, and with four*, that is, with many transgressions (as by one or two we mean *a few*, so by three or four we mean many), where we read of *three things, yea, four*, generally one seems to be more especially intended. (2) That the particular sin which is the fourth, is the sin of persecution.

2. The judgment given against them all is thus far the same, (1) That, their sin having risen to such a height, *God will not turn away the punishment thereof*. Justice shall take its course. (2) That God will *kindle a fire* among them; this is said concerning all these *evil neighbours, v.* 4, 7, 10, 12, 14. God will *send a fire* into their cities.

II. What is peculiar to each of them.

1. Concerning Damascus, the capital of Syria, a kingdom that was often vexatious to Israel. (1) The peculiar sin of Damascus: *They threshed Gilead with threshing-instruments of iron* (*v.* 3), which may be understood literally of their putting to the torture the inhabitants of Gilead whom they got into their hands, as David put the Ammonites under *saws and harrows*, 2 Sam. xii. 31. Or it may be taken figuratively. 2 Kings xiii. 7, He *destroyed them, and made them like the dust by threshing*. (2) The peculiar punishment of Damascus is, [1] That fire shall fasten not on the chief city, but on *the house of Hazael*, which he built; and *it shall devour the palaces of Ben-hadad*. [2] That the enemy shall force his way into the city (*v.* 5): *I will break the bar of Damascus* may be understood figuratively: the strength and safety of that great city shall fail, and prove insufficient. [3] That the people shall be destroyed with the sword: *I will cut off the inhabitant from the plain of Aven*, the *valley of idolatry* (1 Kings xx. 23). [4] That the body of the nation shall be carried off. The *people shall go into captivity unto Kir*, which was in the country of the Medes. We find this fulfilled (2 Kings xvi. 9) about fifty years after.

2. Concerning Gaza, a city of the Philistines. (1) The peculiar sin of the Philistines was *carrying away captive the whole captivity*, either of Israel or Judah, which some think refers to that inroad made upon Jehoram (2 Chron. xxi. 17), or, perhaps, to their seizing those that fled to them for shelter when

Sennacherib invaded Judah, and *selling them to the Grecians* (Joel iii. 4–6), or to the Edomites. (2) The peculiar punishment of the Philistines is that fire shall devour the palaces of Gaza, and that the *inhabitants of the other cities of the Philistines*, Ashdod (or Azotus), Ashkelon, and Ekron, shall all be *cut off*.

3. Concerning Tyre, that famous city, that was itself a kingdom, *v.* 9. (1) The peculiar sin of Tyre is *delivering up the whole captivity to Edom*, that is, selling to the Edomites those of Israel that fled to them for shelter. (2) In the punishment of Tyrus *the palaces thereof* shall be *devoured*, which was done when Nebuchadnezzar took it after thirteen years' siege.

4. Concerning Edom, the posterity of Esau. (1) Their peculiar sin was an unmerciful pursuit of the people of God to do them a mischief, *v.* 11. He did *pursue his brother with the sword*, not only of old (Num. xx. 18), but ever since. Whenever any other enemy had put Judah or Israel to flight, then the Edomites fell upon the rear, slew those that were half dead already, and did *cast off all pity*. (2) In their punishment a *fire* shall be *sent to devour their palaces*.

5. Concerning the Ammonites, *v.* 13–15. The fire of their anger turned against the people of God; they *ripped up the women with child of Gilead*. It was done with a devilish design to extirpate the race of Israel by killing not only all that were born, but all that were to be born. It was *that they might enlarge their border*, that they might make the land of Gilead their own. We find (Jer. xlix. 1) that the Ammonites inherited *Gad* (that is, Gilead) under pretence that Israel had no heirs. (2) See how violently the fire of God's anger burned against them. *Shall not his soul be avenged.* The fire shall be kindled *with shouting in the day of battle*, that is, war shall kindle the fire. It is particularly threatened that *their king and his princes shall go together into captivity*, carried away by the king of Babylon. *Milchom shall go into captivity;* some understand it of the god of the Ammonites, whom they called *Moloch—a king*.

CHAPTER 2

I. God, by the prophet, proceeds with Moab as with other nations, ver. 1–3. II. He shows what quarrel he had with Judah, ver. 4, 5. III. He at length begins his charge against Israel, to which all that goes before is but an introduction. 1. The sins they are charged with—injustice, oppression, whoredom, ver. 6–8. 2. The temporal and spiritual mercies God had bestowed upon them, for which they had made him such ungrateful returns, ver. 9–12. 3. God's complaint of them for their sins (ver. 13) and his threatenings of their ruin, ver. 14–16.

Verses 1–8

I. The judgment of Moab. 1. Moab's fourth transgression was cruelty. The instance given refers not to the people of God: The king of Moab *burnt the bones of the king of Edom into lime*. There was war between the Edomites and the Moabites, in which the king of Moab offered his own son for a burnt-offering, to appease his deity, 2 Kings iii. 26, 27. Afterwards he, or his successors, having an advantage against the *king of Edom*, seized him alive and burnt him to ashes, or slew him and burnt his body, or dug up the bones and *burnt them to lime*. 2. Moab's doom for this transgression is death. *Moab shall die;* the Moabites shall be cut off with the sword. The king, judges and princes, shall be cut off together.

II. Judah also is a near neighbour to Israel, and had made itself like the heathen and mingled with them, and therefore the indictment here runs in the same form: *For three transgressions of Judah, and for four, I will not turn away the punishment thereof.* The sentence is the same (*v.* 5): "*I will send a fire upon Judah*, and it shall *devour the palaces of Jerusalem*,

though it is the holy city, and God has formerly been *known in its palaces for a refuge.*" But the sin charged upon Judah is different from all the rest. The other nations were reckoned with for injuries done to men, but Judah is reckoned with for indignities done to God, *v.* 4. *They have despised the law of the Lord,* and herein they despised the wisdom, justice, and goodness, as well as the authority and sovereignty, of the Lawmaker. They put honour upon his rivals, their idols, here called *their lies*, which *caused them to err.*

III. *The words* which *Amos saw concerning Israel.* He begins with them as with the rest: *For three transgressions of Israel, and for four, I will not turn away the punishment thereof.* Their sins were, 1. Perverting justice. They made nothing of selling a righteous man for a piece of silver; the bribe always turned the scale. Those who will wrong their consciences for anything will come at length to sell justice for a pair of old shoes. 2. Oppressing the poor: *They pant after the dust of the earth on the head of the poor;* they make a prey of those that are in sorrow with dust on their heads, poor orphans in mourning for their parents; to get their estates. 3. Abominable uncleanness, even incest itself. 4. Regaling themselves, and yet pretending to honour their God with that which they had got by oppression and extortion, *v.* 8. They *lay themselves down* at ease upon *clothes laid to pledge*, which they ought to have restored the same night, according to the law, Deut. xxiv. 12, 13. And they *drink the wine of the condemned*, of such as they have fined, spending that in sensuality which they have got by injustice. They think to make atonement for this by *drinking this wine in the house of their God*, in the temples where they worshipped their calves.

Verses 9–16

I. God puts his people Israel in mind of the great things he had done for them, *v.* 9, 10. "Israel, remember God brought thee out of *Egypt*, where thou wouldst otherwise have perished in slavery. He *led thee forty years* through a desert land, and fed thee in a *wilderness.*" He made room for them in Canaan: *I destroyed the Amorite before them.* They were of great stature (*whose height was like the height of the cedars*) and the people of Israel were as shrubs to them; and they were *strong as the oaks. I destroyed his fruit from above and his roots from beneath*, so that the Amorites were no more a nation. Thus highly did God value Israel. How ungrateful then were those who put such contempt upon him!

II. He upbraids them with the spiritual privileges they enjoyed as a holy nation, *v.* 11. They had prophets divinely inspired, and commissioned to make known the mind of God to them. It was an honour that they had children of their own to be God's messengers to them. They had Nazarites that were bright examples of piety. These God raised up to be his witnesses against the impieties of that degenerate age.

III. He charges them with the abuse of the means of grace they enjoyed, *v.* 12. They did what they could to debauch good people: *You gave the Nazarites wine to drink*, contrary to their vow. They did what they could to silence good ministers, and to stop their mouths: *You commanded the prophets, saying, Prophesy not*, and threatened them if they did prophesy (*ch.* vii. 12).

IV. He complains of the wrong they did him by their sins (*v.* 13): "*I am pressed under you*, I am *straitened* by you (Hos. xi. 8, 9). I am loaded and burdened by you (Isa. i. 24). *I am pressed under you* and the load of your sins *as a cart is pressed that is full of sheaves*, is loaded with corn, in the midst of the *joy of harvest.*"

V. He threatens them with unavoidable ruin. And so some read, *v.* 13, "*Behold I will press, or straiten, your place, as a cart full of sheaves presses;* they shall be loaded with judgments till they sink." If God load us daily with his benefits, and we, notwithstanding that, load him with our sins, how can we expect any other than that he should load us with his judgments? When the Assyrian army comes to lay the country waste by sword and captivity none shall escape. *He that is swift of foot shall not deliver himself, v.* 15. Or do they say, *We will flee upon horses,* and *we will ride upon the swift?* Yet they shall be overtaken. It will be in vain to think of fighting it out. *The strong shall not strengthen his force.* And *the mighty* shall not be able to *deliver himself.* And, as the bodily strength shall fail, so shall the weapons of war. *Neither shall he stand that handles the bow. He that is courageous among the mighty,* that used to look danger in the face, shall *flee away naked in that day.*

CHAPTER 3

A stupid, heedless people, are called upon to take notice, I. Of the judgments of God against them and the warnings he gave them, and to be hereby awakened out of their security, ver. 1–8. II. Of the sins that were found among them, by which God was provoked thus to threaten, thus to punish, so that they unless they repented and reformed, might expect no other than that God should proceed, ver. 9–15.

Verses 1–8

The *children of Israel* would not regard the words of counsel that God had spoken to them, and now they shall be made to hear the word of reproof.

I. The gracious cognizance God had taken of them, and the favours he had bestowed, should not exempt them from the punishment due for their sins. Israel is a *family* that God *brought up out of the land of Egypt* (*v.* 1), and it was no more than a family when it went thither; thence God delivered it. It is a family that God has owned in a peculiar manner. *In Judah is God known,* and therefore Judah is known of God. God has covenanted with them, and conversed with them. *Therefore I will punish you for all your iniquities.* The favours of God, if they do not restrain us from sin, shall not exempt us from punishment. It is necessary that God should vindicate his own honour by making it appear that he hates sin and hates it most in those that are nearest to him.

II. They could not expect any comfortable communion with God unless they first made their peace with him (*v.* 3): *Can two walk together except they be agreed?* Where there is not friendship, there cannot be fellowship.

III. The warnings God gave them of judgments approaching were not groundless (*v.* 4): "*Will a lion roar in the forest when he has no prey* in view? No; he roars upon his prey. Nor would God thus give you warning if he were not really about to fall upon you with judgments." The threatenings of the word and providence of God are not bugbears, to frighten children and fools, but are inferences from the sin of man and presages of the judgments of God.

IV. Their own wickedness was the cause of these judgments, *v.* 5. It is their own sin that has entangled them; for *can a bird fall in a snare upon the earth where no gin is for him?* Nothing but their own repentance can disentangle them.

V. All their troubles came from the hand of God's providence (*v.* 6).

VI. Their prophets, who give them warning of judgments approaching, deliver nothing to them but what they have *received from the Lord* (*v.* 7): *Surely the Lord Jehovah will do nothing,* none of that evil in the city spoken of (*v.* 6), *but he reveals it to his servants the prophets.* The *secret* of God is in a peculiar manner with the prophets, to whom the Spirit of prophecy is

a Spirit of revelation. The prophets cannot but make that known to the people which God has made known to them (*v.* 8): *The Lord God has spoken; who can but prophesy?* They received a command from God to deliver what they had been charged with; and they would have been false to their trust if they had not done it.

VII. They ought to tremble before God as they would on the sounding of a trumpet. *Shall a trumpet be blown in the city, and the people not be afraid,* or *run together?* (so some read it, *v.* 6). Yet when God by his prophets gives them notice of their danger it makes no impression.

Verses 9–15

The Israelites are again convicted and condemned.

I. Notice is given of it to their neighbours. The prophet is ordered to *publish it in the palaces of Ashdod,* one of the chief cities of the Philistines; the summons must go even to *the palaces in the land of Egypt.* God's controversies with sinners do not fear a scrutiny; even Philistines and Egyptians will be made to see that *the ways of the Lord are equal,* but *our ways are unequal.*

1. Let them observe the behaviour of the inhabitants of Samaria; and they may see how boisterous they are, and hear how loud the cry of their sin is, as was that of Sodom. In their streets you will see *great tumults in the midst thereof;* reason and justice run down by the fury of an outrageous mob. *The oppressed* are *in the midst thereof,* thrown down and crushed by their oppressors. In their courts of justice, those who preside *know not to do right;* they act as if they had no notion at all of justice. Their treasures and stores are replenished with *violence and robbery,* with that which was unjustly got and unjustly kept.

2. Let them see how heavy the doom is, *v.* 11, 12. Their country *shall be invaded and ruined.* The Assyrian forces shall surround it and break in on every side. They *stored up robbery in their palaces,* and therefore their *palaces shall be spoiled.* Their countrymen shall not escape, *v.* 12. They shall be in the hands of the enemy, as a lamb in the mouth of a lion, devoured and eaten up, and if any do escape, yet they shall be very few, and those of the meanest and least considerable, like *two legs,* or *shanks,* of a lamb, *or a piece of an ear,* which the lion drops, or *the shepherd* takes from him, when he has eaten the body; so, perhaps, here and there one may escape from Samaria and from Damascus, but those shall do so with the utmost hazard, by hiding themselves in the *corner of a bed* or under the *bed's feet,* which intimates that their spirits shall be quite cowed and broken.

II. Notice is given to themselves, *v.* 13. Let this be *testified,* and *heard, in the house of Jacob,* for it is spoken *by the Lord God, the God of hosts.* 1. Woe to *their altars,* for God will *visit* them. He will bring into the account all their superstition and idolatry— *the horns of the altar shall be cut off,* and *fall to the ground,* and with them the altar itself broken to pieces. Some make *the horns of the altar* to signify all those things which they flee to for refuge; they shall all be cut off, so that they shall have nothing to take hold of. 2. Woe to their houses, for God will visit them too. He will enquire into the robbery they have stored up in their houses, and the luxury in which they lived: *and I will smite the winter-house with the summer-house, v.* 15. *The houses of ivory shall perish,* shall be burnt or pulled down; *and the great houses shall have an end;* their extravagance about them will be put to the score of their sins and follies.

CHAPTER 4

I. The oppressors in Israel are threatened for their oppression of the poor, ver. 1–3. II. The idolaters in Israel are given up to their own heart's lusts, ver. 4, 5. III. All the sins of Israel are aggravated from their refusal to return and reform, ver. 6–11. IV. They are invited yet to humble themselves before God, ver. 12, 13.

Verses 1–5

Oppressors shall be humbled and idolaters shall be hardened.

I. Proud oppressors shall be humbled for their oppressions; for *he that does wrong shall receive according to the wrong that he has done.*

1. How their sin is described, *v.* 1. They are compared to the *kine of Bashan*, a breed of cattle very strong, especially if they were fed upon *the mountain of Samaria.* Amos had been a herdsman, and he speaks in the dialect of his calling, comparing the rich men, that lived in luxury and wantonness, to the *kine of Bashan*, which were wanton and unruly, broke through the hedges, and trespassed upon the neighbouring grounds; and not only so, but pushed and gored the smaller cattle. Those that had their summerhouses upon the mountains of Samaria were as mischievous as the kine upon the mountains of Bashan and as injurious to those about them. They oppress the poor and *crush* them, to squeeze something out of them. They are in confederacy with those that do so. They *say to their masters* (to the masters of the poor, that take from them what they have, when they ought to relieve them), *"Bring, and let us drink;* let us feast with you upon the gains of your oppression, and then we will protect you, and stand by you in it, and reject the appeals of the poor against you."

2. How their punishment is described, *v.* 2, 3. God will *take them away with hooks, and their posterity with fish-hooks;* he will send the Assyrian army upon them, that shall not only enclose the body of the nation in their net, but shall angle for particular persons, and take them prisoners as with fish-hooks, shall draw them out of their own land as fish are drawn out of the water. Some shall attempt to escape by flight: *You shall go out at the breaches* made in the wall of the city, *every cow at that which is before her,* to shift for her own safety, and now the unruly kine of Bashan are themselves crushed, as they crushed the poor and needy. Others shall think to shelter themselves: *You shall throw yourselves* (so some read it), or *throw them* (that is your children) *into the palace,* where the enemy will find them ready to be seized.

3. How their sentence to this punishment is ratified: *The Lord God has sworn it by his holiness.* He swears by *his holiness*, that attribute of his which is so much his glory.

II. Obstinate idolaters shall be hardened in their idolatries (*v.* 4, 5): *Come to Bethel, and transgress.* It is spoken ironically: *"Do* so; take your course; *multiply* your *transgressions* by multiplying your sacrifices, *for this liketh you;* but what will you do in the end?" They mimicked God's institutions. They had their *daily sacrifice* at the altar of Bethel, as God had at his altar; they had their *thank-offerings* as God had, only they allowed *leaven* in them. Holy bread would not serve them, unless it were pleasant bread. They are upbraided with it. "Your foolish hearts shall be more and more darkened and besotted, and you shall be quite *given up to* these *strong delusions, to believe a lie."* Thus Christ said to the Jews, *Fill you up the measure of your fathers,* Matt. xxiii. 32.

Verses 6–13

I. God had by several tokens intimated to them his displeasure, but it had no effect.

1. It is five times repeated in these verses, as the burden of the charge, *"Yet have you not returned unto me, saith the Lord;* there is no sign of amendment. This intimates that that which God designed in all his rebukes was to influence them to return to him. If they had returned to their God, they would have been accepted. It is no *pleasure to the Almighty that he should afflict.*

2. He recounts the less judgments with which he had tried to bring them to repentance. There had sometimes been a scarcity of provisions (*v.* 6): *"I have given you cleanness of teeth in all your cities,* for you had no meat to chew." Or, *I have given you emptiness of teeth,* nothing to fill your mouths with. Some think this refers to that *seven years' famine* that was in Elisha's time, which we read of 2 Kings viii. 1. *I have withholden the rain from you.* The rain was withheld *when there were yet three months to the harvest.* Sometimes the fruits of their ground were eaten up by caterpillars, or blasted with mildew, *v.* 9. But they did not take warning: *Yet have you not returned unto me.* Sometimes the plague had raged among them, and the sword of war had cut off multitudes, *v.* 10. It was a *pestilence after the manner of Egypt. In the way of Egypt* (so the margin); when they were making their escape to Egypt, or going thither to seek for aid, the pestilence seized them by the way. The dead carcases of those that were slain either with sword or pestilence were so many that the *stench of their camps came up into their nostrils.* And yet this did not prevail to make them religious. In these judgments some were remarkably cut off, and made monuments of justice, others were remarkably spared, and made monuments of mercy, but it had no effect, *v.* 11. *I have overthrown some of you, as God overthrew Sodom and Gomorrah.* Others very narrowly escaped: *"You were* many of you as a *firebrand plucked out of the burning,* like Lot out of Sodom, and yet you hate sin never the more, nor love God ever the more for the deliverance he wrought for you."

II. God calls upon his people, now in this their day, to understand the things that belong to their peace, before they were hidden from their eyes, *v.* 12, 13. He threatens them with sorer judgments than any they had yet been under. Nothing but reformation will prevent the ruin of a sinful people. *I will punish you yet seven times more, if you will* not *be reformed* (Lev. xxvi. 23, 24). "Resolve therefore to meet him as a humble suppliant, to meet him as *thy God*, in covenant with thee, to submit, and stand it out no longer." Since we cannot flee from God we are concerned to prepare to meet him; and therefore he gives us warning, that we may prepare. He sets forth the greatness and power of God as a reason why we should prepare to meet him, *v.* 13. He that formed the *great mountains* can *make them plain*, when they stand in the way of his people's salvation. He *declares unto man what is his thought.* He makes known by his servants the prophets the thought of his justice against impenitent sinners, and the thought of good he thinks towards those that repent. He knows the thought that is in man's heart; he *understands it afar off.* He *treads upon the high places of the earth*, tramples upon proud men, and upon the idols that were worshipped in the highest places. *Jehovah the God of hosts is his name,* for he has his being of himself, and is the fountain of all being, and all the hosts of heaven and earth are at his command. Let us humble ourselves before this God.

CHAPTER 5

The prophet here tells them, I. What preparation they must make; they must seek the Lord, and not idols (ver. 4–8); they must seek good, and love it, ver. 14, 15. II. Why they must make this preparation to meet their God. 1. Because of the present deplorable condition they were in, ver. 1–3. 2. Because it was by sin that they were brought into such a condition, ver. 7, 10–12. 3. Because it would be their happiness to seek God, and he was ready to be found of them, ver. 8, 9, 14. 4. Because he would proceed to their ruin, if they did not seek him, ver. 5, 6, 13, 16, 17. 5. Because all their confidences would fail them if they did not make him their friend. Their contempt of God's judgments would not secure them, ver. 18–20. Their external services in religion would not avail, ver. 21–24. Their having been long in possession of church-privileges would not be their protection, ver. 25–27. They have therefore no way left them to save themselves but by repentance and reformation.

Verses 1–3

This chapter begins with *Hear this word*. It is the *word which I take up*—not the prophet only, but the God that sent him. It is *the word that the Lord has spoken*, ch. iii. 1, a lamentable account of the present state of the kingdom of Israel, and a prediction of its destruction. *The virgin of Israel has fallen* (*v.* 2), *she has fallen* into contempt, and is universally slighted. *She shall no more rise*, shall never recover her former dignity again. *She is forsaken upon her land*. Those she was in alliance with abroad failed her, but friends at home deserted her; she would not have been carried captive into a strange land if she had not first been *forsaken upon her own land*. Their people, that should have helped them up, were diminished, *v.* 3. The city that had a militia, 1,000 strong, after the battle, shall find but 100 *left*; and, in proportion, the city that sent out 100 shall have but *ten* come back.

Verses 4–15

A message from God to the house of Israel.

I. They are told of their faults. God tells them, in general (*v.* 12), "*I know your manifold transgressions, and your mighty sins;* and you shall be made to know them too." What a multitude of vain and vile thoughts lodge within us! What a multitude of idle, wicked words have been spoken by us! In what a multitude of instances have we indulged our corrupt appetites and passions! And how many are our omissions of duty. He specifies some of these mighty sins. They corrupted the worship of God, and turned to idols; this is implied, *v.* 5. They had *sought to Bethel*, where one of the golden calves was; they had frequented Gilgal, a place where they chose to set up idols. Beer-sheba, famous in the days of the patriarchs, was now another rendezvous of idols. They perverted justice among themselves (*v.* 7): "*You turn judgment to wormwood*, that is, you make your administrations of justice bitter and displeasing to God and man." They trod upon the poor (*v.* 11), and such as they could get nothing by. The judges aimed at nothing but to enrich themselves; and therefore they *took from* the poor *burdens of wheat* by extortion. The poor had no other way to save themselves than by presenting to them horse-loads of corn which they and their families should have had to subsist upon. They took from the poor *debts of wheat*, so some read it. This sin of oppression they are again charged with (*v.* 12): *They afflict the just*, by turning the law against those that are innocent and *quiet in the land*; and he that *departed from evil* thereby *made himself a prey* to them. They take a bribe from the rich to patronise and protect them in oppressing the poor. Thus they *turn aside the poor in the gate*, in the courts of justice, *from their right*. Furthermore they were malicious persecutors of God's faithful ministers and people, *v.* 10. They could not bear to be reproved by the reading and expounding of the law, and the messages which the prophets delivered to them in the name of the Lord. *They hate him that rebukes in the gate*. Though things were generally very bad, yet there were some among them that *spoke uprightly*, and condemned them. For that reason *they abhorred them*; they were such inveterate enemies to honesty that they could not endure the sight of an honest man. Prophets cannot keep silence; the impulse they are under will not allow them to act on prudential considerations; they must *cry aloud, and not spare*. The prudent, who were *wise as serpents*, because they knew not how what they said might be misrepresented, were so cautious as to say nothing. The cautious men will say to a bold reprover, as Erasmus to Luther: "*Abi in cellam, et dic, Miserere mei, Domine—Away to thy cell, and cry, Have mercy on me, O Lord!*" *Evil times* will not bear plain dealing, that is, *evil men* will not.

II. They are told of what judgments they lay exposed to for their sins. The places of their idolatry are in danger of being ruined, *v.* 5. *Gilgal*, the head-quarters of idolatry, *shall go into captivity, and Bethel* with its golden calf *shall come to nought*. The body of the kingdom is in danger of being ruined with them, *v.* 6. There is danger lest, if you seek not God, he *break out like a fire in the house of Joseph and devour it. And there shall be none to quench it in Bethel*. God tells them that when the fire of his judgments should kindle upon them all the gods they served at Bethel should not be able to quench it. What they have got by extortion shall be taken from them (*v.* 11): "*You have built houses of hewn stone*, which you thought would be lasting; *but you shall not dwell in them*, for your enemies shall burn them down, or take you into captivity. *You have planted pleasant vineyards*, but you shall never *drink wine of them*."

III. They are told their duty, and have great encouragement to set about it. The duties here prescribed are godliness and honesty, seriousness in their applications to God and justice in their dealings with men.

1. They are exhorted to be sincere and devout in their addresses to God, *v.* 4. God is not sought truly if he be not sought exclusively: "*Seek you the Lord, and seek not Bethel* (*v.* 5), for you *forsake your own mercies* if you observe those *lying vanities*. But *seek the Lord* (*v.* 6, 8); enquire after him; seek to know his mind as your rule." Seeking God will be *our life*. So he tells them (*v.* 4): *Seek you me, and you shall live*. So the prophet tells them (*v.* 6): *Seek the Lord, and you shall live*. "You shall be delivered from the judgments you are threatened with; your nation shall live, shall recover from its present languishings; your souls shall live; you shall be sanctified and comforted, and made for ever blessed. *You shall live*." God whom we are to *seek* (*v.* 8, 9) is a God of almighty power. Divers instances are here given of God's power as Creator. Compare *ch.* iv. 13. *First*, The stars are the work of his hands (*v.* 26), the *stars of your god*, those stars are God's creatures and servants. He *makes the seven stars and Orion*, two constellations, which Amos, a herdsman, while he kept his cattle by night, had particularly observed. He made them and either *binds* or *looses* the *sweet influences* of *Pleiades* and *Orion*, the two constellations mentioned. See Job xxxviii. 31; ix. 9. *Secondly*, The constant succession of day and night is under his direction. It is he that *turns* the night *into the morning* by the rising of the sun, and by the setting of the sun *makes the day dark with night*; and the same power can, for humble penitents, easily turn affliction and sorrow into prosperity and joy, but can as easily turn the prosperity of presumptuous sinners into darkness. *Thirdly*, The rain rises and falls as he appoints. He *calls for the waters of the sea*; out of them vapours are drawn up by the heat of the sun, which gather into clouds, and are *poured out upon the face of the earth*, to make it fruitful. It is God that has *made these things; Jehovah is his name*. As he is a God of almighty power himself, so he *gives strength and power unto his people* that seek him, and *renews strength* to those that had lost it, if they *wait upon him* for it; for (*v.* 9) he *strengthens the spoiled against the strong*. This is an encouragement to the people to *seek the Lord*, that, if they do so, they shall find him able to retrieve their affairs.

2. They are exhorted to be honest and just in their dealings with men, *v.* 14, 15: *Seek good, and not evil. Hate the evil, and love the good, and establish judgment in the gate;* re-establish it there, whence it has been banished, *v.* 7. If the right course be taken grievances may be redressed and abuses rectified: justice may yet triumph where injustice tyrannizes. In order to this, good must be loved and sought, evil must be hated. We must love good principles, love to do good, love good people; and, whatever good we do, we must do it from a principle of love, and with delight. "He will be with you *as you have spoken,* that is, as you have *gloried.*" Or, "As you have prayed when *you sought the Lord.* Live up to your prayers, and you shall have what you pray for." This is the likeliest way to make the nation happy: "If you seek and love that which is good, you may contribute to the saving of the land from ruin."

Verses 16–20

I. A terrible threatening of destruction approaching, *v.* 16, 17. The threatening is introduced with more than ordinary solemnity, to strike an awe upon them; it is not the word of the prophet only, but it is the Lord Jehovah, it is the *God of hosts,* and it is *Adonai— the Lord,* who has an absolute sovereignty; it is he who can and will make his words good. The land of Israel shall be put in mourning. Look into the cities, and *wailing shall be in all streets.* Look into the country, and *they shall say in all the highways, Alas! alas!* The husbandman shall be called from the plough by the calamities of his country. Even in all vineyards, where there used to be nothing but mirth and pleasure, there shall be general wailing, when a foreign force invades the country. *I will pass through thee,* as the destroying angel passed through the land of Egypt.

II. A reproof to those who made light of these threatenings, *v.* 18. Woe unto you that *desire the day of the Lord,* that really wish for times of war and confusion, as some do who have restless spirits, and long for changes. Or it is spoken to those who, in their lamentations for the calamities, wished they might die. Or, rather, it is spoken to those who speak jestingly of the day of the Lord. Let him do his worst; *let him make speed,* and *hasten his work,* Isa. v. 19. In answer to this, 1. He shows the folly of those who impudently wished for God's judgments: "*To what end is it for you* that the day of the Lord should come? You will find it not a thing to be bantered. *The day of the Lord is darkness, and not light, v.* 18. And, when God makes a day dark, all the world cannot make it light." He shows the folly of those who desire *the day of the Lord,* in hope to better themselves, or, at least, to know the worst. But the prophet tells them that they know not what they ask, *v.* 19. It is *as if a man did flee from a lion and a bear met him,* or as if a man, to escape all dangers abroad, *went into the house for security,* and *leaned his hand on the wall* to rest himself, and there a *serpent bit him.*

Verses 21–27

These verses show how little God valued their shows of devotion while they went on in their sins.

I. How displeasing their hypocritical services were to God. They had their *feast-days* at Bethel, in imitation of those at Jerusalem. They had their *solemn assemblies* for religious worship. They offered to God *burnt-offerings,* to the honour of God, together with the *meat-offerings;* they offered the *peace-offerings,* to implore the favour of God, and they offered the *fat beasts* they had, *v.* 21, 22. In imitation likewise of the temple-music, they had the *noise of their songs* and the *melody of their viols* (*v.* 23). With these services they hoped to obtain leave to go on in sin.

He *hated,* he *despised,* their *feast-days.* Nothing more hateful, more despicable, than hypocrisy. God will not *smell* in *their solemn assemblies,* for there is nothing in them that is grateful to him, but a great deal that is offensive. He will not accept them. Now this intimates, 1. That sacrifice itself is of small account with God in comparison with moral duties; to love God and our neighbour is *better than all burnt-offering and sacrifice.* 2. That the sacrifice of the wicked is really an abomination to him, Prov. xv. 8. Dissembled piety is double iniquity.

II. What it was that he required without which no sacrifice would be acceptable (*v.* 24): *Let judgment run down as waters,* among you, *and righteousness as a mighty stream,* that is, "Let there be a general reformation of manners among you; let religion (God's *judgment*) and *righteousness* have their due influence upon you; let your land be watered with it, and let it bear down all vice and profaneness; let it run wide as overflowing waters, and strong as a mighty stream. Let justice be duly administered, let not the current of it be stopped by partiality and bribery; let it be pure as running waters, not muddied with corruption; let it run *like a mighty stream.*

III. What little stress God had laid upon the law of sacrifices, in comparison with the moral precepts (*v.* 25): "*Did you offer unto me sacrifices in the wilderness forty years?* No, you did not." For part of that time sacrifice was neglected; after the second year, the passover was not kept till they came into Canaan; and yet he never imputed the omission to them as their fault, but continued his kindness to them: it was their murmuring and unbelief for which God was displeased with them. But, though ritual sacrifices may thus be dispensed with, spiritual sacrifices will not; even justice and honesty will not excuse for the want of prayer and praise, a broken heart and the love of God.

IV. What little reason they had to expect that their sacrifices should be acceptable to God, when they and their fathers had been all along addicted to the worship of other gods. So some take *v.* 25, "*Did you offer to me sacrifices,* that is, to me only? No, and therefore not at all to me acceptably." "*But you have borne the tabernacle of your Moloch* (*v.* 26), little shrines that you made to carry. You have had the images of your *Moloch—your king*" (probably representing *the sun,* that sits king among the heavenly bodies), "and *Chiun,* or *Remphan*" (as Stephen calls it, Acts vii. 43, after the LXX), which, it is supposed, represented Saturn. The worship of the sun, moon, and stars, was the most ancient, and most plausible idolatry. They *made to themselves* the *star of their God,* the name of which they gave to their god.

V. What punishment God would inflict upon them for their persisting in idolatry (*v.* 27): *I will cause you to go into captivity beyond Damascus.* Their captivity by the Assyrians was far beyond that by the Syrians. Or the captivity of Israel under Shalmaneser was far beyond that of Damascus under Tiglath-pileser, and much more grievous, which was foretold, *ch.* i. 5.

CHAPTER 6

I. A sinful people studying to put a slight upon God's threatenings and to make them appear trivial (ver. 2, 3), their power (ver. 13), their pleasures, ver. 4–6. II. A serious prophet studying to put a weight upon God's threatenings and to make them appear terrible (ver. 7), God's abandoning them and theirs to death (ver. 8–11), and bringing desolation upon them, ver. 12–14.

Verses 1–7

The first words of the chapter are the contents of these verses: *Woe to those that are at ease!*

I. A description of their pride, security, and sensuality, for which God would reckon with them.

1. They were vainly conceited of their own dignities, and thought those would secure them from the judgments threatened. (1) Those that dwelt in Zion thought that was honour and protection enough. Those that dwelt there doubted not but that God's sanctuary would be a sanctuary to them and would shelter them from his judgments. (2) Those that dwelt *in the mountain of Samaria*, trusted in it, because it was the metropolis of a potent kingdom, and the headquarters of its religion. (3) Both these two kingdoms valued themselves upon their relation to Israel, which they looked upon as making them the *chief of the nations*. The *house of Israel* came to them, that is, was divided into those kingdoms, of which Zion and Samaria were the mother cities. Those that were at ease were the princes and rulers. Great nations and great men are apt to overvalue themselves. But, for a check to their pride, the prophet bids them take notice of those cities that had been as illustrious in their time as ever Zion or Samaria was, and yet were destroyed, *v*. 2. "Go *to Calneh* (an ancient city built by Nimrod, Gen. x. 10), it is now in ruins; so is *Hamath the great*, one of the chief cities of Syria. Gath was likewise made desolate by Hazael, 2 Kings xii. 17. Now *were they better than these kingdoms* of Judah and Israel? Yes, and *their border greater than your border*, so they had more reason than you to be confident of their safety; yet you see what has become of them, and dare you be secure?"

2. They persisted in their wicked courses upon a presumption that they should never be called to an account for them (*v*. 3). You *put it far away*, and therefore you *cause the seat of violence to draw near*.

3. They indulged themselves in all manner of sensual pleasures and delights, *v*. 4–6. That which they are here charged with is not in itself sinful (these things might be soberly and moderately used), but they placed their happiness in the gratification of their carnal appetites. They were extravagant. They were lazy. They *abound in superfluities* (so the margin reads it), when many of their poor brethren wanted necessaries. They must have everything of the best and abundance of it: They ate *the lambs out of the flock* and the *calves out of the midst of the stall*. Some men never show their ingenuity but in their luxury; on that they bestow all their faculty of invention. Or it intimates their profaneness in their mirth; they mimicked the temple-music, and made a jest of that, because, it may be, it was old-fashioned, and they took a pride in bantering it. They drank to excess. They affected the strongest perfumes to make them more in love with their own bodies.

4. They had no concern at all for the interests of the church of God, and of the nation: *They are not grieved for the affliction of Joseph;* the church of God, including both the kingdoms of Judah and Israel (which are called *Joseph*, Ps. lxxx. 1), was in distress, invaded. As to their own kingdom, great breaches were made upon it, upon its peace and welfare; and they were so besotted that they were not aware of them. It is all one to them whether the nation sink or swim, so that they can but live in pleasure. Some think that, in calling the afflicted church *Joseph*, there is an allusion to the story of Pharaoh's butler, who *remembered not Joseph, but forgot him*, Gen. xl. 21, 23. Thus they *drank wine in bowls*, but *were not grieved for the affliction of Joseph*.

II. The doom passed upon them (*v*. 7): *Therefore now shall they go captive with the first that go captive*. Those who lived in luxury shall lose even their liberty. Those who *stretched themselves* shall be made to contract themselves, and to come into a less compass.

Verses 8–14

I. This burden is bound on by *the Lord the God of hosts*.

II. How heavily this burden lies! 1. God will abhor and abandon them, and that implies misery enough. Their temple, altar, and priesthood, were the excellencies of Jacob; but, when these were polluted by sin, God abhorred them, *ch*. v. 21. And, if God abhor them, He will *deliver up the city with all that is therein*, into the hands of the enemy, that will lay it waste, and make a prey of all its wealth. 2. There shall be a great and general mortality among them (*v*. 9). That which makes this judgment the more grievous is that their hearts seem to be hardened under it. 3. Their houses shall be destroyed, *v*. 11. God *will smite the great house with breaches, and the little house with clefts*.

III. How justly they are thus burdened. If we understand the matter aright, we shall say, *The Lord is righteous*. God had sent them his prophets, to *break up their fallow-ground*; but they found them as hard as the rock. Though they are the house of Israel, yet he will *raise up against them a nation* which they had many a time hoped in, even the Assyrians, and this nation shall *afflict them*, from the *entering in of Hamath*, in the north, to *the river of the wilderness*, the river of Egypt, Sihor or Nile, in the south.

CHAPTER 7

I. God contending with Israel. 1. They are threatened with less judgments, but are reprieved at the prayer of Amos, ver. 1–6. 2. God's patience worn out by their obstinacy, and they are sentenced, ver. 7–9. II. Israel contending with God, by the opposition given to his prophet. 1. Amaziah informs against Amos (ver. 10, 11) and does what he can to rid the country of him, ver. 12, 13. 2. Amos justifies himself in what he did as a prophet (ver. 14, 15), the judgments of God against Amaziah his prosecutor (ver. 16, 17).

Verses 1–9

God bears long, but he will not bear always, with a provoking people.

I. Two instances of God's sparing mercy.

1. God is here coming against this sinful nation, first by one judgment and then by another. (1) He begins with the judgment of famine. The prophet saw this in vision. He saw God *forming grasshoppers*, or *locusts*, *v*. 1. God formed these grasshoppers (and the wisdom and power of God appears in the structure of an ant as of an elephant), as instruments of his wrath. These grasshoppers were sent *in the beginning of the shooting up of the latter growth, after the king's mowings*. The judgment was mitigated by the mercy that went before it. God could have sent these insects to eat up the grass at the beginning of the first growth, in the spring, when the grass was most needed; but God suffered that to grow, and suffered them to gather it in. The grasshoppers were commissioned to eat up only the *latter growth* (the edgrew we call it in the country), the after-grass, is of little value in comparison with the former. The remembrance of the mercies of the former growth should make us submissive to the will of God when we meet with disappointments in the latter growth. Some understand this figuratively of a wasting destroying army brought upon them. (2) He proceeds to the judgment of fire (*v*. 4): *The Lord God called to contend by fire*. A fire was kindled among them, by which perhaps is meant a great drought (the heat of the sun scorched it, and burnt up the roots of the grass which the locusts had eaten the spires of), or a raging fever, which was as a fire in their bones, or lightning, fire from heaven, which consumed their houses, as Sodom and Gomorrah were consumed (*ch*. iv. 11), or it was the burning of their cities, either by accident or by the hand of the enemy. Thus were the towns wasted, as the country was by the grasshoppers. This fire *devoured the great deep*, as the fire that fell from heaven on Elijah's altar licked up the water that was in the trench.

2. The prophet, by prayer, seeks to turn away his wrath, *v.* 2. It was the business of prophets to pray for those to whom they prophesied, and so to show they did not *desire the woeful day*.

(1) The prophet's prayer: *O Lord God! Forgive, I beseech thee*, and take away the sin, *v.* 2. He sees sin at the bottom of the trouble, and that the pardon of sin must be at the bottom of the deliverance. *Cease, I beseech thee*, and take away the judgment; *cause thy anger towards us to cease*. Take away the cause and the effect will cease.

(2) The prophet's plea to enforce this prayer: *By whom shall Jacob arise, for he is small? v.* 2. And it is repeated (*v.* 5). It is Jacob that he is interceding for, the professing people of God, called by his name. *Jacob is small*, weakened and brought low by former judgments; if these come, he will be brought to nothing. The people are unable to help themselves or one another. Sin will soon diminish the numerous and weaken the courageous. *By whom shall he arise?* He has no friend to help him, none to raise him, unless the hand of God do it.

3. In answer to the prophet's prayer (*v.* 3): *The Lord repented for this*. He did not change his mind; he changed his way, took another course in mercy. He said, *It shall not be*. And again (*v.* 6), *This also shall not be*. This was not the first time that Israel's life was begged, and so saved. What a blessing praying people, praying prophets, are to a land. Amos moves for a reprieve, and obtains it, because God inclines to grant it. It is the glory of God that he *multiplies to pardon*, that he spares, and forgives, to more than seventy times seven times.

II. The rejection of those at last who had been often reprieved, and yet never reduced to their duty. This is represented to the prophet by a vision (*v.* 7, 8).

1. The vision is of a *plumb-line*, a line with a plummet at the end of it, such as masons and bricklayers use to run up a wall by, that they may work it straight and true. Israel was a wall which God had reared, as a bulwark to his sanctuary. This wall was *made by a plumb-line*, exact and firm. It had long stood fast as a wall of brass. But God now *stands upon it with a plumb-line in his hand*, to take measure of it. Thus God would bring the people of Israel to the trial, would show wherein they erred; and he would set a *plumb-line in the midst of them*, to mark how far their wall must be pulled down.

2. The prediction is of utter ruin, *v.* 9. (1) The body of the people shall be destroyed. They are here called *the house of Isaac* (*v.* 16), some think in allusion to the signification of Isaac's name; it is *laughter*; they shall become a jest among all their neighbours. Their castles they thought safe, and their temples sanctuaries. These shall be *laid waste*, to punish them for their idolatry and their carnal confidences. (2) The royal family shall sink first: Jeroboam the second, was now king of the ten tribes; his family was extirpated in his son Zecharias, 2 Kings xv. 10.

Verses 10–17

Amos is persecuted.

I. The malicious information brought to the king against the prophet Amos, *v.* 10, 11. The informer was *Amaziah the priest of Bethel*, the chief of the priests that ministered to the golden calf there, the *president of Bethel* (so some read it). He complained against Amos because he prophesied against his altars, which would soon be deserted if Amos' preaching could but gain credit. Priests have been bitter persecutors. Amaziah brings an information to Jeroboam against Amos. 1. The crime he is charged with is treason: "*Amos has conspired against thee*, to depose and murder thee; he aims at succeeding thee. *The land is not able to bear his words*."

It is slyly insinuated that the country was exasperated against him. It is no new thing for the accusers of the brethren to misrepresent them as enemies to the king and kingdom, when really they are the best friends to both. 2. The words laid in the indictment for the support of this charge (*v.* 11): *Amos says* (and they have witnesses ready to prove it) *Jeroboam shall die by the sword, and Israel shall be led away captive*. He does not tell the king how Amos had interceded for Israel, and by his intercession had turned away first one judgment and then another. He does not tell him that he had often assured them that if they would repent the ruin should be prevented. It does not appear that Jeroboam took any notice of this information; perhaps he reverenced a prophet, and stood more in awe of the divine authority than Amaziah his priest did.

II. The method he used to persuade Amos to quit the country (*v.* 12, 13); he insinuated himself into his acquaintance, and endeavoured to persuade him to go and prophesy in the *land of Judah*, and not at Bethel. He suggests to him,

1. That Bethel was not a proper place for him to exercise his ministry in, for it was *the king's chapel*, or *sanctuary*, and it was *the king's court*, or *the house of the kingdom*, where the royal family resided and where were set the thrones of judgment. And why not? (1) Because Amos is too plain and blunt a preacher for the court and the king's chapel. (2) Because the worship that is in the king's chapel will be a continual vexation to Amos. (3) Because it was not fit that the king and his house should be affronted in their own court and chapel by reproofs and threatenings in the name of the Lord. (4) Because he could not expect any encouragement there, but, on the contrary, to be ridiculed and threatened. He could not think to persuade any from that idolatry which was supported by the authority and example of the king. To preach his doctrine there was but (as we say) to run his head against a post.

2. He persuades him that the land of Judah was the fittest place for him. *Flee thee away* thither with all speed, and *there eat bread*, and *prophesy there*. There thou wilt be safe; there thou wilt be welcome. (1) How willing wicked men are to get clear of their reprovers. (2) How apt worldly men are to measure others by themselves. Amaziah, as a priest, aimed at nothing but the profits of his place, and he thought Amos, as a prophet, had the same views.

III. The reply which Amos made to these suggestions of Amaziah's. He did not *consult with flesh and blood*, nor was it his care to enrich himself, but to *make full proof of his ministry*, not to sleep in a whole skin, but to keep a good conscience; and therefore he resolved to abide by his post, and, in answer to Amaziah,

1. He justified himself in his adherence to his work and his place (*v.* 14, 15). He had a divine commission: "*I was no prophet, nor prophet's son*, neither born nor bred to the office, as Samuel and Jeremiah, but *I was a herdman*, a keeper of cattle, and *a gatherer of sycamore-fruit*." He was a plain country-man, bred up and employed in country work and used to country fare. God made him a prophet, and a prophet to them, appointed him his work and his post. Therefore he ought not to be silenced, for, (1) He could produce a divine commission for what he did. Men will find it is at their peril if they oppose any that come in God's name. An affront done to an ambassador is an affront to the prince that sends him. (2) The mean character he wore before he received that commission strengthened his warrant. [1] He had no thoughts at all of ever being a prophet, and therefore his prophesying was due to a divine impulse. [2] He was not instructed in the art of prophesying, and therefore he must have his abilities for it immediately from

God, an undeniable proof that he had his mission from him. The apostles, being originally unlearned and ignorant men, evidenced that they owed their knowledge to their having *been with Jesus*, Acts iv. 13. [3] He had an honest calling, by which he could comfortably maintain himself and his family, and therefore did not need to prophesy for bread, as Amaziah suggested (*v.* 12). If God, that sent him, had not strengthened him, he could not thus have *set his face as a flint*, Isa. l. 7. A herdman of Tekoa puts to shame a priest of Bethel, when he receives from God authority to act for him.

2. He condemns Amaziah for the opposition he gave him in the name of the Lord and by authority from him, *v.* 16, 17.

(1) For the opposition he gave to Amos God will bring ruin upon himself and his family. He shall have no comfort in his relations: *His wife shall be a harlot*. His *sons and his daughters shall fall by the sword* of war. He shall be stripped of all his estate. He shall himself perish in a strange country, in a *polluted land*, a heathen country.

(2) Amos was accused for saying, *Israel shall be led away captive* (*v.* 11), but he stands to it, and repeats it. The *burden of the word of the Lord* cannot be shaken off. Stopping the mouths of God's ministers will not stop the progress of God's word, for it shall not return void.

CHAPTER 8

Sinful times are here attended with sorrowful times. I. By the vision of "a basket of summer-fruit" is signified the hastening on of the ruin threatened (ver. 1–3). II. Oppressors are here called to account for their abusing the poor, ver. 4–10. III. A famine of the word of God is here made the punishment of a people that go a-whoring after other gods (ver. 11–14).

Verses 1–3

I. The approach of the threatened ruin is represented by *a basket of summer-fruit* which Amos saw in vision (*v.* 1 and 2). He saw *a basket of summer-fruit* gathered and ready to be eaten, which signified, 1. That they were ripe for destruction, they lay ready to be eaten up. 2. That the year of God's patience was drawing toward a conclusion; it was autumn with them. 3. Those we call *summer-fruits* will not keep till winter, must be used immediately, an emblem of this people, that had nothing consistent in them.

II. The intent and meaning of this vision is no more than this: It signifies that *the end has come upon my people Israel*. What was said *ch.* vii. 8 is here repeated as God's determined resolution, *I will not again pass by them any more*.

III. The consequence of this shall be a universal desolation (*v.* 3). Here in a sinful world, in a sinful nation, 1. Sorrow reigns, reigns to such a degree that *the songs of the temple shall be howlings*. When God's judgments are abroad, they will turn the joy into heaviness, the temple-songs, which used to sound so pleasantly, into loud howlings. 2. Death reigns. There shall be *many dead bodies in every place* (Ps. cx. 6), slain by sword or pestilence. They shall not so much as have the bell tolled, but they shall *cast them forth with silence*.

Verses 4–10

I. They had the character of the unjust judge (Luke xviii. 2) that neither *feared God nor regarded man*.

They do indeed keep up a show of godliness; they observe the *sabbath* and the *new moon*; but they were soon weary of them. They said, *When will the sabbath be gone, that we may sell corn?* They were weary of the restraints of the sabbaths and the new-moons, and wished them over. They were fond of market-days; they longed to be *selling corn* and *setting forth*

wheat. Those are strangers to God, and enemies to themselves, that love market days better than sabbath days, that would rather be selling corn than worshipping God. They neither *do justly* nor *love mercy*. When they *sell their corn* they impose upon the buyer. They measure him the corn by their own measure, but they *make the ephah small*. When they receive his money they weigh it in their own scales, by their own weights. They *make the shekel great*, so that the money, being found too light, must have more added to it. They have in their hearts neither the fear nor the love of that God who has so plainly said that *false weights and balances are an abomination to him*. Another instance of their fraudulent dealing is that they *sell the refuse of the wheat*, and, taking advantage of their neighbours' ignorance or necessity, make them take it at the same price at which they sell the *finest of the wheat*. They are barbarous and unmerciful to the poor: They *swallow up the needy*, and *make the poor of the land to fail*. But he who thus *reproaches the poor despises his Maker*, in whose hands *rich and poor meet together*. They swallowed up the poor by making them hard bargains, and bring them so low that they may have their labour for next to nothing. Thus *they buy the poor for silver*; they bring them and their *children into bondage*. You might buy a poor man to be your slave *for a pair of shoes*. Property was first invaded and then liberty; it is the method of oppressors first to make men beggars and then to make them their vassals.

II. The punishment that shall be inflicted on them for this sin. God will remember their sin against them. He swears, *Surely I will never forget any of their works. I will never forget them* is as much as to say, I will never forgive them. He will bring ruin and confusion upon them. There shall be universal terror and consternation (*v.* 8). When God comes forth against them the waters of trouble and calamity shall *rise up wholly as a flood*, that swells, when it is dammed up, and soon overflows its banks. The whole land *shall be cast out, and drowned*, and laid under water, as the land of Egypt is every year by the overflowing of its river Nile. It shall come upon them when they little think of it (*v.* 9): "*I will cause the sun to go down at noon*, when it is in its full strength and lustre. The *earth* shall be *darkened in the clear day*, when everything looks pleasant and hopeful." It shall change their note, and mar all their mirth (*v.* 10): *I will turn your feasts into mourning*, as (*v.* 3) the *songs of the temple into howlings*. The state of impenitent sinners grows worse and worse, and the last of all will be the worst of all.

Verses 11–14

I. A spiritual famine coming upon the whole land, a *famine of the word of God*, the failing of oracles and the scarcity of good preaching. *The days come* when another kind of darkness shall come upon that land of light. When Amos prophesied, and for a considerable time after, they had great plenty of prophets, abundant opportunities of *hearing the word of God*. God threatens that hereafter he will deprive them of this privilege. They should have plenty of bread and water, and yet their teachers should be removed. Their nation had been great and high, for *to them were committed the oracles of God*; but, when these were taken from them, their beauty was stained and their honour laid in the dust. This was a token of God's highest displeasure against them. We should say at any time that a famine of the word of God is the sorest famine, the heaviest judgment. *They shall wander from sea to sea*, from the sea of Tiberias to the Great Sea, to see if God will send them prophets (*v.* 12). And *in the day* of this famine *the fair virgins and the young men shall faint for thirst* (*v.* 13). The

Jewish churches, and the *masters of their synagogues,* some take to be meant by the *virgins* and the *young men.* Those that trust in their own merit and think they have no need of Christ, others take to be meant by the *fair virgins* and the *choice young men;* they shall *faint for thirst,* when those that *hunger and thirst after the righteousness* of Christ shall be filled.

II. The particular destruction of those that were ringleaders in idolatry, *v.* 14. They *swear by the sin of Samaria,* that is, by the god of Samaria, the idol that was worshipped at Bethel, not far off from Samaria. They say, *Thy God, O Dan! liveth;* that was the other golden calf, a dumb dead idol, and yet caressed as if it had been the living God. They say, *The manner,* or way, of *Beer-sheba liveth;* they swore by the *religion* of Beer-sheba. Those who thus give that honour to idols which is due to God alone *shall fall,* and the gods cannot stand their friends, so they shall *never rise again.*

CHAPTER 9

I. Judgment threatened, which the sinners shall not escape (ver. 1–4), which an almighty power shall inflict (ver. 5, 6), which the people of Israel have deserved, (ver. 7, 8); and yet it shall not be the utter ruin of their nation (ver. 8), for a remnant of good people shall escape, ver. 9. But the wicked shall perish, ver. 10. II. Mercy promised, to be bestowed in the latter days (ver. 11–15), as appears by the application of it to the days of the Messiah, Acts xv. 16.

Verses 1–10

I. Sentence is passed. The prophet saw in vision *the Lord standing upon the altar* (*v.* 1), the altar of burnt-offerings. He is removed from the *mercy-seat* between the *cherubim.* He stands on the altar, to prohibit sacrifice. Now the order given is, *Smite the lintel of the door* of the temple with such a blow *that the posts may shake,* and *cut them,* wound them *in the head, all of them;* break down the door of God's house, in token that he is going out from it, and forsaking it. "*Smite the king, who is* as the lintel of the door, that the princes, who are *as the posts,* may *shake; cut them in the head,* cleave them down, *all of them,* and *I will slay the last of them.*"

II. God's judgments will overtake the swiftest that think to out-run them, *v.* 2. "*Though they dig into hell,* into the centre of the earth, yet *thence shall my hand take them.*" The grave is a hiding-place to the righteous from the malice of the world (Job. iii. 17), but it shall be no hiding-place to the wicked from the justice of God. *The top of Carmel* shall not protect them: "*Though they hide themselves there,* where they imagine nobody will look for them, *I will search, and take them out thence.*" The *bottom of the sea* shall not serve to conceal them. *Thence will I command the serpent, and he shall bite them,* the *crooked serpent,* even *the dragon that is in the sea,* Isa. xxvii. 1. Remote countries will not befriend them, nor less judgments excuse them from greater (*v.* 4). Threatenings are more or less formidable according to the power of him that threatens. We laugh at impotent wrath; but the wrath of God is not so; it is omnipotent wrath. Those who have the Lord of hosts against them, have the whole creation at war with them. He is the Creator and governor of the upper world: *It is he that builds his stories in the heavens,* the celestial orbs, or spheres, one over another as so many stories in a high and stately palace. He has the command of this lower world too, both *earth* and *sea.* Do they think to make a land-fight of it? He *has founded his troop in the earth,* his troop of guards, for the protection of his subjects and the punishment of his enemies. All the creatures on earth make one bundle (as the margin reads it), one bundle of arrows, out of which he takes what he pleases to discharge against the persecutors, Ps. vii. 13. Do they think to make a sea-fight of it? He has the

waters of the sea at command; even its waves, the most tumultuous rebellious waters, do obey him. How justly God passes this sentence upon the people of Israel. He does not destroy them by an act of sovereignty, but by an act of righteousness. *Are you not as children of the Ethiopians unto me, O children of Israel?* A sad change! Those that were trained up in the knowledge and fear of God, and promised fair, throw off their profession and become as bad as the worst. This is an intimation of the rejection of the unbelieving Jews in the days of the Messiah; because they embraced not the doctrine of Christ, the kingdom of God was taken from them, they were unchurched, and cast out of covenant. They thought he would not cast them off, and put them upon a level with other nations, because he had done that for them which he had not done for other nations. "No," says he, "the favours shown to you are not so distinguishing as you think they are: *Have not I brought up Israel out of the land of Egypt?* I have also brought the *Philistines from Caphtor,* or *Cappadocia.*" In like manner the Syrians were brought up from Kir when they had been carried away thither, 2 Kings xvi. 9. If God's Israel lose the peculiarity of their holiness, they lose the peculiarity of their privileges. Though the wicked Israelites shall be as the wicked Ethiopians, and their being called Israelites shall stand them in no stead, yet the pious Israelites shall not be as the *wicked ones.* I will distinguish, as becomes a righteous judge. The house of Israel shall be *sifted as corn is sifted;* but still in the hands of God, as the sieve in the hands of him that sifts (*v.* 9): *I will sift the house of Israel among all nations.* The righteous ones among them, that are as the solid wheat, shall none of them perish; *not the least grain shall fall on the earth,* so as to be lost and forgotten— not the least *stone* (so the word is), for the good corn is weighty as a stone in comparison with that which we call *light corn.*

Verses 11–15

To him to whom all the prophets bear witness this prophet here bears his testimony, and speaks of *that day* in which God will do great things for his church, by the setting up of the kingdom of the Messiah. The promise here may refer to the planting of the Christian church, Acts xv. 15–17. It is promised,

I. That in the Messiah the kingdom of David shall be restored (*v.* 11). The church militant, in its present state, dwelling as in shepherds' tents to feed, as in soldiers' tents to fight, is the *tabernacle of David.* The royal family was so impoverished, its power abridged, for many of that race degenerated, and in the captivity it lost the imperial dignity. So it was with the church of the Jews; in the latter days its glory departed; it was like a tabernacle brought to ruin. By Jesus Christ these tabernacles were raised and rebuilt. In him God's covenant with David had its accomplishment; and the glory of that house revived again. The spiritual glory of the family of Christ far exceeded the temporal glory of the family of David. In him also God's covenant with Israel had its accomplishment, and in the gospel-church the tabernacle of God was set up among men again. This is quoted in the first council at Jerusalem as referring to the calling in of the Gentiles and God's *taking out of them a people for his name.*

II. That that kingdom shall be enlarged (*v.* 12), that the house of David may possess the *remnant of Edom, and of all the heathen,* that is, that Christ may have them given him for his *inheritance,* Ps. ii. 8. Christ died to *gather together in one the children of God that were scattered abroad,* here said to be those that were *called by his name.*

III. That in the kingdom of the Messiah there shall be great plenty (*v.* 13): *The ploughman shall overtake the reaper*, that is there shall be such a plentiful harvest every year, that it shall last all summer, even till autumn, when it is time to begin to plough again. The hills that were dry and barren shall be moistened and shall melt with the *fatness* or *mellowness* (as we call it) of *the soil*. This must be understood of the spiritual blessings with which all those are blessed who are in sincerity added to Christ and his church; they shall have the bread of life, to *strengthen their hearts*, and the wine of divine consolations to *make them glad—meat indeed* and *drink indeed*—all the benefit that comes to the souls of men from the word and Spirit of God. When great multitudes were converted and when the preachers of the gospel were *always caused to triumph in* the success of their preaching, then the *ploughman overtook the reaper*.

IV. That the kingdom of the Messiah shall be well peopled; there shall be mouths for this meat, *v.* 14.

Those that take pains in religion, as men must do about their vineyards and gardens, shall have both the pleasure and the profit of it. The *bringing again* of the *captivity* of God's Israel, which is here promised, may refer to the cancelling of the ceremonial law, and the investing of them in the liberty wherewith Christ came to make his church free, Gal. v. 1.

V. That the kingdom of the Messiah shall take such deep rooting in the world as never to be rooted out of it (*v.* 15): *I will plant them upon their land.* The church may be corrupted, but shall not quite forsake God, may be persecuted, but shall not quite be forsaken of God. Two things secure the perpetuity of the church: 1. God's grants to it: It is *the land which I have given them.* 2. Its interest in him: He is *the Lord thy God*, who has said it, and will make it good, who shall *reign for ever unto all generations.* And because he lives the church shall live also.

THE PROPHECY OF OBADIAH

This is the shortest of all the books of the Old Testament, and yet is not to be passed by, for this penny has Caesar's image and superscription upon it; it is stamped with a divine authority. This book is entitled, *The Vision of Obadiah.* Who this Obadiah was does not appear. Some of the ancients imagined him to be the same with that Obadiah that was steward to Ahab's household (1 Kings xviii. 3); and, if so, he that hid and fed the prophets had indeed a prophet's reward, when he was himself made a prophet. But that is a conjecture which has no ground. This Obadiah, it is probable, was of a later date, some think contemporary with Hosea, Joel, and Amos; others think he lived about the time of the destruction of Jerusalem, when the children of Edom so barbarously triumphed in that destruction. However, what he wrote was what he saw; it is his *vision.* It is a foolish fancy of some of the Jews that because he prophesies only concerning Edom he was himself an Edomite by birth, but a proselyte to the Jewish religion. Other prophets prophesied against Edom, and some of them seem to have borrowed from him in their predictions against Edom, as Jer. xlix. 7, &c.; Ezek. xxv. 12, &c.

This book is wholly concerning Edom, a nation adjoining to Israel, and yet an enemy to the seed of Jacob, inheriting the enmity of their father Esau to Jacob. Now here we have, after the preface, ver. 1, I. Threatenings against Edom, 1. That their pride should be humbled, ver. 2–4. 2. That their wealth should be plundered, ver. 5–7. 3. That their wisdom should be infatuated, ver. 8, 9. 4. That their spiteful behaviour towards God's Israel should be avenged, ver. 10–16. II. Gracious promises to Israel; that they shall be restored and reformed, and shall be victorious over the Edomites (ver. 17–20), and that the kingdom of the Messiah shall be set up by the bringing in of the great salvation, ver. 21.

Verses 1–9

Edom is the nation against which this prophecy is levelled, and which, some think, is put for all the enemies of Israel. Though Edom was mortified in the times of the Maccabees, as it had been before by Jehoshaphat, yet its destruction seems to have been typical, as their father Esau's rejection, and to have had further reference to the destruction of the enemies of the gospel-church. Some have well observed that it could not but be a great trial to the people of Israel, when they saw themselves, the children of beloved Jacob, in trouble, and the Edomites, the seed of hated Esau, triumphing over them in their troubles; and therefore God gives them a prospect of the destruction of Edom, and of a happy issue of their own correction.

I. A declaration of war against Edom (*v.* 1): "*We have heard a rumour,* or rather *an order, from the Lord,* the God of hosts; he has given the word of command that all who do mischief to his people shall certainly bring mischief upon themselves. We have heard a report that God is preparing his throne for judgment; and an *ambassador is sent among the heathen,*" a *herald* rather, to alarm the nations, *Arise ye,* stir up yourselves and one another, and let *us rise up against Edom in battle.* The confederate forces under Nebuchadnezzar prepare to make a descent upon that country: *Gather yourselves together, and come against her.*

II. A prediction of the success of that war. Edom shall certainly be subdued. "*Behold, I have made thee small among the heathen,* so that none of thy neighbours will court an alliance with thee; *thou art greatly despised* among them, as an unfaithful nation." And thus (*v.* 3) *the pride of thy heart has deceived thee.* The fortifications of their country shall deceive them. They *dwelt in the clefts of the rock,* as an eagle in her nest, and their *habitation* was *high,* fortified against their enemies, so high as to be out of the reach of danger. Edom says in the pride of his heart: *Who shall bring me down to the ground?* He speaks with a confidence of his own strength, and a contempt of God's judgments. Carnal security is a sin that most easily besets men in the day of their pomp, power, and prosperity. If men will dare to challenge Omnipotence, their challenge shall be taken up: *Who shall bring me down?* says Edom. "*I will,*" says God. "*Though thou exalt thyself as the eagle* that soars high and builds high, nay, *though thou set thy nest among the stars,* it is but in thy own imagination, and *thence will I bring thee down.*" This we had Jer. xlix. 15, 16. Their money shall rather expose them than protect them; it shall be made a prey to the enemy, and they for the sake of it, *v.* 5, 6. How art thou fallen, and how great is thy fall! *How art thou stupefied!* so the Chaldee words it. The prophet shows that it should be an utter ruin, not a usual calamity; for it is indeed usual for those that have wealth to have it stolen, and to lose a little out of their great deal. *Thieves come to them* and steal no more than they think they can carry away, and out of a great stock it is scarcely missed. It shall not be so with Edom; his wealth shall all be taken away, and nothing shall escape the hands of the destroying army, *v.* 6. *How are his hidden things,* his hidden treasures, plundered, rifled, and *sought up!* Their alliances with neighbouring states and potentates shall fail them (*v.* 7): "*The men of thy confederacy,* all of them, the Ammonites and Moabites, and other allies that were at *peace with thee, did eat thy bread,* were entertained by thee, lived upon thee; they *brought thee even to the border* of thy land, were respectful to thy ambassadors, and brought them on their way home; but then they have *deceived thee;* they flew back and retreated when thou wast in extremity. They have *prevailed against thee;* they were too hard for thee in the treaty imposed upon thee, brought thee into danger, and there left thee an easy prey to thy enemy. They have *laid a wound under thee;* that is, they have laid that under thee for a support, which will prove a wound to thee; not as thorns only, but as swords." If God lay under us the arms of his power and love, these will be firm under us; the God of our covenant will never deceive us. But if we trust to *the men of our confederacy,* and what they will lay under us, it may prove to us a *wound* and *dishonour.* Just censure is passed upon Edom for trusting to those who played tricks with him: "*There is no understanding in him,* or else he would never have put it into their power to betray him by putting such a confidence in them. The politics of their counsellors shall fail them, *v.* 8. Edom had been famous for great statesmen, but now the *counsellors* have become *fools. Shall I not in that day destroy the wise men out of Edom?* This was just punishment of their folly in trusting to an arm of flesh; *There is no understanding in them, v.* 7. It was the forerunner of their destruction. A nation is certainly marked for ruin when God hides the things that belong to its peace from the eyes of those that are entrusted with its counsels. Do they depend upon the strength and courage of their soldiers? They are able-bodied men of spirit and courage, but now (*v.* 9), *Thy mighty men, O Teman! shall be dismayed;* their courage shall fail them, *to the end that every one of the mount of Esau may be cut off by slaughter,* and none escape.

Verses 10–16

Many things were amiss in Edom; they were a sinful people, and *a people laden with iniquity.* But that one single crime which is laid to their charge, as bringing this ruin upon them, is the injury they had done to the people of God (*v.* 10): "It is *for thy violence against thy brother Jacob,* that ancient grudge which thou hast borne to the people of Israel, that all this *shame shall cover thee* and *thou shalt be cut off for ever.*" It is violence *against thy brother,* to whom thou shouldst be a *goël—a redeemer,* whom it is thy duty to right if others wronged him. Thou *slanderest* and *abusest thy own mother's son.* Much more if it is done against one of God's people; "it is thy brother Jacob that is in covenant with God, and dear to him. Thou hatest him whom God has loved."

I. The violence which Edom did against his brother Jacob. That which is laid to their charge is their barbarous conduct towards Judah and Jerusalem when they were in distress, and ready to be destroyed, probably by the Chaldeans. See this is charged upon the Edomites (Ps. cxxxvii. 7), that *in the day of Jerusalem they said, Rase it, rase it,* and Ezek. xxv. 12. Thou *shouldst not have looked,* thou *shouldst not have entered;* but thou didst do so. (*v.* 12–14). Let us see,

1. The case of Judah and Jerusalem when the Edomites insulted over them. With the Edomites it was a day of prosperity when with the Israelites it was a day of calamity, for judgment commonly *begins at the house of God.* Children are corrected when strangers are let alone. It was the day *of their destruction* (*v.* 12), when *foreigners entered into the gates of Jerusalem,* when the great officers of the king of Babylon's army sat in the gates, as judges of the land. It was a day when the *strangers carried away captive his forces* (*v.* 11). The Edomites, their neighbours and brethren, should have pitied them and helped them.

2. The Edomites are here condemned. They looked with pleasure upon the affliction of God's people (*v.* 12, 13), unconcerned. Those have a great deal to answer for that are idle spectators of the troubles and afflictions of their neighbours, when they are capable of being their active helpers. They *rejoiced over the children of Judah in the day of their destruction.* They went further, for they *entered into the gate* of God's people, and *laid hands on their substance.* Though they did not help to conquer them, they helped to plunder them, *v.* 13. They not only robbed their brethren, but murdered them, *v.* 14. When the victorious sword of the Chaldeans was making bloody work among the Jews many made their escape, but the Edomites basely intercepted them, *stood in the cross-way;* some they barbarously cut off; others they delivered up to the pursuers. In all this they joined with the open enemies and persecutors of Israel: *Even thou wast as one of them.*

II. The shame that shall cover them for this violence. When they come to be in the same calamitous condition that Israel is now in, they will be ashamed (*v.* 15): *The day of the Lord is near upon all the heathen,* when God will recompense tribulation to the troublers of his church. *As you have drunk upon my holy mountain* (*v.* 16), that is, as God's professing people have drunk deeply of the cup of affliction, *so shall all the heathen drink* of the same bitter cup. They may expect their case to be worse in the day of distress than that of Israel was in their day. The afflictions of God's people were but for a moment, but their enemies shall *drink continually* the *wine of God's wrath,* Rev. xiv. 10. The dregs of the cup are reserved for the *wicked of the earth* (Ps. lxxv. 8); they shall *drink and swallow down,* or *sup up* (as the margin reads it), shall drink it to the bottom.

Verses 17–21

Precious promises of salvation with which this prophecy concludes, as those of Joel and Amos did, which, however they might be in part fulfilled in the return of the Jews out of Babylon, are yet, doubtless, to have their full accomplishment in that great salvation wrought out by Jesus Christ.

I. There shall be salvation upon Mount Zion: *Upon Mount Zion shall be deliverance, v.* 17. A remnant of Israel, *upon the holy mountain,* shall be saved, *v.* 16.

II. Where there is salvation, there shall be sanctification: *And there shall be holiness,* to prepare and qualify the children of Zion for this deliverance; for wherever God designs glory he gives grace.

III. This salvation and sanctification shall spread, and prevail: The *house of Jacob,* even this *Mount Zion,* with the deliverance and the holiness there wrought, shall *possess their possessions;* that is, the gospel-church shall be set up among the heathen, and shall replenish the earth. When they possess their hearts they shall *possess their possessions,* for those who have given up themselves to the Lord give up all they have to him.

1. How this possession shall be *gained* (*v.* 18): *The house of Jacob shall be a fire, and the house of Joseph a flame,* for their God is a *consuming fire;* and the house of Esau shall be for *stubble.* The gospel, preached in the house of Jacob and Joseph, shall be as a fire and a flame to melt hard hearts, to burn up the dross, that they may be purified with the *spirit of judgment and the spirit of burning.* The word of God in the mouth of his ministers is said to be like fire, and the people as wood to be devoured by it, Jer. v. 14. Those that are not refined as gold by the fire of the gospel shall be consumed as dross by it.

2. How far this possession shall extend, *v.* 19, 20. The *captivity of this host of Israel,* that are still called the *children of the captivity,* these shall recover their own land, and gain ground upon their neighbours adjoining them. Some shall become proselytes and shall incorporate with the Jews, who, by possessing them in a holy communion, possess their land. The kingdom of Israel shall join with that of Judah both in civil and sacred interests, and, as friends and brethren, shall mutually possess and enjoy one another; and both together shall *possess the Canaanites,* even to Zarephath, which *belongeth to Zidon;* and Jerusalem shall possess the *cities of the south,* even to Sepharad. Thus did the Jews enlarge their borders on all sides. But the promise here, no doubt, has a spiritual signification, and had its accomplishment in the setting up of the Christian church, the gospel-Israel, in the world, and shall have its accomplishment more and more in the enlargement of it, till the mystical body is completed.

IV. The kingdom of the Redeemer shall be erected to the comfort of his loyal subjects and the shame of his enemies (*v.* 21): *The kingdom shall be the Lord's*, the Lord Christ's. The mountain of Zion shall be saved; on it *saviours* shall *come*, the preachers of the gospel, called saviours, because their business is to save themselves and those that hear them; and in this they are *workers together with Christ*. The mountain of Esau shall be judged; and the same that come as saviours on Mount Zion shall *judge* the *mountain of Esau*; for the word of the gospel in their mouth, that convinces and condemns them. And in the course of God's providence his scripture is fulfilled; when God raises up friends to the church in her distress, then *saviours come on Mount Zion*, to save it; and when the enemies of the church are brought down, then is the *mount of Esau judged*; and this shall be done in every age in such a way as God thinks best.

THE BOOK OF JONAH

This book of Jonah, though it be placed in the midst of the prophetical books, is rather a history than a prophecy; one line of prediction there is in it, *Yet forty days, and Nineveh shall be overthrown*; the rest of the book is a narrative of the preface to and the consequences of that prediction. Probably Jonah was himself the penman of this book, and he, as other inspired penmen, records his own faults, which is an evidence that in these writings they designed God's glory and not their own. We read of this same Jonah 2 Kings xiv. 25, where we find that he was of Gath-hepher in Galilee, a city that belonged to the tribe of Zebulun, in a remote corner of the land of Israel. He was a messenger of mercy to Israel in the reign of Jeroboam the second; for the *restoring of the coast of Israel*, is said to be *according to the word of the Lord which he spoke by the hand of his servant Jonah the prophet*. The story contains remarkable instances of human infirmity in Jonah, and of God's mercy in pardoning repenting sinners, witness Nineveh, and in bearing with repining saints, witness Jonah.

CHAPTER 1

I. A command given to Jonah to preach at Nineveh, ver. 1, 2. II. Jonah's disobedience to that command, ver. 3. III. The pursuit and arrest of him for that disobedience by a storm, ver. 4–6. IV. The discovery of his disobedience, to be the cause of the storm, ver. 7–10. V. The casting of him into the sea, for the stilling of the storm, ver. 11–16. VI. The miraculous preservation of his life there in the belly of a fish (ver. 17), which was his reservation for further services.

Verses 1–3

1. The honour God put upon Jonah, in giving him a commission to go and prophesy against Nineveh. *Jonah* signifies *a dove*, a proper name for all God's prophets, all his people, who ought to be *harmless as doves*, and to *mourn as doves* for the sins and calamities of the land. His father's name was *Amittai—My truth*; for God's prophets should be sons of truth. To him *the word of the Lord came*—to him it was (so the word signifies). The orders now given were, *Arise, go to Nineveh, that great city*, v. 2. Nineveh was the metropolis of the Assyrian monarchy (Gen. x. 11), *a great city*, great in the number of the inhabitants, great in power and dominion; it was the city that for some time *ruled over the kings of the earth*. But great cities, as well as great men, are under God's government. Nineveh was a heathen city, without the knowledge and worship of the true God. This great city was a wicked city: *Their wickedness has come up before me*; and they sinned with a *high hand*. Jonah must *cry against it*; he must witness against their great wickedness, and must warn them of the destruction that was coming upon them for it. *Cry aloud, spare not.* He must not whisper his message, but publish it in the streets of Nineveh; *he that has ears to hear let him hear* what God has to say by his prophet against that wicked city. He must *go to Nineveh*, and cry there upon the spot against the wickedness of it. Other prophets were ordered to send messages to the neighbouring nations, but Jonah must go and carry the message himself. The dishonour Jonah did to God in refusing to go (*v.* 3): *But Jonah*, instead of rising to go to Nineveh, *rose up to flee to Tarshish*, to *the sea*, not bound for any port, but desirous to get away *from the presence of the Lord*. He *consulted with flesh and blood*, and declined the embassy because he was jealous for the prerogatives of his country, and not willing that any other nation should share in the honour of divine revelation. He owns himself (*ch.* iv. 2) that the reason of his aversion was because he foresaw that the Ninevites would repent, and God would forgive them and take them into favour, which would be a slur upon the people of Israel, who had been so long a peculiar people to God. He went to Joppa, a famous seaport in the land of Israel, in quest of a ship bound for Tarshish, and there he found one. Providence seemed to give him an opportunity to escape. The ready way is not always the right way. He found the ship and set sail for Tarshish. So he *paid the fare thereof*. He went *with them*, the mariners, the passengers, the merchants, whoever they were that were going to Tarshish. Jonah, forgetting his dignity as well as duty, herded with them.

Verses 4–10

I. God sends a pursuer after him, *a mighty tempest in the sea, v.* 4. The effect of this wind was *a mighty tempest*; for when the winds rise the waves rise. The tempest prevailed to such a degree that *the ship was likely to be broken*. This wind was sent after Jonah, to fetch him back again to God and to his duty; and it is a great mercy to be reclaimed and called home when we go astray, though it be by a tempest.

II. The ship's crew were alarmed by this mighty tempest, but Jonah only was unconcerned, *v.* 5. The mariners were *afraid*; though, their business leading them to dangers of this kind, they used to make light of them; yet the oldest and stoutest of them began to tremble, being apprehensive that there was something more than ordinary in this tempest, so suddenly did it rise, so strongly did it rage. They *cried every man unto his god*. Many will not be brought to prayer till they are frightened to it; he that would learn to pray, let him go to sea. Having called upon their gods to help them, they did what they could to help themselves. They *cast forth the wares that were in the ship into the sea, to lighten it of them*, as Paul's mariners in a like case, Acts xxvii. 18, 19, 38. But where is Jonah all this while? One would have expected him busier than any, but we find him gone down into *the hold, between the sides of the ship*, and there he lies, and is *fast asleep*; neither the noise without, nor the sense of guilt within, awoke him.

III. The master of the ship called Jonah up to his prayers, *v.* 6. The *ship-master came to him*, and bade him for shame get up, both to *pray for life* and to *prepare for death. What meanest thou, O sleeper?* We commend the ship-master. We pity Jonah, who needed this reproof; as a prophet of the Lord, if he had been in his place, he might have been reproving the king of Nineveh, but, being out of the way of his duty, he is open to the reproofs of a sorry ship-master. Yet we must admire God's goodness in sending him this seasonable reproof, for it was the first step towards his recovery, as the crowing of the cock was to Peter. "*Arise, call upon thy God;* we are here crying every man to his god, why dost not thou get up and cry to thine?" *If so be that God will think upon us, that we perish not.* It should seem, the many gods they called upon were considered by them only as mediators between them and the supreme God, for the ship-master speaks of one God still, from whom he expected relief.

IV. Jonah is found out to be the cause of the storm. The mariners observed so much peculiar and uncommon in the storm that they concluded it was a messenger of divine justice sent to arrest some-one of those that were in that ship, as having been guilty of some enormous crime (Acts xxviii. 4), and it is for his sake they suffer. *Let us cast lots, that we may know for whose cause this evil is upon us.* They suspected one another, and would find out the man. These mariners desired to know the person that was the dead weight in their ship, that that one man might *die for the people* and that the whole ship *might not be lost.* In order to this they cast lots, by which they appealed to the judgment of God. The *lot fell upon Jonah,* who could have saved them this trouble if he would but have told them what his own conscience told him, *Thou art the man.* We may suppose there were those in the ship who were greater sinners than Jonah, and yet he is the man that the tempest pursues. The storm is sent after Jonah, because God has work for him to do, and it is sent to fetch him back to it. Jonah is brought under examination before the master and mariners. He was a stranger; none of them had anything to lay to his charge, and therefore they must extort a confession from him and judge him *out of his own mouth.* They did not fly outrageously upon him, but calmly enquired into his case. There is a com-passion due to offenders when they are discovered and convicted. *"Tell us for whose cause this evil is upon us;* is it indeed for thy cause, and, if so, *for what cause?* What is the offence for which thou art thus prosecuted?" They enquire concerning his calling: *What is thy occupation? Whence comest thou?* In answer Jonah tells them he is *a Hebrew* (v. 9), and therefore is the more ashamed to own that he is a criminal; for the sins of Hebrews, that make such a profession of religion, are exceedingly sinful. He gives an account of his religion, for that was his calling: *"I fear the Lord Jehovah;* that is the God I worship, even *the God of heaven,* the sovereign Lord of all, that has *made the sea and the dry land* and has the command of both." He owns that he *fled from the presence of the Lord,* that he was here running away from his duty, and the storm was sent to fetch him back. *The men were exceedingly afraid,* and justly, for they perceived that God was angry with one that feared and worshipped him, for running from his work in a particular instance. "If a prophet of the Lord be thus severely punished for one offence, what will become of us that have been guilty of so many, and great, and heinous offences?" They said to him, *"Why hast thou done this?* Why hast thou involved us in the prosecution?"

Verses 11–17

Something more was to be done, for still *the sea wrought and was tempestuous* (v. 11), and (v. 13), it *grew more and more tempestuous* (so the margin reads it).

I. They enquired of Jonah himself what he thought they must do with him (v. 11). He appears to be a delinquent, but he appears also to be a penitent. They would not *cast him into the sea* if he could think of any other expedient by which to *save the ship.*

II. Jonah reads his own doom (v. 12): *Take me up, and cast me forth into the sea.* This is the language of true penitents, who earnestly desire that none but themselves may fare the worse, for their sins and follies. How ready Jonah is to take all the guilt upon himself, and to look upon all the trouble as theirs. "If it is I that have raised the storm, it is not casting the wares into the sea that will lay it again; no, you

must cast me thither." When conscience is awakened, and a storm raised, nothing will turn it into a calm but parting with the sin that occasioned the dis-turbance.

III. The poor mariners did what they could to save throwing Jonah into the sea, but all in vain (v. 13): *They rowed hard to bring the ship to the land,* that, if they must part with Jonah, they might set him safely on shore; *but they could not.*

IV. When they cast Jonah into the sea they first prayed to God that his blood might not lie upon them, v. 14. They prayed to the *God of Israel,* being now convinced, by the providences of God concerning Jonah and the information he had given them, that he is God *alone. "Lord,"* say they, *"let us not perish for this man's life."*

V. Having deprecated the guilt (v. 15): *They took up Jonah,* and cast *him forth into the sea.* When sin is the Jonah that raises the storm, it must thus be cast forth into the sea; we must drown that which otherwise will *drown us.*

VI. The throwing of Jonah into the sea immediately put an end to the storm. If we turn from our sins, God will soon turn from his anger.

VII. The mariners were hereby more confirmed in their belief that Jonah's God was the only true God (v. 16). As evidence they *offered sacrifice* to him when they came ashore again in the land of Israel, and for the present made vows that they would do so, in thankfulness for their deliverance.

VIII. Jonah's life is saved by a miracle. In the midst of judgment God *remembers mercy.* Though he flees from the presence of the Lord, and seems to fall into his avenging hands, yet God has more work for him to do, and therefore has *prepared a great fish to swallow up Jonah* (v. 17), *a whale* our Saviour calls it (Matt. xii. 40), one of the largest sorts of whales, that have wider throats than others, in the belly of which has sometimes been found the dead body of a man in armour. It was of the Lord's mercies that Jonah was not now consumed. Jonah by this preservation was designed to be made, 1. A monu-ment of divine mercy. 2. A successful preacher to Nineveh. 3. An illustrious type of Christ, who was buried and rose again according to the scriptures (1 Cor. xv. 4), for, *as Jonah was three days and three nights in the whale's belly, so was the Son of man three days and three nights in the heart of the earth,* Matt. xii. 40. Was Jonah's grave a strange one, a new one? So was Christ's, one in which never man before was laid. Was Jonah there the best part of three days and three nights? So was Christ; but both in order to their rising again for the bringing of the doctrine of repentance to the Gentile world.

CHAPTER 2

God brings his people through fire, and through water (Ps. lxvi. 12); and by his power, behold, Jonah the prophet is yet alive. In this chapter God hears from him, for we find him praying; in the next Nineveh hears from him, for we find him preaching. In his prayer we have, I. The great distress and danger he was in, ver. 2, 3, 5, 6. II. The despair, ver. 4. III. The encouragement he took to himself, ver. 4, 7. IV. The assurance he had of God's favour to him, ver. 6, 7. V. The warning and instruction he gives to others, ver. 8. VI. The praise and glory of all given to God, ver. 9. In the last verse we have Jonah's deliverance safe and sound upon dry land again.

Verses 1–9

God and his servant Jonah had parted in anger, and the quarrel began on Jonah's side; he fled from his country that he might outrun his work. The reconciliation begins on God's side. In the close of the foregoing chapter we found God returning to Jonah in a way of mercy, *delivering him from going down to the pit,* having *found a ransom;* in this chapter we find Jonah returning to God in a way of duty.

I. When he prayed (*v.* 1): *Then Jonah prayed;* when he was in trouble, under the sense of sin, then he prayed. Then when he was in a hopeful way of deliverance, being preserved alive by miracle, then he prayed.

II. Where he prayed—in *the fish's belly.* No place is amiss for prayer. Wherever God casts us we may find a way open heavenward. He that has Christ dwelling in his heart by faith, wherever he goes carries his altar along with him, that *sanctifies the gift,* and is himself a *living temple.* Men may shut us out from communion with one another, but not from communion with God. Jonah was now in the bottom of the sea, yet *out of the depths he cries to God.*

III. To whom he prayed—*to the Lord his God.* He had been fleeing from God, but now he sees the folly of it, and returns to him.

IV. What his prayer was. He reflects upon the workings of his heart towards God when he was in distress, and the conflict that was then in his breast between faith and sense, between hope and fear. He said, *I cried, by reason of my affliction, unto the Lord.* "*Out of the belly of hell* and the grave *cried I.*" And it was not in vain: *God heard him, heard the voice* of his affliction. How low he was thrown (*v.* 3): *Thou hadst cast me into the deep.* The mariners cast him there; but he saw the hand of God casting him there. How terribly he was beset: *The floods compassed me about.* The channels and springs of the waters of the sea surrounded him on every side; it was high-water with him. *All thy billows and thy waves passed over me.* These words are plainly quoted by Jonah from Ps. xlii. 7, where in the original David's complaint is the same *verbatim.* If ever any man's case was singular, surely Jonah's was, and yet, to his great satisfaction, he finds even the man after God's own heart making the same complaint of God's *waves and billows going over him.* Our path of trouble is no untrodden path. To the same purport, *v.* 5, *The waters compassed me about even to the soul.* And this also is borrowed from David's complaint, Ps. lxix. 1, The *waters have come in unto my soul.* How fast he was held (*v.* 6): *He went down to the bottom of the mountains;* the *earth with her bars was about him;* it was likely to be about him for ever. He began to sink into despair. When the *waters compassed him about even to the soul* no marvel that *his soul fainted within him.* What hopes could he have of deliverance out of a trouble which his *own ways and doings* had *procured to himself?* He says, *I am cast out of thy sight.* Sometimes the condition of God's people may be such in this world that they may think themselves excluded from God's presence, so as no more to see him. But it is only the surmise of unbelief, for God has not *cast away his people whom he has chosen.* He recovered himself from sinking into despair, with some comfortable prospects of deliverance. Faith corrected and controlled the surmises of fear and distrust. Here was a fierce struggle between sense and faith, but faith had the last word and came off conqueror. Jonah's faith said, *Yet I will look again towards thy holy temple.* When Hezekiah desired that he might be assured of his recovery, he asked, *What is the sign that I shall go up to the house of the Lord?* (Isa. xxxviii. 22), as if that were the only thing for the sake of which he wished for health; so Jonah here hopes he shall *look again towards the temple.* How modestly Jonah expresses himself; as one conscious to himself of guilt and unworthiness, he dares not speak of dwelling in God's house, but he hopes he may be admitted to look towards it. Or these words may be taken as Jonah's vow when he was in distress, and he speaks (*v.* 9) of paying what he vowed. His sin for which God pursued him was *fleeing from the presence of the Lord.* He will never again look towards Tarshish, but will again look towards the temple, and will go *from strength to strength* till he appear before God there. When our souls faint we must remember God; and when we think on his name we should call on his name. He reflects upon the favour of God to him when in his distress he sought and trusted him. God graciously accepted his prayer (*v.* 7): *My prayer,* being sent to him, *came in unto him,* even *into his holy temple;* it was heard in the highest heavens, though it was prayed in the lowest deeps. He wonderfully wrought deliverance for him (*v.* 6): *Yet hast thou brought up my life from corruption, O Lord my God!* Some think he said this when he was vomited up on dry ground. *The earth with her bars was about me for ever,* and yet *thou hast brought up my life from the pit,* from the *bars of the pit.* Or we may suppose it spoken while he was yet in the fish's belly, and then it is the language of his faith: "Thou hast kept me alive in the pit, and therefore thou canst, thou wilt, *bring up my life from the pit*"; and he speaks of it with as much assurance as if it were done already: *Thou hast brought up my life.* If the Lord be our God, he will be to us the *resurrection and the life,* will redeem our lives from destruction, from the power of the grave. He gives warning to others to keep close to God (*v.* 8): *Those that observe lying vanities forsake their own mercy.* Those that worship other gods, as the heathen mariners did, and expect relief and comfort from them, *forsake their own mercy;* they turn their back upon their own happiness. Or, those that follow their own inventions, as Jonah himself had done when he *fled from the presence of the Lord* to go to Tarshish, *forsake their own mercy,* that mercy which they might find if they would but keep close to God and their duty. He solemnly binds his soul with a bond that, if God work deliverance for him, the God of his mercies shall be the God of his praises, *v.* 9. Jonah promises, that with the sacrifice of thanksgiving he will *mention the lovingkindness of the Lord,* to his glory, and the encouragement of others. He will honour him by a punctual performance of his vows. Probably his vow was that if God would deliver him he would readily go wherever he should please to send him, though it were to Nineveh. He concludes with an acknowledgement of God as the Saviour of his people: *Salvation is of the Lord;* it *belongs to the Lord,* Ps. iii. 8. Jonah's experience shall encourage others, in all ages, to trust in God as the God of their salvation.

Verse 10

Jonah's discharge from his imprisonment, and his deliverance from death may be considered as an instance of God's mercy to a poor penitent, that in his distress prays to him. When God had him at his mercy he showed him mercy, and did not *contend for ever.* It seems a type and figure of Christ's resurrection. He died and was buried, to lay the storm which our sin had raised, and lay in the grave, as Jonah did, three days and three nights, a prisoner for our debt; but the third day he came forth, by his messengers to preach repentance, and remission of sins, even to the Gentiles.

CHAPTER 3

I. Jonah's mission renewed, and the command a second time given him to go preach at Nineveh, ver. 1, 2. II. Jonah's message to Nineveh faithfully delivered, ver. 3, 4. III. The repentance, humiliation, and reformation of the Ninevites, ver. 5–9. IV. God's gracious revocation of the sentence passed upon them, ver. 10.

Verses 1–4

I. Jonah's commission is renewed and readily obeyed.

God was perfectly reconciled to Jonah, and the commission anew given him was an evidence of the remission of his former disobedience. *The word of the Lord came unto Jonah the second time* (v. 1). After he has been thrown into the sea, and thrown out of it again, God comes and asks him, "Jonah, wilt thou go to Nineveh now?" Jonah shall be trusted. God might justly have said as we should concerning one that had dealt treacherously with us, that though we would not proceed to the rigour of the law against him, yet we would never again repose confidence in him. But, behold! the word of the Lord comes to him again, to show that when God forgives he forgets, and whom he forgives he receives into his family again, and restores them to their former estate. God's making use of us is the best evidence of his being at peace with us. Jonah was reconciled to God, not now *disobedient to the heavenly vision*. He neither endeavoured to avoid hearing the command, nor did he decline obeying it. But now, without murmuring and disputing, *Jonah arose, and went unto Nineveh, according to the word of the Lord*, v. 3. He went directly to Nineveh, though it was a great way off, and a place where, it is likely, he never was before; yet thither he took his journey, *according to the word of the Lord*.

II. The command given him. He was sent in the name of the God of heaven, to proclaim war with Nineveh (v. 2): "*Arise, go up to Nineveh, that great city*," that metropolis, and *preach unto it*, preach *against it*, so the Chaldee. Jonah is sent to Nineveh, which was at this time the chief city of the Gentile world, as an indication of God's gracious intentions to make the light of divine revelation to shine in those dark regions. God knew that if Sodom and Gomorrah, Tyre and Sidon, had had the means of grace, they would have repented, Matt. xi. 21, 23. He knew that if Nineveh had now the means of grace they would repent, and he gave them those means and sent Jonah. Go, and preach (says God) *the preaching that I bid thee*. Tell the men of Nineveh that their wickedness has come up to God, and God's vengeance is coming down upon them. This was the message Jonah was loth to deliver, and flew off and went to Tarshish; but, when he is brought to it the second time, God does not alter the message, to gratify him, or make it the more passable; no, he must now preach the very same that he was then ordered to preach and would not. It was an encouragement to him that God would go with him, that the Spirit of prophecy should abide upon him, when he was at Nineveh, to give him further instructions. Jonah must go with an implicit faith. Admirals, sometimes, when they are sent abroad, are not to open their commission till they have got so many leagues off at sea; so Jonah must go to Nineveh, and, when he comes there, shall be told what to say.

III. He faithfully and boldly delivered his errand. When he came to Nineveh he found it was an *exceedingly great city of three days' journey* (v. 3); a city *great to God*, so the Hebrew phrase is, meaning no more than as we render it, *exceedingly great*. The greatness of Nineveh consisted chiefly in the extent of it; it was much larger than Babylon, such a city, says Diodorus Siculus, as no man ever after built. When he came thither he lost no time; but opened his commission immediately, according to his instructions, and he *cried, and said, Yet forty days, and Nineveh shall be overthrown*. This was the purport of his message. He meant, and they understood him, that it should be overthrown, not by war, but by some immediate stroke, either by an earthquake or by fire and brimstone as Sodom was. So long God will wait to see if, upon this alarm given, they will humble themselves and amend their doings, and so prevent the ruin threatened. But he will wait no longer. Forty days is a long time for a righteous God to defer his judgments, yet it is but a little time for an

unrighteous people to repent and reform. The fixing of the day thus, with all possible assurance, would help to convince them that it was a message from God.

Verses 5–10

I. A wonder of divine grace in the repentance and reformation of Nineveh, upon the warning given them of their destruction approaching. It will *rise up in judgment against the men of* the gospel-*generation, and condemn them; for the Ninevites repented at the preaching of Jonas, but behold, a greater than Jonas is here*, Matt. xii. 41. It did condemn the impenitence and obstinacy of Israel at that time. God sent many prophets to Israel, well known to be *mighty in word and deed*; but to Nineveh he sent only one, and him a stranger, whose aspect was mean, and his *bodily presence weak*, after so long a journey; and yet they repented, but Israel repented not. Jonah preached but one sermon, and we do not find that he gave them any sign or wonder, and yet they were wrought upon, while Israel continued obstinate. Jonah only threatened wrath and ruin; we do not find that he gave them any encouragements to hope that they should find mercy if they did repent, and yet they repented; but Israel persisted in impenitence, though the prophets sent to them drew them *with cords of a man, and with bands of love*. The men of Nineveh *believed God*; they gave credit to the word which Jonah spoke to them in the name of God: they believed that there was but *one living and true God*— that to him they were accountable—that they had sinned against him—that this notice sent them of ruin approaching came from him—that he is a merciful God, and there might be some hopes of the turning away of the wrath threatened, if they did turn away from the sins for which it was threatened. They brought word to the king of Nineveh, who, some think, was at this time Sardanapalus. Jonah is not sent to the court, but to the streets of Nineveh, to make his proclamation. However, an account is brought to the king of Nineveh, not by way of information against Jonah, as a disturber of the public peace, but as a message from heaven, by some that were concerned for the public welfare. The king set them a good example of humiliation, v. 6. When he heard of the *word of God* sent to him he *rose from his throne* in sorrow and shame for sin, by which he and his people had become obnoxious. He laid aside his royal robe, the badge of his imperial dignity, as an acknowledgment that, having not used his power as he ought for the restraining of violence and wrong, and the maintaining of right, he had forfeited his throne and robe to the justice of God. Even the king himself disdained not to put on the garb of a penitent, for he *covered himself with sackcloth, and sat in ashes*. The people *put on sackcloth, from the greatest of them even to the least of them*, v. 5. Though bodily exercise alone profits nothing, and a man's *spreading sackcloth and ashes under him*, if that be all, is but a jest (it is the heart that God looks at, Isa. lviii. 5), yet when God *calls to mourning and girding with sackcloth*, we must by outward expressions of inward sorrow *glorify God with our bodies*, at least by laying aside their ornaments. A general fast was observed throughout that great city, v. 7–9. On the day appointed *let neither man nor beast taste anything*; nor so much as *drink water*. Let them make themselves uneasy in body, to show how uneasy they are in mind, through sorrow for sin and the fear of divine wrath. With their fasting and mourning they must join prayer and supplication to God; for the fasting is designed to fit the body for the service of the soul in the duty of prayer. In prayer we must cry mightily, with a fixedness of thought, firmness of faith, and fervour of pious and devout affections. Yet this is not all. They must to their fasting and praying add reformation and amendment of life: *Let them turn everyone from his evil way*, and particularly *from the violence that is in their hands*; let them restore what they have unjustly taken, and make reparation for what wrong they have done. It is not enough to fast for sin, but we must fast from sin. This fast is proclaimed and religiously observed (*v.* 9). They hope that God will, upon their repenting and turning, revoke his sentence against them. As when we pray for the favour of God we pray for all good, so when we pray against the wrath of God we pray against all evil. Jonah had not told them; they had not among them any other prophets to tell them, yet they had a general notion of the goodness of God's nature, his mercy to man, and from this they raised some hopes that he would spare them; they dare not presume, but they will not despair.

II. Here is a wonder of divine mercy in the sparing of these Ninevites upon their repentance (*v.* 10). God saw that they *turned from their evil way*, and that was the thing he looked for and required. Here were no sacrifices offered to God, that we read of, to make atonement for sin, but the *sacrifice of God is a broken spirit; a broken and contrite heart*, such as the Ninevites now had, is what he *will not despise; it* is what he will give countenance to and put honour upon.

CHAPTER 4

In this chapter we read, with a great deal of uneasiness, concerning the sin of Jonah; and, as there is joy in heaven and earth for the conversion of sinners, so there is grief for the follies and infirmities of saints. In the first chapter we had him fleeing from the face of God; but here we have him flying in the face of God; and there we had an account of his repentance and return to God; but here, though no doubt he did repent, yet no account is left us of his recovering himself; but, while we read with wonder of his perverseness, we read with no less wonder of God's tenderness towards him, by which it appeared that he had not cast him off. I. Jonah's repining at God's mercy to Nineveh, ver. 1–3. II. The gentle reproof God gave him for it, ver. 4. III. Jonah's discontent at the withering of the gourd, ve.. 5–9. IV. God's improving it for his conviction, that he ought not to be angry at the sparing of Nineveh, ver. 10, 11.

Verses 1–4

I. Jonah quarrelled with God for his mercy to Nineveh. This gives us occasion to suspect that Jonah had only delivered the message of wrath against the Ninevites, and had not assisted them in their repentance.

Jonah grudged them the mercy they found (*v.* 1): *It displeased Jonah exceedingly; and he was very angry.* Whatever pleases God should please us, and, though we cannot account for it, yet we must acquiesce in it. He had so little affection to men as to be angry at the conversion of the Ninevites and their reception into the divine favour. It was a point of honour that Jonah stood upon and that made him angry. He was jealous for the honour of his country; the repentance and reformation of Nineveh shamed the obstinacy of Israel that repented not, but *hated to be reformed*; and the favour God had shown to these Gentiles, upon their repentance, was an ill omen to the Jewish nation. He was jealous for his own honour, fearing lest, if Nineveh was not destroyed within forty days, he should be accounted a false prophet, and stigmatized accordingly. He quarrelled with God about it. When his heart was not within him, he *spoke unadvisedly with his lips*; and here he tells us what he said (*v.* 2, 3): He *prayed unto the Lord*, but it is a very awkward prayer. Being in discontent, his corruptions got head of his graces, and, when he should have been praying for benefit by the mercy of God himself, he was complaining of the benefit others had by that mercy. He now begins to justify himself in fleeing *from the presence of the Lord* when he was first ordered to go to Nineveh: "*Lord*," said he, "*was not this my saying when I was in my*

own country? Did I not foresee that if I went to preach to Nineveh they would repent, and thou wouldst forgive them?" What a strange sort of man was Jonah, to dread the success of his ministry! It is unaccountable that that which all the saints had made the matter of their joy and praise Jonah should make the matter of reflection upon God, as if that were an imperfection of the divine nature which is indeed the greatest glory of it—that God is *gracious and merciful*. In a passion, he wishes for death (*v.* 3), "*Now, O Lord! take, I beseech thee, my life from me.* If Nineveh must live, let me die, rather than see thy word and mine disproved, rather than see the glory of Israel transferred to the Gentiles," as if there were not grace enough in God both for Jews and Gentiles. It was very absurd for him to wish he might die when he had a prospect of living to so good a purpose and could be so ill spared. Our business is to get ready to die by doing the work of life, and then to refer ourselves to God to take away our life when and how he pleases.

II. See how justly God reproved Jonah for this heat that he was in (*v.* 4): The Lord said, *Doest thou well to be angry?* See how mildly the great God speaks to this foolish man, to teach us to restore those that have fallen with a *spirit of meekness*, and with *soft answers* to *turn away wrath. Doest thou well?* We should often put this question to ourselves. When passion is up, let it meet with this check, "Do I well to be so soon angry, so often angry, so long angry, to put myself into such a heat, and to give others such ill language in my anger?"

Verses 5–11

Jonah persists here in his discontent.

I. Jonah's sullen expectation of the fate of Nineveh. He retires, *goes out of the city*, sits alone, and keeps silence, because he sees the Ninevites repent and reform, *v.* 5. The forty days were now expiring, or had expired, and Jonah hoped that, if Nineveh was not overthrown, yet some judgment or other would come upon it, sufficient to save his credit. He *made himself a booth* of the boughs of trees.

II. God's gracious provision for his shelter and refreshment when he thus foolishly afflicted himself, *v.* 6. Jonah was sitting in his booth, fretting at the cold of the night and the heat of the day. God looked on him with compassion, as the tender mother does on the froward child. He *prepared a gourd*, a plant with broad leaves, that suddenly grew up, and covered his hut or booth. It was *a shadow over his head, to deliver him from his grief*, that, being refreshed in body, he might the better guard against the uneasiness of his mind. A gourd, one would think, was but a slender fortification at the best, yet Jonah *was exceedingly glad of the gourd*. A gourd in the right place may do us more service than a cedar. A small toy will serve sometimes to pacify a cross child, as the gourd did Jonah.

III. The sudden loss of this provision which God had made for his refreshment, and the return of his trouble, *v.* 7, 8. God *prepared a worm* to destroy the gourd. The gourd withered the next day after it sprang up; our comforts *come forth like flowers and are soon cut down.* A little thing withers them; a small worm at the root destroys a large gourd. Something unseen and undiscerned does it. God did not send an angel to pluck up Jonah's gourd, but sent a worm to smite it. He *prepared a wind* to make Jonah feel the want of the gourd, *v.* 8. It was a *vehement east wind*, which drove the heat of the rising sun violently upon the head of Jonah. Thus poor Jonah lay open to sun and wind.

IV. The further fret that this put Jonah into (*v.* 8). "If the gourd be killed, if the gourd be dead, kill me too, *let me die with the gourd.*" It is just that those who love to complain should never be left without something to complain of, that their folly may be manifested and corrected, and, if possible, cured.

V. The rebuke God gave him for this; he again reasoned with him: *Doest thou well to be angry for the gourd? v.* 9. When afflicting providences deprive us of our relations, possessions, and enjoyments, we must bear it patiently, must not be angry at God, must not be angry *for the gourd.* It is comparatively but a small loss, the loss of a shadow. That which should especially silence our discontent is that though our gourd be gone our God is not gone.

VI. His justification of his passion and discontent is strange, *v.* 9. He said, *I do well to be angry, even unto death.* Passion often over-rules conscience, and forces it to give a false judgment, as Jonah here did. He has so little regard to himself as to abandon his own life, to kill himself with fretting.

VII. He did ill to murmur at the sparing of Nineveh. Out of his own mouth God will judge him; he made no reply, but, we hope, returned to his right mind and recovered his temper. 1. God argued (*v.* 10, 11): "*Thou hast had pity on the gourd,* hast *spared it,* and saidst, *What a pity it is* that this gourd should ever wither! and *should not I then spare Nineveh*? The gourd thou hadst pity on was but one; but the inhabitants of Nineveh, whom I have pity on, are numerous." It is very populous, as appears by the number of the infants, two years old and under, of which there are 120,000 in Nineveh. So many there were in Nineveh not guilty of any transgression, and consequently had not contributed to the common guilt, and yet, if Nineveh had been overthrown, they would all have been involved in the common calamity; "and *shall not I spare* Nineveh then, with an eye to them?" God took notice of the abundance of cattle

too that were in Nineveh, which he had more reason to pity and spare than Jonah had to pity and to spare the gourd, inasmuch as the animal life is more excellent than the vegetable. 2. The gourd which Jonah was concerned for was none of his own; which he made not to grow; but the persons in Nineveh whom God had compassion on were all the *work of his own hands,* he made them, and his they were, and therefore he had much more reason to have compassion on them. 3. The gourd which Jonah had pity on was of a sudden growth, and therefore of less value; it *came up in a night, it was the son of a night* (so the word is); but Nineveh is an ancient city, of many ages standing, and therefore cannot be so easily given up. 4. The gourd which Jonah had pity on *perished in a night*; it withered, and there was an end of it. But the precious souls in Nineveh that God had pity on are immortal. One soul is of more value than the whole world, surely then one soul is of more value than many gourds. It may be that Jonah, after this was well reconciled to the sparing of Nineveh, and was as well pleased with it as ever he had been displeased. Jonah had said, *I do well to be angry,* but he could not prove it. God says and proves it, *I do well to be merciful*; and it is a great encouragement to poor sinners to hope that they shall find mercy with him. Such murmurers shall be made to understand this doctrine, that, how narrow soever their souls, their principles are, and how willing soever they are to engross divine grace to themselves and those of their own way, there is one *Lord over all, that is rich in mercy to all that call upon him,* and in *every nation,* in Nineveh as well as in Israel, *he that fears God and works righteousness is accepted of him*; he that repents, and turns from his evil way, shall find mercy with him.

AN EXPOSITION, WITH PRACTICAL OBSERVATIONS, OF

THE PROPHECY OF MICAH

There is a resemblance between Isaiah's prophecy and this. Compare Isa. ii. 2, 3, with Mic. iv. 1, 2. Isaiah's prophecy is said to be concerning *Judah and Jerusalem*, but Micah's concerning *Samaria and Jerusalem*; for, though this prophecy be dated only by the reigns of the kings of Judah, yet it refers to the kingdom of Israel, the approaching ruin of which, in the captivity of the ten tribes, he foretells and laments. I. To convince sinners of their sins, by charging both Israel and Judah with idolatry, covetousness, oppression, contempt of the word of God, and their rulers both in church and state, with the abuse of their power; and also by showing them the judgments of God. II. To comfort God's people with promises of mercy and deliverance, especially with an assurance of the coming of the Messiah and of the grace of the gospel through him. Two quotations out of it were made publicly upon very solemn occasions, and both refer to very great events. 1. One is a prediction of the destruction of Jerusalem (*ch.* iii. 12), which we find quoted in the Old Testament, by *the elders of the land* (Jer. xxvi. 17, 18), in justification of Jeremiah. "Micah (say they) foretold that *Zion should be ploughed as a field*, and Hezekiah did not put him to death; why then should we punish Jeremiah for saying the same?" 2. Another is a prediction of the birth of Christ (*ch.* v. 2) which we find quoted in the New Testament, by the *chief priests and scribes of the people*, in answer to Herod's enquiry, *where Christ should be born* (Matt. ii. 5, 6).

CHAPTER 1

I. The title of the book (ver. 1) and a preface demanding attention, ver. 2. II. Warning given of judgments hastening upon Israel and Judah (ver. 3, 4), for sin, ver. 5. III. The particulars of the destruction, ver. 6, 7. IV. The greatness of the destruction shown, 1. By the prophets sorrow for it, ver. 8, 9. 2. By the general sorrow that should be for it, in the places that must expect to share in it, ver. 10–16.

Verses 1–7

I. A general account of this prophet and his prophecy, *v.* 1. The prophecy is the *word of the Lord*; a divine revelation. This word of the Lord came to the prophet, and he saw the vision, saw the things themselves which he foretold, as if they had been already accomplished. The prophet is Micah the Morasthite; his name *Micah* is a contraction of Micaiah; his surname, the *Morasthite*, signifies that he was born, or lived, at Moresheth, which is mentioned (*v.* 14), or Mareshah, which is mentioned *v.* 15, and Joshua xv. 44. The date of his prophecy is in the reigns of three kings of Judah—Jotham, Ahaz, and Hezekiah. Ahaz was one of the worst of Judah's kings, and Hezekiah one of the best. The promises and threatenings of this book are interwoven; even in the wicked reign he preached comfort; and in the pious reign he preached conviction, for, however the times change, the word of the Lord is still the same. The prophecy is *concerning Samaria and Jerusalem*, the head cities of the two kingdoms of Israel and Judah.

II. A solemn introduction to the following prophecy (*v.* 2), in which, 1. The people are summoned to draw near. "*Hear you people*" (*all of them*, so the margin reads it). It is an unusual construction; but those words with which Micah begins his prophecy are the same in the original with those wherewith Micaiah ended his, 1 Kings xxii. 28. 2. The earth is called upon, with *all that therein is*, to hear what the prophet has to say: *Hearken, O earth!* If the church, and those in it, will not hear, the earth, and those in it, shall, and shame them. 3. God himself is appealed to in testimony against this people: "*Let the Lord God be witness against you*, a witness that you had fair warning given but you would not take the warning; let the accomplishment of the prophecy prove that it was the word of God, and no word of his shall fall to the ground." He will be a

witness *from his holy temple* in heaven, when he comes down to execute judgment (*v.* 3) against those that turned a deaf ear to his oracles.

III. A terrible prediction of judgments which should come upon Judah and Israel, which had its accomplishment soon after in Israel, and at length in Judah; for it is foretold, 1. That God himself will appear against them, *v.* 3. God's way towards this people had long been a way of mercy, but now he changes his way, he *comes out of his place*, and will come down. 2. That when the Creator appears against them it shall be in vain for any creature to appear for them. High places, set up for the worship of idols or for military fortifications, shall all be trampled into the dust. Neither men of *high degree*, as the mountains, nor *men of low degree*, as the valleys, shall secure either themselves or the land from the judgments of God, when they are sent with commission to lay all waste. This is applied particularly to the head city of Israel (*v.* 6): I *will make Samaria, that is now a rich and populous city, as a heap of the field*, as a heap of stones gathered together to be carried away, and *as plantings of a vineyard*, as hillocks of earth raised to plant vines in. Their *altars* had been as *heaps in the furrows of the fields* (Hos. xii. 11) and now their houses shall be as ruinous heaps.

IV. A charge of sin upon them, as the cause of these judgments (*v.* 5): *For the transgression of Jacob is all this*. All the calamities of Jacob and Israel are owing to their transgressions. But it is asked, *What is the transgression of Jacob?* It is idolatry; it is the *high places*. It is the idolatry of Samaria and Jerusalem, the royal cities of those two kingdoms. These were the royal places that had the greatest influence upon the country, by authority and example. If the transgression of Jacob is Samaria, therefore shall *Samaria become a heap*. Let the ringleaders in sin hear this and fear.

V. The punishment made to answer the sin, *v.* 7. 1. The gods they worshipped shall be destroyed: *The graven images shall be beaten to pieces* by the army of the Assyrians, *and all the idols shall be laid desolate. Samaria and her idols* were ruined together by Sennacherib (Isa. x. 11), and *their gods cast into the fire*, for *they were no gods* (Isa. xxxvii. 19). The gifts that passed between them and their gods shall be destroyed; for *all the hires thereof shall be burnt with fire.* And all this wealth shall become a prey to the idolatrous nations, and so be the *hire of a harlot* again, wages to an army of idolaters.

Verses 8–16

The funeral of a ruined kingdom.

I. The prophet is himself chief mourner (*v.* 8, 9). The prophets usually expressed their own grief for public grievances. It was not out of ill-will that they denounced the judgments of God. They dreaded it more than anything. We ought to lament the punishments of sinners as well as the sufferings of saints in this world; the weeping prophet did so (Jer. ix. 1); so did this prophet. He *makes a wailing like the dragons,* or the *jackals,* ravenous beasts that meet in the night, and *howl,* and make *hideous noises;* he mourns *as the owls,* the *screech-owls,* or *ostriches,* as some read it. Israel's case is desperate: Her *wound is incurable.* She will not by repentance and reformation help herself. There is indeed balm in Gilead and a physician there; but they will not apply to the physician. Judah likewise is in danger. The cup is going round, and is now put into Judah's hand: *The enemy has come to the gate of Jerusalem.* Soon after the destruction of Samaria the Assyrian army, under Sennacherib, laid siege to Jerusalem, came to the gate, but could not force its way any further.

II. Several places are here called upon to mourn; but they must not let the Philistines hear them (*v.* 10): *Declare it not in Gath;* this is borrowed from David's lamentation for Saul and Jonathan (2 Sam. i. 20), for the uncircumcised will triumph in Israel's tears. One would not gratify those that make merry with the sins or the sorrows of God's Israel. But, though it may be prudent not to give way to a noisy sorrow, yet it is duty to admit a silent one when the church of God is in distress. *"Roll thyself in the dust* and so let the house of Judah and every house in Jerusalem become a *house of Aphrah, a house of dust."* Other places are here named that should be sharers in this universal mourning, the names of some of which we do not find elsewhere. Sennacherib's invasion is described by the impressions of terror it should make upon the several cities that fell in his way, Isa. x. 28, 29, &c. 1. *The inhabitants of Saphir,* which *signifies* neat and *beautiful* (*thou that dwellest fairly,* so the margin reads it), shall *pass away* into captivity, or be forced to flee, stripped of all their ornaments *and having their shame naked.* 2. *The inhabitants of Zaanan,* which signifies the *country of flocks,* a populous country, where the people are as numerous as flocks of sheep, shall yet be so taken up with their own calamities, that they shall *not come forth in the mourning of Bethezel,* which signifies a *place near,* shall not bring succour to their neighbours in distress; for *he shall receive of you his standing;* the enemy shall find footing among you. 3. As for *the inhabitants of Maroth* (which, some think, is put for Ramoth, others that it signifies the *rough places*), they *waited carefully for good,* but were disappointed; for *evil came from the Lord unto the gate of Jerusalem,* when the Assyrian army besieged it, *v.* 12. 4. Lachish was a city of Judah, which Sennacherib laid siege to, Isa. xxxvi. 1, 2. The inhabitants of that city are called to *bind the chariot to the swift beast,* to prepare for a speedy flight. God's quarrel with Lachish is that she is *the beginning of sin,* the sin of idolatry, *to the daughter of Zion* (*v.* 13); they had learned it from the ten tribes, their near neighbours, and so infected the two tribes with it. Lachish, having been so much accessory to the sin of Israel, shall certainly be reckoned with: *Thou shalt give presents to Moresheth-gath,* a city of the Philistines, to assist thee, but it shall be in vain, for (*v.* 14) *the houses of Achzib* (a city which joined to Mareshah, or

Moresheth, and is mentioned with it, Joshua xv. 44) *shall be a lie to the kings of Israel.* Achzib signifies *a lie.* 5. Mareshah, that could not, or would not, help Israel, shall herself be made a prey (*v.* 15): *"I will bring an heir* (that is, an enemy) that shall take possession of thy lands, with as much assurance as if he were heir to them, and *The glory of Israel* shall come to be as Adullam, a poor despicable place."* 6. The whole land of Judah seems (*v.* 16) called to weeping and mourning: *"Make thee bald,* by tearing thy hair and shaving thy head; *poll thee for thy delicate children,* that had been tenderly and nicely brought up; *enlarge thy baldness as the eagle* when she casts her feathers and is all over bald; *for they have gone into captivity from thee,* and their captivity will be the more grievous to them because they have not been inured to hardship."*

CHAPTER 2

I. The sins with which the people of Israel are charged—covetousness and oppression, fraudulent and violent practices (ver. 1, 2), dealing barbarously, even with women and children, ver. 8, 9, opposition of God's prophets (ver. 6, 7), and delighting in false prophets, ver. 11. II. The judgments with which they are threatened that they should be humbled, and impoverished (ver. 3–5), and banished, ver. 10. III. Gracious promises of comfort, reserved for the good people among them, in the Messiah, ver. 12, 13.

Verses 1–5

I. The injustice of man contriving the evil of sin, *v.* 1, 2. It is the sin of oppression. 1. They desire that which is not their own—that is the *root of bitterness,* the root of all evil, *v.* 2. They *covet fields and houses,* as Ahab did Naboth's vineyard. 2. They invent ways of accomplishing their desire (*v.* 4). It is bad to do mischief upon a sudden thought, but much worse to do it with deliberation. They devised it *upon their beds,* when they should have been asleep. 3. They practise the iniquity they have devised, *because it is in the power of their hand;* by the help of their wealth, and the authority and interest they have. 4. They are industrious and as soon as the *morning is light* they practise it. 5. They stick at nothing to compass their designs; what they *covet* they *take away*—men's fields by violence, not only by fraud, and colour of law, but by force and with a high hand. They care not to whom they do wrong. They *oppress a man and his house;* they rob those that have families to maintain, though they send them and their wives and children begging. They *oppress a man and his heritage;* take away from men that which they have received from their ancestors, and which they have but in trust, to transmit it to their posterity.

II. The justice of God contriving punishment for this sin (*v.* 3): *Therefore thus saith the Lord, Behold, against this family do I devise an evil,* that is, against the whole kingdom, the *house of Israel,* and particularly those families in it that were cruel and oppressive. 1. He finds them very confident that they shall in some way or other escape judgment, and therefore he tells them, It is *an evil from which they shall not remove their neck.* They were children of *Belial,* that would not endure the easy yoke of God's righteous commands, but *broke those bonds* asunder, and therefore God will lay upon them the heavy yoke of his righteous judgments. 2. He finds them proud, and therefore tells them they shall not go haughtily, with *stretched-forth necks and wanton eyes,* walking and mincing as they go (Isa. iii. 16); for *this time is evil,* and the events of it are very humbling. 3. He finds them jovial, and tells them their laughter shall be turned into mourning and their joy into heaviness (*v.* 4): *In that day,* when God comes to punish you for your oppression, *shall one take up a parable against you,* and *lament with a doleful lamentation,* with a *lamentation of lamentations* (so the word is). Their enemies shall insult over them, and make a jest of their griefs, for they shall *take up a parable against them*. 4. He finds them rich in houses and lands, gained by oppression, and therefore tells them that they shall be stripped of all. They shall say, *We are utterly spoiled; he has changed the portion of my people,* so that it is now in the possession of their enemies: *How has he removed it from me! Turning away* from us in wrath, he *has divided our fields,* and given them into the hands of strangers. The margin reads it, *"Instead of restoring, he has divided our fields."* God shall ratify what they say (*v.* 5): *Thou shalt have none to cast a cord by lot in the congregation of the Lord,* none to divide inheritances, because there shall be no inheritances to divide. It was God's land, a holy land, and therefore it was the more grievous to them to be turned out of it.

Verses 6–11

Two sins charged upon the people of Israel, and judgments for each—persecuting God's prophets and oppressing God's poor.

I. Persecuting God's prophets, suppressing and silencing them, is a sin that provokes God, for his sending prophets to us is a sure token of his goodwill.

1. The opposition which this people gave to God's prophets: They *said to those that prophesy, Prophesy ye not,* as Isa. xxx. 10. They *said to the seers, "See not;* do not trouble us with accounts of what you have seen, nor bring us any such frightful messages." They must either not prophesy at all or prophesy only what is pleasing. Some read it, *Prophesy not; let these prophesy.* Let not those prophesy that tell us of our faults, and threaten us, but *let those prophesy* that will flatter us in our sins, and cry peace to us. If a prophet will but tell them that it is lawful for them to drink as much as they please of their wine and strong drink, that they *shall have peace though they go on and add drunkenness to thirst,* this is a man after their own heart. *He shall even be the prophet of this people;* such a man will not only associate with them in their rioting and revellings, but will pretend to consecrate their sensualities by his prophecies.

2. They are here reproved (*v.* 7): *"O thou that art named the house of Jacob,* wilt thou silence those that prophesy, and forbid them to speak in God's name? *Is the Lord's Spirit straitened?* In silencing the Lord's prophets you do what you can to silence his Spirit too. Can you make the Spirit of God your servant? Will you forbid him to say what is displeasing to you? If you silence the prophets, yet the Spirit of the Lord will find out other ways to reach your consciences? Can your unbelief frustrate the divine counsels?" As Jews: "You are *named the house of Jacob,* and this is your honour; but *are these* the doings of your father Jacob?" Consider how unreasonable the thing is in itself: *Do not my words do good to those that walk uprightly?* God owns the words of the prophets to be his words (they are *my words)* and by them aims and designs to do good to mankind (Ps. cxix. 68); and will you hinder the great benefactor from doing good? It is certainly for the common good of states and kingdoms that religion should be encouraged.

3. They are threatened with punishment for this sin. They shall be deprived of the benefit of a faithful ministry. Since they say, *Prophesy not,* God will take them at their word, and *they shall not prophesy to them.* Let the physician no longer attend the patient that will not be healed, for he will not be ruled. They shall be given up to the blind guidance of an unfaithful ministry. We may understand *v.* 11 as a threatening: *If a man be found walking in the spirit of falsehood, he shall be the prophet of this people.* Since they will not admit the *truth in the*

love of it, God will send them *strong delusions to believe a lie,* 2 Thess. ii. 10, 11.

II. Oppressing God's poor is another sin they are charged with (*v.* 1, 2),

The sin is described, *v.* 8, 9. Those who formerly rose up against the enemies of the nation, now of late *rose up as enemies of the nation,* and, instead of defending it, destroyed it. They made a prey of men, that were travelling on the way, that *pass by securely as men averse from war,* about their lawful occasions. Those they set upon, and *pulled off the robe with the garment from them,* that is, they stripped them. Of women (*v.* 9): *The women of my people have you cast out from their pleasant houses. They devoured widows' houses* (Matt. xxiii. 14), turned them out of the possession of them. Of children, whose age entitles them to a tender usage: *From their children have you taken away my glory for ever.* It was the glory of the Israelites' children that they were free, but they enslaved them, sold them to strangers, sent them into idolatrous countries. The sentence is passed upon them for it (*v.* 10): *"Arise ye, and depart;* prepare to quit this land. You shall have neither contentment nor continuance in it, *because it is polluted* by your wickedness. You shall not only be obliged to depart out of this land, but *it shall destroy you even with a sore destruction;* you shall either be turned out of it or you shall be ruined in it."

Verses 12–13

The chapter concludes, as is usual in the prophets, with promises of mercy, which were in part fulfilled when the Jews returned out of Babylon, and had their full accomplishment in the kingdom of the Messiah. 1. Whereas they were dispersed, they shall be brought together again (*v.* 12): *"I will surely assemble, O Jacob! all of thee,* all that are *named of the house of Jacob* (*v.* 7) now expelled your country, *v.* 10. *I will surely gather the remnant of Israel. I will put them together as the sheep of Bozrah."* Sheep are sociable creatures; they shall be *as the flock in the midst of their fold,* their own fold, where they are safe under the shepherd's eye and care; and *they shall make great noise* (as numerous flocks and herds do, with their bleatings and lowing) *by reason of the multitude of men,* not by reason of their strifes and contentions, but by reason of their great numbers. This was accomplished when Christ by his gospel gathered together in one *all the children of God that were scattered abroad,* and united both Jews and Gentiles in one fold, and under one Shepherd. 2. Whereas God had seemed to desert them, and cast them off, now he will help them through all the difficulties in the way of their return and deliverance (*v.* 13): *The breaker has come up before them,* to break down all opposition, and clear the road for them; and under his guidance *they have broken up, and have passed through the gate,* the door of escape out of their captivity. *Their king shall pass before them,* to head them in the way, even Jehovah (he is their king) *on the head of them,* as he was on the head of the armies of Israel through the wilderness. Christ is the church's King; he is Jehovah; he passes before them, brings them out of the land of their captivity, into the land of their rest. Bishop Pearson applies it to the resurrection of Christ. *The breaker has gone up before us* out of the grave, and has carried away its gates, and by that breach we go out.

CHAPTER 3

Micah is very bold in reproving and threatening the great men that were the ringleaders in sin; and he gives the reason (ver. 8) why he was so bold, because he had commission from God to say what he said, by a higher spirit and power than his own. Magistracy and ministry are two great ordinances of God, but these were both corrupted and the intentions perverted; and upon those that abused them the prophet is very severe, and justly so.

I. He gives them their lesson severally, reproving and threatening princes (ver. 1–4) and false and flattering prophets, ver. 5–7. II. He gives them their lesson jointly as acting in conjunction for the ruin of the kingdom, ver. 9–12.

Verses 1–7

I. Let the princes hear their charge and their doom. The *heads of Jacob, and* the *princes of the house of Israel*, are called upon to *hear* what the prophet has to say to them, *v*. 1. The prophet faithfully discharged his trust: "*And I said, Hear, O princes!* Is it not your business to administer justice impartially, and not to *know faces*" (as the Hebrew phrase for partiality, and respect of persons is), "but to *know judgment*, and the merits of every cause?" Therefore stand still, and hear your own judgment.

2. They had transgressed the rules of judgment, though they knew what they were. They *hate the good and love the evil*. This being their principle, their practice is according to it; they are cruel towards those that are under their power, and whoever lies at their mercy will find that they have none. They fleece the flock they should feed; instead of feeding it, they feed upon it, Ezek. xxxiv. 2. They *eat the flesh of my people*. It is fit that they should be clothed with the wool, but that will not serve: They *flay the skin from them, v*. 3. By imposing heavier taxes and exacting them with rigour, by fines, and corporal punishments, for pretended crimes, they ruined their subjects, took away from some their lives, from others their livelihoods, and were as beasts of prey, rather than shepherds. "They *break their bones* to come at the marrow, and *chop* the flesh *in pieces as for the pot*."

3. How they might expect that God should deal with them. The rule is fixed, Those shall have judgment without mercy that have shown no mercy (*v*. 4). *With the froward God will show himself froward*, and often gives us cruel and unmerciful men into the hands of those who are cruel and unmerciful themselves.

II. Let the prophets hear their charge too; they were such as prophesied falsely, and the princes bore rule by their means.

1. Their sin: They made it their business to flatter and deceive the people. "They make them to err by crying peace, by telling them that all shall be well with them; whereas they are in the paths of sin, and within a step of ruin. They *cry peace*, but they *bite with their teeth*," which perhaps is meant of their biting their own lips, as we are apt to do when we would suppress something. They *bite with their teeth, and cry peace*; that is, they flatter and compliment those that will feed them with good bits, but as for those that *put not into their mouths*, they look upon them as their enemies. They preach either comfort or terror to men, not according as they are to God, but as they are to them.

2. The sentence passed upon them for this sin, *v*. 6, 7. *Night shall be upon them*, a dark cold night of calamity, such as they, in their flattery, led the people to hope would never come. *It shall be dark unto you; the sun shall go down over the prophets;* All comfort shall depart and all hope. Their mind shall be full of confusion, their heads shall be clouded, and their own thoughts shall trouble them. They kept others in the dark, and now God will bring them into the dark. Thereby they shall be silenced, and all their pretensions to prophecy for ever shamed. They never had any true vision; it was all a sham, and they were cheats and impostors. They shall not have so much as a counterfeit vision to produce, they shall be *ashamed*, and *confounded*, and *cover their lips*.

Verses 8–12

I. The prophet experiences a divine power going along with him in his work. He could not but speak the word that God put into his mouth. The false prophets were *sensual, not having the Spirit*, but truly (says Micah) *I am full of power by the Spirit of the Lord, v*. 8. The qualifications with which this prophet was endued: He was *full of power and of judgment, and of might*; he had an ardent love to God and to the souls of men, a deep concern for his glory and their salvation, and a flaming zeal against sin. He had likewise courage to reprove it and witness against it. He was a man of wisdom as well as courage; in all his preaching there was light as well as heat, and a spirit of wisdom as well as of zeal. Those who act honestly may act boldly; and those who are sure that they have a commission from God need not be afraid of opposition from men. He *declared to Jacob his transgression and to Israel his sin*. Since few have meekness enough to receive reproof, those have need of a great deal of boldness, who are to give reproofs, and must pray for a spirit both of wisdom and might.

II. The prophet exerts this power in dealing with the *heads of the house of Jacob*. He repeats the summons (*v*. 9), the same that we had *v*. 1, to the *princes of the house of Israel*, yet he means those of *Judah*; for it appears (Jer. xxvi. 18, 19, where *v*. 12 is quoted) that this was spoken in Hezekiah's kingdom; but, the ten tribes being gone into captivity, Judah is all that is now left of Jacob and Israel. He gives them their titles of *heads* and *princes*. Ministers must be faithful to great men, but they must not be rude and uncivil to them.

1. The great wickedness of the *princes, priests*, and *prophets*; they were covetous, and prostituted their offices to their love of money. (1) The *princes abhorred all judgment*; they *perverted all equity*, when it could not be made pliable to their secular interests. It is laid to their charge (*v*. 10) that they *build up Zion with blood*. "They pretend, in justification of their extortion, that they add new streets and squares to the holy cities, and adorn them. But it is *with blood* and *with iniquity*, and therefore it cannot prosper; nor will their intentions of good to the city of God justify their contradictions to the law of God." *They judge for reward* (*v*. 11). The most righteous cause shall not be carried without a fee, and for a fee the most unrighteous cause shall be carried. The priests' work was to teach the people, but they *teach for hire*, and will be hired to teach anything, which they know will please. The prophets *divine for money*. A man might have what oracle he would from them if he would but pay them for it.

2. They *lean upon the Lord*, and because they are, in profession, his people, think there is neither harm nor danger in their wicked practices. Faith builds upon the Lord, rests in him, and relies upon him, as the soul's foundation; presumption only *leans upon the Lord* as a prop, makes use of him to serve a turn, while still the world is the foundation that is built upon. "*Is not the Lord among us?* Have we not the tokens of his presence with us, his temple, his ark, his lively oracles?" They are *haughty because of the holy mountain* (Zeph. iii. 11), as if their church privileges would palliate the worst of practices. They are confident of their own safety: *No evil can come upon us*. Many are rocked asleep in a fatal security by their church-privileges, as if those would protect them in sin.

3. The doom passed upon them for their wickedness, notwithstanding (*v*. 12): *Therefore shall Zion for your sake be ploughed as a field*. This passage is quoted as a bold word spoken by Micah (Jer. xxvi. 18), which yet Hezekiah and his princes took well; they repented and reformed, and so the execution of this threatening did not come in those days. It is Zion that shall be ploughed as a field, the building burnt to the ground and levelled with it. Some observe

that this was literally fulfilled in the destruction of Jerusalem by the Romans, when the ground on which the city stood was ploughed up in token of its utter desolation. The wickedness of those who preside in them brings the ruin: "It is *for your sake* that *Zion shall be ploughed as a field*; you pretend to build up Zion, but doing it by blood and iniquity, you pull it down."

CHAPTER 4

Zion was ploughed as a field, but the Christian church, was built upon the ruins of it. It is here promised, I. That it shall be enlarged by the accession of the nations to it, ver. 1, 2. II. That it shall be protected in tranquillity and peace, ver. 3, 4. III. That it shall be kept faithful to God, ver. 5. IV. That, under Christ's government, all its grievances shall be redressed, ver. 6, 7. V. That it shall have an ample and flourishing dominion, ver. 8. VI. That its troubles shall be brought to a happy issue, ver. 9, 10. VII. That its enemies shall be destroyed by their attempts against it, ver. 11–14.

Verses 1–7

It is a very comfortable *but* with which this chapter begins. When we sometimes see the corruptions of the church, *Zion ploughed as a field*, we are ready to fear that it will one day perish. But let not our faith fail; out of the ashes of the church another phoenix shall arise. The first words of this chapter bring in *the mountain of the Lord's house* as much dignified by being frequented as ever it had been disgraced by being deserted. Though Zion be ploughed as a field, yet God has not *cast off his people*, but by the fall of the Jews salvation has come to the Gentiles, Rom. xi. 11, 12. This is the mystery which God by the prophet here shows us, the same in the first three verses of this chapter which another prophet said (Isa. ii. 2–4).

I. There shall be a church for God set up in the world, after the defection and destruction of the Jewish church, *in the days of the Messiah*. The people of God shall be incorporated by a new charter, a new spiritual way of worship shall be enacted; better privileges shall be granted by this new charter, and better provision made for establishing the kingdom of God among men than had been made by the Old Testament constitution: *The mountain of the house of the Lord* shall again appear firm ground, *v.* 1. A church shall be set up in the world, to which the Lord will be daily *adding such as shall be saved.*

II. This church shall be firmly founded and well-built: It *shall be established in the top of the mountains*; Christ himself will build it upon a rock.

III. It shall become eminent and conspicuous: It *shall be exalted above the hills*, observed with wonder for its growing greatness from small beginnings. The glory of this latter house is greater than that of the former, Hag. ii. 9. See 2 Cor. iii. 7, 8, &c.

IV. There shall be a great accession of converts to it and succession of converts in it. *People shall flow unto it* as a constant stream of believers flowing in from all parts into the church. In gospel-times many nations shall flow into the church. Ministers shall be sent forth to *disciple all nations*, and they shall not *labour in vain*. "*He will teach us of his ways*, what is the way in which he would have us to walk with him and in which we may depend upon him to meet us graciously."

V. A new revelation shall be published to the world, on which the church shall be founded, and by which multitudes shall be brought into it: *For the law shall go forth of Zion, and the word of the Lord from Jerusalem*. The gospel is here called *the word of the Lord*. It began to be spoken by the Lord Christ himself, Heb. ii. 3. And it is *a law*, a law of faith; we are *under the law to Christ*. This was to go *forth from Jerusalem, from Zion*. Thence the gospel must take rise, to show the connection between the Old Testament and the New, that the gospel is not set up in opposition to the law, but is an explication and illustration of it, and a *branch growing out of its roots*. It was in Jerusalem that Christ preached and wrought miracles; there he died, rose again, and ascended; there the Spirit was poured out; and those that were to preach repentance and remission of sins to all nations were ordered to *begin at Jerusalem*.

VI. A convincing power should go along with the gospel of Christ, in all places where it should be preached (*v.* 3): *He shall judge among many people*.

VII. A disposition to mutual peace and love shall be the happy effect of the setting up of the kingdom of the Messiah, Tit. iii. 2, 3. Those who, before their conversion, did injuries, and would bear none, after their conversion can bear injuries, but will do none. As far as the gospel prevails it makes men peaceable, for such is *the wisdom from above*; it is *gentle and easy to be entreated*; and, if nations were but leavened by it, there would be universal peace. The art of war, instead of being improved (which some reckon the glory of a kingdom), shall be forgotten and laid aside as useless. The gospel men peaceable (*v.* 4): *They shall sit* safely, and none shall disturb them; they shall sit securely, and shall not disturb themselves, every man *under his vine and under his fig-tree*, enjoying the fruit of them, and needing no other shelter than the leaves of them. *None shall make them afraid;* they shall not be disposed to fear.

VIII. The churches shall be constant in their duty, *v.* 5. Peace is a blessing indeed when it strengthens our resolutions to cleave to the Lord. How constant God's people now resolve to be to him: "*We will walk in the name of the Lord our God*, will acknowledge him in all our ways."

IX. Notwithstanding the dispersions, distress, and infirmities of the church, it shall be formed and established, *v.* 6, 7. 1. The state of the church had been low, and very helpless, in the latter times of the Old Testament, partly through the corruptions of the Jewish nation, and partly through the oppressions under which they groaned. They were like *a flock of sheep* that were *maimed, worried, and scattered*, Ezek. xxxiv. 16; Jer. l. 6, 17. It is promised that these grievances shall be redressed. Christ will come himself (Matt. xv. 24), and send his apostles to *the lost sheep of the house of Israel*, Matt. x. 6. From among the Jews God gathered a remnant (*v.* 7). And from among the Gentiles he raised a strong nation. And such a strong nation the gospel-church is, that the gates of hell shall never be able to prevail against it.

X. The *Messiah* shall be the king of this kingdom to the end of time.

Verses 8–13

These verses relate to Zion and Jerusalem, here called the *tower of the flock*, or the *tower of Edor*; we read of such a place (Gen. xxxv. 21) near Bethlehem; and some conjecture it is the same place where the shepherds were keeping their flocks when the angels brought them tidings of the birth of Christ, and some think Bethlehem itself is here spoken of, as *ch.* v. 2. Some think it is a tower at that gate of Jerusalem which is called the *sheep-gate* (Neh. iii. 32), and conjecture that through that gate Christ rode in triumph into Jerusalem. However, it seems to be put for Jerusalem itself, or for Zion the *tower of David*.

I. A promise of the glories of the spiritual Jerusalem, the gospel-church, which is the tower of the flock, that one fold in which all the sheep of Christ are protected under one Shepherd: "*Unto thee shall it come; even the first dominion*, a dignity and power equal to that of David and Solomon, that *kingdom* shall again *come to the daughter of Jerusalem*, which it was deprived of at the captivity." Now this had by no means its accomplishment in Zerubbabel; and therefore it must refer to the kingdom of the *Messiah* and had its accomplishment when God gave to our Lord Jesus *the throne of his father David* (Luke i. 32).

II. This is illustrated by a prediction of the calamities of the literal Jerusalem, to which some favour and relief should be granted, as a type and figure of what God would do for the gospel-Jerusalem.

1. Jerusalem put in pain by the providences of God. "She *cries out aloud*, because there is *no king in her*, none of that honour she used to have. Instead of ruling the nations, she is ruled by them, and has become a captive. Her *counsellors* have *perished. Pangs have taken her*." She is carried captive to Babylon. "She *goes forth out of the city*, and is constrained to *dwell in the field*, exposed to all manner of inconveniences; she *goes even to Babylon*, and there wears out *seventy tedious* years in a miserable captivity, *in pain, as a woman in travail*, waiting to be delivered." When she is delivered out of Babylon, still she is in fear; for *now also*, when Jerusalem is in the rebuilding, *many nations are gathered against her*, *v.* 11. They were so in Ezra's and Nehemiah's time, and did all they could to obstruct the building of the temple and the wall. They were so in the time of the Maccabees; they said, *Let her be defiled.*

2. Jerusalem made easy by the promises of God: "*Why dost thou cry out aloud?*" Jerusalem's pangs are not dying agonies, but travailing throes, which after a while will be forgotten, for joy that a child is born into the world. Let the literal Jerusalem comfort herself with this, that, she shall continue until the coming of the Messiah, for there his kingdom must be first set up, and when at length she is ploughed as a field (as is threatened, *ch.* iii. 12), yet her privileges shall be resigned to the spiritual Jerusalem, and the promises made to her shall be fulfilled. Let Jerusalem be easy then, for, her captivity in Babylon shall have a happy end (*v.* 10). This was done by Cyrus, who acted therein as God's servant; and that deliverance was typical of our redemption by Jesus Christ. The designs of her enemies against her afterwards shall be baffled, *v.* 12, 13. Their coming together against Zion shall be the occasion of their ruin. Zion shall have the honour of being victorious over them, *v.* 13. "*Arise, and thresh, O daughter of Zion!* God will make *thy horn iron*, to push them down, and *thy hoofs brass*, to tread upon them when they are down; and thus thou shalt *beat in pieces many people*, that have long been beating thee in pieces." Thus, when God pleases, *the daughter of Babylon is made a threshing floor*, and the *worm Jacob* is made *a threshing instrument*, with which God will *thresh the mountains, and make them as chaff*, Isa. xli. 14, 15. How strangely are the tables turned, since Jacob was the threshing-floor and Babylon the threshing instrument! Isa. xxi. 10. The spoils gained by Zion's victory shall be brought into the sanctuary, and devoted to God, either in part, as those of Midian (Num. xxxi. 28), or in whole, as those of Jericho, Joshua vi. 17. Some make all this to point at the defeat of Sennacherib when he besieged Jerusalem, others to the destruction of Babylon, others to the successes of the Maccabees; but others think it had its full accomplishment in the Spiritual victories obtained by the gospel of Christ over the powers of darkness that fought against it. The nations thought to ruin Christianity in its infancy, but it was victorious over them.

CHAPTER 5

I. A prediction of the troubles and distresses of the Jewish nation, ver. 1. II. A promise of the Messiah, and of his kingdom, 1. Of the birth of the Messiah, ver. 2, 3. 2. Of his advancement, ver. 4. 3. Of his protection of his people, and his victory over his and their enemies, ver. 5, 6. 4. Of the great increase of the church, and the blessings that shall come to the world by it, ver. 7. 5. Of the destruction of the enemies of the church, both those without and those within, ver. 8–15.

Verses 1–6

I. The abasement and distress of Zion, *v.* 1. The Jewish nation, for many years before the captivity, dwindled: *Now gather thyself in troops, O daughter of troops!* It is a summons to Zion's enemies. Let them *gather in troops*, for, says the prophet, in the name of the inhabitants of Jerusalem, *He has laid siege against us;* the king of Assyria has, the king of Babylon has, and prevail so far as *to smite the judge of Israel*—the king, the chief justice, and the other inferior judges—*with a rod upon the cheek*, having made them prisoners. Complaint had been made of the judges of Israel (*ch.* iii. 11) that they were corrupt and took bribes, and this disgrace came justly upon them for abusing their power.

II. The advancement of Zion's King. Having shown how low the house of David should be brought to encourage the faith of God's people, he adds an illustrious prediction of the Messiah in whom that covenant should be established, and the honours of that house should be revived.

1. How the Messiah is here described. It is he that is to be *ruler in Israel, whose goings forth have been from of old, from everlasting*, from the *days of eternity*, as the word is. This description of Christ's eternal generation, or his going forth as the Son of God, begotten of his Father before all worlds, shows that this prophecy must belong only to him, and could never be verified of any other. The *going forth* is used (Deut. viii. 3) for a *word* which *proceeds out of the mouth*, and is therefore very fitly used to signify the eternal generation of him who is called the *Word of God*, that was *in the beginning with God*, John i. 1, 2. His office as Mediator; he was to be *ruler in Israel*, king of his church; he was to *reign over the house of Jacob for ever*, Luke i. 32, 33. It is a spiritual Israel that he reigns over. In the hearts of these he reigns by his Spirit and grace, and in the society of these by his word and ordinances.

2. What is here foretold concerning him.

(1) That Bethlehem should be the place of his nativity, *v.* 2. *Beth-lehem* signifies *the house of bread*, the fittest place for him to be born in who is *the bread of life*. And, because it was the city of David, by a special providence it was ordered that he should be born there. It is called *Bethlehem-Ephratah*, both names of the same city, as appears Gen. xxxv. 19. It was *little among the thousands of Judah*, not considerable either for the number of the inhabitants or the figure they made. Christ would give honour to the place of his birth, and not derive honour from it.

(2) That in the fulness of time he should be born of a woman (*v.* 3). Though the out-goings of the Messiah were *from everlasting*, yet the *redemption in Jerusalem*, the *consolation of Israel*, must be waited for (Luke ii. 25–38) until the time that *she who should bring forth* (so the virgin Mary is called, as Christ is himself called, *He that shall come*) shall *bring forth*; and in the meantime *he will give them up*. Divine salvations must be waited for until the time fixed for the bringing of them forth.

(3) That *the remnant of his brethren shall then return to the children of Israel*. The remnant of the Jewish nation shall return to the spirit of the true children of Israel, a people in covenant with God. Some understand it of all believers, Gentiles as well as Jews; they shall all be incorporated into the commonwealth of Israel; and, as they are all brethren to one another, so *he is not ashamed to call them brethren*, Heb. ii. 11.

(4) That he shall be a glorious prince, and his subjects shall be happy under his government (*v.* 4):

He shall stand and feed, that is, he shall both teach and rule. He shall do this, not as an ordinary man, but *in the strength of the Lord*, as one clothed with a divine power to go through his work. The prophets prefaced their messages with, *Thus saith the Lord;* but Christ spoke, not as a servant, but as a Son—*Verily, verily, I say unto you.* This was feeding *in the majesty of the name of the Lord his God.* Christ's government shall be happy for his subjects, for *they shall abide. Now shall he be great to the ends of the earth.* Now that he stands and feeds his flock, *now shall he be great.* For Christ reckons it his greatness to do good.

(5) That he shall secure the peace and welfare of his church and people against all the attempts of his and their enemies (*v. 5, 6*): *This man*, as king and ruler, *shall be the peace when the Assyrians shall come into our land.* This refers to the deliverance of Hezekiah and his kingdom from the power of Sennacherib, who invaded them, in the type; but, under the shadow of that, it is a promise of the safety of the gospel-church and of all believers from the designs and attempts of the powers of darkness, Satan and all his instruments, the dragon and his angels, that seek to devour the church of the first-born and all that belong to it. When the Assyrian comes with such a force into a land, can there be any other peace than a tame submission and an unresisted desolation? Yes, even then. Christ is our peace, as a priest, making atonement for sin, and reconciling us to God; and he is our peace as a king, conquering our enemies and commanding down disquieting fears and passions; he *creates the fruit of the lips, peace.* He will find out proper instruments to be employed for their protection and deliverance, and the defeat of their enemies: *Then shall we raise against him seven shepherds and eight principal men, that is, a competent number of persons*, men that shall have the care and tenderness of shepherds and the courage and authority of *principal men*, or *princes of men. Seven* and *eight* are a certain number for an uncertain. Magistrates and ministers are shepherds and principal men, raised in defence of religion's righteous cause against the powers of sin and Satan in the world. The opposition given to the church shall be got over, and the opposers brought down. This is represented by the laying of Assyria and Chaldea waste, which two nations were the most formidable enemies to the Israel of God of any, and the destruction of them signified the making of Christ's enemies his footstool: *They shall waste the land of Assyria with the sword, and the land of Nimrod in the entrance thereof.*

Verses 7–15

Glorious things are here spoken of *the remnant of Jacob*, that remnant which was raised of *her that halted* (*ch.* iv. 7), and it seems to be that *remnant which the Lord our God shall call* (Joel ii. 32), on whom the Spirit shall be poured out, the remnant that shall be saved, Rom. ix. 27.

I. They shall be *as a dew* in the midst of the nations, *v.* 7. God's church is dispersed all the world over; it is *in the midst of many people*, as gold in the ore, wheat in the heap. Israel according to the flesh dwelt alone, but the spiritual Israel lies scattered *in the midst of many people*, as the *salt of the earth*, or as seed sown in the ground, here a grain and there a grain, Hos. ii. 23. Now this remnant shall be *as dew from the Lord, born from above*, not of the earth, savouring the things of the earth. They shall be numerous as the drops of dew in a summer's morning, pure and clear. They shall be as the dew that distils insensibly, such is the way of the Spirit. They shall rely on divine grace, for they are no more than what the free grace of God makes them every day. They

shall be great blessings to those among whom they live, as the dew and the showers are to the grass. They shall be mild and gentle in their behaviour, like their Master, who comes down *like rain upon the new-mown grass*, Ps. lxxii. 6.

II. That they shall be *as a lion among the beasts of the forest*, that *treads down and tears in pieces, v.* 8. As they shall be silent, and gentle, and communicative of all good, to those that receive the truth in the love of it, so they shall be bold as a lion in witnessing against the corruptions of the times and places they live in, and strong as a lion, in the strength of God, to resist and overcome their spiritual enemies.

III. That they shall be brought off from all carnal confidences, which they have relied on, by the providence of God they shall enjoy such a security that they shall not need them. They had trusted in chariots and horses, and multiplied them (Ps. xx. 7); but now God will *cut off their horses*, and *destroy their chariots* (*v.* 10). They depended upon their fortified cities for their security; but God will take care that they be demolished (*v.* 11). They shall have them for habitations, but not for garrisons. Many of them depended much upon the advice of their diviners and fortune-tellers; and those God will cut off (*v.* 12). Many of them had said to the work of their hands, *You are our gods;* but now idolatry shall be abolished and abandoned (*v.* 13). Among other monuments of idolatry, *I will pluck up thy groves out of the midst of thee, v.* 14. These were planted and preserved in honour of their idols, and used in the worship of them. And so *will I destroy their cities*, meaning the cities that were dedicated to the idols.

IV. That those who stand it out against the gospel of Christ, and continue in league with their idolatries and witchcrafts, shall fall under the wrath of God (*v.* 15).

CHAPTER 6

I. God enters an action against his people for their base ingratitude, and the bad returns they had made him for his favours, ver. 1–5. II. He shows the wrong course they took when they were under conviction, and the frivolous proposals they made, in answer to his charge, ver. 6–8. III. He calls upon them to hear the voice of his judgments, and sets the sins in order before them (ver. 9), their injustice (ver. 10–15), and their idolatry (ver. 16), for both which ruin was coming upon them.

Verses 1–5

Here, I. The prefaces to the message are very solemn. *Hear you now what the Lord says. Arise, contend thou before the mountains*, or *with the mountains*, and *let the hills hear thy voice.* Contend with the mountains and hills of Judæa, that is, with the inhabitants of those mountains and hills; some think, reference is to those mountains on which they worshipped idols. It is to be taken more generally, as appears by his call, not only to the mountains, but to the *strong foundations of the earth.* He must speak as vehemently as if to make even the hills hear him. "*Let the hills hear thy voice*, for this senseless, careless people will not hear it. Let the rocks, the *foundations of the earth*, that have no ears, hear, since Israel, will not hear."

II. The message itself is to let all the world know that God has a quarrel with his people. God will plead with his people Israel, that they may be convinced and that he may be justified. In the close of the foregoing chapter he pleaded with the heathen in anger, but here he pleads with Israel in compassion and tenderness, to bring them to repentance, *Come now, and let us reason together.* They had revolted from God and rebelled against him; but had they any cause to do so? (*v.* 3): "*O my people! what have I done unto thee?*" Here is a challenge to all that ever were in God's service to testify against him if they have found him, in anything, a hard

Master, or if they have found his demands unreasonable. He brought them out of Egypt, the land of their bondage, *v.* 4. They were content with their slavery, and almost in love with their chains, for the sake of the garlic and onions they had plenty of; but God *brought them up,* inspired them with an ambition of liberty and animated them with a resolution to shake off their fetters. The Egyptians held them fast, but God *redeemed them* by force, *out of the house of servants, the house of bondage.* When he brought them out of Egypt into a howling wilderness, he sent before them *Moses, Aaron, and Miriam, three prophets* (says the Chaldee paraphrase). We must not forget the mercy of good teachers when we were young. It was God that sent them before us, to prepare the way. God no less glorified himself, and honoured them when he brought them into the land of their rest than when he brought them out of the land of their servitude. Let them remember now what God did for them in baffling and defeating the designs of Balak and Balaam; in bringing them *from Shittim,* their last lodgment out of Canaan, *unto Gilgal,* their first lodgment in Canaan. There it was, between Shittim and Gilgal, that, upon the death of Moses, Joshua, a type of Christ, was raised up to put Israel in possession of the land of promise.

Verses 6–8

The proposal for accommodation between God and Israel. Judgment is given against Israel, and therefore,

I. They express their desires to be at peace with God upon any terms (*v.* 6, 7). Knowing everyone the plague of his own heart, they ask not, *What shall this man do?* But, *What shall I do? What will the Lord be pleased with? What shall I give for my transgressions?*

II. They make proposals such as betray their ignorance, though they show their zeal.

1. They bid high. They offer *thousands of rams.* God required one ram for a sin-offering; they proffer their whole stock, so that they may but be at peace with God. They could be content to part with *their first-born for their transgressions,* if that would be accepted as an atonement, and the *fruit of their body for the sin of their soul.* To those that had become *vain in their imaginations* this seemed a probable expedient of making satisfaction for sin, because our children are pieces of ourselves.

2. Yet they do not bid right. It is true some of these things were instituted by the ceremonial law, but these alone would not recommend them to God. The legal sacrifices had their virtue from the reference they had to Christ the great propitiation; but otherwise, of themselves, it was *impossible that the blood of bulls and goats should take away sin.* All the proposals of peace but those that are according to the gospel are absurd. Some of them are wicked things, as to give our *first-born* and the *fruit of our body* to death. Do they not belong to God? Are they not his already, and born to him? How then can they be a ransom? They could not answer the demands of divine justice, nor would they serve in lieu of the sanctification of the heart and the reformation of the life.

III. God tells them plainly what he demands, *v.* 8. We need not trouble ourselves to make proposals, the terms are already settled and laid down. He whom we have offended has shown it, not only to thee, *O Israel!* but *to thee, O man!* Gentiles as well as Jews—to men, who are rational creatures. What is spoken to *all men everywhere* in general, must by faith be applied to ourselves in particular, as if it were spoken *to thee, O man!* by name, and to no other. The good which God requires of us is not the paying of a price for the pardon of sin. (1) We must *do justly,*

must *render to all their due,* according as our relation and obligation to them are; we must do wrong to none, but do right to all, in their bodies, goods, and good name. (2) We must *love mercy,* not only be just to all we deal with, but kind to all that need us. Nor must we only show mercy, but we must *love mercy.* (3) We must *walk humbly with our God.* This includes all the duties of the first table, as the two former include all the duties of the second table. Enoch's walking with God is interpreted (Heb. xi. 5) his *pleasing God.* We must, in the whole course of our conversation, conform ourselves to the will of God, keep up our communion with God, and study to approve ourselves to him. We must *humble ourselves to walk with God* (so the margin reads it); every thought within us must be brought down, to be brought into obedience to God. This is that which God requires, and without which the most costly services are *vain oblations*; this is more than *all burnt-offerings and sacrifices.*

Verses 9–16

God, having shown them how necessary it was that they should do justly, here shews them how plain it was that they had done unjustly.

I. The action is entered against them, *v.* 9. God speaks to *the city,* to Jerusalem, to Samaria. When the sin of a city cries to God his voice cries against the city. He warns before he wounds, because he is *not willing that any should perish.* 1. How the voice of God is discerned by some: *The man of wisdom will see thy name.* 2. What this voice of God says to all: "*Hear you the rod, and who hath appointed it.* Hear the rod when it is coming; hear it at a distance, before you see it and feel it. Hear the rod when it has come, and you are sensible of the smart of it; hear what cautions it speaks to you." Every rod has a voice, and it is the voice of God that is to be heard in the rod of God. God in every affliction *performs the thing that is appointed for us* (Job xxiii. 14).

II. What is the ground of the action, and the things that are laid to their charge.

1. They are charged with injustice, a sin against the second table. After all the methods that God has taken to teach them to do justly, will they yet deal unjustly? It seems, they will, *v.* 10. And *shall I count them pure? v.* 11. Those that are dishonest in their dealings shall never be reckoned pure. *Treasures of wickedness profit nothing.* A *scant measure,* by which they sold to the poor, cheated them. They had *wicked balances and a bag of false weights.* Those that had wealth and power in their hands abused it. They are *full of violence,* that is, they have their houses full of that which is got by violence. *The inhabitants thereof have spoken lies;* if they are not able to use force and violence, they use fraud and deceit.

2. They are charged with idolatry (*v.* 6): *The statutes of Omri are kept, and all the work of the house of Ahab.* Both these kings were wicked, and the wickedness which they established by a law, was idolatry. The wickedness which they established by their laws and examples remained. Those that make corrupt laws, and bring in corrupt usages, are doing that which perhaps may prove the ruin of the child unborn.

III. The sentence which God had given them warning of (*v.* 9) shall be brought upon them (*v.* 13): *Therefore also I will make thee sick, in smiting thee.* As they had smitten the poor with the rod of their oppressions, so would God in like manner smite them, so as to make them sick of the gains they had unjustly gotten.

1. What they have shall do them no good. Their food shall not nourish them: *Thou shalt eat, but not be satisfied.* Men may be surfeited with the good things of this world and yet not satisfied, Eccles. v. 10;

Isa. lv. 2. Their country shall not harbour and protect them: "*Thy casting down shall be in the midst of thee*, that is, thou shalt be ruined by mischiefs at home, though thou shouldst not be invaded by a foreign force." They shall not be able to preserve what they have from a foreign force: "*Thou shalt take hold* of what is about to be taken from thee, but thou shalt not hold it fast, shalt not retrieve it." Their wives and children whom they resolved not to part with, must go into captivity. What they save for a time shall be reserved for a future stroke: *That which thou deliverest* out of the hand of one enemy *will I give up to the sword* of another enemy. What they have laboured for they shall not enjoy (*v.* 15): "*Thou shalt sow, but thou shalt not reap;* it shall be withered, or an enemy shall reap it for himself, or thou shalt be carried into captivity, and leave it to be reaped by thou knowest not whom. Thou shalt *tread the olives*, but *thou shalt not anoint thyself with oil*, having no heart when all is going to ruin. Thou shalt tread out *the sweet wine*, but *shalt not drink wine*, for many things may fall between the cup and the lip."

2. All they have shall at length be taken from them (*v.* 13): *Thou shalt be made desolate because of thy sins;* and *v.* 16, *a desolation and a hissing*. When a people that have been flourishing are made desolate it is the astonishment of some and the triumph of others. Thus *you shall bear the reproach of my people*. Now that their sins and God's judgments have made their land desolate, their having been once the people of God does but turn so much the more to their reproach; their enemies will say, *These are the people of the Lord*, Ezek. xxxvi. 20.

CHAPTER 7

I. The prophet, in the name of the church, sadly laments the woeful decay of religion in the age wherein he lived, ver. 1–6. II. The prophet, for the sake of the church gives counsel what to do. 1. They must have an eye to God, ver. 7. 2. They must courageously bear up against the insolences of the enemy, ver. 8–10. 3. They must patiently lie down under the rebukes of their God, ver. 9. 4. They must expect that the trouble would continue long, ver. 11–13. 5. They must encourage themselves with God's promises, in answer to the prophet's prayers, ver. 14, 15. 6. They must foresee the fall of their enemies, ver. 16, 17. 7. They must themselves triumph in the mercy and grace of God, and his faithfulness to his covenant (ver. 18–20), and with that comfortable word the prophecy concludes.

Verses 2–6

This description of bad times some take as a prediction of what should be in the reign of Manasseh. But we rather suppose it to be in the reign of Ahaz, or in the beginning of Hezekiah's time, in the best of his days, when he had done his best to purge out corruptions, but still there was much amiss. The prophet bemoans himself that his lot was cast in such a degenerate age, among a people that were ripening apace for a ruin which many a good man would unavoidably be involved in. He laments, 1. That there were so few good people to be found, even among those that were God's people: *The good man has perished out of the earth*, or *out of the land, v.* 2. The *good man* is a *godly man* and a *merciful man;* the word signifies both. Those are completely good men that are devout towards God and compassionate and beneficent towards men, that love mercy and walk with God. There is no such thing as a good man to be met with. This is illustrated by a comparison (*v.* 1): They were *as when they have gathered the summer fruits;* it was as hard a thing to find a good man as to find any of the summer-fruits, the choicest and best, when the harvest is over. You can find no societies of them as bunches of grapes: *There is no cluster to eat;* and the best and fullest grapes are those that grow in large clusters. When we read of the devotion and charity, of the professors of religion

in former ages, and see the reverse of this in the present age, we cannot but wish, with a sigh, *O for primitive Christianity again!* 2. That there were so many wicked people that did all the hurt they could: "*They all lie in wait for blood*, and *hunt every man his brother*. They act as if mankind were in a state of war, and force were the only right. They are as beasts of prey to their neighbours, for *they all lie in wait for blood* as lions for their prey." 3. That the magistrates, who by their office ought to have been the patrons and protectors of right, were the practisers and promoters of wrong: *That they may do evil with both hands earnestly, the prince asketh, and the judge asketh for a reward*, for a bribe, with which they will be hired for carrying on any wicked design *with both hands. So they wrap it up;* they make it intricate (so some understand it), that they may lose equity in a mist, and so make the cause turn which way they please. A sad character is given of them (*v.* 4), *the best of them is as a brier, and the most upright is sharper than a thorn-hedge*. And, when things have come to this pass, *the day of thy watchmen comes*, that is, *the day of thy visitation*, when God will reckon with thee for all this wickedness, which is called *the day of the watchmen*, because their prophets, whom God set as watchmen over them, had often warned them of that day. 4. That there was no faith in man; people had grown universally treacherous, *v.* 5. "Those that have any sense of honour remaining in them, have a firm regard to the laws of friendship; they would not discover what passed in private conversation, nor divulge secrets, to the prejudice of a friend. But those things are now made a jest of. Wise men take it for a rule, *Trust you not in a friend*, for you will find him false. As for him that undertakes to be *your guide* in any business which he professes to understand better than you, you cannot *put a confidence* in him, for he will mislead you if he can get anything by it." Some by a guide understand a husband, who is called *the guide of thy youth*; and that agrees with what follows, "*Keep the doors of thy lips from her that lieth in thy bosom*, from thy own wife; take heed what thou sayest before her, lest she betray thee. 5. That children were abusive to their parents, *v.* 6. It is sad when a man's betrayers and worst enemies are his own children and his best friends.

Verses 7–13

The prophet, having sadly complained of the wickedness of the times, fastens upon some considerations for comfort. The case is bad, but it is not desperate.

I. "Though God be now displeased he shall be reconciled to us, and then all will be well," *v.* 7, 9. At such a time, 1. We must have recourse to God under our troubles (*v.* 7): *Therefore I will look unto the Lord*. All may look bright above him when all looks dark about him. The prophet had been complaining that there was no confidence to be put in friends and relations, and this drives him to his God: *Therefore I will look unto the Lord*. 2. We must submit to the will of God in our troubles: "*I will bear the indignation of the Lord* patiently, without murmuring and repining, *because I have sinned against him*." When we complain to God of the badness of the times we ought to complain against ourselves for the badness of our own hearts. 3. We must depend upon God to work deliverance for us. When things are brought to the last extremity: *My God will hear me;* if the Lord be our God, he will hear our prayers, and grant an answer of peace to them. "*When I sit in darkness*, disconsolate and perplexed, then *the Lord shall be a light to me*, as a light to my eyes, a light to my feet, a light *in a dark place*." *He will plead my cause, and execute judgment for me, v.* 9. "*He will bring me forth to the light. The morning of comfort shall shine forth out of the long and dark night of trouble. *I shall behold his righteousness;* the performance of his promises to me."

II. Though enemies triumph, they shall be put to shame, *v.* 8, 10. The enemies of God's people said, *Where is the Lord their God?* As if because they were afflicted God had forsaken them, and they knew not where to find him with their prayers, and he knew not how to help them with his favours. The people of God by faith bear up under these insults (*v.* 8): "*Rejoice not against me, O my enemy!* I am now down, but shall not be always so, and when my God appears for me then *she that is my enemy shall see it, and be ashamed.*" The deliverance of the church will be the confusion of her enemies.

III. Though the land continue a great while desolate, yet it shall at length be replenished again. Its salvation shall not come *till after it has been desolate;* so the margin reads it, *v.* 13. It must lie long under his rebukes, *because of those that dwell therein.* For this they must expect to smart a great while. When it does come it shall be a complete salvation; and it seems to refer to their deliverance out of Babylon by Cyrus. *The decree shall be far removed.* God's decree concerning their captivity, and Nebuchadnezzar's decree, his resolution never to release them shall be set aside. Jerusalem and the cities of Judah shall be again reared: Then *thy walls shall be built.* All that belong to the land of Israel, whithersoever dispersed, far and wide, shall come flocking to it again (*v.* 12): *He shall come even to thee.* They shall come from all the remote parts, *from sea to sea and from mountain to mountain,* not turning back till they come to Zion.

Verses 14–20

I. The prophet's prayer to God to take care of his own people, *v.* 14. When we see God coming towards us in ways of mercy, we must go forth to meet him by prayer. It is a prophetic prayer, which amounts to a promise of the good prayed for; what God directed his prophet to ask no doubt he designed to give. The people of Israel are here called the *flock of God's heritage.* This flock *dwells solitarily in the wood,* or *forest, in the midst of Carmel,* a high mountain. Israel was a peculiar people, *that dwelt alone,* like a flock of sheep in a wood. They were now a desolate people (*v.* 13), in the land of their captivity as sheep in a forest, in danger from the beasts of the forest. He prays that God would *feed them there with his rod,* that is, that he would take care of them in their captivity, and do the part of a good shepherd to them. "Let them be governed by thy rod, not the rod of their enemies, for they are thy people." He prays that God would in due time bring them back to feed in the plains of Bashan and Gilead. *Let them feed* in their own country again, *as in the days of old.*

Some apply this spiritually, and make it either the prophet's prayer to Christ or his Father's charge to him, to take care of his church, as the great Shepherd of the sheep.

II. God's promise, in answer to this prayer. God answers that he *will show them marvellous things* (*v.* 15), will out-do their hopes and expectations. He will do that which shall be the repetition of the wonders and miracles of former ages—*according to the days of thy coming out of the land of Egypt.* He will do that for them which shall be matter of amazement to the present age, *v.* 16, 17. The *nations about* shall take notice of it. They shall be *confounded at all the might* with which the captives shall now exert themselves, whom they thought for ever disabled. They shall now *lay their hands upon their mouths,* as being ashamed of what they have said. They shall stop their ears, not willing to hear any more of God's wonders wrought for people, whom they had so despised. Those that had impudently confronted God himself shall now be brought, in profession at least, to submit to him (*v.* 17): *They shall lick the dust like a serpent,* as if they were sentenced to the same curse the serpent was laid under (Gen. iii. 14).

III. The prophet's thankful acknowledgment of God's mercy, *v.* 18–20. Pardoning mercy was at the bottom of it. As it was their sin that brought them into bondage, so it was God's pardoning their sin that brought them out of it; Ps. lxxxv. 1, 2, and Isa. xxxiii. 24; xxxviii. 17; xl. 1, 2. This the prophet stands amazed at, while the surrounding nations stood amazed only at those deliverances which were but the fruits of this. The reasons why God pardons sin, and keeps not his anger for ever, are all taken from within himself; it is *because he delights in mercy,* and the salvation of sinners is what he has pleasure in, not their death and damnation. There is *no God like unto him;* no magistrate forgives as God does. In this his thoughts and ways are infinitely above ours; in this he is *God, and not man.* His mercy *endures for ever,* and therefore as he has *shown mercy* so he will, *v.* 19, 20. He will renew us, to prepare and qualify us for his favour: *He will subdue our iniquities;* when he takes away the guilt of sin, that it may not damn us, he will break the power of sin, that it may not have dominion over us. *Thou wilt cast all their sins into the depth of the sea,* as when he brought them out of Egypt he subdued Pharaoh and the Egyptians, and cast them into the depth of the sea. It intimates that when God forgives sin he *remembers it no more.* He casts them into the sea, not near the shore-side, where they may appear again next low water, but into *the depth of the sea,* never to rise again. *All their sins* shall be cast there without exception, for when God forgives sin he forgives all. He with this good work will do all that our case requires and which he has promised (*v.* 20).

AN EXPOSITION, WITH PRACTICAL OBSERVATIONS, OF

THE PROPHECY OF NAHUM

The name of this prophet signifies a *comforter*; for it was a charge given to all the prophets, *Comfort you, comfort you, my people*; and even this prophet, though wholly taken up in foretelling the destruction of Nineveh, is, even in that, comforter to the ten tribes of Israel, who, it is probable, were lately carried captives into Assyria. It is uncertain, but probable that he lived in the time of Hezekiah, and prophesied against Nineveh, after the captivity of Israel by the king of Assyria, which was in the ninth year of Hezekiah, and before Sennacherib's invading Judah, which was in the fourteenth year of Hezekiah, for to that attempt, and the defeat of it, it is supposed, the first chapter has reference. It is the conjecture of Huetius that the two other chapters of this book were delivered by Nahum some years after, perhaps in the reign of Manasseh, and in that reign the Jewish chronologies generally place him, some time before the captivity of Judah.

CHAPTER 1

I. The inscription of the book, ver. 1. II. A magnificent display of the glory of God, in wrath and justice against the wicked, and mercy and grace towards his people, and the discovery of his majesty and power in both, ver. 2–8. III. A particular application of this (as some interpreters think) to the destruction of Sennacherib and the Assyrian army, when they besieged Jerusalem, ver. 9–16.

Verse 1

Nineveh was the place concerned, and the Assyrian monarchy had the royal seat there. Jonah had, in God's name, foretold the speedy overthrow of this great city; but then the Ninevites repented and were spared. The Ninevites then saw clearly how to turn from their evil way; it was the saving of their city; and yet, soon after, they returned to it again; it became worse than ever. Then God sent them this prophecy, to read them their doom, which was now irreversible. It is *the book of the vision of Nahum the Elkoshite*. The burden of Nineveh was what the prophet plainly foresaw, for it was his vision. When he was gone, the event might be compared with the prediction. All the account we have of the prophet himself is that he was an *Elkoshite*, of the town called *Elkes*, which, Jerome says, was in Galilee.

Verses 2–8

Nineveh knows not God, and therefore is here told what a God he is. This glorious description of the Sovereign of the world, like the pillar of cloud and fire, has a bright side towards Israel and a dark side towards the Egyptians.

I. He is a God of inflexible justice; let Nineveh know this, and tremble before him. Their idols are insignificant things; there is nothing formidable in them. But the God of Israel is greatly to be feared. He resents the indignities done him by those that deny his being or any of his perfections, that set up other gods in competition with him, that destroy his laws, ridicule his word, or are abusive to his people. Let such know that Jehovah is jealous for his own honour in the matters of his worship, and will not endure a rival; he is jealous for the comfort of his worshippers, *jealous for his land* (Joel ii. 18), and will not have that injured. He *has fury* (so the word is) not as man has it, in whom it is an ungoverned passion, but he has it in such a way as becomes the righteous God. He is *Lord of anger* (so the Hebrew phrase is for that which we read, *he is furious*); he has anger, but he has it at command and under government. Our anger is often lord over us, as theirs that have *no rule over their own spirits*, but God is always *Lord of his anger* and weighs *a path to it*, Ps. lxxviii. 50. Whoever are his adversaries and enemies among men, he will make them feel his resentments in the day of wrath. He *will not at all acquit the wicked* that sin, and stand to it, and do not repent, *v.* 3. This revelation of the wrath of God against his enemies is applied to Nineveh (*v.* 8), and should be applied by all those that go on still in their trespasses: *With an over-running flood he will make an utter end of the place thereof. Darkness shall pursue his enemies;* terror and trouble shall follow them, whithersoever they go; if they think to flee from the darkness which pursues them they will but fall into that which is before them.

II. He is a God of irresistible power. If we look up into the regions of the air, there we shall find proofs of his power, for *he has his ways in the whirlwind and the storm*. He spoke to Job out of the whirlwind, and even *stormy winds fulfil his word*. If we cast our eye upon the great deeps, we find that the sea is his, for, when he pleases, *he rebukes the sea and makes it dry, drying up all the rivers*. If we look round on this earth, we find proofs of his power, when, either by the extreme heat and drought of summer or the cold and frost of winter, *Bashan languishes, and Carmel, and the flower of Lebanon languishes*. Earthquakes shake the mountains (*v.* 5), melt the hills, and level them with the plains. When he pleases *the earth is burnt at his presence* by the scorching heat of the sun. If God be an almighty God, we may thence infer (*v.* 6), *Who can stand before his indignation?* The Ninevites had once found God *slow to anger* (*v.* 3), and perhaps presumed upon the mercy they had then experienced. It is in vain for the stoutest and strongest of sinners to think to make their part good against the power of God's anger. God's anger is so fierce that it beats down all before it: *The rocks are thrown down on him*. The eruption of subterraneous fires is a faint resemblance of the fierceness of God's anger against sinners whose hearts are rocky. Sinners as stubble before the fire, the wrath of God. *Who can abide in the fierceness of his anger?* Some of the effects of God's displeasure in this world a man may bear up under, but the *fierceness of his anger*, when it fastens immediately upon the soul, who can bear? Let us *fear before him;* let us *stand in awe, and not sin*.

III. He is a God of infinite mercy. *Let the sinners in Zion be afraid*, that go on still in their transgressions, but let not those that trust in God tremble before him. He is *slow to anger* (*v.* 3), ready to show mercy.

When the tokens of his rage against the wicked are abroad he takes care of his own people (*v.* 7): *The Lord is good* to those that are *good*, and to them he will be *a stronghold in the day of trouble*.

Verses 9–15

These verses seem to point at the destruction of the army of the Assyrians under Sennacherib, which may well be reckoned a part of the burden of Nineveh, the head city of the Assyrian empire, and a pledge of the destruction of Nineveh itself about 100 years after.

I. The great provocation which the Assyrians gave to God, the just and jealous God, for which, though *slow to anger*, he would take vengeance (*v.* 11): *There is one come out of thee, that imagines evil against the Lord*—Sennacherib, and his spokesman Rabshakeh. They framed an evil letter and an evil speech, not only against Hezekiah and his people, but against God himself, as level with the gods of the heathen, and unable to protect his worshippers, urging his people to put themselves under the protection of the *great king, the king of Assyria*. To this evil counsel he says (*v.* 9): "*What do you imagine against the Lord?* What a foolish wicked thing it is for you to plot against God, as if you could outwit divine wisdom and overpower omnipotence itself!"

II. The great destruction which God would bring upon them for it, not immediately upon the whole monarchy (the ruin of that was deferred) but,

1. Upon the army; God will *make an utter end* of that; it shall be totally cut off and ruined at one blow. They have laid themselves open to divine wrath by their own act and deed, *v.* 10. They are *as thorns* that entangle one another, and are *folded together*. They make one another worse. God will do with them as the husbandmen does with a bush of thorns when he cannot part them: he puts them all into the fire together. They are *as drunken men*, intoxicated with pride and rage; and such as they shall be destroyed. They shall be *devoured as stubble fully dry*, which is irresistibly and irrecoverably consumed by the flame. This great army (*v.* 12), *though they be quiet and likewise many*, very secure, because *they are numerous*, yet shall they be cut down, as grass and corn when *he shall pass through*.

2. Upon the king. He *imagined evil against the Lord*, and shall he escape? (*v.* 14): "*The Lord has given a commandment concerning thee;* the decree has gone forth, *that thy name be no more sown*, that thy memory perish." The images he worshipped should be cut off from their temple, which, some think, was fulfilled when Sennacherib was slain by his *two sons, as he was worshipping in the house of Nisroch his god*. The temple was looked upon as defiled, and was therefore disused, and the images were cut off. Sennacherib's grave shall be made there, some think in the house of his god; there he is slain, and there he shall be buried, for *he is vile*. Or it may be meant of the ignominious fall of the Assyrian monarchy itself, upon the ruins of which that of Babylon was raised.

III. The great deliverance which God would hereby work for his own people and the city that was called by his name. The siege shall be raised: "*Now will I break his yoke from off thee*, by which thou art kept in servitude, and *will burst thy bonds asunder*, by which thou seemest bound to the Assyrian's wrath." This was a figure of the great salvation, by which the Jerusalem that is above is made free. The enemy shall be so weakened and dispirited that they shall never make any such attempt again. The enemy shall not dare again to attack Jerusalem (*v.* 15): *The wicked shall no more pass through thee as* they have done, to lay all waste. His army is cut off, his spirit cut off, and at length he himself is cut off. The tidings of this great deliverance will be welcomed throughout the kingdom, *v.* 15. While Sennacherib prevailed, and carried all before him, every day brought bad news; but now, *behold, upon the mountains, the feet of him that bringeth good tidings, the feet of the evangelist;* he is seen coming at a distance upon the mountains, as fast as his feet will carry him; and how pleasant a sight is it once more to see a messenger of peace, after we have received so many of Job's messengers! These words are also quoted by the apostle, both from Isaiah and Nahum, and applied to the great redemption wrought for us by our Lord Jesus, and the publishing of it to the world by the everlasting gospel, Rom. x. 15. Christ's ministers are those messengers of good tidings, that preach *peace by Jesus Christ*. During the trouble ordinary feasts had been intermitted. While Jerusalem was *encompassed with armies* they could not go thither to worship; but now they must return to the observance of their feasts. Now that the deliverance is wrought they are called upon to perform their vows.

CHAPTER 2

Nineveh, that great city took not warning by the destruction of her armies and the fall of her king, and therefore may expect, since she persists in her enmity to God, that he will proceed in his controversy with her. Here is foretold, I. The approach of the enemy that should destroy Nineveh, ver. 1–5. II. The taking of the city, ver. 6. III. The captivity of the queen, the flight of the inhabitants, the seizing of all its wealth, ver. 7–10. IV. Its true causes—their sinning against God and God's appearing against them, ver. 11–13. This was fulfilled when Nebuchadnezzar, in the first year of his reign, in conjunction with Cyaxares, or Ahasuerus, king of the Medes, conquered Nineveh, and made himself master of the Assyrian monarchy.

Verses 1–10

I. An alarm of war went to Nineveh, *v.* 1. The prophet speaks of it as just at hand: "Look about thee, and see, *he that dashes in pieces has come up before thy face.* Nebuchadnezzar is noted for dashing nations in pieces, and will disperse thee." The attempt of Nebuchadnezzar upon Nineveh is bold, and daring: "He *has come up before thy face*, avowing his design to ruin thee; therefore stand to thy arms, *O Nineveh!* keep the munition;* secure thy towers and magazines: *watch the way;* set guards upon all the avenues to the city; *make thy loins strong;* encourage thy soldiers; animate thyself and them; *fortify thy power mightily*" (this is spoken ironically); "do the utmost thou canst, yet *there is no counsel or strength against the Lord*."

II. The causes of the war (*v.* 2): *The Lord has turned away the excellency of Jacob, as the excellency of Israel.* The Assyrians have been abusive to Jacob, the two tribes as well as to Israel, the ten tribes, *have emptied them, and marred their vine-branches.* For this God will reckon with them; though done long since. Or, It may mean God is now by Nebuchadnezzar about *to turn away the pride of Jacob* by the captivity of the two tribes, as he did the pride of Israel by their captivity. The enemy that is to do it must begin with Nineveh. God is looking upon proud cities, and abasing them. Samaria is humbled, and Jerusalem is to be humbled, and shall not Nineveh, that proud city, he brought down too? *Emptiers have emptied* the cities, *and marred the vine-branches* in the country of Jacob and Israel.

III. A particular account given of the terrors wherein the invading enemy shall appear against Nineveh. 1. *The shields of his mighty men are made red* as if they were already tinctured with the blood they had shed. 2. *The valiant men are in scarlet;* rich clothes, to intimate the wealth of the army. 3. *The chariots shall be with flaming torches in the day of his preparation;* the wheels shall strike fire upon the stones. Or they carried flaming torches with them in the open chariots, when they made their approach in the night, to be both a guide to themselves to set all on fire wherever they went. 4. *The fir-trees shall be terribly shaken;* the great men of Nineveh, that overtop their neighbours, as the stately firs do the shrubs; or the standing trees shall be made to shake by the concussions which that great army shall cause. 5. The chariots of war shall be very terrible (v. 4): *They shall rage in the streets*, that is, those that drive them shall rage. Even *in the broad ways*, where, one would think, there should be room enough, they shall *jostle one another*; and these iron chariots shall be made so bright that in the beams of the sun *shall they seem like torches* in the night. Nebuchadnezzar's commanders are here called his *worthies*, his *gallants* (so the margin reads it). *His worthies shall remember* (so some read it); they shall be mindful of duty, and the charge they have received, and be so intent upon their business that they *shall stumble in their walks*, for *they shall make haste to the wall thereof*, and the defence, or the covered way, shall be prepared (something to shelter them from the darts of the besieged), and they shall carry on the siege, and with so much vigour, that the *gates of the rivers shall be opened* (v. 6); those gates of Nineveh which open upon the river Tigris (on which Nineveh was built) shall be first forced by the enemy, and by those gates they shall enter. And then the *palace shall be dissolved*, either the king's house or the house of Nisroch his god; the same word signifies both a palace and a temple.

IV. A prediction of the consequences of this. 1. The queen shall fall into the hands of the enemy (v. 7): *Huzzub shall be led away captive;* she that was *established* (so some read it), thought herself safe because she was concealed, shall be *discovered* (so the margin reads it) and shall be led *away captive*, in disgrace. She shall be *brought up* in a mock state, *and her maids* of honour *shall lead her*, because she is weak and faint. They shall be *tabering upon their breasts*, beating their own breasts in grief, as if they were *drumming* upon them, for so the word signifies. 2. The inhabitants, shall none of them be able to stand their ground (v. 8): *Nineveh is of old like a pool of water*, replenished with people as a pool with water. It was long ago a populous city; in Jonah's time there were 120,000 little children in it (Jonah iv. 11). Their commanders shall cry, "*Stand, stand*, have a good heart on it, and we shall do well enough." They shall not have the least spark of courage remaining. They shall not so much as look back to see who calls for them. 3. The wealth of the city shall become a prey, and all its rich furniture shall fall into the hands of the victorious enemy (v. 9). Thus this rich city is empty, and void, and waste, v. 10. 4. The soldiers and people shall have no heart to appear for the defence of the city. *Much pain shall be in all loins*, as is the case in extreme frights, so that they shall not be able to hold up their backs. And the *faces of them all shall gather blackness*, like that of a pot that is every day over the fire; so the word signifies.

Verses 11–13

Nineveh's ruin, 1. Its neighbours now remember against it all the oppressions it had been guilty of in its pomp and prosperity (v. 11, 12): *Where is the dwelling of the lions? Where is the feeding place of the young lions*, where they glutted themselves with prey? The princes of Nineveh had been as lions, beasts of prey. Though nobody loved them, everybody feared them, and that was all they desired. The king made it his business, by violence and extortion to enrich himself and raise his family; he did *tear in pieces enough for his whelps* and he *strangled for his lionesses*. 2. It is avowed by the righteous Judge (v. 13): *Behold, I am against thee, saith the Lord of hosts*. The oppressors in Nineveh thought they only set their neighbours against them, but they set

God against them, who is the asserter of right and the avenger of wrong. These military preparations will stand them in no stead: *I will burn their chariots in the smoke;* he does not say *in the fire*, but, in contempt of them, the very *smoke* of God's indignation shall serve to burn their chariots. Their children the hopes of their families, shall be cut off: *The sword shall devour the young lions*. The wealth they have heaped up by fraud and violence shall not be enjoyed by them: thou shalt not be the better for it and no one else shall. *The voice of thy messengers shall no more be heard*, no more be heeded, which some think refers to Rabshakeh.

CHAPTER 3

I. The sins of that great city are charged upon it, murder (ver. 1), whoredom and witchcraft (ver. 4), and a general extent of wickedness, ver. 19. II. Judgments are here threatened against it, blood for blood (ver. 2, 3), and shame for shameful sins, ver. 5–7. III. Instances are given of like desolations brought upon other places for like sins, ver. 8–11. IV. The overthrow of all those things which they depended upon, is foretold, ver. 12–19.

Verses 1–7

I. Nineveh arraigned and indicted. 1. It is a *city of blood*. 2. *It is all full of lies;* truth is banished from among them; there is no such thing as honesty. 3. It is all full of *robbery* and rapine. 4. There is a *multitude of whoredoms* in it, that is, idolatries, spiritual whoredoms. 5. She is a *mistress of witchcrafts*, and by them she *sells families*, v. 4. That which Nineveh aimed at was a universal monarchy, to be the metropolis of the world, compelling some, deluding others, into subjection to her, and wheedling them as a harlot by her charms. These were her witchcrafts, with which she unaccountably gained dominion.

II. Nineveh condemned to ruin upon this indictment, v. 1.

1. Nineveh had with her cruelties been a terror and destruction to others, and therefore destruction and terror shall be brought upon her. Hear the alarm with which Nineveh shall be terrified, v. 2. It is a formidable army that advances against it; you may hear them at a distance, the *noise of the whip*, the *rattling of the wheels, the prancing horses, and the jumping chariots;* the very noise is frightful. Nineveh shall be laid waste (v. 3), the sword drawn, *the bright sword lifted up and the glittering spear*, the dazzling brightness of which is terrible. See what havoc these make when they are commissioned to slay! The destruction of Sennacherib's army, which, in the morning, were *all dead corpses*, is perhaps looked upon here as a figure of the like destruction that should afterwards be in Nineveh.

2. Nineveh had drawn others to shameful wickedness, and therefore God will load her with contempt (v. 5–7): *The Lord of hosts* is *against her*. When it shall be seen that while she courted her neighbours it was with design to ruin their liberty and property, then her *shame is discovered to the nations*. When her proud pretensions are baffled, then *to see the nakedness of the land do they come*, and it appears ridiculous. Then do they *cast abominable filth upon her*, as upon a carted strumpet, and *make her vile*. Those that formerly looked upon her in hopes of protection from her, now *look upon her and flee from her*, for fear of being ruined with her. When Nineveh is laid waste *who will bemoan her?* Those that showed no pity in the day of their power can expect to find no pity in the day of their fall.

Verses 8–19

I. Nineveh shall fall unpitied and uncomforted and she shall not be able to help herself: *Art thou better than populous No? v.* 8. He quotes precedents. The city mentioned is *No*, a great city in the land of

Egypt (Jer. xlvi. 25), *No-Ammon*, so some read it. Some think it was *Diospolis*, others *Alexandria*. As God said to Jerusalem, *Go, see what I did to Shiloh* (Jer. vii. 12), so to Nineveh, *Go, see what I did to populous No*. Now, concerning No, 1. How firm her standing, *v*. 8. She was fortified both by nature and art, was *situate among the rivers*. Nile watered her fields, guarded her wall. *Her rampart was the sea, the lake of Mareotis*. It was also supported by alliances abroad, *v*. 9. *Ethiopia*, or Arabia, *was her strength*, either by trade or by forces furnished for military service. The whole country of Egypt contributed to this populous city; so that it was *infinite, and there was no end of it* (so it might be rendered); she set no bounds to her ambition and knew no end of her wealth and strength; but it is God's prerogative to be infinite. *Put and Lubim were thy helpers*, two neighbouring countries of Africa, Mauritania and Libya, that is, Libya Cyrenica. 2. How fatal her fall proved to be (*v*. 10): *Yet was she carried away*, and her strength failed her; even she that was so strong, so secure, yet *went into captivity. Her young children were dashed in pieces at the top of all the streets* by the merciless conquerors. *They cast lots for her honourable men* that were made prisoners of war, to be slaves. What a mortification was this to *populous No*. Hence he infers against Nineveh (*v*. 11), "Thou also shalt be intoxicated, drunk with the cup of the Lord's fury, that shall be put into thy hand" (see Jer. xxv. 17, 27). *Thou shalt fall and rise no more*.

II. He shows them that all those things in which they reposed confidence should fail them. 1. Did the men of Nineveh trust to their own bravery? Their hearts should sink and fail them. *They shall be hid*, shall abscond for shame. They shall *seek strength*, shall come sneaking to their neighbours to beg assistance. 2. Did they depend upon the garrisons and strongholds they had? Those shall prove but paper-walls, and *like the first-ripe figs*, which, if you give the tree but a little shake, will *fall into the mouth of the eater* that gapes for them, *v*. 12. They make their strongholds as strong as possible, and are challenged to do their utmost to make them tenable against the invader (*v*. 14): *Draw thee water for the siege;* it is put here for all manner of provision, with which Nineveh is ironically told to furnish herself, in expectation of a siege. "*Go into clay, and tread the mortar*, and *make strong the brick-kiln;* take all the pains thou canst in erecting new fortifications; but it shall be all in vain, for (*v*. 15) there shall *the fire devour thee* if the stronghold be burnt, or *the sword cut thee off* if it be taken by storm." 3. Did they put confidence in the multitude of their in-

habitants? They shall but sink the sooner under the weight of their own numbers (*v*. 13): *Thy people in the midst of thee are women;* they shall be fickle, and fainthearted in danger and distress; adding to their fears by the power of their own imagination. Though they *make themselves many* (*v*. 15), as the *cankerworm* and *as the locust*, that come in vast swarms, *though thou hast multiplied thy merchants above the stars of heaven*, though thy exchange be thronged with wealthy traders, yet their hearts shall fail them too; though they be numerous as caterpillars, yet the fire and sword shall eat them up irresistibly as the cankerworm, *v*. 15. He adds (*v*. 16), *The canker-worm spoils*, or *spreads herself, and flies away*. Both the merchants and the enemies were compared to canker-worms. The enemies shall spoil Nineveh, and carry away the spoil without opposition. Or the rich merchants, who have come from abroad to settle in Nineveh, when they see the country invaded and the city likely to be besieged, will remove to some other place, will *spread their wings* and *fly away* where they may be safe. 4. Did they put a confidence in the strength of their gates and bars? (*v*. 13). *The gates of thy land shall be set wide open unto thy enemies*, the gates of thy rivers (*ch*. ii. 6), the flood-gates, or the passes. *The fire shall devour thy bars, and they shall fly open*. 5. Did they put a confidence in their king and princes? They should do them no service (*v*. 17): *Thy crowned heads are as the locusts;* those that had pomp and power, as crowned heads, were enfeebled. "*Thy captains*, that should lead thy forces look great, but they are as the great *grasshoppers*, they are but grasshoppers, worthless things, that can do no service. *They encamp in the hedges, in the cold day*, the cold weather, *but, when the sun arises, they flee away*, nobody knows whither. So these mercenary soldiers, when any trouble arises, flee away, and shift for their own safety. *The hireling flees, because he is a hireling*." The *king of Assyria* is told that *his shepherds slumber;* they have no spirit to appear for the flock. The *nobles shall dwell in the dust*, and be buried in silence. 6. Did they hope that they should yet rally? In this also they should be disappointed; for, when the shepherds are smitten, the *sheep are scattered;* the people are dispersed *upon the mountains* and *no man gathers them*. The judgment they are under is as a wound, and it is incurable; thy case is desperate (*v*. 19) and thy neighbours shall *clap their hands over thee*, and triumph in thy fall. *Upon whom has not thy wickedness passed continually?* Thou hast been always doing mischief to those about thee; and therefore they shall be far from pitying thee. *The troublers shall be troubled* will be the burden of many, as it is here the burden of Nineveh.

AN EXPOSITION, WITH PRACTICAL OBSERVATIONS, OF

THE PROPHECY OF HABAKKUK

It is a foolish fancy of some of the Jewish rabbin that this prophet was the son of the Shunamite woman that was miraculously raised to life, by Elisha (2 Kings iv), as they say also that the prophet Jonah was the son of the widow of Zaraphath. It is a more probable conjecture that he lived and prophesied in the reign of king Manasseh, when wickedness abounded, and destruction was hastening on, destruction by the Chaldeans, whom this prophet mentions as the instruments of God's judgments; and Manasseh was himself carried to Babylon, as an earnest of what should come afterwards. In the apocryphal story of Bel and the Dragon mention is made of Habakkuk the prophet in the land of Judah, who was carried thence by an angel to Babylon, to feed Daniel in the den; those who give credit to that story take pains to reconcile our prophet's living before the captivity, and foretelling it, with that. And some have imagined that Habakkuk's feeding Daniel in the den is to be understood mystically, that Daniel then *lived by faith*, as Habakkuk had said *the just should do*; he was *fed* by that word, Hab. ii. 4. The prophecy of this book is a mixture of the prophet's addresses to God in the people's name and to the people in God's name; for it is the office of the prophet to carry messages both ways. It is the intercourse and communion between a gracious God and a gracious soul. The whole refers particularly to the invasion of the land of Judah by the Chaldeans.

CHAPTER 1

I. The prophet complains to God of the violence done by the abuse of justice among his own people and the hardships thereby put upon many good people, ver. 1–4. II. God by him foretells the punishment of that abuse of power by the sword of war, and the desolations which the army of the Chaldeans should make, ver. 5–11. III. Then the prophet is grieved that the Chaldeans prevail so far (ver. 12–17), so that he scarcely knows which is more to be lamented, the sin or the punishment of it, for in both many good people are great sufferers. It is well that there is a day of judgment, and a future state, before us, so the present seeming disorders of Providence shall be set to rights.

Verses 1–4

The penman was *a prophet*, a man divinely inspired and commissioned, and the book itself is *the burden which* he *saw*; he was as sure of the truth of it as if he had seen it with his bodily eyes already accomplished. The prophet sadly laments the iniquity of the times. The land was *full of violence*, as the old world was, Gen. vi. 11. The prophet *cries out of violence* (v. 2), *iniquity* and *grievance, spoil* and *violence*. It does not appear that the prophet himself had any great wrong done him (in losing times it fared best with those that had nothing to lose), but it grieved him to see other people wronged. He complains (v. 4) that *the wicked doth compass about the righteous*. One honest man, one honest cause, shall have enemies besetting it on every side. The kingdom was broken into parties and factions that were continually biting and devouring one another. *There are that raise up strife and contention* (v. 3), that foment divisions, and sow discord among brethren. And, if *blessed are the peace-makers*, cursed are such peace-breakers. The torrent of violence and strife ran so strongly as to bid defiance to laws and the administration of justice, v. 4. Because God did not appear against them, nobody else would; *therefore the law is slacked*, is silent; *its pulse beats not* (so, it is said, the word signifies); *and judgment does not go forth*. He complained of this to God, but could not obtain a redress of those grievances: "*Lord*," says he, "*why dost thou show me iniquity?* Why hast thou cast my lot in a time and place when and where it is to be seen?" When God seems to connive at the wickedness of the wicked, and to countenance it, by suffering them to prosper in their wickedness, it shocks the faith of good men. God has reasons for the reprieves of bad men and the rebukes of good men; and therefore we must believe the day will come when the cry of sin will be heard against those that do wrong and the cry of prayer for those that suffer it.

Verses 5–11

An answer to the prophet's complaint. Though God bore long, he would not bear always with this provoking people.

I. The preamble to the sentence (v. 5): *Behold, you among the heathen, and regard*. Since they will not be brought to repentance by the long-suffering of God, he will inflict upon them, 1. A public punishment, at which the neighbouring nations shall stand amazed, see Deut. xxix. 24, 25. Israel will be made a spectacle to the world. 2. An amazing punishment, so strange that it shall not be credited even by those that were eye-witnesses of it when it comes: *You will not believe it; though it be told you*. The punishment of God's professing people cannot but be the astonishment of all about them. 3. A speedy punishment: "*I will work a work in your days*, now quickly; this generation shall not pass till the judgment threatened be accomplished." 4. It shall be a punishment in which the hand of God shall appear. *This is the Lord's doing*. 5. It shall be such a punishment as will typify the destruction to be brought upon the despisers of Christ and his gospel. The ruin of Jerusalem by the Chaldeans for their idolatry was a figure of their ruin by the Romans for rejecting Christ and his gospel.

II. The sentence itself is dreadful and particular (v. 6): *Lo, I raise up the Chaldeans*. When God's professing people quarrel among themselves, snarl, and devour one another, it is just with God to bring the common enemy upon them, that shall make peace by making a devastation. The contending parties in Jerusalem were divided one against another, when the Romans came and *took away their place and nation*.

1. The people that shall be raised up against Israel, to be a scourge to them, are *a bitter and hasty nation*, cruel and fierce. They show no mercy and they spare no pains. *They are terrible and dreadful*, famed for the troops they bring into the field (v. 8); *their horses are swifter than leopards, more fierce* than the *evening wolves;* and wolves are observed to be the most ravenous towards the evening, waiting for

darkness under which *all beasts of the forest creep forth*, Ps. civ. 20. *"Their horsemen shall spread themselves* a great way, for they shall *come from far*, from all parts of their own country. Their own will is a law to them, and they will not be governed by any laws of humanity, equity, or honour: *Their judgment and their dignity shall proceed of themselves*," *v*. 7. Appetite and passion rule them, and not reason nor conscience.

2. A prophecy of the terrible execution that shall be made by this nation: *They shall march through the breadth of the earth*. The Chaldean forces subdued all the nations in those parts, so that they seemed to have conquered the world. Or, through the breadth of *the land* of Israel, which was wholly laid waste by them. *Their faces shall sup up as the east wind;* their very countenances shall be so fierce and frightful that a look will serve to make them masters of all they have a mind to; so that they shall *swallow up* all, as the east wind nips and blasts the buds and flowers. They shall take a vast number of prisoners, and send them into Babylon: *They shall gather the captivity as the sand* for multitude. *They shall scoff* (he shall, so it is in the original, meaning Nebuchadnezzar, who, being puffed up with his successes, shall scoff) *at the kings* and commanders, and *the princes shall be a scorn to them. He shall deride every stronghold*, for to him it shall be weak, and *he shall heap dust, and take it;* a little soil, thrown up for ramparts, shall serve to give him all the advantage that he can desire; he shall make a sport of taking them. By all this he shall be puffed up with an intolerable pride, which shall be his destruction (*v*. 11): *Then shall his mind change* for the worse. *Bel* and *Nebo* were the gods of the Chaldeans, and to them they gave the glory of their successes; they were hardened in their idolatry, and blasphemously argued that because they had conquered Israel their gods were too strong for the God of Israel.

Verses 12–17

The prophet now turns to God, and again addresses him for the ease of his own mind under the burden which he saw. If he look about him, he sees nothing but violence done by Israel; if he look before him, he sees nothing but violence done against Israel. The prospect of the prevalence of the Chaldeans drives the prophet to his knees to plead with God concerning it.

I. The truths which he resolves to abide by, to comfort himself and his friends, under the threatening of the Chaldeans.

1. God is *the Lord our God*, and *our Holy One*. He is *Jehovah*, the fountain of all being, power, and perfection. *Our rock* is not *as theirs*. "He is *my God*." He speaks in the people's name; every Israelite may say, "He is *mine*. Though *all this has come upon us, yet have we not forgotten the name of our God*. We will not entertain any hard thoughts of him, nor of his service, for all this."

2. Our God is from everlasting. If he is from everlasting, he will be to everlasting, and we must have recourse to this first principle, when things seen, which are temporal, are discouraging, that we have hope and help sufficient in a God that is eternal. "Art thou not *from of old*, a God in covenant with thy people?" (so some understand it). "Art thou not the same God still? Thou art God, *and changest not*."

3. While the world stands God will have a church in it. The prophet infers the perpetuity of the church from the eternity of God; for Christ has said, *Because I live*, and therefore as long as I live, *you shall live also*, John xiv. 19. *We shall not die*.

3. It was God that gave the Chaldeans their power. He gave them their commission *to take the spoil and to take the prey*, Isa. x. 6. Herein God appears a

mighty God, that the power of mighty men is derived from him, and is under his cheek; *Hitherto shall it come, and no further*. Those whom God ordains shall do no more than what God has ordained. And he has *ordained them for judgment*, and *for correction*. God's people need correction, and deserve it; but it is for their correction, to drive out the foolishness that is found in their hearts.

5. Though the wicked may prosper for a while, yet God is a holy God, and does not approve of that wickedness (*v*. 13): *Thou art of purer eyes than to behold evil*. The prophet, observing how vicious the Chaldeans were, and yet what great success they had against God's Israel, found a temptation to say it was vain to serve God. But he suppresses the thought, by having recourse to his first principle, That God is not the author or patron of sin; he is *of purer eyes than to behold it* with approbation. There is in the nature of God an antipathy to those practices that are contrary to his holy law; and, though an expedient is happily found out for his being reconciled to sinners, yet he never will, nor can, be reconciled to sin. The mischief done to God's people by their persecutors; though God sees cause to permit it, yet he does not approve of it.

II. The grievances he finds hard to reconcile with these truths: "Since we are sure that thou art a holy God, *Wherefore lookest thou upon the Chaldeans* that deal treacherously with thy people and givest them success? Why dost thou suffer thy sworn enemies, to deal thus cruelly with thy sworn subjects, who desire to fear thy name? What shall we say to this?" This was a temptation to Job (*ch*. xxi. 7; xxiv. 1), to David (Ps. lxxiii. 2, 3), to Jeremiah, *ch*. xii. 1, 2. 1. That God permitted sin, and was patient with the sinners. 2. That his patience was abused, and *because sentence against these evil works and workers was not executed speedily*, therefore *their hearts* were the more *fully set in them to do evil*. They were false and deceitful. They hated and persecuted men because they were better than themselves, as Cain hated Abel because *his own works were evil and his brother's righteous*. They made no more of killing men than of catching fish. The prophet complains that, Providence having delivered up the weaker to be a prey to the stronger, they were, in effect, made as *the fishes of the sea v*. 14. So they had been among themselves, preying upon one another as the greater fishes do upon the less (*v*. 3). They were *as the creeping things*, or *swimming things* (for the word is used for *fish*, Gen. i. 20), *that have no ruler* over them. They are given up to the Chaldeans as fish to the fishermen. Those proud oppressors make no conscience of killing them, any more than men do of pulling fish out of the water. They have various ways of spoiling and destroying, as men have of taking fish. Some they *take up with the angle* (*v*. 15), one by one; others *they catch* in shoals, wholesale, *in their net*, and *gather them in their drag*, their enclosing net. *Their portion is fat, and their meat plenteous*. They live merrily (*v*. 15): *Therefore they rejoice and are glad*, because their wealth is great, and their projects succeed. They are great admirers of their own ingenuity: They *sacrifice to their own net*, and *burn incense to their own drag*.

III. The prophet, in the close, humbly expresses his hope that God will not suffer these destroyers of mankind always to go on and prosper thus (*v*. 17): "*Shall they therefore empty their net?* Shall they empty their net of what they have caught, that they may cast it into the sea again, to catch more? Must the numbers and wealth of nations be sacrificed to their net? Is not God the king of nations, and will he not assert their rights? Is he not jealous for his own honour, and will he not maintain that?" The prophet lodges the matter in God's hand, and leaves it with him, as the psalmist does. Ps. lxxiv. 22, *Arise, O God! plead thy own cause.*

CHAPTER 2

An answer expected by the prophet (ver. 1), and returned by the Spirit of God, to the complaints made of the violences and victories of the Chaldeans. The answer is, I. That after God has served his own purposes by the Chaldeans, has tried the faith and patience of his people, and distinguished between the hypocrites and the sincere, he will humble and bring down, not only that proud monarch Nebuchadnezzar, but that proud monarchy, ver. 2–8. II. That not they only, but all other sinners like them, should perish. 1. Those that are covetous, greedy of wealth and honours, ver. 9, 11. 2. Those that are oppressive, and raise estates by rapine, ver. 12–14. 3. Those that promote drunkenness that they may expose their neighbours to shame, ver. 15–17. 4. Those that worship idols, ver. 18–20.

Verses 1–4

I. The prophet humbly gives his attendance upon God (*v.* 1): "*I will stand upon my watch,* as a sentinel on the walls of a besieged city. I will look up, will look round, will look within, *and watch to see what he will say unto me. I will watch to see what he will say in me*" (so it may be read), "what the Spirit of prophecy in me will dictate to me, by way of answer to my complaints." God not only speaks to us by his word, but speaks in us by our own consciences, whispering to us, *This is the way, walk in it.* Those that expect to hear from God must withdraw from the world, and get above it, must raise their attention, fix their thought, study the scriptures, consult experiences and the experienced, continue instant in prayer, and thus set themselves *upon the tower.* 1. When we are perplexed with doubts concerning the methods of Providence, are tempted to think that it is fate, and not a wise God, that governs the world, then we must set ourselves upon the tower, to see if we can discover that which will silence the temptation and solve the difficulties, must go into the sanctuary of God, and there labour to understand the end of these things. 2. When we have been at prayer, pouring out our complaints and requests before God, we must carefully observe what answers God gives by his word, his Spirit, and his providences.

II. The prophet had complained of the prevalence of the Chaldeans; now, to pacify him concerning it, he here gives him a prospect of their fall and ruin, as Isaiah, before this, when he had foretold the captivity in Babylon, foretold also the destruction of Babylon.

1. The prophet must *write the vision, v.* 2. We have reason to bless God for written visions, that God has written to us the great things of his prophets as well as of his law. He must *write the vision,* and *make it plain upon tables,* must write it legibly, in large characters, so that *he who runs may read it.* God himself has prefixed his *imprimatur* to them; he has said, *Make them plain.*

2. The people must wait for the accomplishment of the *vision* (*v.* 3): "*The vision is yet for an appointed time* to come. You shall now be told of your deliverance by the breaking of the Chaldeans' power, and that the time of it is fixed in the counsel and decree of God." God has an appointed time for his appointed work, and will be sure to do the work when the time comes; it is not for us to anticipate his appointments, but to wait his time.

3. This vision will be such an exercise of faith and patience as will try and discover men what they are, *v.* 4. There are some who will proudly disdain this vision; they think *their own hands sufficient for them,* and God's promise is to them an insignificant thing. Those who are truly good, and whose hearts are upright with God, will value the promise, and venture their all upon it; and will keep close to God and duty in the most difficult trying times, and live comfortably in communion with God, dependence on him, and expectation of him.

Verses 5–14

The prophet having had orders to *write the vision,* the vision itself reads the doom, some think, of Nebuchadnezzar, who was principally active in the destruction of Jerusalem, or of all such proud and oppressive powers as bear hard, especially upon God's people.

I. The charge laid down against this enemy, *v.* 5. The *lusts of the flesh, the lusts of the eye,* and *the pride of life,* are snares; and we find him that led Israel captive, himself led captive by each of these. 1. He is sensual and voluptuous, and given to his pleasures: *He transgresses by wine.* Drunkenness is the cause of abundance of transgression. 2. He is haughty and imperious: *He is a proud man,* and his pride is a certain presage of his fall. When a man is drunk, though he makes himself as a beast, yet he thinks himself as great as a king, and prides himself in that by which he shames himself, Isa. xxviii. 1. 3. He is covetous and greedy of wealth, and this is the effect of his pride. The Chaldean monarchy aimed to be a universal one. He *keeps not at home,* is not content with his own, but thinks it too little. His ambition is his perpetual uneasiness. Though the home be a palace, yet to a discontented mind it is a prison. He *enlarges his desire as hell,* or *the grave,* which daily receives, and yet still cries, *Give, give.* And it is just with God that the desires which are insatiable should still be unsatisfied.

II. The sentence passed upon him (*v.* 6): *Shall not all these take up a parable against him?*

1. Since pride has been his sin, disgrace and dishonour shall be his punishment, and he shall be laughed at and despised by all about him.

2. Since he has been abusive to his neighbours, those very persons whom he has abused shall be the instruments of his disgrace: *All those shall take up a taunting proverb against him. He shall say* (he that draws up the insulting ditty shall say thus), *Ho, he that increases that which is not his! Aha!* what has become of him now? So it may be read in a taunting way. Woe against him for increasing his own possessions by invading his neighbour's rights, *v.* 6–8. He is *lading himself with thick clay.* Riches are but clay, thick clay; what are gold and silver but white and yellow earth? People cry to God, "How long wilt thou suffer this proud oppressor to trouble the nations?" Or they say to one another, "See how long it will last, how long he will be able to keep what he gets thus dishonestly?" What he has got by violence from others, others shall take by violence from him. The Medes and Persians shall make a prey of the Chaldeans, as they have done of other nations, *v.* 7, 8. "There shall be those that will *bite thee* and *vex thee;* those that seemed *asleep,* shall *rise up* and *awake* to be a plague to thee. They shall rise up *suddenly* when thou art most secure. According to the law of retaliation, as *thou hast spoiled many nations* so thou shalt thyself be *spoiled* (*v.* 8); *all the remnant of the people shall spoil thee.*" Woe against him for coveting still more, and aiming to be still higher, *v.* 9–11. *Woe to him that gains an evil gain;* so the margin reads it. There is a lawful gain, which by the blessing of God may be a comfort to a house (*a good man leaves an inheritance to his children's children*), but what is got by fraud and injustice is ill-got, and will be poor gain, will bring poverty and ruin upon it. *Thou hast consulted,* not safety, but shame, *to thy house, by cutting off many people, v.* 10. An estate raised by iniquity is a scandal to a family. "*Thou hast sinned against thy own soul,* and endangered that." But if the sinner pleads, Not guilty, and thinks his frauds cannot be proved upon him, let him know that *the stone shall cry out of the wall* against him, and *the beam out of the timber* in the roof *shall answer it, v.* 11. Woe against him for build-

ing a town and a city by blood and extortion (*v.* 12). So Nebuchadnezzar did (Dan. iv. 30): *Is not this great Babylon that I have built for the house of the kingdom?* But it is built with the blood of his own subjects, whom he has oppressed, and the blood of his neighbours, whom he has invaded; it is *established by iniquity.* The shame of the Chaldeans, who had taken so much pains, and were at such a vast expense, to fortify it (*v.* 13): *Is it not of the Lord of hosts that the people who have laboured so hard to defend that city shall labour in the very fire,* shall labour in vain to save it? There is not a greater drudge in the world than he that is under the power of reigning covetousness. They are but poorly paid for it; for, after all, *they weary themselves for very vanity;* it is worse than vanity, it is *vexation of spirit.*

Verses 15–20

The foregoing articles, upon which the woes here are grounded, are very near akin to each other.

But here are two articles more, of a different nature, which carry a *woe* to those in general to whom they belong, and particularly to the Babylonian monarchs, by whom the people of God were taken and held captives.

I. The promoters of drunkenness stand here condemned. Belshazzar was one of those; he was so, remarkably that very night that the prophecy of this chapter was fulfilled, when he *drank wine before a thousand* of his lords (Dan. v. 1), and forced them to pledge him. The succeeding monarchs of Persia (as we find, Esther i. 8) had seen in the kings of Babylon the mischievous consequences of forcing healths and making people drunk. But the woe here stands firm and fearful against all those, whoever they are, who are guilty of this sin at any time and in any place.

1. The sinner here articled against is he that *makes his neighbour drunk, v.* 15. To give a neighbour drink with design to intoxicate him, that he may expose himself, may make himself ridiculous, may disclose his own secret concerns—this is abominable wickedness; and those who are guilty of it are rebels against God in heaven, and his sacred laws, factors for the devil in hell, and enemies to men on earth.

2. Sentence is here passed upon him. There is a woe to him (*v.* 15), and a punishment (*v.* 16) that shall answer to the sin. (1) Does he put the cup of drunkenness into the hand of his neighbour? The *cup of the Lord's right hand,* shall be *turned unto him;* shall at length be put into the hand of the king of Babylon, as was foretold, Jer. xxv. 15, 16, 18, 26, 27. Does he take a pleasure in putting his neighbour to shame? He shall himself be loaded with contempt: *"Thou art filled with shame for glory, with shame instead of glory.* Thou *also shalt drink* of the cup of trembling, and shalt expose thyself by thy cowardice, which shall be as the *uncovering of thy nakedness,* to thy shame. For *the violence of Lebanon shall cover thee, and the spoil of beasts* (*v.* 17); thou shalt be hunted with as much violence as ever any wild beasts in Lebanon were."

II. The promoters of idolatry stand condemned. Belshazzar, in his revels, *praised his idols.* They are *mad upon their idols;* so the Chaldeans are said to be, Jer. l. 38. They have a great variety of idols, *graven images* and *molten images.* The *maker of the work* has performed his part admirably well, the *fashioner of his fashion* (so it is in the margin). *They lay them over with gold and silver. The maker of the work trusts therein* as his god. They pray to them: *They say to the wood, Awake* for our relief, and to the dumb stone, *"Arise,* and save us." They consult them as oracles, and expect to be directed by them. The folly of this is exposed. Their images are wholly void both of sense and reason, lifeless and speechless, so that the most minute animal, that has but breath and motion, is

more excellent than they. It is not in their power to do their worshippers any good (*v.* 18): *What profits the graven image?* It is so far from profiting them that it keeps them under the power of a strong delusion; they say, *It shall teach,* but it is a *teacher of lies;* for it represents God as having a body, as being finite, visible, and dependent, whereas he is a Spirit, infinite, invisible, and independent. The people of God triumph in him when the idolaters thus shame themselves (*v.* 20): *Our rock is not as their rock,* Deut. xxxii. 31. Theirs are dumb idols; ours is Jehovah, a living god, who is what he is, and not, as theirs, what men please to make him. They have laid waste his temple at Jerusalem; but he has a temple above that is out of the reach of their rage and malice, but within the reach of his people's faith and prayers.

CHAPTER 3

The prophet's prayer, in this chapter, is in imitation of David's psalms, for it is directed "to the chief musician", and is set to musical instruments. The prayer is left upon record for the use of the church, and particularly of the Jews in their captivity, while they were waiting for their deliverance. I. He earnestly begs of God to succour his people in affliction, to hasten their deliverance, and to comfort them in the meantime, ver. 2. II. He calls to mind the experiences which the church formerly had of God's glorious and gracious appearances on her behalf, when he brought Israel out of Egypt through the wilderness to Canaan, and there wrought wonderful deliverances for them, ver. 3–15. III. He affects himself with a holy concern for the present troubles of the church, but encourages himself and others to hope that the issue will be glorious at last, though all visible means fail, ver. 16–19.

Verses 1–2

This chapter is entitled *a prayer of Habakkuk.* It is an intercession for the church. Prophets were praying men, and sometimes they prayed for even those whom they prophesied against. 1. The prophet owns the receipt of God's answer to his former representation, and the impression it made upon him (*v.* 2): *"O Lord! I have heard thy speech, thy hearing"* (so some read it). Those that would rightly order their speech to God must carefully observe his speech to them. The matter of this message made the prophet afraid, when he heard how low the people of God should be brought, under the Chaldeans, and he was afraid lest their spirits should fail, and lest the church should be utterly rooted out and lost at length. 2. He earnestly prays that these *days of trouble* might be *shortened* or moderated, or the people of God supported. He thinks it very long to wait till the *end of the years;* perhaps he refers to the seventy years of the captivity, and therefore, "Lord," says he, "do something on our behalf *in the midst of the years,* though we be not delivered, yet let us not be abandoned and cast off." *Revive thy work,* thy church even when it *walks in the midst of trouble,* Ps. cxxxviii. 7, 8. *Revive the work of thy grace* in us, by sanctifying the trouble to us and supporting us under it, though the time be not yet come for our deliverance out of it. *In the midst of the years make known,* make thyself known, make known thy power, thy pity, thy promise, thy providence, in the government of the world, for the safety and welfare of thy church. When *in the midst of the years* of the captivity God miraculously owned the three children in the fiery furnace, and humbled Nebuchadnezzar, this prayer was answered.

Verses 3–15

God's people, when in distress, help themselves by recollecting their experiences, *considering the days of old.* The prophet here looks as far back as the miracles in Egypt, and through the wilderness. He that thus brought them at first into Canaan can now bring them out of Babylon.

I. God appeared in his glory (*v.* 3, 4): *He came from Teman, even the Holy One from Mount Paran.* This refers to the visible display of the glory of God when he gave the law upon Mount Sinai, Deut. xxxiii. 2. Then *his glory covered the heavens.* The *earth also* was *full of his praise,* or of his *splendour,* as some read it. Or the earth was full of those works of God which were to be praised. Some by the horns, the *two horns* (for the word is dual), *coming out of his hand,* understand the *two tables of the law.* It is added, *And there was the hiding of his power.* The operations of his power, compared with what he could have done, were rather the hiding of it than the discovery of it.

II. God sent plagues on Egypt, for the humbling of proud Pharaoh (*v.* 5): *Before him went the pestilence,* which slew all the first-born of Egypt in one night; and *burning coals went forth at his feet,* when, in the plague of hail, there was *fire mingled with hail—burning diseases* (so the margin reads it). These were *at his feet,* that is, at his coming, for they are at his command; he says to them, Go, and they go, Come, and they come, Do this, and they do it.

III. He divided the land of Canaan to his people Israel, and expelled the heathen (*v.* 6): *He stood, and measured the earth,* measured that land, to assign it for an inheritance to Israel his people, Deut. xxxii. 8, 9. *He beheld, and drove asunder the nations,* though they combined together against Israel. Then *the everlasting mountains were scattered, and the perpetual hills did bow;* the mighty princes of Canaan, that seemed as high and as firmly fixed, as the mountains, were broken to pieces. When he *drove asunder the nations* of Canaan one might have seen the *tents of Cushan in affliction, the curtains of the land of Midian trembling,* and all the inhabitants of the neighbouring countries, *v.* 7.

IV. He divided the Red Sea and Jordan, and yet fetched a river out of a rock when Israel wanted it, *v.* 8. God *rode upon his horses and chariots of salvation,* as a general at the head of his forces, mighty to save. This seems to be referred to again (*v.* 15). *Thou didst walk through the heap,* or mud, *of great waters,* slowly as the children and cattle walked. When they came to enter Canaan, the *overflowing of the water passed by,* that is, Jordan, which at that time overflowed all his banks, was divided, Joshua iii. 15. Then *the deep uttered his voice,* when, the Red Sea and Jordan being divided, the waters roared. They *lifted up their hands,* or sides, *on high* (for the waters *stood up on a heap,* Joshua iii. 16). *Thou didst cleave the earth with rivers;* channels in the wilderness, for the waters out of the rock, to supply the camp of Israel.

V. He arrested the motion of the sun and moon, to befriend Israel's victories (*v.* 11). *At the light,* at the direction, *of thy arrows, they went,* and at *the shining of thy glittering spear;* his spear pointed (the glittering light of which they acknowledged to outshine theirs) that way they directed their march, as when *the stars in their courses fought against Sisera.*

VI. He completed Israel's victories over the nations of Canaan and their kings. This is a plea with God that he would restore them again to that land.

1. Many expressions are here used to set forth the conquest of Canaan. God's *bow was made quite naked,* taken out of the case, to be employed for Israel; *we should say,* his *sword was quite unsheathed.* He *marched through the land* from end to end, *in indignation,* as scorning to let that wicked generation of Canaanites any longer possess so good a land. He *threshed the heathen in anger,* trod them out, as corn in the floor. He *wounded the heads out of the house of the wicked;* he destroyed their princes, cut off the heads, and so *discovered the foundations of them,* even *to the neck.* Some apply this to Christ's victories over Satan and the powers of darkness, in which he *wounded the heads over many countries,* Ps. cx. 6. He *struck through with his staves the head of the villages*

(*v.* 14). Staves shall do the same execution as swords. Pharaoh, when he pursued Israel to the Red Sea, *came out as a whirlwind;* so did the kings of Canaan against Israel. *Their rejoicing was as to devour the poor secretly;* they were as confident of success in their enterprise as ever any great man was of devouring a poor man. But God disappointed them, and their pride did but make their fall more shameful and God's care of his poor more illustrious. He *walked to the sea with his horses* (so some read it, *v.* 15), that is, he carried Israel's victories to the Great Sea, which was opposite to that side of Canaan at which they entered.

2. God would hereby make good his promise to the fathers; it was *according to the oaths of the tribes, even his word, v.* 9. He had sworn to give this land to the *tribes of Israel.* He would hereby show his kindness to *his people,* because of their relation to him, and his interest in them: *Thou wentest forth for the salvation of thy people, v.* 13. He would hereby give a type and figure of the redemption of the world by Jesus Christ. It is *for salvation with thy anointed,* with Joshua, who was a figure of him whose name he bore, even Jesus our Joshua.

Verses 16–19

I. The prophet had foreseen the prevalence of the church's enemies and the sight made him tremble, *v.* 16. Here he goes on with what he had said *v.* 2, "*I have heard thy speech and was afraid. When I heard* what sad times were coming *my belly trembled, my lips quivered at the voice.*" It was no reproach to his courage. *I tremble in myself, that I might rest in the day of trouble.* He that has joy in store for those that *sow in tears* has rest in store for those that tremble before him. *Good hope through grace* is founded in a *holy fear.*

II. He had looked back upon the church in former ages, and had observed what great things God had done for them, and so fell into a transport of holy joy.

1. He supposes the ruin not only of the delights of this life, but even of the necessary supports of it, *v.* 17. Famine is one of the ordinary effects of war. He supposes the fruit-tree to be withered and barren; the *fig-tree* (which used to furnish them with much of their food); he supposes *the labour of the olive* to *fail,* their oil, which was to them as butter is to us; *the fields shall yield no meat. The flock is cut off from the fold, and there is no herd in the stall.*

2. He resolves to delight and triumph in God notwithstanding; when all is gone his God is not gone (*v.* 18): "*Yet will I rejoice in the Lord.*" Those who, when they were full, enjoyed God in all, when they are emptied can *enjoy all in God,* and can sit down upon a melancholy heap of the ruins and even then sing to the praise and glory of God. This is the principal ground of our joy in God, that he is the God of our eternal salvation, the salvation of the soul; and, if he be so, we may rejoice in him in our greatest distresses, since by them our salvation cannot be hindered, but may be furthered. Joy in God is never out of season, nay, it is in a special manner seasonable when we meet with losses and crosses in the world, that it may then appear that our hearts are not set upon these things, nor our happiness bound up in them. He that is the *God of salvation* in another world will be our strength in this world, to carry us on in our journey thither, and help us over the difficulties and oppositions we meet with in our way. Thus the prophet, who began his prayer with fear and trembling, concludes it with joy and triumph, for prayer is heart's ease to a gracious soul. He set his song upon *Shigionoth* (*v.* 1), wandering tunes, *according to the variable songs,* and upon *Neginoth* (*v.* 19), *the stringed instruments.* He that is afflicted, and has prayed aright, may then be so easy, may then be so merry, as to sing psalms.

THE PROPHECY OF ZEPHANIAH

This prophet is placed last, of all the minor prophets before the captivity, and not long before Jeremiah, who lived at the time of the captivity. He foretells the general destruction of Judah and Jerusalem by the Chaldeans, and sets their sins before them, calls them to repentance, threatens the neighbouring nations with the like destructions, and gives encouraging promises of their joyful return out of captivity in due time.

CHAPTER 1

After the title of the book (ver. 1), here is, I. A threatening of the destruction of Judah and Jerusalem by the Chaldeans, ver. 2–4. II. A charge against them for their gross sin (ver. 5, 6); and so he goes on in the rest of the chapter, setting both the judgments before them, that they might prevent them or prepare for them, and the sins that destroy them, that they might judge themselves, and justify God in what was brought upon them. 1. They must hold their peace because they had greatly sinned, ver. 7–9. But, 2. They shall howl because the trouble will be great, ver. 10–18. Such fair and timely warning as this did God give to the Jews of the approaching captivity.

Verses 1–6

I. The title-page of this book (v. 1); it is from heaven, and not of men: It is *the word of the Lord*. *Zephaniah* signifies the *servant of the Lord*, for God *revealed his secrets to his servants the prophets*. The pedigree of Zephaniah goes back four generations, and the highest mentioned is *Hizkiah*; it is the same name in the original with that of Hezekiah king of Judah (2 Kings xviii. 1). This prophet prophesied *in the days of Josiah king of Judah*, who in the twelfth year of his reign carried on a work of reformation, in which he destroyed idols. Now it does not appear whether Zephaniah prophesied in the beginning of his reign; if so, we may suppose his prophesying had a great influence on that reformation.

II. The summary of this book. The general proposition contained in it is, That utter destruction is coming apace upon Judah and Jerusalem for sin. He begins abruptly (v. 2): *By taking away I will make an end of all things from off the face of the land, saith the Lord. I will consume the beasts, the fowls of the heaven, and the fishes of the sea* (v. 3). The expressions are figurative, denoting universal desolation. Those that fly ever so high, those that hide ever so close, shall yet become a prey to them, and be utterly consumed. "*I will consume man; I will cut off man from the land.* The land shall be dispeopled and left uninhabited; I will destroy, not only Israel, but *man.* Though they shall not be cut off from the Lord, yet they shall be *cut off from the land.*" Even Judah, where God is known, and Jerusalem, where his dwelling-place is, if they revolt from him and rebel against him, shall have his hand stretched out against them. "*I will consume the stumbling-blocks with the wicked,* the idols with the idolaters, the offences with the offenders." The Chaldeans would spare none of the images of Baal, or the worshippers of those images. The *Chemarim* shall be *cut off*; we read of them in the history of Josiah's reformation. 2 Kings xxiii. 5, *He put down the idolatrous priests*: the word is the *Chemarim*. The word signifies *black men*, some think because they wore black clothes, others because their faces were black with attending the altars, the fires in which they burnt their children to Moloch. They seem to have been immediate attendants upon the service of Baal. And, among other

idolaters, the *worshippers of the host of heaven upon the house-tops* shall be cut off (v. 5). It will appear as great an offence to God to give divine honours to a star as to give them to a stone or a stock. Those also shall be consumed that halt between God and Baal, and worship between Jehovah and Moloch, and *swear by both*; or, as it might better be read, swear *to the Lord and to Malcham.* Those also shall be consumed that have apostatized from God, together with those that never gave up their names to him, v. 6.

Verses 7–13

Notice is given to Judah and Jerusalem that God is coming against them; *his day*, the day of his judgment is not far off, v. 7. Men have their day now, when they do what they please; but *God's day is at hand*; it is here called his *sacrifice*, reparation to his injured honour.

I. Those that shall be punished in this day of reckoning: The royal family for their pride and affectation (v. 8). They shall be punished, and all such as, like them, are clothed *with strange apparel. The princes and the king's children* send abroad to strange countries for their clothes, which would not please unless they were far-fetched and dear-bought. Pride in apparel is displeasing to God, and a symptom of the degeneracy of a people. *In the same day will I punish those that leap on the threshold,* a phrase which probably signified the invading of their neighbour's rights. They *leap on the threshold*, as much as to say that the house is their own, and, accordingly, they make all in it their own, and so *fill their masters' houses* with goods gotten *by violence and deceit.* Iniquity is found among *the inhabitants of Maktesh*, a low part of Jerusalem, deep like a mortar (for so the word signifies); the *goldsmiths* lived there (Neh. iii. 32) and the merchants; and they are now *cut down*, have shut up their shops, and become bankrupts. *All those that bear silver are cut off* by the invaders. All the careless people that live a loose idle life are next reckoned with (v. 12). God will find them out, and punish them: *At that time I will search Jerusalem with candles*, to discover them. God will punish not only the secret idolaters, but the secret epicures and profane. Their dispositions are sensual: They *are settled on their lees*, intoxicated with their pleasures. Their notions are atheistical. They could not live such loose lives but that they say *in their heart, The Lord will not do good, neither will he do evil*; that is, *He will do nothing.* They deny his providential government of the world. If they were not drowned in sense, they could not be thus senseless.

II. God will punish these sinners. He will silence them (v. 7): *Hold thy peace at the presence of the Lord.* He will *sacrifice* them, for it is *the day of the Lord's sacrifice* (v. 8); he will give them into the hands of their enemies. *In that day there shall be a noise of a cry from the fish-gate*, so called because near to the fish-market. *And a howling from the second*, which was next to that *fish-gate*. The alarm shall go round the walls of Jerusalem from gate to gate; and there shall be *a great crashing from the hills*, from the mountains round about Jerusalem, from the acclamations of the invaders, and the lamentations of the invaded. The inhabitants of the city, even of the closest safest part of the city, shall *howl* (*v.* 11), so clamorous shall the grief be. They shall be stripped of all they have; it shall be a prey to the enemy (*v.* 13): *Their household goods*, and *shop-goods*, shall *become a booty*, and a rich booty they shall be; *their houses shall be* levelled with the ground and be *a desolation*; those of them that have *built* new houses *shall not inherit them*, but the invaders shall get and keep possession of them. And the *vineyards* they have planted they shall not *drink the wine of*, but, instead of having it for the relief of their friends that faint among them, they shall part with it for the animating of their foes that fight against them, Deut. xxviii. 30.

Verses 14–18

The warning given to Judah and Jerusalem of the approaching destruction by the Chaldeans. It is *the great day of the Lord*, a kind of doom's-day, as the last destruction of Jerusalem by the Romans is represented to be in our Saviour's prediction concerning it, Matt. xxiv. 27.

I. This *day of the Lord* is here spoken of as very near. The prophet gives the alarm like one that awakens a family with the cry of *Fire! fire!* when it is at the next door.

II. It is spoken of as a very dreadful day. The very *voice* of this *day of the Lord*, shall make *the mighty men cry there bitterly*. It will be a day of *trouble and distress* to the sinners; they shall see no ways of easing or helping themselves. It is *a day of clouds and thick darkness*; the thick clouds are big with storms and tempests.

III. It is spoken of as a destroying day, *v.* 16, 17. What forts, what fences, can hold out against the wrath of God? "*I will bring distress upon men*, the strongest and stoutest of men; they shall *walk like blind men*, wandering endlessly, *because they have sinned against the Lord*." Those that walk as bad men will justly be left to walk as blind men, always in doubt and danger.

IV. The destruction of that day will be unavoidable and universal, *v.* 18. There shall be no escaping it by ransom: *Neither their silver nor their gold shall be able to deliver them in the day of the Lord's wrath.* There shall be no escaping it by flight or concealment; for the *whole land shall be devoured by the fire of his jealousy*, and where then can a hiding-place be found?

CHAPTER 2

I. An earnest exhortation to the nation to repent and make their peace with God (ver. 1–3). II. The judgments of God against several of the neighbouring nations that had assisted, or rejoiced in, the calamity of Israel. 1. The Philistines, ver. 4–7. 2. The Moabites and Ammonites, ver. 8–11. 3. The Ethiopians and Assyrians, ver. 12–15.

Verses 1–3

The prophet meant in that terrible description of approaching judgments not to drive the people to despair, but to drive them to God and to their duty —not to frighten them out of their wits, but to frighten them out of their sins.

I. The summons to a national assembly (*v.* 1): *Gather yourselves together.* The summons is given to a *nation not desired.* The word signifies either, 1. *Not desiring*, that has not any desire towards God. "Yet *come together*, and see if you can stir up desires in one another." Or, 2. *Not desirable*, nor having

anything which might recommend them to God. God says, "*Gather together*, that you may in a body humble yourselves." Some read it, "*Enquire into yourselves;* examine your consciences; look into your hearts; search and try your ways; *enquire into yourselves*, that you may find out the sin by which God has been provoked."

II. Arguments urged to press them to expedition herein (*v.* 2): "Do it in earnest; do it with all speed before it is too late, *before the decree bring forth, before the day pass.*"

III. Directions prescribed. They are not to gather together in a consternation, but seriously and calmly (*v.* 3): *Seek you the Lord.* If the land be saved, it must be by the intercession of the pious few, the *meek of the earth*, or of *the land.* They must *seek the Lord*, seek his favour and grace. Seek God for the performance of his promises to you, and see to it that you abound yet more in duty to him.

IV. Encouragements given to take these directions: *It may be, you shall be hid in the day of the Lord's anger.* "*Verily it shall be well with thy remnant*, Jer. xv. 11. *It may be, you shall be hid:* if any be hid, you shall." They shall be hid (as Luther says) *aut in cœlo, aut sub cœlo—either in heaven or under heaven*, either in the possession of heaven or under the protection of heaven.

Verses 4–7

The prophet foretells what share the neighbouring nations should have in the destruction made by Nebuchadnezzar. The *day of the Lord* might appear the more dreadful, but though God had seemed to be their enemy, and to fight against them, yet he was still so far their friend, and an enemy to their enemies, that he resented, and would revenge, the indignities done them.

In these verses we have the doom of the Philistines, neighbours, and old enemies, to the people of Israel. They were the *inhabitants of the sea-coasts* (*v.* 5), for their country lay upon the Great Sea. The *nation of the Cherethites* is here joined with them, which bordered upon them (1 Sam. xxx. 14) and fell with them. The Philistines' land is here called *Canaan*, for it belonged to that country which God gave to his people Israel, Joshua xiii. 3. This land is yet to be possessed for so that they wrongfully kept Israel out of the possession of it (Judges iii. 3).

I. It is here foretold that the Philistines, the usurpers, shall be dispossessed and quite extirpated. *Gaza shall be forsaken*, though now a populous city. It was foretold (Jer. xlvii. 5) that *baldness* should come upon Gaza; Alexander the Great razed that city, and we find (Acts viii. 26) that Gaza was a desert. *Ashkelon* shall be *a desolation. Ashdod* shall be *driven out at noon-day;* in the extremity of the scorching heat. They shall be forced away into captivity. *Ekron* likewise shall be *rooted up*, that had been long taking root. The land of the Philistines shall be dispeopled, *v.* 5. The sea-coast, which used to be a harbour for ships and a habitation for merchants, shall now be deserted, and be only *cottages for shepherds* and *folds for flocks* (*v.* 6).

II. It is here foretold that the house of Judah, the rightful owners, shall recover the possession of it, *v.* 7. The remnant of those that shall *return out of captivity* shall *lie down* in safety *in the houses of Ashkelon*.

Verses 8–11

The Moabites and Ammonites were both of the posterity of Lot; their countries joined.

I. They are both charged with reviling the people of God and triumphing in their calamities (*v.* 8). They have *spoken big* (so some read it, *magna locuti* sunt—*they have spoken great things*) *against their border* (v. 8), against those of them that bordered upon their country; they *spoke big against the people of the Lord of hosts* as a deserted abandoned people. "But *I have heard them*" (says God).

II. They are both laid under the same doom. Sentence is pronounced upon them, v. 9. The Moabites and Ammonites *shall be as Sodom and Gomorrah*, the marks of whose ruins in the Dead Sea lay near adjoining to the countries of Moab and Ammon; they shall be laid waste; not again to be inhabited, or not of a long time. The country shall produce *nettles*, instead of corn; and there shall be *brine-pits*, instead of fountains of water. Israel shall *spoil them* of their goods and *possess* their country. And *this shall they have for their pride.*

III. Other nations shall in like manner be humbled. Heathen gods must be abolished. Their worshippers have gloried in them. But *the Lord* will *famish all the gods of the earth*, will starve them out of their strongholds. When the gospel gets ground, by it men shall be brought to worship him who lives for ever, *everyone from his place*; they shall not need to go up to Jerusalem to worship the God of Israel, but, wherever they are, they may have access to him.

Verses 12–15

The Ethiopians, or Arabians, that had sometimes been a terror to Israel (as in Asa's time, 2 Chron. xiv. 9), *shall be slain by my sword*, v. 12. Nebuchadnezzar was God's sword, the instrument with which these enemies were punished, Ps. xvii. 14. The Assyrians, and Nineveh the head city of their monarchy, are next to receive their doom: *He* that is God's sword *will stretch out his hand against the north and destroy Assyria*. Assyria had been the rod of God's anger against Israel, and now Babylon is the rod of God's anger against Assyria, Isa. x. 5. Nineveh was so strong that she feared no evil. She shall be made *a desolation*, v. 13. The melancholy birds, as the *cormorant und bittern*, shall make their nests in what remains of the houses. The *lintels*, or *chapiters* of the pillars, the *windows* and *thresholds*, and all the fine *cedar-work*, shall lie exposed; and on them these rueful ominous birds shall perch, and their *voice shall sing. Everyone that passes by shall hiss* at her, and *wag his hand*—"There is an end of proud Nineveh."

CHAPTER 3

I. Reproof and threatening, for the wickedness that was found in her, ver. 1–7. II. Mercy and grace, which God had yet in reserve for them. Two general promises: 1. That God would bring in a glorious work of reformation among them, cleanse them from their sins, and bring them home to himself, ver. 8–13. 2. That he would bring about a glorious work of salvation for them, when he had thus prepared them for it, ver. 14–20. These promises were to have their full accomplishment in gospel-times and gospel-graces.

Verses 1–7

I. A very bad character given of Jerusalem in general. She shames herself; she is *filthy and polluted* (v. 1), has made herself *infamous* (so some read it), *the gluttonous* city (so the margin), always making provision for the flesh. She wrongs her neighbours and inhabitants; she is *the oppressing city*. She is provoking to her God, v. 2. He had given his law, but *she obeyed not his voice*. Her confidence was placed in her alliances with the nations more than in her covenant with God. She *drew not near to her God*. She stood at a distance, and *said to the Almighty, Depart.*

II. The leading men in it are the great patrons of wickedness, and those that should be her physicians are really her worst disease. *Her princes are* barbarous as *roaring lions*, and are universally hated. *Her judges*

are evening wolves, rapacious, their cruelty and covetousness insatiable: *They gnaw not the bones till the morrow;* they take delight in oppression that when they have devoured a good man they reserve the bones, as it were, for a sweet morsel, Job xxxi. 31. *Her prophets*, who pretend to be special messengers from heaven to them, *are light and treacherous persons*, men of no consistency, in whom one can put no confidence. *Her priests* are false to their trust and betray it. They were to preserve the purity of the *sanctuary*, but they themselves *pollute* it. They *did violence to the law*; they corrupted the sense of it. By forced constructions, they made the law to speak what they pleased, and so, in effect, *made void the law.*

III. General corruption in Jerusalem. They had the tokens of God's presence yet they persisted in their disobedience, v. 5. *"The just Lord is in the midst of thee* as a holy God, and therefore thy pollutions are the more offensive," Deut. xxiii. 14. "A just God will punish the affronts you put upon him, and the wrongs you do to one another." He sent to them his prophets, rising up early and sending them: *Every morning he brings his judgment to light.* He wakens his prophets with the rising sun, to bring to light the things which belong to their peace. God had set before their eyes monuments of his justice, designed for warning (v. 6): *I have cut off the nations*, the seven nations of Canaan, Lev. xviii. 28. Or it may refer to some of the neighbouring nations made desolate for their wickedness. *Their towers were desolate*, their *streets were wasted*, *their cities* were *destroyed* and laid in ruins; *no man* was to be found in them. The enemies did it, but God avows it: *I cut them off*, says he. And God designed this for an admonition to Jerusalem. He had assured them of the continuance of their prosperity if they would fear him and receive instruction, for so *their dwelling would not be cut off* as their neighbour's was. He had made them feel the smart of the rod, though he reprieved them from the sword. They were more resolute and eager in their wicked courses than ever. God *rose up early*, to send them his *prophets*, but they were *up before him*, to shut and bolt the door against them.

Verses 8–13

Things looked bad. Jerusalem has got a very bad name, and seems to be incorrigible, incurable, mercy-proof and judgment-proof. But behold the riches of divine grace. They still grew worse and worse, *therefore wait you upon me, saith the Lord*, v. 8. "Since the *law*, it seems, will *make nothing perfect*, the *bringing in of a better hope shall*. Let those that lament the corruptions of the church *wait upon God*, till he send his Son into the world, to *save his people from their sins*, and to purify to himself a peculiar people both of Jews and Gentiles." And there were those who *waited for redemption* in Jerusalem; and long-looked-for, it came at last, Luke ii. 38.

I. By the gospel of Christ preached to every creature all nations are summoned, as it were, to appear in a body before the Lord Jesus, who is about to set up his kingdom in the world. But, since the greatest part of mankind will not obey the summons, he will *pour upon them his indignation*, for he that *believes not is condemned already*. Then *all the earth shall be devoured with the fire of his jealousy*; both Jews and Gentiles shall be reckoned with for their enmity to the gospel.

II. When God intends the restoration of Israel he makes way for their reformation and the revival of their virtue and piety; for this is God's method, first to make them holy and then to make them happy. These promises were in part accomplished after the return of the Jews out of Babylon. It is promised that there shall be a reformation in men's discourse, which had been generally corrupt, but should now be with grace seasoned with salt (*v.* 9): "*Then will I turn to the people a pure language.*" Converting grace refines the language, not by making the phrases witty, but the substance wise. The Jews, after the captivity, had mingled the language of Canaan with that of Ashdod (Neh. xiii. 24). But that is not all: their language shall be purified from all profaneness, filthiness, and falsehood. I will turn them to a *choice language* (so some read it). Instead of sacrifice and incense, they shall *call upon the name of the Lord.* Prayer is the spiritual offering with which God must be honoured. They shall serve God *with one consent,* with *one shoulder* (so the word is), alluding to oxen in the yoke, that draw even. When Christians are unanimous in the service of God the work goes on cheerfully. Purity is the way to unity; the reformation of manners is the way to a comprehension. Those that were driven from God shall return to him and be accepted of him (*v.* 10). *From beyond the rivers of Ethiopia,* or from some other remote country, they shall be put in mind of him, as the prodigal son was of his father's house, in the far country. The *daughter of his dispersed,* that is *afar off,* will be found among those whom *the Lord our God shall call.* Wherever they are, though *beyond the rivers of Ethiopia,* a great way from his house of prayer, they still are his suppliants. *They shall bring my offering,* shall bring themselves as spiritual sacrifices to God (Rom. xii. 1). *In that day shalt thou not be ashamed for all thy doings.* They shall be ashamed as penitents (see Ezek. xvi. 63), but they shall not be ashamed as sinners that return to folly again. "*I will take away out of the midst of thee,* not only the profane, but the hypocrites, who appear beautiful outwardly, and *rejoice in thy pride,* in the holy city, the holy house." These were *haughty because of the holy mountain,* were conceited, scornful and set even the judgments of God at defiance. That haughtiness is the most offensive to God which is fed by the pretensions of holiness. God will have a remnant of holy, humble, serious people (*v.* 12): *I will leave in the midst of thee an afflicted and poor people.* This select remnant shall be blessed with purity and peace, *v.* 13, both in words and actions: They *shall neither do iniquity nor speak lies.*

Verses 14–20

After the promises of the taking away of sin, here follow promises of the taking away of trouble; for when the cause is removed the effect will cease. Rejoice and sing (*v.* 14): *Sing, O daughter of Zion!* sing for joy; *shout, O Israel!* Those that love God with all their heart have occasion with all their heart to rejoice in him. *In that day it shall be said to Jerusalem* (God will say it by his prophets, by his providences, their neighbours shall say it, they shall say it to one another), "*Fear thou not.* Lift up thy hands in prayer to God; lift up thy hands to help thyself."

I. An end shall be put to all their troubles and distresses (*v.* 15): "*The Lord has taken away thy*

judgments, has removed all the calamities which were the punishments of thy sin; the noise of war shall be silenced, the reproach of famine done away, and the captivity brought back. *He has cast out thy enemy,* that has thrust himself into thy land. He has *swept out thy enemy*" (so some read it). The way to get clear of the evil of trouble is to keep clear from the evil of sin; and to those that do so trouble has no real evil in it.

II. God will give them the tokens of his presence with them. "*The Lord is in the midst of thee, O Zion!* of thee, *O Jerusalem!* as the sun in the centre of the universe, to diffuse his light and influence upon every part. He (*v.* 15) is in the midst of thee as a king in the midst of his people. He is the Lord thy God, thine in covenant, in the midst of thee as thy God, whose thou art. *He will save. He will be Jesus,* will answer the name, for he will save his people from their sins."

III. God will take delight in doing them good. *He will rejoice over thee with joy.* The conversion of sinners and the consolation of saints are the joy of angels, for they are the joy of God himself. He will *rest in his love,* will be *silent in his love,* so the word is.

IV. God will comfort Zion's mourners and will wipe away their tears (*v.* 18): *I will gather those who are sorrowful for the solemn assemblies, to whom the reproach of it was a burden.* Zion is in mourning. Many are her calamities. The city is ruined, and the palaces are demolished; trade is at an end, but all these are nothing to them in comparison with the destruction of the temple and the altar, to attend on which, in solemn feasts, all Israel used to come together three times a year. It is for those sacred solemn assemblies that they are sorrowful. The restraining of public assemblies for religious worship, the scattering of them by their enemies, or the forsaking of them by their friends, is a sorrowful thing to all good people. The reproach of the solemn assemblies is a burden to them.

V. God will recover the captives and bring home the banished that seemed to be expelled, *v.* 19, 20. "*At that time I will undo all that afflict thee,* will break their power, and blast their counsels, so that they shall be forced to surrender the prey they have taken." One act of mercy and grace shall serve both to collect them out of their dispersions and to conduct them to their own land. When the *people's hearts are prepared,* the work will be done suddenly.

VI. God will by all this gain them respect from all about them. When God returns, in mercy, to his church, it is here promised that she shall regain her credit. "*I will get them praise and fame in every land, where they have been put to shame.*" Those that said, "This is Zion whom no man looks after," shall say, "This is Zion whom the great God looks after." So the Jewish church was when *the fear of the Jews* fell upon their neighbours (Esther viii. 17). So the Christian church was when it was made to flourish in the world, for there is that in it which may justly recommend it to the esteem of all people.

AN EXPOSITION, WITH PRACTICAL OBSERVATIONS, OF

THE PROPHECY OF HAGGAI

The captivity in Babylon gave a very remarkable turn to the affairs of the Jewish church both in history and prophecy. Nine of the twelve minor prophets lived and preached before that captivity. But the last three lived and preached after the return out of captivity. Haggai and Zechariah appeared eighteen years after the return, when the building of the temple was both retarded by its enemies, and neglected by its friends. *Then the prophets, Haggai the prophet and Zechariah the son of Iddo, prophesied unto the Jews that were in Jerusalem, in the name of the God of Israel, even unto them* (so we read Ezra v. 1), to encourage them to revive that good work when it had stood still for some time. Haggai began two months before Zechariah. But Zechariah continued longer at the work; for all Haggai's prophecies that are recorded were delivered within four months, in the second year of Darius. But we have Zechariah's prophecies dated above two years after, Zech. vii. 1. The Jews ascribe to these two prophets the honour of being members of the great synagogue, which was formed after the return out of captivity; we think it more certain, and a much greater honour, that they prophesied of Christ. Haggai spoke of him as the *glory of the latter house*, and Zechariah as *the man, the branch*. In them the light of that morning star shone more brightly as they now began to see his day approaching. The LXX make Haggai and Zechariah to be the penmen of Ps. cxxxviii and of Ps. cxlvi, cxlvii and cxlviii.

CHAPTER 1

I. A reproof of the people of the Jews for their dilatoriness in building the temple, with an exhortation to them to resume that good work, in good earnest, ver. 1–11. II. The good success of this sermon, appearing in the people's return and close application to that work, wherein the prophet encouraged them, assuring them that God was with them, ver. 12–15.

Verses 1–11

It was the complaint of the Jews in Babylon that they *saw not their signs*, and there was *no more any prophet* (Ps. lxxiv. 9), which was a judgment for mocking the prophets. We read of no prophets they had in their return. But the lamp of Old Testament prophecy shall yet make some glorious efforts before it expire; and Haggai is the first that appears under the character of a special messenger from heaven. In the reign of Darius Hystaspes, the third of the Persian kings, in the second year of his reign, this prophet was sent; and the word of the Lord came to him, and by him to the leading men among the Jews, v. 1. The chief governor was *Zerubbabel, the son of Shealtiel*, of the house of David, who was commander-in-chief of the Jews, in their return out of captivity. In the church was *Joshua the son of Josedech*, who was now high priest. They were great men and good men. The prophets, who were extraordinary messengers, did not set aside the institutions of magistracy and ministry, but endeavoured to render both more effectual.

I. The sin of the Jews at this time, v. 2. As soon as they came up out of captivity they set up an altar for sacrifice, and within a year after laid the foundations of a temple, Ezra iii. 10. They then seemed very forward in it, but, being served with a prohibition from the Persian court, and charged not to go on with it, they not only yielded to the force, when they were actually under it, but afterwards, when the violence of the opposition had abated, they had no spirit to set about it again, but let it stand still. These Jews continued loitering until they were reminded of their duty. They suggested one to another, "*The time has not come, the time that the Lord's house should be built.* Our losses are not repaired. It is too great an undertaking for beginners as we are; let us first get our own houses up, before we talk of building churches, and in the mean time let a bare altar serve us, as it did our father Abraham." They did not say

that they would not build a temple at all, but, "Not yet; it is all in good time."

II. The judgments of God by which they were punished for this neglect, v. 6, 9–11. That the punishment might answer to the sin, God by his providence kept them still behind-hand, and that poverty which they thought to prevent by not building the temple God brought upon them for not building it. We need the help of God's prophets and ministers to expound, not only the judgments of God's mouth, but the judgments of his hands, that we may understand his mind and meaning in his rod as well as in his word.

1. God did not send them into captivity again, nor bring a foreign enemy upon them, as they deserved, but denied his blessing upon the *seed sown*, and then it never prospered. *They sowed much* (v. 6), kept a great deal of ground in tillage, because their land had long *lain fallow* and had *enjoyed its sabbaths*. Having sown much, they looked for much from it, but they were disappointed: *They bring in little*, very little (v. 6); when they have made the utmost of it, *it comes to little* (v. 9). We are here told how they came to be disappointed (v. 10): *The heaven over you is stayed from dew;* he that has the key of the clouds in his hands shut them up, and withheld the rain, and then of course *the earth is stayed from her fruit*; for, if the heaven be as brass, the earth is as iron. God will make us sensible of our necessary and constant dependence upon him, throughout all the links in the chain of second causes, so that we can at no time say, "Now we have no further occasion for God and his providence." See Hos. ii. 21. *I called for a drought upon the land*, ordered the weather to be extremely hot, and then the fruits of the earth were burnt up. The heat of the sun puts life into the plants and *renews the face of the earth* at spring. And yet, if that go into an extreme, it undoes all again. This drought was *upon the mountains*, which, lying high, were first affected with it. The mountains were their pasture-grounds, and used to be *covered over with flocks*, but now there was no grass for them. It was *upon the corn, the new wine, and the oil*; all failed through the extremity of the hot weather. It inflamed men and put them into fevers. It brought diseases upon cattle too. The bread they ate did not nourish them. When they had the corn in the barn they were not sure of it: *I did blow upon it, saith the Lord of*

hosts (*v.* 9), and it withered. When they had it upon the board it was not that to them that they expected: "*You eat, but you have not enough. You clothe yourselves, but there is none warm. He that earns wages by hard labour, and has it paid him in ready current money, puts it into a bag with holes*; it drops through, and wastes away insensibly. Everything is so scarce and dear that they spend their money as fast as they get it."

2. God thus stopped the current of the favours promised them at their return (Joel ii. 24); they provoked him to do it: *It is because of my house that is waste.* The foundation of the temple is laid, but the building does not go on. "Every man *runs to his own house*, to finish that, and no care is taken about the Lord's house." If God cross us in our temporal affairs, and we meet with trouble and disappointment, we shall find this is the cause of it, the work we have to do for God is left undone, and we *seek our own things more than the things of Jesus Christ*, Phil. ii. 21.

III. The reproof which the prophet gives them for their neglect of the temple-work (*v.* 4): "*Is it time for you, O you! to dwell in your ceiled houses*, to have them beautified and adorned, and your families settled in them?" They were not content with walls and roofs for necessity. "It is high time," says one, "that my house were wainscoted." "It is high time," says another, "that mine were painted." And God's house, all this time, *lies waste*, and nothing is done at it.

IV. The good counsel which the prophet gives to those who thus despised God. *Now therefore consider your ways, v.* 5 and again *v.* 7. Think what you have done that has provoked God and think what you will do to testify your repentance. He would have them reform (*v.* 8): "*Go up to the mountain*, to Lebanon, *and bring wood*, and other materials, *and build the house* with all speed." He assures them: *Build the house, and I will take pleasure in it;* and that was encouragement enough for them to go through with it, whatever it cost them. Those who have long deferred their return to God, if at length they return with all their heart, must not despair of his favour.

Verses 12–15

The foregoing sermon met with the desired success among the people, and their obedience met with due encouragement from God.

I. All those to whom that sermon was preached were wrought upon by it. Zerubbabel, the chief governor, was a man that had been eminently useful in his day, and did not plead his former merits in answer to this reproof for his present remissness. Joshua also, as high priest, willingly received admonition and instruction. *The remnant of the people* all *obeyed the voice of the Lord their God*, and bowed to the yoke of his commands, *v.* 12. They looked upon the prophet to be the Lord's messenger, and the word he delivered to be the Lord's message; and therefore received it *not as the word of man, but as the word of* Almighty God, *v.* 12. Prophecy was a new thing with them; they had had no special messenger from heaven for a great while, and now that they had one, they paid extraordinary regard to him. It is sometimes so; when good preaching is most scarce it does most good, whereas the manna that is rained in plenty is loathed as *light bread.* And, because they so readily received this prophet, God, within a month or two after, raised them up another, Zech. i. 1. When they saw their own sin to be the cause of those judgments, then they feared. *The Lord stirred up* their spirits, *v.* 14. He encouraged them, and with those encouragements enlarged their hearts, Ps. cxix. 32. Lest they should sink under the weight of fear, God stirred them up, and made them cheerful and bold. They

applied to their work with all possible vigour. Everyone, according to his capacity or ability, lent a hand, to further that good work. The consideration of God's covenant-relation to his people by his grace should stir up our spirits to act for him, and for the advancement of the interest of his kingdom among men. It was but on the first day of the sixth month that Haggai preached this sermon, and little more than three weeks after, they were all busy working in the house of the Lord their God, *v.* 15. Those that have lost time have need to redeem time.

II. How God met them in mercy. The same prophet that brought them the reproof brought them a comforting encouraging word (*v.* 13): *Then spoke Haggai, the Lord's messenger, in the Lord's message, saying, I am with you, saith the Lord.* That is all he has to say, and that is enough. *I am with you*, that is, I will forgive your neglects hitherto. *I am with you* to protect you against your enemies, and to prosper you, to strengthen your hands, and bless the work.

CHAPTER 2

Three sermons preached by the prophet Haggai for the encouragement of those that build the temple. In the first he assures the builders that the glory of the house they were now building should, in spiritual respects, though not in outward, exceed that of Solomon's temple, ver. 1–9. In the second he assures them that though their sin, in delaying to build the temple, had retarded the progress of other affairs, yet now that they had set about it in good earnest he would bless them, and give them success ver. 10–19. In the third he assures Zerubbabel that, as a reward of his pious zeal and activity herein, he should be a favourite of Heaven, and one of the ancestors of Messiah the Prince, whose kingdom should be set up on the ruins of all opposing powers, ver. 20–23.

Verses 1–9

I. The date of this message, *v.* 1. It was sent on the twenty-first day of the seventh month, when the builders had been about a month at work. Those that are hearty in the service of God shall receive fresh encouragements from him to proceed in it. Set the wheels going, and God will oil them.

II. The direction of this message, *v.* 2. *Speak to Zerubbabel, and Joshua, and the residue of the people*, the very same that *obeyed the voice of the Lord* (*ch.* i. 12) and whose spirits God stirred up to do so (*ch.* i. 14); to them are sent these words of comfort.

III. The message itself. That which was such a damp upon them, when the foundation of the temple was laid, was still a clog upon them—that they could not build such a temple now as Solomon built, *v.* 3. This fetched tears from the eyes of many, when the dimensions of it were first laid (Ezra iii. 12). It was now about seventy years since Solomon's temple was destroyed, so that there might be some yet alive who could remember to have seen it. One could remember the gold with which it was overlaid, another the precious stones, the porch, the pillars—and where are these now? It is sometimes the fault of old people to discourage the services of the present age by crying up too much the performances and attainments of the former age. *Say not thou that the former days were better than these* (Eccles. vii. 10), but thank God that there is any good in these, bad as they are. The encouragement that is given them to go on in the work, notwithstanding (*v.* 4): *Yet now*, though this house is likely to be inferior to the former, *be strong, O Zerubbabel! and be strong, O Joshua!* Let leading men do as well as they can, when they cannot do so well as they would. The grounds of these encouragements. God himself says to them, *Fear you not* (*v.* 5). The presence of God with us, as the *Lord of hosts*, is enough to silence all our fears. The Jews had hosts against them, but they had the Lord of hosts with them. Though *he chastens them for their transgressions with the rod*, yet he will not make his faithfulness to fail. It was the Spirit of God that stirred up their spirits to come out of Babylon (Ezra i. 5), and now to build the temple, Hag. i. 14. They shall have the Messiah among them shortly—*him that should come, v. 6, 7.* Let the Son of man, when he comes, find faith on the earth. Concerning his coming it is here foretold it shall be introduced by a general shaking (*v.* 6): *I will shake the heavens, and the earth, and the sea, and the dry land.* This is applied to the setting up of Christ's kingdom in the world. God will once again do for his church as he did when he brought them out of Egypt; he shook the heavens and earth at Mount Sinai. This shall be done again when at the birth of Christ, Herod and all *Jerusalem are troubled* (Matt. ii. 3), and he is *set for the fall and rising again of many.* When his kingdom was set up it was with a shock to the nations. The shaking of the nations is often in order to the settling of the church and the establishing of the things that cannot be shaken. The house they are now building shall be filled with glory to such a degree that its glory shall exceed that of Solomon's temple. It is God's prerogative to fill with glory; the glory that comes from him is satisfying, and not vain glory. Moses's tabernacle and Solomon's temple were filled with glory when God in a cloud took possession of them; but this house shall be filled with glory of another nature. Let them not be concerned because this house will not have so much silver and gold about it as Solomon's temple had, *v.* 8. Let them be comforted with this, that, though this temple have less gold in it, it shall have more glory than Solomon's (*v.* 9): *The glory of this latter house shall be greater than of the former.* The presence of the Messiah will be in it, the Son of God presented there, attending there at twelve years old, and afterwards his preaching and working miracles there, and his driving the buyers and sellers out of it. It was necessary, then, that the Messiah should come while the second temple stood; but, that being long since destroyed, we must conclude that our Lord Jesus is the Christ, is *he that should come,* and we are to *look for no other.* It was the *glory of this latter house,* that before the coming of Christ, it was always kept free from idols and idolatries. The purity of the church, and the strict adherence to divine institutions, are much more its glory than external pomp and splendour. After Christ, the gospel was preached in it by the apostles, even all the words of this life, Acts v. 20. In the temple Jesus Christ was daily preached, Acts v. 42. Where Christ is, *behold a greater than Solomon is there,* so the heart in which he dwells, and makes a living temple, is more glorious than Solomon's temple, and will be so to eternity. *In this place will I give peace, saith the Lord of hosts.* But the Jews under the latter temple had so much trouble that we must conclude this promise to have its accomplishment in that spiritual peace which Jesus Christ bequeathed to all believers (John xiv. 27). God will *give peace in this place;* he will give his Son to be the peace, Eph. ii. 14.

Verses 10–19

This sermon was preached two months after that in the former part of the chapter. The people were now going on vigorously with the building of the temple.

I. God sees there are many among them that spoil this good work, by going about it with unsanctified hearts and hands. All are warned thereby to purify the hands they employ in this work. A spiritual use is to be made of the ceremonial law; it was intended, not only as a divine ritual to the Jews, but for *instruction in righteousness* to all. The prophet is ordered to enquire of the priests concerning it (*v.* 11). Haggai himself, though a prophet, must *ask the priests concerning the law.* It was their duty to ex-

pound the ordinances of God, and to give the general rules for the observance of them. The rules of the law, in the cases propounded, are that he that has holy flesh in his clothes cannot by the touch of his clothes communicate holiness (*v.* 12), but he that is ceremonially unclean by the touch of a dead body does by his touch communicate that uncleanness. The law is express (Num. xix. 22). The sum of these two rules is that pollution is more easily communicated than sanctification. The law is here applied (*v.* 14): *So is this people, and so is this nation, before me.* They thought their offering sacrifices on the altar would sanctify them, and excuse their neglect to build the temple. "No," says God, "your holy flesh and your altar will be so far from sanctifying your meat and drink, your wine and oil, to you, that your contempt of God's temple will bring a pollution, not only on your common enjoyments, but even on your sacrifices too." If they be sensual, and morally impure, though they work hard at the temple while it is building, and though they offer many and costly sacrifices there when it is built, yet that shall not serve to sanctify their meat and drink to them; the impurity of their hearts and lives shall make even that work of their hands, and all their offerings, unclean, and an abomination to God.

II. Comfort and encouragement. If their hearts be right with God, and their eye single, God will take away the judgment of famine, and will restore them great plenty. On the twenty-fourth day of the sixth month they began to prepare materials (*ch.* i. 15), and now on the twenty-fourth day of the ninth month they began to *lay a stone upon a stone in the temple of the Lord.* They had gone behind-hand before this day. Let them remember the time when there was waste and decay in all they had, *v.* 16. A man went to his garner, expecting to find *a heap of twenty measures* of corn, but he found it unaccountably diminished, and, when he came to measure it, *there were but ten* measures; it had dried away in the keeping, or vermin had eaten it, or it was stolen. In like manner he went to the *wine-press,* expecting to draw *fifty vessels* of wine; they did not yield as usual, for he could get *but twenty. I smote you with blastings,* winds and frosts, which made every green thing to wither, *and with mildew,* which choked the corn when it was knitting, *and with hail,* which battered it down when it had grown to some maturity; thus they were disappointed *in all the labour of their hands,* while they neglected to lay their hands to the work of God. As long as they continued in neglect of the temple work all their affairs went backward. But they should find that from this day forward God would bless them (*v.* 18, 19): "*Consider now* whether when you begin to change your way towards God you do not find God changing his way towards you." He does not say what they shall be, but, in general, *I will bless you;* they can desire no more to make them happy.

Verses 20–23

After Haggai's sermon *to the people,* here follows one, the same day, *to the magistrates,* particularly to Zerubbabel (*v.* 21): *Speak to Zerubbabel, governor of Judah,* speak to him by himself. Zerubbabel is concerned about the community, about the neighbouring nations, and their governments, and what will become of the few and feeble Jews, and how such a poor prince as he should be able to keep his ground and serve his country. "Go to him," says God, "and tell him it shall be well with him and his remnant."

I. Let him expect to hear of great commotions in the nations (*v.* 21, 22): *I will shake the heavens and the earth.* The world is like the sea, like the wheel, always in motion, but sometimes in a special manner turbulent. But, blessed be God, if the earth be shaken, it is to *shake the wicked out of it*, Job xxxviii. 13. In the apocalyptic visions earthquakes bode no ill to the church. The Chaldean monarchy, which had been the throne of kingdoms was already overthrown; and the powers that are yet to come, shall in like manner be overthrown; their day will come to fall. They *trust in chariots and horses* (Ps. xx. 7), but their *chariots* shall be *overthrown*, and *those that ride in them.* This reads the doom of all the enemies of God's church, and seems likewise designed as a promise of Christ's victory over the powers of darkness; his overthrow of Satan's throne, that *throne of kingdoms.* All opposing *rule, principality, and power*, shall be put down, that the *kingdom* may be *delivered up to God, even the Father.*

II. He shall be safe under the divine protection in the midst of all these commotions, *v.* 23. Zerubbabel was active to build God a house, and therefore God makes the same promise to him as he did to David—

that he would *build him a house*, and establish it, even *in that day* when heaven and earth are shaken. His successors likewise in the government of Judah might take encouragement from it. But this promise has special reference to Christ, who lineally descended from Zerubbabel, and is the sole builder of the gospel-temple. Zerubbabel is here owned as *God's servant. I have chosen thee* to this office. It is promised that, being chosen, God will make him as a *signet.* Jeconiah had been as the *signet on God's right hand*, but was *plucked thence* (Jer. xxii. 24). He shall be near and dear to God, and his family shall continue till the Messiah spring out of it, who is *the signet on God's right hand.* Princes sign their edicts, grants, and commissions, with their signet-rings, Esther iii. 10. Our Lord Jesus is the signet on God's right hand, for all power is given to him and derived from him. By him the great charter of the gospel is signed and ratified, and it is in him that all the promises of God are yea and amen.

AN EXPOSITION, WITH PRACTICAL OBSERVATIONS, OF

THE PROPHECY OF

ZECHARIAH

This prophet was colleague with the prophet Haggai, and a worker together with him in forwarding the building of the second temple (Ezra v. 1). Zechariah began to prophesy some time after Haggai. But he continued longer, soared higher in visions and revelations, and prophesied more particularly concerning Christ, than Haggai had done. He begins with a sermon, expressive of that which was the scope of his prophesying, in the first five verses; but afterwards, to the end of *ch.* vi, he relates the visions he saw, and the instructions he received from heaven by them. At *ch.* vii, from an enquiry made by the Jews concerning fasting, he takes occasion to show them the duty of their present day, and to encourage them to hope for God's favour, after which there are two sermons, both called *burdens of the word of the Lord* (one begins with *ch.* ix, the other with *ch.* xii). The scope of them is to reprove for sin, and threaten God's judgments against the impenitent, and to encourage those that feared God with assurances of the mercy God had in store for his church, and especially of the coming of the Messiah and the setting up of his kingdom in the world.

CHAPTER 1

In this chapter, after the introduction (ver. 1), we have, I. An awakening call to a sinful people to repent and return to God, ver. 2–6. II. Great encouragement given to hope for mercy. 1. By the vision of the horses, ver. 7–11. 2. By the prayer of the angel for Jerusalem, and the answer, ver. 12–17. 3. By the vision of the four carpenters, ver. 18–21.

Verses 1–6

I. The foundation of Zechariah's ministry: *The word of the Lord came to him.* He received a divine commission to be God's mouth to the people. It came in the evidence and demonstration of the Spirit, as a real thing, and not a fancy. The word of the Lord came first to him *in the second year of Darius.* Before the captivity the prophets dated their writings by the reigns of the kings of Judah and Israel; but now by the reigns of the kings of Persia, to whom they were subjects. Zechariah preached his first sermon in the *eighth month* of this *second year* of Darius; Haggai preached his in the sixth month of the same year, Hag. i. 1. *Zechariah was the son of Barachiah, the son of Iddo,* and he was *the prophet,* as Haggai is called *the prophet,* Hag. i. 1.

II. The first-fruits of Zechariah's ministry. Before he published the promises of mercy, he published calls to repentance, for thus *the way of the Lord* must be *prepared.* Law must be first preached, and then gospel. The prophet puts them in mind of the controversy God had had with their fathers (*v.* 2): "*The Lord has been sorely displeased with your fathers.* You have seen with your eyes the woeful remains of it." The judgments of God, which those that went before us were under, should be taken as calls to repentance, that we may cut off the curse and get it turned into a blessing. He calls them, in God's name, to return and make their peace with him, *v.* 3. Let the rebels return to their allegiance, and they shall enjoy all the privileges of good subjects. But that which is most observable here is that God is called here the *Lord of hosts* three times: *Thus saith the Lord of hosts. Turn you to me, saith the Lord of hosts* (this intimates the authority and obligation of the command), *and I will turn to you, saith the Lord of hosts*—this intimates the validity and value of the promise; so that it is no vain repetition. He warns them not to persist in their impenitence, as their fathers had done (*v.* 4): *Be you not as your fathers.* We are apt to be governed very much by precedent. Some argued, "Shall we be wiser than our fathers?

They never minded the prophets, and why then should we mind them? They made laws against them, and why should we tolerate them?" But they are here taught how they should argue: "Our fathers slighted the prophets, and God was sorely displeased with them for it; therefore let us regard what God says to us by his prophets." "*The former prophets cried to your fathers* as men in earnest, in the name of the Lord of hosts; and this was the substance of what they said—*Turn you now from your evil ways, and from your evil doings;* the very same that we now preach to you. A speedy reformation is the only way to prevent an approaching ruin." "What has become both of your fathers and of the prophets that preached to them? They are all dead and gone," *v.* 5. In another world both we and our prophets shall live for ever; and to prepare for that world ought to be our great care and business in this. "The preachers died, and the hearers died, but the word of God died not; that took effect, and not one iota or tittle of it fell to the ground." Though God's prophets could not fasten convictions upon them, the calamities threatened overtook them, and they could not escape them. The unbelief of man cannot make the threatenings of God's word of no effect, but, sooner or later, they will take place, if the prescribed course be not taken to prevent them. *They returned, and said* (they changed their mind, and when it was too late to prevent the ruin of their nation they acknowledged), *Like as the Lord of hosts thought to do unto us according to our ways and doings, so has he dealt with us,* and we must acknowledge both his truth and his justice.

Verses 7–17

Visions and revelations of the Lord; for in that way God chose to speak by Zechariah, to awaken the people's attention. Most of the following visions seem designed for the comfort of the Jews, newly returned out of captivity, and their encouragement to go on with the building of the temple. The scope of this vision (which is an introduction to the rest) is to assure the Jews of the care God took of them, now they seem deserted, and their case deplorable. The vision is dated (*v.* 7) *the twenty-fourth day of the eleventh month,* three months after he preached that sermon (*v.* 1), in which he calls them to repentance. Finding it had a good effect, and that they returned to God in a way of duty, the assurances are confirmed, that God would return to them in a way of mercy.

I. The prophet saw a grove of *myrtle-trees*, a dark shady grove, down *in a bottom*, hidden by the adjacent hills. This represented the low, dark, solitary, melancholy condition of the Jewish church at this time. He saw *a man* mounted upon *a red horse*, standing in the midst of this shady myrtle-grove. This man is no other than the *man Christ Jesus*, the same that appeared to Joshua with *his sword drawn in his hand* as *captain of the host of the Lord* (Joshua v. 13, 14). Though the church was in a low condition, yet Christ was present in the midst of it. He was *riding*, as a man of war, as a man in haste, *riding on the heavens for the help* of his people, Deut. xxxiii. 26. He rode on a *red horse*, as this same victorious prince appeared *red in his apparel*, Isa. lxiii. 1, 2. Red is a fiery colour, denoting that he is *jealous for Jerusalem* (v. 14), and angry at her enemies. Christ, under the law, appeared on a red horse, denoting that he had yet his conflict before him, when he was to *resist unto blood*. But, under the gospel, he appears on a *white horse* (Rev. vi. 2, and again *ch.* xix. 11), denoting that he has now gained the victory. *Behind him there were some red horses, and some speckled, and some white*, angels attending the Lord Jesus, ready to be employed by him for the service of his church, some in acts of judgment, others of mercy, others in varied events. He had an angel talking with him, as his instructor. Zechariah asked him (v. 9), *O my Lord! what are these?* The account given him was, *These are those whom the Lord has sent;* they are his messengers.

II. What the prophet heard, and what instructions were thereby given him. He heard the report which the angels made, v. 11. They had been out abroad, as flying posts, and, having returned, they give this account to the *Angel that stood among the myrtle-trees: We have walked to and fro through the earth, and, behold, all the earth sits still and is at rest.* We find the world of mankind here very careless: *All the earth sits still, and is at rest*, while all the church is made uneasy, *tossed with tempests and not comforted*. Those that are strangers to the church are secure; those that are enemies to it are successful. The Chaldeans and Persians dwell at ease, while the poor Jews are continually alarmed. He heard Christ's intercession with the Father for his afflicted Church, v. 12. The angels related the posture of affairs in this world, but we read not of any prayers they made for the redress of the grievances. It is *the Angel among the myrtle-trees* who is the great intercessor. Upon the report of the angels he immediately turned heavenward, and said, *Lord, wilt thou not have mercy* on thy church? *How long wilt thou not have mercy!* The objects of compassion are Jerusalem, the holy city, and the other cities of Judah that were now in ruins; for God had had *indignation against them* now *threescore and ten years*. So long the indignation lasted, and though *now for a little space grace* had been *shown them from the Lord their God*, to *give them some reviving* (Ezra ix. 8), yet the scars of those seventy years' captivity still remained deep. The captivity went off, as it came on, gradually. "Lord, we are still under the burden of the seventy years' wrath, *and wilt thou be angry with us for ever?*" He heard a gracious reply given to this intercession (v. 13): *The Lord answered the angel*, this angel of the covenant, *with good words and comfortable words*, with promises of mercy and deliverance, and the perfecting of what he had begun. He heard that reply which was given to the angel repeated to himself, with a commission to publish it to the children of his people, for their comfort. Now that God would *speak comfortably to Jerusalem*, Zechariah is *the voice of one crying in the wilderness, Prepare you the way of the Lord.* The voice

said, *Cry*. The prophets must now cry as loudly to show God's people their comforts as ever they did formerly to show them *their transgressions*, Isa. xl. 2, 3, 6. He must proclaim the wrath God has in store for the enemies of Jerusalem, v. 14. The earth *sat still and was at rest* (v. 11), not relenting at all for all the mischief they had done to Jerusalem (v. 15). God is displeased with those who help forward the affliction even of such as suffer justly; for true humanity, in such a case, is good divinity. He must cry, *"Thus saith the Lord, I have returned to Jerusalem with mercies* (v. 16). I was going away in wrath, but I am now returning in love" (v. 17). *The Lord*, even the Lord of hosts, assures them, the temple, though it meet with much discouragement, shall be perfected, and they shall have the tokens of God's presence. Jerusalem shall again be *built as a city compact together. A line shall be stretched forth upon Jerusalem*, in order to the rebuilding of it with exactness and uniformity. The nation shall again become populous and rich. Not only Jerusalem, but other cities that are reduced, shall yet *spread abroad*. The cities that should thus increase God calls his cities; they are *blessed* by him, and they are *fruitful and multiply, and replenish the land*. God has comforts in reserve for Zion and all her mourners. As he first built them up into a people when he brought them out of Egypt, so he will now rebuild them, when he brings them out of Babylon.

Verses 18–21

In this vision (the second which this prophet had), we have an illustration of God's Spirit making a stand, and making head, against the formidable power of the church's adversaries.

I. We have here the enemies of the church threatening to be its death: *I looked and behold four horns* (v. 18), which are explained v. 19. They *are the horns which have scattered Judah, Israel, and Jerusalem*, that is, the Jews both in the country and in the city. They have *tossed them* (so some read it), as furious bulls with their horns toss. They have scattered them, *so that no man did lift up his head*, v. 21. They are *four horns*, for the Jews are surrounded with them on every side. The men of Judah and of Jerusalem, and many of Israel that joined themselves to them, set about building the temple; but enemies from all sides drove them from it. Rehum, and Shimshai, and the other Samaritans that opposed the building of the temple, were these horns, Ezra iv. 8. So were Sanballat and Tobiah, and the Ammonites and Arabians, that opposed the building of the wall, Neh. iv. 7.

II. The friends of the church active and prevailing. The prophet did himself see the four horns, but *the Lord* then *showed him four carpenters*, or *smiths*, who were empowered to cut off these horns, v. 20, 21. With an eye of sense we see the power of the enemies of the church; but it is with an eye of faith that we see it safe, notwithstanding. *Carpenters* or *smiths* (for they are supposed by some to have been horns of iron) were the men who had skill and ability to break the horns. Some by these four carpenters understand Zerubbabel and Joshua, Ezra and Nehemiah, who carried on the work of God in spite of the opposition.

CHAPTER 2

I. Another vision which the prophet saw for the edification of those to whom he was sent, ver. 1, 2. II. A sermon upon it, in the rest of the chapter, 1. By way of explication of the vision, showing it to be a prediction of the replenishing of Jerusalem, ver. 3–5. 2. By way of application. (1) An exhortation to the Jews that were yet in Babylon, pressing them to hasten their return to their own land, ver. 6–9. (2) A consolation to those that were returned, in reference to the many difficulties they had ver. 10–12. (3) A caution to all not to prescribe to God, or limit him, but patiently to wait for him, ver. 13.

Verses 1–5

This prophet was to assure the people (*ch.* i. 16) that a *line should be stretched forth upon Jerusalem.*

I. He sees, in a vision, a man going to measure Jerusalem (*v.* 1, 2): *He lifted up his eyes again, and looked.* In the close of the foregoing chapter he had seen Jerusalem's enemies baffled and broken, so now he begins to hope she shall not be ruined. *The man Christ Jesus,* whom the prophet sees *with a measuring line in his hand,* is the master builder of his church (Heb. iii. 3), and he builds exactly by line and level. Zechariah asked him *whither he was going* with that measuring line. And he readily told him that he was going to *measure Jerusalem,* to take account of the dimensions of it each way, that it might be computed what was necessary for the making of a wall about it, and by comparing its dimensions with the vast numbers that should inhabit it, what additions were necessary to be made. When multitudes flock to Jerusalem (Isa. lx. 4) it is time for her to *enlarge the place of her tent,* Isa. liv. 2.

II. He is informed that this vision means well to Jerusalem. The *angel that talked with* the prophet *went forth,* but *another angel went out to meet him,* to desire that he would first explain this vision to the prophet for his encouragement (*v.* 4): *Jerusalem shall be inhabited as towns without walls;* it shall extend itself far beyond the present dimensions. It shall be extended as freely as if it had no walls at all, and yet shall be as safe as if it had the strongest walls, such a *multitude of men* (which are the best walls of a city) *shall there be therein.* It shall be safe, for God himself will be a *wall of fire round about it.* Jerusalem had no walls about it at this time, but now God will be unto her a wall of fire. Some think it alludes to shepherds that made fires about their flocks, or travellers that made fires about their tents in desert places, to frighten wild beasts from them. He will himself be such a wall; a wall of fire round about on every side. God himself *will be the glory in the midst of it.* Now all this was fulfilled in part in Jerusalem, which in process of time became a very flourishing city, beyond what could have been expected, considering how low it was brought and how long it was ere it recovered itself.

Verses 6–9

One would have thought that Cyrus's proclamation, which gave liberty to the captive Jews to return to their own land, would suffice to bring them all back, but it had not that effect. There were about 40,000 whose spirits God stirred up to go, and they went; but many stayed behind. The land of their captivity was to most of them the land of their nativity; they had taken root there. They had no great affection to their own land, and apprehended the difficulties insuperable. This proceeded from a distrust of the power and promise of God, a love of ease and worldly wealth, and an indifference to the religion of their country and to the God of Israel himself; and it was a tacit censure of those that did return. Here is therefore another proclamation by the God of Israel, commanding all his free-born subjects, wherever dispersed, speedily to return into their own land. They are loudly summoned (*v.* 6): *Ho! ho! come forth, and flee from the land of the north, saith the Lord.* This fitly follows upon the promise of the rebuilding of Jerusalem. If God will build it for them they must come and inhabit it for him and his glory, and not continue sneaking in Babylon. They are now dispersed, but should unite for their mutual common defence (*v.* 6): "*I have spread you abroad as the four winds of heaven,* some into one corner of the world and some into another, and you should now think of coming together again, to help one another." They are now to assert their liberty: "*Deliver thyself, O*

Zion!" When Christ has proclaimed that deliverance to the captives which he has himself wrought, it concerns each of us to *deliver ourselves,* and, since we are under grace, to resolve that *sin shall not have dominion over us. Deliver thyself, O Zion!* by a speedy return to thy own land, and do not destroy thyself by continuing in that polluted land. God now espouses their cause and will plead it with jealousy, *v.* 8, 9. The *angel that talked with* the prophet (that is, Jesus Christ) tells him what he had commission to do for their protection and the perfecting of their salvation. Christ, who is the *Lord of hosts, says, He* (that is, the Father) *has sent me.* He is sent *after the glory.* Christ is sent, in the first place, to the nation and people of the Jews, *to whom pertained the glory,* Rom. ix. 4. But *after the glory,* after his care of them, he is *sent to the nations, to be a light to lighten the Gentiles,* by the power of his gospel to captivate them, and bring them into obedience to himself. He is *sent to the nations that spoiled them,* to take vengeance on them for the wrongs done to Zion. *They shall be a spoil to their servants,* shall be enslaved to those whom they had enslaved. The promise is fulfilled in Christ's victory over our spiritual enemies, his *spoiling principalities and powers and making a show of them openly,* Col. ii. 15. What he will do for his church shall be proof of God's affection for it: *He that touches you touches the apple of his eye.* He takes what is done against her as done against the very apple of his eye, the tenderest part, which nature has put a double guard upon. See (Ps. xvii. 8), *Keep me as the apple of the eye;* and (Prov. vii. 2), *Keep his law as the apple of thy eye.*

Verses 10–13

Joy proclaimed to the church of God, to the *daughter of Zion,* that had separated herself from the *daughter of Babylon.* The Jews that had returned were in distress, their enemies in the neighbourhood were spiteful, their friends that remained in Babylon were cool and declined coming in to their assistance; and yet they are directed to *sing,* and to *rejoice* even in tribulation.

I. God will have a people among them. If their brethren in Babylon will not come to them, those of other nations shall: *Many nations shall be joined to the Lord in that day.* The Jewish nation, after the captivity, multiplied very much, by the accession of proselytes to it, that were naturalized, and entitled to the privileges of native Israelites. It was strange that that should be so great an offence to the Jews in the apostles' times, which was promised as a blessing in the prophets' times.

II. They shall have his presence among them: *Sing and rejoice, for I come.* 1. In the dedication of the temple, in their regularly observing all God's institutions there. Those have God *dwelling in the midst of them.* 2. In the incarnation of Christ. He that promises to dwell among them is that *Lord whom the Lord of hosts has sent* (*v.* 11), and therefore must be the *Lord Jesus,* the eternal *Word,* that was *made flesh, and dwelt among us.*

III. They shall have all their ancient dignities and privileges restored to them again, *v.* 12. Canaan shall be a holy land again. Judah shall be in this holy land, and no longer be scattered in Babylon. Judah shall be God's portion in which he will be glorified. God will protect his people and govern them as a man does his inheritance. He will *choose Jerusalem again,* will continue it a chosen place, till it must resign its honours to the Jerusalem that is from above.

IV. Here is silence proclaimed to all the world besides, *v.* 13. The daughter of Zion must sing, but *all flesh* must *be silent.* God is about to do something unexpected and to plead his people's cause, which had long seemed neglected. Leave it to God to take his own way, and neither prescribe to him what he should do nor quarrel with him whatever he does. *Be still, and know that he is God. Stand still, and see his salvation.*

CHAPTER 3

The vision in the foregoing chapter gave assurances of the re-establishing of the civil interests of the Jewish nation. Now the vision in this chapter concerns their church-state, and their ecclesiastical interests. I. A vision relating to Joshua, as the representative of the church in his time, representing the disadvantages he laboured under, and the people in him, with the redress of the grievances of both. 1. He is accused by Satan, but is brought off by Christ, ver. 1, 2. 2. He appears in filthy garments, but has them changed, ver. 3-5. 3. He is assured of being established in his office if he conduct himself well, ver. 6, 7. II. A sermon relating to Christ, who is here called "The branch", by whom we should have pardon and peace, ver. 8-10.

Verses 1-7

There was a Joshua that was a principal agent in the first settling of Israel in Canaan; here is another of the same name very active in their second settlement there after the captivity; Jesus is the same name, and it signifies *Saviour*; they were both figures of him that was to come, our chief captain and our chief priest. The angel that talked with *Zechariah showed him Joshua the high priest*; it is probable that the prophet saw him frequently, and that there was a great intimacy between them; but then he only saw how he appeared before men; how he stands before the Lord must be shown him in vision. He *stood before the angel of the Lord*, to execute his office. He stood to consult the oracle on behalf of Israel. Guilt and corruption are our two great discouragements when we stand before God obnoxious to his justice and odious to his holiness.

I. Joshua is accused as a criminal, but is justified. 1. A violent opposition is made to him. *Satan stands at his right hand to resist him* as the prosecutor or witness. When God is about to re-establish the priesthood Satan objects the sins that were found among the priests. It is by our own folly that we give Satan advantage against us. We must expect to meet with all the resistance that Satan's subtlety and malice can give us. Let us then resist him and he shall flee from us. 2. A victorious defence is made (*v*. 2): *The Lord* (that is, the Lord Christ) *said unto Satan, The Lord rebuke thee*. It is the happiness of the saints that the Judge is their friend. Satan is here checked by one that has authority. *The Lord said* (that is, the Lord our Redeemer), *The Lord rebuke thee*, that is, the Lord the Creator. The power of God is engaged for the making of the grace of Christ effectual. Satan resists the priest, but his resistance will be to no purpose against Jerusalem, for *the Lord has chosen*. He knew the worst when he chose them. *Is not this a brand plucked out of the fire?* Joshua is so, and the priesthood, and the people, whose representative he is. Christ has that to say for them for which they are to be pitied. One can expect no other than that those who but the other day were captives in Babylon should appear mean and despicable. They have been wonderfully delivered out of the fire, that God might be glorified in them; will he then abandon them?

II. Joshua appears as one polluted, but is purified; for he represents the Israel of God, who are all *as an unclean thing*. *He was clothed*, not only in coarse, but in *filthy garments*, such as did very ill become the dignity of his office, and the sanctity of his work, Exod. xxviii. 2. Joshua's garments were a shame and reproach; yet in them *he stood before the angel of the Lord*; he had no clean linen wherein to minister. This intimates, not only that the priesthood was poor and despised, and loaded with contempt, but that there was iniquity cleaving to the holy things. The returned Jews, because they were free from

idolatry, thought themselves chargeable with no iniquity. But God showed them there were many things amiss in them. There were spiritual enemies warring against them, Ezra x. 18. Yet Joshua was permitted to *stand before the angel of the Lord*. Provision was made for his cleansing. Two things are done for Joshua, representing a double work of divine grace wrought in and for believers: (1) His filthy garments are taken from him, *v*. 4. The meaning of this is given us in what Christ said, and he said it as one having authority, *Behold, I have caused thy iniquity to pass from thee*. When God forgives our sins he *causes our iniquity to pass from us*, he sanctifies the nature and enables us to *put off the old man*, to cast away from us the filthy rags of our corrupt affections and lusts. (2) He is clothed anew, has not only the shame of his filthiness removed, but the shame of his nakedness covered: *I will clothe thee with change of raiment*. Joshua had no clean linen of his own, but he shall appear as lovely as ever he appeared loathsome. Thus those whom Christ makes spiritual priests are clothed with the spotless robe of his righteousness and appear before God in that, and with the graces of his Spirit, which are ornaments to them.

III. Joshua is re-installed and established in his office. 1. The crown of the priesthood is put upon him, *v*. 5. This was done at the request of the prophet. When God designs the restoring or reviving of religion he stirs up his prophets and people to pray for it, and does it in answer to their prayers. Zechariah prayed that the angels might be ordered to set the mitre on Joshua's head, and they did it immediately, and *clothed him with* the priestly *garments*. 2. The covenant of the priesthood is renewed with him, which is called God's *covenant of peace*, Num. xxv. 12. It is *the patent of his office*, which is here declared and delivered to him before witnesses, *v*. 6, 7. Joshua must *walk in God's ways*, must go before the people in the paths of God's commandments, and walk circumspectly. He must also *keep God's charge*, and must see to it that the inferior priests performed the duties of their place. Let him be sure to do his part, and God will own him. The high priest might not make any new laws for God's house, nor ordain any other rites of worship; but he must judge God's house, that is, he must see to it that God's laws and ordinances were observed. "*Thou shalt also keep my courts;* thou shalt have oversight of all the courts of the temple, and keep them in good order for worship to be performed in them." *I will give thee places to walk among those that stand by*. Those that *walk in God's ways* may be said to *walk among the angels* themselves, for they do the will of God as the angels do it that are in heaven, and are their *fellow-servants*, Rev. xix. 10.

Verses 8-10

As the promises made to David often slide insensibly into promises of the Messiah, whose kingdom David's was a type of, so the promises here made to Joshua rise as far upward, and look as far forward, as to Christ, of whose priesthood Joshua's was now a shadow. Christ is a high priest, as Joshua was, for sinners and sufferers.

I. The promise of Christ (*v*. 8): "*Hear now, O Joshua!* Thou hast heard what belongs to thyself; but, behold, a greater than Joshua is at hand. *Hear now* concerning him, *thou* and the rest of the priests, *thy fellows, who sit before thee* as learners." They are set *for signs*, for types and figures of Christ's priesthood. They are *men of wonder*; they are amazed to think how happily their condition is altered.

II. The promise itself consists of several parts designed for the encouragement of Joshua and his friends in that great work of building the temple. 1. The Messiah shall come: *Behold, I will bring forth my servant the branch.* He is the branch; so he was called; Isa. iv. 2, *The branch of the Lord.* Isa. xi. 1, *A branch out of the roots of Jesse.* His beginning was small, as a tender branch, but in time he should become a great tree, Isa. liii. 2, the branch from which all our fruit must be gathered. He is *the stone laid before Joshua,* alluding to the foundation, or chief corner-stone, of the temple, which probably was laid, with great solemnity, in the presence of Joshua. Christ is not only the branch, which is the beginning of a tree, but the foundation, which is the beginning of a building. *Seven eyes shall be upon him.* The eye of his Father was upon him, to protect him, especially in his sufferings. The eyes of all the prophets and Old Testament saints were upon this one stone. The eyes of all believers are upon him; they look unto him and are saved. *I will engrave the graving thereof, saith the Lord of hosts.* This stone the builders refused, as rough and unsightly; but God undertakes to smooth and polish it and to carve it so that it shall be the *head stone of the corner.* This stone is a *precious stone,* though laid for a *foundation;* and the *graving* of it seems to allude to the precious stones in the breastplate of the high priest, Exod. xxviii. 21, 22. By him sin shall be taken away, both the guilt and the dominion of it: *I will remove the iniquity of that land in one day.* When the high priest had the names of Israel engraven on the precious stones he was adorned with he is said to *bear the iniquity of the holy things* (Exod. xxviii. 38). He bore the iniquity of the land, as a type of Christ; but he could not remove it; the doing of that was reserved for Christ, that blessed *Lamb of God, that takes away the sin of the world.* Some make the engravings wherewith God engraved him to signify the wounds and stripes which were given to his blessed body, which he underwent for our *transgression,* and *by which we are healed.* The effect of all this shall be (*v.* 10): *In that day you shall call every man his neighbour under the vine and fig tree.* When iniquity is taken away we repose in tranquillity and are quiet from the fear of evil. We sit down under Christ's shadow with delight, and by it are sheltered from the scorching heat of the curse of the law.

CHAPTER 4

Another vision, which, as it was explained to the prophet, had much in it for the encouragement of the people of God in their present straits. The scope of the vision is to show that God would, by his own power, perfect the work. I. The awakening of the prophet to observe the vision, ver. 1. II. The vision itself, of a candlestick with seven lamps, which were supplied with oil, and kept burning, from two olive-trees that grew by it, one on either side, ver. 2, 3. III. The general encouragement hereby to be given to the builders of the temple to go on in that good work, ver. 4–10. IV. The particular explication of the vision, ver. 11–14.

Verses 1–10

I. The prophet prepared to receive the discovery: *The angel that talked with him came and waked him, v.* 1.

II. The discovery was made to him when he was prepared. He saw a *golden candlestick.* The church is a candlestick for the enlightening of this dark world and the holding of the light of divine revelation to it. The candle is God's; the church is but the candlestick. This golden candlestick had *seven lamps* branching out from it, so many sockets, in each of which was a burning and shining light. The Jewish church was but one, but now, under the gospel, Christ is the centre of unity, and not Jerusalem, or any place. This candlestick had one *bowl,* on the top, into which oil was continually dropping, and from it, by seven pipes, it was diffused to the seven lamps, so that, without any further care, they received oil as fast as they wasted it. They never wanted, nor were ever glutted, and so kept always burning clear. And the

bowl too was continually supplied: without any man; for (*v.* 3) he saw *two olive-trees,* one on each side the candlestick, that of their own accord poured oil continually into the bowl, which by two larger pipes (*v.* 12) dispersed the oil to smaller ones and so to the lamps; so that nobody needed to attend this candlestick, which is to show that God easily can, and often does, accomplish his gracious purposes concerning his church, without the aid of man.

III. The enquiry which the prophet made concerning the meaning of this (*v.* 4): *I answered and spoke to the angel,* saying, *What are these, my lord?* He saw what these *were,* but asked what they *signified.* The angel answered him with a question, *Knowest thou not what these be?* He knew there was a golden candlestick in the tabernacle, which it was the priests' constant business to supply with oil. When therefore he saw such a candlestick, with lamps always kept burning, and yet no priests to attend it, he might discern the meaning of this to be that though God had set up the priesthood again, yet he could carry on his work for his people without them.

IV. The general intention of this vision is to assure the prophet that this work of building the temple should, by Providence, and divine grace, be brought to a happy issue, though the enemies of it were many and the friends few. This vision was to illustrate a word to Zerubbabel, to encourage him to go on with the building of the temple. Let him know that he is a worker together with God, and that it is a work which God will own and crown.

1. God will carry on this work, not by external force, but by internal influences upon the minds of men. He will do it, *not by* human *might or power,* but *by his own Spirit.* It was by the *Spirit of the Lord of hosts* that the people were excited and animated to build the temple; and *therefore* they are said to be *helped by the prophets of God,* because they, as the Spirit's mouth, spoke to their hearts, Ezra v. 2. It was by the same Spirit that the heart of Darius was inclined to favour that good work and that the enemies of it were infatuated so that they could not hinder it. When instruments fail, let us therefore leave it to God to do his work himself by his own Spirit.

2. All the difficulties and oppositions that lie in the way shall be removed, even those that seem insuperable (*v.* 7): *Who art thou, O great mountain? Before Zerubbabel thou shalt become a plain.* The enemies of the Jews are proud and hard as great mountains; but, when God has work to do, the mountains dwindle into mole-hills. Faith will remove mountains and make them plains. Christ is our Zerubbabel; nothing is too hard for his grace to do.

3. The same hand that has begun this good work will perform it: *He shall bring forth the head-stone* (*v.* 7); and again (*v.* 9), *The hands of Zerubbabel have laid the foundation of this house,* and *his hands shall also finish it;* herein he is a type of Christ, who is both the *author* and the *finisher of our faith.* When the work is finished it must be thankfully acknowledged that it was not by any power of our own, but that it was grace that did it—God's goodwill towards us and his good work in us and for us.

4. This shall be a full ratification of the prophecies which went before concerning the Jews' return. When the temple is finished then *thou shalt know that the Lord of hosts has sent me unto you.*

5. This shall effectually silence those that looked with contempt upon the beginning of this work, *v.* 10. In God's work the day of small things is not to be despised. A grain of mustard-seed may become a great tree.

6. Those that despaired of the finishing of the work shall rejoice when they *see the plummet in the hand of Zerubbabel.*

7. This shall magnify God's providence, which is always employed for the good of his church. Zerubbabel does his part, but it is *with those seven, those seven eyes of the Lord* which we read of *ch.* iii. 9. He could do nothing if the gracious providence of God did not go before him and go along with him in it. Those *seven eyes that run through the earth* are all *upon the stone* that Zerubbabel is laying straight with his plummet. And those that have the plummet in their hand must have a constant regard to divine Providence, and act in dependence upon its guidance.

Verses 11–14

Enough is said to Zechariah to encourage him, and to enable him to encourage others, and that was the principal intention of the vision he saw; but still he is inquisitive about the particulars.

I. His enquiry. He understood the meaning of the candlestick with its lamps: It is Jerusalem, it is the temple, and their salvation that is to *go forth as a lamp that burns;* but he wants to know what are these *two olive-trees* (*v.* 11), these *two olive-branches? v.* 12. He took notice not only that the two olive-trees grew, one *on the right side and the other on the left side of the candlestick* (so nigh, so ready, is divine grace to the church), but that the *two olive-branches*, from which in particular the candlestick did receive of *the root and fatness of the olive*, did empty the *golden oil out of themselves through the two golden pipes*, into the *golden bowl* on the head of the candlestick. Our Lord Jesus emptied himself, to fill us; his precious blood is the golden oil in which we are supplied with all we need.

II. Now again the angel obliged him to his own ignorance, before he informed him (*v.* 13): "*Knowest thou not what these are?* If thou knowest the church to be the candlestick, canst thou think the olive-trees, that supply it with oil, to be any other than the grace of God?" 1. If by the candlestick we understand the visible church, particularly that of the Jews at that time, for whose comfort it was primarily intended, these *sons of oil*, that *stand before the Lord of the whole earth*, are the two great ordinances and offices of the magistracy and ministry, at that time lodged in the hands of those two great and good men Zerubbabel and Joshua. Kings and priests were anointed with oil. Their wisdom, courage, and zeal, were continually emptying themselves into the golden bowl, to keep the lamps burning. 2. If by the candlestick we understand the church of the first-born, of true believers, these sons of oil may be meant of Christ and the Spirit, the Redeemer and the Comforter. From Christ, the *olive tree*, by the *Spirit, the olive branch*, all the golden oil of grace is communicated to believers, which keeps their lamps burning.

CHAPTER 5

God's prophets are not only his ambassadors, to treat of peace with the sons of peace, but heralds, to proclaim war against those that delight in war, and persist in their rebellion. In this chapter we have two visions, by which "the wrath of God is revealed against all ungodliness and unrighteousness of men". God will do great and kind things for his people; but "let the sinners in Zion be afraid"; for, I. God will reckon severely with those particular persons that are wicked and profane, and that hated to be reformed in these times of reformation; while God is showing kindness to the body of the nation, they and their families shall lie under the curse, which the prophet sees in a flying roll, ver. 1–4. II. If the body of the nation hereafter degenerate, it shall be carried off with a swift destruction, represented by a talent of lead upon the mouth of an ephah, carried upon the wing I know not where, ver. 5–11.

Verses 1–4

We do not find that the prophet now needed to be awakened, as he did *ch.* iv. 1.

I. He looked up into the air, and *behold a flying roll*. The angel asks him *what he sees?* And he gives him this account of it: *I see a flying roll*, and as near as he can guess by his eye it is *twenty cubits long* (that is ten yards) and *ten cubits broad*, that is five yards. The scriptures of the Old Testament and the New are *rolls*, in which God has *written to us the great things of his law* and gospel. Christ is the Master of the rolls. They are *flying* rolls. God's word *runs very swiftly*, Ps. cxlvii. 15.

II. This flying roll is a *curse*; it contains a declaration of the righteous wrath of God against those who by swearing affront God's majesty or by stealing invade their neighbours' property. This curse *goes forth over the face of the whole earth*, not only of the land of Israel. All mankind are liable to the judgment of God. How welcome then the tidings of a Saviour who came to *redeem us from the curse of the law* by being himself *made a curse for us*, and, like the prophet, *eating this roll*! The world is full of sin: so was the Jewish church at this time. But two sorts of sinners are here specified: (1) Thieves; it is *for everyone that steals*, especially that converts to his own use what was devoted to God, Mal. iii. 8; Neh. xiii. 10. Sacrilege is, without doubt, the worst kind of thievery. (2) Swearers. Sinners of the former class offend against the second table, these against the first. He that swears profanely shall not be held guiltless, much less he that swears falsely (*v.* 4). He that pronounces the sentence will take care to see it executed. Who can put by or resist the curse which a God of almighty power brings forth? The effect is very dreadful: *Everyone that steals shall be cut off*, not corrected, but cut off. He shall be cut off *as on this side* (cut off from this place, that is, from Jerusalem). God will not spare the sinners he finds among his own people, nor shall the holy city be a protection to the unholy. *It shall enter into the house of the thief and of him that swears*. God's curse cannot be kept out by bars or locks. Unless he repent and reform, there is no way to throw it out. It shall *consume it with the timber thereof, and the stones thereof*. Sin is the ruin of houses and families, especially the sins of injury and perjury.

Verses 5–11

The foregoing vision was very plain, but in this are things *dark and hard to be understood*. Some think that it is to foretell the final destruction of the Jewish nation and the dispersion of the Jews, when, by crucifying Christ and persecuting his gospel, they should have filled up the measure of their iniquities.

The prophet was told to turn and he should see greater desolations, *v.* 5. *What is this that goeth forth?* The prophet now, through either the distance or the dimness of his sight, could not well tell what it was, *v.* 6. And the angel tells him both what it is and what it means.

I. He sees an *ephah*, a measure wherewith they measured corn. And *this is their resemblance*, the resemblance of the Jewish nation *over all the earth*, wherever they are now dispersed. And some think that the mentioning of an ephah, which is used in buying and selling, intimates that fraud, and extortion in commerce, were sins abounding among them.

II. He sees a *woman sitting in the midst of the ephah*, representing the sinful church and nation of the Jews in their latter and degenerate age. He that weighs the hills in a balance measures nations and churches as in an ephah; so exact is he in his judicial dealings with them. God's people are called *the corn of his floor*, Isa. xxi. 10. And here he puts this corn into the bushel. The angel says of the woman in the ephah, *This is wickedness;* it is a wicked nation, else God would not have rejected it thus; it is as wicked as *wickedness* itself.

III. He sees the woman thrust down into the ephah, and a *talent*, or large weight, *of lead*, cast upon the *mouth* of it, by which she is made a prisoner in the *ephah*. This is designed to show that the wrath of God against impenitent sinners is what they cannot escape. It is insupportable. Guilt is upon the sinner as a talent of lead.

IV. He sees the ephah, with the woman in it, carried away into some far country. The instruments employed to do it were *two women*, who had *wings like* those *of a stork*, and, to make them fly the more swiftly, they had the *wind in their wings*, denoting the expedition with which the Romans destroyed the Jewish nation. They *lifted it up between the earth and the heaven*, as unworthy of either and abandoned by both. When the prophet enquired whither they carried their prisoner (*v.* 10) he was told that they designed *to build it a house in the land of Shinar*. This intimates that the punishment of the Jews should be a final dispersion; they should be forced to dwell in far countries. There the *ephah* shall be *established, and set upon her own base*. Their calamity shall continue from generation to generation. Their iniquity shall continue too, and their hearts shall be hardened in it.

CHAPTER 6

The two kingdoms of providence and grace are what we are all interested in. All our temporal affairs being in a necessary subjection to divine Providence, and all our spiritual and eternal concerns in a necessary dependence upon divine grace; and these two are represented to us in this chapter—the former by a vision, the latter by a type. Here is, I. God, as King of nations, in the vision of the four chariots, ver. 1–8. II. God, as King of saints, ruling the church by the mediation of Christ, in the figure of Joshua the high priest, ver. 9–15.

Verses 1–8

The prophet *turned and lifted up his eyes and looked*. This was the seventh vision he had had. The sight that the prophet had of *four chariots* drawn by horses of divers colours, *v.* 1–5. Some by the *four chariots* understand the four monarchies; and then they read (*v.* 5), *These are the four winds of the heavens*, and suppose that therein reference is had to Dan. vii. 2. The Babylonian monarchy, they think, is here represented by the *red horses*. The second chariot with the *black horses* is the Persian monarchy, which went forth northward against the Babylonians, and *quieted God's Spirit in the north country*, by executing his judgments on Babylon and freeing the Jews from their captivity. The *white*, the Grecians, go *forth after them* in the north, for they overthrow the Persians. The *grizzled*, the Romans, who conquered the Grecian empire, are said to *go forth towards the south country*, because Egypt, which lay southward was subdued by the Romans. The *bay horses* had been with the *grizzled*, but afterwards went forth by themselves; and by these they understand the Goths and Vandals.

But I incline rather to understand this vision more generally to represent the administration of the kingdom of Providence in the government of this lower world. The *angels* are often called the *chariots of God*, as Ps. lxviii. 17. The various providences of God concerning nations and churches are represented by the different colours of horses, Rev. vi. 2, 4, 5, 8. And so here the counsels and decrees of God are the spring of all events, immovable, as *mountains of brass*. The *chariots* came *from between the two mountains*; for God *performs the thing that is appointed for us*. We could as soon grasp the mountains in our arms as comprehend the divine counsels in our finite understandings, and as soon remove *mountains of brass* as alter any of God's purposes. The works of Providence are as chariots, in which he rides as a prince. His providences

move swiftly as chariots, directed by his infinite wisdom as chariots by their drivers. The holy angels are the ministers of God's providence, and are employed by him, as *the armies of heaven*. They are the *chariots* or the horses that draw the chariots, great in power and might, to carry one prophet to heaven and guard another on earth. The *horses* in the *first chariot* were *red*, signifying war and bloodshed. Those in the *second chariot* were *black*, signifying the dismal melancholy consequences of war. Those in the *third chariot* were *white*, signifying the return of comfort, and peace, and prosperity, after these dark and dismal times. Those in the *fourth chariot* were of a mixed colour, *grizzled* and *bay*; signifying events interwoven, a day of prosperity and a day of adversity set *the one over against the other*. *These are the four spirits of heaven, the four winds* (so some), which seem to blow as they list, from the various points of the compass. Or, rather, These are *the angels* that *go forth from standing before the Lord of all the earth*, to behold his glory in the upper world, which is their blessedness, and to serve his glory in this lower world, which is their business. There is an admirable beauty in Providence, and one event serves for a balance to another (*v.* 6): *The black horses went forth*, carrying with them very dark and melancholy events, but presently *the white went forth after them*, carrying joy to those that mourned. Such are God's dealings with his church and people: if the black horses go forth, the white ones presently go after them; for *as affliction abounds consolation much more abounds*. The *grizzled* and *bay horses* were both in the *fourth chariot* (*v.* 3), and though they went forth, at first, towards the *south country*, yet afterwards they *sought to walk to and fro through the earth*, *v.* 7. If we go to and fro through the earth, we shall find the events of Providence neither all black nor all white, but ash-coloured, or grey, mixed of black and white. Such is the world we live in. God is well-pleased with all the operations of his providence (*v.* 8): *These have quieted my spirit*, these *black horses* which denote extraordinary judgments, and the *white* ones which denote extraordinary deliverances, both which *went towards the north country*. These have *quieted my spirit in the north-country*, which had of late been the most remarkable scene of action with reference to the church.

Verses 9–15

God did not only at *sundry times*, but *in divers manners*, speak in time past by the prophets to his church. In the former part of this chapter he spoke by a vision, which only the prophet himself saw; here, in this latter part, he speaks by a sign, or type, which many saw, and which was a prediction of the Messiah as the priest and king of his church.

I. The *coronation of Joshua* the high priest, *v.* 10, 11. There are two types of Christ in the Old Testament—Joshua the chief captain, a type of Christ the captain of our salvation, and Joshua the chief priest, a type of Christ the high priest of our profession, and both in their day saviours and leaders into Canaan. Joshua was far from being ambitious of a crown, and the people of having a crowned head over them; but the prophet is ordered to crown Joshua as if he had been a king. And Zerubbabel's prudence and piety kept this from being any affront to him. Jews from Babylon brought an offering to the house of God, *some of the captivity* that *came from Babylon* on a visit to Jerusalem. Perhaps they came hearing that the building of the temple went on slowly for want of money, with an offering of gold and silver for the service of the house of God. They thought to bring their present to the priest, but God has a prophet ready to receive them and it, which would be an encouragement to them, who, in their captivity, had so often complained, *We see not our signs, there is no more any prophet.* He was to meet them in the house of Josiah, the son of Zephaniah, who probably kept the treasures of the temple. Crowns are to be *made*, and *put upon the head of Joshua, v.* 11. It is supposed that there were two crowns provided, one of silver and the other of gold; the former (as some think) denoting his priestly dignity, the latter his kingly dignity. The sun shines as gold, when he *goes forth in his strength*; and the beams of the moon, when she *walks in brightness*, we call *silver beams.* Those that worshipped the sun and moon shall now fall down before the golden and silver crowns of the Redeemer, before whom the sun shall be ashamed and the moon confounded.

II. "What is the meaning of Joshua's being crowned thus?" The prophet is ready to tell them.

1. God will, in the fulness of time, raise up a great high priest, like Joshua. Joshua is but the figure of one that is to come, a faint shadow of him (*v.* 12): *Speak unto him* in the name of *the Lord of hosts*, that *the man whose name is The BRANCH* shall *grow up out of his place*, out of the city of David. Though the family be a root in a dry ground, yet this branch shall spring out of it, as when the sun returns, the flowers spring out of the roots, in which they lay buried out of sight and out of mind.

2. Joshua was active in building the temple, so *the man, the branch*, shall be the sole builder of the spiritual temple, the gospel-church. He *shall build the temple of the Lord.*

3. Christ shall bear the glory. Glory is a burden, but not too heavy for him to bear who upholds all things. The cross was his glory, and he bore that; so was the crown *an exceeding weight of glory*, and he bears that. That which he shall undertake, shall be indeed the *glory of Israel.* He shall *lift up the glory* (so it may be read); he shall raise it out of the dust.

4. He shall have a throne, and be both priest and king upon his throne. A throne denotes both dignity and dominion, an exalted honour with an extensive power. Christ, as a priest, ever lives to make intercession for us; but he does it sitting at his Father's right hand, as one having authority, Heb. viii. 1. Christ, who is ordained to offer sacrifices for us, is authorized to give law to us. He will not save us unless we be willing that he should govern us. God has prepared him a throne *in the heavens*; and, if we would have any benefit by that, we must prepare him a throne in our hearts. This king shall be a *priest upon his throne.* With the majesty and power of a king, he shall have the tenderness and simplicity of a priest.

5. *The counsel of peace shall be between them both.* That is, Between *Jehovah* and the *man the branch*, between the Father and the Son; concerning the peace to be made between God and man, by the mediation of Christ. Some think it alludes to the former government of the Jews' state, wherein the king and priest, separate officers, did take counsel one with another, for the maintenance of peace and prosperity in church and state, as did Zerubbabel and Joshua now.

6. There shall be a happy coalition between Jews and Gentiles in the gospel-church, and they shall both meet in Christ, the priest upon his throne, as the centre of their unity (*v.* 15): *Those that are far off shall come and build in the temple of the Lord.*

7. This will be confirmation of the truth of God's word: *You shall know that the Lord of hosts has sent me unto you.* That promise, that those that were afar off should assist them in *building the temple of the Lord*, was *a sign.* This should be fulfilled now very speedily; see Ezra vi. 13, 14. *"For this shall come to pass if you will diligently obey the voice of the Lord your God.* You shall have the help of foreigners in

building the temple, if you will but set about it in good earnest yourselves."

III. *The crowns* that were used were not given to Joshua, but must be *kept for a memorial in the temple of the Lord, v.* 14. Either they were laid up in the temple treasury or (as the Jews' tradition is) they were hung up in the windows of the temple, in the view of all for evidence of the promise of the Messiah.

CHAPTER 7

The prophet sees no more such signs as he had seen, but still "the word of the Lord came to him". I. A case of conscience proposed to the prophet by the children of the captivity concerning fasting, ver. 1-3. II. The answer was given by piece-meal, and, it should seem, at several times, for here are four distinct discourses which have all of them reference to this case, ver. 4-8, and ch. viii. 1, 18. In this chapter, 1. The prophet sharply reproves them for the mismanagements of their fasts, ver. 4-7. 2. He exhorts them to reform their lives, which would be the best way of fasting, ver. 8-14. And then in the next chapter, having searched the wound, he binds it up, and heals it, with gracious assurances of mercy which would turn their fasts into feasts.

Verses 1-7

I. Some persons were sent to enquire of the priests and prophets whether they should continue to observe their yearly fasts, particularly that in the fifth month, as they had done. It is uncertain whether the case was put by those that yet remained in Babylon, or by those that had returned, called the *people of the land, v.* 5. They were *Sherezer* and *Regemmelech*, persons of some rank and figure, for they came *with their men.* They were sent perhaps not with *gold and silver* (as those, *ch.* vi. 10, 11), but upon the two great errands which should bring us all to the house of God, (1) To intercede with God for his mercy. They were sent to *pray before the Lord*, and to *offer sacrifice.* The Jews, in captivity, prayed towards the temple (as appears Dan. vi. 10); but now that it was to be rebuilt they sent their representatives to pray in it. (2) To enquire of God concerning his mind. They spoke *to the priests that were in the house of the Lord and to the prophets.* The priests and the prophets were not jealous one of another, nor had any difference among themselves; let not the people then make differences between them, but thank God they had both. They asked (*v.* 3): *Should I weep in the fifth month, separating myself, as I have done these so many years.* They kept up solemn stated fasts for humiliation and prayer. They mention only one, that of the fifth month; but it appears, *ch.* viii. 19, that they observed four anniversary fasts, one in the fourth month (*June* 17), in remembrance of the breaking up of the wall of Jerusalem (Jer. lii. 6), another in the fifth month (*July* 4), in remembrance of the burning of the temple (Jer. lii. 12, 13), another in the seventh month (*September* 3), in remembrance of the killing of Gedaliah, and another in the tenth month (*December* 10), in remembrance of the beginning of the siege of Jerusalem, 2 Kings xxv. 1. Their present doubt was whether they should continue these fasts or no. The case is put as by a single person: *Should I weep?* A religious fast must be solemnized, not only by abstinence but by a godly sorrow for sin, here expressed by weeping. "Should I still keep such *days to afflict the soul* as *I have done these so many years*?" It is said (*v.* 5) to be seventy years. Something is to be said for the continuance of these fasts. They were still under the tokens of God's displeasure; and it is unwise for the patient to break off his course of physic while he is sensible of remains of his distemper. But there is something to be said for the letting fall of these fasts. God had returned in mercy to them. Now that the bridegroom has returned, why should the *children of the bride-chamber fast?* And as to the fast of the fifth month, that, being kept in remembrance of the burning of the temple, might seem to be superseded because the temple was now in a fair way to be rebuilt.

II. Though the question looked plausible enough, those who proposed it were not conscientious in it, for they were more concerned about the ceremony than about the substance. And therefore the first answer to their enquiry is a very sharp reproof of their hypocrisy. *Did you at all fast unto me, even to me?* He appeals to their own consciences. Was it *to me, even to me?* The repetition intimates what a great deal of stress is laid upon this as the main matter. To fast, and not fast to God, was to mock him and provoke him. If the solemnities of our fasting, though frequent, long, and severe, do not serve to quicken prayer, and to alter the temper of our minds and the course of our lives for the better, God will not accept them as performed to him. They had the same eye to themselves in their fasting that they had in their eating and drinking (*v.* 6). The thing they should have done was left undone (*v.* 7): "*Should you not hear the words which the Lord has cried by the former prophets?* You must do that which you have not yet done; you must repent of your sins and reform your lives. This is what we now call you to, and it is the same that the former prophets called your fathers to." He puts them in mind of the former flourishing state of their country: Jerusalem *was* then *inhabited and in prosperity,* that is now desolate and in distress. But then God *by the prophets cried* to them to amend their ways or else their prosperity would soon be at an end. "Now," says the prophet, "you should have taken notice of that, and, if you do not, all your fasting and weeping signify nothing."

Verses 8–14

Warning to these hypocritical enquirers, who continued their sins when they asked with great preciseness whether they should continue their fasts.

I. This prophet here repeats what former prophets preached to their fathers (*v.* 9, 10). The duties required are not keeping fasts and offering sacrifices, but *doing justly* and *loving mercy.* Magistrates must administer justice impartially. Neighbours must have a tender concern for one another. The infirmities of others, as well as their calamities, are to be looked upon with compassion. *Let none of you imagine evil against his brother in your heart.*

II. He describes the wilfulness and disobedience of their fathers (*v.* 11, 12). If they did hear what was said to them, and seemed inclined at first to comply with it, yet like a bullock unaccustomed to the yoke, *they pulled away the shoulder,* and would not submit to the *easy yoke and light burden* of God's commandments. *They gave a withdrawing shoulder* (so the word is); they seemed to lay their shoulder to the work, but they presently withdrew it again, as those Jer. xxxiv. 10, 11. *They made their hearts as an adamant-stone,* as a *diamond,* the hardest of stones to be wrought upon, or as a *flint.* Nothing is so hard, so unmalleable as the heart of a presumptuous sinner. The reason why men are not good is because they will not be so; they will not consider, will not comply; and therefore God says, *if thou scornest, thou alone shalt bear it.*

III. He shows the fatal consequences to their fathers: *Therefore came great wrath from the Lord of hosts.* As they had turned a deaf ear to God's word, so God turned a deaf ear to their prayers, *v.* 13. As they flew from their allegiance to God, so God dissipated them and threw them about as chaff before a whirlwind: *He scattered them among all the nations whom they knew not, v.* 14. As they violated all the laws of their land, so God took away all the glories of it: *Their land was desolate after them, and no man passed through or returned.* It was not so much the Chaldeans that did it. No; they did it themselves.

Chapter 8

The prophet here is ordered to change his voice, and to speak by way of encouragement to the willing and obedient. In these messages (ver. 1) God promises that Jerusalem shall be restored, reformed (ver. 2–8), that the country shall be rich, their reputation retrieved, and their state the reverse of what it had been for many years past (ver. 9–15); he then exhorts them to reform what was amiss, that they might be ready for these favours designed, ver. 16, 17. In ver. 18 he promises that their fasts should be superseded by the return of mercy (ver. 19), and that they should be strengthened, by the accession of foreigners to them, ver. 20–23.

Verses 1–8

The prophet designed to bring them to repentance not to drive them to despair, so here sets before them the great things God had in store for them.

I. God will appear for Jerusalem, and will be revenged on Zion's enemies (*v.* 2). The great wrath that was against her (*ch.* vii. 12) now turns against her adversaries. "*I have returned to Zion,* after I had seemed so long to stand at a distance, and I will again *dwell in the midst of Jerusalem* as formerly." This secures to them the tokens of his presence in his ordinances and in his providences.

II. There shall be a wonderful reformation in Jerusalem, and religion shall flourish there. *Jerusalem,* that has dealt treacherously both with God and man, shall become so famous for fidelity and honesty that it *shall be called* and known by the name of *a city of truth,* and the inhabitants of it shall be called *children that will not lie.*

III. There shall be in Jerusalem a great increase of people, and all the marks of a profound tranquillity. *In the streets of Jerusalem,* that had been filled with the bodies of the slain, shall now dwell *old men* and *old women,* who have not been cut off by untimely deaths, but have the even thread of their days spun out to a full length; they shall go to their grave in a full age, as a *shock of corn in his season.* The hoary head, as it is a crown of glory to those that wear it, so it is to the places where they live. It is a graceful thing to a city to see abundance of old people in it; it is a sign, not only of the healthfulness of the air, but of the prevalence of virtue and the banishment of vices, a sign, not only that the climate is temperate, but that the people are so. You may look with as much pleasure upon the generation that is rising up in their room (*v.* 5): *The streets of the city shall be full of boys and girls playing in the streets.* Their children shall be healthful, and strong, shall be hearty and cheerful; it is their pleasant playing age; let us not grudge it to them; much good may it do them and no harm. They shall not be terrified with the alarms of war, but enjoy a perfect security.

IV. The scattered Israelites shall be brought together again from all parts whither they were dispersed (*v.* 7): "*I will save my people from the east country, and from the west;* I will save them from being lost, or losing themselves, in Babylon, or in Egypt, or in any other country whither they were driven."

V. God would renew his covenant with them: *They shall be my people and I will be their God.* That is the foundation and crown of all these promises, and is inclusive of all happiness. God will never leave nor forsake them in a way of mercy, as he has promised them; and they shall never leave nor forsake him in a way of duty, as they have promised him. These promises were fulfilled in the flourishing state of the Jewish church, between the captivity and Christ's time; they were to have a further and a fuller accomplishment in the gospel-church, but the fullest accomplishment of all will be in the future state.

All doubts of God's people are silenced with that question (*v.* 6): "*If it be marvellous in the eyes of this people, should it be marvellous in my eyes?* If it seem unlikely to you that ever Jerusalem should be thus repaired, should be thus replenished, is it therefore impossible with God?"

Verses 9–17

God, by the prophet, here gives further assurances of the mercy he had in store for Judah and Jerusalem. These verses contain strong encouragements.

I. These encouragements belong—to those who, in obedience to the call of God by his prophets, applied in good earnest to the building of the temple (*v.* 9). Those, and those only, that are employed for God, may expect to be encouraged by him; those who lay their hands to the plough of duty shall have them strengthened with the promises of mercy.

II. The discouragements they had hitherto laboured under, *v.* 10, are mentioned as a foil to the blessings God was now about to bestow upon them. *Before these days* of reformation began *there was no hire for man, nor any hire for beasts.* The fruits of the earth were thin and poor. Merchants had no goods to export, so that they needed not to hire either men or beasts. There was no such thing as friendship or good neighbourship among them: *I set all men everyone against his neighbour.* In this there was a great deal of sin, for these wars and fightings came from men's lust.

III. "Thus and thus you have been harassed and afflicted, but now God will change his way towards you, *v.* 11. Now that you return to your duty the ebbing tide shall flow again." They shall have great plenty and abundance of all good things (*v.* 12). The *heavens shall give their dew,* without which the earth would not yield her increase, which is a constant intimation to us of the beneficence of the God of heaven to men on earth and of their dependence on him. They shall recover their credit among their neighbours (*v.* 13). The blessed of the Lord are the blessing of the land, and should be so accounted. God himself will determine to do them good, *v.* 14, 15.

IV. Let them take comfort in these promises: *Fear you not* (*v.* 15); *let your hands be strong* (*v.* 9 and *v.* 13). Let them do the duty which those promises call for from them, *v.* 16, 17. "Leave it to God to perform for you what he has promised, in his own way and time, but upon condition that you make conscience of your duty. *These are the things then that you shall do.* You must never tell a lie, but *Speak you every man the truth to his neighbour. Execute the judgment of truth and peace in your gates.* Let the judges that sit in the gates have regard both to truth and to peace. No man must bear malice against his neighbour. Great reverence must be had for an oath, and conscience made of it." The things there forbidden are all of them found among the *seven things which the Lord hates,* Prov. vi. 16–19.

Verses 18–23

These verses contain two precious promises, for the further encouragement of those Jews that were building the temple.

I. Their fasts should be converted into thanksgiving days, *v.* 19. Joyous times will come to the church after troublous times; if weeping endure for more than a night, and joy come not next morning, yet the morning will come that will introduce it at length. Let the truths of God rule in your heads, and let the peace of God rule in your hearts.

II. A great accession should be made to the church by the conversion of many foreigners, *v.* 20–23. This was fulfilled in part when, in the latter times of the Jewish church, there were many proselytes from countries nearby or remote, who came yearly to worship at Jerusalem, which added to the grandeur and wealth of that city, making it considerable before our Saviour's time, though now it was but just peeping out of its ruins. But it would be accomplished much more fully in the conversion of the Gentiles to the faith of Christ, and incorporating them with the believing Jews in one body, under Christ the head (Rom. xvi. 26). The inhabitants of many cities shall embrace the gospel of Christ; *yea, many people and strong nations* (*v.* 22), some of *all languages, v.* 23. They shall come *to pray before the Lord and to seek the Lord of hosts* (*v.* 21). Converts to God and members of the church are such as *seek the Lord of hosts,* such as enquire for *God their Maker,* and are sincerely devoted to his honour and glory. They are such as *pray before the Lord.* They shall be zealous in exciting one another to it (*v.* 21): *The inhabitants of one city shall go to another,* and they shall say, *Let us go speedily to pray before the Lord; I will go also.* Those who are brought into an acquaintance with Christ themselves should do all they can to bring others; thus Andrew invited Peter to Christ and Philip invited Nathanael. True grace hates monopolies. As iron sharpens iron, so may good men sharpen the countenances and spirits one of another in that which is good. They shall join themselves to the church, not for the church's sake, but for his sake who dwells in it (*v.* 23). This intimates the great honour they have for a Jew, as one of the chosen people of God. *We will go with you, for we have heard that God is with you.*

CHAPTER 9

"The burden of the word of the Lord." I. A prophecy against the Jews' unrighteous neighbours—the Syrians, Tyrians, Philistines, and others (ver. 1–6), with an intimation of mercy to some of them, in their conversion (ver. 7), and a promise of mercy to God's people, in their protection, ver. 8. II. A prophecy of their righteous King, the Messiah, and his coming (ver. 9), and of his kingdom, ver. 10. III. An account of the obligation the Jews lay under to Christ for their deliverance out of captivity, ver. 11, 12. IV. A prophecy of the victories God would grant to the Jews over their enemies, as typical of our great deliverance by Christ, ver. 13–15. V. A promise of great plenty and joy, and honour, which God had for his people (ver. 16, 17).

Verses 1–8

I. The Syrians had been bad neighbours to Israel. The word of the Lord shall be a *burden in the land of Hadrach,* that is, of *Syria.* Damascus is the metropolis of that kingdom, and the judgments here threatened shall lie upon it. And the reason of this burden's resting on Damascus is because *the eyes of man, as of all the tribes of Israel* (or rather, *even of all the tribes of Israel*), are *towards the Lord,* because the people of God by faith and prayer look up to him for succour and relief against their enemies. When St. Paul was converted at Damascus, and preached there, and disputed with the Jews, then the word of the Lord might be said to rest there, and then *the eyes of men,* of other men besides *the tribes of Israel,* began to be *towards the Lord;* see Acts ix. 22.

II. Tyre and Zidon come next to be called to account as in other prophecies, *v.* 2–4. Tyrus flourishing, thinking herself very safe, is ready to set God's judgments at defiance. She is *very wise.* It is spoken ironically; she thinks herself very wise! But there is no *wisdom* nor *counsel against the Lord;* nay, it is his honour to take the wise in their own craftiness. *Tyrus did build herself a stronghold,* which she thought could never be brought down nor got over. By her vast trade she has *heaped up silver as the dust,* as common as heaps of sand. Tyre made *fine gold* to be as *the mire of the streets.* Her wisdom, and wealth, and strength, shall not be able to secure her (*v.* 4): *The Lord will cast her out* of that stronghold wherein she has fortified herself, will *make her poor.* God will *smite her power in the sea;* her being surrounded by the water shall not secure her, but *she shall be devoured with fire,* and burnt down to the ground.

III. God next contends with the Philistines, with their great cities that bordered southward upon Israel. Now *Ashkelon shall see* the ruin of her friends and allies, and shall *fear*; *Gaza also shall see it, and be very sorrowful, and Ekron.* What will become of their house when their neighbour's is on fire? They shall themselves be ruined and wasted. *The king shall perish from Gaza. Ashkelon shall not be inhabited.* Foreigners shall take possession of their land (v. 6): *A bastard shall dwell in Ashdod.* And thus God will *cut off the pride of the Philistines.* This prophecy of the destruction of the Philistines, and of Damascus, and Tyre, was accomplished, not long after this, by Alexander the Great, who ravaged all these countries, took the cities, and planted colonies in them. Some understand v. 7 as a promise that God would take away the sins of these nations—*their blood* and *their abominations,* their cruelties and their idolatries. He would preserve a remnant even of these nations, that should be monuments of his mercy and grace. Their birth shall be no bar to their acceptance with God, but a Philistine shall be as acceptable to God, upon gospel-terms, as one of Judah, and a man of Ekron shall be as a Jebusite, or a man of Jerusalem.

IV. In all this God intends mercy for Israel, and it is in kindness to them that God will deal thus with the neighbouring nations. Thus some understand the seventh verse. God would deliver his people from their bloody adversaries, when they were just ready to devour them and make a prey of them: I will *take away his blood* (that is, the blood of Israel) out of the mouth of the Philistines and *from between their teeth* (Amos iii. 12). And *he that remains* (that is, the remnant of Israel) *shall be for our God,* shall be taken into his favour, shall own him and be owned by him, and *he shall be as a governor in Judah.* However it is plainly the sense of v. 8 that God will take his people under his special protection, and *therefore* will weaken their neighbours, that it may not be in their power to do them a mischief: *I will encamp about my house because of the army.* When the times are perilous, when armies are marching, and all bearing ill-will to Zion, then Providence will as it were double its guards upon the church of God, *because of him that passes by and because of him that returns,* that whether he return a conqueror or conquered he may do it no harm. This was fulfilled when, for some time after the struggles of the Maccabees, Judæa was a free and flourishing state, or perhaps when Alexander the Great, struck with an awe of Jaddus the high priest, favoured the Jews, and took them under his protection, when he wasted the neighbouring countries.

Verses 9–11

Here begins a prophecy of the Messiah and his kingdom with express application to Christ's riding in triumph into *Jerusalem,* Matt. xxi. 6; John xii. 15.

I. The approach of the Messiah promised, as matter of great joy to the Old Testament church: *Behold, thy king cometh unto thee.* Christ is a king, a sovereign prince, having all power both in heaven and on earth. In the gospel-church his spiritual kingdom is administered. "This King has been long in coming, but now, *behold, he cometh;* he is at the door. There are but a few ages more to run out, and he that shall come will come."

II. Here is such a description of him as renders his coming to them very acceptable. 1. He is a righteous ruler; *he is just.* 2. He is a powerful protector to all those that bear faith and true allegiance to him, for he *has salvation;* he has it in his power to bestow upon all his subjects. He is a *meek,* humble, tender Father to all his subjects as his children; he is *lowly;* he is *poor* and *afflicted* (so the word signifies); having *emptied himself,* he was *despised and rejected of men.* He is *meek,* not taking state upon him, nor resenting

injuries, but *humbling himself* from first to last. (Matt. xi. 29, *Learn of me, for I am meek and lowly in heart.*) When he made his public entry into his own city (and it was the only passage of his life that had anything in it magnificent in the eye of the world), he chose to ride, not upon a stately horse, or in a chariot, as great men used to ride, but *upon an ass,* nor was it an ass fitted for use, but an *ass's colt,* a little foolish unmanageable thing, likely to disgrace his rider. He had no saddle, no trappings, no equipage, but his disciples' clothes thrown upon the colt; for he *made himself of no reputation* when he visited us in great humility.

III. His kingdom is here set forth in the glory of it. This king has a kingdom, not of this world, but a spiritual kingdom, a *kingdom of heaven.* It shall not be set up by carnal weapons of warfare. No; he *will cut off the chariot from Ephraim and the horses from Jerusalem* (v. 10), in kindness to his people, that they may not cut themselves off from God by putting confidence in them which they should put in the power of God only. He will establish his kingdom by proclaiming peace on earth goodwill towards men. As far as it prevails in the minds of men and has the ascendant over them, it will make them peaceable, and slay all enmities; it will cut off the battle-bow, and *beat swords into plough-shares.* The preachers of the gospel shall carry it from one country to another till the remotest corners of the world are enlightened by it.

IV. The great benefit procured for mankind by the Messiah, is redemption from extreme misery, typified by the deliverance of the Jews out of their captivity in Babylon (v. 11). *I have sent forth thy prisoners,* thy captives out of Babylon, which was to them as *a pit* in which was *no water.* It was part of the covenant that, if in the land of their captivity, they sought the Lord, he would be found of them, Lev. xxvi. 42, 44, 45; Deut. xxx. 4. It was *by the blood of that covenant,* typifying the blood of Christ, in whom all God's covenants with man are yea and amen, that they were released out of captivity; and this was but a shadow of the great salvation wrought out by *thy King, O daughter of Zion!*

Verses 12–17

The prophet, having taught those that had returned out of captivity to attribute their deliverance to the *blood of the covenant* and to the promise of the Messiah, now cheers them with the prospect of a joyful and happy settlement; but these promises have their full accomplishment in the spiritual blessings of the gospel which we enjoy by Jesus Christ.

I. They are invited to look unto Christ, and flee unto him as their city of refuge (v. 12): *Turn you to the stronghold, you prisoners of hope.* The Jews that had returned out of captivity into their own land were *prisoners of hope,* or *expectation,* for God had given them a *little reviving in their bondage,* Ezra ix. 8, 9. Those that continued in Babylon yet lived in hope some time or other to see their own land again. Now both these are directed to turn their eyes upon the Messiah. The promise of the Messiah was the stronghold of the faithful long before his coming; they saw his day at a distance and were glad, Luke ii. 25, 28. This invitation to the stronghold speaks the language of the gospel-call, v. 12. Sinners are prisoners, but they are prisoners of hope; Christ is a stronghold for them.

II. They are assured of God's favour to them: "*I will render double unto thee,* to everyone of you prisoners of hope." As a pledge of this, in the fulness of time God here promises to the Jews victory, plenty, and joy, in their own land, which should be but a type of more glorious victories, riches, and joys, in the kingdom of Christ.

1. *They shall triumph over their enemies.* The Jews, after their return, were surrounded with enemies on all sides. But it is here promised that the Lord would deliver them. They shall be instruments in God's hand for the defeating and baffling of their persecutors: "*I have bent Judah for me, as my bow of steel; that bow I have filled with Ephraim as my arrows, have drawn it up to its full bent, till the arrow be at the head.*" But let them not think that they gain their successes by their own bow, for they themselves are no more than God's bow and his arrows, tools in his hands, which he manages as he pleases. The following words explain this: *I have raised up* and animated *thy sons, O Zion! against thy sons, O Greece!* This was fulfilled when *against Antiochus*, one of the kings of the Grecian monarchy, the people that knew their God were *strong* and *did exploits*, Dan. xi. 32. God will be commander-in-chief in every engagement (*v.* 14): *The Lord shall be seen over them.* Is their army to be mustered, and brought into the field? *The Lord shall blow the trumpet*, to gather the forces together, and to give directions. Whatever enterprise the campaign is opened with, God shall go forth at the head *with whirlwinds of the south*, which were of incredible swiftness and before these whirlwinds thy sons, O Greece! shall be as chaff. Is the army actually engaged? God's *arrows shall go forth as lightning.* He *sent out his arrows and scattered them.* This alludes to that which God had done for Israel of old when he brought them out of Egypt, and into Canaan, and had its accomplishment partly in the wonderful successes which the Jews had in the time of the Maccabees, but perfectly in the glorious victories gained by the cross of Christ over Satan and all the powers of darkness. Did their enemies hope to swallow them up? It shall be turned upon them, and they shall *devour* their enemies, and shall *subdue with sling-stones.* The *stones of the brook*, when God pleases, shall do as great execution as the best train of artillery.

2. *They shall triumph in their God.* They shall take the comfort and give God the glory of their successes. So some read *v.* 15. *They shall eat* (that is, they shall quietly enjoy) what they have got. And, in the fulness of their joy, they shall offer abundance of sacrifices to the honour of God, so that *they shall fill both the bowls and the corners of the altar* with the fat and blood of their sacrifices. They shall triumph in the relation wherein they stand to him, that they are *the flock of his people* and he is their Shepherd, and that they are to him *as the stones of a crown*, very precious and of great value, and kept under a strong guard. And *they shall be lifted up as an ensign upon his land*, as the royal standard is displayed in token of triumph and joy. *For how great is his goodness and how great is his beauty!* This is the burden of the songs wherewith they shall *make a noise* before the Lord. This may refer to the Messiah, to Zion's *King that cometh.* See *that king in his beauty* (Isa. xxxiii. 17), who is the *fairest of ten thousand*, and *altogether lovely.* Though, in the eye of the world, he had no form or comeliness, in the eye of faith how great is his beauty! *How great is his goodness!* How rich in mercy is he! Here is an instance of his goodness to his people: *Corn shall make the young men cheerful and new wine the maids;* that is, God will bless his people with an abundance of the fruits of the earth.

CHAPTER 10

The scope of this chapter is to encourage the Jews that had returned with hopes that though they had been under divine rebukes for their negligence in rebuilding the temple, and were now surrounded with enemies, yet God would make them prosperous at home and victorious abroad. I. They are here directed, both in the evils they suffered and in the comforts they desired,

to acknowledge his hand, ver. 1-4. II. They are encouraged to expect strength and success from him in all their struggles, ver. 5-12.

Verses 1-4

Gracious things and glorious were promised to this poor afflicted people in the foregoing chapter. God intimates to them that he expects they should acknowledge him in all their ways and in all his ways towards them.

I. The prophet directs them to apply to God by prayer for rain in the season thereof. "*Ask you of the Lord rain.* Do not pray to the clouds, nor to the stars, for rain, but *to the Lord.*" The former rain fell at the seed-time, in autumn, the latter fell in the spring, between March and May, which brought the corn to an ear and filled it. If either of these rains failed, it was very bad with that land. We must, in our prayers dutifully attend the course of Providence; we must ask for mercies in their proper time, and not expect that God should go out of his usual way and method for us. *So the Lord shall make bright clouds* (which, though they are without rain themselves, are yet presages of rain)—*lightnings* (so the margin reads it), for *he maketh lightnings for the rain.*

II. He shows them the folly of making their addresses to idols (*v.* 2): *The idols have spoken vanity.* The *diviners*, who were the prophets of those idols, *have seen a lie* (their visions were all a cheat and a sham); and *they have told false dreams*, which proved that they were not from God. They not only got nothing by the false gods, but they lost the favour of the true God, for *therefore they went their way* into captivity *as a flock*, and *they were troubled* as scattered sheep are, *because there was no shepherd.* Those that wandered after strange gods were made to wander into strange nations.

III. He shows them the hand of God in events, both those that made against them and those that made for them, *v.* 3. When everything went cross it was God that walked contrary to them (*v.* 3): "*My anger was kindled against the shepherds* that should have fed the flock, but neglected it, and starved it. I was displeased at the wicked magistrates and ministers, the idol-shepherds." The captivity in Babylon was a token of God's anger against them; in it likewise he *punished the goats*, those of the flock that were filthy and mischievous. When things began to change for the better it was God that gave them the happy turn. "He has now *visited his flock* with favour, and has made them *as his goodly horse in the battle*, managed and made use of them, as a man does the horse he rides on, has made them valuable in themselves and formidable to those about them, *as his goodly horse.*"

IV. He shows them that every creature is to them what God makes it to be (*v.* 4): *Out of him came forth the corner, out of him the nails.* Out of him came the combined force of their enemies; nor could they have had such power unless it had been given them from above. All the power likewise that was engaged for them was derived from him. Out of him came forth *the corner-stone* of the building, the power of magistrates, which keeps the several parts of the state together. Out of him came forth *the nail* that fixed the state (Isa. xxii. 23), the *nail in his holy place*, Ezra ix. 8. Out of him came forth *the battle-bow*, the military power, and out of him *every oppressor.*

Verses 5-12

Precious promises made to the people of God, which look further than to the state of the Jews, and have certain reference to the spiritual Israel of God, the gospel-church, and all true believers.

I. They shall have God's favour and presence, and shall be owned and accepted of him. This is the foundation of all the rest: *The Lord is with them,*

v. 5. Again (v. 6), *I have mercy upon them*. All their dignity and joy are owing purely to God's mercy; and mercy, as it supposes misery, so it excludes merit. *They shall be as though I had not cast them off*. Such favour does God show to returning repenting sinners, such fellowship are they admitted into, and such freedom does he use with them, that they are *as though they had never been cast off. I am the Lord their God*, according to the original contract, the covenant made with their fathers.

II. They shall be victorious over their enemies. (v. 5): *They shall be as mighty men*, that are both strong in body and bold in spirit, effective men. They shall, as mighty men, *tread down their enemies in the battle because the Lord is with them*. Some would argue that they may *therefore* sit still, and do nothing, because the Lord is with them, who can and will do all. No; God's gracious presence with us to help us must not supersede, but quicken and animate, our endeavours to help ourselves. Then *the riders on horses shall be confounded*. The preachers of the gospel of Christ went forth to war a good warfare; they charged bravely, because God was with them; and the *riders on horses* that opposed them *were confounded*. But whence have they all this might? It is in the Lord, and in the power of his might, that they are so (v. 6). God saves us by strengthening us, and works out our happiness by working in us to do our duty.

III. Those of them that are dispersed shall be gathered together into one body (v. 6): *I will bring them again to place them*, bring them from other lands to place them in their own land. In order to this (v. 8) *I will hiss for them*, or, rather, *whistle* for them, as the shepherd with his pipe calls his sheep together, that *know his voice*; and so *I will gather them. I will gather them, for I have redeemed them*. It has its spiritual accomplishment in the gathering in of precious souls out of a bondage worse than that in Egypt or Assyria, and the bringing of them into the glorious liberties of the children of God. All the land of promise is theirs, even Gilead and Lebanon. How shall a people so dispersed be got together? The difficulties seem insuperable, but they shall be got over as effectually as those that lay in the way of their deliverance out of Egypt and their entrance into Canaan: *He shall pass through the sea with affliction*, as of old through the Red Sea. And *all the deeps of the river shall dry up*, as Jordan did to make way for Israel's passage into that good land which God had given them. Does *the pride of Assyria* stand in the way of their deliverance? He shall give check to it who sets bounds to the *proud waves of the sea*. Does the sceptre of Egypt oppose it? That shall *depart away*. When the gospel-church was to be gathered out of all nations by the preaching of the gospel, great opposition was given to it by the enraged powers of earth and hell. But, by divine power it became *mighty to the pulling down of strongholds*, and the conversion and salvation of thousands. Then the sea fled, and Jordan was *driven back at the presence of the Lord*.

IV. They shall greatly multiply, and the church, that new world, shall be replenished (v. 8): *They shall increase as they have increased* formerly in Egypt. *In Judah* only God had been *known*, and his *name was great in Israel* only; here only he revealed his *statutes and judgments*. But in gospel-times that place shall be much too strait; the church's tent must be enlarged. Then *I will sow them among the people*, v. 9. Their scattering shall be like the scattering of seed in the ground, not to bury it, but to increase it. The Jews that came from all parts to worship at Jerusalem fetched thence the gospel light and fire to their own countries, as those Acts ii, and the eunuch, Acts viii. And their own synagogues in the several cities of the Gentiles were the first receptacles of the apostles and their preaching. Thus when God *sowed them among the people* he took care that they should *remember him*, and make mention of his name *in far countries*; and, by keeping up the knowledge of God among them as he had revealed himself in the Old Testament, they would be the more ready to admit the knowledge of Christ as he has revealed himself in the New Testament.

V. God himself will be both their strength and their song. In him they shall be comforted, and shall have abundant satisfaction (v. 7). When we resolutely resist, and so overcome, our spiritual enemies, then our hearts shall rejoice. And with graces joys shall be propagated: *Their children shall see it and be glad, and their hearts* also *shall rejoice in the Lord*. It is good to acquaint children betimes with the delights of religion, and to make the services of it pleasant, that, learning betimes to rejoice in the Lord, they may cleave to him. If God strengthen us (v. 12) we must bestir ourselves, must *walk up and down* in all the duties of the Christian life. To us to live must be Christ; and, *whatever we do in word or deed*, we must *do all in the name of the Lord Jesus*, that we receive not the strengthening grace of God in vain. See Ps. lxxx. 17, 18.

CHAPTER 11

Here is, I. A prediction of the destruction that should come upon the Jewish nation, ver. 1–3. II. The putting of it into the hands of the Messiah. 1. He is charged with the custody of that flock, ver. 4–6. 2. He undertakes it, and bears rule in it, ver. 7, 8. 3. Finding it perverse, he gives it up (ver. 9), breaks his shepherd's staff (ver. 10, 11), resents the indignation done him and the contempt put upon him (ver. 12, 13), and then breaks his other staff, ver. 14. 4. He turns them over into the hands of foolish shepherds, who, instead of preventing, shall complete their ruin, and both the blind leaders and the blind followers shall fall together into the ditch, ver. 15–17.

Verses 1–3

In dark and figurative expressions, as is usual in the scripture predictions of things at a great distance, that destruction of Jerusalem and of the Jewish church and nation is here foretold which our Lord Jesus, when the time was at hand, prophesied of very plainly and expressly. 1. Preparation made for that destruction (v. 1): "*Open thy doors, O Lebanon!* Thou wouldst not open them to let thy king in. Now thou must open them to let thy ruin in. Some by Lebanon here understand the temple, which was built of cedars from Lebanon. It was burnt with fire by the Romans, and its gates were forced open by the fury of the soldiers. Others understand it of Jerusalem, or rather of the whole land of Canaan, to which Lebanon was an inlet on the north. All shall lie open to the invader, and the cedars, the mighty and eminent men, shall be devoured, which cannot but alarm those of an inferior rank, v. 2. If *the cedars* have *fallen* let the *fir-tree howl*. How can the slender fir-trees stand if stately cedars fall? And let the *oaks of Bashan*, that lie exposed to every injury, *howl, for the forest of the vintage* (or the *flourishing vineyard*, that used to be guarded with a particular care) has come down, or (as some read it) when the *defenced forests*, such as Lebanon was, have come down. 2. Lamentation made for the destruction (v. 3): *There is a voice of howling*. Those who have fallen howl for grief and shame, and those who see their own turn coming howl for fear. The great men especially receive the alarm with the utmost confusion. Those great men were by office shepherds, and such should have protected God's flock committed to their charge; it is the duty both of princes and priests. But they were as *young lions*, that made themselves a terror to the flock. The *young lions howl, for the pride of Jordan is spoiled*. The pride of Jordan was the thickets on the banks, in which the lions reposed when the river overflowed, the lions came up from them (as we read Jer. xlix. 19), and they came up roaring.

Verses 4–14

The prophet here is made a type of Christ, as the prophet Isaiah sometimes was; and the scope of these verses is to show that *for judgment Christ came into this world* (John ix. 39), for judgment to the Jewish church and nation, which were, about the time of his coming, corrupted by the worldliness and hypocrisy of their rulers. Christ would have healed them, but they would not be healed.

I. The desperate case of the Jewish church, under the tyranny of their own governors, v. 5. In Zechariah's time we find the rulers and the nobles justly rebuked for *exacting usury of their brethren*, Neh. v. 7, 15. In Christ's time the Sadducees, who were deists, corrupted their judgments. The Pharisees, who were bigots for superstition, corrupted their morals, by making void the commandments of God, Matt. xv. 16. Thus they slew the sheep of the flock, thus they sold them. They affronted God, by giving him thanks. They said, *Blessed be the Lord, for I am rich*, as if, because they prospered in their wickedness God had made himself patron of their unjust practices. Christ had compassion on *the multitude because they fainted and were scattered abroad, as if they had no shepherd* (as really they had worse than none). It is ill for a church when its pastors can look upon the ignorant, the foolish, the wicked, the weak, without pity.

II. The sentence of God's wrath passed upon them for their stupidity. And, as their shepherds pitied them not, so they did not bemoan themselves; therefore God says (v. 6), "*I will no more pity the inhabitants of the land.*" Those who are willing to have their consciences oppressed by those who *teach for doctrines the commandments of men* are often punished by oppression in their civil interests, and justly, for those forfeit their own rights who tamely give up God's rights. He will deliver them into the hand of oppressors, *everyone into his neighbour's hand*. They shall be delivered everyone *into the hand of his king*, whom they chose to submit to rather than to Christ.

III. A trial yet made whether their ruin might be prevented by sending Christ among them as a shepherd, Matt. xxi. 37. Divers of the prophets had spoken of him as the *Shepherd of Israel*, Isa. xl. 11; Ezek. xxxiv. 23. He himself told the Pharisees that he was the *Shepherd of the sheep* (John x. 1, 2, 11), apparently referring to this passage, where we have, 1. The charge he received from his Father to try what might be done with this flock (v. 4); *Thus saith the Lord my God, Feed the flock of the slaughter*. The Jews were God's flock, but they were *the flock of slaughter*, for their enemies had killed them all the day long. 2. His acceptance of this charge, v. 7. Christ will care for these lost sheep; he will go about among them, *teaching* and *healing even you, O poor of the flock!* His disciples, who were his constant attendants, were of the poor of the flock. I *took unto me two staves*, pastoral staves; other shepherds have but one crook, but Christ had two, denoting what he did both for the souls and for the bodies of men. David speaks of God's *rod* and his *staff* (Ps. xxiii. 4), a correcting rod and a supporting staff. One staff he called Beauty, denoting the Temple; the other he called Bands, denoting their civil state. Christ, in his gospel, and in all he did consulted the advancement both of their civil and of their sacred interests. The chief Shepherd *fed the flock* (v. 7), and displaced those under-shepherds that were false to their trust (v. 8): *Three shepherds I cut off in one month.*

IV. Their enmity to Christ. He came to the sheep of his own pasture; it might have been expected that between them and him there would be affection, but they conducted themselves so ill that *his soul loathed them*, was *straitened* towards them (so it may be read). Whatever estrangement there is between God and man, it begins on man's side.

V. The sentence of their rejection passed (v. 9): "*Then said I, I will not feed you.* That which will make itself a prey to the wolf, let it be a prey, and let the rest so far forget their own gentle nature as to *eat the flesh of one another;* let these sheep fight like dogs." A sign of it given (v. 10): *I took my staff, even Beauty, and cut it asunder.* The breaking of this staff signified the breaking of God's covenant which he had *made with all the people*, the covenant of peculiarity made with all the tribes of *Israel*. When Christ told them plainly that the *kingdom of God* should be *taken from them*, and *given to another people*, then he broke the *staff of Beauty*, Matt. xxi. 43. Though Jerusalem and the Jewish nation held up forty years longer, yet from that day we may reckon the staff of Beauty broken, v. 11. It was said before, *Their souls abhorred him;* and here we have an instance of it, their buying and selling him for thirty pieces of silver. This is here foretold in somewhat obscure expressions, lest otherwise the plainness of the prophecy might prevent the accomplishment of it. The Shepherd comes to them for his wages (v. 12): "*If you think good, give me my price;* you are weary of me, pay me off and discharge me; and, *if not, forbear.*" Compare with this what Christ said to Judas when he was going to sell him, "*What thou doest do quickly;* let them either take the bargain or leave it," John xiii. 27. They value him at *thirty pieces of silver*. It was the ordinary price of a slave, Exod. xxi. 32. The silver being no way proportionable to his wrath, it is *thrown to the potter* with disdain: "Let him take it to buy clay with." So the prophet *cast the thirty pieces of silver to the potter in the house of the Lord*. There is a particular accomplishment of this in the history of Christ's sufferings, Matt. xxvii. 9, 10. *Thirty pieces of silver* was the very sum for which Christ was sold to the chief priests; the money was laid out in the purchase of *the potter's field*. The completing of their rejection was the cutting asunder of the other staff, v. 14. The former denoted the ruin of their church, by breaking the covenant between God and them—that defaced their *beauty;* this denotes the ruin of their state, by breaking the brotherhood between Judah and Israel. They shall be crumbled into parties and factions, being thus divided, shall be *brought to desolation*. Nothing ruins a people so inevitably, as the breaking of *the staff of Bands*, and the weakening of the brotherhood among them.

Verses 15–17

God, having shown this people justly abandoned by the good Shepherd, here shows their further misery in being shamefully abused by a foolish shepherd. The prophet is himself to personate this pretended shepherd (v. 15): Take unto thee the *instruments* or accoutrements *of a foolish shepherd*, such a shepherd's coat, and bag, and staff, as a foolish shepherd would appear in; for such a shepherd shall be set over them (v. 16), who, instead of protecting them, shall do them mischief. The description here given of the foolish shepherd suits the character Christ gives of the scribes and Pharisees, Matt. xxiii. They shall be under the tyranny of unmerciful princes. They shall be imposed upon by false Christs and false prophets, as our Saviour foretold, Matt. xxiv. 5.

I. What a curse this foolish shepherd should be to the people, v. 16. He will not *visit those that are cut off*, will take no care of the *young ones*, nor *heal that which was broken*, but let it die of its bruises, when a little thing, in time, would have saved it. He will never do anything to *support the weak* and comfort the *feeble-minded*. Foolish shepherds *eat of the flesh of the fat*; they will have of the best for themselves; when they are in a rage against any of the flock, they *tear their* very *claws in pieces* by overdriving them.

II. What a curse this foolish shepherd should bring upon himself (*v.* 17): *Woe to the idol-shepherd.* His doom is that *the sword* of God's justice shall be *upon his arm* and *his right eye*, so that he shall quite lose the use of both. This was fulfilled when Christ said to the Pharisees, *I have come that those who see may be made blind*, John ix. 39.

CHAPTER 12

The apostle (Gal. iv. 25, 26) distinguishes between "Jerusalem which now is, and is in bondage with her children"—the Jewish church that rejected Christ, and "Jerusalem that is from above, that is free, and is the mother of us all"—the Christian church, the spiritual Jerusalem. In the foregoing chapter we read the doom of the former, and in this chapter, we have many precious promises made to the gospel-Jerusalem by him who (ver. 1) declares his power to make them good. It is promised, I. That the attempts of the church's enemies against her shall be to their own ruin, ver. 2-4, 6. II. That the endeavours of the church's friends and patrons for her good shall be successful, ver. 5. III. That God will strengthen the meanest and weakest that belong to his church, and work salvation for them, ver. 7, 8. IV. That as a pledge, he will pour upon them a spirit of prayer and repentance, ver. 9-14. These promises were of use then to the pious Jews that lived in the troublous times under Antiochus, and oppressors; and they are in every age for the directing of our prayers and the encouraging of our hopes with reference to the gospel-church.

Verses 1–8

I. The title of this charter of promises made to God's Israel; it is the *burden of the word of the Lord*, a divine prediction. But it is *for Israel*; for their comfort and benefit.

II. The title of him that grants this charter: he is the Creator of the world and our Creator, and therefore has irresistible dominion. He *stretches out the heavens* and keeps them stretched out *like a curtain*, and will do so till the end come. He *lays the foundation of the earth*, and keeps it fixed on its own axis, though it is *founded on the seas* (Ps. xxiv. 1, 2), nay, though it is *hung upon nothing*, Job xxvi. 7. He *forms the spirit of man within him*. He *made us these souls*, Jer. xxxviii. 16. He not only breathed into the first man, but still breathes into every man the breath of life.

III. The promises by which the church shall be secured. Whatever attacks the enemies of the church may make upon her purity or peace, they will certainly issue in their own confusion. Jerusalem is in safety, and those are in danger who fight against it. This is here illustrated by three comparisons: 1. *Jerusalem* shall be *a cup of trembling* to all that lay siege to it, *v.* 2. Thus Alexander the Great was struck with amazement when he met Jaddas the high priest, and was deterred from offering any violence to Jerusalem. When Sennacherib laid siege *against Judah* and *Jerusalem* he found them such a cup of stupefying wine as laid all his mighty men asleep, Ps. lxxvi. 5, 6.

2. *Jerusalem* shall be *a burdensome stone* to all that attempt to remove it or carry it away, *v.* 3. Those that are for advancing the kingdom of sin in the world look upon Jerusalem, even the church of God, as the great obstacle to their design, and they must have it out of the way; but they cannot remove it. God will have a church in the world, in spite of them; it is *built upon a rock*, and is as *Mount Zion*, Ps. cxxv. 1. This *stone, cut out of the mountain without hands*, will *break in pieces all that burden themselves* with it, as that stone *smote the image*, Dan. ii. 45. Our Saviour seems to allude to these words when he

speaks of himself as a burdensome stone to those that will not have him for their foundation-stone, which shall *fall upon them and grind them to powder*, Matt. xxi. 44.

3. The governors of Judah shall be among their enemies like *a hearth of fire among the wood, and a torch of fire in a sheaf, v.* 6. Those that contend with them will find it is like an opposition given by briers and thorns to a consuming fire, Isa. xxvii. 4. It will go through them, and burn them together. The enemies thought to be as water to this fire, but God will make them as wood, nay, as a sheaf of corn (which is more combustible), to this fire. The persecutors of the primitive church found this fulfilled in it, witness the confession of Julian the apostate at last, *Thou hast overcome me, O thou Galilean! If you are weary of your life, persecute the Christians*, was once a proverb. It is promised that God will infatuate the counsels and enfeeble the courage of the church's enemies (*v.* 4). The church's infantry shall be too hard for the enemy's cavalry. It is promised that Jerusalem shall be re-peopled and replenished (*v.* 6). They shall have a new Jerusalem upon the same foundation, the same spot of ground. They had so after their return out of captivity, but the gospel-church is a Jerusalem inhabited *in its own place*; for, the gospel being preached to all the world, it may call every place its own. It is promised that the inhabitants of Jerusalem shall be enabled to defend themselves under the divine protection, *v.* 8. God will not only be a *wall of fire* about the city, but he will encompass particular persons with his favour *as with a shield*. He does it by giving them strength and courage to help themselves. In that day the feeblest of the inhabitants of Jerusalem *shall be as David*, as skilful and strong, as serviceable to Jerusalem in guarding it as David himself was in founding it. *The house of David shall be as God*, that is, *as the angel of the Lord, before them.* Zerubbabel was now the top-branch of the house of David; he shall be endued with wisdom and grace, and shall go before the people as an angel, Exod. xxiii. 20. But this was to have its full accomplishment in Christ; now the house of David looked little and mean, and its glory was eclipsed, but in Christ the house of David shone more brightly than ever. It is promised that there shall be a very good understanding between the city and the country. *The governors of Judah*, the magistrates of the country, shall think honourably of the citizens, *the inhabitants of Jerusalem*. It is well with a kingdom when its great men know how to value its good men. God will put signal honour upon Judah, and so save them from the contempt of their brethren. God says (*v.* 4), *I will open my eyes upon the house of Judah*, and (*v.* 7), *the Lord shall save the tents of Judah first.* Those that dwell in tents lie most exposed; but God will deliver them before those that dwell in Jerusalem. Courtiers and citizens ought not to despise country people, those whom God *opens his eyes upon* and who are *first saved*. This promise has a further reference to the gospel-church, in which no difference shall be made between high and low, rich and poor, bond and free, circumcision and uncircumcision, Col. iii. 11.

Verses 9–14

The *day* here spoken of is the day of Jerusalem's defence and deliverance, that glorious day, which, if it refer to the successes which the Jews had against their enemies in the time of the Maccabees, yet certainly looks further, to the *gospel-day*, to Christ's victories over the powers of darkness and the great salvation he has wrought.

I. A glorious work of God to be wrought for his people: "*I will seek to destroy all the nations that come against Jerusalem, v.* 9. Nations come against Jerusalem, but they shall all be destroyed." In Christ's first coming, he *sought to destroy him that had the power of death*, and did destroy him. In his second coming, he will complete their destruction, and *death itself shall be swallowed up in that victory*.

II. A gracious work of God to be wrought in his people. When he seeks to destroy their enemies he will *pour upon them the Spirit of grace and supplication*. When God intends great mercy for his people the first thing he does is to set them praying. But this promise has reference to the graces of the Spirit given to all believers, as that Isa. xliv. 3, *I will pour my Spirit upon thy seed*, which was fulfilled when *Jesus was glorified*, John vii. 39. These blessings are poured on *the house of David*, on the great men; for they are no more, and no better, than the grace of God makes them. But it was given also to *the inhabitants of Jerusalem*, the common people. The church is Jerusalem, the heavenly Jerusalem; all true believers, that have their conversation in heaven, are inhabitants of this Jerusalem, and to them this promise belongs. God will *pour his Spirit upon them*: 1. As a *Spirit of grace*, to sanctify and to make gracious. 2. As a *Spirit of supplications*, instructing and assisting us in the duty of prayer. *I will pour upon them the Spirit of grace*. One effect of the gift is that they shall mourn, for there is a mourning that will end in rejoicing and has a blessing upon it. This mourning is a fruit of the Spirit, an evidence of a work of grace in the soul. It is a mourning grounded upon a sight of Christ: *They shall look on him whom they have pierced, and shall mourn for him*. It is foretold that Christ should be pierced, and this scripture is quoted as that which was fulfilled when Christ's side was pierced upon the cross; see John xix. 37. He is spoken of as one whom we have pierced; it is spoken primarily of the Jews, yet it is true of us all as sinners. Those that truly repent of sin look upon Christ as one who was pierced for their sins and is pierced by them. They shall mourn for sin *as one mourns for an only son*. The sorrow of parents for a child, for a first-born, is natural; it is secret and lasting; such are the sorrows of a true penitent, flowing purely from love to Christ above any other. It shall be *like the mourning of Hadadrimmon in the valley of Megiddon*, where good king Josiah was slain, for whom there was a general lamentation (v. 11). They cried out, *The crown has fallen from our head. Woe unto us, for we have sinned!* Lam. v. 16. Christ is our King; our sins were his death, and, for that reason, ought to be our grief. There shall be not only a mourning of *the land*, by its representatives in a general assembly (as Judges ii. 5, when the place was called *Bochim—A place of weepers*), but: *Every family apart* shall mourn (v. 12), *all the families that remain*, v. 14. Four several families are here specified as examples to others: (1) Two of them are royal families; the *house of David*, in Solomon, and the *house of Nathan*, another son of David, Luke iii. 27–31. (2) Two of them are sacred families (v. 13), *the family of the house of Levi*, which was God's tribe, and in it particularly the family of Shimei, which was a branch of the tribe of Levi (1 Chron. vi. 17). As the princes must mourn for the sins of the magistracy, so must the priests for the *iniquity of the holy things*.

Chapter 13

I. Some further promises relating to gospel-times. Here is a promise of the remission of sins (ver. 1), of the reformation of manners (ver. 2), and particularly of the silencing of false prophets, ver. 2–6. II. A clear prediction of the sufferings of Christ and the dispersion of his disciples (ver. 7), of the destruction of the greater part of the Jewish nation not long after (ver. 8), and of the purifying of a remnant of them, ver. 9.

Verses 1–6

Behold the Lamb of God *taking away the sin of the world*, 1 John iii. 5.

I. He takes away the guilt of sin by the blood of his cross (v. 1): *In that day*, in the gospel-day, *there shall be a fountain opened*, that is, provision made for the cleansing of all those from the pollutions of sin who truly repent. *In that day*, when the Spirit of grace is poured out to set them a mourning for their sins, their consciences shall be purified and pacified by the *blood of Christ, which cleanses from all sin*, 1 John i. 7. This *fountain opened* is the pierced side of Jesus Christ, spoken of just before (ch. xii. 10), for thence came there out *blood and water*, and both for cleansing. Sin is uncleanness; it defiles the mind and conscience, renders us odious to God and uneasy in ourselves, unfit to be employed in the service of God. There is mercy enough in God, and merit enough in Christ, for the forgiving of the greatest sins and sinners, 1 Cor. vi. 11. Under the law there were a brazen laver and a brazen sea to wash in; those were but vessels, but we have a fountain over-flowing, ever-flowing. It is a *fountain opened*; it is opened, not only to *the house of David*, but to *the inhabitants of Jerusalem*, to the poor and mean as well as to the rich and great.

II. He takes away the dominion of sin by the power of his grace. Those that are washed, as they are justified, so they are sanctified. In that day (v. 2): *I will cut off the names of the idols out of the land*. This was fulfilled in the rooted aversion which the Jews had, after the captivity, to idols and idolatry, and still retain to this day; it was fulfilled also in the conversion of many to the faith of Christ, by which they were taken off from making an idol of the ceremonial law. False prophecy shall also be brought to an end. The devil is an *unclean* spirit; and he has his prophets. It is here foretold that false prophets should be brought to punishment even by their nearest relations (v. 3). Holy zeal for God and godliness will make us hate sin, and dread temptation, most in those whom naturally we love best. False prophets should be themselves convinced of their sin (v. 4): "*The prophets shall be ashamed everyone of his vision;* because God has by his grace awakened their consciences and shown them their error, or because the event disproves their predictions. And therefore they shall no longer *wear a rough garment*, or *garment of hair*, as the true prophets used to do, in imitation of Elijah." Let men be really as good as they seem to be, but not seem to be better than really they are. The pretender, as a true penitent shall say, "*I am no prophet*, as I have pretended to be. *I am a husbandman;* I was never taught of God to prophesy, but *taught of man to keep cattle*." We must evince the truth of our repentance by returning to our duty again, though it be the severest mortification to us. "Hast thou not been beaten into this acknowledgment? Was it not the rod and reproof that gave thee this wisdom?" And he shall own, "Yes, it was; these are the *wounds with which I was wounded in the house of my friends*, who bound me, and brought me to my senses." Reduced by stripes, he had the sense and honesty to own that they were his friends, his real friends, who thus wounded him, that they might reclaim him. Some good interpreters think that these are the words of Christ who was wounded in his hands, when they were nailed to the cross. After his resurrection, he had the marks of these wounds; and here he tells how he came by them; he received them as a false prophet, for the chief priests called him a deceiver, but he received them in the house of the Jews, who should have been his friends.

Verses 7–9

Here is a prophecy,

I. Of the sufferings of Christ who was to be pierced, and was to be the fountain opened. *Awake, O sword! against my Shepherd*, v. 7. These are the words of

God the Father, giving commission to the sword of his justice to awake against his Son, when he had voluntarily made his soul an offering for sin; for it *pleased the Lord to bruise him* and *put him to grief;* and *he was stricken, smitten of God, and afflicted,* Isa. liii. 4, 10. Observe, 1. How he calls him. "As God, he is *my fellow*"; for he thought it *no robbery to be equal with God.* He and *the Father are one.* "As Mediator, he is *my Shepherd,* the Shepherd that was to lay down his life for the sheep." 2. How he uses him: *Awake, O sword! against him.* If he will be a sacrifice, he must be slain, for without the shedding of blood, the life-blood, there was no remission. It is not a charge given to a rod to correct him, but to a sword to slay him; for God *spared not his own Son.*

II. Of the dispersion of the disciples thereupon: *Smite the Shepherd, and the sheep shall be scattered.* This our Lord Jesus himself declares to have been fulfilled when *all his disciples were offended because of him* in the n'ght wherein he was betrayed, Matt. xxvi. 31; Mark xiv. 27. They all *forsook him and fled.* They were *scattered everyone to his own, and left him alone,* John xvi. 32. Some think this refers to Christ the *Shepherd* of the Jewish nation; he was smitten; they themselves smote him; and therefore they were dispersed among the nations. These words, *I will turn my hand upon the little ones,* may be understood either as a threatening (as Christ suffered, so shall his disciples), or as a promise that God would gather Christ's scattered disciples together again, and give them the meeting in Galilee.

III. Of the rejection and ruin of the unbelieving Jews (v. 8); and this shall have its accomplishment, in the destruction of the corrupt and hypocritical part of the church.

IV. Of the reformation of the chosen remnant, those of them that believed, and the Christian church in general (*v.* 9): *The third part shall be left.* When Jerusalem and Judæa were destroyed, all the Christians in that country, having the warning Christ gave them to *flee to the mountains,* shifted for their own safety, and were sheltered in a city called *Pella,* on the other side Jordan. *I will bring* that *third part through the fire* of affliction, *and will refine* and *try them* as *silver and gold are refined and tried.* This was fulfilled in the persecutions of the primitive church, the *fiery trial,* 1 Pet. iv. 12. Their communion with God is their triumph: *They shall call on my name, and I will hear them.* They write to God by prayer, and receive from him answers of peace. Their covenant with God is their triumph: "*I will say, It is my people,* whom I have chosen and loved, and will own; *and they shall say, The Lord is my God,* all-sufficient to me."

CHAPTER 14

This chapter speaks of a "day of the Lord that cometh", and ten times in the foregoing chapters, and seven times in this, it is repeated, "in that day"; but what that day is that is here meant is uncertain. Some passages here seem to look as far forward as gospel-times. Now the "day of the Lord" brings with it both judgment and mercy, mercy to his church, judgment to her enemies and persecutors. I. The gates of hell are here threatening the church (ver. 1, 2) and yet not prevailing. II. The power of Heaven appears here for the church, ver. 3, 5. III. The events concerning the church are represented as (ver. 6, 7) issuing well at last. IV. The spreading of knowledge is here foretold, and the setting up of the gospel-kingdom in the world (ver. 8, 9), which shall be the enlargement and establishment of another Jerusalem, ver. 10, 11. V. Those shall be reckoned with that fought against Jerusalem (ver. 12–15) and those that neglect his worship there, ver. 17–19. VI. It is promised that there shall be great resort to the church, and great purity and piety in it, ver. 16, 20, 21.

Verses 1–7

God's providences concerning his church are here represented as strangely changing and strangely mixed.

I. As strangely changing. Sometimes the tide runs high and strong against them, but presently it turns.

1. God here appears against Jerusalem. When the *day of the Lord comes* (v. 1) Jerusalem must pass through the fire to be refined. The *city shall be taken by the* Romans, the houses shall be rifled, and *the women* shall *be ravished. One-half of the city* shall then be carried *into captivity,* to be sold or enslaved.

2. He presently changes his way, and appears for Jerusalem; for, though judgment begin at the house of God, yet, it shall not end there. A remnant shall be spared. *One-half shall go into captivity,* whence they may be fetched back, *and the residue of the people shall not* be cut off *from the city.* Many of the Jews shall receive the gospel, and so shall prevent their being cut off from the city of God, his church upon earth. *Then,* when God has made use of these nations as a scourge to his people, he shall *go forth* and *fight against them* by his judgments. The Roman empire never flourished after the destruction of Jerusalem as it had done before, but in many instances God fought against it. Though Jerusalem and the temple be destroyed, yet God will have a church in the world, into which Gentiles shall be admitted, and with whom the believing Jews shall be incorporated, *v.* 4, 5. God will carefully inspect Jerusalem, even when the enemies of it are laying it waste: *His feet shall stand in that day upon the mount of Olives,* Mark xiii. 3. When the refiner puts his gold into the furnace he stands by to see that it receive no damage; so when Jerusalem, God's gold, is to be refined, he will stand by *upon the mount of Olives;* this was literally fulfilled when our Lord Jesus was often upon this mountain. Thence he *ascended up into heaven,* Acts i. 12. It was the last place on which his feet stood on this earth. By the destruction of Jerusalem this mountain shall be made to *cleave in the midst,* and the Gentiles made one with the Jews by the breaking down of this *middle wall of partition,* Eph. ii. 14. A great mountain the ceremonial law was in the way of the Jews' conversion, yet before Christ and his gospel it was made plain. A new and living way shall be opened to the new Jerusalem. The mountain being divided, one-half *towards the north* and the other half *towards the south,* there shall be *a very great valley,* a broad way of communication between Jerusalem and the Gentile world, by which the Gentiles shall have free admission into the gospel-Jerusalem, and the word of the Lord, that *goes forth from Jerusalem,* shall have a *free course* into the Gentile world. The *valley of the mountains* is the gospel-church, to which there were added of the Jews daily *such as should be saved.* God *makes his mountains a way* (Isa. xlix. 11), by making them a valley. To those that are now separated from God this valley shall reach; for the Gentiles, who are afar off, shall be made nigh, with the Jews, who are a *people near unto him,* and both have a mutual access to each other and a joint access to God as a Father by one Spirit, Eph. ii. 18. God shall appear in his glory for the accomplishing of all this: *The Lord my God shall come, and all the saints with thee;* which may refer to his coming to destroy Jerusalem, or to destroy the enemies of Jerusalem; or his coming to set up his kingdom in the world, which is called the *coming of the son of Man* (Matt. xxiv. 37); or to his last coming, at the end of time; however, it teaches us that the Lord will come. Some think that *v.* 5 may be read as a prayer, *Yet, O Lord my God! come, and bring all the saints with thee.*

II. God's providences appear here strangely mixed (v. 6, 7): *In that day* of the Lord the *light shall not be clear nor dark, not day* nor *night;* but *at evening time it shall be light.* Some refer this to all the time from hence to the coming of the Messiah; the Jewish church had neither perfect peace nor constant trouble, but a cloudy day. But it may be taken more generally to represent the method God usually takes in the administration of the kingdom both of providence and grace. It is so with the church of God in this world; where the Sun of righteousness has risen it cannot be dark night, and yet short of heaven it will not be clear day. *It shall be one day which shall be known to the Lord.* This intimates beauty and harmony in such mixed events; there is one and the same design in all. *At evening-time it shall be light;* it shall be clear light, and no longer dark; we are sure of it in the other world, and we hope for it in this world—at *evening-time,* when things are at the worst and the case of the church is most deplorable.

Verses 8–15

I. Blessings promised to Jerusalem, the gospel-Jerusalem, in the day of the Messiah, and to all the earth.

1. Jerusalem shall be a spring of living waters to the world; it was made so when there the Spirit was poured out upon the apostles, and thence the word of the Lord diffused itself to the nations about (*v.* 8). It was the honour of Jerusalem that *thence the word of the Lord went forth* (Isa. ii. 3). Half of these waters shall go *towards the former sea* and *half towards the hinder sea,* as all rivers bend their course towards some sea or other, some eastward, others westward. The gospel shall spread into all parts of the world. The knowledge of God shall diffuse itself every way and every day. In *summer and in winter it shall be.* And such a divine power goes along with these living waters that they shall not be dried up, either by the droughts in summer or by the frosts in winter.

2. The kingdom of God among men shall be a universal and united kingdom, *v.* 9. *The Lord shall be King over all the earth. There shall be one Lord, and his name one.* All false gods shall be abandoned, and all false ways of worship abolished; and as God shall be the centre of their unity, so the scripture shall be the rule of their unity.

3. The land of Judea, and Jerusalem, its mother-city, shall be repaired and taken under the special protection of Heaven, *v.* 10, 11. Some think this denotes particular favour to the people of the Jews, but it is rather to be understood figuratively of the gospel-church, typified by Judah and Jerusalem. The church shall be like a fruitful country, abounding in all the rich products of the soil. The whole land of Judæa, naturally uneven and hilly, shall be *turned as a plain*; it shall become a smooth level valley, from Gibeah, its utmost border north, to Rimmon, *south of Jerusalem.* The gospel of Christ, where it comes in its power, levels the ground, that the Lord alone may be exalted. As the holy land shall be levelled, so the holy city shall be peopled. *Jerusalem shall be lifted* up out of its low estate, shall be raised out of its ruins. The whole city shall be inhabited. The utmost limits of it are here mentioned, all built upon, from *Benjamin's-gate* north-east to the *corner-gate* north-west and *from the tower of Hananeel* in the south to the *king's wine-presses* in the north. *Those that dwell in it* shall dwell securely, and there shall be no more anathema (as some read it), no more curse.

II. Judgments threatened against the enemies of the church, that *have fought,* or do fight, against Jerusalem. Those that fight against the city of God, and his people, will be found fighting against God, *v.* 12. They shall waste away under grievous and languishing diseases. They shall be dashed in pieces one against another (*v.* 13): *A great tumult from the Lord shall be among them.* Those that are combined against the church will justly be separated, and set against one another; and their tumults raised against God will be avenged in tumults among themselves.

Some think this was fulfilled in the factions and dissensions that were among the Jews, when the Romans were destroying them all. The plunder of their camp shall greatly enrich the people of God, or the spoils of their country (*v.* 14): *Judah also shall eat at Jerusalem* (so one learned interpreter reads it); people shall come from all parts to share in the prey. The *wealth of the sinner is* often *laid up for the just,* and the Israel of God enriched with the spoil of the Egyptians. The very cattle shall share in the plague with which the enemies of God's church shall be cut off (*v.* 15).

Verses 16–21

Three things are here foretold:

I. Those that were left of the enemies of religion shall be so sensible of the mercy of God to them in their narrow escape that they shall apply themselves to the worship of the God of Israel, and pay their homage to him, *v.* 16. As some of Christ's foes shall be made his footstool, so others of them shall be made his friends. They shall *go up to worship* at Jerusalem, because that was the place which God had chosen, and there the temple was, which was a type of Christ and his mediation. Gospel-worship is here represented by the *keeping of the feast of tabernacles,* for the sake of those two great graces which were in a special manner *acted* and *signified* in that feast—contempt of the world, and joy in God, Neh. viii. 17. We must go to Christ our temple with all our offerings, for in him only our *spiritual sacrifices* are acceptable to God, 1 Pet. ii. 5. They shall go up *from year to year,* at the times appointed for this solemn feast. Every day of a Christian's life is a day of the *feast of tabernacles,* and every Lord's day especially.

II. Those who neglect the duties of gospel-worship shall be reckoned with for their neglect. *Upon them there shall be no rain, v.* 17. Some understand it figuratively; the rain of heavenly doctrine shall be withheld, and of the heavenly grace, which should accompany that doctrine. It is a righteous thing with God to withhold the blessings of grace from those that do not attend the means of grace, to deny the *green pastures* to those that attend not the *shepherd's tents.* If we be barren and unfruitful towards God, justly is the earth made so to us. But what shall be done to the defaulters of the land of Egypt, to whom the threatening is no threatening, for they have no rain at any time; the river Nilus waters their land, and makes it fruitful, *v.* 18, 19. There shall be, in effect, the same plague. God can restrain the overflowing of the river, which was equivalent to the shutting up of the clouds. It does not follow that those who can live without rain can therefore live without God. Omissions are sins, and those contract guilt that *go not up to worship* at the times appointed, as they have opportunity.

III. The name and character of holiness shall not be so confined as formerly. *Holiness to the Lord* had been written only upon the high priest's forehead, but now it shall not be so appropriated. All Christians shall be *living temples,* and *spiritual priests,* dedicated to the honour of God and employed in his service. There shall be a more plentiful effusion of the Spirit of holiness and sanctification after Christ's ascension than ever before. There shall be holiness introduced into common things. The furniture of their horses shall be consecrated to God. *"Upon the bells of the horses* shall be engraven *Holiness to the Lord,* or upon the *bridles* of the horses (so the margin) or the *trappings.* Travellers shall have it upon their bridles, with which they guide their horses, to guide themselves by this rule. The furniture of their houses too shall be consecrated to God, to be employed in his service. The common drinking cups they used shall be *like the bowls before the altar*, that were used either to receive the blood of the sacrifices or to present the wine and oil for the *drink-offerings*. The vessels which they used for their own tables shall be used to the glory of God, and their meals shall look like sacrifices; they shall eat and drink, not to themselves, but to him that spread their tables and fills their cups. "*Every pot in Jerusalem and in Judah shall be holiness to the Lord*—the pots in which they boil their meat, the cups out of which they drink. What they eat and drink out of these shall nourish their bodies for the service of God; and out of these they shall give liberally for the relief of the poor"; then are they *Holiness to the Lord*. When there shall be such real holiness people shall not be so concerned about ceremonial holiness: "*Those that sacrifice shall come and take* of these common vessels, *and seethe their sacrifices therein*, making no distinction between them and the *bowls before the altar*." In gospel-times the true worshippers shall worship God *in spirit and in truth*, John iv. 21. One place shall be as acceptable to God as another, and one vessel shall be as acceptable as another. There shall be no unholiness introduced into their sacred things, to corrupt them: *In that day there shall be no more the Canaanite in the house of the Lord of hosts*. Some read it, There shall be no more *the merchant*, for so a Canaanite sometimes signifies; and they think it was fulfilled when Christ once and again drove the buyers and sellers out of the temple. At the end of time, and not before, Christ shall gather out of his kingdom everything that offends.

THE PROPHECY OF
MALACHI

God's prophets were his witnesses to his church, each in his day, for several ages, witnesses for him and his authority, witnesses against sin and sinners, attesting God's providences in his dealings with his people then and his grace concerning his church in the days of the Messiah. The Jews say, Prophecy continued forty years under the second temple, and this prophet they call the *seal of prophecy*, because in him the series or succession of prophets broke off and came to a period. I. The person of the prophet. We have only his name, *Malachi*, and no account of his country or parentage. *Malachi* signifies *my angel*. Prophets were messengers, God's messengers; his name is in the original (*ch.* iii. 1) *my messenger*. The tradition of some of the ancients is that he was of the tribe of Zebulun, and that he died young. II. The scope of the prophecy. Haggai and Zechariah were sent to reprove the people for delaying to build the temple; Malachi was sent to reprove them for the neglect of it when it was built, and for their profanation of the temple-service (for from idolatry and superstition they ran into the other extreme of impiety and irreligion). And now that prophecy was to cease he speaks more clearly of the Messiah, as nigh at hand, and concludes with a direction to the people of God to keep in remembrance the law of Moses, while they were in expectation of the gospel of Christ.

CHAPTER 1

This prophet is sent first to convince and then to comfort, first to discover sin and to reprove and then to promise the coming of him who shall take away sin. And this method the blessed Spirit takes in dealing with souls, John xvi. 8. He first opens the wound and then applies the healing balm. God has provided for the engaging of Israel to himself by providence and ordinances; but it seems that they received the grace of God in vain. I. They were ungrateful to God for his favours, ver. 1-5. II. They were careless and remiss in the observance of his institutions; the priests especially so, ver. 6-14.

Verses 1-5

The prophecy of this book is entitled, *The burden of the word of the Lord* (*v.* 1), which intimates, 1. That it was of great weight and importance. 2. That it ought to be often repeated as the burden of a song. 3. That there were those to whom it was a burden and a reproach. 4. That to them it would prove a burden indeed, to sink them, unless they repented.

This *burden of the word of the Lord* was sent, 1. To Israel. Many prophets God had sent to Israel, and now he will try them with one more. 2. *By Malachi, by the hand of Malachi.*

In these verses, they are charged with ingratitude.

I. God asserts the great kindness he had for them (*v.* 2): *I have loved you, saith the Lord.* Thus abruptly, thus kindly does the sermon begin. In this one word God sums up all his gracious dealings with them.

II. They question his love, *Yet you say, Wherein hast thou loved us?* As God traces up all his favours to them to the fountain, which was his love, so he traces up all their sins against him to the fountain, which was their contempt of his love. "Have we not been wasted, impoverished, and carried captive; and wherein then *hast thou loved us?*"

III. He makes it out, beyond contradiction, that he has loved them. Some read their question, *Wherefore hast thou loved us?* as if they did indeed own that he had loved them, but insinuate that he loved them because their father Abraham had loved him, so that it was not a free love, but a love of debt, to which he replies, *"Was not Esau as near akin to Abraham as you are?* And therefore, if there were any right to a recompence for Abraham's love, Esau had it, and yet *I hated Esau* and *loved Jacob."* What a difference God had made between Jacob and Esau! Esau was Jacob's brother, his twin-brother: "Yet *I loved Jacob* and *I hated Esau*, that is, took Jacob into covenant, but refused and rejected Esau." The

apostle quotes this (Rom. ix. 13). Esau was justly hated, but Jacob freely loved.

1. The Edomites shall be made the monuments of God's justice. For *Esau have I hated; I laid his mountains waste*, the mountains of Seir, which were *his heritage*. When all that part of the world was ravaged by the Chaldean army the country of Edom was laid in ruins, Isa. xxxiv. 6, 11. The Edomites had triumphed in Jerusalem's overthrow (Ps. cxxxvii. 7), and therefore it was just to put the same cup of trembling into their hands. Jacob's cities are laid waste, but they are rebuilt; Edom's are laid waste, and never rebuilt. The sufferings of the righteous will end well; their grievances will be redressed, and their sorrow turned into joy; but the sufferings of the wicked will be as Edom's desolations, *v.* 4. The vain hopes of the Edomites had no promise to build upon. They say, "It is true, *we are impoverished*; it is the common chance, and there is no remedy; but *we will return and build the desolate places*; we are resolved we will" (not so much as asking God leave). They build presumptuously, as Hiel built Jericho in direct contradiction to the word of God (1 Kings xvi. 34), and it shall speed accordingly. They say, *We will build*; but what says *the Lord of hosts*? *They shall build, but I will throw down.* All that see them shall call them *the border of wickedness*, a sinful nation, incurably so, and therefore *the people against whom the Lord has indignation for ever.* Since their wickedness is such as will never be reformed, their desolations shall be such as are never to be repaired.

2. The Israelites shall be made the monuments of his mercy, *v.* 5. "The Edomites shall be stigmatized as a people hated of God, *but your eyes shall see* your doubts concerning his love to you silenced; for you shall have cause to say, *The Lord will be magnified from* every part and border of the land of Israel." When the border of Edom still remains desolate, and the border of Israel is repaired and replenished, then it will appear that God has loved Jacob. God's goodness being his glory, when he does us good we must proclaim him great, for that is magnifying him.

Verses 6-14

The prophet is here calling the priests to account, though they were themselves appointed judges, to call the people to an account. Thus *saith the Lord of hosts to you, O priests! v.* 6.

I. What it was that God expected from them (*v.* 6): *A son honours his father*, because he is his father; nature has written this law in the hearts of children, before God wrote it at Mount Sinai; *a servant*, though his obligation to his master is by voluntary compact, yet thinks it his duty to honour him. But the priests, who are God's children and his servants, do not fear and honour him. They were *fathers* and *masters* to the people, and expected to be called so (Judges xviii. 19, Matt. xxii. 7, 10); but they forgot their Father and Master in heaven, and the duty they owed to him. Our relation to God as our Father and Master strongly obliges us to fear and honour him. If we honour and fear the fathers of our flesh, much more the Father and Master of our spirits, Heb. xii. 9.

II. What the contempt was which the priests put upon God. They despised God's name, his word and ordinances, causing even the *sacrifices of the Lord to be abhorred*, as Eli's sons did. They *profaned God's name*, *v.* 12. They *polluted* it, *v.* 7. They not only made no account of sacred things, but they perverted them to the service of the worst purposes—their own pride, covetousness, and luxury. This is the general charge against them. To this they plead *Not guilty*, and challenge God to prove it upon them. *You say, Wherein have we despised thy name?* (*v.* 6), and *wherein have we polluted thee? v.* 7. Their defence was their offence, and their saying, *Wherein have we despised thy name?* proved them proud and perverse. Justly might they have been condemned upon the general charge, but God shows them very particularly wherein they had despised his name.

1. They despised God's name in what they said: "*You say* in your hearts, *The table of the Lord is contemptible*" (*v.* 7), and again (*v.* 12), "*You say, The table of the Lord is polluted;* it is to be no more regarded than any other table." Either the table in the temple on which the show-bread was placed, is that which they reflect upon, or rather the altar of burnt-offerings is here called the table. This they thought was contemptible in comparison with their own tables, and those of their great men: *The fruit thereof, even his meat, is contemptible.*

2. They despised God's name in what they did, which was of a piece with what they said. They thought anything would serve for a sacrifice, though ever so coarse and mean. With every sacrifice they were to bring a meat-offering of *fine flour mingled with oil*; but they brought *polluted bread* (*v.* 7). And as to the beasts they offered, though the law was express that what was offered in sacrifice should not have a blemish, yet they brought *the blind, and the lame, and the sick* (*v.* 8), and again (*v.* 13), *the torn, and the lame, and the sick*, that was ready to die of itself. Some make *v.* 8 to be a continuation of what the priests profanely said *v.* 7, *You say* to the people, *If you offer the blind for sacrifice, it is not evil; or the lame and the sick, it is not evil.* If we worship God ignorantly, and without understanding, we bring the blind for sacrifice; if we do it carelessly, if we are cold, and dull, and dead, in it, we bring the sick; if we rest in the bodily exercise, and do not make heart-work of it, we bring the *lame*; and, if we suffer vain thoughts and distractions to lodge within us, we bring the torn. Is it not a great affront to God and a great wrong and injury to our own souls? They would do no more of their work than what they were paid for. There is not a man among the priests that would *shut the doors*, or *kindle a fire, for nought*. Their work was a perfect drudgery to them (*v.* 13): *You said also, Behold, what a weariness is it!* They thought the duty of their office toilsome and troublesome, and *snuffed at it* as unreasonable.

III. God expostulates and reasons the case with them. 1. Would they affront an earthly prince thus?

You offer to God *the lame and the sick; offer it now unto thy governor* (*v.* 8), either as tribute or as a present, *will he be pleased with thee?* 2. Could they imagine that such sacrifices as these would be pleasing to God? "*Should I accept this at your hand, saith the Lord?*" (*v.* 13). If God has no pleasure in the person, if the person be not in a justified state, if he be not sanctified, God will not accept the offering. God had respect to Abel first and then to his sacrifice. 3. How could they expect to prevail with God in their intercessions for the people when they thus affronted God in their sacrifices? 4. Had God deserved this at their hands? No, he had provided comfortably for them, and had given them such encouragement in their work as might have engaged them to do it cheerfully and well.

IV. He calls them to repentance for their profanations of his holy name. So we may understand *v.* 9, "*Now, I pray you, beseech God that he will be gracious to us.* Humble yourselves for your sin, cry mightily to God for pardon; for all the rebukes of Providence we are under *are by your means.*"

V. He declares his resolution both to secure the glory of his own name and to reckon with those who profane it. God will magnify his law and make it honourable, though they vilify it and make it contemptible; for (*v.* 11) *from the rising of the sun to the going down of the same my name shall be great among the Gentiles.* Instead of those carnal ordinances, which they profaned, a spiritual way of worship shall be introduced and established: *Incense shall be offered to God's name* (which signifies prayer and praise, Ps. cxli. 2; Rev. viii. 3), instead of the blood and fat of bulls and goats. Instead of his being worshipped and served among the Jews only, a small people in a corner of the world, he will be served and worshipped in all places, *from the rising of the sun to the going down of the same; in every place,* in every part of the world, *incense shall be offered to his name*; nations shall speak of the wonderful works of God, and have them spoken to them in their own language. This is a plain prediction of that great revolution by which the Gentiles, who had been *strangers and foreigners,* came to be *fellow-citizens with the saints and of the household of God,* and welcome to the throne of grace. Profane and careless worshippers are such as *vow and sacrifice to the Lord a corrupt thing* when they have *in their flock a male.* The priests would accept it, though God would not, pretending to be more indulgent than he was. They are *deceivers*; they deal falsely and fraudulently with God. Hypocrites are deceivers, and they will prove self-deceivers, and so self-destroyers. They are *cursed*; they expect a blessing, but will meet with a curse. The heathen paid more respect to their gods, though idols, than the Jews did to theirs, though the only true and living God.

CHAPTER 2

There are two great ordinances which divine wisdom has instituted, the wretched profanation of both of which is sharply reproved in this chapter. I. The ordinance of the ministry, which is peculiar to the church; this was profaned by those who were themselves dignified with the honour of it. The priests profaned the holy things of God; this they are here charged with, ver. 1-9. II. The ordinances of marriage, which is common to the world of mankind, was profaned both by the priests and by the people, in marrying strangers (ver. 11, 12), treating their wives unkindly (ver. 13), putting them away (ver. 16), and herein dealing treacherously, ver. 10, 14, 15.

Verses 1-9

What was said in the foregoing chapter was directed to the priests (*ch.* i. 6): *Thus saith the Lord of hosts to you, O priests! that despise my name.* They might think it some excuse that they offered what the people brought. If the priests had given the people better instructions, the people would have brought better offerings; and therefore the blame returns upon the priests: *And now, O you priests! this commandment is purely for you* (v. 1).

I. A recital of the covenant God made with that sacred tribe, which was their commission for their work: The *Lord of hosts sent a commandment* to them, for the establishing of this covenant (v. 4). Let the sons of Levi know then (and particularly the sons of Aaron) what honour God put upon their family (v. 5): *My covenant was with him of life and peace.* This is called *his covenant of life and peace* because it was intended for the support of religion, which brings life and peace to the souls of men. What is here said of the covenant of priesthood is true of the covenant of grace made with all believers, as spiritual priests; it assures all believers of everlasting peace, everlasting life, all happiness both in this world and in that to come. This covenant was made with the whole tribe of Levi when they were distinguished from the rest of the tribes. These great blessings of life and peace, contained in that covenant, God *gave to him*, to Levi, to Aaron, to Phinehas; he entrusted them with these benefits for the use and behoof of God's Israel; they received that they might give. The tribe of Levi gave a signal proof of their holy fear of God when they appeared so bravely against the worshippers of the golden calf (Exod. xxxii. 26); and for their zeal in that matter God bestowed this blessing upon them. Some read v. 5 not as the consideration of the grant, but as the condition of it: *I gave them to him, provided* that he should *fear before me.* They were hereby made *the messengers of the Lord of hosts*, messengers of that covenant of life and peace, not mediators of it, but only messengers, or ambassadors, employed to treat of the terms of peace between God and Israel. The priests were *God's mouth* to his people. *The priests' lips should keep knowledge*, not keep it from the people, but keep it for them. Ministers must be men of knowledge; they must not only have it, but they must have it ready to be communicated to others as there is occasion. The people *should seek the law at his mouth*; they should consult the priests as God's messengers.

II. The fidelity and zeal of many of their predecessors in the priest's office, are mentioned as an aggravation of their sin in degenerating from such honourable ancestors. The good priest (v. 6) was ready and mighty in the scriptures: *The law of truth was in his mouth*, for the use of those that *asked the law at his mouth.* Truth is a law, it has a commanding power. It is by truth that Christ rules. He lived like a priest that was chosen to *walk before God*, 1 Sam. ii. 30. He walked with God in peace, *in equity. He did turn many away from iniquity*, and God crowned his endeavours with wonderful success; he helped to save many a soul from death, and there are multitudes now in heaven blessing God that ever they knew him. *When the priest is upright many will be upright.*

III. A high charge drawn up against the priests who violated the covenant. Many corruptions had crept into the church of the Jews at this time, mixed marriages, admitting strangers into the house of God, profanation of the sabbath-day, which were all owing to the carelessness and unfaithfulness of the priests. 1. They transgressed the rule: "*You have not kept my ways*, not kept in them yourselves, nor done your part to keep others in them," v. 9. 2. They betrayed their trust: "*You have corrupted the covenant of Levi.* You have managed your office as if it were designed only to feed you fat and make you great, and not for the glory of God and the good of the souls of men." Another instance of their betraying their trust was that they were *partial in the law*, v. 9. In the law they were to lay down to the people they *knew faces* (so the word is); they *accepted persons.*

3. They did mischief to the souls of men, which they should have helped to save: *You have caused many to stumble at the law.* 4. When they were under the rebukes of the word and of the providence of God, they *would not hear.*

IV. The judgments God had brought upon these priests. They had lost their comfort (v. 2): *I have already cursed your blessings.* They had not the comfort of their work, which is the satisfaction of doing good. They had lost their credit (v. 9): *Therefore have I also made you contemptible and base before all the people.* When they forsook the ways of God, and corrupted the covenant of Levi, they thereby made themselves not only mean, but vile, in the eyes even of the common people.

V. A sentence of wrath passed upon them, v. 2, 3. But it is conditional: *If you will not lay it to heart*, implying, "If you will, God's anger shall be turned away." *I will send a curse upon you*, so that you shall neither be blessed yourselves nor blessings to the people, but even your plenty shall be a plague to you and you shall be plagues to your generation." The fruits of the earth should be no comfort to them: "*Behold, I will corrupt your seed;* the corn you sow shall rot under ground." Or it may be understood of the seed of the word which they preached. *Bring no more vain oblations;* your *incense is an abomination* to me.

Verses 10–17

Corrupt practices are the genuine fruit and product of corrupt principles. In these verses we find men dealing falsely with one another, and it is because they think falsely of their God.

I. In general, they *dealt treacherously every man against his brother*, v. 10. It cannot be expected that he who is false to his God should be true to his friend. Two things they are here charged with—taking strange wives of heathen nations, and abusing and putting away the wives they had of their own nation; in both these they violated a sacred covenant. They married strange wives, which was expressly prohibited, and provided against, in that covenant, Deut. vii. 3. God engaged to do them good upon this condition, that they should not mingle with the heathen; this was the covenant made with their fathers, the great charter by which that nation was incorporated. *Have we not all one Father?* Yes, we have, for *has not one God created us?* Are we not all *his offspring?* Here it seems to refer to the Jewish nation: *Have we not all one father*, Abraham, or Jacob? This they prided themselves in, *We have Abraham to our father.* "*Has not one God created us*, that is, formed us into a people, made us a nation by ourselves, and put a life into us, distinct from that of other nations? And should not this oblige us to maintain the dignity of our character?" They were dedicated to God, as well as distinguished from the neighbouring nations. *Israel was holiness to the Lord* (Jer. ii. 3), but by marrying strange wives they profaned this holiness, and laid the honour of it in the dust. *Judah has married the daughter of a strange god.* The harm was not so much that she was the daughter of a strange nation, but that she was the daughter of a strange god. God would reckon with them for it (v. 12): *The Lord will cut off the man that doeth this*, that marries the daughter of a strange god. He has, in effect, cut himself off from the holy nation, and *God will cut him off, him and all that belongs to him;* so the original intimates. God will no more own them as belonging to his nation; and the priest that *offers an offering to the Lord*, if he marry a strange wife (as we find many of the priests did, Ezra x. 18), shall not escape. He shall be cut off from the temple of the Lord, as others from the tabernacles of Jacob. In contempt of the marriage-covenant, which God instituted for the common benefit of mankind, they abused and put away the wives they had of their own nation (*v.* 13). They did not behave as they ought to have done towards their wives. The wives, not daring to make their case known to any other, complained to God, and *covered the altar of the Lord with tears, with weeping, and with crying.* The good Master we serve will not have his altar covered with tears, but compassed with songs. It is a reason given why yoke-fellows should live in holy love and joy—*that their prayers may not be hindered,* 1 Pet. iii. 7. They dealt treacherously with them, *v.* 14–16. They did not perform their promises to them, but took in concubines to share in the affection that was due to their wives only. They *put them away,* gave them a bill of divorce, and turned them off. In all this *they covered violence with their garment;* they abused their wives, and yet, in the sight of others, they pretended to be very loving to them. "*The Lord has been witness between thee and the wife of thy youth* (*v.* 14), has been witness to the marriage-covenant between thee and her, for to him you appealed concerning your sincerity and fidelity. She is *thy wife;* thy own, bone of thy bone and flesh of thy flesh, the nearest to thee of all the relations thou hast in the world, and to cleave to whom thou must quit the rest. She is *the wife of thy youth,* who had thy affections when they were at the strongest. Let not the darling of thy youth be the scorn and loathing of thy age. She is *thy companion;* she has long been an equal sharer with thee in thy cares, and griefs, and joys." The wife is to be looked upon, not as a servant, but as a companion to the husband. "She is *the wife of thy covenant* to whom thou art so firmly bound that, while she continues faithful, thou canst not be loosed from her, for it was a covenant for life." Man and wife should continue together, to their lives' end, in holy love and peace, and neither quarrel with each other nor separate from each other. God has joined them together (*v.* 15): *Did not he make one,* one Eve for one Adam, that Adam might never *take another to her to vex her* (Lev. xviii. 18), nor put her away to make room for another? Designing *Adam a help meet for him,* he made him *one wife;* had he made him more, he would not have had a *meet help.* And wherefore did he make but one woman for one man? It was *that he might seek a godly seed—a seed of God* (so the word is), a seed that should bear the image of God, that *every man having his own wife,* and *but one,* according to the law (1 Cor. vii. 2), they might live in chaste and holy love, and not, as brute beasts, that the children, being born in holy matrimony, which is an ordinance of God, might thus be made a *seed to serve him.* God is much displeased with those who go about to put asunder *what he has joined together* (*v.* 16). The caution inferred from all this (*v.* 15): *Therefore take heed to your spirit, and let none deal treacherously against the wife of his youth;* and again, *v.* 16.

II. How corrupt their principles were, to which were owing all these corrupt practices! Let us trace up the streams to the fountain (*v.* 17): *You have wearied the Lord with your words.* It is a wearisome thing, even to God himself, to hear people insist upon their own justification in their corrupt and wicked practices. They had denied him to be a holy God, and had the impudence to say, *Every one that does evil is good in the sight of the Lord, and he delights in them.* This wicked inference they drew, without any reason, from the prosperity of sinners in their sinful courses (see *ch.* iii. 15). Under pretence of making God not so severe as he was commonly represented, they said he was *altogether such a one as themselves.* They said, "*Where is the God of judgment?* We may do what we please; he sees us not, nor will regard us."

Verses 1–6

The first words of this chapter seem a direct answer to the profane atheistical demand of the scoffers: *Where is the God of judgment?* "Here he is; he is just at the door; the long-expected Messiah is ready to appear; and he says, *For judgment have I come into this world.*"

I. A prophecy of the appearing of his forerunner John the Baptist, which the prophet Isaiah had foretold (*ch.* xl. 3), as the *preparing* of the *way of the Lord.* 1. He is *God's messenger.* John Baptist had his commission *from heaven, and not of men.* All held John Baptist for a prophet, for he was God's messenger, as the prophets were, to call men to repentance and reformation. 2. He is Christ's harbinger: He *shall prepare the way before me,* by taking them off from a confidence in their relation to Abraham *as their father* (which, they thought, would serve their turn without a saviour), and by giving notice that the Messiah was now at hand.

II. A prophecy of the appearing of the Messiah himself: "*The Lord, whom you seek, shall suddenly come to his temple,* even *the God of judgment,* who, you think, has forsaken the earth. The Messiah has been long called *he that should come,* now shortly he will come." 1. He is *the Lord—Adonai,* the basis and foundation on which the world is founded, that one *Lord over all* (Acts x. 36) that has all power committed to him (Matt. xxviii. 18) and is to *reign over the house of Jacob for ever,* Luke i. 33. 2. He is the *Messenger of the covenant,* or the *angel of the covenant,* sent from heaven to negotiate a peace between God and man. Christ is the *angel of this covenant,* by whose mediation it is brought about and established. That covenant which is all our *salvation began to be spoken by the Lord,* Heb. ii. 3. Though he is the *prince of the covenant* (as some read this) yet he condescended to be the *messenger of it.* 3. He it is *whom you seek, whom you delight in,* whom the pious Jews expect and desire. In looking and waiting for him, they *looked for redemption in Jerusalem* and *waited for the consolation of Israel,* Luke ii. 25, 38. Those that seek Jesus shall find pleasure in him. If he be our heart's desire he will be our heart's delight. 4. He *shall suddenly come;* his coming draws nigh, and we see it not at so great a distance as the patriarchs saw it at. 5. He *shall come to his temple,* this temple at Jerusalem, which was lately built. It is his temple, for it is *his Father's house,* John ii. 16.

III. The great ends and intentions of his coming, *v.* 2. He is one whom they seek, and yet *who may abide the day of his coming,* though he comes not to condemn the world, but that the world through him might have life? Even in the days of his flesh there were some emanations of his glory and power, such as none could stand before, witness his transfiguration. The Jewish doctors speak of the *pangs* or *griefs* of the Messiah, meaning (they say) the great afflictions that should be to Israel at the time of his coming. *He shall be like a refiner's fire,* which separates between the gold and the dross by melting the ore, or *like fuller's soap,* which with much rubbing fetches the spots out of the cloth. Christ came to discover men, *that the thoughts of many hearts might be revealed*

(Luke ii. 35), to separate between the precious and the vile, for *his fan is in his hand* (Matt. iii. 12).

1. The gospel shall work good upon those that are disposed to be good, to them it shall be a savour of life unto life (*v.* 3): *He shall sit as a refiner.* He will purge them *as gold and silver*, that is, he will sanctify them inwardly. *He will purge them* with fire, *as gold and silver are purged*, for he *baptizes with the Holy Ghost and with fire* (Matt. iii. 11), with the Holy Ghost working like fire. *That they may offer unto the Lord an offering in righteousness*, that is, that they may be in sincerity converted to God and consecrated. He makes the tree good that the fruit may be good. And then it follows (*v.* 4), *The offering of Judah and Jerusalem shall be pleasant unto the Lord.* It shall no longer be offensive, as when they brought the torn, and the lame, and the sick, for sacrifice; but it shall be *acceptable*. The Messiah will, by his grace in them, make them acceptable; when he has purified and refined them, then they shall offer such sacrifices as God requires and will accept. He will, by his intercession for them, make them accepted.

2. It shall turn for a testimony against those that are resolved to go on in their wickedness, *v.* 5. This is the direct answer to their challenge, "*Where is the God of judgment?* You shall know where he is, and shall know it to your terror and confusion, for *I will come near to you to judgment.*" The sinners that must appear to be judged by the gospel of Christ are the *sorcerers*, who deal in spiritual wickedness, and the *adulterers*, who wallow in the lusts of the flesh; and the *false swearers*, who profane God's name by calling him to witness to a lie; and the oppressors, who *defraud the hireling in his wages* and crush *the widow and fatherless*. That which is at the bottom of all this is, *They fear not me, saith the Lord of hosts. I will come near and will be a swift witness against* them.

IV. The ratification of all this (*v.* 6): *For I am the Lord; I change not; therefore you sons of Jacob are not consumed.* Though the sentence passed against evil works (*v.* 5) be not executed speedily, yet it will be executed for he is *the Lord*; he *changes not*. The people of Israel had reason to say that he was an unchangeable God, for he had been faithful to his covenant with them and their fathers. They had been false and fickle in their conduct to him, and he might justly have abandoned them; but because he *remembered his covenant*, they were preserved. We may apply this to ourselves; because we have to do with a God that *changes not*, therefore it is that *we are not consumed*.

Verses 7–12

God's controversy with the men of that generation for deserting his service and robbing him.

I. They had run away from their Master, and quitted the work he gave them to do (*v.* 7): *You have gone away from my ordinances and have not kept them.* What a gracious invitation God gives them to return and repent: "*Return unto me*, and to your duty, return to your allegiance, return as a traveller that has missed his way, as a soldier that has run his colours, as a treacherous wife that has gone away from her husband; return to me; and then *I will return to you* and will remove the judgments you are under and prevent those you fear." What a peevish answer they return! "*But you said* with disdain to the prophets, to one another, to your own hearts, to stifle the convictions you were under: you said, *Wherein shall we return?*" They take it as an affront to be *told of their faults*, and called upon to amend them. They are so ignorant of themselves, and of the strictness, extent, and spiritual nature, of the divine law, that they think they need no repentance. They are firmly resolved to go on in sin.

II. They had robbed their Master, and embezzled his goods. They stand indicted for robbery, for sacrilege, the worst of robberies: *You have robbed me. Will a man* be so daringly impudent as to *rob God? Will a man do violence to God?* so some read it. *Will a man stint or straighten him?* so others read it. The people plead *Not guilty*, and put God upon the proof of it. They rob God, and know not what they do. They rob him of his honour, rob him of that which is devoted to him, to be employed in his service, rob him of themselves, rob him of sabbath-time, rob him of that which is given for the support of religion, and give him not his dues out of their estates; and yet they ask, *Wherein have we robbed thee?* It is *in tithes and offerings*. They detained them, defrauded the priests of them, would not pay their tithes. They brought not the offerings which God required, or brought the torn, and lame, and sick which were not fit for use. For this they were *cursed with a curse, v.* 9. God punished them with famine and scarcity, through unseasonable weather, or insects that ate up the fruits of the earth. Because God had punished them with scarcity of bread, they made that a pretence for robbing him—that now, being impoverished, they could not afford to bring their tithes and offerings. They are urged to reform in this matter, with a promise that if they did the judgments should be removed. *Bring you all the tithes into the storehouse.* "Bring in the full tithes to the utmost that the law requires, *that there may be meat in God's house* for those that serve at the altar, whether there be meat in your houses or no." "Let God be first served, and then *prove me herewith, saith the Lord of hosts, whether I will not open the windows of heaven.*" The expression is figurative; every good gift coming from above, thence God will plentifully pour out upon them the bounties of his providence. Very sudden plenty is expressed by *opening the windows of heaven*, 2 Kings vii. 2. Here they are opened to *pour down blessings*, to such a degree that there should not be *room enough to receive* them. God will not only be reconciled to sinners that repent and reform, but he will be a bountiful benefactor, to them. God has blessings ready to bestow upon us, but, through the weakness of our faith and narrowness of our desires, we have not room to receive them. Whereas the fruits of their ground had been eaten up by locusts and caterpillars God would now remove that judgment (*v.* 11). Whereas they had lain under the *reproach of famine*, now *all nations shall call them blessed*.

Verses 13–18

I. The angry notice God takes of the impudent blasphemous talk of the sinners in Zion. *Your words have been stout against me, saith the Lord.* They came from their pride, and haughtiness, and contempt of God. They spoke it proudly, and with disdain, scorning to be under the divine check and government. *What have we spoken so much against thee*, so much that there needs all this ado about it? They cannot deny that they have spoken against God, but they make a light matter of it. They said, *It is vain to serve God*, or, "*He is vain that serves God*, that is, he labours in vain and to no purpose; he has his labour for his pains, and therefore is a fool for his labour. We have walked *mournfully*, or *in black*, with great gravity and great grief, *before the Lord of hosts*, have afflicted our souls, and yet we are never the better." They would have it thought that they had served God and had kept his ordinances, whereas it was only the external observance of them that they had kept up, and therefore might say, It is *in vain*. They had *walked mournfully* before God, whereas God had required them to serve him with gladness, and to walk cheerfully before him. They by their own superstitions made the service of God a task and drudgery to themselves, and then complained of it as a hard service. They complained that they had got nothing by their religion; they were still in poverty and affliction. Perhaps this refers to the errors of the Sadducees. They denied a future state, and then said, It is *vain to serve God*, which has indeed some colour in it, for, *if in this life only we had hope in Christ, we were of all men most miserable*, 1 Cor. xv. 19. They maintained that wickedness was the way of prosperity, *v.* 15. The outward prosperity of sinners in their sins, as it has weakened the hands of the godly in their godliness (Ps. lxxiii. 13), so it has strengthened the hands of the wicked in their wickedness. Wait awhile, and you shall see *those that work wickedness set up* as a mark to the arrows of God's vengeance, and *those that tempt God delivered* to the tormentors.

II. Even in this corrupt and degenerate age, when there was so great a decay, so great a contempt, of serious godliness, there were yet some that retained their integrity and zeal for God. They *feared the Lord*—that is the beginning of wisdom and the root of all religion; they reverenced the majesty of God, submitted to his authority. In every age there has been a remnant that feared the Lord, though sometimes but a little remnant. They *thought upon his name*; and meditated upon the discoveries God has made of himself in his word and by his providences. They *spoke often one to another* concerning the God they feared. *Those that feared the Lord* kept together; they spoke kindly one to another, for the promoting of mutual love, that might not *wax cold* when *iniquity* did thus *abound*. They spoke intelligently to one another, for the increasing of faith and holiness. Then, when iniquity was bold and barefaced, the people of God took courage, and stirred up themselves, *the innocent against the hypocrite*, Job xvii. 8. When religion was misrepresented, its friends did all they could to support the credit of it. When seducers were busy to deceive unwary souls with prejudices against religion, those that feared God were industrious to strengthen one another's hands. God countenanced them: *The Lord hearkened and heard it*, and was well pleased with it. When the two disciples, going to Emmaus, were discoursing concerning Christ, he hearkened and heard, and joined himself to them, and made a third, Luke xxiv. 15. *A book of remembrance was written before him*. God remembers the services of his people, that he may say, *Well done; enter thou into the joy of thy Lord*. God has a book for the sighs and tears of his mourners (Ps. lvi. 8). Never was any good word spoken of God, or for God, but it was registered, that it might be recompensed. He promises them a share in his glory hereafter (*v.* 17): *They shall be mine, saith the Lord of hosts, in that day when I make up my jewels. They shall be my segullah—my peculiar treasure* (it is the word used, Exod. xix. 5), *in the day when I make* or *do* what I have said and designed to do; so some read it. The saints are God's jewels; they are a *royal diadem* in his hand, Isa. lxii. 3. There is a day coming when God will *make up his jewels*. They shall be gathered up out of the dirt into which they are now thrown, from all places to which they are now scattered. He promises them a share in his grace now: *I will spare them as a man spares his own son that serves him*. The word usually signifies to spare with compassion, *as a father pities his children*, Ps. ciii. 13. It is our duty to serve God with the disposition of children. We must be his sons, must by a new birth partake of a divine nature. And we must be his servants; God will not have his children trained up in idleness; they must do him service, from a principle of love, with cheerfulness and delight. Nehemiah, when he had done much good, yet, knowing there is not a *just*

man on earth, that does good and sins not, prays, *Lord, spare me according to the greatness of thy mercy*; Neh. xiii. 22. And God as a Father, will show them this mercy. They will thus be distinguished from the children of this world (*v.* 18). You that now speak against God as making no difference between good and bad, and say, *It is in vain to serve him* (*v.* 14), you shall be made to see your error. This manifest difference that was made between the believing Jews and those that persisted in their infidelity, at the time of the destruction of Jerusalem, and of the Jewish church and nation, by the Romans. But it is to have its full accomplishment at the second coming of Jesus Christ. All the children of men are either such as serve God or such as serve him not. In this world it is often hard to *discern between the righteous and the wicked*. There are many who, we think, serve God, who, having not their hearts right with him, will be found none of his servants; and, on the other hand, many will be found his faithful servants, who, because they followed not with us, did not, as we thought, serve him. At the bar of Christ, in the last judgment, it will be easy to *discern between the righteous and the wicked*; for then every man's character will be both perfected and perfectly discovered, every man will then appear in his true colours, and his disguises will be taken off.

CHAPTER 4

I. Concerning the state of recompence and retribution, ver. 1–3. This is represented under a prophecy of the destruction of Jerusalem. II. Concerning the state of trial and preparation they are directed to keep to the law of Moses (ver. 4) and expect a further discovery of God's will by Elijah the prophet, that is, by John Baptist, the harbinger of the Messiah, ver. 5, 6.

Verses 1–3

The great and terrible day of the Lord, like the pillar of cloud and fire, shall have a dark side turned towards the Egyptians that fight against God, and a bright side towards the faithful Israelites that follow him: *The day cometh*, has reference both to the first and to the second coming of Jesus Christ.

I. In both Christ is a consuming fire to those that rebel against him. The day of his coming *shall burn as an oven*; it shall be a day of wrath, of *fiery indignation*. God, that has perfect knowledge of everyone's character, knows who are *the proud*, and of everyone's actions, knows who they are that *do wickedly*; and they shall be as *stubble* to this fire; they shall be consumed by it, and it is wholly owing to themselves that they shall be so, for they make themselves stubble, that is, combustible matter, to this fire. Those that by their unbelief oppose Christ thereby set themselves as *briers and thorns* before a *devouring fire*, Isa. xxvii. 4, 5. *The day that cometh shall burn them up*, and shall *leave them neither root nor branch*. Now this was fulfilled when Christ spoke terror and condemnation to the proud Pharisees and the other Jews that did wickedly, when he sent that fire on the earth which burnt up the chaff of the traditions of the elders and the corrupt glosses they had put upon the law of God. Jerusalem was destroyed by the Romans, and the nation of the Jews, as a nation, blotted out. This seems to be principally intended here; our Saviour says that those should be the *days of vengeance*, Luke xxi. 22. It is certainly applicable also to the day of judgment.

II. In both Christ is a rejoicing light to those who serve him faithfully (*v.* 2). Here are mercy and comfort kept in store for all those who fear the Lord and think on his name. *To you that fear my name shall the Sun of righteousness arise, with healing in his wings.* The day that comes will be a fair and bright day to those who fear God, and reviving as the rising sun is to the earth; and particular notice is taken of the rising of the sun upon Zoar when that was mercifully distinguished from the cities of the plain, Gen. xix. 23. When the hearts of others *fail for fear* let them *lift up their heads for joy, for their redemption draws nigh,* Luke xxi. 28. By the *Sun of righteousness* here we are certainly to understand Jesus Christ. But it is to be applied to the coming of Christ in the flesh to seek and save those that were lost. Christ is the *light of the world.* He is the *light of men* (John i. 4), is to men's souls as the sun is to the visible world, which without the sun would be a dungeon; so would mankind be darkness itself without the *light of the glory of God* shining *in the face of Christ.* He is the *Sun of righteousness,* for he is himself a righteous Saviour. Righteousness sometimes signifies mercy or benignity, and it was in Christ that the *tender mercy of our God* visited us. Those that are governed by a holy fear of God shall have his *love* also *shed abroad in their hearts by the Holy Ghost.* Christ's second coming will be a glorious and welcome sun-rising to all that *fear his name.* Christ came, as *the sun,* to bring not only light to a dark world, but health to a diseased distempered world. The Jews have a proverbial saying, *As the sun riseth, infirmities decrease.* Christ came into the world to be the great physician, and the great medicine too, both the balm in Gilead, and the physician there. When he was upon earth, he went about as the sun in his circuit, doing this good; he *healed all manner of sicknesses and diseases among the people.* His healing bodily diseases was a specimen of his great design in coming into the world to heal the diseases of men's souls. *"You shall go forth,* as those that are healed go abroad and return to their business." The souls shall go forth out of their bodies at death, and the bodies out of their graves at the resurrection, as prisoners out of their dungeons, to see the light and be set at liberty. "You shall likewise *grow up*; being restored to health and liberty, you shall increase in knowledge, and grace, and spiritual strength." Those that by the grace of God are made wise and good are by the same grace made wiser and better. Their growth is compared to that of *the calves of the stall,* which is a quick, strong, and useful growth. Some read it, instead of *You shall grow up,* You shall *move yourselves,* or *leap for joy,* shall be as frolicsome as calves of the stall, when they are let loose in the open field. It shall make them victorious over their enemies (*v.* 3): *You shall tread down the wicked.* When believers by faith *overcome the world,* when they suppress their own corrupt appetites and passions, when the God of peace bruises Satan under their feet, then they *tread down the wicked.* The saints' triumphs are all owing to God's victories; it is not they that do this, but God that does it for them.

Verses 4–6

This is doubtless intended for a solemn conclusion. They were not to expect any more of the dictates of the Spirit of prophecy, till the beginning of the gospel of the Messiah.

Now there are two things required.

I. They must keep up an obedient veneration for the law of Moses (*v.* 4): *Remember the law of Moses my servant,* and observe to do according to it, even that law which *I commanded unto him in Horeb.* Honourable mention is made of *Moses.* God by Malachi calls him *Moses my servant*; for the righteous shall be had in everlasting remembrance. Honourable mention is made of the *law of Moses*; it was what God himself *commanded.* We are concerned to keep the law because God has commanded it and commanded it for us, for we are the spiritual Israel; and, if we expect the benefit of the covenant with Israel (Heb. viii. 10), we must observe the commands given to Israel, those of them that were intended to be of

perpetual obligation. The office of conscience is to bid us *remember the law.* Even when we have made considerable advances in knowledge we must still retain the first principles of practical religion and resolve to abide by them. Those that study the writings of the prophets, and the apocalypse, must still remember the law of Moses and the four gospels. Prophecy was now to cease in the church for some ages, and the Spirit of prophecy not to return till the *beginning of the gospel,* and now they are told to *remember the law of Moses*; let them live by the rules and live upon the promises. As long as we have Bibles, we may keep our communion with God, and keep ourselves in his way. They were to expect the coming of the Messiah, the preaching of his gospel, and the setting up of his kingdom. Let them observe the law of Moses, and then they might expect the benefit of the gospel of Christ, for *to him that has,* and uses what he has well, *more shall be given, and he shall have abundance.*

II. They must keep up a believing expectation of the gospel of Christ, and must look for the beginning of it in the appearing of Elijah the prophet (*v.* 5, 6). The *law and the prophets were until John* (Luke xvi. 16); they continued to be the only lights of the church till that morning-star appeared. The Jewish doctors will have it to be the same Elijah that prophesied in Israel in the days of Ahab—that he shall come again to be the forerunner of the Messiah; yet others of them say not the same person, but another of the same spirit. But we Christians know very well that John Baptist was the Elias that was to come, Matt. xvii. 10–13; and very expressly, Matt. xi. 14, *This is Elias that was to come;* and *v.* 10, the same of whom it is written, *Behold, I send my messenger, ch.* iii. 1. Elijah was a man of great austerity, bold in reproving sin. John Baptist was animated by the same spirit and power, and preached repentance and reformation, as Elias had done. John Baptist gave them fair warning when he told them of the *wrath to come,* and put them into a way of escape from it, and when he told them of the *fan in Christ's hand,* with which Christ would thoroughly purge his floor; see Matt. iii. 7, 10, 12. John Baptist *shall turn the heart of the fathers to their children, and the heart of the children to their fathers;* so *making ready a people prepared for him* (Luke i. 16, 17). It is promised concerning John, 1. That he shall make a bold stand against the strong torrent of sin and impiety. This is called his *coming to restore all things* (Matt. xvii. 11). 2. That he shall preach a doctrine that shall reach men's hearts. Many had their consciences awakened by his ministry. 3. That he shall turn the hearts of the fathers with the children, and of the children with the fathers (for so some read it), to God and to their duty. 4. That thus he shall be an instrument to bind them faster to each other, by bringing and binding them all to their God. He shall prepare the way for that kingdom of heaven which will make all its faithful subjects of *one heart* and *one soul* (Acts iv. 32), which will be a kingdom of love, and will slay all enmities. The body of the Jewish nation, by their impiety and impenitence in it, had laid themselves open to the curse of God. God was ready to smite them with that curse, but he will yet once more try them, and therefore he sends John Baptist to preach repentance to them, that their conversion might prevent their confusion; so unwilling is God that any should perish. Some observe that the last word of the Old Testament is a curse, that we may bid Christ welcome, who comes with a blessing; and it is with a blessing, with the choicest of blessings, that the New Testament ends, and with it let us arm ourselves, or rather let God arm us, against this curse. *The grace of our Lord Jesus Christ be with us all. Amen.*

THE NEW TESTAMENT

AN EXPOSITION, WITH PRACTICAL OBSERVATIONS, OF

THE GOSPEL

ACCORDING TO

ST. MATTHEW

I. *The New Testament of our Lord and Saviour Jesus Christ ;* so this second part of the Holy Bible is entitled: The *new covenant.* But, when it is (as here) spoken of as Christ's act and deed, it is most properly rendered a *testament*, for he is the testator, and it becomes of force *by his death* (Heb. ix. 16, 17). All the grace contained in this book is owing to Jesus Christ as our Lord and Saviour; and, unless we consent to him as our Lord, we cannot expect any benefit by him as our Saviour. This is called a *new* testament, to distinguish it from that which was given by Moses. How carefully do we preserve, and with what attention and pleasure do we read, the last will and testament of a friend, who has therein left us a fair estate, and, with it, high expressions of his love to us! How precious then should this testament of our blessed Saviour be to us, which secures to us all his unsearchable riches! It is *his* testament; for though, as is usual, it was written by others, yet he dictated it; and the night before he died, in the institution of his supper, he signed, sealed, and published it, in the presence of twelve witnesses. In it is declared *the whole counsel of God* concerning our salvation, Acts xx. 27.

II. *The Four Gospels. Gospel* signifies *good news,* or *glad tidings ;* and this history of Christ's coming *into the world to save sinners* is, without doubt, the best news that ever came from heaven to earth; the angel gave it this title (Luke ii. 10), Ἐυαγγελίζομαι ὑμῖν—*I bring you good tidings ; I bring the gospel to you.* And the prophet foretold it, Isa. lii. 7; lxi. 1. *Gospel* is an old Saxon word; it is *God's spell* or *word.* The four books which contain the history of the Redeemer we commonly call *the four gospels*, and the inspired penmen of them *evangelists*, or *gospel-writers.* These four gospels were early and constantly received by the primitive church, and read in Christian assemblies, as appears by the writings of Justin Martyr and Irenæus, who lived little more than a hundred years after the ascension of Christ. A Harmony of these four evangelists was compiled by Tatian about that time, which he called, Τὸ διὰ τεσσάρων—*The Gospel out of the four.* In the third and fourth centuries there were gospels forged by divers sects, and published, one under the name of St. Peter, another of St. Thomas, another of St. Philip, &c. But they were never owned by the church.

III. *The Gospel according to St. Matthew.* The penman was by birth a Jew, by calling a publican, till Christ commanded his attendance, and then he left *the receipt of custom*, to follow him, and was one of those that accompanied him *all the time that the Lord Jesus went in and out, beginning from the baptism of John unto the day that he was taken up,* Acts i. 21, 22. He was therefore a competent witness of what he has here recorded. Doubtless, it was written in Greek, as the other parts of the New Testament were; not in that language which was peculiar to the Jews, whose church and state were near a period, but in that which was common to the world, and in which the knowledge of Christ would be most effectually transmitted to the nations of the earth.

CHAPTER 1

This evangelist begins with the account of Christ's parentage and birth, the ancestors from whom he descended, and the manner of his entry into the world, for it was foretold that he should be the son of David, and should be born of a virgin. I. His pedigree from Abraham in forty-two generations, three fourteens, ver. 1–17. II. An account of the circumstances of his birth, to show that he was born of a virgin, ver. 18–25.

Verses 1–17

Concerning this genealogy of our Saviour,

I. The title of it. It is *the book of the generation of Jesus Christ*, of his ancestors according to the flesh; or, It is the narrative of his birth. It is Βίβλος Γενέσεως —*a book of Genesis.* The Old Testament begins with the book of the generation of the world, but the glory of the New Testament *herein* excelleth, that it begins with *the book of the generation of* him that made the world.

II. The principal intention of it. It is not an endless or needless genealogy. It is like a pedigree given in evidence, to prove a title, and make out a claim; the design is to prove that our Lord Jesus is *the son of David,* and *the son of Abraham*, of that nation and family out of which the Messiah was to arise. Abraham and David were, in their day, the great trustees of the promise relating to the Messiah. It was promised to Abraham that Christ should descend from him (Gen. xii. 3; xxii. 18), and to David that he should

descend from him (2 Sam. vii. 12; Ps. lxxxix. 3, &c.; cxxxii. 11). Christ is here first called *the son of David*, because under that title he was commonly spoken of, and expected, among the Jews. They who owned him to be *the Christ*, called him *the son of David,* ch. xv. 22; xx. 31; xxi. 15. This, therefore, the evangelist undertakes to make out, that he is not only a *son of David*, but that *son of David* on whose *shoulders the government was to be*; not only a *son of Abraham*, but that *son of Abraham* who was to be *the father of many nations.*

In calling Christ *the son of David*, and *the son of Abraham*, he shows that God is faithful to his promise, and will make good every word that he has spoken; and this, 1. Though the performance be long deferred. Delays of promised mercies, though they exercise our patience, do not weaken God's promise. 2. Though it begin to be despaired of. This *son of David*, and *son of Abraham*, who was to be the glory of his Father's house, was born when the seed of Abraham was a despised people, recently become tributary to the Roman yoke, and when the house of David was buried in obscurity; for Christ was to be *a root out of a dry ground.*

III. The particular series of it, drawn in the direct line from Abraham downward, according to the genealogies recorded in the beginning of the books of Chronicles.

Some particulars in this genealogy.

1. Among the ancestors of Christ who had brethren, generally he descended from a younger brother; such Abraham himself was, and Jacob, and Judah, and David, and Nathan, and Rhesa; to show that the pre-eminence of Christ came not from the primogeniture of his ancestors, but from the will of God, who *exalteth them of low degree*, and puts *more abundant honour upon that part which lacked*.

2. Among the sons of Jacob, besides Judah from whom Shiloh came, notice is here taken of *his brethren: Judas and his brethren*. No mention is made of Ishmael the son of Abraham, or of Esau the son of Isaac; because they were shut out of the church; whereas all the children of Jacob were taken in and therefore are mentioned in this genealogy.

3. Phares and Zara, the twin-sons of Judah, are likewise both named, though Phares only was Christ's ancestor, for the same reason that the brethren of Judah are taken notice of.

4. There are four women, and but four, named in this genealogy; two of them were originally *strangers to the commonwealth of Israel*, Rachab a Canaanitess, and a harlot besides, and Ruth the Moabitess; for *in Jesus Christ there is neither Greek nor Jew*; those that are *strangers and foreigners* are welcome, in Christ, to *the citizenship of the saints*. The other two were adulteresses, Thamar and Bathsheba; which was a further mark of humiliation put upon our Lord Jesus. He took upon him *the likeness of sinful flesh* (Rom. viii. 3), and takes even great sinners, upon their repentance, into the nearest relation to himself.

5. Though divers kings are here named, yet none is expressly called a king but David (*v.* 6), because with him the covenant of royalty was made. The Messiah is therefore said to inherit *the throne of his father David*, Luke i. 32.

6. In the pedigree of the kings of Judah, between Joram and Ozias (*v.* 8), there are three left out, namely, Ahaziah, Joash, and Amaziah; and therefore when it is said, *Joram begat Ozias*, it is meant, according to the usage of the Hebrew tongue, that Ozias was lineally descended from him.

7. Some observe what a mixture there was of good and bad in the succession of these kings; as for instance (*v.* 7, 8), wicked *Roboam begat* wicked *Abia*; wicked *Abia begat* good *Asa*; good *Asa begat* good *Josaphat*; good *Josaphat begat* wicked *Joram*. Grace does not run in the blood, neither does reigning sin. God's grace is his own, and he gives or withholds it as he pleases.

8. The captivity in Babylon is mentioned as a remarkable period in this line, *v.* 11, 12. All things considered, it was a wonder that the Jews were not lost in that captivity, as other nations have been; but this intimates the reason why the streams of that people were kept to run pure through that dead sea, because from them, as *concerning the flesh*, Christ was to *come*.

9. *Josias* is said to *beget Jechonias and his brethren* (*v.* 11); by Jechonias here is meant Jehoiakim, who was the first-born of Josias. When Jechonias is said to have been written *childless* (Jer. xxii. 30), it is explained thus: *No man of his seed shall prosper*. *Salathiel* is here said to *beget Zerubbabel*, whereas Salathiel begat Pedaiah, and he begat Zerubbabel (1 Chron. iii. 19): but, as before, the grandson is often called the son.

10. The line is brought down, not to Mary the mother of our Lord, but to *Joseph the husband of Mary* (*v.* 16); for the Jews always reckoned their genealogies by the males; yet Mary was of the same tribe and family with Joseph, so that, both by his mother and by his supposed father, he was of the house of David.

11. The centre in whom all these lines meet is *Jesus, who is called Christ, v.* 16. This is he that was so importunately desired, so impatiently expected. They who do the will of God are in a more honourable relation to Christ than those who were akin to him according to the flesh, *ch.* xii. 50. *Jesus* is called *Christ*, that is, the *Anointed*, the same with the *Hebrew* name *Messiah*.

Lastly, The general summary of all this genealogy we have, *v.* 17, where it is summed up in three fourteens, signalised by remarkable periods. In the first fourteen, we have the family of David rising, and looking forth as the morning; in the second, we have it flourishing in its meridian lustre; in the third, we have it declining and growing less and less, dwindling into the family of a poor carpenter, and then Christ *shines forth* out of it, the *glory of his people Israel*.

Verses 18–25

The mystery of Christ's incarnation is to be adored, not pried into. If we *know not the way of the Spirit* in the formation of common persons, nor *how the bones are formed in the womb of* anyone *that is with child* (Eccles. xi. 5), much less do we know how the blessed Jesus was formed in the womb of the blessed virgin. Some circumstances attending the birth of Christ are not in Luke, though it is more largely recorded there. Here we have,

I. Mary's espousals to Joseph. Mary, the mother of our Lord, *was espoused to Joseph*, not completely married, but contracted. We read of a man who *has betrothed a wife and has not taken her*, Deut. xx. 7. Christ was born of a virgin, but a betrothed virgin, 1. To put respect upon the marriage state, and to recommend it as *honourable among all*. Who more highly favoured than Mary was in her espousals? 2. To save the credit of the blessed virgin, which otherwise would have been exposed. It was fit that her conception should be protected by a marriage, and so justified in the eye of the world. 3. That the blessed virgin might have one to be a help-meet for her. Some think that Joseph was now a widower, and that those who are called the *brethren of Christ* (*ch.* xiii. 55), were Joseph's children by a former wife. Joseph was a *just man*, she a *virtuous woman*. We may also learn, from this example, that it is good to enter into the married state with deliberation, and not hastily —to preface the nuptials with a contract. It is better to *take* time to consider before than to *find* time to repent after.

II. Her pregnancy of the promised seed; *before they came together*, she w*as found with child*, which really was *of the Holy Ghost*. Now we may well imagine, what a perplexity this might justly occasion to the blessed virgin. She herself knew the divine original of this conception; but how could she prove it? She would be *dealt with as a harlot*. Never was any daughter of Eve so dignified as the Virgin Mary was, and yet in danger of falling under the imputation of one of the worst of crimes; yet we do not find that she tormented herself about it; but, being conscious of her own innocence, she kept her mind calm and easy, and committed her cause to *him that judgeth righteously*.

III. Joseph's perplexity, and his care what to do in this case. He is loth to believe so ill a thing of one whom he believed to be so good a woman; and yet the matter, as it is too bad to be excused, is also too plain to be denied.

1. The extremity which he studied to avoid. He was *not willing to make her a public example*. He might have done so, Deut. xxii. 23, 24. How different was the spirit which Joseph displayed from that of Judah, who in a similar case hastily passed that severe sentence, *Bring her forth and let her be burnt!* Gen. xxxviii. 24. How good is it to *think on things*,

as Joseph did here! Were there more of deliberation in our censures and judgments, there would be more of mercy and moderation in them.

Some persons of a rigorous temper would blame Joseph for his clemency: but it is here spoken of to his praise; because *he was a just man*, therefore he was not willing to expose her. He was a *religious, good man*; and therefore inclined to be merciful as God is, and to *forgive* as one that was *forgiven*. It becomes us, in many cases, to be gentle towards those that come under suspicion of having offended. That court of conscience which moderates the rigour of the law we call a *court of equity*. Those who are found faulty were perhaps *overtaken in the fault*, and are therefore to be *restored with the spirit of meekness*.

2. The expedient he found out for avoiding this extremity. He was *minded to put her away privily*, that is, to give a bill of divorce into her hand before two witnesses, and so to hush up the matter among themselves. The necessary censures of those who have offended ought to be managed without noise. Christian love and Christian prudence will *hide a multitude of sins*, and great ones, as far as may be done without having fellowship with them.

IV. Joseph's discharge from this perplexity by an express sent from heaven, *v*. 20, 21. *While he thought on these things* and knew not what to determine, God graciously directed him what to do, and made him easy. Those who would have direction from God must *think on things* themselves, and consult with themselves. It is the *thoughtful*, not the *unthinking*, whom God will guide. When he was at a loss, and had carried the matter as far as he could in his own thoughts, then God came in with advice. God's time to come in with instruction to his people is when they are *nonplussed* and at a stand. The message was sent to Joseph by an *angel of the Lord*. How far God may now, in an invisible way, make use of the ministration of angels, for extricating his people out of their straits, we cannot say; but this we are sure of, they are all *ministering spirits* for their good. This angel appeared to Joseph *in a dream* when he was asleep. When we are most quiet and composed we are in the best frame to receive the notices of the divine will.

1. Joseph is here *directed* to proceed in his intended marriage. It was requisite to put this poor carpenter in mind of his high birth: "Value thyself. Joseph, thou art that *son of David* through whom the line of the Messiah is to be drawn." We may thus say to every true believer, "Fear not, thou son of Abraham, thou child of God; forget not the dignity of thy birth, thy new birth." *Fear not to take Mary for thy wife;* so it may be read.

2. He is here *informed* concerning that *holy thing* with which his espoused wife was now pregnant. That which is conceived in her is of a divine original. Two things he is told,

(1) That she had conceived *by the power of the Holy Ghost;* not by the power of nature. The Holy Spirit, who produced the world, now produced the Saviour of the world, and *prepared him a body*, as was promised him, when he said, *Lo, I come*, Heb. x. 5. He is the *Son of God*, and yet so far partakes of the substance of his mother as to be called *the fruit of her womb*, Luke i. 42. Histories tell us of some who vainly pretended to have conceived by a divine power, as the mother of Alexander; but none ever really did so, except the mother of our Lord. We do not read that the virgin Mary did herself proclaim the honour done to her; but she hid it in her heart, and therefore God sent an angel to attest it.

(2) That she should bring forth *the Saviour of the world* (*v*. 21).

[1] In the name that should be given to her Son: *Thou shalt call his name Jesus, a Saviour*. Jesus is the same name with Joshua, the termination only being changed, for the sake of conforming it to the Greek. Joshua is called *Jesus* (Acts vii. 45; Heb. iv. 8), from the Seventy. Christ is our Joshua; both the *Captain of our salvation*, and the *High Priest of our profession*, and, in both, our Saviour—a Joshua who comes in the stead of Moses, and does that for us which *the law could not do, in that it was weak*. Joshua had been called *Hosea*, but Moses prefixed the first syllable of the name *Jehovah*, and so made it *Jehoshua* (Num. xiii. 16), to intimate that the Messiah, who was to bear that name, should be *Jehovah*; he is therefore *able to save to the uttermost*, neither is there *salvation in any other*.

[2] In the reason of that name: *For he shall save his people from their sins*. Those whom Christ saves he saves *from their sins*; from the guilt of sin by the *merit of his death*, from the dominion of sin by the *Spirit of his grace*. In saving them from sin, he saves them from wrath and the curse, and all misery here and hereafter. Those who leave their sins, and give up themselves to Christ as *his people*, are interested in the Saviour, and the great salvation which he has *wrought out*, Rom. xi. 26.

V. The fulfilling of the scripture in all this. This evangelist, writing among the Jews, more frequently observes this than any other of the evangelists. Here the Old Testament prophecies had their accomplishment in our Lord Jesus. Now the scripture that was fulfilled in the birth of Christ was that promise of a sign which God gave to king Ahaz (Isa. vii. 14), *Behold a virgin shall conceive;* where the prophet, encouraging the people of God to hope for the promised deliverance from Sennacherib's invasion, directs them to look forward to the Messiah, who was to come of the people of the Jews, and the house of David.

1. The sign given is that the Messiah shall be *born of a virgin. A virgin shall conceive*, and, by her, he shall be manifested *in the flesh*. The word *Almah* signifies a *virgin* in the strictest sense, such as Mary professes herself to be (Luke i. 34), *I know not a man*. Christ would be born, not of an *empress* or *queen*, for he appeared not in outward pomp or splendour, but of a virgin, to teach us spiritual purity.

2. The truth proved by this sign is, that he is the Son of God, and the Mediator between God and man; for *they shall call his name Immanuel. Immanuel* signifies *God with us;* a mysterious name, but very precious; God *incarnate* among us, and so God *reconcilable* to us, at peace with us, and taking us into covenant and communion with himself. The people of the Jews had *God with them*, in types and shadows, dwelling between the cherubim; but never so as when the *Word was made flesh*—that was the blessed *Shechinah*. By the light of *nature*, we see God as a God *above us*; by the light of the *law*, we see him as a God *against us*; but by the light of the gospel, we see him as *Immanuel*, God *with us*, in our own nature, and in our interest. Herein consists the salvation he wrought out, in the *bringing of God and man together*; this was what he designed, to bring *God* to be *with us*, which is our great happiness, and to bring *us* to *be with God*, which is our great duty.

VI. Joseph's obedience to the divine precept (*v*. 24). *Being raised from sleep* by the impression which the dream made upon him, *he did as the angel of the Lord had bidden him. He took unto him his wife*. God has still ways of making known his mind in doubtful cases, by hints of providence, debates of conscience, and advice of faithful friends; by each of these, applying the general rules of the written word, we should take direction from God.

VII. The accomplishment of the divine promise (*v*. 25). *She brought forth her first-born son*. The circumstances of it are more largely related, Luke ii.

1, &c. If Christ be *formed* in the soul, God himself has begun the good work which he will perform; what is *conceived* in grace will no doubt be *brought forth* in glory.

Joseph, though he solemnized the marriage with Mary, his espoused wife, *knew her not till she had brought him forth.* Much has been said concerning the perpetual virginity of the mother of our Lord: Jerome was very angry with Helvidius for denying it. It is certain that it cannot be proved from scripture. Dr. *Whitby* inclines to think that when it is said, *Joseph knew her not till she had brought forth her first-born*, it is intimated that, afterward he lived with her, according to the law, Exod. xxi. 10. *Joseph called his name Jesus*, according to the direction given him.

CHAPTER 2

In this chapter, we have the history of our Saviour's infancy. I. The wise men's solicitous enquiry after Christ, ver. 1–8. II. Their devout attendance on him, when they found out where he was, ver. 9–12. III. Christ's flight into Egypt, to avoid the cruelty of Herod, ver. 13–15. IV. The barbarous murder of the infants of Bethlehem, ver. 16–18. V. Christ's return out of Egypt into the land of Israel again, ver. 19–23.

Verses 1–8

It was a *mark of humiliation* put upon the Lord Jesus that, though he was the *Desire of all nations*, yet his coming into the world was little observed and taken notice of, his birth was obscure and unregarded. He *came into the world*, and the *world knew him not*; nay, he *came to his own*, and *his own received him not*. Yet, as afterward, so in his birth, some rays of glory darted forth in the midst of the greatest instances of his abasement.

The first who took notice of Christ after his birth were the shepherds (Luke ii. 15, &c.), who saw and heard glorious things concerning him, and *made them known abroad*, to the amazement of all that heard them, *v.* 17, 18. After that, Simeon and Anna spoke of him, by the Spirit, to all that were disposed to heed what they said, Luke ii. 38. Now, one would think, these hints should have been taken by the men of Judah and the *inhabitants of Jerusalem*, and they should with both arms have embraced the long-looked-for Messiah; but, for aught that appears, he continued nearly two years after at Bethlehem, and no further notice was taken of him till these wise men came. Nothing will awaken those that are resolved to be regardless. Observe,

I. When this enquiry was made concerning Christ. It was *in the days of Herod the king*. This Herod was an Edomite, made king of Judæa by Augustus and Antonius, the then chief rulers of the Roman state, a man made up of falsehood and cruelty; yet he was complimented with the title of *Herod the Great*.

II. Who and what these *wise men* were; they are here called *Magicians*. Some take it in a good sense; the *Magi* among the *Persians* were their philosophers and their priests; others think they dealt in unlawful arts; the word is used of Simon, the sorcerer (Acts viii. 9, 11), and of Elymas, the sorcerer (Acts xiii. 6), nor does the scripture use it in any other sense. Well, whatever sort of wise men they were before, now they began to be *wise men* indeed when they set themselves to enquire after Christ.

This we are sure of, 1. That they were Gentiles, and not belonging to the commonwealth of Israel. The Jews regarded not Christ, but these Gentiles enquired him out. Note, Many times those who are nearest to the means, are furthest from the end. See *ch.* viii. 11, 12. 2. That they were *scholars*. They dealt in arts, curious arts; good scholars should be good Christians, and *then* they complete their *learning* when they *learn Christ*. 3. That they were *men of the east*, who were noted for their *soothsayings*, Isa. ii. 6.

Arabia is called the land of *the east* (Gen. xxv. 6), and the *Arabians* are called *men of the east*, Judges vi. 3. The presents they brought were the products of that country.

III. What induced them to make this enquiry. They, in their country, which was in the *east*, had seen an *extraordinary star*, such as they had not seen before; which they took to be an indication of an extraordinary person born in the land of *Judæa*, over which land this star was seen to hover. This differed so much from anything that was common that they concluded it to signify something uncommon. The birth of Christ was notified to the Jewish shepherds by *an angel*, to the Gentile philosophers by a *star*: to both God spoke in their own language, and in the way they were best acquainted with. The same star which they had seen in the *east* they saw a great while after, leading them to the house where Christ lay, was a candle set up on purpose to guide them to Christ. The idolaters worshipped the stars as the *host of heaven*, especially the *eastern* nations. Thus the stars that had been misused came to be put to the right use, to lead men to Christ; the gods of the heathen became his servants. Others impute their enquiry to the general expectation entertained at that time, in those *eastern* parts, of some great prince to appear. We may suppose a divine impression made upon their minds, enabling them to interpret this star as a signal given by Heaven of the birth of Christ.

IV. How they prosecuted this enquiry. *They came from the* east to Jerusalem, in further quest of this prince. They might have said, "If such a prince be born, we shall hear of him shortly in our own country, and it will be time enough then to pay our homage to him." But so impatient were they to be better acquainted with him, that they took a long journey on purpose to enquire after him. Those who truly desire to know Christ, and find him, will not regard pains or perils in seeking after him.

Their question is, *Where is he that is born king of the Jews?* They do not ask, *whether there were such a one born?* but, *Where is he born?* Those who know *something* of Christ cannot but covet to *know more* of him.

To this question they doubted not but to have a ready answer, and to find all Jerusalem worshipping at the feet of this new king; but no man can give them any information. There is more gross ignorance in the world, and in the church too, than we are aware of. Many that we think should direct us to Christ are themselves strangers to him. They pursue the enquiry, *Where is he that is born king of the Jews?* Are they asked, "Why do ye make this enquiry?" It is because they have *seen his star in the east.* Are they asked, "What business have ye with him? What have the men of the *east* to do with the *King of the Jews?*" They have their answer ready, *We are come to worship him.* Those in whose hearts the day-star is risen, to give them anything of the knowledge of Christ, must make it their business to worship him.

V. How this enquiry was treated at Jerusalem. News of it at last came to court; and *when Herod heard it he was troubled, v.* 3. He could not be a stranger to the prophecies of the *Old Testament*, concerning the Messiah and his kingdom, and the times fixed for his appearing by Daniel's weeks; but, having himself reigned so long and so successfully, he began to hope that those promises would for ever fail, and that his kingdom would be established and perpetuated in spite of them. What a damp therefore must it needs be upon him, to hear talk of this king being born.

But though Herod, an Edomite, was troubled, one would have thought Jerusalem should rejoice greatly to hear that her King comes; yet, it seems, *all Jerusalem were troubled with Herod*, and were apprehensive of I know not what ill consequences of the birth of this new king. The slavery of sin is foolishly preferred by many to the glorious liberty of the children of God, only because they apprehend some present difficulties attending that necessary revolution of the government in the soul. Herod and Jerusalem were thus troubled, from a mistaken notion that the kingdom of the Messiah would clash and interfere with the secular powers; whereas the star that proclaimed him king plainly intimated that his kingdom was heavenly, and not of this lower world.

VI. What assistance they met with in this enquiry from the scribes and the priests, *v.* 4-6. Nobody can pretend to tell where the King of the Jews is, but Herod enquires where it was expected *he should be born.* It was generally known that Christ should be *born at Bethlehem* (John vii. 42); but Herod would have counsel's opinion upon it, and therefore applies himself to the proper persons; *all the chief priests, and all the scribes;* and *demands of them* what was the place, *where Christ should be born?* Many a good question is put with an ill design.

The priests and scribes need not take any long time to give an answer to this query; nor do they differ in their opinion, but all agree that the Messiah must be *born in Bethlehem, the city of David,* here called *Bethlehem of Judæa. Bethlehem* signifies *the house of bread;* the fittest place for him to be born in who is the true manna, *the bread which came down from heaven,* which was *given for the life of the world.* Bethlehem's honour lay not, as that of other cities, in the multitude of the people, but in the magnificence of the princes it produced. Herein it had the pre-eminence above all the cities of Israel, that *the Lord shall count, when he writes up the people, that this man,* even *the man Christ Jesus, was born there,* Ps. lxxxvii. 6. *Out of thee shall come a Governor, the King of the Jews.* Bethlehem was the *city of David,* and David the glory of Bethlehem; there, therefore, must David's son and successor be born. There was a famous well at *Bethlehem,* by the gate, which David longed to drink of (2 Sam. xxiii. 15); in Christ we have not only bread enough and to spare, but may come and take also *of the water of life freely.*

VII. The bloody project and design of Herod, occasioned by this enquiry, *v.* 7, 8. Herod was now an old man, and had reigned thirty-five years; this king was but newly born, and not likely to enterprise anything considerable for many years; yet Herod is jealous of him. Crowned heads cannot endure to think of successors, much less of rivals; and therefore nothing less than the blood of this infant king will satisfy him. Passion has got the mastery of reason and conscience.

1. See how cunningly he laid the project (*v.* 7, 8). *He privily called the wise men,* to talk with them about this matter. He would not openly own his fears and jealousies. Sinners are often tormented with secret fears, which they keep to themselves. Herod learns of the wise men the *time when the star appeared,* and then employs them to enquire further, and bids them bring him an account. All this might look suspicious, if he had not covered it with a show of religion: *that I may come and worship him also.* The greatest wickedness often conceals itself under a mask of piety.

2. See how strangely he was befooled and infatuated in this, that he trusted it with the wise men. It was but seven miles from Jerusalem; how easily might he have sent spies to watch the wise men, who might have been as soon there to destroy the child as they to worship him!

Verses 9–12

We have here the wise men's humble attendance upon this new-born *King of the Jews,* and the honours they paid him. From Jerusalem they went to Bethlehem, resolving to *seek till they should find;* but it is very strange that they went alone. They *came from a far country,* to worship Christ while the Jews, his kinsmen, would not stir a step, would not go to the next town to bid him welcome. We must continue our attendance upon Christ, though we be alone in it; whatever others do, we must *serve the Lord.*

I. See how they found out Christ by the same star that they had seen in their own country, *v.* 9, 10. Observe, 1. How graciously God directed them. By the first appearance of the star they were given to understand where they might enquire for this King, and then it disappeared, and they were left to take the usual methods for such an enquiry. Extraordinary helps are not to be expected where ordinary means are to be had. Well, they had traced the matter as far as they could; they were upon their journey to Bethlehem, but that is a populous town. Where shall they find him when they come thither? Here they were at a loss, at their wit's end, but not at their faith's end; they believed that God would not leave them there; nor did he; for, behold, *the star which they saw in the east went before them.* If we go on as far as we can in the way of our duty, God will direct and enable us to do that which of ourselves we cannot do. The star had left them a great while, yet now returns. They who follow God in the dark shall find that light is sown, is reserved, for them. This star was the token of God's presence with them; for he is light, and goes before his people as their Guide. There is a day-star that arises in the hearts of those that enquire after Christ, 2 Peter i. 19. 2. Observe how joyfully they followed God's direction (*v.* 10). *When they saw the star, they rejoiced with exceeding great joy.* Now they saw they were not deceived, and had not taken this long journey in vain. Now they were sure that God was with them, and the tokens of his presence and favour cannot but fill with joy unspeakable the souls of those that know how to value them. We cannot expect too little from man, nor too much from God. What a transport of joy these wise men were in upon this sight of the star. Now they had reason to hope for a sight of the *Lord's Christ* speedily, of *the Sun of righteousness,* for they see *the Morning Star.* We should be glad of everything that will show us the way to Christ. This star was sent to meet the wise men, and to conduct them into the presence chamber of the King. Now God fulfills his promise of meeting those that are disposed to *rejoice and work righteousness* (Isa. lxiv. 5). God is pleased sometimes to favour young converts with such tokens of his love as are very encouraging to them, in reference to the difficulties they meet with at their setting out in the ways of God.

II. See how they made their address to him when they had found him, *v.* 11. We may well imagine what a disappointment it was to them when they found a cottage was his palace, and his own poor mother all the retinue he had! However, these wise men were so wise as to see through this veil. They did not think themselves baulked or baffled in their enquiry; but, as having found the King they sought, they presented themselves first, and then their gifts, to him.

1. They presented themselves to him: *they fell down, and worshipped him.* We do not read that they gave such honour to Herod, though he was in the height of his royal grandeur; but to this babe they gave this honour, not only as to a king, but as to a God. All that have found Christ fall down before him; they adore him, and submit themselves to him. *He is thy Lord, and worship thou him.*

2. *They presented their gifts to him.* In the eastern nations, when they did homage to their kings, they made them presents. With ourselves, we must give up all that we have to Jesus Christ. Nor are our gifts

accepted, unless we first present ourselves to him living sacrifices. The gifts they presented were, *gold, frankincense, and myrrh,* money, and money's-worth. Providence sent this for a seasonable relief to Joseph and Mary in their present poor condition. These were the products of their own country; what God favours us with, we must honour him with. They offered him *gold,* as a king, paying him tribute; *frankincense,* as God, for they honoured God with the smoke of incense; and *myrrh,* as a Man that should die, for *myrrh* was used in embalming dead bodies.

III. See how they left him when they had made their address to him, *v.* 12. Herod appointed them to *bring him word.* They would have done so, if they had not been countermanded, not suspecting their being thus made his tools in a wicked design. Those that mean honestly and well themselves are easily made to believe that others do so too, and cannot think the world is so bad as really it is. God prevented the mischief Herod designed to the Child Jesus. They were *warned not to return to Herod,* nor to Jerusalem; those were unworthy to have reports brought them concerning Christ, that might have seen with their own eyes, and would not. *They departed into their own country another way,* to bring the tidings to their countrymen; but it is strange that we never hear any more of them.

Verses 13–15

We have here Christ's flight into Egypt to avoid the cruelty of Herod. It was but little respect (compared with what should have been) that was paid to Christ in his infancy: yet even that, instead of honouring him among his people, did but expose him.

I. The command given to Joseph concerning it, *v.* 13. Joseph knew neither the danger the child was in, nor how to escape it; but God, by *an angel,* tells him both *in a dream,* as before he directed him in like manner what to do, *ch.* i. 20. Joseph is here told what their danger was: *Herod will seek the young child to destroy him.* God is acquainted with all the cruel projects and purposes of the enemies of his church. How early was the blessed Jesus involved in trouble! Usually, even those whose riper years are attended with toils and perils have a peaceable and quiet infancy; but it was not so with the blessed Jesus: his life and sufferings began together. He is directed what to do, to escape the danger; *Take the young child, and flee into Egypt.* Thus early must Christ give an example to his own rule (*ch.* x. 23): *When they persecute you in one city, flee to another.* Self-preservation, being a branch of the law of nature, is eminently a part of the law of God. *Flee;* but why *into Egypt*? Egypt was infamous for idolatry, tyranny, and enmity to the people of God. Yet that is appointed to be a place of refuge to the holy child Jesus. God, when he pleases, can make the worst of places serve the best of purposes. This may be considered,

1. As a trial of the faith of Joseph and Mary. They might be tempted to think, "If this child be the Son of God, as we are told he is, has he no other way to secure himself from a man that is a worm, than by such a mean and inglorious retreat as this? They had been lately told that he should be *the glory of his people Israel*; and is the land of Israel so soon become too hot for him? Now it appeared how well God had provided for *the young child and his mother,* in appointing Joseph to stand in so near a relation to them; now the gold which the wise men brought would stand them in stead to bear their charges. God foresees his people's distresses, and provides against them beforehand. God intimates the continuance of his care and guidance, when he saith, *Be thou there until I bring thee word,* so that he must expect to hear from God again, and not stir without fresh orders.

2. As an instance of the humiliation of our Lord Jesus. As there was no room for him in the inn at Bethlehem, so there was no quiet room for him in the land of Judæa. If we and our infants be at any time in straits, let us remember the straits Christ in his infancy was brought into.

3. As a token of God's displeasure against the Jews, who took so little notice of him; justly does he leave those who had slighted him.

II. Joseph's obedience to this command, *v.* 14. The journey would be inconvenient and perilous both to the young child and to his mother; yet Joseph *was not disobedient to the heavenly vision,* made no objection, nor was dilatory in his obedience. As soon as he had received his orders, he immediately *arose,* and went away *by night.* Those that would make *sure* work of their obedience, must make *quick* work of it. Now Joseph went out, as his father Abraham did, with an implicit dependence upon God, *not knowing whither he went,* Heb. xi. 8.

Joseph took the young child and his mother. Some observe, that *the young child* is put first, as the principal person, and Mary is called, not *the wife of Joseph,* but, which was her greater dignity, *the mother of the young child.* They continued in Egypt till the death of Herod. There they were at a distance from the temple and the service of it, and in the midst of idolaters. Though they were far from the temple of the Lord, they had with them the Lord of the temple. A forced absence from God's ordinances, and a forced presence with wicked people, may be the lot, are not the sin, yet cannot but be the grief, of good people.

III. The fulfilling of the scripture in all this—that scripture (Hos. xi. 1), *Out of Egypt have I called my son.* Of all the evangelists, Matthew takes most notice of the fulfilling of the scripture in what concerned Christ. Now this word of the prophet undoubtedly referred to the deliverance of Israel out of Egypt, in which God owned them for his son, his first-born (Exod. iv. 22); but it is here applied, by way of analogy, to Christ, the Head of the church. The scripture has many accomplishments. God is every day fulfilling the scripture. It is no new thing for God's sons to be in Egypt, in a strange land, in a house of bondage; but they shall be fetched out. They may be hid in Egypt, but they shall not be left there.

Verses 16–18

I. Herod's resentment of the departure of the wise men. He waited long for their return; but he hears, upon enquiry, that they are gone off another way, which made him *exceeding wroth*; and he is the more desperate and outrageous for his being disappointed.

II. His politic contrivance, notwithstanding this, to take off him that is *born King of the Jews.* If he could not reach him by a particular execution, he doubted not but to involve him in a general stroke. It was strange that Herod could find any so inhuman as to be employed in such a bloody and barbarous piece of work; but wicked hands never want wicked tools to work with. Herod was now about seventy years old, so that an infant, at this time *under two years old,* was not likely ever to give him any disturbance. It was purely to gratify his own brutish lusts of pride and cruelty that he did this.

Observe, What large measures he took, 1. As to time; He *slew all from two years old and under.* It is probable that the blessed Jesus was at this time not a year old; yet Herod took in all the infants *under two years old,* that he might be sure not to miss his prey. 2. As to place; he kills all the male children, not only *in Bethlehem,* but *in all the coasts thereof,* in all the villages of that city. This was being *overmuch wicked,* Eccles. vii. 17. An unbridled wrath, armed with an unlawful power, often transports men to the most absurd and unreasonable instances of cruelty. We are not to suppose that these children *were sinners above all that were in Israel*, because they suffered such things. But we must look upon this murder of the infants under another character: it was their martyrdom. They shed their blood for him, who afterwards shed his for them. These were the infantry of *the noble army of martyrs*.

III. The fulfilling of the scripture in this (*v.* 17, 18); *Then was fulfilled* that prophecy (Jer. xxxi. 15), *A voice was heard in Ramah*. That prediction was accomplished in Jeremiah's time. But now the prophecy is again fulfilled in the great sorrow that was for the death of these infants. The scripture was fulfilled.

1. In the place of this mourning. The noise of it was heard from Bethlehem to Ramah; for Herod's cruelty extended itself to *all the coasts of Bethlehem*, even into the lot of Benjamin, among the children of Rachel. Rachel's sepulchre was hard by Bethlehem, Gen. xxxv. 16, 19. Compare 1 Sam. x. 2. These mothers were like Rachel, lived near Rachel's grave, and many of them descended from Rachel; and therefore their lamentations are elegantly represented by *Rachel's weeping*.

2. In the degree of this mourning. It was *lamentation and weeping, and great mourning*; all little enough to express the sense they had of this aggravated calamity. There was a great cry in Egypt when the first-born were slain, and so there was here when the youngest was slain; for whom we naturally have a particular tenderness. This sorrow was so great, that they *would not be comforted*. Blessed be God, there is no occasion of grief in this world, no, not that which is supplied by sin itself, that will justify us in refusing to *be comforted*! They *would not be comforted, because they are not*, that is, *they are not* in the land of the living, *are not* as they were, in their mothers' embraces. If, indeed, *they were not*, there might be some excuse for sorrowing as though we had no hope; but we know they are not lost, but gone before; if we forget that *they are*, we lose the best ground of our comfort, 1 Thess. iv. 13. If we look further into this prophecy, we shall find that *the bitter weeping* in Ramah was but a prologue to the greatest joy, for it follows, *Thy work shall be rewarded, and there is hope in thy end*. The worst things are, the sooner they will mend.

Verses 19–23

We have here Christ's return out of Egypt into the *land of Israel* again. Egypt may serve to sojourn in, or take shelter in, for a while, but not to abide in. Christ was *sent to the lost sheep of the house of Israel*, and therefore to them he must return.

I. What it was that made way for his return—the death of Herod, which happened not long after the murder of the infants. Such quick work did divine vengeance make! Of all sins, the guilt of innocent blood fills the measure soonest. So passionate and impatient was he, that he was a torment to himself, and a terror to all that attended him. See what kind of men have been the enemies and persecutors of Christ and his followers! Few have opposed Christianity but such as have first divested themselves of humanity.

II. The orders given from heaven concerning their return, and Joseph's obedience to those orders, *v.* 19–21. God had sent Joseph into Egypt, and there he stayed till the same that brought him thither ordered him thence. In all our removes, it is good to see our way plain, and God going before us; we should not move either one way or the other without order. No place can exclude God's gracious visits. Angels come to Joseph in Egypt, to Ezekiel in Babylon, and to John in Patmos. 1. The angel informs

him of the death of Herod and his accomplices: *They are dead, which sought the young Child's life*. They are dead, but the young Child lives. Persecuted saints sometimes live to tread upon the graves of their persecutors. Thus did the church's King weather the storm, and many a one has the church in like manner weathered. 2. He directs him what to do. He must *go* and return *to the land of Israel*; and he did so without delay. God's people follow his direction whithersoever he leads them, wherever he lodges them.

III. The further direction he had from God, which way to steer, and where to fix in the land of Israel, *v.* 22, 23. God could have given him these instructions with the former, but God reveals his mind to his people by degrees, to keep them still waiting on him, and expecting to hear further from him. These orders Joseph received *in a dream*, probably, as those before, by the ministration of an angel.

Now the direction given this holy, royal family, is,

1. That it might not settle in Judæa, *v.* 22. Joseph might think that Jesus, being *born in Bethlehem*, must be brought up there; yet he is prudently *afraid* for *the young Child*, because *he hears that Archelaus reigns in* Herod's stead, but only over Judæa. See what a succession of enemies there is to fight against Christ and his church! If one drop off, another presently appears, to keep up the old enmity. But for this reason Joseph must not take the young Child into Judæa. God will not thrust his children into the mouth of danger, but when it is for his own glory and their trial.

2. That it must settle in Galilee, *v.* 22. There Philip now ruled, who was a mild, quiet man. Note, The providence of God commonly so orders it, that his people shall not want a quiet retreat from the storm and from the tempest. Thither they were sent, to Nazareth, a city upon a hill, in the centre of the lot of Zebulun; there the mother of our Lord lived, when she conceived that *holy thing*; and, probably, Joseph lived there too, Luke i. 26, 27. Thither they were sent, and there they were well known, and were among their relations; the most proper place for them to be in. There they continued, and from thence our Saviour was called *Jesus of Nazareth*, which was to the Jews a stumbling-block, for, *Can any good thing come* out of *Nazareth?*

In this is said to be fulfilled what was *spoken by the prophets, He shall be called a Nazarene*, which may be looked upon, (1) As a name of honour and dignity, though primarily it signifies no more than a *man of Nazareth*; there is an allusion or mystery in it, speaking Christ to be, [1] The *Man, the Branch*, spoken of, Isa. xi. 1. [2] It speaks him to be the *great Nazarite*. Not that Christ was, *strictly*, a *Nazarite*, for he drank wine, and touched dead bodies; but he was *eminently* so, both as he was singularly holy, and as he was by a solemn designation and dedication set apart to the honour of God in the work of our redemption, as Samson was to save Israel. Or, (2) As a name of reproach and contempt. To be called a *Nazarene*, was to be called a *despicable man*, a man from whom no good was to be expected, and to whom no respect was to be paid. It stuck as a nickname to him and his followers. Let no name of reproach for religion's sake seem hard to us, when our Master was himself called a *Nazarene*.

CHAPTER 3

The story of this chapter, concerning the baptism of John, begins the gospel (Mark i. 1); what went before is but preface or introduction. I. The glorious rising of the morning-star, John the Baptist. II. The more glorious shining forth of the Sun of righteousness, immediately after.

Verses 1–6

We have here an account of the preaching and baptism of John.

I. The time when he appeared. *In those days* (v. 1), or, *after those days*, long after what was recorded in the foregoing chapter, which left the child Jesus in his infancy; *in those days*, in the time appointed of the Father for the beginning of the gospel, when the *fulness of time* was come. Glorious things were spoken both of John and Jesus, at and before their births, which would have given occasion to expect some extraordinary appearances of a divine presence and power with them when they were very young; but it is quite otherwise. Except Christ's disputing with the doctors at twelve years old, nothing appears remarkable concerning either of them, till they were about thirty years old. And this was to show, 1. That even when God is acting as the God of Israel, the *Saviour*, yet *verily he is a God that hideth himself* (Isa. xlv. 15). 2. That our faith must principally have an eye to Christ in his office and undertaking, for there is the *display* of his power; but in his person is the *hiding* of his power.

Matthew says nothing of the conception and birth of John the Baptist, which is largely related by St. Luke, but finds him at full age, as if dropt from the clouds to preach in the wilderness. After Malachi there was no prophet, nor any pretender to prophecy, till John the Baptist.

II. The place where he appeared first. *In the wilderness of Judæa*. It was not an uninhabited desert, but a part of the country not so thickly peopled as other parts were; it was such a wilderness as had six cities and their villages in it. In these cities and villages John preached, for thereabouts he had hitherto lived. The *word of the Lord* found John here in a *wilderness*. No place is so remote as to shut us out from the visits of divine grace. It was in this *wilderness* of Judah that David penned the 63rd Psalm, which speaks so much of the sweet communion he then had with God, Hos. ii. 14. John Baptist was a priest of the order of Aaron, yet we find him preaching in a *wilderness*, and never officiating in the *temple*; but Christ, who was not a son of Aaron, is yet often found in the temple, and sitting there as one having authority. *The Lord whom ye seek shall suddenly come to his temple;* not the *messenger* that was to prepare his way.

The beginning of the gospel in a wilderness, speaks comfort to the deserts of the Gentile world. *The desert shall rejoice,* Isa. xxxv. 1, 2.

III. His preaching. This he made his business. By the foolishness of preaching, Christ's kingdom must be set up.

1. The doctrine he preached was that of repentance (v. 2); *Repent ye*. He preached it, not in Jerusalem, but in the wilderness of Judæa, among the plain country people; for even those who think themselves most out of the way of temptation, and furthest from the vanities and vices of the town, cannot wash their hands in innocency, but must do it in repentance. John Baptist's business was to call men to *repent* of their sins. "*Change your minds;* you have thought amiss; *think again*, and *think aright*." The change of the *mind* produces a change of the *way*. Those who are truly sorry for what they have done amiss, will be careful to do so no more. This repentance is a necessary duty, in obedience to the command of God (Acts xvii. 30); and a necessary preparative and qualification for the comforts of the gospel of Christ. The sore must be searched, or it cannot be cured. *I wound* and *I heal*.

2. The argument he used to enforce this call was, *For the kingdom of heaven is at hand*. It is a *kingdom* of which Christ is the Sovereign. It is a kingdom of *heaven*, not of this world. John preached this as *at hand*; then it was at the door; to us it is come. (1) This is a great *inducement* to us *to repent*. There is nothing like the consideration of divine grace to

break the heart, both *for sin* and *from sin*. Kindness is conquering; abused kindness, humbling and melting. What a wretch was I to sin against such grace, against the law and love of such a kingdom! (2) It is a *great encouragement* to us *to repent*. The proclamation of pardon discovers, and fetches in, the malefactor who before fled and absconded. Thus are we drawn to it with the cords of a man, and the bands of love.

IV. The *prophecy* that was fulfilled in him, v. 3. This is he that was spoken of in the beginning of that part of the prophecy of Esaias, which is mostly evangelical, and which points at gospel-times and gospel-grace; see Isa. xl. 3, 4. John is here spoken of,

1. As the *voice of one crying in the wilderness*. John owned it himself (John i. 23); *I am the voice*, and that is all, God is the Speaker, who makes known his mind by John, as a man does by his voice. John is called the *voice of one crying* aloud, which is startling and awakening. Christ is called *the Word*, which, being distinct and articulate, is more instructive. John as the *voice*, roused men, and then Christ, as the *Word*, taught them.

2. As one whose business it was to *prepare the way of the Lord, and to make his paths straight*. So John prepares the way of the Lord. (1) He himself did so among the men of that generation. In the Jewish church and nation, at that time, all was out of course. The people were, generally, extremely proud of their privileges, insensible of sin; and, though now under the most *humbling* providences, being lately made a province of the Roman Empire, yet they were *unhumbled*. Now John was sent to level these mountains, to take down their high opinion of themselves. (2) His doctrine of repentance and humiliation is still as necessary as it was then. There is a great deal to be done, to make way for Christ into a soul, and nothing is more needful, in order to this, than the discovery of sin, and a conviction of the insufficiency of our own righteousness. That which lets will let, until it be taken out of the way. The way of sin and Satan is a *crooked way*; to prepare a way for Christ, the paths must be *made straight*.

V. The garb in which he appeared, the figure he made, and the manner of his life, v. 4. He shall be *great in the sight of the Lord*, but mean in the eye of the world; and, as Christ himself, having *no form or comeliness*.

1. His *dress* was *plain*. This same John had *his raiment of camel's hair, and a leathern girdle about his loins*; for he lived in a country place, and suited his *habit* to his *habitation*. It is good for us to accommodate ourselves to the place and condition which God, in his providence, has put us in. John appeared in this dress, (1) To show that, like Jacob, he was a *plain man*, and mortified to this world, and the delights and gaieties of it. (2) To show that he was a *prophet*, for prophets wore *rough garments*, as mortified men (Zech. xiii. 4). (3) To show that he was a man of resolution; his girdle was not *fine*, such as were then commonly worn, but it was *strong*.

2. His *diet* was *plain*; his *meat* was locusts and *wild honey*. *Locusts* were a sort of flying insect, very good for food, and allowed as clean (Lev. xi. 22). *Wild honey* was that which *Canaan* flowed with, 1 Sam. xiv. 26. This intimates that he ate *sparingly*, a little served his turn; a man would be long ere he filled his belly with locusts and wild honey. He was so entirely taken up with spiritual things, that he could seldom find time for a set meal. Those whose business it is to call others to mourn for sin, and to mortify it, ought themselves to live a serious life, a life of self-denial. Every day was a *fast-day* with him. A conviction of the vanity of the world, and everything in it, is the best preparative for the entertainment of the

kingdom of heaven in the heart. *Blessed are the poor in spirit.*

VI. The people who attended upon him, and flocked after him (*v.* 5); *Then went out to him Jerusalem, and all Judæa.* Great multitudes came to him from the city, and from all parts of the country. This was a great *honour* put upon John. Frequently those who have most real honour done them, who least court the shadow of it. Men have a secret value and reverence for them, more than one would imagine. This gave John a great opportunity of doing good, and was an evidence that God was with him. It was generally thought that the *kingdom of God* would presently *appear*. They were ready to say of him, that he was *the Christ* (Luke iii. 15). Those who would have the benefit of John's ministry must *go out* to him in the wilderness, sharing in his reproach. They who would learn the doctrine of repentance must *go out* from the hurry of this world, and be still. It appears by the issue, that of the many who came to John's Baptism, there were but few that adhered to it. There may be a multitude of forward hearers, where there are but a few true believers.

VII. The rite, or ceremony, by which he admitted disciples, *v.* 6. Those who received his doctrine, and submitted to his discipline, were *baptized of him in Jordan.* They testified their repentance by *confessing their sins.* The Jews had been taught to *justify* themselves; but John teaches them to *accuse* themselves. A penitent confession of sin is required in order to peace and pardon; and those only are ready to receive Jesus Christ as their Righteousness, who are brought with sorrow and shame to own their guilt, 1 John i. 9. The benefits of the *kingdom of heaven*, now *at hand*, were thereupon sealed to them by baptism. He washed them with water, in token of this—that from all their iniquities God would *cleanse them.* It was *the baptism of repentance*, Acts xix. 4. All Israel were baptized unto Moses, 1 Cor. x. 2. The *ceremonial law* consisted in *divers washings or baptisms* (Heb. ix. 10); but John's baptism refers to the remedial law, the law of repentance and faith. By baptism he obliged them to live a holy life, according to the profession they took upon themselves. Confession of sin must always be accompanied with holy resolutions.

Verses 7–12

The doctrine John preached was that of repentance. Here we have the use of that doctrine. Application is the life of preaching, so it was of John's preaching. To whom he applied it; to the Pharisees and Sadducees that came to his baptism, *v.* 7. The Pharisees were zealots for the ceremonies, and the traditions of the elders; the Sadducees ran into the other extreme, and were little better than deists, denying the existence of spirits and a future state. Many come to ordinances, who come not under the power of them. Note the application was plain and home, and directed to their consciences; he speaks as one that came not to preach *before* them, but to preach *to* them. He was not bashful when he appeared in public, nor did he fear the face of man.

I. Here is a word of conviction and awakening. He begins harshly, calls them not Rabbi, gives them not the titles, much less the applauses, they had been used to. 1. The *title* he gives them is, *O generation of vipers.* Christ gave them the same title; *ch.* xii. 34; xxiii. 33. They were a *viperous brood*, the seed and offspring of such as had been of the same spirit; it was bred in the bone with them. They were a *viperous gang*, they were all alike; though enemies to one another, yet confederate in mischief. It becomes the ministers of Christ to be bold in showing sinners their true character. 2. The *alarm* he gives them is, *Who has warned you to flee from the wrath to come?* This intimates that they were in danger of the wrath to come; that it was next to a miracle to effect anything hopeful among them. "What brings you hither? Who thought of seeing you here? What fright have you been put into, that you enquire after the kingdom of heaven?" (1) There is a *wrath to come.* (2) It is the great concern of everyone of us to flee from this wrath. (3) It is wonderful mercy that we are fairly warned to flee from this wrath; think—*Who has warned us?* God has warned us, who delights not in our ruin. (4) These warnings sometimes startle those who seemed to have been very much hardened in their security and good opinion of themselves.

II. Here is a word of *exhortation* and *direction* (*v.* 8); "*Bring forth therefore fruits meet for repentance. Therefore*, because you profess repentance, and attend upon the doctrine and baptism of repentance, evidence that you are true penitents." Repentance is seated in the heart. There it is as a root; but in vain do we pretend to have it there, if we do not *bring forth the fruits.* Those are not worthy the name of penitents, or their privileges, who say they are sorry for their sins, and yet persist in them. They that profess repentance, as all that are baptized do, must be and act as becomes penitents.

III. Here is a word of caution, not to trust to their external privileges (*v.* 9); *Think not to say within yourselves, We have Abraham to our father.* There is a great deal which carnal hearts are apt to say within themselves, to put by the convincing, commanding power of the word of God. *Please not yourselves* with saying this (so some read it); "rock not yourselves asleep with this, nor flatter yourselves into a fool's paradise." God takes notice of what we say *within* ourselves. Many hide the lie that ruins them, in *their right hand*, and roll it *under their tongue*, because they are ashamed to own it. Now John shows them,

1. What their pretence was; "*We have Abraham to our father;* we are not sinners of the Gentiles; what is this to us?" The word does us no good, when we will not take it as spoken to us, and belonging to us. "Think not that because you are the seed of Abraham, therefore," (1) "You *need not repent*, that there is no occasion for you to change your mind or way." (2) "That therefore you shall *fare well enough*, though you do not *repent.*" It is vain presumption to think that our having good relations will save us, though we be not good ourselves. What will all this avail us, if we do not repent, and live a life of repentance? Multitudes, by resting in the honours and advantages of their visible church-membership, take up short of heaven.

2. How foolish and groundless this pretence was; they thought that being the seed of Abraham, they were the only people God had in the world. John shows them the folly of this conceit; *I say unto you* (whatever you say within yourselves), that *God is able of these stones to raise up children unto Abraham.* He was now baptizing in Jordan at Bethabara (John i. 28), *the house of passage*, where the children of *Israel passed over*; and there were the twelve stones, one for each tribe, which Joshua set up for a memorial, Joshua iv. 20. It is not unlikely that he pointed to those stones, which God could raise to be, more than in representation, the *twelve tribes of Israel.* Whatever comes of the present generation, God will never want a church in the world.

IV. Here is a word of terror to the careless and secure Pharisees and Sadducees, and other Jews, that knew not the signs of the times, nor the day of their visitation, *v.* 10. "Now look about you, now that *the kingdom of God is at hand*, and be made sensible."

1. "How strict and short your trial is; *Now the axe* is *laid to the root of the tree*; now you are marked for ruin, and cannot avoid it but by a speedy and sincere repentance. *Behold, I come quickly.*" Now they were put upon their last trial; now or never.

2. "How sore and severe your doom will be, if you do not improve this." It is now declared with the axe at the root, that *every tree*, however *high* in gifts and honours, however *green* in external professions and performances, if it *bring not forth good fruit*, the fruits meet for repentance, is *hewn down*, disowned as a tree in God's vineyard, unworthy to have room there, and is *cast into the fire* of God's wrath—the fittest place for barren trees: what else are they good for? If not fit for fruit, they are fit for fuel.

V. A word of instruction concerning Jesus Christ. Christ's ministers preach, not themselves, but him.

1. The dignity and pre-eminence of Christ above John. See how meanly he speaks of himself, that he might magnify Christ (*v.* 11); "*I indeed baptize you with water*, that is the utmost I can do. But *he that comes after me is mightier than I.*" John was truly great, great in the sight of the Lord (not a greater was born of woman), yet he thinks himself unworthy to be in the meanest place of attendance upon Christ, *whose shoes I am not worthy to bear.* He sees, (1) How mighty Christ is, in comparison with him. It is a great comfort to faithful ministers, to think that Jesus Christ is mightier than they, his strength is perfected in their weakness. (2) How mean he is in comparison with Christ, not worthy to carry his shoes after him! Those whom God puts honour upon, are thereby made very humble and low in their own eyes, so that Christ may be all.

2. The design and intention of Christ's appearing, which they were now speedily to expect. Christ will come to make a distinction.

(1) By the powerful working of his grace; *He shall baptize you*, that is, some of you, *with the Holy Ghost and with fire*. Note, [1] It is Christ's prerogative to baptize *with the Holy Ghost*. This he did in the extraordinary gifts of the Spirit conferred upon the apostles. This he does in the graces and comforts of the Spirit given to them that ask him. [2] They who are baptized with the Holy Ghost are baptized as *with fire*. Is fire enlightening? So the Spirit is a Spirit of illumination. Is it warming? And do not their hearts burn within them? Is it consuming? And does not the Spirit of judgment, as a *Spirit of burning*, consume the dross of their corruptions? Does fire make all it seizes like itself? And does it move upwards? So does the Spirit make the soul holy like itself, and its tendency is heaven-ward.

(2) By the final determinations of his judgment (*v.* 12); *Whose fan is in his hand.* Now he sits as a Refiner. Observe here, [1] The visible Church is Christ's floor. The temple, a type of the church, was built, upon a threshing-floor. [2] In this floor there is a mixture of wheat and chaff. True believers are as wheat, hypocrites are as chaff; these are now mixed, good and bad, under the same external profession. [3] There is a day coming when the floor shall be purged, and the wheat and chaff shall be separated. But it is the day of the last judgment that will be the great winnowing, distinguishing day, when saints and sinners shall be parted for ever. [4] Heaven is the garner into which Jesus Christ will shortly gather all his wheat, and not a grain of it shall be lost: and there is no chaff among them. They are not only gathered into *the barn* (ch. xiii. 30), but into *the garner*, where they are thoroughly purified. [5] Hell is the *unquenchable fire*, which will burn up the chaff. As we now are in the *field*, we shall be then in the *floor*.

Verses 13–17

Behold, *the Sun of righteousness* rises in glory. *The fulness of time was come* that Christ should enter upon his prophetical office; and he chooses to do it, not at Jerusalem, but there *where John was baptizing*; for to him resorted those who *waited for the consolation of Israel*, to whom alone he would

be welcome. Christ's coming from Galilee *to Jordan, to be baptized*, teaches us not to shrink from pain and toil, that we may have an opportunity of drawing nigh to God in an ordinance. We should be willing to go far, rather than come short of communion with God. They who will find must seek.

Now in this story of Christ's baptism we may observe,

I. How hardly John was persuaded to admit of it, *v.* 14, 15. It was an instance of Christ's great humility, that he would offer himself *to be baptized of John*. As soon as ever Christ began to preach, he preached humility. Christ was designed for the highest honours, yet in his first step he thus abases himself. Those who would rise high must begin low. *Before honour is humility*. Those that honour God he will honour. Now here we have,

1. The objection that John made against baptizing Jesus, *v.* 14. *John forbade him*, as Peter did, when Christ went about to wash his feet, John xiii. 6, 8. Christ's gracious condescensions are so surprising, so deep and mysterious, that even they who know his mind well cannot soon find out the meaning of them. John's modesty thinks this an honour too great for him to receive. John had now obtained a great name, and was universally respected: yet see how humble he is still! God has further honours in reserve for those whose spirits continue low when their reputation rises.

(1) John thinks it necessary that he should be baptized of Christ; *I have need to be baptized of thee* with the baptism of the Holy Ghost, as of fire. [1] Though *John was filled with the Holy Ghost from the womb* (Luke i. 15), yet he acknowledges he had need to be baptized with that baptism. They who have much of the Spirit of God, see that they have need of more. [2] *John has need to be baptized*, though he was the *greatest that ever was born of woman.* The purest souls are most sensible of their own remaining impurity, and seek most earnestly for spiritual washing. [3] He has *need to be baptized of* Christ. The best and holiest of men *have need of* Christ, and the better they are, the more they see of that need. [4] This was said before the multitude, who had a great veneration for John, and were ready to embrace him for the Messiah. It is no disparagement to the greatest of men, to confess that they are undone without Christ and his grace. [5] John was Christ's forerunner, and yet owns that he had *need to be baptized of* him. Even they who were before Christ in time depended on him. [6] While John was dealing with others about their souls, observe how feelingly he speaks of the case of his own soul, *I have need to be baptized of thee*. Take heed to thyself first; *save thyself*, 1 Tim. iv. 16.

(2) He therefore thinks it very preposterous and absurd, that Christ should be baptized by him; *Comest thou to me?* Christ's coming to us may well be wondered at.

2. The overruling of this objection (*v.* 15); *Jesus said, Suffer it to be so now.* Christ accepted his humility, but not his refusal. See,

(1) How Christ insists upon it; It must *be so now.* Everything is beautiful in its season. But why *now*? Why yet? [1] Christ is *now* in a state of humiliation. He is not only *found in fashion as a man*, but is *made in the likeness of sinful flesh*, and thus he *was made sin for us*, though he *knew no sin.* [2] John's baptism is now in reputation, it is that by which God is now doing his work. What we see God owns, and while we see he does so, we must own. [3] It must *be so now*, because now is the time for Christ's appearing in public, and this will be a fair opportunity for it.

(2) The reason he gives for it; *Thus it becomes us to fulfil all righteousness.* [1] There was a propriety in everything that Christ did for us; it was all graceful,

lovely, and of good report. [2] Our Lord Jesus looked upon it as a thing well becoming him, *to fulfil all righteousness. Thus it becomes* him to justify God, and approve his wisdom. *Thus it becomes us* to countenance and encourage everything that is good, by pattern as well as precept. Thus Jesus began *first to do, and then to teach*; and his ministers must take the same method. It became Christ to submit to John's washing with water, because it was a divine appointment.

With the will of Christ, and this reason for it, John was entirely satisfied, and *then he suffered him.* The same modesty which made him at first decline the honour Christ offered him, now made him do the service Christ enjoined him. No pretence of humility must make us decline our duty.

II. How solemnly Heaven was pleased to grace the baptism of Christ with a special display of glory (*v.* 16, 17); *Jesus when he was baptized, went up straightway out of the water.* Others that were baptized stayed to *confess their sins* (*v.* 6); but Christ, having no sins to confess, *went up* immediately. *He went up straightway,* as one that entered upon his work with the utmost cheerfulness and resolution; he would lose no time. *How was he straightened till it was accomplished!*

1. *Lo! the heavens were opened unto him,* so as to discover something above and beyond the starry firmament, at least, to him. This was, (1) To encourage him to go on in his undertaking, with the prospect of the glory and *joy that were set before him.* (2) To encourage us to receive him, and submit to him. Sin shut up heaven, put a stop to all friendly intercourse between God and man; but now Christ *has opened the kingdom of heaven to all believers.* Divine light and love are darted down upon the children of men, and all by Jesus Christ, who is the ladder that has its foot on earth and its top in heaven.

2. *He saw the Spirit of God descending like a dove,* or *as a dove, and* coming or *lighting upon him.* Christ saw it (Mark i. 10), and John saw it (John i. 33, 34), and it is probable that all the standers-by saw it; for this was intended to be his public inauguration.

(1) *The Spirit of God descended, and lighted on him.* In the beginning of the old world, *the Spirit of God moved upon the face of the waters* (Gen. i. 2), *hovered* as a bird upon the nest. So here, in the beginning of this new world *the Spirit of the Lord should rest upon him* (Isa. xi. 2; lxi. 1), and here he did so. [1] He was to be a Prophet; and prophets always spoke by the Spirit of God, who came upon them. [2] He was to be the Head of the church. Christ *received gifts for men,* that he might give *gifts to men.*

(2) He *descended on him like a dove.* If there must be a bodily shape (Luke iii. 22), it must not be that of a man. None therefore was more fit than the shape of one of the fowls of heaven (heaven being now opened), and of all fowl none was so significant as the dove. [1] The Spirit of Christ is a dove-like spirit. *The Spirit descended,* not in the shape of an eagle, which is, though a royal bird, yet a bird of prey, but *in the shape of a dove,* than which no creature is more harmless and inoffensive. Such must Christians be, *harmless as doves.* The dove mourns much (Isa. xxxviii. 14). Christ wept oft; and penitent souls are compared to *doves of the valleys.* [2] The dove was the only fowl that was offered in sacrifice (Lev. i. 14), and Christ *offered himself without spot to God.* [3] The tidings of the decrease of Noah's flood were brought by a dove, with an olive-leaf in her mouth; fitly therefore are the glad tidings of peace with God brought by the Spirit as a *dove.* That God is in Christ reconciling the world unto himself, is a joyful message, which comes to us upon the wing, *the wings of a dove.*

3. To explain and complete this solemnity, *there came a voice from heaven.* The Holy Spirit manifested himself in the likeness of a *dove,* but God the Father by *a voice.*

(1) See here how God owns our Lord Jesus; *This is my beloved Son.* Observe, [1] The relation he stood in to him; He *is my Son.* He is the Son of God by special designation to the work and office of the world's Redeemer. He was sanctified and sealed, and went upon that errand, *brought up with* the Father for it. [2] The affection the Father had for him; He *is my beloved Son.* Particularly as Mediator, and in undertaking the work of man's salvation, he was his *beloved Son.* Because he consented to the covenant of redemption, and delighted to do that *will of God, therefore the Father loved him.* Now know we that he loved us, *seeing he has not withheld his Son, his only Son, his Isaac whom he loved,* but *gave him to be a sacrifice for our sin.*

(2) See here how ready he is to own us in him: He *is my beloved Son,* not only *with* whom, but *in* whom, I am well pleased. He is pleased with all that are in him, and are united to him by faith. Hitherto God had been displeased with the children of men, but now his anger is turned away, and he has made us *accepted in the Beloved,* Eph. i. 6. Out of Christ, God *is a consuming Fire,* but, in Christ, a reconciled Father. This is the sum of the whole gospel. We must by faith cheerfully concur, and say, that he *is our beloved* Saviour, *in whom we are well pleased.*

CHAPTER 4

John Baptist said concerning Christ, He must increase, but I must decrease. He had done what he came to do. As the rising Sun advances, the morning star disappears. Concerning Jesus Christ we have in this chapter, I. The temptation he underwent, ver. 1–11. II. The teaching work he undertook, the places he preached in (ver. 12–16), and the subject he preached on, ver. 17. III. His calling of disciples, Peter and Andrew, James and John, ver. 18–22. IV. His curing diseases (ver. 23, 24), and the great resort of the people to him.

Verses 1–11

We have here the story of a famous duel, fought hand to hand, between Michael and the dragon, the Seed of the woman and the seed of the serpent, nay, the serpent himself in which the seed of the woman suffers, being *tempted,* and so has his heel bruised but the serpent is quite baffled in his temptations, and so has his head broken.

I. The time when it happened. Immediately after *the heavens were opened* to him, and *the Spirit descended on him.* The next news we hear of him is, he is *tempted*; for *then* he is best able to grapple with the temptation. 1. Great privileges, and special tokens of divine favour, will not secure us from being *tempted.* Nay, 2. After great honours put upon us, we must expect something that is humbling. 3. God usually prepares his people for temptation before he calls them to it. 4. The assurance of our sonship is the best preparative for temptation.

Then, when he was baptized, *then* he was *tempted.* After we have been admitted into communion with God, we must expect to be set upon by Satan. The enriched soul must double its guard. The Devil has a particular spite at useful persons, who are not only good, but given to do good, especially at their first setting out. Let young ministers know what to expect, and arm accordingly.

II. The place where it was; *in the wilderness.* After communion with God, it is good to be private awhile, lest we lose what we have received, in the crowd, and hurry of worldly business. Christ withdrew into the wilderness, 1. To gain advantage to himself. Retirement gives an opportunity for meditation and communion with God; even they who are called to the most active life must yet have their contemplative hours, and must find time to be alone with God. Those are not fit to speak of the things of God in public to others, who have not first conversed with those things in secret by themselves. 2. To give advantage to the tempter. Though solitude is a friend to a good heart, yet Satan knows how to improve it against us. Those who, under pretence of sanctity and devotion, retire into dens and deserts, find that they are not out of the reach of their spiritual enemies, and that there they want the benefit of the communion of saints. Christ retired, (1) That Satan might have leave to do his worst. To make his victory the more illustrious, he gave the enemy sun and wind on his side, and yet baffled him. (2) That he might have an opportunity to do his best himself, that he might be exalted in his own strength. Christ entered the lists without a second.

III. The preparatives for it, which were two.

1. He was directed to the combat; he *was led up of the Spirit to be tempted of the Devil*. The Spirit that *descended upon him like a dove* made him meek, and yet made him bold. If God, by his providence, order us into circumstances of temptation, for our trial, we must not think it strange, but double our guard. *Be strong in the Lord, resist steadfast in the faith*, and all shall be well. Whithersoever God leads us, we may hope he will go along with us, and bring us off *more than conquerors*.

Christ *was led to be tempted of the Devil*, and of him only. Others are tempted, *when they are drawn aside of their own lust and enticed* (James i. 14); but our Lord Jesus had no corrupt nature, and therefore he was led, as a champion into the field, *to be tempted purely by the Devil*.

Now Christ's temptation is, (1) An instance of his own condescension and humiliation. Christ submitted because he would humble himself, *in all things to be made like unto his brethren*. (2) An occasion of Satan's confusion. There is no conquest without a combat. Christ was tempted, that he might overcome the tempter. (3) Matter of comfort to all the saints. In the temptation of Christ it appears, that our enemy is not invincible. Though he is *a strong man armed*, yet the Captain of our salvation is *stronger than he*. It is some comfort to us to think that Christ suffered, being *tempted*; for thus it appears that temptations, if not yielded to, are not sins, they are afflictions only. And we have a High Priest who knows, by experience, what it is to be *tempted*, and who therefore is the more tenderly touched with *the feeling of our infirmities* in an hour of temptation.

2. He was dieted for the combat, as wrestlers, who are *temperate in all things* (1 Cor. ix. 25); but Christ beyond any other, for he *fasted forty days and forty nights*. Christ needed not to fast for mortification (he had no corrupt desires to be subdued); yet he *fasted*. If good people are brought low, if they want friends and succours, this may comfort them, that their Master himself was in like manner exercised. A man may want bread, and yet be a favourite of heaven, and under the conduct of the spirit. *When he fasted forty days he was* never hungry; converse with heaven was instead of meat and drink to him, but *he was afterwards an hungred*, to show that he was really and truly man. Man fell by eating, and that way we often sin, and therefore Christ *was an hungred*.

IV. The temptations themselves. That which Satan aimed at, in all his temptations, was, to bring him to *sin against God*, and so to render him for ever incapable of being a Sacrifice for the sin of others. That which he aimed at was, to bring him, 1. To despair of his Father's goodness. 2. To presume upon his Father's power. 3. To alienate his Father's honour, by giving it to Satan. The two former are artful temptations, which there was need of great

wisdom to discern; the last was a strong temptation, which there was need of great resolution to resist.

1. He tempted him to despair of his Father's goodness, and to distrust his Father's care concerning him.

(1) See how the temptation was managed (*v*. 3); *The tempter came to him. The tempter came to* Christ in a visible appearance. If ever the Devil *transformed himself into an angel of light*, he did so now, and pretended to be a good genius, a guardian angel.

Observe the subtlety of *the tempter*, in joining this first temptation with what went before, to make it the stronger. [1] Christ began to be hungry, and therefore the motion seemed very proper, to turn *stones* into *bread* for his necessary support. Want and poverty are a great temptation to discontent and unbelief, and the use of unlawful means for our relief, under pretence that necessity has no law. Those therefore who are reduced to straits, have need to double their guard; it is better to starve to death, than live and thrive by sin. [2] Christ was lately declared to be *the Son of God*, and here the Devil tempts him to doubt of that; *If thou be the Son of God*.

First, "Thou hast now an occasion to question whether *thou be the Son of God* or no; for can it be, that *the Son of God*, who is *Heir of all things*, should be reduced to such straits? Either God is not thy Father, or he is a very unkind one." *a*. The great thing Satan aims at, in tempting good people, is to overthrow their relation to God as a Father. *b*. Outward afflictions, wants and burdens, are the great arguments Satan uses to make the people of God question their sonship. They know how to answer this temptation, who can say with holy Job, *Though he slay me, though he starve me, yet I will trust in him*, and love him as a Friend. *c*. The Devil aims to shake our faith in the word of God. *Has God said* that thou art his *beloved Son*? Surely he did not say so; or if he did it is not true. *d*. The Devil carries on his designs very much by possessing people with hard thoughts of God, as if he were unkind, or unfaithful.

Secondly, "Thou hast now an opportunity to show that thou art *the Son of God. If thou* art *the Son of God*, prove it by this, *command that these stones*" (a heap of which, probably, lay now before him) "*be made bread*," *v*. 3. He does not say, *Pray to thy Father* that he would turn them into *bread*; but *command* it to be done; thy Father hath forsaken thee, set up for thyself, and be not beholden to him. The Devil is for nothing that is humbling, but everything that is assuming.

(2) See how this temptation was resisted and overcome.

[1] Christ refused to comply with it. He would not *command these stones to be made bread*; not because he could not; but he would not. And why would he not? At first view, the thing appears justifiable enough, and the truth is, the more plausible a temptation is, and the greater appearance there is of good in it, the more dangerous it is. This matter would bear a dispute, but Christ was soon aware of the snake in the grass, and would not do anything, *First*, That looked like questioning the truth of the voice he heard from heaven. *Secondly*, That looked like distrusting his Father's care of him. *Thirdly*, That looked like setting up for himself, and being his own carver; or, *Fourthly*, That looked like gratifying Satan, by doing a thing at his motion.

[2] He was ready to reply to it (*v*. 4); *He answered and said, It is written*. This is observable, that Christ answered and baffled all the temptations of Satan with, *It is written*. He put honour upon the scripture, and, to set us an example, he appealed to what was written in the law. The word of God is *the sword of the Spirit*, the only offensive weapon in all the Christian armoury (Eph. vi. 17).

This answer, as all the rest, is taken out of the book of *Deuteronomy*, which signifies *the second law*, and in which there is very little ceremonial; the Levitical sacrifices and purifications, though of divine institution, could not drive away Satan, but moral precepts and evangelical promises, mixed with faith, these are *mighty, through God*, for the vanquishing of Satan. The reason given why God fed the Israelites with manna is, because he would teach them that *man shall not live by bread alone*. This Christ applies to his own case. The Devil would have him question his sonship, because he was in straits; no, says he, Israel was God's son, and it follows there (Deut. viii. 5), *As a man chasteneth his son, so the Lord thy God chasteneth thee*. Christ, *being a Son*, thus *learns obedience*. The Devil would have him distrust his Father's love and care. The Devil would have him, as soon as he began to be hungry, immediately look out for supply. God will have his children, when they want, not only to wait on him, but to wait for him. The Devil would have him to supply himself with bread. "No," says Christ, "what need is there of that? Man may live without bread, as Israel in the wilderness lived forty years upon manna." *Any word proceeding out of the mouth of God*, anything that God shall order and appoint for that end, will be as good a livelihood for man as bread, and will maintain him as well. As we may *have bread*, and yet not be nourished, if God deny his blessing (for though bread is *the staff of life*, it is God's blessing that is *the staff of bread*), so we may *want bread*, and yet be nourished some other way. As in our greatest abundance we must not think to live *without* God, so in our greatest straits we must learn to live *upon* God. Let us learn of Christ here to be at God's finding, rather than at our own. *Jehovah-jireh;* some way or other *the Lord will provide*. It is better to live poorly upon the fruits of God's goodness, than live plentifully upon the products of our own sin.

2. He tempted him to presume upon his Father's power and protection. See what a restless unwearied adversary the Devil is!

Now in this second attempt we may observe,

(1) What the temptation was, and how it was managed. In general, finding Christ so confident of his Father's care of him, in point of nourishment, he endeavours to draw him to presume upon that care in point of safety. Nor are any extremes more dangerous than those of despair and presumption, especially in the affairs of our souls. Some who have obtained a persuasion that Christ is able and willing to save them *from* their sins, are then tempted to presume that he will save them *in* their sins.

Now in this temptation we may observe,

[1] How he made way for it. He took Christ, not by force and against his will, but moved him to go, and went along with him, to Jerusalem. He was *set upon a pinnacle of the temple*. Now observe, *First*, How submissive Christ was, in suffering himself to be hurried thus, that he might let Satan do his worst and yet conquer him. How comfortable is it, that Christ, who let loose this power of Satan against himself, does not in like manner let it loose against us, but restrains it, for he *knows our frame*! *Secondly*, How subtle the Devil was, in the choice of the place for his temptations. He fixes him on a public place in Jerusalem, a populous city, and *the joy of the whole earth*; and in the temple, one of the wonders of the world, continually gazed upon with admiration by some one or other. There he might make himself remarkable, and prove himself the Son of God; not, in the obscurities of a wilderness, but before multitudes.

Observe, *a*. That Jerusalem is here called the *holy city*; for so it was in name and profession. There is no city on earth so holy as to exempt and secure us from the Devil and his temptations. The *holy city*

is the place where he does, with the greatest advantage and success, tempt men to pride and presumption; but, blessed be God, into the Jerusalem above, that holy city, no unclean thing shall enter; there we shall be for ever out of temptation. *b*. That he *set him upon a pinnacle of the temple*. Pinnacles of the temple are places of temptation. (*a*) High places are so; they are slippery places. God casts down, that he may raise up; the Devil raises up, that he may cast down. (*b*) High places *in the church* are, in a special manner, dangerous. They who excel in gifts, who are in eminent stations, and have gained great reputation, have need to keep humble. Those that *stand high* are concerned to *stand fast*.

[2] How he moved it; "*If thou be the Son of God*, now show thyself to the world, and prove thyself to be so; *cast thyself down*, and then," *First*, "Thou wilt be admired, as *under the special protection of heaven*." *Secondly*, "Thou wilt be received, as coming *with a special commission from heaven*. All Jerusalem will see and acknowledge, not only that thou art more than a man, but that thou art that *Messenger*, that *Angel of the covenant*, that should *suddenly come to the temple* (Mal. iii. 1)."

Observe, The Devil said, *Cast thyself down*. The Devil could not cast him down. The power of Satan is a limited power; *hitherto he shall come, and no further*. The Devil can but persuade, he cannot compel; he can but say, *Cast thyself down*; he cannot cast us down. Therefore let us not *hurt ourselves*, and then, blessed be God, no one else can hurt us, Prov. ix. 12.

[3] How he backed this motion with a scripture; *For it is written, He shall give his angels charge concerning thee*. But *is Saul also among the prophets*? Is Satan so well versed in scripture, as to be able to quote it so readily? It seems, he is. Note, It is possible for a man to have his head full of scripture-notions, and his mouth full of scripture-expressions, while his heart is full of reigning enmity to God and all goodness.

First, There was *something right*. It is true, there is such a promise of the ministration of the angels, for the protection of the saints. The devil knows it by experience. The angels guard the saints for Christ's sake, Rev. vii. 5, 11.

Secondly, There was a great deal *wrong in it*; and perhaps the devil had a particular spite against this promise, and perverted it, because it often stood in his way, and baffled his mischievous designs against the saints. See here, 1. How he *misquoted* it; and that was *bad*. The promise is, They shall *keep thee*; but how? *In all thy ways;* not otherwise; if we go *out of our way*, out of the way of our duty, we forfeit the promise, and put ourselves out of God's protection. It is good for us upon all occasions to consult the scriptures themselves, and not to take things upon trust. 2. How he *misapplied* it; and that was *worse*. This promise is firm, and stands good; but the devil made an ill use of it, when he used it as an encouragement to presume upon the divine care. But *shall we continue in sin, that grace may abound*? throw ourselves down, that the angels may bear us up? God forbid.

(2) How Christ overcame this temptation; he resisted and overcame it, as he did the former, with, *It is written*. The Devil's *abusing* of scripture did not prevent Christ from using it, but he presently urges, Deut. vi. 16, *Thou shalt not tempt the Lord thy God*. In the place whence it is quoted, it is in the plural number, *You shall not tempt;* here it is singular, *Thou shalt not*. We are *then* likely to get good by the word of God, when we hear and receive general promises as speaking to us in particular.

If Christ should *cast himself down*, it would be the tempting of God, [1] As it would be *requiring a further confirmation* of that which was so well confirmed.

Christ was abundantly satisfied that God was already his Father, and took care of him. [2] As it would be *requiring a special preservation* of him, in doing that which he had no call to. If we expect that because God has promised not to forsake us, therefore he should follow us out of the way of our duty; that because he has promised to supply our wants, therefore he should humour us, and please our fancies; this is presumption, this is tempting God. This is to affront him whom we ought to honour. We must never promise ourselves any more than God has promised us.

3. He tempted him to the most *black and horrid idolatry*, with the proffer of the *kingdoms of the world, and the glory of them*. (1) The worst temptation was reserved for the last. Whatever temptation we have been assaulted by, still we must prepare for worse.

In this temptation, we may observe,

[1] What he *showed him—all the kingdoms of the world*. In order to this, he took him to an *exceeding high mountain*. The pinnacle of the temple is not high enough; the prince of the power of the air must have him further up into his territories. Hither the blessed Jesus was carried for the advantage of a prospect; as if the devil could show him more of the world than he knew already, who made and governed it. His taking him up into a high mountain, was but to *humour the thing*, and to colour the delusion; in which yet the blessed Jesus did not suffer himself to be imposed upon, but saw through the cheat. Hence, observe, concerning *Satan's temptations*, that, *First*, They often *come in at the eye*. The first sin began in the eye, Gen. iii. 6. We have therefore need to make a covenant with our eyes, and to pray that God would *turn them away from beholding vanity*. *Secondly*, That temptations commonly take rise from the world, and the things of it. *Thirdly*, That it is a *great cheat* which the devil puts upon poor souls, in his temptations. He deceives, and so destroys; he imposes upon men with shadows and false colours; shows the world and the glory of it, and hides from men's eyes the sin and sorrow and death which stain the pride of all this glory. *Fourthly*, That the *glory of the world* is the most *charming* temptation to the *unthinking* and *unwary*, and that by which men are most imposed upon. The *pride of life* is the most dangerous snare.

[2] What he *said to him* (v. 9); *All these things will I give thee, if thou wilt fall down and worship me.* See,

First, How *vain the promise* was. *All these things will I give thee*. He seems to take it for granted, that in the former temptations he had in part gained his point. "Come," says he, "it seems that the God whose Son thou thinkest thyself to be deserts thee, and starves thee—a sign that he is not thy Father; but if thou wilt be ruled by me, I will provide better for thee than so: own me for thy father, and ask my blessing, and *all this will I give thee*." Satan makes an easy prey of men, when he can persuade them to think themselves abandoned of God. The fallacy of this promise lies in that, *All this will I give thee*. The devil's baits are all a sham; they are shows and shadows with which he deceives. The *nations of the earth* had been, long before, promised to the Messiah; if he be *the Son of God*, they belong to him. We must take heed of receiving even that which God hath promised, out of the devil's hand.

Secondly, How *vile the condition* was; *If thou wilt fall down, and worship me*. The devil is fond of being worshipped. What temptation could be more hideous, more black? The best of saints may be tempted to the worst of sins. This is their affliction, but while there is no consent to it, nor approbation of it, it is not their sin; Christ was tempted to worship Satan.

(2) See how Christ warded off the thrust. He rejected the proposal,

[1] With *abhorrence* and *detestation*; Get thee hence, Satan. It appears abominable at the first sight, and therefore is immediately rejected. While Satan tempted Christ to do himself a mischief, by casting himself down, though he yielded not, yet he heard it; but now that the temptation flies in the face of God, he cannot bear it; *Get thee hence, Satan*. It is good to be *peremptory* in resisting temptation, and to *stop our ears* to Satan's charms.

[2] With an argument fetched from scripture. The argument is very suitable, and exactly to the purpose, taken from Deut. vi. 13, and x. 20. *Thou shalt worship the Lord thy God, and him only shalt thou serve*. Our Saviour has recourse to the fundamental law in this case, which is indispensable, and universally obligatory. Religious worship is due to God only. Christ quotes this law concerning religious worship, and quotes it with application to himself; *First*, To show that in his estate of humiliation as man, he did worship God, both publicly and privately. Thus it became him to fulfil all righteousness. *Secondly*, To show that the law of religious worship is of eternal obligation.

V. We have here the end and issue of this combat, *v.* 11.

1. The devil was baffled, and quitted the field; *Then the devil leaveth him*, forced to do so by the power that went along with that word of command, *Get thee hence, Satan*. He made a shameful and inglorious retreat, and came off with disgrace. He despairs of moving him, and begins to conclude that he is the *Son of God*, and that it is in vain to tempt him any further. If we resist the devil, he will flee from us; he will yield, if we keep our ground. When the devil left our Saviour, he owned himself fairly beaten. The devil, though he is an enemy to all the saints, is a conquered enemy. The Captain of our salvation has defeated and disarmed him; we have nothing to do but to *pursue the victory*.

2. The holy angels came and attended upon our victorious Redeemer; *Behold, angels came and ministered unto him*. One angel might have served to bring him food, but here are many attending him, to testify their respect to him, and their readiness to receive his commands. Behold this! It is worth taking notice of; (1) That as there is a world of wicked, malicious spirits that fight against Christ and his church, and all particular believers, so there is a world of holy, blessed spirits engaged and employed for them. (2) That Christ's victories are the angels' triumphs. (3) That the angels ministered to the Lord Jesus, not only food, but whatever else he wanted after this great fatigue. Though God may suffer his people to be brought into wants and straits, yet he will take effectual care for their supply, and will rather send angels to feed them, than see them perish.

Christ was thus succoured after the temptation, [1] For his encouragement to go on in his undertaking. [2] For our encouragement to trust in him. We may expect, not only that he will sympathize with his tempted people, but that he will come in with seasonable relief to them.

Verses 12–17

We have here an account of Christ's preaching in the synagogues of Galilee.

Several passages in the other gospels, especially in that of St. John, are supposed, in the order of the story of Christ's life, to intervene between his temptation and his preaching in Galilee. But Matthew, having had his residence in Galilee, begins his story of Christ's public ministry with his preaching there.

I. The time; *When Jesus had heard that John was cast into prison, then he went into Galilee, v.* 12.

The cry of the saints' sufferings comes up into the ears of the Lord Jesus. If John be cast into prison, Jesus hears it, takes cognizance of it, and steers his course accordingly. 1. Christ did *not* go into the country, *till he heard of* John's imprisonment; for he must have time given him to *prepare the way of the Lord*, before the Lord himself appear. John must be Christ's harbinger, but not his rival. The moon and stars are lost when the sun rises. 2. He *did* go into the country as soon as he heard of John's imprisonment; not only to provide for his own safety, but to supply the want of John Baptist, and to build upon the good foundation he had laid. God will not leave himself without witness, nor his church without guides.

II. The place where he preached; in Galilee, a remote part of the country, that lay furthest from Jerusalem, and was there looked upon with contempt, as rude and boorish. The inhabitants of that country were reckoned stout men, fit for soldiers, but not polite men, or fit for scholars. Observe,

1. The particular city he chose for his residence: not Nazareth, where he had been bred up; no, he left Nazareth; particular notice is taken of that, *v.* 13. And with good reason did he leave Nazareth; for the men of that city *thrust him out* from among them, Luke iv. 29. Christ will not stay long where he is not welcome. Unhappy Nazareth!

But he *came and dwelt in Capernaum*, which was a city of Galilee, but many miles distant from Nazareth, a great city and of much resort. It is said here to be *on the sea coast*, not the *great sea*, but the sea of Tiberias. Hither Christ came, and here he dwelt. However, here he fixed not constantly, for he went about doing good; but this was for some time his headquarters: what little rest he had, was here. And at Capernaum, it should seem, he was welcome. If some reject Christ, yet others will receive him, and bid him welcome. Capernaum is glad of Nazareth's leavings.

2. The prophecy that was fulfilled in this, *v.* 14–16. It is quoted from Isa. ix. 1, 2, but with some variation. The evangelist here takes only the latter clause, which speaks of the return of the light of liberty and prosperity to those countries that had been in the darkness of captivity, and applies it to the appearing of the gospel among them.

The places are spoken of, *v.* 15. Christ came to Capernaum, the gospel came to all those places round about; such diffusive influences did the Sun of righteousness cast.

(1) They were *in darkness*. Those that are without Christ, are in the dark, nay, they are darkness itself. They were *sitting* in this condition. Sitting is a continuing posture; where we sit, we mean to stay. And it is a contented posture; they were in the dark, and they loved darkness. He that is in the dark because it is night, may be sure that the sun will shortly arise; but he that is in the dark because he is blind, will not so soon have his eyes opened. We have the light, but what will that avail us, if we be not light in the Lord? (2) When the gospel comes, light comes; when it comes to any place, when it comes to any soul, it makes day there. Light is discovering, it is directing; so is the gospel.

It is a *great* light. *Great* in comparison with the light of the law, the shadows of which were now done away. It is a *great light*, for it discovers great things and of vast consequence; it will last long, and spread far. And it is a *growing light*, intimated in that word, It is *sprung up*. It was but *spring of day* with them; now the day dawned, which afterward *shone more and more*. The gospel-kingdom, like a grain of mustard-seed or the morning light, was small in its beginnings, gradual in its growth, but great in its perfection.

Observe, The light *sprang up to them*; they did not go to seek it. It came upon them ere they were aware.

III. The text he preached upon (*v.* 17): *From that time* he began to preach.

The subject which Christ dwelt upon now in his preaching (and it was indeed the sum and substance of all his preaching), was the very same that John had preached upon (*ch.* iii. 2); *Repent, for the kingdom of heaven is at hand;* for the gospel is the same for substance under various dispensations; for it is the *everlasting gospel. Fear God, and,* by repentance, *give honour to him*, Rev. xiv. 6, 7. Christ put a great respect upon John's ministry, when he preached to the same purport that John had preached before him. Thus did God confirm the word of his messenger, Isa. xliv. 26. He pitches upon this old, plain text, *Repent, for the kingdom of heaven is at hand.* 1. This he preached *first* upon; he began with this. We need not go up to heaven, nor down to the deep, for matter or language in our preaching. As John prepared Christ's way, so Christ prepared his own, and made way for the further discoveries he designed, with the doctrine of repentance. 2. This he preached *often* upon; wherever he went, this was his subject, and neither he nor his followers ever reckoned it worn threadbare. That which has been preached and heard before, may yet very profitably be preached and heard again; but then it should be preached and heard better. 3. This he preached as gospel. Not only the austere Baptist, who was looked upon as a melancholy, morose man, but the sweet and gracious Jesus, whose lips dropped as a honey-comb, preached repentance. 4. The reason is still the same; The *kingdom of heaven is at hand.* Now that it was so much nearer, the argument was so much the stronger; now is the *salvation nearer*, Rom. xiii. 11.

Verses 18–22

When Christ began to preach, he began to *gather disciples*, who should now be the *hearers*, and hereafter the *preachers.* Now, in these verses, we have an account of the first disciples that he called into fellowship with himself.

And this was an instance, 1. Of *effectual calling* to Christ. In all his preaching he gave a common call to all the country, but in this he gave a special and particular call to those that were given him by the Father. All the country was *called*, but these were *called out.* 2. It was an instance of *ordination*, and appointment to the work of the ministry. When Christ, as a Teacher, set up his great school, one of his first works was to appoint ushers, or under masters, to be employed in the work of instruction.

Now we may observe here,

I. *Where* they were called—by the *sea of Galilee*, where Jesus was walking. Hither he went to call disciples; not to Herod's court (for few mighty or noble are called), not to Jerusalem, among the chief priests and the elders, but to the sea of Galilee; surely Christ sees not as man sees. Galilee was a remote part of the nation, the inhabitants were less cultivated and refined, their very language was broad and uncouth to the curious, their *speech betrayed them.* Yet thither Christ went, to call his apostles that were to be the prime ministers of state in his kingdom, for he *chooses the foolish things of the world, to confound the wise.*

II. *Who* they were. We have an account of the call of two pairs of brothers in these verses—Peter and Andrew, James and John. They had been disciples of John, and so were the better disposed to follow Christ. Those who have submitted to the discipline of repentance, shall be welcome to the joys of faith. We may observe concerning them,

1. That they were *brothers.* It is the honour and comfort of a house, when those that are of the *same* family, are of *God's* family.

2. That they were *fishers*. Being fishers, (1) They were *poor men*: if they had had estates, or any considerable stock in trade, they would not have made fishing their trade, however they might have made it their recreation. Christ does not despise the poor, and therefore we must not. (2) They were *unlearned men*. Yet this will not justify the bold intrusion of ignorant and unqualified men into the work of the ministry. (3) They were *men of business*, who had been bred up to labour. Diligence in an honest calling is pleasing to Christ, and no hindrance to a holy life. Idle people lie more open to the temptations of Satan than to the calls of God. (4) They were men that were accustomed to *hardships* and hazards; the fisher's trade, more than any other, is laborious and perilous; fishermen must be often wet and cold; they must watch, and wait, and toil, and be often in *peril by waters*. Those who have learned to bear hardships, and to run hazards, are best prepared for the fellowship and discipleship of Jesus Christ. Good soldiers of Christ must endure hardness.

III. *What they were doing*. Peter and Andrew were then using their nets, they were fishing; and James and John were *mending their nets*, which was an instance of their industry and good husbandry. They did not go to their father for money to buy new nets, but took pains to mend their old ones. It is commendable to make what we have go as far, and last as long, as may be. James and John were *with their father Zebedee*, ready to assist him. It is a happy and hopeful presage, to see children careful of their parents, and dutiful to them. Observe, 1. They were *all* employed, all very busy, and none idle. When Christ comes, it is good to be found doing. 2. They were *differently* employed; two of them were fishing, and two of them *mending their nets*. Ministers should be always employed, either in teaching or studying; and *mending their nets*, is in its season, as necessary work as fishing.

IV. *What the call was* (v. 19); *Follow me, and I will make you fishers of men*. Even they who have been called to follow Christ, have need to be called to follow on, and to follow nearer. Observe,

1. What Christ intended them for; *I will make you fishers of men*. Let them not be proud of the new honour designed them, they are still but fishers; let them not be afraid of the new work cut out for them, for they have been used to fishing, and fishers they are still. (1) Ministers are *fishers of men*, not to destroy them, but to save them, by bringing them into another element. (2) It is Jesus Christ that makes them so; *I will make you fishers of men*. It is he that qualifies men for this work, calls them to it, authorizes them in it, and gives them success in it.

2. What they must do in order to this; *Follow me*. They must separate themselves to a diligent attendance on him. (1) Those whom Christ employs in any service for him, must first be fitted and qualified for it. (2) Those who would *preach Christ*, must first *learn* Christ, and learn of him. (3) Those who would get an acquaintance with Christ, must be diligent and constant in their attendance on him. There is no learning comparable to that which is got by following Christ. (4) Those who are to fish for men, must therein follow Christ, and do it as he did, with diligence, faithfulness, and tenderness.

V. What was the *success* of this call. Peter and Andrew *straightway left their nets* (v. 20); and James and John *immediately left the ship and their father* (v. 22); *and they all followed him*. Those who would follow Christ aright, must *leave all* to follow him.

1. This instance of the power of the Lord Jesus gives us good encouragement to depend upon the sufficiency of his grace. How strong and effectual is his word! *He speaks, and it is done*.

2. This instance of the pliableness of the disciples, gives us a good example of obedience to the command of Christ. It is the good property of all Christ's faithful servants to come when they are called, and to follow their Master wherever he leads them. Being called, they obeyed, and, like Abraham, *went out not knowing whither they went*, but knowing very well whom they followed.

Verses 23–25

I. What an industrious preacher Christ was; He *went about all Galilee, teaching in their synagogues, and preaching the gospel of the kingdom*. Observe, 1. *What* Christ preached—*the gospel of the kingdom. The kingdom of heaven*, that is, of grace and glory, is emphatically *the kingdom. The gospel* is the charter of that kingdom, containing the King's coronation oath, by which he has graciously obliged himself to pardon, protect, and save the subjects of that kingdom. 2. *Where* he preached—*in the synagogues*; not there only, but there chiefly, because those were the *places of concourse*, where *wisdom* was to *lift up her voice* (Prov. i. 21). 3. *What pains he took* in preaching; He *went about all Galilee, teaching*. He *waits to be gracious*, and comes *to seek and save*. He *went about doing good*. Never was there such an itinerant preacher, such an indefatigable one, as Christ was.

II. What a powerful physician Christ was; he *went about* not only *teaching*, but *healing*,

1. What diseases he cured—all without exception. He *healed all manner of sickness, and all manner of disease*. There are diseases which are called *the reproach of physicians. He healed them*, all, however inveterate.

Three general words are here used to intimate this; he healed every sickness, every *disease*, or languishing, and all *torments*. None was too bad, none too hard, for Christ to heal with a word's speaking.

Three particular diseases are specified; *the palsy*, which is the greatest weakness of the body; *lunacy*, which is the greatest malady of the mind, and *possession of the Devil*, which is the greatest misery and calamity of both, yet Christ healed all.

2. What patients he had. See here, what flocking there was to him from all parts; great multitudes of people came, not only *from Galilee* and the country about, but even *from Jerusalem* and *from Judæa*, which lay a great way off; for *his fame went throughout all Syria. This* is given as the reason why such multitudes came to him, because his fame had spread so widely. What we hear of Christ from others, should invite us to him. The voice of fame is "Come, and see." Christ both *taught and healed*. It is well if anything will bring people to Christ; and they who come to him will find more in him than they expected.

Now concerning the cures which Christ wrought, let us, once for all, observe the *miracle*, the *mercy*, and the *mystery*, of them.

(1) The *miracle* of them. They were wrought in such a manner, as plainly spake them to be the immediate products of a divine and supernatural power, and they were God's seal to his commission. Nature could not do these things. All which proves him *a Teacher come from God*, for, otherwise, none could have done the works that he did, John iii. 2. His healing and his preaching generally went together, for the former confirmed the latter; thus here he *began to* do *and to* teach, Acts i. 1.

(2) The *mercy* of them. The miracles that Christ wrought, were most of them cures, and all of them (except the cursing of the barren fig-tree) blessings and favours; for the gospel dispensation is founded, and built up in love, and grace, and sweetness. Christ designed by his cures to win people, and so

to draw them with the bands of love, Hos. xi. 4. The miracle of them proved his doctrine *a faithful saying*, and convinced men's judgments; the mercy of them proved it *worthy of all acceptation*, and wrought upon their affections. They were not only *great works*, but *good works*, that he *showed them from* his *Father* (John x. 32).

(3) The *mystery* of them. Christ, by curing *bodily diseases*, intended to show, that his great errand into the world was to cure *spiritual maladies*. Sin is the *sickness, disease,* and *torment* of the soul; Christ *came to take away sin*, and so to heal these. And the particular stories of the cures Christ wrought are therefore so to be explained and improved, to the honour and praise of that glorious Redeemer, *who forgiveth all our iniquities, and so healeth all our diseases*.

CHAPTER 5

This chapter, and the two that follow it, are a sermon; the sermon upon the mount. It is the longest and fullest continued discourse of our Saviour that we have upon record. It is a practical discourse. The circumstances of the sermon being accounted for (ver. 1, 2), the sermon itself follows, the scope of which is, not to fill our heads with notions, but to guide and regulate our practice. I. He proposes blessedness as the end, and gives us the character of those who are entitled to blessedness in eight beatitudes, which may justly be called paradoxes, ver. 3–12. II. He prescribes duty as the way, and gives us standing rules of that duty. He directs his disciples, 1. To understand what they are—the salt of the earth, and the lights of the world, ver. 13–16. 2. To understand what they have to do—they are to be governed by the moral law. (1) A general ratification of the law, and a recommendation of it to us, as our rule, ver. 17–20. (2) A particular rectification of divers mistakes, and an authentic explication of divers branches which most needed to be explained and vindicated, ver. 20. Particularly, here is an explication, (1) Of the sixth commandment, ver. 21–26. (2) Of the seventh commandment, ver. 27–32. (3) Of the third commandment, ver. 33–37. (4) Of the law of retaliation, ver. 38–42. (5) Of the law of brotherly love, ver. 43–48.

Verses 1–2

We have here a general account of this sermon.

I. *The Preacher* was our Lord Jesus, the Prince of preachers. The prophets and John had *done virtuously* in preaching, *but* Christ *excelled them all*. He is the eternal Word, by whom God *has in these last days spoken to us*. The many miraculous cures wrought by Christ in Galilee were intended to dispose people to receive instructions from one in whom there appeared so much of a divine power and goodness; and, probably, this sermon was the summary, of what he had preached in the synagogues. His text was, *Repent, for the kingdom of heaven is at hand*.

II. *The place* was a mountain in Galilee. Our Lord Jesus was but ill accommodated; he had no convenient place to preach in, any more than *to lay his head* on. Our Lord Jesus, the great Teacher of truth, is driven out to the desert, and finds no better a pulpit than *a mountain* can afford; and not one of the *holy mountains of Zion*, but a common *mountain*; by which Christ would intimate that it is *the will of God that men should pray* and preach *everywhere*, anywhere, provided it be decent and convenient. Christ preached this sermon, which was an exposition of the law, upon a mountain, because upon *a mountain* the law was given. But observe the difference: when *the law was given*, the Lord *came down* upon the *mountain*; now the Lord *went up*; then, he spoke *in thunder and lightning*; now, *in a still small voice*: then the people were ordered to keep their distance; now they are invited to draw near: a blessed change!

III. *The auditors* were *his disciples*. They followed him for love and learning, while others attended him only for cures. *He taught them*, because they were willing to be *taught*; because they would *understand* what he taught, and because they were to teach others. Though this discourse was directed to the disciples, it was in the hearing of *the multitude*. No bounds were set about *this mountain*, to keep the people off, for, through Christ, we have access to God. Nay, he had an eye to *the multitude*, in preaching this sermon. It is an encouragement to a faithful minister to cast the net of the gospel where there are a great many fishes, in hope that some will be caught. The sight of a *multitude* puts life into a preacher, which yet must arise from a desire of their profit, not his own praise.

IV. *The solemnity* of his sermon is intimated in that word, *when he was set*. This was a set sermon, when he had placed himself so as to be best heard. That phrase, *He opened his mouth*, is only a Hebrew periphrasis of speaking. Yet some think it intimates the solemnity of this discourse; the congregation being large, he raised his voice, and spoke louder than usual. One of the ancients has this remark upon it; Christ *taught* much without *opening his mouth*, that is, by his holy and exemplary life; nay, he *taught*, when, being *led as a lamb to the slaughter, he opened not his mouth*, but now *he opened his mouth, and taught. He taught them*, what was the evil they should abhor, and what the good they should abide and abound in; for Christianity is designed to regulate the temper of our minds and the tenor of our conversations; gospel-time is a time of reformation (Heb. ix. 10); and by the gospel we must be reformed, must be made good, must be made better.

Verses 3–12

Christ begins his sermon with blessings, for *he came into the world to bless us* (Acts iii. 26). He does it *as one having authority*, as one that can *command the blessing, even life for evermore*. The Old Testament ended with a curse (Mal. iv. 6), the gospel begins with a blessing. Each of the blessings Christ here pronounces has a double intention: 1. To show who they are that are to be accounted. 2. What this is wherein true happiness consists.

1. This is designed to rectify the ruinous mistakes of a blind and carnal world. Blessedness is the thing which men pretend to pursue; *Who will make to see good?* Ps. iv. 6. But most mistake the end, and form a wrong notion of happiness; and then no wonder that they miss the way. The general opinion is, *Blessed are they* that are rich, and great, and honourable in the world; that spend their days in mirth, and their years in pleasure; that eat the fat, and drink the sweet, and carry all before them with a high hand. Now our Lord Jesus comes to give us quite another notion of blessedness and blessed people. The beginning of a Christian's practice must be to take his measures of happiness from those maxims, and to direct his pursuits accordingly.

2. It is designed to remove the discouragements of the weak and poor who receive the gospel. Even *the least in the kingdom of heaven*, whose heart was upright with God, was happy in the honours and privileges of that kingdom.

3. It is designed to invite souls to Christ. And those who had seen the gracious cures wrought by his hand (*ch.* iv. 23, 24), and now heard *the gracious words proceeding out of his mouth*, would say that he was all of a piece, made up of love and sweetness.

4. It is designed to settle and sum up the articles of agreement between God and man. The scope of the divine revelation is to let us know what God expects from us, and what we may then expect from him; and nowhere is this more fully set forth in a few words than here. The way to happiness is here opened, and made a *highway* (Isa. xxxv. 8). Some of the wiser heathen had notions of blessedness different from the rest of mankind, and looking toward this of our Saviour. Seneca, undertaking to describe a blessed man, makes it out, that it is only an honest, good man that is to be so called: *In whose estimations nothing is good or evil, but a good or evil heart*.

Our Saviour here gives us eight characters of blessed people; which represent to us the principal graces of a Christian. On each of them a present blessing is pronounced; *Blessed are* they; and to each a future blessedness is promised.

I. *The poor in Spirit* are happy, *v.* 3. There is a poor-spiritedness that is so far from making men blessed that it is a sin and a snare—cowardice and base fear. To be *poor in spirit* is, 1. To be contentedly poor, willing to be empty of worldly wealth, if God orders that to be our lot. Many are poor in the world, but high in spirit, poor and proud, but we must accommodate ourselves to our poverty, must *know how to be abased*, Phil. iv. 12. It is to sit loose to all worldly wealth, and not set our hearts upon it. It is not, in pride or pretence, to make ourselves poor, by throwing away what God has given us. If we be rich in the world we must be *poor in spirit*, that is, we must condescend to the poor and sympathize with them, as being touched with the feeling of their infirmities; we must expect and prepare for poverty; must not inordinately fear or shun it, but must bid it welcome, especially when it comes upon us for keeping a good conscience, Heb. x. 34. Job was *poor in spirit*, when he blessed God in *taking away*, as well as giving. 2. To be humble and lowly in our own eyes. To be *poor in spirit*, is to think meanly of ourselves, of what we are, and have, and do; it is to be as little children in our opinion of ourselves. Paul was rich in *spirituals*, excelling most in gifts and graces, and yet *poor in spirit*, *the least of the apostles*, less than the least of all saints, and *nothing* in his own account. It is to be willing to make ourselves cheap, and mean, and little, to do good; to *become all things to all men*. It is to acknowledge that God is great, and we are mean; that he is holy and we are sinful; that he is all and we are nothing. 3. To come off from all confidence in our own righteousness and strength, that we may depend only upon the merit of Christ and the spirit and grace of Christ. That *broken and contrite spirit* with which the publican cried for mercy to a poor sinner, is this poverty of spirit. We must call ourselves poor, because always in want of God's grace, always begging at God's door, always hanging on in his house.

(1) This poverty in spirit is put first among the Christian graces. The philosophers did not reckon humility among their moral virtues, but Christ puts it first. The foundation of all other graces is laid in humility. Those who would build high must begin low. Those *who are weary and heavy laden*, are *the poor in spirit*, and they shall find rest with Christ.

(2) They are *blessed*. Now they are so, in this world. God looks graciously upon them. Nothing comes amiss to them; while high spirits are always uneasy.

(3) *Theirs is the kingdom of heaven*. The kingdom of *grace* is composed of such; the kingdom of *glory* is prepared for them. The great, high spirits go away with the glory of *the kingdoms of the earth*; but the humble, mild, and yielding souls obtain the glory of *the kingdom of heaven*. The same happiness is promised to those who are usefully rich, as to those who are usefully rich. If I am not able to *spend* cheerfully for his sake, if I can but *want* cheerfully for his sake, even that shall be recompensed.

II. *They that mourn* are happy (*v.* 4); *Blessed are they that mourn*. This is another strange blessing. We are apt to think, Blessed are the *merry*; but Christ, who was himself a great mourner, says, Blessed are the *mourners*. There is a sinful mourning, which is an enemy to blessedness—*the sorrow of the world*. There is a natural mourning, which may prove a friend to blessedness, by the grace of God working with it. But there is a gracious mourning, which qualifies for blessedness. 1. A penitential

mourning for our own sins; this is *godly sorrow*, a sorrow according to God; sorrow for sin, with an eye to Christ. Those are God's mourners, who live a life of repentance, who, out of regard to God's honour, mourn also for the sins of others. 2. A sympathising mourning for the afflictions of others; the mourning of those who *weep with them that weep*, who look with compassion on perishing souls, and *weep over* them, as Christ *over Jerusalem*.

Now these gracious mourners, (1) *Are blessed*. As in vain and sinful *laughter the heart is sorrowful*, so in gracious mourning *the heart* has a serious joy, a secret satisfaction, which *a stranger does not intermeddle with*. (2) *They shall be comforted*. Light is sown for them; and in heaven, it is certain, *they shall be comforted*, as Lazarus, Luke xvi. 25. The happiness of heaven consists in being perfectly and eternally comforted, and in the *wiping away of all tears from their eyes*. Heaven will be heaven indeed to those who go mourning thither; it will be a harvest of joy, the return of a seed-time of tears (Ps. cxxvi. 5, 6).

III. *The meek* are happy (*v.* 5); *Blessed are the meek*. The meek are those who quietly submit themselves to God, and are *gentle towards all men* (Titus iii. 2); who can bear provocation without being inflamed by it; are either silent, or return a soft answer; who can be cool when others are hot; and in their patience keep possession of their own souls, when they can scarcely keep possession of anything else. *They* are the meek, who would rather forgive twenty injuries than revenge one.

These meek ones are here represented as happy, even in this world. 1. They are *blessed*, for they are like the blessed Jesus. They are *blessed*, for they have the most comfortable, undisturbed enjoyment of themselves, their friends, their God; they are fit to live, and fit to die. 2. *They shall inherit the earth*. Not that they shall always have much of *the earth*, much less that they shall be put off with that only; but this branch of godliness has, in a special manner, *the promise of that life that now is*. Meekness, however ridiculed and run down, has a real tendency to promote our health, wealth, comfort, and safety, even in this world. Or, *They shall inherit the land* (so it may be read), *the land of Canaan*, a type of heaven. So that all the blessedness of heaven above, and all the blessings of earth beneath, are the portion of the meek.

IV. *They that hunger and thirst after righteousness* are happy, *v.* 6. Some understand this as a further instance of outward poverty, and a low condition in this world. Yet, *blessed are they*, if they suffer these hardships for and with a good conscience; let them hope in God. Those who contentedly bear oppression, and quietly refer themselves to God to plead their cause, shall in due time be satisfied, abundantly satisfied, in the wisdom and kindness, which shall be manifested in his appearances for them. 1. *Righteousness* is here put for all spiritual blessings. They are purchased for us by *the righteousness of Christ*. To become *a new man*, and to bear the image of God; to have an interest in Christ and the promises —this is *righteousness*. 2. These we must *hunger and thirst after*. We must truly and really desire them. Our desires of spiritual blessings must be earnest and importunate; "*Give me these, or else I die*; give me these, and I have enough, though I had nothing else." *Hunger and thirst* are appetites that return frequently, and call for fresh satisfactions. The quickened soul calls for constant meals of righteousness, grace to do the work of every day in its day. Those who *hunger and thirst* will labour for supplies; so we must not only desire spiritual blessings, but take pains for them in the use of the appointed means.

Those who thus *hunger and thirst shall be filled* with those blessings. (1) They are *blessed* in those desires.

Though all desires of grace are not grace (feigned, faint desires are not), yet such a desire as this is; it is an *evidence* of something *good*, and an *earnest* of something *better*. It is a desire of God's own raising. (2) They *shall be filled* with those blessings. God will give them what they desire to their complete satisfaction. It is God only who can *fill a soul*, whose grace and favour are adequate to its just desires. He *fills the hungry* (Luke i. 53), *satiates* them, Jer. xxxi. 25.

V. The *merciful* are happy, *v.* 7. This, like the rest, is a paradox; for the merciful are not taken to be the wisest, nor are likely to be the richest; yet Christ pronounces them *blessed*. A man may be truly *merciful*, who has not wherewithal to be bountiful or liberal; and then God accepts the willing mind. We must not only bear our own afflictions patiently, but we must, by Christian sympathy, partake of the afflictions of our brethren; pity must be shown (Job vi. 14), and *bowels of mercy put on* (Col. iii. 12). We must have compassion on the souls of others, and help them; pity the ignorant, and instruct them; the careless, and warn them; those who are in a state of sin, and snatch them as *brands out of the burning*. Nay, a *good man is merciful to his beast*.

1. They are *blessed*; so it was said in the Old Testament; *Blessed is he that considers the poor*, Ps. xli. 1. Herein they resemble God, whose goodness is his glory. One of the purest and most refined delights in this world, is that of *doing good*. In this word, *Blessed are the merciful*, is included that saying of Christ, which otherwise we find not in the gospels, *It is more blessed to give than to receive*, Acts xx. 35. 2. *They shall obtain mercy;* mercy *with men*, when they need it (we know not how soon we may stand in need of kindness, and therefore should be kind); but especially mercy *with God*, for *with the merciful he will show himself merciful*, Ps. xviii. 25. The most *merciful* and charitable cannot pretend to *merit*, but must fly to mercy. Whereas *they shall have Judgment without mercy* who have *shown no mercy*.

VI. The *pure in heart* are happy (*v.* 8); *Blessed are the pure in heart, for they shall see God*. This is the most comprehensive of all the beatitudes.

1. Here is the most *comprehensive character* of the blessed; they are the *pure in heart*. True Christianity lies in the heart, in the *purity of the heart*; the *washing* of that *from wickedness*, Jer. iv. 14. We must lift up to God, not only clean hands, but a pure heart, Ps. xxiv. 4, 5; 1 Tim. i. 5. The heart must be *pure*, in opposition to *mixture*—an honest heart that aims well; and pure, in opposition to *pollution* and *defilement*; as wine *unmixed*, as water *unmuddied*. The heart must be kept *pure* from all filthiness of flesh and spirit, all that which comes *out of the heart, and defiles the man*. The heart must be *purified by faith*, and entire for God. *Create in me such a clean heart, O God!*

2. Here is the most *comprehensive comfort* of the blessed; They shall see God. (1) It is the perfection of the soul's happiness to *see God*; *seeing him*, as we may by faith in our present state, is a *heaven upon earth*; and seeing him as we shall in the future state, is the *heaven of heaven*. (2) The happiness of seeing God is promised to those, and those only who are *pure in heart*. None but the *pure* are capable of *seeing* God. What pleasure could an unsanctified soul take in the vision of a holy God? But all that are *pure in heart*, all that are truly sanctified, have desires wrought in them, which nothing but the sight of God will satisfy.

VII. The *peace-makers* are happy, *v.* 9. The wisdom that is from above is first *pure*, and then *peaceable*; the blessed ones are *pure* toward God, and *peaceable* toward men. The *peace-makers* are those who have, 1. *A peaceable disposition*. It is to love, and desire,

and delight in peace; to be in it as in our element. 2. A *peaceable conversation*; industriously, as far as we can, to preserve the peace that it be not broken, and to recover it when it is broken. The *making of peace* is sometimes a *thankless office*, and it is the lot of him who parts a fray, to have *blows on both sides*; yet it is a good office, and we must be forward to it. (1) Such persons are *blessed*. They are working together with Christ, who came into the world to *slay all enmities*, and to proclaim *peace on earth*. (2) *They shall be called the children of God*. God will own them as such. If the peacemakers are blessed, woe to the peace-breakers!

VIII. Those who are *persecuted for righteousness' sake*, are happy. This is the greatest paradox of all, and peculiar to Christianity. This beatitude, like Pharaoh's dream, is doubled, because hardly credited, and yet *the thing is certain*.

1. The case of suffering saints described.

(1) They are persecuted, hunted, pursued, run down, as noxious beasts are, that are sought for to be destroyed; they are abandoned as the *offscouring of all things*.

(2) They are *reviled, and have all manner of evil said against them falsely*. Nicknames, and names of reproach, are fastened upon them, sometimes to make them formidable, that they may be powerfully assailed. Those who have had no power in their hands to do them any other mischief, could yet do this; and those who have had power to *persecute*, have found it necessary to *do this too*, to justify themselves in their barbarous usage of them. *Reviling* the saints is *persecuting* them, and will be found so shortly when *hard speeches* must be accounted for (Jude 15), and *cruel mockings*, Heb. xi. 36. They will say all *manner of evil of you falsely*. There is no evil so black and horrid, which, at one time or other, has not been said falsely, of Christ's disciples and followers.

(3) All this is *for righteousness' sake* (*v.* 10); *for my sake, v.* 11. This precludes those from this blessedness who suffer *justly*, and are evil spoken of *truly* for their real crimes; it is not the *suffering*, but the cause, that makes the martyr. Those suffer *for righteousness' sake*, who suffer for doing that which is good.

2. The comforts of suffering saints laid down.

(1) They *are blessed*; for they now, in their lifetime, receive *their evil things* (Luke xvi. 25), and receive them upon a good account. They are *blessed*, for it is an honour to them; it is an opportunity of glorifying Christ, and of experiencing special comforts and tokens of his presence.

(2) They shall be *recompensed*; Theirs is *the kingdom of heaven*. They have at present a sure title to it, and sweet foretastes of it; and shall ere long be in possession of it. *Great is your reward in heaven:* so great, as far to transcend the service. God will provide that those who lose *for* him, though it be life itself, shall not lose *by* him in the end. This is that which has borne up the suffering saints in all ages—*this joy is set before them*.

(3) "*So persecuted they the prophets that were before you, v.* 12. They were *before you* in excellency, above what you are yet arrived at; they were *before you* in time, that they might be examples to you of *suffering affliction* and *of patience*, James v. 10. Can you expect to go to heaven in a way by yourselves? It is a comfort to see the way of suffering a beaten road, and an honour to follow such leaders. That grace which was *sufficient for them*, to carry them through their sufferings, shall not be *deficient to you*."

(4) Therefore *rejoice and be exceeding glad, v.* 12. It is not enough to be patient and content under these sufferings, but we must rejoice. Not that we must take a *pride* in our sufferings, (that spoils all), but

we must take *a pleasure* in them, as knowing that Christ is herein *beforehand* with us, and that he will not be *behindhand* with us.

Verses 13–16

Christ had lately called his disciples, and told them that they should be *fishers of men*; here he tells them further what he designed them to be—*the salt of the earth*, and *lights of the world*.

I. *Ye are the salt of the earth.* The prophets, who went before them, were the salt of the land of Canaan; but the apostles were the salt of *the whole earth*, for they must *go into all the world to preach the gospel*. What could they do in so large a province as *the whole earth?* But, being to work silently as salt, one handful of that salt would diffuse its savour far and wide; would go a great way, and work insensibly and irresistibly as leaven, *ch.* xiii. 33. The doctrine of the gospel is as *salt*; it is penetrating, it reaches *the heart*, Acts ii. 37. It is cleansing, it is relishing, and preserves from putrefaction. An everlasting covenant is called a *covenant of salt* (Num. xviii. 19); and the gospel is an everlasting gospel. Salt was required in all the sacrifices. Christians, and especially ministers, are the salt of the earth.

1. If they be such as they should be they are *as good salt*, white, and small, and broken into many grains, but very useful and necessary. See in this, (1) What they are to be in themselves—seasoned with the gospel, with the salt of grace. *Have salt in yourselves*, else you cannot diffuse it among others, Mark ix. 50. (2) What they are to be to others; they must not only *be* good but *do* good. (3) What great blessings they are to the world. Mankind, lying in ignorance and wickedness, were a vast heap of unsavoury stuff, ready to putrefy; but Christ sent forth his disciples, by their lives and doctrines, to season it with knowledge and grace, and so to render it acceptable to God. (4) How they must expect to be disposed of. They must be scattered as salt upon the meat, here a grain and there a grain. Some have observed, that whereas it is foolishly called an ill omen to have the salt fall towards us, it is really an ill omen to have this salt fall from us.

2. If they be not, they are as *salt* that has *lost its savour*. If a Christian be so, especially if a minister be so, his condition is very sad; for, (1) He is *irrecoverable*: *Wherewith shall it be salted?* There is no remedy for *unsavoury salt*. (2) He is *unprofitable*: *It is thenceforth good for nothing*. As a man without reason, so is a Christian without grace. (3) He is doomed to ruin and rejection; He shall be *cast out*. He shall be *trodden under foot of men*.

II. *Ye are the light of the world*, v. 14. This also bespeaks them useful, as the former. (*Nothing more useful than the sun and salt*), but more glorious. Truly *the light is sweet*, it is welcome; the light of the first day of the world was so, so is the morning light of every day; so is the gospel, and those that spread it.

1. As *the lights of the world*, they are illustrious and conspicuous, and have many eyes upon them. A city that is *set on a hill cannot be hid*. They are for *signs* (Isa. viii. 18), *men wondered at* (Zech. iii. 8); all their neighbours have an eye upon them. Some admire them, commend them, rejoice in them, and study to imitate them; others envy them, hate them, censure them, and study to blast them. They are concerned therefore to *walk circumspectly*, because of *their observers*.

2. As the *lights of the world*, they are intended to illuminate and give light to others (*v.* 15), and therefore, (1) They shall be *set up* as lights. Christ having lighted these candles, they shall not be put under a bushel. The gospel is so strong a light, and carries with it so much of its own evidence, that, *like a city*

on a hill, *it cannot be hid*, it cannot but appear to be from God. It will *give light to all that are in the house*, to all that will draw near to it, and come where it is. Those to whom it does not give light, must thank themselves; they will not be in the house with it. (2) They must *shine* as lights, [1] By their *good preaching*. The knowledge they have, they must communicate for the good of others; not put it *under a bushel*, but spread it. The disciples of Christ must not muffle themselves up in privacy and obscurity, under pretence of contemplation, modesty, or self-preservation. [2] By their *good living*. They must be *burning and shining lights*.

First, *How* our light must shine—by doing such *good works* as men *may see*. We must do good works *that may be seen* to the edification of others, but not *that they may be seen* to our own ostentation. Those about us must not only *hear* our good words, but *see* our good works.

Secondly, For what *end* our light must shine—"That those who see your good works may be brought, not to glorify *you*, but to *glorify your Father which is in heaven*." The glory of God is the great thing we must aim at in everything we do in religion. We must do all we can to bring others to glorify him. The sight of our *good works* will do this, by furnishing them, 1. With *matter for praise*. 2. With *motives to piety*. The holy, regular, and exemplary conversation of the saints, may do much towards the conversion of sinners. Examples teach. There is a winning virtue in a godly conversation.

Verses 17–20

Those to whom Christ preached had an eye, 1. To the *scriptures* of the *Old Testament* as their *rule*, and therein Christ here shows them they were in the right: 2. To the scribes and Pharisees as their *example*, and therein Christ here shows them they were in the wrong; for,

I. The rule which Christ came to establish exactly agreed with the scriptures of the *Old Testament*, here called *the law* and *the prophets*.

1. He protests against the thought of cancelling and weakening the *Old Testament*; *Think not that I am come to destroy the law and the prophets.* (1) "Let not the pious Jews, who have an affection for the *law and the prophets, fear* that I come to *destroy* them." (2) "Let not the profane Jews, who have a disaffection to the law and the prophets, and are weary of that yoke, hope that I am come to destroy them." The Saviour of souls is the *destroyer* of nothing that comes from God, much less of those excellent dictates which we have from Moses and the prophets. No, he came to *fulfil* them. That is, [1] To obey the commands of the law. He in all respects yielded obedience to the law, and never broke the law in anything. [2] To make good the promises of the law, and the predictions of the prophets. [3] To answer the types of the law. [4] To fill up the defects of it, and so to complete and perfect it. As a picture that is first rough-drawn, displays some outlines only of the piece intended, which are afterwards filled up; so Christ made an improvement of the law and the prophets by his additions and explications. [5] To carry on the same design. The gospel is the *time of reformation* (Heb. ix. 10), not the repeal of the law, but the amendment of it, and, consequently, its establishment.

2. He asserts the perpetuity of it. "*Verily I say unto you*, I, the *Amen*, the faithful Witness, solemnly declare it, that *till heaven and earth pass, one jot, or one tittle, shall in no wise pass from the law till all be fulfilled*." *The word of the Lord endures for ever*, both that of the law, and that of the gospel. The care of God concerning his law extends itself even to those things that seem to be of least account on it, for

whatever belongs to God, and bears his stamp, be it ever so little, shall be preserved.

3. He gives it in charge to his disciples, carefully to preserve the law, and shows them the danger of the neglect and contempt of it (*v.* 19); *Whosoever therefore shall break one of the least commandments of the law of Moses he shall be called the least in the kingdom of heaven. Whosoever shall do and teach them* shall be *called great in the kingdom of heaven.* (1) Among the commands of God there are some less than others; none absolutely little, but comparatively so. (2) It is a dangerous thing, in doctrine or practice, to disannul the least of God's commands. It is something more than transgressing the law, it is making void the law, Ps. cxix. 126. (3) That the further such corruptions as these spread, the worse they are. It is impudence enough to break the command, but it is a greater degree of it to teach men so. He that does so, shall be called *least in the kingdom of heaven,* in the kingdom of glory. Those are truly honourable, and of great account in the church of Christ, who both do and teach that which is good; for those who do not as they teach, pull down with one hand what they build up with the other. Those who speak from experience, who live up to what they preach, are truly great; hereafter they shall shine as the *stars in the kingdom of our Father.*

II. The righteousness which Christ came to establish by this rule, must exceed that of the scribes and Pharisees, *v.* 20. This was strange doctrine to those who looked upon the scribes and Pharisees as having arrived at the highest pitch of religion. It was therefore a great surprise to them, to hear that they must be better than they. The scribes and Pharisees were enemies to Christ and his doctrine, and were great oppressors; and yet it must be owned, that there was something commendable in them. Yet our Lord Jesus here tells his disciples, that the religion he came to establish, did not only exclude the badness, but excel the goodness, of the scribes and Pharisees. We must do more than they, and better than they. They minded only the *outside,* but we must make conscience of *inside* godliness. They aimed at the *praise* and *applause of men,* but we must aim at *acceptance with God*: but we, when we have done all, must *deny ourselves,* and say, We are *unprofitable servants,* and trust only to the *righteousness of Christ.*

Verses 21–26

Christ proceeds to expound the law in some particular instances. He adds not anything new, only limits and restrains some permissions which had been abused: and as to the precepts, shows the breadth, strictness, and spiritual nature of them. In these verses, he explains the law of the sixth commandment, according to the true intent and full extent of it.

I. Here is the *command itself* laid down (*v.* 12). The laws of God are not novel, upstart laws, but were delivered to them of old time; they are ancient laws, but of that nature as never to be *antiquated* nor grow *obsolete. Killing* is here forbidden, killing ourselves, killing any other, directly or indirectly, or being any way accessory to it. The law of God, the God of life, is a hedge of protection about our lives.

II. The exposition of this command which the Jewish teachers contented themselves with; their comment upon it was, *Whosoever shall kill, shall be in danger of the judgment.* Now this gloss of theirs upon this commandment was faulty, for it intimated, That the law of the sixth commandment was only external, and forbade no more than the act of murder, and laid no restraint upon the inward lusts, from which *wars and fightings come.* This was indeed the *fundamental error* of the Jewish teachers, that the divine law prohibited only the sinful act, not the sinful thought.

III. The exposition which Christ gave of this commandment.

1. Christ tells them that *rash anger is heart-murder* (*v.* 22); *Whosoever is angry with his brother without a cause,* breaks the sixth commandment. Anger is a natural passion; there are cases in which it is lawful and laudable; but it is then *sinful,* when we are angry without cause. When it is without any just provocation given; either for no cause, or no good cause, or no great and proportionable cause; when we are angry upon groundless surmises, or for trivial affronts not worth speaking of. When it is without any good end aimed at, then it is in vain, it is to do hurt; whereas if we are at any time angry, it should be to awaken the offender to repentance, and prevent his doing so again. When it exceeds due bounds; when we are outrageous and mischievous, and when we seek the hurt of those we are displeased at. This is a breach of the sixth commandment, for he that is thus angry, would kill if he could and durst; he has taken the first step towards it.

2. He tells them, that giving opprobrious language to our brother is tongue-murder, calling him, *Raca,* and *Thou fool.* When this is done with mildness and for a good end, to convince others of their vanity and folly, it is not sinful. But when it proceeds from anger and malice within, it is the smoke of that fire which is kindled from hell. (1) *Raca* is a scornful word, and comes from pride, "Thou empty fellow." *This people who knoweth not the law, is cursed,* is such language, John vii. 49. (2) *Thou fool,* is a spiteful word, and comes from hatred; looking upon him, not only as mean and not to be honoured, but as vile and not to be loved. The former speaks a man without sense, this (in scripture language) speaks a man without grace; the more the reproach touches his spiritual condition, the worse it is. Malicious slanders and censures are *poison under the tongue,* that kills secretly and slowly. It is an evidence of such an ill-will to our neighbour as would strike at his life, if it were in our power.

3. He tells them, that how light soever they made of these sins, they would certainly be reckoned for; he *that is angry with his brother shall be in danger of the judgment* and anger of God; he that calls him *Raca, shall be in danger of the council,* of being punished by the Sanhedrim for reviling an Israelite; *but whosoever saith, Thou fool,* thou profane person, thou child of hell, *shall be in danger of hell-fire,* to which he condemns his brother. Christ would thus show which sin was most sinful, by showing which was the punishment whereof was most dreadful.

IV. From all this it is here inferred, that we ought carefully to preserve Christian love and peace with all our brethren, and that if at any time a breach happens, we should labour for a reconciliation.

1. Because, till this be done, we are utterly unfit for communion with God in holy ordinances, *v.* 23, 24. If thou *have aught against thy brother,* make short work of it; no more is to be done but to forgive him (Mark xi. 25), and forgive the injury; but if the quarrel began on thy side, and the fault was either at first or afterwards thine, so *that thy brother* has a controversy with *thee, go* and *be reconciled to* him before thou *offer thy gift at the altar,* before thou approach solemnly to God. When we are addressing ourselves to any religious exercises, it is good for us to take that occasion of serious reflection and self-examination. Religious exercises are not acceptable to God, if they are performed when we are in wrath. Prayers made in wrath are written in gall, Isa. i. 15; lviii. 4. Love or charity is so much *better than all burnt-offerings and sacrifice,* that God is content to stay for the gift, rather than have it offered while we are under guilt and engaged in a quarrel. Though we are under guilt and engaged in a quarrel. Though we are unfitted for communion with God, by a continual

quarrel with a brother, yet that can be no excuse for the omission or neglect of our duty. Many give this as a reason why they do not come to church or to the communion, because they are at variance with some neighbour; and whose fault is that? One sin will never excuse another, but will rather double the guilt. Want of charity cannot justify the want of piety. *Therefore* we must *not let the sun go down upon our wrath* any day, because we must go to prayer before we go to sleep; much less let the sun rise *upon our wrath* on a sabbath-day, because it is a day of prayer.

2. Because, till this be done, we lie exposed to much danger, *v.* 25, 26.

(1) Upon a temporal account. If the offence we have done to our brother, in his body, goods, or reputation, be such as will bear an action, in which he may recover considerable damages, it is our wisdom, and it is our duty to our family, to prevent that by a humble submission and a just and peaceable satisfaction; lest otherwise he recover it by law, and put us to the extremity of a prison. It is in vain to contend with the law, and there is danger of our being crushed by it. It is good to agree, for the law is costly. Though we must be merciful to those we have advantage against, yet we must be just to those that have advantage against us. A prison is an uncomfortable place to those who are brought to it by their own pride, and prodigality, their own wilfulness and folly.

(2) Upon a spiritual account. "*Go*, and be *reconciled to thy brother*, be just to him, be friendly with him, because while the quarrel continues, as thou art unfit to *bring thy gift to the altar*, unfit to come to *the table of the Lord*, so thou art unfit to die."

This is very applicable to the great business of our reconciliation to God through Christ; *Agree with him quickly, whilst thou art in the way*. Note, [1] The great God is an Adversary to all sinners. [2] It is our concern to *agree with him*. [3] It is our wisdom to do this *quickly, while we are in the way*. While we are alive, *we are in the way*; after death, it will be too late to do it. [4] They who continue in a state of enmity to God, are continually exposed to the arrests of his justice. Hell is the prison, into which those will be cast that continue in a state of enmity to God. Sinners must remain in it to eternity; they shall not *depart till they have paid the uttermost farthing.*

Verses 27–32

We have here an exposition of the seventh commandment. It is the law against uncleanness, which fitly follows upon the former; *that* laid a restraint upon sinful passions, *this* upon sinful appetites.

I. The command is here laid down (*v.* 17), *Thou shalt not commit adultery*; which includes a prohibition of all other acts of uncleanness, and the desire of them.

II. It is here explained in the strictness of it, in three things.

1. We are here taught, that there is such a thing as *heart-adultery*, adulterous thoughts and dispositions which never proceed to the act of adultery or fornication. *Whosoever looketh on a woman* (not only another man's wife, as some would have it, but any woman), *to lust after her, has committed adultery with her in his heart, v.* 28. This command forbids not only the acts of fornication and adultery, but, (1) All appetites to them. Lust is conscience baffled or biassed: biassed, if it say nothing against the sin; baffled, if it prevail not in what it says. (2) All approaches towards them; feeding the eye with the sight of the forbidden fruit. The eye is both the inlet and outlet of a great deal of wickedness of this kind. What have we the covering of the eyes for, but to restrain corrupt glances, and to keep out their defiling impressions? This forbids also the using of

any other of our senses to stir up lust. If ensnaring looks are forbidden fruit, much more unclean discourses, and wanton dalliances, the fuel and bellows of this hellish fire. These precepts are hedges about the law of heart-purity, *v.* 8. And if looking be lust, they who dress and deck, and expose themselves, with design to be looked at and lusted after are no less guilty. Men sin, but devils tempt to sin.

2. That such looks and such dalliances are so very dangerous and destructive to the soul, that it is better to lose the eye and the hand that thus offend than to give way to the sin. "*It is a hard saying, who can bear it?* Flesh and blood cannot but look with pleasure upon a beautiful woman; and it is impossible to forbear lusting after and dallying with such an object." Such pretences as these will scarcely be overcome by reason, and therefore must be argued against with *the terrors of the Lord*.

(1) It is a severe operation that is here prescribed for the preventing of these fleshly lusts. *If thy right eye offend thee*, or *cause thee to offend*, by wanton glances, or wanton gazings, upon forbidden objects; *if thy right hand offend thee*, or *cause thee to offend*, by wanton dalliances; if there were no other way to restrain them (which, blessed be God, through his grace, there is), it were better for us to *pluck out the eye*, and *cut off the hand* than to indulge them in sin to the ruin of the soul. And if this must be submitted to, at the thought of which nature startles, much more must we resolve to keep a constant watch over our own hearts, and to suppress the first rising of lust and corruption there; to avoid the occasions of sin, to resist the beginnings of it, and to decline the company of those who will be a snare to us, though ever so pleasing; to keep out of harm's way, and abridge ourselves in the use of lawful things, when we find them temptations to us; and to seek unto God for his grace, and depend upon that grace daily, and so to *walk in the Spirit*, as that we may not *fulfil the lusts of the flesh*; and this will be as effectual as *cutting off a right hand or pulling out a right eye*; and perhaps as much against the grain to flesh and blood; it is the destruction of the old man.

(2) It is a startling argument that is made use of to enforce this prescription (*v.* 29). *It is profitable for thee that one of thy members should perish, and not that thy whole body should be cast into hell*. It is not unbecoming a minister of the gospel to preach of hell and damnation; nay, he *must* do it, for Christ himself did it; and we are unfaithful to our trust, if we give not warning of *the wrath to come*. [1] There are some sins from which we need to be *saved with fear*, particularly *fleshly lusts*, which are such *natural brute beasts* as cannot be checked, but by being frightened. [2] Those do not know or do not believe what hell is, that will rather venture their eternal ruin than deny themselves the gratification of a base and brutish lust. [3] Even those duties that are most unpleasant to flesh and blood, are *profitable for us*; and our Master requires nothing from us but what he knows to be for our advantage.

3. That men's divorcing their wives upon dislike, or for any other cause except adultery, was a violation of the seventh commandment, as it opened a door to adultery, *v.* 31, 32. Here observe,

(1) How the matter now stood with reference to divorce. "*Whosoever shall put away his wife, let him give her a bill of divorce;* let him not think to do it by word of mouth, when he is in a passion; let him do it solemnly." Thus the law had prevented rash and hasty divorces.

(2) How this matter was rectified and amended by our Saviour. He reduced the ordinance of marriage to its primitive institution: *They two shall be one flesh*, not to be easily separated, and therefore divorce is not to be allowed, except in case of adultery,

which breaks the marriage covenant; but he that puts away his wife upon any other pretence, *causeth her to commit adultery*, and him also that shall marry her when she is thus divorced.

Verses 33–37

We have here an exposition of the third commandment. *God will not hold him guiltless*, however he may hold himself, who breaks this commandment, by *taking the name of the Lord God in vain*.

I. It is agreed on all hands that it forbids perjury, forswearing, and the violation of oaths and vows, *v.* 33. Perjury is a sin condemned by the light of nature, as a complication of impiety toward God and injustice toward man, and as rendering a man highly obnoxious to the divine wrath. *So help me God;* wishing I may never have any help from God, if I swear falsely. Thus, by the consent of nations, have men cursed themselves, not doubting but that God would curse them, if they lied against the truth then when they solemnly called God to witness to it.

II. It is here added, that the commandment does not only forbid false swearing, but all rash, unnecessary swearing: *Swear not at all*, *v.* 34. Not that all swearing is sinful; so far from that, if rightly done, it is a part of religious worship, and we in it *give unto God the glory due to his name*. In swearing, we pawn the truth of something known, to confirm the truth of something doubtful or unknown; we appeal to a greater knowledge, to a higher court.

Now the mind of Christ in this matter is,

1. That we must *not swear at all*, but when we are duly called to it, and justice or charity to our brother, or respect to the commonwealth, make it necessary for *the end of strife* (Heb. vi. 16). We may be sworn, but we must not swear.

2. That we must not swear lightly and irreverently, in common discourse: it is a very great sin to make a ludicrous appeal to the glorious Majesty of heaven. It is a sin that has no cloak, no excuse for it, and therefore a sign of a graceless heart.

3. That we must in a special manner avoid promissory oaths, of which Christ more particularly speaks here, for they are oaths that are to be performed. The frequent requiring and using of oaths, is a reflection upon Christians, who should be of such acknowledged fidelity, as that their sober words should be as sacred as their solemn oaths.

4. That we must not swear by any creature. It should seem there were some, who, in civility (as they thought) to the name of God, would not make use of that in swearing, but would swear *by heaven* or *earth*, &c. There is nothing we can swear by, but it is some way or other related to God, who is the Fountain of all beings, and therefore it is as dangerous to swear by them, as it is to swear by God himself: it is the verity of the creature that is laid at stake; now that cannot be an instrument of testimony, but as it has regard to God.

(1) *Swear not by the heaven;* "As sure as there is a heaven, this is true;" *for it is God's throne*, where he resides. You cannot *swear by heaven*, but you swear by God himself.

(2) *Nor by the earth, for it is his footstool. The earth is the Lord's;* so that in swearing by it, you swear by its Owner.

(3) *Neither by Jerusalem*, a place for which the Jews had such a veneration, that they could not speak of anything more sacred to *swear by. It is the city of the great King* (Ps. xlviii. 2), *the city of God* (Ps. xlvi. 4), he is therefore interested in it, and in every oath taken by it.

(4) "*Neither shalt thou swear by thy head.* It is more God's than thine; for he made it, and formed all the springs and powers of it; whereas thou thyself canst not, from any natural intrinsic influence, change the colour of *one hair*, so as to make *it white or black*; so that thou canst not *swear by thy head*, but thou swearest by him who is *the Life of thy head*, and *the Lifter up of it*." Ps. iii. 3.

5. That therefore in all our communications we must content ourselves with, *Yea, yea*, and *Nay, nay, v.* 37. *Verily, verily*, was our Saviour's *yea, yea*. So if we deny a thing, let it suffice to say, No. If our fidelity be known, that will suffice to gain us credit; and if it be questioned, to back what we say with swearing and cursing, is but to render it more suspicious. They who can *swallow* a profane oath, will not *strain at a lie*.

The reason is observable; *For whatsoever is more than these cometh of evil*, though it do not amount to the iniquity of an oath. It comes from that deceitfulness which is in men, *All men are liars;* therefore men use these protestations, because they are distrustful one of another, and think they cannot be believed without them. An oath is physic, which supposes a disease.

Verses 38–42

In these verses the law of retaliation is expounded. Observe,

I. What the *Old Testament permission* was, in case of injury. It was not a command, that everyone should of necessity require such satisfaction; but they might lawfully insist upon it, if they pleased; *an eye for an eye, and a tooth for a tooth*. It was a direction, and a restraint to such as have mischief done to them that they may not insist on a greater punishment than is proper: it is not *a life for an eye*, nor *a limb for a tooth*, but observes a proportion.

Now, so far this is in force with us, as a direction to magistrates, to use the sword of justice according to the good and wholesome laws of the land, for the terror of evil-doers, and the vindication of the oppressed. And it is in force as a rule to lawgivers, to provide accordingly, and wisely to apportion punishments to crimes.

II. What the *New Testament precept* is, as to the complainant himself, his duty, is to *forgive the injury* as done to himself, and no further to insist upon the punishment of it than is necessary to the public good.

Two things Christ teaches us here:

1. We must not be revengeful (*v.* 39); *I say unto you, that ye resist not evil;*—the evil person that is injurious to you. We may *avoid evil*, and may *resist* it, so far as is necessary to our own security; but we must not *render evil for evil*, must not bear a grudge, nor avenge ourselves, nor study to be even with those that have treated us unkindly, but we must go beyond them by forgiving them. The law of retaliation must be made consistent with the law of love. It will not justify us in hurting our brother to say that he began, for it is the second blow that makes the quarrel.

Three things our Saviour specifies, to show that Christians must patiently yield to those who bear hard upon them.

(1) A blow on the cheek, which is an injury to me in my body; "*Whosoever shall smite thee on thy right cheek*, which is not only a hurt, but an affront and indignity, *turn to him the other cheek*." Bear it patiently: give not the rude man as good as he brings. Pass it by, and take no further notice of it: there are no bones broken, no great harm done, forgive it and forget it; and if proud fools think the worse of thee, and laugh at thee for it, all wise men will value and honour thee for it, as a follower of the blessed Jesus. Though this may perhaps, with some base spirits, expose us to the like affront another time, and so it is, in effect, to *turn the other cheek*, yet let

not that disturb us. Perhaps, the forgiving of one injury may prevent another, when the avenging of it would but draw on another; some will be overcome by submission, who by resistance would but be the more exasperated.

(2) The loss of a coat, which is a wrong to me in my estate (v. 40); *If any man will sue thee at the law, and take away thy coat.* Though judges be just and circumspect, yet it is possible for bad men who make no conscience of oaths and forgeries, by course of law to force off the coat from a man's back. *Marvel not at the matter* (Eccles. v. 8), but *let him* even *take thy cloak also.* If the matter be small it is good to submit to it for peace' sake. "It will not cost thee so much to buy another cloak, as it will cost thee by course of law to recover that."

(3) The going a mile by constraint, which is a wrong to me in my liberty (v. 41); "*Whosoever shall compel thee to go a mile, go with him two miles.*" Say, "Therefore I will do it, for otherwise there will be a quarrel;" and it is better to serve him, than to serve thy own lusts of pride and revenge. The sum of all is, that Christians must not be litigious; small injuries must be submitted to, and no notice taken of them; and if the injury be such as requires us to seek reparation, it must be for a good end, and without thought of revenge.

2. We must be charitable and beneficent (v. 42); must not only do no hurt to our neighbours, but labour to do them all the good we can. (1) We must be ready to give; "*Give to him that asketh thee.*" If thou hast an ability, look upon the request of the poor as giving thee an opportunity for the duty of almsgiving." Yet the affairs of our charity must be *guided with discretion,* lest we give that to the idle and unworthy, which should be given to those that are necessitous, and deserve well. What God says to us, we should be ready to say to our poor brethren, *Ask, and it shall be given you.* (2) We must be ready to lend. This is sometimes as great a piece of charity as giving; as it not only relieves the present exigence, but obliges the borrower to providence, industry, and honesty. Be easy of access to him *that would borrow*: though he be bashful, and have not confidence to make known his case and beg the favour, yet thou knowest both his need and his desire, and therefore offer him the kindness. It becomes us to be thus forward in acts of kindness, for before we call, God hears us, and *prevents us with the blessings of his goodness.*

Verses 43–48

We have here, lastly, an exposition of that great fundamental law of the second table, *Thou shalt love thy neighbour.*

I. See here how this law was corrupted by the comments of the Jewish teachers, v. 43. God said, *Thou shalt love thy neighbour;* and by *neighbour* they understood those only that they were pleased to look upon as their friends. They were willing to infer what God never designed; *Thou shalt hate thine enemy;* and they looked upon whom they pleased as their enemies. See how willing corrupt passions are to fetch countenance from the word of God, and to *take occasion by the commandment* to justify themselves.

II. See how it is cleared by the command of the Lord Jesus, who teaches us another lesson: "*But I say unto you, Love your enemies,*" v. 44. Though men are ever so bad themselves, and carry it ever so basely towards us, yet that does not discharge us from the great debt we owe them, of love to our kind, love to our kin. It is the great duty of Christians to *love their enemies;* whilst we cannot have complacency in one that is openly wicked and profane, yet we must take notice, with pleasure, of that even in our enemies which

is amiable and commendable; and love that, though they are our enemies. We must have a compassion for them, and a goodwill toward them. We are here told,

1. That we must *speak* well of them: *Bless them that curse you.* When we speak to them, we must answer their revilings with courteous and friendly words, and *not render railing for railing.* They, in whose tongues is *the law of kindness,* can give good words to those who give bad words to them.

2. That we must *do* well to them: *Do good to them that hate you,* and that will be a better proof of love than good words. Be ready to do them all the real kindness that you can, and glad of an opportunity to do it.

3. We must *pray for them*: *Pray for them that despitefully use you, and persecute you.* Christ himself was so treated. When at any time we meet with such usage, we have an opportunity of showing our conformity both to the precept and to the example of Christ, by praying for them who thus abuse us. We must pray that God will forgive them, that they may never fare the worse for anything they have done against us, and that he would make them to be at peace with us. This is *heaping coals of fire on their heads.*

We must do it,

[1] That we may be *like God our Father;* "that ye may be, may approve yourselves to be, *the children of your Father which is in heaven.*" Can we write after a better copy? God *maketh his sun to rise,* and *sendeth rain,* on *the just and unjust,* v. 45. *Sunshine* and *rain* are great blessings to the world, and they come from God. Common mercies must be valued as instances and proofs of the goodness of God, who in them shows himself a bountiful Benefactor. These gifts of common providence are dispensed indifferently to *good* and *evil, just* and *unjust.* The worst of men partake of the comforts of this life in common with others. which is an amazing instance of God's patience and bounty. The gifts of God's bounty to wicked men that are in rebellion against him, teach us to *do good to those that hate us.* Those only will be accepted as the children of God, who study to resemble him, particularly in his goodness.

[2] That we may herein *do more than others,* v. 46, 47. *First, Publicans love their friends.* Nature inclines them to it; interest directs them to it. To do good to them who do good to us, is a common piece of humanity. *Secondly,* We must therefore love our enemies, that we may exceed them. Christianity is something more than humanity. It is a serious question, and which we should frequently put to ourselves, "*What do we more than others? What excelling thing do we do?* God has done more for us, and therefore justly expects more from us than from others; but *what do we more than others?* Wherein do we live above the rate of the children of this world? We cannot expect the reward of Christians, if we rise no higher than the virtue of publicans." Those who promise themselves a reward above others must study to *do more than others.*

Our Saviour concludes this subject with this exhortation (v. 48), *Be ye therefore perfect, as your Father which is in heaven is perfect.* Which may be understood, 1. In general, including all those things wherein we must be *followers of God as dear children.* It is the duty of Christians to desire, and aim at, and press towards a perfection in grace and holiness. Or, 2. In this particular before mentioned, of *doing good to our enemies;* see Luke vi. 36. It is God's perfection to *forgive injuries* and to *entertain strangers,* and to do good to the evil and unthankful, and it will be ours to be like him. We that owe *so much,* that owe *our all,* to the divine bounty, ought to copy it out as well as we can.

CHAPTER 6

Christ, having in the former chapter, armed his disciples against the corrupt doctrines and opinions of the scribes and Pharisees, comes in this chapter to warn them against hypocrisy and worldly-mindedness, sins which, of all others, the professors of religion need most to guard against. We are here cautioned, I. Against hypocrisy, 1. In the giving of alms, ver. 1–4. 2. In prayer, ver. 5–8. We are here taught what to pray for, and how to pray (ver. 9–13); and to forgive in prayer, ver. 14, 15. 3. In fasting, ver. 16–18. II. Against worldly-mindedness, 1. In our choice, which is the destroying sin of hypocrites, ver. 19–24. 2. In our cares, which is the disquieting sin of many good Christians, ver. 25–34.

Verses 1–4

We must watch against hypocrisy, which was the leaven of the Pharisees, as well as against their doctrine, Luke xii. 1. *Almsgiving, prayer,* and *fasting,* are three great Christian duties. Thus we must not only *depart from evil,* but *do good,* and do it well, and so *dwell for evermore.*

We are cautioned against hypocrisy in giving alms. *Take heed* of it. It is a subtle sin; vain-glory insinuates itself into what we do ere we are aware. It is a sin we are in *great danger by.* Take heed of hypocrisy, for if it reign in you, it will ruin you. It is the dead fly that spoils the whole box of precious ointment.

Two things are here supposed,

I. The *giving of alms* is a great duty, and a duty which all the disciples of Christ, according to their ability, must abound in. The Jews called the *poor's box* the *box of righteousness.* It is true, our alms-deeds do not deserve heaven; but it is as true that we cannot go to heaven without them. Christ here takes it for granted that his disciples *give alms,* nor will he own those that do not.

II. That it is such a duty as has a great reward attending it, which is lost if it be done in hypocrisy. It shall be recompensed in the resurrection of the just (Luke xiv. 14), in *eternal riches.*

The riches you impart form the only wealth you will always retain.

1. What was the *practice of the hypocrites* about this duty. They did it indeed, but not from any principle of obedience to God, or love to man, but in pride and vain-glory; not in compassion to the poor, but purely for ostentation. Pursuant to this intention, they chose to give their alms *in the synagogues, and in the streets,* where there was the greatest concourse of people to observe them. Not that it is unlawful to give alms *when men see us;* we may do it, we must do it, but not *that men may see us.* The hypocrites, if they gave alms at their own houses, *sounded a trumpet,* to proclaim their charity, and to have that taken notice of and made the subject of discourse.

Now the doom that Christ passes upon this is very observable: *Verily I say unto you, they have their reward.* Two words in it make it a threatening.

(1) It is a reward, but it is *their* reward; not the reward which God promises to them that do good, but the reward which they promise themselves, and a poor reward it is; they did it to be *seen of men,* and they *are* seen of men.

(2) It is a reward, that it is a *present reward,* they *have* it; and there is none reserved for them in the future state. They now have all that they are likely to have from God. It signifies a *receipt in full.* The world is but for *provision* to the saints, it is their spending-money; but it is *pay* to hypocrites, it is their portion.

2. What is the *precept of our Lord Jesus* about it, *v.* 3, 4. *"Let not thy left hand know what thy right hand doeth* when thou givest alms." The giving of alms with the *right hand,* intimates readiness to it and resolution in it; do it dexterously. But, "whatever kindness thy right hand doeth to the poor, *let not thy left hand know it;* conceal it as much as possible;

industriously keep it private. Do it because it is a good work, not because it will give thee a good name." It is intimated, (1) That we must not let *others* know what we do. (2) That we must not observe it too much *ourselves.* Self-conceit and self-complacency, and an adoring of our own shadow, are branches of pride. We find those had their good works remembered to their honour, who had themselves forgotten them: *When saw we thee an hungered, or athirst?*

3. What is the *promise to those who are thus sincere and humble* in their alms-giving. Let *thine alms be in secret,* and then *thy Father who seeth in secret* will observe them. When we take least notice of our good deeds ourselves, God takes most notice of them. It is a comfort to sincere Christians, that God *sees in secret.* Observe how emphatically it is expressed; *himself shall reward,* he will himself be the Rewarder. Nay, he will *himself be the Reward* (Gen. xv. 1), thine *exceeding great reward.* He will reward thee as thy Father, not as a master who gives his servant just what he earns and no more, but as a father who gives abundantly more, and without stint, to his son that serves him. If the work be not open, the reward shall, and that is better.

Verses 5–8

When thou prayest (v. 5). It is taken for granted that all the disciples of Christ *pray.* You may as soon find a living man that does not breathe, as a living Christian that does not pray. If prayerless, then graceless.

Now there were two great faults they were guilty of in prayer—vain-glory (*v.* 5, 6); and vain repetitions, *v.* 7, 8.

I. We must not be *proud* and *vain-glorious* in prayer, nor aim at the praise of men. And here observe,

1. What was the *way and practice of the hypocrites.* In all their exercises of devotion, it was plain, the chief thing they aimed at was to be commended by their neighbours. When they seemed to *soar upwards* in prayer then their eye was *downwards* upon this as their *prey.* Observe,

(1) What the *places* were which they chose for their devotion; they prayed in the *synagogues,* which were indeed proper places for public prayer, but not for personal. They prayed in *the corners of the streets,* the broad streets (so the word signifies), which were most frequented. It was to cause themselves to be taken notice of.

(2) The *posture* they used in prayer; they prayed standing; this is a lawful and proper posture for prayer, but kneeling being the more humble and reverent gesture, their standing seemed to savour of pride and confidence in themselves (Luke xviii. 11).

(3) Their *pride* in choosing those public places, which is expressed in two things: [1] They *love* to pray there. They did not love prayer for its own sake, but they loved it when it gave them an opportunity of making themselves noticed. [2] It is that they may be *seen of men;* not that God might accept them, but that men might admire and applaud them.

(4) The *product* of all this, *they have their reward;* they have all the recompence they must ever expect from God for their service, and a poor recompence it is. What will it avail us to have the good word of our fellow-servants, if our Master do not say, *Well done?* They did it to be *seen of men,* and they are so; and much good may it do them. What passes between God and our own souls must be out of sight. Public places are not proper for private solemn prayer.

2. What is the *will of Jesus Christ* in opposition to this. *Thou, when thou prayest,* do so and so (v. 6). Personal prayer is here supposed to be the duty and practice of all Christ's disciples.

Observe, (1) The directions here given about it.

[1] Instead of praying in *the synagogues* and in the *corners of the streets*, enter into thy closet, into some place of privacy and retirement. Isaac went into the field (Gen. xxiv. 63), Christ to a mountain, Peter to the house-top. No place amiss in point of ceremony, if it do but answer the end. Yet if the circumstances be such that we cannot possibly avoid being taken notice of, we must not therefore neglect the duty, lest the omission be a greater scandal than the observation of it.

[2] Instead of doing it to be *seen of men, pray to thy Father who is in secret.* The Pharisees prayed rather to men than to God. Do you pray to God, and let that be enough for thee. Pray to him as a Father, as thy Father, ready to hear and answer, graciously inclined to pity, help, and succour thee. Pray to thy Father *who is in secret.* He is there in thy closet when no one else is there; there especially nigh to thee in what thou *callest upon him for.*

(2) The encouragements here given us to it.

[1] Thy Father *seeth in secret.* There is not a secret sudden breathing after God, but he observes it.

[2] He *will reward thee openly*; they have their reward that do it openly, and thou shalt not lose thine for thy doing it in secret. It is called a *reward*, but it is *of grace*, not *of debt.* Sometimes secret prayers are rewarded openly in this world by signal answers to them, which manifests God's praying people in the consciences of their adversaries.

II. We must not *use vain repetitions* in prayer, v. 7, 8. Though the life of prayer lies in *lifting up the soul and pouring out the heart*, yet there is some interest which words have in prayer, especially in joint prayer; for in that, words are necessary. *Use not vain repetitions*, either alone or with others. Now observe,

1. What the *fault* is that is here reproved and condemned; it is making a mere lip-labour of the duty of prayer. (1) *Vain repetitions*—tautology. It is not all repetition in prayer that is here condemned, but vain repetitions. Christ himself prayed, saying the same words (*ch.* xxvi. 44), out of a more than ordinary fervour and zeal, Luke xxii. 44. When we would fain say much, but cannot say much to the purpose; this is displeasing to God and all wise men. (2) *Much speaking*, an affectation of prolixity in prayer, because men love to *hear themselves talk.* Not that all long prayers are forbidden; Christ prayed all night, Luke vi. 12. It is not much *praying* that is condemned; no, we are bid to *pray always*, but much *speaking*; the danger of this error is when we only *say* our prayers, not when we *pray* them.

2. What reasons are given against this.

(1) This is the way of the heathen, *as the heathen do*; and it ill becomes Christians to worship their God as the Gentiles worship theirs. Thinking God altogether such a one as themselves, they thought he needed many words to make him understand what was said to him, or to bring him to comply with their requests. *Lip-labour* in prayer, though ever so well *laboured*, if that be all, is but *lost labour.*

(2) "It need not be your way, *for your Father* in heaven *knoweth what things ye have need of before ye ask him*, and therefore there is no occasion for such abundance of words. It does not follow that therefore ye need not pray; for God requires you by prayer to own your need of him. Open your case, and pour out your hearts before him, and then leave it with him." [1] The God we pray to is our Father. Children do not make long speeches to their parents when they want anything. They need not say many words, that are taught by the Spirit of adoption to say that one aright, *Abba Father.* [2] He is a Father that knows our case and knows our wants better than we do ourselves. *He knows what*

things we have need of. He often gives *before we call* (Isa. lxv. 24), and *more than we ask for* (Eph. iii. 20). We need not be long, nor use many words in representing our case; God knows it better than we can tell him, only he will know it *from us* (*what will ye that I should do unto you?*). The most powerful intercessions are those which are made with *groanings that cannot be uttered*, Rom. viii. 26.

Verses 9–15

Because we know not what to pray for as we ought, he here helps our infirmities, by putting words into our mouths; *after this manner therefore pray ye, v.* 9. Not that we are tied up to the use of this form only, or of this always, as if this were necessary to the consecrating of our other prayers; we are here bid to pray after this manner, with these words, or to this effect. Yet, without doubt, it is very good to use it as a form, and it is a pledge of the communion of saints, it having been used by the church in all ages. It is used acceptably no further than it is used with understanding and without vain repetition.

The Lord's prayer (as indeed every prayer) is a letter sent from earth to heaven. Here is the inscription of the letter, the person to whom it is directed, *our Father*; the place where, *in heaven*; the contents of it in several errands of request; the close, *for thine is the kingdom*; the seal, *Amen*; and if you will, the date, too, *this day.*

I. *The preface, Our Father who art in heaven. Our Father.* Intimating, that we must pray, not only alone and for ourselves, but with and for others. We are here taught *to whom to pray*, to God only, and not to saints and angels. We are taught how to address ourselves to God, and what title to give him, that which speaks him rather beneficent than magnificent, for we are to come boldly to the throne of grace.

1. We must address ourselves to him as *our Father*, and must call him so. Nothing more pleasing to God, nor pleasant, to ourselves, than to call God *Father.* Christ in prayer mostly called God *Father.* If he be our Father, he will pity us under our weaknesses and infirmities (Ps. ciii. 13), will spare us (Mal. iii. 17), will make the best of our performances, though very defective, will deny us nothing that is good for us, Luke xi. 11–13. When we come repenting of our sins, we must eye God as a Father, as the prodigal did (Luke xv. 18), as a loving, gracious, reconciled Father in Christ.

2. As our Father *in heaven*: so in heaven as to be everywhere else, for the heaven cannot contain him; yet so in heaven as there to manifest his glory, for it is his throne (Ps. ciii. 19), and it is to believers a throne of grace: thitherward we must direct our prayers. Thence he has a full and clear view of all our wants and burdens and desires, and all our infirmities. He is not only, as a Father, willing to help us, but as a heavenly Father, able to help us, able to do great things for us, more than we can ask or think; he has wherewith to supply our needs, for every good gift is from above. He is a Father, and therefore we may come to him with boldness, but a Father in heaven, and therefore we must come with reverence. By prayer, we send before us thither, where we profess to be going.

II. *The petitions*, and those are six; the three first relating more immediately to God and his honour, the three last to our own concerns. The method of this prayer teaches us to seek first the *kingdom of God and his righteousness*, and then to hope that *other things shall be added.*

1. *Hallowed be thy name.* (1) We give glory to God. We should give glory to God, before we expect to receive mercy and grace from him. Let him have the praise of his perfections, and then let us have the

benefit of them. (2) We fix our end, that God may be glorified; all our other requests must be in subordination to this, and in pursuance of it. *"Father, glorify thyself* in giving me my daily bread and pardoning my sins," &c. Since all is of him and through him, all must be to him and for him. In prayer our thoughts and affections should be carried out most to the glory of God. "Do so and so for me, *for the glory of thy name,* and as far as is for the glory of it." (3) We desire and pray that the name of God, that is, God himself, in all that whereby he has made himself known, may be sanctified and glorified both by us and others, and especially by himself. "Father, let thy name be glorified as a Father, and a Father in heaven; glorify thy goodness and thy highness, thy majesty and mercy.

2. *Thy kingdom come.* This petition has plainly a reference to the doctrine which Christ preached at this time, *the kingdom of heaven is at hand.* The kingdom of your Father, who is in heaven, this is at hand, pray that it may come. We should turn the word we hear into prayer, our hearts should echo to it; does Christ promise, *surely I come quickly?* our hearts should answer, *Even so, come.* What God has promised we must pray for; for promises are given, not to supersede, but to quicken and encourage prayer.

3. *Thy will be done in earth as it is in heaven.* We pray that God's kingdom being come, we and others may be brought into obedience to all the laws and ordinances of it. We make Christ but a titular Prince, if we call him King, and do not do his will: having prayed that he may rule us, we pray that we may in everything be ruled by him. (1) The thing prayed for, *thy will be done.* In this sense Christ prayed, *not my will, but thine be done.* "Enable me to do what is pleasing to thee; give me that grace that is necessary to the right knowledge of thy will, and an acceptable obedience to it, that we may neither displease God in anything we do nor be displeased at anything God does." (2) The pattern of it, that it may *be done on earth* (where our work must be done, or it never will be done), *as it is done in heaven.* We pray that earth may be made more like heaven by the observance of God's will.

4. *Give us this day our daily bread.* Because our natural being is necessary to our spiritual well-being in this world, therefore, after the things of God's glory, kingdom, and will, we pray for the necessary supports and comforts of this present life.

Every word here has a lesson in it: (1) We ask for *bread*; not dainties, not superfluities; that which is wholesome. (2) We ask for *our* bread; that teaches us honesty and industry. (3) We ask for our *daily* bread; which teaches us not to *take thought for the morrow* (v. 34), but constantly to depend upon divine Providence. (4) We beg of God to *give* it us. The greatest of men must be beholden to the mercy of God for their *daily* bread, (5) We pray, "Give it to us; not to me only, but to others in common with me." This teaches us charity, and a compassionate concern for the poor and needy. (6) We pray that God would give it us *this day*; which teaches us to renew the desire of our souls toward God, as the wants of our bodies are renewed. We could as well go a day without meat, as without prayer.

5. *And forgive us our debts, as we forgive our debtors.* This is connected with the former. *Our daily bread does but feed us as lambs for the slaughter,* if our sins be not pardoned. It intimates, likewise, that we must pray for daily *pardon,* as duly as we pray for daily *bread.*

(1) A petition; *Father in heaven forgive us our debts,* our debts to thee. Our sins are our debts; there is a debt of duty, which, as creatures, we owe to our Creator; we do not pray to be discharged from that, but upon the non-payment of that there arises a

debt of punishment. Our hearts' desire and prayer to our heavenly Father every day should be, that he would *forgive us our debts*; that we may be discharged and have the comfort of it.

(2) An argument to enforce this petition; *as we forgive our debtors.* This is not a plea of merit, but a plea of grace. Our duty is to *forgive our debtors.* We must forbear, and forgive, and forget the affronts put upon us, and the wrongs done us; and this is a moral qualification for pardon and peace; it encourages to hope, that God will *forgive us*; it will be an evidence to us that he has forgiven us, having wrought in us the condition of forgiveness.

6. *And lead us not into temptation, but deliver us from evil. Lead us not into temptation.* Having prayed that the guilt of sin may be removed, we pray, as is fit, that we may never return again to folly, that we may not be tempted to it. *But deliver us from evil*; ἀπὸ τοῦ πονηροῦ—*from the evil one*, the devil, the tempter; keep us, that we may not be assaulted: Or *from the evil thing*, sin, the worst of evils; an evil, an only evil; that evil thing which God hates, and which Satan tempts men to and destroys them by.

III. The conclusion: *For thine is the kingdom, and the power and the glory, for ever. Amen.*

1. It is our duty to plead with God in prayer, to fill our mouth with arguments not to move God, but to affect ourselves; to encourage our faith, to excite our fervency, and to evidence both. Now the best pleas in prayer are those that are taken from God himself, and from that which he has made known of himself. We must wrestle with God in his own strength. *"Thine is the kingdom"*; God gives and saves like a king. *"Thine is the power*, to maintain and support that kingdom, and to make good all thine engagements to thy people." *Thine is the glory*, as the end of all that which is given to, and done for, the saints, in answer to their prayers.

2. It is a form of praise and thanksgiving. The best pleading with God is praising of him; it is the way to obtain further mercy, as it qualifies us to receive it. We praise God, and give him glory, not because he needs it—he is praised by a world of angels, but because he deserves it. Praise is the work and happiness of heaven; and all that would go to heaven hereafter, must begin their heaven now. It becomes us to be copious in praising God. A true saint never thinks he can speak honourably enough of God. Ascribing glory to God *for ever,* intimates an acknowledgment, that it is eternally due, and an earnest desire to be eternally doing it, with angels and saints above, Ps. lxxi. 14.

Lastly, To all this we are taught to affix our *Amen,* so be it. God's *Amen* is a grant; it shall be so: our *Amen* is only a summary desire; let it be so: it is in token of our desire and assurance to be heard, that we say *Amen.* It is good to conclude religious duties with some warmth and vigour, that we may go from them with a sweet savour upon our spirits.

Most of the petitions in the Lord's prayer had been commonly used by the Jews in their devotions, or words to the same effect: but that clause in the fifth petition, *As we forgive our debtors,* was perfectly new, and therefore our Saviour here shows for what reason he added it, from the necessity and importance of the thing itself. God, in forgiving us, has a peculiar respect to our forgiving those that have injured us; and therefore, when we pray for pardon, we must mention our making conscience of that duty, not only to remind ourselves of it, but to bind ourselves to it. Selfish nature is loth to comply with this, and therefore it is here inculcated, v. 14, 15.

1. In a promise. *If ye forgive, your heavenly Father will also forgive.* Not as if this were the only condition required; there must be repentance and faith, and new obedience. He that relents toward his brother

thereby shows that he repents toward his God. It is a good evidence, and a good help of our forgiving others, to call the injuries done us by a mollifying, excusing name. Call them not wilful injuries, but casual inadvertencies; *peradventure it was an oversight*, therefore make the best of it. We must forgive, as we hope to be forgiven; must not upbraid our brother with the injuries he has done us, nor rejoice in any hurt that befalls him, but must be ready to help him and do him good, and if he repent and desire to be friends again, we must be free and familiar with him, as before.

2. In a threatening. *"But if you forgive not"* those that have injured you, that is a bad sign you have not the other requisite conditions, but are altogether unqualified for pardon; and therefore *your Father* will *not forgive you*. And if other graces be sincere, and yet you be defective greatly in forgiving, you cannot expect the comfort of your pardon Those that would find mercy with God must show mercy to their brethren. If we pray in anger, we have reason to fear God will answer in anger. It has been said, Prayers made in wrath are written in gall. What reason is it that God should forgive us the talents we are indebted to him, if we forgive not our brethren the pence they are indebted to us? Christ *came into the world* as the great *Peace-Maker*, not only *to reconcile us to God*, but one to another. It is great presumption and of dangerous consequence, for any to make a light matter of that which Christ here lays such a stress upon. Men's passions shall not frustrate God's word.

Verses 16–18

We are here cautioned against hypocrisy in fasting.

I. It is here supposed that religious fasting is a duty required of the disciples of Christ, when God, in his providence, calls to it, and when the case of their own souls upon any account requires it. Fasting is here put last, because it is not so much a duty for its own sake, as a means to dispose us for other duties. Prayer comes in between almsgiving and fasting, as being the life and soul of both. It was not the Pharisee's fasting *twice in the week*, but his boasting of it, that Christ condemned. It is a laudable practice, and we have reason to lament it, that it is so generally neglected among Christians. It is an act of self-denial and humiliation under the hand of God. The most grown Christians must hereby own, they are so far from having anything to be proud of, that they are unworthy of their daily bread.

II. We are cautioned not to do this *as the hypocrites* did it, lest we lose the reward of it.

Now, 1. The *hypocrites* pretended fasting, when there was nothing of that contrition or humiliation of soul in them, which is the life and soul of the duty. Theirs were mock-fasts, the show and shadow without the substance.

2. They proclaimed their fasting, and managed it so that all who saw them might take notice that it was a fasting-day with them. Even on these days they appeared in the streets, that men might see how often they fasted, and might extol them as devout, mortified men. It is sad that men, who have, in some measure, mastered their pleasure, which is sensual wickedness, should be ruined by their pride, which is spiritual wickedness, and no less dangerous. Here also *they have their reward*, and it is their all.

III. We are directed how to manage a private fast. He does not tell us how often we must fast; the Spirit in the word has left that to the Spirit in the heart; but take this for a rule, whenever you undertake this duty, study therein to approve yourselves to God, and not to recommend yourselves to the good opinions of men. Christ does not direct to abate anything of the reality of the fast; he does not say, "take a little meat, or a little drink, or a little cordial;" no, "let

the body suffer, but lay aside the show and appearance of it. Look pleasant, *anoint thine head and wash thy face*, as thou dost on ordinary days, on purpose to conceal thy devotion; and thou shalt be no loser in the praise of it at last; for though it be not of men, it shall be of God." Fasting is the humbling of the soul; let that therefore be thy principal care. If we be sincere in our solemn fasts, and humble, and trust God's omniscience for our witness, and his goodness for our reward, we shall find, both that he did *see in secret*, and will *reward openly*. Religious fasts, if rightly kept, will shortly be recompensed with an everlasting feast.

Verses 19–24

Christ, having warned us against coveting *the praise of men*, proceeds next to warn us against coveting the wealth of the world; in this also we must take heed, lest we be as the hypocrites are, and do as they do: the fundamental error that they are guilty of is, that they choose the world for *their reward*.

I. In choosing the *treasure* we *lay up*. Something or other every man has which he makes his *treasure*, his portion, which his heart is upon. Something the soul will have, which it looks upon as the best thing. Now Christ designs not to deprive us of our treasure, but to direct us in the choice of it.

1. A *good caution* against making *the things that are seen*, that *are temporal*, our best things, and placing our happiness in them. *Lay not up for yourselves treasures upon earth*. Christ's disciples had left all to follow him, let them still keep in the same good mind. Now we must *not lay up our treasures on earth*, that is, (1) We must not count these things the best things: we must not call them glory, but see and own that they have no glory in comparison with *the glory that excelleth*. (2) We must not covet an abundance of these things, nor be still grasping at more and more of them, as never knowing when we have enough. (3) We must not confide in them for futurity: must not say to the gold, *Thou art my hope*. (4) We must not content ourselves with them, as all we need or desire. It concerns thee to choose wisely, for thou art choosing for thyself, and shalt have as thou choosest. If we know and consider ourselves what we are, what we are made for, how large our capacities are, and how long our continuance, and that our souls are ourselves, we shall see it a foolish thing to *lay up* our *treasures on earth*.

2. Here is a *good reason* given why we should not look upon anything *on earth* as our *treasure*, because it is liable to loss and decay: (1) From corruption within. That which is treasure *upon earth moth and rust do corrupt*. Manna itself bred worms. The *rust and* the *moth* breed in the metal itself and in the garment itself. Worldly riches have in themselves a principle of corruption and decay. (2) From violence without. *Thieves break through and steal*. Every hand of violence will be aiming at the house where *treasure* is laid up; nor can anything be laid up so safe, but we may be spoiled of it. It is folly to make that our *treasure* which we may so easily be robbed of.

3. *Good counsel*, to make the joys and glories of the other world, those *things not seen* that *are eternal*, our best things, and to place our happiness in them. *Lay up for yourselves treasures in heaven*. There are *treasures in heaven*, as sure as there are on this earth; and those in heaven are the only true *treasures*. (1) It is our wisdom to *lay up* our *treasure in* those *treasures*; to give all diligence to make sure our title to eternal life through Jesus Christ, and to depend upon that as our happiness, and look upon all things here below with a holy contempt. If we thus make those *treasures* ours, they are laid up, and we may trust God to keep them safe for us. Let us not

burthen ourselves with the cash of this world. The promises are bills of exchange, by which all true believers return their *treasure* to *heaven*, payable in the future state. (2) It is a great encouragement to us to *lay up* our *treasure in heaven*, for there it is safe; no *moth* nor *rust* will *corrupt* it; *thieves do not break through and steal*. It is a happiness above and beyond the changes and chances of time, *an inheritance incorruptible*.

4. A *good reason* why we should thus choose. *Where your treasure is*, on earth or in heaven, *there will your heart be*. The *heart* follows the *treasure*, as the needle follows the loadstone, or the sunflower the sun. *Where the treasure is there* the value and esteem are, *there* the love and affection are. *Where the treasure is there* our hope and trust are; *there* our joys and delights will be; and *there* our thoughts. The *heart* is God's due and that he may have it, our *treasure* must be laid up with him. Our *treasure* is our alms, prayers, and fastings, and the reward of them; if we have done these only to gain the applause of men, we have *laid up this treasure on earth*. Now it is folly to do this, for *the praise of men* we covet so much is liable to corrupt: a little folly, like a dead fly, will spoil it all, Eccles. x. 1. Slander and calumny are *thieves that break through and steal* it away. Hypocritical services lay up nothing in heaven (Isa. lviii. 3). But if we have prayed and fasted and given alms in truth and uprightness, with an eye to God, we have laid up that treasure *in heaven*; *a book of remembrance is written there* (Mal. iii. 16). Hypocrites are *written in the earth*, but God's faithful ones have their names *written in heaven*, Luke x. 20. His *well done* shall stand for ever; and if we have thus laid up our *treasure* with him, with him our *hearts* will be; and where can they be better?

II. We must take heed of hypocrisy and worldly-mindedness in choosing the *end we look at*. Our concern as to this is represented by two sorts of eyes which men have, a *single eye* and an *evil eye*, v. 22, 23.

1. *The eye*, that is, *the heart* (so some) if that *be single, free and bountiful*, if the heart be liberally affected and stand inclined to goodness and charity, it will direct the man to Christian actions, the whole conversation *will be full of light*, of good works, which are our *light shining before men*; but *if the heart be evil*, covetous, and hard, and envious, griping and grudging, *the body will be full of darkness*, the whole conversation will be heathenish and unchristian. *If the light that is in us be darkness*, if there be not so much as good nature in a man, not so much as a kind disposition, *how great is* the corruption of a man, and the *darkness* in which he sits! Luke xii. 33; 2 Cor. ix. 7.

2. *The eye*, that is, *the understanding* (so some); the practical judgment, the conscience, which is to the other faculties of the soul, as *the eye* is to the *body*, to guide and direct their motions; now *if this eye be single*, if it make a true and right judgment, it will rightly guide the affections and actions, which will all be *full of the light* of grace and comfort; *but if this be evil* and corrupt, the heart and life must needs be *full of darkness*, and the whole conversation corrupt. An error in the practical judgment is fatal, it is that which calls *evil good and good evil* (Isa. v. 20).

3. *The eye*, that is, *the aims and intentions*; by the *eye* we set our end before us. In everything we do in religion, there is something or other that we have in our *eye*. If we aim purely and only at the glory of God, seek his honour and favour, and direct all entirely to him, then *the eye is single, the whole body will be full of light*, all the actions will be regular and gracious, pleasing to God and comfortable to ourselves; *but if this eye be evil*, if, instead of aiming only at the glory of God, and our acceptance with him, we look aside at the applause of men, and while

we profess to honour God, contrive to honour ourselves, and seek our own things under colour of *seeking the things of Christ*, this spoils all. It is of the last importance in religion, that we be right in our aims. The hypocrite is like the waterman, that looks one way and rows another; the true Christian like the traveller, that has his journey's end in his eye. The hypocrite soars like the kite, with his eye upon the prey below. The true Christian soars like the lark, higher and higher, forgetting the things that are beneath.

III. We must take heed of hypocrisy and worldly-mindedness in choosing the master we serve, v. 24. *No man can serve two masters*. Serving *two masters* is contrary to *the single eye*; for *the eye* will be to the master's hand, Ps. cxxiii. 1, 2. Our Lord Jesus here exposes the cheat which those put upon their own souls, who think to divide between God and the world, to have a *treasure on earth*, and a *treasure in heaven* too, to please God and please men too.

1. A general maxim laid down; *No man can serve two masters*, much less two gods; for their commands will some time or other cross or contradict one another. While *two masters* go together, a servant may follow them both; but when they part, you will see to which he belongs. This truth is plain enough in common cases.

2. The application of it to the business in hand. *Ye cannot serve God and Mammon*. *Mammon* is a Syriac word, that signifies gain; so that whatever in this world is, or is accounted by us to be, *gain* (Phil. iii. 7), is *mammon*. *Whatever is in the world, the lust of the flesh, the lust of the eye, and the pride of life*, is *mammon*. Self, the unity in which the world's trinity centres, sensual, secular self, is the *mammon* which cannot be served in conjunction with *God*. He does not say, We *must* not or we *should* not, but we *cannot serve God and Mammon*; we *cannot* love both (1 John ii. 15; James iv. 4); or hold to both, or hold by both in observance, obedience, attendance, trust, and dependence, for they are contrary, the one to the other. Let us not then *halt between God and Baal, but choose ye this day whom ye will serve*, and abide by your choice.

Verses 25–34

There is scarcely any one sin against which our Lord Jesus more largely and earnestly warns his disciples, than the sin of disquieting, distracting, distrustful cares about the things of this life.

I. The prohibition laid down. It is the counsel and command of the Lord Jesus, that we *take no thought* about the things of this world; *I say unto you*. He says it as our Lawgiver, and the Sovereign of our hearts; he says it as our Comforter, and the Helper of our joy. What is it that he says? *Take no thought*. *Be not in care*. It is the repeated command of the Lord Jesus to his disciples, that they should not divide and pull in pieces their own minds which care about the world. There is a *thought* concerning the things of this life, which is not only lawful, but duty.

But the *thought* here forbidden is, 1. A disquieting, tormenting *thought*, which disturbs our joy in God, which breaks the sleep, and hinders our enjoyment of ourselves, of our friends, and of what God has given us. 2. A distrustful, unbelieving *thought*. God has promised to provide for those that are his all things needful for life as well as godliness, *the life that now is*, food and a covering: not dainties, but necessaries. He never said, "They shall be feasted," but, "*Verily, they shall be fed.*" Now an inordinate care for time to come, and fear of wanting those supplies, spring from a disbelief of these promises, and of the wisdom and goodness of Divine Providence. But for the future, we must *cast our care upon God*, and *take no thought*, because it looks like a jealousy of God, who knows how to give what we want when we know not how to get it. Let our souls dwell at ease in him! This gracious carelessness is the same with that sleep which God gives to his beloved.

Take no thought for your life. Life is our greatest concern for this world; *All that a man has will he give for his life;* yet take no thought about it. Refer it to God to *lengthen* or *shorten* it as he pleases; *my times are in thy hand,* and they are in a good hand. Refer it to God to embitter or sweeten it as he pleases. We must not be solicitous, no not about the necessary support of this life, *food* and *raiment;* these God has promised. Say not, *What shall we eat?* Though many good people have the prospect of little, yet there are few but have present support.

Take no thought for the morrow, for the time to come. Be not solicitous for the future. As we must not *boast of* tomorrow, so we must not *care for* tomorrow.

II. The reasons and arguments to enforce this prohibition. To show how much the heart of Christ is upon it, and what *pleasure he takes* in those that *hope in his mercy,* the command is backed with the most powerful arguments. To free us from anxious thoughts and to expel them, Christ here suggests to us *comforting* thoughts, that we may be filled with them. They may be weakened by right reason, but it is by an active faith only that they can be overcome.

1. *Is not the life more than meat, and the body than raiment? v.* 25. Yes, no doubt it is; the thing speaks for itself. Our *life* is a greater blessing than our *livelihood.* Meat and raiment are in order to life, and the *end* is more noble and excellent than the *means.* The daintiest food and finest raiment are from the *earth,* but life from the *breath of God.* This is an encouragement to us to trust God for *food* and *raiment,* and so to ease ourselves of all perplexing cares about them. God has given us life, and given us the body; what cannot he do for us, who did that? —what will he not? If we take care about our souls and eternity, which are more than the body, and its life, we may leave it to God to provide for us food and raiment, which are less. He that guards us against the evils we are exposed to, will supply us with the *good things* we are in need of.

2. *Behold the fowls of the air,* and *consider the lilies of the field.* Here is an argument taken from God's common providence toward the inferior creatures. A fine pass fallen man has come to, that he must be sent to school to the *fowls of the air,* and that they must *teach him!*

(1) Look upon the *fowls,* and learn to trust God for food (*v.* 26). Observe the providence of God concerning them. There are various sorts of fowls; they are numerous, some of them ravenous, but they are all fed, and fed with food convenient for them. The fowls, as they are least serviceable to man, so they are least within his care; men often feed upon them, but seldom feed them; yet they are fed, and it is *your heavenly Father that feeds them;* he *knows all the wild fowls of the mountains,* better than you know the tame ones at your own barn-door. But that which is especially observed here is, that they are fed without any care or project of their own; *they sow not, neither do they reap, nor gather into barns.* Every day, as duly as the day comes, provision is made for them, and their *eyes wait on God,* that great and good Housekeeper, who *provides food for all flesh.* Improve this for your encouragement to trust in God. *Are ye not much better than they?* Yes, certainly you are. The *heirs* of heaven are much better than the *fowls* of heaven; nobler and more excellent beings, and, by faith, they soar higher. He is their Maker and Lord, their Owner and Master; but besides all this, he is your Father; you are his children, his first-born; now he that feeds his birds surely

will not starve his babes. They trust your Father's providence, and will not you trust it? In dependence upon that, they are careless for the morrow; and being so, they live the merriest lives of all creatures; they *sing among the branches.* If we were, by faith, as unconcerned about the morrow as they are, we should sing as cheerfully as they do.

(2) Look upon the *lilies,* and learn to trust God for raiment. That is another part of our care, *what we shall put on.* This care returns almost as often as that for our daily bread. *Consider the lilies of the field;* not only *look upon* them (every eye does that with pleasure), but *consider* them. There is a great deal of good to be learned from what we see every day, if we would but consider it. Consider how *frail* the lilies are; they are the *grass of the field.* Thus *all flesh is grass:* though some in the endowments of body and mind are as lilies, much admired, still they are grass. This grass *today is,* and *tomorrow is cast into the oven;* in a little while the place that *knows us* will *know us no more.* We should not take thought for the morrow, what we shall put on, because, perhaps, by tomorrow, we may have occasion for our grave-clothes. Consider how *free from care* the lilies are: they *toil not* as men do, to earn clothing; *neither do they spin,* as women do, to make clothing. It does not follow that we must therefore neglect, or do carelessly, the proper business of this life. Idleness *tempts* God, instead of *trusting* him. Consider how *fair,* how *fine* the lilies are; *how they grow;* what they *grow from.* The root of the lily is, in the winter, lost and buried under ground, yet, when spring returns, it appears, and starts up in a little time; hence it is promised to God's Israel, that they shall grow *as the lily.* Consider what they *grow to.* Out of that obscurity in a few weeks they come to be so very gay, that even *Solomon, in all his glory, was not arrayed like one of these.* Let him dress himself as fine as he could, he comes far short of the beauty of the lilies, and a bed of tulips outshines him. Let us, therefore, be ambitious of the *wisdom* of Solomon rather than the *glory* of Solomon, in which he was outdone by the lilies. Knowledge and grace are the perfection of man, not beauty, much less fine clothes. Now God is here said thus to *clothe the grass of the field.* All the excellences of the creature flow from God. It was he that gave the horse his strength, and the lily its beauty. Consider how instructive all this is to us, *v.* 30.

First, As to *fine* clothing; this teaches us not to care for it at all, not to covet it, nor to be proud of it, for after all our care in this the lilies will far outdo us; we cannot dress so fine as they do, why then should we attempt to vie with them? Their adorning will soon perish, and so will ours.

Secondly, As to *necessary* clothing; this teaches us to cast the care of it upon God. If he give such fine clothes to the grass, much more will he give fitting clothes to his own children. Observe the title he gives them (*v.* 30), *O ye of little faith.* This may be taken, 1. As an encouragement to true faith, though it be but weak. Great faith shall be commended, and shall procure great things, but little faith shall not be rejected. *Sound* believers shall be provided for, though they be not *strong* believers. The babes in the family are fed and clothed, as well as those that are grown up, and with a special care and tenderness. Or, 2. It is rather a rebuke to weak faith, though it be true. If we had but more faith, we should have less care.

3. *Which of you,* the wisest, the strongest of you, *by taking thought, can add one cubit to his stature?* We did not arrive at the stature we are by our own care and thought, but by the providence of God. An infant of a span long has grown up to be a man of six feet, he grew he knew not how, by the power and goodness of God. Now he that made our bodies,

and made them of such a size, surely will take care to provide for them. The growing age is the thoughtless, careless age, yet we grow; and shall not he who reared us to this, provide for us now we are reared? We cannot alter the stature we are of, if we would. We are not all of a size, yet the difference in stature between one and another is not material, nor of any great account. Now as we do in reference to our bodily stature, so we should do in reference to our worldly estate. We should not covet an abundance of the wealth of this world, any more than we would covet the addition of a cubit to our stature, which is a great deal in a man's height; it is enough to grow by inches; such an addition would but make one unwieldy, and a burden to one's self. We must reconcile ourselves to our state, as we do to our stature; we must set the conveniences against the inconveniences, and so make a virtue of necessity. We cannot alter the disposals of Providence.

4. *After all these things do the Gentiles seek*, v. 32. The *Gentiles* seek *these things*, because they know not *better things*; they are eager for this world, because they are strangers to a better; they seek these things with care and anxiety, because they are *without God in the world*, and understand not his providence. They fear and worship their idols, but know not how to trust them. But it is a shame for Christians, who build upon nobler principles, to walk as Gentiles walk, and to fill their heads and hearts with these things.

5. *Your heavenly Father knows ye have need of all these things;* these necessary things, food and raiment; he knows our wants better than we do ourselves. You think, if such a good friend did but know your wants and straits, you would soon have relief: your God knows them; and he is your Father that loves you and pities you, and is ready to help you. Though he knows our wants, he will know them from us. Therefore, we should ease ourselves of the burthen of care, by casting it upon God, because it is he *that careth for us.* If he cares, why should we care?

6. *Seek first the kingdom of God, and his righteousness, and all these things shall be added unto you*, v. 33. Here is a double argument against the sin of *thoughtfulness*; *take no thought* for your life, the life of the body; for, (1) You have greater and better things to take thought about, the life of your soul, your eternal happiness; that is the *one thing needful* (Luke x. 42), about which you should employ your thoughts. (2) You have a surer and easier, a safer and a more compendious way to obtain the necessaries of this life, and that is, by *seeking first the kingdom of God.*

[1] The great duty required: it is the sum and substance of our whole duty: "*Seek first the kingdom of God.*" Our duty is to seek; *though we have not attained*, but in many things fail and come short, sincere seeking is accepted. We must mind heaven as our end, and holiness as our way. We make nothing of our religion, if we do not make heaven of it. And with the *happiness* of this kingdom, seek the *righteousness* of it; *God's righteousness. Seek first the kingdom of God.* We must seek the things of Christ more than our own things. "Seek these things *first*; first in thy days: let the morning of youth be dedicated to God. Seek this first every day; let waking thoughts be of God." Let him that is the First, have the first.

[2] The gracious promise annexed; *all these things*, the necessary supports of life, *shall be added unto you*; shall be *given over and above*; as he that buys goods has paper and packthread given him into the bargain. *Godliness has the promise of the life that now is*, 1 Tim. iv. 8. We then begin at the right end of our work, when we begin with God. As to all the things of this life, Jehovah-jireh—the Lord will provide as

much of them as he sees good for us, and more we would not wish for. God's Israel were not only brought to Canaan at last, but had their charges borne through the wilderness.

7. *The morrow shall take thought for the things of itself: sufficient unto the day is the evil thereof*, v. 34. Every day brings along with it its own burthen of cares and grievances. It brings along with it its own strength and supply too. *Let the morrow take thought for the things of itself.* If wants and troubles be renewed with the day, there are aids and provisions renewed likewise; *compassions*, that are *new every morning*, Lam. iii. 22, 23. Let us refer it therefore to the morrow's strength to do the morrow's work, and bear the morrow's burthen. This does not forbid a prudent foresight, and preparation accordingly, but a perplexing solicitude, and a prepossession of difficulties and calamities, which may perhaps never come. The meaning is, let us *mind present duty*, and then *leave events to God*; do the *work of the day in its day*, and then let *tomorrow bring its work along with it. Sufficient unto the day is the evil thereof.* This present day has trouble enough attending it, we need not *accumulate* burthens by *anticipating* our trouble, nor borrow perplexities from tomorrow's evils to add to those of this day. Let us not pull that upon ourselves all together at once, which Providence has wisely ordered to be borne by parcels. By our daily prayers we may procure strength to bear us up under our daily troubles, and to arm us against the temptations that attend them, and then let none of these things move us.

CHAPTER 7

This chapter continues and concludes Christ's sermon on the mount. I. Some rules concerning censure and reproof, ver. 1–6. II. Encouragements given us to pray to God for what we need, ver. 7–11. III. The necessity of strictness in conversation urged upon us, ver. 12–14. IV. A caution given us to take heed of false prophets, ver. 15–20. V. The conclusion of the whole sermon, ver. 21–27. VI. The impression which Christ's doctrine made upon his hearers, ver. 28, 29.

Verses 1–6

Our Saviour is here directing us how to conduct ourselves in reference to the faults of others.

I. A caution *against judging*, v. 1, 2. The prohibition; *Judge not.* We must judge ourselves, and judge of our own acts, but we must not judge our brother. We must not sit in the judgment-seat, to make our word a law to everybody. We must not *despise him*, nor *set him at nought*, Rom. xiv. 10. We must not judge rashly. We must not judge uncharitably, unmercifully, nor with a spirit of revenge, and a desire to do mischief. We must not judge the hearts of others, nor their intentions, for it is God's prerogative to try the heart. Nor must we judge of their eternal state, nor call them *hypocrites, reprobates*, and *castaways*; that is stretching beyond our line; what have we to do, thus to judge another man's servant? Counsel him, and help him, but do not judge him. The reason to enforce this prohibition. *That ye be not judged.* This intimates, (1) That if we presume to judge others, we may expect to be ourselves judged. Commonly none are more censured, than those who are most censorious; and no mercy shall be shown to the reputation of those that show no mercy to the reputation of others. Yet that is not the worst of it; they shall be judged of God; from him they shall receive the *greater condemnation*, James iii. 1. Both parties must appear before him (Rom. xiv. 10), who, as he will relieve the *humble sufferer*, will also resist the *haughty scorner*, and give him enough of judging. (2) That if we be modest and charitable in our censures of others, and decline judging them, and judge ourselves rather, *we shall not be judged of the Lord.* As God will forgive those that forgive their brethren; so he will not judge those that will not judge their brethren; the *merciful shall find mercy*.

The judging of those that judge others is according to the law of retaliation; *With what judgment ye judge, ye shall be judged*, v. 2. The righteous God, in his judgments, often observes a rule of proportion. *With what measure ye mete, it shall be measured to you again*; perhaps in this world, so that men may read their sin in their punishment. What would become of us, if God should be as exact and severe in judging us, as we are in judging our brethren; if he should weigh us in the same balance? We may justly expect it, if we be extreme to mark what our brethren do amiss. In this, as in other things, the violent dealings of men return upon their own heads.

II. Some cautions *about reproving*. Because we must not judge others, which is a great sin, it does not therefore follow that we must not reprove others, which is a great duty, and may be a means of *saving a soul from death*.

1. It is not everyone who is fit to reprove. Those who are themselves guilty of the same faults of which they accuse others, or of worse, bring shame upon themselves, and are not likely to do good to those whom they reprove, v. 3–5. Here is,

(1) A just reproof to the censorious, who quarrel with their brother for small faults, while they allow themselves in great ones; who are quick-sighted to spy *a mote* in his eye, but are not sensible of *a beam in their own*. [1] There are degrees in sin: some sins are comparatively but as *motes*, others as *beams*; some as a *gnat*, others as a *camel*: not that there is any sin little, for there is no little God to sin against. [2] Our own sins ought to appear greater to us than the same sins in others, for the sins of others must be extenuated, but our own aggravated. [3] There are many that have *beams in their own eyes*, and yet do not consider it. They are under the guilt and dominion of very great sins, and yet are not aware of it, but justify themselves, as if they needed no repentance nor reformation. With great assurance, they say, *We see*. [4] It is common for those who are most sinful themselves, and least sensible of it, to be most forward and free in judging and censuring others. Pride and uncharitableness are commonly *beams* in the eyes of those that pretend to be critical and nice in their censures of others. Nay, many are guilty of that in secret, which they have the face to punish in others when it is discovered. [5] Men's being so severe upon the faults of others, while they are indulgent of their own, is a mark of hypocrisy. *Thou hypocrite*, v. 5. Whatever such a one may pretend, it is certain that he is no enemy to sin (if he were, he would be an enemy to his own sin), and therefore he is not worthy of praise. This spiritual charity must begin at home; "*For how canst thou say*, how canst thou for shame say, to thy brother, *Let me help to reform thee*, when thou takest no care to reform thyself? [6] The consideration of what is amiss in ourselves, though it ought not to keep us from administering friendly reproof, ought to keep us from magisterial censuring.

(2) Here is a good rule for reprovers, v. 5. Go in the right method, *first cast the beam out of thine own eye*. Our own badness is so far from excusing us in not reproving, that our being by it rendered unfit to reprove is an aggravation of our badness. A man's *off*ence will never be his *def*ence: but I must first reform myself, that I may thereby help to reform my brother, and may qualify myself to reprove him. Those who blame others, ought to be blameless and harmless themselves. The snuffers of the sanctuary were to be of pure gold.

2. It is not everyone that is fit to be reproved; *Give not that which is holy unto the dogs*, v. 6. Our zeal against sin must be guided by discretion, and we must not go about to give instructions, counsels, and rebukes, much less comforts, to hardened scorners. Throw a pearl to a swine, and he will resent it, as if you threw a stone at him; therefore give not to dogs and swine (unclean creatures) holy things. Good counsel and reproof are a holy thing, and a pearl: they are ordinances of God, they are precious. Among the generation of the wicked, there are some that have so long *walked in the way of sinners*, that they have sat down *in the seat of the scornful*; they professedly hate and despise instruction, and set it at defiance. Reproofs of instruction are ill bestowed upon such, and expose the reprover to all the contempt and mischief that may be expected from dogs and swine. Those are to be reckoned such, who *hate reproofs* and reprovers, and fly in the face of those who, in kindness to their souls, show them their sin and danger. These sin against the remedy; who shall heal and help those that will not be healed and helped? *It is not meet to take the children's bread, and cast it to the dogs*. Yet we must be very cautious whom we condemn as dogs and swine. Many a patient is lost, by being thought to be so, who, if means had been used, might have been saved. Our Lord Jesus is very tender of the safety of his people, and would not have them needlessly to expose themselves to the fury of those that will *turn again and rend* them.

Verses 7–11

Our Saviour, in the foregoing chapter, had spoken of prayer as a commanded duty, by which God is honoured. Here he speaks of it as the appointed means of obtaining what we need.

I. Here is a precept in three words to the same purport, *Ask, Seek, Knock* (v. 7); that is, in one word, "Pray; pray, and pray again. *Ask*, as a beggar asks alms." Those that would be rich in grace, must betake themselves to the poor trade of begging, and they shall find it a thriving trade. "*Ask;* represent your wants and burthens to God. *Ask* as a traveller asks the way; to pray is to *enquire of God* (Ezek. xxxvi. 37). *Seek* as for a thing of value that we have lost. *Seek by prayer* (Dan. ix. 3). *Knock*, as he that desires to enter into the house knocks at the door." Sin has shut and barred the door against us; by prayer, we knock; Lord, Lord, open to us. Christ knocks at our door (Rev. iii. 20; Cant. v. 2); and allows us to knock at his, which is a favour we do not allow to common beggars. Seeking and knocking imply something more than asking and praying. We must not only *ask* but *seek*; we must second our prayers with our endeavours; we must, in the use of the appointed means, *seek* for that which we *ask* for, else we tempt God. We must not only *ask*, but *knock*; we must come to God's door, must *ask* importunately; not only pray, but plead and wrestle with God.

II. Here is a promise annexed: *our labour* in prayer, if indeed we do labour in it, *shall not be in vain*: where God finds a praying heart, he will be found a prayer-hearing God; *he shall give thee an answer of peace*.

1. The promise is made, and made so as exactly to answer the precept, v. 7. God will meet those that attend on him; *Ask, and it shall be given you;* not lent you, not sold you, but *given you*; and what is more free than gift? It is but *ask* and have; *ye have not, because ye ask not*, or *ask not aright*: what is not worth asking, is not worth having, and then it is worth nothing. *Seek, and ye shall find*, and then you do not lose your labour; God is himself *found of those that seek* him, and if we find him we have enough. "*Knock, and it shall be opened*; the door of mercy and grace shall no longer be shut against you as enemies and intruders, but opened to you as friends and children. If the door be not *opened* at the first *knock, continue instant in prayer*; it is an affront to a

friend to *knock* at his door, and then go away; though he tarry, yet wait."

2. It is repeated, *v.* 8. It is to the same purport, yet with some addition. It is made to extend to all that pray aright. *Everyone that asketh*, receiveth, whether Jew or Gentile, high or low, they are all alike welcome to *the throne of grace*, if they come in faith: *for God is no respecter of persons.* It is made in words of the present tense, which is more than a promise for the future. *Everyone that asketh*, not only *shall* receive, but *receiveth*; so sure and inviolable are the promises of God, that they do, in effect, give present possession. What we have in hope, according to the promise, is as sure, and should be as sweet, as what we have in hand. Conditional grants become absolute upon the performance of the condition; so here, *he that asketh, receiveth.*

3. It is illustrated, by a similitude taken from earthly parents, and their innate readiness to give their children what they ask, Christ appeals to his hearers, *What man is there of you*, though ever so morose and ill-humoured, *whom if his son ask bread, will he give him a stone? v.* 9, 10. Whence he infers (*v.* 11), *If ye then, being evil*, yet grant your children's requests, *much more will your heavenly Father give you the good things you ask.* Now this is of use,

(1) To *direct* our prayers and expectations. We must come to God, as children to a *Father in heaven.* How naturally does the child in want or distress run to the father with its complaints. We must come to him for *good things*, for those he *gives to them that ask him.* He knows what is good for us, we must therefore leave it with him; *Father, thy will be done.* We often ask that of God which would do us hurt if we had it; he knows this, and therefore does not give it to us. Denials in love are better than grants in anger; we should have been undone ere this if we had had all we desired.

(2) To *encourage* our prayers and expectations. We may hope that we shall not be denied and disappointed: we shall not have *a stone* for *bread*, to break our teeth (though we have a hard crust to employ our teeth), nor *a serpent* for *a fish*, to sting us. God has put into the hearts of parents a compassionate inclination to succour and supply their children, according to their need. No law was ever thought necessary to oblige parents to maintain their legitimate children. He has assumed the relation of a Father to us, and owns us for his children. He compares his concern for his people to that of a father for his children (Ps. ciii. 13), nay, to that of a mother, which is usually more tender, Isa. lxvi. 13; xlix. 14, 15. But here it is supposed, that his love, and tenderness, and goodness, far excel that of any earthly parent; and therefore it is argued with a *much more.* Our earthly fathers have taken care of us; we have taken care of our children; much more will God take care of his. And, *First*, God is more knowing; parents are often foolishly fond, but God is wise, infinitely so. *Secondly*, God is more kind. All the compassions of all the tender fathers in the world compared *with the tender mercies of our God*, would be but as a candle to the sun, or a drop to the ocean. God is more rich, and more ready to give to his children than the fathers of our flesh can be.

Verses 12–14

Our Lord Jesus here presses upon us that righteousness towards men which is an essential branch of true religion, and that religion towards God which is an essential branch of universal righteousness.

I. We must make righteousness our rule, and be ruled by it, *v.* 12. *Therefore*, lay this down for your principle, to do as you would be done by; that you may have the benefit of the foregoing promises. Fitly is the law of justice subjoined to the law of prayer,

for unless we be honest in our conversation, God will not hear our prayers, Isa. i. 15–17; lviii. 6, 9; Zech. vii. 9, 13. We cannot expect to receive *good things from God*, if we do not *fair things*, and that which is *honest*, and *lovely, and of good report* among men.

1. The rule of justice laid down; *Whatsoever ye would that men should do to you, do you even so to them.* Christ came to teach us, not only what we are to know and believe, but what we are to do; what we are to do, not only toward God, but toward men. The golden rule of equity is, to do to others as we would they should do to us. We must not do to others the evil they have done to us, nor the evil which they would do to us, if it were in their power; but what we desire should be done to us. This is grounded upon that great commandment, *Thou shalt love thy neighbour as thyself.* As we must bear the same affection to our neighbour that we would have borne to ourselves, so we must do the same good offices. We must do that to our neighbour which we ourselves acknowledge to be fit and reasonable. We may fear, lest God by his judgments should do to us as we have done to others, if we have not done as we would be done by.

2. A reason given to enforce this rule; *This is the law and the prophets.* It is the summary of that second great commandment, which is one of the two, *on which hang all the law and the prophets, ch.* xxii. 40. We have not this in so many words, either in *the law* or *the prophets*, but it is the concurring language of the whole. Christ has here adopted it into this law; so that both the Old Testament and the New agree in prescribing this to us, to do as we would be done by.

II. We must make religion our business, and be intent upon it. Observe here,

1. The account that is given of the bad way of sin, and the good way of holiness. There are but two ways, right and wrong, good and evil; the way to heaven, and the way to hell; in one of which we are all of us walking: no middle place hereafter, no middle way now.

Here is, (1) An account given us of the way of sin and sinners; both what is the best, and what is the worst of it. That which allures multitudes into it, and keeps them in it; *the gate is wide, and the way broad*, and there are many travellers in that way. *First*, "You will have abundance of liberty, in that way. You may go in at this gate with all your lusts about you; it gives no check to your appetites, to your passions: you may *walk in the way of your heart, and in the sight of your eyes.*" There is choice of sinful ways, contrary to each other, but all paths in this broad way. *Secondly*, "You will have abundance of company in that way: *many there be that go in* at this gate, and walk in this way." If we *follow the multitude*, it will be *to do evil*: if we go with the crowd, it will be the wrong way. It is natural for us to incline to go down the stream, and do as the most do. If many perish, we should be the more cautious. That which should affright us all from it, is that it *leads to destruction.* Whether it be the high way of open profaneness, or the back way of close hypocrisy, if it be the way of sin, it will be our ruin, if we repent not.

(2) Here is an account given us of the way of holiness. What there is in it that frightens many from it. Christ deals faithfully with us, and tells us,

First, That *the gate is strait.* Conversion and regeneration are *the gate*, by which we enter into this way. Out of a state of sin into a state of grace we must pass, by the new birth, John iii. 3, 5. This is a *strait gate*, hard to find, and hard to get through; like a passage between two rocks, 1 Sam. xiv. 4. There must be *a new heart, and a new spirit*, and *old things must pass away.* The bent of the soul must be changed. We must swim against the stream; much opposition must be struggled with, and broken through from without, and from within. It is easier to set a man against all the world than against himself, and yet this must be in conversion. It is a *strait gate*, for we must stoop, or we cannot go in at it; we must become as little children; we must deny ourselves, put off the world, *put off the old man*; we must be willing to forsake all for our interest in Christ. *The gate is strait* to all, but to some straiter than to others; as to the rich. *The gate is strait*; blessed be God, it is not shut up, nor locked against us, nor kept with a flaming sword, as it will be shortly, *ch.* xxv. 10.

Secondly, That *the way is narrow*. We are not in heaven as soon as we have got through *the strait gate*, no, we must go through a wilderness, must travel a *narrow way*, hedged in by the divine law, which *is exceedingly broad*, and that makes *the way narrow*; self must be denied; daily temptations must be resisted; duties must be done that are against our inclination. We must endure hardness, must wrestle and be in an agony, must watch in all things, and walk with care and circumspection. We must go *through much tribulation*. It is a way hedged about with thorns; blessed be God, it is not hedged up. But, as the understanding and will grow more and more sound, it will open and enlarge, and grow more and more pleasant.

Thirdly, The gate being so *strait and the way so narrow*, it is not strange that there are but *few that find it*, and choose it. Many pass it by, through carelessness; they will not be at the pains to find it; they are well as they are, and see no need to change their way. Others look upon it, but shun it; they like not to be so limited and restrained. Those that are going to heaven are but few. This discourages many: they are loth to be singular, to be solitary. However, instead of stumbling at this, say rather, If so few are going to heaven, there shall be more room for me. Let us see what there is in this way, which, notwithstanding this, should invite us all to it; it *leads to life*, to present comfort in the favour of God, which is the life of the soul; to eternal bliss, the hope of which, at the end of our way, should reconcile us to all the difficulties and inconveniences of the road. *The gate is strait and the way narrow* and uphill, but one hour in heaven will make amends for all.

2. The great concern and duty of every one of us, in consideration of all this; *Enter ye in at the strait gate.* The matter is fairly stated; life and death, good and evil, are set before us; both the ways, and both the ends. Choose you this day which you will walk in; nay, the matter determines itself, and will not admit of a debate. Delay not, therefore; deliberate not any longer, but *enter ye in at the strait gate*; *knock* at it by sincere and constant prayers and endeavours, *and it shall be opened.* It is true, we can neither go in, or go on, without the assistance of divine grace; but it is as true, that grace is freely offered, and shall not be wanting to those that seek it, and submit to it.

Verses 15-20

We have here a caution against *false prophets*, to take heed that we be not deceived and imposed upon by them. *Prophets* are properly such as foretell things to come; there are some mentioned in the Old Testament, who pretended to that without warrant, and the event disproved their pretensions. But *prophets* did also teach the people their duty, so that *false prophets* here are false teachers.

They are false teachers and *false prophets*, 1. Who produce false commissions, who pretend to have immediate warrant and direction from God to set up for *prophets*, and to be divinely inspired, when they are not so. 2. Who preach false doctrine in those

things that are essential to religion; who teach that which is contrary to *the truth as it is in Jesus*. Beware of them, suspect them, try them, and when you have discovered their falsehood, avoid them, having nothing to do with them.

I. A good reason for this caution, *Beware of* them, for they are *wolves in sheep's clothing*, v. 15.

1. We have need to be very cautious, because their pretences are very fair and plausible, and such as will deceive us, if we be not upon our guard. They *come in sheep's clothing*, in the habit of *prophets*. We must take heed of being imposed upon by men's dress and garb. Or it may be taken figuratively; they pretend to be sheep, and outwardly appear so innocent, harmless, meek, useful, and all that is good, as to be excelled by none. They and their errors are gilded with the specious pretences of sanctity and devotion. Satan turns himself *into an angel of light*, 2 Cor. xi. 13, 14.

2. Because under these pretensions their designs are very malicious and mischievous; *inwardly they are ravening wolves*. Every *hypocrite* is a *goat* in sheep's clothing; but a *false prophet* is a *wolf* in sheep's clothing. Those that would cheat us of any truth, and possess us with error, whatever they pretend, design mischief to our souls. Paul calls them *grievous wolves*, Acts xx. 29. Now since it is so easy a thing, and withal so dangerous, to be cheated, *Beware of false prophets*.

II. Here is a good rule to go by in this caution; we must *prove all things* (1 Thess. v. 21); *ye shall know them by their fruits*, v. 16-20. Observe,

1. The illustration of this comparison, of the fruit's being the discovery of the tree. You cannot always distinguish them by their bark and leaves, nor by the spreading of their boughs, but *by their fruits ye shall know them.* The fruit is according to the tree. Christ insists upon this, the agreeableness between the fruit and the tree. If you know what the tree is, you may know what fruit to expect. Never look to gather *grapes from thorns, nor figs from thistles*; it is not in their nature to produce such fruits. [1] Corrupt, vicious, unsanctified hearts are like thorns and thistles, which came in with sin, are worthless, vexing, and for the fire at last. [2] Good works are *good fruit*, like grapes and figs, pleasing to God and profitable to men. [3] This *good fruit* is never to be expected from bad men, any more than *a clean thing out of an unclean.* On the other hand, if you know what the fruit is, you may, by that, perceive what the tree is. *A good tree cannot bring forth evil fruit*; and *a corrupt tree cannot bring forth good fruit.* But then that must be reckoned the fruit of the tree which it brings forth naturally, plentifully and constantly and which is its usual product. Men are known, not by particular acts, but by the course and tenor of their conversation, and by the more frequent acts.

2. The application of this to the false prophets.

(1) By way of terror and threatening (*v.* 19). *Every tree that brings not forth good fruit is hewn down.* This very saying John the Baptist had used, *ch.* iii. 10. Christ could have spoken the same sense in other words; but he thought it no disparagement to him to say the same that John had said before him. To write and speak the same things must not be grievous, for it is safe. Note the description of barren trees; they are trees that do *not bring forth good fruit*; though there be fruit, if it be not *good fruit*, the tree is accounted barren. Note also the doom of barren trees: *they are*, that is, certainly they shall be, *hewn down, and cast into the fire*; God will deal with them as men deal with dry trees that cumber the ground.

(2) By way of trial; *By their fruits ye shall know them.*

[1] *By the fruits* of their persons, their words and actions, and the course of their conversation. If

you would know whether they be right or not, observe how they live; their works will testify for them or against them. Those are not taught nor sent of the holy God, whose lives evidence that they are led by the unclean spirit. God puts the treasure into earthen vessels, but not into such corrupt vessels.

[2] *By the fruits* of their doctrine; their fruits as prophets. What do they tend to? What affections and practices will they lead those into, that embrace them? If *the doctrine be of God*, it will tend to promote serious piety, humility, charity, holiness, and love, with other Christian graces; but if, on the contrary, the doctrines these prophets preach have a manifest tendency to make people proud, worldly, and contentious, unjust or uncharitable, and take people off from governing themselves and their families by the strict rules of *the narrow way*, we may conclude, that *this persuasion comes not of him that calleth us*, Gal. v. 8. *This wisdom is not from above*, James iii. 15. *Faith and a good conscience* are held together, 1 Tim. i. 19; iii. 9.

Verses 21–29

We have here the conclusion of this long and excellent sermon, the scope of which is to show the indispensable necessity of obedience to the commands of Christ.

I. He shows, by a plain remonstrance, that an outward profession of religion, however remarkable, will not bring us to heaven, unless there be a correspondent conversation, *v.* 21–23.

1. Christ's law laid down, *v.* 21. *Not every one that saith, Lord, Lord, shall enter into the kingdom of heaven, into the kingdom of* grace and glory. Christ here shows, It will not suffice to say, *Lord, Lord*; in word and tongue to own Christ for our Master, and to make address to him, and professions of him accordingly. But can we imagine that this is enough to bring us to heaven, or that he who knows and requires the heart should be so put off with shows for substance? Compliments among men are pieces of civility that are returned with compliments, but they are never paid as real services; and can they then be of any account with Christ? This is not to take us off from saying, *Lord, Lord*; from professing Christ's name, and being bold in professing it, but from resting in these, in the *form of godliness*, without *the power*. It is necessary to our happiness that we *do the will of* Christ, which is indeed *the will of* his *Father in heaven*. Now this is his will, that we believe in Christ, that we repent of sin, that we live a holy life, that we *love one another. This is his will, even our sanctification*. Saying and doing are two things, often parted in the conversation of men: he that said, *I go, sir*, stirred never a step (*ch.* xxi. 30); but these two things *God has joined* in his command.

2. The hypocrite's plea against the strictness of this law, offering other things in lieu of obedience, *v.* 22. They put in their plea with great importunity, *Lord, Lord*; and with great confidence, appealing to Christ concerning it; *Lord*, dost not thou know, (1) That *we have prophesied in thy name?* Yes, it may be so; Balaam and Caiaphas were overruled to prophesy, and Saul was against his will *among the prophets*, yet that did not save them. These *prophesied* in his *name*, but he did not send them; they only made use of his name to serve a turn. (2) That *in thy name we have cast out devils?* That may be too; Judas *cast out devils*, and yet was a *son of perdition*. A man might *cast devils out* of others, and yet have a devil, nay, and be a devil himself. (3) That *in thy name we have done many wonderful works.* Gifts of tongues and healing would recommend men to the world, but it is real holiness or sanctification that is accepted of God. Grace and love are *a more excellent way* than *removing mountains*, or *speaking with the tongues of*

men and of angels, 1 Cor. xiii. 1, 2. Grace will bring a man to heaven without working miracles, but working miracles will never bring a man to heaven without grace. They had not many good works to plead; they could not pretend to have done many gracious works of piety and charity; one such would have passed better in their account than *many wonderful works*. Miracles have now ceased, and with them this plea; but do not carnal hearts still encourage themselves in their groundless hopes, with the like vain supports? Let us take heed of resting in external privileges and performances, lest *we deceive ourselves*.

3. The rejection of this plea as frivolous. The same that is the Law-Maker (*v.* 21) is here the Judge according to that law (*v.* 23). *I never knew you*, and therefore *depart from me, ye that work iniquity.*— Observe, (1) Why, and upon what ground, he rejects them and their plea—because they were *workers of iniquity*. It is possible for men to have a great name for piety, and yet to be *workers of iniquity*; and those that are so will *receive the greater damnation*. (2) How it is expressed; *I never knew you*. This intimates, that if he had ever known them, as *the Lord knows them that are his*, had ever owned them and loved them as his, he would have known them, and owned them, and *loved them, to the end*; but he *never* did *know* them, for he always knew them to be hypocrites. Those that go no further in Christ's service than a bare profession, he does not accept, nor will he own them in the great day. See from what a height of hope men may fall into the depth of misery! How they may go to hell, by the gates of heaven! At God's bar, a profession of religion will not bear out any man in the practice and indulgence of sin; therefore *let every one that names the name of Christ, depart from all iniquity.*

II. He shows, by a parable, that hearing these sayings of Christ will not make us happy, if we do not make conscience of doing them; but that if we hear them and do them, we are *blessed in our deed, v.* 24–27.

1. The hearers of Christ's word are here divided into two sorts: some that hear, and do what they hear; others that hear and do not.

(1) Some that *hear his sayings and do them*: blessed be God that there are any such, though comparatively few. To hear Christ is not barely to give him the hearing, but to obey him. It is a mercy that we *hear* his *sayings: Blessed are those ears*, ch. xiii. 16, 17. But, if we practise not what we hear, we *receive* that grace in vain. All the *sayings* of Christ, not only the laws he has enacted, but the truths he has revealed, must be done by us. It is not enough to *hear* Christ's *sayings*, and understand them, *hear* them, and remember them, *hear* them, and talk of them, repeat them, dispute for them; but we must *hear, and do* them. *This do, and thou shalt live.* Those only *that hear, and do*, are *blessed* (Luke xi. 28; John xiii. 17), and are akin to Christ (*ch.* xii. 50).

(2) There are others who *hear* Christ's *sayings and do them not*; their religion rests in bare hearing, and goes no further. *They hear* God's *words*, as if they desired to *know his ways*, like a people *that did righteousness, but they will not do them*, Ezek. xxxiii. 30, 31; Isa. lviii. 2. The seed is sown, but it never comes up. Those who only *hear* Christ's *sayings, and do them not*, sit down in the midway to heaven, and that will never bring them to their journey's end.

2. These two sorts of hearers are here represented in their true characters, and the state of their case, under the comparison of two builders; one was *wise*, and *built upon a rock*, and his building stood in a storm; the other *foolish*, and *built upon the sand*, and his building fell. The general scope of this parable teaches us that the only way to make sure work for

our souls and eternity, is to *hear and do the sayings of* the Lord Jesus. They make sure the *good part*, who, like Mary, when they hear the word of Christ, *sit at his feet* in subjection to it: *Speak, Lord, for thy servant heareth*. The particular parts of it teach us divers good lessons. (1) That we have everyone a house to build, and that house is our hope for heaven. It ought to be our chief and constant care, to *make our calling and election sure*. Many never mind this: it is the furthest thing from their thoughts; they are building for this world, as if they were to be here always, but take no care to build for another world. All who take upon them a profession of religion, profess to enquire, what they shall *do to be saved*; how they may get to heaven at last, and may have a well-grounded hope of it in the meantime. (2) That there is *a rock* provided for us to build this house upon, *and that rock is Christ*. He *is our Hope*, 1 Tim. i, 1.

Christ in us is so; we must ground our hopes of heaven upon the fulness of Christ's merit, for the pardon of sin, the power of his Spirit, for the sanctification of our nature, and the prevalency of his intercession, for the conveyance of all that good which he has purchased for us. The church is *built upon his Rock*, and so is every believer. He is strong and immovable as a *rock*; we may venture our all upon him, and shall not be made *ashamed of our hope*. (3) That there is a remnant, who by hearing and doing the *sayings of* Christ, build their hopes *upon* this Rock. Those *build upon* Christ, who make it their constant care to conform to all the rules of his holy religion, and therein depend entirely upon him for assistance from God, and acceptance with him, *and count* every *thing but loss and dung that they may win Christ*, and be found in him. Building *upon a rock* requires care and pains: they that would make their *calling and election sure*, must *give diligence*. They are wise builders who *begin to build* so as they may be *able to finish* (Luke xiv. 30), and therefore lay a firm foundation. (4) That there are many who profess that they hope to go to heaven, but despise this *Rock*, and build their hopes *upon the sand*. Everything besides Christ is sand. Some build their hopes upon their worldly prosperity, as if that were a sure token of God's favour, Hos. xii. 8. Others upon their external profession of religion. They are called Christians, were baptized, go to church, hear Christ's word, say their prayers, and do nobody any harm; but it is all sand, too weak to bear such a fabric as our hopes of heaven. (5) That there is a storm coming, that will try what our hopes are bottomed on. *Rain, and floods, and wind, will beat upon the house;* the trial is sometimes in this world; *when tribulation and persecution arise because of the word*, then it will be seen, who only heard the word, and who heard and practised it. However, when death and judgment come, then the storm comes. Then everything else will fail us but these hopes, and then, if ever, they will be turned into everlasting fruition. (6) That those hopes which are built upon Christ the Rock will stand, and will stand the builder in stead when the storm comes. His comforts will not fail; they will be his strength and song, *as an anchor of the soul, sure and steadfast*. When he comes to the last encounter, those hopes will take off the terror of death and the grave; will be approved by the Judge; will stand the test of the great day; and will be crowned with endless glory, 2 Cor. i. 12; 2 Tim. iv. 7, 8. (7) That those hopes which foolish builders ground upon anything but Christ, will certainly fail them on a stormy day. He shall *lean upon his house, but it shall not stand*, Job. viii. 14, 15. It fell in the storm, when the builder had most need of it, and expected it would be a shelter to him. It was a great disappointment to the builder; the shame and loss were great. The higher men's

hopes have been raised, the lower they fall. It is the sorest ruin of all that attends formal professors.

III. In the two last verses, we are told what impressions Christ's discourse made upon the auditory. *They were astonished at his doctrine;* it is to be feared that few of them were brought by it to follow him: but for the present, they were filled with wonder. It is possible for people to admire good preaching, and yet to remain in ignorance and unbelief; to be astonished, and yet not sanctified. The reason was because he taught them *as one having authority, and not as the scribes*. The scribes pretended to as much authority as any teachers whatsoever, and were supported by all the external advantages that could be obtained. They spake as those that were not themselves masters of what they preached: the word did not come from them with any life or force; they delivered it as a schoolboy says his lesson; but Christ delivered his discourse, as a judge gives his charge. His lessons were laws; his word a word of command. Christ, upon the mountain, showed more true authority than the scribes in Moses' seat. Thus when Christ teaches by his Spirit in the soul, he teaches with authority. He says, *Let there be light, and there is light*.

CHAPTER 8

The evangelist proceeds now to give some instances of the miracles he wrought. I. Christ's cleansing of a leper, ver. 1–4. II. His curing a palsy and fever, ver. 5–18. III. His communing with two that were disposed to follow him, ver. 19–22. IV. His controlling the tempest, ver. 23–27. V. His casting out devils, ver. 28–34.

Verses 1–4

The people that heard him were *astonished at his doctrine*; and the effect was, that *when he came down from the mountain, great multitudes followed him*. They to whom Christ has manifested himself, cannot but desire to be better acquainted with him. They who know much of Christ should covet to know more. It is pleasing to see people so well affected to Christ, as to think they can never hear enough of him. Yet they who gathered to him did not cleave to him. They who followed him closely and constantly were but few, compared with the multitudes that were but followers at large.

In these verses we have an account of Christ's *cleansing a leper*. This is fitly recorded with the first of Christ's miracles, 1. Because the leprosy was looked upon, among the Jews, as a particular mark of God's displeasure; and therefore Christ, to show that he came to turn away the wrath of God, by taking away sin, began with the cure of a leper. 2. Because this disease, as it was supposed to come immediately from the hand of God, so also it was supposed to be removed immediately by his hand, and therefore it was not attempted to be cured by physicians, but was put under the inspection of the priests, the Lord's ministers, who waited to see what God would do. Christ proved himself God, by recovering many from the leprosy, and authorizing his disciples, in his name, to do so too (*ch. x. 8*), and it is put among the proofs of his being, the Messiah, *ch. xi. 5*. He also showed himself to be the Saviour of his people from their sins; for though every disease is both the fruit of sin, and a figure of it, as the disorder of the soul, yet the leprosy was in a special manner so. It is treated, not as a sickness, but as an uncleanness; the priest was to pronounce the party clean or unclean, according to the indications: but the honour of making the lepers clean was reserved for Christ. The law discovered sin (for by the law is the knowledge of sin), and pronounced sinners unclean; but could go no further; it could not *make the comers thereunto perfect*. But Christ takes away sin; cleanses us from it.

I. The leper's address to Christ. We may suppose that the leper, though shut out by his disease from the cities of Israel, yet got within hearing of Christ's sermon, and was encouraged by it to make his application to him; for he that taught *as one having authority*, could heal so. His address is, *Lord, if thou wilt, thou canst make me clean*. The cleansing of him may be considered.

1. As a temporal mercy; a mercy to the body. And so it directs us, not only to apply ourselves to Christ, but it also teaches us in what manner to apply ourselves to him; with an assurance of his power, but with a submission to his will; *Lord, if thou wilt, thou canst*. His *promise* of them is limited by a regard to his glory and our good: when we cannot be sure of his will, we may be sure of his wisdom and mercy, to which we may cheerfully refer ourselves; *Thy will be done*.

2. As a typical mercy. Sin is the leprosy of the soul; it shuts us out from communion with God, it is necessary that we be cleansed from this leprosy. Now, observe, It is our comfort when we apply ourselves to Christ, as the great Physician, that if he will, he can make us clean; and we should, with an humble, believing boldness, go to him and tell him so. (1) We must rest ourselves upon his power; we must be confident of this, that Christ *can* make us clean. (2) We must recommend ourselves to his pity; we cannot demand it as a debt, but we must humbly request it as a favour; "*Lord, if thou wilt*. I throw myself at thy feet, and if I perish, I will perish there."

II. Christ's answer to this address, which was very kind, *v.* 3.

1. *He put forth his hand and touched him.* The leprosy was a noisome, loathsome disease, yet Christ touched him. There was a ceremonial pollution contracted by the touch of a leper; but Christ would show, that when he conversed with sinners, he was in no danger of being infected by them.

2. He said, *I will, be thou clean.* He did not put him upon a tedious, troublesome, chargeable course of physic, but spake the word and healed him. (1) Here is a word of kindness, *I will*; I am as willing to help thee, as thou art to be helped. Christ is a Physician, that does not need to be sought for, he is always in the way; does not need to be urged, while we are yet speaking, he hears; does not need to be paid, he heals, freely, not for price nor reward. He is as willing as he is able to save sinners. (2) A word of power, *Be thou clean*. Both a power of authority, and a power of energy, are exerted in this word. Christ heals by a word of command to us; *Be thou clean*. But there goes along with this a word of command concerning us, a word that does the work; *I will that thou be clean*. The Almighty grace which speaks it, shall not be wanting to those who truly desire it.

III. The happy change hereby wrought: *Immediately his leprosy was cleansed*. Nature works gradually, but the God of nature works immediately; he speaks, it is done.

IV. The after-directions Christ gave him. It is fit that they who are cured by Christ should ever after be ruled by him.

1. *See thou tell no man;* "Tell no man till thou hast shown thyself to the priest, and he has pronounced thee clean; and so thou hast a legal proof, both that thou wast before a leper, and art now thoroughly cleansed." Christ would have his miracles to appear in their full light and evidence, and not to be published till they could appear so.

2. *Go show thyself to the priest*, according to the law, Lev. xiv. 2. Christ took care to have the law observed, lest he should give offence, and to show that he will have order kept up, and good discipline and respect paid to those that are in office.

3. *Offer the gift that Moses commanded*, in token of thankfulness to God, and recompense to the priest for his pains; and this *for a testimony unto them*. It

shall be a testimony, that there is one among them who does that which the high priest cannot do. Let it remain upon record as a witness of my power, and a testimony for me *to* them, if they will use it and improve it; but *against* them, if they will not.

Verses 5–13

We have here an account of Christ's curing the centurion's servant of a palsy. This was done at Capernaum, where Christ now dwelt, *ch.* iv. 13. Christ went about doing good, and came home to do good too; every place he came to was the better for him.

The persons Christ had now to do with were,

1. A *centurion*; he was a supplicant, a Gentile, a Roman, an officer of the army. Though he was a soldier (and a little piety commonly goes a great way with men of that profession), yet he was a godly man. God has his remnant among all sorts of people. No man's calling or place in the world will be an excuse for his unbelief and impiety. And sometimes where grace conquers the unlikely, it is more than a conqueror. Though he was a Roman soldier, and his very dwelling among the Jews was a badge of their subjection to the Roman yoke, yet Christ, who was *King of the Jews*, favoured him; and therein has taught us to do good to our enemies. Though he was a Gentile, yet Christ countenanced him. Now good old Simeon's word began to be fulfilled, that he should be *a light to lighten the Gentiles*, as well as *the glory of his people Israel*. The leprous Jews Christ touched and cured, for he preached personally to them; but the paralytic Gentiles he cured at a distance; for to them he did not go in person, but *sent his word and healed them*; yet in them he was more magnified.

2. *The centurion's servant.* He is as ready to heal the poorest servant, as the richest master; for himself *took upon him the form of a servant*, to show his regard to the meanest.

I. The grace of the centurion working towards Christ. Can any good thing come out of a Roman soldier? Come and see, and you will find abundance of good coming out of this centurion.

1. His affectionate address to Jesus Christ, which speaks,

(1) A pious regard to our great Master, as one able and willing to succour and relieve poor petitioners. He came to him *beseeching him* with cap in hand as a humble suitor. By this it seems that he saw more in Christ than appeared at first view; saw that which commanded respect. The greatest of men must turn beggars, when they have to do with Christ. He owns Christ's sovereignty, in calling him Lord, and referring the case to him, and to his will, and wisdom. He knew he had to do with a wise and gracious Physician, to whom the opening of the malady was equivalent to the most earnest request. A humble confession of our spiritual wants and diseases shall not fail of an answer of peace. Pour out thy complaint, and mercy shall be poured out.

(2) A charitable regard to his poor servant. We read of many that came to Christ for their children, but this is the only instance of one that came to him for a servant: *Lord, my servant lieth at home sick*. It is the duty of masters to concern themselves for their servants, when they are in affliction. The servant could not have done more for the master, than the master did here for the servant. The centurion's servants were very dutiful to him (*v.* 9), and here we see what made them so; he was very kind to them, and that made them the more cheerfully obedient to him. The palsy is a disease in which the physician's skill commonly fails; it was therefore a great evidence of his faith in the power of Christ, to come to him for a cure, which was above the power of natural means

to effect. Observe, How pathetically he represents his servant's case as very sad; he is *sick of the palsy*, a disease which commonly makes the patient senseless of pain, but this person was *grievously tormented*. We should thus concern ourselves for the souls of our children, and servants, that are spiritually sick of the palsy, and bring them to Christ by faith and prayer, bring them to the means of healing and health.

2. Observe his great humility and self-abasement. After Christ had intimated his readiness to come and heal his servant (*v.* 7), he expressed himself with the more humbleness of mind. Humble souls are made more humble, by Christ's gracious condescensions to them. *Lord, I am not worthy that thou shouldst come under my roof* (*v.* 8), which speaks mean thoughts of himself, and high thoughts of our Lord Jesus. He does not say, "My servant is not worthy that thou shouldst come into his chamber, because it is in the garret"; But *I am not worthy that thou shouldst come into my house.* The centurion was a great man, yet he owned his unworthiness before God. Humility very well becomes persons of quality. Christ now made but a mean figure in the world, yet the centurion paid him this respect. We should have a value and veneration for what we see of God, even in those who, in outward condition, are every way our inferiors. In all our approaches to Christ, and to God through Christ, it becomes us to abase ourselves, and to lie low in the sense of our own unworthiness.

3. Observe his great faith. The more humility the more faith. He had an assurance of faith not only that Christ could cure his servant, but,

(1) That he could cure him at a distance. There needed not any physical contact, as in natural operations, not any application to the part affected. We read afterwards of those, who brought the *man sick of the palsy to Christ*, through much difficulty, and set him before him; and Christ commended their faith for a *working* faith. This centurion did not bring his man *sick of the palsy*, and Christ commended his faith for a *trusting* faith: true faith is accepted of Christ, though variously appearing: Christ puts the best construction upon the different methods of religion that people take. Nearness and distance are alike to him. Distance of place cannot obstruct either the knowing or working of him that *fills all places.*

(2) That he could cure him with a *word*, not send him a medicine, much less a charm; but *speak the word only*, and I do not question but *my servant shall be healed.* Herein he owns him to have a divine power. With men, saying and doing are two things; but not so with Christ.

The centurion's faith in the power of Christ he here illustrates by the dominion he had, as a centurion, over his soldiers, as a master over his servants; he says to one, *Go, and he goes*, &c. They were all at his beck and command, so that he could by them execute things at a distance. Thus could Christ speak, and it is done. The centurion had this command over his soldiers, though he was himself a *man under authority*; much more had Christ this power, who is the supreme and sovereign Lord of all. Such servants we all should be to God: we must go and come at his bidding, according to the directions of his word, and the disposals of his providence. When his will crosses our own, his must take place, and our own be set aside. Such servants bodily diseases are to Christ. It is a matter of comfort to all that belong to Christ, that every disease is made to serve the intentions of his grace. They need not fear sickness, nor what it can do, who see it in the hand of so good a Friend.

II. Here is the grace of Christ appearing towards this centurion; for to the gracious he will show himself gracious.

1. He complies with his address at the first word. *I will come and heal him* (*v.* 7); not *I will come and see him*—that had evinced him a kind Saviour; but, *I will come and heal him*—that shows him a mighty, an almighty Saviour. He has *healing under his wings*; his coming is healing. The centurion desired he would heal his servant; he says, *I will come and heal him*; thus expressing more favour than he did either ask or think of. Christ often outdoes the expectations of poor supplicants. He would not go down to see a nobleman's sick child, who insisted upon his coming down (John iv. 47–49), but he proffers to go down to see a sick servant. Christ's humility in being willing to come, gave an example to him, and occasioned his humility, in owning himself unworthy to have him come. Christ's gracious condescensions to us, should make us the more humble and self-abasing before him.

2. He commends his faith, and takes occasion from it to speak a kind word of the poor Gentiles, *v.* 10–12.

(1) As to the centurion himself; he not only approved him and accepted him (that honour have all true believers), but he admired him and applauded him: that honour great believers have.

[1] Christ admired him, not for his greatness, but for his graces. *When Jesus heard it, he marvelled;* not as if it were to him new and surprising, but it was great and excellent, rare and uncommon, and Christ spoke of it as wonderful, to teach us what to admire; not worldly pomp and decorations, but the beauty of holiness. The wonders of grace should affect us more than the wonders of nature or providence, and spiritual attainments more than any achievements in this world.

[2] He *applauded* him in what he said to *them that followed. Verily, I have not found so great faith, no, not in Israel.* Now this speaks, *First, Honour to the centurion;* who, though not a son of Abraham's loins, was an heir of Abraham's faith. The thing that Christ seeks is *faith*, and wherever it is, he finds it, though but *as a grain of mustard seed.* We must be forward, to give those their due praise, that are not within our denomination or pale. *Secondly,* It speaks *shame to Israel.* When *the Son of man comes*, he *finds* little *faith*, and, therefore, he finds so little *fruit.* Christ said this *to those that followed him.* They were Abraham's seed; in jealousy for that honour, let them not suffer themselves to be outstripped by a Gentile, especially in that grace for which Abraham was eminent.

(2) As to others. Christ tells them two things, which could not but be very surprising to them who had been taught that *salvation was of the Jews.*

[1] That *a great many of the Gentiles should be saved, v.* 11. The faith of the centurion was but a specimen of the conversion of the Gentiles. This was a topic our Lord Jesus touched often upon; he speaks with assurance; *I say unto you*, although an intimation of this kind enraged the Nazarenes against him, Luke iv. 27. Christ gives us here an idea, *First*, of the *persons* that shall be *saved*; many *from the east and the west*: he had said (ch. vii. 14), *Few there be that find the way to life*; and yet here *many shall come.* Few at one time, and in one place; yet, when they come altogether, they will be a great many. They shall come *from the east* and *from the west*; places far distant from each other; and yet they shall all meet at the right hand of Christ, the Centre of their unity. God has his remnant in all places. Though they were *strangers to the covenant of promise* now, and had been long, yet who knows what *hidden ones* God had among them then? When we come to heaven, as we shall miss a great many there, that we thought had been going thither, so we shall meet a great many there, that we did not expect. *Secondly*, Christ gives us an idea of the *salvation itself.* They shall

come, shall come together, shall come together to Christ, 2 Thess. ii. 1. 1. They shall be admitted *into the kingdom of grace* on earth; they shall be *blessed with faithful Abraham.* This makes Zaccheus a son of Abraham, Luke xix. 9. 2. They shall be admitted into the *kingdom of glory in heaven.* They shall sit down to rest from their labours, as having done their day's work; sitting denotes *continuance*: while we *stand*, we are *going*; where we *sit*, we mean to *stay*; as *at a table*; that is the metaphor here; they shall sit down to be *feasted*; which denotes both *fulness of communication*, and *freedom* and familiarity of communion, Luke xxii. 30. They shall *sit down with Abraham.* They who in this world were ever so far distant from each other in time, place, or outward condition, shall all meet together in heaven. Holy society is a part of the felicity of heaven.

[2] That a great many of the Jews should perish, *v.* 12. Observe,

First, A strange sentence passed; *The children of the kingdom shall be cast out; the kingdom of God,* of which they boasted that they were *the children,* shall be taken from them. In the great day it will not avail men to have been *children of the kingdom,* either as Jews or as Christians; for men will then be judged, not by what they were *called,* but by what they *were.* Being born of professing parents denominates us *children of the kingdom*; but if we rest in that, and have nothing else to show for heaven but that, we shall be *cast out.*

Secondly, A strange punishment for *the workers of iniquity* described; *They shall be cast into outer darkness,* the darkness of those that are without. *They shall be cast out* from God, and all true comfort, and *cast into darkness.* It is *utter darkness*; without any remainder, or mixture, or hope, of light; not the least gleam or glimpse of it; it is darkness that results from their being shut out of heaven, the land of light.

3. He cures his servant. He grants him that for which he applied, which was a real answer, *v.* 13.

(1) What Christ said to him: he said that which made the cure as great a favour to him as it was to his servant, and much greater; *As thou hast believed, so be it done to thee.* The servant got a cure of his disease, but the master got the confirmation and approbation of his faith. Christ often gives encouraging answers to his praying people, when they are interceding for others. It is kindness to us, to be heard for others. *Be it done as thou believest.* What could he have more? Yet what was said to him is said to us all, *Believe, and ye shall receive; only believe.* See here the power of Christ, and the power of faith. As Christ can *do* what he will, so an active believer may *have* what he will from Christ.

(2) What was the effect of this saying: the prayer of faith was a prevailing prayer, it ever was so, and ever will be so; it appears, by the suddenness of the cure, that it was *miraculous*: *he spake, and it was done*; and this was a proof of his omnipotence, that he has a long arm.

Verses 14–17

I. A particular account of the cure of *Peter's wife's mother,* who was ill *of a fever.*

1. The *case* which was nothing extraordinary; it is recorded as an instance of Christ's peculiar care of, and kindness to, the families of his disciples. Here we find, (1) That Peter had a *wife,* and yet *was called to be an apostle of Christ*; and Christ countenanced the marriage state. (2) That Peter had a *house,* though Christ had not, *v.* 20. Thus was the disciple better provided for than his Lord. (3) That he had a house at Capernaum, though he was originally of Bethsaida; it is probable, he removed to Capernaum, when Christ removed thither, and made that his principal residence. It is worth while to change our quarters,

that we may be near to Christ. (4) That he had his *wife's mother* with him in his family, which is an example to yoke-fellows to be kind to one another's relations as their own. Probably, this good woman was old, and yet was respected and taken care of, as old people ought to be, with all possible tenderness. (5) That she lay ill *of a fever.* The palsy was a chronic disease, the fever an acute disease, but both were brought to Christ.

2. The *cure, v.* 15. (1) How it was *effected*; *He touched her hand;* not to know the disease, as the physicians do, by the pulse, but to heal it. This was an intimation of his kindness and tenderness. The scripture *speaks the word,* the Spirit gives the touch, touches the heart, touches the hand. (2) How it was *evidenced*: this showed that the *fever left her, she arose, and ministered to them.* By this it appears, [1] That the mercy was perfected. They that recover from fevers by the power of nature are commonly weak and feeble. She was immediately so well as to go about the business of the house. [2] That the mercy was sanctified. Though she was thus dignified by a peculiar favour, yet she does not assume importance, but is as ready to wait at table, if there be occasion, as any servant. They must be humble whom Christ has honoured; being thus delivered, she studies what she shall render. It is very fit that they whom Christ hath healed should minister unto him, as his humble servants, all their days.

II. Here is a general account of the many cures that Christ wrought. This cure of Peter's mother-in-law brought him abundance of patients. "He healed such a one; why not me? Such a one's friend, why not mine?" Now we are here told,

1. What he did, *v.* 16. (1) *He cast out devils; cast out the* evil *spirits with his word.* About the time of Christ's being in the world, there seems to have been more than ordinary letting loose of the devil, to possess and vex the bodies of people; and God wisely ordered it so, that Christ might have the fairer and more frequent opportunities of showing his power over Satan. (2) *He healed all that were sick;* all without exception, though the patient was ever so mean, and the case ever so bad.

2. How the scripture was herein fulfilled, *v.* 17. Among other things, it was written of him (Isa. liii. 4), *Surely he hath borne our griefs, and carried our sorrows:* it is referred to, 1 Peter ii. 24, and there it is construed, *he hath borne our sins*; here it is referred to, and is construed, *he hath borne our sicknesses*; our sins make our sicknesses our griefs; Christ bore away sin by the merit of his death, and bore away sickness by the miracles of his life. Many are the diseases and calamities to which we are liable in the body: and there is more, in this one line of the gospels, to support and comfort us under them, than in all the writings of the philosophers. He bore them for us in his *passion,* and bears them with us in *compassion,* being *touched with the feeling of our infirmities*: and thus he bears them off from us. Observe how emphatically it is expressed here: *Himself took our infirmities, and bare our sicknesses;* he was both able and willing to interpose in that matter, and concerned to deal with *our infirmities and sicknesses,* as our Physician.

Verses 18–22

I. Christ's removing to *the other side of the sea of Tiberias,* and his ordering his disciples, whose boats attended him, to get their transport-vessels ready, in order to it, *v.* 18. He must go about to do good; the necessities of souls called to him, *Come over, and help us* (Acts xvi. 9); he removed *when he saw great multitudes about him.* Though by this it appeared that they were desirous to have him there, he knew there were others as desirous to have him with them, and they must have their share of him: his being acceptable and useful in one place was no objection against, but a reason for, his going to another. Many would be glad of such helps, if they could have them at next door, who will not be at pains to follow them to *the other side*.

II. Christ's communication with two, who, upon his remove to *the other side*, were loth to stay behind, and had a mind to follow him, not as others, who were his followers at large, but to come into close discipleship, which the most were shy of.

We have here Christ's managing of two different tempers, one quick and eager, the other dull and heavy; and his instructions are adapted to each of them, and designed for our use.

1. Here is one that was *too hasty in promising*; and he was *a certain scribe* (v. 19), a scholar, a learned man, one of those that studied and expounded the law; generally we find them in the gospels to be men of no good character. They were very seldom following Christ; yet here was one that bid pretty fair for discipleship.

(1) How he expressed his forwardness; *Master, I will follow thee, whithersoever thou goest*. I know not how any man could have spoken better. His profession of a self-dedication to Christ is, [1] Very ready *inclination*: he is not called to it by Christ, of his own accord, he proffers himself to be a close follower of Christ; he is not a pressed man, but a volunteer. [2] Very resolute; he seems to be at a point in this matter. "I am determined, *I will* do it." [3] It was unlimited and without reserve. "*I will follow thee whithersoever thou goest*." Yet it appears, by Christ's answer, that his resolution was rash. There are many resolutions for religion, produced by some sudden pangs of conviction, and taken up without due consideration, that prove abortive, and come to nothing: soon ripe, soon rotten.

(2) How Christ tried his forwardness, whether it was sincere or not, v. 20. He let him know that this *Son of man*, whom he is so eager to follow, *has not where to lay his head*, v. 20. It is strange in itself, that the Son of God, when he came into the world, should put himself into such a very low condition, as to want the convenience of a certain resting-place. See here, *First*, How well provided for the inferior creatures are: *The foxes have holes;* their holes are their castles. *The birds of the air*, though they take no care for themselves, yet are taken care of, and *have nests* (Ps. civ. 17). *Secondly*, How poorly the Lord Jesus was provided for. He had not a settlement, had not a place of repose, not a house of his own, to put his head in, not a pillow of his own, to lay his head on. He and his disciples lived upon the charity of well-disposed people, that *ministered to him of their substance*, Luke viii. 2. Christ submitted to this that he might show us the vanity of worldly wealth, and teach us to look upon it with a holy contempt; that he might purchase better things for us, and so *make us rich*, 2 Cor. viii. 9. It is strange that such a declaration should be made on this occasion. One scribe might be capable of doing him more credit and service than twelve fishermen: but Christ saw his heart, and answered to the thoughts of that, and therein teaches us all how to come to Christ. *First*, The scribe's resolve seems to have been sudden; and Christ would have us, when we take upon us a profession of religion, to *sit down and count the cost* (Luke xiv. 28). It is no advantage to religion, to take men by surprise, ere they are aware. They that take up a profession *in a pang*, will throw it off again *in a fret*; let him that will follow Christ know the worst of it, and expect to lie hard, and fare hard. *Secondly*, His resolve seems to have been from a worldly, covetous principle. He saw what abundance of cures Christ wrought, and concluded that he had

large fees, and would get an estate quickly. He is not for following Christ, unless he can *get by him*.

2. Here is another that was too *slow in performing*. Delay in execution is as bad, on the one hand, as precipitancy in resolution is on the other hand; let it never be said, we left that to be done tomorrow, which we could do today.

(1) The excuse that this disciple made, to defer an immediate attendance on Christ (v. 21); "*Lord, suffer me first to go and bury my father*." His father (some think) was now sick, or dying, or dead; others think, he was only aged, and not likely in a course of nature, to continue long. This seemed a reasonable request, and yet it was not right. He had not the zeal he should have had for the work, and therefore pleaded this, because it seemed a plausible plea. An unwilling mind never wants an excuse. The preference should have been given to Christ.

(2) Christ's disallowing of this excuse (v. 22); *Jesus said to him, Follow me;* and, no doubt, power accompanied this word to him, as to others, and he did *follow Christ*. We are brought to Christ by the force of his call to us, not of our promises to him. When Christ calls, he will overcome, and make the call effectual, 1 Sam. iii. 10. His excuse is laid aside as insufficient; *Let the dead bury their dead. Let the dead* spiritually *bury the dead* corporally; let worldly offices be left to worldly people; do not thou encumber thyself with them. Burying the dead, and especially a dead father, is a good work, but it is not thy work, at this time: thou hast something else to do, and must not defer that. Piety to God must be preferred before piety of parents, though that is a great and needful part of our religion. We must comparatively neglect and disesteem our nearest relations, when they come in competition with Christ, and either our doing for him, or our suffering for him.

Verses 23–27

Christ had given sailing orders to his disciples (v. 18), that they should *depart to the other side of the sea of Tiberias*. He chose to go by water. It had not been much about, if he had gone by land; but he chose to cross the lake. It is a comfort to those *who go down to the sea in ships*, and are often in perils there, to reflect that they have a Saviour to trust in and pray to, who knows what it is to be at sea, and to be in storms there. 2. *His disciples followed him;* the twelve kept close to him. They, and they only, will be found the true disciples of Christ, that are willing to go to sea with him, to follow him into dangers and difficulties. Many would be content to go the landway to heaven, but those that would rest with Christ hereafter must follow him now wherever he leads them, into a ship or into a prison, as well as into a palace.

I. The peril and perplexity of the disciples in this voyage. Those who follow him must count upon difficulties, v. 20.

1. *There arose a very great storm*, v. 24. This storm was *for their sakes*, as John xi. 4. Christ would show that they who are passing with him over the ocean of this world to the other side, must expect storms by the way. It is only the upper region that enjoys a perpetual calm, this lower one is ever and anon disturbed and disturbing.

2. Jesus Christ *was asleep in this storm*. We never read of Christ's sleeping but at this time; this was a sleep, not of security, like Jonah's in a storm, but of holy serenity, and dependence upon his Father. He had no guilt, no fear within to disturb his repose. Those that can lay their heads upon the pillow of a clear conscience, may sleep quietly and sweetly in a storm (Ps. iv. 8), as Peter, Acts xii. 6. He slept at this time, to try the faith of his disciples, whether they could trust him when he seemed to slight them.

3. The poor disciples, though used to the sea, were in a great fright, and in their fear *came to* their Master, *v.* 25. Whither else should they go? It was well they had him so near them. They *awoke him* with their prayers; *Lord, save us, we perish.* They who would learn to pray must go to sea. Imminent and sensible dangers will drive people to him who alone can help in time of need. Their petition is, *Lord, save us.* They believed he *could* save them; they begged he *would.* Christ's errand into the world was *to save,* but those only *shall be saved that call on the name of the Lord,* Acts ii. 21. They call him, *Lord,* and then pray, *Save us.* Christ will save none but those that are willing to take him for their Lord. Their plea is, *We perish;* which was the language of their fear; they had received a sentence of death within themselves, and this they plead, "*We perish,* if thou dost not save us; look upon us therefore with pity." It was the language of their fervency. It becomes us thus to strive and wrestle in prayer; *therefore* Christ slept, that he might draw out this importunity.

II. The power and grace of Jesus Christ put forth for their succour. Christ may sleep when his church is in a storm, but he will not outsleep himself.

1. He rebuked the disciples (*v.* 26); *Why are ye fearful, O ye of little faith?* He does not chide them for disturbing him with their prayers, but for disturbing themselves with their fears. Christ reproved them first, and then delivered them. His dislike of their fears; "*Why are ye fearful?* Ye, my disciples?" His discovery of the cause and spring of their fears; *O ye of little faith.* Many that have true faith are weak in it, and it does but little. By faith we might see through the storm to the quiet shore, and encourage ourselves with hope that we shall weather our point.

2. *He rebukes the wind.* See, (1) How *easily* this was done, with a word's speaking. (2) How *effectually* it was done. *There was a great calm,* all of a sudden. Ordinarily, after a storm, there is such a fret of the waters, that it is a good while ere they can settle; but if Christ speak the word, not only the storm ceases, but all the effects of it, all the remains of it. Great storms of doubt, and fear in the soul sometimes end in a wonderful calm.

3. This excited their astonishment (*v.* 27); *The men marvelled.* They had been long acquainted with the sea, and never saw a storm so immediately turned into a perfect calm, in all their lives. Observe, (1) Their admiration of Christ; *What manner of man is this!* Christ is a Nonsuch; everything in him is admirable: none so wise, so mighty, so amiable, as he. (2) The reason of it; *Even the winds and the sea obey him.* Upon this account, Christ is to be admired, that he has a commanding power even over *winds and seas.* He that can do this, can do anything, can do enough to encourage our confidence and comfort in him, in the most stormy day, within or without, Isa. xxvi. 4.

Verses 28–34

We have here the story of Christ's casting the devils out of two men that were possessed. The scope of this chapter is to show the divine power of Christ. Christ has not only all *power in heaven and earth* and all deep places, but has the keys of hell too. It was observed in general (*v.* 16), that Christ *cast out the spirits with his word;* here we have a particular instance of it. Though Christ was sent chiefly *to the lost sheep of the house of Israel,* yet some sallies he made among the borderers, as here, to gain this victory over Satan. Observe, concerning this legion of devils, What work they made where they *were,* and where they *went.*

I. What work they made where they *were;* which appears in the miserable condition of these two that were possessed by them.

1. They dwelt among *the tombs;* thence they came when they met Christ. Conversing among the graves increased the melancholy and frenzy of the poor possessed creatures, and also made them more formidable to other people, who generally startle at anything that stirs among *the tombs.*

2. They were *exceeding fierce;* not only ungovernable themselves, but mischievous to others, frightening many, having hurt some; *so that no man durst pass that way.* The devil bears malice to mankind, and shows it by making men spiteful and malicious one to another. Mutual enmities, where there should be mutual endearments and assistances, those lusts that war in the members, pride, envy, malice, revenge, make him as unfit for human society, as unworthy of it, and as much an enemy to the comfort of it, as these poor possessed creatures were.

3. They bid defiance to Jesus Christ, and disclaimed all interest in him, *v.* 29. It is an instance of the power of God over the devils, that they could not keep them from meeting Jesus Christ. His chains could hold them, when the chains that men made for them could not. But being brought before him, they protested against his jurisdiction, and broke out into a rage, *What have we to do with thee, Jesus, thou Son of God?* Here is,

(1) *One* word that the devil spoke like a *saint;* he addressed himself to Christ as *Jesus the Son of God;* a *good* word, and at this time, when it was a truth but in the proving, it was a *great* word too. Even the devils know, and believe, and confess Christ to be the *Son of God,* and yet they are devils still. It is not knowledge, but love, that distinguishes saints from devils.

(2) *Two* words that he said like a *devil,* like himself.

[1] A word of defiance; *What have we to do with thee?* It is true that the devils have nothing to do with Christ as a Saviour. O the depth of this mystery of divine love, that fallen man hath so much *to do with Christ,* when fallen angels have nothing *to do with* him! It is possible for men to call Jesus *the Son of God,* and yet have nothing to do with him. It is as true, that the devils desire not to have anything *to do with Christ* as a Ruler; they hate him, they are filled with enmity against him. But it is not true, that the devils have nothing *to do with Christ* as a Judge, for they have, and they know it.

[2] A word of dread and deprecation; "*Art thou come hither to torment us*—to cast us out from these men, and to restrain us from doing the hurt we would do?" To be turned out, and tied up, from doing mischief, is a torment to the devil. Should not we then count it our heaven to be doing well, and reckon that our torment, whether within or without, that hinders us from well-doing?

II. Let us now see what work they made where they *went,* when they were turned out of the men possessed, and that was into *a herd of swine,* which *was a good way off, v.* 30. These Gergesenes, though living on the other side Jordan, were Jews. What had they to do with *swine?*

1. How the devils seized the *swine.* Though they were *a good way off,* yet the devils had an eye upon them.

(1) They *asked* leave to enter *into the swine* (*v.* 31); *they besought him,* with all earnestness, *If thou cast us out, suffer us to go away into the herd of swine.* Hereby, [1] They discover their own inclination to do mischief, and what a pleasure it is to them. If they might not be suffered to hurt men in their bodies, they would hurt them in their goods, and in that too they intend hurt to their souls, by making Christ a burthen to them. [2] They own Christ's power over them; that, without his sufferance and permission, they could not so much as hurt a *swine.* This is comfortable to all the Lord's people, that, though the

devil's power be very great, yet it is limited, and not equal to his malice (what would become of us, if it were?) especially that it is under the control of our Lord Jesus.

(2) They *had* leave. Christ said unto them, *Go* (v. 32), as God did to Satan, when he desired leave to afflict Job. God does often, for wise and holy ends, permit the efforts of Satan's rage, and suffer him to do the mischief he would. Christ permitted this for the punishment of the Gadarenes, who perhaps, though Jews, took a liberty to eat *swine's* flesh, contrary to the law: however, their keeping *swine* bordered upon evil. The devils, in obedience to Christ's command, came out of the men, and having permission, *when they were come out, immediately they went into the herd of swine.* See what an industrious enemy Satan is, and how expeditious; he will lose no time in doing mischief.

2. *Whither they hurried them,* when they had seized them. They were made to *run violently down a steep place into the sea,* where they all perished, to the number of about *two thousand,* Mark v. 13. The possession which the devil gets is for destruction. Thus the devil hurries people to sin, hurries them to that which they have resolved against, and which they know will be shame and grief to them. Thus likewise, he hurries them to ruin.

3. *What effect this had upon the owners.* The report of it was soon brought them by the swine-herds, who seemed to be more concerned for the loss of the swine than anything else, for they went not to tell *what was befallen to the possessed of the devils,* till the swine were lost, v. 33. Christ went not *into the city,* but the news of his being there did.

Now, (1) Their curiosity brought them out to see Jesus. The *whole city came out to meet him.* Thus many go out, in profession, to meet Christ for company, that have no real affection for him, nor desire to know him.

(2) Their covetousness made them *willing to be rid of him.* Instead of inviting him into their city, or bringing their sick to him to be healed, they desired him to *depart out of their coasts.* And now the devils had what they aimed at in drowning the swine; *they* did it, and then made the people believe that *Christ* had done it, and so prejudiced them against him. Thus the devil sows tares in God's fields. There are a great many who prefer their swine before their Saviour, and so come short of Christ, and salvation by him.

CHAPTER 9

We have in this chapter remarkable instances of the power and pity of the Lord Jesus. His power and pity appear here in the good offices he did, I. To the bodies of people, in curing the palsy (ver. 2–8); raising to life the ruler's daughter, and healing the bloody issue (ver. 18–26); giving sight to two blind men (ver. 27–31); casting the devil out of one possessed (ver. 32–34); and healing all manner of sickness, ver. 35. II. To the souls of people; in forgiving sins (ver. 2); calling Matthew, and conversing freely with publicans and sinners (ver. 9–13); considering the frame of his disciples, with reference to the duty of fasting (ver. 14–17); preaching the gospel, and, in compassion to the multitude, providing preachers for them (ver. 35–38). Thus did he prove himself to be, as undoubtedly he is, the skilful, faithful Physician, both of soul and body, who has sufficient remedies for all the maladies of both.

Verses 1–8

The first words of this chapter oblige us to look back to the close of that which precedes it, where we find the Gadarenes so resenting the loss of their swine, that they were disgusted with Christ's company, and besought him to *depart out of their coasts.* Now here it follows, *He entered into a ship, and passed over.* They bid him begone, and he took them at their word. Christ will not tarry long where he is not welcome, but abides with those that covet and court his stay. He did not leave some destroying judgment behind him, to punish them, as they deserved, for their contempt and contumacy. He *entered into a ship, and passed over.* This was the day of his patience; he came not to *destroy men's lives,* but to save them; not to kill, but to cure.

He came *into his own city,* Capernaum, the principal place of his residence at present (Mark ii. 1), and therefore called *his own city.* When the Gadarenes desired Christ to depart, they of Capernaum received him. If Christ be affronted by some, there are others in whom he will be glorious; if one will not, another will.

Now the first occurrence was the cure of the man sick of the palsy.

I. The *faith of his friends* in bringing him to Christ. His distemper was such, that he could not come to Christ himself, but as he was carried. Even the halt and the lame may be brought to Christ, and they shall not be rejected by him. Little children cannot go to Christ themselves, but he will have an eye to the faith of those that bring them, and it shall not be in vain. *Jesus saw their faith,* the faith of the paralytic himself, as well as of them that brought him. Now their faith was, 1. A strong faith; they firmly believed that Jesus Christ both could and would heal him. 2. A humble faith; though the sick man was unable to stir a step, they would not ask Christ to make him a visit, but brought him to attend on Christ. It is fitter that we should wait on Christ, than he on us. 3. An active faith: in the belief of Christ's power and goodness, they brought the sick man to him, *lying on a bed,* which could not be done without a deal of pains. Note, a strong faith regards no obstacles in pressing after Christ.

II. The *favour of Christ,* in what he said to him; *Son, be of good cheer, thy sins be forgiven thee.* This was a sovereign cordial to a sick man. We read not of anything said to Christ. They set him before Christ; that was enough. It is not in vain to present ourselves and our friends to Christ, as the objects of his pity. Misery cries as well as sin, and mercy is no less quick of hearing than justice. Here is, in what Christ said, 1. A kind compellation; *Son.* 2. A gracious encouragement; *"Be of good cheer."* Probably the poor man was afraid of a rebuke for being brought in so rudely: but Christ does not stand upon ceremony; he bids him *be of good cheer.* 3. A good reason for that encouragement; *Thy sins are forgiven thee.* Now this may be considered as an introduction to the cure of his bodily distemper; "Thy sins are *pardoned,* and therefore thou shalt be healed." If we have the comfort of our reconciliation to God, with the comfort of our recovery from sickness, this makes it a mercy indeed to us, as to Hezekiah, Isa. xxxviii. 17. As a reason of the command to *be of good cheer,* whether he were cured of his disease or not; "Though I should not heal thee, wilt thou not say thou hast not sought in vain, if I assure thee that *thy sins are pardoned.*" They who, through grace, have some evidence of the forgiveness of their sins, have reason to be of good cheer, whatever outward troubles or afflictions they are under.

III. The *cavil of the scribes* at that which Christ said (v. 3); They *said within themselves,* in their hearts, *among themselves,* in their secret whisperings, *This man blasphemeth.* See how the greatest instance of heaven's power and grace is branded with the blackest note of hell's enmity.

IV. The conviction which Christ gave them of the unreasonableness of this cavil, before he proceeded.

1. He *charged them with it.* Though they did but say it within themselves he *knew their thoughts.* Note, Our Lord Jesus has the perfect knowledge of all that we say within ourselves. Thoughts are secret and sudden, yet naked and open before Christ. The sins that begin and end in the heart, and go no further, are as dangerous as any other.

2. He *argued them out of it,* v. 5, 6. Where observe,

(1) How he *asserts* his authority in the *kingdom of grace.* He undertakes to make out, that the *Son of Man,* the Mediator, has *power on earth to forgive sins.* What an encouragement is this to poor sinners to repent, that the power of pardoning sin is put into the hands of the *Son of Man,* who is bone of our bone! And if he had this *power on earth,* much more now that he is exalted to the Father's right hand.

(2) How he *proves* it, by his power in the kingdom of nature. Is it not as easy to say, *Thy sins are forgiven thee,* as to say, *Arise and walk?* He that can cure the disease can, in like manner, forgive the sin. This is a general argument to prove that Christ had a divine mission. The *power* that appeared in his cures proved him *sent of God;* and the *pity* that appeared in them proved him sent of God *to heal and save.* The palsy was but a symptom of the disease of sin; now he made it to appear, that he could effectually cure the original disease, by the immediate removal of that symptom. He that had power to remove the punishment, no doubt, had power to remit the sin. His great errand to the world was, to *save his people from their sins.*

V. The immediate cure of the sick man. Christ turned from disputing with them, and spake healing to him. The most necessary arguings must not divert us from doing the good that our *hand finds to do.* He saith to *the sick of the palsy, Arise, take up thy bed, and go to thine house;* and a healing, quickening, strengthening power accompanied this word (v. 7): *he arose and departed to his house.* He sent him to *his house,* to be a blessing to his family, where he had been so long a burthen.

VI. The impression which this made upon the multitude (v. 8); they *marvelled,* and *glorified God.* They glorified God, for what he had done for this poor man. Others' mercies should be our praises, and we should give him thanks for them. They admired him, not as God, or the Son of God, but as a *man* to whom God *had given such power.* God must be glorified in all the power that is *given to men* to do good. For all power is originally his; it is in him, as the Fountain, in men, as the cisterns.

Verses 9–13

In these verses we have an account of the grace and favour of Christ to poor publicans, particularly to Matthew.

I. The call of Matthew, the penman, of this gospel. Mark and Luke call him Levi. Some think Christ gave him the name of Matthew when he called him to be an apostle; as Simon, he surnamed Peter. Matthew signifies, *the gift of God.*

1. The posture that Christ's call found Matthew in. He was *sitting at the receipt of custom,* for he was a publican, Luke v. 27. He was in his calling, as the rest of them whom Christ called, *ch.* iv. 18. As Satan chooses to come, with his temptations, to those that are idle, so Christ chooses to come, with his calls, to those that are employed. It was a calling of ill fame among serious people; because it was attended with so much corruption and temptation, and there were so few in that business that were honest men. God has his remnant among all sorts of people. None can justify themselves in their unbelief, by their calling in the world; for there is no *sinful* calling, but some have been saved *out of it,* and no *lawful calling,* but some have been saved *in it.*

2. The preventing power of his call. We find not that Matthew looked after Christ, or had any inclination to follow him. He is found of those that seek him not. Christ *spoke first;* we have not chosen him, but he hath chosen us. He said, *Follow me.* The call was effectual, for he came at the call; *he arose, and*

followed him immediately; neither denied, nor deferred his obedience. The power of divine grace soon answers and overcomes all objections. He quitted his post, and his hopes of preferment in that way; and, though we find the disciples that were fishers occasionally fishing again afterwards, we never find Matthew at the receipt of custom again.

II. Christ's converse with publicans and sinners upon this occasion; *Jesus sat at meat in the house,* v. 10. The other evangelists tell us, that Matthew made a *great feast,* which the poor fishermen, when they were called, were not able to do. But when he comes to speak of this himself, he neither tells us that it was his own house, nor that it was a feast, but only that he *sat at meat in the house.* It well becomes us to speak sparingly of our own good deeds.

When Matthew invited Christ, he invited his disciples to *come along with him.* Note, They that welcome Christ, must welcome all that are his, for his sake, and let them have a room in their hearts. He invited many publicans and sinners to *meet him.* This was the chief thing Matthew aimed at in this treat, that he might have an opportunity of bringing his old associates acquainted with Christ. They who are effectually brought to Christ themselves, cannot but be desirous that others also may be brought to him, and ambitious of contributing something towards it. True grace will not contentedly eat its morsels alone, but will invite others. And surely some of them will *follow him,* as he *followed Christ.* Thus did Andrew and Philip, John i. 41, 45; iv. 29.

III. The displeasure of the Pharisees at this, v. 11. They cavilled at it; *why eateth your Master with publicans and sinners?* Christ was quarrelled with. It was not the least of his sufferings, that he *endured the contradiction of sinners against himself.* Though he never spoke or did anything amiss, everything he said and did was found fault with. Thus he taught us to expect and prepare for reproach, and to bear it patiently. They that quarrelled with him were the Pharisees. They were very strict in avoiding *sinners,* but not in avoiding *sin;* none greater zealots than they for the *form* of godliness, nor greater enemies to the *power* of it. They brought their cavil, not to Christ himself; they had not the courage to face him with it, but to his disciples. Being offended at the Master, they quarrel with the disciples. It concerns Christians to be able to vindicate and justify Christ, and his doctrines and laws, and to be *ready always to give an answer to those that ask them a reason of the hope that is in them,* 1 Peter iii. 15. While he is an Advocate for us in heaven, let us be advocates for him on earth, and make his reproach our own. The complaint was his *eating with publicans and sinners:* to be intimate with wicked people is against the law of God (Ps. cxix. 115; i. 1); and perhaps by accusing Christ of this to his disciples, they hoped to tempt them from him. To be intimate with publicans was against the *tradition of the elders,* and, therefore, they looked upon it as a heinous thing. They were angry with Christ for this, (1) Because they *wished ill to him.* It is an easy and very common thing to put the worst constructions upon the best words and actions. (2) Because they *wished no good to* publicans and sinners, but envied Christ's favour to them. It may justly be suspected, that they have not the grace of God themselves, who grudge others a share in that grace.

IV. The defence that Christ made for himself and his disciples, in justification of their converse with publicans and sinners. Let him alone to vindicate himself and to plead his own cause, to answer for himself, and for us too. Two things he urges in his defence,

1. The necessity and exigence of the case of the publicans, which called aloud for his help. It was

the extreme necessity of poor, lost sinners, that brought Christ from the pure regions above, to these impure ones; and the same was it, that brought him into this company which was thought impure. He proves the necessity of the case of the publicans: *they that be whole need not a physician, but they that are sick.* The publicans are sick, and they need one to help and heal them, which the Pharisees think they do not. Note, Sin is the sickness of the soul. It is deforming, weakening, disquieting, wasting, killing, but, blessed be God, not incurable. Jesus Christ is the great Physician of souls. Wise and good men should be as physicians to all about them; Christ was so. Sin-sick souls have need of this Physician, for their disease is dangerous; nature will not help itself; no man can help us; such need have we of Christ, that we are undone, eternally undone, without him. There are multitudes who fancy themselves to be sound and whole, who think they have *no need of Christ,* but that they can shift for themselves well enough without him, as Laodicea, Rev. iii. 17. See John ix. 40, 41. He proves, that their necessity did sufficiently justify his conduct, for that necessity made it *an act of charity,* which ought always to be preferred before the formalities of a religious profession, in which *bene*ficence and *muni*ficence are far better than *magni*ficence, as much as substance is better than shows or shadows. If to do well ourselves is better than sacrifice, as Samuel shews (1 Sam. xv. 22, 23), much more to do good to others. To promote the conversion of souls is the greatest act of mercy imaginable; it is *saving a soul from death,* James v. 20. Observe how Christ quotes this, *Go ye and learn what that meaneth.* It is not enough to be acquainted with the letter of scripture, but we must learn to understand the meaning of it. And they have best learned the meaning of the scriptures, that have learned how to apply them as a reproof to their own faults, and a rule for their own practice. This scripture which Christ quoted, served not only to vindicate him, but, [1] To show wherein true religion consists; not in external observances: but in doing all the good we can to the bodies and souls of others; in righteousness and peace. [2] To condemn the Pharisaical hypocrisy of those who place religion in rituals, more than in morals, *ch.* xxiii. 23.

2. The nature and end of his own commission. "*I am not come to call the righteous, but sinners to repentance,* and therefore must converse with publicans." (1) What his errand was; it was to *call to repentance.* A call to us to change our mind and to change our way. (2) With whom his errand lay; not with *the righteous,* but with *sinners.* If the children of men had not been *sinners,* there had been no occasion for Christ's coming among them. Therefore his *greatest business* lies with the *greatest sinners*; the more dangerous the sick man's case is, the more occasion there is for the physician's help. Christ came into the world to *save sinners,* but especially *the chief* (1 Tim. i. 15). Christ came not with an expectation of succeeding among *the righteous,* those who conceit themselves so, and therefore will sooner be sick of their Saviour, than sick of their sins, but among the convinced humble *sinners*; to them Christ will come, for to them he will be welcome.

Verses 14–17

The objections which were made against Christ and his disciples gave occasion to some of the most profitable of his discourses; and thus the wisdom of Christ brings good out of evil. So here, from a reflection upon the conduct of his family, arose a discourse concerning his tenderness for it.

I. The objection which the disciples of John made against Christ's disciples, for not fasting so often as they did; which they are charged with, as another instance of the looseness of their profession, besides that of eating with publicans and sinners. It appears by the other evangelists (Mark ii. 18 and Luke v. 33) that the disciples of the Pharisees joined with them because they, being more in favour with Christ and his disciples, could do it more plausibly. It is no new thing for bad men to set good men together by the ears: if the people of God differ in their sentiments, designing men will take that occasion to sow discord. Now the complaint is, *Why do we and the Pharisees fast often, but thy disciples fast not?* It is a pity the duties of religion, which ought to be the confirmations of holy love, should be made the occasions of strife and contention.

1. How they boasted of their own fasting. *We and the Pharisees fast often.* Fasting has in all ages of the church been consecrated, upon special occasions, to the service of religion; the Pharisees were much in it. The disciples of John *fasted often.* The severer part of religion is often most *minded* by those that are yet under the discipline of the Spirit, as a *Spirit of bondage,* whereas, though these are good in their place, we must pass through them to that life of delight in God and dependence on him, to which these should lead. There is a proneness in professors to brag of their own performances in religion, and not only to boast of them before men, but to plead them before God, and confide in them as a righteousness.

2. How they blamed Christ's disciples for not fasting so often as they did. *Thy disciples fast not.* They could not but know, that Christ had instructed his disciples to keep their fasts private, and to manage themselves so as that they might not *appear unto men to fast.* We must not judge of people's religion by that which falls under the eye and observation of the world. It is common for vain professors to make themselves a standard in religion as if all that did less than they, did too little, and all that did more than they, did too much.

3. How they brought this complaint to Christ. If Christ's disciples, either by omission or commission, give offence, Christ himself will be sure to hear of it, and be reflected upon for it. *O Jesus, are these thy Christians?* The quarrel with Christ was brought to the disciples (v. 11), the quarrel with the disciples was brought to Christ (v. 14), this is the way of sowing discord and killing love, to set people against ministers, ministers against people, and one friend against another.

II. The apology which Christ made for his disciples in this matter. When they had nothing to say for themselves, he had something ready to say for them. What we do according to the precept and pattern of Christ, he will be sure to bear us out in.

Two things Christ pleads in defence of their *not fasting.*

1. That it was not a season proper for that duty (v. 15): *Can the children of the bride-chamber mourn, as long as the bridegroom is with them?* Christ's answer is so framed, as that it might sufficiently justify the practice of his own disciples, and yet not condemn the institution of John, or the practice of his disciples. When at any time we are unjustly censured, our care must be only to clear ourselves, not to recriminate, or throw dirt upon others.

Now his argument is taken from the common usage of joy and rejoicing during the continuance of marriage solemnities, when all instances of melancholy and sorrow are looked upon as improper and absurd. The disciples of Christ were the *children of the bride-chamber,* invited to the wedding-feast, and welcome there. The faithful followers of Christ, who have the Spirit of adoption, have a continual feast, while they who have the spirit of bondage and fear, cannot rejoice for joy, as other people. The disciples of

Christ had *the bridegroom with them*, which the disciples of John had not; their master was now cast into prison and therefore it was seasonable for them to *fast often*. Such a day would come upon the disciples of Christ, when the bridegroom should be taken from them, and *then should they fast*. The thoughts of parting grieved them when he was going, John xvi. 6. Tribulation and affliction befell them when he was gone, and gave them occasion of *mourning* and *praying*, that is, of religious fasting. It is merry or melancholy with the children of the bride-chamber, according as they have more or less of the bridegroom's presence. The presence and nearness of the sun makes day and summer, his absence and distance, night and winter. Christ is all in all to the church's joy. Every duty is to be done in its proper season. See Eccles. vii. 14; James v. 13. There is a time to mourn and a time to laugh, to each of which we should accommodate ourselves, and bring forth fruit in due season.

2. That they had not strength sufficient for that duty. This is set forth in two similitudes, one of putting *new cloth into an old garment*, which does but pull the old to pieces (*v.* 16); the other of putting *new wine into old bottles*, which does but burst the bottles, *v.* 17. Christ's disciples were not able to bear these severe exercises so well as those of John and of the Pharisees. They, being taken immediately from their callings, had not been used to such religious austerities, and were unfit for them, and would by them be rather unfitted for their other work. Some duties of religion are harder and more difficult than others, such as religious fasting and the duties that attend it. The best of Christ's disciples pass through a state of infancy; all the trees in Christ's garden are not of a growth, nor all his scholars in the same form; there are *babes in Christ* and grown men. The weakness and infirmity of young Christians ought to be considered: as the food provided for them must be such as is proper for their age (1 Cor. iii. 2; Heb. v. 12), so must the work be that is cut out for them. Christ would not speak to his disciples that which they could not then bear, John xvi. 12. Young beginners in religion must not be put upon the hardest duties at first, lest they be discouraged. Such as was Jacob's care of his children and cattle, not to overdrive them (Gen. xxxiii. 13), such is Christ's care of the little ones of his family, and the lambs of his flock: he gently leads them. There may be *over*-doing even in *well*-doing, a being *righteous over-much*; and such an *over*-doing as may prove an *un*doing through the subtlety of Satan.

Verses 18–26

We have here two passages of history put together; that of the raising of Jairus's daughter to life, and that of the curing of the woman that had *the bloody issue*, as he was going to Jairus's house, which is introduced in a parenthesis, in the midst of the other; for Christ's miracles were thick sown, and interwoven. He was called to do these good works from speaking the things foregoing, in answer to the cavils of the Pharisees, *v.* 18: *While he spake these things;* and we may suppose it a pleasing interruption given to that unpleasant work of disputation, which, though sometimes needful, a good man will gladly leave, to go about a work of devotion or charity.

I. The ruler's address to Christ, *v.* 18. *A certain ruler*, a ruler of the synagogue, *came and worshipped him. Have any of the rulers believed on him?* Yes, here was one. This ruler had a little daughter, of twelve years old, just dead, and this breach made upon his family comforts was the occasion of his coming to Christ. In trouble we should visit God: the death of our relations should drive us to Christ, who is our life. Now observe,

1. His humility in this address to Christ. He came with his errand to Christ himself. It is no disparagement to the greatest rulers, personally to attend on the Lord Jesus. He *worshipped him*. They that would receive mercy from Christ must give honour to Christ.

2. His faith in this address; "*My daughter is even now dead*," and though any other physician would now come too late, yet Christ comes not too late; he is a Physician after death, for he is *the resurrection and the life*; "*O come* then, *and lay thy hand upon her, and she shall live.*" This was quite above the power of nature, yet within the power of Christ, who has *life in himself, and quickeneth whom he will*. We cannot in faith bring him such a request as this; while there is life, there is hope, and room for prayer; but when our friends are dead, the case is determined. But while Christ was here upon earth working miracles, such a confidence as this was not only allowable but very commendable.

II. The readiness of Christ to comply with his address, *v.* 19. *Jesus immediately arose*, left his company, *and followed him*; he was not only willing to grant him what he desired, in raising his daughter to life, but to gratify him so far as to come to his house to do it. Surely *he never said to the seed of Jacob, Seek ye me in vain*. And observe, when *Jesus followed him, so did his disciples*, whom he had chosen for his constant companions; it was not for state, or that he might come with observation, that he took his attendants with him, but that they might be the witnesses of his miracles, who were hereafter to be the preachers of his doctrine.

III. The healing of the poor woman's bloody issue. I call her a poor woman, not only because her case was piteous, but because, though she had had something in the world, she had *spent it all upon physicians*, for the cure of her distemper, and was never the better; which was a double aggravation of the misery of her condition, that she had impoverished herself for the recovery of her health, and yet had not her health either. This *woman was diseased with a constant issue of blood twelve years* (*v.* 20); a disease, which was not only weakening and wasting, but which also rendered her ceremonially unclean, and shut her *out from the courts of the Lord's house*; but it did not cut her off from approaching to Christ. She applied herself to Christ, and received mercy from him, by the way.

1. The woman's great faith in Christ, and in his power. Her disease was of such a nature, that her modesty would not suffer her to speak openly to Christ for a cure, as others did, but she believed him to have such an overflowing fulness of healing virtue, that the very *touch of his garment* would be her cure. This, perhaps, had something of fancy mixed with faith; for she had no precedent for this way of application to Christ. But what *weakness of understanding* there was in it, Christ was pleased to overlook, and to accept the sincerity and strength of her faith. She believed she should be healed if she did but *touch the* very *hem of his garment*, the very extremity of it. There is virtue in everything that belongs to Christ. Such a fulness of grace is there in Christ, that *from it we may all receive*, John i. 16.

2. Christ's great favour to this woman. He did not suspend his healing influences, but suffered this bashful patient to steal a cure unknown to any one else, though she could not think to do it unknown to him. And now she was well content to be gone, for she had what she came for, but Christ was not willing to let her go so: the triumphs of her faith must be to her praise and honour. He *turned about* to see her (*v.* 22), and soon discovered her. It is great encouragement to humble Christians, that they who hide themselves from men are known to Christ,

who sees in secret their applications to heaven when most private.

(1) He *puts gladness into her heart*, by that word, *Daughter, be of good comfort*. She feared being chidden for coming clandestinely, but she is encouraged. He calls her *daughter*, for he spoke to her with the tenderness of a father, as he did *to the man sick of the palsy* (v. 2), whom he called *son*. He bids her *be of good comfort*. His bidding her *be comforted*, brought comfort with it, as his saying, *Be ye whole*, brought health with it.

(2) He puts honour upon her faith. That grace of all others gives most honour to Christ, and therefore he puts most honour upon it; *Thy faith has made thee whole*. This woman had more faith than she thought she had. She was spiritually healed; that cure was wrought in her which is the proper fruit and effect of faith, the pardon of sin and the work of grace. Her bodily cure was the fruit of faith, of her faith, and that made it a happy, comfortable cure indeed. They out of whom the devils were cast, were helped by Christ's sovereign power; some by the faith of others (as v. 2); but it is *thy faith that has made thee whole*.

IV. The posture in which he found the ruler's house, v. 23.—He *saw the people and the minstrels*, or musicians, *making a noise*. The house was in a hurry: such work does death make, when it comes into a family; and, perhaps, the necessary cares that arise at such a time, when our dead is to be decently buried out of our sight, give some useful diversion to that grief which is apt to prevail and play the tyrant. The people in the neighbourhood came together to condole on account of the loss, to comfort the parents, to prepare for, and attend on, the funeral, which the Jews were not wont to defer long. The musicians were among them, according to the custom of the Gentiles, with their doleful, melancholy tunes, to increase the grief, and stir up the lamentations of those that attended on this occasion. Thus they indulged a passion that is apt enough of itself to grow intemperate, and affected to *sorrow as those that had no hope*. See how religion provides cordials, where irreligion administers corrosives. Heathenism aggravates that grief which Christianity studies to assuage. The parents, who were immediately touched with the affliction, were silent, while *the people and minstrels*, whose lamentations were forced, made such a noise. The loudest grief is not always the greatest; rivers are most noisy where they run shallow. *That grief is most sincere, which shuns observation.*

V. The rebuke that Christ gave to this hurry and noise, v. 24. He said, *Give place*. Note, Sometimes, when *the sorrow of the world* prevails, it is difficult for Christ and his comforts to enter. They that harden themselves in sorrow, and, like Rachel, *refuse to be comforted*, should think they hear Christ saying to their disquieting thoughts, *Give place*. He gives a good reason why they should not thus disquiet themselves and one another; *The maid is not dead but sleepeth*. 1. This was eminently true of this maid, that was immediately to be raised to life; she was really dead, but not so to Christ, who knew within himself what he would do, and could do. This death must be but of short continuance, and therefore is but a sleep, like one night's rest. 2. It is in a sense true of all that die, chiefly of them *that die in the Lord*. (1) Death is a sleep. All nations and languages, for the softening of that which is so dreadful, and withal so unavoidable, and the reconciling of themselves to it, have agreed to call it so. It is not the sleep of the soul; its activity ceases not; but the sleep of the body, which lies down in the grave, still and silent. Sleep is a short death, and death a long sleep. But *the death of the righteous* is in a special manner to be looked upon as a sleep, Isa. lvii. 2.

They sleep in Jesus (1 Thess. iv. 14); they not only rest from the toils and labours of the day, but *rest in hope* of a joyful waking again in the morning of the resurrection, when they shall wake refreshed, wake to a new life, *wake to sleep no more*. (2) The consideration of this should moderate our grief at the death of our dear relations: say not, They *are* lost; no, they are but *gone before*. The apostle speaks of it as an absurd thing to imagine that *they that are fallen asleep in Christ are perished* (1 Cor. xv. 18).

Now could it be thought that such a comfortable word as this, from the mouth of our Lord Jesus, should be ridiculed as it was? *They laughed him to scorn.* The words and works of Christ which cannot be understood, yet are not therefore to be despised. We must adore the mystery of divine sayings, even when they seem to contradict what we think ourselves most confident of. Yet even this tended to the confirmation of the miracle: for it seems she was so apparently dead, that it was thought a very ridiculous thing to say otherwise.

VI. The raising of the damsel to life by the power of Christ, v. 25. *The people were put forth.* Scorners that laugh at what they see and hear that is above their capacity, are not proper witnesses of the wonderful works of Christ, the glory of which lies not in pomp, but in power.

Christ went in and *took her by the hand*, as it were to awake her, and to help her up. The high priest, that typified Christ, was not to come near the dead (Lev. xxi. 10, 11), but Christ *touched the dead*. Christ, having power to raise the dead, is above the infection, and therefore is not shy of touching them. He *took her by the hand, and the maid arose*. So easily, so effectually was the miracle wrought; by a touch. Dead souls are not raised to spiritual life, unless Christ *take them by the hand*. He helps us up, or we lie still.

VII. The general notice that was taken of this miracle, though it was wrought privately; v. 26, the *fame thereof went abroad into all that land:* it was the common subject of discourse. Christ's works are more talked of than considered and improved. Though we at this distance have not seen Christ's miracles, yet blessed *are they that have not seen, and yet have believed*, John xx. 29.

Verses 27–34
In these verses we have an account of two more miracles wrought together by our Saviour.

I. The giving of sight to two blind men, v. 27–31. Christ is the Fountain of light as well as life.

1. The importunate address of the blind men to Christ. He was returning from the ruler's house to his own lodgings, and these *blind men followed him*, as beggars do, with their incessant cries, v. 27. He that cured diseases so easily, so effectually, and, withal, at so cheap a rate, shall have patients enough.

(1) The title which these blind men gave to Christ; *Thou Son of David, have mercy on us*. The promise made to David, that of his loins the Messiah should come, was well known. At this time there was a general expectation of his appearing; these blind men know, and own, and proclaim it in the streets of Capernaum, that he is come, and that this is he. They who, by the providence of God, are deprived of bodily sight, may yet, by the grace of God, have *the eyes of their understanding so enlightened*, as to discern those great things of God, *which are hid from the wise and prudent*.

(2) Their petition, *Have mercy on us*. Whatever our necessities and burthens are, we need no more for supply and support, than a share in the *mercy of our Lord Jesus*. Whether he heal us or no, if he *have mercy on us*, we have enough. They did not each of them say for himself, *Have mercy on me*, but both for one another, *Have mercy on us*. Fellow-sufferers should be

joint-petitioners. In Christ there is enough for all.

(3) Their importunity in this request; they *followed him, crying.* It seems, he did not take notice of them at first, for he would try their faith, which he knew to be strong; would quicken their prayers, and make his cures the more valued, when they did not always come at the first word; and would teach us to *continue instant in prayer, always to pray, and not to faint. When he came into the house,* they *followed him* thither, and *came to him.* Christ's doors are always open to believing and importunate petitioners; it seemed rude in them to rush into the house after him, when he desired to retire; but, such is the tenderness of our Lord Jesus, that they were not more bold than welcome.

2. The confession of faith, which Christ drew from them upon this occasion. When they came to him for mercy, he asked them, *Believe ye that I am able to do this?* Faith is the great condition of Christ's favours. They who would receive the *mercy* of Christ, must firmly believe the *power* of Christ. What we would have him do for us, we must be fully assured that he is *able to do.* Nature may work fervency, but it is only grace that can work faith. They had intimated their faith in the office of Christ as *Son of David,* and in his mercy; but Christ demands likewise a profession of faith in his power. *Believe ye that I am able?* This will amount to their belief of his being not only *the Son of David,* but *the Son of God;* for it is God's prerogative to *open the eyes of the blind* (Ps. cxlvi. 8). Still it is put to us, *Believe we that Christ is able to do for us.* To believe the power of Christ is not only to assure ourselves of it, but to commit ourselves to it, and encourage ourselves in it.

To this question they give an immediate answer, without hesitation: they said, *Yea, Lord.*

3. The cure that Christ wrought on them; he *touched their eyes, v.* 29. He put the cure upon their faith, *According to your faith be it unto you.* When they begged for a cure, he enquired into their faith (*v.* 28), *Believe ye that I am able?* He did not enquire into their wealth, whether they were able to pay him for a cure; but into their faith; and now they had professed their faith he referred the matter to that: "The power you believe in shall be exerted for you; *According to your faith be it unto you.*" It is a great comfort to true believers that Jesus Christ knows their faith, and is well pleased with it. Though it be weak, though others do not discern it, though they themselves are ready to question it, it is known to him. They who apply themselves to Jesus Christ, shall be dealt with *according to their faith*; not according to their *fancies,* nor according to their *profession.* True believers may be sure to find all that favour which is offered in the gospel; and our comforts ebb or flow, according as our faith is stronger or weaker; we are not straitened in Christ, let us not then be straighted in ourselves.

4. The charge he gave them to keep it private (*v.* 30), *See that no man know it.* In the good we do, we must not seek our own praise, but only the glory of God. It must be more our care and endeavour to be useful, than to be known and observed to be so. Some think that Christ, in keeping it private, showed his displeasure against the people of Capernaum, who had seen so many miracles, and yet believed not. It is just in Christ to deny the means of conviction to those that are obstinate in their infidelity; and to shroud the light from those that shut their eyes against it. He did it in discretion, for his own preservation; because the more he was proclaimed, the more jealous would the rulers of the Jews be of his growing interest among the people.

But honour is like the shadow, which, as it flees from those that follow it, so it follows those that flee from it (*v.* 21); *They spread abroad his fame.* Though

it may be excused as honestly meant for the honour of Christ, yet it cannot be justified, being done against a particular charge. Whenever we profess to direct our intention to the glory of God, we must see to it that the action be according to the will of God.

II. The healing of a *dumb man,* that was *possessed with a devil.*

1. His case, which was very sad. He was under the power of the devil in this particular instance, that he was disabled from speaking, *v.* 32. See the calamitous state of this world, and how various the afflictions of the afflicted are! We have no sooner dismissed *two blind men,* but we meet with a *dumb man.* How thankful should we be to God for our sight and speech! When the devil gets possession of a soul, it is made silent as to anything that is good; dumb in prayers and praises. This poor creature *they brought to Christ,* who entertained not only those that came of themselves in their own faith, but those that were *brought to him* by their friends in the faith of others. They brought him in just as *the blind man went out.* See how unwearied Christ was in doing good; how closely one good work followed another! Treasures of mercy, wondrous mercy, are hid in him; which may be continually communicated, but can never be exhausted.

2. His cure, which was very sudden (*v.* 33), *When the devil was cast out, the dumb spake.* Christ's cures strike at the root, and remove the effect by taking away the cause; they open the lips, by breaking Satan's power in the soul.

3. The consequences of this cure.

(1) *The multitudes marvelled;* and well they might; though *few believed, many wondered.* The admiration of the common people is sooner raised than any other affection.

(2) *The Pharisees* blasphemed, *v.* 34. When they could not gainsay the convincing evidence of these miracles, they fathered them upon the devil, as if they had been wrought by compact and collusion: *he casteth out devils* (say they) by *the prince of the devils.* This breathes nothing but malice and falsehood, and hellish enmity in the highest degree; it is diabolism all over. Because the people marvelled, they must say something to diminish the miracle, and this was all they could say.

Verses 35-38

I. A conclusion of the foregoing account of Christ's preaching and miracles (*v.* 35); *He went about all the cities teaching and healing.* This is the same we had before, iv. 23. There it ushers in the more particular record of Christ's preaching (*ch.* v. vi. and vii) and of his cures (*ch.* viii and ix), and here it is elegantly repeated in the close of these instances, as the *quod erat demonstrandum—the point to be proved;* as if the evangelist should say, "Now I hope I have made it out that Christ preached and healed."

Observe how Christ in his preaching had respect,

1. To the private towns. He visited not only the great and wealthy cities, but the poor, obscure villages; there he preached, there he healed. The souls of those that are meanest in the world are as precious to Christ, and should be to us, as the souls of those that make the greatest figure.

2. To the public worship. He taught *in their synagogues,* (1) That he might bear a testimony to solemn assemblies. (2) That he might have an opportunity of preaching there, where people were gathered together, with an expectation to hear.

II. A preface, or introduction, to the account in the following chapter, of his sending forth his apostles. *He* took notice of *the multitude* (*v.* 36); not only of the crowds that *followed him,* but of the vast numbers of people with whom (as he passed along) he observed the country to be replenished: so very populous was that nation now grown; and it was the effect of God's blessing on Abraham.

1. He pitied them, and was concerned for them (v. 36); *He was moved with compassion on them;* not upon a temporal account, as he pitied the blind, and lame, and sick; but upon a spiritual account; he was concerned to see them ignorant and careless, and ready to perish for lack of vision. It was pity to souls that brought him from heaven to earth, and there to the cross. Christ pities those most that pity themselves least; so should we.

See what moved this pity. (1) *They fainted*: they were destitute, vexed, wearied. They wanted help for their souls, and had none at hand that was good for anything. The scribes and Pharisees filled them with vain notions, therefore *they fainted*; for what spiritual health, and life, and vigour can there be in those souls, that are fed with husks and ashes, instead of *the bread of life*? (2) *They were scattered abroad, as sheep having no shepherd.* No creature is more apt to go astray than a sheep, and when gone astray more helpless, shiftless, and exposed, or more unapt to find the way home again: sinful souls *are as lost sheep*; they need the care of shepherds to bring them back. The case of those people is very pitiable, who either have no ministers at all, or those that are as bad as none; that seek their own things, not *the things of Christ*.

2. He excited his disciples to pray for them. It appears (Luke vi. 12, 13) that upon this occasion, before he sent out his apostles, he did himself spend a great deal of time in prayer. Those we pity we should pray for.

(1) How the case stood; *The harvest truly is plenteous, but the labourers are few.* There was a great deal of work to be done, and a great deal of good likely to be done, but there wanted hands to do it. It was an encouragement, that *the harvest* was so *plenteous*. It was not strange, that there were multitudes that needed instruction, but it was what does not often happen, that they who needed it, desired it. It is a blessed thing, to see people in love with good preaching. The valleys are then covered over with corn, and there are hopes it may be well gathered in. A harvest-day should be a busy day. It was a pity when it was so that *the labourers* should be so *few*; that the corn should shed and spoil, and rot upon the ground for want of reapers; loiterers many, but *labourers* very *few*.

(2) What was their duty in this case (v. 38); *Pray ye therefore the Lord of the harvest.* When things look discouraging, we should pray more and then we should complain and fear less. [1] God is *the Lord of the harvest; my Father is the Husbandman,* John xv. 1. It is for him and to him, and to his service and honour that *the harvest* is gathered in. It is very comfortable to those who wish well to *the harvest-work,* that God himself presides in it, who will be sure to order all for the best. [2] Ministers are and should be *labourers* in God's *harvest*; the ministry is a *work* and must be attended to accordingly; it is *harvest-work,* which is needful work; work that requires everything to be done in its season, and diligence to do it thoroughly; but it is pleasant work; they *reap in joy,* and the joy of the preachers of the gospel is likened to the *joy of harvest* (Isa. ix. 2, 3); and *he that reapeth receiveth wages; the hire of the labourers* that reap down God's field, shall not be *kept back,* as theirs was, James v. 4. It is God's work to *send forth labourers;* Christ makes ministers (Eph. iv. 11); the office is of his appointing, the qualifications of his working, the call of his giving. All that love Christ and souls, should show it by their earnest prayers to God, especially when *the harvest is plenteous, that he would send forth* more skilful, faithful, wise, and industrious *labourers into his harvest.* Christ puts his

friends upon praying this, just before he sends apostles forth to labour in *the harvest.* Further observe, that Christ said this to his disciples, who were to be employed as *labourers.* They must pray, First, That God *would send them forth. Here am I, send me,* Isa. vi. 8. Commissions, given in answer to prayer, are most likely to be successful; Paul is a chosen vessel, for *behold he prays,* Acts ix. 11, 15.

CHAPTER 10

This chapter is an ordination sermon, which our Lord Jesus preached, when he advanced his twelve disciples to the degree and dignity of apostles. I. The general commission that was given them, ver. 1. II. The names of the persons to whom this commission was given, ver. 2–4. III. The instructions that were given them. 1. Concerning the services they were to do; their preaching; their working miracles; to whom they must apply themselves; how they must behave themselves; and in what method they must proceed, ver. 5–15. 2. Concerning the sufferings they were to undergo. They are told what they should suffer, and from whom; counsels are given them what course to take when persecuted, and encouragements to bear up cheerfully under their sufferings, ver. 16–42.

Verses 1–4

I. Who they were that Christ ordained to be his apostles or ambassadors; they were his disciples, v. 1. He had called them sometime before to be disciples, and he then told them that they should be made fishers of men, which promise he now performed. Christ commonly confers honours and graces by degrees. All this while Christ had kept these twelve,

1. In a state of probation. Though he knows what is in man, though he knew from the first what was in them (John vi. 70), yet he took this method to give an example to his church. The ministry being a great trust, it is fit that men should be tried for a time, before they are entrusted with it.

2. In a state of preparation. All this while he had been fitting them for this great work. He prepared them by *taking them to be with him.* The best preparative for the work of the ministry, is an acquaintance and communion with Jesus Christ. They that would *serve Christ,* must first be *with him* (John xii. 26). Paul had Christ revealed, not only *to him,* but *in him,* before he went to preach him among the Gentiles, Gal. i. 16. By *teaching them;* they were with him as scholars or pupils, he opened the scriptures to them, and opened their understandings to understand the scriptures: to them it was given to *know the mysteries of the kingdom of heaven,* and to them they were *made plain.* They that design to be teachers must first be learners; they must receive, that they may give. Christ *taught his disciples* before he sent them forth (ch. v. 2), and afterwards, when he enlarged their commission, he gave them more ample instructions, Acts i. 3.

II. What the commission was that he gave them.

1. He *called them to him,* v. 1. He had called them to come *after* him before; now he calls them to come *to* him, admits them to a greater familiarity. The priests under the law were said to *draw near* and *approach* God, nearer than the people; the same may be said of gospel ministers; they are called to draw near to Christ. It is observable, that when the disciples were to be *instructed,* they *came unto* him of their own accord, *ch.* v. 1. But now they were to be *ordained,* he *called them.* It well becomes the disciples of Christ to be more forward to learn than to teach. We must *wait for a call,* a clear call, ere we take upon us to *teach others.*

2. He *gave them power,* ἐξουσίαν, *authority* in his name, to command men to obedience, and for the confirmation of that authority, to command devils too into a subjection. All rightful authority is derived from Jesus Christ. All power is given to him without limitation. Some of his honour he put on his ministers,

as Moses put some of his on Joshua. He gave them *power over unclean spirits,* and over *all manner of sickness.* The design of the gospel was to *conquer the devil* and to *cure the world.*

(1) He gave them power *against unclean spirits, to cast them out.* The power that is committed to the ministers of Christ, is directly levelled against the devil and his kingdom. Christ gave them power to cast him out of the bodies of people; but that was to signify the destruction of his *spiritual kingdom,* and all the works of the devil; for which purpose the *Son of God* was *manifested.*

(2) He gave them power to *heal all manner of sickness.* He authorised them to work miracles for the confirmation of their doctrine, to prove that it was of God; to prove that it is not only faithful, but well *worthy of all acceptation;* that the design of the gospel is to heal and save; but the miracles Christ wrought, and appointed his apostles to work, evince him to be, not only the great Teacher and Ruler, but the Redeemer, of the world. *They were to heal all manner of sickness,* and *all manner of disease,* without exception even of those that are reckoned incurable, and the reproach of physicians. In the grace of the gospel there is a salve for every sore, a remedy for every malady. There is no spiritual disease so malignant, so inveterate, but there is a sufficiency of power in Christ for the cure of it. Let none therefore say there is no hope, or that the breach is wide as the sea, that cannot be healed.

III. The number and names of those that were commissioned; they are made apostles, that is, messengers. An angel, and an apostle, both signify the same thing—one *sent on an errand,* an ambassador. All faithful ministers are sent of Christ, but they that were first, and immediately, sent by him, are eminently called *apostles,* the prime ministers of state in his kingdom. Christ himself is called an apostle (Heb. iii. 1), for he was *sent by the Father,* and so sent them, John xx. 21. The prophets were called God's messengers.

1. Their number was twelve, referring to the number of the tribes of Israel. The gospel church must be the Israel of God; the Jews must be first invited into it; the apostles must be spiritual fathers, to beget a seed to Christ. Israel after the flesh is to be rejected for their infidelity; these twelve, therefore, are appointed to be the fathers of another Israel. These twelve, by their doctrine, were to judge the twelve tribes of Israel, Luke xxii. 30. This was that famous jury (and to make it a grand jury, Paul was added to it) that was impanelled to enquire between the King of kings, and the body of mankind.

2. Their names are here left upon record, and it is their honour; yet in this they had more reason to rejoice, that their names were *written in heaven* (Luke x. 20).

(1) There are some of these twelve apostles, of whom we know no more, from the scripture, than their names; as Bartholomew, and Simon the Canaanite. All the good ministers of Christ are not alike famous, nor their actions alike celebrated.

(2) They are named by couples; for at first they were sent forth *two and two,* because *two are better than one;* they would be serviceable to each other, and the more serviceable jointly to Christ and souls; what one forgot the other would remember. Three couples of them were brethren; Peter and Andrew, James and John, and the other James and Lebbeus. It is an excellent thing, when brethren by nature are brethren by grace, and those two bonds strengthen each other.

(3) Peter is named first, because he was first called; or because he was the most forward man among them, and upon all occasions made himself the mouth of the rest; but that gave him no power

over the rest of the apostles, nor is there the least mark of any supremacy that was given to him, or ever claimed by him, in this sacred college.

(4) Matthew, the penman of this gospel, is here joined with Thomas (*v.* 3), but in two things there is a variation from the accounts of Mark and Luke, Mark iii. 18; Luke vi. 15. There, Matthew is put first, but here, in his own catalogue, Thomas is put first. It well becomes the disciples of Christ in honour to prefer one another. There he is only called Matthew, here Matthew the publican. It is good for those who are advanced to honour with Christ, to look *unto the rock whence they were hewn;* often to remember what they were before Christ called them, that thereby divine grace may be the more glorified. Matthew the apostle was Matthew the publican.

(5) Simon is called the Canaanite, or Simon the Zealot.

(6) Judas Iscariot is always named last, and with that black brand upon his name, *who also betrayed him.* Such spots there have been in our feasts of charity; tares among the wheat, wolves among the sheep; but there is a day of discovery and separation coming, when hypocrites shall be unmasked and discarded.

Verses 5-15

We have here the instructions that Christ gave to his disciples, when he gave them their commission. In this he *commanded them.* With these commands Christ commanded a blessing.

I. The people to whom he sent them.

1. Not to the Gentiles nor the Samaritans. They must not *go into the way of the Gentiles.* As to the Samaritans, their country lay between Judæa and Galilee, so that they could not avoid *going into the way* of the Samaritans, but they must *not enter into any of their cities.* This restraint was upon them only in their first mission, afterwards, they were appointed to go *into all the world,* and teach *all nations.*

2. But *to the lost sheep of the house of Israel.* The first offer of salvation must be made to the Jews, Acts iii. 26. Christ had a particular and very tender concern for the *house of Israel.* He looked with compassion upon them as *lost sheep,* whom he, as a shepherd, was to gather out of the by-paths of sin and error, into which they were gone astray, and in which, if not brought back, they would wander endlessly. Christ gives this description of those to whom they were sent, to quicken them to diligence in their work. They were sent to the house of Israel (of which number they themselves lately were), whom they could not but pity, and be desirous to help.

II. The preaching work which he appointed them. He did not send them forth without an errand; no, *As ye go, preach, v.* 7. They must proclaim the beginning of the gospel, saying, *The kingdom of heaven is at hand.* Not that they must say nothing else, but this must be their text; on this subject they must enlarge. It is said (Mark vi. 12), *they went out, and preached that men should repent;* which was the proper use and application of this doctrine concerning the approach of the *kingdom of heaven.* The preaching of this was like the morning light, to give notice of the approach of the rising sun. This proclaims salvation at hand, *nigh them that fear God; mercy and truth meet together* (Ps. lxxxv. 9, 10), that is, *the kingdom of heaven at hand:* not so much the personal presence of the king; that must not be doated upon; but a spiritual kingdom which is to be set up, when his bodily presence is removed, in the hearts of men.

Now this was the same that John the Baptist and Christ had preached before. People need to have good truths pressed again and again upon them, and if they be preached and heard with new affections, they are as if they were fresh to us. And there is a kingdom of glory yet to come, which we must speak of as at hand, and quicken people to diligence from the consideration of that.

III. The power he gave them to work miracles for the confirmation of their doctrine, *v.* 8. When he sent them to preach the same doctrine that he had preached, he empowered them to confirm it, by the same divine seals, which could never be set to a lie. This is not necessary now the kingdom of God is come; to call for miracles now is to lay again the foundation when the building is reared. They are directed here,

1. To use their power in doing good: *Heal the sick, cleanse the lepers.* They are sent abroad as public blessings, to intimate to the world, that love and goodness were the spirit and genius of that gospel which they came to preach, and of that kingdom which they were employed to set up. By this it would appear, that they were the servants of that God who is good and does good, and whose mercy is *over all his works.* We read not of their raising any to life before the *resurrection of Christ,* yet they were instrumental to raise many to *spiritual life.*

2. In *doing good freely; Freely ye have received, freely give.* They must cure *gratis,* further to exemplify the nature and complexion of the gospel kingdom, which is made up, not only of grace, but of free grace. And the reason is, because *freely you have received.* The consideration of Christ's freeness in doing good to us, should make us free in doing good to others.

IV. The provision that must be made for them in this expedition. As to that,

1. They must make no provision for it themselves, *v.* 9, 10. *Provide neither gold nor silver.* As, on the one hand, they shall not raise estates by their work, so, on the other hand, they shall not spend what little they have of their own upon it. Christ would teach them, (1) To act *under the conduct of human prudence.* They were now to make but a short excursion, therefore, why should they burthen themselves with that which they would have no occasion for? (2) To act in *dependence upon Divine Providence.* They must be taught to live, without *taking thought for life, ch.* vi. 25, &c. They who go upon Christ's errand, have, of all people, most reason to trust him for *food convenient.* Christ's hired servants shall have *bread enough and to spare;* while we abide faithful to God and our duty, and are in care to do our work well, we may cast all our other care upon God.

2. They might expect that those to whom they were sent would *provide for them* what was necessary, *v.* 10. They must not expect to be fed by miracles, as Elijah was: but they might depend upon God to incline the hearts of those they went among, to be kind to them, and provide for them. Ministers are, and must be, workmen, labourers, and they that are so are *worthy of their meat.* Christ would have his disciples, as not to distrust their God, so not to distrust their countrymen, so far as to doubt of a comfortable subsistence among them. If you preach to them, and endeavour to do good among them, surely they will give you meat and drink enough for your necessities; and if they do, never desire dainties; God will pay you your wages hereafter, and it will be running on in the mean time.

V. The proceedings they were to observe in dealing with any place, *v.* 11–15.

1. They are here directed how to conduct themselves toward those that were *strangers to them.*

(1) In *strange towns and cities:* when you come to a town, *enquire who* in it *is worthy.* It is supposed that there were some such in every place, as were better disposed than others to receive the gospel, and the preachers of it. In the worst of times and places,

we may charitably hope that there are some who swim against the stream, and are as wheat among the chaff. There were saints in Nero's household. Enquire who is worthy, who there are that have some fear of God before their eyes. Previous dispositions to that which is good, are both directions and encouragements to ministers, in dealing with people. There is most hope of the word being profitable to those who are already so well inclined, as that it is acceptable to them; and there is here and there one such. They must enquire out such; not enquire for the best inns; public houses were no proper places for them that neither took money with them (*v.* 9), nor expected to receive any (*v.* 8); but they must look out for accommodations in private houses, with those that would entertain them well, and expect no other recompence for it but a prophet's reward, an apostle's reward, their praying and preaching. They that entertain the gospel, must neither grudge the expense of it, nor promise themselves to get by it in this world. Christ's disciples, wherever they come, should ask for the good people of the place, and be acquainted with them; when we took God for our God, we took his people for our people, and like will rejoice in its like. It is implied, that if they did enquire who was worthy, they might discover them. Anyone could tell them, there lives an honest, sober, good man; for this is a character which, like the ointment of the right hand, betrays itself, and fills the house with its odours. In the house of those they found worthy, they must continue. They are justly suspected, as having no good design, that are often changing their quarters. It becomes the disciples of Christ to make the best of that which is, to abide by it, and not be for shifting upon every dislike or inconvenience.

(2) In strange houses. When they had found the house of one they thought worthy, they must at their entrance salute it. "In those common civilities, be beforehand with people. Salute the family, [1] To draw on further discourse, and so to introduce your message." (From matters of common conversation, we may insensibly pass into that communication which is good to the use of edifying.) [2] To try whether you are welcome or not. He that will not receive your salutation kindly, will not receive your message kindly. [3] To insinuate yourselves into their good opinion. *Salute the family,* that they may see that though you are serious, you are not morose. Religion teaches us to be courteous and civil, and obliging to all with whom we have to do. Their instructions were, when they came into a house, not to *command it,* but to *salute* it; for *love's sake rather to beseech,* is the evangelical way, Philemon 8, 9. Souls are first drawn to Christ with the *cords of a man,* and kept to him by the *bands of love,* Hos. xi. 4.

When they had saluted the family after a godly sort, they must, by the return, judge concerning the family; if *the house be worthy, let your peace come and rest upon it; if not, let it return to you, v.* 13. It seems then, that after they had enquired for the *most worthy (v.* 11), it was possible they might light upon those that were unworthy. Though it is wisdom to hearken to, yet it is folly to rely upon, common report and opinion; we ought to use a judgment of discretion, and to see with our own eyes. Now this rule is intended,

First, For satisfaction to the apostles. The common salutation was, *Peace be unto you.* Christ tells them that this gospel prayer (for so it was now become) should be put up for all, as the gospel proffer was made to all indefinitely, and that they should leave it to God to determine the issue of it. If the house be worthy, it will reap the benefit of your blessing; if not, there is no harm done, you will not lose the benefit of it; *it shall return to you.* It becomes us to judge charitably *of all*, to pray heartily *for all*, and to conduct ourselves courteously *to all*, for that is our part.

Secondly, For direction to them. "If, upon your salutation, it appear that they are indeed worthy, let them have more of your company, and so *let your peace come upon them*; preach the gospel to them, peace by Jesus Christ; but if otherwise, if they carry it rudely to you, and shut their doors against you, *let your peace*, as much as in you lies, *return to you*. Retract what you have said, and turn your backs upon them. Great blessings are often lost by a neglect seemingly small and inconsiderable.

2. They are here directed how to carry it towards those that were refusers of them. The case is put (*v*. 14) of those that *would not receive them, nor hear their words*. There would be those that would slight them, and put contempt on them and their message. The best and most powerful preachers of the gospel must expect to meet with some, that will not so much as give them the hearing, nor show them any token of respect. Many turn *a deaf ear*, even to the *joyful sound*. Contempt of the gospel, and contempt of gospel ministers, commonly go together, and they will either of them be construed into a contempt of Christ, and will be reckoned for accordingly. Note.

(1) The directions given to the apostles what to do. They must *depart out of that house or city*. The gospel will not tarry long with those that put it away from them. At their departure they must *shake off the dust of their feet* in detestation of their wickedness. The apostles must not so much as carry away the dust of their city with them, as a denunciation of wrath against them. It was to signify that God would *shake them off*. They who *despise* God and his gospel shall be *lightly esteemed*.

(2) The *doom passed* upon such *wilful recusants, v.* 15. It shall be *more tolerable, in the day of judgment, for the land of* Sodom, as wicked a place as it was. They that would not hear the doctrine that would save them, shall be made to hear the sentence that will ruin them. There are different degrees of punishment in that day. Sodom and Gomorrah were exceedingly wicked (Gen. xiii. 13), and that which filled up the measure of their iniquity, was that they *received not* the angels that were sent to them, but abused them (Gen. xix. 4, 5), and *hearkened not to their words, v.* 14. And yet it will be more tolerable for them than for those who receive not Christ's ministers and hearken not to their words. *Son, remember!* will sound most dreadfully in the ears of such as had a fair offer made them of *eternal life*, and chose death rather.

Verses 16–42

All these verses relate to the sufferings of Christ's ministers in their work, which they are here taught to expect, and prepare for; they are directed also how to bear them, and how to go on with their work in the midst of them. This part of the sermon looks further than to their present mission. They are here forewarned of the troubles they should meet with, when, after Christ's resurrection, their commission should be *enlarged*. Christ tells them, they must expect greater sufferings than they were yet called to. It is good to be told what troubles we may hereafter meet with, that we may provide accordingly, and may not boast, as if we had put off the harness, when we are yet but girding it on.

We have here intermixed, I. Predictions of trouble: and, II. Prescriptions of counsel and comfort, with reference to it.

I. We have here predictions of trouble: which the disciples should meet with in their work: Christ foresaw *their* sufferings as well as his own, and yet will have them go on, as he went on himself; and he

foretold them, not only that the troubles might not be a surprise to them, and so a shock to their faith, but that, being the accomplishment of a prediction, they might be a confirmation to their faith.

He tells them what they should suffer, and from whom.

1. *What they should suffer:* hard things to be sure; for, *Behold, I send you forth as sheep in the midst of wolves, v.* 16. And what may a flock of poor, helpless, unguarded sheep expect, in the midst of a herd of ravenous wolves, but to be worried and torn? They are as *sheep among wolves*, that is frightful; but Christ sends them forth, that is comfortable; for he that sends them forth will protect them, and bear them out.

(1) They must expect to be hated, *v*. 22. *Ye shall be hated for my name's sake:* that is the root of all the rest, and a bitter root it is. Those whom Christ loves, the world hates. *If the world hated Christ without a cause* (John xv. 25), no marvel if it hated those that bore his image and served his interests. It is grievous to be *hated*, and to be the object of so much ill-will, but it is *for thy name's sake*; which, as it speaks the true reason of the hatred, whatever is pretended, so it speaks comfort to them who are thus hated; it is for a good cause, and they have a good friend that shares with them in it, and takes it to himself.

(2) They must expect to be apprehended and arraigned as malefactors. Their restless malice is resistless malice, and they will not only attempt, but will prevail, to *deliver you up to the councils* (*v*. 17, 18). A deal of mischief is often done to good men, under colour of law and justice. They must look for trouble, not only from inferior magistrates in the councils, but from governors and kings, the supreme magistrates. We find this often fulfilled in the *acts of the apostles*.

(3) They must expect to be put to death (*v*. 21); *They shall deliver them to death*. The malice of the enemies rages so high as to inflict this; the faith and patience of the saints stand so firm as to expect this; the wisdom of Christ permits it, knowing how to make the blood of the martyrs *the seal of the truth*, and *the seed of the church*. By this noble army's not loving *their lives to the death*, Satan has been vanquished, and the kingdom of Christ and its interests greatly advanced.

(4) They must expect, in the midst of these sufferings, to be branded with the most odious and ignominious names and characters that could be. Persecutors would be ashamed in this world, if they did not first dress up those in bear-skins whom they thus bait, and represent them in such colours as may serve to justify such cruelties. The blackest of all the ill characters they give them is here stated; they call them Beelzebub, the name of the prince of the devils, *v*. 25. Since every one thinks he hates the devil, thus they endeavour to make them odious to all mankind. Satan's sworn enemies are represented as his friends; the apostles, who pulled down the devil's kingdom, were called devils. Satan's sworn servants would be thought to be his enemies, and they never more effectually do his work, than when they pretend to be fighting against him. Many times they who themselves are nearest akin to the devil, are most apt to father others upon him.

(5) These sufferings are here represented by a sword and division, *v*. 34, 35. *Think not that I am come to send peace*, temporal peace and outward prosperity. Christ came to give us *peace* with God, *peace* in our consciences, *peace* with our brethren, but *in the world ye shall have tribulation*. If all the world would receive Christ, there would then follow a universal *peace*, but while there are and will be so many that reject him, the children of God, that are called out

of the world, must expect to feel the fruits of their enmity.

[1] Look not for *peace, but a sword.* Christ came to give *the sword of the word,* with which his disciples fight against the world, and *the sword of persecution,* with which the world fights against the disciples, being *cut to the heart* with *the sword of the word* (Acts vii. 54), and *cruel* work this sword made. Christ sent that gospel, which gives occasion for the drawing of this sword, and so may be said to send this sword.

[2] Look not for *peace,* but division (*v.* 35), *I am còme to set men at variance.* This effect of the preaching of the gospel is not the fault of the gospel, but of those who do not receive it. The faith of those that believe condemns those that believe not, and, therefore, they have an enmity against them that believe. The most violent and implacable feuds have ever been those that have arisen from difference in religion; no enmity like that of the persecutors, no resolution like that of the persecuted. Christ has dealt fairly and faithfully with us, in telling us the worst we can meet with in his service; and he would have us deal so with ourselves, in sitting down and counting the cost.

2. We are here told from whom, and by whom, they should suffer these hard things. Surely hell itself must be let loose, and devils must become incarnate, ere such spiteful enemies could be found to a doctrine, the substance of which was *goodwill toward men.* No, would you think it? all this mischief arises to the preachers of the gospel from those to whom they came to preach salvation.

These hard things Christ's disciples must suffer,

(1) From men (*v.* 17). *"Beware of men;* you will have need to stand upon your guard." Persecuting rage and enmity turn men into brutes, into devils. It is a sad pass that the world is come to, when the best friends it has, have need to *beware of men.* It aggravates the troubles of Christ's suffering servants, that they arise from those who *are bone of their bone,* made of the same blood. The nature of man, if it be not sanctified, is the worst nature in the world next to that of devils.

(2) From professing men, men that *have a form of godliness,* and make a show of religion. *They will scourge you in their synagogues,* their places of meeting for the worship of God, and for the exercise of their church-discipline: so that they looked upon the scourging of Christ's ministers to be a branch of their religion. Paul was *five times scourged in the synagogues,* 2 Cor. xi. 24. Christ's disciples have suffered much from conscientious persecutors, that *scourge them in their synagogues,* cast them out and kill them, and thi nk *they do God good service* (John xvi. 2).

(3) From great men, and men in authority. The Jews did not only scourge them, which was the utmost their remaining power extended to, but they delivered them up to the Roman powers, as they did Christ, John xviii. 30. *Ye shall be brought before governors and kings* (*v.* 18), who, having more power, are in a capacity of doing the more mischief.

(4) From all men (*v.* 22). *Ye shall be hated of all men,* of all wicked men, and these are the generality of men. So few are there that love, and own, and countenance Christ's righteous cause, that we may say, the friends of it are *hated of all men.* As far as the apostasy from God goes, so far the enmity against the saints goes; sometimes it appears more general than at other times, but there is something of this poison lurking in the hearts of all *the children of disobedience.*

(5) From those of their own kindred. *The brother shall deliver up the brother to death, v.* 21. *A man shall be,* upon this account, *at variance with his own father; the persecuting daughter will be against the believing mother,* where natural affection and filial

duty, one would think, should prevent or soon extinguish the quarrel; and then, no marvel *if the daughter-in-law be against the mother-in-law.* In general, *a man's foes shall be they of his own household* (*v.* 36). They who should be his friends will be incensed against him for embracing Christianity, and especially for adhering to it when it comes to be persecuted, and will join with his persecutors against him. The strongest bonds of relative love and duty have often been broken through, by an enmity against Christ and his doctrine. Sufferings from such are more grievous; nothing cuts more than this, *It was thou, a man, mine equal* (Ps. lv. 12, 13); and the enmity of such is commonly most implacable; *a brother offended is harder to be won than a strong city,* Prov. xviii. 19.

II. With these predictions of trouble, we have here prescriptions of counsels and comforts for a time of trial. Let us gather up what he says,

1. By way of counsel and direction in several things.

(1) *Be ye wise as serpents, v.* 16. A precept, recommending to us that wisdom of the prudent, which is to understand his way, as useful at all times, but especially in suffering times. It is the will of Christ that his people and ministers, being so much exposed to troubles in this world, as they usually are, should not needlessly expose themselves, but use all fair and lawful means for their own preservation. In the cause of Christ we must sit loose to life and all its comforts, but must not be prodigal of them. We must *be wise,* not to pull trouble upon our own heads.

(2) *Be ye harmless as doves.* "Be mild, and meek, and dispassionate; not only do nobody any hurt, but bear nobody any ill will." We must *be wise,* not to wrong ourselves, but rather so than wrong anyone else; must use the harmlessness of the *dove* to bear twenty injuries, rather than the subtlety of the *serpent* to offer or to return one. *The Spirit descended on Christ as a dove,* and all believers partake of *the Spirit of Christ, a dove-like* spirit, made for love, not for war.

(3) *Beware of men, v.* 17. "Be always upon your guard, and avoid dangerous company; take heed what you say and do." It becomes those who are gracious to be cautious. We know not whom to trust. Ever since our Master was betrayed with a kiss, by one of his own disciples, we have need to *beware of men.*

(4) *Take no thought how or what ye shall speak, v.* 19. "When you are brought before magistrates, conduct yourselves decently, but afflict not yourselves with care how you shall come off. A prudent thought there must be, but not an anxious, perplexing, disquieting thought; let this *care be cast upon God.* Affect not quaint expressions, flourishes of wit, and laboured periods, which only serve to gild a bad cause; the gold of a good one needs it not." The disciples of Christ must be more thoughtful how to *do* well than how to *speak* well; how to *keep* their integrity than how to *vindicate* it. *Our lives, no boasting words,* form the best apology.

(5) *When they persecute you in this city, flee to another, v.* 23. "Thus reject them who reject you and your doctrine, and try whether others will not receive you and it. Thus shift for your own safety." In case of imminent peril, the disciples of Christ may and must secure themselves by flight, when God, in his providence, opens to *them a door of escape.* He that flies may fight again. It is no inglorious thing for Christ's soldiers to quit their ground, provided they do not quit their colours: they may go out of the way of *danger,* though they must not go out of the way of *duty.*

(6) *Fear them not* (*v.* 26), because *they can but kill the body* (*v.* 28). They who truly fear God, need not fear man; and they who are afraid of the least sin,

need not be afraid of the greatest trouble. *Yet will we not fear, though the earth be removed*, while we have so good a God, so good a cause, and so *good a hope through grace.*

[1] A good reason against this fear, taken from the limited power of the enemies; they *kill the body*, that is the utmost their rage can extend to; *they are not able to kill the soul*, nor to do it any hurt, and the soul is the man. The soul is killed when it is separated from God and his love, which is its life; now this is out of the reach of their power. *Tribulation, distress, and persecution* may separate us from all the world, but cannot part between us and God, cannot make us either not to love him, or not to be loved by him, Rom. viii. 35, 37. If, therefore, we were more concerned about our souls, as our jewels, we should be less afraid of men. They can but crush the cabinet.

[2] A good remedy against it, and that is, to fear God. *Fear him who is able to destroy both soul and body in hell. Hell* is the destruction both of *soul and body*; not of the *being* of either, but the *well*-being of both. This destruction comes from the power of God: he is *able to destroy*. God is *therefore to be feared*, even by the best saints in this world. The fear of God, and of his power reigning in the soul, will be a sovereign antidote against the fear of man. It is better to fall under the frowns of all the world, than under God's frowns, and therefore, as it is most right in itself, so it is most safe for us, *to obey God rather than men*, Acts iv. 19.

(7) *What I tell you in darkness, that speak ye in light* (v. 27); "whatever hazards you run, go on with your work, publishing and proclaiming the everlasting gospel to all the world; that is your business, mind that. The design of the enemies is not merely to destroy *you*, but to suppress *that*, and, therefore, whatever be the consequence, publish *that*." *What I tell you, that speak ye. Many things Christ spake openly, and nothing in secret* varying from what he preached in public, John xviii. 20. But they must deliver their embassy publicly, *in the light*, and *upon the house-tops*; for the doctrine of the gospel is what all are concerned in. The first indication of the reception of the Gentiles into the church, was *upon a house-top*, Acts x. 9. There is no part of Christ's gospel that needs, upon any account, to be concealed; *the whole counsel of God must be revealed.* In never so mixed a multitude let it be plainly and fully delivered.

2. By way of comfort and encouragement. Here is very much said to that purpose, and all little enough, considering the many hardships they were to grapple with, throughout the course of their ministry, and their present weakness. Christ therefore shows them why they should be of good cheer.

(1) Here is one word peculiar to their present mission, v. 23. *Ye shall not have gone over the cities of Israel, till the Son of man be come.* It was a comfort, [1] That what they said should be made good: they said *the Son of man* is coming, and *behold, he comes. Christ will confirm the word of his messengers.* [2] That it should be made good quickly. It is matter of comfort to Christ's labourers, that their working time will be short, and soon over; the work and warfare will in a little time be accomplished. [3] That then they should be advanced to a higher station. *When the Son of man comes, they shall be endued with greater power from on high.*

(2) Here are many words that relate to their work in general, and the troubles they were to meet with in it; and *they are good words and comfortable words.*

[1] That their sufferings were *for a testimony against them and the Gentiles*, v. 18. When the Jewish consistories transfer you to the Roman governors, that they may have you put to death, your being hurried thus from one judgment-seat to another, will help to make your testimony the more public, and will give you an opportunity of bringing the gospel to the Gentiles, as well as to the Jews. God's people, and especially God's ministers, are his witnesses not only in their *doing* work, but in their *suffering* work. Hence they are called martyrs—*witnesses* for Christ. Now if their sufferings be a testimony, how cheerfully should they be borne!

[2] That upon all occasions they should have God's special presence with them, and the immediate assistance of his Holy Spirit, *it shall be given you* (said Christ) *in that same hour what ye shall speak.* Christ's disciples were chosen *from among the foolish of the world*, unlearned and ignorant men, and, therefore, might justly distrust their own abilities, especially when they were called before great men. First, they are here promised that *it should be given them*, not sometime before, but *in that same hour, what they should speak.* They shall speak *extempore*, and yet shall speak as much to the purpose, as if it had been never so well studied. When God calls us out to speak for him, we may depend upon him to teach us what to say. Secondly, They are here assured, that the blessed Spirit should draw up their plea for them. *It is not ye that speak, but the Spirit of your Father, which speaketh in you*, v. 20. They were not left to themselves upon such an occasion, but God undertook for them; his Spirit of wisdom spoke *in* them. God gave them an ability, not only to speak to the purpose, but what they did say, to say it with holy zeal. The same Spirit that assisted them in the pulpit, assisted them at the bar. They cannot but come off well, who have such an advocate.

[3] That *he that endures to the end shall be saved*, v. 22. Here it is very comfortable to consider, First, that there will be an *end* of these troubles; they may last long, but will not last always. Christ comforted himself with this, and so may his followers; *The things concerning me have an end*, Luke xxii. 37. The troubles may seem tedious, but, blessed be God, they are not everlasting. Secondly, That while they continue, they may be *endured*; they may be borne, and borne *to the end*, because the sufferers shall be borne up under them, in everlasting arms: *The strength shall be according to the day*, 1 Cor. x. 13. Thirdly, Salvation will be the eternal recompence of all those *that endure to the end.* The weather stormy, and the way foul, but the pleasure of home will make amends for all. They who *endure but awhile, and in time of temptation fall away*, have run in vain, and lose all that they have attained; but they who persevere, are sure of the prize, and they only. *Be faithful unto death*, and then thou shalt have the *crown of life.*

[4] That whatever hard usage the disciples of Christ meet with, it is no more than what their Master met with before (v. 24, 25). *The disciple is not above his master.* Here it is given as a reason, why they should not stumble at the hardest sufferings. They are reminded of this saying, John xv. 20. It is a proverbial expression, *The servant is not better than his master*, and, therefore, let him not expect to fare *better.* Jesus Christ our Lord and Master met with very hard usage from the world; they called him Beelzebub, the god of flies, the name of the chief of the devils, with whom they said he was in league. It is hard to say which is here more to be wondered at, the wickedness of men who thus abused Christ, or the patience of Christ, who suffered himself to be thus abused; that Satan's greatest Enemy and Destroyer should be run down as his confederate, and yet *endure such contradiction of sinners.* The consideration of the ill treatment which Christ met with in the world, should engage us to expect and prepare for the like, and to bear it patiently; nor think it hard if they who are shortly to be made *like him in glory*, be now made *like him in sufferings.* Christ began in the *bitter cup*, let us

be willing to pledge him; his bearing the cross made it easy for us.

[5] That *there is nothing covered that shall not be revealed*, v. 26. We understand this, First, Of the revealing of the gospel to all the world. "Do you *publish it* (v. 27), for it shall be published. The truths which are now, as mysteries, hid from the children of men, shall all be made known, to all nations, in their own language," Acts ii. 11. The *ends of the earth must see this salvation*. It is a great encouragement to those who are doing Christ's work, that it is a work which shall certainly be done. It is a plough which God will speed. Or, Secondly, Of the clearing up of the innocency of Christ's suffering servants. However their innocency and excellency are now *covered*, they *shall be revealed*. All their reproach shall be rolled away, and their graces and services, that are now *covered, shall be revealed*, 1 Cor. iv. 5. Let Christ's ministers faithfully reveal his truths, and then leave it to him, in due time, to reveal their integrity.

[6] That the providence of God is in a special manner conversant about the saints, in their suffering, v. 29–31. It is good to have recourse to our first principles, and particularly to the doctrine of God's universal providence, extending itself to all the creatures, and all their actions, even the smallest and most minute.

First, The general extent of providence to all the creatures, even the least, and least considerable, to the *sparrows*, v. 29. These little animals are of so small account, that one of them is not valued; there must go two to be worth *a farthing* (nay, you shall have five for a halfpenny, Luke xii. 6), and yet they are not shut out of the divine care; *One of them shall not fall to the ground without your Father*. They do not light on *the ground* for food, to pick up a grain of corn, but *your* heavenly *Father*, by his providence, laid it ready for them. Now he that feeds the sparrows, will not starve the saints. They do *not fall to the ground* by death, either a natural or a violent death, without the notice of God. Even their death comes within the notice of the divine providence; much more does the death of his disciples. Now this God, who has such an eye to the sparrows, because they are his creatures, much more will have an eye to you, who are his children. If a sparrow die not *without your Father*, surely a man does not,—a Christian,—a minister,—my friend, my child. There is enough in the doctrine of God's providence to silence all the fears of God's people: *Ye are of more value than many sparrows*.

Secondly, The particular cognizance which providence takes of the disciples of Christ, especially in their sufferings (v. 30), *But the very hairs of your head are all numbered*. This is a proverbial expression, denoting the account which God takes and keeps of all the concernments of his people, even of those that are most minute, and least regarded. If God numbers their hairs, much more does he number their heads, and take care of their lives, their comforts, their souls. It intimates, that God takes more care of them, than they do of themselves. God *numbers the hairs of* his people, and *not a hair of their head shall perish* (Luke xxi. 18); not the least hurt shall be done them so precious to God are his saints, and their lives and deaths!

[7] That he will shortly, in the day of triumph, own those who now own him, in the day of trial, when those who deny him shall be for ever disowned and rejected by him, v. 32, 33. It is our duty, and if we do it, it will hereafter be our unspeakable honour and happiness, to *confess Christ before men*. It is our duty, not only to believe in Christ, but to profess that faith, in suffering for him, when we are called to it, as well as in serving him. However this may

expose us to reproach and trouble now, we shall be abundantly recompensed for that, *in the resurrection of the just*. "I will confess him before my Father, when it will do him the most service; I will present him, will represent him to *my Father*." Those who honour Christ he will thus honour. They honour him *before men*; that is a *poor* thing: he will honour them *before* his *Father*; that is a *great* thing. It is a dangerous thing for any to deny and disown *Christ before men*; for they who do so will be disowned by him *in the great day*, when they have most need of him: he will not own them for his servants who would not own him for their Master: *I tell you, I know you not, ch.* vii. 23.

[8] That the foundation of their discipleship was laid in such a temper and disposition, as would make sufferings very light and easy to them; and it was upon the condition of a preparedness for suffering, that Christ took them to be his followers, v. 37–39. He told them at first, that they were *not worthy of* him, if they were not willing to part with all for him. Now, in the Christian profession, they are reckoned unworthy the dignity and felicity of it, that put not such a value upon their interest in Christ, as to prefer that before any other interests. They cannot expect the gains of a bargain, who will not come up to the terms of it. If religion be worth *any*thing, it is worth *every*thing. They who like not Christ on these terms, may leave him at their peril. Whatever we part with for this pearl of price, we may comfort ourselves with this persuasion, that it is well worth what we give for it. The terms are, that we must prefer Christ.

(1) Before our nearest and dearest relations; *father or mother, son or daughter*. Children must love their parents, and parents must love their children; but if they love them better than Christ, they are unworthy of him. As we must not be *deterred* from Christ by the hatred of our relations which he spoke of (v. 21, 35, 36), so we must not be *drawn* from him, by their love.

(2) Before our ease and safety. We must *take up our cross* and *follow him*, else we are *not worthy of* him. Here observe, 1. They who would *follow Christ*, must expect *their cross* and *take it up*. 2. In taking *up the cross*, we must *follow Christ's* example, and bear it as he did. 3. It is a great encouragement to us, when we meet with crosses, that in bearing them we *follow Christ*, who has showed us the way, and that if we follow him faithfully, he will lead us through sufferings like him, to glory with him.

(3) Before life itself, v. 39. *He that findeth his life shall lose it;* he that thinks he has found it when he has saved it, and kept it, by denying Christ, *shall lose it* in an eternal death; but *he that loseth his life for Christ's sake*, that will part with it rather than deny Christ, *shall find it*, to his unspeakable advantage, an eternal life. They are best prepared for the life to come, that sit most loose to this present life.

[9] That Christ himself would so heartily espouse their cause, as to show himself a friend to all their friends, v. 40–42. *He that receiveth you, receiveth me.*

It is here implied, that though the generality would reject them, yet they should meet with some who would receive and entertain them, would bid the message welcome to their hearts, and the messengers to their houses, for the sake of it. Christ's ministers shall not *labour in vain*.

Jesus Christ takes what is done to his faithful ministers, whether in kindness or in unkindness, as done to himself, and reckons himself *treated* as they are *treated*. *He that receiveth you, receiveth me*. See how Christ may still be entertained by those who would testify their respects to him; his people and ministers we have always with us; and he is *with them always*, even to the end of the world. Nay, the honour rises higher, *He that receiveth me, receiveth him that sent me.* By entertaining Christ's ministers, they entertain not *angels unawares,* but Christ, nay, and God himself, and *unawares* too, as appears, *ch.* xxv. 37. *When saw we thee an hungered?*

Though the kindness done to Christ's disciples be never so small, yet if there be occasion for it, and ability to do no more, it shall be accepted, though it be *but a cup of cold water given to one of these little ones, v.* 42. Kindnesses shown to Christ's disciples are valued in Christ's books, not according to the cost of the gift, but according to the love and affection of the giver. On that score the widow's mite not only passed current, but was stamped high, Luke xxi. 3, 4. Thus they who are truly rich in graces may be rich in good works, though poor in the world.

Kindness to Christ's disciples which he will accept, must be done with an eye to Christ, and for his sake. A prophet must be received *in the name of a prophet,* and a *righteous man* in the name of a *righteous man,* and one of those *little ones* in the name of a *disciple;* because they are righteous, and so bear Christ's image. Christ does not interest himself in the matter, unless we first interest him in it.

Kindnesses shown to Christ's people and ministers, shall not only be accepted, but richly and suitably rewarded. He does not say, that they *deserve* a reward; we cannot merit anything as wages, from the hand of God; but they shall *receive a reward* from the free gift of God; and they shall *in no wise lose it.* The reward may be deferred, but it shall in no wise be *lost,* nor shall they be any *losers* by the delay. 2. This is a *prophet's reward,* and a *righteous man's.* That is, either, (1) The reward that God gives to prophets and righteous men; the blessings conferred upon them shall distil upon their friends. Or, (2) The reward he gives by prophets and righteous men; in answer to their prayers (Gen. xx. 7), *He is a prophet, and he shall pray for thee,* that is a prophet's reward. Prophets' rewards are spiritual blessings in heavenly things, and if we know how to value them, we shall reckon them good payment.

CHAPTER 11

In this chapter we have, I. The constant and unwearied diligence of our Lord Jesus, ver. 1. II. His discourse with the disciples of John concerning his being the Messiah, 2–6. III. The honourable testimony that Christ bore to John Baptist, ver. 7–15. IV. The sad account he gives of that generation in general, and of some particular places with reference to the success, both of John's ministry and of his own, ver. 16–24. V. His thanksgiving to his Father for the wise and gracious method he had taken in revealing the great mysteries of the gospel, ver. 25, 26. VI. His gracious call and invitation of poor sinners to come to him, ver. 27–30.

Verses 1–6

The first verse of this chapter some join to the foregoing chapter, and make it (not unfitly) the close of that.

1. The ordination sermon which Christ preached to his disciples in the foregoing chapter is here called his commanding them. Their preaching of the gospel was not only permitted them, but it was enjoined them. *Necessity was laid upon them,* 1 Cor. ix. 16.

2. When Christ had said what he had to say to his disciples, he *departed thence.* It should seem they were very loth to leave their Master, till *he departed* and separated himself from them; as the nurse withdraws the hand, that the child may learn to go by itself. Christ would now teach them how to live, and how to work, without his bodily presence. It was *expedient for them,* that Christ should thus go away for awhile.

3. Christ departed, *to teach and preach* in the cities whither he sent his disciples before him *to work miracles (ch.* x. 1–8), and so to raise people's expectations and to make way for his entertainment. Thus was the *way of the Lord prepared.* When Christ

empowered them to *work miracles,* he employed himself in *teaching* and *preaching,* as if that were the more honourable of the two. That was but in order to do this. Healing the sick was the *saving of bodies,* but preaching the gospel was to the *saving of souls.* Christ had directed his disciples to preach (*ch.* x. 7), yet he did not leave off preaching himself. How unlike are they to Christ, who yoke others only that they may themselves be idle! The increase and multitude of labourers in the Lord's work should be made not an excuse for our negligence, but an encouragement to our diligence. The more busy others are, the more busy we should be, and all little enough, so much work is there to be done. He went to preach *in their cities,* which were populous places; he cast the net of the gospel where there were most fish to be enclosed.

Here is next recorded a message which John Baptist sent to Christ, and his return to it, *v.* 2–6. We heard before that Jesus heard of John's sufferings, *ch.* iv. 12. Now we are told that John, in prison, hears of Christ's doings. He *heard in the prison the works of Christ;* and no doubt he was glad to hear of them. Nothing is more comfortable to God's people in distress, than to *hear of the works of Christ;* especially to experience them in their own souls. This turns a prison into a palace. Some way or other Christ will convey the notices of his love to those that are in trouble for conscience' sake.

Now John Baptist hearing of Christ's works, sent two of his disciples to him; and what passed between them and him we have here an account of.

I. The question they had to propose to him: *Art thou he that should come, or do we look for another?* This was a serious and important question. It is taken for granted that the Messiah should come. They intimate, that if this be not *he,* they would *look for another.* We must not be weary of looking for him that is to come. Though he tarry, wait for him, for he that shall come will come, though not in our time. They intimate likewise, that if they be convinced that this is he, they will not be sceptics, they will be satisfied, and will look *for no other.* They therefore ask, *Art thou he?* John had said for his part, *I am not the Christ,* John i. 20. Some think that John sent this question for his own satisfaction. It is true he had borne a noble testimony to Christ; he had declared him to be the *Son of God* (John i. 34), the Lamb of God (*v.* 29), and he that *should baptize with the Holy Ghost* (*v.* 33), and *sent of God* (John iii. 34), which were great things. But he desired to be further and more fully assured. In matters relating to Christ and our salvation by him, it is good to be sure. Christ appeared not in that external pomp and power in which it was expected he should appear; his own disciples stumbled at this, and perhaps John did so; Christ saw something of this at the bottom of this enquiry, when he said, *blessed is he who shall not be offended in me.* It is hard, even for good men, to bear up against vulgar errors. John's doubt might arise from his own present circumstances. He was a prisoner, and might be tempted to think, if Jesus be indeed the Messiah, whence is it that I, his friend and forerunner, am brought into this trouble, and am left to be so long in it. Doubtless there was a good reason why our Lord Jesus did not go to John in prison, but John construed it into a neglect, and it was perhaps a shock to his faith in Christ. [1] Where there is true faith, yet there may be a mixture of unbelief. The best are not always alike strong. [2] Troubles for Christ, especially when they continue long unrelieved, are such trials of faith as sometimes prove too hard to be borne up against. [3] The remaining unbelief of good men may sometimes, in an hour of temptation, strike at the root, and call in question the most fundamental truths which were thought to be well settled. The best saints have need of the best helps they can get for the strengthening of their faith, and the arming of themselves against temptations to infidelity. Others think that John sent his disciples to Christ with this question, not so much for his own satisfaction as for theirs. Though he was a prisoner they adhered to him, attended on him; they loved him, and would not leave him. They were weak in knowledge, and wavering in their faith, and needed instruction and confirmation; and in this matter they were somewhat prejudiced; being jealous *for their* master, they were jealous *of our* Master; they were loth to acknowledge Jesus to be the Messiah, because he eclipsed John. Good men are apt to have their judgments biassed by their interest. Now John would have their mistakes rectified, and wished them to be as well satisfied as he himself was. John was all along industrious to turn over his disciples to Christ, as from the grammar-school to the academy. Ministers' business is to direct everybody to Christ. And those who would know the certainty of the doctrine of Christ, must apply themselves to him, who is come to give an understanding. They who would grow in grace must be inquisitive.

II. Here is Christ's answer to this question, *v.* 4–6. It was a real answer, an answer in fact. Christ will have us to spell out the convincing evidences of gospel truths, and to take pains in digging for knowledge.

1. He points them to what they heard and saw, which they must tell John. Christ refers us to the things we *hear and see. Go and tell John.*

(1) *What you see* of the *power of Christ's miracles;* you see how, by the word of Jesus, *the blind receive their sight,* the *lame walk,* &c. Christ's miracles were done openly, and in the view of all. *Truth seeks not concealment.* They are to be considered, [1] As the *acts of a divine power.* None but the God of nature could thus overrule and outdo the power of nature. It is particularly spoken of as God's prerogative to *open the eyes of the blind,* Ps. cxlvi. 8. Miracles are therefore the broad seal of heaven, and the doctrine they are affixed to must be of God. However *lying wonders* may be vouched for in proof of *false doctrines, true miracles* evince a divine commission; such Christ's were, and they leave no room to doubt that he was sent of God. [2] As the *accomplishment of a divine prediction.* It was foretold (Isa. xxxv. 5, 6), that our God should come, and that then *the eyes of the blind should be opened.*

(2) Tell him *what you hear* of the *preaching of his gospel.* Faith, though confirmed by seeing, comes by hearing. That *the poor have the gospel preached to them.* The *Old Testament* prophets were sent mostly to kings and princes, but Christ preached to the *congregations of the poor.* Christ's gracious condescensions and compassions to *the poor,* are an evidence that it was he that should bring to the world the tender mercies of our God. Or we may understand it, not so much of the *poor of the world,* as the *poor in spirit,* and so that scripture is fulfilled, Isa. lxi. 1, *He hath anointed me to preach glad tidings to the meek.* It is a proof of Christ's divine mission that his doctrine is gospel indeed; good news to those who are truly humble in the denial of self; to them it is accommodated, for whom God always declared he had mercy in store. That the *poor receive the gospel,* and are wrought upon by it, they receive and entertain the gospel. The wonderful efficacy of the gospel is a proof of its divine original. The poor are *wrought upon* by it. The gospel of Christ made its way into their untutored minds.

2. He pronounces a *blessing* on those that *were not offended in him, v.* 6. They who are not wilfully prejudiced against him, and scandalized in him (so the word is), cannot but receive his doctrine, and so be *blessed in him.* There are many things in Christ which they who are ignorant and unthinking are apt to be offended at. The meanness of his appearance, his education at Nazareth, the poverty of his life, the despicableness of his followers, the slights which the great men put upon him, the strictness of his doctrine, the contradiction it gives to flesh and blood, and the sufferings that attend the profession of his name; these are things that keep many from him, who otherwise cannot but see much of God in him. Thus he is set *for the fall of many,* even in Israel. They are happy who get over these offences. *Blessed are they.* The expression intimates, that it is a difficult thing to conquer these prejudices, and a dangerous thing not to conquer them.

Verses 7–15

Some of Christ's disciples might perhaps take occasion from the question John sent, to reflect upon him, as weak and wavering, and inconsistent with himself, to prevent which Christ gives him this character. We must take all occasions, especially such as discover anything of infirmity, to speak well of those who are praiseworthy. John the Baptist, when he was upon the stage, and Christ in privacy and retirement, bore testimony to Christ; and now that Christ appeared publicly, and John was under a cloud, he bore testimony to John. John had abased himself to honour Christ (John iii. 29, 30, *ch.* iii. 11), had made himself nothing, that Christ might be All, and now Christ dignifies him with this character. They who humble themselves shall be exalted, and those that honour Christ he will honour. John had now *finished his testimony,* and now Christ commends him. Christ reserves honour for his servants when they *have done their work,* John xii. 26.

I. Christ spoke thus honourably of John, not in the hearing of John's disciples, but *as they departed,* just after they were gone, Luke vii. 24. He would not so much as seem to flatter John, nor have these praises of him reported to him. Though we must be forward to give to all their due praise for their encouragement, yet we must avoid everything that looks like flattery. Pride is a corrupt humour, which we must not feed either in others or in ourselves.

II. What Christ said concerning John, was intended not only for his praise, but for the people's profit, to revive the remembrance of John's ministry. "Now, consider, *what went ye out into the wilderness to see?* Put this question to yourselves." 1. John preached *in the wilderness.* If teachers be removed into corners, it is better to go on after them than to be without them. Now if his preaching was worth taking so much pains to hear it, surely it was worth taking some care to recollect it. The greater the difficulties we have broken through to hear the word, the more we are concerned to profit by it. 2. They went out to him to see him; rather for curiosity than for conscience. Many that attend on the word come rather to see and be seen, than to learn and be taught, to have something to talk of, than to be made wise to salvation. Christ puts it to them, *what went ye out to see?* We think when the sermon is done, the care is over; no, then the greatest of the care begins. *What brought you thither?* Was it custom or company, or was it a desire to honour God and get good? *What have you brought thence?* What knowledge, and grace, and comfort? *What went you to see?*

III. Let us see what the commendation of John was. Well, says Christ, "I will tell you what a man John the Baptist was."

1. "He was a firm, resolute man, and not *a reed shaken with the wind.* He was not wavering in his principles, nor uneven in his conversation." When the wind of popular applause on the one hand blew fresh and fair, when the storm of Herod's rage on the

other hand grew fierce and blustering, John was still the same, the same in all weathers. The testimony he had borne to Christ was not the testimony of *a reed*; it was not a weather-cock testimony. The people flocked to him, because he was not as a reed. There is nothing lost in the long run by an unshaken resolution, to go on with our work, neither courting the smiles, nor fearing the frowns of men.

2. He was a *self-denying* man. "Was he a man *clothed in soft raiment?* If so, you would not have gone *into the wilderness* to see him, but to the *court.* You went to see one that had *his raiment of camel's hair*, and a *leathern girdle about his loins*; his clothing agreed with the *wilderness* he lived in, and the doctrine he preached there, that of repentance. Now you cannot think that he who was such a stranger to the pleasures of a court, should be brought to change his mind by the terrors of a prison." They who have lived a life of mortification, are least likely to be driven off from their religion by persecution. He was not a man clothed in *soft raiment*; such *there are*, but they are *in kings' houses.* It becomes people in all their appearances to be consistent with their character and their situation. They who are preachers must not affect to look like courtiers. Prudence teaches us to be *of a piece.*

3. His greatest commendation of all was his office and ministry.

(1) He was *a prophet*, yea, and *more than a prophet* (*v.* 9). John said of himself, he was not *that prophet*, that great prophet, the Messiah himself; and now Christ (a very competent Judge) says of him, that he was *more than a prophet.* The forerunner of Christ was not a king, but a prophet, a *transcendent* prophet, more than an *Old Testament prophet*; they *saw Christ's day* at a distance; but John saw the day dawn, he saw the sun rise. They spake of Christ, but he pointed to him: he said, *Behold the Lamb of God!*

(2) He was the same that was predicted to be Christ's forerunner (*v.* 10); *This is he of whom it is written.* He was prophesied of by the other prophets, and therefore was greater than they. Malachi prophesied concerning John, *Behold, I send my messenger before thy face.* It was great preferment to John above all the prophets, that he was Christ's harbinger. He was a *messenger* sent on a great errand; he is *my messenger* sent *of God*, and sent before the *Son of God.* His business was to *prepare Christ's way.* This he had said of himself (John i. 23) and now Christ said it of him. Much of the beauty of God's dispensations lies in their mutual connection and coherence, and the reference they have one to another. That which advanced John above the *Old Testament* prophets was, that he went immediately before Christ. The nearer any are to Christ, the more truly honourable they are.

(3) There *was not a greater born of women* than John the Baptist, *v.* 11. Christ knew how to value persons according to the degrees of their worth, and he prefers John before all that went before him. Of all that God had raised up and called to any service in his church, John is the most eminent. Many had been born of women that made a great figure in the world, but Christ prefers John before them. Greatness is not to be measured by appearances and outward splendour, but they are the greatest men who are the greatest saints, and the greatest blessings, who are, as John was, *great in the sight of the Lord*, Luke i. 15.

Notwithstanding, he that is least in the kingdom of heaven is greater than he. There are degrees of glory in heaven, some that are less than others there; though every vessel is alike full, all are not alike large and capacious. The least saint in heaven is *greater*, and knows more, and loves more, and does more in praising God, and receives more from him, than the greatest in this world. By the *kingdom of heaven* here, is rather to be understood the *kingdom of grace*, the gospel dispensation in the perfection of its power and purity; and ὁ μικρότερος —*he that is less* in that is *greater than John.* So it agrees with what John the Baptist said (John i. 15), *He that cometh after me is preferred before me.* But it is rather to be understood of the apostles and ministers of the *New Testament.* John preached Christ coming, but they preached Christ not only come, but *crucified* and *glorified.* John came to the dawning of the gospel-day, but he was taken off before the noon of that day, before the rending of the veil, before Christ's death and resurrection, and the pouring out of the Spirit; so that the least of the apostles and evangelists, having greater discoveries made to them, and being employed in a greater embassy, is *greater than John.* All the true greatness of men is derived from, and denominated by, the gracious manifestation of Christ to them. What reason have we to be thankful that our lot is cast in the days of the *kingdom of heaven*, under such advantages of light and love! And the greater the advantages, the greater will the account be, if we *receive the grace of God in vain.*

(4) The great commendation of John the Baptist was, that God owned his ministry, and made it wonderfully successful for the breaking of the ice, and the preparing of people for the *kingdom of heaven. From the days of* the first appearing of *John the Baptist*, until now *the kingdom of heaven suffereth violence*—Βιάζεται—*vim patitur*, like the violence of an army taking a city by storm, or of a crowd bursting into a house, so the *violent take it by force.* Multitudes are wrought upon by the ministry of John, and become his disciples. And it is,

[1] An *improbable* multitude. Those strove for a place in this kingdom, that one would think had no right nor title to it, and so seemed to be intruders. When the *children of the kingdom* are excluded out of it, and many come into it *from the east and the west*, then it *suffers violence.* The publicans and harlots believed John, whom the scribes and Pharisees rejected, and so went into the kingdom of God before them. It is no breach of good manners to go to 'heaven before our betters: and it is a great commendation of the gospel from the days of its infancy, that it has brought many to holiness that were very unlikely.

[2] An *importunate* multitude. This violence denotes a strength, and vigour, and earnestness of desire and endeavour, in those who followed John's ministry. It shows us also, what fervency and zeal are required of all those who design to make heaven of their religion. They who would *enter into the kingdom of heaven* must *strive to enter*; that kingdom suffers a holy violence; we must run, and wrestle, and fight, and be *in an agony*, and all little enough to win such a prize, and to get over such opposition from without and from within. *The violent take it by force.* They who will have an interest in the great salvation are carried out towards it with a strong desire, will have it *upon any terms*, and not think them hard, nor quit their hold without a blessing, Gen. xxxii. 26. The kingdom of heaven was never intended to indulge the ease of triflers, but to be the rest of them that labour. Oh that we could see a greater number with a *holy* contention thrusting themselves into it!

(5) The ministry of John was the *beginning of the gospel.*

[1] In John the Old Testament dispensation began to die, *v.* 13. The discoveries of the Old Testament began to be superseded by the more clear manifestation of the *kingdom of heaven* as *at hand.* When Christ says, *all the prophets and the law prophesied until John*, he shows us, First, How the light of the

Old Testament was set up; it was set up in *the law and the prophets*, who spoke, though darkly, of Christ and his kingdom. Blessed be God that we have both the New Testament doctrine to explain the Old Testament prophecies, and the Old Testament prophecies to confirm and illustrate the New Testament doctrine (Heb. i. 1); like the two cherubim, they look at each other. The scripture is teaching to this day, though the penmen of it are gone. Moses and the prophets are dead; the apostles and evangelists are dead (Zech. i. 5), but the *word of the Lord endures for ever* (1 Pet. i. 25). Secondly, How this light was *laid aside*. Even before the sun rises, the morning light makes candles to shine dim. Their prophecies of a Christ to come became out of date, when John said, *He is come*.

[2] In him the New Testament day began to dawn; for (*v.* 14) *This is Elias, that was for to come.* John was as the loop that coupled the two Testaments. The concluding prophecy of the Old Testament was, *Behold, I will send you Elijah*, Mal. iv. 5, 6. Those words prophesied until John, and then, being turned into a history, they ceased to prophesy. Christ speaks of it as a great truth, that John the Baptist is the Elias of the New Testament; one that should come in the spirit and power of Elias (Luke i. 17), and especially as it is in the prophecy, that should *turn the hearts of the fathers to the children.* Christ suspects the welcome of it, *if ye will receive it.* Not but that it was true, whether they would receive it or not, but he upbraids them with their prejudices. Or, "If *you will receive him*, or if you will receive the ministry of John as that of the promised Elias, he will be an Elias to you, to turn you and prepare you for the Lord." Christ is a Saviour, and John an Elias, to those who will receive the truth concerning them.

Lastly, Our Lord Jesus closes this discourse with a solemn demand of attention (*v.* 15): *He that hath ears to hear, let him hear;* which intimates, that those things were dark and hard to be understood, and therefore needed attention, but of great concern and consequence, and therefore well deserved it. The things of God are of great and common concern: everyone that has *ears to hear* anything, is concerned to hear this. It intimates that God requires no more from us but the right use and improvement of the faculties he has already given us. He requires those to hear that have ears. They do not hear, because, like the deaf adder, they *stop their ears.*

Verses 16–24

Christ was going on in the praise of John the Baptist and his ministry, but here stops on a sudden, and turns that to the reproach of those who enjoyed both that, and the ministry of Christ and his apostles, too, in vain. As to that generation, we may observe to whom he *compares them* (*v.* 16–19), and as to the particular places he instances, we may observe with whom he *compares them, v.* 20–24.

I. As to that *generation*. The generality continued in unbelief and obstinacy. John was a great and good man, but the generation in which his lot was cast was as barren and unprofitable as could be, and unworthy of him. The badness of the places where good ministers live serves for a foil to their beauty. Having commended John, he condemns those who had him among them, and did not profit by his ministry.

This our Lord Jesus here sets forth in a parable. *Whereunto shall I liken this generation?* The similitude is taken from some common custom among the Jewish children at their play, who, as is usual with children, imitated the fashions of grown people at their marriages and funerals, *rejoicing* and *lamenting*; but being all a jest, it made no impression; no more

did the ministry either of John the Baptist or of Christ upon that generation.

The parable will be best explained by opening it and the illustration of it together in these five observations.

Note, 1. The God of heaven uses a variety of proper means and methods for the conversion and salvation of poor souls; he would *have all men to be saved*, and therefore leaves no stone unturned in order to it. In the parable, this is called his *piping* to us, and his *mourning* to us; he hath *piped to us* in the precious promises of the gospel, proper to work upon hope, and mourned to us in the dreadful threatenings of the law, proper to work upon fear. He has *piped to us* in gracious and merciful providences, *mourned to us* in calamitous, afflicting providences.

In the explanation of the parable is set forth the different temper of John's ministry and of Christ's. On the one hand, John came *mourning to them, neither eating nor drinking*. Now this, one would think, should work upon them; for such an austere, mortified life as this, was very agreeable to the doctrine he preached: and that minister is most likely to do good, whose conversation is according to his doctrine; and yet the preaching even of such a minister is not always effectual. On the other hand, *the Son of man came eating and drinking*, and so he *piped unto them*. Christ conversed familiarly with all sorts of people, not affecting any peculiar strictness or austerity. Those who were not awed by John's frowns, would be allured by Christ's smiles; from whom St. Paul learned to become *all things to all men*, 1 Cor. ix. 22. There may be a *great diversity of operations*, where *it is the same God that worketh all in all* (1 Cor. xii. 6), and this *various manifestation of the Spirit is given to every man to profit withal, v.* 7. Observe especially that God's ministers are variously gifted. Some are Boanerges—*sons of thunder;* others, Barnabases—*sons of consolation;* yet *all these worketh that one and the self-same Spirit* (1 Cor. xii. 11), and therefore we ought not to condemn either, but to praise both, and praise God for both.

Note, 2. The various methods which God takes for the conversion of sinners, are with many fruitless and ineffectual: "*Ye have not danced, ye have not lamented.*" Now if people will neither be awakened by the *greatest* things, nor allured by the *sweetest* things, nor startled by the most *terrible* things, nor be made sensible by the *plainest* things; if they will hearken to the voice neither of scripture, nor reason, nor experience, nor providence, nor conscience, nor interest, what more can be done? It is some comfort to faithful ministers, when they see little success of their labours, that it is no new thing for the best preachers and the best preaching in the world to come short of the desired end. *Who has believed our report?*

Note, 3. That commonly those persons who do not profit by the means of grace, are perverse, they do all the hurt they can to others, by raising and propagating prejudices against the word, and the faithful preachers of it. So *this generation* did; because they were resolved not to believe Christ and John, they set themselves to abuse them, and to represent them as the worst. As for John the Baptist, they say, *He has a devil.* They imputed his strictness and reservedness to melancholy, and some kind or degree of a possession of Satan. As for Jesus Christ, they imputed his free and obliging conversation to the more vicious habit of luxury and flesh-pleasing: *Behold a gluttonous man and a wine-bibber.* No reflection could be more foul and invidious; yet none could be more false and unjust; for Christ *pleased not himself* (Rom. xv. 3), nor did ever any man live such a life of self-denial, mortification, and contempt of the world, as Christ lived. The most unspotted innocency, and the most unparalleled excellency, will not always be a fence *against the reproach of tongues*; nay, a man's best gifts and best actions may be made the matter of his reproach. The best of our actions may become the worst of our accusations. It was true in some sense, that Christ was *a Friend to publicans and sinners*, the best Friend they ever had, for he *came into the world to save sinners*; but this is, and will be to eternity, Christ's praise, and they forfeited the benefit of it who thus turned it to his reproach.

Note, 4. They are *like children sitting in the markets*; they are foolish as children, froward as children, mindless and playful as children; would they but *show themselves men* in understanding, there would be some hopes of them. *The market-place they sit in* is to some a place of idleness (*ch.* xx. 3); to others a place of worldly business (James iv. 13); to all a place of noise or diversion. Their heads, and hands, and hearts are full of the world, the cares of which *choke the word*, and choke their souls at last. Thus *in the markets* they are, and there they *sit*; in these things their hearts rest, and by them they resolve to abide.

Note, 5. Though the means of grace be thus slighted and abused by many, by the most, yet there is a remnant that through grace do improve them. *But wisdom is justified of her children.* Christ is *Wisdom*; in him *are hid treasures of wisdom*. The gospel is *wisdom*, it is *the wisdom from above*: true believers are begotten again by it, and born from above too: they are wise *children*. These *children of wisdom justify wisdom*; they comply with the designs of Christ's grace. *The publicans justified God, being baptized with the baptism of John*, and afterwards embracing the gospel of Christ. Paul is *not ashamed of the gospel of Christ*, because, whatever it is to others, *to them that believe it is the power of God unto salvation*, Rom. i. 16. When *the cross of Christ*, which to others is *foolishness* and *a stumbling-block*, is *to them that are called the wisdom of God and the power of God* (1 Cor. i. 23, 24), here is *wisdom justified of her children*. If the unbelief of some reproach Christ by giving him the lie, the faith of others shall honour him by setting to its seal that he is true, and that *he also is wise*, 1 Cor. i. 25. Whether we do it or not, it will be done. That *generation is not passed away*, but remains in a succession of the like; for as it was then, it has been since and is still; *some believe the things which are spoken, and some believe not*.

II. As to the particular *places* in which Christ was most conversant. *Then began he to upbraid them*, *v.* 20. He began to preach to them long before (*ch.* iv. 17), but he did not *begin to upbraid* till now. Rough and unpleasing methods must not be taken, till gentler means have first been used. Christ is not apt *to upbraid. Wisdom* first invites, but when her invitations are slighted, then she *upbraids*. Those do not go in Christ's method, who begin with upbraidings.

1. The sin charged upon them; the most shameful, ungrateful thing that could be, that *they repented not*. Wilful impenitency is the great damning sin of multitudes that enjoy the gospel. The great doctrine that both John the Baptist and Christ, and the apostles preached, was repentance; the great thing designed, both in the *piping* and in the *mourning*, was to prevail with people to change their minds and ways, to leave their sins and turn to God; and this they would not be brought to. Christ reproved them for their other sins, that he might *lead them to repentance*; but when *they repented not, He upbraided them* with it, that they might upbraid themselves, and might at length see the folly of it, as that which alone makes the sad case a desperate one, and the wound incurable.

2. The aggravation of the sin; they were *the cities in which most of his mighty works were done*. By Christ's *mighty works* they should have been prevailed with, not only to receive his doctrine, but to obey his law; the curing of bodily diseases should have

been the healing of their souls, but it had not that effect. The stronger inducements we have to repent, the more heinous is the impenitency and the severer will the reckoning be.

(1) Chorazin and Bethsaida are here instanced (*v.* 21, 22), they have each of them their woe: *Woe unto thee, Chorazin, woe unto thee, Bethsaida.* Christ came *into the world to bless us*; but if that blessing be slighted, he has woes in reserve, and his woes are of all others the most terrible. These two cities were rich and populous places; Bethsaida was lately advanced to a city by Philip the tetrarch; out of it Christ took at least three of his apostles: thus highly were these places favoured! Soon after this they decayed, and dwindled into mean, obscure villages. So fatally does sin ruin cities, and so certainly does the word of Christ take place!

Now Chorazin and Bethsaida are here compared with Tyre and Sidon. Christ, to convince and humble them, here shows,

[1] That Tyre and Sidon would not have been so bad as Chorazin and Bethsaida. If they had had the same word preached, and the same miracles wrought among them, *they would have repented*, and that *long ago*, as Nineveh did, in *sackcloth and ashes*. Christ, who knows the hearts of all, knew that if he had gone and lived among them, and preached among them, he should have done more good there than where he was; yet he continued where he was for some time, to encourage his ministers to do so, though they see not the success they desire. Our repentance is slow and delayed, but theirs would have been speedy; they would have repented long ago. Ours has been slight and superficial; theirs would have been deep and serious, in *sackcloth and ashes*.

[2] That therefore Tyre and Sidon shall not be so miserable as Chorazin and Bethsaida, but it shall be *more tolerable* for them in the *day of judgment, v.* 22. In that judgment, all the means of grace that were enjoyed in the state of probation will certainly come into the account, and it will be enquired, not only how bad we were, but how much better we might have been. If self-reproach be the torture of hell, it must needs be hell indeed to those who had such a fair opportunity of getting to heaven.

(2) Capernaum is here condemned with an emphasis (*v.* 23), "*And thou, Capernaum.*" Christ's miracles here were *daily bread*, and therefore, as the manna of old, were despised and called light bread. Many a sweet and comfortable lecture of grace Christ had read them to little purpose, and therefore here he reads them a dreadful lecture of wrath.

We have here Capernaum's doom, Thou *which are exalted to heaven shalt be brought down to hell*. Those who enjoy the gospel in power and purity, are thereby *exalted to heaven*; they are lifted up *toward heaven*; but if, notwithstanding, they still *cleave to the earth*, they may thank themselves that they are not lifted up *into heaven*. Our external privileges will be so far from saving us, that if our hearts and lives be not agreeable to them, they will but inflame the reckoning: the higher the precipice is, the more fatal is the fall from it. We have it here put in comparison with the doom of Sodom. Christ here tells us, That Capernaum's means would have saved Sodom. If these miracles had been done among the Sodomites, as bad as they were, they would have repented, and *their city would have remained unto this day* a monument of sparing mercy. Upon true repentance through Christ, even the greatest sin shall be pardoned and the greatest ruin prevented. *It shall be more tolerable for the land of Sodom than for that city.*

Verses 25–30

I. Christ here returns thanks to God for his favour to those *babes* who had the mysteries of the gospel *revealed to them* (*v.* 25, 26). *Jesus answered and said.* It is called an answer because it is so comfortable a reply to the melancholy considerations preceding. With this thought therefore he refreshes himself; and to make it the more refreshing, he puts it into a thanksgiving. We may take great encouragement in looking upward to God, when round about us we see nothing but what is discouraging. *Jesus answered and said, I thank thee.* Thanksgiving is a proper answer to dark and disquieting thoughts, and may be an effectual means to silence them. Songs of praise are sovereign cordials to drooping souls. When we have no other answer ready to the suggestions of grief and fear, we may have recourse to this, *I thank thee, O Father*; let us bless God that it is not worse with us than it is.

1. The titles he gives to God: *O Father, Lord of heaven and earth.* In all our approaches to God, by praise as well as by prayer, it is good for us to eye him as a Father. Mercies are then doubly sweet, and powerful to enlarge the heart in praise, when they are received as tokens of a Father's love. It becomes children to be grateful and to say, *Thank you, father*, as readily as, *Pray, father.* When we come to God as a Father, we must withal remember, that he is *Lord of heaven and earth*; which obliges us to come to him with reverence, and yet with confidence, as one able to defend us from all evil and to supply us with all good.

2. The thing he gives thanks for: *Because thou hast hid these things from the wise and prudent, and yet revealed them to babes. These things; the things that belong to our peace,* Luke xix. 42. The great things of the everlasting gospel have been and are hid from many that were *wise and prudent*, that were eminent for learning and worldly policy. *The world by wisdom knew not God*, 1 Cor. i. 21. Men may dive deeply into the mysteries of nature and into the mysteries of state, and yet be ignorant of, and mistaken about, the mysteries of *the kingdom of heaven*, for want of an experience of the power of them. While *the wise and prudent men* of the world are in the dark about gospel mysteries, even the *babes in Christ* have the sanctifying saving knowledge of them: *Thou hast revealed them unto babes.* The learned men of the world were not made choice of to be the preachers of the gospel, but *the foolish things of the world* (1 Cor. ii. 6, 8, 10). This difference between *the prudent* and the *babes* is of God's own making. It is he that has *hid these things from the wise and prudent*; he gave them parts, and learning, and much of human understanding above others, and they were proud of that, and rested in it, and looked no further. Had they honoured God with the wisdom and prudence they had, he would have given them the knowledge of these better things. It is he that has *revealed them unto babes.* Thus *he resists the proud*, and *gives grace to the humble*, James iv. 6. This dispensation must be resolved into the divine sovereignty. Christ himself referred it to that; *Even so, Father, for so it seemed good in thy sight.* Christ here subscribes to the will of his Father in this matter; *Even so.* Let God take what way he pleases to glorify himself. We can give no reason why Peter, a fisherman, should be made an apostle, and not Nicodemus, a Pharisee, and a ruler of the Jews, though he also believed in Christ; but *so it seemed good in God's sight.* This way of dispensing divine grace is to be acknowledged by us with all thankfulness. We must thank God, That *these things* are *revealed.* That they are *revealed to babes*; and this honour put upon those whom the world pours contempt upon. It magnifies the mercy to them, that *these things* are *hid from the wise and prudent*, and divine power and wisdom made to shine the more bright. See 1 Cor. i. 27, 31.

II. Christ here makes a gracious offer of the benefits of the gospel to all.

1. The solemn preface which ushers in this call or invitation. Christ prefixes his authority, produces his credentials.

Two things he here lays before us, *v.* 27.

(1) His commission from the Father: *All things are delivered unto me of my Father.* He is authorised to settle a new covenant between God and man, and to offer peace and happiness to the apostate world, upon such terms as he should think fit. This encourages us to come to Christ, that he is commissioned to receive us, and to give us what we come for, and has *all things delivered to him* for that purpose, by him who is *Lord of all.* All powers, all treasures are in his hand. God has made him the great Referee, the blessed Daysman, to lay his hand upon us both; that which we have to do is to agree to the reference, to submit to the arbitration of the Lord Jesus, for the taking up of this unhappy controversy, and to enter into bonds to stand to his award.

(2) His intimacy with the Father: *No man knoweth the Son but the Father, neither knoweth any man the Father save the Son.* It must therefore be a great encouragement to us to be assured, that they understood one another very well in this affair; that the Father knew the Son, and the Son knew the Father, and both perfectly, so that there could be no mistake in the settling of this matter; as often there is among men, to the overthrow of contracts, and the breaking of the measures taken. *None knows the Father save the Son*, he adds, *and he to whom the Son will reveal him.* The happiness of men lies in an acquaintance with God; it *is life eternal.* Those who would have an acquaintance with God, must apply themselves to Jesus Christ; for the light of the knowledge of the glory of God shines in the face of Christ, 2 Cor. iv. 6.

2. Here is the offer itself that is made to us, and an invitation to accept of it. We are here invited to Christ, as our Priest, Prince, and Prophet, to be saved.

(1) We must come to Jesus Christ as our Rest, and repose ourselves in him (*v.* 28), *Come unto me all ye that labour.* The character of the persons invited; *all that labour, and are heavy laden.* This is a word in season to him that is weary. But it is rather to be understood of the burthen of sin, both the guilt and the power of it. All those, and those only, are invited to rest in Christ, that are sensible of sin as a burthen, and groan under it; that are not only convinced of the evil of sin, of their own sin, but are contrite in soul for it; that are really sick of their sins. This is a necessary preparative for pardon and peace. The Comforter must first convince (John xvi. 8). The invitation itself: *Come unto me.* See here how he holds out *the golden sceptre*, that we may touch the top of it and may live. It is the duty and interest of weary *and heavy laden* sinners to *come to Jesus Christ.* We must accept of him, as our Physician and Advocate, freely willing to be saved by him, in his own way, and upon his own terms. The blessing promised to those that do come: *I will give you rest.* Truly *rest is good*, especially to those *that labour and are heavy laden.* Jesus Christ will give assured rest to those weary souls, that by a lively faith come to him for it; a *rest in God*, in his love.

(2) We must come to Jesus Christ as our Ruler, and submit ourselves to him (*v.* 29). *Take my yoke upon you.* The *rest* he promises is a release from the drudgery of sin, not from the service of God. Christ has a *yoke* for our necks, as well as a *crown* for our heads. To call those who are weary *and heavy laden*, to *take a yoke upon* them, looks like adding *affliction to the afflicted*; but the pertinency of it lies in the word *my*: "You are under a *yoke* which makes you weary: shake that off and try mine, which will make you easy." It is Christ's *yoke*; the *yoke* he has appointed; a *yoke* he has himself drawn in before us,

for *he learned obedience*, and which he does by his Spirit draw in with us, for *he helpeth our infirmities*, Rom. viii. 26. A *yoke* speaks some hardship, but if the beast must draw, the *yoke* helps him.

Now this is the hardest part of our lesson, and therefore it is qualified (*v.* 30). *My yoke is easy and my burden is light*; you need not be afraid of it. The *yoke* of Christ's commands is an *easy yoke*; there is nothing in it to gall the yielding neck, nothing to hurt us, but, on the contrary, much to refresh us. It is a *yoke* that is lined with love. Such is the nature of all Christ's commands, all summed up in one word, and that a sweet word, love. It may be a little hard at first, but it is easy afterwards; the love of God and the hope of heaven will make it *easy*. The *burden* of Christ's cross is a *light burden*, very light. This *burden* in itself is *not joyous, but grievous*; yet as it is Christ's, it is *light*. Paul knew as much of it as any man, and he calls it a *light affliction*, 2 Cor. iv. 17. As afflictions abound, and are prolonged, consolations abound, and are prolonged too.

(3) We must come to Jesus Christ as our Teacher, and set ourselves to learn of him, *v.* 29. Christ has erected a great school, and has invited us to be his scholars. We must enter ourselves, associate with his scholars, and daily attend the instructions he gives by his word and Spirit. We must so *learn of Christ* as to *learn Christ* (Eph. iv. 20), for he is both Teacher and Lesson, Guide and Way, and All in All.

Two reasons are given why we must *learn of Christ*. *I am meek and lowly in heart*. He is *meek*, and can have *compassion on the ignorant*. Many able teachers are hot and hasty, which is a great discouragement to those who are dull and slow; but Christ knows how to bear with such, and to open their understandings. *He is lowly in heart*. He condescends to teach poor scholars, to teach novices. He teaches the first principles, such things as are milk for babes; he stoops to the meanest capacities. It is an encouragement to us to put ourselves to school to such a Teacher. *You shall find rest to your souls*. Rest for the soul is the most desirable rest. The only way, and a sure way to find *rest for our souls*, is to sit at Christ's feet and hear his word. The *understanding* finds *rest* in the *knowledge of* God and Jesus Christ, and is there abundantly satisfied. The affections find rest in the love of God and Jesus Christ, and meet with that in them which gives them an abundant satisfaction; quietness and assurance for ever. This rest is to be had with Christ for all those who learn of him.

CHAPTER 12

I. Christ's clearing of the law of the fourth commandment concerning the sabbath-day, ver. 1–13. II. The prudence, humility, and self-denial of our Lord Jesus in working his miracles, ver. 14–21. III. Christ's answer to the scribes and Pharisees, who imputed his casting out devils to a compact with the devil, ver. 22–27. IV. Christ's reply to the scribes and Pharisees, challenging him to show them a sign from heaven, ver. 38–45. V. Christ's judgment about his kindred and relations, ver. 46–50.

Verses 1–13

The Jewish teachers had corrupted many of the commandments, by interpreting them more loosely than they were intended; but concerning the fourth commandment, they had erred in the other extreme, and interpreted it too strictly.

Now that which our Lord Jesus here lays down is, that the works of necessity and mercy are lawful on the sabbath day.

It is usual to settle the meaning of a law by judgments given upon cases that happen in fact, and in like manner is the meaning of this law settled.

I. Christ, by justifying his disciples in plucking the ears of corn on the sabbath day, shows that *works of necessity* are *lawful* on that day. Now here observe,

1. What it was that the disciples did. They were following their Master one sabbath day through a cornfield and *they were hungry*. Providence ordered it that they *went through the corn*, and there they were supplied. God has many ways of bringing suitable provision to his people when they need it. Being in the cornfields, they began to *pluck the ears of corn*; the law of God allowed this (Deut. xxiii. 25), to teach people to be neighbourly, and not to insist upon property in a small matter whereby another may be benefited. This was but slender provision for Christ and his disciples, but it was the best they had, and they were content with it.

2. What was the offence that the Pharisees took at this. It was but a dry breakfast, yet the Pharisees would not let them eat that in quietness. They did not quarrel with them for taking another man's corn, but for doing it *on the sabbath day*; for plucking and rubbing the ears of corn on that day was expressly forbidden, because it was *a kind of reaping*.

3. What was Christ's answer to this cavil of the Pharisees. The disciples could say little for themselves. But Christ has something to say for them, and justifies what they did.

(1) He justifies them by precedents, which were allowed to be good by the Pharisees themselves. He urges an ancient instance of David: "*Have ye not read* the story (1 Sam. xxi. 6) of David's eating the show-bread, which by the law was appropriated to the priest?" That which bore out David in eating the show-bread was not his dignity but his hunger. The greatest shall not have their lusts indulged, but the meanest shall have their wants considered. That may be done in a case of necessity which may not be done at another time; there are laws which necessity has not, but it is a law to itself. He urges a daily instance of the priests, which they likewise *read in the law. The priests in the temple* did a great deal of servile work on the sabbath day, which in a common case would *have been profaning the sabbath*, because the temple-service required and justified it. This intimates, that those labours are lawful on the sabbath day which are necessary, not only to the *support of life*, but to the *service of the day*; as tolling a bell to call the congregation together, travelling to church, and the like. Sabbath rest is to promote, not to hinder, sabbath worship.

(2) He justifies them by arguments, three cogent ones.

[1] *In this place is one greater than the temple*, *v.* 6. If the temple-service would justify what the priests did in their ministration, the service of Christ would much more justify the disciples in what they did in their attendance upon him. Christ, in a cornfield, was *greater than the temple*.

[2] *God will have mercy and not sacrifice*, *v.* 7. This is quoted from Hos. vi. 6. It was used before, *ch.* ix. 13, in vindication of mercy to the souls of men; here, of mercy to their bodies. The rest of the sabbath was ordained for man's good. *If you had known what this means*, had known what it is to be of a merciful disposition, you would have been sorry that they were forced to do this to satisfy their hunger, and would *not have condemned the guiltless*. It is not enough for us to know the scriptures, but we must labour to *know the meaning* of them. *Let him that readeth understand*. Ignorance of the meaning of the scripture is especially shameful in those who take upon them to teach others.

[3] *The Son of man is Lord even of the sabbath day*, *v.* 8. That law, as all the rest, is put into the hand of Christ, to be altered, enforced, or dispensed with, as he sees good. He was authorised to make such an alteration of that day, as that it should become the Lord's day, the Lord Christ's day.

Christ having thus silenced the Pharisees, and got clear of them (*v.* 9), *departed*, and *went into their synagogue,* the synagogue of these Pharisees, in which they presided, and toward which he was going, when they picked this quarrel with him. We must take heed lest anything that occurs in our way to holy ordinances unfit us for, or divert us from, our due attendance on them. We must not, for the sake of private feuds and personal piques, draw back from public worship. Satan gains this point, if, by sowing discord among brethren, he prevail to drive them, or any of them, from the synagogue, and the communion of the faithful.

II. Christ, by *healing the man that had the withered hand on the sabbath day,* shows that works of mercy are lawful and proper to be done on that day.

Here is, 1. The affliction that this poor man was in. This poor man was in the synagogue. Those who can do but little, or have but little to do for the world, must do so much the more for their souls; as the rich, the aged, and the infirm.

2. A spiteful question which the Pharisees put to Christ upon the sight of this man. *They asked him, saying, Is it lawful to heal?* We read not here of any address this poor man made to Christ for a cure, but they observed Christ began to take notice of him, and knew it was usual for him to be *found of those that sought him not,* and therefore with their badness they anticipated his goodness. Did ever any ask, whether it is lawful for God to heal, to send his word and heal? *Is it lawful to heal?* To enquire into the lawfulness and unlawfulness of actions is very good, and we cannot apply ourselves to any with such enquiring more fitly than to Christ; but they asked here, not that they might be instructed by him, but *that they might accuse him.*

3. Christ's answer to this question, by way of appeal to themselves, and their own opinion and practice, *v.* 11, 12. In case a *sheep* should fall into a pit on the sabbath day, *would they not lift it out?* No doubt they might do it, the fourth commandment allows it; they must do it, for a *merciful man regardeth the life of his beast,* and for their parts they would do it, rather than lose a sheep; does Christ take care for sheep? Yes, he does; he preserves and provides for both man and beast. But here he says it for our sakes (1 Cor. ix. 9, 10), and hence argues, *How much then is a man better than a sheep?* Man, in respect of his being, is a great deal better, and more valuable, than the best of the brute creatures. They do not consider this, who are more solicitous for the education, preservation, and supply of their horses and dogs than of God's poor, or perhaps their own household.

Hence Christ infers a truth that *it is lawful to do well on the sabbath days;* they had asked, *Is it lawful to heal?* Christ proves it is lawful to *do well.* There are more ways of *doing well* upon sabbath days, than by the duties of God's immediate worship; this is *doing good;* and this must be done from a principle of love and charity, and this is *doing well,* and it *shall be accepted.*

4. Christ's curing of the man, notwithstanding the offence which he foresaw the Pharisees would take at it, *v.* 13. Duty is not to be left undone, nor opportunities of doing good neglected, for fear of giving offence. He said to the man, "*Stretch forth thy hand,* exert thyself as well as thou canst;" and he did so, *and it was restored whole.* In order to our cure, he commands us to *stretch forth our hands,* to improve our natural powers, and do as well as we can; to stretch them out in prayer to God, to stretch them out to lay hold on Christ by faith, to stretch them out in holy endeavours. Now this man could not stretch forth his withered hand of himself, yet Christ bid him do it. God's commands to us to do the duty which of ourselves we are not able to do are no more absurd or unjust, than this command to the man with the

withered hand, *to stretch it forth;* for with the command, there is a promise of grace which is given by the word.

Verses 14–21

I. The cursed malice of the Pharisees against Christ (*v.* 14); being enraged at the convincing evidence of his miracles, they *went out, and held a council against him, how they might destroy him.* That which vexed them was, not only that by his miracles his honour eclipsed theirs, but that the doctrine he preached was directly opposite to their pride and hypocrisy, and worldly interest; but they pretended to be displeased at his breaking the sabbath day, which was by the law a capital crime. They took counsel, not to imprison nor banish him, but to destroy him, to be the death of him who came *that we might have life.* What an indignity was hereby put upon our Lord Jesus, to run him down as an outlaw, and the plague of his country, who was the greatest blessing of it, the Glory of his people Israel!

II. Christ's absconding upon this occasion, and the privacy he chose, to decline, not his work, but his danger; because *his hour was not yet come* (*v.* 15), *he withdrew himself from thence.* He could have secured himself by miracle, but chose to do it in the ordinary way of flight and retirement. Herein he humbled himself, that he was driven to the common shift of those who are most helpless; thus also he would give an example to his own rule, *When they persecute you in one city, flee to another.*

Christ did not retire for his own ease, nor seek an excuse to leave off his work. He was even then doing good, when he was forced to flee for the same. Thus he gave an example to his ministers, to do what they can, when they cannot do what they would. The common people crowded after him; *great multitudes followed him* and found him out. But it was really his honour, as it was also the honour of his grace, that the poor were evangelised; that when they received him, he received them and healed them all. Christ came into the world to be a Physician-general, as the sun to the lower world, *with healing under his wings.* Though the Pharisees persecuted Christ for doing good, yet he went on in it. He *healed them all,* and yet (*v.* 16), *charged them that they should not make him known;* which may be looked upon as an act of prudence. Christ though he would not omit doing good, yet would do it with as little noise as possible. Wise and good men, though they covet to do good, yet are far from coveting to have it talked of when it is done; because it is God's acceptance, not men's applause, that they aim at. His withdrawal was also an act of humility and self-denial, to set us an example of humility, and to teach us not to proclaim our own goodness or usefulness, or to desire to have it proclaimed. Christ would have his disciples to be the reverse of those who did all their works *to be seen of men.*

III. The fulfilling of the scriptures in all this, *v.* 17. The scripture here said to be fulfilled is Isa. xlii. 1–4, which is quoted at large, *v.* 18–21. The scope of it is to show how mild and quiet, and yet how successful, our Lord Jesus should be in his undertaking.

1. The pleasure of the Father in Christ (*v.* 18); *Behold, my Servant whom I have chosen, my Beloved in whom my soul is well pleased.* Hence we may learn,

(1) That our Saviour was God's Servant in the great work of our redemption. As a *Servant,* he had a great work appointed him, and a great trust reposed in him. In the work of our salvation he took upon him the form of a servant. The motto of this Prince is, *Ich dien—I serve.*

(2) That Jesus Christ was chosen of God, as the only fit and proper person for the management of the great work of our redemption. He is *my Servant*

whom I have chosen. None but he was able to do the Redeemer's work, or fit to wear the Redeemer's crown. Christ did not thrust himself upon this work, but was duly chosen into it.

(3) That Jesus Christ is God's Beloved, his beloved Son.

(4) That Jesus Christ is one in whom the Father is well pleased. And he is well pleased with us in him; for he has *made us accepted in the Beloved,* Eph. i. 6. All the interest which fallen man has or can have in God is grounded upon and owing to God's *well-pleasedness* in Jesus Christ.

2. The promise of the Father to him in two things.

(1) That he should be every way well qualified for his undertaking; *I will put my Spirit upon him,* as a Spirit of *wisdom and counsel,* Isa. xi. 2, 3. Those whom God calls to any service, he will be sure to fit and qualify for it. He received the Spirit, not by measure, but *without measure,* John iii. 34. Whoever they be that God has chosen, and in whom he is well pleased, he will be sure to *put his Spirit upon them.* Wherever he confers his love, he confers somewhat of his likeness.

(2) That he should be abundantly successful in his undertaking. Those whom God sends he will certainly own.

[1] He shall *show judgment to the Gentiles.* Christ in his own person preached to those who bordered upon the heathen nations (see Mark iii. 6–8), and by his apostle showed his gospel, called here his *judgment,* to the Gentile world. The gospel, which has a direct tendency to the reforming and bettering of men's hearts, and lives, shall be showed to the Gentiles.

[2] *In his name shall the Gentiles trust, v.* 21. He shall so show judgment to them, that they shall heed and observe what he shows them, and be influenced by it to depend upon him. The great design of the gospel, is to bring people to trust in the name of Jesus Christ; his name Jesus, a Saviour. The law we wait for is the law of faith, the law of trusting in his name. This is now his great commandment, that we *believe in Christ,* 1 John iii. 23.

3. The prediction concerning him, and his mild and quiet management of his undertaking, *v.* 19, 20.

(1) That he should carry on his undertaking without noise or ostentation. *He shall not strive, or make an outcry.* Christ and his kingdom *come not with observation,* Luke xvii. 20, 21. He *was in the world and the world knew him not.* He spake in a still small voice, which was alluring to all, but terrifying to none; he did not affect to make a noise, but came down silently like the dew.

(2) That he should carry on his undertaking without severity and rigour (*v.* 20). *A bruised reed shall he not break.* Some understand this of his patience in bearing with the wicked. Others rather understand it of his power and grace in bearing up the weak. In general, the design of his gospel is to establish such a method of salvation as encourages sincerity, though there be much infirmity; it does not insist upon a sinless obedience, but accepts an upright, willing mind. As to particular persons, that follow Christ, observe, How their case is here described—they are like *a bruised reed,* and *smoking flax.* Young beginners in religion are weak as a bruised reed, and their weakness offensive like smoking flax. Christ's disciples were as yet but weak, and many are so that have a place in his family. He will not discourage them, much less reject them or cast them off; the reed that is bruised shall not be broken and trodden down, but shall be supported, and made as strong as a cedar or flourishing palm-tree. The candle newly lighted, though it only smokes and does not flame, shall not be blown out, but blown up. The *day of small things* is the day of *precious* things. The good

issue and success of this, intimated in that, *till he send forth judgment unto victory.* Both the preaching of the gospel in the world, and the power of the gospel in the heart, shall prevail. Grace shall get the upper hand of corruption, and shall at length be perfected in glory. Truth and victory are much the same, for *great is the truth, and will prevail.*

Verses 22–37

I. Christ's glorious conquest of Satan, in the gracious cure of one under his power.

1. The man's case was very sad; he was *possessed with a devil.* This poor man that was possessed was blind and dumb; a miserable case! he could neither see to help himself, nor speak to others to help him. Satan blinds the eye of faith and seals up the lips of prayer.

2. His cure was very strange, and the more so, because sudden; *he healed him.* And the cause being removed, immediately the effect ceased; the *blind and dumb both spake and saw.* When Satan's power is broken in the soul, the eyes are opened to see God's glory, and the lips opened to speak his praise.

II. The conviction which this gave to the people, to *all the people*: they *were amazed.* They inferred from it, *"Is not this the Son of David?"* We may take this, 1. As an *enquiring* question. It was a good question that they started; but, it should seem, it was soon lost, and was not prosecuted. Such convictions as these should be brought to a head, and then they are likely to be brought to the heart. Or, 2. As an *affirming* question; *Is not this the Son of David?* "Yes, certainly it is, it can be no other." So plain and easy was the way made to this great truth of Christ being the Messiah and Saviour of the world, that the common people could not miss it; the *wayfaring men, though fools, could not err therein.* See Isa. xxxv. 8. The world by wisdom knew not God, and by the foolish things the wise were confounded.

III. The blasphemous cavil of the Pharisees, *v.* 24. They were proud of the reputation they had among the people; *that* fed their pride, supported their power, and filled their purses. Those who bind up their happiness in the praise and applause of men, expose themselves to a perpetual uneasiness upon every favourable word that they hear said of any other. The shadow of honour followed Christ, who fled from it, and fled from the Pharisees, who were eager in the pursuit of it. Observe,

1. How scornfully they speak of Christ, *this fellow.* It is a bad thing to speak of good men with disdain because they are poor.

2. How blasphemously they speak of his miracles; they could not deny the matter of fact; it was as plain as the sun, that devils were cast out by the word of Christ. They had no other way to avoid the conclusion, that *this is the Son of David,* than by suggesting that *Christ cast out devils by Beelzebub*; that there was a compact between Christ and the devil; pursuant to that, the devil was not cast out, but did voluntarily retire.

IV. Christ's reply to this base insinuation, *v.* 25–30. *Jesus knew their thoughts.* Jesus Christ knows what we are thinking at any time, knows what is in man; he *understands our thoughts afar off.* Christ's reply is said to be to their thoughts, because he knew that they did not say it in their haste, but that it was the product of a rooted malignity.

Christ's reply to this imputation is copious and cogent.

1. It would be very strange, and highly improbable, that Satan should be cast out by such a compact, because then Satan's *kingdom would be divided against itself, v.* 25, 26.

(1) Here is a known rule laid down, that in all societies a common ruin is the consequence of mutual quarrels: *Every kingdom divided against itself is brought to desolation.* Divisions commonly end in desolations; if we clash, we break; if we divide one from another, we become an easy prey to a common enemy. Churches and nations have known this by sad experience.

(2) The application of it to the case in hand (*v.* 26), *If Satan cast out Satan;* if the prince of the devils should be at variance with the inferior devils, the whole kingdom and interest would soon be broken; nay, if Satan should come into a compact with Christ, it must be to his own ruin; for the manifest design and tendency of Christ's preaching and miracles was to overthrow the kingdom of Satan. If he should fall in with Christ, *how should then his kingdom stand?* He would himself contribute to the overthrow of it. This victory must be obtained by nobler methods. Let the prince of the devils muster up all his forces. Christ will be too hard for his united force, and his kingdom shall not stand.

2. It was not at all strange, or improbable, that devils should be cast out by the Spirit of God.

(1) *How* otherwise *do your children cast them out?* There were those among the Jews who, by invocation of the name of the most high God, or the God of Abraham, Isaac, and Jacob, did sometimes cast out devils. Josephus speaks of some in his time that did it; we read of *Jewish exorcists* (Acts xix. 13), and of some that *in Christ's name cast out devils,* though they did not follow him (Mark ix. 38). These the Pharisees condemned not, but imputed what they did to the Spirit of God. It was therefore merely from spite and envy to Christ, that they would own that others cast out devils by the Spirit of God, but suggest that he did it by compact with Beelzebub. The judgments of envy are made not by reason, but prejudice.

(2) This casting out of devils was a certain token and indication of the approach and appearance of the kingdom of God (*v.* 28); "But if it be indeed that *I cast out devils by the Spirit of God,* the kingdom of the Messiah is now about to be set up among you." Other miracles that Christ wrought proved him *sent of God,* but this proved him sent of God to destroy the devil's kingdom and his works. The destruction of the devil's power is wrought by the Spirit of God. If the devil's interest in a soul be sunk and broken by the Spirit of God, as a Sanctifier, no doubt but *the kingdom of God is come* to that soul, the kingdom of grace, a blessed earnest of the kingdom of the glory.

3. The comparing of Christ's miracles with his doctrine evidenced that he was so far from being in league with Satan, that he was at open enmity and hostility against him (*v.* 29); *How can one enter into a strong man's house, and plunder his goods,* and carry them away, *except he first bind the strong man? And then he* may do what he pleases with his goods. The world was in Satan's possession, and under his power, so is every unregenerate soul; there Satan resides, there he rules. The design of Christ's gospel was to spoil the devil's house, which, as a strong man, he kept in the world; *to turn the people from darkness to light,* from sin to holiness. Pursuant to this design, he bound the strong man, when he cast out unclean spirits by his word. When he showed how easily and effectually he could cast the devil out of people's bodies, he encouraged all believers to hope that, whatever power Satan might usurp and exercise in the souls of men, Christ by his grace would break it. When some of the worst of sinners were sanctified and justified, and became the best of saints, then Christ spoiled the devil's house, and will spoil it more and more.

4. This holy war, which Christ was carrying on with vigour against the devil and his kingdom, was such as would not admit of a neutrality (*v.* 30), *He that is not with me is against me.* In the little differences that may arise between the disciples of Christ among themselves, we are taught to seek peace, by accounting those who *are not against us, to be with us* (Luke ix. 50); but in the great quarrel between Christ and the devil, no peace is to be sought. He that is not hearty *for* Christ, will be reckoned with as really *against* him: he that is cold in the cause, is looked upon as an enemy. We must be entirely, faithfully, and immovably, on Christ's side: it is the *right* side, and will at last be the *rising* side.

The latter clause is to the same purport: *He that gathereth not with me scattereth.* Christ's errand into the world was to gather in his harvest, to gather in those whom the Father had given him, John xi. 52. Christ expects and requires from those who are with him, that they gather with him; gather others to him. If we *gather not with Christ, we scatter;* it is not enough, not to do hurt, but we must do good.

V. Here is a discourse of Christ's upon this occasion, concerning tongue-sins; *Wherefore I say unto you.* He warns the people concerning three sorts of tongue-sins.

1. Blasphemous words against the Holy Ghost are the worst kind of tongue-sins, and unpardonable, *v.* 31, 32.

(1) Here is a gracious assurance of the pardon of all sin upon gospel terms. The greatness of sin shall be no bar to our acceptance with God, if we truly repent and believe the gospel: *All manner of sin and blasphemy shall be forgiven unto men.* Though it *reach up to the heavens,* yet *with the Lord there is mercy, that reacheth beyond the heavens;* mercy will be extended even to blasphemy, a sin immediately touching God's name and honour. Paul obtained mercy, who had *been a blasphemer,* 1 Tim. i. 13. Well may we say, *Who is a God like unto thee, pardoning iniquity?* Micah vii. 18. Even *words spoken against the Son of man shall be forgiven,* as theirs were who reviled him at his death, many of whom repented and found mercy.

(2) Here is an exception of *the blasphemy against the Holy Ghost,* which is here declared to be the only unpardonable sin. What is this sin; it is *speaking against the Holy Ghost.* See what malignity there is in tongue-sins, when the only unpardonable sin is so. *But Jesus knew their thoughts, v.* 25. It is not all speaking against the person or essence of the Holy Ghost, or merely the resisting of his internal working in the sinner himself, that is here meant; for *who then should be saved?* None are excepted by name, nor any by description, but those only *that blaspheme the Holy Ghost.* This blasphemy is excepted, not for any defect of mercy in God, or merit in Christ, but because it inevitably leaves the sinner in infidelity and impenitency. Those who fear they have committed this sin, give a good sign that they have not. Those therefore who blaspheme this dispensation of the Spirit, cannot possibly be brought to believe in Christ; those who shall impute them to a collusion with Satan, as the Pharisees did the miracles, what can convince them? This is such a stronghold of infidelity as a man can never be beaten out of, and is therefore unpardonable, because hereby repentance is hid from the sinner's eyes. See the sentence that is passed upon it: *It shall not be forgiven, neither in this world, nor in the world to come.* There is no cure for a sin so directly against the remedy.

2. Christ speaks here concerning other wicked words, the products of corruption reigning in the heart, and breaking out thence, *v.* 33-35. Our Lord Jesus therefore points to the springs and heals them; let the heart be sanctified and it will appear in our words.

(1) The heart is the *root,* the language is the *fruit*

(v. 33); if the nature of the tree be good, it will bring forth fruit accordingly. Wherever lust reigns in the heart it will break out; diseased lungs make an offensive breath. Men's language discovers what country they are of. "*Either make the tree good, and then the fruit will be good;* get pure hearts and then you will have pure lips and pure lives; or else *the tree will be corrupt, and the fruit* accordingly." You may make a crab-stock to become a good tree, by grafting into it a shoot from a good tree, and then the fruit will be good; but if the tree be still the same, plant it where you will, and water it how you will, the fruit will be still corrupt. Unless the heart be *trans*formed, the life will never be thoroughly *re*formed. It should be more our care to be good really, than to seem good outwardly.

(2) The heart is the fountain, the words are the streams (v. 34); *Out of the abundance of the heart the mouth speaks,* as the streams are the overflowings of the spring. Evil words are the natural, genuine product of an evil heart. Nothing but the salt of grace, cast into the spring, will heal the waters, *season the speech,* and purify the *corrupt communication.* This they wanted, they were evil; *and how can ye, being evil, speak good things?* The people looked upon the Pharisees as a generation of saints, but Christ calls them *a generation of vipers.* Now what could be expected from a *generation of vipers,* but that which is poisonous and malignant? Can the viper be otherwise than venomous? Bad things may be expected from bad people. Christ would have his disciples know what sort of men they were to live among, that they might know what to look for. They are as Ezekiel *among scorpions* (Ezek. ii. 6), and must not think it strange if they be stung and bitten.

(3) The heart is the *treasury,* the words are the things brought out of that treasury (v. 35). It is the character of a *good man,* that he has a *good treasure in his heart,* and from thence *brings forth good things,* as there is occasion. Graces, comforts, experiences, good knowledge, good affections, good resolutions, these are a *good treasure in the heart;* the word of God hidden there, the law of God written there, divine truths dwelling and ruling there, are a treasure there, valuable and suitable, kept safe and kept secret, as the stores of the good householder, but ready for use upon all occasions. Some pretend to good expenses that have not a *good treasure*—such will soon be bankrupts: some hope they have it in them; thank God, whatever their words and actions are, they have good hearts; but *faith without works is dead:* and some have a *good treasure* of wisdom and knowledge, but they are not communicative: they have a talent, but know not how to trade with it. The complete Christian in *this* bears the image of God, that he both *is good, and does good.* It is the character of an *evil man,* that he has an *evil treasure in his heart,* and out of it *bringeth forth evil things.*

3. Christ speaks here concerning *idle words,* and shows what evil there is in them (v. 36, 37). *For every idle word,* or discourse, *that men speak, they shall give account.* God takes notice of every word we say, even that which we ourselves do not notice. Vain, idle, impertinent talk is displeasing to God; it is the product of a vain and trifling heart. We must shortly account for these idle words; they will prove us unprofitable servants, that have not improved the faculties of reason and speech, which are part of the talents we are entrusted with. *By thy words thou shalt be justified or condemned.* The constant tenor of our discourse, according as it is gracious or not gracious, will be an evidence for us, or against us.

Verses 38-45

It is probable that these Pharisees were not the same that cavilled at him (v. 24), and would not credit the signs he gave: but another set of them, who would not content themselves with the signs he gave, unless he would give them such further proof as they should demand.

I. Their address to him, v. 38. They compliment him with the title of *Master,* pretending respect for him, when they intended to abuse him; all are not indeed Christ's servants, who call him *Master.* Their request is, *We would see a sign from thee.* It was highly reasonable that they should see a sign, that he should by miracles prove his divine mission. But it was highly unreasonable to demand a sign now, when he had given so many signs already. It is natural to proud men to *pre*scribe to God, and then to make that an excuse for not *sub*scribing to him; but a man's *of*fence will never be his *de*fence.

II. His answer to this insolent demand.

1. He condemns the demand, as the language of *an evil and adulterous generation,* v. 39. He fastens the charge, not only on the *scribes and Pharisees,* but the whole nation of the Jews. They were an evil generation indeed, that not only hardened themselves against the conviction of Christ's miracles, but set themselves to abuse him, and put contempt on his miracles. They were *an adulterous generation.* As an adulterous brood; so they degenerated from the faith and obedience of their ancestors, that Abraham and Israel acknowledged them not. As an adulterous wife they departed from that God, to whom by covenant they had been espoused: they were guilty of infidelity, they did not look after gods of their own making, but they looked for signs of their own devising; and that was adultery.

2. He refuses to give them any other sign than he has already given them, but *that of the prophet Jonas.* Though Christ is always ready to hear and answer holy desires and prayers, yet he will not gratify corrupt lusts and humours. Those who *ask amiss, ask, and have not.* Signs were granted to those who desired them for the confirmation of their faith, as to Abraham and Gideon; but were denied to those who demanded them for the excuse of their unbelief.

Justly might Christ have said, They shall never see another miracle: but note his wonderful goodness. They shall have one sign of a different kind from all these, and that is, *the resurrection of Christ from the dead by his own power,* called here *the sign of the prophet Jonas.* That was such a sign as surpassed all the rest, completed and crowned them. And yet the unbelief of the Jews found out an evasion to shift off that too, by saying, *His disciples came and stole him away;* for none are so incurably blind as those who are resolved they will not see.

Now this sign of the prophet Jonas he further explains here: (v. 40) *As Jonas was three days and three nights in the whale's belly,* Christ shall be so long in the grave, and then shall rise again. As Jonah on the third day was discharged from his prison, and came to the land of the living again, so Christ on the third day should return to life, and rise out of his grave to send abroad the gospel to the Gentiles.

3. Christ takes this occasion to represent the sad character and condition of that generation in which he lived, a generation that would not be reformed. Persons and things now appear under false colours; characters and conditions are here changeable. Things are really, what they are eternally.

Now Christ represents the people of the Jews,

(1) As a generation that would be condemned by *the men of Nineveh,* whose *repenting at the preaching of Jonas* would *rise up in judgment* against them, v. 41. Christ's resurrection will be the sign of the prophet Jonas to them: but it will not have so happy an effect upon them, as that of Jonas had upon the Ninevites, for they were by it brought to such a repentance as

prevented their ruin; but the Jews will be hardened in an unbelief that shall hasten their ruin. Christ renews his calls, sat and taught, taught in the synagogues. Christ, besides the warning given us of our danger, has shown wherein we must repent, and assured us of acceptance upon our repentance. Christ wrought abundance of miracles, and all miracles of mercy: yet the Ninevites *repented at the preaching of Jonas*, but the Jews were not wrought upon by Christ's preaching. The goodness of some, who have less helps and advantages for their souls, will aggravate the badness of those who have much greater. Those who by the twilight discover *the things that belong to their peace*, will shame those who grope at noon-day.

(2) As a generation that would be condemned by the queen of the south, the queen of Sheba, *v.* 42. The Ninevites would shame them for not repenting, the queen of Sheba for not believing in Christ. She came from a far country to hear the wisdom of Solomon; yet people will not be persuaded to come and hear the wisdom of Christ. The queen of Sheba had no invitation to come to Solomon, nor any promise of being welcome; but we are invited to Christ, to sit at his feet and hear his word. She could not be sure that it would be worth her while to go so far on this errand; but we come not to Christ upon such uncertainties. *She came from the uttermost parts of the earth*, but we have Christ among us, and his word nigh us: *Behold he stands at the door, and knocks.* It should seem the wisdom the queen of Sheba came for was only philosophy and politics; but the wisdom that is to be had with Christ is wisdom to salvation. She could only *hear* Solomon's wisdom; he could not *give* her wisdom: but Christ will give wisdom to those who come to him.

(3) As a generation that were resolved to continue under the power of Satan. They are compared to one out of whom the devil is gone, but returns with double force, *v.* 43–45.

[1] The parable represents his possessing men's bodies: Christ having lately cast out a devil, and they having said *he had a devil*, gave occasion to show how much they were under the power of Satan. Christ's ejectment of him was final, and such as barred a re-entry: we find him charging the evil spirit to *go out, and enter no more*, Mark ix. 25.

[2] The application of the parable makes it to represent the case of the body of the Jewish church and nation: *So it shall be with this wicked generation*, that now resist, and will finally reject, the gospel of Christ. Let this be a warning to all nations and churches, to take heed of leaving their first love, of letting fall a good work of reformation begun among them, and returning to that wickedness which they seemed to have forsaken; *for the last state of such will be worse than the first.*

Verses 46–50

Observe, I. How Christ was interrupted in his preaching by *his mother and his brethren*, that *stood without, desiring to speak with him* (*v.* 46, 47); which desire of theirs was conveyed to him through the crowd.

1. He was as yet talking to the people. Christ's preaching was talking; it was plain, easy, and familiar, and suited to their capacity and case. The opposition we meet with in our work, must not drive us from it. He left off talking with the Pharisees, for he saw he could do no good with them; but continued to talk to the common people.

2. His mother and brethren stood without, desiring to speak with him, when they should have been standing within, desiring to hear him. They had the advantage of his daily converse in private, and

therefore were less mindful to attend upon his public preaching. Familiarity and easiness of access breed some degree of contempt. There is too much truth in that common proverb, "The nearer the church, the further from God"; it is a pity it should be so.

3. They not only would not hear him themselves, but they interrupted others that *heard him gladly*. We often meet with hindrances and obstructions in our work, by our friends that are about us, and are taken off by civil respects from our spiritual concerns. Those who really wish well to us and to our work, may sometimes, by their indiscretion, prove our backfriends, and impediments to us in our duty. Christ once said to his mother, *How is it that ye sought me? Wist ye not, that I must be about my Father's business?* And it was then said, she *laid up that saying in her heart* (Luke ii. 49); but if she had remembered it now, she would not have given him this interruption when he was about his Father's business. There is many a good truth that we thought was well laid up when we heard it, which yet is out of the way when we have occasion to use it.

II. How he resented this interruption, *v.* 48–50.

1. He would not hearken to it. *Who is my mother and who are my brethren?* Not that natural affection is to be put off, but *everything is beautiful in its season*, and the less duty must stand by, while the greater is done. The nearest relations must be comparatively hated, that is, we must love them less than Christ (Luke xiv. 26), and our duty to God must have the preference. And we must not take it ill of our friends, nor put it upon the score of their wickedness, if they prefer the pleasing of God before the pleasing of us. Nay, we must deny ourselves and our own satisfaction, rather than do that which may any way divert our friends from, or distract them in, their duty to God.

2. He took that occasion to prefer his disciples, who were his spiritual kindred, before his natural relations as such. He would rather be profiting his disciples, than pleasing his relations.

(1) The description of Christ's disciples. They are such as *do the will of his Father*; not only hear it, and know it, and talk of it, but *do it*.

(2) The dignity of Christ's disciples: *The same is my brother, and sister, and mother.* His disciples, that had left all to follow him, and embraced his doctrine, were dearer to him than any that were akin to him according to the flesh. It was very endearing and very encouraging for Christ to say, *Behold my mother and my brethren*; yet it was not *their* privilege alone, *this honour have all the saints.* All obedient believers are near akin to Jesus Christ. He loves them, converses freely with them as his relations. He bids them welcome to his table, sees that they want nothing that is fit for them, nor will ever be ashamed of his poor relations, but will confess them before men, before the angels, and before his Father.

CHAPTER 13

I. The favour which Christ did to his countrymen in preaching the kingdom of heaven to them, ver. 1–2. He preached to them in parables, and here gives the reason why he chose that way of instructing, ver. 10–17. And the evangelist gives another reason, ver. 34, 35. 1. Here is one parable to show what are the great hindrances of people's profiting by the word of the gospel, and that is the parable of the four sorts of ground, delivered ver. 3–9, and expounded ver. 18–23. 2. Here are two parables intended to show that there would be a mixture of good and bad: the parable of the tares put forth (ver. 24–30), and expounded at the request of the disciples (ver. 36–43); and that of the net cast into the sea, ver. 47–50. 3. Here are two parables intended to show that the gospel church should be very small at first, but that in process of time it should become a considerable body: that of the grain of mustard-seed (ver. 31, 32), and that of the leaven, ver. 33. 4. Here are two parables intended to show that those who expect salvation by the gospel must be willing to venture all; that of the treasure hid in the field (ver. 44), and that of the pearl of great price, ver. 45, 46. 5. Here is one parable intended for direction to the disciples, to make use of the instructions he had given them for the benefit of others; and that is the parable of the good householder, ver. 51, 52. II. The contempt which his countrymen put upon him on account of the meanness of his parentage, ver. 53–58.

Verses 1–23

1. *When* Christ preached this sermon; it was the same day that he preached the sermon in the foregoing chapter: so unwearied was he in doing good. Christ was for preaching both ends of the day. An afternoon sermon well heard, will be so far from driving out the morning sermon, that it will rather clench it, and fasten the nail in a sure place. Though Christ had been in the morning opposed, disturbed and interrupted, yet he went on with his work; and in the latter part of the day, we do not find that he met with such discouragements. Those who with courage and zeal break through difficulties in God's service, will perhaps find them not so apt to recur as they fear. Resist them, and they will flee.

2. *To whom* he preached; there were *great multitudes gathered together to him*, and they were the auditors. Sometimes there is most of the *power* of religion where there is least of the *pomp* of it. When Christ went to the *sea-side, multitudes* were presently *gathered together to him.* Where the king is, there is the court; where Christ is, there is the church, though it be by the sea-side. Those who would get good by the word, must be willing to follow it in all its removes; when the ark shifts, shift after it.

3. *Where* he preached this sermon. His meeting-place was the sea-side. He went out of the house (because there was no room for the auditory) into the open air. As he had not a house of his own to live in, so he had not a chapel of his own to preach in. By this he teaches us in the external circumstances of worship not to covet that which is stately, but to make the best of the conveniences which God in his providence allots to us. When Christ was born, he was crowded into the stable, and now to the sea-side, upon the strand, where all persons might come to him with freedom. His pulpit was a ship. No place amiss for such a Preacher, whose presence dignified and consecrated any place: let not those who preach Christ be ashamed, though they have mean and inconvenient places to preach in.

4. *What* and *how* he preached. *He spake many things unto them.* Many more it is likely than are here recorded. They were not trifles, but things of everlasting consequence, that Christ spoke of. What he spake was in parables. It was a way of teaching used very much, and it was found very profitable, and the more so from its being pleasant. Our Saviour used it much, and in it condescended to the capacities of people, and lisped to them in their own language.

I. We have here the general reason why Christ taught in parables. The disciples were a little surprised at it, for hitherto, in his preaching, he had not much used them, and therefore they ask, *Why speakest thou to them in parables?* Because they were truly desirous that the people might hear with understanding. They do not say, Why speakest thou to *us?* (they knew how to get the parables explained) but to *them.*

To this question Christ answers largely, *v.* 11–17, where he tells them, that *therefore* he preached by parables, because thereby the things of God were made more plain and easy to them who were willing to be taught, and at the same time more difficult and obscure to those who were willingly ignorant. A parable, like the pillar of cloud and fire, turns a dark side towards Egyptians, which confounds them, but a light side towards Israelites, which comforts them.

1. This reason is laid down (*v.* 11): *Because it is given unto you to know the mysteries of the kingdom of heaven, but to them it is not given.* That is, (1) The

disciples had knowledge, but the people had not. The people are ignorant, are yet but babes, and must be taught as such by plain similitudes: for though they have eyes, they know not how to use them; so some. Or, (2) The disciples were well inclined to the knowledge of gospel mysteries, and would search into the parables, but the carnal hearers that rested in bare hearing, would be never the wiser, and so would justly suffer for their remissness. A parable is a shell that keeps good fruit *for* the diligent, but keeps it *from* the slothful. There are mysteries in the kingdom of heaven. It is graciously given to the disciples of Christ to be acquainted with these mysteries. Knowledge is the first gift of God, it was given to the apostles, because they were Christ's constant followers and attendants. The nearer we draw to Christ, and the more we converse with him, the better acquainted we shall be with gospel mysteries. It is given to all true believers, who have an experimental knowledge of the gospel mysteries, and that is without doubt the best knowledge.

2. This reason is further illustrated by the rule God observes in dispensing his gifts; he bestows them on those who improve them, but takes them away from those who bury them.

(1) Here is a promise to him that has and uses what he has; he shall have more abundance: God's favours are earnests of further favours: where he lays the foundation, he will build upon it.

(2) Here is a threatening to him that has not; that has, but uses not what he has; from him shall be *taken away* that which he has or seems to have. God will *call in* his talents out of their hands that are likely to become bankrupts quickly.

3. This reason is particularly explained, with reference to the two sorts of people Christ had to do with.

(1) Some were willingly ignorant; and such were amused by the parables (*v.* 13); *because they seeing, see not.* They had shut their eyes against the clear light of Christ's plainer preaching, and therefore were now left in the dark. It is just with God to take away the light from those who shut their eyes against it.

Now in this the scripture would be fulfilled, *v.* 14, 15. It is quoted from Isa. vi. 9, 10. It is referred to no less than six times in the New Testament. That which was spoken of the sinners in Isaiah's time was fulfilled in those in Christ's time, and it is still fulfilling every day. Here is,

First. A description of sinners' wilful blindness and darkness, which is their sin. *This people's heart is waxed gross;* it is *fattened,* so the word is; which denotes both sensuality and senselessness. And when the heart is thus heavy, no wonder that the ears are dull of hearing. They shut both the learning senses; for their eyes also they have closed, resolved that they would not see light come into the world, when the Sun of Righteousness arose.

Secondly, A description of that judicial blindness, which is the just punishment of this. "*By hearing, ye shall hear, and shall not understand;* what means of grace you have, shall be to no purpose to you; though in mercy to others, they are continued." The saddest condition a man can be in is to sit under the most lively ordinances with a dead, stupid, untouched heart.

Thirdly, The woeful effect and consequence of this; *Lest at any time they should see. Lest they should be converted, and I should heal them.*

Note, That seeing, hearing, and understanding, are necessary to conversion; for God, in working grace, deals with men as men, as rational agents; he draws with the cords of a man, changes the heart by opening the eyes, and turns *from the power of Satan unto God*, by turning first *from darkness to light,*

Acts xxvi. 18. All those who are truly converted to God, shall certainly be healed by him. "If they be converted I shall heal them, I shall save them."

(2) Others were effectually called to be the disciples of Christ and were truly desirous to be taught of him. By these parables the things of God were made more plain and easy, more intelligible and familiar, and more apt to be remembered (v. 16, 17). *Your eyes see, your ears hear.* Now this Christ speaks of,

[1] As a blessing; "*Blessed are your eyes for they see, and your ears for they hear;* it is your happiness, and it is a happiness for which you are indebted to the peculiar favour and blessing of God." The hearing ear and the seeing eye are God's work. They are a blessed work, which shall be fulfilled with power, when those who *now see through a glass darkly, shall see face to face.* The apostles were to teach others, and therefore were themselves blessed with the clearest discoveries of divine truth.

[2] As a transcendent blessing, desired by, but not granted to, many prophets and righteous men, v. 17. The Old Testament saints, who had some glimpses, some glimmerings of gospel light, coveted earnestly further discoveries. Those who know something of Christ, cannot but covet to know more. There was then, as there is still, a *glory to be revealed*; something in reserve, *that they without us should not be made perfect*, Heb. xi. 40. It is good for us to consider what means we enjoy, and what discoveries are made to us, now under the gospel, above what they had, and enjoyed, who lived under the Old Testament dispensation.

II. One of the parables which our Saviour put forth; it is that of the *sower and the seed.* Christ's parables are borrowed from common, ordinary things, from the most obvious things, that are of every day's observation, and come within the reach of the meanest capacity. Christ chose to do thus, 1. That spiritual things might hereby be made more plain the more easy to slide into our understandings. 2. That we might take occasion from those things which fall so often under our view, to meditate with delight on the things of God; and thus, when our hands are busiest about the world, we may notwithstanding that, but even with the help of that, be led to have our hearts in heaven. Thus the word of God shall talk with us, talk familiarly with us.

The parable of the sower is plain enough, v. 3–9. The exposition of it we have from Christ himself, who knew best what was his own meaning. "*Hear ye therefore the parable of the sower* (v. 18); you have heard it, but let us go over it again." *Then* only we hear the word aright, and to good purpose, when we understand what we hear; it is no hearing at all, if it be not with understanding. It is God's grace indeed that gives the understanding, but it is our duty to give our minds to understand.

Let us therefore compare the parable and the exposition.

(1) The seed sown is the word of God, here called *the word of the kingdom* (v. 19): the kingdom of heaven. This word is the seed sown, which seems a dead, dry thing, but all the product is virtually in it. It is *incorruptible seed* (1 Pet. i. 23).

(2) The sower that scatters the seed is our Lord Jesus Christ, either by himself, or by his ministers; see v. 37. Preaching to a multitude is sowing the corn; we know not where it must light; only see that it be good, that it be clean, and be sure to give it seed enough.

(3) The ground in which this seed is sown is the hearts of the children of men, which are differently qualified and disposed. Man's heart is like soil, capable of improvement, of bearing good fruit; it is a pity it should lie fallow. As it is with the earth; some sort of ground, take ever so much pains with it,

and throw ever so good seed into it, yet it brings forth no fruit to any purpose; while the good soil brings forth plentifully: so it is with the hearts of men, whose different characters are here represented by four sorts of ground, of which *three* are bad, and but *one* good. The number of fruitless hearers is very great, even of those who heard Christ himself.

[1] The highway ground, v. 4–19. They had pathways through their cornfields (*ch.* xii. 1), and the seed that fell on them never entered, and so the birds picked it up.

First, What kind of hearers are compared to *the highway ground*; such as *hear the word and understand it not.* They take no heed to it, take no hold of it; they do not come with any design to get good. They mind not what is said, it comes in at one ear and goes out at the other, and makes no impression.

Secondly, How they come to be unprofitable hearers. The *wicked one*, that is, the devil, *cometh and catcheth away that which was sown.*—Such mindless, careless, trifling hearers are an easy prey to Satan; who, as he is the great murderer of souls, so he is the great thief of sermons. If we break not up the fallow ground, by preparing our hearts for the word, and if we cover not the seed afterwards, by meditation and prayer; if we give not a *more earnest heed to the things which we have heard*, we are as the highway ground.

[2] The *stony ground. Some fell upon stony places* (v. 5, 6), which represents the case of hearers who receive some good impressions of the word, but they are not lasting, v. 20, 21. It is possible we may be a great deal better than some others, and yet not be so good as we should be.

First, How far they went. 1. They *hear the word*; they turn neither their backs upon it, nor a deaf ear to it. Hearing the word will never bring us to heaven. 2. They are *quick in hearing, forthwith it sprung up* (v. 5), it sooner appeared above ground than that which was sown in the good soil. Hypocrites often get the start of true Christians in the shows of profession, and are often too hot to hold. He *receiveth it straightway*, without trying it; swallows it without chewing, and then there can never be a good digestion. 3. They receive it with joy. There are many that are very glad to hear a good sermon, that yet do not profit by it. Many *taste the good word of God* (Heb. vi. 5), and say they find sweetness in it, but some beloved lust is *rolled under the tongue*, which it would not agree with, and so they spit it out again. 4. They *endure for awhile.* Many endure for awhile, that do not endure to the end, they did run well, but something hindered them, Gal. v. 7.

Secondly, How they fell away, so that no fruit was brought to perfection. They have *no root in themselves*, no settled, fixed principles in their judgments, no firm resolution in their wills. It is possible there may be the green blade of a profession, where yet there is not the root of grace. Where there is not a principle, though there be a profession, we cannot expect perseverance. Those who have no root will endure but awhile.

Times of trial come, and then they come to nothing. *When tribulation and persecution arise because of the word, he is offended.* After a fair gale of opportunity usually follows a storm of persecution, to try who have received the word in sincerity, and who have not. It is wisdom to prepare for such a day. When trying times come, those who have no root are soon offended; they first quarrel with their profession, and then quit it. Persecution is represented in the parable by *the scorching sun* (v. 6); the same sun which warms and cherishes that which was well rooted, withers and burns up that which wanted root. Trials which shake some, confirm others, Phil. i. 12. Observe how soon they fall away; a profession taken up without consideration is commonly let fall without it: "Lightly come, lightly go."

[3] The thorny ground, *Some fell among thorns.* This went further than the former, for it had root. Prosperity destroys the word in the heart, as much as persecution does; and more dangerously, because more silently: the stones spoiled the root, the thorns spoil the fruit.

Now what are these choking thorns?

The cares of this world. Care for another world would quicken the springing of this seed, but care for this world chokes it. Worldly cares are fitly compared to thorns. They are entangling, vexing, scratching, and *their end is to be burned,* Heb. vi. 8. These thorns choke the good seed. Worldly cares are great hindrances to our profiting by the word of God. They eat up that vigour of soul which should be spent in divine things. Those who *are careful and cumbered about many things,* commonly neglect *the one thing needful.*

The deceitfulness of riches. Those who, by their care and industry, have raised estates, and from whom the danger that arises from care seems to be over are apt to promise themselves that in riches which is not in them; to rely upon them, and this chokes the word as much as care did. It is not so much riches, as *the deceitfulness of riches,* that does the mischief. We put our confidence in them, and raise our expectations from them, and then it is that they choke the good seed.

[4] The good ground (*v.* 18); *Others fell into good ground,* and it is pity but that good seed should always meet with good soil, and then there is no loss; such are *good hearers of the word, v.* 23.

Now that which distinguished this good ground from the rest, was, in one word, fruitfulness. He does not say that this good ground has no stones in it, or no thorns; but there were none that prevailed to hinder its fruitfulness. Saints, in this world, are not perfectly free from the remains of sin; but happily freed from the reign of it.

The hearers represented by the good ground are,

First, Intelligent hearers; they *hear the word and understand it*; they understand not only the sense and meaning of the word, but their own concern in it; they understand it as a man of business understands his business.

Secondly, Fruitful hearers, which is an evidence of their good understanding: which *also beareth fruit.* We *then* bear fruit, when we practise according to the word, and we do as we are taught.

Thirdly, Not all alike fruitful; *some a hundred-fold, some sixty, some thirty.* Among fruitful Christians, some are more fruitful than others: where there is true grace, yet there are degrees of it; all Christ's scholars are not in the same form. But if the ground be good, and the fruit right, those who bring forth but thirtyfold shall be graciously accepted of God, and it will be fruit abounding to their account.

Lastly, He closes the parable with a solemn call to attention (*v.* 9), *Who hath ears to hear, let him hear.* The sense of hearing cannot be better employed than in hearing the word of God. Some are for hearing sweet melody: there is no melody like that of the word of God; others are for hearing *new things* (Acts xvii. 21): no news like that.

Verses 24–43

I. Another reason given why Christ preached by parables, *v.* 34, 35. *All these things he spoke in parables,* because the time was not yet come for the more clear and plain discoveries of the mysteries of the kingdom. Christ tries all ways and methods to do good to the souls of men. If men will not be instructed and influenced by plain preaching, he will try them with parables. 1. The matter of Christ's

preaching. The mystery of the gospel had been *hid in God,* in his councils and decrees, *from the beginning of the world.* Eph. iii. 9. 2. The manner of Christ's preaching; he preached by parables; wise sayings, but figurative, and which help to engage attention and a diligent search.

II. The parable of the *tares,* and the exposition of it.

1. The disciples' request to their Master to have this parable expounded to them (*v.* 36); *Jesus sent the multitude away;* and it is to be feared many of them went away no wiser than they came. It is sad to think how many go away from sermons with the word of grace in their ears, but not the work of grace in their hearts. Christ *went into the house,* not so much for his own repose, as for particular converse with his disciples. The disciples laid hold on the opportunity, and *they came to him.* Those who would be wise for everything else, must be wise to discern and improve their opportunities, especially of converse with Christ. We lose the benefit of many a sermon by vain and unprofitable discourse after it. See Luke xxiv. 32. Private conference would contribute much to our profiting by public preaching.

The disciples' request to their Master was, *Declare unto us the parable of the tares.* This implied an acknowledgment of their ignorance, which they were not ashamed to make. Those are rightly disposed for Christ's teaching, that are sensible of their ignorance, and sincerely desirous to be taught. Christ had expounded the foregoing parable unasked, but for the exposition of this they ask him. The first light and the first grace are given further degrees of both which must be daily prayed for.

2. The exposition Christ gave of the parable. Now the drift of the parable is, to represent to us the present and future state of the kingdom of heaven, the gospel church: Christ's care of it, the devil's enmity against it, the mixture that there is in it of good and bad in this world, and the separation between them in the other world.

Let us go over the particulars of the exposition of the parable.

(1) *He that sows the good seed is the Son of man.* Jesus Christ is the Lord of the field, *the Lord of the harvest,* the Sower of good seed. Whatever good seed there is in the world, it all comes from the hand of Christ, and is of his sowing: truths preached, graces planted, souls sanctified, are good seed, and all owing to Christ. Ministers are instruments in Christ's hand to sow good seed.

(2) *The field is the world;* the world of mankind, a large field, capable of bringing forth good fruit; the more is it to be lamented that it brings forth so much bad fruit. It is his field, and because it is his he took care to sow it with good seed.

(3) *The good seed are the children of the kingdom,* true saints. Not in profession only, as the Jews were (*ch.* viii. 12), but in sincerity. They are the good seed, precious as seed, Ps. cxxvi. 6. The seed is scattered, so are the saints; dispersed, here one and there another, though in some places thicker sown than in others.

(4) *The tares are the children of the wicked one.* They are the children of the devil. They are tares in the field of this world; they do no good, they do hurt. They are weeds in the garden, have the same rain, and sunshine, and soil, with the good plants, but are good for nothing.

(5) *The enemy that sowed the tares is the devil.* He is an enemy to the field of the world, which he endeavours to make his own, by sowing his tares in it. They were sown *while men slept.* Satan watches all opportunities. We have therefore need to be *sober, and vigilant.* The enemy, when he had sown the tares, *went his way* (*v.* 25), that it might not be

known who did it. When Satan is doing the greatest mischief, he studies most to conceal himself. If the enemy sow the tares, he may even go his way, they will spring up of themselves and do hurt; whereas, when good seed is sown, it must be tended, watered, and fenced, or it will come to nothing. The tares appeared not till *the blade sprung up, and brought forth fruit, v.* 26. There is a great deal of secret wickedness in the hearts of men, which is long hid under the cloak of a plausible profession, but breaks out at last. When a trying time comes, when fruit is to be brought forth, then you will return and discern between the sincere and the hypocrite: then you may say, This is wheat, and that is tares. The servants, when they were aware of it, complained to their master (*v.* 27); *Sir, didst thou not sow good seed in thy field?* No doubt he did; considering the seed which Christ sows, we may well ask, with wonder, *Whence* should *these tares come?* It is sad to see such tares, such weeds, in the garden of the Lord; to see the good soil wasted, the good seed choked, and such a reflection cast on the name and honour of Christ. The Master was soon aware whence it was (*v.* 28); *An enemy has done this.* He does not lay the blame upon the servants; they could not help it. The ministers of Christ, that are faithful and diligent, shall not be judged of Christ, for the mixture of bad with good, hypocrites with the sincere, in the field of the church. *It must needs be that such offences will come;* and they shall not be laid to our charge, if we do our duty. The servants were very forward to have these tares rooted up. "*Wilt thou that we go and do it presently?*" The Master very wisely prevented this (*v.* 29); *Nay, lest while ye gather up the tares, ye root up also the wheat with them.* It is not possible for any man infallibly to distinguish between tares and wheat. It is possible there may be a discipline, either so mistaken in its rules, or so overnice in the application of them, as may prove vexatious to many that are truly godly and conscientious. The tares, if continued under the means of grace, may become good corn; therefore have patience with them.

(6) *The harvest is the end of the world, v.* 39. This world will have an end. At harvest all is ripe and ready to be cut down: both good and bad are ripe at the great day. At harvest every man reaps as he sowed; every man's ground, and seed, and skill, and industry, will be manifested.

(7) *The reapers are the angels.* The angels are servants to Christ, holy enemies to the wicked, and faithful friends to all the saints, and therefore fit to be thus employed.

(8) The *fire*, into which the *tares* shall then be cast.

[1] The tares will then be gathered out: *The reapers* (whose primary work it is to gather in the corn) shall be charged first to *gather out the tares.* Though good and bad are together in this world undistinguished, yet at the great day they shall be parted.

[2] They will then be *bound in bundles, v.* 30. Those who have been associates in sin, will be so in shame and sorrow.

[3] They will *be cast into a furnace of fire*; they are fit for nothing but fire. *There shall be weeping, and gnashing of teeth;* comfortless sorrow, and an incurable indignation at God.

(9) Heaven is the *barn. But gather the wheat into my barn:* so it is in the parable, *v.* 30. All God's wheat shall be lodged together in God's barn. There will be sheaves of corn, as well as bundles of tares: they will then be secured, and no longer exposed to wind and weather, sin and sorrow: no longer afar off, and at a great distance, in the field, but near, in the barn.

In the explanation of the parable, this is gloriously represented (*v.* 43); *Then shall the righteous shine forth as the sun in the kingdom of their Father.* The honour in reserve for them is, that they *shall shine forth as the sun in that kingdom.* Here they are obscure and hidden (Col. iii. 3), their beauty is eclipsed by their poverty, and the meanness of their outward condition; but then they shall shine forth as the sun from behind a dark cloud. They shall shine as the sun, the most glorious of all visible beings. Those who shine as lights in this world, that God may be glorified, shall shine as the sun in the other world, that *they* may be glorified. Our Saviour concludes, as before, with a demand of attention; *Who hath ears to hear, let him hear.*

III. Here is the parable of the *grain of mustard-seed, v.* 31, 32. The scope of this parable is to show, that the beginnings of the gospel *would be small, but that its latter end would greatly increase.*

Now concerning the work of the gospel, observe,

1. That it is commonly very weak and small at first, *like a grain of mustard-seed, which is one of the least of all seeds.* In particular places, the first breaking out of the gospel light is but as *the dawning of the day.* Young converts are like *lambs* that must be *carried in his arms,* Isa. xl. 11.

2. That yet it is growing and coming on. *A grain of mustard-seed* is small, but however, it is seed, and has in it a disposition to grow. Gracious habits confirmed, actings quickened, and knowledge more clear, faith more confirmed, love more inflamed; here is the seed growing.

3. That it will at last come to a great degree of strength and usefulness; *when it is grown to* some maturity, *it becomes a tree.* The church is like a great tree, in which the fowls of the air do lodge; God's people have recourse to it for food and rest, shade and shelter. In particular persons, growing grace will be strong grace, and will bring much to pass. Grown Christians must covet to be useful to others, as the mustard-seed when grown is to the birds.

IV. Here is the parable of the *leaven, v.* 33.

1. *A woman took* this *leaven*; it was her work. Ministers are employed in leavening places, in leavening souls, with the gospel.

2. The leaven was *hid in three measures of meal.* The heart is, as the meal, soft and pliable; it is the tender heart that is likely to profit by the word. It is *three measures of meal,* a great quantity, for *a little leaven leaveneth the whole lump.* The leaven must be *hid in the heart.* We must lay it up, as Mary laid up the sayings of Christ, Luke ii. 51.

3. The leaven thus hid in the dough, works there. The leaven works speedily, so does the word, and yet gradually. It works silently and insensibly (Mark iv. 26), yet strongly and irresistibly. Hide but the leaven in the dough, and all the world cannot hinder it from communicating its taste and relish to it, and yet none sees how it is done, but by degrees *the whole is leavened.* Thus it was in the world. The apostles, by their preaching, hid a handful of leaven in the great mass of mankind, and it had a strange effect; it put the world into a ferment, and in a sense turned it *upside down* (Acts xvii. 6). It was thus effectual, not by outward force, and therefore not by any such force resistible and conquerable, but by *the Spirit of the Lord of hosts, who works, and none can hinder.* Thus it is in the heart. It works a change, not in the substance; the dough is the same, but in the quality. It works a universal change; it diffuses itself into all the powers and faculties of the soul. This change is such as makes the soul to partake of the nature of the word, as the dough does of the leaven. It is a word of faith and repentance, holiness and love, and these are wrought in the soul by it. When the dough is leavened, then to the oven with it; trials and afflictions commonly attend this change; but thus saints are fitted to be bread for our Master's table.

Verses 44-52

I. That of the *treasure hid in the field.* Hitherto he had compared *the kingdom of heaven* to small things. In this parable and the next he represents it as of great value in itself. It is here likened *to a treasure hid in the field,* which, if we will, we may make our own.

1. Jesus Christ is the true Treasure; in him there is an abundance of all that which is rich and useful, and if we have an interest in him, it is all our own.

2. The gospel is the field in which this treasure is hid. It is hid, not *in a garden enclosed,* but *in a field,* an open field. Whatever royal mines we find, they are all our own, if we take the right course.

3. It is a great thing to discover the treasure hid in this field, and the unspeakable value of it. The richest mines are often in grounds that appear most barren. What is the Bible more than other good books? But those who have *searched the scriptures,* so as in them to find Christ and *eternal life* (John v. 39), have discovered such a treasure in this field as makes it infinitely more valuable.

4. Those who discern this treasure in the field, and value it aright, will never be easy till they have made it their own upon any terms. He rejoices in it, though as yet the bargain be not made; he is glad there is such a bargain to be had. He resolves to *buy this field:* they who embrace gospel offers, upon gospel terms, buy this field; they make it their own, for the sake of the unseen treasure in it. And so intent he is upon it, *that he sells all to buy this field:* they who would have saving benefit by Christ, must *count everything but loss, that they may win Christ, and be found in him.*

II. That of *the pearl of price* (v. 45, 46).

1. All the children of men are busy, *seeking goodly pearls:* one would be rich, another would be honourable, another would be learned; but the most are imposed upon, and take up with counterfeits for pearls.

2. Jesus Christ is a *Pearl of great price;* in having him, we have enough to make us happy here and for ever.

3. A true Christian is a spiritual *merchant,* that seeks and finds this pearl of price; and, as one that is resolved to be spiritually rich, trades high: *He went and bought that pearl;* did not only bid for it, but purchased it.

4. Those who would have a saving interest in Christ, must be willing to part with all for him, leave all to follow him. A man may buy gold too dear, but not this pearl of price.

III. That of the *net cast into the sea,* v. 47-49.

1. Here is the parable itself. The world is a vast sea. The preaching of the gospel is the casting of a net into this sea, to catch something out of it. This net gathers of every kind, as large dragnets do. In the visible church there is a deal of trash and rubbish, dirt and weeds and vermin, as well as fish. There is a time coming when this net will be full, and drawn to the shore. The net is now filling; sometimes it fills faster than at other times, but still it fills. When the net is full and drawn to the shore, there shall be a separation between the good and bad that were gathered in it. The good shall be gathered into vessels, as valuable, and therefore to be carefully kept, but the bad shall be cast away. While the net is in the sea, it is not known what is in it; the fishermen themselves cannot distinguish; but they carefully draw it, and all that is in it, to the shore, for the sake of the good that is in it.

2. Here is the explanation of the latter part of the parable, the former is obvious and plain enough: but the latter part refers to that which is yet to come, and is therefore more particularly explained, v. 49, 50. *So shall it be at the end of the world.* We must not look for the net full of all good fish; the vessels will be

so, but in the net they are mixed. (1) The distinguishing of the wicked from the righteous. (2) The doom of the wicked when they are thus severed. They shall be *cast into the furnace.*

IV. Here is the parable of the *good householder,* which is intended to rivet all the rest.

1. The occasion of it was the good proficiency which the disciples had made in learning, and their profiting by this sermon in particular. He asked them, *Have ye understood all these things?* He was ready to explain what they did not understand. It is the will of Christ, that all those who read and hear the word should understand it; for otherwise how should they get good by it? They answered him, *Yea, Lord.* When they did not understand, they asked for an explication, v. 36. And the exposition of that parable was a key to the rest. Good truths mutually explain and illustrate one another.

2. The scope of the parable itself was to give his approbation and commendation of their proficiency. Christ is ready to encourage willing learners in his school, though they are but weak; and to say, *Well done, well said.*

(1) He commends them as *scribes instructed unto the kingdom of heaven.* They were now learning that they might teach. Those who are to instruct others, have need to be well instructed themselves. The instruction of a gospel minister must be in the *kingdom of heaven.* Not instructed to the kingdom of heaven, he will make but a bad minister.

(2) He compares them to a good householder, who *brings forth out of his treasure things new and old;* fruits of last year's growth and this year's gathering, abundance and variety. What should be a minister's furniture, *a treasure of things new and old.* Old experiences, and new observations, all have their use; and we must not content ourselves with old discoveries, but must be adding new. Live and learn. What use he should make of this furniture; he should *bring forth:* laying up is in order to laying out, for the benefit of others. Christ himself received that he might give; so must we, and we shall have more. In bringing forth, things new and old do best together; old truths, but new methods and expressions.

Verses 53-58

We have here Christ in his own country. His own countrymen had rejected him once, yet he came to them again. Christ does not take refusers at their first word, but repeats his offers to those who have often repulsed them. He had a natural affection to his own country. His treatment this time was much the same as before, scornful and spiteful.

I. How they expressed their contempt of him. When he *taught them in their synagogue, they were astonished* that it should be so; looking upon him as unlikely to be such a teacher. Two things they upbraided him with.

1. His want of academical education. They owned that he had wisdom, and did mighty works; but the question was, Whence he had them. Note, Mean and prejudiced spirits are apt to judge of men by their education, and to enquire more into their rise than into their reasons. "*Whence has this man these mighty works?*" If they had not been wilfully blind, they must have concluded him to be divinely assisted and commissioned, who without the help of education gave such proofs of extraordinary wisdom and power.

2. The meanness and poverty of his relations, v. 55, 56. They upbraid him with his father. *Is not this the carpenter's son?* What harm in that? No disparagement to him to be the son of an honest tradesman. This carpenter was *of the house of David* (Luke i. 27), *a son of David* (ch. i. 20); though a carpenter, yet a person of honour. Some sordid

spirits regard no branch, no not the Branch from the stem of Jesse (Isa. xi. 1), if it be not the top branch. They upbraid him with his mother. Why, truly, *his mother is called Mary*, and that was a very common name, and they all knew her, and knew her to be an ordinary person; and this is turned to his reproach, as if men had nothing to be valued by but splendid titles; poor things to measure worth by. They upbraid him with his brethren, whose names they knew, good men but poor men, and therefore despised; and Christ for their sakes. His sisters too are all with us; they should therefore have loved him and respected him the more, because he was one of themselves, but therefore they despised him. They were *offended in him*.

II. See how he resented this contempt, *v.* 57, 58.

1. It did not trouble his heart. He mildly imputes it to the common humour of the children of men, to undervalue excellences that are cheap and common, and home-bred, It is usually so. *A prophet is not without honour, save in his own country.* Prophets should have honour paid them, and commonly have; men of God are great men, and men of honour, and challenge respect. Notwithstanding this, they are commonly least regarded and reverenced in their own country. Familiarity breeds contempt.

2. It did for the present (to speak with reverence), in effect, tie his hands: *He did not many mighty works there, because of their unbelief.* Unbelief is the great obstruction to Christ's favours. So that if mighty works be not wrought in us, it is not for want of power or grace in Christ, but for want of faith in us.

Chapter 14

Here is, I. The martyrdom of John; his imprisonment (ver. 1–5), and the beheading of him, ver. 6–12. II. The miracles of Christ. 1. His feeding five thousand men with five loaves and two fishes, ver. 13–21. 2. Christ's walking on the waves to his disciples in a storm, ver. 22–23. 3. His healing the sick with the touch of the hem of his garment, ver. 34–36.

Verses 1–12

We have here the story of John's martyrdom.

I. The occasion of relating this story here, *v.* 1, 2.

1. The account brought to Herod of the miracles which Christ wrought. Herod the tetrarch or chief governor of Galilee *heard of the fame of Jesus.* At that time, when his countrymen slighted him, upon the account of his meanness and obscurity, he began to be famous at court. The gospel, like the sea, gets in one place what it loses in another. It should seem, Herod had not heard of him till now, and now only heard the fame of him. It is the unhappiness of the great ones of the world, that they are most out of the way of hearing the best things (1 Cor. ii. 8).

2. The construction he puts upon this (*v.* 2); *He said to his servants this is John the Baptist; he is risen from the dead.* John, while he lived, *did no miracle* (John x. 41); but Herod concludes, that, being risen from the dead, he is clothed with a greater power than he had while he was living. Observe here concerning Herod,

(1) How he was disappointed in what he intended by beheading John. He thought if he could get that troublesome fellow out of the way, he might go on in his sins, undisturbed and uncontrolled; yet no sooner is that effected, than he hears of Jesus and his disciples preaching the same pure doctrine that John preached. Ministers may be silenced, and imprisoned, and banished, and slain, but the word of God cannot be run down. Sometimes God raises up many faithful ministers out of the ashes of one.

(2) How he was filled with causeless fears, merely from the guilt of his own conscience. A guilty conscience suggests everything that is frightful and, like a whirlpool, gathers all to itself that comes near

it. Thus *the wicked flee when none pursue* (Prov. xxviii. 1).

(3) How, notwithstanding this, he was hardened in his wickedness. He does not express the least remorse or sorrow for his sin in putting him to death. The devils believe and tremble, but they never believe and repent.

II. The story itself of the imprisonment and martyrdom of John. If Christ's forerunner was thus treated, let not his followers expect to be caressed by the world.

1. John's faithfulness in reproving Herod, *v.* 3, 4. Herod was one of John's hearers (Mark vi. 20), and therefore John might be the more bold with him.

The particular sin he reproved him for was, marrying his brother Philip's wife, not his widow (that had not been so criminal), but his wife. Philip was now living, and Herod inveigled his wife from him, and kept her for his own. For this sin John reproved him: *It is not lawful for thee to have her.* He charges it upon him as a sin: It is not *lawful.* That which by the law of God is unlawful to other people, is by the same law unlawful to princes and the greatest of men. There is no prerogative, no, not for the greatest and most arbitrary kings, to break the laws of God. If princes and great men break the law of God, it is very fit they should be told of it by proper persons, and in a proper manner.

2. The imprisonment of John for his faithfulness, *v.* 3. *Herod laid hold on John, bound him, and put him in prison;* partly to gratify his own revenge, and partly to please Herodias. Faithful reproofs, if they do not profit, usually provoke. It is no new thing for God's ministers to suffer ill for doing well. Troubles abide those most that are most diligent and faithful in doing their duty.

3. The restraint that Herod lay under from further venting of his rage against John, *v.* 5.

(1) He would have put him to death. Perhaps that was not intended at first when he imprisoned him, but his revenge by degrees boiled up to that height.

(2) That which hindered him was his *fear of the multitude, because they counted John as a prophet.* It was not because he feared God (if the fear of God had been before his eyes he would not have imprisoned him), nor because he feared John, but because he feared the people; he was afraid for himself, his own safety. Tyrants have their fears. Wicked men are restrained from the most wicked practices, merely by their secular interest, and not by any regard to God. The danger of sin that appears to sense, or to fancy only, influences men more than that which appears to faith. Men fear being hanged for that which they do not fear being damned for.

4. The contrivance of bringing John to his death. Now here we have an account of his release, not by any other discharge than death, the period of all a good man's troubles.

Herodias laid the plot; her implacable revenge thirsted after John's blood, and would be satisfied with nothing less. Cross the carnal appetites, and they turn into the most barbarous passions. Herodias contrived how to bring about the murder of John so artificially as to save Herod's credit, and so to pacify the people.

(1) The humouring of Herod by the damsel's dancing upon a birthday. In honour of the day, there must needs be, as usual, a ball at court; and, to grace the solemnity, the daughter of Herodias danced before them; who being the queen's daughter, it was more than she ordinarily condescended to do. This young lady's dancing pleased Herod.

(2) The rash and foolish promise which Herod made to this wanton girl, to give her whatsoever she would ask: and this promise confirmed with an oath, *v.* 7. It was a very extravagant obligation which Herod

here entered into, and no way becoming a prudent man.

(3) The bloody demand the young lady made of John the Baptist's head, *v.* 8. She was before instructed of her mother. The case of those children is very sad, whose parents are *their counsellors to do wickedly.*

Herod having given her her commission, and Herodias her instructions, she requires John the Baptist's head in a charger. John must be beheaded then; that is the death by which he must glorify God. Yet this is not enough, the thing must be humoured too, and not only a revenge, but a fancy must be gratified; it must be *given her here in a charger*, served up in blood. It must be given her, and she will reckon it a recompence for her dancing, and desire no more.

(4) Herod's grant of this demand (*v.* 9); *The king was sorry*, at least took on him to be so, but, *for the oath's sake, he commanded it to be given her. The king was sorry.* Many a man sins with regret, that never has any true regret for his sin; sins with reluctancy, and yet goes on to sin. Here is a pretended conscience of his oath, with a specious show of honour and honesty; he must needs do something, for the oath's sake. It is a great mistake to think that a wicked oath will justify a wicked action. No man can lay himself under an obligation to sin, because God has already so strongly obliged every man against sin. Here is a real baseness in compliance with wicked companions. Herod yielded, not so much for the sake of the oath, but because it was public, and in compliment to *them that sat at meat with him*; he granted the demand that he might not seem, before them, to have broken his engagement. A point of honour goes much further with many than a point of conscience. Here is a real malice to John at the bottom of this concession, or else he might have found out evasions enough to have got clear of his promise. *He commanded it to be given her.*

(5) The execution of John, pursuant to this grant (*v.* 10); *He sent and beheaded John in the prison.* He must be beheaded with expedition, to gratify Herodias. It was done in the night. It was done in the prison, not at the usual place of execution, for fear of an uproar. A great deal of innocent blood, of martyr's blood, has thus been huddled up in corners.

Thus was that voice silenced, that burning and shining light extinguished; thus did that prophet, that Elias, of the New Testament, fall a sacrifice to the resentments of an imperious, whorish woman.

5. The disposal of the poor remains of this blessed saint and martyr.

(1) The damsel brought the head in triumph to her mother, as a trophy of the victories of her malice and revenge, *v.* 11.

(2) The disciples *buried the body*, and brought the news in tears to our Lord Jesus.

[1] *They buried the body.* There is a respect owing to the servants of Christ, not only while they live, but in their bodies and memories when they are dead.

[2] *They went and told Jesus;* not so much that he might shift for his own safety as that they might receive comfort from him, and be taken in among his disciples. When anything ails us at any time, it is our duty and privilege to make Christ acquainted with it. It will be a relief to our burthened spirits to unbosom ourselves to a friend we may be free with. When the shepherds are smitten, the sheep need not be scattered while they have the great Shepherd of the sheep to go to, who is still the same, Heb. xiii. 8, 20. Comforts otherwise highly valuable, are sometimes *therefore* taken from us, because they come between us and Christ, and are apt to carry away that love and esteem which are due to him only.

It is better to be drawn to Christ by want and loss, than not to come to him at all.

Verses 13–21

This passage of story, concerning Christ's feeding *five thousand men with five loaves and two fishes*, is recorded by all the four Evangelists.

I. The great resort of people to Christ, when he was retired *into a desert place, v.* 13. He withdrew into privacy when he heard, not of John's death, but of the thoughts Herod had concerning him, that he was *John the Baptist risen from the dead*, he departed further off, to get out of Herod's jurisdiction. In times of peril, when God opens a door of escape, it is lawful to flee for our own preservation, unless we have some special call to expose ourselves. *He departed by ship. When the people heard it, they followed him on foot* from all parts. Such an interest Christ had in the affections of the multitude, that his withdrawing from them did but draw them after him with so much the more eagerness. It should seem, there was more crowding to Christ after John's martyrdom than before. Sometimes *the sufferings of the saints* are made to further the gospel (Phil. i. 12). When Christ and his word withdraw from us, it is best for us (whatever flesh and blood may object to the contrary) to follow it. The presence of Christ and his gospel makes a desert place not only tolerable, but desirable; it makes the wilderness an Eden.

II. The tender compassion of our Lord Jesus towards those who thus followed him, *v.* 14. He went forth, and appeared publicly among them. He went forth from his retirement, when he saw people desirous to hear him, as one willing both to toil himself, and to expose himself, for the good of souls. *When he saw the multitude, he had compassion on them.* The sight of a great multitude may justly move compassion. None like Christ for pity to souls; *his compassions fail not.* He did not only pity them, but he helped them; many of them were *sick, and he, in compassion to them, healed them.* After awhile, they were all hungry, *and he, in compassion to them, fed them.*

III. The motion which the disciples made for the dismissing of the congregation, and Christ's setting aside the motion. They thought there was a good day's work done, and it was time to disperse. Christ's disciples are often more careful to show their discretion, than to show their zeal. Christ would not dismiss them hungry as they were, but orders his disciples to provide for them. Christ all along expressed more tenderness toward the people than his disciples did. See how loth Christ is to part with those who are resolved to cleave to him! *They need not depart.*

But if they be hungry, they have need to depart, for that is a necessity which has no law, therefore *give you them to eat. The Lord is for the body;* it is the *work of his hands*, it is part of his purchase; he was himself clothed with a body, that he might encourage us to depend upon him for the supply of our bodily wants. If we *seek first the kingdom of God*, and make that our chief care, we may depend upon God to *add other things to* us, as far as he sees fit.

IV. The slender provision that was made for this great multitude; and here we must compare the number of invited guests with the bill of fare.

1. The number of the guests was *five thousand of men, besides women and children.* This was a vast auditory that Christ preached to, and we have reason to think an attentive auditory; and yet, it should seem, far the greater part came to nothing; they went off and followed him no more. We would rather perceive the acceptableness of the word by the conversion, than by the crowds, of its hearers; though that also is a good sight and a good sign.

2. The bill of fare was very disproportionable to the number of the guests, but *five loaves and two fishes*. This provision the disciples carried about with them for the use of the family, now they *were retired into the desert*. Here is neither plenty, nor variety, nor dainty; a dish of fish was no rarity to them that were fishermen, but it was food convenient for the twelve; here was no wine or strong drink; fair water from the rivers in the desert was the best they had to drink with their meat; and yet out of this Christ will have the multitude fed. Those who have but a little, yet when the necessity is urgent, must relieve others out of that little, and that is the way to make it more.

V. The liberal distribution of this provision among the multitude (*v.* 18, 19); *Bring them hither to me*. Note, The way to have our creature-comforts, comforts indeed to us, is to bring them to Christ. That is likely to prosper and do well with us, which we put into the hands of our Lord Jesus, that he may dispose of it as he pleases, and that we may take it back from his hand, and then it will be doubly sweet to us.

1. The seating of the guests (*v.* 19); *He commanded them to sit down*. But what shall we do for chairs for them all? Let them *sit down on the grass*. Here is not so much as a cloth spread, no plates or napkins laid, no knives or forks, nor so much as a bench to sit down on; but *he commanded them to sit down on the grass*. By doing everything thus, without any pomp or splendour, he plainly showed *that his kingdom was not of this world*.

2. The craving of a blessing. He himself *looked up to heaven, and blessed, and gave thanks*; he praised God for the provision they had, and prayed to God to bless it to them. Herein he has taught us that good duty of craving a blessing and giving thanks at our meals: God's good creatures must be *received with thanksgiving*. When Christ *blessed, he looked up to heaven*, to teach us, in prayer, to eye God as a *Father in heaven*; and when we receive our creature-comforts to look thitherward, as taking them from God's hand, and depending on him for a blessing.

3. The carving of the meat. The Master of the feast was himself head-carver, for *he brake, and gave the loaves to the disciples, and the disciples to the multitude*. Ministers can never fill the people's hearts, unless Christ first fill their hands: and what he has given to the disciples, they must give to the multitude. And, blessed be God, be the multitude ever so great, there is enough for all, enough for each.

4. The increase of the meat. Here is no mention of any word that Christ spoke, by which the food was multiplied; the purposes and intentions of his mind and will shall take effect, though they be not spoken out: but this is observable, that the meat was multiplied, not in the heap at first, but in the distribution of it. Thus grace grows by being acted, and, while other things perish in the using, spiritual gifts increase in the using. Thus *there is that scattereth, and yet increaseth*.

VI. The plentiful satisfaction of all the guests with this provision.

1. There was enough: *They did all eat, and were filled*. Those whom Christ feeds, he fills. As there was enough for all, *they did all eat*, so there was enough for each, *they were filled*; though there was but a little, there was enough, and that is as good as a feast. The blessing of God can make a little go a great way.

2. There was to spare: *They took up of the fragments that remained, twelve baskets full*, one basket for each apostle: thus what they gave they had again, and a great deal more with it. This was to show that the provision Christ makes for those who are his is not bare and scanty, but rich and plenteous; an over-flowing fulness.

It is the same divine power which multiplies *the seed sown in the ground* every year, and makes *the earth yield her increase*; so that what was brought out by handfuls, is brought home in sheaves. *This is the Lord's doing*.

Verses 22–33

We have here the story of another miracle which Christ wrought for the relief of his friends and followers, his *walking upon the water to his disciples*.

I. Christ's dismissing of his disciples and *the multitude*, after he had fed them miraculously. He *constrained his disciples to get into a ship, and to go before him unto the other side, v.* 22. St. John gives a particular reason for the hasty breaking up of this assembly, because the people were so affected with the miracle of the loaves, that they were about *to take him by force, and make him a king* (John vi. 15).

1. Christ sent the people away. He sent them away with a blessing, with some parting words of caution, counsel, and comfort.

2. He *constrained the disciples to go into a ship* first, for till they were gone the people would not stir. The disciples were loth to go, and would not have gone, if he had not *constrained* them.

II. Christ's retirement hereupon (*v.* 23); *He went up into a mountain apart to pray*. Observe here,

1. That he was alone; *he went apart into a solitary place, and was there all alone*. He chose sometimes to be alone, to set us an example. Those are not Christ's followers that do not care for being alone; that cannot enjoy themselves in solitude, when they have none else to converse with, none else to enjoy, but God and their own hearts.

2. That he was alone at prayer; that was his business in this solitude, to pray. Christ has herein set before us an example of secret prayer, and the performance of it secretly, according to the rule he gave, *ch.* vi. 6. When the disciples went to sea, their Master went to prayer.

3. That he was long alone; *there he was when the evening was come*, and, for aught that appears, there he was till towards morning, *the fourth watch of the night*. *The night* came on, and it was a stormy tempestuous night, yet he continued *instant in prayer*. It is good when we find our hearts enlarged, to continue long in secret prayer.

III. The condition that the poor disciples were in at this time: *Their ship was now in the midst of the sea, tossed with waves, v.* 24.

1. They were got into the midst of the sea when the storm rose. We may have fair weather at the beginning of our voyage, and yet meet with storms before we arrive at the port we are bound for. After a long calm expect some storm or other.

2. The disciples were now where Christ sent them, and yet met with this storm. It is no new thing for Christ's disciples to meet with storms in the way of their duty, and to be sent to sea when their Master foresees a storm; but let them not take it unkindly. Christ designs hereby to manifest himself with the more wonderful grace to them and for them.

3. It was a great discouragement to them now that they had not Christ with them, as they had formerly when they were in a storm. Thus Christ used his disciples first to less difficulties, and then to greater, and so trains them up by degrees to live *by faith*.

4. Though *the wind was contrary*, and they were tossed with waves, yet being ordered by their Master *to the other side*, they did not tack about and come back again, but made the best of their way forward. Though troubles and difficulties may disturb us in our duty, they must not drive us from it.

IV. Christ's approach to them in this condition (*v.* 25); and in this we have an instance,

1. Of his goodness, that he went unto them, as one that took cognizance of their case, and was under a concern about them. The extremity of the church and people of God is Christ's opportunity to visit them and appear for them.

2. Of his power, that he *went unto them, walking on the sea.* This is a great instance of Christ's sovereign dominion over all the creatures. We need not enquire how this was done. It is sufficient that it proves his divine power. Christ can take what way he pleases to save his people.

V. Here is an account of what passed between Christ and his distressed friends upon his approach.

1. Between him and all the disciples. We are here told,

(1) How their fears were raised (*v.* 26); *When they saw him walking on the sea, they were troubled, saying, It is a spirit. It is an apparition;* so it might much better be rendered. These disciples said, *It is a spirit;* when they should have said, *It is the Lord;* it can be no other. Even the appearances and approaches of deliverance are sometimes the occasions of trouble and perplexity to God's people, who are sometimes most frightened when they are least hurt. The appearance of a spirit, or the fancy of it, cannot but be frightful. The more acquaintance we have with God, the Father of spirits, and the more careful we are to keep ourselves in his love, the better able we shall be to deal with those fears. A little thing frightens us in a storm. Most of our danger from outward troubles arises from the occasion they give for inward trouble.

(2) How these fears were silenced, *v.* 27. He delayed his succour for some time; but he hastened his succour against their fright, as much the more dangerous; he straightway laid that storm with his word, *Be of good cheer; it is I; be not afraid.* He rectified their mistake, by making himself known to them, *It is I.* He does not name himself to these disciples, it was enough to say, *It is I;* they *knew his voice, as his sheep* (John x. 4), as Mary Magdalene, John xx. 16. It was enough to make them easy, to understand who it was they saw. A right knowledge opens the door to true comfort, especially the knowledge of Christ. He encouraged them against their fright; *It is I,* and therefore, *Be of good cheer.* If Christ's disciples be not cheerful in a storm, it is their own fault, he would have them so. *Be not afraid;* 1. "Be not afraid of me, now that you know it is I." Christ will not be a terror to those to whom he manifests himself; when they come to understand him aright, the terror will be over. 2. *"Be not afraid* of the tempest, of the winds and waves; fear them not, while I am so near you. I am he that concerns himself for you, and will not stand by and see you perish." Nothing needs be a terror to those that have Christ near them, and know he is theirs; no, not death itself.

2. Between him and Peter, *v.* 28-31.

(1) Peter's courage, and Christ's countenancing that.

[1] It was very bold in Peter, that he would venture to come to Christ *upon the water* (*v.* 28); *Lord, if it be thou, bid me come unto thee.* Courage was Peter's master grace; and that made him so forward above the rest to express his love to Christ, though others perhaps loved him as well.

It is an instance of Peter's affection to Christ, that he desired to come to him. When he sees Christ he is impatient to be with him. He does not say, *Bid me walk on the waters,* as desiring it for the miracle sake; but, *Bid me come to thee,* as desiring it for Christ's sake. True love will break through fire and water to come to Christ. Those that would have benefit by Christ as a Saviour, must thus by faith come to him. When, for a small moment,

Christ has forsaken his people, his returns are welcome and most affectionately embraced.

It is an instance of Peter's caution and due observance of the will of Christ, that he would not come without a warrant. Not, "If it be thou, I will come"; but *If it be thou, bid me come.* The boldest spirits must wait for a call to hazardous enterprises, and we must not rashly and presumptuously thrust ourselves upon them.

It is an instance of Peter's faith and resolution, that he ventured upon the water when Christ bid him. What difficulty or danger could stand before such a faith and such a zeal?

[2] It was very kind in Christ, that he was pleased to own him in it, *v.* 29. Christ knew that it came from a sincere and zealous affection to him, and graciously accepted of it. Christ is well pleased with the expressions of his people's love, though mixed with manifold infirmities, and makes the best of them.

He bid him *come.* When Peter asked a sign, he had it, because he did it with a resolution to trust Christ.

He bore him out when he did come; *Peter walked upon the water.* The communion of true believers with Christ is represented by their being *quickened with him, raised up with him.* Now, methinks, it is represented in this story by their *walking with him on the water.* Through the strength of Christ we are borne up above the world, kept from sinking into it, from being overwhelmed by it, obtain a victory over it (1 John v. 4).

He walked upon the water, not for diversion or ostentation, but to go to Jesus. Nor can we ever come to Jesus, unless we be upheld by his power; which power we must depend upon, as Peter when he *walked upon the water:* and there is no danger of sinking while *underneath are the everlasting arms.*

(2) Here is Peter's cowardice, and Christ's reproving him and succouring him. Christ bid him come, not only that he might walk upon the water, and so know Christ's power, but that he might sink, and so know his own weakness. Peter's great fear (*v.* 30); *He was afraid.* The strongest faith and the greatest courage have a mixture of fear. Those that can say, *Lord, I believe;* must say, *Lord, help my unbelief.* Peter was very stout at first, but afterwards his heart failed him. The lengthening out of a trial discovers the weakness of faith.

The cause of this fear; *He saw the wind boisterous.* While Peter kept his eye fixed upon Christ, and upon his word and power, he *walked upon the water* well enough; but when he took notice withal of the danger he was in, then he feared. Looking at difficulties with an eye of sense more than at precepts and promises with an eye of faith is at the bottom of all our inordinate fears. Peter, *when he saw the wind boisterous,* should have remembered what he had seen (*ch.* viii. 27), when the winds and the sea obeyed Christ.

The effect of this fear; *He began to sink.* While faith kept up, he kept above water: but when faith staggered, *he began to sink.* The sinking of our spirits is owing to the weakness of our faith; we are upheld (but it is as we are saved) *through faith* (1 Pet. i. 5). It was Christ's great mercy to him, that, upon the failing of his faith, he did not leave him to sink outright, to sink to the *bottom as a stone* (Exod. xv. 5), but gave him time to cry, *Lord, save me.* Such is the care of Christ concerning true believers; though weak, they do but begin to sink!

The remedy he had recourse to in this distress, the old, tried, approved remedy, and that was prayer: he cried, *Lord, save me.* 1. The manner of his praying; it is fervent and importunate; *He cried.* When faith is weak, prayer should be strong. 2. The matter of his prayer was pertinent and to the purpose; *He cried,*

Lord, save me. Those that would be saved, must not only *come* to him, but *cry* to him for salvation; but we are never brought to this, till we find ourselves sinking; sense of need will drive us to him.

Christ's great favour to Peter, in this fright.

He saved him. For immediately *he stretched forth his hand, and caught him.* Note, Christ's time to save is, when we sink: he helps at a dead lift. Christ's hand is still stretched out to all believers, to keep them from sinking. Never fear, he will hold his own.

He rebuked him; for as many as he loves and saves, he reproves and chides; *O thou of little faith, wherefore didst thou doubt?* Faith may be true, and yet weak; at first, like a grain of mustard-seed. Peter had faith enough to bring him upon the water, yet, because not enough to carry him through, Christ tells him he had but *little.* Our discouraging doubts and fears are all owing to the weakness of our faith: *therefore* we *doubt,* because we are but *of little faith.* Could we but believe more, we should doubt less. It is true, he doth not cast off weak believers, but it is as true, that he is not pleased with weak faith, no, not in those that are nearest to him. *Wherefore didst thou doubt?* What reason was there for it? There is no good reason why Christ's disciples should be of a doubtful mind, no, not in a stormy day, because he is ready to them, *a very present Help.*

VI. The *ceasing of the storm, v. 32.* When Christ was come into the ship, they were presently at the shore. Christ *walked upon the water* till he came to the ship, and then went into that, when he could as easily have walked to the shore. When Christ came into the ship, Peter came in with him. Companions with Christ in his patience, shall be companions in his kingdom, Rev. i. 9. Those that walk with him shall reign with him.

When they were come into the ship, immediately the storm ceased. When Christ comes into a soul, he makes winds and storms to cease there, and commands peace. Welcome Christ, and *the noise of her waves will soon be quelled.* The way to be still is, to know that he is God, that he is the *Lord with us.*

VII. The adoration paid to Christ hereupon (*v. 33*); *They that were in the ship came and worshipped him, and said, Of a truth, thou art the Son of God.* Two good uses they made of this distress, and this deliverance.

1. It was a confirmation of their faith in Christ. They knew before that he was the Son of God, but now they know it better. Faith, after a conflict with unbelief, is sometimes the more active, and gets to greater degrees of strength by being exercised. Now they *know it of a truth.* Faith *then* grows, when it arrives at a full assurance, when it sees clearly, and saith, *Of a truth.*

2. They took occasion from it to *give him the glory due unto his name. They worshipped Christ.* When Christ manifests his glory for us, we ought to return it to him (Ps. l. 15). Their worship and adoration of Christ were thus expressed, *Of a truth thou art the Son of God.* The matter of our creed may and must be made the matter of our praise. Faith is the proper principle of worship, and worship the genuine product of faith.

Verses 34–36

We have here an account of miracles by wholesale, which Christ wrought on the other side of the water, in the land of Gennesaret. Whithersoever Christ went, he was doing good.

I. The forwardness and faith of *the men of that place.* These were more noble than the Gergesenes, their neighbours. Those *besought Christ to depart* from them, they had no occasion for him; these besought him to help them, they had need of him.

Christ reckons it the greatest honour we can do him, to make use of him. Now here we are told,

1. How *the men of that place* were brought to Christ; they *had knowledge of him.* It is probable that his miraculous passage over the sea might help to make way for his entertainment in those parts; and perhaps it was one thing Christ intended in it, for he has great reaches in what he does. They that know Christ's name, will make their application to him: if Christ were better known, he would not be neglected as he is; he is trusted as far as he is known.

They *had knowledge of him,* that is, of his being among them. The discerning of the day of our opportunities is a good step toward the improvement of it. It is better to know that there *is* a prophet among us than that there *has been one.*

2. How they brought others to Christ; *They sent out into all that country.* Note, those that have got the knowledge of Christ themselves, should do all they can to bring others acquainted with him too. We must not eat these spiritual morsels alone; there is in Christ enough for us all, so that there is nothing got by monopolising. When we have opportunities of getting good to our souls, we should bring as many as we can to share with us. More than we think of would close with opportunities, if they were but called upon and invited to them. Neighbourhood is an advantage of doing good which must be improved.

3. What their business was with Christ; *They brought unto him all that were diseased.* If love to Christ and his doctrine will not bring them to him, yet self-love would. Did we but rightly seek our own things, the things of our own peace and welfare, we should seek the things of Christ.

4. How they made their application to him; *They besought him that they might only touch the hem of his garment, v. 36.* They applied themselves to him, (1) With great importunity; they besought him. The greatest favours and blessings are to be obtained from Christ by entreaty; *Ask, and it shall be given.* (2) With great humility. Their desiring to touch the hem of his garment, intimates that they thought themselves unworthy that he should so much as speak to their case, much less touch them for their cure; but they will look upon it as a great favour, if he will give them leave to *touch the hem of his garment.* (3) With great assurance of the all-sufficiency of his power, not doubting but that they should be healed, even by touching the hem of his garment. They were sure that there was in him such an overflowing fulness of healing virtue, that *they* could not fail of a cure, who were but admitted near him. It was in this country and neighbourhood that the woman with the bloody issue was cured by *touching the hem of his garment,* and was commended for her faith (*ch.* ix. 20–22); and thence, probably, they took occasion to ask this. It is good using those means and methods which others before us have sped well in the use of.

II. The fruit and success of this their application to Christ. It was not in vain for as *many as touched, were made perfectly whole.* Christ's cures are perfect cures. Those that he heals, he heals perfectly. He doth not do his work by halves. There is abundance of healing virtue in Christ for all that apply themselves to him, be they ever so many. The least of Christ's institutions, like the hem of his garment, is replenished with the overflowing fulness of his grace. The healing virtue that is in Christ, is put forth for the benefit of those that by a true and lively faith touch him. Christ is in heaven, but his word is nigh us, and he himself in that word. When we mix faith with the word, submit to its influences and commands, then we touch the hem of Christ's garment. It is but thus touching, and we are made whole.

CHAPTER 15

In this chapter, we have our Lord Jesus, as the great Prophet teaching, as the great Physician healing, and as the great Shepherd of the sheep feeding; as the Father of spirits instructing them: as the Conqueror of Satan dispossessing him; and as concerned for the bodies of his people, providing for them. I. Christ's discourse with the scribes and Pharisees, ver. 1–9. II. His discourse concerning the things that defile a man, ver. 10–20. III. His casting of the devil out of the woman of Canaan's daughter, ver. 21–28. IV. His healing of all that were brought to him, ver. 29–31. V. His feeding of four thousand men, ver. 32–39.

Verses 1–9

I. Here is the cavil of the scribes and Pharisees at Christ's disciples, for *eating with unwashen hands.* They were men of learning and men of business. These scribes and Pharisees here introduced were of Jerusalem; they should therefore have been better than others, but they were worse. External privileges, if they be not duly improved, commonly swell men up the more with pride and malignity.

Now if these great men be the accusers, pray what is the accusation? Nonconformity to the canons of their church (*v.* 2); *Why do thy disciples transgress the tradition of the elders?* This charge they make good in a particular instance; *They wash not their hands when they eat bread.*

Observe, 1. What was the *tradition of the elders*— That people should often wash their hands, and always at meat. This they placed a great deal of religion in, supposing that the meat they touched with unwashen hands would be defiling to them. The Pharisees practised this themselves, and with a great deal of strictness imposed it upon others. Nay, they would not eat meat with one that did not wash before meat.

2. What was the transgression of this tradition or injunction by the disciples; it seems, they did not wash their hands when they ate bread. The custom was innocent enough, and had a decency in its civil use. But when it came to be practised and imposed as a religious rite and ceremony, and such a stress laid upon it, the disciples, though weak in knowledge, yet were so well taught as not to comply with it, or observe it; no not when the scribes and Pharisees had their eye upon them. They had already learned St. Paul's lesson.

3. What was the complaint of the scribes and Pharisees against them. They quarrel with Christ about it. "*Why do thy disciples transgress* the canons of the church?" It was well that the complaint was made to Christ; for the disciples themselves were perhaps not so well able to give a reason for what they did as were to be wished.

II. Here is Christ's answer to this cavil, and his justification of the disciples.

Two ways Christ replies upon them;

1. By way of recrimination, *v.* 3–6. They were spying motes in the eyes of his disciples, but Christ shows them a beam in their own. It is such a censure of their tradition (and the authority of that was what they built their charge upon) as makes not only a non-compliance lawful, but an opposition a duty.

(1) The charge in general is, *You transgress the commandment of God by your tradition.* They call it the *tradition of the elders,* laying stress upon the antiquity of the usage, and the authority of them that imposed it. *You transgress the commandment of God.* Note, Those who are most zealous of their own impositions, are commonly most careless of God's commands.

(2) The proof of this charge is in a particular instance, that of their transgressing the fifth commandment.

[1] Let us see what the command of God is (*v.* 4), what the precept, and what the sanction of the law is. The precept is, *Honour thy father and thy mother;*

this is enjoined by the common Father of mankind. The whole of children's duty to their parents is included in this of honouring them, which is the spring and foundation of all the rest.

The sanction of this law in the fifth commandment, is, a promise, *that thy days may be long*; but our Saviour waives that, lest any should thence infer it to be only a thing commendable and profitable, and insists upon the penalty annexed to the breach of this commandment in another scripture, which denotes the duty to be highly and indispensably necessary; *He that curseth father or mother, let him die the death.* By our Saviour's application of this law, it appears, that denying service or relief to parents is included in cursing them. Though the language be respectful enough, and nothing abusive in it, yet what will that avail, if the deeds be not agreeable?

[2] Let us see what was the contradiction which the tradition of the elders gave to this command. It was not direct and downright, but implicit; their casuists gave them such rules as furnished them with an easy evasion from the obligation of this command, *v.* 5, 6. Observe,

First, What their tradition was; That a man could not in any case bestow his worldly estate better than to give it to the priests, and devote it to the service of the temple: and that when anything was so devoted, it was not only unlawful to alienate it, but all other obligations, though ever so just and sacred, were thereby superseded.

Secondly, How they allowed the application of this to the case of children. When their parents' necessities called for their assistance, they pleaded, that all they could spare from themselves and their children, they had devoted to the treasury of the temple; *It is a gift, by whatsoever thou mightest be profited by me,* and therefore their parents must expect nothing from them. This, they taught, was a good and valid plea, and many undutiful, unnatural children made use of it, and they justified them in it, and said, *He shall be free.* But the absurdity and impiety of this tradition were very evident: for revealed religion was intended to improve, not to overthrow, natural religion; one of the fundamental laws of which is this of honouring our parents. This was *making the command of God of no effect.* To break the law is bad, but to *teach men so,* as the scribes and Pharisees did, is much worse, *ch. v.* 19. To what purpose is the command given, if it be not obeyed?

2. The other part of Christ's answer is by way of reprehension; and that which he here charges them with, is hypocrisy; *Ye hypocrites, v.* 7. It is the prerogative of him who searcheth the heart, and knows what is in man, to pronounce who are hypocrites. The eye of man can perceive open profaneness, but it is only the eye of Christ that can discern hypocrisy, Luke xvi. 15. And as it is a sin which his eye discovers, so it is a sin which of all others his soul hates.

Now Christ fetches his reproof from Isa. xxix. 13. *Well did Esaias prophesy of you.* Isaiah spoke it of the men of that generation to which he prophesied, yet Christ applies it to these scribes and Pharisees. Threatenings directed against others, belong to us, if we be guilty of the same sins. Isaiah prophesied not of them only, but of all other hypocrites, against whom that word of his is still levelled, and stands in force. The prophecies of scripture are every day in the fulfilling.

(1) The description of hypocrites, in two things. In their own performances of religious worship, *v.* 8, when they *draw nigh to God with their mouth, and honour him with their lips, their heart is far from him.*

First, How far a hypocrite goes; he draws nigh to God, and honours him; he is, in profession a worshipper of God. The *Pharisee went up to the temple to pray*; he does not stand at that distance which those are at, who *live without God in the world*. They honour him; that is, they take on them to honour God, they join with those that do so. Some honour God has even from the services of hypocrites.

Secondly, Where he rests and takes up; this is done but with his mouth and with his lips. It is piety but from the teeth outwards; he shows much love, and that is all, there is in his heart no true love. Hypocrites are those that only make a lip-labour of religion and religious worship.

Thirdly, What that is wherein he comes short; it is in the main matter; *Their heart is far from me*, habitually alienated and estranged (Eph. iv. 18), actually wandering and dwelling upon something else. A hypocrite says one thing, but thinks another. The great thing that God looks at and requires is the heart (Prov. xxiii. 26). In their prescriptions to others. This is an instance of their hypocrisy, that *they teach for doctrines the commandments of men*. When men's inventions are tacked to God's institutions, and imposed accordingly, this is hypocrisy, a mere human religion. God will have his own work done by his own rules, and accepts not that which he did not himself appoint. That only comes *to* him, that comes *from* him.

(2) The doom of hypocrites; it is put in a little compass; *In vain do they worship me*. Their worship does not attain the end for which it was appointed; it will neither please God, nor profit themselves. If it be not *in spirit*, it is not *in truth*, and so it is all nothing. Lip-labour is lost labour.

Verses 10-20

I. The solemn introduction to this discourse (*v*. 10); *He called the multitude*. Christ had a regard to the multitude. The humble Jesus embraced those whom the proud Pharisees looked upon with disdain. He turns from them as wilful and unteachable, and turns to the multitude, who, though weak, were humble, and willing to be taught. To them he said, *Hear and understand*. Note, What we hear from the mouth of Christ, we must give all diligence to understand. Not only scholars, but even the multitude, the ordinary people, must apply their minds to understand the words of Christ.

II. The truth itself laid down (*v*. 11), in two propositions.

1. *Not that which goes into the mouth defileth the man*. It is not the kind or quality of our food, nor the condition of our hands, that affects the soul with any moral polution or defilement. *The kingdom of God is not meat and drink*, Rom. xiv. 17. That defiles the man, by which guilt is contracted before God, and the man is rendered offensive to him, and disfitted for communion with him; now what we eat does not this. He was now beginning to teach his followers to *call nothing common or unclean*; and if Peter, when he was bid to *kill and eat*, had remembered this word, he would not have said, *Not so, Lord*, Acts x. 13-15, 28.

2. *But that which comes out of the mouth, this defiles a man*. We are polluted, not by the meat we eat with unwashen hands, but by the words we speak from an unsanctified heart. It is not the disciples that defile themselves with what they eat, but the Pharisees that defile themselves with what they speak spitefully and censoriously of them. Those who charge guilt upon others for transgressing the commandments of men, many times bring greater guilt upon themselves, by transgressing the law of God against rash judging.

III. The offence that was taken at this truth and the account brought to Christ of that offence (*v*. 12);

"The disciples said unto him, Knowest thou that the Pharisees were offended."

1. It was not strange that the Pharisees should be offended at this plain truth. Sore eyes cannot bear clear light; and nothing is more provoking to proud imposers than the undeceiving of those whom they have first blindfolded and then enslaved, great contenders for the formalities of religion, being commonly as great contemners of the substantials of it.

2. The disciples thought it strange that their Master should say that which he knew would give so much offence; he did not use to do so. But he knew what he said, and to whom he said it, and would teach us, that though in indifferent things we must be tender of giving offence, yet we must not, for fear of that, evade any truth or duty. Truth must be owned, and duty done; and if any be offended, it is his own fault; it is scandal, not given, but taken.

Perhaps the disciples themselves stumbled at the word Christ said and therefore objected this to Christ, that they might themselves be better informed. They seem likewise to have a concern upon them for the Pharisees. They would not have the Pharisees go away displeased at anything Christ had said; and therefore, though they do not desire him to retract it, they hope he will explain, correct, and modify it. Weak hearers are sometimes more solicitous than they should be not to have wicked hearers offended.

IV. The doom passed upon the Pharisees and their corrupt traditions. Two things Christ here foretells concerning them.

1. The rooting out of them and their traditions (*v*. 13); *Every plant which my heavenly Father hath not planted, shall be rooted up*. Their sect, and way, and constitution, were plants not of God's planting. The rules of their profession were no institutions of his, but owed their origin to pride and formality. In the visible church, it is no strange thing to find plants that our heavenly Father has not planted. Let the husbandman be ever so careful, his ground will cast forth weeds of itself, more or less, and there is an enemy busy sowing tares. What is corrupt, though of God's permitting, is not of his planting; he sows nothing but *good seed in his field*. Let us not therefore be deceived, as if all must needs be right that we find in the church, and all those persons and things our Father's plants that we find in our Father's garden. *By their fruit you shall know them*. Those plants that are not of God's planting, shall not be of his protecting, but shall undoubtedly be rooted up. What is not of God shall not stand, Acts v. 38. But the gospel of truth is great, and will remain. It cannot be rooted up.

2. The ruin of them; and their followers, *v*. 14.

(1) Christ bids his disciples *let them alone*. "Have no converse with them or concern for them; neither court their favour, nor dread their displeasure; they will take their course, and let them take the issue of it. They are wedded to their own fancies, and will have everything their own way; let them alone. Seek not to please a generation of men that please not God" (1 Thess. ii. 15). The case of those sinners is sad indeed, whom Christ orders his ministers to let alone.

(2) He gives them two reasons for it. *Let them alone; for,*

[1] They are proud and ignorant; two bad qualities that often meet, and render a man incurable in his folly, Prov. xxvi. 12. *They are blind leaders of the blind*. They are grossly ignorant in the things of God, and yet so proud, that they think they see better and further than any, and therefore undertake to be leaders of others, to show others the way to heaven, when they themselves know not one step of the way; and, accordingly, they prescribe to all, and proscribe

those who will not follow them. Though they were blind, if they had owned it, and come to Christ for eye-salve, they might have seen. *Are we blind also?* They were confident that *they themselves were guides of the blind* (Rom. ii. 19, 20), were appointed to be so, and fit to be so; that everything they said was an oracle and a law.

[2] They are posting to destruction; *Both shall fall into the ditch.* This must needs be the end of it, if both be so blind, and yet both so bold, venturing forward, and yet not aware of danger. The blind leaders and the blind followers will perish together. Those that by their cunning craftiness draw others to sin and error, shall not, with all their craft and cunning, escape ruin themselves. If *both fall together into the ditch,* the blind leaders will fall undermost, and have the worst of it. They that have thus mutually increased each other's sin, will mutually exasperate each other's ruin.

V. Instruction given to the disciples concerning the truth Christ had laid down, *v.* 10. Though Christ rejects the wilfully ignorant who care not to be taught, he can have compassion on the ignorant who are willing to learn, Heb. v. 2.

1. Their desire to be better instructed in this matter (*v.* 15); in this request as in many others, Peter was their speaker; *Declare unto us this parable.* What Christ said was plain, yet they call it a parable, and cannot understand it. Weak understandings are apt to turn plain truths into parables, and to seek for a knot in a bulrush. Where a weak head doubts concerning any word of Christ, an upright heart and a willing mind will seek for instruction. The disciples, though offended, sought for satisfaction, imputing the offence, not to the doctrine delivered, but to the shallowness of their own capacity.

2. The reproof Christ gave them for their weakness and ignorance (*v.* 16); *Are ye also yet without understanding?* As many as Christ loves and teaches, he thus rebukes. Two things aggravate their dullness and darkness. That they were the disciples of Christ; "Are *ye* also without understanding? Ye whom I have admitted into so great a degree of familiarity with me, are ye so unskilful in the word of righteousness?" The ignorance and mistakes of those that profess religion, and enjoy the privileges of church-membership, are justly a grief to the Lord Jesus. That they had been a great while Christ's scholars; "Are ye *yet* so, after ye have been so long under my teaching?" Had they been but of yesterday in Christ's school, it had been another matter. Christ expects from us some proportion of knowledge, and grace, and wisdom, according to the time and means we have had. See John xiv. 9.

3. The explication Christ gave them of this doctrine of pollutions. He here shows us,

(1) What little danger we are in of pollution from that which *entereth in at the mouth, v.* 17. An inordinate appetite, intemperance, and excess in eating, come out of the heart, and are defiling; but meat in itself is not so, as the Pharisees supposed. What there is of dregs and defilement in our meat, nature (or rather the God of nature) has provided a way to clear us of it; *it goes in at the belly, and is cast out into the draught,* and nothing remains to us but pure nourishment. By this means nothing defiles; if we eat with unwashen hands, and so anything unclean mix with our food, nature will separate it, and cast it out, and it will be no defilement to us. It may be a piece of cleanliness, but it is no point of conscience, to wash before meat.

(2) What great danger we are in of pollution from that which *proceeds out of the mouth* (*v.* 18). There is no defilement in the products of God's bounty; the defilement arises from the products of our corruption. Now here we have,

[1] The corrupt fountain of that which proceeds out of the mouth; it comes from the heart. It is the heart that is so desperately wicked (Jer. xvii. 9); for there is no sin in word or deed, which was not first in the heart. All evil speakings come forth from the heart, and are defiling.

[2] Some of the corrupt streams which flow from this fountain, specified,

First, Evil thoughts, sins against all the commandments. There is a great deal of sin that begins and ends in the heart, and goes no further.

Secondly, Murders, these come from a malice in the heart against our brother's life, or a contempt of it. Hence he *that hates his brother,* is said to be a *murderer;* he is so at God's bar, 1 John iii. 15.

Thirdly, Adulteries and *fornications,* these come from the wanton, unclean, carnal heart; and the lust that reigns there. There is adultery in the heart first, and then in the act, *ch.* v. 28.

Fourthly, Thefts, cheats, wrongs, rapines, and all injurious contracts. The fountain of all these is in the heart. *Achan coveted, and then took,* Joshua vii. 20, 21.

Fifthly, False witness. If truth, holiness, and love, which God *requires in the inward parts,* reigned as they ought, there would be no false witness bearing.

Sixthly, Blasphemies, speaking evil of God, speaking evil of our neighbour. These are the overflowing of the gall within.

Now *these are the things which defile a man, v.* 20. Sin is defiling to the soul, renders it unlovely and abominable in the eyes of the pure and holy God; unfit for communion with him.

These therefore are the things we must carefully avoid, and all approaches toward them, and not lay stress upon the washing of the hands. He concludes, *To eat with unwashen hands this defileth not a man.* If he wash, he is not the better before God; if he wash not, he is not the worse.

Verses 21–29

We have here that famous story of Christ's *casting the devil out of the woman of Canaan's daughter;* it has something in it singular and very surprising, and which looks favourably upon the poor Gentiles, and is an earnest of that mercy which Christ had in store for them. Here is a gleam of that *light* which was *to lighten the Gentiles,* Luke ii. 32.

I. *Jesus went thence.* Justly is the light taken from those that either play by it, or rebel against it. Though Christ endure long, he will not always *endure, the contradition of sinners against himself.* Wilful prejudices against the gospel, and cavils at it, often provoke Christ to withdraw.

II. When he went thence, he *departed into the coasts of Tyre and Sidon;* not to those cities, but into that part of the land of Israel which lay that way. While he went about doing good, he was never out of his way. The dark corners of the country, which lay most remote, shall have their share of his benign influences. Here it was, that this miracle was wrought, in the story of which we may observe,

1. The address of the woman of Canaan to Christ, *v.* 22. She was a Gentile, *a stranger to the commonwealth of Israel.* God will have his remnant out of all nations, chosen vessels in all coasts, even the most unlikely. If Christ had not now made a visit to these coasts, it is probable that she had never come to him. It is often an excitement to a dormant faith and zeal, to have opportunities of acquaintance with Christ brought to our doors.

Her address was very importunate, she *cried* to Christ, as one in earnest.

(1) She relates her misery; *My daughter is grievously vexed with a devil.* The vexations of children are the trouble of parents. Tender parents very sensibly

feel the miseries of those that are pieces of themselves. "Though vexed with the devil, yet she is my daughter still." The greatest afflictions of our relations do not dissolve our obligations to them, and therefore ought not to alienate our affections from them. It was the distress and trouble of her family, that now brought her to Christ. Because she came in faith, he did not reject her. Though it is need that drives us to Christ, yet we shall not therefore be driven from him.

(2) She requests for mercy; *Have mercy on me, O Lord, thou Son of David.*

Her petition is, *Have mercy on me.* She does not limit Christ, but mercy, mercy is the thing she begs: she pleads not merit, but depends upon mercy. Mercies to the children are mercies to the parents; favours to ours are favours to us. It is the duty of parents to pray for their children, and to be earnest in prayer for them. Bring them to Christ by faith and prayer, who alone is able to heal them.

2. The discouragement she met with in this address; in all the story of Christ's ministry we do not meet with the like. He was wont to countenance and encourage all that came to him, and either to *answer before they called,* or *to hear while they were yet speaking;* but here was one otherwise treated: and what could be the reason of it? Some think that Christ showed himself backward to gratify this poor woman, because he would not give offence to the Jews, by being as free and as forward in his favour to the Gentiles as to them. Or rather, Christ treated her thus, to try her; he knows what is in the heart, knew the strength of her faith, and how well able she was, by his grace, to break through such discouragements; he *therefore* met her with them, *that the trial of her faith might be found unto praise, and honour, and glory,* 1 Pet. i. 6, 7. Many of the methods of Christ's providence, and especially of his grace, in dealing with his people, which are dark and perplexing, may be explained with the key of this story. There may be love in Christ's heart while there are frowns in his face.

Observe the particular discouragements given her:

(1) When she cried after him, *he answered her not a word, v.* 23. His ear was wont to be always open and attentive to the cries of poor supplicants; but to this poor woman he turned a deaf ear, and she could get neither an alms nor an answer. But Christ knew what he did, and *therefore* did not answer, that she might be the more earnest in prayer. By seeming to draw away the desired mercy from her, he drew her on to be so much the more importunate for it. Every accepted prayer is not immediately an answered prayer. Sometimes God seems not to regard his people's prayers, but it is to prove, and so to *improve,* their faith.

(2) When the disciples spake a good word for her, he gave a reason why he refused her, which was yet more discouraging.

It was some little relief, that the disciples interposed on her behalf; they said, *Send her away, for she crieth after us.* The disciples, though wishing she might have what she came for, yet therein consulted rather their own ease than the poor woman's satisfaction; "*Send her away* with a cure, *she cries after us,* and is troublesome to us, and shames us." Continued importunity may be uneasy to men, even to good men; but Christ loves to be cried after.

Christ's answer to the disciples quite dashed her expectations: "*I am not sent, but to the lost sheep of the house of Israel.*" Importunity seldom conquers the settled reason of a wise man. He doth not only not answer her, but he argues against her, and stops her mouth with a reason. It is a great trial, when we have occasion given us to question whether we be of those to whom Christ was sent. But, blessed be God, no room is left for that doubt; the distinction between Jew and Gentile is taken away; we are sure that he *gave his life a ransom for many,* and if for many, why not for me?

When she continued her importunity, he insisted upon the unfitness of the thing, and gave her not only a repulse, but a seeming reproach too (*v.* 26); *It is not meet to take the children's bread and to cast it to dogs.* This seems to cut her off from all hope, and might have driven her to despair, if she had not had a very strong faith indeed. Gospel grace and miraculous cures (the appurtenances of it), were children's bread; and lay not upon the same level with that rain from heaven, and those fruitful seasons, which God gave to the nations whom he suffered *to walk in their own ways* (Acts xiv. 16, 17); no, these were peculiar favours, appropriated to the peculiar people. The Gentiles were looked upon by the Jews with great contempt, were called and counted *dogs.* Christ here seems to allow it, and therefore thinks it not meet that the Gentiles should share in the favours bestowed on the Jews.

Now this Christ urgeth against this woman of Canaan; "How can she expect to eat of the children's bread, who is not of the family?" Those whom Christ intends most signally to honour, he first humbles and lays low in a sense of their own meanness and unworthiness. We must first see ourselves to be as dogs, *less than the least of all God's mercies,* before we are fit to be dignified and privileged with them. Christ delights to exercise great faith with great trials, and sometimes reserves the sharpest for the last, that, *being tried, we may come forth like gold.*

3. Many a one, thus tried, would either have sunk into silence, or broken out into passion. "Here is cold comfort," might she have said, "for a poor distressed creature; as good for me to have stayed at home. Not only to have a piteous case slighted, but to be called a *dog!*" "*Is this the Son of David?*" (might she have said): "Is this he that has such a reputation for kindness, tenderness, and compassion? I am not a dog, I am a woman, and an honest woman, and a woman in misery; and I am sure it is not meet to call me *dog.*" A humble, believing soul, that truly loves Christ, takes everything in good part that he saith and doeth, and puts the best construction upon it.

She breaks through all these discouragements, (1) With an earnestness of desire in prosecuting her petition. This appeared upon the former repulse (*v.* 25); *Then came she, and worshipped him, saying, Lord, help me.* She continued to pray. What Christ said, silenced the disciples; you hear no more of them; they took the answer, but the woman did not. The more sensibly we feel the burthen, the more resolutely we should pray for the removal of it. She improved in prayer. Instead of blaming Christ, or charging him with unkindness, she seems rather to suspect herself. She fears lest she had not been humble and reverent enough, and therefore now *she came, and worshipped him;* or she fears that she had not been earnest enough, and therefore now she cries, *Lord, help me.* When the answers of prayer are deferred, God is thereby teaching us to pray more, and pray better. Disappointments in the success of prayer, must be excitements to the duty of prayer. Christ, in his agony, *prayed more earnestly.* She waives the question, whether she was of those to whom Christ was sent or no; but, "Whether an Israelite or no, I come to the Son of David for mercy, and *I will not let him go, except he bless me.*" Many weak Christians perplex themselves with questions and doubts about their election; such had better mind their errand to God, and continue instant in prayer for mercy and grace; throw themselves by faith at the feet of Christ, and say, *If I perish, I will perish here.* If we cannot *reason* down our unbelief, let us *pray* it down. Her prayer is very short, but comprehensive and fervent, *Lord, help me.* Take this, *First,* As lamenting her case. It is not in vain for broken hearts to bemoan themselves; God looks upon them then. Or, *Secondly,* As begging grace to assist her in this hour of temptation. She found it hard to keep up her faith when it was thus frowned upon, and therefore prays, "*Lord, help me.*" Or, *Thirdly,* As enforcing her original request, "*Lord, help me*; Lord, give me what I come for." She believed that Christ could and would help her. Still she keeps up good thoughts of Christ, and will not quit her hold. *Lord, help me,* is a good prayer, if well put up; and it is pity that it should be turned into a byword, and that we should take God's name in vain in it. (2) With a holy skilfulness of faith, suggesting a very surprising plea. Christ had placed the Jews with the children, *as olive plants round about* God's *table,* and had put the Gentiles with the dogs, under the table. There is nothing got by contradicting any word of Christ, though it bear ever so hard upon us. But this poor woman, since she cannot object against it, resolves to make the best of it (*v.* 27); *Truth, Lord; yet the dogs eat of the crumbs.* Her acknowledgment was very humble: *Truth, Lord.* You cannot speak so meanly and slightly of a humble believer, but he is ready to speak as meanly and slightly of himself. "*Truth, Lord;* I cannot deny it; I am a dog, and have no right to the children's bread." Her improvement of this into a plea was very ingenious; *Yet the dogs eat of the crumbs.* It was by a singular acumen, and spiritual quickness and sagacity, that she discerned matter of argument in that which looked like a slight. A lively, active faith will make that to be for us, which seems to be against us. Faith can find encouragement even in that which is discouraging, and get nearer to God by taking hold on that hand which is stretched out to push it away.

Her plea is, *Yet the dogs eat of the crumbs.* It is true, the full and regular provision is intended for the children only, but the small, casual, neglected crumbs are allowed to the dogs, and are not grudged them. Surely then some of the broken meat may fall to a poor Gentile; "I beg a cure by the by, which is but as a crumb, though of the same precious bread, yet but a small inconsiderable piece, compared with the loaves which they have." When we are ready to surfeit on the children's bread, we should remember how many there are, that would be glad of the crumbs. Our broken meat in spiritual privileges, would be a feast to many a soul.

Her humility and necessity made her glad of crumbs. Those who are conscious to themselves that they deserve nothing, will be thankful for anything. The least of Christ is precious to a believer, and the very crumbs of the bread of life.

Her faith encouraged her to expect these crumbs. Why should it not be at Christ's table, as at a great man's, where the dogs are fed as sure as the children? She calls it their *master's* table; if she were a dog, she was *his* dog. It is good lying in God's house, though we lie at the threshold there.

4. The happy issue and success of all this. She came off with credit and comfort from this struggle; and, though a Canaanite, approved herself a true daughter of Israel; who, *like a prince, had power with God, and prevailed. Then Jesus said, O woman, great is thy faith.* Now he begins to speak like himself, and to put on his own countenance. He commended her faith. *O woman, great is thy faith.* It is her faith that he commends. There were several other graces which shone bright in her conduct of this affair—wisdom, humility, meekness, patience, perseverance in prayer; but these were the product of her faith. Because of all graces faith honours Christ most, therefore of all graces Christ honours faith most. It is the greatness

of her faith. Though the faith of all the saints is alike precious, yet it is not in all alike strong; all believers are not of the same size and stature.

The greatness of faith consists much in a resolute adherence to Jesus Christ, to love him, and trust him, as a Friend, even when he seems to come forth against us as an Enemy. Though weak faith, if true, shall not be rejected, yet great faith shall be commended. He cured her daughter; "*Be it unto thee even as thou wilt:* I can deny thee nothing, take what thou camest for." Great believers may have what they will for the asking. When our will conforms to the will of Christ's precept, his will concurs with the will of our desire. Those that will deny Christ nothing shall find that he will deny them nothing at last, though for a time he seems to hide his face from them.

The event was answerable to the word of Christ; *Her daughter was made whole from that very hour;* the mother's faith prevailed for the daughter's cure. *He spake, and it was done.*

Verses 29–39

I. A general account of Christ's cures, his curing by wholesale. The tokens of Christ's power and goodness are neither scarce nor scanty; for there is in him an overflowing fulness.

1. The place where these cures were wrought; it was *near the sea of Galilee.* We read not of anything he did in the coasts of Tyre and Sidon, but the casting of the devil out of the woman of Canaan's daughter, as if he took that journey on purpose, with that in prospect. Let not ministers grudge their pains to do good, though but to few. He that knows the worth of souls, would go a great way to help to save one from death and Satan's power.

But *Jesus departed thence.* Having let fall that crumb under the table, he here returns to make a full feast for the children. We may do that occasionally for one, which we may not make a constant practice of. Christ steps into the coast of Tyre and Sidon, but he *sits down by the sea of Galilee* (*v.* 29). He *sat down on a mountain,* that all might see him, and have free access to him; for he is an open Saviour. He sat down there as one waiting to be gracious. He settled himself to this good work.

2. The multitudes and maladies that were healed by him (*v.* 30); *Great multitudes came to him.* We are soon sensible of bodily pain and sickness, but few are concerned about their souls and their spiritual diseases. Such was the goodness of Christ, that he admitted all sorts of people; the poor as well as the rich are welcome to Christ. He never looked with contempt upon the vulgar, the *herd,* as they are called; for the souls of peasants are as precious with him as the souls of princes. Such was the power of Christ, that he healed all sorts of diseases; those that came to him, brought their sick relations and friends along with them, and *cast them down at Jesus' feet, v.* 30. We read not of anything they said to him, but they laid them down before him as objects of pity. Their calamities spake more for them than the tongue of the most eloquent orator could. Whatever our case is, the only way to find ease and relief is, to lay it at Christ's feet, and then submit it to him, and refer it to his disposal.

Here were *lame, blind, dumb, maimed, and many others,* brought to Christ. See what work sin has made! What various diseases are human bodies subject to! See what work the Saviour makes! He conquers those hosts of enemies to mankind. *He sent his word, and healed them.* This is an instance of Christ's power, which may comfort us in all our weaknesses; and of his pity, which may comfort us in all our miseries.

3. The influence that this had upon the people, *v.* 31.

(1) They *wondered*, and well they might. Christ's works should be our wonder.

(2) *They glorified the God of Israel*. Miracles, which are the matter of our wonder, must be the matter of our praise; and mercies, which are the matter of our rejoicing, must be the matter of our thanksgiving. If he heal our diseases, all that is within us must bless his holy name; and if we have been graciously preserved from blindness, and lameness, and dumbness, we have as much reason to bless God as if we had been cured. The standers-by glorified God. God must be acknowledged with praise and thankfulness in the mercies of others as in our own.

II. Here is a particular account of his feeding *four thousand men* with *seven loaves, and a few little fishes*, as he had lately fed *five thousand with five loaves*. The guests indeed were now not quite so many as then, and the provision a little more; he wrought his miracles as the occasion required. Both then and now he took as many as were to be fed, and made use of all that was at hand to feed them with. When once the utmost powers of nature are exceeded, we must say, *This is the finger of God;* and it is neither here nor there how far they are outdone.

1. Christ's pity (*v.* 32); *I have compassion on the multitude*. He tells his disciples this, both to try and to excite their compassion. In what he said to them, Observe,

(1) The case of the multitude; *They continue with me now three days, and have nothing to eat*. This is an instance of their zeal, and the strength of their affection to Christ and his word, that they not only left their callings, to attend upon him on weekdays, but underwent a deal of hardship, to continue with him; they wanted necessary food and had scarcely enough to keep life and soul together. They esteemed the words of Christ more than their necessary food. With what tenderness Christ spoke of it; *I have compassion on them*. It had become them to have compassion on him, who took so much pains with them for three days together, and yet for aught that appears he was fasting too. Our Lord Jesus keeps an account how long his followers continue their attendance on him, and takes notice of the difficulty they sustain in it.

Now the exigence the people were reduced to serves to magnify. The mercy of their supply: he fed them when they were hungry; and then food was doubly welcome. The miracle of their supply. If two hungry meals make the third a glutton, what would three hungry days do? And yet *they did all eat and were filled*. There are mercy and grace enough with Christ, to give the most earnest and enlarged desire an abundant satisfaction; *Open thy mouth wide, and I will fill it*.

(2) The care of our master concerning them; *I will not send them away fasting, lest they should faint by the way*. It is the unhappiness of our present state, that when our souls are in some measure elevated and enlarged, our bodies cannot keep pace with them in good duties. The weakness of the flesh is a great grievance to the willingness of the spirit.

2. Christ's power. His pity of their wants sets his power on work for their supply.

(1) How his power was distrusted by his disciples (*v.* 33); *whence should we have so much bread in the wilderness?* They had been not only the witnesses, but the ministers, of the former miracle; the multiplied bread went through their hands; so that it was an instance of great weakness for them to ask, *Whence shall we have bread?* Could they be at a loss, while they had their Master with them? Forgetting former experiences leaves us under present doubts.

Christ knew how slender the provision was, but he would know it from them (*v.* 34); *How many loaves have ye?* Before he would work, he would have it seen how little he had to work on, that his power might shine the brighter. What they had, they had for themselves, and it was little enough, but Christ would have them bestow it all upon the multitude. It becomes Christ's disciples to be generous, their Master was so: what we have, we should be free of. Niggardliness to-day, out of thoughtfulness for tomorrow, is a complication of corrupt affection that ought to be mortified. The disciples asked, *Whence should we have bread?* Christ asked, *How many loaves have ye?* We must not think so much of our wants as of our havings.

(2) How his power was discovered to the multitude.

[1] The provision that was at hand; *seven loaves, and a few little fishes*. It is probable that the fish was such as they had themselves taken. It is comfortable to *eat the labour of our hands* (Ps. cxxviii. 2). And what we have got by God's blessing on our labour we should be free of; for *therefore* we must labour, *that we may have to give*, Eph. iv. 28.

[2] The putting of the people in a posture to receive it (*v.* 35); *He commanded the multitude to sit down on the ground*. They saw but very little provision, yet they must sit down, in faith that they should have a meal's meat out of it.

[3] The distributing of the provision among them. He first *gave thanks*. The word used in the former miracle was *he blessed*. It comes all to one; giving thanks to God is a proper way of craving a blessing from God. He then *broke the loaves and gave to his disciples, and they to the multitude*, Though the disciples had distrusted Christ's power, yet he made use of them now as before; he is not provoked, as he might be, by the weakness and infirmities of his ministers, to lay them aside; but still he gives to them, and they to his people, of the word of life.

[4] The plenty there was among them (*v.* 37). *They did all eat, and were filled*. Those whom Christ feeds, he fills. While we labour for the world, we labour for that which satisfieth not (Isa. lv. 2); but those that duly wait on Christ shall be *abundantly satisfied with the goodness of his house*.

To show that they had all enough, there was a great deal left—*seven baskets full of broken meat;* but enough to show that with Christ *there is bread enough, and to spare*; supplies of grace for more than seek it, and for those that seek more.

[5] The account taken of the guests; not that they might pay their share, but that they might be witnesses to the power and goodness of Christ.

[6] The dismission of the multitude, and Christ's departure to another place (*v.* 39). He *sent away* the people. Though he had fed them twice, they must not expect miracles to be their daily bread. Let them now go home to their callings, and to their own tables.

CHAPTER 16

I. A conference with the Pharisees, ver. 1–4. II. Another with his disciples about the leaven of the Pharisees, ver. 5–12. III. Another with them concerning himself, ver. 13–20. IV. Another concerning his sufferings for them, and theirs for him, ver. 21–28.

Verses 1–4

We have here Christ's discourse with the Pharisees and Sadducees, men at variance among themselves, and yet unanimous in their opposition to Christ. Christ and Christianity meet with opposition on all hands.

I. Their demand, and the design of it.

1. The demand was of a sign from heaven; this they desired him to show them; pretending they were very willing to be satisfied and convinced. That which they pretended to desire was,

(1) Some other sign than what they had yet had. They had great plenty of signs; every miracle Christ

wrought was a sign. But this will not serve; they despised those signs which relieved the necessity of the sick and sorrowful, and insisted upon some sign which would gratify the curiosity of the proud. The evidence that is given is sufficient to satisfy an unprejudiced understanding, but was not intended to please a vain humour. And it is an instance of the deceitfulness of the heart, to think that we should be wrought upon by the means and advantages which we have not, while we slight those which we have.

(2) It must be a sign from heaven. They would have such miracles to prove his commission, as were wrought at the giving of the law upon mount Sinai: thunder, and lightning, and the voice of words were the sign from heaven they required.

2. The design was to tempt him; not to be taught by him, but to ensnare him. If he should show them a sign from heaven, they would attribute it to a confederacy with the *prince of the power of the air.* When they had signs from heaven, they tempted Christ, saying, *Can he furnish a table in the wilderness?* Now that he had furnished a table in the wilderness, they tempted him, saying, *Can he give us a sign from heaven?*

II. Christ's reply to this demand.

1. He condemns their overlooking of the signs they had, *v.* 2, 3. They were seeking for the signs of the kingdom of God, when it was already among them.

To expose this, he observes to them,

(1) Their skilfulness and sagacity in other things, particularly in natural prognostications of the weather. There are common rules drawn from observation and experience, by which it is easy to foretell very probably what weather it will be. We *know not the balancing of the clouds* (Job xxxvii. 16), but we may spell something from the faces of them.

(2) Their sottishness and stupidity in the concerns of their souls; *Can ye not discern the signs of the times?* "Do you not see that the Messiah is come?" The miracles Christ wrought, and the gathering of the people to him, were plain indications that the *kingdom of heaven was at hand*, that this was *the day of their visitation.* It is great hypocrisy, when we slight the signs of God's ordaining, to seek for signs of our own prescribing. "Do not you foresee your own ruin coming for rejecting him?" It is the undoing of multitudes, that they are not aware what will be the end of their refusing Christ.

2. He refuses to give them any other sign (*v.* 4). He calls them *an adulterous generation*; because, while they professed themselves of the true church and spouse of God, they treacherously departed from him, and brake their covenants with him. He refuses to gratify their desire. Christ will not be prescribed to; *we ask, and have not, because we ask amiss.* He refers them to the sign of the prophet Jonas, which should yet be given them; his resurrection from the dead, and his preaching by his apostles to the Gentiles. Though the fancies of proud men shall not be humoured, yet the faith of the humble shall be supported.

This discourse broke off abruptly; *he left them and departed.* Christ will not tarry long with those that tempt him, but justly withdraws from those that are disposed to quarrel with him.

Verses 5–12

We have here Christ's discourse with his disciples concerning bread, in which, as in many other discourses, he speaks to them of spiritual things under a similitude, and they misunderstand him of carnal things. The occasion of it was, their forgetting to victual their ship; usually they carried bread along with them. But now they forgot; we will hope it was because their minds and memories were filled with better things. Christ's disciples are often such as have no great forecast for the world.

I. Here is the caution Christ gave them, to *beware of the leaven of the Pharisees.* Disciples are in most danger from hypocrites; against those that are openly vicious they stand upon their guard, and therefore the caution is doubled, *Take heed, and beware.*

The corrupt principles and practices of the Pharisees and Sadducees are compared to leaven; they fermented wherever they came.

II. Their mistake concerning this caution, *v.* 7. They thought Christ hereby upbraided them with their improvidence and forgetfulness. Or, they took it for a caution, not to be familiar with the Pharisees and Sadducees, not to eat with them, whereas the danger was not in their bread (Christ himself did eat with them, Luke vii. 36; xi. 37; xiv. 1), but in their principles.

III. The reproof Christ gave them for this.

1. He reproves their distrust of his ability and readiness to supply them in this strait (*v.* 8); "*O ye of little faith,* why are ye in such perplexity because ye have *taken no bread,* that ye can mind nothing else?" He does not chide them for their little forecast, as they expected he would. Parents and masters must not be angry at the forgetfulness of their children and servants, more than is necessary to make them take more heed another time; we are all apt to be forgetful of our duty. See how easily Christ forgave his disciples' carelessness; and do likewise. But that which he chides them for is their little faith.

(1) He would have them to depend upon him for supply. Though Christ's disciples be brought into wants and straits, through their own carelessness and incogitancy, yet he encourages them to trust in him for relief. We must not therefore use this as an excuse for our want of charity to those who are really poor, that they should have minded their own affairs better, and then they would not have been in need. It may be so, but they must not therefore be left to starve when they are in need.

(2) He is displeased at their solicitude in this matter. The weakness and shiftlessness of good people in their worldly affairs is that for which men are apt to condemn them; but it is not such an offence to Christ as their inordinate care and anxiety about those things. We must endeavour to keep the mean between the extremes of carelessness and carefulness; but of the two, the excess of thoughtfulness about the world worst becomes Christ's disciples.

(3) The aggravation of their distrust was the experience they had so lately had of the power and goodness of Christ in providing for them, *v.* 9, 10. They had him with them who could provide bread for them. If they had not the cistern, they had the Fountain. *Do ye not yet understand, neither remember?* Christ's disciples are often to be blamed for the shallowness of their understandings, and the slipperiness of their memories. "Remember *how many baskets ye took up.*" These baskets were intended for memorials, by which to keep the mercy in remembrance. He that could furnish them with such an overplus then, surely could furnish them with what was necessary now. We are *therefore* perplexed with present cares and distrusts, because we do not duly remember our former experiences of divine power and goodness.

2. He reproves their misunderstanding of the caution he gave them (*v.* 11); *How is it that you do not understand?* Christ's disciples may well be ashamed of the slowness and dullness of their apprehensions in divine things. *I spake it not unto you concerning bread.* He took it ill, (1) That they should think him as thoughtful about bread as they were; whereas his *meat and drink were to do his Father's will.* (2) That they should be so little acquainted

with his way of preaching, as to take that literally which he spoke by way of parable.

IV. The rectifying of the mistake by this reproof (v. 12); *Then understood they* what he meant. He did not tell them expressly what he meant, but repeated what he had said; and so obliged them to arrive at the sense of it in their own thoughts. Thus Christ teaches by the Spirit of wisdom in the heart, opening the understanding to the Spirit of revelation in the word. And those truths are most precious, which we have thus digged for.

Verses 13–20

We have here a private conference which Christ had with his disciples concerning himself. It was in the coasts of Cæsarea Philippi, there in that remote corner, perhaps, there was less flocking after him than in other places, which gave him leisure for this private conversation with his disciples.

I. He enquires what the opinions of others were concerning him; *Who do men say that I, the Son of man, am?*

1. He calls himself the *Son of man*; which may be taken either, (1) As a title common to him with others. He was called, and justly, *the Son of God*, for so he was (Luke i. 35); but he called himself the Son of man; for he is really and truly "Man, made of a woman." Or, (2) As a title peculiar to him as Mediator.

2. He enquires what people's sentiments were concerning him: "*Who do men say that I am? The Son of man?*" (So I think it might better be read.) "Do they own me for the Messiah?" He asks not, "Who do the *scribes* and *Pharisees* say that I am?" But, "Who do *men* say that I am?" He referred to the common people, whom the Pharisees despised. The common people conversed more familiarly with the disciples than they did with their Master, and therefore from them he might better know what they said. Christ had not plainly said who he was, but left people to infer it from his works, John x. 24, 25. Now he would know what inferences the people drew from *them*.

3. To this question the disciples gave him an answer (v. 14), *Some say, thou art John the Baptist, &c.* They are different opinions; some say one thing, and others another. Truth is one; but those who vary from that commonly vary one from another. Being so noted a Person, everyone would be ready to pass his verdict upon him, and, "Many men, many minds." They are honourable opinions. It is possible for men to have good thoughts of Christ, and yet not right ones, a high opinion of him, and yet not high enough. They all suppose him to be *one risen from the dead*; which perhaps arose from a confused notion they had of the resurrection of the Messiah. They are all false opinions, built upon mistakes.

(1) *Some say, thou art John the Baptist.* Herod said so (*ch.* xiv. 2), and those about him would be apt to say as he said.

(2) *Some Elias;* taking occasion, no doubt, from the prophecy of Malachi (*ch.* iv. 5), *Behold, I will send you Elijah.*

(3) *Others Jeremias.*

(4) Or, *one of the prophets.* This shows what an honourable idea they entertained of the prophets. Rather than they would allow Jesus of Nazareth, one of their own country, to be such an extraordinary Person as his works bespoke him to be, they would say, "It was not he, but *one of the old prophets.*"

II. He enquires what *their* thoughts were concerning him; "*But who say ye that I am?*" v. 15. The disciples had themselves been better taught than others; had, by their intimacy with Christ, greater advantages of getting knowledge than others had. Those who have more acquaintance with Christ

than others, should have truer sentiments concerning him, and be able to give a better account of him than others. The disciples were trained up to teach others, and therefore it was highly requisite that they should understand the truth themselves. This is a question we should every one of us be frequently putting to ourselves, "*Who* do we say, *what* kind of one do we say, that *the Lord Jesus is?*" It is well or ill with us, according as our thoughts are right or wrong concerning Jesus Christ.

Well, this is the question. Peter's answer to this question, v. 16. Peter answers in the name of all the rest, they all consenting to it, and concurring in it. Peter's temper led him to be forward in speaking upon all such occasions, and sometimes he spoke well, sometimes amiss; in all companies there are found some warm, bold men, to whom a precedency of speech falls of course; Peter was such a one.

Peter's answer is short, but it is full, and true, and to the purpose; *Thou art the Christ, the Son of the living God.* This is the conclusion of the whole matter. The people called him *a Prophet, that Prophet* (John vi. 14); but the disciples own him to be the Christ, the anointed One. It was a great thing to believe this concerning one whose outward appearance was so contrary to the general idea the Jews had of the Messiah. He called himself the *Son of Man*; but they owned him to be *the Son of the living God.* They know and believe him to be *the Son of the living God*, and to be the *Life of the world.* Let us then go to Christ; Lord Jesus, *thou art the Christ, the Son of the living God.* Note: Christ's approbation of his answer (v. 17–19).

1. As a believer, v. 17. Christ shows himself well pleased with Peter's confession, that it was so clear and express. Christ shows him whence he received the knowledge of this truth. At the first discovery of this truth in the dawning of the gospel day, it was a mighty thing to believe it.

Peter had the happiness of it; *Blessed art thou, Simon Bar-jona.* He reminds him of his rise and original; he was *Bar-jonas—The son of a dove.* Let him remember *the rock out of which he was hewn*, that he may see he was not born to this dignity, but preferred to it by the divine favour; it was free grace that made him to differ. Having reminded him of this, he makes him sensible of his great happiness as a believer; *Blessed art thou.* True believers are truly blessed, and those are blessed indeed whom Christ pronounces blessed. All happiness attends the right knowledge of Christ.

God must have the glory of it; "*For flesh and blood have not revealed it to thee.*" This light sprang neither from nature nor from education, but from my Father who is in heaven." Saving faith is the gift of God, and, wherever it is, is wrought by him. *Therefore* thou art blessed, because *my Father has revealed it to thee.* Blessed are they that are thus highly favoured.

2. Christ replies to him as an apostle or minister, v. 18, 19. There is nothing lost by being forward to confess Christ; for those who thus honour him, he will honour.

Upon occasion of this great confession made of Christ, which is the church's homage and allegiance, he signed and published this royal, this divine charter, by which that body politic is incorporated.

Now the purport of this charter is,

First, To establish the being of the church; *I say also unto thee.* It is Christ that makes the grant, he who is the church's Head. The grant is put into Peter's hand; "I say it to *thee.*" The New Testament charter is here delivered to Peter as an agent, but to the use and behoof of the church in all ages, according to the purposes therein specified and contained. Now it is here promised, that Christ would build his church upon a rock. This body politic is incorporated by the style and title of *Christ's church*. It is a number of the children of men called out of the world. and set apart from it, and dedicated to Christ. The Builder and Maker of the church is Christ himself; *I will build it. Ye are God's building;* and building is a progressive work; the church in this world is like a house in the building. It is a comfort that Christ, who has divine wisdom and power, undertakes to build it. The foundation on which it is built is, *this Rock.* Let the architect do his part ever so well, if the foundation be rotten, the building will not stand; let us therefore see what the foundation is. The church is built upon a *rock*; a firm, strong, and lasting foundation, which time will not waste, nor will it sink under the weight of the building. Christ would not build his house upon the sand, for he knew that storms would arise. It is built upon *this* rock; thou art *Peter*, which signifies *a stone* or *rock*; Christ gave him that name when he first called him (John i. 42), and here he confirms it. From the mention of this significant name, occasion is taken for this metaphor of *building upon a rock.*

Some by this rock understand Peter himself as an apostle. The church is built upon the foundation of the apostles, Eph. ii. 20. The first stones of that building were laid in and by their ministry. Now Peter being that apostle by whose hand the first stones of the church were laid, both in Jewish converts (Acts ii), and in the Gentile converts (Acts x), he might in some sense be said to be the rock on which it was built.

Others, by this *rock*, understand *Christ*; "Thou art *Peter*, thou hast the name of a *stone*, but *upon this rock*, pointing to himself, *I will build my church.*" He took occasion from Peter, to speak of himself as the Rock.. Christ is both its Founder and its Foundation; he draws souls, and draws them to himself; to him they are united, and on him they rest and have a constant dependence.

Others, by this *rock* understand this confession which Peter made of Christ, and this comes all to one with understanding it of Christ himself. "Now," saith Christ, "this is that great truth *upon which I will build my church.*" Take away this truth itself, and the universal church falls to the ground. If Christ be not the Son of God, Christianity is a cheat. Take away the faith and confession of this truth from any particular church, and it ceases to be a part of Christ's church. This is *articulus stantis et cadentis ecclesiae*—that article, with the admission or the denial of which the church either rises or falls; "the main hinge on which the door of salvation turns"; those who let go this, do not hold the foundation.

Christ here promises to preserve and secure his church, when it is built; *The gates of hell shall not prevail against it.* This implies that the church has enemies that fight against it, and endeavour its ruin and overthrow, here represented by *the gates of hell, that is*, the city of hell; (which is directly opposite to this heavenly city, this *city of the living God*), the devil's interest among the children of men. This assures us that the enemies of the church shall not gain their point. While the world stands, Christ will have a church in it. Somewhere or other the Christian religion shall have a being, though not always in the same degree of purity and splendour, yet so as that the entail of it shall never be quite cut off. The church may be foiled in particular encounters, but in the main battle it shall come off *more than a conqueror.*

The other part of this charter is, to settle the *Second*, Government of the church, *v.* 19. A city without government is a chaos. Now this constituting of the government of the church, is here expressed by the delivering of the keys, and, with them, a power to bind and loose. This invests all the apostles and their successors with a ministerial power to guide and govern the church of Christ, as it exists in particular congregations or churches, according to the rules of the gospel. The keys were first put into Peter's hand, because he was the first *that opened the door of faith to the Gentiles*, Acts. x. 28. Christ, having incorporated his church, hath appointed the office of the ministry for the keeping up of order and government, and to see that his laws be duly served. He doth not say, The keys *shall* be given, but, *I will give* them; for ministers derive their authority from Christ, and all their power is to be used in his name. The power here delegated is a spiritual power; it is a power *pertaining to the kingdom of heaven*, that is, to the church, to the gospel dispensation. It is the *power* of the keys that is given, alluding to the custom of investing men with authority in such a place, by delivering to them the keys of the place. Or as the master of the house gives the keys to the steward, the keys of the stores where the provisions are kept. It is a power to *bind and loose*, that is (following the metaphor of the keys), to shut and open. It is a power which Christ has promised to own the due administration of; *It shall be bound in heaven, and loosed in heaven.* The word of the gospel, in the mouth of faithful ministers, is to be looked upon, not as the word of man, but as the word of God, and to be received accordingly.

Now *the keys of the kingdom of heaven are,*

(1) The key of *doctrine*, called the key of *knowledge*. Now the apostles had an extraordinary power of this kind; some things forbidden by the law of Moses were now to be allowed; some things allowed there were now to be forbidden; and the apostles were empowered to declare this to the world. When Peter was first taught himself, and then taught others, *to call nothing common or unclean*, this power was exercised. There is also an ordinary power hereby conveyed to all ministers, to tell people, in God's name, and according to the scriptures, *what is good, and what the Lord requires of them.* Christ gives his apostles power to shut or open the book of the gospel to people, as the case required. When ministers preach pardon and peace to the penitent, wrath and the curse to the impenitent, in Christ's name, they act then pursuant to this authority of binding and loosing.

(2) The key of *discipline*, which is but the application of the former to particular persons, upon a right estimate of their characters and actions. The judge doth not make the law, but only declares what is law, and gives sentence accordingly. Christ's ministers have a power to admit into the church; "*Go, disciple all nations, baptising them;* those who profess faith in Christ, and obedience to him, admit them by baptism." Ministers are to let in to *the wedding-feast those that are bidden*; and to keep out such as are apparently unfit for so holy a communion. They have a power to expel and cast out such as have forfeited their church-membership. They have a power to restore and to receive in again, upon their repentance, such as had been thrown out; to loose those whom they had bound. The apostles had a miraculous gift of *discerning spirits*; yet even *they* went by the rule of outward appearances, which ministers may still make a judgment upon, if they be skilful and faithful.

Here is the charge which Christ gave his disciples, to keep this private for the present (*v.* 20); *They must tell no man that he was Jesus the Christ.* What they had professed to him, they must not yet publish to the world, for several reasons: Because this was the time of preparation for his kingdom: the great thing now preached, was, that *the kingdom of heaven was at hand.* Everything is beautiful in its season, and it is good advice, *Prepare thy work, and afterwards build*, Prov. xxiv. 27. Christ would have his Messiah-ship proved by his works. He was so secure of the demonstration of his miracles that he waived other witnesses. Christ would not have the apostles preach this, till they had the most convincing evidence ready to allege in confirmation of it. Great truths may suffer damage by being asserted before they can be sufficiently proved. Now the great proof of Jesus being the Christ was his resurrection. It was requisite that the preachers of so great a truth should be furnished with greater measures of the Spirit than the apostles as yet had. When Christ was glorified and the Spirit poured out, we find Peter proclaiming upon the house-tops what was here spoken in a corner. As there is a time to keep silence, so there is a time to speak.

Verses 21–23

I. Christ's foretelling of his sufferings. Some hints he had already given of his sufferings, but now he *began* to show it, to speak plainly and expressly of it. Hitherto he had not touched upon this, because the disciples were weak, but now that they were more ripe in knowledge, and strong in faith, he began to tell them this. Christ reveals his mind to his people gradually, and lets in light as they can bear it, and are fit to receive it.

From that time, when they had made that full confession of Christ, when he found them knowing in one truth, he taught them another. If they had not been well grounded in the belief of Christ's being the Son of God, it would have been a great shaking to their faith. All truths are not to be spoken to all persons at all times, but such as are proper and suitable to their present state. Now observe,

1. What he foretold concerning his sufferings, the particulars and circumstances of them, and all surprising. The place where he should suffer. He must go to Jerusalem, the head city, the holy city, and suffer there. There all the sacrifices were offered, there therefore *he* must die, *who is the great sacrifice.* The persons by whom he should suffer; *the elders, and chief priests, and scribes.* Those that should have been most forward in owning and admiring Christ, were the most bitter in persecuting him. What he should suffer; *he must suffer many things, and be killed.* His enemies' insatiable malice, and his own invincible patience, appear in the variety and multiplicity of his sufferings (he suffered many things) and in the extremity of them; nothing less than his death would satisfy them, he must be killed. What should be the happy issue of all his sufferings; he shall *be raised again the third day.* His rising again the third day proved him to be the Son of God, notwithstanding his sufferings; and therefore he mentions that, to keep up their faith. Thus we must look upon Christ's suffering for us, trace in it the way to his glory; and thus we must look upon our suffering for Christ, look through it to the recompence of reward. *If we suffer with him, we shall reign with him.*

2. Why he foretold his sufferings. His sufferings were no surprise to him, did not come upon him as a snare, but he had a distinct and certain foresight of them, which greatly magnifies his love. To rectify the mistakes which his disciples had imbibed concerning the external pomp and power of his kingdom, here Christ reads them another lesson, tells them of the cross and sufferings. Those that follow Christ must be dealt plainly with, and warned not to expect great things in this world. It was to prepare them for the share, at least, of sorrow and fear, which they must have in his sufferings. When he suffered many things, the disciples could not but suffer some; let them know it before, and, being fore-*warned*, may be fore-*armed*.

II. The offence which Peter took at this: he said, *Be it far from thee, Lord. He took him, and began to rebuke him.*

1. It did not become Peter to contradict his Master, or take upon him to advise him. When God's dispensations are either intricate or cross to us, it becomes us silently to acquiesce in, and not to prescribe to, the divine will; God knows what he has to do, without our teaching.

2. It savoured much of fleshly wisdom. It is the corrupt part of us, that is thus solicitous to sleep in a whole skin. We are apt to look upon sufferings as they relate to this present life, to which they are uneasy; but there are other rules to measure them by. He would have Christ to dread suffering as much as he did; but we mistake, if we measure Christ's love and patience by our own.

III. Christ's displeasure against Peter for this suggestion of his, *v.* 23. We do not read of anything said or done by any of his disciples, at any time, that he resented so much as this. How he expressed his displeasure: *Get thee behind me, Satan.* Just now, he had said, *Blessed art thou, Simon;* but here, *Get thee behind me, Satan;* and there was cause for both. A good man may by a surprise of temptation soon grow very unlike himself. It is the subtlety of Satan, to send temptations to us by the unsuspected hands of our best and dearest friends. Even the kindnesses of our friends are often abused by Satan, and made use of as temptations to us. We should learn to know the devil's voice when he speaks in a saint as well as when he speaks in a serpent. We must be free and faithful in reproving the dearest friend we have. We must not compliment, but rebuke, mistaken courtesies. Why did Christ thus resent a motion that seemed not only harmless, but kind? Two reasons are given:

1. *Thou art my hindrance* (so it may be read); "thou standest in my way." Christ was hastening on in the work of our salvation, and his heart was so much upon it, that he took it ill to be hindered. Peter was not so sharply reproved for disowning and denying his Master in his sufferings as he was for dissuading him from them. Our Lord Jesus preferred our salvation before his own ease and safety; he came into the world, not to spare himself, as Peter advised, but to spend himself. *Thou art an offence to me.* Those that engage in any great and good work must expect to meet with hindrance and opposition from friends and foes, from within and from without. Those that hinder us from doing or suffering for God, when we are called to it, whatever they are in other things, in that they are *Satans, adversaries* to us.

2. *Thou savourest not the things that are of God, but those that are of men.* The things that are of God often clash and interfere with *the things that are of men*, that is, with our own wealth, pleasure, and reputation.

Verses 24–28

Christ, having shown his disciples that *he* must suffer, here shows them that *they* must suffer too.

I. Here is the law of discipleship laid down, and the terms fixed, upon which we may have the honour and benefit of it, *v.* 24.

1. What it is to be a disciple of Christ; it is to come after him. A true disciple of Christ is one that doth follow him in duty, and shall follow him to glory. He is one that comes after Christ, not one that prescribes to him, as Peter now undertook to do. A disciple of Christ comes after him, as the sheep after the shepherd, one that walks in the same way that he walked in, treads in his steps, and *follows the Lamb, whithersoever he goes.*

2. What are the great things required of those that will be Christ's disciples; *If any man will come.*

It denotes a deliberate choice, and cheerfulness and resolution in that choice. Christ will have his people volunteers.

Let him deny himself. Peter had advised Christ to spare himself, but Christ tells them all, they must be so far from *sparing* themselves, that they must *deny* themselves. If self-denial be a hard lesson, and against the grain to flesh and blood it is no more than what our Master learned and practised before us and for us. All the disciples and followers of Jesus Christ must deny themselves. It is the fundamental law of admission into Christ's school; it is both the *strait* gate, and the *narrow* way. We must deny ourselves absolutely, we must not admire our own shadow, nor gratify our own humour; nor seek our own things, nor be our own end. We must deny ourselves comparatively; we must deny ourselves for Christ; we must deny ourselves for our brethren, and for their good; and we must deny ourselves for ourselves, deny the appetites of the body for the benefit of the soul.

Let him take up his cross. The cross is here put for all sufferings, as men or Christians; providential afflictions, persecutions for righteousness' sake, every trouble that befalls us, either for doing well or for not doing ill. It should reconcile us to troubles, and take off the terror of them, that they are what we bear in common with Christ, and such as he hath borne before us. Every disciple of Christ hath his cross, and must count upon it, and everyone feels most from his own burthen. Crosses are the common lot of God's children, but of this common lot each hath his particular share. It is good for us to call the cross we are under *our own*, and entertain it accordingly. We are apt to think we could bear such a one's cross better than our own; but that is best which is, and we ought to make the best of it. Every disciple of Christ must take up that which the wise God hath made his cross. We must not make crosses to ourselves, but must accommodate ourselves to those which God has made for us. Our rule is, not to go a step out of the way of duty, either to meet a cross, or to miss one. We must not by our rashness and indiscretion pull crosses down upon our own heads, but must take them up when they are laid in our way. We must take it up out of our way, and we must then go on with it in our way, though it lie heavy. That which we have to do, is, not only to bear the cross, but we must *take up* the cross, must improve it to some good advantage. We should not say, "This is an evil, and I must bear it, because I cannot help it"; but, "This is an evil, and I will bear it, because it shall work for my good." When we *rejoice in our afflictions, and glory in them,* then we take up the cross.

Let him follow me, in this particular of taking up the cross. Do we bear the cross? We therein follow Christ, who bears it *before* us, bears it *for* us, and so bears it *from* us. He bore the heavy end of the cross, the end that had the curse upon it, that was a heavy end, and so made the other light and easy for us. Or, we may take it in general, we must follow Christ in all instances of holiness and obedience. To do well and to suffer ill, is to follow Christ. Those that come after Christ, must follow after him.

II. Self-denial, and patient suffering, are hard lessons, which will never be learned if we consult with flesh and blood; let us therefore consult with our Lord Jesus, about some considerations proper to these duties of self-denial and suffering for Christ. 1. The weight of that eternity which depends upon our present choice (*v. 25*); *Whosoever will save his life,* by denying Christ, *shall lose it;* and whosoever is content to *lose his life,* for owning Christ, *shall find it.* Here are *life and death, good and evil, the blessing and the curse,* set before us. Observe, The

misery that attends the most plausible apostasy. *Whosoever will save his life* in this world, if it be by sin, he *shall lose it* in another; he that forsakes Christ, to preserve a temporal life and avoid a temporal death, will certainly come short of eternal life, and will be hurt of the second death, and eternally held by it. The life saved is but for a moment, the death shunned is but as a sleep; but the life lost is everlasting, and the death run upon is an endless separation from all good. 2. The advantage that attends the most perilous and expensive constancy; *Whosoever will lose his life for Christ's sake* in this world, *shall find it* in a better. Many a life is lost, for Christ's sake. Christ's holy religion is handed down to us, sealed with the blood of thousands. Though many have been losers for Christ, even of life itself, yet never anyone was, or will be, a loser by him in the end. An assurance of the life they should find, in lieu of the life they hazarded, hath enabled them to triumph over death in all its terrors; to go smiling to a scaffold, and stand singing at a stake. 3. The worth of the soul which lies at stake, and the worthlessness of the world in comparison of it (*v. 26*). *What is a man profited, if he gain the whole world and lose his own soul?* This alludes to that common principle, that, whatever a man gets, if he lose his life, it will do him no good, he cannot enjoy his gains. But it looks higher, and speaks of the soul as immortal, and a loss of it beyond death, which cannot be compensated by the gain of the whole world. Our souls are our own not in respect of dominion and property, but in respect of nearness and concern; our souls are our own, for they are ourselves. It is possible for the soul to be lost, and there is danger of it. The soul is lost when it is eternally separated from all the good, to all the evil that a soul is capable of; when it is separated from the favour of God. If the soul be lost, it is of the sinner's own losing. The *man loses his own soul,* for he does that which is certainly destroying to it, and neglects that which alone would be saving. One soul is worth more than all the world; our own souls are of greater value to us than all the wealth, honour, and pleasures of this present time, if we had them. The winning of the world is often the losing of the soul. Many a one has ruined his eternal interests by his preposterous and inordinate care to secure and advance his temporal ones. The loss of the soul is so great a loss, that the gain of the whole world will not countervail it, or make it up. He that loses his soul, though it be to gain the world, makes a very bad bargain for himself. When he comes to balance the account, and to compare profit and loss, he will find that he is ruined to all intents and purposes, is irreparably broken.

What shall a man give in exchange for his soul? If once the soul be lost, it is lost for ever. It is a loss that can never be repaired, never be retrieved. Therefore it is good to be wise in time, and do well for ourselves. Here are some considerations proper to encourage us in self-denial and suffering for Christ.

(1) The assurance we have of Christ's glory, at his second coming to judge the world, *v. 27.* If we see things as they *will* appear then, we shall see them as they *should* appear now.

The great encouragement to steadfastness in religion is taken from the second coming of Christ, considering it,

[1] As his honour; *The Son of man shall come in the glory of his Father, with his angels.* To look upon Christ in his state of humiliation would discourage his followers from taking any pains, or running any hazards for him; but with an eye of faith to see the Captain of our salvation coming in his glory, will animate us, and make us think nothing too much to do, or too hard to suffer, for him. [2] As our concern;

Then he shall reward every man according to his works. Jesus Christ will come as a Judge, to dispense rewards and punishments. Men will then be rewarded, not according to their gains in this world, but according to their works, according to what they were and did, and the constancy of faithful souls recompensed with a crown of life. The best preparative for that day is to *deny ourselves, and to take up our cross, and follow Christ*; for so we shall make the Judge our Friend. The rewarding of men according to their works is deferred till that day. Here good and evil seem to be dispensed promiscuously; but in that day all will be set to rights.

(2) The near approach of his kingdom in this world, *v.* 28. It was so near, that there were some attending him who should live to see it. At the end of time, he shall come in his Father's glory; but now, in the fulness of time, he was to come in his own kingdom, his mediatorial kingdom. Some little specimen was given of his glory a few days after this, in his transfiguration (*ch.* xvii. 1). The apostles were employed in setting up Christ's kingdom; let them know, for their comfort, that whatever opposition they meet with, yet they shall carry their point. It is a great encouragement to suffering saints to be assured, not only of the safety, but of the advancement of Christ's kingdom among men; not only *notwithstanding* their sufferings, but *by* their sufferings. This shall be done shortly, in the present age. The nearer the church's deliverances are, the more cheerful should we be in our sufferings for Christ. It is spoken as a favour to those that should survive the present cloudy time, that they should see better days.

CHAPTER 17

I. Christ in his pomp and glory transfigured, ver. 1–13. II. Christ in his power and grace, casting the devil out of a child, ver. 14–21. And, III. Christ in his poverty and great humiliation, 1. Foretelling his own sufferings, ver. 22, 23. 2. Paying tribute, ver. 24–27. Thus were the several indications of Christ's gracious intentions admirably interwoven.

Verses 1–13

We have here the story of Christ's transfiguration; he had said that the *Son of man should* shortly *come in his kingdom*, with which promise all the three evangelists industriously connect this story.

When Christ was here in his humiliation, though his state, in the main, was a state of abasement and afflictions, there were some glimpses of his glory intermixed. But the series of his public ministry being a continued humiliation, here, just in the midst of that, comes in this discovery of his glory.

Now concerning Christ's transfiguration, observe,

I. The circumstances of it, which are here noted, *v.* 1.

1. The time; *six days* after he had the solemn conference with his disciples, *ch.* xvi. 21. Nothing is recorded to be said or done by our Lord Jesus for six days before his transfiguration. *Then* when Christ seems to be doing nothing for his church, expect, ere long, something more than ordinary.

2. The place; it was *on the top of a high mountain apart*. Christ chose a mountain, (1) As a secret place. He went apart; Christ chose a retired place to be transfigured in, because his appearing publicly in his glory was not agreeable to his present state; and thus he would teach us that privacy much befriends our communion with God. (2). Those that would maintain intercourse with Heaven, must frequently withdraw, and they will find themselves never less alone than when alone, for the Father is with them. Those that would have a transforming fellowship with God, must not only retire, but ascend; lift up their hearts, and *seek things above*.

3. The witnesses of it. He took with him Peter and James and John. He took three, a competent

number to testify what they should see. Christ makes his appearances certain enough, but not too common that they might be blessed, who have not seen, and yet have believed. He took these three because they were the chief of his disciples. They were afterward to be the witnesses of his agony, and this was to prepare them for that. A sight of Christ's glory, while we are here in this world, is a good preparative for our sufferings with him, as these are preparatives for the sight of his glory in the other world.

II. The manner of it (*v.* 2); *He was transfigured before them*. The substance of his body remained the same; he was not turned into a spirit, but his body, which had appeared in weakness and dishonour, now appeared in power and glory. Now, in his transfiguration, he gave his disciples a glimpse of his glory, which could not but change his form.

Now his transfiguration appeared in two things:

1. *His face did shine as the sun.* The face is the principal part of the body, by which we are known; therefore such a brightness was put on Christ's face. It shone as the sun when he goes forth in his strength, so clear, so bright; the more sensibly glorious, because it suddenly broke out, as it were, from behind a black cloud.

2. *His raiment was white as the light.* The shining of the face of Moses was so weak, that it could easily be concealed by a thin veil; but such was the glory of Christ's body, that his clothes were enlightened by it.

III. The companions of it. There now *appeared unto them Moses and Elias talking with him, v.* 3. There were glorified saints attending him, that, when there were *three to bear record on earth*, Peter, James, and John, these might be some to bear record from heaven too. We see here, that they who are fallen asleep in Christ are not perished. These two were Moses and Elias. The Jews had great respect for the memory of Moses and Elias, and therefore they came to witness of him. In them the law and the prophets honoured Christ, and bore testimony to him. Moses and Elias appeared to the disciples; they saw them, and heard them talk, and they knew them to be Moses and Elias; glorified saints shall know one another in heaven. They talked with Christ. Christ has communion with the blessed.

IV. The great pleasure and satisfaction that the disciples took in the sight of Christ's glory. Peter, as usual, spoke for the rest; *Lord, it is good for us to be here.* Peter here expresses,

1. The delight they had in this converse; *Lord, it is good to be here.* He speaks the sense of his fellow-disciples; It is good not only for *me*, but for *us*. He did not covet to monopolise this favour, but gladly takes them in. He saith this to Christ. The soul that loves Christ, and loves to be with him, loves to go and tell him so; *Lord, it is good for us to be here.* All the disciples of the Lord Jesus reckon it is good for them to be with him in the holy mount. It is good to be here where Christ is; it is good to be here, retired and alone with Christ; to be here, where we may behold the beauty of the Lord Jesus.

2. The desire they had of the continuance of it; *Let us make here three tabernacles.* There was in this, as in many other of Peter's sayings, more zeal than discretion.

(1) Here was a zeal for this converse with heavenly things. Those that by faith *behold the beauty of the Lord* in his house, cannot but desire to *dwell there all the days of their life.* It is good to be in holy ordinances as a man at home, not as a wayfaring man.

(2) Yet in this zeal he betrayed a great deal of weakness and ignorance. What need had Moses and Elias of tabernacles? Christ had lately foretold his sufferings; Peter forgets this, or, to prevent it, will needs be building tabernacles in the mount of

glory, out of the way of trouble. There is a proneness in good men to expect the crown without the cross. We are out in our aim, if we look for a heaven here upon earth. It is not for strangers and pilgrims to talk of building, or to expect a continuing city.

Yet it is some excuse for the incongruity of Peter's proposal, not only that *he knew not what he said* (Luke ix. 33), but also that he submitted the proposal to the wisdom of Christ; *If thou wilt, let us make tabernacles.*

Now to this which Peter said, there was no reply made; the disappearing of the glory would soon answer it.

V. The glorious testimony which God the Father gave to our Lord Jesus.

Now concerning this testimony from heaven to Christ, observe.

1. How it came, and in what manner it was introduced. There was a cloud. We find often in the Old Testament, that a cloud was the visible token of God's presence. He took possession of the tabernacle in a cloud, and afterwards of the temple; where Christ was in his glory, the temple was, and there God showed himself present. It was a bright cloud. Under the law it was commonly a thick and dark cloud that God made the token of his presence. But *we are now come* to the mount that is crowned with a bright cloud. That was a dispensation of darkness, and terror, and bondage, this of light, love, and liberty. It overshadowed them. God, in manifesting himself to his people, considers their frame. This cloud was to their eyes as parables to their understandings, to convey spiritual things by things sensible, as they were able to bear them. *There came a voice out of the cloud,* and it was the voice of God. Here was no thunder, or lightning, or voice of a trumpet, as there was when the law was given by Moses, but only a voice, a still small voice.

2. What this testimony from heaven was; *This is my beloved Son, hear ye him.*

(1) The great gospel mystery revealed; *This is my beloved Son, in whom I am well pleased.* This was the very same that was spoken from heaven at his baptism (*ch.* iii. 17). Moses and Elias were great men, and favourites of Heaven, yet they were but servants; but Christ is *a Son,* and in him God was always well pleased. Moses was a great intercessor, and Elias a great reformer; but in Christ God is reconciling the world; his intercession is more prevalent than that of Moses, and his reformation more effectual than that of Elias.

This repetition of the same voice that came from heaven at his baptism was to show the thing was established. What God hath thus spoken once, yea twice, no doubt he will stand to. Now it was repeated, because he was entering upon his sufferings, to arm him against the terror, and his disciples against the offence, of the cross. When sufferings begin to abound, consolations are given more abundantly.

(2) The great gospel duty required, *Hear ye him.* God is well pleased with none in Christ but those that hear him. It is not enough to give him the hearing (what will that avail us?) but we must hear him, and heed him. Whoever would know the mind of God, must hearken to Jesus Christ; for by him God has in these last days spoken to us. God does here, as it were, turn us over to Christ for all the revelations of his mind.

Christ now appeared in glory; and the more we see of Christ's glory, the more cause we shall see to hearken to him.

Moses and Elias were now with him; the law and the prophets; hitherto it was said, *Hear them,* Luke xvi. 29. No, saith God, *hear him,* and that is enough; him, and not Moses and Elias, hear Christ, and you will not want them.

VI. The fright which the disciples were put into by this voice, and the encouragement Christ gave them.

1. The disciples *fell on their faces, and were sore afraid.* The greatness of the light, and the surprise of it, might have a natural influence upon them, to dispirit them. But that was not all, extraordinary appearances of God have ever been terrible to man, who has been afraid to hear anything immediately from God. It is well for us that God speaks to us by men like ourselves, whose terror shall not make us afraid.

2. Christ graciously raised them up with abundance of tenderness. Observe here, (1) What he did; *he came, and touched them.* His approaches banished their fears. Christ's touches were often healing, and here they were strengthening and comforting. (2) What he said; *Arise, and be not afraid.* It is Christ by his word, and the power of his grace going along with it, that raises up good men from their dejections, and silences their fears; and none but Christ can do it; *Arise, be not afraid.* Causeless fears would soon vanish, if we would not yield to them. Considering what they had seen and heard, they had more reason to rejoice than to fear. Through the infirmity of the flesh, we often frighten ourselves with that wherewith we should encourage ourselves. After they had an express command from heaven to hear Christ, the first word they had from him was, *Be not afraid.*

VII. The disappearing of the vision (*v.* 8); *They lift up themselves,* and then *lift up their eyes,* and *saw no man, save Jesus only.* It is not wisdom to raise our expectations high in this world, for the most valuable of our glories and joys here are vanishing, even those of near communion with God are so, not a continual feast, but a running banquet. Two heavens are too much for those to expect that never deserve one. Now *they saw no man, save Jesus only.* Christ will tarry with us when Moses and Elias are gone.

VIII. The discourse between Christ and his disciples as they came down from the mountain, *v.* 9-13. *They came down from the mountain.* We must come down from the holy mountains, where we have communion with God; even there we have no continuing city. When the disciples came down, Jesus came with them. When we return to the world again after an ordinance, it must be our care to take Christ with us. As they came down, they talked of Christ. Note, When we are returning from holy ordinances, it is good to entertain ourselves and one another with discourse suitable to the work we have been about.

Here is, (1) The charge that Christ gave the disciples to keep the vision very private for the present (*v.* 9); *Tell it to no man till the Son of man is risen.* If they had proclaimed it, the credibility of it would have been shocked by his sufferings, which were now hastening on. But let the publication of it be adjourned till after his resurrection, and then that and his subsequent glory will be a great confirmation of it. Everything is beautiful in its season. Christ's time is the best and fittest for the manifesting of himself and must be attended to by us.

(2) An objection which the disciples made against something Christ had said (*v.* 10); *"Why then say the scribes that Elias must first come?"* When the disciples could not reconcile what Christ said with what they had heard out of the Old Testament, they desired him to explain it to them. When we are puzzled with scripture difficulties, we must apply ourselves to Christ by prayer for his Spirit to open our understandings and to lead us into all truth.

(3) The solving of this objection. *Ask, and it shall be given;* ask instruction, and it shall be given. Christ allows the prediction (*v.* 11); *"Elias truly shall first*

come, and restore all things; so far you are in the right." Christ did not come to alter or invalidate anything foretold in the Old Testament. John Baptist came to restore things spiritually, to revive the decays of religion, which means the same with this, *he shall restore all things.* John preached repentance, and that restores the accomplishment. He asserts the accomplishment. The scribes say true, that *Elias shall come; but I say unto you,* what the scribes could not say, that *Elias is come, v.* 12. God's promises are often fulfilled, and men perceive it not, but enquire, *Where is the promise?* when it is already performed. The scribes busied themselves in criticising upon the scripture, but understood not by the signs of the times the fulfilling of the scripture. It is easier to explain the word of God than to apply it and make a right use of it.

Because they knew him not, *they have done to him whatsoever they listed;* if they had known, they would not have crucified Christ, or beheaded John. He adds, *Likewise also shall the Son of man suffer of them.* When they had imbrued their hands in the blood of John Baptist, they were ready to do the like to Christ. As men deal with Christ's servants, so they would deal with him himself.

(4) The disciples' satisfaction in Christ's reply to their objection (*v.* 13); *They understood that he spake unto them of John the Baptist.* He did not name John, but gives them such a description of him as would put them in mind of what he had said to them formerly concerning him; *This is Elias.* When we diligently use the means of knowledge, how strangely are mists scattered and mistakes rectified!

Verses 14–21

I. A melancholy representation of the case of this child, made to Christ by the afflicted father. This was immediately upon his coming down from the mountain where he was transfigured. Christ's glories do not make him unmindful of us and of our wants and miseries. This poor man's address was very importunate; he came kneeling to Christ. Sense of misery will bring people to their knees. He delights to be thus wrestled with.

Two things the father of the child complains of.

1. The distress of his child (*v.* 15); *Lord, have mercy on my son.* Parents are doubly concerned to pray for their children, not only that are weak and cannot, but much more that are wicked and will not, pray for themselves. (1) The nature of this child's disease was very sad; *He was lunatic and sore vexed.* A lunatic is properly one whose distemper lies in the brain. The child had the falling-sickness, and the hand of Satan was in it. Those whom Satan got possession of, he afflicted by those diseases of the body which do most affect the mind; for it is the soul that he aims to do mischief to. The father, in his complaint, saith, *He is lunatic,* taking notice of the effect; but Christ, in the cure, rebuked the devil, and so struck at the cause. Thus he doth in spiritual cures. (2) The effects of the disease were very deplorable; *He oft falls into the fire, and into the water.*

2. The disappointment of his expectation from the disciples (*v.* 16); *I brought him to thy disciples, and they could not cure him.* Christ gave his disciples power to cast out devils (*ch.* x. 1, 8), and therein they were successful (Luke x. 17); yet at this time they failed in the operation, though there were nine of them together. It is for the honour of Christ to come in with help at a dead-lift, when other helpers cannot help. Sometimes he keeps the cistern empty, that he may bring us to himself, the Fountain. But the failures of instruments shall not hinder the operations of his grace, which will work, if not *by* them, yet *without* them.

II. The rebukes that Christ gave.

1. He chid those about him (*v.* 17); *O faithless and perverse generation!* This is not spoken to the disciples, but to the people, and perhaps especially to the scribes. Christ himself could not do many mighty works among a people in whom unbelief reigned. It was here owing to the faithlessness of this generation, that they could not obtain those blessings from God, which otherwise they might have had; as it was owing to the weakness of the disciples' faith, that they could not do those works for God, which otherwise they might have done.

Two things he upbraids them with. (1) His presence with them so long; *"How long shall I be with you?* Will you always need my bodily presence, and never come to such maturity as to be fit to be left? Must the child be always carried, and will it never learn to go alone?" (2) His patience with them so long; *How long shall I suffer you?* The faithlessness and perverseness of those who enjoy the means of grace are a great grief to the Lord Jesus. He is God, and not man, else he would not suffer so long, nor bear so much, as he doth.

2. He cured the child, and set him to rights again. He called, *Bring him hither to me.* Though the people were perverse, and Christ was provoked, yet care was taken of the child. Though Christ may be angry, he is never unkind. *Bring him to me.* When all other helps and succours fail, we are welcome to Christ.

See here an emblem of Christ's undertaking as our Redeemer.

(1) He breaks the power of Satan (*v.* 18); *Jesus rebuked the devil,* as one having authority. Christ's victories over Satan are obtained by the power of his word. Satan cannot stand before the rebukes of Christ, though his possession has been ever so long.

(2) He redresses the grievances of the children of men; *The child was cured from that very hour.* It was an immediate cure, and a perfect one. This is an encouragement to parents to bring their children to Christ. Not only bring them to Christ by prayer, but bring them to the word of Christ. Christ's rebukes, brought home to the heart, will ruin Satan's power there.

III. Christ's discourse with his disciples hereupon.

1. They ask the reason why they could not cast out the devil at this time (*v.* 19); *They came to Jesus apart.* Ministers, who are to deal for Christ in public, have need to keep up a private communion with him. We should make use of the liberty of access we have to Jesus apart, where we may be free and particular with him. That which is amiss may, when found out, be amended.

2. Christ gives them two reasons why they failed.

(1) It was *because of their unbelief, v.* 20. When he spake to the father of the child and to the people, he charged it upon their unbelief; when he spake to his disciples, he charged it upon theirs; for the truth was, there were faults on both sides. When the preaching of the word seems not to be so successful as sometimes it has been, the people are apt to lay all the fault upon the ministers, and the ministers upon the people; whereas, it is more becoming for each to own his own faultiness, and to say, "It is owing to me." Though they had faith, yet that faith was weak and ineffectual. As far as faith falls short of its due strength, vigour, and activity, it may truly be said, "There is unbelief." Many are chargeable with unbelief, who yet are not to be called *unbelievers.* It is because of our unbelief, that we bring so little to pass in religion, and come short, in that which is good.

Our Lord Jesus takes this occasion to show them the power of faith, *If ye have faith as a grain of mustard-seed,* ye shall do wonders, *v.* 20. Some make the comparison to refer to the quality of the mustard-seed, which is, when bruised, sharp and penetrating;

"If you have an active growing faith, not dead, flat, or insipid, you will not be baffled thus." But it rather refers to the quantity; "If you had but a grain of true faith, though so little that it were like that which is the least of all seeds, you would do wonders." The faith here required, is that which had for its object that particular revelation by which Christ gave his disciples power to work miracles in his name. It was a faith in this revelation that they were defective in. Perhaps their Master's absence with the three chief of his disciples might occasion some doubts concerning their power to do this. It is good for us to be diffident of ourselves and of our own strength; but it is displeasing to Christ, when we distrust any power derived from him or granted by him.

If ye have ever so little of this faith in sincerity *ye shall say to this mountain, Remove.* This is a proverbial expression, denoting that which follows, and no more, *Nothing shall be impossible to you.* They distrusted the power they had received, and so failed. To convince them of this, Christ shows them what they might have done. An active faith can remove mountains, not of itself, but in the virtue of a divine power engaged by a divine promise.

(2) Because there was something in the kind of the malady, which rendered the cure more than ordinarily difficult (*v.* 21); *"This kind goes not out but by prayer and fasting."* The extraordinary power of Satan must not discourage our faith, but quicken us to a greater intenseness in the acting of it, and more earnestness in praying to God for the increase of it. Fasting and prayer are proper means for the fetching in of divine power to our assistance. Fasting is of use to put an edge upon prayer; it is an evidence and instance of humiliation which is necessary in prayer. Fasting must be joined with prayer, to keep under the body.

Verses 22–23

Christ here foretells his own sufferings; he began to do it before (*ch.* xvi. 21); and, finding that it was to his disciples a hard saying, he saw it necessary to repeat it.

1. What he foretold concerning himself—that he should be betrayed and killed.

(1) He tells them that he should *be betrayed into the hands of men.* Men to whom he was allied by nature, and from whom therefore he might expect pity and tenderness; these are his persecutors and murderers.

(2) That *they should kill him*; nothing less than that would satisfy their rage; it was his blood, his precious blood, that they thirsted after. If he be a Sacrifice of atonement, he must be killed; without blood no remission.

(3) That *he shall be raised again the third day.* Still, when he spoke of his death, he gave a hint of his resurrection. This was an encouragement, not only to him, but to his disciples; for if he rise the third day, his absence from them will not be long, and his return to them will be glorious.

2. How the disciples received this; *They were exceedingly sorry.* Herein appeared their love to their Master's person, but with all their ignorance and mistake concerning his undertaking.

Verses 24–27

We have here an account of Christ's paying tribute.

I. Observe how it was demanded, *v.* 24. Christ was now at Capernaum.

1. The tribute demanded was not any civil payment to the Roman powers, but the church-duties, which were required from every person for the service of the temple, and the defraying of the expenses of the worship there.

2. The demand was very modest. Their question is, *Doth not your master pay tribute?* Some think that they sought an occasion against him. It should rather seem, they asked this with respect, intimating, that if he had any privilege to exempt him from this payment, they would not insist upon it.

Peter passed his word for his Master; *"Yes,* certainly; my *Master pays tribute." He was made under the law,* therefore under this law he was paid for at forty days old (Luke ii. 22), and now he paid for himself. Now this tax paid to the temple is called *an atonement for the soul,* Exod. xxx. 15. Christ, that in everything he might *appear in the likeness of sinners,* paid it though he had no sin to atone for. He did this to set us an example: Of *rendering to all their due tribute to whom tribute is due.* Of contributing to the support of the public worship of God in the places where we are. If we reap spiritual things, it is fit that we should return carnal things. If Christ pay tribute, who can pretend an exemption?

II. How it was disputed (*v.* 25), not with the collectors themselves, but with Peter, that he might be satisfied in the reason why Christ paid tribute. He brought the collectors into the house; but Christ anticipated him. The disciples of Christ are never attacked without his knowledge. He appeals to the way of the kings of the earth, which is, to take tribute of strangers. He applies this to himself; *Then are the children free.* Christ is the Son of God, and Heir of all things; and therefore not obliged to pay this tax for the service of the temple. Thus Christ asserts his right. God's children are freed by grace and adoption from the slavery of sin and Satan, but not from their subjection to civil magistrates in civil things; here the law of Christ is express. *Render to Caesar the things that are Caesar's.*

III. How it was paid, notwithstanding, *v.* 27.

1. For what reason Christ waived his privilege, and paid this tribute—*Lest we should offend them.* Christ considers that if he should refuse this payment, it would increase people's prejudice against him and his doctrine, and alienate their affections from him, and therefore he resolves to pay it. Christian prudence and humility teach us, in many cases, to recede from our right, rather than give offence by insisting upon it. We must never decline our duty for fear of giving offence, but we must sometimes deny ourselves in that which is our secular interest, rather than give offence.

2. What course he took for the payment of this tax (*v.* 27).

(1) The poverty of Christ; though he cured so many that were diseased; it seems, he did all gratis.

(2) The power of Christ, in fetching money out of a fish's mouth for this purpose. It was an evidence of his divinity, and that he is Lord of hosts. Those creatures that are most remote from man are at the command of Christ, even the fishes of the sea are under his feet (Ps. viii. 5). Now observe,

[1] Peter must catch the fish by angling. Peter has something to do, and it is in the way of his own calling too; to teach us diligence in the employment we are called *to,* and called *in.* Do we expect that Christ should give to us? Let us be ready to work for him.

[2] The fish came up, with money in the mouth of it. What work we do at Christ's command brings its own pay along with it.

[3] The piece of money was just enough to pay the tax for Christ and Peter. He would teach us not to covet superfluities, but, having enough for our present occasions, therewith to be content, and not to distrust God, though we live but from hand to mouth. Peter fished for this money, and therefore part of it went for his use. Those that are *workers together with Christ* in winning souls shall be sharers

with him in his glory. *Give it for thee and me.* What Christ paid for himself was looked upon as a debt; what he paid for Peter was a courtesy to him. It is a desirable thing, if God so please, to have wherewithal of this world's goods, not only to be just, but to be kind; not only to be charitable to the poor, but obliging to our friends.

CHAPTER 18

We have here, I. Instructions concerning humility, ver. 1-6. II. Concerning offences in general (ver. 7), particularly offences given. 1. By us to ourselves, ver. 8, 9. 2. By us to others, ver. 10-14. 3. By others to us; (1) Scandalous sins, ver. 15-20. (2) Personal wrongs, ver. 21-35.

Verses 1-6

There never was a greater pattern of humility than Christ; he took all occasions to command it, to commend it, to his disciples and followers.

I. The occasion of this discourse concerning humility was an unbecoming contest among the disciples for precedency; *Who is the greatest in the kingdom of heaven?* They mean not, *who* by character but *who* by name. They had heard much, and preached much, of the kingdom of heaven; but as yet they were so far from having any clear notion of it, that they dreamt of a temporal kingdom, and the external pomp and power of it. They expected his kingdom would commence; and now they thought it was time to put in for their places in it; it is good, in such cases, to speak early. Instead of asking how they might have strength and grace to suffer with him, they ask him, "Who shall be highest in reigning with him." Many love to hear and speak of privileges and glory, who are willing to pass by the thoughts of work and trouble.

1. They suppose that all who have a place in that kingdom are great. Those are truly great who are truly good.

2. They suppose that there are degrees in this greatness. All the saints are honourable, but not all alike so.

3. They suppose it must be some of them, that must be prime ministers of state.

4. They strive who it should be, each having some pretence or other to it. We are very apt to amuse and humour ourselves with foolish fancies of things that will never be.

II. The discourse itself, which is a just rebuke to the question, *Who shall be greatest?*

Christ here teacheth them to be humble,

1. By a sign (*v.* 2); *He called a little child to him, and set him in the midst of them.* Humility is a lesson so hardly learned, that we have need by all ways and means to be taught it. When we look upon a little child, we should be put in mind of the use Christ made of this child. *He set him in the midst of them;* not that they might play with him, but that they might learn by him. Grown men, and great men, should not disdain the company of little children. They may either speak to them, and give instruction to them; or look upon them, and receive instruction from them.

2. By a sermon upon this sign; in which he shows them and us,

(1) The necessity of humility, *v.* 3. *Verily I say unto you, Except ye be converted, and become as little children, ye shall not enter into the kingdom of heaven.*

What it is that he requires and insists upon. *First,* "You must be converted, you must be of another mind." Besides the first conversion of a soul there are after-conversions from particular paths of back-sliding. Every step out of the way by sin, must be a step into it again by repentance. *Secondly,* You must *become as little children.* Converting grace makes us like little children. As children, we must be careful

for nothing, but leave it to our heavenly Father to care for us (*ch.* vi. 31). We must be humble as little children; the child of a gentleman will play with the child of a beggar (Rom. xii. 16). The age of childhood is the learning age. What stress he lays upon this; Without this, *you shall not enter into the kingdom of heaven.* The disciples, when they put that question (*v.* 1), thought themselves sure of the kingdom of heaven. They were ambitious of being *greatest in the kingdom of heaven;* Christ tells them, that except they came to a better temper, they should never come thither. Our Lord designs here to show the great danger of pride and ambition. Pride threw the angels that sinned out of heaven, and will keep us out, if we be not converted from it.

(2) He shows the honour and advancement that attend humility (*v.* 4). He that humbles himself as a little child *the same is greatest in the kingdom of heaven.* The humblest Christians are the best Christians and most like to Christ, and highest in his favour, and fittest to serve God in this world, and enjoy him in another.

(3) The special care Christ takes for those that are humble.

Those that thus humble themselves will be afraid, [1] That nobody will receive them; but (*v.* 5), *Whoso shall receive one such little child in my name, receiveth me.* Whatever kindnesses are done to such, Christ takes as done to himself. Though it be but one such little child that is received in Christ's name, it shall be accepted. The less they are in themselves, to whom we show kindness, the more there is of good will in it to Christ; the less it is for their sakes, the more it is for his; and he takes it accordingly.

[2] They will be afraid that everybody will abuse them. This objection he obviates (*v.* 6), where he warns all people not to offer any injury to one of Christ's little ones. This word makes a wall of fire about them; he that touches them, touches the apple of God's eye.

The crime supposed; *offending one of these little ones that believe in Christ.* Their believing in Christ unites them to him, so that, as they partake of the benefit of his sufferings, he also partakes in the wrong of theirs. Even the little ones that believe have the same privileges with the great ones. The best men have often met with the worst treatment in this world.

The punishment of this crime; intimated in that word, *Better for him that he were drowned in the depth of the sea.* The sin is so heinous, and the ruin proportionably so great, that he had better undergo the sorest punishments inflicted on the worst of malefactors, which can only kill the body.

Verses 7-14

Our Saviour here speaks of offences, or scandals,

I. In general, *v.* 7. That is an offence, 1. Which occasions guilt. 2. Which occasions grief. Christ here tells them,

(1) That they were certain things; *It must needs be, that offences come.* When we are sure there is danger, we should be the better armed. Not that Christ's word necessitates any man to offend, but it is a prediction upon a view of the causes. It is morally impossible but that there should be offences. Let us stand upon our guard.

(2) That they would be woeful things.

[1] A woe to the careless and unguarded, to whom the offence is given; *Woe to the world because of offences.* This present world is an evil world, it is so full of offences, of sins, and snares, and sorrows; a dangerous road we travel, full of stumbling-blocks, precipices, and false guides. Woe to the world. As for those whom God hath chosen they are preserved by the power of God, are helped over all these stones of stumbling.

[2] A woe to the wicked, who wilfully give the offence; *But woe to that man by whom the offence comes.* Though it must needs be, that the offence will come, that will be no excuse for the offenders. The guilt will be laid at the door of those who give the offence, though they also fall under a woe who take it. The righteous God will reckon with those who ruin the eternal interests of precious souls, and the temporal interests of precious saints. Men will be reckoned with, not only for their doings, but for the fruit of their doings.

II. In particular, Christ here speaks of offences given,

1. By us to ourselves, which is expressed by our hand or foot offending us; in such a case, it must be *cut off, v.* 8, 9. This Christ had said before (*ch. v.* 29, 30). Those hard sayings of Christ need to be repeated to us again and again, and all little enough. What it is that is here enjoined. We must part with an *eye,* or a *hand,* or a *foot,* whatever it is, which is dear to us, when it proves unavoidably an occasion of sin to us. Many prevailing temptations to sin arise from within ourselves; if there were never a devil to tempt us, we should be drawn away of our own lust. We must, as far as lawfully we may, part with that which we cannot keep without being entangled in sin by it. It is certain, the inward lust must be mortified. Corrupt inclinations and appetites must be checked and crossed. The outward occasions of sin must be avoided, though we thereby put as great a violence upon ourselves as it would be to cut off a hand, or pluck out an eye. We must think nothing too dear to part with, for the keeping of a good conscience. Upon what inducement this is required; *It is better for thee to enter into life maimed, than, having two hands, to be cast into hell.* The argument is the same with that of the apostle, Rom. viii. 13. *If we live after the flesh, we shall die. If we through the Spirit mortify the deeds of the body, we shall live;* that is meant by our *entering into life maimed,* that is, the body of sin maimed. They that are Christ's have nailed the flesh to the cross, but it is not yet dead; its life is prolonged, but its *dominion taken away.*

2. Concerning offences given by us to others.

(1) The caution itself; *Take heed that ye despise not one of these little ones.* He will be displeased with the great ones of the church, if they despise the little ones of it. We may understand it literally of little children; of them Christ was speaking, *v.* 2, 4. Or, figuratively; true but weak believers are these little ones, who are like little children, the lambs of Christ's flock. We must not despise them, not think meanly of them. We must not make a jest of their infirmities, not conduct ourselves scornfully or disdainfully toward them, as if we cared not what became of them. We must not impose upon the consciences of others. There is a respect owing to the conscience of every man who appears to be conscientious. We must take heed that we do not despise them; and be very cautious what we say and do, lest we should through inadvertency give offence to Christ's little ones.

(2) The reasons to enforce the caution. We must not look upon these little ones as contemptible. Let not those be looked upon by us with disdain, whom God has put honour upon. To prove that the little ones which believe in Christ are worthy to be respected, consider,

[1] The ministration of the good angels about them; *In heaven their angels always behold the face of my Father.* Two things he lets us know concerning them.

First, That they are the little ones' angels. God's angels are theirs. They can look by faith on the heavenly hosts, and call them theirs. It is bad being enemies to those who are so guarded; and it is good having God for our God, for then we have his angels for our angels.

Secondly, That *they always behold the face of the Father in heaven.* This bespeaks, 1. The angels' continual felicity and honour. The happiness of heaven consists in the vision of God, beholding his beauty. 2. It bespeaks their continual readiness to minister to the saints. They behold the face of God, expecting to receive orders from him what to do for the good of the saints. If we would behold the face of God in glory hereafter, we must behold the face of God now, in readiness to our duty.

[2] The gracious design of Christ concerning them (*v.* 11); *For the Son of man is come to save that which was lost.* This is a reason, *First,* Why the little ones' angels have such a charge concerning them, and attend upon them; it is in pursuance of Christ's design to save them. *Secondly,* Why they are not to be despised; because Christ came to save them, to save them that are lost. Our souls by nature are lost souls; as a traveller is lost, that is out of his way. Christ's errand into the world was to *save that which was lost,* to put us into the right way that leads to our great end. This is a good reason why the least and weakest believers should not be despised or offended. If Christ put such a value upon them, let us not undervalue them.

[3] The tender regard which our heavenly Father has to these little ones, and his concern for their welfare. This is illustrated by a comparison, *v.* 12–14.

Here is, *First,* The comparison, *v.* 12, 13. The owner that had lost one sheep out of a hundred diligently enquires after it, is greatly pleased when he has found it, and has in that a sensible and affecting joy, more than in the ninety and nine that wandered not. Now this is applicable, 1. To the state of fallen man in general; he is strayed like a lost sheep. Wandering man is sought upon the mountains, which Christ, in great fatigue, traversed in pursuit of him, and he is found; which is matter of joy. Greater joy there is in heaven for returning sinners than for remaining angels. 2. To particular believers, God is graciously concerned, not only for his flock in general, but for every lamb, or sheep, that belongs to it. Though they are many, yet out of those many he can easily miss one, for he is a *great* Shepherd, but not so easily lose it, for he is a *good* Shepherd.

Secondly, The application of this comparison (*v.* 14); *It is not the will of your Father, that one of these little ones should perish.* It is his will, that these little ones should be saved; it is the will of his design and delight. This care extends itself to every particular member of the flock, even the meanest.

Observe, Christ called God, *v.* 19, *my Father which is in heaven;* he calls him, *v.* 14, *your Father which is in heaven;* intimating that he is not ashamed to call his poor disciples *brethren.* This intimates likewise the ground of the safety of his little ones; that God is their Father. A father takes care of all his children, but is particularly tender of the little ones.

Verses 15–20

Christ, having cautioned his disciples not to give offence, comes next to direct them what they must do in case of offences given them.

I. Let us apply it to the quarrels that happen, upon any account, among Christians.

1. *Go, and tell him his fault between thee and him alone.* Do not suffer thy resentments to ripen into a secret malice (like a wound, which is most dangerous when it bleeds inwardly), but give vent to them in a mild and grave admonition, let them so spend themselves, and they will expire the sooner. If he has indeed done thee a considerable wrong, endeavour to make him sensible of it, but let the rebuke be private,

between thee and him alone; if thou wouldest convince him, do not expose him, for that will but exasperate him. "*If he shall hear thee*, well and good, *thou hast gained thy brother*, there is an end of the controversy, and it is a happy end; let no more be said of it, but let the falling out of friends be the renewing of friendship."

2. "*If he will not hear thee*, if he will not own himself in a fault, yet do not despair, but try what he will say to it, if thou take *one or two more*, not only to be witnesses of what passes, but to reason the case further with him."

3. "*If he shall neglect to hear them*, and will not refer the matter to their arbitration, then *tell it to the church*, and do not presently appeal to the magistrate, or fetch a writ for him." This is fully explained by the apostle (1 Cor. vi), where he reproves those that went to law before the unjust, and not before the saints (*v.* 1). This rule was then in a special manner requisite, when the civil government was in the hands of such as were not only aliens, but enemies.

4. "If he will not *hear the church* but persists in the wrong he has done thee *let him be to thee as a heathen man, and a publican*. Thou mayest, if thou wilt, break off thy friendship and familiarity with him; though thou must by no means study revenge, yet thou mayest choose whether thou wilt have any dealings with him. Thou wouldest have preserved his friendship, but he would not, and so has forfeited it." If a man cheat and abuse me once, it is his fault; if twice, it is my own.

II. Let us apply it to scandalous sins. Christ, designing to erect a church for himself in the world, here took care of the preservation, 1. Of its purity. 2. Of its peace and order.

(1) What is the case supposed? *If thy brother trespass against thee.* Church discipline is for church members. *Them that are without God judges.* Christ and believers have twisted interests; what is done against them Christ takes as done against himself, and what is done against him they cannot but take as done against themselves.

(2) What is to be done in this case.

[1] The rules prescribed, *v.* 15–17.

First, "*Go and tell him his fault between thee and him alone.* Do not stay till he comes to thee, but go to him, as the physician visits the patient. *Tell him his fault*, remind him of what he has done, and of the evil of it." People are loth to see their faults, and have need to be told of them. Great sins often amuse conscience, and for the present stupefy and silence it; and there is need of help to awaken it.

"*Tell him his fault*, ἔλεγξον αὐτόν—*argue the case with him*" (so the word signifies). Where the fault is plain and great, and the person proper to deal with, we must with meekness and faithfulness tell people of what is amiss in them. Christian reproof is an ordinance of Christ for the bringing of sinners to repentance. "Let the reproof be private that it may appear you seek not his reproach, but his repentance." It is a good rule not to speak of our brethren's faults to others, till we have first spoken of them to themselves; this would make less reproaching and more reproving. It will be likely to work upon an offender, when he sees his reprover concerned not only for his salvation, in telling him his fault, but for his reputation in telling him of it privately.

"*If he shall hear thee, thou hast gained thy brother;* thou hast helped to save him from sin and ruin, and it will be thy credit and comfort," James *v.* 19, 20. If the loss of a soul be a great loss, the gain of a soul is sure no small gain.

Secondly, If that doth not prevail, *then take with thee one or two more, v.* 16. We must not be weary of well-doing, though we see not presently the good

success of it. "If he will not hear thee, yet do not give him up as in a desperate case; but go on in the use of other means."

"*Take with thee one or two more;* 1. To assist thee; they may speak some pertinent convincing word which thou didst not think of, and may manage the matter with more prudence than thou didst." Christians should see their need of help in doing good, as in other things, so in giving reproofs. 2. "To affect him; he will be the more likely to be humbled for his fault, when he sees it witnessed against by *two or three.*" Though in such a world as this it is rare to find one good whom *all men speak well of*, yet it is more rare to find one good whom *all men speak ill of.* 3. "To be witnesses of his conduct, in case the matter should afterward be brought before the church."

Thirdly, If he neglect to hear them, and will not be humbled, *then tell it to the church, v.* 17. There are some stubborn spirits to whom the likeliest means of conviction prove ineffectual; yet such must not be given over as incurable. Private admonitions must always go before public censures; if gentler methods will do the work, those that are more rough and severe must not be used. Those that will be reasoned out of their sins, need not be shamed out of them. Let God's work be done effectually, but with as little noise as may be. Where private admonition does not prevail, there public censure must take place.

Tell it to the church. What church must be told—is the great question. By what follows, *v.* 18, it is plain that he means a Christian church, which, though not yet formed, was now in the embryo. "*Tell it to the church*, that particular church in the communion of which the offender lives. Tell it to the guides and governors of the church; let them examine the matter and, if they find the complaint frivolous and groundless, let them rebuke the complainant; if they find it just, let them rebuke the offender, and call him to repentance."

Fourthly, "*If he neglect to hear the church, let him be unto thee as a heathen man and a publican;* let him be cast out of the communion of the church." Those who put contempt on the orders and rules of a society, and bring reproach upon it, forfeit the honours and privileges of it. But observe, he doth not say, "Let him be to thee as a devil," but "as a heathen and a publican, as one in a capacity of being restored and received in again." But when by this he is humbled and reclaimed, he must be welcomed into communion again, and all shall be well.

[2] Here is a warrant signed for the ratification of all the church's proceedings according to these rules, *v.* 18. What was said before to Peter is here said to all the disciples. While ministers preach the word of Christ faithfully, and in their government of the church strictly adhere to his laws, they may be assured that he will own them, and stand by them. He will own them,

First, In their sentence of suspension; *Whatsoever ye shall bind on earth shall be bound in heaven.* If the censures of the church duly follow the institution of Christ, his judgments will follow the censures of the church, for Christ will not suffer his own ordinances to be trampled upon. Christ will not own those as his, nor receive them to himself, whom the church has duly delivered to Satan; but, if through error or envy the censures of the church be unjust, Christ will graciously find those who are so cast out, John ix. 34, 35.

Secondly, In their sentence of absolution; *Whatsoever ye shall lose on earth shall be loosed in heaven.* No church censures bind so fast, but that, upon the sinner's repentance and reformation, they may and must be loosed again. Sufficient is the punishment which has attained its end, and the offender must then be forgiven and comforted. Those who, upon their repentance, are received by the church into communion again may take the comfort of their absolution in heaven, if their hearts be upright with God.

Now it is a great honour which Christ here puts upon the church.

(1) God's readiness to answer the church's prayers (*v.* 19); *If two of you shall agree* harmoniously, *touching any thing that they shall ask, it shall be done for them.* Apply this,

[1] In general, to all the requests of the faithful praying seed of Jacob; they shall not *seek God's face in vain.* Many promises we have in scripture of a gracious answer to the prayers of faith, but this gives a particular encouragement to joint-prayer. No law of heaven limits the number of petitioners. If they join in the same prayer, or, though at a distance, agree in some particular matter of prayer, they shall speed well.

[2] In particular, to those requests that are put up to God about binding and loosing. The power of church discipline is not here lodged in the hand of a single person, but two, at least, are supposed to be concerned in it. Heats and animosities, among those whose work it is to remove offences, will be the greatest offence of all. Prayer must evermore go along with church discipline. Pass no sentence, which you cannot in faith ask God to confirm. Prayer must go along with all our endeavours for the conversion of sinners; see James v. 16. The unanimous petitions of the church of God, for the ratification of their just censures, shall be heard in heaven. God will set his fiat to the appeals and applications you make to him. God doth especially own and accept us, when we are praying for those that have offended him and us. *The Lord turned the captivity of Job,* not when he prayed for himself, but when he prayed for his friends who had trespassed against him.

(2) The presence of Christ in the assemblies of Christians, *v.* 20. Assemblies of Christians for holy purposes are hereby appointed, directed, and encouraged. They are hereby appointed; the church of Christ in the world exists most visibly in religious assemblies; it is the will of Christ that these should be set up, and kept up. If there be no liberty and opportunity for large and numerous assemblies, yet then it is the will of God that two or three should gather together. When we cannot do what we would in religion, we must do as we can, and God will accept us. They are hereby directed to gather together in Christ's name. In the exercise of church discipline, they must *come together in the name of Christ.* In meeting for worship, we must have an eye to Christ; and in communion with all that in every place call upon him. When we come together to worship God in a dependence upon the Spirit and grace of Christ, having an actual regard to him as our Way to the Father, and our Advocate with the Father, then we are met together in his name. They are hereby encouraged with an assurance of the presence of Christ; *There am I in the midst of them.* Where his saints are, his sanctuary is, and there he will dwell. He is in the midst of them, that is, in their hearts; it is a spiritual presence, the presence of Christ's Spirit with their spirits, that is here intended. *There am I,* not only *I will be* there, but *I am there*; as if he came first, is ready before them, they shall find him there.

Though but two or three are met together, Christ is among them; this is an encouragement to the meeting of a few, when it is either, *First,* Of choice. There may be occasion sometimes for two or three to come together, either for mutual assistance in conference or joint assistance in prayer; there Christ

will be present. Or, *Secondly,* By constraint; when there are not more than two or three to come together, or, if there be, they dare not. It is not the multitude, but the faith and sincere devotion, of the worshippers, that invites the presence of Christ; and though there be but two or three, the smallest number that can be, yet, if Christ make one among them, who is the principal one, their meeting is as honourable and comfortable as if they were two or three thousand.

Verses 21–35

I. Peter's question concerning this matter (*v.* 21); *Lord, how oft shall my brother trespass against me, and I forgive him?* Will it suffice to do it *seven times*?

1. He takes it for granted that he must forgive. He knows that he must not only not bear a grudge against his brother, or meditate revenge, but be as good a friend as ever, and forget the injury.

2. He thinks it a great matter to forgive till seven times; he means not *seven times a day,* as Christ said (Luke xvii. 4), but seven times in his life. There is a proneness in our corrupt nature to stint ourselves in that which is good, and to be afraid of doing too much in religion, particularly of forgiving too much, though we have so much forgiven us.

II. Christ's direct answer to Peter's question; *I say not unto thee, Until seven times,* but *Until seventy times seven*; a certain number for an indefinite one, but a great one. It does not look well for us to keep count of the offences done against us by our brethren. There is something of ill-nature in scoring up the injuries we forgive, as if we would allow ourselves to be revenged when the measure is full. It is necessary to pass by injuries, without reckoning how often; to forgive, and forget. God multiplies his pardons, and so should we. We should make it our constant practice to forgive injuries, and should accustom ourselves to it till it becomes habitual.

III. A further discourse of our Saviour's, by way of parable, to show the necessity of forgiving the injuries that are done to us. The parable is a comment upon the fifth petition of the Lord's prayer, *Forgive us our trespasses, as we forgive them that trespass against us.* Those, and those only, may expect to be forgiven of God, who forgive their brethren.

There are three things in the parable.

1. The master's wonderful clemency to his servant who was indebted to him; he forgave him ten thousand talents, out of pure compassion to him, *v.* 23–27. Where observe,

(1) Every sin we commit is a debt to God; not like a debt to an equal, contracted by buying or borrowing, but to a superior; like a debt to a prince when a recognizance is forfeited, or a penalty incurred by a breach of the law. We are all debtors; we owe satisfaction, and are liable to the process of the law.

(2) There is an account kept of these debts. This king *would take account of his servants.* God now reckons with us by our own consciences; conscience is an auditor for God in the soul, to call us to account, and to account with us. One of the first questions that an awakened Christian asks, is, *How much owest thou unto my Lord?* And unless it be bribed, it will tell the truth, and not write fifty for a hundred.

(3) The debt of sin is a very great debt; and some are more in debt, by reason of sin, than others. When he *began to reckon,* one of the first defaulters appeared to owe *ten thousand talents.* The debt was ten thousand talents, a vast sum, a king's ransom or a kingdom's subsidy. See what our sins are, [1] For the heinousness of their nature; they are talents, the greatest denomination that ever was used in the account of money or weight. [2] For the vastness of their number; they are ten thousand, a myriad.

(4) The debt of sin is so great, that we are not able to pay it; *He had not to pay*. Sinners are insolvent debtors.

(5) If God should deal with us in strict justice, we should be condemned as insolvent debtors. Justice demands satisfaction. The servant had contracted this debt by his wastefulness and wilfulness, and therefore might justly be left to lie by it. *His lord commanded him to be sold; his wife and children to be sold, and all that he had, and payment to be made.* See here what every sin deserves; this is *the wages of sin.* Thus he would have *payment to be made*, that is, something done towards it; though it is impossible that the sale of one so worthless should amount to the payment of so great a debt.

(6) *The servant fell down* at the feet of his royal master, *and worshipped him*; or, as some copies read it, *he besought him*; his address was very submissive and very importunate; *Have patience with me, and I will pay thee all*, v. 26. The servant knew before that he was so much in debt, and yet was under no concern about it, till he was called to an account. Sinners are commonly careless about the pardon of their sins, till they come under the arrests of some awakening word, some startling providence, or approaching death. The stoutest heart will fail, when God sets the sins in order before it. He begs time; *Have patience with me.* Patience and forbearance are a great favour, but it is folly to think that these alone will save us; reprieves are not pardons. He promises payment; *Have patience* awhile, *and I will pay thee all.* He that *had nothing to pay* with (v. 25) fancied he could pay *all.* See how close pride sticks, even to awakened sinners; they are convinced, but not humbled.

(7) The God of infinite mercy is very ready, out of pure compassion, to forgive the sins of those that humble themselves before him (v. 27); *The lord of that servant*, since he could not be satisfied by the payment of the debt, would be glorified by the pardon of it. The servant's prayer was, *Have patience with me;* the master's grant is a discharge in full. The pardon of sin is owing to the mercy of God, to his tender mercy (Luke i. 77, 78); *He was moved with compassion.* There is forgiveness with God for the greatest sins, if they be repented of. Though the debt was vastly great, he *forgave it all*, v. 32. The forgiving of the debt is the loosing of the debtor; *He loosed him.* The obligation is cancelled, the judgment vacated. Though he discharged him from the penalty as a debtor, he did not discharge him from his duty as a servant. The pardon of sin doth not slacken, but strengthen, our obligations to obedience.

2. The servant's unreasonable severity toward his fellow-servant, notwithstanding his lord's clemency toward him, *v.* 28–30. This represents the sin of those who are rigorous and unmerciful in demanding that which is their own, to the utmost of right, which sometimes proves a real wrong. To exact satisfaction for debts of injury purely for revenge, though the law may allow it, savours not of a Christian spirit.

See here, (1) How small the debt was, how very small, compared with the *ten thousand talents* which his lord forgave him; *He owed him a hundred pence.* Offences done to men are nothing to those which are committed against God. Not that *therefore* we may make light of wronging our neighbour, for that is also a sin against God; but *therefore* we should make light of our neighbour's wronging us, and not aggravate it, or study revenge.

(2) How severe the demand was; *He laid hands on him, and took him by the throat.* What needed all this violence? The debt might have been demanded without taking the debtor by the throat. How lordly is this man's carriage, and yet how base and servile is his spirit! If he had been himself going to prison for his debt he might have had some pretence for going to this extremity in requiring his own; but frequently pride and malice prevail more to make men severe than the most urgent necessity would do.

(3) How submissive the debtor was; *His fellow servant fell down at his feet*, and humbled himself to him for this trifling debt, as much as he did to his lord for that great debt. The poor man's request is, *Have patience with me;* he honestly confesses the debt, only begs time. Forbearance, though it be no acquittance, is sometimes a piece of needful and laudable charity. As we must not be hard, so we must not be hasty, in our demands, but think how long God bears with us.

(4) How implacable and furious the creditor was (v. 30); *He would not have patience with him*, but without mercy *cast him into prison.* How insolently did he trample upon one as good as himself, that submitted to him!

(5) How much concerned the rest of the servants were; *They were very sorry* (v. 31). The sins and sufferings of our fellow-servants should be matter of grief and trouble to us. To see a fellow-servant, either raging like a bear or trampled on like a worm, cannot but occasion great regret to all that have any jealousy for the honour either of their nature or of their religion.

(6) How notice of it was brought to the master; *They came, and told their lord.* They durst not reprove their fellow-servant for it, he was so unreasonable and outrageous; but they went to their lord. Let our complaints both of the wickedness of the wicked and of the afflictions of the afflicted, be brought to God, and left with him.

3. The master's just resentment of the cruelty his servant was guilty of.

(1) How he reproved his servant's cruelty (v. 32, 33); *O thou wicked servant.* Note, Unmercifulness is wickedness, it is great wickedness. He upbraids him with the mercy he had found with his master; *I forgave thee all that debt.* Those that will use God's favours, shall never be upbraided with them, but those that abuse them, may expect it. The greatness of sin magnifies the riches of pardoning mercy: we should think *how much has been forgiven us*, Luke vii. 47. He thence shows him the obligation he was under to be merciful to his fellow-servant; *Shouldst not thou also have had compassion on thy fellow-servant, even as I had pity on thee?* It is justly expected, that such as have received mercy, should show mercy. He shows him, *First*, That he should have been more compassionate to the distress of his fellow servant, because he had himself experienced the same distress. What we have had the feeling of ourselves, we can the better have the fellow feeling of with our brethren. *Secondly*, That he should have been more conformable to the example of his master's tenderness. The comfortable sense of pardoning mercy tends much to the disposing of our hearts to forgive our brethren. We must have compassion on our brethren, as God has on us.

(2) How he revoked his pardon (v. 34); *He delivered him to the tormentors, till he should pay all that was due unto him.* Though the wickedness was very great, his lord laid upon him no other punishment than the payment of his own debt. See how the punishment answers the sin; he that would not forgive shall not be forgiven. Our debts to God are never compounded; either all is forgiven or all is exacted; glorified Saints in heaven are pardoned all, through Christ's complete satisfaction.

Lastly, Here is the application of the whole parable (v. 35); *So likewise shall my heavenly Father do also unto you.* If God's governing be fatherly, it follows thence, that it is righteous, but it does not therefore follow that it is not rigorous. When we pray to God as *our Father in heaven*, we are taught to ask for *the forgiveness of sins, as we forgive our debtors*. We must *from our hearts* forgive. We do not forgive our offending brother aright, nor acceptably, if we do not forgive from the heart; for that is it that God looks at. No malice must be harboured there, nor ill will to any person. Yet this is not enough; we must from the heart desire and seek the welfare even of those that have offended us. The danger of not forgiving; *So shall your heavenly Father do*. This is not intended to teach us that God reverses his pardons to any, but that he denies them to those that are unqualified for them. Intimations enough we have in scripture of the forfeiture of pardons, for caution to the presumptuous; and yet we have security enough of the continuance of them, for comfort to those that are sincere, but timorous; that the one may fear, and the other may hope. Those that do not *forgive their brother's trespasses*, did never truly repent of their own, and therefore that which is *taken away* is only what *they seemed to have*. This is intended to teach us, that *they shall have judgment without mercy, that have showed no mercy*, James ii. 13. It is indispensably necessary to pardon and peace, that we not only *do justly*, but *love mercy*.

CHAPTER 19

I. Christ changing his quarters, ver. 1, 2. II. His dispute with the Pharisees about divorce, and his discourse with his disciples upon occasion of it, ver. 3–12. III. The kind entertainment he gave to some little children which were brought to him, ver. 13–15. IV. An account of what passed between Christ and a hopeful young gentleman that applied himself to him, ver. 16–22. V. His discourse with his disciples upon that occasion, ver. 23–30.

Verses 1, 2

1. He left Galilee. There he had been brought up, and had spent the greatest part of his life in that remote despicable part of the country. In this, as in other things, he appeared in a mean state, that he would go under the character of a Galilean, a north-countryman, the least polite and refined part of the nation. Now, having *finished these sayings, he departed from Galilee*, and it was his final farewell; for he never came to Galilee again till after his resurrection.

2. *He came into the coasts of Judæa, beyond Jordan*, that *they* might have their day of visitation as well as Galilee, for they also belonged *to the lost sheep of the house of Israel*.

3. *Great multitudes followed him*. When Christ departs, it is best for us to follow him. He *went about doing good*; for so it follows, *he healed them there*. This shows what they followed him for, to have their sick healed; and they found him as able and ready to help here, as he had been in Galilee.

Verses 3–12

We have here the law of Christ in the case of divorce, occasioned, as some other declarations of his will, by a dispute with *the Pharisees*.

I. The case proposed by the Pharisees (*v.* 3); *Is it lawful for a man to put away his wife?* This they asked, tempting him, not desiring to be taught by him. If he would declare himself now against divorce, they would make use of it for the prejudicing and incensing of the people of this country against him, who would look with a jealous eye upon one that attempted to cut them short in a liberty they were fond of. If he should say that divorces were not lawful, they would reflect upon him as an enemy to the law of Moses, which allowed them; if he should say that they were, they would represent his doctrine as not having that perfection in it which was expected in the doctrine of the Messiah, since though divorces were tolerated, they were looked upon by the stricter sort of people as not of good report.

Their question is, *Whether a man may put away his wife for every cause*. That it might be done for some cause, even for that of fornication, was granted; but may it be done, as now it commonly was done, by the looser sort of people, for any cause that a man shall think fit to assign, though ever so frivolous?

II. Christ's answer to this question; though it was proposed to tempt him, was a full one, not a direct one, but an effectual one. Now his argument is this: "If husband and wife are by the will and appointment of God joined together in the strictest and closest union, then they are not to be lightly, and upon every occasion, separated." He urges three things.

1. The creation of Adam and Eve, concerning which he appeals to their own knowledge of the scriptures; *Have ye not read? Ye have read* (but have not considered) *that he which made them at the beginning, made them male and female*, Gen. i. 27; v. 2. *He made them male and female*, one female for one male; so that Adam could not divorce his wife, and take another, for there was no other to take. It likewise intimated an inseparable union between them; Eve was a rib out of Adam's side, so that he could not put her away, but he must put away a piece of himself.

2. The fundamental law of marriage, which is, that *a man shall leave father and mother, and shall cleave to his wife, v.* 5. The relation between husband and wife is nearer than that between parents and children; now, if the filial relation may not easily be violated, much less may the marriage union be broken. May a child desert his parents, or may a parent abandon his children, for any cause, for every cause? No, by no means.

3. The nature of the marriage contract; it is a union of persons; *They twain shall be one flesh*, so that (*v.* 6) *they are no more twain, but one flesh*. A man's children are pieces of himself, but his wife is himself. As the conjugal union is closer than that between parents and children, so it is in a manner equivalent to that between one member and another in the natural body.

From hence he infers, *What God hath joined together, let not man put asunder*. Husband and wife are of God's joining together; συνέζευξεν—*he hath yoked them together*, so the word is. God himself instituted the relation between husband and wife. Though marriage be not peculiar to the church, but common to the world, yet it ought to be managed *after a godly sort, and sanctified by the word of God, and prayer*. A conscientious regard to God in this ordinance would have a good influence upon the duty, and consequently upon the comfort, of the relation. Husband and wife, being joined together by the ordinance of God, are not to be put asunder by any ordinance of man.

III. An objection started by the Pharisees against this (*v.* 7); "*Why did Moses command to give a writing of divorcement*, in case a man did put away his wife?" He urged scripture reason against divorce; they allege scripture authority for it. The seeming contradictions that are in the word of God are great stumbling-blocks to men of corrupt minds.

IV. Christ's answer to this objection.

1. He rectifies their mistake concerning the law of Moses; they called it a *command*, Christ calls it but a *permission*, a *toleration*. Carnal hearts will take an ell if but an inch be given them.

But Christ tells them there was a reason for this toleration, not at all for their credit; *It was because of the hardness of your hearts*, that you were permitted to *put away your wives*. Moses complained of the people of Israel in his time, that *their hearts were hardened*, hardened against God; this is here meant of their being hardened against their relations. There is not a greater piece of hard-heartedness in the world than for a man to be harsh, and severe with his own wife. The Jews, it seems, were infamous for this, and therefore were allowed to put them away; better divorce them than do worse. A little compliance, to humour a madman, or a man in a frenzy, may prevent a greater mischief. The law of Moses considered the hardness of men's hearts, but the gospel of Christ cures it. By the law was the knowledge of sin, but by the gospel was the conquest of it.

2. He reduces them to the original institution; *But from the beginning it was not so.* Corruptions that are crept into any ordinance of God must be purged out by having recourse to the primitive institution. If the copy be vicious, it must be examined and corrected by the original.

3. He settles the point by an express law; *I say unto you* (*v.* 9); and it agrees with what he said before (*ch.* v. 32). Now, in both these places he allows divorce, in case of adultery, the reason of the law against divorce being this, *They two shall be one flesh.* If the wife play the harlot, and make herself one flesh with an adulterer, the reason of the law ceases, and so does the law. He disallows it in all other cases; *Whosoever puts away his wife, except for fornication, and marries another, commits adultery.* This is a direct answer to their query, that it is not lawful. There will be no occasion for divorces, if we *forbear one another, and forgive one another, in love,* as those that are, and hope to be, forgiven. No need of divorces, if *husbands love their wives, and wives be obedient to their husbands,* and they live together as heirs of the grace of life.

V. Here is a suggestion of the disciples against this law of Christ (*v.* 10); *If the case of the man be so with his wife, it is better not to marry.* It seems, the disciples themselves were loth to give up the liberty of divorce, thinking it a good expedient for preserving comfort in the married state. Unless they may have a liberty of divorce, they think it is good for a man not to marry. Corrupt nature is impatient of restraint. It is a foolish, peevish thing for men to abandon the comforts of this life, because of the crosses that are commonly woven in with them. No, whatever our condition is, we must bring our minds to it, be thankful for its comforts, submissive to its crosses, and make the best of that which is. If the yoke of marriage may not be thrown off at pleasure, it does not follow that *therefore* we must not come under it; but *therefore,* when we do come under it, we must resolve to comport with it, by love, and meekness, and patience, which will make divorce the most unnecessary undesirable thing that can be.

VI. Christ's answer to this suggestion (*v.* 11, 12). He allows it good for some not to marry; *He that is able to receive it, let him receive it.* Christ allowed what the disciples said, *It is good not to marry,* as giving them a rule that they who have the gift of continence do best if they continue single. The increase of grace is better than the increase of the family, and fellowship with the Father and with his Son Jesus Christ is to be preferred before any other fellowship. He disallows it, as utterly mischievous, to forbid marriage, because *all men cannot receive this saying.*

Christ here speaks of a twofold unaptness to marriage.

1. That which is a calamity by the providence of God; such as those labour under who are born eunuchs, or made so by men.

2. That which is a virtue by the grace of God; such is theirs who *have made themselves eunuchs for the kingdom of heaven's sake.* This is meant of an unaptness for marriage, not in body but in mind. Those have thus made themselves eunuchs who have attained a holy indifference to all the delights of the

married state, have a fixed resolution, in the strength of God's grace, wholly to abstain from them. These are they that *can receive* this saying. This affection to the single state must be given of God; for none can receive it, *save they to whom it is given.* Continence is a special gift of God to some, and not to others. The single state must be chosen for the kingdom of heaven's sake. When it is for religion's sake, then it is approved and accepted of God. That condition is best for us, and to be chosen and stuck to accordingly, which is best for our souls, and tends most to the preparing of us for, and the preserving of us to, the kingdom of heaven.

Verses 13–15

I. The faith of those that brought them. The account here given of it, is, that *there were brought unto him little children, that he should put his hands on them, and pray, v.* 13. They testified their respect to Christ, and the value they had for his favour and blessing. They did a kindness to their children. Others brought their children to Christ, to be healed when they were sick; but these children were under no present malady, only they desired a blessing for them. It is a good thing when we come to Christ ourselves, and bring our children to him, before we are driven to him (as we say) by woe-need.

They desired that he would put his hands on them, and pray. Imposition of hands was a ceremony used especially in paternal blessings. It intimates something of love and familiarity mixed with power and authority and bespeaks an efficacy in the blessing. We cannot do better for our children than to commit them to the Lord Jesus, to be wrought upon, and prayed for, by him. We can but beg a blessing for them, it is Christ only that can command the blessing.

II. The fault of the disciples in rebuking them. They discountenanced the address as vain and frivolous, and reproved them that made it as impertinent and troublesome. It is well for us, that Christ has more love and tenderness in him than the best of his disciples have. And let us learn of him not to discountenance any willing well-meaning souls in their enquiries after Christ, though they are but weak. If *he* do not break the bruised reed, *we* should not.

III. The favour of our Lord Jesus.

1. He rebuked the disciples (*v.* 14); *Suffer little children, and forbid them not;* and he rectifies the mistake they went upon, *Of such is the kingdom of heaven.* The children of believing parents belong to the kingdom of heaven, and are members of the visible church. For this reason they are welcome to Christ, who is ready to entertain those who, when they cannot come themselves, are brought to him. And this, (1) In respect to the little children themselves, whom he had upon all occasions expressed a concern for. (2) With an eye to the faith of the parents who brought them. Parents are trustees of their children's wills. Therefore Christ accepts their dedication of them as their act and deed. (3) Therefore he takes it ill of those who forbid them, and exclude those whom he has received.

2. *He received the little children,* and did as he was desired; *he laid his hands on them,* that is, *he blessed them.* The strongest believer lives not so much by apprehending Christ as by being apprehended of him (Phil. iii. 12), and this the least child is capable of. If they cannot stretch out their hands to Christ, yet he can lay his hands on them, and so make them his own, and own them for his own.

Verses 16–22

Here is an account of what passed between Christ and a hopeful young gentleman; he is said to be a *young man* (*v.* 20); and I called him a *gentleman,* not only because he had great possessions, but because he was a ruler (Luke xviii. 18).

Now concerning this young gentleman, we are told how fair he bid for heaven and came short.

I. How fair he bid for heaven, and how kindly and tenderly Christ treated him.

1. The gentleman's serious address to Jesus Christ (v. 16); *Good Master, what good thing shall I do, that I may have eternal life?* Not a better question could be asked, nor more gravely.

(1) He gives Christ an honourable title, *Good Master*. It signifies not a ruling, but a teaching Master. His calling him *Master*, bespeaks his submissiveness, and willingness to be taught; and *good Master*, his affection and peculiar respect to the Teacher. It is a good thing when men's quality and dignity increase their civility and courtesy. It was gentleman-like to give this title of respect to Christ. It was not usual among the Jews to accost their teachers with the title of *good*; and therefore this bespeaks the uncommon respect he had for Christ.

(2) He comes to him upon an errand of importance (none could be more so), and he came not to tempt him, but sincerely desiring to be taught by him. His question is, *What good thing shall I do, that I may have eternal life?* He was convinced that there is a happiness prepared for those in the other world, who are prepared for it in this world. It was a rare thing for one of his age and quality to appear so much in care about another world. The rich are apt to think it below them to make such an enquiry as this; and young people think it time enough yet; but here was a young man, and a rich man, solicitous about his soul and eternity. He was sensible something must be done, some good thing, for the attainment of this happiness. We must be doing, and doing that which is good. The blood of Christ is the only purchase of eternal life (he merited it for us), but obedience to Christ is the appointed way to it, Heb. v. 9. Those that know what it is to have eternal life, and what it is to come short of it, will be glad to accept of it upon any terms. Such a holy violence does the kingdom of heaven suffer. Our great enquiry should be, *What shall we do, that we may have eternal life?* For this world has not that in it that will make us happy.

2. The encouragement that Jesus Christ gave to this address. It is not his manner to send any away without an answer, that come to him on such an errand, for nothing pleases him more, v. 17.

(1) He tenderly assists his faith; for, doubtless, he did not mean it for a reproof, when he said, *Why callest thou me good?* He intended no more than to own and honour him as a good man, but Christ would lead him to own and honour him as a good God; for *there is none good but one, that is God.* As Christ is graciously ready to make the best that he can of what is said or done amiss; so he is ready to make the most that can be of what is well said and well done. His constructions are often better than our intentions. All crowns must lie before his throne. God only is good. We in our language call him *God*, because he is good.

(2) He plainly directs his practice. Now Christ's answer is, in short, this, *If thou wilt enter into life, keep the commandments.* The end proposed is, entering into life. The young man, in his question, spoke of eternal life. Christ, in his answer, speaks of *life*; to teach us, that eternal life is the only true life. He desired to know how he might *have* eternal life; Christ tells him how he might *enter into it.* The way of *entering into it*, is, by obedience, and Christ directs us in that. Christ, who is our Life, is the Way to the Father. He is the only Way, but duty, and the obedience of faith, are the way to Christ. The way prescribed is, keeping the commandments. Keeping

the commandments of God, according as they are revealed and made known to us, is the only way to life and salvation. *Keeping the commandments* includes *faith in Jesus Christ*, for that is the great commandment (1 John iii. 23). It is not enough for us to *know* the commandments of God, but we must *keep* them, keep in them as our way, keep to them as our rule. At his further instance and request, he mentions some particular commandments which he must keep (v. 18, 19); *The young man saith unto him, Which?*

In answer to this, Christ specifies several, especially the commandments of the second table. *First*, That which concerns our own and our neighbour's life; *Thou shalt do no murder.* *Secondly*, Our own and our neighbour's chastity, *Thou shalt not commit adultery.* *Thirdly*, Our own and our neighbour's wealth and outward estate, *Thou shalt not steal.* *Fourthly*, That which concerns truth, and our own and our neighbour's good name; *Thou shalt not bear false witness.* *Fifthly*, That which concerns the duties of particular relations; *Honour thy father and mother.* *Sixthly*, That comprehensive law of love in which they are all fulfilled, *Thou shalt love thy neighbour as thyself* (Gal. v. 14; Rom. xiii. 9), that *royal* law, James ii. 8.

Our Saviour here specifies second-table duties only; not as if the first were of less account, but, 1. Because they that now sat in Moses's seat, either wholly neglected, or greatly corrupted, these precepts in their preaching. While they pressed the tithing of *mint, anise, and cummin—judgment, and mercy, and faith*—the summary of second-table duties, were overlooked, ch. xxiii. 23. Their preaching ran out all in rituals and nothing in morals. 2. Because he would teach him, and us all, that moral honesty is a necessary branch of true Christianity. Though a mere moral man comes short of being a complete Christian, yet an immoral man is certainly no true Christian. Nay, though first-table duties have in them more of the essence of religion, yet second-table duties have in them more of the evidence of it. Our light *burns* in love to God, but it *shines* in love to our neighbour.

II. See here how he came short and wherein he failed.

1. By pride, and a vain conceit of his own merit and strength. When Christ told him what commandments he must keep, he answered very scornfully, *All these things have I kept from my youth up*, v. 20. Christ knew it, for he did not contradict him; nay, it is said in Mark, *He loved him*; and so far he was very good and pleasing to Christ. His observance of these commands was universal; *All these have I kept*: it was early and constant; *from my youth up.* A man may be free from gross sin, and yet come short of grace and glory.

It was commendable also, that he desired to know further what his duty was; *What lack I yet?* He was convinced that he wanted something to fill up his works before God, and was therefore desirous to know it, because, if he was not mistaken in himself, he was willing to do it. Having not yet attained, he thus seemed to press forward. And he applied himself to Christ. Who could bid fairer? Even in this that he said, he discovered his ignorance and folly. Had he been acquainted with the extent and spiritual meaning of the law, instead of saying, *All these have I kept; what lack I yet?* he would have said, with shame and sorrow, "All these have I broken, what shall I do to get my sins pardoned?" Take it how you will, what he said savoured of pride and vain-glory, and had in it too much of that boasting which is excluded by the law of faith (Rom. iii. 27). That word, *What lack I yet?* perhaps was not so much a desire of further instruction as a demand of the praise of his present fancied perfection.

2. He came short by an inordinate love of the world, and his enjoyments in it. This was the fatal rock on which he split. Observe,

(1) How he was tried in this matter (*v.* 21); *Jesus said unto him, If thou wilt be perfect, go and sell that thou hast.* Christ waived the matter of his boasted obedience to the law, and let that drop, because this would be a more effectual way of discovering him than a dispute of the extent of the law. What Christ said to him, he thus far said to us all, that, if we would approve ourselves Christians indeed, and would be found at last the heirs of eternal life, we must do these two things:

[1] We must practically prefer the heavenly treasures before all the wealth and riches in this world. Now, as an evidence of this, *First,* We must dispose of what we have in this world, for the honour of God, and in his service: "*Sell that thou hast, and give to the poor.* Sell what thou canst spare for pious uses, all thy superfluities; if thou canst not otherwise do good with it, sell it. Sit loose to it, be willing to part with it for the honour of God, and the relief of the poor." In those that have wherewithal, giving of alms is as necessary an evidence of that contempt of the world, and compassion to our brethren. When we embrace Christ, we must let go the world, for we cannot serve God and mammon. Christ knew that covetousness was the sin that did most easily beset this young man, that, though what he had he had got honestly, yet he could not cheerfully part with it, and by this he discovered his insincerity. *Secondly,* We must depend upon what we hope for in the other world as an abundant recompence for all we have left, or lost, or laid out, for God in this world; *Thou shalt have treasure in heaven.* Trust God for a happiness out of sight, which will make us rich amends for all our expenses in God's service. Christ immediately annexes this assurance of a treasure in heaven. Christ's promises make his precepts easy, and his yoke not only tolerable, but pleasant, and sweet, and very comfortable.

[2] We must devote ourselves entirely to the conduct and government of our Lord Jesus; *Come, and follow me.* It seems here to be meant of a close and constant attendance upon his person, but of us it is required that we follow Christ, strictly conform to his pattern, and keep his laws, and all this from a principle of love to him, and dependence on him, and with a holy contempt of everything else in comparison of him. This is to *follow Christ fully.* To sell all, and give to the poor, will not serve, unless we come, and follow Christ. If I give all my goods to feed the poor, and have not love, it profits me nothing.

(2) See how he was discovered. This touched him in a tender part (*v.* 22); *When he heard that saying, he went away sorrowful, for he had great possessions.* He was a rich man, and loved his riches, and therefore went away. Those who have much in the world are in the greatest temptation to love it. Such is the bewitching nature of worldly wealth, that those who want it least desire it most. The reigning love of this world keeps many from Christ, who seem to have some good desires toward him. A great estate, as to those who are got above it, is a great furtherance, so to those who are entangled in the love of it, it is a great hindrance, in the way of heaven.

Yet something of honesty there was in it. He went away, and would not pretend to that, which he could not find in his heart to come up to the strictness of. Since he could not be a complete Christian, he would not be a hypocrite. Yet he was a thinking man, and well-inclined, and therefore *went away sorrowful.* He had a leaning toward Christ, and was loth to part with him. Many a one is ruined by the sin he commits with reluctance; leaves Christ sorrowfully, and yet is never truly sorry for leaving him, for, if he were, he would return to him.

Verses 23–30

We have here Christ's discourse with his disciples upon occasion of the rich man's breaking with Christ.

I. Christ took occasion from thence to show the difficulty of the salvation of rich people, *v.* 23–26.

1. That it is a very hard thing for a rich man to get to heaven. From the harms and falls of others it is good for us to infer that which will be of caution to us. This is vehemently asserted by our Saviour, *v.* 23, 24. He said this to his disciples, who were poor. The less they had of worldly wealth, the less hindrance they had in the way to heaven. This saying is ratified, *v.* 23. *Verily I say unto you.* It is repeated, *v.* 24. *Again I say unto you.* Thus he speaks once, yea, twice, that which man is loth to perceive and more loth to believe. He saith that it is a hard thing for a rich man to enter into the kingdom of heaven, either here or hereafter. The way to heaven is to all a narrow way, and the gate that leads into it, a strait gate, but it is particularly so to rich people. Rich people have great temptations to resist, and such as are very insinuating; it is hard not to be charmed with a smiling world. It must be a great measure of divine grace that will enable a man to break through these difficulties. He saith that the conversion and salvation of a rich man is so extremely difficult, that *it is easier for a camel to go through the eye of a needle, v.* 24. Nothing less than the almighty grace of God will enable a rich man to get over this difficulty. It is very rare for a man to be rich, and not to set his heart upon his riches; and it is utterly impossible for a man that sets his heart upon his riches, to get to heaven. The way to heaven is very fitly compared to a *needle's eye,* which is hard to hit and hard to get through. A rich man is fitly compared to a *camel,* a beast of burthen, for he has riches, as a camel has his load. This truth is very much wondered at, and scarcely credited by the disciples (*v.* 25); *They were exceedingly amazed, saying, Who then can be saved?* Many surprising truths Christ told them, which they were astonished at, and knew not what to make of. It was not on contradiction to Christ, but for awakening to themselves, that they said, *Who then can be saved?* When we think how good God is, it may seem a wonder that so *few* are his; but when we think how bad man is, it is a more wonder that so *many* are. *Who then can be saved?* Since so many are rich, and have great possessions, and so many more would be rich, and are well affected, to great possessions; who can be saved? This is a good reason why rich people should strive against the stream.

2. That, though it be hard, yet it is not impossible for the rich to be saved (*v.* 26); *Jesus beheld them, turned and looked wistfully upon his disciples, and he said unto them, with men this is impossible, but with God all things are possible.* This is a great truth in general. Nothing is too hard for God. When men are at a loss, God is not; but this truth is here applied, (1) To the salvation of any. *Who can be saved?* say the disciples. None, saith Christ, by any created power. *With men this is impossible.* It is a creation, it is a resurrection, and with men this is impossible; but *with God all things are possible.* (2) To the salvation of rich people especially; it is impossible with men that such should be saved, but with God even this is possible. The sanctification and salvation of such as are surrounded with the temptations of this world are not to be despaired of; it is possible. In this word of Christ there is an intimation of mercy Christ had yet in store for this young gentleman, who was now gone away sorrowful; it was not impossible to God yet to recover him.

II. Peter took occasion from hence to enquire what *they* should get by it, who had left all to follow him, *v.* 27, &c.

1. We have their expectations from Christ; *Behold, we have forsaken all, and have followed thee; what shall we have therefore?* Peter desires to know,

(1) Whether they had sufficiently come up to those terms: they had not sold all (for they had many of them wives and families to provide for), but they had *forsaken all.* When we hear what are the characters of those that shall be saved, it concerns us to enquire whether we, through grace, answer those characters.

Lord, saith Peter, *we have forsaken all.* Alas! it was but a poor *all* that they had forsaken; and yet observe how Peter there speaks of it, as if it had been some mighty thing; *Behold, we have forsaken all.* We are too apt to make the most of our services and sufferings, our expenses and losses, for Christ, and to think we have made him much our debtor. However, Christ does not upbraid them with this. It was their *all*, like the widow's two mites, and was as dear to them as if it had been more, and therefore Christ took it kindly that they left it to follow him.

(2) Whether therefore they might expect *that treasure* which the young man shall have if he will sell all. All people are for what they can get; and Christ's followers are allowed to consult their own true interest, and to ask, *What shall we have?* Christ encourages us to ask what we shall gain by leaving all to follow him; that we may see he doth not call us to our prejudice, but unspeakably to our advantage. It is of a hoping, trusting faith, to ask, "What shall we *have?*" The disciples had never till now asked, *What shall we have?* They were so well assured of his goodness, that they knew they should not lose by him at last, and therefore minded their work, and asked not what should be their wages. It honours Christ, to trust him and serve him, and not to bargain with him.

2. We have here Christ's promises to them, and to all others that tread in the steps of their faith and obedience.

(1) To his immediate followers, *v.* 28. To them he promises not only *treasure*, but *honour. Ye which have followed me in the regeneration shall sit upon twelve thrones.* Observe, The *preamble* to the patent, or the *consideration* of the grant, which, as usual, is a recital of their services; "You have followed me in the regeneration, and therefore this will I do for you." The disciples had followed Christ when the gospel temple was but in the framing. Now they followed Christ with constant fatigue, when few did; and therefore on them he will put particular marks of honour. Christ hath special favour for those who begin early with him, who trust him further than they can see him. Peter spoke of their forsaking *all*, to follow him, Christ only speaks of their *following* him, which was the main matter. The *date* of their honour, *when the Son of man shall sit in the throne of his glory.* All that partake of the regeneration in grace shall partake of the regeneration in glory.

Now their honour being adjourned till the Son of man's sitting in the throne of his glory, intimates, *First*, That they must stay for their advancement till then. As long as our Master's glory is delayed, it is fit that ours should be so too. We must live, and work, and suffer, in faith, and hope, and patience. *Secondly*, That they must share with Christ in his advancement. They having suffered with a suffering Jesus, must reign with a reigning Jesus. The longest voyages make the richest returns. The honour itself hereby granted; *Ye also shall sit upon twelve thrones, judging the twelve tribes of Israel.*

The general intendment of this promise is, to show the glory and dignity reserved for the saints in heaven, which will be abundant recompence for the disgrace they suffered here in Christ's cause. There are higher degrees of glory for those that have done and suffered most. Here *bonds, and afflictions, and deaths, did abide them*, but there they *shall sit on thrones of glory.* And will not this be recompence enough to make up all their losses and expenses for Christ? The ratification of this grant; it is firm, it is inviolably immutably sure; for Christ hath said, "*Verily I say unto you.*"

(2) Here is a promise to all others that should in like manner leave all to follow Christ. *This honour have all his saints.* Christ will take care they shall none of them lose by him (*v.* 29). Losses for Christ are here supposed. Christ had told them that his disciples must deny themselves. Now here he specifies particulars; for it is good to count upon the worst. If they have not forsaken all, yet they have forsaken a great deal, houses suppose, or dear relations, that would not go with them, to follow Christ; these are particularly mentioned, as hardest for a tender gracious spirit to part with; *brethren, or sisters, or father, or mother, or wife, or children*; and *lands* are added in the close, the profits of which were the support of the family.

The loss of these things is supposed to be *for Christ's name's sake*; else he doth not oblige himself to make it up. Many forsake brethren, and wife, and children, in humour and passion; that is a sinful desertion. But if we forsake them *for Christ's sake*, because we must either quit them, or quit our interest in Christ; if we do not quit our concern for them, or our duty to them, but our comfort in them, and will do it rather than deny Christ, this is that which shall be thus recompenced. It is not the suffering, but the cause, that makes both the martyr and the confessor.

It is supposed to be a great loss; and yet Christ undertakes to make it up. A recompence of these losses is here secured. Thousands have dealt with Christ, and have trusted him far; but never anyone lost by him, never anyone but was an unspeakable gainer by him.

A hundred-fold in this life; sometimes in *kind*, in the things themselves which they have parted with. God will raise up for his suffering servants more friends, that will be so to them for Christ's sake, than they have left that were so for their own sakes. The apostles, wherever they came, met with those that were kind to them, and entertained them, and opened their hearts and doors to them. However, they *shall receive a hundred-fold*, in *kindness*. Their graces shall increase, their comforts abound, they shall have tokens of God's love, and then they may truly say they have received a hundred times more comfort in God and Christ than they could have in *wife, or children.*

Eternal life at last. The former is reward enough, if there were no more. But this comes in over and above, as it were, into the bargain. Now, if we could but mix faith with the promise, and trust Christ for the performance of it, surely we should think nothing too much to do, nothing too hard to suffer, nothing too dear to part with, for him. *Many that are first, shall be last, and the last, first, v.* 30. God will cross his hands. The heavenly inheritance is not given as earthly inheritances commonly are, by seniority of age, and priority of birth, but according to God's pleasure. This is the text of another sermon, which we shall meet with in the next chapter.

CHAPTER 20

I. The parable of the labourers in the vineyard, ver. 1-16. II. A prediction of Christ's approaching sufferings, ver. 17-19. III. The petition of two of the disciples, by their mother, reproved, ver. 20-28. IV. The petition of the two blind men granted, ver. 29-34.

Verses 1-16

This parable of the labourers in the vineyard is intended,

I. To represent to us *the kingdom of heaven* (v. 1). The laws of that kingdom are not wrapt up in parables, but plainly set down, as in the sermon upon the mount. The notions of it are more necessary to be illustrated than the duties of it; which is that which parables are designed for.

II. In particular, to represent to us that concerning the kingdom of heaven, which he had said in the close of the foregoing chapter, that *many that are first shall be last, and the last, first*.

The parable shows us, 1. That God is debtor to no man; a great truth. 2. That many who begin last, and promise little in religion, sometimes, by the blessing of God, arrive at greater attainments in knowledge, grace, and usefulness, than others whose entrance was more early, and who promised fairer. John is swifter of foot, and comes *first to the sepulchre*: but Peter has more courage, and goes *first into it*. Thus *many that are last, shall be first*. Some make it a caution to the disciples. Let them look to it, that they keep up their zeal; else their good beginnings will avail them little; they that seemed to be *first*, would be *last*. Sometimes those that are converted later in their lives, outstrip those that are converted earlier. 3. That *the recompence of reward* will be given to the saints, not according to the time of their conversion; not according to the seniority, but *according to the measure of the stature of the fulness of Christ*. Sufferers for Christ in the latter days, shall have the same reward with the martyrs and confessors of the primitive times, though they are more celebrated; and faithful ministers now, the same with the first fathers.

We have two things in the parable; the *agreement* with the labourers, and the *account* with them.

(1) Here is the agreement made with the labourers (v. 1–7); and here it will be asked, as usual, Who hires them? *A man that is a householder*. God is the great Householder; as a householder, he has work that he will have to be done, and servants that he will have to be doing. God hires labourers in kindness to them, to save them from idleness and poverty, and pay them for working for themselves. Whence are they hired? Out of *the market-place*, where, till they are hired into God's service, they *stand idle* (v. 3), *all the day idle* (v. 6). The soul of man stands ready to be hired into some service or other; it was (as all the creatures were) created to work, and is either a *servant to iniquity*, or a *servant to righteousness*. The devil, by his temptations, is *hiring labourers* into his field, to *feed swine*. God, by his gospel, is *hiring labourers into his vineyard, to dress it, and keep it*, paradise-work. We are put to our choice. Till we are hired into the service of God, we are standing all the day idle. The gospel call is given to those that *stand idle in the market-place*. The market-place is *a place of concourse*; it is a place of sport, there the *children are playing* (ch. xi. 16); it is a place of business, of noise and hurry. "Come, come from this market-place." What are they hired to do? To labour in his vineyard. The church is God's vineyard; it is of his planting, watering, and fencing. We are all called upon to be labourers in this vineyard. We have each of us our own vineyard to keep, our own soul; and it is God's, and to be kept and dressed for him. In this work we must not be slothful, not loiterers, but *labourers*, working. Work for God will not admit of trifling. A man may go idle to hell; but he that will go to heaven, must be busy. What shall be their wages? He promises, *First, A penny*, v. 2. A day's wages for a day's work, and the wages sufficient for a day's maintenance. This doth not prove that the reward of our obedience to God is *of works*, or *of debt*. It is to signify that there is a reward set before us, and a sufficient one. *Secondly, Whatsoever is right*, v. 4–7. God will be sure not to be behind-hand with any for the service they do him: never any lost by working for God. For what term are they hired? For *a day*. It is but a day's work that is here done. The time of life is the day. It is a short time; the reward is for eternity, the work is but for *a day*. This should quicken us to expedition and diligence in our work, that we have but a little time to work in. It should also encourage us in reference to the hardships and difficulties of our work, that it is but for *a day*; the approaching *shadow* will bring with it both rest, and *the reward of our work*. Hold out, faith, and patience, yet a little while. Notice is taken of the several hours of the day, at which the labourers were hired.

This may be, and commonly is, applied to the several ages of life, in which souls are converted to Christ. The effectual call is particular, and it is *then* effectual when we come to the call.

First, Some are effectually called, and begin to work in the vineyard when they are very young; are sent in early in the morning. Those that have such a journey to go, had need set out betimes, the sooner the better.

Secondly, Others are savingly wrought upon in middle age; *Go work in the vineyard, at the third, sixth, or ninth hour*. The power of divine grace is magnified in the conversion of some, when they are in the midst of their pleasures and worldly pursuits, as Paul. God has work for all ages; no time amiss to turn to God. The time past of our life may suffice that we have served sin; *Go ye also into the vineyard*. God turns away none that are willing to be hired.

Thirdly, Others are hired into the vineyard in old age, at *the eleventh hour*, when *the day of life is far spent*, and there is but *one hour* of the twelve remaining. "While there is life, there is hope." There is hope *for* old sinners; true repentance is never too late. There is hope *of old sinners*, that they may be brought to true repentance; nothing is too hard for Almighty grace to do, it can set those to work, who have contracted a habit of idleness. Nicodemus may *be born again when he is old*.

Yet let none, upon this presumption, put off their repentance till they are old. These were *sent into the vineyard*, it is true, *at the eleventh hour*; but nobody had hired them, or offered to hire them, before.

(2) Here is the account with the labourers. When the account was taken; *when the evening was come*, then, as usual, the day-labourers were called and paid. Evening time is the reckoning time. Faithful labourers shall receive their reward when they die; it is deferred till then, that they may wait with patience for it. Ministers call them into the vineyard, to do their work; death calls them out of the vineyard, to receive their penny: and those to whom the call into the vineyard is effectual, the call out of it will be joyful. They did not come for their pay till they were called; we must with patience wait God's time for our rest and recompence; go by our master's clock. What the account was; and in that observe, The general pay (v. 9, 10); *They received every man a penny*. Though there be degrees of glory in heaven, yet it will be to all a complete happiness. In heaven, every vessel will be full, brimful, though every vessel is not alike large and capacious.

The giving of a whole day's wages to those that had not done the tenth part of a day's work, is designed to show that God distributes his rewards by *grace* and *sovereignty*, and not of *debt*. Because *we are under grace*, and *not under the law*, even such defective services, done in sincerity, shall not only be accepted, but by free grace richly rewarded. Note the particular pleading with those that were offended with this distribution in gavelkind.

1. The offence taken (v. 11, 12); *They murmured at the good man of the house;* not that there is, or can

be, any discontent or murmuring in heaven, but there may be, and often are, discontent and murmuring concerning heaven and heavenly things, while they are in prospect and promise in this world. These labourers quarrelled with their master, and found fault, not because they had not enough, so much as because others were made *equal* with them. They boast of their good services; *We have borne the burthen and heat of the day.* Now *these last have worked but one hour,* and that too in the cool of the day; and yet *thou hast made them equal with us.* There is a great proneness in us to think that we have too little, and others too much, of the tokens of God's favour. Very apt we all are to undervalue the deserts of others, and to overvalue our own. Perhaps, Christ here gives an intimation to Peter, not to boast too much, as if, because he and the rest of them had borne the burthen and heat of the day thus, they must have a heaven by themselves. It is hard for those that do or suffer more than ordinary for God, not to be elevated too much with the thought of it.

2. The offence removed. Three things the master of the house urges.

(1) That the complainant had no reason at all to say he had any wrong done to him, *v.* 13, 14. *Friend, I do thee no wrong.* He calls him *friend,* for in reasoning with others we should use soft words and hard arguments. It is incontestably true, that God can do no wrong. Whatever God does to us, or withholds from us, he does us no wrong. If God gives that grace to others, which he denies to us, it is kindness to them, but no injustice to us; and bounty to another, while it is no injustice to us, we ought not to find fault with.

To convince the murmurer that he did no wrong, he refers him to the bargain: "*Didst not thou agree with me for a penny?* Thou shalt have that we agreed for." It is good for us often to consider what it was that we agreed with God for. Worldlings agree with God for their penny in this world; they chose *their portion in this life* (Ps. xvii. 14). Believers agree with God for their penny in the other world, and they must remember that they have so agreed.

He therefore ties him to his bargain (*v.* 14); *Take that thine is, and go thy way.* If we understand it of that which is ours by *gift,* the free gift of God, it teaches us *to be content with such things as we have.* If God be better in any respect to others than to us, yet we have no reason to complain while he is so much better to us than we deserve. He tells him that those he envied should fare as well as he did; "*I will give unto this last, even as unto thee.*"

(2) He had no reason to quarrel with the master; for what he gave was absolutely his own, *v.* 15. As before he asserted his justice, so here his sovereignty; *Is it not lawful for me to do what I will with my own?* He may therefore give or withhold his blessings, as he pleases. What God has, is his own; and this will justify him, in all the disposals of his providence; when God takes from us that which was dear to us we must silence our discontents with this; *May he not do what he will with his own? Absulit, sed et dedit.* —*He hath taken away; but he originally gave.* We are in his hand, as clay in the hands of a potter; and it is not for us to prescribe to him, or strive with him.

(3) He had no reason to be angry that he came into the vineyard no sooner; for he was not sooner called; he had no reason to be angry that the master had given him wages for the whole day. *Is thine eye evil, because I am good?* The nature of envy; It is an evil eye. The eye is often both the inlet and the outlet of this sin. It is an evil eye, which is displeased at the good of others, and desires their hurt, and see the aggravation of it; "It is because I am good." Envy is unlikeness to God, who is good,

and doeth good, and delighteth in doing good. It is a direct violation of both the two great commandments at once; both that of love to God, in whose will we should acquiesce, and love to our neighbour, in whose welfare we should rejoice.

Lastly, Here is the application of the parable (*v.* 16), in that observation which occasioned it (*ch.* xix. 30); *So the first shall be last, and the last first.* Christ, to obviate and silence their boasting, here tells them,

1. That they might possibly be outstripped by their successors in profession, and, might be found inferior to them in knowledge, grace, and holiness. Who knows but that the church, in its old age, may be more fat and flourishing than ever. What *labourers* may be *sent into the vineyard in the eleventh hour,* and what plentiful effusions of the Spirit may then be, above what has been yet, who can tell?

2. That they had reason to fear, lest they themselves should be found hypocrites at last; for *many are called but few chosen.* As to the outward call; *many are called,* and yet refuse (Prov. i. 24). There are but few *chosen* Christians, in comparison with the many that are only *called* Christians.

Verses 17–19

This is the third time that Christ gave his disciples notice of his approaching sufferings.

I. The privacy of this prediction; *He took the twelve disciples apart in the way.* His secret was with them, as his friends. It was a hard saying, and if any could bear it, they could. It was requisite that they should know of it, that, being fore-warned, they might be fore-armed. It was not fit to be spoken publicly as yet, because many that were cool toward him, would hereby have been driven to turn their backs upon him; because many that were hot for him, would hereby be driven to take up arms in his defence, and it might have occasioned *an uproar among the people* (*ch.* xxvi. 5). He never countenanced anything which had a tendency to prevent his sufferings.

II. The prediction itself, *v.* 18, 19.

1. It is but a repetition of what he had once and again said before, *ch.* xvi. 21; xvii. 22, 23. This intimates that he not only saw clearly what troubles lay before him, but that his heart was upon his suffering-work; it filled him, not with fear but with desire and expectation; he spoke thus frequently of his sufferings, because through them he was to enter into his glory.

2. He is more particular here in foretelling his sufferings than any time before. He had said (*ch.* xvi. 21), that he *should suffer many things, and be killed;* here he adds, that he shall be *condemned, and delivered to the Gentiles, that they shall mock him, and scourge him, and crucify him.* The more clearly he foresaw his sufferings, the more cheerfully he went forth to meet them. He foretells by whom he should suffer, by the *chief priests and the scribes;* so he had said before, but here he adds, *They shall deliver him to the Gentiles.* He was to suffer for the salvation both of Jews and Gentiles; both had a hand in his death, because he was to reconcile both by his cross, Eph. ii. 16.

3. Here, as before, he annexes the mention of his resurrection and his glory to that of his death and sufferings; *The third day he shall rise again.* He still brings this in to encourage himself in his sufferings, and to carry him cheerfully through them. *He endured the cross for the joy set before him;* he foresaw he should rise again, and rise quickly, the third day. The reward is not only sure, but very near. It was also to encourage his disciples, and comfort them, and to direct us, under all *the sufferings of this present time* to look at *the things that are not seen, that are eternal,* which will enable us to call the present afflictions light, and but for a moment.

Verses 20–28

Here is, first, the request of the two disciples to Christ, *v.* 20–23. The sons of Zebedee were James and John, two of the first three of Christ's disciples; Peter and they were his favourites; John was the disciple whom Jesus loved; yet none were so often reproved as they; whom Christ loves best he reproves most, Rev. iii. 19.

I. Here is the ambitious address they made to Christ, *v.* 20, 21. It was a great degree of faith, that they were confident of his kingdom, but a great degree of ignorance, that they still expected a temporal kingdom, with worldly pomp and power. In this they expected to be grandees. They ask not for employment in this kingdom, but for honour only. It is probable that the last word in Christ's foregoing discourse gave occasion to this request, that *the third day he should rise again.* What Christ said to comfort them, they thus abused. Some cannot bear comforts, but they turn them to a wrong purpose; as sweetmeats in a foul stomach produce bile. There was policy in the management of this address, that they put their mother on to present it, that it might be looked upon as her request, and not theirs. She was one of those women that attended Christ, and ministered to him; and they thought that he could deny her nothing, and therefore they made her their advocate. It was their mother's weakness thus to become the tool of their ambition. Those that are wise and good, would not be seen in an ill-favoured thing. In gracious requests, we should learn this wisdom, to desire the prayers of those that have an interest at the throne of grace; we should beg of our praying friends to pray for us, and reckon it a real kindness. There was pride at the bottom of it. Pride is a sin that most easily besets us, and which it is hard to get clear of. It is a holy ambition to strive to excel others in grace and holiness; but it is a sinful ambition to covet to exceed others in pomp and grandeur.

II. Christ's answer to this address (*v.* 22, 23), directed not to the mother, but to the sons that set her on. He reproved the ignorance and error of their petition; *Ye know not what ye ask.* They were much in the dark concerning the kingdom they had their eye upon. They knew not what it was to sit on his right hand, and on his left; they talked of it as blind men do of colours. Our apprehensions of that glory which is yet to be revealed, are like the apprehensions which a child has of the preferments of grown men. What it will be in the performance, eye has not seen, nor ear heard. They were much in the dark concerning the way to that kingdom. *They* know not what they ask, who ask for the end, but overlook the means. The disciples thought, when they had left what little *all* they had for Christ, all their service and sufferings were over, and it was now time to ask, *What shall we have?* They imagined their warfare was accomplished when it was scarcely begun, and they had yet but run with the footman. We know not what we ask, when we ask for the glory of wearing the crown, and ask not for grace to bear the cross in our way to it. See how he repressed the vanity and ambition of their request.

(1) He leads them to the thoughts of their sufferings, which they were not so mindful of as they ought to have been. Therefore he thinks it necessary to put them in mind of the hardships that were before them, that they might be no surprise or terror to them.

Observe, [1] How fairly he puts the matter to them. *Are you able to drink of the cup that I shall drink of?* Are you able to hold out to the end of it? Put the matter seriously to yourselves. They were not aware what was amiss in their spirits when they were lifted up with ambition. Christ sees that pride in us which we discern not in ourselves.

Note, That to suffer for Christ is *to drink of a cup,* and *to be baptised with a baptism.* It is supposed to be a bitter cup, those waters of a full cup, that are wrung out to God's people (Ps. lxxiii. 10). It is supposed to be a baptism, a washing with the waters of affliction; some are dipped in them; others have but a sprinkling of them; both are baptisms, some are overwhelmed in them, as in a deluge, others ill wet, as in a sharp shower. Even in this, *consolation doth more abound.* It is but a cup, bitter perhaps, but we shall see the bottom of it; it is a cup in the hand of a Father (John xviii. 11). It is but a baptism; if dipped, that is the worst of it, not drowned; perplexed, but not in despair. It is to drink of the same cup that Christ drank of, and to be baptised with the same baptism that he was baptised with. Christ is beforehand with us in suffering. 1. It bespeaks the condescension of a suffering Christ, that he would drink of such a cup (John xviii. 11); that he would be baptised with such a baptism. 2. It bespeaks the consolation of suffering Christians, that they do but pledge Christ in the bitter cup. It is good for us to be often putting it to ourselves, whether we are able to drink of this cup, and to be baptised with this baptism. We must expect suffering. Are we able to suffer cheerfully. What can we afford to part with for Christ? The truth is, Religion, if it be worth anything, is worth everything; but it is worth little, if it be not worth suffering for. Now let us sit down, and count the cost of dying for Christ rather than denying him, and ask, Can we take him upon these terms?

[2] See how boldly they engage for themselves; they said, *We are able;* but at the same time they fondly hoped that they should never be tried. As before they knew not what they asked, so now they knew not what they answered. But those are commonly most confident that are least acquainted with the cross.

[3] See how plainly and positively their sufferings are here foretold (*v.* 23); *Ye shall drink of my cup.* Sufferings foreseen will be the more easily borne. Christ will have us know the worst, that we may make the best of our way to heaven; *Ye shall drink;* that is, ye shall suffer.

(2) He leaves them in the dark about the degrees of their glory. To carry them cheerfully through their sufferings, it was enough to be assured that they should have *a place in his kingdom.* The lowest seat in heaven is an abundant recompence for the greatest sufferings on earth. "*To sit on my right hand and on my left is not mine to give,* and therefore it is not for you to ask it or to know it; *but it shall be given to them for whom it is prepared of my Father.*" It is not mine to give to those that seek and are ambitious of it, but to those that by great humility and self-denial are prepared for it.

III. Here are the reproof and instruction which Christ gave to the other ten disciples for their displeasure at the request of James and John.

1. The fret that the ten disciples were in (*v.* 24). *They were moved with indignation against the two brethren;* not because they were desirous to be preferred, but because they were desirous to be preferred *before them.* Many seem to have indignation at sin; but it is not because it is sin, but because it touches them. These disciples were angry at their brethren's ambition, though they themselves, nay *because* they themselves, were as ambitious. It is common for people to be angry at those sins in others which they allow of and indulge in themselves. Nothing makes more mischief among brethren, or is the cause of more indignation and contention, than ambition.

2. The check that Christ gave them. He had reproved this very sin before (*ch.* xviii. 3), and told them they must be humble as little children; yet they

relapsed into it, and yet he reproved them for it thus mildly.

He called them unto him, which intimates great tenderness and familiarity. He did not, in anger, bid them get out of his presence, but called them, in love, to come into his presence.

(1) They must not be *like the princes of the Gentiles*. Christ's disciples must not be like Gentiles, no not like princes of the Gentiles.

Observe, What is the way of the princes of the Gentiles (*v.* 25); to *exercise dominion and authority* over their subjects. That which bears them up in it is, that they are great, and great men think they may do anything. What is the will of Christ in this matter. "*It shall not be so among you*. You are to teach the subjects of this kingdom, to take pains with them, and suffer with them; you are not to *lord it over God's heritage* (1 Pet. v. 3), but to labour in it." The pomp and grandeur of the princes of the Gentiles ill become Christ's disciples. How then shall it be among the disciples of Christ? Something of greatness among them Christ himself had intimated, and here he explains it; "*He that will be great among you*, that *will be chief, let him be your minister, your servant*," *v.* 26, 27. It is the duty of Christ's disciples to serve one another, for mutual edification. This includes both humility and usefulness. It is the dignity of Christ's disciples faithfully to discharge this duty. The way to be great and chief is to be humble and serviceable. Those are to be best accounted of, and most respected, that are most humble and self-denying, and lay out themselves most to do good. These honour God most, and those he will honour. As he must become a fool that would be wise, so he must become a servant that would be chief.

(2) They must be like the Master himself. The *Son of man came not to be ministered to, but to minister, and to give his life a ransom for many*, *v.* 28. Our Lord Jesus here sets himself before his disciples as a pattern of those two things before recommended, humility, and usefulness.

[1] Never was there such an example of humility and condescension as there was in the life of Christ, who came not to be *ministered unto, but to minister*. He was indeed ministered to as a poor man, but he was never ministered to as a great man. He once washed his disciples' feet, but we never read that they washed his feet. He came to minister help to all that were in distress; he made himself a servant to the sick and diseased; was as ready to their requests as ever any servant was at the beck of his master, and took as much pains to serve them.

[2] Never was there such an example of beneficence and usefulness as there was in the death of Christ, who *gave his life a ransom for many*. He lived as a servant, and went about doing good; but he died as a sacrifice, and in that he did the greatest good of all. He came into the world on purpose to give his life a ransom. He gives his honour and life too a ransom for his subjects. It was a ransom for many, sufficient for all, effectual for many; and, if for many, then, saith the poor doubting soul, "Why not for me?"

Now this is a good reason why we should not strive for precedency, because the cross is our banner, and our Master's death is our life. It is a good reason why we should study to do good. The nearer we are all concerned in, and the more we are advantaged by, the humility and humiliation of Christ, the more ready and careful we should be to imitate it.

Verses 29–34

I. Their address to Christ, *v.* 29, 30.

1. The circumstances of it are observable. It was as Christ and his disciples departed from Jericho;

of that devoted place, which was rebuilt under a curse, Christ took his leave with this blessing. It was in the presence of *a great multitude that followed him*; Christ had a numerous attendance, and did good to them. This multitude that followed Christ was a mixed multitude. Some followed him for loaves, and some for love, some for curiosity, very few with desire to be taught their duty; yet, for the sake of those few, he confirmed his doctrine by miracles wrought in the presence of great multitudes. Two blind men concurred in their request; for joint-prayer is pleasing to Christ, *ch.* xviii. 19. Being companions in the same tribulation, they were partners in the same supplication. It is good for those that are labouring under the same calamity, or infirmity of body or mind, to join together in the same prayer to God for relief, that they may quicken one another's fervency, and encourage one another's faith. There is mercy enough in Christ for all the petitioners. These blind men were *sitting by the way-side*. It is good thus to way-lay Christ, to be in his road.

They heard that Jesus passed by. Though they were blind, they were not deaf. Seeing and hearing are the learning senses. These blind men had heard of Christ by the hearing of the ear, but they desired that their eyes might see him. *When they heard that Jesus passed by*, they asked no further questions, but immediately *cried out*. It is good to improve the present opportunity. These blind men did so, and did wisely; for we do not find that Christ ever came to Jericho again. *Now is the accepted time*.

2. The address itself is more observable; *Have mercy on us, O Lord, thou Son of David*, repeated again, *v.* 31. Four things are recommended to us for an example in this address.

(1) Here is an example of importunity in prayer. They cried out as men in earnest; men in want are earnest, of course. Cold desires do but beg denials. When they were discountenanced in it, they cried the more. The stream of fervency, if it be stopped, will rise and swell the higher. This is wrestling with God in prayer, and makes us the fitter to receive mercy; for the more it is striven for, the more it will be prized and thankfully acknowledged.

(2) Of humility in prayer; in that word, *Have mercy on us*, not specifying the favour, or prescribing what; "Only have mercy." They ask not for silver and gold, though they were poor, but mercy, mercy. This is that which our hearts must be upon.

(3) Of faith in prayer; in the title they gave to Christ, which was in the nature of a plea; *O Lord, thou Son of David*; they confess that *Jesus Christ is Lord*. Thus they take their encouragement in prayer from his power, as in calling him the Son of David they take encouragement from his goodness, as Messiah, of whom so many kind and tender things had been foretold. It is of excellent use, in prayer, to eye Christ in the grace and glory of his Messiahship; to remember that he is the Son of David, whose office it is to help, and save.

(4) Of perseverance in prayer, notwithstanding discouragement. *The multitude rebuked them* and bid them *hold their peace*. In following Christ with our prayers, we must expect to meet with hindrances and manifold discouragements. Such rebukes are permitted, that faith and fervency, patience and perseverance, may be tried. These poor blind men were rebuked by the multitude that followed Christ. But they would not be beaten off so; when they were in pursuit of such a mercy. *They cried the more*. Men *ought always to pray, and not to faint;* to pray with all perseverance (Luke xviii. 1).

II. The answer of Christ to this address of theirs. The multitude rebuked them; but Christ encouraged them. It were sad for us, if the Master were not more kind and tender than the multitude. He will not suffer his humble supplicants to be run down, and put out of countenance.

1. *He stood still, and called them, v.* 32. He was now going up to Jerusalem, and yet he stood still to cure these blind men. When we are ever so much in haste about any business, yet we should be willing to stand still to do good. *He called them.* Christ not only enjoins us to pray, but invites us; holds out the golden sceptre to us, and bids us come touch the top of it.

2. He enquired further into their case; *What will ye that I shall do unto you?* "Here I am; let me know what you would have, and you shall have it." What would we more? *Ask, and it shall be given you.* One would think this a strange question, anyone might tell what they would have. Christ knew well enough; but he would know it from them, whether they begged only for an alms, as from a common person, or for a cure, as from the Messiah. The waterman in the boat, who with his hook takes hold of the shore, does not thereby pull the shore to the boat, but the boat to the shore. So in prayer we do not draw the mercy to ourselves, but ourselves to the mercy.

They soon made known their request to him; *Lord, that our eyes may be opened.* The wants and burthens of the body we are soon sensible of, and can readily relate. O that we were but as apprehensive of our spiritual maladies, and could as feelingly complain of them, especially our spiritual blindness! Lord, that the eyes of our mind may be opened! Were we but sensible of our darkness, we should soon apply ourselves to him. *Lord, that our eyes may be opened.*

3. He cured them. What he did was an instance,

(1) Of his pity; *He had compassion on them.* Misery is the object of mercy. It was the tender mercy of our God, that gave light and sight to them that sat in darkness, Luke i. 78, 79.

(2) Of his power. He did it easily, he touched their eyes; he did it effectually, *Immediately their eyes received sight.* These blind men, when they had received sight, *followed him.* None follow Christ blindfold. He first by his grace opens men's eyes, and so draws their hearts after him.

CHAPTER 21

The history of his sufferings, even unto death, and his rising again, is more particularly recorded by all the evangelists than any other part of his story; and to that this evangelist now hastens apace. Now at length he is come up to Jerusalem; and here we have, I. The public entry which he made into Jerusalem, ver. 1–11. II. The authority he exercises there, in cleansing the temple, ver. 12–16. III. The emblem he gave of the state of the Jewish church, in cursing the barren fig-tree, and his discourse with his disciples thereupon, ver. 17–22. IV. His justifying his own authority, ver. 23–27. V. His shaming the chief priests and elders, with the repentance of the publicans, illustrated by the parable of the two sons, ver. 29–32. VI. The parable of the vineyard let out to unthankful husbandmen, ver. 33–46.

Verses 1–11

All the four evangelists take notice of this passage of Christ's *riding in triumph into Jerusalem,* five days before his death. He had lodged at Bethany, a village not far from Jerusalem, for some time; at a supper there the night before Mary had *anointed his feet,* John xii. 3. Our Lord Jesus travelled much, and his custom was to travel on foot from Galilee to Jerusalem; many a dirty weary step he had when *he went about doing good.* How ill does it become Christians to be inordinately solicitous about their own ease and state. Yet once in his life he rode in triumph, and it was now when he went into Jerusalem, to suffer and die.

I. The provision that was made for this solemnity; and it was very poor and ordinary.

1. The preparation was sudden and off-hand. For his glory in the other world was the glory his heart was upon; his glory in this world he was dead to.

They were come to Bethphage, a long scattering street that lay toward the mount of Olives; when he entered upon that *he sent two of his disciples* to fetch him an ass.

2. It was very mean. He sent only for an ass and her colt, *v.* 2. Asses were much used in that country for travel; horses were kept only by great men, and for war. In his state of humiliation, he *rides upon an ass.*

3. It was not his own, but borrowed. He had nothing of this world's goods but what was given him or lent him.

The disciples who were sent to borrow this ass are directed to say, *The Lord has need of him.* In the borrowing of this ass,

(1) We have an instance of Christ's knowledge. Christ could tell his disciples where they should find an ass tied, and a colt with her.

(2) We have an instance of his power over the spirits of men. Christ asserts his right to use the ass, in bidding them bring it to him; but he foresees some hindrance which the disciples might meet with in this service; *If any man say aught to you, ye shall say, The Lord hath need of him.* What Christ sets us to do, he will bear us out in the doing of; *Straightway he will send them.*

(3) We have an example of justice and honesty, in not using the ass without the owner's consent.

II. The prediction that was fulfilled in this, *v.* 4, 5. Our Lord Jesus, in all that he did and suffered, had very much his eye upon this, *That the scriptures might be fulfilled.* This particularly which was written of him, Zech. ix. 9, where it ushers in a large prediction of the kingdom of the Messiah, *Tell ye the daughter of Sion, Behold, thy King cometh,* must be accomplished.

1. How the coming of Christ is foretold; *Tell ye the daughter of Sion, Behold, thy King cometh unto thee.* Jesus Christ is the church's King. Christ, the King of his church, came to his church, even in this lower world. Notice was given to the church beforehand of the coming of her King; *Tell the daughter of Sion.* Christ will have his coming looked for, and waited for, and his subjects big with expectation of it.

2. How his coming is described. When a king comes, something great and magnificent is expected. But there is nothing of that here; *Behold, he cometh to thee, meek, and sitting upon an ass.* When Christ would appear in his glory, it is in his meekness, not in his majesty. His temper is very mild. He is meek to suffer the greatest injuries and indignities for Sion's cause. He is easy of access, easy to be entreated. His government is mild and gentle, and his laws not written in the blood of his subjects, but in his own. His yoke is easy. As an evidence of this, his appearance is very mean, sitting upon an ass, a creature made not for state, but service, not for battles, but for burthens; slow in its motions, but sure, and safe and constant. Sion's King comes riding, not on a prancing horse, which the timorous petitioner dares not come near, or a running horse, which the slow-footed petitioner cannot keep pace with, but on a quiet ass, that the poorest of his subjects may not be discouraged in their access to him.

III. The procession itself. His equipage; *The disciples did as Jesus commanded them (v.* 6). Christ's commands must not be disputed, but obeyed; and those that sincerely obey them, shall not be baulked or baffled in it; *They brought the ass and the colt.* They had not so much as a saddle for the ass, but the disciples threw some of their clothes upon it, and that must serve for want of better accommodations. We ought not to be nice or curious, or to affect exactness in outward conveniences. A holy indifference or neglect well becomes us in these things. The disciples furnished him with the best they had, and did not object the spoiling of their clothes when *the Lord had need of them.* We must not think the clothes on our backs too dear to part with for the service of Christ, for the clothing of his poor destitute and afflicted members. Christ stripped himself for us. His retinue; there was nothing in this stately or magnificent. He has his attendants, *a very great multitude;* they were only the common people, the mob (the *rabble* we should have been apt to call them), that graced the solemnity of Christ's triumph, and none but such. Christ is honoured by the multitude, more than by the magnificence, of his followers; for he values men by their souls, not by their preferments, names, or titles of honour.

Now, concerning this great multitude, we are here told, what they did; according to the best of their capacity, they studied to do honour to Christ. *They spread their garments in the way,* that he might ride upon them. When Jehu was proclaimed king, the captains put their garments under him, in token of their subjection to him. Those that take Christ for their King must lay their all under his feet; the clothes, in token of the heart. How shall we express our respects to Christ? What honour and what dignity shall be done to him? *Others cut down branches from the trees, and strewed them in the way,* as they used to do at the feast of tabernacles, in token of liberty, victory, and joy. What they said; *They that went before, and they that followed, cried, saying, Hosanna to the Son of David, v.* 9. When they carried branches about at the feast of tabernacles, they were wont to cry *Hosanna,* and from thence to call their bundles of branches their *hosannas. Hosanna* signifies, *Save now, we beseech thee;* referring to Ps. cxviii. 25, 26.

The hosannas with which Christ was attended bespeak two things: Their welcoming his kingdom. *Hosanna* bespeaks the same with, *Blessed is he that cometh in the name of the Lord. All nations shall call him blessed* (Ps. lxxii. 17); these here began, and all true believers in all ages concur in it, and call him blessed: it is the genuine language of faith. Well may we say, *Blessed is he;* for it is in him that we are blessed. Well may we follow *him* with our blessings, who meets us with his. Their wishing well to his kingdom was intimated in their *Hosannas;* earnestly desiring that it might be a victorious kingdom. If they understood it of a temporal kingdom it was their mistake, which a little time would rectify; however, their good-will was accepted. It is our duty earnestly to desire and pray for the prosperity and success of Christ's kingdom in the world. This we mean when we pray, *Thy kingdom come.* They add, *Hosanna in the highest.* Let him have a name above every name, a throne above every throne. We have here his entertainment in Jerusalem (*v.* 10); *When he was come into Jerusalem, all the city was moved;* everyone took notice of him, some were moved with wonder at the novelty of the thing, others with laughter at the meanness of it; some perhaps were moved with joy; others, of the Pharisaical class, were moved with envy and indignation. So various are the motions in the minds of men upon the approach of Christ's kingdom!

Upon this commotion we are further told,

1. What the citizens said; *Who is this?* They were, it seems, ignorant concerning Christ. The Holy One unknown in the holy city! In places where the clearest light shines, and the greatest profession of religion is made, there is more ignorance than we are aware of. Yet they were inquisitive concerning him. *Who is this King of glory?*

2. How the multitude answered them; *This is Jesus, v.* 11. In the account they give of him they were right in calling him *the Prophet, that great Prophet.* Yet they missed it, in saying he was *of Nazareth:* and it helped to confirm some in their prejudices against him. Some that are willing to honour Christ, and bear their testimony to him, yet labour under mistakes concerning him.

Verses 12–17

It is in holy things that he rules, in the temple of God that he exercises authority. Now, what did he do there?

I. Thence he drove the buyers and sellers. Abuses must first be purged out before that which is right can be established. Here we are told,

1. What he did (*v.* 12); *He cast out all them that sold and bought;* he had done this once before (John ii. 14, 15). Buyers and sellers driven out of the temple, will return and nestle there again. The abuse was, buying and selling, and changing money, in the temple. Lawful things, ill timed, and ill placed, may become sinful things. They sold beasts for sacrifice, for the convenience of those that could more easily bring their money with them than their beast; and they changed money for those that wanted the half shekel. This might pass for the outward business of the house of God; and yet Christ will not allow of it. Great corruptions and abuses come into the church by the practices of those whose *gain is godliness,* that is, who make worldly gain the end of their godliness, and counterfeit godliness their way to worldly gain (1 Tim. vi. 5). The purging out of this abuse. Christ *cast them out that sold.* He did it before *with a scourge of small cords* (John ii. 15); now he did it with a look, with a frown, with a word of command. Some reckon this none of the least of Christ's miracles, that he should himself thus clear the temple. It is an instance of his power over the spirits of men, and the hold he has of them by their own consciences. *He overthrew the tables of the money-changers;* he did not take the money to himself, but scattered it, threw it to the ground, the fittest place for it.

2. What he said, to justify himself, and to convict them (*v.* 13); *It is written.* The eye must be upon the scripture, and that must be adhered to as the rule, the pattern in the mount.

(1) He shows, from a scripture prophecy, what the temple should be, and was designed to be; *My house shall be called the house of prayer;* which is quoted from Isa. lvi. 7. All the ceremonial institutions were intended to be subservient to moral duties; the house of sacrifices was to be a house of prayer, for that was the substance and soul of all those services.

(2) He shows how they had abused the temple, and perverted the intention of it; *Ye have made it a den of thieves.* Markets are too often dens of thieves, so many are the corrupt and cheating practices in buying and selling; but markets in the temple are certainly so, for they rob God of his honour, the worst of thieves.

II. There, in the temple, *he healed the blind and the lame, v.* 14. When he had driven the buyers and sellers out of the temple, he invited the blind and lame into it. It is good coming to the temple, when Christ is there, who, as he shows himself jealous for the honour of his temple, in expelling those who profane it, so he shows himself gracious to those who humbly seek him. *The blind and the lame* were debarred David's palace, but were admitted into God's house. The temple was profaned and abused when it was made a market-place, but it was graced and honoured when it was made an hospital; to be doing good in God's house, is more honourable, and better becomes it, than to be getting money there. Christ's healing was a real answer to that question, *Who is this?* His works testified of him more than the *hosannas.*

There also he silenced the offence which the chief priests and scribes took at the acclamations with which he was attended, *v.* 15, 16. They that should have been most forward to give him honour, were his worst enemies. They were inwardly vexed at the wonderful things that he did. If they had any sense, they could not but own the miracle of them; and if any good nature, could not but be in love with the mercy of them: yet, because they were resolved to oppose him, for these they envied him, and bore him a grudge. They openly quarrelled at the children's hosannas; they thought that hereby an honour was given him, which did not belong to him. Proud men cannot bear that honour should be done to any but to themselves, and are uneasy at nothing more than at the just praises of deserving men. When Christ is most honoured, his enemies are most displeased.

Here we have him (*v.* 16), taking part with the children against priests and scribes.

(1) The children were in the temple. It is good to bring children betimes to the house of prayer, *for of such is the kingdom of heaven.* Let children be taught to keep up the form of godliness, it will help to lead them to the power of it. Christ has a tenderness for the lambs of his flock.

(2) They were there *crying Hosannas to the Son of David.* This they learned from those that were grown up. Little children say and do as they hear others say, and see others do; so easily do they imitate; and therefore great care must be taken to set them good examples, and no bad ones. Children will learn of those that are with them, either to curse and swear, or to pray and praise.

(3) Our Lord Jesus not only allowed it, but was very well pleased with it, and quoted a scripture which was fulfilled in it (Ps. viii. 2), or, at least, may be accommodated to it; *Out of the mouth of babes and sucklings thou hast perfected praise.* Christ is so far from being ashamed of the services of little children, that he takes particular notice of them (and children love to be taken notice of), and is well pleased with them. Praise is perfected out of the mouth of such; it has a peculiar tendency to the honour and glory of God for little children to join in his praises; the praise would be accounted defective and imperfect, if they had not their share in it; which is an encouragement for children to be good betimes, and to parents to teach them to be so. In the psalm it is, *Thou hast ordained strength. God perfecteth praise,* by *ordaining strength out of the mouths of babes and sucklings.* When great things are brought about by weak and unlikely instruments, God is thereby much honoured, for his *strength is perfected in weakness.* Christ, having thus silenced them, forsook them, *v.* 17. By repining at Christ's praises we drive him from us. *He left them* and he *went out of the city to Bethany,* which was a more quiet retired place; not so much that he might *sleep* undisturbed as that he might *pray* undisturbed.

Verses 18–22

I. Christ *returned in the morning to Jerusalem, v.* 18. Having work to do there, he returned.

II. *As he went, he hungered.* He was a man, and submitted to the infirmities of nature. He was a poor man, and had no present supply.

Christ *therefore* hungered, that he might have occasion to work this miracle and therein might give us an instance of his justice and his power.

1. See his *justice, v.* 19. He went to it, expecting fruit, because it had leaves; but, finding none, he sentenced it to a perpetual barrenness. All Christ's miracles hitherto were wrought for the good of men, and proved the power of his grace and blessing. Now, at last he would give a specimen of the power of his wrath and curse; yet this not on any man, woman or child, but on an inanimate tree; that is set forth for an example. This cursing of the barren fig-tree, represents the state of hypocrites in general; and so it teaches us, (1) That the fruit of fig-trees may justly be expected from those that have the leaves. Christ looks for the power of religion from those that make profession of it. (2) Christ's just expectations from flourishing professors are often frustrated and disappointed. Many have a name to live, and are not alive indeed. (3) The sin of barrenness is justly punished with the curse and plague of barrenness; *Let no fruit grow on thee henceforward for ever.* As one of the chiefest blessings, and which was the first, is, *Be fruitful;* so one of the saddest curses is, *Be no more fruitful.* (4) A false and hypocritical profession commonly withers in this world; the fig-tree that had no fruit, soon lost its leaves. Hypocrites may look plausible for a time, but, their profession will soon come to nothing; the gifts wither, common graces decay, and the falseness and folly of the pretender are manifested to all men. It represents the state of the nation and people of the Jews in particular; they were a fig-tree planted in Christ's way. They gave disappointment to our Lord Jesus. He came among them, expecting to find some fruit, something that would be pleasing to him. But his expectations were frustrated; he found nothing but leaves. They professed themselves expectant of the promised Messiah, but, when he came, they did not receive and entertain him. So we see the doom he passed upon them, *that never any fruit should grow upon them from henceforward for ever.* Never any good came from them (except the particular persons among them that believed), after they rejected Christ; they became worse and worse; blindness and hardness happened to them, and grew upon them. How soon did their fig-tree wither away, after they said, *His blood be on us, and on our children!*

2. See the *power* of Christ.

(1) The disciples admired the effect of Christ's curse (*v.* 20); *They marvelled.* They marvelled at the suddenness of the thing; *How soon is the fig-tree withered away!*

(2) Christ empowered them by faith to do the like (*v.* 21, 22). The description of this wonder-working faith; *If ye have faith, and doubt not.* Doubting of the power and promise of God is the great thing that spoils the efficacy and success of faith. As certain as the promise is, so confident our faith should be. The power and prevalence of it expressed figuratively; *If ye shall say to this mountain, Be thou removed, it shall be done.* This is a proverbial expression; intimating that we are to believe that nothing is impossible with God, and therefore that what he has promised shall certainly be performed, though to us it seem impossible. The ways and means of exercising this faith; *All things whatsover ye shall ask in prayer, believing ye shall receive.* Faith is the soul, prayer is the body; both together make a complete man for any service. Faith, if it be right, will excite prayer; and prayer is not right, if it do not spring from faith. This is the condition of our receiving—we must *ask in prayer, believing.* The requests of prayer shall not be denied; the expectations of faith shall not be frustrated. It is but ask and have, believe and receive; and what would we more? Observe, How comprehensive the promise is—*all things whatsoever ye shall ask. All things,* in general; *whatsoever,* brings it to particulars. Such is the folly of our unbelief, that, though we think we assent to promises in the general, yet we fly off when it comes to particulars, and therefore, it is thus copiously expressed, *All things whatsoever.*

Verses 23–27

Our Lord Jesus (like St. Paul after him) preached his gospel *with much contention;* and here, just before he died, we have him engaged in controversy. The great contenders with him, were, *the chief priests and the elders*, the judges of two distinct courts, the chief priests presided in the ecclesiastical court, the elders of the people were judges of the civil courts. These joined to attack Christ, thinking they should find or make him obnoxious either to the one or to the other. Here we have them disturbing him when he was preaching, *v.* 23. They would neither receive his instructions themselves, nor let others receive them.

I. As soon as he came into Jerusalem, he went to the temple, though he had been affronted there the day before, was there in the midst of enemies and in the mouth of danger.

II. In the temple he was teaching; he had called it *a house of prayer* (*v.* 13), and here we have him preaching there. Praying and preaching must go together, and neither must encroach upon, or jostle out, the other. To make up communion with God, we must not only speak to him in prayer, but hear what he has to say to us by his word; ministers must *give themselves both to the word and to prayer*.

III. When Christ was teaching the people, the priests and elders came upon him, and challenged him to produce his orders. Yet good was brought out of the evil, for hereby occasion was given to Christ to dispel the objections that were advanced against him; and, while his adversaries thought by their power to have silenced him, he by his wisdom silenced them.

1. How he was assaulted by their insolent demand; *By what authority doest thou these things, and who gave thee this authority?* Had they duly considered his miracles, and the power by which he wrought them, they needed not to have asked this question. It is good for all that take upon them to act with authority, to put this question to themselves, "Who gave us that authority?" They who run before their warrant, run without their blessing.

Christ had often said it, and proved it beyond contradiction, that he was *a teacher sent of God* (John iii. 2); yet, at this time of day, when that point had been so fully cleared and settled, they come to him with this question. (1) In the ostentation of their own power. How haughtily do they ask, *Who gave thee this authority?* Intimating that he could have no authority, because he had none from them. It is common for the greatest abusers of their power to be the most rigorous assertors of it, and to take a pride and pleasure in any thing that looks like the exercise of it. (2) It was to ensnare and entangle him. Should he refuse to answer this question, they would insinuate to the people, that his silence was a tacit confessing of himself to be a usurper: should he plead an authority from God, they would, as formerly, demand a sign from heaven, or accuse him of blasphemy for it.

2. How he answered this demand with another, which would help them to answer it themselves (*v.* 24, 25); *I also will ask you one thing.* He declined giving them a direct answer, lest they should take advantage against him; but answers them with a question.

How this question is concerning John's baptism, here put for his whole ministry; "Was this *from heaven, or of men?* One of the two it must be." This question was not at all shuffling, to evade theirs; but, if they answered this question, it would answer theirs: should they say, against their consciences, that John's baptism was of men, yet it would be easy to answer, *John did no miracle* (John x. 41), Christ did many; but should they say, as they could not but own, that John's baptism was from heaven then their demand was answered, for he bare testimony to Christ. If they refused to answer it, that would be a good reason why he should not offer proofs of his

authority to men that were obstinately prejudiced against the strongest conviction.

3. How they were hereby baffled and run aground.

(1) How *they reasoned with themselves*, not concerning the merits of the cause; no, their care was, how to make their part good against Christ. Two things they considered and consulted—their credit, and their safety; the same things which *they* principally aim at, who *seek their own things*.

[1] They consider their own credit, which they would endanger if they should own John's baptism to be of God; for then Christ would ask them, before all the people, *Why did ye not believe him?*

[2] They consider their own safety, if they should say that John's baptism was of men; *We fear the people, for all hold John as a prophet.* It seems, then, *First*, That the people had truer sentiments of John than the chief priests and the elders had. This people, of whom they said in their pride that they *knew not the law, and were cursed* (John vii. 49), it seems, knew the gospel, and were blessed. *Secondly*, That the chief priests and elders stood in awe of the common people, which is an evidence that things were in disorder among them. If they had kept their integrity, and done their duty, they had kept up their authority, and needed not to fear the people. *Thirdly*, That it is usually the temper even of common people, to be zealous for the honour of that which they account sacred and divine. Hence the hottest contests have been about holy things. *Fourthly*, That the chief priests and elders were kept from an open denial of the truth, not by the fear of God, but purely by the fear of the people. Many bad people would be much worse than they are, if they durst.

(2) How they replied to our Saviour, and so dropped the question. They fairly confessed *We cannot tell*; that is, "We will not"; The more shame for them. When they would not confess their knowledge, they were constrained to confess their ignorance. And observe, by the way, when they said, *We cannot tell*, they told a lie, for they knew that John's baptism was of God. There are many who are more afraid of the *shame* of lying than of the *sin*, and therefore scruple not to speak that which they knew to be false concerning their own thoughts and apprehensions, because in those things they know nobody can disprove them.

Thus Christ avoided the snare they laid for him, and justified himself in refusing to gratify them; *Neither tell I you by what authority I do these things.* They were not fit to be discoursed with concerning Christ's authority; for men of such a disposition could not be convinced of the truth. Those that imprison the truths they know, in unrighteousness are justly denied the further truths they enquire after. Take away the talent from him that buried it; those that *will not* see, *shall not* see.

Verses 28–32

As Christ instructed his disciples by parables, so sometimes he convinced his adversaries by parables, which bring reproofs more close, and make men, or ever they are aware, to reprove themselves. This Christ designs here, as appears by the first words (*v.* 28), *But what think you?*

I. The parable itself, which represents two sorts of persons; some that prove better than they promise; others that promise better than they prove.

1. They had both one and the same father. There are favours which all alike receive from him, and obligations which all alike lie under to him. Yes, and yet there is a vast difference between men's characters.

2. They had both the same command given them; *Son, go work today in my vineyard.* God sets his children to work, though they are all heirs. (1) The

work of religion, which we are called to engage in, is vineyard work, creditable, profitable, and pleasant. By the sin of Adam we were turned out to work upon the common, and to eat the herb of the field; but by the grace of our Lord Jesus we are called to work again in the vineyard. (2) The gospel call to work in the vineyard, requires present obedience; *Son, go work* today. We were not sent into the world to be idle, nor had we daylight given us to play by. (3) The exhortation speaketh unto us *as unto children, Son, go work*. It is the command of a Father, which carries with it both authority and affection, a Father that is very tender of *his Son that serves him*.

3. Their conduct was very different. One of the sons did better than he said, proved better than he promised. His answer was bad, but his actions were good. Here is the untoward answer that he gave to his father; he said, flat and plain, *I will not*. Excuses are bad, but downright denials are worse; yet such peremptory refusals do the calls of the gospel often meet with. Some love their ease, and will not work. Their hearts are so much upon their own fields, that they are not for working in God's vineyard. They love the business of the world better than the business of their religion. Here is the happy change of his mind, and of his way, upon second thoughts; *Afterward he repented, and went. Afterward he repented.* Repentance is μετανοία—*an after-wit*: and μεταμελεία—*an after-care*. Better late than never. When he repented, he went; that was the *fruit meet for repentance*. The only evidence of our repentance for our former resistance, is, immediately to comply, and set to work; and then what is past, shall be pardoned, and all shall be well. Our God *waits to be gracious*, and, notwithstanding our former follies, if we repent and mend, will favourably accept of us; blessed be God, we are under a covenant that leaves room for such a repentance. The other son said better than he did; his answer was good but his actions bad. To him the father *said likewise, v.* 30. The gospel call, though very different, is, in effect, the same to all. Observe,

(1) How fairly this other son promised; *He said, I go, sir.* He gives his father a title of respect, *sir*. He professes a ready obedience, *I go*; not, "I will go by and by," but, "Ready, sir, you may depend upon it, I go just now."

(2) How he failed in the performance; *He went not.* Saying and doing are two things; and many there are that say, and do not. Many with their mouth show much love, but their heart goes another way. Buds and blossoms are not fruit.

II. A general appeal upon the parable; *Whether of the twain did the will of his father? v.* 31. They both had their faults, one was rude, and the other was false. But the question is, Which was the better of the two, and the less faulty? And it was soon resolved; the first, because his actions were better than his words, and his latter end than his beginning. The tenor of the whole scripture gives us to understand that those are accepted as doing their Father's will, who, wherein they have missed it, are sorry for it, and do better.

III. A particular application of it to the matter in hand, *v.* 31, 32. The primary scope of the parable is, to show how the publicans and harlots entertained the doctrine, and submitted to the discipline, of John the Baptist, his forerunner, when the priests and elders slighted John the Baptist, and ran counter to the designs of his mission.

In Christ's application of this parable, observe,

1. How he proves that John's baptism was *from heaven, and not of men*. "If you *cannot* tell," saith Christ, "you *might* tell."

(1) By the scope of his ministry; *John came unto you in the way of righteousness*. Remember the rule

of trial, *By their fruits ye shall know them*; the fruits of their doctrines, the fruits of their doings. Now it was evident that John came *in the way of righteousness*. In his ministry, he taught people to repent, and to work the works of righteousness.

(2) By the success of his ministry; *The publicans and the harlots believed him*. If God had not sent John the Baptist, he would not have crowned his labours with such wonderful success. The people's profiting is the minister's best testimonial.

2. How he reproves them for their contempt of John's baptism. To shame them for it, he sets before them the faith, repentance, and obedience, of the publicans and harlots, which aggravated their unbelief and impenitence.

(1) The publicans and harlots were like the first son in the parable, from whom little of religion was expected. They promised little good, and those that knew them promised themselves little good from them. And yet many of them were wrought upon by the ministry of John.

(2) The scribes and Pharisees, the chief priests and elders, and indeed the Jewish nation in general, were like the other son that gave good works. A hypocrite is more hardly convinced and converted than a gross sinner. It was an aggravation of their unbelief, [1] That John was such an excellent person. The better the means are, the greater will the account be, if not improved. [2] That, when they saw the publicans and harlots go before them into the kingdom of heaven, they did not afterward repent and believe. Through the pride of their countenance, they would not seek after God, after Christ.

Verses 33–46

This parable plainly sets forth the sin and ruin of the Jewish nation.

I. We have here the privileges of the Jewish church, represented by the letting out of a vineyard to the husbandmen. Observe,

1. How God established a church for himself in the world. The kingdom of God upon earth is here compared to a vineyard, furnished with all things requisite to an advantageous management and improvement of it. (1) He planted this vineyard. The church is *the planting of the Lord*. The earth of itself produces thorns and briars; but vines must be planted. (2) He hedged it round about. God's church in the world is taken under his special protection. It is *a hedge round about*. He will not have his vineyard to lie in common, that those who are without, may thrust in at pleasure; not to lie at large that those who are within, may lash out at pleasure. (3) He *digged a wine-press and built a tower*. God instituted ordinances in his church, for the due oversight of it, and for the promoting of its fruitfulness.

2. How he entrusted these visible church-privileges with the nation and people of the Jews; he let it out to them as husbandmen, because he would try them, and be honoured by them. And then he *went into a far country*. When God had in a visible appearance settled the Jewish church at mount Sinai, he did in a manner withdraw; they had no more such open vision, but were left to the written word.

II. God's expectation of rent from these husbandmen, *v.* 34. It was a reasonable expectation. 1. His expectations were not hasty, but staid *till the time of the fruit drew near*. God waits to be gracious, that he may give us time. 2. They were not high. He sent his *servants to them*, to remind them of their duty, and of the rent-day, and to help them in gathering in the fruit, and making return of it. 3. They were not hard; it was only to *receive the fruits*. He did not demand more than they could make of it, but some fruit of that which he himself planted—an observance of the laws and statutes he gave them.

III. The husbandmen's baseness in abusing the messengers that were sent to them.

1. When he sent them his servants, they abused them. The calls and reproofs of the word, if they do not engage, will but exasperate. See here what hath all along been the lot of God's faithful messengers, more or less; (1) To suffer; *so persecuted they the prophets.* They not only despised and reproached them, but treated them as the worst of malefactors. If they that *live godly in Christ Jesus* themselves shall *suffer persecution,* much more they that press others to it. (2) It has been their lot to suffer from their Master's own tenants; they were the husbandmen that treated them thus.

Now see, [1] How God persevered in his goodness to them. He sent other servants, more than the first; though the first sped not, but were abused. [2] How they persisted in their wickedness. They *did unto them likewise.* One sin makes way for another of the same kind.

2. At length, he sent them his Son; we have seen God's goodness in sending, and their badness in abusing, the servants; but in the latter instance both these exceed themselves.

(1) Never did grace appear more gracious than in *sending the Son.* This was done *last of all.* He was sent last; for if nothing else would work upon them, surely this would. *Surely they will reverence my Son,* and therefore I will send him. If they will but reverence the Son, the point is gained. *Surely they will reverence my Son,* for he comes with more authority than the servants could.

(2) Never did sin appear more sinful than in the abusing of him.

[1] How it was plotted (v. 38); *When they saw the Son.* This touched their copyhold, and they were resolved to make one bold push for it, and to preserve their wealth and grandeur by taking *him* out of the way. *This is the heir, come, let us kill him.* Pilate and Herod, the princes of this world, *knew not.* But the *chief priests and elders* knew that *this was the heir,* and therefore, *Come, let us kill him.* Many are killed for what they have. The chief thing they envied him, and for which they hated and feared him, was his interest in the people. Therefore *let us kill him;* and then, as if the premises must of course go to the occupant, *let us seize on his inheritance.* They thought, if they could but get rid of this Jesus, they should carry all before them. While they thought to kill him, and so to seize on his inheritance, he went by his cross to his crown.

[2] How this plot was executed, v. 39. No wonder they soon *caught him, and slew him.* Nay, looking upon him to be as unworthy to live, as they were unwilling he should, *they cast him out of the vineyard,* and out of the holy city, for he was crucified *without the gate,* Heb. xiii. 12. As if *He* had been the shame and reproach, who was the greatest glory, of his people Israel.

IV. Here is their doom read out of their own mouths, v. 40, 41. He puts it to them, *When the Lord of the vineyard cometh, what will he do unto these husbandmen?* He puts it to themselves, for their stronger conviction. God's proceedings are so unexceptionable, that there needs but an appeal to sinners themselves concerning the equity of them. They could readily answer, *He will miserably destroy those wicked men.* Many can easily prognosticate the dismal consequences of other people's sins, that see not what will be the end of their own.

1. Our Saviour, in his question, supposes that *the lord of the vineyard will come,* and reckon with them. Persecutors say in their hearts, He *delays his coming.* Though he bear long with them, he will not bear always.

2. They, in their answer, suppose that it will be a terrible reckoning.

(1) That he will *miserably destroy those wicked men.* Let men never expect to do ill, and fare well. This was fulfilled upon the Jews, in that miserable destruction which was brought upon them by the Romans.

(2) That he will *let out his vineyard to other husbandmen.* God will have a church in the world. The unbelief and frowardness of man shall not make the word of God of no effect.

V. The further illustration and application of this by Christ himself, telling them, in effect, that they had rightly judged.

1. He illustrates it by referring to a scripture fulfilled in this (v. 42); *Did ye never read in the scriptures?* The scripture he quotes is Ps. cxviii. 22, 23, the same context out of which the children fetched their hosannas. The same word yields matter of praise and comfort to Christ's friends and followers, which speaks conviction and terror to his enemies. Such a two-edged sword is the word of God.

(1) The builders' rejecting of the stone is the same with the husbandmen's abusing of the son that was sent to them. They would not allow Christ a place in their building; they threw him aside as a despised broken vessel, a stone that would serve only for a stepping-stone, to be trampled upon.

(2) The advancing of this stone to be the head of the corner is the same with *letting out the vineyard to other husbandmen.* He who was rejected by the Jews was embraced by the Gentiles; and to that church, *Christ is all, and in all.*

(3) The hand of God was in all this; *This is the Lord's doing. It is marvellous in our eyes.* The wickedness of the Jews that rejected him is marvellous. The honour done him by the Gentile world is marvellous; that he whom men despised and abhorred, should be adored by kings! But *it is the Lord's doing.*

2. He applies it to them, and application is the life of preaching. He applies the sentence which they had passed (v. 41), and turns it upon themselves; not the former part of it, concerning the miserable destruction of the husbandmen (he could not bear to speak of that), but the latter part, of *letting out the vineyard to others.* Know then,

(1) That the Jews shall be unchurched; *The kingdom of God shall be taken from you.* To the Jews had long pertained *the adoption and the glory* (Rom. ix. 4); and the sacred trust of revealed religion, and bearing up of God's name in the world; but now it shall be so no longer. They were not only unfruitful in the use of their privileges, but opposed the gospel of Christ, and so forfeited them.

(2) That the Gentiles shall be taken in. Though his vine be plucked up in one place, he will find another to plant it in. The fall of Israel was the riches of the Gentiles. They shall bring forth the fruits better than the Jews had done. When he changes, it shall not be to his loss. He applies the scripture which he had quoted (v. 42), to their terror, v. 44. We have here the doom of two sorts of people. Some, through ignorance, stumble at Christ in his estate of humiliation; they, through their blindness and carelessness, fall on it, fall over it, and *they shall be broken.* The unbelief of sinners will be their ruin. Others oppose Christ, and bid defiance to him in his estate of exaltation, when this Stone is advanced to the head of the corner; and on them *it shall fall,* for they pull it on their own heads, and *it will grind them to powder.* Christ's kingdom will be a burthensome stone to all those that attempt to overthrow it, or heave it out of its place. None ever hardened his heart against God and prospered.

1. *They perceived that he spake of them* (v. 45), and that in what they said (v. 41) they had but read their

own doom. A guilty conscience needs no accuser.

2. *They sought to lay hands on him.* When those who hear the reproofs of the word, perceive that it speaks of them, if it do not do them a great deal of good, it will certainly do them a great deal of hurt.

3. They durst not do it, *for fear of the multitude, who took him for a prophet.* God has many ways of restraining the remainders of wrath, as he has of making that which breaks out redound to his praise.

CHAPTER 22

This chapter is a continuation of Christ's discourses in the temple. I. Instruction given, by the parable of the marriage-supper, concerning the rejection of the Jews (ver. 1–10), and the danger of hypocrisy in the profession of Christianity, ver. 11–14. II. Disputes, 1. Concerning paying tribute to Caesar, ver. 15–22. 2. Concerning the resurrection of the dead, and the future state, ver. 23–33. 3. Concerning the great commandment of the law, ver. 34–40. 4. Concerning the relation of the Messiah to David, ver. 41–46.

Verses 1–14

We have here the parable of the guests invited to *the wedding-feast.* In this it is said (*v.* 1), *Jesus answered,* not to what his opposers *said,* but to what they *thought.* Christ knows how to answer men's thoughts, for he is a discerner of them. This parable represents the gospel offer, and the entertainment it meets with.

I. Gospel preparations are here represented by a feast which a king made *at the marriage of his son.*

1. Here is *a marriage made for his son.* Christ is the Bridegroom, the church is the bride. The gospel covenant is a marriage covenant betwixt Christ and believers.

2. Here is *a dinner prepared for this marriage, v.* 4. All the blessings of the new covenant, pardon of sin, the favour of God, peace of conscience, the promises of the gospel, the comforts of the Spirit, and a well-grounded hope of eternal life. These are the preparations for this feast, a heaven upon earth now, and a heaven in heaven shortly.

(1) It is *a feast. Oxen and fatlings are killed* for this feast; no niceties, but substantial food; enough, and enough of the best. A feast was made for love, it is a reconciliation feast. It was made *for laughter,* it is a rejoicing feast. It was made for fulness; the design of the gospel was to fill every *hungry soul with good things.* It was made for fellowship.

(2) It is a *wedding feast.* Wedding feasts are usually rich, free, and joyful. The first miracle Christ wrought, was, to make plentiful provision for a wedding feast (John ii. 7); and surely then he will not be wanting in provision for his own wedding feast.

(3) It is a *royal wedding feast*; it is *the feast of a king,* at the marriage, not of a servant, but of a son. The provision made for believers in the covenant of grace, is such as it becomes *the King of glory* to give. He gives like himself; for he gives himself, a feast indeed for a soul.

II. Gospel calls and offers are represented by an invitation to this feast. Those that make a feast will have guests to grace the feast with. God's guests are the children of men. *Lord, what is man,* that he should be thus dignified!

Now, 1. The guests *are called, bidden* to the wedding. All that are within hearing of the joyful sound of the gospel, to them is the word of this invitation sent. None are excluded but those that exclude themselves.

2. The guests are called upon; for in the gospel there are not only gracious proposals made, but gracious persuasives. See how much Christ's heart is set upon the happiness of poor souls! He not only provides for them, in consideration of their want, but sends to them, in consideration of their weakness

and forgetfulness. When the invited guests were slack in coming, the king *sent forth other servants, v.* 4. One would think it had been enough to give men an intimation that they had leave to come, and should be welcome; that, during the solemnity of the wedding, the king kept open house. *Behold, the dinner is prepared, the oxen and fatlings are killed, and all things are ready;* pardon is ready, peace is ready, comfort is ready; the promises are ready, and heaven, at last, is ready to receive us. Is all this ready; and shall we be unready? Is all this preparation made for us; and is there any room to doubt of our welcome?

III. The cold treatment which the gospel of Christ often meets with among the children of men, represented by the cold treatment that this message met with and the hot treatment that the messengers met with.

1. The message was basely slighted (*v.* 3); *They would not come.* The reason why sinners come not to Christ and salvation by him is, not because they *cannot,* but because *they will not.* But this was not all (*v.* 5); *they made light of it;* they thought it not worth coming for; they could feast as well at home. Multitudes perish eternally through mere carelessness, who have not any direct aversion, but a prevailing indifference, to the matters of their souls.

And the reason why *they made light of the marriage feast* was, because they had other things that they minded more, and had more mind to; *they went their ways, one to his farm, and another to his merchandise.* None turn their back on the feast, but given some plausible excuse or other, Luke xiv. 18. The country people have their farms to look after, about which there is always something or other to do; the town's people must tend their shops, and be constant upon the exchange. It is true, that both farmers and merchants must be diligent in their business, but not so as to keep them from making religion their main business. Both the city and the country have their temptations, the merchandise in the one, and the farms in the other; so that, whatever we have of the world in our hands, our care must be to keep it out of our hearts, lest it come between us and Christ.

2. The messengers were basely abused; *The remnant, the scribes and Pharisees, and chief priests;* these were the persecutors, these *took the servants, and treated them spitefully, and slew them.* In the application of the parable, it was matter of fact. The prophets and John the Baptist had been thus abused already, and the apostles and ministers of Christ must count upon the same.

IV. The utter ruin that was coming upon the Jewish church and nation is here represented by the revenge which the king, in wrath, took on these insolent recusants (*v.* 7); *He was wroth.*

1. What was the crying sin that brought the ruin; it was their being *murderers.* He does not say, he destroyed those *despisers of his call,* but *those murderers of his servants*; as if God were more jealous for the lives of his ministers than for the honour of his gospel. Persecution of Christ's faithful ministers fills the measure of guilt more than anything.

2. What was the ruin itself, that was coming; *He sent forth his armies.* The Roman armies were his armies, of his raising. God is the Lord of men's hosts, and makes what use he pleases of them, to serve his own purposes. It is set forth for an example to all that should oppose Christ and his gospel.

V. The bringing in of the Gentiles, is here represented by the furnishing of the feast with guests *out of the highways, v.* 8–10.

Here is, 1. The complaint of the master of the feast concerning those that were first bidden (*v.* 8), *The wedding is ready, but they which were bidden,* that is, the Jews, *were not worthy,* they were utterly unworthy, and had forfeited all the privileges they were invited to. It is not owing to God, that sinners perish, but to themselves.

2. The commission he gave to the servants, to invite other guests. The inhabitants of the *city* (v. 7) had refused; *Go into the highways* then; into *the way of the Gentiles*, which at first they were to decline, *ch.* x. 5. Thus by the fall of the Jews salvation is come to the Gentiles. Christ will have a *kingdom in the world*, though many reject the grace, and resist the power, of that kingdom. The offer of Christ and salvation to the Gentiles was, (1) Unlooked for and unexpected; such a surprise it would be to wayfaring men upon the road to be met with an invitation to a wedding feast. To the Gentiles it was all new, what they had never heard of before (Acts xvii. 19, 20), and, consequently, what they could not conceive of as belonging to them. (2) It was universal and undistinguishing; *Go, and bid as many as you find.* The highways are public places. "Ask them that go by the way, ask anybody, tell them all, that they shall be welcome, whoever will, let him come, without exception."

3. The success of this second invitation (v. 10); *They gathered together all, as many as they found.* The design of the gospel is, (1) To gather souls together; not the nation of the Jews only, but *all the children of God* who were *scattered abroad* (John xi. 52), *the other sheep that were not of that fold,* John x. 16. (2) To gather them together to the wedding-feast to partake of the privileges of the new covenant. Where the dole is, there will the poor be gathered together.

Now the guests that were gathered were a multitude, *all, as many as they found;* so many, that the guest-chamber was filled. A mixed multitude, *both bad and good*; some that before their conversion were sober and well-inclined; others that had run to an excess of riot; *Such were some of you;* or, some that after their conversion proved bad; others that were upright and sincere, and proved of the right class. Ministers, in casting the net of the gospel, enclose *both good* fish *and bad*.

VI. The case of hypocrites, who are *in* the church, but not *of* it, is represented by *the guest that had not on a wedding garment*; one of the bad that were gathered in. Concerning this hypocrite observe,

1. His discovery, how he was found out, v. 11.

(1) *The king came in to see the guests*, to bid those welcome who came prepared, and to turn those out who came otherwise. Let this be a warning to us against hypocrisy, that disguises will shortly be stripped off, and an encouragement to us in our sincerity, that God is a witness to it. This hypocrite was never discovered to be without *a wedding garment*, till *the king himself came in to see the guests.* It is God's prerogative to know who are sound at heart in their profession, and who are not. We may be deceived in men, either one way or other; but He cannot.

(2) As soon as he came in, *He saw there a man which had not on a wedding garment;* he soon had his eye upon him; there is no hope of being hid in a crowd from the arrests of divine justice; he had not on a wedding garment; he had not his best clothes on. If the gospel be the wedding feast, then the wedding garment is a frame of heart, and a course of life agreeable to the gospel. This man was not naked, or in rags; some raiment he had, but not a wedding garment. Those, and those only, who *put on the Lord Jesus*, and to whom he is all in all, have the wedding garment.

2. His trial (v. 12). How he was arraigned (v. 12); *Friend, how camest thou in hither, not having a wedding garment?* A startling question to one that was priding himself in the place he securely possessed at

the feast. *Friend!* That was a cutting word; a seeming friend, under manifold ties and obligations to be a friend. *How camest thou in hither?* He does not chide the servants for letting him in, but he checks his presumption in crowding in, when he knew that his heart was not upright. Despised sabbaths and abused sacraments must be reckoned for. "How camest thou to the Lord's table, at such a time, unhumbled and unsanctified? *How camest thou in?* Not by the door, but *some other way, as a thief and a robber.*" It is good for those that have a place in the church, often to put it to themselves, "How came I in hither? Have I a wedding-garment?" If we would thus *judge ourselves, we should not be judged.* How he was convicted; *he was speechless:* the man stood mute, upon his arraignment, being convicted and condemned by his own conscience. They who never heard a word of this wedding feast will have more to say for themselves; their sin will be more excusable than theirs who came to the feast without the wedding garment, and so sin against the clearest light and dearest love.

3. His sentence (v. 13); *Bind him hand and foot,* &c.

(1) He is ordered to be pinioned, as condemned malefactors are, to be manacled and shackled. These that will not work and walk as they should, may expect to be bound hand and foot. They can neither resist nor outrun their punishment.

(2) He is ordered to be carried off from the wedding feast; *Take him away.* This bespeaks the punishment of loss in the other world; they shall be taken away from the king, from the kingdom, from the wedding feast. Those that walk unworthy of their christianity, forfeit all the happiness they presumptuously laid claim to.

(3) He is ordered into a doleful dungeon; *Cast him into utter darkness.* Hell is utter darkness, it is darkness out of heaven, the land of light; or it is extreme darkness, darkness to the last degree, without the least ray or spark of light, or hope of it. *There shall be weeping, and gnashing of teeth. Weeping,* an expression of great sorrow and anguish; and the *gnashing of teeth* is an expression of the greatest rage and indignation.

Lastly, The parable is concluded with that remarkable saying which we had before (*ch.* xx. 16), *Many are called, but few are chosen,* v. 14. Many called to the wedding feast, but few chosen to the wedding garment.

Verses 15–22

In these verses, we have him attacked by the Pharisees and Herodians with a question about paying tribute to Cæsar.

I. What the design was; *They took counsel to entangle him in his talk.* Now he is set upon from another quarter; the Pharisees will try whether they can deal with him by their learning in the law. It is in vain for the best and wisest of men to think that, by their ingenuity, or interest, or industry, or even by their innocence and integrity, they can escape the hatred and ill will of bad men, or screen themselves from *the strife of tongues.* See how unwearied the enemies of Christ and his kingdom are in their opposition!

1. *They took counsel.* The more there is of contrivance and consultation about sin, the worse it is. The more there is of the wicked wit in the contrivance of a sin, the more there is of the wicked will in the commission of it.

2. That which they aimed at was *to entangle him in his talk.* They saw him free and bold in speaking his mind, and hoped by that to get an advantage against him. It has been the old practice of Satan's agents and emissaries, to make a man an offender for

a word, a word misplaced, or mistaken, or misunderstood; a word, though innocently designed, yet perverted by strained innuendos.

There are two ways by which the enemies of Christ might be revenged on him, and be rid of him; either by law or by force. By law they could not do it, unless they could make him obnoxious to the civil government. By force they could not do it, unless they could make him obnoxious to the people, but the people took Christ for a Prophet, and therefore his enemies could not raise the mob against him. The design was, to bring him into such a dilemma, that he must make himself liable to the displeasure either of the Jewish multitude, or of the Roman magistrates; let him take which side of the question he will. So they will gain their point, and make his own tongue to fall upon him.

II. The question which they put to him, *v.* 16, 17.

1. The persons they employed; they did not go themselves, but they sent their disciples, who would look less like tempters, and more like learners. Wicked men will never want wicked instruments to be employed in carrying on their wicked counsels. With them they sent the Herodians, a party among the Jews, who made it their business to reconcile people to that government, and pressed all to pay their tribute. They went with the Pharisees to Christ, with this blind upon their plot, that while the Herodians demanded the tax, and the Pharisees denied it, they were both willing to refer it to Christ, as a proper Judge to decide the quarrel. Now, if he should countenance the paying of tribute, the Pharisees would incense the people against him; if he should discountenance or disallow it, the Herodians would incense the government against him. It is common for those that oppose one another, to continue in an opposition to Christ and his kingdom. Samson's foxes looked several ways, but met in one firebrand.

2. The preface; it was highly complimentary to our Sáviour (*v.* 16); *Master, we know that thou art true, and teachest the way of God in truth.* Note, It is a common thing for the most spiteful projects to be covered with the most specious pretences. Had they come to Christ with the most serious enquiry, and the most sincere intention, they could not have expressed themselves better. What they said of Christ was right that Jesus Christ was a faithful Teacher; *Thou art true, and teachest the way of God in truth.* He is the Truth itself. As for his doctrine, the matter of his teaching was the way of God that leads to happiness. The manner of it was in truth; he showed people *the right way.* That he was a bold Reprover. In preaching, he *cared not for any*; he valued no man's frowns or smiles, he did not court, he did not dread, either the great or the many. He *reproved with equity*, and never with partiality. Though what they said was true for the matter of it, yet there was nothing but flattery and treachery in the intention of it. They called him *Master*, when they were contriving to treat him as the worst of malefactors; they pretended respect for him, when they intended mischief against him; and they affronted his wisdom when they imagined that they could impose upon him with these pretences.

3. The proposal of the case; *What thinkest thou?* As if they had said, "Many men are of many minds in this matter; it is a case which relates to practice, and occurs daily; let us have thy thoughts freely in the matter, *Is it lawful to give tribute to Cæsar, or not?*" This implies a further question; Has Cæsar a right to demand it?

Now the question was, Whether it was lawful to pay these taxes voluntarily or, Whether they should not insist upon the ancient liberty of their nation, and rather suffer themselves to be distrained upon?

However, by this question they hoped to entangle Christ, and, which way soever he resolved it, to expose him to the fury either of the jealous Jews, or of the jealous Romans.

III. The breaking of this snare by the wisdom of the Lord Jesus.

1. He discovered it (*v.* 18); *He perceived their wickedness.* A temptation perceived is half conquered, for our greatest danger lies from snakes under the green grass; *and he said, Why tempt ye me, ye hypocrites?* Whatever vizard the hypocrite puts on, our Lord Jesus sees through it. He cannot be imposed upon, as we often are, by flatteries and fair pretences. *Why tempt ye me, ye hypocrites?* Those that presume to tempt Christ will certainly find him too hard for them, and that he is of more piercing eyes than not to see, and more pure eyes than not to hate the disguised wickedness of hypocrites, that dig deep to hide their counsel from him.

2. He evaded it. (Such captious malicious questions deserve a reproof, not a reply): but our Lord Jesus gave a full answer to their question, and introduced it by an argument sufficient to support it.

(1) He forced them, ere they were aware, to confess Cæsar's authority over them, *v.* 19, 20. In dealing with those that are captious, it is good to give our reasons, and, if possible, reasons of confessed cogency, before we give our resolutions. Thus the evidence of truth may silence gainsayers by surprise, while they only stood upon their guard against the truth itself, not against the reason of it; *Show me the tribute-money.* The Romans demanded their tribute in their own money, which was current among the Jews at that time: that therefore is called the *tribute-money.* *A penny*, a Roman penny in silver, the most common piece then in use: it was stamped with the emperor's image and superscription, which was the warrant of the public faith for the value of the pieces so stamped.

Christ asked them, *Whose image is this?* They owned it to be Cæsar's.

(2) From thence he inferred the lawfulness of paying tribute to Cæsar (*v.* 21); *Render therefore to Cæsar the things that are Cæsar's;* not, "*Give* it him" (as they expressed it, *v.* 17), but, "Restore it; if Cæsar fill the purses, let Cæsar command them. When once a relation is admitted, the duty of it must be performed. *Render to all their due*, and particularly *tribute to whom tribute is due.*" Now by this answer, No offence was given. He did not interpose as a Judge or a Divider in matters of this nature. Christ discusses not the emperor's title, but enjoins a peaceable subjection to *the powers that be.* The government therefore had no reason to take offence at his determination, but to thank him, for it would strengthen Cæsar's interest with the people, who held him for a Prophet. As to the people, the Pharisees could not accuse him to them, because they themselves had, before they were aware, yielded the premises. Though truth seeks not a fraudulent concealment, yet it sometimes needs a prudent management, to prevent the offence which may be taken at it. His adversaries were reproved. Many excuse themselves from that which they must do, by arguing whether they may do it or no. They all withheld from God his dues, and are reproved for that. His disciples were instructed.

First, That the Christian religion is no enemy to civil government, but a friend to it.

Secondly, It is the duty of subjects to tender to magistrates that which, according to the laws of their country, is their due. The higher powers, being entrusted with the public welfare, are entitled, in consideration thereof, to a just proportion of the public wealth. It is doubtless a greater sin to cheat the government than to cheat a private person. My coat is my coat, by the law of man; but he is a thief, by the law of God, that takes it from me.

Thirdly, We must remember withal to render to God the things that are God's. If our purses be Cæsar's, our consciences are God's; we must render to God that which is his due, out of our time and out of our estates; from them he must have his share as well as Cæsar his; and if Cæsar's commands interfere with God's *we must obey God rather than men*.

Lastly, Observe how they were nonplussed by this answer; they *marvelled, and left him, and went their way*, *v.* 22. They admired his sagacity in discovering and evading a snare which they thought so craftily laid. One would think they should have marvelled and followed him; no, they marvelled and left him. There are many in whose eyes Christ is marvellous, and yet not precious. They admire his wisdom, but will not be guided by it. *They went their way*, as persons ashamed, and made an inglorious retreat. They quitted the field. There is nothing got by contending with Christ.

Verses 23–33

We have here Christ's dispute with the Sadducees concerning the resurrection.

I. The opposition which the Sadducees made to a very great truth of religion; they say, *There is no resurrection*. They lie under heavy censures among the writers of their own nation, as men of base and debauched conversations. They were the fewest in number of all the sects among the Jews, but generally persons of some rank. They said, There is no future state, no life after this; that, when the body dies, the soul is annihilated, and dies with it. They maintained, that, except God, there is no spirit (Acts xxiii. 8). The Pharisees and Sadducees were contrary to each other, and yet confederates against Christ.

II. The objection they made against the truth, which was taken from a supposed case of a woman that had seven husbands successively; now they take it for granted, that, if there be a resurrection, it must be a return to such a state as this we are now in; and if so, it is an invincible absurdity for this woman, in the future state to have seven husbands, or else an insuperable difficulty which of them should have her, he whom she had first, or he whom she had last, or he whom she loved best, or he whom she lived longest with.

1. They suggest the law of Moses in this matter (*v.* 24), that the next of kin should marry the widow of him that died childless (Deut. xxv. 5). It was a political law to preserve the distinction of families and inheritances.

2. They put a case upon this statute. If it had not really occurred, yet possibly it might. Now this case supposes,

(1) The desolations that death sometimes makes in families. It often sweeps away a whole fraternity in a little time.

(2) The obedience of these seven brothers to the law. The seventh, who ventured last to marry the widow (many a one would say) was a *bold* man. I would say, if he did it purely in obedience to God, he was a *good* man, and one that made conscience of his duty.

But, *last of all, the woman died also*. Survivorship is but a reprieve. Death's bitter cup goes round, and, sooner or later, we must all pledge in it.

3. They propose a doubt upon this case (*v.* 28); "*In the resurrection, whose wife shall she be of the seven?* You cannot tell whose; and therefore we must conclude *there is no resurrection*." The Pharisees, who professed to believe a resurrection, had very gross and carnal notions concerning the future state; expecting to find there the delights and pleasures of

the animal life, which perhaps drove the Sadducees to deny the thing itself. While those that are erroneous deny the truth, those that are superstitious betray it to them. Let truth be set in a clear light, and then it appears in its full strength.

III. Christ's answer to this objection.

1. He reproves their ignorance (*v.* 29); *Ye do err*. Those do greatly err, in the judgment of Christ, who deny the resurrection and a future state. Here Christ reproved with the meekness of wisdom, and is not so sharp upon them (whatever was the reason) as sometimes he was upon the chief priests and elders; *Ye do err, not knowing*. Ignorance is the cause of error; those that are in the dark, miss their way. Ingorance is the cause of error about the resurrection and the future state. *What* it is in its particular instances, the wisest and best know not; it doth not yet appear what we shall be, it is a glory that is to be revealed. But that *is* a thing about which we are not left in the dark, blessed be God, we are not. *They know not the power of God;* which would lead men to infer that there *may be a* resurrection and a future state. The ignorance, disbelief, or weak belief, of God's power, is at the bottom of many errors, particularly theirs who deny the resurrection. When we are told of the soul's existence and agency in a state of separation from the body, we are ready to say, *How can these things be?* If a man die, shall he live again? And vain men, because they cannot comprehend the *way* of it, question the *truth* of it. This therefore we must fasten upon, in the first place, that God is omnipotent, and can do what he will; and then no room is left for doubting but that he will do what he has promised. His power far exceeds the power of nature. *They know not the scriptures*, which decidedly affirm that there shall be a resurrection and a future state. Now the scriptures speak plainly, that the soul is immortal, and there is another life after this. Christ rose again *according to the scriptures* (1 Cor. xv. 3); and so shall we. Ignorance of the scripture is the rise of abundance of mischief.

2. He rectifies their mistake and (*v.* 30) corrects those gross ideas which they had of the resurrection and a future state. It is not like the state we are now in upon earth; *They neither marry, nor are given in marriage*. In our present state marriage is necessary. All civilised nations have had a sense of the obligation of the marriage covenant. But, in the resurrection, there is no occasion for marriage. In heaven, *where there shall be no more deaths* (Rev. xxi. 4), there need be no more births.

It is like the state angels are now in, in heaven; *They are as the angels of God in heaven*. Man in his creation was *made a little lower than the angels* (Ps. viii. 5); but in his complete redemption and renovation will be as the angels; pure and spiritual as the angels, knowing and loving, ever praising God like them and with them. We should *therefore* desire and endeavour to do the will of God now as the angels do it in heaven, because we hope shortly to be like the angels who always behold our Father's face.

IV. Christ's argument to confirm this great truth; the matters being of great concern, he did not think it enough to discover the fallacy and sophistry of the objections, but backed the truth with a solid argument.

1. Whence he fetched his argument—from the scripture. *It is written* is Goliath's sword. *Have ye not read that which was spoken to you by God?* What the scripture speaks God speaks. What was spoken to Moses was spoken to us. It concerns us to read and hear what God hath spoken, because it is spoken to us. The latter prophets have more express proofs of a future state than the law of Moses has. No express revelation of it is made by the law of Moses; because so much of that law was peculiar to that people; but

our Saviour finds a very solid argument for the resurrection even in the writings of Moses. Much scripture treasure lies underground, that must be digged for.

2. What his argument was (*v.* 32); *I am the God of Abraham.* This was not an express proof, and yet it was really a conclusive argument. Consequences from scripture, if rightly deduced, must be received as scripture,; for it was written for those that have the use of reason.

Now the drift of the argument is to prove,

(1) That there is a future state, another life after this. This is proved from what God said; *I am the God of Abraham.* For God to be anyone's God supposes some very extraordinary privileges and happiness. The God *of* Israel is a God *to* Irsael, a spiritual Benefactor; an all-sufficient Benefactor, a God that is enough, a complete Good, and an eternal Benefactor; for he is himself an everlasting God, and will be to those that are in covenant with him an everlasting Good. It is manifest that these good men had no such extraordinary happiness, in *this* life, as might look anything like the accomplishments of so great a word as that. They were strangers in the land of promise; they had not a foot of ground of their own but a burying-place, which directed them to look for something beyond this life. In present enjoyments they came far short of their neighbours that were strangers to this covenant. What was there in this world to distinguish them from other people, any whit proportionable to the dignity and distinction of this covenant? Therefore there must certainly be a future state, in which, as God will ever live to be eternally rewarding, so Abraham, Isaac, and Jacob, will ever live to be eternally rewarded.

(2) That the soul is immortal, and the body shall rise again, to be united; if the former point be gained, these will follow; but they are likewise proved by considering the time when God spoke this; it was to Moses at the bush, long after Abraham, Isaac, and Jacob were dead and buried; and yet God saith, not, "*I was,*" or "*have been,*" but, *I am the God of Abraham.* Now '*God is not the God of the dead, but of the living.* Which proves the immortality of the soul in a state of bliss; and that, by consequence, infers the resurrection of the body.

Lastly, We have the issue of this dispute. The Sadducees were *put to silence* (*v.* 34), and so put to shame. But the multitude *were astonished at his doctrine, v.* 33. 1. Because it was new to them. They had sorry scribes, or this had been no news to them. 2. Because it had something in it very good and great. Truth often shows the brighter, and is the more admired, for its being opposed.

Verses 34–40

I. The combination of the Pharisees against Christ, *v.* 34. They heard *that he had put the Sadducees to silence*; and they were *gathered together,* not to return him the thanks of their party, for his effectually asserting and confirming of the truth against the Sadducees, but to *tempt him,* in hopes to get the reputation of puzzling him who had puzzled the Sadducees. They were more vexed that Christ was honoured, than pleased that the Sadducees were silenced. It is an instance of Pharisaical envy and malice, to be displeased at the maintaining of a confessed truth, when it is done by those we do not like.

II. The lawyer's question, which he put to Christ. The lawyers were students in, and teachers of the law of Moses, as the scribes were. This lawyer *asked him a question, tempting him*; not with any design to ensnare him, as appears by St. Mark's relation of the story, where we find that this was he to whom Christ said, *Thou art not far from the kingdom of God,* Mark xii. 34, but only to see what he would say, and to draw on discourse with him, to satisfy his own and his friend's curiosity.

1. The question was, *Master,* which is the greatest commandment of the law? It is true, there are some commands that are the principles of the oracles of God, more extensive and inclusive than others.

2. The design was to try him not so much his knowledge as his judgment. It was a question disputed among the critics in the law. Now they would try what Christ said to this question; and if he should magnify one commandment, they would reflecton him as vilifying the rest. The question was harmless enough; and it appears by comparing Luke x. 27, 28, that it was an adjudged point among the lawyers, that the *love of God* and our *neighbour* is the great commandment, and the sum of all the rest.

III. Christ's answer to this question. Now Christ recommends to us as the great commandments, not those which are so exclusive of others, but, which are *therefore* great because inclusive of others. Observe,

1. Which these great commandments are (*v.* 37–39); the love of God and our neighbour, which are the spring and foundation of all the rest, which (these being supposed) will follow of course.

(1) All the law is fulfilled in one word, and that is, *love.* See Rom. xiii. 10. All obedience begins in the affections, and nothing in religion is done right, that is not done there first. Love is the leading affection, and therefore that, as the main fort, is to be first secured and garrisoned for God. Man is a creature cut out for love; thus therefore is the law written in the heart, that it is a *law of love.* Love is a short and sweet word; and, if that be *the fulfilling of the law,* surely the yoke of the command is very easy. Love is the rest and satisfaction of the soul; if we walk in this good old way, we shall find rest.

(2) The *love of God* is the first and great commandment of all. Now God, being good infinitely, originally, and eternally, is to be loved in the first place, and nothing loved beside him, but what is loved for him. *Love* is the first and great thing that God demands from us, and therefore the first and great thing that we should devote to him.

Now here we are directed,

[1] To love God as ours; *Thou shalt love the Lord thy God* as thine. To love God as ours is to love him because he is ours, and to conduct ourselves to him as ours, with obedience to him, and dependence on him.

[2] To love him *with all our heart, and soul, and mind.* Some make these to signify one and the same thing, to love him with all our powers; others distinguish them; the heart, soul, and mind, are the will, affections, and understanding. Our love of God must be a sincere love, and not in word and tongue only. It must be a strong love, we must love him in the most intense degree. It must be a singular and superlative love, we must love him more than anything else; this way the stream of our affections must entirely run. The heart must be united to love God, in opposition to a divided heart. All our love is too little to bestow upon him, and therefore all the powers of the soul must be engaged for him, and carried out toward him. *This is the first and great commandment;* for obedience to this is the spring of obedience to all the rest; which is only acceptable, when it flows from love.

(3) *To love our neighbour as ourselves* is the *second great commandment* (*v.* 39); *It is like unto that first;* it is inclusive of all the precepts of the second table, as that is of the first. It is *like* it, for it is founded upon it, and flows from it. It is implied, that we do, and should, love ourselves. There is a self-love which is corrupt, and it must be put off and mortified: but there is a self-love which is natural, and the rule of the greatest duty, and it must be preserved and

sanctified. We must love ourselves, that is, we must have a due regard to the dignity of our own natures, and a due concern for the welfare of our own souls and bodies. It is prescribed, that we *love our neighbour as ourselves.* We must honour and esteem all men, and must wrong and injure none; and, as we have opportunity, must do good to all. We must love our neighbour as ourselves, as truly and sincerely as we love ourselves, and in the same instances; nay, in many cases we must deny ourselves for the good of our neighbour.

2. Observe what the weight and greatness of these commandments is (*v.* 40); *On these two commandments hang all the law and the prophets.* All hang upon the law of love; take away this, and all falls to the ground, and comes to nothing. Love is the more excellent way. This is the spirit of the law, which animates it; it is the root and spring of all other duties, the compendium of the whole Bible, not only of the law and the prophets, but of the gospel too. All hangs on these two commandments. *Love never faileth.* Into these two great commandments therefore let our hearts be delivered as into a mould; in the defence and evidence of these let us spend our zeal, and not in notions, names, and strifes of words. To the commanding power of these let everything else be made to bow.

Verses 41–46

Many questions the Pharisees had asked Christ, but now let him ask them a question; and he will do it when they are gathered together, *v.* 41. He took them all together, when they were in confederacy and consulting against him. God delights to baffle his enemies when they most strengthen themselves; he gives them all the advantages they can wish for, and yet conquers them.

I. Christ proposes a question to them, which they could easily answer; it was a question in their own catechism; "*What think ye of Christ? Whose Son is he?*" This they could easily answer, *The Son of David.* It was the common periphrasis of the Messiah; they called him *the Son of David.*

What think ye of Christ? They had put questions to him, one after another, out of the law; but he comes and puts a question to them upon the promise. Many are so full of the law, that they forget Christ, as if their duties would save them without his merit and grace. It concerns each of us seriously to ask ourselves, What think we of Christ? Some think not of him at all, some think meanly, and some think hardly, of him; but *to them that believe he is precious*; and *how precious then are the thoughts of him!*

II. He starts a difficulty upon their answer, which they could not so easily solve, *v.* 43–45. Many can so readily affirm the truth, that they think they have knowledge enough to be proud of, who, when they are called to confirm the truth, show they have ignorance enough to be ashamed of. The objection Christ raised was, *If Christ be David's son, how then doth David, in spirit, call him Lord?* He did not hereby design to ensnare them, as they did him, but to instruct them.

1. It is easy to see that David calls Christ *Lord.* Now, to prove that David, in spirit, called Christ *Lord,* he quotes Ps. cx. 1, which psalm the scribes themselves understood of Christ. It is a prophetical summary of the doctrine of Christ, it describes him executing the offices of a Prophet, Priest, and King.

Christ quotes the whole verse, which shows the Redeemer in his exaltation; (1) *Sitting at the right hand of God.* His sitting denotes both rest and rule; his sitting at God's right hand denotes superlative honour and sovereign power. (2) Subduing his enemies. There he shall sit, till they be all made either his friends or his footstool.

But that which this verse is quoted for is, that David calls the Messiah *his Lord; the Lord,* Jehovah, *said unto my Lord.*

2. It is not so easy for those who believe not the Godhead of the Messiah, to clear this from an absurdity, if Christ be David's son. If David call him *Lord,* that is laid down (*v.* 45) as the *more evident truth.* We must hold this fast, that he is David's Lord, and by that explain his being David's son.

III. We have here the success of this gentle trial which Christ made of the Pharisees' knowledge, in two things.

1. It puzzled them (*v.* 46); *No man was able to answer him a word.* Either it was their ignorance that they did not know, or their impiety that they would not own, the Messiah to be God; which truth was the only key to unlock this difficulty. Christ, as God, was David's *Lord*; and Christ, as Man, was David's *son.* This he did not now himself explain, but reserved it till the proof of it was completed by his resurrection.

2. It silenced them, and all others that sought occasion against him, *Neither durst any man, from that day forth, ask him any more questions.* Many are convinced, that are not converted, by the word. Had these been converted, they would have asked him more questions, especially that great question, What must we do to be saved? But since they could not gain their point, they would have no more to do with him.

<h2 style="text-align:center">CHAPTER 23</h2>

In the foregoing chapter, we had our Saviour's discourses with the scribes and Pharisees; here we have his discourse concerning them. I. He allows their office, ver. 2, 3. II. He warns his disciples not to imitate their hypocrisy and pride, ver. 4-12. III. He exhibits a charge against them for divers high crimes and misdemeanours; and to each article he prefixes a woe, ver. 13-33. IV. He passes sentence upon Jerusalem, ver. 34-39.

Verses 1–12

We find not Christ, in all his preaching, so severe upon any sort of people as upon these *scribes and Pharisees.* Yet these were the idols and darlings of the people, who thought, if but two men went to heaven, one would be a Pharisee. Now Christ directs his discourse here *to the multitude, and to his disciples* (*v.* 1), to rectify their mistakes concerning these scribes and Pharisees, by painting them out in their true colours. It is good to know the true characters of men, that we may not be imposed upon by great and mighty names, titles, and pretensions to power. Even the disciples need these cautions; for good men are apt to have their eyes dazzled with worldly pomp.

I. Christ allows their office as expositors of the law; *The scribes and Pharisees sit in Moses' seat* (*v.* 2), as public teachers and interpreters of the law. They were as judges, or a bench of justices; teaching and judging seem to be equivalent. Or, we may apply it, not to the Sanhedrim, but to the other Pharisees and scribes, that expounded the law, and taught the people how to apply it to particular cases. Moses had those in every city (so the expression is, Acts xv. 21), who preached him; this was their office, and it was just and honourable; it was requisite that there should be some at whose mouth the people might *enquire the law.* Many a good place is filled with bad men. The men are not so much honoured by the seat as the seat is dishonoured by the men. Good and useful offices and powers are not *therefore* to be condemned and abolished, because they fall sometimes into the hands of bad men, who abuse them.

Hence he infers (*v.* 3), "*Whatsoever they bid you observe, that observe and do.* As far as they *sit in Moses' seat,* that is, read and preach the law that was given by Moses, so far you must hearken to them." Now Christ would have the people to make use of the helps they gave them for the understanding of the scripture, and do accordingly. As long as their comments did illustrate the text, did make plain, and not *make void, the commandment of God*; so far they must be observed and obeyed. We must not think the worse of good truths for their being preached by bad ministers; nor of good laws for their being executed by bad magistrates. Though it is most desirable to have our food brought by angels, yet, if God send it to us by ravens, if it be good and wholesome, we must take it, and thank God for it.

II. He condemns the men. He had ordered the multitude to do as they taught; not to do as they did, to beware of their leaven; *Do not ye after their works.* As we must not swallow corrupt doctrines for the sake of any laudable practices of those that teach them, so we must not imitate any bad examples for the sake of the plausible doctrines of those that set them.

Our Saviour here, and in the following verses, specifies divers particulars of their works, wherein we must not imitate them. In general, they are charged with hypocrisy, dissimulation, or double-dealing in religion.

Four things are in these verses charged upon them.

1. Their saying and doing were two things. *They say, and do not;* they teach out of the law that which is good, but their conversation gives them the lie. Those are of all sinners most inexcusable that allow themselves in the sins they condemn in others, or in worse. This doth especially touch wicked ministers; for what greater hypocrisy can there be, than to press that upon others, which they themselves disbelieve and disobey; pulling down in their practice what they build up in their preaching; when in the pulpit, preaching so well that it is a pity they should ever come out; but, when out of the pulpit, living so ill that it is a pity they should ever come in; like bells, that call others to church, but hang out of it themselves.

It is applicable to all others that say, and do not; that make a plausible profession of religion, but do not live up to that profession. Great talkers, but little doers.

2. They were very severe in imposing upon others those things which they were not themselves willing to submit to the burthen of (*v.* 4); *They bind heavy burthens, and grievous to be borne;* not only insisting upon the minute circumstances of the law, but by imposing their own inventions and traditions, under the highest penalties. They loved to show their authority and to exercise their domineering faculty. But see their hypocrisy; *They themselves will not move them with one of their fingers.* They pressed upon the people a strictness in religion which they themselves would not be bound by. They indulged their pride in giving law to others; but consulted their ease in their own practice. They would not ease the people in these things, nor put a finger to lighten their burthen, when they saw it pinched them.

3. They were all for show, and nothing for substance, in religion (*v.* 5); *All their works they do, to be seen of men.* We must do such good works, that they who see them may glorify God; but we must not proclaim our good works, with design that others may see them, and glorify us. All their end was to be praised of men, and therefore all their endeavour was to be seen of men. The *form* of godliness will get them a name to live, which is all they aim at, and therefore they trouble not themselves with the *power* of it, which is essential to a life indeed. He that does all to be seen does nothing to the purpose.

He specifies two things which they did to be seen of men.

(1) *They made broad their phylacteries.* Those were little scrolls of paper or parchment, wherein were written, with great niceness, these four paragraphs of the law, Exod. xiii. 2–11; xiii. 11–16; Deut. vi. 4–9; xi. 13–21. These were sewn up in leather, and worn upon their foreheads and left arms. Now the Pharisees made broad these phylacteries, that they might be thought more holy, and strict, and zealous for the law, than others. It is a gracious ambition to covet to be really more holy than others, but it is a proud ambition to covet to appear so. It is good to excel in real piety, but not to exceed in outward shows.

(2) *They enlarged the borders of their garments.* God appointed the Jews to make borders or fringes upon their garments (Num. xv. 38), to be a memorandum to them of their being a peculiar people; but the Pharisees were not content to have these borders like other people's; they must be larger than ordinary, to answer their design of making themselves to be taken notice of; as if they were more religious than others.

4. They much affected pre-eminence and superiority. Pride was the darling reigning sin of the Pharisees. He describes their pride, *v.* 6, 7. They courted, and coveted places of honour and respect. In all public appearances, as *at feasts, and in the synagogues*, they expected, and had, to their hearts' delight, *the uppermost rooms and the chief seats.* They took place of all others, and precedency was adjudged to them, as persons of the greatest note and merit. It is not possessing the uppermost rooms, nor sitting in the chief seats, that is condemned (somebody must sit uppermost), but *loving* them. What is that but making an idol of ourselves, and then falling down and worshipping it—the worst kind of idolatry! It is bad anywhere, but especially in the synagogues. *There* to seek honour to ourselves, where we appear in order to give glory to God, and to humble ourselves before him, is indeed to mock God instead of serving him. It savours much of pride and hypocrisy, when people do not care for going to church, unless they can look fine and make a figure there.

Titles of honour and respect. They *loved greetings in the markets*, loved to have people put off their hats to them, and show them respect when they met them in the streets. This was meat and drink and dainties to them. The *greetings* would not have done them half so much good, if they had not been in the markets, where everybody might see how much they were respected, and how high they stood in the opinion of the people. For him that is taught in the word to give respect to him that teaches is commendable enough in him that gives it; but for him that teaches to love it, and demand it, is sinful and abominable; and, instead of teaching he has need to learn the first lesson in the school of Christ, which is humility. He cautions his disciples against being herein like them; "But be not ye called so, for ye shall not be of such a spirit," *v.* 8, &c.

Here is, A prohibition of pride. They are here forbidden to challenge titles of honour and dominion to themselves, *v.* 8–10. It is repeated twice; *Be not called Rabbi, neither be ye called Master* or *Guide.* Christ's ministers must not affect the name of *Rabbi* or *Master*, by way of distinction from other people; it is not agreeable to the simplicity of the gospel. They must not assume the authority and dominion implied in those names. The reasons for this prohibition are,

(1) *One is your Master, even Christ, v.* 8, and again, *v.* 10. Christ only is our Master, ministers are but ushers in the school.

(2) *All ye are brethren.* Ye are brethren, as ye are all disciples of the same Master. School-fellows are brethren, and, as such, should help one another in getting their lesson; but it will by no means be allowed that one of the scholars step into the master's seat, and give law to the school. They are forbidden to ascribe such titles to others (*v.* 9); "*Call no man your*

father upon the earth; constitute no man the father of your religion." God only must be allowed as *the Father of our spirits,* Heb. xii. 9. Our religion must not be derived from, or made to depend upon, any man. We must not pin our faith on any man's sleeve, because we know not whither he will carry it. St. Paul calls himself *a Father* (1 Cor. iv. 15; Phil. 10); but he uses that title to denote, not authority, but affection: therefore he calls them not his *obliged,* but his *beloved,* sons, 1 Cor. iv. 14.

The reason given is, *One is your Father, who is in heaven.* He is the Fountain of it, and its Founder; the Life of it, and its Lord; from whom alone, as the Original, our spiritual life is derived, and on whom it depends. Christ having taught us to say, *Our Father, who art in heaven*; let us *call no man Father upon earth.* Here is a precept of humility and mutual subjection (*v.* 11); *He that is greatest among you shall be your servant.* Take it as a promise; "*He* shall stand highest in the favour of God, that is most submissive and serviceable": or as a precept; "He that is advanced to any place of dignity, *let him be your servant.*" *He that is greatest* is not a lord, but a minister. Here is a good reason for all this, *v.* 12. Consider,

First, The punishment intended for the proud; *Whosoever shall exalt himself shall be abased.* If God give them repentance, they will be abased in their own eyes, and will abhor themselves for it; if they repent not, sooner or later they will be abased before the world.

Secondly, The preferment intended for the humble; *He that shall humble himself shall be exalted.* In this world the humble have the honour of being accepted with the holy God, and respected by all wise and good men; of being qualified for, and often called out to, the most honourable services; for honour is like the shadow, which flees from those that pursue it, and grasp at it, but follows those that flee from it. However, in the other world, they that have humbled themselves in contrition for their sin, shall be exalted to inherit the throne of glory.

Verses 13–33

In these verses we have eight woes levelled directly against the scribes and Pharisees by our Lord Jesus Christ, like so many claps of thunder, or flashes of lightning, from mount Sinai. Here are *eight* woes, in opposition to the eight beatitudes, Matt. v. 3. These woes are the more remarkable because of the meekness and gentleness of him that denounced them. He came to bless, and loved to bless; but, if his wrath be kindled, there is surely cause for it.

This is here the burthen of the song, and it is a heavy burthen; *Woe unto you, scribes and Pharisees,* hypocrites. The scribes and Pharisees are hypocrites; that is it in which all the rest of their bad characters are summed up. A hypocrite is a stage-player in religion (that is the primary signification of the word); he personates or acts the part of one that he neither is nor may be, or perhaps that he neither is nor would be.

Now each of these woes against the scribes and Pharisees has a reason annexed to it, justifying the judgment of Christ upon them; for his woes, his curses, are never causeless.

I. They were sworn enemies to the gospel of Christ, and consequently to the salvation of the souls of men (*v.* 13); *They shut up the kingdom of heaven, against men.* Christ came to *open the kingdom of heaven* to bring men to be subjects of that kingdom. Now the scribes and Pharisees, who sat in Moses's seat, and pretended to the key of knowledge, ought to have contributed their assistance herein. They that undertook to expound Moses and the prophets should have showed the people how they testified of Christ. Thus

they might have facilitated that great work, and have helped thousands to heaven; but, instead of this, they shut up the kingdom of heaven; they made it their business to beget and nourish up in the minds of the people prejudices against Christ and his doctrine.

1. They would not go in themselves; *Have any of the rulers,* or *of the Pharisees, believed on him?* John vii. 48. No; they were too proud to stoop to his meanness; they did not like a religion which insisted so much on humility. Repentance was the door of admission into this kingdom, and nothing could be more disagreeable to the Pharisees than to repent. Therefore they *went not in themselves*; but that was not all.

2. They would not *suffer them that were entering to go in.* It is bad to keep away from Christ ourselves, but it is worse to keep others from him. Their not going in themselves was a hindrance to many; multitudes rejected the gospel only because their leaders did. They opposed both Christ's entertaining of sinners (Luke vii. 39), and sinners' entertaining of Christ; and used all their wit and power to serve their malice against him; and thus they *shut up the kingdom of heaven,* so that *they who would enter* into it must *suffer violence* (*ch.* xi. 12), and *press into it* (Luke xvi. 16).

II. They made religion and the form of godliness a cloak and stalking-horse to their covetous practices and desires, *v.* 14. Observe here,

1. What their wicked practices were; they *devoured widows' houses,* either by quartering themselves and their attendants upon them for entertainment; or by insinuating themselves into their affections, and so getting to be the trustees of their estates, which they could make an easy prey of. The thing they aimed at was to enrich themselves. And doubtless they did all this under colour of law; for they did it so artfully that it passed uncensured.

2. What was the cloak with which they covered this wicked practice; *For a pretence they made long prayers;* very long indeed, if it be true which some of the Jewish writers tell us, that they spent three hours at a time in the formalities of meditation and prayer, and did it thrice every day. By this craft they got their wealth, and maintained their grandeur. Christ doth not here condemn long prayers, as in themselves hypocritical. Christ himself *continued all night in prayer to God.* Where there are many sins to be confessed, and many wants to pray for the supply of, and many mercies to give thanks for, there is occasion for long prayers. But the Pharisees' long prayers were for a *pretence*; by them they got the reputation of pious devout men, that loved prayer, and were the favourites of Heaven; and by this means people were made to believe it was not possible that such men as they should cheat them. Thus, while they seemed to soar heaven-ward, upon the wings of prayer, their eye, like the kite's, was all the while upon their prey on the earth, some widow's house or other that lay convenient for them. It is no new thing for the show and form of godliness to be made a cloak to the greatest enormities.

3. The doom passed upon them for this; *Therefore ye shall receive the greater damnation.* The pretences of religion, with which hypocrites disguise or excuse their sin now, will aggravate their condemnation shortly.

III. They shut up the kingdom of heaven against those that would turn to Christ, but at the same time *compassed sea and land to make proselytes* to themselves, *v.* 15.

1. Their commendable industry in making proselytes to the Jewish religion; for this, for one such, though but one, they compass sea and land. And what did they aim at? Not the glory of God, and the good of souls; but that they might have the credit of

making them proselytes. The making of proselytes, if it be to the truth and serious godliness, and be done with a good design, is a good work. Such is the value of souls, that nothing must be thought too much to do, to save a soul from death. The industry of the Pharisees herein may show the negligence of many who would be thought to act from better principles, but will be at no pains or cost to propagate the gospel.

2. Their cursed impiety in abusing their proselytes when they were made. "*Ye make him twofold more the child of hell than yourselves.*" They are called *children of hell*, because of their rooted enmity to the kingdom of heaven, which was the principle and genius of Pharisaism. Perverted proselytes are commonly the greatest bigots; the scholars outdid their masters, (1) In fondness of ceremony. Weak heads commonly admire those shows and ceremonies which wise men cannot but think meanly of. (2) In fury against Christianity. Paul, a disciple of the Pharisees, was *exceedingly mad against the Christians* (Acts xxvi. 11), when his master, Gamaliel, seems to have been more moderate.

IV. They led the people into dangerous mistakes, particularly in the matter of oaths; which have been by all nations accounted sacred (*v.* 16); *Ye blind guides.* Christ denounces a woe to the blind guides that have the blood of so many souls to answer for.

(1) He lays down the doctrine they taught. They distinguished between an oath by *the temple* and an oath by the *gold of the temple*; an oath by *the altar* and an oath by *the gift upon the altar*; making the latter binding, but not the former. Here was a double wickedness; *First*, That there were some oaths which they dispensed with, and made light of, and reckoned a man was not bound by to assert the truth, or perform a promise. That doctrine cannot be of the God of truth which gives countenance to the breach of faith in any case whatsoever. Oaths are edge-tools and are not to be jested with. *Secondly*, That they preferred the gold before the temple, and the gift before the altar, to encourage people to bring gifts to the altar, and gold to the treasures of the temple, which they hoped to be gainers by.

(2) He shows the folly and absurdity of this distinction (*v.* 17–19); *Ye fools, and blind.*

To convict them of folly, he appeals to themselves, *Whether is greater, the gold or the temple that sanctifies the gold; the gift, or the altar that sanctifies the gift?* They that sware by the gold of the temple had an eye to it as holy; but what was it that made it holy but the holiness of the temple, to the service of which it was appropriated? And therefore the temple cannot be less holy than the gold, but must be more so.

(3) He rectifies the mistake (*v.* 20–22), by reducing all the oaths they had invented to the true intent of an oath, which is, By the name of the Lord: so that though an oath by the temple, or the altar, or heaven, be formally bad, yet it is binding. He that swears by the altar shall be interpreted by it and by all things thereon. And, the things thereon being offered up to God, to swear by it and them was, in effect, to call God himself to witness: for it was the altar of God; and he that went to that, went to God. He that swears by the temple, if he understand what he does, cannot but apprehend that the ground of such a respect to it is because it is the house of God, the place which he has chosen to put his name there; and therefore he swears *by it, and by him that dwells therein.* If a man swears by heaven, he sins (*ch.* v. 34); yet he shall not therefore be discharged from the obligation of his oath; no, God will make him know that the heaven he swears by, is his throne (Isa. lxvi. 1); and he that swears by the throne, appeals to him that sits upon it.

V. They were very strict and precise in the smaller matters of the law, but as careless and loose in the weightier matters, *v.* 23, 24. They were *partial in the law.* Sincere obedience is universal, and he that from a right principle obeys any of God's precepts, will have respect to them all. The partiality of the scribes and Pharisees appears here, in two instances.

1. They observed smaller duties, but omitted greater; they were very exact in paying tithes, when it came to *mint, anise,* and *cummin,* their exactness in tithing of which would not cost them much, but would be cried up, and they should buy reputation cheap. The Pharisee boasted of this, *I give tithes of all that I possess,* Luke xviii. 12. Paying tithes was their duty; Christ tells them they ought not to leave it undone. All ought in their places to contribute to the support and maintenance of a standing ministry. They that *are taught in the word,* and do not *communicate to them that teach them,* that love a cheap gospel, come short of the Pharisees.

But that which Christ here condemns them for, is, that they *omitted the weightier matters of the law, judgment, mercy, and faith.* All the things of God's law are weighty, but those are most weighty, which are most expressive of inward holiness in the heart. Judgment and mercy toward men, and faith toward God, are the weightier matters of the law, the *good things* which the *Lord our God requires* (Mic. vi. 8), to do justly, and love mercy, and humble ourselves by faith to walk with God. This is the obedience which is better than sacrifice or tithe. Mercy also is preferred before sacrifice, Hos. vi. 6. Nor will judgment and mercy serve without faith in divine revelation; for God will be honoured in his truths as well as in his laws.

2. They avoided lesser sins, but committed greater (*v.* 24); *Ye blind guides;* so he had called them before (*v.* 16), for their corrupt teaching; here he calls them so for their corrupt living. They were blind and partial; they *strained at a gnat, and swallowed a camel.* In their doctrine they strained at gnats, warned people against every least violation of the tradition of the elders. In their practice they strained at gnats, heaved at them, with a seeming dread, as if they had a great abhorrence of sin, and were afraid of it in the least instance; but they made no difficulty of those sins which, in comparison with them, were as a camel to a gnat. It is not the scrupling of a little sin that Christ here reproves, if it be a sin, though but a gnat, it must be strained at, but the doing of that, and then swallowing a camel.

VI. They were all for the outside, and not at all for the inside, of religion. This is illustrated by two similitudes.

1. They are compared to a vessel that is clean washed on the outside, but all dirt within, *v.* 25, 26. Now what a foolish thing would it be for a man to wash only the outside of a cup, which is to be looked at, and to leave the inside dirty, which is to be used; so they do who only avoid scandalous sins, that would spoil their reputation with men, but allow themselves in heart-wickedness, which renders them odious to the pure and holy God. In reference to this, observe,

(1) The practice of the Pharisees; they made clean the outside. In those things which fell under the observation of their neighbours, they seemed very exact; people generally took them for very good men. But within they were *full of extortion and excess.* While they would seem to be godly, they were neither sober nor righteous. And that we are really, which we are inwardly.

(2) The rule Christ gives, in opposition to this practice, *v.* 26. Those are blind, in Christ's account, who are strangers, and no enemies, to the wickedness of their own hearts; who see not, and hate not, the

secret sin that lodgeth there. Self-ignorance is the most shameful and hurtful ignorance. The rule is, *Cleanse first that which is within.* The main business of a Christian lies within, to get cleansed from the *filthiness of the spirit.'* Those sins must be conscientiously abstained from, which the eye of God only is a witness to, who searcheth the heart. *Cleanse first that which is within;* not that *only,* but that *first;* because, if due care be taken concerning that, the outside will be clean also. If renewing, sanctifying grace make clean the inside, that will have an influence upon the outside, for the commanding principle is within. If the heart be well kept, all is well, for *out of it are the issues of life.* First cleanse that which is within; we then make sure work, when this is our first work.

2. They are compared to *whited sepulchres, v.* 27, 28.

(1) They were fair without, like sepulchres, *which appear beautiful outward.* Some make it to refer to the custom of the Jews to whiten graves, that people might avoid them, because of the ceremonial pollution contracted by the touch of a grave. The formality of hypocrites doth but make all wise and good men the more careful to avoid them. It rather alludes to the custom of whitening the sepulchres of eminent persons, for the beautifying of them. It is said here (*v.* 29), that they *garnished the sepulchres of the righteous.* Now the righteousness of the scribes and Pharisees was like the ornaments of a grave, only for show. The top of their ambition was to *appear righteous before men,* and to be applauded and had in admiration by them.

(2) They were *foul* within, like sepulchres, *full of dead men's bones, and all uncleanness.* Thus were they full of hypocrisy and iniquity. It is possible for those that have their hearts full of sin, to have their lives free from blame, and to appear very good. But what will it avail us, to have the good work of our fellow-servants, if our Master doth not say, *Well done?*

VII. They pretended a deal of kindness for the memory of the prophets that were dead and gone, while they hated and persecuted those that were present with them. God is jealous for his honour in his laws and ordinances; but he has often expressed an equal jealousy for his honour in his prophets and ministers. Therefore, when our Lord Jesus comes to this head, he speaks more fully than upon any of the other (*v.* 29–37).

1. The respect which the scribes and Pharisees pretended for the prophets that were gone, *v.* 29, 30.

(1) They honoured the relics of the prophets, they built their tombs, and garnished their sepulchres. *The memory of the just is blessed,* when the names of those that hated and persecuted them shall be covered with shame. This is an instance of the hypocrisy of the scribes and Pharisees, who paid their respect to them. They can pay respect to the writings of the dead prophets, which tell them what they *should be;* but not the reproofs of the living prophets, which tell them what they *are.*

(2) They protested against the murder of them (*v.* 30); *If we had been in the days of our fathers, we would not have been partakers with them.* No, not they, they would sooner have lost their right hands than have done any such thing. And yet they were at this time plotting to murder Christ, *to whom all the prophets bore witness.* The deceitfulness of sinners' hearts appears very much in this, that, while they go down the stream of the sins of their own day, they fancy they should have swum against the stream of the sins of the former days; that, if they had had other people's opportunities, they should have improved them more faithfully. We are sometimes thinking, if we had lived when Christ was upon earth, how constantly we would have followed him; we

would not have despised and rejected him, as they then did; and yet Christ in his Spirit, in his word, in his ministers, is still no better treated.

2. Their enmity and opposition to Christ and his gospel, notwithstanding, and the ruin they were bringing upon themselves and upon that generation thereby, *v.* 31–33. Observe here,

(1) The indictment proved; *Ye are witnesses against yourselves.* Sinners cannot hope to escape the judgment of Christ for want of proof against them, when it is easy to find them witnesses against themselves. By their own confession, it was the great wickedness of their forefathers, to kill the prophets. They who condemn sin in others, and yet allow the same or worse in themselves, are of all others most inexcusable, Rom. i. 32–ii. 1. By their own confession, these notorious persecutors were their ancestors; *Ye are the children of them.* Christ turns it upon them, that they were so by spirit and disposition. They are, as you say, *your* fathers, and you *take after your fathers;* it is the sin that runs in the blood among you.

(2) The sentence passed upon them. Christ here proceeds,

[1] To give them up to sin as irreclaimable (*v.* 32); *Fill ye up then the measure of your fathers.* Christ knew they were now contriving his death, and in a few days would accomplish it; "Well," saith he, "go on with your plot, walk in the way of your heart and in the sight of your eyes, and see what will come of it. You will but fill up the measure of guilt. *First,* There is a measure of sin to be filled up. God will bear long, but the time will come when he can *no longer forbear. Secondly,* Children fill up the measure of their father's sins when they are gone, if they persist in the same or the like. That national guilt which brings national ruin is made up of the sin of many in several ages. God justly visits the iniquity of the fathers upon the children that tread in the steps of it. *Thirdly,* Persecuting Christ, and his people and ministers, is a sin that fills the measure of a nation's guilt sooner than any other. *Fourthly,* It is just with God to give those up to their own heart's lusts, who obstinately persist in the gratification of them.

[2] He proceeds to give them up to ruin as irrecoverable, to a personal ruin in the other world (*v.* 33); *Ye serpents, ye generation of vipers, how can ye escape the damnation of hell?* These are strange words to come from the mouth of Christ, into whose lips grace was poured. But he can and will speak terror.

Here is, *First,* Their description; *Ye serpents.* Doth Christ call names? Yes, but this doth not warrant us to do so. He infallibly knew what was in man. They were a *generation of vipers;* they and those that joined with them, were a generation of envenomed, enraged, spiteful adversaries to Christ and his gospel. Christ calls them *serpents* and *vipers;* for he gives men their true characters, and delights to put contempt upon the proud.

Secondly, Their doom. *How can ye escape the damnation of hell?* Christ himself preached hell and damnation, for which his ministers have often been reproached by those that care not to hear of it. This doom coming from Christ, was more terrible than coming from all the prophets and ministers that ever were, for he is the Judge, into whose hands the keys of hell and death are put. There is a way of escaping this damnation. Repentance and faith are necessary to that escape; and how will *they* be brought to these, who are so conceited of themselves, and so prejudiced against Christ and his gospel, as they were? Publicans and harlots, who were sensible of their disease and applied themselves to the Physician, were more likely to escape the damnation of hell than those who, though they were in the high road to it, were confident they were in the way to heaven.

Verses 34–39

We have left the blind leaders fallen into the ditch; let us see what will become of the blind followers, and particularly Jerusalem.

I. Jesus Christ designs yet to try them with the means of grace; *I send unto you prophets, and wise men, and scribes.* One would think it should follow, "Therefore you shall never have a prophet sent to you any more;" but no, *"Therefore I will send unto you prophets,* to see if you will yet at length be wrought upon, or else to leave you inexcusable."

1. It is Christ that sends them; *I send.* By this he avows himself to be God, having power to gift and commission prophets. It is an act of kingly office. After his resurrection, he made this word good, when he said, *So send I you,* John xx. 21.

2. He sends them to the Jews first; "I send them to *you.*" They began at Jerusalem; and, wherever they went, they observed this rule, to make the first tender of gospel grace *to the Jews,* Acts xiii. 46.

3. Those he sends are called *prophets, wise men,* and *scribes,* Old Testament names for New Testament officers. We may take the apostles and evangelists for the prophets and wise men, and the pastors and teachers for the scribes, *instructed to the kingdom of heaven* (*ch.* xiii. 52); for the office of a scribe was honourable till the men dishonoured it.

II. He foresees and foretells the ill usage that his messengers would meet with among them; *"Some of them ye shall kill and crucify,* and yet I will send them." Christ knows beforehand how ill his servants will be treated, and yet sends them; yet he loves them never the less, for he designs to glorify himself by their sufferings, and them after them; he will counter-balance them, though not prevent them.

1. The cruelty of these persecutors; *Ye shall kill and crucify them.* It is no less than the blood, the life-blood, that they thirst after. Thus did the members partake of the sufferings of the Head, he was killed and crucified, and so were they. Christians must expect to resist unto blood.

2. Their unwearied industry; *Ye shall persecute them from city to city.* As the apostles went from city to city, to preach the gospel, the Jews dodged them, and haunted them, and stirred up persecution against them, Acts xiv. 19; xvii. 13.

3. The pretence of religion in this; they scourged them in their synagogues, so that they did it as a piece of service to the church.

III. He imputes the sin of their fathers to them, because they imitated it; *That upon you may come all the righteous blood shed upon the earth,* v. 35, 36. Though God bear long with a persecuting generation, he will not bear always; and patience abused, turns into the greatest wrath.

Observe, 1. The extent of this imputation; it takes in *all the righteous blood shed upon the earth,* that is, the blood shed for righteousness' sake. He dates the account *from the blood of righteous Abel.* How early did martyrdom come into the world! He extends it *to the blood of Zacharias, the son of Barachias* (v. 36), as is most probable, *Zechariah the son of Jehoiada,* who was *slain in the court of the Lord's house,* 2 Chron. xxiv. 20, 21. His father is called *Barachias,* which signifies much the same with Jehoiada; and it was usual among the Jews for the same person to have two names; *whom ye slew,* ye of this nation, though not of this generation.

2. The effect of it; *All these things shall come;* all the guilt of this blood, all the punishment of it, it shall *all come upon this generation.* The destruction shall be so dreadful, as if God had once for all arraigned them for all the righteous blood shed in the world. It shall *come upon this generation;* which intimates, that it shall come quickly; some here shall live to see it. The sorer and nearer the punishment of sin is, the louder is the call to repentance and reformation.

IV. He laments the wickedness of Jerusalem, and justly upbraids them with the many kind offers he had made them, *v.* 37. See with what concern he speaks of that city; *O Jerusalem, Jerusalem!* The repetition is emphatic, and bespeaks abundance of commiseration. A day or two before Christ had wept over Jerusalem, now he sighed and groaned over it. Jerusalem, *the vision of peace* (so it signifies), must now be the seat of war and confusion. But wherefore will the Lord do all this to Jerusalem? Why? *Jerusalem hath grievously sinned.*

1. She persecuted God's messengers; *Thou that killest the prophets, and stonest them that are sent unto thee.* This sin is especially charged upon Jerusalem; because there the Sanhedrim, or great council, sat, who took cognizance of church matters, and therefore a prophet could not perish but in Jerusalem, Luke xiii. 33. They killed the prophets in popular tumults, mobbed them, as Stephen, and put the Roman powers on to kill them. At Jerusalem, where the gospel was first preached, it was first persecuted (Acts viii. 1), and that place was the headquarters of the persecutors; and thither the saints were brought bound, Acts ix. 2. *Thou stonest them.* There was abundance of other wickedness in Jerusalem; but this was the sin that made the loudest cry, and which God had an eye to more than any other.

2. She refused and rejected Christ, and gospel offers. The former was a sin *without* remedy, this *against* the remedy. The wonderful grace and favour of Jesus Christ toward them; *How often would I have gathered thy children together, as a hen gathers her chickens under her wings!* The favour proposed was the gathering of them. Christ's design is to gather poor souls, gather them in from their wanderings, gather them home to himself. It is here illustrated by a humble similitude; *as a hen* clucks *her chickens together.* Christ would have gathered them, *First,* With such a tenderness of affection as the hen does, which has, by instinct, a peculiar concern for her young ones. Christ's gathering of souls, comes from his love, Jer. xxxi. 3. *Secondly, For the same end. The hen gathered her chickens under her wings,* for protection and safety, and for warmth and comfort. The chickens naturally run to the hen for shelter, when they are threatened by the birds of prey; perhaps Christ refers to that promise (Ps. xci. 4), *He shall cover thee with his feathers.* There is *healing under Christ's wings;* that is more than the hen has for her chickens. The forwardness of Christ to confer this favour. His offers are, *First,* Very free; *I would have done it. Secondly,* Very frequent; *How often!* Christ often came up to Jerusalem, preached, and wrought miracles there. As often as we have heard the sound of the gospel, as often as we have felt the strivings of the Spirit, so often Christ would have gathered us. Their wilful refusal of this grace and favour; *Ye would not.* I would, and *ye would not.* He was willing to save them, but they were not willing to be saved by him.

V. He reads Jerusalem's doom (v. 38, 39); *Therefore behold your house is left unto you desolate.* Both the city and the temple, God's house and their own, all shall be laid waste. But it is especially meant of the temple, which they boasted of, and trusted to.

1. Their house shall be *deserted; It is left unto you.* Christ was now departing from the temple, and never came into it again. They doated on it, would have it to themselves; Christ must have no room or interest there. "Well," saith Christ, "it is left to you; take it, and made your best of it; I will never hav

anything more to do with it." Their city also was left to them, destitute of God's presence and grace.

2. It shall be *desolate; It is left unto you desolate.* It was immediately, when Christ left it, in the eyes of all that understood themselves, a very dismal melancholy place. Christ's departure makes the best furnished, best replenished place a wilderness. For what comfort can there be where Christ is not? This comes of men's rejecting Christ, and driving him away from them. It was, not long after, destroyed and ruined, and *not one stone left upon another.* The temple, that holy and beautiful house, became desolate. When God goes out, all enemies break in.

Lastly, Here is the final farewell that Christ took of them and their temple; *Ye shall not see me henceforth, till ye shall say, Blessed is he that cometh.* This bespeaks,

3. His departure from them. The time was at hand, when *he should leave the world, to go to his Father,* and be seen no more. *After his resurrection, he was seen only by a few chosen witnesses,* and they saw him not long, but he soon removed to the invisible world, and there will be *till the time of the restitution of all things,* when his welcome at his first coming will be repeated with loud acclamations; *Blessed is he that cometh in the name of the Lord.* Would we have our lot in that day with those that say, *Blessed is he that cometh?* let us be with them now, with them that truly worship, and truly welcome, Jesus Christ.

4. Their continued blindness and obstinacy; *Ye shall not see me,* that is, not see the light of the truth concerning me, nor *the things that belong to your peace, till ye shall say, Blessed is he that cometh.* Wilful blindness is often punished with judicial blindness. If they *will* not see, they *shall* not see. With this word he concludes his public preaching. When *the Lord comes with ten thousand of his saints,* he will convince all. They who now reproach and ridicule the hosannas of the saints will be of another mind shortly; it were therefore better to be of that mind now.

CHAPTER 24

In this chapter, we have a prophetical discourse, intended, not to gratify the curiosity of his disciples, but to guide their consciences. I. The occasion of his discourse, ver. 1–3. II. The discourse itself, in which we have, 1. The prophecy of divers events, especially referring to the destruction of Jerusalem; the prefaces to that destruction, the concomitants and consequences of it; yet looking further, to Christ's coming at the end of time, and the consummation of all things, ver. 4–31. 2. The practical application of this prophecy, ver. 32–51.

Verses 1–3

I. Christ's quitting *the temple,* and his public work there. He had said, in the close of the foregoing chapter, *Your house is left unto you desolate;* and here he made his words good; *He went out, and departed from the temple.* He departed from it, never to return to it any more; and then immediately follows a prediction of its ruin. That house is left desolate indeed, which Christ leaves. But Christ departed not till they drove him away; did not reject them, till they first rejected him.

II. His private discourse with his disciples; he left the temple, but he did not leave the twelve. When he left the temple, his disciples left it too, and came to him. It is good being where Christ is, and leaving that which he leaves.

1. *His disciples came to him, to show him the buildings of the temple.* It was a stately and beautiful structure. It was richly furnished with gifts and offerings. They showed Christ these things, and desired him to take notice of them, either,

(1) As being greatly pleased with them themselves, and expecting he should be so too. They had lived mostly in Galilee, at a distance from the temple,

had seldom seen it, and therefore were the more struck with admiration at it, and thought he should admire as much as they did *all this glory.* Even good men are apt to be too much enamoured with outward pomp and gaiety, and to overvalue it, even in the things of God. The temple was indeed glorious, but, [1] Its glory was sullied and stained with the sin of the priests and people. [2] Its glory was eclipsed and outdone by the presence of Christ in it.

Or, (2) As grieving that this house should be left desolate; they showed him the buildings, as if they would move him to reverse the sentence. Christ had lately looked upon *the precious souls, and wept for them,* Luke xix. 41. The disciples look upon the pompous buildings, and are ready to weep for them. In this, as in other things, *his thoughts are not like ours.*

2. Christ, hereupon, foretells the utter ruin and destruction that were coming upon this place, *v.* 2. A believing foresight of the defacing of all worldly glory will help to take us off from overvaluing it. *See ye not all these things?* They would have Christ look upon them, and be as much in love with them as they were. There is such a sight of these things as will do us good; so to see them as to see through them and see to the end of them.

Christ, instead of reversing the decree, ratifies it; *Verily, I say unto you, there shall not be left one stone upon another.* He speaks of it as a certain ruin; "*I say unto you.*" I, that know what I say. He speaks of it as an utter ruin. The temple shall not only be stripped, and plundered, and defaced, but utterly demolished and laid waste; *Not one stone shall be left unto another.* Though Titus, when he took the city, did all he could to preserve the temple, yet he could not restrain the enraged soldiers from destroying it utterly; and it was done to that degree, that Turnus Rufus ploughed up the ground on which it had stood.

3. The disciples enquire more particularly of the time when it should come to pass, and the signs of its approach, *v.* 3.

(1) Where they made this enquiry; privately, *as he sat upon the mount of Olives;* probably, he was returning to Bethany, and there sat down by the way, to rest him; the mount of Olives directly faced the temple, and from thence he might have a full prospect of it at some distance.

(2) What the enquiry itself was; *When shall these things be; and what shall be the sign of thy coming, and of the end of the world?* Here are three questions.

[1] Some think these questions do all point at one and the same thing—the destruction of the temple. Or, they thought the destruction of the temple must needs be the end of the world.

[2] Others think their question, *When shall these things be?* refers to the destruction of Jerusalem, and the other two to the end of the world. They had very confused thoughts of future events; so that perhaps it is not possible to put any certain construction upon this question of theirs.

Verses 4–31

The disciples had asked concerning the times, *When shall these things be?* Christ gives them no answer to that. But they had asked, *What shall be the sign?* That question he answers fully. Now the prophecy primarily respects the events near at hand; but as the prophecies of the Old Testament, which have an immediate reference to the affairs of the Jews, do certainly look further, to the gospel church and the kingdom of the Messiah, and are so expounded in the New Testament, so this prophecy, under the type of Jerusalem's destruction, looks as far forward as the general judgment. What Christ here saith to his disciples tends more to engage their caution than to satisfy their curiosity; more to prepare them for the events that should happen than to give them a distinct idea of the events themselves.

I. Christ begins with a caution, *Take heed that no man deceive you.* They expected to be told when these things should be, to be let into that secret; but this caution is a check to their curiosity, "*What is that to you?* Mind you your duty, follow me, and be not seduced from following me." Seducers are more dangerous enemies to the church than persecutors.

Three times in this discourse he mentions the appearing of *false prophets*, which was, 1. A presage of Jerusalem's ruin. Justly were they who killed the true prophets, left to be ensnared by false prophets; and they who crucified the true Messiah, left to be deceived and broken by false Christs and pretended Messiahs. 2. It was a trial to the disciples of Christ, and therefore agreeable to their state of probation, *that they which are perfect, may be made manifest.*

Now concerning these deceivers, observe here,

(1) The pretences they should come under. Satan acts most mischievously, when he appears as an angel of light: the colour of the greatest good is often the cover of the greatest evil. There should appear *false prophets* (v. 11–24); the deceivers would pretend to divine inspiration, when it was all a lie. Some think, the seducers here pointed to were such as had been settled teachers in the church, and revolted to error; and from such the danger is the greater, because least suspected. One false traitor in the garrison may do more mischief than a thousand avowed enemies without. There should appear *false Christs, coming in Christ's name* (v. 5), assuming to themselves the name peculiar to him, and saying, *I am Christ, pseudo-christs, v.* 24. There was at that time a general expectation of the appearing of the Messias; they spoke of him; as *he that should come*; but when he did come, the body of the nation rejected him; which those who were ambitious of making themselves a name, took advantage of, and set up for Christs. These false Christs and false prophets would have their agents and emissaries busy in all places to draw people unto them, *v.* 23. *Then* when public troubles are great and threatening, and people will be catching at anything that looks like deliverance, then Satan will take the advantage of imposing on them; then they will say, *Lo, here is a Christ, or there* is one. The true Christ did not strive, nor cry; nor was it said of him, *Lo, here! or Lo, there!* (Luke xvii. 21). Christ is All in all, not here or there, but meets his people with a blessing *in every place where he records his name.*

(2) The proof they should offer for the making good of these pretences; *They shall show great signs and wonders* (v. 24), not true miracles, those are a divine seal, and with those the doctrine of Christ stands confirmed. It is not said, *They shall work miracles*, but, *They shall show great signs*; they are but a show.

(3) The success they should have in these attempts, *They shall deceive many* (v. 5), and again, *v.* 11. The devil and his instruments may prevail far in deceiving poor souls; few find the strait gate, but many are drawn into the broad way. *They shall deceive, if it were possible, the very elect, v.* 24. This bespeaks, *First,* The strength of the delusion; it is such as many shall be carried away by (so strong shall the stream be), even those that were thought to stand fast. Nothing but the almighty grace of God, pursuant to his eternal purpose, will be a protection. *Secondly,* The safety of the elect in the midst of this danger, which is taken for granted in that parenthesis, *If it were possible,* plainly implying that it is not possible, for they are *kept by the power of God.* Used proverbially by Galen; when he would express a thing very

difficult and morally impossible, he saith, "You may sooner draw away a Christian from Christ."

(4) The repeated cautions which our Saviour gives; *therefore* he gave them warning, that they might watch (v. 25); *Behold, I have told you before.* He that is told before where he will be assaulted, may save himself. Christ's warnings are designed to engage our watchfulness. We are kept through faith, faith in Christ's word, which he has told us before. We must not believe those who say, *Lo, here is Christ;* or, *Lo, he is there, v.* 23. We believe that the true Christ is at the right hand of God, and that his spiritual presence is *where two or three are gathered together in his name.* There is not a greater enemy to true faith than vain credulity. The simple believeth every word, and runs after every cry. We must not go forth after those that say, *He is in the desert,* or, *He is in the secret chambers, v.* 26. We must not follow everyone that puts up the finger to point us to a new Christ, and a new gospel. Many a man's vain curiosity to go forth hath led him into a fatal apostasy.

II. He foretells wars and great commotions among the nations, *v.* 6, 7. When Christ was born, there was a universal peace in the empire, the temple of Janus was shut; but *think not that Christ came to send,* or continue such a *peace* (Luke xii. 51); no, his city and his wall are to be built even in troublesome times, and even wars shall forward his work.

1. A prediction of the event of the day; You will now shortly *hear of wars, and rumours of wars.* When wars are, they will be heard. See how terrible it is. Even the quiet in the land cannot but hear the rumours of war. See what comes of refusing the gospel! Those that will not hear the messengers of peace, shall be made to hear the messengers of war.

2. A prescription of the duty of the day; *See that ye be not troubled.* Is it possible to hear such sad news, and not be troubled? Yet, where the heart is fixed, trusting in God, it is kept in peace, and is not afraid. It is against the mind of Christ, that his people should have troubled hearts even in troublous times.

We must not be troubled, for two reasons.

(1) Because we are bid to expect this: the Jews must be punished; by this the justice of God and the honour of the Redeemer must be asserted; and therefore *all those things must come to pass.* God is but performing the thing that is appointed for us. Let us therefore acquiesce. The old house must be taken down (though it cannot be done without noise, and dust, and danger), ere the new fabric can be erected: the things that are shaken (and ill shaken they were) *must be removed, that the things which cannot be shaken may remain,* Heb. xii. 27.

(2) Because we are still to expect worse; *The end is not yet;* the end of time is not, and, while time lasts, we must expect trouble, or, "The end of these troubles is not yet. Do not give way to fear and trouble, sink not under the present burthen, but rather gather in all the strength and spirit you have, to encounter what is yet before you." If running with the footmen weary us, how shall we contend with horses? And if we be frightened at a little brook in our way, what shall we do in the swellings of Jordan? Jer. xii. 5.

III. He foretells other judgments more immediately sent of God—*famines, pestilences, and earthquakes.* These were the three judgments which David was to choose one out of; and he was in a great strait, for he knew not which was the worst. Beside war (and that is enough), there shall be, *Famine,* signified by the *black horse* under the *third seal,* Rev. vi. 5, 6. The sorest famine was in Jerusalem during the siege. *Pestilences,* signified by the *pale horse, and death upon him,* and *the grave at his heels,* under the *fourth seal,* Rev. vi. 7, 8. *Earthquakes in divers places.* Great desolations have sometimes been made by earth-quakes, they have been the death of many, and the terror of more. But here they are spoken of as dreadful judgments, and yet but *the beginning of sorrows*.

IV. He foretells the persecution of his own people and ministers, and a general apostasy and decay in religion thereupon, *v.* 9, 10, 12.

1. The *cross* itself foretold, *v.* 9. Of all future events we are as much concerned, though commonly as little desirous, to know of our own sufferings as of anything else. Christ had told his disciples what hard things they should suffer; but they had hitherto experienced little of it, and therefore he reminds them again.

(1) They shall be *afflicted* with bonds and imprisonments.

(2) They shall be *killed*.

(3) They shall be *hated of all nations for Christ's name's sake*, as he had told them before, *ch.* x. 22. The world was generally leavened with enmity and malignity to Christians. What shall we think of this world, when the best men had the worst usage in it? It is the cause that makes the martyr, and comforts him; it was for Christ's sake that they were thus hated.

2. *The offence of the cross, v.* 10–12. Three ill effects of persecution are here foretold.

(1) The *apostasy* of some. When the profession of Christianity begins to cost men dear, *then shall many be offended*, shall first fall out with, and then fall off from, their profession. It is no new thing (though it is a strange thing) for those that have known the way of righteousness, to turn aside out of it. Suffering times are shaking times; and those fall in the storm, that stood in fair weather. Many will follow Christ in the sunshine, who will shift for themselves, and leave him to do so too, in the cloudy dark day.

(2) The *malignity* of others. Then *they shall betray one another*, that is, "Those that have treacherously deserted their religion, shall hate and betray those who adhere to it." Apostates have commonly been the most bitter and violent persecutors. Persecuting times are discovering times. Wolves in sheep's clothing will then throw off their disguise, and appear wolves: they shall *betray one another, and hate one another*.

(3) The general *declining* and *cooling* of most, *v.* 12. Expect these two things,

[1] The *abounding* of iniquity; though the world always lies in wickedness, yet there are some times in which it may be said, that *iniquity doth* in a special manner abound.

[2] The *abating* of love; this is the consequence of the former; *Because iniquity shall abound the love of many shall wax cold*. Understand it in general of true serious godliness, which is all summed up in *love*; it is too common for professors of religion to grow cool in their profession, when the wicked are hot in their wickedness. Or, it may be understood more particularly of brotherly love. When iniquity abounds, seducing iniquity, persecuting iniquity, this grace commonly waxes cold. Christians begin to be shy and suspicious one of another, and so love comes to nothing.

This gives a melancholy prospect of the times, that there shall be such a great decay of love; but, *First*, It is of the love of *many*, not of *all*. In the worst of times, God has his remnant that hold fast their integrity, and retain their zeal, as in Elijah's days, when he thought himself left alone. *Secondly*, This love is grown cold, but not dead. There is life in the root, which will show itself when the winter is past.

3. Comfort administered in reference to this offence of the cross, for the support of the Lord's people

under it (*v.* 13); *He that endures to the end, shall be saved*. It is comfortable to those who wish well to the cause of Christ in general, that, though many are offended, yet some shall endure to the end. It is comfortable to those who do thus endure to the end, and suffer for their constancy, that they shall be saved. Perseverance wins the crown, through free grace, and shall wear it. *They shall be saved*. The crown of glory will make amends for all. Choose rather to die at a stake with the persecuted, than to live in a palace with the persecutors.

V. He foretells the preaching of the gospel in all the world (*v.* 14); *This gospel shall be preached, and then shall the end come*. It is called *the gospel of the kingdom*, because it reveals the kingdom of grace, which leads to the kingdom of glory. This gospel, sooner or later, is to be preached in all the world, to every creature. The gospel is preached *for a witness to all nations*, that is, a faithful declaration of the mind and will of God.

1. It is intimated that the gospel should be, if not heard, yet at least heard of, throughout the then known world, before the destruction of Jerusalem. Within forty years after Christ's death, the *sound of the gospel was gone forth to the ends of the earth*, Rom. x. 18. St. Paul *fully preached the gospel from Jerusalem, and round about unto Illyricum*; and the other apostles were not idle. The persecuting of the saints at Jerusalem helped to disperse them, so that they *went everywhere, preaching the word*, Acts viii. 1–4.

2. It is likewise intimated that even in times of temptation, trouble, and persecution, the gospel of the kingdom shall force its way through the greatest opposition. Though the enemies of the church grow very hot, and many of her friends very *cool*, yet the gospel shall be preached. Then the people that do know their God, shall be strengthened to do the greatest exploits of all.

3. That which seems chiefly intended here, is, that the end of the world shall be *then*, and not till then, when the gospel has done its work in the world. When the mystery of God shall be finished, the mystical body completed, *then shall the end come*, of which he had said before (*v.* 6, 7), *not yet*.

VI. He foretells more particularly the ruin that was coming upon the people of the Jews, their city, temple, and nation, *v.* 15, &c. What he said here, would be of use to his disciples, both for their conduct and for their comfort, in reference to that great event.

1. The Romans *setting up the abomination of desolation in the holy place, v.* 15. Some understand by this an image, or statue, set up in the temple by some of the Roman governors, which was very offensive to the Jews. Since the captivity in Babylon, nothing was, nor could be, more distasteful to the Jews than an image in the holy place. Others choose to expound it by the parallel place (Luke xxi. 20), *when ye shall see Jerusalem compassed with armies*. Jerusalem was the holy city, Canaan the holy land, the Mount Moriah, which lay about Jerusalem, for its nearness to the temple was, they thought, in a particular manner holy ground; on the country lying round about Jerusalem the Roman army was encamped, that was the abomination that made desolate. Now this is said to be *spoken of by Daniel, the prophet*, who spoke more plainly of the Messiah and his kingdom than any of the Old Testament prophets did. Christ refers them to that prophecy of Daniel, that they might see how the ruin of their city and temple was spoken of in the Old Testament, which would confirm his prediction. As Christ by his precepts confirmed the law, so by his predictions he confirmed the prophecies of the Old Testament, and it will be of good use to compare both together.

Reference being here had to a prophecy, which is commonly dark and obscure, Christ inserts this memorandum, "*Whoso readeth, let him understand.*" Those that read the scriptures, should labour to understand the scriptures, else their reading is to little purpose; we cannot use that which we do not understand. And we must not despair of understanding even dark prophecies; the great New-Testament prophecy is called a *revelation*, not a *secret*. Now *things revealed belong to us*, and therefore must be humbly and diligently searched into.

2. The means of preservation which thinking men should betake themselves to (*v.* 16, 20); *Then let them which are in Judæa, flee.* We may take this, as a prediction of the ruin itself; that it should be irresistible; that it would be impossible for the stoutest hearts to make head against it, but they must have recourse to the last shift, getting out of the way. Christ here, to show how fruitless it would be to stand it out, bids everyone make the best of his way. We may take it as a direction to the followers of Christ what to do. Let them acquiesce in the decree that was gone forth, and with all speed quit the city and country, as they would quit a falling house or a sinking ship, as Lot quitted Sodom. He shows them, whither they must flee—from Judæa *to the mountains.* In times of imminent peril and danger, it is not only lawful, but our duty, to seek our own preservation by all good and honest means; and if God opens a door of escape, we ought to make our escape, otherwise we do not trust God but tempt him. While we only go out of the way of danger, not out of the way of duty, we may trust God to provide. He that flees, may fight again. See what haste they must make, *v.* 17, 18. The life will be in danger; and therefore he *that is on the house-top,* when the alarm comes, let him not *come down into the house,* but go the nearest way down, to make his escape; and so he that shall be *in the field,* will find it his wisest course to run immediately, for two reasons, *First,* Because the time which would be taken up in packing up his things, would delay his flight. When death is at the door, delays are dangerous. *Secondly,* Because the carrying of his clothes, and his other moveables and valuables with him, would but burthen him, and clog his flight. The Syrians, in their flight, *cast away their garments,* 2 Kings vii. 15. Those who carried off least, were safest in their flight. He that has grace in his heart carries his all along with him, when stripped of all.

Now those to whom Christ said this immediately, did not live to see this dismal day, none of all the twelve but John only; but they left the direction to their successors in profession, who pursued it, and it was of use to them; for when the Christians in Jerusalem and Judæa saw the ruin coming on, they all retired to a town called *Pella,* on the other side Jordan, where they were safe, so that of the thousands that perished in the destruction of Jerusalem, there was not so much as one Christian. Note, whom it would go hard with at that time (*v.* 19); *Woe to them that are with child, and to them that give suck.* To this same event that saying of Christ at his death refers (Luke xxiii. 29), They shall say, *Blessed are the wombs that never bare, and the paps that never gave suck.* To them the famine would be most grievous. To them the sword would be most terrible, when in the hand of worse than brutal rage. To them also the flight would be most afflictive; the women with child cannot make haste, or go far; the sucking child cannot be left behind, or, if it should, *can a woman forget it, that she should not have compassion on it?* If it be carried along, it retards the mother's flight, and so exposes her life. What they should pray against at that time—*that your flight be not in the winter, nor on the sabbath*

day, v. 20. In general, it becomes Christ's disciples, in times of public trouble and calamity, to be much in prayer; that is a salve for every sore, never out of season. There is no remedy but you must flee, the decree is gone forth. Labour to make the best of that which is; and when you cannot in faith pray that you may not be forced to flee, yet pray that the circumstances of it may be graciously ordered, that, though the cup may not pass from you, yet the extremity of the judgment may be prevented. God has the disposing of the circumstances of events, which sometimes makes a great alteration one way or other; and therefore in those our eyes must be ever toward him. Christ's bidding them pray for this favour, intimates his purpose of granting it to them; and in a general calamity we must see and own wherein it might have been worse. When trouble is in prospect, at a great distance, it is good to lay in a stock of prayers beforehand; they must pray, *First, That their flight, if it were the will of God, might not be in the winter,* when the days are short, the weather cold, the ways dirty, and therefore travelling very uncomfortable, especially for whole families. Though the ease of the body is not to be *mainly* consulted, it ought to be *duly* considered; though we must take what God sends, and when he sends it, yet we may pray against bodily inconveniences, and are encouraged to do so. *Secondly,* That it might not be *on the sabbath day.* For the sabbath he often showed a concern. It intimates likewise that the sabbath is ordinarily to be observed as a day of rest from travel and worldly labour; but that works of necessity were lawful on the sabbath day, as this of fleeing from an enemy to save our lives. But it intimates, likewise, that it is very uneasy and uncomfortable to a good man, to be taken off by any work of necessity from the solemn service and worship of God on the sabbath day. We should pray that we may have quiet undisturbed sabbaths, and may have no other work than sabbath work to do on sabbath days; that we may attend upon the Lord without distraction. To flee in the winter is uncomfortable to the body; but to flee on the sabbath day is so to the soul.

3. The greatness of the troubles which should immediately ensue (*v.* 21); *Then shall be great tribulation;* when the measure of iniquity is full, then come the troubles. *There shall be great tribulation.* Great, indeed, when within the city plague and famine raged, and (worse than either) faction and division, so that every man's sword was against his fellow; then and there it was that the hands of the pitiful women flayed their own children. Josephus's *History of the Wars of the Jews,* has in it more tragical passages than perhaps any history whatsoever.

(1) It was a desolation unparalleled, such as *was not since the beginning of the world, nor ever shall be.* Many a city and kingdom has been made desolate, but never any with a desolation like this. No wonder that the ruin of Jerusalem was an unparalleled ruin, when the sin of Jerusalem was an unparalleled sin—even their crucifying Christ. The nearer any people are to God in profession and privileges, the greater and heavier will his judgments be upon them.

(2) It was a desolation which, if it should continue long, would be intolerable, so that *no flesh should be saved, v.* 22. *No flesh shall be saved;* he doth not say, "No *soul* shall be saved," for the destruction of the flesh may be for *the saving of the spirit in the day of the Lord Jesus.*"

But here is one word of comfort in the midst of all this terror—that *for the elects' sake these days shall be shortened,* not made shorter than what God had determined, but shorter than what he might have decreed, if he had dealt with them according to their sins. In times of common calamity God manifests his favour to the elect remnant; his peculiar treasure, which he will secure when the lumber is abandoned to the spoiler. The shortening of calamities is a kindness God often grants. Instead of complaining that our afflictions last so long, if we consider our defects, we shall see reason to be thankful that they do not last always; when it is bad with us, it becomes us to say, "Blessed be God that it is no worse."

And now comes in the repeated caution to take heed of being ensnared by false Christs, and false prophets (v. 23, &c.). Times of great trouble are times of great temptation and therefore we have need to double our guard then. Do not heed them, it is all but talk.

VII. He foretells the sudden spreading of the gospel in the world, about the time of these great events (v. 27, 28); *As the lightning comes out of the east, so shall the coming of the Son of man be.*

1. It seems primarily to be meant of his coming to set up his spiritual kingdom in the world. The gospel would be remarkable for two things.

(1) Its swift spreading; it shall fly as the lightning. The gospel is light (John iii. 19); and it is not in this as the lightning, that it is a sudden flash, and away, for it is sunlight, and daylight. It is as lightning in these respects:

[1] It is light from heaven, as the lightning. It is God, and not man, that sends the lightnings, and summons them.

[2] It is visible and conspicuous as the lightning. Truth seeks no corners, however it may sometimes be forced into them. Christ preached his gospel openly (John xviii. 20), and his apostles on *the housetop* (*ch.* x. 27).

[3] It was sudden and surprising to the world as the lightning. The powers of darkness were dispersed and vanquished by the gospel lightning.

[4] It spread far and wide, and that quickly and irresistibly, like the lightning, which comes, suppose, out of the east (Christ is said to ascend *from the east*), and lighteneth to the west. Gospel light rose with the sun, and went with the same, so that the beams of it reached to the ends of the earth. Though it was fought against, it could never be cooped up in a desert, or in a secret place, as the seducers were; but by this, according to Gamaliel's rule, proved itself to be *of God*, that it *could not be overthrown*, Acts v. 38, 39. How soon did the gospel lightning reach this island of Great Britain! Tertullian, who wrote in the second century, takes notice of it, *The fastnesses of Britain, though inaccessible to the Romans, were occupied by Jesus Christ.* This was the Lord's doing.

(2) Another thing remarkable concerning the gospel, was, its strange success in those places to which it was spread; it gathered in multitudes. The *lifting up of Christ from the earth*, that is, the preaching of Christ crucified, which, one would think, should drive all men from him, will *draw all men to him* (John xii. 32). Whither should the soul go but to Jesus Christ, who *has the words of eternal life*? Those who have spiritual senses exercised, will know the voice of the good Shepherd from that of a thief and a robber. Saints will be where the true Christ is, not the false Christs. A living principle of grace is a kind of natural instinct in all the saints, drawing them to Christ to live upon him.

2. Some understand these verses of the coming of the Son of man *to destroy Jerusalem.*

Now here are two things intimated concerning it.

(1) That to the most it would be as unexpected as a flash of lightning, which indeed gives warning of the clap of thunder which follows, but is itself surprising.

(2) That it might be as justly expected as that the eagle should fly to the carcases. The desolation will come as certainly as the birds of prey to a dead carcase. The Jews were so corrupt and degenerate that they were become a carcase, obnoxious to the righteous judgment of God. The Romans were as an eagle, and the ensign of their armies was an eagle. The destruction shall find out the Jews wherever they are, as the eagle scents the prey.

3. It is very applicable to the day of judgment, the coming of our Lord Jesus Christ in that day. Now see here,

(1) How he shall come; *as the lightning.* Therefore those that enquire after Christ must not go into the desert or the secret places, nor listen to everyone that will put up the finger to invite them to a sight of Christ; but let them look upward, for the heavens must contain him, and thence *we look for the Saviour.*

(2) How the saints shall be gathered to him with the greatest swiftness and alacrity imaginable.

VIII. He foretells his second coming at the *end of time*, v. 29–31. *The sun shall be darkened*, &c.

1. Some think this is to be understood only of the destruction of Jerusalem and the Jewish nation; the darkening of the sun, moon, and stars, denotes the eclipse of the glory of that state. The *sign of the Son of man* (v. 30) means a signal appearance of the power and justice of the Lord Jesus in it, and the gathering *of his elect* (v. 31) signifies the delivering of a remnant from this sin and ruin.

2. It seems rather to refer to Christ's second coming. The only objection against this, is, that it is said to be *immediately after the tribulation of those days*; but as to that, (1) It is usual in the prophetical style to speak of things great and certain as near and just at hand, only to express the greatness and certainty of them. (2) *A thousand years are* in God's sight *but as one day*, 2 Pet. iii. 8. It is there urged, with reference to this very thing, and so it might be said to be immediately after.

Now concerning Christ's second coming, it is here foretold,

[1] That there shall be then a great and amazing change of the creatures, and particularly the *heavenly bodies* (v. 29). *The sun shall be darkened, and the moon shall not give her light. The stars shall fall; and the powers of heaven shall be shaken.* This intimates,

First, That there shall be a great change, in order to the making of all things new.

Secondly, It shall be a visible change, and such as all the world must take notice of; for such the darkening of the sun and moon cannot but be: and it would be an amazing change. The days of heaven, and the continuance of the sun and moon, are used to express that which is lasting and unchangeable, yet they shall thus be shaken.

Thirdly, It shall be a universal change. Nature shall sustain a general shock and convulsion, which yet shall be no hindrance to the joy and rejoicing of heaven and earth *before the Lord, when he cometh to judge the world.*

Fourthly, The sun was darkened at the death of Christ, for then was in one sense *the judgment of this world* (John xii. 31).

Fifthly, The glorious appearance of our Lord Jesus, will darken the sun and moon, as a candle is darkened in the beams of the noon-day sun.

Sixthly, The sun and moon shall be then darkened, because there will be no more occasion for them. To the saints that had their treasure above, such light of joy and comfort will be given as shall supersede that of the sun and moon, and render it useless.

[2] That *then shall appear the sign of the Son of man in heaven* (v. 30), the Son of man himself, as it follows here, *They shall see the Son of man coming in the clouds.* At his first coming, he was *set for a Sign that should be spoken against* (Luke ii. 34), but at his second coming, a sign that should be admired.

[3] That *then all the tribes of the earth shall mourn,* v. 30. Some of all the tribes and kindreds of the earth shall mourn, while the chosen remnant shall lift up their heads with joy, knowing that their redemption draws nigh, and their Redeemer. Penitent sinners look to Christ, and mourn after a godly sort; and they who sow in those tears, shall shortly reap in joy.

[4] That *then they shall see the Son of man coming in the clouds of heaven, with power and great glory. First,* The judgment of the great day will be committed to the Son of man. *Secondly,* The Son of man will at that day come in the clouds of heaven. Much of the intercourse between heaven and earth is by the clouds; drawn by heaven from the earth, distilled by heaven upon the earth. Christ went to heaven in a cloud, and *will in like manner come again,* Acts i. 9, 11. *Thirdly,* He will *come with power and great glory*: his first coming was in weakness and great meanness (2 Cor. xiii. 4). *Fourthly, Therefore* the Son of man will be the Judge, that he may be seen, that sinners thereby may be the more confounded. "Is this he whom we have slighted, and rejected, and rebelled against; whom we have crucified to ourselves afresh; who might have been our Saviour, but is our Judge?"

[5] That *he shall send his angels with a great sound of a trumpet,* v. 31. The angels shall be attendants upon Christ at his second coming; they shall be obliged to wait upon him. They are now ministering Spirits sent forth by him (Heb. i. 14), and will be so then. Their ministration will be ushered in with a great sound of a trumpet. Very fitly therefore shall there be the sound of a trumpet at the last day, when the saints shall enter upon their eternal jubilee.

[6] That *they shall gather together his elect from the four winds.* At the second coming of Jesus Christ, there will be a general meeting of all the saints. The gifts of love to eternity follow the thoughts of love from eternity; and *the Lord knows them that are his.* The angels shall be employed to bring them together, as Christ's servants, and as the saints' friends. They *shall be gathered from one end of heaven to the other*; the elect of God are scattered abroad (John xi. 52), but when that great gathering day comes, there shall not one of them be missing; distance of place shall keep none out of heaven, if distance of affection do not.

Verses 32–51

We have here the practical application of the foregoing prediction; in general, we must expect and prepare for the events here foretold.

I. We must expect them; "*Now learn a parable of the fig-tree,* v. 32, 33. Now learn what use to make of the things you have heard; that you may provide accordingly." The parable of the fig-tree is no more than this, that its budding and blossoming are a presage of summer. Thus when God begins to fulfil prophecies, he will make an end. After *the branch grows tender,* we expect the March winds, and the April showers, before the summer comes; however, we are sure it is coming; "so likewise ye, when the gospel day shall dawn, the perfect day will come. *Know that it is near.*" When the trees of righteousness begin to bud and blossom, when God's people promise faithfulness, it is a happy presage of good times. In them God begins his work, first prepares their heart, and then he will go on with it.

Now touching the events foretold here, which we are to expect,

1. Christ here assures us of the certainty of them (v. 35); *Heaven and earth shall pass away; but my words shall not pass away.* The word of Christ is more sure and lasting than heaven and earth. We may build with more assurance upon the word of Christ than we can upon the pillars of heaven, or the strong foundations of the earth; for, when they shall be no more, the word of Christ shall remain. In God's time, which is the best time, and in God's way, which is the best way, it shall certainly be fulfilled. Every word of Christ is very pure, and therefore very sure.

2. He here instructs us as to the time of them, v. 34, 36.

(1) As to *these things,* especially the ruin of the Jewish nation; "*This generation shall not pass away, till all these things be fulfilled* (v. 34); there are those now alive, that shall see Jerusalem destroyed. Because it might seem strange, he backs it with a solemn asseveration; "*Verily, I say unto you.* You may take my word for it, these things are at the door."

(2) But as to *that day and hour* which will put a period to time, *that knoweth no man,* v. 36. There is a certain day and hour fixed for the judgment to come; it is called *the day of the Lord.* That day and hour are a great secret. *No man knows it;* not the wisest by their sagacity, not the best by any divine discovery. None *knows but my Father only.* The uncertainty of the time of Christ's coming, is, to those who are watchful, *a savour of life unto life,* and makes them more watchful; but to those who are careless, it is *a savour of death unto death,* and makes them more careless.

II. To this end we must expect these events, that we may prepare for them, v. 37–41. In these verses we have such an idea given us of the judgment day, as may serve to startle and awaken us.

It will be a surprising day, and a separating day.

1. It will be a surprising day, as the deluge was to the old world, v. 37–39. Besides his first coming, to save, he has other comings to judge. He saith (John ix. 39), *For judgment I am come;* and for judgment he will come.

Now this here is applicable,

(1) To *temporal judgments,* particularly that which was now hastening upon the nation and people of the Jews; though they had fair warning given them of it, yet it found them secure, crying, *Peace and safety.* Men's unbelief shall not make God's threatenings of no effect.

(2) To *the eternal judgment*; so the judgment of the great day is called, Heb. vi. 2. Now Christ here shows what were the temper and posture of the old world when the deluge came.

[1] They were sensual and worldly; *they were eating and drinking, marrying and giving in marriage.* They were all of them, except Noah, over head and ears in the world, and regardless of the word of God, and this ruined them. Universal neglect of religion is a more dangerous symptom to any people than particular instances here and there of daring irreligion. *Eating and drinking* are necessary to the preservation of man's life; *marrying and giving in marriage* are necessary to the preservation of mankind. They were unreasonable in it, inordinate and entire in the pursuit of the delights of sense. They were in these things as in their element, as if they had their being for no other end than to *eat and drink.* They were unreasonable in it; they were entire and intent upon the world and the flesh. They were eating and drinking, when they should have been repenting and praying.

[2] They were secure and careless; *they knew not, until the flood came,* v. 39. *Knew not!* Surely they could not but know. Did he not call them to repentance while his long-suffering waited? Their *not knowing* is joined with their *eating, and drinking, and marrying*; for, *First, Therefore* they were sensual, because they were secure. *Secondly, Therefore* they were secure, because they were sensual; were so taken up with things seen and present, that they

had neither time nor heart to mind the things not seen as yet, which they were warned of. *They knew not, until the flood came.* The flood did come, though they would not foresee it. The evil day is never the further off for men's putting it far off from them. They did not know it till it was too late to prevent it. Judgments are most terrible and amazing to the secure, and those that have made a jest of them.

The application of this, concerning the old world, we have in these words; *So shall the coming of the Son of man be.* Security and sensuality are likely to be the epidemical diseases of the latter days. All are off their watch, and at their ease. As the flood took away the sinners of the old world, irresistibly and irrecoverably; so shall secure sinners, that mocked at Christ and his coming, be taken away.

2. It will be a separating day (*v.* 40, 41); *Then shall two be in the field.*

(1) We may apply it to the success of the gospel, especially at the first preaching of it; it divided the world; *some believed the things which were spoken,* and were taken to Christ; *others believed not,* and were left to perish in their unbelief.

When ruin came upon Jerusalem, a distinction was made by Divine Providence, according to that which had been before made by divine grace; for all the Christians among them were saved from perishing in that calamity. If we are safe when thousands fall on our right hand and our left, are not consumed when others are consumed round about us, so that we are as brands plucked out of the fire, we have reason to say, *It is of the Lord's mercies,* and it is a great mercy.

(2) We may apply it to the second coming of Jesus Christ, and the separation which will be made in that day. He had said before (*v.* 31), that the elect will be *gathered together.* Here it is applied to them who shall be found alive. Christ will come unlooked for, will find people busy at their usual occupations, *in the field, at the mill.* And it speaks abundance of comfort to the Lord's people. Are they mean and despised in the world, as the man-servant in the field, or the maid at the mill (Exod. xi. 5)? Yet they shall not be forgotten or overlooked in that day. Are they dispersed in distant and unlikely places, where one would not expect to find the heirs of glory, *in the field, at the mill?* Yet the angels will find them there. A very great change it will be, to go to heaven from ploughing and grinding. Are they weak, and unable of themselves to move heavenward? They shall be taken. Those whom Christ has once apprehended and laid hold on, he will never lose his hold of. Are they intermixed with others, linked with them in the same habitations, societies, employments? Let not that discourage any true Christian; God knows how to separate the wheat and chaff in the same floor.

III. Here is a general exhortation to us, *to watch, and be ready,* v. 42, &c.

1. The duty required; *Watch, and be ready,* v. 42, 44.

(1) *Watch therefore,* v. 42. It is the great duty and interest of all the disciples of Christ to watch, to be awake and keep awake. As a sinful state or way is compared to *sleep,* senseless and inactive, so a gracious state or way is compared to *watching* and *waking.* We must watch for our Lord's coming. To watch implies not only to believe that our Lord will come, but to desire that he would come, to be often thinking of his coming. To watch for Christ's coming, is to maintain that gracious temper and disposition of mind which we should be willing that our Lord, when he comes, should find us in. Watching is supposed to be in the night, which is sleeping time; while we are in this world, it is *night* with us, and we must take pains to keep ourselves awake.

(2) *Be ye also ready,* We wake in vain, if we do not get ready. It is not enough to *look* for such things;

but we must therefore *give diligence.* There is an inheritance which we then hope to enter upon, and we must have ourselves ready, made meet to partake of it.

2. The reasons to induce us to this watchfulness; which are two.

(1) Because the time of our Lord's coming is very uncertain. Let us consider then,

[1] That *we know not what hour he will come,* v. 42. We cannot know that we have a long time to live; nor can we know how little a time we have to live, for it may prove less than we expect.

[2] That he may *come at such an hour as we think not,* v. 44. Though we know not *when* he will come, we are sure he *will* come. *In such an hour as you think not,* that is, such an hour as they who are unready and unprepared, think not (*v.* 50); nay, such an hour as the most lively expectants perhaps thought least likely.

[3] That the children of this world are thus wise in their generation. This he shows in a particular instance, v. 43. If the master of a house had notice that a thief would come such a night, and such a watch of the night, though it were the midnight-watch, when he was most sleepy, yet he would be up, and listen to every noise in every corner, and he ready to give him a warm reception. Though we know not *just when* our Lord will come, yet, knowing that he *will* come, it concerns us to watch always. The day of the Lord comes *by surprise, as a thief in the night.* If Christ, when he comes, finds us asleep and unready, our house will be broken up, and we shall lose all we are worth. *Be ye also ready;* as ready at all times as the good man of the house would be at the hour when he expected the thief.

(2) Because the issue of our Lord's coming will be very happy and comfortable to those that shall be found ready, but very dismal and dreadful to those that shall not, v. 45, &c. This is represented by the different state of good and bad servants, when their lord comes to reckon with them. Now this parable seems especially intended as a warning to ministers; for the servant spoken of is a *steward.* Now observe what Christ here saith,

[1] Concerning the *good servant;* he shows here what he is—*a ruler of the household;* what, being so, he should be—*faithful* and *wise;* and what, if he be so, he shall be eternally—*blessed.*

First, We have here his place and office. He is one whom *his Lord has made ruler over his household, to give them meat in due season.* The church of Christ is his household, or family, standing in relation to him as the Father and Master of it. Gospel ministers are appointed *rulers* in this household; not as princes but as stewards, or other subordinate officers; not as lords, but as guides. They are rulers by Christ; what power they have is derived from him. The work of gospel ministers is to give to Christ's household their meat in due season, as stewards. Their work is *to give,* not take to themselves, but give to the family what the Master has bought, to *dispense* what Christ has *purchased.* It is to give *meat;* not to give *law* (that is Christ's work), but to deliver those doctrines to the church which, if duly digested, will be nourishment to souls. They must give the meat that is *sound* and *wholesome.* It must be given *in due season,* that is, whenever any opportunity offers itself; or time after time, according as the duty of every day requires.

Secondly, His right discharge of this office. The good servant will be a good *steward.*

1. He is *faithful;* stewards must be so. He that is *trusted,* must be trusty; and the greater the trust is, the more is expected from them. It is a great good thing that is committed to *ministers;* and they must be faithful. Christ counts those ministers, and those only, that are *faithful.* A faithful minister of Jesus

Christ is one that sincerely designs his master's honour, not his own; regards the meanest, reproves the greatest, and doth not respect persons.

2. He is wise to understand his duty. In guiding of the flock there is need, not only of the integrity of the heart, but the skilfulness of the hands. Honesty may suffice for a good *servant*, but wisdom is necessary to a *good steward*.

3. He is doing. The ministry is a good work, and they whose office it is, have always something to do; they must not indulge themselves in ease, but be doing, and doing to the purpose; not *talking*, but *doing*.

4. He is *found doing* when his Master comes; which intimates, (1) Constancy at his work. At what hour soever his Master comes, he is found busy at the work of the day. As with a good God the end of one mercy is the beginning of another, so with a good man, a good minister, the end of one duty is the beginning of another. (2) Perseverance in his work till the Lord come.

Thirdly, The recompence of reward intended him for this.

1. He shall be taken notice of. This is intimated in these words, Who then is that *faithful and wise servant*? Which supposes that there are but few who answer this character. Those who thus distinguish themselves now, Christ will in the great day both dignify and distinguish by the glory conferred on them.

2. He shall be blessed? *Blessed is that servant*. All the dead that die in the Lord are blessed, Rev. xiv. 13. But there is a peculiar blessedness secured to them that approve themselves faithful stewards, and are found so doing. Next to the honour of those who die in the field of battle, suffering for Christ as the martyrs, is the honour of those that die in the field of service, ploughing, and sowing, and reaping, for Christ.

3. He shall be preferred (*v.* 47); *He shall make him ruler over all his goods*. Great men, if the stewards of their house conduct themselves well in that place, commonly prefer them to be the managers of their estates. But the greatest honour which the kindest master ever did to his most tried servants in this world, is nothing to that weight of glory which the Lord Jesus will confer upon his faithful watchful servants in the world to come.

[2] Concerning the *evil* servant. Here we have,

First, His description given (*v.* 48, 49). The vilest of creatures is a wicked man, the vilest of men is a wicked Christian, and the vilest of them a wicked minister.

1. The cause of his wickedness; He hath *said in his heart, My Lord delays his coming*; and therefore he begins to think he will never come. The delay of Christ's coming, though it is a gracious instance of his patience, is greatly abused by wicked people. They that walk by sense, are ready to say of the unseen Jesus, as the people did of Moses when he tarried in the mount upon their errand, *We wot not what is become of him*, and therefore *up, make us gods*, the world a god, the belly a god, anything but him that should be.

2. The particulars of his wickedness; he is a slave to his passions and his appetites.

(1) Persecution is here charged upon him. He begins to *smite his fellow servants*. It is no new thing to see evil servants smiting their fellow servants; both private Christians and faithful ministers. He smites them, either because they reprove him, or because they will not bow, and do him reverence. The steward, when he smites his fellow servants, does it under colour of his Master's authority, and in his name; but he shall know that he could not put a greater affront upon his Master.

(2) Profaneness and immorality; *He begins to eat and drink with the drunken*. He associates with the worst of sinners. The drunken are the merry and jovial company, and those he is for, and thus he hardens them in their wickedness. He does like them; *eats, and drinks, and is drunken*. This is an inlet to all manner of sin. Drunkenness is a leading wickedness; they who are slaves to that, are never masters of themselves in anything else. Well, this is the description of a wicked minister, who yet may have the common gifts of learning and utterance above others; and, as hath been said of some, may preach so well in the pulpit, that it is a pity he should ever come out, and yet live so ill out of the pulpit, that it is a pity he should ever come in.

Secondly, His doom read, *v.* 50, 51. Observe,

1. The surprise that will accompany his doom (*v.* 50); *The Lord of that servant will come*. Our putting off the thoughts of Christ's coming will not put off his coming. Whatever fancy he deludes himself with, his Lord will come. The coming of Christ will be a most dreadful surprise to secure and careless sinners, especially to wicked ministers; He shall *come in a day when he looketh not for him*. Behold, he has told us before.

2. The severity of his doom, *v.* 51. It is not more severe than righteous, but it is a doom that carries in it utter ruin.

(1) Death. His Lord shall *cut him asunder*, "he shall cut him off from the land of the living," from the congregation of the righteous, shall separate him unto evil. Death cuts off a good man, as a choice imp is cut off to be grafted in a better stock; but it cuts off a wicked man, as a withered branch is cut off for the fire. Or, as we read it, *shall cut him asunder*, that is, part body and soul. The soul and body of a godly man at death part fairly, the one cheerfully lifted up to God, the other left to the dust; but the soul and body of a wicked man at death are cut asunder, torn asunder.

(2) Damnation. He *shall appoint him his portion with the hypocrites*, and a miserable portion it will be, for *there shall be weeping*. There is a place and state where there is nothing but *weeping and gnashing of teeth*; which speaks the soul's tribulation and anguish under God's indignation and wrath. The divine sentence will appoint this place and state as the portion of those who by their own sin were fitted for it. He that is now *the Saviour*, will then be *the Judge*, and the everlasting state of the children of men will be as he appoints. When Christ would express the most severe punishment in the other world, he calls it *the portion of hypocrites*. Wicked ministers will have their portion in the other world with the worst of sinners, even with the hypocrites, and justly, for they are the worst of hypocrites. *Son, remember*, will be as cutting a word to a minister if he perish as to any other sinner whatsoever. Let them therefore who preach to others, fear, lest they themselves should be castaways.

CHAPTER 25

This chapter continues and concludes our Saviour's discourse concerning his second coming and the end of the world. This was his farewell sermon of caution. The application of that discourse was, Watch therefore, and be ye also ready. We have three parables, the scope of which is the same—to quicken us all with the utmost care and diligence to get ready for Christ's second coming. I. That we may then be ready to attend upon him; and this is shown in the parable of the ten virgins, ver. 1–13. II. That we may then be ready to give up our account to him; and this is shown in the parable of the three servants, ver. 14–30. III. That we may then be ready to receive from him our final sentence, and that it may be to eternal life; and this is shown in a more plain description of the process of the last judgment, ver. 31–46.

Verses 1–13

I. That in general which is to be illustrated is, *the kingdom of heaven*. Some of Christ's parables had shown us what it is like now in the present reception of it, as *ch.* xiii. This tells us what it shall be like, when the mystery of God shall be finished, and that kingdom delivered up to the Father.

II. That by which it is illustrated, is, a marriage solemnity. It was a custom sometimes used among the Jews on that occasion, that the bridegroom came, attended with his friends, late in the night, to the house of the bride, where she expected him, attended with her bride-maids; who, upon notice given of the bridegroom's approach, were to go out with lamps in their hands, to light him into the house with ceremony and formality, in order to the celebrating of the nuptials with great mirth.

1. The *Bridegroom* is our Lord Jesus Christ. It bespeaks his singular and superlative love to, and his faithful and inviolable covenant with, his spouse the church.

2. The virgins are the professors of religion, members of the church; but here represented as *her companions.*

3. The office of these virgins is to meet the bridegroom, which is as much their happiness as their duty. They come to wait *upon* the bridegroom when he appears, and in the meantime to wait *for* him. As Christians, we profess ourselves to be, (1) Attendants upon Christ, to do him honour. Hold up the name, and hold forth the praise of the exalted Jesus; this is our business. (2) Expectants of Christ, and of his second coming. The second coming of Christ is the centre in which all the lines of our religion meet, and to which the whole of the divine life hath a constant reference and tendency.

4. Their chief concern is to have lights in their hands, when they attend the bridegroom, thus to do him honour and do him service. Christians are children of light.

Now concerning these ten virgins, we may observe,

(1) Their different character, with the proof and evidence of it. Their character was, that *five were wise, and five foolish* (*v.* 2). Those of the same profession and denomination among men, may yet be of characters vastly different in the sight of God. Those are wise or foolish indeed, that are so in the affairs of their souls. True religion is true wisdom; sin is folly. The evidence of this character was in the very thing which they were to attend to.

First, It was the folly of the foolish virgins, that they *took their lamps, and took no oil with them, v.* 3. They had just oil enough to make their lamps burn for the present, to make a show with, as if they intended to meet the bridegroom; but no cruse or bottle of oil with them for a recruit if the bridegroom tarried; thus hypocrites.

[1] They have no principle within. They have a lamp of profession in their hands, but have not in their hearts that stock which is necessary to carry them through the services and trials of the present state.

[2] They have no prospect of, nor make provision for, what is to come. They took lamps for a present show, but not oil for after use. They do not provide for hereafter, as the ant does, nor *lay up for the time to come,* 1 Tim. vi. 19.

Secondly, It was the wisdom of the wise virgins, that *they took oil in their vessels with their lamps, v.* 4. They had a good principle within, which would maintain and keep up their profession. The heart is the vessel, which it is our wisdom to get furnished; for, out of a good treasure there, good things must be brought; but if that root be rottenness, the blossom will be dust. Grace is the *oil* which we must have in this *vessel.* Our light must shine before men, in good works, but this cannot be, or not long, unless there be a fixed active principle in the heart, of faith in Christ, and love to God and our brethren. They

that took oil in their vessels, did it upon supposition that perhaps the bridegroom might tarry. In looking forward it is good to prepare for the worst, to lay in for a long siege.

(2) Their common fault, during the bridegroom's delay; *They all slumbered and slept, v.* 5. The bridegroom tarried, that is, he did not come out so soon as they expected. What we look for as certain, we are apt to think is very near. Christ, as to us, *seems* to tarry, and yet really *does not.* But though Christ tarry past *our* time, he will not tarry past the *due* time. While he tarried, those that waited for him, grew careless, and forgot what they were attending; *They all slumbered and slept;* as if they had given over looking for him. Those that inferred the suddenness of it from its certainty, when that answered not their expectation, were apt from the delay to infer its uncertainty. The wise virgins kept their lamps burning, but did not keep themselves awake. Too many good Christians, when they have been long in profession, grow remiss, their graces are not lively, nor their works found perfect before God; and though all *love* be not lost, yet the *first* love is left.

(3) The surprising summons given them, to attend the bridegroom (*v.* 6); *At midnight there was a cry made, Behold, the bridegroom cometh.* Though Christ tarry long, he will come at last; though he seem slow, he is sure. His friends shall find, to their comfort, that *the vision is for an appointed time.* The year of the redeemed is fixed, and it will come. Christ's coming will be at our midnight, when we least look for him. His coming for the relief and comfort of his people, often is when the good intended seems to be at the greatest distance. Christ will come when he pleases, to show his sovereignty, and will not let us know when, to teach us our duty. When Christ comes, we must *go forth to meet him. Go ye forth to meet him,* is a call to those who are habitually prepared, to be actually ready. The notice given of Christ's approach, and the call to meet him, will be awakening; *There was a cry made.* His first coming was not with any observation at all, nor did they say, *Lo, here is Christ,* or *Lo, he is there; he was in the world, and the world knew him not;* but his second coming will be with the observation of all the world.

(4) The address they all made to answer this summons (*v.* 7); *They all arose, and trimmed their lamps,* snuffed them and supplied them with oil, and went about with all expedition to receive the bridegroom. This, in the wise virgins, bespeaks an actual preparation for the Bridegroom's coming. Even those that are best prepared for death, have work to do, to get themselves actually ready, that they may be *found in peace* (2 Pet. iii. 14), *found doing* (*ch.* xxiv. 46), and not *found naked,* 2 Cor. v. 3. It will be a day of search and enquiry; and it concerns us to think how we shall then be found. In the foolish virgins, it denotes a vain confidence, and conceit of the goodness of their state, and their readiness for another world.

(5) The distress which the foolish virgins were in, for want of *oil, v.* 8, 9. This bespeaks, [1] The apprehensions which some hypocrites have of the misery of their state, even on this side death, when God opens their eyes to see their folly. Or, however, [2] The real misery of their state on the other side death, and in the judgment.

First, Their lamps are gone out. The lamps of hypocrites often go out in this life; when they who have begun in the spirit, end in the flesh. The profession withers, and the credit of it is lost; the hopes fail, and the comfort of them is gone. The gains of a hypocritical profession will not follow a man to judgment, *ch.* vii. 22, 23.

Secondly, They wanted oil to supply them when they were going out. An external profession well humoured may carry a man far, it may light him along this world, but the dams of the valley of the shadow of death will put it out.

Thirdly, They would gladly be beholden to the wise virgins for a supply out of their vessels; *Give us of your oil.* Those who now hate the strictness of religion, will, at death and judgment, wish for the solid comforts of it. Those who care not to live the life, yet would die the death, of the righteous. *Give us of your oil;* that is, "Speak a good word for us"; so some; but there is no occasion for vouchers in the great day, the Judge knows what is every man's true character. Those will see their need of grace hereafter, when it should save them, who will not see their need of grace now, when it should sanctify and rule them. It comes too late. There is no buying when the market is over, no bidding when the inch of candle is dropped.

Fourthly, They were denied a share in their companions' oil. *The wise answered, Not so;* that peremptory denial is not in the original, but supplied by the translators: these wise virgins would rather give a reason without a positive refusal, than (as many do) give a positive refusal without a reason. They were well inclined to help their neighbours in distress; but, We must not, we cannot, we dare not, do it, *lest there be not enough for us and you;* charity begins at home; but *go, and buy for yourselves.* Those that would be saved, must have grace of their own. Though we have benefit by the communion of saints, and the faith and prayers of others, yet our own sanctification is indispensably necessary to our own salvation. Every man shall give account of himself; for he cannot get another to muster for him in that day. Those that have most grace, have none to spare; all we have, is little enough for ourselves to appear before God in. The best have need to borrow from Christ, but they have none to lend to any of their neighbours. These wise virgins do not upbraid the foolish with their neglect, but give them the best advice the case will bear, *Go ye rather to them that sell.* When ministers attend such as have been mindless of God and their souls all their days, but are under death-bed convictions; and direct them to repent, and turn to God, and close with Christ; they do but as these wise virgins did by the foolish, even make the best of bad. They can but tell them what is to be done. It is good advice now, if it be taken in time, *Go to them that sell, and buy for yourselves.*

(6) The coming of the bridegroom, and the issue of all this.

[1] *While they went out to buy, the bridegroom came.* With regard to those that put off their great work to the last, it is a thousand to one, that they have not time to do it then. Getting grace is a work of time, and cannot be done in a hurry. While the poor awakened soul addresses itself, upon a sick bed, to repentance and prayer, in awful confusion, it scarcely knows which end to begin at. This comes of having oil to buy when we should burn it, and grace to get when we should use it.

The bridegroom came. Our Lord Jesus will come to his people, at the great day, as a Bridegroom; will come in pomp and rich attire, attended with his friends.

[2] *They that were ready, went in with him to the marriage.* To be eternally glorified is to be in his immediate presence, and in the most intimate fellowship and communion with him. Those, and those only, shall go to heaven hereafter, that are made ready for heaven here.

[3] *The door was shut,* as is usual when all the company are come. The door was shut, *First,* To secure those that were within. Adam was put into paradise, but the door was left open and so he went out again; but when glorified saints are put into the heavenly paradise, they are shut in. *Secondly,* To exclude those that were out. Now the gate is strait, yet it is open; but then it will be shut and bolted, and *a great gulf fixed.*

[4] The foolish virgins came when it was *too late* (v. 11); *Afterward came also the other virgins.* There are many that will seek admission into heaven when it is too late; as profane Esau, who *afterward would have inherited the blessing.* The vain confidence of hypocrites will carry them very far in their expectations of happiness. They go to heaven-gate, and demand entrance, and yet are shut out.

[5] They were *rejected*, as Esau was (v. 12); *I know you not.* We are all concerned to *seek the Lord while he may be found.* Time was, when, Lord, Lord, open to us, would have sped well, by virtue of that promise, *Knock, and it shall be opened to you;* but now it comes too late.

Lastly, Here is a practical inference drawn from this parable (v. 13); *Watch therefore.* We had it before (ch. xxiv. 42), and here it is repeated as the most needful caution. Our great duty is to watch. Be awake, and be wakeful. It is a good reason for our watching, that the time of our Lord's coming is very uncertain; *we know neither the day nor the hour.*

Verses 14–30

We have here the parable of the *talents* committed to three servants; this implies that we are in a state of work and business, as the former implies that we are in a state of expectancy. *That* showed the necessity of habitual preparation, *this* of actual diligence in our present work and service. 1. The *Master* is Christ. 2. The *servants* are Christians, his own servants, so they are called.

We have three things, in general, in this parable.

I. The trust committed to these servants; Their master *delivered to them his goods*: having appointed them to work (for Christ keeps no servants to be idle), he left them something to work upon. 1. Christ's servants have and receive their all from him; nor have anything they can call their own but sin. 2. Our receiving from Christ is in order to our working for him. 3. Whatever we receive to be made use of for Christ, still the property is vested in him.

(1) On what occasion this trust was committed to these servants; The master was *travelling into a far country. When he ascended on high, he gave gifts unto men.* When Christ went to heaven, he was as a man *travelling into a far country.* When he went, he took care to furnish his church with all things necessary for it during his personal absence. Thus Christ, at his ascension, left his goods to his church.

(2) In what proportion this trust was committed. He gave *talents.* Christ's gifts are rich and valuable, the purchases of his blood inestimable, and none of them mean. He gave to some more, to others less; to everyone according to his several ability. When Divine Providence has made a difference in men's ability, grace dispenses spiritual gifts accordingly, but still the ability itself is from him. Everyone had some one talent at least, and that is not a despicable stock for a poor servant to begin with. A *soul* of our own is the *one* talent we are every one of us entrusted with, and it will find us with work. *It is the duty of a man to render himself beneficial to those around him. He that is useful to others, may be reckoned a common good.* All had not alike, for they had not all alike abilities and opportunities. Some are cut out for service in one kind, others in another, as the members of the natural body.

II. The different management and improvement of this trust, v. 16–18.

1. Two of the servants did well.

(1) They were diligent and faithful; *They went, and traded*; as soon as ever their master was gone, they immediately applied themselves to their business.

Those that have so much work to do, as every Christian has, need to set about it quickly, and lose no time. *They went, and traded.* A true Christian is a spiritual tradesmen. A tradesman is one who, having made his trade his choice, and taken pains to learn it, makes it his business to follow it, makes all other affairs bend to it, and lives upon the gain of it. We have no stock of our *own* to trade with, but trade as factors with our master's stock. The endowments of the mind—the enjoyments of the world—must be improved for the honour of Christ. The ordinances of the gospel, and our opportunities of attending them, must be improved for the end for which they were instituted, and communion with God kept up by them, and the gifts and graces of the Spirit must be exercised.

(2) They were successful; they doubled their stock. The hand of the diligent makes rich in graces, and comforts, and treasures of good works. There is a great deal to be got by industry in religion. The returns were in proportion to the receivings. The greater gifts any have, the more pains they ought to take, as those must that have a large stock to manage. From those to whom he has given but two talents, he expects only the improvement of two; if they lay out themselves to do good according to the best of their capacity and opportunity, they shall be accepted, though they do not so much good as others.

2. The third did ill (*v.* 18); *He that had received one talent, went, and hid his lord's money.* The unfaithful servant was he that had but *one talent*: doubtless there are many that have five talents, and bury them all; great abilities, great advantages, and yet do no good with them: but Christ would hint to us, (1) That if he that had but one talent, be reckoned with thus for burying that one, much more will they be accounted offenders, that have more, that have many, and bury them. (2) That those who have least to do for God, frequently do least of what they have to do. Some make it an excuse, because they have not wherewithal to do what they say they would, they will not do what we are sure they can, and so sit down and do nothing; it is really an aggravation of their sloth, that when they have but one talent to take care about, they neglect that one.

He digged in the earth, and hid the talent, for fear it should be stolen. Money is like manure (so my Lord Bacon used to say), good for nothing in the heap, but it must be spread; and so it is in spiritual gifts; many have them, and make no use of them for the end for which they were given them.

He hid his *lord's money*; had it been his *own,* he might have done as he pleased. His fellow-servants were busy and successful in trading, and their zeal should have provoked his. Are others active, and shall we be idle?

III. The account of this improvement, *v.* 19. The account is deferred; it is not *till after a long time* that they are reckoned with. Yet the day of account comes at last; *The lord of those servants reckoneth with them.* We must all be reckoned with—what good we have got to our own souls, and what good we have done to others.

1. The good account of the faithful servants. The servants *giving up the account* (*v.* 20, 22); "*Lord, thou deliveredst to me five talents,* and to me *two*; behold, *I have gained five talents,* and I *two* talents *more.*"

Christ's faithful servants acknowledge with thankfulness his vouchsafements to them; *Lord, thou deliveredst to me* such and such things. It is good to remember what we have received, that we may know what is expected from us, and may render according to the benefit. We must never look upon our improvements but with a general mention of God's favour to us, of the honour he has put upon us, in entrusting us with his goods. For the truth is, the more we do for God, the more we are indebted to him for making use of us.

They produce, as an evidence of their faithfulness, what they have gained. God's good stewards have something to show for their diligence; *Show me thy faith by thy works.* He that is a good man, *let him show it,* James iii. 13. And it is observable that he who had but *two* talents, gave up his account as cheerfully as he who had *five*; for our comfort, in the day of account, will be according to our faithfulness, our sincerity, not our success; according to the uprightness of our hearts, not according to the degree of our opportunities.

The master's acceptance and approbation of their account, *v.* 21, 23.

First, He commended them; *Well done, good and faithful servant.* Those that own and honour God now, he will own and honour shortly. Christ will give them their just characters, of *good and faithful.* Their performances will be accepted; *Well done.* Christ will call those, and those only, *good servants,* that have done well. If we do that which is good, and do it well, we shall have *praise of the same.* Some masters are so morose, that they will not commend their servants; it is thought enough not to chide: but Christ will commend his servants that do well; whether their praise be of men or no, it is of him. If he saith, *Well done,* we are happy.

Secondly, He rewards them. All their work and labour of love shall be rewarded.

Now this reward is here expressed two ways.

(1) In one expression agreeable to the parable; *Thou hast been faithful over a few things, I will make thee ruler over many things.* It is usual in the courts of princes, and families of great men, to advance those to higher offices, that have been faithful in lower. Christ is a master that will prefer his servants who acquit themselves well. Christ has honour in store for those that honour him. Here they are beggars; in heaven they shall be rulers.

Observe the disproportion between the work and the reward; there are but few things in which the saints are serviceable to the glory of God, but there are many things wherein they shall be glorified with God. What charge we receive from God, what work we do for God in this world, is but little, very little, compared with *the joy set before us.*

(2) In another expression, which slips out of the parable into the thing signified by it; *Enter thou into the joy of thy Lord.* The state of the blessed is a state of joy. Where there are the vision and fruition of God, a perfection of holiness, and the society of the blessed, there cannot but be a fulness of joy. This joy is the *joy of thy Lord*; the joy which he himself has purchased and provided for them; the joy of the redeemed, bought with the sorrow of the Redeemer. Christ admits his faithful stewards into his own joy, to be joint-heirs with him. Glorified saints shall enter into this joy, shall have a full and complete possession of it, as they that were ready, *went* in to the marriage feast. Shortly they shall enter into it, shall be in it to eternity, as in their element.

2. The bad account of the slothful servant.

(1) His apology for himself, *v.* 24, 25. Though he had received but *one* talent, for that one he is called to account. None shall be called to an account for more than they have received; but for what we have, we must all account.

First, What he confides in. "*Lo, there thou hast that is thine;* if I have not made it more, as the others have done, yet this I can say, I have not made it less." This, he thinks, may serve to bring him off, if not with praise, yet with safety. Slothful professors, that are afraid of doing too much for God, yet hope to come off as well as those that take so much pains in religion. This servant thought that this account would pass well enough, because he could say, *There thou hast that is thine*. Many that are called Christians, build great hopes for heaven upon their being able to make such an account; as if no more were required, or could be expected.

Secondly, What he confesses. He owns the burying of his talent; *I hid thy talent in the earth*. He speaks as if that were no great fault; nay, as if he deserved praise for his prudence in putting it in a safe place, and running no hazards with it.

Thirdly, What he makes his excuse; *I knew that thou wert a hard man, and I was afraid*. Good thoughts of God would beget love, and that love would make us diligent and faithful; but hard thoughts of God beget fear, and that fear makes us slothful and unfaithful. His excuse bespeaks,

[1] The sentiments of an enemy; *I knew thee, that thou art a hard man*. Thus his *defence* is his *offence*. Observe how confidently he speaks; *I knew thee to be so*. How could he know him to be so? Does not all the world know the contrary, that he is so far from being a hard master, that *the earth is full of his goodness*, so far from reaping where he sowed not, that he sows a great deal where he reaps nothing? For he *causes the sun to shine, and his rain to fall, upon the evil and unthankful, and fills their hearts with food and gladness* who say to the Almighty, *Depart from us*. This suggestion bespeaks the common reproach which wicked people cast upon God, as if all the blame of their sin and ruin lay at his door, for denying them his grace. But if we perish, it is owing to ourselves.

[2] The spirit of a slave; *I was afraid*. This ill affection toward God arose from his false notions of him. Hard thoughts of God drive us from, and cramp us in his service. Those who think it impossible to please him, and in vain to serve him, will do nothing to purpose in religion.

(2) His Lord's answer to this apology. His plea is made to turn against him, and he is struck speechless with it.

First, His conviction, *v*. 26, 27. Two things he is convicted of.

[1] Slothfulness; *Thou wicked and slothful servant*. Slothful servants are wicked servants. He that is careless in God's work, is near akin to him that is busy in the devil's work. Omissions are sins, and must come into judgment; slothfulness makes way for wickedness. When the house is empty, the unclean spirit takes possession. When men sleep, the enemy sows tares.

[2] Self-contradiction (*v*. 26, 27); *Thou knewest that I reap where I sowed not: thou oughtest therefore to have put my money to the exchangers*. Three ways this may be taken; *a*. "Suppose I had been so hard a master, shouldest not thou therefore have been the more diligent and careful to please me, if not for *love*, yet for *fear*?" *b*. "If thou didst think me to be a hard master, and therefore durst not trade with the money thyself, for fear of losing by it, yet thou mightest have brought it to the bank, and then at my coming I should have received *my own with usury*." If we could not find in our hearts to venture upon more difficult and hazardous services, yet will that justify us in shrinking from those that were more safe and easy? Something is better than nothing; if we fail of showing our courage in bold enterprises, yet we must not fail to testify our goodwill in honest endeavours. *c*. "Suppose I did reap *where I sowed not*, yet that is nothing to thee, for I had sowed upon thee, and the talent was my money which thou wast entrusted with, not only to keep, but to improve."

Secondly, His condemnation. The slothful servant is sentenced,

[1] To be deprived of his talent (*v*. 28, 29); *Take therefore the talent from him*. And the meaning of this

part of the parable we have in the reason of the sentence (*v*. 29), *To every one that hath shall be given*. This may be applied, *a*. To the blessings of this life —worldly wealth and possessions. These we are entrusted with, to be used for the glory of God, and the good of those about us. But *from him that hath not*, that is, that hath these things as if he had them not, they *shall be taken away*. *b*. We may apply it to the means of grace. They who are diligent in improving the opportunities they have, God will enlarge them. *c*. We may apply it to the common gifts of the Spirit. He that hath these, and doeth good with them, shall have abundance; these gifts improve by exercise, and brighten by being used; the more we do, the more we may do, in religion; but those who stir not up the gift that is in them their gifts rust, and decay, and go out like a neglected fire.

[2] He is sentenced to be *cast into outer darkness*, *v*. 30.

(1) His character is that of an *unprofitable servant*. Slothful servants will be reckoned with as unprofitable servants. A slothful servant is a withered member in the body, he is good for nothing. In one sense, we are all *unprofitable servants* (Luke xvii. 10); we cannot *profit God*. It is not enough not to do hurt, but we must do good, must bring forth fruit, and though thereby God is not profited, yet he is glorified, John xv. 8.

(2) His doom is, to be *cast into outer darkness*. Their state is, [1] Very dismal; it is outer darkness. In the dark *no man can work*, a fit punishment for a slothful servant. It is *outer* darkness, *out* from the light of heaven, *out* from the joy of their Lord, into which the faithful servants were admitted; *out* from the feast. [2] Very doleful; there is weeping and gnashing of teeth. This will be the portion of the slothful servant.

Verses 31–46

We have here a description of the process of the last judgment in the great day. It is, as it were, the explanation of the former parables.

I. The placing of the judge upon the judgment-seat (*v*. 31); *When the Son of man shall come*.

1. That there is a judgment to come, in which every man shall be sentenced according to what he did in this world of trial and probation.

2. The administration of the judgment of the great day is committed to the Son of man. Here, as elsewhere, when the last judgment is spoken of, Christ is called *the son of man*, because he is to judge the sons of men (and, being himself of the same nature, he is the more unexceptionable).

3. Christ's appearing to judge the world will be splendid and glorious. Christ will come to the judgment-seat in real glory; and all the world shall see what the saints only do now believe—that he is the brightness of his Father's glory. His first coming was under a black cloud of obscurity; his second will be in a bright cloud of glory.

4. When Christ comes in his glory to judge the world, he will bring all his holy angels with him. This glorious person will have a glorious retinue, his holy myriads.

5. He will then sit upon the throne of his glory. He is *now* set down with the Father upon his throne; and it is a throne of grace, to which we may come boldly; but *then* he will sit upon the throne of glory, the throne of judgment. Christ, in the days of his flesh, was arraigned as a prisoner at the bar; but at his second coming, he will sit as a judge upon the bench.

II. The appearing of all the children of men before him (*v*. 32); *Before him shall be gathered all nations*. The judgment of the great day will be a general judgment. All must be summoned before Christ's tribunal; all nations, all those nations of men that are made of one blood, to dwell on all the face of the earth.

III. The distinction that will then be made; *He shall separate them one from another*, as the tares and wheat are separated at the harvest, the good fish and the bad at the shore, the corn and chaff in the floor. Wicked and godly here dwell together and are not certainly distinguishable one from another: but in that day they will be separated, and parted for ever. They cannot separate themselves one from another in this world (1 Cor. v. 10), nor can anyone else separate them (*ch.* xiii. 29); but the Lord knows them that are his, and he can separate them. This is compared to a shepherd's dividing between the sheep and the goats. 1. Jesus Christ is the great Shepherd; he now feeds his flock like a shepherd, and will shortly distinguish between those that are his, and those that are not. 2. The godly are like sheep—innocent, mild, patient, useful: the wicked are like goats, a baser kind of animal, unsavoury and unruly. The sheep and goats are here feeding all day in the same pasture, but will be coted at night in different folds. Being thus divided, he will set the *sheep on his right hand*, and the *goats on his left*, *v.* 33. Christ puts honour upon the godly, as we show respect to those we set on our right hand. All other divisions and subdivisions will then be abolished; but the great distinction of men into saints and sinners, sanctified and unsanctified, will remain for ever.

IV. The process of the judgment concerning each of these.

1. Concerning the godly, on the right hand. Observe here,

(1) The *glory* conferred upon them (*v.* 34); *The king shall say unto them.* He that was the Shepherd (which bespeaks the care and tenderness wherewith he will make this disquisition), is here the King. Where the word of this King is, there is power. Here are two things in this sentence:

[1] The acknowledging of the saints to be the blessed of the Lord; *Come, ye blessed of my Father.* He pronounces them *blessed*; and his saying they are blessed, makes them so. *Blessed of his Father*; reproached and cursed by the world, but blessed of God. All our blessings in heavenly things flow to us from God, as the Father of our Lord Jesus Christ, Eph. i. 3. He calls them *to come*: this *come* is, in effect, "*Welcome*, ten thousand welcomes, to the blessings of my Father; come to me, come to be for ever with me; you that followed me bearing the cross, now come along with me wearing the crown." We now come boldly to the throne of grace, but we shall then come boldly to the throne of glory.

[2] The admission of the saints into the blessedness and kingdom of the Father; *Inherit the kingdom prepared for you.*

First, The happiness they shall be possessed of is very rich.

a. It is a *kingdom*; which is reckoned the most valuable possession on earth, and includes the greatest wealth and honour. They that here are beggars, prisoners, accounted as the off-scouring of all things, shall then inherit a kingdom.

b. It is a kingdom *prepared*: the happiness must needs be great, for it is the product of the divine counsels.

c. It is prepared *for them.* This bespeaks, (*a*) The suitableness of this happiness. (*b*) Their property and interest in it. It is prepared on purpose for them; not only for such as you, but for you, you by name.

d. It is prepared *from the foundation of the world.* This happiness was designed for the saints, and they for it, before time began, from all eternity, Eph. i. 4.

Secondly, The tenure by which they shall hold and possess it is very good, they shall come and *inherit it.* It is God that makes heirs, heirs of heaven. We come to an inheritance by virtue of our sonship, our adoption; *if children, then heirs.* A title by inheritance is the sweetest and surest title. Saints, in this world, are as heirs under age, tutored and governed till the time appointed of the Father (Gal. iv. 1, 2); and then they shall be put in full possession of that which now through grace they have a title to; *Come,* and inherit it.

(2) The ground of this (*v.* 35, 36), *For I was an hungered, and ye gave me meat.* We cannot hence infer that any good works of ours merit the happiness of heaven; but it is plain that Jesus Christ will judge the world by the same rule by which he governs it, and therefore will reward those that have been obedient to that law. This happiness will be adjudged to obedient believers, upon the promise of God purchased by Jesus Christ. It is the purchase and promise that give the title, the obedience is only the qualification of the person designed.

Now the good works here mentioned are such as we commonly call works of charity to the poor, and it teaches us this in general, that faith working by love is all in all in Christianity; *Show me thy faith by thy works.* The good works here described imply three things, which must be found in all that are saved.

[1] Self-denial, and contempt of the world; reckoning the things of the world no further good things, than as we are enabled to do good with them: and those who have not wherewithal to do good, must show the same disposition, by being contentedly and cheerfully poor.

[2] Love to our brethren; which is the second great commandment. We must give proof of this love by our readiness to do good, and to communicate; good wishes are but mockeries without good works. Those that have not to give, must show the same disposition some other way.

[3] A believing regard to Jesus Christ. That which is here rewarded is the relieving of the poor for Christ's sake, out of love to him. Those good works shall then be accepted which are done in the name of the Lord Jesus, Col. iii. 17.

I was hungry, and *you gave them meat.* It is no new thing for those that are feasted with the dainties of heaven to be hungry and thirsty, and to want daily food; for those that are at home in God, to be strangers in a strange land; for those that have put on Christ, to want clothes to keep them warm; for those that have healthful souls, to have sickly bodies, and for those to be in prison, that Christ has made free. Works of charity and beneficence, according as our ability is, are necessary to salvation. These must be the proofs of our love, and of our professed subjection to the gospel of Christ. But they that show no mercy, shall have judgment without mercy.

Now this reason is modestly excepted against by the righteous, but is explained by the Judge himself.

a. It is questioned by the righteous, *v.* 37–39. Not as if they were loth to inherit the kingdom, or were ashamed of their good deeds. Christ has a mighty regard to works of charity, and is especially pleased with kindnesses done to his people for his sake. They bespeak the humble admiration which glorified saints will be filled with, to find such poor and worthless services, as theirs are, so highly celebrated, and richly rewarded: *Lord, when saw we thee an hungered, and fed thee?* Gracious souls are apt to think meanly of their own good deeds; especially as unworthy to be compared with the glory that shall be revealed. Saints in heaven will wonder what brought them thither, and that God should so regard them and their services. *"When saw we thee an hungered? We have seen the poor in distress many a time; but when saw we thee?"* Christ is more among us than we think he is.

b. It is explained by the Judge himself (*v.* 40); *Inasmuch as ye have done it to these my brethren,* to the least, to one of the least of them, *ye have done it unto me.* The good works of the saints, when they are produced in the great day, (*a*) Shall all be remembered; and not the least overlooked, no not a cup of cold water. (*b*) They shall be interpreted most to their advantage. As Christ makes the best of their infirmities, so he makes the most of their services.

But what will become of the godly poor, that had not wherewithal to do so? Must they be shut out? No, Christ will own them, even the least of them, as his brethren; he will not be ashamed, nor think it any disparagement to him, *to call them brethren.* In the height of his glory, he will not disown his poor relations. He will take the kindness done to them, as done to himself; *Ye have done it unto me*; which shows a respect to the poor that were relieved, as well as to the rich that did relieve them.

2. Here is the process concerning the wicked, those on the left hand. And in that we have,

(1) The sentence passed upon them, *v.* 41. He shall say to them, *Depart from me, ye cursed.*

[1] To be so near to Christ was some satisfaction, though under his frowns; but that will not be allowed, *Depart from me.* In this world they were often called to come to Christ, to come for life and rest, but they turned a deaf ear to his calls. Here they said to the Almighty, *Depart from us*; then he will say to them, *Depart from me.*

[2] If they must depart, and depart from Christ, might they not be dismissed with a blessing, with one kind and compassionate word at least? No, *Depart, ye cursed.* They that would not come to Christ, to inherit a blessing, must depart from him under the burthen of a curse. The righteous are called *the blessed of my Father*; for their blessedness is owing purely to the grace of God and his blessing, but the wicked are called only *ye cursed*, for their damnation is of themselves.

[3] If they must depart may they not go into some place of ease and rest? Will it not be misery enough for them to bewail their loss? They must depart into *fire.* This fire is the wrath of the eternal God.

[4] If into fire, prepared fire, O let it be but of short continuance, let them but pass *through* fire. No for the streams of mercy and grace being for ever excluded, there is nothing to extinguish it.

[5] If they must be doomed to such a state of endless misery, yet may they not have some good company there? No, none but *the devil and his angels.* They served the devil while they lived, and therefore are justly sentenced to be where he is, as those that served Christ, are taken to be with him where he is.

The reason of this sentence assigned.

[1] All that is charged upon them, on which the sentence is grounded, is, omission; as, before, the servant was condemned, not for wasting his talent, but for burying it. "When I was in these distresses, you were so selfish that you did not *minister* as you might have done to my relief and succour." Omissions are the ruin of thousands.

[2] It is the omission of works of charity to the poor; for omitting the weightier matters of the law, *judgment, mercy, and faith.* Uncharitableness to the poor is a damning sin. *They shall have judgment without mercy, that have showed no mercy.* Sinners will be condemned, at the great day, for the omission of that good which it was in the power of their hand to do. Now this reason of the sentence is,

First, Objected against by the prisoners (*v.* 44); *Lord, when saw we thee an hungered, or athirst?* Condemned sinners, though they have no plea that will bear them out, will yet in vain offer excuses. *When saw we thee hungry, or thirsty, or naked?* They care not to repeat the full charge, as conscious to themselves of their own guilt. The matter of their plea bespeaks their former inconsideration of that which they might have known, but would not till now that it was too late. They imagined it was only a company of poor, weak, silly, and contemptible people that they put those slights upon; but they who do so, will be made to know that it was *Jesus whom they persecuted.*

Secondly, Justified by the Judge. He goes by this rule (*v.* 45); *Inasmuch as ye did it not to one of the least of these, ye did it not to me.* What is done against the faithful disciples and followers of Christ, even the least of them, he takes as done against himself. *In all their afflictions he is afflicted.* He that touches them, touches him in a part no less tender than the apple of his eye.

Lastly, Here is the execution of both these sentences, *v.* 46.

a. The wicked shall go away into everlasting punishment. Sentence will then be executed speedily. It can neither be thought that sinners should change their own natures, nor that God should give his grace to change them, when in this world the day of grace was misspent.

b. The righteous shall go away into life eternal; that is, they shall *inherit the kingdom, v.* 34. Heaven is life, it is all happiness. It is *eternal* life. There is no death to put a period to the life itself, nor old age to put a period to the comfort of it, or any sorrow to embitter it. Thus life and death, good and evil, the blessing and the curse, are set before us, that we may choose our way; and so shall our end be.

CHAPTER 26

The narrative of the death and sufferings of Christ is more particularly and fully recorded by all the four evangelists than any part of his history. And this chapter begins that memorable narrative. In this chapter, we have, I. The preliminaries, or prefaces, to Christ's sufferings. 1. The previous notice given by him to his disciples, ver. 1, 2. 2. The rulers' conspiracy against him, ver. 3–5. 3. The anointing of his head at a supper in Bethany, ver. 6–13. 4. Judas's bargain with the priests to betray him, ver. 14–16. 5. Christ eating the passover with his disciples, ver. 17–25. 6. His instituting the Lord's supper, and his discourse with his disciples, after it, ver. 26–35. II. His entrance upon them, and some of the particulars of them. 1. His agony in the garden, ver. 36–46. 2. The seizing of him by the officers, with Judas's help, ver. 47–56. 3. His arraignment before the chief priest, and his condemnation in his court, ver. 57–68. 4. Peter's denying him, ver. 69–75.

Verses 1–5

Here is, 1. The notice Christ gave his disciples of the near approach of his sufferings, *v.* 1, 2. He had often told them of his sufferings at a distance, now he speaks of them as at the door; *after two days.* Observe,

(1) The *time* when he gave this alarm; *when he had finished all these sayings.* Christ's witnesses die not till they have finished their testimony. He had bid his disciples to expect sad times, bonds and afflictions, and then tells them, *The Son of man is betrayed*; to intimate that they should fare no worse than he should, and that his sufferings should take the sting out of theirs.

(2) The thing itself he gave them notice of; *The Son of man is betrayed.* The thing was not only so sure, but so near, that it was as good as done. It is good to make sufferings that are yet to come, as present to us.

2. The plot of the chief priests, and scribes, and elders of the people, against the life of our Lord Jesus,

v. 3–5. Many consultations had been held against the life of Christ; but this plot was laid deeper than any yet, for the grandees were all engaged in it. (1) The *place* where they met; *in the palace of the high priest.* (2) The plot itself; to *take Jesus by subtlety, and kill him*; nothing less than his blood, his lifeblood, would serve their turn. (3) The policy of the plotters; *Not on the feastday. Lest there should be an uproar among the people.* They were awed, not by the fear of God, but by the fear of the people; all their concern was for their own safety, not God's honour.

Verses 6–13

I. The singular kindness of a good woman to our Lord Jesus in anointing his head, *v.* 6, 7. It was *in Bethany*, a village hard by Jerusalem, and *in the house of Simon the leper.* Probably he was one who had been miraculously cleansed from his leprosy by our Lord Jesus, and he would express his gratitude to Christ by entertaining him; nor did Christ disdain to come in to him, and sup with him. The woman that did this, is supposed to have been Mary, the sister of Martha and Lazarus. She had a *box of ointment very precious*, which she *poured upon the head* of Christ as he sat at meat. This, among us, would be a strange sort of compliment. But it was then accounted the highest piece of respect. Now this may be looked upon,

1. As an act of faith in our Lord Jesus, the Christ, the Messiah, the anointed.

2. As an act of love and respect to him. Some think that this was she who *loved much* at first, and *washed Christ's feet with her tears* (Luke vii. 38, 47). Where there is true love in the heart to Jesus Christ, nothing will be thought too good, no, nor good enough, to bestow upon him.

II. The offence which the disciples took at this. They *had indignation* (*v.* 8, 9).

1. See how they expressed their offence at it. They said, *To what purpose is this waste?* Now this bespeaks,

(1) Want of tenderness toward this good woman, in interpreting her over-kindness (suppose it was so) to be wastefulness. Charity teaches us to put the best construction upon everything that it will bear. It is true, there may be over-doing in well-doing; but thence we must learn not to be censorious of others; because that which we may impute to the want of prudence, God may accept as an instance of abundant love. We must not say, Those do too much in religion, that do more than we do, but rather aim to do as much as they.

(2) Want of respect to their Master. It did not become them to call it *waste*, when they perceived that he admitted and accepted it as a token of his friend's love. We must take heed of thinking anything waste, which is bestowed upon the Lord Jesus, either by others or by ourselves.

2. See how they excused their offence at it; *This ointment might have been sold for much, and given to the poor.*

III. The reproof Christ gave to his disciples for the offence at this good woman (*v.* 10, 11); *Why trouble ye the woman?* Note, It is a great trouble to good people to have their good works censured and misconstrued; and it is a thing that Jesus Christ takes very ill. He here took part against all his disciples; so heartily does he espouse the cause of the *offended little ones*, ch. xviii. 10.

Observe his reason; *You have the poor always with you.*

1. There are some opportunities of doing and getting good which are constant, and which we must give constant attendance to the improvement of. Those who have a heart to do good, never need complain for want of opportunity.

2. There are other opportunities of doing and getting good, which come but seldom, and which ought to be preferred before the other; "*Me ye have not always, therefore use me while ye have me.*" Sometimes special works of piety and devotion should take place of common works of charity.

IV. Christ's approbation and commendation of the kindness of this good woman. He calls it a *good work* (*v.* 10), and says more in praise of it than could have been imagined; particularly,

1. That the meaning of it was mystical (*v.* 12); *She did it for my burial.* Some think that she *intended* it so, and that the woman better understood Christ's frequent predictions of his death and sufferings than the apostles did. Christ interpreted it so; and he is always willing to make the best, to make the most of his people's well-meant words and actions.

2. That the memorial of it should be honourable (*v.* 13); *This shall be told for a memorial.* This act of faith and love was so remarkable, that the preachers of Christ crucified, and the inspired writers of the history of his passion, could not choose but take notice of this passage. None of all the trumpets of fame sound so loud and so long as the everlasting gospel. Though the honour of Christ is principally designed in the gospel, yet the honour of his saints and servants is not altogether overlooked. The memorial of this woman was to be preserved by mentioning her faith and piety in the preaching of the gospel, for example to others.

Verses 14–16

Immediately after an instance of the greatest kindness done to Christ, follows an instance of the greatest unkindness; such mixture is there of good and bad among the followers of Christ.

I. The traitor was Judas Iscariot; he is said to be *one of the twelve*, as an aggravation of his villainy. When the *number of the disciples was multiplied* (Acts vi. 1), no marvel if there were some among them that were a shame and trouble to them; but when there were but twelve, and one of them was *a devil*, surely we must never expect any society perfectly pure on this side heaven. The twelve were Christ's chosen friends, and yet one of them betrayed him. No bonds of duty or gratitude will hold those that have a devil.

II. Here is the proffer which he made to the chief priests; he *went to them, and said, What will ye give me? v.* 15. They did not send for him, nor make the proposal to him; they could not have thought that one of Christ's own disciples should be false to him.

1. What Judas promised; "*I will deliver him unto you*; that you may seize him without noise, or danger of an uproar." In their conspiracy against Christ, this was it they were at a loss about, *v.* 4, 5. They durst not meddle with him in public, and knew not where to find him in private. Here the matter rested, and the difficulty was insuperable, till Judas came, and offered them his services. Those that give up themselves to be led by the devil, find him readier than they imagine to help them at a dead lift. Though the rulers, by their power and interest, could kill him when they had him in their hands, yet none but a disciple could betray him.

I will deliver him unto you. He did not offer himself to be a witness against Christ, though they wanted evidence, *v.* 59. This is an evidence of the innocency of our Lord Jesus, that his own disciple, who was false to him, could not charge him with anything criminal, though it would have served to justify his treachery.

2. What he asked in consideration of this undertaking; *What will ye give me?* This was the only thing that made Judas betray his Master; he hoped to get money by it. It was not the hatred of his

Master, nor any quarrel with him, but purely the love of money; that, and nothing else, made Judas a traitor.

What will ye give me? Why, what did he want? Neither bread to eat, nor raiment to put on; neither necessaries nor conveniences. This covetous wretch could not be content, but comes basely cringing to the priests with, *What will ye give me?* It is not the *lack* of money, but the *love* of money, that is the root of all evil.

III. Here is the bargain which the chief priests made with him; *they covenanted with him for thirty pieces of silver.* By the law (Exod. xxi. 32), thirty pieces of silver was the price of a slave—a goodly price, at which Christ was valued! They *covenanted with him—they paid it down,* so some; gave him his wages in hand, to secure him and to encourage him.

IV. Here is the industry of Judas, in pursuance of his bargain (v. 16); *he sought opportunity to betray him,* his head was still working to find out how he might do it effectually. It is a very wicked thing to seek opportunity to sin, and to devise mischief; for it argues the heart fully set in men to do evil. He had time to repent; but now by his covenant the devil tells him that he must be true to his word, though ever so false to his Master.

Verses 17–25

We have here an account of Christ's keeping the passover.

I. The time when Christ ate the passover, was the usual time appointed by God, and observed by the Jews (v. 17); *the first day of the feast of unleavened bread.*

II. The place was particularly appointed by himself to the disciples, upon their enquiry (v. 17): they asked, *Where wilt thou that we prepare the passover?*

1. They took it for granted that their Master would eat the passover, though he was at this time persecuted by the chief priests, and his life sought; they knew that he would not be put by his duty, either by frightenings without or fears within.

2. They knew very well that there must be preparation made for it, and that it was their business; *Where wilt thou that we prepare?* Before solemn ordinances there must be solemn preparation.

3. They knew that he had no house of his own wherein to eat the passover.

4. They would not pitch upon a place without direction from him, and from him they had direction; he sent them to *such a man* (v. 18), who probably was a friend and follower of his, and to his house he invited himself and his disciples.

(1) Tell him, *My time is at hand;* he means the time of his death. He knew when it was at hand, and was busy accordingly; we *know not our time* (Eccles. ix. 12), and therefore must never be off our watch; *our time is always ready* (John vii. 6), and therefore we must be always ready. When our Lord Jesus invited himself to this good man's house, he sent him this intelligence, that his time was at hand. Christ's secret is with them that entertain him in their hearts.

(2) Tell him, *I will keep the passover at thy house.* This was an instance of his authority, as *the Master;* he did not beg, but command, the use of his house for this purpose. Thus, when Christ by his Spirit comes into the heart, he demands admission, as one whose own the heart is and cannot be denied. His people shall be willing, for he makes them so. *I will keep the passover with my disciples.* Wherever Christ is welcome, he expects that his disciples should be welcome too. When we take God for our God, we take his people for our people.

III. The preparation was made by the disciples (v. 19); *They did as Jesus had appointed. They made ready the passover;* they got the lamb killed, and everything set in readiness for such a sacred solemn feast.

IV. They ate the passover according to the law (v. 20); *He sat down.* His sitting down, denotes the composedness of his mind, when he addressed himself to this solemnity; *He sat down with the twelve,* Judas not excepted. By the law, they were to *take a lamb for a household;* Christ's disciples were his household. They whom God has charged with families, must have their houses with them in serving the Lord.

V. We have here Christ's discourse with his disciples at the passover-supper. The usual subject was the deliverance of Israel out of Egypt (Exod. xii. 26, 27); but the great Passover is now ready to be offered, and the discourse of that swallows up all talk of the other.

1. The general notice Christ gives his disciples of the treachery that should be among them (v. 21); *One of you shall betray me.* Christ knew it. We know not what troubles will befall us, nor whence they will arise: but Christ knew all his. It magnifies his love, that he knew all things that should befall him, and yet did not draw back. When there was occasion, he let those about him know it. He had often told them that the Son of man should be betrayed; now he tells them that one of them should do it.

2. The disciples' feelings on this occasion, v. 22.

(1) *They were exceedingly sorrowful.* It troubled them much to hear that their Master should be betrayed. When Peter was first told of it, he said, *Be it far from thee.* It troubled them more to hear that one of them should do it. Gracious souls grieve for the sins of others, especially of those that have made a more than ordinary profession of religion. It troubled them most of all, that they were left at uncertainty which of them it was.

(2) *They began every one of them to say, Lord, is it I?* They were not apt to suspect Judas. Though he was *a thief,* yet, it seems, he had carried it so plausibly, that none of them so much as looked upon him, much less said, *Lord, is it Judas?* It is possible for a hypocrite to go through the world, not only undiscovered, but unsuspected; like bad money so ingeniously counterfeited that nobody questions it.

They were apt to suspect themselves; *Lord, is it I?* They feared the worst, and asked Him who knows us better than we know ourselves, *Lord is it I?* We know not how strongly we may be tempted, nor how far God may leave us to ourselves, and therefore have reason, *not to be high-minded, but fear.*

3. Further information given them concerning this matter (v. 23, 24), where Christ tells them, (1) That the traitor was a familiar friend; *He that dippeth his hand with me in the dish,* that is, One of you that are now with me at the table. It is base ingratitude to dip with Christ in the dish, and yet betray him. (2) That this was according to the scripture, which would take off the offence at it. The more we see of the fulfilling of the scripture in our troubles, the better we may bear them. (3) That it would prove a very dear bargain to the traitor; *Woe to that man by whom the Son of man is betrayed.* Though God can serve his own purposes by the sins of men, that doth not make the sinner's condition the less woeful; *It had been good for that man, if he had not been born.*

4. The conviction of Judas, v. 25. He asked, *Is it I?* to avoid coming under the suspicion of guilt by his silence. He knew very well that it was he, and yet wished to appear a stranger to such a plot. Note, Many whose consciences condemn them are very industrious to justify themselves before men, and put a good face on it, with, *Lord, is it I?* Christ soon answered this question; *Thou hast said.* It was

enough to convict him, and, if his heart had not been wretchedly hardened, to have broken the neck of his plot, when he saw it discovered to his Master, and discovered by him.

Verses 26–30

We have here the institution of the great gospel ordinance of the Lord's supper.

I. The time when it was instituted—*as they were eating.* At the latter end of the passover-supper, before the table was drawn, because it was to come in the room of that ordinance. Christ is to us the Passover-sacrifice by which atonement is made (1 Cor. v. 7); *Christ our Passover is sacrificed for us.*

II. The institution itself. A sacrament must be instituted; it has both its being and significancy from the institution, from a divine institution. Hence the apostle (1. Cor. xi. 23, &c.), in that discourse of his concerning this ordinance, all along calls Jesus Christ *the Lord,* because, as *Lord,* he appointed this ordinance.

1. The body of Christ is signified and represented by bread; he had said formerly (John vi. 35), *I am the bread of life.* As the life of the body is supported by bread, so the life of the soul is supported and maintained by Christ's mediation.

(1) *He took bread—the loaf;* some loaf that lay ready at hand, fit for the purpose. His taking the bread was a solemn action, and was, probably, done in such a manner as to be observed by them that sat with him.

(2) *He blessed it;* set it apart for this use by prayer and thanksgiving. We do not find any set form of words used by him upon this occasion. Christ could command the blessing, and we, in his name, are emboldened to beg the blessing.

(3) *He brake it;* which denotes, [1] The breaking of Christ's body for us, that it might be fitted for our use; *He was bruised for our iniquities.* [2] The breaking of Christ's body to us, as the father of the family breaks the bread to the children.

(4) *He gave it to his disciples,* as the Master of the family, and the Master of this feast. *To the disciples,* because all the disciples of Christ have a right to this ordinance; and those shall have the benefit of it who are his disciples indeed; yet he gave it to them as he did the multiplied loaves, by them to be handed to all his other followers.

(5) *He said, Take, eat; this is my body,* v. 26. He here tells them,

[1] What they should do with it; *"Take, eat;* accept of Christ as he is offered to you, receive the atonement, approve of it, consent to it." Believing on Christ is expressed by *receiving him* (John i. 12), and *feeding upon him,* John vi. 57, 58. Meat looked upon, or the dish ever so well garnished, will not nourish us; it must be fed upon: so must the doctrine of Christ.

[2] What they should have with it; *This is my body,* not ὄντος—*this bread,* but τοῦτο—*this eating and drinking.* Believing carries all the efficacy of Christ's death to our souls. *This is my body,* spiritually and sacramentally; this signifies and represents my body. He employs sacramental language. We partake of the sun, not by having the bulk and body of the sun put into our hands, but the beams of it darted down upon us; so we partake of Christ by partaking of his grace, and the blessed fruits of the breaking of his body.

2. The blood of Christ is signified and represented by the wine (v. 27, 28); *He took the cup,* the grace-cup, which was set ready to be drank, after thanks returned, according to the custom of the Jews at the passover. *He gave thanks,* to teach us, not only in every ordinance, but in every part of the ordinance, to have our eyes up to God.

This cup he gave to the disciples,

(1) With a command; *Drink ye all of it.* Thus he welcomes his guests to his table, obliges them all to drink of his cup.

(2) With an explication; *For this is my blood of the New Testament.* Hitherto the blood of Christ had been represented by the blood of beasts, real blood: but, after it was actually shed, it was represented by the blood of grapes, metaphorical blood.

[1] *It is my blood of the New Testament.* The covenant God is pleased to make with us, and all the benefits and privileges of it, are owing to the merits of Christ's death.

[2] *It is shed;* it was not shed till next day, but it was now upon the point of being shed, it is as good as done.

[3] *It is shed for many.* Christ came to confirm *a covenant with many.* The blood of the Old Testament was shed for a few. But Jesus Christ is a propitiation *for the sins of the whole world,* 1 John ii. 2.

[4] *It is shed for the remission of sins,* that is, to purchase remission of sins for us. The new covenant which is procured and ratified by the blood of Christ, is a charter of pardon, an act of indemnity, in order to a reconciliation between God and man. The pardon of sin is that great blessing which is, in the Lord's supper, conferred upon all true believers; it is the foundation of all other blessings, and the spring of everlasting comfort, *ch.* ix. 2, 3. A farewell is now bidden to the fruit of the vine, *v.* 29. How good to be here! Never such a heaven upon earth as was at this table; but it was not intended for a perpetuity.

First, He takes leave of such communion; *I will not drink henceforth of this fruit of the vine.* Farewell *this fruit of the vine,* this passover-cup, this sacramental wine. Dying saints take their leave of sacraments, and the other ordinances of communion which they enjoy in this world, with comfort, for the joy and glory they enter into supersede them all; when the sun rises, farewell the candles.

Secondly, He assures them of a happy meeting again at last. *Until that day when I drink it new with you.* Some understand it of the interviews he had with them after his resurrection. Others understand it of the joys and glories of the future state, which the saints shall partake of in everlasting communion with the Lord Jesus. Christ will himself partake of those pleasures; it was *the joy set before him,* which he had in his eye, and all his faithful friends and followers shall partake with him.

Lastly, Here is the close of the solemnity with a hymn (*v.* 30); *They sang a hymn* or psalm. Singing of psalms is a gospel-ordinance. It is very proper after the Lord's supper, as an expression of our joy in God through Jesus Christ, and a thankful acknowledgment of that great love wherewith God has loved us in him. It is not unseasonable, no, not in times of sorrow and suffering. Our spiritual joy should not be interrupted by outward afflictions.

When this was done, they *went out into the mount of Olives.* He would not stay in the house to be apprehended, lest he should bring the master of the house into trouble; but he retired into the adjacent country, the mount of Olives. They had the benefit of moonlight for this walk, for the passover was always at the full moon. After we have received the Lord's supper, it is good for us to retire for prayer and meditation, and to be alone with God.

Verses 31–35

We have here Christ's discourse with his disciples upon the way.

I. A prediction of the trial which both he and his disciples were now to go through. He here foretells,

1. A dismal scattering storm just arising, *v.* 31.

(1) That they should *all be offended because of Christ that very night*; they would not have the courage to cleave to him but would all basely desert him. Offences will come among the disciples of Christ in an hour of trial and temptation; it cannot be but they should, for they are weak. Even they whose hearts are upright may sometimes be overtaken with an offence. There are some temptations and offences, the effects of which are general, *All you shall be offended.* Though there will be but one traitor, they will be all deserters. We have need to prepare for sudden trials, which may come to extremity in a very little time. How soon may a storm arise! The cross of Christ is the great stumbling-block to many that pass for his disciples.

(2) That herein the scripture would be fulfilled; *I will smite the Shepherd.* It is quoted from Zech. xiii. 7. Here is the smiting of the Shepherd in the sufferings of Christ, and the scattering of the sheep, thereupon, in the flight of the disciples. It was each one's care to shift for himself, and happy he that could get furthest from the cross.

2. He gives them the prospect of a comfortable gathering together again after this storm (*v.* 32); "*After I am risen again, I will go before you.* Though you will forsake me, I will not forsake you; though you fall, I will take care you shall not fall finally: we shall have a meeting again in Galilee, *I will go before you,* as the shepherd before the sheep." The captain of our salvation knows how to rally his troops, when, through their cowardice, they have been put into disorder.

II. The presumption of Peter (*v.* 33); *Though all men be offended, yet will I never be offended.* Peter had a great stock of confidence, and was upon all occasions forward to speak; sometimes it did him a kindness, but at other times it betrayed him, as it did here.

1. How he bound himself with a promise, that he would never be offended in Christ. Before the Lord's supper, Christ's discourse led his disciples to *examine* themselves with, *Lord, is it I?* For that is our preparatory duty; after the ordinance, his discourse leads them to an *engaging* of themselves to close walking, for that is the subsequent duty.

2. How he fancied himself better armed against temptation than anyone else, *Though all men shall be offended yet will not I.* Peter supposes it possible that *some,* nay that *all,* might be offended, and yet he escape better than any. We should rather say, If it be possible that others may be offended, there is danger that I may be so.

III. The particular warning Christ gave Peter of what he would do, *v.* 34. He imagined that in the hour of temptation he should come off better than any of them, and Christ tells him that he should come off worse. "*Verily, I say unto thee; take my word for it, who know thee better than thou knowest thyself.*" He tells him,

1. That he should deny him. He said, "Though all men, yet not I"; and he did it sooner than any.

2. How quickly he should do it; *this night,* before to-morrow, nay, *before cock-crowing.* As we know not how near we may be to trouble, so we know not how near we may be to sin; if God leave us to ourselves, we are always in danger.

3. How often he should do it; *thrice.* Christ tells him that he would do it again and again; for, when once our feet begin to slip, it is hard to recover our standing again.

IV. Peter's repeated assurances of his fidelity (*v.* 35); *Though I should die with thee.* He knew what he *should* do—rather die with Christ than deny him; and he thought what he *would* do—never be false to his Master, whatever it cost him; yet, it proved, he was. It is easy to talk boldly and carelessly of death

at a distance; but it is not so soon done as said, when it comes to the setting-to, and death shows itself in its own colours.

What Peter said the rest subscribed to; *likewise also said all the disciples.* There is a proneness in good men to be over-confident of their own strength and stability. Those often fall soonest and foulest that are most confident of themselves. Those are least safe that are most secure.

Verses 36–46

In these verses we have the story of his agony in the garden. The clouds had been gathering a good while, and looked black. But now the storm began in good earnest.

I. The place where he underwent this mighty agony; it was *in a place called Gethsemane.* The name signifies *an olive-mill,* a press for olives, like a wine-press, where they *trod the olives.* There our Lord Jesus began his passion; there it pleased the Lord to bruise him, and crush him, that fresh oil might flow to all believers from him.

II. The company he had with him, when he was in this agony.

1. He took all the twelve disciples with him to the garden, except Judas, who was at this time otherwise employed.

2. He took only Peter, and James, and John, with him into that corner of the garden where he suffered his agony. He left the rest at some distance, with this charge, *Sit ye here, while I go and pray yonder.* Christ went to pray alone, though he had lately prayed with his disciples, John xvii. 1. He took these three with him, because they had been the witnesses of his glory in his transfiguration (*ch.* xvii. 1, 2), and that would prepare them to be the witnesses of his agony. Those are best prepared to suffer with Christ, that have by faith beheld his glory. If we hope to reign with him, why should we not expect to suffer with him?

III. The agony itself that he was in; *He began to be sorrowful, and very heavy.* It is called an agony (Luke xxii. 44), a conflict. It was not any bodily pain or torment that he was in, it was from within; he troubled himself, John xi. 33. The words here used are very emphatical; he began *to be sorrowful, and in a consternation.* He had like a weight of lead upon his spirits.

But what was the cause of all this? What was it that put him into this agony? *Why art thou cast down,* blessed Jesus, and *why disquieted?* Certainly, it was nothing of despair or distrust of his Father, much less any conflict or struggle with him. As the Father loved him because he laid down his life for the sheep, so he was entirely subject to his Father's will in it. But,

1. He engaged in an encounter with the powers of darkness; so he intimates (Luke xxii. 53). *As the Father gave me commandment, so I do;* however it be, I must have a struggle with him, therefore *arise, let us go hence,* let us hasten to the field of battle, and meet the enemy. Christ, when he works salvation, is described like a champion taking the field, Isa. lix. 16–18.

2. He was now *bearing the iniquities* which the Father laid upon him, and, by his sorrow and amazement, he accommodated himself to his undertaking. The sufferings he was entering upon were for our sins; they were all made to meet upon him, and he knew it. As we are obliged to be sorry for our particular sins, so was he grieved for the sins of us all.

3. He had a full and clear prospect of all the sufferings that were before him. He foresaw the treachery of Judas, the unkindness of Peter, the malice of the Jews, and their base ingratitude. Death in its most dreadful appearances, death in

pomp, attended with all its terrors, looked him in the face; and this made him sorrowful, especially because it was the wages of our sin, which he had undertaken to satisfy for. It is true, the martyrs have suffered for Christ without any such sorrow and consternation. But then, (1) Christ was now denied the supports and comforts which they had; that is, he denied them to himself. Their cheerfulness under the cross was owing to the divine favour, which, for the present, was suspended from the Lord Jesus. (2) His sufferings were of another nature from theirs. On the saints' cross there is a blessing pronounced, which enables them to rejoice under it (*ch.* v. 10, 12); but to Christ's cross there was a curse annexed, which made him sorrowful and very heavy under it. And his sorrow under the cross was the foundation of their joy under it.

IV. His complaint of this agony. He goes to his disciples (*v.* 38), and,

1. He acquaints them with his condition; *My soul is exceedingly sorrowful, even unto death.* It gives some little ease to a troubled spirit, to have a friend ready to unbosom itself to, and give vent to its sorrows. Christ here tells them, (1) What was the seat of his sorrow; it was his soul that was now in an agony. Christ suffered in soul as well as in body. (2) What was the degree of his sorrow. He was *exceedingly sorrowful.* It was sorrow in the highest degree, even unto death; it was a killing sorrow, such sorrow as no mortal man could bear and live. (3) The duration of it; it will continue even unto death. He now *began* to be sorrowful, and never ceased to be so till he said, *It is finished.* It was prophesied of Christ, that he should be *a Man of sorrows* (Isa. liii. 3).

2. He bespeaks their company and attendance; *Tarry ye here, and watch with me.* Surely he was destitute indeed of help, when he entreated theirs, who, he knew, would be but miserable comforters. It is good to have, and therefore good to seek, the assistance of our brethren, when at any time we are in an agony.

V. What passed between him and his Father when he was in this agony; *Being in an agony, he prayed.* Prayer is never out of season, but it is especially seasonable in an agony.

1. The place where he prayed; *He went a little further,* withdrew from them. He retired for prayer; a troubled soul finds most ease when it is alone with God, who understands the broken language of sighs and groans. Christ has hereby taught us that secret prayer must be made secretly.

2. His posture in prayer; *He fell on his face;* his lying prostrate denotes, (1) The agony he was in, and the extremity of his sorrow. (2) His humility in prayer.

3. The prayer itself; wherein we may observe three things.

(1) The title he gives to God; *O my Father.* Thick as the cloud was, he could see God as a Father through it. It is a pleasing string to harp upon at such a time, *My Father;* whither should the child go, when anything grieves him, but to his father?

(2) The favour he begs; *If it be possible, let this cup pass from me.* He calls his sufferings a *cup;* not a river, not a sea, but a cup, which we shall soon see the bottom of. When we are under troubles, we should make the best, the least, of them, and not aggravate them. He begs that this cup might *pass from him,* that is, that he might avoid the sufferings now at hand; or, at least, that they might be shortened. This intimates no more than that he was really and truly Man, and as a Man he could not but be averse to pain and suffering. A prayer of faith against an affliction, may very well consist with the patience of hope under affliction. But observe the proviso; *If it be possible.* If God may be glorified, man saved,

and the ends of his undertaking answered, without his drinking of this bitter cup, he desires to be excused; otherwise not. What we cannot do with the securing of our great end, we must reckon to be in effect impossible; Christ did so.

(3) His entire submission to, and acquiescence in, the will of God; *Nevertheless, not as I will, but as thou wilt.* Our Lord Jesus, though he had a quick sense of the extreme bitterness of the sufferings he was to undergo, yet was freely willing to submit to them for our redemption and salvation. The reason of Christ's submission to his sufferings, was, his Father's will; *as thou wilt, v.* 39. He grounds his own willingness upon the Father's will. He did what he did, and did it with delight, because it was the will of God. This he had often referred to, as that which put him upon, and carried him through, his whole undertaking. In conformity to this example of Christ, we must drink of the bitter cup which God puts into our hands, be it ever so bitter; though nature struggle, grace must submit.

4. The repetition of the prayer; *He went away again the second time, and prayed* (*v.* 42), and again the third time (*v.* 44). Though we may pray to God to prevent and remove an affliction, yet our chief errand must be, that he will give us grace to bear it well. It should be more our care to get our troubles sanctified, and our hearts satisfied under them, than to get them taken away. *He prayed, saying, Thy will be done.* Prayer is the offering up, not only of our desires, but of our resignations, to God. The third time he *said the same words.* It should seem by *v.* 40 that he continued *an hour* in his agony and prayer; but, whatever more he said, it was to this effect, deprecating his approaching sufferings, and yet resigning himself to God's will in them.

But what answer had he to this prayer? Certainly it was not made in vain; he that heard him *always,* did not deny him *now.* It is true, the cup did not pass from him, but he had an answer to his prayer; for, *He was strengthened with strength in his soul;* and that was a real answer, Luke xxii. 43. In answer to his prayer, God provided that he should not fail or be discouraged.

VI. What passed between him and his three disciples at this time.

1. The fault they were guilty of; that when he was in his agony, they were so little concerned, that they could not keep awake; he comes, and *finds them asleep, v.* 40. Much more should their love to their Master, and their care concerning him, have obliged them to a more close and vigilant attendance on him; yet they were so dull, that they could not keep their eyes open. What had become of us, if Christ had been now as sleepy as his disciples were? Christ engaged them to watch with him, as if he expected some succour from them, and yet they slept; surely it was the unkindest thing that could be. His enemies, who watched for him, were wakeful enough (Mark xiv. 43); but his disciples, who should have watched with him, were asleep.

2. Christ's favour to them, notwithstanding. Persons in sorrow are too apt to be cross and peevish with those about them, but Christ in his agony is as meek as ever and is not apt to take things ill.

When Christ's disciples put this slight upon him, (1) *He came to them,* as if he expected to receive some comfort from them. They added grief to his sorrow; and yet he came to them, more careful for them than they were for themselves; when he was most engaged, yet he came to look after them; for those that were given him, were upon his heart, living and dying.

(2) He gave them a gentle reproof; he directed it to Peter, who used to *speak* for them; let him now *hear* for them. *What! could ye not watch with me*

one hour? He speaks as one amazed to see them so stupid. Consider, [1] Who *they* were; "Could not *ye* watch—ye, my disciples and followers? From you I expected better things." [2] Who *he* was; "Watch with *me*." He awoke out of his sleep, to help them when they were in distress (*ch.* viii. 36); and could not they keep awake, at least to show their goodwill to him? [3] How small a thing it was that he expected from them—only to *watch with him*. If he had bid them do some great thing, or die with him, they thought they could have done it; and yet they could not do it, when he only desired them to *watch with him.* [4] How short a time it was that he expected it—but *one hour*; they were not set upon the guard whole nights, only *one hour.*

(3) He gave them good counsel; *Watch and pray, that ye enter not into temptation, v.* 41. There was an hour of temptation drawing on, and very near; the troubles of Christ were temptations to his followers to disbelieve and distrust him, to deny and desert him, and renounce all relation to him. There was danger of their entering into the temptation, as into a snare or trap. He therefore exhorts them to watch and pray; *Watch with me, and pray with me.* While they were sleeping, they lost the benefit of joining in Christ's prayer. "Watch *yourselves*, and pray *yourselves. Pray* that you may *watch*; beg of God by his grace to keep you awake, now that there is occasion."

(4) He kindly excused for them; *The spirit indeed is willing, but the flesh is weak.* We do not read of one word they had to say for themselves; but then he had a tender word to say on their behalf; in this he sets us an example of that love *which covers a multitude of sins.* He considered their frame, and did not chide them, for he remembered that they were but flesh; *and the flesh is weak, though the spirit be willing.* It is the unhappiness and burthen of Christ's disciples, that their bodies cannot keep pace with their souls in works of piety and devotion, but are many a time a cloud and clog to them; that, when the spirit is free and disposed to that which is good, the flesh is averse and indisposed. Yet it is our comfort, that our Master graciously considers this, and accepts the willingness of the spirit, and pities and pardons the weakness and infirmity of the flesh; for *we are under grace, and not under the law.*

(5) Though they continued dull and sleepy, he did not any further rebuke them for it; for, though we daily offend, yet he will not always chide. When he came to them the second time, we do not find that he said anything to them (*v.* 43); *he findeth them asleep again.* One would have thought that he had said enough to them to keep them awake; but it is hard to recover from a spirit of slumber. *Their eyes were heavy*, which intimates that they strove against it as much as they could, but were overcome by it, and therefore their Master looked upon them with compassion. When he came the third time, he left them to be alarmed with the approaching danger (*v.* 45, 46); *Sleep on now, and take your rest.* See here how Christ deals with those that suffer themselves to be overcome by security, and will not be awakened out of it. Sometimes he gives them up to the power of it; *Sleep on now.* He that will sleep, let him sleep still. The curse of spiritual slumber is the just punishment of the sin of it. Many times he sends some startling judgment. Those who will not be alarmed by reasons and arguments, had better be alarmed by swords and spears than left to perish in their security. Let those that would not believe, be made to feel.

As to the disciples here, their Master gave them notice of the near approach of his enemies. *The Son of man is betrayed into the hands of sinners.* And again, *He is at hand that doth betray me.* Christ's sufferings were no surprise to him. He called them

to rise, and be going: not, "Rise, and let us flee from the danger"; but, "Rise, and let us go meet it". He intimates to them their folly, in sleeping away the time which they should have spent in preparation; now the event found them unready, and was a terror to them.

Verses 47–56

We are here told how the blessed Jesus was seized, and taken into custody; this followed immediately upon his agony, *while he yet spake*; for from the beginning to the close of his passion he had not the least intermission or breathing-time.

Now concerning the apprehension of the Lord Jesus,

I. Who the persons were, that were employed in it. Here was *Judas, one of the twelve*, at the head of this infamous guard: *he was guide to them that took Jesus* (Acts i. 16); without his help they could not have found him in this retirement. Here was *with him a great multitude.* This multitude was made up partly of a detachment out of the guards, these were Gentiles, *sinners*, as Christ calls them, *v.* 45. The rest were the servants and officers of the High Priest, and they were Jews; they that were at variance with each other, agreed against Christ.

II. How they were armed for this enterprise.

1. What weapons they were armed with; They came *with swords and staves.* They were not regular troops, but a tumultuous rabble. But wherefore is this ado? His hour being come for him to give up himself, all this force was needless. When a butcher goes into the field to take out a lamb for the slaughter, does he raise the militia, and come armed? No, he needs not; yet is there all this force used to seize the Lamb of God.

2. What warrant they were armed with; *They came from the chief priests, and elders of the people.* He was taken up by a warrant from the great sanhedrim, as a person obnoxious to them. Pilate, the Roman governor, gave them no warrant; but they were men who pretended to religion, and presided in the affairs of the church, that were active in this prosecution, and were the most spiteful enemies Christ had. Pilate upbraided him with it; *Thine own nation and the chief priests delivered thee to me,* John xviii. 35.

III. The manner how it was done, and what passed at that time.

1. How Judas betrayed him; he did his business effectually, and his resolution in this wickedness may shame us who fail in that which is good.

(1) The instructions he gave to the soldiers (*v.* 48). He *gave them a sign*, lest by mistake they should seize one of the disciples instead of him. *That same is he;* and when they had him in their hands, not to lose him—*Hold him fast;* for he had sometimes escaped from those who thought to secure him; as Luke iv. 30. And Judas by his kiss intended not only to distinguish him, but to detain him, while they came behind him, and laid hands on him.

(2) The dissembling compliment he gave his Master. He came close up to Jesus; surely when he comes to look him in the face, he will either be awed by its majesty, or charmed by its beauty. Dares he to come into his very sight and presence, to betray him? Peter denied Christ, but when *the Lord turned and looked* upon him, he relented presently; but Judas comes up to his Master's face, and betrays him. He said, *Hail, Master; and kissed him.* A kiss is a token of allegiance and friendship. But Judas, when he broke all the laws of love and duty, profaned this sacred sign to serve his purpose.

(3) The entertainment his Master gave him, *v,* 50. He calls him *friend.* He would teach us under the greatest provocation to forbear bitterness. He calls

him _friend_, because he furthered his sufferings, and so _befriended_ him; whereas, he called Peter _Satan_ for attempting to hinder them. He asks him, "_Wherefore art thou come?_ Is it peace, Judas? Explain thyself; if thou come as an enemy, what means this kiss? If as a friend, what mean these swords and staves? _Wherefore art thou present?_ Why hadst thou not so much shame left thee, as to keep out of sight, which thou mightest have done, and yet have given the officers notice where I was?"

2. How the officers and soldiers secured him; _Then came they, and laid hands on Jesus, and took him;_ they made him their prisoner. We may well imagine what rude and cruel hands they were, which this barbarous multitude laid on Christ; and now, it is probable, they handled him the more roughly for their being so often disappointed when they sought to lay hands on him. They could not have taken him, if he had not surrendered himself, and been _delivered by the determinate counsel and foreknowledge of God_, Acts ii. 23.

Our Lord Jesus was made a prisoner, because he would in all things be treated as a malefactor, punished for our crime. He became a prisoner, that he might set us at liberty; for he said, _If ye seek me, let these go their way_ (John xviii. 8); and those are free indeed, whom he makes so.

3. How Peter fought for Christ, and was checked for his pains. It is here only said to be _one of them that were with Jesus in the garden_; but in John xviii. 10, we are told that it was Peter who signalized himself upon this occasion.

(1) Peter's rashness (v. 51); He _drew his sword_. They had but two swords among them all (Luke xxii. 38), and one of them, it seems, fell to Peter's share; and now he thought it was time to draw it. But all the execution he did was the cutting off an ear from a servant of the High Priest; designing, it is likely, to cleave him down the head, he missed his blow. Peter had talked much of what he would do for his Master, he would _lay down his life for him_; yea, that he would; and now he would be as good as his word, and venture his life to rescue his Master. He had a great _zeal_ for Christ, and his honour and safety; but it was not _according to knowledge_, nor guided by discretion; he did it without warrant. We must see not only our cause good, but our call clear, before we draw the sword. He indiscreetly exposed himself and his fellow-disciples to the rage of the multitude; for what could they with two swords do against a band of men?

(2) The rebuke which our Lord Jesus gave him (v. 52); _Put up again thy sword into its place._ He commands Peter to put up his sword, does not chide him indeed for what he had done, because done out of goodwill, but stops the progress of his arms. Christ's errand into the world was to make peace. As Christ forbade his disciples the sword of justice (ch. xx. 25, 26), so here the sword of war. Christ bade Peter put up his sword, and never bade him draw it again.

Three reasons Christ gives to Peter for this rebuke:

[1] His drawing the sword would be dangerous to himself and to his fellow-disciples; _They that take the sword, shall perish with the sword;_ they that use violence, fall by violence; and men hasten and increase their own troubles by blustering bloody methods of self-defence. Grotius gives another, and a probable sense of this blow, making those that take the sword to be, not Peter, but the officers and soldiers that come with swords _to take Christ_; They shall _perish with the sword_. They took the Roman sword to seize Christ with, and by the Roman sword, not long after, they and their place and nation were destroyed.

[2] It was needless for him to draw his sword in defence of his Master, who, if he pleased, could summon into his service all the hosts of heaven (v. 53); "_Thinkest thou that I cannot now pray to my Father, and he shall send_ from heaven effectual succours? Peter, if I would put by these sufferings, I could easily do it without thy hand or thy sword." Note, God has no need of us, of our services, much less of our sins, to bring about his purposes. God can do his work without us. Though Christ was crucified through weakness, it was a voluntary weakness; he submitted to death, not because he could not, but because he would not contend with it. Christ here lets us know,

First, What a great interest he had in his Father; _I can pray to my Father, and he will send me help._ It is a great comfort to God's people, when they are surrounded with enemies on all hands, that they have a way open heavenward; if they can do nothing else, they can pray to him that can do everything. And they who are much in prayer at other times, have most comfort in praying when troublesome times come. Christ saith, not only that God could, but that, if he insisted upon it, he would do it. He might yet have gone out free from the service, but he loved it, and would not; so that it was only with the cords of his own love that he was bound to the altar.

Secondly, What a great interest he had in the heavenly hosts; _He shall presently give me more than twelve legions of angels_. _a_. There is an _innumerable company of angels_, Heb. xii. 22. _b_. This innumerable company of angels are all at the disposal of our heavenly Father, and do his pleasure, Ps. ciii. 20, 21. _c_. These angelic hosts were ready to come in to the assistance of our Lord Jesus in his sufferings, if he had needed or desired it. _He shall give them me;_ therefore angels are not to be prayed to, but the Lord of the angels. He shall _presently_ give them me. See how ready his Father was to hear his prayer.

[3] It was no time to make any defence at all, or to offer to put by the stroke; _For how then shall the scriptures be fulfilled, that thus it must be?_ v. 54. It was written, that Christ should be _led as a lamb to the slaughter_, Isa. liii. 7. In all difficult cases, the word of God must be conclusive against our own counsels, and nothing must be done, nothing attempted, against the fulfilling of the scripture. We ought to say, "Let God's word and will take place, let his law be magnified and made honourable, whatever becomes of us." Thus Christ checked Peter, when he set up for his champion, and captain of his life-guard.

4. We are next told how Christ argued the case with them that came to take him (v. 55); though he did not resist them, yet he did reason with them. It will consist with Christian patience under our sufferings, calmly to expostulate with our enemies and persecutors. _Are ye come out_, (1) With rage and enmity, _as against a thief_, as if I were an enemy to the public safety, and deservedly suffered this? If he had been the plague of his country, he could not have been prosecuted with more heat and violence. (2) With all this power and force, as against the worst of thieves, that dare the law, bid defiance to public justice, and add rebellion to their sin?

He further expostulates with them, by reminding them how he had behaved himself hitherto toward them, and they toward him. _I sat daily with you in the temple teaching. Ye laid no hold on me._ How comes then this change? They were very unreasonable, in treating him as they did. He had given them no occasion to look upon him as a thief, for he had taught in the temple. Such gracious words as came from his mouth, were not the words of a thief, nor of one that had a devil. Nor had he given them occasion to look upon him as one that absconded, or fled from justice, that they should come in the night to seize him. They might find him every day in the temple, and there they might do as they pleased with him; for the chief priests had the custody of the temple. To come upon him thus clandestinely, in the place of his retirement, was base and cowardly. Thus the greatest hero may be villainously assassinated in a corner, by one that in open field would tremble to look him in the face.

But all this was done (so it follows, *v.* 56) *that the scriptures of the prophets might be fulfilled.* It is hard to say, whether these are the words of the sacred historian, as a comment upon this story, or, whether they are the words of Christ himself, that the scriptures of the prophets might be fulfilled, to which he had just now referred himself, *v.* 54.

5. How he was, in the midst of this distress, shamefully deserted by his disciples; *They all forsook him, and fled, v.* 56.

(1) This was their sin; and it was a great sin for them who had left all to follow him, now to leave him for they knew not what. There was unkindness in it. There was unfaithfulness in it, for they had solemnly promised to adhere to him, and never to forsake him.

(2) It was a part of Christ's suffering, it added affliction to his bonds, to be thus deserted. They should have stayed with him, to minister to him, and, if need were, to be witnesses for him at his trial. Christ, as a sacrifice for sins, stood thus abandoned. The deer that by the keeper's arrow is marked out to be hunted and run down, is immediately deserted by the whole herd. Christ, as the Saviour of souls, stood thus alone. He bore all, and did all himself.

Verses 57–68

We have here the arraignment of our Lord Jesus in the ecclesiastical court, before the great sanhedrim. Observe,

I. The sitting of the court; the scribes and the elders were assembled, though it was in the dead time of the night; yet, to gratify their malice against Christ, they sat up all night, to be ready to fall upon the prey.

1. Who they were, that were assembled; the *scribes,* the principal teachers, and *elders,* the principal rulers, of the Jewish church: these were the most bitter enemies to Christ our great teacher and ruler. 2. Where they were assembled; *in the palace of Caiaphas the High Priest*; there they assembled two days before, to lay the plot (*v.* 3), and there they now convened again, to prosecute it. His house should have been the sanctuary of oppressed innocency, but it is become the throne of iniquity; and no wonder, when even God's house of prayer was made a den of thieves.

II. The setting of the prisoner to the bar; they that had *laid hold on Jesus, led him away,* hurried him, no doubt, with violence. He was brought into Jerusalem through that which was called the *sheepgate,* for that was the way into town from the mount of Olives; and it was so called because the sheep appointed for sacrifice were brought that way to the temple; very fitly therefore is Christ led that way.

III. The cowardice and faint-heartedness of Peter (*v.* 58).

1. He followed him, but it was *afar off.* Some sparks of love and concern for his Master there were in his breast, and therefore he followed him; but fear and concern for his own safety prevailed, and therefore he followed afar off. It looks ill, and bodes worse, when those that are willing to be Christ's disciples, are not willing to be known to be so. To follow him afar off, is by little and little to go back from him. There is danger in drawing back, nay, in looking back.

2. He followed him, but he *went in, and sat with the servants.* He went in where there was a good

fire, and sat with the servants, not to silence their reproaches, but to screen himself. It was presumption in Peter thus to thrust himself into temptation; he that does so, throws himself out of God's protection.

3. He followed him, but it was only to *see the end,* led more by his curiosity than by his conscience; he attended as an idle spectator rather than as a disciple. He went in, only to look about him; it is not unlikely that Peter went in, expecting that Christ would have made his escape miraculously out of the hands of his persecutors; having so lately struck them down, who came to seize him; and this he had a mind to see: if so, it was folly for him to think of seeing any other end than what Christ had foretold, that he should be put to death. It is more our concern to prepare for the end, whatever it may be, than curiously to enquire what the end will be. The event is God's, but the duty is ours.

IV. The trial of our Lord Jesus in this court.

1. They examined witnesses against him. The crimes properly cognizable in their court, were, false doctrine and blasphemy; these they endeavoured to prove upon him.

(1) Their search for proof; *They sought false witness against him*; they had seized him, bound him, abused him, and after all have to seek for something to lay to his charge, and can show no cause for his commitment. They made proclamation, that, if any-one could give information against the prisoner at the bar, they were ready to receive it, and presently many bore false witness against him (*v.* 60).

(2) Their success in this search; in several attempts they were baffled, they sought false testimonies among themselves, others came in to help them, and yet they found none.

But at last they met with *two* witnesses, who, it seems, agreed in their evidence, and therefore were hearkened to, in hopes that now the point was gained. The words they swore against him, were, that he should say, *I am able to destroy the temple of God, and to build it in three days, v.* 61. Now by this they designed to accuse him, [1] As an enemy to the temple, and one that sought for the destruction of it. [2] As one that dealt in witchcraft, or some such unlawful arts, by the help of which he could rear such a building in three days. Now, as to this, *First,* The words were mis-recited; he said, *Destroy ye this temple* (John ii. 19); they come, and swear that he said, *I am able to destroy* this temple, as if the design against it were his. He said, *In three days I will raise it up,* a word properly used of a living temple; *I will raise it to life.* They come, and swear that he said, *I am able to build it*; which is properly used of a house temple. *Secondly,* The words were misunderstood; *he spoke of the temple of his body* (John ii. 21), but they swore that he said the *temple of God,* meaning this holy place. There have been, and still are, such as *wrest* the sayings of Christ *to their own destruction.* He was accused, that we might not be condemned; and if at any time we suffer thus, have all manner of evil, not only said, but *sworn, against us falsely,* let us remember that we cannot expect to fare better than our Master.

(3) Christ's silence under all these accusations, to the amazement of the court, *v.* 62. The High Priest, the judge of the court, arose in some heat, and said, *"Answerest thou nothing?* Come, you the prisoner at the bar; you hear what is sworn against you, what have you now to say for yourself?" *But Jesus held his peace* (*v.* 63), not because he wanted something to say, or knew not how to say it, but that the scripture might be fulfilled (Isa. liii. 7); *As the sheep is dumb before the shearer,* and before the butcher, *so he opened not his mouth.* He was silent, because *his hour was come*; he would not deny the charge, because he was willing to submit to the sentence. He

stood mute at this bar, that we might have something to say at God's bar.

2. They examined our Lord Jesus himself upon an oath. They will try, contrary to the law of equity, to make him accuse himself.

Here is the interrogatory put to him by the High Priest. The question itself; *Whether thou be the Christ, the Son of God?* That is, Whether thou pretend to be so? For they will by no means admit it into consideration, whether he be really so or no. They only wished him to confess that he called himself so, that they might on that indict him as a deceiver. What will not pride and malice carry men to? The solemnity of the proposal of it; *I adjure thee by the living God, that thou tell us.* Not that he had any regard to the living God, but took his name in vain; only thus he hoped to gain his point with our Lord Jesus. If he should refuse to answer when he was thus adjured, they would charge him with contempt of the blessed name of God.

Christ's answer to this interrogatory (*v.* 64), in which,

(1) He owns himself to be *the Christ the Son of God. Thou hast said;* that is, "It is as thou hast said"; for in St. Mark it is, *I am.* Hitherto, he seldom professed himself expressly to be the Christ, the Son of God; but now he would not omit to make a confession of it, *First,* Because that would have looked like a disowning of that truth which he came into the world to bear witness to. *Secondly,* It would have looked like declining his sufferings. He thus confessed himself, for example and encouragement to his followers, when they are called to it, to *confess him before men,* whatever hazards they run by it.

(2) He refers himself, for the proof of this, to his second coming. It is probable that they looked upon him with a scornful disdainful smile, when he said, *I am.* To that this *nevertheless* refers. "Though now you see me in this low and abject state, *nevertheless* the day is coming when I shall appear otherwise." *Hereafter ye shall see the Son of man sitting on the right hand of power, to judge the world;* of which his coming shortly to judge and destroy the Jewish nation would be a type and earnest. *First,* Whom they should see; *the Son of man.* Having owned himself the Son of God, even now in his estate of humiliation, he speaks of himself as the Son of man, even in his estate of exaltation; for he had these two distinct natures in one person. He is *Immanuel,* God with us. *Secondly,* In what posture they should see him; *Sitting on the right hand of power.* Though now he stood at the bar, they should shortly see him sit on the throne. *Coming in the clouds of heaven.* He had spoken of this day to his disciples, a while ago, for their comfort, and had bid them *lift up their heads* for joy in the prospect of it, Luke xxi. 27, 28. Now he speaks of it to his enemies, for their terror.

V. His conviction upon this trial; *The High Priest rent his clothes,* according to the custom of the Jews, when they heard or saw anything done or said which they looked upon to be a reproach to God.

1. The crime he was found guilty of; *blasphemy. He hath spoken blasphemy.* Christ, when *he was made Sin for us,* was condemned as a blasphemer for the truth he told them.

2. The evidence upon which they found him guilty; *Ye have heard the blasphemy;* why should we trouble ourselves to examine *witnesses* any further? Thus was he *judged out of his own mouth* at their bar, because we were liable to be so judged at God's bar. There is no need of witnesses against us; our own consciences are against us instead of a thousand witnesses.

VI. His sentence passed, upon this conviction, *v.* 66.

Here is, 1. Caiaphas's appeal to the bench; *What think ye?* When he had already prejudged the cause, and pronounced him a blasphemer, then, as if he were willing to be advised, he asks the judgment of his brethren. He knew that by the authority of his place he could sway the rest, and therefore declares his judgment, and presumes they are all of his mind.

2. Their concurrence with him; they said, *He is guilty of death;* perhaps they did not all concur: it is certain that Joseph of Arimathea, if he was present, dissented (Luke xxiii. 51); so did Nicodemus, and, it is likely, others with them; however, the majority carried it that way. The judgment was, *"He is guilty of death;* by the law he deserves to die." Though they had not power now to put any man to death, yet by such a judgment as this they made a man an *outlaw* among his people, and so exposed him to the fury either of a popular tumult, as Stephen was, or to be clamoured against before the governor, as Christ was.

VII. The abuses and indignities done to him after sentence passed (*v.* 67, 68); *Then,* when he was found guilty, they *spat in his face.* Because they had not power to put him to death, and could not be sure that they should prevail with the governor to be their executioner, they would do him all the mischief they could, now that they had him in their hands. When they had passed sentence upon our Lord Jesus, he was treated as if he were not only *worthy of death,* but as if that were too good for him. See how they abused him.

1. *They spat in his face.* It is an expression of the greatest contempt and indignation possible; looking upon him as more despicable than the very ground they spit upon. Yet Christ submitted to it. Thus was confusion poured upon his face, that ours might not be filled with everlasting shame and contempt.

2. *They buffeted him, and smote him with the palms of their hands.* This added pain to the shame, for both came in with sin. Here the margin reads it, *They smote him with rods;* for so ἐρράπισαν signifies, and this he submitted to.

3. They challenged him to tell who struck him, having first blindfolded him; *Prophesy unto us, thou Christ, who is he that smote thee?* They made sport of him, as the Philistines did with Samson; it is grievous to those that are in misery, for people to make merry *about* them, but much more to make merry *with* them and their misery. They had heard him called a *prophet;* this they upbraided him with, and pretended to make a trial of; as if the divine omniscience must stoop to a piece of children's play.

Verses 69-75

We have here the story of Peter's denying his Master, and it comes in as a part of Christ's sufferings. Observe how he fell, and how he got up again by repentance.

I. His sin. The immediate occasion of Peter's sin. He sat without in the palace, among the servants of the High Priest. Bad company is to many an occasion of sin; and those who needlessly thrust themselves into it, go upon the devil's ground; they scarcely can come out of such company, without guilt or grief, or both. The temptation came, when he was challenged as a retainer to Jesus of Galilee. First one maid, and then another, and then the rest of the servants, charged it upon him; *Thou also wert with Jesus of Galilee, v.* 69. And again, *This fellow was with Jesus of Nazareth, v.* 71. And again (*v.* 73), *Thou also art one of them, for thy speech betrayeth thee* to be a Galilean. Happy he whose speech betrays him to be a disciple of Christ. Observe how scornfully they speak of Christ—Jesus *of Galilee,* and *of Nazareth,* upbraiding him with the country he was of: and how disdainfully they speak of Peter—

This fellow; as if they thought it a reproach to them to have such a man in their company. The sin itself. When he was charged as one of Christ's disciples, he denied it, was ashamed and afraid to own himself so. Upon the first mention of it, he said, *I know not what thou sayest.* This was a shuffling answer; he pretended that he did not understand the charge. It is a fault to pretend that we do not understand, or did not think of, or remember, that which yet we do apprehend, and did think of, and remember; this is a species of lying which we are more prone to than any other, because in this a man is not easily disproved. It is yet a greater fault to be shy of Christ, to dissemble our knowledge of him; it is, in effect, to *deny* him. Upon the next attack, he said, flat and plain, *I know not the man,* and backed it with an oath, *v.* 72. This was, in effect, to say, I will not own him. Why, Peter? Canst thou look upon yonder Prisoner at the bar, and say thou dost not know him? Hast thou forgotten all the kind and tender looks thou hast had from him, and all the intimate fellowship thou hast had with him? Canst thou look him in the face, and say that thou dost not know him? Upon the third assault, *he began to curse and to swear, saying, I know not the man, v.* 74. This was worst of all, for the way of sin is downhill. He cursed and swore, 1. To back what he said, and to gain credit to it, and yet what he said, was false. We have reason to suspect the truth of that which is backed with rash oaths and imprecations. None but the devil's sayings need the devil's proofs. 2. He designed it to be an evidence for him, that he was none of Christ's disciples, for this was none of their language.

This is written for warning to us, that we sin not after the similitude of Peter's transgression; that we never, either directly or indirectly, deny Christ the Lord, dissembling our knowledge of him, and being ashamed of him and his words. This sin was aggravated considering who he was; an apostle, one of the first three. The greater profession we make of religion, the greater is our sin if in anything we walk unworthily. What fair warning his Master had given him of his danger. How solemnly he had promised to adhere to Christ in this night of trial; he had said again and again, "*I will never deny thee.*" How soon he fell into this sin after the Lord's supper. There to receive such an inestimable pledge of redeeming love, and yet the same night, before morning, to disown his Redeemer, was indeed *turning aside quickly.* How weak comparatively the temptation was; it was not the judge, nor any of the officers of the court, that charged him with being a disciple of Jesus, but a silly maid or two. How often he repeated it; even after the cock had crowed once he continued in the temptation, and a second and third time relapsed into the sin.

Thus was his sin aggravated; but on the other hand there is this to extenuate it, that, what he said he said *in his haste.* He fell into the sin by surprise, not as Judas, with design; his heart was against it.

II. Peter's repentance for this sin, *v.* 75.

1. What it was, that brought Peter to repentance. (1) *The cock crew* (*v.* 74). The word of Christ can put a significancy upon whatever sign he shall please to choose. The crowing of a cock is to Peter instead of a John Baptist, the voice of one calling to repentance. Conscience should be to us as the crowing of the cock, to put us in mind of what we had forgotten. Where there is a living principle of grace in the soul, though for the present overpowered by temptation, a little hint will serve, when God sets in with it, to recover it from a by-path. Here was the crowing of a cock made a happy occasion of the conversion of a soul. Christ comes sometimes in mercy *at cock-crowing.*

(2) *He remembered the words of the Lord;* this was it that brought him to himself, a sense of his ingratitude to Christ. Nothing grieves a penitent more than that he has sinned against the grace of the Lord Jesus and the tokens of his love.

2. How his repentance was expressed; *He went out, and wept bitterly.*

(1) His sorrow was secret; he went out, out of the High Priest's hall, vexed at himself that ever he came into it. He went out into the porch before (*v.* 71); and if he had gone quite off then, his second and third denial had been prevented; but then he came in again, now he went out and came in no more.

(2) His sorrow was serious; *He wept bitterly.* Sorrow for sin must not be slight, but great and deep. Those that have sinned sweetly, must weep bitterly; for, sooner or later, sin will be bitterness. This deep sorrow is requisite to evidence that there is a real change of mind. Peter, who wept so bitterly for denying Christ, never denied him again, but *confessed* him often and openly, and in the mouth of danger. True repentance for any sin will be best evidenced by our abounding in the contrary grace and duty. Some of the ancients say, that as long as Peter lived, he never heard a cock crow but it set him a weeping. Those that have truly sorrowed for sin, will sorrow upon every remembrance of it; yet not so as to hinder, but rather to increase, their joy in God and in his mercy and grace.

CHAPTER 27

It is a very affecting story which is recorded in this chapter concerning the sufferings and death of our Lord Jesus. But considering the design and fruit of Christ's sufferings, it is gospel, it is good news, and there is nothing we have more reason to glory in than the cross of Christ. I. How he was prosecuted. 1. The delivering of him to Pilate, ver. 1, 2. 2. The despair of Judas, ver. 3–10. 3 The arraignment and trial of Christ before Pilate, ver. 11–14. 4. The clamours of the people against him, ver. 15–25. 5. Sentence passed, and the warrant signed for his execution, ver. 26. II. How he was executed. 1. He was barbarously used, ver. 27–30. 2. Led to the place of execution, ver. 31–33. 3. There he had all possible indignities done him, ver. 34–44. 4. Heaven frowned upon him, ver. 45–49. 5. Many remarkable things attended his death, ver. 50–56. He was buried and a watch set on his grave, ver. 57–66.

Verses 1–10

We left Christ in the hands of the chief priests and elders, condemned to die, but they could only show their teeth. The Romans had taken from the Jews the power of capital punishment; they could put no man to death, and therefore early in the morning another council is held, to consider what is to be done.

I. Christ is delivered up to Pilate, that he might execute the sentence they had passed upon him. Pilate is characterized by the Roman writers of that time, as a man of a rough and haughty spirit; the Jews had a great enmity to his person, and were weary of his government, and yet they made use of him as the tool of their malice against Christ.

1. They *bound* Jesus. Having found him guilty, they tied his hands behind him, as they usually do with convicted criminals. He was already bound with the bonds of love to man, and of his own undertaking, else he had soon broken these bonds, as Samson did his.

2. They *led him away* in a sort of triumph, led him *as a lamb to the slaughter.* It was nearly a mile from Caiaphas's house to Pilate's. All that way they led him through the streets of Jerusalem, when in the morning they began to fill, to make him a spectacle to the world.

3. They *delivered him to Pontius Pilate*; according to that which Christ had often said, that he should be *delivered to the Gentiles.* Christ was to be the Saviour both of Jews and Gentiles; and therefore

Christ was brought into the judgment both of Jews and Gentiles, and both had a hand in his death.

II. The money which they had paid to Judas for betraying Christ, is by him delivered back to them, and Judas, in despair, hangs himself. The chief priests and elders supported themselves with *this*, in prosecuting Christ, that his own disciple betrayed him to them; but now, in the midst of the prosecution, that string failed them, and even *he* is made to them a *witness* of Christ's innocency, which served, 1. For glory to Christ in the midst of his sufferings, and a specimen of his victory over Satan who had entered into Judas. 2. For warning to his persecutors, and to leave them the more inexcusable.

(1) See here how Judas *repented*: not like Peter, who repented, believed, and was pardoned: no, he repented, despaired, and was ruined.

[1] What induced him to repent. It was *when he saw that he was condemned*. Judas, it is probable, expected that Christ would have made his escape out of their hands, and then Christ would have had the honour, the Jews the shame, and he the money, and no harm done. This he had no reason to expect, because he had so often heard his Master say that he must be *crucified*. Those who measure actions by the consequences of them rather than by the divine law, will find themselves mistaken in their measures. The way of sin is down-hill; and if we cannot easily stop ourselves, much less can we stop others whom we have set going in a sinful way. He *repented himself*. When he was tempted to betray his Master, the thirty pieces of silver looked very fine and glittering. But when the thing was done, and the money paid, the silver was become dross. Now his conscience flew in his face; "What have I done! What a fool, what a wretch, am I, to sell my Master for such a trifle! It is owing to me, that he is bound and condemned, spat upon and buffeted. I little thought it would have come to this, when I made that wicked bargain." The remembrance of his Master's goodness to him, steeled his convictions, and made them the more piercing. Now he found his Master's words true; *It were better for that man, that he had never been born*. Sin will soon change its taste.

[2] What were the indications of his repentance. *First*, He made restitution; *He brought again the thirty pieces of silver to the chief priests*. Now the money burned in his conscience, and he was as sick of it as ever he had been fond of it. That which is ill gotten, will never do good to those that get it. If he had repented, and brought the money back before he had betrayed Christ, he might have done it with comfort; but now it was too late, now he cannot do it without horror. What is unjustly gotten, must not be kept; for that is a continuance in the sin by which it was got. He brought it to those from whom he had it, to let them know that he repented his bargain.

Secondly, He made confession (*v.* 4); *I have sinned, in that I have betrayed innocent blood*. 1. To the *honour of Christ*, he pronounces his blood *innocent*. He, freely and without being urged to it, pronounces him innocent, to the face of those who had pronounced him *guilty*. 2. To *his own shame*, he confesses that he had sinned, in betraying this blood. He does not lay the blame on anyone else, but takes it all to himself; "I have sinned, in doing it." Thus far Judas went toward his repentance, yet it was *not to salvation*. He confessed, but not to God, did not go to him, and say, *I have sinned, Father, against heaven*.

(2) See here how the chief priests and elders entertained Judas's penitential confession; they said, *What is that to us? See thou to that*.

[1] See here how carelessly they speak of the betraying of Christ. *What is that to us?* Was it nothing to them that they had thirsted after this blood,

and hired Judas to betray it, and had now condemned it to be shed unjustly?

[2] See here how carelessly they speak the sin of Judas; he said, *I have sinned*, and they said, *"What is that to us?* What are we concerned in thy sin, that thou tellest us of it?" It is folly for us to think that the sins of others are nothing to us, especially those sins that we are any way accessory to, or partakers in. The guilt of sin is not so easily transferred as some people think it is. If there were guilt in the matter, they tell Judas that he must *look to it*, he must *bear it*. *First*, Because he had betrayed him to them. His was indeed *the greater sin* (John xix. 11); but it did not therefore follow, that theirs was no sin. *Secondly*, Because he knew and believed him to be innocent. "If he be innocent, see thou to it. We have adjudged him *guilty*, and therefore may justly prosecute him as such." Wicked practices are buoyed up by wicked principles, and particularly by this, That sin is sin only to those that think it to be so; that it is no harm to persecute a good man, if we take him to be a bad man.

[3] See how carelessly they speak of the conviction, terror, and remorse, that Judas was under. They were glad to make use of him in the sin, and were then very fond of him. But now they slighted him, had nothing to say to him, but turned him over to his own terrors. Those that are resolvedly impenitent, look with disdain upon the penitent. When they had brought him into the snare, they not only left him, but laughed at him. Sinners, under convictions, will find their old companions in sin, but miserable comforters. It is usual for those that love the treason, to hate the traitor.

(3) Here is the utter despair that Judas was hereby driven into. He grew desperate, *v.* 5.

[1] *He cast down the pieces of silver in the temple*. The chief priests would not take the money, for fear of taking thereby the whole guilt to themselves. Judas would not keep it, it was too hot for him to hold, he therefore threw it down in the temple, that, whether they would or no, it might fall into the hands of the chief priests.

[2] *He went, and hanged himself. First*, He retired; he withdrew into some solitary place. Woe to him that is in despair, and is alone. If Judas had gone to Christ, or to some of the disciples, perhaps he might have had relief, bad as the case was. *Secondly*, He became his own executioner; *He hanged himself*. Judas had a *sight* and *sense* of sin, but no apprehension of the mercy of God in Christ. His sin, we may suppose, was not in its own nature unpardonable: but he concluded, as Cain, that his iniquity was greater than could be forgiven. And some have said, that Judas sinned more in *despairing* of the mercy of God, than in *betraying* his Master's blood. He throws himself into the fire, to avoid the flame; but miserable is the case when a man must go to hell for ease. 1. We have an instance of the wretched end of those into whom Satan enters, and particularly those that are given up to the love of money. 2. We have an instance of the wrath of God. As in the story of Peter we behold the goodness of God, and the triumphs of Christ's grace in the conversion of some sinners; so in the story of Judas we behold the severity of God. 3. We have an instance of the direful effects of despair; it often ends in self-murder. Let us think as bad as we can of sin, provided we do not think it unpardonable; let us despair of help in ourselves, but not of help in God. And self-murder, though prescribed by some of the heathen moralists, is certainly a remedy worse than the disease, how bad soever the disease may be.

(4) The disposal of the money which Judas brought back, *v.* 6–10. It was laid out in the purchase of a field, called *the potter's field*. And this field was to

be a burying-place for strangers. It looks like an instance of their humanity, that they took care for the *burying of strangers*. It was no instance of their humility that they would bury strangers in a place by themselves. Strangers must keep their distance, alive and dead, and that principle must go down to the grave.

This buying of the potter's field took place not long after; for Peter speaks of it soon after Christ's ascension; yet it is here recorded.

First, To show the hypocrisy of the chief priests and elders. They scruple to put that money into the treasury, or *corban*, of the temple, with which they had hired the traitor. They would not put that money into it, which was the price of blood. The hire of a traitor they thought parallel to the hire of a whore, and the price of a malefactor (such a one they made Christ to be) equivalent to the price of a dog, neither of which was to be *brought into the house of the Lord*. Thus they that *swallowed a camel, strained at a gnat*. They think to *atone* for what they had done, by this public good act of providing a burying-place for strangers, though not at their own charge.

Secondly, To signify the favour intended by the blood of Christ to *strangers*, and sinners of the Gentiles. Through the price of his blood, a resting place is provided for them after death. The *grave* is the potter's field, but Christ by his blood *purchased* it. He has altered the property of it (as a purchaser doth), so that now death is ours, the grave is ours, a bed of rest for us.

Thirdly, To perpetuate the infamy of those that bought and sold the blood of Christ. This field was commonly called *Aceldama—the field of blood*; not by the chief priests, they hoped in this burying-place to bury the remembrance of their own crime; but by the people. They fastened this name upon the field *in perpetuam rei memoriam—for a perpetual memorial*.

Fourthly, That we may see how the scripture was fulfilled (v. 9, 10); *Then was fulfilled that which was spoken by Jeremy the prophet*. The words quoted are found in the prophecy of Zechariah, *ch. xi. 12*. How they are here said to be spoken by Jeremy is a difficult question. The Syriac version, which is ancient, reads only, *It was spoken by the prophet*, not naming any. The Jews used to say, *The spirit of Jeremiah was in Zechariah*. Here that is really acted, which was there but figuratively expressed. The sum of money is the same—*thirty pieces of silver*; this they *weighed for his price*, and this was *cast to the potter in the house of the Lord*; which was here literally accomplished.

The giving of the price of him that was valued, not for him, but for the *potter's field*, bespeaks, 1. The high value that ought to be put upon Christ. He cannot be *valued with the gold of Ophir*, nor this unspeakable Gift *bought with money*. 2. The low value that was put upon him. *They of the children of Israel* did strangely undervalue him, when his price did but reach to buy a potter's field, a pitiful sorry spot of ground, not worth looking upon. *Cast it to the potter*, so it is in Zechariah; a contemptible petty chapman, not the merchant that deals in things of value. He gave kings' ransoms for them, but they gave a slave's ransom for him (see Exod. xxi. 32), and valued him but at the rate of a potter's field. But all this was *as the Lord appointed*.

Verses 11–25

We have here an account of what passed in Pilate's judgment-hall.

I. The trial Christ had before Pilate.

1. His arraignment; *Jesus stood before the governor*, as the prisoner before the judge. We could not stand before God because of our sins, if Christ had not been thus made sin for us. He was arraigned that we might be discharged.

2. His indictment; *Art thou the king of the Jews?* Now they thought that whoever was the Christ, must be the *king of the Jews*, and must deliver them from the Roman power, and restore to them a temporal dominion. They accused our Lord Jesus, as making himself king of the Jews, in opposition to the Roman yoke. They assuring the governor that, if he made himself Christ, he made himself king of the Jews, the governor takes it for granted, that he goes about to pervert the nation, and subvert the government. *Art thou a king?*

3. His plea; *Jesus said unto him, "Thou sayest*. It is as thou sayest, though not as thou meanest; I am a king, but not such a king as thou dost suspect me to be."

4. The evidence (v. 12); He was *accused of the chief priests*. Pilate found *no fault in him*; whatever was said, nothing was proved, and therefore what was wanting in matter they made up in noise and violence.

5. The prisoner's silence as to the prosecutors' accusations; *He answered nothing*. Because there was no occasion; nothing was alleged but what carried its own confutation along with it. His hour was come, and he submitted to his Father's will; *Not as I will, but as thou wilt*. Pilate pressed him to make some reply (v. 13); *Hearest thou not how many things they witness against thee?* Pilate, having no malice at all against him, was desirous he should clear himself, urges him to it. He wondered at his silence. Pilate is not said to be angry at it, but to have *marvelled greatly* at it, as a thing very unusual. He thought it strange that he had not one word to say for himself.

II. The outrage and violence of the people, in pressing the governor to crucify Christ. The chief priests by the power of the mob gained the point which they could not otherwise carry. Now here are two instances of their outrage.

1. Their preferring Barabbas before him, and choosing to have him released rather than Jesus.

(1) It seems it was grown into a custom with the Roman governors, for the humouring of the Jews, to grace the feast of the passover with the release of a prisoner, (v. 15).

(2) The prisoner put in competition with our Lord Jesus was Barabbas; he is here called a *notable prisoner* (v. 16). *Treason, murder*, and *felony*, are the three most enormous crimes that are usually punished by the sword of justice; and Barabbas was guilty of all three, Luke xxiii. 19; John xviii. 40. A *notable prisoner* indeed, whose crimes were so complicated.

(3) The proposal was made by Pilate the governor (v. 17); *Whom will ye that I release unto you?* Pilate proposed to them to have Jesus *released*; he was convinced of his innocency, and that the prosecution was malicious; yet had not the courage to acquit him, as he ought to have done, by his own power, but would have him released by the people's election, and so he hoped to satisfy both his own *conscience*, and the *people* too. But such little tricks and artifices as these are the common practice of those that seek more to please men than God. *What shall I do then*, saith Pilate, *with Jesus, who is called Christ?* He puts the people in mind of this, that this *Jesus*, whose release he proposed, was looked upon by some among them as the Messiah.

The reason why Pilate *laboured* thus to get Jesus *discharged* was because he knew that *for envy the chief priests had delivered him up* (v. 18); that it was not his *guilt*, but his goodness, that they were provoked at. Anyone that heard the *hosannas* with which Christ was but a few days ago brought into Jerusalem, would have thought that Pilate might safely have referred this matter to the commonalty. But it proved otherwise.

(4) While Pilate was thus labouring the matter, he was confirmed in his unwillingness to condemn Jesus, by a message sent him from his wife (v. 19), by way of caution; *Have thou nothing to do with that just man, for I have suffered many things this day in a dream because of him.* Observe, The special providence of God, in sending this dream to Pilate's wife; it is not likely that she had heard anything, before, concerning Christ. Perhaps she was one of the *devout and honourable women*, and had some sense of religion. She *suffered many things* in this dream. It seems that it was a frightful dream, and her thoughts *troubled her.* See the tenderness and care of Pilate's wife, in sending this caution, thereupon, to her husband; *Have nothing to do with that just man.* This was an honourable testimony to our Lord Jesus, witnessing for him that he was a *just man.* When his friends were afraid to appear in defence of him, God made even those that were strangers and enemies, to speak in his favour; when Peter denied him, Judas confessed him; when the chief priests pronounced him guilty of death, Pilate declared he *found no fault* in him; when the women that loved him stood afar off, Pilate's wife, who knew little of him, showed a concern for him. It was a fair warning to Pilate; *Have nothing to do with him.* God has many ways of giving checks to sinners in their sinful pursuits, and it is a great mercy to have such checks. It is also our great duty to hearken to them. Pilate's lady sent him this warning, out of the love she had to him; let him take it how he would, she would give him the caution. It is an instance of true love to our friends and relations, to do what we can to keep them from sin; and the nearer any are to us, and the greater affection we have for them, the more solicitous we should be. The best friendship is friendship to the soul.

(5) The chief priests and the elders were busy, all this while, to influence the people in favour of Barabbas, *v.* 20. They *persuaded the multitude that they should ask Barabbas, and destroy Jesus.* Thus they managed the mob, who otherwise were well affected to Jesus, and, if they had not been so much at the beck of their priests, would never have done such a preposterous thing as to prefer Barabbas before Jesus. We cannot but look upon these wicked priests with indignation. Great power put into their hands they wretchedly abused, and the leaders of the people caused them to err. We cannot but look upon the deluded people with pity; *I have compassion on the multitude*, to see them hurried thus violently to so great wickedness.

(6) Being thus over-ruled by the priests, at length they made their choice, *v.* 21. *Whether of the twain* (saith Pilate) *will ye that I release unto you?* He hoped that he had gained his point, to have Jesus released. But, to his great surprise, they said *Barabbas.* Were ever men that pretended to reason or religion, guilty of such prodigious madness, such horrid wickedness! This was it that Peter charged so home upon them (Acts iii. 14); *Ye desired a murderer to be granted to you.*

2. Their pressing earnestly to have Jesus crucified, *v.* 22, 23. Pilate, being amazed at their choice of Barabbas puts it to them, *"What shall I do then with Jesus?" They all said, Let him be crucified.* That death they desired he might die, because it was looked upon as the most scandalous and ignominious; and they hoped thereby to make his followers ashamed to own him, and their relation to him. Malice and rage made them forget all rules of order and decency, and turned a court of justice into a *riotous, tumultuous,* and *seditious assembly.* See what a change was made upon the mind of the populace in a little time: when he *rode in triumph* into Jerusalem, so *general* were the *acclamations of praise*, that one would have thought

he had *no enemies*; but now when he was *led in triumph* to Pilate's judgment-seat, so *general* were the *outcries* of enmity, that one would think he had *no friends.* Such revolutions are there in this changeable world, through which our way to heaven lies, as our Master's did, *by honour and dishonour, by evil report, and good report.*

Now, as to this demand, we are further told,

(1) How Pilate objected against it; *Why, what evil hath he done?* A proper question for a judge to ask before he pass a sentence of death. It is much for the honour of the Lord Jesus, that, though he suffered as an evil-doer, yet neither his judge nor his prosecutors could find that he had done any evil. This repeated assertion of his unspotted innocency, plainly intimates that he died to satisfy for the sins of others; for if it had not been for our transgressions that he was thus wounded, and for our offences that he was delivered up, and that upon his own voluntary undertaking to atone for them, I see not how these extraordinary sufferings of a person that had never thought, said, or done, anything amiss, could be reconciled with the justice and equity of that providence that governs the world, and at least *permitted* this to be done in it.

(2) How they *insisted* upon it; *They cried out the more, Let him be crucified.* They do not go about to show any evil he had done, but, right or wrong, he must be *crucified.* This unjust judge was wearied by importunity into an unjust sentence, as he in the parable into a just one (Luke xviii. 4, 5), and the cause carried purely by noise.

III. Here is the *devolving* of the *guilt* of Christ's blood upon the *people* and *priests.*

1. Pilate endeavours to transfer it from himself, *v.* 24. He sees it *to no purpose to contend.* What he said, (1) Would do no good; *he could prevail nothing.* See how strong the stream of lust and rage sometimes is; neither authority nor reason will prevail to give check to it. Nay, (2) It was more likely to *do hurt*; he saw that rather a *tumult was made.* This rude and brutish people fell to high words, and began to threaten Pilate what they would do if he did not gratify them. Now this turbulent tumultuous temper of the Jews contributed more than anything to the ruin of that nation not long after; for their frequent insurrections provoked the Romans to destroy them, and their inveterate quarrels among themselves made them an easy prey to the common enemy. Thus their sin was their ruin.

The priests were apprehensive that their endeavours to *seize* Christ would have caused an uproar, especially *on the feast day*; but it proved that Pilate's endeavour to *save* him, caused an uproar, and that on the feast day; so uncertain are the sentiments of the crowd. This puts him into a *great strait*, betwixt the peace of his own mind, and the peace of the city. Had he steadily and resolutely adhered to the sacred laws of justice, he had not been in any perplexity. A man in whom was found *no fault*, ought not to be crucified, upon any pretence whatsoever, nor must an unjust thing be done, to gratify any man or company of men in the world. Pilate thinks to trim the matter, and to pacify both the people and his own conscience too, by *doing it*, and yet *disowning it.*

Now Pilate endeavours to clear himself from the guilt,

[1] By a *sign*; He *took water, and washed his hands before the multitude*; not as if he thought thereby to cleanse himself from any guilt contracted before God, but to acquit himself before the people. He *borrowed* the ceremony from that law which appointed it to be used for the clearing of the country from the guilt of an undiscovered murder (Deut. xxi. 6, 7); and he used it the more to affect the people with the conviction he was under of the prisoner's innocency.

[2] By a *saying*; in which, *First*, He *clears* himself; *I am innocent of the blood of this just person*. What nonsense was this, to condemn him, and yet protest that he was innocent of his blood! For men to protest against a thing, and yet to practise it, is only to proclaim that they sin against their consciences. *Secondly*, He casts it upon the priests and people; "*See ye to it*"; do you answer it before God and the world. Sin is a brat that nobody is willing to own; and many deceive themselves with this, that they shall bear no blame if they can but find any to lay the blame upon; but it is not so easy a thing to transfer the guilt of sin as many think it is. The priests threw it upon Judas; *See thou to it*; and now Pilate throws it upon them; *See ye to it*.

2. The priests and people *consented* to take the guilt *upon themselves*; they all said, "*His blood be on us, and on our children*". They, in the heat of their rage, agreed to it, rather than lose the prey they had in their hands, and cried, *His blood be upon us*. By this they designed to indemnify Pilate. But those that are themselves bankrupts and beggars will never be admitted security for others. None could bear the sin of others, except him that had none of his own to answer for; it is a bold undertaking, and too big for any creature, to become bound for a sinner to Almighty God. But they did really imprecate wrath and vengeance upon themselves and their posterity. Christ had lately told them, that upon them would come *all the righteous blood shed upon the earth*, from that of the righteous Abel; but as if that were too little, they here imprecate upon themselves the guilt of that blood which was more precious than all the rest, and the guilt of which would lie heavier. Observe, How *cruel* they were in their *imprecation*. They imprecated the punishment of this sin, not only upon themselves, but upon *their children* too. It was madness to pull it upon themselves, but the height of barbarity to entail it on their posterity. See what enemies wicked men are to their own children and families. From the time they imprecated this blood upon them, they were followed with one judgment after another. Yet on some of them, and some of theirs, this blood came, not to *condemn* them, but to *save* them; divine mercy, upon their repenting and believing, cut off this entail, and then *the promise* was again *to them, and to their children*. God is better to us and ours than we are.

Verses 26–32

I. The sentence passed, and the warrant signed for his execution; and this *immediately*, the same hour.

1. Barabbas was released; to intimate that Christ was condemned for this purpose, that sinners, even the chief of sinners, might be *released*; he was *delivered up*, that we might be delivered. In this *unparalleled* instance of divine grace, the *upright* is a *ransom for the transgressors*, the just for the unjust.

2. Jesus was *scourged*; this was an ignominious cruel punishment, especially as it was inflicted by the Romans, who were not under the moderation of the Jewish law, which forbade scourgings, above forty stripes.

3. He was then *delivered to be crucified*; a kind of death used only among the Romans; the manner of it is such, that it seems to be the result of wit and cruelty in combination, to make death in the highest degree terrible and miserable. A cross was set up in the ground, to which the hands and feet were nailed, on which nails the weight of the body hung, till it died of the pain. It was a bloody death, a painful, shameful, cursed death; it was so miserable a death, that merciful princes appointed those who were condemned to it by the law, to be strangled first, and then nailed to the cross.

II. The barbarous treatment which the soldiers gave him. When he was condemned, he ought to have had some time allowed him to prepare for death. There was a law made by the Roman senate that the execution of criminals should be deferred at least *ten days* after sentence. But there were scarcely allowed so many minutes to our Lord Jesus. The storm continued without any intermission.

When he was *delivered* to be *crucified*, that was enough; they that *kill the body*, yield that there is no more that they *can do*, but Christ's enemies will *do more*. His guards set themselves to abuse him. Perhaps it was not so much in spite to him, as to make *sport* for themselves, that they thus abused him. They understood that he *pretended to a crown*; to *taunt* him with that gave them some diversion, and an opportunity to make themselves and one another merry.

Observe, 1. *Where* this was done—in the *common hall*. The *governor's house*, which should have been a shelter to the wronged and abused, is made the theatre of this barbarity. Those in authority will be accountable, not only for the wickedness which they *do*, or *appoint*, but for that which they do not restrain.

2. *Who* were concerned in it. They gathered the *whole band*, the soldiers that were to attend the execution.

3. *What* particular indignities were done him.

(1) They *stripped him*, v. 28. The shame of nakedness came in with sin (Gen. iii. 7).

(2) They *put on him a scarlet robe*, some old red cloak, such as the Roman soldiers wore, in imitation of the *scarlet robes* which kings and emperors wore; thus upbraiding him with his being called *a King*. This *sham* of majesty they put upon him in his dress, only to expose him to the spectators, as the more *ridiculous*.

(3) They *platted a crown of thorns, and put it upon his head*, v, 29. This was to carry on the humour of making him a *mock-king*; yet, had they intended it only for a *reproach*, they might have *platted a crown of straw*, or *rushes*, but they designed it to be painful to him. Thorns signify afflictions. These Christ put into a *crown*; so much did he alter the property of them to them that are his, giving them cause to *glory in tribulation*, and making it to work for them a weight of glory. Christ was crowned with thorns, to show that *his kingdom was not of this world*, nor the glory of it worldly glory, but is attended here with bonds and afflictions, while the glory of it is *to be revealed*.

(4) They *put a reed in his right hand*; this was intended for a *mock-sceptre*, another of the *insignia* of the majesty they jeered him with; as if this were a sceptre good enough for such a King. Like sceptre, like kingdom, both weak and wavering, and withering and worthless; but they were quite mistaken, for his throne is *for ever and ever*.

(5) They *bowed the knee before him, and mocked him, saying, Hail, King of the Jews!* Having made him a sham King, they thus make a jest of doing homage to him, thus ridiculing his pretensions to sovereignty.

(6) They *spit upon him*; thus he had been abused in the High Priest's hall, *ch.* xxvi. 67. In doing homage, the subject kissed the sovereign, in token of his allegiance; but they, in this mock-homage, instead of kissing him, spit in his face. It is strange that the sons of men should ever do such a piece of *villainy*, and that the Son of God should ever *suffer* such a piece of *ignominy*.

(7) They *took the reed, and smote him on the head*. That which they had made the *mock-ensign* of his royalty, they now make the real instrument of *their* cruelty, and *his* pain. They smote him, it is probable, upon the *crown of thorns*, and so struck them into

his head, which made the most sport for them, to whom his pain was the greatest pleasure. All this misery and shame he underwent, that he might purchase for us everlasting life, and joy, and glory.

III. The conveying of him to the place of execution. After they had mocked and abused him, as long as they thought fit, they then *took the robe off from him*; and they put his own raiment on him, because that was to fall to the soldiers' share, that were employed in the execution. No mention is made of their taking off the *crown of thorns*, whence it is commonly supposed (though there is no certainty of it) that he was crucified with that on his head.

1. They *led him away* to be *crucified*; he was led *as a lamb to the slaughter*, as a sacrifice to the altar. We may well imagine how they hurried him on, and dragged him along, with all the speed possible. They led him away *out of the city*; for Christ, that he might sanctify the people with his own blood, *suffered without the gate* (Heb. xiii. 12).

2. They compelled Simon of Cyrene *to bear his cross*, v. 32. It seems, at first he *carried the cross* himself. And this was intended, as other things, both for pain and shame to him. But after a while they *took the cross* off from him, either, (1) In compassion to him, because they saw it was too great a load for him. We can hardly think that they had any consideration of that. But, (2) Perhaps it was because he could not, with the cross on his back, go forward so fast as they would have him. Or, (3) They were afraid, lest he should faint away under the load of his cross, and die, and so prevent what their malice further intended to do against him. Taking the cross off from him, they *compelled* one Simon of Cyrene to bear it. It was a reproach, and none would do it but by compulsion. Some think that this Simon was a disciple of Christ, at least a well-wisher to him, and that they knew it, and therefore put this upon him. All that will approve themselves disciples indeed, must follow Christ, *bearing his cross.*

Verses 33–49

We have here the crucifixion of our Lord Jesus.

I. The place where our Lord Jesus was put to death.

1. They came to a place called *Golgotha*, near adjoining to Jerusalem, probably the common place of execution. But now in the same place where criminals were sacrificed to the justice of the government, was our Lord Jesus sacrificed to the justice of God. Some think that it was called *the place of a skull*, because it was the common charnel-house, where the bones and skulls of dead men were laid together out of the way, lest people should touch them, and be defiled thereby. When by dying Christ would destroy death, he added this circumstance of honour to his victory, that he triumphed over death upon his own dunghill.

2. There they *crucified* him (v. 35), nailed his hands and feet to the cross, and then reared it up, and him hanging on it; for so the manner of the Romans was to crucify. Let our hearts be touched with the feeling of that exquisite pain which our blessed Saviour now endured. And when we behold what manner of death he died, let us in that behold with *what manner of love* he *loved us*.

II. The barbarous and abusive treatment they gave him. As if death, so great a death, were not bad enough, they contrived to add to the bitterness and terror of it.

1. By the drink they provided for him before he was nailed to the cross, v. 34. It was usual to have a cup of spiced wine for those to drink of, that were to be put to death. But with that cup which Christ was to drink of, they mingled *vinegar and gall*, to make it sour and bitter. He *tasted thereof*, and so had the *worst* of it, took the bitter taste into his mouth; now he was *tasting* death in its full bitterness. He *would not drink it*, because he would not have the *best of it*; would have nothing like an opiate to lessen his sense of pain, for he would die so as to *feel himself die*.

2. By the dividing of his garments, v. 35. When they nailed him to the cross, they *stripped* him of his garments. If we be at any time stripped of our comforts for Christ, let us bear it patiently; he was stripped for us. Enemies may strip us of our *clothes*, but cannot strip us of our *best comforts*; cannot take from us the *garments of praise*. The clothes of those that are executed are the executioner's fee: four soldiers were employed in crucifying Christ, and they must each of them have a share; his upper garment, if it were divided, would be of no use to any of them, and therefore they agreed to *cast lots* for it. Perhaps they had heard of those that had been cured by touching the hem of his garment, and they thought it valuable for some magic virtue in it. Or, It was for diversion; to pass away the time while they waited for his death, they would play a game at dice for the clothes. but, whatever they designed, the word of God is herein accomplished. In that famous *psalm*, the first words of which Christ made use of upon the cross, it was said, *They parted my garment among them, and cast lots upon my vesture*, Ps. xxii. 18. Christ stripped himself of his glories, to divide them among us.

They now *sat down, and watched him*, v. 36. But Providence so ordered it, that those who were appointed to *watch* him, thereby became unexceptionable witnesses for him; having the opportunity to see and hear that which extorted from them that noble confession (v. 54), *Truly this was the Son of God.*

3. By the *title* set up over his head, v. 37. It was usual not only by a crier to proclaim before them, but by a writing also over their heads to notify what was the crime for which they suffered; so they set up over Christ's head his accusation written, *This is Jesus the King of the Jews*. Here was no crime alleged against him. It is not said that he was a pretended Saviour, or a usurping King, but, *This is Jesus, a Saviour*; surely that was no crime; and, *This is the King of the Jews*; nor was that a crime; for they expected that the Messiah should be so. Here was a very glorious truth asserted concerning him—that he is *Jesus the King of the Jews*, that King whom the Jews expected and ought to have submitted to. Pilate, instead of accusing Christ as a Criminal, proclaimed him a *King*, and that *three times*, in three inscriptions. Thus God makes men to serve *his* purposes, quite beyond *their own.*

4. By his companions with him in suffering, v. 38. There were *two thieves crucified with him* at the same time, in the same place, under the same guard; two highway-men, or robbers upon the road, as the word properly signifies. It is probable that this was appointed to be *execution-day*. However it was, the scripture was fulfilled in it (Isa. liii. 12), *He was numbered with the transgressors.*

(1) It was a reproach to him, that he was *crucified with them*. He was made to partake with the vilest malefactors in their plagues, as if he had been a partaker with them in their sins. He was, at his death, numbered among the transgressors, that we, at our death, might be *numbered among the saints.*

(2) It was an additional reproach, that he was crucified *in the midst, between them*, as if he had been the worst of the three, the principal malefactor; for among *three* the *middle* is the place for the chief. Every circumstance was contrived to his dishonour, as if the great Saviour were of all others the *greatest sinner*. It was also intended to ruffle and discompose

him, in his last moments, with the shrieks, and groans, and blasphemies, of these malefactors. But thus would Christ affect himself with the miseries of sinners, when he was suffering for their salvation.

5. By the blasphemies and revilings with which they loaded him when he was hanging upon the cross. One would have thought that, when they had nailed him to the cross, they had done their worst. A dying man, though an infamous man, should be treated with compassion. For aught that appears, not one of his friends, who the other day cried *Hosanna* to him, durst be seen to show him any respect.

(1) The common *people, that passed by, reviled him.* His extreme misery and exemplary patience under it, did not make them to relent; but they who by their outcries brought him to this, now think to justify themselves in it by their reproaches, as if they *did well* to *condemn* him. They *reviled* him.

[1] The persons that reviled him; *they that passed by,* the travellers that went along the road; they were possessed with prejudices against him by the reports and clamours of the High Priest's creatures. It is a hard thing to keep up a good opinion of persons and things that are *everywhere* run down, and spoken against. Every one is apt to say as the most say, and to throw a stone at that which is put into an ill name.

[2] The gesture they used, in contempt of him— *wagging their heads;* which signifies their triumph in his fall, and their insulting over him.

[3] The taunts and jeers they uttered. These are here recorded.

First, They upbraided him with his *destroying of the temple.* They industriously spread it among the people, to bring an *odium* upon him, that he had a design to destroy the temple; than which nothing would more *incense* the people against him. "*Thou that destroyest the temple,* that vast and strong fabric, try thy strength now in plucking up that *cross,* and drawing those *nails,* and so *save thyself;* if thou hast the power thou hast boasted of, this is a proper time to exert it, and give proof of it." He was *crucified in weakness* (2 Cor. xiii. 4), so it seemed to them; but indeed Christ crucified is the *Power of God.*

Secondly, They upbraided him with his saying that he was *the Son of God;* If thou be so, say they, *come down from the cross.* Now they take the devil's words out of his mouth, with which he tempted him in the wilderness (*ch.* iv. 3, 6), and renew the same assault; *If thou be the Son of God.* They think that now, or never, he must prove himself to be the *Son of God;* forgetting that he had proved it by the miracles he wrought; and unwilling to wait for the complete proof of it by his own resurrection, to which he had so often referred. This comes of judging things by the present aspect of them, without a due remembrance of what is *past,* and a patient expectation of *what may further be produced.*

(2) The *chief priests and scribes, v.* 41. They did not think it enough to invite the rabble to do it. They should have been in the temple at their devotion, for it was the first day of the feast of unleavened bread. but they were here at the place of execution, spitting their venom at the Lord Jesus. Did they disparage themselves thus, to do despite to Christ, and shall we be afraid of disparaging ourselves, by joining with the multitude to *do him honour?*

Two things the priests and elders upbraided him with.

[1] That he could not *save himself, v.* 42. *First,* They take it for granted that he *could not* save himself, and therefore had not the power he pretended to, when really he *would not* save himself, because he would die to *save us. Secondly,* They would insinuate that, because he did not now save himself, therefore all his pretence to save others was but sham and

delusion. *Thirdly,* They upbraid him with being *the King of Israel.* Many people would like the *King of Israel* well enough, if he would but *come down from the cross.* But the matter is settled; if no cross, then no Christ, no crown. Those that would reign with him, must be willing to suffer with him, for Christ and his cross are *nailed together* in this world. *Fourthly,* They challenged him to *come down from the cross.* But his unchangeable love and resolution set him above, and fortified him against, this temptation, so that he did not *fail,* nor was *discouraged. Fifthly,* They promised that, if he would *come down from the cross, they would believe him.* When they had formerly demanded a sign, he told them that the sign he would give them, should be not his *coming down from the cross,* but, which was a greater instance of his power, his *coming up from the grave.* But to promise ourselves that we would believe, if we had such and such means and motives of faith as we ourselves would prescribe, is not only a gross instance of the deceitfulness of our hearts, but the sorry *refuge,* or *subterfuge* rather, of an obstinate destroying infidelity.

[2] That God, *his Father,* would *not save him* (*v.* 43); *He trusted in God,* for he said, *I am the Son of God.* Those who call God *Father,* and themselves *his children,* thereby profess to put a confidence in him, Ps. ix. 10. Now they suggest, that he did but deceive himself and others; for, if he had been the Son of God he would not have been *abandoned to* all this misery, much less *abandoned* in it. It was intended, *First,* To *vilify* him, and to make the standers-by think him a deceiver and an imposter. *Secondly,* To *terrify* him, and drive him to distrust and despair of his Father's power and love.

(3) To complete the reproach, the *thieves also that were crucified with him* were not only not reviled as he was, as if they had been saints compared with him, but *cast the same in his teeth;* that is, one of them did, who said, *If thou be the Christ, save thyself and us,* Luke xxiii. 39. One would think that of all people this thief had *least cause,* and should have had *least mind,* to banter Christ.

Well, thus our Lord Jesus having undertaken to satisfy the justice of God for the wrong done him in his honour by sin, he did it by suffering *in his honour;* by submitting to the utmost indignity that could be done to the worst of men; because he was made sin for us, he was thus made a curse for us.

III. We have here the frowns of heaven, which our Lord Jesus was under, in the midst of all these injuries and indignities from men. Concerning which, observe,

1. How this was signified—by an extraordinary and miraculous eclipse of the sun, which continued for *three hours, v.* 45. An extraordinary light gave intelligence of the birth of Christ (*ch.* ii. 2), and therefore it was proper that an extraordinary darkness should notify his death, for he is the *Light of the world.* This surprising, amazing, darkness was designed to stop the mouths of those blasphemers, who were reviling Christ as he hung on the cross. Though their hearts were not changed, yet they were silent, and stood doubting what this should mean, till after *three hours* the darkness *scattered,* and then (as appears by *v.* 47), like Pharaoh when the plague was over, they hardened their hearts. But that which was principally intended in this darkness, was, (1) Christ's present *conflict* with the *powers of darkness.* He fights them on their own ground; gives them all the advantage they could have against him by this darkness, lets them take the *wind* and *sun,* and yet baffles them, and so becomes more than a conqueror. (2) His present *want* of heavenly comforts. This darkness signified that dark cloud which the human soul of our Lord Jesus was now under. God makes his sun

to shine upon the just and upon the unjust; but even the light of the sun was withheld from our Saviour, when he was *made sin for us*. When earth denied him a drop of cold water, heaven denied him a beam of light; having to deliver us from *utter darkness*, he did himself, in the depth of his sufferings, walk in darkness, and had no light. During the *three hours* that this darkness continued, we do not find that he said *one word*, but passed this time in a silent retirement into his own soul. Never were there three such hours since the day that God created man upon the earth, never such a dark and awful scene; the *crisis* of that great affair of man's redemption and salvation.

2. How he complained of it (*v.* 46); *About the ninth hour*, when it began to clear up, after a long and silent conflict. *Jesus cried, Eli, Eli, lama sabachthani?* The words are related in the Syriac tongue, in which they were spoken, for the sake of the perverse construction which his enemies put upon them, in putting *Elias*, for *Eli*. Now observe here,

(1) Whence he borrowed this complaint—from Ps. xxii. 1. This, and that other word, *Into thy hands I commit my spirit*, he fetched from David's psalms to teach us of what use the word of God is to us, to direct us in prayer, which will *help our infirmities*.

(2) How he uttered it—*with a loud voice*; which bespeaks the extremity of his pain and anguish, the strength of nature remaining in him, and the great earnestness of his spirit in this expostulation.

(3) What the complaint was—*My God, My God, why hast thou forsaken me?* A strange complaint to come from the mouth of our Lord Jesus, who, we are sure, was one in whom he was always *well pleased*. The Father now loved him, nay, he knew that *therefore he loved him, because he laid down his life for the sheep*; what, and yet forsaken of him, and in the midst of his sufferings too! Surely never sorrow was like unto that sorrow which extorted such a complaint as this. No wonder that such a complaint as this made the earth to quake, and rent the rocks.

Note, [1] That our Lord Jesus was, in his sufferings, for a time, *forsaken by his Father*. So he saith himself, who we are sure was under no mistake concerning his own case. Not as if there were any abatement of his Father's love to him, or his to his Father; but his Father forsook him. He delivered him up into the hands of his enemies, and did not appear to deliver him out of their hands. No angel is sent from heaven to deliver him, no friend on earth raised up to appear for him. When *his soul* was first *troubled*, he had a *voice from heaven* to comfort him (John xii. 27, 28); when he was in his agony in the garden, there appeared an angel from heaven strengthening him; but now he had neither the one nor the other. God hid his face from him. Christ was made *Sin* for us, a *Curse* for us; and therefore, though God loved him as a Son, he frowned upon him as a Surety.

[2] That Christ's being *forsaken* of his Father was the most grievous of his sufferings. Here he laid the most doleful accents. When his Father stood at a distance, he cried out thus; for this was it that *put wormwood and gall* into the affliction and misery.

[3] That our Lord Jesus, even when he was thus forsaken of his Father, kept hold of him as his God, notwithstanding; *My God, my God*; though forsaking me, yet *mine*. This supported him, and bore him up, that even in the depth of his sufferings God was his God, and this he resolves to keep fast hold of.

(4) See how his enemies impiously bantered and ridiculed this complaint (*v.* 47); *They said, This man calleth for Elias*. Some think that this was the ignorant mistake of the Roman soldiers, who knew not the signification of *Eli, Eli*, and so made this blundering comment upon these words of Christ. Many of

the reproaches cast upon the word of God and the people of God, take rise from gross mistakes. Those that hear by the halves, pervert what they hear. But others think that it was the wilful mistake of some of the Jews, who knew very well what he said, but were disposed to abuse him, and to misrepresent him as one who, being forsaken of God, was driven to trust in creatures. It is no new thing for the most pious devotions of the best men to be ridiculed and abused by profane scoffers. Christ's words were so, though he spoke as never man spoke.

IV. The cold comfort which his enemies ministered to him in this agony.

1. Some *gave him vinegar to drink* (*v.* 48); instead of some cordial-water to revive and refresh him under this heavy burthen. *One of them ran* to fetch it.

2. Others, with the same purpose of disturbing and abusing him, refer him to Elias (*v.* 49); "*Let be, let us see whether Elias will come to save him.* Come, let him alone, he has appealed to Elias, and *to Elias let him go.*"

Verses 50-56

We have here, at length, an account of the death of Christ.

I. The *manner* how he breathed his last (*v.* 50); between the third and the sixth hour, that is, between nine and twelve o'clock, as we reckon, he was nailed to the cross, and soon after the ninth hour, that is, between three and four o'clock, in the afternoon, he *died*. That was the time of the offering of the evening sacrifice, and the time when the paschal lamb was killed; and Christ our Passover was sacrificed for us.

Two things are here noted concerning the manner of Christ's dying.

1. That he *cried with a loud voice*, as before, *v.* 46. Now,

(1) This was a sign, that, after all his pains and fatigues, his life was *whole* in him, and nature *strong*. The voice of dying men is one of the first things that fails; with a panting breath and a faltering tongue, a few broken words are hardly spoken, and more hardly heard. But Christ, just before he expired, spoke like a man *in his full strength*, to show that his life was not forced from him, but was freely *delivered* by him into his Father's hands.

(2) It was significant. His crying with a loud voice when he died, signified that his death should be published and proclaimed to all the world. Christ's loud cry was like a trumpet blown over the sacrifices.

2. That then he *yielded up the ghost*. This is the usual periphrasis of dying; to show that the Son of God upon the cross did truly and properly die by the violence of the pain he was put to. His *soul* was separated from his *body*, and so his body was left really and truly dead. He had undertaken to make his soul an *offering for sin*.

II. The miracles that attended his death. So many miracles being wrought *by him* in his life, we might well expect some to be wrought concerning him at his death.

1. *Behold, the veil of the temple was rent in twain.* Just as our Lord Jesus expired, at the time of the offering of the evening sacrifice, *the veil of the temple was rent* by an invisible power; that veil which parted between the *holy place* and the *most holy*. In this, as in others of Christ's miracles, there was a mystery.

(1) It was in correspondence with the temple of Christ's body, which was now in the dissolving. Death is the rending of the veil of flesh which interposes between us and the holy of holies; the death of Christ was so, the death of true Christians is so.

(2) It signified the revealing and unfolding of the mysteries of the Old Testament. The veil of the temple was for concealment, for it was highly penal for any person to see the furniture of the most holy place,

except the High Priest, and he but once a year, with great ceremony and through a cloud of smoke. But now, at the death of Christ, all was laid open, the mysteries were unveiled, so that now he that runs may read the meaning of them.

(3) It signified the uniting of Jew and Gentile, by the removing of the partition wall between them, which was the ceremonial law. Christ, in his death, repealed the ceremonial law, took it out of the way, nailed it to his cross. Christ died, to rend all dividing veils, and to make all his one, John xvii. 21.

(4) It signified the consecrating and laying open of *a new and living way* to God. The veil kept people off from drawing near to the most holy place, where the *Shechinah* was. But the rending of it signified that Christ by his death opened a way to God, [1] *For himself*. Having offered his sacrifice in the outer court, the blood of it was now to be sprinkled upon the mercy-seat within the veil. Though he did not personally ascend into the holy place not made with hands till above forty days after, yet he immediately acquired a right to enter, and had a virtual admission. [2] *For us in him:* so the apostle applies it, Heb. x. 19, 20. He died, to *bring us to God*, and, in order thereunto, to rend that veil of guilt and wrath which interposed between us and him. We have free access through Christ to the throne of grace, or mercy-seat, now, and to the throne of glory hereafter, Heb. iv. 16. *When Christ had overcome the sharpness of death, he opened the kingdom of heaven to all believers.* Nothing can obstruct or discourage our access to heaven.

2. The *earth did quake*. This earthquake signified two things.

(1) The *horrible* wickedness of *Christ's crucifiers*. The earth, by trembling under such a load, bore its testimony to the innocency of him that was persecuted, and against the impiety of those that persecuted him.

(2) The *glorious* achievements of *Christ's cross*. This *earthquake* signified the mighty shock, nay, the fatal blow, now given to the devil's kingdom. God shakes all nations, when the Desire of all nations is to come.

3. The *rocks rent*; the hardest and firmest part of the earth was made to feel this mighty shock. Christ had said, that if the children should cease to cry *Hosanna, the stones would immediately cry out*; and now, in effect, they did so, proclaiming the glory of the suffering Jesus. Jesus Christ is *the Rock*; and the rending of *these* rocks, signified the rending of *that* rock, (1) That in the clefts of it we may be *hid*, as Moses in the cleft of the rock at Horeb, that there we may *behold the glory of the Lord*, as he did. (2) That from the cleft of it *rivers of living water* may flow, and follow us in this wilderness. When we celebrate the memorial of Christ's death, our hard and rocky hearts must be *rent*—the heart, and not the garments. That heart is harder than a rock, that will not *yield*, that will not *melt*, where Jesus Christ is *evidently set forth crucified*.

4. The *graves were opened*. It should seem, the same earthquake that rent the rocks, *opened the graves*, and many bodies of *saints which slept, arose*. Death to the saints is but the *sleep* of the body, and the *grave* the bed it *sleeps in*; they awoke by the power of the Lord Jesus, and (v. 53) came *out of the graves after his resurrection, and went into Jerusalem, the holy city, and appeared unto many*. We may raise many enquiries concerning it, which we cannot resolve: as, [1] *Who* these *saints* were, that *did arise*. Some think, the *ancient patriarchs*, that were in such care to be buried in the land of Canaan. Others think, these that arose were *modern saints*, such as had seen Christ in the flesh, but died before him. What if we should suppose that they were the *martyrs*, who

in the Old Testament times had sealed the truths of God with their blood. Sufferers with Christ shall *first* reign with him. [2] It is uncertain whether (as some think) they arose to life, now at the death of Christ, but did not *go into the city* till after his resurrection; or whether they did not *revive* and *rise* till after the resurrection; only, for brevity-sake, it is mentioned here, upon the mention of the *opening of the graves*. [3] Some think that they arose only to bear witness of Christ's resurrection to those to whom they appeared, and, having finished their testimony, retired to their graves again. But it is more agreeable, both to Christ's honour and theirs, to *suppose* that they arose as Christ did, to *die no more*. Surely on them who did partake of his first resurrection, a *second* death had no power. [4] To whom they appeared, whether enemies or friends, in what manner they appeared, how often, what they said and did, are secret things which belong not to us. The relating of this matter so briefly, is a plain intimation to us, that we must not look that way for a confirmation of our faith; we have a more sure word of prophecy.

Yet we may learn many good lessons from it. [1] That even those who lived and died before the death and resurrection of Christ, had saving benefit thereby, as well as those who have lived since. [2] That Jesus Christ, by dying, conquered, disarmed, and disabled, death. These saints that arose, were the present trophies of the victory of Christ's cross over the powers of *death*. [3] That, in virtue of Christ's resurrection, the bodies of all the saints shall, in the fulness of time, *rise again*. This was an earnest of the general resurrection at the last day.

III. The conviction of his enemies that were employed in the execution, *v*. 54.

1. The persons convinced; *the centurion, and they that were with him watching Jesus*. (1) They were *soldiers*, whose profession is commonly hardening, and whose breasts are commonly not so susceptible as some others of the impressions either of fear or pity. But there is no spirit too big, too bold, for the power of Christ to break and humble. (2) They were *Romans, Gentiles*, yet they only were convinced. Here were the Gentiles *softened*, and the Jews *hardened*. (3) They were the persecutors of Christ, and those that just before had reviled him, as appears Luke xxiii. 36. How soon can God, by the power he has over men's consciences, alter their language.

2. The means of their conviction; they perceived *the earthquake*, which frightened them, and saw the other *things that were done*. These had their end on these soldiers, whatever they had on others.

3. The expressions of this conviction, in two things.

(1) The *terror* that was *struck* upon them; they *feared greatly*; feared lest they should have been buried in the darkness, or swallowed up in the earthquake. God can easily frighten the most daring of his adversaries. Guilt puts men into fear. Whereas there are those who will not fear, *though the earth be removed*, Ps. xlvi. 1, 2.

(2) The *testimony* that was *extorted* from them; they said, *Truly this was the Son of God*. It was the great matter now in dispute, the point upon which he and his enemies had *joined issue*, ch. xxvi. 63, 64. His disciples believed it, but at this time durst not confess it; our Saviour himself was tempted to question it, when he said, *Why hast thou forsaken me?* The Jews, now that he was dying upon the cross, looked upon it as plainly determined against him. And yet now this centurion and the soldiers make this voluntary confession of the Christian faith, *Truly this was the Son of God*. The best of his disciples could not have said more at any time, and at this time they had not faith and courage enough to say thus much.

IV. The attendance of his friends, that were witnesses of his death, v. 55, 56.

1. Who they were; *many women who followed him from Galilee*. Not his apostles (only elsewhere we find John by the cross, John xix. 26), their hearts failed them, they durst not appear. But here were a company of women, some would have called them *silly* women, that *boldly* stuck to Christ, when the rest of his disciples had basely deserted him. Even those of the weaker sex are often, by the grace of God, made strong in faith. There have been women martyrs, famous for courage and resolution in Christ's cause. Now of these women it is said, (1) That they had *followed Jesus from Galilee*, out of the great love they had to him. The males only were obliged to come up, to worship at the feast. Now having followed him such a long journey they resolved not to forsake him now. Our former services and sufferings for Christ should be an argument with us, faithfully to persevere to the end in our attendance on him. (2) That they *ministered to him* of their substance. How gladly would they have ministered to him now, if they might have been admitted! When we are restrained from doing what we *would*, we must do what we can, in the service of Christ. (3) Some of them are particularly named. They were such as we have several times met with *before*, and it was their praise, that we meet with them *to the last*.

2. What they did; they were *beholding afar off*.

(1) They stood *afar off*. It was an aggravation of the sufferings of Christ, that his *lovers and friends stood aloof from his sore*. Perhaps they might have come nearer, if they would; but good people, when they are in sufferings, must not think it strange, if some of their best friends be shy of them. If we be thus looked strangely upon, remember, our Master was so before us.

(2) They were there *beholding*; when they were debarred from doing any other office of love to him, they looked a look of love toward him. It was a *sorrowful* look. We may well imagine how it cut them to the heart, to see him in his torment. Let us with an eye of faith behold Christ and him crucified, and be affected with that great love wherewith he loved us. It was no more than a look; they beheld him, but they could not *help him*. When Christ was in his sufferings, the best of his friends were but spectators and lookers on.

Verses 57–66

We have here an account of Christ's *burial*. 1. The *kindness* and *goodwill* of his friends that *laid him in the grave*. 2. The *malice* and *ill will* of his enemies that were very solicitous to keep him there.

I. His friends gave him a *decent burial*.

1. Jesus Christ was *buried*; when his precious soul was gone to paradise, his blessed body was deposited in the chambers of the grave. He was buried, to make his death the more certain, and his resurrection the more illustrious. Pilate would not deliver his body to be buried, till he was well assured that he was really dead. He was *buried*, that he might take off the terror of the grave, and make it easy to us, might warm and perfume that cold noisome bed for us, and that we might be *buried with him*.

2. The particular circumstances of his burial here related.

(1) The time *when* he was buried; *when the evening was come*; the same evening that he died, before sunset, as is usual in burying malefactors. It was not deferred till the next day, because it was *the sabbath*.

(2) The person that took care of the funeral was Joseph of Arimathea. The apostles had all fled. The women that followed him durst not move in it; then did God stir up this good man to do it; for what work God has to do, he will find out instruments to do it. Joseph was a fit man, for, [1] He had wherewithal to do it, being a *rich man*. Most of Christ's disciples were poor men; but here was one that was a *rich man*, ready to be employed in a piece of service which required *a man of estate*. Worldly wealth in some services to be done for Christ is an advantage and an opportunity, and it is well for those who have it, if withal they have a heart to use it for God's glory. [2] He was well affected to our Lord Jesus, for he was himself *his disciple*, though he did not openly profess it. Christ has more secret disciples than we are aware of.

(3) The grant of the dead body procured from Pilate, v. 58. Joseph *went to* Pilate, the proper person to be applied to on this occasion. Pilate was willing to give the body to one that would inter it decently. In Joseph's petition, and Pilate's ready grant of it, *honour* was done to Christ, and a testimony borne to his *integrity*.

(4) The dressing of the body in its graveclothes (v. 59); though he was an honourable counsellor, yet he himself *took the body*, as it should seem, into his own arms, from the infamous and accursed tree (Acts xiii. 29); for where there is true love to Christ, no service will be thought too mean to stoop to for him. Having taken it, he wrapped it in a *clean linen cloth*; for burying in linen was then the common usage. This common act of humanity, if done after a *godly sort*, may be made an acceptable piece of Christianity.

(5) The depositing of it in the sepulchre, v. 60. A private funeral did best befit him whose kingdom came not with observation. He was laid in a *borrowed* tomb, in Joseph's burying place; as he had not a house of his own, wherein to *lay his head* while he lived, so he had not a grave of his own, wherein to *lay his body* when he was dead. The grave is the peculiar heritage of a *sinner*. There is nothing we can truly call our own but our sins and our graves. When we go to the grave, we go to our own place; but our Lord Jesus, who had no sin of his own, had no grave of his own; dying under imputed sin, it was fit that he should be buried in a *borrowed* grave. He was laid in a *new tomb*, which Joseph, it is likely, designed *for himself*; it would, however, be *never the worse* for his lying in it, who was to rise so quickly, but a *great deal the better* for *his* lying in it, who has altered the property of the grave. It was a tomb *hewn out of a rock*. Christ's sepulchre should be in a solid entire rock, that no room might be left to suspect his disciples had access to it to steal the body; for there was no access to it but by the door, which was watched. A *great stone was rolled to the door of his sepulchre*; this also was according to the custom of the Jews in burying their dead, as appears by the description of the grave of Lazarus (John xi. 38). If the grave were his prison, now was the prison-door locked and bolted. The rolling of the stone to the grave's mouth, was with them as filling up the grave is with us, it completed the funeral. It is the most melancholy circumstance in the funerals of our Christian friends, when we have laid their bodies in the dark and silent grave to go home, and leave them behind; but alas, it is not we that *go home*, and *leave them behind*, no, it is they that are gone to the better home, and have left us behind.

(6) The company that attended the funeral; and that were very *small* and *mean*. Some good women that were true mourners—*Mary Magdalene, and the other Mary*, v. 56. These, as they had attended him *to the cross*, so they followed him *to the grave*. True love to Christ will carry us through to the utmost, in following him. Death itself cannot quench that divine fire.

II. His enemies did what they could to prevent his resurrection; what they did herein was *the next day that followed the day of the preparation, v.* 62. That was the seventh day of the week, the Jewish *sabbath*. All that day, Christ lay dead in the grave. On that day, the *chief priests and Pharisees*, when they should have been at their devotions, asking pardon for the sins of the week past, were dealing with Pilate about securing the sepulchre.

(1) Their address to *Pilate*. They desire a guard may be set on the sepulchre.

[1] Their petition sets forth, that *that deceiver had said, After three days I will rise again*. He had said so, and his disciples *remembered* those very words for the confirmation of their faith, but his persecutors remember them for the provocation of their rage and malice. Thus the same word of Christ to the one was a savour of life unto life, to the other of death unto death.

[2] It further sets forth their jealousy; *lest his disciples come by night, and steal him away, and say, He is risen*.

First, That which *really* they were afraid of, was, his *resurrection*; that which is most Christ's honour and his people's joy, is most the terror of his enemies. So the chief priests and Pharisees laboured to defeat the predictions of Christ's resurrection; if he should rise, that would break all their measures. Christ's enemies, even when they have gained their point, are still in fear of losing it again. Perhaps the priests were surprised at the respect shown to Christ's dead body by Joseph and Nicodemus, two honourable counsellors, nor can they forget his raising Lazarus from *the dead*, which so confounded them.

Secondly, That which they took on them to be afraid of, was, lest *his disciples should come by night, and steal him away*, which was a very improbable thing. They had not the courage to own him while he lived, and it was not likely that his death should put courage into such cowards. What could they promise themselves by stealing away his body, and making people believe he was risen. What good would it do them, to carry on a cheat upon themselves, to steal away his body, and say, *He is risen*? The chief priests apprehend that if the doctrine of Christ's resurrection be once preached and believed, the *last error will be worse than the first*. Those that oppose Christ and his kingdom, will see not only their attempts baffled, but themselves miserably *plunged* and *embarrassed*, their errors each worse than other, and the last worst of all.

[3] In consideration hereof, they humbly move to have a guard set upon the sepulchre till the third day; *Command that the sepulchre be made sure*. One would think that death's prisoners needed no other guard, and that the grave were *security* enough to itself.

(2) Pilate's answer to this address (*v.* 65); *Ye have a watch, make it sure, as sure as you can*. He was ready to gratify Christ's friends, in allowing them the body, and his enemies, in setting a guard upon it, being desirous to please all sides, looking upon the hopes of one side and the fears of the other to be alike ridiculous. *Ye have a watch*; but, as if ashamed to be himself seen in such a thing, he leaves the management of it wholly to them. Methinks that word, *Make it as sure as you can*, looks like a banter, either, [1] Of their *fears*; "Be sure to set a strong guard upon the dead man"; or rather, [2] Of their *hopes*; "Do your worst, but if he be of God, he will rise, in spite of you and all your guards." Tertullian, speaking of Pilate, saith, *In his conscience he was a Christian*; and it is possible that he might be under such convictions, yet never be thoroughly persuaded, any more than Agrippa or Felix was, to be a Christian.

(3) The wonderful care they took, hereupon, to secure the sepulchre (*v.* 66); *They sealed the stone*. But not trusting too much to that, withal they *set a watch*, to keep *his disciples* from coming to *steal him away*. God brought this good out of it, that they who were set to *oppose* his resurrection, thereby had an opportunity to observe it, and did so, and told the chief priests what they observed. To guard the sepulchre against the poor weak disciples, was folly, because *needless*; but to think to guard it against the power of God was folly, because *fruitless* and to no purpose.

CHAPTER 28

In the foregoing chapters we saw the Captain of our salvation engaged with the powers of darkness; victory seemed to hover between the combatants; nay, at length, it inclined to the enemies' side, and our Champion fell before them. But then the Lord awaked as one out of sleep. The Prince of our peace is in this chapter rallying again, coming out of the grave, a Conqueror. Now the resurrection of Christ being one of the main foundations of our religion, it is requisite that we should have infallible proofs of it; four of which proofs we have in this chapter. Luke and John give a larger account of the proofs of Christ's resurrection than Matthew and Mark do. Here is, I. The testimony of the angel to Christ's resurrection, ver. 1-8. II. His appearance himself to the women, ver. 9, 10. III. The confession of the adversaries that were upon the guard, ver. 11-15. IV. Christ's appearance to the disciples in Galilee, and the commission he gave them, ver. 16-20.

Verses 1-10

For the proof of Christ's resurrection, we have here the testimony of *the angel*, and of *Christ* himself. Let us not prescribe to Infinite Wisdom, which ordered that the witnesses of his resurrection should see him *risen*, but not see him *rise*. His incarnation was a mystery; so was this *second incarnation*.

I. The *coming* of the *good women* to the *sepulchre*.

1. *When* they came; *in the end of the sabbath, as it began to dawn toward the first day of the week, v.* 1. This fixes the time of Christ's resurrection.

(1) He arose the *third day* after his death. He was buried in the evening of the sixth day of the week, and arose in the morning of the first day of the following week.

(2) He arose *after the Jewish sabbath*, and it was the passover-sabbath. Christ on *the sixth day finished* his work; he said, *It is finished*; on the seventh day he rested, and then on the first day of the next week did as it were begin a new world, and enter upon new work. The time of the saints' lying in the grave, is a sabbath to them for there they *rest from their labours* (Job iii. 17).

(3) He arose upon the *first day of the week*; on the first day of the first week God *commanded the light to shine out of darkness*; on this day therefore did he who was to be the Light of the world, shine out of the darkness of the grave. It arose again in the first-day sabbath, called the *Lord's day* (Rev. i. 10), and no other day of the week is from henceforward mentioned in all the New Testament than this. The sabbath was instituted in remembrance of the *perfecting* of the work of creation, Gen. ii. 1. Man by his revolt made a breach upon that *perfect work*, which was never perfectly repaired till Christ arose from the dead. He who on that day arose from the dead, is the same by whom, and for whom, all things were at first created, and now anew created.

(4) He arose *as it began to dawn* toward that day; as soon as it could be said that the *third day* was come, he *arose*. Christ arose *when the day began to dawn*, because then the day-spring from on high did again visit us, Luke i. 78. His passion began in the night; when he hung on the cross the sun was darkened; he was laid in the grave in the dusk of the evening; but he arose from the grave when the sun was near rising, for he is the *bright and morning Star* (Rev. xxii. 16), the *true Light*.

2. Who they were, that came to the sepulchre; *Mary Magdalene and the other Mary*, the same that attended the funeral, and *sat over against the*

sepulchre, as before they *sat over against the cross*; still they studied to express their love to Christ. Their attendance on Christ not only *to* the grave, but *in* the grave, represents his like care for those that are his. As Christ in the grave was beloved of the *saints*, so the saints in the grave are beloved of Christ; for death and the grave cannot slacken that bond of love which is between them.

3. What they *came to do*: the other evangelists say that they came to anoint the body; Matthew saith that they came to *see the sepulchre*. They went, to show their goodwill in another visit to the dear remains of their beloved Master. Visits to the grave are of great use to Christians, especially visits to the grave of our Lord Jesus, where we may see sin buried out of sight, and the great proof of redeeming love shining illustriously even in that *land of darkness*.

II. The appearance of an angel of the Lord to them, *v.* 2–4. We have here an account of the manner of the resurrection of Christ.

1. There was a *great earthquake*. When he died, the earth that *received him*, shook for fear; now that he arose, the earth that *resigned him*, leaped for joy in his exaltation. It was the *signal* of Christ's victory. Those who are sanctified, and thereby raised to a spiritual life, while it is in the doing find an earthquake in their own bosoms, as Paul, who *trembled* and was *astonished*.

2. The *angel of the Lord descended from heaven*. The angels frequently attended our Lord Jesus, but upon the cross we find no angel attending him: when his Father *forsook him*, the angels withdrew from him; but now that he is resuming the glory, behold, the *angels of God worship him*.

3. He came, and rolled back the stone from the door, and sat upon it. The *stone* of our sins was *rolled* to the door of the grave of our Lord Jesus, but to demonstrate that divine justice was satisfied, an angel was commissioned to roll back the stone. All the powers of death and darkness are under the control of the God of light and life. An angel from heaven has power to *break the seal*, though it were the *great seal of Israel*, and is able to *roll away the stone*, though ever so great. The angel's *sitting* upon the *stone*, when he had *rolled it away*, is very observable. There he sat, defying all the powers of hell to roll the stone to the grave again. The angel sat as a guard to the grave, having frightened away the enemies' *black* guard; he sat, expecting the women, and ready to give them an account of his resurrection.

4. That his *countenance was like lightning, and his raiment white as snow, v.* 3. His look upon the keeper was like flashes of lightning. The *whiteness* of his raiment was an emblem, not only of purity, but of joy and triumph. When Christ died, the court of heaven *went into deep mourning*, signified by the *darkening of the sun*; but when he arose, they again put on the *garments of praise*. The glory of this angel represented the glory of Christ, to which he was now risen, for it is the same description that was given of him in his transfiguration (*ch.* xvii. 2); but when he conversed with his disciples after his resurrection, he drew a veil over it.

5. That *for fear of him the keepers did shake, and became as dead men, v.* 4. They were *soldiers*, that thought themselves hardened against fear, yet the very sight of an angel struck them with terror. The resurrection of Christ, as it is the joy of his friends, so it is the terror and confusion of his enemies. *They did shake;* the word is the same with that which was used for the earthquake, *v.* 2. When the *earth* shook, these *children of the earth*, that had their portion in it, *shook too;* whereas, those that have their happiness in things above, *though the earth be removed, yet are without fear*. They were posted here, to keep a dead man in his grave—as easy a piece of service

surely as was ever assigned them, and yet it proves too hard for them.

III. The message which this angel delivered to the women, *v.* 5–7.

1. He *encourages them against their fears, v.* 5. To come near to graves and tombs, especially in silence and solitude, has something in it *frightful*, much more was it so to those women, to find an angel at the sepulchre; but he soon makes them easy with the word, *Fear not ye*. The keepers shook, and became as dead men, but, *Fear not ye*. "Let not the news I have to tell you, be any surprise to you; let it be no terror to you, for his resurrection will be your consolation. *Fear not ye, for I know that ye seek Jesus*. I do not come to frighten you, but to encourage you." Those that *seek Jesus*, have no reason to be *afraid*; for, if they seek him diligently they shall *find him. Ye seek Jesus that was crucified*. He mentions his being crucified, the more to commend their love to him; "You seek him still, though *he was crucified*." True believers love and seek Christ, not only *though* he was crucified, but *because* he was so.

2. He *assures them of the resurrection of Christ*; and there was enough in that to silence their fears, *v.* 6. To be told *He is not here*, would have been no welcome news to those who sought him, if it had not been added, *He is risen*. We must not hearken to those who say, *Lo, here is Christ, or, Lo, he is there*, for he is not *here*, he is not *there*, he is *risen*. We must seek him as one *risen*. They that make pictures and images of Christ, forget that *he is not here, he is risen;* our communion with him must be spiritual, by faith in his word. We must seek him with great *reverence* and *humility*, and an awful regard to his glory, for *he is risen*. We must seek him with a *heavenly mind;* when we are ready to make this world our home, and to say, *It is good to be here*, let us remember our Lord Jesus *is not here, he is risen*, and therefore let not our *hearts* be *here*, but let them *rise* too.

Two things the angel refers these women to, for the confirmation of their faith.

(1) To his *word* now *fulfilled*, which they might remember; *He is risen, as he said*. "He said that he *would rise*, why should you be backward to *believe* that which he told you would be?" Let us never think that strange, of which the word of Christ has raised our expectations. If we remember what Christ hath said *to us*, we shall be the less surprised at what he does *with us*.

(2) To his *grave* now *empty*, which they might look into; "Come, see the place where the Lord lay. Compare what you have *heard*, with what you *see*, and, putting both together, you will *believe*." It may have a good influence upon us, to come, and with an eye of faith *see the place where the Lord lay*. When we look into the grave, where we expect we must lie, to take off the terror of it, let us look into the grave where the Lord lay; the place where *our Lord* lay.

3. He *directs them* to go *carry the tidings* of it to his disciples (*v.* 7); Go *quickly, and tell his disciples*. It was good to be here, but they have other work appointed them. They must not have the *monopoly* of it, must not hold their peace. They must go *tell the disciples*. Public usefulness to others must be preferred before the pleasure of secret communion with God ourselves.

(1) The *disciples* of Christ must first be *told the news;* not, Go, tell the *chief priests* and the *Pharisees*, that they may be *confounded;* but, Tell the disciples, that they may be *comforted*. God anticipates the joy of his friends more than the *shame* of his enemies. *Tell his disciples;* [1] That they may encourage themselves under their present sorrows and dispersions. It was a dismal time with them, between grief and fear;

what a cordial would this be to them now, to hear, *their Master is risen!* [2] That they may enquire further into it themselves. This was to set them on seeking him, and to prepare them for his appearance to them. General hints excite to closer searches. They shall now hear of him, but shall very shortly see him.

(2) The *women* are sent to tell it to them. This was a recompence for their constant affectionate adherence to him, at the cross, and in the grave, and a rebuke to the disciples who forsook him. As *the woman was first in the transgression*, so these women were first in the belief of the redemption from transgression by Christ's resurrection.

(3) They were bid to *go quickly* upon this errand. Why, what haste was there? Would not the news keep cold, and be welcome to them at any time? Yes, but they were now overwhelmed with grief, and Christ would have this cordial hastened to them. We must always be ready and forward to do good to our brethren, and to carry comfort to them, now, quickly.

(4) They were directed to appoint the disciples to *meet him in Galilee*. Now this general rendezvous was appointed in Galilee, eighty or a hundred miles from Jerusalem; [1] *In kindness* to those of his disciples that remained in Galilee, and *did not* (perhaps they *could not*) come up to Jerusalem. Christ knows where his disciples dwell, and will visit there. Even to them that are at a distance from the plenty of the means of grace he will graciously *manifest himself*. [2] In consideration of the weakness of his disciples that were now at Jerusalem, who as yet were *afraid of the Jews*, and durst not appear publicly. Christ knows our fears, and considers our frame, and made his appointment where there was least danger of disturbance.

Lastly, The angel solemnly affirms upon his word the truth of what he had related to them; "*Lo, I have told you,* you may be assured of it." This angel was *now* sent to certify the resurrection of Christ to the disciples, and so leave it in their hands to be published to the world. "*I have done my errand,* I have faithfully delivered my message, *I have told you.*" Those messengers from God, that discharge their trust faithfully, may take the comfort of that, whatever the success be.

IV. The women's *departure* from the *sepulchre*, to bring notice to the disciples, *v.* 8.

1. What frame and temper of spirit they were in; They *departed with fear and great joy*; a strange mixture, fear and joy at the same time, in the same soul. To hear that Christ was risen, was matter of joy; but to be led into his grave, and to see an angel, and talk with him about it, could not but cause fear. It was good news, but they were *afraid* that it was too *good* to be true. It is said of their *joy,* it was *great* joy; it is not said so of their fear. Holy fear has joy attending it. It is only perfect love and joy that will cast out all fear.

2. What haste they made; *They did run.* The fear and joy together quickened their pace, and added wings to their motion. Those that are sent on God's errand must not loiter, or lose time.

3. What errand they went upon; They ran, to *bring his disciples word.* They ran, to comfort them with the same comforts wherewith they themselves were comforted of God. The disciples of Christ should be forward to communicate to each other their experiences, should tell others what God had *done for their souls*, and spoken to them. Joy in Christ Jesus will betray itself.

V. Christ's appearing to the women, to confirm the testimony of the angel, *v.* 9, 10. These zealous good women, not only heard the first tidings of him, but had the first sight of him, after his resurrection.

Jesus Christ is often better than his word, but never worse; often anticipates, but never frustrates, the believing expectations of his people.

1. Christ's surprising appearance to the women; *As they went to tell his disciples, behold, Jesus met them.* God's gracious visits usually meet us in the way of duty, and to those who use what they have for others' benefit, more shall be given. This interview with Christ was unexpected. Christ is nearer to his people than they imagine. Christ was *nigh them,* and still in *the word is nigh us.*

2. The salutation wherewith he accosted them; *All hail*—χαίρετε. We use the old *English form of salutation,* wishing *all health* to those we meet; for so *All hail* signifies. And it bespeaks, (1) The goodwill of Christ to us and our happiness. (2) The freedom and holy familiarity which he used in his fellowship with his disciples; for he called them *friends.* But the Greek word signifies, *Rejoice ye.* They were affected both with *fear* and *joy*; what he said to them tended to encourage their joy (*v.* 9), *Rejoice ye,* and to silence their fear (*v.* 10), *Be not afraid.* It is the will of Christ that his people should be a cheerful joyful people, and his resurrection furnishes them with abundant matter for joy.

3. The affectionate respect they paid him; *They came, and held him by the feet, and worshipped him.* Thus they expressed, (1) The *reverence* and *honour* they had *for* him. (2) The *love* and *affection* they had *to* him; they *held him, and would not let him go.* (3) The *transport of joy* they were in, now that they had this further assurance of his resurrection.

4. The encouraging words Christ said to them, *v.* 10. We do not find that they said anything to him, their affectionate embraces and adorations spoke plainly enough; and what he said to them was no more than what the angel had said (*v.* 5, 7). Now observe here,

(1) How he rebukes their fear; *Be not afraid.* The news, though strange, was both *true* and *good.* Christ arose from the dead, to silence his people's fears, and there is enough in that to silence them.

(2) How he repeats their message; "*Go, tell my brethren,* that they must prepare for a journey into Galilee, and there *they shall see me.*" If there be any communion between our souls and Christ, it is he that *appoints the meeting,* and he will observe the appointment. But that which is especially observable here, is, that he calls his disciples *his brethren.* He never called them so till after his resurrection, here and John xx. 17. Christ did not now converse so constantly and familiarly with his disciples as he had done before his death; but he gives them this endearing title, *Go to my brethren.* They had shamefully *deserted* him in his sufferings; but he not only continues his purpose to *meet* them, but calls them *brethren.*

Verses 11–15

We have here the confession of the adversaries that were upon the guard; and there are two things which strengthen this testimony—that they were *eye-witnesses*—and that they were *enemies,* set there to oppose and obstruct his resurrection.

I. How this testimony was *given in* to the chief priests (*v.* 11). *Some of the watch came into the city,* and brought to those who employed them, the report of their disappointment. *They showed to the chief priests all the things that were done;* told them of the earthquake, the descent of the angel, the rolling of the stone away, and the coming of the body of Jesus alive out of the grave. So the utmost means of conviction were afforded them. It might justly have been expected that they should now have believed in Christ, but they were obstinate in their infidelity, and therefore sealed up under it.

II. How it was baffled and stifled by them. They called an assembly, and considered what was to be done. For their own parts, they were resolved not to believe that Jesus was risen; but their care was, to keep others from believing.

The result of their debate was, that those soldiers must by all means be bribed off, and hired not to tell tales. They *put money into their hands*. They *gave large money* unto *the soldiers*. These chief priests loved their money as well as most people did, and were as loth to part with it; and yet, to carry on a malicious design against the gospel of Christ, they were very prodigal of it. Here was *large money* given for the advancing of that which they knew to be a lie, yet many grudge a little money for the advancement of that which they know to be the truth. Let us never starve a good cause, when we see a bad one so liberally supported. They *put a lie into their mouths* (*v.* 13); *Say ye, His disciples came by night, and stole him away while we slept;* a sorry shift is better than none, but this is a sorry one indeed. (1) The sham was *ridiculous*, and carried along with it its own confutation. If *they slept*, how could they know anything of the matter, or say who came? But had it been ever so plausible, (2) It was a wicked thing for these priests and elders to hire those soldiers to tell a deliberate lie.

But lest the soldiers should object the penalty they incurred by the Roman law for *sleeping upon the guard*, which was very severe (Acts xii. 19), they promised to interpose with the governor; "*We will persuade him, and secure you.*" If really these soldiers had slept, and so suffered the disciples to steal him away, the priests and elders would certainly have been the forwardest to solicit the governor to punish them for their treachery; so that *their* care for the soldiers' safety plainly gives the lie to the story.

Well, thus was the plot laid; now what success had it?

[1] Those that were *willing to deceive*, took the money, and did as they were taught. They *took the money*; that was it they aimed at, and nothing else. Money is a bait for the blackest temptation; mercenary tongues will sell the truth for it.

The great argument to prove Christ to be the Son of God, is, his resurrection and none could have more convincing proofs of the truth of that than these soldiers had; they saw the angel descend from heaven, saw the stone rolled away, saw the body of Christ come out of the grave, and yet they were so far from being convinced by it themselves, that they were hired to belie him, and to hinder others from believing in him. The most sensible evidence will not convince men, without the concurring operation of the Holy Spirit.

[2] Those that were willing to be deceived, not only credited, but propagated, the story; This *saying is commonly reported among the Jews until this day*. The sham took well enough, and answered the end. The Jews, when they were pressed with the argument of Christ's resurrection, had this still ready to reply, *His disciples came, and stole him away*. When once a lie is raised, none knows how far it will spread, nor how long it will last, nor what mischief it will do.

Verses 16–20

This evangelist passes over several other appearances of Christ, recorded by Luke and John, and hastens to this, which was of all other the most solemn, as being promised and appointed again and again before his death, and after his resurrection.

I. How the disciples attended his appearance, according to the appointment (*v.* 16); *They went into Galilee*, a long journey to go for one sight of Christ, but it was worth while.

1. Because he appointed them to do so. Though it seemed a needless thing to go into Galilee, yet they had learned to obey Christ's commands and not object against them. Those who would maintain communion with Christ, must attend him there where he has appointed.

2. Because that was to be a public and general meeting. The place was a *mountain in Galilee*, probably the same mountain on which he was transfigured. There they met, for privacy, and perhaps to signify the exalted state into which he was entered.

II. How they were affected with the appearance of Christ to them, *v.* 17. We are told,

1. That they *worshipped him;* many of them did so, nay, it should seem, they all did that, they gave divine honour to him. All that see the Lord Jesus with an eye of faith are obliged to *worship him*.

2. But *some doubted*. Even among those that *worship* there are some that *doubt*. The faith of those that are sincere, may yet be very weak and wavering. *They hung in suspense*, as the scales of the balance, when it is hard to say which preponderates. It tended much to the honour of Christ, that the disciples *doubted* before they *believed;* so that they cannot be said to be credulous, and willing to be imposed upon; for they first *questioned*, and *proved all things*, and then *held fast* that which was *true*, and which they found to be so.

III. What Jesus Christ said to them (*v.* 18–20); *Jesus came, and spoke unto them*. He did not stand at a distance, but *came near*, and gave them such convincing proofs of his resurrection, as turned the wavering scale, and made their faith to triumph over their doubts. *He came, and spoke* familiarly *to them*, as one friend speaks to another. Christ now delivered to his apostles the great charter of his kingdom in the world, was sending them out as his ambassadors, and here gives them their credentials.

In opening this great chapter, we may observe two things.

1. The commission which our Lord Jesus received himself from the Father. Being about to *authorize* his apostles, here he tells us, *All power is given unto me in heaven and in earth*. Hereby he asserts his universal dominion as Mediator. He has *all power*. (1) *Whence* he hath this power. It was *given* him, by a grant from him who is the Fountain of all being, and consequently of all power. As God, equal with the Father, all power was originally and essentially *his;* but as Mediator, as God-man, *all power* was *given him*. He had this *power* given him *over all flesh*, that he might *give eternal life to as many as were given him* (John xvii. 2). This power he was now more signally invested in, upon his resurrection. (2) *Where* he has this power; in *heaven and earth*, comprehending the universe. He is *Lord of all*. He has all *power in heaven*. He has power of dominion over the angels. He has power of intercession with his Father, he intercedes not as a suppliant, but as a demandant; *Father, I will*. He has *all power on earth* too; he prevails with men, and deals with them as one having authority, by the ministry of reconciliation. All souls are his, and to him *every heart and knee must bow*, and *every tongue confess* him to be the *Lord*. This our Lord Jesus tells them to take off the offence of the cross; they had no reason to be ashamed of *Christ crucified*, when they saw him *thus glorified*.

2. The commission he gives to those whom he sent forth; *Go ye therefore*. This commission is given, (1) To the *apostles* primarily, the architects that laid the foundation of the church. It is not only a word of command, like that, *Son, go work*, but a word of encouragement, *Go, and fear not, have I not sent you?* They must go, and bring the gospel to their doors, *Go ye. As an eagle stirs up her nest,*

flutters over her young, to excite them to fly (Deut. xxxii. 11), so Christ stirs up his disciples, to disperse themselves over all the world. (2) It is given to their successors, the ministers of the gospel, whose business it is to transmit the gospel from age to age, to the end of the world in time. Christ, at his ascension, gave not only apostles and prophets, but *pastors and teachers*, Eph. iv. 11. Now observe,

How far his commission is extended; to *all nations*. Go, and disciple *all nations*. Now this plainly signifies it to be the will of Christ, *First*, That the covenant of peculiarity, made with the Jews, should now be cancelled and disannulled. Whereas the apostles, when first sent out, were forbidden to go into the way of the Gentiles, now they were sent to *all nations*. *Secondly*, That salvation by Christ should be offered to all, and none excluded that did not by their unbelief and impenitence exclude themselves. The salvation they were to preach is a *common salvation*. *Thirdly*, That Christianity should be twisted in with national constitutions, that the kingdoms of the world should become Christ's kingdoms, and their kings the church's nursing-fathers.

What is the principal intention of this commission; to *disciple* all nations. "*Admit them disciples;* do your utmost to make the nations Christian nations"; Christ the Mediator is setting up a kingdom in the world, bring the nations to be his subjects; setting up a school, bring the nations to be his scholars; raising an army, enlist the nations of the earth under his banner. The work which the apostles had to do, was, to set up the Christian religion in all places, and it was honourable work; the achievements of the mighty heroes of the world were nothing to it. They conquered the nations for themselves, and made them miserable; the apostles conquered them for Christ, and made them happy.

Their instructions for executing this commission. *First*, They must *admit disciples* by the *sacred rite of baptism*; "Go into all nations, preach the gospel to them, work miracles among them, and persuade them to come in themselves, and bring their children with them, into the church of Christ, and then admit them and theirs into the church, by washing them with water." *Secondly*, This baptism must be administered *in the name of the Father, and of the Son, and of the Holy Ghost*. That is, 1. *By authority from heaven*, and not *of man*; for his ministers act by authority from the three persons in the Godhead. 2. *Calling upon the name* of the Father, Son, and Holy Ghost. Everything is sanctified by prayer, and particularly the waters of baptism. But, 3. It is *into the name* (εἰς τὸ ὄνομα) of *Father, Son, and Holy Ghost*; this was intended as the *summary* of the first principles of the Christian religion. By our being baptized, we solemnly profess, (1) Our *assent* to the scripture-revelation concerning *God, the Father, Son, and Holy Ghost*. (2) Our *consent* to a covenant-relation to God, *the Father, Son, and Holy Ghost*. Baptism is a *sacrament*, that is, it is *an oath*. It is an oath of *abjuration*, by which we renounce the world and the flesh, as rivals with God for the throne in our hearts; and an oath of *allegiance*, by which we resign and give up *ourselves* to God, to be *his, body, soul, and spirit*, to be governed by his will, and made happy in his favour; *we become his men*, so the form of homage in our law runs. [1] It is into the name of *the Father*, believing him to be the *Father of our Lord Jesus Christ*, and *our Father*, as our Creator, Preserver, and Benefactor, to whom therefore we resign ourselves, to rule us, as free agents, by his law; and as our *chief good*, and *highest* end. [2] It is into the name of *the Son*, the *Lord Jesus Christ*, the *Son of God*. In baptism we *assent*, as Peter did, *Thou art Christ, the Son of the living God* (*ch*. xvi. 16), and *consent*, as Thomas did, *My Lord,*

and my God, John xx. 28. We take Christ to be our Prophet, Priest, and King, and give up ourselves to be taught, and saved, and ruled, by him. [3] It is into the name of *the Holy Ghost*. We give up ourselves to his conduct and operation, as our sanctifier, teacher, guide and comforter. *Thirdly*, Those that are thus baptized, and enrolled among the disciples of Christ, must be taught (*v*. 20); *Teaching them to observe all things, whatsoever I have commanded you*. This denotes two things. The duty of *disciples*, of all *baptized Christians*; they must observe all things whatsoever Christ has commanded, and, in order to that, must submit to the teaching of those whom he sends. He *enlists* soldiers that he may *train them* up for his service.

All that are baptized, are thereby obliged, (1) To make the command of Christ their rule. We are by baptism *bound*, and must *obey*. (2) To *observe* what Christ has commanded. Due *obedience* to the commands of Christ requires a diligent observation. (3) To observe *all things*, that he has commanded, without exception; all the *moral* duties, and all the *instituted* ordinances. (4) To confine themselves to the commands of Christ, and as not to *diminish* from them, so not to *add* to them. (5) To learn their duty according to the law of Christ, from those whom he has appointed to be teachers in his school. The duty of the apostles of Christ, and his ministers; and that is, to *teach* the commands of Christ. They must teach *them*, and in the knowledge of *them* Christians must be *trained up*. The heirs of heaven, till they come to age, must be *under tutors and governors*. Here is the assurance he gives them of his spiritual presence with them in the execution of this commission; *And lo, I am with you always, even unto the end of the world*. Observe,

(1) The favour promised them; *I am with you*. Not, *I will be* with you, but *I am*. He was now about to leave them; his bodily presence was now to be removed from them, and this grieved them; but he assures them of his *spiritual* presence, *I am with you*; that is, "My Spirit is with you, the Comforter shall *abide with you*, John xvi. 7. I am *with you*, and not *against* you: with you to take your part, to be on your side. I am *with you*, and not *absent from you*, not at a distance; I am a very *present help*," Ps. xlvi. 1. Christ was now sending them to set up his kingdom in the world. And then doth he seasonably promise them his presence with them, [1] To *carry them* on through the difficulties they were likely to meet with. "I am with you, to *bear you up*, to plead your cause; with you in all your services, in all your sufferings." [2] To *succeed* this great undertaking; "Lo, *I am with you*, to make your ministry effectual for the discipling of the nations." It was an unlikely thing that they should persuade people to become the disciples of a *crucified* Jesus; but *lo, I am with you*, and therefore you shall *gain your point*.

(2) The continuance of the favour, *always, even unto the end of the world*.

[1] They shall have his *constant* presence; *always*, πάσας τὰς ἡμέρας—*all days*, every day. "I will be with you on sabbath days and week days, fair days and foul days, winter days and summer days." Since his resurrection he had appeared to them *now and then*. But he assures them that they shall have his spiritual presence continued to them without intermission. The *God of Israel*, the *Saviour*, is sometimes *a God that hideth himself* (Isa. xlv. 15), but never a God that absenteth himself; sometimes *in the dark*, but never *at a distance*.

[2] They shall have his perpetual presence, even to *the end of the world*. This is hastening towards its period; and even till then the Christian religion shall, in one part of the world or other, he *kept up*, and the presence of Christ continued with his

ministers. I am with you *to the end of the world, First,* With *you and your writings.* There is a divine power going along with the scriptures of the New Testament, not only preserving them in being, but producing strange effects by them, which will continue to the end of time. *Secondly,* With you and *your successors*; with all who thus *baptize* and thus *teach.* This is an encouraging word to all the faithful ministers of Christ, that what was said to the apostles, was said to them all, *I will never leave thee, nor forsake thee.*

Two solemn farewells we find our Lord Jesus giving to his church, and his parting word at both of them is very encouraging; one was here, "*Lo, I am with you always;* I leave you, and yet still I am with you"; the other was, "*Surely, I come quickly.*

I leave you for awhile, but I will be with you again shortly," Rev. xxii. 20. By this it appears that he did not part in anger, but in love, and that it is his will we should keep up both our communion with him and our expectation of him.

There is one word more remaining, which must not be overlooked, and that is *Amen*; which is not a cipher, intended only for a concluding word, like *finis* at the end of a book. It bespeaks Christ's confirmation of this promise, *Lo, I am with you.* It is his *Amen,* in whom all the promises are *Yea and Amen.* It bespeaks the church's concurrence with it, in their desire, and prayer, and expectation. It is the evangelist's *Amen—So be it,* blessed Lord. Our *Amen* to Christ's promises turns them into prayers.

AN EXPOSITION, WITH PRACTICAL OBSERVATIONS, OF

THE GOSPEL

ACCORDING TO

ST. MARK

We have heard the evidence given in by the first witness to the doctrine and miracles of our Lord Jesus; and now here is another witness produced, who calls for our attention.

I. Concerning *this witness*. His name is *Mark*. *Marcus* was a Roman name, and a very common one, and yet we have no reason to think, but that he was by birth a Jew; but as Saul took the Roman name of *Paul*, so he of *Mark*. We read of John whose surname was *Mark*, sister's son to Barnabas, whom Paul was displeased with (Acts xv. 37, 38), but afterward had a great kindness for, and not only ordered the churches to receive him (Col. iv. 10), but sent for him to be his assistant, with this encomium, *He is profitable to me for the ministry* (2 Tim. iv. 11); and he reckons him among his fellow-labourers, Philem. 24. We read of Marcus whom Peter calls his *son* (1 Pet. v. 13); whether that was the same with the other is altogether uncertain. It is a tradition very current among the ancients, that St. Mark wrote this gospel under the direction of St. Peter, and that it was con- firmed by his authority; so Hieron. *Mark, the disciple and interpreter of Peter, being sent from Rome by the brethren, wrote a concise gospel;* and Tertullian saith—*Mark, the interpreter of Peter, delivered in writing the things which had been preached by Peter.* It is true Mark was no apostle, yet we think that both he and Luke were of the number of the seventy disciples. St. Jerome saith that, after the writing of this gospel, he went into Egypt, and was the first that preached the gospel at Alexandria, where he founded a church, to which he was a great example of holy living.

II. Concerning *this testimony*. Mark's gospel, 1. Is but short, much shorter than Matthew's, not giving so full an account of Christ's sermons as that did, but insisting chiefly on his miracles. 2. It is very much a repetition of what we had in Matthew; many remarkable circumstances being added to the stories there related, but not many new matters. It was fit that such great things as these should be spoken and written, once, yea twice, because man is so *unapt* to *perceive* them, and so *apt* to *forget* them. Though it was written at Rome it was written in Greek, as was St. Paul's epistle to the Romans, the Greek being the more universal language.

CHAPTER 1

Mark's narrative does not take rise so early as those of Matthew and Luke do, but from John's baptism. I. The office of John Baptist illustrated by the prophecy of him (ver. 1–3), and by the history of him, ver. 4–8. II. Christ's baptism, and his being owned from heaven, ver. 9–11. III. His temptation, ver. 12, 13. IV. His preaching, ver. 14, 15, 21, 22, 38, 39. V. His calling disciples, ver. 16–20. VI. His praying, ver. 35. VII. His working miracles. 1. His rebuking an unclean spirit, ver. 23–28. 2. His curing Peter's mother-in-law, who was ill of a fever, ver. 29–31. 3. His healing all that came to him, ver. 32, 34. 4. His cleansing a leper, ver. 40–45.

Verses 1–8

I. What the New Testament is. It is *the gospel of Jesus Christ the Son of God*, v. 1. 1. It is *gospel*. It is a *good word*, and well *worthy of all acceptation*; it brings us glad tidings. 2. It is the *gospel of Jesus Christ*. The foregoing gospel began with the *genera- tion of Jesus Christ*—that was but preliminary, this comes immediately to the business—*the gospel of Christ*. 3. This Jesus is the *Son of God*. That truth is the foundation on which the gospel is built, and which it is written to demonstrate.

II. What the *reference* of the New Testament is to the Old. The gospel of Jesus Christ *begins*, and so we shall find it *goes on*, just *as it is written in the prophets*, v. 2. which was most proper and powerful for the conviction of the Jews, who believed the Old Testament prophets to be sent of God, but it is of use to us all, for the confirmation of our faith both in the Old Testament and in the New.

Quotations are here borrowed from two prophecies —that of Isaiah, and that of Malachi, both of whom spoke to the same purport concerning *the beginning of the gospel of Jesus Christ*, in the ministry of John.

1. Malachi spoke very plainly (*ch.* iii. 1) concerning John Baptist. *Behold, I send my messenger before thy face*, v. 2. Christ himself had taken notice of this, and applied it to John (Matt. xi. 10), who was God's *messenger*, sent to *prepare Christ's way*.

2. Isaiah, the most evangelical of all the prophets, *begins* the evangelical part of his prophecy with this, which points to the *beginning of the gospel of Christ*, (Isa. xl. 3); *The voice of him that crieth in the wilder- ness*, v. 3. Matthew had taken notice of this, and applied it to John, *ch.* iii. 3. Such is the corruption of the world, that there is something to do to *make room* for him. When God sent his Son into the world, he *took care*, and when he sends him into the heart, he *takes care*, effectual care, to *prepare his way before him*. The mistakes of the judgment are rectified, and the *crooked ways* of the affections; then way is made for Christ's comforts. It is in a *wilderness*, for such this world is, that *Christ's way* is prepared, and theirs that follow him, like that which Israel passed through to Canaan. They that are sent to *prepare the way of the Lord*, in such a vast howling wilderness as this is, have need to cry *aloud*.

III. What the *beginning* of the New Testament was. The gospel began in John Baptist. His baptism was the dawning of the *gospel day*.

1. In John's way of *living* there was the beginning of a *gospel spirit*; for it bespoke great self-denial, mortification of the flesh, a holy contempt of the world, and nonconformity to it. The more we sit loose to the body, and live above the world, the better we are prepared for Jesus Christ.

2. In John's *preaching* and *baptizing* there was the beginning of the *gospel doctrines and ordinances*. (1) He preached the *remission of sins*, which is the

great gospel privilege. (2) He preached *repentance*, in order to it; he told people that there must be a renovation of their hearts and a reformation of their lives. (3) He preached Christ, and directed his hearers to *expect him* speedily to appear, and to *expect great things* from him. He preached, [1] The great *pre-eminence* Christ is *advanced to*; so high, so great, is Christ, that John thinks himself unworthy to be employed in the meanest office about him, even to *stoop down*, and *untie his shoes*. [2] The great *power* Christ is *invested with*; He *comes after me* in time, but he is *mightier than I*, for he is able to *baptize with the Holy Ghost*. [3] The great *promise* Christ makes in his gospel to those who have *repented*, and have had their sins forgiven them; They shall be *baptized* with the Holy Ghost. And, *lastly*, All those who received his doctrine, and submitted to his institution, he *baptized with water*, as the manner of the Jews was to admit proselytes, in token of their *cleansing themselves* by repentance and reformation, and of God's *cleansing them* both by remission and by sanctification.

3. In the success of John's preaching, and the disciples he admitted by baptism, there was the *beginning of a gospel church*. He baptized *in the wilderness*, but *there went out unto him all the land of Judæa, and they of Jerusalem, and were all baptized of him*. They entered themselves his disciples, and bound themselves to his discipline; in token of which, they *confessed their sins*; he admitted them his disciples, in token of which, he *baptized* them. Many of these afterward became followers of Christ, and preachers of his gospel, and this grain of mustard-seed became a *tree*.

Verses 9–13

We have here a brief account of Christ's baptism and temptation.

I. His *baptism*, which was his first public appearance, after he had long lived obscurely *in Nazareth*.

1. See how *humbly* he *owned* God, by coming to be *baptized of* John. Though he was perfectly pure and unspotted, yet he was *washed* as if he had been *polluted*.

2. See how *honourably* God owned him, when he submitted to John's *baptism*.

(1) He *saw the heavens opened*; thus he was owned to be the Lord from heaven. Matthew saith, *The heavens were opened to him*. Mark saith, *He saw them opened*. Many have the heavens opened to receive them, but they do not see it.

(2) He *saw the Spirit like a dove descending upon him*. It is an ancient tradition, that *a great light shone round the place*.

(3) He heard a voice which was intended for his encouragement to proceed in his undertaking, and therefore it is here expressed as directed *to him*, *Thou art my beloved Son*. God is *well pleased* in him, and so well pleased in him, as to be well pleased *with us* in him.

II. His *temptation*. The *good Spirit* that descended upon him, *led him into the wilderness*, *v*. 12. Retirement from the world is an opportunity of more free converse with God, and therefore must sometimes be chosen. Mark observes this circumstance of his being *in the wilderness*—that he was *with the wild beasts*. It was an instance of his Father's care of him, that he was preserved from being torn in pieces by the wild beasts. Special protections are earnests of seasonable supplies. In that wilderness,

1. The *evil spirits* were *busy with him*; he *was tempted of Satan*. Christ himself was tempted, not only to teach us, that *it is no sin to be tempted*, but to direct us whither to go for succour when we are tempted, even to him that *suffered*, being *tempted*.

2. The *good spirits* were *busy about him*; the *angels ministered to him*. The ministration of the good angels about us, is matter of great comfort in reference to the malicious designs of the evil angels against us.

Verses 14–22

I. A general account of Christ's preaching in Galilee.

1. When Jesus began to preach in Galilee; *After that John was put in prison*. When he had *finished* his testimony, then Jesus *began* his.

2. What he preached; *The gospel of the kingdom of God*. Christ came to set up the kingdom of God among men, and he set it up by the preaching of his gospel, and a power going along with it.

(1) The great *truths* Christ preached; *The time is fulfilled, and the kingdom of God is at hand*. Christ gives them notice of it; "The time prefixed is now *at hand*; glorious discoveries of divine light, life, and love, are now to be made." God keeps time; when *the time is fulfilled*, the *kingdom of God is at hand*.

(2) The great *duties* inferred from thence. Christ gave them to *understand the times*, that they might know *what Israel ought to do*; they fondly expected the Messiah to appear in external pomp and power, and therefore thought, when that *kingdom of God* was *at hand*, they must prepare for war, and for victory. Christ tells them, in the prospect of that kingdom approaching, they must *repent, and believe the gospel*. By repentance we must lament and forsake our sins, and by faith we must receive the forgiveness of them. Both these must go together: we must not think either that reforming our lives will save us without trusting in the righteousness and grace of Christ, or that trusting in Christ will save us without the reformation of our hearts and lives. Christ hath joined these two together, and let no man think to put them asunder. Thus the preaching of the gospel began, and thus it continues; still the call is, Repent, and believe, and live a *life of repentance* and *a life of faith*.

II. Christ appearing as a teacher, here is next his *calling of disciples, v*. 16–20. Observe, 1. Christ will have followers. If he set up a school, he will have scholars; if he set up his standard, he will have soldiers; if he preach, he will have hearers. 2. The instruments Christ chose to employ in setting up his kingdom, were the *weak* and *foolish things of the world*; not called from the great sanhedrim, or the schools of the rabbin, but picked up from among the tarpaulins *by the sea-side*. 3. Though Christ needs not the help of man, yet he is pleased to make use of it in setting up his kingdom. 4. Christ puts honour upon those who are *diligent in their business*, and *loving to one another*; so those were, whom Christ called. He found them *employed*, and employed *together*. Industry and unity are *good* and *pleasant*, and there the Lord Jesus commands the blessing. 5. The business of ministers is to *fish for souls*, and *win them to Christ*. Ministers, in preaching the gospel, *cast the net* into the waters, Matt. xiii. 47. Some are enclosed and brought to shore, but far the greater number escape. If many a draught brings home nothing, yet they must go on. 6. Those whom Christ calls, must *leave all*, to follow him; and by his grace he inclines them to do so. We must sit loose to the world, and forsake everything that is inconsistent with our duty to Christ. Mark takes notice of James and John, that they left not only *their father* (which we had in Matthew), but *the hired servants*, being their *fellow-labourers* and pleasant comrades; not only relations, but companions, must be left for Christ, and old acquaintance.

III. Here is a particular account of his preaching in Capernaum. 1. When Christ *came into Capernaum*, he *straightway* applied himself to his work there, and took the *first* opportunity of preaching the gospel. Those will think themselves concerned not to *lose time*, who consider what a deal of work they have to do, and what a little time to do it in. 2. Christ religiously observed the sabbath day. 3. Sabbaths are to be sanctified in *religious assemblies*, if we have opportunity; it is a *holy day*. 4. In *religious assemblies* on sabbath-days, the gospel is to be preached. 5. Christ was a non-such preacher; he did not preach *as the scribes*, who expounded the law of Moses by rote; it came not *from the heart*, and therefore came not *with authority*. But Christ taught *as one that had authority*.

Verses 23–28

As soon as Christ began to preach, he began to work miracles for the confirmation of his doctrine.

I. Christ's *casting the devil* out of a man that was possessed, in the synagogue at Capernaum. *There was in the synagogue a man with an unclean spirit,* εν πνεύματι ἀκαθάρτψ—*in an unclean spirit;* for the spirit had the man in his possession, and led him captive at his will. This man *was in the synagogue*; he did not come either to be taught or to be healed.

1. The rage which the unclean spirit expressed at Christ; *He cried out*, as one in an agony, at the presence of Christ. We are told what he said, *v.* 24, where he doth not *make terms*, but speaks as one that knew his doom. (1) He calls him *Jesus of Nazareth;* for aught that appears, he was the first that called him so. (2) Yet a confession is extorted from him—that he is *the holy One of God*. Those who have only a *notion* of Christ, and have no faith in him, or love to him, go no further than the devil doth. (3) He in effect acknowledgeth that he could not stand before the power of Christ; "*Let us alone; for* if thou take us to task, we are undone, thou canst *destroy us.*" (4) He desires to have *nothing to do* with Jesus Christ; for he *despairs* of being *saved* by him, and *dreads* being *destroyed* by him.

2. The victory which Jesus Christ obtained over the unclean spirit. It is in vain for Satan to beg and pray, *Let us alone;* his power must be broken, and the poor man must be relieved. (1) Jesus *commands*. As he taught, so he healed, *with authority*. Jesus re-buked him; *Hold thy peace;* φιμώθητι—*be muzzled.* Christ has a muzzle for that unclean spirit when he *fawns* as well as when he *barks*. But this is not all, he must not only *hold his peace*, but he must *come out of the man*. (2) The unclean spirit *yields*, for there is no remedy (*v.* 26); He *tore him*, put him into a *strong convulsion*. When he would not *touch* Christ, in fury at him he grievously disturbed this poor creature. Thus, when Christ by his grace delivers poor souls out of the hands of Satan, it is not without a grievous toss and tumult in the soul. He *cried with a loud voice*, to frighten the spectators, and make himself seem terrible.

II. The impression which this miracle made upon the minds of the people, *v.* 27, 28.

1. It astonished them that saw it; *They were all amazed*. This was surprising to them, and put them upon considering with themselves, and enquiring of one another, "*What is this new doctrine?* For it must certainly be of God, which is thus confirmed." The Jewish exorcists pretended by charm or invocation to drive away evil spirits; but this was quite another thing, *with authority he commands them*. Surely it is our interest to make *him* our Friend, who has the control of infernal spirits.

2. It raised his reputation among all that heard it; *Immediately his fame spread abroad into the whole adjacent region of Galilee*. The story was presently got into everyone's mouth, together with the remark made upon it, *What new doctrine is this?* So that it was universally concluded, that he was a *Teacher come from God*. Thus he *prepared his own way*, now that John, who was his harbinger, was clapped up.

Verses 29–39

In these verses, we have,

I. A particular account of one miracle that Christ wrought, in the cure of Peter's wife's mother.

1. When Christ had done that which *spread his fame* throughout all parts, he did not then sit still, as some think that they may *lie in bed* when their *name is up*. No, he continued to *do good*. Those who are in reputation, had need be busy and careful to keep it up.

2. When he *came out of the synagogue*, where he had taught and healed with a divine authority, yet he conversed familiarly with the poor fishermen that attended him.

3. He went into Peter's house, probably invited thither to such entertainment as a poor fisherman could give him, and he accepted of it.

4. He cured his mother-in-law, who was sick. Wherever Christ comes, he comes to do good, and will be sure to pay richly for his entertainment. The same hand that *healed* her, *strengthened* her, so that she was able to *minister* to them; the cure is in order to that, to fit for action.

II. A general account of many cures he wrought—diseases healed, devils expelled. It was on the *evening of the sabbath*, when the *sun did set*, or *was set*; perhaps many scrupled bringing their sick to him, till the sabbath was over.

1. How *numerous* the patients were; *All the city was gathered at the door*, as beggars for a dole. That one cure in the synagogue occasioned this crowding after him. Others speeding well with Christ should quicken us in our enquiries after him. Christ was flocked after in a *private house*, as well as in the *synagogue*; wherever he is, there let his servants, his patients, be.

2. How *powerful* the Physician was; he *healed all* that were brought to him, though ever so many. Nor was it some one particular disease, that Christ set up for the cure of, but he healed those that were *sick of divers* diseases. And that miracle particularly which he wrought in the synagogue, he *repeated in the house* at night; for he *cast out many devils*, and *suffered not the devils to speak*.

III. His *retirement* to his *private devotion* (*v.* 35); *He prayed*, prayed alone; to set us an example of secret prayer. Though as God he was *prayed to*, as man he *prayed*. He found time to be alone with his Father.

1. The time *when* Christ prayed. (1) It was *in the morning*, the morning after the *sabbath day*. We must go to the *throne of grace*, every day in the week. This *morning* was the morning of the *first day of the week*, which afterward he sanctified, and made remarkable, by another sort of *rising early*. (2) It was early, *a great while before day*. When others were asleep in their beds, he was *praying*. When our spirits are most fresh and lively, then we should take time for *devout* exercises.

2. The place *where* he prayed; He *departed into a solitary place*. Secret prayer must be made secretly. Those that have the most business in public, and of the best kind, must sometimes be *alone with God*.

IV. His *return* to his *public* work. The disciples thought they were *up early*, but found their Master was up *before them, followed him* to his *solitary place*, and there *found him* at prayer, *v.* 36, 37. They told him that he was much wanted, *All men seek for thee.* They were proud that their Master was become so popular already, and would have him appear *in public*, yet more in that place, because it was *their own city.* "No," saith Christ, "*Let us go into the next towns, the villages, that I may preach there also, for therefore came I forth*, to go about doing good." He *preached in their synagogues throughout all Galilee*, and, to illustrate and confirm his doctrine, *he cast out devils.*

Verses 40–45

We have here the story of Christ's *cleansing a leper.* It teaches us,

1. *How to apply ourselves to Christ;* come as this leper did, (1) With great *humility*; this leper came *beseeching him, and kneeling down to him* (*v.* 40); it teaches us that those who would receive grace and mercy from Christ, must approach to him with humility and reverence. (2) With a firm belief of *his power; Thou canst make me clean.* He believes it with application, not only in general, *Thou canst do everything* (as John xi. 22), but, *Thou canst make me clean.* What we believe of the power of Christ we must bring home to our particular case; *Thou canst do this for me.* (3) With submission to the will of Christ; *Lord, if thou wilt.* With the modesty that became a poor petitioner, he refers his own particular case to him.

2. *What to expect from Christ;* that according to our faith it shall be to us. His address is not in the form of prayer, yet Christ answered it as a request. (1) Christ was *moved with compassion.* This is added here, in Mark, to show that Christ's power is employed by his pity for the relief of poor souls. Our *misery* makes us the objects of his *mercy.* And what he does for us he does with all possible tenderness. (2) He *put forth his hand, and touched him.* In healing souls, Christ *toucheth them.* Christ *toucheth and healeth too.* (3) He said, *I will, be thou clean.* The poor leper put an *if* upon the will of Christ; *If thou wilt;* but that *doubt* is soon put *out of doubt; I will.* Christ most readily *wills* favours to those that most readily *refer* themselves to his will. He was confident of Christ's *power;* Thou *canst make me clean;* and Christ will show how much his power is drawn out into act by the faith of his people, *Be thou clean.* And power accompanied this word, and the cure was perfect in an instant; *Immediately his leprosy* vanished, and there remained no more sign of it, *v.* 42.

3. *What to do when we have received mercy from Christ.* We must with his favours receive his commands. When Christ had cured him, *he strictly charged him.* I am apt to think that this refers not to the directions he gave him to conceal it (*v.* 44), for those are mentioned by themselves; but that this was such a charge as he gave to the impotent man whom he cured, John v. 14, *Sin no more, lest a worse thing come unto thee.* He also appointed him, (1) To *show himself to the priest.* (2) Till he had done that, not to *say anything* of it *to any man.* He must not *proclaim* it, because that would much increase the crowd that followed Christ, which he thought was too great already; not as if he were unwilling to *do good to all*, to as many as came; but he would do it with as little *noise* as might be. What to think of the leper's *publishing* it, and *blazing it abroad*, I know not. The leper ought to have observed his orders; yet, no doubt, it was with a good design that he *proclaimed* the cure, and it had no other ill effect than that it increased the multitudes which followed Christ, to that degree, that he *could no more openly enter into the city*, which obliged him to go into *desert places.* This shows how *expedient* it was for us, that Christ should go *away*, for his bodily presence could be but in one place at a time. By his spiritual presence he is with his people wherever they are, and comes to them to *every quarter.*

CHAPTER 2

I. Christ's healing a man that was sick of a palsy, ver.- 1–12. II. His calling of Matthew from the receipt of custom, and his eating with publicans and sinners, ver. 13–17. III. His justifying his disciples in not fasting so much as those of the Pharisees did, ver. 18–22. IV. His justifying them in plucking the ears of corn on the sabbath day, ver. 23–38.

Verses 1–12

Christ having been for some time preaching about in the country, here returns to Capernaum, his headquarters.

I. The great resort there was to him. Though he was *in the house* yet people came to him as soon as it was *noised* that he was in town. *Straightway many were gathered together to him.* Where the king is, there is the court. *There was no room to receive them*, they were so numerous, *no not so much as about the door.* A blessed sight, to see people thus flying like a cloud to Christ's house.

II. The good entertainment Christ gave them; he *preached the word unto them, v.* 2. Many of them perhaps came only for cures, and many perhaps only for curiosity, to get a sight of him; but when he had them together he *preached to them.* He thought it not at all amiss to preach in a house, on a week day; though some might reckon it both an improper place and an improper time.

III. The presenting of a poor cripple to him, to be helped by him. The patient was one *sick of the palsy*, but perfectly disabled, so that he was *borne of four*, was carried upon *a bed*, as if he had been upon *a bier.* It was his misery, that he needed to be so carried, it was their charity, who did so carry him. These kind relations or neighbours thought, if they could but carry this poor man once to Christ, they should not need to carry him any more; and therefore made hard shift to get him to him, they *uncovered the roof where he was, v.* 4. It had no *upper room*, but the *ground-floor* was open to the roof: and these petitioners for the poor paralytic, when they could not get through the crowd at the door, got their friend by some means or other to the roof of the house, took off some of the tiles, and so let him down upon his bed with cords into the house where Christ was preaching. This bespoke both their *faith* and their *fervency.* Hereby it appeared that they were in earnest, and would not go away, nor *let Christ go without a blessing*, Gen. xxxii. 26.

IV. The kind word Christ said to this poor patient; *He saw their faith; theirs* that brought him. He commended *their faith*, because they did bring their friend through so much difficulty. True faith and strong faith may work variously, conquering sometimes the objections of reason, sometimes those of sense; but, however manifested, it shall be accepted and approved by Jesus Christ. Christ said, *Son, thy sins be forgiven thee.* The *compellation* is very *tender—Son.* Christ owns true believers as his sons: *a son*, and yet sick of the palsy; *Thy sins are forgiven thee.* The *cordial* is very rich; *Thy sins are forgiven thee.* The word of Christ was to take his thoughts off from the disease, which was the effect, and to lead them to the sin, the cause, that he might be more concerned about that, to get that pardoned. Recovery from sickness is *then* a mercy indeed, when way is made for it by the pardon of sin. The way to remove the effect, is, to take away the cause. Pardon of sin strikes at the root of all diseases, and either cures them, or alters their property.

V. The cavil of the scribes at that which Christ said. They were expositors of the law, and their doctrine was *true.* But their application was *false.* It is *true, None can forgive sins but God only*; but it is false that therefore Christ cannot. But Christ *perceived in his spirit that they so reasoned within them-*

selves; this proves him to be God. God's royalties are inseparable, and he that could *know thoughts*, could *forgive sins*. Now he proves his power to *forgive sin*, by demonstrating his power to cure the *man sick of the palsy*, v. 9–11. He would not have pretended to do *the one*, if he could not have done *the other*; *that ye may know that the Son of man has power on earth to forgive sin, Thou that art* sick of the palsy, *arise, take up thy bed*. He could not have cured the disease, which was the effect, if he could not have taken away the sin, which was the cause. He that could by a word accomplish the sign, could doubtless perform the thing signified. It was proper enough to appeal, whether it is easier to say, *Thy sins are forgiven thee*, or to say, *Arise, and walk?* The removing of the punishment as such, was the remitting of the sin; he that could go so far in the cure, no doubt could perfect it.

VI. The cure of the sick man, and the impression it made upon the people, v. 12. He not only *arose* out of his bed, perfectly well, but *he took up his bed and went forth before them all*; and *they were all amazed*, and *glorified God* saying, "*We never saw it on this fashion.*" Christ's works were without precedent. When we see what he does in healing souls, we must own that we *never saw the like*.

Verses 13–17

I. Christ preaching by the *sea-side* (v. 13), whither he went *for room*. Upon the strand there might come as many as would. It should seem by this, that our Lord Jesus had a strong voice, and could and did speak loud.

II. His calling Levi; the same with Matthew, who had a place in the custom-house at Capernaum, from which he was denominated a *publican*; his place fixed him by the waterside, and thither Christ went to meet with him. It is probable that Matthew was but a loose extravagant young man, or else, being a Jew, he would never have been a publican. Christ called him to *follow him*. With God, through Christ, there is mercy to pardon the greatest sins, and grace to sanctify the greatest sinners. Matthew, that had been a publican, became an evangelist. Great sin and scandal before conversion, are no bar to great gifts, graces, and advancements, after; nay, God may be the more glorified. In bodily cures, ordinarily, he was *sought unto*, but in these spiritual cures, he was *found of them that sought him not*. For this is the great evil and peril of the disease of sin, that those who are under it, desire not to be *made whole*.

III. His familiar converse with *publicans and sinners*, v. 15. We are here told, 1. That Christ *sat at meat in Levi's house*, who invited *him and his disciples* to the farewell feast he made to his friends, when he left all to attend on Christ. 2. That *many publicans and sinners* sat with Christ in Levi's house, and *they followed him*. They followed Levi; so some understand it. I rather take it, that they *followed Jesus* because of the report they had heard of him. They did not *for conscience-sake* leave all to follow him, but *for curiosity-sake* they came to Levi's feast, to see him. The publicans are here and elsewhere ranked with *sinners*, the worst of *sinners*. (1) Because commonly they were *such*; so general were the corruptions in the execution of that office, oppressing, exacting, and taking bribes or fees to extortion, and *accusing falsely*. (2) Because the Jews had a particular antipathy to them and their office, as an affront to the liberty of their nation, and thought it scandalous to be seen in their company. Such as these our blessed Lord was pleased to converse with, when he appeared *in the likeness of sinful flesh*.

IV. The *offence* which the scribes and Pharisees took at this, v. 16. They would not come to hear him preach, which they might have been convinced

and edified by; but they would come themselves to *see him* sit with publicans and sinners, which they would be provoked by. They endeavoured to put the disciples out of conceit with their Master, and therefore put the question to them. *How is it, that he eateth and drinketh with publicans and sinners?*

V. Christ's justification of himself in it, v. 17. He stood to what he did, and would not withdraw. Those are too tender of their own *good name*, who, to preserve it with some nice people, will decline a *good work*. Christ would not do so. They thought the publicans were to be *hated*. "No," saith Christ, "they are to be *pitied*, they are *sick* and *need a physician*; they are sinners, and need a Saviour." They thought Christ's character should separate him from them; "No," saith Christ, "*I came not to call the righteous, but sinners to repentance*. It is to a *sinful world* that I am sent, and therefore my business lies most with those that are the greatest sinners in it." Or thus; "*I am not come to call the righteous*, the proud Pharisees that think themselves righteous, but poor publicans, that own themselves to be sinners, and are glad to be invited and encouraged to repent." It is good dealing with those that there is hope of.

Verses 18–28

Here he is put to justify his disciples; and in what they do according to his will he will justify them, and bear them out.

I. He justifies them in their *not fasting*. Why do the Pharisees and the disciples of John fast? They *used to fast*, the Pharisees fasted *twice in the week* (Luke xviii. 12), and probably the disciples of John did so too. Thus apt are strict professors to make their own practice a standard, and to censure and condemn all that do not fully come up to it. They invidiously suggest that if Christ went among sinners to do them *good*, yet the disciples went to indulge their appetites, for they never knew what it was to fast. Ill-will always suspects the worst.

Two things Christ pleads in excuse of his disciples *not fasting*.

1. That these were *easy days* with them, and fasting was not so *seasonable* now as it would be hereafter, v. 19, 20. There is a time for all things.

2. That these were *early days* with them, and they were not so able for the severe exercises of religion as hereafter they would be. The Pharisees had long accustomed themselves to such austerities; and John Baptist himself came neither eating nor drinking. But it was not so with Christ's disciples; their Master came *eating and drinking*, and had not bred them up to the difficult services of religion as yet. To put them upon such frequent fasting at first, would be a discouragement to them, it would be of as ill consequence as *putting new wine into old casks*, or sewing *new cloth* to that which is worn thin and threadbare, v. 21, 22. God graciously *considers the frame of young Christians, that are weak* and *tender*, and so must we; nor must we expect more than the *work of the day in its day*, and that day according to the strength. Weak Christians must take heed of *over-tasking* themselves, and of making the yoke of Christ otherwise than it is, easy, and sweet, and pleasant.

II. He justifies them in *plucking the ears of corn on the sabbath day*, which, I will warrant you, a disciple of the Pharisees would not dare to have done; for it was contrary to an express tradition of their elders. They reflect upon the discipline of Christ's school, as too easy, so common it is for those who deny the *power of godliness*, to be jealous for the *form*, and censorious of those who affect not *their* form.

Observe, 1. What a poor breakfast Christ's disciples had on a sabbath-day morning, when they were going to church (v. 23); they *plucked the ears* of corn, and that was the best they had. They were so intent upon spiritual dainties, that they forget even their *necessary food*.

2. How even this was *grudged them* by the Pharisees, upon supposition that it was not lawful to *pluck the ears of corn* on the sabbath day, that that was as much a servile work as *reaping* (v. 24); *Why do they on the sabbath day that which is not lawful?* If Christ's disciples do that which is unlawful, Christ will be reflected upon. It is observable, that when the Pharisees thought Christ did amiss, they told the disciples (v. 16); and now when they thought the disciples did amiss, they spoke to Christ.

3. How Christ defended them.

(1) By example. They had a good precedent for it in David's eating the *showbread* (v. 25, 26); *Have ye never read?* Ritual observances must give way to moral obligations; and that may be done in a case of necessity, which otherwise may not be done.

(2) By argument. To reconcile them to the disciples' *plucking the ears of corn*, let them consider whom the sabbath was *made for* (v. 27); *it was made for man, and not man for the sabbath*. The sabbath is a sacred and divine institution; but we must receive and embrace it as a privilege and a benefit, not as a task and a drudgery. God never designed it to be an *imposition* upon us, and therefore we must not make it so to ourselves. Man was made *for God*, and for his honour and service, but he was not *made for the sabbath*. God did design it to be an *advantage* to us. He made it *for man*. He had *some* regard to our *bodies* in the institution, that they might rest, and not be tired out with the constant business of this world. He had *much more* regard to our *souls*. The sabbath was made a day of rest, only in order to its being a day of holy work, a day of communion with God, a day of praise and thanksgiving; and the rest from worldly business is *therefore* necessary, that we may closely apply ourselves to this work. See here, [1] What a *good Master* we serve, all whose institutions are for our own benefit. It is not he, but we, that are gainers by our service. [2] What we should aim at in our *sabbath work*. If the sabbath was made for man, we should then ask ourselves at night, "What am I the better for this sabbath day?" [3] What care we ought to take not to make those exercises of religion burthens to ourselves or others, which God ordained to be blessings. Consider whom the sabbath was *made by* (v. 28); "*The Son of man is Lord also of the sabbath.*" The sabbath days are *days of the Son of man*; he is the Lord of the day, and to his honour it must be observed. The shifting of it one day forward to the first day of the week, was to be in remembrance of *his* resurrection, and therefore the Christian sabbath was to be called *the Lord's day*.

CHAPTER 3

I. Christ's healing a man that had a withered hand, on the sabbath day, ver. 1–6. II. The universal resort of people to him from all parts, to be healed, ver. 7–12. III. His ordaining his twelve apostles, ver. 13–21. IV. His answer to the scribes, who imputed his power to cast out devils to a confederacy with the prince of the devils, ver. 22–30. V. His owning his disciples for his nearest and dearest relations, ver. 31–35.

Verses 1–12

Here, as before, we have our Lord Jesus busy at work *in the synagogue* first, and then by *the seaside*; to teach us that his presence should not be confined either to the one or to the other, but, wherever any are gathered together in his name there is he in the midst of them.

I. When he *entered again into the synagogue*, he improved the opportunity he had there, of doing good.

1. The patient's case was piteous; he had a *withered hand*, by which he was disabled to work for his living; let those be helped that cannot help themselves.

2. The spectators were very unkind, both to the patient and to the Physician; instead of interceding for a poor neighbour, they did what they could to hinder his cure: for they intimated that if Christ cured him now on the sabbath day, they would accuse him as a *Sabbath breaker*.

3. Christ dealt very fairly with the spectators, and dealt with them *first*, if possible to *prevent* the offence.

(1) He laboured to convince their judgment. He bade the man *stand forth* (v. 3), that by the sight of him they might be moved with compassion. And then he appeals to their own consciences; "*Is it lawful to do good on the sabbath days, or to do evil?* Whether is better to *save life* or to *kill?*" What fairer question could be put? And yet, because they saw it would turn against them, *they held their peace*.

(2) When they rebelled against the light, he *lamented their stubbornness* (v. 5); *He looked round about on them with anger, being grieved for the hardness of their hearts*. The *sin* he had an eye to, was, the *hardness of their hearts*. We hear what is said amiss, and see what is done amiss; but Christ looks at the *root of bitterness* in the heart, the blindness and hardness of *that*. [1] How he was *provoked* by the sin; he looked *round upon them*; and he looked *with anger*; his anger, it is probable, appeared in his countenance. The sin of sinners is very displeasing to Jesus Christ; and the way to be angry, and not to sin, is to be angry, as Christ was, at nothing but sin. [2] How he *pitied* the sinners; he was *grieved for the hardness of their hearts*. It is a great grief to our Lord Jesus, to see sinners bent upon their own ruin, for he would not that any should perish. This is a good reason why the hardness of our own hearts and of the hearts of others, should be a grief to us.

4. Christ dealt very kindly with the patient; he bade him *stretch forth his hand*, and it was immediately *restored*. Christ has hereby taught us to go on with resolution in the way of our duty, how violent soever the opposition is, that we meet with in it. We must not deny ourselves the satisfaction of serving God, and doing good, though offence may unjustly be taken at it. None could be more tender of giving offence than Christ; yet, rather than send this poor man away uncured, he would venture offending all the scribes and Pharisees that compassed him about. He hath hereby given us a *specimen* of the cures wrought by his grace upon *poor souls*; our hands are spiritually *withered*, the powers of our souls weakened by sin. Though our hands are withered, and we cannot of ourselves *stretch them forth*, we must attempt it, must, as well as we can, *lift them up* to God in prayer, *lay hold* on Christ and eternal life, and employ them in good works; and if we do our endeavour, power goes along with the word of Christ, he effects the cure. If we will not offer to *stretch them out*, it is our own fault that we are not healed.

5. The enemies of Christ dealt very barbarously with him. Such a work of *mercy* should have engaged their love *to him*, and such a work of *wonder* their faith *in him*. But, instead of that, the Pharisees and the Herodians, *took counsel together against him, how they might destroy him*.

II. When he withdrew *to the sea*, he did good there. He quitted the place; to teach us in troublous times to shift for our own safety.

1. How he was followed into his retirement. When some had such an enmity to him, that they drove him out of their country, others had such a value for him, that they followed him wherever he went. *Great multitudes* followed him from all parts of the nation. (1) What induced them to follow

him; it was the report they heard of the *great things he did*. Some wished to *see* one that had done such *great things*, and others hoped he would do great things *for them*. The consideration of the *great things* Christ has done, should engage us to *come to him*. (2) What they followed him for (*v.* 10); They *pressed upon him, to touch him, as many as had plagues*. Diseases are here called *plagues*, corrections, chastisements. Those that were under these *scourgings* came to Jesus; this is the errand on which sickness is sent, to quicken us to enquire after Christ, and apply ourselves to him as our Physician. They *pressed upon him*, each striving which should get *nearest to him*, and which should be *first served*. They desired leave but to *touch him*, having faith to be healed, not only by *his* touching *them*, but by *their* touching him. (3) What provision he made to be ready to attend them (*v.* 9); He *spoke to his disciples*, that a *small ship should wait on him*, to carry him from place to place on the same coast; without pressing through the crowds of people that followed him for curiosity. Wise men, as much as they can, decline a crowd.

2. What abundance of good he did in his retirement. He did not withdraw to be idle, nor did he send back those who rudely crowded after him when he withdrew, but took it kindly, and gave them what they came for; for he never said to any that sought him diligently, *Seek ye me in vain*. (1) Diseases were effectually cured. He *healed many*. (2) *Devils* were effectually *conquered*; those whom unclean spirits had got possession of, *when they saw him*, trembled at his presence, and they also *fell down before him*, not to supplicate his favour, but to deprecate his wrath. (3) Christ sought not applause to himself in doing those great things, for *he strictly charged* those for whom he did them, *that they should not make him known* (*v.* 12); that they should not be *industrious* to spread the notice of his cures, as it were by advertisements in the newspapers, but let them leave *his own works to praise him*, and let the report of them *diffuse itself*, and make its own way. Let the *standers-by* carry away the intelligence of it.

Verses 13–21

I. The choice Christ made of the *twelve apostles* to be his constant followers and attendants.

1. The introduction to this *call* or *promotion* of disciples; He *goes up into a mountain*, and his errand thither was *to pray*.

2. The rule he went by in his choice, and that was his own good pleasure; He *called unto him whom he would*. Not such as we should have thought *fittest to be called*; but such as he *thought fit* to call, and determined ¸to *make fit* for the service to which he called them. Christ calls *whom he will*.

3. The efficacy of the call; He *called them* to separate themselves from the crowd, and stand by him, and they *came unto him*. Those whom it was his *will* to call, he made *willing to come*.

4. The end and intention of this call; He *ordained them that they should be with him* constantly, to be witnesses of *his doctrine, manner of life, and patience*, that they might *fully know it*; they must be *with him*, to receive instructions *from him*, that they might be qualified to give instructions *to others*. It would *require time* to fit them for that which he designed them for. Christ's ministers must be much *with him*.

5. The power he gave them to work miracles. He ordained them to *heal sicknesses and to cast out devils*. This showed that the power which Christ has to work these miracles was an *original* power; that he had it not *as a Servant*, but *as a Son in his own house*. Our Lord Jesus had *life in himself*, and the Spirit without measure; for he could give this power even to the *weak* and *foolish things* of the world.

6. Their number and names; He *ordained twelve*, according to the number of the twelve tribes of Israel. They are here named not just in the same order as they were in Matthew, but as there, so here, Peter is put first and Judas last. Here Matthew is put before Thomas; but in that catalogue which Matthew himself drew up, he puts himself after Thomas. But that which Mark only takes notice of in this list of the apostles, is, that Christ called James and John *Boanerges*, which is, *The sons of thunder*; perhaps they were remarkable for a loud commanding voice, they were thundering preachers; or, rather, it denotes the zeal and fervency of their spirits. Yet John, one of those *sons of thunder*, was full of love and tenderness, as appears by his epistles, and was the beloved disciple.

7. Their retirement with their Master, and close adherence to him; *They went into a house*. Now that this jury was impanelled, they *stood together, to hearken to their evidence*.

II. The continual crowds that attended Christ's motions (*v.* 20); The *multitude cometh together again*, unsent for, and unseasonably pressing upon him, so that he and his disciples could not get time *so much as to eat bread*. Yet he did not shut his doors against the petitioners, but bade them welcome. They whose hearts are enlarged in the work of God, can easily bear with great inconveniences to themselves, *in the* prosecution of it. It is happy when zealous *hearers* and zealous *preachers* thus *meet*, and encourage one another. This was a gale of opportunity worth improving. It is good striking while the iron is hot.

III. The care of his relations concerning him (*v.* 21); *When his friends* in Capernaum heard how he was followed they *went out, to lay hold on him*, and fetch him home, for they said, *He is beside himself*. 1. Some understand it of an absurd preposterous care, which had more in it of reproach to him than of respect; and so we must take it as we read it, *He is beside himself*. His kindred were willing to hearken to this ill construction which some put upon his great zeal, and to conclude him crazed in his intellects. 2. Others understand it of a *well-meaning* care; and then they read ἐξέστη—"*He fainteth*, he has no time to *eat bread*, and therefore his strength will fail him; he will be stifled with the crowd of people. Therefore let us use a friendly violence with him, and get him a little *breathing-time*." They who go on with vigour and zeal in the work of God, must expect to meet with hindrances, both from the groundless disaffection of their enemies, and the mistaken affections of their friends.

Verses 22–30

Here is, I. The impudent impious brand which the scribes fastened upon Christ's casting out devils. These *scribes came down from Jerusalem, v.* 22. It should seem they came this long journey on purpose to hinder the progress of the doctrine of Christ. Coming from Jerusalem, where were the most polite and learned scribes, they were in the greater capacity to do mischief; the reputation of scribes from Jerusalem would have an influence not only upon the *country people*, but upon the *country scribes*. They could not deny but that he cast out devils, but they insinuated that *he had Beelzebub* on his side, and by *the prince of the devils cast out devils*. There is a trick in the case; Satan is not *cast out*, he only *goes out* by consent.

II. The rational answer which Christ gave to this objection.

1. Satan is so *subtle*, that he will never voluntarily quit his possession; *If Satan cast out Satan, his kingdom is divided against itself*, and it *cannot stand*, *v.* 23–26. He *called them to him*, he vouchsafed to reason the case with them, *that every mouth may be*

stopped. It was plain that the doctrine of Christ *made war* upon the devil's kingdom, and had a direct tendency to break his power, and it was as plain that the casting of him out of the bodies of people confirmed that doctrine. Everyone knows that Satan is no *fool*, nor will act so directly against his own interest.

2. Christ is so *wise*, that, being engaged in war with him, he will attack his forces wherever he meets them, whether in the bodies or souls of people, *v.* 27. It is plain, Christ's design is to *enter into the strong man's house*, and to *spoil his goods*. Therefore it is natural to suppose that he will thus *bind the strong man*, and thus show that he has gained a victory over him.

III. The awful warning Christ gave them to take heed how they spoke such dangerous words as these; however they might make light of them, as only conjectures, and the language of *free-thinking*, if they persisted in it, it would be of fatal consequence to them; it would be found a sin against the last remedy, and consequently *unpardonable*. It is true, the gospel *promiseth*, because Christ hath *purchased*, forgiveness for the greatest sins and sinners, *v.* 28. Many of those who reviled Christ on the cross found mercy, and Christ himself prayed, *Father, forgive them*; but this was *blaspheming the Holy Ghost*, for it was by the Holy Spirit that he *cast out* devils, and they said, It was *by the unclean spirit, v.* 30.

Verses 31–33

Here is, 1. The *disrespect* which Christ's *kindred, according to the flesh*, showed to him when he was preaching; they not only *stood without*, but they sent in a message to *call him out to them* (*v.* 31, 32).

2. The *respect* which Christ showed to his spiritual kindred upon this occasion. Now, as at other times, he put a *comparative neglect* upon his mother. He looked upon those that *sat about* him, and pronounced those of them that not only heard, but did, the will of God, to be to him as *his brother, and sister, and mother*; as much esteemed, loved, and cared for, as his nearest relations, *v.* 33–35. This is a good reason why we should *honour those that fear the Lord*, that we may share with the saints in this honour.

Chapter 4

I. The parable of the seed, and the four sorts of ground (ver. 1–9), with the exposition of it (ver. 10–20), and the application of it, ver. 21–25. II. The parable of the seed growing gradually, ver. 26–29. III. The parable of the grain of mustard-seed, ver. 30–34. IV. The miracle of Christ's sudden stilling a storm at sea, ver. 35–41.

Verses 1–20

The foregoing chapter began with Christ's *entering into the synagogue* (*v.* 1); this chapter begins with Christ's *teaching again by the seaside*. Thus he changed his method, that if possible all might be reached and wrought upon.

Here seems to be a new convenience found out, which had not been used before, and that was—his standing *in a ship*, while his hearers *stood upon the land*.

I. The *way of teaching* that Christ used with the multitude (*v.* 2); He *taught them many things*, but it was *by parables*, which would *tempt them to hear*; for people love to be spoken to in their own language, and careless hearers will catch at a plain comparison borrowed from common things. Unless they would take pains to search into it, it would but amuse them; *seeing they would see, and not perceive* (*v.* 12). They wilfully shut their eyes against the light, and therefore justly did Christ put it into the dark lantern of a parable, which had a bright side toward those who applied it to themselves, but to those who were only *willing for a season to play with it*, it only gave a flash of light now and then, but sent them away in the dark.

II. The way of *expounding* that he used with his *disciples*; *When he was alone* by himself, not only the *twelve*, but others that were *about him with the twelve*, took the opportunity to *ask him* the meaning of the parables, *v.* 10. And he told them what a distinguishing favour it was to them, that they were made acquainted with the *mystery of the kingdom of God, v.* 11. That *instructed* them, which others were only *amused* with. Those who know the *mystery* of the *kingdom of heaven*, must acknowledge that it is *given to them*; they receive both the light and the sight from Jesus Christ.

1. The parable of the sower, as we had it, Matt. xiii. 3, &c. He begins (*v.* 3), with, *Hearken*, and concludes (*v.* 9) with, *He that hath ears to hear, let him hear*. The words of Christ demand attention; even that which as yet we do not *thoroughly* understand, or not *rightly*, we must carefully attend to. We shall find more in Christ's sayings than at first there seemed to be.

2. The exposition of it to the disciples. Here is a question Christ put to them before he expounded it, which we had not in Matthew (*v.* 13); "*Know ye not this parable?* Know ye not the meaning of it? How then will ye know all parables?*" "If ye know not this, which is so plain, how will ye understand other parables, which will be more dark and obscure?" This should quicken us both to prayer and pains that we may get knowledge. If we understand not the plain truths of the gospel, how shall we master those that are more difficult? This parable is to teach you to be attentive to the word, and affected with it, that you may *understand* it. "If ye receive not this, ye will not know how to use the key by which ye must be let into all the rest." Before Christ expounds the parable, (1) He shows them how sad *their* case was, who were not let into the meaning of the doctrine of Christ; *To you it is given, but not to them*. It will help us to put a value upon the privileges we enjoy as disciples of Christ, to consider the deplorable state of those who want such privileges, *lest they should be converted, and their sins should be forgiven them, v.* 12. Those only who are *converted*, have *their sins forgiven them*. (2) He shows them what a shame it was, that they needed such particular explanations of the word they heard, and did not apprehend it at first. Those that would improve in knowledge, must be made sensible of their ignorance.

He gives them the interpretation of the parable of the sower, as we had it before in Matthew. Let us only observe here,

First, That in the great field of the church, the word of God is dispensed to all promiscuously; *The sower soweth the word* (*v.* 14), sows it at a venture, not knowing where it will light, or what fruit it will bring forth. He *scatters* it, in order to the *increase* of it. Christ was awhile *sowing* himself, when he went about teaching and preaching; now he sends his ministers and sows by their hand.

Secondly, That of the many that hear the word of the gospel, there are, comparatively, but few that receive it, so as to bring forth the fruits of it; here is but one in four, that comes to good. It is sad to think, how much of the precious seed of the word of God is lost, and *sown in vain*; but there is a day coming when *lost sermons* must be accounted for.

Thirdly, Many are much affected with the word for the present, who yet receive no abiding benefit by it. The motions of soul they have, answerable to what they hear, are but a mere flash, like the crackling of thorns under a pot. Those represented here by the stony ground, received the word *with gladness*, and yet came to nothing.

Fourthly, The reason why the word doth not leave commanding, abiding, impressions upon the minds of the people. The fault is in themselves, not in the word; some are careless forgetful hearers, and these get *no good at all* by the word; it comes in at one ear, and goes out at the other; others have their convictions overpowered by their corruptions, and they lose the good impressions the word has made upon them, so that they get no *abiding* good by it.

Fifthly, The devil is very busy about loose, careless hearers, as the fowls of the air go about the seed that lies above ground. *Like the fowls*, he comes swiftly, and carries away the word ere we are aware. Though we cannot keep them from hovering over our heads we may not let them nestle in our hearts.

Sixthly, Many that are not openly *scandalized*, so as to throw off their profession, as they on the stony ground did, yet have the efficacy of it secretly *choked* and stifled, so that it comes to nothing.

Seventhly, Impressions that are not *deep*, will not be *durable*. Many that keep their profession in fair days, lose it in a storm; and as those that go to sea only for pleasure, come back again when the wind arises. It is the ruin of hypocrites, that they *have no root*; they do not act from a living fixed principle. He is the Christian, that is *one inwardly*.

Eighthly, Many are hindered from profiting by the word of God, by their abundance of the world. Many a good lesson is choked and lost by that prevailing complacency in the world, which *they* are apt to have, on whom it smiles.

Ninthly, Those that are not encumbered with the cares of the world, and the deceitfulness of riches, may yet lose the benefit of their profession by the *lusts of other things*; this is added here in Mark; an inordinate appetite toward those things that are pleasing to sense or to the fancy. Those that have but little of the world, may yet be ruined by an indulgence of the body.

Tenthly, Fruit is the thing that God expects and requires from those that enjoy the gospel: fruit according to the *seed*; a temper of mind, and a course of life, agreeable to the gospel. This is *fruit*, and it will abound to our account.

Lastly, No good fruit is to be expected but from good seed. If the seed be sown on *good ground*, if the heart be humble, and holy, and heavenly, there will be *good fruit*, and it will *abound* sometimes even to a *hundredfold*.

Verses 21–34

I. Those who *are good* ought to *do good*; that is to *bring forth fruit*. God expects a grateful return of his gifts to us, and a useful improvement of his gifts in us; for (v. 21), *Is a candle brought to be put under a bushel, or under a bed?* No, but that it may be *set on a candlestick*. All Christians, as they have *received the gift*, must *minister the same*. Gifts and graces make a man *as a candle*; the most eminent are but candles, poor lights, compared with the *Sun of righteousness*. A candle gives light but a *little way*, and but a *little while*, and is easily blown out, and continually burning down and wasting. Many who are *lighted* as candles, put themselves *under a bed, or under a bushel*: they do not *manifest* grace themselves, nor *minister* grace to others. Like a taper in an urn, they burn to themselves. Those who are lighted as candles, should set themselves *on a candlestick*; that is, should improve all opportunities of doing good. We are not born for ourselves.

The reason given for this, is, because *there is nothing hid, which shall not be manifested, v. 22*. There is no treasure of gifts and graces lodged in any but with design to be communicated; nor was the gospel made a *secret* to the apostles. It should *come abroad*, and be divulged to all the world.

Though Christ expounded the parables to his disciples privately, yet it was with design to make them the more publicly useful; they were *taught*, that they might teach.

II. It concerns those who hear the word of the gospel, to *mark* what they hear, and to *make a good use* of it, *If any man have ears to hear, let him hear*, v. 23. It is added (v. 24), *Take heed what ye hear*, and give a due regard to that which ye do hear; *Consider what ye hear*. What we hear, doth us no good, unless we consider it; those especially that are to teach others must themselves be very observant of the things of God. We must likewise *take heed what we hear*, by *proving* all things, that we may *hold fast that which is good*. As we deal with God, God will deal with us, "*With what measure ye mete, it shall be measured to you.*" As we improve the talents we are entrusted with, we shall increase them; if we make use of the knowledge we have, it shall sensibly grow, as stock in trade both by being turned; *Unto you that hear, shall more be given; to you that have, it shall be given*, v. 25. Gifts and graces multiply by being exercised.

If we do not *use*, we *lose*, what we have; *From him that hath not shall be taken even that which he hath*. Burying a talent is the betraying of a trust, and amounts to a forfeiture; and gifts and graces *rust* for want of *wearing*.

III. The good seed of the gospel sown in the world, and sown in the heart, doth by degrees produce wonderful effects, but without noise (v. 26, &c.); *So is the kingdom of God*.

1. It will *come up;* though it seem lost and buried under the clods, it will find or make its way through them. The seed *cast into the ground will spring*. After a field is sown with corn, how soon is the surface of it altered! How gay and pleasant doth it look, when it is covered with green!

2. The husbandman cannot describe how it comes up; it is one of the mysteries of nature; It *springs and grows up, he knows not how, v. 27*. Thus we know not how the Spirit by the word makes a change in the heart, any more than we can account for the blowing of the wind, which we can hear the sound of, but cannot tell whence it comes, or whither it goes.

3. The husbandman, when he hath sown the seed, doth nothing toward the springing of it up; *He sleeps, and rises, night and day*, and perhaps never so much as thinks of the corn he hath sown, and yet *the earth brings forth fruit of itself*, according to the ordinary course of nature. Thus the *word of grace*, when it is received in faith, is in the heart a *work of grace*.

4. It grows gradually; *first the blade, then the ear, after that the full corn in the ear, v. 28*. When it is sprung up, it will go forward; nature will have its course, and so will grace. Christ's interest, is, and will be, a *growing* interest; and though *the beginning be small, the latter end will greatly increase*. Though at first it is but a tender *blade*, which the frost may nip, or the foot may crush, yet it will increase to *the ear*, to the *full corn in the ear*. God carries on his work insensibly and without noise, but insuperably and without fail.

5. It comes to perfection at last (v. 29); *When the fruit is brought forth, then he puts in the sickle*. From the fruit of the gospel taking place and working in the soul, Christ *gathers in* a harvest. When those that receive the gospel aright, have finished their course, the harvest comes, when they shall be gathered as *wheat into God's barn* (Matt. xiii. 30).

IV. The work of grace is small in its beginnings, but comes to be great and considerable at last (v. 30–32); "*Whereunto shall I liken the kingdom of God?* How shall I make you to understand the designed method of it?" It is *like a grain of mustard-seed*; he had compared it before to *seed sown*, here to *that seed*, intending thereby to show,

1. That the beginnings of the *gospel kingdom* would be very small, like that which is *one of the least of all seeds*. The work of grace in the soul, is, at first, but the *day of small things*; a *cloud* no *bigger than a man's hand*. Never were there such great things undertaken by such an inconsiderable handful, as that of the discipling of the nations by the ministry of the apostles.

2. That the perfection of it will be very great; *When it grows up, it becomes greater than all herbs*. The gospel kingdom in the world, shall increase and spread to the remotest nations of the earth. The difference between a *grain of mustard seed* and a *great tree*, is nothing to that between a *young convert* on earth and a *glorified saint* in heaven.

With many such parables he spoke the word unto them (v. 33). He spoke in parables, *as they were able to hear them*; he fetched his comparisons from those things that were familiar to them. His manner of expression was easy, and such as they might hereafter recollect to their edification. But, for the present, *without a parable spoke he not unto them*, *v. 34*. The disciples themselves understood those sayings of Christ afterward, which at first they did not rightly take the sense of. But these parables *he expounded to them, when they were alone*. We cannot but wish we had had that exposition, as we had of the parable of the sower.

Verses 35–41

This miracle which Christ wrought for the relief of his disciples, in stilling the storm, we had before (Matt. viii. 23, &c.); but it is here more fully related.

1. It was *the same day, when the even was come*, *v. 35*. When he had been *labouring in the world and doctrine* all day, instead of *reposing* himself, he *exposeth* himself. The end of a toil may perhaps be but the beginning of a toss.

2. He himself proposed putting to sea at night, because he would lose no time; *Let us pass over to the other side*; he has work to do there. Christ went about doing good, and no difficulties in his way should hinder him.

3. They did not put to sea, till *they had sent away the multitude*, that is, answered all their requests; for he sent none home complaining that they had attended him *in vain*.

4. They took him *even as he was*, without any cloak to throw over him, which he ought to have had, to keep him *warm*, when he went to sea at night. We may learn hence not to be over nice and solicitous about the body.

5. The storm was so great, that the ship was *full of water* (v. 37). The ship being little, the waves beat into it so that *it was full*.

6. There were *with him other little ships*, which, no doubt, shared in the distress and danger. The *multitude went away* when he put to sea, but some there were, that would venture upon the water with him. One may boldly and cheerfully put to sea in Christ's company, yea though we foresee a storm.

7. Christ was asleep in this storm. It was *in the hinder part of the ship*, the pilot's place: he lay at the helm.

He had a *pillow* there. And he *slept*, to try the faith of his disciples and to stir up prayer: upon the trial, their faith appeared *weak*, and their prayers *strong*. Sometimes when the church is in a storm, Christ seems as if he were asleep, unconcerned in the troubles of his people, and regardless of their prayers. When he sleeps he doth not sleep; the keeper of Israel doth not so much as slumber (Ps. cxxi. 3, 4); he slept, but his heart was awake.

8. His disciples encouraged themselves with their having his presence, and thought it the best way to improve that, and appeal to that, and ply the oar of prayer rather than their other oars. Their confidence lay in this, that they had their Master with them; and the ship that has Christ in it, though it may be *tossed*, cannot *sink*. They *awoke Christ*. When Christ seems as if he slept in a storm, he is awakened by the prayers of his people; we may be at our wits' end, but not at our faith's end, while we have such a Saviour to go to. Their address to Christ is here expressed very emphatically; *Master, carest thou not that we perish?* I confess this sounds somewhat harsh, rather like chiding him for sleeping than begging him to awake. I know no excuse for it, but the present distress they were in, which put them into such a fright, that they knew not what they said. They do Christ a deal of wrong, who suspect him to be *careless* of his people in distress.

9. The word of command with which Christ rebuked the storm, we have here, and had not in Matthew, *v. 39*. He says, *Peace, be still—be silent, be dumb*. Let not the wind any longer roar, nor the sea rage. The noise is threatening and terrifying; let us hear no more of it. This is, (1) A word of command to us; when our wicked hearts are *like the troubled sea which cannot rest* (Isa. lvii. 20); let us think we hear the law of Christ, saying, *Be silent, be dumb*. Think not confusedly, speak not unadvisedly; but *be still*. (2) A word of comfort to us, that, be the storm of trouble ever so loud, ever so strong, Jesus Christ can lay it with a word's speaking. He that made the seas, can make them *quiet*.

10. The reproof Christ gave them for their fears, is here carried further than in Matthew. There it is, *Why are ye fearful?* Here, *Why are ye so fearful?* There it is, *O ye of little faith*. Here it is, *How is it that ye have no faith?* Not that the disciples were without faith. But at this time their fears prevailed so that they seemed to *have no faith* at all. It was out of the way, when they had occasion for it, and so it was as if they had not had it. Those may suspect their faith, who can entertain such a thought as that Christ *careth not* though his *people perish*.

Lastly, The impression this miracle made upon the disciples, is here differently expressed. In Matthew it is said, *The men marvelled;* here it is said, *They feared greatly*. Now their fear was rectified by their faith. When they feared the winds and the seas, it was for want of the reverence they ought to have had for Christ. But now that they saw a demonstration of his power over them, they feared *them* less, and *him* more. They had *feared* the power and wrath of the Creator in the storm, and that fear had torment and amazement in it; but now they feared the power and grace of the Redeemer in the calm; and it had pleasure and satisfaction in it. They said, *What manner of man is this?* Surely more than a man, *for even the winds and the seas obey him*.

CHAPTER 5

In this chapter, we have, I. Christ's casting the legion of devils out of the man possessed, and suffering them to enter into the swine, ver. 1–20. II. Christ's healing the woman with the bloody issue, in the way as he was going to raise Jairus's daughter to life, ver. 21–43.

Verses 1–20

We have here an instance of Christ's dispossessing the strong man armed. This he did when he was come *to the other side*, whither he went through a storm; his business there was to rescue this poor creature out of the hands of Satan.

I. The miserable condition that this poor creature was in; he was under the power of an *unclean spirit*; he was raving mad; his condition seems to have been worse than any of the possessed, that were Christ's patients.

1. He had *his dwelling among the tombs*, among the graves of dead people. Their tombs were out of the cities, in *desolate places*. Perhaps the devil drove him to *the tombs*. The touch of a grave was polluting. The *unclean spirit* drives people into that company that is *defiling*, and so keeps possession of them. Christ, by rescuing souls out of Satan's power, *saves the living from among the dead*.

2. He was very strong and ungovernable; *No man could bind him*. Not only cords would not hold him, but *chains* and *fetters of iron* would not, *v.* 3, 4. This sets forth the sad condition of those souls in which the devil has dominion. Some notoriously wilful sinners are like this madman. The commands and curses of the law are as *chains* and *fetters*, to restrain sinners from their wicked courses; but they *break those bonds in sunder*.

3. He was a terror and torment to himself and to all about him, *v.* 5. The devil is a *cruel* master. This wretched creature was *night and day in the mountains and in the tombs, crying, and cutting himself with stones*. What is a man, when reason is dethroned and Satan enthroned?

II. His application to Christ (*v.* 6); *When he saw Jesus afar off*, coming ashore, he *ran, and worshipped him*. He usually *ran upon* others with *rage*, but he *ran to* Christ with *reverence*. That was done by an invisible hand of Christ, which could not be done with chains and fetters; his fury was all on a sudden curbed. The poor man came, and *worshipped Christ*, in a sense of the need he had of his help, the power of Satan in and over him being, for this instant, suspended.

III. The word of command Christ gave (*v.* 8); *Come out of him, thou unclean spirit*. He made the man desirous to be relieved, when he enabled him to *run*, and *worship him*, and then put forth his power for his relief. If Christ *work in us* heartily to pray for a deliverance from Satan, he will work for us that deliverance.

IV. The dread which the devil had of Christ. The *man ran*, and *worshipped Christ*; but it was the devil in the man, that *cried with a loud voice* (making use of the poor man's tongue), *What have I to do with thee? v.* 7. 1. He calls God the *most high God*, above all other gods. 2. He owns Jesus to be the *Son of God*. It is no strange thing to hear the best words drop from the worst mouths. Piety from the teeth outward is an easy thing. The most fair-spoken hypocrite cannot say better than to call Jesus the Son of God and yet that the devil did. 3. He disowns any design against Christ; "*What have I to do with thee?*" 4. He deprecates his wrath; *I adjure thee*, that, though those drive me out hence, yet that thou *torment me not*.

V. The account Christ took from this unclean spirit of his name. This we had not in Matthew. Christ asked him, *What is thy name? My name is Legion, for we are many*. Now this intimates that the devils are, 1. *Military* powers. The devils war against God and his glory, Christ and his gospel, men and their holiness and happiness. 2. That they are *numerous*; he *owns*, or rather he *boasts*—*We are many*; as if he hoped to be *too many* for Christ himself to deal with. 3. That they are *unanimous*; they are *many* devils, and yet but *one legion* engaged in the same wicked cause. 4. That they are very *powerful*; Who can stand before a *legion?* We are not a match for our spiritual enemies, in our own strength; but *in the Lord, and in the power of his might*, we shall be able to *stand against them*.

VI. The request of this legion, that Christ would suffer them to go into a herd of swine that was *feeding nigh unto the mountains* (*v.* 11). Their request was, 1. That he *would not send them away out of the country* (*v.* 10); not only that he would not *torment them before the time*; but that he would not *banish* them *that country*. They seem to have had a particular affection for *that country*; or, rather, a particular spite to it. 2. That he would suffer them to *enter into the swine*.

VII. The permission Christ gave them to enter into the swine, and the immediate destruction of the swine thereby; *He gave them leave* (*v.* 13). Immediately the *unclean spirits entered into the swine*, which by the law were unclean creatures. Those that, like the swine, delight in *the mire* of sensual lusts, are fit habitations for Satan. The consequence of the devils entering into the swine, was, that they all *ran mad* presently, and ran headlong into the adjoining sea, where they were all drowned, to the number of *two thousand*.

VIII. The report of all this dispersed through the country immediately. They that *fed the swine*, hastened to the owners, to give an account of their charge, *v.* 14. This drew the people together, to see what was done. When they saw how wonderfully the poor man was cured, they hence conceived a *veneration for Christ*, *v.* 15. They saw him that was *possessed with the devil sitting clothed and in his right mind*; when Satan was cast out, he came to himself, and was his own man presently. Those who are grave and sober, and live by rule and with consideration, thereby make it appear that by the power of Christ the devil's power is broken in their souls. The sight of this *made them afraid*; it astonished them, and forced them to own the power of Christ, and that he is *worthy to be feared*. When they found that their swine were lost, they thence conceived a *dislike of Christ*, they prayed him to *depart out of their coasts*, for they think not any good he can do them sufficient to make them amends for the loss of so many swine, fat swine, it may be, and ready for the market. Now the devils had what they would have; for by no handle do these evil spirits more effectually manage sinful souls than by that of the love of the world. If they would but part with their sins, he had life and happiness for them; but, being loth to quit either their sins or their swine, they chose rather to abandon their Saviour. Thus they do, who, rather than let go a base lust, will throw away their interest in Christ. They wished him further off.

IX. An account of the conduct of the poor man after his deliverance. 1. He *desired that he might go along with Christ* (*v.* 18). 2. Christ *would not suffer him* to go with him. He had other work for him to do; he must go home to his friends, and tell them what *great things the Lord had done for him*, and his neighbours and friends might be edified, and invited to believe in Christ. He must take particular notice rather of Christ's *pity* than of his *power*; he must tell them what *compassion* the Lord had had on him in his misery. 3. The man, in a transport of joy, proclaimed, all the country over, what *great things Jesus had done for him*, *v.* 20. And see what was the effect of it; *All men did marvel*, but few went any further. Many that cannot but wonder at the works of Christ, yet do not, as they ought, *wonder after him*.

Verses 21–34

The Gadarenes having desired Christ to leave their country, he did not stay to trouble them long, but presently went by water, back *to the other side* (*v.* 21), and there *much people gathered to him*. If there be some that reject Christ, yet there are others that receive him, and bid him welcome.

I. Here is one, that comes *openly* to *beg* a cure for a sick child; and it is no less a person than one of the *rulers of the synagogue*. He was not named in Matthew, he is here, *Jairus*, or *Jair*, Judges x. 3.

He addressed himself to Christ with great humility and reverence; *When he saw him, he fell at his feet,* and with great importunity, he *besought him greatly,* as one in earnest. He has a *little daughter,* about twelve years old, the darling of the family, and she *lies a-dying;* but he believes that if Christ will but come, and *lay his hands upon her,* she will return even from the gates of the grave. He said, at first, when he came, *She lies a-dying* (so Mark); but afterward, *She is even now dead* (so Matthew); but he still prosecutes his suit. Christ readily agreed, and went with him, *v.* 24.

II. Here is another, that comes *clandestinely* to *steal* a cure (if I may so say) for herself; and she got the relief she came for. This cure was wrought by *the way,* as he was going to raise the ruler's daughter. Many of his discourses, and some of his miracles, are dated *by the way-side;* we should be doing good, not only when we *sit in the house,* but when we *walk by the way.*

1. The piteous case of this poor woman. She had a constant *issue of blood* upon her, for *twelve years.* She had had the best advice of physicians, that she could get, and had made use of the many medicines and methods they prescribed; but now that she had spent all she had among them, they gave her up as incurable. It is usual with people not to apply themselves to Christ, till they have tried in vain all other helpers, and find them, as certainly they will, *physicians of no value.* And he will be found a *sure refuge,* even to those who make him their *last refuge.*

2. The strong faith that she had in the power of Christ to heal her; *If I may but touch his clothes, I shall be whole, v.* 28. A private cure was what she wished for, and her faith was suited to her case.

3. The wonderful effect produced by it; *She came in the* crowd *behind* him, and with much ado got to touch his *garment,* and immediately she felt the cure wrought, *v.* 29. The flux of blood was *dried up,* and she felt herself perfectly well all over her in an instant. Those whom Christ heals of the disease of sin, that bloody issue, cannot but experience in themselves a universal change for the better.

4. Christ's enquiry after his concealed patient, and the encouragement he gave her; Christ *knew in himself that virtue had gone out of him, v.* 30. Being desirous to see his patient, he asked, not in displeasure, as one affronted, but in tenderness, as one concerned, *Who touched my clothes?* The disciples almost ridiculed his question (*v.* 31); *The multitudes throng thee, and sayest thou, Who touched me?* Christ passed by the affront, and *looks around* to *see her that had done this thing;* not that he might *blame* her for her presumption, but that he might *commend* and *encourage* her faith, and by his own act and deed might *warrant* and *confirm* the cure. As secret acts of sin, so secret acts of faith, are known to the Lord Jesus, and are under his eye. The poor woman, hereupon, presented herself to the Lord Jesus (*v.* 33), *fearing and trembling,* not knowing how he would take it. Christ's patients are often trembling, when they have reason to be triumphing. She might have come boldly, *knowing what was done in her;* yet, *knowing that,* she *fears* and *trembles.* It was a *surprise,* and was not yet, as it should have been, a *pleasing* surprise. However, she *fell down before him.* There is nothing better for those that fear and tremble, than to throw themselves at the feet of the Lord Jesus. And she *told him all the truth.* We must not be ashamed to own the secret transactions between Christ and our souls; but, when called to it, mention what he has done for our souls, and the experience we have had of *healing virtue* derived from him. What an encouraging word he gave her (*v.* 34); *Daughter, thy faith hath made thee whole.* God's grace will set the seal of its *amen* to the prayers and hopes of faith, saying, "So be it, and so it shall be, to thee." And therefore, "*Go in peace.*"

Verses 35–43

Christ, having healed an incurable disease, here goes on to triumph over death.

I. The melancholy news is brought to Jairus, that his *daughter is dead.* While there is life, there is hope, and room for the use of means; but when life is gone, it is past recall; *Why troublest thou the Master any further? v.* 35. Ordinarily, the proper thought in this case, is, "The matter is determined, the will of God is done, and I submit, I acquiesce; *The Lord gave, and the Lord hath taken away.*" But here the case was extraordinary; the death of the child doth not, as usually, put an end to the narrative.

II. Christ encourageth the afflicted father yet to hope. Christ had stayed to work a cure by the way, but he shall be no sufferer by that, nor loser by the gain of others; *Be not afraid, only believe.* We may suppose Jairus at a pause, whether he should ask Christ to go on or no; but have we not as much occasion for the grace of God, and his consolations, when death is in the house, as when sickness is? Christ therefore soon determines this matter; "*Be not afraid* that my coming will be to no purpose, only believe that I will make it turn to a good account." *Only believe.* Keep up a confidence in Christ, and a dependence upon him, and he will do what is for the best. Believe the resurrection, and then be not afraid.

III. He went with a select company to the house where the dead child was. Now he shook off the crowd, and *suffered no man to follow him* but his three bosom-disciples, Peter, and James, and John.

IV. He raised the dead child to life. Here we may observe,

1. That the child was extremely well beloved, for the relations and neighbours *wept and wailed greatly.*

2. That it was evident beyond dispute, that the child was really and truly dead. Their *laughing* Christ to *scorn,* for saying, *She is not dead, but sleepeth,* serves for the proof of this.

3. That Christ put those out as unworthy to be witnesses of the miracle, who were so ignorant in the things of God, as not to understand him when he spoke of death as a *sleep,* or so scornful, as to ridicule him for it.

4. That he took the parents of the child to be witnesses of the miracle, and designed it for *their* comfort, who were the *true,* for they were the *silent* mourners.

5. That Christ raised the child to life by a word of power, which is recorded here, and recorded in Syriac, in the language in which Christ spoke, for the greater certainty of the thing; *Talitha, cumi; Damsel, I say unto thee, Arise.* Christ said, *Arise from the dead;* meaning, *I command* that thou arise; nay, there is more in it—the dead have not power to arise, therefore power goes along with this word, to make it effectual. Christ works while he commands, and works by the command, and therefore may command what he pleaseth, even the dead to arise. Such is the gospel call to those that are by nature dead in trespasses and sins, and can no more rise from that death by their own power, than this child could.

6. That the damsel, as soon as life returned, *arose, and walked, v.* 42. Spiritual life will appear by our *rising* from the bed of sloth and carelessness, our walking *up and down* in Christ's name and strength.

7. That all who saw it, and heard of it, admired the miracle, and him that wrought it; *They were astonished with a great astonishment.* They could not but acknowledge that there was something in it extraordinary and very great, and yet they knew not what to make of it, or to infer from it.

8. That Christ endeavoured to conceal it; *He charged them straitly, that no man should know it.* It was sufficiently known to a competent number, but he would not have it as yet *proclaimed* any further.

9. That Christ took care something should be *given her to eat.* By this it appeared that she was raised not only to life, but to a good state of health, that she had an appetite to her meat. Where Christ hath given *spiritual life*, he will provide food for the support and nourishment of it unto life eternal, for he will *never forsake*, or be wanting to, the *work of his own hands.*

CHAPTER 6

I. Christ contemned by his countrymen, because he was one of them, ver. 1–6. II. The just power he gave his apostles over unclean spirits, ver. 7–13. III. A strange notion which Herod and others had of Christ, upon which occasion we have the story of the martyrdom of John Baptist, ver. 14–29. IV. Christ's retirement into a desert place; the crowds that followed him; and his feeding five thousand of them with five loaves and two fishes, ver. 30–44. V. Christ's walking upon the sea to his disciples, and the abundance of cures he wrought on the other side of the water, ver. 45–56.

Verses 1–6

I. Christ makes a visit to *his own country*, that was *Nazareth*; where his relations were. He had been in danger of his life among them (Luke iv. 29), and yet he came among them again; so strangely doth he wait to be gracious.

II. There he *preached* in their *synagogue*, on the *sabbath day*, v. 2. On sabbath days, the word of God is to be preached according to Christ's example.

III. They could not but own that which was very honourable concerning him. 1. That he spoke with great *wisdom.* 2. That he did *mighty works.* They acknowledged the two great proofs of the divine original of his gospel—the *divine wisdom*, and the *divine power*, and yet, though they could not deny the premises, they would not admit the conclusion.

IV. They studied to disparage him. All this *wisdom*, and all these *mighty works*, shall be of no account. *Is not this the Carpenter?* In Matthew, they upbraid him with being the carpenter's son. But, it seems, they could say further, *Is not this the Carpenter?* 1. He would thus *humble himself* as one that had taken upon him the form of a servant. 2. He would thus teach us to *abhor idleness*, and to find *ourselves something to do* in this world. Nothing is more pernicious for young people than to get a *habit of sauntering.* The Jews had a good rule for this—that their young men who were designed for scholars, were yet bred up to some trade, as Paul was a tent-maker, that they might have some business to fill up their time with. 3. He would thus put an honour upon despised mechanics, and encourage those who eat the labour of their hands, though great men look upon them with contempt.

Another thing they upbraided him with, was, the meanness of his relations; "*He is the son of Mary; his brethren and sisters are here with us; we know his family and kindred;*" and therefore, though they were *astonished* at his doctrine (v. 2), yet they were *offended* at his person (v. 3), and for that reason would not receive his doctrine.

V. Let us see how Christ bore this contempt.

1. He partly *excused* it (v. 4); *A prophet is not despised anywhere but in his own country.* Doubtless many have got over this prejudice, but ordinarily it holds good, that ministers are seldom so acceptable and successful in their own country as among strangers; *familiarity* in the younger years breeds a contempt, the advancement of one that was an inferior begets *envy*, and men will hardly set those among the guides of their souls whose fathers they were ready to set with the dogs of their flock.

2. He did *some good* among them, notwithstanding the slights they put upon him, for he is kind even to the evil and unthankful; *He laid his hands upon a few sick folks, and healed them.*

3. Yet he *could there do* no such mighty works as in other places, because of the unbelief that prevailed among the people, v. 5. It is a strange expression, as if unbelief tied the hands of omnipotence itself; he *would have done* as many miracles there as he had done elsewhere, but he could not. They forfeited the honour of having them wrought for them. By unbelief and contempt of Christ men stop the current of his favours to them, and put a bar in their own door.

4. He *marvelled because of their unbelief*, v. 6. We never find Christ wondering but at the *faith* of the Gentiles that were strangers, as the *centurion* (Matt. viii. 10), and the woman of Samaria, and at the unbelief of Jews that were his own countrymen.

5. He *went round about the villages, teaching.* If we cannot do good where we would, we must do it where we can, though but in the villages. Sometimes the gospel of Christ finds better entertainment in the country villages, than in the populous cities.

Verses 7–13

I. The commission given to the twelve apostles, to preach and work miracles. Hitherto they had been conversant with Christ, and had sat at his feet, had heard his doctrine, and seen his miracles. They had *received*, that they might *give*, had *learned*, that they might *teach*; and therefore now he *began to send them forth.* They must not always be studying in the academy, to get knowledge. Though they were not as yet so well accomplished as they were to be, yet, according to their present ability and capacity, they must be set to work, and make further improvements afterward. Now observe here,

1. That Christ sent them forth *by two and two*; this Mark takes notice of. They went two and two to a place that they might be company for one another when they were among strangers, and might strengthen the hands, and encourage the hearts, one of another; might help one another. It is an approved maxim, *Two are better than one.* Christ would thus teach his ministers to associate, and both lend and borrow help.

2. That he *gave them power over unclean spirits.* He commissioned them to attack the devil's kingdom, and empowered them to cast him out of the bodies of those that were possessed.

3. That he *commanded them* not to take provisions along with them, neither *victuals* nor *money*, that they might appear, wherever they came, to be poor men. When afterward he bid them *take purse and scrip* (Luke xxii. 36), that did not intimate that his care of them was abated from what it had been; but, that they should meet with worse times and worse entertainment than they met with at their first mission. In Matthew and Luke they are forbidden to *take staves* with them, that is, fighting staves; but here in Mark they are bid to take nothing save a *staff only*, that is, a walking staff, such as pilgrims carried. They must not put on *shoes*, but *sandals* only; they must go in the readiest plainest dress they could, and must not so much as have *two coats.* What they wanted, those they preached to would cheerfully accommodate them with.

4. He directed them, whatever city they came to, to make that house their headquarters, which happened to be their first quarters (v. 10); "*There abide till ye depart from that place.* And since ye know ye come on an errand sufficient to make you welcome, have such charity for your friends that first invited you, as to believe they do not think you burthensome.*"

5. He pronounces a very heavy doom upon those that rejected the gospel they preached (*v.* 11); "*Whosoever shall not receive you,* or will not so much as *hear you, depart thence,* and *shake off the dust under your feet, for a testimony against them.*" That dust, like the dust of Egypt (Exod. ix. 9), shall turn into a plague to them; and their condemnation in the great day, will be more intolerable than *that of Sodom.*

II. The apostles' conduct in pursuance of their commission. Though they were conscious to themselves of great weakness, yet, in obedience to their Master's order, and in dependence upon his strength, they *went out* as Abraham, not knowing whither they went.

1. The doctrine they preached; *They preached that men should repent* (*v.* 12); that they should change their minds, and reform their lives. The great design of gospel preachers, and the great tendency of gospel preaching, should be, to bring people to repentance, to a *new heart* and a *new way.* They did not amuse people with curious speculations, but told them that they must repent of their sins, and turn to God.

2. The miracles they wrought. The power Christ gave them *over unclean spirits,* was not ineffectual, nor did they receive it in vain, but used it, for they *cast out many devils* (*v.* 13); and they *anointed with oil many that were sick, and healed them.*

Verses 14–29

I. The wild notions that the people had concerning our Lord Jesus, *v.* 15. His own countrymen could believe nothing great concerning him, because they knew his poor kindred; but others were yet willing to believe anything rather than the truth. They said, He is Elias, whom they expected; or, *He is the prophet,* one of the Old Testament prophets raised to life; or *as one of the prophets,* a prophet now newly raised up.

II. The opinion of Herod concerning him. He said, "It is certainly John Baptist, *v.* 14. *It is John whom I beheaded, v.* 16. He is *risen from the dead;* he is come again with greater power, and *now mighty works do show forth themselves in him.*"

1. Where there is an *idle faith,* there is commonly a *working fancy.* The people said, It is a prophet risen from the dead; Herod said, *It is John Baptist risen from the dead.* It seems by this, that the *rising of a prophet from the dead,* to do *mighty works,* was thought neither impossible nor improbable, and it was now readily suspected when it was *not true;* but afterward, when *it was true* concerning Christ, it as obstinately gainsaid and denied. Those who most wilfully disbelieve the truth, are commonly most credulous of errors and fancies.

2. They who fight against the cause of God, will find themselves baffled, even when they think themselves conquerors.

3. A guilty conscience needs no accuser or tormentor but itself. *I beheaded him;* and the terror of it made him imagine that Christ was John risen. He feared John while he lived, and now, fears him ten times worse when he is dead. One might as well be haunted with ghosts and furies, as with the horrors of an accusing conscience.

4. There may be the terrors of strong conviction, where there is not the truth of a saving conversion.

III. A narrative of Herod's putting John Baptist to death.

1. The great value and veneration which Herod had some time had for John Baptist, which is related only by this evangelist, *v.* 20.

(1) He *feared John, knowing that he was a just man, and a holy.* It is possible that a man may have a great reverence for good men, and especially for good ministers, yea, and for that in them that is good, and yet himself be a bad man. [1] John was a *just man, and a holy;* to make a complete good man, both justice and holiness are necessary; holiness toward God, and justice toward men. [2] Herod knew this by personal acquaintance with him. Those that have but little justice and holiness themselves, may yet discern it with respect in others. [3] He therefore *feared* him, he honoured him. Many that are not good themselves, have respect for those that are.

(2) He *observed* him; he took notice of that in him that was praiseworthy, and commended it in the hearing of those about him; he made it appear that he observed what John said and did.

(3) He *heard him* preach; which was great condescension.

(4) He *did many of those things* which John in his preaching taught him. He was not only a *hearer of the word,* but in part a *doer of the work.* But it will not suffice to do *many* things, unless we have *respect to all* the commandments.

(5) He *heard him gladly.* There is a flashy joy, which a hypocrite may have in hearing the word. The *stony ground received the word with joy,* Luke viii. 13.

2. John's faithfulness to Herod, in telling him of his faults. Herod had married his brother Philip's wife, *v.* 17. John *reproved* him, told him plainly, *It is not lawful for thee to have thy brother's wife.* This was Herod's own iniquity, which he could not leave, when he did many things that John taught him. Though he were a king, he would not spare him, any more than Elijah did Ahab. Though it was dangerous to offend Herod, and much more to offend Herodias, yet John would run the hazard rather than be wanting in his duty. Those ministers that would be found faithful in the work of God, must not be afraid of the face of man.

3. The malice which Herodias bore to John for this (*v.* 19). She *has a quarrel with him, and would have him killed;* but when she could not obtain that, she got him committed to prison, *v.* 17. Many that pretend to honour prophesying, are for smooth things only, and love good preaching, if it keep far enough from their beloved sin. But it is better that sinners persecute ministers now for their faithfulness, than curse them eternally for their unfaithfulness.

4. The plot laid to take off John's head. *When a convenient day was come* (*v.* 21). There must be a ball at court, upon the king's birthday. To grace the solemnity, the daughter of Herodias must *dance* publicly, and Herod must take on him to be wonderfully charmed with her dancing. The king hereupon must make her an extravagant promise, to give her *whatever she would ask,* even to the *half of the kingdom.* This promise is bound with an oath; *He sware unto her, Whatsoever thou shalt ask, I will give.* She, being instructed by Herodias her mother, asked the *head of John Baptist;* and she must have it brought her *in a charger,* as a pretty thing for her to play with (*v.* 24, 25); and there must be no delay, no time lost, she must have it *by and by.* Herod granted it, and the execution was done immediately while the company were together. But he takes on him, (1) To be very backward to it, and that he would not for all the world have done it, if he had not been surprised into such a promise; *The king was exceeding sorry.* He could not do it but with great regret and reluctancy; natural conscience will not suffer men to sin easily. (2) He takes on him to be very sensible of the obligation of his oath. The promise was rashly made, and could not bind him to do an unrighteous thing. Sinful oaths must be repented of, and therefore not performed. He was hurried into the doing of it by those about him, only to carry on the humour; for he did it *for*

their sakes who sat with him. Thus do princes make themselves slaves to those whose respect they covet. The king sent an *executioner,* a soldier of his guard. Bloody tyrants have executioners ready to obey their most cruel and unrighteous decrees.

5. The effect of this is, that Herod's wicked court is *all in triumph,* the head is made a present of *to the damsel,* and by her to her *mother, v.* 28. And John Baptist's sacred college is *all in tears.* When they *heard of it,* they came, and took up the neglected *corpse,* and *laid it in a tomb.*

Verses 30–44

I. The return to Christ of the apostles whom he had sent forth (*v.* 7). They *gathered themselves together,* and came to Jesus to give him an account of what they had done. They *told him all things,* both *what they had done, and what they had taught.* Ministers are accountable both for what they *do,* and for what they *teach.* Let them not either *do* anything, or *teach* anything, but what they are willing should be related and repeated to the Lord Jesus.

II. The tender care Christ took for their repose, after the fatigue they had (*v.* 31); *He said unto them, Come ye yourselves apart into a desert place, and rest awhile.* It should seem that John's disciples came to Christ with the mournful tidings of their master's death, much about the same time that his own disciples came to him. Christ takes cognizance of the *frights* of some, and the *toils* of others, of his disciples, and provides suitable relief for both, rest for those that are tired, and refuge for those that are terrified. With what kindness and compassion doth Christ say to them, *Come, and rest!* The most active servants of Christ cannot be always upon the stretch of business, but have bodies that require some relaxation, some breathing-time. And the Lord is for the body, considers its frame, and not only allows it time for rest, but puts it in mind of resting. Those that work diligently and faithfully, may cheerfully retire to rest. 1. Christ calls them to come *themselves apart;* if they must *rest,* they must be *alone.* 2. He invites them not to some pleasant country-seat, but *into a desert place.* No wonder that he who had but a ship for his preaching place, had but a desert for his resting place. 3. He calls them only to rest *awhile;* only to *get breath,* and then to go to work again. 4. The reason given for this, is, *for there were many coming and going, and they had no leisure so much as to eat.* Let but proper time be set, and kept for everything, and a great deal of work may be done with a great deal of ease; but if people be continually coming and going, a little work will not be done without a deal of trouble. 5. They withdrew, accordingly, *by ship, v.* 32. Going *by water* was much less toilsome than going *by land* would have been. They went away *privately.* The most public persons cannot but wish to be private sometimes.

III. The diligence of the people to follow him. They are not blamed for it, nor bid to go back, but bid welcome. A failure in good manners will easily be excused in those who follow Christ, if it be but made up in a fulness of good affections. They followed him *out of the cities,* quitted their houses and shops, their callings and affairs. They followed him *afoot,* though he was gone by sea. They stuck to him. They *ran* afoot, and made such haste, that they *out-went* the disciples. Nay they followed him, though it was into a *desert place.* The presence of Christ will turn a wilderness into a paradise.

IV. The entertainment Christ gave them (*v.* 34); *When he saw much people,* instead of being moved with displeasure, he was *moved with compassion toward them,* because *they were as sheep having no shepherd,* they seemed to be well-inclined, and manageable as sheep. But they had *no shepherd,* none to lead and guide them in the right way, and therefore, in compassion to them, he not only *healed their sick,* as it is in Matthew, but he *taught them many things.*

V. The provision he made for them all; all his hearers he generously made his guests, and treated them at a *splendid* entertainment: so it might truly be called, because a *miraculous* one.

1. The disciples moved that they should be *sent home.* When *the day was now far spent* they said, *This is a desert place,* and *much time is now past; send them away to buy bread, v.* 35, 36. This the disciples suggested to Christ; but we do not find that the multitude themselves did. The disciples thought it would be a kindness to them to dismiss them. Willing minds will do more, and hold out longer, in that which is good, than one would expect from them.

2. Christ ordered that they should all be fed (*v.* 37); *Give ye them to eat.* To teach us to be kind to those who are rude to us, he ordered provision to be made for them; that bread which Christ and his disciples took with them into the desert, that they might make a quiet meal of it for themselves, he will have them to partake of. Thus was he given to hospitality. They attended on the spiritual food of his word, and then he took care that they should not want corporal food. The way of duty, as it is the way of safety, so it is the way to supply. Providence, not *tempted,* but duly *trusted,* never yet failed any of God's faithful servants, but has refreshed many with seasonable and surprising relief.

3. The disciples objected against it as impracticable; *Shall we go, and buy two hundred penny-worth of bread, and give them to eat?* Instead of waiting for directions from Christ, they perplex the cause with projects of their own. Christ would let them see their folly in forecasting for themselves, that they might put the greater value upon his provision for them.

4. Christ effected it, to universal satisfaction. They had brought with them *five loaves,* and *two fishes,* and that is the bill of fare. This was but a little for Christ and his disciples, and yet this they must give away. We often find Christ entertained at other people's tables, but here we have him supping a great many at his own charge.

(1) The provision was *ordinary.* Here were no rarities. If we have for necessity, it is no matter though we have not for delicacy and curiosity. The promise to them that fear the Lord, is, that verily they shall be fed; he doth not say, They shall be *feasted.*

(2) The guests were *orderly;* for they *sat down by companies on the green grass* (*v.* 39), they *sat down in ranks by hundreds and by fifties* (*v.* 40), for God is the God of order, and not of confusion.

(3) A blessing was craved upon the meat; *He looked up to heaven, and blessed.* Christ did not call one of his disciples to crave a blessing, but did it himself (*v.* 41); and by virtue of this blessing the bread strangely multiplied, and so did the fishes, for they did *all eat, and were filled,* though they were to the number of *five thousand, v.* 42–44. Christ came into the world, to be the great feeder as well as the great healer; and in him there is enough for all that come to him. None are sent empty away from Christ, but those that come to him full of themselves.

(4) Care was taken of the fragments that remained, with which they filled *twelve baskets.* Though Christ had bread enough at command, he would hereby teach us, not to make waste.

Verses 45–56

I. The dispersing of the assembly; Christ *constrained his disciples* to go before by ship to Bethsaida. The people were loth to scatter. For now that they had got a good supper, they were in no haste to leave him.

II. Christ departed *into a mountain, to pray*. He *prayed*; he was much in prayer; he prayed often, and prayed long. He went *alone*, to pray, to set us an example, and to encourage us in our *secret* addresses to God, he prayed *alone*. A good man is never less alone than when alone with God.

III. The disciples were in distress at sea; *The wind was contrary* (v. 48), so that they *toiled in rowing*. This was a specimen of the hardships they were to expect, when hereafter he should send them abroad to preach the gospel. The church is often like a ship at sea, *tossed with tempests, and not comforted*; we may have Christ for us, and yet wind and tide against us; but it is a comfort to Christ's disciples in a storm, that their Master is in the heavenly mount, interceding for them.

IV. Christ made them a kind visit upon the water. He chose to help them in the most endearing manner possible, and therefore came to them himself.

1. He did not come till the *fourth watch of the night*, not till after three o'clock in the morning; but then he came. If Christ's visits to his people be deferred long, yet at length he will come.

2. He came, walking upon the waters. The sea was now tossed with waves, and yet Christ came, walking upon it. No difficulties can obstruct Christ's gracious appearances for his people. He will either find, or force, a way through the most tempestuous sea, for their deliverance.

3. He *would have passed by them*. Providence, when it is acting designedly and directly for the succour of God's people, yet sometimes seems as if it were *giving them the go-by*. They thought that *he would*, but we may be sure that he would not, *have passed by them*.

4. They were frightened at the sight of him, supposing him to have been an apparition; *They all saw him, and were troubled* (v. 50). We often perplex and frighten ourselves with phantasms, the creatures of our own fancy and imagination.

5. He encouraged them, and silenced their fears, by making himself known to them; *Be of good cheer, it is I; be not afraid*. We know not Christ till he is pleased to reveal himself to us. "*It is I;* I your Master, I your friend." The knowledge of Christ, as he is in himself, and near to us, is enough to make the disciples of Christ cheerful even in a storm, and no longer fearful. Christ's presence with us in a stormy day, is enough to make us of good cheer, though clouds and darkness be round about us. He doth not tell them who he was, they knew his voice, as the sheep know the voice of their own shepherd. When Christ said to those that came to apprehend him by force, *I am he*, they were struck down by it, John xviii. 6. When he saith to those that come to apprehend him by faith, *I am he*, they are raised up by it, and comforted.

6. He *went up to them into the ship*. Let them but have their Master with them, and all is well. And as soon as he was come into the ship, *the wind ceased*. The wind ceased all of a sudden. Though we hear not the command given, yet, if thus the wind cease, and we have the comfort of a calm, say, It is because Christ is in the ship.

7. They were more surprised and astonished at this miracle than did become them, *They were sore amazed in themselves*. But why all this confusion about it? It was because they *considered not the miracle of the loaves*; had they given that its due weight they would not have been so much surprised at this; for his multiplying the bread was as great an instance of his power as his walking on the water. It is for want of a right understanding of Christ's former works, that we are transported at the thought of

his present works, as if there never were the like before.

V. When they came to the land of Gennesaret the people bid them very welcome; *The men of that place knew Jesus* (v. 53), and knew what mighty works he did wherever he came, they knew likewise that he used to stay but a little while at a place, and therefore, *They ran through that whole region round about*, with all possible expedition, and *began to carry about in beds those that were sick*, there was no danger of their getting cold when they hoped to get a cure, v. 55. Let him go where he would, he was crowded with patients, they *laid the sick in the streets*, to be in his way, and begged leave for them to touch if it were but *the border of his garment, and as many as touched, were made whole*. We do not find that they were desirous to be taught by him, only to be healed. If ministers could now cure people's bodily diseases, what multitudes would attend them! But it is sad to think how much more concerned the most of men are about their bodies than about their souls.

CHAPTER 7

I. Christ's dispute with the scribes and Pharisees about eating meat with unwashen hands (ver. 1–13); and the needful instructions he gave to the people on that occasion, ver. 14–23. II. His curing of the woman of Canaan's daughter, ver. 24–30. III. The relief of a man that was deaf, and had an impediment in his speech, ver. 31–37.

Verses 1–23

One great design of Christ's coming, was, to set aside the ceremonial law which God made, and to put an end to it; to make way for which he begins with the ceremonial law which men had made, and added to the law of God's making. These Pharisees and scribes with whom he had this argument, are said to *come from Jerusalem* down to Galilee—fourscore or a hundred miles, to pick quarrels with our Saviour there.

I. What the tradition of the elders was: by it all were enjoined to *wash their hands* before meat; a cleanly custom, and no harm in it; but they placed religion in it. They interposed their authority, and commanded all to do it upon pain of excommunication; this they kept up as a *tradition of the elders*.

We have here an account of the practice of the Pharisees and *all the Jews*, v. 3, 4. 1. They *washed their hands oft*. 2. They particularly washed before they *ate bread*; for that was the rule; they must be sure to wash before they ate the bread on which they begged a blessing, else he was thought to be defiled. 3. They took special care, when they came in *from the markets*, to wash their hands. It signifies any place of concourse where there were people of all sorts, and, it might be supposed, some heathen or Jews under a ceremonial pollution, by coming near to whom they thought themselves polluted. They say, The rule of the rabbis was—That, if they washed their hands well in the morning, the first thing they did, it would serve for all day, provided they kept alone; but, if they went into company, they must not, at their return, either eat or pray till they had washed their hands. 4. They added to this the washing of *cups* and *pots*, and *brazen vessels*, nay, and the very *tables* on which they ate their meat. There were many cases in which, by the law of Moses, washings were appointed; but they *added* to them, and enforced the observation of their own impositions as much as of God's institutions.

II. What the practice of Christ's disciples was; they knew what the law was, and the common usage; but they would not be bound up by it: they ate bread with *defiled*, that is, with *unwashen hands*, v. 2. The disciples knew (it is probable) that the Pharisees had their eye upon them, and yet they would not humour them by a compliance with their traditions, and ate bread with *unwashen* hands; and herein *their righteousness*, however it might seem to come short, did really *exceed, that of the scribes and Pharisees,* Matt. v. 20.

III. The offence which the Pharisees took at this; They *found fault* (v. 3). They brought a complaint against them to their Master, expecting that he should check them, and order them to conform. They do not ask, Why do not thy disciples *do as we do?* But, Why do not they *walk according to the tradition of the elders?* v. 5.

IV. Christ's vindication of them; in which,

1. He argues with the Pharisees concerning the authority by which this ceremony was imposed; but this he did not speak of publicly to the multitude (as appears by his *calling the people* to him, v. 14) lest he should have seemed to stir them up to faction; but addressed it as a reproof to the persons concerned.

(1) He reproves them for their hypocrisy in pretending to honour God, when really they had no such design in their religious observances (v. 6, 7); *They honour me with their lips,* they pretend it is for the glory of God, but really *their heart is far from God.* They rested in the outside of all their religious exercises, and their hearts were not right with God in them, and this was worshipping God in vain; for neither was he pleased with such sham-devotions, nor were they profited by them.

(2) He reproves them for placing religion in the inventions and injunctions of their elders and rulers; They *taught for doctrines the traditions of men.* They were enforcing the canons of their church, and judged of people's being Jews or no, according as they did, or did not, conform to them, without any consideration had, whether they lived in obedience to God's laws or no. Instead of providing the substance, they presumptuously added to the ceremony, and were very nice in *washing pots and cups;* and observe, he adds, *Many other suchlike things ye do,* v. 8. Superstition is an endless thing.

(3) He reproves them for *laying aside the commandment of God,* and overlooking that, and in their discipline conniving at the violation of that, as if that were no longer of force, v. 8. It is the mischief of impositions, that too often they who are zealous for them, have little zeal for the essential duties of religion. Nay, they *rejected the commandment of God,* v. 9. Ye *do fairly disannul and abolish the commandment of God;* and even *by* your traditions *make the word of God of no effect,* v. 13. They were entrusted to expound the law, and to enforce it; and, under pretence of using that power, they violated the law, and dissolved the bonds of it.

This he gives them a particular instance of, and a flagrant one—God commanded children to *honour their parents,* not only by the law of Moses, but by the law of nature; and whoso *revileth,* or *speaketh evil of,* father or mother, *let him die the death,* v. 10. It is the duty of children, if their parents be poor, to relieve them, according to their ability; and if those children are worthy to die, that curse their parents, much more those that starve them. But they will find him out an expedient by which he may be discharged from this obligation, v. 11. If his parents be in want, and he has wherewithal to help them, but has no mind to do it, let him swear by the *Corban* that is, by the *gold of the temple,* and the *gift upon the altar,* that his parents shall not be profited by him, and, if they ask anything of him, let him tell them this, and it is enough; as if by the obligation of this wicked vow he had discharged himself from the obligation. He concludes, *And many such things do ye.* Where will men stop, when once they have made the word of God give way

to their tradition? These eager imposers of such ceremonies, at first only *made light* of God's commandments *in comparison* with their traditions, but afterward *made void* God's commandments, if they stood *in competition* with them.

2. He instructs the people concerning the principles upon which this ceremony was grounded. It was requisite that this part of his discourse should be public, he therefore *called the people unto him* (v. 14), and bid them *hear and understand.* It is not enough for the common people to *hear,* but they must *understand* what they hear. Corrupt customs are best cured by rectifying corrupt notions.

Now that which he goes about to set them right in, is, what the pollution is, which we are in danger of being damaged by, v. 15. (1) Not by the *meat we eat,* that is but from without, and goes through a man. But, (2) It is by the breaking out of the corruption that is in our hearts. We become odious in the sight of God by that which *comes out* of us; our wicked thoughts and affections, words and actions, these defile us, and these only. Our care must therefore be, to *wash our heart from wickedness.*

3. He gives his disciples, in private, an explication of the instructions he gave the people. They *asked him concerning the parable* (v. 17). (1) He reproves their dulness; *"Are ye so without understanding also?"* He doth not expect they should understand everything; "But are ye so weak as not to understand *this?"* (2) He explains this truth to them, that they might *perceive* it, and then they would *believe* it. [1] That that which we eat and drink cannot defile us, so as to call for any religious washing; it *goes into the stomach,* and what there may be in it that is defiling is voided and gone. But, [2] It is that which *comes out from* the heart, the corrupt heart, that defiles us. What comes out from the *mind* of a man is that which defiles him before God, and calls for a religious washing (v. 21); *From within, out of the heart of men,* thence that which defiles proceeds, thence comes all the mischief. As a corrupt fountain sends forth corrupt streams, so doth a corrupt heart. Divers particulars are specified, as in Matthew; we had one there, which is not here, and that is, *false witness-bearing;* but *seven* are mentioned here, to be added to those we had there. *First, Covetousnesses,* for it is plural; *immoderate desires* of more of the wealth of the world, and the gratifications of sense, and still more, still crying, Give, give. *Secondly, Wickedness,* malice, hatred, and ill-will, a desire to do mischief, and a delight in mischief done. *Thirdly, Deceit;* which is wickedness covered and disguised, that it may be the more securely and effectually committed. *Fourthly, Lasciviousness;* that filthiness and foolish talking which the apostle condemns; the eye full of adultery, and all wanton dalliances. *Fifthly,* The *evil eye;* the envious eye, and the covetous eye, grudging others the good we give them, or grieving at the good they do or enjoy. *Sixthly, Pride;* exalting ourselves in our own conceit above others, and looking down with scorn and contempt upon others. *Seventhly, Foolishness;* imprudence, inconsideration; some understand it especially of vainglorious boasting. *Ill-thinking* is put first, as that which is the spring of our own *com*missions, and *un*thinking put last, as that which is the spring of all our *om*issions. Of all these he concludes (v. 23), 1. That they *come from within,* from the corrupt nature. 2. That they *defile the man;* they render a man unfit for communion with God, they bring a stain upon the conscience.

Verses 24–30

I. How *humbly* Christ was pleased to *conceal himself.* Never man was so cried up as he was in Galilee, and therefore, to teach us not to be fond of popular applause, he arose from thence, and went into the borders of Tyre and Sidon, where he was little known; and there he entered *into a private house*, and he *would have no man to know it*. As there is a time to *appear*, so there is a time to *retire*. Or, he would not be known, because he was among Gentiles, to whom he would not be so forward to show himself as to the tribes of Israel.

II. How *graciously* he was pleased to *manifest himself*, notwithstanding. Though he would not carry a harvest of miraculous cures into those parts, he let fall this one which we have here an account of. *He could not be hid;* for, though a candle may be put under a bushel, the sun cannot. Christ was too well known to be long *hid*, anywhere.

1. The application made to him by a poor woman in distress and trouble. She was a Gentile, a Greek, *an alien to the covenant of promise*; she was by extraction a Syrophenician; she had a *daughter*, a *young* daughter, that was possessed *with the devil*. Her address was, (1) Very humble, pressing, and importunate; *She heard of him*, and *came, and fell at his feet*. Christ never put any from him, that fell at his feet, which a poor trembling soul may do, that has not boldness and confidence to throw itself into his arms. (2) It was very particular; she tells him what she wanted. She besought him that he would *cast forth the devil out of her daughter*, v. 26. The greatest blessing we can ask of Christ for our children is, that he would break the power of Satan, that is, the power of sin, in their souls.

2. The discouragement he gave to this address (v. 27); He said unto her, "*Let the children first be filled;* let the Jews have all the miracles wrought for them, that they have occasion for, and let not that which was intended for them, be thrown to those who are not of God's family, and who are as *dogs in comparison of them*, and who are as *dogs* to them, snarling at them, and ready to worry them." Where Christ knows the faith of poor supplicants to be strong, he sometimes delights to try it, and put it to the stretch. But his saying, *Let the children first be filled*, intimates that there was mercy in reserve for the Gentiles, and not far off; for the Jews began already to be surfeited with the gospel of Christ, and some of them had desired him to *depart out of their coasts*. The children begin to play with their meat, and their leavings would be a feast for the Gentiles.

3. The turn she gave to this word of Christ, which made against her, and her improvement of it, to make it for her, v. 28. She said, "*Yes, Lord*, I own it is true that the *children's bread* ought not to be cast to the dogs, but they were never denied the *crumbs*, and they are allowed a place *under the table*, that they may be ready to receive them. I ask not for a *loaf*, no, nor for a *morsel*, only for a *crumb*; do not refuse me that." This she speaks, magnifying the abundance of miraculous cures with which she heard the Jews were feasted, in comparison with which a single cure was but as a crumb. Perhaps she had heard of Christ's feeding five thousand lately at once, after which, there could not but be some crumbs left for the dogs.

4. The grant Christ thereupon made of her request. For *this saying*, *Go thy way*, thou shalt have what thou camest for, *the devil is gone out of thy daughter*, v. 29. This encourages us to *pray* and not to *faint*, not doubting but to prevail at last. Christ's saying that it *was done*, did it effectually, for (v. 30) she *came to her house*, depending upon the word of Christ, and so she *found it*, the *devil was gone out*. Christ can conquer Satan at a distance. She found her daughter not in any toss or agitation, but very quietly *laid on the bed*, and reposing herself; waiting for her mother's return, to rejoice with her, that she was so *finely well*.

Verses 31–37

Our Lord Jesus seldom stayed long in a place. When he had cured the woman of Canaan's daughter, he had done what he had to do in that place, and returned *to the sea of Galilee*. He did not come directly thither, but fetched a compass *through the midst of the coasts of Decapolis*, which lay mostly on the other side Jordan.

Now here we have the story of a cure that Christ wrought, which is not recorded by any other of the evangelists; it is of one that was *deaf* and *dumb*.

I. His case was sad, *v. 32*. There were those that brought to him one that was *deaf*; and he had an *impediment in his speech*. He was perfectly unfit for conversation, and deprived both of the pleasure and of the profit of it; he had not the satisfaction either of hearing other people talk, or of telling his own mind. Let us take occasion from hence to give thanks to God for preserving to us the sense of hearing, especially that we may be capable of hearing the word of God; and the faculty of speech, especially that we may be capable of speaking God's praises. They that brought this poor man to Christ, besought him that he would *put his hand upon him*. It is not said, They besought him to *cure him*, but to *put his hand upon him*, to take cognizance of his case, and put forth his power to do to him as he pleased.

II. His cure was solemn, and some of the circumstances of it were singular.

1. Christ *took him aside from the multitude*, v. 33. Ordinarily, he wrought his miracles publicly, but this he did privately. Let us learn of Christ to do good where no eye sees, but his.

2. He used more significant actions, in the doing of this cure, than usual. (1) He *put his fingers into his ears*. (2) He spit upon his own finger, and then *touched his tongue*, and so loosened that with which his tongue was tied; these were no causes that could in the least contribute to his cure, but only signs for the encouraging of his faith and theirs that brought him.

3. He *looked up to heaven*. Thus he signified that it was by a divine power. He also hereby directed his patient who could *see*, though he could not *hear*, to look up to heaven for relief.

4. He sighed; not as if he found any difficulty in working this miracle; thus he expressed his pity for the miseries of human life, and his sympathy with the afflicted in their afflictions, as one that was himself *touched with the feeling of their infirmities*.

5. He said, *Ephphatha*; that is, *Be opened*. *Be opened*, served both parts of the cure; "Let the *ears* be *opened*, let the *lips* be *opened*, let him hear and speak freely," and the effect was answerable (*v. 35*); *Straightway his ears were opened, and the string of his tongue was loosed*. Happy he who, as soon as he had his hearing and speech, had the blessed Jesus so near him, to converse with.

Now this cure was, (1) A proof of Christ's being the Messiah; for it was foretold that by his power the *ears of the deaf should be unstopped*, and the *tongue of the dumb* should be made to *sing*, Isa. xxxv. 5, 6. (2) It was a specimen of the operations of his gospel upon the minds of men. The great command of the gospel, and grace of Christ to poor sinners, is *Ephphatha—Be opened*. He *opens the heart*, and thereby opens the ear to receive the word of God, and opens the mouth in prayer and praises.

6. He ordered it to be kept very private, but it was made very public. It was his humility, that he *charged them they should tell no man*, v. 36. Most men will proclaim their own goodness, or, at least, desire that others should proclaim it. We should take pleasure in doing good, but not in its being known. It was their zeal, that they published it, before Christ would have had it published. But they

meant honestly, and therefore it is to be reckoned rather an act of indiscretion than an act of disobedience, *v.* 36. But they that told it, and they that heard it, were *beyond measure astonished.* This was said by everybody, it was the common verdict, *He hath done all things well* (*v.* 37). They are ready to witness for him, not only that he has done no evil, but that he has done a great deal of good, and has done it well, and all gratis, *without money and without price.* He *maketh both the deaf to hear, and the dumb to speak;* and that is *well,* and therefore *they* are inexcusable who will speak ill of him.

CHAPTER 8

I. Christ's miraculous feeding of four thousand with seven loaves and a few small fishes, ver. 1–9. II. His refusing to give the Pharisees a sign from heaven, ver. 10–13. III. His cautioning his disciples to take heed of the leaven of Pharisaism and Herodianism, ver. 14–21. IV. His giving of sight to a blind man at Bethsaida, ver. 22–26. V. Peter's confession of him, ver. 27–30. VI. The notice he gave his disciples of his own approaching sufferings (ver. 31–33), and the warning he gave them to prepare for sufferings likewise, ver. 34–38.

Verses 1–9

We had the story of a miracle very like this before, in this gospel (*ch.* vi. 35), and of this same miracle (Matt. xv. 32).

1. Our Lord Jesus was greatly followed; *The multitude was very great* (*v.* 1); the common people, who had more honesty, and therefore more true wisdom, than their leaders, kept up their high thoughts of him. With such Christ conversed, and was familiar; this encouraged the meanest to come to him for life and grace.

2. *They were with him three days, and had nothing to eat;* that was hard service. Never let the Pharisee say, that *Christ's disciples fast not.* Yet they continued with Christ, and did not speak of leaving him till he spoke of dismissing them. True zeal makes nothing of hardships in the way of duty. It was an old saying among the Puritans, *Brown bread and the gospel are good fare.*

3. Christ said, *I have compassion on the multitude.* Whom the proud Pharisees looked upon with disdain, the humble Jesus looked upon with pity and tenderness. But that which he chiefly considers, is, *They have been with me three days, and have nothing to eat.* Whatever losses we sustain, or hardships we go through, for Christ's sake, and in love to him, he will take care that they shall be made up to us one way or other. Observe with what sympathy Christ saith (*v.* 3), *If I send them away fasting to their own houses, they will faint by the way.* He considered that *many of them came from afar,* and had a great way home. When we see *multitudes* attending upon the word preached, it is comfortable to think that Christ knows whence they all come, though we do not. Christ would by no means have them go home fasting, for it is not his manner to send those *empty* away from him, that in a right manner attend on him.

4. The doubts of Christians are sometimes made to work for the magnifying of the power of Christ. The disciples could not imagine whence so many men should be *satisfied with bread* here in this wilderness, *v.* 4. That therefore must needs be *wonderful,* which the disciples looked upon as *impossible.*

5. Christ's time to act for the relief of his people, is, when things are brought to the last extremity. That he might not invite them to follow him for the *loaves,* he did not supply them but when they were utterly reduced, and then he *sent them away.*

6. The bounty of Christ is inexhaustible. Christ *repeated* this miracle. His favours are renewed, as our wants and necessities are. In the former miracle, Christ used all the bread he had, which was *five loaves,* and fed all the guests he had, which were *five thousand.*

He might have said, "If five loaves would feed five thousand, four may feed four thousand"; he took all the seven loaves, and fed with them the four thousand; for he would teach us to use what we have, and make the best of that which is.

7. In our Father's house *there is bread enough, and to spare.* Those need not fear wanting, that have Christ to live upon.

8. It is good for those that follow Christ, *to keep together.* Christ fed them all. Christ's sheep must abide by the flock, and verily they shall be fed.

Verses 10–21

Still Christ is upon motion; now he visits the parts of Dalmanutha. Meeting with occasions of dispute, there, and not with opportunities of doing good, he *entered into the ship again* (*v.* 13), and came back.

I. How he refused to gratify the Pharisees, who challenged him to give them a *sign from heaven.* They *came forth* on purpose to *question with him,* that they might ensnare him.

1. They demanded of him a *sign from heaven,* as if the signs he gave them on earth were not sufficient. They demanded this sign, *tempting him;* not in hopes that he would give it them, that they might imagine themselves to have a pretence for their infidelity.

2. He denied them their demand; He *sighed deeply in his spirit, v.* 12. He *groaned* (so some), being grieved for the *hardness of their hearts.* It troubles him, that sinners should thus stand in their own light, and put a bar in their own door. He expostulates with them upon this demand; "*Why doth this generation seek after a sign;* this generation, that is so unworthy to have the gospel brought to it, and to have any sign accompanying it; *this generation,* that has had such plenty of sensible and merciful signs given them in the cure of their sick? What an absurdity is it for them to desire a sign!" (2) He refuses to answer their demand; *Verily, I say unto you, there shall no sign be given to this generation.* He denied them, and then *left them,* as men not fit to be talked with; if they will not be convinced, they shall not; leave them to their strong delusions.

II. How he warned his disciples against the leaven of the Pharisees and of Herod. Observe here,

1. What the caution was (*v.* 15); "*Take heed, beware,* lest ye partake of the *leaven of the Pharisees.*" Matthew adds, *and of the Sadducees;* Mark adds, *and of Herod.* The leaven of both was the same; they were unsatisfied with the signs they had, and would have others of their own devising; "Take heed of *this leaven*" (saith Christ), "be convinced by the miracles ye have seen."

2. How they misunderstood this caution. It seems, at their putting to sea this time, they had *forgotten to take bread,* and *had not in their ship more than one loaf, v.* 14. They *reasoned among themselves,* what should be the meaning of this caution, and concluded "*It is because we have no bread.*" They *reasoned it,* they *disputed* about it; one said, "It was owing to you"; and the other said, "It was owing to you, that we are so ill provided for this voyage." Thus distrust of God makes Christ's disciples quarrel among themselves.

3. The reproof Christ gave them for their uneasiness in this matter. The reproof is given with some warmth, for he knew their hearts, and knew they needed to be thus soundly chidden; "*Perceive ye not yet, neither understand? Have ye your hearts yet hardened? Having eyes, see ye not? Having ears, hear ye not?* How strangely stupid and senseless are ye! *Do ye not remember when I broke the five loaves among the five thousand,* and soon after, the *seven loaves among the four thousand?* Do ye not remember how many baskets full ye took up of the fragments?*" Yes, they did remember, and could tell that they took

up *twelve* baskets full one time, and *seven* another; "Why, then," saith he, "*how is it that ye do not understand?* As if he that multiplied *five* loaves, and *seven*, could not multiply one." They seemed to suspect that that one was not matter enough to work upon. As if it were not all alike to the Lord, to save by many or few, and as easy to make one loaf to feed five thousand as five. It was therefore proper to remind them, not only of the sufficiency, but of the overplus, of the former meals. The experiences we have had of God's goodness to us in the way of duty, greatly aggravate our distrust of him. Our *not understanding* of the true intent and meaning of God's favours to us, is equivalent to our not remembering of them. We are *therefore* overwhelmed with present cares and distrusts, because we do not *understand*, and remember, what we have known and seen of the power and goodness of our Lord Jesus. When we thus *forget the works of God*, and distrust him, we should chide ourselves severely for it, as Christ doth his disciples here.

Verses 22–26

This cure is related only by this evangelist.

I. Here is a *blind man* brought to Christ by his friends, with a desire that he would *touch him, v.* 22. Here appears the faith of those that brought him; but the man himself showed not that earnestness for, or expectation of, a cure that other blind men did. If those that are spiritually blind, do not pray for themselves, yet let their friends and relations pray for them, that Christ would be pleased to *touch them.*

II. Here is Christ *leading* this blind man, *v.* 23. He did not bid his friends lead him, he himself *took him by the hand, and led him.* Never had poor blind man such a Leader. He led him *out of the town.* Had he herein only designed privacy, he might have led him into a house, into an inner chamber, and have cured him there. Perhaps Christ took the blind man *out of the town,* that he might have a larger prospect in the *open fields,* to try his sight with, than he could have in the *close streets.*

III. Here is the cure of the blind man. In this cure we may observe, 1. That Christ used a *sign*; he *spat on his eyes,* and *put his hand upon him.* He could have cured him, as he did others, with a word, but thus he was pleased to assist his faith which was very weak, and to help him against his *unbelief.* 2. That the cure was wrought *gradually,* which was not usual in Christ's miracles. He *asked him if he saw aught, v.* 23. And he *looked up*; and he said, *I see men as trees walking;* he could not distinguish men from trees, otherwise than that he could discern them to move. He had some glimmerings of sight, and betwixt him and the sky could perceive a man erect like a tree. 3. It was soon completed; Christ never doeth *his work* by the halves. He *put his hands again upon his eyes,* to disperse the remaining darkness, and then bade him look up again, and he *saw every man clearly, v.* 25. Now Christ took this way, (1) Because he would not *tie himself to a method.* He did not cure by *rote.* Providence gains the same end in different ways, that men may attend its motions with an *implicit faith.* (2) Because it should be to the patient *according to his faith*; and perhaps this man's faith was at first very weak, but afterward gathered strength, and accordingly his cure was. (3) Thus Christ would show how, and in what method, those are healed by his grace, who by nature are *spiritually blind*; at first, their knowledge is confused, they see *men as trees walking*; but like the light of the morning, it *shines more and more to the perfect day,* and then they *see all things clearly.*

IV. The directions Christ gave the man he had cured, not to *tell it to any in the town* of Bethsaida, nor so much as to *go into the town.* Christ doth not forbid him to tell it to others, but he must not tell it to *any in the town.* Slighting Christ's favours is forfeiting them; and Christ will make those know the worth of their privileges by the want of them, that would not know them otherwise. They will not see, and therefore shall not see.

Verses 27–38

We have read a great deal of the doctrine Christ preached, and the miracles he wrought. It is now time for us to pause a little, and to consider what these things mean. What shall we think of them? Is the record of these things designed only for an amusement, or to furnish us with matter for discourse? No, certainly *these things are written, that we may believe that Jesus is the Christ the Son of God* (John xx. 31). Three things we are here taught to infer from the miracles Christ wrought.

I. They *prove* that he is the Son of God, and Saviour of the world. This his disciples, who were the eye-witnesses of those works, here profess their belief of.

1. Christ enquired of them: *Who do men say that I am? v.* 27. Though it is a small thing for us to be judged of men, yet it may sometimes do us good to know what people say of us, not that we may seek our own glory, but that we may hear of our faults.

2. The account they gave him, was such as plainly intimated the *high opinion* the people had of him. Though they came short of the truth, yet they were convinced by his miracles that he was an extraordinary person, with a divine commission. None of the people said that he was a Deceiver, but some said that *he was John Baptist,* others *Elias,* others *one of the prophets, v.* 28. All agreed that he was one *risen from the dead.*

3. The account they gave him of their own sentiments concerning him. *But whom say ye that I am?* To this they have an answer ready, *Thou art the Christ,* the Messiah often promised, and long expected, *v.* 29. This they knew, and must shortly publish and maintain; but for the present they must keep it secret (*v.* 30), till the proof of it was completed, and they were completely qualified to maintain it.

II. These miracles of Christ *take off the offence of the cross,* and assure us that Christ was, in it, not conquered, but a Conqueror. Now that the disciples are convinced that Jesus is the Christ, they may bear to hear of his sufferings, *v.* 31.

1. Christ *taught* his disciples that he must *suffer many things,* Though they had got over the vulgar error of the Messiah's being a temporal Prince, yet still they retained it, so far as to expect that he would *shortly restore the kingdom to Israel.* Christ here gives them a prospect of the contrary, that he must be *rejected of the elders, and the chief priests,* and the scribes; that, instead of being crowned, *he must be killed,* he must be crucified, and *after three days he must rise again* to a heavenly life, and to be *no more in this world.* This he spoke openly (*v.* 32). He said it freely and plainly, and did not wrap it up in ambiguous expressions. He spoke it cheerfully and without any terror, and would have them to hear it so: he spoke that saying *boldly,* as one that not only knew he *must* suffer and die, but made it his own act and deed.

2. Peter opposed it; *He took him, and began to rebuke him.* Here Peter showed more love than discretion, a zeal for Christ, and his safety, but not according to knowledge. He took hold of him, as it were to stop and hinder him, took him in his arms, and embraced him (so some understand it); or he took him aside privately, and *began to rebuke* him. This was not the language of the least authority, but

of the greatest affection. Our Lord Jesus allowed his disciples to be free with him, but Peter here took too great a liberty.

3. Christ checked him for his opposition (*v.* 33); He *turned about*, and *looked on his disciples*, to see if the rest of them were of the same mind, and he said, *Get thee behind me, Satan*. Peter little thought to have had such a sharp rebuke, but perhaps expected as much commendation now for his love as he had lately had for his faith. Christ knows what manner of spirit we are of, when we ourselves do not. (1) Peter spoke as one that did not rightly understand the purposes and counsels of God. The most potent enemies could not overpower him whom diseases and deaths, whom winds and waves and devils themselves, were forced to obey and yield to. He looked upon his death only as a *martyrdom* which he thought might be prevented. He knew not that the thing was necessary for the glory of God, the destruction of Satan, and the salvation of man, that the Captain of our salvation must be *made perfect through sufferings*. The wisdom of man is perfect folly, when it pretends to give measures to the divine counsels. The cross of Christ was to some a stumbling-block, and to others foolishness. (2) Peter spoke as one that did not rightly understand the nature of Christ's kingdom; he took it to be *temporal* and *human*, whereas it is *spiritual* and *divine. Thou savourest not the things that are of God, but those that are of men.* Peter seemed to mind more the things that relate to the lower world, than those which relate to the upper world, and the life to come. Minding the *things of men* more than the *things of God*, and his glory and kingdom, is a very great sin, and the root of much sin, and very common among Christ's disciples. *Thou art not wise* (so it may be read) *in the things of God*, but in the *things of men.* It seems policy to shun trouble, but if with that we shun duty it will be folly in the end.

III. These miracles of Christ should engage us all to *follow him*, whatever it cost us, not only as they were *confirmations* of his *mission*, but as they were *explications* of his *design*; plainly intimating that by his Spirit he would do that for our blind, deaf, lame, leprous, diseased, possessed *souls*, which he did for the *bodies* of those many who in those distresses applied themselves to him. This is written, that we may believe that he is the great Physician of souls, and may become his patients. He *called all the people to him*, to hear this. This is that which all are concerned to know, and consider, if they expect Christ should heal *their souls*.

1. They must not be *indulgent* of the *ease of the body*; for (*v.* 34), "*Whosoever will come after me, let him deny himself*, and live a life of self-denial; let him not pretend to be his own physician, and let him *take up his cross*, and thus let him continue to *follow me.*" Those that will be Christ's patients must attend on him, converse with him, receive instruction and reproof from him, and must resolve they will never forsake him.

2. They must not be *solicitous*, no, not for *the life of the body*, when they cannot keep it without quitting Christ, *v.* 35. Are we invited by the words and works of Christ to follow him? Let us sit down, and count the cost, whether we can prefer our advantages by Christ before life itself. When the devil is drawing away disciples and servants after him, he conceals the worst of it. What there is of trouble and danger in the service of Christ, he tells us of it before, and is not afraid that we should know the worst; because the *advantages* of his service abundantly suffice to *balance the discouragements*, if we will but impartially set the one over against the other.

(1) We must *not dread the loss of our lives in the cause of Christ* (v 35); *Whosoever will save his life*,

by declining Christ, or by disowning him after he has in profession come to Christ, he shall *lose it*, and all his hopes of eternal life; such a bad bargain will he make for himself. But whosoever *shall lose his life*, shall be truly willing to lose it, when he cannot keep it without denying Christ, he shall *save it*, he shall be an unspeakable gainer. It is looked upon to be some kind of recompence to those who lose their lives in the service of their prince and country, to have their memories honoured and their families provided for; but what is that to the recompence which Christ makes in eternal life to all that die for him?

(2) We must *dread the loss of our souls* (v. 36, 37); *For what shall it profit a man, if he should gain the whole world*, by denying Christ, and *lose his own soul?* "True it is," said Bishop Hooper, the night before he suffered martyrdom, "that *life is sweet*, and *death is bitter*, but *eternal death is more bitter*, and *eternal life is more sweet.*" The gain of all the world *in sin*, is not sufficient to countervail the ruin of the soul *by sin.*

What that is that men do, to *save their lives*, and *gain the world*, he tells us (v. 38), *Whosoever therefore shall be ashamed of me, and of my words, in his adulterous and sinful generation, of him shall the Son of man be ashamed.* The disadvantage that the cause of Christ labours under in this world, is, that it is to be owned and professed in an *adulterous and sinful generation*. Some ages, some places, are more especially sinful, as that was in which Christ lived; in such a *generation* the cause of Christ is opposed and run down, and those that own it, are exposed to reproach and contempt, and everywhere ridiculed and *spoken against*. There are many, who, though they cannot but own that the cause of Christ is a righteous cause, are *ashamed* of it. They are *ashamed* of their relation to Christ. They cannot bear to be frowned upon and despised, and therefore throw off their profession. There is a day coming, when the cause of Christ will appear as bright and illustrious as now it appears mean and contemptible. *They* shall not share with him in his glory then, that were not willing to share with him in his disgrace now.

CHAPTER 9

I. Christ's transfiguration upon the mount, ver. 1–13. II. His casting the devil out of a child, when the disciples could not do it, ver. 14–29. III. His prediction of his own sufferings and death, ver. 30–32. IV. The check he gave to his disciples for disputing who should be greatest (ver. 33–37); and to John for rebuking one who cast out devils in Christ's name, and did not follow with them, ver. 38–41. V. Christ's discourse with his disciples of the danger of offending one of his little ones (ver. 42), and of indulging that in ourselves, which is an offence and an occasion of sin to us (ver. 43–50).

Verses 1–13

I. A prediction of Christ's kingdom now near approaching, *v.* 1. That which is foretold is, 1. That the *kingdom of God* would *come*, and would come so as to be *seen*. 2. That it would come *with power*, and bear down the opposition that was given to it. 3. That it would come while some now *present were alive*; There are some *standing here, that shall not taste of death*, till they *see* it.

II. A specimen of that kingdom in the transfiguration of Christ, *six days* after Christ spoke that prediction. He gives them this glimpse of his glory, to show that his sufferings were voluntary, and to prevent the *offence of the cross*.

1. It was on the top of a *high mountain*. Tradition saith, It was on the top of Mount Tabor that Christ was transfigured.

2. The witnesses of it were Peter, James, and John; these were the *three* that were to *bear record on earth*, answering to Moses, Elias, and the *voice from heaven*.

As there are distinguishing favours which are given to disciples and not to the world, so there are to some disciples and not to others. All the saints are a people *near to Christ*, but some lie in his bosom. James was the first of all the twelve that died for Christ, and John survived them all, to be the last eye-witness of this glory; he bore record (John i. 14); *We saw his glory:* and so did Peter, 2 Pet. i. 16–18.

3. The manner of it; *He was transfigured before them.* See what a great change human bodies are capable of, when God is pleased to put an honour upon them. His *raiment became shining, exceeding white as snow*, beyond what the fuller's art could do toward whitening it.

4. His companions in this glory were Moses and Elias (*v.* 4); They appeared *talking with him*, to *testify* to him. Moses and Elias lived at a great distance of time one from another, but that breaks no squares in heaven, where the *first shall be last, and the last first*, that is, all one in Christ.

5. The great delight that the disciples took in seeing this sight, and hearing this discourse, is expressed by Peter; *He said, Master, it is good for us to be here, v.* 5. Though Christ was transfigured, and was in discourse with Moses and Elias, yet he gave Peter leave to speak to him. Many, when they are in their greatness, oblige their friends to keep their distance; but even to the glorified Jesus true believers have access with boldness. Even in this heavenly discourse there was room for Peter to put in a word; and this is it, "*Lord, it is good to be here, for let us make tabernacles.*" Gracious souls reckon it *good to be* in communion with Christ, good to be *in the mount* with him. If it is good to be with Christ transfigured only upon a mountain with Moses and Elias, how good will it be to be with Christ glorified in heaven with all the saints! But observe, While Peter was for staying here, he forgot what need there was of the presence of Christ among the people. At this very time, the other disciples wanted them greatly, *v.* 14. When it is well with us, we are apt to be mindless of others. It was a weakness in Peter to prefer private communion with God before public usefulness. Peter talked of making three distinct tabernacles for Moses, Elias, and Christ, which was not well-contrived. One tabernacle will hold them all; they dwell together in unity. But whatever was incongruous in what he said, he may be excused, for they were all *sore afraid*; and he, for his part, *wist not what to say* (*v.* 6).

6. The voice that came from heaven, was an attestation of Christ's mediatorship, *v.* 7. *There was a cloud that overshadowed them.* Peter had talked of making tabernacles for Christ and his friends; but *while he yet spoke* God created his tabernacle *not made with hands.* Now out of this cloud it was said, *This is my beloved Son, hear him.* God owns him, and accepts him, as his beloved Son.

7. The vision disappeared (*v.* 8); *Suddenly when they had looked round about* all was gone, *they saw no man any more.* Jesus only remained with them, and he not transfigured, but as he used to be. Christ doth not leave the soul, when extraordinary joys and comforts leave it. Christ's disciples have, and shall have, his ordinary presence with them always, even to the end of the world. Let us thank God for *daily bread*, and not expect a continual feast on this side heaven.

8. The discourse between Christ and his disciples, as they came down from the mount.

(1) He charged them to keep this matter very private, till he was *risen from the dead, v.* 9. He, being now in a state of humiliation, would have nothing publicly taken notice of, that might seem disagreeable to such a state. This enjoining of silence to the disciples, would likewise be of use to them,

to prevent their boasting. It is a mortification to a man, to be tied up from telling of his advancements, and may help to hide pride from him.

(2) The disciples were at a loss what the *rising from the dead* should mean. Here is another thing that embarrasses them (*v.* 11). *Why say the Scribes, Elias must first come?* But Elias was gone, and Moses too. The scribes taught them to expect the person of Elias, whereas the prophecy intended one *in the spirit and power of Elias.*

(3) Christ gave them a key to the prophecy concerning Elias (*v.* 12, 13); "It is indeed prophesied that Elias will come, and will *restore all things.* It is also prophesied of the *Son of man* that he must *suffer many things*, and be *set at nought.* Though the scribes do not tell you so, the *scriptures* do, and you have as much reason to expect that as the other. But as to Elias, I tell you *he is come*; and if you consider a little, you will understand whom I mean, it is one to whom they have *done whatsoever they listed.*" The true Elias, as well as the true Messiah promised, is come, and we are to look for *no other.* He is come, and hath been, and done, according as was *written of him.*

Verses 14–29

We have here the story of Christ's casting the devil out of a child.

I. Christ's return to his disciples, and the perplexity he found them in. Christ's glory above does not make him forget the concerns of his church below, *v.* 14. And he came very seasonably, when the disciples were embarrassed and run a-ground. A child possessed with a devil was brought to them, and they could not cast out the devil, whereupon the scribes triumphed as if the day were their own. He *found the scribes questioning with them.* Christ's return was very welcome, no doubt, to the disciples, and *unwelcome* to the scribes. But particular notice is taken of its being very surprising to the people. When they *beheld him* coming to them again, they were *greatly amazed*; and *running to him*, they saluted him. It is easy to give a reason why they should be glad to see him; but why were they *amazed, greatly amazed*, when they beheld him? Probably, there might remain something unusual in his countenance. Instead of seeming *fatigued*, there appeared a wonderful briskness and sprightliness in his looks, which *amazed* them.

II. The case which perplexed the disciples, brought before him. He asked the scribes, "*What question ye with them?* What is the quarrel now?" The scribes made no answer, for they were confounded at his presence; the disciples made none, for they were comforted, and now left all to him. But the father of the child opened the case, *v.* 17, 18. 1. His child is possessed with a *dumb spirit*, and in his fits *is speechless*; wheresoever the fit takes him, the spirit *tears* him, throws him into such violent convulsions as almost pull him to pieces; and, *he foams* at the mouth, and *gnashes with his teeth.* Though the fits go off presently, yet they leave him so weak, that he *pines away*, is worn to a skeleton. 2. The disciples cannot give him any relief; "I desired they would *cast him out*, but *they could not*; and therefore thou couldest never have come in better time; *Master, I have brought him to thee.*"

III. The rebuke he gave to them all (*v.* 19); *O faithless generation, how long shall I be with you? How long shall I suffer you?* Them he calls a *faithless generation*, and speaks as one weary of *being with* them, and of *bearing with* them. "How long shall I be among these *faithless people*, and suffer them?"

IV. The deplorable condition that the child was actually in, when he was brought to Christ, and the doleful representation which the father made of it.

When the child saw Christ, he fell into a fit; *The spirit straightway tore him*, as if the devil would set Christ at defiance, and hoped to be too hard for him too, and to keep possession in spite of him. The child *fell* on the *ground, and wallowed foaming*. Christ asked, *How long since this came to him?* And, it seems, the disease was of long standing; it came to him *of a child* (v. 21), which made the case the more sad, and the cure the more difficult.

V. The pressing instances which the father of the child makes with Christ for a cure (v. 22); *Oft-times it hath cast him into the fire, and into the waters, to destroy him.* But *if thou canst do anything, have compassion on us, and help us.* The leper was confident of Christ's power, but put an *if* upon his will (Matt. viii. 2); *If thou wilt, thou canst.* This poor man referred himself to his goodwill, but put an *if* upon his power.

VI. The answer Christ gave to his address (v. 23); *If thou canst believe, all things are possible to him that believeth.* He tacitly checks the weakness of his faith. The sufferer put it upon Christ's power, *If thou canst do anything*; but Christ turns it upon him, and puts him upon questioning his own faith, and will have him impute the disappointment to the want of that; *If thou canst believe.* He graciously encourages the strength of his desire; "*All things are possible to him that believes* the almighty power of God, to which all things are possible." In dealing with Christ, very much is put upon our believing, and very much promised to it. *Canst thou believe?* Darest thou believe? *If thou canst believe*, it is possible that thy hard heart may be softened, thy spiritual diseases may be cured; and that, weak as thou art, thou mayest be able to hold out to the end.

VII. The *profession of faith* which the poor man made hereupon (v. 24); He cried out, "*Lord, I believe;* my cure shall not be prevented by the want of faith; *Lord, I believe.*" He adds a prayer for grace to enable him more firmly to rely upon Christ to save; *Help thou my unbelief.* Those that complain of unbelief, must look up to Christ for grace to *help* them against it, *and his grace* shall be *sufficient for them.* "*Help mine unbelief*; help out what is wanting in my faith with thy grace, the strength of which is perfected in our weakness."

VIII. The cure of the child. Christ *saw the people come running together*, and therefore kept them in suspense no longer, but *rebuked the foul spirit.* 1. What the charge was which Christ gave to this unclean spirit; "*Thou dumb and deaf spirit come out of him* immediately, and *enter no more into him.* Let him not only be brought out of this fit, but let his fits never return." Whom Christ cures, he cures effectually. Satan may *go out himself*, and yet recover possession; but if Christ *cast* him out, he will *keep* him out. 2. How the unclean spirit took it; he grew yet more outrageous, he *cried*, and *rent him sore*, gave him such a twitch at parting, that he was *as one dead. Many said, He is dead.* 3. How the child was perfectly restored (v. 27); *Jesus took him by the hand, took fast hold of him*, and strongly bore him up, and he arose and recovered, and all was well.

IX. The reason he gave to the disciples why they could not cast out this devil. They *enquired* of him privately *why they could not*, and he told them (v. 29), *This kind can come forth by nothing* but *prayer and fasting.* The disciples must not think to do their work always with a like ease; but Christ can do that with a word's speaking, which they must prevail for the doing of by *prayer and fasting.*

Verses 30–40

I. Christ foretells his own approaching sufferings. He *passed through Galilee*, and *would not that any man should know it* (v. 30). The time of his sufferings drew nigh, and therefore he was willing to converse only with his disciples, to prepare them for the approaching trial, v. 31. He said to them, *The Son of man is delivered into the hands of men* (v. 31), and *they shall kill him.* That *men*, who have *reason*, and should have *love*, that they should be thus spiteful to the *Son of man*, who came to redeem and save them, is unaccountable. But still it is observable that when Christ spoke of his death, he always spoke of his resurrection. But they *understood not that saying*, v. 32. The words were plain enough, but they could not be reconciled to the thing, and they were *afraid to ask him.* Many remain ignorant because they are ashamed to enquire.

II. He rebukes his disciples for magnifying themselves. When he came to Capernaum, he privately asked his disciples what it was that they *disputed among themselves by the way*, v. 33. As our other discourses among ourselves by the way, so especially our disputes, will be all called over again, and we shall be called to an account about them. Of all disputes, Christ will be sure to reckon with his disciples for their disputes about precedency and superiority: that was the subject of the debate here, *who should be the greatest*, v. 34. Nothing could be more contrary to the two great laws of Christ's kingdom, which are *humility* and *love*, than *desiring* preferment in the world, and *disputing* about it. This ill temper he took all occasions to check. They were willing to *cover this fault* (v. 34); they *held their peace.* As they would not *ask* (v. 32), because they were ashamed to own their ignorance, so here they would not *answer* because they were ashamed to own their pride. He was willing to *amend this fault* in them, and therefore *sat down*, that he might have a solemn and full discourse with them. He *called the twelve to him*, and told them, 1. That ambition, instead of gaining them preferment in his kingdom, would but postpone their preferment; *If any man desire* and aim *to be first*, he shall *be last*; he that exalteth himself, shall be abased. 2. That there is no preferment to be had under him, but an opportunity for, and an obligation to, so much the more labour and condescension. 3. That those who are most humble and self-denying, do most resemble Christ, and shall be most tenderly owned by him. *He took a child in his arms.* "Look you," saith he; "*whosoever shall receive* one like this child, *receives me.* Those of a humble, meek, mild disposition are such as I will own and countenance, and so will my *Father* too, for he who thus *receiveth me, receiveth him that sent me.*"

III. While they are striving which of them should be greatest, they will not allow those who are not in communion with them to be anything.

1. The account which John gave him, of the restraint they had laid upon one from making use of the name of Christ, because he was not of their society. *Master*, saith John, *we saw one casting out devils in thy name, but he followeth not us*, v. 38. (1) It was strange that one who was not a professed disciple and follower of Christ, should yet have power to *cast out devils*, in his name, for that seemed to be peculiar to those whom he called. And why might not he receive that power from Christ, whose *Spirit*, like the wind, *blows where it listeth*, without such an outward call as the apostles had? And perhaps there were many more such. Christ's grace is not tied to the visible church. (2) It was strange that one who *cast out devils* in the name of Christ, did not join himself to the apostles, and follow Christ with them, but should continue to act in *separation* from them. I know of nothing that could hinder him from following them, unless because he was loth to leave all to follow them. The thing did not look well, and therefore the disciples *forbade him* to make use of Christ's name as they did, unless he would follow

him as they did. Thus apt are we to imagine that those do not follow Christ at all, who do not follow him *with us*, and that those do nothing well, who do not just as we do. But the *Lord knows them that are his*, however they are dispersed.

2. The rebuke he gave to them for this (*v.* 39); *Jesus said, "Forbid him not."* That which is good, and doeth good, must not be prohibited, though there may be some defect or irregularity in the manner of doing it. If Christ be preached, Paul therein doth, and will rejoice, though he be eclipsed by it, Phil. i. 18. Two reasons Christ gives why such should not be forbidden. (1) Because we cannot suppose that any man who makes use of Christ's name in working miracles, should blaspheme his name, as the scribes and Pharisees did. (2) Because those that differed in communion, while they agreed to fight against Satan under the banner of Christ, ought to look upon one another as on the same side. *He that is not against us is on our part.* As to the great controversy between Christ and Beelzebub, he had said, *He that is not with me is against me*, Matt. xii. 30. He that will not own Christ, owns Satan. But as to those that own Christ, that follow him, though *not with us*, we must reckon that they are not against us, and therefore are *on our part*.

Verses 41–50

I. Christ promiseth a reward to all those that are any way kind to his disciples (*v.* 41); *"Whosoever shall give you a cup of water because you belong to Christ, he shall not lose his reward."* It is the honour and happiness of Christians, that they *belong to Christ*; they wear his livery as retainers to his family; nay, they are more nearly related, they are *members of his body*. The relieving of Christ's poor in their distresses, is a good deed; he accepts it, and will reward it. What kindness is done to Christ's poor, must be done them *for his sake*, and *because they belong to him*; for that is it that sanctifies the kindness. This is a reason why we must not discountenance and discourage those who are serving the interests of Christ's kingdom, though they are not in everything of our mind and way. If Christ reckons *kindnesses to us* services to *him*, we ought to reckon *services to him* kindnesses to us, and to encourage them, though done by those that follow not with us.

II. He threatens those that *offend* his *little ones*, *v.* 42. Whosoever shall grieve any true Christians, though they be of the weakest, shall either restrain them from doing good, or draw them in to commit sin, it were *better for him that a millstone were hanged about his neck, and he were cast into the sea*: his punishment will be very great.

III. He warns all his followers to take heed of ruining their own souls. This charity must begin at home; if we must take heed of doing anything to hinder others from good, much more careful must we be to avoid everything that will take us off from our duty, or lead us to sin; and that which doth so we must part with, though it be ever so dear to us. Observe,

1. The case supposed, that our own *hand*, or *eye*, or *foot*, *offends us*; that the impure *corruption* we indulge is as dear to us as an eye or a hand. Suppose the beloved is become a sin, or the sin a beloved. Suppose we must part with it, or part with Christ and a good conscience.

2. The duty prescribed in that case; *Pluck out the eye, cut off the hand and foot*, mortify the darling lust, crucify it. Let the idols that have been *delectable* things, be cast away as *detestable* things. It is necessary that the part which is gangrened should be taken off for the preservation of the whole. Self must be denied, that it may not be destroyed.

3. The necessity of doing this. The flesh must be mortified, that we may *enter into life* (*v.* 43, 45), into the kingdom of God, *v.* 47. Though, by abandoning sin, we may, for the present, feel ourselves as if we were *halt* and *maimed*, yet it is for *life*; and all that men have, they will give for their lives. These *halts* and *maims* will be the *marks of the Lord Jesus*, will be in that kingdom *scars of honour*.

4. The danger of not doing this. The matter is brought to this issue, that either sin must die, or we must die. If we be *ruled* by sin, we shall inevitably be *ruined* by it. With what an emphasis of terror are those words repeated three times here, *Where their worm dieth not, and the fire is not quenched!* The reflections and reproaches of the sinner's own conscience are the *worm that dieth not*. The wrath of God fastening upon a guilty and polluted conscience, is the *fire* that is *not quenched*; for it is the wrath of the living God, into whose hands it is a fearful thing to fall. Philo saith, The punishment of the wicked is *to live for ever dying*.

The last two verses are somewhat difficult, and interpreters agree not in the sense of them; *for every-one* shall be *salted with fire, and every sacrifice shall be salted with salt. Therefore have salt in yourselves*. It was appointed by the law of Moses, that every sacrifice should be *salted with salt*, not to *preserve* it but because it was the food of God's table. The nature of man, being *corrupt*, and as such being called *flesh*, some way or other must be *salted*, in order to its being a sacrifice to God. Our chief concern is, to present ourselves *living sacrifices* to the grace of God (Rom. xii. 1), and, in order to our acceptableness, we must be *salted with salt*. We must have in our souls a savour of grace. Those that have the salt of grace, must make it appear that they have it; that they *have salt in themselves*, a living principle of grace in their hearts, which works out all corrupt dispositions. Our *speech* must be *always with grace seasoned with* this salt, that no *corrupt communication* may *proceed out of our mouth*, but we may loathe it as much as we would to put putrid meat into our mouths. As this gracious salt will keep our own consciences void of offence, so it will keep our conversation with others so, that we may not offend any of Christ's little ones. We must not only have this salt of grace, but we must always retain the relish and savour of it; for if this *salt lose its saltness, wherewith will ye season it?* They who will not be *salted with the salt* of divine grace, will be *salted with fire*. The pleasures they have lived in, *shall eat their flesh, as it were fire*. Now since this will certainly be the doom of those that do not crucify the flesh with its affections and lusts, let us, knowing this *terror of the Lord*, be *persuaded* to do it.

CHAPTER 10

I. Christ's dispute with the Pharisees concerning divorce, ver. 1–12. II. The kind entertainment he gave to the little children that were brought to him to be blessed, ver. 13–16. III. His trial of the rich man that enquired what he must do to get to heaven, ver. 17–22. IV. His discourse with his disciples, upon that occasion (v. 23–27), and the advantage of being impoverished for his sake, ver. 28–31. V. The repeated notice of his sufferings and death approaching, ver. 32–34. VI. The counsel he gave to James and John, to think of suffering with him, ver. 15–45. VII. The cure of Bartimæus, ver. 46–52.

Verses 1–12

Our Lord Jesus did not continue long in a place, for the whole land of Canaan was his parish, and therefore he would visit every part of it. Here we have him in the *coasts* of Judæa, eastward, as we found him, not long since, in the utmost borders westward, near Tyre and Sidon. Thus was his circuit like that of the sun, from whose light and heat nothing is hid.

I. *Resorted to* by the *people*, v. 1. They came to him *again*, and, *as he was wont, he taught them again.* He did *as he was wont.* In Matthew it is said, *He healed them*; here it is said, *He taught them.* His *teaching* was *healing* to poor souls. He *taught them again.* Such is the fulness of the Christian doctrine, that there is still more to be learned; and such our forgetfulness, that we need to be reminded of what we do know.

II. *Disputed with* by the Pharisees.

1. A question they started concerning divorce (v. 2); *Is it lawful for a man to put away his wife?* They proposed it, *tempting him,* seeking an occasion against him, which side soever he should take of the question. Ministers must stand upon their guard, lest, under pretence of being advised with, they be ensnared.

2. Christ's reply to them with a question (v. 3); *What did Moses command you?* This he asked them, to testify his respect to the law of Moses, and to show that he came not to destroy it.

3. The fair account they gave of the law of Moses, expressly concerning divorce, v. 4. Christ asked, *What did Moses command you?* They own that Moses only *suffered,* or *permitted,* a man to write his wife a *bill of divorce,* and to put *her away,* Deut. xxiv. 1.

4. The answer that Christ gave to their question, in which he abides by the doctrine he had formerly laid down in this case (Matt. v. 32), *That whosoever puts away his wife, except for fornication, causeth her to commit adultery.* He here shows,

(1) That the reason why Moses, in his *law,* permitted divorce, was only *for the hardness of their hearts* (v. 5).

(2) That the account which Moses, in this *history,* gives of the institution of marriage, affords such a reason against divorce, as amounts to a prohibition of it.

Moses tells us, God made man *male and female, one* male, and *one* female; so that *Adam could not* put away his wife and take another. The law was, That a man must *leave his father and mother, and cleave to his wife* (v. 7); which intimates not only the nearness of the relation, but the perpetuity of it. The result of the relation is, that, though they are *two,* yet they are *one,* they are *one flesh,* v. 8. The union between them is a sacred thing that must not be violated. God himself has *joined them together*; he has in wisdom and goodness appointed them who are thus joined together, to live together in love till death parts them. Marriage is not an invention of men, but a divine institution. The bond which God himself has tied, is not to be lightly untied.

5. Christ's discourse with his disciples, in private, about this matter, v. 10-12. It was an advantage to them, that they had opportunity of personal converse with Christ, not only about gospel mysteries, but about moral duties. No more is here related of this private conference, than the law Christ laid down in this case—That it is adultery for a man to put away his wife, and marry another; it is adultery *against the wife* he puts away, v. 11. He adds, *If a woman shall put away her husband,* and *be married to another,* she *commits adultery* (v. 12). Wisdom and grace, holiness and love, reigning in the heart, will make those commands easy which to the carnal mind may be as a heavy yoke.

Verses 13–16

It is looked upon as the indication of a kind and tender disposition to take notice of little children, and this was remarkable in our Lord Jesus, which is an encouragement not only to little children to

apply themselves to Christ, but to grown people, who are conscious to themselves of weakness and childishness, and of being helpless and useless, like little children.

I Little children brought to Christ, v. 13. It doth not appear that they needed any bodily *cure,* nor were they capable of being *taught.* They that had the care of them were mostly concerned *about their souls,* their better part. They believed that Christ's blessing would do their souls good; and therefore to him they brought them, that he might *touch* them, knowing that he could reach their hearts, when nothing their parents could say to them, or do for them, would reach them. We may present our children to Christ, now that he is in heaven, and therein we may act faith upon the fulness and extent of his grace, and the promise *to us and to our children.*

II. The *discouragement* which the disciples gave to the bringing of children to Christ; *They rebuked them that brought them.*

III. The *encouragement* Christ gave to it. He took it very ill that his disciples should keep them off; *When he saw it, he was much displeased,* v. 14. Christ is very angry with his own disciples, if they discountenance any in coming to him themselves, or in bringing their children to him. He ordered that they should be *brought to him*; suffer *little children* to *come to me.* Little children are welcome betimes to the throne of grace with their Hosannas. He came to set up the *kingdom of God* among men, and took this occasion to declare that that kingdom admitted *little children* to be the subjects of it. There must be something of the temper and disposition of little children found in all that Christ will own and bless. We must *receive the kingdom of God as little children* (v. 15); that is, we must stand affected to Christ and his grace as little children do to their parents, nurses, and teachers. We must be *inquisitive.* as children, must learn as children and in learning must *believe.* The mind of a child is white paper, you may write upon it what you will; such must our minds be to the pen of the blessed Spirit. Children are under government; so must we be. Little children depend upon their parents' wisdom and care, are carried in their arms, and take what they provide for them; and thus must we receive the *kingdom of God,* with a humble resignation of ourselves to Jesus Christ, and an easy dependence upon him. He received the children, and gave them what was desired (v. 16); *He took them up in his arms, put his hands upon them,* and *blessed them.* They begged he would touch them, but he did more. He *took them in his arms. He shall gather the lambs in his arms, and carry them in his bosom.* Time was, when Christ himself was taken up in old Simeon's arms, Luke ii. 28. And now he took up these children, not complaining of the burthen, but pleased with it. He *put his hands upon them.* He *blessed* them. Our children are happy, if they have but the *Mediator's blessing* for their portion.

Verses 17–31

I. Here is a *hopeful meeting* between Christ and a *young man*; such he is said to be (Matt. xix. 20, 22), and a *ruler* (Luke xviii. 18).

1. He came *running* to Christ; he laid aside the gravity and grandeur of a ruler; he manifested his earnestness and importunity; he *ran* as one *in haste.* He had now an opportunity of consulting this great Prophet, and he would not let slip the opportunity.

2. He came to him when he was *in the way,* in the midst of company.

3. He *kneeled to him,* in token of the great value and veneration he had for him, and his earnest desire to be taught by him. He *bowed the knee,* as one that meant to *bow the soul* to him.

4. His address to him was serious and weighty; *Good Master, what shall I do, that I may inherit eternal life?* He thinks it a thing possible, that he may *inherit eternal life*, looking upon it not only as set before us, but as offered to us. Most men enquire for good to be *had* in this world, he asks for *good to be done* in this world; not, Who will make us to *see good?* But, "Who will make us to *do good?*" He enquires for *happiness* in the way of *duty*. Now this was, (1) A very serious question. *Then* there begins to be some hope of people, when they begin to enquire solicitously, what they shall do to get to heaven. (2) It was proposed to a right person, one that was every way fit to answer it, being himself *the Way, the Truth,* and *the Life;* who came *from heaven* on purpose, first to make, and then to make known, the way *to heaven.* It is peculiar to the Christian religion, both to show eternal life, and to show the way to it. (3) It was proposed with a good design—to be instructed. We find this same question put by a lawyer (Luke x. 25), with a bad design; he *tempted him, saying, Master, what shall I do?* It is not so much the good *words* as the good *intention* of them that Christ looks at.

5. Christ encouraged this address by *assisting his faith, v.* 18. He called him *good Master;* Christ would have him mean thereby, that he looked upon him to be *God,* since there is none good but *one,* that is *God.* Our English word *God* doubtless hath affinity with *good.* Further, he directed his practice (*v.* 19); *Keep the commandments.* He mentions the six commandments of the second table, which prescribe our duty to our neighbour. The fifth commandment is here put last, as that which should especially be remembered and observed, to keep us to all the rest.

6. The young man bid fair for heaven, having been free from any open gross violations of the divine commands. *Master, all these have I observed from my youth.* He thought he had, and his neighbours thought so too. He that could say he was free from scandalous sin, went further than many in the way to eternal life.

7. Christ had a kindness for him; *Jesus, beholding him, loved him, v.* 21. Christ particularly *loves* to see young people, and rich people, *asking the way to heaven, with their faces thitherward.*

II. Here is a *sorrowful parting* between Christ and this young man.

1. Christ gave him a command of trial. Has he indeed his heart upon it? Bring him to the touchstone. Can he find in his heart to *part with his riches* for the service of Christ? Let him know the worst now; if he will not come up to these terms, let him quit his pretensions; as good at first as at last. "*Sell whatsoever thou hast;* and be a *father to the poor.*" Every man, according to his ability, must relieve the poor. Worldly wealth is given us as a *talent,* to be used and employed for the glory of our great Master in the world, who hath so ordered it, that the poor we should have always with us as his receivers. Can he find in his heart to go through the hardest, costliest services he may be called to as a disciple of Christ, and depend upon him for a recompence *in heaven?* Doth he really believe there is a treasure in heaven sufficient to make up all he can leave, or lose, or lay out, for Christ? Is he willing to deal with Christ *upon trust?* Can he give him credit for all he is worth; and be willing to bear a present cross, in expectation of a future crown?

2. Upon this he flew off (*v.* 22); *He was sad at that saying;* was sorry that he could not be a follower of Christ upon any easier terms, that he could not *lay hold* on eternal life, and *keep hold* of his temporal possessions too. But since he could not come up to the terms of discipleship, he was so fair as not to pretend to it; *He went away grieved.* Here appeared

the truth of that (Matt. vi. 24), *Ye cannot serve God and mammon;* while he held to mammon he did in effect *despise* Christ. He bids for what he has a mind for in the market, yet goes away grieved, and leaves it, because he cannot have it at his own price.

III. Here is Christ's discourse with his disciples. We are tempted to wish that Christ had *mollified* that saying and taken off the hardness of it: but he knew all men's hearts; he would not court him to be his follower, because he was a *rich man* and a ruler; but, if he will go, let him go. Christ will keep no man against his will.

1. The difficulty of the salvation of those who have an abundance of this world; because there are few who have a *deal to leave,* that can be *persuaded to leave it* for Christ.

(1) Christ asserts this here; *He looked about* upon his *disciples; How hardly shall they who have riches enter into the kingdom of God! v.* 23. They have many temptations to grapple with, and many difficulties to get over, which lie not in the way of poor people. But he explains himself, *v.* 24, where he calls the disciples *children,* because as such they should be *taught* by him. Whereas he had said, *How hardly will those who have riches get to heaven;* here he tells them, that the danger arose not so much from their *having* riches as from their *trusting to them.* They that have such a value as this for the wealth of the world, will never be brought to put a right value upon Christ and his grace. They that *have* ever so much riches, but do not *trust in them,* have got over the difficulty, and can easily part with them for Christ: but they that have ever so little, if they set their hearts upon that little, it will keep them from Christ. He enforces this assertion with, *v.* 25, *It is easier for a camel to go through the eye of a needle, than for a rich man to enter into the kingdom of God.* [1] Some imagine there might be some wicket-gate, or door, to Jerusalem, commonly known by the name of *the needle's eye,* for its straitness, through which a camel could not be got, unless he were unloaded. So a rich man cannot get to heaven, unless he be willing to part with the burthen of his worldly wealth, and stoop to the duties of a humble religion. [2] Others suggest that the word we translate a *camel,* sometimes signifies a *cable-rope.* A rich man, compared with the poor, is as a cable to a single thread, and it will not go through the *needle's eye,* unless it be untwisted. So the rich man must be loosed and disentangled from his riches, that thread by thread he may be got through the eye of the needle, otherwise he is good for nothing but to cast anchor in the earth.

(2) This truth was very surprising to the disciples; *They were astonished at his words, v.* 24. They were *astonished out of measure, and said among themselves, Who then can be saved?* They knew what abundance of promises there were, in the Old Testament, of temporal good things; they knew likewise that they who are rich have so much the larger opportunities of doing good, and therefore were amazed to hear that it should be so hard for rich people to go to heaven.

(3) Christ reconciled them to it, by referring it to the almighty power of God, to help even rich people over the difficulties that lie in the way of their salvation (*v.* 27); *He looked upon them: "With men it is impossible,* but the grace of God can do it, for *with him all things are possible."*

2. The greatness of the salvation of those that have but a little of this world, and leave it for Christ. This he speaks of, upon occasion of Peter's mentioning what he and the rest of the disciples had left to follow him; *Behold* (saith he), *we have left all to follow thee, v.* 28. "You have *done well,*" saith Christ, "you

shall be abundantly recompensed, and not only you shall be *reimbursed*, who have left but a little, but those that have ever so much, though it were so much as this young man had." (1) The loss is supposed to be very great; he specifies, Worldly wealth; *houses* are here put first, and *lands* last: a man may quit his *house*, which should be for his habitation, and his *land*, which should be for his maintenance; or his dear relations. *Father and mother, wife and children, brethren and sisters.* Without these the world would be a wilderness; yet, when we must either forsake these or Christ, we must remember that we stand in nearer relation to Christ than we do to any creature. The greatest trial of a good man's constancy is, when his love to Christ comes to stand in competition with a love that is lawful, nay, that is his duty. It is easy to such a one to forsake a *lust* for Christ; but to forsake a *father*, a *brother*, a *wife*, for Christ, that is, to forsake those whom he knows he must love, is hard. And yet he must do so, rather than deny or disown Christ. It is not the *suffering*, but the *cause*, that makes the *martyr.* And therefore, (2) The advantage will be great. *They shall receive a hundred-fold in this time, houses, and brethren, and sisters.* He shall have abundance of comfort while he lives, sufficient to make up all his losses. Suffering Christians shall have a *hundred-fold* in the comforts of the Spirit sweetening their creature comforts. It is added here in Mark, *with persecutions.* Even when they are gainers by Christ, let them still expect to be sufferers for him. They shall have *eternal life in the world to come.* If they receive a hundred-fold in this world, one would think they should not be encouraged to expect any more. Yet, as if that were a small matter, they shall have *life eternal* into the bargain. But because they talked so much, and really more than became them, of *leaving all* for Christ, he tells them, though they were *first called*, that there should be disciples called after them, that should be preferred before them. Then the *first* were *last*, and the last *first.*

Verses 32–45

I. Christ's prediction of his own sufferings.

1. See here how bold he was; when they were going up to Jerusalem, *Jesus went before them, v.* 32. Now that the time was at hand, more than ever, he *pressed forward. Jesus went before them, and they were amazed.* They began now to consider what imminent danger they ran themselves into, when they went to Jerusalem; and they were ready to tremble at the thought of it. To hearten them, therefore, Christ *went before them.* When we see ourselves entering upon sufferings, it is encouraging to see our Master go before us. Or, *He went before them,* and *therefore* they were *amazed*; they admired to see with what cheerfulness and alacrity he went on. Christ's courage and constancy are, and will be, the wonder of all his disciples.

2. See here how timorous and faint-hearted his disciples were; *As they followed, they were afraid.* Their Master's courage should have put spirit into them.

3. See here what method he took to silence their fears. He did not go about to make the matter better than it was, but told them *again* the *things that should happen to him.* He knew the worst of it, and therefore went on thus boldly, and he will let them know the worst of it. Come, *be not afraid.* He *shall rise again*; the issue of his sufferings will be glorious to himself, and advantageous to all that are his, *v.* 33, 34. The method and particulars of Christ's sufferings are more largely foretold here than in any other of the predictions. Christ had a perfect foresight, not only of his own death, but of all the aggravating circumstances of it; and yet he thus went forth to meet it.

II. The check he gave to two of his disciples for their ambitious request. This story is much the same here as we had it Matt. xx. 20. Only there they are said to have made their request by their mother, here they are said to make it themselves. As, on the one hand, there are some that do not *use*, so, on the other hand, there are some that *abuse*, the great encouragements Christ has given us in prayer. It was a culpable presumption in these disciples to make such a boundless demand upon their Master; *We would that thou shouldst do for us whatsoever we shall desire.* We had much better leave it to him to do for us what he sees fit, and he will do more than we can desire, Eph. iii. 20. We must be cautious how we make general promises. *What would ye that I should do for you?* He would have them go on with their suit, that they might be made ashamed of it. James and John conclude, If Christ *rise again*, he must be a king, and if he be a king, his apostles must be peers, and one of these would willingly be the *first peer of the realm*, and the other next him. To *be good* should be more our care than to *look great*, or to have the pre-eminence. Our weakness and short-sightedness appear as much in our prayers as in any thing. It is folly to *prescribe* to God, and wisdom to *subscribe.* It is the will of Christ that we should prepare for sufferings, and leave it to him to recompense us for them. Our care must be, that we may have wisdom and grace to know how to suffer with him, and then we may trust him to provide in the best manner how we shall reign with him.

III. The check he gave to the rest of the disciples, for their uneasiness at it. *They began to be much displeased*, to have indignation about James and John, *v.* 41. They were angry at them for affecting precedency, because each of them hoped to have it himself. So these discovered their own ambition, in their displeasure at the ambition of James and John; and Christ took this occasion to warn them against it, *v.* 42–44. He *called them to him* in a familiar way, to give them an example of condescension. He shows them,

1. That dominion was generally *abused in the world* (*v.* 42); *They that seem to rule over the* Gentiles, *they exercise lordship over them*, that is all they study and aim at. Their care is, what they shall get by their subjects to support their own pomp and grandeur, not what they shall do for them.

2. That therefore it ought not to be *admitted into the church;* "*It shall not so be among you;* those that shall be put under your charge, must be as sheep under the charge of the *shepherd*, who is to tend them and feed them, and be a servant to them, not as horses under the command of the driver, that works them and beats them, and gets his pennyworths out of them. He that affects to be great and chief, *he shall be servant of all.* He that would be *truly* great and chief, he must lay out himself to do good to all. Those not only shall be most *honoured* hereafter, but are most *honourable* now, who are most useful." To convince them of this, he sets before them his own example (*v.* 45). He takes upon him *the form of a servant*, comes not to be *ministered to*, and waited upon, but *to minister.* He becomes *obedient to death*, for he *gives his life a ransom for many.*

Verses 46–52

This passage of story agrees with that in Matt. xx. 29, &c. Only that there we were told of *two* blind men; here, and* Luke xviii. 35, only of *one*: but if there were *two*, there was *one.* This one is named here; he was called *Bartimæus*, that is, the *son of Timæus.*

I. This blind man sat *begging.* Those who are disabled to get a livelihood by their own labour, are the most proper objects of charity; and particular care ought to be taken of them.

II. He cried out; *Have mercy on me, O Lord, thou Son of David.* Misery is the object of mercy.

III. Christ encouraged him, for he *stood still, and commanded him to be called.* We must never reckon it a hindrance to us in our way, to *stand still,* when it is to do a good work. Those about him, who had discouraged him at first, perhaps were now the persons that signified to him the gracious call of Christ; *"Be of good comfort, rise, he calls thee."* The gracious invitations Christ gives us to come to him, are great encouragements to our hope, that we shall have what we come for.

IV. The poor man, hereupon, *cast away his* loose upper *garment,* and came to Jesus (*v.* 50); he cast away everything that might be in danger of throwing him down, or might any way hinder him. Those who would come to Jesus must cast away the garment of their own sufficiency, and the sin that, like long garments, doth *most easily beset them,* Heb. xii. 1.

V. The particular favour he begged, was, that his *eyes might be opened;* that so he might be able to work for his living, and might be no longer burthensome to others.

VI. This favour he received; his eyes were opened (*v.* 52). *"Thy faith hath made thee whole;* not thy importunity, but *thy faith,* setting Christ on work, or rather Christ setting thy faith on work." Those supplies are most comfortable, that are fetched in by our faith. When he had *received his sight,* he *followed Jesus by the way.* By this he made it appear that he was thoroughly cured, that he no more needed one to lead him. When he had his sight, he made this use of it. It is not enough to *come to Christ* for spiritual healing, but, when we are healed, we must continue to follow him. Those that have spiritual eye-sight, see that beauty in Christ, that will effectually draw them to *run after him.*

CHAPTER 11

We are now come to the Passion-Week, and the great occurrences of that week. I. Christ's riding in triumph into Jerusalem, ver. 1–11. II. His cursing the barren fig-tree, ver. 12–14. III. His driving those out of the temple that turned it into an exchange, ver. 15–19. IV. His discourse with his disciples on occasion of the withering of the fig-tree he cursed, ver. 20–26. V. His reply to those who questioned his authority, ver. 27–33.

Verses 1–11

We have here the story of the public entry Christ made into Jerusalem. And he came into town thus remarkably, 1. To show that he was not afraid of the power and malice of his enemies in Jerusalem. He did not steal into the city *incognito,* as one that durst not show his face. 2. To show that he was not cast down or disquieted at the thoughts of his approaching sufferings. He came, not only publicly, but cheerfully.

I. The *outside* of this triumph was very *mean;* he rode upon an ass's *colt.* This *colt* was borrowed too. Christ went upon the water in a *borrowed* boat, ate the passover in a *borrowed* chamber, was buried in a *borrowed* sepulchre, and here rode on *borrowed* ass. Let not Christians scorn to be beholden one to another, and, when need is, to go borrowing, for our Master did not. He had no rich trappings; they threw their clothes upon the colt, and so he *sat upon him, v.* 7. All the show they could make was, by *spreading their garments in the way,* and *strewing branches of trees in the way* (*v.* 8), as they used to do at the feast of tabernacles. They are instructions to us, not to *mind high things,* but to *condescend to them of low estate.* How ill doth it become Christians to *take state,* when Christ was so far from affecting it!

II. The *inside* of this triumph was very *great.* Christ showed his knowledge of things distant, and his power over the wills of men, when he sent his disciples for the colt, *v.* 1–3. He showed his dominion over the *creatures* in riding on *a colt that was never backed.* Perhaps Christ, in riding the ass's colt, would give a shadow of his power over the spirit of man, who is born as *the wild ass's colt,* Job xi. 12. The colt was brought from a place *where two ways met* (*v.* 4), as if Christ would show that he came to direct those into the right way, who had *two ways* before them, and were in danger of taking the wrong. Christ received the joyful *hosannas* of the people. It was God that put it into the hearts of these people to cry *Hosanna.*

(1) They *welcomed* his *person* (*v.* 9); *Blessed is he that cometh,* so often promised, so long expected; he comes *in the name of the Lord; Blessed be he:* let him have our applauses, and best affections; he is a *blessed* Saviour, and brings blessings to us, and blessed be he that sent him.

(2) They *wished well* to his *interest, v.* 10. They believed that he had a *kingdom,* that it was the kingdom of *their father David;* a kingdom that came *in the name of the Lord. Blessed be this kingdom;* let it come in the power of it. Let it go on *conquering, and to conquer. Hosanna* to this kingdom; all happiness attend it.

Christ, thus *attended,* thus *applauded,* came into the city, and went directly *to the temple.* He came to the temple, and took a view of the present state of it, *v.* 11. He *looked round about upon all things,* but as yet said nothing. He let things be as they were for this night, intending the next morning to apply himself to the necessary reformation. We may be confident that God sees all the wickedness that is in the world, though he do not presently reckon for it, nor cast it out. Christ, having made his remarks upon what he saw in the temple, retired in the evening to a friend's house at Bethany.

Verses 12–26

I. Christ's cursing the fruitless fig-tree. He returned in the morning, at working-time; and so intent was he upon his work, that he went out from Bethany without breakfast, and *was hungry* (*v.* 12). He went to a *fig-tree,* being well *adorned* with green leaves which he hoped to find *enriched* with some fruit. But he *found nothing but leaves;* he hoped to find some fruit, *for* though *the time of* gathering in *figs* was near, it *was not yet.* There was not so much as one fig to be found upon it, though it was so full of leaves. However, Christ was willing to make an example of it, not to the *trees,* but to the *men,* of that generation, and therefore cursed it. He said unto it, *Never let any man eat fruit of thee hereafter for ever, v.* 14. This was intended to be a type and figure of the doom passed upon the Jewish church, to which he came, *seeking fruit, but found none* (Luke xiii. 6, 7). The *disciples heard* what sentence Christ passed on this tree, and took notice of it. Woes from Christ's mouth are to be observed and kept in mind, as well as blessings.

II. His clearing the temple of the market people that frequented it, and of those that made it a thoroughfare. He came, hungry as he was, to Jerusalem, and went straight to the temple, and began to reform those abuses which the day before he had marked out. He came not, as he was falsely accused, to *destroy* the temple, but to purify and refine it.

1. He cast out the *buyers* and *sellers, overthrew the tables of the money-changers* (and threw the money to the ground, the fitter place for it), and threw down the *seats of them that sold doves.* And he did it without opposition; for what he did, was manifested to be right and good, even in the consciences of those that had connived at it, and countenanced it, because they got money by it. It may be some encouragement to zealous reformers, that frequently

the purging out of corruptions, and the correcting of abuses, prove an easier piece of work than was apprehended. Prudent attempts sometimes prove successful beyond expectation.

2. He *would not suffer that any man should carry any vessel through the temple*, v. 16. The Jews owned that it was one of the instances of honour due to the temple, not to make the mountain of the house, or the court of the Gentiles, a road, or common passage, or to come into it with any bundle.

3. He gave a good reason for this; because it was written, *My house shall be called of all nations, The house of prayer*, v. 17. It shall pass among all people under that character. *It shall be the house of prayer to all nations;* it was so in the first institution of it. Christ will have the temple to be, (1) A *house of prayer.* After he had turned out the oxen and doves, which were things for sacrifice, he revived the appointment of it as a *house of prayer.* (2) That it should be so *to all nations*, and not to the people of the Jews only; for *whosoever shall call on the name of the Lord, shall be saved.* When Christ drove out the buyers and sellers at the beginning of his ministry, he only charged them with making the temple *a house of merchandise* (John ii. 16); but now he chargeth them with making it a *den of thieves.* Those that suffer vain worldly thoughts to lodge within them when they are at their devotions, turn the *house of prayer* into a *house of merchandise;* but they that make long prayers for a pretence to devour widows' houses, turn it into a *den of thieves.*

4. The scribes and the chief priests were extremely nettled at this, v. 18. They hated him, and yet they *feared him*, lest he should next overthrow *their* seats, and expel *them.* They found that *all the people were astonished at his doctrine*, and that everything he said was an oracle and a law to them; and what durst *he* not attempt, being thus supported? They therefore sought, not how they might make their peace with him, but *how they might destroy him.* They care not what they do, to support their own power and grandeur.

III. His discourse with his disciples, upon occasion of the fig-tree's withering away. At *even*, as usual, he *went out of the city* (v. 19), to Bethany. The next morning, as they *passed by*, they observed the *fig-tree dried up from the roots*, v. 20. The curse was no more than that it should never bear fruit again, but the effect goes further, *it is dried up from the roots.* If it bear no fruit, it shall bear no leaves to cheat people.

1. How the disciples were affected with it. Peter remembered Christ's words, and said, with surprise, *Master, behold, the fig-tree which thou cursedst is withered away*, v. 21. Christ's curses have wonderful effects, and make those to wither that flourished like the green bay-tree. And this seemed very strange to the disciples. They could not imagine how that *fig-tree* should *so soon wither away*: but this comes of rejecting Christ, and being rejected by him.

2. The good instructions Christ gave them from it; for of *those* even this *withered* tree was *fruitful.*

(1) Christ teacheth them from hence to *pray in faith* (v. 22); *Have faith in God.* They admired the power of Christ's word of command; "Why," saith Christ, "a lively active faith would put as great a power into your prayers, v. 23, 24. *Whosoever shall say to this mountain, Be removed, and be cast into the sea; and if he shall not doubt in his heart, but shall believe that those things which he saith shall come to pass, he shall have whatsoever he saith.*" Through the strength and power of God in Christ, the greatest difficulty shall be got over, and the thing shall be effected. And therefore (v. 24), "*What things soever ye desire, when ye pray believe that ye shall* receive them; nay, believe that ye *do receive them*, and he that has power to give them, saith, *Ye shall have them.*

I say unto you, Ye shall, v. 24. *Verily* I say unto you, Ye shall," v. 23. Now this is to be applied, [1] To that *faith of miracles* which the apostles and first preachers of the gospel were endued with. [2] It may be applied to that *miracle of faith*, which all true Christians are endued with. *It justifies* us (Rom. v. 1), and so removes mountains of guilt, and casts them into the *depths of the sea.* It *purifies* the heart (Acts xv. 9), and so removes mountains of corruption. It is by faith that the world is conquered, Satan's fiery darts are quenched, a soul is crucified with Christ, and yet lives.

(2) To this is added here that necessary qualification of the prevailing prayer, that we freely forgive, and be in charity with all men (v. 25, 26); *When ye stand praying*, forgive. When we are at prayer, we must remember to pray for others, particularly for our enemies, and those that have wronged us. If we have injured others before we pray, we must go and *be reconciled to them*, Matt. v. 23, 24. But if they have injured us, we go a nearer way to work, and must immediately from our hearts *forgive* them; because this is a *good step* towards obtaining the *pardon* of our own sins: *Forgive*, that *your Father may forgive you;* because the want of this is a certain bar to the obtaining of the pardon of our sins; "*If ye do not forgive, neither will your Father forgive your trespasses.*" This ought to be remembered in prayer, because one great errand we have to the throne of grace, is, to pray for the pardon of our sins. Our Saviour often insists on this, for it was his great design to engage his disciples to love one another.

Verses 27–33

We have here Christ examined by the great Sanhedrim concerning his authority. They came to him when he was *walking in the temple, teaching* the people. The cloisters, in the courts of the temple, were fitted for this purpose. The great men *came to him*, and did as it were arraign him at the bar with this question, *By what authority doest thou these things?* v. 28.

I. How they designed hereby to run him aground, and embarrass him. If they could make it out before the people, that he had not a *legal mission*, that he was not duly *ordained*, they would tell the people that they *ought not to hear him.* This they made the last refuge of an obstinate unbelief; they were resolved to find some flaw or other in his commission. This is indeed a question, which all that act either as magistrates or as ministers, ought to be furnished with a good answer to, *By what authority do I these things? For how can men preach except they be sent?*

II. How he effectually ran them aground, and embarrassed them, with this question, "What are your thoughts concerning the *baptism of John?* Was it from heaven, or of men? Answer me*," v. 30. By the resolving of *their* question into *this*, our Saviour intimates how near akin his doctrine and baptism were to John's; they had the same design and tendency—to introduce the gospel kingdom.

They knew what they *thought* of this question; they could not but think that *John Baptist* was a man sent of God. But the difficulty was, what they should *say to it* now.

1. If they own the baptism of John to be *from heaven*, they *shame themselves;* for Christ will presently turn it upon them, *Why did ye not then believe him?* They could not bear that Christ should say this, but they could bear it that their own consciences should say so.

2. If they say, "*It is of men*, he was not sent of God," they *expose themselves;* the people will be ready to do them a mischief; for *all men counted John that he was a prophet indeed.* There is a carnal slavish fear, which not only wicked subjects but wicked rulers likewise are liable to. (1) They were confounded and

forced to make a dishonourable retreat; to pretend ignorance—*We cannot tell.* What Christ did by his wisdom we must labour to do by our well doing—*put to silence the ignorance of foolish men,* 1 Pet. ii. 15. (2) Christ justified himself in refusing to give them an answer to their imperious demand; *Neither tell I you by what authority I do these things.* They did not deserve to be told; nor did *he* need to *tell them,* since no man could do those miracles which he did unless God were with him.

Chapter 12

I. The parable of the vineyard let out to unthankful husbandmen, ver. 1–12. II. A question about paying tribute to Caesar, ver. 13–17. III. His silencing the Sadducees, ver. 18–27. IV. His conference with a scribe about the first and great command of the law, ver. 28–34. V. A question about Christ's being the Son of David, ver. 35–37. VI. The caution he gave the people, to take heed of the scribes, ver. 38–40. VII. His commendation of the poor widow that cast her two mites into the treasury, ver. 41–44.

Verses 1–12

Christ had formerly in parables showed how he designed to set up the gospel church; now he begins in parables to show how he would lay aside the Jewish church.

I. They that enjoy the privileges of the visible church, have a vineyard let out to them, from the occupiers of which rent is justly expected. Members of the church are God's tenants, and they have both a good Landlord and a good bargain, and may live well upon it, if it be not their own fault.

II. Those whom God lets out his vineyard to, he sends his servants to, to put them in mind of his just expectations from them, *v.* 2.

III. It is sad to think what base usage God's faithful ministers have met with, in all ages. The Old Testament prophets were persecuted. They *beat them,* and *sent them empty away* (*v.* 3); that was bad: they *wounded them,* and *sent them away shamefully entreated* (*v.* 4); that was worse: nay, at length, they came to such a pitch of wickedness, that they *killed* them, *v.* 5.

IV. It was no wonder if those who abused the prophets, abused Christ himself. God did at length send them his Son, his *well-beloved.* And it might be expected that he whom their Master *loved,* they also should respect and love (*v.* 6); "*They will reverence my son.*" But, instead of *reverencing* him because he was the son and heir, they *therefore* hated him, *v.* 7. They were the more enraged against him, and determined to put him to death, that all the respect might be paid to them only; "*The inheritance shall be ours.*" There is an *inheritance,* which, if they had duly *reverenced the Son,* might have been theirs, a heavenly inheritance. So they *took him, and killed him*; and they *cast him out of the vineyard.*

V. For such sinful and shameful doings nothing can be expected but a fearful doom (*v.* 9); *What shall therefore the Lord of the vineyard do?*

1. He will *come, and destroy the husbandmen.* When they killed his servants, and his Son, he determined to *destroy* them; and this was fulfilled when Jerusalem was laid waste.

2. He will *give the vineyard to others.* This was fulfilled in the taking in of the Gentiles, and the abundance of fruit which the *gospel brought forth in all the world,* Col. i. 6. If some from whom we expected well, prove bad, it doth not follow but that others will be better.

3. Their opposition to Christ's exaltation shall be no obstruction to it (*v.* 10, 11); *The stone which the builders rejected,* is *become the Head of the corner.* God will set Christ as *his King,* upon his *holy hill of Zion.* And all the world shall see and own this to be *the Lord's doing.*

Now what effect had this parable upon the chief priests and scribes? They knew *he spoke this parable against them, v.* 12. They could not but see their own faces in the glass of it. (1) They *sought to lay hold on him,* and make him their prisoner immediately, and so to fulfil what he had just now said they would do to him, *v.* 8. (2) Nothing restrained them from it but the awe they stood in of the people; they did not *reverence* Christ, nor had any *fear of* God before their eyes. (3) They *left him, and went their way*; if they could not do hurt to him, they resolved he should not do good to them, and therefore they got out of the hearing of his powerful preaching. If men's prejudices be not conquered by the evidence of truth, they are but confirmed. If the gospel be not a *savour of life unto life,* it will be a *savour of death unto death.*

Verses 13–17

Here we have him tempted, or *at*tempted rather, with a question about the lawfulness of paying tribute to Caesar.

I. The persons they employed were the *Pharisees* and the *Herodians, v.* 13. The Pharisees were great sticklers for the liberty of the Jews, and, if he should say, It is lawful to give tribute to Caesar, they would incense the common people against him. The Herodians were great sticklers for the Roman power, and, if he should discountenance the paying of tribute to Caesar, they would incense the governor against him. It is no new thing for those that are at variance in other things, to join in a confederacy against Christ.

II. The pretence they made was, that they desired him to resolve them a case of conscience, *v.* 14. They complimented him at a high rate, called him *Master,* owned him for a Teacher of the *way of God,* a Teacher of it *in truth,* who would not be brought by smiles or frowns to depart a step from the rules of equity and goodness; "*Thou carest for no man,* nor *regardest the person of men; thou art right,* and dost in a right manner declare good and evil, truth and falsehood." They knew that he taught the way of God in truth, and yet rejected the counsel of God against themselves.

III. The question they put was, *Is it lawful to give tribute to Caesar, or not?* They would be thought desirous to know their duty. Really they desired nothing but to know what he would say, in hopes that, which side soever he took of the question, they might take occasion from it to accuse him. They seemed to refer the determining of this matter to Christ; they put the question fairly, *Shall we give, or shall we not give?* They seemed resolved to stand to his award. Many seem desirous to know their duty, who are no ways disposed to do it.

IV. Christ determined the question, and evaded the snare, *v.* 15–17. He *knew their hypocrisy.* Hypocrisy, though ever so artfully managed, cannot be concealed from the Lord Jesus. He sees the *potsherd* that is *covered* with the *silver dross.* He knew they intended to ensnare him, and therefore contrived the matter so as to ensnare them. He made them acknowledge that the current money of their nation was Roman money, had the emperor's image on one side, and his *superscription* on the reverse; and if so, 1. *Caesar* might command their money for the public benefit. *Render to Caesar the things that are Caesar's.* The circulation of the money is from him as the fountain, and therefore it must return to him. 2. Caesar might not command their consciences, nor did he pretend to it. "Pay your tribute, therefore, without murmuring or disputing, but be sure to *render to God the things that are God's.*" Many that seem careful to give to men their due, are in no care to give to God *the glory due to his name.* All that heard Christ, *marvelled* at the discretion of his answer, but I doubt none were brought by it, as they ought to be, to render to God themselves and their devotions. Many will commend the wit of a sermon, that will not be commanded by the divine laws of a sermon.

Verses 18–27

The Sadducees, who were the deists of that age, here attack our Lord Jesus. They were not bigots and persecutors, but sceptics and infidels, and their design was upon his doctrine. They denied that there was any resurrection, any world of spirits, any state of rewards and punishments on the other side of death; now those great and fundamental truths which they denied, Christ had made it his business to establish and prove, and therefore they set themselves to perplex his doctrine.

I. See here the method they take to entangle it; they quote the ancient law, by which, if a man died without issue, his brother was obliged to marry his widow, *v.* 19. They suppose a case to happen that, according to that law, seven brothers were, successively, the husbands of one woman, *v.* 20. Probably, these Sadducees intended hereby to ridicule that law. Those who deny divine truths, commonly set themselves to disparage divine laws and ordinances. Their design was to expose the doctrine of the resurrection; for they suppose that if there be a future state, it must be such a one as this, and then the doctrine, they think, is clogged either with this invincible absurdity, that a woman in that state must have seven husbands, or else with this insolvable difficulty, whose wife she must be. See with what subtlety these heretics *undermine* the truth; they do not *deny* it, they do not seem to doubt of it. They pretend to own the truth, as if they were not Sadducees. They take it for granted that there is a resurrection, and would be thought to desire instruction concerning it, when really they are designing to give it a fatal stab, and think that they shall do it. It is the common artifice of heretics and Sadducees to perplex and entangle the truth, which they have not the impudence to deny.

II. See here the method Christ takes to clear and establish this truth. This was a matter of moment, and therefore Christ does not pass it over lightly, but enlarges upon it.

1. He charges the Sadducees with *error*, and charges that upon their *ignorance. Do ye not therefore err?* Ye cannot but be sensible of it yourselves, and that the cause of your error is, (1) Because ye do not *know the scriptures.* Not but that the Sadducees had read the scriptures, and perhaps were ready in them; yet they might be truly said not to *know the scriptures,* because they did not know the sense and meaning of them, but put false constructions upon them. A right knowledge of the scripture, as the fountain whence all revealed religion now flows, and the foundation on which it is built, is the best preservative against error. Keep the truth, the scripture-truth, and it shall keep thee. (2) Because ye *know not the power of God.* They could not but know that God is almighty, but they would not apply that doctrine to this matter, but gave up the truth to the objections of the impossibility of it. The power of God, seen in the return of the spring (Ps. civ. 30), in the reviving of the corn (John xii. 24), in the restoring of an abject people to their prosperity (Ezek. xxxvii. 12–14), in the raising of so many to life, miraculously, both in the Old Testament and in the New, and especially, in the resurrection of Christ (Eph. i. 19, 20), are all earnests of our resurrection by the same power (Phil. iii. 21); *according to the mighty working whereby he is able to subdue all things to himself.*

2. He sets aside all the force of their objection, by setting the doctrine of the future state in a true light

(*v.* 25); *When they shall rise from the dead, they neither marry, nor are given in marriage.* It is a folly to ask, *Whose wife shall she be of the seven?* It is no wonder if we confound ourselves with endless absurdities, when we measure our ideas of the world of spirits by the affairs of this world of sense.

III. He builds the doctrine of the future state, and of the blessedness of the righteous in that state, upon the covenant of God with Abraham, which God was pleased to own, after Abraham's death, *v.* 26, 27. He appeals to the scriptures; *Have ye not read in the book of Moses?* Now that which he refers them to is, what God said to Moses at the bush, I *am the God of Abraham*; not only, I *was* so, but I *am* so. It is absurd to think that God's relation to Abraham should be continued, and thus solemnly recognized, if Abraham was annihilated, or that the *living God* should be the portion and happiness of a man that is dead, and must be for ever so. You must conclude, 1. That Abraham's soul exists and acts in a state of separation from the body. 2. That therefore, some time or other, the body must rise again. Upon the whole matter, he concludes, *Ye therefore do greatly err.* Those that deny the resurrection, greatly err, and ought to be told so.

Verses 28–34

Only we have here an account of *one* of them, a scribe, who had so much civility in him as to take notice of Christ's answer to the Sadducees, and to own that he had *answered well,* and much to the purpose (*v.* 28). We have his application to Christ for instruction, and it was such as became him; not tempting Christ, but desiring to improve his acquaintance with him.

I. He enquired, *Which is the first commandment of all? v.* 28. He doth not mean the first in *order,* but the first in *weight* and *dignity.* Not that any commandment of God is little, but some are greater than others, moral precepts than rituals, and of some we may say, They are the *greatest of all.*

II. Christ gave him a direct answer to this enquiry, *v.* 29–31. Those that sincerely desire to be instructed concerning their duty, Christ will *guide in judgment,* and *teach his way.* He tells him,

1. That the great commandment of all, which is indeed inclusive of all, is, that of *loving God with all our hearts.* Where this is the commanding principle in the soul, there is a disposition to every other duty. Love is the leading affection of the soul; the love of God is the leading grace in the renewed soul. Where this is not, nothing else that is good is done. Loving God with all our heart, will effectually take us off from all those things that are rivals with him for the throne in our souls. No commandment will be grievous where this principle commands, and has the ascendant. Now here in Mark, our Saviour prefixes to this command the great doctrinal truth upon which it is built (*v.* 29); *Hear, O Israel, The Lord our God is one Lord;* if we firmly believe this, it will follow, that we shall love him *with all our heart.* If he be one, our hearts must be one with him, and since there is no God besides, no rival must be admitted with him upon the throne.

2. That the second great commandment is, to *love our neighbour as ourselves* (*v.* 31), and we must show it by *doing as we would be done by.* As we must therefore love God better than ourselves, so we must *love our neighbour as ourselves,* because he is of the same nature with ourselves; and if a fellow-Christian, and of the same sacred society, the obligation is the stronger. *Hath not one God created us?* Has not one Christ redeemed us? Well might Christ say, There is no other commandment greater than these; for in these all the law is fulfilled, and if we make conscience of obedience to these, all other instances of obedience will follow of course.

III. The scribe consented to what Christ said, *v.* 32, 33. 1. He commends Christ's decision of this question; *Well, Master, thou hast said the truth.* It shall be brought in evidence against those who persecuted Christ, as a deceiver, that one of themselves confessed that he *said the truth*, and said it *well*. And thus must we subscribe to Christ's sayings, must set to our seal that they are true. 2. He comments upon it. Christ had quoted that great doctrine, that *the Lord our God is one Lord*; and this he not only assented to, but added, "*There is none other but he.*" This excludes all rivals with him, and secures the throne in the heart entire for him. Christ had laid down that great law, of loving God *with all our heart*; and this also he explains—that it is loving him *with the understanding*. Our love to God, as it must be an *entire*, so it must be an *intelligent*, love; we must love him with *all* the understanding; our rational powers and faculties must all be set on work to lead out the affections of our souls toward God. Christ had said, "To love God and our neighbour is the greatest commandment of all"; "Yea," saith the scribe, "it is *more than all whole-burnt offerings and sacrifices*, more acceptable to God." There were those who held, that the law of *sacrifices* was the *greatest commandment* of all; but this scribe readily agreed with our Saviour in this—that the law of love to God and our neighbour is greater than that of *sacrifice*, even than that of *whole-burnt-offerings*.

IV. Christ approved of what he said, and encouraged him to proceed in his enquiries of him, *v.* 34. 1. He owned that he understood well, as far as he went; so far, so good. *Jesus saw that he answered discreetly*, and was the more pleased with it, because he had of late met with so many that answered *indiscreetly*. He answered as *one that had a mind*; as one that had his wits about him; whose judgment was not biassed. He answered as one that allowed himself liberty and leisure to consider, and as one that had considered. 2. He owned that he stood fair for a further advance; "*Thou art not far from the kingdom of God*, the kingdom of grace and glory." There is hope of those who make a good use of the light they have, and go as far as that will carry them, that by the grace of God they will be led further. What became of this scribe we are not told, but would willingly hope that he took the hint Christ hereby gave him, and that he proceeded to enquire of him what was the great commandment of the gospel too. Yet, if he did not, we are not to think it strange; for there are many who are *not far from the kingdom of God*, and yet never come thither. *No man, after that, durst ask him any question;* those that desired to *learn*, were *ashamed* to ask, and those that designed to *cavil*, were *afraid* to ask.

Verses 35–40

I. Christ shows the people how weak and defective the scribes were in their preaching, and how unable to solve the difficulties that occurred in the scriptures of the Old Testament. Of this he gives an instance, which is not so fully related here as it was in Matthew.

1. They told the people that the Messiah was to be the *Son of David* (*v.* 35), and they were in the right. The people took it as what the scribes said; whereas the truths of God should rather be quoted from our Bibles than from our ministers, for there is the original of them.

2. Yet they could not tell them how to call him *his Lord*, as he doth, Ps. cx. 1. They had taught the people that concerning the Messiah, which would be for the honour of their nation—that he should be a branch of their royal family; but they had not taken care to teach them that he should be the Son of God, and, as such, and not otherwise, *David's Lord*. If any should object, *How then doth David himself call him Lord?* they would not know how to avoid the force of the objection. Note, Those are unworthy to sit in Moses's seat, who, though they are able to preach the truth, are not in some measure able to defend it when they have preached it, and to convince gainsayers.

Now this galled the scribes, to have their ignorance thus exposed; but the *common people heard him gladly*, *v.* 37. What he preached was surprising and affecting, and they had never heard such preaching. Probably there was something more than ordinarily commanding and charming in his voice and way of delivery which recommended him to the affections of the common people; for we do not find that any were wrought upon to *believe* in him, and to *follow* him. And perhaps some of these cried, *Crucify him*, as Herod heard John Baptist gladly, and yet cut off his head.

II. He cautions the people to take heed of suffering themselves to be imposed upon by the scribes; *He said unto them in his doctrine,* "*Beware of the scribes*" (*v.* 38).

1. They affect to appear *very great*; for they go in *long clothing*, as princes, or judges. Their going in such clothing was not sinful, but their *loving* to go in it, this was a product of pride. Christ would have his disciples go with *their loins girt*.

2. They affect to appear *very good*; for they pray, they make *long prayers*. They took care it should be known that they prayed, that they prayed long. This they did *for a pretence*, that they might seem to love prayer.

3. They coveted applause, and were fond of it; they loved *salutations in the market-places*, and the *chief seats in the synagogues, and the uppermost rooms at feasts*. To have these given them, they thought, expressed the value *they* had for them, who did know them, and gained them respect for those who did not.

4. They herein aimed to *enrich* themselves. They *devoured widows' houses*; it was to screen themselves from the suspicion of dishonesty, that they put on the mask of piety; and that they might not be thought as bad as the worst, they were studious to seem as good as the best. Let not prayers, no nor *long prayers*, be thought the worse of, if made in humility and sincerity, for their having been by some thus abused. Iniquity, thus disguised with a show of piety, is *double* iniquity, so its doom will be doubly heavy; *These shall receive greater damnation.*

Verses 41–44

This passage of story was not in Matthew, but is here and in Luke; it is Christ's commendation of the poor widow, that cast *two mites* into the treasury.

I. There was a *public fund* for charity, a poor's-box, and this in *the temple*; for works of charity and works of piety very fitly go together. We often find *prayers* and *alms* in conjunction, as Acts x. 2, 4. It is good for those to *lay by as God has prospered them* (1 Cor. xvi. 2), that they may have something ready to give when an object of charity offers itself.

II. Jesus Christ has *an eye* upon it; *He sat over against the treasury, and beheld how the people cast money into it.* Our Lord Jesus takes notice of what we contribute to pious and charitable uses; whether we give liberally or sparingly; whether we do it as unto the Lord, or only to be seen of men.

III. He saw *many that were rich cast in much*: and it was a good sight to see rich people charitable, to see *many* rich people so, and to see them cast in *much*. Those that are rich, ought to give richly; if God give abundantly to us, he expects we should give abundantly.

IV. There was a *poor widow that cast in two mites, which make a farthing* (*v.* 42); and our Lord Jesus highly commended her; *called his disciples* to him, and bid them take notice of it (*v.* 43); told them that she could very ill spare that which she gave, it was *all her living*. He reckoned it more than all that put together, which the rich people threw in; for they did *cast in of their abundance, but she of her want, v.* 44. Now many would have been ready to censure this *poor widow*; why should she give to others, when she had little enough for herself? Charity begins at home. It is so rare a thing to find any that would not blame this widow, that we cannot expect to find any that will imitate her; and yet our Saviour commends her. We must hence learn, 1. That *giving alms*, is an excellent good thing, and highly pleasing to the Lord Jesus; he will graciously accept of it, though in some circumstances there may not be all the discretion in the world. 2. Those that have but a *little*, ought to give alms out of *their little*. We should in many cases pinch ourselves, that we may supply the necessities of others; this is loving our neighbours as ourselves. 3. Public charities should be encouraged, and though there may be some mismanagement of them, yet that is not a good reason why we should not bring in our *quota* to them. 4. Though we can give but *a little* in charity, it shall be accepted of Christ, who requires *according to what a man has, and not according to what he has not*; two mites shall be put upon the score, and brought to account, if given in a right manner, as if they had been two pounds. 5. It is much to the praise of charity, when we give not only *to our power*, but *beyond our power*, as the Macedonian churches, whose *deep poverty abounded to the riches of their liberality*, 2 Cor. viii. 2, 3, and trust God to provide for us some other way, *this is thank-worthy*.

CHAPTER 13

That prophetical sermon which our Lord Jesus preached, pointing at the destruction of Jerusalem, and the consummation of all things; preached only to four of his disciples. I. His disciples' admiring the buildings of the temple (ver. 1, 2), and their enquiry concerning the time of the desolation of them, ver. 3, 4. II. The predictions themselves, 1. Of the rise of deceivers, ver. 5, 6, 21–23. 2. Of the wars of the nations, ver. 7, 8. 3. Of the persecution of Christians, ver. 9–13. 4. Of the destruction of Jerusalem, ver. 14–20. 5. Of the end of the world, ver. 24–27. III. Some general intimations concerning the time of them, ver. 28–32. IV. Some practical inferences from all, ver. 33–37.

Verses 1–4

I. How apt many of Christ's own disciples are to idolize things that look *great*, and have been long looked upon as *sacred*. One of them said to him, "Look, Master, *what manner of stones, and what buildings are here* (*v.* 1). We never saw the like in Galilee; O do not leave this fine place."

II. How little Christ values external pomp, where there is not real purity; "*Seest thou these great buildings*" (saith Christ)? "I tell thee, the time is at hand when *there shall not be left one stone upon another, that shall not be thrown down*," *v.* 2. He looks with *pity* upon the ruin of precious souls, and weeps over them, for on them he has put a great value; but we do not find him look with any pity upon the ruin of a magnificent house, when he is driven out of it by sin. With what little concern doth he say, *Not one stone shall be left on another!* While any part remained standing, there might be some hopes of the repair of it; but what hope is there, when not one stone is *left upon another*?

III. How natural it is to us to desire to know things to come, and the times of them; more inquisitive we are apt to be about that than about our duty. His disciples knew not how to *digest* this doctrine, and therefore they were in pain till they got him alone, and got more out of him concerning this matter. As he was returning to Bethany therefore, he *sat upon the mount of Olives, over against the temple*; and

there four of them agreed to *ask him privately*, what he meant by the destroying of the temple. Probably, Christ's discourse, in answer to it, was in the hearing of the rest of the disciples, yet *privately*, that is, apart from the multitude. Their enquiry is, *When shall these things be?* They will not question whether they shall be or no, but are willing to hope it is a great way off. "Tell us *what shall be the sign, when all these things shall be fulfilled?*"

Verses 5–13

Our Lord Jesus, in reply to their question, sets himself, not so much to satisfy their curiosity as to direct their consciences; but gives them the cautions which were needful, with reference to the events that should now shortly come to pass.

I. They must take heed that they be not *deceived* by the *seducers* and *impostors* that should now shortly arise (*v.* 5, 6); "*Take heed lest any man deceive you. Many shall come in my name*, saying, *I am Christ.*" After the Jews had rejected the true Christ, they were imposed upon by many false Christs. Those false Christs *deceived many*; Therefore *take heed lest they deceive you*. When many are deceived, we should thereby be awakened to look to ourselves.

II. They must take heed that they be not *disturbed* at the noise of wars, which they should be alarmed with, *v.* 7, 8. At some times the nations are more distracted and wasted with wars than at other times; so it shall be now; Christ was born into the world when there was a general peace, but soon after he went out of the world there were general wars; *Nation shall rise against nation, and kingdom against kingdom.* "But *be not troubled at it.* Let it be no *surprise* to you; *such things must needs be.* Let it be no *terror* to you, you have no concern in them, and therefore need not be apprehensive of any damage by them." Those that despise the smiles of the world, and do not court and covet them, may despise the frowns of the world, and need not fear them. "Let it not be looked upon as an omen of the approaching period of the world, for the *end is not yet* (*v.* 7). Think not that these *wars* will bring the world to a period. Let it not be looked upon as if in them God had done his worst. Be not troubled at the wars you shall hear of, for they are but *the beginnings of sorrows*, and therefore, you ought to *prepare for worse*; for there shall also be *earthquakes in divers places*, and there *shall be famines* and *troubles.* The world shall be full of *troubles*, but *be not ye troubled*; but *fear not ye their fear*." The disciples of Christ may enjoy a holy security and serenity of mind, when all about them is in the greatest disorder.

III. They must take heed that they be not *drawn away* from Christ by the sufferings they should meet with for Christ's sake. Again, he saith, "*Take heed to yourselves, v.* 9. Though you may escape the *sword of war*, better than some of your neighbours, yet be not secure; you will be exposed to the *sword of justice* more than others. *Take heed* therefore lest you *deceive* yourselves with the hopes of outward prosperity, when it is *through many tribulations* that *you must enter into the kingdom of God.* Take heed what you say and do, for you will have many eyes upon you."

1. What the trouble is which they must expect. They shall be *hated of all men*; trouble enough! The thoughts of *being hated* are grievous to a tender spirit. Those that are *malicious*, will be *mischievous*. It was not for anything amiss in them, or done amiss by them, that they were *hated*, but for Christ's name's sake. The world hated them because he loved them. Their own *relations* shall *betray them*, those to whom they were most nearly allied, and on whom therefore they depended for protection. Their *church-rulers* shall inflict *their censures* upon them; "You shall be

delivered up, and shall be *beaten in the synagogues* with forty stripes at a time, as offenders against the law." It is no new thing for the church's artillery, through the treachery of its officers, to be turned against some of its best friends. *Governors* and *kings* shall use their power against them. They shall *cause you to be put to death*, as enemies to the empire. They must resist unto blood and still resist.

2. What they shall have to comfort themselves with.

(1) That the work they were called to should be carried on and prosper (v. 10); "*The gospel shall, for all this, be published among all nations*, and the *sound* of it shall *go forth into all the earth*." It is comfort to those who suffer for the gospel, that, though they may be crushed and borne down, the gospel cannot; it shall keep its ground, and carry the day.

(2) That their sufferings, instead of obstructing their work, should forward it; "*Your being brought before governors and kings* shall be for *a testimony of them* (so some read it, v. 9); it shall give you an opportunity of preaching the gospel to those before whom you are brought as criminals." Or, as we read it, It shall be for a testimony *against them*, against both the judges and the prosecutors. The gospel is a testimony to us concerning Christ and heaven. If we receive it, it will be a testimony for us: it will justify and save us; if not, it will be a testimony *against* us in the great day.

(3) That, when they were brought before kings and governors for Christ's sake, they should have special assistance from heaven (v. 11); "*Take no thought beforehand what ye shall speak*, but *whatsoever shall be given you in that hour* that *speak ye*, and fear not the success of it, because it is *offhand*, for *it is not ye that speak*, but it is *the Holy Ghost*." When we are engaged in the service of Christ, we may depend upon the aids of the Spirit of Christ.

(4) That heaven at last would *make amends for all*; *he that shall endure to the end, the same shall be saved*," v. 13. Perseverance gains the crown. The salvation here promised is more than a deliverance from evil, it is an everlasting blessedness.

Verses 14–23

The Jews, in rebelling against the Romans, and in persecuting the Christians, were setting both God and man against them. Now here we have a prediction of that ruin which came upon them within less than forty years after this.

I. What is here foretold concerning it.

1. That the Roman *armies* should make a descent upon Judæa, and invest Jerusalem, the holy city. These were the *abomination of desolation*. They had rejected Christ as an *abomination*, who would have been their *salvation*; and now God brought upon them an abomination that would be their *desolation*. This army stood *where it ought not*, in and about the *holy city*, which the heathen ought not to have approached. Sin made the breach, at which the glory went out, and the abomination of desolation broke in, *and stood where it ought not*.

2. That when the Roman *army* should come into the country, there would be no safety anywhere but by quitting the country, and that with all possible expedition. A man cannot have so much as his life given him for a prey, but by *fleeing to the mountains* out of Judæa; and let him take the first alarm, and make the best of his way. If he be *on the house-top*, and spies them coming, let him not *go down to take anything out of the house*, for it will occasion his losing of time. If he be in the field, let him get away as he is, and not *turn back again, to take up his garment*, v. 16. If he can save his life, let him reckon it a good bargain, though he can save nothing else, and be

thankful to God, that, though he is cut short, he is not cut off.

3. That it would go very hard at that time with poor mothers and nurses (v. 17); "*Woe to them that are with child*, that cannot shift for themselves, nor make haste as others can. And *woe to them that give suck*, that know not how either to leave the tender infants behind them, or to carry them along with them." The time may often be, when the greatest comforts may prove the greatest burthens. It would likewise be very uncomfortable, if they should be forced to flee *in the winter* (v. 18). If there be no remedy but that trouble must come, yet we may desire and pray that the circumstances of it may be so ordered as to be a mitigation of the trouble; and when things are bad, we ought to consider they might have been worse.

4. There should be such destruction and desolation made, as could not be paralleled in any history (v. 19); *In those days shall be affliction, such as was not from the beginning of the creation which God created unto this day, neither shall be*. It threatened a universal slaughter of all the people of the Jews; so barbarously did they devour one another, and the Romans devour them all, that, if their wars had continued a little longer, *no flesh could have been saved*. But in the midst of wrath God remembered mercy. He *shortened the days*. Many particular persons had their lives given them for a prey, by the storm's subsiding when it did. It was *for the elects' sake* that those days were shortened; *many* among them fared the better for the sake of the *few* among them that believed in Christ. There was a promise, that *a remnant* should be saved (Isa. x. 22). God's own *elect cry day and night to him*, and their prayers must be answered, Luke xviii. 7.

II. What directions are given to the disciples with reference to it.

1. They must shift for the safety of *their lives*; "When you see the country invaded, and the city invested, without further deliberation or delay, *let them that are in Judæa, flee to the mountains*, v. 14. Do you go out of the ship when you see it sinking"

2. They must provide for the safety of *their souls*. Then, *if any man shall* say unto you, Lo, *here is Christ*, or, Lo, *he is there*, *believe them not*; for *false christs, and false prophets, shall arise*, v. 22. *False christs* shall *rise*, and false prophets that shall preach them up; or such, as set up for *prophets*, and they shall *show signs* and lying *wonders*. They *shall seduce, if it were possible, the very elect*; so plausible shall their pretences be, that they shall draw away many that were forward and zealous professors of religion, many that were very likely to have persevered. They *shall seduce, if it were possible, the very elect*. In consideration hereof, let the disciples be cautious whom they give credit to (v. 23); But *take ye heed*. Christ knew that they were of the *elect*, and yet he said to them, *Take heed*. An assurance of persevering, and cautions against apostasy, will very well consist with each other. God will keep them, but they must keep themselves. "*I have foretold you all things*; that, being *forewarned*, you may be *fore-armed*."

Verses 24–27

These verses seem to point at Christ's second coming, to judge the world; the disciples, in their question, had confounded the *destruction* of Jerusalem and the *end of the world* (Matt. xxiv. 3), which was built upon a mistake, as if the temple must needs stand as long as the world stands; this mistake Christ rectifies. And here he foretells,

1. The final dissolution of the present frame and fabric of the world; *The sun shall be darkened*, and the *moon* shall no more *give her light*. The *stars of heaven* shall fall as leaves in autumn; and the *powers that are in heaven shall be shaken*.

2. The visible appearance of the Lord Jesus, to whom the judgment of that day shall be committed (*v.* 26); *Then shall they see the Son of man coming in the clouds.* He shall come with *great power and glory. Every eye shall then see him.*

3. The gathering together of all the elect to him (*v.* 27); He shall *send his angels,* and *gather together his elect* to him. They shall be fetched *from the uttermost parts of the earth,* most remote from the place where Christ's tribunal shall be set, and shall be brought to the *uttermost part of heaven.* A faithful Israelite shall be carried safely, though it were from the utmost border of the land of bondage to the utmost border of the land of promise.

Verses 28–37

We have here the application of this prophetical sermon.

I. "As to the *destruction* of Jerusalem, *expect* it to come very *shortly*; as when the *branch of the fig-tree becomes soft,* and the *leaves sprout forth,* ye expect that summer will come shortly, *v,* 28. So when *ye see these things come to pass,* when ye see the Jewish nation embroiled in wars, distracted by false christs and prophets, and drawing upon them the displeasure of the Romans, then say that their *ruin is nigh, even at the door.*" The disciples themselves were indeed all of them, except John, taken away from the evil to come, but the next generation would live to see it. "*This generation* that is now rising up, shall not all be worn off before *all these things* come to pass. And as this destruction is near and within ken, so it is sure." Christ doth not speak these things, merely to frighten them; no, they are the declarations of God's fixed purpose; "*Heaven and earth shall pass away*; but *my words shall not pass away*" (*v.* 31).

II. "As to the *end of the world,* do not enquire when it will come, for of *that day,* and *that hour, knoweth no man*; it is not revealed by any word of God, either to *men* on earth, or to *angels in heaven.*" But it follows, *neither the Son*; but is there anything which the Son is ignorant of? There were those in the primitive times, who taught from this text, that there were some things that Christ, as man, was *ignorant* of; they said, "It was no more absurd to say so, than to say that his human soul suffered grief and fear." Christ, as God, could not be ignorant of anything; but the divine wisdom which dwelt in our Saviour, did communicate itself to his human soul, according to the divine pleasure, so that his human nature might sometimes not know some things; therefore Christ is said to grow in wisdom (Luke ii. 52).

III. "As to both, your duty is to *watch and pray* (*v.* 33); *Take ye heed* of everything that would indispose you for your Master's coming; *watch* for his coming, that it may not at any time be a surprise to you, and *pray* for that grace which is necessary to qualify you for it, for *ye know not what the time is*; and you are concerned to be ready for that *every day,* which may come *any day.*" This he illustrates, in the close, by a parable.

1. Our Master is gone away, and left us something which we must give account of, *v.* 34. He is *as a man taking a far journey*; he has *left his house on earth,* and left his servants in their offices, given *authority* to some, and *work* to others. They that have *authority* given them, in that had *work* assigned them, for those that have the greatest *power* have the most *business*; and to them to whom he gave *work,* he gave *authority,* to do that work. And when he took his last leave, he *appointed the porter to watch,* to be sure to be ready to open to him at his return. Thus our Lord Jesus, when he *ascended on high,* left something for all his servants to do. *All* are appointed to work, and some authorized to rule.

2. We ought to be always upon our watch, in expectation of his return, *v.* 35–37. Our Lord *will come,* and will come as the *Master of the house,* to take account of his servants. We know not *when he will come.* This is applicable to his coming to us in particular, at our death, as well as to the general judgment. Our present life is a *night,* a dark night, compared with the other life; we know not in which watch of the night our Master will come, whether in the days of youth, or middle age, or old age; but as soon as we are born, we begin to die, and therefore, as soon as we are capable of expecting anything, we must expect death. Our great care must be, that, whenever our Lord comes, he does not *find us sleeping,* secure in ourselves, off our guard, *ready* to say, He will not come, and *unready* to meet him. His coming will indeed be *coming suddenly.* It is therefore the indispensable duty of all Christ's disciples, to *watch,* to be awake, and keep awake; "*What I say unto you* four (*v.* 37), I *say unto all,* what I say to you of this generation, I say to all that shall believe in me, in every age, *Watch, watch,* expect my second coming, prepare for it, that you may be found in peace, without spot, and blameless."

Chapter 14

In this chapter begins the account of the death and sufferings of our Lord Jesus. I. The plot of the chief priests and scribes against Christ, ver. 1, 2. II. The anointing of Christ's head at a supper in Bethany, ver. 3–9. III. The contract Judas made to betray him, ver. 10, 11. IV. Christ's eating the passover with his disciples, his instituting the Lord's supper, and his discourse with his disciples, ver. 12–31. V. Christ's agony in the garden, ver. 32–42. VI. The betraying of him by Judas, and the apprehending of him by the chief priests' agents, ver. 43–52. VII. His arraignment before the high priests, his conviction, and the indignities done him, ver. 53–65. VIII. Peter's denying him.

Verses 1–11

We have here instances,

I. Of the *kindness of Christ's friends.* Some friends he had, even in and about Jerusalem, that loved him, and never thought they could do enough for him.

1. Here was *one friend,* that was so kind as to *invite him to sup with him, v.* 3. Though he had a prospect of his death approaching, yet he did not abandon himself to a melancholy retirement from all company.

2. Here was *another friend,* that was so kind as to *anoint his head* with very precious ointment as he *sat at meat.* This was an extraordinary piece of respect paid him by a good woman that thought nothing too good to bestow upon Christ. Did he pour out his soul unto death for us, and shall we think any box of ointment too precious to pour out upon him? It is observable that she took care to pour it all out upon Christ's head; she *broke the box.* Christ must be honoured with *all we* have. Do we give him the *precious ointment* of our best affections? Let him have them *all*; love him *with all the heart.*

(1) There were those that put a *worse construction* upon this than it *deserved.* They called it a *waste of the ointment, v.* 4. The *liberal* and *bountiful* ought not to be called *wasteful.* They pretended it might have been *sold,* and *given to the poor, v.* 5. A common charity to the poor will not excuse from a particular act of piety to the Lord Jesus.

(2) Our Lord Jesus put a *better construction* upon it than, for aught that appears, was *designed.* Christ makes it to be an act of *great faith,* as well as *great love* (*v.* 8); "*She is come aforehand, to anoint my body to the burying.*" See how Christ's heart was filled with the thoughts of his death, how familiarly he spoke of it upon all occasions. It is usual for those who are *condemned to die,* to have their coffins prepared, and other provision made for their funerals, while they are yet alive; and *so* Christ accepted *this.* Christ never rode in triumph into Jerusalem, but

when he came thither to suffer; nor had ever his head anointed, but for *his burial*.

(3) He recommended this piece of heroic piety to all ages; *Wherever this gospel shall be preached, it shall be spoken of, for a memorial of her, v. 9.* Thus was this good woman repaid for her box of ointment. *She lost neither her oil nor her labour.* She got by it that good name which is *better than precious ointment*, Those that *honour* Christ *he will honour*.

II. Of the *malice of Christ's enemies*.

1. The chief priests consulted how they might *put him to death, v. 1, 2.* The feast of the *passover* was now at hand, and at *that* feast he must be crucified, (1) That his death and sufferings might be the more public. (2) That the anti-type might answer to the type. Christ, our Passover, was sacrificed for us, at the same time that the paschal lamb was sacrificed, and Israel's deliverance out of Egypt was *commemorated*.

Now see, How *spiteful* Christ's enemies were, for they aimed not only to *silence* him, but to be revenged on him for all the good he had done. How *subtle* they were; *Not on the feast-day, Lest there should be an uproar (v.* 2); lest they should rise, and rescue him. They who *desired* nothing more than the *praise* of men, dreaded nothing more than the rage and displeasure of men.

2. Judas, his *disguised enemy*, contracted with them for the betraying of him, *v.* 10, 11. He *went to the chief priests*, to tender his service in this affair.

(1) That which he proposed to them, was, to *betray Christ* to them without making an *uproar among the people*, which they were afraid of. Did they know that he had a mind to serve them, and make court to him? No, they could not imagine that any of his intimates should be so base. The spirit that works in all the children of disobedience, knows how to bring them in to the assistance one of another in a wicked project.

(2) That which he proposed to himself, was, to *get money* by the bargain; *they promised to give him money*. Covetousness was Judas's master-lust. They promised him *money*. Perhaps it was Judas's covetousness that brought him at first to *follow Christ*, having a promise that he should be cashkeeper, or purser, to the society, and he loved in his heart to be fingering money; and now that there was money to be got on the other side, he was as ready to betray him as ever he had been to follow him.

(3) Having secured the money, he set himself to make good his bargain; he sought *how he might conveniently betray him*. See what need we have to be careful that we do not ensnare ourselves in sinful engagements. It is a rule in our law, as well as in our religion, that an *obligation* to do an *evil thing* is *null* and *void*; it binds to repentance, not to performance. See how the way of sin is down-hill— when men are *in*, they must *on*.

Verses 12–31

I. Christ's eating the passover with his disciples, the night before he died. No apprehension of trouble, come or coming, should put us out of frame for our attendance on holy ordinances.

1. Christ ate the passover at the *usual time*, when the other Jews did. It was on the first day of that feast, which was called, *The feast of unleavened bread*, even that day when they *killed the passover, v.* 12.

2. He directed his disciples how to find the place where he intended to eat the passover. *"Go into the city and there shall meet you a man bearing a pitcher of water; follow him, go in* where he goes, enquire for his master, *the good man of the house (v.* 14), and desire him to show you a room."* No doubt, the inhabitants of Jerusalem had rooms fitted up to be *let out*, for this occasion, to those that came out of the country to keep the passover and one of those Christ made use of. Probably he went where he was not known, that he might be *undisturbed* with his disciples. Perhaps he notified it by *a sign*, and by *such a sign* to intimate that he will dwell in the *clean heart*, that is, *washed* as with *pure water*. Where he designs to come, a pitcher of water must go before him.

3. He ate the passover in an *upper room furnished*. In eating his common meals he chose that which was homely, sat down on the grass: but, when he was to keep a sacred feast, in honour of that he would be at the expense of as good a room as he could get.

4. He ate it *with the twelve*. If Christ came *with the twelve*, then Judas was with them, though he was at this time contriving to betray his Master; and it is plain by what follows (*v.* 20), that he was there: he did not absent himself, lest he should have been suspected. Christ did not *exclude* him from the feast, though he *knew* his wickedness, for it was not as yet become public.

II. Christ's discourse with his disciples, as they were *eating* the passover.

1. They were *pleasing* themselves with the society of *their Master*; but he tells them that they must now presently lose him; *The Son of man is betrayed*. If he be *betrayed*, the next news you will hear of him, is, that he is *crucified* and *slain; The Son of man goes, as it is written of him, v.* 21.

2. They were *pleasing* themselves with the society *one of another*, but Christ casts a damp upon the joy of that, by telling them, *One of you that eateth with me shall betray me, v.* 18. Christ said this, if it might be, to startle the conscience of Judas, and to awaken him to repent of his wickedness, and to draw back from the brink of the pit. But for aught that appears, he who was *most concerned* in the warning, was *least concerned at* it. All the rest were affected with it. They began to be *sorrowful*. Here were the *bitter herbs*, with which this *passover-feast* was taken. They began to be *suspicious* of themselves; they said one by one, *Is it I? And another said, Is it I?* They were more jealous of themselves than of *one another*. It is the law of charity, to *hope the best* (1 Cor. xiii. 5–7), because we assuredly *know*, therefore we may justly *suspect*, more evil by ourselves than by our brethren. They trusted more to *his words* than to *their own hearts*; and therefore do not say, "I am sure *it is not I*", but, "*Lord, is it I?*"

Now, in answer to their enquiry, Christ saith that, [1] Which would make them easy; "It is not *you*, nor *you*; it is this that now *dips with me in the dish*." [2] Which, one would think, should make Judas very uneasy. If he go on in his undertaking, it is upon the sword's point, for *woe to that man by whom the Son of man is betrayed*; it were *better for him that he had never been born*. It is very probable that Judas encouraged himself in it with *this* thought, that his Master had often said he must be betrayed; "And if it must be done, surely God *will not find fault* with him that doth it." But Christ tells him that this will be no shelter or excuse to him; *The Son of man indeed goes, as it is written of him*, but *woe to that man by whom he is betrayed*. Christ was delivered indeed by *the determinate counsel and fore-knowledge of God*; but, notwithstanding that, it is *with wicked hands that he is crucified and slain*, Acts ii. 23.

III. The institution of the Lord's supper.

1. It was instituted in the close of a *supper*. In the Lord's supper there is no *bodily repast* intended. It is food for *the soul* only, and therefore a very little of that which is for the body, as much as will serve for a *sign*, is enough.

2. It was instituted by the *example* of Christ himself; by the practice of our Master himself, because intended for those who are already his disciples.

3. It was instituted with *blessing* and *giving of thanks*; the gifts of common providence are to be so received much more the gifts of special grace. He *blessed* (v. 22), and *gave thanks*, v. 23.

4. It was instituted to be a *memorial* of his *death*; and therefore he *broke* the bread, to show how it pleased the Lord to *bruise him*; and he called the *wine*, which is the blood of the grape, the *blood of the New Testament*. Frequent mention is made of the *blood*, the *precious blood*, as the price of our redemption. It is called the *blood of the New Testament*; for the covenant of grace became a *testament*, and of force by the death of Christ, the testator. It is said to be *shed for many*, to bring *many* sons to glory, Heb. ii. 10. It was sufficient for *many*, being of infinite value; we read of a great multitude which no man could number, that had all *washed their robes, and made them white in the blood of the Lamb* (Rev. vii. 9–14); and still it is a *fountain opened*. How comfortable is this that the blood of Christ is *shed for many*! And if for *many*, why not for *me*? If for sinners, sinners of the Gentiles, the chief of sinners, then *why not for me*?

5. It was a sign of the conveyance of those benefits to us, which were purchased for us by his death; and therefore he broke the bread *to them* (v. 22), and said, *Take eat* of it: he gave the cup *to them*, and ordered them to *drink of it*, v. 23.

6. It was instituted with an eye to the happiness of heaven, and to be an earnest and foretaste of that, and thereby to put our mouths out of taste for all the pleasures and delights of sense (v. 25); *I will drink no more of the fruit of the wine*. Lord, hasten the day, when I shall *drink* it *in the kingdom of God*.

7. It was closed with a *hymn*, v. 26. This was Christ's *swan-like* song, which he sung just before he entered upon his agony; probably, that which was usually sung, Ps. cxiii to cxviii.

IV. Christ's discourse with his disciples, as they were returning to Bethany by moonlight. When they had *sung the hymn*, presently they *went out*. The Israelites were forbidden to go out of their houses the night that they ate the passover, for fear of the sword of the destroying angel. But because Christ, the *great shepherd*, was to be *smitten*, he *went out* purposely to expose himself to the sword, as a champion; they *evaded* the destroyer, but Christ *conquered* him.

1. Christ here foretells that in his sufferings he should be *deserted* by all his disciples; "*You will all be offended because of me, this night*." Christ knew this before, and yet welcomed them at his table. Nor should we be discouraged from coming to the Lord's supper, by the fear of relapsing into sin afterward; but, the greater our danger is, the more need we have to fortify ourselves by the diligent conscientious use of holy ordinances. Christ tells them that they would be *offended in him*. Hitherto, they had *continued with him in his temptations*; though they had sometimes offended him, yet they had not been *offended in him*; but now the storm would be so great, that they would all *slip their anchors*, and be in danger of *shipwreck*. The *smiting* of the shepherd is often the *scattering* of the sheep: the whole flock suffers for it, and is endangered by it.

But Christ encourages them with a promise that they shall rally again, shall return both to their duty and to their comfort (v. 28); "*After I am risen* I will go *before you into Galilee*."

2. He foretells that he should be *denied* particularly by Peter. When they *went out* to go to the mount of Olives, we may suppose that they dropped Judas (he stole away from them). But Christ tells them that they would have no reason to boast of their constancy. Though God keeps us from being as bad as the worst, yet we may well be ashamed to think that we are not better than we are.

(1) Peter is confident that he should not *do so ill* as the rest of the disciples (v. 29); *Though all should be offended, yet will not I*. He supposes himself to be able to receive the shock of a temptation, and bear up against it, *all alone*; to *stand*, though nobody stood *by him*. It is bred in the bone with us, to *think well* of ourselves, and *trust* to *our own hearts*.

(2) Christ tells him that he will *do worse* than any of them. They will all *desert* him, but he will *deny* him; not once, but *thrice*; and that presently; "*This day, even this night before the cock crow twice*, thou wilt *deny* that ever thou hadst any knowledge of me."

(3) He stands to his promise; "*If I should die with thee, I will not deny thee*": and, no doubt, he thought as he said. Judas said nothing like this, when Christ told him he would betray him. He sinned by contrivance, Peter by surprise; Peter was *overtaken in this fault*. It was ill done of Peter, to contradict his Master. If he had said, with fear and trembling, "Lord, give me grace to keep me from denying thee," it might have been prevented: but they were all thus confident; they who said, *Lord, is it I?* now said, *It shall never be me*. Being acquitted from their fear of betraying Christ, they were now secure. But he that thinks he stands, must learn to take heed lest he fall.

Verses 32–42

Christ is here entering upon his sufferings, and begins with those which were the sorest of all his sufferings, those in his *soul*. Here we have him in his *agony*.

I. He retired for prayer; *Sit ye here* (saith he to his disciples), while I go a little further, and *pray*. He had lately prayed *with them* (John xvii); and now he appoints them to withdraw while he goes to his Father upon an errand peculiar to himself.

II. Even into that retirement he took with him Peter, *and James, and John* (v. 33), three competent witnesses of this part of his humiliation. These three had boasted most of their ability and willingness to suffer with him; Peter here, in this chapter, and James and John (*ch.* x. 39); and therefore Christ takes them to stand by, and see what a struggle he had, to convince them that they knew not what they said. It is fit that they who are most confident, should be *first* tried, that they may be made sensible of their folly and weakness.

III. There he was in a tremendous agitation (v. 33); *He began to be sore amazed*—a word not used in Matthew, but very significant; it bespeaks something like that *horror of great darkness*, which *fell upon Abraham* (Gen. xv. 12). Never was *sorrow* like unto *his* at that time. Yet there was not the least disorder or irregularity in this commotion of his spirits; for he had no corrupt nature to mix with them, as we have. If water have a sediment at the bottom, though it may be clear while it stands still, yet, when shaken, it grows muddy; so it is with our affections: but pure water in a clean glass, though ever so much stirred, continues clear; and so it was with Christ.

IV. He made a sad complaint of this agitation. He said, *My soul is exceeding sorrowful*. He was *made sin for us*, and therefore was thus *sorrowful*; he fully knew the *malignity* of the *sins* he was to *suffer for*; and having the highest degrees of love to God, who was *offended* by them, and of love to *man*, who was damaged and endangered by them, no marvel that *his soul* was *exceeding sorrowful*. He was *made a curse* for us; the curses of the law were transferred to him as our surety and representative. He now *tasted death* (as he is said to do, Heb. ii. 9), he *drank up* even the dregs of the cup; he *tasted* all the bitterness of it.

Now the consideration of Christ's sufferings in *his soul*, and his *sorrows* for us, should be of use to us,

(1) To *embitter our sins*. Can we ever entertain a *favourable* or so much as a *slight* thought of sin, when we see what impression sin made upon the Lord Jesus? Shall that *sit light* upon our souls, which sat *so heavy* upon his? Was Christ in such an agony for our sins, and shall we never be in an agony about them? If Christ thus suffered for sin, let us *arm ourselves with the same mind*.

(2) To *sweeten our sorrows*; if our souls be at any time *exceeding sorrowful*, let us remember that our Master was so before us, and the *disciple is not greater than his Lord*. Why should we affect to *drive away* sorrow, when Christ for our sakes, submitted to it, and thereby not only took out the *sting* of it, but put *virtue* into it, and made it *profitable*, nay, and put *sweetness* into it, and made it comfortable. Blessed Paul was *sorrowful*, and yet *always rejoicing*.

V. He ordered his disciples to keep with him; he said to them, *Tarry ye here and watch*. He had said to the other disciples nothing but, Sit ye here (*v.* 32); but these three he bids to tarry *and watch*, as expecting more from them than from the rest.

VI. He addressed himself to God by prayer (*v.* 35); He *fell on the ground, and prayed*. It was but a little before this, that in prayer he *lifted up his eyes* (John xvii. 1); but here, being in an agony, he *fell upon his face*. As *Man*, he deprecated his sufferings, that, *if it were possible, the hour might pass from him* (*v.* 35). We have his very words (*v.* 36), *Abba, Father*. The Syriac word is here retained, which Christ used, and which signifies *Father*, to intimate what an emphasis our Lord Jesus, in his *sorrows*, laid upon it, and would have us to lay. Father, *all things are possible to thee*. Even that which we cannot expect to be done for us, we ought yet to believe that God is *able to do*; and when we submit to his will, it must be with a believing acknowledgment of his power, that *all things are possible to him*. As *Mediator*, he acquiesced in the will of God concerning them; "*Nevertheless, not what I will, but what thou wilt*."

VII. He roused his disciples, who were dropped asleep while he was at prayer, *v.* 37, 38. He comes to look after them, since they did not look after him; and he *finds them asleep*. This carelessness of theirs was a presage of their further offence in deserting him. He had so lately commended them for *continuing with him in his temptations*, though they had not been without their faults. They had lately promised not to be *offended in him*; what! and yet mind him so little? He particularly upbraided Peter with his drowsiness; *Simon, sleepest thou? Couldest thou not watch one hour?* He did not require him to watch *all night* with him, only for *one hour*. He doth not over-task us, nor weary us.

As those whom Christ *loves* he *rebukes* when they do amiss, so those whom he *rebukes* he counsels and comforts. It was a very wise and faithful word of advice which Christ here gave to his disciples; *Watch and pray, lest ye enter into temptation, v.* 38. It was bad to *sleep* when Christ was in his agony, but if they did not stir up themselves, and fetch in grace and strength from God by prayer, they would *do worse*; and so they did, when they all forsook him, and fled. It was a very kind and tender excuse that Christ made for them; "*The spirit truly is willing*; you would willingly *keep awake*, but you cannot." *The flesh is weak*, and if you do not *watch* and *pray*, you may be overcome, notwithstanding. The consideration of the *weakness* and infirmity *of our flesh* should engage and quicken us to *prayer* and *watchfulness*.

VIII. *He repeated* his address to his Father (*v.* 39); *He went again, and prayed*, saying *the same word*; he spoke to the same purport, and again *the third time*. This teaches us, that *men ought always to pray, and not to faint*, Luke xviii. 1. Though the answers to our prayers do not come quickly, yet we must renew our requests. Paul, when he was *buffeted by a messenger of Satan, besought the Lord thrice*, as Christ did here, before he obtained an answer of peace, 2 Cor. xii. 7, 8. He must come a second and a third time, for the visits of God's grace, in answer to prayer, come sooner or later, according to the pleasure of his will.

IX. He *repeated* his visits to his disciples. Thus he gave a specimen of his continued care for his church on earth, even when it is *half asleep*. He came the *second time* to his disciples, and *found them asleep again, v.* 40. See how the infirmities of Christ's disciples *return* upon them, and *overpower* them, and what clogs those bodies of ours are to our souls. This second time he spoke to them as before, but *they wist not what to answer him*. Like men between sleeping and waking, they knew not where they were, or what they said. But, the *third time*, they were bid to *sleep* if they would (*v.* 41); "*Sleep on now, and take your rest*." It is enough; we had not that word in Matthew. "You have had warning enough to keep awake, and would not take it. Now *the hour is come*, in which I knew you would all forsake me." The *Son of man* is now *betrayed into the hands of sinners*. "Come, *rise up. Let us go*, for lo, he that betrayeth me is at hand."

Verses 43–52

We have here the *seizing* of our Lord Jesus by the officers of the chief priests. He began first to suffer *in his soul*, but afterward suffered in his body.

I. Here is a band of rude miscreants employed to *take* our Lord Jesus; *a great multitude with swords and staves*. At the head of this rabble is Judas, *one of the twelve*. It is no new thing for a very fair and plausible profession to end in a shameful and fatal apostasy.

II. Men of no less figure than the *chief priests, and the scribes*, and *the elders*, sent them, and set them on work, who pretended to expect the Messiah, and to be ready to welcome him; and yet, when he *is come*, they set themselves against him, and resolve to run him down.

III. Judas betrayed him *with a kiss*. He called him, *Master, Master, and kissed him*. It is enough to put one for ever out of conceit with being called of men *Rabbi, Rabbi* (Matt. xxiii. 7), since it was with this compliment that Christ was betrayed.

IV. They arrested him, and made him their prisoner (*v.* 46); *They laid their hands on him*, rude and violent hands, and *took him* into custody.

V. Peter laid about him in defence of his Master, and wounded one of the assailants. He was *one of them that stood by*, of them that *were with him* (so the word signifies). He *drew a sword*, and aimed, it is likely, to cut off the head, but missed his blow, and only *cut off the ear*, of a servant of the high priest, *v.* 47. It is easier to *fight* for Christ, than to *die* for him; but Christ's good soldiers overcome, not by taking away other people lives, but by laying down their own.

VI. Christ shows them the absurdity of their proceedings against him. 1. That they came out *against him*, as against a *thief*, whereas he was *innocent* of any crime; he *taught daily in the temple*, and if he had any wicked design, there it would some time or other have been discovered. By his fruits he was known to be a good tree; why then did they come out against him *as a thief*? 2. That they came to take him thus *privately*, whereas he was neither *ashamed* nor *afraid* to appear *publicly* in the temple. He was none of those *evil-doers* that *hate the light*, neither come *to the light*, John iii. 20. To come upon him thus at midnight, and in the place of his retirement, was base and cowardly. But this was not all. 3. They came *with swords and staves*, as if he had been in arms against the government. There was no occasion for those weapons; but they made this ado, (1) To secure themselves from the rage of some; they came armed, because they *feared the people*. (2) To expose him to the rage of others. By coming *with swords and staves to take him*, they represented him to the people as a dangerous turbulent man.

VII. He reconciled himself to all this injurious, ignominious treatment, by referring himself to the Old Testament predictions of the Messiah. I am hardly used, *but* I submit, for *the scriptures must be fulfilled, v.* 49. See here what a regard Christ had to the *scriptures*; he would bear anything rather than that the least jot or tittle of the word of God should fall to the ground. See what use we are to make of the Old Testament; we must search for Christ, the true *treasure hid in that field*.

VIII. All Christ's disciples, hereupon, deserted him (*v.* 50); *They all forsook him, and fled*. They were very confident that they should adhere to him; but even good men know not what they will do, till they are tried. If it was such a comfort to him as he had lately intimated, that they had hitherto *continued with him* in his lesser trials (Luke xxii. 28), we may well imagine what a grief it was to him, that they deserted him now in the greatest. Let not those that suffer for Christ, think it strange, if they be thus deserted, and if all the herd shun the wounded deer. When St. Paul was in peril, none *stood by him*, but *all men forsook him*, 2 Tim. iv. 16.

IX. The noise disturbed the neighbourhood, *v.* 51, 52. This passage of story we have not in any other of the evangelists. Here is an account of a *certain young man*, who, as it should seem, was no disciple of Christ, who *followed him* to see what would become of him. Now observe concerning him,

1. How he was *frightened out of his bed*, to be a *spectator* of Christ's sufferings. Such a *multitude*, so armed, could not but produce a great stir; this alarmed our *young man*, who had the curiosity to go, and see what the matter was, and was in such haste to inform himself, that he could not stay to dress himself, but threw a sheet about him. When all his disciples had quitted him, he continued to *follow him*, desirous to *hear* what he would say, and *see* what he would do.

2. See how he was *frightened into his bed* again, when he was in danger of being made a *sharer* in Christ's sufferings. His own disciples had run away from him; but this young man thought he might securely attend him, especially being so far from being armed, that he was not so much as clothed; but *the young men*, the Roman soldiers, who were called to assist, *laid hold of him*. Finding himself in danger, he *left the linen cloth* by which they had *caught hold of him*, and *fled away naked*. This passage is recorded to show what a narrow escape the disciples had of falling into their hands, out of which nothing could have kept them but their Master's care of them; *If ye seek me, let these go their way*, John xviii. 8. It also intimates that there is *no hold* of those who are led by curiosity only, and not by faith and conscience, to follow Christ.

Verses 53–65

We have here Christ's arraignment, trial, conviction, and condemnation, before the great sanhedrim, of which the *high priest* was president, the same Caiaphas that had lately adjudged it expedient he should be put to death, guilty or not guilty (John xi. 50), and who therefore might justly be excepted against as partial.

I. Christ is hurried away to his *house*. And there though in the dead of the night, *all the chief priests, and elders, and scribes*, that were in the secret, were *assembled*, ready to receive the prey; so sure were they of it.

II. *Peter followed* at a distance, *v.* 54. But when he came to the high priest's palace, he *sat with the servants*. The high priest's fire side was no proper place, nor his servants proper company for Peter, but it was his *entrance into a temptation*.

III. Great diligence was used to procure, for love or money, false witnesses against Christ. They had seized him as a malefactor, and now they had him they had no indictment to prefer against him, but they *sought for witnesses against him*, if they *would accuse him, v.* 55, 56. The chief priests and elders were by the law entrusted with the prosecuting and punishing of *false witnesses* (Deut. xix. 16, 17). It is time to cry, *Help, Lord*, when the physicians of a land are its troublers, and those that should be the conservators of peace and equity, are the corrupters of both.

IV. He was at length charged with words which, as they were represented, seemed to threaten *the temple* (*v.* 57, 58), but the witnesses to this matter did not agree (*v.* 59). *Their testimony was not sufficient*, nor equal to the charge of a capital crime; they did not accuse him of that upon which a *sentence of death* might be founded.

V. He was urged to be his own accuser (*v.* 60); The *high priest stood up* and said, *Answerest thou nothing?* This he said under pretence of justice and fair dealing, but really with a design to ensnare him, that they might *accuse him*. We may well imagine with what an air of haughtiness and disdain this proud high priest brought our Lord Jesus to this question. Pleased to think that *he* seemed silent, who had so often silenced those that picked quarrels with him. Still Christ *answered nothing*, that he might set us an example, 1. Of *patience* under calumnies and false accusations. 2. Of *prudence*, when a man shall be made an *offender for a word*, and our *de*fence made our *of*fence.

VI. When he was asked *whether he was the Christ*, he confessed, and denied not, that *he was, v.* 61, 62. He asked, *Art thou the Son of the Blessed?* that is, the Son of *God*? And for the proof of his being the *Son of God*, he binds them over to his second coming; "*Ye shall see the Son of man sitting on the right hand of power*; that *Son of man* that now appears so mean you shall shortly see and *tremble before.*" Now, one would think that such a word as this should have startled the court, and at least, in the opinion of some of them, should have amounted to a *demurrer*, or *arrest of judgment*. When Paul at the bar reasoned of the *judgment to come*, the judge *trembled*, and adjourned the trial, Acts. xxiv. 25.

VII. The high priest, upon this confession of his, convicted him as *a blasphemer* (*v.* 63); He *rent his clothes*. If Saul's rending Samuel's mantle was made to signify the rending of the kingdom from him (1 Sam. xv. 27, 28), much more did Caiaphas's rending his own clothes signify the rending of the priesthood from him, as the rending of the veil, at Christ's death, signified the throwing off all open.

VIII. They agreed that he was a blasphemer, and, as such, was guilty of a capital crime, *v.* 64. So they *all condemned him* to be *guilty of death*; what friends he had in the great sanhedrim, did not appear, it is probable that they had not notice.

IX. They set themselves to abuse him and to make sport with him, *v.* 65. It should seem that some of the priests themselves so far forgot the dignity, and the gravity which became them, that they helped their servants in playing the fool with a condemned prisoner. This they made their diversion, while they *waited for the morning*. If they did not think it below them to abuse Christ, shall we think anything below us, by which we may do him honour.

Verses 66–72

We have here the story of Peter's denying Christ.

1. It began in *keeping at a distance* from him. Peter had followed *afar off* (v. 54). Those that are *shy* of Christ, are in a fair way to *deny* him.

2. It was occasioned by his associating with the high priest's servants. They that think it dangerous to be in company with Christ's disciples, because thence they may be drawn in to *suffer for him*, will find it much more dangerous to be in company with his enemies, because there they may be drawn into *sin against him*.

3. The temptation was, his being charged as a disciple of Christ; *Thou also wert with Jesus of Nazareth*, v. 67. *This is one of them* (v. 69), *for thou art a Galilean*, one may know that by thy speaking broad, v. 70. It doth not appear that he was *challenged* upon it, but only *bantered* upon it, and in danger of being ridiculed as a fool for it. Sometimes the cause of Christ seems to fall so much on the losing side, that everybody has a stone to throw at it. Yet, all things considered, the temptation could not be called *formidable*; it was only a *maid* that casually cast her eye upon him, and said, *Thou art one of them*, to which he needed not to have made any reply.

4. The sin was very great; he *denied Christ before men*, at a time when he ought to have confessed and owned him. Christ had often given notice to his disciples of his own sufferings; yet, when they came, they were to Peter as great a surprise and terror as if he had never heard of them before. When Christ was admired and flocked after, he could readily own him; but now that he is deserted, and despised, and run down, he is ashamed of him, and will own no relation to him.

5. His repentance was very speedy. He repeated his denial thrice, and the third was worst of all, for then he *cursed* and *swore*, to confirm his denial. Then the *cock crew* the second time, which put him in mind of his Master's words, the warning he had given him, with that particular circumstance of the *cock crowing twice*; and when he thought thereon, he wept. Some observe that this evangelist, who wrote, as some have thought, by St. Peter's direction, speaks as fully of Peter's sin as any of them, but more briefly of his *sorrow*, which Peter, in modesty, would not have to be magnified, and because he thought he could never sorrow enough for so great a sin. *Fixing his mind upon it*, he wept. It is not a transient thought of that which is humbling, that will suffice, but we must dwell upon it.

CHAPTER 15

Here we have him, I. Arraigned and accused before Pilate the Roman governor, ver. 1–5. II. Cried out against by the common people, ver. 6–14. III. Condemned to be crucified immediately, ver. 15. IV. Bantered and abused, by the Roman soldiers, ver. 16–19. V. Led out to the place of execution, ver. 20–24. VI. Nailed to the cross between two thieves, ver. 25–28. VII. Reviled and abused by all that passed by, ver. 29–32. VIII. Forsaken for a time by his father, ver. 33–36. IX. Dying, and rending the veil, ver. 37, 38. X. Attested and witnessed to by the centurion and others, ver. 39–41. XI. Buried in the sepulchre of Joseph of Arimathea, ver. 42–47.

Verses 1–14

I. A *consultation* held by the great Sanhedrim for the effectual prosecution of our Lord Jesus. They met *early in the morning* about it; they lost no time, but followed their blow in good earnest. The unwearied industry of wicked people in doing that which is evil, should shame us for our backwardness and slothfulness in that which is good.

II. The delivering of him up a prisoner to Pilate; they *bound him*. Christ was bound, to make bonds easy to us, and enable us, as Paul and Silas, to sing in bonds. It is good for us often to *remember the bonds* of the Lord Jesus, as bound with him who was

bound for us. They led him through the streets of Jerusalem, to expose *him* to contempt, and we may well imagine how miserably he looked after such a night's usage as he had had. They voluntarily betrayed him that was *Israel's crown*, to them that were *Israel's yoke*.

III. The examining of him by Pilate upon interrogatories (v. 2); *"Art thou the king of the Jews?"* "Yea," saith Christ, "it is as *thou sayest*, I am that Messiah."

IV. The articles of impeachment exhibited against him, and his silence under the charge and accusation. The chief priests turned informers, and did in person *accuse Christ of many things* (v. 3), and witness against him, v. 4. Wicked priests are generally the worst of men. The better anything is, the worse it is when it is corrupted. These priests were very eager and noisy in their accusation; but Christ *answered nothing*, v. 3. While Pilate urged him to clear himself, and was desirous he should (v. 4), yet still he stood mute (v. 5), he *answered nothing*, which Pilate thought very strange. He gave Pilate a direct answer (v. 2), but would not answer the prosecutors and witnesses, because the things they alleged, were notoriously false, and he knew Pilate himself was convinced they were so. As Christ *spoke* to admiration, so he *kept silence* to admiration.

V. The proposal Pilate made to the people, to have Jesus released to them, since it was the custom of the feast to grace the solemnity with the release of one prisoner. The people expected and demanded that he should do *as he had ever done to them* (v. 8). Now Pilate perceived that the chief priests delivered up Jesus *for envy*, v. 10. It was easy to see that it was not his *guilt*, but his *goodness*, that they were provoked at. He thought that he might safely appeal from the priests to the people. Let them demand him to be *released*, and Pilate will readily do it. There was indeed another prisoner, *one Barabbas*, that had an interest, and would have some votes; but he questioned not but Jesus would out-poll him.

VI. The unanimous outrageous clamours of the people to have *Christ put to death*, and particularly to have him *crucified*. It was a great surprise to Pilate, when he found that they all agreed to desire that Barabbas might be *released*, v. 11. Pilate opposed it all he could; *"What will ye that I shall do to him whom ye call the King of the Jews?"* v. 12. They say, *Crucify him*. When Pilate objected, *Why, what evil has he done?* they did not pretend to answer it, but *cried out the more exceedingly*, *Crucify him, crucify him*. Now the priests promised themselves that it would influence Pilate two ways to condemn him. 1. It might incline him to believe Christ *guilty*, when there was so general an out-cry against him. "Surely," might Pilate think, "he must needs be a bad man, whom all the world is weary of." It has been the common artifice of Satan, to put Christ and his religion into an ill name, and so to run them down. But let us *judge* of persons and things by their merits, and not prejudge by common fame and the cry of the country. 2. It might induce him to condemn Christ, to *please* the people, and indeed for *fear* of *displeasing* them. Though he was not so *weak* as to be governed by their opinion, to believe him guilty, yet he was so *wicked* as to be swayed by their outrage, to condemn him, though he believed him innocent. Our Lord Jesus dying as a *sacrifice* for the *sins of many*, he fell a sacrifice to the *rage of many*.

Verses 15–21

I. Pilate, to gratify the Jews' malice, delivers Christ to be *crucified*, v. 15. *Willing to content the people*, he *released Barabbas unto them*, and *delivered Jesus* to be *crucified*. Though he *had scourged him* before, hoping that would *content* them, and then not designing to crucify him, yet he went on to that.

He who could persuade himself to *chastise* one that was innocent (Luke xxiii. 16), could by degrees persuade himself to *crucify* him.

Christ was *crucified*, for that was, 1. A *bloody* death, and *without blood no remission*, Heb. ix. 22. Christ was to lay down *his life* for us, and therefore shed *his blood*. 2. It was a *painful* death. Christ died, so as that he might *feel himself die*. Christ would meet death in its greatest terror, and so conquer it. 3. It was a *shameful* death, the death of slaves, and the vilest malefactors. The *cross* and the *shame* are put together. Christ makes *satisfaction* by submitting to the greatest reproach and ignominy. Yet this was not the worst. 4. It was a *cursed* death; thus it was branded by the Jewish law (Deut. xxi. 23). Now that Christ has submitted to be *hanged upon a tree*, the reproach and curse of that kind of death are quite rolled away.

II. Pilate, to gratify the gay humour of the Roman soldiers, delivered him to them, to be abused and spitefully treated. They called together *the whole regiment* that was then in waiting, and they went into an inner hall, where they ignominiously abused our Lord Jesus, as a king. 1. Do kings wear robes of purple or scarlet? They *clothed him with purple*. 2. Do kings wear *crowns*? They *platted a crown of thorns*, and *put it on his head*. A crown of straw, or rushes, would have been banter enough; but this was pain also. He wore the crown of thorns which we had deserved, that we might wear the crown of glory which he merited. 3. Are kings attended with the acclamations of their subjects, *O king, live for ever?* That also is mimicked; they saluted him with "*Hail, King of the Jews.*" 4. Kings have *sceptres* put into their hand, marks of dominion; to imitate this, they put a *reed in his right hand*. Those who despise the authority of the Lord Jesus do, in effect, *put a reed in his hand*; nay, and, as these here, *smite him on the head* with it. 5. Subjects, when they swear allegiance, were wont to *kiss* their sovereign; but, instead of that, *spit upon him*. 6. Kings used to be addressed upon the *knee*; and this also they brought into the jest, they *bowed the knee, and worshipped him*; this they did in scorn, to make themselves and one another laugh. He was thus mocked, not in *his own clothes*, but in another's, to signify that he suffered not for his own sin; the crime was ours, the shame his. Those that bow the knee to Christ, but do not bow the soul, put the same affront upon him that these here did.

III. The soldiers, at the hour appointed, led him away from Pilate's judgment-hall to the place of execution (*v.* 20). They compelled one Simon of Cyrene to carry his cross for him. He *passed by, coming out of the country*, not thinking of any such matter. We must not think it strange, if crosses come upon us suddenly, and we be surprised by them. The cross was a very troublesome unwieldly load: but he that carried it a few minutes, had the honour to have his name upon record in the book of God. Wherever this gospel is preached, there shall this be told for a memorial of him.

Verses 22–32

We have here the *crucifixion* of our Lord Jesus.

I. The *place where* he was crucified; it was called *Golgotha—the place of a skull*: it was the common place of execution, for he was in all respects numbered with the transgressors.

II. The *time when* he was crucified; it was the *third* hour, *v.* 25. At the *third hour*, according to the Jews' way of reckoning, that is, about nine of the clock in the morning, or soon after, they nailed him to the cross.

III. The indignities that were done him, when he was nailed to the cross.

1. It being the custom to give *wine* to persons that were to be *put to death*, they *mingled* his with *myrrh*,

which was *bitter*; he *tasted* it, but would not drink it; was willing to admit the bitterness of it, but not the benefit of it.

2. The garments of those that were crucified, being, as with us, the executioners' fee, the soldiers *cast lots* upon his garments (*v.* 24), so making themselves merry with his misery.

3. They set a superscription over his head, *The king of the Jews*, *v.* 26. Here was no crime alleged, but his sovereignty owned. Perhaps Pilate meant to cast disgrace upon Christ as a baffled king, or upon the Jews, as a people that deserved no better a king: however, God intended it to be the proclaiming even of Christ upon the cross, the *king of Israel*; though Pilate knew not what he wrote, any more than Caiaphas what he said, John xi. 51. Whenever we look unto Christ crucified, we must remember the inscription over his head, that he is a king.

4. They crucified *two thieves* with him, *one on his right hand, the other on his left*, and him in the midst as the worst of the three (*v.* 27). While he lived he has *associated* with sinners, to do them good; and now when he died, he was for the same purpose joined with them, for he *came into the world*, and went out of it, to *save sinners*. But this evangelist takes particular notice of the fulfilling of the scriptures in it, *v.* 28. In that famous prediction of Christ's sufferings (Isa. liii. 12), it was foretold that he should be numbered with the *transgressors*.

5. The spectators instead of condoling with him in his misery, added to it by insulting over him.

(1) Even they that *passed by railed on him*, *v.* 29. They taunted him, and expressed themselves with the utmost detestation of him, and indignation at him. The chief priests, no doubt, put these sarcasms into their mouths, *Thou that destroyest the temple, and buildest it in three days, now*, if thou canst, *save thyself*, and *come down from the cross*.

(2) Even the chief priests, who, being *taken from among men* and ordained for men, should be tender of those that are suffering and dying (Heb. v. 1, 2), yet they *mocked him, they said, He saved others, himself he cannot save*. They challenged him to *come down from the cross*, if he could, *v.* 22. Let them but *see* that, and they would *believe*.

(3) Even they that were crucified with him, reviled him (*v.* 32).

Verses 33–41

Here we have an account of Christ's dying.

I. There was a thick *darkness* over *the whole land* for three hours. The Jews had often demanded of Christ a *sign from heaven*; and now they had one, but such a one as signified the blinding of their eyes. It was a sign of the darkness that was come, and coming, upon the nation. This intimated to them, that the things which belonged to their peace, were now *hid from their eyes*. It was the power of darkness that they were now under, the works of darkness that they were now doing.

II. Toward the close of this darkness, our Lord Jesus, in the agony of his soul, cried out, *My God, my God, why hast thou forsaken me? v.* 34. The darkness signified the present cloud which the human soul of Christ was under, when he was making it an *offering for sin*. Our Lord Jesus was denied the light of the sun, when he was in his sufferings, to signify the withdrawing of the light of God's countenance. And this he complained of more than anything; he did not complain of his disciples' forsaking him, but of his Father's, 1. Because this *wounded his spirit*; and that is a thing *hard to bear*. 2. Because in this especially he was *made sin for us*. These symptoms of divine wrath were like that fire from heaven which had been sent sometimes, to consume the sacrifices; and it was always a token of God's acceptance. The fire that should have fallen upon the *sinner*, if God had not been pacified, fell upon the *sacrifice*, as a token that he was so; therefore it now fell upon Christ. When Paul was to be *offered* as a sacrifice for *the service of saints*, he could *joy* and *rejoice* (Phil. ii. 17); but it is another thing to be offered as a sacrifice for *the sin of sinners*.

III. Christ's prayer was bantered by them that stood by (*v*. 35, 36); because he cried, *Eli, Eli*, or (as Mark has it, according to the Syriac dialect) *Eloi, Eloi*, they said, *He calls for Elias*, though they knew very well what he said, and what it signified, *My God, My God*. One of them *filled a sponge with vinegar*, and reached it up to him upon a reed, *v*. 36. This was intended for a further affront and abuse to him; and whoever it was that checked him who did it, did but add to the reproach; "*Let him alone; let us see whether Elias will come to take him down;* and if not, we may conclude that he also hath abandoned him."

IV. Christ did again *cry with a loud voice*, and so *gave up the ghost, v*. 37. He was now commanding his soul into his Father's hand. Though speech fails, that we cannot *cry with a loud voice*, as Christ did, yet if God be the *strength of the heart*, that will not fail. Christ was really and truly *dead*, for he *gave up the ghost*; his human soul departed to the world of spirits, and left his body a breathless clod of clay.

V. Just at that instant that Christ died upon *mount Calvary*, the veil of the *temple* was *rent in twain from the top to the bottom, v*. 38. This bespoke a great deal, 1. Of terror to the unbelieving Jews; for it was a presage of the utter destruction of their church and nation, which followed not long after. 2. It bespeaks a great deal of comfort to all believing Christians, for it signifies the consecrating and laying open to us of a *new and living way into the holiest* by the *blood of Jesus*.

VI. The centurion who commanded the detachment which had the oversight of the execution was convinced, and confessed that this Jesus was the *Son of God, v*. 39. One thing that satisfied him, was, that he *so cried out, and gave up the ghost*. He said, to the honour of Christ, and the shame of those that abused him, *Truly this man was the Son of God*. But what reason had he to say so? 1. He had reason to say that he suffered *unjustly*. He suffered for saying that he was *the Son of God*; so that if he suffered unjustly, then what he said was true, and he was indeed the *Son of God*. 2. He had reason to say that he was a *favourite of heaven*, seeing how Heaven did thus honour him at his death. "Surely," thinks he, "this must be some divine person, highly beloved of God." Our Lord Jesus, even in the depth of his sufferings and humiliation, was the Son of God, and was declared to be so *with power*.

VII. There were some of his friends, the good women especially, that attended him (*v*. 40, 41); *There were women looking on afar off:* the men durst not be seen at all. The women durst not come near, but stood at a distance, overwhelmed with grief. Some of these women are here named. *Mary Magdalene* was one; she owed all her comfort to his power and goodness, which rescued her out of the possession of seven devils, in gratitude for which she thought she could never do enough for him. *Mary* also was there, *the mother of James the little*. This Mary was the wife of Cleophas or Alpheus, sister to the virgin Mary. These women had followed Christ *from Galilee*, though they were not required to attend the feast, as the males were. Now to see *him* upon a cross, whom they thought to have seen upon a throne, could not but be a great disappointment to them. Those that follow Christ, in expectation of great things in this world by him, may probably live to see themselves sadly disappointed.

Verses 42–47

We are here attending the funeral of our Lord Jesus.

I. How the body of Christ was *begged*. It was at the disposal of the government. We are here told,

1. When the body of Christ was begged, and why such haste was made with the funeral; *The even was come*, and it was the *preparation*, that is, *the day before the sabbath, v*. 42. The Jews were more strict in the observation of the sabbath than of any other feast; and therefore, though this day was itself a *feast-day*, yet they observed it more religiously as the *eve of the sabbath*. The day before the sabbath should be a day of preparation for the sabbath. We should get ready for it a day before; nay, the whole week should be divided between the improvement of the foregoing sabbath and the preparation for the following sabbath.

2. Who it was that begged the body; it was *Joseph of Arimathea*, who is here called an *honourable counsellor* (*v*. 43), a person of character and distinction; he was one of the *great Sanhedrim*. But here is a more shining character put upon him; he was one that *waited for the kingdom of God*. Those who *wait for the kingdom of God*, and hope for an interest in the privileges of it, must show it by their forwardness to own Christ's cause. This man God raised up for this necessary service, when none of Christ's disciples could, or durst, undertake it. *Joseph went in boldly to Pilate;* though he knew how much it would affront the chief priests, yet he *put on courage;* perhaps at first he was a little afraid.

3. What a surprise it was to Pilate, to hear that he was *dead*, especially that he was *already dead*. Pilate doubted whether he was yet dead or no, fearing lest he should be imposed upon, and the body should be *taken down alive*. He therefore called the centurion, his own officer, and asked him *whether he had been any while dead* (*v*. 44). The centurion could assure him of this, for he had particularly observed how he *gave up the ghost, v*. 39. There was a special providence in it, that there might be no pretence to say that he was buried alive, and so to take away the truth of his resurrection. Thus the truth of Christ gains confirmation, sometimes, even from its enemies.

II. How the body of Christ was *buried*. Pilate gave Joseph leave to take down the body, and do what he pleased with it.

1. Joseph bought *fine linen* to wrap the body in, though in such a case old linen might have been thought sufficient.

2. He *took down* the body, mangled and macerated as it was, and *wrapt it in the linen* as a treasure of great worth.

3. He *laid it in a sepulchre* of his own, in a private place. This sepulchre belonged to Joseph. Abraham when he had no other possession in the land of Canaan, yet had a burying-place, but Christ had not so much as that. This sepulchre was *hewn out of a rock*, for Christ died to make the grave a *refuge* and shelter to the saints.

4. He *rolled a stone to the door of the sepulchre*, for so the manner of the Jews was to bury.

5. Some of the good women attended the funeral, and *beheld where he was laid*, that they might come after the sabbath to anoint the dead body, because they had not time to do it now. When our great Mediator and Lawgiver was buried, special notice was taken of his sepulchre, because he was to *rise again*: and the care taken of his body, bespeaks the care which he himself will take concerning his body the church. Our meditations on Christ's burial should lead us to think of our own, and should help to make the grave familiar to us, and so to render that bed easy which we must shortly make in the darkness.

CHAPTER 16

A short account of the resurrection and ascension of the Lord Jesus. I. Christ's resurrection notified by an angel to the women that came to the sepulchre to anoint him, ver. 1–8. II. His appearance to Mary Magdalene, ver. 9–11. III. His appearance to the two disciples, going to Emmaus, ver. 12, 13. IV. His appearance to the eleven, ver. 14–18. V. His ascension into heaven, ver. 19, 20.

Verses 1–8

Never was there such a *sabbath* since the sabbath was first instituted as this was; during all this sabbath our Lord Jesus lay in the grave. It was *to him* a sabbath of *rest*, but a *silent* sabbath; it was to his disciples a melancholy sabbath, spent in tears and fears. Well, this sabbath is over, and the first day of the week is the first day of a new world.

I. The affectionate visit which the good women that had attended Christ, now made to his sepulchre. They set out from their lodgings *very early in the morning*, so that it was *sun-rising* by the time they got to the sepulchre. They had *bought sweet spices* too, and came not only to *bedew* the dead body with their tears, but to *perfume* it with their *spices, v.* 1. Nicodemus had bought a very large quantity of *dry spices, myrrh* and *aloes*, John xix. 39. But these good women did not think that enough; they bought spices, some perfumed oils, to *anoint him*. The respect which others have showed to Christ's name, should not hinder us from showing our respect to it.

II. The care they were in about the rolling away of the stone, and the superseding of that care (*v.* 3, 4); *They said among themselves*, as they were coming along, and now drew near the sepulchre, *Who shall roll us away the stone from the door of the sepulchre? For it was very great*, more than they with their united strength could move. And there was another difficulty much greater than this, to be got over, which they knew nothing of, to wit, a guard of soldiers set to *keep* the sepulchre; who, had they come before they were frightened away, would have frightened them away. But their gracious love to Christ carried them to the sepulchre; and see how by the time they came thither, both these difficulties were removed, both the *stone* which they *knew of*, and the *guard* which they *knew not of*. They saw *that the stone was rolled away*. They who seek Christ diligently, will find the difficulties that lie in their way strangely to vanish, and themselves helped over them beyond their expectation.

III. The assurance that was given them by an angel, that the Lord Jesus was risen from the dead, and had left him there to tell those so who came thither to enquire after him.

1. They *entered into the sepulchre*, and saw that the body of Jesus was not there. He, who by his death undertook to pay our debt, in his resurrection took out our acquittance, and the matter in dispute was determined by an incontestable evidence that he was the Son of God.

2. They saw a *young man sitting on the right side* of the sepulchre. The angel appeared in the likeness of *a man*, of a *young man*; for angels grow not *old*. This angel was *sitting* on *the right hand* as they went into the sepulchre, *clothed with a long white garment*, a garment down to the feet. The sight of him might justly have encouraged them, but they were *affrighted*. Thus many times that which should be matter of comfort to us, through our own mistakes and misapprehensions proves a terror to us.

3. He silences their fears by assuring them that here was cause enough for triumph, but none for trembling (*v.* 6); *He saith to them, Be not affrighted*. Be not affrighted, for, (1) "Ye are faithful lovers of Jesus Christ, and therefore, instead of being con-founded, ought to be *comforted*. *Ye seek Jesus of Nazareth, which was crucified*." He speaks of Jesus as one that *was crucified*; "The thing is *past*, that

scene is over, ye must not dwell so much upon the sad circumstances of his crucifixion as to be unapt to believe the joyful news of his resurrection." He *was* crucified, but he *is* glorified. After his entrance upon his glory, he never drew any veil over his sufferings, nor was shy of having his cross spoken of. (2) "It will therefore be good news to you, to hear that, instead of anointing him dead, you may rejoice in him living. *He is risen, he is not here*, not dead, but alive again. And you may here see *the place where they laid him*. You see he is gone hence, not stolen either by his enemies or by his friends, but *risen*."

4. He orders them to give speedy notice of this to his disciples. Thus they were made the apostles of the apostles, which was a recompence of their affection in attending him on the cross, to the grave, and in the grave. They first came, and were first served; no other of the disciples durst come near his sepulchre. None came near him but a few women, who were not able so much as to *roll away the stone*.

(1) They must tell the *disciples*, that *he is risen*. It is a dismal time with them, their dear Master is dead, and all their hopes and joys are buried in his grave; so that there remains no more spirit in them, they are perfectly at their wits' end. "O, go quickly to them," saith the angel, "tell them that *their Master is risen*; this will keep them from sinking into despair." Christ is not ashamed to own his poor disciples; his preferment doth not make him shy of them, for he took early care to have it *notified* to them. Christ is not extreme to mark what *they* do amiss, whose hearts are upright with him.

(2) They must be sure to tell Peter. This is particularly taken notice of by this evangelist, who is supposed to have written by Peter's direction. He is particularly named: *Tell Peter*, for, [1] It will be good news to him, more welcome to him than to any of them; for he is in sorrow for sin. [2] He will be afraid, lest the joy of this good news do not belong to him. Had the angel said only, *Go, tell his disciples*, poor Peter would have been ready to sigh, and say, "But I doubt I cannot look upon myself as one of them, for I disowned him, and deserve to be disowned by him"; to obviate that, "Go to Peter by name, and tell him, he shall be as welcome as any of the rest to *see* him in Galilee." A sight of Christ will be very welcome to a true penitent, and a true penitent shall be very welcome to a sight of Christ, for there is joy in heaven concerning him.

(3) They must appoint them all, and Peter by name, to give him the meeting in Galilee, as *he said unto you*, Matt. xxvi. 32. All the meetings between Christ and his disciples are of his own appointing. Christ never forgets his appointment. In all meetings between Christ and his disciples, he is the most forward. *He goes before you.*

IV. The account which the women did bring of this to the disciples (*v.* 8); They *went out quickly*, and *ran from the sepulchre, trembling* and *amazed*. Christ had often told them, that *the third day he would rise again*; had they given that its due notice and credit, they would have come to the sepulchre, expecting to have found him risen, and would have received the news of it with a joyful assurance, and not with all this terror and amazement. They showed not anything of it to any man that they *met by the way*, for *they were afraid*, afraid it was too good news to be true.

Verses 9–13

We have here a very short account of two of Christ's appearances.

I. He appeared to Mary Magdalene, to her first in the garden, which we have a particular narrative of, John xx. 14. It was she *out of whom he had cast seven devils*; and she *loved much*; and this honour Christ did her, that she was the first that saw him after his resurrection. The closer we cleave to Christ, the sooner we may expect to see him, and the more to see of him.

1. She brings notice of what she had seen, to the disciples; not only to the *eleven*, but to the rest that followed him, *as they mourned and wept*, v. 10. And it was an evidence of their great love to Christ. But when their *weeping* had *endured a night* or two, comfort returned, as Christ had promised them; *I will see you again, and your heart shall rejoice.* Better news cannot be brought to disciples in tears, than to tell them of Christ's resurrection.

2. They could not give credit to the report she brought them. They heard that *he was alive*, and had been seen of her. Yet *they believed not*. They fear that she is *imposed upon*, and that it was but a fancy that she *saw him*. Had they believed the *frequent* predictions of it from his own mouth, they would not have been now so incredulous of the report of it.

II. He appeared to two of the disciples, *as they went into the country*, v. 12. This refers, no doubt, to that which is largely related (Luke xxiv. 13, &c.), of what passed between Christ and the two disciples *going to Emmaus*. He is here said to have appeared to them in *another form*, in another dress than what he usually wore.

1. These *two* witnesses gave in their *testimony* to this proof of Christ's resurrection; *They went and told it to the residue*, v. 13. Being *satisfied* themselves, they were desirous to give their brethren the *satisfaction* they had, that they might be comforted as they were.

2. This did not gain credit with all; *Neither believed they them*. Now there was a wise providence in it, that the proofs of Christ's resurrection were given in thus *gradually*, and admitted thus *cautiously*. We have the more reason to believe those who did themselves believe so slowly: had they swallowed it presently, they might have been thought *credulous*, and their testimony the less to be *regarded*; but their *disbelieving* at first, shows that they did not believe it afterward but upon a full conviction.

Verses 14–18

I. The *conviction* which Christ gave his apostles of the truth of his resurrection (v. 14); He *appeared to them* himself, when they were all together, *as they sat at meat*, which gave him an opportunity to *eat and drink with them*, for their full satisfaction; see Acts x. 41. And still, when he appeared to them, he *upbraided them with their unbelief and hardness of heart*. The evidences of the truth of the gospel are so full, that those who receive it not, may justly be *upbraided* with their unbelief; and it is owing to the *hardness of their heart*, its senselessness and stupidity. Though they had not till now seen him themselves, they are justly blamed *because they believed not them who had seen him after he was risen*. It will not suffice for an excuse of our infidelity in the great day, to say, "*We did not see him* after he was risen," for we ought to have believed the testimony of those who did see him.

II. The *commission* which he gave them to set up his kingdom among men by the preaching of his *gospel*.

1. *To whom* they were to preach *the gospel*. Hitherto they had been sent only to *the lost sheep of the house of Israel*, and were forbidden to go into the *way of the Gentiles*, or into any city of the Samaritans; but now they are authorized to *go into all the world*, and to *preach the gospel* of Christ to *every creature*, to the Gentiles as well as to the Jews; to every human creature that is capable of receiving it. These eleven men could not themselves preach it to all the world, much less to *every creature* in it; but they and the other disciples, with those who should afterward be added to them, must *disperse* themselves several ways, and, wherever they went, carry the gospel along with them. They must make it the business of their lives to send those glad tidings *up and down*

the world with all possible fidelity and care, not as an amusement or entertainment, but as a solemn message from God to men, and an appointed means of making men happy.

2. What is the *summary of the gospel* they are to preach (v. 16); "Set before the world life and death, good and evil. Now go and tell them," (1) "That if they *believe the gospel*, and give up themselves to be Christ's disciples; if they *renounce* the devil, the world, and the flesh, and be *devoted* to Christ, they *shall be saved* from the guilt and power of sin, it shall not *rule* them, it shall not *ruin* them. He that is a true Christian, shall be saved through Christ." *Baptism* was appointed to be the *inaugurating* rite, by which those that embraced Christ owned him. (2) "*If they believe not they shall be damned*, by the sentence of a *despised* gospel, added to that of a broken law." And even this is *gospel*, it is good news, that nothing else but unbelief shall damn men, which is a sin against the remedy.

3. What power they should be endowed with, for the confirmation of the doctrine they were to preach (v. 17); *These signs shall follow them that believe*. They shall do wonders *in Christ's name*, the same name into which they were baptized, in the virtue of power derived from him, and fetched in by prayer. Some particular signs are mentioned; (1) They shall *cast out devils*; this power was more common among Christians than any other. (2) They shall *speak with new tongues*, which they had never learned, or been acquainted with; and this was both a *miracle* for the confirming of the truth of the gospel, and a *means* of spreading the gospel among those nations that had not heard it. (3) They shall *take up serpents*. This was fulfilled in Paul, who was not hurt by the *viper* that *fastened on his hand*, which was acknowledged a great miracle by the barbarous people, Acts xxviii. 5, 6. (4) If they be compelled by their persecutors to *drink any deadly* poisonous thing, *it shall not hurt them*. (5) They shall not only be preserved from hurt themselves, but they shall be enabled to do good to others; *They shall lay hands on the sick*, and they *shall recover*. Many of the elders of the church had this power, as appears by James v. 14, where they are said to *anoint* the sick *with oil in the name of the Lord*. With what assurance of success might they go about the executing of their commission, when they had such credentials as these to produce!

Verses 19–20

1. Christ *welcomed* into the *upper world* (v. 19): *After the Lord had spoken* what he had to say to his disciples, he *went up into heaven*, in a cloud; which we have a particular account of (Acts i. 9); he was *received up*, and he *sat on the right hand of God*. Now he is glorified with the glory he had before the world.

2. Christ *welcomed* in this *lower world*. (1) We have here the apostles working diligently for him; they *went forth, and preached everywhere* far and near. Though the doctrine they preached was directly contrary to the *spirit* and *genius* of the world, though it met with abundance of opposition, yet the preachers of it were neither *afraid* nor *ashamed*. (2) We have here God *working* effectually *with them*, to make their labours successful, by *confirming the word with signs following*, partly by the miracles that were wrought upon the *bodies* of people, and partly by the influence it had upon the *minds* of people. These were properly *signs following* the word—the reformation of the world, the destruction of idolatry, the conversion of sinners, the comfort of saints; and these signs still follow it, and that they may do so more and more, for the honour of Christ and the good of mankind, the evangelist prays, and teaches us to say *Amen*. Father in heaven, thus let thy name be hallowed, and let thy kingdom come.

AN EXPOSITION, WITH PRACTICAL OBSERVATIONS, OF

THE GOSPEL

ACCORDING TO

ST. LUKE

We are now entering into the labours of another evangelist; his name *Luke*. Some think that he was the only one of all the penmen of the scripture that was not of the seed of Israel. He was a Jewish proselyte, and, as some conjecture, converted to Christianity by the ministry of St. Paul; and after his coming into Macedonia (Acts xvi. 10) he was his constant companion. He had employed himself in the study and practice of physic; hence, Paul calls him *Luke the beloved Physician*, Col. iv. 14. Some of the pretended ancients tell you that he was a painter, and drew a picture of the virgin Mary. He is supposed to have written this gospel when he was associated with St. Paul. Some think that this is *the brother* whom Paul speaks of (2 Cor. viii. 18), *whose praise is in the gospel throughout all the churches of Christ*. His way and manner of writing are accurate and exact, his style polite and elegant, yet perspicuous. He expresses himself in a vein of purer Greek than is to be found in the other writers of the holy story. Thus he relates divers things more copiously than the other evangelists; and thus he especially treats of those things which relate to the priestly office of Christ. It is uncertain when, or about what time, this gospel was written. Some think that it was written at Rome, a little before he wrote his history of the *Acts of the Apostles* (which is a continuation of this), when he was there with Paul, while he was a prisoner, and preaching in *his own hired house*, with which the history of the Acts concludes; and then Paul saith that *only Luke was with him*, 2 Tim. iv. 11. When he was under that voluntary confinement with Paul, he had leisure to compile these two histories (and many excellent writings the church has been indebted to a prison for). Jerome says, He died when he was eighty-four years of age, and was never married.

CHAPTER 1

The narrative which this evangelist gives us of the life of Christ begins earlier than either Matthew or Mark. I. Luke's preface to his gospel, ver. 1–4. II. The prophecy and history of the conception of John Baptist, ver. 5–25. The annunciation of the virgin Mary, ver. 26–38. IV. The interview between Mary the mother of Jesus and Elisabeth the mother of John, ver. 39–56. V. The birth and circumcision of John Baptist, ver. 57–66. VI. Zacharias's song of praise, ver. 67–79. VII. A short account of John Baptist's infancy, ver. 80.

Verses 1–4

Complimental prefaces and dedications, the language of flattery and the food and fuel of pride, are justly condemned by the wise and good; but it doth not therefore follow, that such as are useful and instructive are to be run down; such is this. It is not certain who this Theophilus was; the name signifies a *friend of God*; some think that it does not mean any particular person, but everyone that is a *lover of God*. But it is rather to be understood of some particular person, probably a magistrate; because Luke gives him here the same title of respect which St. Paul gave to Festus the governor, Acts xxvi. 25. Religion does not destroy civility and good manners, but teaches us, according to the usages of our country, to *give honour to them to whom honour is due*.

I. Why St. Luke wrote this gospel. It is certain that he was moved by the Holy Ghost, not only *to* the writing, but *in* the writing of it; but in both he was moved as a reasonable creature, and not as a mere machine; and he was made to consider,

1. That the things he wrote of were things that were *most surely believed among all Christians*, and therefore things which they ought to be instructed in. He will not write about things of *doubtful disputation*, but the things which are, and ought to be, most *surely believed*. Though it is not the foundation of our faith, yet it is a support to it, that the articles of our creed are things that have been long *most surely believed*. The doctrine of Christ is what thousands

of the wisest and best of men have *ventured their souls upon*.

2. That it was requisite there should be a *declaration made in order* of those things; that the history of the life of Christ should be *methodized*. When things are *put in order*, we know the better where to *find them* for *our own* use, and how to *keep* them for the benefit of *others*.

3. That there were *many who had undertaken* to *publish* narratives of the *life of Christ*. Others' services to Christ must not be reckoned to supersede ours, but rather to quicken them.

4. That the truth of the things he had to write was *confirmed* by the *concurring testimony* of those who were competent and unexceptionable witnesses of them. What he was now about to publish, agreed with that which had been delivered by word of mouth, over and over, by those who from the beginning were *eye-witnesses and ministers of the word, v.* 2. (1) The apostles were *ministers of the word* of Christ, or of the doctrine of Christ; they, having received it themselves, ministered it to others, 1 John i. 1. They had not a gospel to make as masters, but a gospel to preach as ministers. (2) The *ministers of the word* were *eye-witnesses*. They did themselves *hear* the doctrine of Christ, and *see* his miracles, and had them not by report, at second hand. (3) They were so *from the beginning* of Christ's ministry, *v.* 2. He had his disciples with him when he wrought his *first miracle*, John ii. 11. They *companied with him all the time that he went in and out among them*, Acts i. 21. (4) The *written* gospel, which we have to *this day*, exactly agrees with the gospel which was *preached* in the *first days* of the church. (5) That he himself had a *perfect understanding* of the *things* he wrote of, *from the first, v.* 3. He asserts his own ability for this undertaking: "It seemed good to me, agreed attained to the exact knowledge of all things." He had diligently *searched* into these things. He had made it his business to inform himself concerning

particulars. He had received his intelligence, not only by tradition, but by revelation. He wrote his history of things *reported* by tradition, but *ratified* by inspiration. He could therefore say that he had a *perfect understanding* of these things. He knew them, *accurately*, exactly.

II. Observe why he sent it to *Theophilus*: "I wrote unto thee these things *in order, that thou mightest know the certainty of those things wherein thou hast been instructed.*" It is implied that he had been *instructed* in these things either before his baptism, or since, or both, according to the rule, Matt. xxviii. 19, 20. *Concerning which thou hast been catechized;* so the word is; the most knowing Christians began with being catechized. It was intended that he should *know the certainty of those things.* There is a *certainty* in the gospel of Christ, there is that therein which we may build upon; and those who have been well instructed in the things of God should give diligence to *know the certainty* of those things, to know not only what we believe, but why we believe it, that we may be able to give a *reason of the hope that is in us.*

Verses 5-25

The two preceding evangelists begin the gospel with the baptism of John and his ministry. This evangelist, designing to give a more particular account than had been given of our Saviour's conception and birth, determines to do so of John Baptist.

I. The account given of *his parents* (v. 5): They lived *in the days of Herod the king*, who was a foreigner, and a deputy for the Romans, who had lately made Judæa a province of the empire. This is taken notice of to show that the sceptre was quite departed from Judah. Israel is enslaved, yet then comes the glory of Israel.

Now the father of John Baptist was a priest, a son of Aaron; his name *Zacharias*. No families in the world were ever so honoured of God as those of Aaron and David; with one was made the covenant of priesthood, with the other that of royalty. Christ was of David's house, his forerunner of Aaron's. This Zacharias was *of the course of Abia.* When in David's time the family of Aaron was multiplied, he divided them into twenty-four courses, for the more regular performance of their office. The eighth of those was that of *Abia* (1 Chron. xxiv. 10), who was descended from Eleazar, Aaron's eldest son. The wife of this Zacharias was of the daughters of Aaron too, and her name was *Elisabeth*, the very same name with *Elisheba*, the wife of Aaron, Exod. vi. 23. The priests were very careful to marry within their own family.

Now that which is observed concerning Zacharias and Elisabeth is,

1. That they were a very religious couple (v. 6): *They were both righteous before God;* they were sincerely and really so. They *approved* themselves *to him.* It is a happy thing when those who are joined to each other in marriage are both *joined to the Lord. They walked in all the commandments and ordinances of the Lord, blameless.* They showed it, not by their talk, but by their *works;* by the way they walked in and the rule they walked by. They walked not only in the *ordinances* of the Lord, which related to divine worship, but in the *commandments* of the Lord, which have reference to all the instances of a good conversation. Not that they never did in anything *come short* of their duty, but it was their constant care and endeavour to *come up* to it. Though they were not *sinless*, yet they were *blameless*; nobody could charge them with any open scandalous sin; they lived *honestly* and *inoffensively.*

2. That they had been long *childless*, v. 7. Children are a *heritage of the Lord.* They are valuable desirable blessings; yet many there are, who are *righteous*

before God, who yet are not thus blessed. Elisabeth was *barren*, and they began to despair of ever having children, for they were both now *well stricken in years.* Many eminent persons were born of mothers that had been long childless, as Isaac, Jacob, Joseph, Samson, Samuel, and so here John Baptist, to make their birth the more remarkable and the blessing of it the more valuable to their parents.

II. The appearing of an angel to his father Zacharias, as he was ministering in the temple, v. 8-11. Observe,

1. How Zacharias was employed in the service of God (v. 8): He *executed the priest's office, before God, in the order of his course*; it was his *week of waiting*, and he was *upon duty.* Now it fell to Zacharias's lot to burn incense morning and evening for that week of his waiting, as other services fell to other priests *by lot* likewise. It was the burning of the daily incense at the *altar of incense* (v. 11), which was *in the temple* (v. 9), not in the most holy place, into which the high priest entered. The Jews say that one and the same priest burned not incense twice in all his days (there were such a multitude of them), at least never more than one week.

While Zacharias was burning incense in the temple, *the whole multitude of the people were praying without*, v. 10. These all addressed themselves to their devotions (in mental prayer, for their voice was not heard), when by the tinkling of a bell they had notice that the priest was gone in to burn incense. Now observe here, (1) That the true Israel of God always were a *praying* people. (2) That *then*, when ritual and ceremonial appointments were in full force, as this of *burning incense*, yet moral and spiritual duties were required to go along with them. David knew that when he was at a distance from the altar his prayer might be heard *without incense.* But, when he was *compassing the altar*, the incense could not be accepted *without prayer*, any more than the shell without the kernel. (3) That it is not enough for us to be where God is worshipped, if our hearts do not join in the worship. (4) All the prayers we offer up to God here in his courts are acceptable and successful only in virtue of the incense of Christ's intercession in the temple of God above. We cannot expect an interest in Christ's intercession if we do not *pray*, and pray *with our spirits*, and continue instant in prayer.

2. How, when he was thus employed, he was *honoured* with a messenger sent from heaven to him (v. 11): *There appeared unto him an angel of the Lord.* This angel stood on the right side of the altar of incense, on Zacharias's right hand. Zacharias had a good angel standing *at his right hand*, to encourage him.

3. What impression this made upon Zacharias (v. 12): *When Zacharias saw him* he was *troubled*, and *fear fell upon him*, v. 12. Though he was *righteous before God*, and *blameless* in his conversation, yet he could not be without some apprehensions. Ever since man sinned, his mind has been unable to bear the glory of such revelations and his conscience afraid of evil tidings brought by them. And for this reason God chooses to speak to us by men like ourselves, whose *terror* shall *not make us afraid.*

III. The message which the angel had to deliver to him, v. 13. He began his message, as angels generally did, with, *Fear not.* Perhaps when he saw the angel he was afraid lest he came to rebuke him for some mistake or miscarriage; "No," saith the angel, "*Fear not*, but compose thyself, that thou mayest with a sedate and even spirit receive the message I have to deliver to thee." Let us see what that is.

1. The *prayers* he has often made shall now receive an *answer of peace*: *Fear not, Zacharias, for thy prayer is heard.* If he means his particular prayer

for a son, it must be the prayers he had formerly made for that mercy, when he was likely to have children. God will now, in giving this mercy, look a great way back to the prayers that he had made long since for and with his wife. Prayers of faith are *filed* in heaven, and are not *forgotten*, though the thing prayed for is not presently *given* in. If he means the prayers he was *now making*, we may suppose that those were according to the duty of his place, for the Israel of God and their welfare, and the performance of the promises made to them concerning the Messiah and the coming of his kingdom: "This prayer of thine is now *heard*; for thy wife shall shortly conceive him that is to be the Messiah's forerunner." Some of the Jewish writers themselves say that the priest, when he burnt incense, prayed for the *salvation of the whole world*; and now that prayer shall be heard. In general, "The prayers thou *now* makest, and all thy prayers, are accepted of God, and this shall be the sign that thou art accepted of God, Elisabeth shall *bear thee a son*."

2. He shall have a son in his old age, by Elisabeth his wife, who had been long barren. He is directed what name to give his son: *Call him John*, in Hebrew *Johanan*, a name we often meet with in the Old Testament: it signifies *gracious*.

3. This son shall be the joy of his family and of all his relations, *v.* 14. He shall be a *welcome child. Thou* for thy part *shalt have joy and gladness*. Mercies that have been long *waited for*, when they *come at last*, are the more acceptable. "He shall be such a son as thou shalt have reason to rejoice in; many parents, if they could foresee what their children will prove, instead of *rejoicing* at their birth, would wish they had *never been*; but I will tell thee what thy son will be, and then thou wilt not need to *rejoice with trembling* at his birth, as the best must do, but mayest rejoice with triumph at it. Nay, and *many shall rejoice at his birth*; all the relations of the family will rejoice in it, and all its well-wishers, because it is for the honour and comfort of the family," *v.* 58.

4. This son shall be a distinguished *favourite of Heaven*, and a distinguished *blessing to the earth*. The honour of having *a son* is nothing to the honour of having *such a son*.

(1) He shall be *great in the sight of the Lord*. God will *set him before his face* continually. He shall be a prophet, yea *more than a prophet*. He shall be *much*, he shall be *great, in the sight of the Lord*.

(2) He shall be a Nazarite, set apart to God from everything that is *polluting*; in token of this, according to the law of Nazariteship, he *shall drink neither wine nor strong drink*. He shall be a Nazar te for life. Which intimates that those that would be *eminent* servants of God, and employed in *eminent* services, must learn to live a life of self-denial and mortification, must be dead to the pleasures of sense, and keep their minds from everything that is darkening and disturbing to them.

(3) He shall be abundantly fitted and qualified for those great and eminent services. *He shall be filled with the Holy Ghost, even from his mother's womb.* [1.] Those that would be filled with the Holy Ghost must be sober and temperate, and very moderate in the use of wine and strong drink. *Be not drunk with wine*, but *be filled with the Spirit*, Eph. v. 18. [2.] It is possible that infants may be wrought upon by the *Holy Ghost*, even from their *mother's womb*; for John Baptist even then was *filled with the Holy Ghost*. God has promised to *pour out his Spirit* upon the *seed* of believers, Isa. xliv. 3.

(4) He shall be instrumental for the conversion of many souls to God, and the preparing of them to receive and entertain the gospel of Christ, *v.* 16, 17. He shall be sent to the *children of Israel*, and not to the Gentiles; to the *whole* nation, and not to the

family of *the priests only*. He shall go before *the Lord their God*, that is, before the Messiah. John shall *go before him*, a little before him, to give notice of his approach, and to prepare people to receive him. He shall go *in the spirit and power of Elias*. That is, *First*, He shall be such a man as Elias was, and do such works as Elias did—shall, like him, preach the necessity of repentance and reformation to a very corrupt and degenerate age—shall like him, be bold and zealous in reproving sin and witnessing against it even in the greatest, and be hated and persecuted for it. He shall be carried on. in his work, as Elijah was, by a divine *spirit* and *power*, which shall crown his ministry with wonderful success. John Baptist went before Christ and his apostles, and introduced the gospel dispensation by preaching the substance of the gospel doctrine and duty, *Repent, with an eye to the kingdom of heaven. Secondly*, He shall be that very person who was prophesied of by Malachi under the name of Elijah (Mal. iv. 5), who should be *sent before the coming of the day of the Lord*. He shall *turn many of the children of Israel to the Lord their God*. Whatever has a tendency to *turn us from iniquity*, will turn us to Christ as *our Lord and our God*; for those who through grace are wrought upon to shake off the yoke of sin, will soon be persuaded to take upon them the yoke of the *Lord Jesus*. Hereby he shall *turn the hearts of the fathers to the children*, that is, of the Jews to the Gentiles; shall help to conquer the rooted prejudices which the Jews have against the Gentiles, which was begun to be done by John Baptist, who baptized and taught Roman soldiers as well as Jewish Pharisees, and who cured the pride and confidence of those Jews who gloried in their having Abraham to their father, and told them that God would *out of stones raise up children unto Israel*, Matt. iii. 9. When the Jews that embraced the faith of Christ were brought to join in communion with the Gentiles that did so too, then the heart of the fathers was turned to the children. And the effect of this will be, that enmities will be slain and discord made to cease; and they that are at variance, being united in his baptism, will be better reconciled one to another. This agrees with the account Josephus gives of John Baptist, *Antiq. lib.* 18. *cap*, 7. "That he was a good man, and taught the Jews the exercise of virtue, in piety towards God, and righteousness towards one another." And he saith, "The people flocked after him, and were exceedingly delighted in his doctrine." Thus he turned the hearts of fathers and children to God and one another, by *turning the disobedient to the wisdom of the just. First*, True religion is *the wisdom of just men*. It is both our wisdom and our duty to be religious; there is both equity and prudence in it. *Secondly*, It is not impossible but that those who have been unbelieving and *disobedient* may be turned to the *wisdom of the just*; divine grace can conquer the greatest ignorance and prejudice. *Thirdly*, The great design of the gospel is to bring people *home* to God, and to bring them nearer to *one another*. Hereby he shall *make ready a people prepared for the Lord*. All that are to be *devoted* to the Lord, and *made happy* in him, must first be *prepared* and *made ready* for him. Nothing has a more direct tendency to prepare people for Christ than the doctrine of repentance. When sin is thereby made grievous, Christ will become very precious.

IV. Zacharias's unbelief of the angel's prediction, and the rebuke he was laid under. We are here told,

1. What his unbelief spoke, *v.* 18. *Whereby shall I know this?* There are many instances in the Old Testament of those that had children when they were old, yet he cannot believe that he shall have this child of promise: "*For I am an old man*, and my wife is now well *stricken in years*. Therefore he must have

a sign given him, or he will not believe." Though he had this notice given him in the temple, though it was given him when he was praying, and burning incense, and though a firm belief that God has an almighty power, and with him *nothing is impossible,* was enough to silence all objections, yet considering his own body and his wife's too much, unlike a son of Abraham, he *staggered at the promise.*

2. How his unbelief was *silenced,* and he *silenced* for it.

(1) The angel *stops his mouth.* Doth he ask, *Whereby shall I know this?* Let him know it by this, *I am Gabriel, v.* 19. He puts his name to his prophecy. This angel readily saith, *I am Gabriel,* which signifies *the power of God,* or, the *mighty one of God.* He is Gabriel, who *stands in the presence of God.* "Though I am now talking with thee here, yet *I stand in the presence of God. I am sent to speak to thee,* sent on purpose to *show thee these glad tidings,* which, being so well worthy of all acceptation, thou oughtest to have received cheerfully."

(2) The angel *stops his mouth* indeed. "That thou mayest object no more, *behold thou shalt be dumb, v.* 20. If thou wilt have a sign for the support of thy faith, it shall be such a one as shall be also the punishment of thine unbelief; thou *shalt not be able to speak till the day that these things shall be performed," v.* 20. Thou shalt be both *dumb* and *deaf;* the same word signifies both, and it is plain that he lost his hearing as well as his speech, for his friends *made signs* to him (*v.* 62) as well as he to them, *v.* 22. God dealt *justly* with him, because he had objected against God's word. God dealt *kindly* with him, and very tenderly and graciously. For, *First,* Thus he prevented his speaking any more such distrustful unbelieving words. It is better not to speak at all than to *speak wickedly. Secondly,* Thus he *confirmed* his faith; and, by his being disabled to *speak,* he is enabled to *think* the better. *Thirdly,* Thus he was kept from divulging the vision, and boasting of it. *Fourthly,* It was a great mercy that God's words should be fulfilled in their season, notwithstanding his sinful distrust. He shall not be for ever *dumb,* but only *till the day that these things shall be performed,* and then thy *lips* shall be *opened,* that thy *mouth* may *show forth God's praise.*

V. The return of Zacharias to the people, and at length to his family, and the conception of this child of promise.

1. The people staid, expecting Zacharias to come out of the temple, because he was to pronounce the blessing upon them in the name of the Lord. Though he staid beyond the usual time, yet they did not hurry away without the blessing, but *waited* for him, marvelling that he *tarried so long in the temple,* and afraid lest something was amiss, *v.* 21.

2. When he came out, he was *speechless, v.* 22. He was now to have dismissed the congregation with a blessing, but was dumb and not able to do it.

3. He made a shift to give them to understand that he had *seen a vision,* for he *beckoned to them,* and *remained speechless, v.* 22. The Old Testament speaks by signs; it *beckons to us,* but *remains speechless.* It is the gospel that speaks to us articulately, and gives us a clear view of that which in the Old Testament was seen *through a glass darkly.*

4. He staid out the *days of his ministration;* for, his lot being to *burn incense,* he could do that, though he was *dumb* and *deaf.* When we cannot perform the service of God so well as we would, yet, if we perform it as well as we can, God will accept of us in it.

5. He then returned to his family, and his *wife conceived, v.* 23, 24. *She hid herself five months,* and kept in private. (1) Lest she should do herself any

prejudice. (2) Lest she should contract any ceremonial pollution which might intrench upon the Nazariteship of her child. (3) Some think it was in an excess of modesty that she *hid herself.* Or, it was in token of her humility, that she might not seem to boast of the honour God had put upon her. (4) She *hid herself* for devotion. She gives this reason for her retirement, *"For thus hath the Lord dealt with me;* he hath *taken away my reproach among men."* Fruitfulness was looked upon to be so great a blessing among the Jews that it was a great reproach to be barren; and those who were so were concluded to be guilty of some great sin *unknown.* Now Elisabeth triumphs, that not only this reproach is taken away, but great glory is put upon her instead of it: *Thus hath the Lord dealt with me in the days wherein he looked on me.*

Verses 26-38

We have here notice given us of all that it was fit we should know concerning the incarnation and conception of our blessed Saviour. The same angel, Gabriel, that was employed in making known to Zacharias God's purpose concerning *his son,* is employed in this also; for in this, the same glorious work of redemption, which was *begun* in that, is carried on.

I. We have here an account given of the mother of our Lord.

1. Her name was *Mary,* the same name with *Miriam,* the sister of Moses and Aaron; the name signifies *exalted.*

2. She was a daughter of the royal family, lineally descended from David, and she herself and all her friends knew it, for she went under the title and character of the *house of David.* She was enabled by God's providence, and the care of the Jews, to preserve their genealogies, to *make it out,* and as long as the promise of the Messiah was to be fulfilled it was *worth keeping;* but for those now, who are brought low in the world, to have descended from persons of honour, is not worth mentioning.

3. She was *a virgin,* but *espoused* to one of the same royal stock, like her, however, of low estate. His name was Joseph; he also was *of the house of David,* Matt. i. 20. Christ's mother was a *virgin.* But he was born of a *virgin espoused,* made up to be married, and contracted, to put honour upon the married state.

4. She lived in Nazareth, a *city of Galilee,* a remote corner of the country, and in no reputation for religion or learning, but which bordered upon the heathen, and therefore was called *Galilee of the Gentiles.* The angel was sent to her from Nazareth. No distance or disadvantage of place shall be a prejudice to those for whom God has favours in store.

II. The *address* of the angel to her, *v.* 28. He surprised her with this salutation, *Hail, thou that art highly favoured.* This was intended to raise in her, 1. A value for *herself.* In some, who like Mary pore only on their *low estate,* there is occasion for it. 2. An expectation of great news, not from abroad, but from above. *Hail, thou, χαῖρε—rejoice thou;* it was the usual form of salutation.

(1) She is dignified: "Thou art *highly favoured.* God, in his choice of thee to be the mother of the Messiah, has put an honour upon thee peculiar to thyself."

(2) She has the presence of God with her: *"The Lord is with thee."* Nothing is to be despaired of, not the performance of any service, not the obtaining of any favour, though ever so great, if we have *God with us.*

(3) She has the blessing of God upon her: *"Blessed art thou among women;* not only thou shalt be

accounted so by men, but thou shalt be so. Thou that art so *highly favoured* in this instance mayest expect in other things to be *blessed*." She explains this herself (v. 48), *All generations shall call me blessed.*

III. The consternation she was in, upon this address, v. 29. *When she saw him* she is *confounded* at it, as not conscious to herself of anything that either *merited* or *promised* such great things; and she *cast in her mind what manner of salutation this should be.* Was it from heaven or of men? Her thoughtfulness upon this occasion gives a very useful intimation to young people of her sex, when addresses are made to them, to consider and *cast in their minds* what manner of *salutations* they are.

IV. The message itself which the angel had to deliver to her. He went on with his errand, v. 30. To what he had said she made no reply; he therefore confirms it: "*Fear not, Mary, thou hast found favour with God* more than thou thinkest of, as there are many who think they are more favoured of God than really they are." Doth God favour thee? Is he for thee? No matter who is against thee.

1. Though she is a *virgin*, she shall have the honour of being a *mother*: "*Thou shalt conceive in thy womb, and bring forth a son, thou shalt call his name Jesus,*" v. 31.

2. Though she lives in *poverty* and *obscurity*, yet she shall have the honour to be the mother of the Messiah; her son shall be named *Jesus—a Saviour.* He v ill be very *nearly allied* to the *upper world.* He *shall be great*, truly great, for he shall be called *the Son of the Highest.* He shall be *called*, and not miscalled, the *Son of the Highest.* Those who are the children of God, are *truly great*, and therefore are concerned to be *very good*, 1 John iii. 1, 2. He will be very *highly preferred* in the *lower world*; for, though appearing in the form of a servant, yet the *Lord God shall give unto him the throne of his father David,* v. 32. His people will not *give him that throne*, but the *Lord God* shall give him a right to *rule them*, and set him as *his king* upon the *holy hill of Zion.* He assures her, (1) That his kingdom shall be *spiritual*: he shall *reign over the house of Jacob.* It must therefore be a *spiritual* kingdom, the house of Israel *according to promise*, that he must *rule over.* (2) That it shall be eternal: he shall reign *for ever*, and *of his kingdom there shall be no end.* Other crowns endure not *to every generation*, but Christ's doth.

V. The further information given her, upon her enquiry.

1. It is a just enquiry which she makes: "*How shall this be?*" v. 34. She knew that the Messiah must be born of *a virgin*; and, if she must be his mother, she desires to know how. This was not the language of her distrust, but of a desire to be further instructed.

2. It is a satisfactory answer that is given to it, v. 25. (1) She shall conceive by *the power of the Holy Ghost.* A divine power will undertake it, the power of *the Holy Ghost* himself.

(2) She must *ask no questions* concerning the way and manner how it shall be wrought; for the Holy Ghost, as the *power of the Highest*, shall *overshadow* her. The formation of every babe in the womb, and the entrance of the spirit of life into it, is a mystery in nature. We were *made in secret.* Much more was the formation of the child Jesus a *mystery.*

(3) The child she shall conceive is a *holy thing*, and therefore must not be conceived by *ordinary generation.* He is spoken of emphatically, *That Holy Thing*, such as never was; and he shall be called *the Son of God.* His human nature must be so produced, as it was fit that should be which was to be taken into union with the divine nature.

3. It was a further encouragement to her faith to be told that *her cousin Elisabeth*, though stricken in years, was *with child*, v. 36. Here is an age of wonders

beginning. *This is the sixth month with her that was called barren.* The angel assures Mary of this, to encourage her faith, and concludes with that great truth, of undoubted certainty and universal use, *For with God nothing shall be impossible* (v. 37), and, if nothing, then not this. No *word* of God must be *incredible to us*, as long as no *work* of God is *impossible to him.*

VI. Her acquiescence in the will of God concerning her, v. 38. She owns herself, 1. A believing subject to the divine authority: "*Behold, the handmaid of the Lord.* Lord, I am at thy service." She leaves the issue with God, and submits entirely to his will. 2. A believing expectant of the divine favour. She is not only content that it should be so, but humbly desires that it may be so: *Be it unto me according to thy word.* We must, as Mary here, *guide* our desires by the word of God, and *ground* our hopes *upon* it. Be it unto me *according to thy word*; just so, and no otherwise.

Hereupon, *the angel departed from her*; having completed the errand he was sent upon, he returned.

Verses 39–56

We have here an interview between the two happy mothers, Elisabeth and Mary. Sometimes it may prove a better piece of service than we think to bring good people together, to compare notes.

I. The visit which Mary made to Elisabeth, v. 39. She *arose*, and left her affairs, to attend this greater matter: *in those days, at that time.* She went *with care, diligence*, and *expedition.* She went *to a city of Judah in the hill-country*; thither Mary hastened, though it was a long journey, some scores of miles.

It is generally supposed that she went thither for the confirming of her faith, and to rejoice with her sister-favourite. And, besides, she went thither, perhaps, that she might be more retired from company, or else might have more agreeable company than she could have in Nazareth. We may suppose that she did not acquaint any of her neighbours at Nazareth with the message she had received from heaven, yet longed to *talk over* a thing she had a thousand times *thought over*, and knew no person in the world with whom she could *freely* converse concerning it but her cousin Elisabeth. It is very beneficial and comfortable for those that have a good work of grace begun in their souls, to consult those who are in the same case. They will find that, as in water face answers to face, so doth the heart of man to man, of Christian to Christian.

II. The meeting between Mary and Elisabeth. Mary entered into the house of Zacharias. She *saluted Elisabeth* (v. 40), told her that she was come to make her visit, and *rejoice with her* in her joy.

1. The babe *leaped in her womb*, v. 41. It is very probable that she had often felt the child stir; but this was a more than ordinary motion of the child, which alarmed her to expect something very extraordinary. The *babe leaped* as it were to give a signal to his mother that *he* was now at hand whose forerunner he was to be.

2. Elisabeth was herself *filled with the Holy Ghost*, or a Spirit of prophecy, by which she was given to understand that the Messiah was at hand. The uncommon motion of the babe in her womb was a token of the extraordinary emotion of her spirit under a divine impulse.

III. The welcome which Elisabeth, by the Spirit of prophecy, gave to Mary, the mother of our Lord.

1. She congratulates her on her honour. She *spoke with a loud voice.* She said, *Blessed art thou among women*, the same word that the angel had said, v. 28. But Elisabeth adds a reason, *Therefore blessed art thou* because *blessed is the fruit of thy womb.* Elisabeth was the wife of a priest, and in years, yet she *grudges*

not that her kinswoman, who was many years younger than she, should have the honour of conceiving in her virginity, and being the mother of the Messiah, whereas the honour put upon her was *much less*; she *rejoices* in it. While we cannot but own that we are more *favoured* of God than we deserve, let us by no means envy that others are *more highly* favoured than we are.

2. She acknowledges her condescension, in making her this visit (v. 43): *Whence is this to me, that the mother of my Lord should come to me?* She calls the virgin Mary the *mother of her Lord.* She not only bids her welcome to her house, but reckons this visit a great favour, which she thought herself unworthy of. *Whence is this to me?* Those that are filled with the Holy Ghost have *low thoughts* of their own merits, and high thoughts of God's favours.

3. She acquaints her with the concurrence of the babe in her womb, in this welcome to her (v. 44): "*As soon as the voice of thy salutation sounded in my ears,* not only my heart *leaped for joy,* but the *babe in my womb did so* too." He *leaped* as it were *for joy* that the Messiah, whose harbinger he was to be, would himself come so soon after him. This would serve very much to strengthen the faith of the virgin, that there were such assurances as these given to others.

4. She commends her faith, and encourages it (v. 45): *Blessed is she that believed.* Believing souls are blessed souls. They are *blessed* who *believe* the word of God, for that word will not fail them; *there shall,* without doubt, *be a performance of those things which are told her from the Lord.* The faithfulness of God is the blessedness of the faith of the saints. Those that have experienced the performance of God's promises themselves should encourage others to hope that he will be as good as his word to them also.

IV. Mary's song of praise, upon this occasion. Elisabeth's prophecy was an echo to the virgin Mary's salutation, and this song is yet a stronger *echo* to that prophecy. We may suppose the blessed virgin to come in, very much *fatigued* with her journey; yet she forgets that, and is inspired with new life, and vigour, and joy, upon the confirmation she here meets with of her faith.

1. Here are the expressions of joy and praise, and God alone the object of the praise and centre of the joy. Observe how Mary here speaks of God.

(1) With great reverence of him, as *the Lord*: "*My soul doth magnify the Lord.*" Those, and those only, are *advanced* in mercy, who are thereby brought to think the more *highly* and *honourably* of God. The more honour God has any way put upon us, the more honour we must study to give to him; and *then* only are we accepted in magnifying the Lord, when our *souls* magnify him, and *all that is within us.* Praising work must be soul work.

(2) With great complacency in him as *her Saviour: My spirit rejoiceth in God my Saviour.* This seems to have reference to the Messiah, whom she was to be the mother of. She calls him *God her Saviour*; for the angel had told her that he should be the *Son of the Highest,* and that his name should be *Jesus, a Saviour*; this she fastened upon, with application to herself: *He is God my Saviour.* Even the mother of our Lord had need of an interest in him as her Saviour, and would have been undone without it.

2. Here are just causes assigned for this joy and praise.

(1) Upon *her own* account, v. 48, 49. Her *spirit rejoiced in the Lord,* because of the *kind* things he had done for her. *He has regarded the low estate of his handmaiden.* "He has chosen me to this honour, notwithstanding my great meanness, poverty, and obscurity." And, if God *regards her low estate,* he not only thereby gives a specimen of his favour to the whole race of mankind, whom he *remembers in their low estate,* but secures a lasting honour to her (for such the honour is that God bestows, honour that fades not away): "*From henceforth all generations shall call me blessed.*" Elisabeth had once and again called her *blessed*: "But that is not all," saith she, "all generations of Gentiles as well as Jews shall call me so." Her *soul magnifies* the Lord (v. 49): *He that is mighty has done to me great things.* A great thing indeed, that a *virgin* should *conceive.* A great thing indeed, that Messiah should now at length be born. It is the *power of the Highest* that appears in this. She adds, *and holy is his name.* He that is *mighty,* even he whose name is holy, has *done to me great things.* Glorious things may be expected from him that is both *mighty* and *holy*; who *can do everything,* and *will* do everything *well* and *for the best.*

(2) Upon the account of *others.* The virgin Mary, as the mother of the Messiah, is become a kind of public person, and therefore *looks abroad,* looks *about her,* looks *before her,* and takes notice of God's various dealings with the children of men, v. 50, &c. It is a certain truth that *God has mercy in store,* mercy in reserve. But never did this appear so as in sending his Son into the world to save us (v. 50): *His mercy is on them that fear him;* it has always been so. But he hath manifested this *mercy,* so as never before, in sending his Son to bring in an everlasting righteousness, and work out an everlasting salvation, for them that fear him, and this *from generation to generation;* for there are gospel privileges transmitted by entail, and intended for perpetuity. In him *mercy* is settled upon all that *fear God,* pardoning mercy, healing mercy, accepting mercy, crowning mercy, *from generation to generation,* while the world stands. It has been a common observation that God in his providence puts *contempt* upon the *haughty* and *honour* upon the *humble.* As God had, with his *mercy* to her, shown himself *mighty* also (v. 48, 49), so he had, with his *mercy on them that fear him, shown strength* likewise *with his arm.* In the course of his providence, it is his usual method to *cross the expectations of men. Proud men* expect to carry all before them, but he *scatters them in the imagination of their hearts,* and brings them low. The *mighty* think to secure themselves by might *in their seats,* but he *puts them down,* while, on the other hand, those of *low degree* are wonderfully *exalted.* This observation concerning *honour* holds likewise concerning *riches*; many who were so poor that they had not bread for themselves and their families, by some surprising turn of Providence in favour of them, come to be *filled with good things*; while, on the other hand, those who were rich, are strangely impoverished, and *sent away empty.* God takes a pleasure in *disappointing* their expectations who promise themselves *great things* in the world, and in *out-doing* the expectations of those who promise themselves but *a little.* As a *good* God, it is his glory to exalt those who humble themselves, and to speak comfort to those who fear before him. The gospel grace is shown

1. In the *spiritual honours* it dispenses. When the proud Pharisees were rejected, and Publicans and sinners went *into the kingdom of heaven* before them,— when the Jews, who *followed after the law of righteousness,* did not attain it, and the Gentiles, who never thought of it, attained to righteousness (Rom. ix. 30, 31),—when God chose not the *wise men after the flesh,* not the *mighty,* or the *noble,* to preach the gospel, and plant Christianity in the world, but the *foolish* and *weak* things of the world, and things that were despised (1 Cor. i. 26, 27)—then he *scattered the proud,* and *put down the mighty,* but *exalted them of low degree.*

2. In the *spiritual riches* it dispenses, v. 53. (1) Those who see their need of Christ, he *fills* with *good things*, with the *best things*; he gives liberally to them, and they are *abundantly satisfied*. Those who are weary and heavy-laden shall find rest with Christ, and those who thirst are called to *come to him and drink*. (2) Those who are rich, who, like Laodicea, think they have *need of nothing*, are full of themselves, and think they have a sufficiency in themselves, those he *sends away* from his door; he sends them *empty* away; they come *full of self*, and are sent away *empty of Christ*.

It was always expected that the Messiah should be the strength and glory of his people Israel, and so he is in a peculiar manner (v. 54): *He hath helped his servant Israel*. He hath taken them by the hand, and *helped them up* that were fallen and could not help themselves. The sending of the Messiah, on whom *help* was laid for poor sinners, was the greatest kindness that could be done and that which magnifies it is,

First, That it is *in remembrance of his mercy*. While this blessing was deferred, his people were often ready to ask, *Has God forgotten to be gracious?* But now he made it appear that he had not forgotten, but *remembered*, his mercy. He remembered the days of old.

Secondly, That it is *in performance of his promise*. It is a mercy not only designed, but declared (v. 55); it was *what he spoke to our fathers*, and particularly to Abraham, that *in his seed all the families of the earth shall be blessed* with the blessings that are *for ever*. What God hath spoken he will perform; what he hath spoken to the fathers will be performed to their seed.

Lastly, Mary's return to Nazareth (v. 56), after she had continued with Elisabeth about *three months*. Those in whose hearts Christ is formed take more delight than they used to do in *sitting alone* and *keeping silence*.

Verses 57–66

I. The birth of John Baptist, v. 57. *Elisabeth's full time came, that she should be delivered*, and then *she brought forth a son*. Promised mercies are to be expected when the *full time* for them is come, and not before.

II. The great joy that was among all the relations of the family, upon this extraordinary occasion (v. 58): *Her neighbours and her cousins heard of it*. Now these here discovered, 1. A *pious* regard to God. They acknowledged that *the Lord had magnified his mercy to her*, so the word is. Many things concurred to make the mercy *great*—that she had been long barren, was now old, but especially that the child should be *great in the sight of the Lord*. 2. A *friendly* regard to Elisabeth. When she rejoiced, they *rejoiced with her*. We ought to take *pleasure* in the prosperity of our neighbours and friends, and to be thankful to God for *their* comforts as for our own.

III. The dispute that was among them concerning the naming him (v. 59): *On the eighth day they came together, to circumcise the child*. They that rejoiced in the birth of the child came together to the circumcising of him. The greatest comfort we can take in our children is in *giving them up to God*. The baptism of our children should be more our joy than their birth.

Now it was the custom, when they circumcised their children, to *name them*, and it is not unfit that they should be left *nameless* till they are by name *given up to God*.

1. *Some* proposed that he should be called by his father's name, *Zacharias*. They intended hereby to do honour to the father, who was not likely to have another child.

2. The *mother* opposed it, and would have him called *John*; having learned that God appointed this to be his name (v. 60): *He shall be called Johanan—Gracious*, because he shall introduce the gospel of Christ, wherein God's grace shines more brightly than ever.

3. The *relations* objected against that (v. 61): "*There is none of thy kindred that is called by that name;* and therefore let him have the name of some of his kindred."

4. They appealed to the *father*, for it was his office to *name the child*, v. 62. They *made signs* to him, by which it appears that he was *deaf* as well as *dumb*. However, they gave him to understand what the dispute was which he only could determine; whereupon he made signs to them to give him a *table-book*. He wrote these words, *His name is John*, v. 63. Not, "It shall be so," or, "I would have it so," but, "It is so." The matter is determined already. When Zacharias could not *speak*, he *wrote*. When ministers have their mouths stopped, that they cannot preach, yet they may be doing good as long as they have not their hands tied, that they cannot write. Zacharias's pitching upon the same name that Elisabeth had chosen was a great surprise to the company: *They marvelled all*.

5. He thereupon recovered the use of his speech (v. 64): *His mouth was opened immediately*. The time prefixed for his being silenced was *till the day that these things shall be fulfilled*, v. 20. That time was now expired, whereupon the restraint was taken off, and God gave him the *opening of the mouth again*. Infidelity closed his mouth, and now believing opens it again. *His mouth was opened, and he spake, and praised God*. When God opens our lips, our mouths must *show forth his praise*. As good be without our speech as not use it in *praising God*.

6. These things were told all the country over, to the great amazement of all that heard them, v. 65, 66. We are here told, (1) That *these sayings were discoursed of*, and were the common talk all about the *hill-country of Judæa*. (2) That most people who heard of these things were put into consternation by them: *Fear came on all them that dwelt round about* there. (3) It raised the expectations of people concerning this child. They *laid up these* presages *in their hearts*. What we hear, that may be of use to us, we should *treasure* up, that we may be able to bring forth, for the benefit of others, things new and old, and may be able to look back and to say, "It was what we might expect." They said *within* themselves, and said *among* themselves, "*What manner of child shall this be?* What will be the fruit when these are the buds?"

Lastly, It is said, *The hand of the Lord was with him*; that is, he was taken under the special protection of the Almighty, from his birth, as one designed for something great. God has ways of operating upon children in their infancy, which we cannot account for. God never made a soul but he knew how to sanctify it.

Verses 67–80

We have here the song wherewith Zacharias *praised God* when his *mouth was opened*; in it he is said to *prophesy*, v. 67.

I. How he was qualified for this: *He was filled with the Holy Ghost*; he was divinely inspired. God not only *forgave* him his unbelief and distrust, he *filled him* with the *Holy Ghost*.

II. What the matter of his song was. Here is nothing said of the private concerns of his own family, the rolling away of the reproach from it, but in this song he is wholly taken up with the kingdom of the Messiah. The Old Testament prophecies are often expressed in *praises* and *new songs*, so is this beginning of New Testament prophecy: *Blessed be the Lord*

God of Israel. Zacharias, speaking of the work of redemption, called him the *Lord God of Israel,* because to Israel the prophecies, promises, and types, of the redemption had hitherto been given, and to them the first proffers and proposals of it were now to be made.

Now Zacharias here blesses God,

1. For the work of *salvation* that was to be wrought out by the Messiah himself, *v.* 68–75.

(1) In sending the Messiah, God has *made a gracious visit* to his people; he hath *visited them* as a friend, to take cognizance of their case.

(2) He has *wrought out redemption* for them: *He has redeemed his people.* This was the errand on which Christ *came into the world,* to redeem those that were *sold for* sin, and *sold under* sin. Christ redeems them by *price* out of the hands of God's justice, and redeems them by *power* out of the hands of Satan's tyranny.

(3) He has fulfilled the *covenant of royalty* made with the most famous *Old Testament prince,* that is, David. Glorious things had been said of his family, that on him, as a *mighty one, help* should be *laid.* But that family had been long in a manner *cast off.* Now here it is gloried in, that, according to the promise, the *horn* of David should again be *made to bud;* he *hath raised up a horn of salvation for us in the house of his servant David* (*v.* 69), there, where it was promised and expected to arise. There is in Christ, and in him only, *salvation for us,* and it is a *horn of salvation.* It is an *honourable* salvation. It is *raised up* above all other salvations, none of which are to be compared with it. It is a *plentiful salvation.* It is a *cornucopia—a horn of plenty.* It is a *powerful salvation.* He has raised up such a salvation as shall *pull down* our spiritual enemies, and *protect* us from them.

(4) He has fulfilled all the precious promises made to the church by the most famous *Old Testament prophets* (*v.* 70): *As he spoke by the mouth of his holy prophets.* His doctrine of salvation by the Messiah is confirmed by an appeal to the prophets. God is now *doing* that which he has long ago *spoken of.* See, [1] How *sacred* the prophecies of this salvation were. The prophets who delivered them were *holy prophets,* and it was the *holy God* himself that *spoke by* them. [2] How *ancient* they were: ever *since the world began.* God having promised, when the world began, that the *Seed of the woman should break the serpent's head.* [3] What a wonderful *harmony* and *concert* we perceive among them. God spoke the same thing by them all.

Now what is this *salvation* which was prophesied of?

First, It is a *rescue* from the malice of *our enemies; a salvation out of our enemies,* from among them, and *out of the power of them that hate us* (*v.* 71); it is a salvation from sin. He shall *save his people from their sins,* that they may not have dominion over them, Matt. i. 21.

Secondly, It is a *restoration* to the *favour of God;* it is to *perform the mercy promised to our forefathers, v.* 72. The Redeemer shall *reinstate* us in the *mercy of God* and *re-establish* us in *his covenant;* which was signified by the *promises* made to the patriarchs, and the *holy covenant* made with them, *the oath which he sware to our Father Abraham, v.* 73. That which was promised to the fathers, and is performed to us, is *mercy,* pure mercy; nothing in it is owing to our *merit.* He loved us because he would love us. God herein had an eye to his *holy* covenant, that covenant with Abraham: *I will be a God to thee and thy seed.* This his seed had *really forfeited* by their transgressions; this he *seemed to have forgotten* in the calamities brought upon them; but he will now *remember* it.

Thirdly, It is a qualification for, and an encouragement to, the service of God. Thus was *the oath he sware to our Father Abraham,* That he would *give us* power and grace to *serve him,* in an acceptable manner to him and a comfortable manner to ourselves, *v.* 74, 75. The great design of gospel grace is not to discharge us from, but to engage us to, and encourage us in, the service of God. We are *therefore* delivered from the iron yoke of sin, that our necks may be put under the sweet and easy yoke of the Lord Jesus. *The very bonds which he has loosed do bind us faster unto him.* We are hereby enabled, 1. To serve God *without fear—ἀφόβως.* We are *therefore* put into a state of *holy safety* that we might serve God with a *holy security* and *serenity of mind,* as those that are *quiet from the fears of evil.* God must be served with a *filial fear,* a reverent obedient fear, an awakening quickening fear, but not with a *slavish fear,* like that of the slothful servant, who represented him to himself as a *hard master,* and unreasonable. 2. To serve him in *holiness and righteousness,* which includes the whole duty of man towards God and our neighbour. 3. To serve him, *before him,* in the duties of his *immediate* worship, to serve him as those that have an eye always upon him, and see his eye always upon us, upon our inward man. 4. To serve him *all the days of our life.* Christ *loved us to the end,* and thereby engaged us to *love him to the end.*

2. He *blessed God* for the work of *preparation* for this salvation, which was to be done by John Baptist (*v.* 76): *Thou child* shalt be called *the prophet of the Highest.* Jesus Christ is *the Highest.* John Baptist was *his prophet.* Prophecy had now long ceased, but in John it *revived.* John's business was,

(1) To prepare people for the salvation: *Thou shalt go before the face of the Lord* to *prepare his ways.* Let everything that may obstruct his progress, or embarrass it, or hinder people from coming to him, be taken away: see Isa. xl. 3, 4.

(2) To give people a general idea of the salvation, for the doctrine he preached was that the *kingdom of heaven* is at hand. There are two things in which you must know that this salvation consists:—

[1] The *forgiveness* of what we have *done amiss.* It is salvation *by the remission of sins, v.* 77. John Baptist gave people to understand that, though their case was sad, it was not desperate, for pardon might be obtained *through the tender mercy of our God:* there was nothing in us but a *piteous case* to recommend us to the divine compassion.

[2] *Direction* to *do better* for the time to come. The gospel salvation sets up a clear and true light, by which we may order our steps aright. In it *the day-spring hath visited us from on high* (*v.* 78); and this also is owing to the *tender mercy of our God.* Christ is *the morning Light,* the *rising Sun.* The gospel brings *light* with it, leaves us not to wander in the darkness of Pagan ignorance, or in the moonlight of the Old Testament types or figures, but in it the day dawns; in John Baptist it began to break, but increased apace, and *shone more and more to the perfect day.* We have as much reason to welcome the gospel day as those have to welcome the morning who had long waited for it. *First,* The gospel is *discovering;* it is to *give light to them that sit in darkness, the light of the knowledge of the glory of God in the face of Jesus Christ. Secondly,* It is *reviving;* it brings light to them that sit *in the shadow of death,* as condemned prisoners in the dungeon, to bring them the tidings of a *pardon,* at least of a *reprieve* and opportunity of producing a pardon. How pleasant is that light! *Thirdly,* It is *directing;* it is to *guide our feet in the way of peace.* It guides us into the way of making our peace with God; that *way of peace* which as sinners we have wandered from and *have not known,* nor could ever have known of ourselves.

In the last verse, we have a short account of the younger years of John Baptist. We are here told,

1. Of his *eminence* as to the *inward man*: The *child grew* in the capacities of his mind, so that he *waxed strong in spirit*, had a strong judgment and strong resolution. Those that are strong in the Lord are *strong in spirit*.

2. Of his *obscurity* as to the *outward man*: *He was in the deserts*. There he spent most of his time, in contemplation and devotion, and had not his education in the schools, or at the feet of the rabbin. Many a one is qualified for great usefulness, who yet is buried alive; and many are long so buried who are designed, and are thereby in the fitting, for so much greater usefulness at last; as John Baptist, who was *in the desert* only *till the day of his showing to Israel*. There is a time fixed for the *showing* of those favours to Israel which are reserved.

CHAPTER 2

In this chapter, we have an account of the birth and infancy of our Lord Jesus. I. The place and other circumstances of his birth, ver. 1–7. II. The notifying of his birth to the shepherds in that neighbourhood by an angel, and the spreading of the report of it by the shepherds, ver. 8–20. III. The circumcision of Christ, and the naming of him, ver. 21. IV. The presenting of him in the temple, ver. 22–24. V. The testimonies of Simeon, and Anna the prophetess, concerning him, ver. 25–39. VI. Christ's growth and capacity, ver. 40–52. VII. His observing the passover at twelve years old, and his disputing with the doctors in the temple, ver. 41–51.

Verses 1–7

The *fulness of time* was now come, when God would send forth his Son, and it was foretold that he should be born at Bethlehem. Now here we have an account of the time, place, and manner of it.

I. The time when our Lord Jesus was born.

1. He was born at the time when the *fourth monarchy* was in its height. He was born *in the days* of Augustus Cæsar, when the Roman empire extended itself further than ever before or since, including Parthia one way, and Britain another way; so that it was then called *Terrarum orbis imperium—The empire of the whole earth*; and here that empire is called *all the world* (*v.* 1), for there was scarcely any part of the civilized world, but what was dependent on it.

2. He was born when Judæa was become a province of the empire, and tributary to it; as appears evidently by this, that when all the Roman empire was taxed, the Jews were taxed among the rest. Jerusalem was taken by Pompey the Roman general, about sixty years before this. Judæa was ruled by Cyrenius the Roman governor of Syria (*v.* 2). This was the *first taxing* that was made in Judæa, the first badge of their servitude.

3. There is another circumstance, as to the time, which is, that there was now universal peace in the empire. The temple of Janus was now shut, which it never used to be if any wars were on foot; and now it was fit for the Prince of peace to be born.

II. The place where our Lord Jesus was born is very observable. He was born at *Bethlehem*; so it was foretold (Mic. v. 2), the scribes so understood it (Matt. ii. 5, 6), so did the common people, John vii. 42. The name of the place was significant. Bethlehem signifies *the house of bread*; a proper place for him to be born in who is the Bread of life, the Bread that *came down from heaven*. Bethlehem was the city of David, where he was born, and therefore there *he* must be born who was the *Son of David*. Zion was also called *the city of David*, yet Christ was not born there; for Bethlehem was that city of David where he was born in meanness, to be a *shepherd*; and this our Saviour chose for the place of his birth; not Zion, where he ruled in power and prosperity. Now when the virgin Mary was with child, and near her time, Providence so ordered it that, by order

from the emperor, all the subjects of the *Roman empire* were to be *taxed*; that is, they were to be *registered* and *enrolled*, according to their families, which is the proper signification of the word here used.

That which Augustus designed was either to gratify his *pride* in knowing the numbers of his people, and proclaiming it to the world, or he did it in *policy*, to make his government appear the more formidable; but Providence had another reach in it. All the world shall be at the trouble of being *enrolled*, only that Joseph and Mary may. This brought them up from Nazareth in Galilee to Bethlehem in Judæa, because they were *of the stock and lineage of David*, *v.* 4, 5. Divers ends of Providence were served by this.

1. Hereby the virgin Mary was brought, *great with child*, to Bethlehem, to be *delivered* there, according to the prediction. See how *man purposes and God disposes*.

2. Hereby it appeared that Jesus Christ was of the *seed* of David; for what brings his mother to Bethlehem, now, but because she *was of the stock and lineage of David*?

3. Hereby it appeared that he was *made under the law*; for he became a subject of the Roman empire as soon as he was born. Instead of having kings tributaries to him, when he came into the world he was himself a tributary.

III. The circumstances of his birth, which were very mean. He was indeed a *first-born son*; but it was poor honour to be the first-born of such a poor woman as Mary was, who had no inheritance but what was *in nativity*.

1. He was under some abasements in common with other children; he was *wrapped in swaddling clothes*, as other children are when they are new-born, as if he could be bound, or needed to be kept straight. The Ancient of days became an infant of a span long.

2. He was under some abasements peculiar to himself.

(1) He was born *at an inn*. Christ was born *in an inn*, to intimate that he came into the world but to sojourn here for awhile, as in an inn. An inn receives all comers, and so does Christ. He hangs out the banner of love for his sign, and whoever comes to him, he will in no wise cast out; only, unlike other inns, he welcomes those that come *without money and without price*.

(2) He was born *in a stable*; so some think the word signifies which we translate *a manger*. Because there was *no room in the inn*, and for want of conveniences, nay for want of necessaries, he was laid *in the manger*, instead of a cradle. His being born in a stable and laid in a manger was an instance, [1] Of the poverty of his parents. Had they been rich, room would have been made for them. [2] Of the corruption and degeneracy of manners in that age. If there had been any common humanity among them, they would not have turned a woman in travail into a stable. [3] It was an instance of the humiliation of our Lord Jesus. We were become by sin like an outcast infant, helpless and forlorn; and such a one Christ was.

Verses 8–20

The meanest circumstances of Christ's humiliation were all along attended with some discoveries of his glory, to balance them. When we saw him *wrapped in swaddling clothes* and *laid in a manger*, we were tempted to say, "Surely this cannot be the *Son of God*." But see his birth attended with a choir of angels, and we shall say, "Surely it can be no other than the *Son of God*."

We had in Matthew an account of the notice given to the wise men, who were Gentiles, by a star;

here we are told of the notice given of it to the shepherds who were Jews, by an angel: to each God chose to speak in the language they were most conversant with.

I. How the shepherds were employed; they were *abiding in the fields* and *keeping watch over their flocks by night*, v. 8. The angel was not sent to the chief priests or the elders, but to a company of poor shepherds. The patriarchs were shepherds and by this instance God would show that he had still a favour for those of that innocent employment. They were not *sleeping* in their beds, when this news was brought them, but *abiding in the fields*, and *watching*. They were broad awake, and therefore could not be deceived in what they saw and heard, so as those may be who are half asleep. They were employed now, not in acts of devotion, but in the business of their calling; they were *keeping watch over their flock*. We are not out of the way of divine visits when we are sensibly employed in an honest calling, and abide with God in it.

II. How they were surprised with the appearance of an angel (v. 9): *Behold, an angel of the Lord came upon them*, of a sudden. The angel's *coming upon them* intimates that they little thought of such a thing, or expected it. Gracious visits are made us from heaven, *or ever we are aware*. They saw and heard the *glory of the Lord round about them*; such as made the night as bright as day. This made them *sore afraid*, as fearing some evil tidings. While we are conscious to ourselves of so much guilt, we have reason to fear lest every express from heaven should be a messenger of wrath.

III. What the message was which the angel had to deliver to the shepherds, v. 10–12. "*Fear not*, you *need not* fear your enemies, and *should not* fear your friends." He furnishes them with abundant matter for joy: "Behold, I *evangelize to you great joy*. It shall bring *joy to all people*; that *unto you is born this day a Saviour which is Christ the Lord, in the city of David*," v. 11. "The Saviour *is born this day*; and, since it is matter of *great joy to all people*, you may proclaim it. He is born in the place where it was foretold he should be born, in the *city of David*; and he is born *to you*; to you Jews he is sent in the first place, to *bless you*, to you shepherds, though poor and mean in the world." This refers to Isa. ix. 6. *Unto us a child is born, unto us a son is given*. This is matter of *joy* indeed to all people, great joy. Long-looked for is come at last. He gives them a sign for the confirming of their faith in this matter. "You will find him by this token: he is lying in a *manger*, where surely never any new-born infant was laid before. You will find him wrapped in *swaddling clothes*, and *laid in a manger*.

IV. The angels' *doxology* to God, and *congratulations* of men, upon this solemn occasion, v. 13, 14. The message was no sooner delivered by one angel than suddenly there was with that angel *a multitude of the heavenly hosts praising God*. Let God have the honour of this work: *Glory to God in the highest*; *Glory to God*, whose kindness and love designed this favour, and whose wisdom contrived it. Other works of God are for his glory, but the redemption of the world is for his *glory in the highest*. Let men have the joy of it: *On earth peace, goodwill toward men*. If God be at peace with us, all peace results from it. Peace is here put for *all good*. All the *good* we have, or hope, is owing to God's *goodwill*; and, if we have the comfort of it, he must have the glory of it. Here was the *peace proclaimed* with great solemnity; whoever will, let them come and take the benefit of it. It is on earth peace, to *men of goodwill* (so some copies read it), ἀνθρώποις εὐδοκίας; to men who have a *goodwill to God*; or to men whom God has a *goodwill to*. This is a *faithful saying*, and well *worthy of all*

acceptation, *That the goodwill of God toward men is glory to God in the highest, and peace on the earth*.

V. The visit which the shepherds made to the new-born Saviour. 1. They consulted about it, v. 15. While the angels were singing their hymn, they could attend to that only; but, *when they were gone away from them into heaven, the shepherds said one to another, Let us go to Bethlehem*. And it is no reflection upon the testimony of angels, no nor upon a divine testimony itself, to get it corroborated by observation and experience. These shepherds do not speak doubtfully, "Let us go see whether it be so or no"; but with assurance, *Let us go see this thing which is come to pass*; for what room was left to doubt of it, when *the Lord had* thus *made it known to them*? 2. They immediately made the visit, v. 16. They lost no time, but *came with haste* to the place, and there *they found Mary and Joseph*, and *the babe lying in the manger*. The poverty and meanness in which they found *Christ the Lord* were no shock to their faith, who themselves knew what it was to live a life of comfortable communion with God in very poor and mean circumstances. We have reason to think that the shepherds told Joseph and Mary of the vision of the angels they had seen, and the song of the angels they had heard, which was a great encouragement to them, more than if a visit had been made them by the best ladies in the town.

VI. The care which the shepherds took to spread the report of this (v. 17): *When they had seen it* they made *known abroad* the whole story of what was *told them*, both by the *angels*, and by Joseph and Mary, *concerning this child*, that he was the Saviour, even *Christ the Lord*, that in him there is *peace on earth*. This they told everybody, and agreed in their testimony concerning it. What impression did it make upon people? Why truly, *All they that heard it wondered at those things which were told them by the shepherds*, v. 18. They wondered, but never *enquired* any further about the Saviour, but let the thing drop as a *nine days' wonder*.

VII. The use which those made of these things, who did believe them. 1. The virgin Mary made them the matter of her *private meditation*. She said little, but *kept all these things*, and *pondered them in her heart*, v. 19. As she had silently left it to God to clear up her virtue, when that was suspected, so she silently leaves it to him to publish her honour, now when it was veiled; and it is satisfaction enough to find that, if no one else takes notice of the birth of her child, angels do. The truths of Christ are worth keeping; and the way to keep them safe is to *ponder them*. Meditation is the best help to memory. 2. The shepherds made them the matter of their more *public praises*. If others were not affected with those things, yet they themselves were (v. 20): They *returned, glorifying and praising God*. God would accept the thanksgivings they offered to him. They praised God for what *they had heard* from the angel, and for what *they had seen*, the babe *in the manger*, as it had been spoken to them. They thanked God that they had seen Christ. As afterwards the cross of Christ, so now his *manger*, was to some *foolishness* and a *stumbling-block*, but others saw in it, and admired, and praised, the wisdom *of God* and the *power of God*.

Verses 21–24

Our Lord Jesus, being *made of a woman*, was *made under the law*, Gal. iv. 4. As the son of a daughter of Abraham he was made under the law of *Moses*.

Now here we have two instances of his being *made under* that *law*, and submitting to it.

I. He was *circumcised* on the very day that the law appointed (v. 21): *When eight days were accomplished* they *circumcised* him. Though it was a *painful* operation, yet Christ would undergo it for us. Though it supposed him a *stranger*, that was by that ceremony to be admitted into covenant with God, though it supposed him a *sinner, yet* he submitted to it; nay, *therefore* he submitted to it, because he would be made in the likeness, not only of *flesh*, but of *sinful flesh*, Rom. viii. 3. Though thereby he made himself a *debtor to the whole law* (Gal. v. 3), yet he submitted to it. Christ was circumcised, that he might own himself of the seed of Abraham; that he might own himself a surety for our sins, and an undertaker for our safety; that he might justify the dedication of the infant seed of the church to God, by that ordinance which is the instituted seal of the covenant, as circumcision was (Rom. iv. 11), and baptism is.

At his circumcision he had his name given him; he was called *Jesus* or *Joshua*, for he was *so named of the angel* to his mother Mary *before he was conceived in the womb* (Luke i. 31) and to his supposed father Joseph after, Matt. i. 21. It was a *common name* among the Jews, and in this he would be made *like unto his brethren.* It was the name of two eminent types of him in the Old Testament, Joshua, the successor of Moses; and Joshua, the high priest, Zech. vi. 11, 13. It was very significant of his undertaking. Jesus signifies a *Saviour.* He *brings salvation.*

II. He was *presented* in the temple. This was done at the time appointed by the law, when he was forty days old, *when the days of her purification were accomplished, v.* 22. Now, according to the law,

1. The child Jesus, being a first-born son, was *presented to the Lord.* The law is here recited (*v.* 23): *Every male that opens the womb shall be called holy to the Lord.* Christ was the *first-born* among many brethren, and was *called holy to the Lord*, so as never any other was; yet he was *presented to the Lord* as other first-born were, and no otherwise. But, according to the law, he was *redeemed*, Num. xviii. 15. *The first-born of man shalt thou redeem*, and *five shekels* was the value, Lev. xxvii. 6; Num. xviii. 16. But probably in case of poverty the priest was allowed to take less, or perhaps nothing; for no mention is made of it here.

2. The mother brought her offerings, *v.* 24. So *it is said in the law of the Lord*, that law which was yet in force, she must offer *a pair of turtle-doves*, or *two young pigeons*; had she been of ability, she must have brought a *lamb for a burnt-offering*, and a *dove for a sin-offering*; but, being poor, and not able to reach the price of a lamb, she brings *two doves*, one for a *burnt-offering and the other for a sin-offering* (see Lev. xii. 6, 8). Christ was not *conceived* and *born* in sin, as others are, yet, because he was made under the law, he complied with it. *Thus it became him to fulfil all righteousness.*

Verses 25–40

Even when he humbles himself, still Christ has honour done him. Simeon and Anna now do him honour, by the inspiration of the Holy Ghost.

I. A very honourable testimony is born to him by Simeon. Now observe here,

1. The account that is given us concerning this Simeon, or Simon. He dwelt now in Jerusalem, and was eminent for his piety and communion with God. Some learned men, who have been conversant with the Jewish writers, find that there was at this time one Simeon, a man of great note in Jerusalem. The Jews say that he was endued with a *prophetical* spirit. One thing objected against this conjecture is that at this time his father Hillel was living, and that he himself lived many years after this; but, as to that, he is not here said to be old; and his saying *Now let thy servant depart* intimates that he was willing to die *now*, but does not conclude that therefore he did die quickly. Another thing objected is that the son

of Simeon was Gamaliel, a Pharisee, and an enemy to Christianity; but, as to that, it is no new thing for a faithful lover of Christ to have a son a bigoted Pharisee.

The account given of him here is, (1) That he was *just* and *devout, just* towards men and *devout* towards God; these two must always go together, and each will befriend the other, but neither will atone for the defect of the other. (2) That he *waited for the consolation of Israel*, that is, for the coming of the Messiah. Christ is not only the author of his people's comfort, but the matter and ground of it. He was long coming, and they who believed he would come continued *waiting, desiring* his coming, and *hoping* for it with *patience*; I had almost said, with some degree of *impatience* waiting till it came. The consolation of Israel is to be waited for, and it is worth waiting for, and it will be very welcome to those who have *waited* for it, and continue waiting. (3) That the *Holy Ghost* was upon him, not only as a Spirit of holiness, but as a Spirit of prophecy; he was *filled with the Holy Ghost.* (4) That he had a gracious promise made him, that before he died he should have a sight of the Messiah, *v.* 26. He received *this oracle* (for so the word signifies), *that he should not see death before he had seen* the Messiah, the Lord's *Anointed.* Those, and those only, can with courage *see death*, and look it in the face without terror, that have had by faith a sight of Christ.

2. The seasonable coming of Simeon into the temple, at the time when Christ was presented there, *v.* 27. Just then, when Joseph and Mary brought in the child, Simeon came, by direction of *the Spirit*, into the temple. The same Spirit that had provided for the support of his hope now provided for the transport of his joy. Those that would see Christ must go to his temple; for there *the Lord, whom ye seek*, shall suddenly come to *meet you*, and there you must be ready to *meet him.*

3. The abundant satisfaction wherewith he welcomed this sight: *He took him up in his arms (v.* 28), he *embraced* him, laid him in his bosom, as near his heart as he could, which was as full of joy as it could hold. He *took him up in his arms*, to present him to the Lord. When we receive the record which the gospel gives us of Christ with a lively faith, and the offer it makes us of Christ with love and resignation, then we *take Christ in our arms.* It was promised him that he should have a sight of Christ; but more is *performed* than was *promised*: he has him in his arms.

4. The solemn declaration he made hereupon: *He blessed God*, and said, *Lord, now let thou thy servant depart in peace, v.* 29–32.

(1) He has a pleasant prospect *concerning himself*, he is arrived at a holy contempt of life, and desire of death: *"Lord, now let thou thy servant depart*, for mine eyes have seen the salvation I was promised a sight of before I died."* Here is, [1] An acknowledgment that God had been *as good as his word.* Never any that hoped in God's word were made ashamed of their hope. [2] A thanksgiving for it. He *blessed God* that he saw that salvation in his arms. [3] A confession of his faith, that this child in his arms was the *Saviour*, the *Salvation* itself; *thy salvation*, the salvation of thine appointing, the salvation *which thou hast prepared.* [4] It is a farewell to this world: *"Now let thy servant depart."* The eye is not satisfied with seeing till it hath *seen Christ*, and then it is. What a poor thing doth this world look to one that hath Christ in his arms and salvation in his eye! [5] It is a welcome to death: *Now let thy servant depart.* Simeon is promised that he should not *see death* till he had *seen Christ*; and he is willing to construe what was expressed, as an intimation that, when he had seen Christ, he should

die: *Lord, be it so,* saith he, *now let me depart.* See here, *First,* How *comfortable* the death of a good man is; he departs *as God's servant* from the place of his toil to that of his rest. He departs *in peace,* peace with God, peace with his own conscience; in *peace* with death. *Secondly,* What is the ground of this comfort? *For mine eyes have seen thy salvation.* It bespeaks a believing expectation of a happy state on the other side death, through this salvation he now had a sight of, which not only takes off the terror of death, but makes in *gain,* Phil. i. 21. Those that have welcomed Christ may welcome death.

(2) He has a pleasant prospect concerning the world, and concerning the church. This salvation shall be a blessing to the world. It is *prepared before the face of all people,* to be a *light to lighten the Gentiles* that now sit in darkness. This has reference to Isa. xlix. 6, *I will give thee for a light to the Gentiles;* for Christ came to be the light of the world, not a candle in the Jewish candlestick, but the *Sun of righteousness;* a blessing to the church: *the glory of thy people Israel.* Of those who were Israelites indeed, of the spiritual Israel, he was indeed *the glory,* and will be so to eternity. They shall *glory* in him. When Christ ordered his apostles to preach the gospel to all nations, therein he made himself a *light to lighten the Gentiles;* and when he added, *beginning at Jerusalem,* he made himself *the glory of* his people Israel.

5. The prediction concerning this child, which he delivered to Joseph and Mary. They *marvelled at those things* which were still more and more fully and plainly spoken concerning this child, *v.* 33. And because they were affected with, and had their faith strengthened by, that which was said to them, here is more said to them.

(1) Simeon shows them what reason they had to *rejoice;* for he *blessed them* (*v.* 34). He *prayed* for them that God would *bless* them, and would have others do so too. He is set *for the rising again of many in Israel,* that is, for the conversion of many to God that are dead and buried in sin, and for the consolation of many in God that are sunk and lost in sorrow and despair. Those whom he is set *for the fall of* may be the same with those whom he is set for the *rising again of; For their fall, in order to their rising again.* He wounds and then heals, Paul *falls,* and rises again.

(2) He shows them likewise what reason they had to *rejoice with trembling.* Lest Joseph and Mary especially, should be *lifted up* with the abundance of the revelations, here is a *thorn in the flesh* for them, and it is what we sometimes need. It is true, Christ shall be a blessing to Israel; but there are those in Israel whom he is *set for the fall of,* who will be prejudiced and enraged against him, and offended. As it is pleasant to think how many there are to whom Christ and his gospel are a savour of life unto life, so it is sad to think how many there are to whom he is a savour of death unto death. He is set for *a sign,* to be admired by some, but by others, by many, spoken against. He had many *eyes upon him,* he was a *sign,* but he had many *tongues against* him. The effects of this will be that the *thoughts of many hearts will be revealed* (*v.* 35). The secret good affections and dispositions in the minds of some will be revealed by their embracing Christ, and closing with him; the secret corruptions and vicious dispositions of others will be revealed by their enmity to Christ and their rage against him. Men will be judged of by the thoughts of their hearts, their thoughts concerning Christ. The *word of God* is a discerner of the *thoughts* and *intents of the heart.* It is true, Christ shall be a comfort to his mother; but be not thou too proud of it, for *a sword shall pass through thine own soul also.* He shall be a suffering

Jesus. "Thou *shalt suffer with him,* by sympathy, because of the nearness of thy relation, and strength of affection, to him." When he was abused, it was *a sword in her bones.* When she stood by his cross, and saw him dying, we may well think her inward grief was such that it might truly be said, *A sword pierced through her soul,* it cut her to the heart. Thou shalt *suffer for him.* Many understand it as a prediction of her martyrdom.

II. He is taken notice of by one *Anna,* a *prophetess.*

1. The account here given of this Anna, who she was. She was *A prophetess.* Perhaps no more is meant than that she was one who had understanding in the scriptures above other women, and made it her business to instruct the *younger women* in the things of God. God *left not himself without witness.* She was *the daughter of Phanuel* and her name signifies *gracious.* She was of *the tribe of Asher,* which was in Galilee. She was of *a great age,* a widow of about eighty-four years. She never married again, but continued a widow to her dying day, which is mentioned to her praise. She was a constant resident *in* or at least attendant *on* the temple. Some think she had lodgings in the courts of the temple; others think her not *departing from the temple* means no more, than that she was constantly there at the time of divine service; when any good work was to be done, she was ready to join in it. She *served God with fastings and prayers night and day;* she gave up herself wholly to her devotions, and spent that time in religious exercises which others spent in eating and drinking and sleeping. And in these she *served* God; that was it that put a value upon them and an excellency into them. She *served God,* and aimed at his honour, in *fasting and praying.* Other duties are in season now and then, but we must *pray always.* It is a pleasant sight to see aged Christians abounding in acts of devotion, as those that are not *weary of well-doing,* but that take more and more pleasure in them. Anna is now at length abundantly recompensed for her attendance so many years in the temple.

2. The testimony she bore to our Lord Jesus (*v.* 38): *She came in at that instant,* she, who was so *constant* to the temple, could not miss the opportunity. She *gave thanks likewise to the Lord,* just as Simeon, perhaps like him, wishing now to depart in peace. We should be excited to our duty by the praises and thanksgiving of others; why should not we *give thanks likewise,* as well as they? She, as a prophetess, instructed others concerning him: She *spoke of him to all them* that believed the Messiah would come, and with him *looked for redemption in Jerusalem.* Some there were in Jerusalem that *looked for redemption;* yet but a few, for Anna, it should seem, had acquaintance with all. She knew where to find them, or they where to find her, and she told them all the good news, that she had seen the Lord. Those that have an acquaintance with Christ *themselves* should do all they can to bring *others* acquainted with him.

Lastly, Here is a short account of the infancy and childhood of our Lord Jesus. *Where* he spent it, *v.* 39. They *returned into Galilee.* Luke relates no more concerning them, till they were returned into Galilee; but it appears by St. Matthew's gospel (*ch.* ii) that from Jerusalem they returned to Bethlehem, and there they continued till they were directed to flee into Egypt, and, returning thence when Herod was dead, they were directed to go to their old quarters in Nazareth. It is here called *their own city.* *How* he spent it, *v.* 40. In all things *it behoved him to be made like unto his brethren,* and therefore he passed through infancy and childhood as other children did. As other children, he *grew in stature* of body, and the improvement of understanding in his human soul. Whereas other children are weak in understanding and resolution, he was *strong in spirit*. By the Spirit of God his human soul was endued with extraordinary vigour. Whereas other children have *foolishness bound in their hearts*, he was *filled with wisdom*. Everything he said and did was wisely said, and wisely done, above his years. Whereas other children show that the corruption of nature is in them, and *the tares of sin* grow up with the *wheat of reason*, he made it appear that nothing but *the grace of God was upon him*. He was *greatly beloved*, and high in the favour of God.

Verses 41–52

We have here the only story recorded concerning our blessed Saviour, from his infancy to the day of his showing to Israel, and therefore we are concerned to make much of this, for it is in vain to wish we had more.

I. Christ's *going up with his parents* to Jerusalem, at the feast of the passover, v. 41, 42. It was their constant practice to attend there, according to the law, though it was a long journey, and they were poor. Public ordinances must be frequented, and we must not *forsake the assembling of ourselves together*. They *went up* thither, *after the custom of the feast*. The child Jesus, at *twelve years old*, went up with them. The Jewish doctors say that at twelve years old children must begin to fast from time to time, and that at thirteen years old a child begins to be *a son of the commandment*, having been from his infancy, by virtue of his circumcision, *a son of the covenant*. Those children that are forward in other things should be put forward in religion. Those children that were in their infancy dedicated to God should be called upon, when they are grown up, to come to the *gospel passover*, to the Lord's supper, that they may make it their own act and deed to join themselves to the Lord.

II. Christ's *tarrying behind his parents at Jerusalem*, unknown to them.

1. His parents did not return till they had *fulfilled the days*; they had stayed there all the seven days at the feast, though it was not absolutely necessary that they should stay longer than the two first days. It is good to stay to the conclusion of an ordinance, as becomes those who say, *It is good to be here*, and not to hasten away.

2. The child *tarried behind in Jerusalem*, not because he was loth to go home, or shy of his parents' company, but because he had business to do there, and would let his parents know that he had a *Father in heaven*, whom he was to be *observant* of more than of *them*; and respect to *him* must not be construed disrespect *to them*. It is good to see young people willing to *dwell in the house of the Lord*; they are then like Christ.

3. His parents went the *first day's journey* without any suspicion that he was left behind, for they *supposed him to have been in the company*, v. 44. On these occasions, the crowd was very great, and they concluded that he came along with some of their neighbours, and they *sought him among their kindred and acquaintance*. Pray did *you* see our Son? or, Did *you* see him? They *found him not*, v. 45. There are many, too, many who are our kinsfolk and acquaintance, that we cannot avoid conversing with, among whom we find little or nothing of Christ: When they could not hear of him, yet they hoped they should meet with him at the place where they lodged that night; but *there* they could learn no tidings of him.

4. When they found him not at their quarters at night, they *turned back again*, next morning, to *Jerusalem, seeking him*. Those that would find Christ must *seek till they find*; for he will at length be found of those that seek him. Those that have lost their comforts in Christ, must bethink themselves where, and when, and how, they lost them, and must *turn back again* to the place where they last had them.

5. The *third day* they found him *in the temple*. There they found him *sitting in the midst of them* (v. 46), not standing as a *catechumen* to be examined or instructed by them. This is an instance, not only that he was *filled with wisdom* (v. 40), but that he had both a desire to increase it and a readiness to communicate it; and herein he is an example to children and young people, who should learn of Christ to delight in the company of those they may get good by, and choose to *sit in the midst of* the doctors rather than in the midst of the players. Many a youth at Christ's age now would have been playing with the *children in the temple*, but he was sitting with the *doctors in the temple*. He *heard* them. Those that would *learn* must be *swift to hear*. He *asked them questions*; whether, as a teacher (he had authority so to ask) or as a learner (he had humility so to ask) I know not. He returned *answers* to them, which were very surprising and satisfactory, v. 47. And his wisdom and *understanding* appeared as much in the questions he asked as in the answers he gave, so that all who heard him *were astonished*: they never heard one so young, nor indeed any of their greatest doctors, talk sense at the rate that he did. He *gave them a taste* (says Calvin) of his divine wisdom and knowledge. *They understood not;* they were only *astonished*.

6. His mother talked with him privately about it. v. 48. Joseph and Mary were both *amazed* to find him there, and to find that he had so much respect showed him as to be admitted to *sit among the doctors*. His mother told him how ill they took it: *"Son, why hast thou thus dealt with us?* Why didst thou put us into such a fright?" *Thy father and I have sought thee, sorrowing*. Those may have leave to complain of their losses that think they have lost Christ. They did not sorrow and sit down in despair, but sorrowed and *sought*. They that thus seek him in sorrow shall find him, at length, with so much the greater joy. He gently reproved their inordinate solicitude about him (v. 49): *"How is it that you sought me?* Wist ye not that I *ought* to be, ἐν τοῖς τοῦ πατρός μου;—*in my Father's house?"* so some read it. *"Under my Father's care* and protection." *"At my Father's work"* (so we take it): I must be *about my Father's business*, and therefore could not go home as soon as you might. *Wist ye not?* It was his errand into the world, and his meat and drink in the world, to do his Father's will, and finish his work: and yet at that time his parents *understood not this saying*, v. 50.

Lastly, Here is their return to Nazareth. He did not urge his parents either to come and settle at Jerusalem, but very willingly retired into his obscurity at Nazareth, where for many years he was, as it were, buried alive. But here we are told,

1. That he was *subject to his parents*; as it should seem, worked with his father at the trade of a carpenter. Herein he hath given an example to children to be dutiful and obedient to their parents in the Lord. Though his parents were poor and mean, though he was *strong in spirit*, and *filled with wisdom*, yet he was subject to his parents; how then will *they* answer it who, though foolish and weak, yet are disobedient to their parents?

2. That his mother, though she did not perfectly understand her son's sayings, yet *kept them in her heart*. However we may neglect men's sayings because they are obscure, yet we must not think so of God's sayings. That which at first is dark, so that we know not what to make of it, may afterwards become plain and easy. We may find use for that another time which now we see not how to make useful to us.

3. That he improved, and came on, to admiration (v. 52): *He increased in wisdom and stature.* This is meant of his human nature, his body increased in *stature* and bulk, he grew in the growing age; and his soul increased *in wisdom*, and in all the endowments of a human soul. As the faculties of his human soul grew more and more capable, the gifts it received from the divine nature were more and more communicated. And he increased in *favour with God and man.* The image of God shone brighter in him, when he grew up to be a youth, than it did, or could, while he was an *infant* and a *child*.

CHAPTER 3

Nothing is related concerning our Lord Jesus from his twelfth year to his entrance on his thirtieth year. In this chapter we have, I. The beginning of John's baptism, ver. 1–6. His exhortation to the multitude (ver. 7–9), and the particular instructions he gave to those who desired to be told their duty, ver. 10–14. II. The notice he gave them of the approach of the Messiah (ver. 15–18), to which is added the mention of his imprisonment, ver. 19–20. III. Christ coming to be baptized of John, ver. 21, 22. IV. His pedigree and genealogy recorded up to Adam, ver. 23–38.

Verses 1–14

John's baptism introducing a new dispensation, it was requisite that we should have a particular account of it. Glorious things were said of John (*ch.* i. 15, 17); but we lost him in the deserts, and there he remains until *the day of his showing unto Israel, ch.* i. 80.

I. The date of the beginning of John's baptism; this is here taken notice of, which was not by the other evangelists, that the truth of the thing might be confirmed by the exact fixing of the time. And it is dated,

1. By the government of the heathen, which the Jews were under.

(1) It is dated by the reign of the Roman emperor; it was in the fifteenth year of Tiberius Cæsar, the third of the twelve Cæsars, a very bad man. The people of the Jews, after a long struggle, were of late made a province of the empire, and were under the dominion of this Tiberius; an inconsiderable despicable part of the Roman empire.

(2) It is dated by the governments of the viceroys that ruled in the several parts of the Holy Land under the Roman emperor, which was another badge of their servitude, for they were all foreigners. Pilate is here said to be the governor, president, or procurator, of Judæa. This character is given of him by some other writers, that he was a wicked man, and one that made no conscience of a lie. He reigned ill, and at last was displaced and sent to Rome, to answer for his maladministrations. The other three are called *tetrarchs*, some think from the countries which they had the command of, each of them being over a *fourth part* of that which had been entirely under the government of Herod the Great.

2. By the government of the Jews among themselves, v. 2. Annas and Caiaphas were the high priests. God had appointed that there should be but one high priest at a time, but here were two, to serve some ill turn or other.

II. The origin and tendency of John's baptism.

1. The origin of it was *from heaven*: *The word of God came unto John, v.* 2. It is the same expression that is used concerning the Old Testament prophets (Jer. i. 2); for John was a prophet, yea, more than a prophet. John is here called *the son of Zacharias*, to refer us to what the angel said to his father. The word of the Lord came to him *in the wilderness*; for those whom God *fits* he will find out, wherever they are. As the word of the Lord is not *bound* in a *prison*, so it is not *lost* in a *wilderness*. John was the *son of a priest*, now entering upon the thirtieth year of his age; and therefore, according to the custom of

the temple, he was now to be admitted into the temple-service. But God had called him to a more honourable ministry.

2. The scope and design of it were to bring all the people of his country off from their sins and home to their God, v. 3. *He came* first *into all the country about Jordan*, that part of the country which Israel took possession of first; there was the banner of the gospel first displayed. John resided in the most solitary part of the country; but, when the word of the Lord came to him, he quitted his deserts, and came into the inhabited country. Those that are *best pleased* in their retirements must cheerfully *exchange* them, when God calls them into places of concourse. *He came into all the country, preaching* a new *baptism.* The sign or ceremony, was such as was ordinarily used among the Jews, *washing with water*, by which proselytes were sometimes admitted, but the meaning of it was, *repentance for the remission of sins.*

(1) They were thereby obliged to *repent of their sins*, to be *sorry* for what they had done amiss, and to *do so no more.* The former they *professed*, and were concerned to be *sincere* in their professions; the latter they *promised*, and were concerned to *make good* what they promised. He bound them to change their mind, and change their way, and to *make them new hearts* and to live new lives.

(2) They were thereby assured of the pardon of their sins, upon their repentance. As the baptism he administered bound them not to submit to the power of sin, so it sealed to them a gracious and pleadable discharge from the guilt of sin.

III. The fulfilling of the scriptures in the ministry of John. The other evangelists had referred us to the same text that is here referred to, that of Esaias, *ch.* xl. 3. It is *written in the book of the words of Esaias the prophet.* Among them it is found that there should be *the voice of one crying in the wilderness*; and John is that voice; he cries, *Prepare ye the way of the Lord, and make his paths straight.* Luke goes further on with the quotation than Matthew and Mark had done, and applies the following words likewise to John's ministry (v. 5, 6), *Every valley shall be filled.* 1. The humble shall by it be *enriched* with grace. 2. The proud shall by it be humbled; *Every mountain and hill shall be brought low.* 3. Sinners shall be converted to God; *The crooked ways* and the *crooked* spirits shall be *made straight.* God by his grace can make that straight which sin hath made crooked. 4. Difficulties that were hindering and discouraging in the way to heaven shall be removed: *The rough ways shall be made smooth.* The gospel has made the way to heaven *plain* and easy to be *found*, smooth and easy to be *walked in.* 5. The great salvation shall be more fully discovered than ever, and the discovery of it shall spread further (v. 6): *All flesh shall see the salvation of God;* not the Jews only, but the Gentiles. All shall *see* it, and some of all sorts shall *see* it, enjoy it, and have the benefit of it.

IV. The general warnings and exhortations which he gave to those who submitted to his baptism, v. 7–9. In Matthew he is said to have preached these same things to *many of the Pharisees and Sadducees*, that *came to his baptism* (Matt. iii. 7–10); but here he is said to have spoken them *to the multitude, that came forth to be baptized of him, v.* 7. This was the purport of his preaching to all that came to him. As he did not flatter the *great*, so neither did he compliment the *many*, but gave the same reproofs of sin and warnings of wrath to the *multitude* that he did to the Sadducees and Pharisees; for, if they had not the same faults, they had others as bad. Now observe here,

1. That the guilty corrupted race of mankind is become a *generation of vipers*; not only poisoned, but poisonous; hateful to God, hating one another.

2. This generation of vipers is fairly warned to *flee from the wrath to come*, which is certainly before them if they continue such. We are not only warned of this wrath, but are put into a way to escape it, if we look about us in time.

3. There is no way of *fleeing from the wrath to come*, but by *repentance*.

4. Those that profess repentance are highly concerned to live like penitents (*v.* 8): *Bring forth therefore fruits meet for repentance*, else you cannot escape the wrath to come. By the change of our way must be evidenced the change of our mind.

5. If we be not really holy, both in heart and life, our profession of religion will stand us in no stead at all: *Begin not* now to frame excuses from this great duty of repentance, by *saying within yourselves, We have Abraham to our father*.

6. We have therefore no reason to depend upon our external privileges and professions of religion, because God can effectually secure his own honour and interest without us. If we were cut off and ruined, he could raise up to himself a church out of the most unlikely,—*children to Abraham* even *out of stones*.

7. The greater professions we make of repentance, and the greater assistances and encouragements are given us to repentance, the nearer and the sorer will our destruction be if we do not *bring forth fruits meet for repentance*. Now that the kingdom of heaven is at hand, *now* that the *axe is laid to the root of the tree*, threatenings to the wicked and impenitent are now more terrible than before, as encouragements to the penitent are now more comfortable.

8. Barren trees will be cast into the fire at length; it is the fittest place for them: *Every tree* that doth not bring forth fruit, *good fruit*, is *hewn down*, and *cast into the fire*.

V. The particular instructions he gave to several sorts of persons, that enquired of him concerning their duty: the *people*, the *publicans*, and the *soldiers*. Some of the Pharisees and Sadducees came to his baptism; but we do not find them asking, *What shall we do?* They thought they knew. But the *people*, the *publicans*, and the *soldiers*, who knew that they had done amiss, and were conscious to themselves of great ignorance and unacquaintedness with the divine law, were particularly inquisitive: *What shall we do?* Those that are *baptized* must be *taught*. Those that profess and promise repentance in general must evidence it by particular instances of reformation. They that would do their duty must desire to know their duty. These here enquire, not, *What shall this man do?* but, What shall *we* do? What *fruits meet for repentance* shall we *bring forth?* Now John gives answer to each, according to their place and station.

(1) He tells the *people* their duty, and that is to be charitable (*v* 11): *He that has two coats*, let him *give*, or *lend* at least, *to him that has none*, to keep him warm. The gospel requires *mercy*, and not sacrifice; and the design of it is to engage us to do all the good we can. Food and raiment are the two supports of life; he that hath *meat* to spare, let him give to him that is destitute of *daily food*. What we have we are but stewards of, and must use it, accordingly, as our Master directs.

(2) He tells the *publicans* their duty, the collectors of the emperor's revenue (*v.* 13): *Exact no more than that which is appointed you*. They must do justice between the government and the merchant, and not oppress the people in levying the taxes. They must not think that because it was their office to take care that the people did not defraud the prince they might therefore, by the power they had, bear hard upon the people, as those that have ever so little a branch of power are apt to abuse it: "Collect

for Cæsar the things that are Cæsar's, and do not enrich yourselves by taking more." The public revenues must be applied to the public service, and not to gratify the avarice of private persons. He does not direct the publicans to quit their places, the employment is in itself lawful and necessary, but let them be just and honest in it.

(3) He tells the *soldiers* their duty, *v.* 14. Some think that these soldiers were Romans; and then it is an early instance of Gentiles embracing the gospel and submitting to it. Military men seldom seem inclined to religion; yet these submitted even to the Baptist's strict profession, and desired to receive the *word of command* from him: *What must we do?* In answer to this enquiry, John does not bid them lay down their arms, but cautions them against the sins that soldiers were commonly guilty of. They must not be injurious to *the people* among whom they were quartered: "*Do violence to no man*. Your business is to keep the peace, do not you *do violence* to any. *Shake no man*" (so the word signifies); "do not put people into fear; the sword of war, as well as that of justice, is to be a terror only to evil doers, but a protection to those that do well." Nor must they *accuse any falsely* to the government, thereby to make themselves formidable, and get bribes. They must not be injurious to their *fellow-soldiers*; for some think that caution, not to *accuse falsely*, has special reference to them: "Be not forward to complain one of another to your superior officers, that you may be revenged on those whom you have a pique against." They must not be given to mutiny, or contend with their generals about their pay: "*Be content with your wages*. While you have what you agreed for, do not murmur that it is not more." It is discontent with what they have that makes men oppressive and injurious. It is wisdom to make the best of that which is.

Verses 15–20

I. How the people took occasion, from the ministry and baptism of John, to think of the Messiah, and to think of him as at the door. Thus the way of the Lord was *prepared*. When men's expectations are raised, that which they are in expectation of becomes doubly acceptable. Now when they observed what an excellent doctrine John Baptist preached, 1. They began presently to consider that now was the time for the Messiah to appear. Never did the corrupt state of the Jews more need a reformation, nor their distressed state more need a deliverance, than now. 2. Their next thought was, "Is not this he that should come?" *All* thinking *men mused*, or reasoned, *in their hearts*, concerning John, *whether he were the Christ or not*. His life was holy and strict, his preaching powerful and with authority, and therefore "why may we not think that he is the Messiah?" That which puts people upon considering, reasoning with themselves, prepares the way for Christ.

II. How John disowned all pretensions to the honour of being himself the Messiah, but confirmed them in their expectations of him that really was the Messiah, *v.* 16, 17. John's office, as a crier or herald, was to give notice that the *kingdom of God was at hand*; and therefore, when he had told all manner of people severally what they must do, he tells them one thing more which they must all do: they must expect the Messiah now shortly to appear. And this serves as an *answer* to their *musings* and debates concerning himself.

1. He declares that the utmost he could do was to *baptize* them *with water*. He could only exhort them to *repent*, and assure them of forgiveness, upon repentance.

2. He consigns them, and turns them over, as it were, to Jesus Christ, for whom he was sent to

prepare the way, and would have them no longer to *debate* whether John was the Messiah or no, but to look for him that was really so.

(1) John owns the Messiah to have a greater *excellency* than he had; he is one the *latchet of whose shoe* he does not think himself *worthy to loose*. John was *a prophet*, yea *more than a prophet*, more so than any of the Old Testament prophets; but Christ was a prophet more than John. This was a great truth which John came to preach; but the manner of his expressing it bespeaks his humility, and in it he not only *does justice* to the Lord Jesus, but *does him honour* too. Thus highly does it become us to speak of Christ, and thus humbly of ourselves.

(2) He owns him to have a greater *energy* than he had: "He is *mightier than I*." They thought that a wonderful power went along with John; but what was that compared with the power which Jesus would come clothed with? John can do no more than *baptize with water*, in token of this, that they ought to purify and cleanse themselves; but Christ can, and will, *baptize with the Holy Ghost*; he can give the *Spirit* to cleanse and purify the heart. John can only preach a *distinguishing* doctrine, and by word and sign *separate between the precious and the vile*; but Christ hath his *fan in his hand*, with which he can, and will, perfectly separate between the wheat and the chaff. He *will thoroughly purge his floor*. John can only *speak comfort* to those that receive the gospel, but Jesus Christ will *give them comfort*. John can only promise them that they shall be safe; but Christ will make them so. John can only *threaten* hypocrites, and tell the *barren trees* that they shall be *hewn down* and *cast into the fire*; but Christ can execute that threatening; those that are as *chaff*, light, and vain, and worthless, *he will burn with fire unquenchable*.

The evangelist concludes his account of John's preaching with an *et cetera* (*v.* 18): *Many other things in his exhortation preached he unto the people.* First, John was an *affectionate* preacher. He was *exhorting*, beseeching; he pressed things home upon his hearers, as one in earnest. *Secondly*, He was a *practical* preacher. Much of his preaching was *exhortation*, quickening them to their duty, directing them in it, and not amusing them with matters of nice speculation. *Thirdly*, He was a *popular* preacher. He addressed himself *to the people, to the laity*, and accommodated himself to their capacity, as promising himself best success among them. *Fourthly*, He was an *evangelical* preacher, *he preached the gospel* to the people; in all his *exhortations*, he directed people to Christ, and excited and encouraged their expectations of *him*. *Fifthly*, He was a *copious* preacher: *Many other things he preached, many things, and different.* He *varied* in his preaching, that those who were not reached, and touched, and wrought upon by one truth, might be by another.

III. How full a stop was put to John's preaching. When he was in the midst of his usefulness he was imprisoned by the malice of Herod (*v.* 19, 20): *Herod the tetrarch being reproved by him*, not only for living in incest with his brother Philip's wife, but for the many other *evils which Herod had done* (for those that are wicked in one instance are commonly so in many others), he could not *bear it*, and *added* this wickedness to all the rest, that he *shut up John in prison*. Because he could not bear his reproofs, others should be deprived of the benefit of his instructions and counsels. Must he be silenced who is the *voice of one crying in the wilderness*? But thus the faith of his disciples must be tried; thus the unbelief of those who rejected him must be punished; thus he must be Christ's forerunner in suffering as well as preaching. He must now give way to him, and, the Sun being risen, the morning-star must of course disappear.

Verses 21–38

The evangelist mentioned John's imprisonment before Christ's being baptized, though it was nearly a year after it, because he would finish the story of John's ministry, and then introduce that of Christ.

I. A short account of Christ's baptism. Jesus came, to be baptized of John, and he was so, *v.* 21, 22.

1. It is here said that, *when all the people were baptized*, then *Jesus was baptized*. Christ would be baptized last, among the common people, and in the rear of them. He saw what multitudes were hereby prepared to receive him, and then he appeared.

2. Notice is here taken of Christ's *praying* when he was *baptized*, which was not in Matthew: being baptized, and *praying*. He *prayed*, as others did, for he would thus keep up communion with his Father. He prayed for the discovery of his Father's favour to him, and the descent of the Spirit. What was promised to Christ, he must obtain by prayer: *Ask of me and I will give thee*, &c.

3. When he prayed, *the heaven was opened*. Sin had shut up heaven, but Christ's prayer opened it again. Prayer is an ordinance that *opens heaven*: *Knock, and it shall be opened unto you*.

4. *The Holy Ghost descended in a bodily shape like a dove upon him*. When he begins to preach, *the Spirit of the Lord is upon him*. Now this is here expressed by a sensible evidence for his encouragement in his work, and for the satisfaction of John the Baptist; for he was told before that by this sign it should be notified to him which was the Christ.

5. There came *a voice from heaven* from the *excellent glory* (so it is expressed, 2 Pet. i. 17), *Thou art my beloved Son*. Here, and in Mark, it is expressed as spoken *to* Christ; in Matthew as spoken *of* him: *This is my beloved Son*. It comes all to one. It was foretold concerning the Messiah, *I will be his Father, and he shall be my Son*, 2 Sam. vii. 14. It was also foretold that he should be God's *elect, in whom his soul delighted* (Isa. xlii. 1); and, accordingly, it is here declared, *Thou art my beloved Son, in whom I am well pleased*.

II. A long account of Christ's pedigree, which had been more briefly related by St. Matthew.

1. His age: *He now began to be about thirty years of age*. At this age the priests were to enter upon the full execution of their office, Num. iv. 3.

2. His pedigree, *v.* 23, &c. Matthew had given us somewhat of this. He goes no higher than Abraham, but Luke brings it as high as Adam. Matthew designed to show that Christ was the son of Abraham, in whom *all the families of the earth are blessed*, and that he was heir to the throne of David; and therefore he begins with Abraham, and brings the genealogy down to Jacob, who was the father of Joseph, an heir-male of the house of David: but Luke, designing to show that Christ was the *seed of the woman*, that should break the serpent's head, traces his pedigree upward as high as Adam, and begins it with Eli, or Heli, who was the father, not of Joseph, but of the virgin Mary. Matthew draws the pedigree from Solomon, whose natural line ending in Jechonias, the legal right was transferred to Salathiel, who was of the house of Nathan, another son of David, which line Luke here pursues, and so leaves out all the kings of Judah. It is well for us that our salvation doth not depend upon our being able to solve all these difficulties. It is further worthy of observation, that, when those records of the Jewish genealogies had continued thirty or forty years after these extracts out of them, they were all lost and destroyed with the Jewish state and nation; for now there was no more occasion for them.

The genealogy concludes with this, *who was the son of Adam, the son of God*. He was both the *Son of Adam* and the *Son of God*, that he might be a proper

Mediator between God and the sons of Adam, and might bring the sons of Adam to be, through him, the *sons of God.*

CHAPTER 4

In this chapter, we have, I. A further preparation of him for his public ministry by his being tempted in the wilderness (ver. 1–13). II. His entrance upon his public work in Galilee (ver. 14, 15), particularly, 1. At Nazareth (ver. 16–30), which we had no account of before in Matthew. 2. At Capernaum, where, having preached to admiration (ver. 31–32), he cast the devil out of a man that was possessed (ver. 33–37), cured Peter's mother-in-law of a fever (ver. 38, 39), and many others that were sick and possessed, (ver. 40, 41) and then went and did the same in other cities of Galilee, ver. 42–44.

Verses 1–13

In this story of Christ's temptation, observe,

I. How he was *prepared* and *fitted* for it.

1. He was *full of the Holy Ghost,* who had *descended* on him *like a dove.* Those are well armed against the strongest temptations that are *full of the Holy Ghost.*

2. He was newly *returned from Jordan,* where he was baptized, and owned by a voice from heaven to be the beloved Son of God. When we have had the most comfortable communion with God, and the clearest discoveries of his favour to us, we may expect that Satan will set upon us (the richest ship is the pirate's prize), and that God will suffer him to do so, that the power of his grace may be manifested and magnified.

3. He was *led by the Spirit into the wilderness.* His being *led into the wilderness gave* some advantage to the tempter; for there he had him alone. *Woe to him that is alone! He might* give Satan advantage, who knew his own strength; *we may not,* who know our own weakness. He *gained* some advantage to himself, during his forty days, fasting in the wilderness. We may suppose that he was wholly taken up in proper meditation, that he spent all his time in immediate, intimate converse with his Father, as Moses in the mount. And this prepared him for Satan's assaults, and hereby he was fortified against them.

4. He continued fasting (*v.* 2): *In those days he did eat nothing.* As by retiring into the *wilderness* he showed himself perfectly indifferent to the *world,* so by his *fasting* he showed himself perfectly indifferent to the *body;* and Satan cannot easily take hold of those who are thus loosened from, and dead to, the *world* and the *flesh.*

II. How he was assaulted by one temptation after another, and how he defeated the design of the tempter in every assault. During the *forty days,* he was *tempted of the devil* (*v.* 2). But at the end of the forty days he did as it were close with him, when he perceived *that he was hungry, v.* 2.

1. He tempted him to *distrust his Father's* care of him, and to *set up for himself* (*v.* 3): *If thou be the Son of God, command this stone to be made bread.* (1) "I counsel thee to do it; for God, if he be thy Father, has forgotten thee." If we begin to think of living by our own forecast, without depending upon divine Providence, we must look upon it as a temptation of Satan's, and reject it accordingly; it is Satan's counsel to think of an independence upon God. (2) "I *challenge* thee to do it, if thou canst; if thou dost not do it, I will say thou art *not the Son of God.*" Christ yielded not to the temptation. *First,* Because he would not do what Satan bade him do. We must not do anything that looks like *giving place to the devil.* Miracles were wrought for the confirming of faith, and the devil had no faith to be confirmed. *Secondly,* He wrought miracles for the ratification of his doctrine, and therefore till he began to *preach* he would not begin to work miracles. *Thirdly,* He would not work miracles *for himself* and

his own supply. He would rather turn *water into wine,* for the credit and convenience of his friends, than *stones into bread,* for his own *necessary supply. Fourthly,* He would reserve the proof of his being the Son of God for hereafter. *Fifthly,* He would not do anything that looked like distrust of his Father. He would, like the other children of God, live in a dependence upon the divine Providence and promise. He returned a scripture-answer to it (*v.* 4): *It is written.* This is the first word recorded as spoken by Christ after his instalment in his prophetical office; and it is a quotation out of the Old Testament. The word of God is our *sword,* and faith in that word is our *shield;* we should therefore be *mighty in the scriptures.* The text of scripture he makes use of is quoted from Deut. viii. 3: "*Man shall not live by bread alone.* I need not turn the stone into bread; man can live *by every word of God,* by whatever God will appoint that he shall live by." God has many ways of providing for his people, without the ordinary means of subsistence; and therefore he is not at any time to be distrusted, but at all times to be depended upon, in the way of duty. She was an active believer who said that she had made many a meal's meat of the promises when she wanted bread.

2. He tempted him to *accept from him* the kingdom and to *do him homage, v.* 5–7. This evangelist puts this temptation second, which Matthew had put last, and which, it should seem, was really the last. Now observe,

(1) How Satan *managed* this temptation.

[1] He gave him a prospect of *all the kingdoms of the world in a moment of time.* He *took him up* for this purpose *into a high mountain.* It was done *in a moment of time;* whereas, if a man take a prospect of but one country, he must do it successively. Thus the devil thought to impose upon our Saviour with a fallacy; and, by making him believe that he could *show him all the kingdoms of* the world, would draw him into an opinion that he could *give him* all those kingdoms.

[2] He boldly alleged that these kingdoms were *all delivered to him,* that he had power to dispose of them and all their *glory,* and to give them to *whomsoever he would* (*v.* 6), but clogged with this condition, that he should *fall down and worship him.*

[3] He demanded of him homage and adoration: *If thou wilt worship me, all shall be thine, v.* 7. He would have him worship him himself. He would indent with him, that, when he had got possession of the kingdoms of this world, he should make no alteration of religions in them. Then let him take all the power and glory of the kingdoms if he pleased. Let who will take the wealth and grandeur of this earth, Satan has all he would have if he can but have men's hearts and adorations.

(2) How our Lord Jesus *triumphed* over this temptation. He gave it a peremptory repulse, rejected it with abhorrence (*v.* 8): "*Get thee behind me, Satan.*" Such a temptation as this was not to be *reasoned with,* but immediately refused; it was presently knocked on the head with one word, *It is written, Thou shalt worship the Lord thy God;* and not only so, but *him only,* him and *no other.* Men must be *turned from the power of Satan unto God,* from the worship of devils to the worship of the only living and true God. This is the great divine law that Christ will re-establish among men, and reduce men to the obedience of, *That God only is to be served and worshipped.*

3. He tempted him to a presumptuous confidence of his Father's protection.

(1) What he designed in this temptation: *If thou be the Son of God, cast thyself down, v.* 9. He would have him seek for a new proof of his being the Son of God, as if that which his Father had given him by

the voice from heaven, and the descent of the Spirit upon him, were not sufficient. He would have him seek a new method of proclaiming and publishing this to the world. If he would now declare from *the pinnacle of the temple*, among all the great people who attend the temple service, that he was the Son of God, and then, for proof of it, throw himself down unhurt, he would presently be received by everybody as a messenger sent from heaven. Or the fall might be his death, and then he should have got him finely out of the way.

(2) How he backed and enforced this temptation. He suggested, *It is written*, v. 10. Christ had quoted scripture against him; and he thought he would be quits with him, and would show that he could quote scripture as well as he. *He shall give his angels charge over thee*, and *in their hands they shall bear thee up*. It is true, God has promised the protection of angels, to encourage us to trust him, not to tempt him; as far as the promise of God's presence with us, so far the promise of the angels' ministration goes, but no further.

(3) How he was baffled and defeated in the temptation, *v*. 12. Christ quoted Deut. vi. 16, where it is said, *Thou shalt not tempt the Lord thy God*, by desiring a sign for the proof of divine revelation, when he has already given that which is sufficient.

III. What was the result and issue of this combat, *v*. 13. Our victorious Redeemer kept his ground, and came off a conqueror, not for himself only, but for us also.

1. The devil emptied his quiver: *He ended all the temptation*. Did Christ suffer, being tempted, till all the temptation was ended? And must not we expect also to pass all our trials, to go through the *hour of temptation* assigned us?

2. He then quitted the field: He *departed from him*. He saw it was to no purpose to attack him, he had no blind side, no weak or unguarded part in his wall. If we resist the devil, he will flee from us.

3. Yet he continued his malice against him; he departed but *for a season*, till the season when he was again to be let loose upon him, but as a *persecutor*, to bring him to *suffer*. He *departed now* till that season came which Christ calls the *power of darkness* (ch. xxii. 53), and when the prince of this world would again *come*, John xiv. 30.

Verses 14–30

Having defended himself against the devil's assaults, he now begins to act *offensively*, and to make those attacks upon him, by his preaching and miracles, which he could not resist or repel.

I. What is here said in general of his preaching, and the entertainment it met with *in Galilee*. Thither he came *in the power of the Spirit*. He was not to wait for a call from men, for he had light and life in himself. There he *taught in their synagogues*, their places of public worship, where they met, not, as in the temple, for ceremonial services, but for devotion. These came to be more frequent since the captivity, when the ceremonial worship was near expiring. This he did so as that he gained a great reputation. *A fame of him went through all that region* (v. 14), and it was a good fame; for (v. 15) he *was glorified of all*. Now, at first, he met with no contempt or contradiction; all *glorified* him, and there were none as yet that vilified him.

II. Of his preaching at Nazareth, the city where he was brought up. And here we are told how he *preached* there, and how he was *persecuted*.

1. How he preached there.

(1) The opportunity he had for it: *He came to Nazareth* when he had gained a reputation in other places. There he took occasion to preach, [1] In the *synagogue*, where it had been *his custom* to attend

when he was a private person, *v*. 16. But, now that he was entered upon his public ministry, there he preached. [2] On the sabbath day, the proper time which the pious Jews spent, not in a mere ceremonial rest from worldly labour, but in the duties of God's worship.

(2) The call he had to it. He *stood up to read*. They had in their synagogues seven readers every sabbath, the first a priest, the second a Levite, and the other five Israelites of that synagogue. We often find Christ *preaching* in other synagogues, but never *reading*, except in this synagogue at Nazareth, of which he had been many years a member. The *book of the prophet Esaias* was *delivered to him*. The second lesson for *that* day being in the prophecy of Esaias, they gave him that volume to read in.

(3) The text he preached upon. He *stood up to read*. Now the book being *delivered to him*, [1] He *opened* it. The books of the Old Testament were in a manner *shut up* till Christ opened them, Isa. xxix. 11. [2] He *found* the place which was appointed to be read *that day*. Now his text was taken out of Isa. lxi. 1, 2, which is here quoted at large, *v*. 18, 19. There was a providence in it that that portion of scripture should be read that day, which speaks so very plainly of the Messiah. This text gives a full account of Christ's undertaking, and the work he came into the world to do.

First, How he was qualified for the work: *The Spirit of the Lord is upon me*. All the gifts and graces of the Spirit were conferred upon him, not by measure, as upon other prophets, but without measure, John iii. 34.

Secondly, How he was commissioned: *Because he has anointed me, and sent me*. His being *anointed* signifies both his being fitted for the undertaking and called to it.

Thirdly, What his work was. He was qualified and commissioned.

(*a*). To be a great *prophet*. He was *anointed to preach*; that is three times mentioned here. To *whom* he was to preach: to the *poor*; to those that were *poor in the world*; to those that were *poor in spirit*, to the meek and humble, and to those that were truly sorrowful for sin. *What* he was to preach. In general, he must preach *the gospel*. He is sent to *evangelize* them; not only to preach to them, but to make that preaching effectual; to bring it, not only to their ears, but to their hearts. Three things he is to preach:

(*i*) *Deliverance to the captives*. The gospel is a proclamation of liberty, like that to Israel in Egypt and in Babylon. It is a deliverance from the worst of thraldoms, which all those shall have the benefit of that are willing to make Christ their Head.

(*ii*) *Recovering of sight to the blind*. He came not only by the word of his gospel to bring *light* to them that sat *in the dark*, but by the power of his grace to give sight to those that were *blind*. Christ came to tell us that he has *eye-salve* for us, which we may have for the asking: that, if our prayer be, *Lord, that our eyes may be opened*, his answer shall be, *Receive your sight*.

(*iii*) *The acceptable year of the Lord*, v. 19. He came to let the world know that the God whom they had offended was willing to be reconciled to them, and to *accept* of them upon new terms. It alludes to the year of *release*, or that of *jubilee*, which was an *acceptable year*. It was an acceptable time, for it was a day of salvation.

(*b*) Christ came to be a great *Physician*; for he was sent to *heal the broken-hearted*, to give peace to those that were troubled and humbled for sins, and to bring them to rest who were weary and heavy-laden, under the burden of guilt and corruption.

(*c*) To be a great *Redeemer*. He not only proclaims liberty to the captives, but he sets at liberty them that are bruised. The prophets could but *proclaim liberty*, but Christ, as one having authority, as one that had *power on earth to forgive sins*, came to *set at liberty*; and therefore this clause is added here.

(4) Here is Christ's *application* of this text to himself (*v.* 21): When he had read it, he *rolled up the book*, and gave it again *to the minister*, or *clerk*, that attended, and *sat down*, according to the custom of the Jewish teachers. Now he *began* his discourse thus, "*This day is this scripture fulfilled in your ears.*" It now began to be fulfilled in Christ's entrance upon his public ministry; *now*, in the report they heard of his preaching and miracles in other places; *now*, in his preaching to them in their own synagogue. Many other gracious words proceeded out of his mouth, which these were but the *beginning* of; for Christ often preached long sermons, which we have but a short account of. This was enough to introduce a great deal: *This day is this scripture fulfilled.* The works of God are the accomplishment not only of his secret word, but of his word revealed; and it will help us to understand both the scriptures and the providences of God to compare them one with another.

(5) Here is the *attention* and *admiration* of the auditors.

[1] Their *attention* (*v.* 20): *The eyes of all them that were in the synagogue were fastened on him.* It is good, in hearing the word, to keep the eye fixed upon the minister by whom God is speaking to us; for, as the eye affects the heart, so, usually, the heart follows the eye, and is wandering, or fixed, as that is.

[2] Their *admiration* (*v.* 22): *They all bore him witness* and *wondered at the gracious words that proceeded out of his mouth*; and yet, as appears by what follows, they did not *believe in him.* They admired the *gracious words which proceeded out of his mouth.* Christ's words are *words of grace.* And these words of grace are to be *wondered at*; Christ's name was Wonderful, and in nothing was he more so than in his grace, in the words of his grace, and the power that went along with those words. Their wonder increased as they *said, Is not this Joseph's son?* Some from this suggestion took occasion perhaps so much the more to admire his *gracious words*, concluding he must needs be *taught of God*, while others perhaps with this consideration corrected their wonder at his gracious words, and concluded there could be nothing *really* admirable in them, whatever appeared, because he was the *Son of Joseph.*

(6) Christ's anticipating an objection which he knew to be in the minds of many of his hearers. Observe,

[1] What the objection was (*v.* 23): "*You will surely say to me, Physician, heal thyself.* You will expect that I should work miracles among you, as I have done in other places." Most of Christ's miracles were *cures*;—"Now why should not the sick in thine own city be *healed* as well as those in other cities?" They were designed to cure people of their unbelief:—"Now why should not the disease of unbelief be cured in those of thine own city as well as in those of others? *Whatsoever we have heard done in Capernaum, do here also in thine own country.*" They were pleased with *Christ's gracious words*, only because they hoped they were but the introduction to some *wondrous works* of his. They thought their own town as worthy to be the stage of miracles as any other. And why should not his neighbours and acquaintance have the benefit of his preaching and miracles, rather than any other?

[2] How he answers this objection against the course he took.

First, By a plain and positive reason why he would not make Nazareth his headquarters (*v.* 24), because it generally holds true *that no prophet is accepted in his own country*. Experience seals this. Familiarity

breeds contempt; and we are apt to think meanly of those whose conversation we have been accustomed to. That is most esteemed that is *far-fetched* and *dear-bought*, above what is *home-bred*, though really more excellent. Christ declined working miracles, or doing anything extraordinary, at Nazareth, because of the rooted prejudices they had against him there.

Secondly, By pertinent examples of two of the most famous prophets of the Old Testament. Elijah maintained a *widow of Sarepta*, a *city of Sidon*, one that was a stranger to the commonwealth of Israel, when there was a *famine in the land*, *v.* 25, 26. As God would hereby show himself a *Father of the fatherless*, and a *Judge of the widows*, so he would show that he was rich in mercy to all, even to the Gentiles. Elisha cleansed Naaman the Syrian of his leprosy, though he was a Syrian, and not only a foreigner, but an enemy to Israel (*v.* 27): *Many lepers were in Israel in the days of Eliseus.* And yet we do not find that Elisha cleansed them, but only this Syrian; for none besides had faith to apply himself to the prophet for a cure. Christ himself often met with greater faith among Gentiles than in Israel. Christ wrought his miracles, though not among his townsmen, yet among Israelites, whereas these great prophets wrought theirs among Gentiles.

2. How he was *persecuted* at Nazareth.

(1) That which provoked them was his taking notice of the favour which God by Elijah and Elisha showed to the Gentiles: *When they heard these things, they were filled with wrath* (*v.* 28), a great change since *v.* 22, when they *wondered at the gracious words that proceeded out of his mouth*; thus uncertain are the opinions and affections of the multitude, and so very fickle. If they had mixed faith with those gracious words of Christ which they wondered at, they would have been awakened by these latter words of his. Those only *pleased the ear*, and went no further, and therefore these *grated on the ear*. But that which especially exasperated them was that he intimated some kindness God had in reserve for the Gentiles. Their pious ancestors pleased themselves with the hopes of adding the Gentiles to the church; but this degenerate race hated to think that any others should be taken in.

(2) They were provoked to that degree that they made an attempt upon his life. They *rose up* in a tumultuous manner against him. They *thrust him out of the city.* They thrust from them the Saviour and the salvation. They *led him to the brow of the hill*, with a purpose to *throw him down headlong.* Though they had heard such a fame of him and had but just now themselves *admired his gracious words*, yet they hurried him away in a popular fury, or frenzy rather, to put him to death in a most barbarous manner.

(3) Yet he escaped, because his hour was not yet come: He *passed through the midst of them*, unhurt. They *drove* him from them, and he *went his way.* He would have gathered Nazareth, but they *would not*, and therefore their house is *left to them desolate.* But now, though they *received him not*, there were those that did.

Verses 31–44

When Christ was expelled from Nazareth, he came to Capernaum, another city of Galilee.

I. His preaching: He *taught them on the sabbath days*, *v.* 31. Christ's preaching much affected the people (*v.* 32); they were *astonished at his doctrine*, there was weight in every word he said, and admirable discoveries were made to them by it. *His word was with power;* there was a commanding force in it, and a working power went along with it to the consciences of men.

II. His miracles.

1. Two particularly specified, showing Christ to be,

(1) A *controller* and *conqueror* of *Satan* by his power to cast him out of the bodies of those he had taken possession of. [1] The devil is an *unclean spirit*, his nature directly contrary to that of the pure and *holy* God. [2] This unclean spirit works in the children of men. [3] It is possible that those who are very much under the power and working of Satan may yet be found *in the synagogue*. [4] Even the devils *know and believe* that *Jesus Christ is the Holy One of God*. [5] They believe and *tremble*. This unclean spirit *cried out with a loud voice*, apprehensive that Christ was now come to destroy him. [6] The devils have *nothing to do with Jesus Christ*, nor desire to have anything to do with him. [7] Christ has the devil under check: *He rebuked him*, saying, *Hold thy peace*; and this word he spoke *with power*; *Be muzzled*. Christ did not only enjoin him silence, but stopped his mouth. [8] In the breaking of Satan's power, both the enemy that is conquered shows his malice, and Christ, the conqueror, shows his overruling grace. The devil showed what he would have done, when he *threw the man in the midst*, as if he would have dashed him to pieces. Christ showed what a power he had over him, in that he not only forced him to leave him, but to leave him without so much as *hurting* him. Whom Satan cannot *destroy*, he will do all the *hurt* he can to; but this is a comfort, he can harm them no further than Christ permits; nay, he shall not do them any real harm. He *came out*, and *hurt him not*. [9] Christ's power over devils was universally acknowledged and adored, *v.* 36. They were *all amazed, saying, What a word is this*! They that pretended to cast out devils did it with abundance of charms and spells, but Christ commanded them *with authority and power*. [10] This, as much as anything, gained Christ a reputation, and spread his fame. This instance of his power, magnified, and was looked upon as greatly magnifying him (*v.* 37); upon the account of this, *the fame of him went out*, more than ever, *into every place of the country round about*. Our Lord Jesus, when he set out at first in his public ministry, was greatly talked of, more than afterwards, when people's admiration wore off with the novelty of the thing.

(2) Christ showed himself to be *a healer of diseases*. In the former, he struck at the root of man's misery, which was Satan's enmity: in this, he strikes at one of the most spreading branches of it, one of the most common calamities of human life, and that is bodily diseases. These our Lord Jesus came to take away the sting of. Of all bodily diseases none are more common or fatal to grown people than *fevers*. Now here we have Christ's curing a fever with a word's speaking; the place was in Simon's house, his patient was Simon's wife's mother, *v.* 38, 39. [1] Christ is a guest that will pay well for his entertainment; those that bid him welcome into their hearts and houses shall be no losers by him; he comes with healing. [2] Even families that Christ visits may be visited with sickness. Houses that are blessed with his *distinguishing favours* are liable to the *common calamities* of this life. Simon's wife's mother was *ill* of a *fever*. [3] Even good people may sometimes be exercised with the sharpest afflictions. She was *taken with a great fever*, very acute, and high, and threatening. [4] No age can exempt from diseases. [5] When our relations are sick, we ought to apply ourselves to Christ, by faith and prayer, on their account: *They besought him for her*. [6] Christ has a tender concern for his people when they are in sickness and distress: *He stood over her*, as one concerned for her. [7] Christ had, and still has, a sovereign power over bodily diseases: *He rebuked the fever*, and *it left her*. [8] This proves Christ's cures to be miraculous, that they were done in an instant: *Immediately she arose*. [9] Where Christ gives a

new life he designs and expects that it should be a new life indeed, spent more than ever in his service. If distempers be rebuked, and we arise from a bed of sickness, we must set ourselves to minister to Jesus Christ. [10] Those that minister to Christ must be ready to minister to all that are his for his sake: She *ministered to them*, not only to *him* that had cured her, but to them that had *besought him for her*.

2. A general account of many other miracles which Christ did. He *cured many that were diseased*, and it was *when the sun was setting* (*v.* 40); in the evening of that sabbath day which he had spent in the synagogue. It is good to abound in the work of the day, in some good work or other, even till sunset; as those that call the sabbath, and the business of it, *a delight*. He cured *all that were sick* of divers *diseases*. He had a remedy for every malady. The sign he used in healing was *laying his hands* on the sick. He healed by his own power. He cast the devil out of many that were possessed, *v.* 41. They said, *Thou art Christ the Son of God*. Christ *rebuked them*, and did not *suffer them to say that they knew him to be the Christ*.

3. Here is his removal from Capernaum, *v.* 42, 43.

(1) He *retired* for awhile into a place of *solitude*. It was but a little while that he allowed himself for sleep. *When it was day*, he went *into a desert place* to be sometimes *alone with God*, as even those should be, and contrive to be, that are most engaged in public work. They will find themselves never *less alone* than when *thus alone*.

(2) He *returned* again to the places of *concourse* and to the work he had to do there. Though a *desert place* may be a convenient *retreat*, yet it is not a *convenient residence*, because we were not sent into this world to *live to ourselves*. He was earnestly solicited to stay at Capernaum. The people were exceedingly fond of him. *They sought him*, and, though it was in a *desert place*, they *came unto him*. A desert is no desert if we be *with Christ* there. They *detained him that he should not depart from them*. It ought not to discourage the ministers of Christ that some reject them, for they will meet with others that will welcome them and their message. He chose rather to *diffuse* the light of his gospel to *many* places than to fix it to *one*. Though he was welcome at Capernaum, yet he is *sent to preach the gospel to other cities also*. They that enjoy the benefit of the gospel must be willing that others also should share in that benefit, and not covet the *monopoly* of it. Christ, though he preached not in vain in the synagogue at Capernaum, yet would not be tied to that, but *preached in the synagogues of Galilee*, *v.* 44. It is well for us that our Lord Jesus has not tied himself to any one place or people, but, wherever two or three are gathered in his name, he will be in the midst of them.

CHAPTER 5

In this chapter, we have, I. Christ preaching to the people out of Peter's ship, ver. 1–3. II. The recompence he made to Peter for the loan of his boat, in a miraculous draught of fishes, ver. 4–11. III. His cleansing the leper, ver. 12–15. IV. A short account of his private devotion and public ministry, ver. 16, 17. V. His cure of the man sick of the palsy, ver. 18–26. VI. His calling Levi the publican, and conversing with publicans on that occasion, ver. 27–32. VII. His justifying his disciples in not fasting so frequently as the disciples of John and his Pharisees did, ver. 33–39.

Verses 1–11

This passage of story is the same with that which was more briefly related by Matthew and Mark, of Christ's calling Peter and Andrew to be *fishers of men*, Matt. iv. 18, and Mark i. 16. They had not related this miraculous draught of fishes at that time, having only in view the calling of his disciples;

but Luke gives us that story as one of the many signs which Jesus did, which *had not been written* in the foregoing books.

I. What vast *crowds* attended Christ's preaching: *The people pressed upon him to hear the word of God* (v. 1). The people *flocked about him* (so the word signifies); they showed respect to his preaching, though not without some rudeness to his person, which was very excusable, for they *pressed upon him*. Some would reckon this a discredit to him when none of the *rulers* or of *the Pharisees believed in him*. Their souls were as precious as the souls of the grandees, and it is his aim to bring not so much the mighty as the *many sons* to God. See how the people relished *good preaching*: they pressed to *hear the word of God*; they could perceive it to be the *word of God*, and therefore they coveted to hear it.

II. What poor *conveniences* Christ had for preaching: *He stood by the lake of Gennesaret* (v. 1), upon a level with the crowd, so that they could neither see him nor hear him; he was lost among them, he was crowded, and in danger of being crowded into the water: what must he do? *There were two ships*, or *fishing boats* brought to shore, one belonging to Simon and Andrew, the other to Zebedee and *his sons*, v. 2. At first, Christ saw Peter and Andrew fishing at some distance (so Matthew tells us, *ch.* iv. 18); but he waited till they came to land, and till the *fishermen*, that is, the servants, were *gone out of them*. Christ *entered* into that *ship* that belonged to Simon, and begged of him that he would lend it him for a pulpit; and *prayed him* that he would *thrust out a little from the land*, which would be the worse for his being *heard*, but Christ would have it so, that he might the better be *seen*; and it is his being *lifted up* that *draws men to him*. It intimates that Christ had a strong voice (strong indeed, for he made the *dead* to hear it). There he *sat down*, and *taught the people* the good knowledge of the Lord.

III. What a particular acquaintance Christ, hereupon, fell into with these fishermen, They had had some conversation with him before, which began at John's baptism (John i. 40, 41); they were with him at *Cana of Galilee* (John ii. 2), and in Judæa (John iv. 3); but as yet they were not called to attend him constantly. Now it was that they were called into a more intimate fellowship with Christ.

1. When Christ had done preaching, he ordered Peter to apply himself to the business of his calling again: *Launch out into the deep, and let down your nets*, v. 4. It was not the sabbath day, and therefore, as soon as the lecture was over, he set them to work. With what cheerfulness may we go about the duties of our calling when we have been *in the mount* with God. It is our wisdom and duty so to manage our religious exercises as that they may befriend our worldly business, and so to manage our worldly business as that it may be no enemy to our religious exercises.

2. Peter having *attended* upon Christ in his *preaching*, Christ will *accompany* him in his *fishing*. He stayed with Christ at the shore, and now Christ will *launch out* with him *into the deep*.

3. Christ ordered Peter and his ship's crew to *cast their nets into the sea*, which they did, in obedience to him, though they had been hard at it all night, and had *caught nothing*, v. 4, 5. We may observe here,

(1) How melancholy their business had now been: "*Master, we have toiled all the night and have taken nothing*." One would have thought that this should have excused them from hearing the sermon; but it was more refreshing and reviving to them than the softest slumbers. But they mention it to Christ, when he bids them go a fishing again. Some *callings* are much more *toilsome* than others are, and more perilous; yet Providence has so ordered it for the

common good that there is no useful calling so discouraging but some or other have a genius for it. Those who follow their business, and get abundance by it with a great deal of ease, should think with compassion of those who cannot follow theirs but with a great fatigue, and hardly get a bare livelihood by it. Be the calling ever so laborious, it is good to see people diligent in it. These fishermen, that were thus *industrious*, Christ singled out for his favourites. Even those who are most diligent in their business often meet with disappointments; they who *toiled all night* yet *caught nothing*. We must do our duty, and then leave the event to God. When we are tired with our worldly business, and crossed in our worldly affairs, we are welcome to come to Christ, and spread our case before him.

(2) How ready their obedience was to the command of Christ: *Nevertheless, at thy word, I will let down the net*. Though they had *toiled all night*, yet, if Christ bid them, they will renew their toil. For every fresh service they shall have a fresh supply of *grace sufficient*. Though they have *taken nothing*, yet, if Christ bid them *let down for a draught*, they will hope to take *something*. We must not abruptly quit the callings wherein we are called because we have not the success in them we promised ourselves. The ministers of the gospel must continue to *let down* that net, though they have perhaps *toiled long and caught nothing*; and this is thankworthy, to continue unwearied in our labours, though we see not the success of them. In this they have an eye to the *word of Christ*: "*At thy word, I will let down the net*." We are *then* likely to speed well when we follow the guidance of Christ's word.

4. The draught of fish they caught was so much beyond what was ever known that it amounted to a miracle (v. 6): They *enclosed a great multitude of fishes*, so that *their net broke*. It was so great a *draught* that they had not hands sufficient to draw it up; but they were obliged to beckon to their partners to come and help them, v. 7. But the greatest evidence of the vastness of the draught was that they filled both the ships with fish, to such a degree that they overloaded them, and they *began to sink*.

Now by this vast draught of fishes, Christ intended to show his *dominion* in the *seas* as well as on the *dry land*, over its *wealth* as over its *waves*. He intended hereby to confirm the doctrine he had just now preached out of Peter's ship. We may suppose that the people on shore stayed halting about there, to see what he would do next; and this miracle immediately following would be a confirmation to their faith, of his being at least *a teacher come from God*. He intended hereby to repay Peter for the loan of his boat. Christ's recompences for services done to his name are abundant, they are superabundant. He intended hereby to give a specimen, to those who were to be his ambassadors to the world, of the success of their embassy, that though they might for a time, and in one particular place, *toil* and *catch nothing*, yet they should be instrumental to bring in many to Christ, and enclose many in the gospel net.

5. The impression made upon Peter was very remarkable.

(1) All *concerned* were *astonished*, and the more *astonished* for their being *concerned*. All the boat's crew were *astonished* at the draught of fishes which they had taken (v. 9); they were all surprised. So were also *James* and *John*, who were partners with Simon (v. 10). Now they were the more *affected* with it, because they *understood* it better than others did. They that were well acquainted with this sea had never seen such a draught of fishes fetched out of it, and therefore they could not be tempted to diminish it, by suggesting that it was what might as

well have happened at *any time*. It greatly corroborates the evidence of Christ's miracles that those who were best *acquainted* with them most *admired* them. Because they were most *interested* in it, and *benefited* by it. Peter and his part-owners were gainers by this great draught of fishes; their *joy* was a *helper* to their *faith*. When Christ's works of wonder are to us, in particular, works of grace, then especially they command our faith in his doctrine.

(2) Peter was astonished to such a degree that he *fell down at Jesus's knees*, as he sat in the stern of his boat, and said, *Depart from me, for I am a sinful man, O Lord, v.* 8. He thought himself unworthy of the favour of Christ's presence in his boat. It was the language of Peter's humility and self-denial, and had not the least tincture of the devils' dialect, *What have we to do with thee, Jesus, thou Son of God?* His acknowledgment was very just, and what it becomes us all to make: *I am a sinful man, O Lord.* Even the *best men* are *sinful men*, and should be ready upon all occasions to own it, and especially to own it to Jesus Christ. His inference from it was what *might have been* just, though really it was not so. If I be a *sinful man*, as indeed I am, I ought to say, "*Come to me, O Lord*, or let me come to thee, or I am undone, *for ever undone*." Peter may well be excused, if, in a sense of his own sinfulness and vileness, he cried out on a sudden, *Depart from me.* Those whom Christ designs to admit to the most *intimate acquaintance* with him he first makes sensible that they deserve to be set at the *greatest distance* from him. We must all own ourselves *sinful men*, and that therefore Jesus Christ might justly *depart from us*; but we must *therefore fall down at his knees*, to pray him that he would not depart.

6. The occasion which Christ took from this to intimate to Peter (*v.* 10), and soon after to James and John (Matt. iv. 21), his purpose to make them his apostles. He *said unto Simon*, "Thou shalt both see and do greater things than these; *fear not, henceforth thou shalt catch men.* That shall be a more *astonishing* miracle, and infinitely more *advantageous* than this."

Lastly, The fishermen's farewell to their calling, in order to their constant attendance on Christ (*v.* 11): *When they had brought their ships to land* they *forsook all and followed him.* It is observable that they *left all to follow Christ*, when their calling prospered in their hands more than ever it had done. When *riches increase*, and we are therefore most in temptation to *set our hearts* upon them, then to quit them for the service of Christ, this is *thankworthy*.

Verses 12–16

I. The cleansing of a leper, *v.* 12–14. This narrative we had both in Matthew and Mark. It is here said to have been *in a certain city* (*v.* 12); it was in Capernaum. This man is said to be *full of leprosy*; he had that distemper in a high degree. Let us learn here,

1. What we must do in the sense of our spiritual leprosy. We must *seek Jesus*. We must humble ourselves before him, as this leper, seeing Jesus, *fell on his face.* We must be *ashamed* of our pollution, and blush to lift up our faces before the *holy Jesus*. We must earnestly desire to be *cleansed*. We must firmly believe Christ's ability and sufficiency to cleanse us; Lord, *thou canst make me clean*, though I be *full of leprosy*. No doubt is to be made of the merit and grace of Christ. We must be importunate in prayer: *He fell on his face and besought him;* they that would be cleansed must reckon it a favour worth wrestling for. We must refer ourselves to the goodwill of Christ: *Lord, if thou wilt, thou canst.* This is not so much the language of his *diffidence*, or *distrust* of the goodwill of Christ, as of his submission to the goodwill of Jesus Christ.

2. What we may expect from Christ, if we thus apply ourselves to him. We shall find him very forward to take cognizance of our case (*v.* 13): He *put forth his hand and touched him.* His *touching the leper* was wonderful condescension; but it is much greater to us when he is himself *touched with the feeling of our infirmities.* We shall find him very compassionate, and ready to relieve us; he said, "*I will*, whosoever comes to me to be healed, *I will in no wise cast him out.*" We shall find him all-sufficient, and able to heal and cleanse us, though we be ever so full of this loathsome leprosy. One word, one touch, from Christ, did the business: *Immediately the leprosy departed from him.*

3. What he requires from those that are cleansed, *v.* 14. We must be very *humble* (*v.* 14): He charged *him to tell no man.* He must not tell it to his own honour. Those whom Christ hath healed and cleansed must know that he hath done it in such a way as for ever excludes boasting. We must be very *thankful*: Go, *and offer for thy cleansing.* Christ did not require him to give him a fee, but to bring the sacrifice of praise to God. We must *keep close to our duty;* go *to the priest.* The man whom Christ had made whole he *found in the temple*, John v. 14. Those who by any affliction have been detained from public ordinances should, when the affliction is removed, attend on them the more diligently.

4. Christ's *public serviceableness* to men and his *private communion* with God.

(1) Though never any had so much *pleasure* in his *retirements* as Christ had, yet he was *much in a crowd*, to do good, *v.* 15. Though the leper should altogether hold his peace, yet the thing could not be hid, *so much the more went there a fame abroad of him.* For honour is like a shadow, which flees from those that pursue it, but follows those that decline it. The less good men say of themselves, the more will others say of them. But Christ reckoned it a small honour to him that his *fame went abroad*; it was much more so that hereby multitudes were brought to receive benefit by him. By his preaching. They came together to *hear* him. By his miracles. They came *to be healed by him* of their infirmities.

(2) Though never any did so much *good in public*, yet he found time for *pious* and *devout retirements* (*v.* 16): He *withdrew himself into the wilderness, and prayed.* It is likewise our wisdom so to order our affairs as that our public work and our secret work may not interfere with one another. Secret prayer must be performed secretly; and those that have ever so much to do of the best business in this world must keep up constant stated times for it.

Verses 17–26

I. A general account of Christ's preaching and miracles, *v.* 17. He was *teaching on a certain day*, not on the sabbath day, but on a *week-day.* Preaching and hearing the word of *God* are *good works*, if they be *done well*, any day in the *week.* It was in a *private house*; for even there where we ordinarily converse with our friends it is not improper to give and receive good instruction. *And the power of the Lord was to heal them.* It was *mighty* to heal them; to heal their souls, to give them a new life, a new nature. It may be meant (and so it is generally taken) of the healing of those who were *diseased in body*, who came to him for cures. Whenever there was occasion, Christ had not *to seek* for his power, it was *present to heal.* There were Pharisees, and doctors of the law, *sitting by;* not sitting *at his feet*, to learn of him. But, by what follows (*v.* 21), it appears that they were *not healed*, but cavilled at Christ. They sat by as spectators, censors, and spies, to pick up something on which to ground a reproach or accusation. How many are there in the midst of our assemblies that do not *sit under* the word, but *sit by*! It is to them as a *tale* that is *told them*, not as a *message* that is *sent them*; they are willing that we should preach *before them*, not that we should preach *to them*. These Pharisees and scribes *came out of every town of Galilee, and Judæa, and Jerusalem*; they came from all parts of the nation. Christ went on with his work of *preaching* and *healing*, though he saw these Pharisees *sitting by*, who, he knew, *despised* him, and watched to *ensnare him*.

II. A particular account of the cure of the man *sick of the palsy*.

1. The doctrines that are taught us and confirmed to us by the story of this cure. (1) That sin is the fountain of all sickness, and the forgiveness of sin is the only foundation upon which a recovery from sickness can comfortably be built. They presented the *sick man* to Christ, and he said, "*Man, thy sins are forgiven thee* (v. 20), that is the blessing thou art most to prize and seek." The cords of our iniquity are the bands of our affliction. (2) That Jesus Christ has power on earth to *forgive sins*. This was the thing intended to be proved (v. 24): *That ye may know* and believe *that the Son of man hath power to forgive sins*, he *saith to the sick of the palsy, Arise, and walk*; and he is cured immediately. Christ claims one of the prerogatives of the King of kings when he undertakes to *forgive sin*, and it is justly expected that he should produce a good proof of it. "Well," saith he, "I will put it upon this issue: here is a man struck with a palsy, and *for his sin*; if I do not with a word's speaking cure his disease, then say that I am not entitled to the prerogative of forgiving sin: but, if I do, you must own that *I have power to forgive sins*." Thus it was put upon a fair trial, and one word of Christ determined it. He did but say, *Arise, take up thy couch*, and that *chronical* disease had an *instantaneous* cure; *immediately he arose before them*. They must all own that there could be no cheat or fallacy in it. (3) That Jesus Christ is God. He appears to be so, [1] By *knowing the thoughts* of the scribes and Pharisees (v. 22). [2] By doing that which their thoughts owned none could do but God only (v. 21): *Who can forgive sins*, say they, *but only God*? "I will prove," saith Christ, "that I can forgive sins"; and what follows then but that *he is God*?

2. The duties that are taught us, and recommended to us, by this story. (1) In our applications to Christ, we must be very *pressing* and *urgent*. They that were the friends of this sick man *sought means to bring him in before Christ* (v. 18); and, when they were baffled in their endeavour, they did not give up their cause; but when they could not get in by *the door*, it was so crowded, they untiled the house, and let the poor patient down through the roof, *into the midst before Jesus*, v. 19. In this Jesus Christ *saw their faith*, v. 20. When the centurion and the woman of Canaan were in no care at all to bring the patients they interceded for into Christ's presence, but believed that he could cure them *at a distance*, he commended *their faith*. In *these* there seemed to be an apprehension that it was requisite the *patient* should be *brought into his presence*, yet he did not *censure* and *condemn* their weakness, did not ask them, "Are you under such a degree of infidelity as to think I could not have cured him, though he had been out of doors?" But he made the best of it, and even in *this* he saw *their faith*. It is a comfort to us that we serve a Master that is willing to *make the best* of us. (2) When we are sick, we should be more in care to get our sins pardoned than to get our sickness removed. (3) The mercies which we have the comfort of, God must have the praise of. The man *departed to his own house, glorifying God*, v. 25. (4) The miracles which Christ wrought were *amazing* to those that saw them, and we ought to *glorify* God in them, v. 26.

They said, "*We have seen strange things today*." They *glorified* God, who had sent into their country such a benefactor to it; and were *filled with fear*, with a reverence of God.

Verses 27–35

All this, except the last verse, we had before in Matthew and Mark; it is not the story of any *miracle in nature* wrought by our Lord Jesus, but it is an account of some of the *wonders of his grace*.

I. It was a wonder of his grace that he would call a *publican*, from the *receipt of custom*, to be his disciple and follower, v. 27. By this he *exposed himself*, and got the invidious character of a *friend of publicans and sinners*.

II. It was a wonder of his grace that the call was made *effectual*, v. 28. This publican, though those of that employment commonly had little inclination to religion, *rose up, and followed Christ*. There is no heart too hard for the Spirit and grace of Christ to work upon, nor any difficulties in the way of a sinner's conversion insuperable to his power.

III. It was a wonder of his grace that he would not only admit a converted publican into his family, but would keep company with unconverted publicans. Here is a wonder of grace indeed, that Christ undertakes to be the Physician of souls *distempered* by sin, and ready to *die* of the distemper (he is a Healer by office, v. 31)—that he came to call *sinners*, the worst of sinners, to repentance, and to assure them of pardon, upon repentance, v. 32. These are glad tidings of great joy indeed.

IV. It was a wonder of his grace that he did so patiently bear the *contradiction of sinners* against himself and his disciples, v. 30. He did not express his resentment of the cavils of the scribes and Pharisees, but answered them with reason and meekness.

V. It was a wonder of his grace that, in the discipline under which he trained up his disciples, he *considered their frame*, and proportioned their services to their strength. It was objected that he did not make *his disciples* to *fast* so often as those of the *Pharisees* and John Baptist did, v. 33. He insisted most upon that which is the *soul of* fasting, the living of a life of self-denial, which is as much better than fasting and corporal penances as *mercy* is better than *sacrifice*.

VI. It was a wonder of his grace that Christ reserved the trials of his disciples for their latter times, when by his grace they were in some good measure better prepared and fitted for them. Now they were as the *children of the bride-chamber*, when the *bridegroom is with them*, when they have plenty and joy, and every day is a festival. But this will not last always. *The days will come* when the *bridegroom shall be taken away from them*, v. 35. When Christ shall leave them with their hearts full of sorrow, their hands full of work, and the world full of enmity and rage against them, *then shall they fast*.

VII. It was a wonder of his grace that he proportioned their exercises to their strength. He would not put *new cloth upon an old garment* (v. 36), nor *new wine into old bottles* (v. 37, 38); he would not, as soon as ever he had called them out of the world, put them upon the strictnesses and austerities of discipleship, lest they should be tempted to *fly off*. Christ would train up his followers gradually to the discipline of his family; for no man, having *drank old wine*, will *of a sudden*, straightway, *desire new*, or relish it, but will say, *The old is better*, because he has been *used to it*, v. 39. The disciples will be tempted to think their old way of living better, till they are by degrees trained up to this way whereunto they are called. Christ's disciples, though they had not so much of the *form of godliness*, had more of the *power of it*.

Chapter 6

I. Here is a proof of the lawfulness of works of necessity and mercy on the sabbath day, the former in vindication of his disciples' plucking the ears of corn, the latter in vindication of himself healing the withered hand on that day, ver. 1–11. II. His retirement for secret prayer, ver. 12. III. His calling his twelve apostles, ver. 13–16. IV. His curing the multitudes of those under various diseases, ver. 17–19. V. The sermon that he preached to his disciples and the multitude, instructing them in their duty both to God and man, ver. 20–49.

Verses 1–11

I. Christ justifies his disciples in a *work of necessity* for themselves on that day, and that was *plucking the ears of corn*, when they were hungry on that day. This story here has a date, which we had not in the other evangelists; it was *on the second sabbath after the first* (v. 1), that is, the *first sabbath after the second day of unleavened bread*, from which day they reckoned the *seven weeks* to the feast of pentecost. We may observe, 1. Christ's disciples ought not to be nice and curious in their diet, but take up with what is easiest got, and be thankful. These disciples *plucked the ears of corn, and did eat* (v. 1); a little served them, and that which had no delicacy in it. 2. Many are forward to censure others for the most innocent and inoffensive actions, v. 2. The Pharisees quarrelled with them as doing that which it *was not lawful to do on the sabbath days*, when it was their own practice to feed deliciously on sabbath days. 3. Jesus Christ will justify his disciples, and will own and accept of them in many a thing which men tell them *it is not lawful for them to do*. 4. Ceremonial appointments may be dispensed with, in cases of necessity, v. 3, 4. And, if God's own appointments might be thus set aside for a greater good, much more may the traditions of men. 5. Works of necessity are particularly allowable on the sabbath day. 6. Jesus Christ, though he allowed works of necessity on the sabbath day, will notwithstanding have us to know and remember that it is his day (v. 5): *The Son of man is Lord also of the sabbath.* In the kingdom of the Redeemer, the sabbath day is to be turned into a *Lord's day*. In token of this, it shall not only have a new name, the *Lord's day*, but shall be transferred to a new day, the first day of the week.

II. He justifies himself in doing *works of mercy* for others on the sabbath day. 1. Christ on the sabbath day *entered into the synagogue*. It is our duty, as we have opportunity, to sanctify sabbaths in religious assemblies. Our place must not be empty without very good reason. 2. In the synagogue, on the sabbath day, *he taught*. Christ took all opportunities to teach, not only his disciples, but the multitude. 3. Christ's patient was one of his hearers. *A man whose right hand was withered* came. Those that would be *cured* by the grace of Christ must be willing to *learn* the doctrine of Christ. 4. Among those who were the hearers and the eye-witnesses, there were some who came with no other design than to pick quarrels with him, v. 7. The scribes and Pharisees *watched him*, as the lion does his prey, whether he would *heal on the sabbath day, that they might find an accusation against him.* 5. Jesus Christ was neither ashamed nor afraid to own the purposes of his grace, v. 8. He bade the man *rise, and stand forth*, hereby to try the patient's faith and boldness. 6. He appealed to his adversaries themselves, whether it was the design of the fourth commandment to restrain men from doing good on the sabbath day, that good which their hand finds to do, and which cannot so well be put off to another time (v. 9): *Is it lawful to do good, or evil, on the sabbath days?* 7. He healed the poor man, though he knew that his enemies would not only take offence at it, but take advantage against him for it, v. 10. 8. His adversaries were hereby enraged so much the more against him, v. 11. Instead

of being brought to be in love with him as a benefactor to mankind,—they were *filled with madness*, vexed that they could not frighten him from doing good. They were *mad* at Christ, *mad* at the people, *mad* at themselves. When they could not prevent his working this miracle, they *communed one with another what they might do to Jesus*, what other way they might take to run him down.

Verses 12–19

In these verses, we have our Lord Jesus in *secret*, in *his family*, and in *public*; and in all three acting like himself.

I. In *secret* we have him *praying to God*, v. 12. This evangelist takes frequent notice of Christ's retirements, to give us an example of secret prayer, without which it is impossible that the soul should prosper. *In those days*, when his enemies were filled with madness against him, he went out to *pray*. He was *alone* with God; he *went out into a mountain, to pray*, where he might have no disturbance or interruption given him. He was *long* alone with God: *He continued all night in prayer.* We think one half hour a great deal, but Christ continued a *whole night* in meditation and secret prayer. We have a great deal of *business* at the throne of grace, and we should take a great *delight* in communion with God, and by both these we may be kept sometimes long at prayer.

II. We have him nominating his immediate attendants, that should be the constant auditors of his doctrine and eye-witnesses of his miracles, that hereafter they might be sent forth as *apostles*, his *messengers* to the world, v. 13. After he had *continued all night in prayer*, one would have thought that, when it was day, he should have reposed himself. No, as soon as anybody was stirring, he *called unto him his disciples*. In serving God, our great care should be, not to *lose time*, but to make the end of one good duty the beginning of another. Ministers are to be ordained with *prayer* more than ordinarily *solemn*. The number of the apostles was *twelve*. Their names are here recorded; it is the *third time* that we have met with them, and in each of the *three* places the *order* of them differs. Never were men so privileged, and yet one of them had a devil, and proved a traitor (v. 16); yet Christ, when he chose him, was not deceived in him.

III. In *public* we have him *preaching* and *healing*, the two great works between which he divided his time, v. 17. He came down with the twelve from the mountain, and *stood in the plain*, and there were presently gathered about him, not only the *company of his disciples*, but also a great *multitude of people*, a mixed multitude *out of all Judæa and Jerusalem*. They came also from the *sea-coast of Tyre and Sidon*. Though they bordered upon Canaanites, yet there were some well affected to Christ; such there were dispersed in all parts, here and there one. They *came to hear him*, and he *preached* to them. It is worthwhile to go a great way to hear the word of Christ, and to go out of the way of other business for it. They came to be *cured* by him, and he *healed* them. Some were troubled *in body*, and some *in mind*; some had *diseases*, some had *devils*; but both the one and the other, were *healed*, for he has power over *diseases* and *devils* (v. 17, 18). Nay, it should seem, those who had no *particular diseases* to complain of yet found it a great confirmation and renovation to their bodily *health* and *vigour* to partake of the *virtue that went out of him*; for (v. 19) *the whole multitude sought to touch him*, and they were all, one way or other, the better for him: he *healed them all*; and who is there that doth not need, upon some account or other, to be *healed?* There is a *fulness of grace* in Christ, that is enough for all, enough for each.

Verses 20–26

Here begins a practical discourse of Christ, most of which is found in the *sermon upon the mount*, Matt. v. and vii.

I. Blessings pronounced upon *suffering saints* (*v.* 20): He *lifted up his eyes upon his disciples*, not only the *twelve*, but the whole *company of them* (*v.* 17), and directed his discourse to them. There he *sat*, as one having authority; thither *they come to him* (Matt. v. 1).

1. "You are *poor*, you have *left all to follow me*. But you are blessed in your poverty, nay, you are blessed *for* it, for *yours is the kingdom of God*, all the comforts and graces of his kingdom here and all the glories and joys of his kingdom hereafter; yours it *shall be*, nay, yours *it is*."

2. "You *hunger now* (*v.* 21), you are not *fed to the full* as others are, you are glad of a few *ears of corn* for a meal's meat; thus you hunger now in this world, but in the other world *you shall be filled*."

3. "You *weep now*. But *blessed are you*; your present sorrows are no *prejudices* to your future joy, but *preparatories* for it: *You shall laugh*. You are but *sowing in tears*, and shall shortly *reap in joy*," Ps. cxxvi. 5, 6. God is treasuring up comforts for them; and the day is coming when their *mouth shall be filled with laughing and their lips with rejoicing*, Job. viii. 21.

4. "You now undergo *the world's ill will*. You must expect all the base treatment that a spiteful world can give you for Christ's sake, because you serve him and his interests. Wicked men will *hate you*, because your doctrine and life convict and condemn them. *They will reproach you*, will charge you with the blackest crimes, which you are perfectly innocent of, will fasten upon you the blackest characters, which you do not deserve; they will *cast out your name as evil*. *Blessed are you* when you are so used. It is an honour to you, as it is to a brave hero to be employed in the wars, in the service of his prince; and therefore *rejoice you in that day, and leap for joy*, *v.* 23. Do not only *bear it*, but *triumph* in it. You are treated as the prophets were before you, and therefore not only need not be ashamed of it, but may justly rejoice in it. You will for this be abundantly *recompensed*. *Your reward is great in heaven*. Though you may be losers for Christ, you shall not be losers by him in the end."

II. *Woes* denounced against *prospering sinners as miserable people*, though the world *envies them*. These we had not in Matthew. It should seem, the best exposition of *these woes*, compared with the foregoing *blessings*, is the parable of the rich *man* and Lazarus. Here is a *woe* to them that are *rich*, that is, that *trust in riches*; woe to them, for *they have received their consolation*, that which they placed their happiness in, *v.* 24. They in their lifetime received *their good things*, which, in their account, were the *best things*. "You that are *rich* are in temptation to *set your hearts* upon a *smiling world*, and to say, *Soul, take thine ease* in the embraces of it." It is the *folly* of carnal worldlings that they make the things of this world *their consolation*, which were intended only for their *convenience*. They please themselves with them; and to them the *consolations of God* are small, and of no account. It is their misery that they are *put off* with them as *their consolation*. Here is a *woe* to them that are *full* (*v.* 25), and have *more than heart could wish*. They are *full of themselves*, without God and Christ. Woe to such, for *they shall hunger*, they shall shortly be *stripped* and *emptied* of all the things they are so proud of. Here is a *woe* to them that *laugh now*, that have always a *disposition to be merry*, and always something to *make merry with*, and are always entertaining themselves with the laughter of the fool.

Woe unto such, for it is but *now*, for a little time, that they *laugh*; they shall *mourn and weep* shortly. Here is a *woe* to them *whom all men speak well of*, that is, who make it their great and only care to gain the praise and applause of men (*v.* 26): "*Woe unto you;* it would be a bad sign that you were not faithful to your trust, and to the souls of men, if you preached so as that nobody would be disgusted; for your business is to tell people of their faults. The false prophets indeed, that flattered your fathers in their wicked ways, were caressed and spoken well of. We should desire to have the approbation of those that are wise and good; but, as we should despise the reproaches, so we should also despise the praises, of the fools in Israel.

Verses 27–36

These verses agree with Matt. v. 38, to the end of that chapter: *I say unto you that hear* (*v.* 27), to all you that hear, for these are lessons of universal concern. *He that has an ear, let him hear*. Now the lessons Christ here teaches us are,

I. That we must render to all their due, and be honest and just in all our dealings (*v.* 31): *As ye would that men should do to you, do ye also to them likewise;* for this is *loving your neighbour as yourselves*. We must *put our souls into their souls' stead*, and then pity and succour them, as we should desire and justly expect to be ourselves pitied and succoured.

II. That we must be free in *giving* to them that *need* (*v.* 30): "*Give to every man that asketh of thee*, that wants necessaries, which thou hast wherewithal to supply out of thy superfluities. Give to those that are not able to help themselves." Christ would have his disciples ready to distribute, and willing to communicate, *to their power* in ordinary cases, and beyond their power in extraordinary.

III. That we must be generous in *forgiving* those that have been any way injurious to us.

1. We must not be *extreme* in *demanding* our right, when it is denied us: "*Him that taketh away thy cloak, forbid him not to take thy coat also* (*v.* 29). Let him have that too, rather than fight for it. And (*v.* 30) *of him that taketh thy goods*, of such do not *exact them*; if Providence have made such insolvent, do not take the advantage of the law against them, but rather lose it than *take them by the throat*," Matt. xviii. 28.

2. We must not be rigorous in revenging a wrong when it is done us: "*Unto him that smiteth thee on the one cheek, offer also the other*. If anyone *smite thee on the cheek*, rather than give another blow to him, be ready to receive another from him"; that is, "leave it to God to plead thy cause, and do thou sit down silent under the affront."

3. Nay, we must *do good to them that do evil to us*. This is that which our Saviour chiefly designs to teach us, as a law peculiar to his religion, and a branch of the perfection of it. We must be kind to those from whom we have *received injuries*. We must not only *love our enemies*, and bear a good will to them, but we must *do good* to them. We must study to make it appear, by positive acts, that we bear them no malice, nor seek revenge. Do they *curse us*, speak ill of us, and wish ill to us? Do they *despitefully use us*, in word or deed? Do they endeavour to make us contemptible or odious? Let us *bless them*, and *pray for them*, speak well of them, the best we can, wish well to them, and be intercessors with God for them. This is repeated, *v.* 35: *Love your enemies*, and *do them good*. To recommend this difficult duty to us, it is represented as a generous thing, and an attainment few arrive at. *To love those that love us* has nothing *uncommon* in it, nothing peculiar to Christ's disciples, for *sinners will love those that love them*. It is but following nature and puts no force at all upon it

(v. 32). "And (v. 33) *if you do good to them that do good to you, what thanks have you?* What credit are you to the name of Christ, or what reputation do you bring to it? for *sinners also do even the same.* But it becomes you to do something more excellent and eminent, to do that which sinners will not do: you must *render good for evil*"; *then* we are to our God *for a name and a praise,* and he will have the thanks. We must be kind to those from whom we expect no manner of advantage (v. 35): *Lend, hoping for nothing again.* We must *lend* though we have reason to suspect that what we *lend* we *lose,* lend to those who are so poor that it is not probable they will be able to pay us again. Here are two motives to this generous charity. It will redound to our profit; for our *reward shall be great,* v. 35. What is lent and lost on earth, from a true principle of charity, will be made up to us. "You shall not only be *repaid,* but *rewarded,* greatly rewarded; it will be said to you, *Come, ye blessed, inherit the kingdom.*" It will redound to our honour; for herein we shall resemble God in his goodness, which is the greatest glory: "*Ye shall be the children of the Highest.*" It is the glory of God that he is *kind to the unthankful and to the evil.* Hence he infers (v. 36), *Be merciful,* as *your Father is merciful;* this explains Matt. v. 48, "*Be perfect, as your Father is perfect.* Imitate your Father in those things that are his brightest perfections." Those that are *merciful* as God is *merciful,* even *to the evil and the unthankful,* are *perfect* as God is *perfect.* This should strongly engage us to be merciful to our brethren, not only that God is so to others, but that he is so to us, though we have been, and are, evil and unthankful; it is of his mercies that *we* are not consumed.

Verses 37–49

All these sayings of Christ we had before in Matthew. They were sayings that Christ often used. We need not be critical here in seeking for the coherence: they are golden sentences, like Solomon's proverbs or parables.

I. We ought to be very candid in our censures of others, because we need grains of allowance ourselves: "Therefore *judge not* others, because then *you* yourselves *shall not be judged*; therefore *condemn not* others, because then *you* yourselves *shall not be condemned,* v. 37. God will not *judge* and *condemn* you, men will not." They that are merciful to other people's names shall find others merciful to theirs.

II. If we are of a *giving* and a *forgiving* spirit, we shall ourselves reap the benefit of it: *Forgive and you shall be forgiven.* If we forgive the injuries done to us by others, others will forgive our inadvertencies. If we forgive others' trespasses against *us,* God will forgive our trespasses against *him.* And he will be no less mindful of the *liberal* that *devise liberal things* (v. 38): *Give, and it shall be given to you. Men* shall *return it into your bosom;* for God often makes use of *men* as instruments, not only of his *avenging,* but of his *rewarding* justice. God will incline the hearts of others to give to us when we need, and to give liberally, *good measure pressed down and shaken together.* Whom God recompenses he recompenses *abundantly.*

III. We must expect to be dealt with ourselves as we deal with others: *With the same measure that ye mete it shall be measured to you again.* Those that deal *hardly* with others may expect to be paid in their own coin; but they that deal *kindly* with others have reason to hope that God will raise them up friends who will deal kindly with them.

IV. Those who put themselves under the guidance of the ignorant and erroneous are likely to perish with them (v. 39): *Can the blind lead the blind? Shall not both fall* together *into the ditch?* How can they expect any other? Those that are led by the common opinion, course, and custom, of this world, are themselves blind, and are led by the blind.

V. Christ's followers cannot expect better treatment in the world than their Master had, v. 40. Let them not promise themselves more honour or pleasure in the world than Christ had. Let each live a life of labour and self-denial as his Master doth, and make himself a servant of all; let him stoop, and let him toil, and do all the good he can, and then he will be a complete disciple.

VI. Those who take upon them to rebuke and reform others are concerned to look to it that they be themselves without rebuke, v. 41, 42. It is very absurd for any to pretend to be so quick-sighted as to spy small faults in others, like a mote in the eye, when they are themselves so perfectly past feeling as not to perceive *a beam in their own eye.* How canst thou offer thy service to thy brother, to *pull out the mote from his eye,* which requires a good eye as well as a good hand, when thou thyself hast a *beam in thine own eye.* To help to pull the mote out of our brother's eye is a good work, but then we must qualify ourselves for it by beginning with ourselves; reforming our own lives.

VII. We may expect that men's words and actions will be according as *they* are.

1. The heart is the *tree,* and the words and actions are fruit according to the nature of the tree, v. 43, 44. If a man be really a *good man,* though perhaps he may not abound in fruit, and though he may be sometimes like a tree in winter, yet he does not *bring forth corrupt fruit*; though he may not do you all the good he should, yet he will not do you hurt. If he cannot reform ill manners, he will not *corrupt good manners.* If the fruit that a man brings forth be *corrupt* you may be sure that he is not a *good tree.* On the other hand, a *corrupt tree doth not bring forth good fruit,* though it may bring forth green leaves. So neither can you expect any *good conduct* from those who have justly a *bad character.* If the fruit be good, you may conclude that the tree is so; for *every tree is known by its fruit.*

2. The heart is the *treasure,* and the words and actions are the produce from that treasure, v. 45. The reigning love of God and Christ in the heart is *a good treasure in the heart*: it enriches a man, it furnishes him with a good stock to spend upon, for the benefit of others. Out of such a *good treasure* a man may bring forth that which is good. But where the love of the world and the flesh reign there is an *evil treasure* in the heart, out of which an *evil man* is continually bringing forth *that which is evil. Of the abundance of the heart the mouth speaks;* what the mouth ordinarily speaks generally agrees with what is innermost and uppermost in the heart. Not but that a good man may possibly drop a bad word, and a wicked man make use of a good word to serve a bad turn; but, for the most part, the heart is as the words are, *vain* or *serious*; it therefore concerns us to get our hearts filled, not only with *good,* but with *abundance* of it.

VIII. It is not enough to *hear* the sayings of Christ, but we must *do* them.

1. It is putting an *affront upon him* to call him *Lord, Lord,* if we do not make conscience of conforming to his will. We do but mock Christ, as they that in scorn said, *Hail, King of the Jews,* if we call him ever so often *Lord, Lord,* and yet walk in the way of our own hearts.

2. It is *putting a cheat* upon ourselves if we think that *hearing* the sayings of Christ will bring us to heaven, without *doing* them. This he illustrates by a similitude (v. 47–49), which shows,

(1) That those only make sure work for their souls and eternity who do not only *come* to Christ as his

scholars, and *hear his sayings*, but do them. They are like a *house built on a rock*. These are they that *take pains* in religion, as they do that *build on a rock*,— that *begin low*, as they do,—that *dig deep*, that found their hope upon Christ, who is the Rock of ages (and other foundation can no man lay). They who do thus do well for themselves; for, [1] They shall keep their integrity, in times of temptation and persecution; when others fall from their own steadfastness they shall *stand fast in the Lord*. [2] They shall keep their comfort, and peace, and hope, and joy, in the midst of the greatest distresses. The *storms* and *streams* of affliction shall not shock them, for their feet are *set upon a rock*. [3] Their everlasting welfare is secured. Obedient believers are *kept by the power of Christ, through faith, unto salvation*, and shall never perish.

(2) That those who rest in a bare hearing of the sayings of Christ, and do not live up to them, are but preparing for a fatal disappointment: *He that heareth and doeth not*, he is like a man that *built a house without a foundation*. His hopes will fail him when he most needs the *comfort* of them. When the *stream beats vehemently* upon his house, it is gone, the sand it is built upon is washed away, and *immediately it falls*.

CHAPTER 7

I. Christ confirming the doctrine he had preached with two glorious miracles—the curing of one at a distance, and that was the centurion's servant (ver. 1–10), and the raising of one to life that was dead, the widow's son at Nain, ver. 11–18. II. Christ confirming the faith of John who was now in prison in answer to a question he received from him (ver. 19–23), to which he adds an honourable testimony concerning John, ver. 24–35. III. Christ comforting a poor penitent that applied herself to him, assuring her that her sins were pardoned, and justifying himself in the favour he showed her, ver. 36–50.

Verses 1–10

Some difference there is between this story of the cure of the centurion's servant as it is related here and as we had it in Matt. viii. 5, &c. There it was said that the centurion came to Christ; here it is said that he sent to him first some of the *elders of the Jews* (v. 3), and afterwards some other *friends*, v. 6.

This miracle is here said to have been wrought by our Lord Jesus *when he had ended all his sayings in the audience of the people*, v. 1. What Christ said he said *publicly; In secret have I said nothing*, John xviii. 20.

I. The centurion's servant that was sick was *dear to his master*, v. 2. It was the praise of the servant that by his diligence and faithfulness, he recommended himself to his master's esteem and love. Servants should study to *endear* themselves to their masters. It was likewise the praise of the master that, when he had a good servant, he knew how to value him. Many masters think it favour enough to the best servants they have not to rate them, whereas they ought to be kind to them, and tender of them, and solicitous for their welfare and comfort.

II. The master, *when he heard of Jesus*, v. 3, begged that *Christ would come and heal his servant*.

III. He sent some of the *elders of the Jews* to Christ, thinking that a greater piece of respect to Christ than if he had come himself. For that reason he sent Jews. And not ordinary Jews either, but *elders of the Jews*, that the dignity of the messengers might give honour to him to whom they were sent.

IV. The elders of the Jews were hearty intercessors for the centurion: *They besought him instantly* (v. 4), pleading for the centurion that which he would never have pleaded for himself, *that he was worthy for whom he should do this*. The centurion said, *I am not* so much as *worthy* of a visit (Matt. viii. 8), but the elders of the Jews thought him worthy of the cure. But that which they insisted upon in particular was, that, though he was a Gentile, yet he was a

hearty well-wisher to the Jewish nation and religion, v. 5. *He loveth our nation* (which few of the Gentiles did). Even conquerors, and those *in power*, ought to keep up an affection for the conquered, and those they have *power over*. He was well-affected to their worship: *He built them a* new *synagogue* at Capernaum. Hereby he testified his veneration for the God of Israel, and his desire to have an interest in the prayers of God's Israel. Building places of meeting for religious worship is a very *good work*, and those who do good works of that kind are *worthy of double honour*.

V. Jesus Christ was very ready to show kindness to the centurion. He presently *went with them* (v. 6), though he was a Gentile. The centurion did not think himself worthy to visit Christ (v. 7), yet Christ thought him worthy to be visited by him.

VI. The centurion gave further proofs both of his humility and of his faith. *When he was now not far from the house he sends friends* to meet him with fresh expressions, 1. Of his *humility*: "Lord, trouble *not thyself*, for I am unworthy of such an honour." This bespeaks not only his low thoughts of himself, notwithstanding the greatness of his figure; but his high thoughts of Christ, notwithstanding the meanness of his figure in the world. 2. Of his *faith*: "Lord, *trouble not thyself*; thou canst *cure* my servant without coming *under my roof. Say in a word, and my servant shall be healed.*" He illustrates this faith of his by a comparison taken from his own profession, and is confident that Christ can as easily command away the distemper as he can command any of his soldiers, as he can send a soldier on an errand, v. 8.

VII. Our Lord Jesus was wonderfully well pleased with the faith of the centurion, and the more surprised at it because he was a Gentile; and, the centurion's faith having thus honoured Christ, see how he honoured it (v. 9): *He turned him about* and *said to the people that followed him, I have not found so great faith, no not in Israel*. Christ will have those that follow him to observe and take notice of the great examples of faith—especially when any such are found among those that do not follow Christ so closely as they do in profession—that we may be shamed by the strength of their faith out of the weakness and waverings of ours.

VIII. The cure was *presently* and *perfectly* wrought (v. 10): *They that were sent* went back, and found the servant well. Christ will take cognizance of the distressed case of poor servants, for there *is no respect of persons with him*. Nor are the Gentiles excluded from the benefit of his grace.

Verses 11–18

We have here the story of Christ's raising to life a widow's son at Nain, which Matthew and Mark had made no mention of.

I. Where, and when, this miracle was wrought. It was the *next day after* he had cured the centurion's servant, v. 11. It was done at the gate of a small city, or town, called *Nain*, not far from Capernaum.

II. Who were the witnesses of it. It was done in the sight of two crowds that met in or near the gate of the city. There was a crowd of *disciples* and other *people* attending Christ (v. 11), and a crowd of relations and neighbours attending the funeral of the young man, v. 12.

III. How it was wrought by our Lord Jesus. The person raised to life was a *young man*. This young man was the *only son of his mother*, and *she a widow*. She depended upon him to be the staff of her old age, but he proves a broken reed; every man at his best estate is so. We may well think how deep the *sorrow* of this poor mother was for her *only son*, and it was the deeper in that she was a *widow*. *Much people of the city was with her, condoling* with her loss, to *comfort* her. Christ showed both his *pity* and his *power* in raising him to life. See how *tender* his *compassions* are towards the afflicted (v. 13): *When the Lord saw* the poor widow following her son to the grave, *he had compassion on her.* Here was no application made to him for her. *Purely from the goodness of his nature*, he was troubled for her. The case was piteous, and he looked upon it with pity. He *said unto her, Weep not.* What a pleasing idea does this give us of the compassions of the Lord Jesus, and the multitude of his *tender mercies.* Christ said, *Weep not;* and he could give her a reason for it which no one else could: "Weep not for a *dead son*, for he shall presently become a *living one.*" This was a reason peculiar to her case; yet there is a reason common to all that sleep in Jesus, that they shall rise again, shall rise in glory; and therefore we must *not sorrow as those that have no hope*, 1 Thess. iv. 13. Let our *passion* at such a time be checked and calmed by the consideration of Christ's *compassion.* See how *triumphant* his *commands* are over even death itself (v. 14): *He came, and touched the bier.* Hereby he intimated to the bearers that they should not proceed. Hereupon *they that bore him stood still*, and then with solemnity, as one that had authority, he said, *Young man, I say unto thee, Arise.* Power went along with that word to *put life* into him. Christ's dominion over death was evidenced by the immediate effect of his word (v. 15): *He that was dead sat up.* Have we grace from Christ? Let us show it. Another evidence of life was that he *began to speak;* for whenever Christ gives us spiritual life he *opens the lips* in prayer and praise. He *delivered him to his mother*, to attend her as became a dutiful son. Now she was *comforted*, according to the time in which she had been afflicted.

IV. What influence it had upon the people (v. 16): *There came a fear on all;* they were all struck with wonder at this miracle, and *glorified God.* The Lord and his goodness, as well as the Lord and his greatness, are to be feared. The inference they drew from it was, "*A great prophet is risen up among us*, and in him *God hath visited his people.*" This would be *life from the dead* indeed to all them that waited for the consolation of Israel. The report of this miracle was carried, in general, all the country over (v. 17): *This rumour of him went forth through all Judæa*, which lay a great way off, and throughout all Galilee, which was the *region round about.* Many have the *rumour* of Christ's gospel in their ears that have not the *savour* and *relish* of it in their souls. In particular, it was carefully brought to John Baptist, who was now in prison (v. 18): *His disciples came*, and gave him an account of all things, that he might know that though *he* was bound yet *the word of the Lord was not bound*; God's work was going on, though he was laid aside.

Verses 19–35

I. We have here the message John Baptist sent to Christ, and the return he made to it. The great thing we are to enquire concerning Christ is whether he be he that should come, or whether we are to look for another, v. 19, 20. We are sure that God has promised that a Saviour shall come; we are as sure that what he has promised he will perform. If this Jesus be that promised Messiah, we will receive him; but, if not, we will continue our expectations, and will wait for him. The faith of John Baptist himself wanted to be *confirmed* in this matter. The great men of the Jewish church had not owned him. Nothing of that power and grandeur was to be seen about him in which it was expected that the Messiah would appear; and therefore it is not strange that they should ask, *Art thou the Messiah?* Christ left it to his own works to praise him. While John's

messengers were with him, he wrought many miraculous cures, *in that same hour*, v. 21. *He cured many of their infirmities and plagues* in body, and of *evil spirits*, and *unto many that were blind he gave sight.* He multiplied the cures, that there might be no ground left to suspect a fraud; and then (v. 22) he bade them *go and tell John what they had seen.* And he and they might easily argue, as even the common people did (John vii. 31), *When Christ cometh, will he do more miracles than these which this man hath done?* You see that Jesus does this to the bodies of people, and therefore must conclude this is he that should come to do it to the souls of people, and you are to *look for no other.* To his miracles in the kingdom of nature he adds this in the kingdom of grace (v. 22), *To the poor the gospel is preached*, which they knew was to be done by the Messiah. Judge, therefore, whether you can look for any other that will more fully answer the characters of the Messiah. He gave them an intimation of the danger people were in of being prejudiced against him (v. 23): *Blessed is he whosoever shall not be offended in me*, or *scandalized* at me. Christ's education at Nazareth, his residence at Galilee, the meanness of his family and relations, his poverty, and the despicableness of his followers—these and the like were stumbling-blocks to many. He is *blessed*, for he is wise, humble, and well disposed, that is not overcome by these prejudices. It is a sign that God has *blessed* him, *and he shall be blessed* indeed, blessed in Christ.

II. We have here the high encomium which Christ gave of John Baptist; *when they were departed* (v. 24). Let them now consider *what they went out into the wilderness to see.* "Come," saith Christ, "I will tell you."

1. He was a man of steadiness and constancy. He was not a *reed shaken with the wind*; he was *firm* as a *rock*, not *fickle* as a *reed.*

2. He was a man of unparalleled *self-denial.* He was not *a man clothed in soft raiment*, nor did he *live delicately* (v. 25); but, on the contrary, he lived in a wilderness and was clad and fed accordingly.

3. He was *a prophet.* Nay, he was *more*, he was *much more than a prophet* (v. 26), than any of the prophets of the Old Testament; for they spoke of Christ as at a distance, he spoke of him as at the door.

4. He was the harbinger and forerunner of the Messiah, and was himself prophesied of in the Old Testament (v. 27): *This is he of whom it is written* (Mal. iii. 1), *Behold, I send my messenger before thy face.* Before he sent the Master himself, he sent a messenger, to give notice of his coming. It was a *previous* indication, plain enough, of the *spiritual* nature of Christ's kingdom, that the messenger he sent before him to *prepare his way* did it by preaching repentance and reformation. Certainly that kingdom was not of this world which was thus ushered in.

5. He was so great that really there was not a *greater prophet* than he. Prophets were the *greatest* that were *born of women*, and John was the *greatest* of all the *prophets.* And yet *he that is least in the kingdom of God is greater than he.* The meanest of those that *follow the Lamb* far excel the greatest of those that went before him. Those therefore who live under the gospel dispensation have so much the more to answer for.

III. We have here the just censure of the men of that generation.

1. Christ here shows what contempt was put upon John Baptist, while he was preaching and baptizing. Those who did show him any respect were but the common ordinary sort of people, v. 29. *The people* indeed, the vulgar herd, of whom it was said, *This people, who know not the law, are cursed* (John vii.

49), and the publicans, these were *baptized with his baptism*, and became his disciples. By their repentance and reformation they *justified God* in appointing such a one as John Baptist to be the forerunner of the Messiah: they hereby made it to appear that it was the best method that could be taken, for it was not in vain to *them*, whatever it was to others. The great men of their church and nation heard him indeed, but they were not *baptized of him, v.* 30. The Pharisees and the lawyers *rejected the counsel of God against themselves*; if they had closed with the counsel of God, it had been *for themselves*; but they *rejected it*, and it was *against themselves*, it was to their own ruin.

2. He here shows the strange perverseness of the men of that generation, and the prejudices they conceived. They made but a jesting matter of the methods God took to do them good (*v.* 31): "*Whereunto shall I liken the men of this generation?* They are, then, *like children sitting in the market-place*, that mind nothing that is serious, but are as full of play as they can hold. As if God were but in jest with them, as children are with one another in the market-place (*v.* 32), they turn it all off with a banter." This is the ruin of multitudes, they can never persuade themselves to be *serious* in the concerns of their souls. O the amazing stupidity and vanity of the blind and ungodly world! The Lord awaken them out of their security. They still found something or other to carp at. John Baptist was a reserved austere man, lived much in solitude, and ought to have been hearkened to as a man of thought and contemplation; but this, which was his praise, was turned to his reproach. Because he came *neither eating nor drinking you say*, "*He has a devil*; he is a melancholy man, he is possessed." Our Lord Jesus was of a more free and open conversation; he *came eating and drinking*, *v.* 34. He would go and dine with Pharisees, and with publicans. In hopes of doing good both to the one and the other, he conversed familiarly with them. By this it appears that the ministers of Christ may be of very different tempers and dispositions, very different ways of preaching and living, and yet all good and useful. Therefore none must make themselves a standard to all others, nor judge hardly of those that do not do just as they do. John Baptist bore witness to Christ, and Christ applauded John Baptist, though they were the reverse of each other in their way of living. But the common enemies of them both reproached them both. The very same men that had represented John as *crazed in his intellects*, represented our Lord Jesus as *corrupt in his morals*; *he is a gluttonous man, and a wine-bibber*. Ill-will never speaks well.

3. He shows that, notwithstanding this, God will be glorified in the salvation of a chosen remnant (*v.* 35): *Wisdom is justified of all her children.* Wisdom's children are herein unanimous, one and all, they have all a complacency in the methods of grace which divine wisdom takes, and think never the worse of them for their being ridiculed by some.

Verses 36–49

When and where this passage of story happened does not appear, but it comes in here, upon occasion of Christ's being reproached as *a friend to publicans and sinners*. Who this woman was that here testified so great an affection to Christ does not appear.

I. The civil entertainment which a Pharisee gave to Christ (*v.* 36): *One of the Pharisees desired him that he would eat with him.* It appears that this Pharisee did not believe in Christ, for he will not own him to be a *prophet* (*v.* 39), and yet our Lord Jesus accepted his invitation, *went into his house, and sat down to meat.* And those may venture further into the society of such as are prejudiced against Christ,

who have wisdom and grace sufficient to instruct and argue with them, than others may.

II. The great respect which a poor penitent sinner showed him. It was a woman in the city *that was a sinner*, a *harlot*, and infamous. She *knew that Jesus sat at meat in the Pharisee's house*, and she came to acknowledge her obligations to him, having no opportunity of doing it in any other way than by *washing* his feet, and anointing them with some sweet ointment that she brought with her for that purpose. Now this woman did not look Christ in the face, but came *behind him*, and did the part of a *maidservant*.

Now in what this good woman did, we may observe,

1. Her *deep humiliation* for sin. She stood behind him *weeping*; her eyes had been the inlets and outlets of sin, and now she makes them fountains of tears. Her face is now foul with weeping, which perhaps used to be covered with paints. Her hair now made a towel of, which before had been plaited and adorned. We have reason to think that she had before sorrowed for sin; but now that she had an opportunity of coming into the presence of Christ, her sorrow was renewed.

2. Her *strong affection* to the Lord Jesus. This was what our Lord Jesus took special notice of, that she *loved much, v.* 42, 47. She *washed his feet*, she washed them with *her tears*, tears of joy; she was in a transport, to find herself so near her Saviour, whom her soul loved. She *kissed his feet*. It was a kiss of adoration as well as affection. *She wiped them with her hair*. Her eyes shall yield water to wash them, and her hair be a towel to wipe them; and she *anointed* his feet *with the ointment*. All true penitents have a dear love to the Lord Jesus.

III. The offence which the Pharisee took at Christ, for admitting the respect which this poor penitent paid him (*v.* 39): *He said within himself, This man, if he were a prophet,* would then have so much *knowledge* as to perceive that *this woman is a sinner*, and so much *sanctity* as *therefore* not to suffer her to come so near him. See how apt proud and narrow souls are to think that others should be as haughty and censorious as themselves.

IV. Christ's justification of the woman in what she did to him, and of himself in admitting it. Christ knew what the Pharisee spoke *within himself*, and made answer to it: *Simon, I have something to say unto thee, v.* 40. Simon is willing to give him the hearing: *He saith, Master, say on.* Now Christ, in his answer to the Pharisee, reasons thus:—It is true this woman has been a sinner: he knows it; but she is a *pardoned* sinner, which supposes her to be a *penitent* sinner. What she did to him was an expression of her *great love* to her Saviour. If she was pardoned, who had been *so great a sinner*, it might reasonably be expected that she should love her Saviour more than others, and if this was the fruit of her love, and flowing from a sense of the pardon of her sins, it became him to accept of it, and it ill became the Pharisee to be offended at it.

1. He by a parable forces Simon to acknowledge that the greater sinner this woman had been the greater love she ought to show to Jesus Christ when her *sins* were *pardoned, v.* 41–43. A man had *two debtors* that were both insolvent, but one of them owed him *ten times* more than the other. He very freely *forgave them both*, and did not take the advantage of the law against them. Now they were both sensible of the great kindness they had received; but *which of them will love him most?* Certainly, saith the Pharisee, he to *whom he forgave most.* Hence learn the duty between debtor and creditor.

(1) The *debtor*, if he have *anything to pay*, ought to make satisfaction to his *creditor*.

(2) If God in his providence have disabled the debtor to pay his debt, the creditor ought not to be severe with him, but *freely to forgive him.*

(3) The debtor that has found his creditors merciful ought to be very grateful to them; and ought to love them. Some insolvent debtors, instead of being *grateful*, are *spiteful*, to their creditors that lose by them, and cannot give them a good word. But this parable speaks of God (or rather of the Lord Jesus himself, for he it is that forgives) and sinners are the debtors: and so we may learn here, [1] That *sin is a debt*, and *sinners are debtors* to God Almighty. As creatures, we owe a debt, a debt of obedience. We have not paid our rent; nay, we have wasted our Lord's goods, and so we become debtors. [2] That some are deeper in debt to God, by reason of sin, than others are: *One owed five hundred pence and the other fifty.* The Pharisee was the less debtor, yet he a debtor too, which was more than he thought himself. This woman was the *greater debtor.* Some sinners are in themselves greater debtors than others. [3] That, whether our debt be more or less, it is *more* than we are able to pay: *They had nothing to pay*, nothing at all to make a composition with. No righteousness of our own will pay it, no, not our repentance and obedience for the future; for it is what we are already bound to. [4] That the God of heaven is *ready* to forgive, *frankly to forgive*, poor sinners. If we repent, and believe in Christ, our iniquity shall not be laid to our charge. God has proclaimed his name gracious and merciful, and ready to forgive sin. [5] That those who have their sins *pardoned* are obliged to *love him* that pardoned them; and the more is forgiven them, the more they should love him. The *greater sinners* any have been before their conversion, the *greater saints* they should be after. When a *persecuting Saul* became a preaching Paul he *laboured more abundantly.*

2. He applies this parable to the different temper and conduct of the Pharisee and the sinner. Christ seems rea ly to allow that he was one *forgiven*, though to him *less was forgiven.* He did indeed show some love to Christ, but nothing to what this poor woman showed. "Observe," saith Christ to him, "she is one that has much forgiven her, and therefore, she should love much more than thou dost, and so it appears. *Seest thou this woman?* (v. 44). Consider how much kinder a friend she is to me than thou art; should I then accept thy kindness, and refuse hers? Thou didst not so much as order a basin of water to be brought, to wash my feet in, but she has done much more: *she has washed my feet with tears*, and has *wiped them with the hairs of her head*, in token of her great love to me. Thou didst not so much as kiss my cheek, but *this woman has not ceased to kiss my feet* (v. 45). Thou didst not provide me a little common oil, as usual, to anoint my head with; but she has bestowed a box of precious *ointment* upon *my feet* (v. 46)." The reason why some people blame the pains and expense of zealous Christians, in religion, is because they are not willing themselves to come up to it, but resolve to rest in a *cheap* and *easy* religion.

3. He silenced the Pharisee's cavil: *I say unto thee*, Simon, *her sins, which are many, are forgiven*, v. 47. He owns that she had been guilty of *many sins*: "But they are *forgiven* her, *for she loved much.*" It should be rendered, *therefore she loved much*; for it is plain that her loving much was not the *cause*, but the *effect*, of her pardon. We love God because he *first loved us;* he did not forgive us because we first loved him. "But to *whom little is forgiven*, as is to thee, *the same loveth little*, as thou dost." Instead of grudging greater sinners the mercy they find with Christ we should be stirred up by their example to examine ourselves whether we be indeed forgiven, and do love Christ.

4. He silenced her fears. Christ said unto her, *Thy sins are forgiven*, v. 48. She was dismissed with this word from Christ, *Thy sins are forgiven!* and what an effectual prevention would this be of her return to sin again! Though there were those present who quarrelled with Christ, in their own minds, for presuming to forgive sin, and to pronounce sinners absolved (v. 49), yet he *stood to what he had said.* He would now show that he had *pleasure in forgiving sin;* he loves to speak pardon and peace to penitents: *He said to the woman, Thy faith hath saved thee*, v. 50. All these expressions of sorrow for sin, and love to Christ, were the effects and products of faith. As faith of all graces doth most honour God, so Christ doth of all graces put most honour upon faith.

CHAPTER 8

Most of this chapter is a repetition of divers passages which we had before in Matthew and Mark. I. A general account of Christ's preaching, ver. 1–3. II. The parable of the sower, ver. 4–18. III. The preference which Christ gave to his obedient disciples before his nearest relations, ver. 19–21. IV. His stilling a storm at sea, ver. 22–25. V. His casting a legion of devils out of a man, ver. 26–40. VI. His healing the woman that had the bloody issue, and raising Jairus's daughter to life, ver. 41–56.

Verses 1–3

I. *What* Christ *made* the *constant business* of his *life*—it was *preaching;* in that work he was indefatigable, and went about doing good (v. 1). 1. *Where* he preached: *He went about.* He was an *itinerant* preacher, did not confine himself to one place, but diffused the beams of his light. He went about *through every city*, that none might plead ignorance. Hereby he set an example to his disciples; they must traverse the nations of the earth, as he did the cities of Israel. Nor did he confine himself to the *cities*, but went into the *villages*, among the plain country-people. 2. What he preached: *He showed the glad tidings of the kingdom of God.* Tidings of the *kingdom of God* are *glad tidings*, and those Jesus Christ came to bring. It was *glad tidings* to the world that there was hope of its being *reformed* and *reconciled.* 3. Who were his attendants: *The twelve were with him* to learn from him what and how to preach hereafter.

II. *Whence* he *had* the *necessary supports* of life: He lived upon the kindness of his friends. There were *certain women* that *ministered to him of their substance*, v. 2, 3. Some of them are named; but there were *many others.*

1. They were such, for the most part, as were the monuments of his power and mercy; they had been *healed by him of evil spirits and infirmities.* We are bound in *interest* to attend him, that we may be ready to apply ourselves to him for help in case of a relapse; and we are bound in *gratitude* to serve him and his gospel, who hath *saved* us, and saved us *by it.*

2. One of them was Mary Magdalene, out of whom had been *cast seven devils.* Some think that she was one that had been *very wicked*, and then we may suppose her to be the woman that *was a sinner* mentioned just before, *ch.* vii. 37. Upon her repentance and reformation she found mercy, and became a zealous disciple of Christ. The worse any have been before their conversion the more they should study to do for Christ after. This Mary Magdalene was attending on Christ's cross and his sepulchre.

3. Another of them was *Joanna the wife of Chuza, Herod's steward.* Her *husband*, though preferred in Herod's court, had received the gospel, and was very willing that his wife should be both a hearer of Christ and a contributor to him.

4. There were many of them that *ministered to Christ of their substance.* Though he was rich, yet for our sakes *he became poor*, and lived upon alms. Christ would rather be beholden to his known friends

for a maintenance for himself and his disciples than be burdensome to strangers. It is the duty of those who are taught in the word to *communicate to them who teach them in all good things.*

Verses 4–21

The former paragraph began with an account of Christ's industry in *preaching* (v. 1); this begins with an account of the people's industry in hearing, v. 4. He *went into every city*, to preach; but there were those here that came *to him out of every city*, would not stay till he came to *them*, nor think that they had enough when he left *them*, but *met him* when he was coming towards them, and *followed him* when he was going from them.

Much people were gathered together, abundance of fish to cast his net among; and he was as ready and willing to *teach* as they were to be *taught*.

I. Necessary and excellent rules and cautions for hearing the word, in the parable of *the sower*. When Christ had put forth this parable, the disciples were *inquisitive* concerning the meaning of it, v. 9. They asked him, *What might this parable be?* We should covet earnestly to know the true *int*ent, and full *ext*ent, of the word we hear. They had opportunity of acquainting themselves with the mystery and meaning of his word, which others had not: *Unto you it is given*, v. 10. Happy are we, and for ever indebted to free grace, if the same thing that is a *parable* to others, with which they are only *amused*, is a *plain truth* to us.

Now from the parable itself, and the explication of it, observe,

1. The *heart of man* is as *soil* to the *seed of God's word*; it is capable of receiving it, and bringing forth the fruits of it; but, unless that seed be sown in it, it will bring forth nothing valuable. Our care therefore must be to bring the *seed* and the *soil* together.

2. The *success* of the *seeding* is very much according to the nature and temper of the *soil*. The word of God *is to us*, as *we are, a savour of life unto life*, or *of death unto death.*

3. The devil is a subtle and spiteful enemy. He takes the word out of the hearts of *careless* hearers, *lest they should believe and be saved*, v. 12. This is added here to teach us that we cannot be *saved* unless we *believe*. That therefore the devil does all he can to keep us from *believing*, to make us not believe the word when we read and hear it; or, if we heed it for the present, to make us forget it again, and let it slip (Heb. ii. 1); or, if we remember it, to create prejudices in our minds against it, or *divert* our minds from it to something else; and all is *lest we should believe and be saved.*

4. Where the word of God is heard *carelessly* there is commonly a *contempt* put upon it too. It is added here in the parable that the seed which fell by the wayside was *trodden down*, v. 5.

5. Those on whom the word makes *some* impressions, but they are not *deep* and *durable* ones; as the seed sown upon the rock, where it gains no root, v. 13. These *for awhile believe*, their profession promises something, but in *time of temptation they fall away* from their good beginnings.

6. The *pleasures of this life* are as dangerous and mischievous thorns to choke the good seed of the word. This is added here (v. 14), which was not in the other evangelists. The delights of sense may ruin the soul, even lawful delights, indulged, and too much delighted in.

7. It is not enough that the fruit be brought forth, but it must be *brought to perfection*, it must be fully ripened. If it be not, it is as if there was no fruit at all brought forth; for that which in Matthew and Mark is said to be *unfruitful* is the same that here is said to *bring forth none to perfection.*

8. The good ground, which brings forth *good fruit*, is an *honest* and *good heart* (v. 15); a heart firmly fixed for God and duty, an upright heart, a tender heart, is an honest and good heart, which, having heard the word, *understands* it (so it is in Matthew), *receives* it (so it is in Mark), and *keeps* it (so it is here), as the soil not only *receives*, but keeps, the seed.

9. Where the word is well kept there is fruit brought forth *with patience*. This also is added here; Patience to continue to the end in well-doing.

10. In consideration of all this, we ought to take *heed how we hear* (v. 18); take heed of those things that will hinder our profiting by the word we hear; take heed *lest* we hear carelessly and slightly; and take heed after we have heard the word, lest we lose what we have gained.

II. Needful instructions given to those that are appointed to preach the word, and to those also that have heard it. Those that have *received the gift* must *minister the same*. People that have profited by the word must look upon themselves as *lighted candles*. A *candle* must not be *covered with a vessel* nor *put under a bed*, v. 16. Ministers and Christians are to be lights in the world. Their light must shine before men; they must not only *be good*, but *do good*. What is now done *in secret* will shortly be *manifested* and *made known*, v. 17. What is committed to you *in secret* should be made manifest *by you*; for your Master did not give you talents to be buried, but to be traded with. The gifts we have will either be continued to us, or taken from us, according as we do, or do not, make use of them for the glory of God: *Whosoever hath, to him shall be given*, v. 18. He that hath gifts, and does good with them, shall have more; he that *buries his talent* shall lose it. From him that hath not shall be taken away even *that which he hath*, so it is in Mark; that which he *seemeth to have*, so it is in Luke. The grace that is lost was but *seeming* grace, was never *true*. Men do but *seem* to have what they do not *use.*

III. Great encouragement given to those that prove themselves faithful *hearers of the word*, by being *doers of the work*, in a particular instance of Christ's respect to his disciples, in preferring them even before his nearest relations (v. 19–21). Observe what crowding there was after Christ. There was no coming near for the throng of people that attended him. Some of his nearest kindred were least solicitous to hear him preach. Instead of getting *within*, desiring to *hear him*, they stood *without*, desiring to *see him*. Jesus Christ would rather be busy at his work than conversing with his friends. Christ is pleased to own those as his nearest and dearest relations that *hear the word of God and do it.*

Verses 22–39

We have here two illustrious proofs of the power of our Lord Jesus—his power over the *winds*, and his power over the *devils*. See Mark iv. and v.

I. His power over the winds.

1. Christ ordered his disciples to put to sea: *He went into a ship with his disciples*, v. 22. If Christ sends his disciples, he goes *with them*. And those may safely and boldly venture anywhere that have Christ accompanying them. He said, *Let us go over unto the other side.*

2. Those that put to sea in a calm, yea, and at Christ's word, must yet *prepare for a storm*. There came down a *storm of wind on the lake* (v. 23), and presently their ship was so tossed that it was filled with water, and they were in jeopardy of their lives.

3. Christ was *asleep* in the storm, v. 23. Some bodily refreshment he must have. The disciples of Christ may really have his gracious presence with them at sea, and in a storm, and yet he may seem as if he were *asleep*; he may not immediately appear for

their relief. Thus he will try their faith and patience and make their deliverance the more welcome when it comes at last.

4. A complaint to Christ of our danger is enough to engage him to awake, and appear for us, *v.* 24. They cried, *Master, master, we perish!* The way to have our fears silenced is to bring them to Christ. Those that in sincerity call upon him as *their Master,* may be sure that he will not let them *perish.*

5. Christ's business is to *lay storms,* as it is Satan's business to *raise* them. He delights to do it: for he came to *proclaim peace on earth.* He rebuked the *wind and the raging of the water,* and immediately *they ceased* (*v.* 24); all of a sudden, *there was a great calm.*

6. When our dangers are over, it becomes us to take to ourselves the shame of our own fears and to give to Christ the glory of his power. Christ gives them a rebuke for their inordinate fear: *Where is your faith? v.* 25. Many that have *true faith* have it to seek when they have occasion to use it. A little thing disheartens them; and *where is their faith* then? They give him the glory of his power: *They, being afraid, wondered.* Those that had feared the storm feared him that had stilled it, and *said one to another, What manner of man is this!*

II. His power over *the devil.* Presently after the winds were stilled they were brought to their desire'd haven, and *arrived at the country of the Gadarenes,* and there went ashore (*v.* 26, 27).

1. These *malignant* spirits are very *numerous.* They that had taken possession of this one man called themselves *Legion* (*v.* 30), because *many devils were entered into him:* he had *had devils a long time, v.* 27. They either were, or at least would be thought to be, a *legion.*

2. They have an *inveterate enmity* to man. This man in whom the devils had got possession *wore no clothes, neither abode in any house* (*v.* 27). They forced this man to *abide in the tombs,* to make him so much the more a terror to himself and to all about him.

3. They are very *strong, fierce,* and unruly, and hate and scorn to be restrained: *He was kept bound with chains and in fetters,* but he *broke the bands, v.* 29. Those that are *ungovernable* by any other thereby show that they are under Satan's government. *He was driven of the devil.* Those that are under Christ's government are *sweetly led* with the bands of love; those that are under the devil's government are *furiously driven.*

4. They are much enraged against our Lord Jesus, and have a great dread and horror of him: *When the man saw Jesus, he roared out* and *fell down before him,* and owned him to be *the Son of God most high,* that was infinitely above him and too hard for him; but protested against having any league or confederacy with him: *What have I to do with thee?* The devils have neither inclination to do service to Christ nor expectation to receive benefit by him. But they dreaded his power and wrath: *I beseech thee, torment me not.* They do not say, *I beseech thee, save me,* but only, *Torment me not.* See whose language *they* speak that have only a dread of hell but no desire of heaven as a place of holiness and love.

5. They are perfectly *at the command,* a⌄d under *the power,* of our Lord Jesus; and they knew it, for they *besought him that he would not command them to go into the deep.* O what a comfort is this to the Lord's people, that all the powers of darkness are under the check and control of the Lord Jesus! He can send them to *their own place,* when he pleaseth.

6. They delight in *doing mischief.* When they found there was no remedy, but they must quit their hold of this poor man, they begged they might have leave to take possession of a *herd of swine, v.* 32. When he could not destroy the man, he would destroy the swine. If he could not hurt them in their bodies, he would hurt them in their goods, which sometimes prove a great temptation to men to draw them from Christ, as here. Christ *suffered them to enter into the swine.* They entered into the *swine;* and no sooner had they entered into them than the herd ran violently *down a steep place into the lake,* and were *drowned.*

7. When the devil's power is broken in any soul that soul recovers itself: *The man out of whom the devils were departed sat at the feet of Jesus, v.* 35. While he was under the devil's power he was ready to *fly in the face* of Jesus; but now he *sits at his feet.* If God has possession of us, he preserves to us the government and enjoyment of ourselves; but, if Satan has possession of us, he robs us of both. We are never more our own than when we are Christ's.

Let us now see what was the effect of this miracle.

(1) What effect it had upon the people of that country: *The swineherds went and told it* both *in city and country* (*v.* 34). They told *by what means he that was possessed of the devils was healed* (*v.* 36), that it was by sending the devils into the swine, as if Christ could not have delivered the man out of their hands, but by delivering the swine into them. *The people came out,* to *see what was done,* and *they were afraid* (*v.* 35); they were *taken with great fear* (*v.* 37). They thought more of the destruction of the swine than of the deliverance of their poor afflicted neighbour, and therefore *the whole multitude besought Christ to depart from them.* None need to be afraid of Christ that are willing to forsake their sins and give up themselves to him. But Christ took them at their word: *He went up into the ship, and returned back again.* Those lose their Saviour, and their hopes in him, that love their swine better.

(2) What effect it had upon the poor man. He *desired* Christ's company as much as others *dreaded* it: he besought Christ that *he might be with him,* as others were *that have been healed by him of evil spirits and infirmities* (*v.* 2). He was loth to stay among those rude and brutish Gadarenes that desired Christ to depart from them. But Christ sent him home, to publish among those that knew him the great things God had done for him, that so he might be a blessing to his country, as he had been a burden to it. We must sometimes deny ourselves the satisfaction even of spiritual benefits and comforts, to gain an opportunity of being serviceable to the souls of others.

Verses 40–56

Christ was driven away by the *Gadarenes.* But when he returned to the *Galileans,* they *gladly received* him, *wished* and *waited* for his return, and *welcomed* him with all their hearts, *v.* 40. He returned, and found work to do in the place whence he came, fresh work. The needy you have always with you.

We have here two miracles interwoven, as they were in Matthew and Mark.

I. A *public address* made to Christ by *a ruler of the synagogue,* whose name was *Jairus,* on the behalf of a little daughter of his, that was very ill. Jairus, though a *ruler, fell down at Jesus's feet.* He *besought* him that he would *come into his house;* not having the *faith* of the centurion, who desired Christ only to *speak the* healing *word* at a distance. But Christ complied with his request; *he went along* with him. Strong faith shall be applauded, and yet weak faith shall not be rejected. When Christ was going *the people thronged him.* Let us not complain of a crowd, and a throng, and a hurry, as long as we are in the way of our duty, and *doing good;* but otherwise it is what every wise man will keep himself out of as much as he can.

II. Here is a *secret application* made to Christ by a woman ill of a *bloody issue,* which had been the consumption of her body and the consumption of her purse too; for *she had spent all her living upon physicians*, and was never the better, *v.* 43. The nature of her disease was such that she did not care to make a public complaint of it and therefore she took this opportunity of coming to Christ *in a crowd*. Her *faith* was very *strong*; for she doubted not but that by the *touch of the hem of his garment* she should derive from him healing virtue, looking upon him to be such a full fountain of mercies that she should *steal* a cure and he not *miss it*. Thus many a poor soul is *healed*, and *helped*, and *saved*, by Christ, that is *lost in a crowd*. The woman found an immediate change for the better in herself, and that her disease was cured, *v.* 44. Believers have comfortable communion with Christ *incognito*.

III. Here is a *discovery* of this secret cure.

1. Christ takes notice that there is a cure wrought: *Virtue is gone out of me, v.* 46. Those that have been healed by virtue derived from Christ must *own* it, for he *knows it*. It was his delight that *virtue* was gone out of him to do any good, and he did not grudge it to the meanest; they were as welcome to it as to the light and heat of the sun.

2. The poor patient owns her case, and the benefit she had received: *When she saw that she was not hid, she came, and fell down before him, v.* 47. She came *trembling*, and yet *her faith saved her, v.* 48. There may be *trembling* where yet there is saving faith. She *declared before all the people for what cause she had touched him*, because she believed that a touch would cure her, and it did so.

3. The great physician confirms her cure, and sends her away with the comfort of it: *Be of good comfort: thy faith hath made thee whole, v.* 48. It was obtained *surreptitiously* and *underhand*, but it was secured and seconded *aboveboard*. She *is* healed, and she *shall be* healed.

IV. Here is an *encouragement* to Jairus not to distrust the power of Christ, *though his daughter was now dead*, and they that brought him the tidings advised him not to give *the Master any further trouble* about her: *Fear not*, saith Christ, *only believe*. Our *faith in Christ* should be bold and daring. Though the child is dead, yet *believe*, and all shall be well.

V. The *preparatives* for the raising of her to life again. 1. The *choice* Christ made of witnesses that should see the miracle wrought. A *crowd* followed him, but perhaps they were rude and noisy; however, it was not fit to let such a multitude come into a gentleman's house, especially now that the family was all in sorrow; *therefore* he sent them back. He took none with him but Peter, and James, and John, designing these three, with the parents, to be the only spectators of the miracle. 2. The *check* he gave to the mourners. *They all wept, and bewailed her.* But Christ bids them *not weep; for she is not dead, but sleepeth.* He means, as to her peculiar case, that she was not dead for good and all; it would be to her friends as if she had been but a few hours asleep. But it is applicable to all that die in the Lord; therefore we should not sorrow for them as those that have *no hope*, because death is but a *sleep*. This was a comfortable word which Christ said to these mourners, yet they wickedly ridiculed it, and *laughed him to scorn* for it. They *knew that she was dead*, they were certain of it, and therefore nothing less than a *divine power* could restore her to life. But he *put them all out, v.* 54. They were unworthy to be the witnesses of this work of wonder.

VI. Her return to life: *He took her by the hand* (as we do by one that we would awake out of sleep, and help up), and he called, saying, *Maid, arise, v.* 55. Here that is expressed which was only implied in the other evangelists, that *her spirit came again.* Where the soul of this child was in this interval we

are not told; it was in the hand of the *Father of spirits*. When *her spirit came again* she arose, and made it appear that she was alive by her motion, as she did also by her appetite; for Christ *commanded to give her meat*. In the last verse, we need not wonder to find *her parents astonished*.

CHAPTER 9

I. The commission Christ gave to his twelve apostles, ver. 1–6. II. Herod's terror at the growing greatness of our Lord Jesus, ver. 7–9. III. The apostles' return to Christ, his retirement with them, the great resort of people to them notwithstanding, and his feeding five thousand men, ver. 10–17. IV. His discourse with his disciples concerning himself and his own sufferings for them, ver. 18–27. V. Christ's transfiguration, ver. 28–36. VI. The cure of a lunatic child, ver. 37–42. VII. The repeated notice of his approaching sufferings, ver. 43–45. VIII. His check to the ambition of his disciples (ver. 46–48), and to their monopolizing the power over devils to themselves, ver. 49, 50. IX. The rebuke he gave them for an undue resentment of an affront given him by a village of the Samaritans, ver. 51–56. X. The answers he gave to several that were inclined to follow him, ver. 57–62.

Verses 1–9

I. The method Christ took to spread his gospel. He had *himself* travelled about; but he could be only in one place at a time, and therefore now he *sent* his twelve disciples abroad. Let them disperse themselves, some one way and some another, to *preach the kingdom of God*. For the confirming of their doctrine he empowered them to work miracles (*v.* 1, 2): He *gave them authority over all devils*, to dispossess them, and cast them out. He authorized and appointed them likewise to *cure diseases*, and to *heal the sick*, which would not only convince people's judgments, but gain their affections. This was their commission.

1. What Christ directed them to do, in prosecution of this commission. (1) They must not be solicitous to recommend themselves to people's esteem by their outward appearance. They must *go as they were*, and not change their clothes, or so much as put on a pair of new shoes. (2) They must depend upon Providence, and the kindness of their friends. They must not take with them *either bread or money*. Christ would not have his disciples *shy* of receiving the kindnesses of their friends, but rather to *expect* them. (3) They must not change their lodgings, as suspecting that those who entertained them were *weary* of them; "*Whatsoever house ye enter into there abide* (*v.* 4), that people may know where to find you; *there abide* till you *depart* out of that city; stay with those you are used to." (4) They must put on authority, and speak *warning* to those who *refused* them as well as comfort to those that *received* them, *v.* 5. "If there be any place that will not entertain you, bind them over to the judgment of God for it; *shake off the dust of your feet* for a *testimony against them*."

2. What they did, in prosecution of this commission (*v.* 6): *They departed* from their Master's presence; they *went through the towns, preaching the gospel, and healing everywhere.* Their work was the same with their Master's, doing good both to souls and bodies.

II. We have here Herod's perplexity and vexation at this. The communicating of Christ's power to those who were sent forth in his name was an *amazing* and *convincing* proof of his being the Messiah. That he could not only work miracles *himself*, but empower others to work miracles too, this spread his fame more than anything. *They had been with Jesus*, Acts iv. 13. When the country sees such as these *healing the sick* in the name of Jesus it gives it an alarm.

1. The *various speculations* it *raised* among the *people*, who, though they thought not *rightly*, yet could not but think *honourably*, of our Lord Jesus, and that he was one come from the other world;

that either John Baptist or *one of the old prophets* was *risen again*; or that Elias *had appeared*, *v.* 7, 8.

2. The *great perplexity* it *created* in the mind of Herod: *When he had heard of all that was done* by Christ, he was ready to conclude with them that *John was risen from the dead.* "What shall I do now?" saith Herod. "John *have I beheaded, but who is this*? Is he carrying on John's work, or is he come to avenge John's death?" Those who oppose God will find themselves more and more *embarrassed.* He *desired to see him*; and why did he not go and see him? He desired to see him, but we do not find that ever he did, till he saw him at his bar.

Verses 10–17

I. The account which the twelve gave their Master of the success of their ministry. *When they returned, they told him all that they had done.*

II. Their *retirement*, for a little *breathing*: He *took them, and went aside privately into a desert place.* He that hath appointed our man-servant and maid-servant to rest would have his servants to rest too. Those in the most public stations, must sometimes go aside privately, both for the repose of their bodies, and for the furnishing of their minds by meditation for further public work.

III. The *resort* of the people to him, and the kind *reception* he gave them. They *followed* him, though it was into a *desert place.* He *welcomed* them, *v.* 11. Pious zeal may excuse a little rudeness; it did with Christ, and should with us. Though they came unseasonably, yet Christ gave them what they came for. He *spoke unto them of the kingdom of God.* He *healed them that had need of healing.* Christ hath still a power over bodily diseases, and heals his people that *need healing.* Sometimes he sees that we need the *sickness* for the good of our souls, more than the *healing* for the ease of our bodies. Death is the servant, to heal the saints of *all diseases.*

IV. The plentiful provision Christ made for the multitude that attended him. With *five loaves* of bread, and *two fishes*, he fed *five thousand men.* This narrative we had twice before, and shall meet with it again; it is the only miracle of our Saviour's that is recorded by all the four evangelists. Let us only observe out of it, 1. Those who diligently attend upon Christ in the way of duty, and therein deny or expose themselves, are taken under his particular care. He will not see those that fear him, and serve him faithfully, want any good thing. 2. Our Lord Jesus was of a free and generous spirit. His disciples said, *Send them away, that they may get victuals;* but Christ said, "No, *give ye them to eat;* let what we have go as far as it will reach, and they are welcome to it." Thus he has taught both ministers and Christians to *use hospitality without grudging.* Those that have but a little, let them do what they can with that little, and that is the way to make it more. 3. Jesus Christ has not only physic, but food. He not only *heals them that need healing*, but feeds them too that need feeding. Christ has provided not only to save the soul from perishing by its diseases, but to nourish the soul unto life eternal. 4. All the gifts of Christ are to be received in a regular orderly manner: *Make them sit down by fifties in a company*, *v.* 14. 5. When we are receiving our creature-comforts, we must *look up to heaven.* Christ did so, to teach us to do so. We receive them from God, we depend upon God's blessing upon them to make them serviceable to us, and desire that blessing. 6. The blessing of Christ will make a little go a great way. 7. Those whom Christ *feeds* he *fills*; as there is in him enough for *all*, so there is enough for *each.* Here were *fragments taken up*, to assure us that in our Father's house there is *bread enough, and to spare.* We are not straitened or stinted, in him.

Verses 18–27

One circumstance of this discourse is taken notice of here which we had not in the other evangelists—that Christ was *alone praying*, and his *disciples with him*, when he entered into this discourse, *v.* 18. He found some time to be *alone* in private, for converse with himself, with his Father, and with his disciples. When Christ was alone he was *praying.* It is good for us to improve our solitude for devotion, that, *when we are alone*, we may *not be alone*, but may have *the Father with us.* When Christ was alone, praying, his *disciples were with him*, to join with him in his prayer. Christ *prayed* with them before he *examined* them. Those we give instructions to we should put up prayers for and with. He discourses with them,

I. Concerning himself; and enquires,

1. What *the people* said of him: *Who say the people that I am?* They tell him what conjectures concerning him they had heard in their converse with the common people. Ministers would know better how to suit their instructions, reproofs, and counsels, to the case of ordinary people, if they did but converse more frequently and familiarly with them. The more conversant the physician is with his patient, the better he knows what to do for him. Some said that he was John Baptist, who was beheaded but the other day; others Elias, or *one of the old prophets*; anything but what he was.

2. What *they* said of him. Saith Peter, "We know that thou art *the Christ of God*, the *Anointed* of God." Now one would have expected that Christ should have charged his disciples to publish it to everyone they met with; but no, he *strictly charged them to tell no man that thing* as yet. After his resurrection, which completed the proof of it, Peter made the temple ring of it, that *God had made this same Jesus both Lord and Christ* (Acts ii. 36); but as yet the evidence was not ready to be summed up, and therefore it must be concealed.

II. Concerning his own *sufferings* and *death.* Now that his disciples were well established in the belief of his being the Christ, and able to bear it, he speaks of them expressly, *v.* 22. They must not yet preach that he was *the Christ*, because the wonders that would attend his death and resurrection would be the most convincing proof of his being *the Christ of God.*

III. Concerning their sufferings for him.

1. We must *accustom* ourselves to all instances of *self-denial* and *patience*, *v.* 23. We must not indulge our ease and appetite, for then it will be hard to bear toil, and weariness, and want, for Christ. We frequently meet with crosses in the way of duty; and, though we must not pull them upon our own heads, yet, when they are laid for us, we must *take them up*, carry them after Christ, and make the best of them.

2. We must *prefer the salvation and happiness of our souls* before any *secular concern* whatsoever. Reckon upon it, (1) That he who to preserve his liberty or estate, nay, or to save his life, denies Christ and his truths, will be, not only not a *saver*, but an unspeakable *loser*, in the issue. *He that will save his life upon these terms will lose it*, will lose that which is of infinitely more value, his precious soul. (2) We must firmly believe also that, if we lose our life for cleaving to Christ, we shall *save* it to our unspeakable advantage. We shall have it again a new and an eternal life. (3) That the gain of all the world, if we should forsake Christ, would be so far from countervailing the eternal loss and ruin of the soul that it would bear no manner of proportion to it, *v.* 25. If we could be supposed to gain all the wealth, honour, and pleasure, in the world, by denying Christ, yet when, by *so doing*, we *lose ourselves* to all eternity, and are *cast away* at last, what good will our worldly

gain do us? In Matthew and Mark the dreadful issue is a man's *losing his own soul*, here it is *losing himself*, which plainly intimates that *our souls are ourselves. The soul is the man;* and it is well or ill with us according as it is well or ill with our souls. The body cannot be happy if the soul be miserable in the other world; but the soul may be happy though the body be greatly afflicted and oppressed in this world.

3. We must therefore *never be ashamed* of Christ and his gospel, *v.* 26. *For whosoever shall be ashamed of me and of my words, of him shall the Son of man be ashamed*, and justly. He can expect no other than that in the great day, when his case calls for Christ's appearance on his behalf, Christ will be ashamed to own such a cowardly, worldly, sneaking spirit, and will say, "He is none of mine; he belongs not to me." As Christ had a state of *humiliation* and of *exaltation*, so likewise has his cause. They, and they only, that are willing to suffer with it when it suffers, shall reign with it when it reigns. Observe here, How Christ, to support himself and his followers under present disgraces, speaks *magnificently* of the lustre of his second coming. He shall come *in his own glory*. This was not mentioned in Matthew and Mark. He shall come *in his Father's glory*. He shall come in *the glory of the holy angels*. What a figure will the blessed Jesus make in that day! Did we believe it, we should never be ashamed of him or his words now.

Lastly, To encourage them in suffering for him, he assures them that *the kingdom of God* would now *shortly be set up, v.* 27. "The kingdom of God shall come in its power in the present age, while some here present are alive." They *saw the kingdom of God* when the Spirit was poured out, when the gospel was preached to all the world and nations were brought to Christ by it.

Verses 28–36

We have here the narrative of Christ's transfiguration which was designed for a specimen of that glory of his of which he had lately been speaking, and, consequently, an encouragement to his disciples to suffer for him, and never to be ashamed of him. We had this account before in Matthew and Mark.

I. Here is one circumstance of the narrative that seems to differ from the other two evangelists. They said that it was *six days* after the foregoing sayings; Luke says that it was *about eight days after*, that is, it was that day sevennight, six whole days intervening, and it was the eighth day.

II. Here are divers circumstances added and explained.

1. We are *here* told that Christ had this honour put upon him when he was *praying*: He *went up into a mountain to pray* (*v.* 28), and *as he prayed he was transfigured*. When Christ *humbled* himself to pray, he was thus *exalted*. Christ himself must *sue out* the favours that were purposed for him, and promised to him. And thus he intended to put an *honour* upon the duty of prayer, and to *recommend* it to us. It is a transfiguring, transforming duty. By prayer we fetch in the wisdom, grace, and joy, which *make the face to shine*.

2. Luke does not use the word *transfigured* (which Matthew and Mark used), but makes use of a phrase equivalent, *the fashion of his countenance was another thing from what it had been*; and *his raiment was white and glistening*; it was *bright like lightning* (a word used only here), so that he seemed to be arrayed all with light, to *cover himself with light as with a garment*.

3. It was said in Matthew and Mark that Moses and Elias *appeared to them*; here it is said that they *appeared in glory*. He being in glory, they *appeared with him in glory*.

4. We are here told what was the subject of the discourse between Christ and the two great prophets of the Old Testament: *They spoke of his decease, which he should accomplish at Jerusalem. His departure;* that is, *his death.* (1) The death of Christ is here called his *exit*, his *going out*, his *leaving the world*. The death of the saints is their *exodus*, their departure out of the Egypt of this world, their release out of a *house of bondage*. (2) This departure of his he *must accomplish*; for thus it was determined in the counsel of God, and could not be altered. (3) He must accomplish it at Jerusalem. (4) Moses and Elias spoke of this, to intimate that the *sufferings* of Christ, and his *entrance into his glory*, were what Moses and the prophets had *spoken of*; see Luke xxiv. 26, 27. (5) Our Lord Jesus, even in his transfiguration, was willing to enter into a discourse concerning his death and sufferings. In our greatest glories on earth, let us remember that here *we have no continuing city*.

5. We are here told, which we were not before, that the disciples were *heavy with sleep, v.* 32. Perhaps it was owing to a sinful carelessness: when Christ was at prayer with them, they did not regard his prayer as they should have done, and, to punish them for that, they were left to *sleep on now*, and so lost an opportunity of seeing how that work of wonder was wrought. These three were now asleep, when Christ was in *his glory*, as afterwards they were, when he was in *his agony*. Nothing could be more affecting to these disciples, one would think, than the *glories* and the *agonies* of their Master, and both in the highest degree; and yet neither the one nor the other would serve to *keep them awake*. What need have we to pray to God for quickening grace, to make us not only *alive*, but *lively*! After awhile they *recovered themselves*, and then they took an exact view of all those glories, so that they were able to give a particular account, as we find one of them does, of all that passed when they were with Christ *in the holy mount*, 2 Pet. i. 18.

6. It is here observed that it was when Moses and Elias were now about to *depart* that Peter said, *Lord, it is good to be here, let us make three tabernacles.* Thus we are often not sensible of the worth of our mercies till we are about to lose them; nor do we covet and court their continuance till they are upon the departure. Peter said this, *not knowing what he said.*

7. It is here added, concerning the *cloud* that *overshadowed them*, that they *feared as they entered into the cloud*. This cloud was a token of God's more peculiar presence. Then no wonder that the disciples were *afraid to enter into it*. But never let any be afraid to enter into a cloud with Jesus Christ; for he will be sure to bring them safely through it.

8. The *voice* which came from heaven is here, and in Mark, related not so fully as in Matthew: *This is my beloved Son, hear him*: though those words, *in whom I am well pleased*, which we have both in Matthew and Peter, are not expressed, they are implied in that, *This is my beloved Son*.

Lastly, The apostles are here said to have kept this vision private. They *told no man in those days*. As there is a time *to speak*, so there is a time to *keep silence*. Everything is beautiful and useful in its season.

Verses 37–42

This passage of story in Matthew and Mark follows immediately upon that of Christ's transfiguration, and his discourse with his disciples after it; but here it is said to be *on the next day, as they were coming down from the hill*. It was not till next day that they came down from the hill, and then he found things in some disorder among his disciples. 1. How forward the people were to receive Christ at his return to them.

Much people met him, as, at other times, much people *followed* him. 2. How importunate the father of the lunatic child was with Christ for help for him (v. 38): *I beseech thee, look upon my son;* this is his request; one compassionate look from Christ is enough to set everything to rights. Let us bring ourselves and our children to Christ, to be *looked upon.* His plea is, *He is my only child.* They that have many children may balance their affliction in one with their comfort in the rest. 3. How *deplorable* the case of the *child* was, v. 39. He was under the power of an evil spirit, that *took him*; when the fit seized him, he suddenly *cried out*, and many a time his shrieks had pierced the heart of his tender father. This malicious spirit *tore him*, and *bruised* him, and *departed not from him* but with great difficulty. What mischief doth Satan do where he gets possession! But happy they that have access to Christ! 4. How defective the disciples were in their faith. Though Christ had given them *power over unclean spirits*, yet they *could not* cast out this *evil spirit*, v. 40. Either they distrusted the power they were to fetch in strength from, or they did not exert themselves in prayer as they ought; for this Christ reproved them. 5. How effectual the cure was, which Christ wrought upon this child, v. 42. Christ can do that for us which his disciples cannot: *Jesus rebuked the unclean spirit.* The devil *threw the child down, and tore him,* as if he would have pulled him to pieces. But one word from Christ *healed the child,* and made good the damage the devil had done him. He *delivered him again to his father.* When our children are recovered from sickness, we must receive them as delivered to us again, receive them as life from the dead. It is comfortable to receive them from the hand of Christ: "Here, take this child, and be thankful; take it, and bring it up for me, for thou hast it again from me." With such cautions as these, parents should receive their children *from Christ's hands,* and then with comfort put them again *into his hands.*

Verses 43–50

I. The impression which Christ's miracles made upon all that beheld them (v. 43): *They were all amazed at the mighty power of God.* Their wonder was universal: they wondered *every one.* The causes of it were universal: they wondered at *all things which Jesus did*; all his actions had something uncommon and surprising in them.

II. The notice Christ gave to his disciples of his approaching sufferings: *The Son of man shall be delivered into the hands of men.* That is here *implied* which is *expressed* by the other evangelists: *They shall kill him.* But that which is peculiar here is, 1. The connection of this with what goes next before, of the admiration with which the people were struck at beholding Christ's miracles (v. 43): *While they all wondered at all things which Jesus did, he said this to his disciples.* They had a fond conceit of his temporal kingdom, and that he should reign, in secular pomp and power; and now they thought that this *mighty power* of his would easily effect the thing. Therefore Christ takes this occasion to tell them again that he was so far from having men *delivered into his hands* that he must be *delivered into the hands of men.* 2. The solemn preface with which it is introduced: "*Let these sayings sink down into your ears.* Admit what I say, and submit to it." *Let it sink down into your hearts;* so the Syriac and Arabic read it. The word of Christ does us no good, unless we let it sink down into our heads and hearts. 3. The unaccountable stupidity of the disciples. It was said in Mark, *They understood not that saying.* It was plain enough, but they *would not understand it* in the literal sense; and they *could not* understand it in any other, *and were afraid to ask him* lest they should be

undeceived and awaked out of their pleasing dream. But it is here added that *it was hidden from them, that they perceived it not.* We cannot think that it was *in mercy* hidden from them, lest they should be swallowed up with overmuch sorrow at the prospect of it; but that it was a paradox, because they *made it so* to themselves.

III. The rebuke Christ gave to his disciples for their disputing among themselves which should be greatest, v. 46–48. This passage we had before, and, the more is the pity, we shall meet with the like again.

1. Ambition of honour, and strife for superiority and precedency, are sins that most easily beset the disciples of our Lord Jesus. They flow from corruptions which they are highly concerned to subdue and mortify, v. 46. They that expect to be *great* in this world commonly aim high, and nothing will serve them short of being *greatest*; this exposes them to a great deal of temptation and trouble, which they are safe from that are content to be *little*, to be *least*, to be *less than the least.*

2. Jesus Christ is perfectly acquainted with the thoughts and intents of our hearts: He *perceived their thoughts*, v. 47. Thoughts are *words* to him, and *whispers* are loud cries.

3. Christ will have his disciples to aim at that honour which is to be obtained by a quiet humility, and not at that which is to be obtained by a restless and aspiring ambition. Christ *took a child, and set him by him*, v. 47 (for he always expressed a tenderness and kindness for little children). (1) Let them be of the *temper* of this child, *humble* and *quiet*, and *easy* to itself. Let them be willing to be *the least*, if that would contribute anything to their usefulness. (2) Let them assure themselves that this was the way to preferment. They that loved Christ would *therefore receive* them *in his name*, because they did most resemble him. Christ would take the kindnesses done to them as done to himself: *Whosoever shall receive one such child receiveth me;* and *whosoever receiveth me, receiveth him that sent me;* and what greater honour can any man attain to in this world than to have God and Christ own themselves received and welcomed in him?

IV. The rebuke Christ gave to his disciples for discouraging one that honoured him and served him, but was not of their communion, but, upon occasional hearing of Christ, believed in him, and made use of his name with faith and prayer in a serious manner, for the casting out of devils. This man they *rebuked and restrained*; they would not let him pray and preach, though it was to the honour of Christ. He did not *follow Christ with them.* Jesus Christ chid them for what they did: "*Forbid him not* (v. 50), but rather encourage him, for he is carrying on the same design that you are. He will meet you in *the same end*, though he does not accompany you in *the same way.* *He that is not against us is for us*, and therefore ought to be countenanced by us." We need not lose any of our friends, while we have so few, and so many enemies. Those may be found faithful followers of Christ, and, as such, may be accepted of him, though they do not follow *with us.*

Verses 51–56

This passage of story we have not in any other of the evangelists. Here they were for putting infidels to death. Christ reprimanded them, for a spirit of bigotry and persecution is directly contrary to the spirit of Christ.

I. The *readiness* and *resolution* of our Lord Jesus, in prosecuting his great undertaking for our redemption and salvation. Of this we have an instance, v. 51: *When the time was come that he should be received up, he steadfastly set his face to go to Jerusalem.* There was a time fixed for the sufferings and death of our Lord Jesus, and he knew well enough when it was. Then he appeared most publicly of all, and was most busy, knowing that his time was short. When he saw his death and sufferings approaching, he looked through them and beyond them, to the glory that should follow, when he should be *received up into glory* (1 Tim. iii. 16). All good Christians may frame to themselves the same notion of death, and may call it their being *received up*, to be with Christ where he is. On this prospect of the joy set before him, he *steadfastly set his face to go to Jerusalem*. He was fully *determined* to go, and would not be dissuaded; he went *directly* to Jerusalem. He went cheerfully and courageously thither. He *did not fail nor was discouraged*, *knowing* that he should be not only *justified*, but glorified, not only not *run down*, but *received up*. How should this shame us *for*, and shame *us out of*, our backwardness to do and suffer for Christ!

II. The *rudeness* of the Samaritans in a *certain village* who would not *receive him*. 1. How *civil* he was to them: *He sent messengers before his face*, that went to take up lodgings, and to know whether he might have leave to accommodate himself and his company among them. He sent some to *make ready* for him that his coming might be no surprise. 2. How *uncivil* they were to him, *v*. 53. They did not *receive him*, would not suffer him to come into their village. He would have been the greatest blessing that ever came to their village, and yet they forbid him entrance. Now the reason was *because his face was as though he would go to Jerusalem*. The great controversy between the Jews and the Samaritans was about the place of worship—whether Jerusalem or mount Gerizim near Sychar; see John iv. 20. And so hot was the controversy between them that the *Jews would have no dealings with the Samaritans*, nor they with them, John iv. 9. They were particularly incensed against Christ, who was a celebrated teacher, for owning and adhering to the temple at Jerusalem. They would not show him the common civility which probably they used formerly to show him in his journey thither.

III. The *resentment* which James and John expressed of this affront, *v*. 54. When these two heard this message brought, they were all in a flame presently, and nothing will serve them but Sodom's doom upon this village.

1. Here indeed was something commendable, for they showed, (1) A great confidence in the power they had received from Jesus Christ. They could with a word's speaking fetch *fire from heaven*. *Wilt thou that we speak the word*, and the thing will be done. (2) A great zeal for the honour of their Master. They took it very ill that he who did good wherever he came and found a hearty welcome should be denied the liberty of the road by a parcel of paltry Samaritans. (3) A submission, notwithstanding, to their Master's goodwill and pleasure. They will not offer to do such a thing, unless Christ give leave: *Wilt thou that we do it?* (4) A regard to the examples of the prophets that were before them. It is doing *as Elias did*. They thought that this *precedent* would be their *warrant*; so apt are we to misapply the examples of good men.

2. But though there was something right in what they said, yet there was much more amiss for (1) This was not the first time, by a great many, that our Lord Jesus had been thus affronted, yet he never called for any judgment upon them, but patiently put up with the injury. (2) These were Samaritans, from whom better was not to be expected, and perhaps they had heard that Christ had forbidden his disciples to *enter into any of the cities of the Samaritans* (Matt. x. 5), and therefore it was not so bad in them as in others who knew more of Christ. (3) Perhaps it was only some few of the town that sent that rude message to him, while, for aught they knew, there were many in the town who would have gone to meet him and welcomed him. (4) Their Master had never yet upon any occasion called for *fire from heaven*. James and John were the two disciples whom Christ had called *Boanerges*—sons of thunder (Mark iii. 17); and will not that serve them, but they must be *sons of lightning* too? (5) The example of Elias did not reach the case. Elijah was sent to display the terrors of the law, but it is a dispensation of grace that is now to be introduced, to which such a terrible display of divine justice will not be at all agreeable.

IV. The *reproof* he gave to James and John (*v*. 55): He *turned* and *rebuked them*; for *as many as he loves he rebukes and chastens*, particularly for what they do, that is irregular and unbecoming them, under colour of zeal for him.

1. He shows them in particular their mistake: *Ye know not what manner of spirit ye are of*. (1) "You *are not aware* how much there is of pride, and passion, and personal revenge, covered under this pretence of zeal for your Master." There may be much corruption lurking, nay, and stirring too, in the hearts of good people, and they themselves not be sensible of it. (2) "You *do not consider* what a *good spirit* you *should be of*. Surely you have yet to learn what the spirit of Christ is. Have you not been taught to *love your enemies*, and to *bless them that curse you*, and to call for grace from heaven, not fire from heaven, upon them? You are under the dispensation of love, and liberty, and grace, which was ushered in with a proclamation of *peace on earth* and *goodwill toward men*."

2. He shows them the general design and tendency of his religion (*v*. 56): *The Son of man is not himself come to destroy men's lives, but to save them*. He designed to propagate his holy religion by love and sweetness, and everything that is inviting and endearing, not by fire and sword, by miracles of healing, not by plagues and miracles of destruction, as Israel was brought out of Egypt. Christ came to *slay all enmities*, not to foster them. Christ came, not only to save men's *souls*, but to save their *lives* too. Christ would have his disciples do good to all, but hurt to none, to draw men into his church with the *cords of a man and the bands of love*, but not think to drive men into it.

V. His *retreat* from this village. Christ would not only not punish them for their rudeness but quietly and peaceably *went to another village*, where they were not so stingy. If some be very rude, instead of revenging it, we should try whether others will not be more civil.

Verses 57–62

We have here an account of three several persons that offered themselves to follow Christ.

I. Here is one that is extremely forward to follow Christ immediately, but seems to have been too rash and not to have set down and counted the cost.

1. He makes Christ a very large promise (*v*. 57): *As they went in the way* one said to him, Lord, I will *follow thee whithersoever thou goest*. This must be the resolution of all that will be found Christ's disciples indeed; they *follow the Lamb whithersoever he goes*.

2. Christ gives him a necessary caution, not to promise himself great things in the world, in following him; for *the Son of man has not where to lay his head*.

We may look upon this, (1) As *setting forth* the very low condition that our Lord Jesus was in, in this world. He not only wanted the delights and ornaments that great princes usually have, but even such accommodations for mere necessity as the *foxes* have, and the *birds of the air*. He that made all did not make a dwelling-place for himself, not a house of his own to put his head in. He here calls himself the *Son of man*, a Son of Adam, partaker of flesh and blood. He glories in his condescension towards us, to testify his love to us, and to teach us a holy contempt of the world, and a continual regard to another world. Christ was thus poor, to sanctify and sweeten poverty to his people. We may well be content to fare as Christ did. (2) As proposing this to the consideration of those who intend to be his disciples. If we mean to follow Christ, we must not reckon upon making anything *more than heaven* of our religion. Christ tells this man what he must count upon if he followed him, to lie cold and uneasy, to fare hard, and live in contempt; if he could not submit to this, let him not pretend to follow Christ. This word sent him back, for aught that appears; but it will be no discouragement to any that know what there is in Christ and heaven to set in the scale against this.

II. Here is another, that seems *resolved* to follow Christ, but he *begs a day*, v. 59. To this man Christ first gave the call; he said to him, *Follow me*. This man to whom Christ gave a call, though he hesitated at first, yet, as it should seem, afterwards yielded. It is not of *him that willeth*, nor *of him that runneth* (as that forward spark in the foregoing verses), but of God that showeth mercy, that *gives* the call.

1. The excuse he made: "*Lord, suffer me first to go and bury my father*. I have an aged father at home, who cannot live long, and will need me while he does live; let me go and attend on him until he is dead, and then I will do anything." We may here see three temptations. (1) We are tempted to *rest* in a *discipleship at large*, in which we may be *at a loose end*, and not to come *close*. (2) We are tempted to *defer* the doing of that which we know to be our duty, and to put it off to some other time. When we have got clear of such a care and difficulty, then we will begin to think of being religious; and so we are cozened out of all our time, by being cozened out of the present time. (3) We are tempted to think that our duty to our relations will excuse us from our duty to Christ. The *kingdom of God and the righteousness thereof* must be sought and minded *in the first place*.

2. Christ's answer to it (v. 60): "*Let the dead bury their dead. Thou hast other work to do; go thou, and preach the kingdom of God.*" Not that Christ would have his followers or his ministers to be *unnatural*; our religion teaches us to be kind and good in every relation. But we must not make these offices an excuse from our duty to God. If the nearest and dearest relation we have in the world stand in our way to keep us from Christ, it is necessary that we have a zeal that will make us forget *father and mother*. No excuses must be admitted against a present obedience to the call of Christ.

III. Here is another that is willing to follow Christ, but he must have a *little time* to *talk with his friends* about it.

1. His request for a dispensation, v. 61. He said, "*Lord, I will follow thee; but let me first go bid them farewell that are at home.*" *Let me go and set in order my household affairs*, so some understand it. Now that which was amiss in this is, (1) That he looked upon his following Christ as a melancholy, troublesome, dangerous thing; it was to him as if he were *going to die*, and therefore he must take *leave* of all his friends; whereas in following Christ, he might be more a comfort and blessing to them than if he had continued with them. (2) That he seemed to have his worldly concerns more upon his heart than would consist with a close attendance to his duty as a follower of Christ. He seemed to hanker after his relations and family concerns; they stuck to him.

It may be he had bidden them *farewell* once, but *Loth to depart bids oft farewell*, and therefore he must bid them *farewell* once more, for they are *at home at his house*. (3) That he was willing to enter into a temptation from his purpose of following Christ. To go and bid them *farewell* that were *at home at his house* would be to expose himself to the strongest solicitations imaginable to alter his resolution; for they would all *beg* and *pray* that he would not *leave them*. Those that resolve to follow their Redeemer, must resolve that they will not so much as parley with their tempter.

2. The rebuke which Christ gave him for this request (v. 62): "*No man, having put his hand to the plough*, will *look back*, or look behind him, for then he makes balks with his plough, and the ground he ploughs is *not fit* to be sown; so thou, if thou hast a design to follow me, yet if thou *lookest back* to a worldly life again and hankerest after that, *thou art not fit for the kingdom of God*. Thou art not a *sower* fit to *scatter* the good seed of the kingdom if thou canst *hold the plough* no better." Ploughing is in order to sowing. Those are not fit to be employed in sowing who know not how to break up the fallow ground, but, when they have *laid their hand to the plough*, upon every occasion look back and think of quitting it. Looking back inclines to *drawing back*, and *drawing back* is to *perdition*. Those are not fit for heaven, who, having set their faces heavenward, face about. But he, and he only, that *endures to the end*, *shall be saved*.

CHAPTER 10

I. The ample commission which Christ gave to the seventy disciples to preach the gospel, and to confirm it by miracles; and the full instructions he gave them, ver. 1–16. II. The report which the seventy disciples made, and his discourse thereupon, ver. 17–24. III. Christ's discourse with a lawyer concerning the way to heaven, and the instructions Christ gave him by a parable to look upon every one as his neighbour, ver. 25–37. IV. Christ's entertainment at Martha's house, the reproof he gave to her for her care about the world, and his commendation of Mary, ver. 38 42.

Verses 1–16

We have here the sending forth of seventy disciples, two and two. This is not taken notice of by the other evangelists: but the instructions here given them are much the same with those given to the twelve.

I. Their number: they were seventy. As in the choice of twelve apostles Christ has an eye to the twelve patriarchs, the twelve tribes, and the twelve princes of those tribes, so here he seems to have an eye to the *seventy* elders of Israel.

1. We are glad to find that Christ had so many followers fit to be sent forth; his labour was not altogether in vain, though he met with much opposition. These *seventy*, though they did not attend him so closely and constantly as the *twelve* did, were nevertheless the constant hearers of his doctrine, and witnesses of his miracles, and believed in him. These seventy are those of whom Peter speaks as "*the men who companied with us all the time that the Lord Jesus went in and out among us*," and were part of the one hundred and twenty there spoken of, Acts i. 15, 21. Many of those that were the companions of the apostles, whom we read of in the Acts and the Epistles, we may suppose, were of these seventy disciples.

2. We are glad to find there was work for so many ministers, hearers for so many preachers: thus the grain of mustard-seed began to *grow*, and the savour of the leaven began to diffuse itself in the meal.

II. Their work and business: He sent them *two and two*, that they might strengthen and encourage one another. He sent them, not to all the cities of Israel, as he did the *twelve*, but only *to every city and place whither he himself would come* (v. 1), as his harbingers. Two things they were ordered to do, the same that Christ did wherever he came: 1. They must *heal the sick* (v. 9), heal them *in the name of Jesus*, which would make people long to see this Jesus, and ready to entertain him whose name was so powerful. 2. They must publish the approach of the kingdom of God: *The kingdom of God is come nigh to you.* It is good to be made sensible of our advantages and opportunities, that we may lay hold of them. When the *kingdom of God comes nigh us,* it concerns us to go forth to meet it.

III. The instructions he gives them.

1. They must set out with prayer (v. 2). They must be duly affected with the necessities of the souls of men. They must *look about,* and see how *great the harvest was.* There was corn ready to shed and be lost for want of hands to gather it in. They must likewise be concerned that the *labourers were so few.* It is common for tradesmen not to care how few there are of their own trade; but Christ would have the labourers in his vineyard reckon it a matter of complaint when the *labourers are few.* They must earnestly desire to receive their mission from God, that *he* would send them forth as *labourers into his harvest,* and that he would send others forth; for, if God send them forth, they may hope he will go along with them and give them success.

2. They must set out with an expectation of trouble and persecution: *"Behold, I send you forth as lambs among wolves;* but *go your ways.* Your enemies will be as *wolves.* But you must be as *lambs,* peaceable and patient, though made an easy prey of." It would have been very hard thus to be sent forth as *sheep among wolves,* if he had not endued them with his spirit and courage.

3. They must not encumber themselves, as if they were going a long voyage, but depend upon God and their friends to provide: "Carry neither a *purse* for money, nor a *scrip* or knapsack for clothes or victuals, nor new *shoes* (as before to the twelve, *ch.* ix. 3); and *salute no man by the way.*" (1) They must go as men *in haste,* must not hinder or retard themselves with needless ceremonies or compliments. (2) They must go as *men of business,* business that relates to another world, and therefore must not entangle themselves with conversation about secular affairs. (3) They must go as *serious* men.

4. They must show, not only *their goodwill,* but *God's goodwill,* to all to whom they came, v. 5, 6.

(1) The charge given them was, Whatsoever *house* they *entered into,* they must say, *Peace be to this house.* Here, [1] They are supposed to enter into *private houses;* for, being not admitted into the synagogues, they were forced to preach where they could have liberty. And, as their public preaching was driven into houses, so thither they carried it. Christ's church was at first very much *a church in the house.* [2] They are instructed to say, "*Peace be to this house.* Salute *no man by the way* in compliment, but to those into whose house ye enter, say, *Peace be to you,* with seriousness and in reality." Christ's ministers go into all the world, to say, in Christ's name, *Peace be to you.* We are to *propose* peace to all, to *preach peace by Jesus Christ, peace on earth,* and to invite the children of men to come and take the benefit of it. We are to *pray* for peace to all.

(2) The success was to be different, according to the different dispositions of those whom they preached to and prayed for. According as the inhabitants were sons of peace or not, so their peace should or should not *rest upon the house.* "You will meet with some that are the *sons of peace,* that are ready to admit the word of the gospel in the light and love of it. As to those, *your peace* shall find them out and *rest upon them;* your prayers for them shall be heard, the promises of the gospel shall be *confirmed* to them. You will meet with others that are no ways disposed

to hear or heed your message, whole houses that have not one *son of peace* in them." Now it is certain that our peace shall *not come* upon *them.* But it shall *return to us again;* that is, we shall have the comfort of having done our duty to God and discharged our trust. Our peace shall return to us again, not only to be enjoyed by ourselves, but to be communicated to others, them that are *sons of peace.*

5. They must *receive* the kindnesses of those that should *entertain* them and *bid them welcome,* v. 7, 8. "Those that receive the gospel will receive you that preach it, and give you entertainment." (1) "Be not *shy;* do not suspect your welcome, nor be afraid of being troublesome, but *eat and drink* heartily *such things as they give.* You will deserve it, for *the labourer is worthy of his hire,* and it is not an act of charity, but of justice, in those who are *taught in the word to communicate to those that teach them.*" (2) "Be not *nice* and *curious* in your diet: *Eat and drink such things as they give* (v. 7), *such things as are set before you,* v. 8. Be thankful for plain food, and do not find fault, though it be not dressed according to art." It ill becomes Christ's disciples to be *desirous of dainties.* Probably, Christ here refers to the traditions of the elders about their meat, but Christ would not have them to regard those things, but eat what was given them, *asking no question for conscience' sake.*

6. They must *denounce* the judgments of God against those who should *reject* them and their *message:* "If you *enter into a city,* and they *do not receive you,* leave them, v. 10. If they will not *give you welcome* into their houses, do you *give them warning* in their streets." He orders them to (*ch.* ix. 5) do as he had ordered the apostles to do: "Say to them: *Even the dust of your city, which cleaveth on us, we do wipe off against you,* v. 11. From them do not receive any kindnesses at all, be not beholden to them." It shall be a witness for Christ's messengers that they had been there according to their Master's order; *tender* and *refusal* were a discharge of their trust. "But tell them plainly, and bid them *be sure* of it, *The kingdom of God is come nigh to you.* Here is a fair offer made you; if you have not the benefit of it, it is your own fault. Now that the *kingdom of God is come nigh to you,* if you will not come up to it, and come into it, your sin will be inexcusable." The fairer offers we have of grace and life by Christ, the more we shall have to answer for another day, if we slight these offers: *It shall be more tolerable for Sodom than for that city,* v. 12. The Sodomites indeed rejected the warning given them by Lot; but rejecting the gospel is a more heinous crime.

Upon this occasion, the evangelist repeats,

(1) The particular doom of those cities wherein most of Christ's mighty works were done, which we had, Matt. xi. 20, &c. [1] They enjoyed greater privileges. Christ's *mighty works were done in them.* They were hereby *exalted to heaven.* They were brought as near heaven as external means could bring them. [2] God's design in favouring them thus was to bring them to *repentance* and *reformation* of life, *to sit in sackcloth and ashes.* [3] Their frustrating this design, and their receiving the grace of God therein in vain. It is implied that they *repented not;* they did not bring forth fruits agreeable to the advantages they enjoyed. [4] There was reason to think, morally speaking, that, if Christ had gone to Tyre and Sidon, Gentile cities, they would have repented *long ago,* so speedy would their repentance have been, and that in *sackcloth and ashes,* so deep would it have been. [5] The doom of those who thus receive the grace of God in vain will be very fearful. They that were *thus exalted,* not making use of their elevation, will be *thrust down to hell.* [6] In the day

of judgment Tyre and Sidon will fare better, and it will be more tolerable for them than for these cities.

(2) The general rule which Christ would go by, as to those to whom he sent his ministers: He will reckon himself treated according as they treated his ministers, v. 16. "*He that heareth you, heareth me.* He that *despiseth you* doth in effect *despise me,* nay, he *despiseth him that sent me.*" And they who *despise* the faithful ministers of Christ, and turn their backs upon their ministry, will be reckoned with as despisers of God and Christ.

Verses 17–24

I. What account they gave him of the success of their expedition: *They returned again with joy* (v. 17); not complaining of the fatigue of their journeys, but rejoicing in their success, especially in casting out unclean spirits: *Lord, even the devils are subject unto us through thy name.* They give Christ the glory of this: It is *through thy name.* All our victories over Satan are obtained by power derived from Jesus Christ. We must *in his name* enter the lists with our spiritual enemies. If the work be done *in* his name, the honour is due *to* his name. They speak of it with an air of exultation: *Even the devils* are *subject to us.* If devils are *subject to us,* what can stand before us?

II. How he received this account.

1. He confirmed what they said, as agreeing with his own observation (v. 18): I *saw Satan fall as lightning from heaven.* Satan and his kingdom fell before the preaching of the gospel. He falls *as lightning falls from heaven,* so suddenly, so irrecoverably. Satan *falls from heaven* when he falls from the throne in men's hearts. And Christ foresaw that the preaching of the gospel would wherever it went pull down Satan's kingdom. *Now is the prince of this world cast out.*

2. He repeated, ratified, and enlarged their commission: *Behold I give you power to tread on serpents,* v. 19. They had employed their power vigorously against Satan, and now Christ entrusts them with greater power. (1) An *offensive* power, power to *tread on serpents and scorpions,* devils and malignant spirits, the old serpent. As the devils have now been *subject to you,* so they shall still be. (2) A *defensive* power: "*Nothing shall by any means hurt you;* not *serpents* nor *scorpions.* If wicked men be as *serpents* to you, and you *dwell* among those *scorpions,* you may despise their rage, and *tread* upon it. They may *hiss,* but they cannot *hurt.*"

3. He directed them to turn their joy into the right channel (v. 20): "*Notwithstanding in this rejoice not, that the spirits are subject unto you.* Do not rejoice in this *only,* or in this *chiefly,* but *rather rejoice because your names are written in heaven,* because you are the children of God through faith." Christ could tell them that their *names were written in heaven,* for it is the *Lamb's book of life* that they are written in. Power to become the children of God is to be valued more than a power to work miracles; for we read of those who did *in Christ's name cast out devils,* and yet will be disowned by Christ in the great day. But they whose *names are written in heaven* shall never perish; they are *Christ's sheep,* to whom he will *give eternal life.* Holy love is *a more excellent way* than speaking with tongues.

4. He offered up a solemn thanksgiving to his Father, v. 21, 22. This we had before (Matt. xi. 25–27), only here it is prefixed that *in that hour Jesus rejoiced.* In *that hour* in which he saw Satan fall, *in that hour he rejoiced.* Christ's joy was a solid substantial joy, an inward joy: *he rejoiced in spirit.* Before he applied himself to *thank his Father,* he stirred up himself to *rejoice;* for, as *thankful praise* is the genuine language of *holy joy,* so *holy joy* is the

root and spring of *thankful praise.* Two things he gives thanks for:

(1) For what was *revealed* by the *Father* through the *Son: I thank thee, O Father, Lord of heaven and earth,* v. 21. Now that which he gives thanks for is, [1] That the counsels of God concerning man's reconciliation to himself were *revealed* to some of the children of men, who might be fit also to *teach others;* he has *revealed* that which had been *kept secret* from the beginning of the world. [2] That they were revealed to *babes,* to those who were but *children in understanding,* till God by his Spirit elevated their faculties. We have reason to thank God, not so much for the honour he has hereby put upon babes, as for the honour he has hereby done himself in perfecting strength *out of weakness.* [3] That, at the same time when he revealed them unto babes, he *hid them from the wise and prudent,* the Gentile philosophers, the Jewish rabbin. He *did not reveal* the things of the gospel to them, nor employ them in preaching up his kingdom. Paul indeed was bred a scholar among the wise and prudent; but he became a *babe* when he became an apostle, and made neither show nor use of any other knowledge than that of *Christ and him crucified,* 1 Cor. ii. 2, 4. [4] That God herein acted by way of sovereignty: *Even so, Father, for so it seemed good in thy sight.* If God gives his grace and the knowledge of his son to some that are less likely, and does not give it to others whom we should think better able to deliver it with advantage, this must satisfy. He chooses to entrust the dispensing of his gospel in the hands of those who with a *divine energy* will give it the *setting on,* rather than in theirs who with *human art* will give it the *setting off.*

(2) For what was *secret* between the *Father* and *the Son,* v. 22. [1] The vast *confidence* that the Father *puts* in the Son: *All things are delivered to me of my Father.* In him all fulness must *dwell,* and from him it must be *derived:* he is the great *trustee* that manages all the concerns of God's kingdom. [2] The good understanding that there is between the Father and the Son: *No man knows who the Son is but the Father,* nor *who the Father is but the Son, and he to whom the Son* by the Spirit *will reveal him.*

5. He told his disciples how well it was for them that they had these things revealed to them, v. 23, 24. He *turned to his disciples,* designing to make them sensible how much it was for their happiness, that they knew the mysteries of the kingdom and were employed to lead others into the knowledge of them. (1) What a step it is *towards* something better. Though the bare knowledge of these things is not saving, yet it puts us in the way of salvation: *Blessed are the eyes which see the things which we see.* (2) What a step it is *above* those that went before them: "*Many prophets and righteous men*" (so it is in Matt. xiii. 17), "*many prophets and kings*" (so it is here), "have *desired* to see and hear those things which you are daily and intimately conversant with, and *have not seen* and *heard* them." The honour and happiness of the New Testament saints far exceed those even of the *prophets* and *kings* of the Old Testament. The general ideas which the Old Testament saints had of the graces and glories of the Messiah's kingdom, made them wish a thousand times that they might see the substance of those things of which they had faint shadows.

Verses 25–37

We have here Christ's discourse with a lawyer about some points of conscience, which we are all concerned to be rightly informed in, and are so here, from Christ.

I. We are concerned to know what that good is which we should do in *this* life, in order to our attaining *eternal life*. A question to this purport was proposed to our Saviour by a *certain lawyer*, only with a design to *try* him, v. 25. The lawyer *stood up*, and *asked him, Master, what shall I do to inherit eternal life?* If Christ had anything peculiar to prescribe, by this question he would get it out of him; if not, he would expose his doctrine as needless; or, perhaps, he had no malicious design against Christ, only he was willing to have a little talk with him, just as people go to church to hear what the minister will say. This was a good question: *What shall I do to inherit eternal life?* But it lost all its goodness when it was proposed with an ill design. It is not enough to speak of the things of God, and to enquire about them, but we must do it with a suitable concern.

1. How Christ turned him over to the divine law. Though he knew the thoughts and intents of his heart, he did not answer him according to the folly of that, but according to the wisdom and goodness of the question he asked. He answered him with a question: *What is written in the law? How readest thou?* v. 26. Christ will catechize him, and make him know himself. The studies of his profession would inform him; let him practise according to his knowledge, and he should not come short of *eternal life*. It will be of great use to us, in our way to heaven, to consider *what is written in the law*, and *what we read* there. We must have recourse to our bibles, to the law, as it is now in the hand of Christ, and walk in the way that is shown us there. Having it *written*, it is our duty to read it, to read it with understanding so that, when there is occasion, we may be able to tell *what is written in the law*, and *how we read*.

2. What a good account he gave of the law, of the principal commandments of the law. He did not, like a Pharisee, refer himself to the tradition of the elders, but fastened upon the two first and great commandments of the law, which included all the rest, v. 27. We must *love God with all our hearts*, must look upon him as the best of beings, in himself most amiable, and infinitely perfect and excellent. Our love to him must be sincere, hearty, and fervent; it must be a superlative love, a love that is as strong as death, but an intelligent love. It must be an *entire* love; he must have our *whole* souls, and must be served with *all that is within us*. We must love our neighbours as *ourselves*, which we shall easily do, if we, as we ought to do, love God *better than ourselves*. We must do all the good we can in the world and no hurt, and must fix it as a rule to ourselves to do to others as we would they should do to us; and this is to love our neighbour *as ourselves*.

3. Christ's approbation of what he said, v. 28. What he said that was good Christ commended: *Thou hast answered right*. Christ himself fastened upon these as the two great commandments of the law (Matt. xxii. 37). So far is right; but the hardest part of this work yet remains: *"This do, and thou shalt live; thou shalt inherit eternal life."*

4. His care to avoid the conviction which was now ready to fasten upon him. When Christ said, *This do, and thou shalt live*, he began to be aware that Christ intended to draw from him an acknowledgment that he *had not done this*. He was *willing to justify himself*, and therefore cared not for carrying on that discourse. Many ask good questions with a design rather to *justify themselves* than to *inform themselves*, rather proudly to show what is good in them than humbly to see what is bad in them.

II. We are concerned to know who is our neighbour. This is another of this lawyer's queries. As to loving God, he was willing to say no more of it; but, as to his *neighbour*, he was sure that there he had come up to the rule, for he had always been very kind and respectful to all about him. Now observe,

1. What was the corrupt notion of the Jewish teachers in this matter. "Where he saith, *Thou shalt love thy neighbour, he excepts all Gentiles*, for they are not *our neighbours*, but those only that are of our own nation and religion." If they saw a Gentile in *danger of death*, they thought themselves under no obligation to help to *save his life*.

2. How Christ corrected this inhuman notion, and showed, by a parable, that whomsoever we *have need* to receive kindness *from*, and *find ready* to show us the kindness *we need*, we cannot but look upon as *our neighbour*.

(1) The parable itself, which represents to us a poor Jew in distressed circumstances, succoured and relieved by a good Samaritan. Let us see here,

[1] How he was *abused* by his *enemies*. The honest man was travelling peaceably upon his lawful business in the road, and it was a great road that led from Jerusalem to Jericho, v. 30. Probably it happened lately, just as it is here related. This poor man *fell among thieves*. They were very *barbarous*: they not only took his money, but stripped him of his clothes, and they *wounded him*, and left him *half dead*, ready to die of his wounds. What reason have we to thank God for our preservation from perils by robbers!

[2] How he was *slighted* by those who should have been his friends, one a priest and the other a Levite, men of professed sanctity, whose offices obliged them to tenderness and compassion, who ought to have taught others their duty in such a case as this. Many of the courses of the priests had their residence in Jericho, and thence came up to Jerusalem, and so back again, which occasioned abundance of *passing* and *repassing* of priests that way, and Levites their attendants. They came *this way*, and saw the poor wounded man. The Levite not only saw him, but *came and looked on him*, v. 32. But they *passed by on the other side*; when they saw his case, they got as far off him as ever they could.

[3] How he was *succoured* and *relieved* by a *stranger*, a *certain Samaritan*, of that nation which of all others the Jews most despised and detested and would have no dealings with. This man had some humanity in him, v. 33. The priest had his heart hardened against one of *his own people*, but the Samaritan had his opened towards one of *another* people. *When he saw him he had compassion on him*. Though he was a Jew, he was a man, and a man in *misery*, and the Samaritan has learned to honour all men; and therefore pities him, as he himself would desire and expect to be pitied in the like case. The *compassion* of this Samaritan was not an idle compassion; but, when he *drew out his soul*, he *reached forth his hand* also to this poor *needy* creature. See how friendly this good Samaritan was. He *went to* the poor man, whom the priest and Levite kept at a distance from. He did the surgeon's part, for want of a better. He *bound up his wounds*, making use of his own linen, it is likely, for that purpose; and poured *in oil and wine*; wine to wash the wound, and oil to mollify it, and close it up. He did all he could as one whose heart bled with them. He *set him on his own beast*, and went on foot himself, and *brought him to an inn*. We suppose this Samaritan went upon business; but he understood that both his own business and God's sacrifice too must give place to such an act of mercy as this. He *took care of him* in the inn, got him to bed, had food for him that was proper, and due attendance, and, it may be, prayed with him. As if he had been his own child, when he left him next morning, he left money with the landlord, and passed his word for what he should spend more. *Twopence* of their money would go a great way; however, here it was an earnest of satisfaction to the full of all demands. All this was kind and generous, and as much as one could have expected from a friend or a

brother; and yet here it is done by a stranger and foreigner.

Now this parable is applicable to another purpose than that for which it was intended; and does excellently set forth the kindness and love of God our Saviour towards sinful miserable man. We were like this poor distressed traveller. The law of Moses *passes by on the other side*, as having neither pity nor power to help us; but then comes the blessed Jesus, that good Samaritan; he has compassion on us. He takes care of us. This magnifies the riches of his love, and obliges us all to say, "How much are we indebted, and what shall we render?"

(2) The application of the parable. [1] The truth contained in it is extorted from the lawyer's own mouth. Saith Christ, *"Which of these three was neighbour to him that fell among thieves (v. 36). Which of these did the neighbour's part?"* To this the lawyer would not answer, "Doubtless, the Samaritan was"; but, *"He that showed mercy on him; doubtless, he was a good neighbour to him."* [2] The duty inferred from it is pressed home upon the lawyer's own conscience: *Go, and do thou likewise.* If a Samaritan does well that helps a distressed Jew, certainly a Jew does not well if he refuses in like manner to help a distressed Samaritan. "And therefore *go thou and do as the Samaritan did*, whenever occasion offers: show mercy to those that need thy help, and do it freely, and with concern and compassion, though they be not of thy own nation." This lawyer thought to have puzzled Christ himself; but Christ sends him to school to a Samaritan, to learn his duty: "Go, and do like him." It is the duty of everyone of us to succour, help, and relieve all that are in distress and necessity, and of lawyers particularly.

Verses 38–42

I. The entertainment which Martha gave to Christ and his disciples at her house, *v.* 38.

1. Christ's coming to the village where Martha lived: *As they went he entered into a certain village.* This village was *Bethany*, nigh to Jerusalem. Christ honoured the country-villages with his presence and favour, and not the great and populous cities only; for, as he *chose privacy*, so he *countenanced poverty.*

2. His reception at Martha's house: *A certain woman, named Martha, received him into her house*, and made him welcome. There were some who were Christ's particular friends, whom he loved more than his other friends, and them he visited most frequently. He *loved* this family (John xi. 5), and often invited himself to them. It is called Martha's house, for, probably, she was a widow, and was the housekeeper. Though at this time it was grown dangerous to entertain him, especially so near Jerusalem, yet she cared not what hazard she ran for his name's sake. Though there were many that rejected him, and would not entertain him, yet there was one that would bid him welcome.

II. The attendance which Mary, the sister of Martha, gave upon the word of Christ, *v.* 20. 1. She *heard his word.* It seems, our Lord Jesus, as soon as he came into Martha's house, addressed himself to his great work of preaching the gospel. A good sermon is never the worse for being preached in a house. Since Christ is forward to speak, we should be *swift to hear.* She *sat* to hear, which denotes a close attention. Her mind was composed, and she resolved not to catch a word now and then, but to receive all that Christ delivered. If we sit with him at his feet now, we shall sit with him on his throne shortly.

III. The care of Martha about her domestic affairs: But Martha *was cumbered about much serving (v.* 40), and that was the reason why she was not where Mary was. Housekeepers know what care and bustle there must be when a great entertainment is to be made. Observe here,

1. Something *commendable*, which must not be overlooked. Here was a commendable *respect to our Lord Jesus.* It was not for ostentation, but purely to testify her goodwill to him, that she made this entertainment. Here was a commendable *care of her household affairs.* It is the duty of those who have the charge of families to *look well to the ways of their household.* The affectation of state and the love of ease make many families neglected.

2. Here was something *culpable.* She was for *much serving.* Her heart was upon it, to have a very sumptuous and splendid entertainment. She was in care, *concerning much attendance.* It does not become the disciples of Christ to affect *much serving*; what need is there of *much serving*, when much less will serve? She was *cumbered* about it; she was just *distracted* with it. Note, Whatever cares the providence of God casts upon us we must not be *cumbered* with them. *Care* is good and duty; but *cumber* is sin and folly. She was *then cumbered about much serving* when she should have been with her sister, sitting at Christ's feet to hear his word.

IV. The *complaint* which Martha made to Christ against her sister Mary (*v.* 40): *"Lord, dost thou not care that my sister has left me to serve alone? Bid her come and help me."*

1. This complaint of Martha's may be considered as a *discovery* of her *worldliness*; it was the language of her inordinate care and cumber. The inordinacy of worldly cares and pursuits is often the occasion of disturbance in families and of strife and contention among relations. Martha, being angry at her sister, appealed to Christ, and would have him say that she *did well to be angry. Lord, dost thou not care that my sister has left me to serve alone?* When Martha was caring, she must have Mary, and Christ and all, to *care* too, or else she is not pleased. Those are not always in the right that are most forward to appeal to God; we must therefore take heed, lest at any time we expect that Christ should espouse our unjust and groundless quarrels. The cares which he casts upon us we may cheerfully cast upon him, but not those which we foolishly draw upon ourselves.

2. It may be considered as a discouragement of Mary's piety and devotion. Her sister should have *commended* her for it, but, instead of this, she *condemns* her as wanting in her duty. It is no strange thing for those that are zealous in religion to meet, not only with opposition from enemies, but with blame and censure from their friends.

V. The reproof which Christ gave to Martha for her inordinate care, *v.* 41. *Martha, Martha, thou art careful and troubled about many things*, whereas but *one thing is needful.*

1. He reproved her, though he was at this time her guest. *As many as Christ loves he rebukes and chastens.* Even those that are dear to Christ, if anything be amiss in them, shall be sure to hear of it.

2. When he reproved her, he called her by her name, *Martha.* He repeated her name, *Martha, Martha*; he speaks as one in earnest, and deeply concerned for her welfare. Those that are *entangled* in the cares of this life are not easily *disentangled.*

3. That which he reproved her for was her being *careful and troubled about many things.* Christ reproves her, both for the *intenseness* of her care ("Thou art *careful and troubled, divided* and *disturbed* by thy care"), and for the *extensiveness of it*, "about *many things.* Poor Martha, thou hast many things to fret at, and this puts thee out of humour, whereas less ado would serve." Inordinate care or trouble about many things in this world is a common fault among Christ's disciples. If they fret for no just cause, it is just with him to order them something to fret at.

4. That which aggravated the sin and folly of her care was that *but one thing is needful. The one thing needful* is certainly meant of that which Mary made her choice—*sitting at* Christ's feet, to hear his word. She was troubled about *many things*, when she should have applied herself to one; godliness *unites* the heart, which the world had *divided*. The *many things* she was troubled about were *needless*, while the *one thing* she neglected was *needful*. Martha's care and work were good in their proper season and place; but now she had something else to do, which was unspeakably more needful. She expected Christ to have blamed Mary for not doing as she did, but he blamed her for not doing as Mary did. The day will come when Martha will wish she had set where Mary did.

VI. Christ's approbation and commendation of Mary for her serious piety: *Mary hath chosen the good part.*

1. She had justly given the preference to that which best deserved it; for *one thing is needful*, this one thing that she has done. Serious godliness is a *needful* thing, it is the *one thing needful*. Nothing but this will go with us into another world.

2. She had herein wisely done well for herself. Christ *justified Mary* against her sister's clamours. Sooner or later, Mary's choice will be justified, and all those who make that choice, and abide by it. But this was not all; he *applauded* her for her wisdom: *She hath chosen the good part;* for she chose to be with Christ, and took a better way of *honouring* Christ and of *pleasing* him, by receiving his word into her heart, than Martha did by providing for his entertainment in her house. (1) A *part with Christ* is a *good part*; it is a part for the soul and eternity. (2) It is a part that shall *never be taken away from those that have it. Nothing shall separate us from the love of Christ*, and our part in that love. Men and devils *cannot* take it away from us, and God and Christ *will not*. (3) It is the wisdom and duty of everyone of us to choose this *good part*. Mary was at her choice whether she would partake with Martha in her care, and get the reputation of a fine *housekeeper*, or sit at the feet of Christ and approve herself a *zealous disciple*; and, by her choice in this particular, Christ judges of her general choice.

CHAPTER 11

I. Christ teaches his disciples to pray, ver. 1–13. II. The blasphemous imputation of the Pharisees, who charged him with casting out devils by confederacy with Beelzebub, ver. 14–26. III. He shows the honour of obedient disciples to be greater than that of his own mother, ver. 27, 28. IV. He upbraids the men of that generation for their infidelity and obstinacy, ver. 29–36. V. He severely reproves the Pharisees and lawyers, ver. 37–54.

Verses 1–13

Prayer is one of the great laws of natural religion. One great design therefore of Christianity is to *assist us in prayer*, to enforce the duty upon us, to instruct us in it, and encourage us to expect advantage by it.

I. We find Christ himself *praying in a certain place.* This evangelist has taken particular notice of Christ's *praying often*, more than any other of the evangelists: when he was baptized (*ch.* iii. 21); he was *praying;* he *withdrew into the wilderness, and prayed* (*ch.* v. 16); he *went out into a mountain to pray, and continued all night in prayer* (*ch.* vi. 12); he was *alone praying* (*ch.* ix. 18); soon after, he *went up into a mountain to pray*, and *as he prayed he was transfigured* (*ch.* ix. 28, 29); and here he was *praying in a certain place.*

II. His disciples applied themselves to him for direction in prayer. When he was praying, they asked, *Lord, teach us to pray.* They came to him with this request, *when he ceased;* for they would not disturb him when he was at prayer. *One of his disciples* said, *Lord, teach us.* Though Christ is *apt to teach*, yet he will for this be enquired of.

1. Their request is, *"Lord, teach us to pray."* It becomes the disciples of Christ to apply themselves to him for instruction in prayer. *Lord, teach us to pray*, is itself a good prayer, and a very needful one, for it is a hard thing to *pray well*; and it is Jesus Christ only that can *teach us*, by his word and Spirit, *how to pray*. "Give me a mouth and wisdom in prayer, that I may speak as I ought; *teach me what I shall say.*"

2. Their plea is, *"As John also taught his disciples.* He took care to instruct his disciples in this necessary duty, and we would be taught as they were." Whereas the Jews' prayers were generally adorations, and praises of God, and doxologies, John taught his disciples such prayers as were more filled up with petitions and requests. "Now, Lord, teach us this, to be added to those benedictions of the name of God which we have been accustomed to from our childhood." Christ did there teach them a prayer consisting wholly of petitions, and even omitting the doxology which had been affixed; and the *Amen.*

III. Christ gave them direction, much the same as he had given them before in his sermon upon the mount, Matt. vi. 9, &c. They would find all their requests couched in these few words, and would be able, in words of their own, to expatiate and enlarge upon them.

1. There are some differences between the Lord's prayer in Matthew and in Luke. There is a difference in the fourth petition. In Matthew we pray, "Give us daily bread *this day*": here, "Give it us *day by day*. Give us *each day* the bread which our bodies require, as they call for it." Let us have bread *today* for *today*, and t*omorrow* for t*omorrow*; for thus we may be kept in a *continual dependence* upon God, as children upon their parents, and may find ourselves under *fresh* obligations to do the work of every day in the day, according as the *duty of the day requires*, because we have from God the supplies of every day in the day, according as the *necessity of the day requires*. Here is likewise some difference in the fifth petition. In Matthew it is, *Forgive us our debts*, as we forgive: here it is, *Forgive us our sins. For we forgive.* This is a very necessary qualification for forgiveness, and, if God have wrought it in us, we may plead that work of his grace for the enforcing of our petitions for the pardon of our sins: "Lord, forgive us, for thou hast thyself inclined us to forgive others." There is another addition here; we plead not only in general, We forgive *our debtors*, but in particular, "We profess *to forgive everyone that is indebted to us.*" Here also the doxology in the close is wholly omitted, and the *Amen.* He left a vacuum here, to be filled up by a doxology more peculiar to the Christian institutes, ascribing glory to *Father, Son and Holy Ghost.*

2. Yet it is, for substance, the same; and we shall therefore here only gather up some general lessons from it.

(1) That in prayer we ought to come to God as children to *a Father*, a common Father to us and all mankind.

(2) That at the same time, and in the same petitions, which we address to God for *ourselves*, we should take in with us all the children of men. A rooted principle of *catholic charity* should go along with us throughout this prayer, which is so worded as to be accommodated to that noble principle.

(3) That in order to the confirming of the habit of heavenly-mindedness in us, we should, with an eye of faith look *heavenward*, and view the God we pray to as our Father *in heaven.*

(4) That in every prayer we must *seek first the kingdom of God and the righteousness thereof*, by ascribing honour to his name, his *holy* name, and power to his government. O that both the one and the other may be more manifested.

(5) That the *principles* and *practices* of the *unseen* world (which therefor by *faith* only we are *apprized of*), are the *great original—the* ἀρχέτυπον, to which we should desire that the principles and practices of this *lower* world may be more conformable. Those words, *As in heaven, so on earth*, refer to all the first three petitions.

(6) That those who faithfully and sincerely mind the kingdom of God may humbly hope that *all other things shall be added to them*, and they may in faith pray for them. If our first chief desire and care be that God's name may be sanctified, his kingdom come, and his will be done, we may then come boldly to the throne of grace for our *daily bread*.

(7) That in our prayers for temporal blessings we must *moderate* our desires, and confine them to a *competency*. The expression here used of *day by day* is the very same with our *daily bread*.

(8) That sins are debts which we are daily contracting, and which therefore we should every day pray for the forgiveness of. Every day adds to the score of our guilt, and it is a miracle of mercy that we have so much encouragement given us to come every day to the throne of grace, to pray for the pardon of our sins of daily infirmity. God *multiplies to pardon* beyond seventy times seven.

(9) That we have no reason to expect that God would forgive our sins against him, if we do not *sincerely* forgive those that have at any time affronted us or been injurious to us.

(10) That temptations to sin should be as much dreaded and deprecated by us as ruin by sin. We must be as earnest with God that we may not be led into it as that we may not be led by that to sin, and by sin to ruin.

(11) That God is to be depended upon for our deliverance *from all evil*; and we should pray, not only that we may not be left to ourselves to run into evil, but that we may not be left to Satan to bring evil upon us.

IV. He stirs up and encourages importunity, fervency, and constancy, in prayer, by showing,

1. That importunity will go far in our dealings with men, *v.* 5–8. Suppose a man, upon a sudden emergency, goes to borrow a loaf or two of bread of a neighbour, at an unseasonable time of night, not for himself, but for his friend that came unexpectedly to him. His neighbour will be loth to accommodate him, for he has wakened him with his knocking, and put him out of humour, and he has a great deal to say in his excuse. But his neighbour will have no nay, therefore he continues *knocking* still, and tells him he will do so till he has what he comes for; so that he must give it to him, to be rid of him: *He will rise and give him as many as he needs, because of his importunity.* We prevail with men by importunity because they are *displeased* with it, but with God because he is *pleased* with it. Now this similitude may be of use to us to *direct* us in prayer. (1) We must come to God with *boldness* and *confidence* for what we need, as a man does to the house of his neighbour or friend, who, he knows, loves him, and is inclined to be kind to him. (2) We must come for *bread*, for that which is *needful*. (3) We must come to him by prayer *for others* as well as *for ourselves*. This man did not come for bread for himself, but for his friend. We cannot come to God upon a more pleasing errand than when we come to him for grace to enable us to do good. (4) We may come with the more boldness to God in a strait, if it be a strait that we have not brought ourselves into by our own folly and carelessness, but Providence has led us into it. This man would not have wanted bread if his friend had not come in *unexpectedly*. The care which Providence casts upon us, we may with cheerfulness cast back upon Providence.

If importunity could prevail thus with *a man* who was angry at it, much more with a God who is infinitely more kind, and is not angry at our importunity, but accepts it. If he do not answer our prayers presently, yet he will in due time, if we continue to pray.

2. That God has promised to give us what we ask of him. We have not only the goodness of nature to take comfort from, but the word which he has spoken (*v.* 9, 10): "*Ask, and it shall be given you.*" *I say unto you.* We have it from Christ's own mouth. We must not only *ask*, but we must *seek*, must second our prayers with our endeavours; and, in *asking* and *seeking*, we must continue *pressing*, still knocking at the same door, and we shall at length prevail. *Every one that asketh receiveth*, even the meanest saint that asks in faith. When we ask of God those things which Christ has here directed us to ask, that his name may be sanctified, that his kingdom may come, and his will be done, in these requests we must be importunate.

V. He gives us both instruction and encouragement in prayer from the consideration of our relation to God as a Father.

1. An *appeal* to the *bowels* of *earthly fathers*: "Let any of you that *is a father* tell me, if his son *ask bread*, will he give him a stone? If he ask a fish will he *for a fish give him a serpent*? Or, *if he shall ask an egg* for his supper (an egg and to bed), *will he offer him a scorpion*? You know you could not be so unnatural to your own children," *v.* 11, 12.

2. An *application* of this to the *blessings* of our *heavenly Father* (*v.* 13): *If ye then, being evil, give good gifts to your children, much more shall God give you the Spirit.* He shall give *good things*; so it is in Matthew. Observe,

(1) The direction he gives us what to *pray for*. We must ask for the *Holy Spirit*, not only as necessary in order to our *praying well*, but as inclusive of all the good things we are to pray for.

(2) The *encouragement* he gives us to hope that we shall speed in this prayer: *Your heavenly Father will give*. It is *in his power* to give the Spirit; he has all good things to bestow, wrapped up in that one; but that is not all, it is *in his promise*. If our earthly parents, though *evil*, be yet so kind, if they, though *weak*, be yet so *knowing*, that they not only give, but give with discretion, give what is best, much more will our *heavenly Father* give us his *Holy Spirit*.

Verses 14–26

The substance of these verses we had in Matt. xii. 22, &c. Christ is here giving a general proof of his divine mission, by a particular proof of his power over Satan. Here too he gives an earnest of the success of that undertaking. He is here casting out *a devil* that made the poor possessed man *dumb*: in Matthew we are told that he was *blind* and *dumb*. When the devil was forced out by the word of Christ, the *dumb* spoke immediately, and the lips were opened to show forth his praise.

I. Some were *affected* with this miracle. The people *wondered*; they admired the power of God.

II. Others were *offended* at it, and suggested that it was by virtue of a league with Beelzebub, the prince of the devils, that he did this, *v.* 15. Some, to *corroborate* this suggestion and *confront* the evidence of Christ's miraculous power, challenged him to *give them a sign from heaven* (*v.* 16), to confirm his doctrine. As if a *sign from heaven* could not have been given them as well by a compact and collusion with *the prince of the power of the air*, as the *casting out of a devil*. Obstinate infidelity will never be at a loss for something to say in its own excuse, though ever so frivolous and absurd. Christ here returns a full and direct answer in which he shows,

1. That it can by no means be imagined that such a subtle prince as Satan is should ever agree to measures that had such a direct tendency to his own overthrow, v. 17, 18. Jesus *knew their thoughts*, even when they industriously thought to conceal them, and he said, "You yourselves cannot but see the groundlessness of this charge; for it is an allowed maxim that no interest can stand that is divided against itself; not the more *public* interest of a *kingdom*, nor the *private* interest of a house or family; if either the one or the other be *divided against itself*, it cannot stand. Now, if Satan should thus be *divided against himself*, he would hasten his own overthrow."

2. That it was a very partial ill-natured thing for them to impute that in him to a compact with Satan which yet they applauded and admired in others that were of their own nation (v. 19): "*By whom do your sons cast them out?* Some of your own *kindred*, some of your own *followers*, have undertaken, in the name of the God of Israel, to cast out devils, and they were never charged with such a hellish combination." It is gross hypocrisy to *condemn* that in those who *reprove* us which yet we *allow* in those that *flatter* us.

3. That, in opposing the conviction of this miracle, they were enemies to themselves, for they thrust from them the kingdom of God (v. 20): "*If I with the finger of God cast out devils, no doubt the kingdom of God is come upon you*, and if you receive it not, it is at your peril." In Matthew it is *by the Spirit of God*, here *by the finger of God*. He needed not make bare his *everlasting arm*; that roaring lion, when *he* pleases, is crushed, like a moth, with a touch of *a finger*.

4. That his casting out devils was really the destroying of them and their power, v. 21, 22. When Christ cast out devils he was *stronger than they*, and could do it *by force*, and did it so as to ruin Satan's power. Now this is applicable to Christ's victories over Satan both in the world and in the hearts of particular persons. And so we may observe here,

(1) The miserable condition of an unconverted sinner. In his heart, which was fitted to be a habitation of God, the devil has his palace; and all the powers and faculties of the soul are *his goods*. The heart is a *palace*, a noble dwelling; but the unsanctified heart is the *devil's palace*. The devil, as a *strong man armed, keeps* this palace. All the prejudices with which he hardens men's hearts against truth and holiness are the *strongholds* which he erects for the *keeping of his palace*. There is a kind of *peace* in the palace of an unconverted soul, while the devil, as a *strong man armed*, keeps it. The sinner has a good opinion of himself, is very secure and merry; he flatters himself in his own eyes, and cries peace to himself. Before Christ appeared, all was quiet, because all *went one way*; but the preaching of the gospel disturbed the peace of the devil's palace.

(2) The wonderful change that is made in conversion. *Satan* is a *strong man armed;* but our Lord Jesus is *stronger than he*, see the manner of this victory: *He comes upon him* by surprise, when his *goods are in peace* and *overcomes* him. See the evidences of this victory. *First*, He *takes from him all his armour wherein he trusted*. Christ disarms him. When the power of sin and corruption in the soul is broken then Satan's *armour is taken away*. *Secondly*, He *divides the spoils*; he *takes possession* of them for himself. All the endowments of mind and body are now converted to Christ's service. Yet this is not all; he *makes a distribution* of them among his followers, and gives to all believers the benefit of that victory. Hence Christ infers that, since the whole drift of his doctrine and miracles was to break the power of the devil, it was the duty of all to join with him, to receive his gospel and come heartily into the interests of it;

for otherwise they would justly be reckoned as siding with the enemy (v. 23): *He that is not with me is against me*.

5. That there was a vast difference between the devil's *going out* by compact and his being *cast out* by compulsion. Those out of whom Christ *cast him* he never entered into again, for so was Christ's charge (Mark ix. 25); whereas, if he had *gone out*, whenever he saw fit he would have made a re-entry, v. 24–26. Christ, as he gives a *total*, so he gives a *final*, defeat to the enemy. Here we have,

(1) The condition of a *formal hypocrite*, his *bright side* and his *dark side*. His heart still remains the *devil's house*, and yet [1] The *unclean spirit is gone out*. He was not *driven out*, but he *went out*, withdrew for a time, so that the man seemed not to be under the power of Satan as formerly. [2] The *house is swept* from common pollutions by a partial reformation. The house is *swept*, but it is not *washed*; the house must be *washed*, or it is *none of his*. Sweeping takes off only the loose dirt, while the sin that *besets* the sinner, is untouched. It is swept from the filth that lies open to the eye of the world, but it is not searched and ransacked for secret filthiness. It is *swept*, but the *leprosy is in the wall*. [3] The house is *garnished* with common gifts and graces. It is not *furnished* with any true grace, but *garnished* with the pictures of all graces. It is all paint and varnish, not real, not lasting. The house is *garnished*, but the property is not altered; it was never surrendered to Christ.

(2) Here is the condition of a *final apostate*, into whom the devil returns after he had *gone out*: *Then goes he, and takes seven other spirits more wicked than himself* (v. 26). These *enter in* without any difficulty or opposition; they are welcomed, and they *dwell there*; and the *last state of that man is worse than the first*. Hypocrisy is the high road to apostasy. Where secret haunts of sin are kept up conscience is debauched, and the *close* hypocrite commonly proves an *open* apostate. The last state of such is *worse than the first*, in respect both of sin and punishment. Apostates are usually the worst of men; their consciences are seared, and their sins of all others the most aggravated. In the other world they will *receive the greater damnation*.

Verses 27, 28

We had not this passage in the other evangelists.

1. The applause which an affectionate, honest, well-meaning woman gave to our Lord Jesus, upon hearing his excellent discourses. This good woman admired them: *As he spoke these things* (v. 27), a *certain woman of the company* was so pleased that she could not forbear crying out, "*Blessed is the womb that bore thee*. Happy the woman that has thee for her son. I should have thought myself very happy to have been the mother of one that *speaks as never man spoke*, that has so much of the grace of heaven in him, and is so great a blessing to this earth." To all that believe the word of Christ the person of Christ is precious.

2. The occasion which Christ took from this to pronounce *them* more happy who are his faithful and obedient followers than she was who bore and nursed him. *Yea, rather, blessed are they that hear the word of God, and keep it*, v. 28. This is intended partly as a *check* to her, for doting so much upon his bodily presence, partly as an *encouragement* to her to hope that she might be as happy as his own mother, if she would *hear the word of God and keep it*. Those only are truly blessed that hear it and *keep* it.

Verses 29–36

I. What is the *sign* we may *expect* from God for the *confirmation* of our *faith*. The great and most convincing proof of Christ's being sent of God was the resurrection of Christ from the dead.

1. A reproof to the people for demanding other signs than what had already been given them in great plenty: *The people were gathered thickly together* (v. 29), a vast crowd of them. Christ knew what brought such a multitude together; they came *seeking a sign*, they came to gaze, to have something to talk of when they went home.

2. A promise that yet there should be *one sign* more given them, even the *sign of Jonas the prophet*, which in Matthew is explained as meaning the *resurrection of Christ*. But, if this do not work upon them, let them look for nothing but utter ruin: *The Son of man shall be a sign to this generation* (v. 30), a sign speaking to them, though a sign spoken against by them.

3. A warning to them to improve this sign. The *queen of Sheba* would *rise up in judgment against them*, and condemn *their unbelief*, v. 31. She was a stranger to the commonwealth of Israel, and yet she came from the uttermost parts of the earth to *hear his wisdom*, not only to satisfy her curiosity, but to inform her mind; and, behold, a *greater than Solomon is here*. Yet these wretched Jews will give no manner of regard to what Christ says to them, though he be in the midst of them. The Ninevites would rise up in judgment against them (v. 32): They *repented at the preaching of Jonas*; but here is preaching which far exceeds that of Jonas, and yet none are startled by it, to turn *from their evil way*, as the Ninevites did.

II. What is the *sign* that God *expects* from us for the *evidencing* of our faith, and that is the serious practice of that religion which we profess to believe.

1. They had *the light*. For God, having *lighted the candle* of the gospel, did not put it in a *secret place*, or *under a bushel*; Christ did not preach in corners. It is a great privilege that the light of the gospel is put on a *candlestick*, so that all that come in may *see it*, and may *see by it*.

2. Having the *light*, their concern was to have the *sight*. Be the *object* ever so *clear*, if the *organ* be not right, we are never the better: *The light of the body is the eye* (v. 34). So the light of the soul is its power of discerning between good and evil, truth and falsehood. Now, according as this is, so the light of divine revelation is to us, and our benefit by it. (1) If this eye of the soul be *single*, if it see *clear*, if it aim at *truth* only, and seek it for its own sake, the *whole body*, that is, the whole soul, is *full of light*. If our understanding admits the gospel in its full light, it fills the soul, and it has enough to *fill it*. And if the soul be thus *filled, having no part dark*, then *the whole soul shall be full of light*. It was darkness itself, but is now light in the Lord, *as when the bright shining of a candle doth give thee light*, v. 36. The gospel will come into those souls whose doors and windows are thrown open to receive it. (2) If the *eye of the* soul be *evil*, it is no wonder that the *whole body*, the whole soul, should be *full of darkness*, v. 34. The inference hence therefore is, *Take heed that the light which is in thee be not darkness*, v. 35. Be sincere in your enquiries after truth, and ready to receive the light, and love, and power of it; and not as the men of *this generation* to whom Christ preached, who never sincerely *desired* to know God's will, nor *designed* to do it, and therefore no wonder that they *walked on in darkness*.

Verses 37–54

Christ here says many of those things to a Pharisee and his guests, in a *private* conversation at table, which he afterwards said in a *public* discourse in the temple (Matt. 23); for what he said in public and private was *of a piece*.

I. Christ's going to dine with a Pharisee that very civilly invited him to his house (v. 37): *As he spoke a certain Pharisee* interrupted him with a request to him to come and *dine with him*. We know not the mind of this Pharisee; but, whatever it was, Christ knew it: if he meant ill, he shall know Christ does not fear him; if well, he shall know Christ is willing to do him good: so *he went in, and sat down to meat*. Christ's disciples must learn of him to be *conversable*, and not *morose*. Though we have need to be *cautious* what company we keep, yet we need not be *rigid*.

II. The offence which the Pharisee took at Christ for not *washing before dinner*, v. 38. He wondered that a man of his sanctity should sit down to meat, and not first *wash his hands*; the Pharisee himself and all his guests, no doubt, *washing*. The ceremonial law consisted in *divers washings*, but this was none of them, and therefore Christ would not practise it, though he knew that offence would be taken at his omitting it.

III. The sharp reproof which Christ gave to the Pharisees.

1. He reproves them for placing religion so much in those instances of it which are only external, and fall under the eye of man, while those were not only *postponed*, but quite *expunged*, which respect the soul, and fall under the eye of God, v. 39, 40. (1) The absurdity they were guilty of: "*You Pharisees make clean the outside* only, you wash your hands with water, but do not *wash your hearts from wickedness*." Those can never be reckoned *cleanly* servants that wash only the *outside of the cup* or the *platter*, and take no care to make clean the *inside*. The frame or temper of the mind in every religious service is as the *inside* of the cup and platter; the impurity of this *infects* the services. To live under the dominion of spiritual wickedness, is as great an affront to God as it would be for a servant to give the cup into his master's hand, clean wiped from all the dust on the outside, but *within* full of cobwebs and spiders. *Ravening* and *wickedness* are the dangerous damning sins of many who have made the *outside of the cup* clean from the more gross, and scandalous, and inexcusable sins of whoredom and drunkenness. (2) A particular instance of the absurdity of it, "*Ye fools, did not he that made that which is without make that which is within also? (v. 40).* Did not that God who in the law of Moses appointed divers ceremonial washings, appoint also that you should cleanse and purify your hearts? He who made laws for that which is *without*, did not he even in those laws further intend something within. Did not God, who made us these bodies, make us *these souls* also? Now, if he made both, he justly expects we should take care of both; and therefore not only wash the *body*, but wash the spirit, which he is the Father of, and get the leprosy in the heart cleansed?"

To this he subjoins a rule for making our creature-comforts clean to us (v. 41): "Instead of *washing your hands* before you go to meat, *give alms of such things as you have*, let the poor have their share out of them, and then *all things are clean to you*, and you may use them comfortably." Here is a plain allusion to the law of Moses, by which it was provided that certain portions of the increase of their land should be given *to the Levite, the stranger, the fatherless, and the widow*; and, when that was done, what was reserved for their own use was *clean to them*. Deut. xxvi. 12–15. *Then* we can with comfort enjoy the gifts of God's bounty ourselves when we *send portions to them for whom nothing is prepared*. What we have is not our own, unless God have his dues out of it; and it is by *liberality to the poor* that we clear up to ourselves our *liberty* to make use of our creature-comforts.

2. He reproves them for laying stress upon trifles, and neglecting the weighty matters of the law, v. 42. Those laws which related only to the *means of religion* they were very exact in the observance of: *Ye pay tithe of mint and rue*, pay it in kind and to the full. By this they would gain a reputation with the people as strict observers of the law. Now Christ does not condemn them for being so exact in paying tithes (*these things ought ye to have done*), but for thinking that this would atone for the neglect of their greater duties. Those laws which relate to the *essentials of religion* they made nothing of: *You pass over judgment and the love of God*, you make no conscience of giving men their *dues* and God your *hearts*.

3. He reproves them for their pride and vanity (v. 43): "*Ye love the uppermost seats in the synagogues, and you love greetings in the markets.*" It is not sitting uppermost, or being greeted, that is reproved, but *loving* it.

4. He reproves them for their hypocrisy (v. 44): "*You are as graves overgrown with grass, which therefore appear not*, and *the men that walk over them are not aware of them*, and so they contract the ceremonial pollution which by the law arose from the *touch of a grave*." These Pharisees were *within* full of *abominations*, as a grave of putrefaction; and yet they concealed it so artfully that it did not appear, so that they who conversed with them, and followed their doctrine, were infected with their corruptions and ill morals, and yet suspected no danger by them. The contagion *insinuated* itself, and was *insensibly* caught, and those that caught it thought themselves never the worse.

IV. The testimony which he bore also against the lawyers or scribes, who made it their business to *expound* the law, as the Pharisees did to *observe* the law.

1. There was one of that profession who resented what he said against the Pharisees (v. 45): "*Master, thus saying thou reproachest us also.*" It is the folly of those who are wedded to their sins, and resolved not to part with them, to make an *ill use* of the faithful and friendly admonitions given them, which come from love, and to have their passions provoked by them as if they were intended for *reproaches*. This lawyer espoused the Pharisee's cause, and so made himself partaker of his sins.

2. Our Lord Jesus thereupon took them to task (v. 46): *Woe unto you also, ye lawyers;* and again (v. 52): *Woe unto you, lawyers.* They blessed themselves in the reputation they had among the people, but Christ denounced *woes* against them, for he sees not as man sees. Those who quarrel with the reproofs of others, and suspect them to be reproaches to them, do but get *woes of their own* by so doing.

(1) The lawyers are reproved for making the services of religion more *burdensome* to others, but more *easy* to themselves, than God had made them (v. 46): "*You lade men with burdens grievous to be borne, but you yourselves touch them not with one of your fingers*"; that is, [1] "You will not *burden* yourselves with them, nor be yourselves bound by those restraints with which you hamper others." [2] "You will not *lighten* them, *you will not touch them*, that is, either to repeal them or to dispense with them when you find them to be burdensome and grievous to the people." They would come in with *both hands* to dispense with a command of God, but not with a *finger* to mitigate the rigour of any of the traditions of the elders.

(2) They are reproved for pretending a veneration for the memory of the prophets whom their fathers killed, when yet they hated and persecuted those in their own day who were sent to them on the same errand, v. 47–49. [1] These hypocrites *built the sepulchres of the prophets*; that is, they erected monu-

ments over their graves, in honour of them. They were not so superstitious as to enshrine their relics, or to think their devotions the more acceptable to God for being offered at the *tombs of the martyrs*; but, as if they owned themselves the *children of the prophets*, they *repaired* and *beautified* the monuments sacred to their *pious memory*. [2] Notwithstanding this, they had an inveterate *enmity* to those in their *own day* that came to them in the *spirit* and *power* of those prophets. For the *Wisdom of God said* that they would *slay* and *persecute* the prophets and apostles that would be sent them. The *Wisdom of God* would thus make trial of them by sending them prophets, to reprove them for their sins and warn them of the judgments of God. "*I will send them prophets* under the style and title of apostles, and these they shall not only contradict and oppose, but *slay* and *persecute*, and put to death." [3] Therefore God will justly put another construction upon their *building* the *tombs* of the prophets, and it shall be interpreted their *allowing the deeds of their fathers* (v. 45); the *building* of *their sepulchres* shall have this sense put upon it, that they resolved to keep them in their graves whom their fathers had hurried thither. [4] They must expect no other than to be reckoned with, as the *fillers up* of the *measure* of persecution, v. 50, 51. It shall all be *required of this generation* whose sin in persecuting Christ's apostles would exceed any of the sins of that kind that their fathers were guilty of. Their destruction by the Romans was so terrible that it might well be reckoned the completing of God's vengeance upon that persecuting nation.

(3) They are reproved for opposing the gospel of Christ, v. 52. They had not, according to the duty of their place, faithfully expounded to the people those scriptures of the Old Testament which pointed at the Messiah. Instead of that, they had perverted those texts by their corrupt glosses upon them, and this is called *taking away the key of knowledge*; instead of *using* that key for the people, and helping them to use it aright, they *hid it* from them; this is called, in Matthew, *shutting up the kingdom of heaven against men*, Matt. xxiii. 13. They themselves did not embrace the gospel of Christ, though by their acquaintance with the Old Testament they could not but know that the *time was fulfilled*, and the *kingdom of God was at hand*, and yet would not themselves *enter into it*. Them that without any guidance or assistance of theirs were *entering in* they did all they could to *hinder* and discourage, by threatening to *cast them out of the synagogue*. It is bad for people to be averse to revelation, but much worse to be adverse to it.

Lastly, In the close of the chapter we are told how spitefully and maliciously the scribes and *Pharisees* contrived to draw him into a snare, v. 53, 54. They could not bear those cutting reproofs which they must own to be just, as if, because his reproofs were warm, they hoped to stir him up to some intemperate heat and passion, so as to put him off his guard, they *began to urge him vehemently*, and to *provoke him to speak of many things, laying wait* for something which might serve the design they had of making him either *odious* to the people, or *obnoxious* to the government, or both. Faithful reprovers of sin must expect to have many enemies. That we may bear trials of this kind with patience, and get through them with prudence, let us *consider him who endured such contradiction of sinners against himself.*

CHAPTER 12

In this chapter we have divers excellent discourses of our Saviour's upon various occasions, many of which are to the same purport with what we had in Matthew, and we need thus to have precept upon precept, line upon line. I. Christ warns his disciples to take heed of hypocrisy, and of cowardice, ver. 1–12. II. He gives a caution against covetousness, and illustrates that caution by a parable of a rich man suddenly cut off by death, ver. 13–21. III. He encourages his disciples to cast all their care upon God, ver. 22–34. IV. He stirs them up to watchfulness for their Master's coming, ver. 35–48. V. He bids them expect trouble and persecution, ver. 49–53. VI. He warns the people to observe and improve the day of their opportunities, ver. 54–59.

Verses 1–12

I. A vast auditory that was got together to hear Christ preach. The *scribes* and *Pharisees* sought *to accuse him*, but the people still *admired* him, attended on him, and did him honour. *In the meantime* (*v.* 1), while he was in the Pharisee's house, the people got together for an afternoon sermon, a sermon after dinner, after dinner with a Pharisee; and he would not disappoint them. Though in the morning sermon, when they were *gathered thickly together* (*ch.* xi. 29), he had severely reproved them, yet they renewed their attendance on him; so much better could the people bear *their* reproofs than the Pharisees *theirs*. The more the Pharisees strove to drive the people from Christ, the more flocking there was to him. Here was an *innumerable multitude of people gathered together, so that they trode one upon another*. It is a good sight to see people thus forward to hear the word. When the net is cast where there is such a multitude of fish, it may be hoped that some will be enclosed.

II. The instructions which he gave his followers.

1. He began with a caution against *hypocrisy*. This he said *to his disciples first of all*. These were his more peculiar charge, and therefore he particularly *warned* them as his *beloved sons*; they made more profession of religion than others, and hypocrisy in *that* was the sin they were most in danger of. Hypocrisy would be worse in them than in others. Christ's disciples were, for aught we know, the *best men* then in the world, yet they needed to be cautioned against hypocrisy. Christ said this to the disciples, *in the hearing* of this great multitude, to add the greater weight to the caution, and to let the world know that he would not countenance hypocrisy, no, not in *his own disciples*.

(1) The description of that sin which he warns them against: *It is the leaven of the Pharisees*. It is *leaven*; it is *spreading* as leaven, *insinuating* itself into the whole man, and all that he does; it is *swelling* and *souring* as leaven, for it puffs men up with pride, embitters them with malice, and makes their service unacceptable to God. It is the leaven of the Pharisees: "It is the sin they are most of them found in. Take heed of imitating them; do not dissemble in Christianity as they do in Judaism."

(2) A good reason against it: "*For there is nothing covered that shall not be revealed*, *v.* 2, 3. Sooner or later, truth will come out. If you *speak in darkness* that which is inconsistent with your public professions, *it shall be heard in the light*; some way or other it shall be discovered, and your folly and falsehood will be *made manifest*." If men's religion prevail not to conquer and cure the wickedness of their hearts, it shall not always serve for a cloak. The day is coming when hypocrites will be stripped of their fig-leaves.

2. To this he added a charge to them to be faithful to the trust reposed in them, and not to betray it, through cowardice or base fear. "Whether men will *hear*, or whether they will *forbear*, tell them the *truth*, the *whole* truth, and *nothing but* the truth; what has been spoken to you *privately*, that do you preach *publicly*, whoever is offended." It was likely to be a *suffering* cause, though never a *sinking* one; let them therefore arm themselves with courage; and divers arguments are furnished here to steel them with a holy resolution in their work.

(1) "The power of your enemies is a limited power (*v.* 4): *I say unto you, my friends*" (Christ's disciples

are his friends, he calls them *friends*, and gives them this *friendly* advice), "*be not afraid.*" Those whom Christ owns for *his friends* need not be afraid of any enemies. "*Be not afraid*, no, not of them that *kill the body; after that there is no more that they can do.*" Those can do Christ's disciples no real harm who can but *kill the body*, for they only send that to its rest, and the soul to its joy, the sooner.

(2) God is to be feared more than the most powerful men: "*I will forewarn you whom you shall fear* (*v.* 5). By *owning Christ* you may incur the wrath of men, but by *denying* Christ, and disowning him, you will incur the wrath of God, which has power to send *you* to hell. Therefore *I say unto you, Fear him.*" "It is true," said that blessed martyr, Bishop Hooper, "life is sweet, and death bitter; but eternal life is more sweet, and eternal death more bitter."

(3) The lives of good Christians and good ministers are the particular care of divine Providence, *v.* 6, 7. Providence takes cognizance of the *meanest creatures*, even of *the sparrows*. "Though they are of such small account that *five* of them are sold for *two farthings*, yet not one of them is *forgotten of God*. Now, *you are of more value than many sparrows*, and therefore you may be sure you *are not forgotten*." Providence takes cognizance of the *meanest interest* of the disciples of Christ: "*Even the very hairs of your head are all numbered* (*v.* 7); much more are your sighs and tears numbered, and the drops of your blood, which you shed for Christ's name's sake."

(4) "You will be owned or disowned by Christ, according as you now own or disown him," *v.* 8, 9. To engage us to *confess Christ before men*, how dear soever it may cost us, we are assured that they who *confess Christ* now shall be owned by him in the great day *before the angels of God*. Jesus Christ will *confess*, not only that he suffered for them, but that they suffered *for him*, and what greater honour can be done them? To deter us from *denying Christ* we are here assured that those who *deny Christ*, whatever they may save by it, though it were life itself, and whatever they may *gain* by it, will be vast losers at last, for they shall be *denied before the angels of God*; Christ will not know them, will not own them.

(5) The errand they were shortly to be sent out upon was of the highest and last importance, *v.* 10. Let them be bold in preaching the gospel, for a sorer and heavier doom would attend those that rejected them (after the Spirit was poured upon them, which was to be the *last* method of conviction) than those that now rejected Christ himself. "*Whosoever shall speak a word against the Son of man*, it is capable of some excuse: *Father, forgive them, for they know not what they do*. But unto him that *blasphemes the Holy Ghost*, the privilege of the *forgiveness of sins* shall be denied; he shall have no benefit by Christ and his gospel." There were hopes of those who, though not convinced by them at first, yet admired them, but those who *blasphemed* them were given over.

(6) Whatever trials they should be called out to, they should be sufficiently furnished for them, and honourably brought through them, *v.* 11, 12. The faithful martyr for Christ has not only *sufferings* to *undergo*, but a *testimony* to bear, a *good confession* to *witness*, and is concerned to do that *well*, so that the cause of Christ may not suffer, though he suffer for it; and, if this be his care, let him cast it upon God: "When they *bring you into the synagogues*, or before *magistrates and powers*, to be examined about your doctrine, *take no thought what ye shall answer*," [1] "That you may *save yourselves*. If it be the will of God that you should come off, and your time is not yet come, he will bring it about effectually." [2] "That you may *serve your Master*; aim at this, but do not perplex yourselves about it, for *the Holy Ghost*, as a Spirit of wisdom, *shall teach you what*

you ought to say, and how to say it, so that it may be for the honour of God and his cause."

Verses 13–21

I. The application that was made to Christ by one of his hearers, desiring him to interpose *between him and his brother* in a matter that concerned the estate of the family (*v.* 13): "*Master, speak to my brother that he divide the inheritance with me.*" Some think that his brother *did him wrong*, and that he appealed to Christ to *right him*. Such brethren there are in the world, who have no sense at all either of *natural equity* or *natural affection*. They who are so wronged have a God to go to, who will *execute* judgment and justice for *those that are oppressed*. Others think that he had a mind to *do his brother wrong*, and would have Christ to *assist him*; that, whereas the law gave the elder brother a double portion of the estate, he would have Christ to *alter that law*, and oblige his brother to *divide the inheritance* equally *with him*. It was not a lawful desire of getting his own, but a *sinful* desire of getting more than his own.

II. Christ's refusal to interpose this in matter (*v.* 14): *Man, who made me a judge or divider over you?* Christ will not assume either a *legislative* power, or a *judicial* power. He corrects the man's mistake. If he had come to him to desire him to assist his pursuit of the heavenly inheritance, Christ would have given him his best help; but as to this matter he has nothing to do. Whatever he did, he could tell by what authority he did it, and who gave him that authority. Now this shows us what is the nature and constitution of Christ's kingdom. It is a spiritual kingdom, and not of this world. 1. It does not interfere with civil powers. Christianity leaves the matter as it found it, as to civil power. 2. It does not intermeddle with civil rights; it obliges all to do justly, according to the settled rules of equity. 3. It does not *encourage* our *expectations* of worldly advantages by our religion. 4. It does not *encourage* our *contests* with our brethren, and our being rigorous and high in our demands.

III. The necessary caution which Christ took occasion from this to give to his hearers.

1. The caution itself (*v.* 15): *Take heed and beware of covetousness*; ὁρᾶτε—"*Observe yourselves*, keep a *jealous eye* upon your own hearts, lest covetous principles steal into them; and φυλάσσεσθε—*preserve yourselves*, keep a *strict hand* upon your own hearts, lest covetous principles rule and give law in them."

2. An argument to enforce this caution: *For a man's life consisteth not in the abundance of the things which he possesseth;* that is, "our happiness and comfort do not depend upon our having a great deal of the wealth of this world." The life of the *soul*, undoubtedly, does not depend upon it. The things of the world will not suit the nature of a soul, nor supply its needs, nor satisfy its desires. Even the life of the body and the happiness of that do not consist in an *abundance* of these things; for many live very contentedly and easily, who have but a little of the wealth of it (a dinner of herbs with holy love is better than a *feast of fat things*); and, on the other hand, many live very miserably who have a great deal of the things of this world.

3. The illustration of this by a parable, which is intended for the enforcing of that necessary caution to us all, to *take heed of covetousness*. The parable gives us the life and death of a *rich man*, and leaves us to judge whether he was a *happy* man.

(1) Here is an account of his worldly wealth and abundance (*v.* 16): *The ground of a certain rich man brought forth plentifully.* His wealth lay much in the fruits of the earth. He had a great deal of ground, and his ground was *fruitful*; much would have *more*, and he *had more*.

(2) Here are the workings of his heart. We are here told what *he thought within himself, v.* 17. The God of heaven knows and observes whatever we think within ourselves, and we are accountable to him for it. Let us here observe,

[1] What his *cares* and *concerns* were. When he saw an extraordinary crop upon his ground, instead of *thanking God* for it, or rejoicing in the opportunity it would give him of doing the more good, he afflicts himself with this thought, *What shall I do, because I have no room where to bestow my fruits?* He speaks as one at *a loss*, and full of perplexity. *What shall I do now?* The poorest beggar in the country, that did not know where to get a meal's meat, could not have said a more anxious word. Even the *abundance* of the rich will not suffer them to *sleep*, for thinking what they shall do with what they have. The rich man seems to speak it with a sigh, *What shall I do?* And if you ask, Why, what is the matter? Truly he has *abundance* of wealth, and wants a place to *put it in*, that is all.

[2] What his *projects* and *purposes* were (*v.* 18): "*This will I do, I will pull down my barns, and I will build greater, and there will I bestow all my fruits and my goods*, and then I shall be at ease." It was folly for him to call the fruits of the ground *his* fruits and *his* goods. What we have is but *lent* us for our use, the property is still in God; we are but stewards of our *Lord's goods*. It was folly for him to *hoard up* what he had, and then to think it *well bestowed*. There will I bestow it *all*; as if none must be bestowed upon the poor, and *the stranger*, the *fatherless and the widow*, but all in the great barn. It was folly for him to let his *mind* rise with his *condition*; to talk of bigger barns, as if the next year must needs be as fruitful as this, and much more abundant, whereas the barn might be as much too big the next year as it was too little this. It was folly for him to think to ease his care by building new barns, for the building of them would but increase his care; those know this who know anything of the spirit of building. It was folly for him to contrive and resolve all this *absolutely* and *without reserve*. This *I will do. I will*; without so much as that necessary proviso, *If the Lord will, I shall live*, James iv. 13–15. Peremptory projects are foolish projects; for our times are in God's hand, and not in our own, and we do not so much as *know what shall be on the morrow*.

[3] What his *pleasing hopes* and *expectations* were. "Then *I will say to my soul, Soul, thou hast much goods laid up for many years; now take thine ease, eat, drink, and be merry*," *v.* 19. Here also appears his folly. It was folly for him to put off his comfort in his abundance till he had compassed his projects concerning it. When he has built bigger barns, then he will *take his ease*; and might he not as well have *done that now*? It was folly for him to be confident that his goods were *laid up for many years*, whereas in an hour's time they might be burnt to the ground and all that was laid up in them, perhaps by lightning. A few years may make a great change; *moth and rust may corrupt, or thieves break through and steal*. It was folly for him to count upon certain *ease*, whereas there are many things that may make people uneasy in the midst of their greatest abundance. One dead fly may spoil a whole pot of precious ointment; and one thorn a whole bed of down. Pain and sickness of body, disagreeableness of relations, and especially a guilty conscience, may rob a man of his ease, who has ever so much of the wealth of this world. It was folly for him to think of making no other use of his plenty than to *eat* and *drink*, and to *be merry*; to indulge the flesh, and gratify the sensual appetite, without any thought of doing good to others: as if

we *lived* to *eat*, and did not *eat* to *live*. It was the greatest folly of all to say all this to his *soul*. If he had said, *Body, take thine ease*, for *thou hast goods laid up for many years*, there had been sense in it; but the soul was no way interested in a barn full of corn or a bag full of gold. If he had had the *soul of a swine*, he might have *blessed it* with the satisfaction of *eating* and *drinking*. It is the great absurdity which the children of this world are guilty of that they portion their souls in the wealth of the world and the pleasures of sense.

(3) Here is God's sentence upon all this. He said to himself, *Take thine ease*. If God had said so too, the man had been happy. *But God said* quite otherwise; God said he did ill for himself: *Thou fool, this night thy soul shall be required of thee*, v. 20. *God said to him*, that is, decreed this concerning him. This was said when he was *in the fulness of his sufficiency*, when his eyes were held waking upon his bed with his cares and contrivances about enlarging his barns. When he was forecasting this, and then lulled himself asleep again with a pleasing dream of many years' enjoyment, *then* God said this to him. Now observe what God said,

The character he gave him: *Thou fool*, thou *Nabal*, alluding to the story of Nabal, that *fool* (Nabal is his name, and folly is with him). Carnal worldlings are fools, and the day is coming when God will call them by their own name, *Thou fool*, and they will call themselves so.

The sentence he passed upon him, a sentence of death: *This night thy soul shall be required of thee*; and then *whose shall those things be which thou hast provided*? He thought he had goods that should be his for many years, but he must part from them *this night*; he thought he should enjoy them himself, but he must leave them to he knows not who.

First, It is a *force*, an *arrest*; it is the *requiring of the soul*; what hast thou to do with a soul, who canst use it no better? Thy soul shall be *required*. A good man cheerfully resigns his soul at death, and gives it up; but a worldly man has it *torn* from him with violence. *They shall require thy soul*. God shall require it; he shall require an account of it. "Man, woman, what hast thou done with thy soul. Give an account of that stewardship."

Secondly, It is a *surprise*, an *unexpected* force. It is in *the night*. The time of death is day-time to a good man; it is his morning. But it is night to a worldling, a dark night. It is *this night*, this *present* night, without delay. This *pleasant* night, when thou art promising thyself many years to come, now thou must die. In the midst of all, here is an end of all.

Thirdly, It is the leaving of all *those things* behind which they have provided. All that which they have placed their happiness in, and built their hope upon, they must leave behind.

Fourthly, It is leaving them to they *know not who*: "Then *whose shall those things be*? Not *thine* to be sure, and thou knowest not what *they* will prove for whom thou didst design them, thy children and relations, whether they will be *wise* or *fools* (Eccles. ii. 18, 19), whether such as will bless thy memory or curse it, be a credit to thy family or a blemish, do good or hurt with what thou leavest them." If many a man could have foreseen to whom his house would have come after his death, he would rather have burned it than beautified it.

Fifthly, It is a demonstration of his folly. *At his end he shall be a fool*, for then it will appear that he took pains to lay up treasure in a world he was hastening from, but took no care to lay it up in the world he was hastening to.

Lastly, Here is the application of this parable (v. 21): *So is he* that *layeth up treasure for himself, and is not rich towards God*. This is the way and this is the end of such a man.

1. The description of a worldly man: He *lays up treasure for himself*, for *himself* in opposition to God, for that *self* that is to be *denied*. It is his error that he counts his *flesh himself*, as if the *body* were the *man*. It is his error that he makes it his business to *lay up for the flesh*, which he calls laying up *for himself*. It is his error that he counts those things his *treasure* which are thus *laid up* for the world, and the body, and the life that now is. The greatest error of all is that he is in no care to be *rich towards God*, rich in the *things of God*. Many who have abundance of this world are wholly destitute of that which will enrich their souls, which will make them rich towards God, rich for eternity.

2. The folly and misery of a worldly man: *So is he*. Our Lord Jesus Christ has here told us what his end will be. It is the unspeakable folly of the most of men to mind that which is merely for the body and for time, more than that which is for the soul and eternity.

Verses 22–40

"*Therefore*, because there are so many that are ruined by covetousness, *I say unto you*, my disciples, take heed of it." *Thou, O man of God, flee these things*, as well as thou, O man of the world, 1 Tim. vi. 11.

I. He charges them not to afflict themselves with disquieting perplexing cares about the necessary supports of life: *Take no thought for your life*, v. 22. In the foregoing parable he had given us warning against that branch of covetousness of which rich people are most in danger. He here warns them against another branch of covetousness, which they are most in temptation to that have but a little of this world, and that was, an *anxious solicitude* about the necessary supports of life: "*Take no thought for your life what ye shall eat* or *what ye shall put on*." This is the caution he had largely insisted upon, Matt. vi. 25, &c.; and the arguments here used are much the same.

1. God, who has done the greater for us, may be depended upon to do the less. He has given us *life* and a *body*, and therefore we may cheerfully leave it to him to provide *meat* for the support of that life, and *raiment* for the defence of that body.

2. God, who provides for the inferior creatures, may be depended upon to provide. "Trust God for *meat*, for he *feeds the ravens* (v. 24); they *neither sow nor reap*, and yet they are *fed*. Now consider how *much better ye are than the fowls*, than the ravens. Trust God for clothing, for he clothes the lilies (v. 27, 28); they *toil not*, they *spin not*, and yet, as the flower grows up, it appears wonderfully *beautified*. Now, if God has so clothed the flowers, *shall he not much more clothe* you?" Then let them not be *of little faith*. Our inordinate cares are owing to the weakness of our faith; for a powerful practical belief of the all-sufficiency of God would be mighty, through God, to the pulling down of the strongholds of these disquieting perplexing imaginations.

3. Our cares are fruitless, vain, and insignificant. They will not gain us our wishes, and therefore ought not to hinder our repose (v. 25): "*Which of you by taking thought can add to his stature one cubit?* Now if ye be *not able to do that which is least*, if it be not in your power to alter your statures, why should you perplex yourselves about other things, which are as much out of your power?" As in our *stature*, so in our *state*, it is our wisdom to take *it as it is*, and make the best of it; for fretting and vexing, carping and caring will not mend it.

4. An inordinate anxious pursuit of the things of this world, even necessary things, very ill becomes the disciples of Christ (v. 29, 30): "*Seek not ye what*

ye shall eat, *or what ye shall drink;* do not you afflict yourselves with perplexing cares." Let not the disciples of Christ thus *seek* their food, but ask it of God day by day; let them not be *of doubtful mind;* blown hither and thither with every wind. Be even and steady, and have your hearts fixed; *live not in careful suspense;* let not your minds be continually perplexed between hope and fear, ever upon the rack. Let not the children of God make themselves uneasy; for,

(1) This is to make themselves like the children of this world: "*All these things do the nations of the world seek after,* v. 30. They that take care for this world only, and not for the other, look no further than what they shall *eat* and *drink.* But it ill becomes you to do so. When inordinate cares prevail over us, we should think, "What am I, a Christian or a heathen? If a Christian, shall I rank myself with Gentiles, and join with them in their pursuits?"

(2) It is needless for them to disquiet themselves with care about the necessary supports of life: "*Your Father knows that you have need of these things,* and will supply your needs *according to his riches in glory*; for he is *your Father,* and therefore will take care that you *want no good thing.*"

(3) They have better things to mind and pursue (v. 31): "*But rather seek ye the kingdom of God,* and mind this, you, my disciples, who are to *preach the kingdom of God.* Let all that have souls to save *seek the kingdom of God,* in which only they can be *safe.* Then *all these things shall be added to you.* Mind the affairs of your souls with diligence and care, and then trust God with all your other affairs."

(4) They have better things to expect and hope for: *Fear not, little flock,* v. 32. When we frighten ourselves with an apprehension of evil to come, we put ourselves upon the stretch of care how to avoid it, when after all perhaps it is but the creature of our own imagination. Therefore *fear not, little flock,* for *it is your Father's good pleasure to give you the kingdom.* This comfortable word we had not in Matthew. [1] Christ's flock in this world is a *little flock.* The church is a vineyard, a garden, a small spot, compared with the wilderness of this world. [2] Though it be a little flock, quite *over-numbered* by its enemies, yet it is the will of Christ that they should not *be afraid*: "*Fear not, little flock,* but see yourselves safe under the protection and conduct of the great and good Shepherd." [3] God has *a kingdom* in store for all that belong to Christ's *little flock,* a crown of glory (1 Pet. v. 4). [4] The kingdom is given according to the *good pleasure* of the Father: *It is your Father's good pleasure;* it is given not of debt, but of grace. [5] The believing hopes and prospects of *the kingdom* should silence and suppress the fears of Christ's little flock in this world. "Fear no trouble; for, though it should come, it shall not come between you and the kingdom." (That is not an evil worth trembling at the thought of which cannot separate us from the love of God.)

II. He charged them to make sure work for their souls, by laying up their treasure in heaven, v. 33, 34.

1. "*Sell that ye have,* and *give alms,*" that is, "rather than want wherewith to relieve those that are truly *necessitous,* sell what you have that is *superfluous,* and give it *to the poor. Sell what you have,* if you find it a hindrance from, or incumbrance in, the service of Christ. Do not sell to *hoard up* the money, or because you can make more of it by usury, but *sell and give alms*; what is given in alms, in a right manner, is put out to the *best* interest, upon the *best* security."

2. "*Set your hearts upon the other world. Provide yourselves bags that wax not old.*" Grace will *go with us* into another world, for it is *woven in* the soul; and our good works will *follow us.* These will be *treasures in heaven,* that will enrich us to eternity. (1)

It is treasure that will not be *exhausted*; we may spend upon it to eternity; there is no danger of seeing the bottom of it. (2) It is treasure that we are in no danger of being robbed of; what is laid up in heaven is out of the reach of enemies. (3) It is treasure that will not *spoil* with *keeping,* any more than it will *waste* with *spending*; the *moth* does not *corrupt* it. We have laid up our treasure in heaven if our *hearts* be *there* while we are *here* (v. 34). But, if your hearts be set upon the earth and the things of it, it is to be feared that you have your treasure and portion in it, and are undone when you leave it.

III. He charges them to get ready, and to keep in a readiness for Christ's coming, v. 35, &c.

1. Christ is our *Master,* and we are his *servants,* not only *working* servants, but *waiting* servants. We must be as men that *wait for their Lord,* that sit up late while he stays out late, to be ready to receive him.

2. Christ our Master, though now *gone from us,* will *return again.* Christ's servants are now in a state of expectation, *looking for their Master's glorious appearing.* He *will come* to take cognizance of his servants, and they shall either stay with him or be turned out of doors, according as they are found in that day.

3. The time of our Master's return is uncertain; it will be *far* in the night, when he has long *deferred* his coming; in the *second watch,* just before midnight, or in the *third watch,* next after midnight, v. 38. *The Son of man cometh at an hour that ye think not* (v. 40). This bespeaks the prevailing security of the greatest part of men, who are *unthinking,* so that, whenever he comes, it is *in an hour that they think not.*

4. That which he expects and requires from his servants is that they be *ready to open to him immediately* (v. 36), that is, that they be found *as* his servants, with their *loins girded about,* having their long garments tucked up (which otherwise would hang about them, and hinder them), and *their lights burning,* with which to light their master into the house.

5. Those servants will be happy who shall be found ready when their Lord shall come (v. 37): *Blessed are those servants* who, after having waited long, are then found awake and aware of his first approach, of his first knock; and again (v. 38): *Blessed are those servants.* He *will make them sit down to meat, and will serve them.* For the bridegroom to wait upon his bride at table is not uncommon, but to wait upon his servants is not *the manner of men*; yet Jesus Christ did once, to show his condescension, *gird himself,* and *serve them,* when he *washed their feet* (John xiii. 4, 5).

6. We are *therefore* kept at uncertainty concerning the precise time of his coming that we may be always ready: *The good man of the house, if he had known what hour the thief would have come,* though he were ever so careless a man, *would yet have watched,* v. 39. But we do not know at what hour the alarm will be given us, and therefore are concerned never to be off our guard. Or this may intimate the miserable case of those who are careless and unbelieving in this great matter. We have notice of the day of the Lord's coming, *as a thief in the night,* and yet do not thus *watch.* If men will take such care of their houses, O let us be thus wise for our souls: *Be ye therefore ready also,* as ready as the good man of the house would be *if he knew what hour the thief would come.*

Verses 41–53

I. Peter's question, which he put to Christ upon occasion of the foregoing parable (v. 41): "*Lord, speakest thou this parable to us, or also to all*—to all the hearers?" Peter was now, as often, spokesman for the disciples. We have reason to bless God that there are some such forward men; let those that are such take heed of being proud. Now Peter desires Christ to explain himself. Lord, said Peter, was it intended for *us*, or for *all*? To this Christ gives a direct answer (Mark xiii. 37): *What I say unto you, I say unto all.* Yet here he seems to show that the apostles were primarily concerned in it. *Speakest thou this to us?* Doth this word belong to me? Speak it to *my heart*.

II. Christ's reply to this question, directed to Peter and the rest of the disciples. This that follows is peculiarly adapted to ministers, who are the *stewards* in Christ's house.

1. What was their *duty* as *stewards*, and what the *trust* committed to them. They are made *rulers of God's household*, under Christ, whose own the house is; ministers derive an authority from Christ. Their business is to give God's children and servants *their portion of meat*, that which is proper for them; convictions and comfort to those to whom they respectively belong; to give it to them *in due season*; a word *in season* to him *that is weary*. Herein they must approve themselves *faithful* and *wise*; *faithful* to their Master, and faithful to their fellow-servants; and *wise*. Ministers must be both *skilful* and *faithful*.

2. What would be their happiness if they approved themselves faithful and wise (*v.* 43): *Blessed is that servant*, (1) That is *doing*, and is not idle. (2) That is *so* doing, doing as he should be, by public preaching and personal application. (3) That is *found* so doing when his Lord comes. Now his happiness is illustrated by the preferment of a steward that has approved himself within a lower and narrower degree of service; he shall be preferred to a larger and higher (*v.* 44): *He will make him ruler over all that he has.* Ministers that obtain mercy of the Lord to be faithful shall obtain further mercy to be abundantly rewarded for their faithfulness in the day of the Lord.

3. What a dreadful reckoning there would be if they were treacherous and unfaithful, *v.* 45, 46. We had all this before in Matthew, and therefore shall here only observe, (1) *He saith in his heart, My Lord delays his coming*. Christ's patience is very often misinterpreted as *delay*, to the *discouragement* of his people, and the *encouragement* of his enemies. (2) The persecutors of God's people are commonly abandoned to security and sensuality; *they beat their fellow-servants*, and then *eat and drink with the drunken*, altogether unconcerned either at their own sin or their brethren's sufferings. (3) Death and judgment will be very terrible to all wicked people, but especially to wicked ministers. It will be a surprise to them: *At an hour when they are not aware.*

4. What an aggravation it would be of their sin and punishment that they knew their duty, and did not do it (*v.* 47, 48): *That servant that knew his lord's will, and did it not, shall be beaten with many stripes*; and *he that knew not shall be beaten with few stripes*, his punishment shall be mitigated. Here seems to be an allusion to the law, which made a distinction between sins committed through ignorance, and presumptuous sins (Num. xv. 29, 30). (1) Ignorance of our duty is an extenuation of sin. He *that knew not his lord's will*, and *did things worthy of stripes*, he shall *be beaten*, because he might have known his duty better, but *with few stripes*; his ignorance excuses in part, but not wholly. Thus *through ignorance* the Jews put Christ to death, and Christ pleaded that ignorance in their excuse: *They know not what they do*. (2) The knowledge of our duty is an aggravation of our sin: *That servant that knew his lord's will* shall be *beaten with many stripes*. God will justly inflict more upon him because it argues a great degree of wilfulness and contempt to sin against knowledge. Here is a good reason for this added: *To whomsoever*

much is given, of him shall be much required. Those that have greater capacities of mind than others, more knowledge and learning, more acquaintance and converse with the scriptures, to them *much is given*, and their account will be accordingly.

III. A further discourse concerning his own sufferings, and concerning the sufferings of his followers. In general (*v.* 49): *I am come to send fire on the earth*. By this some understand the preaching of the gospel, and the pouring out of the Spirit, holy fire; and it was *already kindled*. But, by what follows, it seems rather to be understood of the fire of persecution. Christ is not the Author of it, as it is the sin of the incendiaries, the *persecutors*; but he *permits* it as a *refining* fire for the *trial* of the persecuted.

1. He must himself suffer many things; he must pass through this fire that was already kindled (*v.* 50): *I have a baptism to be baptized with*. Afflictions are compared both to *fire* and *water*, Ps. lxvi. 12. Christ's sufferings were both. He calls them a *baptism* (Matt. xx. 22); for he was watered or sprinkled with them, and dipped into them, as Israel was baptized *in the sea*, 1 Cor. x. 2. Christ's *foresight* of his sufferings: *I am to be baptized with a baptism*. He calls his sufferings by a name that *mitigates* them; it is a baptism, not a deluge; I must be *dipped* in them, not *drowned* in them; and by a name that *sanctifies* them, for baptism is a sacred rite. Christ's *forwardness* to his sufferings: *How am I straitened till it be accomplished!* He longed for the time when he should suffer and die, having an eye to the glorious issue of his sufferings. Christ's sufferings were the *travail of his soul*, which he cheerfully underwent. So much was his heart set upon the redemption and salvation of man.

2. He tells those about him that they also must bear with hardships and difficulties (*v.* 51): "*Suppose ye that I came to give peace on earth?*" It is intimated that they went upon this supposition, that the gospel would meet with a *universal* welcome, that people would *unanimously* embrace it, that Christ would at least give them *peace*. "But," saith Christ, "you will be mistaken, the event will declare the contrary, and therefore do not flatter yourselves into a fool's paradise. You will find:

(1) "That the effect of the preaching of the gospel will be *division*." Not but that the design of the gospel and its proper tendency are to unite the children of men to one another, to knit them together in holy love, and, if all would receive it, this would be the effect of it; but there being multitudes that not only will not receive it, but oppose it, it proves, though not the *cause*, yet the *occasion* of division. While *the strong man armed kept his palace*, in the Gentile world, *his goods were at peace*. The sects of philosophers agreed well enough, so did the worshippers of different deities; but when the gospel was preached, and many were turned from the power of Satan to God, then there was a disturbance. Some *distinguished* themselves by embracing the gospel, and others were angry that they did so. Yea, and among them that received the gospel there would be *division*; and Christ permits it for holy ends, that Christians may learn and practise mutual forbearance.

(2) "That this *division* will reach into private families" (*v.* 53): *The father shall be divided against the son, and the son against the father*, when the one turns Christian and the other does not; for the one that does turn Christian will be zealous by arguments and endearments to turn the other too. The one that continues in unbelief will be provoked, and will hate and persecute the one that by his faith and obedience witnesses against, and condemns, his unbelief and disobedience. Even *mothers* and *daughters* fall out about religion; and those that believe not are ready to deliver up those that believe, though

otherwise very near and dear to them. We find in the *Acts* that, wherever the gospel came, *persecution was stirred up*; it was *everywhere spoken against*, and there was *no small stir about that way*. Therefore let not the disciples of Christ promise themselves *peace upon earth*.

Verses 54–59

Having given his disciples *their* lesson in the foregoing verses, here Christ turns to *the people*, and gives them *theirs*, *v.* 54. In general, he would have them be as wise in the affairs of their souls as they are in their outward affairs.

I. Let them learn to *discern the way of God towards them*, that they may *prepare* accordingly. They were *weather-wise*, could foresee when there would be *rain* and when there would be *hot weather* (*v.* 54, 55). Even in regard to changes of the weather God gives warning to us what is coming, and art has improved the notices of nature in weather-glasses. From what *has been* we conjecture what *will be*. See the benefit of experience; by *taking notice* we may come to *give notice*. Whoso is wise will *observe* and *learn*.

1. The particulars of the presages: "*When you see a cloud arising out of the west*, perhaps it is at first *no bigger than a man's hand* (1 Kings xviii. 44), but you say, There is a shower in the womb of it, and it proves so. When you *observe* the *south wind blow*, you say, *There will be heat*, and it usually *comes to pass*"; yet nature has not tied itself to such a track but that *sometimes* we are mistaken in our prognostics.

2. The inferences from them (*v.* 56): "*Ye hypocrites*, who pretend to be wise, but really are not so, *how is it that you do not discern this time?* Why are you not aware that you have now an opportunity which you *will not have long*, and which you *may never have again*?" *Now is the accepted time*, now or never. It is the folly and misery of man that he *knows not his time*. This was the ruin of the men of that generation, that they *knew not the day of their visitation*, ch. xix. 44. He adds, "*Yea, and why even of yourselves, judge ye not what is right?*" *v.* 57. If men would allow themselves the liberty of *judging what is right*, they would soon find that all Christ's precepts concerning all things are right, and that there is nothing more equitable in itself, than to submit to them and be ruled by them.

II. Let them hasten to *make their peace with God* in time, before it be too late, *v.* 58, 59. This we had upon another occasion, Matt. v. 25, 26. 1. We reckon it our wisdom in our temporal affairs to *compound* with those with whom we cannot *contend*. "*When thou goest with thine adversary to the magistrate*, and thou art in danger of being cast, thou knowest it is the most prudent course to make the matter up between yourselves; *as thou art in the way, give diligence to be delivered from him.*" Wise men will not let their quarrels go to an extremity, but accommodate them in time. 2. Let us do thus in the affairs of our souls. We have by sin made God our *adversary*, and he has both *right* and *might* on his side. Christ, to whom all judgment is committed, is the magistrate before whom we are hastening to appear: if we stand a trial before him, the cause will certainly go against us, the *Judge* will *deliver* us to the *officer*, and we shall be *cast into the prison* of hell, *till the last mite be paid*, which will not be to all eternity. Christ's sufferings were short, yet the *value* of them made them fully satisfactory. Now, in consideration of this, let us give diligence to be delivered *out of* the hands of God as an adversary, into his hands as a Father, and this *as we are in the way*, which has the chief stress laid upon it here. While we are alive, we are *in the way*; and *now* is our *time*, by repentance and faith, to get the quarrel made up,

while it may be done, before it be too late. Let us take hold on the arm of the Lord stretched out in this gracious offer, that we may make peace.

CHAPTER 13

I. The good improvement Christ made of a piece of news that was brought him concerning some Galileans, that were lately massacred by Pilate, ver. 1–5. II. The parable of the fruitless fig-tree, ver. 6–9. III. Christ's healing a poor infirm woman on the sabbath day, ver. 11–17. IV. A repetition of the parables of the grain of mustard-seed, and the leaven, ver. 18–22. V. His answer to the question concerning the number of the saved, ver. 23–30. VI. The slight he put upon Herod's malice and menaces, and the doom of Jerusalem read, ver. 31–35.

Verses 1–5

We have here, I. Tidings brought to Christ of the death of some Galileans lately, whose blood *Pilate had mingled with their sacrifices*, *v.* 1.

1. What this tragical story was. It is briefly related here, and is not met with in any of the historians of those times. The Galileans being Herod's subjects, it is probable that this outrage committed upon them by Pilate occasioned the quarrel that was between Herod and Pilate, which we read of in *ch.* xxiii. 12. We are not told what number they were, perhaps *but a few*; but the circumstance remarked is that he *mingled their blood with their sacrifices*. Though perhaps they had reason to fear Pilate's malice, yet they would not keep away from Jerusalem, whither the law obliged them to go up with their sacrifices. Neither the holiness of the place nor of the work would be a protection to them from the fury of an unjust judge, *who neither feared God nor regarded man*. The altar, which used to be a sanctuary and place of shelter, is now become a snare and a trap, a place of danger and slaughter.

2. Why it was related *at this season* to our Lord Jesus. Perhaps merely as a matter of news, which they supposed he had not heard before, and as a thing which they lamented and believed he would do so too. Perhaps it was intended as a confirmation of what Christ had said in the close of the foregoing chapter, concerning the necessity of making our peace with God in time, "Master, here is a fresh instance of some that were very suddenly *delivered to the officer*, that were taken away by death when they little expected it; and therefore we have all need to be ready." It will be of good use to us both to explain the word of God and to enforce it upon ourselves by observing the providences of God. Perhaps they would stir him up, being himself of Galilee, and a prophet, to find out a way to revenge the death of these Galileans upon Herod. Perhaps this was told Christ to *deter* him from going up to Jerusalem, to worship (*v.* 22), lest Pilate should serve him as he had served those Galileans. Now, lest Pilate, when his hand was in, should proceed further, they think it advisable that Christ should for the present keep out of the way. Christ's answer intimates that they told him this with a spiteful *innuendo*, that without doubt they were secretly bad men, else God would not have permitted Pilate thus barbarously to cut them off. It was very invidious; rather than they would allow them to be martyrs they would, without any colour of proof, suppose them to be malefactors. This fate of theirs was capable not only of a favourable, but an honourable construction.

II. Christ's reply to this report.

1. He seconded it with another story, which, like it, gave an instance of people's being taken away by sudden death. It is not long since *the tower of Siloam fell*, and there were eighteen persons killed and buried in the ruins of it. It was a sad story; yet such melancholy accidents we often hear of. Towers, that were built for safety, often prove men's destruction.

2. He cautioned his hearers not to make an ill use of these and similar events, nor take occasion thence to censure *great sufferers*, as if they were *therefore* to be accounted *great sinners*: *Suppose ye that these Galileans were sinners above all the Galileans, because they suffered such things? I tell you nay, v.* 2, 3. Perhaps they that told him the story of the Galileans were Jews, and were glad of anything that furnished them with matter of reflection upon the Galileans, and therefore Christ retorted upon them the story of the *men of Jerusalem*, that came to an untimely end. "Now suppose ye that *those eighteen* who met with their death from the tower of Siloam, while perhaps they were expecting their cure from the pool of Siloam, were *debtors* to divine justice *above all men that dwelt at Jerusalem? I tell you nay.*" We cannot judge of men's *sins* by their *sufferings* in this world; for many are thrown into the furnace as gold to be purified, not as dross and chaff to be consumed. We must therefore not be harsh in our censures of those that are afflicted more than their neighbours, lest we add sorrow to the sorrowful. If we will be judging, we have enough to do to judge ourselves. And we might as justly conclude that the *oppressors on whose side are power* and success, are the greatest saints, as that the *oppressed* are the *greatest sinners*. Let us, in our censures of others, do as we would be done by; for as we do we shall be done by: *Judge not, that ye be not judged*, Matt. vii. 1.

3. On these stories he founded a call to repentance, adding to each of them this awakening word, *Except ye repent, ye shall all likewise perish, v.* 3–5. (1) This intimates that we all deserve to *perish* as much as *they did*. It must moderate our censures, not only that we are *sinners*, but that we are as great sinners as they, have as much sin to repent of as they had to suffer for. (2) That therefore we are all concerned to *repent*, to be sorry for what we have done amiss, and to do so no more. The judgments of God upon others are loud calls to us to *repent*. (3) That repentance is the way to escape perishing, and it is a sure way. (4) That, if we repent not, we shall certainly perish, as others have done before us. Except we repent, we shall perish eternally, as they perished out of this world. The same Jesus that calls us to *repent because the kingdom of heaven is at hand*, bids us *repent* because otherwise we shall perish; so that he has set before us life and death, good and evil, and put us to our choice.

Verses 6–9

This parable is intended to enforce that word of warning immediately going before, "*Except ye repent, ye shall all likewise perish.*"

I. This parable primarily refers to the nation and people of the Jews. God chose them for his own, made them a people near to him, expected answerable returns of duty and obedience from them, which he would have accounted *fruit*; but they disappointed his expectations; they were a reproach instead of being a credit to their profession. Upon this, he justly determined to abandon them; but, upon Christ's intercession, he graciously gave them further time and further mercy; tried them, as it were, another year, by sending his apostles among them, to call them to repentance, and in Christ's name to offer them pardon. Some of them were wrought upon to *repent*, and bring forth fruit, and with them all was well; but the body of the nation continued impenitent and unfruitful, and ruin without remedy came upon them.

II. Yet it has a further reference, and is designed for the awakening of all that enjoy the means of grace to see to it that the temper of their minds and the tenor of their lives be answerable to their opportunities, for that is the *fruit* required.

1. The advantages which this fig-tree had. It was *planted in a vineyard*, in better soil, and where it had more care taken of it than other fig-trees had, that commonly grew by the *way-side*, Matt. xxi. 19. This fig-tree belonged to a *certain man*. The church of God is *his vineyard*. We are *fig-trees planted* in this vineyard. It is a distinguishing favour.

2. The owner's expectation from it: *He came, and sought fruit thereon.* He did not *send*, but came himself. Christ came into this world, *came to his own*, seeking fruit. The God of heaven requires and expects *fruit* from those that have a place in his vineyard. *Leaves* will not serve, crying, *Lord, Lord*; *blossoms* will not serve, beginning well and promising fair; there must be *fruit*. Our thoughts, words, and actions must be according to the gospel, light and love.

3. The disappointment of his expectation: *He found none*, not one fig. It is sad to think how many enjoy the privileges of the gospel, and yet do nothing at all to the honour of God.

(1) He here complains of it to the dresser of the vineyard: I come, *seeking fruit*, but am disappointed— *I find none.*

(2) He aggravates it, with two considerations: [1] That he had waited long, and yet was disappointed. As he was not *high* in his expectations, he only expected fruit, not *much* fruit, so he was not *hasty*, he came *three years*, year after year. In general, it teaches us that the patience of God is stretched out to longsuffering with many that enjoy the gospel, and do not bring forth the fruits of it. How many times three years has God come to many of us, *seeking fruit*, but has *found none*. [2] That this fig-tree did not only not bring forth fruit, but did hurt; it *cumbered the ground*; it took up the room of a fruitful tree, and was injurious to all about it. Those who do not *do good* commonly *do hurt* by the influence of their bad example. And the mischief is the greater, and the ground the more cumbered, if it be a high, large, spreading tree, and if it be an old tree of long standing.

4. The doom passed upon it: *Cut it down*. No other can be expected concerning barren trees than that they should be *cut down*. And with good reason, for *why cumbers it the ground?* What reason is there why it should have a place in the vineyard to no purpose?

5. The dresser's intercession for it. Christ is the great Intercessor. Ministers are intercessors; those we *preach to* we should *pray for*.

(1) What it is he prays for, and that is a reprieve: *Lord, let it alone this year also.* He doth not pray, "Lord, let it never be cut down," but, "Lord, not now." It is desirable to have a barren tree reprieved. Some have not yet *grace to repent*, yet it is a mercy to them to have *space to repent*. We owe it to Christ, the great Intercessor, that *barren* trees are not cut down immediately. We are encouraged to pray to God for the merciful reprieve of barren fig-trees: "Lord, *let them alone*; bear with them a little longer, and wait to be gracious." Thus must we stand in the gap, to turn away wrath. Reprieves of mercy are but for a time: *Let it alone this year also.* When God has borne long, we may hope he will bear yet a little longer, but we cannot expect he should bear always. *Reprieves* may be obtained by the prayers of others for us, but not *pardons*; there must be our own faith, and repentance, and prayers.

(2) How he promises to improve this reprieve: *Till I shall dig about it, and dung it.* In general, our prayers must always be seconded with our endeavours. Thus in all our prayers we must request God's grace, with a humble resolution to do our duty, else we mock God, and show that we do not rightly value the mercies we pray for. The dresser of the vineyard

engages to do *his* part, and therein teaches ministers to do *theirs*. He will *dig about* the tree and will *dung* it. Unfruitful Christians must be *awakened* by the terrors of the law, which *break up the fallow ground*, and then encouraged by the promises of the gospel, which are warming and fattening, as manure to the tree. Both methods must be tried; the one prepares for the other, and all little enough.

(3) Upon what foot he leaves the matter: "Let us try what we can do with it one year more, *and, if it bear fruit, well,*" v. 9. The word *well* is not in the original, but the expression is abrupt: *If it bear fruit!* —supply it how you please, so as to express how wonderfully well-pleased both the owner and dresser will be. Unfruitful professors of religion, if after long unfruitfulness they will repent, and amend, and bring forth fruit, shall find *all is well*. God will be *pleased*, ministers' hands will be strengthened. Nay, there will be joy in heaven for it; the ground will be no longer cumbered, but bettered, the vineyard beautified, and the good trees in it made better. As for the tree itself, it is *well* for it; it shall *receive blessing from God* (Heb. vi. 7); it shall be *purged*, and *shall bring forth more fruit*.

But he adds, *If not, then after that thou shalt cut it down*. Though God bear long, he will not bear always. Barren trees will certainly be *cut down* at last, and *cast into the fire*. The longer God has *waited* the greater will their destruction be: to be cut down *after that* will be sad indeed. Cutting down, though it is work that shall be done, is work that God does not take pleasure in. Those that now intercede for barren trees, if they persist in their unfruitfulness will be even content to see them cut down. Their best friends will acquiesce in the righteous judgment of God.

Verses 10–17

I. The miraculous cure of a woman that had been long under a spirit of infirmity. Our Lord Jesus spent ᷾is *sabbaths* in the *synagogues*, v. 10. We should make conscience of doing so, and not think we can spend the sabbath as well at home in reading a good book. And, when he was in the synagogues on the sabbath day, *he was teaching there*. He was in his element when he was teaching. Now to confirm the doctrine he preached, he wrought a miracle, a miracle of mercy.

1. The object of charity was a woman in the synagogue that had *a spirit of infirmity eighteen years*, v. 11. She had an infirmity which was such that she was *bowed together*, and could *in no wise lift up herself*; she could not stand erect. Though she was under this infirmity, yet she went to the *synagogue on the sabbath day*. Even bodily infirmities, unless they be very grievous indeed, should not keep us from public worship on sabbath days; for God can help us, beyond our expectation.

2. The offer of this cure to one that sought it not bespeaks the preventing mercy and grace of Christ: *When Jesus saw her, he called her to him*, v. 12. Before she called he answered. She came to him to be *taught*, and to get good to her soul, and then Christ gave this relief to her bodily infirmity. Those whose first and chief care is for their souls do best befriend the true interests of their bodies likewise.

3. The cure effectually and immediately wrought bespeaks his almighty power. He *laid his hands on her*, and said, "*Woman, thou art loosed from thine infirmity*." Though *she could in no wise lift up herself*, Christ could lift her up, and enable her to lift up herself. She that had been *crooked* was *immediately made straight*. This cure represents the work of Christ's grace upon the souls of people, in the *conversion* of sinners. Unsanctified hearts are under this *spirit of infirmity*; they are distorted. They can

in no wise *lift up themselves* to God and heaven; the bent of the soul is the quite contrary way. Such crooked souls seek not to Christ; but he calls them to him, speaks a healing word to them, by which he *looses them from their infirmity*, makes the soul *straight*. The grace of God can make that straight which the sin of man has made crooked. In the *consolation* of good people. Many of the children of God are long under a *spirit of infirmity*, a spirit of bondage. Christ, by his Spirit of adoption, looses them from this infirmity in due time.

4. The present effect of this cure upon the *soul* of the patient as well as upon her *body*. She *glorified God*. When crooked souls are made straight, they will show it by their glorifying God.

II. The offence that was taken at this by the *ruler of the synagogue*. He *had indignation* at it, because it was *on the sabbath day*, v. 14. What light can shine so clear, so strong, that a spirit of bigotry will not serve to shut men's eyes against it? He said *to the people*, reflecting upon Christ in what he said, *There are six days in which men ought to work, in them therefore come and be healed, and not on the sabbath day*. See here how light he made of the miracles Christ wrought, as if they were *things of course*: "You may *come* and be healed any day of the week." Christ's cures were become, in his eyes, cheap and common things. This was evidently *the work of God*; and, when God tied us out from working that day, did he tie himself out? The same word in Hebrew signifies both *godly* and *merciful* (*chesed*), to intimate that works of *mercy* and *charity* are in a manner works of *piety* and therefore very proper on sabbath days.

III. Christ's justification of himself in what he had done (v. 15): *The Lord then answered him, Thou hypocrite*. We *must* judge charitably, and *can* judge only according to the outward appearance. Christ knew that he had a real enmity to him and to his gospel, that he did but cloak this with a pretended zeal for the sabbath day. Christ could have told him this, but he vouchsafes to reason the case with him.

1. He *appeals* to the common practice among the Jews, which was never disallowed, that of *watering* their cattle on the sabbath day. Those cattle that are kept up in the stable are constantly *loosed from the stall on the sabbath day, and led away to watering*. It would be a barbarous thing not to do it. Letting the cattle *rest* on the sabbath day, would be worse than working them, if they must be made to fast on that day.

2. He applies this to the present case (v. 16): "Must the *ox* and the *ass* have compassion shown them on the sabbath day, and shall not this woman be *loosed* from a much *greater* grievance? She is *a daughter of Abraham*; she is *your sister*, and shall she be denied a favour that you grant to an ox or an ass? She is *a daughter of Abraham*, and therefore is entitled to the Messiah's blessings. She is one whom Satan *has bound*. Therefore it was not only an act of charity to the poor woman, but of piety to God, to break the power of the devil. She has been in this deplorable condition *lo, these eighteen years*, and therefore, now that there is an opportunity of delivering her, it ought not to be deferred *a day* longer. Any of you would have thought eighteen years' affliction full long enough."

IV. The different effect that this had upon those that heard him.

1. What a confusion this was to the malice of his persecutors: *When he had said these things, all his adversaries were ashamed* (v. 17). It was not a shame that worked repentance, but rather indignation.

2. What a confirmation this was to the faith of his friends: *All the people rejoiced for all the glorious things that were done by him*. The shame of his foes was the joy of his followers. The things Christ did

were *glorious things*, and we ought to rejoice in them.

Verses 18–22

I. The gospel's progress foretold in two parables, which we had before, Matt. xiii. 31–33. Christ undertakes here to show *what the kingdom of God is like* (v. 18): "*Whereunto shall I liken the kingdom of God?* v. 20. It will be quite another thing from what you expect. You expect it will appear *great*, and will arrive at its perfection all of a sudden; but you are mistaken, *it is like a grain of mustard-seed*, a little thing, makes but a little figure, and promises but little; yet, when sown it *waxes a great tree*, v. 19." Many perhaps were prejudiced against the gospel, because its beginning was so small. Christ would remove this prejudice, by assuring them that though *its beginning was small its latter end should greatly increase*; so that many should come upon the wing, to lodge in the branches of it. "You expect it will make its way by *external* means, but it shall work *like leaven*, silently and insensibly, and without any force or violence," v. 21. A little leaven leaveneth the whole lump; so the doctrine of Christ will strangely *diffuse* its relish into the world of mankind. But you must *give it time*, and you will find it does wonders. By degrees *the whole will be leavened*.

II. Christ's progress towards Jerusalem recorded: *He went through the cities and villages, teaching and journeying*, v. 22. Here we find Christ journeying towards Jerusalem, to the feast of dedication, which was *in the winter*, when travelling was uncomfortable.

Verses 23–30

I. A question put to our Lord Jesus. Who it was that put it we are not told, whether a friend or a foe. The question was, *Are there few that are saved? v.* 23. Perhaps it was a *captious* question. If he should say that many would be saved, they would reproach him as too loose; if few, they would reproach him as precise and strait-laced. In nothing do men more betray their ignorance than in judging of the salvation of others. Perhaps it was a *curious* question, a nice speculation. Many are more inquisitive respecting who shall be saved, and who not, than respecting what they shall do to be saved. Perhaps it was an *admiring* question. He had taken notice how strict the law of Christ was, and how bad the world was, and, comparing these together, cries out, "How few are there that will be saved!" We have reason to wonder that of the many to whom the word of salvation is sent there are so few to whom it is indeed a saving word. Perhaps it was an *enquiring* question: "*If there be few that be saved*, what then? What influence should this have upon me?"

II. Christ's answer to this question. Our Saviour did not give a direct answer to this enquiry, for he came to *guide* men's *consciences*, not to *gratify* their *curiosity*. Not, "What shall become of such and such?" But, "What shall I do, and what will become of me?"

1. A quickening exhortation and direction: *Strive to enter in at the strait gate*. This is directed not to him only that asked the question, but to all: *Strive ye*. All that will be saved must *enter in at the strait gate*, and must submit to a strict discipline. Those that would enter in at the strait gate must *strive to enter*. It is a hard matter to get to heaven, and a point that will not be gained without a great deal of care and pains. "*Be in an agony;* strive as those that run for a prize; excite and exert ourselves to the utmost."

2. Divers awakening considerations.

(1) Think how many take *some pains* for salvation and yet perish because they do not take *enough*. *Many will seek to enter in, and shall not be able;* they *seek*, but they do not *strive*. The reason why many come short of grace and glory is because they rest in a *lazy seeking*. They have a *good mind to happiness*, and a *good opinion of holiness*, and take some *good steps* towards both. But their convictions are weak; their desires are cold, and their endeavours feeble, and there is no strength or steadiness in their resolutions; and thus they *come short*.

(2) Think of the *distinguishing* day that is coming and the *decisions* of that day: The *Master of the house* will *rise up, and shut to the door*, v. 25. Now he seems as if he left things at large; but the day is coming when he will *rise up, and shut to the door*. What door? A door of *distinction*. Now, within the temple of the church there are *carnal* professors who worship in the *outer-court*, and *spiritual* professors who worship *within the veil*; between these the door is now open. But, when the *Master of the house is risen up*, the door will be shut between them, that those who are in the *outer-court* may be kept out. As to those *that are filthy*, shut the door upon them, that those who are within may be kept within, that those who are *holy may be holy still*. The door is shut to *separate* between the *precious* and the *vile*. A door of *denial* and exclusion. The door of *mercy* and grace has long *stood open* to them, but they would *not come in by it;* they hoped to get to heaven by their own merits, and therefore when the Master of the house is risen up he will justly *shut that door*.

(3) Think how many who were very *confident* that they should be *saved* will be rejected in the day of trial, and you will say that there are *few* that *shall be saved* and that we are all concerned to *strive*. Consider,

[1] How far their hope carried them, even to *heaven's gate*. There they *stand and knock*, knock as those that belong to the house, *saying*, "*Lord, Lord, open to us*, for we think we have a right to enter." Many are ruined by an ill-grounded hope of heaven, which they never distrusted or called in question. They call Christ, *Lord*; they are desirous now to enter in by that door which they had formerly made light of.

[2] What *grounds* they had for this *confidence*. Let us see what their plea is, v. 26. They had been *Christ's guests* and had shared in his favours: *We have eaten and drunk in thy presence*, at thy table. They had been *Christ's hearers*: "*Thou hast taught in our streets*. Wouldest thou teach us, and not save us?"

[3] How their confidence will fail them. Christ will say to them, *I know you not whence you are*, v. 25. And again (v. 27), *I tell you, I know you not, depart from me. First*, He *disowns* them: "*I know you not;* you do not belong to my family." *The Lord knows them that are his*, but them that are not he does not know, he has nothing to do with them. *Secondly*, He *discards* them: *Depart from me.* "Depart from my door, here is nothing for you." *Thirdly*, He gives them such a character as is the reason of this doom: *You are workers of iniquity.* This is their ruin, that, under a pretence of piety, they did the devil's drudgery in Christ's livery.

[4] How terrible their punishment will be (v. 28): *There shall be weeping and gnashing of teeth*, the utmost degree of grief and indignation: *You shall see the patriarchs and prophets in the kingdom of God, and yourselves thrust out.* The *Old Testament saints* are in the kingdom of God; they *saw his day* at a distance and it reflected comfort upon them. *New Testament sinners* will be *thrust out* of the kingdom of God. They shall be *thrust out* with shame, as having no part or lot in the matter. The sight of the saint's glory will be a great aggravation of sinner's misery.

(4) Think who are they that shall be saved, notwithstanding: *They shall come from the east and the west; and the last shall be first*, v. 29, 30. By what

Christ said, it appears that but *few shall be saved* of those who we think most likely. Yet do not say then that the gospel is preached in vain. There shall come many from all parts of the Gentile world that shall be admitted. When we come to heaven, we shall meet a great many there whom we little thought to have met there, and miss a great many thence whom we verily expected to have found there. Those who *sit down in the kingdom of God* are such as had taken pains to get thither, for they came from far—*from the east and from the west, from the north and from the south.* This shows that they who would enter into that kingdom must *strive.* Many who stood fair for heaven came short, and others who seemed cast behind will win and wear this prize, and therefore it concerns us to *strive to enter.* Shall I, who started first, and stood nearest, miss of heaven, when others, less likely, enter into it? If it be got by striving, why should not I strive?

Verses 31–35

I. A suggestion to Christ of his danger from Herod, now that he was in Galilee, within Herod's jurisdiction (*v.* 31): *Certain of the Pharisees came* to Christ, and said, *Get thee* out of this country, and *depart hence*, for otherwise *Herod will kill thee.* Some think that these Pharisees had no ground at all for this, but that they framed this lie, to drive him out of Galilee, and to drive him into Judea, where they knew there were those that really sought his life. But, Christ's answer being directed to Herod himself, it should seem that the Pharisees had ground for what they said, and that Herod was enraged against Christ, and designed him a mischief. Herod was willing to get rid of Christ. He hoped to *frighten him away* by sending him this threatening message.

II. His defiance of Herod's rage: *Go you, and tell that fox* so, *v.* 32. In calling him a *fox*, he gives him his true character; for he was subtle as a fox, noted for his craft, and treachery, and baseness. And, though it is a black and ugly character, yet it did not ill become Christ to give it to him. For Christ was a prophet, and prophets always had a liberty of speech in reproving princes and great men. Therefore it became him to call this proud king by his own name: "Go, and tell *that* fox that *I do not fear him.* I know that I must die, and must die shortly; I expect it, *the third day*," that is, "very shortly; my hour is at hand. If Herod should kill me, he will not surprise me. Tell him I do not fear him; when I die, *I shall be perfected*; I shall have completed my business"; *I shall be consecrated.* When Christ died, he is said to have *sanctified himself*; he consecrated himself to his priestly office with his own blood. "I know that neither he nor any one else can kill me *till I have done my work. I will cast out devils, and do cures, today and tomorrow*, in spite of him and all his threats. It is not in his power to hinder me. I must *go about* preaching and healing, *today, and tomorrow, and the day following*." It is good for us to look upon the time we have before us as but a little, that we may thereby be quickened to *do the work of the day in its day.* And it is a comfort to us, in reference to the power and malice of our enemies, that they can have no power to take us off as long as God has any work for us to do. "I know that Herod can do me no harm, not only because *my time* is not yet come, but because the place appointed for my death is Jerusalem, which is not within his jurisdiction: *It cannot be that a prophet perish out of Jerusalem.*" Now none undertook to try prophets, but the great sanhedrim, which always sat at Jerusalem; and therefore, if a *prophet* be *put to death*, it must be at Jerusalem.

III. His lamentation for Jerusalem, and his denunciation of wrath against that city, *v.* 34, 35. This we had in Matt. xxiii. 37–39. 1. The wickedness of persons and places that more eminently than others profess relation to God is in a particular manner provoking and grieving to the Lord Jesus. How pathetically does he speak of the sin and ruin of that holy city! *O Jerusalem! O Jerusalem!* 2. Those that enjoy great plenty of the means of grace, if they are not profited by them, are often prejudiced against them. If men's corruptions are not conquered, they are provoked. 3. Jesus Christ has shown himself willing to receive and entertain poor souls that come to him: *How often would I have gathered thy children together*, as a hen gathereth her brood under her wings, with such care and tenderness! 4. *I would*, I often would, and *ye would not.* Christ's willingness aggravates sinners' unwillingness. 5. The house that Christ leaves is *left desolate.* The temple is desolate if Christ has deserted it. He leaves it *to them*; let them take it to themselves, and make their best of it, Christ will trouble it no more. 6. Christ justly withdraws from those that drive him from them. They would not be *gathered* by him, and therefore, saith he, "*You shall not see me* any more." 7. The judgment of the great day will effectually convince unbelievers that would not now be convinced: "Then you will say, *Blessed is he that cometh*"—"you *will not see me* to be the Messiah till then when it is too late."

CHAPTER 14

I. The cure which our Lord Jesus wrought upon a man that had the dropsy, on the sabbath day, ver. 7–11. III. A lesson of humility, ver. 7–11. III. A lesson of charity, ver. 12–14. IV. The success of the gospel offer foretold in the parable of the guests invited to a feast, ver. 15–24. V. The great law of discipleship laid down, ver. 25–35.

Verses 1–6

I. *The Son of man came eating and drinking*, conversing familiarly with all sorts of people. Here he *went into the house of one of the chief Pharisees to eat bread on the sabbath day, v.* 1. See how favourable God is to us, that he allows us time, even on his own day, for bodily refreshments; and how careful we should be not to abuse that liberty. Christ went only to *eat bread*, to take such refreshment as was necessary on the sabbath day. Our sabbath meals must, with a particular care, be guarded against all manner of excess.

II. He *went about doing good.* Here was *a certain man before him who had the dropsy, v.* 2. Christ *prevented him* with the blessings of his goodness, and *before he called* he answered him. It is a happy thing to be where Christ is. This man had the *dropsy*, it is probable, in a high degree.

III. He *endured the contradiction of sinners against himself: They watched him, v.* 1. The Pharisee that invited him, it should seem, did it with a design to pick some quarrel with him. When Christ asked them *whether* they thought it *lawful to heal on the sabbath day* they would say neither *yea* nor *nay*, for their design was to *inform against him*, not to be *informed by him.* They would not say it *was lawful to heal*, they could not for shame say it was *not lawful.* Good men have often been persecuted for doing that which even their persecutors could not but own to be lawful and good. Many a *good work* Christ did, for which they *cast stones* at him and his name.

IV. Christ would not be hindered from *doing good* by the *opposition* and *contradiction* of sinners. He *took him, and healed him, and let him go, v.* 4. He *took him*, that is, he *laid hands* on him, to cure him; *he embraced him*, took him in his arms, big and unwieldly as he was (for so dropsical people generally are), and reduced him to shape. Christ cured even *that* disease, perfectly cured it, in a moment. He then let him go, lest the Pharisees should fall upon him for *being healed*, for what absurdities would not such men as they were be guilty of?

V. Our Lord Jesus *did nothing but what he could justify, v.* 5, 6. He still answered their thoughts, and made them *hold their peace* for *shame* who before held their peace for *subtlety*, by an appeal to their own practice. *Which of you shall have an ass or an ox fallen into a pit, and will not pull him out on the sabbath day*, and that straightway, not deferring it till the sabbath be over, lest it perish? It is not so much out of *compassion to the poor creature* that they do it as a concern for their own interest. It is *their own ox*, and *their own ass*, that is worth money, that they will dispense with the law of the sabbath for the *saving of*. Many can easily dispense with that, for their own interest, which they cannot dispense with for God's glory and the good of their brethren. This question *silenced* them: *They could not answer him again to these things, v.* 6. Christ will be justified when he speaks.

Verses 7–14

Our Lord Jesus here sets us an example of profitable edifying discourse at our tables, when we are in company with our friends. When he was in company with strangers, nay, with enemies that *watched him*, he took occasion to reprove what he saw amiss in them, and to instruct them. We must not only not allow any corrupt communication at our tables, but we must go beyond common harmless talk, and should take occasion from God's goodness to us at our tables to speak well of him, and learn to *spiritualise* common things. Our Lord Jesus was among persons of quality, yet, as one that had not respect of persons,

I. He takes occasion to reprove *the guests* for striving to *sit uppermost.*

1. He observed how these lawyers and Pharisees affected the *highest seats, v.* 7. He had charged that sort of men with this in general, *ch.* xi. 43. Here he brings home the charge to particular persons. He *marked* how they *chose out the chief rooms*; every man, as he came in, got as near the best seat as he could. Even in the common actions of life, Christ's eye is upon us, and he *marks* what we do.

2. He observed how those who were thus aspiring often exposed themselves, and came off *with a slur*; whereas those who were modest, and seated themselves in the lowest seats, often *gained respect* by it. Those who assume the highest seats, may perhaps be *degraded*, and forced to *come down* to give place to one *more honourable, v.* 8, 9. It ought to check our high thoughts of ourselves to think how many there are that are *more honourable* than we, not only in respect of worldly dignities, but of personal merits and accomplishments. The master of the feast will marshal his guests, and will not see the *more honourable* kept out of the seat that is his due, and therefore will make bold to take him lower that usurped it: *Give this man place.* Pride will have *shame*, and will at last have a *fall*. Those who content themselves with the lowest seats, are likely to be preferred (*v.* 10): "Go, and *seat thyself in the lowest room*, as taking it for granted that thy friend has guests to come that are of better rank and quality than thou art; but perhaps it may not prove so, and then it will be said to thee, *Friend, go up higher.*" The way to *rise high* is to *begin low*: "*Thou shalt have honour and respect before those that sit with thee.* They will see thee to be an *honourable man.* Honour appears the brighter for shining *out of obscurity.* They will likewise see thee to be a *humble man*, which is the greatest honour of all." A parable out of one of the rabbin is somewhat like this. "Three men," said he, "were bidden to a feast; one sat highest, For, said he, I am a prince;

the other next, For, said he, I am a wise man; the other lowest, For, said he, I am a humble man. The king seated the humble man highest, and put the prince lowest."

3. He applied this generally, and would have us all learn not to *mind high things.* Pride and ambition are disgraceful before men: for *whosoever exalteth himself shall be abased*; but humility and self-denial are really honourable: *he that humbleth himself shall be exalted, v.* 11.

II. He takes occasion to reprove the master of the feast for inviting so many *rich people*, when he should rather have *invited the poor.* Our Saviour here teaches us that the using of what we have in works of charity is better than using it in magnificent house-keeping.

1. "Covet not to *treat the rich*; invite not *thy friends, and brethren, and neighbours, that are rich," v.* 12. This does not *prohibit* the entertaining of such, for the cultivating of friendship among relations and neighbours. "Do not make a common custom of it. One feast for the rich will make a great many meals for the poor. Be not *proud of it.*" Many *make feasts* only to *make a show*, and thus rob their families, to please their fancies. "Aim not at being paid again in your own coin." This is that which our Saviour blames in making such entertainments: "You commonly do it in hopes that you will be invited by them, and so *a recompense will be made you.*"

2. "Be forward to *relieve the poor* (*v.* 13, 14): *When thou makest a feast* invite *the poor and maimed*, such as have nothing to live upon, nor are able to work for their living. These are objects of charity; they want necessaries; furnish them, and they will recompense thee with their prayers. They will go away, and thank God for thee. Say not that thou art a *loser*, because *they cannot recompense thee*, for *thou shalt be recompensed at the resurrection of the just.*" Works of charity perhaps may not be rewarded *in this world*, for the things of this world are not the *best things*, but they shall *in no wise lose their reward.* It will be found that the longest voyages make the richest returns.

Verses 15–24

I. The occasion of the discourse was given by one of the guests, who said to him, *Blessed is he that shall eat bread in the kingdom of God* (*v.* 15).

1. But with what design does this man bring it in here? (1) Perhaps this man, fearing he should put the company out of humour, started this, to *divert* the discourse to something else. Or, (2) Admiring the good rules which Christ had now given, but despairing to see them lived up to, he longs for *the kingdom of God*, and pronounces them *blessed* who shall have a place in that kingdom. Or, (3) Christ having mentioned *the resurrection of the just*, he here confirms what he said, "Yea, Lord, they that shall be recompensed in the resurrection of the just, shall *eat bread in the kingdom.*" Or, (4) Observing Christ to be silent, he was willing to draw him in again to further discourse; and he knew nothing more likely to engage him than to mention the *kingdom of God.* Even those that are not of ability to carry on good discourse themselves ought to put in a word now and then, to help it forward.

2. Now what this man said was a plain and acknowledged truth, and it was quoted very *appositely* now that they were *sitting at meat.* This thought will be very seasonable when we are partaking of bodily refreshments: *Blessed are they that shall eat bread in the kingdom of God.* (1) In the kingdom of grace. Christ promised his disciples that they should *eat and drink with him in his kingdom.* (2) In the kingdom of glory. Blessed are they that shall sit down at that table, whence they shall rise no more.

II. The parable which our Lord Jesus put forth upon this occasion, v. 16, &c. "But who are they that shall enjoy that privilege? You Jews will generally reject it, and the Gentiles will be the greatest sharers in it." Now in the parable we may observe,

1. The free grace and mercy of God, shining in the gospel of Christ; it appears,

(1) In the rich provision he has made for poor souls (v. 16): *A certain man made a great supper*. It is called a *supper*, because in those countries supper time was the chief feasting time.

(2) In the gracious invitation given us to come and partake of this provision. A general invitation given: He *bade many*. Christ invited the whole nation and people of the Jews to partake of the benefits of his gospel. Christ in the gospel, as he keeps a *good* house, keeps an *open* house. A particular memorandum given; the servant was sent round to put them in mind of it: *Come, for all things are now ready*. This is the call now given to us: "*All things are now ready*, now is the *accepted time*; and therefore *come now*; do not delay; accept the invitation; believe yourselves welcome."

2. The cold entertainment which the grace of the gospel meets with. The invited guests declined coming. *They all with one consent began to make excuse*, v. 18. They all found out some pretence or other to shift off their attendance. This bespeaks the general neglect of the Jewish nation to close with Christ. It also intimates the backwardness there is in most people to close with the gospel call. They cannot for shame avow their refusal, but they desire to be *excused*. They were *unanimous* in it; *with one voice*. Here were *two* that were *purchasers*. One had *bought a piece of ground* which was represented to him to be a good bargain, and he must needs *go and see* whether it was so or no; and therefore *I pray thee have me excused*. But what a frivolous excuse was this! He might have deferred going to see his piece of ground till the next day, and have found it in the same place and plight it was now in. Another had purchased *stock* for his land. "*I have bought five yoke of oxen* for the plough, and I must just now go and *prove them*, and therefore excuse me for this time." The former intimates that inordinate *complacency* in the world, this the inordinate *care* and *concern* about the world, which keep people from Christ and his grace. It is very criminal, when we are called to any duty, to make excuses for our neglect of it: it is a sign that there are convictions that it is duty, but no inclination to it. These things here were, [1] *Little things*. It had better become them to have said, "I am invited *to eat bread in the kingdom of God*, and therefore must be excused from going to see the *ground* or the *oxen*." [2] *Lawful things*. Things lawful in themselves, when the heart is too much set upon them, *prove fatal* hindrances in religion. Here was one that was *newly married* (v. 30): *I have married a wife, and therefore, in short, I cannot come*. He pretends that he *cannot*, when the truth is he *will not*. Thus many pretend *inability* for the duties of religion when really they have an *aversion* to them. Our affection to our relations often proves a hindrance to us in our duty to God. He might have gone and taken his wife along with him; they would both have been welcome.

3. The account which was brought to the master of the feast of the affront put upon him by his friends, who now showed how little they valued him (v. 21): *That servant came, and showed his lord these things*, told him with surprise that he was likely to sup alone. He made the matter neither better nor worse, but related it just as it was. Ministers must give account of the success of their ministry. They must do it now at the throne of grace. If they see of *the travail of their soul*, they must go to God with their *thanks*;

if they *labour in vain*, they must go to God with their *complaints*. The apostle urges this as a reason why people should give ear to the word of God sent them by his ministers; for *they watch for your souls, as those that must give account*, Heb. xiii. 17.

4. The master's just resentment of this affront: *He was angry*, v. 21. The ingratitude of those that slight gospel offers, and the contempt they put upon the God of heaven thereby, are a very great provocation to him, and justly so. Abused mercy turns into the greatest wrath. *None of the men that were bidden shall taste of my supper*. Grace despised is grace forfeited, like Esau's birthright. They that will not have Christ when they *may* shall not have him when they *would*.

5. The care that was taken to furnish the table with guests, as well as meat. "Go" (saith he to the servants), "*go first into the streets and lanes of the city* that you may invite those that will be glad to come, bring in *hither the poor and the maimed, the halt and the blind*; pick up the common beggars." They soon gather an abundance of such guests: *Lord, it is done as thou hast commanded*. Many of the Jews are brought in, not of the scribes and Pharisees, but publicans and sinners; these are *the poor and the maimed*. But *yet there is room* for more guests. "Go, then, *secondly, into the highways and hedges*. Go out into the country, and pick up the vagrants, or those that are returning now in the evening from their work in the field, and *compel them to come in*, not by force of arms, but by force of arguments. Be earnest with them; for in this case it will be necessary to convince them that the invitation is sincere. They will hardly believe that they shall be welcome, and therefore do not leave them till you have prevailed with them." This refers to the *calling of the Gentiles*, and with them the church was filled. (1) The provision made for precious souls in the gospel of Christ shall appear not to have been made *in vain*; for, if some *reject it*, yet others will thankfully *accept* the offer of it. (2) Those that are very poor and low in the world shall be as welcome to Christ as the rich and great. Christ here plainly refers to what he had said just before, to invite to our tables *the poor and maimed, the lame and blind*, v. 13. His condescensions and compassions towards them should engage ours. (3) Many times the gospel has the *greatest success* among those that are *least likely* to have the benefit of it. The publicans and harlots went into the kingdom of God before the scribes and Pharisees; *so the last shall be first, and the first last*. Let us not be *confident* concerning those that are most forward, nor despair of those that are least promising. (4) Christ's ministers must be both very expeditious and very importunate in inviting to the gospel feast: "*Go out quickly* (v. 21); lose no time, because *all things are now ready*." (5) Though many have been brought in to partake of the benefits of the gospel, yet still *there is room for more*. There is in him enough for all, and enough for each; and the gospel excludes none that do not exclude themselves. (6) Christ's house, though it be *large*, shall at last be *filled*.

Verses 25–35

He is in these verses directing his discourse to the multitudes that crowded after him, and his exhortation to them is to understand the terms of discipleship.

I. How zealous people were in their attendance on Christ (v. 25): *There went great multitudes with him*, many for love and more for company. Here was a *mixed multitude*.

II. How *considerate* he would have them to be in their *zeal*. Those that undertake to follow Christ must count upon the worst, and prepare accordingly.

1. He tells them what the worst is that they must

count upon. He takes it for granted that they had a mind to be *his disciples*. They expected that he should say, "If any man come to me, and be my disciple, he shall have wealth and honour in abundance." But he tells them quite the contrary.

(1) They must be willing to *quit* that which was *very dear*, rather than quit their interest in Christ, *v.* 26. A man cannot be Christ's disciple but he must *hate father, and mother, and his own life*. He is not *sincere*, he will not be *constant* and persevering, unless he love Christ better than anything in this world. Mention is not made here of *houses* and *lands*; philosophy will teach a man to look upon these with contempt; but Christianity carries it higher. Every good man loves *his relations*; and yet, if he be a disciple of Christ, he must comparatively *hate them*. Not that their persons must be in any degree hated, but our comfort and satisfaction in them must be lost and swallowed up in our love to Christ. When our duty to our parents comes in competition with our evident duty to Christ, we must give Christ the preference. If we must either *deny Christ* or be *banished* from our families and relations (as many of the primitive Christians were), we must rather lose their society than his favour. Every man loves *his own life*, no man ever yet *hated it*; and we cannot be Christ's disciples if we do not love him better than our own lives. The experience of the pleasures of the *spiritual life*, and the believing hopes and prospects of *eternal life* will make this *hard saying* easy. When tribulation and persecution arise because of the word, then chiefly the trial is. Yet even in *days of* peace this matter is sometimes brought to the trial. Those that are ashamed to confess him, for fear of disobliging a relation or friend, or losing a customer, give cause to suspect that they love him better than Christ.

(2) That they must be willing to *bear* that which was very *heavy* (*v.* 27): *Whosoever doth not bear his cross*, and so *come after me*, he *cannot be my disciple*. Though the disciples of Christ are not *all crucified*, yet they all *bear their cross*. They must be content to be put into an ill name, for no name is more ignominious than *Furcifer—the bearer of the gibbet*. He must bear his cross, and *come after Christ*; that is, he must bear it in the way of his duty, whenever it lies in that way. He must bear it when Christ calls him to it, and live in hope of a recompense with him.

2. He bids them count upon it, and then consider of it. It is better never to begin than not to proceed; and therefore before we begin we must consider what it is to proceed. This is to act rationally, and as becomes men. The cause of Christ will bear a scrutiny. Satan shows the best, but hides the worst. This considering of the case is necessary to perseverance. Our Saviour here illustrates the necessity of it by two similitudes. We are like a man that undertakes to *build a tower*, and therefore must consider the *expense of it* (*v.* 28–30): *Which of you, intending to build a tower sitteth not down first, and counteth the cost?* Let him compare the charge with his purse, lest he make himself to be laughed at, by *beginning to build* what he is *not able to finish*. All that take upon them a profession of religion undertake to *build a tower*. Begin low, and lay the foundation deep, lay it on the rock, and make sure work, and then aim as high as heaven. Those that intend to build this tower must *sit down and count the cost*. Let them consider that it *will cost them* a life of self-denial and watchfulness. It *may*, perhaps, *cost them* their reputation among men, and all that is dear to them in this world, even life itself. And if it should cost us all this, what is it in comparison with what it cost Christ? Many that begin to *build this tower* do not *go on with it*, nor persevere in it, and it is their folly. It is true, we have none of us in ourselves

sufficient to finish this tower, but Christ hath said, *My grace is sufficient for thee*. Nothing is more *shameful* than for those that have begun well in religion to break off.

(2) When we undertake to be Christ's disciples we are like a man that *goes to war*, and therefore must consider the *hazard* of it, *v.* 31, 32. A king that declares war against a neighbouring prince considers whether he has strength wherewith to make his part good, and, if not, he will lay aside his thoughts of war. *Is not the Christian life a warfare?* We must fight every step we go, so restless are our spiritual enemies in their opposition. We ought to consider whether we can *endure the hardness* which a good soldier of Jesus Christ must expect and count upon, before we enlist ourselves under Christ's banner. Of the two it is better to make the best terms we can with the world than pretend to renounce it and afterwards *return to it*. That *young man* that could not find in his heart to part with his possessions for Christ did better to go away from Christ *sorrowing* than to have stayed with him *dissembling*.

This parable is another way applicable, and may be taken as designed to teach us to begin *speedily* to be religious, rather than to begin *cautiously*; and may mean the same with Matt. v. 25, *Agree with thine adversary quickly*. Those that persist in sin make war against God. The proudest and most daring sinner is no equal match for God. In consideration of this, it is our interest to make peace with him. We need not send to *desire conditions of peace*; they are offered to us, and are unexceptionable. Let us acquaint ourselves with them, and be at peace; do this in time, *while the other is yet a great way off*.

But the application of this parable here (*v.* 33) is to the consideration that ought to be exercised when we take upon us a profession of religion. Enter upon a profession of religion, as those that know that *except you forsake all you have you cannot be Christ's disciples*.

3. He warns them against apostasy, for that would make them utterly useless, *v.* 34, 35. Good Christians are *the salt of the earth*, and good ministers especially (Matt. v. 13); *salt is good* and of great use. Degenerate Christians, who, rather than part with what they have in the world, will throw up their profession, are like *salt that has lost its savour*, that is the most useless worthless thing in the world; it has no manner of virtue or good property in it. It can never be recovered: *Wherewith shall it be seasoned?* You cannot salt it. This intimates that it is extremely difficult, and next to impossible, to recover an apostate, Heb. vi. 4–6. It is of no use. It is *not fit*, as dung is, *for the land*, to manure that, nor will it be the better if it be laid in the dunghill to rot. A professor of religion whose mind and manners are depraved is the most *insipid* animal that can be. It is abandoned: *Men cast it out*, they will have no more to do with it. Such scandalous professors ought to be cast out of the church, because there is danger that others will be infected by them. Our Saviour concludes this with a call to all to take notice of it, and to take warning: *He that hath ears to hear, let him hear*.

CHAPTER 15

The murmuring of the scribes and Pharisees at the grace of Christ, and the favour he showed to publicans and sinners, gave occasion for a more full discovery of that grace than perhaps otherwise we should have had in these three parables which we have in this chapter, the scope of all of which is the same, to show, not only what God had said and sworn in the Old Testament, that he had no pleasure in the death and ruin of sinners, but that he has great pleasure in their return and repentance. I. The offence which the Pharisees took at Christ, ver. 1, 2. II. His justifying himself in it, as the bringing of them to repent and reform their lives, than which there could not be a more pleasing and acceptable service done to God, which he shows in the parables, 1. Of the lost sheep that was brought home with joy, ver. 4–7. 2. Of the lost silver that was found with joy, ver. 8–10. 3. Of the lost son that had been a prodigal, but returned to his father's house, and was received with great joy, though his elder brother, like these scribes and Pharisees, was offended at it, ver. 11–32.

Verses 1–10

Here is, I. The diligent attendance of the publicans and sinners upon Christ's ministry. *Great multitudes* of Jews *went with him* (*ch.* xiv. 25), with such an assurance of admission into the kingdom of God that he found it requisite to say that to them which would shake their vain hopes. Here multitudes of *publicans* and *sinners* drew near to him, with a humble modest fear of being *rejected* by him, and to them he found it requisite to give encouragement. The *publicans* were perhaps some of them *bad men*, but they were all industriously put into an *ill name*, because of the prejudices of the Jewish nation against their office. They are sometimes ranked with *harlots* (Matt. xxi. 32); here and elsewhere with *sinners*. They drew near to him, not, as some did, for curiosity to *see him*, nor as others did, to solicit for cures, but to hear his excellent doctrine. In all our approaches to Christ we must have this in our eye, to *hear him*; to hear the instructions he gives us, and his answers to our prayers.

II. The offence which the *scribes* and *Pharisees* took at this. They murmured, *This man receiveth sinners, and eateth with them, v.* 2. 1. They were angry that *publicans* and *heathens* had the means of grace allowed them, and were encouraged to hope for pardon upon repentance. 2. They thought it inconsistent with the dignity of his character, to make himself familiar with such sort of people, and to *eat with them*. They could not, for shame, condemn him for *preaching to them*, and therefore they reproached him for *eating with them*, which was more expressly contrary to the tradition of the elders.

III. Christ's justifying himself in it, by showing that the worse these people were, the more glory would redound to God, and the more joy there would be in heaven, if by his preaching they were brought to repentance. It would be a more pleasing sight in heaven to see publicans and sinners live an orderly sort of life than to see *scribes* and *Pharisees* go on in living such a life. This he here illustrates by two parables.

1. The parable of the *lost sheep*. Something like it we had in Matt. xviii. 12. There it was designed to show the care God takes for the preservation of saints; here it is designed to show the pleasure God takes in the conversion of sinners. We have here,

(1) The case of a sinner that goes on in sinful ways. He is like a *lost sheep*, a sheep *gone astray*; he is *lost* to God; *lost* to the flock; *lost* to himself: he knows not where he is, wanders endlessly, is continually exposed to the beasts of prey, subject to frights and terrors, taken from under the shepherd's care, and wanting the green pastures; and he cannot of himself find the way back to the fold.

(2) The care the God of heaven takes of poor wandering sinners. There is a particular care to be taken of this lost sheep; and though he has a hundred sheep, yet he will not *lose* that *one*, but he goes after it, and shows abundance of care in *finding it out*. He follows it, looking about for it, until he *finds* it. God follows backsliding sinners until at length they are wrought upon to think of returning. Though he finds it *weary* and not able to bear being driven home, yet he does not leave it to perish, but *lays it on his shoulders*, and, with a great deal of tenderness and labour, brings it to the fold. God sends his Son to *seek and save that which was lost, ch.* xix. 10. Christ is said to *gather the lambs in his arms*, and carry *them in his bosom*, denoting his pity and tenderness. Here he is said to bear them

upon his shoulders; those can never perish whom he carries upon his shoulders.

(3) The pleasure that God takes in repenting returning sinners. He *lays it on his shoulders rejoicing*, and the joy is the greater because he began to be out of hope of finding it; and he *calls his friends and neighbours, saying, Rejoice with me.* Observe, he calls it *his sheep*, though a *stray*, a wandering sheep. Therefore he looks after it himself: *I have found it*; he did not send a servant, but his own Son, the great and good Shepherd, who will find what he seeks, and will be found of those that seek him not.

2. The parable of the *lost piece of silver*. (1) The *loser* is here supposed to be *a woman*. She has *ten pieces of silver*, and out of them loses only one. Notwithstanding the sinfulness and misery of the world of mankind there are nine to one, nay, in the foregoing parable there are ninety-nine to one, that retain their integrity, in whom God *is* praised, and never *was* dishonoured. (2) That which is lost is a piece of silver. The soul is *silver*, of intrinsic worth and value; not base metal, as iron or lead, but *silver*. It is *silver coin*. It is stamped with God's *image* and *superscription*. This silver was lost *in the dirt*; a soul plunged in the world is like a piece of money in the dirt; anyone would say, It is a thousand pities that it should *lie there*. (3) Here is a great deal of care and pains taken in quest of it. The woman *lights a candle, sweeps the house*, and *seeks diligently till she finds it*. This represents the various means and methods God makes use of to bring lost souls home to himself: he has *lighted the candle* of the gospel, not to show himself the way to us, but to show us the way to him; his heart is upon it, to bring lost souls to himself. (4) Here is a great deal of joy for the finding of it: *Rejoice with me, for I have found the piece which I had lost, v.* 9. Those that rejoice desire that others should rejoice with them. The pleasing surprise of finding it put her, for the present, into a kind of transport—*I have found, I have found*, is the language of joy.

3. The explication of these two parables is to the same purport (*v.* 7, 10): *There is joy in heaven, joy in the presence of the angels of God, over one sinner that repenteth*, more than *over* a great number of *just persons, who need no repentance*.

(1) The *repentance* and *conversion of sinners* on earth are *matter of joy* and rejoicing *in heaven*. It is possible that the greatest sinners may be brought to repentance. While there is life there is hope, and the worst are not to be despaired of. God will *delight* to show them mercy. There is always *joy in heaven*. God *rejoiceth in all his works*, but particularly in the works of his grace. He rejoiceth to do good to penitent sinners. He rejoiceth not only in the conversion of nations, but even over *one sinner that repenteth*, though but *one*. The good angels will be glad that mercy is shown them. The redemption of mankind was matter of joy in the presence of the angels; for they sung, *Glory to God in the highest, ch.* ii. 14.

(2) There is more joy over *one sinner that repenteth* than there is *over ninety-nine just persons, who need no repentance*. More joy for the conversion of the sinners of the Gentiles, and of those publicans that now heard Christ preach, than for all the praises and devotions, and all the *God I thank thee*, of the Pharisees, and the other self-justifying Jews, who thought that they *needed no repentance*. Christ tells them that God was more praised *in*, and pleased *with*, the penitent broken heart of one of those despised, envied sinners, than all the long prayers which the scribes and Pharisees made, who could not see anything amiss in themselves; more joy for the conversion of one such great sinner than for the regular conversion of one that had always conducted himself decently and well, and comparatively *needs no repentance*.

Not but that it is best not to go astray; but the grace of God is more manifested in the *reducing* of great sinners than in the *conducting* of those that never went astray. And many times those that have been great sinners before their conversion prove more eminently and zealously good after. They to whom much is forgiven will love much. We are moved with a more sensible joy for the recovery of what we had lost than for the continuance of what we had always enjoyed, for health *out of* sickness than for health *without* sickness. A constant course of religion may in itself be more valuable, and yet a sudden return from an evil course and way of sin may yield a more surprising pleasure.

Verses 11–32

We have here the parable of the prodigal son, the scope of which is the same with those before. But the circumstances of the parable do much more largely and fully set forth the riches of gospel grace, and it has been, and will be while the world stands, of unspeakable use to poor sinners.

I. The parable represents God as a *common Father* to all mankind. He is *our Father*, for he has the *educating* and *portioning* of us. Our Saviour hereby intimates to those proud Pharisees that these publicans and sinners, whom they thus despised, were their brethren, and therefore they ought to be glad of any kindness shown them.

II. It represents the children of men as of *different* characters. He had *two sons*, one of them a solid grave youth, *reserved* and *austere*, sober himself, but not at all *good-humoured* to those about him; such a one would adhere to his education, and not be easily drawn from it; but the other *volatile* and *mercurial*, and impatient of restraint, roving, and willing to try his fortune, and, if he fall into ill hands, likely to be a rake. Now this latter represents the publicans and sinners, and the Gentiles. The former represents the Jews in general, and particularly the Pharisees.

The *younger son* is the prodigal.

1. His *riot* and *ramble* when he was a prodigal, and the extravagances and miseries he fell into.

(1) What his request to his father was (v. 12): *He said to his father, "Father, give me"*—he might have put a little more in his mouth, and have said, *Pray give me*, or, *Sir, if you please, give me*, but he makes an imperious demand—"*give me the portion of goods that falleth to me;* that which falls to me as *my due.*" It is bad, and the beginning of worse, when men look upon God's gifts as debts. "*Give it me all* at present in possession, and I will never expect anything in *reversion*, anything *hereafter*." The great folly of sinners is being content to have *their portion in hand*, now in this lifetime to *receive their good things*. They look only at the things that are seen, and covet only a present gratification, but have no care for a future felicity. And why did he desire to have his portion in his own hands? [1] He was *weary* of his *father's government*, and was fond of liberty falsely so called. See the folly of many young men, who never think themselves their own masters till they have broken all God's bands in sunder, and, instead of them, bound themselves with the cords of their own lust. Here is the original of the apostasy of sinners from God; they will not be tied up to the rules of *God's government*; they will themselves *be as gods*, knowing no other *good and evil* than what themselves please. [2] He was willing to get *from under his father's eye*. A shyness of God, and a willingness to disbelieve his omniscience, are at the bottom of the wickedness of the wicked. [3] He was distrustful of his *father's management*. He would have his *portion of goods* himself, for he thought that his father would limit him in his present expenses, and that he did not like. [4] He was *proud of himself*, and had a *great*

conceit of his own sufficiency. He thought that if he had put his portion in his own hands he could manage it better than his father did, and make a better figure with it. There are more young people ruined by *pride* than by any one lust whatsoever.

(2) How kind his father was to him: *He divided unto them his living*. He computed what he had to dispose of between his sons, and gave the younger son *his share*, and offered the elder his; but, it should seem, he desired his father to keep it in his own hands still, and we may see what he got by it (v. 31): *All that I have is thine*. He gave the younger son what he asked. He had as much as he expected, and perhaps more. [1] Thus he might *now see his father's kindness*, how willing he was to please him and make him easy. [2] Thus he would in a little time be made to see *his own folly*, and that he was not such a wise manager for himself.

(3) How he managed himself when he had got his portion in his own hands. He set himself to spend it as fast as he could, and, in a little time he made himself a beggar: *not many days after*, v. 13. That which the younger son determined was to *be gone* presently, and, in order to that, he *gathered all together*.

Now the condition of the prodigal in this ramble of his represents to us a *sinful state*, into which man has fallen.

[1] A sinful state is a state of *departure* and *distance* from God. It is the *sinfulness* of sin that it is an apostasy from God. He *took his journey* from his father's house. Sinners are fled from God. They get as far off him as they can. The world is the *far country* in which they take up their residence. It is the misery of sinners that they are afar off from God, and are going further and further from him. What is hell itself, but being *afar off* from God?

[2] A sinful state is a *spending* state: There he *wasted his substance with riotous living* (v. 13), devoured it *with harlots* (v. 30), and in a little time *he had spent all*, v. 14. He bought fine clothes, associated with those that helped him to make an end of what he had in a little time. But this is to be applied spiritually. Wilful sinners *waste* their patrimony; for they misemploy their thoughts and all the powers of their souls, do not only bury, but embezzle; the talents they are entrusted to trade with, and the gifts of Providence, which were intended to enable them to serve God and to do good with, are made the food and fuel of their lusts. The soul that is made a drudge, either to the world or to the flesh, *wastes its substance*, and *lives riotously*.

[3] A sinful state is a *wanting* state: *When he had spent all there arose a mighty famine in that land*, and he *began to be in want*, v. 14. Wilful waste brings woeful want. Riotous living in time, perhaps in a little time, brings men to a *morsel of bread*, especially when *bad times* hasten on the consequences of *bad husbandry*. This represents the misery of *sinners*, who have thrown away *their own mercies*. These they *gave away* for the pleasure of sense, and the wealth of the world, and then are ready to perish for want of them. Sinners want necessaries for their souls; they have neither food nor raiment for them, nor any provision for hereafter. A sinful state is like a land where *famine reigns*. Sinners are *wretchedly* and *miserably poor*, and, what aggravates it, they brought themselves into that condition.

[4] A sinful state is *a vile servile state*. When this young man's riot had brought him to want his want brought him to servitude. *He went, and joined himself to a citizen of that country*, v. 15. The same wicked life that before was represented by *riotous living* is here represented by *servile living*. How did this young gentleman debase and disparage himself, when he hired himself into such a service and under such a

master as this! He *sent him into the fields*, not to feed sheep but to *feed swine*. The business of the devil's servants is to *make provision for the flesh, to fulfil the lusts thereof*, and that is no better than feeding greedy, dirty, noisy swine; and how can rational immortal souls more disgrace themselves?

[5] A sinful state is a state of *perpetual dissatisfaction. He would fain have filled his belly with the husks which the swine did eat, v.* 16. A fine pass my young master had brought himself to, to be fellow-commoner with the swine! That which sinners, when they *depart from God*, promise themselves *satisfaction in*, will certainly disappoint them; they are *labouring for that which satisfieth not*, Isa. lv. 2. Husks are food for swine, but not for men. The wealth of the world and the entertainments of sense will serve for bodies; but what are these to *precious souls*? They neither suit their nature, nor satisfy their desires, nor supply their needs.

[6] A sinful state is a state which *cannot expect relief from any creature*. This prodigal, when he would not earn his bread by *working*, took to *begging*; but *no man gave unto him*. Those who depart from God cannot be helped by any creature. In vain do we cry to the world and the flesh; they have that which will *poison* a soul, but have nothing to give it which will *feed* and *nourish* it.

[7] A sinful state is a *state of death: This my son was dead, v.* 23, 32. A sinner is not only dead in law, as he is under a sentence of death, but dead in trespasses and sins, destitute of spiritual life; no union with Christ, no living to God, and therefore *dead*. The prodigal in the *far country* was *dead* to his father and his family, and it is his own doing.

[8] A sinful state is a *lost state: This my son was lost*—lost to everything that was good—lost to his father's house. Souls that are separated from God are *lost* souls; lost as a *traveller* that is out of his way, and, if infinite mercy prevent not, will soon be lost irrecoverably.

[9] A sinful state is a state of *madness* and *frenzy*. This is intimated in that expression (*v.* 17), *when he came to himself*, which intimates that he had been *beside himself*. Surely he was so when he left his father's house, and much more so when he joined himself to the citizen of that country. Sinners, like those that are *mad*, destroy themselves with *foolish lusts*, and yet at the same time deceive themselves with foolish *hopes*.

2. We have here his *return* from this *ramble*. Now observe here,

(1) What was the *occasion* of his return and repentance. It was his *affliction*; when he was in *want*, then he *came to himself*. Afflictions, when they are sanctified by divine grace, prove happy means of turning sinners from the error of their ways. When we find the insufficiency of creatures to make us happy, and have tried all other ways of relief for our poor souls in vain, then it is time to think of returning to God. When we see what miserable comforters, what physicians of no value, all but Christ are; no *man gives unto us* what we need, then surely we shall apply ourselves to Jesus Christ.

(2) What was the *preparative* for it; it was *consideration*. He said within himself when he recovered his right mind, *How many hired servants of my father's have bread enough!* Consideration is the first step towards conversion. He considered how bad his condition was: *I perish with hunger*. Not only, "I am *hungry*," but, "*I perish with hunger*." Sinners will not come to the service of Christ till they are brought to see themselves just ready to perish in the service of sin. And though we be thus driven to Christ he will not think himself dishonoured by our being forced to him, but rather honoured by his being applied to in a desperate case.

He considered how much better it might be made if he would but return: *How many hired servants of my father's have bread enough, and to spare*, such a good house does he keep! In our *Father's house* there is bread for all his family. There is *enough* and to *spare*, enough for all, enough for each, enough and *to spare* for *charity*. There are *crumbs* that fall from his table, which many would be glad of, and thankful for. Even the *hired servants* in God's family are well provided for. The consideration of this should encourage sinners, that have gone astray from God, to think of returning to him.

(3) What was the *purpose* of it. His consideration issues, at length, in this conclusion: *I will arise, and go to my father*. Good purposes are good things, but still good performances are all in all. He determined what to do: *I will arise and go to my father*. Though he be in a *far country*, a great way off from his father's house, yet, far as it is, he will return; every step of backsliding from God must be a step back again in return to him. Observe with what resolution he speaks: "*I will arise, and go to my father;* I am resolved I will, whatever the issue be." He determined what to say. True repentance is a *rising*, and *coming* to God. But what words shall we take with us? In all our addresses to God, it is good to deliberate with ourselves beforehand what we shall say, that we may *order our cause before him*. Let us observe what he purposed to say.

First, He would confess his fault and folly: *I have sinned*. Forasmuch as we have all sinned, it behoves us to own that we have sinned. The confession of sin is required and insisted upon, as a necessary condition of peace and pardon. If we plead *not guilty*, we put ourselves upon a trial. If *guilty*, with a contrite, penitent, and obedient heart, we refer ourselves to the covenant of grace, which offers forgiveness to those that *confess their sins*.

Secondly, He would be so far from extenuating the matter that he would *lay a load* upon himself for it: I have sinned *against Heaven*, and *before thee*. Let those that are *undutiful* to their *earthly parents* think of this; they sin *against Heaven, and before God*. Offences against them are offences against God. Sin is committed in contempt of God's authority over us: *We have sinned against Heaven*. The malignity of sin aims high; it is *against Heaven*. Yet it is *impotent* malice, for we cannot hurt the heavens. Nay, it is foolish malice; what is shot *against the heavens* will return upon the head of him that shoots it. It is committed in contempt of God's eye upon us: "I have sinned *against Heaven*, and yet *before thee*."

Thirdly, He would acknowledge himself to have forfeited all the privileges of the family: *I am no more worthy to be called thy son, v.* 19. He does not deny the relation (for that was all he had to trust to), but he owns that his father might justly deny the relation. He had, at his own demand, the portion of goods that belonged to him, and had reason to expect no more. It becomes sinners to acknowledge themselves unworthy to receive any favour from God.

Fourthly, He would nevertheless sue for admission into the family, though it were into the meanest post there: "*Make me as one of thy hired servants;* that is good enough, and too good for me." If it be imposed on him as a mortification to sit with the servants, he will not only submit to it, but count it a preferment in comparison with his present state. "*Make me as a hired servant*, that I may show I love my father's house as much as ever I slighted it."

Fifthly, In all this he would have an eye to his father as a father: "*I will arise, and go to my father, and will say unto him, Father*. Eyeing God as a Father, and our Father, will be of great use in our repentance and return to him. It will make our sorrow for sin genuine, our resolutions against it strong, and encourage us to hope for pardon. God delights to be called *Father* both by penitents and petitioners.

(4) What was the performance of this purpose: *He arose, and came to his father.* His good resolve he put in execution without delay; he struck while the iron was hot. Have we said that we will arise and go? Let us immediately arise and come. He did not come halfway, and then pretend that he was tired and could get no further, but, weak and weary as he was, he made a thorough business of it.

3. We have here his reception and entertainment with his father: *He came to his father;* but was he welcome? Yes, heartily welcome. And, by the way, it is an example to parents whose children have been foolish and disobedient, if they repent, not to be harsh and severe with them, but to be governed by the wisdom that is from above, which is *gentle and easy to be entreated.* But it is chiefly designed to set forth the grace and mercy of God to poor sinners that repent and return to him, and his readiness to forgive them. Now here observe,

(1) The great love and affection wherewith the father received the son: *When he was yet a great way off his father saw him, v.* 20. He expressed his kindness before the son expressed his repentance. Even *before we call he answers;* for he knows what is in our hearts. How lively are the images presented here! [1] Here were *eyes of mercy,* and those eyes quick-sighted: *When he was yet a great way off his father saw him,* as if from the top of some high tower he had been looking that way which his son was gone, with such a thought as this, "O that I could see yonder wretched son of mine coming home!" This intimates God's desire of the conversion of sinners, and his readiness to meet them that are coming towards him. He is aware of the first inclination towards him. [2] Here were *bowels of mercy,* yearning at the sight of his son: *He had compassion.* Misery is the object of pity, even the misery of a sinner; though he has brought it upon himself, yet God compassionates. [3] Here were *feet of mercy,* and those feet quick-paced: *He ran.* The prodigal son came slowly, under a burden of shame and fear; but the tender father ran to meet him with his encouragements. [4] Here were *arms of mercy,* and those arms stretched out to embrace him: *He fell on his neck.* Though guilty and deserving to be beaten, though dirty and newly come from feeding swine, yet he thus takes him in his arms, and lays him in his bosom. Thus dear are true penitents to God, thus welcome to the Lord Jesus. [5] Here were *lips of mercy,* He *kissed him.* This kiss not only *assured* him of his *welcome,* but *sealed his pardon;* his former follies shall be all forgiven, nor is one word said by way of upbraiding.

(2) The penitent submission which the poor prodigal made to his father (*v.* 21): He *said unto him, Father, I have sinned.* As it commends the good father's kindness that he showed it before the prodigal expressed his repentance, so it commends the prodigal's repentance that he expressed it after his father had shown him so much kindness. When he had received the kiss which sealed his pardon, yet he said, *Father, I have sinned.* Even those that have received the pardon of their sins must have in their hearts a sincere contrition for it. The more we see of God's readiness to *forgive us,* the more difficult it should be to us to *forgive ourselves.*

(3) The splendid provision which this kind father made for the returning prodigal. One word we find in his purpose to say (*v.* 19) which we do not find that he did say (*v.* 21), and that was, *Make me as one of thy hired servants.* We cannot think that he forgot it, much less that he changed his mind, but his father interrupted him, prevented his saying it: "Hold, son, thou art heartily welcome, and, though

not *worthy to be called a son,* shalt be treated as a *dear son.*" He who is thus entertained at first needs not ask to be made *as a hired servant,* It is strange that here is not one word of rebuke: "You could never find the way home till beaten hither with your own rod." No, here is nothing like this; which intimates that, when God forgives the sins of true penitents, he forgets them, he remembers them no more. But this is not all; here is rich and royal provision made for him, far beyond what he did or could expect. He would have thought it sufficient if his father had but taken notice of him, and bid him go to the kitchen, and get his dinner with his servants; but God does for those who cast themselves upon his mercy, abundantly above what they are able to ask or think. The prodigal came home between hope and fear, fear of being rejected and hope of being received; but his father was not only better to him than his fears, but better to him than his hopes.

[1] He came home *in rags,* and his father not only *clothed* him, but *adorned* him. He *said to the servants, Bring forth the best robe, and put it on him.* The worst old clothes in the house might have served; but the father calls not for a *coat,* but for a *robe,* the *best robe.* "That robe, that principal robe, you know which I mean. Bring hither that robe, and put it on him; he will be ashamed to wear it, and think that it ill becomes him who comes home in such a dirty pickle, but *put it on him,* and *put a ring on his hand,* a signet-ring, with the arms of the family, in token of his being owned as a branch of the family." He came home barefoot, his feet perhaps sore with travel, and therefore, "Put *shoes on his feet.*" Thus does the grace of God provide for true penitents. *First,* The *righteousness of Christ* is the robe with which they are clothed; they *put on the Lord Jesus Christ.* A *new nature* is this *best robe;* true penitents are clothed with this. *Secondly,* The *earnest* of the Spirit is the *ring on the hand.* "*Put a ring on his hand,* to be before him a constant memorial of his father's kindness, that he may never forget it." *Thirdly,* The *preparation of the gospel of peace* is as *shoes for our feet* (Eph. vi. 15). It intimates that they shall go on cheerfully, and with resolution, in the way of religion, as a man does when he has shoes on his feet, above what he does when he is barefoot.

[2] He came home *hungry,* and his father not only *fed him,* but *feasted him* (*v.* 23): "*Bring hither the fatted calf* and *kill it,* that my son may be satisfied with the best we have." The fatted calf can never be better bestowed. It was a great change with the prodigal, who just before *would fain have filled his belly with husks.* How sweet will the supplies of the new covenant be, to those who have been *labouring in vain* for satisfaction in the creature! Now he found his own words made good, *In my father's house there is bread enough and to spare.*

(4) The great joy and rejoicing occasioned by his return. The bringing of the fatted calf was designed to be not only a *feast* for him, but a *festival* for the family: "*Let us all eat, and be merry,* for it is a good day; for *this my son was dead;* we thought that he was dead, but behold *he lives; he was lost,* we gave him up for lost, but *he is found.*" The conversion of a soul from sin to God is the raising of that soul from death to life, and the finding of that which seemed to be lost: it is a great, and wonderful, and happy change. It is such a change as that upon the face of the earth when the spring returns. The conversion of sinners is greatly pleasing to the God of heaven, and all that belong to his family ought to rejoice in it; those in heaven *do,* and those on earth *should.* It was *the father* that began the joy, and set all the rest on rejoicing. The family complied with the master: *They began to be merry.* God's children and servants ought to be affected with things as he is.

4. We have here the *repining and envying of the elder brother*, which is described by way of reproof to the scribes and Pharisees. He represents it so as not to aggravate the matter, but as allowing them still the privileges of elder brethren. Christ, when he reproved them for their faults, yet accosted them mildly, to smooth them into a good temper towards the poor publicans. But by the *elder brother* here we may understand those who are really good, and never went astray, who *comparatively* need no repentance; and to such these words in the close, *Son, thou art ever with me*, are applicable without any difficulty, but not to the scribes and Pharisees. Now concerning the elder brother, observe,

(1) How *foolish* and *fretful* he was upon occasion of his brother's reception, and how he was disgusted at it. It seems he was abroad *in the field* when his brother came, and by the time he had returned home the *mirth* was *begun: When he drew nigh to the house he heard music and dancing*, v. 25. He enquired *what these things meant* (v. 26), and was informed that his brother was come, and his father had made him a feast for his *welcome home*, and great joy there was because he had received him *safe and sound*, v. 27. It is but one word in the original, he had *received* him ὑγιαίνοντα—*in health*, well both in body and mind. He received him not only well in body, but a penitent, returned to his *right mind*, cured of his vices, else he had not been received *safe* and *sound*. Now this offended him to the highest degree: *He was angry, and would not go in* (v. 28), because he would intimate to his father that he should have kept out his younger brother. This shows what is a common fault,

[1] In men's families. Those who have always been a comfort to their parents think they should have the monopoly of their parents' favours, and are apt to be *too sharp* upon those who have transgressed.

[2] In God's family. Those who are comparatively *innocents* seldom know how to be compassionate towards those who are manifestly *penitents*. The language of such we have here, in what the *elder brother* said (v. 29, 30). First, He *boasted* of *himself* and *his own virtue* and *obedience*. *Lo, these many years do I serve thee, neither transgressed I at any time thy commandment*. It is too common for those that are better than their neighbours to boast of it. I am apt to think that this elder brother said more than was true, that he had never *transgressed his father's commands*, for then I believe he would not have been so obstinate as now he was to *his father's entreaties*. Those that have long served God, and been kept from gross sins, have a great deal to be humbly thankful for, but nothing proudly to boast of. Secondly, He *complained of his father*: *Thou never gavest me a kid, that I might make merry with my friends*. He was out of humour now, else he would not have made this complaint; for, no question, if he had asked such a thing at any time, he might have had it at the first word. The *killing of the fatted calf* put him upon making this peevish reflection. When men are *in a passion* they are apt to reflect in a way they would not if they were in their right mind. He had many a time been merry with him and the family; but his father had never given him so much as a kid, which was but a small token of love compared with the *fatted calf*. Those that think *highly* of themselves and their services are apt to think *hardly* of their master and meanly of his favours. We ought to own ourselves utterly unworthy of those mercies which God has thought fit to give us, and therefore we must not *complain*. He would have had a kid, to *make merry with his friends* abroad, whereas the *fatted calf* was given to his brother, not to *make merry with his friends* abroad, but *with the family* at home: the mirth of God's children should

be with their father and his family, and not with *any other friends*. Thirdly, He was very *ill-humoured* towards his younger brother. Some good people are apt to be overtaken in this fault, to look with disdain upon those who have not preserved their reputation so clean as they have done, though they have given very good evidence of their repentance and reformation. This is not the Spirit of Christ, but of the Pharisees. Let us observe the instances of it. 1. He *would not go in*; one house shall not hold him and his own brother, no, not his *father's house*. Though we are to shun the society of those sinners by whom we are in danger of being infected, yet we must not be shy of the company of penitent sinners, by whom we may get good. He saw that his father had *taken him in*, and yet he would not *go in* to him. We think too well of ourselves, if we cannot find in our hearts to *receive* those whom God *hath received*, and who are taken into friendship and fellowship with him. 2. He would not call him *brother*; but *this thy son*, which sounds arrogant, and not without reflection upon his father. Let us give our relations the titles that belong to them. Let the rich call the poor *brethren*, and let the innocents call the penitents so. 3. He *aggravated his brother's faults*, and made the worst of them: He *is thy son, who hath devoured thy living with harlots*. He had spent his own portion foolishly enough (whether *upon harlots* or no we are not told before, perhaps that was only the language of the elder brother's jealousy and ill will), but that he had devoured *all his father's living* was false; the father had still a good estate. Now this shows how apt we are to *make the worst* of everything, and to set it out in the blackest colours, which is not doing as we would be done by, nor as our heavenly Father does by us. 4. He *grudged* him the *kindness* that his father *showed him*: *Thou hast killed for him the fatted calf*. It is a wrong thing to *envy* penitents the grace of God. As we must not envy those that *are* the worst of sinners the gifts of common providence, so we must not envy those that *have been* the worst of sinners the gifts of covenant love upon their repentance; we must not envy them any extraordinary gift which God bestows upon them. Paul, before his conversion, had been a prodigal, yet when after his conversion he had greater measures of grace given him than the other apostles, they who were the elder brethren did not envy him his visions and revelations, nor his more extensive usefulness, but *glorified God in him*, which ought to be an example to us, as the reverse of this elder brother.

(2) Let us now see how *favourable* and *friendly* his father was in *his carriage towards him* when he was thus sour and ill-humoured. This is as surprising as the former. Methinks the mercy and grace of our God in Christ shine almost as brightly in his tender and gentle bearing with *peevish saints*, as before in his reception of prodigal sinners upon their repentance. The disciples of Christ themselves had many infirmities, and were men subject to like passions as others, yet Christ bore with them.

[1] When he would not come in, his *father came out, and entreated him*, accosted him mildly, gave him good words, and desired him to come in. He might justly have said, "If he will not come in, let him stay out. Is not the house my own? and may I not do what I please in it? Is not the fatted calf my own? and may I not do what I please with it?" No, as he went to meet the younger son, so now he goes to court the elder. This is designed to represent to us the goodness of God; how strangely gentle and winning he has been towards those that were strangely froward and provoking. It is to teach all superiors to be mild and gentle with their inferiors, even when they are in a fault and passionately justify themselves in it. Even in that case let fathers *not provoke their*

children to more wrath, and let *masters forbear threatening,* and both show all *meekness.*

[2] His father assured him that the kind entertainment he gave his younger brother was neither any reflection upon him nor should be any prejudice to him (v. 31): "*Son, thou art ever with me;* the reception of him is no rejection of thee, nor what is laid out on him any sensible diminution of what I design for thee; *all that I have is thine,* by an indefeasible title." If he had not *given him a kid to make merry with his friends,* he had allowed him to eat bread at his table continually; and it is better to be *happy with our Father* in heaven than *merry* with any *friend* we have in this world. *First,* It is the unspeakable happiness of all the children of God, that they are, and shall be, ever with him. All that he has is theirs; for, *if children, then heirs,* Rom. viii. 17. *Secondly, Therefore* we ought not to envy others God's grace to them because we shall have never the less for their sharing in it. If we be true believers, all that God is, all that he has, is *ours;* and, if others come to be true believers, all that he is, and all that he has, is theirs too, and yet we have not the less, as they that walk in the light and warmth of the sun have all the benefit they can have by it, and yet not the less for others having as much.

[3] His father gave him a good reason, *It was meet that we should make merry and be glad, v. 32.* He might have insisted upon his own authority: "It was *my will* that the family should make merry and be glad." But it does not become even those that have authority to be vouching and appealing to it upon every occasion, which does but make it cheap and common; it is better to give a convincing reason, as the father does here: *It was meet that we should make merry* for the return of a prodigal son, more than for the perseverance of a dutiful son; for, though the latter is a greater blessing to a family, yet the former is a more sensible pleasure. Any family would be much more transported with joy at the raising of a dead child to life, than for the continued life and health of many children. We do not find that the elder brother made any reply to what his father said, which intimates that he was well reconciled to his prodigal brother; and his father put him in mind that he was his brother: *This thy brother.* A good man, though he have not such a command of himself at all times as to *keep his temper,* yet will, with the grace of God, *recover his temper.*

CHAPTER 16

The scope of Christ's discourse in this chapter is to awaken and quicken us all so to manage all our possessions and enjoyments here as that they may make for us, and may not make against us, in the other world. I. If we do good with them we shall reap the benefit of it in the world to come; and this he shows in the parable of the unjust steward. The parable itself we have, ver. 1–8; the explanation and application of it, ver. 9–13; and the contempt which the Pharisees put upon the doctrine Christ preached to them, for which he sharply reproved them, adding some other weighty sayings, ver. 14–18. II. If, instead of doing good with our worldly enjoyments, we make them the food and fuel of our luxury and sensuality, and deny relief to the poor, we shall certainly perish eternally. This he shows in the other parable of the rich man and Lazarus, ver. 19–31.

Verses 1–18

We mistake if we imagine that the design of Christ's doctrine and holy religion was either to amuse us with notions of divine mysteries or to entertain us with notions of divine mercies. No, the divine revelation of both these in the gospel is intended to engage and quicken us to the practice of Christian duties, to the duty of beneficence and doing good to those who stand in need of anything that either we have or can do for them. We are but *stewards of the manifold grace of God.* It is our wisdom to think how we may make what we have in the world turn to a good account. If we would act wisely, we must be as diligent and industrious to employ our riches in the acts of piety and charity, in order to promote our future and eternal welfare, as worldly men are in laying them out to the greatest temporal profit.

I. The parable itself, in which all the children of men are represented as *stewards* of what they have in this world. Whatever we have, the property of it is God's; we have only the use of it.

1. Here is the *dishonesty* of this *steward.* He *wasted his lord's goods,* and for this he was *accused to his lord,* v. 1. We are all *liable* to the same charge. We have not made a due improvement of what God has entrusted us with in this world. That we may not be for this *judged of our Lord,* it concerns us to *judge ourselves.*

2. His *discharge* out of his place. His lord *called for him,* and said, "*How is it that I hear this of thee?*" He speaks as one sorry to find himself disappointed in him: it troubles him to hear it; but the steward cannot deny it, and therefore there is no remedy, he must make up his accounts, and be gone in a little time, v. 2. Now this is designed to teach us, (1) That we must all of us shortly be discharged from *our stewardship* in this world. Death will come, and *dismiss* us from our stewardship, others will come in our places. (2) That our discharge from our stewardship at death is *just,* and what we have deserved, for we have wasted our Lord's goods. (3) That when our stewardship is taken from us we must *give an account* of it to our Lord.

3. His *after-wisdom.* Now he began to consider, *What shall I do? v. 3.* He would have done well to have considered this before, but it is better to *consider* late than never. He must live; which way shall he have a livelihood? (1) He knows that he has not such a degree of industry in him as to get his living by work: "*I cannot dig.*" But why can he not dig? The truth is, he is *lazy.* His *cannot* is a *will not;* it is not a natural but a moral disability that he labours under. He *cannot dig,* for he was never used to it. (2) He knows that he has not such a degree of *humility* as to get his bread by begging: *To beg I am ashamed.* This was the language of his pride, as the former of his slothfulness. This steward had more reason to be ashamed of cheating his master than of begging his bread. (3) He therefore determines to make friends of his lord's debtors: "*I am resolved what to do (v. 4).* I am acquainted with my lord's tenants, have done them many a good turn, and now I will do them one more, which will so oblige them that they will bid me welcome to their houses. Till I can better dispose of myself, I will quarter upon them, and go from one good house to another." Accordingly, he sent for one, who owed his lord *a hundred measures of oil: Take thy bill,* said he, and *sit down quickly, and write fifty (v. 6);* so he reduced his debt to the one half. "*Sit down quickly,* and do it, lest we be taken treating, and suspected." He took another, who owed his lord *a hundred measures of wheat,* and bade him write *fourscore (v. 7).* See here what uncertain things our worldly possessions are; they are most so to those who have most of them, who devolve upon others all the care concerning them, and so put it into their power to *cheat them.* See also what treachery is to be found even among those in whom trust is reposed. Though this steward is turned out for dealing dishonestly, yet still he does so. So rare is it for men to mend of a fault, though they smart for it.

4. The approbation of this: *The lord commended the unjust steward, because he had done wisely, v. 8.* It may be meant of *his lord,* the lord of that servant, who yet was pleased with his ingenuity and policy for himself; but, taking it so, the latter part of the verse must be the words of *our Lord,* and therefore I think

the whole is meant of him. He does not commend him because he had done *falsely* to his master, but because he had done *wisely* for himself. Yet perhaps herein he did well for his master too, and but justly with the tenants. He knew what *hard bargains* he had *set them*, so that they could not *pay their rent*. He now, at going off, did as he ought to do both in justice and charity. He had been *all for his lord*, but now he begins to consider the tenants, that he might have *their favour* when he had lost *his lord's*. Now this forecast of his, for a comfortable subsistence in this world, shames our improvidence for another world: *The children of this world are wiser for their generation*, better consult their worldly interest and advantage, than the *children of light*, in *their generation*, that is, in the concerns of their souls and eternity. (1) The wisdom of worldly people in the concerns of this world is to be *imitated* by us in the concerns of our souls: it is their principle to improve their opportunities, to do that first which is most needful. O that we were thus wise in our spiritual affairs! (2) The children of light are commonly *outdone* by the children of this world. Not that the children of this world are *truly wise*; it is only *in their generation*. But in that they are *wiser than the children of light in theirs*. We live as if we were to be *here always* and as if there were not *another life after this*. Though as *children of the light* we cannot but see *another world* before us, yet we do not prepare for it, do not send our best effects and best affections thither, as we should.

II. The application of this parable, and the inferences drawn from it (v. 9): "*I say unto you*, you my disciples" (for to them this parable is directed, *v.* 1), "though you have but little in this world, consider how you may do good with that little." Observe,

1. What it is that our Lord Jesus here exhorts us to: "*Make to yourselves friends of the mammon of unrighteousness*." It is the wisdom of the men of this world so to manage their money as that they may have the benefit of it hereafter, and not for this present only. Now we should learn of them to make use of our money so as that we may be the better for it hereafter in another world, as they do in hopes to be the better for it hereafter in this world. And in our case, though whatever we have *are our Lord's goods*, yet, as long as we dispose of them among *our Lord's tenants* and for their advantage, it is so far from being reckoned a wrong to our Lord, that it is a duty to him as well as policy for ourselves. (1) The things of this world are the *mammon of unrighteousness*, or the false *mammon*. Riches are perishing things, and will disappoint those that raise their expectations from them. (2) Though this *mammon of unrighteousness* is not to be *trusted* for a happiness, yet it may and must be *made use of* in subserviency to our pursuit of that which is our happiness. Though we cannot find true satisfaction in it, yet we may *make to ourselves friends* with it. (3) At death we must all *fail*, ὅταν ἐκλίπητε—*when ye suffer an eclipse*. Death eclipses us. A tradesman is said to *fail* when he becomes a *bankrupt*. We must all thus fail shortly; death shuts up the shop, seals up the hand. (4) It ought to be our great concern to make it sure to ourselves, that *when we fail* at death we may be *received into everlasting habitations* in heaven. Christ is gone before, to prepare a place for those that are his, and is there ready to *receive them*. See 1 Tim. vi. 17–19, which explains this here.

2. With what arguments he presses this exhortation.
(1) If we do not make a right use of the *gifts of God's providence*, how can we expect from him the *gifts of his spiritual grace*? Our unfaithfulness in the use of them may be justly reckoned a *forfeiture* of that grace which is necessary to bring us to glory, *v.* 10–14. The riches of this world are the *less*; grace and glory are the *greater*. Now if we be unfaithful

in the less, it may justly be feared that we should be so in the gifts of God's grace, and therefore they will be denied us: *He that is faithful in that which is least is faithful also in much*, He that serves God, and does good, with his money, will serve God, and do good, with the more noble and valuable talents of wisdom and grace, but he that buries the *one talent* of this world's wealth will never improve the *five talents* of spiritual riches. The riches of this world are the *unrighteous mammon*, which is hastening from us apace, and, if we would make any advantage of it, we must bestir ourselves quickly; if we do not, how can we expect to be entrusted with spiritual riches, which are the only *true riches*? *v.* 11. Let us be convinced of this, that those are *truly* rich, and *very* rich, who are rich in *faith*, and rich *towards God*, rich in Christ, the *kingdom of God and the righteousness thereof*. If other things be added to us, by using them well we may take the faster hold of the *true riches*, and may be qualified to receive yet *more grace* from God. To a man that is *faithful in the unrighteous mammon*, he gives the *true riches*. The riches of this world are *another man's*. They are not *our own*; for they are God's. They are *another man's*; we have them from others; we use them for others; and we must shortly leave them to others. But spiritual and eternal riches are *our own inseparably*; they are a good part that will never be taken away from us. If we make Christ our own, and the promises our own, and heaven our own, we have that which we may truly call *our own*. But how can we expect God should *enrich us* with these if we do not serve him with our worldly possessions, of which we are but stewards?

(2) We have no other way to prove ourselves the servants of God than by giving up ourselves so entirely to his service as to make all our worldly gain serviceable to us in his service (*v.* 13): *No servant can serve two masters*. If a man will *love* the world, and *hold to that*, it cannot be but he will *hate God* and *despise* him. But, on the other hand, if a man will *love God*, and *adhere* to him, he will comparatively *hate* the world, and the things of the world shall be made to help him in serving God and working out his salvation. The matter is here laid plainly before us: *Ye cannot serve God and mammon*. So divided are their interests that their services can never be *compounded*.

3. We are here told what entertainment this doctrine of Christ met with among the Pharisees.
(1) They wickedly *ridiculed* him, *v.* 14. *The Pharisees, who were covetous, heard all these things*, and could not contradict him, but *they derided him*. Let us consider this as their *sin*, and the fruit of their *covetousness*, which was their reigning sin. Many that make a great profession of religion and abound in the exercise of devotion, are yet ruined by the love of the world. These covetous Pharisees could not bear to have that *touched*, which was their *Delilah*, their darling lust; for this they derided him, *they snuffled up their noses at him*, or blew their noses on him. It is an expression of the utmost scorn and disdain imaginable. They laughed at him for going so contrary to the opinion and way of the world. It is common for those to *make a jest* of the word of God who are resolved that they will not be ruled by it. Our Lord Jesus endured not only the *contradiction* of sinners, but their *contempt*. He that spoke as never man spoke was bantered and ridiculed, that his faithful ministers, whose preaching is unjustly *derided*, may not be disheartened at it. It is no disgrace to a man to be laughed at, but to deserve to be laughed at.

(2) He justly reproved them for *deceiving* themselves with the shows and colours of piety, *v.* 15. Here is,

[1] Their *specious outside*. *First*, They *justified themselves before men*; they denied whatever ill was laid to their charge. They claimed to be looked upon as men of singular sanctity and devotion: "*You are they that* make it your business to court the opinion of men, and will justify yourselves before the world; you are *notorious* for this." *Secondly*, They were *highly esteemed among men*. Men did not only *acquit* them, but *applauded* them, not only as *good men*, but as the *best of men*.

[2] Their *odious inside*, which was under the eye of God: "He *knows your heart*, and it is in his sight an *abomination*." It is folly to *justify ourselves before men*, and to think this enough to bear us out, that men *know no ill* of us; for God, who knows our hearts, knows that ill of us which no one else can know. This ought to check our value for ourselves, that *God knows our hearts*, for we have reason to abase and distrust ourselves. It is folly to judge of persons and things by the opinion of men concerning them, and to go down with the stream of vulgar estimate; for that which is *highly esteemed among men* is perhaps *an abomination in the sight of God*, who sees things as they are. There are those whom men despise and condemn who yet are accepted and approved of God, 2 Cor. x. 18.

(3) He turned from them to the publicans and sinners, as more likely to be wrought upon by his gospel than those covetous conceited Pharisees (*v.* 16): "The *law and the prophets were* indeed *until John*; but since John Baptist appeared *the kingdom of God is preached*. *Every man presses* into the gospel kingdom, Gentiles as well as Jews. It is not as the Jewish economy was, when *salvation was of the Jews*; but it is made a particular personal concern, and therefore *every man* that is convinced he has a soul to save, thrusts to get in, lest he should come short." Some give this sense of it; they derided Christ for speaking in contempt of riches, for, thought they, were there not many promises of riches and other temporal good things in the *law and the prophets?* "It is true," saith Christ, "so it was, but now that the kingdom of God is begun to be preached, blessed are the poor, and the mourners, and the persecuted. Now that the *gospel is preached* the eyes of the people are opened, they *press* with a holy violence into the kingdom of God." Those that would go to heaven must take pains, must strive against the stream, must press against the crowd that are going the contrary way.

(4) Yet still he protests against any design to invalidate the law (*v.* 17): *It is easier for heaven and earth to pass than for one tittle of the law to fail.* The moral law is confirmed and ratified; the duties enjoined by it are duties still; the sins forbidden by it are sins still. The ceremonial law is perfected in the gospel, and its shades are filled up with the gospel colours; not *one tittle* of that *fails*, for it is found printed off in the gospel. There were some things which were connived at by the law, for the preventing of greater mischiefs, the permission of which the gospel has indeed taken away, but without any detriment or disparagement to the law, as in the case of divorce (*v.* 18), which we had before, Matt. v. 32; xix. 9. His gospel is intended to strike at the bitter root of men's corrupt appetites and passions, to kill them, and pluck them up; and therefore they must not be so far *indulged* as that permission *did* indulge them, for the more they are indulged the more impetuous and headstrong they grow.

Verses 19–31

As the parable of the prodigal son set before us the grace of the gospel, so this sets before us the *wrath to come*, and is designed for our awakening. The tendency of the gospel of Christ is both to reconcile us to poverty and affliction and to arm us against temptations to worldliness and sensuality. Now this parable goes very far in prosecuting those two great intentions. This parable is not like Christ's other parables, in which spiritual things are represented by similitudes borrowed from worldly things, as those of the sower and the seed. But here the spiritual *things themselves* are represented in a narrative or description of the different state of good and bad in this world and the other. It is *matter of fact* that is true every day, that poor godly people die away out of their miseries, and go to heavenly bliss and joy; and that rich epicures, who live in luxury, and are unmerciful to the poor, die, and go into a state of insupportable torment. Is this a parable? What similitude is there in this? Our Saviour came to bring us acquainted with another world, and here he does it. In this description (for so I shall choose to call it) we may observe,

I. The different condition of a *wicked rich man*, and a *godly poor man*, in this world. The Jews of old were ready to make prosperity one of the marks of a good man so that they could hardly have any favourable thoughts of a *poor man*. This mistake Christ, upon all occasions, set himself to correct, and here very fully, where we have,

1. A wicked man, and one that will be for ever miserable, in the height of prosperity (*v.* 19): *There was a certain rich man*. From the Latin we commonly call him *Dives—a rich man*; but he has no name given him, as the poor man has. Now we are told concerning this rich man,

(1) That he was *clothed in purple and fine linen*, and that was his *adorning*. He had *fine linen* for *pleasure*, and clean, no doubt, every day; nightlinen, and day-linen. He had *purple* for *state*. He never appeared abroad but in great magnificence.

(2) He *fared sumptuously every day*. His table was furnished with all the varieties and dainties that nature and art could supply; his side-table richly adorned with plate; his servants, who waited at table, in rich liveries; and the guests at his table, no doubt, such as he thought *graced* it. Well, and what harm was there in all this? It is no sin to be rich, no sin to wear purple and fine linen, nor to keep a plentiful table, if a man's estate will afford it. Nor are we told that he got his estate by fraud, oppression, or extortion, no, nor that he was drunk, or made others drunk. [1] Christ would hereby show that a man may have a great deal of the wealth, and yet lie and perish for ever under God's wrath and curse. We cannot infer from men's living great either that God loves them *in* giving them so much, or that they love God *for* giving them so much. [2] That plenty and pleasure are very *dangerous*. This man might have been happy if he had not had great possessions and enjoyments. [3] That the indulgence of the body, and the ease and pleasure of that, are the ruin of many a soul. It is true, eating good meat and wearing good clothes are lawful; but they often become the food and fuel of pride and luxury, and so turn into sin to us. [4] That feasting ourselves and our friends, and, at the same time, forgetting the distresses of the poor and afflicted, are very provoking to God and damning to the soul.

2. Here is a godly man in the depth of adversity and distress (*v.* 20): *There was a certain beggar*, named *Lazarus*. This poor man was reduced to the last extremity, as miserable as you can suppose a man to be in this world.

(1) His body was *full of sores*, like Job. To be sick and weak in body is a great affliction; but sores are more *painful* to the patient, and more *loathsome* to those about him.

(2) He was forced to beg his bread. He was so sore and lame that he could not go himself, but was carried by some compassionate hand or other, and *laid at the rich man's gate*. Tnose that are not able to help the poor with their *purses* should help them with their *pains*; those that cannot lend them *a penny* should lend them *a hand*. Lazarus, in his distress, had nothing of his own to subsist on.

[1] His expectations from the rich man's table: *He desired to be fed with the crumbs, v.* 21. He did not look for a mess from off his table, though he ought to have had one, but would be thankful for the crumbs from under the table, nay, the leavings of his dogs. Now this is taken notice of to show, *First,* What was the distress, and what the disposition, of the poor man. He was *poor,* but he was *poor in spirit,* contentedly poor. He did not lie at the rich man's gate complaining, and bawling, but silently and modestly desiring to be *fed with the crumbs.* Here is a child of wrath and an heir of hell sitting in the house, faring sumptuously; and a child of love and an heir of heaven lying at the gate, perishing for hunger. And is men's spiritual state to be judged of then by their outward condition? *Secondly,* What was the temper of the rich man towards him. We are not told that he abused him, but it is intimated that he slighted him. Here was a *real* object of charity, and a very *moving* one, which spoke for itself; it was presented to him at *his own gate.* A *little* thing would be a *great* kindness to him, and yet he took no cognizance of his case, but let him lie there. It is not enough not to oppress and trample upon the poor; we shall be found unfaithful stewards of our Lord's goods if we do not succour and relieve them. The reason given for the most fearful doom is, *I was hungry, and you gave me no meat.* I wonder how those rich people who have read the gospel of Christ, and say that they believe it, can be so unconcerned as they often are in the necessities and miseries of the poor and afflicted.

[2] The usage he had from the dogs: *The dogs came and licked his sores.* The rich man kept a kennel of hounds, it may be, or other dogs, and these were fed to the full, when poor Lazarus could not get enough to keep him alive. Those will have a great deal to answer for hereafter that feed their dogs, but neglect the poor. Those offend God, nay, and they put a contempt upon human nature, that pamper their dogs and horses, and let the families of their poor neighbours starve. Now those dogs *came and licked the* sores of poor Lazarus, which may be taken, *First,* As an aggravation of his misery. His sores were *bloody,* which tempted the dogs to come and lick them. The dogs were like their master, and thought they fared sumptuously when they regaled themselves with human gore. Or, it may be taken, *Secondly,* as some relief to him in his misery; the master was *hard-hearted* towards him, *but* the dogs came and licked his sores, which mollified and eased them. The dogs were more kind to him that their master was.

II. The *different condition* of this *godly poor man,* and this *wicked rich man,* at and *after death.*

1. They both died (*v.* 22): The *beggar died*; the *rich man also died.* Death is the common lot of rich and poor, godly and ungodly; there they meet together. Saints die, that they may bring their sorrows to an end, and may enter upon their joys. Sinners die, that they may go to give up their account. It concerns both rich and poor to prepare for death, for it waits for them both.

2. The beggar *died first.* God often takes godly people out of the world, when he leaves the wicked to flourish still. Since he could find no other shelter or resting-place, he was *hid in the grave.*

3. The rich man *died and was buried.* Nothing is said of the interment of the poor man. They dug a hole anywhere, and tumbled his body in. But the rich man had a pompous funeral; probably he had a funeral oration in praise of him, and his generous way of living, and the good table he kept, which those would commend that had been feasted at it. How foreign is the ceremony of a funeral to the happiness of the man!

4. The beggar died and was *carried by angels into Abraham's bosom.* How much did the honour done to his soul, by this convoy of it to its rest, exceed the honour done to the rich man, by the carrying of his body with so much magnificence to its grave! (1) His soul *existed* in a state of separation from the body. It did not *die,* or *fall asleep,* with the body. (2) His soul *removed* to another world, it returned to God who gave it, to its native country. The spirit of a man goes upward. (3) Angels took care of it; it was *carried by angels.* They are ministering spirits to the heirs of salvation, not only while they live, but when they die. The soul of man, if not chained to this earth and clogged by it as unsanctified souls are, has in itself an elastic virtue, by which it *springs upward* as soon as it gets clear of the body; but Christ will not trust those that are his to that, and therefore will send special messengers to fetch them to himself. Saints shall be brought home, not only safely, but honourably. What were the bearers at the rich man's funeral, though, probably, those of the first rank, compared with Lazarus's bearers? (4) It was carried *into Abraham's bosom.* Abraham was the *father of the faithful*; and whither should the souls of the faithful be gathered but to him. He was carried *to his bosom,* that is, to feast with him. The *saints in heaven* sit *down with Abraham, and Isaac, and Jacob.* Abraham was a great and rich man, yet in heaven he does not disdain to lay poor Lazarus in his bosom. Rich saints and poor meet in heaven. *He* is laid in the bosom of Abraham, whom the rich glutton scorned to *set with the dogs of his flock.*

5. The next news you hear of the *rich man* is that *in hell he lifted up his eyes, being in torment, v.* 23. (1) His state is very miserable. *He is in hell,* in *hades,* in the state of separate souls, and there he is in *the utmost misery* and *anguish* possible. As the souls of the faithful, immediately *after they are delivered from the burden of the flesh, are in joy and felicity,* so wicked and unsanctified souls, immediately after they are fetched from the pleasures of the flesh by death, are in misery and torment endless, useless, and remediless. This *rich man* had entirely devoted himself to the pleasures of the *world of sense,* and therefore was wholly unfit for the pleasures of the *world of spirits*; to such a carnal mind as his they would indeed be no pleasure, and therefore he is of course excluded from them. (2) The misery of his state is aggravated by his knowledge of the happiness of Lazarus: He *lifts up his eyes,* and *sees Abraham afar off,* and *Lazarus in his bosom.* He now began to consider what is become of Lazarus. He does not find him where he himself is, nay, he plainly sees him afar off in the bosom of Abraham. [1] He saw *Abraham afar off.* To see Abraham we should think a pleasing sight; but to see him afar off was a tormenting sight. [2] He saw *Lazarus in his bosom.* The sight of him brought to his mind his own cruel and barbarous conduct towards him; and the sight of him in that happiness made his own misery the more grievous.

III. An account of what passed between the rich man and Abraham in the separate state.

1. The request which the rich man made to Abraham for some mitigation of his present misery, *v.* 24. See- ing Abraham afar off, *he cried to him.* He that used to *command* aloud now *begs* aloud. The songs of his

riot and revels are all turned into lamentations. Observe here,

(1) The title he gives to Abraham: *Father Abraham.* There are many in hell that can call Abraham *father.* Perhaps this rich man, in his carnal mirth, had ridiculed Abraham and the story of Abraham, as the scoffers of the latter days do; but now he gives him a title of respect, *Father Abraham.* The day is coming when wicked men will be glad to scrape acquaintance with the righteous, and to claim kindred to them, though now they slight them.

(2) The representation he makes to him of his present deplorable condition: *I am tormented in this flame.* It is the torment of his soul that he complains of, and therefore it is such a fire as will operate upon souls; and such a fire the *wrath of God* is, fastening upon a guilty conscience; such a fire horror of mind is, and the reproaches of a self-accusing self-condemning heart.

(3) His request to Abraham, in consideration of this misery: *Have mercy on me.* The day is coming when those that make light of divine mercy will beg hard for it. He that had no mercy on Lazarus, yet expects Lazarus should have mercy on him; "for," thinks he, "Lazarus is better natured than ever I was." The particular favour he begs is, *Send Lazarus, that he may dip the tip of his finger in water, and cool my tongue.* [1] Here he complains of the torment of his *tongue* particularly. The *tongue* is one of the organs of speech, and by the torment of that he is put in mind of all the wicked words that he had spoken against God and man, all his *hard speeches,* and *filthy speeches*; by his words *he is condemned,* and therefore in his tongue he is tormented. The tongue is also one of the organs of *tasting,* and therefore the torments of that will remind him of his inordinate relish of the delights of sense. [2] He desires a *drop of water to cool his tongue.* He asks as small a thing as could be asked, *a drop of water to cool his tongue for one moment.* [3] He desires that Lazarus might bring it. He *names* him, because he *knows* him, and thinks Lazarus will not be unwilling to do him this good office for old acquaintance' sake. There is a day coming when those that now hate and despise the people of God would gladly receive kindness from them.

2. The reply which Abraham gave to this request. In general, he did not grant it. See how justly this rich man is paid in his own coin. He that denied a crumb is denied a drop. Now it is said to us, *Ask, and it shall be given you;* but, if we let slip this accepted time, we may ask, and it shall not be given us.

(1) He calls him *son,* a kind and civil title. He had been a son, but a rebellious one, and now an abandoned disinherited one.

(2) He puts him in mind of what had been both his own condition and the condition of Lazarus, in their *life-time: Son, remember;* this is a cutting word. Now sinners are called upon to *remember,* but they do not, they will not. "*Son, remember* thy Creator, thy Redeemer, remember thy latter end"; but they can forget that for which they have their memories. "*Son, remember* the many warnings that were given thee, remember the fair offers made thee of eternal life and glory, which thou wouldest not accept!" But that which he is here put in mind of is, [1] That *thou in thy life-time receivedst thy good things.* He does not tell him that he had *abused* them, but that he had *received* them: "Remember what a bountiful benefactor God has been to thee; thou canst not therefore say he owes thee anything, no, not a *drop of water.* What he gave thee *thou receivedst,* and that was all. Thou hast been the grave of God's blessings, in which they were buried, not the field of them, in which they were sown. Thou receivedst *thy good things.* They were the things which thou didst choose

for *thy good things,* which were in thine eye the *best things.* Thou wast for the *good things of thy life-time,* and hadst no thought of better things in another life. The day of thy *good things* is past and gone." [2] "What *evil things Lazarus received.* Think what a large share of miseries he had in *his life-time.* Thou hadst as *much good* as could be thought to fall to the lot of so *bad a man,* and he as *much evil* as could be thought to fall to the lot of so *good a man.* He *received* his evil things; he *received* them as physic appointed for the cure of his spiritual distempers, and the cure was effected." As wicked people have *good things* in this life only, godly people have evil things only *in this life.* Now Abraham awakens his conscience to remind him how he had behaved towards Lazarus; he cannot forget that then he would not help Lazarus, and how then could he expect that Lazarus should now help him?

(3) He puts him in mind of Lazarus's present bliss, and his own misery: *Now he is comforted, and thou art tormented.* Heaven is *comfort,* and hell is *torment*: heaven is *joy,* hell is *weeping, and wailing.* Heaven will be heaven indeed to those that go thither through many and great calamities in this world. When they are fallen asleep in Christ, you may truly say, "Now *they are comforted*; now *all their tears are wiped away.*" In heaven there is everlasting consolation. And, on the other hand, hell will be hell indeed to those that go thither from the midst of the enjoyment of all the delights and pleasures of sense.

(4) He assures him that it was to no purpose to think of having any relief by the ministry of Lazarus; for (*v.* 26), *Besides all this, between us and you there is a great gulf fixed,* a great chasm. The kindest saint in heaven cannot make a visit to the congregation of the dead and damned, to comfort or relieve any there who once were their friends. "*They that would pass hence to you cannot.*" The most daring sinner in hell cannot force his way out of that prison. *They cannot pass to us that would come thence.* In this world, blessed be God, there is no gulf fixed between a state of nature and grace, but we may pass from the one to the other, from sin to God. It might have been prevented *in time,* but it cannot now be remedied *to eternity.* A stone is rolled to the door of the pit, which cannot be rolled back.

3. The further request he had to make to his father Abraham. having an opportunity of speaking to Abraham, he will improve it for his relations whom he has left behind.

(1) He begs that Lazarus might be *sent to his father's house. I pray thee therefore, father, v.* 27. Again he calls upon Abraham. Surely thou wilt be so compassionate as not to deny this. Send him back *to my father's house*; he knows well enough where it is, has been there many a time. He knows I have *five brethren* there; they will *know him,* and will regard what he saith. Let him *testify to them*; let him tell them what condition I am in. Let him warn them not to tread in my steps *lest they also come into this place of torment, v.* 28. He does not say, "Give me leave to go to them, that I may testify to them"; his going would frighten them out of their *wits*; but, "Send Lazarus, whose address will be less terrible, and yet his testimony sufficient to frighten them out of their *sins.*" Now he desired the preventing of their ruin, in tenderness to *them,* for whom he could not but retain a *natural affection.*

(2) Abraham denies him this favour too. There is no request granted in hell. Abraham leaves them to the testimony of Moses and the prophets. Here is their privilege: *They have Moses and the prophets;* and their duty: "*Let them hear them,* and mix faith with them, and that will be sufficient to keep them from this place of torment."

(3) He urges his request yet further (v. 30): *"Nay, father Abraham, they have Moses and the prophets, yet it may be hoped, if one went to them from the dead, they would repent,* that would be a more sensible conviction to them. They are used to Moses and the prophets; but this would be a *new thing,* and more startling; surely this would bring them to *repent."* Foolish men are apt to think any method of conviction better than that which God has chosen and appointed.

(4) Abraham insists upon the denial of it (v. 31): *"If they hear not Moses and the prophets, neither will they be persuaded though one rose from the dead."* The same strength of corruption that breaks through the convictions of the written word would certainly triumph over those by a witness *from the dead.* The scripture is now the ordinary way of God's making known his mind to us, and it is sufficient.

CHAPTER 17

I. Christ teaches them to take heed of giving offence, and to forgive the injuries done them (ver. 1–4), encourages them to pray for the increase of their faith (ver. 5, 6), and then teaches them humility, ver. 7–10. II. His cleansing ten lepers, and the thanks he had from one of them only, and he a Samaritan, ver. 11–19. III. His discourse with his disciples when the kingdom of God should appear, ver. 20–37.

Verses 1–10

Note, I. That the *giving of offences* is a *great sin, v.* 1, 2. We can expect no other than that offences will come. *It is* almost *impossible but that offences will come,* and therefore we are concerned to provide accordingly; but *woe to him through whom they come,* his doom will be heavy (v. 2). They perish under a load of guilt more *ponderous* than that of *millstones.* This includes a woe, 1. To persecutors who offer any injury to the least of Christ's *little ones.* 2. To seducers, who corrupt the truths of Christ, and so *trouble the minds of the disciples.* 3. To those who live scandalously, and thereby weaken the hands and sadden the hearts of God's people.

II. That the *forgiving of offences* is a *great duty* (v. 3): *Take heed to yourselves.* This may refer either to what goes before, or to what follows: *Take heed that you offend not one of these little ones.* Or, "When *your brother trespasses against you, take heed to yourselves at such a time,* lest you be put into a passion."

1. If you are permitted to *rebuke him,* you are advised to do so. Smother not the resentment, but give it vent. *Tell him his faults;* and, it may be, you will perceive that you mistook him, that it was not a *trespass against you,* but an *oversight,* and then you will beg his pardon for misunderstanding him.

2. You are commanded, upon his repentance, to forgive him: *If he repent, forgive him;* forget the injury, never think of it again. Though he do not repent, you must not therefore bear malice to him, nor meditate revenge.

3. You are to repeat this every time he repeats his trespass, v. 4. If he could be supposed to be either so negligent as to *trespass against thee seven times in a day,* and as often profess himself sorry for his fault, continue to *forgive him.* Christians should be of a forgiving spirit, willing to make the best of everybody, and they should contrive as much to show that they have forgiven an injury as others to show that they resent it.

III. That we have all need to get our *faith* strengthened, because, as that grace grows, all other graces grow. 1. The address which the disciples made to Christ, for the strengthening of their faith, v. 5. *The apostles* themselves yet acknowledged the weakness and deficiency of their faith, and saw their need of Christ's grace for the improvement of it; they said unto the Lord, *"Increase our faith."* The increase of our faith is what we should earnestly desire. They put up this prayer to Christ upon occasion of his pressing upon them the duty of forgiving injuries: *"Lord, increase our faith,* or we shall never be able to practise such a difficult duty as this." Faith in God's pardoning mercy will enable us to get over the greatest difficulties that lie in the way of our forgiving our brother. 2. The assurance Christ gave them of the wonderful efficacy of true faith (v. 6): *"If ye have faith as a grain of mustard-seed, so small* as mustard-seed, or so *sharp as mustard-seed,* so pungent, so exciting to all other graces, nothing would be too hard for you, that was fit to be done for the glory of God, yea, though it were the *transplanting of a tree* from the earth *to the sea."* As with God *nothing is impossible,* so are all *things possible to him that can believe.*

IV. That, whatever we do in the service of Christ, we must be very humble. Even the apostles themselves, who did so much more for Christ than others, must not think that they had thereby made him their debtor. 1. We are all *God's servants.* Our whole strength and our whole time are to be employed for him. 2. As God's servants, it becomes us to fill up our time with duty, we ought to make the end of one service the beginning of another. The servant that has been *ploughing,* or *feeding cattle, in the field,* when he *comes home* at night has work to do still; he must *wait at table, v.* 7, 8. When we have been *working for God,* still we must be *waiting on God.* 3. Our principal care here must be to do the duty of our relation, and leave it to our Master to give us the comfort of it. No servant expects that his master should say to him, *Go and sit down to meat;* it is time enough to do that when we have *done our day's work.* Let us be in care to finish our work, and then the reward will come in due time. 4. It is fit that Christ should be served before us: *Make ready wherewith I may sup, and afterwards thou shalt eat and drink.* 5. Christ's servants, when they are to wait upon him, must *gird themselves,* must free themselves from everything that is entangling and encumbering. We must then *gird ourselves,* to attend him. This is expected from servants, and Christ might require it from us, but he does not insist upon it. He was *among his disciples as one that served,* and came not *to be ministered unto, but to minister;* witness his washing his disciples' feet. 6. Christ's servants do not so much as merit his thanks for any service they do him: *"Does he thank that servant?"* No good works of ours can merit anything at the hand of God. 7. Whatever we do for Christ, it is no more than is our duty to do. Though we should *do all things that are commanded us,* and alas! in many things we come short of this, it is but what we are bound to by that first and great commandment of *loving God* with *all our heart and soul.* 8. The best servants of Christ must humbly acknowledge that they are *unprofitable servants.* God cannot be a *gainer* by our services, and therefore cannot be made a *debtor* by them. It becomes us therefore to call ourselves *unprofitable servants,* but to call his service a profitable service.

Verses 11–19

We have here an account of the cure of ten lepers, which we had not in any other of the evangelists. The leprosy was a disease which the Jews supposed to be, more than other diseases, a mark of God's displeasure; and therefore Christ, who came to take away sin, took particular care to cleanse the lepers that fell in his way. Christ was now in his way to Jerusalem, about the mid-way. He was now in the frontier-country, the marches that lay between Samaria and Galilee.

I. The address of these lepers to Christ. They were ten in a company; for, though they were shut out from society with others, yet those that were infected were at liberty to converse with one another. 1. They *met* Christ *as he entered into a certain village.* They did not stay till he had refreshed himself, but met him as he *entered* the town, weary as he was; and yet he did not put them off. 2. They *stood afar off.* A sense of our spiritual leprosy should make us very humble in all our approaches to Christ. Who are we, that we should draw near to him that is infinitely pure? 3. Their request was unanimous, and very importunate (v. 13): *They lifted up their voices* and cried, *Jesus, Master, have mercy on us.* Those that expect help from Christ must take him for their Master. If he be *Master,* he will be *Jesus, a Saviour.* They ask not in particular to be cured of their leprosy, but, *Have mercy on us;* and it is enough to refer ourselves to the compassions of Christ, for they *fail not.*

II. Christ sent them to *the priest,* to be *inspected* by him. He did not tell them positively that they should be *cured,* but bade them *go show themselves to the priests,* v. 14. This was a trial of their obedience. Those that expect Christ's favours must take them in his way and method. They all *went to the priest.* As the ceremonial law was yet in force, Christ took care that it should be observed.

III. *As they went, they were cleansed.* Then, we may expect God to meet us with mercy when we are found in the way of duty. If we do what we can, God will not be wanting to do that for us which we cannot. Though the means will not heal thee of themselves, God will heal thee in the diligent use of those means.

IV. One of them, and but one, *returned, to give thanks,* v. 15. When he *saw that he was healed* he *turned back* towards him who was the Author of his cure, whom he wished to have the glory of it. He appears to have been very hearty and affectionate in his thanksgivings: *With a loud voice he glorified God,* v. 13. Those that have received mercy from God should publish it to others. But he also made a particular address of thanks to Christ (v. 16): *He fell down at his feet,* and *gave him thanks.* We ought to give thanks for the favours Christ bestows upon us, and particularly for recoveries from sickness. It becomes us also to be very humble in our thanksgivings, as well as in our prayers.

V. Christ took notice of this one that had thus distinguished himself; for, it seems, he was a Samaritan whereas the rest were Jews, v. 16. The Samaritans had not the pure knowledge and worship of God among them that the Jews had, and yet it was one of them that *glorified God,* when the Jews forgot.

1. The particular notice Christ took of him, and the ingratitude of those that were sharers with him in the mercy—that he who was a *stranger* was the only one that *returned to give glory to God,* v. 17, 18. (1) How *rich* Christ is in *doing good:* Were there not *ten cleansed?* Here was a cure by *wholesale,* a whole *hospital* healed with *one* word's speaking. We shall have never the less grace for others sharing it. (2) How *poor* we are in our returns: *"Where are the nine?"* Ingratitude is a very common sin. Of the many that receive mercy from God, there are but few, very few, that *return to give thanks.* (3) How those often prove most grateful from whom it was least expected. A Samaritan gives thanks, and a Jew does not. This serves here to aggravate the ingratitude of those Jews of whom Christ speaks.

2. The great encouragement Christ gave him, v. 19. The rest had their *cure,* and had it not *revoked,* but he had his cure confirmed particularly; *Thy faith hath made thee whole.* The rest were *made whole* by the power of Christ, in compassion to their distress; but he was made whole *by his faith,* by which Christ saw him distinguished from the rest.

Verses 20–37

I. Here is the demand of the Pharisees concerning it, which occasioned this discourse. They asked *when the kingdom of God should come.* They understood, perhaps, that Christ had taught his disciples to pray for the coming of it, and they had long preached that it was *at hand.* "Now," say the Pharisees, "when will that glorious view open?"

II. Christ's reply to this demand, directed to the Pharisees first, and afterwards to his own disciples (v. 22); what he said to both, he saith to us.

1. That the kingdom of the Messiah was to be a *spiritual kingdom.* They asked *when* it would come. "You know not what you ask," saith Christ; "it may come, and you not be aware of it." For it has not an *external show,* as other kingdoms have, the advancements and revolutions of which fill the newspapers. "No," saith Christ, "it will have a silent entrance; it *cometh not with observation."* They desired to have their curiosity satisfied concerning the *time* of it. Christ will have their mistakes rectified concerning the nature of it. When Messiah the Prince comes to set up his kingdom, they shall not say, *Lo here,* or *Lo there,* as when a prince goes in progress to visit his territories. Christ will not come with all this talk; it will not be set up in this or that particular place. Those who confine Christianity and the church to this place or that party, cry, *Lo here,* or *Lo there;* so do they who make prosperity and external pomp a mark of the true church. "It has a *spiritual* influence: *The kingdom of God is within you."* It is not of this world. Its glory does not strike men's fancies, but affects their spirits, and its power is over their souls and consciences. The *kingdom of God* will not change men's outward condition, but their hearts and lives. Then it *comes* when it makes those humble, and serious, and heavenly, that were proud, and vain; and therefore look for the kingdom of God in the revolutions of the heart. The kingdom of God is *among you;* so some read it. "You enquire when it will come, and are not aware that it is already begun to be set up *in the midst of you.* It is *in your* nation, though not in your hearts." It is the folly of many curious enquirers concerning the times to come that they look for that *before them* which is already *among them.*

2. That the setting up of this kingdom was a work that would meet with a great deal of *opposition* and *interruption,* v. 22. The *disciples* thought they should carry all before them, but Christ tells them it would be otherwise: *"The days will come when you shall desire to see one of the days of the Son of man, and shall not see it.* At first, indeed, you will have wonderful success (so they had, when *thousands* were added to the church *in a day);* "but do not think it will be always so; people will grow cool to it." This looks forward to his disciples in after-ages; they must expect much disappointment. Ministers and churches will sometimes be under *outward restraints.* Then they will wish to see such days of opportunity as they have formerly enjoyed. God teaches us to know the worth of such mercies by the want of them. Sometimes they will be under *inward restraints.* Then they shall wish to see such *victorious triumphant* days as they have sometimes seen. We must not think that Christ's church and cause are lost because not always alike visible and prevailing.

3. That Christ and his kingdom are not to be looked for in this or that particular place, but his appearance will be general in all places at once (v. 23, 24): *"They will say to you, See here, or, See there. Go not after them, nor follow them.* The kingdom of God was not designed to be the glory of one people only, but to *give light to the Gentiles;* for *as the lightning that lightens out of one part under heaven, and shines* all on a sudden irresistibly *to the*

other part under heaven, so shall also the Son of man be in his day. The gospel that is to set up Christ's kingdom in the world shall *fly like lightning* through the nations. The kingdom of the Messiah is not to be a *local* thing, but is to be dispersed far and wide over the face of the whole earth." The design of the setting up of Christ's kingdom was not to make one *nation great,* but to make *all nations good*—some, at least, of all nations.

4. That the Messiah must *suffer* before he must *reign* (v. 25): "*First must he suffer many things* and *be rejected of this generation;* and, if he be thus treated, his disciples must expect no other than to *suffer* and be *rejected* too for his sake. We must go by the cross to the crown. The *Son of man must suffer many things.* Pain, and shame, and death, are those *many things.* He must be *rejected by this generation* of unbelieving Jews, before he be embraced by another generation of believing Gentiles."

5. That the setting up of the kingdom of the Messiah would introduce the destruction of the Jewish nation. Observe,

(1) How it had been with sinners formerly. Think how it was with the men of Sodom, who were *wicked, and sinners before the Lord exceedingly.* Now observe, [1] That they had *fair warning given them.* Noah was a *preacher of righteousness* to the old world; so was Lot to the Sodomites. [2] That they did not regard the warning given them. They were very secure. They were all very merry, and yet very busy too. When they should have been, as the men of Nineveh, *fasting and praying, repenting and reforming,* they were going on securely, *eating flesh,* and *drinking wine.* [3] That they continued in their security and sensuality, till the threatened judgment came. [4] That God took care for the preservation of those that were his. Noah entered *into the ark,* and there he was safe; Lot went out of Sodom, and so went out of harm's way. [5] That they were surprised with the ruin which they would not fear. The *flood came,* and destroyed all the sinners of the old world; *fire and brimstone* came, and *destroyed* all the sinners of Sodom. But that which is especially intended here is to show what a dreadful surprise destruction will be to those who are secure and sensual.

(2) How it will be with sinners still (v. 30): *Thus shall it be in the day when the Son of man is revealed.* They have warning given by Christ now, and will have it repeated to them by the apostles after him; but it will be all *in vain.* One would have thought that this discourse of our Saviour's, which was public, should have awakened them; but it did not.

6. That it ought to be the care of his disciples and followers to distinguish themselves from the unbelieving Jews in that day, and, leaving them, to flee at the signal given, according to the direction that should be given. This flight of theirs from Jerusalem must be *expeditious,* and must not be retarded by any concern about their worldly affairs (v. 31): "*He that shall be on the house-top, let him not come down, to take his stuff away.*" It will be better to leave his stuff behind him than to stay to look after it, and *perish with them that believe not.* It will be their concern to do as Lot and his family were charged to do: *Escape for thy life. Save yourselves from this untoward generation.* When they have made their escape, they must not think of returning (v. 32): "*Remember Lot's wife* and do not *look back,* as she did; be not loth to leave a place marked for destruction." Let them not *look back,* lest they should be tempted to *go back;* nay, lest that be construed a *going back in heart,* or an evidence that the heart was left behind. There would be no other way of saving their lives (v. 33): "*Whosoever shall seek to save his life,* he shall *lose it;* but whosoever is willing to venture his

life, he shall *preserve* his life, for he shall make sure of *eternal life.*"

7. That all good Christians should certainly escape, but many of them very *narrowly,* v. 34–36. When God's judgments are laying all waste, he will take an effectual course to preserve those that are his: *two in a bed, one taken and the other left.* Sooner or later it shall be made to appear that the Lord knows them that are his and them that are not.

8. That this distinguishing, dividing, discriminating work shall be done in all places, as far as the kingdom of God shall extend, v. 37. *Where, Lord?* They had enquired concerning the time, and he would not gratify their curiosity, they therefore tried him with another question: "*Where, Lord?*" The answer is proverbial: *Wheresoever the body is, thither will the eagles be gathered together.* (1) Wherever the wicked are, they shall *be found out* by the judgments of God; as wherever a dead carcase is, the birds make a prey of it. The judgments of God shall fasten upon them, as the eagles do upon the prey. (2) Wherever the godly are, who are marked for preservation, they *shall be found* happy in the enjoyment of Christ. Wherever Christ is, believers will flock to him, and meet in him, as eagles about the prey, by the instinct of the new nature. *Wherever the body is,* wherever the gospel is preached, thither will pious souls resort, there they will find Christ. Wherever Christ records his name he will meet his people, and bless them.

CHAPTER 18

I. The parable of the importunate widow, ver. 1–8. II. The parable of the Pharisee and publican, designed to teach us humiliation for sin, in prayer, ver. 9–14. III. Christ's favour to little children that were brought to him, ver. 15–17. IV. The trial of a rich man that had a mind to follow Christ, whether he loved better Christ or his riches, ver. 18–30. V. Christ's foretelling his own death and sufferings, ver. 31–34. VI. His restoring sight to a blind man, ver. 35–43.

Verses 1–8

This parable has its key hanging at the door. Christ spoke it to teach us that *men ought always to pray and not to faint,* v. 1. It supposes that all God's people are *praying* people; all God's children send to him *stately,* and upon *every emergency.* It is our privilege and honour that we *may* pray. It is our duty; we *ought to pray.* It is to be our constant work; we ought *always* to pray. We must pray, and never grow weary of praying, till it comes to be swallowed up in everlasting praise. But that which seems particularly designed here is to teach us constancy and perseverance in our requests for some spiritual mercies that we are in pursuit of, relating either to ourselves or to the church of God. When we are praying for strength against our spiritual enemies, our lusts and corruptions, we must continue instant in prayer, must pray and *not faint,* for we shall not *seek God's face in vain.*

I. Christ shows, by a parable, the *power of importunity* among men. He gives you an instance of an honest cause that succeeded before an unjust judge, not by the equity or compassionableness of it, but purely by *dint of importunity.* 1. The bad character of the judge that was in a certain city. He *neither feared God nor regarded man;* he took no care to do his duty either to God or man; he was a perfect stranger both to godliness and honour. It is not strange if those that have cast off the fear of their Creator be altogether regardless of their fellow-creatures; where no *fear of God* is no good is to be expected. Such a prevalency of irreligion and inhumanity is bad in any, but very bad in a *judge.* Instead of doing good with his power he will be in danger of doing hurt. 2. The distressed case of a poor widow. She had manifestly right on her side; but, it should seem, she tied not herself to the formalities of the law, but made personal application to the judge from day to day, still crying, *Avenge me of mine adversary*, that is, *Do me justice against mine adversary*. Magistrates are particularly charged, not only not to do *violence to the widow* (Jer. xxii. 3), but to *judge the fatherless*, and *plead for the widow* (Isa. i. 17). 3. The difficulty and discouragement she met with in her cause: *He would not for awhile*. According to his usual practice, he took no notice of her cause; for she had no bribe to give him, so that he did not at all incline to redress her grievances. 4. The gaining of her point by continually *dunning* this unjust *judge* (v. 5): "*Because this widow troubleth me* I will hear her cause, and do her justice, lest by her clamour to me she weary me; for she is resolved that she will give me no rest till it is done, and therefore I will do it, to save myself further trouble; as good at first as at last." Thus she got justice done her by continual craving.

II. He applies this for the encouragement of God's praying people.

1. He assures them that God will at length be gracious to them (v. 6): *Hear what the unjust judge saith, and shall not God avenge his own elect?* Observe,

(1) What it is that they desire and expect: that God would *avenge his own elect*. There are a people in the world that are God's people, his *own elect*. And this he has an eye to in all he does for them. God's own elect meet with a great deal of trouble and opposition in this world; there are *many adversaries*. That which is wanted and waited for is God's preserving and protecting them.

(2) What it is that is required of God's people: they must *cry day and night to him*. This he has made their duty, and to this he has promised mercy. We ought to be particular in praying against our spiritual enemies, like this importunate widow. Lord, mortify *this* corruption. Lord, arm me against *this* temptation. We ought to concern ourselves for the persecuted and oppressed churches, and to pray that God would do them justice. We must *cry* with earnestness; we must cry *day and night*; we must *wrestle with God*. God's praying people are told to *give him no rest*, Isa. lxii. 6, 7.

(3) What discouragements they may perhaps meet with in their prayers. He may *bear long with them*. He *exercises patience towards* the adversaries of his people, and he *exercises the patience of his people*,

(4) What assurance they have that mercy will come at last, though it be delayed. If this widow prevail by being importunate, much more shall God's elect prevail. [1] This widow was a *stranger*, but God's praying people are his own elect, whom he knows, and loves. [2] She was but *one*, but the praying people of God are *many*. Saints on earth besiege the throne of grace with their united prayers. [3] She came to a *judge* that bade her *keep her distance*; we come to a *Father* that bids us *come boldly* to him. [4] She came to an *unjust judge*; we come to a *righteous Father*. [5] She came to this judge purely upon her own account; but God is himself engaged in the cause which we are soliciting. [6] She had no friend to speak for her, but we have an *Advocate with the Father*, his own Son, who *ever lives to make intercession* for us. [7] She had no encouragement given her to ask; but we have a promise that it shall be given to us. [8] She could have access to the judge only at some certain times; but we may cry to God *day and night*, at all hours. [9] Her importunity was provoking to the judge, but our importunity is pleasing to God, and therefore we may hope, shall avail much, if it be an effectual fervent prayer.

2. He intimates to them that, notwithstanding this, they will begin to be weary of waiting for him (v. 8):

"*Nevertheless, when the Son of man cometh, shall he find faith on the earth?*" Now, when he comes, will he find faith on the earth? The question implies a strong negation: No, he will not; he himself foresees it.

(1) It supposes that *faith* is the great thing that Jesus Christ *looks for*. He does not ask, Is there innocency? but, *Is there faith?*

(2) It supposes that if there were faith, though ever so little, he would *find it out*.

(3) It is foretold that, when Christ comes he will find but *little faith*. [1] In general, he will find but *few good people*. Many that have the form and fashion of godliness, but few that have faith, that are sincere and honest. [2] In particular, he will find few that have *faith* concerning his coming. It intimates that Christ may, and will, delay his coming so long as that, *First*, Wicked people will begin to *defy it*, and his delay will harden them in their wickedness. *Secondly*, Even his own people will begin to *despair* of it. But this is our comfort, that, when the time appointed comes, it will appear that the unbelief of man has not made the promise of God of no effect.

Verses 9–14

The scope of this parable likewise is prefixed to it. He designed it for the conviction of some who *trusted in themselves that they were righteous, and despised others*. 1. They were such as had a great conceit of themselves; they thought themselves as holy as they needed to be, and holier than all their neighbours. 2. They had a confidence in themselves before God. They *trusted in themselves as being righteous*; they thought they had made God their debtor. 3. They despised others. This is called a *parable*, though the e be nothing of similitude in it. It is matter of fact every day.

I. Here are both these addressing themselves to the duty of prayer at the same place and time (v. 10): *Two men went up into the temple to pray*. It was not the hour of public prayer, but they went thither to offer up their personal devotions. The *Pharisee* and the *publican* both went to *the temple to pray*. Among the worshippers of God there is a mixture of good and bad. The Pharisee, proud as he was, could not think himself above prayer; nor could the publican, humble as he was, think himself shut out from the benefit of it. The Pharisee went *to the temple* to pray because it was a *public* place, and therefore he should have many eyes upon him. The character Christ gave of the Pharisees, that *all their works they did to be seen of men*, gives us occasion for this suspicion. There are many whom we see *every day* at the temple, whom, it is to be feared, we shall not see in the great day at Christ's right hand. The Pharisee came to the temple upon a *compliment*, the publican upon business; the Pharisee to make his appearance, the publican to make his request. God sees with what disposition and design we come to wait upon him.

II. Here is the Pharisee's address to God (for a prayer I cannot call it): He *stood* and *prayed thus with himself* (v. 11, 12); *standing by himself, he prayed thus*, so some read it; he was wholly intent upon himself, had nothing in his eye but *self*, not God's glory. That which he is here supposed to say is that which shows,

1. That he *trusted to himself that he was righteous*. A great many good things he said of himself, which we will suppose to be true. He was not an *extortioner*. He was not *unjust* in any of his dealings; he did no man any wrong; he was *no adulterer*. Yet this was not all: he *fasted twice in the week*. Thus he glorified God with his body: yet that was not all; he *gave tithes of all that he possessed*, and so glorified God with his worldly estate. Yet he was not accepted; and why was he not? (1) His giving God thanks for this seems to be a mere formality. He does not say,

By the grace of God I am what I am, as Paul did, but turns it off with a slight, *God, I thank thee.* (2) He makes his boast of this as if all his business to the temple was to tell God Almighty how very good he was. (3) He *trusted* to it as a righteousness. (4) Here is not one word of prayer in all he saith. He went *up to the temple to pray,* but forgot his errand. He thought he had need of nothing, no, not of the favour and grace of God, which, it would seem, he did not think worth asking.

2. That he *despised others.* (1) He thought meanly of all mankind but himself: *I thank thee that I am not as other men are.* We may have reason to thank God that we are not as *some men* are, but to speak as if *we* only were good, is to judge by wholesale. (2) He thought meanly in a particular manner of this publican. He knew that he was a publican, and therefore very uncharitably concluded that he was an *extortioner, unjust,* and all that is naught. Suppose it had been so, what business had he to take notice of it? Could not he *say his prayers* without reproaching his neighbours? And was he as much pleased with the publican's badness as with his own goodness?

III. Here is the publican's address to God, which was the reverse of the Pharisee's, as full of *humility* and *humiliation* as his was of *pride* and *ostentation;* as full of *repentance* for sin, and *desire* towards God, as his was of *confidence* in *himself.*

1. He expressed his repentance and humility in *what he did.* (1) He *stood afar off.* The publican *kept at a distance* under a sense of unworthiness to draw near to God. Hereby he owned that God might justly *behold him afar off,* and that it was a great favour that God was pleased to admit him *thus nigh.* (2) He *would not lift up so much as his eyes to heaven.* He did *lift up his heart* to God in the heavens, in *holy desires,* but, through prevailing shame and humiliation, he did not lift up his eyes in *holy confidence* and *courage.* The dejection of his looks is an indication of the dejection of his mind at the thought of sin. (3) He *smote upon his breast.* The sinner's heart first smites him in a penitent rebuke. Sinner, what hast thou done? And then he smites his heart with penitent remorse: *O wretched man that I am!*

2. He expressed it *in what he said.* His prayer was *short.* Sighs and groans swallowed up his words; but what he said was to the purpose: *God, be merciful to me a sinner.* And blessed be God that we have this prayer upon record as an answered prayer. (1) He owns himself *a sinner* by nature, by practice, guilty before God. The Pharisee denies himself to be a *sinner.* But the publican gives himself no other character than that of a *sinner.* (2) He has no dependence but upon the *mercy of God.* The Pharisee had insisted upon the *merit* of his fastings and tithes; but the poor publican disclaims all thought of merit, and flies to mercy as his city of refuge. "Justice condemns me; nothing will save me but mercy, mercy." (3) He earnestly prays for the benefit of that mercy: *"O God, be merciful,* be *propitious, to me."* He comes as a beggar for an alms, when he is ready to perish for hunger. Probably he repeated this prayer with renewed affections, but still this was the burden of the song: *God, be merciful to me a sinner.*

IV. Here is the publican's *acceptance with God.* There were those who would cry up the Pharisee, and who would look with contempt upon this sneaking whining publican. But our Lord Jesus assures us that this poor, penitent, broken-hearted publican *went to his house justified, rather than the other.* The Pharisee thought that if one of them must be justified, and not the other, certainly it must be he rather than the publican. "No," saith Christ, *"I tell you* it is the publican rather than the Pharisee." The proud Pharisee goes away rejected of God; he is *not justified.* He is not accepted as righteous in God's sight, because he is so righteous in his own sight; but the publican obtains the remission of his sins, and he whom the Pharisee would not set *with the dogs of his flock* God sets with the *children of his family.* Proud men, who *exalt themselves,* are *rivals with God,* and therefore *they shall* certainly be *abased.* Humble men, who *abase themselves,* are *subject to God,* and they shall be *exalted.* See how the punishment answers the sin: *He that exalteth himself shall be abased.* See how the recompense answers the duty: *He that humbles himself shall be exalted.* See also the power of God's grace in bringing good out of evil; the publican had been a great sinner, and out of the greatness of his sin was brought the greatness of his repentance. It was good that the Pharisee was no extortioner, nor unjust; but the devil made him proud of this, to his ruin.

Verses 15–17

1. Those who are themselves blessed in Christ should desire to have their children also blessed in him. They brought to him *infants,* very young, not able to go, sucking children, as some think. None are too little, too young, to bring to Christ. 2. One gracious touch of Christ's will make our children happy. They *brought infants to him, that he might touch them.* 3. It is no strange thing for those who make their application to Jesus Christ, for themselves or for their children, to meet with discouragement: *When the disciples saw it* they *rebuked them.* 4. Many whom the disciples rebuke the Master invites: *Jesus called them unto him.* 5. It is the mind of Christ that *little children* should be brought to him: *"Suffer little children to come to me, and forbid them not;* let nothing be done to hinder them, for they shall be as welcome as any." 6. The children of those who belong to the kingdom of God do likewise belong to that kingdom, as the children of freemen are freemen. 7. Those grown people are most welcome to him who have in them most of the disposition of children (*v.* 17): *Whosoever shall not receive the kingdom of God as a little child,* that is, receive the benefits of it with humility and thankfulness, gladly owning himself indebted to free grace for them; unless a man be brought to this self-denying frame he shall *in no wise enter* into that kingdom.

Verses 18–30

I. Christ's discourse with a ruler, that had a good mind to be directed by him in the way to heaven.

1. Luke takes notice of it that he was a *ruler.* Few of the rulers had any esteem for Christ, but here was one that had.

2. The great thing we are everyone of us concerned to enquire after is, *what we shall do to inherit eternal life.*

3. Those who would inherit eternal life must apply themselves to Jesus Christ as their *Master,* their *teaching* Master, and their *ruling* Master. There is no learning the way to heaven but in the school of Christ.

4. Those who come to Christ as their Master must believe him to have not only a *divine mission,* but a *divine goodness.* *"Why callest thou me good? Thou knowest there is none good but one, that is, God."*

5. Our Master, Christ himself, has not altered the way to heaven from what it was before his coming, but has only made it more plain, and easy, and comfortable. *Thou knowest the commandments.* Wouldest thou inherit eternal life? Govern thyself by the commandments.

6. The duties of the second table must be conscientiously observed. Nor is it enough to keep ourselves free from the gross violations of these commandments, but we must *know these commandments* in their extent and spiritual nature.

7. Men think themselves *innocent* because they are *ignorant*; so this ruler did. He said, *All these have I kept from my youth up*, v. 21. He boasts that he began *early* in a course of virtue, that he had continued in it to this day, and that he had not in any instance transgressed. Had he been acquainted with the nature of the divine law, and with the workings of his own heart,—had he been but Christ's disciple awhile, he would have said quite the contrary: *"All these have* I broken from my youth up."

8. The great things are how we stand affected to Christ and to our brethren, to this world and to the other. If he have a true *affection to Christ*, he will *come and follow him* whatever it cost him. None shall inherit eternal life who are not willing to follow the Lamb whithersoever he goes. If he have a true *affection to his brethren*, he will *distribute to the poor*. If he think meanly of *this world* he will not stick at *selling what he has* for the relief of God's poor. If he think highly of the other world, he will desire no more than to have *treasure in heaven*.

9. There are many that have a great deal in them that is very commendable, and yet they perish *for lack of some one thing*; so this *ruler* here; he broke with Christ upon this, which would part between him and his estate.

10. Many that are loth to leave Christ, yet do leave him. Their corruptions carry the day at last. If one must be quitted, it shall be their God, not their worldly gain.

II. Christ's discourse with his disciples upon this occasion, in which we may observe, 1. Riches are a great hindrance to many in the way to heaven. He *saw that he was very sorrowful*, and was sorry for him; but thence he infers, *How hardly shall they that have riches enter into the kingdom of God! v.* 24. Having a great estate, it had a great influence upon him, and he chose rather to take his leave of Christ than to lay himself under an obligation to dispose of his estate in charitable uses. Christ asserts the difficulty of the salvation of rich people very emphatically: *It is easier for a camel to go through a needle's eye than for a rich man to enter into the kingdom of God, v.* 25. 2. It is really very hard for any to get to heaven. If we must *sell all*, or break with Christ, *who then can be saved? v.* 26. They do not find fault with what Christ required as hard and unreasonable. But they know how closely the hearts of most men cleave to this world, and are ready to despair of their being ever brought to this, 3. There are such difficulties in the way of our salvation as could never be got over but by that grace of God which is almighty. The *things which are impossible with men*, these things are *possible with God*. His grace can work upon the soul, so as to alter the bent and bias of it, and give it a contrary ply. 4. There is an aptness in us to speak too much of what we have left and lost for Christ. This appears in Peter: *Lo we have left all, and followed thee, v.* 28. When it came in his way, he could not forbear magnifying his own and his brethren's affection to Christ, in *quitting* all to follow him. 5. Whatever we have left for Christ, it shall without fail be abundantly made up to us in this world and that to come (*v.* 29, 30): *No man has left the comfort of his estate or relations for the kingdom of God's sake, who shall not receive manifold more in this present time*, in the pleasures of communion with God and of a good conscience, advantages which will abundantly countervail all their losses. In the world to come they *shall receive life everlasting*, which is the thing that the ruler seemed to have his eye and heart upon.

Verses 31–34

I. The notice Christ gave to his disciples of his sufferings and death approaching, and of the glorious issue of them. Two things are here which we had not in the other evangelists:—1. The *sufferings* of Christ are here spoken of as the *fulfilling of the scriptures. All things that are written by the prophets concerning the Son of man shall be accomplished.* This proves that the scriptures are the *word* of God, for they had their exact and full accomplishment; and that Jesus Christ was *sent of God*, for they had their accomplishment *in him*. This makes the *offence of the cross to cease*, and puts an honour upon it. *Thus it was written, and thus it behoved Christ to suffer.* 2. The ignominy and disgrace done to Christ in his sufferings are here most insisted upon. The other evangelists had said that he should be *mocked*; but here it is added, *He shall be spitefully treated*, shall have all possible reproach put upon him. But here, as always, when Christ spoke of his sufferings and death, he foretold his resurrection as that which took off both the terror and reproach of his sufferings: *The third day he shall rise again.*

II. The confusion that the disciples were hereby put into. This was so contrary to the notions they had had of the Messiah and his kingdom that *they understood none of these things, v.* 34. Their prejudices were so strong that they *would not* understand them literally, and they *could not* understand them otherwise, so that they did not understand them at all. This saying was *hidden from them*, they could not receive it. They were so intent upon those prophecies that spoke of his glory that they overlooked those that spoke of his *sufferings. Therefore* it is that people run into mistakes, because they *read their Bibles by the halves*, and are as partial in the prophets as they are *in the law.* Thus now we are too apt, in reading, the prophecies that are yet to be fulfilled, to have our expectations raised of the glorious state of the church in the latter days. But we overlook its wilderness sackcloth state, and are willing to fancy that is over.

Verses 35–43

Christ came not only to bring *light* to a *dark* world, and so to set before us the *objects* we are to have in view, but also to give *sight* to blind *souls*, to enable them to view those objects. We have now an account of one to whom he *gave sight* near Jericho. Mark gives us an account of one, and names him, whom he cured *as he went out of Jericho*, Mark x. 46. Matthew speaks of two whom he cured *as they departed* from Jericho, Matt. xx. 30. Luke says it was *when he was near to Jericho*.

I. This poor blind man *sat by the wayside, begging, v.* 35. It seems, he was not only *blind*, but *poor*; the fitter emblem of the world of mankind which Christ came to heal and save. He sat begging, for he was blind, and could not work for his living. Such objects of charity *by the wayside* ought not to be overlooked by us. Christ here cast a favourable eye upon a *common beggar.*

II. Hearing the noise of a multitude passing by, he asked *what it meant, v.* 36. This we had not before. It teaches us that it is good to be *inquisitive*, and that those who are so some time or other find the benefit of it. Those who want their *sight* should make so much the better use of their *hearing*, and, when they cannot see with their own eyes, should, by *asking questions*, make use of other people's eyes. So this blind man did, and by that means came to understand that Jesus of Nazareth *passed by, v.* 37.

III. His prayer has in it a great deal both of faith and fervency: *Jesus, thou Son of David, have mercy on me, v.* 38. He believes he is able to help and succour him, and earnestly begs his favour: "*Have mercy on me." Have mercy on us;* for Christ's mercy includes all.

IV. Those who are in good earnest for Christ's favours and blessings will not be put by from the pursuit of them, though they meet with opposition and rebuke. They who went along chid him as troublesome to the Master, noisy and impertinent, and bade him *hold his peace*. The check given him was but as a dam to a full stream, which makes it swell so much the more: he *cried the louder, Thou Son of David, have mercy on me*.

V. Christ encourages poor beggars and invites them to come to him: *He commanded him to be brought to him*. Christ has more tenderness and compassion for distressed supplicants than any of his followers have. Those who had checked him must now lend him their hands to lead him to Christ.

VI. Though Christ knows all our wants, he will know them from us (*v.* 41): *What wilt thou that I shall do unto thee?* This man poured out his soul before Christ, when he said, *Lord, that I may receive my sight.*

VII. The prayer of faith shall not be in vain (*v.* 42); Christ said, *Receive thy sight, thy faith hath saved thee*. True faith will produce fervency in prayer, and both together will fetch in abundance of the fruits of Christ's favour.

VIII. The *grace of Christ* ought to be thankfully acknowledged, *v.* 43. 1. The poor beggar himself, that had his sight restored, *followed Christ, glorifying God*. Those whom he healed *pleased him* best when they *praised God*, as those shall *please God* best who *praise Christ* and do him honour. 2. The *people that saw it* could not forbear *giving praise to God*. We must give praise to God for his mercies to others as well as for mercies to ourselves.

Chapter 19

I. The conversion of Zaccheus the publican at Jericho, ver. 1–10. II. The parable of the pounds which the king entrusted with his servants, and of his rebellious citizens, ver. 11–27. III. Christ's riding in triumph into Jerusalem; and his lamentation in prospect of the ruin of that city, ver. 28–44. IV. His teaching in the temple, and casting the buyers and sellers out of it, ver. 45–48.

Verses 1–10

Many, no doubt, were converted to the faith of Christ of whom no account is kept in the gospels; but the conversion of some, whose case had something in it extraordinary, is recorded, as this of Zaccheus. Christ passed through Jericho, *v.* 1. This city was built under a curse, yet Christ honoured it with his presence, for the gospel *takes away the curse*.

I. Who, and what, this Zaccheus was. His name bespeaks him a Jew. 1. His calling, and the post he was in: *He was the chief among the publicans*. Here was one that was *chief* of the publicans, that enquired after him. God has his remnant among all sorts. Christ came to save even the *chief of sinners*, and therefore even the *chief of publicans*. 2. His circumstances in the world were very considerable: *He was rich*. Christ had lately shown how *hard* it is for *rich people to enter into the kingdom of God*, yet presently produces an instance of one rich man that had been lost, and was found, and that not as the prodigal by being reduced to want.

II. How he came in Christ's way. 1. He had a great *curiosity to see Jesus, v.* 3. It is natural to us to come in sight, if we can, of those whose fame has filled our ears; at least, we shall be able to say hereafter that we have seen such and such *great men*. We should now *seek to see Jesus* with an eye of faith, to see *who he is; We would see Jesus*. 2. He could not get his curiosity gratified in this matter because he was *little*, and the crowd was *great*. Christ did not study to *show himself*. As *one of us*, he was *lost in a crowd*. Many that are little of stature have large souls, and are lively in spirit. 3. Because he would not disappoint his curiosity he *forgot his gravity*, and *ran before*, like a boy, and *climbed up into a sycamore-tree, to see him*. Those that sincerely desire

a sight of Christ will use the proper means for gaining a sight of him. Those that find themselves *little* must take all the advantages they can get to *raise themselves* to a sight of Christ. Let not dwarfs despair, with good help, by aiming high to reach high.

III. The notice Christ took of him, the call he gave him to a further acquaintance (*v.* 5), and the efficacy of that call, *v.* 6. 1. Christ *invited himself* to Zaccheus's house. Christ *looked* up into the tree, and *saw* Zaccheus. He came to look upon Christ, but little thought of being taken notice of by Christ. See how Christ *prevented* him with the blessings of his goodness, and *outdid* his expectations; and see how he *encouraged* very weak beginnings. He that had a mind to know Christ shall be *known of him*; he that only courted to see him shall be admitted to converse with him. And sometimes those that come to hear the word of Christ, as Zaccheus did, only for curiosity, have their consciences awakened, and their hearts changed. Christ called him *by name, Zaccheus*. He bade him *make haste, and come down*. Zaccheus must not hesitate, but hasten. He must *come down*, for Christ intends this day to *bait at his house*, and *stay* an hour or two with him. 2. Zaccheus was *overjoyed* to have such an honour put upon his house (*v.* 6): *He made haste, and came down, and received him joyfully;* and his receiving him *into his house* was an indication and token of his receiving him *into his heart*. How often has Christ said to us, *Open to me*, when we have made excuses! Zaccheus's forwardness to receive Christ will shame us.

IV. The offence which the people took. Those narrow-souled censorious Jews *murmured*, saying that he was *gone to be a guest with a man that is a sinner*; and were not they themselves sinful men? Was it not Christ's errand to seek and save *men* that are *sinners*? Now this was very unjust to blame Christ for going to *his house*: 1. Though he was a *publican*, and many of the publicans were *bad men*, it did not therefore follow that they were *all so*. We must take heed of condemning men in the lump, for at God's bar every man will be judged as he is. 2. Though he *had been a sinner*, it did not therefore follow that he was now as bad as he had been. God allows room for repentance, and so must we. 3. Though he was *now a sinner*, they ought not to blame Christ for going to him. Whither should the physician go but to the sick?

V. The proofs which Zaccheus gave publicly that he was now a *penitent, v.* 8. By his *good works* he will evidence the *sincerity* of his *faith* and *repentance*. He *stood*, which denotes his saying it deliberately and with solemnity, in the nature of a vow to God. He addressed himself to Christ in it, not to the people, but to the Lord. He makes it appear that there is a change *in his heart* (and that is repentance), for there is a change in his way.

1. Zaccheus had a good estate. He resolves that for the future he will be all towards God, and do good to others with it: *Behold, Lord, the half of my goods I give to the poor*. "I *do* give it now," saith Zaccheus; "though hitherto I have been uncharitable to the poor, now I will relieve them, and give so much the more for having neglected the duty so long, even the *half of my goods*." Zaccheus would give one moiety to the poor, which would oblige him to retrench all his extravagant expenses. This he mentions here as a fruit of his repentance.

2. Zaccheus was conscious to himself that he had not gotten all he had honestly and fairly. He promises to make restitution: "If *I have taken anything from any man by false accusation*, exacting more than was appointed, I promise to restore him *four-fold*." (1) He seems plainly to own that he had *done wrong*. True penitents will own themselves not only in general guilty before God, but will particularly reflect upon

that which, by reason of their business and employment in the world, has most easily beset them. (2) He admits that he had done wrong *by false accusation*. They had the ear of the government, which gave them an opportunity of gratifying their revenge if they bore a man an ill will. (3) He promises to restore *four-fold*. He does not say, "If I be sued, and compelled to it, I will make restitution" (some are *honest* when they cannot help it); but he will do it *voluntarily*. Those who are convinced of having done wrong cannot evidence the sincerity of their repentance but by *making restitution*. He does not think that his giving half his estate to the poor will atone for the wrong he has done. It is no charity, but hypocrisy, to give that which is *none of our own*; and we are not to reckon that our own which we have not come honestly by.

VI. Christ's *approbation* and *acceptance* of Zaccheus's conversion, *v.* 9, 10.

1. Zaccheus is declared to be now a *happy man. This day is salvation come to this house.* Now that he is *converted* he is in effect *saved.* Christ is come *to his house,* and, where Christ comes, he brings salvation along with him. Yet this is not all. Salvation this day *comes to his house.* (1) When Zaccheus becomes a convert, he will be, more than he had been, a *blessing to his house.* He will bring the means of grace and salvation to his house. He that is charitable to the poor does a kindness to his own house, and brings a blessing upon it. (2) When Zaccheus is brought to Christ himself his *family* also become related to Christ, and so *salvation comes to his house,* for that he is *a son of Abraham,* that *blessing* of Abraham which comes upon the publicans, *upon the Gentiles,* through faith, that God will be a God *to them and to their children.* Zaccheus is by birth a son of Abraham, but, being a publican, he was deemed a heathen. Being a true penitent, he is become as good a son of Abraham as if he had never been a publican.

2. What Christ had done was consonant to the great design and intention of his coming into the world, *v.* 10. With the same argument he had before justified his conversing with publicans, Matt. ix. 13. There he pleaded that he came to *call sinners to repentance;* now that he came to *seek and save that which was lost.* (1) The *deplorable case* of the *sons of men:* they were *lost.* The whole world of mankind, by the fall, is become a *lost world:* as a traveller is lost when he has missed his way in a wilderness, as a sick man is lost when his disease is incurable. (2) The *gracious design* of the *Son of God:* he came to *seek and save,* to seek in order to saving. He came from heaven to earth (a long journey), to *seek* that which was *lost* (which had *wandered and gone astray*), and to bring it back (Matt. xviii. 11, 12), and to *save* that which was lost, which was perishing. Christ undertook the cause when it was given up for *lost.* Christ *came* into this lost world to seek and save it. His design was to *save.* In prosecution of that design, he *sought,* took all probable means to effect that salvation. He seeks those that sought him not, and asked not for him, as Zaccheus here.

Verses 11–27

Our Lord Jesus is now upon his way to Jerusalem, to his last passover.

I. How the expectations of his friends were *raised* upon this occasion: *They thought that the kingdom of God would immediately appear, v.* 11. The Pharisees expected it about this time (*ch.* xvii. 20), and, it seems, so did Christ's own disciples. The disciples thought that their Master would introduce it, but with temporal pomp and power. Jerusalem, they concluded, must be the seat of his kingdom, and therefore, now that he is going directly thither, they doubt not but in a little time to see him upon the throne there. Even good men are subject to mistakes concerning the kingdom of Christ.

II. How their expectations were *checked,* and the mistakes *rectified;* and this he does in three things:—

1. They expected that he should appear in his glory now *presently,* but he tells them that he must not be publicly installed in his kingdom for a great while yet. He is like *a certain nobleman,* he *goes into a far country, to receive for himself a kingdom.* He must receive the kingdom, and then *return.* Christ returned when the Spirit was poured out, when Jerusalem was destroyed. But his chief return here meant is that at the great day, of which we are yet in expectation.

2. They expected that his apostles and immediate attendants should be advanced to dignity and honour, that they should all be made princes and peers, privy-counsellors and judges, and have all the pomp and preferments of the court and of the town. But Christ here tells them that, instead of this, he designed them to be *men of business;* they must expect no other preferment in this world than that of the trading end of the town; he would set them up with a stock under their hands, that they might employ it themselves, in serving him and the interest of his kingdom among men. That is the true honour of a Christian and a minister which will enable us to look upon all temporal honours with a holy contempt. The apostles had dreamed of *sitting on his right hand and on his left in his kingdom,* and were pleasing themselves with this dream; but Christ tells them that which would fill them with serious thoughts, instead of those *aspiring* ones.

(1) They have a *great work* to do now. Their Master leaves them, and, at parting, he gives each of them a *pound.* This signifies the same thing with the talents in the parable that is parallel to this (Matt. xxv). But perhaps it is in the parable thus represented to make them the more humble; their honour in this world is only that of *traders,* and that not of first-rate merchants. He gave these pounds to his servants, with this charge: *Occupy till I come.* Or, as it might much better be translated, *Trade till I come—Be busy.* So the word properly signifies. "Now," saith he, "mind your business, and make a business of it; set about it in good earnest, and stick to it." All Christians have *business* to do for Christ in this world, and ministers especially; the former were not *baptized,* nor the latter *ordained, to be idle.* Those that are called to business for Christ he furnishes with gifts necessary for their business; and, on the other hand, from those to whom he gives power he expects service. He delivers the *pounds* with this charge, Go work, go trade. We must continue to mind our business *till our Master comes.*

(2) They have a *great account* to make shortly. These servants are *called to him that he might know what every man had gained by trading.* They that trade diligently and faithfully in the service of Christ shall be *gainers.* Many a labouring tradesman has been a loser; but those that trade for Christ shall be *gainers.* The conversion of souls is the *winning* of them; every true convert is clear gain to Jesus Christ. Ministers are but factors for him, and to him they must give account what fish they have enclosed in the gospel-net, that is, what they have *gained by trading.*

First, The *good account* which was given by *some* of the servants, and the master's approbation of them. Two such are instanced, *v.* 16, 19. 1. They had both made considerable improvements, but not both *alike;* one had gained *ten pounds* by his trading, and another *five.* All that are alike *faithful* are not alike *successful.* And perhaps, though they were both faithful, one of them took more pains, and applied himself more closely to his business, than the other, and sped accordingly. 2. They both acknowledged their obligations to their Master: Lord, it is not *my* industry, but *thy* pound, that has gained *ten pounds*. God must have all the glory of all our gains. 3. They were both commended for their fidelity and industry: *Well done, thou good servant, v.* 17. And to the other he *said likewise, v.* 19. If he says *Well done*, the matter is not great who says otherwise. 4. They were *preferred* in proportion to the improvement they had made: "*Because thou hast been faithful in a very little, have thou authority over ten cities.*" Those are in a fair way to rise who are content to begin low. Two things are hereby promised the apostles: (1) That when they have taken pains to *plant* many churches they shall have great respect paid them, and have a great interest in the love and esteem of good Christians. (2) That, when they have served their generation, according to the will of Christ, in the other world they shall reign as kings with Christ. The happiness of heaven will be a much greater advancement to a good minister or Christian than it would be to a poor tradesman to be made governor of ten cities. He that had gained but *five pounds* had dominion over *five cities*. There are *degrees of glory* in heaven; every vessel will be alike *full*, but not alike *large*. And the degrees of glory there will be according to the degrees of usefulness here.

Secondly, The *bad account* that was given by *one* of them, and the sentence passed upon him, *v.* 20, &c. 1. He owned that he had not *traded* with the pound with which he had been entrusted (*v.* 20): "*Lord, behold, here is thy pound;* it is true, I have not made it *more*, but withal I have not made it *less*; I have kept it safely *laid up in a napkin*." This represents the carelessness of those who have gifts, but never lay out themselves to do good with them. It is all one to them whether the interests of Christ's kingdom sink or swim, go backward or forward; for their parts, they will take no care about it. Those are the servants that lay up their pound *in a napkin* who think it enough to say that they have done no hurt in the world, but *did no good*. 2. He justified himself with a plea that made the matter worse and not better (*v.* 21): *I feared thee, because thou art an austere man. Austere* is the Greek word itself: a *sharp* man: *Thou takest up that which thou laidst not down.* He thought that it was *reaping where he did not sow*; whereas really it was reaping where he *had sown*. He had no reason to *fear* his master's austerity. This was a mere sham, a frivolous groundless excuse for his idleness. 3. His excuse is turned upon him: *Out of thine own mouth will I judge thee, thou wicked servant, v.* 22. He will be *condemned* by his crime, but *self-condemned* by his plea. If thou hadst had any regard to my interest, thou mightest have put my money *into the bank*, that I might have had, not only *my own*, but my own *with usury*. If he durst not *trade* for fear of *losing* the principal, yet that would be no excuse for his not setting it out to interest, where it would be sure. Whatever may be the pretences of slothful professors, the true reason of it is a reigning indifference to the interests of Christ and his kingdom. They care not whether religion gets ground or loses ground, so long as they can but live at ease. 4. His pound is taken from him, *v.* 34. It is fit that those should *lose* their gifts who will not *use* them. *Take from him the pound*. 5. It is given to him that had the *ten pounds*. When this was objected against because he had so much already (*Lord, he has ten pounds, v.* 25), it is answered (*v.* 26), *Unto everyone that hath shall be given*. It is the rule of justice, (1) That those should be most encouraged who have been most industrious. To him that hath gotten shall more be given, that he may be in a capacity to get more. (2) That those who have their gifts, as if they had

them not, should be deprived of them. To those who endeavour to increase the grace they have, God will impart more; those who neglect it, and suffer it to decline, can expect no other than that God should do so too.

3. Another thing they expected was, that, when the kingdom of God should appear, the body of the Jewish nation would immediately fall in with it. Christ tells them that, after his departure, the generality of them would persist in their obstinacy and rebellion. This is shown here,

(1) In the message which his citizens sent after him, *v.* 14. When he was gone to be invested in his kingdom, then they continued their enmity to him, and said, *We will not have this man to reign over us.* This was fulfilled in the prevailing infidelity of the Jews after the ascension of Christ. They would not submit their necks to his yoke. It speaks the language of all unbelievers; they could be content that Christ should *save them*, but they will not have him to *reign over them*.

(2) In the sentence passed upon them at his return: *Those mine enemies bring hither, v.* 27. When his faithful subjects are preferred and rewarded, then he will take vengeance on his enemies. When the *kingdom of God appeared* then vengeance was taken on those irreconcilable enemies to Christ and his government; they were *brought forth and slain before him*. But this is applicable to all others who *persist* in their infidelity. Utter ruin will certainly be the portion of all Christ's enemies. *Bring them hither*, to have their frivolous pleas overruled, and to receive sentence according to their merits. Those that *will not have Christ to reign over them* shall be reputed and dealt with as his enemies. Those will be accounted so that will not submit to Christ's yoke, but will be their own masters. Whoever will not be *ruled* by the grace of Christ will inevitably be ruined by the wrath of Christ.

Verses 28–40

We have here the same account of Christ's riding in some sort of triumph (such as it was) into Jerusalem which we had before in Matthew and Mark.

I. Jesus Christ was forward and willing to suffer and die for us. He went forward *to Jerusalem* knowing very well the *things* that should *befall him there*, and yet *he went before, ascending up to Jerusalem, v.* 28. He was the foremost of the company. Was he so forward to suffer and die for us, and shall we draw back from any service we are capable of doing for him?

II. It was no ways inconsistent either with Christ's humility or with this present state of humiliation to make a *public entry* into Jerusalem a little before he died. The ignominy of his death might appear the greater.

III. Christ is entitled to a dominion over all the creatures. Christ sent to fetch an *ass* and her *colt* from their *owner's* and *master's crib*, when he had occasion for their service.

IV. Christ has all men's hearts both under his eye and in his hand. He could influence those to whom the ass and the colt belonged to consent to their taking them away, as soon as they were told that the Lord had occasion for them.

V. Those that go on Christ's errands are sure to speed (*v.* 32). It is a comfort to Christ's messengers that they shall bring what they are sent for, if indeed the Lord has occasion for it.

VI. The disciples of Christ, who fetch that for him from others which he has occasion for, should not think that enough, but, whatever they have themselves wherewith he may be served, they should be ready to serve him with it. Those disciples not only fetched the ass's colt for him, but *cast their own garments upon the colt.*

VII. Christ's triumphs are the matter of his disciples' praises. When Christ came nigh to Jerusalem, God put it of a sudden into the hearts of the *whole multitude of the disciples,* not of the twelve only, *to rejoice and praise God* (v. 37), and the *spreading of their clothes in the way* (v. 36) was a common expression of joy. Observe, What was the matter or occasion of their joy and praise. They praised God *for all the mighty works they had seen,* especially the *raising of Lazarus,* which is particularly mentioned, John xii. 17, 18. See how they expressed their joy and praise (v. 38): *Blessed be the king that cometh in the name of the Lord.* Christ is *the king;* he *comes in the name of the Lord. Blessed be he.* Let us *praise him,* let God *prosper him. Peace in heaven.* Let the God of heaven send peace and success to his undertaking, and then there will be *glory in the highest.* Compare this song of the saints on earth with that of the angels, ch. ii. 14. They both agree to give glory to God in the highest. The angels say, *On earth peace.* The saints say, *Peace in heaven.* Such is the communion we have with the holy angels that, as *they* rejoice in the *peace on earth,* so *we* rejoice in the *peace in heaven.*

VIII. Christ's triumphs, and his disciples' joyful praises of them, are the vexation of proud Pharisees. There were some Pharisees among *the multitude* who were enraged at them. They thought that he would not admit such acclamations as these, and therefore expected that he should *rebuke his disciples,* v. 39. As he despises the contempt of the proud, so he accepts the praises of the humble.

IX. Whether men praise Christ or no he will, and shall, and must be praised (v. 40): *If these should hold their peace the stones would immediately cry out,* rather than that Christ should not be praised. Pharisees would silence the praises of Christ, but they cannot gain their point; for as God can *out of stones raise up children unto Abraham,* so he can out of the mouths of those children perfect praise.

Verses 41–48

The great Ambassador from heaven is here making his public entry into Jerusalem, not to be *respected* there, but to be *rejected.* See here two instances of his love to that place and his concern for it.

I. The *tears he shed* for the *approaching ruin* of the *city* (v. 41): *When he was come near, he beheld the city, and wept over it.* Probably, it was when he was coming down the descent of the hill from the *mount of Olives,* where he had a full view of the city, and his eye affected his heart, and his heart his eye again. See here,

1. What a tender spirit Christ was of; we never read that he laughed, but we often find him in tears.

2. That Jesus Christ *wept* when all about him were *rejoicing,* to show how little he was elevated with the applause and acclamation of the people.

3. That he *wept over Jerusalem.* There are cities to be wept over, and none to be more lamented than Jerusalem. But why did Christ weep at the sight of Jerusalem? He himself gives us the reason of his tears.

(1) Jerusalem has not improved the day of her opportunities. He wept, and said, *If thou hadst known, even thou at least in this thy day, the things that belong to thy peace*—but thou *dost not know the day of thy visitation,* v. 44. The manner of speaking is abrupt: *If thou hadst known! O that thou hadst,* so some take it. Or, *If thou hadst known, well;* like that of the *fig-tree,* ch. xiii. 9. How happy had it been for thee! What he says lays all the blame of Jerusalem's impending ruin upon herself. [1] There

are things which *belong to our peace,* which we are all concerned to *know* and *understand.* The things that belong to our peace are those things that relate to our present and future welfare; these we must know with application. [2] There is a *time of visitation* when those things which *belong to our peace* may be *known by us.* When we enjoy the means of grace in great plenty, and have the word of God powerfully preached to us—then is the *time of visitation.* [3] With those that have long neglected the time of their visitation, if at last their eyes be opened, and they bethink themselves, all will be well yet. Those shall not be refused that come into the vineyard *at the eleventh hour.* [4] It is the amazing folly of multitudes that enjoy the means of grace, that they do not improve the day of their opportunities. The *things of their peace* are revealed to them, but are not minded or regarded by them; they *hide their eyes* from them. They are not aware of the *accepted time* and the *day of salvation,* and so let it slip and perish through mere carelessness. None are so *blind* as those that will not *see.* [5] The sin and folly of those that persist in a contempt of gospel grace are a great grief to the Lord Jesus, and should be so to us. He looks with weeping eyes upon lost souls, that continue impenitent. He had rather that they would *turn and live* than *go on and die,* for he is not willing that any should perish.

(2) Jerusalem cannot escape the day of her desolation. The *things of her peace* are now in a manner hidden from her eyes. Not but that after this the gospel was preached to them by the apostles, and multitudes were convinced and converted. But as to the body of the nation, and the leading part of it, they were sealed up under unbelief. They were justly given up to *judicial* blindness and hardness. Neglecting the great salvation often brings temporal judgments upon a people; it did so upon Jerusalem. [1] The Romans besieged the city, *cast a trench about it, compassed it round,* and *kept their* inhabitants in on *every side.* [2] They *laid it even with the ground* (*thy children within thee*), by the cruel slaughters that were made of them: and there was scarcely one stone *left upon another.* This was because they *knew not the day of their visitation.*

II. The *zeal he showed* for the *present purification of the temple.*

1. Christ cleared it of those who profaned it. He went straight to the temple, and *began to cast out the buyers and sellers,* v. 45. Its purity was more its glory than its wealth was. Christ gave a reason for his dislodging the temple-merchants, v. 46. The temple is a *house of prayer,* set apart for communion with God: the *buyers* and *sellers* made it a *den of thieves* by the fraudulent bargains they made there. It would be a distraction to those who came there to pray.

2. He put it to the best use that ever it was put to, for he *taught daily in the temple,* v. 47. Now, when Christ preached in the temple, observe here, (1) How spiteful the church-rulers were against him (v. 47): *The chief priests and scribes, and the chief of the people, sought to destroy him.* (2) How respectful the common people were to him. They were *very attentive to hear him.* The people paid him great respect, attended on his preaching with diligence. Some read it, *All the people, as they heard him, took his part;* and so his enemies *could not find what they might* do against him. Till his hour was come his interest in the common people protected him; but, when his hour was come, the chief priests' influence upon the common people delivered him up.

CHAPTER 20

I. Christ's answer to the chief priests' question concerning his authority, ver. 1–8. II. The parable of the vineyard, let out to unjust and rebellious husbandmen, ver. 9–19. III. Christ's answer to the question proposed to him concerning the lawfulness of paying tribute to Caesar, ver. 20–26. IV. His vindication of that great fundamental doctrine—the resurrection of the dead and the future state, ver. 27–39. V. His puzzling the scribes with a question concerning the Messiah's being the Son of David, ver. 39–44. VI. The caution he gave his disciples to take heed of the scribes, ver. 46–47.

Verses 1–8

Nothing is added here to what we had in the other evangelists; but only in the first verse, where we are told,

I. That he was now *teaching the people in the temple,* and *preaching the gospel.* Christ was a preacher of his own gospel. He not only *purchased* the salvation for us, but *published* it to us. This likewise puts an honour upon the preachers of the gospel. It puts an honour upon the *popular preachers* of the gospel; Christ condescended to the capacities of the *people* in preaching the gospel, and *taught them.*

II. That his enemies are here said to *come upon him.* The word is used only here, and it intimates,

1. That they thought to surprise him with this question; they *came upon him* suddenly.

2. That they thought to frighten him with this question. From this story itself we may learn, (1) That it is not to be thought strange, if even that which is evident be disputed and called in question by those that shut their eyes against the light. Christ's miracles plainly showed *by what authority he did these things.* (2) Those that question Christ's authority will have their folly made manifest unto all men. Christ answered these priests and scribes with a question concerning the baptism of John: *Was it from heaven or of men?* They all knew it was *from heaven.* And this question gravelled them, and ran them aground, and served to shame them before the people. (3) It is not strange if those that are governed by reputation and secular interest imprison the plainest truths, as these priests and scribes did who would not own that John's baptism was *from heaven,* and had no other reason why they did not say it was *of men* but because they *feared the people.* What good can be expected from men of such a spirit? (4) Those that bury the knowledge they have are justly denied further knowledge, *v.* 7, 8.

Verses 9–19

Christ spoke this parable against those who were resolved not to own his authority.

I. The parable has nothing added here to what we had before in Matthew and Mark. The scope of it is to show that the Jewish nation had provoked God to abandon them to ruin. It teaches us, 1. That those who enjoy the privileges of the visible church are as tenants and farmers that have a vineyard to look after, and rent to pay for it. God, by setting up revealed religion, hath planted a vineyard, which he lets out, *v.* 9. And they have *vineyard work* to do, needful and constant work, but pleasant and profitable. They have also *vineyard-fruits* to present to the Lord of the vineyard. There are rents to be paid and services to be done. 2. That the work of God's ministers is to call upon those who enjoy the privileges of the church to *bring forth fruit* accordingly. They are God's rent-gatherers, *v.* 10. 3. That it has often been the lot of God's faithful servants to be wretchedly abused by his own tenants. They that are resolved not to do their duty to God cannot bear to be called upon to do it. 4. That God sent his Son into the world to *gather the fruits of the vineyard.* The prophets spoke as *servants,* but Christ *as a Son;* to send him, one would have thought, should have won upon

them. 5. That those who reject Christ's ministers would reject Christ himself. They said, *This is the heir, come let us kill him.* When they slew the servants, there were other servants sent. "But, if we can but be the death of the son, there is never another son to be sent; we may have a quiet possession of the vineyard for ourselves." Therefore they took the bold step, they *cast him out of the vineyard, and killed him.* 6. That the putting of Christ to death filled up the measure of the Jewish iniquity. No other could be expected than that God should *destroy those wicked husbandmen.* Those that live in the neglect of their duty to God know not what degrees of sin and destruction they are running themselves into.

II. To the application of the parable is added here, which we had not before, their deprecation of the doom included in it (*v.* 16): *When they heard it, they said, God forbid—Let not this be done,* so it should be read. And see what a cheat they put upon themselves, to think to avoid it by a cold *God forbid,* when they do nothing towards the preventing of it. Now observe what Christ said. 1. He *beheld them.* This is taken notice of only by this evangelist, *v.* 17. He *looked upon* them with pity and compassion. He *beheld them,* to see if they would blush at their own folly. 2. He referred them to the scripture: "*What is this then that is written? The stone which the builders rejected is become the head of the corner.*" The Lord Jesus will be exalted to the Father's right hand. Even those that stumble at him *shall be broken*—it will be their ruin; but as to those that not only reject him, but hate and persecute him, he will fall upon them and crush them to pieces—will *grind them to powder.*

Lastly, We are told how the chief priests and scribes were exasperated by this parable (*v.* 19): *They perceived that he had spoken this parable against them.* They fall into a rage at him and *sought to lay hands on him.* And it was only because they *feared the people,* that they did not now fly in his face, and take him by the throat. They were just ready to make his words good: *This is the heir, come let us kill him.* Christ tells them that instead of *kissing the Son* of God they would *kill him.* They do, in effect, say this: "And so we will; have at him now." And, though they deprecate the punishment of the sin, in the next breath they are projecting the commission of it.

Verses 20–26

We have here Christ's evading a snare which his enemies laid for him, by proposing a question to him about tribute.

I. The mischief designed him. The plot was to *deliver him unto the power and authority of the governor, v.* 20. They could not themselves put him to death by course of law, nor otherwise than by a *popular tumult.* They hoped to gain their point, if they could but incense the governor against him. Thus Christ's word must be fulfilled that he should be *delivered into the hands of the Gentiles.*

II. The persons they employed. They were *spies, who should feign themselves just men.* It is no new thing for *bad men* to feign themselves *just men.* A spy must go in disguise. These spies must take on them to have a value for Christ's judgment, and therefore must desire his advice in a case of conscience.

III. The question they proposed. Their preface is very courtly: *Master, we know that thou sayest and teachest rightly, v.* 21. Thus they thought to flatter him into an incautious freedom and openness with them. They were much mistaken who thought thus to impose upon the humble Jesus. He *accepts not the person of any,* but it is as true that he knows the hearts of all, and knew theirs, though they *spoke fair.* It was certain that he *taught the way of God truly;*

but he knew that they were unworthy to be taught by him, who came to *take hold of his words*, not to be *taken hold of* by them. Their case is very nice: "Is it lawful *for us*" (this is added here in Luke), "*to give tribute to Caesar?*" Their pride and covetousness made them loth to pay taxes, and then they would have it a question whether it was lawful or no. Now if Christ should say that *it was lawful* the people would take it ill. But if he should say that *it was not lawful* as they expected he would, then they should have something to accuse him of to the governor.

IV. His evading the snare which they laid for him: *He perceived their craftiness, v. 23.* He did not give them a direct answer, but reproved them for offering to impose upon him—*Why tempt ye me? Show me a penny;* he asked them whose money it was, whose stamp it bore, who coined it. They owned, "It is Caesar's money." "Why then," saith Christ, "you should first have asked whether it was lawful to *pay* and *receive* Caesar's money among yourselves, and to admit that to be the instrument of your commerce. You must therefore *render to Caesar the things that are Caesar's.* But in sacred things God only is your King. You must *render to God the things that are God's.*"

V. The confusion they were hereby put into, *v. 26.* The snare is broken: *They could not take hold of his words before the people.* They *marvelled at his answer*, it was so discreet and unexceptionable. Their mouths are stopped; they *held their peace.* They durst ask him nothing else, lest he should shame and expose them.

Verses 27–38

I. In every age there have been men of corrupt minds, that have endeavoured to subvert the fundamental principles of revealed religion. The Sadducees deny that *there is any resurrection*, any *future state*, no world of spirits, no state of recompense and retribution for what was done in the body. Take away this, and all religion falls to the ground.

II. It is common for those that design to undermine any truth of God to perplex it. So these Sadducees did when they would weaken people's faith in the doctrine of the resurrection. The case perhaps was matter of fact of a woman that had *seven husbands.* Now in the resurrection *whose wife shall she be?*

III. There is a great deal of difference between the state of the children of men on earth and that of the children of God in heaven.

1. The children of men in this world *marry, and are given in marriage.* Much of our business in this world is to raise and build up families, and to provide for them. Much of our pleasure in this world is in our relations, our wives and children; nature inclines to it. Marriage is instituted for the comfort of human life.

2. The world to come is quite another thing; it is called *that world*, by way of emphasis and eminency.

(1) Who shall be the inhabitants of *that world*: They that shall be *accounted worthy to obtain it.* They have not a *legal* worthiness, but an *evangelical* worthiness. It is a worthiness imputed by which we are glorified, as well as a righteousness imputed by which we are justified. They are by grace made and *counted worthy to obtain that world*; it intimates some *difficulty* in reaching after it, and danger of coming short. We must *so run* as that we may obtain. They shall obtain the *resurrection from the dead*, that is, the blessed resurrection.

(2) What shall be the happy state of the inhabitants of that world we cannot express or conceive, 1. Cor. ii. 9. See what Christ here says of it. [1] They *neither marry nor are given in marriage.* Those that have entered into the joy of their Lord are entirely taken up with that. Into that *new Jerusalem* there enters

nothing that defiles. [2] They cannot *die any more*; and this comes in as a reason why they do not *marry.* Where there are no burials, there is no need of weddings. This crowns the comfort of that world that there is no more death there. Here death reigns, but thence it is for ever excluded. [3] They are *equal unto the angels.* In the other evangelists it was said, They are *as the angels*, but here they are said to be *equal to the angels—angels' peers*; they have a glory and bliss no way inferior to that of the holy angels. Saints, when they come to heaven, shall be *naturalised.* They have in all respects equal privileges with them that are free-born, the angels that are the natives and aborigines of that country. [4] They *are the children of God*, and so they are as the angels. We have the nature and disposition of sons, but that will not be *perfected* till we come to heaven. [5] They are the *children of the resurrection*, that is, they are made capable of the employments and enjoyments of the future state. They are the *children of God*, being the *children of the resurrection.*

IV. It is an undoubted truth that there is another life after this (*v. 37, 38*): *Moses showed this, as it was shown to Moses at the bush*, when he *calleth the Lord*, the *God of Abraham, and the God of Isaac, and the God of Jacob. Abraham, Isaac, and Jacob*, were then *dead* as to our world; they had departed out of it many years before; how then could God say, not *I was*, but *I am the God of Abraham?* We must therefore conclude that they were then in being in another world; for *God is not the God of the dead, but of the living.* Luke here adds, *For all live unto him*, that is, all who, like them, are true believers; though they are dead, yet they *do live.* But there is more in it yet; when God called himself *the God* of these patriarchs, he meant that he was their felicity and portion, their *exceeding great reward*, Gen. xv. 1. Therefore there must be another life after this, in which he will do that for them that will amount to a *discharge in full* of that promise.

Verses 39–47

The scribes were *students* in the law, and *expositors* of it to the people, men in reputation for wisdom and honour, but the generality of them were enemies to Christ and his gospel.

I. We have them here commending the reply which Christ made to the Sadducees: *Certain of the scribes said, Master, thou hast well said, v. 39.* Even the scribes commended his performance, and owned that he said well. Many that call themselves Christians come short even of this spirit.

II. We have them here struck with an awe of Christ, and of his wisdom and authority (*v. 40*): *They durst not ask him any questions at all.* His own disciples, being willing to receive his doctrine, durst *ask him any question*; but the Sadducees durst ask him none.

III. We have them here *puzzled* and run aground with a question concerning the Messiah, *v. 41.* It was plain by many scriptures that Christ was to be the *Son of David*; even the blind man knew this (*ch.* xviii. 39); and yet it was plain that David called the Messiah *his Lord* (*v. 42, 44*): *The Lord said to my Lord*, Ps. cx. 1. Now if he be *his Son*, why doth he call him *his Lord?* If he be *his Lord*, why do *we* call him *his Son?* They could not reconcile this seeming contradiction; thanks be to God, we can; that Christ, *as God*, was David's Lord, but Christ, *as man*, was David's Son.

IV. We have them here described in their black characters, *v. 45–47.* Christ bids his disciples *beware of the scribes*, that is,

1. "Take heed of being drawn *into sin* by them; beware of such a spirit as they are governed by."

2. "Take heed of being *brought into trouble* by them," in the same sense that he had said (Matt. x.

17), *"Beware of men, for they will deliver you up to the councils; beware of the scribes, for they will do so. Beware of them, they are proud and haughty. They desire to* walk about the streets *in long robes,* as those that are above business, and as those that take state, and take place." They loved in their hearts to have people make their obeisance to them *in the markets.* They *loved the highest seats in the synagogues* and *the chief rooms at feasts,* and looked upon themselves with great conceit and upon all about them with great contempt. "They are *covetous and oppressive,* and make their religion a cloak and cover for crime. They *devour widows' houses. For a show they make long prayers."*

Christ reads them their doom in a few words: *These shall receive a more abundant judgment,* a double damnation. *Dissembled piety is double iniquity.*

CHAPTER 21

I. The notice Christ took of a poor widow that cast two mites into the treasury, ver. 1–4. II. A prediction of future events, ver. 5–7. 1. Of what should happen between that and the destruction of Jerusalem, ver. 8–19. 2. Of that destruction itself, ver. 20–24. 3. Of the second coming of Jesus Christ to judge the world, ver. 25–33. III. A practical application of this (ver. 34–36), and an account of Christ's preaching and the people's attendance on it, ver. 37, 38.

Verses 1–4

This short passage of story we had before in Mark. It is thus recorded twice, to teach us, 1. That *charity* to the poor is a *main matter* in religion. Our Lord Jesus took all occasions to commend it and recommend it. 2. That Jesus Christ has his eye upon us, to observe what we give to the poor. Christ, though intent upon his preaching, looked up, to see what *gifts were cast into the treasury, v.* 1. He observes whether we give largely and liberally, in proportion to what we have, or whether we be sneaking and paltry in it. He observes whether we give charitably and with a willing mind, or grudgingly and with reluctance. And this should encourage us to be abundant in it. He sees in secret, and will reward openly. 3. That Christ observes and accepts the charity of the poor in a particular manner. Those that have nothing *to give* may yet *do* a great deal in charity by ministering to the poor, and helping them. But here was one that was herself poor and yet *gave* what little she had to the treasury. It was but *two mites,* which make a farthing; but Christ magnified it as a piece of charity exceeding all the rest: *She has cast in more than they all.* Christ does not blame her for indiscretion; but commended her liberality, which proceeded from a belief of and dependence upon God's providence to take care of her. 4. That, whatever may be called *the offerings of God,* we ought to have a respect for, and to our power, yea, and beyond our power, to contribute cheerfully to.

Verses 5–19

See here, I. With what admiration some spoke of the external pomp and magnificence of the temple. They took notice of it to him *how it was adorned with goodly stones and gifts, v.* 5. They thought their Master should be as much affected with those things as they were. When we *speak of the temple,* it should be of the presence of God in it.

II. Christ spoke of their being all made desolate very shortly (*v.* 6): *"As for those things which you behold, the days will come in which there shall not be left one stone upon another.* This building shall yet be utterly ruined."

III. With what curiosity those about him enquire concerning the time when this great desolation should be: *Master, when shall these things be? v.* 7. It is

natural to us to covet to know future things, when we are more concerned to ask what is our duty in the prospect of these things, and how we may prepare for them. They enquire *what sign there shall be when these things shall come to pass.* They ask not for a *present* sign, to confirm the prediction itself, but what the future signs will be of the approaching accomplishment of the prediction.

IV. With what clearness and fulness Christ answers their enquiries.

1. They must expect to hear of false Christs and false prophets appearing (*v.* 8): *Many shall come in my name,* usurping the title and character of the Messiah. They shall say, *I am he.* To encourage people to follow them, they added, *"The time draws near* when the kingdom shall be restored to Israel." When they asked solicitously and eagerly, *Master, when shall these things be?* the first word Christ said was, *Take heed that you be not deceived.* Those that are most *inquisitive* in the things of God (though it is very good to be so) are in most danger of being imposed upon. *"Go you not after them."* If we are sure that Jesus is the Christ, and his doctrine is the *gospel of God,* we must be deaf to all intimations of another Christ and another gospel.

2. They must expect to hear of great commotions in the nations. There shall be *bloody wars* (*v.* 10): *Nation shall rise against nation.* There shall be *earthquakes, in divers places.* There shall be *famines* and *pestilences.* God has various ways of punishing a provoking people. Though spiritual judgments are more commonly inflicted in gospel times, yet God makes use of temporal judgments also. There shall be *fearful sights* and *great signs from heaven.* "Be *not terrified.* Others will be frightened at them, but be not you frightened, *v.* 2. As to the *fearful sights,* let them not be fearful to you. You fall into the hands of God. Trust therefore in him, and *be not afraid.* It is your interest to *make the best of that which is,* for all your fears cannot alter it: *these things must first come to pass.* There is *worse behind. The end is not by and by,* not *suddenly.* Be not *terrified,* for, if you begin so quickly to be discouraged, how will you bear up under what is yet before you?"

3. They must expect to be themselves for *signs* and *wonders* in Israel. *"Before all these, they shall lay their hands on you.* This must be considered not only as the *suffering* of the *persecuted,* but as the *sin* of the *persecutors."* The ruin of a people is always introduced by their sin.

(1) Christ tells them what hard things they should suffer for his name's sake. They should *sit down and count the cost.* The Christians, having themselves been originally Jews, might expect fair quarter with them; but Christ bids them not expect it: *They shall deliver you up to the synagogues* to be scourged there. They shall *deliver you into prisons, that* you may be *brought before kings and rulers for my name's sake.* "Your own relations will betray you (*v.* 16), *your parents, brethren, and kinsfolks, and friends.* You will be called to *resist unto blood. Some of you shall they cause to be put to death. You shall be hated of all men for my name's sake."* This is worse than death itself. They were hated of *all men,* that is, of all bad men, who could not bear the light of the gospel (because it discovered their evil deeds). The wicked world, which hated to be reformed, hated Christ, the great Redeemer, and all that were his, for his sake.

(2) He encourages them to bear up under their trials, and to go on in their work. God will bring glory both to himself and them out of their sufferings: *"It shall turn to you for a testimony, v.* 13. Your being set up thus for a mark, and publicly *persecuted,* will make you the more taken notice of. Your being

brought *before kings and rulers* will give you an opportunity of preaching the gospel to them. Your suffering such severe things, and being so hated by the worst of men, will be a testimony that you are good. Your courage, and cheerfulness, and constancy under your sufferings will be a testimony for you, that you believe what you preach, that you are supported by a divine power. God will stand by you, and own you, and assist you, and you shall be well furnished with instructions, *v.* 14, 15. *Settle it in your hearts, not to meditate before what you shall answer;* do not *depend* upon your own wit and ingenuity, and do not *distrust* or *despair* of the immediate and extraordinary aids of the divine grace. I promise you the special assistance of divine grace: *I will give you a mouth and wisdom."* A *mouth* and *wisdom* together completely fit a man both for services and sufferings; *wisdom* to know what to say, and a *mouth* wherewith to say it. Those that plead Christ's cause may depend upon him to give them a *mouth and wisdom* to enable them to answer for themselves. They are enabled to say that both for him and themselves which *all their adversaries are not able to gainsay or resist,* Acts iv, v and vi. "You shall suffer no real damage by all the hardships they shall put upon you (*v.* 18): *There shall not a hair of your head perish."* Shall some of them lose their heads, and yet not lose a hair? Take it figuratively in the same sense that Christ saith, *He that loseth his life for my sake shall find it.* To this end he had said (Matt. x. 30), *The hairs of your head are all numbered.* We do not reckon that *lost* or *perishing* which is laid out for good purposes. If we drop the body itself for Christ's name's sake, it does not perish, but is well bestowed. "It shall be abundantly recompensed." Though we may be losers for Christ, we shall not, we cannot, be losers by him in the end. "It is therefore your duty and interest to maintain a holy sincerity and serenity of mind, which will keep you always easy (*v.* 19): *In your patience possess ye your souls."* It is our duty and interest at all times, especially in perilous times, to secure the possession of our own souls, that they be not distempered now, nor our possession of them disturbed and interrupted. *"Possess your souls,* be your own men. Keep under the tumults of passion, that neither grief nor fear may tyrannise over you." It is by patience, Christian patience, that we keep possession of our own souls. "Set patience upon the guard, and keep out all those impressions which would ruffle you and put you out of temper."

Verses 20–28

He here comes to show them what all those things would issue in at last, namely, the destruction of Jerusalem, which would be a little day of judgment, a type and figure of Christ's second coming.

I. He tells them that they should see Jerusalem besieged, *compassed with armies* (*v.* 20), and, when they saw this, they might conclude that *its desolation was nigh.*

II. He warns them, upon this signal given, to shift for their own safety (*v.* 21): *"Then let them that are in Judæa flee to the mountains; let them that are in the midst of it depart out,* and let not them that are in the countries and villages about enter into the city. Do you abandon a city and country which you see God has abandoned and given up to ruin."

III. He foretells the terrible havoc that should be made of the Jewish nation (*v.* 22): *Those are the days of vengeance* so often spoken of by the Old Testament prophets. All their predictions must now be fulfilled. *All things that are written must be fulfilled* at length. Reprieves are not pardons. The greatness of that destruction is set forth. It is *wrath upon this people,* the wrath of God. Of particular terror it would be to women with child, and poor mothers that are

nurses. There should be general confusion all the nation over.

IV. He describes the issue of the struggles between the Jews and the Romans. Multitudes of them *shall fall by the edge of the sword.* The siege of Jerusalem was, in effect, a military execution. The rest shall be *led away captive;* not into *one* nation, but *into all nations.* Jerusalem itself was *trodden down of the Gentiles.* The Romans laid it quite waste.

V. He describes the great frights that people should generally be in. Many frightful *sights* shall be *in the sun, moon, and stars,* and here in this lower world, the *sea and the waves roaring.* The effect of this shall be universal confusion and consternation *upon the earth, distress of nations with perplexity, v.* 25. *Men's hearts shall fail them for fear* (*v.* 26), dying away for fear, still trembling for fear of worse, and *looking after those things which are coming upon the world.* The *powers of heaven shall be shaken,* and then the pillars of the earth cannot but tremble. As that day was all terror and destruction to the unbelieving Jews, so the great day will be to all unbelievers.

VI. He makes this to be a kind of *appearing of the Son of man: Then shall they see the Son of man coming in a cloud, with power and great glory, v.* 27. The destruction of Jerusalem was in a particular manner an act of Christ's judgment, so that it might justly be looked upon as *a coming of the Son of man, in power and great glory,* but *in the clouds.* Now this was, 1. An *evidence* of the first coming of the Messiah. Those that would not have him to *reign over them* shall have him to *triumph over them.* 2. It was an *earnest* of his second coming.

VII. He encourages all the faithful disciples (*v.* 28) *"When these things begin to come to pass, then* do you look *up,* look heavenward, in faith, hope, and prayer, and *lift up your heads for your redemption draws nigh."* When Christ came he came to redeem the Christians that were persecuted and oppressed. When he comes to judge the world at the last day, he will *redeem* all that are his, from all their grievances. When they see that day approaching, they can *lift up their heads with joy,* knowing that *their redemption draws nigh.*

VIII. Here is one word of prediction that looks further than the destruction of the Jewish nation, which is not easily understood; we have it in *v.* 24: *Jerusalem shall be trodden down of the Gentiles, till the times of the Gentiles be fulfilled.* 1. Some understand it of what is past. The Gentiles shall keep possession of it, and it shall be purely Gentile, till a great part of the Gentile world shall have become Christian. 2. Others understand it of what is yet to come. Jerusalem shall be possessed by the Gentiles, till the time come when the kingdoms of this world shall become Christ's kingdoms, and then all the Jews shall be converted.

Verses 29–38

I. Christ appoints his disciples to observe the signs of the times, which they might judge by, as they could judge of the approach of summer by the budding forth of the trees, *v.* 29–31. As in the kingdom of nature there is a chain of causes, so in the kingdom of providence there is a consequence of one event upon another. When we see the ruin of persecuting powers hastening on, we may thence infer that *the kingdom of God is nigh at hand.*

II. He charges them to look upon those things as *sure* and very *near.* The destruction of the Jewish nation, 1. Was *near* (*v.* 32): *This generation shall not pass away till all be fulfilled.* There were some now alive that should see it. 2. It was *sure;* the decree was gone forth (*v.* 33): *"Heaven and earth shall pass away* sooner than any word of mine: but *my words shall not.*"

III. He cautions them against security and sensuality (v. 34, 35): *Take heed to yourselves.* This is the word of command given to all Christ's disciples. We cannot be *safe* if we be *secure.* It concerns us at *all* times, but especially at *some* times, to be very cautious. 1. What our *danger* is: that *the day* of death and judgment should *come upon us unawares,* when we do not *expect* it, and are not *prepared* for it, lest it *come upon us as a snare.* 2. What our *duty* is: we must *take heed lest our hearts be overcharged.* Two things we must watch against, lest our hearts be overcharged with them: (1) The indulging of the appetites of the body: *Take heed lest you be overcharged with surfeiting and drunkenness,* the immoderate use of meat and drink. They stupefy the conscience, and cause the mind to be *unaffected* with those things that are most *affecting.* (2) The inordinate pursuit of the good things of this world. The heart is overcharged with the *cares of this life.* This is the snare of the men of business, that *will be rich.*

IV. He counsels them to prepare and get ready for this great day, *v.* 36. Here see, 1. What should be *our aim:* that we may be *accounted worthy to escape all these things.* Yet we must aim not only to *escape that,* but to *stand before the Son of man;* not only to stand *acquitted* before him as our Judge, but to *stand before him,* to attend on him as our Master, and serve him day and night, always to *behold his face.* The saints are here said to be *accounted worthy,* as before, *ch.* xx. 35. God, by the goodwill of his grace towards them, *accounts them worthy* of it. A great part of our worthiness lies in an acknowledgment of our own unworthiness. 2. What should be our *actings* in these aims: *Watch therefore, and pray always.* Watching and praying must go together. Those that would make sure of the joys to come, must *watch* and *pray.* (1) To keep a guard upon themselves. "Watch against sin, watch to every duty. Be awake, and keep awake." (2) To keep up their communion with God: "*Pray always.*" Those shall be accounted worthy to live a life of praise in the other world that live a life of prayer in this world.

V. In the last two verses we have an account how Christ disposed of himself during those three or four days between his riding in triumph into Jerusalem and the night in which he was betrayed. 1. He was *all day teaching in the temple.* He was an indefatigable preacher; he preached in the face of opposition, and in the midst of those that he knew sought occasion against him. 2. At night he went out to lodge at a friend's house, in the mount of Olives. 3. Early in the morning he was in the temple again, and the people were forward to hear one that they saw forward to preach (*v.* 38): *They all came early in the morning to hear him.* Sometimes the taste and relish which serious, honest, plain people have of good preaching are more to be valued and judged by than the opinion of the witty and learned.

CHAPTER 22

All the evangelists give us a particular account of the death and resurrection of Christ, this evangelist as fully as any, and with many circumstances and passages added which we had not before. I. The plot to take Jesus, and Judas's coming into it, ver. 1–6. II. Christ's eating the passover with his disciples, ver. 7–18. III. The instituting of the Lord's supper, ver. 19, 20. IV. Christ's discourse with his disciples after supper, ver. 21–38. V. His agony in the garden, ver. 39–46. VI. The apprehending of him, ver. 47–53. VII. Peter's denying him, ver. 54–62. VIII. The indignities done to Christ, and his trial and condemnation in the ecclesiastical court, ver. 63–71.

Verses 1–6

Christ is here delivered up, *when the feast of unleavened bread drew nigh, v.* 1. Here we have,

I. His sworn enemies contriving it (*v.* 2), *the chief priests,* and the scribes, *seeking how they might kill him.* Could they have had their will, it had been soon done, but they *feared the people.*

II. A treacherous disciple joining in with them, Judas surnamed *Iscariot.* He is here said to be *of the number of the twelve.* One would wonder that one of *that number,* who could not but *know Christ,* should be so base as to betray him. How he who knew Christ so well yet came to betray him we are here told: *Satan entered into Judas, v.* 3. It was the devil's work. Whoever betrays Christ, or his truths or ways, it is Satan that puts them upon it. Judas knew how desirous the chief priests were to get Christ into their hands. He therefore went himself, and made the motion to them, *v.* 4. When you see Judas communing with the *chief priests,* be sure some mischief is hatching.

III. The issue of the treaty between them. 1. Judas must *betray Christ to them,* and this they would be *glad of.* 2. They must give him a sum of money for doing it, and this he would be glad of (*v.* 5): *They covenanted to give him money.* Judas sought opportunity to betray him. He gained the advantage he sought, and fixed the time and place where it might be done, *in the absence of the multitude,* and *without tumult.*

Verses 7–20

I. The preparation that was made for Christ's eating the passover with his disciples, upon the very *day of unleavened bread, when the passover must be killed* according to the law, *v.* 7. He sent Peter and John to *prepare the passover.* He directed those whom he employed whither they should go (*v.* 9, 10): *they must follow a man bearing a pitcher of water,* and he must be their guide to the house. He directed them thus, to teach them to depend upon the conduct of Providence, and to follow that, *step by step.* Being come to the house, they must desire the master of the house to show them a room (*v.* 11), and he will readily do it, *v.* 12. The disciples found their guide, and the house, and the room, just as he had said to them (*v.* 13). They got everything in readiness for *the passover, v.* 11.

II. The solemnizing of the passover. When *the hour was come he sat down,* and *the twelve apostles with him,* Judas not excepted. Though Judas has already been guilty of an *overt act* of treason, yet, it not being publicly known, Christ admits him to sit down with the rest at the passover. Now observe.

1. How Christ *bids this passover welcome* (*v.* 15): "*With desire I have desired* to eat this passover with *you before I suffer.*" He knew it was to be the prologue to his sufferings, and *therefore* he desired it, because it was in order to his Father's glory and man's redemption. Shall we be *backward* to any service for him who was so *forward* in the work of our salvation? See the love he had to his disciples; he desired to eat it *with them,* that he and they might have a little time together for private conversation. He was now about to leave them, but was very desirous to *eat this passover with them before he suffered,* as if the comfort of that would carry him the more cheerfully through his sufferings.

2. How Christ in it *takes his leave of all passovers* (*v.* 16): "*I will not any more eat thereof until it be fulfilled in the kingdom of God.*" (1) It was fulfilled when *Christ our Passover was sacrificed for us.* (2) It was fulfilled in the *Lord's supper,* an ordinance of the gospel kingdom, in which the passover had its accomplishment. They ate of it, and Christ might be said to eat with them, because of the spiritual communion they had with him in that ordinance.

(3) The complete accomplishment of that commemoration of liberty will be in the kingdom of glory. What he had said of his eating of the paschal lamb, he repeats concerning his drinking of the *passover wine*, the cup of *blessing*, or of thanksgiving. This cup *he took*, according to the custom, and *gave thanks* and then said, *Take this, and divide it among yourselves, v.* 17. This is not said afterwards of the sacramental cup, which, being the *New Testament in his blood*, he might give into everyone's hand, to teach them to make a particular application of it to their own souls; but, as for the paschal cup, it is enough to say, "*Take it, and divide it among yourselves, v.* 18. *I will not drink of the fruit of the vine any more, till the kingdom of God shall come.*" Christ dying next day was its fulfilment.

III. The institution of the Lord's supper, *v.* 19, 20. The *passover* and the *deliverance* out of Egypt were *typical* and *prophetic signs* of a Christ to come, who should by dying deliver us from sin and death, and the tyranny of Satan. Therefore the Lord's supper is instituted to be a commemorative sign or memorial of a Christ already come, that *has* by dying delivered us.

1. The *breaking of Christ's body* as a *sacrifice for us* is here commemorated by the *breaking of bread*: *This is my body which is given for you.* This bread that was given for us is given *to us* to be food for our souls, this bread that was *broken* and *given for us*, to satisfy for the guilt of our sins, is *broken* and *given to us*, to satisfy the desire of our souls. And this we do in *remembrance* of what he did for us, when he died for us, and for a *memorial* of what we *do*, in making ourselves *partakers of him*, and joining ourselves to him in an everlasting covenant.

2. The *shedding* of *Christ's blood*, by which the atonement was made, as represented by the wine in the cup. It *commemorates* the purchase of the covenant by the blood of Christ, and *confirms* the promises of the covenant. In all our commemorations of the shedding of Christ's blood, we must have an eye to it as shed for us; *who loved me, and gave himself for me.*

Verses 21-38

We have here Christ's discourse with his disciples after supper, much of which is new here; and in St. John's gospel we shall find other additions.

I. He discoursed with them concerning him that should betray him. 1. He signifies to them that the traitor was now among them, and one of them, *v.* 21. By placing this after the institution of the Lord's supper, though in Matthew and Mark it is placed before it, it seems plain that Judas did receive the Lord's supper, did *eat of that bread* and *drink of that cup*; for, after the solemnity was over, Christ said, *Behold, the hand of him that betrayeth me is with me on the table.* 2. He foretells that the treason would take effect (*v.* 22): *Truly the Son of man goes as it was determined*; for he is delivered up by the counsel and foreknowledge of God. Christ was not driven to his sufferings, but cheerfully *went to them.* 3. He threatens the traitor: *Woe to that man by whom he is betrayed.* Though God has *determined* that Christ shall be betrayed, and he himself has cheerfully submitted to it, yet Judas's sin or punishment is not at all the less. 4. He frightens the rest of the disciples into a suspicion of themselves, by saying that it was one of them (*v.* 23): *They began to enquire among themselves who it was that should do this thing.*

II. Concerning the strife that was among them for precedency or supremacy.

1. See what the dispute was: *Which of them should be accounted the greatest.* How inconsistent is this with that in the verse before! There they were enquiring which would be the traitor, and here which should be the prince. What a self-contradiction is the deceitful heart of man!

2. See what Christ said to this dispute. He was not sharp upon them but mildly showed them the sin and folly of it.

(1) This was to make themselves like the *kings of the Gentiles, v.* 25. They *exercise lordship* over their subjects. The *exercising of lordship* better becomes the *kings of the Gentiles* than the ministers of Christ. *They that exercise authority*, they are called *Benefactors*, they call themselves so, and so their flatterers call them. However they may really serve themselves, they would be thought to *serve their country.* One of the Ptolemies was surnamed *The Benefactor.* Now our Saviour, by taking notice of this, intimates, [1] That to *do good* is much more honourable than to *look great.* By their own confession, a benefactor to his country is much more valued than a ruler of his country. [2] That to *do good* is the surest way to be great. He would have his disciples believe, that their greatest honour would be to do all the good they could in the world. If they have that which is confessedly the *greater* honour, of being benefactors, let them despise the less, of being rulers.

(2) It was to make themselves unlike Christ himself: "*You shall not be so,*" *v.* 26, 27. "It was never intended that you should *rule* any otherwise than by the power of truth and grace, but that you should *serve.*" Here is the rule Christ gave to his disciples: He that is *greater among you*, that is *senior*, let him be as the *younger.* Their age and honour, instead of warranting them to take their ease, bind them to double work. And he *that is chief*, let him be *as he that* serves. Here is the example which he himself gave to this rule: *Whether is greater, he that sitteth at meat or he that serveth?* He was ready to do any office of kindness and service for them; witness his *washing* their feet.

(3) They ought not to strive for worldly honour and grandeur, because he had better honours in reserve for them, a *kingdom, a feast*, a *throne*, wherein they should all share alike, *v.* 28-30.

[1] Christ's commendation of his disciples for their faithfulness to him. It is spoken with an air of encomium and applause: "*You are they who have continued with me in my temptations*, you are they who have stood by me and stuck to me." His disciples continued with him, and were afflicted in all his afflictions. It was but little help that they could give him; nevertheless, he took it kindly that they *continued with him*, and he here owns their kindness. Christ's disciples had been very defective in their duty. We find them guilty of many mistakes and weaknesses: yet their Master passes all by and forgets it. *You are they who have continued with me.* Thus does he praise at parting, to show how willing he is to make the best of those whose hearts he knows to be upright with him.

[2] The recompence he designed them for their fidelity: *I appoint unto you a kingdom.* Understand it, *First*, Of what should be done for them in this world. God gave his Son a *kingdom among men*, the gospel church. This *kingdom* he *appointed* to his apostles and their successors in the ministry of the gospel. This is the honour reserved for you. Or, *Secondly*, Of what should be done for them in the other world. God will give them *the kingdom.* They shall *eat and drink at Christ's table in his kingdom*, of which he had spoken, *v.* 16, 18. They shall partake of those joys and pleasures which were the recompence of his services and sufferings. The *highest dignities*: "You shall *sit down with me on my throne*," Rev. iii. 21.

III. Concerning Peter's denying him.

1. The general notice Christ gives to Peter of the devil's design upon him and the rest of the apostles (*v.* 31): *The Lord said, Simon, Simon, Satan hath*

desired to have you, that he may sift you as wheat.
Peter, who used to be the *mouth* of the rest in speaking
to Christ, is here made the *ear* of the rest; and what
is designed for warning to them all (*all you shall be
offended, because of me*) is directed to Peter, being in
a particular manner struck at by the tempter: *Satan
has desired to have you.* "Give me leave to try them,"
saith Satan, "and Peter particularly." He desired to
have them, *that he might sift them,* that he might
show them to be chaff, and not wheat. Satan could
not sift them unless God gave him leave: He *desired
to have them,* "*He has challenged you* to prove you a
company of hypocrites, and Peter especially, the
forwardest of you."

2. The particular encouragement he gave to Peter:
"*I have prayed for thee:* thou wilt be most violently
assaulted, *but I have prayed for thee, that thy faith
fail not.*" Though there may be many failings in the
faith of true believers, yet there shall not be a total
and final failure of their faith. It is owing to the
mediation and intercession of Jesus Christ that the
faith of his disciples, though sometimes sadly shaken,
yet is not sunk. They are *kept by the power of God*
and the prayer of Christ.

3. The charge he gives to Peter to help others:
"*When thou art converted, strengthen thy brethren;*
when thou hast found thy faith kept from failing,
labour to confirm the faith of others; when thou
hast found mercy with God thyself, encourage others
to hope that they also shall find mercy." Those
that have fallen into sin must be *converted from it.*
Those that through grace are converted from sin
must do what they can to strengthen their brethren
that stand, and to prevent *their falling;* see Ps. li.
11–13.

4. Peter's declared resolution to cleave to Christ,
whatever it cost him (*v.* 33): *Lord, I am ready to go
with thee, both into prison and to death.* This was a
great word, and yet I believe no more than he meant
at this time, and thought he should *make good* too.
All the true disciples of Christ sincerely desire and
design to *follow him, withersoever he goes.*

5. Christ's express prediction of his denying him
thrice (*v.* 34): "*I tell thee, Peter, the cock shall not
crow this day before thou even deny that thou knowest
me.*" Christ knows us better than we know ourselves.
It is well for us that Christ knows where we are weak
better than we do, and therefore where to come in
with grace sufficient.

IV. Concerning the condition of all the disciples.
1. He appeals to them concerning what had been,
v. 35. He had owned that they had been faithful
servants to him, *v.* 28. *When I sent you without
purse, lacked you anything?* He owns that he had
sent them out in a very poor and bare condition.
If God thus send us out into the world, let us remember that better than us have thus begun low. Notwithstanding this, they had *lacked nothing;* and they
readily acknowledged it: "*Nothing, Lord.*" It is
good for us often to review the providences of God,
and to observe how we have got through the straits
and difficulties we have met with. Christ is a good
Master, and his service a good service; for though his
servants may sometimes be brought low, yet he will
help them. We must reckon ourselves well done by
if we have had the necessary supports of life, though
we have lived from hand to mouth. They had wanted
nothing.

2. He gives them notice of a very great change of
their circumstances now approaching. He that was
their Master was now entering upon his sufferings,
which he had often foretold (*v.* 37): "*Now that which
is written must be fulfilled in me. He was numbered
among the transgressors.* This is *yet to be accomplished,* and then *the things concerning me* will have
an end; then I shall say, *It is finished.*" It may be the

comfort of suffering Christians, as it was of a suffering Christ, that their sufferings were foretold. They
will have an end, and will end well, everlastingly well.
They must now in some degree suffer *with* their Master;
and, when he is gone, they must expect to suffer
like him. They must not now expect that their friends
would be so kind and generous to them as they had
been; and therefore, *He that has a purse, let him take
it.* They must now expect that their enemies would
be more fierce upon them than they had been, and
they would need magazines as well as stores: *He that
has no sword* will find a great want of it, and will be
ready to wish that he had sold his garment and
bought one. But the *sword of the Spirit* is the sword
which the disciples of Christ must furnish themselves
with. *Christ having suffered for us,* we must *arm
ourselves* with the same mind, with a holy resignation
to the will of God, and then we are better prepared
than if we had sold a coat to buy a sword. The
disciples hereupon enquire what strength they had,
and find they had among them *two swords* (*v.* 38), of
which one was Peter's. But he intimates how little
he would have them depend upon this when he saith,
It is enough. Two swords are sufficient for those
who need more, having God himself to be *the shield
of their help and the sword of their excellency.*

Verses 39–46

We have here the awful story of Christ's *agony in
the garden.* In it Christ entered the lists with the
powers of darkness, and yet conquered them.

I. What we have in this passage which we had
before is, 1. That when Christ went out, *his disciples*
(eleven of them, for Judas had given them the slip)
followed him. Having continued with him hitherto
in his temptations, they would not leave him now.
2. That he went to the place *where he was wont* to be
private, which intimates that Christ was often alone,
to teach us to be so. 3. That he exhorted his disciples
to *pray* that, though the approaching trial could not
be avoided, yet they might not in it *enter into temptation* to sin. 4. That he withdrew from them, and prayed
himself. He withdrew about a *stone's cast,* and there
he *kneeled down* (so it is here); but the other evangelists
say that afterwards he *fell on his face,* and there
prayed that, if it were the will of God, this cup of
suffering might be *removed from him.* 5. That he,
knowing it to be his Father's will that he should
suffer and die, withdrew that petition, resigned himself to his heavenly Father's will: "*Nevertheless not
my will be done,* not the will of my human nature,
but the will of God, let that be done." 6. That his
disciples were *asleep* when he was at prayer, and when
they should have been themselves praying, *v.* 45.
When he *rose from prayer,* he *found them sleeping.*
See what a favourable construction is here put upon
it, which we had not in the other evangelists—they
were *sleeping for sorrow.* This teaches us to make the
best of our brethren's infirmities, and, if there be
one cause better than another, charitably impute
them to that. 7. That when he awoke them, then he
exhorted them to pray (*v.* 46): "*Why sleep ye? Rise
and pray.*" When we find ourselves entering into
temptation, it concerns us to *rise and pray,* Lord,
help me in this *time of need.*

II. There are three things in this passage which
we had not in the other evangelists:
1. That when Christ was in his agony, *there appeared* to him *an angel from heaven, strengthening
him, v.* 43. When he was not delivered from his
sufferings, yet he was *strengthened* and supported
under them, and that was *equivalent.* If God proportion the shoulders to the burden, we shall have no
reason to complain, whatever he is pleased to lay
upon us. The angels ministered to the Lord Jesus in
his sufferings. He could have had legions of them

to rescue him; but he made use of his ministration only to *strengthen him.*

2. That, *being in an agony, he prayed more earnestly, v.* 44. As his sorrow and trouble grew upon him, he grew more importunate in prayer. Prayer, though never out of season, is in a special manner seasonable when we are in an agony; and the stronger our agonies are the more lively and frequent our prayers should be.

3. That, in this agony, *his sweat was as it were great drops of blood falling down to the ground.* There is some dispute among the critics whether this *sweat* is only *compared to* drops of *blood,* or whether *real* blood mingled with it, so that it was in colour like blood, and might truly be called a *bloody sweat;* the matter is not great. Every pore was as it were a bleeding wound, and his blood stained all his raiment. This showed the *travail of his soul.*

Verses 47–53

I. The marking of him by Judas. Here a numerous party appears, and Judas at the head of them, for he was *guide to them that took Jesus;* they knew not where to *find him,* but he brought them to the place: when they were there, they knew not which was he, but Judas told them that whomsoever he should kiss, that same was he; so he *drew near to him to kiss him.* Luke takes notice of the question Christ asked him, which we have not in the other evangelists: *Judas, betrayest thou the Son of man with a kiss? v.* 48. Must one of his own disciples betray him? Must he be betrayed with a kiss? Was ever a love-token so desecrated and abused?

II. The effort which his disciples made for his protection (*v.* 49): *When they saw what would follow,* they said, "*Lord, shall we smite with the sword? Thou didst allow us to have* two swords, shall we now make use of them?" But they were in too much *haste* and too much *heat* to stay for an answer. Peter, aiming at the head of one of the servants of the *high priest,* missed his blow, and *cut off his right ear.* The other evangelists tell us what was the check Christ gave to Peter for it. Luke here tells us, 1. How Christ excused the blow: *Suffer ye thus far, v.* 51. He said this to his enemies who came to take him, to pacify them, that they might not be provoked by it to fall upon the disciples. He *speaks them fair,* and, as it were, *begs their pardon* for an assault made upon them by one of his followers, to teach us to give good words even to our enemies. 2. How he cured the wound: *He touched his ear, and healed him;* fastened his ear on again. Christ hereby gave them a proof, (1) Of his power. He that could *heal* could *destroy* if he pleased. (2) Of his mercy and goodness. Christ here gave an illustrious example to his own rule of *doing good to them that hate us,* as afterwards he did of *praying for them that despitefully use us.* Those who render good for evil do as Christ did.

III. Christ's expostulation with the officers to show what an absurd thing it was for them to make all this rout and noise, *v.* 52, 53. Luke tells us that it was said to the *chief priests and captains of the temple,* so that they were all ecclesiastics, retainers to the temple, who were employed in this odious piece of service.

1. How Christ *reasons* with them concerning their proceedings. What occasion was there for them to come out in the dead of the night, and *with swords and staves?* They knew that he was one that would not *resist.* Why then *are ye come out as against a thief?* They knew he was one that would not *abscond,* for he was daily with them in the temple, in the midst of them.

2. How he reconciles himself to their proceedings; and this we had not before: "*But this is your hour, and the power of darkness.* How hard soever it may

seem that I should be thus exposed, I submit, for so it is determined. Now the *power of darkness,* Satan, *the ruler of the darkness of this world,* is permitted to do his worst. Let him do his worst." It is *the power of darkness* that *rides master,* and darkness must give way to light, and the power of darkness be made to truckle to the prince of light.

Verses 54–62

We have here the melancholy story of Peter's denying his Master. Notice is not taken here, as was in the other evangelists of Christ's being now upon his examination before the high priest, only of his being brought into *the high priest's house, v.* 54. But the manner of expression is observable. They *took him, and led him, and brought him,* which methinks intimates that they were in confusion. Struck with inward terror upon what they had seen and heard, they took him the furthest way about, such a hurry were they in in their own bosoms.

I. Peter's falling. It began in *sneaking.* He *followed Christ;* this was well. But he followed *afar off.* He thought to trim the matter, to *follow Christ,* and so to satisfy his conscience, but to follow *afar off,* and so to save his reputation, and sleep in a whole skin. It proceeded in associating himself with the high priest's servants. The *servants kindled a fire in the midst of the hall* and *sat down together.* Peter *sat down among them,* as if he had been one of them. His fall itself was disclaiming all acquaintance with Christ, because he was now in distress and danger. He was charged by a sorry simple maid with being retainer to this *Jesus.* She *looked wistfully* upon him as he *sat by the fire; and this man was with him,* saith she. And Peter, as he had not the courage to *own* the charge, so he had not the wit and presence of mind to *turn it off,* and therefore flatly and plainly denies it: *Woman, I know him not.* His fall was repeated a second time (*v.* 58): *After a little while another saw him,* and said, "*Even thou art one of them." Not I,* saith Peter; *Man, I am not.* And a *third* time, about the space of an hour after another confidently affirms, *strenuously* asserts it. "*Of a truth this fellow also was with him,* let him deny it if he can, for you may all perceive *he is a Galilean."* Peter now not only denies that he is a disciple of Christ, but that he knows anything of him (*v.* 60): "*Man, I know not what thou sayest."*

II. Peter's getting up again. See how happily he recovered himself.

1. The *cock crew,* and this startled him and put him upon thinking. Small accidents may involve great consequences.

2. *The Lord turned and looked upon him.* This circumstance we had not in the other evangelists, but it is a very remarkable one. Though Christ had now his back upon Peter, and was upon his trial, yet he knew all that Peter said. Christ takes more notice of what we say and do than we think he does. When Peter disowned Christ, yet Christ did not disown him. It is well for us that Christ does not deal with us as we deal with him. Christ *looked upon Peter,* for he knew that, though he had denied him with his lips, yet his eye would still be towards him. He only gave him *a look,* which none but Peter would understand the meaning of. (1) It was a *convincing* look. Peter said that he did not *know* Christ. Christ *turned, and looked upon him,* as if should say, "Dost thou not know me, Peter?" (2) It was a *chiding* look. (3) It was an *expostulating* upbraiding look: "What Peter, art thou he that disownest me now? Thou that wast the most forward to confess me to be the Son of God, and didst solemnly promise thou wouldest never disown me?" (4) It was a *compassionate* look; he looked upon him with tenderness. "Poor Peter! How art thou fallen and undone if I do not help thee!" (5) It

was a *directing* look. Christ *guided him with his eye*
to *retire*, and bethink himself a little. (6) It was a
significant look: it signified the conveying of grace to
Peter's heart. The crowing of the cock would not
have brought him to repentance without this look.
Power went along with this look to change the heart
of Peter.

3. *Peter remembered the words of the Lord.*

4. Then *Peter went out, and wept bitterly.* One look
from Christ melted him into tears of godly sorrow
for sin.

Verses 63–71

I. How our Lord Jesus was *abused* by the servants
of the high priest. They that *held Jesus mocked him*,
and *smote him* (v. 63). They made sport with him:
this sorrowful night to him shall be a merry night
to them. They *hood-winked* him and then, they
struck him on the face, and continued to do so till
he named the person that smote him (v. 64), intending
hereby an affront to his prophetical office. *Many
other things blasphemously spoke they against him*,
v. 65.

II. How he was accused and condemned by the
great sanhedrim, consisting of the *elders of the people,
the chief priests, and the scribes*, who were all up betimes, and got together *as soon as it was day*, to
prosecute this matter. They would not have been up
so early for any good work.

1. They ask him, *Art thou the Christ?* They could
not prove it upon him that he had ever said so *in
so many words*, and therefore urged him to own it
to them, v. 67. If they had asked him this question
with a willingness to admit that he was the Christ,
it had been *well*; but they asked it with a resolution
not to believe him, but a design to ensnare him.

2. He justly complained of their unfair and unjust
usage of him, v. 67, 68. "But," saith he, "*If I tell you
that I am the Christ, you will not believe.* Why should
the cause be brought on before you who have already
prejudged it? *If I ask you* what you have to object
against the proofs I produce, *you will not answer me.
You will neither answer me nor let me go;* if I be *not*
the Christ, you ought to *answer* the arguments with
which I prove that I am; if I be, you ought to *let me
go*; but you will do neither."

3. He referred them to his second coming, for the
full proof of his being the Christ (v. 69): "*Hereafter
shall the Son of man sit on the right hand of the power
of God*, and then you will not need to ask whether
he be the Christ or no."

4. Hence they inferred that he set up himself as the
Son of God, and asked him *whether he were so or no*
(v. 70): *Art thou then the Son of God?* He called
himself the *Son of man*, referring to Daniel's vision of
the *Son of man*, Dan. vii. 13, 14. But they understood
so much as to know that if he was *that Son* of man,
he was also the *Son of God*.

5. He owns himself to be the Son of God: *Ye say
that I am;* that is, "I am, as ye say."

6. Upon this they ground his condemnation (v. 71):
What need we any further witness? It was true, they
needed not any further witness to prove that he said
he was *the Son of God*, they had it from *his own mouth*.
They cannot think it possible that he should be the
Messiah, if he appear not, as they expect, in worldly
pomp and grandeur.

CHAPTER 23

This chapter carries on and concludes the history of Christ's
sufferings and death. I. His arraignment before Pilate the Roman
governor, ver. 1–5. II. His examination before Herod, ver. 6–12.
III. Pilate's struggle with the people to release Jesus, but his
yielding at length, and condemning him to be crucified, ver.
13–25. IV. An account of what passed as they led him to be
crucified, and his discourse to the people that followed, ver.
26–31. V. An account of what passed at the place of execution,

ver. 32–38. VI. The conversion of one of the thieves, as Christ
was hanging on the cross, ver. 39–43. VII. The death of Christ,
ver. 44–49. VIII. His burial, ver. 50–56.

Verses 1–12

Our Lord Jesus was condemned as a blasphemer
in the spiritual court. When they had *condemned* him,
they knew they could not *put him to death*, and therefore took another course.

I. They accused him before Pilate. The *whole
multitude of them arose, led him unto Pilate*, and they
demanded justice against him, not as a blasphemer
(that was no crime that he took cognizance of), but
as one disaffected to the Roman government, which
they in their hearts did not look upon as any crime
at all.

1. Here is the indictment drawn up against him
(v. 2). They misrepresented him, (1) As making the
people *rebel against Caesar*. It was true, and Pilate
knew it, that there was a general uneasiness in the
people under the Roman yoke. They would have
Pilate believe that this Jesus was active to foment
that general discontent: *We have found him perverting
the nation*. Christ had particularly taught that they
ought to give tribute to Caesar, and yet he is here
falsely accused as *forbidding to give tribute to Caesar*.
Innocency is no fence against calumny. (2) As making
himself a *rival with Caesar*, though the very reason
why they rejected him was because he did not offer
to do anything against Caesar; yet this is what they
charged him with, that he said, *he himself is Christ
a king*.

2. His pleading to the indictment: *Pilate asked him,
Art thou the king of the Jews?* v. 3. To which he
answered, *Thou sayest it;* that is, "It is as thou sayest."
Christ's kingdom is wholly spiritual, and will not
interfere with Caesar's jurisdiction. All that knew
him knew that he never pretended to be the *king of
the Jews*, in opposition to Caesar as supreme.

3. Pilate's declaration of his innocency (v. 4): He
*said to the chief priests, and the people, "I find no
fault in this man."*

4. The continued fury and outrage of the prosecutors, v. 5. Instead of being moderated by Pilate's
declaration of his innocency they were the more
exasperated, more exceedingly *fierce*. We do not
find that they have any particular fact to produce,
but they resolve to carry it with noise and confidence:
*He stirs up the people, teaching throughout all Judæa,
beginning from Galilee to this place.* He did *stir up
the people*, but it was to everything that was virtuous
and praiseworthy. He did *teach*, but they could not
charge him with teaching any doctrine that tended to
disturb the public peace.

II. They accused him before Herod. 1. Pilate
removed him and his cause to Herod's court. The
accusers mentioned Galilee. "Why," said Pilate, "is
he of that country? Is he a Galilean?" v. 6. "Yes,"
said they. "Let us send him to Herod then," said
Pilate, "since he belongs to Herod's jurisdiction."
Pilate was already sick of the cause, and desirous to
rid his hands of it. 2. Herod was very willing to have
the examining of him (v. 8): *When he saw Jesus he
was exceedingly glad.* He had *heard many things of
him* in Galilee, and he *longed to see him*, but purely
out of curiosity; and it was only to gratify this that he
hoped to have seen some miracle done by him. In order
to this, he *questioned with him in many things.* But
Jesus *answered him nothing;* nor would he gratify
him so much as with the performance of one miracle.
The poorest beggar, that asked a miracle for the
relief of his necessity, was *never denied*; but this proud
prince, is denied. He might have seen Christ and his
wondrous works many a time in Galilee, and *would
not*. Now he would see them, and *shall not*; because
he knew not the day of his visitation. Miracles must
not be made cheap, nor Omnipotence be at the beck

of the greatest potentate. 3. His prosecutors appeared against him before Herod. *They stood, and vehemently accused him* (v. 10), *impudently* and *boldly,* so the word signifies. 4. Herod was very *abusive* to him: He, with *his men of war, set him at nought.* They *made nothing* of him; so the word is. They laughed at him as one that had lost his power, and was become weak as other men. Herod was more *abusive* to Christ than Pilate was. Herod arrayed Christ in a *gorgeous robe,* as a mock-king; and so he taught Pilate's soldiers afterwards to do him the same indignity. 5. Herod sent him back to Pilate, and it proved an occasion of the making of them friends. Herod would not condemn him as a malefactor, and therefore *sent him again to Pilate* (v. 11), and so returned Pilate's civility and respect; and this mutual obligation brought them to a better understanding one of another, v. 12. They had been *at enmity between themselves.* Observe how those that quarrelled with one another yet could unite against Christ. Christ is the great peacemaker; both Pilate and Herod owned his innocency, and their agreeing in this cured their disagreeing in other things.

Verses 13–25

We have here the blessed Jesus run down by the mob, and hurried to the cross in the storm of a popular noise and tumult.

I. Pilate solemnly protests that he believes he has done nothing worthy of death or of bonds. And, if he did believe so, he ought immediately to have *discharged* him. But, being himself a bad man, he had no kindness for Christ, and was afraid of displeasing the people; and therefore, for want of integrity, he *called together the chief priests, and rulers, and people,* and will hear what they have to say (v. 14): "*You have brought,*" said he, "*this man to me,* and *I have examined him before you,* and have heard all you have to allege against him, and I can make nothing of it: *I find no fault in him.*"

II. He appeals to Herod concerning him (v. 15): "*I sent you to him,* and he has *sent him back*; in his opinion, his crimes are not capital. He has laughed at him as a weak man, but has not stigmatized him as a dangerous man." He thought Bedlam a fitter place for him than Tyburn.

III. He proposes to release him, if they will but consent to it. He ought to have done it without asking leave of them. But the fear of man brings many into this snare, that, they will do an unjust thing rather than pull an old house about their ears. To please the people, 1. He will release him under the notion of a malefactor, because *of necessity he must release one* (v. 17). 2. He will *chastise* him, and release him. If *no fault* is to be *found in him,* why should he be chastised?

IV. The people choose rather to have Barabbas released. He was imprisoned for a *sedition made in the city,* and for *murder,* yet this was the criminal that was preferred before Christ: *Away with this man, and release unto us Barabbas,* v. 18, 19.

V. When Pilate urged the second time that Christ should be released, they cried out, *Crucify him, crucify him,* v. 20, 21. Nothing less will serve but he must be crucified: *Crucify him, crucify him.*

VI. When Pilate the third time reasoned with them they were the more peremptory and outrageous (v. 22): "*Why? What evil hath he done?* Name his crime. *I have found no cause of death, I will chastise him and let him go.*" But they were *instant with loud voices,* not requesting, but *requiring, that he might be crucified*; as if they had as much right to demand the crucifying of one that was innocent as the release of one that was guilty.

VII. Pilate's yielding, at length. The voice of the people and of the *chief priests* prevailed. He gave *sentence that it should be as they required,* v. 24. This is repeated, in v. 25, with the aggravating circumstance of the release of Barabbas: *He released unto them him that for sedition and murder was cast into prison,* because *him they had desired*; but he *delivered Jesus to their will,* and he could not deal more barbarously with him than to deliver him to *their will.*

Verses 26–31

It is strange with what expedition they went through his trial. He was brought before the chief priests at break of day (*ch.* xxii. 66), after that to Pilate, then to Herod, then to Pilate again; and there seems to have been a long struggle between Pilate and the people about him. He was scourged, and crowned with thorns, and contumeliously used, and all this was done in four or five hours' time, or six at most, for he was crucified between nine o'clock and twelve. Never anyone was so *chased out of the world* as Christ was. Now as they led him away to death we find,

I. One that was a *bearer,* that carried his cross, *Simon* by name, *a Cyrenian.* They laid Christ's cross upon him, that he might *bear it after Jesus* (v. 26), lest Jesus should faint under it. It was pity, but a *cruel pity,* that gave him this ease.

II. Many that were *mourners.* The common people, were moved with compassion towards him, because they had reason to think he suffered unjustly. This drew a great crowd after him, as is usual at executions. *A great company of people followed him,* especially of women (v. 27); they *also bewailed and lamented him.* Though there were many that reproached and reviled him, yet there were some that valued him, and pitied him. Many bewail Christ that do not believe in him, and lament him that do not love him above all. He found time and heart to take cognizance of their tears. Christ *died lamented.* He *turned to them,* and bade them *not weep for him, but for themselves,* v. 28.

1. He gives them a general direction concerning their lamentations: *Daughters of Jerusalem, weep not for me.* They must not weep for him only, but rather let them *weep for themselves and for their children.* When with an eye of faith we behold Christ crucified we ought to weep, not for him, but for ourselves. The death of Christ was a thing peculiar; it was his victory and triumph over his enemies; it was our deliverance, and the purchase of eternal life for us. And therefore let us weep, not for him, but for our own sins, and the sins of our children, that were the cause of his death.

2. He gives them a particular reason why they should *weep for themselves and for their children*: "*For behold* sad times are coming upon your city." He had lately wept over Jerusalem himself, and now he bids them weep over it. Christ's tears should set us weeping. Now the destruction of Jerusalem is here foretold by two proverbial sayings, which both bespeak it very terrible, that what people commonly dread they would then desire, to be *written childless* and to be *buried alive.* (1) They would wish to be *written childless.* They will envy those that have none, and say, *Blessed are the barren, and the wombs that never bare.* (2) They would wish to be *buried alive*: *They shall begin to say to the mountains, Fall on us, and to the hills, Cover us,* v. 30. They shall wish to be hid in the darkest caves, that they may be out of the noise of these calamities. They will be willing to be sheltered upon any terms, though with the hazard of being crushed to pieces.

3. He shows how natural it was for them to infer this desolation from his sufferings. *If they do these things in a green tree, what shall be done in the dry?* v. 31. Christ was a *green tree,* fruitful and flourishing; now, if such things were done to him, we may thence infer what would have been done to the whole race of

mankind if he had not *interposed*, and what shall be done to those that continue dry trees, notwithstanding all that is done to make them fruitful. The consideration of the bitter sufferings of our Lord Jesus should engage us to stand in awe of the justice of God. The best saints, compared with Christ, are *dry trees*; if he suffer, why may not they expect to suffer?

Verses 32–43

I. Divers passages which we had before in Matthew and Mark concerning Christ's sufferings. 1. That there were *two others, malefactors, led with him* to the place of execution. 2. That he was crucified at a place called *Calvary—the place of a skull*. He was *crucified*. This was a painful and shameful death above any other. 3. That he was crucified *in the midst between two thieves*. Thus he was not only treated as a transgressor, but *numbered with them*. 4. That the soldiers who were employed in the execution seized his garments as their fee, and divided them among themselves *by lot*: *They parted his raiment and cast lots*. 5. That he was reviled and reproached: *The people stood beholding*, and *the rulers* stood among the rabble, *and derided him*, and they said, *He saved others, let him save himself*. They challenged him to save himself from the cross, when he was saving others by the cross: *If he be the Christ, the chosen of God*, let him save himself. They *mocked him* (v. 36, 37); they made sport with him, and made a jest of his sufferings. And they said, *If thou be the king of the Jews, save thyself*. 6. That the superscription over his head, setting forth his crime, was, *This is the King of the Jews*, v. 38. He is put to death for pretending to be the king of the Jews; but God intended it to be a declaration of what he really was: he is *the king of the Jews*, and his cross is the way to his crown. This was written in those that were called the three learned languages, *Greek, and Latin, and Hebrew*. It was written in these three languages that it might be known and read of all men. In these three languages is Jesus Christ *proclaimed king*.

II. Here are two passages which we had not before, and they are very remarkable ones.

1. Christ's prayer for his enemies (v. 34): *Father, forgive them*. Seven remarkable words Christ spoke after he was nailed to the cross, and before he died, and this is the first. As soon as ever he was fastened to the cross, or while they were nailing him, he prayed this prayer, in which observe,

(1) The petition: *Father, forgive them*. The sin they were now guilty of might justly have been made unpardonable. No, these are particularly *prayed for*. Now he made intercession for transgressors. Now the sayings of Christ upon the cross as well as his sufferings had a further intention than they seemed to have. This was explicatory of the intent and meaning of his death: "*Father, forgive them*, not only these, but all that shall repent, and believe the gospel." The great thing which Christ died to purchase and procure for us is the forgiveness of sin. His blood speaks this: *Father, forgive them*. Though they were his persecutors and murderers, he prayed, Father, forgive *them*.

(2) The plea: *For they know not what they do;* for, *if they had known*, they would not have crucified him. The crucifiers of Christ *know not what they do*. There is a kind of ignorance that does in part excuse sin: ignorance through want of the means of knowledge or of a capacity to receive instruction. The crucifiers of Christ were kept in ignorance by their rulers, and had prejudices against him instilled into them, so that in what they did against Christ and his doctrine they thought they did God service. Such are to be pitied and prayed for. We must in prayer call God *Father*. The great thing we must beg of God, both for ourselves and others, is the forgiveness of sins.

We must pray for *our enemies*, and those that hate and persecute us; and we must be earnest with God in prayer for the forgiveness of their sins, their sins against us. This is Christ's example to his own rule (Matt. v. 44, 45, *Love your enemies*). If Christ loved and prayed for such enemies, what enemies can we have that we are not obliged to *love* and *pray for*?

2. The conversion of the thief upon the cross. Christ was crucified between two thieves, and in them were represented the different effects which the cross of Christ would have upon the children of men. Now the cross of Christ is to some a *savour of life unto life*, to others of *death unto death*.

(1) Here was one of these malefactors that was *hardened to the last*. Near to the cross of Christ, he *railed on him*, as others did (v. 39): he said, *If thou be the Christ save thyself and us*. Though he was now in pain and agony, yet this did not humble his proud spirit, nor teach him to give good language, no, not to his fellow-sufferer. He challenges Christ to *save both himself and them*. There are some that have the impudence to rail at Christ, and yet the confidence to expect to be saved by him.

(2) Here was the other of them that was *softened at the last*. This malefactor was snatched as a brand out of the burning, and made a monument of divine mercy and grace. This gives no encouragement to any to put off their repentance, for, though it is certain that true repentance is never too late, it is as certain that late repentance is seldom true. He never had any offer of Christ, nor day or grace, before now: he was designed to be made a singular instance of the power of Christ's grace. Christ, having conquered Satan in the destruction of Judas and the preservation of Peter, erects this further trophy of his victory over him. We shall see the case to be extraordinary if we observe,

[1] The extraordinary operations of God's grace upon him, which appeared in what he said.

First, See what he said to the other malefactor, v. 40, 41. 1. He reproved him for railing at Christ, as destitute of the *fear of God*: *Dost not thou fear God?* This implies that it was the fear of God which restrained him from following the multitude to do this evil. "If thou hadst any humanity in thee, thou wouldest not insult over one that is thy fellow-sufferer; *thou art in the same condition;* thou art a *dying man* too." 2. He owns that he deserves what was done to him: *We indeed justly. We received the due reward of our deeds*. True penitents acknowledge the justice of God in all the punishments of their sin. God has *done right*, but *we have done wickedly*. 3. He believes Christ to have suffered *wrongfully*. This penitent thief is convinced, by his conduct in his sufferings, that *he has done nothing amiss*. The chief priests would have him crucified *between* the malefactors, as *one of them*; but this thief has more sense than they.

Secondly, See what he said to our Lord Jesus: *Lord, remember me when thou comest into thy kingdom*, v. 42. This is the prayer of a *dying sinner* to a *dying Saviour*. It was the honour of Christ to be *thus prayed to*. It was the happiness of the thief *thus to pray*; perhaps he never prayed before, and yet now was heard, and saved at the last gasp. Observe his *faith* in this prayer. In his confession of sin (v. 41) he discovered *repentance towards God*. In this petition he discovered *faith towards our Lord Jesus Christ*. He owns him to be *Lord*, and to have a *kingdom*, and that he was going to that kingdom, and that those should be happy whom he favoured; and to *believe* and *confess* all this was a *great thing* at this time of day. He believed *another life* after this, and desired to be happy in *that* life, not as the other thief, to be *saved from the cross*, but to be well provided for when the cross had done its worst. Observe his humility in this prayer. All he begs is, *Lord, remember me,* referring himself to Christ in what way to remember him. Christ remembered this thief. There is an air of importunity and fervency in this prayer. He does, as it were, breathe out his soul in it: *"Lord, remember me;* I desire no more; into thy hands I commit my case." To be remembered by Christ, now that he is in his kingdom, is what we should earnestly desire and pray for, and it will be enough to secure our welfare living and dying.

[2] The extraordinary grants of Christ's favour to him: *Jesus said unto him*: *"Verily I say unto thee,* I say *Amen* to this prayer: nay, thou shalt have more than thou didst ask, *This day thou shalt be with me in paradise,"* v. 43.

First, To whom this was spoken: to the penitent thief. Though Christ himself was now in the greatest struggle and agony, yet he had a word of comfort to speak to a poor penitent. Even great sinners, if they be true penitents, shall, through Christ, obtain not only the pardon of their sins, but a place in the paradise of God.

Secondly, By whom this was spoken. This was another mediatorial word which Christ spoke to explain the true intent and meaning of his sufferings; as he died to purchase the *forgiveness of sins* for us (v. 34), so also to purchase *eternal life* for us. By this word we are given to understand that Jesus Christ died to *open the kingdom of heaven to all penitent obedient believers.* 1. Christ here lets us know that he was going to paradise himself. He went by the cross to the crown, and we must not think of going any other way. 2. He lets all penitent believers know that when they die they shall go to be with him there. See here how the happiness of heaven is set forth to us. (1) It is *paradise,* a garden of pleasure, the *paradise of God* (Rev. ii. 7). (2) It is being *with Christ* there. That is the happiness of heaven. (3) It is immediate upon death: *This day shalt thou be with me,* tonight, before tomorrow.

Verses 44–49

I. Christ's dying *magnified* by the *prodigies* that attended it. 1. The *darkening of the sun at noon-day.* It was now about the *sixth hour,* that is, twelve o'clock at noon; and there was a *darkness over all the earth until the ninth hour.* 2. The *rending of the veil of the temple.* The former prodigy was in the *heavens,* this in the *temple;* for both these are the houses of God. By this rending of the veil was signified the taking away of the ceremonial law, and of all other difficulties and discouragements in our approaches to God, so that now we may *come boldly to the throne of grace.*

II. Christ's dying *explained* (v. 46) by the words with which he breathed out his soul. Jesus *had cried* with a loud voice when he said, *Why hast thou forsaken me?* So we are told in Matthew and Mark, and, it should seem, it was with a *loud voice* that he said this too. He said, *Father, into thy hands I commend my spirit.* He borrowed these words from his father David (Ps. xxxi. 5). Christ died with scripture in his mouth. In this address to God he calls him *Father.* When he complained of being forsaken, he cried, *Eli, Eli, My God, my God;* but, to show that that dreadful agony of his soul was now over, he here calls God *Father.* Christ made use of these words in a sense peculiar to himself as Mediator. He was now to *make his soul an offering for our sin* (Isa. liii. 10), to *give his life a ransom for many* (Matt. xx. 28). Now by these words he *offered up the sacrifice,* did, as it were, lay his hand upon the head of it, and surrender it. "I *deposit* it, I pay it down into thy hands. Father, accept of my life and soul instead of the lives and souls of the sinners I die for." *The goodwill of the offerer* was requisite to the acceptance

of the offering. He commends his spirit into his Father's hand, to be *received* into paradise, and *returned* the third day. Christ has fitted those words of David to the purpose of dying saints, and hath, as it were, sanctified them for their use. We must show that we are freely willing to die, that we firmly believe in another life after this, by saying, *Father, into thy hands I commend my spirit.*

III. Christ's dying improved by the impressions it made upon those that attended him.

1. The centurion that had command of the guard was much affected with what he saw, v. 47. He was a Roman, a Gentile, and yet he *glorified God.* And he bore a testimony to the patient sufferer: *"Certainly this was a righteous man."* His testimony in Matthew and Mark goes further: *Truly this was the Son of God.*

2. The disinterested spectators could not but be concerned. This is taken notice of only here, v. 48. *All the people that came together to that sight, beholding the things which were done,* could not but go away very serious. *They smote their breasts, and returned.* They laid the thing very much to heart for the present. Probably these very people were of those that had cried, *Crucify him, crucify him,* and, when he was nailed to the cross, reviled and blasphemed him; but now they had not only their mouths stopped, but their consciences startled. Yet, it should seem, the impression soon wore off: *They smote their breasts, and returned.* They did not show any further token of respect to Christ, but went home; and we have reason to fear that in a little time they quite forgot it. Thus many that see Christ evidently set forth crucified among them in the word and sacraments are a little affected for the present, but it does not continue. They see Christ's face and admire him; but they *go away, and straightway forget what manner of man he is,* and what reason they have to love him.

3. His own friends and followers were obliged to keep their distance, and yet got as near as they could and durst, to see what was done (v. 49): *All his acquaintance stood afar off;* this was part of his sufferings. And *the women that followed him from Galilee were beholding these things.* Now was Christ *set for a sign that should be spoken against,* as Simeon foretold, that the thoughts of many hearts might be revealed, ch. ii. 34, 35.

Verses 50–56

We have here an account of Christ's burial.

I. Who buried him. His acquaintance *stood afar off;* but God raised up a *man named Joseph,* v. 50. His character is that he was *a good man and a just,* a man of unspotted reputation for virtue and piety, not only *just* to all, but good to all that needed him; he was a person of quality, a counsellor, a member of the sanhedrim, one of the elders of the Jewish church. Though he was of that body of men who had put Christ to death, yet he *had not consented to their counsel and deed* (v. 51). Nay, he not only *dissented* openly from those that were enemies to Christ, but he *consented* secretly with those that were his friends: *He himself waited for the kingdom of God.* There are many who, though they do not make any show in their outward profession, yet will be more ready to do him a piece of real service, than others who make a greater figure and noise.

II. What he did towards the burying of him. 1. He *went to Pilate* and *begged the body of Jesus.* 2. He *took it down, it should seem,* with his own hands, and *wrapped it in linen.* It was the manner of the Jews to *roll* the bodies of the dead, as we do little children in their *swaddling-clothes,* so that the piece of fine linen, which he bought whole, he cut into many pieces for this purpose.

III. Where he was buried. *In a sepulchre that was hewn in stone.* But it was *a sepulchre in which never man before was laid.*

IV. When he was buried. *On the day of the preparation, when the sabbath drew on, v.* 54. This is given as a reason why they made such haste with the funeral, because the *sabbath drew* on. Weeping must not hinder sowing. Though they were in tears for the death of Christ, yet they must apply themselves to the sanctifying of the sabbath.

V. Who attended the funeral; not any of the disciples, but only *the women that came with him from Galilee* (*v.* 55), who, as they stayed by him while he hung on the cross, so they *followed* him, and *beheld the sepulchre*, and *how his body was laid in it.* They were led to this, not by their curiosity, but by their affection to the Lord Jesus.

VI. What preparation was made for the embalming of his body after he was buried (*v.* 56): *They returned, and prepared spices and ointments,* which was more an evidence of their love than of their faith; for had they *remembered* and *believed* that he should *rise again the third day,* they would have spared their *cost* and *pains* herein. But, busy as they were in this preparation, they *rested on the sabbath day.*

Chapter 24

Our Lord Jesus went gloriously down to death, but he rose again more gloriously, and the proofs and evidences of Christ's resurrection are more fully related by this evangelist than they were by Matthew and Mark. I. Assurance given by two angels, to the women who visited the sepulchre (ver. 1–7), and the report of this to the apostles, ver. 8–11. II. The visit which Peter made to the sepulchre, ver. 12. III. Christ's conference with the two disciples that were going to Emmaus, ver. 13–35. IV. His appearing to the eleven disciples themselves, the same day at evening, ver. 36–49. V. The farewell he gave them, his ascension into heaven, and the joy and praise of his disciples whom he left behind, ver. 50–53.

Verses 1–12

The *infallible proofs* of his resurrection are *things revealed which belong to us and to our children.* Some of them we have here in these verses.

I. We have here the affection and respect which the good women that had followed Christ showed to him, after he was dead and buried, *v.* 1. As soon as ever they could, after the sabbath was over, they *came to the sepulchre,* to embalm his body, to anoint the head and face, and perhaps the wounded hands and feet, and to scatter sweet spices upon and about the body as it is usual with us to strew flowers upon the dead bodies and graves of our friends. The zeal of these good women for Christ did continue. The spices they had prepared the evening before the sabbath, they brought to the sepulchre on the morning after the sabbath, early, very early. What is prepared for Christ, let it be used for him. Notice is taken of the names of these women, *Mary Magdalene,* and *Joanna,* and *Mary* the Mother of James. Notice is also taken of certain others with them, *v.* 1, and again, *v.* 10. These, who had not joined in preparing the spices, would yet go along with them to the sepulchre; as if the number of Christ's friends increased when he was dead.

II. The surprise they were in, when they found the stone rolled away and the grave empty (*v.* 2, 3); they were *much perplexed* at that (*v.* 4), that *the stone was rolled away from the sepulchre,* and that they *found not the body of the Lord Jesus.* Good Christians often perplex themselves about that with which they should comfort and encourage themselves.

III. The plain account which they had of Christ's resurrection from two angels, who appeared to them *in shining garments.* The women, when they saw the angels, *were afraid,* they *bowed down their faces to the earth,* to look for their dear Master in the grave.

They would rather find him in his *grave-clothes* than angels themselves in their *shining-garments.* They upbraid the women with the absurdity of the search they were making: *Why seek ye the living among the dead? v.* 5. Witness is hereby given to Christ that he is *living,* and it is the comfort of all the saints, *I know that my Redeemer liveth;* for because he lives we shall live also. But a reproof is given to those that look for him *among the dead.* They assure them that he is risen from the dead (*v.* 6): "*He is not here, but is risen;* he has quitted his grave." They refer them to his own words: *Remember what he spoke to you, when he was yet in Galilee.* If they had duly believed and observed the prediction of it, they would easily have believed the thing itself when it came to pass. The angels repeat to them what Christ had often said in their hearing, *The Son of man must be delivered into the hands of sinful men.* He told them that he *must be crucified.* Would not this bring to their mind that which always followed, *The third day he shall rise again?* These angels from heaven bring not any *new gospel,* but put them in mind of the sayings of Christ, and teach them how to improve and apply them.

IV. Their satisfaction in this account, *v.* 8. They *remembered his words,* when they were thus put in mind of them, and thence concluded that if he was risen it was no more than they had reason to expect. A seasonable remembrance of the words of Christ will help us to a right understanding of his providence.

V. The report they brought of this to the apostles: *They returned from the sepulchre, and told all these things to the eleven, and to all the rest* of Christ's disciples, *v.* 9. In a little time, that morning, they all had notice of it. But we are told (*v.* 11) how the report was received: *Their words seemed to them as idle tales, and they believed them not.* They thought it was only the fancy of the women, and imputed it to the power of imagination; for they also had forgotten Christ's words. One cannot but be amazed at the stupidity of these disciples,—who had themselves so often professed that they believed Christ to be the Son of God, had been so often told that he must die and rise again, and then enter into his glory, had seen him more than once raise the dead,— that they should be so backward to believe.

VI. The enquiry which Peter made hereupon, *v.* 12. It was Mary Magdalene that brought the report to him, as appears, John xx. 1, 2, where this story of his running to the sepulchre is more particularly related. 1. Peter hastened to the sepulchre upon the report. Perhaps, he had not been so ready to go thither now if the women had not told him that *the watch was fled.* Many that are *swift-footed* enough when there is no danger are but *cow-hearted* when there is. 2. He looked into the sepulchre, and took notice how orderly the linen clothes in which Christ was wrapped were taken off, and folded up, and laid by themselves, but the body gone. He was very particular in making his observations, as if he would rather credit his own eyes than the testimony of the angels. 3. He went away *wondering in himself; at that which was come to pass.* He is only amazed with the thing, and knows not what to make of it. There is many a thing puzzling and perplexing to us which would be both plain and profitable if we did but rightly understand the words of Christ.

Verses 13–35

This appearance of Christ to the *two disciples* going to Emmaus was mentioned, and but just mentioned, before (Mark xvi. 12); here it is largely related. It happened the same day that Christ rose, the first day of the new world that rose with him. One of these two disciples was *Cleopas;* who the other was is not certain. It was one of those that were associated with the eleven, mentioned *v.* 9.

I. The *walk* and *talk* of these two disciples: *They went to a village called Emmaus*, which is reckoned to be about two hours' walk from Jerusalem, *v.* 13. The accounts brought them that morning of their Master's resurrection seemed to them *as idle tales.* But as they travelled they *talked together of all those things which had happened*, *v.* 14. They *talked over these things*, reasoning with themselves concerning the probabilities of Christ's resurrection.

II. The good company they met with upon the road, when Jesus himself came, and joined himself to them (*v.* 15): *They communed together, and reasoned. Jesus himself drew near*, as a stranger, who, seeing them travel the same way that he *went*, told them that he should be *glad of their company.* Where but two together are well employed in work of that kind Christ will come to them, and make a third. Two thus twisted in faith and love become a *threefold cord, not easily broken.* They in their communings and reasonings together were searching for Christ, and now Christ comes to them. They who seek Christ shall find him. But, though they had Christ with them, they were not at first aware of it (*v.* 16): *Their eyes were held, that they should not know him.* No matter *how* it was, but *so* it was they did not *know him*, Christ so ordering it that they might the more freely discourse with him and he with them.

III. The conference that was between Christ and them, when he knew them, and they knew not him. Now Christ and his disciples, as is usual when friends meet incognito, or in a disguise, are here crossing questions.

1. Christ's first question to them is concerning *their* present *sadness: What manner of communications are these that you have one with another as you walk, and are sad? v.* 17.

(1) They *were sad.* They had lost their dear Master, and were, in their own apprehensions, quite disappointed in their expectations from him. They had given up the cause, and knew not what course to take to retrieve it. Though he was risen from the dead, yet either they did not know it or did not believe it, and so they were still in sorrow. Christ's disciples are often sad and sorrowful even when they have reason to rejoice. They had *communications one with another* concerning Christ. It becomes Christians to talk of Christ, not only of God and his providence, but of Christ and his grace and love. Good company and good converse are an excellent antidote against prevailing melancholy. Giving *vent* to the grief may perhaps give *ease* to the grieved. Joint mourners should be mutual comforters; comforts sometimes come best from such.

(2) Christ came up to them, and enquired into the matter of their talk: *What manner of communications are these?* Though Christ had now entered into his state of exaltation, yet he continued tender of his disciples. Our Lord Jesus takes notice of the sorrow and sadness of his disciples, and is afflicted in their afflictions. Christ has thereby taught us to be *conversable.* It does not become Christians to be morose and shy, but to take pleasure in good society. We are hereby taught to be *compassionate.* When we see our friends in sorrow and sadness, we should, like Christ here, take cognizance of their grief.

2. In answer to this, they put a question to him concerning *his strangeness. Art thou only a stranger in Jerusalem, and hast not known the things that are come to pass there in these days?* Cleopas gave him a civil answer. We ought to be civil to those who are civil to us. It was a dangerous time now with Christ's disciples; yet he was not jealous of this stranger, that he had any design upon them, to inform against them. He is full of Christ himself and of his death and sufferings, and wonders that everybody else is not so too: "What! art thou such a stranger in

Jerusalem as not to know what has been done to our Master there?" He is very willing to inform this stranger concerning Christ. He would not have anyone that had the face of a man to be ignorant of Christ. And it is observable that these disciples, who were so forward to instruct the stranger, were instructed by him; for to him that has, and uses what he has, shall be given. It appears, by what Cleopas says, that the death of Christ made a great noise in Jerusalem, so that it could not be imagined that any man should be such a stranger in the city as not to know of it.

3. Christ, by way of reply, asked concerning *their knowledge* (*v.* 19): *He said unto them, What things?* thus making himself yet more a stranger. Jesus Christ made light of his own sufferings, in comparison with the joy set before him. See with what unconcernedness he looks back upon his sufferings. He had reason to know what things; for to him they were bitter things, and heavy things, and yet he asks, *What things?* They must tell him *what things* they know, and then he will tell them what was the meaning of these things, and lead them into the mystery of them.

4. They, hereupon, gave him a particular account concerning Christ. Observe the story they tell, *v.* 19, &c.

(1) Here is a summary of Christ's *life* and *character.* The *things* they are full of are concerning *Jesus of Nazareth*, who *was a prophet*, a teacher come from God. He confirmed it by many glorious miracles, miracles of mercy, so that he was *mighty in deed and word before God and all the people.* He had great acceptance with God, and a great reputation in the country. Many are *great before all the people*, who are not so *before God*, but Christ was mighty *before God and all the people.* Those were strangers in Jerusalem that did not know this.

(2) Here is a modest narrative of his sufferings and death, *v.* 20. "The *chief priests and our rulers delivered him to be condemned to death*, and *they have crucified him.*" It is strange that they did not lay a greater load upon those that had been guilty of crucifying Christ.

(3) Here is an intimation of their disappointment in him, as the reason of their sadness: "*We trusted that it had been he who should have redeemed Israel,*" *v.* 21; great things expected from him, by them that *looked for redemption*, and in it for the consolation of Israel. Now, if *hope deferred makes the heart sick*, hope disappointed, especially such a hope, kills the heart. *We trusted* (say they) *that it had been he that should have redeemed Israel.* And is it not he that doth redeem Israel? Nay, is he not by his death paying the price of their redemption? So that now, since that most difficult part of his undertaking was got over, they had more reason than ever to *trust* that *this was he that should deliver Israel.*

(4) Here is an account of their present amazement. "*This is the third day* since he was crucified and died, and that was the day when it was expected, if ever, that he should rise again and show himself as publicly in honour as he had been shown three days before in disgrace, but all is silent." They own that there was a report among them that he was risen, but they seem to speak of it very slightly (*v.* 22, 23): "*Certain women also of our company made us astonished*, who were *early at the sepulchre*, and found the body gone, and they said that they had *seen a vision of angels, who said that he was alive;* but we are ready to think it was only their fancy. Women are easily imposed upon." They acknowledge that some of the apostles had visited the sepulchre, and found it empty, *v.* 24. "But *him they saw not*, and therefore we have reason to fear that he *is not risen*, for, if he be, surely he would have *shown himself* to them; so that we have

no great reason to think that he is risen. Our hopes were all nailed to his cross, and buried in his grave."

(5) Our Lord Jesus, though not known by face to them, makes himself known to them by his word.

[1] He reproves them for the weakness of their faith in the scriptures of the Old Testament: *O fools, and slow of heart to believe, v.* 25. Christ called them *fools,* not as it signifies *wicked men,* but as it signifies *weak men.* That which is condemned in them as their *foolishness* is, *First,* Their *slowness to believe.* Christ tells us that those are *fools* who are *slow of heart to believe,* and are kept from it by prejudices never impartially examined. *Secondly,* Their slowness to believe *the writings of the prophets.* Were we but more *conversant* with the scripture, and the divine counsels as far as they are made known in the scripture, we should not be subject to such perplexities as we often *entangle* ourselves in.

[2] He shows them that the sufferings of Christ were really the appointed way to his glory, and he could not go to it any other way (*v.* 26): "*Ought not the Christ to have suffered these things, and to enter into his glory?*" The cross of Christ was that to which they could not reconcile themselves; now here he shows them two things which take off the offence of the cross: *First,* That the Messiah *ought to suffer* these things; and therefore his sufferings were not only no objection against his being the Messiah, but really a proof of it. He could not have been a *Saviour,* if he had not been a *sufferer. Secondly,* That, when he had suffered these things, he should *enter into his glory,* which he did at his resurrection. It is called *his* glory, and it was the glory he had before the world was. He *ought* to suffer first, and then to enter into his glory. We are directed to expect the crown of *thorns* and then that of *glory.*

[3] He expounded to them the scriptures of the Old Testament, and showed them how they were fulfilled in Jesus of Nazareth (*v.* 27): *Beginning at Moses* he went in order through *all the prophets,* and *expounded to them the things concerning himself,* showing that the sufferings he had now gone through were the accomplishment of them. There are things dispersed throughout *all the scriptures* concerning Christ. You cannot go far in any part of scripture but you meet with something that has reference to Christ, some prophecy, some promise, some prayer, some type or other. A golden thread of gospel grace runs through the whole web of the Old Testament. The things concerning Christ need to be *expounded.* They were delivered darkly, according to that dispensation: but now that the veil is taken away the New Testament expounds the Old. Jesus Christ is himself the best expositor of scripture, particularly the scriptures concerning himself. In *studying* the scriptures, it is good to be *methodical,* for the Old Testament light shone *gradually* to the *perfect day,* and it is good to observe how at *sundry times,* and in *divers manners,* God spoke to the fathers *concerning* his Son, by whom he has now *spoken* to us. Some begin their bible at the wrong end, who study the Revelation first.

IV. Here is the discovery which Christ at length made of himself to them. One would have given a great deal for a copy of the sermon Christ preached to them by the way, of that exposition of the bible which he gave them. The disciples are so charmed with it, that they think they are come too soon to their journey's end; but so it is: *They drew nigh to the village whither they went* (*v.* 28). And now,

1. They courted his stay with them: *He made as though he would have gone further;* he did not *say* that he would but he seemed to them to be going further. He would have gone further if they had not courted his stay. Those that would have Christ dwell with them must invite him, and be importunate with him. If he seem to *draw off* from us, it is but

to draw out our importunity; as here, *they constrained him;* with a kind and friendly violence, saying, *Abide with us.* Those that have experienced the pleasure and profit of communion with Christ cannot but covet more of his company, and beg of him, not only to *walk with them* all day, but to *abide with them* at night. Christ yielded to their importunity: He *went in, to tarry with them.* He has promised that *if any man open the door,* to bid him welcome, he will *come in to him,* Rev. iii. 20.

2. He manifested himself to them, *v.* 30, 31. We may suppose that he continued his discourse with them, which he began upon the road. While supper was getting ready (which perhaps was soon done, the provision was so small and mean), it is probable that he entertained them. But still they little thought that it was Jesus himself that was all this while talking with them, till at length he was pleased to throw off his disguise. They began to suspect it was he, when, as they *sat down to meat: He took bread, and blessed it,* and *brake it, and gave to them.* This was not a *miraculous* meal like that of the five loaves, nor a *sacramental* meal like that of the eucharist, but a *common* meal; yet Christ here did the same as he did in those, to teach us to keep up our communion with God through Christ in common providences as well as in special ordinances. Wherever we *sit down to eat,* let us set Christ at the upper end of the table, take our meat as *blessed to us* by him, and *eat and drink* to his glory, and receive contentedly and thankfully what he is pleased to *carve* out to us, be the fare ever so coarse and mean. *Their eyes were opened,* and then they saw who it was, and *knew him* well enough. The mists were scattered, the veil was taken off, and then they made no question but it was their Master. He might put on the shape of another, but no other could put on his; and therefore it must be he. See how Christ by his Spirit and grace makes himself known. The work is completed by the opening of the eyes of their mind. If he that gives the revelation do not give the understanding, we are in the dark still.

3. He immediately disappeared: *He vanished out of their sight.* He *became not visible by them.* As soon as he had given his disciples one glimpse of him he was gone. Such short and transient views have we of Christ in this world; we see him, but in a little while lose the sight of him again.

V. Here is the reflection which these disciples made upon this conference, and the report which they made of it to their brethren at Jerusalem.

1. The reflection they each of them made upon the influence which Christ's discourse had upon them (*v.* 32): *They said one to another, Did not our hearts burn within us?* Thus do they not so much compare *notes* as compare *hearts,* in the review of the sermon Christ had preached to them. They found the preaching powerful, even when they knew not the preacher. It made things very plain and clear to them; and, which was more, brought a *divine heat* with a *divine light* into their souls. Now this they take notice of, for the confirming of their belief, that it was indeed, as at last they saw, *Jesus himself* that had been talking with them all along. See here, (1) What *preaching* is likely to *do good*—such as Christ's was, *plain preaching*—he talked with us by the way; and scriptural preaching—*he opened to us the scriptures.* Ministers should show people their religion in their bibles, they must show that they make that the fountain of their knowledge and the foundation of their faith. (2) What *hearing* is likely to *do good*—that which makes the *heart burn;* when we are much affected with the things of God, especially with the love of Christ in dying for us, and have our hearts thereby drawn out in love to him, and drawn up in holy desires and devotions, then our hearts *burn within us.*

2. The report they brought of this to their brethren at Jerusalem (v. 33): *They rose up the same hour*, so transported with joy at the discovery Christ had made of himself to them that they could not stay to make an end of their supper, but returned with all speed to Jerusalem, though it was towards evening. Now that they had seen Christ they could not rest till they had brought the good news to the disciples, both for the confirmation of their trembling faith and for the comfort of their sorrowful spirits. It is the duty of those to whom Christ has manifested himself to let others know what he has done for their souls. These disciples were *full* of this matter themselves, and must go to their brethren, to give vent to their joys. (1) How they found them relating another proof of the resurrection of Christ. They found the eleven, and those that were their usual companions, *gathered together* late in the night, and they found them *saying* among themselves, and when these two came in, they repeated to them with joy and triumph, *The Lord is risen indeed, and hath appeared to Simon*, v. 34. That Peter had a sight of him before the rest of the disciples had appears 1 Cor. xv. 5, where it is said, *He was seen of Cephas, then of the twelve*. The angel having ordered the women to tell Peter of it particularly (Mark xvi. 7), for his comfort, it is highly probable that our Lord Jesus did himself the same day appear to Peter, though we have no particular narrative of it. This he had related to his brethren; but, observe, Peter does not here proclaim it, and boast of it, himself, but the other disciples speak of it with exultation, *The Lord is risen indeed*. He has appeared not only to the women, but to Simon. (2) How they seconded their evidence with an account of what they had seen (v. 35): *They told what things were done in the way*. The words that were spoken by Christ to them in the way are here called the *things* that were *done in the way*; for the words that Christ speaks are not an empty sound, wondrous things are *done* by them, done *by the way*, by the by as it were, where it is not expected. They told also how he was at length *known to them in the breaking of bread*.

Verses 36–49

Five times Christ was seen the same day that he rose: by Mary Magdalene alone in the garden (John xx. 14), by the women as they were going to tell the disciples (Matt. xxviii. 9), by Peter alone, by the two disciples going to Emmaus, and now at night by the eleven.

I. The great *surprise* which his appearing gave them. He came in among them very *seasonably*, as they were comparing notes concerning the proofs of his resurrection: *As they thus spoke, Jesus himself stood in the midst of them*, and *put it out of question*. 1. The *comfort* Christ spoke to them: *Peace be unto you*. This intimates in general that it was a kind visit which Christ now paid them, a visit of love and friendship. They did not *credit* those who had seen him; therefore he *comes himself*. He had promised that after his resurrection he *would see them in Galilee*; but so desirous was he to see them that he anticipated the appointment and *sees them at Jerusalem*. Christ is often *better than his word*, but never worse. Now his first word to them was, *Peace be to you*. Thus Christ would at the first word intimate to them that he did not come to quarrel with Peter for *denying* him and the rest for *running away* from him; no, he came peaceably, to signify to them that he had forgiven them. 2. The *fright* which they put themselves into upon it (v. 37): They were *terrified*, supposing that *they had seen a spirit*, because he was in the midst of them ere they were aware. The word used (Matt. xiv. 26), when they said *It is a spirit*, is a *spectre*, an *apparition*; but the word here used properly

signifies a *spirit*; they supposed it to be a spirit not clothed with a real body.

II. The great *satisfaction* which his discourse gave them, wherein we have,

1. The reproof he gave them for their causeless fears: *Why are you troubled, and why do thoughts arise in your hearts?* v. 38. Observe here, (1) That when at any time we are *troubled*, *thoughts* are apt to *rise in our hearts* that do us hurt. Sometimes the trouble is the effect of the *thoughts* that *arise in our hearts*. Sometimes the thoughts arising in the heart are the effect of the trouble, without are fightings and then within are fears. (2) That many of the troublesome thoughts with which our minds are disquieted arise from our mistakes concerning Christ. They here thought that they had *seen a Spirit*, when they saw Christ. When Christ is by his Spirit convincing and humbling us, when he is by his providence trying and converting us, we *mistake him*, as if he designed our hurt, and this troubles us. (3) That all the troublesome thoughts which rise in our hearts at any time are known to the Lord Jesus. He chid his disciples for such *thoughts*, to teach us to chide ourselves for them.

2. The proof he gave them of his resurrection, both for the *silencing* of their *fears* and for the *strengthening* of their *faith*. Two proofs he gives them:

(1) He shows them his body, particularly *his hands and his feet*. "*Behold my hands and my feet;* you see I have *hands* and *feet*, and therefore have a *true* body; and you see the marks of the nails in my hands and feet, and therefore it is *my own* body, the *same* that you saw crucified, and not a *borrowed* one." He lays down this prinicple—that a *spirit has not flesh and bones*. Now hence he infers, "*It is I myself*, whom you have been so intimately acquainted with, and have had such familiar conversation with; it is *I myself*, whom you have reason to rejoice in, and not to be afraid of." [1] He appeals to their *sight*, *shows* them *his hands* and *his feet*, which were pierced with the nails. Christ retained the marks of them in his glorified body, that they might be proofs that it was he himself; and he was willing that they should be *seen*. He afterwards showed them to Thomas, for he is not ashamed of his sufferings for us; little reason then have we to be ashamed of them, or of ours for him. [2] He appeals to their *touch*: *Handle me, and see*. He would not let Mary Magdalene touch him at that time, John xx. 17. But the disciples here are entrusted to do it, that they who were to preach his resurrection, and to suffer for doing so, might be themselves abundantly satisfied concerning it. He bade them *handle him*, that they might be convinced that he was not a *spirit*. There were many heretics in the primitive times who said that Christ had never any substantial body, was neither really born nor truly suffered. Blessed be God, these heresies have long since been *buried*; and we know and are sure that Jesus Christ was no *spirit* or *apparition*, but had a true and real body, even after his resurrection.

(2) He *eats* with them, to show that he had a real and true body. Peter lays a great stress upon this (Acts x. 41): We *did eat and drink with him after he rose from the dead*.

[1] When they *saw his hands and his feet, They believed not for joy, and wondered*, v. 41. It was their infirmity that they *believed not*, that *yet* they believed not. This very much corroborates the truth of Christ's resurrection that the disciples were so slow to believe it. Instead of stealing away his body, and saying, *He is risen*, when he is not, as the chief priests suggested they would do, they are ready to say again and again, *He is not risen*, when he is. When afterwards they did believe it, and venture their all upon it, it was not but upon the fullest demonstration of the thing that could be. But, though it was their

infirmity, yet it was an excusable one; for it was not from any contempt of the evidence offered them that they believed not. They *believed not for joy*; they thought it too good news to be true. They *wondered*; they thought it not only *too good*, but *too great*, to be true.

[2] For their further conviction and encouragement, he *called for some meat*. He here did actually *eat* with *them* and *the rest*, to show that his body was really and truly *returned to life*. They gave him a *piece of a broiled fish, and of a honey-comb*, v. 42. This was mean fare; yet, if it be the fare of the disciples, their Master will fare as they do, because in the kingdom of our Father they shall fare as he does.

3. The *insight* he gave them into the word of God. He refers them to the *word* which they had *heard* from him when he was with them (v. 44): *These are the words which I said unto you while I was yet with you.* We should better *understand* what Christ *does*, if we did but better *remember* what he hath *said*. He refers them to the *word* they had read in the Old Testament: *All things must be fulfilled which were written.* Whatever they found written concerning the Messiah in the Old Testament must be fulfilled in him, what was written concerning his sufferings as well as what was written concerning his kingdom. *All things* must be fulfilled, even the *hardest*, even the *heaviest*. The several parts of the Old Testament are here mentioned, as containing each of them things concerning Christ: *The law of Moses*, the *prophets*, the *Psalms*. See in what various ways of writing God did of old reveal his will. By an immediate present work upon their minds he gave them to apprehend the true intent and meaning of the Old Testament prophecies of Christ: *Then opened he their understanding, that they might understand the scriptures*, v. 45. In his discourse with the two disciples he took the veil from off the text, by *opening* the scriptures; here he took the veil from off the heart, *by opening the mind*. Jesus Christ by his Spirit operates on the minds of men. He has access to our Spirits and can immediately influence them. Even good men need to have their *understandings opened*; for though they are not *darkness*, yet in many things they are *in the dark*. Christ's way of working faith in the soul is by *opening the understanding*. Thus he comes into the soul by the *door*. The design of opening the understanding is *that we may understand the scriptures*; not that we may be *wise above what is written*, but that we may be *wiser in what is written*. Christ's scholars never learn *above their bibles* in this world; but they need to be learning still more and more *out of their bibles*.

4. The instructions he gave them as *apostles*: "*You are* to be *witnesses of these things* (v. 48), to carry the notice of them to all the world. You are fully assured of these things yourselves, you are eye and ear-witnesses of them; go, and assure the world of them."

(1) *What they must preach.* They must preach the gospel. They must take their bibles along with them, and must show people how it was written of old concerning the Messiah, and the glories and graces of his kingdom, and then must tell them how all this was fulfilled in the Lord Jesus. The great *gospel truth* concerning the *death* and *resurrection* of Jesus Christ must be *published* to the children of men (v. 46): *Thus it was written*, and therefore, *thus it behoved Christ to suffer.* "Go, and tell the world that Christ *suffered*, as it was written of him. Go, preach *Christ crucified*; be not ashamed of his cross, not ashamed of a suffering Jesus. Tell them that it *behoved him to suffer*, that it was necessary to the taking away of the sin of the world. That he rose from the dead on *the third day*. In this also the *scriptures* were *fulfilled*. Go, and tell them, then, that he that *was dead is*

alive, and *lives for evermore*, and *has the keys of death and the grave.*" The great *gospel duty* of repentance must be *pressed* upon the children of men. *Repentance for sin* must be preached in *Christ's name*, and by his authority, v. 47. "Go, and tell all people that they must turn to the service of God in Christ. Their hearts and lives must be changed." The great *gospel privilege* of the *remission of sins* must be *proposed* to all, and assured to all that *repent*, and *believe the gospel*. "Go, tell a guilty world that *there is hope* concerning them."

(2) *To whom they must preach.* They must preach this *among all nations.* They must disperse themselves and carry this light along with them wherever they go. The prophets had preached *repentance* and *remission* to the Jews, but the apostles must preach them to *all the world*. None are *exempted* from the obligations the gospel lays upon men to *repent*, nor are any *excluded* from those inestimable benefits. They must *begin at Jerusalem*. There the gospel day must dawn. And why must they begin there? *First*, Because *thus it was written*, and therefore it *behoved them* to take this method. *The word of the* Lord must go forth from Jerusalem, Isa. ii. 3. *Secondly*, Because there the matters of fact on which the gospel was founded were transacted; and therefore there they were first attested. So strong, so bright, is the first shining forth of the glory of the risen Redeemer that it dares face those daring enemies of his and sets them at defiance. *Thirdly*, Because he would give us a further example of forgiving enemies. The first offer of gospel grace is made to Jerusalem, and thousands there are in a little time brought to partake of that grace.

(3) What *assistance they should have in preaching. Behold, I send the promise of my Father upon you*, and *you shall be endued with power from on high*, v. 49. He here assures them that in a little time the Spirit should be poured out upon them in greater measures than ever, and they should thereby be furnished with all those gifts and graces which were necessary to their discharge of this great trust. Those who *receive the Holy Ghost* are thereby *endued with a power from on high*. Christ's apostles could never have planted his gospel, and set up his kingdom in the world, as they did, if they had not been endued with such a power. *This power from on high* was the *promise of the Father*. And, if it be the *promise of the Father*, we may be sure that the promise is *inviolable* and the thing promised *invaluable*. Christ's ambassadors must stay till they have their powers. Though, one would think, never was such haste as now for the preaching of the gospel, yet the preachers must tarry till they be endued with power from on high.

Verses 50–53

His ascension into heaven, of which we have a very brief narrative in these verses.

I. How solemnly Christ took leave of his disciples. He had business to do in both worlds, and accordingly came from heaven to earth in his incarnation, to despatch his business here, and, having finished this, he returned to heaven, to reside there. 1. Whence he ascended: from *Bethany*, near Jerusalem, adjoining to the *mount of Olives*. There was the *garden* in which his sufferings began, there he was in his agony; and Bethany signifies *the house of sorrow*. Those that would go to heaven must ascend thither from the house of sufferings and sorrow. And here it was that awhile ago he began his triumphant entry into Jerusalem, *ch.* xix. 29. 2. Who were the witnesses of his ascension: *He led out his disciples* to see him. The disciples did not see him rise out of the grave, because his resurrection was capable of being proved by their seeing him alive afterwards; but they saw him *ascend* into heaven, because they could not otherwise have an *ocular* demonstration of his ascension. 3. What was the farewell he gave them: *He lifted up his hands, and blessed them.* He did not go away in displeasure, but in love; he left a blessing behind him. He blessed them to show that, having loved his own which were in the world, he loved them unto the end. 4. How he left them: *While he was blessing them, he was parted from them;* to intimate that his being parted from them did not put an end to his blessing them. He *began* to bless them on earth, but he went to heaven to *go on* with it. 5. How his ascension is described. (1) He was *parted from them.* Those that love us, and pray for us, and instruct us, must be *parted from us.* Those that knew him after the flesh must now henceforth know him so no more. (2) He was *carried up into heaven.* There needed no chariot of fire, nor horses of fire; he knew the way.

II. How cheerfully his disciples continued their attendance on him. They paid their homage to him at his going away: *They worshipped him,* v. 52. He *blessed them,* in token of gratitude for which they *worshipped him.* The cloud that received him out of their sight did not put them or their services out of his sight. They *returned to Jerusalem with great joy.* Thither they went, and there they stayed *with great joy.* This was a wonderful change. When Christ told them that he must leave them sorrow filled their hearts; yet now that they see him go they are *filled with joy.* They abounded in acts of devotion while they were in expectation of the promise of the Father, v. 53. They attended the temple-service at the hours of prayer. *They were continually in the temple,* as their Master was when he was at Jerusalem. Temple-sacrifices, they knew, were superseded by Christ's sacrifice, but the temple-songs they joined in. Nothing better prepares the mind for the receiving of the Holy Ghost than holy joy and praise. Fears are silenced, sorrows sweetened and allayed, and hopes kept up. *Amen.* Let him be continually praised and blessed.

AN EXPOSITION, WITH PRACTICAL OBSERVATIONS, OF

THE GOSPEL

ACCORDING TO

ST. JOHN

It is not material to enquire when and where this gospel was written; we are sure that it was given to John, the brother of James, one of the twelve apostles, distinguished by the honourable character of *that disciple whom Jesus loved*. The ancients tell us that John lived longest of all the twelve apostles, and was the only one of them that died a natural death. Some of them say that he wrote this gospel at Ephesus in opposition to the heresy of the Ebionites, who held that our Lord was a *mere man*. It is clear that he wrote last of the four evangelists, and, comparing his gospel with theirs, we may observe, 1. That he *relates* what they had *omitted; he brings up the rear*, gleans up what they had passed by. 2. That he gives us more of the *mystery* of that of which the other evangelists gave us only the *history*. Some of the ancients observe that the other evangelists wrote more of the *bodily* things of Christ; but John writes of the *spiritual* things of the gospel, the life and soul of it.

CHAPTER 1

The scope and design of this chapter is to confirm our faith in Christ as the eternal Son of God, and the true Messiah and Saviour of the world. In order to this, we have here I. The inspired penman himself, fairly laying down, in the beginning, what he designed his whole book should be the proof of, ver. 1–5; and again, ver. 10–14; and again, ver. 16–18. II. The testimony of John Baptist concerning him (ver. 6–9; and again, ver. 15); but most fully and particularly, ver. 19–37. III. His own manifestation of himself to Andrew and Peter (ver. 38–42), to Philip and Nathanael, ver. 43–51.

Verses 1–5

Let us enquire what there is in those strong lines. The evangelist here lays down the great truth he is to prove, that Jesus Christ is God, one with the Father.

I. Of whom he speaks—*The Word*—ὁ λόγος. This is an idiom peculiar to John's writings. Even the vulgar Jews were taught that the *Word of God* was the same with God. The evangelist, in the close of his discourse (*v.* 18), plainly tells us why he calls Christ *the Word*—because he is the only begotten Son, *who is in the bosom of the Father, and has declared him. Word* is two-fold: *Word conceived*, and *word uttered*. 1. There is the *word conceived*, that is, *thought*, which is the first and only immediate product and conception of the soul. And thus the second person in the Trinity is fitly called *the Word*; for he is the *first-begotten of the Father*. There is nothing we are more sure of then *that we think*, yet nothing we are more in the dark about then *how we think*. Surely then the generations and births of the eternal mind may well be allowed to be great mysteries of godliness, the bottom of which we cannot fathom, while yet we adore the depth. 2. There is the *word uttered*, and this is *speech*, the chief and most natural indication of the mind. And thus Christ is *the Word*, for *by him* God has in *these last days spoken to us*. He has made known God's mind to us, as a man's word or speech makes known his thoughts. John Baptist was *the voice*, but Christ *the Word*.

II. What he saith of him.

1. His existence in the beginning: *In the beginning was the Word*. This bespeaks his existence, not only before his incarnation, but before all time. The world was *from* the beginning, but the Word was *in* the beginning. The Word had a being before the world had a beginning. He that *was* in the beginning *never* began, and therefore was *ever*.

2. His co-existence with the Father: *The Word was with God, and the Word was God*. It is repeated in *v.* 2: *the same* was *in the beginning with God*, that is, he was so from eternity. In the beginning the world was *from God*, but the Word was *with God*, as ever with him. The Word was with God, (1) In respect of *essence* and *substance*; for the *Word was God*. (2) In respect of *complacency* and *felicity*. There was a glory and happiness which Christ had *with God* before the world was (*ch.* xvii. 5). (3) In respect of *counsel* and *design*. So that this grand affair of man's reconciliation to God was concerted between the Father and Son from eternity.

3. His agency in making the world, *v.* 3. This is here, (1) Expressly asserted: *All things were made by him*. He was *with God*, active in the divine operations in the beginning of time. Not as the workman cuts by his axe, but as the body sees by the eye. (2) The contrary is denied: *Without him was not anything made that was made*, from the highest angel to the meanest worm. God the Father did nothing without him in that work. This proves that *he is God*. This proves the excellency of the Christian religion, that the author and founder of it is the same that was the author and founder of the world. This shows how well qualified he was for the work of our redemption and salvation. He is appointed the author of our bliss who was the author of our being.

4. The original of life and light that is in him: *In him was life*, *v.* 4. This further proves that he is God. (1) He has *life in himself*; not only the *true God*, but the *living God*. (2) All living creatures have their life in him; all the *life* too that is in the creation is derived from him. He is that Word by which man lives more than by bread, Matt. iv. 4. (3) Reasonable creatures have their *light* from him; that *life* which is *the light of men* comes from him. Life in man is something greater and nobler than it is in other creatures; it is *rational*, and not merely *animal*. The *spirit of a man is the candle of the Lord*, and it was the eternal Word that lighted this candle. The light of reason, as well as the life of sense, is derived from him. From whom may we better expect the light of divine revelation than from him who gave us the light of human reason?

5. The manifestation of him to the children of men. Whence is it that he has been so little taken

notice of and regarded? To this he answers (v. 5), *The light shines, but the darkness comprehends it not.*

(1) The discovery of the eternal Word to the lapsed world, even before he was manifested in the flesh: *The light shineth in darkness.* [1] The eternal Word, *as God,* shines in *the darkness* of *natural conscience.* Something of the power of the divine Word all mankind have an innate sense of. [2] The eternal Word shone in the darkness of the Old Testament prophecies and promises. He that had commanded the light of this world to shine out of darkness was himself long a light *shining in darkness.*

(2) The disability of the degenerate world to receive this discovery: *The darkness comprehended it not.* The darkness of error and sin overpowered and quite eclipsed this light. The Jews who had the light of the Old Testament, yet comprehended not Christ in it. It was therefore requisite that Christ should come, both to rectify the errors of the Gentile world and to improve the truths of the Jewish church.

Verses 5–14

The evangelist designs to bring in John Baptist bearing an honourable testimony to Jesus Christ. Now in these verses, before he does this,

I. He gives us some account of the witness he is about to produce. His name was *John,* which signifies *gracious.*

1. We are here told concerning him, in general, that he was a *man sent of God.* He was a *man,* a mere man. God is pleased to speak to us by men like ourselves. He was *sent from God,* he was God's *messenger.* God gave him both his mission and his message. John wrought no miracle, but the strictness and purity of his life and doctrine, were plain indications that he was *sent of God.*

2. We are here told what his office and business were (v. 7): *The same came for a witness, for a testimony.* The legal institutions had been long a testimony for God, in the Jewish church. But now divine revelation is to be turned into another channel. There was a profound silence concerning him, till John Baptist came for a witness to him. (1) The matter of his testimony: *He came to bear witness to the light.* Light is a thing which witnesses for itself. Christ's light needs not man's testimony, but the world's darkness does. John was like the night watchman that goes round the town, proclaiming the approach of the morning light to those that have closed their eyes. He was sent of God to proclaim that dispensation at hand which would bring life and immortality to light. (2) The design of his testimony: *That all men through him might believe;* not in him, but in Christ. He taught men to look through him, and pass through him, to Christ. If they would but receive this witness of man, they would soon find that the witness of God was greater. It was designed that all men through him might believe, excluding none that did not exclude themselves.

3. We are here cautioned not to mistake him for the light who only came to bear witness to it (v. 8): *He was not that light.* He was a star, like that which guided the wise men to Christ, a morning star; but he was not the Sun. The evangelist here, when he speaks very honourably of him, yet shows that he must give place to Christ. He was great as the prophet of the Highest, but not the Highest himself. We must take heed of over-valuing ministers, as well as of under-valuing them; they are not our lords, but ministers by whom we believe. Those who usurp the honour of Christ forfeit the honour of being the servants of Christ; yet John was very serviceable as a witness to the light, though he was not that light. Those may be of great use to us who yet shine with a borrowed light.

II. Before he goes on with John's testimony, he returns to give us a further account of this Jesus, to show the graces of his incarnation.

1. Christ was the *true Light* (v. 9). Christ is the great light that deserves to be called so. Other lights are but figuratively and equivocally called so: Christ is the true light. But how does Christ enlighten every man that comes into the world? (1) By his creating power he enlightens every man with the light of reason; all the beauty it puts upon us, are from Christ. (2) By the publication of his gospel to all nations he does in effect enlighten every man. John Baptist was a light but he lightened only Jerusalem and Judæa, like a candle that enlightens one room; but Christ is the true light, for he is a light to enlighten the Gentiles. Divine revelation is not now to be confined, as it had been, to one people, but to be diffused to all people, Matt. v. 15. Whatever light any man has, he is indebted to Christ for it, whether it be natural or supernatural.

2. Christ *was in the world, v.* 10. This speaks of his being in the world when he took our nature upon him, and dwelt among us. *I am come into the world.* He left a world of bliss and glory, and was here in this melancholy miserable world. He was in the world, but not of it. The greatest honour that ever was put upon this world was that the Son of God was once *in the world.* It should reconcile us to our present abode in *this* world that once Christ was *here.* What reason Christ had to expect the most affectionate and respectful welcome possible in this world; for *the world was made by him. Therefore* he came to save a lost world because it was a world of his own making. The world was *made by him,* and therefore ought to do him homage. What cold entertainment he met with, notwithstanding: *The world knew him not.* The ox *knows his owner,* but the more brutish world did not. They did not own him, did not bid him welcome, because they did not *know him.* When he shall come as a Judge the world shall *know him.*

3. He *came to his own* (v. 11); not only to the world, which was *his own,* but to the people of Israel, that were peculiarly *his own.* To them he was *first sent.* He came to his own, to seek and save them, because they were *his own.* The generality *rejected* him: *His own received him not.* He had reason to expect that those who were his own should have bidden him welcome. He came among them himself, introduced with signs and wonders, and himself the greatest; and therefore it is not said of them, as it was of the world (v. 10), that they *knew him not;* but *his own,* though they could not but know him, yet *received him not.* Many who in profession are *Christ's own,* yet do not *receive him,* because they will not part with their sins, nor have him to *reign over them.* Yet there was a remnant who *owned* him, and were faithful to him. There were those that *received* him (v. 12): *But as many as received him.* There were many of *them* that were wrought upon to submit to Christ, and many more that *were not of that fold.* The true Christian's *description* and *property;* and that is, that he *receives* Christ, and *believes on his name.* Believing in Christ's name is *receiving* him as a gift from God. We must receive his doctrine as true and good; and we must receive the image of his grace, and impressions of his love, as the governing principle of our affections and actions. The true Christians' dignity and privilege are twofold:

First, The *privilege of adoption: To them gave* 'he *power to become the sons of God.* Hitherto, the adoption pertained to the Jews only; but now, by faith in Christ, Gentiles are the *children of God.* To them gave he a *right; this power have all the saints.* It is the unspeakable privilege of all good Christians, that they are become the *children of God.* If they be the *children of God,* they *become* so, are *made* so.

Behold what manner of love is this, 1 John iii. 1. God calls them *his children,* they call him *Father.* The privilege of adoption is entirely owing to *Jesus Christ;* he *gave* this power to them that believe on his name. The Son of God became a Son of man, that the sons and daughters of men might become the sons and daughters of God Almighty.

Secondly, The *privilege of regeneration* (*v.* 13): *Which were born.* All the children of God are born again; all that are adopted are regenerated. Now here we have an account of the original of this new birth. 1. Negatively. (1) It is *not of blood, not of the will of the flesh,* nor of *corruptible seed.* We do not become the children of God as we become the children of our natural parents. Grace does not run in the blood, as corruption does. (2) It is not *produced* by the natural power of our own will. As it is not of *blood,* nor of *the will of the flesh,* so neither is it of the *will of man.* It is the grace of God that makes us willing to be *his.* But, 2. Positively: it is of *God.* This new birth is owing to the word of God as the means and to the Spirit of God as the great and sole author. True believers are *born of God,* 1 John iii. 9; v. 1.

4. The *word was made flesh, v.* 14. This expresses Christ's incarnation more clearly than what went before. Now that the fulness of time was come he was sent forth after another manner, *made of a woman.*

(1) The *human nature of Christ* with which he was veiled. *The word was made flesh. Forasmuch as the children* who were to become the sons of God, *were partakers of flesh and blood, he also himself likewise took part of the same,* Heb. ii. 14. John here saith, *He was God,* but *He was made flesh.* Compare *v.* 1 with this. He subjected himself to the miseries and calamities of the human nature. *Flesh* bespeaks *man tainted with sin,* and Christ appeared *in the likeness of sinful flesh* (Rom. viii. 3), and was made *sin for us,* 2 Cor. v. 21, and *condemned sin in the flesh,* Rom. viii. 3. The *Word of the Lord,* who was made flesh, *endures for ever;* when made flesh, he ceased not to be the Word of God. He *dwelt among us.* Having taken upon him the nature of man, he put himself into the place and condition of other men. Having taken a *body* of the same mould with ours, in it he came, and resided in the same world with us. He *dwelt among us,* us worms of the earth, us that were *corrupt* and *depraved,* and revolted from God. When we look upon the upper world, how mean and contemptible does this flesh, this body, appear, which we carry about with us, and this world in which our lot is cast. But that the eternal Word was *made flesh,* and dwelt in this world as we do should make us willing to abide in the flesh while God has any work for us to do. He dwelt *among* the Jews. Though the Jews were unkind to him, yet he continued to dwell among them. He *dwelt* among us. He was in the world, not as a wayfaring man that tarries but for a night, but he *dwelt* among us. The original word is observable, he dwelt *as in a tabernacle,* which intimates, that he dwelt here in very *mean* circumstances, as shepherds that dwell in tents. That his stay among us was not to be perpetual. He dwelt here as *in a tent,* not as at *home.* That as of old God dwelt in the tabernacle of Moses, so now he dwells in the human nature of Christ. And we are to make all our addresses to God through Christ.

(2) The *beams of his divine glory* that *darted* through this *veil of flesh: We beheld his glory, the glory as of the only begotten of the Father, full of grace and truth.* The sun is still the fountain of light, though eclipsed or clouded; so Christ was still the brightness of his Father's glory. There were those that saw through the veil.

[1] Who were the witnesses of this glory: *we,* his disciples and followers, we among whom he *dwelt.*

Other men discover their weaknesses to those that are most familiar with them, but it was not so with Christ; those that were most intimate with him saw most of his glory. They saw the glory of his divinity, while others saw only the veil of his human nature.

[2] What evidence they had of it: *We saw it.* They had not their evidence by report, at secondhand, but were themselves eyewitnesses, *We saw it.* The word signifies a fixed abiding sight. This apostle himself explains this: *What we declare unto you* of the Word of life is what we have *seen with our eyes,* and what *we have looked upon,* 1 John i. 1.

[3] What the glory was: *The glory as of the only begotten of the Father.* The glory of the *Word made flesh* was such a glory as became the only *begotten Son of God,* and could not be the glory of any other. Jesus Christ is the only begotten of the Father. Believers are the children of God by the special favour of adoption and the special grace of regeneration. They are in a sense *of a like nature,* and have the image of his perfections; but Christ is *of the same nature.* He was evidently declared to be the only begotten of the Father, by that which was seen of his glory when he dwelt among us. His divine glory appeared in the holiness and heavenliness of his doctrine; in his miracles; it appeared in the purity, goodness, and beneficence, of his whole conversation. God's goodness is his glory, and he went about doing good. Perhaps the evangelist had a particular regard to the glory of his *transfiguration,* of which he was an eyewitness.

[4] What advantage those he dwelt among had from this. In the old tabernacle wherein God dwelt was the *law,* in *this* was grace; in that were *types,* in this was *truth.* He was *full of grace and truth,* the two great things that fallen man stands in need of. He was full *of grace,* and therefore qualified to intercede for us; and full *of truth,* and therefore fit to instruct us. He had a fulness of knowledge and a fulness of compassion.

Verses 15–18

I. The evangelist begins again to give us John Baptist's testimony concerning Christ, *v.* 15.

1. *How he expressed* his testimony: He *cried,* according to the prediction that he should be *the voice of one crying.* The Old Testament prophets cried aloud, to show people their *sins;* this New Testament prophet cried aloud, to show people their *Saviour.* It was an open *public* testimony, proclaimed, that all manner of persons might take notice of it. He was free and hearty in bearing this testimony. He *cried* as one that was both *well assured* of the truth to which he witnesses and *well affected* to it.

2. What his *testimony* was. He appeals to what he had said at the beginning of his ministry, when he had directed them to expect one that should *come after him,* whose forerunner he was. Now what he had then said he applies to this Jesus whom he had lately baptized: *This was he of whom I spoke.* In *this* he went beyond all the Old Testament prophets that he particularly specified the person.

(1) He had given the preference to this Jesus: *He that comes after me* is preferred before me as the prince or peer that *comes after* is preferred before the harbinger or gentleman-usher that makes way for him. Jesus Christ, who was to be called the *Son of the highest* (Luke i. 32), was preferred before John Baptist, who was to be called only the *prophet of the Highest,* Luke i. 76. John was a great man, yet he was forward to give the preference to him to whom it belonged. All the ministers of Christ must prefer him and his interest before themselves and their own interests. He comes *after me,* and yet is *preferred before me.* God dispenses his gifts according to his good pleasure, and many times crosses hands, as

Jacob did. Paul far outstripped those that were in Christ before him.

(2) He gives here a good reason for it: *For he was before me.* In respect of *seniority*: he was *before me*, for he was before Abraham, *ch.* viii. 58. I am but of yesterday, he from eternity. In respect of supremacy: he is my Master, I am his minister and messenger."

II. He returns again to speak of Jesus Christ, and cannot go on with John Baptist's testimony till *v.* 19. The 16th verse has a manifest connection with *v.* 14, where the incarnate Word was said to be *full of grace and truth.* He has a fountain of fulness overflowing: *We all have received. All we* believers; as many as received him (*v.* 16), received from him. All true believers receive from Christ's fulness, the best and greatest saints cannot live without him, the meanest and weakest may live by him. This excludes proud boasting, that we have nothing but *we have received it*; and silences perplexing fears, that we want nothing but *we may receive it.*

1. We have received *grace for grace.* Our receivings by Christ are all summed up in this one word, *grace*; so great a gift, so rich, so invaluable; we have received *no less* than grace. It is repeated, *grace for grace.*

(1) The blessing received. It is *grace*; the goodwill of God towards us, and the good work of God in us. God's goodwill works the good work, and then the good work qualifies us for further tokens of his good will. As the cistern receives water from the fulness of the fountain, the branches sap from the fulness of the root, and the air light from the fulness of the sun, so we receive grace from the fulness of Christ.

(2) The manner of its reception: *Grace for grace.* The phrase is singular, and interpreters put different senses upon it, each of which will be of use to illustrate the unsearchable riches of the grace of Christ. *Grace for grace* bespeaks, [1] The *freeness* of this grace. It is grace for grace' sake. We receive grace, not for *our sakes.* It is grace *to us* for the sake of Jesus Christ. [2] The *fulness* of this grace. *Grace for grace* is abundance of grace, grace upon grace. It is a blessing poured out, that there shall not be room to receive it: one grace a pledge of more grace. [3] The *serviceableness* of this grace. *Grace for grace* is grace for the promoting and advancing of grace. Gracious vouchsafements for gracious performances; grace is a talent to be traded with. [4] The *substitution* of New Testament grace *in the room and stead* of Old Testament grace. And this sense is confirmed by what follows (*v.* 17); for the Old Testament had grace in type, the New Testament has grace in truth. This is grace instead of grace. [5] It bespeaks the *augmentation* and *continuance of grace. Grace for grace* is one grace to improve, confirm, and perfect another grace. [6] *Grace for grace* is grace in us answering to grace in him, as the impression upon the wax answers the seal line for line. The grace we receive from Christ *changes us into the same image.*

2. We have received *grace and truth, v.* 17. He had said (*v.* 14) that Christ was *full of grace and truth*; now here he says that by him *grace and truth* came to us. From Christ we *receive grace*; this is a string he delights to harp upon, he cannot go off from it. Two things he further observes in this verse concerning this grace: (1) Its *preference* above the law of Moses: *The law was given by Moses*, and it was a glorious discovery; but the gospel of Christ is a much clearer discovery. That which was given by Moses was purely terrifying and threatening, but that which is given by Jesus Christ has all the beneficial uses of the law, but not the terror, for it is *grace.* The endearments of love are the genius of the gospel, not the affrightments of law and the curse. (2) Its *connection* with truth: *grace and truth.* In the gospel we have the discovery of the greatest *truths* to be embraced by the understanding, as well as of the richest *grace* to be embraced by the will and affections. It is *grace and truth* with reference to the *law* that was *given by Moses.* For it is, [1] The performance of all the Old Testament promises. [2] It is the substance of all the Old Testament types and shadows. He is the *true* paschal lamb, the *true* scape-goat, the true *manna.* They had grace in the picture; we have grace in the person. *Grace and truth came, was made;* the same word that was used (*v.* 3) concerning Christ's *making all things.* By him this *grace and truth* do *consist.*

3. Another thing we receive from Christ is a clear revelation of God to us (*v.* 18): He hath *declared* God to us, whom *no man hath seen at any time.*

(1) The insufficiency of all other discoveries: *No man hath seen God at any time.* This intimates, [1] That the nature of God being *spiritual*, he is invisible to bodily eyes. We have therefore need to *live by faith*, by which we *see him that is invisible*, Heb. xi. 27. [2] That the revelation which God made of himself in the Old Testament was very short and imperfect, in comparison with that which he has made by Christ: *No man hath seen God at any time.* But *this* recommends Christ's holy religion to us that it was founded by one that had seen God, and knew more of his mind than anyone else ever did.

(2) The all-sufficiency of the gospel discovery proved from its author: *The only-begotten Son, who is in the bosom of the Father, he has declared him.* Observe here, How *fit* he was to make this discovery. He is *the only-begotten Son*; and who so likely to know the Father as the Son? or in whom is the Father better known than in the Son? Matt. xi. 27. He is *in the bosom of the Father.* 1. In the bosom of his *special love*, dear to him, in *whom he was well pleased.* 2. In the bosom of his *secret counsels.* None so fit as he to make known God, for none knew his mind as he did.

(3) How *free* he was in making this discovery: *He hath declared.* Not only that which was hid *of God*, but that which was hid *in* God. It signifies a plain, clear, and full discovery. He that runs may now read the will of God and the way of salvation. This is the *grace*, this the *truth*, that came by Jesus Christ.

Verses 19–28

We have here the testimony of John, which he delivered to the messengers who were sent from Jerusalem to examine him.

I. Who they were that sent to him, and who they were that were sent. They that sent to him were *the Jews at Jerusalem.* One would think that they should have understood the times so well as to know that the Messiah was at hand, and therefore have known him that was his forerunner, but, instead of this, they sent messengers to *cross questions* with him. Secular learning, honour, and power, seldom dispose men's minds to the reception of divine light. They that were sent were, (1) *Priests and Levites.* John Baptist was himself a priest of the seed of Aaron, and therefore it was not fit that he should be examined by any but priests. (2) They were *of the Pharisees* that thought they needed no repentance.

II. On what errand they were sent; it was to enquire concerning John and *his baptism.* They did not send for John; they thought it was good to keep him at a distance. They enquire concerning him, 1. To satisfy their curiosity. The doctrine of repentance was to them strange doctrine. 2. It was to show their authority. 3. It was with a design to *suppress* him and silence him.

III. What was the answer he gave them, and his account, both concerning himself and concerning his baptism.

1. *Concerning himself.* They asked him, *Thou, who art thou?* John's appearing in the world was surprising. His spirit, his converse, his doctrine, had something in them which commanded and gained respect; but he did not give out himself to be *some great one.* He was more industrious to *do good* than to *appear great.* He answers their interrogatory,

Negatively. He was not that great one whom some took him to be. God's faithful witnesses stand more upon their guard *against undue respect* than against *unjust contempt.* John disowns himself to be *the Christ* (v. 20): *He said, I am not the Christ.* Observe how emphatically this is here expressed concerning John: He *confessed, and denied not, but confessed;* it denotes his vehemence and constancy in making this protestation. *I am not the Christ, not I;* another is at hand, who is he, but I am not, His disowning himself to be the Christ is called his *confessing* and not *denying* Christ. He disowns himself to be Elias, v. 21. The Jews expected the person of Elias to return from heaven. Hearing of John's character, doctrine, and baptism, and observing that he appeared as one dropped from heaven, it is no wonder that they were ready to take him for this Elijah; but he disowned this honour too. He was indeed prophesied of under the name of Elijah (Mal. iv. 5), and he came in the *spirit and power of Elias* (Luke i. 17), and was the Elias that was to come (Matt. xi. 14); but he was not the person of Elias. He was the Elias that God had promised, not the Elias that they foolishly dreamed of. Elias did come, and *they knew him not* (Matt. xvii. 12); because they had promised themselves such an Elias as God never promised them. He disowns himself to be *prophet. First,* He was not *that* prophet which Moses said *the Lord* would *raise up to them of their brethren. Secondly,* He was not such a prophet as they expected and wished for, who would interpose in public affairs, and rescue them from under the Roman yoke. *Thirdly,* He was not one of the old prophets raised from the dead.

The committee sent to examine him pressed for a positive answer (v. 22), urging the authority of *those that sent them*: "*Tell us, What art thou?* that we may *give an answer* to those that sent us." John was looked upon as a man of sincerity, and therefore they believed he would be fair and above-board, and give a plain answer to a plain question: *What sayest thou of thyself?* And he did so, *I am the voice of one crying in the wilderness.* He gives his answer in the words of scripture, to show that the scripture was fulfilled in him. He gives his answer in very humble, modest, self-denying expressions. He chooses to apply that scripture to himself which bespeaks him little: *I am the voice, mere voice.* He gives such an account of himself as might awaken them to hearken to him; for he *was the voice* (see Isa. xl. 3), a voice to alarm, an articulate voice to instruct. Ministers are but the *voice,* by which God is pleased to communicate his mind. *First,* He was a *human* voice. The people were prepared to receive the law by the voice of thunders; but they were prepared for the gospel by the voice of a man like ourselves, *a still small voice. Secondly,* He was the voice of *one crying,* which denotes, 1. His *earnestness* and *importunity*; he *cried aloud, and did not spare.* Ministers must preach as those that are in earnest. Those words are not likely to *thaw* the hearers' hearts that *freeze* between the speaker's lips. 2. His *open publication* of the doctrine he preached. *Thirdly,* It was in the *wilderness* that this voice was crying; in a place of silence and solitude, out of the noise of the world and the hurry of its business. *Fourthly,* That which he cried was, *Make straight the way of the Lord.* He came to *rectify* the mistakes of people concerning the ways of God. The scribes and Pharisees had made

them crooked. Now John Baptist calls people to return to the original rule.

2. Here is his testimony concerning *his baptism.*

(1) The enquiry which the committee made about it: *Why baptizest thou, if thou be not the Christ, nor Elias, nor that prophet? v.* 25. They readily apprehended baptism to be fitly and properly used as a sacred rite or ceremony, to signify the cleansing of them from the pollutions of their former state. That sign was made use of in the Christian church. Christ did not affect novelty, nor should his ministers. They expected it would be used in the days of the Messiah. It is taken for granted that Christ, and Elias, and *that prophet,* would baptize, when they came to *purify a polluted world.* Divine grace has provided for the cleansing of this new world *from its filth.* They would therefore know by what authority John baptized. His denying himself to be Elias, or *that prophet,* subjected him to this further question, *Why baptizest thou?*

(2) The account he gave of it, v. 26, 27. He owned himself to be only the minister of the outward sign: "*I baptize with water, and that is all.* I cannot confer the spiritual grace signified by it." He directed them to one who was greater than himself, and would do that for them which he could not do. John gave the same account to this committee that he had given to the people (v. 15): *This was he of whom I spoke.* He tells them of Christ's *presence among them* now at this time: *There stands one among you, whom you know not.* Christ stood among the common people, and was as one of them. Much true worth lies hid in this world; obscurity is often the lot of real excellency. God himself is often nearer to us than we are aware of. The kingdom of God was abroad and already *among them,* Luke xvii. 21. He tells them of Christ's *preference above himself*: He comes *after me,* and yet is *preferred before me,* "Whose *shoe-latchet I am not worthy to loose.*" If so great a man as John accounted himself unworthy of the honour of being near Christ, how unworthy then should we account ourselves! Now, one would think, these chief priests and Pharisees, should presently have asked who, and where, this excellent person was. No, they came to molest John, not to receive any instructions from him. They might have known Christ, and would not. Notice is taken of the place where all this was done: *In Bethabara beyond Jordan, v.* 28. Bethabara signifies the *house of passage;* there was opened the way into the gospel state by Jesus Christ. He made this confession in the same place where he was *baptizing,* that all those who attended his baptism might be witnesses of it.

Verses 29–36

We have in these verses an account of John's testimony concerning Jesus Christ, which he witnessed to his own disciples that followed him. As soon as ever Christ was *baptized* he was immediately hurried into the wilderness, to be *tempted*; and there he was forty days. During his absence John had continued to bear testimony to him, but now at last he *sees Jesus coming to him.* Now here are *two testimonies* borne by John to Christ, but those two *agree in one.*

I. Here is his testimony to Christ, and here four things are witnessed by him concerning Christ.

1. That he is *the Lamb of God which taketh away the sin of the world, v.* 29. Let us learn here,

(1) That Jesus Christ is the *Lamb of God,* which bespeaks him the great sacrifice, by which atonement is made for sin, and man reconciled to God. Of all the legal sacrifices he chooses to allude to the *lambs* that were offered with a special reference to the *daily sacrifice,* which was offered every morning and evening continually, and that was always a *lamb*; to the *paschal lamb,* the blood of which secured the

Israelites from the stroke of the destroying angel. Christ is *our passover*. Christ, who was to make atonement for sin, is called the *Lamb of God*.

(2) That Jesus Christ, as the *Lamb of God, takes away the sin of the world*. John Baptist had called people to repent of their sins, in order to the remission of them. Now here he shows how and by whom that remission was to be expected. This ground of hope we have—Jesus Christ is *the Lamb of God*. [1] He *takes away sin*. He came to take away the guilt of sin by the merit of his death. To take away the power of sin by the Spirit of his grace. *He is taking away* the sin of the world, which denotes it a continued act. He is always *taking away* sin. [2] He takes away the *sin of the world*; purchases pardon for all of what country, nation, or language, soever they be. The Lamb of God was offered to be a propitiation for the *sin of the whole world*; see 1 John ii. 2. If Christ takes away the sin of the world, then why not my sin? [3] He does this by *taking it upon himself*. He is the Lamb of God, that *bears the sin of the world*; so the margin reads it. He bears it *from us*; he *bore the sin of many*, as the scape-goat had the sins of Israel put upon his head, Lev. xvi. 21. God has found out a way of abolishing the sin, and yet sparing the sinner, by making his Son *sin for us*.

(3) That it is our duty to *behold* the Lamb of God thus taking away the *sin of the world*. See him taking away sin, and let that increase our hatred of sin. Let it increase our love to Christ.

2. That this was he of whom he had spoken before (v. 30, 31): *This is he of whom I said, After me cometh a man*. This honour John had above all the prophets, that, whereas they spoke of him as one that should come, he saw him already come. Such a difference there is between present *faith* and future *vision*. He refers to what he had himself said of him before: *This is he of whom I said*. Though Christ appeared not in any external pomp or grandeur, yet John is not ashamed to own, *This is he whom I* meant, who is *preferred before me*. And it was necessary that John should thus show them the person, otherwise they could not have believed that one who made so mean a figure should be he of whom John had spoken such great things. He protests against any confederacy or combination with this Jesus: *And I knew him not*. There was no acquaintance at all between them; John had no personal knowledge of Jesus till he saw him come to his baptism. They who are taught believe and confess one whom they have not seen, and blessed are they who *yet have believed*. The great intention of John's ministry and baptism was to introduce Jesus Christ. That he should be *made manifest to Israel, therefore am I come baptizing with water*. Though John did not know Jesus by face, yet he knew that he should be made manifest. We may know the certainty of that which yet we do not fully know the nature and intention of. The general assurance John had that Christ *should be made manifest* served to carry him with diligence and resolution through his work: *Therefore am I come*. God reveals himself to his people by degrees. At first, John knew no more concerning Christ but that he should be made manifest; and now he is favoured with a sight of him.

3. That this was he *upon whom the Spirit descended from heaven like a dove*. For the confirming of his testimony concerning Christ, he here vouches the extraordinary appearance at his baptism, in which God himself bore witness to him. We are here told (v. 32–34),

(1) That John Baptist saw it: He *bore record*; attested it, with all the seriousness and solemnity of *witness-bearing*. He made affidavit of it: *I saw the Spirit descending* from heaven. John could not see the *Spirit*, but he saw the dove which was a sign and representation of the Spirit. God's children are made manifest by their *graces*; their glories are reserved for their future state. He descended *like a dove*—an emblem of meekness, and wildness, and gentleness. The dove brought the olive-branch of peace, Gen. viii. 11. The Spirit that descended upon Christ *abode upon him*. The *Spirit did not* move him at times, but *at all times*.

(2) That he was *told to expect it*. It was an *instituted* sign given him before, by which he might certainly know it (v. 33): *I knew him not. He that sent me to baptize* gave me this sign, *Upon whom thou shalt see the Spirit descending, the same is he*. See here what sure grounds John went upon. He did not run *without sending*: God *sent him to baptize*. He had a warrant from heaven for what he did. When a minister's call is clear, his comfort is sure, though his success is not always so. He did not run *without speeding*; for, when he was sent to *baptize with water*, he was directed to one that should *baptize with the Holy Ghost*. It is a great comfort to Christ's ministers, that he whose ministers they are can put life, and soul, and power into their ministrations; can speak to the heart what they speak to the ear, and *breathe* upon the dry bones to which they *prophesy*. God had before given him a sign: "On whom thou shalt see the Spirit descend, *that same is he*." This not only prevented any mistakes, but gave him boldness in his testimony. When he had such assurance as this given him, he could speak with assurance.

4. That he is *the Son of God*. This is the conclusion of John's testimony, that in which all the particulars centre (v. 34): *I saw, and bore record, that this is the Son of God*. The truth asserted is, *that this is the Son of God*. This was the peculiar Christian creed, that Jesus is the Son of God (Matt. xvi. 16), and here is the first framing of it. John's testimony to it: "*I saw, and bore record*." What he *saw* he was forward to *bear record* of. What he *bore record* of was what he *saw*. Christ's witnesses were eyewitnesses.

II. Here is John's testimony to Christ, the next day after, v. 35, 36. *John stood looking upon Jesus as he walked*. It should seem, John was in close conversation with *two* of his disciples. He saw Jesus *walking*. He was *looking upon Jesus*; he looked stedfastly, and fixed his eyes upon him. Those that would lead others to Christ must be diligent and frequent in the *contemplation* of him themselves. 2. He repeated the same testimony which he had given to Christ the day before. Christ's sacrifice for the taking away of the sin of the world ought especially to be insisted upon by all good ministers: Christ, the Lamb of God, *Christ and him crucified*. 3. He intended this especially for his two disciples that stood with him; he was willing to turn them over to Christ. He did not reckon that he lost those disciples who went over from him to Christ, any more than the schoolmaster reckons that scholar lost whom he sends to the university. John gathered disciples, not for himself, but for Christ. Humble, generous souls will give others their due praise without fear of diminishing themselves by it.

Verses 37–42

We have here the turning over of two disciples from John to Jesus, and one of them fetching in a third, and these are the first-fruits of Christ's disciples.

I. Andrew and another with him were the two that John Baptist had directed to Christ, v. 37. Who the other was we are not told.

1. Here is their readiness to go over to Christ. They heard him speak of Christ as the *Lamb of God, that takes away the sin of the world*, and this made them *follow him*.

2. The kind notice Christ took of them, v. 38. He was soon aware of them, and *turned*, and *saw*

them following. Christ takes early cognizance of the first motions of a soul towards him. He did not stay till they begged leave to speak with him, but spoke first. When there is communion between a soul and Christ, it is he that *begins the discourse*. He saith unto them, "*What seek ye?*" It is a kind invitation of them into his acquaintance: "Come, what have you to say to me?" Those whose business it is to instruct people in the affairs of their souls should be humble, and mild, and easy of access. The question Christ put to them is what we should all put to ourselves when we begin to follow Christ: "*What seek ye? What do we design and desire? Do we seek a teacher, ruler, and reconciler? In following Christ, do we seek the favour of God and eternal life?*"

3. Their modest enquiry concerning the place of his abode: *Rabbi, where dwellest thou?* In calling him *Rabbi*, they intimated that their design in coming to him was to be *taught by him*; *rabbi* signifies a *master*, a teaching master. These came to Christ to be his scholars, so must all those that apply themselves to him. In asking *where he dwelt*, they intimate a desire to be better acquainted with him. They would attend him at some seasonable time, when he should appoint. Civility and good manners well become those who follow Christ. They hoped to have more from him than they could have now by the way. They resolved to make a business, not a by-business of conversing with Christ. Those that have had some communion with Christ cannot but desire a *further communion* with him; a *fixed communion* with him; where they may sit down at his feet. It is not enough to take a turn with Christ now and then, but we must *lodge with him*.

4. The courteous invitation Christ gave them to his lodgings: *He saith unto them, Come and see.* He invites them to come to his lodgings: the nearer we approach to Christ, the more we see of his beauty. Deceivers maintain their interest in their followers by keeping them at a distance, but that which Christ desired to recommend him to the esteem and affections of his followers was that they would *come and see*. He invites them to come *immediately* and without delay. There is never a better time. It is best taking people when they are in a good mind; strike while the iron is hot. It is wisdom to embrace the present opportunities: *Now is the accepted time.*

5. Their cheerful and (no doubt) thankful acceptance of his invitation: *They came and saw where he dwelt*, and *abode with him that day*. They readily went along with him. Gracious souls cheerfully accept Christ's gracious invitations. It is good being where Christ is, wherever it be. They *abode with him that day* ("Master, it is good to be here"); and he bade them welcome. It was about the tenth hour.

II. Andrew brought his brother Peter to Christ. Andrew had the honour first to be acquainted with Christ, and to be the instrument of bringing Peter to him.

1. The *information* which Andrew gave to Peter.

(1) *He first finds his own brother Simon;* his finding implies his seeking him. *He first findeth Simon* who came only to attend on John, but has his expectations out-done; he meets with Jesus.

(2) He told him whom they had found: *We have found the Messias*. He speaks *humbly*; not, "I have found," but "*We* have," rejoicing that he had shared with others in it. He speaks *exultingly*: *We have found*. He proclaims it, for he knows that he shall have never the less in Christ for others sharing. He speaks *intelligently*: *We have found the Messias*, which was more than had yet been said. He speaks more clearly concerning Christ than ever *his teacher* had done.

(3) He *brought him to Jesus*, brought him to the fountain-head. Now this was an instance of true love to his brother. We ought with a particular concern

and application to seek the spiritual welfare of those that are related to us; for their relation to us adds both to the *obligation* and to the *opportunity* of doing good to their souls. It was an effect of his day's conversation with Christ. Hereby it appeared that Andrew had *been with Jesus* that he was so full of him. He knew there was enough in Christ for all; and, having tasted that he is gracious, he could not rest till those he loved had tasted it too. True grace hates monopolies, and loves not to eat its morsels alone.

2. The *entertainment* which Jesus Christ gave to Peter, *v*. 42.

(1) Christ called him by his name: *When Jesus beheld him, he said, Thou art Simon, the son of Jona*. Some observe the signification of these names: *Simon—obedient, Jona—a dove*. An obedient dove-like spirit qualifies us to be the disciples of Christ.

(2) He gave him a new name: *Cephas*. His giving him a name intimates *Christ's favour* to him. By this Christ adopted him into his family as one of his own. The name which he gave him bespeaks his *fidelity* to Christ: *Thou shalt be called Cephas* (that is Hebrew for *a stone:*), *which is by interpretation Peter.* Peter's natural temper was stiff, and hardy, and resolute, which I take to be the principal reason why Christ called him *Cephas—a stone*. When Christ afterwards prayed for him, that his faith might not fail, that so he might be firm to Christ himself, then he *made him* what he here called him, *Cephas—a stone*. Those that come to Christ must come with a fixed resolution to be firm and constant to him, *like a stone*, and it is by his grace that they are so.

Verses 43–51

We have here the call of Philip and Nathanael.

I. Philip was called immediately by Christ himself, not as Andrew, who was directed to Christ by John or Peter, who was invited by his brother. God has various methods of bringing his chosen ones home to himself. *Jesus findeth Philip*. Christ sought us, and found us, before we made any enquiries after him. The name *Philip* is of Greek origin, and much used among the Gentiles, yet Christ changed not his name. He was called the *day following*. When work is to be done for God, we must not *lose a day*. Jesus *would go forth into Galilee*. Christ will find out all those that are given to him. Philip was brought to be a disciple by the power of Christ going along with that word, *Follow me*. We are told that Philip was of Bethsaida, and Andrew and Peter were so too, *v*. 44. Bethsaida was a wicked place (Matt. xi. 21), yet even *there* was a remnant, according to the election of grace.

II. Nathanael was invited to Christ by Philip.

1. What passed between Philip and Nathanael.

(1) The joyful news that Philip brought to Nathanael, *v*. 45. Philip, though newly come to an acquaintance with Christ himself, yet steps aside to seek Nathanael. O, saith Philip, *we have found him of whom Moses and the prophets did write*. What a transport of joy Philip was in, upon this new acquaintance with Christ: "We have found him whom we have so long wished and waited for; at last, *he is come, he is come*, and *we* have found him!" What an advantage it was to him that he was so well acquainted with the scriptures of the Old Testament, which prepared his mind for the reception of evangelical light. It was his weakness to say, *We have found him*, for Christ found them before they found Christ. He did not yet *apprehend*, as Paul did, how he was *apprehended of Christ Jesus*.

(2) The objection which Nathanael made against this, *Can any good thing come out of Nazareth? v*. 46. [1] His *caution* was commendable; our rule is, *Prove all things*. [2] His objection arose from ignorance. If he meant that the Messiah, that great good thing,

could not come out of Nazareth, so far he was right, but then he was ignorant of the matter of *fact*, that this Jesus was born at Bethlehem; so that the blunder Philip made, in calling him *Jesus of Nazareth*, occasioned this objection.

(3) The short reply which Philip gave to this objection: *Come and see*. We may *know* enough to *satisfy* ourselves, and yet not be able to *say* enough to *silence* a subtle adversary. It was his *wisdom* and zeal that, when he could not answer the objection himself, he would have him go to one that could: *Come and see*. Not, *Go and see*, but, "*Come, and I will go along with thee*." Many people are kept from the ways of religion by the unreasonable prejudices they have conceived against religion, upon the account of some foreign circumstances which do not at all touch the merits of the case.

2. What passed between Nathanael and our Lord Jesus. He came and *saw*, not in vain.

(1) *Jesus saw him* coming. He said of him to those about him, *Behold an Israelite indeed*. He *commended* him; not to flatter him, but perhaps because he knew him to be a *modest* man. Nathanael had objected against Christ; but Christ hereby showed that he excused it, because he knew his heart was upright. He commended him for his *integrity*. *Behold an Israelite indeed*. *All are not Israel that are of Israel;* here, however, was *an Israelite indeed*. A sincere follower of the good example of Israel. He was a genuine son of *honest Jacob*. A sincere professor of the faith of Israel: he was really as good as he seemed, and his practice was *of a piece* with his profession. He is the Jew that is one *inwardly*, so is he *the Christian*. He is one in whom is *no guile: no guile* towards men; a man that one may trust; *no guile* towards God, sincere in his repentance for sin. He does not say without *guilt*, but without *guile*. An Israelite indeed, a miracle of divine grace.

(2) Nathanael is much surprised at this.

[1] Here is Nathanael's modesty: "*Whence knowest thou me*, me that am unworthy of thy cognizance?" This was an evidence of his sincerity, that he did not catch at the praise he met with. Doth Christ know us? Let us covet to know him.

[2] Here is Christ's further *manifestation* of himself to him: *Before Philip called thee, I saw thee. First,* He gives him to understand that he *knew him*, and so manifests his divinity. *Secondly,* That before Philip called him he saw him under the fig-tree. Christ has knowledge of us before we have any knowledge of him. His eye was upon him when he was *under the fig-tree;* this was a private token which nobody understood but Nathanael: "When thou wast retired *under the fig-tree* I had then my eye upon thee, and saw that which was very acceptable." It is most probable that Nathanael under the fig-tree was employed in meditation, and prayer, and communion with God. *Sitting under the* fig-tree denotes quietness and composedness of spirit, which much befriend communion with God.

(3) Nathanael hereby obtained a full assurance of faith in Jesus Christ (*v.* 49): *Rabbi, thou art the Son of God, thou art the king of Israel;* that is, in short, thou art the true Messiah. Observe here, how *firmly* he believed *with the heart*. Now he asks no more, *Can any good thing come out of Nazareth?* How *freely* he confessed *with the mouth*. He confesses Christ's prophetical office, in calling him *Rabbi*. He confesses his divine nature and mission, in calling him the Son of God. He confesses, "*Thou art the king of Israel*." If he be the Son of God, he is king of the Israel of God.

(4) Christ hereupon raises the hopes and expectations of Nathanael to something further and greater than all this, *v.* 50, 51.

[1] He here signifies his acceptance, and (it should seem) his admiration, of the ready faith of Nathanael:

Because I said, I saw thee under the fig-tree, believest thou? It was a sign that Nathanael's heart was prepared beforehand, else the work had not been done so suddenly.

[2] He promises him much greater helps for the confirmation and increase of his faith.

First, In general: "*Thou shalt see greater things than these*"; the miracles of Christ, and his resurrection. Those who truly believe the gospel will find its evidences grow upon them. Whatever discoveries Christ is pleased to make of himself here in this world, he hath still greater things than these to make known to them.

Secondly, In particular: "Not thou only, but you, all you my disciples, you *shall see heaven opened*." *Verily, verily I say unto you*, which commands both a *fixed attention* to what is said as very weighty, and a *full assent* to it as undoubtedly true. None used this word at the beginning of a sentence but Christ, though the Jews often used it at the close of a prayer. It is a solemn asseveration. Now see what it is that Christ assures them of: *Hereafter*, or *ere long*, ye shall see heaven opened. *The Son of man* is a title frequently applied to him in the gospel, but always by himself. Nathanael had called him the *Son of God* and *king of Israel*: he calls himself *Son of man* to express his *humility*, and to teach his *humanity*. They are great things which he here foretells: *You shall see heaven opened*, and *the angels of God ascending and descending upon the Son of man*. It was fulfilled in the many ministrations of the angels to our Lord Jesus, especially that at his ascension, when heaven was opened to receive him, and the angels *ascended* and *descended*, and this in the sight of the disciples. Christ's ascension was the great proof of his mission, and much confirmed the faith of his disciples. We may understand it of Christ's *miracles*. Christ is now beginning a dispensation of miracles. Immediately after this, Christ began to work miracles, *ch.* ii. 11.

CHAPTER 2

In this chapter, we have, I. The account of the first miracle which Jesus wrought at Cana of Galilee (ver. 1–11), and his appearing at Capernaum, ver. 12. II. The account of the first passover he kept at Jerusalem after he began his public ministry; his driving the buyers and sellers out of the temple (ver. 13–17); and the sign he gave to those who quarrelled with him for it (ver. 18–22), with an account of some almost believers (ver. 23–25.)

Verses 1–11

We have here the story of Christ's miraculous conversion of water into wine at a marriage in Cana of Galilee. He could have wrought miracles before, but, miracles being designed for the sacred and solemn seals of his doctrine, he began not to work any till he began to preach.

I. The occasion of this miracle. Maimonides observes it to be to the honour of Moses that all the signs he did in the wilderness he did *upon necessity;* we needed food, he brought us manna, and so did Christ.

1. The time: the *third day* after he came into Galilee. The evangelist keeps a journal of occurrences. Our Master filled up his time better than his servants do, and never lay down at night complaining that he had *lost a day*.

2. The place: it was at Cana in Galilee. Christ began to work miracles in an obscure corner of the country. His doctrine and miracles would not be so much opposed by the plain and honest Galileans as they would be at Jerusalem.

3. The occasion itself was a *marriage*. The *mother of Jesus* is said to be *there*. The honour which Christ hereby put upon the ordinance of marriage, that he graced the solemnity of it, not only with his presence, but with his first miracle. There was a *marriage*, a

marriage-feast, to grace the solemnity. Marriages were usually celebrated with festivals.

4. Christ and his mother and disciples were principal guests at this entertainment. *The mother of Jesus was there;* no mention being made of Joseph, we conclude him dead before this. Jesus was *called*, and he came, and feasted with them. Christ was to come in a way different from that of John Baptist, who came *neither eating nor drinking. There was a marriage, and Jesus was called.* It is very desirable, when there is a *marriage*, to have Jesus Christ *present* at it; to have the marriage owned and blessed by him: the *marriage* is then *honourable* indeed. They that would have Christ with them at their marriage must invite him by prayer; that is the messenger that must be sent to heaven for him; and he will come. And he will turn the water into wine. The disciples also were invited. They had thrown themselves upon his care, and they soon found that, though he had no wealth, he had good friends. Those that *follow* Christ shall *feast* with him, they shall *fare* as he *fares.* Love to Christ is testified by a love to those that are his.

II. The miracle itself.

1. They *wanted wine, v.* 3. There was *want* at a *feast*; though much was provided, yet all was spent. While we are in this world we sometimes find ourselves *in straits*, even then when we think ourselves in the *fulness of our sufficiency.* If always *spending*, perhaps all is spent ere we are aware. There was want at a *marriage feast.* It should seem, Christ and his disciples were the occasion of this want, but they who straiten themselves for Christ shall not lose by him.

2. The *mother of Jesus* solicited him to assist her friends. We are told (*v.* 3–5) what passed between Christ and his mother.

(1) She acquaints him with the difficulty they were in (*v.* 3): *She saith unto him, They have no wine.* Some think that she did not expect from him any miraculous supply (he having as yet wrought no miracle). But, most probably, she looked for a miracle. The bridegroom might have sent out for more wine, but she was for going to the fountain-head. We ought to be concerned for the wants and straits of our friends. In our own and our friends' straits it is our wisdom and duty to apply ourselves to Christ by prayer. In our addresses to Christ, we must not prescribe to him, but humbly spread our case before him.

(2) He gave her a reprimand for it. Here is,

[1] The rebuke itself: *Woman, what have I to do with thee?* As many as Christ loves, he rebukes and chastens. He calls her *woman*, not *mother.* When we begin to be assuming, we should be reminded what we are, *men* and *women*, frail, foolish, and corrupt. Now this was intended to be, *First*, A check to his mother for interposing in a matter which was the act of his Godhead, which had no dependence on her, and which she was not the mother of. The greatest advancements must not make us forget ourselves and our place, nor the familiarity to which the covenant of grace admits us breed contempt, irreverence, or any kind of degree of presumption. *Secondly*, It was an instruction to others of his relations that they must never expect him to have any regard to his kindred according to the flesh, in his working miracles, who in this matter were no more to him than other people. In the things of God we must not *know faces.*

[2] The reason of this rebuke: *Mine hour is not yet come.* For everything Christ did, and that was done to him, he had *his hour*, the *fixed* time and the *fittest* time. "Mine hour for *working miracles* is not yet come." Yet afterwards he wrought this, before the hour, because he foresaw it would confirm the faith of his infant disciples (*v.* 11): so that this was an earnest of the many miracles he would work when his *hour was come.* His mother moved him to help them *when the wine began to fail* (so it may be read, *v.* 3), but his hour was not yet come till it was quite spent. This teaches us that man's extremity is God's opportunity. Then *his hour is come* when we are reduced to the utmost strait, and know not what to do. The delays of mercy are not to be construed the denials of prayer.

(3) Notwithstanding this, she encouraged herself with expectations, that he would help, for she bade the servants *observe his orders, v.* 5. She took the reproof very submissively, and did not reply to it. It is best not to deserve reproof from Christ, but next best to be meek and quiet under it, and to count it a kindness. She kept her hope in Christ's mercy. When we come to God in Christ for any mercy, two things discourage us: Sense of *our own follies* and infirmities and fear of *our Lord's frowns and rebukes.* Afflictions are continued, deliverances delayed, and God seems angry at our prayers. This was the case of the mother of our Lord here, and yet she encourages herself with hope that he will at length give an answer of peace, to teach us to wrestle with God even when he seems in his providence to walk contrary to us. She directed the servants to have an eye *to him*, and not to make their applications to her. She directed them punctually to observe his orders: "*Whatsoever he saith unto you, do it.*" Those that expect Christ's *favours* must with an implicit obedience observe his *orders.* The way of duty is the way to mercy; and Christ's methods must not be objected against.

(4) Christ did at length miraculously supply them; for he is often better than his word, but never worse.

[1] The miracle itself was *turning water into wine*; the substance of water acquiring a new form, and having all the accidents and qualities of wine. By this Christ showed himself to be the God of nature, who maketh the earth to bring forth wine. The beginning of Christ's miracles was turning water into wine; the blessing of the gospel turns water into wine. Christ hereby showed that his errand into the world was to heighten and improve creature-comforts to all believers, and make them comforts indeed.

[2] The circumstances of it magnified it and freed it from all suspicion of cheat.

First, It was done in water-pots (*v.* 6): *There were set there six water-pots of stone.* 1. For what use these water-pots were intended: for the legal purifications enjoined by the law of God, and many more by the tradition of the elders. They used much water in their washing, for which reason here were six large water-pots provided. It was a saying among them—*He who uses much water in washing will gain much wealth in this world.* 2. To what use Christ put them; to be the receptacles of the miraculous wine. Thus Christ came to bring in the grace of the gospel, which is as *wine*, instead of the shadows of the law, which were as water. These were *water-pots*, that had never been used to have wine in them; and of *stone*, which is not apt to retain the scent of former liquors, if ever they had had wine in them. They contained *two or three firkins apiece*; the quantity is uncertain, but very considerable. Christ gives like himself, gives abundantly, according to his riches in glory.

Secondly, The water-pots were filled *up to the brim* by the servants at Christ's word, *v.* 7.

Thirdly, The miracle was wrought suddenly, and in such a manner as greatly magnified it.

a. As soon as they had filled the water-pots, he said, *Draw out now* (*v.* 8), and it was done. Without any ceremony, in the eye of the spectators. He sits still in his place, says not a word, but *wills* the thing, and so works it. Christ does great things and marvellous *without noise*, works manifest changes in a hidden way, without any hesitation or uncertainty in his own breast. With the greatest assurance imaginable, though it was his *first miracle*, he recommends it to the master of the feast *first*. As he knew what he *would* do, so he knew what he *could* do. All was good, very good, even in the beginning.

b. Our Lord Jesus directed the servants, (*a*) *To draw it out;* to be drank. Christ's works are all *for use.* Has he turned thy water into wine, given thee knowledge and grace? It is to *profit withal;* and therefore *draw out now.* Those that would know Christ must make trial of him. (*b*) *To present it to the governor of the feast.* Though he was not treated as the Master of the feast, he kindly approved himself a friend to the feast, and, if not its founder, yet its best benefactor. This *governor* was the monitor of the feast, whose office it was to see that each had enough, and none did exceed, and that there were no indecencies or disorders. Feasts have need of governors, because too many, when they are at feasts, have not the government of themselves. Some think that this *governor* was priest or Levite that craved a blessing and gave thanks, and Christ would have the cup brought to him, that he might bless it, and bless God for it; for the extraordinary tokens of Christ's presence and power were not to supersede, or jostle out, the ordinary rules and methods of piety and devotion.

Fourthly, The wine which was thus miraculously provided was of the best and richest kind, which was acknowledged by the governor of the feast, *v.* 9, 10. 1. It was certain that this was *wine.* The governor knew this when he drank it, though he knew not *whence it was;* the servants knew whence it was, but had not yet tasted it. 2. That it was the best wine. Christ's works commend themselves even to those that know not their author. The products of miracles were always the best in their kind. This the governor of the feast takes notice of to the bridegroom, with an air of pleasantness, as *uncommon.* The common method was otherwise. Good wine is brought out to the best advantage at the beginning of a feast, but *when they have well drank,* good wine is but thrown away upon them, worse will serve then. See the vanity of all the pleasures of sense; they soon surfeit, but never satisfy; the longer they are enjoyed, the less pleasant they grow. *Thou hast kept the good wine until now;* not knowing to whom they were indebted for this good wine, he returns the thanks of the table to the bridegroom. Christ, in providing thus plentifully for the guests, though he hereby allows a sober cheerful use of wine, especially in times of rejoicing (Neh. viii. 10), yet he does not invalidate his own caution, which is, that our hearts be not *at any time,* no not at a marriage feast, *overcharged with surfeiting and drunkenness,* Luke xxi. 34. Temperance *per force* is a thankless virtue; but if divine providence gives us abundance of the delights of sense, and divine grace enables us to use them moderately, this is self-denial that is praiseworthy. Two considerations, drawn from this story, may be sufficient at any time to fortify us against temptations to intemperance: *First,* That our meat and drink are the *gifts of God's bounty* to us. It is therefore ungrateful and impious to abuse them. *Secondly,* That, wherever we are, Christ has his eye upon us. He has given us a specimen of the method he takes in dealing with those that deal with him, which is, to reserve the *best* for the *last,* and therefore they must *deal upon trust.* The pleasures of sin give their colour in the cup, but *at the last bite;* but the pleasures of religion will be *pleasures for evermore.*

III. In the conclusion of this story (*v.* 11) we are told, 1. That this was *the beginning of miracles* which

Jesus did. He himself was the greatest miracle of all; but this was the first that was wrought *by* him. He had power, but there was a *time of the hiding of his power.* 2. That herein he *manifested his glory;* hereby he proved himself to be the Son of God. 3. That *his disciples believed on him.* Those whom he had called (*ch.* i), now saw this, shared in it, and had their faith strengthened by it. Even the faith that is true is at first but weak. The strongest men were once babes, so were the strongest Christians.

Verses 12–22

I. The short visit Christ made to Capernaum, *v.* 12. It is called *his own city* (Matt. ix. 1), because he made it his headquarters in Galilee, and what little rest he had was there. It was a place of concourse, and *therefore* Christ chose it, that the fame of his doctrine and miracles might thence spread the further.

1. The company that attended him thither: *his mother, his brethren, and his disciples.* Wherever Christ went, (1) He *would not* go alone, but would take those with him who had put themselves under his guidance. (2) He *could not* go alone, but they would follow him, because they liked the sweetness either of his doctrine or of his wine, *ch.* vi. 26. His mother, yet followed him; not to intercede with him, but to learn of him. His *brethren,* who were at the marriage, and *his disciples,* attended him wherever he went. It should seem, people were more affected with Christ's miracles at first than they were afterwards, when custom made them seem less strange.

2. His continuance there, which was at this time *not many days.* Christ was still upon the remove, would not confine his usefulness to *one* place, because *many* needed him. He did not stay long at Capernaum because the passover was at hand, and he must attend it at Jerusalem.

II. The passover he kept at Jerusalem; it is the *first* after his baptism. Christ, being *made under the law,* observed the passover at Jerusalem. He went up to Jerusalem when *the passover was at hand,* that he might be there *with the first.* Christ kept the passover at Jerusalem yearly, ever since he was twelve years old, but now that he has entered upon his public ministry we may expect something more from him than before; and two things he did there:

1. He *purged the temple, v.* 14–17.

(1) The first place we find him in at Jerusalem was the *temple,* and, it should seem, he did not make any public appearance till he came thither.

(2) The first work we find him at in the temple was the *purging* of it. He first *purged out* what was amiss and then taught them to do well. He expects that all who come to him should reform their hearts and lives. And this he has taught us by purging the temple. See here, What were the corruptions that were to be purged out. He found a market in one of the courts of the temple, that which was called the *court of the Gentiles.* They sold *oxen, and sheep, and doves,* for sacrifice; not for common use, but for the convenience of those who came out of the country, and could not bring their sacrifices *in kind* along with them. This *market* was admitted into the temple by the chief priests, for filthy lucre. Great corruptions in the church owe their rise to the love of money. They *changed money,* for the convenience of those that were to pay a half-shekel for the service of the tabernacle, and no doubt they got by it. See what course our Lord took to purge out those corruptions. He did not complain to the chief priests, for he knew they countenanced those corruptions. But he himself,

First, Drove out the sheep and oxen, and those that *sold them.* He never used *force* to drive any *into* the temple, but only to drive those out that profaned it. He made a scourge of *small cords*, which probably they had led their sheep and oxen with. Sinners prepare the scourges with which they themselves will be driven out from the temple of the Lord.

Secondly, He *poured out the changers' money*. In *pouring out* the money, he showed his contempt of it. In *overthrowing* the tables, he showed his displeasure against those that make religion a matter of worldly gain. Money-changers in the temple are the scandal of it.

Thirdly, He said to them that sold doves (sacrifices for the poor), *Take these things hence*. The sparrows and swallows were welcome, that were left to God's providence (Ps. lxxxiv. 3), but not the doves, that were appropriated to man's profit. God's temple must not be made a pigeon-house.

Fourthly, He gave them a good reason for what he did: *Make not my Father's house a house of merchandise*.

a. Here is a reason why they should not profane the temple, because it was the *house of God*. Merchandise is a good thing in the exchange, but not in the temple. It was *sacrilege*; it was robbing God. It was to debase that which was solemn and awful, and to make it mean. It was to make the business of religion subservient to a secular interest. Those make God's house a house of merchandise whose minds are filled with cares about the worldly business when they are attending on religious exercises, as those who perform divine offices for filthy lucre.

b. Here is a reason why he was concerned to purge it, because it was *his Father's house*. Therefore he had authority to purge it, as a Son *over his own house*. Therefore he had a zeal for the purging of it: "It is *my Father's house*, and therefore I cannot bear to see it profaned, and *him* dishonoured." Christ's purging the temple thus may justly be reckoned among his *wonderful works*. Considering, (*a*) That he did it without the *assistance* of any of his *friends*. (*b*) That he did it without the *resistance* of any of his *enemies*. The corruption was too plain to be justified; sinners' own consciences are reformers' best friends; yet that was not all, there was a divine power put forth herein, a power over the spirits of men.

Fifthly, Here is the remark which his disciples made upon it (*v.* 17): *They remembered that it was written, The zeal of thine house hath eaten me up*. One scripture came to their thoughts, which taught them to reconcile this action both with the meekness of the *Lamb of God* and with the majesty of the *King of Israel*; for David, speaking of the Messiah, takes notice of his *zeal for God's house*, as so great that it even *ate him up*. 1. The disciples came to understand the meaning of what Christ did, by remembering the scriptures: *They remembered* now *that it was written*. The word of God and the works of God do mutually explain and illustrate each other. See of what great use it is to the disciples of Christ to be *ready* and *mighty* in the scriptures, and to have their memories well stored with scripture truths. 2. The scripture they remembered was very apposite: *The zeal of thine house hath eaten me up*. All the graces that were to be found among the Old Testament saints were eminently in Christ, and particularly this of zeal for the house of God. Zeal for the house of God forbids us to consult our own credit, ease, and safety, when they come in competition with Christ's service, and sometimes carries on our souls in our duty so far and so fast that our bodies cannot keep pace with them.

2. Christ gave a sign to those who demanded it to prove his authority for so doing.

(1) Their demand of a sign: *Then answered the Jews*, that is the multitude of the people, with their leaders. When they could object nothing against the thing itself, they questioned his authority to do it: "*What sign showest thou unto us.*" What had he to do to undertake it, who was in no office there? But was not the thing itself sign enough?

(2) Christ's answer to this demand, *v.* 19. A sign in something *to come*, the truth of which must appear by the event. The sign that he gives them is his own *death* and *resurrection*. He refers them to that which would be. He foretells his death and resurrection, not in plain terms, but in figurative expressions: *Destroy this temple, and in three days I will raise it up*. Thus he spoke in parables to those who were willingly ignorant, that *they might not perceive*, Matt. xiii. 13, 14. Those that will not see shall not see. Nay, this figurative speech used here proved such a *stumbling-block* to them that it was produced in evidence against him at his trial, Matt. xxvi. 60, 61. He foretells his death by the Jews' malice, in these words, *Destroy you this temple*. Christ, even at the beginning of his ministry, had a clear foresight of all his sufferings at the end of it, and yet went on cheerfully in it. He foretells his resurrection by his own power: In *three days I will raise it up*. There were others that *were raised*, but Christ raised himself. He chose to express this by *destroying* and *re-edifying* the temple. *First*, Because he was now to justify himself in purging the temple, which they had profaned: "You that defile one temple will destroy another; and I will prove my authority to *purge* what you have defiled by *raising* what you will *destroy*."

(3) "*Forty and six years was this temple in building, v.* 20. Temple work was always slow work and canst thou make such quick work of it?" They show *some knowledge*; they could tell how long the temple was in building. They show *more ignorance, First*, Of the *meaning of Christ's words. Secondly*, Of *the almighty power of Christ*, as if he could do no more than another man.

(4) A vindication of Christ's answer from their cavil. *He spoke of the temple of his body, v.* 21. Some think that when he said, Destroy *this* temple, he pointed to his own body; however, it is certain that he *spoke of the temple of his body*. Like the temple it was built by immediate divine direction. Like the temple, it was a *holy house*; it is called *that holy thing*. It was, like the temple, the habitation, of God's glory; there the eternal Word dwelt. He is *Emmanuel*—*God with us*. Worshippers looked *towards* that house. So we must worship God with an eye to Christ.

(5) A reflection which the disciples made upon this, long after (*v.* 22): *When he was risen from the dead his disciples remembered that he had said this*. The memories of Christ's disciples should be like the treasure of the good householder, furnished with things both *new* and *old*, Matt. xiii. 52. *They remembered* that saying *when he was risen from the dead*. They laid up the saying in their hearts, and afterwards it became both intelligible and useful. The juniors in years and profession should treasure up those truths of which at present they do not well understand either the meaning or the use, for they will be serviceable to them hereafter. This saying of Christ revived in the memories of his disciples *when he was risen from the dead*; and why then? Because *then* the Spirit was poured out to bring things to their remembrance which Christ had said to them. That very day that Christ rose from the dead he *opened their understandings*, Luke xxiv. 45. Because then this saying of Christ was fulfilled. When the temple of his body had been *destroyed* and was *raised again*, and that upon the *third day*, then they remembered this. See what use they made of it: *They believed the scripture, and the word that Jesus had said*. They were slow of heart to believe (Luke xxiv. 25), but they were *sure*. The *scripture* and the *words of Christ* are here put together, because they mutually illustrate and strengthen each other.

Verses 23–25

I. Our Lord Jesus, when he was at Jerusalem at the passover, did preach and work miracles. The time was holy time, *the feast-day*, and Christ took that opportunity of preaching, when the concourse of people was great.

II. Hereby many were brought to *believe in his name*, to acknowledge him a *teacher come from God*, as Nicodemus did (*ch.* iii. 2).

III. Yet *Jesus did not commit himself unto them* (*v.* 24): Christ did not see cause to repose any confidence in these new converts at Jerusalem, either, 1. Because they were *false*, at least some of them. He had more disciples that he could trust among the Galileans than among the dwellers at Jerusalem. Or, 2. Because they were *weak*. (1) They were *timorous*, and wanted zeal and courage. In times of difficulty and danger, cowards are not fit to be trusted. Or, (2) They were *tumultuous*, and wanted discretion and management.

IV. The reason why he did not *commit himself* to them was because he *knew* them (*v.* 25), knew the wickedness of some and the weakness of others. The evangelist takes this occasion to assert Christ's omniscience. He *knew all men*, not only their names and faces, as it is possible for us to know many, but their nature, dispositions, affections, designs, as we do not know *any man*, scarcely *ourselves*. He knows them that are truly his, knows their integrity and knows their infirmity too. He *needed not that any should testify of man*. His knowledge was not by information from others, but by his own infallible intuition. He *knew what was in man*. We know what is done *by men*; Christ knows what is *in them*. How fit is Christ to be the *Saviour of men*, very fit to be the physician, who has such a perfect knowledge of the patient's state and case, temper and distemper; knows what is in him! How fit also to be the *Judge of all*! The Lord comes to his temple, and none come to him but a parcel of weak simple people, that he can neither have *credit* from nor put *confidence* in.

CHAPTER 3

In this chapter we have, I. Christ's discourse with Nicodemus, a Pharisee, ver. 1–21. II. John Baptist's discourse with his disciples concerning Christ (ver. 22–36), in which he fairly and faithfully resigns all his honour and interest to him.

Verses 1–21

We found, in the close of the foregoing chapter, that few were brought to Christ at Jerusalem; yet here was *one*, a considerable one.

I. Who this Nicodemus was. Not many mighty and noble are called; yet some are, and here was one. *Not many* of the *rulers, or of the Pharisees*. This was a *man of the Pharisees*, bred to learning, a scholar. Let it not be said that all Christ's followers are *unlearned and ignorant men*. He was a *ruler of the Jews*, and a member of the great sanhedrim, a man of authority in Jerusalem. Bad as things were, there were some rulers *well inclined*. Nicodemus continued in his place, and did what he *could*, when he could not do what he *would*.

II. His solemn address to our Lord Jesus Christ, *v.* 2.

1. When he came: *He came to Jesus by night*, did not think it enough to hear his public discourses. He resolved to talk with him by himself, where he might be free with him. He made this address *by night*, which may be considered, (1) As an act of *prudence* and *discretion*. Christ was engaged all day in *public* work, and he would not interrupt him then, but observed *Christ's hour*, and waited on him when he was *at leisure*. Christ had many enemies, and therefore Nicodemus came to him *incognito*, lest being known to the chief priests they should be the

more enraged against Christ. (2) As an act of *zeal*. He would rather take time from the diversions of the *evening*, or the rest of the *night*, than not converse with Christ. When others were sleeping, he was getting knowledge. He knew not how soon Christ might leave the town, nor what might happen betwixt that and another feast, and therefore would lose no time. In the night his converse with Christ would be more free, and less liable to disturbance. (3) As an act of *fear* and *cowardice*. He was afraid, or ashamed, to be *seen* with Christ, and therefore came *in the night*. Though he came by night, Christ bade him welcome, accepted his integrity, and pardoned his infirmity, and hereby taught his ministers to encourage good beginnings, though weak. Though now he came *by night*, yet afterwards he owned Christ *publicly*, *ch.* vii. 50; xix. 39. The grace which is at first but a grain of mustard-seed may grow to be a great tree.

2. What he said. He comes immediately to the business; he calls Christ *Rabbi*, which signifies a *great man*. There are hopes of those who have a respect for Christ, and think and speak honourably of him. He tells Christ how far *he had attained*: We *know that thou art a teacher*. (1) His *assertion* concerning Christ: *Thou art a teacher come from God;* supported with divine inspiration and divine authority. He came first to be a *teacher*; for he would rule by the power of truth, not of the sword. (2) His *assurance* of it: *We know, not only I*, but *others*; so he took it for granted, the thing being so plain and self-evident. (3) The ground of this assurance: *No man can do those miracles that thou doest, except God be with him*. Here was Nicodemus, a judicious, sensible, inquisitive man, one that had all the *reason* and *opportunity* imaginable to examine them, so fully satisfied that they were real miracles that he was wrought upon by them to go contrary to the stream of those of his own rank. We are directed what inference to draw from Christ's miracles: Therefore we are to receive him as a *teacher come from God*.

III. The discourse between Christ and Nicodemus hereupon, see *v.* 11, 12. Four things our Saviour here discourses of:

1. Concerning the *necessity and nature of regeneration* or the *new birth*, *v.* 3–8. Now we must consider this,

(1) As *pertinently answered* to Nicodemus's address. Jesus *answered*, *v.* 3. It was not enough for him to admire Christ's miracles, and acknowledge his mission, but he must be *born again*. It is plain that he expected the *kingdom of heaven* now shortly to appear. He is betimes aware of the dawning of that day. But Christ tells him that he can have no benefit by that *change of the state*, unless there be a *change of the spirit*, equivalent to a new birth. When Nicodemus owned Christ a *teacher come from God*, he plainly intimated a desire to know what this revelation was, and Christ declares it.

(2) As *positively* and *vehemently* asserted by our Lord Jesus: *Verily, verily, I say unto thee, except a man be born again he cannot see the kingdom of God*. Observe,

[1] What it is that is required: to be *born again*. We must *live a new life*. Birth is the beginning of life; to be *born again* is to begin anew. We must not think to patch up the old building, but begin from the foundation. We must *have a new nature*, new principles, new affections, new aims. We must be born ἄνωθεν, which signifies both *again*, and *from above*. We must be born *anew*. Our souls must be *fashioned* and *enlivened* anew. We must be born *from above*. This new birth has its rise *from heaven*, it is to be born to a *divine* and *heavenly* life.

[2] The indispensable necessity of this: "Except *a man be born again, he cannot see the kingdom of*

God." Except we be *born from above,* we cannot *see* this. We cannot *understand* the *nature* of it. We cannot *receive* the *comfort* of it. Regeneration is absolutely necessary to our happiness here and hereafter. It will appear, in the nature of the thing, that we must be *born again,* because it is impossible that we should be *happy* if we be not *holy.*

This great truth of the necessity of regeneration being thus solemnly laid down,

a. It is objected against by Nicodemus (v. 4): *How can a man be born when he is old? Can he enter the second time into his mother's womb, and be born?* Herein appears, (a) His weakness in knowledge; what Christ spoke spiritually he seems to have understood after a corporal and carnal manner, as if there was such a connection between the soul and the body that there could be no fashioning the *heart anew* but by forming the *bones anew.* It is a great surprise to him to hear of being *born again.* Could he be better bred and born than bred and born an Israelite. They that are proud of their *first birth* are hardly brought to a *new birth.* (b) His willingness to be taught. He does not turn his back upon Christ because of his hard saying, but ingenuously acknowledges his ignorance. "Lord, make me to understand this, for it is a riddle to me; I am such a fool as to know no other way for a man to be born than of his mother." When we meet with that in the things of God which is *dark,* and *hard to be understood,* we must continue our attendance upon the means of knowledge.

b. It is opened and further explained by our Lord Jesus, v. 5–8. From the objection he takes occasion to repeat and confirm what he had said (v. 5): "*Verily, verily I say unto thee,* the very same that I said before." Though Nicodemus understood not the mystery of regeneration, yet Christ asserts the necessity of it as positively as before. It is folly to think of evading the obligation of evangelical precepts, by pleading that they are unintelligible. To expound and clear what he had said he further shows,

(a) The *author* of this blessed change, and who it is that works it. To be born again is to be *born of the Spirit,* v. 5–8. The change is not wrought by any wisdom or power of our own, but by the power and influence of the blessed Spirit of grace.

(b) The *nature* of this change, and what that is which is wrought; it is *spirit,* v. 6. Those that are regenerated are made *spiritual.* The dictates and interests of the rational and immortal soul have retrieved the dominion they ought to have over the flesh.

(c) The *necessity* of this change. Christ here shows that it is necessary in the *nature of the thing: That which is born of the flesh is flesh,* v. 6. 1. We are here told *what we are:* We are *flesh.* The soul is still a spiritual substance, but so wedded to the flesh, so captivated by the will of the flesh, that it is justly called *flesh.* And what communion can there be between God, who is a *spirit,* and a soul in this condition? 2. How we *came to be so;* by being *born of the flesh.* It is a corruption that is bred *in the bone* with us. The corrupt nature, which is *flesh,* takes rise from our *first birth;* and therefore the new nature, which is *spirit,* must take rise from a second birth. Nicodemus spoke of entering again into his mother's womb, and being born; but, if he could do so, to what purpose? If he were born of his mother a hundred times, that would not mend the matter, for still that *which is born of the flesh is flesh.* Corruption and sin are woven into our nature; we are *shapen in iniquity.* It is not enough to put on a new coat or a new face, but we must put on the *new man.* Christ makes it further necessary, by his own word: *Marvel not that I said unto thee, You must be born again,* v. 7. Christ hath said it. He who is the great Physician of souls,

knows their case, and what is necessary to their cure,— he hath said, *You must be born again.* We are not to marvel at it; for when we consider the holiness of the God with whom we have to do, the depravity of our nature, we shall not think it strange that so much stress is laid upon this as the one thing needful, that *we must be born again.*

(d) This change is illustrated by two comparisons. *First,* The regenerating work of the Spirit is compared to *water,* v. 5. To be born again is to be *born of water* and of the Spirit. That which is primarily intended here is to show that the Spirit, in sanctifying a soul, (1) *Cleanses* and purifies it as water, takes away its filth. (2) Cools and refreshes it, as water does the hunted hart and the weary traveller. It is probable that Christ had an eye to the ordinance of baptism, which John had used and he himself had begun to use, "You must be born again of the Spirit," which regeneration by the Spirit should be signified by washing with water, as the visible sign of that spiritual grace. *Secondly,* It is compared to *wind: The wind bloweth where it listeth, so is every one that is born of the Spirit,* v. 8. The same word signifies both the wind and the Spirit. The Spirit, in regeneration, works *arbitrarily,* and as a free agent. The Spirit dispenses his influences where, and when, on whom, and in what measure and degrees, he pleases. He works *powerfully,* and with evident effects: *Thou hearest the sound thereof;* though its causes are hidden, its effects are manifest. He works *mysteriously,* and in secret hidden ways. *Thou canst not tell whence it comes, nor whither it goes.* How it gathers and how it spends its strength is a riddle to us; so the manner and methods of the Spirit's working are a mystery.

2. The *certainty and sublimity of gospel truths.*

(1) The objection which Nicodemus still made (v. 9): *How can these things be?* Christ's explication of the doctrine of the necessity of regeneration, it should seem, made it never the clearer to him. The corruption of nature which makes it *necessary,* and the way of the Spirit which makes it *practicable,* are as much mysteries to him as the thing itself. Thus many will neither believe the truths of Christianity nor submit to the laws of it further than *they please.* Christ shall be their teacher, provided they may choose their lesson. Nicodemus owns himself ignorant of Christ's meaning, after all: "*How can these things be?* They are things I do not understand, my capacity will not reach them." Because this doctrine was *unintelligible* to him he questions the truth of it. Many think that that cannot be *proved* which they cannot *believe.*

(2) The reproof which Christ gave him for his dullness and ignorance: "*Art thou a master in Israel,* and yet not only unacquainted with the doctrine of regeneration, but incapable of understanding it?" This word is a reproof, [1] To those who undertake to teach others and yet are ignorant and unskilful in the world of righteousness themselves. [2] To those that spend their time in notions and ceremonies in religion, niceties and criticisms in the scripture, and neglect that which is practical. Two words in the reproof are very emphatic: *First,* The place where his lot was cast: in *Israel,* where divine revelation was. He might have learned this out of the Old Testament. *Secondly,* The things he was thus ignorant in: *these* things, these *necessary* things, these *great* things, these *divine* things.

(3) Christ's discourse, hereupon, of the certainty and sublimity of gospel truths (v. 11–13). Observe here,

[1] That the truths Christ taught were very *certain* and what we may venture upon (v. 11): *We speak that we do know.* The truths of Christ are of undoubted certainty. We have all the reason in the world to be assured that the sayings of Christ are

faithful sayings, and such as we may venture our souls upon. Whatever Christ spoke, he spoke *of his own knowledge*. The things are thus sure, thus clear; and yet *you receive not our witness*.

[2] The truths Christ taught, though communicated in language and expressions borrowed from common and earthly things, yet were most sublime and heavenly; this is intimated, *v.* 12: "*I have told them earthly things*, that is, have told them the great things of God in similitudes taken from earthly things, to make them the more easy and intelligible, as that of the *new birth* and the *wind*, and lisped to you in your own language, and cannot make you to understand my doctrine. If such *familiar expressions* be stumbling-blocks, what would *abstract ideas* be, and spiritual things painted *proper?*" The things of the gospel are *heavenly* things, out of the road of the enquiries of human reason, and much more out of the reach of its discoveries. He considers our *frame*, that we are *of* the earth, and our *place*, that we are *on* the earth, and therefore speaks to us earthly things, and makes things sensible the vehicle of things spiritual, to make them the more easy and familiar to us. Earthly things are despised because they are *vulgar*, and heavenly things because they are *abstruse*; and so, whatever method is taken, still some fault or other is found with it.

[3] Our Lord Jesus, and he alone, was fit to reveal to us a doctrine thus certain, thus sublime: *No man hath ascended up into heaven but he*, *v.* 13. None but Christ was able to reveal to us the will of God for our salvation. Nicodemus addressed Christ as a prophet; but he must know that he is greater than all the Old Testament prophets, for none of them *had ascended into heaven*. No man hath attained to the certain knowledge of God and heavenly things as Christ has. It is not for us to send to heaven for instructions; we must wait to receive what instructions Heaven will send to us. Jesus Christ is able to reveal the will of God to us; for it is *he that came down from heaven* and *is in heaven*. He had said (*v.* 12), *How shall ye believe, if I tell you of heavenly things?* He gives them an instance of those *heavenly things* when he tells them of one that *came down from heaven*, and yet is the *Son of man*. If the regeneration of the *soul of man* is such a mystery, what then is the incarnation of the *Son of God?* We have here an intimation of Christ's two distinct natures in one person. He gives them a proof of his ability to speak to them *heavenly things* by telling them, (1) That *he came down from heaven*. The intercourse settled between God and man began *above*. We love him, and send to him, because he first loved us, and sent to us. Now this intimates, [1] Christ's divine nature. [2] His intimate acquaintance with the divine counsels. [3] The *manifestation of God*. The New Testament shows us God *coming down* from heaven, to teach and save us. Herein he commended his love. (2) That *he is the Son of man*, by which the Jews always understand to be meant the Messiah. (3) That he *is in heaven*. Now at this time, when he is talking with Nicodemus on earth, yet, as God, he is *in heaven*.

3. Christ here discourses of the *great design of his own coming into the world, and the happiness of those that believe in him*, *v.* 14–18. Here we have the very marrow and quintessence of the whole gospel, that Jesus Christ came to seek and to save the children of men from death, and recover them to life. This saving here is opposed to condemning, *v.* 16–18.

(1) Jesus Christ came to save us by *healing* us, as the children of Israel that were stung with fiery serpents were cured and *lived* by looking up to the brazen serpent.

First, The *deadly* and *destructive* nature of *sin*, which is implied here. The guilt of sin is like the

pain of the biting of a fiery serpent; the power of corruption is like the *venom* diffused thereby. The curses of the law are as fiery serpents, so are all the tokens of divine wrath.

Secondly, The powerful remedy provided against this fatal malady. The case of poor sinners is deplorable; but is it desperate? Thanks be to God, it is not. The *Son of man is lifted up*, as the *serpent of brass* was by Moses. It was a *serpent of brass* that cured them. It was made in the shape of a *fiery serpent*, and yet had no poison, no sting, fitly representing Christ; as harmless as a serpent of brass. It was lifted up upon a pole, and so *must* the Son of man be lifted up. Christ is lifted up, [1] In his *crucifixion*. He was lifted up upon the cross. His death is called his being *lifted up*, ch. xii. 32, 33. [2] In his *exaltation*. He was lifted up to the Father's right hand. He was lifted up to the cross, to be further lifted up to the crown. [3] In the *publishing* and *preaching* of his everlasting gospel. Being thus lifted up, it was appointed for the cure. He that sent the plague provided the remedy. It was God himself that *found the ransom*. He whom we have offended is *our peace*.

Thirdly, The way of *applying* this remedy, and that is by *believing*. Everyone that *looked up to it* did well, Num. xxi. 9. He hath said, *Look, and be saved* (Isa. xlv. 22), look and live.

Fourthly, The great encouragements given us by faith to look up to him. *a*. It was for this end that he was *lifted up*, that his followers might be saved. *b*. The offer that is made of salvation by him is general, *whosoever believes* without exception. *c*. The salvation offered is complete. They *shall not perish*. They shall *have eternal life*.

• (2) Jesus Christ came to save us by *pardoning us*, *v.* 16, 17. Here is *gospel* indeed, good *news*, the best that ever came from heaven to earth.

First, Here is God's *love*, in *giving his Son for the world* (v. 16). [1]. The great *gospel mystery* revealed: *God so loved the world that he gave his only-begotten Son*. *a*. Jesus Christ is the *only-begotten Son of God*. Now know we that he loves us, when he has given his *only-begotten Son for us*. *b*. In order to the redemption and salvation of man, it pleased God to *give his only-begotten Son*. He *gave him*, that is, he gave him up to suffer and die for us. His enemies could not have *taken him* if his Father had not *given* him. *c*. Herein God has commended his *love to the world*; God so *loved the world*, so really, so richly. Behold, and wonder, that the *great God* should love such a *worthless* world; that the *holy God* should love such a *wicked* world. The Jews vainly conceited that the Messiah should be sent only in love to *their nation*; but Christ tells them that he came in love to the *whole world*, Gentiles as well as Jews. Through him there is a *general offer* of life and salvation made to all. So *far God loved the world* that he sent his Son with this fair proposal, that *whosoever believes in him shall not perish*. *Salvation* has been *of the Jews*, but now Christ is *known as salvation to the ends of the earth*. [2]. Here is the great *gospel duty*, and that is to *believe in Jesus Christ*. [3]. Here is the great gospel benefit: *That whosoever believes in Christ shall not perish*. God has taken away their sin, they shall not die; a pardon is purchased. They are entitled to the joys of heaven: they shall *have everlasting life*.

Secondly, Here is God's design in sending his Son into the world: it was *that the world through him might be saved*. He came into the world with salvation in *his eye*, with salvation *in his hand* (v. 17): *God sent his Son into the world*; sent him as his agent or ambassador, as resident. We are concerned to enquire on what errand he comes: *Is it peace?* And this scripture returns the answer, *Peaceably*. He did not come to *condemn the world*. We had reason enough to expect that he should, for it is a guilty world; it is *convicted*. Justly may such a world as this be *condemned*. He came with full powers indeed to *execute judgment* (*ch.* v. 22, 27), but did not begin with a judgment of condemnation, but put us upon a new trial before a *throne of grace*. He came *that the world through him might be saved*. God was in Christ *reconciling the world to himself*, and so *saving* it. This is good news to a convinced conscience, healing to broken bones and bleeding wounds, that Christ, our judge, came not to *condemn*, but to *save*.

(3) From all this is inferred the happiness of true believers: *He that believeth on him is not condemned*, v. 18. This denotes more than a reprieve; he is *not condemned*, that is, he is acquitted; and if he be not condemned he is discharged. *Who is he that condemns? It is Christ that died.* The cross perhaps lies heavy upon him, but he is saved from the curse: condemned *by the world*, it may be, but not *condemned with the world*, Rom. viii. 1.

4. The *deplorable condition of those that persist in unbelief and wilful ignorance*, v. 18–21.

(1) Read here the doom of those that will not *believe in Christ*: they *are condemned already*. [1] How great the *sin* of unbelievers is. They *believe not in the name of the only-begotten Son of God*, who is infinitely *true*, and deserves to be believed, *infinitely good*, and deserves to be embraced. God sent one to save us that was *dearest* to himself; and shall not he be *dearest to us*? [2] How great the *misery* of unbelievers is: they *are condemned already*. A *certain* condemnation. A *present* condemnation. They are condemned already, for their own hearts condemn them. A condemnation *grounded upon their former guilt*. *He is condemned already, because he has not believed.* Unbelief is a sin against the *remedy*.

(2) Read also the doom of those that would not so much as *know him*, v. 19. And *this is the condemnation, that light is come into the world, and they loved darkness rather*. The gospel is light, and, when the gospel came, *light came into the world*. Light is *self-evidencing*, so is the gospel; it proves its own divine origin. Light is *discovering*, and *truly the light is sweet*. A dark place indeed the world would be without it. It is the unspeakable folly of the most of men that they loved darkness rather than *this* light. Sinners that were wedded to their lusts loved their ignorance and mistakes rather than the truths of Christ. Wretched man is in love with his sickness, in love with his slavery, and will not be made *free*, will not be *made whole*. The true reason why men love darkness rather than light is *because their deeds are evil*. Their case is sad, and, because they are resolved that they will not *mend* it, they are resolved that they will not *see* it. Wilful ignorance is so far from excusing sin that it will be found to aggravate the condemnation: *This is the condemnation, that they* shut their eyes against the light, and will not so much as admit a parley with Christ and his gospel. We must account in the judgment not only for the knowledge we *sinned against*, but for the knowledge we *sinned away*. It is a common observation that *everyone that doeth evil hateth the light*, v. 20. Evil-doers seek concealment, out of a sense of shame and fear of punishment. *They come not to this light*, but keep as far off it as they can, *lest their deeds should be reproved*. The light of the gospel is sent into the world to *reprove the evil deeds* of sinners; to *show* people *their transgressions*, to show that to be sin which was not thought to be so, *that sin by the new commandment* might appear *exceeding sinful*. The gospel has its convictions, to make way for its consolations. It is for this reason that evil-doers *hate the light* of the gospel. There were those who *had done evil* and were sorry for it, who bade this light welcome, as the *publicans and harlots*. But he

that *does evil*, and resolves to go on in it, *hateth the light*. Christ is hated because sin is loved. They who do not *come to the light* thereby evidence a secret *hatred* of the light. On the other hand, upright hearts bid this light welcome (v. 21): *He that doeth truth cometh to the light*. As it *convinces* and *terrifies* evildoers, so it *confirms* and *comforts* those that walk in their integrity. The character of a *good man*. He is one that *doeth truth*. Though sometimes he comes short of *doing good*, the good he would do, yet he *doeth truth*, he aims honestly; he has his infirmities, but holds fast his integrity. He is one that *cometh to the light*. He that *doeth truth* is willing to know the *truth* by himself, and to *have his deeds made manifest*. He is solicitous to *know* what the will of God is, and resolves to *do* it, though ever so contrary to his own will and interest. Here is the character of a *good work*: it is *wrought in God*. Our works are *then* good, when the will of God is the rule of them and the glory of God the end of them; when they are done in his strength and for his sake. Nicodemus, though he was puzzled at first, yet afterwards became a faithful disciple of Christ.

Verses 22–36

I. Christ's removal into the land of Judæa (v. 22). Our Lord Jesus, after he entered upon his public work, travelled much, and removed often. Many a weary step he took to do good to souls. The *Sun of righteousness* took a large circuit to diffuse his light and heat, Ps. xix. 6. He was not wont to stay long at Jerusalem. *After these things*, after he had had this discourse with Nicodemus, he came into the land of Judæa; not so much for *greater privacy* as for *greater usefulness*. His preaching and miracles, perhaps, made *most noise* at Jerusalem, the fountain-head of news, but did *least good* there. When he came into the land of Judæa his *disciples came with him*. There he *tarried with them*. Those that are ready to *go with Christ* shall find him as ready to *stay with them*. There he *baptized*. John began to baptize in the land of Judæa (Matt. iii. 1), therefore Christ began there. He himself *baptized* not, with his own hand, but his disciples by his orders and directions, as appears, *ch.* iv. 2. Holy ordinances are Christ's, though administered by weak men.

II. John's continuance in his work, as long as his opportunities lasted, v. 23, 24. Here we are told,

1. That *John was baptizing*. Christ's baptism, was, for substance, the same with John's, and therefore they did not at all clash or interfere with one another. (1) Christ began the work of preaching and baptizing before *John laid it down*, so the wheels might be kept going. It is a comfort to useful men, when they are going off the stage, to see those rising up who are likely to fill up their place. (2) John continued the work of preaching and baptizing though Christ had *taken it up*. There was still work for John to do, for Christ was not yet *generally known*, nor were the minds of people *thoroughly prepared* for him by repentance. He goes on with his work, till Providence lays him aside. The greater gifts of some do not *render* the labours of others, that come short of them, *needless* and *useless*; there is work enough for all hands. They are sullen that will sit down and do nothing when they see themselves outshone.

2. That he baptized in Ænon near Salim, places we find nowhere else mentioned. Wherever it was, it seems that John removed from *place to place*. Ministers must follow their opportunities. He chose a place where there was much water, that is, many *streams* of water; so that wherever he met with any that were willing to submit to his baptism water was at hand to baptize.

3. That thither people *came to him* and *were baptized*. Some refer this both to John and to Jesus:

some came to John, some to Jesus, and, as their baptism was one, so were their hearts.

4. It is noted (*v.* 24) that *John was not yet cast into prison.* John never desisted from his work as long as he had his liberty.

III. A contest between *John's disciples and the Jews about purifying, v.* 25. 1. Who were the disputants: *some of John's disciples, and the Jews* who had not submitted to his baptism of repentance. Penitents and impenitents divide this sinful world. 2. What was the matter in dispute: *about purifying,* about *religious washing.* We may suppose that John's disciples cried up his baptism, his purifying, and gave the preference to that as perfecting and superseding all the purifications of the Jews, and they were in the right. No doubt the Jews with as much assurance applauded the *purifyings* that were in use among them. It is very likely that the Jews in this dispute, when they could not *deny* the excellent nature and design of John's baptism, raised an objection against it from Christ's baptism, which gave occasion for the complaint that follows here (*v.* 26). Thus objections are made against the gospel from the advancement and improvement of gospel light, as if childhood and manhood were contrary to each other, and the superstructure were against the foundation.

IV. A complaint which John's disciples made to their master concerning Christ and his baptizing, *v.* 26. They come to their master, and tell him, "*Rabbi, he that was with thee*; he *baptizeth, and all men come to him.*" They suggest that Christ's setting up a baptism of his own was a piece of presumption, as if John, having first set up this rite of baptizing, must have, as it were, a patent for the invention: "*He that was with thee beyond Jordan, behold, the same, baptizes.*" They suggest that it was a piece of ingratitude to John. He *to whom thou barest witness* baptizes; as if Jesus owed all his reputation to the honourable character John gave of him. But Christ needed not John's testimony, *ch.* v. 36. He reflected more honour upon John than he received from him. John was *just* to Christ, in bearing witness to him; and Christ's answering his testimony did rather enrich than impoverish John's ministry. They conclude that it would be a total eclipse to John's baptism: "*All men come to him.*" Aiming at the monopoly of honour and respect has been in all ages the bane of the church, and the shame of its members and ministers. We mistake if we think that the excelling gifts and graces, and labours and usefulness, of one, are a diminution and disparagement to another that has obtained mercy to be faithful. We must leave it to God to choose, employ, and honour his own instruments as he pleaseth.

V. Here is John's answer, *v.* 27, &c. It was no *disturbance* to him, but what he wished for. He therefore checked the complaint, and took this occasion to confirm the testimonies he had formerly borne to Christ as superior to him.

1. John here *abases himself in comparison with Christ, v.* 27–30.

(1) John *acquiesces* in the divine disposal (*v.* 27): *A man can receive nothing except it be given him from heaven.* Different employments are according to the direction of divine Providence, different endowments according to the distribution of the divine grace. We should not *envy* those that have a larger share of gifts than we have, or move in a larger sphere of usefulness. John reminds his disciples that Jesus would not have thus excelled him *except he had received it from heaven,* and, if God gave him *the Spirit without measure* (*v.* 34), shall they grudge at it? We should not be *discontented,* though we be inferior to others in gifts and usefulness, and be eclipsed by their excellencies. John was ready to own that it was God that gave him the interest he

had in the love and esteem of the people; and, if now his interest decline, God's will be done! When he has fulfilled his ministry, he can contentedly see it go out of date.

(2) John appeals to the testimony he had formerly given concerning Christ (*v.* 28). I said, again and again, *I am not the Christ, but I am sent before him.* Neither the frowns of the chief priests, nor the flatteries of his own disciples, could make him change his note. Now this serves here, [1] As a *conviction* to his disciples of the unreasonableness of their complaint. "Now," saith John, "do you not remember what the testimony was that I did bear? Did I not say, *I am not the Christ*? Did I not say, *I am sent before him*? Why then does it seem strange to you that I should stand by and give way to him?" [2] As a *comfort* to himself that he had never *given* his disciples *any occasions* thus to set him up in competition with Christ; but, on the contrary, had particularly *cautioned* them against this mistake. John had not only not encouraged them to hope that he was the Messiah, but had plainly told them the contrary. It is a common excuse for those who have undue honour paid them—*If the people will be deceived, let them;* but that is an ill maxim for those to go by whose business it is to *undeceive* people.

(3) John professes the great satisfaction he had in the advancement of Christ, he *rejoiced* in it. This he expresses (*v.* 29) by an elegant similitude. He compares our Saviour to the *bridegroom*: "*He that hath the bride is the bridegroom.* Do *all men come to him*? It is his right." As far as particular souls are devoted to him in faith and love, so far the bridegroom has the bride. He compares himself to the *friend of the bridegroom,* assists him in prosecuting the match, speaks a good word for him, rejoices most of all when he *has the bride. The friend of the bridegroom stands, and hears him; rejoices with joy because of the bridegroom's voice.* Faithful ministers are friends of the bridegroom, to recommend him to the children of men; to bring letters and messages from him, for he courts by proxy. The friends of the bridegroom must *stand, and hear the bridegroom's voice;* must receive instructions from him, and attend his orders. The espousing of souls to Jesus Christ, in faith and love, is the fulfilling of the joy of every good minister. Surely they have *no greater joy.*

(4) He owns it highly fit and necessary that the reputation and interest of Christ should be advanced, and his own diminished (*v.* 30): *He must increase, but I must decrease.* John speaks of Christ's increase and his own decrease as highly *just* and *agreeable,* and affording him entire satisfaction. He was *well pleased* to see the kingdom of Christ getting ground: "*He must increase.*" The kingdom of Christ is, and will be, a growing kingdom, like the light of the morning, like the grain of mustard-seed. He was not at all *displeased* that the effect of this was the diminishing of his own interest: *I must decrease.* The shining forth of the glory of Christ eclipses the lustre of all other glory. As the light of the morning increases, that of the morning star decreases. We must cheerfully be content to be *anything,* to be *nothing,* so that Christ may be *all.*

2. John Baptist here *advances* Christ, and instructs his disciples concerning him.

(1) Concerning the *dignity of Christ's person* (*v.* 31): *He that cometh from above is above all.* He supposes his divine origin, that he *came from above,* from *heaven.* None but he that came from heaven was fit to show us the will of heaven, or the way to heaven. Hence he infers his sovereign authority: he is *above all,* above all things and all persons. When we come to speak of the honours of the Lord Jesus, we can say but this, *He is above all.* This he further illustrates by the meanness of those who stood in competition

with him: *He that is of the earth, is earthly*, has his converse with earthly things, and his concern is for them. The prophets and apostles were of the same mould with other men; they were but *earthen vessels*, though they had a rich treasure lodged in them.

(2) Concerning the *excellency and certainty of his doctrine*. He, for his part, *spoke of the earth*, and so do all those that are *of the earth*. The prophets were men; *of themselves* they could not speak but *of the earth*. The preaching of the prophets and of John was but low and flat compared with Christ's preaching; as heaven is high above the earth, so were his thoughts above theirs. But he that cometh from heaven is above all the prophets that ever lived on earth. The doctrine of Christ is here recommended to us,

First, As infallibly *sure* and *certain*, and to be entertained accordingly (*v.* 32): *What he hath seen and heard, that he testifieth.* 1. Christ's divine knowledge; he testified nothing but *what he had seen and heard.* What he discovered of the divine nature was what he had *seen*; what he revealed of the mind of God was what he had *heard* immediately from him. The prophets testified what was made known to them in dreams and visions, but not what they had seen and heard. The gospel of Christ is not a doubtful opinion, like an hypothesis or new notion in philosophy, but it is a revelation of the mind of God, which is of *eternal truth* in itself. 2. His divine grace and goodness. Christ's preaching is here called his *testifying*, to denote, (1) The *convincing evidence* of it; it was not *reported* as news by hearsay, but it was *testified* as evidence given in court. (2) The affectionate earnestness of the delivery of it.

From the *certainty* of Christ's doctrine, John takes occasion, to lament the infidelity of the most of men. They receive it not, they will not hear it, or give credit to it. This he speaks of not only as a matter of *wonder* but as a matter of *grief*; John's disciples grieved that *all men came to Christ* (*v.* 26); they thought his followers too many. But John grieves that *no man came to him*; he thought them too few. The unbelief of sinners is the grief of saints. He takes occasion to commend the faith of the chosen remnant (*v.* 33): *He that hath received his testimony* hath *set to his seal that God is true*. God is true, though we do not *set our seal to it*; his truth needs not our faith to support it, but by faith we do ourselves the honour and justice to subscribe to his truth. God's promises are all *yea* and *amen*; by faith we put our *amen* to them. By believing in Christ we set to our seal that God is true to all the promises which he has made *concerning Christ*. That he is true to all the promises he has made *in Christ*. Being satisfied that he is *true*, we are willing to deal with him *upon trust*.

Secondly, It is recommended to us as a *divine* doctrine (*v.* 34): *For he whom God hath sent speaketh the word of God, for God giveth not the Spirit by measure unto him*. 1. He spoke the *words of God*. Both substance and language were divine. He proved himself *sent of God* (ch. iii. 2), and therefore his words are to be received as the words of God. 2. He spoke as no other prophet did; for *God giveth not the Spirit by measure to him*. The Old Testament prophets had the Spirit, and in different degrees. But, whereas God gave them the Spirit by *measure*, he gave him to Christ *without measure*. The Spirit was not in Christ as in a vessel, but as in a fountain, as in a bottomless ocean.

(3) Concerning *the power and authority he is invested with*. He is the *beloved Son of the Father* (*v.* 35): *The Father loveth the Son*. The prophets were faithful as servants, but Christ as a Son. He continued his love to him even in his estate of humiliation, loved him never the less for his poverty, and sufferings. He is *Lord of all*. The Father *hath given*

all things into his hand. Love is generous. Having given *him the Spirit without measure*, he gave him *all things*. All *power*; so it is explained, Matt. xxviii. 18. He has *power over all flesh*, the heathen given *him for his inheritance*. Both the golden sceptre and the iron rod are given into his hand. All *grace* is given into his hand as the channel of conveyance. We are unworthy that the Father should give those things *into our hands*. The things he intended for us he gives *into his hands*, who is worthy. They are given *into his hands*, by him to be given into ours. The riches of the new covenant are deposited in so sure, so kind, so good a hand, the hand of him that purchased them for us.

He is the object of that faith which is made the great condition of eternal happiness: *He that believeth on the Son, hath life, v.* 36. It is the *conclusion of the whole matter*. As God offers and conveys good things to us by the *testimony* of Jesus Christ, so we receive and partake of those favours by *believing* the testimony. This way of *receiving* fitly answers that way of *giving*. We have here the sum of that gospel which is to be preached to every creature. Here is,

First, The blessed state of all true Christians: *He that believes on the Son hath everlasting life*. Not only *believes him*, that what he saith is true, but believes *on him*, and confides in him. The benefit of true Christianity is no less than *everlasting life*. True believers, even now, *have* everlasting life; not only they shall have it hereafter, but they have it now. They have the Son of God, and in him *they have life*. Grace is glory begun.

Secondly, The wretched and miserable condition of unbelievers: *He that believeth not the Son* is undone. The word includes both *incredulity* and *disobedience*. They *cannot be happy* in this world, nor that to come: *He shall not see life*, that life which Christ came to bestow. They *cannot but be miserable*: *The wrath of God abides upon* an unbeliever.

CHAPTER 4

We have Christ, I. Departing out of Judæa, ver. 1–3. II. Passing through Samaria. 1. His coming into Samaria, ver. 4–6. 2. His discourse with the Samaritan woman at a well, ver. 7–26. 3. The notice which the woman gave of him to the city, ver. 27–30. 4. Christ's talk with his disciples in the meantime, ver. 31–38. 5. The good effect of this among the Samaritans, ver. 39–42. III. For some time in Galilee (ver. 43–46), and his curing a nobleman's son there, ver. 46–54.

Verses 1–3

Now he left Judæa four months before harvest (*v.* 35).

I. He *made disciples*. His ministry was successful, notwithstanding the opposition it met with. It is Christ's prerogative to *make disciples*, to form and fashion them to his will. *The Christian is made such, not born such*.

II. He *baptized* those whom he *made disciples*; not himself, but by the ministry of his disciples, *v.* 2. Because he would put a difference between his baptism and that of John, who baptized all himself, He would put honour upon his disciples, and so train them up to further services. He would teach us that what is done by his ministers, according to his direction, he owns as done by himself.

III. He made and baptized *more disciples than John*. Christ's converse was more winning than John's.

IV. The Pharisees were informed of this. When the Pharisees thought they had got rid of John, Jesus appears. That which grieved them was that Christ made so many disciples. The success of the gospel exasperates its enemies.

V. Our Lord Jesus knew very well what informations were given in against him. None can dig so deep as to *hide their counsels from the Lord*.

VI. Hereupon our Lord Jesus *left Judæa* and *departed again* to go to Galilee. He *left Judæa*, because he was likely to be persecuted there even to the death. Christ quitted the country, and went where what he did would be less provoking than just under their eye. His hour was not yet come. He had not finished his testimony, and therefore would not surrender or expose himself. The disciples he had gathered in Judæa were not able to bear hardships, and therefore he would not expose them. Hereby he gave an example to his own rule: *When they persecute you in one city, flee to another.* We are not called to suffer, while we may avoid it without sin; and therefore we may change our place. He departed into Galilee, because he had work to do there, and many friends and fewer enemies.

Verses 4–26

We have here an account of the good Christ did in Samaria. The Samaritans, both in *blood* and *religion*, were *mongrel Jews.* They worshipped the God of Israel only, to whom they erected a temple on mount Gerizim. The Samaritans would not admit Christ, when they saw he was going to Jerusalem (Luke ix. 53); the Jews thought they could not give him a worse name than to say, *He is a Samaritan.*

I. Christ's coming into Samaria. He charges his disciples not to *enter into any city of the Samaritans* (Matt. x. 5), nor did he here preach publicly, or work any miracle, his eye being to *the lost sheep of the house of Israel.* What kindness he here did them was only a *crumb* of the children's bread that casually *fell from the master's table.*

1. His *road* from Judæa to Galilee lay through the *country* of Samaria (*v.* 4): *He must needs go through Samaria.* There was no other way, unless he would have fetched a compass on the other side *Jordan*, a great way about. We should not go into places of temptation but when we *needs must*; and then we should not reside in them, but *hasten through* them. It was happy for Samaria that it lay *in Christ's way.* 2. His baiting place happened to be at a *city of Samaria.* The place is described. It was called *Sychar*; probably the same with *Sichem*, or *Shechem.* Shechem yielded the first proselyte that ever came into the church of Israel (Gen. xxxiv. 24), and now it is the first place where the gospel is preached out of the commonwealth of Israel. Abimelech was made king here; it was Jeroboam's royal seat; but the evangelist takes notice of Jacob's interest there, which was more its honour than its crowned heads. Here lay Jacob's ground, the *parcel of ground which Jacob gave to his son Joseph.* Here was Jacob's well. *Being wearied with his journey, he sat thus on the well.* We have here our Lord Jesus labouring under the common fatigue of travellers. He was *wearied with his journey. Because* it was the sixth hour, the time of the heat of the day, therefore he was weary. He was a *true man*, and subject to the common infirmities of the human nature. He was a *poor man*, else he might have travelled on horseback or in a chariot. When we are carried easily, let us think on the weariness of our Master. It should seem that he was not of a robust constitution; it should seem, his disciples were not tired, for they went into the town without any difficulty. Bodies of the finest mould are most sensible of fatigue, and can worst bear it. We have him betaking himself to the common relief of travellers: *Being wearied, he sat thus on the well.* He sat *thus*, in an *uneasy posture.*

II. His discourse with a Samaritan woman. This discourse is reducible to four heads:

1. They discourse *concerning the water, v.* 7–15.

(1) Notice is taken of the *circumstances* that gave occasion to this discourse. There comes a *woman* of Samaria to *draw water.* She had no servant to be a *drawer of water*; she would do it herself. See here, How the divine Providence brings about glorious purposes by events which seem to us fortuitous and accidental. His disciples were *gone away into the city to buy meat.* Christ did not go into the city to eat, but sent his disciples to fetch his meat thither; not because he scrupled eating in a Samaritan city, but, [1] Because he had a good work to do at that well. [2] Because it was more private and retired, more cheap and homely, to have his dinner brought him thither, than to go into the town for it. Christ could eat his dinner as well upon a *draw well* as in the best inn in the town. He often preached to multitudes yet here he condescends to teach a single person, a woman, a poor woman, a stranger, a Samaritan, to teach his ministers to do likewise, as those that know what a glorious achievement it is to help to save, though but *one soul*, from death.

(2) Let us observe the *particulars* of this discourse. Jesus begins with a *modest request* for a draught of water: *Give me to drink.* He that *for our sakes became poor* here becomes a beggar. Christ asked for it because he would draw on further discourse with her. Christ is still begging in his poor members, and a *cup of cold water*, given to them in his name, shall not lose its reward. The woman quarrels with him because he did not carry on the humour of his own nation (*v.* 9): *How is it?* Observe, *First*, What a mortal feud there was between the Jews and the Samaritans: *The Jews have no dealings with the Samaritans.* Quarrels about religion are usually the most implacable of all quarrels. They plainly show that however their religion may be *true* they are not truly religious. *Secondly*, How ready the woman was to upbraid Christ with the haughtiness and ill nature of the Jewish nation: *How is it that thou, being a Jew, askest drink of me?* Moderate men of all sides are *men wondered at.* Two things this woman wonders at: That he should *ask* this kindness; for it was the pride of the Jews that they would endure any hardship rather than be beholden to a Samaritan. We must, like our Master, put on *goodness* and *kindness*, though it should be ever so much the genius of our country, or the humour of our party, to be morose and ill-natured. This woman expected that Christ should be as other Jews were. No rule but has some exceptions. She wonders that he should *expect to receive* this kindness from her that was a Samaritan. Christ takes this occasion to instruct her in divine things: *If thou knewest the gift of God, thou wouldst have asked, v.* 10. He waives her objection of the feud between the Jews and Samaritans. Some differences are best *healed* by avoiding all occasions of *entering into dispute* about them. Christ will convert this woman, showing her her need of a Saviour. He fills her with an apprehension that she had now an opportunity of gaining that which would be of unspeakable advantage to her. Christ tells her expressly that she had now a season of grace.

[1] He hints to her what she *should know*, but was ignorant of: *If thou knewest the gift of God, who it is that saith, Give me to drink.* She saw him to be a Jew, a poor weary traveller; but he would have her know something more concerning him. Jesus Christ is the *gift of God*, the richest token of God's love to us. It is an unspeakable privilege to have this gift of God proposed and offered to us. It is he that saith, *Give me to drink;* this gift comes begging to thee.

[2] He hopes concerning her, what she would have done if she had known him: *Thou wouldst have asked.* Those that would have any benefit by Christ must ask for it. Those that have a right knowledge of Christ will seek to him. Christ knows what they that want the means of knowledge would have done if they had had them.

[3] He assures her what he would have done for her if she had applied to him: "He *would have given thee living water.*" By this living water is meant the *Spirit*, who is not like the water in the bottom of the well, but like *living* or *running* water. The Spirit of grace is as *living water*. Jesus Christ *can* and *will* give the Holy Spirit to them that ask him. The woman cavils at the gracious intimation which Christ gave her (v. 11, 12): *Thou hast nothing to draw with;* and besides, *Art thou greater than our father Jacob?* What he spoke figuratively, she took literally; Nicodemus did so too. She does not think him capable of furnishing her with any water: *Thou hast nothing to draw with*, and *the well is deep*. But there are those who will not believe his promise, unless the means of the performance of it be *visible*; as if he could not draw water without our buckets. She asks scornfully, "*Whence hast thou this living water?* I see not whence thou canst have it." The fountain of life is hid with Christ. Christ has enough for us, though we see not whence he has it. She does not think it possible that he should furnish her with any better water, *Art thou greater than our father Jacob, who gave us the well?*

[4] We will suppose the tradition true, that Jacob *himself, and his children, and cattle, did drink of this well*. And we may observe from it, the power and providence of God, in the continuance of the fountains of water from generation to generation.

[5] Yet, allowing that to be true, she was out in several things. In calling Jacob *father*. What authority had the Samaritans to reckon themselves of the seed of Jacob? She is out in claiming this well as Jacob's gift. But thus we are apt to call the *messengers* of God's gifts the *donors* of them, and to look so much at the hands they *pass through* as to forget the hand they *come from*. She was out in speaking of Christ as not worthy to be compared with our father Jacob. An over-fond veneration for antiquity makes God's graces, in the good people of our own day, to be slighted. Christ makes it out that the *living water* he had to give was far better than that of Jacob's well, v. 13, 14. Christ did not cast her off, but encouraged her. He shows her that the water of Jacob's well yielded but a *transient* satisfaction: "*Whoso drinketh of this water shall thirst again.* It is no better than other water; it will quench the present thirst, but the thirst will return." This intimates, *a*. The *infirmities* of our bodies in this present state; they are ever *craving*. Life is a fire, a *lamp*, which will soon go out, without continual supplies of fuel and oil. *b*. The *imperfections* of all our comforts in this world; they are not lasting. Yesterday's meat and drink will not do to-day's work. But the living waters he would give should yield a lasting satisfaction and bliss, v. 14. Whoever partakes of the Spirit of grace,

(*a*) He shall *never thirst*. A ˙*desiring* thirst he has, nothing more *than* God, still more and more *of* God; but not a *despairing* thirst.

(*b*) He shall never thirst, because this water that Christ gives *shall be in him a well of water*. He can never be reduced to extremity that has in himself a *fountain* of supply and satisfaction, *ever ready*, for it shall be *in him*. He needs not sneak to the world for comfort. Believers have in them a *well of water*, overflowing, ever flowing. It is *springing up*, ever in motion. If good truths *stagnate* in our souls, like standing water, they do not answer the end of our receiving them. It is springing up *unto everlasting* life, which intimates the *aims* of gracious actings. Spiritual life springs up towards its own perfection in eternal life. It will continue springing up till it come to perfection, eternal life at last. And now is not this water better than that of Jacob's well? The woman begs of him to give her some of this

water (v. 15): *Give me this water, that I thirst not*. Some think that she speaks *tauntingly*, and ridicules what Christ had said as mere stuff. "A rare invention; it will save me a great deal of *pain* if I *thirst not*, and a great deal of *pains* if I never *come hither to draw*." Others think that it was a *well-meant* but weak and ignorant desire. *Whatever it be*, let me have it. *Ease*, or saving of labour, is a valuable good to poor labouring people. Even those that are weak and ignorant may yet have some faint and fluctuating desires towards Christ and his gifts.

2. The next subject of discourse with this woman is *concerning her husband, v. 16–18*. It was not to let fall the discourse of the water of life that Christ started this, but it was with a gracious design. Waiving the discourse about the living water, he sets himself to awaken her conscience, and then she would more easily apprehend the remedy by grace. And this is the method of dealing with souls; they must first be made *weary* and *heavy-laden* under the burden of sin, and then brought to Christ for rest. This is the course of spiritual physic.

(1) How discreetly and decently Christ introduces this discourse (v. 16): *Go, call thy husband, and come hither*. The order Christ gave her had a *very good colour*: "*Call thy husband*, that he may teach thee, and help thee to understand these things. *Call thy husband*, that he may learn with thee: that then you may be *heirs together of the grace of life*." As it had a good colour, so it had a *good design*; for hence he would take occasion to call her sin to remembrance. There is need of art and prudence in giving reproofs.

(2) How industriously the woman seeks to evade the conviction, and yet insensibly convicts herself. She said, *I have no husband*.

(3) How closely our Lord Jesus brings home the conviction to her conscience. It is probable that he said more than is here recorded, for she thought that he told her all that ever she did (v. 29). A *surprising narrative* of her *past conversation: Thou hast had five husbands*. A severe reproof of her present state of life: *He whom thou now hast is not thy husband*. So that, in short, *she lived in adultery*. Yet observe how mildly Christ tells her of it; *He with whom thou livest is not thy husband:* and then leaves it to her own conscience to say the rest. Yet in this he puts a better construction than it would well bear upon what she said: *Thou hast well said I have no husband;* and again, *In that saidst thou truly*. What she intended as a *denial of the fact* he favourably interpreted as a *confession of the fault*. Those who would win souls should *make the best* of them, whereby they may hope to *work* upon their *good-nature;* for, if they *make the worst* of them, they certainly *exasperate* their *ill-nature*.

3. The next subject of discourse with this woman is concerning *the place of worship, v. 19–24*.

(1) A case of conscience concerning the place of worship, v. 19, 20.

[1] The inducement she had to put this case: *Sir, I perceive that thou art a prophet*. She does not deny the truth of what he had charged her with, nor is she put into a passion by it, as many are when they are touched in a sore place, but (which is a rare thing) can bear to be told of a fault. She goes further: *First*, She speaks respectfully to him, calls him *Sir*. This was the effect of Christ's meekness in reproving her; he gave her no ill language, and then she gave him none. *Secondly*, She acknowledges him to be a *prophet*. *Thirdly*, She desires some further instruction from him.

[2] The case itself that she propounded concerning the *place of religious worship in public*. She knew she must worship God, and desired to do it aright; and therefore, meeting with a prophet, begs his direction.

It was agreed between the Jews and the Samaritans that God is to be worshipped (even those who were such fools as to worship *false* gods were not such brutes as to worship none). But the matter in variance was *where* they should worship God. Observe how she states the case:

As for the Samaritans: *Our fathers worshipped in this mountain*; there the Samaritan temple was built by Sanballat. Whatever the temple was the place was holy; it was mount *Gerizim*, the mount on which the blessings were pronounced. It might plead prescription: *Our fathers* worshipped here. She thinks they have antiquity, tradition, and succession, on their side. As to the Jews: *You say* that *in Jerusalem is the place where men ought to worship*. The Samaritans governed themselves by the five books of Moses. Now, though they found frequent mention there of the place God would choose, yet they did not find it named there; and therefore thought themselves at liberty to set up another place.

(2) Christ's answer to this case of conscience, *v.* 21, &c. He puts *a slight* upon the question concerning the place of worship (*v.* 21): "*Woman, believe me;* that which thou hast been taught to lay so much weight on shall be set aside as a thing *indifferent." The hour comes when you shall neither in this mountain nor yet at Jerusalem worship the Father.* A period shall be put to all niceness and all differences about the place of worship. It shall be a thing perfectly indifferent whether in either of these places or any other men worship God, for they shall not be tied to any place; neither *here* nor *there*, but *both*, and *anywhere*, and *everywhere*. He *lays a stress* upon other things. When he made so light of the place of worship he did not intend to lessen our concern about the thing itself. As to the present state of the controversy, he *determines* against the Samaritan worship, *v.* 22. The Samaritans were certainly *in the wrong*, because they were out in the object of their worship. *But you worship you know not what.* Ignorance is so far from being the *mother* of devotion that it is the *murderer* of it. That the Jews were certainly *in the right.* "*We know what we worship.* We go upon sure grounds in our worship." Those who by the scriptures have obtained some knowledge of God may worship him *comfortably* to themselves, and *acceptably* to him, for they *know what they worship.* Worship may be *true* where yet it is not *pure* and *entire.* Our Lord Jesus was pleased to reckon himself among the *worshippers* of God: *We worship.* Let not the greatest of men think the worship of God below them, when the Son of God himself did not. *Salvation is of the Jews;* and therefore they know what they worship, and what grounds they go upon in their worship. The author of eternal salvation comes of the Jews, and is sent first to *bless* them. The means of eternal salvation are afforded to them. The *word of salvation* was *of the Jews.* Having shown that the place is *indifferent*, he comes to show what is *necessary* and *essential*—that we worship God *in spirit and in truth, v.* 23, 24. The stress is upon the state of *mind* in which we worship him. It concerns us to be right, not only in the *object* of our worship, but in the *manner* of it; and it is this which Christ here instructs us in.

[1] The revolution which should introduce this change: *The hour cometh, and now is.* The *perfect day is coming*, and now it *dawns.*

[2]. The blessed change itself. *True worshippers shall worship the Father in spirit and in truth.* As creatures, we worship the Father of *all*: as Christians, we worship *the Father of our Lord Jesus.* Now the change shall be in the *nature* of the worship. Christians shall worship God, not in the ceremonial observances of the Mosaic institution, but in *spiritual* ordinances; in the *temper* and *disposition* of the worshippers. All

should, and they will, worship God *in spirit and in truth.* It is spoken of (*v.* 23) as their character, and (*v.* 24) as their duty. It is required of all that worship God that they worship him *in spirit and in truth.* We must worship God *in spirit*, Phil. iii. 3. We must depend upon *God's Spirit* for strength and assistance. We must worship him with fixedness of thought and a flame of affection, with *all that is within us. In truth*, that is, in *sincerity.* We must mind the power more than the form. God must be thus worshipped, because they only are accounted the *true* worshippers. The gospel erects a spiritual way of worship, so that the professors of the gospel do not live up to gospel light and laws, if they do not worship God *in spirit and in truth.* For the *Father seeketh such worshippers of him.* Such worshippers are very rare. The gate of spiritual worshipping is strait. Such worship is necessary, and what the God of heaven insists upon. God is greatly well pleased with and graciously accepts such worship and such worshippers. His *seeking* such worshippers implies his *making* them such. Christ came to *declare God* to us (*ch.* i. 18), and this he has declared concerning him; he declared it to this poor Samaritan woman, for the meanest are concerned to know God. *God is a spirit.* It is easier to say what God is not than what he is. The spirituality of the divine nature is a very good reason for the spirituality of divine worship. If we do not worship God, who is *a spirit, in the spirit*, we miss the *end* of worship.

4. The last subject of discourse with this woman is concerning the Messiah, *v.* 25, 26.

(1) The faith of the woman, by which she expected the Messiah: *I know that Messias cometh—and he will tell us all things.* She had nothing to object against what Christ had said; his discourse was what might become the Messiah; but *from him* she would receive it, and in the meantime she thinks it best to suspend her belief. Thus many have no heart to the price *in their hand*, because they think they have a better *in their eye.* Whom she expects: *I know that Messias cometh.* The Jews and Samaritans agreed in the expectation of the Messiah and his kingdom. Those who knew least knew this, that Messias was to come. *Messias, who is called Christ.* The evangelist, though he retains the Hebrew word *Messias*, takes care to render it by a Greek word of the same signification, *who is called Christ—Anointed.* What she expects from him: "*He will tell us all things.* He will tell us the mind of God fully and clearly, and keep back nothing." Now this implies an acknowledgment, *First*, Of the imperfection of the discovery they now had of the divine will, and the rule they had of the divine worship. *Secondly*, Of the sufficiency of the Messiah to make this change: "*He will tell us all things* which we want to know, and about which we wrangle in the dark."

(2) The favour of our Lord Jesus in making himself known to her: *I that speak to thee am he, v.* 26. Christ did never make himself known so expressly to any as he did here to this poor Samaritan, and to the blind man (*ch.* ix. 37). Christ would thus put an honour upon such as were poor and despised. This woman had never had any opportunity of seeing Christ's miracles, which were then the ordinary method of conviction. God can make the light of grace shine *into the heart* even where he doth not make the light of the gospel shine *in the face.* This woman was better prepared to receive such a discovery than others were. Christ will manifest himself to those who with an honest humble heart desire to be acquainted with him: *I that speak to thee am he.* See here, How near Jesus Christ was to her, when she knew not who he was, Gen. xxviii. 16. Many are lamenting Christ's absence, and longing for his presence, when at the same time he is speaking to

them. Christ makes himself known to us by *speaking* to us: *I that speak unto thee, I am he.*

Verses 27–42

I. The *interruption given to this discourse* by the disciples' coming. Just when the discourse was brought to a head, *then came the disciples.* They wondered at Christ's converse with this woman, marvelled that he talked thus earnestly with a woman, a strange woman alone, especially with a Samaritan woman. They wondered he should condescend to talk with such a poor contemptible woman, forgetting what despicable men they themselves were when Christ first called them. Yet they acquiesced in it; they knew it was for some good reason, and therefore none of them asked, *What seekest thou?* or, *Why talkest thou with her?* All is well which Jesus Christ saith and doeth. Whatever they *thought*, they said *nothing*.

II. The notice which the woman gave to her neighbours, *v.* 28, 29. Observe here,

1. How she *forgot her errand to the well, v.* 28. She *went her way*. She withdrew, in civility to Christ, that he might have leisure to *eat his dinner*. She delighted in his discourse, but would not be *rude*. She supposed that Jesus would go forward in his journey, and therefore hastened to tell her neighbours. See how she improved time. When opportunities of *getting good* cease we should seek opportunities of *doing good*. Notice is taken of her *leaving her waterpot* or pail. She left it in kindness to Christ, that he might have water to drink with his dinner. She left it that she might make the more haste into the city. She left her water-pot, as one *careless of it*, being wholly taken up with better things.

2. How she *minded her errand to the town*. She *went into the city*, and said to *the men*, to every man she met in the streets: *Come, see a man who told me all things that ever I did. Is not this the Christ?* Observe,

(1) How *solicitous* she was to *have her friends and neighbours* acquainted with Christ. When she had found that treasure, she *called together her friends and neighbours* (as Luke xv. 9), not only to *rejoice with her*, but to share with her. Has he done us the honour to make himself known to us? Let us do him the honour to make him known to others; nor can we do ourselves a greater honour. This woman becomes an apostle. I have most *opportunity*, and therefore lie under the greatest *obligations*, to do good to those that live near me.

(2) How fair and ingenuous she was in the notice she gave them concerning this stranger. She *tells them* plainly what induced her to admire him: *He has told me all things that ever I did*. No more is recorded than what he told her of her husbands. He told her that which none knew but God and her own conscience. Two things affected her: *First, the extent of his knowledge*. We ourselves cannot tell *all things that ever we did. Secondly, The power of his word*. This made a great impression upon her, that he told her her *secret sins*. "*Come see a man* that has told me of my sins." She fastens upon that part of Christ's discourse which one would think she would have been most shy of repeating. That *knowledge of Christ* into which we are led by the conviction of sin and humiliation is most likely to be *sound* and *saving*. She *invites them* to *come and see* him. Not barely, "Come and look upon him" (she does not invite them to him as a *show*), but "Come and converse with him; come and *hear his wisdom*, as I have done." She would not undertake to manage the arguments which had convinced her, in such a manner as to convince others; all that see the evidence of truth themselves are not able to make others see it. Jesus was now at the town's end. "Now come see him." Shall we not go over the threshold to see

him, whose day prophets and kings desired to see? She resolves to *appeal to themselves, Is this not the Christ?* She does not peremptorily say, "He is the Messiah." She will not impose her faith upon them, but only propose it to them. By such fair but forcible appeals as these men's judgments and consciences are sometimes taken hold of ere they are aware.

(3) What success she had in this invitation: *They went out of the city, and came to him, v.* 30. They *came unto him*; did not send for him into the city to them, they *went out to him*. Those that would know Christ must meet him where he records his name.

III. Christ's discourse with his disciples while the woman was absent, *v.* 31–38. See how industrious our Lord Jesus was to *redeem time*, to husband every minute of it. It were well if we could *thus* gather up the fragments of time. Two things are observable in this discourse:

1. How Christ *expresses the delight* which he himself had in his work. Now with this work we here find him wholly taken up. For,

(1) *He neglected his meat and drink for his work*. When he sat down upon the well, he was *weary*, and needed refreshment; but this opportunity of saving souls made him forget his weariness and hunger. And he minded *his food* so little that his disciples were forced to invite him to it: *They prayed him, Master, eat*. It was an instance of their *love to him* that they invited him; but it was a greater instance of his *love to souls* that he needed invitation. He minded it so little that they suspected he had had meat brought him in their absence (*v.* 33): *Has any man brought him aught to eat?* He had so little appetite for his dinner that they were ready to think he had dined already.

(2) He *made his work his meat and drink*. The work he *had done* in instructing the woman, the work he *had to do* among the Samaritans, this was *meat and drink* to him. Never did a hungry man, or an epicure, expect a plentiful feast with so much desire, nor feed upon its dainties with so much delight, as our Lord Jesus expected and improved an opportunity of doing good to souls. It was such *meat* as the disciples *knew not of*. This may be said of good Christians too, that they have meat to eat which others know not of, joy with which a stranger does not intermeddle. Now this word made them ask, *Has any man brought him aught to eat?* The reason why his work was his meat and drink was because it was his Father's work, his Father's will: *My meat is to do the will of him that sent me, v.* 34. The salvation of sinners is the *will of God*, and the instruction of them in order thereunto is *his work*. He made this work his business and delight. When his body needed food, his mind was so taken up with this that he forgot both hunger and thirst, both meat and drink. He was *earnest* and in care to go *through* it, and to *finish his work*. He resolved never to quit it, nor lay it down, till he could say, *It is finished*. Many have zeal to carry them *out* at first, but not zeal to carry them *on* to the last.

2. See here how Christ excites his disciples to diligence in *their* work; they were workers *with him*, and therefore should be workers *like him*. The work they had to do was to *preach the gospel*. Now this work he here compares to *harvest work, v.* 35–38. Harvest time is *busy* time; all hands must be then at work. Harvest time is *opportunity*, a short and limited time, and harvest work is work that must be done *then* or not at all. Now he here suggests three things to them to quicken them to diligence:

(1) That it was *necessary work*, and the *occasion* for it very urgent and pressing (*v.* 35): *You say, It is four months to harvest*; but I say, *The fields are already white*. [A saying concerning the *corn-harvest*; there

are yet *four months, and then comes harvest.* "You say, for the encouragement of the sower at seed-time, that it will be but four months to the harvest."] God has not only promised us a harvest every year, but has appointed the *weeks of harvest;* so that we know *when to expect it.* Christ's saying concerning the *gospel harvest: Look, the fields are already white unto the harvest.* Here in *this* place there was harvest work for *him* to do. They would have him to *eat,* v. 31. "Eat!" saith he, "I have other work to do, that is more needful; *look* what crowds of Samaritans are coming that are ready to receive the gospel." People's forwardness to hear the word is a great excitement to ministers' diligence and liveliness in preaching it. There are multitudes as ready to receive the gospel as a field of corn that is fully ripe is ready to be reaped. The fields were now made *white to the harvest.* It is a great encouragement to us to engage in any work for God, if we understand by the signs of the times that this is the proper season for that work. John Baptist had *made ready a people prepared for the Lord.* Since he began to preach the kingdom of God *every man pressed into it,* Luke xvi. 16. This, therefore, was a time to *thrust in their sickle.* It was *necessary* to work now. If the corn that is *ripe* be not reaped, it will *shed* and be lost. If souls that are under convictions be not helped now, their hopeful beginnings will come to nothing.

(2) That it was *profitable* and *advantageous* work, which they themselves would be gainers by (v. 36): "*He that reapeth receiveth wages.*" Christ's reapers never have cause to say they served a hard Master. His work is *its own wages.* Christ's reapers have *fruit: He gathereth fruit unto life eternal;* that is, he shall both save himself and those that hear him. This is the comfort of faithful ministers, that their work has a tendency to the eternal salvation of precious souls: They have *joy: That he that sows and they that reap may rejoice together.* The minister who is the happy instrument of beginning a good work is *he that sows;* he that is employed to carry it on and perfect it is *he that reaps:* and both shall rejoice together. The reapers share in the *joy of harvest.*

(3) That it was *easy* work, and work that was half done to their hands by those that were gone before them: *One soweth, and another reapeth,* v. 37, 38. Moses, and the prophets, and John Baptist, had *paved* the way to the gospel. *I sent you to reap that whereupon you bestowed* no *labour.* This intimates *two things* concerning the Old Testament ministry: It was very much *short* of the New Testament ministry. Moses and the *prophets* sowed, but they could not be said to *reap.* Their writings have done much more good since they left us than ever their preaching did. It was very *serviceable* to the New Testament ministry, and made way for it. Had it not been for the seed sown by the prophets, this Samaritan woman could not have said, *We know that Messias cometh.* This also intimates *two things* concerning the ministry of the *apostles of Christ.* It was a *fruitful* ministry: they were reapers that gathered in a great harvest. It was much *facilitated* by the writings of the prophets. The prophets *sowed in tears,* crying out, *We have laboured in vain;* the apostles *reaped in joy,* saying, *Thanks be to God, who always causeth us to triumph.* From the labours of ministers that are dead and gone much good fruit may be reaped by the people that *survive* them and the ministers that *succeed* them. See what reason we have to bless God for those that are *gone before us.* We are *entered into their labours.*

IV. The *good effect* which this visit Christ made to the Samaritans had upon them, v. 39–42. See what impressions were made on them,

1. By the *woman's testimony* concerning *Christ;* and the testimony no more than this, *He told me all that ever I did.* And *two things* they were brought to:

(1) To *credit* Christ's *word* (v. 39): *Many of the Samaritans of that city believed on him for the saying of the woman.* Who they were that believed: *Many of the Samaritans,* who were not of the house of Israel. Their faith was an *earnest* of the *faith* of the Gentiles. Upon what inducement they believed: *For the saying of the woman.* See here, *First,* How God is sometimes pleased to use very weak and unlikely instruments for the beginning and carrying on of a good work. *Secondly,* How great a matter a little fire kindles. Our Saviour, by instructing one poor woman, spread instruction to a whole town. Let not ministers be either *careless* in their preaching, or *discouraged* in it, because their hearers are *few* and *mean;* for, by doing good to *them,* good may be conveyed to *more.* See how good it is to speak *experimentally* of Christ. Those are most likely to do good that can tell what God has done *for their souls.*

(2) To *court his stay* among them (v. 40): When they were come to him *they besought him that he would tarry with them.* Upon the woman's report, they believed him to be a prophet, and *came to him;* and, when they *saw* him, they respected him as a prophet. They begged he would tarry with them that they might *testify their respect* to him; that they might receive instruction from him. Many would have flocked to one that would tell them *their fortune,* but these flocked to one that would tell them *their faults.* The Jews drove him from them: while the Samaritans invited him to them. The *proof* of the gospel's success is not always according to the *probability,* nor what is *experienced* according to what is *expected.* Christ granted their request. He *abode there.* When he had an opportunity of doing good, he *abode there.* We are told what impressions were made upon them by Christ's own word (v. 41, 42), what he *said* and *did* there is not related. He said and did that which convinced them that he was the Christ; and the labours of a minister are best told by the good fruit of them. *Now their eyes saw him;* and the effect was, [1] That their number grew (v. 41): *Many more believed.* [2] That their faith grew. Those who had been wrought upon by the report of the woman now saw cause to say, *Now we believe, not because of thy saying,* v. 42. Here are three things in which their *faith grew: a.* In the matter of it. Upon the testimony of the woman, they believed him to be a *prophet;* but now that they have conversed with him they believe that he is *the Christ,* the *Anointed One,* and that, being the *Christ,* he is the *Saviour of the world.* They believed him to be the Saviour not only of the Jews, but *of the world,* which they hoped would take them in, though Samaritans. *b.* In the *certainty* of it; their faith now grew up to a full assurance: *We know* that this is indeed the *Christ. c.* In the *ground* of it: *Now we believe, not because of thy saying, for we have heard him ourselves.* They had before believed for her saying: "*Now we believe because we have heard him ourselves.* We are abundantly satisfied and assured that *this is the Christ.*" In this instance we may see how *faith comes by hearing.* Faith comes *to the birth* by hearing the *report of men.* The instructions of parents and preachers *recommend* the doctrine of Christ *to our acquaintance.* Faith *comes to its growth,* by hearing the testimony of Christ himself; and this goes further, and recommends his doctrine *to our acceptance.* We were induced to look into the scriptures *by the saying* of those who told us that in them they had found eternal life; now we believe, *not for their saying,* but because we have searched them ourselves: and our faith *stands not in the wisdom of men, but in the power of God.*

Thus was the seed of the gospel sown in Samaria.

Verses 43–54

I. Christ's *coming* into Galilee, *v.* 43. *After two days* he left them because *he must preach to other cities,* Luke iv. 43. *He went into Galilee.*

1. Whither Christ went; into Galilee, but not to Nazareth, which was strictly *his own* country. He went among the villages, but declined going to Nazareth, for a reason here given, which *Jesus himself testified*: That a *prophet has no honour in his own country.* The honour due to the Lord's prophets has very often been denied them. This *due* honour is most frequently denied them *in their own country.* Christ's near kinsmen spoke most slightly of him, *ch.* vii. 5. Men's pride and envy make them scorn to be instructed by those who once were their school-fellows and play-fellows. It is just with God to deny his gospel to those that despise the ministers of it. They that mock the messengers forfeit the benefit of the message.

2. What entertainment he met with among the Galileans in the country (*v.* 45): They *received him.* Christ and his gospel are not sent in vain; if they have not honour with *some,* they shall have with *others.* Now the reason given why these Galileans were so ready to receive Christ is because they had seen *the miracles he did at Jerusalem, v.* 45. They went up to Jerusalem at the feast, the feast of the passover. They *went up to the feast,* and there they became acquainted with Christ. They that are diligent and constant in attending on public ordinances some time or other meet with more spiritual benefit than they expect. At Jerusalem they *saw* Christ's miracles. The miracles were wrought for the benefit of those at Jerusalem; yet the Galileans got more advantage by them than they did for whom they were chiefly designed. Thus the word preached to a *mixed multitude* may perhaps edify *occasional* hearers more than the constant auditory.

3. What city he went to. He chose to go to Cana of Galilee, *where he had made the water wine* (*v.* 46). The evangelist mentions this miracle here to teach us to keep in remembrance what we *have seen of the* works of Christ.

II. His *curing* the *nobleman's son.* This story is not recorded by any other of the evangelists.

1. Who the *petitioner* was, and who the *patient*: the petitioner was a *nobleman*; the patient was his son: *There was a certain nobleman.* The father a nobleman and yet the son sick; for dignities and titles of honour will be no security from the assaults of sickness and death. It was fifteen miles from Capernaum to Cana, where Christ now was; yet this affliction in his family sent him so far to Christ.

2. How the petitioner made *his application* to the physician. He *went to him* himself, and *besought him to come and heal his son, v.* 47. See here, His *tender affection* to his son, that when he was sick he would spare no pains to get help for him. His *great respect* to our Lord Jesus, that he would come himself to wait upon him, and that he *besought him,* when, as a man in authority, he might have ordered his attendance. The greatest men, when they come to God, must become beggars. As to the errand he came upon, we may observe a mixture in *his faith.* There was *sincerity* in it; he did believe that Christ could heal his son. Yet there was *infirmity* in his faith; he thought he could not heal him at a distance, and therefore he besought him that he would *come down* and heal him. We are encouraged to *pray,* but we are not allowed to prescribe: Lord, heal me; but, whether with a word or a touch, *thy will be done.*

3. The gentle rebuke he met with in this address (*v.* 48): *Jesus said to him, "Except you see signs and wonders, you will not believe."* Though he was a *nobleman,* and now in *grief* about his son, yet Christ gives him a reproof. Christ first shows him his sin

and weakness, to prepare him for mercy, and then grants his request. Those whom Christ intends to honour with his *favours* he first *humbles* with his *frowns.* Whereas they had heard by credible and incontestable report of the miracles he had wrought in other places, they could not believe except they saw them with their own eyes. They must be *honoured,* and they must be *humoured,* or they will not be *convinced.* Whereas they had seen divers miracles which sufficiently proved Christ to be a teacher come from God, they would go no further in believing than they were *driven* by signs and wonders. The *spiritual* power of the word did not *affect them,* did not *attract* them, but only the *sensible* power of miracles.

4. His continued importunity in his address (*v.* 49): *Sir, come down ere my child die.* He took the reproof patiently; he spoke to Christ respectfully. And, as he did not take the reproof for an affront, so he did not take it for a denial, but still prosecuted his request, and continued to wrestle till he prevailed. He is so wholly taken up with concern about his child that he can mind nothing else. He still discovered the weakness of his faith in the power of Christ. He must have Christ to come down, thinking that else he could do the child no kindness. He believes that Christ could heal a *sick* child, but not that he could raise a *dead* child, "O *come down, ere my child die,"* as if then it would be too late. He forgot that Elijah and Elisha had raised dead children; and is Christ's power inferior to theirs? Observe what haste he is in: *Come down, ere my child die;* as if there were danger of Christ's slipping his time.

5. The answer of peace which Christ gave (*v.* 50): *Go thy way, thy son liveth.* Christ here gives us an instance of his *power,* that he not only could heal, but could heal with so much ease. Here is nothing *said,* nothing *done,* nothing *ordered* to be done, and yet the cure wrought. This nobleman would have Christ *come down and heal his son*; Christ will heal his son, and not *come down.* And thus the cure is the sooner wrought, the nobleman's mistake rectified, and his faith confirmed; so that the thing was better done in Christ's way. When he denies what we ask, he gives what is much more to our advantage. He observed the nobleman to be *in pain* about his son, and therefore Christ dropped the reproof, and gave him assurance of the recovery of his child; for he knows how a father *pities his children.*

6. The nobleman's belief of the word of Christ: He *believed,* and *went away.* He is satisfied with the method Christ took. Now he *sees no sign or wonder,* and yet *believes* the wonder done. Christ said, *Thy son liveth,* and the man *believed* him. Christ said, *Go thy way;* and, as an evidence of the sincerity of his faith, he *went his way.*

7. The further confirmation of his faith, by comparing notes with his servants at his return. His servants met him with the agreeable news of the child's recovery, *v.* 51. Christ said, *Thy son liveth*; and now the servants say the same. Good news will meet those that hope in God's word. He enquired what hour the child began to recover (*v.* 52). He was desirous to have his faith confirmed. The diligent comparison of the works of Christ with his word will be of great use to us for the confirming of our faith. This was the course the nobleman took: He *enquired of the servants the hour when he began to amend;* and they told him, *Yesterday at the seventh hour* the *fever left him*; not only he began to amend, but he was perfectly well on a sudden; so *the father knew that it was at the same hour* when Jesus said to him, *Thy son liveth.* Two things would help to confirm his faith: *First,* That the child's recovery was *sudden* and not *gradual.* They name the precise time to an hour: *Yesterday,* not *about,* but *at* the seventh hour, *the fever left him.* The word of Christ did not work

like physic, which must have time to operate, and produce the effect, and perhaps *cures by expectation* only; no, with Christ it was *he spoke and it was done;* not, He spoke and it was *set a-doing. Secondly,* That it was just at the same time that Christ spoke to him: *at that very hour.* The synchronisms and co-incidents of events add very much to the beauty and harmony of Providence. In men's works, distance of place is the delay of time and the retarding of business; but it is not so in the works of Christ.

8. The *happy effect and issue of this.* The bringing of the cure to the family brought salvation to it. The nobleman *himself believed.* He had before *believed* the word of Christ; but now he *believed in Christ.* Christ has many ways of gaining the heart, and by the grant of a *temporal* mercy may make way for *better* things. His *whole house* believed likewise. Because of the *interest* they all had in the miracle, which preserved the *blossom* and *hopes* of the family; this affected them all, and endeared Christ to them. This was a *nobleman,* and probably he had a *great household;* but, when he comes into Christ's school, he brings them all along with him. What a blessed change was here in this house, occasioned by the sickness of the child! This should reconcile us to afflictions; we know not what good may follow from them.

9. Here is the evangelist's remark upon this cure (*v.* 54); *This is the second miracle,* referring to *ch.* ii. 11. In Judæa he had wrought many miracles. They had the first offer; but, being driven thence, he wrought miracles in Galilee. Somewhere or other Christ will find a welcome. People may, if they please, shut the sun out of *their own houses,* but they cannot shut it *out of the world.* This is noted to be the *second miracle,* to remind us of the first. *Fresh* mercies should revive the remembrance of *former mercies,* as former mercies should encourage our hopes of further mercies. Probably, the patient being a person of quality, when this nobleman applied himself to Christ, multitudes followed. What abundance of good may great men do, if they be good men!

CHAPTER 5

We have in the gospels a faithful record of all that Jesus began both to do and to teach, Acts i. 1. These two are interwoven, because what he taught explained what he did, and what he did confirmed what he taught. Accordingly, we have in this chapter a miracle and a sermon. I. The miracle was the cure of an impotent man that had been diseased thirty-eight years, ver. 1–16. II. The sermon was Christ's vindication of himself, when he was prosecuted as a criminal for healing the man on the sabbath day. 1. He asserts his authority as Messiah, ver. 17–29. 2. He proves it and condemns the Jews for their unbelief, ver. 30–47.

Verses 1–16

This miraculous cure is not recorded by any other of the evangelists, who confine themselves mostly to the miracles wrought in Galilee, but John relates those wrought at Jerusalem.

I. *The time when* this cure was wrought: it was at a *feast of the Jews,* that is, the passover, for that was the most celebrated feast. Christ, though residing in Galilee, yet *went up to Jerusalem* at the feast, *v.* 1. It was an *opportunity of good;* there were great numbers gathered together there at that time; it was a general rendezvous, from all parts of the country, besides proselytes from other nations. It was to be hoped that they were in a *good frame,* for they came together to *worship God.* Now a mind *inclined to devotion lies very open* to the further discoveries of divine light and love.

II. The *place where* this cure was wrought: at the *pool of Bethesda,* which had a miraculous healing virtue in it, *v.* 2–4.

1. Where it was situated: *At Jerusalem, by the sheep-market.* Some think it was near the temple, and, if so, it yielded a melancholy but profitable

spectacle to those that went up to the temple to pray.

2. How it was called: It was a *pool which is called in Hebrew, Bethesda—the house of mercy;* for therein appeared much of the *mercy of God* to the sick and diseased. In a world of so much misery as this is, it is well that there are some *Bethesdas.*

3. How it was fitted up: It had *five porches* in which the sick lay. Thus the charity of men concurred with the mercy of God for the relief of the distressed. Nature has provided *remedies,* but men must provide *hospitals.*

4. How it was frequented with sick and cripples (*v.* 3): *In these lay a great multitude of impotent folks.* How many are the afflictions of the afflicted in this world! It may do us good to visit the hospitals sometimes, that we may take occasion, from the calamities of others, to thank God for our comforts. The evangelist specifies three sorts of diseased people that lay here, *blind, halt,* and *withered.* These are mentioned because, being least able to help themselves into the water, they lay longest waiting in the *porches.* O that men were as wise for their souls, and as solicitous to get their spiritual diseases healed!

5. What virtue it had for the cure of these impotent folks (*v.* 4): *An angel went down,* and *troubled the water;* and *whoso first stepped in was made whole.* The virtue this pool had was supernatural.

(1) The *preparation* of the medicine by an angel, who *went down into the pool,* and *stirred the water.* See what mean offices the holy angels condescend to. If we would do the will of God as the angels do it, we must think nothing below us but sin. The *troubling of the water* was the signal given of the descent of the angel. The waters of the sanctuary are then *healing* when they are put in *motion.* Ministers must *stir up the gift* that is in them. When they are cold and dull in their ministrations, the waters *settle* and are not apt to *heal.* The angel descended, to *stir the water at a certain season.*

(2) The *operation* of the medicine: *Whoever first stepped in was made whole.* What disease soever it was, this water cured it. The power of miracles *succeeds* where the power of nature *succumbs.* He that first stepped in had the benefit, not those that lingered and came in afterwards. This teaches us to observe and improve our opportunities, that we slip not a season which may never return.

Now this is all the account we have of this *standing* miracle. It was a *token* of God's goodwill to that people, and an indication that, though they had been long without prophets and miracles, yet God had not *cast them off.* It was a type of the Messiah that arises *with healing under his wings.*

III. The patient on whom this cure was wrought (*v.* 5): one that *had been infirm thirty-eight years.* His *disease* was grievous: He had an *infirmity;* he had lost the use of his limbs. It is sad to have the body so disabled that instead of being the soul's instrument, it is become, even in the affairs of this life, its burden. What reason have we to thank God for bodily strength, to use it for him. The *duration* of it was tedious: *Thirty-eight years.* He was lame longer than most live. Shall we complain of one wearisome night, or one fit of illness, who perhaps for many years have scarcely known what it has been to be a day sick, when many others, better than we, have scarcely known what it has been to be a day well?

IV. The cure and the circumstances of it briefly related, *v.* 6–9.

1. *Jesus saw him lie.* Observe, When Christ came up to Jerusalem he visited not the palaces, but the hospitals, an *indication* of his great design in coming into the world, which was to seek and save the sick

and wounded. There was a great multitude of poor cripples here at Bethesda, but Christ fastened his eye upon this one. Christ delights to help the helpless. He had often been disappointed of a cure; therefore Christ took him for his patient: it is his honour to side with the weakest.

2. He knew and considered *how long he had lain* in this condition.

3. He asked him, *Wilt thou be made whole?* A strange question to be asked one that had been so long ill. Some indeed would not be made whole, because their sores serve them to beg by. Christ put it to him, to *express* his own pity and concern for him. Christ is tenderly inquisitive concerning the desires of those that are in affliction, to teach them to value the mercy, and to excite in them desires after it. In spiritual cases, people are not willing to be cured of their sins. If people were willing to be *made whole*, the work were half done, for Christ is willing to heal, if we be but willing to be healed.

4. The poor impotent man takes this opportunity to set forth the misery of his case: *Sir, I have no man to put me into the pool, v.* 7. He complains for want of friends to help him in: "*I have no man*, no friend to do me that kindness." One would think that some of those who had been themselves healed should have lent him a hand. To the sick and impotent it is as true a piece of charity to work for them as to relieve them. He bewails his infelicity, that very often when *he* was coming *another stepped in before him*. But a step between him and a cure, and yet he continues impotent. There is no getting over the old maxim, *Every one for himself.* Having been so often disappointed, he begins to despair, and now is Christ's time to come to his relief. And observe further, to his praise, that, though he had waited so long in vain, yet still he continued lying by the pool-side, hoping that sometime or other help would come.

5. Our Lord Jesus hereupon cures him with a word.

(1) The word he said: *Rise, take up thy bed, v.* 8. He is bidden to *rise and walk*; a strange command to be given to an *impotent* man, that had been long disabled. He must *rise and walk*, that is, attempt to do it, and in the *essay* he should receive strength to do it. If he had not attempted to help himself, he had not been cured, yet it does not therefore follow that, when he did rise and walk, it was by his own strength; no, it was by the power of Christ. He is bidden to *take up his bed. First*, To make it to appear that it was a *perfect cure*, and purely miraculous; for he did not recover strength by degrees, but from the extremity of weakness and impotency he suddenly stepped into the highest degree of bodily strength. He, who this minute was not able to turn himself in his bed, the next minute was able to carry his bed. *Secondly*, It was to *proclaim* the cure. Being the sabbath day, whoever carried a burden through the streets made himself very remarkable, and everyone would enquire what was the meaning of it. Christ would thus witness against the tradition of the elders. The case may be such that it may become a work of *necessity*, or *mercy*, to carry a bed on the sabbath day; but here it was more, it was a work of *piety*. He would hereby try the faith and obedience of his patient. Those that have been *healed by Christ's word* should be *ruled by his word*.

(2) The efficacy of this word (*v.* 9). *Immediately he was made whole.* What a joyful surprise was this to the poor cripple, to find himself all of a sudden so easy, so strong, so able to help himself! What a new world was he in, in an instant! He *took up his bed and walked*, and did not care who blamed him or threatened him for it.

V. What became of the poor man after he was cured.

1. What passed between him and the Jews who saw him carry his bed on the sabbath day. The Jews quarrelled with the man, telling him that *it was not lawful, v.* 10. Thus far was commendable, that, while they knew not by *what authority* he did it, they were jealous for the honour of the sabbath. The man justified himself in what he did by a warrant that would bear him out, *v.* 11. "I do not do it in contempt of the law and the sabbath. He that could work such a miracle as to *make me whole* no doubt might give me such a command as to carry *my bed*. He that was so kind as to make me whole would not be so unkind as to bid me do what is sinful." The Jews enquired further who it was that gave him this warrant (*v.* 12): *What man is that?* How industriously they *overlooked* that which might be a ground of their *faith in Christ*. They resolve to look upon Christ as a *mere man: What man is that?* They were resolved that they would never own him to be the *Son of God*. They resolve to look upon him as a *bad man*. He who bade this man carry his bed was certainly a delinquent. The poor man was unable to give them any account of him: *He wist not who he was, v.* 13. Christ was *unknown* to him when he healed him. Christ does many a good turn for those that know him not. He enlightens, strengthens, quickens, comforts us, and we *wist not who he is*. For the present he *kept himself unknown*; for as soon as he had wrought the cure he *conveyed himself away, a multitude being in that place*. This is mentioned to show, either, *First, How* Christ conveyed himself away—by retiring into the crowd, so as not to be distinguished from a common person. Or, *Secondly, Why* he conveyed himself away, because there was *a multitude* there, and he industriously avoided both the *applause* of those who would admire the miracle and *cry that up*, and the censure of those who would censure him as a sabbath-breaker, and *run him down*. Christ left the miracle to commend itself, and the man on whom it was wrought to justify it.

2. What passed at their next interview, *v.* 14.

(1) Where Christ found him: *in the temple.* Christ *went to the temple.* The man that was cured *went to the temple.* There Christ found him. Thither he straightway went because he had, *by his infirmity*, been so long *detained* thence. Perhaps he had not been there for thirty-eight years. His first visit shall be to the temple. Because he had *by his recovery* a good errand thither; he went up to the temple to return thanks to God for his recovery. Because he had, by *carrying his bed*, seemed to put a contempt on the sabbath, he would thus show that he had an honour for it. Works of necessity and mercy are allowed; but when they are over we must *go to the temple*.

(2) What he said to him. He now applies himself to the healing of his soul. He gives him a *memento* of his cure: *Behold thou art made whole.* Christ calls his attention to it. Let the impressions of it abide, and never be lost. He gives him a caution against sin, *Being made whole, sin no more.* This implies that his disease was the punishment of sin. While those chronical diseases lasted, they prevented the outward acts of many sins, and therefore watchfulness was the more necessary when the disability was removed. When the trouble which only dammed up the current is over, the waters will return to their old course. It is common for people, when they are sick, to *promise much*, when newly recovered to *perform something*, but after awhile to *forget all*. He gives him warning of his danger: *Lest a worse thing come to thee.* Christ knew that he was one of those that must be *frightened* from sin. There is something *worse* that will come to him if he relapse into sin after God has *given him such a deliverance*.

VI. The notice which the poor simple man gave to the Jews concerning Christ, *v.* 15. He told them it was Jesus that had *made him whole*. The rage and enmity of the Jews against him: *Therefore did the rulers of the Jews persecute Jesus*. See, (1) How absurd and unreasonable their enmity to Christ was. *Therefore*, because he had made a poor sick man well, they persecuted him, because he did good in Israel. (2) How bloody and cruel it was: *They sought to slay him*. (3) How it was varnished over with a colour of zeal for the honour of the sabbath; for this was the pretended crime, *Because he had done these things on the sabbath day*. Thus hypocrites often cover their real enmity against the *power* of godliness with a pretended zeal for the *form of it*.

Verses 17–30

We have here Christ's discourse upon occasion of his being accused as a sabbath-breaker.

I. The doctrine laid down, by which he justified what he did on the sabbath day (*v.* 17): *He answered them, My father worketh hitherto, and I work*. Waving all other pleas, he insists upon that which was *equivalent to the whole*, and abides by it, which he had mentioned, Matt. xii. 8. *The Son of man is Lord even of the sabbath day*. 1. He pleads that he was the *Son of God*, plainly intimated in his calling *God his Father*. 2. That he was a worker together with God. *My Father worketh hitherto*. But I also *work with him*. As God created all things by Christ, so he supports and governs all by him. He that does all is Lord of all, and therefore *Lord of the sabbath*.

II. The offence that was taken at his doctrine (*v.* 18): *The Jews sought the more to kill him*. His defence was made his offence. They sought to kill him,

1. Because he had broken the sabbath.

2. He had said also *that God was his Father*. Now they pretend a jealousy for *God's honour*, and charge Christ with it as a heinous crime that he made himself equal with God. This was justly inferred from what he said, that he was the *Son of God*, and that God was *his Father*. He had said that he worked with his Father, and hereby he made himself equal with God. Yet it was unjustly imputed to him as an offence that he equalled himself with God, for he was and is God. Therefore Christ, in answer to this charge, makes out his claim and proves that he is equal with God in power and glory.

III. Christ's discourse upon this occasion. In these verses he explains, and afterwards confirms, his commission, as Mediator. And, as the honours he is hereby *entitled to* are such as it is not fit for any creature to receive, so the work he is hereby entrusted with is such as it is not possible for any creature to go through with, and therefore he is God.

1. *In general*. He is one with the Father in all he does as Mediator. It is ushered in with a solemn preface (*v.* 19): *Verily, verily, I say unto you*. This intimates that the things declared are, (1) Very awful and great. (2) Very sure. (3) That they are matters purely of divine revelation, which we could not otherwise have come to the knowledge of. Two things he saith in general concerning the Son's oneness with the Father in working:

[1] That the Son *conforms to the Father* (*v.* 19): *The Son can do nothing of himself but what he sees the Father do;* for *these things does the Son*. The Lord Jesus, as Mediator, is *Obedient to his Father's will*. Christ was so entirely devoted to his Father's will that it was impossible for him in anything to act separately. He is *observant of his Father's counsel*; he can, he will, do nothing *but what he sees the Father do*. No man can *find out the work of God*, but the only-begotten Son, sees what he does, is intimately acquainted with his purposes, and has the plan of them ever before him. What the Father did in his counsels, the Son had ever in his view, and still he had his eye upon it. Yet he is *equal* with the Father

in *working*; for *what things soever* the Father does *these also does the Son likewise*; he did the *same* things, not *such* things, but the *same things*; and he did them in the *same manner*, with the same authority, the same energy and efficacy.

[2] That the Father *communicates* to the Son, *v.* 20.

First, The inducement to it: *The Father loveth the Son*. Christ was now hated of men, but he comforted himself with this, that his Father loved him.

Secondly, The instances of it. He shows it, 1. In what he *does* communicate to him: *He shows him all things that himself doth*. He shows him all things *which he does*, that is, which the *Son* does; all that the Son does is by direction from the Father; he *shows* him. 2. In what he *will* communicate; he will *show him greater works than these*. Works of greater *power* than the *curing of the impotent man*; for he should raise the dead, and should himself rise from the dead. Many are brought to marvel at Christ's works, whereby he has the honour of them, who are not brought to believe, by which they would have the benefit of them.

2. *In particular*. He proves his equality with the Father, by specifying some of those works which he does that are the peculiar works of God. This is enlarged upon, *v.* 21–30.

(1) Observe what is here said concerning the Mediator's power to *raise the dead* and *give life*. [1] His *authority* to do it (*v.* 21): *As the Father raiseth up the dead, so the Son quickeneth whom he will*. It is God's prerogative to raise the dead, and give life. A *resurrection from the dead* never lay in the common road of nature, nor ever fell within the thought of those that studied only the compass of nature's power. It is purely the work of a divine power, and the knowledge of it purely by divine revelation. The Mediator is invested with this prerogative: *He quickens whom he will*. He does not enliven things by natural necessity, as the sun does, whose beams revive of course; but he acts as a free agent. As he has the power, so he has the wisdom and sovereignty, of a God; has the *key of the grave and of death*.

[2] His *ability* to do it, because *he has life in himself, as the Father has*, *v.* 26. It is certain that the Father *has life in himself*. He is a sovereign giver of life; he has the disposal of life in himself; and of all good (for so *life* sometimes signifies). He is to his creatures the fountain of life, and all good. It is as certain that he has *given to the Son to have life in himself*. The Son, as Redeemer, is the original of all spiritual life and good; is that to the church which the Father is to the world. The kingdom of grace, and all the life in that kingdom, are as fully and absolutely in the hand of the Redeemer as the kingdom of providence is in the hand of the Creator.

[3] His *acting* according to this authority and ability. There are two resurrections performed by his powerful word, both which are here spoken of:

A resurrection that *now is* (*v.* 29), a resurrection from the depth of sin to the life of righteousness. *The hour is coming, and now is*. It is a resurrection begun already. This is plainly distinguished from that in *v.* 28, which speaks of the resurrection at the end of time. Some think this was fulfilled in those whom he miraculously raised to life. I rather understand it of the power of the doctrine of Christ, for the recovering and quickening of those that were *dead in trespasses and sins*, Eph. ii. 1. The *hour* was *coming* when dead souls should be made alive by the *preaching* of the gospel: nay, it *then was*, while Christ was upon earth. It is to be applied to all the wonderful success of the gospel, among both Jews and Gentiles; an hour which still *is*, and is still *coming*. Sinners are spiritually *dead*, miserable, but neither sensible of their misery nor able to help themselves out of it.

The conversion of a soul to God is its resurrection from death to life; then it begins to live when it begins to *live to God*. It is by the *voice of the Son of God* that souls are raised to spiritual life. *The dead shall hear the voice of the Son of God.*

The voice of Christ must be heard by us, that we may live by it. A resurrection yet *to come*; this is spoken of, *v.* 28, 29. When this resurrection shall be: *The hour is coming.* It is *not yet* come, it is not the hour spoken of at *v.* 25, that is coming, and *now is.* It *will certainly* come, it is coming on, nearer every day. How far off it is we know not. Who shall be raised: *All that are in the graves.* Christ here tells us that *all* must appear before the Judge, and therefore *all* must be raised. The grave is the prison of dead bodies, where they are *detained.* Yet, in prospect of their resurrection, we may call it their *bed*, where they sleep to be *awaked* again. How they shall be raised. (*a*) The efficient of this resurrection: *They shall hear his voice.* A divine power shall go along with the voice, to put life into them, and enable them to obey it. (*b*) The effect of it: *They shall come forth* out of their graves. They shall *appear* before Christ's tribunal. To what they shall be raised; to a different state of happiness or misery, according to their different character.

(*a*) *They that have done good shall come forth to the resurrection of life;* they shall live again, to live for ever. It will be well in the great day with those only that have *done good.* They shall be *admitted* into the presence of God, and that is life, it is better than life.

(*b*) *They that have done evil to the resurrection of damnation;* they shall live again, to be for ever dying.

(2) Observe what is here said concerning the Mediator's *authority to execute judgment, v.* 22–24, 27. As he has an almighty power, so he has a sovereign jurisdiction. Christ's commission or delegation to the office of a judge, which is twice spoken of here (*v.* 22): *He hath committed all judgment to the Son;* and again (*v.* 27): *He hath given him authority.*

First, The *Father judges no man*; he is pleased to govern by Jesus Christ. He does not *rule* us by the *mere* right of *creation.* Having made us, he *may* do what he *pleases* with us, as the potter with the clay; yet he does not take advantage of this. The Mediator having undertaken to make a *vicarious* satisfaction, the matter is referred to him.

Secondly, He has committed all judgment to the Son. It is God in Christ that reconciles the world, and to him he has given power to confer eternal life. The book of life is the Lamb's book; by his award we must stand or fall. He is constituted sole manager of the judgment of the great day. The final and universal judgment is committed to the Son of Man.

Thirdly, He has *given him authority to execute judgment also, v.* 27. He that *executes judgment* upon them is the same that would have *wrought salvation* for them. Whence he has that authority: the Father *gave it to him.* Now all this redounds very much to the honour of Christ, and very much to the comfort of all believers, who may with the greatest assurance venture their all in such hands. He has all judgment committed to him for two reasons:

First, Because he is the *Son of man*; which denotes these three things: 1. His humiliation and gracious condescension. To this low estate he stooped. Because he condescended to be the *Son of Man,* his Father made him *Lord of all*, Phil. ii. 8, 9. 2. His affinity and alliance to us. Being the *Son of man*, he is of the same nature with those whom he is *set over.* 3. His being the Messiah promised. He is the Messiah, and therefore is invested with all this power. Christ usually called himself the *Son of man*, which was the more humble title, and bespeaks him a prince and

Saviour, not to the Jewish nation only, but to the whole race of mankind.

Secondly, That all men should honour the Son, v. 23. The honouring of Jesus Christ is here spoken of as God's great design, and as man's great duty. We must *honour the Son*, must *confess that he is Lord*, and worship him; must honour him who was dishonoured for us. *Even as they honour the Father.* This *supposes* it to be our duty to *honour the Father*, and *directs* us to *honour the Son.* To enforce this law, it is added, *He that honours not the Son honours not the Father* who has sent him. Some pretend a reverence for the Creator, and speak *honourably* of him, who make light of the Redeemer, and speak *contemptibly* of him. Indignities done to the Lord Jesus reflect upon God himself. The Father counts himself struck as through him. The reason of this is because it is the *Father who hath sent him.* Affronts to an ambassador are justly resented by the prince that sends him. Here is the rule by which the Son goes in executing this commission (*v.* 24): *He that heareth and believeth* hath *everlasting life.* Here we have the substance of the whole gospel.

First, The *character* of a Christian: *He that heareth my word, and believeth on him that sent me.* To be a Christian indeed is to *hear the word of Christ.* It is not enough to be within hearing of it, we must hear and obey, it must abide by the gospel of Christ as the fixed rule of our faith and practice. *To believe on him that sent him*; for Christ's design is to *bring us to God.* Christ is our *way*; God is our rest.

Secondly, The *charter* of a Christian. A charter of pardon: *He shall not come into condemnation.* The grace of the gospel is a full discharge from the curse of the law. A charter of privileges: *He is passed out of death to life. Hear and live, believe and live,* is what we may venture our souls upon. Here is the righteousness of his proceedings (*v.* 30). *My judgment is just.* His judgments are certainly just, for they are directed by the Father's *wisdom: I can of my ownself* do nothing, but *as I hear I judge*, as he had said before (*v.* 19). The Son *can do nothing but what he sees the Father do*; so here, nothing but what he hears the Father *say: As I hear, 1.* From the secret eternal counsels of the Father, *so I judge.* Would we know what we may depend upon in our dealing with God? *Hear the word of Christ.* What Christ has adjudged is an exact copy or counterpart of what the Father has decreed. 2. From the published records of the Old Testament. Christ, in all the execution of his undertaking, had an eye to the scripture. *As it was written in the volume of the book.* By the Father's *will: My judgment is just, because I seek not my own will*, but *his who sent me.* Not as if the will of Christ were contrary to the will of the Father. Christ has, as man, the natural and innocent affections of the human nature, *sense of pain* and *pleasure*, an inclination to life, an aversion to death: yet he *pleased not himself*, but acquiesced entirely in the will of his Father. What he did as Mediator was not the result of any *peculiar* or *particular* purpose and design of his own, but he was therein guided by his Father's will.

Verses 31–47

I. He *sets aside* his own testimony of himself (*v.* 31): *"If I bear witness of myself*, though it is infallibly true (*ch.* viii. 14), you will not admit it."

II. He produces other witnesses that bear testimony to him that he was sent of God.

1. The Father himself bore testimony to him (*v.* 32): *There is another that beareth witness.* I take this to be meant of God the Father. The seal which the Father put to his commission: He *beareth witness of me*, not only has done so by a voice from heaven, but still does so by the tokens of his presence with

me. The satisfaction Christ had in this testimony: "*I know that the witness which he witnesseth of me is true.*"

2. John Baptist witnessed to Christ, *v.* 33, &c. John came to *bear witness of the light* (*ch.* i. 7).

(1) Now the testimony of John was a *solemn* and public testimony: You sent an embassy of priests and Levites to John, which gave him an opportunity of publishing what he had to say. It was a *true* testimony: *He bore witness to the truth.* Christ does not say, *He bore witness to me*, but, like an honest man, *He bore witness to the truth.*

(2) Two things are added concerning John's testimony:

[1] That it was a testimony *more than he needed to vouch* (*v.* 34): *I receive not testimony from man.* Christ needs no testimonials or certificates, but what his own worth and excellency bring with him; why then did Christ here urge the testimony of John? Why, *these things I say, that you may be saved.* This he aimed at in all this discourse, to save not his own life, but the souls of others. Christ desires and designs the salvation even of his enemies and persecutors.

[2] That it was a testimony *to the man*, because John Baptist was one whom *they* had a respect for (*v.* 35).

First, The character of John Baptist: *He was a burning and a shining light.* He was a *light*, not *light* (so Christ was *the* light), but a *luminary*, a derived subordinate light. He was a *burning* light, which denotes *sincerity*; painted fire may be made to shine, but that which *burns* is true fire. It denotes also his *activity*, zeal, and fervency. Fire is always working on itself or something else, so is a good minister. He was a *shining* light, which denotes either his *exemplary conversation*, in which our light should shine (Matt. v. 16), or an *eminent* diffusive influence.

Secondly, The affections of the people to him: *You were willing for a season to rejoice in his light.* 1. It was a *transport* that they were in, upon the appearing of John: "*You delighted to rejoice in his light;* you were very proud that you had such a man among you. You were willing to *dance*, and make a noise about this light, as boys about a bonfire." 2. It was but *transient*, and soon over: "You were fond of him for *a season*, as little children are fond of a new thing, but soon grew weary of him, and said that *he had a devil*, and now you have him in prison." It is common for forward and noisy professors to cool and fall off. These here rejoiced in John's light, but never walked in it. Christ mentions their respect to John, to *condemn* them for their present opposition to himself. If they had continued their veneration for John they would have embraced Christ.

3. Christ's own works witnessed to him (*v.* 36): *I have a testimony greater than that of John;* for *if we believe the witness of men, the witness of God is greater*, 1 John v. 9. We must be glad of all the supports that offer themselves for the confirmation of our faith, though they may not amount to a demonstration; we have occasion for them all. Now this greater testimony was that of the *works* which *his Father had given him to finish.* In general the whole course of his life and ministry. All that work of which he said when he died, *It is finished*; all he said and did was *holy* and *heavenly*, and a divine purity, power and grace shone in it, proving abundantly that he was *sent of God*. In particular, the miracles he wrought for the proof of his divine mission witnessed of him. Now it is here said, (1) That these works were *given him by the Father*, that is, he was both *appointed* and *empowered* to work them. (2) They were given to him to *finish*; and his finishing them proves a divine power. (3) These works did *bear witness of him*, did prove that he was sent of God. That the Father had sent him as *a Father*, not as a master sends his servant on an errand, but as a father sends his son to take possession for himself.

4. He produces, more fully than before, his Father's testimony concerning him (*v.* 37): *The Father that sent me hath borne witness of me.* God was pleased to bear witness of his Son himself by a voice from heaven at his baptism (Matt. iii. 17): *This is my beloved Son.* Those whom God *sends* he will *bear witness* of; where he gives a commission, he will not fail to seal it. Where God demands belief, he will not fail to give sufficient *evidence*, as he has done concerning Christ. If God himself thus bore witness of Christ, how came it to pass that he was not universally received by the Jewish nation and their rulers? To this Christ here answers that it was for two reasons: (1) Because they were not acquainted with such extraordinary revelations of God and his will: *You have neither heard his voice at any time, nor seen his shape*, or *appearance*. They showed themselves to be as ignorant of God as we are of a man we never either saw or heard. Ignorance of God is the true reason of men's rejecting the record he has given concerning his Son. (2) Because they were not affected with the ordinary ways by which God had revealed himself to them: *You have not his word abiding in you*, v. 38. *First*, The word of God was not in them; it was *among them*, but not *in them*, in their hearts: not ruling in their souls, but only shining in their eyes and sounding in their ears. What did it avail them that they had the oracles of God *committed* to them (Rom. iii. 2), when they had not these oracles *commanding* in them? If they had, they would readily have embraced Christ. *Secondly*, It did not *abide*. Many have the word of God coming into them, and making some impressions for awhile, but it does not *abide* with them; it is not constantly in them, as a man at home, but only now and then, as a *wayfaring man*. But how did it appear that they *had not the word of God abiding in them?* It appeared by this, *Whom he hath sent, him ye believe not.* The indwelling of the word, and Spirit, and grace of God in us, is best tried by its effects, particularly by our *receiving what he sends*, especially Christ whom he hath sent.

5. The next witness he calls is the Old Testament, and to it he appeals (*v.* 39, &c.): *Search the scriptures.*

(1) This may be read, either, [1] "*You search the scriptures*, and you do well to do so." Christ owns that they did indeed search the scriptures, but it was in search of their *own glory*. It is possible for men to be very studious in the letter of the scripture, and yet to be strangers to the power and influence of it. Or, [2] As we read it: *Search the scriptures.* It was spoken to *them* in the nature of an *appeal*. When appeals are made to the scriptures they must be searched. Search the whole book of scripture *throughout*, compare one passage with another, and explain one by another. We must likewise search particular passages *to the bottom*, and see not what they *seem* to say, but what they say *indeed*. It is spoken to *us* in the nature of an *advice*. All those who would *find Christ* must *search the scriptures*, which denotes, 1. *Diligence* in seeking, close application of mind. 2. *Desire* and *design* of finding. We must often ask, "What am I now searching for?" We must search as those that *sink* for gold or silver, or that *dive* for pearl.

(2) Now there are two things which we are here directed to have in our eye, in our searching the scripture: *heaven* our end, and *Christ* our way. [1] *For in them you think you have eternal life.* The scripture assures us of an eternal state set before us, and offers to us an eternal life in that state. But to the Jews Christ saith only, *You think* you have *eternal life* in the scriptures. They looked for it by the bare reading and studying of the scripture. It was a common but corrupt saying among them, *He that has the words of the law has eternal life.* [2] We must *search the scriptures* for *Christ*, as the new and living *way* that

leads to this *end*. These are *they that testify of me*. The scriptures, even those of the Old Testament, *testify* of Christ, and by them God *bears witness* to him. The Jews knew very well that the Old Testament testified of the Messiah, and were critical in their remarks upon the passages that looked that way; and yet were careless, and wretchedly overseen, in the application of them. *Therefore* we must *search the scriptures*, because they testify of Christ; for this is *life eternal, to know him*. Christ is the treasure hid in the field of the scriptures, the water in those wells.

(3) To this testimony he annexes a reproof in four instances.

[1] Their *neglect of him* and his doctrine: "*You will not come to me, that you might have life*," *v.* 40. Their estrangement from Christ was the fault not so much of their *understandings* as of their *wills*. Christ offered life, and it was not accepted. There is *life* to be had with Jesus Christ for poor souls. Life is the perfection of our being, and inclusive of all happiness; and Christ is our life. Those that would have this life must *come* to Jesus Christ for it, we may have it for the coming for. The only reason why sinners die is because they *will not come* to Christ; it is not because they *cannot*, but because they *will* not. They will not be cured, for they will not observe the methods of cure. Those words (*v.* 41), *I receive not honour from men*, come in in a parenthesis, to obviate an objection against him, as if he sought his own glory in obliging all to come to *him*. He did not *covet* nor *court* the applause of men. He *had not* the applause of men. Instead of *receiving honour* from men, he received a great deal of *dishonour* and disgrace from men. He *needed* not the applause of men; it was no addition to his glory.

[2] Their *want of the love of God* (*v.* 42): "*I know you that you have not the love of God in you*." The reason why people *slight Christ* is because they do not *love God*. He charged them (*v.* 37) with *ignorance* of God, and here with want of love to him; *therefore* men have not the love of God because they desire not the knowledge of him. The crime charged upon them: *You have not the love of God in you*. They pretended a great love to God, and thought they proved it by their zeal for the law, and yet they were really without the love of God. There are many who make a great profession of religion who yet show they want the love of God by their neglect of Christ. They hate his holiness and undervalue his goodness. It is the love of God *in us*, that love seated *in the heart*, that God will *accept*; the love *shed abroad* there. The proof of this charge, is given by the personal knowledge of Christ. *I know you*. Christ sees through all our disguises, and can say to each of us, *I know thee*. Christ knows men better than *their neighbours know them*. Christ knows men better than *they know themselves*. We may deceive ourselves, but we cannot deceive him.

[3] Another charge is their readiness to entertain false christs and false prophets (*v.* 43): *I am come in my Father's name, and you receive me not. If another shall come in his own name, him you will receive*. They would not receive Christ, who came in his Father's name. They hearken to everyone that will set up in his own name. They forsake their own mercies, which is bad enough; and it is for *lying vanities*, which is worse. Those are false prophets who come in their own name. It is just with God to suffer those to be deceived with false prophets who receive not the truth. They that shut their eyes against the true light are given up to wander endlessly after *false lights*, and to be led aside after every *ignis fatuus*. They loathe manna, and at the same time *feed upon ashes*.

[4] They are charged with pride and vain-glory, and unbelief, and the effect of them, *v.* 44. They *therefore*

slighted and undervalued Christ because they *admired* and *overvalued themselves*.

First, their ambition of worldly honour. Christ despised it, *v.* 41. They set their hearts upon it: *You receive honour one of another*. "You desire to receive it, and aim at this in all you do. You give honour to others, and applaud them, only that they may return it, and may applaud you. What respect is shown to you you *receive* yourselves, and do not transmit to God."

Secondly, Their neglect of spiritual honour, called here *the honour that comes from God only*. *This honour have all the saints*. All that believe in Christ, through him receive the honour that comes from God. This honour that comes from God we must *seek*; we must account it *our reward*, as the Pharisees accounted the praise of men.

Thirdly, The influence this had upon their infidelity. *How can you believe* who are thus affected? The ambition and affectation of worldly honour are a great hindrance to faith in Christ. How can they believe, the summit of whose ambition is to *make a fair show in the flesh*?

6. The last witness here called is Moses, *v.* 45, &c. Christ here shows them,

(1) That Moses was a witness against the unbelieving Jews: *There is one that accuses you, even Moses*. This may be understood either, [1] As showing the difference between the law and the gospel. Moses, that is, the law, *accuses you*, for by the law is the knowledge of sin; it *condemns* you. But it is not the design of Christ's gospel to *accuse* us: *Think not that I will accuse you*. He came to be an advocate, not an accuser; to reconcile God and man. Or, [2] As showing the manifest unreasonableness of their infidelity: "Think not that I will appeal from your bar to God's and challenge you to answer there for what you do against me, as injured innocency usually does." Instead of *accusing* his crucifiers to his Father, he prayed, *Father, forgive them*. Nor let them mistake concerning Moses, as if he would stand by them in rejecting Christ; no, *There is one that accuses you, even Moses in whom you trust*. The Jews *trusted* in Moses, and thought their having his laws and ordinances would save them. Those that confide in their privileges will find that those very privileges will be witnesses against them.

(2) That Moses was a witness for Christ and to his doctrine (*v.* 46, 47): *He wrote of me*. The ceremonies of the law of Moses were *figures of him that was to come*. Christ here shows that Moses was so far from writing against Christ that he wrote *for him*, and *of him*. Christ here charges it on the Jews that they *did not believe Moses*. He had said (*v.* 45) that they *trusted* in Moses, they trusted to his name, but they did not receive his doctrine in its true sense and meaning. He proves this charge from their disbelief of him: *Had you believed Moses, you would have believed me*. Many say that they believe, whose actions give their words the lie. Those who rightly believe one part of scripture will receive every part. From their disbelief of Moses he infers that it was not strange that they rejected him: *If you believe not his writings, how shall you believe my words?* "If you do not believe sacred *writings*, those oracles which are in black and white, which is the most certain way of conveyance, *how shall you believe my words*, words being usually less regarded? If you believe not what Moses spoke and wrote of me, how shall you believe me and my mission?" If we admit not the premises, how shall we admit the conclusion. If therefore we believe not the divine inspiration of those writings, how shall we receive the doctrine of Christ?

Thus ends Christ's plea for himself. Their *mouths* were *stopped* for the present, and yet their *hearts* were *hardened*.

CHAPTER 6

I. The miracle of the loaves, ver. 1–14. II. Christ's walking upon the water, ver. 15–21. III. The people's flocking after him to Capernaum, ver. 22–25. IV. His conference with them, occasioned by the miracles of the loaves (ver. 26, 27), showing them how they must labour for spiritual food (ver. 28, 29), and what that spiritual food is, ver. 30–59. V. Their discontent at what he said, ver. 60–65. VI. The apostasy of many from him, ver. 66–71.

Verses 1–14

We have here an account of Christ's feeding five thousand men with five loaves and two fishes. It is the only passage of the actions of *Christ's life* that is recorded by all the four evangelists. John relates this, because of the reference the following discourse has to it.

I. The *place* and *time* where and when this miracle was wrought.

1. The country that Christ was in (*v.* 1): *He went over the sea of Galilee.* Christ did not go directly over but made a *coasting* voyage to another place on the same side.

2. The company that he was attended with: *A great multitude followed him, because they saw his miracles, v.* 2. Our Lord Jesus, while he went about *doing good,* lived continually in *a crowd.* Good and useful men must not complain of a *hurry* of business, when they are serving God. It will be time enough to *enjoy ourselves* when we come to that world where we shall *enjoy* God. Christ's miracles drew many *after him* that were not effectually drawn *to him.*

3. Christ's posting himself advantageously to entertain them (*v.* 3): *He went up into a mountain,* and there he *sat with his disciples,* Christ was now driven to be a *field preacher*; but his word was never the worse for that to those who followed him still, not only when he *went out* to a desert place, but when he *went up* to a mountain, though *up-hill* be *against heart.* Whoever would might come, and find him there. He sat *with his disciples.*

4. The time when it was. *After those things.* We are told (*v.* 4) that it was *when the passover was nigh.* It was a custom with the Jews religiously to observe the approach of the passover *thirty days* before. Perhaps, the approach of the passover, when everyone knew Christ would go up to Jerusalem, and be absent for some time, made the multitude attend the more diligently on him. The prospect of losing our opportunities should quicken us to improve them with double diligence.

II. The miracle itself.

1. The notice Christ took of the crowd that attended him (*v.* 5): He *lifted up his eyes,* and *saw a great company come to him.* Christ showed himself pleased with their attendance, and concerned for their welfare, to teach us to *condescend to those of low estate,* and not to *set* those *with the dogs of our flock* whom Christ hath set with the lambs of his.

2. The enquiry he made concerning the way of providing for them. He directed himself to Philip, who had been his disciple from the first, and had seen all his miracles, and particularly that of his turning water into wine. Those that have been witnesses of Christ's works, and have shared in the benefit of them, are inexcusable if they say, *Can he furnish a table in the wilderness?* Philip was of Bethsaida, in the neighbourhood of which town Christ now was, and therefore he was most likely to help them to provision at the best hand. Now Christ asked, *Whence shall we buy bread, that these* may eat? He takes it for granted that they must all *eat with him.* One would think that when he had taught and healed them he had done his part; yet he is solicitous to entertain them. Those that will accept Christ's spiritual gifts, instead of *paying* for them, shall be *paid* for their acceptance of them. His enquiry is, *Whence shall we*

buy bread? He will buy to give, and we must *labour* that we may give, Eph. iv. 28.

3. The design of this enquiry; it was only to try the faith of Philip, *for he himself knew what he would do, v.* 6. When we know not, he *himself knows what he will do.* When Christ is pleased to *puzzle* his people, it is only with a design to *prove* them.

4. Philip's answer to this question: "*Two hundred pennyworth of bread is not sufficient, v.* 7. Neither will the country afford so much bread, nor can we afford to lay out so much money." Philip would go as near hand as he could, would have *everyone to take a little.* Christ might now have said to him, as he did afterwards, Have I *been so long with you, and yet hast thou not known me, Philip?* We are apt thus to distrust God's power when visible and ordinary means fails, that is, to trust him no further than we can see him.

5. The information which Christ received concerning the provision they had. It was Andrew who acquainted Christ with what they had at hand; and in this we may see,

(1) The *strength* of his *love* to those for whom he saw his Master concerned, in that he was willing to bring out all they had, though he knew not but they might want themselves, and anyone would have said, *Charity begins at home.* He did not go about to conceal it. It was *five barley loaves,* and two small fishes. The provision was *coarse* and *ordinary*; they were *barley loaves.* Christ and his disciples were glad of barley-bread. It does not follow hence that we should tie ourselves to such coarse fare, and place religion in it (when God brings that which is finer to our hands, let us receive it, and be thankful). Barley-bread is what Christ *had,* and better than we *deserve.* It was but *short* and *scanty*; there were but *five loaves,* and those so small that one little lad carried them all. There were but two fishes, and those *small* ones. The provision of *bread* was *little,* but that of *fish* was *less* in proportion to it, so that many a bit of dry bread they must eat before they could make a meal. Well, Andrew was willing that the people should have this, as far as it would go. A distrustful fear of wanting ourselves should not hinder us from needful charity to others.

(2) See here the *weakness* of his *faith* in that word, "*But what are they among so many?*" Philip and he had not that actual consideration of the power of Christ which they should have had.

6. The directions Christ gave the disciples to seat the guests (*v.* 10): "*Make the men sit down.*" This was like *sending providence* to *market,* and going to buy without money. (1) The furniture of the dining-room: *there was much grass in that place.* Here was this plenty of grass where Christ was preaching; the gospel brings other blessings along with it. This plenty of grass made the place the more commodious for those that must sit on the ground, and served them for cushions, and, considering what Christ says of the grass of the field (Matt. vi. 29, 30), these excelled those of Ahasuerus: nature's pomp is the most glorious. (2) The number of the guests: *About five thousand*: a great entertainment, representing that of the gospel, which is a *feast for all nations* (Isa. xxv. 6), a feast for all *comers.*

7. The distribution of the provision, *v.* 11. It was done with thanksgiving: *He gave thanks.* We ought to give thanks to God for our food, for it is a mercy to have it. Though our provision be coarse and scanty, though we have neither plenty nor dainty, yet we must give thanks to God for what we have. It was distributed from the hands of Christ by the hands of his disciples, *v.* 11. All our comforts come to us *originally* from the hand of Christ; whoever *brings* them, it is he that *sends* them. It was done to universal satisfaction. They did not everyone take

a little, but all had *as much as they would.* How agreeable this miraculous food may be supposed to have been, above common food. Those whom Christ feeds with the bread of life he does not stint. There were but *two small fishes,* and yet they had *of them* too *as much as they would.* Those who call feeding upon fish *fasting,* reproach the entertainment Christ here made, which was a *full feast.*

8. The care that was taken of the broken meat. The orders Christ gave concerning it (*v.* 12): *When they were filled* Christ *said to the disciples, Gather up the fragments.* We must always take care that we make no waste of any of God's good creatures; for the grant we have of them is with this proviso, *wilful waste only excepted.* It is just with God to bring us to the want of that which we make waste of. When we are filled we must remember that others want, and we may want. Those that would have wherewith to be *charitable* must be *provident.* Christ did not order the broken meat to be gathered up till all were filled; we must not begin to hoard and lay up till all is laid out that ought to be. The observance of these orders (*v.* 13): *They filled twelve baskets with the fragments,* which was an evidence not only of the *truth* of the miracle, that they were fed, but of the *greatness* of it; they were not only filled, but there was all this over and above. See how large the divine bounty is; bread enough, and to spare, in our Father's house. The fragments filled twelve baskets, one for each disciple; they were thus repaid with interest for their willingness to part with what they had for public service.

III. Here is the influence which this miracle had upon the people (*v.* 14): *They said, This is of a truth that prophet.* Even the vulgar Jews with great assurance expected the Messiah to come into the world, and to be a *great prophet.* The Pharisees despised them as *not knowing the law;* but, it should seem, they knew more of him that is the *end of the law* than the Pharisees did. The miracles which Christ wrought did clearly demonstrate that he was the *Messiah* promised, a teacher come from God, the great prophet. There were many who were convinced he was that prophet that should come into the world who yet did not cordially receive his doctrine. It is possible for men to acknowledge that Christ is that prophet, and yet to turn a deaf ear to him.

Verses 15–21

I. Christ's retirement from the multitude.

1. What induced him to retire; because he perceived that those who acknowledged him to be that prophet would come, and *take him by force, to make him a king, v.* 15. Now here we have an instance,

(1) Of the irregular zeal of some of Christ's followers; nothing would serve but they would make him *a king.* This was *an act of zeal* for the honour of Christ. They were concerned to see so great a benefactor to the world so little esteemed in it; and therefore they would make him a king. Those whom Christ has feasted with the royal dainties of heaven should, in return for his favour, make him *their* king, and set him upon the throne in their souls. It was an *irregular* zeal. It was grounded upon a mistake concerning the nature of Christ's kingdom, as if it were to be *of this world,* and he must appear with outward pomp. Such a king as this they would make him, which was as great a disparagement to his glory as it would be to lacker gold or paint a ruby. Right notions of Christ's kingdom would keep us to right methods for advancing it. It was excited by the love of the flesh; they would make *him* their king who could feed them so plentifully without their toil, and save them from the curse of *eating their bread in the sweat of their face.* It was intended to carry on a *secular* design; they hoped this might be a fair

opportunity of shaking off the Roman yoke. Thus is religion often prostituted to a secular interest, and Christ is served only to *serve a turn. Jesus is usually sought after for something else, not for his own sake.* It was contrary to the mind of our Lord Jesus himself; for they would take him *by force,* whether he would or no.

(2) Of the humility of the Lord Jesus, that he *departed;* so far was he from countenancing the design that he effectually quashed it. Herein he has left a testimony against ambition and affectation of worldly honour. Let us not then covet to be the *idols of the crowd,* nor be *desirous of vain-glory.* It is a testimony also against faction and sedition, treason and rebellion, and whatever tends to disturb the peace of kings and provinces. *Whither* he retired: *He departed again into a mountain, into the* mountain, the mountain where he had preached (*v.* 3), and then returned to it alone, to be private. Christ chose sometimes to be alone for the more free converse with God, and our own souls are *never less alone, than when alone.*

II. The disciples' distress at sea.

1. Here is their *going down to the sea* in a ship (*v.* 16, 17): *When even was come,* and they had done their day's work, it was time to look homeward, and therefore they went aboard, and set sail for Capernaum.

2. Here is the *stormy wind* arising. They had lately been feasted at Christ's table; but after the sunshine of comfort expect a storm. *It was now dark.* Sometimes the people of God are in trouble, and cannot see their way out; in the dark concerning the cause of their trouble, concerning the design and tendency of it, and what the issue will be. Jesus *was not come to them.* The absence of Christ is the great aggravation of the troubles of Christians. The *sea rose by reason of a great wind.* It was calm and fair when they put to sea, but it arose when they were *at sea.* In times of tranquillity we must prepare for trouble, for it may arise when we little think of it. Clouds and darkness sometimes surround the children of the light, and of the day.

3. Here is Christ's seasonable approach to them, *v.* 19. *They had rowed about twenty-five or thirty furlongs.* And, when they were got off a good way at sea, they *see Jesus walking on the sea.* The power Christ has over the laws and customs of nature. Christ walked *upon* the water as upon dry land. The concern Christ has for his disciples in distress: *He drew nigh to the ship.* He will not leave them comfortless when they seem to be *tossed with tempests* and *not comforted.* The relief Christ gives to his disciples in their fears. They *were afraid,* more afraid of an apparition (for so they supposed him to be) than of the winds and waves. When they thought a demon haunted them, they were more terrified than they had been while they saw nothing in it but what was natural. Our real distresses are often much increased by our imaginary ones. We are often not only *worse frightened than hurt,* but *then* most *frightened* when we are ready to be *helped.* How affectionately did Christ silence their fears with that compassionate word (*v.* 20), *It is I, be not afraid!* Nothing more powerful to comfort saints than this, "*I am Jesus whom thou lovest;* be not afraid of me, nor of the storm." When trouble is nigh Christ is nigh.

4. Here is their speedy arrival at the port they were bound for, *v.* 17. They *welcomed* Christ into the ship; they *willingly received him.* Christ's absenting himself for a time is but so much the more to *endear himself,* at his return, to his disciples. Christ brought them safely to the shore: *Immediately the ship was at the land whither they went.* The ship of the church may be much shattered and distressed, yet it shall come safe to the harbour at last. The disciples

had rowed hard, but could not make their point till they had got Christ in the ship, and then the work was *done suddenly*. If we have received Christ Jesus the Lord, though the night be dark and the wind high, yet we may comfort ourselves with this, that we shall be at shore shortly, and are nearer to it than we think we are.

Verses 22–27

I. The careful enquiry which the people made after Christ, *v.* 23, 24. They saw Christ retire to the mountain. They way-laid his return, and *the day following*,

1. They were *much at a loss* for him. He was gone, and they knew not what was become of him. They saw there was *no boat there* but that in which the disciples went off. They observed also that *Jesus did not go with his disciples*, but that they went off alone.

2. They were very *industrious in seeking* him. They searched the places thereabouts, and when *they saw that Jesus was not there, nor his disciples*, they resolved to search elsewhere. Those whom Christ has feasted with the bread of life should have their souls carried out in earnest desires towards him. Much would have more, in communion with Christ. They resolved to go to Capernaum in quest of him. Thither his disciples were gone; and they knew he would not be long absent from *them*. Providence favoured them with an opportunity of going thither, for there came *other boats from Tiberias*, nigh to the place where they did *eat bread*. Those that in sincerity seek Christ are commonly owned and assisted by Providence in those pursuits. The evangelist adds, *After that the Lord had given thanks*, v. 11. So much were the disciples affected with their Master's giving thanks that they could never forget the impressions made upon them by it. This was the grace and beauty of that meal, and made it remarkable; their hearts burned within them.

3. *They also took shipping, and came to Capernaum, seeking for Jesus.* Their convictions being strong, and their desires warm, they followed him. Good motions are often crushed, and come to nothing, for want of being *prosecuted* in *time*. They came to Capernaum, and, for aught that appears, had a *calm* and *pleasant* passage, while his sincere disciples had a *rough* and *stormy* one. It is not strange if it fare worst with the best men in this evil world. They *came, seeking Jesus*.

II. The success of this enquiry: *They found him on the other side of the sea*, v. 25. It is worth while to cross a sea to seek Christ, if we may but find him at last. These people appeared afterwards to be unsound, and not actuated by any good principle, and yet were thus zealous. If men have *no more* to show for their love to Christ than their running after sermons and prayers, and their pangs of affection to good preaching, they have reason to suspect themselves no better than this *eager crowd*. But though these people were no better principled, and Christ knew it, yet he was willing to be found of them.

III. The question they put to him: *Rabbi, when camest thou hither?* It should seem by *v.* 59 that they found him *in the synagogue*. There they found him, and all they had to say to him was, *Rabbi, when camest thou hither?* Their enquiry refers not only to the *time*, but to the *manner*, of his conveying himself thither; not only *When*, but "*How* camest thou hither?" They were curious in asking concerning Christ's motions, but not solicitous to observe their own.

IV. The answer Christ gave them, such an answer as their case required.

1. He discovers the *corrupt principle* they *acted from* in following him (*v.* 26): "*Verily, verily, I say unto you. You seek me;* that is well, but it is not from a good principle." Christ knows not only *what*

we do, but *why* we do it. *Not because you saw the miracles*. It was for their own bellies' sake: *Because you did eat of the loaves, and were filled;* not because he taught them, but because he fed them. He had given them a *full* meal's meat: *They did eat, and were filled;* and some of them perhaps were so poor that they had not known of a long time before now what it was to have enough, to eat and leave. A *cheap* meal's meat, that cost them nothing. Many follow Christ for *loaves*, and not for *love*. These people *complimented* Christ with Rabbi, yet he told them thus faithfully of their hypocrisy; his ministers must hence learn not to flatter those that flatter them, but to give faithful reproofs where there is cause for them.

2. He directs them to better principles (*v.* 27): *Labour for that meat which endures to everlasting life*. His design is,

(1) To moderate our worldly pursuits: *Labour not for the meat that perishes*. We must not make the things of this world our chief care and concern. The things of the world are *meat that perishes*. Worldly wealth, honour, and pleasure, are *meat*; they *feed the fancy* (and many times this is all) and *fill the belly*. These are things which men *hunger* after as *meat*. Those that have the largest share of them are not sure to have them while they live, but are sure to leave them and lose them when they die. It is therefore folly for us inordinately to labour after them. We must not make these perishing things our *chief good*.

(2) To quicken and excite our gracious pursuits: "*Labour for that meat* which belongs to the soul." It is *unspeakably desirable*: It is meat which *endures to everlasting life*; it is a happiness which will last as long as we must, which not only itself endures eternally, but will nourish us up to everlasting life. It is *undoubtedly attainable*. It is that *which the Son of man shall give*. First, Who gives this meat: the Son of man, who has power to give eternal life, with all the means of it. We are told to *labour for it*, as if it were to be got by our own industry, and sold upon that valuable consideration. But, when we have laboured ever so much for it, we have not merited it as our *hire*, but the Son of man *gives it*. And what more free than gift? Secondly, What authority he has to give it; for *him has God the Father sealed*. He has *sealed him*, that is, has given him full authority to deal between God and man, as God's *ambassador* to man and man's *intercessor* with God, and has proved his commission by miracles.

Verses 28–59

He gave them leave to ask him questions, and did not resent the interruption as an affront. Those that would be apt to teach must be swift to hear, and study to answer.

I. They enquire what work they must do, and he answers them, *v.* 28, 29. Their *enquiry* was *pertinent* enough (*v.* 28): *What shall we do, that we may work the works of God?* A humble serious question, showing them to be, at least for the present, in a good mind, and willing to know and do their duty. They were convinced that those who would obtain this everlasting meat, (1) Must aim to do something great. Those who *look high* in their expectations, must *aim high* in those endeavours, and study to *do the works of God*, distinguished from the works of worldly men in their worldly pursuits. It is not enough to speak the words of God, but we must do the works of God. (2) Must be willing to do anything: *What shall we do?* Lord, I am ready to do whatever thou shalt appoint. Christ's answer was plain enough (*v.* 29): *This is the work of God that ye believe*. The work of faith is the work of God. They enquire after the *works* of God (in the plural number), being careful about *many things*; but Christ directs them to the one thing needful; that *you believe*. Without faith you cannot please God. That faith is the work of God which closes with Christ; to *rest* upon him, and *resign ourselves* to him.

II. Christ having told them that the *Son of man* would *give them this meat*, they enquire concerning him.

1. Their enquiry is after *a sign* (v. 30): *What sign showest thou?* Thus far they were right, that, since he required them to give him *credit*, he should produce his *credentials*. But *herein* they missed it,

(1) That they overlooked the many miracles which they had seen wrought by him. Is this a time of day to ask, "What sign showest thou?" especially at Capernaum, where he had done so *many mighty works*. Were not these very persons but the other day miraculously fed by him? None so blind as they that will not see.

(2) That they preferred the miraculous feeding of Israel in the wilderness before all the miracles Christ wrought (v. 31): *Our fathers did eat manna in the desert*. They quote a scripture for it: *He gave them bread from heaven*. What a good use might be made of this story to which they here refer! Yet see how these people perverted it, and made an ill use of it. Christ reproved them for their fondness of the miraculous bread, and bade them not set their hearts upon *meat which perisheth*. Under colour of *magnifying* the miracles of Moses, they tacitly *undervalue* this miracle of Christ. Christ fed them but once, and then reproved those who followed him in hope to be still fed. Moses fed his followers forty years, and miracles were not their rarities, but their daily bread: Christ fed them with bread out of *the earth*, barley-bread, and fishes out of *the sea*; but Moses fed Israel with bread *from heaven*, angel's food. Thus big did these Jews talk of the *manna* which *their fathers did eat*; but their fathers had slighted it, and called it *light bread*, Num. xxi. 5. Thus apt are we to slight and overlook the appearances of God's power and grace in our own times, while we pretend to admire the wonders of which *our fathers told us*.

2. Here is Christ's reply to this enquiry. It was true that their fathers did eat *manna* in the desert. But, it was not Moses that gave it to them, he was but the instrument, and therefore they must look beyond him to God. Moses gave them not either *that* bread or *that* water. He *informs* them concerning the *true* manna: *But my Father giveth you the true bread from heaven*; the *bread from heaven* is *now given*, not to *your fathers*, but *to you*, for whom the *better things were reserved*: he is *now giving* you that *bread from heaven*, which is *truly* so called.

III. Christ, having replied to their enquiries, takes further occasion to discourse of *himself* under the similitude of *bread*, and of *believing* under the similitude of *eating and drinking*; to which, together with his putting both together in the *eating* of *his flesh* and *drinking* of his *blood*, and with the remarks made upon it by the hearers, the rest of this conference may be reduced.

1. Christ having spoken of *himself* as the great *gift of God*, and the *true bread* (v. 32), largely *explains* and *confirms* this. He here shows that he is the *true bread*; this he repeats again and again, v. 33, 35, 48–51. Observe, (1) That Christ is *bread*, is that to the soul which bread is to the body; *it is the staff of life*. Our bodies could better live without food than our souls without Christ. (2) That he is the *bread of God* (v. 33), divine bread; the bread of God's family, his *children's bread*. (3) That he is the *bread of life* (v. 35, and again, v. 48), *that* bread of life. Christ is the bread of life, for he is the fruit of the *tree of life*. He is the *living bread* (so he explains himself, v. 51): *I am the living bread*. Bread is itself a dead thing, but Christ is himself *living bread*, and

nourishes by his own power. Christ is ever living, everlasting bread. The doctrine of Christ crucified is now as strengthening and comforting to a believer as ever it was. *He gives life unto the world* (v. 33). The *manna* did only preserve and support life. Christ *gives* life to those that were dead in sin. The manna was ordained only for the life of the Israelites, but Christ is given for the *life of the world*. (4) That he is the *bread which came down from heaven*; this is often repeated here, v. 33, 50, 51, 58. This denotes, the divinity of Christ's person; the divine original of all that good which flows to us through him. (5) That he is *that bread* of which the *manna* was a type and figure (v. 58), the true bread, v. 32. There was *manna* enough for them all; so in Christ a fulness of grace for all believers; he that *gathers much* of this *manna* will have none to spare when he comes to use it, and he that gathers little, when his grace comes to be perfected in glory, shall find that *he has no lack*. He here shows what his undertaking was, giving us an account of his business among men, v. 38–40. He came from heaven upon his Father's business (v. 38), not to *do his own will, but the will of him that sent him*. He *came from heaven*; we may well ask with wonder, "What moved him to such an expedition?" Here he tells us that he came to do, not *his own will*, but the will of his Father. "I am come to *do the will of him that sent me*." He came into the world as God's great agent and the world's great physician. The scope of his whole life was to glorify God and do good to men. He acquaints us, in particular, with that will of the Father which he came to do.

First, The *private instructions* given to Christ to save all the chosen remnant; and this is the *covenant of redemption* between the Father and the Son (v. 38): *This is the Father's will, who hath sent me; that of all whom he hath given me I should lose none*. There is a certain number of the children of men *given* by the Father to Jesus Christ, to be his care, and so to be to him for a name and a praise. Those whom God chose to be the objects of his special love he lodged as a trust in the hands of Christ. Jesus Christ has undertaken that he will *lose none* of those that were thus *given him* of the Father. Christ's undertaking for those that are given him extends to the resurrection of their bodies. *I will raise it up again at the last day*. Christ's undertaking will never be accomplished till the resurrection. The spring and original of all this is the *sovereign will of God*.

Secondly, The *public instructions* which were to be given to the children of men, upon what terms, they might obtain salvation by Christ; and this is the *covenant of grace* between God and man. Who the particular persons were that were given to Christ is a *secret*. Though their names are concealed, their characters are published. An offer is made that by it those that were given to Christ might be brought to him (v. 40): "*This is the will of him that sent me, that every one that sees the Son, and believes on him, may have everlasting life, and I will raise him up*." Is it not reviving to hear this? *Eternal life* may be had, if it be not our own fault. The crown of glory is set before us as the prize of our high calling, which we may run for and obtain. Every one may have it. This everlasting life is sure to all those who believe in Christ. He that *sees the Son*, and *believes on him*, shall be saved. I rather understand *seeing* here to mean the same thing with *believing*. Everyone that *sees the Son*, that is, *believes on him*, sees him with an eye of faith. It is not a *blind* faith that Christ requires, that we should be willing to have our *eyes put out*, and then follow him, but that we should *see him*, and see what ground we go upon in our faith. Those who believe in Jesus Christ, shall be raised up by his power at the last day. He had it in charge as his Father's will (*v.* 39), and here he solemnly makes it his own undertaking: *I will raise him up.*

2. Now Christ discoursing thus concerning himself, as the *bread of life* that came down from heaven, let us see what remarks his hearers made upon it.

(1) When they heard of such a thing as the *bread of God*, which *gives life*, they heartily prayed for it (*v.* 34): *Lord, evermore give us this bread.* I take this request to be made, though ignorantly, yet honestly, and to be well meant. General and confused notions of divine things produce some kind of desires towards them. Those who have an indistinct knowledge of the things of God, who see men as trees walking, make, as I may call them, *inarticulate* prayers for spiritual blessings. They think the favour of God a *good thing*, and heaven a *fine place*, while they have no value nor desire at all for that holiness which is necessary.

(2) But, when they understood that by this *bread of life* Jesus meant *himself*, then they *despised* it. *They murmured* at him. This comes in immediately after that solemn declaration which Christ had made of God's will and his own undertaking concerning man's salvation (*v.* 39, 40), which certainly were some of the most weighty and gracious words that ever proceeded out of the mouth of our Lord Jesus. One would think that when they heard that God had thus *visited* them, they should have *bowed their heads and worshipped*; but on the contrary, they *murmured*, quarrelled with what Christ said. Many that will not professedly contradict the doctrine of Christ yet say in their hearts that they *do not like it.* That which offended them was Christ's asserting his origin to be *from heaven, v.* 41, 42. How is it that he saith, *I came down from heaven?* That which they thought justified them herein was that they knew his extraction on earth: *Is not this Jesus the son of Joseph, whose father and mother we know?* They took it amiss that he should say that he came down from heaven, when he was *one of them.*

3. Christ, having spoken of faith as the great *work of God* (*v.* 29), discourses largely concerning this work.

(1) He shows what it is to *believe in Christ.* He that *comes to* me is the same with him that *believes in me* (*v.* 35), and again (*v.* 37): *He that comes unto me;* so *v.* 44, 45. Repentance towards God is *coming to him* as our chief good and highest end; and so faith towards our Lord Jesus Christ is coming to him as our prince and Saviour, and our way to the Father. When he was here on earth it was more than barely coming where he was; so it is now more than coming to his word and ordinances. It is to *feed upon Christ* (*v.* 51): *If any man eat of this bread.* The former denotes applying ourselves to Christ; this denotes applying Christ to ourselves.

(2) He shows what is to be got by believing in Christ. What shall we be the better if we *feed upon him*? *Want* and *death* are the chief things we dread. They shall never want, *never hunger, never thirst, v.* 35. Desires they have, earnest desires, but these so abundantly satisfied, that they cannot be called hunger and thirst, which are uneasy and painful. They shall *never die*, not die eternally. He that believes on Christ *has everlasting life* (*v.* 47). Union with Christ and communion with God in Christ are *everlasting life* begun. Whereas they that did *eat manna* died, Christ is such bread as a man may eat of and never die, *v.* 49, 50. [1] The insufficiency of the typical manna: *Your fathers did eat manna in the wilderness, and are dead.* Those that did eat manna, angel's food, died, like other men. Many of them died for their unbelief and murmurings. Their eating manna was no security to *them* from the *wrath of God*, as believing in Christ is to *us.* The rest of them died in a course of nature, and their carcases fell in that

wilderness where they did *eat manna.* Let them not then boast so much of *manna.* [2] The all-sufficiency of the true *manna: This is the bread that cometh down from heaven, that a man may eat thereof and not die. Not die*, that is, not perish, not come short of the heavenly Canaan. *If any man eat of this bread, he shall live for ever, v.* 51. This is the meaning of this *never dying*: though he go down to *death*, he shall pass through it to that world where there shall be *no more death.* To *live for ever* is not to *be* for ever, but to be *happy* for ever.

(3) He shows what encouragements we have to believe in Christ. Christ here speaks of some who *had seen him and yet believed not, v.* 36. Faith is not always the effect of sight; the soldiers were eye-witnesses of his resurrection, and yet, instead of *believing* in him, they *belied* him. Two things, to encourage our faith: That the Son will bid all those welcome that come to him (*v.* 37): *Him that cometh to me I will in no wise cast out.* How welcome should this word be to our souls which bids us welcome to Christ! The duty required is a pure gospel duty: to *come to Christ*, that we may come to God by him. His beauty and love must *draw* us to him; sense of need and fear of danger must *drive* us to him; anything to bring us to Christ. The promise is a pure gospel promise: *I will in no wise cast out.* There are two negatives: *I will not, no, I will not.* Much favour is expressed here. We have reason to fear that he should *cast us out.* We may justly expect that he should frown upon us, and shut his doors against us; but he obviates these fears with this assurance, he *will not* do it; will not reject us though we are sinful. More favour is implied than is expressed; when it is said that he will not cast them out the meaning is, He will receive them, and give them all that which they come to him for. That the Father will, without fail, bring all those to him in due time that were given him.

First, He here *assures* us *that* this shall be done: *All that the Father giveth me shall come to me, v.* 37. Christ had complained (*v.* 36) of those who, though they had *seen* him, yet would not believe on him; and then he adds this for *their* conviction and awakening. How can we think that God gave us to Christ if we give ourselves to the world and the flesh? For *his own* comfort and encouragement he adds : *All that the Father gives him shall come to him.* Here we have, (*a*) The election described: *All that the father giveth me*, and all that belongs to them; all their services, all their interests. As all that he has is *theirs*, so all that they have is *his.* God was now about to *give him the heathen for his inheritance* (Ps. ii. 8). And though the Jews, who *saw* him, *believed not* on him, yet these (saith he) shall *come to me*; the other sheep, which are not of this fold, shall be *brought, ch.* x. 15, 16. (*b*) The effect of it secured: *They shall come to me.* This is not in the nature of a *promise*, but a *prediction.* None of them shall be forgotten; not a grain of God's corn shall be lost. They are by nature *alienated* from Christ, and averse to him, and yet *they shall come.* Not, They shall be *driven* to me, but, They shall come freely, shall be made *willing.*

Secondly, How shall those who are given to Christ be brought to him? Two things are to be done in order to it:

a. Their *understandings* shall be *enlightened*; this is promised, *v.* 45, 46. It is written in the prophets, *And they shall be all taught of God; they shall all know me.* In order to our *believing in Jesus Christ*, it is necessary that we be *taught of God.* That there be a *divine revelation made to us.* There are some things which *even nature teaches*, but to bring us to Christ there is need of a higher light. That there be a *divine work wrought in us.* God, in giving us reason, teaches us more than the *beasts of the earth*; but in giving us faith he teaches more than the *natural man.* All that are *genuine,* are *taught of God;* he hath undertaken their education. It follows then, by way of inference from this, that *every man that has heard and learned of the Father comes to Christ, v.* 45. Except God by his grace enlighten our minds and not only *tell* us, that we may *hear,* but teach us, that we may *learn* the truth as it is in Jesus, we shall never be brought to believe in Christ. Those who do not *come to Christ* have never *heard* nor *learned* of the Father; for, if they had, doubtless they would have come to Christ. In vain do men pretend to be *taught of God* if they believe not in Christ. But lest any should dream of a visible appearance of God the Father, he adds (*v.* 46): *Not that any man hath seen the Father.* God, in enlightening men's eyes and teaching them, works in a spiritual way. The Father of spirits hath access to, and influence upon, men's spirits, undiscerned. Those that have not seen his face have felt his power. Those that *learn of the Father* must learn of Christ, who alone hath seen him.

b. Their *wills* shall be *bowed.* In the depraved soul of fallen man there is a rebellion of the will against the right dictates of the understanding. It is therefore requisite that there be a work of grace wrought upon the will, which is here called *drawing* (*v.* 44): *No man can come to me except the Father, who hath sent me, draw him.* The Jews murmured at the doctrine of Christ. Christ said (*v.* 43), "*Murmur not among yourselves;* lay not the fault of your dislike of my doctrine one upon another. Your antipathies to the truths of God are so strong that nothing less than a divine power can conquer them. *No man can come to me except the Father, who hath sent me, draw him,*" *v.* 44. (*a*) The nature of the work: It is *drawing,* which denotes not a *force* put upon the will, but a *change* wrought in the will. A new bias is given to the soul, by which it inclines to God. He that *formed the spirit of man* knows how to new-mould the soul. (*b*) The necessity of it: *No man,* in this weak and helpless state, can come to Christ without it. (*c*) The author of it: The *Father who hath sent me.* The Father would not send him on a fruitless errand. So, having sent Christ to save souls, he sends souls to him to be saved by him. (*d*) The crown and perfection of this work: And *I will raise him up at the last day.* This is four times mentioned in this discourse. If he undertakes this, surely he *can* do anything. Let our expectations be carried out towards a happiness reserved for the *last day.*

4. Christ comes more particularly to show *what of himself* is this bread, *v.* 51–58, where he still prosecutes the metaphor of food. *The bread that I will give is my flesh* (*v.* 51), *the flesh of the Son of man and his blood, v.* 53. *His flesh is meat indeed, and his blood is drink indeed, v.* 53. We must *eat the flesh of the Son of man and drink his blood* (*v.* 53); and again (*v.* 54), *Whoso eateth my flesh and drinketh my blood;* and the same words (*v.* 56, 57), he that *eateth me.*

(1) Let us see how this discourse of Christ was liable to mistake and misconstruction. It was misconstrued by the carnal *Jews* (*v.* 52): *They strove among themselves: How can this man give us his flesh to eat?* Christ spoke (*v.* 51) of giving his flesh *for us,* to suffer and die; but they understood it of his giving it *to us,* to be eaten. It is misunderstood by many who hence infer that, if they take the sacrament when they die, they shall certainly go to heaven.

(2) Let us see how this discourse of Christ is to be understood.

[1] What is meant by the *flesh and blood of Christ.* It is called (*v.* 53), *The flesh of the Son of man, and his blood.* It is said to be *given for the life of the world,* that is, *First, Instead* of the *life of the world,*

which was *forfeited* by sin, Christ gives his own flesh as a ransom. *Secondly,* In *order to* the *life of the world,* to purchase a *general* offer of eternal life to all the world. So that the *flesh and blood* of the Son of man denote Christ and *him crucified,* and the redemption wrought out by him. The promises of the covenant, and eternal life; these are called *the flesh and blood* of Christ, 1. Because they are purchased by the breaking of his body, and the shedding of his blood. 2. Because they are meat and drink to our souls. He had before compared himself to *bread,* which is necessary food; here to *flesh,* which is delicious. It is *meat indeed,* and *drink indeed;* in opposition to the shows and shadows with which the world shams off those that feed upon it.

[2] What is meant by *eating this flesh* and *drinking* this *blood.* It is certain that it means neither more nor less than believing in Christ. *Believing in Christ* includes these four things, which *eating and drinking* do: *First,* It implies an *appetite* to Christ. This spiritual eating and drinking begins with *hungering* and *thirsting* (Matt. v. 6): "Give me Christ or else I die." *Secondly,* An *application* of Christ to ourselves. Meat *looked upon* will not nourish us, but meat *fed upon.* We must so accept of Christ as to appropriate him to ourselves. *Thirdly,* A *delight* in Christ and his salvation. The doctrine of Christ crucified must be *meat and drink* to us, most pleasant and delightful. *Fourthly,* A *derivation of nourishment* from him and a dependence upon him for the support and comfort of our spiritual life, and the strength, growth, and vigour of the new man. It is to live upon him as we do upon our meat. When afterwards he would institute some outward sensible signs, by which to represent our *communicating* of the benefits of his death, he chose those of *eating* and *drinking,* and made them *sacramental* actions.

(3) Having thus explained the general meaning of this part of Christ's discourse, the particulars are reducible to two heads:

[1] The *necessity* of our *feeding upon Christ* (*v.* 53): *Except you eat the flesh of the Son of man, and drink his blood, you have no life in you. First,* It is a certain sign that you *have no* spiritual *life* in you if you have no *desire* towards Christ, nor *delight* in him. If the soul does not *hunger* and *thirst,* certainly it does not *live. Secondly,* It is certain that you *can have* no spiritual life, unless you derive it from Christ by faith; separated from him you can do nothing. Our bodies may as well live without meat as our souls without Christ.

[2] The *benefit* and *advantage* of it, in two things: *First,* We shall be *one with Christ* (*v.* 56): *He that eats my flesh, and drinks my blood, he dwelleth in me, and I in him.* By faith we have a close and intimate union with Christ; he is *in us,* and we *in him.* Such is the union between Christ and believers that he shares in their griefs, and they share in his graces and joys; he *sups* with them upon their bitter herbs, and *they with him* upon his *rich dainties.*

Secondly, We shall *live,* shall live eternally, *by him.* We shall *live by him* (*v.* 57): *As the living Father hath sent me, and I live by the Father, so he that eateth me, even he shall live by me.* True believers receive this divine life by virtue of their union with Christ. *He that eateth me,* or feeds on me, *even he shall live by me:* those that live *upon* Christ shall live *by* him. Because he lives, we shall live also. We shall live *eternally* by him (*v.* 54): *Whoso eateth my flesh, and drinketh my blood, he hath eternal life.* He shall live *for ever, v.* 58.

Lastly, The historian concludes with an account *where* Christ had this discourse with the Jews (*v.* 59): *In the synagogue as he taught.* This was that in his discourse which was new. Christ pleaded this upon his trial (ch. xviii. 20): *I ever taught in the synagogue.*

Verses 60-71

We have here an account of the effects of Christ's discourse.

I. To some it was a *savour of death unto death*; not only to the Jews, but even to many of *his disciples*.

1. Their murmurings at the doctrine they heard (*v.* 60); not a few, but many of them, were offended at it. See what they say to it (*v.* 60): *This is a hard saying, who can hear it?* They do not like it themselves. Now, when they found it a hard saying, if they had humbly begged of Christ to have *declared unto them this parable*, he would have opened it, and their understandings too. They think it impossible that anyone else should like it: "*Who can hear it?* Surely none can." Thus the scoffers at religion are ready to undertake that all the intelligent part of mankind concur with them. Thanks be to God, thousands have *heard* these sayings of Christ, and have found them not only easy, but pleasant.

2. Christ's animadversions upon their murmurings.

(1) He well enough knew their murmurings, *v.* 61. Christ *knew* them; he saw them, he heard them. He knew it *in himself*, not by any information given him, but by his own divine omniscience. Thoughts are words to Christ; we should therefore take heed not only what we say and do, but what we think.

(2) He well enough knew how to answer them: "*Doth this offend you?*" We may justly wonder that so much offence should be taken at the doctrine of Christ for so little cause. Christ speaks of it here with wonder: "*Doth this offend you?*" He gives them a hint of his ascension into heaven, as that which would give an irresistible evidence of the truth of his doctrine (*v.* 62): *What and if you shall see the Son of man ascend up where he was before?* If this be so hard a saying that you cannot hear it, how will you digest it when I tell you of my returning *to* heaven, whence I came down? Those who stumble at smaller difficulties should consider how they will get over greater. "You think I take too much upon me when I say, *I came down from heaven*, for it was with this that you quarrelled (*v.* 42); but will you think so when you see me return to heaven?" Christ did often refer himself thus to *subsequent* proofs. He gives them a general key to this and all such parabolical discourses, teaching them that they are to be understood spiritually: *It is the spirit that quickeneth, the flesh profiteth nothing, v.* 63. The bare participation of ordinances, unless the Spirit of God work with them, and quicken the soul by them, *profits nothing*; the word and ordinances, if the Spirit works with them, arc as food to a living man, if not, they are as food to a dead man. The doctrine of eating Christ's flesh and drinking his blood, if it be understood literally, *profits nothing.* The spiritual sense of meaning of it quickens the soul, makes it *alive* and *lively: The words that I speak unto you, they are spirit, and they are life.* To believe that Christ died for me, to derive from that doctrine strength and comfort, this is the *spirit and life* of that saying, and, construing it thus, it is an excellent saying. The reason why men *dislike* Christ's sayings is because they *mistake* them. The literal sense of a parable does us no good, we are never the wiser for it. *The flesh profits nothing;* but the *Spirit quickeneth.* They found fault with Christ's sayings, whereas the fault was in themselves; it is only to *sensual* minds that spiritual things are *senseless* and *sapless,* spiritual minds *relish* them, see 1 Cor. ii. 14, 15. He gives them an intimation of his *knowledge of them,* and that he had expected no better from them, though they called themselves his disciples, *v.* 64, 65.

First, They did not *believe his report.* Among those who are *nominal Christians,* there are many who are *real infidels.* The unbelief of hypocrites is naked and open before the eyes of Christ. He *knew from the beginning* who they were that *believed,* and who of the twelve should betray him; who were sincere, as Nathanael (*ch.* i. 47), and who were not. It is Christ's prerogative to *know the heart;* he knows who they are that *believe not,* but dissemble in their profession. If we pretend to judge men's hearts, we step into Christ's throne. We are often deceived in men, and see cause to change our sentiments of them.

Secondly, The reason why they did not believe his report was because the *arm of the Lord* was not *revealed* to them (*v.* 65): *Therefore said I unto you that no man can come to me, except it be given unto him of my Father;* referring to *v.* 44. There he had said that none could *come to him, except the Father draw him;* here he saith, *except it be given him of my Father,* which shows that God *draws* souls by giving them grace and strength, and a heart to come.

3. We have here their final apostasy from Christ hereupon: *From that time many of his disciples went back, and walked no more with him, v.* 66: the *backsliding* of these *disciples.* They had entered themselves in Christ's school, but they *went back,* did not only play truant for once, but took leave of him. Here were *many* that *went back.* It is often so; when some backslide many backslide with them; the disease is infectious. The occasion of this backsliding: *From that time,* from the time that Christ preached this comfortable doctrine, that he is the *bread of life,* and that those who by faith feed *upon him* shall live *by him.* The corrupt and wicked heart of man often makes that an occasion of offence which is indeed matter of the greatest comfort. That which is the undoubted word and truth of Christ must be faithfully delivered, whoever may be offended at it. Men's humours must be captivated to God's word, and not God's word accommodated to men's. The degree of their apostasy: *They walked no more with him,* returned no more to him and attended no more upon his ministry.

II. This discourse was to others a *savour of life unto life. Many went back,* but, thanks be to God, all did not.

1. The affectionate question which Christ put to the twelve (*v.* 67): *Will you also go away?* He saith nothing to those who went back. It was no great *loss* of those whom he never *had;* lightly come, lightly go; but he takes this occasion to speak to the twelve, to confirm them: *Will you also go away?* (1) "It is *at your choice* whether you will or no; if you will forsake me, now is the time, when so many do." Christ will detain none with him against their wills; his soldiers are volunteers, not pressed men. The twelve had now had time enough to try how they liked Christ and his doctrine. He here allows them a power of revocation, and leaves them at their liberty. (2) "It is *at your peril* if you do go away." They have not been so intimate with me as you have been, nor received so many favours from me; they are gone, but will *you* also go? The nearer we have been to Christ and the longer we have been with him, the more mercies we have received from him the greater will be our sin if we desert him. (3) "I have reason *to think you will not. I hope better things of you,* for *you are they that have continued with me,*" Luke xxii. 28. Christ and believers know one another too well to part upon every displeasure.

2. The believing reply which Peter, in the name of the rest, made to this question, *v.* 68, 69. Peter was upon all occasions the *mouth of the rest,* not so much because he had more of his Master's ear than they, but because he had more tongue of his own; and what he said was sometimes approved and sometimes reprimanded (Matt. xvi. 17, 23)—the common lot of those who are swift to speak. Here is a good resolution to adhere to Christ: "*Lord, to whom shall we go?* No, Lord, we like our choice too well

to change." Those who leave Christ would do well to consider to whom they will go. "*Whither shall we go?* Shall we make our court to the world? It will certainly *deceive* us. Shall we return to sin? It will certainly *destroy* us. Shall we leave the *fountain of living waters* for *broken cisterns*?" The disciples resolve to continue their pursuit of life and happiness, and will adhere to Christ as their guide. "If ever we find the way to happiness, it must be in following thee." Let those who find fault with this religion find a better before they quit it. Here is a good reason for this resolution. It was not the inconsiderate resolve of a blind affection, but the result of mature deliberation. The disciples were resolved never to go away from Christ because of the *advantage* they promised themselves by him: *Thou hast the words of eternal life.* The word of his doctrine showed the way to *eternal life,* and directed us what to do, that we might inherit it. His *having the words of eternal life* is the same with his having *power to give eternal life.* He had in the foregoing discourse assured *eternal life* to his followers; these disciples fastened upon this plain saying, and therefore resolved to stick to him, when the others overlooked this, and fastened upon the *hard sayings,* and therefore forsook him. Though we cannot account for every mystery, every obscurity, in Christ's doctrine, yet we know that it is the word of eternal life, and therefore must live and die by it. Because of the assurance they had concerning him (*v.* 69): *We believe, and are sure, that thou art that Christ.* The *doctrine* they believed: that this Jesus was the Messiah promised to the fathers, and that he was not a mere man, but the Son of the living God. The *degree* of their faith: it rose up to a full assurance: *We are sure.* When we have so strong a faith in the gospel of Christ as boldly to venture our souls *upon it,* then, and not till then, we shall be willing to venture everything else for it.

3. The melancholy remark which our Lord Jesus made upon this reply of Peter's (*v.* 70, 71): *Have not I chosen you twelve, and one of you is a devil?* And the evangelist tells us whom he meant: *he spoke of Judas Iscariot.* Peter had undertaken for them all that they would be faithful to their Master. Now Christ does not condemn his charity (it is always good to hope the best), but he tacitly corrects his confidence. We must not be too sure concerning any. God knows those that are his; we do not. Hypocrites and betrayers of Christ are no better than devils. Judas, into whose *heart* Satan entered, and filled it, is called a *devil.* Many that are *seeming* saints are *real* devils. It is *strange,* and to be wondered at; *Christ* speaks of it with wonder: *Have not I?* It is *sad,* and to be lamented. The disguises of hypocrites however they may deceive men cannot deceive Christ. Christ's *divine sight,* far better than any *double sight,* can see spirits. There are those who are chosen by Christ to special services who yet prove false to him: *I have chosen you* and yet one of *you* is a devil. In the most *select* societies on this side heaven it is no new thing to meet with those that are corrupt. Of the twelve that were chosen to an intimate conversation with an *incarnate Deity,* one was an *incarnate devil.* The historian lays an emphasis upon this, that Judas was *one of the twelve* that were so dignified and distinguished. Let us not reject the twelve because *one of them is a devil.* There is a society within the veil into which no unclean thing shall enter.

CHAPTER 7

I. Christ's declining for some time to appear publicly in Judæa, ver. 1. II. His design to go up to Jerusalem at the feast of tabernacles, and his discourse with his kindred in Galilee concerning his going up to this feast, ver. 2–13. III. His preaching publicly in the temple at that feast. 1. In the midst of the feast, ver. 14, 15. (1) Concerning his doctrine, ver. 16–18. (2) Concerning the crime of sabbath-breaking laid to his charge, ver. 19–24. (3) Concerning himself, both whence he came and whither he was going, ver. 25–36. 2. On the last day of the feast. (1) His gracious invitation to poor souls to come to him, ver. 37–39. (2) The reception that it met with. [1] Many of the people disputed about it, ver. 40–44. [2] The chief priests would have brought him into trouble for it (ver. 45–49), but were silenced by one of their own court, ver. 50–53.

Verses 1–13

I. The reason given why Christ spent more of his time in Galilee than in Judæa (*v.* 1): *because the Jews,* the people in Judæa and Jerusalem, sought to *kill him,* for curing the impotent man on the sabbath day, *ch.* v. 16. It is not said, He *durst not,* but, He *would not,* walk in Jewry; it was not through fear and cowardice that he declined it, but in *prudence,* because his hour was not yet come. Christ will withdraw from those that drive him from them. In times of imminent peril it is not only *allowable,* but *advisable,* to *withdraw,* and to choose the service of those places which are least perilous, Matt. x. 23. If the providence of God casts persons of *merit* into places of obscurity and little note, it must not be thought strange; it was the lot of our Master himself. He did not sit still in Galilee, but *walked;* he went about doing good. When we cannot do *what* and *where* we *would,* we must do *what* and *where* we *can.*

II. The approach of the *feast of tabernacles* (*v.* 2), one of the three solemnities which called for the personal attendance of all the males at Jerusalem. This feast was still religiously observed. Divine institutions are never antiquated, nor go out of date, by length of time: nor must wilderness mercies ever be forgotten.

III. Christ's discourse with his *brethren.* They interposed to advise him in his conduct.

1. Their ambition and vain-glory in urging him to make a more public appearance than he did: "*Depart hence,*" said they, "*and go into Judæa*" (*v.* 3).

(1) They give two reasons for this advice: That it would be an encouragement to those in and about Jerusalem. They would have had the disciples *there* particularly countenanced, and thought the time he spent among his Galilean disciples wasted and thrown away, and his miracles turning to no account unless those at Jerusalem saw them. That it would be for the advancement of his name, *There is no man that does anything in secret* if he himself *seeks to be known* openly. They took it for granted that Christ sought to make himself known: "*If thou do these things,* venture abroad, and *show thyself to the world.* It is high time to think of being *great.*"

(2) The evangelist notes it is an evidence of their infidelity: *For neither did his brethren believe in him* (*v.* 5). They that hear his word and keep it are the kindred he values. There were those who were akin to Christ according to the flesh who did believe in him, and yet others did not believe in him.

(3) What was there amiss in the advice which they gave him? It was a sign that they *did not believe him* able to guide them, when they did not think him sufficient to guide himself. They discovered a great carelessness about his safety, when they would have him go to Judæa, where they knew the Jews sought to kill him. Perhaps they were weary of his company in Galilee, and this was, in effect, a desire that he would *depart out of their coasts.* They tacitly reproach him as *mean-spirited,* that he durst not trust himself upon the stage of public action, which, if he had any courage and *greatness of soul,* he would do, and not sneak thus and skulk in a corner. They seem to question the truth of the miracles he wrought, in saying, "*If thou do these things,* if they will bear the test of a public scrutiny in the courts above, produce them there." They think Christ altogether such a one as themselves, and as desirous as they to *make a fair show in the flesh.* Self was at the bottom of all;

if he would make himself as great as he might, they, being his kinsmen, should share in his honour. Many go to public ordinances, only to *show themselves,* and all their care is to make a *good appearance.*

2. The prudence and humility of our Lord Jesus, *v.* 6–8. Though there were so many base insinuations in it, he answered them mildly. We should learn of our Master to reply with meekness, and where it is easy to find much amiss, to seem not to see it, and wink at the affront.

(1) He shows the difference between himself and them, in two things: [1] His *time* was *set,* so was not *theirs*: *My time is not yet come, but your time is always ready.* Those who live useless lives have *their time always ready*; they can go and come when they please. But those whose *time* is filled up with *duty* will often find themselves *straitened,* and they have *not yet time* for that which others can do *at any time.* The confinement of business is a thousand times better than the liberty of idleness. We, who are ignorant and short-sighted, are apt to prescribe to him. The present time is *our* time, but he is fittest to judge, and, it may be, *his time is not yet come.* Therefore wait with patience for *his time.* [2] His *life* was *sought,* so was not *theirs, v.* 7. They, in *showing themselves* to the world, did not expose themselves: "*The world cannot hate you,* for you are *of the world.*" Unholy souls, whom the holy God *cannot love,* the world that lies in wickedness *cannot hate*; but Christ, in showing himself to the world, laid himself open to the greatest danger; for *me it hateth.* Christ was not only *slighted,* but *hated.* But why did the world hate Christ? "Because" (saith he), "*I testify of it, that the works of it are evil.*" The works of an evil world are *evil works*; as the tree is, so are the fruits. It is a great uneasiness and provocation to the world to be convicted of the evil of its works. Whatever is *pretended,* the *real* cause of the world's enmity to the gospel is the testimony it bears against sin and sinners. It is better to incur the world's hatred, by testifying against its wickedness, than gain its good-will by going down the stream with it.

(2) He dismisses them, with a design to stay behind for some time in Galilee (*v.* 8): *Go you up to this feast, I go not up yet.* He allows their going to the feast. He denies them his company. Those who go to ordinances for ostentation, or to serve some secular purpose, go without Christ, and will speed accordingly. If the presence of Christ go not with us, to what purpose should we go up? When we are going to, or coming from, solemn ordinances, it becomes us to be careful what company we *have* and *choose,* lest the coal of good affections be quenched by corrupt communications. *I go not up yet to this feast;* he does not say, I will not go up at all, but not yet. The reason he gives is, *My time is not yet fully come.*

3. Christ's continuance in Galilee till his *full time* was come, *v.* 9. He, saying these things to them, *abode still in Galilee.* He would not depart from his own purpose. It becomes the followers of Christ thus to be *steady,* and not to *use lightness.*

4. His going up to the feast when his time was come. (1) *When* he went: *When his brethren were gone up.* He went up *after them.* His carnal brethren went up *first,* and then he went. It is not, Who comes *first*? that will be the question, but, Who come *fittest*? If we bring our hearts *with us,* it is no matter who gets *before us.* (2) *How* he went, *as if he were hiding himself: not openly, but as it were in secret.* Provided the work of God be done effectually, it is best done when done with *least noise.* We may do the work of God *privately,* and yet not do it *deceitfully.*

5. The great expectation that there was of him among the Jews at Jerusalem, *v.* 11–14. They could not but think of him (*v.* 11): *The Jews sought him at the feast, and said, Where is he?* They hoped the feast would bring him to Jerusalem, and then they should see him. If an opportunity of acquaintance with Christ come to their door, they can like it well enough. They *sought him at the feast.* Those who would *see* Christ at a feast must *seek* him there. Perhaps it was his enemies that were thus waiting an opportunity to seize him. They said, *Where is he?—where is that fellow?* Thus scornfully and contemptibly do they speak of him. When they should have welcomed the feast as an opportunity of serving God, they were glad of it as an opportunity of persecuting Christ. The people differed much in their sentiments concerning him (*v.* 12): *There was much murmuring,* or *muttering,* rather *among the people concerning him.* The enmity of the rulers against Christ caused him to be so much the more talked of. This ground the gospel of Christ has got by the opposition made to it. By being *everywhere spoken against,* it has come to be everywhere *spoken of,* and by this means has been spread the further. This murmuring was not *against* Christ, but *concerning* him; some murmured at the rulers, because they did not countenance and encourage him: others murmured at them, because they did not silence and restrain him. Christ and his religion have been, and will be, the subject of much controversy, and debate, Luke xii. 51, 52. But the noise and rencounter of liberty and business are preferable, surely, to the silence and agreement of a prison. Some said, *He is a good man.* This was a truth, but it was far short of being the *whole truth.* He was the *Son of God.* Many who have no *ill* thoughts of Christ have yet *low* thoughts of him, they do not *say enough.* Even those who would not believe him to be the Messiah could not but own he was a *good man.* Others said, *Nay, but he deceiveth the people*; if this had been true, he had been a very bad man. It must be taken for granted that there was some undiscovered cheat at the bottom, because it was the interest of the chief priests to oppose him and run him down. They were frightened by their superiors from speaking much of him (*v.* 13): *No man spoke openly of him, for fear of the Jews.* Either, they durst not openly speak *well* of him. Or they durst not speak *at all* of him openly. Because nothing could justly be said *against* him, they would not suffer anything to be said *of* him.

Verses 14–36

I. Christ's public preaching in the temple (*v.* 14): He *went up into the temple, and taught.* His sermon is not recorded. But that which is observable here is that it was *about the midst of the feast.* Why did he not go to the temple *sooner,* to preach? Because the people would have more leisure to hear him when they had spent some days in their booths. Because he would choose to appear when both his friends and his enemies had done looking for him. But why did he appear thus publicly now? Surely it was to *shame* his persecutors. By showing that he did not fear them; by taking their work out of their hands. Their office was to teach the people in the temple. But they taught for doctrines the commandments of men, and therefore he goes up to the temple and teaches the people.

II. His discourse with the Jews hereupon.

1. Concerning *his doctrine.*

(1) How the Jews *admired* it (*v.* 15): *They marvelled,* saying, *How knoweth this man letters, having never learned?* Our Lord Jesus was not educated in the schools of the prophets, or at the feet of the rabbin. Having received the Spirit *without measure,* he needed not to receive any knowledge *from man, or by man.* Christ *had letters,* though he had never *learned* them. It is necessary that Christ's ministers should have *learning,* and since they cannot expect to have it by inspiration, they must take pains to get it in an

ordinary way. Christ's having learning, though he had not been taught it, made him truly great and wonderful. Some, it is likely, took notice of it to his honour. Others, probably, mentioned it in disparagement and contempt of him: Whatever he *seems* to have, he cannot really have any true learning, for he was never at the university, nor took his degree. Some perhaps suggested that he had got his learning by magic arts. Since they know not how he could be a scholar, they will think him a conjuror.

(2) What he *asserted* concerning it; three things:

[1] That his *doctrine* is *divine* (v. 16): *My doctrine is not mine, but his that sent me.* They were offended because he undertook to *teach* though he had never learned, in answer to which he tells them that his doctrine was such as was not to be *learned*. It was a *divine revelation*. "*My doctrine is not mine*, but *his that sent me*; it does not centre in myself, nor lead ultimately to myself, but to him that sent me."

[2] That the most competent judges are those that with a sincere and upright heart desire and endeavour to do the will of God (v. 17): *If any man be willing to do the will of God he shall know of the doctrine whether it be of God or whether I speak of myself. First,* What the question is, concerning the doctrine of Christ, *whether it be of God* or no. Christ himself was willing to have his doctrine enquired into, much more should his ministers. *Secondly,* Who are likely to succeed in this search: those that *do the will of God,* at least are desirous to do it. Who they are that *will do the will of God.* Such as are resolved by the grace of God, when they find out what the will of God is, to conform to it. Whence it is that such a one shall know of the truth of Christ's doctrine. Christ has promised to *give knowledge* to such; he hath said, *He shall know.* Those who improve the light they have shall be secured by divine grace. He that is inclined to submit to the rules of the divine law is disposed to admit the rays of divine light.

[3] That hereby it appeared that Christ, as a teacher, did not speak *of himself,* v. 18. See here the character of a deceiver: he *seeketh his own glory,* which is a sign that he *speaks of himself.* Here is the description of the *cheat:* they *speak of themselves,* and have no commission nor instructions from God; no warrant but their own will, no inspiration but their own imagination. They consult purely *their own glory;* self-seekers are self-speakers. Those who speak *from God* will speak *for God,* and for his glory. See the contrary character Christ gives of himself and his doctrine: *He that seeks his glory that sent him, he is true.* He was *sent of God.* Those teachers, and those only, who are sent of God, are to be received and entertained by us. He *sought the glory of God.* It was both the tendency of his doctrine and the tenor of his whole conversation to *glorify God.* This was a proof that he was *true.* False teachers are most *unrighteous;* they are unjust to God whose name they abuse, and unjust to the souls of men whom they impose upon. But Christ made it appear that he was *true,* that he was really what he said he was.

2. They discourse concerning the *crime* that was laid to his charge for curing the impotent man, and bidding him carry his bed on the sabbath day. He argues against them by way of *recrimination,* v. 19. How could they for shame censure him for a breach of the law of Moses, when they themselves were such notorious breakers of it? *Did not Moses give you the law?* But it was their wickedness that *none of them* kept the law. Their neglect of the law was universal: *None of you keepeth* it. They boasted of the law, and pretended a zeal for it, and yet none of them kept it; like those who say that they are for the church, and yet never go to church. It was an aggravation of their wickedness, in persecuting Christ; "*None of you keepeth the law,* why then go ye about to kill me for

not keeping it?" Those are commonly most censorious of others who are most faulty themselves. Those that support themselves and their interest by persecution and violence, whatever they pretend, are not keepers of the law of God.

Here the *people* rudely interrupted him (v. 20): *Thou hast a devil; who goes about to kill thee?* This intimates the *good opinion* they had of their rulers, who, they think, would never attempt so atrocious a thing as to kill him. The *ill opinion* they had of our Lord Jesus: "*Thou hast a devil,* thou art possessed with a lying spirit, and art a *bad man* for saying so"; so some: or rather, "Thou art melancholy, and art a *weak man;* thou frightenest thyself with causeless fears." Not only open frenzies, but silent melancholies were then commonly imputed to the power of Satan. "Thou art crazed, hast a distempered brain." Let us not think it strange if the best of men are put under the worst of characters. Those who would be like Christ must put up with affronts, must not *regard* them, much less *resent* them, and least of all *revenge* them. He argues by way of appeal and vindication.

(1) He appeals to *their own sentiments* of this miracle: "*I have done one work, and you all marvel,* v. 21. You cannot choose but marvel at it as truly great."

(2) He appeals to their own practice in other instances: "*I have done one work* on the sabbath, and you all marvel, you make a mighty strange thing of it, that a religious man should dare do such a thing. If it be lawful for you, nay, and your duty, to circumcise a child on the sabbath day, much more was it lawful and good for me to heal a diseased man on that day."

First, The rise and origin of circumcision: *Moses gave you circumcision.* Circumcision is said to *be given,* and (v. 23) they are said to *receive it.* The ordinances of God, and particularly those which are seals of the covenant, are *gifts given to men,* and are to be received as such. Moses did not give it them, but God; nay, it was not of Moses first, but *of the fathers,* v. 22. It was ordained long before, for it was a seal of the righteousness of faith, and was part of that blessing of Abraham which was to come upon the Gentiles.

Secondly, The respect paid to the law of circumcision above that of the sabbath. If a child was born one sabbath day it was without fail circumcised the next.

Thirdly, The inference Christ draws hence in justification of himself (v. 23): *A man-child on the sabbath day receives circumcision, that the law of circumcision might not be broken.* "Now, if this be allowed by yourselves, how unreasonable are you, who are angry with me because I have made a man every whit whole on the sabbath day!*" It was a spiteful anger, anger with gall in it. It is very absurd and unreasonable for us to condemn others for that in which we justify ourselves. Observe the comparison Christ here makes between their *circumcising a child* and his *healing a man* on the sabbath day. Circumcision was but a ceremonial institution. What Christ did was a good work by the law of nature. Circumcision *made sore;* but what Christ did made whole. Whereas, when they had circumcised a child, their care was only to heal up that part which was circumcised, which might be done and yet the child remain under other illnesses, Christ had made this man *every whit whole. I have made the whole man healthful* and sound. The *whole body* was *healed.* Nay, Christ not only healed his body, but his soul too, by that admonition, *Go, and sin no more,* and so indeed made the *whole man* sound.

He concludes this argument with that rule (v. 24): *Judge not according to the appearance, but judge righteous judgment.* This may be applied, either,

First, In particular, to this work. Be not partial in your judgment; judge not *with respect of persons.* Or, *Secondly*, In general, to Christ's person and preaching, which they were offended at. Those things that are false commonly appear best when they are judged of *according to the outward appearance*, they appear most plausible *prima facie—at the first glance.* It was this that gained the Pharisees such an interest and reputation, that they *appeared right* unto men (Matt. xxiii. 27, 28), and men judged of them by that appearance. "But," saith Christ, "be not too confident that all are real saints who are seeming ones." Those who undertook to judge whether he was the Son of God or no by his *outward appearance* were not likely to *judge righteous judgment.* If a divine power accompanied him, and God bore him witness, and the scriptures were fulfilled in him, they ought to receive him, and to judge by faith, and not by the sight of the eye. We must not judge concern-cerning any by their *outward appearance*, not by their titles, the figure they make in the world, and their fluttering show, but by their intrinsic worth, and the gifts and graces of God's Spirit in them.

3. Christ discourses with them here concerning *himself*, whence he came, and whither he was going, *v.* 25–36.

(1) *Whence he came, v.* 25–31.

[1] The objection concerning this stated by some of the inhabitants of Jerusalem, who seem to have been of all others most prejudiced against him, *v.* 25. Our Lord Jesus has often met with the least welcome from those that one would expect the best from. But it was not without some just cause that it came into a proverb. *The nearer the church the further from God.*

First, Reflecting on the rulers, because they let him alone: *Is not this he whom they seek to kill?* "Why do they not do it then? Lo, *he speaketh boldly*, and *they say nothing to him*; do *the rulers know indeed that this is the very Christ?*" *v.* 26. Here they slyly and maliciously insinuate two things, to exasperate the rulers against Christ. *a.* That by conniving at his preaching they *brought their authority into contempt.* "If our rulers will suffer themselves to be thus trampled upon, they may thank themselves if none stand in awe of them." The worst of persecutions have often been carried on under colour of the necessary support of authority and government. *b.* That hereby they brought *their judgment* into *suspicion*: *Do they know that this is the Christ?* It is spoken ironically. "How came they to change their mind?" When religion and the profession of Christ's name are *out of fashion*, and consequently *out of repute*, many are strongly tempted to persecute and oppose them, only that they may not be thought to favour them and incline to them. It was strange that the rulers, thus irritated, did not seize Christ; but his hour was not yet come; and God can tie men's hands to admiration, though he should not turn their hearts.

Secondly, By their exception against his being the Christ, in which appeared more malice than matter, *v.* 27. "We have this argument against it, that *we know this man, whence he is; but when Christ comes no man knows whence he is.*" They *despised him* because they knew *whence he was.* Familiarity breeds contempt, and we are apt to disdain the *use* of those whom we know the *rise of.* Christ's own received him not, because he was *their own*, for which very reason they should the rather have loved him.

[2] Christ's answer to this objection, *v.* 28, 29. He spoke freely and boldly, he *cried in the temple, as he taught*; to express his earnestness, being *grieved for the hardness of their hearts.* There may be a vehemency in contending for the truth where yet there is no intemperate heat nor passion. We may

instruct gainsayers with warmth, and yet with *meek-ness.* Whoever has ears to hear, let him hear this. His answer to their cavil is, *a.* By way of *concession*, "*You both know me, and you know whence I am. You know me*, you think you know me; but you are mistaken; you take me to be the carpenter's son, and born at Nazareth, but it is not so." *b.* By way of *negation*, denying that that which they did see in him, and know of him, was all that was to be known. He will tell them what they knew not, *from whom* he came. (*a*) That he did not *come of himself.* (*b*) That he was sent of his Father; this is twice mentioned. (*c*) That he was *from his Father* as the beams from the sun. (*d*) *That the Father who sent him is true;* he had promised to give the Messiah. He that made the promise is *true*, and has performed it. He *is true*, and will fulfil the promise in the calling of the Gentiles. (*e*) That these unbelieving Jews did *not know the Father*: *He that sent me, whom you know not.* There is much ignorance of God even with many that have a *form of knowledge*; and the true reason why people reject Christ is because they do not *know God.* (*f*) Our Lord Jesus was intimately acquainted with the Father that *sent him: but I know him.* He was not at all *in doubt* concerning his mission from him, nor at all *in the dark* concerning the work he had to do.

[3] The provocation which this gave to his enemies, *v.* 30. *They sought therefore to take him.* But nobody touched him, *because his hour was not yet come.* God has wicked men in a chain. The malice of persecutors is *impotent* even when it is most *impetuous*, and, when Satan *fills their hearts*, yet God *ties their hands.* God's servants are sometimes wonderfully protected by indiscernible unaccountable means. Christ had *his hour* set. So have all his people and all his ministers. Nor can all the powers of hell and earth prevail against them, until they have *finished their testimony.*

[4] The good effect which Christ's discourse had upon some of his hearers (*v.* 31): *Many of the people believed on him.* Even where the gospel meets with opposition there may yet be a great deal of good done. *Who* they were that believed; not a few, but many, more than one would have expected when the stream ran so strongly the other way. But these *many* were *of the people.* We must not measure the prosperity of the gospel by its success among the great ones; nor must ministers say that they labour in vain, though none but the *poor* receive the gospel. What *induced* them to believe: the *miracles which he did.* How *weak* their faith was: they do not positively assert, as the Samaritans did, *This is indeed the Christ*, but they only argue, *When Christ comes will he do more miracles than these?* "Therefore why may not this be he?" They *believe* it, but have not courage to own it. Even weak faith may be true faith, and so *accepted*, by the Lord Jesus.

(2) *Whither he was going, v.* 32–36.

[1] The design of the Pharisees and chief priests against him, *v.* 32. The provocation given them was that they had information brought them by their spies, that *the people murmured such things concerning him*, that there were many who had a respect and value for him. Though the people did but whisper these things, yet the Pharisees were enraged at it. The Pharisees were sensible that if Christ did thus *increase* they must *decrease.* The project they laid hereupon was to seize Jesus, and take him into custody: *They sent officers to take him.* The most effectual way to disperse the flock is to *smite the shepherd.* The Pharisees *as such*, had no power, and therefore they got the *chief priests* to join with them. As *the world by wisdom knew not God*, so the Jewish church by their wisdom knew not Christ.

[2] The discourse of our Lord Jesus hereupon (*v.* 33, 34): *Yet a little while I am with you, and then*

I go to him that sent me; you shall seek me, and shall not find me; and where I am, thither you cannot come. These words, like the pillar of cloud and fire, have a *bright* side and a *dark* side.

First, They have a *bright side* towards our Lord Jesus himself. Three things Christ here comforted himself with: That he had but *a little time* to continue here in this troublesome world. His warfare will shortly be accomplished. Whomsoever we are *with* in this world, friends or foes, it is but a *little while* that we shall be with them. We must be *awhile* with those that are pricking briars and grieving thorns; but thanks be to God, it is but a little while, and we shall be out of their reach. That he should *go to him that sent him.* When I have done my work with you, then, and not till then, I go to him *that sent me.* Let those who suffer for Christ comfort themselves with this, that they have a God to go to, and are going to him, to be for ever with him. That none of their persecutions could follow him to heaven: *You shall seek me, and shall not find me.* It adds to the happiness of glorified saints that they are out of the reach of the devil and all his wicked instruments.

Secondly, These words have a *black and dark side* towards those that hated and persecuted Christ. They now longed to be rid of him. According to their choice so shall their doom be. He will not trouble them long, yet a little while and he will *depart* from them. They that are weary of Christ need no more to make them miserable than to have *their wish.* They would certainly repent their choice when it was too late. They should in vain seek the presence of the Messiah: "*You shall seek me, and shall not find me.*" Those who now seek Christ shall find him, but the day is coming when those who now refuse him *shall seek him, and shall not find him.* They should in vain expect a place in heaven: *Where I am, and where all believers shall be with me, thither ye cannot come.* They are disabled by their own iniquity and infidelity: *You cannot come,* because you *will not.* Indeed heaven would be no heaven to them.

[3] Their descant upon this discourse (*v.* 35, 36): *They said among themselves; Whither will he go? First,* Their wilful ignorance and blindness. He had expressly said whither he would go—to him that sent him, to his Father in heaven, and yet they ask, *Whither will he go?* and, *What manner of saying is this? Secondly,* Their daring contempt of Christ's threatenings. Instead of trembling at that terrible word, *You shall seek me, and not find me,* they banter it and make a jest of it. *Thirdly,* Their inveterate malice and rage against Christ. All they dreaded in his *departure* was that he would be out of the reach of their power: "*Whither will he go, that we shall not find him?*" *Fourthly,* Their proud disdain of the Gentiles, whom they here call the *dispersed of the Gentiles.* Will he make his court to them? "Will he go and *teach the Gentiles*? Will he carry his doctrine to them?" So common is it for those who have lost the power of religion to be very jealous for the monopoly of the the name. They now made a *jest* of his going *to teach the Gentiles*; but not long after he did it *in good earnest* by his apostles and ministers.

Verses 37–44

I. Christ's discourse, with the explication of it, *v.* 37–39. It is probable that these are only short hints of what he enlarged upon, but they have in them the substance of the whole gospel; here is a *gospel invitation* to *come to Christ,* and a *gospel promise* of comfort and happiness in him.

1. *When* he gave this invitation: *On the last day* of the feast of tabernacles, *that great day.* Much people were gathered together, and, if the invitation were given to *many,* it might be hoped that *some* would accept of it. The people were now returning to their homes, and he would give them this to carry away with them as his parting word. When a great congregation is about to scatter, it is affecting to think that in all probability they will never come all together again in this world, and therefore, if we can say or do anything to help them to heaven, that must be the time. It is good to be lively at the close of an ordinance. Christ made this offer *on the last day of the feast.* He will try them once more, and, if they will yet hear his voice, they shall live. It would be half a year before there would be another feast, and in that time they would many of them be in their graves. *Behold now is the accepted time.*

2. *How* he gave this invitation: *Jesus stood and cried,* which denotes his great earnestness and importunity. Love to souls will make preachers lively. His desire was that all might take notice, and take hold of this invitation. He *stood,* and *cried,* that he might the better be heard. The heathen oracles were delivered privately by them that *peeped and muttered*; but the oracles of the gospel were proclaimed by one that *stood, and cried.*

3. The invitation itself is very general: *If any man thirst,* whoever he be, he is invited to Christ. It is also very *gracious*: "*If any man thirst, let him come to me and drink.* If any man desires to be truly and eternally happy, let him apply himself to me."

(1) The persons invited are such as *thirst,* which may be understood, either, [1] Of the *indigence* of their cases; either as to their *outward* condition (let his poverty and afflictions draw him to Christ for that peace which the world can neither give nor take away), or as to their *inward* state: "If any man want spiritual blessings, he may be supplied by me." Or, [2] Of the *inclination* of their souls and their desires towards a spiritual happiness. If any man hunger and thirst after righteousness.

(2) The invitation itself: *Let him come to me.* Let him *go to Christ* as the fountain of living waters.

(3) The satisfaction promised: Let him come *and drink,* he shall have that which will not only *refresh,* but *replenish.*

4. A gracious promise annexed to this gracious call (*v.* 38): *He that believeth on me, out of his belly shall flow*: (1) See here what it is to come to Christ: It is *to believe on him, as the scripture hath said.* We must not frame a Christ according to our fancy, but believe in a Christ according to the scripture. (2) See how thirsty souls, that come to Christ, shall be made *to drink.* Israel drank of the *rock that followed them,* but believers drink of a rock *in them,* Christ in them. Provision is made not only for their *present* satisfaction, but for their *continual perpetual* comfort. *Living water, running* water, which the Hebrew language calls *living,* because still in motion. The graces and comforts of the Spirit are compared to *living* (meaning *running*) *water*: Rivers of living water. The comfort flows in both *plentifully* and *constantly* as a river; strong as a stream to bear down the oppositions of doubts and fears. These flow out of his heart or soul. There *gracious principles* are planted; and out of the heart, in which the Spirit dwells, flow the *issues of life.* Where there are *springs* of grace and comfort in the soul they will *send forth streams.* Grace and comfort will *evidence themselves.* A holy heart will be seen in a holy life; the tree is known by its fruits, and the fountain by its streams. They will *communicate themselves* for the benefit of others; a good man is a common good.

Those words, *as the scripture hath said,* seem to refer to some promise in the Old Testament to this purport, and there are many. It was a custom of the Jews which they received by tradition, *the last day of the feast* of tabernacles to have a solemnity, which they called *the pouring out of water.* They fetched a golden vessel of water from the pool of Siloam, brought it into the temple with sound of trumpet and other ceremonies, and, upon the ascent to the altar, poured it out before the Lord with all possible expressions of joy. It is thought that our Saviour might here allude to this custom. Believers shall have the comfort, not of a vessel of water fetched from a pool, but of a river flowing from themselves.

5. Here is the evangelist's exposition of this promise (v. 39): *This spoke he of the Spirit*, of the gifts, graces, and comforts of the Spirit. It is promised to *all that believe* on Christ that they shall *receive the Holy Ghost*. Some received his miraculous gifts; all receive his sanctifying graces. The Spirit dwelling and working in believers is as a *fountain of living running water*, out of which plentiful streams flow, cooling and cleansing as water, mollifying and moistening as water, making them fruitful, and others joyful. This plentiful effusion of the Spirit was yet the matter of a promise; for *the Holy Ghost was not yet given, because Jesus was not yet glorified*. It was certain that he should be glorified, but he was as yet in a state of humiliation and contempt. And, if Christ must wait for his glory, let not us think it much to wait for ours. *The Holy Ghost was not yet given.* If we compare the clear knowledge and strong grace of the disciples of Christ themselves, after the day of Pentecost, with their darkness and weakness before, we shall understand in what sense *the Holy Ghost was not yet given*; the earnests and first-fruits of the Spirit were given, but the full harvest was not yet come. The *Holy Ghost* was *not yet given* in such rivers of living water as should issue forth to water the whole earth, even the Gentile world. The reason why the *Holy Ghost was not given* was because *Jesus was not yet glorified*. The death of Christ is sometimes called his glorification; for in his cross he conquered and triumphed. The gift of the Holy Ghost was purchased by the blood of Christ: the Holy Ghost was not given. There was not so much need of the Spirit, while Christ himself was here upon earth, as there was when he was gone. Though the Holy Ghost was not yet given, yet he was *promised*. Though the gifts of Christ's grace are *long deferred*, while we are waiting for the good promise, we have the promise to live upon.

II. The consequents of this discourse. In general, it occasioned differences: *There was a division among the people because of him*, v. 43. There were diversities of opinions, and those managed with heat and contention; various sentiments, and those such as set them at *variance*. Think we that Christ came to send peace. No, the effect of the preaching of his gospel would be *division*, for, while some are *gathered to it* others will be *gathered against it*. This is no more the fault of the gospel than it is the fault of a wholesome medicine that it stirs up the *peccant* humours in the body, in order to the discharge of them.

1. Some were *taken with him*: *Many of the people, when they heard this saying*, could not but think highly of him. Some of them said, *Of a truth this is the prophet*, the harbinger and forerunner of the Messiah. Others went further, and said, *This is the Christ* (v. 41), the Messiah himself. We do not find that these people became his disciples and followers; a good opinion of Christ is far short of a lively faith in Christ; many give Christ a good word that give him no more.

2. Others were *prejudiced against him*. No sooner was this great truth started, that *Jesus is the Christ*, than immediately it was contradicted and argued against. That his rise and origin were (as they took it for granted) out of Galilee, was thought enough to answer all the arguments for his being the Christ. For, *shall Christ come out of Galilee? Has not the scripture said that Christ comes of the seed of David?* See here, (1) A laudable knowledge of the scripture.

This even the common people knew by the traditional expositions which their scribes gave them. Many that espouse some corrupt notions, seem to be very ready in the scriptures, when indeed they know little more than those scriptures which they have been taught to *pervert*. (2) A culpable ignorance of our Lord Jesus. They speak of it as certain and past dispute that *Jesus was of Galilee*, whereas by enquiring they might have known that he was the Son of David, and a native of Bethlehem.

3. Others were *enraged against him*, and they *would have taken him*, v. 44. Though what he said was most sweet and gracious, yet they were exasperated against him for it. They *would have taken him*; but no man *laid hands on him*, because his hour was not come. As the malice of Christ's enemies is always *unreasonable*, so sometimes the suspension of it is *unaccountable*.

Verses 45–53

The chief priests and Pharisees are here contriving how to suppress Christ; though this was the *great day of the feast*, they attended not the religious services of the day. They sat in the council-chamber, expecting Christ to be brought a prisoner to them, as they had issued out warrants for apprehending him, v. 32.

I. What passed between them and their own officers, who returned without him.

1. The reproof they gave the officers for not executing the warrant they gave them: *Why have you not brought him?* It vexed them that those who were their own creatures should thus disappoint them.

2. The reason which the officers gave: *Never man spoke like this man*, v. 46. This was a very great truth, that *never any man spoke with* that wisdom, and power, and grace, that convincing clearness, and that charming sweetness, wherewith Christ spoke. The very officers that were sent to take him were taken with him, and acknowledged this. They could not but prefer him before all those that sat in Moses's seat. Thus Christ was preserved by the power God has upon the consciences even of bad men. They said this to their lords and masters, who could not endure to hear anything that tended to the honour of Christ and yet could not avoid hearing this. Their own officers, who could not be suspected to be biassed in favour of Christ, are witnesses against them.

3. The Pharisees endeavour to secure their officers to their interest, and to beget in them prejudices against Christ. They suggest two things: (1) That if they embrace the gospel of Christ they will *deceive themselves* (v. 47): *Are you also deceived?* Christianity has, from its first rise, been represented to the world as a great cheat upon it, and they that embraced it as men *deceived*, then when they began to be *undeceived*, observe what a *compliment* the Pharisees paid to these officers: "*Are you also deceived?* What! men of your sense?" They endeavour to prejudice them against Christ by persuading them to think well of themselves. (2) That they will *disparage themselves*. Most men, even in their religion, are willing to be governed by the example of those of the *first rank*; these officers therefore, are desired to consider,

(1) That, if they become disciples of Christ, they go contrary to those who were persons of quality and reputation: "*Have any of the rulers, or of the Pharisees, believed on him?*" Some of the rulers did embrace Christ and more believed in him, but wanted courage to confess him (ch. xii. 42); but, when the interest of Christ runs low in the world, it is common for its adversaries to represent it as lower than really it is. The cause of Christ has seldom had rulers and Pharisees on its side. *Self-denial* and the *cross* are hard lessons to *rulers* and *Pharisees*. This has confirmed many in their prejudices against Christ, that the rulers and Pharisees have been no friends. If *rulers*

and *Pharisees* do not believe in Christ, they that do believe in him will be the most singular, unfashionable, ungenteel people in the world. Thus are people foolishly willing to be damned for fashion-sake.

(2) That they will link themselves with the despicable vulgar sort of people (*v.* 43): *But this people, who know not the law, are cursed.* First, How scornfully and disdainfully they speak of them: *This people.* As the wisdom of God has often chosen base things, and things which are despised, so the folly of men has commonly debased and despised those whom God has chosen. *Secondly,* How unjustly they reproach them: *They know not the law.* Perhaps many of those whom they thus despised *knew the law,* and the prophets too, better than they did. Many a plain, honest, unlearned disciple of Christ attains to a more clear, sound, and useful knowledge of the word of God, than some great scholars with all their wit and learning. Whose fault was it but theirs, who should have *taught them better? Thirdly,* How magisterially they pronounce sentence upon them: they are *cursed.* We are unable to *try,* and therefore unfit to *condemn,* and our rule is, *Bless, and curse not.* They use this odious word, they are *cursed,* to express their own indignation, and to frighten their officers from having anything to do with them.

II. What passed between them and Nicodemus, *v.* 50, &c.

1. The just and rational objection which Nicodemus made against their proceedings.

(1) Who it was that appeared against them; it was Nicodemus, *he that came to Jesus by night, being one of them, v.* 50. Though he had been with Jesus, and taken him for his teacher, yet he retained his place in the council, and his vote among them. Some impute this to his *weakness* and cowardice. It seems rather to have been his *wisdom* not immediately to throw up his place, because there he might have opportunity of serving Christ, and stemming the tide of the Jewish rage. God has his remnant among all sorts, and many times finds, or puts, or makes, some good in the worst places and societies. Though at first he came to Jesus *by night,* for fear of being known; yet, when there was occasion, he boldly appeared in defence of Christ, and opposed the whole council. Thus many believers who at first were timorous have at length, by divine grace, grown courageous. Let none justify the disguising of their faith by the example of Nicodemus, unless, like him, they be ready openly to appear in the cause of Christ, though they stand alone in it; for so Nicodemus did here, and *ch.* xix. 39.

(2) What he alleged against their proceedings (*v.* 51): *Doth our law judge any man before it hear him* and *know what he doeth?* He prudently argues from the principles of their own law, and an incontestable rule of justice, that no man is to be condemned *unheard.* Whereas they had reproached the people, as *ignorant of the law,* he here tacitly retorts the charge upon themselves. The law is here said to *judge,* and *hear,* and *know.* It is highly fit that none should come under the *sentence* of the law, till they have first undergone the *scrutiny* of it. Judges have two ears, to remind them to hear both sides. Persons are to be judged, not by what is *said* of them, but by what they *do.* Facts, and not faces, must be known in judgment; and the *scale* of justice must be used before the *sword* of justice.

2. What was said to this objection. Here is no direct reply given to it. What was lacking in *reason* they made up in railing and reproach. Whoever are *against reason* give cause to suspect that *reason* is *against them.* See how they taunt him: *Art thou also of Galilee?* (*v.* 52).

(1) How *false* the grounds of their arguing were. They suppose that Christ was of Galilee, and this was false. They suppose that because most of his disciples were Galileans they were all such. They suppose that out of Galilee no prophet had *risen,* yet this was false too.

(2) How *absurd* their arguings were upon these grounds. Is any man of worth and virtue ever the worse for the poverty and obscurity of his country? Supposing no prophet had risen out of Galilee, yet it is not impossible that any should arise thence.

3. The hasty adjournment of the court hereupon. They broke up the assembly in confusion, and with precipitation, and *every man went to his own house.* All the policy of the close cabal was broken to pieces with one plain honest word. They were not willing to hear Nicodemus, because they could not answer him.

CHAPTER 8

I. Christ's evading the snare which the Jews laid for him, in bringing to him a woman taken in adultery, ver. 1–11. II. Divers discourses or conferences of his with the Jews. 1. Concerning his being the light of the world, ver. 12–20. 2. Concerning the ruin of the unbelieving Jews, ver. 21–30. 3. Concerning liberty and bondage, ver. 31–37. 4. Concerning his Father and their father, ver. 38–47. 5. Here is his discourse in answer to their blasphemous reproaches, ver. 48–50. 6. Concerning the immortality of believers, ver. 51–59.

Verses 1–11

I. His retirement in the evening out of the town (*v.* 1): *He went unto the mount of olives.* He went out of Jerusalem, perhaps because he had no friend there that had either kindness or courage enough to give him a night's lodging; while his persecutors had *houses* of their own to go to (*ch.* vii. 53). In the daytime, when he had work to do in the temple, he willingly exposed himself. But in the night, he withdrew into the country, and sheltered himself there.

II. His return in the morning to the temple, and to his work there, *v.* 2.

1. What a diligent preacher Christ was: *Early in the morning he came again, and taught.* Three things were taken notice of here concerning Christ's preaching. (1) The time: *Early in the morning.* When a day's work is to be done for God and souls it is good to take the day before us. (2) The place: *In the temple;* not so much because it was a *consecrated* place as because it was not a *place of concourse.* (3) His posture: *He sat down,* and taught, as one having authority.

2. How diligently his preaching was attended upon: *All the people came unto him.* Though the rulers were displeased at those that came to hear him, yet they would come; and *he taught them,* though they were angry at *him* too.

III. His dealing with those that brought to him the *woman taken in adultery, tempting him.*

1. The case proposed to him by the scribes and Pharisees, who herein contrived to pick a quarrel with him, *v.* 3–6.

(1) They set the prisoner to the bar (*v.* 3): they brought him *a woman taken in adultery.* Those that were *taken in adultery* were by the Jewish law to be put to death. The scribes and Pharisees bring her to Christ, and set her in the midst of the assembly, as if they would leave her wholly to the judgment of Christ.

(2) They prefer an indictment against her: *Master, this woman was taken in adultery, v.* 4. Here they call him *Master* whom but the day before they had called a *deceiver.* The crime for which the prisoner stands indicted is no less than adultery. The Pharisees seemed to have a great zeal against the sin, when it appeared afterwards that they themselves were not free from it. It is common for those that are indulgent to their own sin to be severe against the sins of others. The proof of the crime, an incontestable

proof; she was *taken in the act.* Sometimes it proves a mercy to sinners to have their sin brought to light. Better our sin should *shame* us than *damn* us.

(3) They produce the statute in this case upon which she was indicted, *v. 5.* Moses in the law commanded *that such should be stoned.* Adultery is an exceedingly sinful sin. It is the violation of a divine institution in innocency, by the indulgence of one of the basest lusts of man in his degeneracy.

(4) They pray his judgment in the case: "*But what sayest thou,* who pretendest to be a teacher come from God to repeal old laws and enact new ones?" If they had asked this question in sincerity, it had been very commendable. But *this they said tempting him, that they might have to accuse him, v. 6.* If he should confirm the sentence of the law, they would censure him as inconsistent with himself (he having received publicans and harlots) and with the character of the Messiah, who should be meek, and have salvation. If he should acquit her they would represent him, *First,* As an enemy to the law of Moses. *Secondly,* As a friend to sinners, and, consequently a favourer of sin; than which no reflection could be more invidious upon one that professed the strictness, purity, and business of a prophet.

2. The method he took to resolve this case, and so to break this snare.

(1) He seemed to slight it, and turned a deaf ear to it: He *stooped down, and wrote on the ground.* It is impossible to tell, and therefore needless to ask, what he wrote; but this is the only mention made in the gospels of Christ's writing. Christ by this teaches us to be slow to speak when difficult cases are proposed to us, not quickly to shoot our bolt. Think twice before we speak once. But, when Christ seemed as though he heard them not, he made it appear that he not only heard their words, but knew their thoughts.

(2) He turned the conviction of the prisoner upon the prosecutors, *v. 7.*

[1] They *continued asking him,* and his seeming not to take notice of them made them the more vehement; for now they thought sure enough that they had run him aground. Therefore they pushed on their appeal to him with vigour; whereas they should have construed his disregard of them as a check to their design, and an intimation to them to desist.

[2] At last he put them all to shame and silence with one word: *He lifted up himself* and *said unto them, He that is without sin among you, let him first cast a stone at her.* He neither reflected upon the law nor excused the prisoner's guilt, nor did he on the other hand encourage the prosecution or countenance their heat. When we cannot make our point by steering a direct course, it is good to fetch a compass. They came with design to accuse him, but they were forced to accuse themselves. He here refers to that rule which the law of Moses prescribed in the execution of criminals, that the *hand of the witnesses must be first upon them* (Deut. xvii. 7), as in the stoning of Stephen, Acts vii. 58. Christ puts it to them whether, according to their own law, they would dare to be the executioners. Durst they take away that life with their hands which they were now taking away with their tongues? He builds upon an uncontested maxim in morality. They are not better than self-condemned who judge others, and yet themselves do the same thing: "If there be any of you who is *without sin,* let him cast the first stone at her." Whenever we find fault with others, we ought to reflect upon ourselves, and to be more severe against sin in ourselves than in others. We ought to be favourable, though not to the sins, yet to the persons, of those that offend, considering ourselves and our own corrupt nature. Let this restrain us from *throwing stones* at our

brethren. Those that are any way obliged to animadvert upon the faults of others are concerned to look well to themselves, and keep themselves pure. If you are without sin, stand to the charge, and let the adulteress be executed; but, if not, though she be guilty, while you that present her are equally so, according to your own rule she shall be free. He aimed to bring, not only the prisoner to repentance, by showing her his mercy, but the prosecutors too, by showing them their sins. They sought to ensnare him; he sought to convince and convert them.

[3] Having given them this startling word, he left them to consider of it, *and again stooped down,* and *wrote on the ground, v. 8.* The matter was lodged in their own breasts, let them make the best of it there. Some Greek copies here read, He *wrote on the ground, the sins of everyone of them.* But he does not write men's sins *in the sand;* no, they are written as with a *pen of iron* (Jer. xvii. 1), never to be forgotten till they are forgiven.

[4] The scribes and Pharisees were so strangely thunderstruck with the words of Christ that they let fall their persecution of Christ, whom they durst no further tempt, and their prosecution of the woman, whom they durst no longer accuse (*v. 9*): *They went out one by one.* Perhaps his writing on the ground frightened them, as the handwriting on the wall frightened Belshazzar. Happy they who have no reason to be afraid of Christ's writing! What he said frightened them by sending them to their own consciences; he had *shown them to themselves,* and they were afraid his next word would show them to the world. They went out *one by one,* that they might go out *softly;* they went away by *stealth,* as *people being ashamed.* The order of their departure is taken notice of, *beginning at the eldest.* If the eldest quit the field, and retreat ingloriously, no marvel if the younger follow them. 1. The *force* of the word of Christ for the conviction of sinners: *They who heard it were convicted by their own consciences.* Conscience is God's deputy in the soul, and one word from him will set it on work, Heb. iv. 12. Even scribes and Pharisees are by the power of Christ's word made to retire with shame. 2. The *folly* of sinners under these convictions. It is folly for those that are under convictions to make it their principal care to *avoid shame.* Our care should be more to save our souls than to save our credit. The scribes and Pharisees had the wound *opened,* and now they should have been desirous to have it *searched,* and then it might have been *healed.* It is folly for those that are under convictions to *get away from Jesus Christ,* for he is the only one that can heal the wounds of conscience. To whom will they go?

[5] When the *self-conceited* prosecutors quitted the field, the *self-condemned* prisoner stood her ground: *Jesus was left alone and the woman standing in the midst,* where they set her, *v. 3.* She did not seek to make her escape. Her prosecutors had appealed unto Jesus, and to him she would go. Those whose cause is brought before our Lord Jesus will never have occasion to remove it into any other court. Our cause is lodged in the gospel court; we are *left with Jesus alone,* it is with him only that we have now to deal. Let his gospel *rule us,* and it will infallibly *save us.*

[6] Here is the conclusion of the trial: *Jesus lifted up himself, and he saw none but the woman, v. 10, 11.* The woman, it is likely, stood trembling at the bar, as one doubtful of the issue. Christ was *without sin,* and might cast the first stone; but though none more severe than he against sin, none more compassionate than he to sinners, for he is infinitely gracious and merciful, and this poor malefactor finds him so. The prosecutors are called: *Where are those thine accusers? Hath no man condemned thee?* He asked, that he

might shame them, who declined his judgment, and encourage her who resolved to abide by it. They do not appear when the question is asked: *Hath no man condemned thee?* She said, *No man, Lord.* She speaks respectfully to Christ, calls him *Lord*, but is silent concerning her prosecutors. She does not triumph in their retreat nor insult over them as witnesses against themselves, not against her. But she answered the question which concerned herself. *Has no man condemned thee?* True penitents find it enough to give an account of themselves to God, and will not undertake to give account of other people. The prisoner is therefore discharged: *Neither do I condemn thee; go, and sin no more.* 1. Her discharge from the temporal punishment: "If they do not condemn thee to be *stoned to death*, neither *do I*." Christ would not condemn this woman, (*a*) Because it was *none of his business*; would not intermeddle in secular affairs. (*b*) Because she was prosecuted by those that were more guilty than she and could not for shame insist upon their demand of justice against her. When Christ dismissed her, it was with this caution, *Go, and sin no more.* The fairer the escape was, the fairer the warning was to go and sin no more. Those who help to save the life of a criminal should, as Christ here, help to save the soul with this caution. 2. Her discharge from the eternal punishment. For Christ to say, *I do not condemn thee* is, in effect, to say, *I do forgive thee*; and the *Son of man had power on earth to forgive sins.* He knew the tenderness and sincere repentance of the prisoner, and therefore said that which would comfort her. Those are truly happy whom Christ *doth not condemn.* Christ will not condemn those who, though they have sinned, will *go and sin no more.* Christ's favour to us in the remission of the sins that are past should be a prevailing argument with us to *go and sin no more.*

Verses 12–20

The rest of the chapter is taken up with debates between Christ and contradicting sinners. There were other Pharisees (*v.* 13) to confront Christ, who had brass enough in their foreheads to keep them in countenance.

I. A great doctrine laid down, with the application of it.

1. The doctrine is, *That Christ is the light of the world* (*v.* 12): *Then spoke Jesus again unto them.* They had turned a deaf ear to what he said, and yet he *spoke again to them*, saying, *I am the light of the world.* He was expected to be a *light to enlighten the Gentiles* (Luke ii. 32), and so the *light of the world.* The visible light of the world is the sun. One sun enlightens the whole world, so does one Christ, and there needs no more. What a dungeon would the world be without the sun. So would it be without Christ by whom *light came into the world.* 2. The inference from this doctrine is, *He that followeth me shall not walk in darkness, but shall have the light of life.* It is our duty to *follow him.* Christ is the *true light.* It is not enough to *look at* this light, and to *gaze* upon it, but we must follow it, believe in it, and walk in it, for it is a light to *our feet*, not *our eyes* only. It is the happiness of those who follow Christ that they *shall not walk in darkness.* They shall have the *light of life*, the light of spiritual life in this world and of everlasting life in the other world. Follow Christ, and we shall follow him to heaven.

II. The objection which the Pharisees made against this doctrine: *Thou bearest record of thyself; thy record is not true, v.* 13. The objection was very unjust, for they made that his crime which in the case of one who introduced a divine revelation was necessary and unavoidable. Did not Moses and all the prophets bear witness of themselves when they avouched themselves to be God's messengers?

Futhermore they overlooked the testimony of all the other witnesses. Had he only borne record of himself, his testimony had indeed been *suspicious*, and the belief of it might have been *suspended.*

III. Christ's reply to this objection, *v.* 14. He is the light of the world, and it is the property of light to be self-evidencing. First principles prove themselves. He urges three things to prove that his testimony, though of himself, was true and cogent.

1. That he was conscious to himself of his own authority. He did not speak as one at uncertainty. *I know whence I came, and whither I go.* He knew that he came *from the Father*, and was going *to him*, came *from glory*, and was going *to glory.*

2. That they are very incompetent judges of him. Because they were *ignorant*: *You cannot tell whence I came, and whither I go.* He had told them of his coming from heaven and returning to heaven, but it was *foolishness to them*, they *received it not.* They took upon them to judge of that which they did not understand. Because they were *partial* (*v.* 15): *You judge after the flesh.* The judgment cannot be right when the rule is wrong. The Jews judged of Christ and his gospel by outward appearances, and thought it impossible he should be the light of the world; as if the sun under a cloud were no sun. Because they were *unjust* and *unfair* towards him, intimated in this "*I judge no man;* I neither make nor meddle with your political affairs." He thus *judged no man.* It was very unreasonable for them to *judge him after the flesh.*

3. That his testimony of himself was sufficiently supported and corroborated by the testimony of his Father *with him and for him* (*v.* 16): *And yet, if I judge, my judgment is true.* Consider him then,

(1) As a judge: "*If I judge, my judgment is true. If I should judge*, my judgment must be true, and then you would be condemned." Now that which makes his judgment unexceptionable is his Father's concurrence with him: *I am not alone, but I and the Father.* He did not act *separately*, but in his own name and his Father's. His Father's commission was to him: "It is the Father that *sent me.*" No doubt his *judgment* was *true* and valid.

(2) Look upon him as *a witness.* As such his testimony was true and unexceptionable; this he shows, *v.* 17, 18. He quotes a maxim of the Jewish law, *v.* 17: That *the testimony of two men is true.* If nothing appear to the contrary it is taken for granted to be *true.* He applies this to the case in hand (*v.* 18): *I am one that bear witness of myself, and the Father that sent me bears witness of me.* Behold two witnesses! Now if the testimony of two distinct persons, that are *men*, and therefore may deceive or be deceived, is conclusive, much more ought the testimony of the Son of God concerning himself, backed with the testimony of his Father concerning him, to command assent. In conclusion, we are told how their tongues were let loose, and their hands tied.

First, How their tongues were let loose, *v.* 19. They set themselves to *cross question* with him.

a. How they evaded the *conviction. Then said they unto him, Where is thy Father?* They might easily have understood that when he spoke of his *Father* he meant no other than God himself; yet they pretend to understand him of a common person. They bid him *call his witness*, and challenge him, if he can, to produce him: *Where is thy Father?* Thus, as Christ said of them (*v.* 15), they *judge after the flesh.* Thus they turned it off with a taunt.

b. How he evaded the *cavil* with a further *conviction*; he charged them with wilful ignorance: "*You neither know me nor my Father.* It is to no purpose to discourse to you about divine things, who talk of them as blind men do of colours." He charges them with ignorance of God: "*You know not my Father.*" Their eyes were darkened that they could not see the light of his glory shining *in the face of Jesus Christ*. The *little children* of the Christian church *know the Father*, but these rulers of the Jews did not, because they would not so know him. He shows them the true cause of their ignorance of God: *If you had known me, you would have known my Father also*. The reason why men are ignorant of God is because they are unacquainted with Jesus Christ. In knowing him we should know the Father. If we *knew Christ* better, we should *know the Father* better.

Secondly, See how their hands were tied, though their tongues were thus let loose. *These words spoke Jesus in the treasury*. Now the priests might easily, with the assistance of the janizaries that were at their beck, either have seized him and exposed him to the rage of the mob, or, at least, have *silenced* him. Yet even *in the temple*, where they had him in their reach, *no man laid hands on him*, for *his hour was not yet come*. 1. The restraint laid upon his persecutors by an invisible power. God can set bounds to the wrath of men, as he does to the waves of the sea. 2. The reason of this restraint: *His hour was not yet come*. The frequent mention of this, intimates how much the time of our departure out of the world depends upon the fixed counsel and decree of God. It *will* come, it is coming; not yet come, but it is at hand. *My times are in thy hands;* and better there than in our own.

Verses 21–30

Christ here gives fair warning to the careless unbelieving Jews to consider what would be the consequence of their infidelity.

I. The wrath threatened (*v*. 21): *Jesus said again unto them*. He continued to teach, in kindness to those few who received his doctrine, which is an example to ministers to go on with their work, notwithstanding opposition, because a remnant shall be saved. Here Christ changes his voice; he had *piped to them* in the offers of his grace, and they *had not danced*; now he mourns to them in the denunciations of his wrath, to try if they would lament. He said *I go my way, and you shall seek me, and shall die in your sins. Whither I go you cannot come*. Every word is terrible, and bespeaks spiritual judgments, which are the sorest of all judgments. Four things are here threatened against the Jews.

1. Christ's departure from them: *I go my way*. But woe to those from whom Christ departs. He *bade often farewell*, as one *loth to depart*, and willing to be invited.

2. Their enmity to the true Messiah, and their infatuated enquiries after another Messiah when he was gone away. *You shall seek me*, which intimates either, (1) Their *enmity* to the *true Christ*: "You shall seek to ruin my interest, by persecuting my doctrine and followers." Or, (2) Their *enquiries* after *false Christs*: "You shall continue your expectations of the Messiah, of a Christ to come, when he is already come."

3. Their final impenitency: *You shall die in your sins*. Here it is meant especially of the sin of unbelief. Those that live in unbelief are for ever undone if they die in unbelief. Many that have long lived in sin are, through grace, saved by a timely repentance from *dying in sin*.

4. Their eternal separation from Christ. *Whither I go you cannot come*. When Christ left the world he went to paradise. Thither he took the penitent thief with him, that did not die in his sins; but the impenitent not only *shall not* come to him, but they *cannot*; for heaven would not be heaven to those that die unsanctified and unmeet for it.

II. The jest they made of this threatening. They turned it into ridicule (*v*. 22): *Will he kill himself?*

What slight thoughts they had of Christ's threatenings; they could make themselves and one another merry with them. What ill thoughts they had of Christ's meaning, as if he had an inhuman design upon his own life. They had put a much more favourable construction upon this word of his (*ch*. vii. 34, 35): *Will he go to the dispersed among the Gentiles?* But see how indulged malice grows more and more malicious.

III. The confirmation of what he had said.

1. He had said, *Whither I go you cannot come* (*v*. 23): *You are from beneath, I am from above; you are of this world, I am not of this world*. You are *of those things which are beneath*. You are *in with these things*, how can you come where I go, when your spirit and disposition are so directly contrary to mine? The *spirit of the Lord Jesus* was—not of *this world*, but from *above*. None shall be with him but those who are *born from above* and have their *conversation in heaven*. How contrary to this *their* spirit was: "*You are from beneath*." What communion could Christ have with them?

2. He had said, *You shall die in your sins*, and here he stands to it. He gives this further reason for it, *If you believe not that I am he, you shall die in your sins*, *v*. 34. (1) What we are required to believe: *that I am he;* he that should come, he that you expect the Messias to be. I do not only call myself so, but I *am he*. True faith does not *amuse* the soul with an empty sound of words, but *affects* it. (2) How necessary it is that we believe this. If we have not this faith, *we shall die in our sins*. We cannot be saved from the power of sin while we live, and therefore shall certainly continue in it to the last. None but the Spirit of Christ's grace will be an agent powerful enough to turn us from sin to God. If Christ do not cure us, our case is desperate, and we shall *die in our sins*. Without faith we cannot be saved from the punishment of sin when we die. This implies the great gospel promise: *If we believe that Christ is he*, and receive him accordingly, *we shall not die in our sins*. Believers die in Christ, in his love, in his arms.

IV. Here is a further discourse concerning *himself*, *v*. 25–29.

1. The question which the Jews put to him (*v*. 25): *Who art thou?* He had said, You must believe that *I am he*. His not saying expressly who he was, they turned to his reproach, as if he knew not what to say of himself: "*Who art thou?*"

2. His answer to this question, wherein he directs them three ways for information:

(1) He refers them to *what he had said* all along: "Do you ask who I am? *Even the same that I said unto you from the beginning*." I am *the same that I said to you from the beginning* of time in the scriptures of the Old Testament; *from the beginning* of my public ministry. The account he had already given of himself he resolved to *abide by*. To this he refers them for an answer to their question.

(2) He refers them to his Father's judgment (*v*. 26): "*I have many things to say, and to judge of you. I speak to the world* (to which I am sent as an ambassador) *those things which I have heard of him*."

[1] He suppresses his accusation of them. He had *many things* to charge them with, but for the present he had said enough.

[2] He enters his appeal against them to his Father: *He that sent me*. Here two things comfort him: *First*, That he had been *true to his Father*, and to the trust reposed in him: *I speak to the world* (for his gospel was to be preached to every creature) *those things which I have heard of him*. *Secondly*, That his Father would be *true to him*. Though he should not *accuse* them to his Father, yet the Father, who sent him, would undoubtedly reckon. Christ would not accuse them; "for," saith he, "he that sent me is

true, and will pass judgment on them." Upon this part of our Saviour's discourse the evangelist has a melancholy remark (*v.* 27): *They understood not that he spoke to them of the Father.* Though Christ spoke so plainly of God as his Father in heaven, yet they did not understand whom he meant. Day and night are alike to the blind.

(3) He refers them to *their own convictions* hereafter, *v.* 28, 29. Now observe here,

[1] *What* they should ere long be *convinced of:* "*You shall know that I am he.* You shall be made to know it in your own consciences, the convictions of which, though you may *stifle,* yet you cannot *baffle.*" Two things they should be convinced of, *First,* That he did nothing *of himself,* of himself without the Father. Of false prophets it is said that they prophesied *out of their own hearts,* and followed *their own spirits. Secondly,* That as *his Father taught him* so he *spoke these things,* that he was not *self-taught,* but *taught of God.*

[2] *When* they should be convinced of this: *When you have lifted up the Son of man,* lifted him up upon the cross, as the brazen serpent upon the pole (*ch.* iii. 14). Or the expression denotes that his death was his exaltation. They *lifted him up* to the cross, but then he lifted up himself to his Father. Observe with what tenderness and mildness Christ here speaks to those who he certainly knew would put him to death. Christ speaks of his death as that which would be a powerful conviction of the infidelity of the Jews. *When you have lifted up the Son of man, then shall you know* this. Careless and unthinking people are often taught the worth of mercies by the want of them. The guilt of their sin would so awaken their consciences that they would be put upon serious enquiries after a Saviour, and then would know that Jesus was he who alone could save them. And so it proved, when, being told that with wicked hands they had *crucified and slain* the Son of God, they cried out, *What shall we do?* (Acts ii. 36). There would be such signs and wonders attending his death as would give a stronger proof of his being the Messiah than any that had been yet given. By the death of Christ the pouring out of the Spirit was purchased, who would convince the world that *Jesus is he.* The judgments which the Jews brought upon themselves, by putting Christ to death, were a sensible conviction to the most hardened among them that *Jesus was he.*

[3] What supported our Lord Jesus in the mean time (*v.* 29): *He that sent me is with me, for the Father hath not left me alone,* for *I do always those things that please him.* The assurance which Christ had of his Father's *presence* with him: *He that sent me is with me.* This greatly *emboldens* our faith in Christ and our reliance upon his word. The King of kings accompanied his own ambassador, and *never left him alone,* either solitary or weak; it also *aggravated* the wickedness of those that opposed him. The ground of this assurance: *For I do always those things that please him.* His whole undertaking is called the *pleasure of the Lord* (Isa. liii. 10). His management of that affair was in nothing *displeasing* to his Father. Our Lord Jesus never offended his Father in anything, he *fulfilled all righteousness.* God's servants may *then* expect God's presence with them when they *choose* and do *those things that please him.*

V. Here is the good effect which this discourse of Christ's had upon some of his hearers (*v.* 30): *As he spoke these words many believed on him.* There is a remnant who *believe to the saving of the soul.* If Israel, the whole body of the people, *be not gathered,* yet there are those of them in whom Christ will be *glorious.* When Christ told them that if they *believed not* they should *die in their sins,* they thought it was time to look about them. Sometimes there is a *wide door opened,* and an *effectual* one, even where there are *many adversaries.* The gospel sometimes gains great victories where it meets with great opposition. Let this encourage God's ministers to preach the gospel, though it be with *much contention,* for they shall not *labour in vain.* Many may be *secretly* brought home to God by those endeavours which are openly contradicted.

Verses 31-37

I. A comfortable doctrine laid down concerning the *spiritual liberty* of Christ's disciples. Christ, knowing that his doctrine began to work upon some of his hearers addressed himself to those *weak* believers.

1. How graciously the Lord Jesus looks to those that *tremble at his word,* and are ready to receive it; and will not pass by those who set themselves in his way, without speaking to them.

2. How carefully he cherishes the beginnings of grace. In what he said to them, we have two things, which he saith to all that should at any time believe: (1) The character of a true disciple of Christ: *If you continue in my word, then are you my disciples indeed.* He lays down this for a settled rule, that he would own none for his disciples but those that *continued in his word.* It highly concerns those that are not *strong in faith* to see to it that they be *sound in the faith.* Let those who have thoughts of covenanting with Christ have no thoughts of reserving a power of revocation. Children are sent to school, and bound apprentices, only for a *few years*; but those only are Christ's who are willing to be bound to him *for the term of life.* Those only that *continue in Christ's word* shall be accepted as his *disciples indeed.* It is *to dwell* in Christ's word, as a man does at home, which is his centre, and rest, and refuge.

(2) The privilege of a true disciple of Christ. Here are two precious promises, *v.* 32. "*You shall know the truth.*" Even those who are true believers may be, and are, much in the dark concerning many things which they should know. God's children are but children, and understand and speak as children. Did we not need to be taught, we should not need to be disciples. It is a very great privilege to *know the truth.* Christ's scholars are sure to be well taught. *The truth shall make you free;* that is, *First,* The truth which Christ teaches tends to make men free, Isa. lxi. 1. It makes us *free from* our spiritual enemies, free *in* the service of God, free *to* the privileges of sons. *Secondly,* The knowing, entertaining, and believing, of this truth does actually *make us free,* free from prejudices, mistakes, and false notions, free from the dominion of lust and passion; and restores the soul to the government of itself. The mind, by admitting the truth of Christ is vastly enlarged, and has scope and compass given it and never acts with so true a liberty as when it acts under a divine command, 2 Cor. iii. 17.

II. The offence which the carnal Jews took at this doctrine. They cavilled at it, *v.* 33. With a great deal of pride and envy they answered him, "*We Jews are Abraham's seed,* and therefore are *free-born; we were never in bondage to any man; how sayest thou then, You shall be made free?*"

1. What it was that they were grieved at; it was an *innuendo* in those words, *You shall be made free,* as if the Jewish nation were in some sort of bondage.

2. What it was that they alleged against it. (1) "We are Abraham's seed." It is common for a sinking decaying family to boast of the glory and dignity of its ancestors, and to borrow honour from that name to which they repay disgrace; so the Jews here did. It is the common fault and folly of those that have pious parentage and education to trust to their privilege, and boast of it, as if it would atone for the want of real holiness. Saving benefits are not

conveyed by *entail* to us and our issue, nor can a title to heaven be made by *descent*. They are not all Israel that are of Israel. (2) *We were never in bondage to any man.* How false this allegation was. I wonder how they could have the assurance to say a thing in the face of a congregation which was so notoriously *untrue*. Were they not at this time tributaries to the Romans, and, though not in a *personal*, yet in a *national* bondage to them, and groaning to be made free? How foolish the application was. Christ had spoken of a liberty wherewith the *truth* would make them free, which must be meant of a *spiritual* liberty, for truth as it is the enriching, so it is the *enfranchising* of the mind, and the *enlarging* of that from the captivity of error and prejudice; and yet they plead against the offer of *spiritual* liberty that they were never in *corporal* thraldom. Carnal hearts are sensible of no other grievances than those that molest the body and injure their secular affairs. Discourse to them of the bondage of sin, a captivity to Satan, and a liberty by Christ—and *you bring certain strange things to their ears.*

III. Our Saviour's vindication of his doctrine, *v.* 34–37, where he does these four things:

1. He shows that it was possible that they might be in a state of bondage (*v.* 34): *Whosoever commits sin is the servant of sin.* Christ further explains what he had said for their edification. (1) The preface is very solemn: *Verily, verily, I say unto you.* The style of the prophets was, *Thus saith the Lord,* for they were *faithful* as *servants*; but Christ, being a Son, speaks in his own name: *I say unto you.* He pawns his veracity upon it.

(2) The truth is of universal concern: *Whosoever commits sin is the servant of sin,* and sadly needs to be made free. See who it is on whom this brand is fastened—on him that *commits sin.* There is not a *just man* upon earth, that *lives, and sins not*; yet every one that sins is not a *servant* of sin, for then God would have no servants; but he that *makes sin,* that *makes choice* of sin, who walks after the flesh, and *makes a trade* of sin. See what the brand is which Christ fastens upon those that thus *commit sin.* He stigmatizes them, gives them a mark of servitude. They are *servants of sin.* He does the work of sin, supports its interest, and accepts its wages, Rom. vi. 16.

2. He shows them that their having a place in the house of God would not entitle them to the inheritance of sons: for (*v.* 35) *the servant abideth not in the house for ever, but the son* of the family abideth ever. (1) This points primarily at the rejection of the Jewish church and nation. Israel had been *God's son,* his *first-born.* Christ tells them that having made themselves servants they should not *abide in the house for ever.* "Think not to be made free from sin by the rites and ceremonies of the law of Moses, for Moses was but a servant. But, if the Son make you free, it is well," *v.* 36. (2) It looks further, to the rejection of all that are the *servants of sin.* True believers only are accounted free, and shall abide for ever in the house.

3. He shows them the way of deliverance. The case of those that are the servants of sin is sad, but thanks be to God it is not helpless, it is not hopeless. He who is *the Son* has a power both of manumission and of adoption (*v.* 36): *If the Son shall make you free, you shall be free indeed.*

(1) Jesus Christ in the gospel offers us *our freedom.* [1] To *discharge prisoners;* this he does in *justification,* by making satisfaction for *our guilt,* and for *our debts.* Christ, as our surety, compounds with the creditor, answers the demands of injured justice with more than an *equivalent.* [2] He has a power to rescue *bond-slaves,* and this he does in *sanctification;* by the powerful operations of his Spirit, he breaks

the power of corruption in the soul, rallies the scattered forces of reason and virtue, and so the soul is made free. [3] He has a power to *naturalize strangers and foreigners,* and this he does in *adoption.* This is a further act of grace. There is a charter of privileges as well as pardon.

(2) Those whom Christ makes free are *free indeed.* It is not the word used (*v.* 31) for disciples *indeed,* but *really.* The truth and certainty of the promise, the liberty which the Jews boasted of was an *imaginary* liberty; but the liberty which Christ gives is a certain thing, it is real. The servants of sin promise themselves liberty and fancy themselves free, but they cheat themselves. None are *free indeed* but those whom Christ *makes free.* The singular excellency of the freedom promised; it is a freedom that deserves the name. It is a *glorious* liberty. It is *substance,* while the things of the world are shadows.

4. He applies this in answer to their boasts of relation to Abraham (*v.* 37): "*I know that you are Abraham's seed, but now you seek to kill me, because my word hath no place in you.*"

(1) The dignity of their extraction admitted: "*I know that you are Abraham's seed.*" They boasted of their descent from *Abraham,* as that which *aggrandized* their names; whereas really it did but *aggravate* their crimes.

(2) The inconsistency of their practice with this dignity: *But you seek to kill me.* They had attempted it several times, and were now designing it, which quickly appeared (*v.* 58), when they *took up stones to cast at him.*

(3) The reason of this inconsistency. It is because *my word hath no place in you.* Some of the critics read it, *My word does not penetrate into you;* it descended as the rain, but it came upon them as the rain upon the rock, which it runs off, and did not soak into their hearts, as the rain upon the ploughed ground. Our translation is very significant: *It has no place in you.* The words of Christ ought to have a place in us, the innermost and uppermost place,—a *dwelling* place, as a man at home, and not as a stranger or sojourner,—a *working* place; it must have room to operate, to work sin out of us, and to work grace in us; it must have a *ruling* place, its place must be *upon the throne.* There are many that make a profession of religion in whom *the word of* Christ has no place; they will not *allow* it a place, for they do not like it. Other things possess the place it should have in us. Where the word of God has no place no good is to be expected, for room is left there for all wickedness.

Verses 38–47

Here Christ and the Jews are still at issue.

I. He here traces the difference between his sentiments and theirs to a different rise and origin (*v.* 38): *I speak that which I have seen with my Father,* and *you do what you have seen with your father.*

1. Christ's *doctrine* was from *heaven. I speak that which I have seen.* The discoveries Christ has made to us of God and another world are not grounded upon guess and hearsay. It is what I have seen *with my Father.* The doctrine of Christ is not a plausible hypothesis, supported by probable arguments. It was not only what he had *heard from* his Father, but what he had *seen with him.* It was Christ's prerogative to have *seen* what he *spoke,* and to *speak* what he had *seen.*

2. Their *doings* were from hell: "*You do that which you have seen with your father.*" As a child that is trained up with his father learns his father's words and fashions, and grows like him by imitation as well as by a natural image, so these Jews made themselves as like the devil as if they had industriously set him before them for their pattern.

II. He answers their vain-glorious boasts of relation to Abraham and to God as their fathers.

1. They pleaded relation to Abraham, and he replies to this plea. *They said, Abraham is our father,* v. 39. In this they intended, (1) To do honour to themselves, and to make themselves look great. (2) They designed to cast an odium upon Christ as if he reflected upon the patriarch Abraham, in speaking of their father as one they had learned evil from. Now Christ overthrows this plea by a plain and cogent argument: "Abraham's children will do the works of Abraham, but you do not do Abraham's works, therefore you are not Abraham's children." The proposition is plain: *If you were Abraham's children* then you would *do the works of Abraham.* Those only are reckoned the seed of Abraham, who *tread in the steps of* his faith and obedience. Those who would approve themselves Abraham's seed must not only be of Abraham's faith, but do Abraham's works (James ii. 21, 22). The assumption is evident likewise: *But you do not do* the works of Abraham, for *you seek to kill me, a man that has told you the truth, which I have heard of God; this did not Abraham,* v. 40. He shows them what their work was which they were now about; they *sought to kill him.* They were so *unnatural* as to seek the life of *a man* who had done them no harm, nor given them any provocation. They were so *ungrateful* as to seek the life of one who had *told them the truth.* They were so *ungodly* as to seek the life of one who told them the truth *which he had heard from God.* He shows them that this did not become the children of Abraham; for *this did not Abraham.* "He did nothing like this." He was famous for his humanity, and for his piety. Abraham believed God; they were obstinate in unbelief. "He would not have done thus if he had lived now, or I had lived then." The conclusion follows of course (v. 41): "You are not Abraham's children, but father yourselves upon another family (v. 41); there is *a father whose deeds you do.*" He does not *yet* say plainly that he means the devil. He tried whether they would suffer their own consciences to infer from what he said that they were the devil's children.

2. So far were they from owning their unworthiness of relation to Abraham that they pleaded relation to God himself as their Father: "We are *not born of fornication, we have one Father, even God.*"

(1) Some understand this literally. They were Hebrews of the Hebrews; and, being born in *lawful* wedlock, they might call God *Father.*

(2) Others take it figuratively. They begin to be aware now that Christ spoke of a *spiritual* father, of the father of their religion. They deny themselves to be a generation of idolaters: "We are *not born of fornication*, are not the children of idolatrous parents." If they meant no more than that they themselves were not idolaters, what then? A man may be free from idolatry, and yet perish in another iniquity. They boast themselves to be true worshippers of the true God. We have not many fathers, as the heathens had. *The Lord our God is one Lord and one Father,* and therefore it is well with us. Now our Saviour gives a full answer to this fallacious plea (v. 42, 43), and proves, by two arguments, that they had no right to call God Father.

First, They did not love Christ: *if God were your Father, you would love me.* He had disproved their relation to Abraham by their going about to kill him (v. 40), but here he disproves their relation to God by their not loving and owning him. All that have God for their Father have a true love to Jesus Christ. God has taken various methods to prove us, and this was one: he sent his Son into the world, concluding that all that called him Father would bid *him* welcome. By this our adoption will be proved or disproved—Did we love Christ, or no? If they

were God's children they would *love him.* He was the *Son of God.* Now this could not but recommend him to the affections of all that were *born of God.* He was *sent of God.* Observe the emphasis he lays upon this: *I came from God; neither came I of myself, but he sent me.* He came to *gather together in one the children of God* (ch. xi. 52). And would not all God's children embrace with both arms a messenger sent from their Father on *such* errands?

Secondly, They did not understand him. They did not understand the language and dialect of the family: *You do not understand my speech* (v. 43). Those that had made the word of the Creator familiar to them needed no other key to the dialect of the Redeemer. And the reason why they did not understand Christ's speech made the matter much worse: *Even because you cannot hear my word,* that is, "You cannot persuade yourselves to hear it without prejudice, as it should be heard." The meaning of this *cannot* is an obstinate *will not.* They do not like it nor love it, and therefore they will not understand it. *You cannot hear my words,* for you have *stopped your ears.*

III. He comes next to tell them plainly whose children they were: *You are of your father the devil,* v. 44. If they were not God's children, they were the devil's.

This is a high charge, and sounds very harsh and horrid, and therefore our Saviour fully proves it,

1. By a general argument: *The lusts of your father you will do.* (1) "You *do* the devil's lusts, the lusts which he would have you to fulfil, and are *led captive by him at his will.*" The peculiar lusts of the devil are *spiritual wickedness*; pride and envy, and wrath and malice; enmity to that which is good, and enticing others to that which is evil; these are lusts which the devil fulfils. (2) You *will do* the devil's lusts. The more there is of the *will* in these lusts, the more there is of the devil in them. "The lusts of your father you *delight to do,*" they are rolled under the tongue as a sweet morsel.

2. By two particular instances, wherein they manifestly resembled the devil—*murder* and *lying.*

(1) He was *a murderer from the beginning.* He was a *hater of man,* and so in disposition a murderer of him. He was man's tempter to *that* sin which brought death into the world. The great tempter is the great destroyer. The Jews called the devil *the angel of death.* If the devil had not been very strong in Cain, he could not have done such an unnatural thing as to kill his own brother. Now herein these Jews were followers of him, and were murderers, like him; murderers of souls, sworn enemies of Christ, and now ready to be his betrayers and murderers. *Now you seek to kill me.*

(2) He was *a liar.* He is a *deserter* from the truth; he *abode not in the truth.* The truth which Christ was now preaching, and which the Jews opposed; herein they did *like their father the devil.* He is *destitute* of the truth: *There is no truth in him.* There is no truth, nothing you can confide in, in him, nor in anything he says or does. He is a friend and patron of lying: *When he speaketh a lie he speaketh of his own.* Three things are here said of the devil with reference to the sin of lying: *First,* That he is *a liar*; his oracles were lying oracles, his prophets lying prophets. All his temptations are carried on by lies, calling *evil good and good evil. Secondly,* That when he *speaks a lie* he *speaks of his own.* It is the proper *idiom* of his language. *Thirdly,* That he is the *father of it.* He is the author and founder of all lies. He is the father of *every liar.* God made men with a disposition to truth. It is congruous to reason and natural light, that we should speak truth; but the devil, the author of sin, is the father of liars, who begat them, who trained them up in the *way of lying,* whom they resemble and obey.

IV. Christ, having thus proved all murderers and all liars to be the devil's children, comes in the following verses to assist them in the application of it to themselves. Two things he charges upon them:

1. That they would not *believe the word of truth* (v. 45).

(1) Two ways it may be taken: [1] "Though I tell you the truth, yet you will not believe me." They would not believe that he told them the truth. The greatest truths with some gained not the least credit; for they *rebelled against the light*. Or, [2] *Because I tell you the truth* (so we read it) therefore *you believe me not*. They would not receive him, nor entertain him as a prophet, because he showed them their faces in a glass that would not flatter them. Miserable is the case of those to whom the light of divine truth is become a torment.

(2) Now, to show them the unreasonableness of their infidelity, he condescends to put the matter to this fair issue, *v.* 46. If *he* were in an error, why did they not convince him? But (saith Christ) *which of you convinceth me of sin*? Their accusations were malicious groundless calumnies, and *utterly false*. The very judge that condemned him owned he *found no fault in him*. The only way not to be convicted of sin is not to sin. If *they* were in an error, why were they not convinced by him? "*If I say the truth, why do you not believe me*? If you cannot convince me of error, you must own that I *say the truth*, and why do you not then *give me credit*?" It will be found that the reason why we believe not in Jesus Christ is because we are not willing to part with our sins, and deny ourselves, and serve God faithfully.

2. Another thing charged upon them is that they would not hear the words of God (v. 47).

(1) A doctrine laid down: *He that is of God heareth God's words*. He is *willing* and *ready* to hear them, is sincerely desirous to know what the mind of God is, and cheerfully embraces whatever he knows to be so. He *apprehends* and *discerns* them, he so hears them as to perceive the *voice of God* in them, as they of the family know the master's tread, and the master's knock, as the sheep know the voice of their shepherd from that of a stranger.

(2) The application of this doctrine: *You therefore hear them not, because you are not of God*. Your being thus deaf and dead to the words of God is a plain evidence that you are *not of God*. Or, their not being of God was the reason why they did not profitably *hear the words of God*, which Christ spoke. If the word of the kingdom do not bring forth fruit, the blame is to be laid upon the soil, not upon the seed.

Verses 46–50

I. Hitherto they had cavilled at his doctrine, but, having shown themselves uneasy when he complained (v. 43, 47) that they would not hear him, now at length they fall to downright railing, v. 48. The scribes and Pharisees scornfully turned off the conviction with this: *Say we not well that thou art a Samaritan, and hast a devil?*

1. The blasphemous character commonly given of our Lord Jesus among the wicked Jews. (1) That he was a Samaritan. Thus they exposed him to the ill will of the people, with whom you could not put a man into a worse name than to call him a Samaritan. They had often enough called him a Galilean—*a mean man*; they will have him a Samaritan—*a bad man*. Great endeavours have in all ages been used to make good people odious by putting them under black characters, and it is easy to run that down with a crowd and a cry which is once put into an ill name. (2) That *he had a devil*; that he was *in league with the devil*. That he was possessed with a devil, that he was a melancholy man, whose brain was *clouded*, or a mad man, whose brain was *heated*,

and that which he said was no more to be believed than the extravagant rambles of a distracted man.

2. How they undertook to justify this character: *Say we not well that thou art so?* Their hearts were more hardened and their prejudices confirmed. They value themselves on their enmity to Christ, as if they had never spoken *better* than when they spoke the worst they could of Jesus Christ. It is bad to say and do ill, but it is worse to *stand to it*.

II. The meekness and mercifulness of Heaven shining in Christ's reply, *v.* 49, 50.

1. He denies their charge against him: *I have not a devil*. The imputation is unjust; "I am neither actuated by a devil, nor in compact with one."

2. He asserts the sincerity of his own intentions: But *I honour my Father*. It also proves that he *had not a devil*; for, if he had, he would not honour God.

3. He complains of the wrong they did him by their calumnies: *You do dishonour me*. By this it appears that, as man, he had a tender sense of the disgrace and indignity done him. Christ honoured his Father so as never man did, and yet was himself dishonoured so as never man was; for, though God has promised that those who honour him he will honour, he never promised that men should honour them.

4. He clears himself from the imputation of vain glory, *v.* 50. His *contempt* of worldly honour: *I seek not mine own glory*. He did not aim at this nor covet preferment in the world. "*You do dishonour me*, but cannot disturb me, for I *seek not my own glory*." Those who are dead to men's praise can safely bear their contempt. His *comfort* under worldly dishonour: *There is one that seeketh and judgeth*. In two things Christ made it appear that he *sought not his own glory*. (1) He did not *court* men's respect. In reference to this he saith, "There is one that seeketh". God will seek *their* honour that do not seek *their own*; for before honour is humility. (2) He did not *revenge* men's affronts, and in reference to this he saith, "*There is one that judgeth*, that will vindicate my honour." If we be humble appellants and patient expectants, we shall find, to our comfort, *there is one that judgeth*.

Verses 51–59

I. The doctrine of the immortality of believers laid down, *v.* 51. It is ushered in with the usual solemn preface, *Verily, verily, I say unto you, If a man keep my sayings, he shall never see death*. 1. The *character* of a believer: he is one that *keeps the sayings of the Lord Jesus*—*my word*. This we must not only *receive*, but *keep*; not only *have*, but *hold*. We must keep it in mind and memory, keep it in love and affection, keep it as our way, keep it as our rule. 2. The *privilege* of a believer: *He shall by no means see death for ever;* so it is in the original. Not as if the bodies of believers were secured from the stroke of death. How then is this promise made good that they *shall not see death*? The property of death is so altered to them that they do not see it as death, they do not see the terror of death. Their sight does not *terminate* in death, they look so clearly, so comfortably, through death, and beyond death, that they overlook death, and *see it not*. They shall not see death *for ever*. The day will come when *death shall be swallowed up in victory*. They are perfectly delivered from *eternal death*. They shall have their everlasting lot where there will be *no more death*, where they *cannot die any more*.

II. The Jews cavil at this doctrine. They lay hold of this occasion to reproach him that makes them so kind an offer: *Now we know that thou hast a devil. Abraham is dead*.

1. Their *railing*: "*Now we know that thou hast a devil*." If he had not abundantly proved himself a *teacher come from God*, his promises of immortality to his credulous followers might justly have been ridiculed, and charity itself would have imputed

them to a crazed fancy; but his doctrine was evidently divine, his miracles confirmed it, and the Jews' religion taught them to expect such a prophet, and to believe in him.

2. Their *reasoning*. They look upon him as guilty of an insufferable piece of arrogance, in making himself greater than *Abraham and the prophets: Abraham is dead*, and *the prophets*, they are dead too. It is true that Abraham and the prophets were great men, great in the favour of God, and great in the esteem of all good men. It is true that they *kept God's sayings*. It is true that they *died*; they never pretended to *have*, much less to *give*, immortality. It was their honour that they *died in faith*, but die they must. Why should a good man be afraid to die when Abraham is dead, and the prophets are dead? They have *tracked* the way through that darksome valley, which should reconcile us to death and help to take off the terror of it. Now they think Christ talks madly when he saith, *If a man keep my sayings, he shall never taste death*. Now their arguing goes upon two mistakes: [1] They understood Christ of an immortality in this world. God is still the *God of Abraham* and the *God of the holy prophets*. God is not the God of the dead, but of the living; therefore Abraham and the prophets are still alive, and, as Christ meant it, they had not *seen* nor *tasted* death. [2] They thought none could be greater than Abraham and the prophets, whereas they could not but know that the Messiah would be greater than Abraham or any of the prophets. Instead of inferring from Christ's making himself greater than Abraham that he had a *devil*, they should have inferred that he was the Christ; but their eyes were blinded. They scornfully asked, *Whom makest thou thyself?*

III. Christ's reply; still he vouchsafes to reason with them. This was the *day of his patience*.

1. In his answer he insists not upon his own testimony concerning himself, but waives it as not sufficient nor conclusive (v. 54): *If I honour myself, my honour is nothing*. Honour of our own creating is a mere chimera, has nothing in it, and therefore is called *vain-glory*. Self-admirers are self-*deceivers*.

2. He refers himself to *his* Father, God; and to *their* father, Abraham.

(1) To his Father, *God: It is my Father that honoureth me*. He *derived* from his Father all the honour he now claimed. He *depended* upon his Father for all the honour he further *looked for*. Christ and all that are his depend upon God for their honour; and he that is sure of honour where he is known cares not though he be slighted where he is in disguise.

First, He here takes occasion to show the reason of *their* incredulity, and this was their *unacquaintedness* with God; You *say of him that he is your God, yet you have not known him*. The profession they made of relation to God: "*You say that he is your God*." Many pretend to have an interest in God, and say say that he is *theirs*, who yet have no just cause to say so. What will it avail us to say, He is *our* God, if we be not in sincerity *his people*. Their ignorance of him: *Yet you have not known him. You know him not at all*. Or, *You know him not aright;* and this is as bad as not knowing him at all, or worse. Men may be able to dispute subtly concerning God, and *not know him*. It is only the name of God which they have learned to talk of. They knew not God; and therefore perceived not the image of God, nor the voice of God in Christ. The reason why men receive not the *gospel of Christ* is because they have not the *knowledge of God*.

Secondly, He gives them the reason of *his* assurance that his Father would *honour* him and *own* him: *But I know him;* and again, *I know him*; which bespeaks his *confidence* in him. He *professes* his knowledge of his Father, with the greatest certainty: If

I should say I know him not, I should be a liar like unto you. He would not deny his relation to God, to humour the Jews. If he should, he would be found a false witness against God and himself. He *proves* his knowledge of his Father: *I know him and keep his sayings*, or *his word*. He kept *his Father's* word, and *his own word* with the Father. Christ requires of us (v. 51) that we *keep his sayings*; and he has set before us a copy of obedience: he *kept his Father's sayings*; well might he who *learned obedience* teach it. Christ by this evinced that he knew the Father.

(2) Christ refers them to *their* father, and that was Abraham.

[1] Christ asserts Abraham's prospect of him, and respect to him: *Your father Abraham rejoiced to see my day, and he saw it, and was glad*, v. 56. Two things he here speaks of as instances of that patriarch's respect to the promised Messiah:

First, The ambition he had to *see his day: He rejoiced—he leaped at it*. The word must here signify a transport of *desire* rather than of *joy*, for otherwise the latter part of the verse would be a tautology; he *saw it, and was glad*. The notices he had received of the Messiah to come had raised in him an expectation of something *great*, which he earnestly longed to know more of. Those who rightly know anything of Christ cannot but be earnestly desirous to know more of him. Those who discern the dawning of the light of the Sun of righteousness cannot but wish to see his rising. Abraham desired to see Christ's day, though it was at a great distance; but this degenerate seed of his discerned not his day, nor bade it welcome when it came.

Secondly, The satisfaction he had in what he did see of it: *He saw it, and was glad*.

a. How God gratified the pious desire of Abraham; he longed to see Christ's day, and he *saw it*. He saw something of it, more *afterwards* than he did at first. To him that desires and prays for more of the knowledge of Christ, God will give more. But how did Abraham see Christ's day? Some understand it of the sight he had of it in the other world. The longings of gracious souls after Jesus Christ will be fully satisfied when they come to heaven, and not till then. It is more commonly understood of some sight he had of *Christ's day* in this world. They that *received not the promises*, yet *saw them afar off*. There is room to conjecture that Abraham had some vision of Christ and his day, which is not recorded in his history.

b. How *Abraham* entertained these discoveries of Christ's day: *He saw, and was glad*. He was glad of what he *saw* of God's favour to himself, and glad of what he *foresaw* of the mercy God had in store for the world. A believing sight of Christ and his day will put gladness into the heart. No joy like the joy of faith; we are never acquainted with true pleasure till we are acquainted with Christ.

[2] The Jews cavil at this, and reproach him for it (v. 57): *Thou art not yet fifty years old, and hast thou seen Abraham?* They suppose it a very absurd thing for him to pretend to have seen Abraham, who was *dead* so many ages before he was born. Now this gave them occasion to *despise his youth*, as if he were *but of yesterday, and knew* nothing: *Thou art not yet fifty years old*.

[3] Our Saviour gives an effectual answer to this cavil, by a solemn assertion of his own seniority even to Abraham himself (v. 58): "*Verily, verily, I say unto you;* I say it to your faces, take it how you will: *Before Abraham was, I am. Before Abraham was made or born, I am*." The change of the word is observable, and bespeaks Abraham a creature, and himself the Creator. *Before Abraham he was*, as God. *I am*, is the name of God. He does not say, *I was*, but *I am*, for he is the first and the last. He was the appointed Messiah, long before Abraham.

[4] This great word ended the dispute *abruptly*: they could bear to hear no more from him, and he needed to say no more to them. Their inveterate prejudice against the holy spiritual doctrine and law of Christ, baffled all the methods of conviction. They were *enraged* at Christ for what he said: *They took up stones to cast at him, v.* 59. Perhaps they looked upon him as a blasphemer, and such were indeed to be stoned, but they must be first legally tried and convicted. Farewell justice and order if every man pretend to execute a law at his pleasure. Who would think that ever there should be such wickedness as this in men? Thus everyone has a stone to throw at his holy religion. He made his *escape* out of their hands. Jesus *hid himself.* Not that Christ was afraid or ashamed to stand by what he had said, but his *hour was not yet come*, and he would countenance the flight of his ministers and people in times of persecution. He *departed*, he *went out of the temple*, going *through the midst of them*, undiscovered, and *so passed by.* This was not a cowardly inglorious flight, nor such as argued either guilt or fear. It was an instance of his power over his enemies, and that they could do no more against him than he gave them leave to do. They now thought they had made sure of him and yet he *passed through the midst* of them, and thus he left them to fume. It was an instance of his prudent provision for his own safety. Thus he gave an example to his own rule, *When they persecute you in one city flee to another.* It was a righteous deserting of those who stoned him from among them. Christ will not long stay with those who bid him be gone. Christ now *went through* the midst of the Jews, and none of them courted his stay, nor stirred up himself to take hold of him, but were even content to let him go. God never forsakes any till they have first provoked him to withdraw, and will have none of him. When Christ left them it is said that he passed by silently and unobserved; so that they were not aware of him. Christ's departures from a church, or a particular soul, are often *secret.* As *the kingdom of God comes not*, so it *goes not, with observation.* Thus it was with these forsaken Jews, God left them, and they never missed him.

CHAPTER 9

In this chapter we have, I. The miraculous cure of a man that was born blind, ver. 1–7. II. The discourses which were occasioned by it. 1. A discourse of the neighbours among themselves, and with the man, ver. 8–12. 2. Between the Pharisees and the man, ver. 13–34. 3. Between Christ and the poor man, ver. 35–38. 4. Between Christ and the Pharisees, ver. 39 to the end.

Verses 1–7

I. The notice which our Lord Jesus took of the piteous case of this poor blind man (*v.* 1): *As Jesus passed by he saw a man which was blind from his birth.* Though the Jews had so basely abused him, yet he did not miss any opportunity of doing good among them. The cure of this blind man was a kindness to *the public*, enabling him to work for his living who before was a charge and burden to the neighbourhood. It is noble, and generous, and Christ-like, to be willing to *serve the public.* Though he was in his flight from a threatening danger, and escaping for his life, yet he willingly halted and stayed awhile to show mercy to this poor man. We make more haste than good speed when we out-run opportunities of doing good. Christ took this poor blind man in his way, and cured him *as he passed by.* Thus should we take occasions of doing good, even as we *pass by*, wherever we are. The condition of this poor man was very sad. He was *blind*, and had been so *from his birth.* He that is *blind* has no *enjoyment* of the light, but he that is *born blind* has no *idea* of it. Methinks such a one would give a great deal to have his curiosity

satisfied with but one day's sight of light and colours, shapes and figures, though he were never to see them more. Let us bless God that it was not our case. The eye is one of the most curious parts of the body, its structure exceedingly nice and fine. What a mercy is it that there was no miscarriage in the making of ours! Christ cured many that were blind by disease or accident, but here he cured one that was *born blind*; that he might give an instance of his power to help in the most desperate cases. That he might give a *specimen* of the work of his grace, upon the souls of sinners, which gives sight to those that were by nature blind. The compassions of our Lord Jesus towards him were very tender. He *saw him*; and looked upon him with concern. Others saw him, but not as he did. Christ is often found of those that seek him not, nor see him.

II. The discourse between Christ and his disciples concerning this man.

1. The question which the disciples put to their Master, *v.* 2. When Christ looked upon him, they had an eye to him too; Christ's compassion should kindle ours. But they did not move Christ to heal him. Instead of this, they started a very odd question concerning him: *Rabbi, who sinned, this man or his parents, that he was born blind?* Now this question of theirs was,

(1) *Uncharitably censorious.* They take it for granted that this extraordinary calamity was the punishment of some uncommon wickedness. The greatest sufferers are not *therefore* to be looked upon as the greatest sinners. The grace of repentance calls our own afflictions *punishments*, but the grace of charity calls the afflictions of others *trials.*

(2) It was *unnecessarily curious.* They ask, *Who were the criminals, this man or his parents?* And what was this to them? Or what good would it do them to know it? We are apt to be more inquisitive concerning other people's sins than concerning our own. To judge ourselves is our duty, but to judge our brother is our sin. They enquire, [1] Whether this man was punished thus for some sin of his own, either committed or foreseen before his birth. The Pharisees seem to have had the same opinion of his case when they said, *Thou wast altogether born in sin* (*v.* 34). Or, [2] Whether he was punished for the wickedness of his parents, which God sometimes *visits upon the children.* It is a good reason why parents should take heed of sin, lest their children smart for it when they are gone. Being at a loss what construction to put upon this providence, they desire to be informed. The equity of God's dispensations is always certain, but not always to be accounted for, for his *judgments are a great deep.*

2. Christ's answer to this question.

(1) He gives the reason of this poor man's blindness: *"Neither has this man sinned nor his parents, but he was born blind, that now at last the works of God should be made manifest in him," v.* 3. Here Christ told them two things concerning such uncommon calamities: That they are not always inflicted as punishments of sin. Many are made much more *miserable* than others in this life who are not at all more *sinful.* It was not any uncommon guilt that God had an eye to in inflicting this upon him. Misfortunes are sometimes intended purely *for the glory of God*, and the *manifesting of his works.* If God be glorified, either by us or in us, we were not made *in vain.* This man was *born blind, that the works of God might be manifest in him. First*, That the *attributes of God* might be made manifest in him, especially that his extraordinary power and goodness might be manifested in curing him. The difficulties of providence, otherwise unaccountable, may be resolved into this—God intends in them to *show* himself. Those who regard him not in the ordinary

course of things are sometimes alarmed by things extraordinary. *Secondly*, That the counsels of God might be manifested in him. He was *born blind* that our Lord Jesus might prove himself sent of God to be the true light to the world. It was now a great while since this man was born blind, and yet it never appeared till now *why* he was so. The sentences in the book of providence are sometimes *long*, and you must read a great way before you can apprehend the sense of them.

(2) He gives the reason of his own forwardness and readiness to help and heal him, *v.* 4, 5. *I must work the works of him that sent me while it is day; the night cometh, when no man can work.* It was the sabbath day, on which works of necessity might be done, and he proves this to be a work of necessity.

[1] It was his Father's will: *I must work the works of him that sent me.* Whom God sends he employs, for he sends none to be idle. He was a worker together with God. He was pleased to lay himself under the strongest obligations to do the business he was sent about: I *must work.* Christ laid out himself with the utmost vigour and industry in his work. He *worked the works* he had to do. It is not enough to look at our work, and talk over it, but we must work it.

[2] Now was his opportunity. I must work *while it is day*, while the light lasts which is given to work by. Christ himself had *his day.* All the work he had to do *in his own person* here on earth was to be done *before his death*; the time of his living in this world is *the day* here spoken of. The time of our life is our day. Day-time is the proper season for work; during the day of life we must be busy, not waste day-time, nor play by *daylight*; it will be time enough to rest when our day is done.

[3] The period of his opportunity was at hand, and therefore he would be busy: *The night comes when no man can work.* It will come certainly, may come suddenly, is coming nearer and nearer. We cannot compute how nigh our sun is, it may go down at noon: nor can we promise ourselves a twilight between the day of life and the night of death. When the night comes we *cannot work.* When night comes, *call the labourers*; we must then *show our work*, and receive according to the things done. It is too late to *bid* when the inch of candle is *dropped.*

[4] His business in the world was to enlighten it (*v.* 5): *As long as I am in the world, I am the light of the world.* He had said this before, *ch.* viii. 12. Christ would cure this blind man, the representative of a blind world, because he came to be *the light of the world*, not only to give *light*, but to give *sight.* Now this gives us a great *encouragement* to come to him. Which way should we turn our eyes, but to the light? We partake of the sun's light, and so we may of Christ's grace, without money and without price. A good *example* of usefulness in the world. What Christ saith of himself, he saith of his disciples: *You are lights in the world*, and, if so, *Let your light shine.* What were candles made for but to burn?

III. The manner of the cure of the blind man, *v.* 6, 7. The circumstances of the miracle are singular, and no doubt significant. *When he had thus spoken* he addressed himself to the opening of the blind man's eyes. He did not defer it till the sabbath was past, when it would give less offence. What good we have opportunity of doing we should do quickly; he that will never do a good work till there is nothing to be objected against it will leave many a good work for ever undone.

1. The preparation of the eye-salve. Christ *spat on the ground, and made clay of the spittle.* He made clay of his own spittle, because there was no water near; and he would teach us to be willing to take up with that which is *next hand*, if it will but serve the

turn. Why should we *go about* for that which may as well be had and done a *nearer way?*

2. The application of it to the place: *He anointed the eyes of the blind man with the clay.* Like a tender physician; he did it himself with his own hand, though the patient was a beggar. Daubing clay on the eyes would *close them* up, but never *open them.* The power of God often works by contraries. The design of the gospel is to *open men's eyes.* Now the eye-salve that does the work is of Christ's preparing. We must come to Christ for *the eye-salve.* He only is *able*, and he only is *appointed*, to make it up. The means used in this work are very weak, and unlikely, and are made effectual only by the power of Christ. And the method Christ takes is first to make men feel themselves blind, and then to give them sight.

3. The directions given to the patient, *v.* 7. His physician said to him, *Go, wash in the pool of Siloam.* Christ would hereby try his obedience, and whether he would with an implicit faith obey the orders of one he was so much a stranger to. He would likewise try how he stood affected to the tradition of the elders, which taught that it was not lawful to wash the eyes on the sabbath day. He would hereby represent the method of spiritual healing, in which, though the effect is owing purely to his power and grace, there is duty to be done by us. Go, search the scriptures, attend upon the ministry, converse with the wise; this is like washing in the pool of Siloam. Promised graces must be expected in the way of instituted ordinances. Concerning the pool of Siloam observe that it was supplied with water from Mount Zion, living waters, which were *healing.* The evangelist takes notice of the signification of the name, its being interpreted *sent.* Christ is often called the *sent of God*, so that when Christ sent him to the pool of Siloam he did in effect send him to himself. *Go, wash in the fountain opened*, a fountain of life, not a *pool.*

4. The patient's obedience to these directions: *He went his way therefore*, and *he washed his eyes.* In confidence of Christ's power, as well as in obedience to his command, he went, and washed.

5. The cure effected: *He came seeing.* So when the pangs and struggles of the new birth are over, the bands of sin fly off with them, and a glorious light and liberty succeed. Such is the power of Christ. What cannot *he* do who could do *this*, and do it *thus?* This man let Christ do what *he* pleased, and did what he appointed him to do, and so was cured. Those that would be healed by Christ must be ruled by him. He *came back* from the pool wondering and wondered at; he came *seeing.* This represents the benefit gracious souls find in attending on instituted ordinances, according to Christ's appointment; they have gone trembling, and come away triumphing; have gone *blind*, and come away *seeing*, come away singing.

Verses 8-12

Such a wonderful event as the giving of sight to a man born blind could not but be the talk of the town. Here we are told what the neighbours said of it, for the confirmation of the matter of fact. That which at first was not believed without *scrutiny* may afterwards be admitted without *scruple.*

I. Whether this was the same man that had before been blind, *v.* 8.

1. The neighbours could not but be amazed when they saw that he had his eyesight, and they said, *Is not this he that sat and begged?* When he could not labour, his parents not being able to maintain him, he *begged.* Those who cannot otherwise subsist must not be *ashamed to beg*; let no man be ashamed of anything but sin. There are some common beggars that are objects of charity, that should be distinguished; and we must not let the bees starve for the sake of

the drones or wasps that are among them. The truth of the miracle was the better attested, and there were more to witness against those infidel Jews who would not believe *that he had been blind* than if he had been maintained in his father's house. Note, Christ's condescension. When it was for the advantage of his miracles that they should be wrought on those that were remarkable, he pitched upon those that were made so by their poverty and misery, not by their dignity.

2. Some said, *This is he*, the very same man; and these are witnesses to the truth of the miracle, for they had long known him stone-blind. Others said, *He is not he, but is like him*, and so, by their confession, if it be he, it is a great miracle that is wrought upon him. Think, [1] Of the wisdom and power of Providence in ordering such a universal variety of the faces of men and women, so that no two are so alike but that they may be distinguished, which is necessary to society, and commerce, and the administration of justice. [2] Of the wonderful change which the converting grace of God makes upon some who before were very wicked and vile, but are thereby so universally and visibly altered that one would not take them to be the same person.

3. This controversy was soon decided by the man himself: *He said, I am he*, "I am he that was blind, but now see, and am a monument of the mercy and grace of God." Those who are savingly enlightened by the grace of God should be ready to own what they were before.

II. How he came to have his eyes opened, *v. 10–12*. They will now turn aside, and *see this great sight*, and enquire further concerning it. Two things these neighbours enquire after:

1. The manner of the cure: *How were thine eyes opened?* It is good to observe the way and method of God's works, and they will appear the more wonderful. In answer to this enquiry the poor man gives them a plain and full account of the matter: *A man that is called Jesus made clay—and I received sight, v. 11.* Those who have experienced God's power and goodness, in temporal or spiritual things, should be ready upon all occasions to communicate their experiences. It is a debt we owe to our benefactor, and to our brethren. God's favours are lost *upon* us, when they are lost *with us*, and go no further.

2. The author of it (*v. 12*): *Where is he?* Some perhaps asked this question out of curiosity. "Where is he, that we may see him?" Others, perhaps, asked out of ill-will. "Where is he, that we may *seize* him?" The unthinking crowd will have ill thoughts of those that are put into an ill name. Some, we hope, asked this question out of *goodwill*. "Where is he, that we may be acquainted with him?" In answer to this, he could say nothing: *I know not*. As soon as Christ had sent him to the pool of Siloam, it should seem, he withdrew immediately. The man had never seen Jesus, for by the time that he had gained his sight he had lost his Physician. None of all the new and surprising objects that presented themselves could be so grateful to him as one sight of Christ, but as yet he knew no more of him than that he was called *Jesus—a Saviour*. Thus in the work of grace wrought upon the soul we see the change, but see not the hand that makes it.

Verses 13–34

One would have expected that such a miracle as Christ wrought upon the blind man would have silenced and shamed all opposition, but it had the contrary effect; instead of being embraced as a prophet for it, he is prosecuted as a criminal.

I. *They brought to the Pharisees him that aforetime was blind, v. 13.* Some think that those who brought this man to the Pharisees did it with a *good design*,

to show them that this Jesus was not what they represented him, but one that gave considerable proofs of a divine mission. It should seem, rather, that they did it with an *ill design*.

II. That which is good was never maligned but under the imputation of something evil. And the crime objected here (*v. 14*) was that *it was the sabbath day when Jesus made the clay, and opened his eyes*. The traditions of the Jews had made that to be a violation of the law of the sabbath which was far from being so. But it may be asked, "Why would Christ not only work miracles on the sabbath day, but work them in such a manner as he knew would give offence to the Jews? Could he not have cured this blind man without making clay?" He would not seem to yield to the usurped power of the scribes and Pharisees. Christ was made under the law of God, but not under their law. He did it that he might, both by word and action, expound the law of the fourth commandment. Works of necessity and mercy are allowed, and the sabbath-rest to be kept, not so much for its own sake as in order to the sabbath-work.

III. The trial and examination of this matter by the Pharisees, *v. 15*. So much passion, prejudice, and ill-humour, and so little reason, appear here, that the discourse is nothing but crossing questions. Their enmity to Christ had divested them of all manner of humanity, and divinity too. Let us see how they teased this man.

1. They interrogated him concerning the cure itself. They *did not believe* that he was *born blind*. This was not a prudent caution, but a prejudiced infidelity. However, it was a good way that they took for the clearing of this: *They called the parents of the man who had received his sight*. This they did in hopes to disprove the miracle. God so ordered and overruled this counsel of theirs that it turned to the more effectual proof of the miracle, and left them under a necessity of being either convinced or confounded. Now in this part of the examination we have the questions that were put to them (*v. 19*): They *asked them, "Is this your son? Do you say he was born blind? How then doth he now see?* That is impossible, and therefore you had better unsay it." Those who cannot bear the light of truth do all they can to *eclipse* it, and hinder the discovery of it. Their answers to these interrogatories. They fully attest that which they could safely say in this matter (*v. 20*): *We know that this is our son*, and we know that he was *born blind*. It had cost them many a sad thought, and many a careful troublesome hour, about him. Those who are ashamed of their children because of their bodily infirmities, may take a reproof from *these* parents, who freely owned, This is *our son*, though he was *born blind*. They cautiously decline giving any evidence concerning his cure. They were not themselves eye-witnesses of it, and could say nothing to it *of their own knowledge*. Observe how warily they express themselves (*v. 21*): *"By what means he now seeth we know not*, or *who has opened his eyes we know not.*" Now these parents of the blind man were bound in gratitude to have borne their testimony to the honour of the Lord Jesus, who had done their son so great a kindness; but they had not courage to do it, and then thought it might serve to atone for their not appearing in favour of him that they said nothing to his prejudice. They refer themselves and the court to him: *He is of age, ask him, he shall speak for himself.* This man, though he was *born blind*, seems to have been of quick understanding above many. Thus God often by a kind providence makes up in the mind what is wanting in the body. His parents' turning them over to him was only to save themselves from trouble. See the reason why they were so cautious (*v. 22, 23*): *Because*

they feared the Jews. Because they would shift trouble off from themselves. Near is my friend, and near is my child, and perhaps near is my religion, but *nearer is myself.* Note,

(1) The *late law* which the sanhedrim had made. If any man within their jurisdiction did *confess* that Jesus *was Christ, he should be put out of the synagogue.* [1] The crime designed to be punished, and that was embracing Jesus of Nazareth as the promised Messiah, and confessing of him. They themselves did expect a Messiah, but they could by no means bear to think that this Jesus should be he. *First,* Because his precepts were all so contrary to their traditional *laws.* The spiritual worship he prescribed overthrew their formalities. Humility and mortification, repentance and self-denial, were lessons new to them and sounded harsh and strange in their ears. *Secondly,* Because his promises and appearances were so contrary to their traditional hopes. Now to hear of a Messiah whose outward circumstances were all mean and poor, and at the same time bade his followers expect the cross, and count upon persecution; this was such a disappointment to all their hopes, that they could never be reconciled to it. Right or wrong, it must be *crushed.*

[2] The penalty to be inflicted for this crime. If any should own himself a disciple of Jesus, he should therefore be *put out of the synagogue,* as one that had rendered himself unworthy of the honours, and incapable of the privileges, of their church. Nor was this merely an ecclesiastical censure. It was, in effect, an *outlawry.* Christ's holy religion, from its first rise, has been opposed by penal laws made against the professors of it. The church's artillery, when the command of it has fallen into ill hands, has often been turned against itself. It is no new thing to see those cast out of the synagogue that were the greatest ornaments and blessings of it. They had already agreed it. Thus early were they aware of his growing interest, and already agreed to do their utmost to suppress it.

(2) The influence which this law had upon the parents of the blind man. They declined saying anything of Christ, *because they feared the Jews.* Christ had incurred the frowns of the government to do their son a kindness, but they would not incur them to do him any honour. Let us now go on with the examination of the man himself.

(3) They enquired of *him* concerning the *manner* of *the cure, v.* 15, 16.

[1] The same question which his neighbours had put to him *now again the Pharisees asked him, how he had received his sight.* This they enquired not with any sincere desire to find out the truth, but with a desire to find an occasion against Christ.

[2] The same answer, in effect, which he had before given to his neighbours, he here repeats to the Pharisees: *He put clay upon mine eyes, and I washed, and do see.* In the former account he said, *I washed, and received sight;* but lest they should think it was only a glimpse, he now says, "*I do see;* it is a complete and lasting cure."

[3] The remarks made upon this story were very different, and occasioned a debate in the court, *v.* 16.

First, Some took this occasion to censure and condemn Christ. Some of the Pharisees said, *This man is not of God, because he keepeth not the sabbath day.* The doctrine upon which this censure is grounded is very true—that those *are not of God* who do not *keep the sabbath day.* Those that are of God will *keep the commandments of God;* and this is his commandment, that we sanctify the sabbath. The application of it to our Saviour is very unjust, for he did religiously observe the sabbath day, never did otherwise than *well* on the sabbath day. He did not

keep the sabbath according to the tradition of the elders, but he kept it according to the command of God. Much unrighteousness and uncharitable judging is occasioned by men's making the rules of religion more strict than God has made them, and adding their own fancies to God's appointments. Everything that we take for a rule of practice must not presently be made a rule of judgment.

Secondly, Others spoke in his favour, and very pertinently urged, *How can a man that is a sinner do such miracles?* There were some that were witnesses for Christ, even in the midst of his enemies. The matter of fact was plain, that this was a true miracle. Such things as these could never be done by a *man that is a sinner.* Such a one may indeed show some *signs and lying wonders,* but not such signs and true wonders as Christ wrought. Thus there was a *division among them.* Thus God defeats the counsels of his enemies by dividing them.

2. Their enquiry concerning the *author* of it.

(1) What the man said of him. They ask him (*v.* 17), "*What sayest thou of him, seeing that he has opened thine eyes?*" If he should speak *slightly* of Christ, in answer to this, as he might be tempted to do, to please them, they would have triumphed in it. Nothing confirms Christ's enemies in their enmity to him so much as the slights put upon him by those that have passed for his friends. But if he should speak honourably of Christ, they would prosecute him. They would make him an example. Or perhaps Christ's friends proposed to have the man's own sentiments concerning his physician, since he appeared to be a sensible man. Those whose eyes Christ has opened know best what to say of him. What think we of Christ? To this question the poor man makes a short, plain, and direct answer: *He is a prophet.* It should seem, this man had not any thoughts that Christ was the Messiah, the great prophet. This blind man thought well of Christ according to the light he had, though he did not think well enough of him. This poor blind beggar had a clearer judgment of the things pertaining to the kingdom of God than the *masters in Israel.*

(2) What they said of him, in reply to the man's testimony. Finding that indeed a *notable miracle was wrought,* and they *could not deny it,* they do all they can to shake the good opinion the man had of him that opened his eyes, and to convince him that Christ was a bad man (*v.* 24): *Give God the praise, we know that this man is a sinner.* Two ways this is understood: By way of *advice,* to take heed of ascribing the praise of his cure to a sinful man, but to give it all to God. When God makes use of men that are sinners as instruments of good to us, we must *give God the glory,* and yet there is gratitude owing to the instruments. It was a good word, *Give God the praise,* but here it was ill used. By way of *adjuration;* "We know that this man is *a sinner;* this we are sure of, therefore *give God praise.* In God's name, man, tell the truth." See how basely they speak of the Lord Jesus: *We know that this man is a sinner,* is a man of sin. Their insolence and pride. They know very well that he is a sinner, and nobody can convince them of the contrary. He had challenged them to their faces (*ch.* viii. 46) to *convince him of sin,* and they had nothing to say; but now behind his back they speak of him as a malefactor. Thus false accusers make up in confidence what is wanting in proof. The injury and indignity hereby done to the Lord Jesus. When he became man, he took upon him the form not only of a *servant,* but of a *sinner.* Being *made sin for us,* he despised even this shame.

3. The debate that arose between the Pharisees and this poor man concerning Christ. They say, *He is a sinner;* he says, *He is a prophet.* It is an encouragement to those who are called out to witness

for Christ to find with what prudence and courage this man managed his defence, according to the promise, *It shall be given you in that same hour what you shall speak.* Now in the parley we may observe three steps:

(1) He sticks to the certain matter of fact the evidence of which they endeavour to shake. He adheres to that which to himself, at least, was past dispute (*v.* 25): "*Whether he be a sinner or no I know not,*" or, as it might better be rendered, "*If he be a sinner, I know it not,* for this *one thing I know, that whereas I was blind, now I see,* and therefore he is a *prophet;* I am both able and bound to speak well of him.*"* He tacitly reproves their great assurance of the ill character they gave of the blessed Jesus: "I, who know him as well as you do, cannot give him any such character." He boldly relies upon his own experience of the power and goodness of the holy Jesus, and resolves to abide by it. There is no disputing against experience. As Christ's mercies are most valued by those that have felt the want of them, so the most powerful and durable affections to Christ are those that arise from an experimental knowledge of him. Thus in the work of grace in the soul, though we cannot tell when and how, the blessed change was wrought, yet we may take the comfort of it if we can say, through grace, "*Whereas I was blind, now I see.*" A needless repetition of their enquiries into it (*v.* 26): *What did he to thee? How opened he thine eyes?* They asked these questions, because they wanted something to say, and would rather speak *impertinently* than seem to be silenced; because they hoped, by putting the man upon repeating his evidence, to catch him tripping in it.

(2) He upbraids them with their invincible prejudices, and they revile him as a disciple of Jesus, *v.* 27–29.

[1] Their wilful and unreasonable opposition to the evidence of this miracle, *v.* 27. He would not gratify them with a repetition of the story: *I have told you already, and you did not hear, wherefore would you hear it again, will you also be his disciples?* Some think that he spoke *seriously,* and really expecting that they would be convinced. But it rather seems to be spoken *ironically:* "*Will you be his disciples?* No, I know you abhor the thoughts of it." Those that wilfully shut their eyes against the light, as these Pharisees here did, *First,* Make themselves contemptible and base. *Secondly,* They forfeit all the benefit of further instruction. They that have been told once, and *would not hear,* why should they be told it again? *Thirdly,* They hereby *receive the grace of God in vain.* This is implied in that, "*Will you be his disciples?*" Those who will not see cause to embrace Christ, and join with his followers, yet, one would think, should see cause enough not to hate and persecute him and them.

[2] For this they scorn and revile him, *v.* 28. When they could not resist the wisdom and spirit by which he spoke, they broke out into a passion. The method commonly taken by unreasonable man is to make out with railing what is wanting in truth and reason.

First, They taunted this man for his affection to Christ; they said, *Thou art his disciple.* They *reviled him.* The Vulgate reads it, *they cursed him;* and what was their curse? It was this, *Be thou his disciple.* "May such a curse" (saith St. Austin here) "ever be on us and on our children!" They had no reason to call this man a *disciple of* Christ. He had spoken favourably of a kindness Christ had done him, and this they could not bear.

Secondly, They gloried in their relation to Moses as their Master: "*We are Moses's disciples.*" These Pharisees had before boasted of their good parentage: *We are Abraham's seed;* here they boast of their good education, *We are Moses's disciples;* as if these would save them. There was a perfect harmony between

Christ and Moses; they might be disciples of Moses and become the disciples of Christ too; and yet they here put them in opposition. If we rightly understand the matter, we shall see God's grace and man's duty meet together and kiss and befriend each other.

Thirdly, They gave some sort of reason for their adhering to Moses against Christ (*v.* 29): *We know that God spoke unto Moses; as for this fellow, we know not whence he is.* But did they not know that they must expect another prophet, and a further revelation of the mind of God? yet, when our Lord Jesus did appear, they not only forfeited, but forsook, their own mercies. In this argument of theirs observe,

a. How impertinently they allege that which none of his followers ever denied: *We know that God spoke unto Moses,* and, thanks be to God, we know it too. Moses was a prophet, it is true, and might not Jesus be a prophet also? *b.* How absurdly they urge their ignorance of Christ as a reason to justify their contempt of him: *As for this fellow.* Thus scornfully do they speak of the blessed Jesus, as if they did not think it worth while to charge their memories with a name so inconsiderable. *As for this fellow,* this sorry fellow, *we know not whence he is.* It was not long ago that the Jews had made the contrary to this an objection against Christ (*ch.* vii. 27): *We know this man whence he is, but when Christ comes no man knows whence he is.* Thus they could with the greatest assurance either affirm or deny the same thing, according as they saw it would serve their turn. See the absurdity of infidelity. Men will not know the doctrine of Christ because they are resolved they will not believe it, and then pretend they do not believe it because they do not know it.

4. He reasons with them, and they excommunicate him.

(1) The poor man, finding that he had reason on his side, grows more bold. He wonders at their obstinate infidelity (*v.* 30). He bravely answered, "*Why, herein is a marvellous thing,* that *you know not whence he is,* and yet he has opened mine eyes.*"* Two things he wonders at: [1] That they should be strangers to a man so *famous.* He that could open the eyes of the blind must certainly be a considerable man, and worth taking notice of. That they should talk as if they thought it below them to take cognizance of such a man as this, this is a strange thing indeed. There are many who pass for learned and knowing men, who have no concern, no, not so much as a curiosity, to acquaint themselves with that which the *angels desire to look into.* [2] That they should question the divine mission of one that had undoubtedly wrought a divine miracle. "Now this is strange," saith the poor man, "that the miracle wrought upon me has not convinced you, that you should thus shut your eyes against the light." Had Christ opened the eyes of the Pharisees, they would not have doubted his being a prophet. He argues strongly against them, *v.* 31–33. The man here proves not only that he was *not a sinner* (*v.* 31), but that he was *of God, v.* 33.

a. He argues here, (*a*) With great knowledge. Though he could not read a letter of the book, he was well acquainted with the scripture; he had wanted the sense of seeing, yet had well improved that of hearing, by which faith cometh. (*b*) With great zeal for the honour of Christ. (*c*) With great boldness, and courage. Those that are ambitious of the favours of God must not be afraid of the frowns of men.

b. His argument may be reduced into form, somewhat like that of David, Ps. lxvi. 18–20. *If I regard iniquity in my heart, God will not hear me. But verily God hath heard me; blessed be God.*

(*a*) He lays it down for an undoubted truth that none but good men are the favourites of heaven (*v.* 31): *Now we know that God heareth not sinners* but *if any man be a worshipper of God, and does his will, him he heareth.* The assertions, rightly understood, are true. Be it spoken to the terror of the wicked, *God heareth not sinners.* This bespeaks no discouragement to repenting returning sinners, but to those that go on still in their trespasses. God will not *hear* them. Be it spoken to the comfort of the righteous, *If any man be a worshipper of God, and does his will, him he heareth.* The complete character of a good man: he is one that *worships God*, and *does his will.* The unspeakable comfort of such a man: him *God hears*; hears his prayers, and answers them.

(*b*) He magnifies the miracles which Christ had wrought, to strengthen the argument the more (*v.* 32): *Since the world began was it not heard that any man opened the eyes of one that was born blind.* It was a true miracle, and above the power of nature; it was never heard that any man, by the use of natural means, had cured one that was *born blind.* It was an extraordinary miracle, and beyond the precedents of former miracles. Moses wrought miraculous plagues, but Christ wrought miraculous cures.

(*c*) He therefore concludes, *If this man were not of God, he could do nothing.* What Christ did on earth sufficiently demonstrated what he was in heaven. We may each of us know by this whether we are of God or no: *What do we?* What do we more than others?

(2) The Pharisees fell foul upon him, and broke off the discourse, *v.* 34. What they *said.* Having nothing to reply to his argument, they reflected upon his person: *Thou wast altogether born in sin, and dost thou teach it?* [1] How they despised him: "*Thou wast not only born in sin,* as every man is, but altogether so, and bearing about with thee in thy body as well as in thy soul the marks of that corruption; thou waste one whom nature *stigmatized.*" It was most unjust to take notice of it now that the cure had not only rolled away the reproach of his blindness, but had *signalised* him as a favourite of Heaven. [2] How they *disdain* to learn of him: *Dost thou teach us?* A mighty emphasis must be laid here upon *thou* and *us.* "What! wilt *thou*, a silly sorry fellow, ignorant and illiterate, wilt thou pretend to teach *us*, that sit in Moses's chair. Proud men scorn to be taught, especially by their inferiors, whereas we should never think ourselves too old, nor too wise, nor too good, to learn. Those that have much wealth would have more; and why not those that have much knowledge? What they did: They *cast him out.* Some understand it only of a rude and scornful dismission of him from their council-board. But it seems rather to be a judicial act; they excommunicated him.

Verses 35–38

I. The tender care which our Lord Jesus took of this poor man (*v.* 35): *When Jesus heard that they had cast him out,* then he *found him,* which implies his seeking him and looking after him, that he might encourage and comfort him, 1. Because he had spoken so very well, so bravely, so boldly, in defence of the Lord Jesus. Jesus Christ will be sure to stand by his witnesses, and own those that own him and his truth and ways. It shall redound not only to our credit hereafter, but our comfort now. 2. Because the Pharisees had cast him out. Here was one poor man suffering for Christ, and he took care that as his afflictions abounded his consolations should *much more abound.* Happy are they who have a friend from whom men cannot debar them. Jesus Christ will graciously find and receive those who for his sake are unjustly rejected and cast out by men.

II. The comfortable converse Christ had with him. Christ gives him further instruction; for he that is faithful in a little shall be entrusted with more, Matt. xiii. 12.

1. Our Lord Jesus examines his faith: "*Dost thou believe on the Son of God?*" The Messiah is here called the *Son of God.* Christ, that he might give us an idea of his kingdom, as purely spiritual and divine, calls himself the *Son of God.*

2. The poor man solicitously enquires concerning the Messiah he was to believe in, professing his readiness to embrace him (*v.* 36): *Who is he, Lord, that I may believe on him?* Some think he did know that Jesus, who cured him, was the Son of God, but did not know which was Jesus, and therefore, supposing this person that talked with him to be a follower of Jesus, desired him to do him the favour to direct him to his master. Others think he did know that this person who talked with him was Jesus, whom he believed a great and good man and a prophet, but did not yet know that he was the Son of God. "Thou who hast given me bodily sight, tell me, O tell me, who and where this Son of God is." The question was rational and just: *Who is he, Lord, that I may believe on him?*

3. Our Lord Jesus graciously reveals himself to him as that Son of God: *Thou hast both seen him, and it is he that talketh with thee, v.* 37. We do not find that Christ did thus expressly, and in so many words, reveal himself to any other as to this man here and to the woman of *Samaria.* He left others to find out by arguments who he was. Christ here describes himself to this man by two things: (1) *Thou hast seen him.* Now he was made sensible, more than ever, what an unspeakable mercy it was to be cured of his blindness, that he might see the Son of God. The greatest comfort of bodily eyesight is its serviceableness to our faith and the interests of our souls. Can we say that by faith we have seen Christ, seen him in his beauty and glory? Let us give him the praise, who opened our eyes. (2) *It is he that talketh with thee.* Great princes are willing to be *seen* by those whom yet they will not vouchsafe to *talk with.* But Christ talks with those whose desires are towards him, and manifests himself to them, as he did to the two disciples, when he talked their hearts warm, Luke xxiv. 32. This poor man was solicitously enquiring after the Saviour, when at the same time he saw him, and was talking with him. Jesus Christ is often nearer the souls that seek him than they themselves are aware of.

4. The poor man readily entertains this surprising revelation and said, *Lord, I believe, and he worshipped him.* He professed his faith in Christ: *Lord, I believe thee to be the Son of God.* He would not dispute anything that *he* said who had shown such mercy to him, and wrought such a miracle for him. Believing with the heart, he thus confesses with the mouth; and now the bruised reed was become a cedar. He paid his homage to him: *He worshipped him.* In worshipping Jesus he owned him to be God. Those who believe in him will see all the reason in the world to worship him. We never read any more of this man.

Verses 39–41

I. The account Christ gives of his design in coming into the world (*v.* 39): *For judgment I am* come. What Christ spoke, he spoke not as a preacher in the pulpit, but as a king upon the throne, and a judge upon the bench.

1. His business in the world was *great.* He came *for judgment.* To preach a doctrine and a law which would try men, and effectually discover and distinguish them. To put a difference between men, by revealing the thoughts of many hearts, and laying open men's true characters.

2. This great truth he explains by a metaphor borrowed from the miracle which he had lately wrought. That *those who see not might see, and that those who see might be made blind.* (1) This is applicable to nations and people. The Gentiles see a great

light, while blindness is *happened unto Israel*, and their eyes are darkened. (2) To particular persons. Christ came into the world, [1] Intentionally and designedly to give sight to those that were spiritually blind; by his word to reveal the object, and by his Spirit to heal the organ, that many precious souls might be turned *from darkness to light*. [2] Eventually, and in the issue, *that those who see might be made blind*; that those who have a high conceit of their own wisdom, and set up that in contradiction to divine revelation, might be sealed up in ignorance. The preaching of the cross was foolishness to those who by wisdom *knew not God*.

II. The Pharisees' cavil at this. They said, *Are we blind also?* When Christ said that *those who saw* should by his coming be made blind, they apprehended that he meant them, who were the *seers* of the people, and valued themselves on their *insight* and *foresight*. "We know that the common people are blind; but *are we blind also*?" Frequently those that need reproof most, and deserve it best, though they have wit enough to discern a *tacit* one, have not grace enough to bear a *just* one. These Pharisees took this reproof for a reproach.

III. Christ's answer to this cavil, which, if it did not convince them, yet silenced them: *If you were blind you should have no sin; but now you say, We see, therefore your sin remaineth*. They gloried that they were not blind, but would *see with their own eyes*, having abilities, as they thought, sufficient for their own guidance. This very thing which they gloried in, Christ here tells them, was their shame and ruin.

1. *If you were blind, you would have no sin*. If you were blind you would have had comparatively *no sin*. The times of ignorance God *winked at*. It will be more tolerable with those that perish for lack of vision than with those that *rebel against the light*. "If you had been sensible of your own blindness you would soon have accepted Christ as your guide, and then you would *have had no sin*." Those that are convinced of their disease are in a fair way to be cured, for there is not a greater hindrance to the salvation of souls than self-sufficiency.

2. "*But now you say, We see;* now that you have knowledge, and are instructed out of the law, and now that you think you see your way better than anybody can show it you, *therefore your sin remains*." And as those are most blind who *will not see*, so their blindness is most dangerous who fancy they do see. Hearest thou the Pharisees say, *We see? There is more hope of a fool*, of a publican and a harlot, than of such.

Chapter 10

I. Christ's parabolical discourse concerning himself as the door of the sheepfold and the shepherd of the sheep, ver. 1–18. II. The various sentiments of people upon it, ver. 19–21. III. The dispute Christ had with the Jews in the temple at the feast of dedication, ver. 22–39. IV. His departure into the country thereupon, ver. 40–42.

Verses 1–18

The Pharisees supported themselves in their opposition to Christ with this principle, that they were the *pastors of the church*, and that Jesus was an intruder and an imposter, and therefore the people were bound in duty to stick to *them*, against *him*. In opposition to this, Christ here describes who were the false shepherds, and who the true, leaving them to infer what they were.

I. Here is the parable or similitude proposed (*v*. 1–5). *Verily, verily, I say unto you,—Amen, amen.* This vehement asseveration intimates the certainty and weight of what he said.

1. In the parable we have, (1) A thief and a robber, that comes to do mischief to the flock, and damage to the owner, *v*. 1. *He enters not by the door*, as having

no lawful cause of entry, but *climbs up some other way*. How industrious are wicked people to do mischief! This should shame us out of our slothfulness and cowardice in the service of God. (2) The character that distinguishes the rightful owner. *He enters in by the door* (*v*. 2), and he comes to do them some good office or other. Sheep need man's care, and, in return for it, are serviceable to man, they clothe and feed those by whom they are coted and fed. (3) The ready entrance that the shepherd finds: *To him the porter openeth*, *v*. 3. (4) The care he takes. The *sheep hear his voice*, and, which is more, he *calls his own sheep by name*, so exact is the notice he takes of them, and he leads them out from the fold to the green pastures (*v*. 4, 5). He does not drive them, but (such was the custom in those times) he goes before them, and they, being used to it, *follow him*, and are safe. (5) The strange attendance of the sheep upon the shepherd: *They know his voice*, and *a stranger will they not follow*, but will flee from him, not *knowing his voice*.

2. Good men are fitly compared to sheep. Men, as creatures depending on their Creator, are called the *sheep of his pasture*. The church of God in the world is a *sheepfold*, into which the *children of God* that were scattered abroad are *gathered together* (*ch*. xi. 52). This sheepfold lies much exposed to thieves and robbers; *wolves* in sheep's clothing, Matt. vii. 15. The great Shepherd of the sheep takes wonderful care of the flock and of all that belong to it. God is the great Shepherd, Ps. xxiii. 1. The under-shepherds, who are entrusted to feed the flock of God, ought to be careful and faithful in the discharge of that trust. Ministers must serve them in their spiritual interests, must *feed their souls* with the word of God. They must know the members of their flocks by name, and watch over them; must lead them into the pastures of public ordinances, be their mouth to God and God's to them. Those who are truly the sheep of Christ will be very observant of their Shepherd, and very cautious and shy of strangers. *They follow their Shepherd*, for they *know his voice*, having both a discerning ear, and an obedient heart. *They flee from a stranger*, and dread following him, because they know not his voice.

II. The Jews' ignorance of the drift and meaning of this discourse (*v*. 6): *Jesus spoke this parable* to them, but they *understood not what the things were which he spoke unto them*. The Pharisees had a great conceit of their own knowledge, and yet they had not sense enough to *understand the things that Jesus spoke of*; they were above their capacity. Frequently the greatest pretenders to knowledge are most ignorant in the things of God.

III. Christ's explication of this parable. Christ, in the parable, had distinguished the shepherd from the robber by this, that he *enters in by the door*. He makes himself to be both *the door* by which the shepherd enters and the shepherd that enters in by the door.

1. Christ is *the door*. He saith it to the Jews, who would be thought God's only sheep, and to the Pharisees, who would be thought their only shepherds: *I am the door* of the sheepfold.

(1) In general, he is as a *door shut*, to keep out thieves and robbers, and such as are not fit to be admitted. He is as a *door open* for passage and communication. By Christ, as the door, we have our first admission into the flock of God. By him God comes to his church, visits it, and communicates himself to it. By him, as the door, the sheep are at last admitted into the heavenly kingdom.

(2) More particularly,

[1] Christ is the door of *the shepherds*, so that none who come not in by him are to be accounted pastors, but *thieves and robbers* (though they pretended to be *shepherds*); but the *sheep did not hear*

them. The character given of them: they are *thieves and robbers* (v. 8); all that *went before him*, that assumed a precedency and superiority above him. They condemned our Saviour as a thief and a robber, because he did not come in by them as the door, but he shows that they ought to have been admitted by him. The care taken to preserve the sheep from them: *But the sheep did not hear them*. Those that were spiritual and heavenly could by no means approve of the traditions of the elders, nor relish their formalities.

[2] Christ is the door of *the sheep* (v. 9): *By me if any man enter into the sheepfold, he shall be saved; he shall go in and out. First,* Plain directions how to come into the fold: we must come in *by Jesus Christ* as the door. By faith in him we come into covenant and communion with God. *Secondly,* Precious promises to those who observe this direction. They *shall be saved hereafter*; this is the privilege of *their home*. They shall be *for ever happy*. In the meantime they shall *go in and out and find pasture*; this is the privilege of *their way*. True believers are *at home* in Christ; when they go out, they are not *shut out* as strangers, but have liberty to come in again; when they come in, they are not *shut in* as trespassers, but have liberty to go out. They go out to the field in the morning, they come into the fold at night; and they *find pasture* in both: grass in the field, fodder in the fold.

2. Christ is the *shepherd*, v. 11, &c. God has constituted his Son Jesus to be our *shepherd*; and here again and again he owns the relation. He expects all that attendance and observance which the shepherds in those countries had from their flocks.

(1) Christ is *a shepherd*, and not as the thief. The mischievous design of the thief (v. 10): *The thief cometh not* but *to steal, and to kill, and to destroy*. Those whom they *steal*, whose hearts and affections they steal from Christ and his pastures, they *kill and destroy* spiritually. Deceivers of souls are murderers of souls. The gracious design of the shepherd; he is come,

First, To *give life to the sheep*. Christ saith, *I am come among men*, [1] That *they might have life*. He came to put life into the flock, the church in general, which had seemed rather like a valley full of dry bones than like a pasture covered over with flocks. He came to *give life* to particular believers. Life is inclusive of all good. [2] That they might have it *more abundantly*, that they might have a life *more abundant* than could have been expected or than we are *able to ask or think*. But it may be construed that *they might have abundance*. Christ came to give life and *something more*, something *better*, life with advantage. Life in abundance is *eternal life*, life and *much more*.

Secondly, To *give his life for the sheep*, and this that he might give life *to them* (v. 11): *The good shepherd giveth his life for the sheep*. It is the property of every good shepherd to hazard and expose his life for the sheep. It was the prerogative of the great Shepherd to give his life to purchase his flock.

(2) Christ is *a good shepherd*, and not as a hireling. There were many that were not thieves, yet were very careless in the discharge of their duty, and through their neglect the flock was greatly damaged. Christ here *calls himself the good shepherd* (v. 11), and again (v. 14). Jesus Christ is the best of shepherds, none so skilful, so faithful, so tender, as he. He *proves himself* so, in opposition to all hirelings, v. 12-14. The carelessness of the unfaithful shepherd described (v. 12, 13); he that is a hireling, *whose own the sheep are not, sees the wolf coming*, and *leaves the sheep*, for in truth he *careth not for them*. Evil shepherds, magistrates and ministers, are here described both by their bad principles and their bad practices. Their

bad principles, the root of their bad practices. What makes those that have the charge of souls in trying times to betray their trust, and in quiet times not to mind it? It is because they are *hirelings*, and *care not for the sheep*. The wealth of the world is the chief of their good; it is because they are *hirelings*. They undertook the shepherds' office, as a trade to live and grow rich by. It is the love of money, and of their own bellies, that carries them on in it. Those are *hirelings* that love the wages more than the work. The work of their place is the least of their care. They *value not the sheep*, are unconcerned in the souls of others. They *seek their own things*. What can be expected but that they will flee when *the wolf comes*. He *careth not for the sheep*, for he is one *whose own the sheep are not*. Their *bad practices*, the effect of these bad principles, v. 12. How basely the hireling deserts his post; when he sees *the wolf coming* he *leaves the sheep and flees*. Those who mind their safety more than their duty are an easy prey to Satan's temptations. How fatal the consequences are! *The wolf catches them*, and *scatters the sheep*, and woeful havoc is made of the flock. See here the grace and tenderness of the good Shepherd. The Lord Jesus is, and will be, as he ever has been, *the good Shepherd*. Here are two great instances of the shepherd's goodness.

[1] His *acquainting* himself with his flock.

a. He is acquainted with all that *are now of his flock* (v. 14, 15), as the good Shepherd (v. 3, 4): *I know my sheep and am known of mine*. They know one another very well, and knowledge notes affection. Christ *knows his sheep*. He knows who are his sheep, and who are not; he knows the sheep under their many infirmities, and the goats under their most plausible disguises. He *knows* them, that is, he approves and accepts of them. He is *known of them*. They observe him with an eye of faith. It is not so much our knowing him as our being known of him that is our happiness. Upon this occasion Christ mentions (v. 15) the mutual acquaintance between his Father and himself: *As the Father knoweth me, even so know I the Father. First,* As the *ground* of that intimate acquaintance and relation which subsist between Christ and believers. The Lord Jesus *knows whom he hath chosen*, and is sure of them (ch. xiii. 18), and they also *know whom they have trusted*, and are sure of him (2 Tim. i. 12), and the ground of both is the perfect knowledge which the Father and the Son had of one another's mind. *Secondly,* As an apt similitude, illustrating the intimacy that is between Christ and believers. It may be connected with the foregoing words, thus: *I know my sheep, and am known of mine, even as the Father knows me, and I know the Father*. As the Father knew the Son, and loved him, so Christ knows his sheep, and has a watchful tender eye upon them. As the Son knew the Father, loved and obeyed him, so believers know Christ.

b. He is acquainted with those that are *hereafter to be of this flock* (v. 16): *Other sheep I have, which are not of this fold; them also I must bring.*

(a) The eye that Christ had to the poor Gentiles. He had sometimes intimated his special concern for *the lost sheep of the house of Israel*, but, saith he, *I have other sheep*. Those who in process of time should believe in Christ, from among the Gentiles, are here called *sheep*. Christ has a right to many a soul of which he has not yet the possession. Christ speaks of those *other sheep* to take off the contempt that was put upon him, as having but a *little flock*, and therefore, if a *good* shepherd, yet a *poor* shepherd: "But," saith he, "I have more sheep than you see."

(b) The purposes and resolves of his grace concerning them: *"Them also I must bring."* But why *must* he bring them? What was the necessity? The

necessity of their case required it. Like sheep, they will never come back, of themselves. The *necessity of his own engagements* required it; he must bring them, or he would not be faithful to his trust.

(*c*) The happy effect and consequence of this. "They shall hear my voice. It shall be heard *by them*; I will speak, and give to them to hear." Faith comes by hearing. *There shall be one fold and one shepherd.* As there is one shepherd, so there shall be one fold. Both Jews and Gentiles shall be incorporated in one church. Being united to Christ, they shall unite in him; two sticks shall become one in the hand of the Lord.

[2] Christ's *offering up himself for his sheep v.* 15, 17, 18.

a. He declares his purpose of *dying for his flock* (*v.* 15): *I lay down my life for the sheep.* He laid down his life not only for the good of the sheep, but *in their stead.* Thousands of sheep had been offered in sacrifice for their shepherds, as sin-offerings, but here, by a surprising reverse, the shepherd is sacrificed for the sheep. Though the smiting of the shepherd be for the present the *scattering* of the flock, it is in order to the gathering of them in.

b. He takes off the offence of the cross by four considerations.

(*a*) That his *laying down his life for the sheep* entitled him to the honours and powers of his exalted state (*v.* 17): "*Therefore doth my Father love me, because I lay down my life.*" He was *therefore* beloved of the Father because he undertook to *die for the sheep.* Did he think God's love recompence sufficient for all his services and sufferings, and shall we think it too little for ours, and court the smiles of the world to make it up?

(*b*) That his laying down his life was in order to his resuming it: *I lay down my life, that I may receive it again.* God loved him too well to leave him in the grave. He yielded to death, as if he were smitten before it, that he might the more gloriously conquer death, and triumph over the grave.

(*c*) That he was perfectly voluntary in his sufferings and death (*v.* 18). "I freely *lay it down of myself,* for I *have power to lay it down, and to take it again.*" See here the power of Christ, as the Lord of life. He had power to *keep his life* against all the world. Though Christ's life seemed to be taken by storm, yet really it was surrendered, otherwise it had been impregnable. *No man taketh my life from me.* He had power to *lay down his life.* [*a*] He had ability to do it. He could, when he pleased, slip the knot of union between soul and body. Having voluntarily *taken up* a body, he could voluntarily lay it down again. [*b*] He had authority to do it. We are not at liberty to do it; but Christ had a sovereign authority to dispose of his own life as he pleased. He had power to *take it again*; we have not. Our life, once laid down, is *as water spilt upon the ground*; but Christ, when he laid down his life, still had it within reach, and could resume it. See here the grace of Christ; he *laid it down of himself* for our redemption. He offered himself to be the Saviour.

(*d*) That he did all this by the express order and appointment of his Father: *This commandment have I received of my Father.*

Verses 19–21

The people's different sentiments concerning Christ. There was a division, a *schism,* among them. Such a ferment as this they had been in before (*ch.* vii. 43; ix. 16); and where there has once been a division a little thing will make a division again. Rents are sooner made than made up or mended. But it is better that men should be *divided* about the doctrine of Christ than *united* in the service of sin.

I. Some upon this occasion spoke ill of Christ and of his sayings. They said, *He has a devil, and is mad, why do you hear him?* They reproach him as a demoniac. He is a distracted man, no more to be heard than the rambles of a man in bedlam. They ridicule his hearers: "*Why hear you him?*" Men would not thus be laughed out of their necessary food, and yet suffer themselves to be laughed out of what is more necessary.

II. Others stood up in defence of him, and, though the stream ran strong, dared to swim against it. They could not bear to hear him thus abused. If they could say no more of him, this they would maintain, that he was a man in his wits, that he had not a devil, that he was neither senseless nor graceless. Two things they plead: 1. The excellency of his doctrine: "*These are not the words of him that hath a devil.* These are not the words of one that is either violently possessed with a devil or voluntarily in league with the devil." So much of holiness there is in the words of Christ that we may conclude they are *not the words of one that has a devil,* and therefore are the words of one that was sent of God. 2. The power of his miracles: *Can a devil open the eyes of the blind?* Neither mad men nor bad men can work miracles. The devil will sooner put out men's eyes than open them. Therefore Jesus *had not a devil.*

Verses 22–38

It is hard to say which is more strange, the gracious words that came out of his mouth or the spiteful ones that came out of theirs.

I. *It was at the feast of dedication, and it was winter,* a feast that was annually observed by consent, in remembrance of the dedication of a new altar and the purging of the temple, by Judas Maccabæus. The return of their liberty was to them as life from the dead, and, in remembrance of it, they kept an annual feast about the beginning of *December,* and seven days after. The celebrating of it was not confined to Jerusalem, but every one observed it in his own place, not as a *holy time,* but as a *good time.*

II. The place where it was (*v.* 23): *Jesus walked in the temple in Solomon's porch. He walked,* ready to give audience to any that should apply to him, and to offer them his services. Those that have anything to say to Christ may find him in the temple and walk with him there.

III. The conference itself.

1. A weighty question put to him by the Jews, *v.* 24. They *came round about him,* to tease him; he was waiting for an opportunity to do them a kindness. Ill-will for good-will is no rare and uncommon return. They came about him pretending an impartial and importunate enquiry after truth, but intending a general assault upon our Lord Jesus: *How long dost thou make us to doubt? If thou be the Christ tell us.* They quarrel with him, as if he had unfairly held them in suspense hitherto. "*How long dost thou keep us in suspense?* How long are we kept debating whether thou be the Christ or no?" It was the effect of their infidelity, and powerful prejudices. The struggle was between their convictions, which told them he was Christ, and their corruptions, which said, No, because he was not such a Christ as they expected. They laid the blame of their doubting upon Christ himself, as if he *made them to* doubt by inconsistency with himself. Christ would make us to believe; we make ourselves to *doubt.* They challenge him to give a direct and categorical answer: "*If thou be the Christ, tell us plainly, in so many words,* either that thou art the Christ, or, as John Baptist, that thou art not," *ch.* i. 20. Now this pressing query of theirs was *seemingly good*; but it was *really bad,* and put with an ill design. Everyone knew the Messiah was to be a king, and therefore whoever pretended to be the Messiah would be prosecuted as a traitor, which was the thing they would have been at.

2. Christ's answer to this question.

(1) He justifies himself, referring them, [1] To what he had said: *I have told you.* He had told them that he was the Son of God, the Son of man. And is not this the Christ then? *You believed not.* They pretended that they only doubted, but Christ tells them that they did not believe. It is not for us to teach God how he should teach us, but to be thankful for divine revelation as we have it. [2] He refers them to his works, to the example of his life, and especially to his miracles. No man could do those miracles except God were with him, and God would not be with him to attest a forgery.

(2) He condemns them for their obstinate unbelief: "*You believed not.*" But the reason he gives is very surprising: "*You believed not, because you are not of my sheep.* You are not disposed to be my followers, you will not herd yourselves with my sheep, will not come and see, come and hear my voice." Rooted antipathies to the gospel of Christ are the bonds of iniquity and infidelity.

(3) He takes this occasion to describe both the gracious disposition and the happy state of those that are his sheep.

[1] To convince them that they were not his sheep, he tells them what were the characters of his sheep. They *hear his voice* (v. 27), for they know it to be his (v. 4), and he has undertaken that they shall hear it, v. 16. They discern it. They delight in it. They do according to it. Christ will not account those his sheep that are deaf to his calls, deaf to his charms. They *follow him.* The word of command has always been, *Follow me.* We must *tread in his steps—follow the Lamb whithersoever he goes.* In vain do we *hear his voice* if we do not *follow him.*

[2] To convince them that it was their great unhappiness and misery not to be of Christ's sheep, he here describes the blessed state and case of those that are. Our Lord Jesus *takes cognizance* of his sheep: They *hear my voice,* and *I know them.* He distinguishes them from others (2 Tim. ii. 19), has a particular regard to every individual (Ps. xxxiv. 6). He has provided a happiness for them: *I give unto them eternal life,* v. 28. Man has a living soul; therefore the happiness provided is life. Man has an immortal soul: therefore the happiness provided is eternal life. *Life eternal* is the felicity and chief good of a *soul immortal. I give it* to them; it is given by the free grace of Jesus Christ. Not *I will* give it, but *I do* give it; it is a present gift. He gives the assurance of it, heaven in the seed, in the bud, in the embryo. He has undertaken for their security and preservation to this happiness. *They shall by no means perish for ever;* so the words are. As there is an eternal life, so there is an eternal destruction. They shall not *come into condemnation.* Shepherds that have large flocks often lose some of the sheep and suffer them to perish; but Christ has engaged that none of his sheep shall perish, not one. They cannot be kept from their *everlasting happiness.* His own power is engaged for them: *Neither shall any man pluck them out of my hand.* The Shepherd is so careful of their welfare that he has them not only within his fold, but *in his hand,* and taken under his special protection. Yet their enemies are so daring that they attempt to pluck them out of his hand; but they cannot, they shall not do it. Those are safe who are in the hands of the Lord Jesus. His Father's power is likewise engaged for their preservation, v. 29. *a.* The power of the Father: *My Father is greater than all;* greater than all the other *friends* of the church, all the other shepherds, magistrates or ministers. Those shepherds slumber and sleep, but he keeps his flock day and night. He is greater than all the enemies of the church. He is *greater than all* the combined force of hell and earth. The devil and his angels have had

many a push, many a pluck for the mastery, but have never yet prevailed. *b.* The interest of the Father in the sheep: "It is my Father *that gave them to me,*" and therefore God will still look after them. All the divine power is engaged for the accomplishment of all the divine counsels. *c.* The safety of the saints inferred from these two. *None* (neither man nor devil) is *able to pluck them out of the Father's hand.* Christ had himself experienced the power of his Father *upholding* and *strengthening* him, and therefore puts all his followers into his hand too. He that secured the glory of the Redeemer will secure the glory of the redeemed. Further to corroborate the security, he asserts: "*I and my Father are one.*" The Jews understood him as hereby making himself God (v. 33), and he did not deny it. None could pluck them out *of his hand* because they could not pluck them out *of the Father's hand.*

IV. The rage of the Jews. *The Jews took up stones again,* v. 31. It is not the word that is used before (ch. viii. 59), but *they carried stones*—great stones, such as they used in stoning malefactors. The absurdity of this insult will appear if we consider that they had *imperiously,* not to say *impudently,* challenged him to tell them plainly whether he was the Christ or no; and yet now they condemned him as a malefactor. If the preachers of the truth propose it *modestly,* they are branded as cowards; if *boldly,* as insolent. When they had before made a similar attempt it was in vain; he *escaped through the midst of them* (ch. viii. 59); yet they repeat their baffled attempt. Daring sinners will throw stones at heaven, though they return upon their own heads.

V. Christ's tender expostulation with them (v. 32): *Jesus answered* what they *did,* for we do not find that they *said anything.* He mildly replied, *Many good works have I shown you from my Father: for which of those works do you stone me?* Words so very tender that one would think they should have melted a heart of stone. In dealing with his enemies he still argued from his works (men evidence what they *are* by what they *do*), his *good works;* the expression signifies both *great works* and *good works.*

1. The divine power of his works convicted them of the most obstinate infidelity. They were works *from his Father.* These works he *showed* them; he did them openly before the people. He did not show his works by candle-light, as those that are concerned only for *show,* but he showed them at noon-day before the world, ch. xviii. 20. His works were an incontestable *demonstration* of the validity of his commission.

2. The divine grace of his works convicted them of the most base ingratitude. The works he did among them were not only works of wonder to amaze them, but works of love and kindness to do them good, and so make them good. "*Now, for which of these do you stone me?* If therefore you will pick a quarrel with me, it must be for some good work; tell me for which." When he asks, *For which of these do you stone me?* as he intimates the abundant satisfaction he had in his own innocency, so he puts his persecutors upon considering what was the true reason of their enmity, and asking: *Why persecute we him?*

VI. Their vindication of the attempt they made upon Christ, v. 33.

1. They would not be thought such enemies to their country as to persecute him for a good work: *For a good work we stone thee not.* For indeed they would scarcely allow any of his works to be so. But, if he had done any good works, they would not own that they stoned him *for them.* Thus, though most absurd, they could not be brought to own their absurdities.

2. They would be thought such friends to God as to prosecute him for blasphemy: *Because that thou, being a man, makest thyself God.*

(1) A pretended zeal for the law. They seem mightily concerned for the honour of the divine majesty. A blasphemer was to be *stoned*, Lev. xxiv. 16. The vilest practices are often varnished with plausible pretences. As nothing is more *courageous* than a well-informed conscience, so nothing is more *outrageous* than a mistaken one.

(2) A real enmity to the gospel by representing Christ as a blasphemer. It is no new thing for the worst of characters to be put upon the best of men, by those that resolve to give them the worst of treatment. The crime laid to his charge is *blasphemy.* The proof of the crime: *Thou, being a man, makest thyself God.* As it is God's glory that *he is God*, so it is his glory that *besides him there is no other.* Thus far they were in the right, that what Christ said of himself amounted to this—that he was God, for he had said that he was *one with the Father* and that he would *give eternal life*; and Christ does not deny it. They were much mistaken when they looked upon him as a *mere man*, and that the Godhead he claimed was of his own making.

VII. Christ's reply to their accusation and his making good those claims which they imputed to him as blasphemous (*v.* 34, &c.), by two arguments:

1. By an argument taken from *God's word.* It is written (Ps. lxxxii. 6), *I have said, You are gods.* If they were gods, much more am I.

(1) How he explains the text (*v.* 35): *He called them gods to whom the word of God came, and the scripture cannot be broken.* We are sure that the scripture *cannot be broken* or found fault with. Every word of God is *right.*

(2) How he applies it. *Say you of him whom the Father hath sanctified, Thou blasphemest?* [1] The honour done him by the *Father*: He *sanctified him*, and *sent him into the world.* Our Lord Jesus was himself the *Word*, and had the *Spirit without measure.* He was sent *into the world* as Lord of all. The Father's sanctifying and sending him is here vouched as a sufficient warrant for his calling himself the *Son of God.* [2] The dishonour done him by the Jews, that he was a *blasphemer*, because he called himself the *Son of God*: "*Say you of him* so and so? Dare you say so? Have you brow and brass enough to tell the God of truth that he lies? What! say you of the Son of God that *he is a blasphemer?*" If devils, whom he came to condemn, had said so of him, it had not been so strange; but that *men*, whom he came to teach and save, should say so of him, *be astonished, O heavens! at this.*

2. By an argument taken from *his own works.* He here makes out his own claims, and proves that he and the Father are one (*v.* 37, 38): *If I do not the works of my Father, believe me not.*

(1) *From what* he argues—from his works. As he proved himself sent of God by the *divinity* of his works, so we must prove ourselves allied to Christ by the *Christianity* of ours. [1] The argument is very cogent; for the works he did were the *works of his Father*, which the Father only could do, and which could not be done in the ordinary course of nature. The miracles which the apostles wrought in his name corroborated this argument, and continued the evidence of it when he was gone. [2] It is proposed as fairly as can be desired, and put to a short issue. *If I do not the works of my Father, believe me not.* He does not demand an assent to his divine mission further than he gave proof of it. Christ is no hard master, who expects to reap in assents where he has not sown in arguments. "But if I do *the works of my Father, though you believe not me*, yet *believe the works;* believe your own eyes, your own

reason." The invisible things of the Redeemer were seen by his miracles, and by all his works both of power and mercy; so that those who were not convinced by these works were *without excuse.*

(2) *For what* he argues—*that you may know and believe* that *the Father is in me and I in him;* which is the same with what he had said (*v.* 30): *I and my Father are one.* This we must *know*; not know and *explain*, but know and *believe* it; acknowledging and adoring the depth, when we cannot find the bottom.

Verses 39–42

We have here the issue of the conference with the Jews. Here we are told,

I. How they attacked him by force. Therefore *they sought again to take him, v.* 39. Because he persevered in the same testimony concerning himself, they persisted in their malice against him. They express the same resentment, and justify their attempt to stone him by another attempt to take him.

II. How he avoided them by flight. He *escaped out of their hands*, not by the interposal of any friend that helped him, but by his own wisdom he *got clear* of them. And he who knew how to *deliver himself* no doubt knows how to *deliver the godly out of temptation*, and to make *a way for them to escape.*

III. How he disposed of himself in his retirement: He *went away again beyond Jordan, v.* 40.

1. What *shelter* he found there. He went into a private part of the country, and *there he abode*; there he found some rest and quietness, when in Jerusalem he could find none. Christ and his gospel have often found better entertainment among the plain country-people than among *the wise, the mighty, the noble*, 1 Cor. i. 26, 27.

2. What *success* he found there. He chose to go thither, where John at first baptized (*ch.* i. 28), because there could not but remain some impressions of John's ministry and baptism thereabouts, which would dispose them to receive Christ. The event in some measure answered expectation; for we are told,

(1) That they flocked after him (*v.* 41): *Many resorted to him.* The return of the means of grace to a place, commonly occasions a great stirring of affections.

(2) That they reasoned in his favour as much as those at Jerusalem sought objections against him. They said, *John did no miracle, but all things that John spoke of this man were true.* Two things they considered: That Christ far exceeded John Baptist's power, for *John did no miracle*, but Jesus does many; whence it is easy to infer that Jesus is greater than John. How great then is this Jesus! Christ is best known and acknowledged by such a comparison with others as sets him superlatively above others. That Christ exactly answered John Baptist's testimony. All things that *John said of this man were true.* Great things John had said of him, which raised their expectations. They acknowledged him as great as John had said he would be. When we get acquainted with Christ, and come to know him experimentally, we find that the reality exceeds the report, 1 Kings x. 6, 7. John Baptist was now dead and gone, and yet his hearers profited by what they had heard formerly. They were confirmed in their belief that *John was a prophet*, who foretold such things. They were prepared to believe that *Jesus was the Christ.* The success and efficacy of the words preached are not confined to the life of the preacher, nor do they expire with his breath.

(3) That many believed on him there. They gave up themselves to him as his disciples, *v.* 42. They were *many.* It was where John had had great success; *there* many believed on the Lord Jesus. Where the preaching of the doctrine of repentance has had

success, there the preaching of the doctrine of reconciliation is most likely to be prosperous. Where John had been acceptable, Jesus will not be unacceptable.

CHAPTER 11

The raising of Lazarus to life, which is recorded only by this evangelist; for the other three confine themselves to what Christ did in Galilee, and scarcely ever carried their history into Jerusalem till the passion-week: whereas John's memoirs relate chiefly to what passed at Jerusalem. It is more largely recorded than any other of Christ's miracles because it was an earnest of that which was to be the crowning proof of all—Christ's own resurrection. I. The tidings sent to our Lord Jesus of the sickness of Lazarus, ver. 1–16. II. The visit he made to Lazarus's relations when he had heard of his death, ver. 17–32. III. The miracle, ver. 33–44. IV. The effect wrought by this miracle upon others, ver. 45–57.

Verses 1–16

I. A particular account of the parties principally concerned in this story, *v.* 1, 2. They lived at *Bethany*, a village not far from Jerusalem, where Christ usually lodged when he came up to the feasts. It is here called the *town of Mary and Martha*. Here was a brother named *Lazarus*. Here were two sisters, *Martha* and *Mary*, who seem to have been the housekeepers. Here was a decent, happy, well-ordered family, and a family that Christ was very much conversant with. One of the sisters is particularly described to be *that Mary which anointed the Lord with ointment, v.* 2. It refers to that anointing of Christ which this evangelist relates (*ch.* xii. 3). This was she *whose brother Lazarus was sick*; and the sickness of those we love is our affliction. The more friends we have the more frequently we are thus afflicted by sympathy. The multiplying of our comforts is but the multiplying of our cares and crosses.

II. The tidings that were sent to our Lord Jesus of the sickness of Lazarus, *v.* 3. *His sisters* knew where Jesus was, and they sent a special messenger to him, in which they manifest, 1. The affection and concern they had for their brother. They showed their love to him now that he was sick, for a *brother is born for adversity*, and so is a sister too. 2. The regard they had to the Lord Jesus, whom they were willing to make acquainted with all their concerns. The message they sent was very short, barely relating the case with the tender insinuation of a powerful plea, *Lord, behold, he whom thou lovest is sick*. They do not say, Lord, behold, he *who loveth thee*, but *he whom thou lovest*. Our love to him is not worth speaking of, but his to us can never be enough spoken of. It is no new thing for those whom Christ loves to be sick: all things come alike to all. It is a great comfort to us, when we are sick, to have those about us that will pray for us. We have reason to love and pray for those whom we have reason to think Christ loves and cares for.

III. An account how Christ entertained the tidings brought him.

1. He prognosticated the event and issue of the sickness. Two things he prognosticates:

(1) *This sickness is not unto death.* It was mortal, proved *fatal*, and no doubt but Lazarus was truly dead for four days. It came not, as in a common case, to be a summons to the grave. That was not the final effect of this sickness. He *died*, and yet it might be said he did not *die*. Death is an everlasting farewell to this world; and in this sense it was *not unto death*. The sickness of good people, how threatening soever, is *not unto death*. The body's death to this world is the soul's birth into another world.

(2) *But it is for the glory of God.* The afflictions of the saints are designed for the glory of God. The sweetest mercies are those which are occasioned by trouble. Let this reconcile us to the darkest dispensations of Providence, they are all for the glory of

God; and, if God be glorified, we ought to be satisfied. It was *that the Son of God might be glorified thereby*, as it gave him occasion to work that glorious miracle, the *raising of him from the dead*. Let this comfort those whom Christ loves under all their grievances that the design of them all is that *the Son of God may be glorified thereby*.

2. He deferred visiting his patient, *v.* 5, 6. They had pleaded, *Lord, it is he whom thou lovest*, and the plea is allowed (*v.* 5): *Jesus loved Martha, and her sister, and Lazarus.* Now one would think it should follow, *When he heard therefore that he was sick* he made all the haste that he could to him. But he took the contrary way to show his love. Instead of coming post to him, he abode *two days still in the same place where he was.* (1) He *loved them* and therefore he deferred coming to them, that he might try them, that their trial might at last *be found to praise and honour.* (2) He *loved them*, that is, he designed to do something great and extraordinary for them. Therefore he delayed coming to them, that Lazarus might be *dead* and *buried* before he came. Deferring his relief so long, he had an opportunity of doing more for him than for *any*. God hath gracious intentions even in seeming delays. Christ's friends at Bethany were not out of his thoughts, though he made no haste to them.

IV. The discourse he had with his disciples, *v.* 7–16. Two things he discourses about—his own *danger* and Lazarus's *death*.

1. His own danger in going into Judæa, *v.* 7–10.

(1) He saith (*v.* 7): "*Let us go into Judæa again.*" Now this may be considered, [1] As a purpose of his kindness to his friends at Bethany. When he knew they were brought to the last extremity, "Now," saith he, "let us go to Judæa." Christ will arise in favour of his people when *the time to favour them, yea, the set time, is come*; and the worst time is commonly the set time. In the depths of affliction, let this therefore keep us out of the depths of despair, that man's extremity is God's opportunity. [2] As a trial of the courage of the disciples, whether they would venture to follow him thither. To go to Judæa, which was so lately made *too hot* for them, was a saying that *proved them. Let us go.* Christ never brings his people into any peril but he accompanies them in it.

(2) Their objection against this journey (*v.* 8): *Master, the Jews of late sought to stone thee, and goest thou thither again?* They remind him of the danger he had been in there not long since. Christ's disciples are apt to make a greater matter of sufferings than their Master does. The rememberance of the fright was fresh in their minds. They marvel that he will *go thither again.* "Wilt thou favour those with thy presence that have expelled thee out of their coasts? *Goest thou thither again*, where thou hast been so ill used?" Had Christ been inclined to shift off suffering, he did not want friends to persuade him to it. They discover at the same time a distrust of his power, as if he could not secure both himself and them now in Judæa as well as he had done formerly; a secret fear of suffering themselves, for they count upon this if he suffer.

(3) Christ's answer to this objection (*v.* 9, 10): *Are there not twelve hours in the day?* Divine Providence has given us daylight to work by. Man's life is a *day*; this day is divided into divers ages, states, and opportunities, as into hours; the consideration of this should make us not only *very busy*, as to the *work* of life, but also *very easy* as to the perils of life; our day shall be lengthened out till our work be done. He shows the comfort and satisfaction which a man has while he keeps in the way of his duty: *If any man walk in the day, he stumbles not.* He does not *hesitate* in his own mind, but, *walking uprightly, walks*

surely. As he that walks in the day stumbles not, but goes on steadily and cheerfully in his way, *because he sees the light of this world,* and by it sees his way before him; so a good man, relies upon the word of God as his rule, and regards the glory of God as his end, *because he sees* those two great lights. He is furnished with a faithful guide in all his doubts, and a powerful guard in all his dangers. Christ, wherever he went, walked *in the day,* and so shall we, if we follow his steps. He shows the pain and peril a man is in who walks not according to this rule (v. 10): *If a man walk in the night, he stumbles.* If a man walk in the way of his heart, and according to the course of this world—he falls into temptations and snares. He stumbles, *because there is no light in him,* for light in us is that to our moral actions which light about us is to our natural actions.

2. The death of Lazarus v. 11–16.

(1) The notice Christ gave his disciples of the death of Lazarus, *v.* 11. He then gives them plain intelligence of the death of Lazarus: *Our friend Lazarus sleepeth.* See here how Christ calls a believer and a believer's death. He calls a believer his friend: *Our friend Lazarus.* Those whom Christ is pleased to own as his friends all his disciples should take for *theirs.* Christ speaks of Lazarus as their common friend: *Our friend.* Death itself does not break the bond of friendship between Christ and a believer. Lazarus is dead, and yet he is still *our friend.* He calls the death of a believer a *sleep: he sleepeth.* It is good to call death by such names and titles as will help to make it more *familiar* and less *formidable* to us. Why should not the believing hope of that resurrection to eternal life make it as easy to us to put off the body and die as it is to put off our clothes and go to sleep? A good Christian, when he dies, does but sleep: he rests from the labours of the day past, and is refreshing himself for the next morning. To the godly it is a bed, and all its bands as the soft and downy fetters of an easy quiet sleep. It is but putting off our clothes to be mended and trimmed up for the marriage day. Particular intimations of his favourable intentions concerning Lazarus: *but I go, that I may awake him out of sleep.* Christ had no sooner said, *Our friend sleeps,* but presently he adds, *I go, that I may awake him.* When Christ tells his people at any time how bad the case is he lets them know in the same breath how easily, how quickly, he can mend it. Christ's telling his disciples that this was his business to Judæa might help to take off their fear of going with him thither; and, besides, it was to do a kindness to a family to which they were all obliged.

(2) Their mistake, and the blunder they made about it (v. 12, 13): They said, *Lord, if he sleep, he shall do well.* This intimates, [1] *Some concern they* had for their friend Lazarus; they hoped he would recover. Now that they heard he slept they concluded the worst was past. Sleep is often nature's physic. This is true of the sleep of death; if a good Christian so *sleep,* he shall do well. [2] A *greater concern* for themselves. It was now needless for Christ to go to him, and expose himself and them. Thus we are willing to hope that the good work which we are called to do will do itself if there be peril in the doing of it.

(3) This mistake of theirs rectified (v. 13): *Jesus spoke of his death.* How dull of understanding Christ's disciples as yet were. Frequently death is called a sleep in the Old Testament. They should have understood Christ when he spoke scripture language. What Christ undertakes to do, we may be sure, is something great and uncommon, and a work *worthy of himself.* How carefully the evangelist corrects this error: *Jesus spoke of his death.*

(4) The plain and express declaration which Jesus made to them of the death of Lazarus, and his resolution to go to Bethany, *v.* 14, 15. He gives them notice of the death of Lazarus; what he had before said darkly he now says plainly: *Lazarus is dead, v.* 14. He gives them the reason why he had delayed so long: *I am glad for your sakes that I was not there.* Now that he went and raised him from the dead, as there were many brought to *believe on him* who before did not (v. 45), so there was much done towards the perfecting of what was lacking in the faith of those that did, which Christ aimed at: *To the intent that you may believe.* He resolves now to go to Bethany, and take his disciples along with him: *Let us go unto him.* Death cannot separate us from the love of Christ, nor put us out of the reach of his calls. Perhaps those who said, If he sleep there is *no need* to go, were ready to say, If he be dead it is to *no purpose* to go.

(5) Thomas exciting his fellow-disciples cheerfully to attend their Master's motions (v. 16): *Thomas, who is called Didymus.* Thomas in Hebrew and Didymus in Greek signify a *twin.* Probably Thomas was a *twin.* He said *to his fellow-disciples* very courageously, *Let us also go that we may die with him; with him,* that is,

[1] With Lazarus, who was now dead; so some take it. Perhaps Thomas had a particular intimacy with him. "If we *survive,* we know not how to *live without him.*" Thus we are sometimes ready to think our lives bound up in the lives of some that were dear to us: but God will teach us to live, and to live comfortably, upon himself, when those are gone without whom we thought we could not live. "If we die, we hope to be *happy with him.*" Such a firm belief he has of a happiness on the other side death that he is willing they should all go and *die with him.* The more of our friends are translated hence, the fewer cords we have to bind us to this earth, and the more to draw our hearts heavenwards.

[2] "Let us go and die *with our Master,*" and so I rather think it is meant. "If he will go into danger, let us also go, according to the command we received, *Follow me.*" Thomas knew so much of the malice of the Jews against Christ that it was no foreign supposition that he was now going to die. Thomas manifests a gracious readiness to die with Christ himself, flowing from strong affections to him. A zealous desire to help his fellow-disciples into the same frame: "*Let us go* and *die with him;* who would desire to survive such a Master?" Thus, in difficult times, Christians should animate one another.

Verses 17–32

The matter being determined, that Christ will go to Judæa, and his disciples with him, they address themselves to their journey.

At length, he comes near to Bethany, which is said to be about *fifteen furlongs* from Jerusalem, *v.* 18. Notice is taken of this, that this miracle was in effect wrought *in Jerusalem.*

I. What posture he found his friends there in. When we part from our friends we know not what changes may affect us or them before we meet again.

1. He found his friend Lazarus *in the grave, v.* 17. Lazarus had been *four days buried.* Promised salvations, though they always come surely, yet often come slowly.

2. He found his friends that survived *in grief.* Many of the Jews came to Martha and Mary to comfort them. Ordinarily, where death is there are *mourners.* Here was Martha's house, a house where the fear of God was, and on which his blessing rested, yet made a *house of mourning.* Grace will keep sorrow from the heart (ch. xiv. 1), not from the house. Where there are mourners there ought to be

comforters. It is a duty we owe to those that are in sorrow to mourn with them, and to comfort them. They comforted them *concerning their brother,* that is, by speaking to them of him, not only of the good name he left behind, but of the happy state he was gone to. We have reason to be comforted concerning those who are gone before us to a happiness where they have no need of us. This visit which the Jews made to Martha and Mary is an evidence that they were persons of distinction. There was also a providence in it, that so many Jews should come together, just at this time, that they might be unexceptionable witnesses of the miracle.

II. What passed between him and his surviving friends. His departures endear his returns, and his absence teaches us how to value his presence.

1. The interview between Christ and Martha.

(1) We are told that she *went and met him, v.* 20. It should seem that Martha was earnestly expecting Christ's arrival, and enquiring for it. However it was, she heard of his coming before it arrived. Martha, when the good news was brought that Jesus was coming, threw all aside, and *went and met him.* When Martha went to meet Jesus, Mary *sat still in the house.* Some think she did *not* hear the tidings, while Martha, who was busied in the household-affairs, had early notice of it. Others think she *did* hear that Christ was come, but was so overwhelmed with sorrow that she did not care to stir. Comparing this story with that in Luke x. 38, &c., we may observe the different tempers of these two sisters. Martha's natural temper was active and busy; she loved to be here and there, and at the end of everything; and this had been a snare to her when by it she was not only careful and cumbered about many things, but hindered from the exercises of devotion: but now in a day of affliction this active temper did her a kindness, kept the grief from her heart, and made her forward to meet Christ, and so she received comfort from him the sooner. On the other hand, Mary's natural temper was contemplative and reserved. This had been formerly an advantage to her, when it was placed at her Christ's feet, to hear his word, and enabled her there to attend upon him without those distractions with which Martha was cumbered; but now in the day of affliction that same temper proved a snare to her, made her less able to grapple with her grief, and disposed her to melancholy. See here how much it will be our wisdom carefully to watch against the temptations, and improve the advantages, of our natural temper.

(2) Here is fully related the discourse between Christ and Martha.

[1] Martha's address to Christ, *v.* 21, 22.

First, She complains of Christ's long absence and delay. *Lord, if thou hadst been here, my brother had not died.* Here is, 1. Some evidence of faith. She believed Christ's *power,* that he could have prevented his death. She believed his *pity,* that if he had but seen Lazarus in his extreme illness, he would have had compassion. 2. Here are sad instances of unbelief. Her faith was true, but weak as a bruised reed, for she limits the power of Christ, in saying, *If thou hadst been here;* whereas she ought to have known that Christ could cure at a distance. She reflects likewise upon the wisdom and kindness of Christ, that he did not hasten to them when they sent for him, and now might as well have stayed away.

Secondly, Yet she corrects and comforts herself. At least, she blames herself for blaming her Master, and for suggesting that he comes too late: *for I know that even now, whatsoever thou wilt ask of God, God will give it to thee.* 1. How *willing* her hope was. She humbly recommends the case to the wise and compassionate consideration of the Lord Jesus. When we know not what in particular to ask or expect, let us

in general refer ourselves to God. 2. How *weak* her faith was. She should have said, "Lord, thou canst do whatsoever thou wilt"; but she only says, "Thou canst obtain whatsoever thou prayest for." His power is always predominant, his intercession always prevalent.

[2] The comfortable word which Christ gave to Martha (*v.* 23): *Jesus saith unto her, Thy brother shall rise again.* Martha, in her complaint, looked back. We are apt, in such cases, to add to our own trouble, by fancying what *might have been.* Christ directs Martha, and us in her, to look forward, and to think what *shall be. Thy brother shall rise again.* This was true of Lazarus in a sense peculiar to him: he was now presently to be raised. It is applicable to all the saints. Think you hear Christ saying, "Thy parent, thy child, thy yoke-fellow, shall rise again."

[3] The faith which Martha mixed with this word, and the unbelief mixed with this faith, *v.* 24. She accounts it a *faithful saying* that *he shall rise again at the last day.* Yet she seems to think this saying not so well worthy of all acceptation as really it was. *I know that he shall rise again at the last day;* and is not this enough? She seems to think it is not. Thus, by our discontent under present crosses, we greatly undervalue our future hopes.

[4] The further instruction and encouragement which Jesus Christ gave her. He said to her, *I am the resurrection and the life, v.* 25, 26. Two things Christ possesses her with the belief of.

First, The power of Christ, his sovereign power: *I am the resurrection and the life.* Martha believed that at his prayer God would give any thing, but he would have her know that by his word he could work any-thing. It is an unspeakable comfort to all good Christians that Jesus Christ is the resurrection and the life, and will be so to them. *Resurrection* is a return to life; Christ is the author of that return, and of that life to which it is a return.

Secondly, The promises of the new covenant. To whom these promises are made—to those that believe in Jesus Christ. The condition of the latter promise is thus expressed: *Whosoever liveth and believeth in me,* which may be understood, either, of *natural* life: *Whosoever lives in this world,* whether he be Jew or Gentile, if he believes in Christ, he shall live by him. Or, of *spiritual* life. He that *lives* and *believes* is he that by faith is born again to a heavenly and divine life. What the promises are (*v.* 25): *Though he die, yet shall he live, nay, he shall never die, v.* 26.

a. For the *body;* here is the promise of a *blessed resurrection.* Though the body be dead because of sin yet it *shall live again.* The body shall be raised a glorious body.

b. For the *soul;* here is the promise of a *blessed immortality.* He that *liveth and believeth* shall *never die.* That spiritual life shall never be extinguished, but perfected in eternal life. The *mortality* of the body shall at length be *swallowed up of life;* but the life of the soul shall be immediately at death swallowed up of immortality. Christ asks her, *"Believest thou this? Canst thou take my word for it?"* Martha was doting upon her brother's being raised to life in this world; before Christ gave her hopes of this, he directed her thoughts to another life, another world. The crosses and comforts of this present time would not make such an impression upon us as they do if we did but believe the things of eternity as we ought.

[5] Martha's unfeigned assent yielded to what Christ said, *v.* 27. We have here Martha's creed, the good confession she witnessed. And it is the *conclusion of the whole matter.*

First, Here is the *guide of her faith,* and that is the word of Christ. She takes it entire as Christ had said it: *Yea, Lord.* Faith is an echo to divine revelation, returns the same words.

Secondly, The *ground of her faith,* and that is the authority of Christ. She has recourse to the foundation, for the support of the superstructure. "*I have believed* that thou art Christ, and therefore *I do believe* this." What she believed and confessed concerning Jesus. That he was the Christ; that he was the *Son of God;* that it was *he who should come.* That blessing of blessings she embraced as *present.* What she inferred hence. If she admits this, that Jesus is the Christ, there is no difficulty in believing that he is the resurrection and the life. He is the fountain of light and truth, and we may take all his sayings for faithful and divine. He is the fountain of life and blessedness, and we may therefore depend upon his ability.

2. The interview between Christ and Mary.

(1) The notice which Martha gave her of Christ's coming (v. 28): *When she had so said, she went her way,* and *called Mary her sister.* Time was when Martha would have drawn Mary from Christ, to come and help her in *much serving* (Luke x. 40). Here she is industrious to draw her to Christ. She called her *secretly.* She called her by order from Christ: *The Master is come, and calleth for thee.* She triumphs in his arrival: *The Master is come.* He whom we have long wished and waited for, *he is come, he is come;* this was the best cordial in the present distress. She invites her sister to go and meet him: "*He calls for thee.*" When Christ our Master comes, he *calls for us.* He calls for thee in particular, for thee *by name.* If he calls thee, he will cure thee, he will comfort thee.

(2) The haste with which Mary made to Christ (v. 29): *As soon as she heard* that the *Master was come,* she *arose quickly,* and came to him. She little thought how near he was to her, for he is often nearer to them that mourn in Zion than they are aware of. The least intimation of Christ's gracious approaches is enough to a lively faith, which stands ready to take the hint, and answer the first call. She did not consult her neighbours, the Jews that were *with her, comforting her;* she left them all, to come to him.

(3) We are told (v. 30) where she found the Master; *in that place where Martha met him.* Christ's love to his work. He stayed near the place where the grave was, that he might be ready to go to it. Mary's love to Christ; still she *loved much.* Though Christ had seemed unkind in his delays, yet she could take nothing amiss from him.

(4) The misconstruction which the Jews made of her going away so hastily (v. 31): They said, *She goes to the grave, to weep there.* Martha bore up better under this affliction than Mary did, who was a woman of tender and sorrowful spirit; such was her natural temper. These comforters therefore concluded when she went out, it was to go *to the grave and weep there.* [1] What often is the folly and fault of mourners; they contrive how to aggravate their own grief, and to make bad worse. We are apt to fasten upon those things that aggravate the affliction, when it is our duty to reconcile ourselves to the will of God in it. [2] What is the wisdom and duty of comforters; and that is, to prevent as much as may be, the revival of the sorrow, and to divert it. Those Jews that followed Mary were thereby led to Christ, and became the witnesses of one of his most glorious miracles. It is good cleaving to Christ's friends in their sorrows, for thereby we may come to know him better.

(5) Mary's address to our Lord Jesus (v. 32): She came and *fell down at his feet* and said with many tears (as appears v. 33), *Lord, if thou hadst been here, my brother had not died,* as Martha said before. *She fell down at his feet,* which was more than Martha did, who had a greater command of her passions. This Mary had sat *at Christ's feet to hear his word* (Luke x. 39), and here we find her there on another errand. Those that in a day of peace place themselves at Christ's feet, to receive instructions from him, may with comfort and confidence in a day of trouble cast themselves at his feet with hope to find favour with him. Mary hereby made profession of the Christian faith as truly as Martha did, and in effect said, *I believe that thou art the Christ.* This she did in presence of *the Jews* that attended her, who, though friends to her and her family, yet were bitter enemies to Christ. Let them resent it as they pleased, she falls at his feet. Her address is very pathetic: *Lord, if thou hadst been here, my brother had not died.* Christ's delay was designed for the best, and proved so; yet both the sisters very indecently *cast the same in his teeth,* and in effect charge him with the death of their brother. Mary added no more, as Martha did. She said less than Martha, but wept more; and tears of devout affection have a voice, in the ears of Christ; no rhetoric like this.

Verses 33–44

I. Christ's tender *sympathy* with his afflicted friends, which appeared three ways:—

1. By the inward groans and troubles of his spirit (v. 33): *Jesus saw Mary weeping* and the *Jews that came with her weeping; he groaned in the spirit, and was troubled.* The griefs of the sons of men represented in the tears of Mary and her friends. What an emblem was here of this world, this vale of tears! Religion teaches us likewise to *weep with them that weep,* as these Jews wept with Mary. Those that truly love their friends will share with them in their joys and griefs; for what is friendship but a communication of affections? The grace of the Son of God and his compassion towards those that are in misery. *In all their afflictions he is afflicted,* Isa. lxiii. 9. When Christ saw them all in tears, He *groaned in the spirit.* This was an expression of his feeling sense of the calamitous state of human life, and the power of death. Having now to make a vigorous attack upon death and the grave, he thus stirred up himself to the encounter. It was an expression of his kind sympathy with his friends that were in sorrow. Christ not only seemed concerned, but he *groaned in the spirit;* he was inwardly and sincerely affected with the case. Christ's was a deep and a hearty sigh. He was *troubled.* He *troubled himself;* so the phrase is, very significantly. He was never troubled, but when he *troubled himself,* as he saw cause. He often *composed* himself to trouble, but was never discomposed or disordered by it.

2. His concern for them appeared by his *kind enquiry,* (v. 34): Where *have you laid him?* He would thus divert the grief of his mourning friends, by raising their expectations of something great.

3. It appeared by *his tears.* Those about him desired him to *come and see.*

(1) As he was going to the grave, *Jesus wept,* v. 35. A very short verse, but it affords many useful instructions. Jesus Christ was really and truly man, susceptible of the impressions of joy, and grief. Christ gave this proof of his humanity, in both senses of the word; that, as a man, he could weep, and, as a merciful man, he *would weep,* before he gave this proof of his divinity. He was *a man of sorrows,* and *acquainted with grief,* as was foretold, Isa. liii. 3. We never read that he laughed, but more than once we have him in tears. Tears of compassion well become Christians, and make them most to resemble Christ.

(2) Different constructions were put upon Christ's weeping. Some made a kind and candid interpretation of it (v. 36): *Then said the Jews, Behold how he loved him!* They seem to wonder that he should have so strong an affection for one to whom he was not related. It becomes us, according to this example of Christ, to show our love to our friends, both living and dying. Though our tears profit not the dead,

they embalm their memory. When he only dropped a tear over Lazarus, they said, *See how he loved him!* Much more reason have we to say so, for whom he hath laid down his life: *See how he loved us!* Others make a peevish unfair reflection upon it (*v.* 37): *Could not this man, who opened the eyes of the blind, have prevented the death of Lazarus?* If he could have prevented it he would, and therefore because he *did not* they incline to think that he *could not.* Therefore it might justly be questioned whether he did indeed *open the eyes of the blind.* His not working this miracle they thought enough to invalidate the former. Christ soon convinced these *whisperers,* by raising Lazarus from the dead, which was the greater work, that he could have prevented his death.

II. Christ's approach to the grave.

1. Christ repeats his groans (*v.* 38): *Again groaning in himself, he comes to the grave;* he groaned, (1) Being displeased at the unbelief of those who spoke doubtingly of his power, and blamed him for not preventing the death of Lazarus. He never groaned so much for his own pains and sufferings as for the sins and follies of men. (2) Being affected with the fresh lamentations which, it is likely, the mourning sisters made, when they came near the grave, his tender spirit was sensibly touched with their wailings. Ministers, when they are sent by the preaching of the gospel to raise dead souls, should be much affected with the deplorable condition of those they preach to and pray for, and groan in themselves to think of it.

2. The grave wherein Lazarus lay is here described: *It was a cave, and a stone lay upon it;* and such was the sepulchre in which Christ was buried. They reckoned the solemnity of the funeral ended when the stone was rolled to the grave, or, as here, *laid upon it.*

3. Orders are given to remove the stone (*v.* 39): *Take away the stone.* He would have this stone removed, that all the standers-by might see the body lie dead in the sepulchre, and that way might be made for its coming out, and it might appear to be a true body, and not a *ghost* or *spectre.* It is a good step towards the raising of a soul to spiritual life when prejudices are removed and got over and way made for the word to the heart.

4. An objection made by Martha against the opening of the grave: *Lord, by this time he stinketh, for he has been dead four days.* Probably Martha perceived the body to smell, as they were removing the stone, and therefore cried out thus.

(1) It is easy to observe hence the nature of human bodies: four days are but a little while, yet what a great change will this time make with the body of man. Christ rose the third day because he was not to *see corruption.*

(2) Some think she said it in a due tenderness to the dead body. She did not care that it should be thus publicly shown and made a spectacle of. Others think she said it out of a concern for Christ. If there were any thing noisome she would not have her Master near it; but he was none of those tender and delicate ones that cannot bear an ill smell; if he had, he would not have visited the world of mankind, which sin had made a perfect dunghill. It should seem, by Christ's answer, that it was the language of her unbelief and distrust: "Lord, it is too late now. It is impossible that this putrid carcase should *live.*" She gives up his case as helpless and hopeless. This distrustful word of hers served to make the miracle both the more evident and the more illustrious. Her suggesting that it *could not be done* puts the more honour upon him that *did it.*

5. The gentle reproof Christ gave to Martha (*v.* 40): *Said I not unto thee that if thou wouldest believe thou shouldest see the glory of God?* Our Lord Jesus has given us all the assurances imaginable that a sincere faith shall at length be crowned with a blessed vision. If we will take Christ's word, and rely on his power and faithfulness, we shall see the glory of God, and be happy in the sight. We have need to be often reminded of these *sure mercies* with which our Lord Jesus hath encouraged us. We are apt to forget what Christ has spoken, and need him to put us in mind of it by his Spirit: "*Said I not unto thee* so and so? And dost thou think that he will ever unsay it?"

6. The opening of the grave, notwithstanding Martha's objection (*v.* 41): *Then they took away the stone.* If we will see the glory of God, we must let Christ take his own way. *They took away the stone,* and this was all they could do; Christ only could *give life.*

III. The miracle itself wrought.

1. He applies himself to his *living Father in heaven.* The gesture he used was very significant: *He lifted up his eyes.* What is prayer, but the ascent of the soul to God, and the directing of its affections and motions heavenward? He *lifted up* his eyes, looking beyond the grave where Lazarus lay, and overlooking all the difficulties that arose thence. His address to God was with great assurance: *Father, I thank thee that thou hast heard me.* He has here taught us, by his own example, *First,* In prayer to call God Father. *Secondly,* In our *prayers* to *praise him,* and thankfully to acknowledge former favours. But our Saviour's thanksgiving here was intended to express the unshaken assurance he had of the effecting of this miracle. He speaks of this as his own act (*v.* 11): *I go, that I may awake him;* yet he speaks of it as what he had obtained by prayer, for his Father *heard him.* Christ speaks of this miracle as an answer to prayer. He was pleased thus to *honour prayer,* making it the key wherewith even he unlocked the treasures of divine power and grace. Christ, being assured that his prayer was answered, professes,

(1) His thankful acceptance of this answer: *I thank thee that thou hast heard me.* He triumphs before the victory. We may by faith in the promise have a prospect of mercy before it be actually given in, and give God thanks for it. Mercies in answer to prayer ought in a special manner to be acknowledged with thankfulness. Besides the grant of the mercy itself, we are to value it as a great favour to have our poor prayers taken notice of. As God *answers* us with mercy, even *before we call,* so we should answer him with praise even before he grants.

(2) His cheerful assurance of a ready answer at any time (*v.* 42): *And I know that thou hearest me always.* "I *gave thanks*" (saith he) "for being heard in this, because I am sure to be heard in every thing." The Father *heard him always,* which may encourage us to depend upon his intercession, and put all our petitions into his hand, for we are sure that him the Father *hears always.* The confidence he had: *I knew it.* We cannot have such a particular assurance as he had; but this we know, that *whatsoever we ask according to his will he heareth us,* 1 John v. 14, 15. But why should Christ give this public intimation of his obtaining this miracle by prayer? It is *because of the people who stand by, that they may believe that thou hast sent me;* for *prayer may preach.* It was to obviate the objections of his enemies. It was blasphemously suggested by the Pharisees that he wrought his miracles by compact with the devil; now, to evidence the contrary, he openly made his address to God, using *prayers,* and not *charms,* with elevated eyes and voice professing his dependence on Heaven. It was to corroborate the faith of those that were well inclined to him: *That they may believe that thou hast sent me.* Christ proves his mission by raising to life one that was dead.

2. He now applies himself to his *dead friend.* He *cried with a loud voice, Lazarus come forth.*

(1) He could have raised Lazarus by a silent exertion of his power and will, but he did it by a call, a loud call.

[1] To be significant of the power then put forth for the raising of Lazarus. The soul of Lazarus, which was to be called back, was at a distance, not hovering about the grave, as the Jews fancied, but removed to Hades. It is natural to speak loud when we call to those at a distance. The body of Lazarus, which was to be called up, was *asleep*, and we usually speak loud when we would awake any out of sleep.

[2] To be typical of other works of wonder which the power of Christ was to effect. This loud call was a figure, *First*, Of the gospel call, by which dead souls were to be brought out of the grave of sin. *Secondly*, Of the sound of the archangel's trumpet at the last day, with which they that sleep in the dust shall be awakened when Christ shall *descend with a shout*.

(2) This *loud call* was but *short*, yet *mighty through God*. He calls him by name, Lazarus, as we call those by their names whom we would wake out of a fast sleep. He calls him *out of the grave*. He does not say unto him, *Live;* but he saith to him, *Move*, for when by the grace of Christ we live spiritually we must stir up ourselves to *move;* the grave of sin and this world is no place for those whom Christ has quickened, and therefore they must *come forth*. The event was according to the intention: *He that was dead came forth*, v. 44. Power went along with the word of Christ to reunite the soul and body of Lazarus, and then he came forth. The miracle is described, not by its invisible springs, to satisfy our curiosity, but by its visible effects, to confirm our faith. If any ask whether Lazarus, after he was raised, could give an account or description of his soul's removal out of the body or return to it, or what he saw in the other world, I suppose both these changes were so unaccountable to himself that it was not lawful nor possible to express it. Let us not covet to be wise above what is written, and this is all that is written concerning the resurrection of that Lazarus, that *he that was dead came forth.*

(3) This miracle was wrought, [1] *Speedily*. Nothing intervenes between the command, *Come forth*, and the effect, *He came forth*. [2] *Perfectly*. He was so thoroughly revived that he got up out of his grave as strongly as ever he got up out of his bed, and returned not only to life, but health. He was not raised to serve a present turn, but to live as other men. He came out of his grave, though he was fettered with his grave-clothes, with which he was *bound hand and foot*, and *his face bound about with a napkin* (for so the manner of the Jews was to bury); and he came forth in the same dress wherein he was buried, that it might appear that it was he himself and not another. The standers-by, in unbinding him, would *handle him, and see him, that it was he himself*, and so be witnesses of the miracle. How little we carry away with us, when we leave the world—only a winding-sheet and a coffin; there is no change of raiment in the grave, nothing but a single suit of grave-clothes. Lazarus being *come forth*, hampered and embarrassed with his grave-clothes, we may well imagine that those about the grave were exceedingly surprised and frightened at it. Christ, to make the thing familiar, sets them to work: "*Loose him*, slacken his grave-clothes, that they may serve for day-clothes till he comes to his house."

Verses 45–57

We have here an account of the consequences of this glorious miracle.

I. Some were invited by it, and induced to believe. Many of the Jews, when they *saw the things that Jesus did*, *believed on him*. They had often heard of his miracles, and yet evaded the conviction of them, by calling in question the matter of fact; but now that they had themselves seen this done their unbelief was conquered. These were some of those Jews that came to Mary, to comfort her. When we are doing good offices to others we put ourselves in the way of receiving favours from God.

II. Others were irritated by it, and hardened in their unbelief.

1. The *informers* were so (v. 46): *Some of them went to the Pharisees and told them what things Jesus had done*, with a spiteful design to excite those who needed no spur the more vigorously to prosecute him. A most *obstinate infidelity*, refusing to yield to the most powerful means of conviction. A most *inveterate enmity*. If they would not be satisfied that he was to be believed in as the Christ, yet one would think they should have been mollified, and persuaded not to persecute him.

2. The judges, *the blind leaders*, of the people were no less exasperated by the report made to them.

(1) A special council is called and held (v. 47): *Then gathered the chief priests and Pharisees a council*. This council was called, not only for joint advice, but for mutual irritation; that so they might exasperate and inflame one another with enmity and rage against Christ.

(2) The case is proposed, and shown to be weighty and of great consequence.

[1] The matter to be debated was what course they should take with this Jesus; they said, *What do we? For this man doeth many miracles*. They own the truth of Christ's miracles, and that he had wrought many of them; they are therefore witnesses against themselves, for they acknowledge his credentials and yet deny his commission. They consider what is to be done, and chide themselves that they have not done something sooner effectually to crush him. They do not take it at all into their consideration whether they shall not receive him and own him as the Messiah; but they take it for granted that he is an enemy, and as such is to be run down: "*What do we?* Shall we be always talking, and bring nothing to pass?"

[2] That which made this matter weighty was the peril they apprehended their church and nation to be in from the Romans (v. 48): "If we do not silence him, *all men will believe on him*; and, this being the setting up of a new king, the Romans *will come* and *take away our place and nation*." See what an opinion they have of their own *power*. They speak as if they thought Christ's progress depended upon their connivance; as if it were in their power to conquer him who had conquered death.

a. They take on them to prophecy that if he have liberty to go on, *all men will believe on him*. Thus do they now make his interest formidable, though, to serve another turn, these same men strove to make it contemptible, *ch*. vii. 48, *Have any of the rulers believed on him?* This was the thing they were afraid of, that men would *believe on him*.

b. They foretell that if the generality of the nation be *drawn after him*, the rage of the Romans will be *drawn upon them*. They *will come and take away our place*. Here appeared a cowardice. Had they kept their integrity, they needed not to have feared the Romans; but they speak like a dispirited people. When men lose their piety they lose their courage. It was false that there was any danger of the Romans' being irritated against their nation by the progress of Christ's gospel. He taught men to give tribute to Cæsar, and not to *resist evil*. The Roman governor, at his trial, could *find no fault in him*. Pretended fears are often the colour of malicious designs. The enemies of Christ and his gospel have often coloured their enmity with a seeming care for the *public good* and the *common safety*, and have branded his prophets and ministers as men that *turn the world upside down*.

Carnal policy commonly sets up *reasons of state*, in opposition to *rules of justice*. That calamity which we seek to escape by sin we take the most effectual course to bring upon our own heads.

(3) Caiaphas makes a malicious but mystical speech in the council.

[1] The *malice* of it appears evident at first view, *v.* 49, 50. He, being the high priest, took upon him to decide the matter. "*You know nothing at all*. It is soon determined, if you consider that received maxim, *That it is expedient for us that one man should die for the people.*"

First, The counsellor was Caiaphas, who was *high priest that same year.*

Secondly, the drift of the advice was, in short, this, That some way or other must be found out to put Jesus to death. Caiaphas does not say, Let him be silenced, but *die he must.*

Thirdly, This is plausibly insinuated. He suggests his own sagacity. How scornfully does he say, "*You know nothing*, who are but common priests. Thus it is common for those in authority to impose their corrupt dictates by virtue of that; and, because they *should be* the wisest and best, to expect that everybody should believe they *are so*. He takes it for granted that the case is plain and past dispute. Reason and justice are often run down with a high hand. *Truth is fallen in the streets*, and, when it is down, down with it; and *equity cannot enter*, and, when it is out, out with it. He insists upon a maxim in politics, That the welfare of communities is to be preferred before that of particular persons. *It is expedient for us* that *one man die for the people*. Caiaphas craftily insinuates that the greatest and best man ought to think his life well spent, nay well lost, to save his country from ruin. The case ought to have been put thus: Was it expedient for them to bring upon themselves and upon their nation the guilt of blood, for the securing of their civil interests? Carnal policy, while it thinks to *save all* by sin, *ruins all* at last.

[2] The *mystery* that was in this counsel of Caiaphas does not appear at first view, but the evangelist leads us into it (*v.* 51, 52): *This spoke he not of himself*. In these words he prophesied, though he himself was not aware of it, *that Jesus should die for that nation*. Here is a precious comment upon a pernicious text. Charity teaches us to put the most favourable construction upon men's words and actions that they will bear; but piety teaches us to make a good improvement of them. If wicked men *are God's hand* to humble and reform us, why may they not be God's mouth to instruct and convince us? As the hearts of all men are in God's hand, so are their tongues.

(4) The evangelist explains and enlarges upon Caiaphas's words.

[1] He explains what he said. He did not *speak it of himself*. As it was an artifice to stir up the council against Christ, he spoke it of himself, but as it was an *oracle*, declaring it the purpose and design of God, he did not speak it of himself.

First, He *prophesied*, and those that prophesied did not, in their prophecying, *speak of themselves*. But is Caiaphas also among the prophets? He is so, *this once*. God can and often does make wicked men instruments to serve his own purposes, even contrary to their own intentions. Words of prophecy in the mouth are no infallible evidence of a principle of grace in the heart. *Lord, Lord, have we not prophesied in thy name?* will be rejected as a frivolous plea.

Secondly, He prophesied, *being high priest that year;* not that his being high priest did at all dispose or qualify him to be a prophet. Being high priest, God was pleased to put this significant word into his mouth rather than into the mouth of any other, that it might be the more observed or the non-observance of it the more aggravated.

Thirdly, The matter of his prophecy was *that Jesus should die for that nation*. He meant by *that nation* those in it that obstinately adhered to Judaism, but God meant those in it that would receive the doctrine of Christ, and become followers of him. It is a great thing that is here prophesied: That Jesus should *die*, die for others, not only *for their good*, but *in their stead*. If the whole nation of the Jews had unanimously believed in Christ, and received his gospel, they had been not only saved eternally, but saved as a nation from their grievances.

[2] The evangelist enlarges upon this word of Caiaphas (*v.* 52), *not for that nation only*, but *that also he should gather together in one the children of God that were scattered abroad.*

First, The persons Christ died for: *Not for the nation* of the Jews *only*. He must die for *the children of God that were scattered abroad*. Some understand it of the children of God that were then *in being*, scattered abroad in the Gentile world, *devout men* of every nation that *feared God* and worshipped him. Christ died to incorporate these in one great society. Others take in with these all that belong to the election of grace, who are called the children of God. There are those that *fear him throughout all generations*; to all these he had an eye in the atonement he made. As he prayed, so he died, for *all that should believe on him.*

Secondly, The purpose and intention of his death: he died to *gather in* those who wandered, and to *gather together in one* those who were scattered. Christ's dying is, 1. The great *attractive of our hearts;* for this end he is lifted up, to draw men to him. His love in dying for us is the great lodestone of our love. 2. The great *centre of our unity*. He gathers them together *in one*. All the saints in all places and ages meet in Christ.

(5) The result of this debate (*v.* 53): *From that day they took counsel together, to put him to death*. They now understood one another's minds, and so each was fixed in his own, that Jesus must die. What before they had thought of *severally* now they *jointly* concurred in, and so strengthened the hands one of another in this wickedness. Evil men confirm and encourage themselves and one another in evil practices, by comparing notes; then the wickedness which before seemed impracticable appears not only possible, but easy to be effected. What before they wished done, but *wanted a colour for*, now they are furnished with a plausible pretence to justify themselves in.

(6) Christ hereupon absconded, *v.* 54. *He walked no more openly among the Jews*. He withdrew into an obscure part of the country, so obscure that the name of the town he retired to is scarcely met with anywhere else. He went to a country *near the wilderness*. He entered into a city called Ephraim. Thither his disciples went with him; neither would they leave him in solitude, nor would he leave them in danger. But why would Christ abscond now? It was not because he either feared the power of his enemies or distrusted his own power. He retired to put a mark of his displeasure upon Jerusalem and the people of the Jews. They rejected him and his gospel; justly therefore did he remove himself and his gospel from them. It was a sad presage of that thick darkness which was shortly to come upon Jerusalem, because she knew not the day of her visitation. It was to render the cruelty of his enemies the more inexcusable. He would try whether their anger would be turned away by his retirement into privacy. His hour was *not yet come*, and therefore he declined danger. His retirement, for awhile, was to make his return into Jerusalem the more remarkable and illustrious. This swelled the acclamations of joy with which his well-wishers welcomed him when he rode triumphantly into the city.

(7) The strict enquiry made for him during his recess, *v.* 55–57.

[1] The occasion of it was the approach of the passover, at which they expected his presence, according to custom (*v.* 55): *The Jews' passover was nigh at hand*, a festival which shone bright in their calendar. Now the passover being at hand, *many went out of* all parts of *the country to Jerusalem, to purify themselves.* This was either: A *necessary purification* of those who had contracted any ceremonial pollution. Or: A *voluntary purification*, by fasting and prayer, and other religious exercises, which many spent some time in before the passover.

[2] The enquiry was very solicitous: *They said, What think you, that he will not come to the feast? v.* 56. Some think this was said by those who wished well to him, and expected his coming. Those who came early out of the country, that they might purify themselves, were very desirous to meet with Christ, and perhaps came up the sooner with that expectation. They enquired what news of Christ? It should rather seem that they were his enemies who made this enquiry after him. When they should have been assisting those that came to purify themselves, according to the duty of their place, they were plotting against Christ. Their asking, *What think you? Will he not come up to the feast?* implies, *a.* An invidious reflection upon Christ, as if he would omit his attendance on the feast of the Lord for fear of exposing himself. It is sad to see holy ordinances prostituted to such unholy purposes. *b.* A fearful apprehension that they had of missing their game: *"Will he not come up to the feast? If he do not, our measures are broken."*

[3] The orders for the apprehending of him were very strict, *v.* 57. The great sanhedrim issued out a proclamation, strictly charging and requiring that if any person *knew where he was* they should show it, that he might be taken. See, *First*, How intent they were upon this prosecution. *Secondly*, How willing they were to involve others in the guilt with them. It is an aggravation of the sins of wicked rulers that they commonly make those that are under them instruments of their unrighteousness.

CHAPTER 12

Let us see what honours were heaped on the head of the Lord Jesus, even in the depths of his humiliation. I. Mary did him honour, by anointing his feet at the supper in Bethany, ver. 1–11. II. The common people did him honour, with their acclamations of joy, when he rode in triumph into Jerusalem, ver. 12–19. III. The Greeks did him honour, by enquiring after him with a longing desire to see him, ver. 20–26. IV. God the Father did him honour, by a voice from heaven, ver. 27–36. V. He had honour done him by the Old Testament prophets, ver. 37–41. VI. He had honour done him by some of the chief rulers, though they had not courage to own it, ver. 42, 43. VII. He claimed honour to himself, by asserting his divine mission, ver. 44–50.

Verses 1–11

I. The *kind visit* our Lord Jesus paid to his friends at Bethany, *v.* 1. He came up out of the country, *six days before the passover*, and took up at Bethany. He lodged here with his friend Lazarus, whom he had lately *raised from the dead*. His coming to Bethany now may be considered.

1. As a preface to the passover he intended to celebrate, to which reference is made in assigning the date of his coming: *Six days before the passover.*

2. As a voluntary exposing of himself to the fury of his enemies; now that his hour was at hand he came within their reach. Our Lord Jesus was voluntary in his sufferings; his life was not *forced* from him, but *resigned.* As the strength of his persecutors could not overpower him, so their subtlety could not surprise him. As there is a time when we are allowed to shift for our own preservation, so there is a time when we are called to hazard our lives in the cause of God.

3. As an instance of his kindness to his friends at Bethany, whom he loved. This was a farewell visit.

Bethany is here described to be the town *where Lazarus was, whom he raised from the dead.* The miracle wrought here put a new honour upon the place, and made it remarkable. Where he has sown plentifully, he observes whether it comes up again.

II. The *kind entertainment* which his friends there gave him: They *made him a supper* (*v.* 2). It is queried whether this was the same with that which is recorded, Matt. xxvi. 6, &c., in the house of Simon. Most commentators think it was. Let us see the account of this entertainment. They *made him a supper;* for with them, ordinarily, supper was the best meal. This they did in token of their respect and gratitude, for a feast is made for *friendship;* and that they might have an opportunity of free and pleasant conversation with him, for a feast is made for *fellowship.* Martha *served.* She did not think it below her to *serve*, when Christ sat at meat; nor should we think it a dishonour to stoop to any service whereby Christ may be honoured. Christ had formerly reproved Martha for being *troubled with much serving.* But she did not therefore leave off serving, as some, who, when they are reproved for one extreme, peevishly run into another; no, still she *served.* Better be a *waiter* at Christ's table than a *guest* at the table of a prince. Lazarus was *one of those that sat at meat.* It proved the truth of his resurrection, as it did of Christ's, that there were those who did *eat and drink with him*, Acts x. 41. He *sat at meat*, as a momument of the miracle Christ had wrought. Those whom Christ has *raised up* to a spiritual life are made to *sit together with him.*

III. The particular respect which Mary showed him, *v.* 3. She had a *pound of ointment of spikenard, very costly*, and with this she *anointed the feet of Jesus*, and she *wiped them with her hair*, and *the house was filled with the odour of the ointment.* Doubtless she intended this as a token of her love to Christ. By this her love to Christ appears to have been a *generous* love. If she had anything more valuable than another, that must be brought out for the honour of Christ. Those who love Christ truly love him so much better than this world as to be willing to lay out the best they have for him. A *condescending* love; she not only bestowed her ointment upon Christ, but with her own hands poured it upon him. Nay, she did not, as usual, anoint his *head* with it, but his *feet.* True love, as it does not spare charges, so it does not spare pains, in honouring Christ. A *believing* love; there was faith working by this love, faith in Jesus as the Messiah, the Christ, the Anointed. *God's Anointed* should be *our Anointed.* Let us pour on him the ointment of our best affections. The *filling of the house* with the pleasant *odour of the ointment.* Those who entertain Christ in their hearts and houses bring a sweet odour into them.

IV. Judas's dislike of Mary's token of her respect to Christ, *v.* 4, 5.

1. The person that carped at it was Judas, *one of his disciples;* not one of their nature, but only one of their number. Judas was an apostle, a preacher of the gospel, and yet one that discouraged this instance of pious affection. It is sad to see the life of religion discountenanced by such as are bound by their office to assist and encourage it. But this was he that should *betray Christ.*

2. The pretence with which he covered his dislike (*v.* 5): *"Why was not this ointment sold for three hundred pence, and given to the poor?"* Here is worldly wisdom passing a censure upon pious zeal. Those who value themselves upon their *secular policy*, and undervalue others for their *serious piety*, have more in them of the spirit of Judas than they would be thought to have. Here is charity to the poor secretly made a cloak for covetousness. Many excuse themselves from *laying out* in charity under pretence of *laying up* for charity. Judas asked, *Why was it not*

given to the poor? We must not conclude that those do no acceptable piece of service who do not do it in our way. Proud men think all ill-advised who do not advise with them.

3. The detection and discovery of Judas's hypocrisy herein, v. 6. *This he said, not that he cared for the poor, but because he was a thief, and had the bag.* It did not come from a principle of charity: *Not that he cared for the poor*. What were the poor to him any further than he might serve his own ends? Thus some warmly contend for the *power* of the church, as others for its *purity*, when perhaps it is all one to them whether its *true interest* sink or swim, but under the pretence of this they are advancing themselves. It did come from a principle of covetousness. The truth of the matter was, he would rather have had it in money, to be put in the common stock, and then he knew what to do with it.

(1) Judas was treasurer of Christ's household. See what *estate* Jesus and his disciples had to live upon. Only a *bag*, wherein they kept just enough for their subsistence, giving the overplus, if any were, to the poor. This bag was supplied by the contributions of good people, and the Master and his disciples had all *in common*; for our sakes he *became poor*. See who was the *steward* of the little they had; it was Judas, he was purse-bearer. He was the least and lowest of all the disciples; it was not Peter nor John that was made steward. Secular employments, as they are a digression, so they are a degradation to a minister of the gospel. He was desirous of the place. He loved in his heart to be fingering money, and therefore had the moneybag committed to him. The bag he chose, and the bag he had. Strong inclinations to sin within are often justly punished with strong temptations to sin without. We have little reason to be fond of the bag, or proud of it, for at the best we are but stewards of it.

(2) Being trusted with the bag, he was *a thief*. The reigning love of money is *heart-theft* as much as anger and revenge are *heart-murder*. Those to whom the management and disposal of public money is committed have need to be governed by steady principles of justice and honesty, that no blot cleave to their hands. Judas, who had betrayed his trust, soon after betrayed his Master.

V. Christ's justification of what Mary did (v. 7, 8): *Let her alone*. Hereby he intimated his acceptance of her kindness. As it was a token of her goodwill, he signified himself well-pleased with it. Christ would not have those censured nor discouraged who sincerely design to please him, though in their honest endeavours there be not all the discretion that may be. Christ puts a favourable construction upon what she did, which those that condemned it were not aware of: *Against the day of my burying she has kept this.* "The day of my burying is now at hand, and she has anointed a body that is already *as good as dead*." Providence does often so open a door of opportunity to good Christians, that the expressions of their pious zeal prove to be more *seasonable*, and more *beautiful*, than any foresight of their own could make them. He gives a sufficient answer to Judas's objection, v. 8. It is so ordered in the kingdom of Providence that *the poor we have always with us*. It is so ordered in the kingdom of grace that the church should not always have the bodily presence of Jesus Christ: "*Me you have not always*." Opportunities are to be improved, and those opportunities first and most vigorously which are likely to be of the shortest continuance. That good duty which may be done *at any time* ought to give way to that which cannot be done but *just now*.

VI. The public notice which was taken of our Lord Jesus here at this supper in Bethany (v. 9): *Much people of the Jews knew that he was there*, and *they came* flocking thither. They came to see Jesus, whose name was very much magnified by the late miracle he had wrought in raising Lazarus. They came, not to hear him, but to gratify their curiosity with a sight of him. It being known where Christ was, multitudes came to him. They came to see Lazarus and Christ together, which was a very inviting sight. Some came for the confirmation of their faith in Christ. Others came only for the gratifying of their curiosity, that they might say they had seen a man who had been dead and buried, and yet lived again; so that Lazarus served for a *show*.

VII. The indignation of the chief priests at the growing interest of our Lord Jesus (v. 10, 11): They *consulted how they might put Lazarus also to death*, because that *by reason of him many of the Jews went away, and believed on Jesus*. Here observe,

1. How vain and unsuccessful their attempts against Christ had hitherto been. They had done all they could to alienate the people from him, and yet many of the Jews were so overcome by the convincing evidence of Christ's miracles that they *went away* from the party of the priests, *and believed* on *Jesus*; and it was by reason of Lazarus; his resurrection put life into their faith. What was impossible to him that could raise the dead?

2. How absurd and unreasonable that Lazarus must be put to death. It was a sign that they *neither feared God nor regarded man*. If they had feared God, they would not have done such an act of defiance to him. God will have Lazarus to live by a miracle, and they will have him to die by malice. Lazarus is singled out to be the object of their special hatred, because God has distinguished him by the tokens of his peculiar love. One would think that they should rather have consulted how they might have joined in friendship with Lazarus and his family, and by their mediation have reconciled themselves to this Jesus whom they had persecuted. If they had regarded man, they would not have done such an act of injustice to Lazarus, an innocent man, to whose charge they could not pretend to lay any crime.

Verses 12–19

I. The respect that was paid to our Lord Jesus by the common people, v. 12, 13.

1. Who they were that paid him this respect: *much people—a great crowd* of those that came up to the feast; not the inhabitants of Jerusalem, but the country people. The nearer the temple of the Lord, the further from the Lord of the temple. They were such as *came up to the feast*. Perhaps they had been Christ's hearers in the country, and great admirers of him there, and therefore were forward to testify their respect to him at Jerusalem. Perhaps they were those more *devout Jews* that came up to the feast some time before, to purify themselves, that were more inclined to religion than their neighbours, and these were they that were so forward to honour Christ. They were not the rulers, nor the great men, that went out to meet Christ, but the commonalty. But Christ is honoured more by the multitude than by the magnificence of his followers; for he values men by their souls, not their names and titles of honour.

2. On what occasion they did it: *They heard that Jesus was coming to Jerusalem.* They had enquired for him (ch. xi. 55, 56): *Will he not come up to the feast?* Now when they heard he was coming, they bestirred themselves, to give him an agreeable reception.

3. In what way they expressed their respect. Such as they had they gave him; and even this despicable crowd was a faint resemblance of that glorious company which John saw *before the throne, and before the Lamb*, Rev. vii. 9, 10. Though these were not before the throne, they were before the Lamb. There it is said of that celestial choir,

(1) That they had palms in their hands, and so had these *branches of palm-trees*. The palm-tree has ever been an emblem of victory and triumph. Christ was now by his death to conquer principalities and powers. Though he was but girding on the harness, yet he could boast as though he had put it off.

(2) That they *cried with a loud voice, saying, Salvation to our God* (Rev. vii. 10); so did these here, they shouted before him, *Hosanna, blessed is the king of Israel, that comes in the name of the Lord;* and *hosanna* signifies *salvation*. [1] They acknowledge our Lord Jesus to be the king of Israel, that comes *in the name of the Lord*. They own him to be a king, which bespeaks both his dignity and honour, which we must adore; and his dominion and power, to which we must submit. A rightful king, coming in *the name of the Lord*. The promised and long-expected king, Messiah the prince, for he is *king of Israel*. [2] They heartily wish well to his kingdom, which is the meaning of hosanna. In crying hosanna they prayed for three things: That his kingdom might come in the light and knowledge of it, and in the power and efficacy of it. That it might conquer. That it might continue. Hosanna is, *Let the king live for ever*. [3] They bid him welcome in Jerusalem: "*Welcome is he that cometh; come in thou blessed of the Lord*." Thus we must every one of us bid Christ welcome into our hearts. Faith saith, *Blessed is he that cometh*.

II. The posture Christ puts himself into for receiving the respect that was paid him (*v.* 14): *When he had found a young ass*, he *sat thereon*. It was but a poor sort of figure he made, he alone upon an ass, and a crowd of people about him shouting *Hosanna*. This was much more of state than he used to take; he used to travel on foot, but now was mounted. Yet it was much less of state than the great ones of the world usually take. His kingdom was not of this world, and therefore came not with outward pomp.

III. The fulfilling of the scripture in this; *As it is written, Fear not, daughter of Sion, v.* 15.

1. It was foretold that Zion's king should come, should come *thus, sitting on an ass's colt*. Though he comes but slowly (an ass is slow-paced), yet he comes surely, and with such expressions of condescension as greatly encourage his loyal subjects. Humble supplicants may reach to speak with him.

2. The daughter of Zion is therefore called upon to *behold her king*. *Fear not*. In the prophecy, Zion is told to rejoice greatly, and to shout, but here it is rendered, *Fear not*. Unbelieving fears are enemies to spiritual joys; if they be cured, if they be conquered, joy will come of course. If the case be so that we cannot reach to the exultations of joy, yet we should labour to get from under the oppressions of fear. *Rejoice greatly;* at least, *fear not*.

IV. The remark respecting the disciples (*v.* 16): *They understood not at first*, but when *Jesus was glorified* they remembered that *these things were written of him*, and that they and others had *done these things to him*.

1. See here the imperfection of the disciples; *they understood not these things at first*. They did not consider that they were performing the ceremony of the inauguration of Zion's king. The scripture is often fulfilled by the agency of those who have not themselves an eye to the scripture in what they do. That which afterwards is clear was at first dark and doubtful. It well becomes the disciples of Christ to reflect upon the follies and weaknesses of their first beginning, that they may have compassion on the ignorant. *When I was a child, I spoke as a child*.

2. See here the improvement of the disciples in their adult state.

(1) When they understood it: *When Jesus was glorified*. Till then they did not rightly apprehend the nature of his kingdom. Till then the Spirit was not poured out, who was to lead them into all truth.

(2) How they understood it; they compared the prophecy with the event. *Then remembered they that these things were written of him*. The remembrance of what is written will enable us to understand what is done, and the observation of what is done will help us to understand what is written.

V. The reason which induced the people to pay this respect to our Lord Jesus. It was because of the illustrious miracle he had lately wrought in raising Lazarus.

1. See here what account and what assurance they had of this miracle; no doubt, the city rang of it. Those who considered it as a proof of Christ's mission, and a ground of their faith in him, traced the report to those who were eye-witnesses of it, that they might *know the certainty* of it. *The people therefore that stood by when he called Lazarus* out of his grave, *bore record, v.* 17. They unanimously averred the thing to be true, beyond dispute or contradiction. The truth of Christ's miracles was evidenced by incontestable proofs.

2. What influence it had upon them (*v.* 18): *For this cause the people met him*. Some, out of curiosity, were desirous to see one that had done such a wonderful work. Others, out of conscience, studied to do him honour, as the one sent of God.

VI. The indignation of the Pharisees at all this. They own that they had got no ground against him; that they *prevailed nothing*. Those who oppose Christ, will be made to perceive that they prevail nothing. God will accomplish his own purposes in spite of them, and the little efforts of their impotent malice. *You prevail nothing, you profit nothing*. There is nothing got by opposing Christ. They own that he had got ground: *The world is gone after him*. Yet here, like Caiaphas, ere they were aware, they prophesied that *the world would go after him*. 1. Thus they *express* their own vexation; their envy makes them fret. Considering how great these Pharisees were, one would think they needed not grudge Christ so inconsiderable a piece of honour as was now done him; but proud men would monopolize honour, and have none share with them. 2. Thus they excite themselves, and one another, to a more vigorous carrying on of the war against Christ. Thus the enemies of religion are made more resolute and active by being baffled; and shall its friends be disheartened with every disappointment, who know its cause is righteous and will at last be victorious?

Verses 20–26

Honour is here paid to Christ by certain Greeks that enquired for him.

I. We are told who they were that paid this honour to our Lord Jesus: *Certain Greeks among* the people who *came up to worship at the feast, v.* 20. Some think they were *Jews of the dispersion*, that were scattered among the Gentiles, and were called *Greeks*. Others think they were Gentiles, those whom they called *proselytes of the gate*, such as the eunuch and Cornelius. There were devout worshippers of the true God even among those that were strangers to the commonwealth of Israel. Though these Greeks, if uncircumcised, were not admitted to eat the passover, yet they came to *worship at the feast*. We must thankfully use the privileges we have, though there may be others from which we are shut out.

II. What was the honour they paid him: they desired to be acquainted with him, *v.* 21. Having a desire to see Christ, they were industrious in the use of proper means. They did not rest in bare wishes, but resolved to try what could be done. They made their application to Philip, one of his disciples. Some think that they had acquaintance with him formerly.

It is good to know those who know the Lord. I think that they applied to him only because they saw him a close follower of Christ. Those that would see Jesus by faith now that he is in heaven must apply to his ministers, whom he has appointed for this purpose, to guide poor souls in their enquiries after him. The bringing of these Greeks to the knowledge of Christ by the means of Philip signified the agency of the apostles, and the use made of their ministry in the conversion of the Gentiles. Their address to Philip was in short this: *Sir, we would see Jesus.* They gave him a title of respect, because he was in relation to Christ. Their business is, they would *see Jesus*; not only see his face, that they might be able to say, when they came home, they had seen one that was so much talked of; but they would have some free conversation with him, and be taught by him. Now that they were come to worship at the feast, they would see Jesus. In our attendance upon holy ordinances, and particularly the gospel passover, the great desire of our souls should be to see Jesus. We miss of our end in coming if we do not see Jesus. The report which Philip made of this to his Master, *v.* 22. He tells Andrew. They agree that it must be made; but then he would have Andrew go along with him. Christ's ministers should be helpful to one another and concur in helping souls to Christ. It should seem that Andrew and Philip brought this message to Christ when he was teaching in public, for we read (*v.* 29) of the *people that stood by*.

III. Christ's acceptance of this honour. He foretells both the honour which he himself should have in being followed (*v.* 23, 24) and the honour which those should have that followed him, *v.* 25, 26.

1. He foresees that plentiful harvest, in the conversion of the Gentiles, of which this was as it were the first-fruits, *v.* 23. *The hour is come when the Son of man shall be glorified.* The end designed hereby, and that is the glorifying of the Redeemer: "And is it so? Do the Gentiles begin to enquire after me? Then the hour is come for the *glorifying of the Son of man.*" This was no surprise to Christ, but a paradox to those about him. The calling of the Gentiles greatly redounded to the glory of the Son of man. The multiplying of the redeemed was the magnifying of the Redeemer. There was a time, a set time, for the glorifying of the Son of man, and he speaks of the approach of it with exultation and triumph: *The hour is come.* The strange way in which this end was to be attained, and that was by the death of Christ, intimated in that similitude (*v.* 24): "*Verily, verily, I say unto you, except a corn of wheat fall into the ground and die, it abideth alone, and you never see any more of it; but if it die it bringeth forth much fruit.*" The necessity of Christ's humiliation intimated. He would never have been the living quickening head and root of the church if he had not descended from heaven to this accursed earth and ascended from earth to the accursed tree, and so accomplished our redemption. He must *pour out his soul unto death.* The advantage of Christ's humiliation illustrated. He *fell to the ground* in his incarnation; but this was not all: *he died.* He lay in the grave like seed under the clods; but as the seed comes up again green, and fresh, and flourishing, and with a great increase, so one dying Christ gathered to himself thousands of living Christians. The salvation of souls hitherto, and henceforward to the end of time, is all owing to the dying of this *corn of wheat.*

2. He promises an abundant recompence to those who should cordially embrace him, and should make it appear that they do so by their faithfulness.

(1) In suffering for him (*v.* 25): *He that loves his life shall lose it;* but he that hates *his life in this world,* shall *keep it unto life eternal.* The great design of his religion is to wean us from this world, by setting before us another world.

[1] See here the fatal consequences of an inordinate love of life; many a man hugs himself to death, and loses his life by overloving it. He that so loves his animal life shall thereby shorten his days, shall lose the life he is so fond of, and another infinitely better. He that is so much in love with the life of the body, as to deny Christ, he shall lose it, that is, lose a real happiness in the other world, while he thinks to secure an imaginary one in this. He that gives his soul, his God, his heaven, for it, buys life too dear.

[2] See also the blessed recompence of a holy contempt of life. He that so hates the life of the body as to venture it for the preserving of the life of his soul shall find both in eternal life. It is required of the disciples of Christ that they hate *their life in this world.* Our life in this world includes all the enjoyments of our present state. We must hate, that is, despise them as vain and insufficient to make us happy, and cheerfully part with them whenever they come in competition with the service of Christ. See here much of the *power of godliness*—that it conquers the strongest natural affections; and much of the *mystery of godliness*—that it is the greatest wisdom, and yet makes men hate their own lives. Those who, in love to Christ, hate their own lives in this world, shall be abundantly recompenced in the resurrection of the just. *He that hateth his life shall keep it.*

(2) In serving him (*v.* 26): *If any man* profess *to serve me,* let him *follow me*; and *where I am,* there *let my servant be*; so some read it, as part of the duty. We read it as part of the promise, *there shall he be* in happiness with me. And, lest this should seem a small matter, he adds, *If any man serve me, him will my Father honour.* The Greeks desired to see Jesus (*v.* 21), but Christ lets them know that it was not enough to see him, they must *serve him.* In taking servants it is usual to fix both the work and the wages; Christ does both here.

[1] Here is the work which Christ expects from his servants. Let them attend their Master's movements: *If any man serve me, let him follow me.* Christians must follow Christ, *do the things that he says, walk as he also walked.* We must go whither he leads us, and in the way he leads us. Let them attend their Master's repose: *Where I am, there let my servant be,* to wait upon me. Christ is where his church is; and *there let his servants be,* to present themselves before him, and receive instructions from him.

[2] Here are the wages which Christ promises to his servants.

First, They shall be happy with him: *Where I am, there shall also my servant be.* Doubtless, he means being with him in paradise. Christ speaks of heaven's happiness as if he were already in it: Where *I am*; because he was sure of it, and near to it. And the same joy and glory which he thought recompence enough for all his services and sufferings are proposed to his servants as the recompence of theirs. Those that follow him in the way shall be with him in the end.

Secondly, They shall be honoured by his Father; he will make them amends for all their pains and loss, by conferring an honour upon them, far beyond what such worthless worms of the earth could expect to receive. The reward is honour, true lasting honour, the highest honour; it is the honour that comes from God. Those that wait on Christ God will put honour upon. Those that serve Christ must humble themselves, and are commonly vilified by the world, in recompence of both which they shall be exalted in due time.

What became of those Greeks we are not told, but are willing to hope that those who thus asked the way to heaven, with their faces thitherward, found it, and walked in it.

Verses 27–36

Honour is here done to Christ by his Father in a voice from heaven, which gave occasion to a further conference with the people.

I. Christ's address to his Father, upon occasion of the trouble which seized his spirit at this time: *Now is my soul troubled, v.* 27. A strange word to come from Christ's mouth, and at this time surprising, for it comes in the midst of divers pleasing prospects, in which, one would think, he should have said, Now is my soul *pleased.* Trouble of soul sometimes follows after great enlargements of spirit.

1. Christ's dread of his approaching sufferings: *Now is my soul troubled.* Now were the first throes of the travail of his soul. The sin of our soul was the trouble of Christ's soul. The trouble of his soul was designed to ease the trouble of our souls. Christ was *now* troubled, but it would not be so always, it would not be so long. The same is the comfort of Christians in their troubles; they are but *for a moment,* and will be turned into joy.

2. The strait he seems to be in hereupon: *And what shall I say?* Christ speaks like one at a loss, as if what he should choose he wot not. There was a struggle between the work he had taken upon him, which required sufferings, and the nature he had taken upon him, which dreaded them; between these two he here pauses with, *What shall I say?*

3. His prayer to God in this strait: *Father, save me from this hour, out of this hour,* praying, not so much that it might not come as that he might be brought through it. This was the language of innocent nature, and its feelings poured forth in prayer. Christ was voluntary in his sufferings, and yet prayed to be saved from them. Prayer against a trouble may very well consist with patience under it and submission to the will of God in it. The time of his suffering was, (1) A set time. (2) A short time. An hour is soon over, so were Christ's sufferings; he could see through them to the *joy set before him.*

4. His acquiescence in his Father's will, notwithstanding. *But for this cause came I to this hour.* Innocent nature got the first word, but divine wisdom and love got the last. Those who would proceed regularly must go upon second thoughts. With the second thought he checked himself: *For this cause came I to this hour;* he does not silence himself with this, that he could not avoid it, but satisfies himself with this, that he would not avoid it. This should reconcile us to the darkest hours of our lives.

5. His regard to his Father's honour herein. *Father, glorify thy name,* to the same purport with *Father, thy will be done;* for God's will is for his own glory. This expresses more than barely a submission to the will of God; it is a consecration of his sufferings to the glory of God. It was a mediatorial word, and was spoken by him as our surety, who had undertaken to satisfy divine justice for our sin. Our Lord Jesus interposed, undertook to satisfy God's injured honour, and he did it by his humiliation. Now here he makes a tender of this satisfaction as an equivalent: *"Father, glorify thy name;* let the debt be levied upon me." Thus he restored that which he took not away.

II. The Father's answer to this address. 1. How this answer was given. By a voice from heaven. 2. What the answer was. It was an express return to that petition, *Father, glorify thy name: I have glorified it already,* and *I will glorify it yet again.* (1) The name of God had been glorified in the life of Christ, in his doctrine and miracles, and all the examples he gave of holiness and goodness. (2) It should be further glorified in the death and sufferings of Christ. His wisdom and power, his justice and holiness, his truth and goodness, were greatly glorified. God accepted the satisfaction, and declared himself well pleased. What God has done for the glorifying of his own

name is an encouragement to us to expect what he will yet further do.

III. The opinion of the standers-by concerning this voice, *v.* 29. Some of them said that *it thundered;* others said that certainly *an angel spoke to him.* Now this shows, 1. That it was a real thing. 2. That they were loth to admit so plain a proof of Christ's divine mission. They would rather say that it was this, or that, or any thing, than that God spoke to him in answer to his prayer.

IV. The account which our Saviour himself gives of this voice.

1. Why it was sent (*v.* 30): "It came *not because of me, but for your sakes,* that all you who heard it may *believe that the Father hath sent me.*" What is said from heaven concerning our Lord Jesus, is said for our sakes, that we may be brought to rest upon him. "That you my disciples, who are to follow me in sufferings, may therein be comforted with the same comforts that carry me on."

2. What was the meaning of it. Two things God intended when he said that he would *glorify his own name:*—

(1) That by the death of Christ Satan should be conquered (*v.* 31): *Now is the judgment.* He speaks with a divine exultation and triumph. "Now the year of my redeemed is come: now, now, that great work is to be done which has been so long thought of in the divine counsels." The matter of the triumph is, [1] That *now is the judgment of the world;* take it as a medical term: "Now is the *crisis* of this world." The sick and diseased world is now upon the turning point; this is the critical day upon which the trembling scale will turn for life or death, to all mankind. Or, rather, it is a law term, "Now, judgment is entered." The death of Christ was the *judgment of this world. First,* It is a judgment of discovery and distinction. Now is the trial of this world, for men shall have their character according as the cross of Christ is to them. By this men are judged, what they think of the death of Christ. *Secondly,* It is a judgment of favour and absolution. Christ upon the cross interposed between a righteous God and a guilty world. It was as it were the judgment of this world, for an everlasting righteousness was thereby brought in, not for Jews only, but the whole world. *Thirdly,* It is a judgment of condemnation given against the powers of darkness; see *ch.* xvi. 11. Satan's dominion is declared to be a usurpation. The judgment of this world is, that it belongs to Christ, and not to Satan. That *now is the prince of this world cast out.* It is the devil that is here called the *prince of this world,* because he rules over the men of the world by the things of the world. He is said to be *cast out,* to be now cast out. Christ reconciling the world to God by the merit of his death, broke the power of death, and cast out Satan as a destroyer; Christ, reducing the world to God by the doctrine of his cross, broke the power of sin, and cast out Satan as a deceiver. With what assurance Christ here speaks of the victory over Satan; it is as good as done, and even when he yields to death he triumphs over it.

(2) That by the death of Christ souls should be converted, and this would be the casting out of Satan (*v.* 32): *If I be lifted up from the earth, I will draw all men unto me.* Here observe two things:—

[1] The great design of our Lord Jesus, which was to *draw all men to him,* not the Jews only, but the Gentiles also. Observe here how Christ himself is all in all in the conversion of a soul. It is Christ that draws. He does not drive by force, but draws as the loadstone; the soul is *made willing.* It is to Christ that we are drawn. He that was shy and distrustful of him is brought to love him and trust in him—drawn up to his terms, into his arms.

[2] The strange method he took to accomplish his design by *being lifted up from the earth. This he spoke*

signifying by what death he should die, the death of the cross. He that was crucified was first nailed to the cross, and then lifted up upon it. The word here used signifies an honourable advancement: *If I be exalted;* he reckoned his sufferings his honour. Now Christ's drawing all men to him followed his being *lifted up from the earth.* It followed after it in time. The great increase of the church was after the death of Christ. It followed upon it as a blessed consequence of it. The cross of Christ, though to some a *stumbling-stone*, is to others a *loadstone.* Some make it an allusion to the lifting up of the brazen serpent in the wilderness, which drew all those to it who were stung with fiery serpents. O what flocking was there to it! So there was to Christ, when salvation through him was preached to all nations; see *ch.* iii. 14, 15. Perhaps it has some reference to the posture in which Christ was crucified, with his arms stretched out, to invite all to him, and embrace all that come.

V. The people's exception against what he said, *v.* 34. Though they had heard the voice from heaven, they object, and pick quarrels with him. Christ had called himself the *Son of man* (*v.* 23), which they knew to be one of the titles of the Messiah. He had also said that the *Son of man must be lifted up*, which they understood of his dying.

1. They alleged those scriptures of the Old Testament which speak of the perpetuity of the Messiah, from all which they inferred that the Messiah should not die. Their perverseness in opposing this to what Jesus had said will appear if we consider: That, when they vouched the scripture to prove that the Messiah *abideth for ever*, they took no notice of those texts which speak of the Messiah's death and sufferings. Had they never heard out of the law that he should *pour out his soul unto death* (Isa. liii. 12), and particularly that his *hands and feet* should be pierced? Why then do they make so strange of the *lifting up of the Son of man?* That, when they opposed what Christ said concerning the sufferings of the Son of man, they took no notice of what he had said concerning his glory and exaltation. In the doctrine of Christ there are paradoxes, which to men of corrupt minds are stones of stumbling.

2. They asked hereupon, *Who is this Son of man?* "Thou sayest, *The Son of man must die*; we have proved the Messiah must not, and where is then thy Messiahship?" They would rather have no Christ than a suffering one.

VI. What Christ said to this exception. They might, if they pleased, answer it themselves: man dies, and yet is immortal, and abideth for ever, so the *Son of man.* He gives them a serious caution to take heed of trifling away the day of their opportunities (*v.* 35, 36): "*Yet a little while is the light with you; therefore walk while you have the light.*"

1. In general, we may observe here: The concern Christ has for the souls of men, and his desire of their welfare. With what tenderness does he here admonish those to look well to themselves who were contriving ill against him! The method he takes with these objectors, *with meekness instructing those that opposed themselves*, 2 Tim. ii. 25.

2. Particularly we have here,

(1) The advantage they enjoyed in having Christ and his gospel among them, with the shortness and uncertainty of their enjoyment of it: *Yet a little while is the light with you.* Christ is this light. His dying upon the cross was as consistent with his *abiding for ever* as the setting of the sun every night is with his perpetuity. The Jews at this time had the *light with them*; they had Christ's bodily presence. It was to be but a little while with them; Christ would shortly leave them. It is good for us all to consider what a little while we are to have the light with us. Time is short, and perhaps opportunity not so long.

(2) The warning given them to make the best of this privilege while they enjoyed it: *Walk while you have the light;* as travellers who make the best of their way forward, that they may not be benighted in their journey. It is our business to walk, to press forward towards heaven. The best time of walking is while we have the light. The day is the proper season for work, as the night is for rest. We are highly concerned thus to improve our opportunities, for fear lest our day be finished before we have finished our day's work and our day's journey: "*Lest darkness come upon you.*"

(3) The sad condition of those who have sinned away the gospel. *They walk in darkness*, and know neither *where* they go, nor *whither* they go. Set aside the instructions of the Christian doctrine, and we know little of the difference between good and evil. He is going to destruction, and knows not his danger, for he is either sleeping or dancing at the pit's brink.

(4) The great duty and interest of every one of us inferred from all this (*v.* 36): *While you have light, believe in the light.* This is an admonition to them not to out-stand their market, but to accept the offer when it was made to them: the same Christ saith to all who enjoy the gospel. It is the duty of every one of us *to believe in the gospel light*, to subscribe to the truths it discovers, for it is a light to our eyes, and to follow its guidance, for it is a light to our feet. We are concerned to do this while we have the light. Those that have God for their Father are children of light, for God is light.

VII. Christ's retiring from them, hereupon: *These things spoke Jesus and departed, and did hide himself from them.* 1. For their conviction and awakening. If they will not regard what he hath said, he will have nothing more to say to them. Christ justly removes the means of grace from those that quarrel with him. 2. For his own preservation. He hid himself from their rage and fury. What he said irritated and exasperated them, and they were made worse by that which should have made them better.

Verses 37–41

We have here the honour done to our Lord Jesus by the Old Testament prophets, who foretold and lamented the infidelity of the many that believed not on him. Two things are here said concerning this untractable people, and both were forefold by the evangelical prophet Isaiah, that they *did not* believe, and that they *could not* believe.

I. They did not believe (*v.* 37): *Though he had done so many miracles before them.*

1. The abundance of the means of conviction. He did miracles, *so many miracles;* both so many and so great. Two things concerning them he here insists upon:—The number of them; they were *many*, and every new miracle confirmed the reality of all that went before. Being all *miracles of mercy*, the more there were the more good was done. The notoriety of them. He wrought these miracles *before them*, not in a corner, but before many witnesses.

2. The inefficacy of these means: *Yet they believed not on him.* These *saw*, and yet *believed not.*

3. The fulfilling of the scripture in this (*v.* 38): *That the saying of Esaias might be fulfilled.* The more improbable any event is, the more does a divine foresight appear in the prediction of it. One could not have imagined that the kingdom of the Messiah, supported with such pregnant proofs, should have met with so much opposition among the Jews, and therefore their unbelief is called a *marvellous work, and a wonder*, Isa. xxix. 14. Christ himself *marvelled at it*, but it was what Isaiah foretold (Isa. liii. 1). The gospel is here called *their report: Who has believed* our *hearing*, which we have heard from God, and which you have heard from us. Many hear it, but few heed

it and embrace it: *Who hath believed it?* Here and there one, but none to speak of. It is spoken of as a thing to be greatly lamented that so few believe the report of the gospel. The reason why men believe not the report of the gospel is because *the arm of the Lord* is not *revealed* to them. They saw Christ's miracles, but did not see the *arm of the Lord revealed in them.*

II. They could not believe, *because Esaias said, He hath blinded their eyes.* This is a hard saying, who can explain it? God damns none by mere sovereignty; yet it is said, *They could not believe.*

1. They *could not* believe, that is, they *would not*; they were obstinately resolved in their infidelity. This is a *moral* impotency, like that of one that is accustomed to do evil, Jer. xiii. 23.

2. They could not because Esaias had said, *He hath blinded their eyes.* It is certain that God is not the author of sin, and yet,

(1) There is a righteous hand of God sometimes to be acknowledged in the blindness of those who persist in impenitency and unbelief, by which they are justly punished for their former resistance of the divine light. If God withhold abused grace, and give men over to indulged lusts, then he *blinds their eyes*, and *hardens their hearts*, and these are spiritual judgments. Observe the method of conversion implied here. Sinners are brought to *see with their eyes*, to discern the reality of divine things. *To understand with their heart*, not only to assent and approve, but to consent and accept. To be *converted*, and effectually turned from sin to Christ. Then God will *heal* them; will *pardon* their sins, and mortify their corruptions, which are as lurking diseases.

(2) Judicial blindness and hardness are in the word of God threatened against those who wilfully persist in wickedness. Known unto God are all his works, and all ours too. Christ knew before who would betray him.

(3) What God has foretold will certainly come to pass, and so it might be said that *therefore* they *could not believe.* Such is the knowledge of God that he cannot be deceived in what he foresees, and such his truth that he cannot deceive in what he foretells. Yet be it observed that the prophecy did not name particular persons. It pointed at the body of the Jewish nation; yet still reserving a remnant, which reserve was sufficient to keep a door of hope open to particular persons; for each one might say, Why may not I be of that remnant?

Lastly, The evangelist, having quoted the prophecy, shows (*v.* 41) that its principal reference was to the days of the Messiah: *These things said Esaias when he saw his glory, and spoke of him.* We read in the prophecy that this was said to Esaias, Isa. vi. 8, 9. But here we are told that it was said *by him* to the purpose. For nothing was said by him as a prophet which was not first said to him; nor was anything said to him which was not afterwards said by him to those to whom he was sent. The vision which the prophet there had of the *glory of God* is here said to be his *seeing the glory* of Jesus Christ; He *saw his glory.* It is said that the prophet there *spoke of him.* It might be objected against his doctrine, If it was from heaven, why did not the Jews believe it? It was not for want of evidence, but because their *ears were heavy.* It was spoken of Christ, that he should be glorified in the ruin of an unbelieving multitude, as well as in the salvation of a distinguished remnant.

Verses 42–43

Some honour was done to Christ by these rulers: for they *believed on him*; but they did not do him honour enough, for they had not courage to own their faith in him. Many professed more kindness for Christ than really they had; these had more kindness for him than they were willing to profess.

I. See the power of the word in the convictions that many of them were under. They *believed on him* as Nicodemus, received him as a teacher come from God. Many cannot but approve of that in their hearts which yet outwardly they are shy of. It may be, there are more good people than we think there are. Some are really better than they seem to be. Their faults are known, but their repentance is not; a man's goodness may be concealed by a *culpable* yet pardonable weakness, which he himself truly repents of. Nor have all who are good the same faculty of appearing to be so.

II. See the power of the world in the smothering of these convictions. They believed in Christ, but because of the Pharisees they durst not confess him. Wherein they failed and were defective: They did not *confess* Christ. There is cause to question the sincerity of that faith which is either afraid or ashamed to show itself. What they feared: being *put out of the synagogue*, which they thought would be a disgrace and damage to them. What was at the bottom of this fear: *They loved the praise of men*, chose it as a more valuable good than the *praise of God.* They set these two in the scale one against the other. 1. They set the praise of men in one scale, and considered how good it was to give praise to men and receive praise from men. They would not confess Christ, lest they should thereby derogate from the reputation of the Pharisees, and forfeit their own. Besides, the followers of Christ were put into an *ill name*, and were looked upon with contempt, which those who had been used to honour could not bear. Each one thought that if he should declare himself in favour of Christ he should stand alone, whereas, if anyone had had resolution to *break the ice*, he would have had more *seconds* than he thought of. 2. They put the praise of God in the other scale. They were sensible that by confessing Christ they should both give praise to God, and have praise from God; but, 3. They gave the preference to the praise of men, and this turned the scale. Many come short of the glory of God by having a regard to the applause of men. Love of the praise of men, as a by-end in that which is good, will make a man a hypocrite when religion is in fashion. Love of the praise of men, as a base principle in that which is evil, will make a man an apostate when religion is in disgrace.

Verses 44–50

We have here the honour Christ not assumed, but asserted, to himself, in the account he gave of his mission. As this evangelist records it, it was his last public discourse; all that follows was private with his disciples. He *cried and said.* The raising of his voice and crying intimate, 1. His boldness in speaking. Though they had not courage openly to profess faith in his doctrine, he had courage openly to publish it; if they were ashamed of it, he was not. 2. His earnestness in speaking. He cried as one that was importunate, and in good earnest in what he said. 3. It denotes his desire that all might take notice of it. This being the last time of the publication of his gospel by himself in person, he makes proclamation. Now what is this closing summary of all Christ's discourses? It is much like that of Moses (Deut. xxx. 15): *See, I have set before you life and death.* So Christ here takes leave of the temple, with a solemn declaration of three things:—

I. The privileges and dignities of those that believe.

1. By believing in Christ we are brought into an *honourable acquaintance with God* (v. 44, 45): *He that believes on me, believes on him that sent me.* He does not believe in a mere man, but he believes in one that is the Son of God. His faith does not terminate in Christ, but through him it is carried out to the Father, to whom we come by Christ as our way. This is illustrated, v. 45. He that *sees me sees him that sent*

me; in getting an acquaintance with Christ, we come to the knowledge of God. God makes himself known in the face of Christ (2 Cor. iv. 6). All that have a believing sight of Christ are led by him to the knowledge of God. God is pleased to deal with fallen man by proxy.

2. We are hereby brought into a comfortable enjoyment of ourselves (v. 46): *I am come a light into the world, that whoever believes in me should not abide in darkness.* (1) The character of Christ: *I am come a light into the world*, to be a light to it. (2) The comfort of Christians: They *do not abide in darkness.* They do not continue in that dark condition in which they were by nature; they are *light in the Lord.* Light is sown for them. They are delivered from that darkness which *abideth for ever.*

II. The peril and danger of those that believe not, (v. 47, 48): "*If any man hear my words, and believe not, I judge him not; though I judge him not, there is one that judgeth him.*"

1. Who they are whose unbelief is here condemned: those who *hear Christ's words* and yet *believe them not.* Those shall not be condemned for their infidelity that never had, nor could have, the gospel; every man shall be judged according to the dispensation of light he was under.

2. What is their unbelief: not receiving Christ's word; it is interpreted (v. 48) a *rejecting* of Christ. Where the banner of the gospel is displayed, no neutrality is admitted.

3. The wonderful patience and forbearance of our Lord Jesus: *I judge him not.* He had work of another nature to do first, and that was to *save the world.* To offer salvation to all the world, and thus far to save them that it is their own fault if they be not saved.

4. The certain and unavoidable judgment of unbelievers at the great day, the day of the revelation of the righteous judgment of God. There is *one that judgeth them.* Nothing is more dreadful than abused patience, and grace trampled on. Their final judgment is reserved to the *last day.* The word of Christ will judge them then: *The words that I have spoken, the same shall judge* the unbeliever *in the last day.* Christ's words will judge unbelievers. As the evidence of their crime, they will convict them. As the rule of their doom, they will condemn them.

III. A solemn declaration of the authority Christ had to demand our faith, v. 49, 50.

1. The commission which our Lord Jesus received from the Father (v. 49): *I have not spoken of myself; but the Father gave me a commandment what I should say.* This is the same with what he said *ch.* vii. 16. *My doctrine is, Not mine, for I have not spoken of myself.* It was his that sent him. God the Father gave him his commission. His instructions are called a *commandment.* Our Lord Jesus learned obedience himself, before he taught it to us, though he was a Son. *The Lord God commanded* the first Adam, and he by his disobedience ruined us; he commanded the second Adam, and he by his obedience saved us.

2. The scope of this commission: *I know that his commandment is life everlasting,* v. 50. The commission given to Christ had a reference to the everlasting state of the children of men, and was in order to their everlasting life and happiness in that state. The command given him was life everlasting. This Christ says he knew: "I know it is so." Those who disobey Christ despise everlasting life, and renounce it.

3. Christ's exact observance of the commission and instructions given him: *Whatsoever I speak,* it is *as the Father said unto me.* As the faithful witness delivers souls, so did he, and spoke the truth, the whole truth, and nothing but the truth. This is a great encouragement to faith; the sayings of Christ, rightly understood, are what we may venture our souls upon. It is a great example of obedience. Christ said as he

was bidden. This is the honour he values himself upon, that what the Father had said to him that he spoke. By an unfeigned belief of every word of Christ, and an entire subjection of soul to it, we must give him the glory due to his name.

CHAPTER 13

Our Saviour having finished his public discourses, now applies himself to a private conversation with his friends. Henceforward we have an account of what passed between him and his disciples. I. He washes his disciples' feet, ver. 1–17. II. He foretells who should betray him, ver. 18–30. III. He instructs them in the great doctrine of his own death, and the great duty of brotherly love, ver. 31–35. IV. He foretells Peter's denying him, ver. 36–38.

Verses 1–17

It has generally been taken for granted by commentators that Christ's washing his disciples' feet, and the discourse that followed it, were the same night in which he was betrayed, and at the same sitting wherein he ate the passover and instituted the Lord's supper. This evangelist, making it his business to gather up those passages which the others had omitted, industriously omits those which the others had recorded, which occasions some difficulty in putting them together. It is here said (v. 1) to be *before the feast of the passover.*

In these verses we have the story of Christ's washing his disciples' feet. But why would Christ do this? A wise man will not do a thing that looks odd and unusual, but for very good causes and considerations. The transaction was very solemn, and four reasons are here intimated why Christ did this: 1. That he might testify his love to his disciples, v. 1, 2. 2. That he might give an instance of his own voluntary humility, v. 3–5. 3. That he might signify to them spiritual washing, which is referred to in his discourse with Peter, v. 6–11. 4. That he might set them an example, v. 12–17.

I. Christ washed his disciples' feet that he might give a proof of that great love wherewith he loved them, v. 1, 2.

1. Our Lord Jesus, *having loved his own that were in the world, loved them to the end,* v. 1.

(1) This is true of the disciples that were his immediate followers, in particular the twelve. These were his own in the world, his bosom-friends. These he loved, he called them into fellowship with himself, was always tender of them. He allowed them to be very free with him, and bore with their infirmities. He loved them to the end; he never took away his loving kindness. Though there were some persons of quality that espoused his cause, he did not lay aside his old friends, but still stuck to his poor fishermen. Though he reproved them often, he never ceased to love them and take care of them.

(2) It is true of all believers. Our Lord Jesus has a people in the world that are his own. *His own;* where *his own* were spoken of that *received him not,* as a man's cattle are his own, which yet he may, when he pleases, dispose of. But here it is, *his own persons,* as a man's wife and children are his own. Christ has a cordial love for his own that are in the world. He was now going to his own in heaven; but he seems most concerned for his own on earth, because they most needed his care: the sickly child is most indulged. Those whom Christ loves *he loves to the end.* Nothing can separate a believer *from the love of Christ*; he loves his own *unto perfection.*

2. Christ manifested his love to them by washing their feet. Thus he would show that as his love to them was constant so it was condescending, would put honour upon them as great and surprising as for a lord to serve his servants. The disciples had just now betrayed the weakness of their love to him, in grudging the ointment that was poured upon his head (Matt.

xxvi. 8), yet he presently gives this proof of his love to them. Our infirmities are foils to Christ's kindnesses, and set them off.

3. He chose this time to do it, for two reasons:

(1) Because now *he knew that his hour was come when he should depart out of this world to the Father.* The change that was to pass over our Lord Jesus; he must *depart*. As Christ himself, so all believers, when they depart out of the world, *go to the Father*. It is a departure *out of the world*, and it is a going *to the Father* and the fruition of him as ours. The time of this change: *His hour was come.* It is sometimes called his enemies' hour (Luke xxii. 53), the hour of their triumph; sometimes his hour, the hour of his triumph. His foresight of it: He *knew that his hour was come;* he knew from the beginning that it would come, but now he knew that it *was come.*

(2) Because the *devil had now put it into the heart of Judas to betray him, v. 2.* These words in a parenthesis may be considered, [1] As tracing Judas's treason to its origin. What way of access the devil has to men's hearts we cannot tell. But there are some sins in their own nature so exceedingly sinful, that it is plain Satan lays the egg of them in a heart disposed to be the nest to hatch them in. [2] As intimating a reason why Christ now washed his disciples' feet. Judas being now resolved to betray him, the time of his departure could not be far off. The more malicious we perceive our enemies to be against us, the more industrious we should be to prepare for the worst that may come. Judas being now got into the snare, and the devil aiming at Peter and the rest of them (Luke xxii. 31), Christ would fortify his own against him. If the wolf has seized one of the flock, it is time for the shepherd to look well to the rest. Antidotes must be stirring, when the infection is begun. Judas, who was now plotting to betray him, was *one of the twelve.* Now Christ would hereby show that he did not design to cast them all off for the faults of one. Though one had a devil, and was a traitor, yet they should fare never the worse for that. Christ had still a kindness for his disciples though there was a Judas among them and he knew it.

II. Christ washed his disciples' feet that he might let all the world know how low he could stoop in love to his own. This is intimated, *v. 3–5. Jesus knowing that the Father had given all things into his hand, rises from supper,* and, to the great surprise of the company, *washed his disciples' feet.*

1. Here is the rightful advancement of the Lord Jesus. *The Father had given all things into his hands;* had given him a power over all. See Matt. xi. 27. He is *heir of all things.* He *came from God.* This implies that he was in the beginning with God. He came from God as the Son of God, and the sent of God. He *went to God.* That which comes from God shall go to God; those that are born from heaven are bound for heaven. He *knew* all this; was not like a prince in the cradle, that knows nothing of the honour he is born to. He had a full view of all the honours of his exalted state, and yet stooped thus low. But how does this come in here? It may come in as that which supported him under his sufferings. Judas was now betraying him, and he knew it, yet, knowing also *that he came from God and went to God,* he did not draw back. It seems to come in as a foil to his condescension. That is given as an inducement to Christ to stoop which should rather have been a reason for his taking state; for God's thoughts are not as ours.

2. Here is the voluntary abasement of our Lord Jesus. A well-grounded assurance of heaven and happiness, instead of puffing a man up with pride, will make and keep him very humble. Now that which Christ humbled himself to was to *wash his disciples' feet.* The action itself was mean and servile, and that which servants of the lowest rank were employed in.

If he had washed their hands or faces, it had been great condescension; but for Christ to stoop to such a piece of drudgery as this may well excite our admiration. He did this for his own disciples, who in themselves were of a low and despicable condition, not curious about their bodies; their feet, it is likely, were seldom washed, and therefore very dirty. They were his servants, and such as should have washed his feet. Many of great spirits otherwise will do a mean thing to curry favour with their superiors; they rise by stooping, and climb by cringing; but for Christ to do this to *his disciples* could be no act of policy, but pure humility. He *rose from supper* to do it. Though we translate it (*v. 2*) *supper being ended,* it might be better read, *there being a supper made,* for he sat down again (*v. 12*), and we find him dipping a sop (*v. 26*), so that he did it in the midst of his meal, and thereby taught us, (1) Not to reckon it a disturbance to be called from our meal to do God or our brother any real service. Christ would not leave his preaching to oblige his nearest relations (Mark iii. 33), but would leave his supper to show his love to his disciples. (2) Not to be over nice about our meat. It would have turned many a squeamish stomach to wash dirty feet at supper-time; but Christ did it, not that we might learn to be rude and slovenly (cleanliness and godliness will do well together), not to indulge, but mortify, the delicacy of the appetite, giving good manners their due place, and no more. He put himself into the garb of a servant, to do it: he *laid aside* his *garments.* We must address ourselves to duty as those that in earnest buckle to business. He did it with all the humble ceremony that could be. He *girded himself with the towel;* he *poured water into the basin,* and then *washed their feet* and *wiped them.* Nothing appears to the contrary but that he washed the feet of Judas, for he was present, *v. 26.* Jesus here washed the feet of a sinner, the worst of sinners, who was at this time contriving to betray him.

III. Christ washed his disciples' feet that he might signify to them the cleansing of the soul from the pollutions of sin. This is plainly intimated in his discourse with Peter upon it, *v. 6–11*:

1. The surprise Peter was in (*v. 6*): *Then cometh he to Simon Peter,* and bids him put out his feet to be washed. It is most probable that when he *went about* this service (which is all that is meant by his *beginning* to wash, *v. 5*)he took Peter first, and that the rest would not have suffered it, if they had not first heard it explained in what passed between Christ and Peter. Peter was startled at the proposal: *Lord* (saith he) *dost thou wash my feet?* What *thou,* our Lord and Master, whom we know and believe to be the Son of God, do this for *me,* a worthless worm of the earth, *a sinful man, O Lord?* Shall those hands wash my feet which with a touch have cleansed lepers, given sight to the blind, and raised the dead? Very willingly would Peter have taken the basin and towel, and washed his Master's feet, and been proud of the honour. For *my Master* to wash my feet is such a paradox as I cannot understand.

2. The immediate satisfaction Christ gave. This was at least sufficient to silence his objections (*v. 7*): *What I do, thou knowest not now, but thou shalt know hereafter.* Here are two reasons why Peter must submit:

(1) Because he was at present in the dark concerning it, and ought not to oppose what he did not understand. Christ would teach Peter an *implicit obedience*: "*What I do thou knowest not now,* and therefore art no competent judge of it."

(2) Because there was something considerable in it, of which he should hereafter know the meaning: "*Thou shalt know hereafter.* Our Lord Jesus does many things the meaning of which even his own disciples do not for the present know, but they *shall*

know afterwards. Subsequent providences explain preceding ones; and we see afterwards the kind tendency of events that seemed most cross; and the way which we thought was *about* proved the *right way.* We must let Christ take his own way, and we shall find in the issue it was the best way.

3. Peter's peremptory refusal to let Christ wash his feet (*v.* 8): *Thou shalt by no means wash my feet; no, never.* It is the language of a fixed resolution. Here was a show of humility and modesty. Peter herein seemed to have, and no doubt he really had, a great respect for his Master. Under this show of humility there was a real contradiction to the will of the Lord Jesus. It is not humility, but infidelity, to put away the offers of the gospel, as if too rich to be made to us or too good news to be true.

4. Christ's insisting upon his offer: *If I wash thee not, thou hast no part with me.* A severe caution against disobedience: "*If I wash thee not,* if thou continue refractory, thou shalt not be owned as one of my disciples." If Peter will dispute the commands he ought to obey, he does in effect renounce his allegiance. A declaration of the necessity of spiritual washing: "*If I wash not* thy soul from the pollution of sin, *thou hast no part with me.*" All those, and those only, that are spiritually washed by Christ, have a part in Christ. It is that *good part* the having of which is the *one thing needful.* It is necessary to our having a part in Christ that he wash us.

5. Peter's more than submission, his earnest request, to be washed by Christ, *v.* 9: *Lord, wash not my feet only, but also my hands and my head.* How soon is Peter's mind changed! Let us therefore not be peremptory in any resolve, because we may soon see cause to retract it, but cautious in taking up a purpose we will be tenacious of.

(1) How ready Peter is to recede from what he had said: "Lord, what a fool was I to speak such a hasty word!" Now that the washing of him appeared to be an act of Christ's grace he admits it; but disliked it when it seemed only an act of humiliation. Good men, when they see their error, will not be loth to recant it.

(2) How importunate he is for the purifying grace of the Lord Jesus, and the universal influence of it, even upon his hands and head. An exclusion from having a part in him, is the most formidable evil in the eyes of all that are enlightened. And for fear of this we should be earnest with God in prayer, that he will wash us. "*Lord, wash not my feet only* from the gross pollutions that cleave to them, *but also my hands and my head* from the spots which they have contracted, and the undiscerned filth which proceeds by perspiration from the body itself."

6. Christ's further explication of this sign.

(1) With reference to his disciples that were faithful to him (*v.* 10): *He that is washed* all over in the bath, *needeth not save to wash his feet,* his hands and head having been washed, and he having only dirtied his feet in walking home. Peter had gone from one extreme to the other. At first he would not let Christ wash his feet; and now he overlooks what Christ had done for him in his baptism, and what was signified thereby. See here what is the privilege and comfort of such as are in a justified state; they are washed by Christ, and are *clean every whit.* The heart may be swept and garnished, and yet still remain the devil's palace; but, if it be washed, it belongs to Christ, and he will not lose it. See what ought to be the daily care of those who through grace are in a justified state, and that is to wash their feet; to cleanse themselves from the guilt they contract daily through infirmity and inadvertence, by the renewed exercise of repentance. We must also wash our feet by constant watchfulness against everything that is defiling. The provision made for our cleansing should not make us presumptuous, but the more cautious. From yesterday's pardon we

should fetch an argument against this day's temptation.

(2) With reflection upon Judas: *And you are clean, but not all, v.* 10, 11. He washed them himself, and then said, *You are clean;* but he excepts Judas: *not all.* Many have the sign that have not the thing signified. Christ sees it necessary to let his disciples know that they are not all clean; that we may all be jealous over ourselves (*Is it I? Lord, is it I* that am among the clean, yet not clean?)

IV. Christ washed his disciples' feet to set before us an example. This explication he gave of what he had done, when he had done it, *v.* 12–17.

1. With what solemnity he gave an account of the meaning of what he had done (*v.* 12): *After he had washed their feet,* he said, *Know you what I have done?*

(1) He adjourned the explication until he had finished the transaction: To try their submission and implicit obedience, that they might learn to acquiesce in his will when they could not give a reason for it. Because it was proper to finish the riddle before he unriddled it.

(2) Before he explained it, he asked them if they could construe it: *Know you what I have done to you?* He puts this question to them, not only to make them sensible of their ignorance, but to raise their desires and expectations of instruction.

2. Upon what he grounds that which he had to say (*v.* 13): "*You call me Master and Lord,* and *you say well,* for *so I am.*" He that is our Redeemer and Saviour is, in order to that, our Lord and Master. He is our Master—our teacher and instructor. He is our Lord—our ruler and owner. It becomes the disciples of Christ to call him Master and Lord, not in compliment, but in reality; not by constraint, but with delight. Our calling Christ Master and Lord is an obligation upon us to receive and observe the instructions he gives us. We are bound in honour and honesty to be observant of him.

3. The lesson which he hereby taught: *You also ought to wash one another's feet, v.* 14.

(1) Some have understood this literally, that Christians should, in a solemn religious manner, *wash one another's feet,* in token of their condescending love to one another. St. Ambrose took it so, and practised it in the church of Milan. St. Austin saith that those Christians who did not do it with their hands, yet (he hoped) did it with their hearts in humility; but he saith, It is much better to do it with the hands also. What Christ has done Christians should not disdain to do.

(2) But doubtless it is to be understood figuratively. Three things our Master hereby designed to teach us: [1] A humble condescension. We must learn of our Master to be *lowly in heart* (Matt. xi. 29). Christ had often taught his disciples humility, and they had forgotten the lesson; but now he teaches them in such a way as surely they could never forget. [2] A condescension to be serviceable. To wash one another's feet is to stoop to the meanest offices of love, for the real good and benefit one of another. We must not grudge to take care and pains, and to spend time, for the good of those to whom we are not under any particular obligations, even of our inferiors. The duty is *mutual;* we must both accept help from our brethren and afford help to our brethren. [3] A serviceableness to the sanctification one of another: *You ought to wash one another's feet,* from the pollutions of sin. We cannot satisfy for one another's sins, but we may help to purify one another from sin. We must in the first place wash ourselves; this charity must begin at home, but it must not end there; we must sorrow for the failings and follies of our brethren, must wash our brethren's polluted feet in tears.

4. Here is the enforcing of this command from the example of what Christ had now done: *If I your Lord*

and Master have done it to you, you ought to do it *to one another.* I am *your Master,* and therefore you ought to *learn of me* (*v.* 15); for in this, *I have given you an example,* that *you should do* to others, *as I have done* to you. What a good teacher Christ is. He teaches by example as well as doctrine, and for this end came into this world, that he might set us a copy; and it is a copy without one false stroke. What good scholars we must be. We must *do as he hath done;* he gave us a copy, that we should write after it. Christ's example herein is to be followed by ministers in particular, in whom the graces of humility and holy love should especially appear. When Christ sent his apostles abroad, it was with this charge: *become all things to all men,* 1 Cor. ix. 22. What I have done to your dirty feet that do you to the polluted souls of sinners; *wash them.* Christians likewise are here taught to condescend to each other in love, unasked, unpaid; we must not be mercenary in the services of love. I am *your Master,* and you are my disciples (*v.* 16), *the servant is not greater than his Lord, neither he that is sent greater than he that sent him.* Christ had urged this (Matt. x. 24, 25) as a reason why they should not think it strange if they suffered as he did; here he urges it as a reason why they should not think it much to humble themselves as he did. What he did not think a disparagement to him, they must not think a disparagement to them. Christ reminds them of their place as his servants; they were not better men than their Master. We need to be put in mind of this, that we are not *greater than our Lord.* Christ, by humbling himself, has dignified humility. We commonly say to those who disdain to do such or such a thing, As good as you have done it; and true indeed it is, if our Master has done it. When we see our Master serving, we cannot see but how ill it becomes us to be domineering.

5. Our Saviour closes this part of his discourse: *If you know these things, happy are you if you do them.* Most people think, Happy are those that rise and rule. Washing one another's feet will never get estates and preferments; but Christ saith, notwithstanding this, Happy are those that stoop and obey. Since they had such excellent precepts given them, recommended by such an excellent pattern, it will be necessary to the completing of their happiness that they practise accordingly. This is applicable to the commands of Christ in general. Though it is a great advantage to know our duty, yet we shall come short of happiness if we do not do our duty. Knowing is in order to doing, James iv. 17. It is knowing and doing that will demonstrate us of *Christ's kingdom,* and wise builders. It is to be applied especially to this command of humility. Nothing is better known than this, that we should be humble. Few will own themselves to be proud, for it is as inexcusable a sin, and as hateful, as any other; and yet how little is to be seen of true humility. Most know these things so well as to expect that others should do accordingly to them, but not so well as to do so themselves.

Verses 18–30

We have here the discovery of Judas's plot to betray his Master. Christ knew it from the beginning; but now first he discovered it to his disciples.

I. Christ gives them a general intimation of it (*v.* 18): *I speak not of you all,* for *I know whom I have chosen,* but the scripture will be fulfilled (Ps. xli. 9), *He that eateth bread with me hath lifted up his heel against me.*

1. He intimates to them that they were not all right. He had said (*v.* 10), *You are clean, but not all.* So here, *I speak not of you all.* What is said of the excellencies of Christ's disciples cannot be said of all that are called so. There is a mixture of bad with good in the best societies, a Judas among the apostles.

2. He himself knew who were right, and who were not: *I know whom I have chosen.* Those that are chosen, Christ himself had the choosing of them. Those that are chosen are known to Christ, for he never forgets any whom he has once had in his thoughts of love, 2 Tim. ii. 19.

3. In the treachery of him that proved false to him the scripture was fulfilled. Christ took one into his family whom he foresaw to be a traitor, *that the scripture might be fulfilled.* This our Saviour applies to Judas. Judas, as an apostle, was admitted to the highest privilege: he did *eat bread with Christ.* He was favoured by him, one of those with whom he was intimately conversant. He saith, He did *eat bread with me;* such as he had, his disciples had their share of, Judas among the rest. Wherever he went, Judas was welcome with him, sat at table with his Master, and in all respects fared as he fared. He ate miraculous bread with him, when the loaves were multiplied, ate the passover with him. All that eat bread with Christ are not his disciples indeed. Judas was guilty of the basest treachery: he *lifted up the heel* against Christ. He forsook him, *v.* 30. He despised him. He became an enemy to him. It is no new thing for those that were Christ's seeming friends to prove his real enemies.

II. He gives them a reason why he told them beforehand of the treachery of Judas (*v.* 19): "*Now I tell you before it come, that when it is come to pass you may* be confirmed in your *belief that I am he.*" By his clear and certain foresight of things to come, of which he gave incontestable proof, he proved himself to be the true God. By this application of the types and prophecies of the Old Testament to himself, he proved himself to be the true Messiah.

III. He gives a word of encouragement to his apostles, and all his ministers whom he employs in his service (*v.* 20): *He that receiveth whomsoever I send receiveth me.* Christ had told his disciples that they must humble and abase themselves. "Now," saith he, "though there may be those that will despise you for your condescension, yet there will be those that will do you honour, and shall be honoured for so doing." Those who know themselves dignified by Christ's commission may be content to be vilified in the world's opinion. As Christ will think never the worse of them for Judas's crime, so he will own them, and will raise up such as shall receive them. Those that had received Judas when he was a preacher were never the worse, though he afterwards proved a traitor; for he was one whom Christ sent. Those who appear to be sent of Christ we must receive, till the contrary appear. Though some, by entertaining strangers, have entertained robbers unawares, thereby some have entertained angels. The abuses put upon our charity, will neither justify our uncharitableness, nor lose us the reward of our charity. We are here encouraged to receive ministers as *sent of Christ:* "*He that receiveth whomsoever I send,* though weak and poor, yet if he deliver my message, he that entertains him shall be owned as a friend of mine." It is *receiving Christ Jesus the Lord* himself. We are here encouraged to receive Christ as sent of God: *He that* thus *receiveth me,* receiveth the Father also. *He that receiveth me* as his prince and Saviour receiveth *him that sent me* as his portion and felicity.

IV. Christ more particularly notifies to them the plot (*v.* 21): *When Jesus had thus said,* he was *troubled in spirit,* and *he testified,* he solemnly declared it: "*One of you shall betray me.*" This did not determine Judas to the sin by any fatal necessity; for, though the event did follow according to the prediction, yet not from the prediction. Christ is not the author of sin. As to this heinous sin of Judas, 1. Christ foresaw it. He *knows what is in men* better than they do themselves, and therefore sees what will be done by them. 2. He foretold it, not only for the sake of the rest of the disciples, but for the sake of Judas himself, that he might take warning. Traitors proceed not in their plots when they find they are discovered; surely Judas, when he finds that his Master knows his design, will retreat in time. 3. He spoke of it with a manifest concern; he was *troubled in spirit* when he mentioned it. The falls of the disciples of Christ are a great trouble of spirit to their Master; the sins of Christians are the grief of Christ. "What! *One of you betray me?*" This went to his heart, as the undutifulness of children grieves those who have *nourished and brought them up.*

V. The disciples quickly take the alarm; and therefore *looked one upon another*, with a manifest concern, *doubting of whom he spoke.* It struck such a horror upon them that they knew not well which way to look, nor what to say. They saw their Master troubled, and therefore they were troubled. That which grieves Christ is, and should be, a grief to all that are his. Hereby they endeavoured to *discover* the traitor. Christ thus perplexed his disciples for a time, that he might *humble them, and prove them*, might excite in them a jealousy of themselves. It is good for us sometimes to be put to a gaze, to be put to a pause.

VI. The disciples were solicitous to get their Master to explain himself.

1. Of all the disciples John was most fit to ask, because he was the favourite, and sat next his Master (v. 23): *There was leaning on Jesus's bosom one of the disciples whom Jesus loved.* It appears that this was John, by comparing *ch.* xxi. 20, 24. The particular kindness which Jesus had for him; he was *the disciple whom Jesus loved.* He loved them all (v. 1), but John was particularly dear to him. His name signifies *gracious.* Among the disciples of Christ some are dearer to him than others. His place at this time: He was *leaning on Jesus's bosom.* It seems to be an extraordinary expression of endearment. Those who lay themselves at Christ's feet, he will lay in his bosom. Yet he conceals his name. He puts this instead of his name, to show that he was pleased with it; it is his title of honour, that he was *the disciple whom Jesus loved.*

2. Of all the disciples Peter was most forward to know, *v.* 24. Peter, sitting at some distance, beckoned to John to ask. Peter was generally the leading man. Where men's natural tempers lead them to be thus bold in answering and asking, if kept under the laws of humility and wisdom, they make men very serviceable. God gives his gifts variously; but it must be noted that it was not Peter, but John, that was the beloved disciple. The reason why Peter did not himself ask was because John had a much fairer opportunity to whisper the question into the ear of Christ, and to receive a like private answer. It is good to improve our interest in those that are near to Christ. Do we know any that we have reason to think lie in Christ's bosom? Let us beg of them to speak a good word for us.

3. The question was asked accordingly (v. 25): *He then, lying at the breast of Jesus, saith unto him, Lord, who is it?* Now here John shows: A regard to his fellow-disciple. Those who lie in Christ's bosom may often learn from those who lie at his feet and be reminded of that which they did not of themselves think of. A reverence of his Master. Though he whispered this in Christ's ear, yet he called him Lord; the familiarity he was admitted to did not at all lessen his respect for his Master. The more intimate communion gracious souls have with Christ, the more sensible they are of his worthiness and their own unworthiness.

4. Christ gave a speedy answer to this question, but whispered it in John's ear; for it appears (v. 29) that the rest were still ignorant of the matter. *He it is to*

whom I shall give a sop, when I have dipped it. And *when he had dipped the sop, he gave it to Judas.* Christ notified the traitor by a sign. He could have told John by name who he was. The false brethren we are to stand upon our guard against are not made known to us by words, but by signs; they are to be known to us by *their fruits.* That sign was a sop. Christ sometimes gives sops to traitors; worldly riches, honours, and pleasures are sops (if I may so speak), which Providence sometimes gives into the hands of wicked men. We must not be outrageous against those whom we know to be very malicious against us. Christ carved to Judas as kindly as to any at the table, though he knew he was then plotting his death.

VII. Judas himself, instead of being convinced hereby of his wickedness, was the more confirmed in it.

1. The devil hereupon took possession of him (v. 27): *After the sop, Satan entered into him.* Satan entered into him to possess him with a prevailing prejudice against Christ, and a contempt of him, to excite in him a covetous desire of the wages of unrighteousness and a resolution to stick at nothing for the obtaining of them. Was not Satan in him before? How then is it said that now *Satan entered into him?* Judas was all along a devil (*ch.* vi. 70), but now Satan gained a more full possession of him. Though the devil is in every wicked man that does his works, yet sometimes he enters more manifestly and more powerfully than at other times. How came Satan to enter into him *after the sop?* Perhaps he was aware that it was the discovery of him, and it made him desperate in his resolutions. Many are made worse by the gifts of Christ's bounty, and are confirmed in their impenitency by that which should have led them to repentance.

2. Christ hereupon dismissed him: *Then said Jesus unto him, What thou doest, do quickly.* Abandoning him to the conduct and power of Satan. Christ knew that Satan had entered into him, and had peaceable possession; and now he gives him up as hopeless. The various methods Christ had used for his conviction were ineffectual. When the evil spirit is willingly admitted, the good Spirit justly withdraws. Challenging him to do his worst: "I do not fear thee, I am ready for thee."

3. Those that were at table understood not what he meant (v. 28, 29): *No man at table knew for what intent* he spoke this to him. They did not suspect that Christ said it to Judas as a traitor, because it did not enter into their heads that Judas was such a one, or would prove so. Christ's disciples were so well taught to love one another that they could not easily learn to suspect one another. They therefore took it for granted that he said it to him as treasurer of the household, giving him orders for the laying out of some money. In works of piety: *Buy those things that we have need of against the feast.* Or in works of charity: *That he should give something to the poor.* Our Lord Jesus, though he lived upon alms himself (Luke viii. 3), yet gave alms to the poor, a little out of a little. Though he might very well be excused, not only because he was poor himself, but because he did so much good in other ways, curing so many *gratis*; yet, to set us an example, he gave for the relief of the poor. The time of a religious feast was thought a proper time for works of charity. When he celebrated the passover he ordered something for the poor. When we experience God's bounty to us, this should make us bountiful to the poor.

4. Judas hereupon sets himself vigorously to pursue his design against him: He *went away.*

(1) His speedy departure: *He went out presently.* For fear of being more plainly discovered to the company. He went out as one weary of Christ's company and the society of his apostles. Christ needed not to

expel him, he expelled himself. *He went out* to prosecute his design. Now that Satan had got into him he hurried him on.

(2) The time of his departure: *It was night.* [1] Though it was night, he made no difficulty of the coldness and darkness of the night. This should shame us out of our slothfulness and cowardice in the service of Christ, that the devil's servants are so earnest and venturous in his service. [2] Because it was night, and this gave him advantage of privacy and concealment. Those whose deeds are evil love darkness rather than light.

Verses 31–35

This and what follows, to the end of *ch.* xiv., was Christ's table-talk with his disciples. When supper was done, Judas went out. Christ begins this discourse. Those especially that by their place, reputation, and gifts, *command the company,* to whom *men give ear,* ought to use the opportunity of doing them good.

I. Concerning the great mystery of his own death and sufferings, about which they were as yet so much in the dark, much less did they understand the meaning of it. Christ did not begin this discourse until Judas was gone out. The presence of wicked people is often a hindrance to good discourse. When Judas *was gone out,* Christ said, *Now is the Son of man glorified.* Christ is glorified by the purifying of Christian societies: corruptions in his church are a reproach to him. Now Judas was gone to set the wheels a-going, in order to his being put to death: *Now is the Son of man glorified,* meaning, *Now he is crucified.*

1. Here is something which Christ instructs them in, concerning his sufferings, that was very *comforting.*

(1) That he should himself be glorified in them. Now the Son of man is to be exposed to the greatest ignominy, and dishonoured both by the cowardice of his friends and the insolence of his enemies; yet *now he is glorified.* Now he is to obtain a glorious victory over Satan and all the powers of darkness. Now he is to work out a glorious deliverance for his people, by his death to reconcile them to God, and bring in an everlasting righteousness and happiness for them. Now he is to give a glorious example of self-denial and patience under the cross, and love to the souls of men, such as will make him to be for ever admired. Christ had been glorified in many miracles he had wrought, and yet he speaks of his being glorified *now* in his sufferings, as if that were more than all his other glories.

(2) That God the Father should be glorified in them. The sufferings of Christ were: The satisfaction of God's justice, and so God was glorified in them. They were the manifestation of his holiness and mercy. God is love, and herein he hath commended his love.

(3) That he should himself be greatly glorified after them, in consideration of God's being greatly glorified by them, *v.* 32. [1] He is sure that God will glorify him. Hell and earth set themselves to vilify Christ, but God resolved to glorify him. He glorified him in his sufferings by the amazing signs and wonders which attended them, and extorted even from his crucifiers an acknowledgment that he was the Son of God. [2] That he will glorify him *in himself.* In Christ himself. He will glorify him in his own person. This supposes his speedy resurrection. [3] That he will glorify him straightway. He looked upon the joy and glory set before him, not only as great, but as near. Good services done to earthly princes often remain long unrewarded; but Christ had his preferments presently. [4] All this in consideration of God's being glorified in and by his sufferings: *Seeing God is glorified in him,* God shall in like manner glorify him in himself. Those who mind the business of glorifying God no doubt shall have the happiness of being glorified with him.

2. Here is something which was *awakening,* for as yet they were slow of heart to understand it (*v.* 33). Two serious words:

(1) That his stay in this world they would find to be very short. *Little children.* This compellation does not bespeak so much their weakness as his tenderness. Know this, then, that *yet a little while I am with you.* Let them improve the advantage they now had. We must make the best of the helps we have for our souls while we have them. Let them not dote upon his bodily presence. They must think of living without it; not be always little children, but go alone, without their nurses.

(2) That their following him to the other world they would find to be very difficult. What he had said to the Jews (*ch.* vii. 34) he saith to his disciples. Christ tells them here, [1] That when he was gone they would feel the want of him: *You shall seek me.* We are often taught the worth of mercies by the want of them. The presence of the Comforter was not such a *sensible* satisfaction as his bodily presence would have been. But observe, Christ said to the Jews, You shall seek me and *not find me;* but to the disciples he only saith, *You shall seek me.* They should find that which was tantamount, and should not seek in vain. [2] That whither he went they *could not come.* Christ tells them that they could not follow him only to quicken them to so much the more diligence and care. They could not follow him to his cross, for they had not courage and resolution. Nor could they follow him to his crown.

II. He discourses with them concerning the great duty of brotherly love (*v.* 34, 35): *You shall love one another.* Now that they must expect such treatment as their Master had, it concerned them by brotherly love to strengthen one another's hands. Three arguments for mutual love are here urged:

1. The command of their Master (*v.* 34): *A new commandment I give unto you.* He not only commends it, not only counsels but commands it, and makes it one of the fundamental laws of his kingdom. It is *a new commandment.* It is a renewed commandment. It is like an old book in a new edition corrected and enlarged. This commandment has been so corrupted that when Christ revised it, it might well be called a *new commandment.* The law of brotherly love was forgotten as obsolete and out of date; so that as it came from Christ new, it was new to the people. It is an everlasting command; so strangely new as to be always so. It shall be new to eternity, when faith and hope are antiquated. As Christ gives it, it is *new.* Before it was, *Thou shalt love thy neighbour;* now it is, You shall love *one another;* it is pressed in a more winning way when it is thus pressed as mutual duty owing to one another.

2. The example of their Saviour is another argument for brotherly love: *As I have loved you.* It is this that makes it a *new commandment.* Understand this of all the instances of Christ's love to his disciples. Thus he *had* loved them, and thus they *must* love one another, and love *to the end.* It may be understood of the special instance of love which he was now about to give, in laying down his life for them. *Greater love hath no man than this, ch.* xv. 13. We must love one another in some respects after the *same manner;* we must set this before us as our copy. It must be love *to the souls* one of another. We must also love one another from *this motive,* and upon this consideration —because Christ has loved us.

3. The reputation of their profession (*v.* 35): *By this shall all men know that you are my disciples, if you have love one to another.* We must have love, not only show love, but have it in the root and habit of it; have it *ready.* Brotherly love is the badge of Christ's disciples. This is the livery of his family; this he would have them *noted for,* as that wherein they excelled all others —their loving one another. This was what their Master

was famous for; and therefore, if you see any people more affectionate one to another than what is common, say, "Certainly these are the followers of Christ, they have been with Jesus." The heart of Christ was very much upon it. In this they must be *singular*; whereas the way of the world is to be *every-one for himself*, they should be hearty for one another. He does not say, *By this shall men know* that you are my disciples—if you *work miracles*, for a worker of miracles is but a cipher without charity (1 Cor. xiii. 1, 2). It is the true honour of Christ's disciples to excel in brotherly love. Christians were known by their affection to one another. Their adversaries took notice of it, and said, *See how these Christians love one another*. If the followers of Christ do not love one another, they give just cause to suspect their own sincerity. When our brethren stand in need of help from us, when they are any ways rivals with or provoking to us, and so we have an occasion to forgive, in such cases as this it will be known whether we have this badge of Christ's disciples.

Verses 36–38

In these verses we have,

I. Peter's curiosity.

1. Peter's question was bold and blunt (*v.* 36): *Lord, whither goest thou?* referring to what Christ had said (*v.* 33), *Whither I go, you cannot come.* It is a common fault among us to be more desirous to have our curiosity gratified than our consciences directed. It is easy to observe it in the converse of Christians, how soon a discourse of that which is plain and edifying is dropped, and no more said to it; which in a matter of doubtful disputation runs into an endless strife of words.

2. Christ's answer. He did not gratify him, but said what he had said before (*v.* 36): Let this suffice, *thou canst not follow me now, but thou shalt follow me hereafter.* We may understand it of his following him to the cross. When Christ was seized, he provided for the safety of his disciples. *Let these go their way,* because they could not *follow him now.* Christ considers the frame of his disciples. The day shall be as the strength is. Peter, though designed for martyrdom, cannot follow Christ now, but he *shall follow him hereafter*; he shall be crucified at last, like his Master. Let him not think that because he escapes suffering now he shall never suffer. We may be reserved for greater trials than we have yet known. We may understand it of his following him to the crown: "No," saith Christ, "*thou canst not follow me now. Thou shalt follow me afterwards*, after thou hast fought the good fight." There is a wilderness between the Red Sea and Canaan.

II. Peter's confidence.

1. Peter makes a daring protestation of his constancy. "*Lord, why cannot I follow thee now? I will lay down my life for thy sake.*" Having heard his Master so often speak of his own sufferings, surely he could not understand him any otherwise than of his going away by death; and he resolves as Thomas did that he will *go and die with him*; and better die with him than live without him. What an affectionate love Peter had to our Lord Jesus: "*I will lay down my life for thy sake.*" Peter spoke as he thought, and though he was inconsiderate he was not insincere. How ill he took it to have it questioned: "*Lord, why cannot I follow thee now?* Dost thou suspect my fidelity to thee?" It is with regret that true love hears its own sincerity arraigned. We are apt to think that we can do anything, and take it amiss to be told that this and the other we cannot do, whereas without Christ we can do nothing.

2. Christ gives him a surprising prediction of his inconstancy, *v.* 38. He upbraids Peter with his confidence: *Wilt thou lay down thy life for my sake?* Christ

hereby puts Peter upon second thoughts, that he might insert into it that necessary proviso, "Lord, *thy grace enabling me*, I will lay down my life for thy sake." "Wilt thou undertake to die for me? What! thou that trembledst to walk upon the water to me? It was an easy thing to leave thy boats and nets to follow me, but not so easy to lay down thy life." It is good for us to shame ourselves out of our presumptuous confidence in ourselves. What a fool am I to talk so big. He plainly foretells his cowardice in the critical hour. Christ solemnly asserts it with, *Verily, verily, I say unto thee, the cock shall not crow till thou hast denied me thrice: the cock shall not crow*, shall not have crowed his crowing out, till thou hast again and again denied me. The crowing of the cock is to be the occasion of his repentance. Christ not only foresaw that Judas would betray him, but he foresaw that Peter would deny him though he did not design it, but the contrary. He knows not only the wickedness of sinners but the weakness of saints. Christ told Peter that he would deny him. That he would do this not once only by a hasty slip of the tongue, but would repeat it a second and a third time. We may well imagine what a mortification it was to Peter's confidence of his own courage to be told this. The most secure are commonly the least safe; and those most shamefully betray their own weakness that most confidently presume upon their own strength, 1 Cor. x. 12.

CHAPTER 14

When he had convicted and discarded Judas, he set himself to comfort the rest. The general scope of this chapter is in the first verse; it is designed to keep trouble from their hearts. Let them consider, I. Heaven as their everlasting rest, ver. 2, 3. II. Christ himself as their way, ver. 4–11. III. The great power they shall be clothed with by the prevalency of their prayers, ver. 12–14. IV. The coming of another comforter, ver. 15–17. V. The fellowship and communion that should be between him and them after his departure, ver. 18–24. VI. The instructions which the Holy Ghost should give them, ver. 25, 26. VII. The peace Christ bequeathed to them, ver. 27. VIII. Christ's own cheerfulness in his departure, ver. 28–31.

Verses 1–3

I. A general caution which Christ gives to his disciples against *trouble of heart* (*v.* 1): *Let not your heart be troubled.*

1. How Christ took notice of it. Perhaps it was apparent in their looks; at least it was intelligible to the Lord Jesus, who is acquainted with all our secret undiscovered sorrows, with the wound that bleeds inwardly. He takes cognizance of all the trouble which his people are at any time in danger of being overwhelmed with. Many things concurred to trouble the disciples now.

(1) Christ had just told them of the unkindness he should receive from some of them, and this troubled them all. Christ comforts them; though a godly jealousy over ourselves is of great use to keep us humble and watchful, yet it must not prevail to the disquieting of our spirits and the damping of our holy joy.

(2) He had just told them of his own departure from them, that he should not only go away, but go away in a cloud of sufferings. When we now look upon Christ pierced, we cannot but *mourn and be in bitterness*, though we see the glorious issue and fruit of it; much more grievous must be the sight to them, who could then look no further. If Christ depart from them, [1] They will think themselves shamefully disappointed; for they looked that this had been he that should have delivered Israel. [2] They will think themselves sadly deserted and exposed. Now, in reference to all these, *Let not your hearts be troubled.* Here are three words, upon any of which the emphasis may significantly be laid. Upon the word *troubled.* Be not *like the troubled sea when* it cannot rest. He does not say, "Let not your hearts be sensible of the

griefs, or sad because of them," but, "Be not ruffled and discomposed." Upon the word *heart*: "*Let not your heart be troubled.*" Keep possession of your own souls when you can keep possession of nothing else. The heart is the main fort; whatever you do, keep trouble from this. Upon the word *your*: "You that are my disciples and followers, be not you so, for you know better." Herein Christ's disciples should *do more than others*, should keep their minds quiet, when everything else is unquiet.

2. The remedy he prescribes; in general, *believe*. (1) Some read it in both parts imperatively, "*Believe in God*, and his perfections and providence, *believe also in me*, and my mediation." (2) We read the former as an acknowledgment that they did believe in God. "But, if you would effectually provide against a stormy day, *believe also in me.*" By believing in Christ as the Mediator between God and man, our belief in God becomes comfortable. Those that rightly believe in God will believe in Jesus Christ, and believing in God through Jesus Christ is an excellent means of keeping trouble from the heart. The joy of faith is the best remedy against the griefs of sense.

II. Here is a particular direction to act faith upon the promise of eternal life, *v*. 2, 3. But what must they trust God and Christ for? Trust them for a happiness to come, for a happiness to last as long as the immortal soul and the eternal world shall last. The saints have encouraged themselves with this in their greatest extremities. *That heaven would make amends for all.* Let us see how this is suggested here.

1. Believe and consider that really there is such a happiness: *In my Father's house there are many mansions; if it were not so, I would have told you*, *v*. 2.

(1) See under what notion the happiness of heaven is here represented: as *mansions*. Heaven is a house, not a tent or tabernacle. It is a Father's house: *my Father's house*; and his Father is our Father. All true believers shall be welcome to that happiness as to their home. There are *mansions* there. Distinct dwellings, an apartment for each. Our individuality shall not be lost there. Durable dwellings. The house itself is lasting; our estate in it is not for a term of years, but a perpetuity. Here we are as in an inn; in heaven we shall gain a settlement. There are *many* mansions, for there are many sons to be brought to glory.

(2) See what assurance we have of the reality of the happiness itself: "*If it were not so, I would have told you.*" The assurance is built: Upon the veracity of his word. Upon the sincerity of his affection to them. As he is true, and would not impose upon them himself, so he is kind, and would not suffer them to be imposed upon. He loves us too well, and means us too well, to disappoint the expectations of his own raising.

2. Believe and consider that the design of Christ's going away was to prepare a place in heaven for his disciples. He went to prepare a place for us; to take possession for us, as our advocate or attorney, and so to secure our title as indefeasible; to make provision. The happiness of heaven yet must be further fitted up for man. It consisting much in the presence of Christ there, it was therefore necessary that he should *go before*. Heaven would be an *unready* place for a Christian if Christ were not there.

3. Believe and consider that *therefore* he would certainly come again (*v*. 3): "*If I go and prepare a place for you, I will come again, and receive you to myself, that where I am there you may be also.*" Now these are comfortable words indeed. (1) That Jesus Christ will come again; intimating the certainty of it. We say, We are coming, when we are busy in preparing for our coming, and so he is. (2) That he will come again to receive all his faithful followers to himself. The coming of Christ is in order to our gathering *together unto him*. (3) *That where he is there they shall be also.* This

intimates that the quintessence of heaven's happiness is being with Christ *there*. *That where I am;* where I am to be shortly, where I am to be eternally; there you shall be shortly, there you shall be eternally: not only spectators of his glory, but sharers in it. (4) That this may be inferred from his *going to prepare a place* for us, for his preparations shall not be in vain. He will not build and furnish lodgings, and let them stand empty. If he has prepared the place for us, he will prepare us for it, and in due time put us in possession of it.

Verses 4–11

Christ, having set the happiness of heaven before them as the end, here shows them himself as the way to it. *You know*, 1. "You may know; it is none of the *secret things* which belong not to you, but one of the *things revealed.*" 2. "You do know; you know that which is the home and which is the way, though perhaps not as the home and as the way. You have been told it, and cannot but know."

I. Thomas enquired concerning the way (*v*. 5).

He said, "*Lord, we know not whither thou goest, and how can we know the way?*" Christ's testimony concerning their knowledge made them more sensible of their ignorance, and more inquisitive after further light. Thomas here shows more modesty than Peter. Peter was the more solicitous to know *whither Christ went*. Thomas here seems more solicitous to know *the way*. His confession of his ignorance was commendable enough. If good men be in the dark, and know it but in part, yet they are willing to own their defects. The cause of his ignorance was culpable. They knew not whither Christ went, because they dreamed of a temporal kingdom. Their fancy ran upon his going to some remarkable city or other, there to be anointed king. Where these castles in the air were to be built, east, west, north, or south, they could not tell, and therefore knew not the way. Had Thomas understood, that Christ was going to the invisible world, he would not have said, *Lord, we do not know the way.*

II. Now to this complaint of their ignorance Christ gives a full answer, *v*. 6, 7. Thomas had enquired both whither he went and what was the way, and Christ answers both these enquiries. They knew him, and he was the way; they knew the Father, and he was the end; and therefore, *whither I go you know, and the way you know.* Believe in God as the end, and in me as the way (*v*. 1).

(1) He speaks of himself as the way, *v*. 6. *I am the way; no man comes to the Father but by me.*

[1] The nature of his mediation: He is *the way, the truth, and the life.* Let us consider these first distinctly. Christ is *the way*. In him God and man meet, and are brought together. We could not get to the tree of life in the way of innocency; but Christ is another way to it. The disciples followed him, and Christ tells them that while they continued following him, they would never be out of their way. He is *the truth*; as truth is opposed to falsehood and error. When we enquire for truth, we need learn no more than *the truth as it is in Jesus*; as truth is opposed to fallacy and deceit; as true as truth itself. He is *the life*; for we are *alive unto God* only in and *through Jesus Christ*. Let us consider these jointly. Christ is *the way, the truth, and the life.* He is the beginning, the middle, and the end. He is *the true and living way*; there are *truth and life* in the way, as well as at the end of it. He is *the true way to life.* Other ways may seem right, but the end of them is *the way of death*.

[2] The necessity of his mediation: *No man cometh to the Father but by me.* Fallen man cannot come to him as a Father, otherwise than by Christ as Mediator.

(2) He speaks of his Father as the end (*v*. 7): "*If you had known me, you would have known my Father*

also; and henceforth you know him and have seen him."
A tacit rebuke to them for their dullness and carelessness in not acquainting themselves with Jesus Christ:
If you had known me——. They knew him, and yet did
not know him so well as they might and should have
known him. Christ had said to the Jews (*ch.* viii. 19):
*If you had known me, you would have known my Father
also;* and here the same to his disciples; for it is hard
to say which is the more strange, the wilful ignorance
of those that are enemies to the light, or the defects
and mistakes of *the children of light.* He was well satisfied concerning their sincerity, notwithstanding the
weakness of their understanding: "*And henceforth you
know him, and have seen him,*" for in the face of Christ
we see the glory of God. Many of the disciples of
Christ have more knowledge and more grace than they
think they have. Those that know God do not all at
once know that they know him.

III. Philip enquired concerning the Father (*v.* 8), and
Christ answered him, *v.* 9–11.

1. Philip's request for some extraordinary discovery
of the Father. From an earnest desire of further light,
he cries out, *Show us the Father.* "That is what we
want, that is what we would have: *Show us the Father
and it sufficeth us.*" This supposes an earnest desire of
acquaintance with God as a Father. The petition is,
"*Show us the Father.*" The plea is, *It sufficeth us.* Grant
us but one sight of the Father, and we have enough.
In the knowledge of God as our Father the soul is
satisfied; a sight of the Father is a heaven upon earth.
"Let us see the Father with our bodily eyes, as we see
thee, *and it sufficeth us.*" It manifests not only the
weakness of his faith, but his ignorance of the gospel
way of manifesting *the Father.* Christ's institutions
have provided better for the confirmation of our faith
than our own inventions would.

2. Christ's reply, *v.* 9–11.

(1) He refers him to what he had seen, *v.* 9. "*Have
I been so long time with you, and yet hast thou not
known me, Philip?* Now, *he that hath seen me hath seen
the Father; and how sayest thou then, Show us the
Father?*" He reproves him for two things: [1] For not
improving his acquaintance with Christ to a clear and
distinct knowledge of him: "*Hast thou not known me,
Philip?*" Philip, the first day he came to him, declared
that he knew him to be the Messiah (*ch.* i. 45), and yet
to this day did *not know the Father* in him. Many
know Christ, who yet do not know what they might
know of him, nor see what they should see in him. *I
have been so long time with thee.* Christ expects that
our proficiency should be in some measure according
to our standing, that we should not be always babes.
[2] For his infirmity in the prayer made, *Show us the
Father.* Herein appears much of the weakness of
Christ's disciples that they *know not what to pray for
as they ought* (Rom. viii. 26), but often *ask amiss*
(Jas. iv. 3). He instructs him, and gives him a maxim
which justifies what he had said (*v.* 7): *You know
the Father, and have seen him;* and answered what
Philip had asked, *Show us the Father. He that hath
seen me hath seen the Father.* All that saw *Christ in the
flesh* might *have seen the Father* in him. All that saw
Christ by faith did *see the Father* in him, though they
were not suddenly aware that they did so. The holiness
of God shone in the spotless purity of Christ's life,
and his grace in all the acts of grace he did.

(2) He refers him to what he had reason to believe
(*v.* 10, 11): "*Believest thou not that I am in the Father,
and the Father in me,* and therefore that in *seeing me*
thou hast *seen the Father?*" What it is which we are to
believe: *That I am in the Father, and the Father in me;*
that is, as he had said (*ch.* x. 30), *I and my Father are
one.* In knowing Christ we know the Father; and in
seeing him we see the Father. What inducements we
have to believe this. We must believe it: For his word's
sake: *The words that I speak to you, I speak not of*

myself. He spoke not of himself only, but the mind of
God according to the eternal counsels. For his works'
sake: *The Father that dwelleth in me, he doeth them;*
and therefore *believe me for their sake.* The Father is
said to *dwell* in him. The Father so dwells in Christ
that in him he may *be found,* as a man where he dwells.
Seek ye the Lord, seek him in Christ, and *he will be
found,* for in him he dwells. *He doeth the works.* Many
works of power, and works of mercy, Christ did, and
the Father did them in him. We are bound to believe
this, *for the very works' sake.* Christ's miracles are
proofs of his divine mission, not only for the conviction of infidels, but for the confirmation of the faith
of his own disciples.

Verses 12–14

The disciples, as they were full of grief to think of
parting with their Master, so they were full of care
what would become of themselves when he was
gone. If he leave them, they will be *as sheep having
no shepherd.* Christ here assures them that they
should be clothed with powers sufficient to bear them
out.

I. Great power on earth (*v.* 12): *He that believeth on
me, the works that I do shall he do also.* This magnifies
his power more than anything, that he not only
wrought miracles himself, but gave power to others to
do so too.

1. Two things he assures them of:

(1) That they should be enabled to do such works
as he had done. Did Christ *heal the sick, cleanse the
leper, raise the dead?* So should they. Did he convince
and convert sinners, and draw multitudes to him? So
should they. Though he should depart, the work should
not cease, nor fall to the ground; and it is still in the
doing.

(2) That they should do *greater works than these.*
In the kingdom of nature they should work greater
miracles. No miracle is little, but some to our apprehension seem greater than others. Christ wrought
miracles for two or three years in one country, but
his followers wrought miracles in his name for many
ages in divers countries. In the kingdom of grace,
they should obtain greater victories by the gospel
than had been obtained while Christ was upon earth.
The truth is, the captivating of so great a part of the
world to Christ, was the miracle of all.

2. The reason Christ gives for this is, *Because I
go unto my Father.* "*Because I go,* it will be requisite
that you should have such a power. *Because I go to
the Father,* I shall be in a capacity to furnish you with
such a power."

II. Great *power in heaven:* "*Whatsoever you shall
ask, that will I do*" (*v.* 13, 14).

1. In what way they were to derive power from him,
when he was gone to the Father—by prayer. When
dear friends are to be removed to a distance from
each other, they provide for the settling of a correspondence; thus, when Christ was going to his Father,
he tells his disciples how they might write to him
upon every occasion, and send their epistles by a safe
and ready way of conveyance. "Let me hear from
you by prayer, and you shall hear from me by the
Spirit." And it is still open to us. Humility prescribed: *You shall ask.* They could demand nothing
of him as a debt, but must be humble supplicants,
beg or starve, beg or perish. Liberty allowed: "Ask
anything, anything that is good and proper for you;
anything, provided you know what you ask." Occasions vary, but they shall be welcome to the throne of
grace upon every occasion.

2. In what name they were to present their petitions:
Ask in my name. They were to plead his merit and
intercession, and to depend upon it. If we ask *in our own
name,* we cannot expect to speed, for, being strangers,
we have *no name* in heaven; being sinners, we have an

ill name there; but Christ's is a good name, well known in heaven.

3. What success they should have in their prayers: "What you ask, *that will I do,*" *v.* 13. And again (*v.* 14), "*I will do it.* You may be sure I will: not only it shall be done, but *I will do it.*" By faith in his name we may have what we will for the asking.

4. For what reason their prayers should speed so well: *That the Father may be glorified in the Son. Hallowed be thy name* is an answered prayer, and is put first, because, if the heart be sincere in this, it does in a manner *consecrate* all the other petitions. This Christ will aim at in granting, and for the sake of this will do what they ask. The wisdom, power, and goodness of God were magnified in the Redeemer when his apostles and ministers were enabled to do such great things, both in the proofs of their doctrine and in the successes of it.

Verses 15–17

Christ here promises to send the Spirit, whose office it should be to be their Comforter, to *impress* these things upon them.

I. He premises to this a memento of duty (*v.* 15): *If you love me, keep my commandments.* We must not expect comfort but in the way of duty. When they were in care what would become of them now, he bids them *keep his commandments.* In difficult times our care concerning the events of the day should be swallowed up in a care concerning the duty of the day. When they were showing their love to Christ by their grieving to think of his departure, and the sorrow which filled their hearts, he bids them, if they would show their love to him, do it, not by these weak and feminine passions, but by a universal obedience to his commands; this is better than sacrifice, better than tears. When Christ has given them precious promises he lays down this as a limitation of the promises, "Provided you keep my commandments, from a principle of love to me."

II. He promises this great and unspeakable blessing to them, *v.* 16, 17.

1. It is promised that they shall have *another comforter.* This is the great New Testament promise; a promise adapted to the present distress of the disciples, who were in sorrow, and needed a comforter.

(1) The blessing promised. The word is used only here in these discourses of Christ's, and 1 John ii. 1, where he translates it an *advocate.* You shall have another *advocate.* The office of the Spirit was to be Christ's advocate with them and others, to plead his cause, and take care of his concerns, on earth. When Christ was with them he spoke for them; but now that he is leaving them, the Spirit of the Father shall speak in them, Matt. x. 19, 20. And the cause cannot miscarry that is pleaded by such an advocate. You shall have another *master* or *teacher,* another *exhorter.* While they had Christ with them he excited and exhorted them to their duty; but now he leaves one with them that shall do this as effectually. Another *comforter.* Christ comforted his disciples when he was with them, and now that he was leaving them in their greatest need he promises them *another.*

(2) The giver of this blessing: *The Father* shall give him. The same that gave the Son to be our Saviour will give his Spirit to be our comforter.

(3) How this blessing is procured—by the intercession of the Lord Jesus: *I will pray the Father.* When Christ saith, *I will pray the Father,* it does not suppose that the Father is unwilling, but only that the gift of the Spirit is a fruit of Christ's mediation.

(4) The continuance of this blessing: *That he may abide with you for ever.* "*With you, as long as you live.* You shall never know the want of a comforter." There are everlasting consolations provided for us. They must disperse, and therefore a comforter that

would be with them all, in all places alike, was alone fit to be with them for ever: "With your successors, when you are gone, to the end of time."

2. This comforter is the *Spirit of truth, whom you know, v.* 16, 17.

(1) The comforter promised is *the Spirit,* one who should do his work in a spiritual way and manner.

(2) He is the *Spirit of truth.* He will be true to you, and to his undertaking for you. He will *teach you the truth.* The Spirit of truth shall not only *lead you into all truth,* but others by your ministry. Christ is the truth, and he is the Spirit of Christ.

(3) He is one *whom the world cannot receive;* but *you know him. Therefore he abideth with you.* The disciples of Christ are here distinguished from the world; they are the children and heirs of another world, not of this. It is the misery of those that are invincibly devoted to the world that they *cannot receive* the Spirit of truth. Where the spirit of the world has the ascendant, the Spirit of God is excluded. Therefore men *cannot receive the Spirit of truth* because they *see him not, neither know him.* The comforts of the Spirit are *foolishness to them,* as much as ever the cross of Christ was. Speak to the children of this world of the operations of the Spirit, and you are as a barbarian to them. The best knowledge of the Spirit of truth is that which is got by experience: *You know him, for he dwelleth with you.* Christ had dwelt with them, and by their acquaintance with him they could not but know *the Spirit of truth.* The experiences of the saints are the explications of the promises. He *dwelleth with you, and shall be in you,* for the blessed Spirit doth not use to shift his lodging. Those that know him know how to invite him and bid him welcome; and therefore he shall be in them, as the light in the air, as the sap in the tree, and their union with him inseparable. The gift of the Holy Ghost is a peculiar gift, bestowed upon the disciples of Christ in a distinguishing way—upon them, and not the world. No comforts are comparable to those which make no show, make no noise.

Verses 18–24

When friends are parting, it is a common request they make to each other, "Pray let us hear from you as often as you can": this Christ engaged to his disciples, that out of sight they should not be out of mind.

I. He promises that he would continue his care of them (*v.* 18): "*I will not leave you orphans,* or *fatherless; I will come to you.*" His departure from them was neither total nor final. Not total. "Though I leave you without my bodily presence, yet I do not leave you without comfort." The case of true believers, though sometimes it may be sorrowful, is never comfortless, because they are never orphans: for God is their Father. Not final: *I will come to you.* "I will come speedily to you at my resurrection." He had often said, *The third day I will rise again.* "I will be coming daily to you in my Spirit"; in the tokens of his love, and visits of his grace, he is still coming. The consideration of Christ's coming to us saves us from being comfortless in his removals from us.

II. He promises that they should continue their acquaintance with him (*v.* 19, 20): *Yet a little while, and the world sees me no more.* The malignant world thought they had seen enough of him, and *cried, Away with him, crucify him;* and so shall their doom be; they shall see him no more. But his disciples have communion with him in his absence.

1. *You see me.* They saw him with their bodily eyes after his resurrection. And *then were the disciples glad when they saw the Lord.* They saw him with an eye of faith after his ascension; saw that in him which the world saw not.

2. *Because I live, you shall live also*. That which grieved them was, that their Master was dying, and they counted upon nothing else but to die with him. No, saith Christ, *I live*. Not only, I shall live, as he saith of them, but, I do live. We are not comfortless, while *we know that our Redeemer lives*. Therefore *you shall live also*. The life of Christians is bound up in the life of Christ; as sure and as long as he lives, those that by faith are united to him shall live also. This life is hid with Christ; if the head and root live, the members and branches live also.

3. You shall have the assurance of this (*v.* 20): *At that day you shall know* that *I am in my Father, and you in me, and I in you*. These glorious mysteries will be fully known in heaven. Now it appears not *what we shall be*, but then it will appear what we were. They were more fully known after the pouring out of the Spirit upon the apostles; at that day divine light should shine, and their eyes should see more clearly, like the blind man's at the second touch of Christ's hand, who at first only *saw men as trees walking*. They are known by all that receive the Spirit of truth. They know that *Christ is in the Father*, is one with the Father, by their experience of what he has wrought for them and in them. That Christ is in them. That they are in Christ, for the relation is mutual. Christ in them and they in Christ, which speaks an intimate and inseparable union. Union with Christ is the life of believers. The knowledge of this union is their unspeakable joy and satisfaction.

III. He promises that he would love them, and manifest himself to them, *v.* 21–24.

1. Who they are whom Christ will accept as lovers of him; those that *have his commandments, and keep them*. The kind things he here said to his disciples were intended not for those only that were *now* his *followers*, but for all that should *believe in him through their word*. The duty of those who claim the dignity of being disciples. Having Christ's commandments, we must keep them. Having them in our heads, we must keep them in our hearts and lives. The dignity of those that do the duty of disciples. Not those that have the greatest wit and know how to talk for him, or the greatest estate to lay out for him, but those that *keep his commandments*. The surest evidence of our love to Christ is obedience to the laws of Christ.

2. What returns he will make to them for their love. (1) They shall have the Father's love: *He that loveth me shall be loved of my Father*. We could not love God if he did not first give us his grace to love him. He loves them, and lets them know that he loves them. God so loves the Son as to love all those that love him. (2) They shall have Christ's love: *And I will love him*. God will love him as a Father, and I will love him as a brother, an elder brother. In the nature of God, nothing shines more brightly than this, that *God is love*. And in the undertaking of Christ nothing appears more glorious than this, that *he loved us*. Christ was now leaving his disciples, but promises to continue his love to them. He bears them on his heart, and ever lives interceding for them. (3) They shall have the comfort of that love: *I will manifest myself to him*. Being promised to all that *love him and keep his commandments*, it must be construed so as to extend to them.

3. What occurred upon Christ's making this promise.

(1) One of the disciples expresses his wonder and surprise at it, *v.* 22. [1] Who it was that said this— *Judas, not Iscariot*. Two of Christ's disciples were of that name: one of them was the traitor, the other was the brother of James (Luke vi. 16). There was a very good man, and a very bad man, called by the same name; for names commend us not to God, nor do they make men worse. Judas the apostle was never the worse, nor Judas the apostate ever the

better, for being namesakes. The evangelist carefully distinguishes between them. Take heed of mistaking; let us not confound the precious and the vile. [2] What he said—*Lord how is it? First*, The weakness of his understanding. He expected the temporal kingdom of the Messiah, that it should appear in external pomp and power. "*What is the matter* now, that thou wilt not show thyself openly as is expected." *Secondly*, The strength of his affections. *Lord, how is it?* He is amazed at the condescensions of divine grace. What is there in us to deserve so great a favour? It is justly *marvellous in our eyes*; for it is unaccountable, and must be resolved into free and sovereign grace.

(2) Christ explains and confirms what he had said, *v.* 23, 24.

[1] He further explains the condition of the promise, which was loving him, and keeping his commandments. Love is the root, obedience is the fruit. Where a sincere love to Christ is in the heart, there will be obedience: "*If a man love me* indeed, he will *keep my words*." Where love is, duty follows of course, is easy and natural, and flows from a principle of gratitude. Where there is no true love to Christ there will be no care to obey him: *He that loveth me not keepeth not my sayings, v.* 24. Certainly those do not love him that believe not his truths, and obey not his laws, to whom Christ's sayings are but as idle tales, which he heeds not, or hard sayings, which he likes not. Why should Christ be familiar with those that will be strange to him?

[2] He further explains the promise (*v.* 23): *If a man thus love me, I will manifest myself to him. My Father will love him;* this he had said before (*v.* 21), and here repeats it for the confirming of our faith. Jude wondered that Christ should *manifest himself to them. We will come unto him, and make our abode with him.* Not only, *I will*, but *We will, I and the Father.* Wherever Christ is formed the image of God is stamped. Not only, "*I will show myself to him* at a distance," but, "*We will come to him*, to be near him, to be with him." Not only, "I will give him a transient view of me, or make him a short and running visit," but, *We will take up our abode with him.* God will not only love obedient believers, but he will rest in love to them. He will be with them as at his home.

[3] He gives a good reason both to bind us to observe the condition and encourage us to depend upon the promise. *The word which you hear is not mine, but his that sent me, v.* 24. To this purport he had often spoken (*ch.* vii. 16). The stress of duty is laid upon the precept of Christ as our rule. The stress of our comfort is laid upon the promise of Christ. It concerns us to enquire whether the security be sufficient for us to venture our all upon; and this satisfies us that it is, that the promise is not Christ's bare word, but the Father's which sent him.

Verses 25–27

Two things Christ here comforts his disciples with:

I. That they should be under the tuition of his Spirit, *v.* 25, 26. Christ would have them reflect upon the instructions he had given them: *These things have I spoken unto you being yet present with you.* What he had said he did not retract. What he had spoken he had spoken, and would abide by it. Christ should find out a way of speaking to them after his departure from them, *v.* 26.

(1) On whose account he should be sent: "The Father will send him *in my name*; that is, for *my sake*." He came in his Father's name: the Spirit comes in his name to carry on his undertaking.

(2) On what errand he should be sent: *He shall teach you all things*. He shall teach them all things necessary for them either to learn themselves, or to teach others; for those that would teach the things

of God must first themselves be taught of God. *He shall bring all things to your remembrance whatsoever I have said unto you.* Many a good lesson Christ had taught them, which they had forgotten. The Spirit shall not teach them a new gospel, but bring to their minds that which they had been taught, by leading them into the understanding of it. To all the saints the Spirit of grace is given to be a remembrancer.

II. That they should be under the influence of his peace (v. 27): *Peace I leave with you.* When Christ was about to leave the world he *made his will.* His soul he committed to his Father; his body he bequeathed to Joseph, to be decently interred; his clothes fell to the soldiers; his mother he left to the care of John: but what should he leave to his poor disciples, that had left all for him? Silver and gold he had none; but he left them that which was infinitely better, *his peace.* "*I leave you,* but I leave *my peace* with you." He did not part in anger, but in love; for this was his farewell, *Peace I leave with you.*

1. The legacy that is here bequeathed: *Peace, my peace.* Peace is put for all good. Peace is put for reconciliation and love; the peace bequeathed is peace with God. Peace *in our own bosoms* seems to be especially meant. It is the peace on which the angels congratulated men at his birth, Luke ii. 14.

2. To whom this legacy is bequeathed: "To you, my disciples and followers." This legacy was left to them and their successors, to them and all true Christians in all ages.

3. In what manner it is left: *Not as the world giveth, give I unto you.* "I do not compliment you with *Peace be unto you*; no, it is not a mere formality, but a real blessing. The gifts I give to you are not such as this world gives." The world's gifts concern only the body and time; Christ's gifts enrich the soul for eternity. The peace which Christ gives is infinitely more valuable than that which the world gives. As is the difference between a killing lethargy and a reviving refreshing sleep, such is the difference between Christ's peace and the world's.

4. What use they should make of it: *Let not your heart be troubled, neither let it be afraid.* This comes in here as the conclusion of the whole matter; he had said (v. 1), *Let not your heart be troubled,* and here he repeats it as that for which he had now given sufficient reason.

Verses 28–31

Christ here gives his disciples another reason why their hearts should not be troubled for his going away; and that is, because his heart was not. He comforted himself,

I. That, though he went away, he should *come again*: "*You have heard how I have said, I go away, and come again.*" Christ encouraged himself with *this,* in his sufferings and death, that he should *come again,* and the same should comfort us in our departure at death; we go away to come again; the leave we take of our friends at that parting is only a good night, not a final farewell.

II. That he *went to his Father*: "*If you loved me, you would rejoice* because, though I leave you, *I go unto the Father*; for *my Father is greater than I.*" It is matter of joy. His departure had a bright side as well as a dark side. The reason of this is, because *the Father is greater than he.* His state with his Father would be much more excellent and glorious than his present state. Christ raises the thoughts and expectations of his disciples to something greater than that in which now they thought all their happiness bound up. The kingdom of the Father will be greater than the mediatorial kingdom. The disciples of Christ should show that they love him by their rejoicing in the glories of his exaltation. Many that

love Christ, let their love run out in a wrong channel; they think if they love him they must be continually in pain because of him; whereas those that love him should *rejoice in Christ Jesus.*

III. That his going away would be a means of confirming the faith of his disciples (v. 29): *I have told you before it come to pass, that, when it is come to pass, you might believe.* See this reason, ch. xiii. 19; xvi. 4. Christ told his disciples of his death because it would afterwards redound to the confirmation of their faith. He who foretold these things had a divine prescience. The things foretold were according to the divine purpose. Let them therefore not be troubled at that which would be for the confirmation of their faith.

IV. That he was sure of a victory over Satan (v. 30): "*Henceforth I will not talk much with you.*" He had a great deal of good talk with them after this (ch. xv. and xvi.), but, in comparison with what he had said, it was not much. One reason why he would not talk much with them was because he had now other work to apply himself to: *The prince of this world comes.* He called the devil the *prince of this world,* ch. xii. 31. Christ tells them that the *prince of this world* was his enemy. But *he has nothing in me.* 1. The prospect Christ had of an approaching conflict, not only with men, but with the powers of darkness. The devil had set upon him with his temptations (Matt. iv), had offered him the *kingdoms of this world. Then the devil departed from him for a season.* "But now," says Christ, "I see him rallying again." The foresight of a temptation gives us great advantage in our resistance of it; for, being forewarned, we should be forearmed. 2. The assurance he had of good success in the conflict: *He hath nothing in me.* There was no guilt in Christ. Christ having done no evil, Satan, though he prevailed to crucify him, could not prevail to terrify him; though he hurried him to death, yet not to despair. When Satan comes to disquiet us, he has something in us to perplex us with, for we have all sinned; but, when he would disturb Christ, he found no occasion against him. There was no corruption in Christ. Such was the spotless purity of his nature that he was above the possibility of sinning.

V. That his departure was in obedience to his Father. *That the world may know that I love the Father, v. 31.*

1. Confirming what he had often said, that his undertaking, as Mediator, was a demonstration to the world, of his compliance with the Father. As it was an evidence of his love to man that he died for his salvation, so it was of his love to God that he died for his glory. It demonstrates also his obedience to his Father: "*As the Father gave me commandment, even so I do.*" The best evidence of our love to the Father is our doing as he hath given us commandment. The command of God is sufficient to bear us out in that which is most disputed by others, and therefore should be sufficient to bear us up in that which is most difficult to ourselves.

2. Concluding what he had now said; *that the world may know that I love the Father.* You shall see how cheerfully I can meet the appointed cross: "*Arise, let us go hence.*" When we talk of troubles at a distance, it is easy to say, *Lord, I will follow thee whithersoever thou goest.* When an unavoidable cross lies in the way of duty, then to say, "*Arise, let us go* to meet it," instead of going out of our way to miss it, this lets *the world know that we love the Father.* In these words he gives his disciples an encouragement to follow him. He does not say, *I must go;* but, *Let us go.* He calls them out to no hardships but what he himself goes before them in as their leader. He gives them an example, teaching them at all times to sit loose to all things here below, and often to think

and speak of leaving them. When we sit down under Christ's shadow with delight, and say, *It is good to be here;* yet we must think of rising and going hence; going down from the mount.

CHAPTER 15

It is generally agreed that Christ's discourse in this and the next chapter was at the close of the last supper. What he chooses to discourse of is very pertinent to the present sad occasion of a farewell. There are four words to which his discourse in this chapter may be reduced: 1. Fruit, ver. 1–8. 2. Love, ver. 9–17. 3. Hatred, ver. 18–25. 4. The Comforter, ver. 26, 27.

Verses 1–8

Here Christ discourses concerning the fruit, *the fruits of the Spirit,* under the similitude of a vine.

I. The doctrine of this similitude.

1. Jesus Christ is *the vine, the true vine.* He is pleased to speak of himself under low and humble comparisons. He is *the vine,* planted in the vineyard, and not a spontaneous product; planted in the earth, for he is *the Word made flesh.* The vine is a spreading plant, and Christ will be known as *salvation to the ends of the earth.* The fruit of the vine honours God and cheers man, so does the fruit of Christ's mediation. He is *the true vine,* as truth is opposed to pretence and counterfeit. Unfruitful trees are said to *lie,* but Christ is a vine that will not deceive.

2. Believers are branches of this vine, which supposes that Christ is the root of the vine. The root bears the tree (Rom. xi. 18), diffuses sap to it, and is all in all to its flourishing and fruitfulness; and in Christ are all supports and supplies. The branches of the vine are many, yet, meeting in the root, are all but one vine; thus all good Christians, though in place and opinion distant from each other, yet meet in Christ, the centre of their unity.

3. *The Father is the husbandman, the land-worker.* Though *the earth is the Lord's,* it yields him no fruit unless he work it. God has not only a propriety in, but a care of, the vine and all the branches. Never was any husbandman so wise, so watchful, about his vineyard, as God is about his church, which therefore must needs prosper.

II. The duty taught us by this similitude.

1. We must be fruitful. From a vine we look for grapes, and from a Christian we look for Christianity; this is the *fruit,* a Christian temper and disposition, a Christian life and conversation. We must honour God, and do good, and this is bearing fruit. The disciples here must be fruitful, as Christians, in all *the fruits of righteousness,* and as apostles, in diffusing the savour of the knowledge of Christ.

(1) The doom of the unfruitful (*v.* 2): They are *taken away.* It is here intimated that there are many who pass for *branches* in Christ who yet do *not bear fruit.* Being only tied to him by the thread of an outward profession, though they seem to be branches, they will soon be seen to be dry ones. Unfruitful professors are unfaithful professors; professors, and no more. It is here threatened that they shall be *taken away.*

(2) The promise made to the fruitful: *He purgeth them, that they may bring forth more fruit.* Further fruitfulness is the blessed reward of forward fruitfulness. Even fruitful branches, in order to their further fruitfulness, have need of purging or pruning. The best have that in them which is peccant; some notions, passions, or humours, that want to be purged away. These shall be taken off by degrees in the proper season. The purging of fruitful branches is the care and work of the great husbandman.

(3) The benefits which believers have. *Now you are clean, v.* 3. Their society was clean, now that Judas was expelled. Till they were got clear of him *they were not all clean.* They were each of them clean,

that is, sanctified, by the truth of Christ (*ch.* xvii. 17). Apply it to all believers. The word of Christ is spoken to them; there is a cleansing virtue in that word. It cleanses as fire cleanses the gold from its dross, and as physic cleanses the body from its disease.

(4) The glory that will redound to God by our fruitfulness, *v.* 8. If we *bear much fruit,* herein our Father will be glorified. The fruitfulness of all Christians is to the glory of God. By the eminent good works of Christians many are brought to *glorify our Father who is in heaven.* So shall we be Christ's disciples indeed. So shall we both evidence our discipleship and adorn it, and be to our Master *for a name and a praise.* And the more fruit we bring forth, the more we abound in that which is good, the more he is glorified.

2. In order to our fruitfulness, we must abide in Christ.

(1) The duty enjoined (*v.* 4): *Abide in me, and I in you.* Those that are come to Christ must abide in him: "*Abide in me, and I in you. Abide in me,* and then fear not but I will *abide in you*"; for the communion between Christ and believers never fails on his side. The knot of the branch abides in the vine, and the sap of the vine abides in the branch, and so there is a constant communication between them.

(2) The necessity of our abiding in Christ, in order to our fruitfulness (*v.* 4, 5): "*You cannot bring forth fruit, except you abide in me;* but, if you do, you *bring forth much fruit; for without me you can do nothing.*" So necessary is it to our happiness that we be fruitful, that the best argument to engage us to abide in Christ is, that otherwise we cannot be fruitful. Abiding in Christ is necessary in order to our doing much good. He that is constant in the exercise of faith in Christ and love to him, *bringeth forth much fruit.* A life of faith in the Son of God is incomparably the most excellent life a man can live in this world. It is necessary to our doing any good. It is the root and spring of all good: "*Without me you can do nothing:* not only no great thing, but nothing." *Without Christ we can do nothing* aright, nothing that will be fruit pleasing to God or profitable to ourselves. We depend upon Christ, not only as the vine upon the wall, for support; but, as the branch on the root, for sap.

(3) The fatal consequences of forsaking Christ (*v.* 6): *If any man abide not in me, he is cast forth as a branch.* This is a description of the fearful state of hypocrites that are *not in Christ.* They are cast forth as dry and withered branches, which are plucked off because they cumber the tree. It is just that those who reject him should be rejected by him. Those that abide not in Christ shall be abandoned by him. They are withered, as a branch broken off from the tree. Those that abide not in Christ in a little time wither and come to nothing. Those that bear no fruit after a while will bear no leaves. *Men gather them.* Satan's agents and emissaries pick them up, and make an easy prey of them. *They are burned;* this follows, of course, but it is here added very emphatically, and makes the threatening very terrible.

(4) The blessed privilege which those have that *abide in Christ* (*v.* 7): *If my words abide in you, you shall ask what you will and it shall be done.* How our union with Christ is maintained: *If you abide in me;* he had said before, *and I in you;* here he explains himself, *and my words abide in you.* It is in the word that we receive and embrace him; and so where the *word of Christ dwells richly* there Christ dwells. If the word be in us as at home, then we abide in Christ, and he in us. How our communion with Christ is maintained: *You shall ask what you will, and it shall be done to you.* And what can we desire more than to have what we will for the asking? Those that abide in Christ as their heart's delight shall

have, through Christ, their heart's desire. If we abide in Christ, and his word in us, we shall not ask anything but what is proper to be done for us. The promises abiding in us lie ready to be turned into prayers; and the prayers so regulated cannot but speed.

Verses 9–17

Christ, who is love itself, is here discoursing concerning love, a fourfold love.

I. Concerning the Father's love to him. 1. The Father did love him (v. 9): *As the Father hath loved me.* He was the Son of his love. And yet God so *loved the world* as to deliver him up for us all. Those whom God loves as a Father may despise the hatred of all the world. 2. He abode in his Father's love, v. 10. Because he continued to love his Father, he went cheerfully through his sufferings, and therefore his Father continued to love him. 3. Therefore he abode in his Father's love because he kept his Father's law: *I have kept my Father's commandments,* and so *abide in his love.* Christ satisfied for us by obeying the law of redemption, and so he abode in his love, and restored us to it.

II. Concerning his own love to his disciples. Though he leaves them, he loves them.

1. The pattern of this love: *As the Father has loved me, so have I loved you.* As the Father loved him, who was most worthy, he loved them, who were most unworthy. The Father loved him as his Son, and he loves them as his children. The Father was well pleased with him, that he might be well pleased with us in him; and loved him, that in him, as beloved, he might *make us accepted.*

2. The proofs and products of this love.

(1) Christ loved his disciples, for he laid down his life for them (v. 13): *Greater love hath no man than this,* to *lay down his life for his friend.* And this is the love wherewith *Christ hath loved us.* See the extent of the love of the children of men to one another. The highest proof of it is laying down one's life for a friend, to save his life. It is love in the highest degree, which is *strong as death.* See the excellency of the love of Christ. He has not only equalled, but exceeded, the most illustrious lovers. Others have thus laid down their lives for their friends, but Christ laid down his for us *when we were enemies,* Rom. v. 8, 10. *Those hearts must be harder than iron or stone which are not softened by such incomparable sweetness of divine love.*—Calvin.

(2) Christ loved his disciples, for he took them into a covenant of friendship with himself, v. 14, 15. The followers of Christ are the friends of Christ. Those that do the duty of his servants are admitted and advanced to the dignity of his friends. This honour have all Christ's servants. Christ takes believers to be his friends. Though they often show themselves unfriendly, he is a friend that loves at all times. He will not *call them servants.* He will *call them his friends*; he will not only love them, but will let them know it. Though Christ called *them his friends,* they called themselves *his servants*: Peter, *a servant of Christ* (1 Pet. i. 1), and so James, *ch.* i. 1. The more honour Christ puts upon us, the more honour we should study to do him; the higher in his eyes, the lower in our own.

(3) Christ loved his disciples, for he was very free in communicating his mind to them (v. 15). "*All things that I have heard of my Father I have declared unto you.*" Jesus Christ has faithfully handed to us what he received of the Father, Matt. xi. 27. The great things relating to man's redemption Christ declared to his disciples, that they might declare them to others.

(4) Christ loved his disciples, for he chose and ordained them (v. 16): *I have chosen you, and ordained you.* His love to them appeared,

[1] In their election to their apostleship: *I have chosen you twelve.* It did not begin on their side: *You have not chosen me,* but I first *chose you.* It is fit that Christ should have the choosing of his own ministers; still he does it. Though ministers make that holy calling their own choice, Christ's choice is prior to theirs and directs and determines it.

[2] In their ordination: *I have ordained you;* "*I have put you* into commission." It was a mighty confidence he reposed in them. The treasure of the gospel was committed to them that it might be propagated; *that you may go* from place to place all the world over, and *bring forth fruit.* They were ordained, not to sit still, but to go about. They were ordained, not to beat the air, but to be instrumental for the bringing of nations into obedience to Christ. Those whom Christ ordains shall not labour in vain. The church of Christ was not to be a short-lived thing. It did not *come up in a night,* nor should it *perish in a night.* As one generation of ministers and Christians has passed away, still another has come. Thus *their fruit remains* to this day, and shall do while the earth remains.

[3] His love to them appeared in the interest they had at the throne of grace: *Whatsoever you shall ask of my Father, in my name, he will give it you.* Probably this refers in the first place to the power of working miracles, which was to be drawn out by prayer. "Whatever help from heaven you have occasion for at any time, it is but ask and have." We have a God to go to who is a Father. We come in a good name. Whatever errand we come upon to the throne of grace, we may with a humble boldness mention Christ's name in it. An answer of peace is promised us. What you come for shall be given you.

III. Concerning the disciples' love to Christ. Three things he exhorts them to:

1. To continue in his love, v. 9. "Continue in your love to me, and in mine to you." All that love Christ should continue in their love to him. *Continue in my love.* Keep up your love to me, and then all the troubles you meet with will be easy. Let not the troubles you meet with for Christ's sake quench your love to Christ, but rather quicken it.

2. To let his joy remain in them, and fill them, v. 11.

(1) That his joy might remain in them. That *my joy in you may remain.* If they bring forth much fruit, and continue in his love, he will continue to rejoice in them as he had done. Fruitful and faithful disciples are the joy of the Lord Jesus. That *my joy,* that is, your joy in me, *may remain.* It is the will of Christ that his disciples should constantly and continually rejoice in him, Phil. iv. 4. The joy of those who abide in Christ's love is a continual feast.

(2) *That your joy might be full;* not only that you might be full of joy, but that your joy in me and in my love may rise higher and higher, till it come to perfection. Those and those only that have Christ's joy remaining in them have their joy full; worldly joys soon surfeit but never satisfy. The design of Christ in his word is to *fill the joy* of his people.

3. To evidence their love to him by keeping his commandments: *If you keep my commandments, you shall abide in my love,* v. 10. The promise: *You shall abide in my love* as in a dwelling place, at home in Christ's love; as in a resting-place, at ease in Christ's love; as in a stronghold, safe in it. "*You shall abide in my love,* you shall have grace and strength to persevere in loving me." The condition of the promise: *If you keep my commandments.* The disciples were to keep Christ's commandments, not only by a constant conformity to them themselves, but by a faithful delivery of them to others; they were to keep them as trustees.

To induce them to keep his commandments, he urges his own example: *As I have kept my Father's commandments, and abide in his love.* The necessity of it to their interest in him (v. 14): "*You are my friends if you do whatsoever I command you.*" Those only will be accounted Christ's faithful friends that approve themselves his obedient servants. It is universal obedience to Christ that is the only acceptable obedience.

IV. Concerning the *disciples' love one to another*. We must keep his commandments, and this is his commandment, that we *love one another*, v. 12, and again, v. 17. No one duty of religion is more frequently inculcated, nor more pathetically urged upon us, by our Lord Jesus, than that of mutual love. It is here recommended by Christ's pattern (v. 12): *as I have loved you.* We should love one another, as, and because, Christ has loved us. *Go you and do likewise.* It is required by his precept. Observe how differently it is expressed in these two verses, and both very emphatic. 1. *This is my commandment* (v. 12), as if this were the most necessary of all the commandments. Christ, foreseeing the addictedness of the Christian church to uncharitableness, has laid most stress upon this precept. 2. *These things I command you,* v. 17. He speaks as if he were about to give them many things in charge, and yet names this only, *that you love one another.*

Verses 18–25

Here Christ discourses concerning *hatred*, which is the character and genius of the devil's kingdom, as love is of the kingdom of Christ.

I. Who they are in whom this hatred is found—the world, the children of this world, as distinguished from the children of God. The calling of these *the world* intimates, 1. Their number; there were a world of people that opposed Christ and Christianity. I fear, if we should put it to the vote between Christ and Satan, Satan would out-poll us quite. 2. Their confederacy. Jews and Gentiles, that could agree in nothing else, agreed to persecute Christ's ministers. 3. Their spirit and disposition; they are *men of the world.* The people of God are taught to hate the sins of sinners, yet not their persons, but to love and do good to all men. A malicious, spiteful, envious spirit, is not the spirit of Christ, but of the world.

II. Who they are against whom this hatred is levelled—against the disciples of Christ, against Christ himself, and against the Father.

1. The world hates the disciples of Christ: *The world hateth you* (v. 19).

(1) Observe how this comes in here. Christ had expressed the great kindness he had for them as friends; but there was given them a *thorn in the flesh,* reproaches and persecutions for Christ's sake. He had appointed them their work, but tells them what hardships they should meet with in it. He had charged them to *love one another,* and need enough they had to love one another, for the world would hate them. Those that are in the midst of enemies are concerned to hold together.

(2) Observe what is here included. The world's enmity against the followers of Christ: it *hateth them.* Whom Christ blesseth the world curseth. The favourites and heirs of heaven have never been the darlings of this world. The fruits of that enmity, v. 20. They will persecute you. It is the common lot of those who will live godly in Christ Jesus to *suffer persecution.* He sent them forth as sheep in the midst of wolves. Another fruit of their enmity is implied, that they would reject their doctrine. When Christ says, *If they have kept my sayings, they will keep yours,* he means, They will keep yours, and regard yours, no more than they have regarded and

kept mine. The causes of that enmity. The world will hate them,

First, Because they do not belong to it (v. 19): "*If you were of the world,* of its spirit, *the world would love you* as its own." We are not to wonder if those that are devoted to the world are caressed by it as its friends. Nor are we to wonder if those that are delivered from the world are maligned by it as its enemies. The reason why Christ's disciples are not of the world is because Christ hath chosen them out of it. This is the reason why the world hates them. The glory which they are designed for sets them above the world, and so makes them the objects of its envy. The grace which they are endued with sets them against the world. They witness against it, and are not conformed to it. This would support them under all the calamities which the world's hatred would bring upon them, that they were hated because they were the chosen ones of the Lord Jesus. This was no just cause for the world's hatred of them. If men hate us for that for which they should love and value us, we have reason to pity them. This was just cause for their own joy. Those hug themselves whom the world hates, but whom Christ loves.

Secondly, Another cause will be because you do belong to Christ (v. 21): *For my name's sake.* Whatever is pretended, this is the ground of the quarrel, they hate Christ's disciples because they *bear his name,* and *bear up his name* in the world. It is the character of Christ's disciples that they stand up for his name. It has commonly been the lot of those that appear for Christ's name to suffer for so doing, to suffer *all these things. If you be reproached for the name of Christ, happy are you* (1 Pet. iv. 14). *If we suffer with Christ,* and for Christ, *we shall reign with him.*

Thirdly. It is the world's ignorance that is the true cause of its enmity to the disciples of Christ (v. 21): *Because they know not him that sent me.* They know not God. They know not God as him that sent our Lord Jesus. We do not rightly know God if we do not know him in Christ.

2. The world hates Christ himself. And this is spoken of here for two ends:

(1) To mitigate the trouble of his followers, arising from the world's hatred (v. 18): *You know that it hated me before you.* We read it as signifying priority of time. But it may be read as expressing his superiority over them: "*You know* that it hated me, *your first,* your chief and captain." If Christ was hated, can we expect that any virtue or merit of ours should screen us from malice. If our Master, the founder of our religion, met with so much opposition in the planting of it, his servants and followers can look for no other in propagating and professing it. For this he refers them (v. 20) to his own word: *Remember the word that I said unto you.* A plain truth: *The servant is not greater than his Lord.* The servant is inferior to his lord. The plainest truths are sometimes the strongest arguments for the hardest duties. A proper inference drawn from it: "*If they have persecuted me they will also persecute you;* you may expect it, for," [1] "You will do the same that I have done to provoke them; you will reprove them for their sins, and give them strict rules of holy living, which they will not bear." [2] "You cannot do more than I have done to oblige them. Let none wonder if they suffer ill for doing well. *If they have kept my sayings, they will keep yours also;* as there have been a few that have been wrought upon by my preaching, so there will be by yours a few."

(2) To aggravate the wickedness of this unbelieving world, and to discover its exceeding sinfulness. The world is generally in an ill name in scripture, and nothing can put it into a worse name than this, that it hated Jesus Christ. Two things he insists upon

to aggravate the wickedness of those that hated him:

[1] That there was the greatest reason imaginable why they should love him.

First, His words were such as merited their love (*v.* 22): "*If I had not spoken unto them they had not had sin.* But now they have no pretence, no excuse for their sin." The advantage which those have that enjoy the gospel; Christ in it comes and speaks to them; he spoke in person to the men of that generation, and is still speaking to us. Every word of his carries with it a condescending tenderness, able, one would think, to charm the deafest adder. The excuse which those have that enjoy not the gospel: "*If I had not spoken to them they had not had sin.*" Not this kind of sin. They had not been chargeable with a contempt of Christ. As *sin is not imputed where there is no law*, so unbelief is not imputed where there is no gospel. Not such a degree of sin. If they had not had the gospel among them, their other sins had not been so bad. The aggravated guilt which those lie under to whom Christ has *come and spoken in vain. They have no cloak for their sin;* they are altogether inexcusable. The word of Christ strips sin of its cloak, that it may appear sin.

Secondly, His works were such as merited their love (*v.* 24): "*If I had not done among them* such works as *no other man ever did, they had not had sin;* their unbelief and enmity had been excusable." But he produced satisfactory proofs of his divine mission, *works which no other man did.* His miracles, his mercies, works of wonder and works of grace, prove him sent of God, and sent on a kind errand. Christ's works were such as *no man ever did.* No common person that had not a commission from heaven, and God with him, could work miracles, *ch.* iii. 2. They were all good works, works of mercy. One that was so universally useful should have been universally beloved, and yet even he is hated. The works of Christ enhance the guilt of sinners' enmity to him. If they had only heard his words, and not seen his works, unbelief might have pleaded want of proof. They saw Christ to be studious to do them a kindness; yet they hated him. And we see in his word that great love wherewith he loved us, and yet are not wrought upon by it.

[2] That there was no reason at all why they should hate him (*v.* 25): "*This comes to pass that the word might be fulfilled which is written in their law, They hated me without a cause.*" Those that hate Christ hate him without any just cause; enmity to Christ is unreasonable enmity. Christ was the greatest blessing imaginable to his country, and yet was hated. He testified indeed that *their works were evil*, with a design to make them good, but to hate him for this cause was to hate him without cause. Herein the scripture was fulfilled. Those that hated Christ did not design therein to fulfil the scripture; but God, in permitting it, confirms our faith in Christ as the Messiah that even this was foretold concerning him, and, being foretold, was accomplished in him. And we must not think it strange or hard if it have a further accomplishment in us.

3. In Christ the world hates God himself; this is twice said here (*v.* 23): *He that hateth me hates my Father also.* And again, *v.* 24, They have *seen and hated both me and my Father.* There are those that hate God. Those who cannot bring themselves to deny that there is a God, and yet wish there were none, they see and hate him. Hatred of Christ will be adjudged hatred of God. What entertainment the Son has, that the Father has. Let an unbelieving world know that their enmity to the gospel of Christ will be looked upon as an enmity to the blessed God himself; and let all that suffer for righteousness' sake take comfort from this; if God himself be hated in

them, they need not be either ashamed of their cause or afraid of the issue.

Verses 26–27

Christ having spoken of the great opposition which his gospel was likely to meet with here intimates what effectual provision was made for supporting it, both by the principal testimony of the Spirit (*v.* 26), and the subordinate testimony of the apostles (*v.* 27).

I. It is here promised that the blessed Spirit shall maintain the cause of Christ in the world. "*When the Comforter is come, who proceedeth from the Father*, and *whom I will send, he shall testify of me.*" We have more in this verse concerning the Holy Ghost than in any one verse besides in the Bible.

1. Here is an account of him. In his essence He is *the Spirit of truth, who proceedeth from the Father.* He is spoken of as a distinct person; as a divine person, that *proceedeth from the Father.* The spirit or breath of man, called the *breath of life*, proceeds from the man, and by it invigorated he sometimes exerts his strength to *blow out* what he would extinguish, and *blow up* what he would excite. Thus the blessed Spirit is the emanation of divine light, and the energy of divine power.

2. In his mission. He will come in a more plentiful effusion of his gifts, graces, and powers, than had ever yet been. *I will send him to you from the Father.* He had said (*ch.* xiv. 16), *I will pray the Father, and he shall send you the Comforter.* Here he says, *I will send him.* The Spirit was sent, (1) By Christ as Mediator, now *ascended on high* to *give gifts unto men.* (2) From the Father: "Not only from heaven, my Father's house, but according to my Father's will and appointment." (3) To the apostles to instruct them in their preaching.

3. In his office and operations, which are two: One implied in the title given to him; he is the *Comforter*, or *Advocate*. An advocate for Christ, to maintain his cause against the world's infidelity, a comforter to the saints against the world's hatred. Another expressed: *He shall testify of me.* He is not only an advocate, but a witness for Jesus Christ. The power of the ministry is derived from the Spirit, for he qualifies ministers; and the power of Christianity too, for he sanctifies Christians, and in both testifies of Christ.

II. It is here promised that the apostles also should have the honour of being Christ's witnesses (*v.* 27): *And you also shall bear witness of me.*

1. The apostles were appointed to be witnesses for Christ in the world. When he had said, *The Spirit shall testify*, he adds, *And you also shall bear witness.* The Spirit's working is not to supersede, but to engage and encourage ours. Though the Spirit testify, ministers also must bear their testimony. The work cut out for them; they were to attest the truth, the whole truth, and nothing but the truth, concerning Christ. Though Christ's disciples fled upon his trial before the high priest and Pilate, yet after the Spirit was poured out upon them they appeared courageous in vindication of the cause of Christ. The truth of the Christian religion was to be proved very much by the evidence of matter of fact, especially Christ's resurrection, of which the apostles were in a particular manner chosen witnesses (Acts x. 41). Christ's ministers are his witnesses. The honour put upon them hereby—that they should be *workers together with God*. "The *Spirit shall testify of me*, and you also *shall bear witness.*" This might encourage them against the hatred and contempt of the world, that Christ had honoured them.

2. They were qualified to be so: *You have been with me from the beginning.* They not only heard his public sermons, but had constant private converse with him. Others saw the wonderful and merciful

works that he did in their own town and country only, those that went about with him were witnesses of them all. Those are best able to bear witness for Christ that have themselves been with him, by faith, hope, and love. Ministers must first learn Christ, and then preach him. Those speak best of the things of God that speak experimentally. It is particularly a great advantage to have been acquainted with Christ *from the beginning*. To have been with him from the beginning of our days. An early acquaintance and constant converse with the gospel of Christ will make a man like a good householder.

CHAPTER 16

I. Here are wounding words in the notice he gives them of the troubles that were before them, ver. 1–6. II. Here are healing words in the comforts he administers to them for their support, which are five: 1. That he would send them the Comforter, ver. 7–15. 2. That he would visit them again at his resurrection, ver. 16–22. 3. That he would secure to them an answer of peace to all their prayers, ver. 23–27. 4. That he was now but returning to his Father, ver. 28–32. 5. That, whatever troubles they might meet with they should be sure of peace in him, ver. 33.

Verses 1–6

Christ dealt faithfully with his disciples when he sent them forth. He told them the worst, that they might sit down and count the cost.

I. He gives them a reason why he alarmed them thus: *These things have I spoken unto you, that you should not be offended, v.* 1. The disciples of Christ are apt to be offended at the cross; and the offence of the cross is a dangerous temptation, even to good men, to turn back from the ways of God. Our Lord Jesus, by giving us notice of trouble, designed to take off the terror of it, that it might not be a surprise to us. We can easily welcome a guest we expect, and *being forewarned are forearmed.*

II. He foretells particularly what they should suffer (*v.* 2): "Those that have power to do it shall *put you out of their synagogues; they shall kill you.*" *Behold two swords* drawn against the followers of the Lord Jesus.

1. The sword of ecclesiastical censure. They shall *cast you out of their synagogues.* At first, they scourged them in their synagogues as contemners of the law (Matt. x. 17), and at length cast them out as incorrigible. "They shall cast you out of the congregation of Israel, put you into the condition of an outlaw," *to be knocked on the head, like another wolf.* Many a good truth has been branded with an anathema.

2. The sword of civil power. When you are expelled as heretics, they will *kill you, and think they do God service.* You will find them really cruel: They will *kill you.* The twelve apostles (we are told) were all put to death, except John. You will find them *seemingly conscientious;* they will think they do God service. It is possible for those that are real enemies to God's service to pretend a mighty zeal for it. The devil's work has many a time been done in God's livery. It is common to patronise an enmity to religion with a colour of duty to God. God's people have suffered the greatest hardships from conscientious persecutors. This does not at all lessen the sin of the persecutors, but it does enhance the sufferings of the persecuted, to die under the character of being enemies to God.

III. He gives them the true reason of the world's enmity and rage against them (*v.* 3): "*These things will they do unto you, because they have not known the Father, nor me.*" Many that pretend to know God are wretchedly ignorant of him. Those that are ignorant of Christ cannot have any right knowledge of God. Those are very ignorant indeed of God and Christ that think it an acceptable piece of service to persecute good people.

IV. He tells them why he gave them notice of this now, and why not sooner. Why he told them of it now (*v.* 4), not to discourage them, but that, "when *the time shall come* you may *remember that I told you.*" When suffering times come it will be of use to us to remember what Christ has told us of sufferings. The trouble may be the less grievous, for we were told of it before. So that it ought not to be a surprise to us. Why he did not tell them of it sooner: "*I spoke not this to you from the beginning* because *I was with you.*" While he was with them, he bore the shock of the world's malice, and stood in the front of the battle. But we do find that from the beginning he bade them prepare for sufferings.

V. He expresses a very affectionate concern for the present sadness of his disciples (*v.* 5, 6): "*Now I go my way to him that sent me;* and *none of you asketh me, Whither goest thou?* But, instead of enquiring after that which would comfort you, you pore upon that which looks melancholy."

1. He had told them that he was about to leave them: *Now I go my way.* He was not driven away by force, but voluntarily departed. He went *to him that sent him,* to give an account of his negotiation.

2. He had told them what hard things they must suffer when he was gone. They would be tempted to think they had made a sorry bargain of it. Their Master sympathizes with them, yet blames them, (1) They were careless of the means of comfort: *None of you asks me, Whither goest thou?* Peter had started this question (*ch.* xiii. 36), and Thomas had seconded it (*ch.* xiv. 5), but they did not pursue it. See what a compassionate teacher Christ is. Many a teacher will not endure that the learner should ask the same question twice; if he cannot take a thing quickly, let him go without it; but our Lord Jesus knows how to deal with babes, that must be taught with *precept upon precept.* Enquiry into the design and tendency of the darkest dispensations of Providence would help to reconcile us to them. It will silence us to ask, Whence come they? but will abundantly satisfy us to ask, Whither go they? for we know they *work for good,* Rom. viii. 28.

(2) They were too intent upon the occasions of their grief: *Sorrow has filled their hearts.* By looking at that only which made against them, and overlooking that which made for them, they were so full of sorrow that there was no room left for joy. It is the common fault and folly of melancholy Christians to dwell only upon the dark side of the cloud. That which filled the disciples' hearts with sorrow was too great an affection to this present life. They were big with hopes of their Master's external kingdom and glory. Nothing is a greater prejudice to our joy in God than *the love of the world;* and *the sorrow of the world,* the consequence of it.

Verses 7–15

Three things we have here concerning *the Comforter's coming:*

I. Christ's departure was absolutely necessary to the Comforter's coming, *v.* 7. Christ saw cause to assert it with a more than ordinary solemnity: *I tell you the truth.*

1. *It is expedient,* not only for me, but *for you* also, *that I go away.* Our Lord Jesus is always for that which is most expedient for us, and gives us the physic we are loth to take, because he knows it is good for us.

2. *It was therefore expedient* because it was in order to the sending of the Spirit.

(1) Christ's going was in order to the Comforter's coming. *If I go not away, the Comforter will not come.* He that gives freely may recall one gift before he bestows another, while we would fondly hold all. The sending of the Spirit was to be the fruit of Christ's purchase, and that purchase was to be made by his

death. It was to be an answer to his intercession within the veil. See *ch.* xiv. 16. Thus must this gift be both paid for, and prayed for, by our Lord Jesus. The disciples must be weaned from his bodily presence before they were duly prepared to receive the spiritual aids and comforts of a new dispensation. *If I depart I will send him to you.* Though he *departs, he sends the Comforter*; nay, he departs on purpose to send him.

(2) The presence of Christ's Spirit in his church is so much more desirable than his bodily presence, that it was really expedient for us that he should go away. His corporal presence could be but in one place at one time, but his Spirit is wherever *two or three are gathered in his name.* Christ's bodily presence draws men's eyes, his Spirit draws their hearts.

II. The coming of *the Spirit* was absolutely necessary to the carrying on of Christ's interests on earth (*v.* 8): *And when he is come he will reprove,* or, *he will convince the world,* concerning *sin, righteousness, and judgment.*

1. See here on what errand he is sent. To *reprove.* The Spirit, by the word and conscience, is a reprover. To *convince.* It is a law-term, and speaks the office of the judge in summing up the evidence. He shall *convince,* that is, "He shall put to silence the adversaries of Christ and his cause." Convincing work is the Spirit's work; man may open the cause, but it is the Spirit only that can open the heart. The Spirit is called the *Comforter* (*v.* 7), and here it is said, *He shall convince.* One could think this were cold comfort, but it is the method the Spirit takes, first to convince, and then to comfort; first to lay open the wound, and then to apply healing medicines.

2. See who they are whom he is to reprove and convince: *The world.* He shall give the world the most powerful means of conviction, the gospel, fully proved. He shall sufficiently provide for the silencing of the objections and prejudices of the world against the gospel. He shall savingly convince many in the world, some in every age, in every place. Even this malignant world the Spirit shall work upon; and the conviction of sinners is the comfort of faithful ministers.

3. See what the Spirit shall convince the world of.

(1) *Of sin* (*v.* 9), *because they believe not on me.* The Spirit is sent to convince sinners of sin, not barely to tell them of it; in conviction there is more than this; it is to prove it upon them, and force them to own it. The Spirit convinces of the fact of sin, of the fault of sin, of the folly of sin, of the filth of sin, and, lastly, of the fruit of sin, that the end thereof is death. The Spirit, in conviction, fastens especially upon the sin of unbelief, their not believing in Christ, *First,* As the great reigning sin. There was, and is, a world of people, that believe not in Jesus Christ, and they are not sensible that it is their sin. Those transgress who, when *God speaketh to us by his Son, refuse him that speaketh. Secondly,* As the great ruining sin. Every sin is so in its own nature. It is a sin against the remedy. *Thirdly,* As that which is at the bottom of all sin. The Spirit shall convince the world that the true reason why sin reigns among them is because they are not by faith united to Christ.

(2) *Of righteousness, because I go to my Father, and you see me no more, v.* 10. We may understand this, [1] Of Christ's personal righteousness. He shall convince the world that Jesus of Nazareth was Christ the righteous, as the centurion owned (Luke xxiii. 47), *Certainly this was a righteous man.* Now by what medium or argument will the Spirit convince men of the sincerity of the Lord Jesus? Their *seeing him no more* will contribute something towards the removal of their prejudices. His *going to the Father* would be a full conviction of it. The coming of the Spirit, according to the promise, was a proof of Christ's exaltation to God's *right hand* (Acts ii. 33), and this

was a demonstration of his righteousness. Christ's righteousness communicated to us fc justification and salvation. The Spirit shall con men of this righteousness. Having shown them need of a righteousness, lest this should drive th to despair he will show them where it is to be ha It was hard to convince those of this righteousnes that *went about to establish their own,* but the Spirit will do it. Christ's ascension is the great argument proper to convince men of this righteousness: *I go to the Father, and you shall see me no more.* Now that we are sure he is *at the right hand of God* we are sure of being justified through him.

(3) *Of judgment, because the prince of this world is judged, v.* 11. The devil, *the prince of this world,* was judged, was discovered to be a great deceiver and destroyer. He was cast out of the souls of people by the grace of God working with the gospel of Christ. The Spirit convinces the world of judgment. By *the judgment of the prince of this world,* it appears that Christ is stronger than Satan. He shall show that Christ's errand into the world was to set things to right in it. All will be well when his power is broken who made all the mischief. If Satan be thus subdued by Christ, we may be sure no other power can stand before him.

III. The coming of the Spirit would be of unspeakable advantage to the disciples themselves. The Spirit has work to do, not only on the enemies of Christ, but upon his servants and agents, and therefore it was *expedient for them that he should go away.*

1. The tender sense he had of their present weakness (*v.* 12): *I have yet many things to say unto you, but you cannot bear them now.* See what a teacher Christ is. None like him for copiousness. Treasures of wisdom and knowledge are hid in him. None like him for compassion; he would have told them more of *the things pertaining to the kingdom of God,* but they could not bear it, it would have confounded and stumbled them, rather than have given them any satisfaction.

2. He assures them of sufficient assistances. *"But when he, the Spirit of truth, is come,* all will be well." He shall undertake to guide the apostles, and glorify Christ.

(1) To guide the apostles. That they do not miss their way: *He will guide you.* The Spirit is given us to be our guide, to go along with us. That they do not come short of their end: *He will guide them into all truth,* as the skilful pilot guides the ship into the port it is bound for. To be led *into a truth* is more than barely to know it; it is to be intimately and experimentally acquainted with it. It denotes a gradual discovery of truth shining more and more. But how into *all truth?* Into the whole truth relating to their embassy; whatever was needful or useful for them to know; what truths they were to teach others the Spirit would teach them. Into nothing but the truth. All that *he shall guide you into* shall be *truth.* [1] "The Spirit shall teach nothing but the truth, *for he shall not speak of himself, but whatsoever he shall hear, that,* and that only, *shall he speak.*" The testimony of the Spirit, in the word and by the apostles, is what we may rely upon. We may venture our souls upon the Spirit's word. The testimony of the Spirit always concurs with the word of Christ, *for he does not speak of himself.* Men's word and spirit often disagree, but the eternal Word and the eternal Spirit never do. [2] "He shall teach you all truth, for *he will show you things to come.*" The Spirit was in the apostles a Spirit of prophecy. This was a great satisfaction to their own minds, and of use to them in their conduct. We should not grudge that the Spirit does not now *show us things to come* in this world, let it suffice that the Spirit in the word

shown us things to come in the other world, ... are our chief concern.

...) The Spirit undertook to glorify Christ, v. 14, 15. ...en the sending of the Spirit was the glorifying of ...rist. It was the honour of the Redeemer that the ...pirit was both sent in his name and sent on his ...rrand, to carry on and perfect his undertaking. All the gifts and graces of the Spirit, all the preaching and all the writing of the apostles, the tongues, and miracles, were to glorify Christ. The Spirit glorified Christ by leading his followers into *the truth as it is in Jesus. First*, The Spirit should communicate the things of Christ to them: *He shall receive of mine, and shall show it unto you*. All that the Spirit shows us, all that he gives us for our strength and quickening, did all belong to Christ, and was had from him. The Spirit came not to erect a new kingdom, but to advance and establish the same kingdom that Christ had erected. *Secondly*, Herein the things of God should be communicated to us. *All things that the Father hath are mine*. All that *grace and truth* which God designed to show to us be lodged in the hands of the Lord Jesus. Spiritual blessings in heavenly things are given by the Father to the Son for us, and the Son entrusts the Spirit to convey them to us.

Verses 16–22

I. Observe the intimation he gave them of the comfort he designed them, v. 16.

1. That they should now shortly lose the sight of him: *A little while, and you shall not see me;* and therefore, if they had any good question to ask him, they must ask quickly. It is good to consider how near to a period our seasons of grace are, that we may be quickened to improve them. They lost the sight of Christ at his death. The most that death does to our Christian friends is to take them out of our sight, only out of sight, and then not out of mind. At his ascension, when he withdrew from them, *out of their sight*; *a cloud received* him, and *they saw him no more.*

2. That yet they should speedily recover the sight of him: *Again a little while, and you shall see me.* His farewell was not a final farewell. (1) At his resurrection, soon after his death, when *he showed himself alive*, by many infallible proofs. (2) By the pouring out of the Spirit, soon after his ascension. The Spirit's coming was Christ's visit to his disciples, not a transient but a permanent one. (3) At his second coming.

3. He assigns the reason: "*Because I go to the Father.*" This refers rather to his going away at death, and return at his resurrection, than his going away at his ascension, and his return at the end of time; for it was his death that was their grief, not his ascension. Thus we may say of our ministers and Christian friends, *Yet a little while, and we shall not see them.* It is certain that we must part shortly, and yet not part for ever. It is but a good night to those whom we hope to see with *joy in the morning.*

II. The perplexity of the disciples. They were at a loss what to make of it (v. 17, 18): *Some of them said among themselves, What is this that he saith to us?* Though Christ had often spoken to this purport before, yet still they were in the dark. 1. The disciples' weakness, in that they could not understand so plain a saying. Having told them so often in plain terms that he should *be killed*, *and the third day rise again;* yet, say they, *We cannot tell what he saith. Sorrow had filled their heart*, and made them unapt to receive the impressions of comfort. Mistakes cause griefs, and then griefs confirm mistakes. The notion of Christ's secular kingdom was so deeply rooted in them. When we think the scripture must be made to agree with the false ideas we have imbibed, no wonder that we complain of its

difficulty; but, when our reasonings are captivated to revelation, the matter becomes easy. It should seem, that which puzzled them was the *little while*. They could not conceive how he should leave them quickly. Thus it is hard for us to represent to ourselves that change as near which yet we know will come certainly, and may come suddenly. 2. Their willingness to be instructed. When they were at a loss about the meaning of Christ's words, they conferred together upon it. By mutual converse about divine things we both borrow the light of others and improve our own. We must revolve what we cannot explain, and wait *till God shall reveal even this unto us.*

III. The further explication of what Christ had said.

1. See here *why* Christ explained it (v. 19); because he *knew they were desirous to ask him*. The knots we cannot untie we must bring to him. Christ *knew they were desirous to ask him*, but were bashful and ashamed to ask. Christ instructed those who he *knew were desirous to ask him*, though they did not ask. Who they are that Christ will teach. The humble, that confess their ignorance. The diligent, that use the means they have: "*Do you enquire?* You shall be taught."

2. See here *how* he explained it. He explains it by their sorrowing and rejoicing, because we commonly measure things according as they affect us (v. 20): *You shall weep and lament, but the world shall rejoice and you shall be sorrowful, but your sorrow will be turned into joy.* Believers have joy or sorrow according as they have or have not a sight of Christ.

(1) What Christ says here, and v. 21, 22, of their sorrow and joy, is primarily to be understood of the present state of the disciples. Their grief foretold: *You shall weep and lament, and you shall be sorrowful.* They wept for him because they loved him; the pain of our friend is a pain to ourselves. They wept for themselves, and their own loss. Christ has given notice to his disciples beforehand to expect sorrow, that they may treasure up comforts accordingly. The world's rejoicing: *But the world shall rejoice.* That which is the grief of saints is the joy of sinners. Those that are *strangers to Christ* will continue in their carnal mirth. Those that are *enemies to Christ* will rejoice because they hope they have conquered him. Let it be no surprise to us if we see others triumphing, when we are *trembling for the ark.* The return of joy. *But your sorrow shall be turned into joy.* The sorrow of the true Christian, *is but for a moment. The disciples were glad when they saw the Lord.* His resurrection was *life from the dead* to them, and their sorrow for Christ's sufferings was turned into joy. They were *sorrowful, and yet always rejoicing* (2 Cor. vi. 10), had sorrowful lives and yet joyful hearts.

(2) It is applicable to all the faithful followers of the Lamb.

[1] Their condition and disposition are both mournful. Those that are acquainted with Christ must, as he was, be *acquainted with grief.* They mourn with sufferers that mourn, and mourn for sinners that mourn not for themselves.

[2] The world, at the same time, goes away with all the mirth. Mirth and pleasures are surely none of the best things, for then the worst men would not have so large a share of them, and the favourites of heaven be such strangers to them.

[3] Spiritual mourning will shortly be turned into eternal rejoicing. Their sorrow will not only be followed with joy, but turned into it. It is the will of Christ that his people should be a comforted people.

First, Here is the parable itself (v. 21): *A woman, when she is in travail, hath sorrow because her hour is come, but as soon as she is delivered of the child she remembers no more the anguish, for joy that a man is born into the world.* The fruit of the curse according to the sentence (Gen. iii. 16), *In sorrow shalt thou bring forth*. See what this world is; all its roses are surrounded with thorns. This comes of sin. The fruit of the blessing, in *the joy there is for a child born into the world*. The fruit of a blessing is matter of joy; the birth of a living child is the parents' joy. Though children are certain cares, uncertain comforts, and often prove the greatest crosses, yet it is natural to us to rejoice at their birth. Now this is very proper to set forth, (*a*) The sorrows of Christ's disciples in this world; they are sure and sharp, but not to last long, and in order to a joyful product. (*b*) Their joys after these sorrows, which will *wipe away all tears*. When they reap the fruit of all their services and sorrows, the toil and anguish of this world will be no more remembered.

Secondly, The application of the similitude (*v.* 22): "*You now have sorrow, but I will see you again*."

a. Here again he tells them of their *sorrow*: "*You now therefore have sorrow; therefore*, because I am leaving you." Christ's withdrawings are just cause of grief to his disciples. When the sun sets, the sunflower will hang the head.

b. He, more largely than before, assures them of a return of joy. Three things recommend the joy: The cause of it: "*I will see you again*." Christ will graciously return to those that wait for him. Men, when they are exalted, will scarcely look upon their inferiors; but the exalted Jesus will visit his disciples. Christ's returns are returns of joy to all his disciples. The cordiality of it: *Your heart shall rejoice*. Joy in the heart is solid, and not flashy; it is secret, it is sweet, it is sure, and not easily broken in upon. The continuance of it: *Your joy no man taketh from you*. They would if they could; but they shall not prevail. Some understand it of the eternal joy of those that are glorified. Our joys on earth we are liable to be robbed of by a thousand accidents, but heavenly joys are everlasting. I rather understand it of the spiritual joys of those that are sanctified. They could not rob them of their joy, because they could not *separate them from the love of Christ*, could not rob them of their God, nor of their *treasure in heaven*.

Verses 23–27

An answer to their askings is here promised. Now there are two ways of asking: asking by way of enquiry, which is the asking of the ignorant; and asking by way of request, which is the asking of the indigent. Christ here speaks of both.

I. By way of enquiry, they should not need to ask (*v.* 23): "*In that day you shall ask me nothing*. You shall not need to enquire." In the story *of the apostles' Acts* we seldom find them asking questions, for they were constantly under a divine guidance. Asking questions supposes us at a loss, or at least at a stand, and the best of us have need to ask questions.

Now for this he gives a reason (*v.* 25): "*These things have I spoken unto you in proverbs, but the time cometh when I shall show you plainly of the Father*, so that you shall not need to ask questions."

1. The great thing Christ would lead them into was the knowledge of God: "*I will show you the Father*." When Christ would express the greatest favour intended for his disciples, he tells them that he would *show them plainly of the Father*; for what is the happiness of heaven, but immediately and everlastingly to see God?

2. Of this he had hitherto spoken to them in proverbs. Christ had expounded his parables privately to the disciples. (1) Considering their dullness, and unaptness to receive what he said to them, he might be said to speak in proverbs; what he said to them was as a book sealed. (2) Comparing the discoveries he had made to them with what he would make to them, all hitherto had been but proverbs. (3) Confining it to what he had said of *the Father*, what he had said was very dark, compared with what was shortly to be revealed.

3. He would speak to them *plainly* of the Father. When the Spirit was poured out, the apostles attained to a much greater knowledge of divine things than they had before. But this promise will have its full accomplishment in heaven, where we shall see the Father as he is. While we are here, we have many questions to ask, but in that day we shall see all things clearly, and *ask no more questions*.

II. He promises that by way of request they should ask nothing in vain. It is taken for granted that all Christ's disciples give themselves to prayer. Their instruction, direction, strength, and success, must be fetched in by prayer.

1. Here is an express promise of a grant, *v.* 23. The preface to this promise leaves no room to question it: "*Verily, verily, I say unto you*." The golden sceptre is here held out to us, with this word, *What is thy petition, and it shall be granted?* For he says, *Whatsoever you shall ask the Father in my name, he will give it to you*. What would we more? The promise is as express as we can desire. (1) We are here taught how to seek; we must *ask the Father in Christ's name*. Asking of the Father includes a sense of spiritual wants and a desire of spiritual blessings, with a conviction that they are to be had from God only. Asking in Christ's name includes an acknowledgment of our own unworthiness, and an entire dependence upon Christ. (2) We are here told how we shall speed: *He will give it to you*. What more can we wish for? Christ had promised them great illumination by the Spirit, but they must pray for it. They must continue praying. Perfect fruition is reserved for the land of our rest; asking and receiving are the comfort of the land of our pilgrimage.

2. Here is an invitation for them to petition. Great men permit addresses, but Christ calls upon us to petition, *v.* 24.

(1) He looks back upon their practice hitherto: *Hitherto have you asked nothing in my name*. This refers either, [1] To the matter of their prayers: "You have asked nothing comparatively, nothing to what you might have asked." See what a generous benefactor our Lord Jesus is; he gives liberally, and is so far from upbraiding us with the frequency and largeness of his gifts that he rather upbraids us with the seldomness and straitness of our requests. Or, [2] To the name in which they prayed. They prayed many a prayer, but never so expressly in the name of Christ as now he was directing them to do; for he had not as yet offered up that great sacrifice in the virtue of which our prayers were to be accepted, the incense whereof was to perfume all our devotions.

(2) He looks forward to their practice for the future: *Ask, and you shall receive, that your joy may be full*. He directs them to ask for all that which they needed and he had promised. He assures them that they shall *receive*. What we ask from a principle of grace God will graciously give, that hereby *their joy shall be full*. This denotes, *First*, The blessed effect of the *prayer of faith*; it helps to fill up the *joy of faith*. When we are told to *rejoice evermore*, it follows immediately, *Pray without ceasing*. See how high we are to aim in prayer—not only at peace, but joy. Or, *Secondly*, The blessed effects of the *answer of peace*: "Ask, and you shall receive that which will *fill your joy*."

3. Here are the grounds upon which they might hope to speed (*v.* 26, 27), which are summed up in short by the apostle (1 John ii. 1): "*We have an advocate with the Father*."

(1) We have an advocate: "*I say not unto you that I will pray the Father for you*." He speaks as if they

needed not any further favours, when he had prevailed for the gift of the Holy Ghost to *make intercession within them*; as if they had no further need of him to pray for them now; but we shall find that he does more for us than he says he will.

(2) We have to do with a Father: *For the Father himself loveth you.* The disciples of Christ are the beloved of God himself. Observe what an emphasis is laid upon this: "*The Father himself loveth you.*" The Father himself, whose favour you have forfeited, and with whom you need an advocate, he himself now loves you. Why the Father loved the disciples of Christ: *Because you have loved me, and have believed that I came out from God*, that is, because you are my disciples indeed. The character of Christ's disciples; they love him, because they *believe he came out from God.* Faith in Christ works by love to him. If we believe him to be our Saviour, we cannot but love him as the most kind to us. Observe with what respect Christ is pleased to speak of his disciples' love to him; he speaks of it as that which recommended them to his Father's favour. What advantage Christ's faithful disciples have, the Father loves them, and that because they love Christ. What encouragement this gave them in prayer. They need not fear speeding when they came to one that loved them. This cautions us against hard thoughts of God. When we are taught in prayer to plead Christ's merit and intercession, it is not as if all the kindness were in Christ only. We owe Christ's merit to God's mercy in giving him for us. Let it cherish and confirm in us good thoughts of God. Believers, that love Christ, ought to know that God loves them.

Verses 28–33

Two things Christ here comforts his disciples with:

I. With an assurance that, though he was leaving the world, he was returning to his Father, v. 28–32.

1. A plain declaration of Christ's mission from the Father, and his return to him (v. 28): *I came forth from the Father, and am come into the world. Again, I leave the world and go to the Father.* This is the conclusion of the whole matter.

(1) These two great truths are here, [1] Contracted. Brief summaries of Christian doctrine are of great use to young beginners. The principles of the oracles of God brought into a little compass in creeds and catechisms have, like the beams of the sun contracted in a burning glass, conveyed divine light and heat with a wonderful power. [2] Compared. There is an admirable harmony in divine truths; they both corroborate and illustrate one another; Christ's coming and his going do so. Christ had commended his disciples for believing that he came forth from God (v. 27), and thence infers the necessity of his returning to God again. The due improvement of what we know and own would help us into the understanding of that which seems difficult and doubtful.

(2) If we ask concerning the Redeemer *whence he came*, and *whither he went*, we are told, [1] That he *came from the Father*, and he came into this world, this world of mankind. Here his business lay, and hither he came to attend it. He left his home for this strange country; his palace for this cottage. [2] That, when he had done his work on earth, he left the world, and went back to his Father. That still he is spiritually present with his church, and will be to the end.

2. The disciples' satisfaction in this declaration (v. 29, 30): *Lo, now speakest thou plainly.* It should seem, this one word of Christ did them more good than all the rest. Two things they improved in.

(1) In knowledge: *Lo, now speakest thou plainly.* Divine truths are most likely to do good when they are spoken plainly. When Christ is pleased to speak

plainly to our souls we have reason to rejoice in it.

(2) In faith: *Now are we sure.*

[1] What was the matter of their faith: *We believe that thou camest forth from God.* He had said (v. 27) that they did believe this; "Lord" (say they) "we do believe it."

[2] What was the motive of their faith—his omniscience. This proved him a teacher come from God, and more than a prophet, that he knew all things. Those know Christ best that know him by experience, that can say of his power, It works in me; of his love, He loved me. This confirmed the faith of the disciples here. *And needest not that any man should ask thee.* Christ's aptness to teach. He prevents us with his instructions and needs not to be importuned. His ability to teach. The best of teachers can only answer what is spoken, but Christ can answer what is thought.

3. The gentle rebuke Christ gave the disciples, v. 31, 32. Observing how they triumphed in their attainments, he said, "*Do you now believe?* Alas! you know not your own weakness; you will very shortly *be scattered every man to his own*," &c.

(1) A question, designed to put them upon consideration: *Do you now believe?* "If now, why not sooner?" Those who are at last persuaded to believe have reason to be ashamed that they stood it out so long. "If now, why not ever? When an hour of temptation comes, where will your faith be then?"

(2) A prediction of their fall. In a little time they would all desert him, which was fulfilled that very night. They were scattered from one another; they shifted everyone for his own safety. Scattered from him: *You shall leave me alone.* They should have been witnesses for him upon his trial, but they were ashamed of his chain, and afraid of sharing with him in his sufferings, and left him alone. Many a good cause, when it is distressed by its enemies, is deserted by its friends. Those that are tried, do not always prove trusty. If we at any time find our friends unkind to us, let us remember that Christ's were so to him. When they left him alone, they were scattered *every man to his own.* Everyone went his own way, where he fancied he should be most safe. Christ knew before that his disciples would thus desert him in the critical moment, and yet he was still tender of them. We are ready to say of some, "If we could have foreseen their ingratitude, we would not have been so prodigal of our favours to them"; Christ did foresee theirs, and yet was kind to them. He told them of it: "*Do you now believe?* Be not high-minded, but fear." Even when we are taking the comfort of our graces, it is good to be reminded of our danger from our corruptions. When our faith is strong, our love flaming, and our evidences are clear, yet we cannot infer thence that *tomorrow shall be as this day.* Even when we have most reason to think we stand, yet we have reason enough to take heed lest we fall. He spoke of it as a thing very near. *The hour was* already *come* when they would be as shy of him as ever they had been fond of him.

(3) An assurance of his own comfort notwithstanding: *Yet I am not alone. The Father is with me.* We may consider this as a privilege peculiar to the Lord Jesus. The divine nature did not desert the human nature, but supported it. Even when he complained of his Father's forsaking him, yet he called him *My God*, and was so well assured of his favourable presence with him as to commit his Spirit into his hand. This he had comforted himself with all along (ch. viii. 29), *He that sent me is with me, the Father hath not left me alone.* As a privilege common to all believers. When they are alone, they are *not alone*, but *the Father is with them.* When solitude is their choice—Nathaniel under the fig-tree,

Peter upon the house-top, meditating and praying—the Father is with them. Those that converse with God in solitude are never less alone than when alone. A good God and a good heart are good company at any time. When solitude is their affliction, they are not so much alone as they are thought to be, *the Father is with them.* While we have God's favourable presence with us, we are happy, though all the world forsake us.

II. He comforts them with a promise of peace in him, by virtue of his victory over the world, whatever troubles they might meet with in it (*v.* 33): *"These things have I spoken, that in me you might have peace; for in the world you shall have tribulation. I have overcome the world."*

1. The end Christ aimed at: *That in him they might have peace.* His departure from them was really for the best. It is the will of Christ that his disciples should have peace within, whatever their troubles may be without. Peace in Christ is the only true peace. Through him we have peace with God, and so in him we have peace in our own minds. The word of Christ aims at this, *that in him we may have peace.*

2. The entertainment they were likely to meet with in the world. It has been the lot of Christ's disciples to have more or less tribulation in this world. Men persecute them because they are so good, and God corrects them because they are no better. So between both *they shall have tribulation.*

3. The encouragement Christ gives them: *"But be of good cheer,* have a good heart on it, all shall be well." In the midst of the tribulations of this world it is the duty and interest of Christ's disciples to be of good cheer; as sorrowful indeed, in compliance with the temper of the climate, and yet always rejoicing, always cheerful, even *in tribulation,* Rom. v. 3.

4. The ground of that encouragement: *I have overcome the world.* Christ's victory is a Christian triumph. When he sends his disciples to preach the gospel to all the world, "Be *of good cheer,"* says he, *"I have overcome the world."* He overcame the evil things of the world by submitting to them; he endured the cross, despising it and the shame of it; and he overcame the good things of it by being wholly dead to them. Never was there such a conqueror of the world as Christ was, and we ought to be encouraged by it. Christ has overcome the world before us; so that we may look upon it as a conquered enemy. He has conquered it for us, as the captain of our salvation. By his cross the world is *crucified to us,* which bespeaks it completely conquered. Christ having overcome the world, believers have nothing to do but to pursue their victory, and this we do by faith. *We are more than conquerors through him that loved us.*

CHAPTER 17

This chapter is a prayer, the Lord Christ's prayer. This was properly and peculiarly his, and yet is of use to us both for instruction and encouragement in prayer. I. The circumstances of the prayer, ver. 1. II. The prayer itself. 1. He prays for himself, ver. 1–5. 2. He prays for those that are his. (1) The general pleas with which he introduces his petitions for them, ver. 6–10. (2) The particular petitions he puts up for them, [1] That they might be kept, ver. 11–16. [2] That they might be sanctified, ver. 17–19. [3] That they might be united, ver. 11 and 20–23. [4] That they might be glorified, ver. 24–26.

Verses 1–5

I. The circumstances of this prayer, *v.* 1. None of his prayers are recorded so fully as this.

1. The time when he prayed this prayer; when he had *spoken these words,* had given the foregoing farewell to his disciples. (1) It was a prayer after sermon; when he had spoken from God to them, he turned to speak to God for them. Those we preach to we must pray for. The word preached should be prayed over, for God *gives the increase.* (2) It was a prayer after sacrament. He closed the solemnity with this prayer, that God would preserve the good impressions of the ordinance upon them. (3) It was a family prayer. Christ's disciples were his family, and, to set a good example before masters of families, he blessed his household, prayed for them and with them. (4) It was a parting prayer. When we and our friends are parting, it is good to part with prayer, Acts xx. 36. (5) It was a prayer that was a preface to his sacrifice, which he was now about to offer on earth. Christ prayed then as a priest now offering sacrifice, in the virtue of which all prayers were to be made. (6) It was a prayer that was a specimen of his intercession, which he ever lives to make for us within the veil.

2. The outward expression of fervent desire which he used in this prayer: He *lifted up his eyes to heaven.* He was pleased thus to sanctify this gesture to those that use it, and justify it against those that ridicule it. *Sursum corda* was anciently used as a call to prayer, *Up with your hearts,* up to heaven.

II. The first part of the prayer itself, in which Christ prays for himself.

1. He prays to God as a Father: He *lifted up his eyes, and said, Father.* If God be our Father, we have liberty of access to him, and great expectations from him. Christ calls him here *holy Father* (*v.* 11), and *righteous Father, v.* 25. For it will be of great use to us in prayer to call God as we hope to find him.

2. He prayed for himself first. Though Christ, as God, was prayed to, Christ, as man, prayed. What he had purchased he must ask for; and shall we expect to have what we never merited, but have a thousand times forfeited, unless we pray for it? It gives great encouragement to praying people. Time was when he that is advocate for us had a cause of his own to solicit, and this he was to solicit in the same method that is prescribed to us, *by prayers and supplications* (Heb. v. 7). Christ began with prayer for himself, and afterwards prayed for his disciples; this charity must begin at home, though it must not end there. Christ was much shorter in his prayer for himself than in his prayer for his disciples. Our prayers for the church must not be crowded into a corner of our prayers. Now here are two petitions which Christ puts up for himself, and these two are one. This one petition, *Glorify thou me,* is twice put up, because it has a double reference. To the prosecution of his undertaking further: *Glorify me, that I may glorify thee, v.* 1–3. And to the performance of his undertaking hitherto: *"Glorify me, for I have glorified thee.* I have done my part, and now, Lord, do thine," *v.* 4, 5.

(1) Christ here prays to be *glorified,* in order to his glorifying God (*v.* 1): *Glorify thy Son that thy Son may glorify thee.*

[1] What he prays for—that he might be glorified in this world. The Father glorified the *Son* upon earth; even in his sufferings, by the signs and wonders which attended them. Then the Father not only justified, but glorified the Son; even by his sufferings; when he was crucified, he was magnified, he was glorified. It was in his cross that he conquered Satan and death; his thorns were a crown. Much more after his sufferings. The Father glorified the Son when he *raised him from the dead.*

[2] What he pleads to enforce this request.

First, He pleads relation: *Glorify thy Son.* Those that have received the adoption of sons may in faith pray for the inheritance of sons; if sanctified, then glorified.

Secondly, He pleads the time: *The hour is come.* He had often said his hour was not yet come; but now it was come, and he knew it. He calls it *this hour* (*ch.* xii. 27), and here *the hour.* The hour of the

Redeemer's death, which was also the hour of the Redeemer's birth, was the most signal and remarkable hour, and, without doubt, the most critical, that ever was since the clock of time was first set going. 1. "*The hour is come* in the midst of which I need to to be owned." The decisive battle between heaven and hell is now to be fought. "*Now glorify thy Son,* now give him victory, now let thy Son be so upheld as not to fail nor be discouraged." He *glorified his Son* when he made the cross his triumphant chariot. 2. *The hour is come* when I am *to be glorified.* Good Christians in a trying hour, particularly a dying hour, may thus plead: "*Now the hour is come,* stand by me, now or never: now *the earthly tabernacle is to be dissolved, the hour is come that I should be glorified,*" 2 Cor. v. 1.

Thirdly, He pleads the Father's own interest and concern herein: *That thy Son may also glorify thee;* that he might glorify the Father two ways: By *the death of the cross. Father, glorify thy name,* expressed the great intention of his sufferings. "Father, own me in my sufferings, that I may honour thee by them." By the doctrine of the cross now shortly to be published to the world. If God had not glorified Christ crucified, *by raising him from the dead,* his whole undertaking had been crushed; therefore *glorify me, that I may glorify thee.* Now hereby he hath taught us what to eye and aim at in our prayers—that is, the honour of God. "Do this and the other for thy servant, that thy servant may glorify thee. Give me health, that I may glorify thee with my body; success, that I may glorify thee with my estate," &c. *Hallowed be thy name* must be our first petition, which must fix our end in all other petitions, 1 Pet. iv. 11. He hath taught us what to expect and hope for. If we sincerely set ourselves to glorify our Father, he will give us the grace he knows sufficient, and the opportunity he sees convenient. But, if we secretly honour ourselves more than him, instead of honouring ourselves, we shall shame ourselves.

Fourthly, He pleads his commission (*v.* 2, 3); he desires to glorify his Father, in conformity to the commission given him. Now see here the power of the Mediator.

a. The origin of his power: *Thou hast given him power;* he has it from God, *to whom all power belongs.* The church's king is no usurper, as the prince of this world is; Christ's right to rule is incontestable.

b. The extent of his power: He has *power over all flesh.* Over all mankind. Being now mediating between God and man, he here *pleads his power over all flesh.* They were men whom he was to subdue and save; out of that race he had a remnant given him, and therefore all that rank of beings are *put under his feet.* Over mankind considered as corrupt and fallen. If man had not in this sense been flesh, he had not needed a Redeemer. Over this sinful race the Lord Jesus has all power; and *all judgment is committed to him.* Whom he does not rule, he over-rules.

c. The grand intention and design of this power: *That he should give eternal life to as many as thou hast given him.* Here is the Father making over the elect to the Redeemer, and giving them to him as the crown and recompence of his undertaking. Here is the Son undertaking to secure the happiness of those that were given him, that he would *give eternal life to them.* He has lives and crowns to give, eternal lives that never die, immortal crowns that never fade. Now consider how great the Lord Jesus is, and how gracious he is. He sanctifies them in this world, gives them the spiritual life which is eternal life in the bud and embryo. Grace in the soul is heaven in that soul. He will glorify them in the other world; their happiness shall be completed in the vision and fruition of God. We are *called to his kingdom and glory,* and *begotten to the inheritance.* What is last in execution was first

in intention, and *that is eternal life.* Christ's dominion over the children of men is in order to the salvation of the children of God. The administration of the kingdoms of providence and grace are put into the same hand, that all things may be made to concur for good to the called.

d. Here is a further explication of this grand design (*v.* 3): "*This is life eternal, to know thee the only true God.*" Here is,

(*a*) The great end which the Christian religion sets before us, and that is, eternal life. This he was to reveal to all, and secure to all that were given him. By the gospel *life and immortality are brought to light,* are brought to hand.

(*b*) The sure way of attaining this blessed end, which is, by the right knowledge of God and Jesus Christ: "*This is life eternal, to know thee,* which may be taken two ways: [*a*] *Life eternal* lies in the knowledge of God and Jesus Christ. Those that are brought into union with Christ, and live a life of communion with God in Christ, will say, "If this be heaven, heaven is sweet." [*b*] The knowledge of God and Christ leads to life eternal. The Christian religion shows us the way to heaven, *First,* By directing us to God, for Christ died to *bring us to God.* He is the true God, the only true God; the service of him is the only true religion. *Secondly,* By directing us to Jesus Christ: *Jesus Christ whom thou hast sent.* If man had continued innocent, the knowledge of the only true God would have been life eternal to him; but now that he is fallen there must be something more. We are therefore concerned to know Christ as our Redeemer. It is life eternal to believe in Christ; and this he has undertaken to give. Those that are acquainted with God and Christ are already in the suburbs of life eternal.

(2) Christ here prays to be glorified in consideration of his having glorified the Father hitherto, *v.* 4, 5. The meaning of the former petition was, Glorify me in this world; the meaning of the latter is, Glorify me in the other world.

[1] With what comfort Christ reflects on the life he had lived on earth: *I have glorified thee, and finished my work.* He pleases himself in reviewing the service he had done his Father. This is here recorded for the honour of Christ, that his life upon earth did in all respects fully answer the end of his coming into the world. 1. Our Lord Jesus had work given him to do. His Father gave him his work, both appointed him to it and assisted him in it. 2. *The work that was given him to do* he finished. It was as good as done, he was giving it its finishing stroke. 3. Herein he glorified his Father. It is the glory of God that *his work is perfect,* and the same is the glory of the Redeemer; what he is the author of he will be the finisher of. It is recorded for example to all, *that we may follow his example.* We must make it our business to do the work God has appointed us to do. We must aim at the glory of God in all. We must persevere herein to the end of our days; we must not sit down till we have finished our work. It is recorded for encouragement to all those that rest upon him. If he has *finished the work that was given him to do,* then he is a complete Saviour, and did not do his work by the halves.

[2] See with what confidence he expects *the joy set before him* (*v.* 5): *Now, O Father, glorify thou me.*

First, See here what he prayed for: *Glorify thou me,* as before, *v.* 1. What his Father had promised him yet he must pray for; promises are not designed to supersede prayers, but to be the guide of our desires and the ground of our hopes. 1. It is a glory with God; not only, *Glorify my name on earth,* but, *Glorify me with thine own self.* The prayers of the lower world draw out grace and peace *from God our Father and our Lord Jesus Christ* in conjunction; and thus the Father has glorified him with himself.

2. It is *the glory he had with God before the world was.*
(1) Jesus Christ, as God, had a being *before the world
was.* Our religion acquaints us with one that *was
before all things, and by whom all things consist.*
(2) His glory with the Father is from everlasting.
Christ undertook the work of redemption, not
because he needed glory, for he had a glory *with the
Father before the world,* but because we needed glory.
(3) Jesus Christ in his state of humiliation divested
himself of this glory. He was *God manifested in the
flesh,* not in his glory. (4) In his exalted state he
resumed this glory. He does not pray to be glorified
with the princes and great men of the earth: no; he
that knew both worlds, chose it in the glory of the
other world, as far exceeding all the glory of this.
*Let the same mind be in us. Father, glorify thou me with
thine own self.*

Secondly, See here what he pleaded: *I have glorified
thee;* and now, *glorify thou me.* There was an equity
in it, and an admirable becomingness, that, *if God
was glorified in him, he should glorify him in himself.*
If the Father was a gainer in his glory by the Son's
humiliation, it was fit the Son should be no loser
by it, at long run, in his glory. It was according to
the covenant between them. It was *for the joy set
before him* that *he endured the cross.* He still expects
the completing of his exaltation, because he perfected his undertaking. By the glorifying of Christ
we are satisfied that God was satisfied, and therein a
real demonstration was given that his Father was well
pleased in him as his beloved Son. Thus we must
be taught that those, and only those who glorify
God on earth shall be glorified with the Father,
when they must be no more in this world.

Verses 6–10

Christ, having prayed for himself, comes next to
pray for those that are his.

I. Whom he did not pray for (*v.* 9): *I pray not for
the world.* It is not meant of the world of mankind
in general (he prays for that here, *v.* 21, *That the
world may believe that thou hast sent me*). Take the
world for a heap of unwinnowed corn in the floor, and
God loves it, Christ prays for it, and dies for it,
for a blessing is in it. Then take the world for the
remaining heap of rejected, worthless chaff. For these
Christ does not pray; not but that there are some
things which he intercedes with God for on their
behalf, as the dresser for the reprieve of the barren
tree; but he does not pray for them in this prayer.
He does not say, I pray against the world, but, *I
pray not for them,* I pass them by, and leave them
to themselves. We that know not who are chosen,
and who are passed by, must *pray for all men,* 1 Tim.
ii. 1, 4. While there is life, there is hope, and room
for prayer.

II. Whom he did pray for; the children of men.
He prays *for those that were given him,* who receive
and believe the words of Christ, *v.* 6, 8. He prays *for
all that should believe on him* (*v.* 20). Not only the
petitions that follow, but those also which went
before, must be construed to extend to all believers,
in every place and every age.

III. What are the general pleas with which he
introduces his petitions for them. They are five:

1. The charge he had received concerning them:
Tnine they were, and thou gavest them me (*v.* 6), and
again (*v.* 9), *Those whom thou hast given me.* This
is meant primarily of the disciples that then were.
They were given in order to their being the publishers
of his gospel and the planters of his church. When
they left all to follow him, this was the secret spring
of that strange resolution: they were given to him,
else they had not given themselves to him. The
apostleship and ministry, which are Christ's gift to
the church, were first the Father's gift to Jesus Christ.

Christ received this gift for men, that he might give
it to men. It lays a mighty obligation upon the
ministers of the gospel to devote themselves entirely
to Christ's service, as being *given to him,* but it is
designed to extend to all the elect, for they are elsewhere said to be given to Christ (*ch.* vi. 37, 39).

(1) The Father had authority to give them: *Thine
they were,* his own in three ways: *First,* They were
creatures, and their lives and beings were derived
from him. *Secondly,* They were criminals, and their
lives and beings were forfeited to him. It was a remnant of fallen mankind that was given to Christ
to be redeemed, that might have been made sacrifices
to justice when they were pitched upon to be the
monuments of mercy. Thirdly, They were chosen; they
were set apart for God. This he insists upon again
(*v.* 7): *All things whatsoever thou hast given me are
of thee;* they *are all of thee,* and therefore, Father,
I bring them all to thee, that they may be all for thee.

(2) He did accordingly give them to the Son:
Thou gavest them to me, as sheep to the shepherd,
to be kept; as patients to the physician, to be cured;
children to a tutor, to be educated. They were
delivered to Christ, that the election of grace might
not be frustrated, *that not one,* no not *of the little
ones, might perish,* that the undertaking of Christ
might not be fruitless. He should *see of the travail
of his soul and be satisfied* (Isa. liii. 10, 11).

2. The care he had taken of them to teach them
(*v.* 6): *I have manifested thy name to them. I have
given to them the words which thou gavest to me,
v.* 8. Observe here, The great design of Christ's
doctrine, which was to manifest God's name, to
declare him that he might be better loved and worshipped. His faithful discharge of this undertaking:
I have done it. His fidelity appears in the truth of
his doctrine. It agreed exactly with the instructions
he received from his Father. Ministers, in wording
their message, must have an eye to *the words which
the Holy Ghost teaches.* In the tendency of his
doctrine, which was to manifest God's name, He did
not seek himself, but aimed to magnify his Father.
It is Christ's prerogative to manifest God's name to
the souls of the children of men. He only has acquaintance with the Father, and so is able to open
the truth; and he only has access to the spirits of
men, and so is able to open the understanding.
Ministers may *publish the name of the Lord,* but Christ
only can manifest that name. Ministers may speak
the words of God to us, but Christ can give us his
words, can put them in us. Sooner or later, Christ
will manifest God's name to all that were given him.

3. The good effect of the care he had taken of them
(*v.* 6): *They have kept thy word* (*v.* 7), *they have known
that all things are of thee* (*v.* 8); *they have received
thy words, and have known surely that I came out
from thee, and have believed that thou didst send me.*

(1) What success the doctrine of Christ had among
those *that were given to him.* "They have received
the words which I gave them, as the ground receives
the seed, and the earth drinks in the rain." The
word was to them an *ingrafted word. "They have
kept thy word;* they have conformed to it." Christ's
commandment is then only kept when it is obeyed.
It was requisite that these should *keep what was committed to them,* for it was to be transmitted by them
to every place for every age. "They have understood
the word, They have been aware *that all things
whatsoever thou hast given me are of thee.*" All
Christ's offices and powers, all the gifts of the Spirit,
all his graces and comforts, were all from God,
designed by his grace, for his own glory in man's
salvation. We may therefore venture our souls upon
Christ's mediation. If the righteousness be of God's
appointing, we shall be justified; if the grace be of his
dispensing, we shall be sanctified. They have set their

seal to it: *They have known surely that I came out from God*, v. 8. What it is to believe; it is to *know surely*, to know *that it is so of a truth*. We may know surely that which we neither do nor can know fully. *We walk by faith*, which knows surely, *not yet by sight*, which knows clearly. What it is we are to believe: *that Jesus Christ came out from God*, and that God did send him. Therefore all the doctrines of Christ are to be received as divine truths, and all his promises depended upon as divine securities.

(2) How Jesus Christ here speaks of this: As pleased with it himself. Their constant adherence to him, their gradual improvements, and their great attainments at last, were his joy. Christ is a Master that delights in the proficiency of his scholars. He accepts the sincerity of their faith, and graciously passes by the infirmity of it. As pleading it with his Father. He is praying for *those that were given to him*; and he pleads that they had given themselves to him. Those that keep Christ's word, and believe on him, let Christ alone to commend them, and, which is more, to recommend them to his Father.

4. He pleads the Father's own interest in them (*v.* 9): *I pray for them, for they are thine. All mine are thine, and thine are mine.*

(1) The plea particularly urged for his disciples: *They are thine.* The consigning of the elect to Christ was so far from making them less the Father's that it was in order to making them the more so. Christ has *redeemed us*, not to himself only, but *to God*. This is a good plea in prayer, Christ here pleads it, *They are thine;* we may plead it for ourselves, *I am thine, save me*; and for others: "*They are thy people. They are thine.* Wilt thou not secure them, that they may not be run down by the devil and the world? *They are thine*, own them as thine."

(2) The foundation on which this plea is grounded: *All mine are thine, and thine are mine.* This bespeaks the Father and Son to be one in essence and one in interest. What the Father has as Creator is delivered over to the Son. *All things are delivered to him* (Matt. xi. 27); nothing is excepted but *he that did put all things under him*. What the Son has as Redeemer is designed for the Father. All the benefits of redemption purchased by the Son are intended for the Father's praise: *All mine are thine.* The Son owns none for his that are not devoted to the service of the Father. In a limited sense, every true believer may say, *All thine are mine*. In an unlimited sense every true believer does say, Lord, *all mine are thine*; all laid at his feet, to be serviceable to him. "Lord, take care of what I have, for it is *all thine.*"

5. He pleads his own concern in them: *I am glorified in them.* (1) *I have been glorified in them.* What little honour Christ had in this world was among his disciples, and therefore *I pray for them.* (2) "*I am to be glorified in them*; they are to bear up my name. *I am glorified in them*, therefore, I concern myself for them. Therefore I commit them to the Father, who has engaged to glorify the Son, and, upon this account, will have a gracious eye to those in whom he is glorified."

Verses 11–16

After the general pleas follow the particular petitions he puts up for them. They all relate to spiritual blessings in heavenly things. The prosperity of the soul is the best prosperity. They are such blessings as were suited to their present state and case. Christ's intercession is always pertinent. Our *advocate with the father* is acquainted with all the particulars of our wants. He is large and full in the petitions, to teach us fervency and importunity in prayer, wrestling as Jacob, *I will not let thee go, except thou bless me.*

Now the first thing Christ prays for is their preservation. Keeping supposes danger, and their

danger arose *from the world; the evil* of this he begs they might be kept from.

I. The request itself: *Keep them from the world.* There were two ways of their being delivered from the world:

1. By taking them out of it; and he does not pray that they might be so delivered: *I pray not that thou shouldest take them out of the world.*

(1) "I pray not that they may be speedily removed by death." If the world will be vexatious to them, the readiest way to secure them would be to hasten them out of it. Send chariots and horses of fire for them, to fetch them to heaven. Christ would not pray so for his disciples. Because he came to conquer those intemperate passions which make men impatient of life, it is his will that we should take up our cross, and not outrun it. Because he had work for them to do in the world, the world could ill spare them. In pity therefore to this dark world, Christ would not have these lights removed out of it, especially for the sake of those in the world that were to *believe in him through their word.* They must each in his own order die a martyr, but not till they have finished their testimony. The taking of good people out of the world is a thing by no means to be desired. Though Christ loves his disciples, he does not presently send for them to heaven, but leaves them for some time in this world, that they may be ripened for heaven. Many good people are spared to live, because they can ill be spared to die.

(2) "I pray not that they may be exempted from the troubles of this world, and taken out of the toil and terror of it." *Not that, being freed from all trouble, they may bask in luxurious ease, but that by the help of God they may be preserved in a scene of danger;* so Calvin. Not that they may be kept from all conflict with the world, but that they may not be overcome by it. It is more the honour of a Christian soldier by faith to *overcome the world* than by a monastical vow to retreat from it; and more for the honour of Christ to serve him in a city than to serve him in a cell.

2. By keeping them from the corruption that is in the world, *v.* 11, 15. Here are three branches of this petition:

(1) *Holy Father, keep those whom thou hast given me.* Christ was now leaving them. He does here commit them to the custody of his Father. It is the unspeakable comfort of all believers that Christ himself has committed them to the care of God. Those cannot but be safe whom the almighty God keeps, and he cannot but keep those whom the Son of his love commits to him. He here puts them under the divine protection. To this prayer is owing the wonderful preservation of the gospel ministry and gospel church in the world unto this day. He puts them under the divine tuition. We need God's power not only to put us into a state of grace, but to keep us in it. The titles he gives to him he prays to, and them he prays for, enforce the petition. He speaks to God as a *holy Father.* If he be a holy God and hate sin, he will make those holy that are his, and keep them from sin, which they also hate and dread as the greatest evil. If he be a Father, he will take care of his own children; who else should? He speaks of them as those whom the Father had *given him.* What we receive as our Father's gifts, we may comfortably remit to our Father's care.

(2) *Keep* them *through thine own name:* keep them for his name's sake. Those may with comfort plead it that are indeed more concerned for the honour of God's name than for any interest of their own. Keep them in thy name. "Keep them in the knowledge and fear of thy name; keep them in the profession and service of thy name, whatever it cost them." Keep

them by or through thy name. "Keep them by thine own power, in thine own hand. Let thy name be their strong tower."

(3) *Keep them from the evil*, or out of the evil. He had taught them to pray daily, *Deliver us from evil*, and this would encourage them to pray. "Keep them from the evil one. Keep them from Satan as a tempter, that their faith may not fail. Keep them from him as a destroyer. Keep them from the evil thing, that is, sin. Keep them, that they do no evil. Keep them from the evil of the world, and of their tribulation in it, so that it may have no sting in it." Not that they might be kept from affliction, but kept through it.

II. The reasons with which he enforces these requests, which are five:

1. He pleads that hitherto he had kept them (*v.* 12): "*While I was with them in the world, I have kept them in thy name*, they are all safe, and none of them missing, *but the son of perdition*; he is lost, that the scripture might be fulfilled."

(1) Christ's faithful discharge of his undertaking: *While he was with them, he kept them*, and his care concerning them was not in vain. Many that followed him awhile took offence at something or other, and went off; but he kept the twelve that they should not go away. *While he was with them*, he kept them in a visible manner. When he was gone from them, they must be kept in a more spiritual manner. Comforts and supports are sometimes given and sometimes withheld; but, when they are withdrawn, yet they are not left comfortless. What Christ here says is true of all the saints while they are here in this world; Christ keeps them *in God's name*. They are weak, and cannot keep themselves. They are, in God's account, valuable and worth the keeping; his treasure, his jewels. Their salvation is designed, for to this it is that they are kept, 1 Pet. i. 5. The righteous are preserved for the day of bliss. They are the charge of the Lord Jesus; he keeps them, and exposed himself like the good shepherd for the preservation of the sheep.

(2) The comfortable account he gives of his undertaking: *None of them is lost*. Jesus Christ will certainly keep all that were given to him; they may think themselves lost, and may be nearly lost (in imminent peril); but it is the Father's will that he should *lose none*, and none he will lose.

(3) A brand put upon Judas, as none of those whom he had undertaken to keep. He was among those that were given to Christ, but not of them. But the apostasy and ruin of Judas were no reproach at all to his Master, or his family. He was *the son of perdition*, and therefore not one of those that were given to Christ to be kept. It is an awful consideration that one of the apostles proved a son of perdition. No man's place or name in the church will secure him from ruin, if his heart be not right with God. The scripture was fulfilled; the sin of Judas was foreseen and foretold, and the event would certainly follow after the prediction as a consequent, though it cannot be said necessarily to follow from it as an effect.

2. He pleads that he was now under a necessity of leaving them (*v.* 11): "Keep them now. Keep them, *that they may be one* with us *as we are* with each other."

(1) With what pleasure he speaks of his own departure. He expresses himself concerning it with an air of triumph and exultation, with reference both to the world he left and the world he removed to. "*Now I am no more in the world*. Now farewell to this provoking troublesome world. Now the welcome hour is at hand when I shall be *no more in it*." It should be a pleasure to those that have their home in the other world to think of being *no more in this*

world. What is there here that should court our stay? *Now I come to thee*. To get clear of the world is but the one half of the comfort of a dying Christ, of a dying Christian; the far better half is to think of going to the Father. Those who love God cannot but be pleased to think of coming to him, though it be through the valley of the shadow of death. It is to be *present with the Lord*, like children fetched home from school to their father's house.

(2) With what a tender concern he speaks of those whom he left behind: "*But these are in the world. Holy Father, keep them;* they will want my presence, let them have thine. They have now more need than ever to be kept, and will be lost if thou do not keep them." When our Lord Jesus was going to the Father, he carried with him a tender concern for *his own that are in the world*. When he is out of their sight they are not out of his, much less out of his mind. When Christ would express the utmost need his disciples had of divine preservation, he only says, *They are in the world;* this bespeaks danger enough to those who are bound for heaven.

3. He pleads what a satisfaction it would be to them to know themselves safe, and what a satisfaction it would be to him to see them easy: *I speak this, that they may have my joy fulfilled in themselves, v.* 13.

(1) Christ earnestly desired the fulness of the joy of his disciples, for it is his will that they should rejoice evermore. When they thought their joy in him was brought to an end, then was it advanced nearer to perfection than ever it had been, and they were fuller of it. We are here taught to found our joy in Christ. Christ is a Christian's joy, his chief joy. Joy in the world is withering with it; joy in Christ is everlasting, like him. To build up our joy with diligence. No part of the Christian life is pressed upon us more earnestly, Phil. iii. 1; iv. 4. To aim at the perfection of this joy.

(2) In order hereunto, he did thus solemnly commit them to his Father's care and keeping: *These things I speak in the world*. Saying this in the world would be a greater satisfaction and encouragement to them, and would enable them to *rejoice in tribulation*. Christ has not only treasured up comforts for his people, but has given out comforts to them. He here condescended to publish his last will and testament, and (which many a testator is shy of) lets them know what legacies he had left them, and how well they were secured. Christ's intercession for us is enough to fulfil our joy in him; nothing more effectual to silence all our fears and mistrusts than this, that he always appears in the presence of God for us. See Heb. vii. 25.

4. He pleads the ill usage they were likely to meet with in the world, for his sake (*v.* 14): "*I have given them thy word, and they have received it*, and therefore the world hath hated them, because they are *not of the world*, any more than I." The world's enmity to Christ's followers. While Christ was with them it hates them, much more would it do so when by their more extensive preaching of the gospel they would *turn the world upside down*. "Father, stand their friend," says Christ. "Let them have thy love, for the world's hatred is entailed upon them." It is God's honour to take part with the weaker side, and to help the helpless. The reasons of this enmity, which strengthen the plea. One reason is because they had received the word of God by the hand of Christ, when the greatest part of the world rejected it. Those that receive Christ's goodwill and good word must expect the world's ill and ill word. Gospel ministers have been in a particular manner hated by the world, because they call men out of the world, and separate them from it, and so condemn the world. "*Father, keep them*, they are sufferers for thee." Those that keep the word of Christ's

patience are entitled to special protection in the hour of temptation. That cause which makes a martyr may well make a joyful sufferer. Another reason is more express; the world hates them, because they *are not of the world.* Those to whom the word of Christ comes in power are not of the world, and therefore the world bears them a grudge.

5. He pleads their conformity to himself in a holy non-conformity to the world (*v.* 16): "Father, keep them, *they are not of the world, even as I am not of the world.*" Those may in faith commit themselves to God's custody, who are *as Christ was in this world.* God will love those that are like Christ. (1) Jesus Christ was not of this world; he never had been of it. This intimates, *First,* His state; he was none of the world's favourites nor darlings; worldly possessions he had none, not even *where to lay his head*; nor worldly power. *Secondly,* His Spirit; he was perfectly dead to the world, the prince of this world had nothing in him. (2) Therefore true Christians are not of this world. It is their lot to be despised by the world; they are not in favour with the world any more than their Master before them was. It is their privilege to be delivered from the world. It is their duty and character to be dead to the world. Christ's disciples were weak, and had many infirmities; yet this he could say for them, They were not of the world and therefore he recommends them to the care of Heaven.

Verses 17–19

The next thing he prayed for them was that they might be sanctified; not only kept from evil, but made good.

I. Here is the petition (*v.* 17): *Sanctify them through thy truth; thy word is truth.* He desires they may be sanctified,

1. As Christians, 1 Thess. v. 23.

(1) The grace desired—sanctification. He prays, *Father, sanctify them.* "Confirm the work of sanctification in them, rivet their good resolutions. Carry on that good work in them; let the *light shine more and more.* Complete it, sanctify them throughout and to the end." He cannot for shame own them as his, either here or hereafter, or present them to his Father, if they be not sanctified. Those that through grace are sanctified have need to be sanctified more and more. Not to go forward is to go backward; *he that is holy must be holy still,* more holy still. It is God that sanctifies as well as God that justifies.

(2) The means of conferring this grace—*through thy truth, thy word is truth.* Divine revelation, as it now stands in the written word, is not only pure truth without mixture, but entire truth without deficiency. This word of truth should be the outward and ordinary means of our sanctification. It is the seed of the new birth, and the food of the new life.

2. As ministers. "*Sanctify them,* let their call to the apostleship be ratified in heaven. Qualify them for the office, with Christian graces and ministerial gifts. Separate them to the office. I have called them, they have consented; Father, say *Amen* to it. Own them in the office; let thy hand go along with them. Sanctify them to thy truth, to be the preachers of thy truth to the world." Jesus Christ intercedes for his ministers with a particular concern, and recommends to his Father's grace those stars he carries in his right hand. The great thing to be asked of God for gospel ministers is that they may be sanctified, entirely devoted to God, and experimentally acquainted with the influence of that word upon their own hearts which they preach to others.

II. We have here two pleas to enforce the petition,

1. The mission they had from him (*v.* 18): "*As thou hast sent me into the world,* so now *have I sent them into the world.*"

(1) Christ speaks with great assurance of his own mission: *Thou hast sent me into the world.* He was sent of God to say what he said, and do what he did, and be what he is to those that believe on him.

(2) He speaks of the commission he had given his disciples: "*So have I sent them* on the same errand"; to preach the same doctrine that he preached. He gave them their commission (*ch.* xx. 21) with a reference to his own, and it magnifies their office that it comes from Christ, and that there is some affinity between the commission given to the ministers of reconciliation and that given to the Mediator. Only they are sent as servants, he as a Son. Christ was concerned so much for them, because he had himself put them into a difficult office, which required great abilities for the due discharge of it. Whom Christ sends he will stand by. What he calls us out to he will fit us out for, and bear us out in. He committed them to his Father, because he was concerned in their cause, their mission being in prosecution of his. The Father *sanctified him* when *he sent him into the world, ch.* x. 36. Now, they being sent as he was, let them also be sanctified.

2. The merit he had for them is another thing here pleaded (*v.* 19): *For their sakes I sanctify myself.* (1) Christ's designation of himself to the work and office of Mediator: *I sanctified myself.* He entirely devoted himself to the undertaking, and all the parts of it, especially that which he was now going about— the *offering up of himself without spot unto God, by the eternal Spirit.* This he pleads with his Father, for his intercession is made in the virtue of his satisfaction. (2) Christ's design of kindness to his disciples herein; it is *for their sakes,* that *they may be sanctified,* that they may be saints and ministers, duly qualified and accepted of God. The office of the ministry is the purchase of Christ's blood, and one of the blessed fruits of his satisfaction. The real holiness of all good Christians is the fruit of Christ's death. He *gave himself for his church,* to *sanctify it.* And he that designed the end designed also the means, that they might be sanctified *by the truth.* The word of truth receives its sanctifying virtue and power from the death of Christ. And this Christ has prayed for, for all that are his; for *this is his will, even their sanctification,* which encourages them to pray for it.

Verses 20–23

Next to their purity he prays for their unity.

I. Who are included in this prayer (*v.* 20): "*Not these only,* but *for those also who shall believe on me through their word.* I pray *for them all.*" Those, and those only, are interested in the mediation of Christ, that believe in him. They that lived then, *saw and believed,* but they in after ages *have not seen,* and yet *have believed.* It is *through the word* that souls are brought to believe on Christ. He does not here pray at a venture. Christ knew very well whom he prayed for. Jesus Christ intercedes not only for great and eminent believers, but for the meanest and weakest. The Good Shepherd has an eye even to *the poor of the flock.* Jesus Christ in his mediation had an actual regard to those that were yet unborn, the *other sheep* which he *must yet bring.*

II. What is intended in this prayer (*v.* 21): *That they all may be one.* The same was said before (*v.* 11), *that they may be one as we are,* and again, *v.* 22. The heart of Christ was much upon this. Let them be not only of *one heart,* but of *one mouth,* speaking the same thing. The oneness prayed for in *v.* 21 respects all believers. It is the prayer of Christ for all that are his—*that they all may be one,* one in us (*v.* 21), one *as we are one* (*v.* 22), made *perfect in one, v.* 23.

1. That they might all be *incorporated in one body.* "Father, look upon them all as one. Though they

live in distant places, and in several ages, yet let them be united in me their common head." As Christ died, so he prayed, to *gather them all in one.*

2. That they might all be animated by one Spirit. This is plainly implied in this—*that they may be one in us.* Let them all be stamped with the same image and superscription, and influenced by the same power.

3. That they might all be *knit together* in the bond of love and charity, all of one heart. *That they all may be one.* In judgment and sentiment; not in every little thing—this is neither possible nor needful, but in the great things of God, and in them, by the virtue of this prayer. In disposition and inclination. They have all a new heart, and it is *one heart.* In their designs and aims. In their desires and prayers; though they differ in words and the manner of expressions, yet they pray for the same things in effect. In love and affection. That which Christ here prays for is that *communion of saints* which we profess to believe. But this prayer of Christ will not have its complete answer till all the saints come to heaven, for then, and not till then, they shall be *perfect in one.*

III. What is intimated by way of plea to enforce this petition.

1. The oneness that is between the Father and the Son, which is mentioned again and again, *v.* 11, 21–23. It is taken for granted that the Father and Son are one, one in mutual endearments. The *Father loveth the Son,* and the Son always pleased the Father. They are one in design. The intimacy of this oneness is expressed in these words, *thou in me, and I in thee.* This is insisted on in Christ's prayer for his disciples' oneness, (1) As the pattern of that oneness. Believers are one in some measure as God and Christ are one; they are united by a divine nature, by the power of divine grace, in pursuance of the divine counsels. It is a holy union, for holy ends; not a body politic for any secular purpose. It is a complete union. (2) As the centre of that oneness; that they may be *one in us.* There is *one God* and *one Mediator.* That is a conspiracy, not a union, which doth not centre in God as the end, and Christ as the way. All who are truly united to God and Christ, who *are one,* will soon be *united one to another.* (3) As a plea for that oneness. The Creator and Redeemer are one in interest and design; but to what purpose are they so, if all believers be not one body with Christ, and do not jointly receive grace for grace from him, as he has received it for them? Those words, *I in them, and thou in me,* show what that union is which is so necessary, not only to the beauty, but to the very being, of his church. Union with Christ: *I in them.* Union with God through him: *Thou in me,* so as by me to be in them. Union with each other, resulting from these: *that they* hereby *may be made perfect in one.* We are complete in him.

2. The design of Christ in all his communications of light and grace to them (*v.* 22): "*The glory which thou gavest me, I have* accordingly *given them, that they may be one, as we are one;* so that those gifts will be in vain, if they be not one." Now these gifts are either, (1) Those that were conferred upon the apostles. The glory of being God's ambassadors to the world, and erecting the throne of God's kingdom among men—this glory was given to Christ, and some of the honour he put upon them when he sent them to *disciple all nations.* Or, (2) Those that are given in common to all believers. The glory of being in covenant with the Father was the glory which the Father gave to the Redeemer, and he has confirmed it to the redeemed. This honour he says he *hath given them.* He gave it to them, that they *might be one,* to entitle them to the privilege of unity. The gift of the Spirit, that great glory which the Father gave to the Son, by him to be given to all believers, makes them one, to engage them to the duty of unity. That in consideration of what they have in one God and one Christ, and of what they hope for in one heaven, they may be of one mind and one mouth. Worldly glory sets men at variance; for if some be advanced others are eclipsed. The more Christians are taken up with the glory Christ has given them, the less desirous they will be of vain-glory, and, consequently, the less disposed to quarrel.

3. He pleads the happy influence their oneness would have upon others. This is twice urged (*v.* 21): *That the world may believe that thou hast sent me.* And again (*v.* 23): *That the world may know it.* Believers must know what they believe, and why and wherefore they believe it. Those who believe *at a venture,* venture too far. Now Christ here shows,

(1) His goodwill to the world of mankind in general. Herein he is of his Father's mind, that he would have all men to be saved. Therefore it is his will that no stone be left unturned, for the conviction and conversion of the world. We must in our places do our utmost to further men's salvation.

(2) The good fruit of the church's oneness; it will be an evidence of the truth of Christianity, and a means of bringing many to embrace it. In general, it will recommend Christianity to the world. The embodying of Christians in one society will greatly promote Christianity. When the world shall see so many of those that were its children changed from what they themselves sometimes were, they will be ready to say, *We will go with you, for we see that God is with you.* The uniting of Christians in love and charity is the beauty of their profession, and invites others to join with them. When Christianity, instead of causing quarrels about itself, makes all other strifes to cease,—when it disposes men to be kind and loving, studious to preserve and promote peace, this will recommend it to all that have anything either of natural religion or natural affection in them. In particular, it will beget in men good thoughts of Christ: They will know and believe that *thou hast sent me.* By this it will appear that Christ was sent of God, in that his religion prevails to join so many of different capacities, tempers, and interests in other things, in one body by faith, with one heart by love. Of Christians: They will *know that thou hast loved them as thou hast loved me.* 1. The privilege of believers: *the Father* himself loveth them with a love resembling his love to his Son, for they are loved in him with an everlasting love. 2. The evidence, that of their being one: it will appear that God loves us, if we *love one another with a pure heart.* See how much good it would do to the world to know better how dear to God all good Christians are. Those that have so much of God's love would have more of ours.

Verses 24–26

I. A petition for the glorifying of all those that were given to Christ (*v.* 24): *Father, I will that they may be with me.*

1. The connection of this request with those foregoing. He had prayed that God would sanctify them; and now he prays that he would crown all his gifts with their glorification. In this method we must pray, first for grace, and then for glory; for in this method God gives.

2. The manner of the request: *Father, I will.* Here, as before, he addresses himself to God as a Father, and therein we must do likewise; but when he says, *I will,* he speaks a language such as does not become ordinary petitioners. This intimates the authority of his intercession in general; his word was with power in heaven, as well as on earth. It intimates his particular authority in this matter; he had a power to *give eternal life* (*v.* 2), and, pursuant to that power, he says, *Father, I will.*

3. The request itself—that all the elect might come to be with him in heaven at last.

(1) Under what notion we are to hope for heaven? Wherein does that happiness consist? Three things make heaven: It is to be where Christ is: *Where I am*, am to be shortly, am to be eternally. In this world we are but *on our passage*; there we truly are where we are to be for ever. It is to be with him where he is. The happiness of the place will consist in his presence. The very heaven of heaven is to be with Christ. It is to *behold his glory, which the Father* has given him. The glory of the Redeemer is the brightness of heaven. The Lamb is the light of the new Jerusalem, Rev. xxi. 23. God shows his glory there, as he does his grace here, through Christ. The felicity of the redeemed consists very much in the beholding of this glory. They will see into those springs of love from which flow all the streams of grace. They shall *be changed into the same image, from glory to glory*.

(2) Upon what ground we are to hope for heaven; because he hath said, *Father, I will*. Our sanctification is our evidence, but it is the will of Christ that is our title. Christ speaks here as if he did not count his own happiness complete unless he had his elect to share with him in it.

4. The argument to back this request: *for thou lovedst me before the foundation of the world*. This is a reason, (1) Why he expected this glory himself. Thou wilt *give it to me, for thou lovedst me. The Father loves the Son*, is infinitely well pleased in his undertaking, and *therefore has given all things into his hands*. He is said to love him as Mediator *before the foundation of the world*. Or, (2) Why he expected that those who *were given to him* should be with him to share in his glory: "*Thou lovedst me*, and them in me, and canst deny me nothing I ask for them."

II. The conclusion of the prayer.

1. The respect he had to his Father, *v.* 25.

(1) The title he gives to God: *O righteous Father*. When he prayed that they might be sanctified, he called him *holy Father*; when he prays that they may be glorified, he calls him *righteous Father*.

(2) The character he gives of the world: *The world has not known thee*. Ignorance of God overspreads the world of mankind; this is the darkness they sit in. These disciples needed the aids of special grace, both because of the necessity of their work, and also because of the difficulty of their work—therefore keep them. They were qualified for further peculiar favours, for they had that knowledge of God which the world had not.

(3) The plea he insists upon for himself: *But I have known thee*. Christ knew the Father as no one else ever did, and therefore, in this prayer, came to him with confidence, as we do to one we know. When he had said, *The world has not known thee*, one would expect it should follow, *but they have known thee;* no, their knowledge was not to be boasted of, *but I have known thee*. There is nothing in us to recommend us to God's favour, but all our interest in him, and intercourse with him, result from Christ's interest and intercourse. We are unworthy, but he is worthy.

(4) The plea he insists upon for his disciples: *And they have known that thou hast sent me*. Hereby they are distinguished from the unbelieving world. To know and believe in Jesus Christ, in the midst of a world that persists in ignorance and infidelity, shall certainly be crowned with distinguishing glory. Singular faith qualifies for singular favours. Hereby they partake of the benefit of his acquaintance with the Father: "*I have known thee*, and these *have known that thou hast sent me*." Knowing Christ as sent of God, they have, in him, known the Father. "Father, look after them for my sake."

2. The respect he had to his disciples (*v.* 26): "I have led them into the knowledge of thee, *that the love wherewith thou hast loved me may be in them, and I in them*."

(1) What Christ had done for them: *I have declared unto them thy name*. This he had done for those that were his immediate followers. This he has done for all that believe on him. We are indebted to Christ for all the knowledge we have of the Father's name. Those whom Christ recommends to the favour of God he first leads into an acquaintance with God.

(2) What he intended to do yet further for them: *I will declare it*. To the disciples he designed to give further instructions after his resurrection (Acts i. 3), by the pouring out of the Spirit after his ascension; and to all believers, into whose hearts he hath shined, he shines more and more.

(3) What he aimed at in all this; to secure and advance their real happiness in two things:

[1] Communion with God: "Therefore I have given them the knowledge of thy name, *that thy love, wherewith thou hast loved me, may be in them*. Let the Spirit of love, with which thou hast filled me, *be in them*." Christ declares his Father's name to believers, that with that divine light darted into their minds a divine love may be shed abroad in their hearts, that they may partake of a divine nature. When God's love to us comes to be in us, it is like the virtue which the loadstone gives the needle, inclining it to move towards the pole; it draws out the soul towards God. Let them not only be interested in the love of God, let them have the comfort of that interest; that they may not only know God, but *know that they know him*. It is *the love of God* thus *shed abroad in the heart* that fills it with joy, Rom. v. 3, 5. We may not only be satisfied with his loving kindness, but be satisfied of it. This we must press after; if we have it, we must thank Christ for it; if we want it, we may thank ourselves.

[2] Union with Christ in order hereunto: *And I in them*. There is no getting into the love of God but through Christ, nor can we keep ourselves in that love but by abiding in Christ. It is *Christ in us* that is *the* only *hope of glory* that will *not make us ashamed*, Col. i. 27. All our communion with God, the reception of his love to us with our return of love to him again, passes through the hands of the Lord Jesus. Christ had said but a little before, *I in them* (*v.* 23), and here it is repeated, and the prayer closed with it, to show how much the heart of Christ was set upon it. "*I in them;* let me have this, and I desire no more." Let us therefore make sure our union with Christ, and then take the comfort of his intercession. *This* prayer had an end, but *that* he ever lives to make.

CHAPTER 18

Hitherto this evangelist has recorded little of the history of Christ, only so far as was requisite to introduce his discourses; but now he is very particular in relating the circumstances of his sufferings. This chapter relates, I. How Christ was arrested in the garden, ver. 1–12. II. How he was abused in the high priest's court, and how Peter, in the meantime, denied him, ver. 13–27. III. How he was prosecuted before Pilate, and put in election with Barabbas for the favour of the people, and lost it, ver. 28–40.

Verses 1–12

The hour was now come that *the captain of our salvation*, who was to be *made perfect by sufferings*, should engage the enemy. *Let us turn aside now, and see this great sight*.

I. Our Lord Jesus, like a bold champion, takes the field first (*v.* 1, 2): *When he had spoken these words*, he would lose no time, but *went forth with his disciples*, and *he went over the brook Cedron where was a garden*.

1. Our Lord Jesus entered upon his sufferings *when he had spoken these words*. Christ had said all he had to say as a prophet, and now he addresses himself to the discharge of his office as a priest,

to *make his soul an offering for sin*; and, when he had gone through this, he entered upon his kingly office. Having by his sermon prepared his disciples for this hour of trial, and by his prayer prepared himself for it, he then courageously went out to meet it. When he had put on his armour, he entered the lists, and not till then. Christ will not engage those that are his in any conflict, but he will first do that for them which is necessary to prepare them for it. We may, with an unshaken resolution, venture through the greatest hardships in the way of duty.

2. *He went forth with his disciples.* He would do as he was wont to do, and not alter his method, either to meet the cross or to miss it, when his hour was come. It was his custom when he was at Jerusalem to retire at night *to the mount of Olives.* This being his custom, he would not be put out of his method by the foresight of his sufferings. He was as unwilling that there should be *an uproar among the people* as his enemies were. If he had been seized in the city, and a tumult raised thereby, mischief might have been done, and a great deal of blood shed, and therefore he withdrew. When we find ourselves involved in trouble, we should be afraid of involving others with us. It is no disgrace to the followers of Christ to fall tamely. Those who aim at honour from men value themselves upon a resolution to sell their lives as dearly as they can; but those who know that their blood is precious to Christ need not stand upon such terms. He would set us an example of retirement from the world. We must lay aside, and leave behind, the crowds, and cares, and comforts, of cities, even holy cities, if we would cheerfully take up our cross.

3. He went *over the brook Cedron.* He must go over this to go to *the mount of Olives*, but the notice taken of it intimates that there was something in it significant. *The brook Cedron, the black brook*, so called either from the darkness of the valley it ran through or the colour of the water, tainted with the dirt of the city. The godly kings of Judah had burnt and destroyed the idols they found at *the brook Cedron.* Into that brook the abominable things were cast. Christ began his passion by the same brook.

4. He entered into a garden. This circumstance is taken notice of only by this evangelist, that Christ's sufferings began in a garden. In the garden of Eden sin began; there the Redeemer was promised. Christ was buried also in a garden. Let us, when we walk in our gardens, take occasion thence to meditate on Christ's sufferings in a garden, to which we owe all the pleasure we have in our gardens. When we are in the midst of our possessions and enjoyments, we must keep up an expectation of troubles, for our gardens of delight are in a vale of tears.

5. He had his disciples with him. They must be witnesses of his sufferings, and his patience under them, that they might with the more assurance and affection preach them to the world, and be themselves prepared to suffer. He would take them into the danger to show them their weakness. Christ sometimes brings his people into difficulties that he may magnify himself in their deliverance.

6. Judas the traitor *knew the place.* A solitary garden is a proper place for meditation and prayer, that we may pray over the impressions made and the vows renewed, and clench the nail. Mention is made of Judas's knowing the place, (1) To aggravate the sin of Judas, that he would betray his Master, and that he would make use of his familiarity with Christ, as giving him an opportunity of betraying him; a generous mind would have scorned to do so base a thing. (2) To magnify the love of Christ, that, though he knew where the traitor would seek him, thither he went to be found of him. Thus he showed himself willing to suffer and die for us. It was late in the night (we may suppose eight or nine o'clock)

when Christ went out to the garden. When others were going to bed, he was going to prayer, going to suffer.

II. *The captain of our salvation* having taken the field, the enemy attacks him (*v.* 3): Judas with his men comes thither. This evangelist passes over Christ's agony, because the other three had fully related it.

1. The persons employed in this action—*a band of men and officers from the chief priests, with Judas.* (1) Here is a multitude engaged against Christ—*a band of men.* Christ's friends were few, his enemies many. (2) Here is a mixed multitude; the band of men were Gentiles, Roman soldiers, the *officers of the chief priests.* The officers of their courts were Jews; these had an enmity to each other, but were united against Christ. (3) It is a commissioned multitude who have received orders *from the chief priests*, and it is likely that they had a warrant to take him up, *for they feared the people.* See what enemies Christ and his gospel have had, and are likely to have, numerous and potent; ecclesiastical and civil powers combined against them. (4) All under the direction of Judas. He *received* this *band of men.* He thought himself wonderfully preferred from coming in the rear of the contemptible twelve to be placed at the head of these formidable hundreds.

2. The preparation they had made for an attack: They came *with lanterns, and torches, and weapons.* If Christ should abscond, though they had moonlight, they would have occasion for their lights. It was folly to light a candle to seek the Sun by. If he should resist, they would have occasion for their arms. *The weapons of his warfare were spiritual*, and at these *weapons* he had often beaten them, therefore they have now recourse to other *weapons, swords and staves.*

III. Our Lord Jesus gloriously repulsed the first onset of the enemy, *v.* 4–6.

1. How he received them.

(1) He met them with a very soft and mild question (*v.* 4): *Knowing all things that should come upon him*, undisturbed and undaunted, he *went forth* to meet them, and softly asked, *"Whom seek you?"* See here, Christ's foresight of his sufferings: he knew *all those things that should come upon him.* We should not covet to know what shall come upon us; it would but anticipate our pain; *sufficient unto the day is the evil thereof:* yet it will do us good to expect sufferings in general. "It is but the cost we sat down and counted upon." Christ's forwardness to his sufferings. When the people would have forced him to a crown, he withdrew, and hid himself (*ch.* vi. 15); but, when they came to force him to a cross, he offered himself; for he came to this world to suffer and went to the other world to reign. This will not warrant us needlessly to expose ourselves to trouble, but we are called to suffering when we have no way to avoid it but by sin.

(2) He met them with a very calm and mild answer when they told him whom they were in quest of, *v.* 5. They said, *Jesus of Nazareth;* and he said, *I am he.* It is highly probable that at least the officers of the temple had often seen him. Judas knew him well enough, and yet none of them could pretend to say, *Thou art the man* we seek. In their enquiries for him they called him *Jesus of Nazareth.* It was a name of reproach given him, to darken the evidence of his being the Messiah. By this it appears that they knew him not, whence he was. He fairly answers them: *I am he.* Though they called him Jesus of Nazareth, he answered to the name, for he despised the reproach; he might have said, *I am not he*, for he was *Jesus of Bethlehem.* He has hereby taught us to own him, whatever it cost us; not to be *ashamed of him or his words.* Particular notice is taken *that Judas*

stood with them. He that used to stand with those that followed Christ now stood with those that fought against him. This is mentioned: To show the impudence of Judas. One would wonder where he got the confidence with which he now faced his Master, and *was not ashamed.* To show that Judas was particularly aimed at in the power which went along with that word, *I am he,* to foil the aggressors.

2. See how he terrified them, and obliged them to retire (*v.* 6): *They went backward, and fell to the ground.* This word, *I am he,* had revived his disciples, and raised them up, but the same word strikes his enemies down. Hereby he showed plainly,

(1) What he could have done with them. When he struck them down, he could have struck them dead. But he would not do so. He would only show that his life was not forced from him, but *he laid it down of himself,* as he had said. He would give an instance of his patience and forbearance and his compassionate love to his very enemies. In striking them down, and no more, he gave them both a call to repent and space to repent.

(2) What he will do at last with all his implacable enemies, *that will not repent to give him glory; they shall flee, they shall fall before him.*

IV. Having given his enemies a repulse, he gives his friends a protection, *v.* 7–9.

1. He continued to expose himself to their rage, *v.* 7. When they were down, one would have thought Christ should have made his escape; when they were up again, one would have thought they should have let fall their pursuit. They are as eager as ever to seize him. They cannot imagine what ailed them, but will impute it to anything rather than Christ's power. There are hearts so very hard in sin that nothing will work upon them to reduce and reclaim them. He is as willing as ever to be seized. When they were fallen before him, he asked them the same question, *Whom seek you?* And they gave him the same answer, *Jesus of Nazareth.* In their repeating the same answer, they showed an obstinacy in their wicked way; they still call him *Jesus of Nazareth,* with as much disdain as ever, and Judas is as unrelenting as any of them.

2. He contrived to secure his disciples from their rage. When he shows his courage with reference to himself, *I have told you that I am he,* he shows his care for his disciples, *Let these go their way.* This aggravated the sin of the disciples in forsaking him, and particularly Peter's in denying him. When Christ said, *Let these go their way,* he intended,

(1) To manifest his affectionate concern for his disciples. When he exposed himself, he excused them, because they were not as yet fit to suffer. It would have been as much as their souls, and the lives of their souls, were worth, to bring them into sufferings now. And, besides, they had other work to do; they must go their way, for they are to go into all the world, to preach the gospel. Christ gives us a great encouragement to follow him. He considers our frame, will wisely time the cross, and proportion it to our strength. He gives us a good example of love to our brethren. We must not consult our own ease and safety only, but others' as well as our own, and in some cases more than our own.

(2) To give a specimen of his undertaking as Mediator. When he offered himself to suffer and die, it was that we might escape.

3. He confirmed the word which he had spoken a little before (*ch.* xvii. 12), *Of those whom thou gavest me, I have lost none.* Though Christ's keeping them was meant especially of the preservation of their souls from sin, yet it is here applied to the preservation of their natural lives. Christ will preserve the natural life for the service to which it is designed. It shall be held in life as long as any use is to be made of it.

This preservation of the disciples was a spiritual preservation. They were now so weak in faith and resolution that in all probability, if they had been called out to suffer at this time, some of them, at least the weaker of them, would have been lost; and therefore, that he might *lose none,* he would not expose them.

V. He rebukes the rashness of one of them, and represses the violence of his followers, *v.* 10, 11.

1. Peter's rashness. He had a sword. They had two swords among them all (Luke xxii. 38), and Peter, being entrusted with one, drew it; and *he smote one of the high priest's servants,* and *cut off his right ear. The servant's name,* for the greater certainty of the narrative, is recorded; it *was Malchus.*

(1) We must here acknowledge Peter's goodwill; he had an honest zeal for his Master, though now misguided. He had lately promised to venture his life for him, and would now make his words good.

(2) Yet we must acknowledge Peter's ill conduct; and, though his good intention did excuse, yet it would not justify him. [1] He had no warrant from his Master for what he did. Christ's soldiers must wait the word of command, and not outrun it. [2] He resisted the powers that were, which Christ had never countenanced, but forbidden (Matt. v. 39). [3] He opposed his Master's sufferings. Thus, while he seemed to fight for Christ, he fought against him. [4] He broke the capitulation his Master had lately made with the enemy. When he said, *Let these go their way,* he in effect passed his word for their good behaviour; this Peter heard, and yet would not be bound by it. [5] He foolishly exposed himself and his fellow disciples to the fury of this enraged multitude. Many have been guilty of self-destruction, in their zeal for self-preservation. [6] Peter played the coward so soon after this (denying his Master) that we have reason to think his courage failed him; whereas the true Christian hero will appear in the cause of Christ, not only when it is prevailing, but when it seems to be declining; will be on the right side, though it be not the rising side.

(3) We must acknowledge God's overruling providence in giving Christ an opportunity to manifest his power and goodness in healing the hurt, Luke xxii. 51.

2. The rebuke his Master gave him (*v.* 11): *Put up thy sword into the sheath.* It is a gentle reproof, because it was his zeal that carried him beyond the bounds of discretion. Many think their being in grief and distress will excuse them if they be hot and hasty with those about them; but Christ has here set us an example of meekness in sufferings.

3. The reason for this rebuke: *The cup which my Father has given me, shall I not drink it?* Christ gives us, (1) A full proof of his own submission to his Father's will. Of all that was amiss in what Peter did, he seems to resent nothing so much as that he would have hindered his sufferings now that his *hour was come.* He was willing to drink of this cup, though it was a bitter cup. He drank it, that he might put into our hands the cup of salvation. He is willing to drink it, because *his Father put it into his hand.* (2) A fair pattern to us of submission to God's will. We must *pledge* Christ in the cup that he drank of (Matt. xx. 23). It is but a *cup;* a small matter comparatively. It is a cup that is given us; sufferings are gifts. It is given us by a Father, who has a Father's affection, and means us no hurt.

VI. He calmly surrendered, and yielded himself a prisoner, not because he could not have made his escape, but because he would not.

1. How they seized him: *They took Jesus.* Only some few of them could lay hands on him, but it is charged upon them all, for they were all aiding and abetting. In treason there are no accessories; all are

principals. They had so often been frustrated in their attempts to seize him that now we may suppose they flew upon him with so much the more violence.

2. How they secured him: *They bound him.* This particular of his sufferings is taken notice of only by this evangelist, that, as soon as ever he was taken, he was bound, pinioned, handcuffed.

(1) This shows the spite of his persecutors. They bound him, that they might torment him, and put him in pain; that they might disgrace him, and put him to shame; that they might prevent his escape. They bound him as one already condemned, for they were resolved to prosecute him to the death. Christ had bound the consciences of his persecutors with the power of his word, which galled them; and, to be revenged on him, they laid these bonds on him.

(2) Christ's being bound was very significant. Before they bound him, he had bound himself to the work and office of a Mediator. He was already bound to the horns of the altar with the cords of his own love to man, and duty to his Father. Guilt is a bond on the soul, by which we are bound over to the judgment of God; corruption is a bond on the soul, by which we are bound under the power of Satan. Christ, to free us from those bonds, himself submitted to be bound for us. To his bonds we owe our liberty. Thus the Son maketh us free. Christ was bound, that he might bind us to duty and obedience. His bonds for us are bonds upon us, by which we are for ever obliged to love him and serve him. Christ's bonds for us were designed to make our bonds for him easy to us, to sanctify and sweeten them; these enabled Paul and Silas to sing in the stocks.

Verses 13–27

We have here an account of Christ's arraignment before the high priest, and some circumstances that occurred therein which were omitted by the other evangelists. Peter's denying him, of which the other evangelists had given the entire story by itself, is interwoven with the other passages. The crime laid to his charge having relation to religion, the judges of the spiritual court took it to fall directly under their cognizance. Both Jews and Gentiles seized him, and so both Jews and Gentiles tried and condemned him, for he died for the sins of both.

I. Having seized him, they *led him away to Annas first,* v. 13. 1. They *led him away,* led him in triumph, as a trophy of their victory. They hurried him away with violence, as if he had been the worst and vilest of malefactors. We had been led away of our own impetuous lusts, and led captive by Satan at his will, and, that we might be rescued, Christ was led away, led captive by Satan's agents and instruments. 2. They led him away to their masters that sent them. It was now about midnight, and one would think they should have put him in ward till it was a proper time to call a court; but he is hurried away immediately, not to the justices of peace, to be committed, but to the judges to be condemned; so extremely violent was the prosecution. 3. They led him to Annas first. Probably his house lay in the way. To gratify him therefore with the assurance of their success, they produce their prisoner before him. Christ, the great sacrifice, was presented to him, and sent away bound, as approved and ready for the altar. This Annas was father-in-law to Caiaphas the high priest. Acquaintance and alliance with wicked people are a great confirmation to many in their wicked ways.

II. Annas being as willing as any of them to have the prosecution pushed on, sent him bound to Caiaphas.

1. The power of Caiaphas intimated (v. 13). He was *high priest that same year.* The high priest's commission was during life; but there were now such frequent changes that it was become almost an annual office. While they were undermining one another, God was overturning them all. Caiaphas was high priest that same year when Messiah was to be cut off. When a bad thing was to be done by a high priest, Providence so ordered it that a bad man should be in the chair to do it. It was the ruin of Caiaphas that he was high priest that year, and so became a ringleader in the putting of Christ to death. Many a man's advancement has lost him his reputation, and he had not been dishonoured if he had not been preferred.

2. The malice of Caiaphas, which is intimated (v. 14) by the repeating of what he had said some time before, that *it was expedient that one man should die for the people.* This was that Caiaphas that governed himself and the church by rules of policy, in defiance of the rules of equity. His case was adjudged before it was heard, and they were already resolved what to do with him; *he must die;* so that his trial was a jest. It is a testimony to the innocence of our Lord Jesus, from the mouth of one of his worst enemies, who owned that he fell a sacrifice to the public good, and that it was not just he should die, but *expedient* only.

3. The concurrence of Annas in the prosecution of Christ. He made himself a partaker in guilt, (1) With the captain and officers, by continuing him bound when he should have loosed him. It was more excusable in the rude soldiers to bind him than in Annas, who should have known better, to continue him bound. (2) With the chief priest and council. This Annas was not present with them, yet thus he became a *partaker of their evil deeds.*

III. In the house of Caiaphas, Simon Peter began to deny his Master, v. 15–18.

1. It was with much ado that Peter got into the hall where the court was sitting, an account of which we have, v. 15, 16.

(1) Peter's kindness to Christ, which (though it proved no kindness) appeared in two things: [1] That he *followed Jesus* when he was *led away;* though at first he fled with the rest, yet afterwards he took heart a little, and followed at some distance, calling to mind the promises he had made to adhere to him, whatever it should cost him. Those that truly love and value Christ will follow him all weathers and all ways. [2] When he could not get in where Jesus was in the midst of his enemies, he *stood at the door without,* willing to be as near him as he could, and waiting for an opportunity to get nearer. As it proved, he did but run himself into a snare. Christ, who knew him better than he knew himself, had expressly told him (ch. xiii. 36), *Whither I go thou canst not follow me now,* and had told him again and again that he would deny him; and he had lately had experience of his own weakness in forsaking him.

(2) The other disciple's kindness to Peter, which yet, as it proved, was no kindness either. St. John several times in this gospel speaking of himself as another disciple, many interpreters have been led by this to fancy that this other disciple here was John. But I see no reason to think that this other disciple was John, or one of the twelve; other sheep Christ had, which were not of the fold. As there are many who seem disciples and are not so, so there are many who are disciples and seem not so. There are good people hid in courts, even in Nero's, as well as hid in crowds. This other disciple showed a respect to Peter, in introducing him, not only to gratify affection, but to give him an opportunity of being serviceable to his Master upon his trial. But this kindness proved no kindness, nay a great diskindness; by letting him into the high priest's hall, he let him into temptation, and the consequence was bad.

2. Peter, having got in, was immediately assaulted with the temptation, *v.* 17.

(1) How slight the attack was. It was but a silly maid, of so small account that she was set to keep the door, that challenged him, and she only asked him carelessly, *Art not thou one of this man's disciples?* Peter would have had some reason to take the alarm if Malchus had set upon him, and had said, "This is he that cut off my ear, and I will have his head for it."

(2) How speedy the surrender was. Without taking time to recollect himself, he suddenly answered, *I am not.* All his care being for his own safety, he thought he could not secure this but by a peremptory denial.

(3) Yet he goes further into the temptation: *And the servants and officers stood there, and Peter with them, v.* 18.

[1] See how the servants made much of themselves; the night being cold, they made a fire in the hall. They cared not what became of Christ; all their care was to sit and warm themselves.

[2] See how Peter herded himself with them. *He sat and warmed himself.* It was a fault bad enough that he did not attend his Master, and appear for him at the upper end of the hall. He might have been a witness for him, at least, he might have been a witness to him. He might have learned by his Master's example how to carry himself when it should come to his turn to suffer thus; yet neither his conscience nor his curiosity could bring him into the court. It was much worse that he joined himself with those that were his Master's enemies: *He stood with them, and warmed himself.* A little thing will draw those into bad company that will be drawn to it by the love of a good fire. If Peter's zeal for his Master had not frozen, but had continued in the heat it seemed to be of but a few hours before, he had not had occasion to warm himself now. Peter was much to be blamed, 1. Because he associated with these wicked men. Doubtless they were diverting themselves with this night's expedition, scoffing at Christ; and what sort of entertainment would this give to Peter? If Peter had not so much courage as to appear publicly for his Master, yet he might have had so much devotion as to retire into a corner, and weep in secret for his Master's sufferings, and his own sin in forsaking him. 2. Because he desired to be thought *one of them.* Is this Peter? It is ill warming ourselves with those with whom we are in danger of burning ourselves.

IV. Peter, Christ's friend, having begun to deny him, the high priest, his enemy, begins to accuse him, *v.* 19–21. It should seem, the first attempt was to prove him a teacher of false doctrine, which this evangelist relates; and, when they failed in the proof of this, then they charged him with blasphemy, which is related by the other evangelists.

1. The articles or heads upon which Christ was examined (*v.* 19): concerning *his disciples and his doctrine.*

(1) The irregularity of the process; it was against all law and equity. Now that he is their prisoner they have nothing to *lay to his charge.* Against all reason and justice, he is put on to be his own accuser.

(2) The intention. The *high priest then* examined him upon those interrogatories which would touch his life. [1] Concerning his disciples, that he might charge him with sedition. Some think his question concerning his disciples was, "What is now become of them all? Why do they not appear?" upbraiding him with their cowardice in deserting him, and thus adding to the affliction of it. [2] Concerning his doctrine, that they might charge him with heresy. This was a matter properly cognizable in that court, therefore a prophet could not perish but at Jerusalem, where that court sat. They said nothing to him concerning his miracles, by which he had done so much

good, because of these they were sure they could take no hold.

2. The appeal Christ made, in answer to these interrogatories. As to his disciples, he said nothing, because it was an impertinent question. His having disciples was no more than what was practised and allowed by their own doctors. If Caiaphas designed to ensnare them, it was in kindness to them that Christ said nothing of them, for he had said, *Let these go their way.* If he meant to upbraid him with their cowardice, no wonder that he said nothing. He would say nothing to condemn them, and could say nothing to justify them. As to his doctrine, he said nothing in particular, but in general referred himself to those that heard him, *v.* 20, 21.

[1] He tacitly charges his judges with illegal proceedings. He appeals to the settled rules of their own court, whether they dealt fairly by him. *Why ask you me?* Which implies two absurdities in judgment: *First*, "*Why ask you me now* concerning my doctrine, when you have already condemned it?" They had made an order of court for excommunicating all that owned him (*ch.* ix. 22), and now they come to ask what his doctrine is! *Secondly*, "*Why ask you me?* Must I accuse myself?"

[2] He insists upon his fair and open dealing with them in the publication of his doctrine. Christ clears himself very fully. *First*, As to the manner of his preaching. He spoke openly *with freedom and plainness of speech.* Christ explained himself fully, with, *Verily, verily, I say unto you. Secondly*, As to the persons he preached to: *He spoke to the world*, to all that had *ears to hear*, and were willing to hear him, high or low, learned or unlearned, Jew or Gentile, friend or foe. *Thirdly*, As to the places he preached in. When he was in the country, he preached ordinarily in the synagogues; when he came up to Jerusalem, he preached the same doctrine in the temple. Though he often preached in private houses, and on mountains, and by the seaside, yet what he preached in private was the very same with what he delivered publicly. The doctrine of Christ needs not be ashamed to appear in the most numerous assembly, for it carries its own strength and beauty along with it. *Fourthly*, As to the doctrine itself. *In secret have I said nothing.* He sought no corners, for he feared no colours, nor said anything that he needed to be ashamed of; what he did speak in private to his disciples he ordered them to proclaim on the house-tops, Matt. x. 27.

[3] He appeals to those that had heard him, and desires that they might be examined: "*Ask those that heard me what I said unto them.*" He means not his friends and followers, who might be presumed to speak in his favour, but, Ask any impartial hearer. The doctrine of Christ may safely appeal to all that know it. Those who will judge impartially cannot but witness to it.

V. While the judges were examining him, the servants that stood by were abusing him, *v.* 22, 23.

1. It was a base affront which one of the officers gave him; this insolent fellow *struck him with the palm of his hand*, saying, Answerest thou the high priest so?

(1) He *struck him—he gave him a blow.* It was unjust to strike one that neither said nor did amiss; it was cowardly to strike one that had his hands tied; and barbarous to strike a prisoner at the bar. Here was a breach of the peace in the face of the court, and yet the judges countenanced it.

(2) He checked him in a haughty imperious manner: *Answerest thou the high priest so?* As if the blessed Jesus were not good enough to speak to his master, but, like a rude and ignorant prisoner, must be controlled by the jailer, and taught how to behave. It was done to please the high priest, and to curry favour with him; for what he said implied a jealousy for the dignity

of the high priest. Wicked rulers will not want wicked servants, who will *help forward the affliction* of those whom their masters persecute.

2. Christ bore this affront with wonderful meekness and patience (*v.* 23): "*If I have spoken evil, bear witness of the evil.* But if well, *why smitest thou me?*" Christ did not here *turn the other cheek*, by which it appears that that rule, Matt. v. 39, is not to be understood literally. Comparing Christ's precept with his pattern, we learn that in such cases we must not be our own avengers, nor judges in our own cause. Our resentment of injuries done us must always be rational, and never passionate; such Christ's here was.

VI. While the servants were thus abusing him, Peter was proceeding to deny him, *v.* 25-27.

1. He repeated the sin the second time, *v.* 25. While he was warming himself with the servants, they asked him, *Art not thou one of his disciples?* He, perhaps, fearing he should be seized, if he should own it, flatly denied it, and said, *I am not.*

(1) It was his great folly to thrust himself into the temptation, by continuing in the company. He stayed to warm himself; but those that warm themselves with evil doers grow cold towards good people and good things, and those that are fond of the devil's fire-side are in danger of the devil's fire.

(2) It was his great unhappiness that he was again assaulted by the temptation. [1] The subtlety of the tempter in running down one whom he saw falling; not a maid now, but all the servants. Yielding to one temptation invites another, and perhaps a stronger. Satan redoubles his attacks when we give ground. [2] The danger of bad company. We commonly study to approve ourselves to those with whom we choose to associate. As we choose our people we choose our praise; we are therefore concerned to make the first choice well.

(3) It was his great weakness to yield to the temptation, and to say, *I am not one* of his disciples, as one ashamed of that which was his honour. When Christ was admired and treated with respect, Peter prided himself, in this, that he was a disciple of Christ. Thus many who seem fond of the reputation of religion when it is in fashion are ashamed of the reproach of it.

2. He repeated the sin the third time, *v.* 26, 27. Here he was attacked by one of the servants, who was kinsman to Malchus, who gave him the lie with great assurance: "*Did not I see thee in the garden with him?*" Peter then denied again.

(1) Before his relation to Christ was only suspected, here it is proved upon him by one that saw him with Jesus. Those who by sin think to help themselves out of trouble do but entangle and embarrass themselves the more. Dare to be brave, for truth will out. Notice is taken of this servant's being akin to Malchus, because this circumstance would make it the more a terror to Peter. We should not make any man in particular our enemy if we can help it. He that may need a friend should not make a foe. Though here was sufficient evidence against Peter to have prosecuted him, yet he escapes, has no harm done him. We are often drawn into sin by groundless causeless fears, which a small degree of wisdom and resolution would make nothing of.

(2) His yielding to it was no less base than the former: *He denied again.* The nature of sin in general: *the heart is hardened by the deceitfulness of it,* Heb. iii. 13. *The beginning of sin is as the letting forth of water,* when once the fence is broken men easily go from bad to worse. Of the sin of lying in particular; it is a fruitful sin; one lie needs another to support it, and that another.

(3) *Immediately the cock crew;* and this is all that is here said of his repentance, it being recorded by the other evangelists. The crowing of the cock to others was an accidental thing, and had no significancy, but to Peter it was the voice of God.

Verses 28-40

We have here an account of Christ's arraignment before Pilate, the Roman governor, in the praetor's house, or *hall of judgment;* thither they hurried him, to get him condemned in the Roman court, and executed by the Roman power. They took this course, 1. That he might be put to death the more legally and regularly; not stoned in a popular tumult, as Stephen, but put to death with the present formalities of justice. 2. That he might be put to death the more safely. If they could engage the Roman government in the matter, there would be little danger of an uproar. 3. That he might be put to death with more reproach to himself. *The death of the cross,* being of all deaths the most ignominious, they were desirous by it to put an indelible mark of infamy upon him. This therefore they harped upon, *Crucify him.* 4. That he might be put to death with less reproach to them. It was an invidious thing to put one to death that had done so much good, and therefore they were willing to throw the odium upon the Roman government. Thus many are more afraid of the scandal of a bad action than of the sin of it. (1) Their industry in the prosecution: *It was early,* when most people were in their beds. Now that they had him in their hands, they would lose no time till they had him upon the cross. (2) Their superstition and vile hypocrisy: *The chief priests and elders went not into the judgment-hall lest they should be defiled,* but kept out of doors, *that they might eat the passover,* and therefore would not go into the court, for fear of touching a Gentile, and thereby contracting, not a legal, but only a traditional pollution. This they scrupled, but made no scruple of breaking through all the laws of equity to persecute Christ to the death.

I. Pilate's conference with the prosecutors. They were called first, and stated what they had to say against the prisoner, *v.* 29-32.

1. The judge calls for the indictment. Because they would not come into the hall, *he went out to them.* Here are three things commendable in him: (1) His diligent and close application to business. Men in public trusts must not love their ease. (2) His condescending to the humour of the people. He might have said, "If they be so nice as not to come in to me, let them go home as they came"; but Pilate insists not upon it, and goes out to them. (3) His adherence to the rule of justice, in demanding the accusation: "*What accusation bring you against this man?* What is the crime you charge him with, and what proof have you of it?"

2. The prosecutors demand judgment against him upon a general surmise that he was a criminal (*v.* 30): *If he were not a malefactor we would not have delivered him to thee.* This bespeaks them, (1) Very rude and uncivil to Pilate. He put the most reasonable question to them that could be; but, if it had been the most absurd, they could not have answered him with more disdain. (2) Very spiteful and malicious towards our Lord Jesus. They will presume him guilty who could prove himself innocent. They say, "He is an evil-doer." He an evil-doer who *went about doing good!* It is no new thing for the best of benefactors to be branded and run down as the worst of malefactors. (3) Very proud and conceited of themselves, and their own judgment and justice.

3. The judge remands him to their own court (*v.* 31): "*Take you him, and judge him according to your own law.*" Some think Pilate herein complimented them, acknowledging the remains of their power, and allowing them to exert it. Saith Pilate, "Go as far as your law will allow you, and, if you go

further, it shall be connived at." This he said, willing to do the Jews a pleasure, but unwilling to do them the service they required. (2) Others think he upbraided them with their present state of weakness and subjection. Saith Pilate, "You have found him guilty by your own law, condemn him, if you dare, by your own law." Some think Pilate here reflects upon the law of Moses, as if it allowed them what the Roman law would by no means allow—the judging of a man unheard.

4. They disown any authority as judges: "*It is not lawful for us to put any man to death.*" Some think they had lost their power to give judgment in matters of life and death only by their own carelessness. Others think their power was taken from them by the Romans. Their acknowledgment of this they designed for a compliment to Pilate, and to atone for their rudeness (*v.* 30). However, there was a providence in it, *That the saying of Jesus might be fulfilled, which he spoke, signifying what death he should die*, *v.* 32. Even those who designed the defeating of Christ's sayings were made serviceable to the fulfilling of them by an overruling hand of God. Those sayings of Christ in particular were fulfilled which he had spoken concerning his own death. Two sayings of Christ concerning his death were fulfilled, by the Jews declining to *judge him according to their law*. *First*, He had said that he should be *delivered to the Gentiles*, and that *they should put him to death* (Matt. xx. 19; Mark x. 33; Luke xviii. 32, 33). *Secondly*, He had said that he should be crucified (Matt. xx. 19; xxvi. 2), *lifted up*, ch. iii. 14; xii. 32. Now if they had *judged him by their law*, he had been stoned. It was therefore necessary that Christ should be put to death by the Romans. As the Roman power had brought him to be born at Bethlehem, so now to die upon a cross, and both according to the scriptures.

II. Here is Pilate's conference with the prisoner, *v.* 33, &c.

1. The prisoner set to the bar. Pilate, after he had conferred with the chief priests at his door, entered into the hall, and called for Jesus to be brought in. Pilate entered into judgment with him, that God might not enter into judgment with us.

2. His examination. The other evangelists tell us that his accusers had laid it to his charge that *he perverted the nation, forbidding to give tribute to Caesar*.

(1) Here is a question put to him, with a design to find out something upon which to ground an accusation: "*Art thou the king of the Jews?*" Some think Pilate asked this with an air of scorn and contempt: "What! *art thou a king? Art thou the king of the Jews*, by whom thou art thus hated and persecuted?" Since it could not be proved he ever said it, he would constrain him to say it now, that he might proceed upon his own confession.

(2) Christ answers this question with another as an intimation to Pilate to consider upon what grounds he went (*v.* 34): "*Sayest thou this thing of thyself or did others tell it thee of me?* It is plain that thou hast no reason to *say this of thyself*." Pilate was bound by his office to take care of the interests of the Roman government, but he could not say that this was in any danger, or suffered any damage, from anything our Lord Jesus had ever said or done. [2] "If others *tell it of me* thou oughtest to consider whether those who represent me as an *enemy to Caesar* are not really such themselves." If Pilate had been as inquisitive as he ought to have been in this matter, he would have found that the true reason why the chief priests were outrageous against Jesus was because he did not set up a temporal kingdom in opposition to the Roman power. Not answering this expectation of theirs, they charged that upon

him of which they were themselves most notoriously guilty—disaffection to and design against the present government.

(3) Pilate resents Christ's answer, and takes it very ill, *v.* 35. This is a direct answer to Christ's question, *v.* 34. Christ had asked him whether he spoke of himself. "No," says he; "*am I a Jew?*" Observe with what disdain Pilate asks, *Am I a Jew?* A man of sense and honour reckoned it a scandal to be counted a Jew. Christ had asked him whether others told him. "Yes," says he, "and those *thine own people*, and *the priests*; and therefore I have nothing to do but to proceed upon their information." Christ had declined answering that question, *Art thou the king of the Jews?* And therefore Pilate puts another question: "*What hast thou done?* Surely there cannot be all this smoke without some fire, what is it?"

(4) Christ, in his next reply, gives a more full answer to Pilate's former question, *Art thou a king?* explaining in what sense he was a king, *v.* 36.

[1] An account of the nature and constitution of Christ's kingdom: It *is not of this world*. Christ is a king, and has a kingdom, but *not of this world*. Its rise is not from this world. Its nature is not worldly; it is a kingdom within men, set up in their hearts and consciences. Its guards and supports are not worldly; its weapons are spiritual. Its tendency and design are not worldly. Its subjects, though they are in the world, yet *are not of the world*. They are neither the world's pupils nor its darlings, neither governed by its wisdom nor enriched with its wealth.

[2] An evidence of the spiritual nature of Christ's kingdom produced. *If my kingdom were of this world, then would my servants fight, that I should not be delivered to the Jews.* His followers did not offer to fight; there was no uproar, no attempt to rescue him. He did not order them to fight; nay, he forbade them, knowing that what would have been the destruction of any worldly kingdom would be the advancement and establishment of his. *Now* you may see *my kingdom is not from hence*; in the world, but not of it.

(5) In answer to Pilate's further query, he replies yet more directly, *v.* 37. Pilate's plain question: "*Art thou a king then?* Thou speakest of a kingdom thou hast; art thou then, in any sense, a king? Explain thyself." The good confession which our Lord Jesus witnessed before Pontius Pilate: *Thou sayest that I am a king*, that is, It is as thou sayest, I am a king. He grants himself to be a king, though not in the sense that Pilate meant. Though Christ *took upon him the form of a servant*, yet even then he justly claimed the honour and authority of a king. He explains himself, and shows how he is a king, as *he came to bear witness of the truth*; he rules in the minds of men by the power of truth. *He came to be a witness*, a witness for the God that made the world, and against sin that ruins the world, and by this *word of his testimony* he sets up and keeps up, his kingdom. Christ's errand into the world, and his business in the world, were *to bear witness to the truth*. To reveal it, to discover to the world that which otherwise could not have been known concerning God and his *goodwill to men*, ch. xvii. 26. To confirm it. By his miracles *he bore witness to the truth* of religion, *that all men through him might believe*. Now by doing this he is a king, and sets up a kingdom. The spirit and genius, of Christ's kingdom, is truth, divine truth. When he said, *I am the truth*, he said, in effect, I am a king. He conquers by the convincing evidence of truth; he rules by the commanding power of truth. He came *a light into the world*, and rules as the sun by day. The subjects of this kingdom are those that are *of the truth*. All that are in love with truth will hear the voice of Christ, for greater, better, surer,

sweeter truths can nowhere be found than are found in Christ, by whom *grace and truth came*.

(6) Pilate, hereupon, puts a good question to him, but does not stay for an answer, *v.* 38. He said, *What is truth?* and *immediately went out again*. It is certain that this was a good question. Truth is that *pearl of great price* which the human understanding is in quest of; for it cannot rest but in that which is, or at least is apprehended to be, truth. But many put this question that have not patience enough to persevere in their search after truth, or not humility and sincerity enough to receive it when they have found it. It is uncertain with what design Pilate asked this question. Perhaps he spoke it as a learner, as one that began to think well of Christ. Some think he spoke it as a judge, enquiring further into the cause: "Tell me what the truth of it is, the true state of this matter." Others think he spoke it as a scoffer: "Thou talkest of truth; canst thou tell what truth is, or give me a definition of it?" Like men of no religion, who take a pleasure in bantering all religions, he ridicules both sides; and therefore Christ made him no reply. But, though Christ would not tell Pilate what is truth, he has told his disciples, and by them has told us, *ch.* xiv. 6.

III. The result of both these conferences with the prosecutors and the prisoner (*v.* 38–40).

1. The judge appeared his friend.

(1) He publicly declared him innocent, *v.* 38. *I find in him no fault at all*. Nothing criminal appears against him. This solemn declaration of Christ's innocency was, [1] For the justification and honour of the Lord Jesus. Though he was treated as the worst of malefactors he had never merited such treatment. [2] For explaining the design and intention of his death, that he did not die for any sin of his own, and therefore he died as a sacrifice for our sins, and that, *one man should die for the people, ch.* xi. 50. [3] For aggravating the sin of the Jews that prosecuted him with so much violence. Our Lord Jesus, though brought in not guilty, is still run down as a malefactor, and his blood thirsted for.

(2) He proposed an expedient for his discharge (*v.* 39): *You have a custom, that I should release to you a prisoner at the passover;* shall it be this king of the Jews. It was an appeal to the people, as appears, Matt. xxvii. 15. Probably he had heard how this Jesus had been attended but the other day with the hosannas of the common people, and therefore he made no doubt but they would demand the release of Jesus. He allows their custom, in honour of the passover, which was a memorial of their release. He offers to release Jesus to them, according to the custom. If he *found no fault in him*, he was bound in conscience to discharge him. But he was willing to trim the matter, and please all sides, being governed more by worldly wisdom than by the rules of equity.

2. The people appeared his enemies (*v.* 40): *They cried all again, Not this man, but Barabbas*. Observe how fierce and outrageous they were. Pilate proposed the thing to them calmly, but they resolved in it a heat, and gave in their resolution with clamour and noise. There is cause to suspect a deficiency of reason and justice on that side which calls in the assistance of popular tumult. How foolish and absurd they were, as is intimated in the short account here given of the other candidate: *Now Barabbas was a robber*, and therefore, [1] A breaker of the law of God; and yet he shall be spared. [2] An enemy to the public safety and personal property. The clamour of the town is wont to be against robbers, yet here it is for one. Thus those do who prefer their sins before Christ. Sin is a robber, and yet foolishly chosen rather than Christ, who would truly enrich us.

CHAPTER 19

When he comes to the sufferings and death of Christ he repeats what had been before related, with considerable enlargements, as one that desired to know nothing but Christ and him crucified. I. The remainder of Christ's trial before Pilate, ver. 1–15. II. Sentence given, and execution done upon it, ver. 16–18. III. The title over his head, ver. 19–22. IV. *The parting of his garment*, ver. 23, 24. V. The care he took of his mother, ver. 25–27. VI. The giving him vinegar to drink, ver. 28, 29. VII. His dying word, ver. 30. VIII. The piercing of his side, ver. 31–37. IX. The burial of his body, ver. 38–42.

Verses 1–15

Here is a further account of the unfair trial which they gave to our Lord Jesus. The prosecutors carried it on with great confusion among the people, and the judge with great confusion in his own breast.

I. The judge abuses the prisoner, though he declares him innocent, and hopes therewith to pacify the prosecutors.

1. He ordered him to be whipped as a criminal, *v.* 1. *Pilate*, being disappointed in his project of releasing him upon the people's choice, *took Jesus, and scourged him*. Matthew and Mark mention his scourging after his condemnation, but here it appears to have been before. Luke speaks of Pilate's offering to *chastise him, and let him go*, which must be before sentence. This scourging of him was designed only to pacify the Jews. The Roman scourgings were ordinarily very severe, not limited, as among the Jews, to *forty stripes*; yet this pain and shame Christ submitted to for our sakes. (1) *That the scripture might be fulfilled*, which spoke of *the chastisement of our peace* being *upon him* (Isa. liii 5). He himself likewise had foretold it, Matt. xx. 19; Mark x. 34; Luke xviii. 33. (2) *That by his stripes we might be healed*. The physician scourged, and so the patient healed. (3) That stripes, for his sake, might be sanctified and made easy to his followers. Christ's stripes take out the sting of theirs.

2. He turned him over to his soldiers, to be ridiculed and made sport with as a fool (*v.* 2, 3): *The soldiers put a crown of thorns upon his head; they put on him a purple robe;* and they complimented him with, *Hail, king of the Jews*, and then *smote him with their hands*.

(1) See here the baseness and injustice of Pilate. Pilate did this: To oblige his soldiers' merry humour, and perhaps his own too. *Herod*, as well as *his men of war*, had just before done the same, Luke xxiii. 11. It was as good as a stage-play to them, now that it was a festival time. To oblige the Jews' malicious humour.

(2) See here the rudeness and insolence of the soldiers. Thus hath Christ's holy religion been basely misrepresented, dressed up by bad men at their pleasure, and so exposed to contempt and ridicule. They clothe him with a mock-robe. And as Christ is here represented as a king in conceit only, so is his religion as a concern in conceit only, and God and the soul, sin and duty, heaven and hell, are with many all chimeras. They crown him with thorns, as if to submit to the control of God and conscience were to thrust one's head into a thicket of thorns; but this is an unjust imputation; *thorns and snares are in the way of the froward*, but roses and laurels in religion's ways.

(3) See here the wonderful condescension of our Lord Jesus. Great and generous minds can bear anything better than ignominy, yet this the great and holy Jesus submitted to for us. See and admire, the invincible patience of a sufferer, the invincible love and kindness of a Saviour. Herein he commended his love, that he would not only die for us, but die as a fool dies. He *endureth the pain*; not the pangs of death only, but, as if these were too little, he submitted to those previous pains. Shall we complain of a thorn in the flesh, and of being

buffeted by affliction. Christ humbled himself to bear those thorns in the head, and those buffetings, to save and teach us. He *despised the shame*, the shame of a fool's coat, and the mock-respect paid him, with, *Hail, king of the Jews*. He that bore these sham honours was recompensed with real honours, and so shall we, if we patiently suffer shame for him.

II. Pilate presents him to the prosecutors in hope that they would now be satisfied, *v.* 4, 5. Here he proposes two things to their consideration:

1. That he had not found anything in him which made him obnoxious to the Roman government (*v.* 4): *I find no fault in him.* If he found no fault in him, why did he bring him out to his prosecutors, and not immediately release him, as he ought to have done? Thinking to trim the matter, to please the people by scourging Christ, and save his conscience by not crucifying him, behold he does both. It is common for those who think to keep themselves from greater sins by venturing upon less sins to run into both.

2. That he had done that to him which would make him the less dangerous to them and to their government, *v.* 5. He brought him out to them, wearing the crown of thorns, his head and face all bloody, and said, *Behold the man*, treating him as a slave, and exposing him to contempt, after which he supposed the people would never look upon him with any respect. Little did Pilate think with what veneration even these sufferings of Christ would in after ages be commemorated by the best and greatest of men. Our Lord Jesus shows himself dressed up in all the marks of ignominy. He came forth, willing to be made a spectacle. Did he go forth thus bearing our reproach? Let us go forth to him *bearing his reproach*. Pilate saith unto them, with a design to appease them, *Behold the man*; not so much to move their pity, Behold a man worthy your compassion, as to silence their jealousies, Behold a man not worthy your suspicion. The word however is very affecting: *Behold the man.* It is good for everyone of us to behold the man Christ Jesus in his sufferings. "Behold him, and mourn because of him. Behold him, and love him; be still *looking unto Jesus.*"

III. The prosecutors were but the more exasperated, *v.* 6, 7.

1. Their clamour and outrage. *The chief priests cried out*, and their officers joined with them in crying, *Crucify him, crucify him.* The common people perhaps would have acquiesced in Pilate's declaration of his innocency. Their malice against Christ was unreasonable and most absurd, in that they offer not to make good their charge against him; but, though he be innocent, he must be crucified. It was insatiable and very cruel. Neither the extremity of his scourging, nor his patience under it, could mollify them in the least. It was violent and exceedingly resolute; they will have it their own way. Were they so violent in running down our Lord Jesus, and in crying, *Crucify him, crucify him?* and shall not we be vigorous and zealous in crying, *Crown him, Crown him?* Shall not our love to him quicken our endeavours for him and his kingdom?

2. The check Pilate gave to their fury: "*Take you him and crucify him.*" He knew they could not, they durst not, crucify him; but it is as if he should say, "You shall not make me a drudge to your malice." A good resolve, if he would but have stuck to it. He found no fault in him, and therefore should not have continued to parley with the prosecutors. Those that would be safe from sin should be deaf to temptation. Nay, he should have secured the prisoner from their insults. But Pilate had not courage enough to act according to his conscience.

3. The further colour which the prosecutors gave to their demand (*v.* 7): *We have a law, and by our law*

he ought to die, because he made himself the Son of God. They *made their boast of the law*. They had indeed an excellent law, but in vain did they boast of their law, when they abused it to such bad purposes. They discover a restless and inveterate malice against our Lord Jesus. They urged this, that he pretended himself a God. Thus they turn every stone to take him off. They pervert the law, and make that the instrument of their malice. It was true that blasphemers were to be put to death. Whoever falsely pretended to be the Son of God was guilty of blasphemy. It was false that Christ pretended to be the Son of God, for he really was so. That which was his honour, and might have been their happiness, they impute to him as a crime, for which he ought to die; yet he ought not to be crucified, for this was no death inflicted by their law.

IV. The judge brings the prisoner again to his trial, upon this new suggestion.

1. The concern Pilate was in, when he heard this alleged (*v.* 8): When he heard that his prisoner pretended not to royalty only, but to deity, he was *the more afraid*. There was the more danger of offending the people if he should acquit him. Though he might hope to pacify their rage against a pretended king, he could never reconcile them to a pretended God. There was the more danger of offending his own conscience if he should condemn him. "Is he one" (thinks Pilate) "that makes himself *the Son of God*? and what if it should prove that he is so? What will become of me then?"

2. His further examination of our Lord Jesus thereupon, *v.* 9. He resumed the debate, went into the judgment-hall, and asked Christ, *Whence art thou?*

(1) The place he chose for this examination: He *went into the judgment-hall* for privacy, that he might be out of the noise and clamour of the crowd. Those that would find out the truth as it is in Jesus must get out of the noise of prejudice, and retire as it were into the judgment-hall, to converse with Christ alone.

(2) The question he put to him: *Whence art thou?* Art thou from men or from heaven? From beneath or from above?

(3) The silence of our Lord Jesus; but *Jesus gave him no answer.* This was not a sullen silence, in contempt of the court, nor was it because he knew not what to say. It was a patient silence. This silence loudly bespoke his submission to his Father's will in his present sufferings. He was silent, because he would say nothing to hinder his sufferings. It was a prudent silence. When the chief priests asked him, *Art thou the Son of the Blessed?* he answered, *I am*; but when Pilate asked him he knew he did not understand his own question, having no notion of the Messiah, and of his being the *Son of God*, and therefore to what purpose should he reply to him whose head was filled with the pagan theology?

(4) The haughty check which Pilate gave him for his silence (*v.* 10): "*Speakest thou not unto me? Knowest thou not that I have power to crucify thee, and have power to release thee?*" Observe here how Pilate magnifies himself, and boasts of his own authority. Men in power are apt to be puffed up with their power, and the more absolute and arbitrary it is the more it gratifies and humours their pride. How he tramples upon our blessed Saviour: *Speakest thou not unto me?* He reflects upon him as if he were undutiful and disrespectful to those in authority or as if he were ungrateful to one that had been tender of him, as if he were unwise for himself. If Christ had indeed sought to save his life, now had been his time to have spoken.

(5) Christ's pertinent answer to this check, *v.* 11.

[1] He boldly rebukes his arrogance: "*Thou couldest have no power at all against me, except it were given*

thee from above." Though Christ did not think fit to answer him when he was impertinent, yet he did think fit to answer him when he was imperious. When Pilate used his power, Christ silently submitted to it; but, when he grew proud of it, he made him know himself: "All the power thou hast is given thee from above." His power in general, as a magistrate, was a limited power, and he could do no more than God would suffer him to do. Let the proud oppressors know that there is *a higher than they.* And let this silence the murmurings of the oppressed, let it comfort them that their persecutors can do no more than God will let them. Pilate never fancied himself to look so great as now, when he sat in judgment upon such a prisoner as this, who was looked upon by many as the *Son of God* and king of Israel. But Christ lets him know that he was herein but an instrument in God's hand.

[2] He mildly excuses his sin, in comparison with the sin of the ringleaders: "*Therefore he that delivered me unto thee* lies under greater guilt." It is plainly intimated that what Pilate did was sin, a great sin, and that the forces which the Jews put upon him would not justify him. The guilt of others will not acquit us, nor will it avail in the great day to say that others were worse than we. Yet theirs that delivered him to Pilate was the greater sin. By this it appears that all sins are not equal, but some more heinous than others. *He that delivered Christ to Pilate* was either, 1. The people of the Jews, who cried out, *Crucify him, crucify him.* They had seen Christ's miracles, which Pilate had not, and therefore it was much worse in them to appear against him than in Pilate. 2. Or Caiaphas in particular, who first advised his death, *ch.* xi. 49, 50. The sin of Caiaphas was abundantly greater than the sin of Pilate. Caiaphas prosecuted Christ from pure enmity and of malice prepense. Pilate condemned him purely for fear of the people, and it was a hasty resolution which he had not time to cool upon. 3. Some think Christ means Judas. The sin of Judas was, upon many accounts, greater than the sin of Pilate. The sin of Judas was a leading sin, and let in all that followed. He was a *guide to them that took Jesus.*

V. Pilate struggles with the Jews to deliver Jesus out of their hands, but in vain.

1. Pilate seems more zealous than before to get Jesus discharged (*v.* 12): *Thenceforth,* though Christ found fault with him, he still continued to find no fault in Christ, but *sought to release him.* If Pilate's policy had not prevailed above his justice, he would not have been long seeking to release him, but would have done it.

2. The Jews were more violent to get Jesus crucified. Still they carry on their design with noise and clamour as before. They laboured to get him cried down by a multitude, and it is no hard matter to pack a mob. A few madmen may out-shout many wise men, and then fancy themselves to speak the sense (when it is but the nonsense) of a nation, but it is not so easy a thing to change the sense of the people as it is to misrepresent it. In this outcry they sought: To blacken the prisoner as an enemy to Caesar. They will have it that he *speaks against Caesar.* It has always been the artifice of the enemies of religion to represent it as hurtful to kings and provinces, when it would be highly beneficial to both. To frighten the judge, as no friend to Caesar: "If thou *let this man go thou art not Caesar's friend.*" They intimate a threatening that they would inform against him, and here they touched him in a sensible and very tender part. A pretended zeal for that which is good often serves to cover a real malice against that which is better.

3. Pilate slightly endeavoured to banter them out of their fury, and yet, in doing this, yielded to the rapid stream, *v.* 13–15. After he had seemed now as

if he would have made a vigorous resistance upon this attack (*v.* 12), he basely surrendered.

(1) What it was that shocked Pilate (*v.* 13): "*When he heard that saying,* that he could not be sure of Caesar's favour, if he did not put Jesus to death, then he thought it was time to look about him." Those that bind up their happiness in the favour of men make themselves an easy prey to the temptations of Satan.

(2) What preparation was made for a definitive sentence upon this matter: *Pilate brought Jesus forth,* and then *sat down in the judgment-seat.* Christ was condemned with all the ceremony that could be. Notice is here taken of the place and time. The place where Christ was condemned: in a *place called the Pavement, but in Hebrew, Gabbatha,* probably the place where he used to sit to try causes or criminals. The time, *v.* 14. It was the preparation of the passover, and *about the sixth hour.* 1. The day: It was the preparation of the passover, that is, for the passover-sabbath. It was when they should have been purging out the old leaven, to get ready for the passover; but the better the day the worse the deed. 2. The hour: *It was about the sixth hour.* Some ancient Greek and Latin manuscripts read it about the third hour, which agrees with Mark xv. 25. And it appears by Matt. xxvii. 45 that he was upon the cross before the sixth hour. From the third to the sixth hour (which was, as we call it, church-time) on that day, they were employed in this wickedness; so that for this day, though they were priests, they dropped the temple-service.

(3) The rencounter Pilate had with the Jews, endeavouring in vain to stem the tide of their rage. He saith unto the Jews: "*Behold your king,* that is, him whom you accuse as a pretender to the crown. Is this a man likely to be dangerous to the government?" Pilate, though he was far from meaning so, seems as if he were the voice of God to them. Christ, now crowned with thorns, is, as a king at his coronation, offered to the people: "*Behold your king.*" They cried out with the greatest indignation, *Away with him, away with him.* "*Take him,* he is none of ours; we disown him; *away with him* out of our sight." Had not Christ been thus rejected of men, we had been for ever rejected of God. It shows how we ought to treat our sins. We are often in scripture said to crucify sin, in conformity to Christ's death. With a pious indignation we should run down sin in us, as they with an impious indignation ran him down who was made sin for us. Pilate, willing to have Jesus released, asks them, *Shall I crucify your king?* To stop their mouths, by showing them how absurd it was for them to reject one who offered himself to them to be their king. Though he saw no cause to fear him, they might see cause to hope for something from him. To stop the mouth of his own conscience. "If this Jesus be a king" (thinks Pilate), "he is only king of the Jews. If they refuse him, and will have their king crucified, what is that to me?" The chief priests cried out, *We have no king but Caesar.* This they knew would please Pilate, and so they hoped to carry their point, though at the same time they hated Caesar and his government. What a righteous thing it was with God to bring upon them that ruin by the Romans which followed not long after. They adhere to Caesar, and to Caesar they shall go. God soon gave them enough of their Caesars. Henceforward they were rebels to the Caesars, and the Caesars tyrants to them, and their disaffection ended in the overthrow of their place and nation. It is just with God to make that a scourge and plague to us which we prefer before Christ.

Verses 16–18

We have here sentence of death passed upon our Lord Jesus, and execution done soon after. A mighty struggle Pilate had had within him; but at length his convictions yielded, and his corruptions prevailed, the fear of man having a greater power over him than the fear of God.

I. *Pilate gave judgment* against Christ and signed the warrant for his execution, *v.* 16. Pilate sinned against his conscience; he had again and again pronounced him innocent, and yet at last condemned him as guilty. He was a man of a haughty and implacable spirit. Fearing therefore that he should be complained of, he was willing to gratify the Jews. Now this makes the matter much worse. For a man that was so wilful in other things, and of so fierce a resolution, to be overcome in a thing of this nature, shows him to be a bad man indeed, that could better bear the wronging of his conscience than the crossing of his humour. He endeavoured to transfer the guilt upon the Jews. He *delivered him* to the prosecutors, the chief priests and elders; so excusing the wrong to his own conscience with this, that it was but a permissive condemnation, and that he did not put Christ to death, but only connived at those that did it.

II. Judgment was no sooner given than the prosecutors, having gained their point, resolved to lose no time lest Pilate should change his mind. And also lest there should be *an uproar among the people.* It were well if we would be thus expeditious in that which is good, and not stay for more difficulties.

1. They immediately hurried away the prisoner. The chief priests greedily flew upon the prey which they had been long waiting for. Or *they*, that is, the soldiers, took him and led him away. Both the priests and the soldiers joined in leading him away. By the law of Moses the prosecutors were to be the executioners. And the priests here were proud of the office. He was led forth for us, that we might escape.

2. To add to his misery, they obliged him to carry his cross (*v.* 17), according to the custom among the Romans. Their crosses did not stand up constantly. Everyone that was crucified had a cross of his own. Christ's carrying his cross may be considered as a part of his sufferings; he endured the cross literally. The blessed body of the Lord Jesus was tender; it had now lately been harassed and tired out; his shoulders were sore with the stripes they had given him; every jog of the cross would renew his smart, and be apt to strike the thorns he was crowned with into his head; yet all this he patiently underwent. He was made a curse for us, and therefore on him was the cross. Our Master hereby taught all his disciples to take up their cross, and follow him. Whatever cross he calls us out to bear at any time, we must remember that he bore the cross first. He bore that end of the cross that had the curse upon it; this was the heavy end; and hence all that are his are enabled to call their afflictions for him *light.*

3. They brought him to the place of execution: He *went forth*, not dragged against his will, but voluntary in his sufferings. He went forth out of the city, for he was *crucified without the gate*, Heb. xiii. 12. And, to put the greater infamy upon his sufferings, he was brought to the common place of execution, a place called *Golgotha, the place of a skull.* There Christ suffered, because he was *made sin for us.*

4. There they crucified him, and the other malefactors with him (*v.* 18): *There they crucified him.* (1) What death Christ died; the death of the cross, a bloody, painful, shameful death, a cursed death. He was lifted up as the brazen serpent. His hands were stretched out to invite and embrace us. (2) In what company he died: *Two others with him.* This exposed him much to the people's contempt and hatred, who are apt to judge of persons by the lump, and are not curious in distinguishing, and would conclude him not only a malefactor because he was yoked with malefactors, but the worst of the three because

put in the midst. But thus the scripture was fulfilled, *He was numbered among the transgressors.* He died among the criminals, and mingled his blood with theirs who were sacrificed to public justice.

And now let us pause awhile, and with an eye of faith look upon Jesus. Was ever sorrow like unto his sorrow? See him bleeding, see him struggling, see him dying, see him and love him, love him and live to him, and study what we shall render.

Verses 19–30

Here are some remarkable circumstances of Christ's dying more fully related than before.

I. The title set up over his head.

1. The inscription itself which Pilate wrote, and ordered to be fixed to the top of the cross, declaring the cause for which he was crucified, *v.* 19. It was this, *Jesus of Nazareth, the King of the Jews.* Pilate intended this for his reproach, that he, being *Jesus of Nazareth*, should pretend to be king of the Jews, and set up in competition with Caesar. But God overruled this matter: That it might be a further testimony to the innocence of our Lord Jesus; for here was an accusation which, as it was worded, contained no crime. That it might show forth his dignity and honour. This is Jesus a Saviour, dying for the good of his people, as Caiaphas had foretold.

2. The notice taken of this inscription (*v.* 20): *Many of the Jews read it*, not only those of Jerusalem, but those from other countries, that came up to worship at the feast. Multitudes read it, and it occasioned a great variety of reflections and speculations. Christ himself was set for a sign, a title. The title was so much read: Because the place where Jesus was crucified, though without the gate, was yet *nigh the city.* It is an advantage to have the means of knowing Christ brought to our doors. Because it was written in Hebrew, and Greek, and Latin; they all understood one or other of these languages. Everyone would be curious to enquire what it was which was so industriously published in the three most-known languages. In each of these Christ is proclaimed king. It was intimated thereby that Jesus Christ should be a Saviour to all nations, and not to the Jews only; and also that every nation should hear *in their own tongue the wonderful works* of the Redeemer. It teaches us that the knowledge of Christ ought to be diffused throughout every nation in their own tongue, that people may converse as freely with the scriptures as they do with their neighbours.

3. The offence which the prosecutors took at it, *v.* 21. They would not have it written, *the king of the Jews*; but that he said *I am the king of the Jews.* Here they show themselves: Very spiteful and malicious against Christ. To justify themselves they thought themselves concerned to represent him as a usurper of honours and powers that he was not entitled to. Foolishly jealous of the honour of their nation. They scorned to have it said that this was their king. Very impertinent and troublesome to Pilate. They could not but be sensible that they had forced him, against his mind, to condemn Christ. Though they had charged him with pretending to be the king of the Jews, yet they had not proved it

4. The judge's resolution to adhere to it: *"What I have written I have written."*

1. Hereby an affront was put upon the chief priests. By this inscription he insinuates: That, notwithstanding their pretences, they were not sincere in their affections to Caesar and his government. That such a king as this, so mean and despicable, was good enough to be the king of the Jews. That they had been very unjust in prosecuting this Jesus, when there was no fault to be found in him.

2. Hereby honour was done to the Lord Jesus. Pilate stuck to it with resolution, that he was the

king of the Jews. When the Jews reject Christ Pilate, a Gentile, sticks to it that he is a king, which was an earnest of what came to pass soon after, when the Gentiles submitted to the kingdom of the Messiah.

II. The dividing of his garments among the executioners, v. 23, 24. Four soldiers were employed, who, *when they had crucified Jesus*, had nailed him to the cross, and lifted it up, and him upon it, and nothing more was to be done than to wait his expiring, went to make a dividend of his clothes. And so they *made four parts*, as nearly of the same value as they could, *to every soldier a part*; but *his coat, without seam, woven from the top throughout*, they *cast lots for it*. 1. The shame they put upon our Lord Jesus. The shame of nakedness came in with sin. He therefore who was made sin for us bore that shame. 2. The wages with which these soldiers paid themselves for crucifying Christ. They were willing to do it for his old clothes. Nothing is to be done so bad, but there will be found men bad enough to do it for a trifle. 3. The sport they made about his seamless coat. We read not of anything about him valuable or remarkable but this. Tradition says, his mother wove it for him, and adds this further, that it was made for him when he was a child. But this is a groundless fancy. The soldiers thought it a pity to rend it for then it would unravel; they would *therefore cast lots for it*. While Christ was in his dying agonies, they were merrily dividing his spoils. The preserving of Christ's seamless coat is commonly alluded to to show the care all Christians ought to take that they rend not the church of Christ with strifes and divisions. 4. The fulfilling of the scripture in this. David, in spirit, foretold this very circumstance of Christ's sufferings, in that passage, Ps. xxii. 18. *These things therefore the soldiers did.*

III. The care that he took of his poor mother.

1. His mother attends him to his death (v. 25): *There stood by the cross his mother*, and some of his relations and friends with her. At first, they stood near, as it is said here; but afterwards, it is probable, the soldiers forced them to stand afar off, as it is said in Matthew and Mark. See here the tender affection of these pious women. When all his disciples, except John, had forsaken him, they continued their attendance on him. They were not deterred by the fury of the enemy nor the horror of the sight; they could not rescue him nor relieve him, yet they attended him. We may easily suppose what an affliction it was to these poor women to see him thus abused, especially to the blessed virgin. Now was fulfilled Simeon's word, *A sword shall pierce through thy own soul*, Luke ii. 35. His torments were her tortures, and her heart bled with his wounds. We may justly admire the power of divine grace in supporting these women, especially the virgin Mary. We do not find his mother wringing her hands or making an outcry; but *standing by the cross*, and her friends with her. Surely she and they were strengthened by a divine power to this degree of patience. We know not what we can bear till we are tried, and then we know who has said, *My grace is sufficient for thee.*

2. He tenderly provides for his mother. It is probable that Joseph was long since dead, and that her son Jesus had supported her, and now that he was dying what would become of her? He saw her standing by, and he saw John standing not far off, and so he settled a new relation between his beloved mother and his beloved disciple: "*Woman, behold thy son*," and to him, "*Behold thy mother*." And so *from that hour that disciple took her to his own home.*

(1) The care Christ took of his dear mother. He was not so much taken up with a sense of his sufferings as to forget his friends. He had no other way to provide for his mother than by his interest in a

friend, which he does here. He calls her *woman*, not mother, because mother would have been a cutting word to her that was already wounded to the heart with grief. He directs her to look upon John as her son. An instance of divine goodness. Sometimes, when God removes one comfort from us, he raises up another for us, perhaps where we looked not for it. Let none therefore reckon all gone with one cistern dried up, for from the same fountain another may be filled. An instance of filial duty. Christ has here taught children to provide for the comfort of their aged parents. Children at their death, according to their ability, should provide for their parents, if they survive them, and need their kindness.

(2) The confidence he reposed in the beloved disciple. It is to him he says, *Behold thy mother*. This was an honour put upon John, and a testimony both to his prudence and to his fidelity. It is a great honour to be employed for Christ, and to be entrusted with any of his interest in the world. It would be a care and some charge to John; but he cheerfully accepted it, *and took her to his own home*. Those that truly love Christ, and are beloved of him, will be glad of an opportunity to do any service to him or his.

IV. The fulfilling of the scripture, in the giving of him vinegar to drink, v. 28, 29.

1. How much respect Christ showed to the scripture (v. 28): *Knowing that all things were accomplished, that the scripture might be fulfilled, he saith, I thirst.*

(1) It was not at all strange that he was thirsty. Well might he thirst after all the toil and hurry which he had undergone, and being now in the agonies of death, ready to expire purely by the loss of blood and extremity of pain.

(2) But the reason of his complaining of it is somewhat surprising; it is the only word he spoke that looked like complaint of his outward sufferings. He cried, *I thirst*. He would thus express *the travail of his soul*. He thirsted after the accomplishment of the work of our redemption. He would thus take care to see the scripture fulfilled. Hitherto, all had been accomplished, and he knew it. The scripture had foretold his thirst, and therefore he himself related it, because it could not otherwise be known, saying, *I thirst*. The scripture had foretold that in his thirst he should have vinegar given him to drink, Ps. lxix. 21.

2. See how little respect his persecutors showed to him (v. 29): *There was set a vessel full of vinegar*, probably according to the custom at all executions of this nature; with this *they filled a sponge, and they put it upon hyssop*, a hyssop-stalk, and with this heaved it to his mouth. A drop of water would have cooled his tongue better than a draught of vinegar. When heaven denied him a beam of light earth denied him a drop of water, and put vinegar in the room of it.

V. The dying word wherewith he breathed out his soul (v. 30): *When he had received the vinegar he said, It is finished;* and, with that, *bowed his head, and gave up the ghost.*

1. What he said, and we may suppose him to say it with triumph and exultation—*It is finished. It is finished*, that is, the malice and enmity of his persecutors had now done their worst. (2) *It is finished*, that is, the counsel and commandment of his Father concerning his sufferings were now fulfilled. He had said, when he entered upon his sufferings, *Father, thy will be done;* and now he saith with pleasure, *It is done*. (3) *It is finished*, that is, all the types and prophecies of the Old Testament, which pointed at the sufferings of the Messiah, were accomplished and answered. (4) *It is finished*, that is, the ceremonial law is abolished. The substance is now come, and all the shadows are done away. (5) *It is finished*, that is, sin is finished, and an end made of transgression.

The Lamb of God was sacrificed to take away the sin of the world, and it is done. (6) *It is finished*, that is, his sufferings were now finished. The storm is over, the worst is past, and he is just entering upon *the joy set before him*. Let all that *suffer for Christ*, and with Christ, comfort themselves with this, *that yet a little while* and they also shall say, *It is finished*. (7) *It is finished*, that is, his life was now finished, he was just ready to breathe his last. This we must all come to shortly. (8) *It is finished*, that is, the work of man's redemption and salvation is now completed, a fatal blow given to the power of Satan, a fountain of grace opened that shall ever flow. *He that has begun a good work will perform it;* the mystery of God shall be finished.

2. What he did: *He bowed his head, and gave up the ghost. He gave up the ghost.* His life was not forcibly extorted from him, but freely resigned. He had said, *Father, into thy hands I commit my spirit,* and, accordingly, he did give up his spirit, paid down the price of pardon and life at his Father's hands. *He bowed his head.* Those that were crucified, in dying stretched up their heads to gasp for breath, and did not drop their heads till they had breathed their last; but Christ *bowed his head* first, composing himself, as it were, to fall asleep.

Verses 31–37

This passage concerning the piercing of Christ's side after his death is recorded only by this evangelist.

I. Observe the superstition of the Jews, which occasioned it (*v.* 31): *Because it was the preparation for the sabbath, and that sabbath day was a high day*, they would *not have the dead bodies to remain on the crosses on the sabbath-day*, but *besought Pilate that their legs might be broken*, and that then they might be buried out of sight. 1. The esteem they would be thought to have for the approaching sabbath. Every sabbath day is a holy day, and a good day, but this was a high day, *a great day*. Sacrament-days, supper-days, communion-days are high days, and there ought to be more than ordinary preparation for them. 2. The reproach which they reckoned it would be to that day if the dead bodies should be left hanging on the crosses. Dead bodies were not to be left at any time. Many strangers from all parts being then at Jerusalem, it would have been an offence to them; nor could they well bear the sight of Christ's crucified body. 3. Their petition to Pilate, that their bodies, now as good as dead, might be despatched by the breaking of their legs, which would carry them off in the most exquisite pain. The pretended sanctity of hypocrites is abominable. They made no conscience of bringing an innocent and excellent person to the cross, and yet scrupled letting a dead body hang upon the cross.

II. The despatching of the *two thieves that were crucified with him*, *v.* 32. Pilate gave orders as they desired; *and the soldiers came and broke the legs of the two thieves.* One of these thieves was a penitent, and had received from Christ an assurance that he should shortly be with him in paradise, and yet died in the same pain and misery that the other thief did. The extremity of dying agonies is no obstruction to the living comforts that wait for holy souls on the other side death.

III. The trial that was made whether Christ was dead or no.

1. They supposed him to be dead, and therefore *did not break his legs, v.* 33. Jesus died in less time than persons crucified ordinarily did. It was to show that he laid down his life of himself. He yielded to death, yet he was not conquered. His enemies were satisfied he was really dead.

2. Because they would be sure he was dead they would put it past dispute. *One of the soldiers with a spear pierced his side and forthwith came thereout blood and water, v.* 34.

(1) The soldier hereby designed to decide the question whether he was dead or no, and by this honourable wound in his side to supersede the ignominious method of despatch they took with the other two. Tradition says that this soldier's name was *Longinus.*

(2) But God had a further design herein. To give an evidence of the truth of his death, in order to the proof of his resurrection. He was certainly dead, for this spear broke up the very fountains of life. To give an illustration of the design of his death. There was much of mystery in it, and its being so solemnly attested (*v.* 35) intimates there was something miraculous in it. It was very significant; this same apostle refers to it as a very considerable thing, 1 John v. 6, 8. The opening of his side was significant. When we would protest our sincerity, we wish there were a window in our hearts, that the thoughts and intents of them might be visible to all. Through this window, opened in Christ's side, you may look into his heart, and see love flaming there, love strong as death. *The blood and water* that flowed out of it were significant. They signified the two great benefits which all believers partake of through Christ —blood for atonement, water for purification. Guilt contracted must be expiated by blood; stains contracted must be done away by *the water of purification*. These two must always go together. Christ has joined them together, and we must not think to put them asunder. They both flowed from the pierced side of our Redeemer. They signified the two great ordinances of baptism and the Lord's supper. It is not the water in the font that will be to us *the washing of regeneration*, but the water out of the side of Christ; not the blood of the grape that will refresh the soul, but the blood out of the side of Christ.

IV. The attestation of the truth of this by an eyewitness (*v.* 35), the evangelist himself.

1. What a competent witness he was of the matters of fact. What he bore record of he saw; he was an eye-witness of it. What he saw he faithfully bore record of; he told not only the truth, but the whole truth. *His record is* undoubtedly *true*, for he wrote from the dictates of the Spirit of truth. He had himself a full assurance of the truth of what he wrote: *He knows that he saith true.* He *therefore* witnessed these things, *that we might believe*; to draw men to believe the gospel in order to their eternal welfare.

2. What care he showed in this particular instance. Let this silence the fears of weak Christians, and encourage their hopes. There came both water and blood out of Christ's pierced side, both to justify and sanctify them; and if you ask, How can we be sure of this? you may be sure, for *he that saw it bore record.*

V. The accomplishment of the scripture in all this (*v.* 36): *That the scripture might be fulfilled.*

1. The scripture was fulfilled in the preserving of his legs from being broken; therein that word was fulfilled, *A bone of him shall not be broken.* There was a promise of this made indeed to all *the righteous*, but principally pointing at *Jesus Christ the righteous* (Ps. xxxiv. 20). There was a type of this in the paschal lamb (Num. ix. 12): *You shall not break any bone of it.* He is *the Lamb of God* (ch. i. 29), and, as the true passover, his bones were kept unbroken. There was a significancy in it; the strength of the body is in the bones. The Hebrew word for the bones signifies the strength. Though *he be crucified in weakness* his strength to save is not at all broken. Sin breaks our bones but it did not break Christ's bones; he stood firm under the burden, mighty to save.

2. *The scripture was fulfilled* in *the piercing of his side* (v. 27): *They shall look on me whom they had pierced;* so it is written, Zech. xii. 10. It is here implied that the Messiah shall be pierced; and here it had a more full accomplishment than in *the piercing of his hands and feet.* It is promised that *when the Spirit is poured out they shall look on him and mourn.* This was in part fulfilled when many of those that were his betrayers and murderers *were pricked to the heart,* and brought to believe in him. We have all been guilty of piercing the Lord Jesus, and are all concerned with suitable affections to look on him.

Verses 38–42

We have here an account of the burial of the blessed body of our Lord Jesus. Come and see a burial that conquered the grave, and buried it, a burial that beautified the grave and softened it for all believers.

I. The body begged, *v.* 38. This was done by *Joseph of Arimathea,* of whom no mention is made in all the New Testament story, but only in the narrative which each of the evangelists gives us of Christ's burial. 1. The character of this Joseph. He was a disciple of Christ *in secret,* a better friend to Christ than he would willingly be known to be. It was his honour that he was a disciple of Christ; and some such there are, that are themselves great men, and unavoidably linked with bad men. But it was his weakness that he was so secretly. Christ may have many that are his disciples sincerely, though secretly; better secretly than not at all, especially, if like Joseph, here, they grow stronger and stronger. Some who in less trials have been timorous, yet in greater have been very courageous; so Joseph here. To Pilate the governor he *went boldly,* and yet *feared the Jews.* The impotent malice of those that can but censure, and revile, is sometimes more formidable even to wise and good men than one would think. 2. The part he bore in this affair. He, having access to Pilate, desired leave of him to dispose of the body. His disciples were gone; if nobody appeared, the Jews or soldiers would bury him with the thieves. When God has work to do he can find out such as are proper to do it, and embolden them for it. Observe it as an instance of the humiliation of Christ, that his dead body lay at the mercy of a heathen judge, and must be begged before it could be buried.

II. The embalming prepared, *v.* 39. This was done by Nicodemus, another person of quality, and in a public post. He brought a *mixture of myrrh and aloes.* 1. The character of Nicodemus, which is much the same with that of Joseph; he was a secret friend to Christ. He at first *came to Jesus by night,* but now owned him publicly, as before, *ch.* vii. 50, 51. That grace which at first is like a bruised reed may afterwards become like a strong cedar. It is a wonder that Joseph and Nicodemus, men of such interest, did not appear sooner, and solicit Pilate not to condemn Christ. Begging his life would have been a nobler piece of service than begging his body. 2. The kindness of Nicodemus. Joseph served Christ with his interest, Nicodemus with his purse. Probably, they agreed it between them, because they were straightened in time. But why did they made this ado about Christ's dead body? Some think we may see in it the weakness of their faith. What need of such furniture of the grave for one that, like a way-faring man, did but turn aside into it, to *tarry for a night or two?* However, we may plainly see in it the strength of their love. Hereby they showed the value they had for his person and doctrine, and that it was not lessened by the reproach of the cross. They showed not only the charitable respect of committing his body to the earth, but the honourable respect shown to

great men. This they might do, and yet believe and look for his resurrection. Since God designed honour for this body, they would put honour upon it.

III. The body got ready, *v.* 40. They *took it,* and, having washed it from blood and dust, *wound it in linen clothes,* with the spices, as *the manner of the Jews is to bury.* Here was care taken of Christ's body: It was *wound in linen clothes.* Among clothing that belongs to us, Christ put on even the grave-clothes, to make them easy to us, and to enable us to call them our wedding-clothes. Dead bodies and graves are noisome and offensive. No ointment or perfume can rejoice the heart so as the grave of our Redeemer does, where there is faith to perceive the fragrant odours of it. In conformity to this example, we ought to have regard to the dead bodies of Christians; not to enshrine and adore their relics, but carefully to deposit them, the dust in the dust, as those who believe that the dead bodies of the saints are still united to Christ. The resurrection of the saints will be in virtue of Christ's resurrection, and therefore in burying them we should have an eye to Christ's burial.

IV. The grave pitched upon, in a garden which belonged to Joseph of Arimathea, very near the place where he was crucified. There was a sepulchre not yet used.

1. Christ was buried without the city, for thus the manner of the Jews was to bury. There was then a peculiar reason for it, because the touching of a grave contracted a ceremonial pollution: but now that the resurrection of Christ has altered the property of the grave, we need not keep at such a distance from it. Those that would not superstitiously, but by faith, visit the holy sepulchre, must go forth out of the noise of this world.

2. Christ was buried in a garden. Joseph had his sepulchre in his garden that it might be a memento: To himself while living. The garden is a proper place for meditation, and a sepulchre there may furnish us with a proper subject for meditation. To his heirs and successors when he was gone. It is good to acquaint ourselves with the *place of our fathers' sepulchres;* and perhaps we might make our own less formidable if we made theirs more familiar. In a sepulchre in a garden Christ's body was laid. In the garden of Eden death and the grave first received their power, and now in a garden they are conquered.

3. He was buried in a new sepulchre. This was so ordered, (1) For the honour of Christ. He that was born from a virgin-womb must rise from a virgin-tomb. (2) For the confirming of the truth of his resurrection, that it might not be suggested that it was not he, but some other that rose. He that has *made all things new* has new-made the grave for us.

V. The funeral solemnized (*v.* 42): *There laid they Jesus.* There they laid him because it was the preparation day.

1. The deference which the Jews paid to the sabbath, and to the day of preparation. This day had been ill kept by the chief priests, who called themselves the church, but was well kept by the disciples of Christ, who were branded as dangerous to the church; and it is often so. They would not put off the funeral till the sabbath day, because the sabbath is to be a day of holy rest and joy. They would not drive it too late on the day of preparation for the sabbath.

2. The convenience they took of an adjoining sepulchre; the sepulchre they made use of was *nigh at hand.* It was so ordered that he should be laid in a sepulchre nigh at hand: Because he was to lie there but awhile, as in an inn, and therefore he took the first that offered itself. Because this was a new sepulchre. Those that prepared it little thought who

should handsel it. We are hereby taught not to be over-curious in the place of our burial. Where the tree falls, why should it not lie? For Christ was buried in the sepulchre that was next at hand.

Thus without pomp or solemnity is the body of Jesus laid in the cold and silent grave. Here lies death itself slain, and the grave conquered. *Thanks be to God, who giveth us the victory.*

CHAPTER 20

This evangelist, though he began not his gospel as the rest did, yet concludes it as they did, with the history of Christ's resurrection; not of the thing itself, but of the proofs and evidences of it. The proofs of Christ's resurrection, which we have in this chapter, are, I. Such as occurred immediately at the sepulchre. 1. The sepulchre found empty, ver. 1–10. 2. Two angels appearing to Mary Magdalene at the sepulchre, ver. 11–13. 3. Christ himself appearing to her, ver. 14–18. II. Such as occurred afterwards at the meetings of the apostles. 1. At one, the same day at evening that Christ rose, when Thomas was absent, ver. 19–25. 2. At another, that day seven-night, when Thomas was with them, ver. 26–31.

Verses 1–10

There was no one thing of which the apostles were more concerned to produce substantial proof than the resurrection of their Master, 1. Because it was that which he himself appealed to as the last and most cogent proof of his being the Messiah. And therefore enemies were most solicitous to stifle the notice of this. 2. Because it was upon this the performance of his undertaking for our redemption and salvation did depend. 3. Because he never showed himself alive after his resurrection to all the people, Acts x. 40, 41. But the demonstrations of his resurrection should be reserved as a favour for his particular friends, and by them be published to the world, that those might be blessed who have not seen, and yet have believed.

In these verses we have the first step towards the proof of Christ's resurrection, which is, that the sepulchre was found empty.

I. Mary Magdalene, coming to the sepulchre, finds the *stone taken away.* This evangelist does not mention the other women that went with Mary Magdalene, but her only. Much was forgiven her, therefore she loved much. She had shown her affection to him while he lived, attended his doctrine, ministered to him of her substance, Luke viii. 2, 3. The continued instances of her respect to him at and after his death prove the sincerity of her love. Love to Christ, if it be cordial, will be constant. Her love to Christ was *strong as death,* the death of the cross, for it stood by that.

1. She *came to the sepulchre,* to wash the dead body with her tears, for she *went to the grave, to weep there,* and to *anoint it with the ointment* she had prepared. It must be an extraordinary affection to the person which will endear his grave to us. It is especially frightful to the weak and timorous sex. Love to Christ will take off the terror of death and the grave. If we cannot come to Christ but through that darksome valley, even in that, if we love him, we shall *fear no evil.*

2. She came as soon as she could. Upon the *first day of the week,* as soon as ever the sabbath was gone. This was the first Christian sabbath, and she begins it accordingly with enquiries after Christ. She came *early, while it was yet dark.* Those who would seek Christ so as to find him must seek him early. Seek him solicitously; be up early for fear of missing him. Seek him industriously. Seek him betimes. That day is in a fair way to be well ended that is thus begun. Those that diligently enquire after Christ *while it is yet dark* shall have such light given them concerning him as shall shine *more and more.*

3. She found the stone taken away, which she had seen *rolled to the door of the sepulchre.* Now this was, (1) A surprise to her. Christ crucified is

the fountain of life. His grave is one of the wells of salvation; if we come to it in faith, we shall find the stone rolled away and free access to the comforts of it. Surprising comforts are the frequent encouragements of early seekers. (2) The beginning of a glorious discovery; the Lord was risen, though she did not at first apprehend it so. Those that are most constant in their adherence to Christ have commonly the first and sweetest notices of the divine grace. Mary Magdalene, who followed Christ to the last in his humiliation, met him with the first in his exaltation.

II. Finding the stone taken away, she hastens back to Peter and John: *"They have taken the Lord out of the sepulchre, and we know not where they have laid him."* She found the stone gone, looked into the grave, and saw it empty. Now one would expect that the first thought that offered itself would have been, Surely the Lord is risen; for whenever he had told them that he should be crucified, he still subjoined in the same breath that *the third day he should rise again.* Could she now see the grave empty, and yet have no thought of the resurrection enter into her mind? When we come to reflect upon our own conduct in a *cloudy and dark day,* we shall stand amazed at our dulness and forgetfulness, that we could miss of such thoughts as afterwards appear obvious. She suggested, *They have taken away the Lord.* Whatever was her suspicion, it seems it was a great vexation and disturbance to her that the body was gone; whereas, if she had understood it rightly, nothing could be more happy. Weak believers often make that the matter of their complaint which is really just ground of hope, and matter of joy. She did not stand poring upon the grief herself, but acquaints her friends with it. The communication of sorrows is one good improvement of the communion of saints. Peter, though he had denied his Master, had not deserted his Master's friends; by this appears the sincerity of his repentance. And the disciples' keeping up their intimacy with him as formerly, teaches us to restore those that have been faulty. If God has received them upon their repentance, why should not we?

III. Peter and John go with all speed to the sepulchre, *v.* 3, 4. Some think that the other disciples were with Peter and John when the news came; for they *told these things to the eleven,* Luke xxiv. 9. Yet none of them went to the sepulchre but Peter and John, who were often distinguished from the rest by special favours. It is well when those that are more honoured than others with the privileges of disciples are more active than others in the duty of disciples, more willing to take pains and run hazards. See here what use we should make of the experience of others. When Mary told them what she had seen, they would go and see with their own eyes. Do others tell us of the comfort and benefit of ordinances? Let us be engaged thereby to make trial of them. See how ready we should be to share with our friends in their cares and fears. Peter and John hastened to the sepulchre. See what haste we should make in a good work. Peter and John consulted neither their ease nor their gravity, but ran to the sepulchre. See what a good thing it is to have good company in a good work. See what a laudable emulation it is among disciples to strive which shall excel in that which is good. It was no breach of ill manners for John to outrun Peter. We must do our best, and neither envy those that can do better, nor despise those that do as they can, though they come behind. He that got foremost in this race was *the disciple whom Jesus loved.* Sense of Christ's love to us, kindling love in us to him again, will make us to excel in virtue. He that was cast behind was Peter, who had denied his Master, and was in sorrow and shame for it. When conscience is offended we lose ground.

IV. Peter and John, having come to the sepulchre, prosecute the enquiry.

1. John went no further than Mary Magdalene had done. He had the curiosity to look into the sepulchre, and saw it was empty. He *stooped down*, and *looked in*. Those that would find the knowledge of Christ must stoop down, and look in. Yet he had not courage to go into the sepulchre. The warmest affections are not always accompanied with the boldest resolutions.

2. Peter went in first and made a more exact discovery than John had done, *v.* 6, 7. While John was with much caution looking in, he came, and with great courage *went into the sepulchre*. The boldness of Peter, and how God dispenses his gifts variously. John could out-run Peter, but Peter could out-dare John. Some disciples are quick, and they are useful to quicken those that are slow; others are bold, and they are useful to embolden those that are timorous. Those who in good earnest seek after Christ must not frighten themselves with bugbears and foolish fancies. Good Christians need not be afraid of the grave, since Christ has lain in it. Let us therefore not indulge, but conquer, the fear we are apt to conceive upon the sight of a dead body, or being alone among the graves. We must be willing to go through the grave to Christ; that way he went to his glory, and so must we. If we cannot see God's face and live, better die than never see it. The posture in which he found things in the sepulchre. Christ had left his grave-clothes behind him there. He laid them aside because he arose to die no more. Lazarus came out with his grave-clothes on, for he was to use them again. When we arise from the death of sin to the life of righteousness, we must leave our grave-clothes behind us, must put off all our corruptions. Christ left those in the grave, as it were, for our use; if the grave be a bed to the saints, thus he hath sheeted that bed, and made it ready for them. The grave-clothes were found in very good order, which serves for an evidence that his body was not stolen away while men slept. Peter's boldness encouraged John; now he took heart and ventured in (*v.* 8), and *he saw and believed*. He began to believe that Jesus was risen to life again.

(1) John followed Peter in venturing. He durst not have gone into the sepulchre if Peter had not gone in first. It is good to be emboldened in a good work by the boldness of others. The dread of difficulty and danger will be taken off by observing the resolution and courage of others. Perhaps John's quickness had made Peter run faster, and now Peter's boldness makes John venture further. John not only associated with Peter, but thought it no disparagement to follow him.

(2) John got the start of Peter in believing. Peter saw and wondered (Luke xxiv. 12), but John saw and believed. A mind disposed to contemplation may perhaps sooner receive the evidence of divine truth than a mind disposed to action. But what was the reason that they were so slow of heart to believe? The evangelist tells us (*v.* 9), as yet they *knew not the scripture* that he must *rise again from the dead*. *First*, How unapt the disciples themselves were, at first, to believe the resurrection of Christ, which confirms the testimony they afterwards gave with so much assurance concerning it; for, by their backwardness to believe it, it appears that they were not credulous concerning it, nor of those simple ones that believe every word. It was to them as a strange thing, and one of the furthest things from their thoughts. Peter and John were so shy of believing it at first that nothing less than the most convincing proof could bring them to testify it afterwards with so much assurance. Hereby it appears that they were not only honest men, who would not deceive others,

but cautious men, who would not themselves be imposed upon. *Secondly*, The reason of their slowness to believe; because as yet they *knew not the scripture*. This seems to be the evangelist's acknowledgment of his own fault among the rest.

3. Peter and John pursued their enquiry no further, hovering between faith and unbelief (*v.* 10): *The disciples went away to their own home*. For fear of being taken up upon suspicion of a design to steal away the body, or of being charged with it now that it was gone. In difficult dangerous times it is hard even for good men to go on in their work with the resolution that becomes them. Because they were at a loss, and knew not what to do next, nor what to make of what they had seen; which is an instance of their weakness as yet. It is probable that the rest of the disciples were together; to them they return, to make report of what they had discovered. It is observable that before Peter and John came to the sepulchre an angel had appeared there, rolled away the stone, frightened the guard, and comforted the women; as soon as they were gone from the sepulchre, Mary Magdalene here sees two angels in the sepulchre (*v.* 12), and yet Peter and John come to the sepulchre, and go into it, and see none. Angels appear and disappear at pleasure, according to the orders and instructions given them. They may be, and are really, where they are not visibly. This favour was shown to those who were early and constant in their enquiries after Christ, and was the reward of those that came first and stayed last, but denied to those that made a transient visit.

Verses 11–18

I. The constancy and fervency of Mary Magdalene's affection to the Lord Jesus, *v.* 11.

1. She stayed at the sepulchre, when Peter and John were gone, because there her Master had lain. This good woman, though she has lost him, will abide by his grave for his sake, and continue in his love even when she wants the comfort of it.

2. She stayed there weeping, and these tears loudly bespoke her affection to her Master. Those that have lost Christ have cause to weep. Those that seek Christ must weep, not for him, but for themselves.

3. *As she wept, she looked into the sepulchre*. When we are in search of something that we have lost we look again and again in the place where we last left it, and expected to have found it. Weeping must not hinder seeking. Though she wept, she *stooped down and looked in*.

II. The vision she had of two angels in the sepulchre, *v.* 12.

1. The description of the persons she saw. They were *two angels in white, sitting* one *at the head*, and the other at the *feet*, of the grave. Their nature. They were angels, messengers from heaven, sent on purpose: To honour the Son. Now that the Son of God was again to be brought into the world, the angels have a charge to attend him, as they did at his birth. To comfort the saints, and, by giving them notice that the Lord was risen, to prepare them for the sight of him. Their number: *two*, not a *multitude of the heavenly host*, to sing praise, only two, to bear witness. Their array: They were *in white*, denoting their purity and holiness. Glorified saints, when they come to be as the angels, shall *walk with Christ in white*. Their posture and place: They sat in Christ's grave. These angels went into the grave, to teach us not to be afraid of it. Matters are so ordered that the grave is not much out of our way to heaven. These angelic guards, keeping possession of the sepulchre, when they had frightened away the guards, represents Christ's victory over the powers of darkness. Their sitting to face one another, one at his bed's head, the other at his bed's feet, may also

remind us of the two cherubim, placed one at either end of the mercy-seat, looking one at another. Christ crucified was the great propitiary, at the head and feet of which were these two cherubim, not with flaming swords, to keep us from, but welcome messengers, to direct us to, the way of life.

2. Their compassionate enquiry into the cause of Mary Magdalene's grief (*v.* 13): *Woman, why weepest thou?* A rebuke to her weeping: "*Why weepest thou,* when thou hast cause to rejoice?" Many of the floods of our tears would *dry away* before such a search as this into the fountain of them. It was designed to show how much angels are concerned at the griefs of the saints. Christians should thus sympathize with one another. It was only to make an occasion of informing her of that which would turn her mourning into rejoicing.

3. The melancholy account of her present distress: *Because they have taken away* the blessed body I came to embalm, *and I know not where they have laid it.* (1) The weakness of her faith. We often perplex ourselves needlessly with imaginary difficulties, which faith would discover to us as real advantages. (2) The strength of her love. Mary Magdalene is not diverted from her enquiries by the surprise of the vision, nor satisfied with the honour of it; but still she harps upon the same string: *They have taken away my Lord.* A sight of angels and their smiles will not suffice without a sight of Christ and God's smiles in him. Nay, the sight of angels is but an opportunity of pursuing her enquiries after Christ. The angels asked her, *Why weepest thou?* I have cause enough to weep, says she, for *they have taken away my Lord.* None know, but those who have experienced it, the sorrow of a deserted soul, that has had comfortable evidences of the love of God in Christ, but has now lost them, and walks in darkness.

III. Christ's appearing to her while she was talking with the angels. Christ himself steps in. Mary would fain know where her Lord is, and behold he is at her right hand. Those that will be content with nothing short of a sight of Christ shall be put off with nothing less. Christ, in manifesting himself to those that seek him, often outdoes their expectations. Mary longs to see the dead body of Christ, and behold she sees him alive. Thus he does for his praying people more than they are able to ask or think.

(1) He did at first conceal himself from her.

[1] He stood as a common person, and she looked upon him accordingly, *v.* 14. She *turned herself back* from talking with the angels, and *sees Jesus himself* standing, and yet she *knew not that it was Jesus. The Lord is nigh unto them that are of a broken heart* (Ps. xxxiv. 18), nearer than they are aware. Those that seek Christ, though they do not see him, may yet be sure he is not far from them. Those that diligently seek the Lord will turn every way in their enquiry after him. *Mary turned herself back,* in hopes of some discoveries. It was her earnest desire in seeking that made her turn every way. Christ is often near his people, and they are not aware of him. She *knew not that it was Jesus.*

[2] He asked her a common question, and she answered him accordingly, *v.* 15.

First, The question he asked her was what anyone would have asked her: "*Woman, why weepest thou? Whom seekest thou?*" It should seem, this was the first word Christ spoke after his resurrection: "*Why weepest thou?*" Christ takes cognizance: Of his people's griefs, and enquires, *Why weep you?* Of his people's cares, and enquires, *Whom seek you, and what would you have?* When he knows they are seeking him, yet he will know it from them.

Secondly, The reply she made him is natural enough. *Supposing him to be the gardener, Sir, if thou hast*

carried *him hence,* pray *tell me where thou hast laid him, and I will take him away.* 1. The error of her understanding. She supposed our Lord Jesus to be the gardener. Troubled spirits, in a cloudy and dark day, are apt to misrepresent Christ to themselves. 2. The truth of her affection. See how her heart was set upon finding Christ. She puts the question to everyone she meets. When she speaks of Christ, she does not name him; but, *If thou have borne him hence,* taking it for granted that this gardener was full of thoughts concerning this Jesus as well as she. Another evidence of the strength of her affection was that, wherever he was laid, she would undertake to remove him. Such a body was much more than she could pretend to carry; but true love thinks it can do no more than it can, and makes nothing of difficulties. Christ needs not to stay where he is thought a burden.

(2) How Christ at length made himself known to her, and gave her infallible assurances of his resurrection.

[1] How Christ discovered himself to this good woman (*v.* 16): *Jesus saith unto her, Mary.* It was said with that air of kindness with which he was wont to speak to her. Now he changed his voice, and spoke like himself, not like the gardener. Christ's *sheep know his voice, ch.* x. 4. This one word, *Mary,* was like that to the disciples in the storm, *It is I.*

[2] How readily she received this discovery. She turned herself and said, *Rabboni, My Master.* The title of respect she gives him: *My Master. Rabbon* was with them a more honourable title than *Rabbi;* and therefore Mary chooses that, and adds a note of appropriation, *My great Master.* Notwithstanding the freedom of communion which Christ is pleased to admit us to, he is our *Master.* With what liveliness of affection she gives this title to Christ. *She turned* from the angels to look unto Jesus. We must take off our regards from all creatures, even the brightest and best, to fix them upon Christ. When *she thought it had been the gardener,* she looked another way while speaking to him; but now that she knew the voice of Christ *she turned herself.*

[3] The further instructions that Christ gave her (*v.* 17): "*Touch me not,* but go and carry the news to the disciples."

First, He diverts her from the expectation of familiar society and conversation with him at this time: *Touch me not, for I am not yet ascended.* Mary was ready to express her joy by affectionate embraces of him, which Christ here forbids at this time. *Touch me not* for I am to ascend to heaven. He bade the disciples touch him, for the confirmation of their faith. She must believe him, and adore him, but must not expect to be familiar with him as formerly. He forbids her to dote upon his bodily presence, and leads her to the spiritual communion which she should have with him after he was ascended to his Father. Though *I am not yet ascended, go to my brethren, and tell them, I am to ascend.* As before his death, so now after his resurrection, he still harps upon this. They must look higher than his bodily presence, and look further than the present state of things. "*Touch me not,* stay not now to make any further enquiries, or give any further expressions of joy, for *I am not yet ascended.* The best service thou canst do now is to carry the tidings to the disciples; lose no time therefore, but go away with all speed." Mary must not stay to talk with her Master, but must carry his message; for it is a day of good tidings.

Secondly, He directs her what message to carry to his disciples: *But go to my brethren, and tell them that I ascend.* To whom this message is sent: *Go to my brethren* with it. He was now entering upon his glory, yet he owns his disciples as his brethren. He had called them friends, but never brethren till now.

Though Christ be high, yet he is not haughty. Notwithstanding his elevation, he disdains not to own his poor relations. He had never seen them together since *they all forsook him and fled*. He forgives, he forgets, and does not upbraid. By whom it is sent: by *Mary Magdalene, out of whom had been cast seven devils*. This was her reward for her constancy in adhering to Christ; she becomes an apostle to the apostles. What the message itself is: *I ascend to my Father*.

a. Our joint-relation to God, resulting from our union with Christ, is an unspeakable comfort. He says, He is *my Father, and your Father*; *my God, and your God*. It is the great dignity of believers that *the Father of our Lord Jesus Christ* is, in him, *their Father*. He is ours by a gracious adoption; yet even this warrants us to call him, as Christ did, *Abba, Father*. It is the great condescension of Christ that he is pleased to own the believer's God for his God: *My God, your God;* the God of the Redeemer, to support him, that he might be the God of the redeemed, to save them.

b. Christ's ascension into heaven is likewise an unspeakable comfort: "Tell them I must shortly ascend." (*a*) A word of caution to these disciples, not to expect the continuance of his bodily presence on earth. "I am risen, not to stay with them, but to go on their errand to heaven." Thus those who are raised to a spiritual life must reckon that they rise to ascend. Let them not think that this earth is to be their home and rest; no, being born from heaven, they are bound for heaven. I ascend, therefore must I seek things above. (*b*) A word of comfort to them, and to all *that shall believe in him through their word*; he was then ascending, he is now *ascended to his Father, and our Father*. He says it with triumph, that those who love him may rejoice. He ascended as our forerunner, *to prepare a place for us*, and to be ready to receive us.

Some make these words, *I ascend to my God and your God*, to include a promise of our resurrection. *Because I live, you shall live also*.

IV. Here is Mary Magdalene's faithful report to the disciples (*v.* 18): *She came and told the disciples that she had seen the Lord*. Peter and John had left her seeking him carefully with tears, and would not stay to seek him with her. Now she found it was a living body and a glorified one; so that she found what she sought, and, what was infinitely better, she had joy in her sight of the Master herself. When God comforts us, it is with this design, that we may comfort others. And as she told them what she had seen, so also what she had heard; *that he had spoken these things unto her* as a message to be delivered to them.

Verses 19-25

The infallible proof of Christ's resurrection was his *showing himself alive*, Acts i. 3. In these verses, we have an account of his first appearance to the college of the disciples, on the day on which he rose. He had sent them the tidings of his resurrection, but to confirm their faith in him, he came himself, that they might not have it by hearsay only, but might themselves be eye-witnesses of his being alive.

I. When and where this appearance was, *v.* 19. It was *the same day, being the first day of the week*.

There are three secondary ordinances (as I may call them) instituted by our Lord Jesus, to continue in his church; these are, the Lord's day, solemn assemblies, and a standing ministry. The mind of Christ concerning each of these is plainly intimated to us in these verses: of the first two, here, in the circumstances of this appearance, the other *v.* 21.

1. Here is a Christian sabbath observed by the disciples, and owned by our Lord Jesus. The visit Christ made to his disciples was on *the first day of the week*. And the first day of the week is (I think) the only day of the week, or month, or year, that is ever mentioned by number in all the New Testament; and this is several times spoken of as a day religiously observed. Thus, in effect, he blessed and sanctified that day.

2. Here is a Christian assembly solemnized by the disciples, and also owned by the Lord Jesus. Probably the disciples met here for some religious exercise, to pray together. They met to know one another's minds, strengthen one another's hands, and concert proper measures to be taken in the present critical juncture. This meeting was private, because they durst not appear publicly. They met in a house, but they kept the door shut, that they might not be seen together, and that none might come among them but such as they knew; for they feared the Jews. Those *sheep of the flock were scattered* in the storm; but sheep are sociable, and will come together again. It is no new thing for the assemblies of Christ's disciples to be driven into corners, and forced into the wilderness. God's people have been often obliged to *enter into their chambers, and shut their doors,* as here, *for fear of the Jews*.

II. What was said and done in this visit Christ made to his disciples. When they were assembled, Jesus came among them. *Where two or three are gathered together in his name, he will be in the midst of them*. He came, though *the doors were shut*. It is a comfort to Christ's disciples, when their solemn assemblies are reduced to privacy, that no doors can shut out Christ's presence from them. We have five things in this appearance of Christ:

1. His kind and familiar salutation of his disciples: *He said, Peace be unto you*. The phrase was common, but the sense was now peculiar. *Peace be unto you* is as much as, All good be to you, all peace always by all means. Christ had left them his peace for their legacy, *ch.* xiv. 27. He here makes prompt payment of the legacy: *Peace be unto you*. Peace with God, peace in your own consciences, peace with one another; all this peace be with you; not peace with the world, but peace in Christ. His sudden appearing in *the midst of them*, could not but put them into some disorder and consternation, the noise of which waves he stills with this word, *Peace be unto you*.

2. His clear and undeniable manifestation of himself to them, *v.* 20. And here observe: The method he took to convince them of the truth of his resurrection. None could desire a further proof than the scars or marks of the wounds in the body. The marks of the wounds remained in the body of the Lord Jesus even after his resurrection, that they might be demonstrations of the truth of it. Conquerors glory in the marks of their wounds. Christ's wounds were to speak on earth that it was he himself, and therefore he arose with them; they were to speak in heaven, in the intercession he must ever live to make, and therefore he ascended with them. These marks he showed to his disciples, for their conviction. They had not only the satisfaction of seeing him look with the same countenance, and hearing him speak with the same voice, but they had the further evidence of these peculiar marks: he opened his hands to them, that they might see the marks of the wounds on them; he opened his breast, to show them the wound there. The exalted Redeemer will ever show himself open-handed and open-hearted to all his faithful friends and followers. The impression it made upon them. They were convinced that they saw the Lord; so was their faith confirmed. Thus many true believers, who, while they were weak, feared their comforts were but imaginary, afterwards find them, through grace, real and substantial. *Then they were*

glad. The evangelist seems to write it with somewhat of transport and triumph. *Then! then! were the disciples glad, when they saw the Lord.* How would it revive the heart of these disciples to hear that Jesus is again alive! It is life from the dead to them. Now that word of Christ was fulfilled (*ch.* xvi. 22), *I will see you again, and your heart shall rejoice.* This wiped away all tears from their eyes.

3. The commission he gave them to be his agents in the planting of his church, *v.* 21.

(1) The preface to their commission, which was the solemn repetition of the salutation before: *Peace be unto you.* The former salutation was to still the tumult of their fear, that they might calmly attend to the proofs of his resurrection; this was to reduce the transport of their joy, that they might sedately hear what he had further to say to them. To encourage them to accept of the commission he was giving them. In the issue, it would be peace to them. Christ was now sending the disciples to publish peace to the world, and he here not only confers it upon them but commits it to them as a trust to be by them transmitted.

(2) The commission itself: *As my Father hath sent me, even so send I you.* It is easy to understand how Christ sent them; he appointed them to go on with his work upon earth. He sent them authorized with a divine warrant, armed with a divine power. Hence they were called *apostles*—men *sent.* But how Christ sent them as the Father sent him is not so easily understood; certainly their commissions and powers were infinitely inferior to his. [1] Their work was of the same kind with his, and they were to go on where he left off. As he was sent to bear witness to the truth, so were they; not to be mediators of the reconciliation, but only preachers and publishers of it. As the Father sent him *to the lost sheep of the house of Israel,* so he sent them into all the world. [2] He had a power to send them equal to that which the Father had to send him. By the same authority that the Father sent me do I send you. Had he an incontestable authority, and an irresistible ability, for his work? so had they for theirs. *As the Father hath sent me:* by virtue of the authority given him as a Mediator, he gave authority to them, to act for him, and in his name, so that those who received them, or rejected them, received or rejected him, and him that sent him, *ch.* xiii. 20.

4. The qualifying of them (*v.* 22): *He breathed on them, and said, Receive ye the Holy Ghost.*

(1) The sign he used: *He breathed on them;* not only to show them, by this breath of life, that he himself was really alive, but to signify to them the spiritual life and power which they should receive from him. As *the breath of the Almighty* gave life to man and began the old world, so the breath of the mighty Saviour gave life to his ministers, and began a new world. The Spirit is the breath of Christ, *proceeding from the Son. The breath of God* is put for the power of his wrath, but the breath of Christ signifies the power of his grace; the breathing of threatenings is changed into the breathings of love by the mediation of Christ. The Spirit is the gift of Christ. The apostles communicated the Holy Ghost by the laying on of hands, for they could only carry it as messengers; but Christ conferred the Holy Ghost by breathing, for he is the author of the gift.

(2) The solemn grant he made: "*Receive ye the Holy Ghost.*" *First,* Christ hereby gives them assurance of the Spirit's aid in their future work: "*I send you,* and you shall have the Spirit to go along with you." Whom Christ employs he will clothe with his Spirit, and furnish with all needful powers. *Secondly,* He hereby gives them experience of the Spirit's influences in their present case. He had shown them his hands and his side, to convince them of the truth of his resurrection. "Therefore *receive ye the Holy Ghost,* to work faith in you." They were now in danger of the Jews: "Therefore receive ye the Holy Ghost, to work courage in you." What Christ said to them he says to all true believers, *Receive ye the Holy Ghost.*

5. One particular branch of the power given them particularized (*v.* 23): "*Whosesoever sins you remit,* they are remitted to them; *and whosesoever sins you retain, they are retained.*" How this follows upon their receiving the Holy Ghost; for, if they had not had an extraordinary spirit of discerning, they had not been fit to be entrusted with such an authority. Yet it must be understood as a general charter to the church and her ministers, encouraging the faithful stewards of the mysteries of God to stand to the gospel they were sent to preach, for that God himself will stand to it. Christ, being risen for our justification, sends his gospel heralds to proclaim the act of indemnity now passed. Those whom the gospel acquits shall be acquitted, and those whom the gospel condemns shall be condemned, which puts immense honour upon the ministry, and should put immense courage into ministers. Two ways, and both as having authority: (1) By sound doctrine. They are commissioned to tell the world that salvation is to be had upon gospel terms, and no other. (2) By a strict discipline, applying the general rule of the gospel to particular persons.

III. The incredulity of Thomas, which introduced Christ's second appearance.

1. Here is Thomas's absence, *v.* 24. He is said to be *one of the twelve,* though now eleven. They were but eleven, and one of them was missing: Christ's disciples will never be all together till the general assembly at the great day. By his absence he missed the satisfaction of seeing his Master risen, and of sharing with the disciples in their joy upon that occasion.

2. The account which the other disciples gave him, *v.* 25. They *said unto him, We have seen the Lord.* It seems, though Thomas was then from them, he was not long from them; absentees for a time must not be condemned as apostates for ever: Thomas is not Judas. With what exultation they speak it. "*We have seen the Lord,* and we wish thou hadst been here, to see him too." The disciples of Christ should endeavour to *build up one another in their most holy faith,* both by repeating what they have heard to those that were absent, and also by communicating what they have experienced. Those that by faith have seen the Lord, and tasted that he is gracious, should tell others what God has done for their souls; only let boasting be excluded.

3. The objections Thomas raised against the evidence. "*Except I shall* not only *see in his hands the print of the nails,* but put my finger into it, *and thrust my hand* into the wound *in his side, I will not believe.*" Some conjecture him to have been a man of a rough, morose temper, apt to speak peevishly; for all good people are not alike happy in their temper. There was certainly much amiss in his conduct. He had either not heeded, or not duly regarded, what Christ had so often said, that he would *rise again the third day.* He did not pay a just deference to the testimony of his fellow-disciples. They all ten of them concurred in the testimony with great assurance; and yet he could not persuade himself to say that *their record was true.* It was not, however, their veracity that he questioned, but their prudence; he feared they were too credulous. He tempted Christ when he would be convinced by his own method, or not at all. Thomas ties up his faith to this evidence. Either he will be humoured, and have his fancy gratified, or he will not believe. The open avowal of this in the presence of the disciples was an offence

and discouragement to them. As one coward makes many, so does one unbeliever, one sceptic. His proclaiming his infidelity, and that so peremptorily, might be of ill consequence to the rest.

Verses 26–31

We have here an account of another appearance of Christ, when Thomas was now with them.

I. When it was: *After eight days*, which must therefore be, as that was, *the first day of the week*.

1. He deferred his next appearance for some time, to show his disciples that he was as one that belonged to another world, and visited this only now and then, when there was occasion. In the beginning of his ministry he had been forty days unseen, tempted by the evil Spirit. In the beginning of his glory he was forty days, for the most part unseen, attended by good spirits.

2. He deferred it so long as seven days. That he might put a rebuke upon Thomas for his incredulity. He cannot have such another opportunity for several days. He that slips one tide must stay a good while for another. A very melancholy week Thomas had of it, while the other disciples were full of joy. That he might try the faith and patience of the rest. They had gained a great point when they were satisfied that they had seen the Lord. He would try whether they could keep the ground they had got. He would gradually wean them from his bodily presence, which they had depended too much upon. That he might put an honour upon the first day of the week, and give a plain intimation of his will, that it should be observed in his church as the Christian sabbath. The religious observance of that day has been thence transmitted down to us through every age of the church.

II. Where, and how, Christ made them this visit. It was at Jerusalem, for the doors were shut now, as before, for fear of the Jews. Thomas was with them; though he had withdrawn himself once, yet not a second time. When we have lost one opportunity, we should give the more earnest heed to lay hold on the next. It is a good sign if such a loss whet our desires, and a bad sign if it cool them. The disciples admitted him among them. They did not receive him to doubtful disputation, but bade him welcome to come and see. Christ did not appear to Thomas till he found him in society with the rest of his disciples. He would have all the disciples witnesses of the rebuke he gave to Thomas, and yet withal of the tender care he had of him. Christ *came* in among them, and *stood in the midst*. See the condescension of our Lord Jesus. For the benefit of his church, he lingered on earth, and visited the little private meetings of his poor disciples, and is in the midst of them. He saluted them all as he had done before; he said, *Peace be unto you*. This was no vain repetition, but significant of the abundant peace which Christ gives, and of the continuance of his blessings.

III. What passed between Christ and Thomas at this meeting; and that only is recorded.

1. Christ's gracious condescension to Thomas, *v.* 27. He singled him out from the rest: "*Reach hither, thy finger*, and *behold my hands, the print of the nails; reach hither thy hand*, and *thrust it into my side.*" (1) An implicit rebuke of Thomas's incredulity, in the plain reference to what Thomas had said, answering it word for word. There is not an unbelieving word on our tongues, no, nor thought in our minds, but it is known to the Lord Jesus. (2) An express condescension to his weakness. He suffers his wisdom to be prescribed to. Christ is pleased here to accommodate himself even to Thomas's fancy in a needless thing, rather than leave him in his unbelief. He suffers his wounds to be raked into, allows Thomas even to thrust his hand into his side, if then at last he would

believe. Thus, for the confirmation of our faith, he has instituted an ordinance on purpose to keep his death in remembrance. And in that ordinance wherein we *show the Lord's death* we are called, as it were, to put our finger *into the print of the nails. Reach hither thy hand* to him, who reacheth forth his helping, inviting, giving hand to thee.

It is an affecting word with which Christ closes up what he had to say to Thomas: *Be not faithless but believing.* This warning is given to us all: *Be not faithless;* for, if we are faithless, we are Christless and graceless, hopeless and joyless.

2. Thomas's believing consent to Jesus Christ. He is now ashamed of his incredulity, and cries out, *My Lord and my God, v.* 28. We are not told whether he did put his finger into the print of the nails. Christ says (*v.* 29), *Thou hast seen, and believed;* seeing sufficed. And now faith comes off a conqueror.

(1) Thomas is now fully satisfied of the truth of Christ's resurrection. His slowness and backwardness to believe may help to strengthen our faith.

(2) He therefore believed him to be Lord and God, and we are to believe him so. [1] We must believe his deity—that he is God; not a man made God, but God made man. [2] His mediation—that he is Lord, the one Lord, to settle the great concerns that lie between God and man, and to establish the correspondence that was necessary to our happiness.

(3) He consented to him as his Lord and his God. We must accept of Christ to be that to us which the Father hath appointed him. This is the vital act of faith, He is mine.

(4) He made an open profession of this. He says it to Christ, *Thou art* my Lord and my God; or, speaking to his brethren, *This is* my Lord and my God. Do we accept of Christ as our *Lord God*? We must go to him, and tell him so, tell others so, as those that triumph in our relation to Christ. Thomas speaks with an ardency of affection as one that took hold of Christ with all his might, *My Lord* and *my God*.

3. The judgment of Christ upon the whole (*v.* 29): "*Thomas, because thou hast seen me, thou hast believed*; but *blessed are those that have not seen, and yet have believed.*" Christ owns Thomas a believer. Sound and sincere believers, though they be slow and weak, shall be graciously accepted of the Lord Jesus. No sooner did Thomas consent to Christ than Christ gives him the comfort of it, and lets him know that he believes. He upbraids him with his former incredulity. He had been so backward to believe, and came so slowly to his own comforts. Those that in sincerity have closed with Christ see a great deal of reason to lament that they did not do it sooner. It was not without much ado that he was brought to believe at last. If no evidence must be admitted but that of our own senses, and we must believe nothing but what we ourselves are eyewitnesses of, how must the world be converted to the faith of Christ? He is therefore justly blamed for laying so much stress upon this.

He commends the faith of those who believe upon easier terms. Thomas, as a believer, was truly blessed; but rather *blessed are those that have not seen* Christ's miracles, and especially his resurrection; blessed are those that see not these, and yet believe in Christ. This may look forward upon those who should afterwards believe, the Gentiles, who had never seen Christ in the flesh. This faith is more praiseworthy than theirs who saw and believed. It evidences a better temper of mind in those that do believe. He that believes upon that sight has his resistance conquered by a sort of violence; but he that believes without it is more noble. It is a greater instance of the power of divine grace. Flesh and blood contribute more to their faith that see and believe, than to theirs who see not and yet believe.

IV. The remark which the evangelist makes like an historian drawing towards a conclusion, *v.* 30, 31.

1. He assures us that many other things occurred, which are *not written in the book*; *many signs.* There were other signs, many others, for the confirmation of our faith. Those that recorded the resurrection of Christ were not put to fish for evidence, to take up such short and scanty proofs as they could find, and make up the rest with conjecture. No, they had evidence enough and to spare. The disciples, in whose presence these other signs were done, were to be preachers of Christ's resurrection to others, and therefore it was requisite they should have proofs of it *in abundance.* We need not ask why they were not all written, or why not more than these, or others than these. Had this history been a mere human composition, it had been swelled with a multitude of depositions and affidavits, to prove the contested truth of Christ's resurrection; but, being a divine history, the penmen write with a noble security, sufficient to convince those that were willing to be taught and to condemn those that were obstinate in their unbelief; and, if this satisfy not, more would not. Men produce all they have to say, that they may gain credit; but God does not, for he can give faith. Had this history been written for the entertainment of the curious, it would have been more copious, but it was written to bring men to believe, and enough is said to answer that intention.

2. He instructs us in the design of recording what we do find here (*v.* 31): "*That you might believe* upon these evidences; that you might believe that Jesus is the Christ, the Son of God."

(1) The design of those that wrote the gospel. The evangelists wrote without any view of temporal benefit to themselves or others, but to bring men to Christ and heaven, and to persuade men to believe.

(2) The duty of those that read and hear the gospel. It is their duty to believe, to embrace, the doctrine of Christ. [1] What the great gospel truth is which we are to believe—that *Jesus is that Christ*, that *Son of God.* He is the Christ, *anointed* of God to be a prince and a Saviour. He is the Son of God, endued with the power of God and entitled to the glory of God. [2] What the great gospel blessedness is which we are to hope for—*That believing we shall have life through his name.* This is: To direct our faith. Life through Christ's name is what we must propose to ourselves as the fulness of our joy. To encourage our faith. Upon the prospect of some great advantage, men will venture far; and greater advantage there cannot be than that which is offered by the *words of this life.* It includes both spiritual life and eternal life. Both are through Christ's name and both indefeasibly sure to all true believers.

Chapter 21

The evangelist seemed to have concluded his history. New matter occurring, he begins again. He had said that there were many other signs which Jesus did. And in this chapter he mentions one, Christ's appearance to some of his disciples at the sea of Tiberias. I. How he discovered himself to them as they were fishing, filled their net, and then very familiarly came and dined with them upon what they had caught, ver. 1–14. II. What discourse he had with Peter after dinner. 1. Concerning himself, ver. 15–19. 2. Concerning John, ver. 20–23. III. The solemn conclusion of this gospel, ver. 24, 25.

Verses 1–14

We have here an account of Christ's appearance to his disciples at the sea of Tiberias. 1. Let us compare this appearance with those that *went before.* In those Christ showed himself to his disciples when they were met upon a Lord's day, and when they were all together; but in this he showed himself to some of them upon a week-day, when they were fishing. Christ has many ways of making himself known to his

people; sometimes by his Spirit he visits them when they are employed in common business. 2. Let us compare it with that which followed at the mountain in Galilee, where Christ had appointed them to meet him, Matt. xxviii. 16. Now this appearance was while they were waiting for that, that they might not be weary of waiting.

I. Who they were to whom Christ now showed himself (*v.* 2): not to all the twelve, but to seven of them only. Nathanael is mentioned as one of them, whom we have not met with since *ch.* i. But some think he was the same with Bartholomew. It is good for the disciples of Christ to be much together; in common conversation, and about common business. Christ chose to manifest himself to them when they were together, that they might be joint witnesses of the same matter of fact. Thomas was one of them, and is named next to Peter, as if he now kept closer to the meetings of the apostles than ever.

II. How they were employed, *v.* 3.

1. Their agreement to go a-fishing. For my part, says Peter, *I will go a-fishing*; *We will go with thee* then, say they. Though commonly two of a trade cannot agree, yet they could. They did it, (1) To redeem time, and not to be idle. The hour for entering upon action was not come. Now, in the meantime, rather than do nothing, they would go a-fishing; not for recreation, but for business. It is an instance likewise of their industry, and bespeaks them good husbands of their time. While they were waiting, they would not be idling. Those who would give an account of their time with joy should contrive to fill up the vacancies of it. (2) That they might help to maintain themselves and not be burdensome to any.

2. Their disappointment in their fishing. That night they caught nothing. The hand of the diligent often returns empty. Even good men may come short of desired success in their honest undertakings. Providence so ordered it that all that night they should catch nothing, that the miraculous draught of fishes in the morning might be the more acceptable. In those disappointments which to us are very grievous God has often designs that are very gracious.

III. After what manner Christ made himself known to them. It is said (*v.* 1), *He showed himself.* Four things are observable in the appearance of Christ to them:

1. He showed himself to them seasonably (*v.* 4): *When the morning was now come*, Jesus *stood on the shore.* Christ's time of making himself known to his people is when they are most at a loss. When they think they have lost themselves, he will let them know that they have not lost him. Christ appeared to them, not *walking upon the water*, but *standing upon the shore*, because now they were to make towards him. It is a comfort to us, when our passage is rough and stormy, that our Master is at shore, and we are hastening to him.

2. He showed himself to them gradually. The disciples *knew not*, all at once, *that it was Jesus.* Christ is often nearer to us than we think he is.

3. He showed himself to them by an instance of his pity, *v.* 5. He called to them, *Children*, "*Lads have you any meat?*" (1) The compellation is very familiar; he speaks unto them with the care and tenderness of a father: *Children.* They were not children in age, but they were his children, the children which God had given him. (2) The question is very kind: *Have you any meat? The Lord is for the body*, 1 Cor. vi. 13. Christ takes cognizance of the temporal wants of his people, and has promised them not only grace sufficient, but food convenient. Christ looks into the cottages of the poor, and asks, *Children, have you any meat?* Christ takes care of them, takes care for them. Christ has herein set us an

example of compassionate concern for our brethren. There are many poor householders disabled for labour, or disappointed in it, that are reduced to straits, whom the rich should enquire after thus, *Have you any meat?* For the most necessitous are commonly the least clamorous. The disciples gave a short answer. They said, *No.* Christ put the question to them, not because he did not know their wants, but because he would know them *from them.* Those that would have supplies from Christ must own themselves empty and needy.

4. He showed himself to them by an instance of his power (*v.* 6): he ordered them to *cast the net on the right side of the ship.* And then they, who were going home empty-handed, were enriched with a great draught of fishes. (1) The orders Christ gave them, and the promise annexed to those orders: *Cast the net* there in such a place, and *you shall find.* Divine providence extends itself to things most minute, and they are happy that know how to take hints thence in the conduct of their affairs. (2) Their obedience of these orders, and the good success of it. As yet *they knew not that it was Jesus*; however, they were willing to be advised by anybody. In being thus observant of strangers, they were obedient to their Master unawares. And it sped wonderfully well; now they had a draught that paid them for all their pains. There is nothing lost by observing Christ's orders. Now the draught of fishes may be considered, [1] As a miracle in itself. Christ manifests himself to his people by doing that for them which none else can do. [2] As a mercy to them. When their ingenuity and industry failed them, the power of Christ came in opportunely for their relief. [3] As the memorial of a former mercy, with which Christ had formerly recompensed Peter for the loan of his boat, Luke v. 4, &c. Both that and this affected him much, as meeting him in his own element, in his own employment. Latter favours are designed to bring to mind former favours, that eaten bread may not be forgotten. [4] As a mystery, and very significant of that work to which Christ was now sending them forth. When, soon after this, three thousand were converted in one day, then the net was *cast on the right side of the ship.* It is an encouragement to Christ's ministers to continue their diligence in their work. One happy draught, at length, may be sufficient to repay many years of toil at the gospel net.

IV. How the disciples received this discovery, *v.* 7, 8.

1. John was the most intelligent and quick-sighted disciple. He whom Jesus loved was the first that said, *It is the Lord.* His secret is with his favourites. When John was himself aware that it was the Lord, he communicated his knowledge to those with him. Those that know Christ themselves should endeavour to bring others acquainted with him; we need not engross him, there is enough in him for us all. John tells Peter particularly, knowing he would be glad to see him above any of them.

2. Peter was the most zealous and warmhearted disciple; for as soon as he heard it was the Lord the ship could not hold him, but into the sea he throws himself that he might come first to Christ. He showed his respect to Christ by *girding his fisher's coat* about him, that he might appear before his Master in the best clothes he had, and he girt it to him that he might make the best of his way through the water to Christ. He showed the strength of his affection to Christ by casting himself into the sea; and either wading or swimming to shore, to come to him. *He cast himself into the sea* with precipitation; sink or swim, he would show his goodwill and aim to be with Jesus. Peter had had much forgiven, and made it appear he loved much by his willingness to run hazards, to come to him. Those that have been

with Jesus will be willing to swim through a stormy sea to come to him.

3. The rest of the disciples were careful and honest hearted. They hastened in the boat to the shore, and made the best of their way (*v.* 8). (1) How variously God dispenses his gifts. Some excel, as Peter and John; are very eminent in gifts and graces; others are but ordinary disciples, that mind their duty, and are faithful to him, and yet both the one and the other, the eminent and the obscure, shall sit down together with Christ in glory; nay, and perhaps *the last shall be first.* Some, like John, are eminently contemplative, have great gifts of knowledge, and serve the church with them; others, like Peter, are eminently active and courageous, and are thus very serviceable to their generation. Some are useful as the church's eyes, others as the church's hands, and all for the good of the body. (2) What a great deal of difference there may be between some good people and others in the way of their honouring Christ, and yet both *accepted of him.* Peter ought not to be censured for casting himself into the sea, but commended for his zeal and the strength of his affection; and so must those be who, in love to Christ, quit the world, with Mary, to *sit at his feet.* But others serve Christ more in the affairs of the world. They continue in that ship, drag the net, and bring the fish to shore, as the other disciples here; and such ought not to be censured as worldly, for they, in their place, are as truly serving Christ as the other, even in serving tables. Christ was well placed with both, and so must we be.

V. What entertainment the Lord Jesus gave them.

1. He had provision ready for them. When they came to land, wet and cold, weary and hungry, they found a good fire there to warm them and dry them, and fish and bread. We need not be curious in enquiring whence this fire, and fish, and bread. Here was nothing stately or delicate. We should be content with mean things, for Christ was. We may be comforted in this instance of Christ's care of his disciples. He kindly provided for those fishermen, when they came weary from their work. It is encouraging to Christ's ministers that they may depend upon him who employs them to provide for them. Let them content themselves with what they have here; they have better things in reserve.

2. He called for some of that which they had caught, *v.* 10, 11.

(1) The command Christ gave them to bring their draught of fish to shore: "Bring of the fish hither, which you have now caught." He would have them eat the labour of their hands. What is got by God's blessing on our own industry and honest labour hath a peculiar sweetness in it. Christ would hereby teach us to use what we have. He would have them taste the gifts of his miraculous bounty. The benefits Christ bestows upon us are not to be buried and laid up, but to be used and laid out. He would give a specimen of the spiritual entertainment he has for all believers— that *he sups with them, and they with him.* Ministers, who are fishers of men, must bring all they catch to their Master.

(2) Their obedience to this command, *v.* 11. It was said (*v.* 6), *They were not able to draw the net to shore, for the multitude of fishes.* Thus the fishers of men, when they have enclosed souls in the gospel net, cannot bring them to shore, and complete the good work begun, without the continued influence of the divine grace. Who it was that was most active in landing the fishes: it was Peter, who, as in the former instance (*v.* 7), had shown a more zealous affection to his Master's person than any of them, so in this he showed a more ready obedience to his Master's command; but all that are faithful are not alike forward. The number of the fishes

that were caught. They were in all a *hundred and fifty and three*, and all *great fishes*. A further instance of Christ's care of them: *For all there were so many and great fishes* too, *yet was not the net broken;* so that they lost none of their fish, nor damaged their net. The net of the gospel has enclosed multitudes, three thousand in one day, and yet is not broken; it is still as mighty as ever to bring souls to God.

3. He invited them to dinner. Observing that they were afraid to ask him, Who art thou? because they *knew it was their Lord*, he called to them very familiarly, *Come and dine*.

(1) See here how free Christ was with his disciples; he treated them as friends. *Come, and dine* with me. The call Christ gives his disciples into communion with him in grace here. Christ is a friend; come, dine with him, he will bid you welcome. The call he will give them into the fruition of him in glory hereafter. Christ has wherewithal to dine all his friends and followers; there is room and provision enough for them all.

(2) See how reverent the disciples were before Christ. They were somewhat shy of using the freedom he invited them to. *None of them durst ask him, Who art thou?* Either, because they would not be so bold with him. They had very good reason to think it was he, and could be no other. Or, because they would not so far betray their own folly. They must be stupid indeed if they questioned whether it was he or no. We should be ashamed of our distrusts. Groundless doubts must be stifled, and not started.

4. He carved for them, as the master of the feast, v. 13. *He comes, and takes bread himself*, and *gives them, and fish likewise*. The entertainment here was but ordinary; it was only a fish-dinner, plain and homely. Hunger is the best sauce. Christ *showed himself alive by eating*, not showed himself a prince by feasting. Christ himself began. He would show that he had a true body, which was capable of eating. The apostles produced this as one proof of his resurrection, that *they had eaten and drank with him*, Acts x. 41. He gave the meat about to all his guests. He not only provided it for them, but he himself divided it among them, and put it into their hands. Thus to him we owe the application, as well as the purchase, of the benefits of redemption.

The evangelist leave them at dinner, and makes this remark (v. 14): *This is now the third time that Jesus showed himself alive to his disciples*. Though he had appeared to Mary, to the women, to the two disciples, and to Cephas, yet he had but twice before this appeared to any company of them together. This is taken notice of, (1) For confirming the truth of his resurrection; the vision was doubled, was trebled, for the thing was certain. (2) As an instance of Christ's continued kindness to his disciples; once, and again, and a third time, he visited them. It is good to keep account of Christ's gracious visits. *This is now the third;* have we made a due improvement of *the first and second?* This is the third, perhaps it may be the last.

Verses 15–19

We have here Christ's discourse with Peter after dinner.

I. He examines his love to him, and gives him a charge concerning his flock, v. 15–17.

1. When Christ entered into this discourse with Peter.—It was after they had dined. Christ foresaw that what he had to say to Peter would give him some uneasiness. Peter was conscious to himself that he had incurred his Master's displeasure, and could expect no other than to be upbraided with his ingratitude. Twice, if not thrice, he had seen his

Master since his resurrection, and he said not a word to him of it. We may suppose Peter full of doubts upon what terms he stood with his Master; sometimes hoping the best, yet not without some fears. But now, at length, his Master put him out of his pain. *When they had dined* together, in token of reconciliation, then discoursed he with him about it as with a friend. Peter had reproached himself for it, and therefore Christ did not reproach him for it. Being satisfied in his sincerity, the offence was not only forgiven, but forgotten; and Christ let him know that he was as dear to him as ever. Herein he has given us an encouraging instance of his tenderness towards penitents.

2. What was the discourse itself. Here was the same question three times asked, the same answer three times returned, and the same reply three times given. The same thing was repeated by our Saviour, the more to affect Peter. It is repeated by the evangelist, the more to affect us, and all that read it.

(1) Three times Christ asks Peter whether he loves him or no. The first time the question is, *Simon, son of Jonas, lovest thou me more than these?* Now he calls him: *Simon, son of Jonas*. He speaks to him by name, the more to affect him, as Luke xxii. 31. *Simon, Simon*. He does not call him *Cephas*, nor *Peter*, the name he had given him, but his original name, *Simon*. Yet he gives him no hard language, but as he had called him when he pronounced him blessed, *Simon Bar-jona*, Matt. xvi. 17. How he catechises him: *Lovest thou me more than these?*

First, Lovest thou me? If we would try whether we are Christ's disciples indeed, this must be the enquiry, Do we love him? 1. His fall had given occasion to doubt of his love: "Peter, I have cause to suspect thy love; for if thou hadst loved me thou wouldst not have been ashamed and afraid to own me in my sufferings." We must not reckon it an affront to have our sincerity questioned, when we ourselves have done that which makes it questionable. The question is affecting: "Dost thou love me? Give but proof of this, and the affront shall be passed by, and no more said of it." Peter had professed himself a penitent, witness his tears; he was now upon his probation as a penitent; but the question is not, "Simon, how much hast thou wept?" but, "Dost thou love me?" It is this that will make the other expressions of repentance acceptable. *Much is forgiven her*, not because *she wept much*, but because *she loved much*. 2. His function would give occasion for the exercise of his *love*. Before Christ would commit his *sheep* to his care, he asked him, *Lovest thou me?* Christ has such a tender regard to his flock that he will not trust it with any but those that love him. Those that do not truly love Christ will never truly love the souls of men; nor will that minister love his work that does not love his Master. Nothing but the love of Christ will constrain ministers to go cheerfully through the difficulties and discouragements they meet with in their work. But this love will make their work easy, and them in good earnest in it.

Secondly, Lovest thou me more than these? 1. "Lovest thou me more than thou dost lovest these?" Dost thou love me more than thou dost James or John, or Andrew? Those do not love Christ aright that do not love him better than the best friend they have in the world. 2. "*Lovest thou me more than these love me*," more than any of the rest of the disciples love me? And then the question is intended to upbraid him with his vain-glorious boast, *Though all men should deny thee, yet will not I*. Or, to intimate to him that he had now more reason to love him than any of them had, for more had been forgiven to him than to any of them. It is no breach of the peace to strive which shall love Christ best.

Thirdly, The second and third time that Christ put this question, 1. He left out the comparison *more than these,* because Peter modestly left it out, not willing to compare himself with his brethren, much less to prefer himself before them. Though we cannot say, *We* love Christ more than others do, yet we shall be accepted if we can say, We love him indeed. 2. In the last he altered the word. In the first two enquiries, the original word is: *Dost thou retain a kindness for me?* In answer to which Peter uses another word, more emphatic, *I love thee dearly.* In putting the question the last time, Christ uses that word.

(2) Three times Peter returns the same answer to Christ: *Yea, Lord, thou knowest that I love thee.* [1] Peter does not pretend to love Christ more than the rest of the disciples did. Though we must aim to be better than others, yet we must, *in lowliness of mind, esteem others better than ourselves;* for we know more evil of ourselves than we do of any of our brethren. [2] Yet he professes again and again that he loves Christ: *Yea, Lord,* surely *I love thee.* He had a grateful sense of his kindness, his desire was towards him, and his delight in him, as one he should be unspeakably happy in. This amounts to a profession of repentance for his sin, for it grieves us to have affronted one we love; and to a promise of adherence to him for the future: *Lord, I love thee,* and *will never leave thee.* Christ *prayed that his faith might not fail* (Luke xxii. 32), and, because his faith did not fail, his love did not; for faith will work by love. Christ puts his trial upon this issue: *Dost thou love me?* And Peter joins issue upon it: *Lord, I love thee.* [3] He appeals to Christ himself for the proof of it: *Thou knowest that I love thee;* and *the third time* yet more emphatically: *Thou knowest all things, thou knowest that I love thee.* He calls Christ himself to witness. Peter was sure that Christ knew all things, and particularly that he knew the heart. Peter was satisfied of this, that Christ, who knew all things, knew the sincerity of his love to him. It is a terror to a hypocrite to think that Christ knows all things. But it is a comfort to a sincere Christian. Christ knows us better than we know ourselves. Though we know not our own uprightness, he knows it. [4] *He was grieved* when Christ asked him the *third time, Lovest thou me? v.* 17. It put him in mind of his threefold denial of Christ. Every remembrance of past sins, even pardoned sins, renews the sorrow of a true penitent. It put him in fear lest his Master foresaw some further miscarriage of his. "Surely," thinks Peter, "my Master would not thus put me upon the rack if he did not see some cause for it. What would become of me if I should be again tempted?"

(3) Three times Christ committed the care of his flock to Peter: *Feed my lambs; feed my sheep; feed my sheep.* Those whom Christ committed to Peter's care were his lambs and his sheep. In this flock some are lambs, others are sheep. The Shepherd here takes care of both, and of the lambs first, for upon all occasions he showed a particular tenderness for them. The charge he gives him concerning them is to feed them. The word used in *v.* 15, 17, strictly signifies to *give them food*; but the word used in *v.* 16 signifies more largely to do all the offices of a shepherd to them. It is the duty of all Christ's ministers to feed his lambs and sheep. *Feed them,* that is, teach them. *Feed them,* that is, "Lead them to the green pastures, ministering all the ordinances to them. Feed them by personal application to their respective state and case; not only lay meat before them, but feed those with it that are wilful and will not, or weak and cannot feed themselves." But why did he give this charge particularly to Peter? The particular application to Peter here was designed to restore him to his apostleship, now that he repented. This commission given to Peter was an evidence that Christ was reconciled to him, else he would never have reposed such a confidence in him. Christ, when he forgave Peter, trusted him with the most valuable treasure he had on earth. It was designed to quicken him to a diligent discharge of his office as an apostle. Peter was always forward to speak and act, and, lest he should be tempted to take upon him the directing of the shepherds, he is charged to feed the sheep. If he will be doing, let him do this, and pretend no further. What Christ said to him he said to all his disciples; he charged them all, not only to be fishers of men by the conversion of sinners, but feeders of the flock, by the edification of saints.

II. Having confirmed to him the honour of an apostle, he now tells him of further preferment designed him—the honour of a martyr.

1. How his martyrdom is foretold (*v.* 18): *Thou shalt stretch forth thy hands* and *another shall gird thee* (as a prisoner that is pinioned) *and carry thee whither thou wouldest not.*

(1) He prefaces the notice he gives to Peter of his sufferings with a solemn asseveration, *Verily, verily, I say unto thee.* It was not spoken of as a thing probable, but as a thing certain, *I say it to thee.* As Christ foresaw all his own sufferings, so he foresaw the sufferings of all his followers. Having charged him to feed his sheep, he bids him not to expect ease and honour in it, but trouble and persecution.

(2) He foretells particularly that he should die by the hands of an executioner. The tradition of the ancients informs us that Peter was crucified at Rome under Nero. The pomp and solemnity of an execution add much to the terror of death. Death, in these horried shapes, has often been the lot of Christ's faithful ones. It was a violent death that he should be carried to, such a death as even innocent nature could not think of without dread. He that puts on the Christian does not put off the man. Christ himself prayed against the bitter cup. A natural aversion to pain and death is well reconcilable with a holy submission to the will of God in both.

(3) He compares this with his former liberty. "Time was when *thou girdedst thyself and walkedst whither thou wouldest.*" Where trouble comes we are apt to fret the more at the grievances of restraint, sickness, and poverty, because we have known the sweets of liberty, health, and plenty. But we may turn it the other way: "How many years of prosperity have I enjoyed more than I deserved and improved? And, having received good, shall I not receive evil also?" What a change may possibly be made with us, as to our condition in this world! What a change is presently made with those that leave all to follow Christ! They must no longer walk whither they will, but whither he will.

(4) Christ tells Peter he should suffer thus in his old age. His enemies would hasten him out of the world violently when he was about to retire out of it peaceably. God would shelter him from the rage of his enemies till he should come to be old, that he might be made the fitter for sufferings, and the church might the longer enjoy his services.

2. The explication of this prediction (*v.* 19), *This spoke he* to Peter, *signifying by what death he should glorify God.* It is not only *appointed to all once to die,* but it is appointed to each what death he shall die. There is one way into the world, but many ways out, and God has determined which way we should go. It is the great concern of every good man, whatever death he dies, to glorify God in it. When we die patiently, die cheerfully, and die usefully, we glorify God in dying. The death of the martyrs was in a special manner for the glorifying of God. The blood of the martyrs has been the seed of the church.

Those who thereby at such an expense honour him he will honour.

3. The word of command he gives him hereupon: *When he had spoken thus, he saith unto him, Follow me.* This word, *Follow me*, was a further confirmation of his restoration to his Master's favour, for *Follow me* was the first call. It was an explication of the prediction of his sufferings. *Follow me:* "Expect to be treated as I have been, *for the disciple is not greater than his Lord.*" It was to encourage him in faithfulness and diligence in his work as an apostle. He had told him to *feed his sheep*, and let him set his Master before him as an example. Herein they did follow him, and it was their present honour; who would be ashamed to follow such a leader? Hereafter they should follow him, and that would be their future happiness. Those that faithfully follow Christ in grace shall certainly follow him to glory.

Verses 20–25

I. The conference Christ had with Peter concerning John.

1. The eye Peter cast upon him (*v.* 20): Peter followed him, and *turning about he sees the disciple whom Jesus loved following* likewise. (1) How John is described. He does not name himself, but gives such a description of himself as sufficiently informs us whom he meant. *He was the disciple whom Jesus loved.* It is probable that mention is here made of John's having *leaned on Jesus's breast* and his enquiring concerning the traitor, which he did at the instigation of Peter (*ch.* xiii. 24), as a reason why Peter made the following enquiry concerning him. Then John was in the favourite's place, and he improved the opportunity to oblige Peter. And now that Peter was in the favourite's place, called to take a walk with Christ, he thought himself bound in gratitude to put such a question for John as he thought would oblige him, we all being desirous to know things to come. As we have interest at the throne of grace, we should improve it for the benefit of one another. This is the *communion of saints.* (2) What he did: He also followed Jesus; where he was there also would this servant of his be. What Christ said to Peter he took as said to himself; for that word of command, *Follow me*, was given to all the disciples. (3) The notice Peter took of it: *He, turning about, seeth him.* [1] A culpable diversion from following his Master. The best men find it hard to *attend upon the Lord without distraction.* A needless and unseasonable regard to our brethren often diverts us from communion with God. Or, [2] A laudable concern for his fellow-disciples. He was not so elevated with the honour his Master did him as to deny a kind look to one that followed.

2. The enquiry Peter made concerning him (*v.* 21): "*Lord, and what shall this man do?* What shall be his work, and his lot?" Now this may be taken as the language, (1) Of concern for John, and kindness to him. Here comes thy beloved disciple, hast thou nothing to say to him? Wilt thou not tell how he must be employed, and how he must be honoured? (2) Or of uneasiness at what Christ had said to him concerning his sufferings: "Lord, must I alone be *carried whither I would not?* Must this man have no share of the cross?" (3) Or of curiosity, and a fond desire of knowing things to come. It seems, by Christ's answer, there was something amiss in the question. He seems more concerned for another than for himself. So apt are we to be busy in other men's matters, but negligent in the concerns of our own souls—quick-sighted abroad, but dim-sighted at home. He seems more concerned about events than about duty. We need not ask, "What shall be the lot of those that shall come after us?" Scripture-predictions must be eyed for the directing of our consciences, not the satisfiying or our curiosity.

3. Christ's reply to this enquiry (*v.* 22), "*If I will that he tarry till I come, what is that to thee. Follow thou me.*"

(1) There seems to be here an intimation of Christ's purpose concerning John. That he should not die a violent death, like Peter, but should tarry till Christ himself came by a natural death to fetch him to himself. The most credible of the ancient historians tell us that John was the only one of all the twelve that did not actually die a martyr. He at length died in his bed in a good old age. Though the crown of martyrdom is bright and glorious, yet the beloved disciple comes short of it.

(2) Others think that it is only a rebuke to Peter's curiosity. "Suppose I should design that John should never die, what does that concern thee? I have told thee how thou must die; it is enough for thee to know that, *Follow thou me.*" It is the will of Christ that his disciples should mind their own present duty, and not be curious about future events concerning either themselves or others. There are many things we are apt to be solicitous about that are nothing to us. Other people's characters are nothing to us; it is out of our line to judge them. Other people's affairs are nothing to us to intermeddle in. What do you think will become of such and such? is a common question, which may easily be answered with another: *What is that to me?* To his own Master he stands or falls. Secret things belong not to us. The great thing that is all in all to us is duty, and not event; for duty is ours, events are God's. Now all our duty is summed up in this one of following Christ. And, if we will closely attend to the duty of following Christ, we shall find neither heart nor time to meddle with that which does not belong to us.

4. The mistake which arose from this saying of Christ, that *that disciple should not die.*

(1) The easy rise of a mistake in the church by misconstruing the sayings of Christ. Because John must not die a martyr, they conclude he must not die at all. They were inclined to expect it because they could not choose but desire it. We are apt to dote too much on men and means, instruments and external helps; whereas God will change his workmen, and yet carry on his work. There is no need of immortal ministers to be the guides of the church, while it is under the conduct of an eternal Spirit. Perhaps they were confirmed in their expectations when they now found that John survived all the rest of the apostles. However, it took rise from a saying of Christ's, misunderstood, and then made a saying of the church. Hence learn the uncertainly of human tradition, and the folly of building our faith upon it. Here was a tradition, an apostolical tradition, a saying that *went abroad among the brethren.* It was early; it was common; it was public; and yet it was false. Let the scripture be its own interpreter and explain itself. The aptness of men to misinterpret the sayings of Christ. The scriptures themselves have been wrested by the unlearned and unstable.

(2) The easy rectifying of such mistakes by adhering to the word of Christ. So the evangelist here corrects that saying among the brethren, by repeating the very words of Christ. He said, *If I will that he tarry till I come, what is that to thee?* He said so, and no more. Let the words of Christ speak for themselves. The best end of men's controversies would be to keep to the express words of scripture. Scripture language is the safest and most proper vehicle of scripture truth. As the scripture itself is the best weapon wherewith to wound all dangerous errors, so the scripture itself is the best weapon-salve to heal the wounds that are made by different modes of expression concerning the same truths. Those that cannot agree

in the same logic and metaphysics, may yet agree in the same scripture terms, and then may agree to love one another.

II. We have here the conclusion of this gospel, *v.* 24, 25.

1. This gospel concludes with an account of the penman of it (*v.* 24): *This is the disciple which testifies of these things* to the present age, and wrote these things for the benefit of posterity. Those who wrote the history of Christ were not ashamed to put their names to it. John here does in effect subscribe his name. The record of Christ's life and death was drawn up by men of known integrity, who were ready to *seal it with their blood.* Those who wrote the history of Christ wrote upon their own knowledge. The penman of this history was a disciple, one that had leaned on Christ's breast, that had himself heard his sermons, had seen his miracles, and the proofs of his resurrection. This is he who testifies what he was well assured of. Those who wrote the history of Christ, as they testified what they had seen, so they wrote what they had first testified. It was published by word of mouth, with the greatest assurance, before it was committed to writing. What they wrote they wrote as an affidavit, which they would abide by. It was graciously appointed that the history of Christ should be put into writing, that it might spread to every place, and last through every age.

2. It concludes with an attestation of the truth of what had been here related: *We know that his testimony is true.* The testimony of one who is an eye-witness, is of unspotted reputation, and puts it into writing for the greater certainty, is an unexceptionable evidence. *We know,* that is, All the world knows, that the testimony of such a one is valid. The truth of the gospel comes confirmed by all the evidence we can rationally desire or expect. Then let the doctrine recommend itself, and let the miracles prove it to be of God. It expresses the satisfaction of the churches *at that time* concerning the truth of what is here related. Not as if an inspired writing needed any attestation from men, but hereby they recommended it to the notice of the churches. Or, it expresses the evangelist's own assurance of the truth of what he wrote. The evangelists themselves were entirely satisfied of the truth of what they have testified and transmitted to us. They ventured both this life and the other upon it; threw away this life, and depended upon another.

3. It concludes with an *et cetera,* with a reference to *many other things* said and done by our Lord Jesus, *v.* 25. If they should be written at large, even the world itself could not contain the books that might be written. If it be asked why the gospels are not larger, it may be answered,

(1) It was not because they had exhausted their subject, and had nothing more to write that was worth writing. Everything that Christ said and did was worth our notice. His miracles were many, very many, of many kinds, and the same often repeated. The repetition of the miracles before a great variety of witnesses, helped very much to prove them true miracles. Every new miracle rendered the report of the former the more credible; and the multitude of them renders the whole report incontestable. When we speak of Christ, we have a copious subject before us; the reality exceeds the report, and, after all, *the one half is not told us.* St. Paul quotes one of Christ's sayings, which is not recorded by any of the evangelists (Acts xx. 35), and doubtless there were many more.

(2) But it was for these three reasons: Because it was not needful to write more. What is written is a sufficient revelation of the doctrine of Christ and the proof of it. If we do not believe and improve what is written, neither should we if there had been much more. It was not possible to write all. It would be such a large and overgrown history as never was; such as would jostle out all other writings, and leave us no room for them. It would have been an endless thing. It was not advisable to write much; for *the world,* in a moral sense, *could not contain the books that should be written. The world could not contain.* It is the word that is used, *ch.* viii. 37, "My word *has no place* in you." They would have been so many that they would have found no room. All people's time would have been spent in reading, and other duties would thereby have been crowded out. Much is overlooked of what is written, much forgotten, and much made the matter of doubtful disputation; this would have been the case much more if there had been such a world of books. Especially since it was requisite that what was written should be meditated upon and expounded, which God wisely thought fit to leave room for. Let us be thankful for the books that are written, and not prize them the less for their plainness and brevity, and long to be above, where our capacities shall be so elevated and enlarged that there will be no danger of their being over-loaded.

The evangelist, concluding with *Amen,* thereby sets to his seal, and let us set to ours, an *Amen* of faith, that it is true, all true; and an *Amen* of satisfaction in what is written, as able to make us wise to salvation. *Amen;* so be it.

AN EXPOSITION, WITH PRACTICAL OBSERVATIONS, OF

THE ACTS
OF THE APOSTLES

We have with an abundant satisfaction seen the foundation of our holy religion laid in the history of our blessed Saviour. Upon this rock the Christian church is built. How it began to be built upon this rock comes next to be related in this book.

The history of this book may be considered,

I. As looking back to the preceding gospels. The promises there made we here find made good, particularly the great promises of the descent of the Holy Ghost. The powers there lodged in them we here find exerted in miracles wrought on the bodies of people—miracles of mercy, miracles of judgment, and much greater miracles wrought on the minds of people. The proofs of Christ's resurrection with which the gospels closed are here abundantly corroborated according to the word of Christ, that his resurrection should be the most convincing proof of his divine mission. Christ had told his disciples that they should be his witnesses, and this book brings them in witnessing for him. That day-spring from on high the first appearing of which we there discerned we here find shining more and more. *The kingdom of heaven,* which was then *at hand,* is here set up. Christ's predictions of the virulent persecutions which the preachers of the gospel should be afflicted with we here find abundantly fulfilled, and also the assurances he gave them of extraordinary supports and comforts under their sufferings. This latter part of the history of the New Testament exactly answers to the word of Christ in the former part of it: and thus they mutually confirm and illustrate each other.

II. As looking forward to the following epistles. This book introduces them and is a key to them. We are members of the Christian church, that *tabernacle of God among men.* Now this book gives us an account of the framing and rearing of that tabernacle. The four gospels showed us how the foundation of that house was laid; this shows us how the superstructure began to be raised; Among the Jews and Samaritans; among the Gentiles.

Two things more are to be observed concerning this book: (1) The penman of it. It was written by Luke, who wrote the third of the four gospels, which bears his name. This Luke was very much a companion of Paul in his services and sufferings. *Only Luke is with me,* 2 Tim. iv. 11. We may know by his style in the latter part of this book when and where he was with him, for then he writes, We did so and so, as *ch.* xvi. 10; xx. 6. (2) The title of it: *The Acts of the Apostles.* [1] It is the history of the apostles; yet there is in it the history of Stephen, Barnabas, and some other apostolical men. It is the history of Peter and Paul only that is here recorded; Peter the apostle of the circumcision, and Paul the apostle of the Gentiles, Gal. ii. 7. [2] It is called their *acts,* or *doings.* The apostles were active men; and though the wonders they did were by the word, yet they are fitly called *their acts*; they spoke, *and it was done.*

CHAPTER 1

The inspired historian begins his narrative of the Acts of the Apostles, I. With a reference to his gospel, inscribing this, as he had done that, to his friend Theophilus, ver. 1, 2. II. With a summary of the proofs of Christ's resurrection, his conference with his disciples, and the instructions he gave them during the forty days of his continuance on earth, ver. 3–5. III. With a particular narrative of Christ's ascension into heaven, ver. 6–11. IV. With a general idea of the embryo of the Christian church, ver. 12–14. V. With a particular account of the filling up of the vacancy that was made in the sacred college by the death of Judas, by the electing of Matthias in his room, ver. 15–26.

Verses 1–5

I. Theophilus is put in mind, and we in him, of St. Luke's gospel, which it will be of use for us to cast an eye upon.

1. His patron, to whom he dedicates this book, is Theophilus, *v.* 1. The directing some of the books of the scripture so is an intimation to each of us to receive them as if directed to us in particular, to us by name.

2. His gospel is here called *the former treatise which he had made.* He made the former treatise, and now is divinely inspired to make this, for Christ's scholars must *go on towards perfection,* and not think that their former labours will excuse them from further labours. St. Luke, because he had laid the foundation in a former treatise, will build upon it in this. Let not new sermons and new books make us forget old ones, but put us in mind of them, and help us to improve them.

3. The contents of his gospel were *that, all that, which Jesus began both to do and teach.* (1) Christ both did and taught. Those are the best ministers that both do and teach, whose lives are a constant sermon. (2) *He began both to do and teach;* he laid the foundation. His apostles were to carry on and continue what he began. Christ set them in, and then left them to go on, but sent his Spirit to empower them. It is a comfort to those who are endeavouring to carry on the work of the gospel that Christ himself began it. (3) The four evangelists, and Luke particularly, have handed down to us *all that Jesus began both to do and to teach*; not all the particulars; but all the heads, that by them we may judge of the rest.

4. The period of the evangelical story is fixed *to the day in which he was taken up, v.* 2. Then it was that he left this world, and his bodily presence was no more in it.

II. The truth of Christ's resurrection is maintained and evidenced, *v.* 3. The great evidence of his resurrection was that *he showed himself alive to his apostles*; and *he was seen of them.* 1. The proofs were infallible, both that he was *alive* (he walked and talked with them, he ate and drank with them) and that *it was he himself, and not another*; for he showed them again and again the marks of *the wounds in his hands, and feet, and side.* 2. They were many, and often repeated: *He was seen by them forty days,* not constantly residing with them, but frequently appearing to them.

III. A general hint given of the instructions he furnished his disciples with. He instructed them concerning the work they were to do: *He gave commandments to the apostles whom he had chosen.* Those whom he elected into the apostleship expected he should give them preferments, instead of which *he gave them commandments. He gave them commandments through the Holy Ghost.* In giving them the Holy Ghost, he gave them his commandments; for the Comforter will be a commander. He instructed them concerning the doctrine they were to preach: *He spoke to them of the things pertaining to the kingdom of God.* He had given them a general idea of that kingdom, but here he instructed them more in the nature of it, as a kingdom of grace in this world and of glory in the other, to prepare them to receive the Holy Ghost, and to go through that which they were designed for. It was one of the proofs of Christ's resurrection; the disciples, to whom *he showed himself alive,* knew that it was he, not only by what he showed them, but by what he said to them. None but he could speak thus clearly, thus fully, *of the things pertaining to the kingdom of God.*

IV. A particular assurance given them that they should now shortly receive the Holy Ghost (*v.* 4, 5).

1. The command he gives them to wait. This was to raise their expectations. They must wait till the time appointed, which is now *not many days hence.* Those that by faith hope promised mercies will come must with patience wait till they do come. They must wait in the place appointed, *in Jerusalem.* There Christ was put to shame, there he will have this honour done him, and this favour is done to Jerusalem to teach us to forgive our enemies and persecutors. The apostles were now to put on a public character. Jerusalem was the fittest candlestick for those lights to be set up in.

2. The assurance he gives them that they shall not wait in vain.

(1) The blessing designed them shall come: *You shall be baptized with the Holy Ghost.* They had already been breathed upon with the Holy Ghost (John xx. 22), and they had found the benefit of it; but now they shall have larger measures of his gifts, graces, and comforts. "You shall be cleansed and purified by the Holy Ghost," as the priests were baptized and washed with water, when they were consecrated to the sacred function: "They had the sign; you shall have the thing signified. You shall hereby be more effectually than ever engaged to your Master. You shall be tied so fast to Christ that you shall never forsake him again."

(2) Now this gift of the Holy Ghost he speaks of,

[1] As *the promise of the Father, which they had heard of him,* and might therefore depend upon. *First,* The Spirit was given by promise. The Spirit of God is not given as the spirit of men is given us, but by the word of God. That the gift may be the more valuable. That it may be the more sure. That it may be of grace, and may be received by faith. As Christ, so the Spirit, is received by faith. *Secondly,* It was *the promise of the Father,*—of Christ's Father; of our Father. He will give the Spirit as *the Father of mercies;* it is *the promise of the Father. Thirdly,* This promise of the Father they had heard from Christ many a time. He assured them, again and again, that *the Comforter* should come. This confirms the promise of God that we have heard it from Jesus Christ.

[2] As the prediction of John Baptist (*v.* 5): "You have not only heard it from me, but you had it from John; he said (Matt. iii. 11), *I indeed baptize you with water, but he that comes after me shall baptize you with the Holy Ghost.*" It is a great honour that Christ now does to John. Thus *he confirmeth the word of his servants, his messengers.* But Christ can

do more than any of his ministers. It is an honour to them to be employed in dispensing the means of grace, but it is his prerogative to give *the Spirit of grace.*

(3) Now this gift of the Holy Ghost thus promised is that which we find the apostles received in the next chapter, for in that this promise had its full accomplishment. Other scriptures speak of *the gift of the Holy Ghost* to ordinary believers; this speaks of that particular power which the first preachers of the gospel were endued with. By virtue of this promise we receive the New Testament as of divine inspiration.

Verses 6–11

They came together to be *the witnesses* of his ascension.

I. The question they asked him at this interview. *Lord, wilt thou at this time restore again the kingdom to Israel?* Two ways this may be taken:

1. "Surely thou wilt not at all restore it to the present rulers of Israel. What! Shall those that hate and persecute thee and us be trusted with power?" Or rather,

2. "Surely thou wilt now restore it to the Jewish nation, as far as it will submit to thee." Now two things were amiss in this question:

(1) Their expectation of the thing itself. They thought Christ would *restore the kingdom to Israel,* whereas Christ came to set up his own kingdom, and that a kingdom of heaven, not to *restore the kingdom to Israel,* an earthly kingdom. See here, [1] How apt even good men are to place the happiness of the church too much in external pomp and power. We are told to expect the cross in this world, and to wait for the kingdom in the other world. [2] How apt we are to retain what we have imbibed, and how hard it is to get over the prejudices of education. The disciples were long before they could be brought to have any idea of his kingdom as spiritual. [3] How naturally we are biased in favour of our own people. The kingdoms of this world were to become his whether Israel should sink or swim. [4] How apt we are to misunderstand scripture and to expound scripture by our schemes, whereas we ought to form our schemes by the scriptures.

(2) Their enquiry concerning the time of it: "*Lord, wilt thou* do it *at this time?*" They were inquisitive into that which their Master had never encouraged them to enquire into. They were impatient for the setting up of that kingdom in which they promised themselves so great a share. Christ had told them that they should *sit on thrones* (Luke xxii. 30), and now nothing will serve them but they must be in the throne immediately.

II. The check which Christ gave to this question, *v.* 7: *It is not for you to know the times and seasons.* That mistake would soon be rectified by the pouring out of the Spirit, after which they never had any more thoughts of the temporal kingdom. There is a sense of the expectation which is true, the setting up of the gospel kingdom in the world. But he checks their enquiry after the time.

1. The knowledge of this is not allowed to them: *It is not for you to know.* (1) Christ is now parting from them, and yet he gives them this rebuke; a caution to his church to take heed of splitting upon the rock which was fatal to our first parents—an inordinate desire of forbidden knowledge. (2) Christ had given his disciples a great deal of knowledge above others. He here lets them understand that there were some things which it was not for them to know. We shall see how little reason we have to be proud of our knowledge when we consider how many things we are ignorant of. (3) Christ had given his disciples instructions sufficient for the discharge of their duty, and in this knowledge he will have them

to be satisfied. (4) Christ had himself told his disciples *the things pertaining to the kingdom of God,* and had promised that the Spirit should *show them things to come.* He had likewise given them *signs of the times.* But they must not expect nor desire to know either all the particulars of future events or the exact times of them. As to the times and seasons of the year, we know, in general, there will be summer and winter counterchanged, but we know not particularly which day will be fair or which foul, either in summer or in winter. What this or that particular *day will bring forth* we cannot tell, but must accommodate ourselves to it, whatever it is, and make the best of it.

2. The knowledge of it is reserved to God; it is what *the Father hath put in his own power.* None besides can reveal the times and seasons to come. He has not thought fit to let you know the times and seasons. He hath not said that he will not give you to know something more than you do of the times and seasons, but he has put it in his own power to do it or not, as he thinks fit.

III. He appoints them their work, and with authority assures them of success in it. "Know this (*v.* 8) that you shall receive a spiritual *power,* by the *descent of the Holy Ghost upon you, you shall be witnesses unto me;* and your testimony shall be received here in Jerusalem, in the country about, and all the world over," *v.* 8. If Christ make us serviceable to his honour in our own day and generation, let this be enough for us. Christ here tells them,

1. That their work should be honourable and glorious: *You shall be witnesses unto me.* They shall proclaim him king. They must openly and solemnly preach his gospel to the world. They shall confirm their testimony, not as witnesses do, with an oath, but with the divine seal of miracles and supernatural gifts: *You shall be martyrs to me;* for they attested the truth of the gospel with their sufferings, even unto death.

2. That their power for this work should be sufficient. They had not strength of their own for it, nor wisdom nor courage enough. "*But you shall receive the power of the Holy Ghost coming upon you.* You shall have power to preach the gospel, and to confirm it both by miracles and by sufferings." Those whom he employs in his service he will qualify for it.

3. That their influence should be great and very extensive: "*You shall be witnesses: In Jerusalem;* there you must begin. Your light shall thence shine throughout all Judæa. Thence you shall proceed *to Samaria.* Your usefulness shall reach *to the uttermost part of the earth.*"

IV. Having left these instructions with them, he leaves them (*v.* 9): *When he had spoken these things he blessed them* (so we were told, Luke xxiv. 50); and *while they beheld him, he was taken up, and a cloud received him out of their sight.* He began his ascension in the sight of his disciples, even *while they beheld.* They saw him go up towards heaven, and had actually their eye upon him with so much care and earnestness of mind that they could not be deceived. He *vanished out of their sight, in a cloud.* It was a bright cloud that overshadowed him in his transfiguration, and most probably this was so, Matt. xvii. 5. By the clouds there is a sort of communication kept up between the upper and lower world; in them the vapours are sent up from the earth, and the dews sent down from heaven. Fitly therefore does he ascend in a cloud who is *the Mediator between God and man,* by whom God's mercies come down upon us and our prayers come up to him. This was the last that was seen of him.

V. The disciples, when he had gone out of their sight, yet still continued *looking up steadfastly to*

heaven (*v.* 10). 1. Perhaps they hoped that Christ would come back to them again, so much did they still dote upon his bodily presence, though he had told them that *it was expedient for them that he should go away.* 2. Perhaps they expected to see some change in the visible heavens now upon Christ's ascension. Christ had told them that hereafter they should *see heaven opened* (John i. 51), and why should not they expect it now?

VI. Two angels appeared to them. To show how much Christ had at heart the concerns of his church on earth, he sent back to his disciples two of those that came to meet him, who appear as *two men in white apparel.* Now we are told what the angels said to them, 1. To check their curiosity: *You men of Galilee, why stand you gazing up into heaven?* What would you see? You have seen all that you were called together to see, and why do you look any further? *Why stand you gazing?* Christ's disciples should never stand at a gaze, because they have a sure rule to go by. 2. To confirm their faith concerning Christ's second coming. Their Master had often told them of this: "*This same Jesus, who is taken up from you into heaven will come in like manner thence, as you have seen him go thither.*" (1) "*This same Jesus,* who came once in disgrace to be judged, will come again in glory to judge." (2) "*He shall come in like manner.* He is gone away in a *cloud.* You have now lost the sight of him in the clouds; and *whither he is gone you cannot follow him now,* but shall then." When we stand gazing and trifling, the consideration of our Master's second coming should quicken and awaken us; and, when we stand gazing and trembling, the consideration of it should comfort and encourage us.

Verses 12–14

I. When Christ ascended—*from the mount of Olives* (*v.* 12). There he began his sufferings, and therefore there he rolled away the reproach of them by his glorious ascension. Thus would he enter upon his kingdom in the sight of Jerusalem. This mount is here said to be near Jerusalem, *a sabbath day's journey* from it; no further than devout people used to walk out on a sabbath evening, after the public worship was over, for meditation. Some reckon it a thousand paces; some seven furlongs. Thus far it is a rule to us, not to journey on the sabbath any more than in order to the sabbath work; and as far as is necessary to this we are not only allowed, but enjoined.

II. Whither the disciples returned: They came to Jerusalem, according to their Master's appointment. It should seem that though immediately after Christ's resurrection they were watched, yet after it was known that they were gone into Galilee no notice was taken of their return to Jerusalem. God can find out hiding-places for his people in the midst of their enemies. At Jerusalem they *went up into an upper room, and there abode.* There they assembled every day, in expectation of the descent of the Spirit. *They were continually in the temple* (Luke xxiv. 53), but that was in *the courts of the temple, at the hours of prayer,* where they could not be hindered from attending; but, it should seem, this upper room was in a private house.

III. Who the disciples were, that kept together. The eleven apostles are here named (*v.* 13), so is Mary the mother of our Lord (*v.* 14), and it is the last time that ever any mention is made of her. There were others, the brethren of our Lord, and, to make up *the hundred and twenty* spoken of (*v.* 15), we may suppose that all or most of the *seventy disciples* were with them.

IV. How they spent their time: *They all continued with one accord in prayer and supplication.* They prayed, *and made supplication.* All God's people are praying people. It was now a time of trouble and danger, and, *Is any afflicted? Let him pray.* They had new work before them, and, before they entered upon it, *they were instant in prayer to God.* Before they were first sent forth Christ spent time in prayer for them, and now they spent time in prayer for themselves. Those are in the best frame to receive spiritual blessings that are in a praying frame. God will be enquired of for promised mercies, and the nearer the performance seems to be the more earnest we should be in prayer for it. *They continued in prayer.* It is said (Luke xxiv. 53), *They were praising and blessing God;* here, *They continued in prayer and supplication.* Praise for the promise is a decent way of begging for the performance, and praise for former mercy of begging further mercy. They did this *with one accord.* Those who so keep *the unity of the Spirit in the bond of peace* are best prepared to receive the *comforts of the Holy Ghost.*

Verses 15–26

The sin of Judas made a vacancy in the college of the apostles. If they were but eleven, it would occasion everyone to enquire what had become of the twelfth; therefore care was taken, to fill up the vacancy.

I. The persons concerned in this affair. The house consisted of *about a hundred and twenty.* This was *the number of the names,* that is, the persons. Here was the beginning of the Christian church: this hundred and twenty was the grain of mustard-seed that grew into a tree, the leaven that leavened the whole lump. The speaker was Peter, who had been, and still was, the most forward man. Peter, being designed to be the apostle of the circumcision, while the sacred story stays among the Jews, he is still brought in, as afterwards, when it comes to speak of the Gentiles, it keeps to the story of Paul.

II. The proposal which Peter made for the choice of another apostle. He *stood up in the midst of the disciples, v.* 15.

1. The account he gives of the vacancy made by the death of Judas, in which he is very particular, and takes notice of the fulfilling of the scriptures in it.

(1) The power to which Judas had been advanced (*v.* 17): *He was numbered with us, and had obtained part of this ministry.* What will it avail us to be added to the number of Christians, if we partake not of the spirit and nature of Christians?

(2) The sin of Judas. He was *guide to those that took Jesus.* He had the impudence to appear openly at the head of the party that seized him. He went before them to the place, and gave the word of command: *That same is he, hold him fast.* Ringleaders in sin are the worst of sinners.

(3) The ruin of Judas by this sin. Perceiving the chief priests to seek the life of Christ and his disciples, he thought to save his by going over to them, and not only so, but to get an estate under them. [1] He lost his money shamefully enough (*v.* 18): *He purchased a field* with the *thirty pieces of silver,* which were the *reward of his iniquity.* He thought to have purchased a field for himself, but it proved the purchase of a field to bury strangers in; and what was he or any of his the better for this? [2] He lost his life more shamefully. We were told (Matt. xxvii. 5) that he *went away* in despair; here it is added, he *fell headlong.* He *burst asunder in the midst,* so that *all his bowels tumbled out.* Bowelling is part of the punishment of traitors.

(4) The public notice that was taken of this: *It was known to all the dwellers in Jerusalem.* It was, as it were, put into the newspapers, and was all the talk of the town, as a remarkable judgment of God upon him that betrayed his Master, *v.* 19. It was in everybody's mouth, and nobody disputed the truth of the fact. *It was known,* that is, it was known to be true. Here is one proof of the notoriety of the thing mentioned, that the field was called *Aceldama* —*the field of blood,* because it was bought with the *price of blood.*

(5) The fulfilling of the scriptures in this, *that it must needs be fulfilled, v.* 16. Let none be surprised nor stumble at it, for David had not only foretold his sin, but had also foretold his punishment: *Let his habitation be desolate.* The substitution of another in his room. His *bishopric,* or *his office shall another take.* We are not to think the worse of any office that God has instituted either for the wickedness of any that are in that office or for the ignominious punishment of that wickedness; nor will God suffer any purpose of his to be frustrated, or any work of his to be undone, for the miscarriages of those that are entrusted therewith. Judas is hanged, but his bishopric is not lost. Christ's cause shall never be lost for want of witnesses.

2. The motion he makes for the choice of another apostle, *v.* 21, 22. (1) How the person must be qualified that must fill up the vacancy. It must be one of *these men that have companied with us all the time that the Lord Jesus went in and out among us, beginning from the baptism of John, unto that same day that he was taken up from us.* Those that have been diligent in the discharge of their duty in a lower station, are fittest to be preferred to a higher; those that have been faithful in a little shall be entrusted with more. None shall be an apostle but one that has companied with the apostles, and that continually. (2) To what work he is called. He must be *a witness with us of his resurrection.* By this it appears that others of the disciples were with the eleven when Christ appeared to them. The great thing which the apostles were to attest to the world was Christ's resurrection. See what the apostles were ordained to, not to a secular dignity and dominion, but to preach Christ, and the power of his resurrection.

III. The nomination of the person that was to succeed Judas.

1. Two, who were known to have been Christ's constant attendants, were set up as candidates for the place (*v.* 23): *They appointed two.* The two they nominated were *Joseph* and *Matthias,* of neither of whom do we read elsewhere. These two were both of them so well qualified for the office, that they could not tell which of them was the fitter, but all agreed it must be one of these two.

2. They applied to God by prayer for direction, *which of these two? v.* 24, 25. (1) They appeal to God as the searcher of hearts: "*Thou, Lord, who knowest the hearts of all men.*" When an apostle was to be chosen he must be chosen by his heart and the temper and disposition of that. It is comfortable to us, in our prayers for the welfare of the church and its ministers, that the God to whom we pray *knows the hearts of all men,* can make them fit for his purpose by giving them another spirit. (2) They desire to know which of these *God* had chosen: Lord, show us this. It is fit that God should choose his own servants. (3) They are ready to receive him as a brother whom God hath chosen, to *take part of this ministry and apostleship from which Judas by transgression fell,* that he might go *to his own place,* the place of a traitor, the fittest place for him. Those that betray Christ, as they fall from the dignity of relation to him, so they fall into all misery. Our Saviour had said that Judas's own place should be such that *it had been better for him that he had never been born* (Matt. xxvi. 24). (4) The doubt was determined by lot (*v.* 26), which is an appeal to God, and lawful to be used for determining matters not otherwise determinable, provided it be done in a solemn religious

manner, and with prayer, the prayer of faith. Thus the number of the apostles was made up.

CHAPTER 2

Between the promise of the Spirit and his coming there were but a few days; and during those days the apostles lay perfectly wind-bound, and not offering to preach. But in this chapter the north wind and the south wind awake, and then they awake, and we have them in the pulpit presently. Here is, I. The descent of the Spirit on the day of pentecost, ver. 1–4. II. The various speculations among the people that were now met in Jerusalem from all parts, ver. 5–13. III. The sermon which Peter preached wherein he shows that this pouring out of the Spirit was the accomplishment of an Old Testament promise (ver. 14–21), that it was a confirmation of Christ's being the Messiah (ver. 22–32), and that it was a fruit and evidence of his ascension into heaven, ver. 23–36. IV. The good effect of this sermon in the conversion of many to the faith of Christ, ver. 37–41. V. The eminent piety and charity of those primitive Christians, ver. 42–47.

Verses 1–4

We have here an account of the descent of the Holy Ghost.

I. When, and where, this was done.

1. It was *when the day of pentecost was fully come.* (1) The Holy Ghost came down at the time of a solemn feast, because there was then a great concourse of people to Jerusalem from all parts, which would make the fame of it to be spread the sooner and further. Thus now, as before at the passover, the Jewish feasts served to toll the bell for gospel services. (2) This feast of pentecost was kept in remembrance of the giving of the law upon Mount Sinai. Fitly, therefore, is the Holy Ghost given at that feast, in fire and in tongues, for the promulgation of the evangelical law, not as that to one nation, but to every creature. (3) This feast of pentecost happened on the *first day of the week,* which was a confirmation of it to be the Christian sabbath, to be a standing memorial in his church of those two great blessings—the resurrection of Christ, and the pouring out of the Spirit. Every Lord's day in the year, I think, there should be a full and particular notice taken in our prayers and praises of these.

2. It was when *they were all with one accord in one place.* What place it was we are not told particularly. But it was at Jerusalem, because this had been the place which God chose, and the prophecy was that thence the word of the Lord should go forth. Here God had promised to meet them and bless them; here therefore he meets them with this blessing of blessings. He did this honour to Jerusalem, to teach us not to fall out with places, for God has his remnant in all places; he had this in Jerusalem. Here the disciples were in one place. And here they were *with one accord.* They had prayed more together of late than usual (*ch.* i. 14), and this made them love one another better. By his grace he thus prepared them for the gift of the Holy Ghost; for that blessed dove comes not where there is noise and clamour, but moves upon the face of the still waters, not the rugged ones. Would we have the Spirit *poured out upon us from on high*? Let us all be of one accord; let us agree to love one another.

II. How, and in what manner, the Holy Ghost came upon them. We often read in the Old Testament of God's coming down in a cloud. And Christ went up to heaven in a cloud. But the Holy Ghost did not descend in a cloud; for he was to dispel and scatter the clouds that overspread men's minds.

1. Here is an audible summons given them to awaken their expectations, *v.* 2. It came *suddenly,* but was at the height immediately. It came sooner than they expected, and startled even those that were now together waiting. It was *a sound from heaven.* It was the sound of a wind, for the way of the Spirit is like that of the wind (John iii. 8), *thou hearest the sound thereof, but canst not tell whence it comes nor whither it goes.* It was a *rushing mighty wind*; it was strong and violent, and came with great force, as if it would bear down all before it. This was to signify the powerful influences and operations of the Spirit of God. *It filled* not only the room, but *all the house where they were sitting.* This wind filling the house would strike an awe upon the disciples, and help to put them into a very serious frame, for the receiving of the Holy Ghost. Thus the convictions of the Spirit make way for his comforts; and the rough blasts of that blessed wind prepare the soul for its soft and gentle gales.

2. Here is a visible sign of the gift. They saw *cloven tongues, like as of fire* (*v.* 3), and *it sat,* rested upon each of them. There is a meteor which naturalists call *ignis lambens—a gentle flame,* not a devouring fire; such was this.

(1) There was an outward sensible sign, for the confirming of the faith of the disciples themselves.

(2) The sign given was fire, that John Baptist's saying concerning Christ might be fulfilled, *He shall baptize you with the Holy Ghost and with fire.* They were now celebrating the memorial of the giving of the law upon mount Sinai; and as that was given in fire, so is the gospel. The Spirit, like fire, melts the heart, burns up the dross, and kindles pious and devout affections in the soul. This is that fire which Christ came to send upon the earth.

(3) This fire appeared in cloven tongues. The operations of the Spirit were many; that of speaking with divers tongues was one, and to that this sign had a reference. They were tongues. By him Christ would speak to the world, and he gave the Spirit to the disciples to endue them with a power to publish and proclaim to the world what they knew. These tongues were cloven. The tongues were divided, and yet they still continued all of one accord; for there may be a sincere unity of affections where yet there is a diversity of expression.

(4) This fire sat upon them to denote the constant residence of the Holy Ghost with them. The disciples of Christ had the gifts of the Spirit always with them, though the sign, we may suppose, soon disappeared.

III. What was the immediate effect of this? 1. *They were all filled with the Holy Ghost.* They were filled with the graces of the Spirit, and were more than ever under his sanctifying influences. They were more filled with the comforts of the Spirit, rejoiced more than ever in the love of Christ and the hope of heaven. They were also filled with the gifts of the Holy Ghost. They were endued with miraculous powers for the furtherance of the gospel. It seems evident that not only the twelve apostles, but all the hundred and twenty disciples were *filled with the Holy Ghost* alike at this time. The *all* here must refer to the *all* that were together, *v.* 1. 2. *They began to speak with other tongues,* besides their native language. They spoke not matters of common conversation, but the word of God, and the praises of his name, *as the Spirit gave them utterance.* We may suppose that they understood not only themselves but one another too. They spoke not from any previous thought or meditation, but *as the Spirit gave them utterance;* he furnished them with the matter as well as the language. Now this was, (1) A very great miracle; it was a miracle upon the mind, for in the mind words are framed. They had not only never learned these languages, for aught that appears, they had never so much as heard these languages spoken. They were neither scholars nor travellers. Peter indeed was forward enough to speak in his own tongue, but the rest of them were no spokesmen. He that made man's mouth new-made theirs. (2) A very proper, needful, and serviceable miracle. The language the disciples spoke was Syriac, a dialect of the Hebrew. They were commissioned to preach the gospel to every creature, to disciple all nations. But here is an insuperable difficulty at the threshold. And therefore, to prove that Christ could give authority to preach to the nations, he gives ability to preach to them in their own language. This may well be reckoned, all things considered, a greater work than the miraculous cures Christ wrought. It was the first effect of the *pouring out of the Spirit* upon them.

Verses 5–13

We have here an account of the public notice that was taken of this extraordinary gift.

I. The great concourse of people that there was now at Jerusalem. *There were dwelling at Jerusalem* Jews that were *devout men, out of every nation under heaven*, denoting that there were some from most of the then known parts of the world. Jerusalem at that time was a rendezvous of religious people. 1. We may here see what were some of those countries whence those strangers came (*v.* 9–11), some from the eastern countries, as the *Parthians, Medes, Elamites, and dwellers in Mesopotamia*; thence we come in order to Judæa. Next come the inhabitants of Cappadocia, Pontus, and that country which was particularly called *Asia*. Next come the dwellers in *Phrygia and Pamphylia*, which lay westward, also the *strangers of Rome*; there were some also that dwelt in the southern parts of *Egypt, in the parts of Libya about Cyrene*; there were also some from the island of Crete, and some from the deserts of Arabia; but they were all either Jews originally, or *proselytes* to the Jewish religion. The Jewish writers about this time speak of the Jews as *dwelling everywhere through the whole earth*; and that *there is not a people upon earth among whom some Jews do not inhabit.* 2. We may enquire what brought all those Jews and proselytes together to Jerusalem at this time? for they are said to dwell there. There was at this time a general expectation of the appearing of the Messiah. This brought those who were most zealous and devout to Jerusalem, to sojourn there.

II. The amazement with which these strangers were seized when they heard the disciples speak in their own tongues.

1. They observe that the speakers are all Galileans, that knew no other than their mother tongue (*v.* 7). God chose the weak and foolish things of the world to confound the wise and mighty.

2. They acknowledge that they spoke intelligibly and readily their own language; *We hear every man in our own tongue wherein we were born* (*v.* 8). *We do hear them speak in our tongues the wonderful works of God, v.* 11. It was not only a surprise, but a pleasing surprise, to them to hear the language of their own country spoken. (1) The things they heard the apostles discourse of were the *wonderful works of God, the great things of God.* It is probable that the apostles spoke of Christ, and redemption by him, and the grace of the gospel; and these are indeed the *great things of God.* (2) They heard them both praise God for these great things and instruct the people concerning these things, *in their own tongue.* Now though, perhaps they were got to be so much masters of the Jewish language that they could have understood the meaning of the disciples if they had spoken that language, yet this was more strange, and helped to convince their judgment, that this doctrine was of God. It was more kind, and helped to engage their affections. And this is to us a plain intimation of the mind and will of God, that the scriptures should be read, and public worship performed, in the vulgar languages of the nations.

3. They wonder at it (*v.* 12): *They were all amazed; they were in doubt what the meaning of it was. They asked themselves and one another—What is the tendency of this?* They will *turn aside, and see this great sight.*

III. The scorn which some made of it, probably the scribes and Pharisees, and chief priests; they said, *These men are full of new wine*, they have drunk too much this festival-time, *v.* 13. These, being native Jews, knew not, as the others did, that what was spoken was really the languages of other nations, and therefore took it to be gibberish and nonsense, such as drunkards sometimes talk. And, if they called the Master of the house a wine-bibber, no marvel if they so called those of his household.

Verses 14–36

We have here the first-fruits of the Spirit, in the sermon which Peter preached immediately, directed to the Jews, even to those that mocked; for he begins with the notice of that (*v.* 15), and addresses his discourse (*v.* 14) *to the men of Judæa and the inhabitants of Jerusalem.* It was not by Peter's preaching only, but that of all, *that three thousand souls were* that day converted, but Peter's sermon only is recorded. He that had sneakingly denied Christ now as courageously confesses him.

I. His introduction: *Peter stood up* (*v.* 14) *with the eleven.* Those that were of greatest authority stood up to speak to the scoffing Jews. Thus among Christ's ministers, some of greater gifts are called out to instruct those that oppose themselves, to take hold of sword and spear. *Peter lifted up his voice*, as one that was both well assured of what he said, and was neither afraid nor ashamed to own it. He applied himself to *the men of Judæa*, "and you especially *that dwell at Jerusalem, be this known unto you, and hearken to my words.*"

II. His answer to their blasphemous calumny (*v.* 15): "*These men are not drunken, as you suppose.*" These disciples of Christ, that now *speak with other tongues*, speak good sense, and know what they say. You cannot think they are drunk, for *it is but the third hour of the day*," nine of the clock in the morning; and before this time, on the sabbaths and solemn feasts, the Jews did not eat nor drink.

III. His account of the miraculous effusion of the Spirit. Two things he resolves it into: that it was the fulfilling of the scripture, and the fruit of Christ's resurrection and ascension.

1. That it was the accomplishment of the prophecies of the Old Testament. He specifies one, that of *the prophet Joel, ch.* ii. 28. It is observable that though Peter *was filled with the Holy Ghost*, yet he did not set aside the scriptures, nor think himself above them. Christ's scholars never learn above their Bible.

(1) The text itself that Peter quotes, *v.* 17–21. It refers to *the last days*, the times of the gospel, which are called *the last days* because the dispensation of God's kingdom among men, which the gospel sets up, is the last dispensation of divine grace. "It was prophesied of and promised, and therefore you ought to expect it, and not to be surprised at it; to desire it, and bid it welcome." The apostle quotes the whole paragraph, for it is good to take scripture entire; now it was foretold,

[1] That there should be a more plentiful and extensive effusion of the Spirit of grace from on high than had ever yet been. Now *the Spirit shall be poured out*, not only upon the Jews, but *upon all flesh*, Gentiles as well as Jews. The Jewish doctors taught that the Spirit came only upon wise and rich men, and such as were of the seed of Israel; but God will not tie himself to their rules.

[2] That the Spirit should be in them a Spirit of prophecy. This power shall be given without distinction of sex—not only *your sons*, but *your daughters shall prophesy*; without distinction of age—both *your young men and your old men shall see visions, and*

dream dreams, the *servants and handmaids* shall receive of *the Spirit, and shall prophesy* (v. 18); men and women, whom God calls his servants and his handmaids. The mention of *the daughters* (v. 17) and *the handmaidens* (v. 18) would make one think that *the women* (ch. i. 14) received the extraordinary gifts of the Holy Ghost, as well as the men.

[3] That one great thing which they should prophesy of should be the judgment that was coming upon the Jewish nation. Those that would not submit to the power of God's grace should fall and lie under the pourings out of the vials of his wrath. Those shall break that will not bend. *First*, The destruction of Jerusalem, which was about forty years after Christ's death, is here called *that great and notable day of the Lord*. The desolation itself was such as was never brought upon any place or nation, either before or since. It was *the day of the Lord*, for it was the day of his vengeance upon that people for crucifying Christ. It was a little day of judgment; it was a *notable day*. The destruction of the Jews was the deliverance of the Christians. *Secondly*, The terrible presages of that destruction are here foretold: *There shall be wonders in heaven above, the sun turned into darkness and the moon into blood; and signs* too *in the earth beneath, blood and fire*. Josephus, in his preface to his history of the wars of the Jews, speaks of the signs and prodigies that preceded them, terrible thunders, lightnings, and earthquakes; there was a fiery comet that hung over the city for a year, and a flaming sword was seen pointing down upon it. *The fire and vapour of smoke* literally came to pass in the burning of their cities, and towns, and synagogues, and temple at last. *Thirdly*, The signal preservation of the Lord's people is here promised (v. 21): *Whosoever shall call upon the name of the Lord Jesus shall be saved*. In the destruction by the Romans not one Christian perished. The saved remnant are a praying people: *they call on the name of the Lord*. It is *the name of the Lord* which *they call upon* that is *their strong tower*.

(2) The application of this prophecy to the present event (v. 16): *This is that which was spoken by the prophet Joel*. This is that effusion of the Spirit upon all flesh which should come, and we are to look for no other. This Spirit of grace, the Advocate, or Comforter, that was given now, according to the promise, will, according to the same promise, continue with the church on earth to the end.

2. That it was the gift of Christ. From this *gift of the Holy Ghost*, he takes occasion to preach unto them Jesus (v. 22): "*You men of Israel, hear these words*."

(1) An abstract of the history of the life of Christ, v. 22. He calls him *Jesus of Nazareth*. He was a *man approved of God among you*, censured and condemned by men, but approved of God: *a man marked out by God*. "You yourselves are witnesses how he became famous by *miracles, wonders, and signs, which God did by him; for no man could do such works unless God were with him*." See what a stress Peter lays upon Christ's miracles. The matter of fact was not to be denied: "They were done *in the midst of you, as you yourselves also know*. You have been eyewitnesses of his miracles." The inference from them cannot be disputed; certainly God approved him, *declared him to be the Son of God* and *the Saviour of the world*.

(2) An account of his death and sufferings. This was the greatest miracle of all, that a man approved of God should thus seem to be abandoned of him; and a man thus approved among the people, should be thus abandoned by them too. But both these mysteries are here explained (v. 23). As God's act; and in him it was an act of wonderful grace and wisdom. He *delivered him to death*. And yet there was nothing in this that signified the disapproving

of him; for it was done by *the determinate counsel and foreknowledge of God*. This reconciled him to the cross: *Father, thy will be done;* and *Father, glorify thy name*. As the people's act; and in them it was an act of prodigious sin and folly. It was their voluntary act and deed, from a principle morally evil, and therefore "they were *wicked hands with which you have crucified and slain* him." It is probable that some of those were here present who had cried, *Crucify him, crucify him*. He charges it particularly on them the more effectually to bring them to faith and repentance.

(3) An attestation of his resurrection (v. 24): *Whom God raised up;* the same that delivered him *to death* delivers him *from death*.

[1] He describes his resurrection: God *loosed the pains of death, because it was impossible that he should be holden of it*. From *these pains and sorrows of soul the Father loosed him*, when at his death he said, *It is finished*. Most refer this to the resurrection of Christ's body. Christ was imprisoned for our debt, was thrown into the bands of death; but it was not possible he should be detained there, for he had life in himself and had conquered the prince of death.

[2] He attests the truth of his resurrection (v. 32): *God hath raised him up, whereof we all are witnesses*. They *received power*, by *the descent of the Holy Ghost upon them*, on purpose that they might be skilful, faithful, and courageous witnesses.

[3] He showed it to be the fulfilling of the scripture, it *was impossible that he should be holden* by *death* and *the grave; for David speaks* of his being raised.

First, The text quoted at large (v. 25–28). 1. The constant regard that our Lord Jesus had to his Father: *I foresaw the Lord before me continually*. He set before him his Father's glory as his end in all—*for he saw* that his sufferings would redound abundantly to the honour of God. 2. The assurance he had of his Father's presence and power: "*He is on my right hand, that I should not be moved*." If God be at our right hand we shall not be moved. 3. The cheerfulness with which our Lord Jesus went on in his work. "*I shall not be moved*, therefore *doth my heart rejoice, and my tongue is glad*." It was a constant pleasure to our Lord Jesus to look *to the end of his work*, it does his heart good to think how the issue would answer the design. 4. The happy issue of his death and sufferings. *My flesh shall rest; it shall rest in hope, that thou wilt not leave my soul in hell;* what follows is the matter of his hope. (1) The soul shall not continue in a state of separation from the body: "*Thou wilt not leave my soul in hell*" (in *hades*, in *the invisible state*, so *hades* properly signifies). (2) The body shall lie but a little while in the grave: *Thou wilt not suffer thy Holy One to see corruption*. He must die, but he must *not see corruption*. (3) His death and sufferings should be an inlet to a blessed immortality: "*Thou hast made known to me the ways of life*, and by me made them known to the world, and laid them open." (4) That all his sorrows and sufferings should end in perfect felicity: *Thou shalt make me full of joy with thy countenance*. The reward set before him was *joy, a fulness of joy*, and that in God's *countenance*. That is *the joy of our Lord*, into which all his shall enter, and in which they shall be for ever happy.

Secondly, The comment upon this text. He addresses himself to them with a title of respect, *Men and brethren*, v. 29. "Give me leave *freely to speak to you concerning the patriarch David*. David cannot be understood here as speaking of himself, but of the Christ to come." He could not say *that of himself*, for *he died, and was buried, and his sepulchre remained in Jerusalem till now*. He could never say of himself that he *should not see corruption*; for it was plain he did see corruption. Therefore certainly he spoke *it as a prophet*, with an eye to the Messiah. David knew that the Messiah should descend from his loins (*v.* 30), *that God had sworn to him, that of the fruit of his loins, according to the flesh, he would raise up Christ to sit on his throne.* When our Lord Jesus was born, it was promised *that the Lord God would give him the throne of his Father David*, Luke i. 32. *According to the spirit*, and by his divine nature, he was *to be David's Lord*, not his son. When he says that *his soul should not be left in its separate state, nor his flesh see corruption*, without doubt he must be understood to speak of the resurrection of Christ, *v.* 31. And as *Christ died*, so *he rose again, according to the scriptures;* and *that he did so we are witnesses*. Here is a glance at his ascension too. As David did not rise from the dead, so neither did he *ascend into the heavens, v.* 34. And further, in another psalm, he plainly shows that he spoke of another person, and such another as was his Lord (Ps. cx. 1): *"The Lord said unto my Lord, Sit thou at my right hand until I make thy foes thy footstool," v.* 35.

(4) The application of this discourse.

[1] This explains the meaning of the present wonderful effusion of the Spirit. Some of the people had asked (*v.* 12), *What meaneth this?* I will tell you the meaning of it, says Peter. *This Jesus being exalted by the right hand of God*, and *having received of the Father the promise of the Holy Ghost, hath shed forth this which you now see and hear. The gift of the Holy Ghost* was a performance of divine promises already made; this is the promise that includes all the rest. It was a pledge of all divine favours further intended; what you now see and hear is but an earnest of greater things.

[2] This proves that Christ Jesus is the true Messiah and Saviour of the world; this he closes his sermon with (*v.* 36): *Therefore let all the house of Israel know assuredly that God has made that same Jesus whom you have crucified both Lord and Christ.* They were charged to *tell no man that he was Jesus the Christ* till after his resurrection (Matt. xvii. 9); but now it must be *proclaimed*. It is not proposed as probable, but deposed as certain: *Let them know it assuredly. First*, That God has glorified him *whom they have crucified*. God had glorified him, and the indignities they had done him served as a foil to his lustre. *Secondly*, That he has glorified him to such a degree as to make him *both Lord and Christ.* This is the great truth of the gospel *that that same Jesus that was crucified at Jerusalem* is Lord and Christ.

Verses 37–41

We have seen the wonderful effect of the pouring out of the Spirit, in its influence upon the preachers of the gospel. We are now to see another blessed fruit of the pouring out of the Spirit in its influence upon the hearers of the gospel. From the first delivery of that divine message, it appeared that there was a divine power going along with it. We have here the first-fruits of that vast harvest of souls which by it were gathered in to Jesus Christ. Let us see the method of it.

I. They were put upon a serious enquiry, *v.* 37. *When they heard they were pricked to the heart*, and, under a deep concern applied themselves to the preachers with this question, *What shall we do?* It was very strange that such impressions should be made upon such hard hearts all of a sudden. Peter had charged them with having a hand, a *wicked hand*, in his death, which was likely to have exasperated them against him; yet, when they heard this plain scriptural sermon, they were much affected with it.

1. It put them in pain: *They were pricked in their hearts.* Peter awakened their consciences, touched them to the quick. Sinners, when their eyes are opened, cannot but be *pricked to the heart* for sin.

2. It put them upon enquiry.

(1) To whom they thus addressed themselves: *To Peter and to the rest of the apostles.* By them they had been convinced, and therefore by them they expect to be counselled and comforted. They call them *men* and *brethren*, as Peter had called them (*v.* 29): it is a style of friendship and love. Ministers are spiritual physicians, and it is good for people to be free and familiar with those ministers, as men and their brethren, who deal for their souls as for their own.

(2) What the address is: *What shall we do?* [1] They speak as men at a stand, that did not know what to do: *"Is that Jesus* whom we have crucified both *Lord and Christ?* Then what will become of us who crucified him?" No way of being happy but by seeing ourselves miserable. When we find ourselves in danger of being lost for ever, there is hope of our being made for ever. [2] They speak as men at a point, that were resolved to do anything they should be directed to immediately. Those that are convinced of sin would gladly know the way to peace and pardon.

II. Peter and the other apostles direct them in short what they must do, *v.* 38, 39. Sinners convinced must be encouraged; though their case is sad it is not desperate, there is hope for them.

1. He here shows them the course they must take. *Repent;* this is a plank after shipwreck. This was the same duty that John the Baptist and Christ had preached, and it is still insisted on: *"Repent, repent;* change your mind, change your way." *Be baptized every one of you in the name of Jesus Christ;* that is, "firmly believe the doctrine of Christ, and make an open solemn profession of this, and renounce your infidelity." They must be baptized *in the name of Jesus Christ.* Believe in the name of Jesus, that he is the Christ, the Messias promised to the fathers. They must be baptized *in his name* for the *remission of sins.* This is pressed upon each particular person: *Every one of you.* "Even those of you that have been the greatest sinners, if they repent and believe, are welcome to be baptized. There is grace enough in Christ for everyone of you, be you ever so many, and grace suited to the case of everyone."

2. He gives them encouragement to take this course: (1) "It shall be for *the remission of sins.*" Repent of your sin, and it shall not be your ruin; be baptized into the faith of Christ, and in truth you shall be justified. Aim at this, and depend upon Christ for it, and this you shall have. (2) "You shall *receive the gift of the Holy Ghost* as well as we." All that receive the remission of sins *receive the gift of the Holy Ghost.* (3) "Your children shall still have an interest in the covenant, for the promise of the remission of sins, and the gift of the Holy Ghost, is *to you and to your children," v.* 39. Now it is proper for an Israelite to ask, "What must be done with my children? Must they be thrown out, or taken in with me?" "Taken in" (says Peter) "by all means; for the promise is as much to you and to your children now as ever it was." (4) "Though the promise is still extended to your children, yet it is not confined to you and them, but the benefit of it is *designed* for *all that are afar off."* To this general the following limitation must refer, *even as many of them*, as many particular persons in each nation, *as the Lord our God shall call.* God can make his call to reach those that are ever so far off.

III. These directions are followed with a needful caution (*v.* 40): *With many other words did he testify.* He had said much in a little (*v.* 38, 39), yet he had more to say. When we have heard those words which have done our souls good, we cannot but wish to hear more. Among other things he said, *Save yourselves from this untoward generation.* "Give diligence to save yourselves from their ruin. *Repent, and be baptized;* and then you shall not be sharers in destruction with those with whom you have been sharers in sin. In order to this continue not with them in their sin. *Save yourselves* from this *untoward generation.* Partake not with them in their sins, that you share not with them in their plagues." To separate ourselves from wicked people is the only way to save ourselves from them. If we consider whither they are hastening, we shall see it is better to have the trouble of swimming against their stream than the danger of being carried down their stream. Those that repent of their sins, and give up themselves to Jesus Christ, must evidence their sincerity by breaking off all intimate society with wicked people.

IV. Here is the happy success and issue of this, *v.* 41. The Spirit wrought with the word, and wrought wonders by it. These same persons that had many of them been eye-witnesses of the death of Christ, were yet wrought upon by the preaching of the word. They received the word; and *then* only the word does us good, when we do receive it, and bid it welcome. They gladly received it. Herod *heard* the word gladly, but these gladly *received* it. They were baptized and enrolled themselves among the disciples of Christ by that sacred rite and ceremony which he had instituted. Those that receive the Christian covenant ought to receive the Christian baptism. Hereby there were added to the disciples to the number of about *three thousand souls that same day.* All those that had received the Holy Ghost had their tongues at work to preach, and their hands at work to baptize; for it was time to be busy, when such a harvest was to be gathered in. The conversion of these three thousand with these words was a *greater work* than the feeding of four or five thousand with a few loaves. These were *added to them.* When we take God for our God, we must take his people to be our people.

Verses 42-47

In these verses we have the history of the *truly primitive church,* its state of infancy indeed, but, like that, the state of its greatest *innocence.*

I. They kept close to holy ordinances. Christianity will dispose the soul to communion with God in all those ways wherein he has appointed us to meet him and promised to meet us.

1. They were diligent and constant in their attendance upon the *preaching of the word.* They *continued in the apostles' doctrine.* Those who have given up their names to Christ must make conscience of hearing his word.

2. They kept up the *communion of saints.* They continued *in fellowship* (v. 42), and *continued daily with one accord in the temple,* v. 46. They were much together. Wherever you saw one disciple, you would see more, like *birds of a feather.* See how these Christians love one another. They had fellowship with one another in religious worship. They met *in the temple*: there was their rendezvous; for joint-fellowship with God is the best fellowship we can have with one another. They were daily in the temple. Worshipping God is to be our daily work. They were *with one accord*; not only no discord nor strife, but a great deal of holy love among them.

3. They frequently joined in the ordinance of the Lord's supper. They continued *in the breaking of bread.* They broke bread *from house to house*; they administered that ordinance in private houses; and they went from one to another of these little synagogues or domestic chapels, and there celebrated the eucharist with those that usually met there to worship God.

4. They continued *in prayers. After* the Spirit was poured out, as well as before, they continued instant in prayer; for prayer will never be superseded till it comes to be swallowed up in everlasting praise.

5. They abounded in thanksgiving; were continually *praising God,* v. 47. This should have a part in every prayer, and not be crowded into a corner.

II. They were loving one to another and their joining together in holy ordinances very much endeared them to one another.

1. They had frequent meetings for Christian converse (*v.* 44): *All that believed were together.* They associated together, and so both expressed and increased their mutual love.

2. They had *all things common.* There was such a readiness to help one another that it might be said, They had *all things common,* according to the law of friendship.

3. They were very cheerful; they did *eat their meat with gladness and singleness of heart.* They brought the comforts of *God's table* along with them to *their own.* It made them very pleasant, and enlarged their hearts with holy joy. None have such cause to be cheerful as good Christians have; it is a pity but that they should always have hearts to be so. It made them very liberal to their poor brethren. They did *eat their meat with singleness of heart—with liberality of heart;* so some: they did not eat their morsels alone, but bade the poor welcome to their table. It becomes Christians to be open-hearted and open-handed.

4. They raised a fund for charity (*v.* 45): They *sold their possessions and goods,* and *parted* the money to their brethren, *as every man had need.* This was to destroy not property, but selfishness. Herein, probably, they had an eye to the command which Christ gave to the rich man, as a test of his sincerity, *Sell that thou hast, and give to the poor.* Not that this was intended for an example to be a constant binding rule. But here the case was extraordinary. They were under no obligation of a divine command to do this, as appears by what Peter said to Ananias (*ch.* v. 4): *Was it not in thine own power?* But it was a very commendable instance of their love to their brethren, their compassion to the poor, and their great zeal for the encouraging of Christianity, and the nursing of it in its infancy. Our rule is, to give according as God has blessed us.

III. God owned them, and gave them signal tokens of his presence with them (*v.* 43): *Many wonders and signs were done by the apostles.*

But the Lord's giving them power to work miracles was not all he did for them; he *added to the church daily.* The word in their mouths *did wonders,* and God blessed their endeavours.

IV. The people were influenced by it. They *feared them* (v. 43): *Fear came upon every soul.* They had abundance of spiritual gifts that were truly honourable, which possessed men with an inward reverence for them. The *souls* of people were strangely influenced by their awful preaching and living. They *favoured them.* Though we have reason to think there were those that despised them, yet far the greater part of the common people had a kindness for them— they *had favour with all the people.* Here we find them *in favour with them all,* by which it appears that their prosecuting Christ was a sort of force put upon them by the artifices of the priests; now they returned to their wits, to their right mind. Undissembled piety and charity will command respect; and cheerfulness in serving God will recommend religion to those that are without. They *fell over* to them. Some or other were daily coming in, and they were such as *should be saved.*

CHAPTER 3

In this chapter we have a miracle and a sermon. I. The miracle was the healing of a man that was lame from his birth (ver. 1–8), and the impression which this made upon the people, ver. 9–11. II. The scope of the sermon which was to bring people to Christ, to repent of their sin in crucifying him (ver. 12–19), to believe in him now that he was glorified ver. 20–26.

Verses 1–11

We were told in general (*ch.* ii. 43) that *many signs and wonders were done by the apostles.* Here we have one given us for an instance.

I. The persons by whose ministry this miracle was wrought were Peter and John.

Peter and John had each of them a brother among the twelve, yet now they seem to be knit together more closely than either of them to his brother, for the bond of friendship is sometimes stronger than that of relation. Peter and John seem to have had a peculiar intimacy after Christ's resurrection more than before. It was good evidence of Peter's accept-ance with God, upon his repentance, that Christ's favourite was made his bosom friend.

II. The time and place are here set down. It was in *the temple,* whither *Peter and John went up together.* There were the shoals of fish among which the net of the gospel was to be cast. It is good to go up to the temple, to attend on public ordinances; and it is comfortable to go up together to the temple. The best society is society in worshipping God. It was *at the hour of prayer.* There must be a house of prayer and an hour of prayer. It is of use for private Christians so far to have their hours of prayer as may serve, though not to bind, yet to remind, conscience.

III. The patient on whom this miraculous cure was wrought, *v.* 2. He was a poor lame beggar at the temple gate. 1. He was a cripple, not by accident, but born so. He was *lame from his mother's womb.* Such piteous cases show us what we all are by nature spiritually: *without strength,* lame from our birth, unable to work or walk in God's service. 2. He was a beggar. Being unable to work for his living, he must live upon alms; such are God's poor. He was *laid daily* at *one of the gates of the temple* to *ask alms of those that entered into the temple.* Those that need, and cannot work, must not be ashamed to beg. Our prayers and our alms should go together. Objects of charity should be in a particular manner welcome to us when we go up to the temple to pray; it is a pity that common beggars at church doors should any of them be of such a character as to discourage charity; but they ought not always to be overlooked: some there are surely that merit regard, and better feed ten drones, yea, and some wasps, than let one bee starve. The gate of the temple at which he was laid is here named: it was called *Beautiful.* It was no diminution to the beauty of this gate that a poor man lay there begging. 3. He begged of Peter and John (*v.* 3), begged an alms; this was the utmost he expected from them. He *asked an alms,* and had a cure.

IV. We have here the method of the cure.

1. His expectations were raised. Peter, instead of turning his eyes from him, *fastened his eyes upon him, v.* 4. John did so too, they said, *Look on us.* This gave him cause to expect that he should *receive something from them,* and therefore he *gave heed to them, v.* 5. We must come to God with hearts fixed and expecta-tions raised. We must look up to heaven and expect to receive.

2. His expectation of an alms was disappointed. *Peter said, "Silver and gold have I none."* It is not often that Christ's friends and favourites have abund-ance of the wealth of this world. Peter and John had abundance of money laid at their feet, but this was appropriated to the maintenance of the poor of the church. Public trusts ought to be strictly and faithfully observed. Many who are well inclined to works of charity are yet not in a capacity of doing any-thing considerable, while others, who have where-withal to do much, have not a heart to do anything.

3. His expectations were quite outdone. Peter had no money to give him. He had that which was better, such a power from heaven, as to be able to cure his disease. Those who are poor in the world may yet be rich, very rich, in spiritual gifts. He gave him that which was better—the cure of his disease. This would enable him to work for his living, so that he would not need to beg any more; nay, he would *have to give to those that needed.* When Peter had no silver and gold to give, yet (says he) *such as I have I give thee.* Those who have not silver and gold may have their limbs and senses, and with these may be serviceable to the blind, and lame, and sick, and if they be not, neither would they give to them if they had silver and gold. How the cure was wrought. Peter bids a lame man *rise up and walk,* which would have been a banter upon him if he had not premised *in the name of Jesus Christ of Nazareth.* He bids the cripple *rise up and walk.* If he attempt to rise and walk, and depend upon a divine power to enable him to do it, he shall be enabled; and by rising and walking he must evidence that that power has wrought upon him; and then let him take the comfort, and let God have the praise. Peter lent his hand, and helped him (*v.* 7): *He took him by the right hand and lifted him up.* When God by his word commands us to rise, and walk in the way of his commandments, he will give his Spirit to take us by the hand, and lift us up. If we set ourselves to do what we can, God has promised his grace to enable us to do what we cannot. *His feet and ankle-bones received strength;* he does his part, and Peter does his, and yet it is Christ that does all: it is he that puts strength into him.

V. Here is the impression which this cure made upon the patient himself. He leaped up, in obedience to the command, *Arise.* He started up, as one re-freshed with sleep, that questioned not his own strength. The incomes of strength were sudden, and he was no less sudden in showing them. He stood, and walked. He trod strongly, and moved steadily; and this was to manifest the cure. Those who have had experience of the working of divine grace upon them should evidence what they have experienced. Has God put strength into us? Let us stand up resolutely for him, and walk cheerfully with him. He *held Peter and John, v.* 11. We need not ask why he held them. I believe he scarcely knew himself: but it was in a transport of joy that he embraced them. Thus he testified his affection to them; he held them, and would not let them go. Those whom God hath healed love those whom he made instruments of their healing, and see the need of their further help. He *entered with them into the temple.* His strong affection to them held them; but it could not hold them so fast as to keep them out of the temple. He is resolved to go with them, and the rather because they are going into the temple. Like the impotent man whom Christ cured, was presently found in the temple, John v. 14. He was there *walking, and leaping, and praising God.* The strength God has given us, both in mind and body, should be made use of to his praise. This man, as soon as he could leap, leaped for joy in God, and praised him. All true converts walk and praise God; but perhaps young converts leap more in his praises.

VI. How the people that were eye-witnesses of this miracle were influenced by it. 1. They were entirely satisfied in the truth of the miracle. *They knew it was he that sat begging at the beautiful gate of the temple, v.* 10. He had sat there so long that they all knew him. They now saw him *walking and praising God* (*v.* 9). He was now as loud in praising God as he had before been in begging relief. Mercies are then perfected, when they are sanctified. 2. They were astonished at it: They were *filled with wonder and amazement* (*v.* 10); *greatly wondering, v.* 11. There seems to have been this effect of the pouring out of the Spirit, that the people were much more affected with the miracles the apostles wrought than they had been with those that had been wrought by Christ himself. 3. They gathered about Peter and John: *All the people ran together unto them in Solomon's porch.* Here the people met, to see this great sight.

Verses 12–26

We have here the sermon which Peter preached. *When Peter saw it.* When he saw the people got together in a crowd, he took that opportunity to preach Christ to them. When he saw the people affected with the miracle, he sowed the gospel seed in the ground which was thus prepared to receive it. When he saw the people ready to adore him and John, he diverted their respect from them, that it might be directed to Christ only.

I. He humbly disclaims the honour of the miracle. He addresses himself to them as *men of Israel*, men to whom pertained, not only the law and the promises, but the gospel and the performances. Two things he asks them: 1. Why they were so surprised at the miracle itself: *Why marvel you at this?* It was indeed marvellous, but it was no more than what Christ had done many a time. It was but a little before that Christ had *raised Lazarus from the dead*; and why should this then seem so strange? Stupid people think that strange now which might have been familiar to them if it had not been their own fault. Christ had lately risen from the dead himself; why did they not marvel at this? 2. Why they gave so much of the praise of it to them, who were only the instruments of it: *Why look you so earnestly on us?* It was certain that they *had made this man to walk*, by which it appeared that the apostles not only were sent of God, but were sent to be blessings to the world. Yet they did not do it by any *power or holiness of their own.* The power they did it by was wholly derived from Christ. The power which Christ gave them to do it they had not deserved: it was not by their own holiness. Peter was a sinful man. Yet he wrought miracles in Christ's name. It was the people's fault that they attributed it to their power and holiness. The instruments of God's favour to us, must not be idolized. It was the praise of Peter and John that they would not take the honour of this miracle to themselves, but carefully transmitted it to Christ. Useful men must see to it that they be very humble.

II. He preaches Christ to them.

1. He preaches Christ, as the true Messiah promised to the fathers (*v.* 13). He is Jesus the Son of God. He is *his Son Jesus*; to him dear as a Son; to us, *Jesus*, a Saviour. God hath glorified him, in raising him up. He hath glorified him as the *God of our fathers, the God of Abraham, of Isaac, and of Jacob.* God sent him into the world, pursuant to the promises made to those patriarchs. The gospel they preached was the revelation of the mind and will of the God of Abraham.

2. He charges them flatly and plainly with the murder of this Jesus: *"You delivered him up,* and you of the common people were influenced to clamour against him, as if he had been a public grievance." *You denied him,* and you disowned him, could not look upon him as the Messiah, because he came not in external pomp and power; *you denied him in the presence of Pilate.* "You were worse than Pilate, for he would have released him, if you had let him follow his own judgment. *You denied the holy One and the Just."* The holiness and justice of the Lord Jesus, which are something more than his innocency, were a great aggravation of the sin of those that put him to death. *"You desired a murderer to be released,* and Christ crucified." *You killed the prince of life.* "You preserved *a murderer*, a destroyer of life; and destroyed the Saviour, *the author of life. You killed the prince of life,* and so not only forsook, but rebelled against your own mercies."

3. He attests his resurrection as before, *ch.* ii. 32. "You thought *the prince of life* might be deprived of his life. *But of his resurrection we are all witnesses."*

4. He ascribes the cure of this impotent man to the power of Christ (*v.* 16): *His name, through faith in his name, has made this man strong.* He repeats it again, *The faith which is by him hath given him this soundness.* (1) He appeals to themselves concerning the truth of the miracle; the man on whom it was wrought is one *whom you see, and know.* The miracle was wrought publicly, *in the presence of you all,* in the gate of the temple. The cure is complete; it is a *perfect soundness;* you see the man walks and leaps. (2) He acquaints them with the power by which it was wrought. It is done by the name of Christ. That name which Christ has above every name; his authority, his command has done it; as writs run in the king's name, though it is an inferior officer that executes them. The power of Christ is fetched in *through faith in his name,* and it is for his sake, that he may have the glory of it. Those that wrought this miracle by faith derived power from Christ to work it, and therefore returned all the glory to him. Peter both confirmed the great gospel truth they were to preach to the world—that Jesus Christ is the fountain of all power and grace, and the great healer and Saviour—and recommended the great gospel duty of faith in him as the only way of receiving benefit by him. Thus does Peter preach unto them Jesus, and him crucified.

III. He encourages them to hope that they might find mercy; he does all he can to convince them, yet is careful not to drive them to despair. 1. He mollifies their crime by a candid imputation of it to their ignorance. He saw it needful to mitigate the rigour of the charge by calling them *brethren;* and well might he call them so, for he had been himself a brother with them in this iniquity: he had *denied the Holy One and the Just,* and sworn that he did not know him. *I know that through ignorance you did it,* as did also *your rulers, v.* 17. This was the language of Peter's charity, and teaches us to make the best of those whom we desire to make better. He has the example of his Master's praying for his crucifiers, and pleading in their behalf that they knew not what they did. Perhaps some of the rulers, and of the people did it through malice; but the generality went down the stream, and did it through ignorance. 2. He mollifies the effects of their crime, it was *according to the scriptures (v.* 18). So he himself saith: *Thus it is written, and thus it behoved Christ to suffer.* "You fulfilled the scripture, and did not know it; *God,* by your hands, *hath fulfilled what he showed by the mouth of all his prophets, that Christ should suffer;* this was his design but you had views of your own, and were altogether ignorant of this design. God was fulfilling the scripture when you were gratifying your own passions." This is no extenuation at all of their sin in hating and persecuting Christ *to the death,* yet it was an encouragement to them to repent, and hope for mercy. The death and sufferings of Christ were for *the remission of sins,* and the ground of that display of mercy for which he now encouraged them to hope.

IV. He exhorts them all to turn Christians.

1. He tells them what they must believe. They must believe that Jesus Christ is the promised seed, *v.* 25. *Jesus,* who was of *the seed of Abraham, according to the flesh,* and *in him all the families of the earth are blessed,* and not the families of Israel only. They must believe that Jesus Christ is a prophet, *that prophet like unto Moses* whom God had promised to *raise up to them from among their brethren, v.* 22. Christ is a prophet, for by him God speaks unto us. He is a *prophet like unto Moses.* He was a deliverer

of his people out of bondage, like Moses. Moses was *faithful as a servant*, Christ *as a Son*. Moses was a pattern of meekness and patience, so is Christ. *There was no prophet like unto Moses*, but a greater than Moses is here where Christ is. He is a prophet of God's raising up. He was raised up unto Israel in the first place. They had the first offer of divine grace made to them; and therefore he was *raised up from among them*. If he come to his own, one would think, they should receive him. The Old Testament church was blessed with many prophets from *Samuel, and those that follow after*, *v.* 24; but, these servants being abused, last of all God sent them his Son. They must believe *that times of refreshing will come from the presence of the Lord* (*v.* 19), and that they will be *the times of the restitution of all things*, *v.* 21. The absence of the Lord occasions many of the securities of sinners and the distrusts of saints; but his presence is hastening on, which will for ever silence both. The presence of the Lord will introduce, (1) *The restitution of all things* (*v.* 21); the renovation of the whole creation; that *end of all things which God hath spoken of by the mouth of all his holy prophets since the world began*. This is more clearly and plainly revealed in the New Testament than it had been before. (2) With this will come *the times of refreshing* (*v.* 19), like a cool shade to those *that have borne the burden and heat of the day*. All Christians look for *a rest that remains for the people of God*, after the travails and toils of their present state. The refreshing that then *comes from the presence of the Lord* will continue eternally in the presence of the Lord.

2. He tells them what they must do. They must *repent*; they must begin anew. Peter, who had himself denied Christ, repented, and he would have them to do so too. They must *be converted*, must face about; they must *return to the Lord their God*. It is not enough to repent of sin, but we must be converted from it, and not return to it again. They must hear Christ, the great prophet: "*Him shall you hear in all things whatsoever he shall say unto you*. Hear him with a divine faith, as prophets should be heard. *Hear him in all things;* let his laws govern all your actions. Whatever he saith to you, bid it welcome." It is at our peril if we turn a deaf ear to his call (*v.* 23): *Every soul that will not hear that prophet shall be destroyed from among the people*. Those that will not be advised by the Saviour can expect no other than to fall into the hands of the destroyer.

3. He tells them what they might expect.

(1) That they should have the pardon of their sins (*v.* 19): *Repent, and be converted, that your sins may be blotted out*. The remission of sin is the blotting of it out. When God forgives sin he remembers it no more against the sinner; it is forgotten, as that which is blotted out. We cannot expect our sins should be pardoned unless we repent of them, and turn from them to God. If no repentance, no remission. Hopes of the pardon of sin upon repentance should be a powerful inducement to us to repent. This was the first and great argument, *Repent, for the kingdom of heaven is at hand*. The most comfortable fruit of the forgiveness of our sins will be *when the times of refreshing shall come*. During these times of toil and conflict (doubts and fears within, troubles and dangers without) we cannot have that full satisfaction of our pardon, and in it, that we shall have when the refreshing times come, which shall wipe away all tears.

(2) That they should have the comfort of Christ's coming (*v.* 20, 21): "*He shall send Jesus Christ, that before was preached unto you. If you repent and be converted*, you shall find no want of him; some way or other he shall be seen of you." We must not expect Christ's personal presence with us in this world;

for the heavens, which received him out of the sight of the disciples, must retain him till the end of time. We must live by that faith in him which is *the evidence of things not seen*. Yet it is promised that he shall be sent to all that repent and are converted (*v.* 20): "*He shall send Jesus Christ, who was preached to you*. You shall have his spiritual presence. He that is sent into the world shall be sent to you; you shall have the comfort of his being sent. The sending of Christ to judge the world, at the end of time, will be a blessing to you." It seems to refer to this, for till then *the heavens must receive him, v.* 21.

4. He tells them what ground they had to expect these things, if they were converted to Christ.

(1) As Israelites they were, above any other, God's favourite nation. *You are the children of the prophets and of the covenant*. A double privilege. [1] They were *the children of the prophets*. You are of that people from among whom prophets were raised up, and to whom prophets were sent. Those of the latter ages of the church, when prophecy had ceased, might yet be fitly called *the children of the prophets*, because they heard *the voices of the prophets, which were read in their synagogues every sabbath day*, ch. xiii. 27. Now this should quicken them to embrace Christ. Those that are blessed with prophets and prophecy (as all are that have the scriptures) are concerned not to receive the grace of God therein in vain. [2] They were *the children*, that is, the heirs, *of the covenant which God made with our Fathers*. "The promise of the Messiah was made to you, and therefore you may hope it shall be made good to you." If all the kindreds of the earth were to be blessed in Christ, much more that kindred, *his kinsmen according to the flesh*.

(2) As Israelites, they had the first offer of the grace of the New Testament. To them the Redeemer was first sent, which was an encouragement to them to hope that if they did repent, and were converted, he should be yet further sent for their comfort (*v.* 20): *He shall send Jesus Christ, for to you first he hath sent him, v.* 26. *Unto you first, God, having raised up his Son Jesus from the dead, sent him to bless you*, especially that great blessing of *turning every one of you from your iniquities*. [1] We are here told whence Christ had his mission: *God raised up his Son Jesus, and sent him*. God raised him up when he constituted him a prophet. He sent him to bear witness of the truth, sent him to seek and save lost souls. Some refer *the raising of him up to the resurrection*. Though having raised him up, he seemed presently to take him from us, yet he did really send him afresh to us in his gospel and Spirit. [2] To whom he was sent: "*Unto you first, you that are the children of the prophets, and of the covenant.*" The personal ministry of Christ, as that of the prophets, was confined to the Jews; *to the lost sheep of the house of Israel*, and he forbade the disciples he then sent forth to go any further. After his resurrection, he was to be preached indeed to all nations, but they must *begin at Jerusalem*, Luke xxiv. 47. And, when they went to other nations, they first preached to the Jews they found therein. So far were they from being excluded for their putting Christ to death, that, when he is risen, he is first sent to them. [3] On what errand he was sent: "*He is sent to you first, to bless you*; not to condemn you, as you deserve, but to justify you." Christ's errand into the world was to bless us, and, when he left the world, he left a blessing behind him, for he was *parted from the disciples as he blessed them*, Luke xxiv. 51. It is by Christ that God sends blessings to us, and through him only we can expect to receive them. The great blessing was the turning of us away from our iniquities, that we may be qualified to receive all other blessings. Sin is that to which naturally we cleave; the design of divine grace is to

turn us from it, nay, to turn us against it, that we may not only forsake it, but hate it. "Therefore, do your part: *repent, and be converted*, because Christ is ready to do his, *in turning you from your iniquities*, and so blessing you."

CHAPTER 4

Here, I. Peter and John are taken up and committed to jail, ver. 1–4. II. They are examined by a committee of the great sanhedrim, ver. 5–7. III. They bravely avow what they have done, and preach Christ to their persecutors, ver. 8–12. IV. Their persecutors enjoin them silence, and so dismiss them, ver. 13–22. V. They apply to God by prayer, for the further operations of that grace which they had already experienced, ver. 23–30. VI. God owns them by manifest tokens of his presence with them, ver. 31–33. VII. The believers had their hearts knit together in holy love, and the church flourished more than ever, ver. 33–37.

Verses 1–4

We have here the powers of darkness appearing against them to put a stop to them. Let Christ's servants be ever so resolute, Satan's agents will be spiteful; and therefore, let Satan's agents be ever so spiteful, Christ's servants ought to be resolute.

I. The apostles, Peter and John, went on in their work, and did not labour in vain.

1. The preachers faithfully deliver the doctrine of Christ: *They spoke unto the people*, v. 1. *They taught the people;* taught those that as yet did not believe, for their conviction and conversion; and taught those that did believe, for their comfort and establishment. *They preached through Jesus the resurrection from the dead.* The doctrine of the resurrection of the dead was verified in Jesus. They preached the resurrection of Christ as their warrant for what they did. It is secured by him to all believers. This *they preached through Jesus Christ*, attainable through him, and through him only. They meddled not with matters of state, but kept to their business, and preached to the people heaven as their end and Christ as their way.

2. The hearers cheerfully receive it (v. 4): *Many of those who heard the word believed, to the number of about five thousand.* Though the preachers were persecuted, the word prevailed; for sometimes the church's suffering days have been her growing days: the days of her infancy were so.

II. The chief priests and their party did what they could to crush them; their hands were tied awhile, but their hearts were not in the least changed. 1. Who they were that appeared against the apostles. They were *the priests*. With them was joined *the captain of the temple*, who, it is supposed, was a Roman officer. Still here were both Jews and Gentiles confederate against Christ. *The Sadducees* also, who denied *the being of spirits* and *the future state*, were zealous against them. 2. How they stood affected to the apostles' preaching: *They were grieved that they taught the people*, v. 2. It grieved them, both that the gospel doctrine was preached, and that the people were so ready to hear it. It vexed them to see that his gospel got ground, instead of losing it. Miserable is their case to whom the glory of Christ's kingdom is a grief. It grieved them that the apostles *preached through Jesus the resurrection from the dead.* The Sadducees were grieved that the resurrection from the dead was preached; for they opposed that doctrine. The chief priests were grieved that they preached the resurrection of the dead through Jesus; they would rather give up that important article than have it preached and proved to be through Jesus. 3. How far they proceeded against the apostles (v. 3): *They laid hands on them*, and *put them in hold* until the next day. See how God trains up his servants for sufferings by degrees; now they resist unto bonds only, but afterwards to blood.

Verses 5–14

We have here the trial of Peter and John before the judges of the ecclesiastical court.

I. Here is the court set. An extraordinary court, it should seem, was called on purpose upon this occasion. 1. The time when the court sat (v. 5)—*on the morrow*. They adjourned it to the morrow, and no longer; for they were impatient to get them silenced. 2. The place where—in Jerusalem (v. 6), where there were so many that looked for redemption before it came, yet there were more that would not look upon it when it did come. 3. The judges of the court. (1) Their general character: they were *rulers, elders,* and *scribes*, v. 5. The scribes were men of learning. The rulers and elders were men in power. The gospel of Christ had both the learning and power of the world against it. (2) The names of some of them, who were most considerable. Here were Annas and Caiaphas, ringleaders in this persecution; Annas the president of the sanhedrim, and Caiaphas the high priest (though Annas is here called so). However they were both equally malignant against Christ and his gospel. There were others likewise that were *of the kindred of the high priest*, who having dependence on him, would be sure to say as he said. Great relations, and not good, have been a snare to many.

II. The prisoners are arraigned, v. 7. They are brought to the bar; they *set them in the midst*, for the sanhedrim sat in a circle. The question they asked them was, "*By what power, or by what name, have you done this?* Who commissioned you to preach such a doctrine as this, and empowered you to work such a miracle as this?" They knew very well that they preached Jesus (v. 2), yet they asked them, to tease them, and try if they could get anything out of them that looked criminal.

III. The plea they put in, not so much to clear and secure themselves as to advance the name and honour of their Master.

1. By whom this plea was drawn up: it was dictated by the Holy Ghost. The apostles set themselves to preach Christ and then Christ made good to them his promise, that the Holy Ghost should *give them in that same hour what they should speak.* Christ's faithful advocates shall never want instructions, Mark xiii. 11.

2. To whom it was given in: Peter addresses himself to the judges of the court, as the *rulers of the people, and elders of* Israel; for the wickedness of those in power does not divest them of their power, but the consideration of the power they are entrusted with should prevail to divest them of their wickedness.

3. What the plea is.

(1) What they did was in the name of Jesus Christ, which was a direct answer to the question the court asked them (v. 9, 10): "*If we this day be examined for a good deed done to the impotent man, by what means*, or by whom, *he is made whole*, we have an answer ready. *Be it known to you all*, and not to you only, but *to all the people of Israel that by the name of Jesus Christ, whom you crucified*, and *whom God hath raised from the dead, even by him doth this man stand here before you whole*, a monument of the power of the Lord Jesus." He justifies what he and his colleague had done in curing the lame man. It was a *good deed*. "Now, if we be reckoned with for this good deed, we have no reason to be ashamed. Let those be ashamed who bring us into trouble for it." It is no new thing for good men to suffer ill for doing well. He transfers all the praise and glory of this good deed to Jesus Christ. "It is by him, and not by any power of ours, that this man is cured. Let the Lord alone be exalted, no matter what becomes of us." He charges it upon the judges themselves, that they had been the murderers of this Jesus: "It is he *whom you crucified*." He endeavours to

convince them of sin, of that sin which was most likely to startle conscience—their putting Christ to death. Peter will miss no occasion to tell them of it. He attests the resurrection of Christ as the strongest testimony for him, and against his persecutors: "God *raised him from the dead*; they took away his life, but God gave it to him again." He preaches this to all the bystanders: "*Be it known to you all,* to *all the people of Israel,* that wonders are wrought in the name of Jesus, not by repeating it as a charm, but believing in it as a divine revelation of grace and goodwill to men.

(2) The name of this Jesus is that name alone by which we can be saved. It is not an indifferent thing, but of absolute necessity, that people believe in this name, and call upon it. We are obliged to it in duty to God, and in compliance with his designs (*v.* 11): "*This is the stone which was set at nought of you builders,* you that are *the rulers of the people, and the elders of Israel,* that should be the builders of the church. Here was a stone offered you, to be put in the chief place of the building; but you rejected it, threw it by as good for nothing. But this stone is *now become the head of the corner.*" Probably St. Peter here chose to make use of this quotation because Christ had himself made use of it not long before this, Matt. xxi. 42. Scripture is a tried weapon in our spiritual conflicts: let us therefore stick to it. We are obliged to it for our own interest. We cannot be saved but by Jesus Christ (*v.* 12): *Neither is there salvation in any other.* As there is no other name by which diseased bodies can be cured, so there is no other by which sinful souls can be saved. Our salvation is our chief concern. Our salvation is not in ourselves; we can destroy ourselves, but we cannot save ourselves. This is the honour of Christ's name, that it is the only name whereby we must be saved. This name is *given.* God has appointed it. It is given *under heaven.* He has all power both in the upper and in the lower world. It is given *among men,* who need salvation. We may be saved by his name, and we cannot be saved by any other. How far those may find favour with God who have not the knowledge of Christ, yet live up to the light they have, it is not our business to determine. Whatever saving favour such may receive it is upon the account of Christ, and for his sake only; so that still *there is no salvation in any other.*

IV. The stand that the court was put to, *v.* 13, 14.

1. They could not deny the cure of the lame man to be both a good deed and a miracle. They had *nothing to say against it* (*v.* 14).

2. They could not face down Peter and John. This was a miracle not inferior to the cure of the lame man. They see *the boldness of Peter and John, v.* 13. They appeared not only undaunted by the rulers, but daring and daunting to them. The courage of Christ's faithful confessors has often been the confusion of their cruel persecutors. (1) What increased their wonder: *They perceived that they were unlearned and ignorant men.* They enquired and found that they were born in Galilee, that they were bred fishermen, and had no learned education. And yet speak to them of the Messiah and his kingdom, and they speak so pertinently and so fluently, and are so ready in the scriptures that the most learned judge upon the bench is not able to answer them. They were *ignorant men*—men that had not any public character or employment, which made them wonder to see what freedom they took. (2) What made their wonder in a great measure to cease: they *took knowledge of them that they had been with Jesus.* When they understood that *they had been with Jesus* they knew what to impute their boldness to. Those that *have been with Jesus* should conduct themselves, in everything, so that those who converse with them may

take knowledge of them that they have been with Jesus. One may know that they have been in the mount by the shining of their faces.

Verses 15–22

We have here the issue of the trial. They came off now with flying colours.

I. Here is the consultation of the court and their proceeding thereupon.

1. The prisoners were ordered to withdraw (*v.* 15): They *commanded them to go aside out of the council,* willing enough to get clear of them (they spoke so home to their consciences). The designs of Christ's enemies are carried on in close cabals, as if they would hide their counsels from the Lord.

2. A debate arose upon this matter: *They conferred among themselves.* The question proposed was, *What shall we do to these men? v.* 16. If they would have yielded to the convincing commanding power of truth, it had been easy to say what they should do to these men. But, when men will not be persuaded to do what they should do, it is no marvel that they are ever and anon at a loss what to do.

3. They came at last to a resolution, in two things:

(1) That it was not safe to punish the apostles. Now they could not find how they might punish Peter and John, *because of the people.* They knew it would be an unrighteous thing to punish them, and therefore should have been restrained from it by the fear of God; but they considered it only as a dangerous thing, and therefore were held in from it only by the fear of *the people.* [1] The people were convinced of the truth of the miracle; it was a *notable miracle—a known miracle.* This was a known instance of the power of Christ, and a proof of his doctrine. That it was wrought for the confirmation of the doctrine they preached, was *manifest to all that dwelt in Jerusalem:* it was an opinion universally received. They themselves, with all the craftiness and all the effrontery they had, *could not deny* it to be a true miracle; everybody would have hooted at them if they had. They could easily deny it to their own consciences, but not to the world. [2] All men *glorified God for that which was done.* Even those that were not persuaded by it to believe in Christ could not but give praise to God for it.

(2) That it was nevertheless necessary to silence them for the future, *v.* 17, 18. All their care is that the doctrine of Christ *spread no further among the people;* as if that healing institution were a plague begun, the contagion of which must be stopped. To prevent the further spreading of this doctrine, [1] They charge the apostles never to preach it any more, that *no man speak at all nor teach in the name of Jesus, v.* 18. "Not only that you do not preach this doctrine publicly, but that you *speak henceforth to no man,* not to any particular person privately, *in this name," v.* 17. There is not a greater service done to the devil's kingdom than the silencing of faithful ministers, and putting those under a bushel that are the lights of the world. [2] They threaten them if they do: it is at their peril. Christ had not only charged them to preach the gospel to every creature, but had promised to bear them out in it. Those who know how to put a just value upon Christ's promises know how to put a just contempt upon the world's threatenings.

II. Here is the courageous resolution of the prisoners to go on in their work, and their declaration of this resolution, *v.* 19, 20. Peter and John jointly put in the answer: "*Whether it be right in the sight of God to hearken unto you more than unto God, judge you; for we cannot forbear speaking the things which we have seen and heard.*" The prudence of the serpent would have directed them to be silent. But the boldness of the lion directed them thus to set their persecutors at defiance. They justify themselves in it with two things: 1. The command of God: "You charge us not to preach the gospel; he has charged us to preach it; now whom must we obey, God or you?" Nothing can be more absurd than to hearken unto weak and fallible men more than unto a God that is infinitely wise and holy. The case is so plain and self-evident, that we will venture to leave it to yourselves to judge of it. Can you think it *right in the sight of God* to break a divine command in obedience to a human injunction? 2. The convictions of their consciences. They *could not but speak those things which they had seen and heard.* (1) They felt the influence of it upon themselves, what a blessed change it had wrought upon them. Those speak the doctrine of Christ best that have felt the power of it. (2) They knew the importance of it to others. They look with concern upon perishing souls, and know that they cannot escape eternal ruin but by Jesus Christ, and therefore will be faithful to them in giving them warning. They are things *which we have seen and heard*, and therefore are fully assured of ourselves: and things which we only have seen and heard, and therefore, if we do not publish them, who will? Who can?

III. Here is the discharge of the prisoners (v. 21): *They further threatened them*, and then *let them go*. 1. Because they durst not contradict the people, who *glorified God for that which was done*. As rulers by the ordinance of God are made a terror and restraint to wicked people, so people are sometimes by the providence of God made a terror and restraint to wicked rulers. 2. Because they could not contradict the miracle: For (v. 22) *the man was above forty years old on whom this miracle of healing was shown*. The miracle was so much the greater, he having been lame *from his mother's womb, ch.* iii. 2. If those that have been long accustomed to evil, are cured of their spiritual impotency to good, the power of divine grace is therein so much the more magnified. The truth of it was so much the better attested; for *the man being above forty years old*, he was able when he was asked, to *speak for himself*.

Verses 23–31

We hear no more at present of the chief priests, but are to attend those *two witnesses*.

I. Their return to their brethren (v. 23): *Being let go, they went to their own company*. As soon as ever they were at liberty, they went to their old friends. 1. Though God had highly honoured them, in calling them out to be his witnesses, yet they were not puffed up with the honour done them, but *went to their own company*. No advancement in gifts or usefulness should make us think ourselves above either the duties or the privileges of the communion of saints. 2. Though their enemies had severely threatened them, yet they *went to their own company*. Christ's followers do best in company, provided it be in their own company.

II. The account they gave them of what had passed: They *reported all that the chief priests and elders had said to them*. They related it to them, 1. That they might know what to expect both from men and from God. From men they might expect everything that was terrifying, but from God everything that was encouraging. 2. That they might have it recorded for the confirmation of our faith touching the resurrection of Christ. These apostles told the chief priests to their faces that God had *raised up Jesus from the dead*. They had not the confidence to deny it, but, in the silliest and most sneaking manner imaginable, bade the apostles not to tell anybody of it. 3. That they might now join with them in prayers and praises.

III. Their address to God upon this occasion: *When they heard they lifted up their voice to God with one accord*, v. 24. One in the name of the rest *lifted up his voice to God* and the rest joined with him, *with one mind* (so the word signifies); their hearts went along with him, and so, though but one spoke, they all prayed.

1. Their adoration of God as the Creator of the world (v. 24). They *said*, "*O Lord. thou art God our Master and sovereign Ruler*" (so the word signifies), "thou art the God *who hast made heaven and earth, and the sea*." The heathen worship gods which they have made, we are worshipping the God that made us and all the world. And it is very proper to begin our prayers, as well as our creed, with the acknowledgment of this, that God is the *Father almighty, Maker of heaven and earth, and of all things visible and invisible*. The Christian religion was intended to confirm and improve, not to eclipse nor jostle out, the truths and dictates of natural religion. It is a great encouragement to God's servants that they serve the God that made all things, and is able to strengthen them under all their difficulties.

2. Their reconciling themselves to the present dispensations of Providence, by reflecting upon the Old Testament, v. 25, 26. *Thus he spoke by the mouth of his servant David*. Let it not therefore be a surprise to them, for the *scripture must be fulfilled*. It was foretold, Ps. ii. 1, 2. (1) That the heathen would rage at Christ and his kingdom. (2) That the people would imagine all the things that could be against it. (3) That the kings of the earth, particularly, would stand up in opposition to the kingdom of Christ. (4) That the rulers would gather together against God and Christ. Where the power is in many rulers, councils, and senates, they *gather together against the Lord and against his Christ*. What is done against Christ, God takes as done against himself. Christianity was opposed and fought against by them, and yet it made its way.

3. Their representation of the present accomplishment of those predictions. What was foretold we see fulfilled, v. 27, 28. It is *of a truth* that Herod and Pilate, the two Roman governors with the *people of Israel*, were *gathered together against thy holy child Jesus whom thou hast anointed*. (1) The wise and holy designs God had concerning Christ. He is here called the *child Jesus*. The word signifies both a son and a servant. He was the Son of God; and yet in the work of redemption he acted as his Father's servant. It was he whom God anointed, and thence he was called the Lord's Christ, v. 26. God that anointed Christ determined what should be done to him. He was anointed to be a Saviour, and therefore it was determined he should be a sacrifice to make atonement for sin. He must die. God wisely determined before by what hands it should be done. He must therefore be *delivered into the hands of sinners. God's hand and his counsel determined it*. His hand and his counsel always agree: for *whatsoever the Lord pleased that did he*. (2) The wicked and unholy instruments that were employed in the executing of this design. Herod and Pilate, Gentiles and Jews, who had been at variance with each other, united against Christ. Sin is not the less evil for God's bringing good out of it, but he is by this the more glorified.

4. Their petition with reference to the case at this time.

(1) That God would take cognizance of the malice of their enemies: *Now, Lord, behold their threatenings*, v. 29. And now, *Lord*; there is an emphasis upon the *now*. Then is God's time to appear for his people, when the power of their enemies is most daring and threatening. They do not dictate to God what he shall do, but refer themselves to him. To thee we appeal, *behold their threatenings*, and either tie their

hands or turn their hearts. It is a comfort to us that if we be unjustly threatened we may make ourselves easy to spreading the case before the Lord, and leaving it with him.

(2) That God, by his grace, would keep up their spirits: *Grant unto thy servants that with all boldness they may speak thy word.* Their prayer is not, *"Lord, behold their threatenings, and frighten them,"* but, *"Behold their threatenings, and animate us."* They do not pray, "Lord, give us a fair opportunity to retire from our work, now that it is become dangerous"; but, "Lord, give us grace to go on in our work, and not to be afraid." Those that are sent on God's errands ought to deliver their message with boldness, not doubting of what they say, nor of being borne out in saying it. God is to be sought unto for an ability to speak his word with boldness. The threatenings of our enemies should rather stir us up to so much the more courage. Are they daring that fight against Christ? For shame, let not us be sneaking that are for him.

(3) That God would still give them power to work miracles for the confirmation of the doctrine they preached: *Lord, grant us boldness, by stretching forth thy hand to heal.* Nothing emboldens faithful ministers more in their work than the tokens of God's presence with them. They pray: *That signs and wonders might be done by the name of the holy child Jesus,* which would be convincing to the people, and confounding to the enemies. It is the honour of Christ that they aim at that the wonders might be done by the name of Jesus.

IV. The gracious answer God gave. God gave them a sign of the acceptance of their prayers (v. 31): *When they had prayed, the place was shaken where they were assembled together.* This shaking of the place was designed to awaken and raise their expectations, and to give them a sensible token that God was with them of a truth. This was to show them what reason they had to fear God more, and then they would fear man less. The place was shaken, that their faith might be established and unshaken. God gave them greater degrees of his Spirit. Their prayer, without doubt, was accepted, for it was answered: *They were all filled with the Holy Ghost,* by which they were not only encouraged, but enabled to speak the word of God with boldness. The Holy Ghost taught them not only *what* to speak, but *how* to speak. They were *filled with the Holy Ghost* at the bar (v. 8), and now *filled with the Holy Ghost* in the pulpit. We have here an instance of the performance of that promise, *that God will give the Holy Spirit to those that ask him* (Luke xi. 13), for it was in answer to prayer that *they were filled with the Holy Ghost:* we have also an example of the improvement of that gift; have it and use it, use it and have more of it. *They spoke the word with all boldness.* Talents must be traded with, not buried.

Verses 32–37

I. The disciples loved one another dearly. *The multitude of those that believed were of one heart, and of one soul* (v. 32). 1. There were multitudes that believed; even in Jerusalem *there were three thousand* converted on one day, and *five thousand* on another, and, besides these, *there were added to the church daily.* The increase of the church is the glory of it. 2. They were *all of one heart, and of one soul.* Though there were many, very many, of different ages, tempers, and conditions, in the world, they were unanimous in the faith of Christ, and, being all *joined to the Lord, they were joined to one another in holy love.* This was the blessed fruit of Christ's dying precept to his disciples, to *love one another,* and his dying prayer for them, *that they all might be one. They were all of one heart, and one soul.* Thus it

was then, and we may not despair of seeing it so again.

II. The ministers went on in their work with great vigour and success (v. 33). *With great power gave the apostles witness of the resurrection of the Lord Jesus.* The resurrection of Christ, rightly understood, will let us into the great mysteries of religion. By the great power wherewith the apostles attested the resurrection may be meant the great vigour, spirit, and courage, with which they published this doctrine; they did it not softly and diffidently, but with liveliness and resolution. Or it may mean the miracles which they wrought to confirm their doctrine. God himself, in them, *bearing witness* too.

III. The beauty of the Lord our God shone upon them: *Great grace was upon them all,* grace that had something *great* in it (magnificent and very extraordinary) *was upon them all.* Christ poured out abundance of *grace upon them.* There were evident fruits of this grace in all they said and did. Some think it includes the favour they were in with the people. Everyone saw a beauty and excellency in them, and respected them.

IV. They were very liberal to the poor.

1. They insisted not upon property, which even children seem to have a sense of and a jealousy for, and which worldly people triumph in. *No man said that aught of the things which he possessed was his own, v.* 32. They did not take away property, but they were indifferent to it. They did not call it their own, because they had, in affection, forsaken all for Christ. We can call nothing our own but sin. *No man said that what he had was his own;* for he was *ready to distribute, willing to communicate.* Those that had estates were not solicitous to lay up, but very willing to lay out, and would straiten themselves to help their brethren. *Meum—mine,* and *tuum—thine,* are the great makebates. Men's holding their own, and grasping at more than their own, are the rise of wars and fightings.

2. They abounded in charity, *they had all things common;* for (v. 34) *there was not any among them that lacked.* As there were many poor that received the gospel, so there were some rich that were able to maintain them, and the grace of God made them willing. The gospel hath laid *all things common,* not so that the poor are allowed to rob the rich, but so that the rich are appointed to relieve the poor.

3. They did many of them sell their estates: *As many as had possession of lands or houses sold them, v.* 34. We are here told what they did with the money that was so raised: They *laid it at the apostles' feet*— they left it to them to be disposed of as they thought fit. *Distribution was made unto every man according as he had need.* Great care ought to be taken in the distribution of public charity. That it be given to such as have need. Those who have real need, above all, those that are reduced to want for well doing ought to be taken care of, and provided for. That it be given *to every man according as he has need,* without partiality or respect of persons.

Here is one particular person mentioned: *Barnabas,* afterwards Paul's colleague. [1] The account here given concerning him, *v.* 36. His name was *Joses;* he was of *the tribe of Levi.* He was born in Cyprus, a great way off from Jerusalem. Notice is taken of the apostles' changing his name after he associated with them. He was respected by the apostles, who, in token of their value for him, gave him a name, *Barnabas. A son of consolation* (so we read it)— a cheerful Christian, and this enlarged his heart in charity to the poor; eminent for comforting the Lord's people; he had an admirable facility that way. There were two among the apostles that were called *Boanerges—sons of thunder* (Mark iii. 17); but here was a *son of consolation* with them. Each had his several gift. Let the one search the wound, and then let the other heal it and bind it up. [2] Here is an account of his great generosity. This is particularly taken notice of, because of the eminency of his services afterwards in the church of God. Or perhaps this is mentioned because it was a leading card, and an example to others: *He having land, he sold it, brought the money, and laid it at the apostles' feet.* And he lost nothing upon the balance of the account, when he himself was, in effect, numbered among the apostles, by that word of the Holy Ghost, *Separate me Barnabas and Saul for the work whereunto I have called them,* ch. xiii. 2. Thus, for the respect he showed to the apostles as apostles, he had an apostle's reward.

CHAPTER 5

I. The sin and punishment of Ananias and Sapphira, ver. 1–11. II. The flourishing state of the church, ver. 12–16. III. The imprisonment of the apostles, and their miraculous discharge out of prison, ver. 17–26. IV. Their arraignment before the great sanhedrim, ver. 27–33. V. Gamaliel's counsel concerning them, and their concurrence, for the present, with this advice, ver. 34–40. VI. The apostles' cheerful progress in their work.

Verses 1–11

The chapter begins with a melancholy *but.* As every man, so every church, in its best state has its *but.* The disciples seemed to be all exceedingly good; *but* there were hypocrites among them. There is a mixture of bad with good in the best societies of this side heaven; tares will grow among the wheat until the harvest. They came up to that perfection which Christ recommended to the rich young man—they *sold what they had, and gave to the poor*; *but* even that proved a cloak and cover of hypocrisy. The signs and wonders which the apostles wrought were hitherto miracles of mercy; *but* now comes in a miracle of judgment that God may be both loved and feared.

I. The sin of Ananias and Sapphira his wife. 1. They were ambitious of being thought eminent disciples when really they were not true disciples. They *sold a possession, and brought the money to the apostles' feet,* that they might not seem to be behind the very chief of believers. It is possible that hypocrites may deny themselves in one thing, but then it is to serve themselves in another. Ananias and Sapphira would take upon them a profession of Christianity, *and make a fair show in the flesh* with it, when they knew they could not go through with the Christian profession. It is often of fatal consequence for people to go a greater length in profession than their inward principle will admit of. 2. They were covetous of the wealth of the world, and distrustful of God and his providence: *They sold their land,* and in a pang of zeal, designed to dedicate the whole of the purchase-money to pious uses; but, when the money was received, their heart failed them, and *they kept back part of the price* (v. 2), because they loved the money. They could not take God's word that they should be provided for, but thought they would play a wiser part than the rest had done, and lay up for a rainy day. As if there were not an all-sufficiency in God to make up the whole to them. If they had been thorough-paced worldlings, they would not have sold their possession; and, if they had been thorough-paced Christians, they would not have detained part of the price. 3. They thought to deceive the apostles, and make them believe they brought the whole purchase-money. They came and *laid the money at the apostles' feet,* as if it were their all.

II. The indictment of Ananias, which proved both his condemnation and execution for this sin. When he brought the money Peter took him to task about it. He charges him peremptorily with the crime, showing it to him in its own colour, *v.* 3, 4. The Spirit of God in Peter not only discovered the fact but likewise discerned the principle of reigning infidelity in the heart of Ananias, which was at the bottom of it. Had it been a sin of infirmity, through the surprise of a temptation, Peter would have bidden him go home, and repent of his folly. He here showed him,

1. The origin of his sin: *Satan filled his heart;* he not only suggested it to him, and put it into his head, but hurried him on with resolution to do it.

2. The sin itself: *He lied to the Holy Ghost;* a sin of such a heinous nature that he could not have been guilty of it if Satan had not filled his heart. We read it, *to lie unto the Holy Ghost,* which reading is countenanced by *v.* 4, *Thou hast not lied unto men, but unto God.* Ananias told a lie; he told Peter that he had sold a possession and this was the purchase-money. He did as the rest did who brought the whole price, and would be thought to do so, and expected the praise those had that did so. Many are brought to gross lying by reigning pride, and affectation of the applause of men, particularly in works of charity to the poor. Those that boast of good works they never did, or promise good works they never do, or make the good works they do more or better than really they are, come under the guilt of Ananias's lie. He told this lie *to the Holy Ghost.* It was not so much to the apostles as to the Holy Ghost in them that the money was brought, and that was said which was said, *v.* 4, *Thou hast not lied unto men but thou hast lied unto God.*

3. The aggravations of the sin (v. 4): *While it remained, was it not thine own? And, after it was sold, was it not in thine own power?* (1) "Thou wast under no temptation *to keep back part of the price;* before it was sold it was thy own, and when it was sold it was in thy own power to dispose of the money at thy pleasure." Or, (2) "Thou wast under no necessity of selling thy land at all, nor bringing any of the money to the apostles' feet. Thou mightest have kept the money, if thou hadst pleased, and the land too." It is better not to vow than to vow and not to pay, so better had it been for him not to have pretended to do the good work than thus to do it by the halves. *"When it was sold, it was in thine own power;* but it was not so when it was vowed." Thus, in giving our hearts to God, we are not admitted to divide them. Satan, like the mother whose own the child was not, would take up with a half; but God will have all or none.

4. All this guilt is charged upon him: *Why hast thou conceived this thing in thine heart?* He is said to have conceived it in his own heart, which shows that we cannot extenuate our sins by laying the fault of them upon the devil; he tempts, but he cannot force. The close of the charge is very high, but very just: *Thou hast not lied unto men, but unto God.* If we think to put a cheat upon God, we shall prove in the end to have put a fatal cheat upon our own souls.

III. The death and burial of Ananias, *v.* 5, 6.

1. He died upon the spot: *Ananias, hearing these words, was speechless:* he had nothing to say for himself; but this was not all. He *fell down, and gave up the ghost.* See the power of the word of God in the mouth of the apostles. As there are those whom the gospel justifies, so there are those whom it condemns. This punishment of Ananias may seem severe, but we are sure it was just. It was a great affront which Ananias put upon the Holy Ghost, as if he could be imposed upon. It was designed to deter others from the like presumptions. The doing of this by the ministry of Peter, who himself with a lie denied his Master, intimates that it was not the resentment of a wrong done to himself; for then he would have forgiven this affront, and endeavoured to bring this offender to repentance;

but it was the act of the Spirit of God in Peter: to him the indignity was done, and by him the punishment was inflicted.

2. He was buried immediately, for this was the manner of the Jews (*v.* 6): *The young men wound up the dead body in grave-clothes, carried it out* and *buried it.*

IV. The reckoning with Sapphira, the wife of Ananias. *She came in about three hours after, for she knew not what had been done.*

1. She was found guilty of sharing with her husband in his sin, by a question that Peter asked her (*v.* 8): *Tell me whether you sold the land for so much?* Saith she, "We had no more, but that was every farthing we received." Ananias and his wife agreed to tell the same story; they thought they might safely stand in the lie, and should gain credit to it. It is sad to see those relations who should quicken one another to that which is good harden one another in that which is evil.

2. Sentence was passed upon her, that she should partake in her husband's doom, *v.* 9.

(1) Her sin is opened: *How is it that you have agreed together to tempt the Spirit of the Lord?* Before he passes sentence he shows her the evil of her sin. They tempted the Spirit of the Lord. They saw that the apostles had the gift of tongues; but had they the gift of discerning spirits? Those that presume upon security and impunity in sin tempt the Spirit of God. They agreed together to do it. It is hard to say which is worse between yoke-fellows and other relations—a discord in good or concord in evil.

(2) Her doom is read: *Behold, the feet of those who have buried thy husband are at the door, and they shall carry thee out.*

3. The sentence executed itself. *Then she fell down straightway at his feet.* Some sinners God makes quick work with, while others he bears long with; for which difference, doubtless, there are good reasons; but he is not accountable to us for them. And many instances there are of sudden deaths which are not to be looked upon as the punishment of some gross sin, like this. We must not think that all who die suddenly are sinners above others; perhaps it is in favour to them, that they have a quick passage: however, it is forewarning to all to be always ready. But here it is plain that it was in judgment. Some put the question concerning the eternal state of Ananias and Sapphira, and incline to think that the destruction of the flesh was that *the spirit might be saved in the day of the Lord Jesus.* But secret things belong not to us. It is said, *She fell down at Peter's feet.* The *young men* coming in *found her dead. They carried her out and buried her by her husband.* Some ask whether the apostles kept the money which they did bring. What they brought was not polluted to those to whom they brought it; but what they kept back was polluted to those that kept it back.

V. The impression that this made upon the people. Notice is taken of this in the midst of the story (*v.* 5): *Great fear came upon all that heard these things.* And again (*v.* 11), *Great fear came upon all the church, and upon as many as heard these things.* Those that had joined themselves to the church were thereby struck with an awe of God and of his judgments. It was not a damp or check to their holy joy, but it taught them to be serious in it, and to rejoice with trembling.

Verses 12–16

I. Here is a general account of the miracles which the apostles wrought (*v.* 12): *By the hands of the apostles were many signs and wonders wrought among the people.* God had come out of his place to punish, but now returns to his place, to his mercy-seat again. The miracles they wrought proved their divine mission.

They were signs and wonders, such wonders as were confessedly signs of a divine presence and power.

II. We are here told what were the effects of these miracles.

1. The church was hereby kept together: *They were all with one accord in Solomon's porch.* They met in the temple, Solomon's porch. Those who permitted buyers and sellers could not for shame prohibit such preachers and healers there. They all met in public worship. They were there with one accord. The separation of hypocrites should make the sincere cleave so much the closer to each other.

2. It gained the apostles very great respect. *Of the rest* of their company *durst no man join himself to them,* as their equal or an associate with them. All *the people magnified them.* Though the chief priests did all they could to make them contemptible, this did not hinder the people from magnifying them. The apostles were far from magnifying themselves, and yet the people magnified them; for those that humble themselves shall be exalted, and those honoured that honour God only.

3. The church increased in number (*v.* 14): *Believers were the more added to the Lord,* even *multitudes both of men and women.* They were so far from being deterred by the example that was made of Ananias and Sapphira that they were rather invited by it into a society that kept such a strict discipline. Many have been brought to the Lord, and yet there is room for others to be added to him, added to the number of those that are united to him. Notice is taken of the conversion of *women* as well as *men.* As among those that followed Christ while he was upon earth, so among those that believed on him after he went to heaven, great notice was taken of the good women.

4. The apostles had abundance of patients, and gained abundance of reputation by the cure of them all, *v.* 15, 16. So many *signs and wonders were wrought by the apostles* that all manner of people put in for the benefit of them, both in city and country, and had it. In the city: They *brought forth their sick into the streets.* And they *laid them on beds and couches that at least the shadow of Peter, passing by, might overshadow some of them,* though it could not reach them all; and it had the desired effect, as the woman's touch of the hem of Christ's garment had; and in this that word of Christ was fulfilled, *Greater works than these shall you do.* And, if such miracles were wrought by Peter's shadow, we have reason to think they were so by the other apostles, as by the handkerchiefs from Paul's body (*ch.* xix. 12). In the country towns: Multitudes came to Jerusalem from *the cities round about, bringing sick folks* and *those that were vexed with unclean spirits,* and they were *healed every one;* distempered bodies and distempered minds were set to rights. Thus opportunity was given to the apostles, both to convince people's judgments of the heavenly origin of the doctrine they preached, and also to engage people's affections both to them and it.

Verses 17–25

Never did any good work go on with any hope of success, but it met with opposition. It would have been strange if the apostles had gone on thus teaching and healing and had had no check. In these verses we have the malice of hell and the grace of heaven struggling about them, the one to drive them off from this good work, the other to animate them in it.

I. The priests were enraged at them, and shut them up in prison, *v.* 17, 18. 1. Who their enemies and persecutors were. The high priest was the ringleader, Annas or Caiaphas. Those that were most forward to join with the high priest herein were the *sect of the Sadducees,* who had a particular enmity to the gospel of Christ, because it confirmed the resurrection of the dead, and the future state, which they denied. 2. How they were affected towards them, ill affected, and exasperated to the last degree. They *rose up* in a passion, being *filled with indignation* at the apostles for preaching the doctrine of Christ, and curing the sick,—at the people for hearing them, and bringing the sick to them to be cured. 3. How they proceeded against them (v. 18): *They laid their hands on them*, and *put them in the common prison*, among the worst of malefactors. (1) To put a restraint upon them. While they had them in prison they kept them from going on in their work, and this they reckoned a good point gained. (2) To put a terror upon them, and so to drive them off from their work. The last time they had them before them, they only threatened them (*ch.* iv. 21); but, now they imprisoned them, to make them afraid of them. (3) To put a disgrace upon them, and therefore they chose to clap them up in the common prison.

II. God sent his angel to release them out of prison. The powers of darkness fight against them, but the Father of lights fights for them. The Lord will never desert his witnesses, his advocates, but will certainly stand by them.

1. The apostles are discharged from their imprisonment (v. 19): *The angel of the Lord by night opened the prison doors*, and, in spite of the keepers that *stood without before the doors, brought forth* the prisoners (see v. 23). There is no prison so dark, so strong, but God can both visit his people in it, and fetch them out of it.

2. They are charged to· go on with their work. The angel bade them, *Go, stand, and speak in the temple to the people all the words of this life*, v. 20. When they were miraculously set at liberty it was that they might go on with their work with so much the more boldness. Recoveries from sickness, releases out of trouble, are granted us, not that we may enjoy the comforts of our life, but that God may be honoured with the services of our life. Where they must preach: *Speak in the temple.* One would think it had been prudent to go on with it in a more private place. No; "Speak in the temple, for this is the place of concourse, this is your Father's house." It is not for the preachers of Christ's gospel to retire into corners, as long as they can have any opportunity of preaching in the great congregation. To whom they must preach: "*Speak to the people*, who are willing and desirous to be taught, and whose souls are as precious to Christ as the souls of the greatest." How they must preach: *Go, stand, and speak*, which intimates, not only that they must speak publicly, but that they must speak boldly and resolutely. What they must speak: *All the words of this life.* "Go, and preach the same to the world, that others may be comforted with the same comforts with which you yourselves are comforted of God. Of this life emphatically; this heavenly, divine life, in comparison with which the present earthly life does not deserve the name." The gospel is concerning matters of life and death, and ministers must preach it and people hear it accordingly. They must speak *all the words of this life*, and not conceal any. Christ's witnesses are sworn to speak the whole truth.

III. They went on with their work (v. 21): *When they heard this* they *returned to Solomon's porch*, v. 12. It was a great satisfaction to them to have these fresh orders. Now that the angel ordered them to go preach in the temple, their way was plain, and they ventured without any difficulty, entered into the temple, and feared not the face of man. If we may but be satisfied concerning our duty, our business is to keep close to this, and then we may cheerfully trust God with our safety. They set themselves immediately to execute them. They *entered into the temple early in the morning*, and taught them the gospel of the kingdom: and did not at all fear what

man could do unto them. The whole treasure of the gospel is lodged in their hands; if they be silent now the springs are shut up, and the whole work falls to the ground and is made to cease. When God gives opportunity of doing good, though we be under the restraint and terror of human powers, we should venture far rather than let go such an opportunity.

IV. The high priest and his party went on with their prosecution, v. 21. They *called the council together*, a great and extraordinary council, for they summoned *all the senate of the children of Israel*.

1. How they were prepared to crush the gospel of Christ and the preachers of it, for they raised the whole posse. The last time they had the apostles in custody they convened them only before a committee of those that were of the kindred of the high priest, but now they called together *all the eldership.* Thus God ordered it, that the confusion of the enemies, and the apostles' testimony against them, might be more public, and that those might hear the gospel who would not hear it otherwise than from the bar.

2. How they were disappointed, and had their faces filled with shame. An officer is despatched immediately to fetch the prisoners to the bar. (1) The officers come and tell them that they are not to be found in the prison, v. 22, 23. They were gone, and the report which the officers make is, "*The prison-door truly found we shut with all safety, the keepers standing without before the doors*, but when we went in *we found no man* therein." Which way the angel fetched them we are not told; however it was, they were gone. The Lord knows, though we do not, how to deliver the godly out of temptation, and how to loose those that are in bonds for his name's sake, and he will do it, as here, when he has occasion for them (v. 24): *When the high priest, and the captain of the temple*, and the *chief priests, heard these things*, they were all at a plunge, and looked one upon another, *doubting what this thing should be.* They were at their wits' end, having never been so disappointed in all their lives of anything they were so sure of. Those often distress and embarrass themselves that think to distress and embarrass the cause of Christ. (2) Their doubt is, in part, determined; and yet their vexation is increased by another messenger, who brings them word that their prisoners are preaching in the temple (v. 25): "*Behold, the men whom you put in prison are now standing in the temple*, under your nose and in defiance of you, *teaching the people.*" Now this confounded them more than anything. Common malefactors may have art enough to break prison; but those are uncommon ones that have courage enough to avow it when they have so done.

Verses 26–42

We are not told what it was that the apostles preached to the people; but what passed between them and the council we have here an account of; for in their sufferings there appeared more of a divine power and energy than even in their preaching.

I. The seizing of the apostles a second time. They brought them without violence. One would think they had reason to do so, in reverence to the temple, and for fear of the apostles, lest they should strike them, as they did Ananias. But all that restrained their violence was their fear of the people, who had such a veneration for the apostles that they would have stoned the officers if they had offered them any abuse. 2. Yet they brought them to those who were resolved to take violent courses with them (v. 27): They *brought them, to set them before the council.* Thus the powers that should have been a terror to evil works and workers became so to the good.

II. Their examination. The high priest told them what it was they had to lay to their charge, v. 28. 1. They had disobeyed the commands of authority (v.

28): "*Did not we* strictly charge and command you *that you should not teach in this name?* But you have disobeyed our commands." *Did not we command you?* Yes, they did; but did not Peter at the same time tell them that God's authority was superior to theirs, and his commands must take place of theirs? And they had forgotten this. 2. They had spread false doctrine among the people. "*You have filled Jerusalem with your doctrine*, and thereby have disturbed the public peace." 3. They had a malicious design against the government, as having made itself justly odious both to God and man: "*You intend to bring this man's blood*, the guilt of it before God, the shame of it before men, *upon us*." See here how those who with a great deal of presumption will do an evil thing yet cannot bear to hear of it afterwards. When they were in the heat of the persecution they could cry daringly enough, "*His blood be upon us and upon our children*." But now they take it as a great affront to have his blood laid at their door.

III. Their answer to the charge exhibited against them: *Peter and the other apostles* all spoke to the same purport; they spoke as one and the same Spirit gave them utterance.

1. They justified themselves in their disobedience (*v.* 29): *We ought to obey God rather than men.* God had commanded them to teach in the name of Christ, and therefore they ought to do it, though the chief priests forbade them. Those rulers have a great deal to answer for, who punish men for disobedience to them in that which is their duty to God.

2. They justified themselves in doing what they could to fill Jerusalem with the doctrine of Christ, and if they thereby bring his blood upon them they may thank themselves.

(1) The chief priests are told to their faces the indignities they did to this Jesus: "*You slew him and hanged him on a tree.*" People's being unwilling to hear of their faults is no good reason why they should not be faithfully told of them. It is a common excuse made for not reproving sin that the times will not bear it. But those whose office it is to reprove must not be awed by this; the times must bear it, and shall bear it.

(2) They are told also what honours God put upon this Jesus, and then let them judge who was in the right, the persecutors of his doctrine or the preachers of it. He calls God the *God of our fathers.* The God of *Abraham, Isaac,* and *Jacob,* is the *God and Father of our Lord Jesus Christ*; see what honour he did him. [1] He *raised him up.* "You put him to death, but God has restored him to life, so that God and you are manifestly contesting about this Jesus; and which must we side with?" [2] He *exalted him with his right hand.* "You loaded him with disgrace, but God has crowned him with honour; and ought we not to honour him whom God honours? God has *given him a name above every name.*" [3] "He has appointed him to be *a prince and a saviour.*" There is no having Christ to be our Saviour, unless we be willing to take him for our prince. We cannot expect to be redeemed and healed by him, unless we give up ourselves to be ruled by him. Faith takes an entire Christ, that came, not to save us in our sins, but to save us from our sins. [4] He is appointed to *give repentance to Israel and remission of sins.* Therefore they must preach in his name to the people of Israel, for his favours were designed primarily and principally for them. Why should the rulers and elders of Israel oppose one who came with no less a blessing to Israel than repentance and pardon? But repentance and remission of sins are blessings they neither value nor see their need of. Repentance and remission go together; wherever repentance is wrought remission is without fail granted. On the other hand, no remission without repentance. It is Jesus Christ that gives both repentance and remission. Are we appointed to repent? Christ is appointed to give repentance. The new heart is his work, and the broken spirit a sacrifice of his providing; and, when he has given repentance, if he should not give remission he would *forsake the work of his own hands.* [5] All this is well attested, *First,* by the apostles themselves. "*We are his witnesses,* and if we should be silent, as you would have us, we should betray a trust." When a cause is trying, witnesses ought not to be silenced, for the issue of the cause depends on their testimony. *Secondly,* By the Spirit of God. *The Holy Ghost is witness,* a witness from heaven. For this end the Holy Ghost is given us, whose operations we cannot stifle. The giving of the Holy Ghost to obedient believers, not only to bring them to the obedience of faith, but to make them eminently useful therein, is a very strong proof of the truth of Christianity. *Lastly,* The giving of the Holy Ghost to those that obey Christ is a plain evidence that it is the will of God that Christ should be obeyed; "judge then whether we ought to obey you in opposition to him."

IV. The impression which the apostles' defence of themselves made upon the court. Surely such fair reasoning could not but clear the prisoners, and convert the judges. They raged against it, and were filled, 1. With indignation: They were *cut to the heart*, angry to see their own sin set in order before them; stark mad to find that the gospel of Christ had so much to say for itself. When a sermon was preached to the people to this purport, they were *pricked to the heart*, in remorse and godly sorrow, *ch.* ii. 37. These here were *cut to the heart* with rage and indignation. 2. With malice against the apostles themselves. Since they see they cannot stop their mouths any other way than by stopping their breath, they *take counsel to slay them.* While the apostles went on in the service of Christ, with a holy security and serenity of mind, their persecutors went on in their opposition to Christ, with a constant perplexity and perturbation of mind, and vexation to themselves.

V. The grave advice which Gamaliel gave upon this occasion. This Gamaliel is here said to be a *Pharisee* by his profession and sect, and by office a *doctor of the law.* Paul was brought up at his feet (*ch.* xxii. 3). He is here said to be *in reputation among all the people.* He was a moderate man, and not apt to go in with furious measures. Men of temper and charity are justly had in reputation, for checking the incendiaries that otherwise would set the world on fire.

1. The necessary caution he gives to the council: *He commanded to put the apostles forth a little while. You men of Israel,* saith he, *take heed to yourselves,* consider what you do, or *intend to do, as touching these men, v.* 25. He calls them *men of Israel,* to enforce this caution: "You are men, that should be governed by reason; you are men of Israel, that should be governed by revelation. *Take heed to yourselves.*" The persecutors of God's people had best look to themselves, lest they fall into the pit which they dig.

2. The cases he cites. Two instances he gives of factious seditious men, whose attempts came to nothing of themselves; whence he infers that if these men were indeed such as they represented them their cause would sink with its own weight.

(1) There was one *Theudas, boasting himself to be somebody.* He observes here (*v.* 26) concerning him, how far he prevailed: "*A number of men, about four hundred* in all, joined themselves to him." How soon his pretensions were all dashed: "When *he was slain, all, as many as obeyed him, were scattered.* Now compare that case with this. You have slain Jesus, the ringleader of this faction. Now if he was an impostor and pretender, his death will be the death of his cause."

(2) The case was the same with *Judas of Galilee*, *v*. 37. [1] The attempt he made. It is said to be *after this*, which some read, *besides this*. It is not easy to determine particularly when these events happened. It is probable that they were cases which lately happened, and were fresh in memory. This *Judas drew away much people after him*. [2] Here is the defeat of his attempt, *he also perished, and all, even as many as obeyed him*, were dispersed.

3. His opinion upon the whole matter.

(1) That they should not persecute the apostles (*v*. 38): *Now I say unto you, "Refrain from these men; let not our hand be upon them."* It is uncertain whether he spoke this out of policy. The apostles did not attempt anything by outward force. Why should any outward force be used against them? Or, whether it was only the language of a mild quiet spirit. Or, whether God put this word into his mouth beyond his own intention. We are sure there was an overruling Providence in it, that the servants of Christ might not only come off, but come off honourably.

(2) That they should refer this matter to Providence: "Wait the issue. *If it be of men, it will come to nought* of itself; *if of God, it will stand*, in spite of all your powers and policies." That which is apparently wicked and immoral must be suppressed, but that which has a show of good, and it is doubtful whether it be of God or men, it is best to let it alone, and let it take its fate. Christ rules by the power of truth, not of the sword. [1] "If this *counsel, and this work, be of men, it will come to nothing*. If it be the counsel and work of foolish crack-brained men, they will run themselves out of breath. They will make themselves ridiculous. If it be the counsel and work of politic and designing men, let them alone awhile, and their knavery will be manifest to all men. Providence will never countenance it. *It will come to nothing* in a little time; there is no occasion to kill that which, if you give it a little time, will die of itself. The unnecessary use of power is an abuse of it." [2] "If it should prove *that this counsel and this work is of God*, then what do you think of persecuting them, of this attempt of yours (*v*. 33) *to slay them?* You must conclude it to be a fruitless attempt against them: *If it be of God, you cannot overthrow it.*" It may be the comfort of all who are sincerely on God's side, that whatsoever is of God cannot be overthrown totally and finally, though it may be very vigorously opposed; it may be run upon, but cannot be run down. "A dangerous attempt to yourselves. Pray let it alone, *lest haply you be found even to fight against God.*" Those that hate and abuse God's faithful people, that restrain and silence his faithful ministers, fight against God. Well, this was the advice of Gamaliel: we wish it were duly considered by those that persecute for conscience' sake.

VI. The determination of the council upon the whole matter, *v*. 40. Thus far they agreed with Gamaliel that they let fall the design of putting the apostles to death. Yet they could not forbear giving some vent to their rage. *They beat them*, scourged them as malefactors, and notice is taken (*v*. 41) of the ignominy of it. Thus they thought to make them ashamed of preaching, and the people ashamed of hearing them. *They commanded them that they should not speak* any more *in the name of Jesus*.

VII. The wonderful courage and constancy of the apostles. *They departed from the council*, and we do not find one word they said by way of reflection upon the court, *but committed their cause to him* to whom Gamaliel had referred it.

1. They bore their sufferings with an invincible cheerfulness (*v*. 41): When *they went out*, instead of being ashamed of Christ, *they rejoiced that they were counted worthy to suffer shame for his name*. They were men that had never done anything to make themselves vile, and therefore could not but have a sense of the shame they suffered, which was more grievous to them than the smart, as it usually is to ingenuous minds; but they considered that it was for the name of Christ that they were thus abused, and their sufferings should be made to contribute to the further advancement of his name. They reckoned it an honour *that they were counted worthy to suffer shame, that they were honoured to be dishonoured for Christ*. Reproach for Christ is true preferment. They rejoiced in it, remembering what their Master had said to them at their first setting out (Matt. v. 11, 12): *When men shall revile you, and persecute you, rejoice and be exceedingly glad*. They rejoiced *that they suffered shame*. If we suffer ill for doing well, provided we suffer it well, we ought to rejoice in that grace which enables us so to do.

2. They went on in their work with indefatigable diligence (*v*. 42): They were commanded *not to preach*, and *yet they ceased not to teach and preach*. When they preached—*daily*; every day, as duly as the day came. Where they preached—both publicly *in the temple*, and privately *in every house*. Though in the temple they were under the eye of their enemies, yet they did not confine themselves to their own houses, but ventured into the post of danger; and though they had the liberty of the temple, yet they made no difficulty of preaching in houses, in every house, even the poorest cottage. What was the subject matter of their preaching: *They preached Jesus Christ*. They did *not preach themselves, but Christ*. This was the preaching that gave most offence to the priests, but they would not alter their subject to please them. It ought to be the constant business of gospel ministers to preach Christ; *Christ, and him crucified; Christ, and him glorified*.

CHAPTER 6

I. The discontent that was among the disciples about the distribution of the public charity, ver. 1. II. The election and ordination of seven men, who should take care of that matter, ver. 2–6. III. The increase of the church, ver. 7. IV. A particular account of Stephen. 1. His great activity for Christ, ver. 8. 2. The opposition he met with from the enemies of Christianity, ver. 9, 10. 3. The convening of him before the great sanhedrim, ver. 11–14. 4. God's owning him upon his trial, ver. 15.

Verses 1–7

I. An unhappy disagreement among some of the church members was prudently taken up in time (*v*. 1): *When the number of the disciples was multiplied there arose a murmuring*.

1. It does our hearts good to find that *the number of the disciples is multiplied*, as, no doubt, it vexed *the priests and Sadducees* to see it. The opposition that the preaching of the gospel met with contributed to the success of it. The preachers were beaten, threatened, and abused, and yet the people received their doctrine, invited thereto by their wonderful patience and cheerfulness under their trials.

2. Yet it casts a damp upon us to find that the multiplying of the disciples proves an occasion of discord. Now that they were multiplied they began to murmur. *There arose a murmuring*, not an open falling out, but a secret heart-burning.

(1) The complainants were *the Grecians against the Hebrews*—the Jews that were scattered in Greece, and other parts, many of whom being at Jerusalem at the feast embraced the faith of Christ. These complained against the Hebrews, the native Jews. Some of each of these became Christians, and their joint-embracing of the faith of Christ did not prevail to extinguish the little jealousies they had one of another before their conversion. But all are alike welcome to Christ, and should be, for his sake, dear to one another.

(2) The complaint of these Grecians was *that their widows were neglected in the daily administration*.

The first contention in the Christian church was about a money-matter. A great deal of money was gathered for the relief of the poor, but, as often happens in such cases, it was impossible to please everybody in the laying of it out. *The apostles* no doubt designed to do it with the utmost impartiality, and yet here they are complained to, and tacitly complained of, *that the Grecian widows were neglected.* Perhaps this complaint was groundless and unjust. Those who, upon any account, lie under disadvantages (as the Grecian Jews did, in comparison with those that were Hebrews of the Hebrews) are apt to be jealous that they are slighted when really they are not so; and it is the common fault of poor people that they are querulous and clamorous, and apt to find fault that more is not given them. There are envy and covetousness to be found among the poor as well as among the rich. We will suppose there might be some occasion for their complaint. As those that have the administration of public justice ought in a particular manner to protect widows from injury, so those that have the administration of public charity ought in a particular manner to provide for widows what is necessary. In the best-ordered church in the world there will be something amiss, some grievances, or at least some complaints; those are the best that have the least and the fewest.

II. The happy accommodating of this matter. The apostles had hitherto the directing of the matter. Some persons must be chosen to manage this matter who have more leisure to attend to it than the apostles had.

1. How the method was proposed by the apostles: They *called the multitude of the disciples unto them.* The twelve themselves would not determine anything without them. Those might be best able to advise who were more conversant in the affairs of this life than the apostles were.

(1) The apostles could by no means admit so great a diversion from their great work (*v.* 2): *It is not reasonable that we should leave the word of God and serve tables.* This was foreign to the business which the apostles were called to. They were *to preach the word of God.* They thought that was work enough for a whole man. If they serve tables, they must, in some measure, *leave the word of God.* They will no more be drawn from their preaching by the money laid at their feet than they will be driven from it by the stripes laid on their backs. Preaching the gospel is the best work that a minister can be employed in. He must not entangle himself in the affairs of this life, no, not in the outward business of the house of God.

(2) They therefore desire *that seven men* might be chosen whose business it should be *to serve tables, v.* 2. The business must be minded, must be better minded than it had been, and than the apostles could mind it; and therefore proper persons must be chosen, that everything might be done decently and in order, and no person nor thing neglected. The persons must be duly qualified. The people are to choose, and the apostles to ordain. *Look out seven men.* These must be *of honest report,* men free from scandal, that were looked upon by their neighbours as men of integrity, that might be trusted, well spoken of for everything that is virtuous. They must be *full of the Holy Ghost.* They must not only be honest men, but they must be men of ability and men of courage, hereby appearing to be *full of the Holy Ghost.* They must be *full of wisdom.* It was not enough that they were honest, good men, but they must be discreet, judicious men, that could not be imposed upon: *full of the Holy Ghost, and wisdom,* that is, of the Holy Ghost as a Spirit of wisdom. Those must be full of wisdom who are entrusted with public money, that it may be disposed of, not only with

fidelity, but with frugality. The people must nominate the persons: "*Look you out among yourselves seven men.*" They might be presumed to know better, or at least were fitter to enquire, what character men had, than the apostles. The apostles will ordain them to the service, will give them their charge, and give them their authority. *Whom we may appoint over this business,* to take care of it, and to see that there be neither waste nor want.

(3) The apostles engage to addict themselves wholly to their work as ministers, if they can but get fairly quit of this troublesome office (*v.* 4): *We will give ourselves continually to prayer, and to the ministry of the word.* See here, [1] What are the two great gospel ordinances—*the word, and prayer.* By these two the kingdom of Christ must be advanced, and additions made to it. [2] What is the great business of gospel ministers—to give themselves continually to prayer, and to the ministry of the word. They must be God's mouth to the people in the ministry of the word, and the people's mouth to God in prayer. In order to the conviction and conversion of sinners, and the edification and consolation of saints, we must not only offer up our prayers for them, but we must minister the word to them. Nor must we only minister the word to them, but we must pray for them. God's grace can do all without our preaching, but our preaching can do nothing without God's grace. Those ministers, without doubt, are the successors of the apostles, who give themselves continually to prayer, and to the ministry of the word.

2. How this proposal was agreed to by the disciples. It was not imposed, but proposed. *The saying pleased the whole multitude, v.* 5.

(1) They pitched upon the persons. The majority of votes fell upon the persons here named; and the rest both of the candidates and the electors acquiesced. The overseers of the poor were chosen by the suffrage of the people, in which yet a regard is to be had to the providence of God. We have a list of the persons chosen. We may conjecture, concerning these seven, [1] That they were such as had sold their estates, and brought the money into the common stock; those were fittest to be entrusted with the distribution of it who had been most generous in the contribution to it. [2] That these seven were all of the Grecian or Hellenist Jews, for they have all Greek names, and this would be most likely *to silence the murmurings of the Grecians. Nicolas,* it is plain, was one of them, for he was *a proselyte of Antioch.* The first named is *Stephen, a man full of faith and of the Holy Ghost, full of fidelity, full of courage* (so some), for he was *full of the Holy Ghost,* of his gifts and graces. He was an extraordinary man, and excelled in everything that was good: his name signifies *a crown. Philip* is put next, afterwards ordained to the office of an evangelist, a companion and assistant to the apostles, for so he is expressly called, *ch.* xxi. 8. And his preaching and baptizing (which we read of *ch.* viii. 12) were certainly not as a deacon, but as an evangelist. The last named is *Nicolas,* who, some say, afterwards degenerated (as the Judas among these seven) and was the founder of *the sect of the Nicolaitans* which we read of (Rev. ii. 6, 15), and which Christ there says, once and again, was a thing he hated. But some of the ancients clear him from this charge, and tell us that, though that vile impure sect denominated themselves from him, yet it was unjustly, and because he only insisted much upon it *that those that had wives should be as though they had none,* thence they wickedly inferred *that those that had wives should have them in common,* which therefore Tertullian, when he speaks of the community of goods, particularly excepts: *Omnia indiscreta apud nos, præter uxores—All things are common among us, except our wives*—Apol. cap. 39.

(2) The apostles appointed them to this work of

serving tables for the present, *v.* 6. They prayed with them, and for them. All that are employed in the service of the church ought to be committed to the conduct of the divine grace by the prayers of the church. *They laid their hands on them.* Having by prayer implored a blessing upon them, they did by the laying on of hands assure them that the blessing was conferred in answer to the prayer; and this was giving them authority to execute that office.

III. The advancement of the church hereupon. When things were thus put into good order in the church then religion got ground, *v.* 7. *The word of God increased.* Now that the apostles resolved to stick more closely than ever to their preaching, it spread the gospel further. Ministers disentangling themselves from secular employments, and addicting themselves entirely to their work, will contribute very much, as a means, to the success of the gospel. Christians became numerous: *The number of the disciples multiplied in Jerusalem greatly.* When Christ was upon earth, his ministry had least success in Jerusalem; yet now that city affords most converts. God has his remnant even in the worst of places. *A great company of the priests were obedient to the faith.* Then is the word and grace of God greatly magnified when those are wrought upon by it that were least likely. It should seem, they came *in a body*; many of them agreed together, for the keeping up of one another's credit, and the strengthening of one another's hands, to join at once in giving up their names to Christ: *a great crowd of priests* were by the grace of God helped over their prejudices, and *were obedient to the faith.* They embraced the doctrine of the gospel; their understandings were captivated to the power of the truths of Christ. They evinced the sincerity of their believing the gospel of Christ by a cheerful compliance with all the rules and precepts of the gospel.

Verses 8–15

Stephen, no doubt, was diligent and faithful in the discharge of his office. Being called to that office, he did not think it below him to do the duty of it. And, being faithful in a little, he was entrusted with more. We find him here called out to very honourable services, and owned in them.

I. He proved the truth of the gospel, by working miracles in Christ's name, *v.* 8. He was *full of faith and power.* Those that are full of faith are full of power, because by faith the power of God is engaged for us. By faith we are emptied of self, and so are filled with Christ. Being so *he did great wonders and miracles among the people,* openly, and in the sight of all; for Christ's miracles feared not the strictest scrutiny.

II. He pleaded the cause of Christianity against those that opposed it (*v.* 9, 10); he served the interests of religion as a disputant, in the high places of the field, while others were serving them as vinedressers and husbandmen.

1. We are here told who were his opponents, *v.* 9. They were Jews, but Hellenist Jews. It was with difficulty that they retained the practice of it in the country where they lived, and not without great expense and toil that they kept up their attendance at Jerusalem, and this made them more active sticklers for Judaism than those were whose profession of their religion was cheap and easy. They were *of the synagogue which is called the synagogue of the Libertines*; the Romans called those *Liberti*, or *Libertini*, who, slaves by birth, were manumitted, or made freemen. Some think that these Libertines were such of the Jews as had obtained the Roman freedom, as Paul had (*ch.* 27, 28). There were others that belonged to the synagogue of the Cyrenians and Alexandrians, and others who were of Cilicia and Asia. The Jews

that were born in other countries, and had concerns in them, had frequent occasion to reside in Jerusalem. Each nation had its synagogue, as in London there are French, and Dutch, and Danish churches. Now those that were in these synagogues, being confident of the goodness of their cause, and their own sufficiency to manage it, would undertake to run down Christianity by force of argument. It was a fair and rational way of dealing with it, and what religion is always ready to admit. But why did they dispute with Stephen? And why not with the apostles themselves? Some think because they despised the apostles as *unlearned and ignorant men*; but Stephen was bred a scholar, and they thought it their honour to meddle with their match. Others think it was because they stood in awe of the apostles. Perhaps, they having given a public challenge, Stephen was chosen by the disciples to be their champion. Stephen, who was only a deacon in the church, and a very sharp young man, of bright parts, was appointed to this service. It is probable that they disputed with Stephen because he was zealous to argue with them and convince them, and this was the service to which God had called them.

2. We are here told how he carried the point in this dispute (*v.* 10): *They were not able to resist the wisdom and the Spirit by which he spoke.* They could neither support their own arguments nor answer his. Though they were not convinced, yet they were confounded. It is not said, They were not able to resist him, but, They were not able to resist the *wisdom and the Spirit by which he spoke.* They thought they had only disputed with Stephen; but they were disputing with the Spirit of God in him, for whom they were an unequal match.

III. At length, he sealed it with his blood. When they could not answer his arguments as a disputant, they prosecuted him as a criminal, and suborned witnesses against him, to swear blasphemy upon him. They suborned men, that is, instructed them what to say, and then hired them to swear it.

1. How they incensed both the government and the mob against him (*v.* 12): *They stirred up the people* against him, that, if the sanhedrim should still think fit to let him alone, yet they might run him down by a popular tumult; they also found means to stir up the elders and scribes against him, that, if the people should countenance him, they might prevail by authority. Thus they doubted not but to gain their point, when they had two strings to their bow.

2. How they got him to the bar: *They came upon him and caught him and brought him to the council.* They came upon him in a body, and flew upon him as a lion upon his prey; so the word signifies.

3. How they were prepared with evidence ready to produce against him. They had *heard him speak blasphemous words against Moses and against God* (*v.* 11)—against this *holy place and the law* (*v.* 13); for they heard him say what Jesus would do to their place and their customs, *v.* 14. Those who swore it against him are called *false witnesses,* because though there was something of truth in their testimony, yet they put a wrong and malicious construction upon what he had said, and perverted it. The general charge exhibited against him—that he *spoke blasphemous words*; and, to aggravate the matter, "He *ceases not to speak blasphemous words.*" It intimates likewise something of contumacy and contempt of admonition. "He has been warned against it, and yet ceases not to talk at this rate." Stephen's persecutors would be thought to have a deep concern upon them for the honour of God's name, and to do this in a jealousy for that. He is said to have spoken blasphemous words *against Moses and against God.* But did Stephen blaspheme Moses? By no means. Christ, and the preachers of his gospel, never said anything

that looked like blaspheming Moses. Very unjustly therefore is Stephen indicted for blaspheming Moses. How this charge is supported and made out. All they can charge him with is that *that he hath spoken blasphemous words against this holy place and the law.* Thus does the charge dwindle when it comes to the evidence. He is charged with blaspheming *this holy place.* Christ was condemned as a blasphemer for words which were thought to reflect upon the temple, even when they by their wickedness had profaned it. He is charged with blaspheming *the law.* The charge dwindles again; for all they can accuse him of is that *they had heard him say* that this *Jesus of Nazareth shall destroy this place, and change the customs which Moses delivered to us.* He could not be charged with having said anything to the disparagement either of the temple or of the law. He had said, *Jesus of Nazareth shall destroy this place,* destroy the temple, destroy Jerusalem. It is probable that he might say so; and what blasphemy was it against the holy place to say that it should not be perpetual. And is he a blasphemer, then, who tells them that Jesus of Nazareth will bring a just destruction upon their place and nation, and they may thank themselves? He had said, *This Jesus shall change the customs which Moses delivered to us.* Christ came, *not to destroy,* but to fulfil, the law; and, if he changed some customs it was to introduce and establish those that were much better.

IV. We are here told how God owned him (*v.* 15): *All that sat in the council, looking steadfastly on him, saw his face as it had been the face of an angel.* It is usual for judges to observe the countenance of the prisoner, which sometimes is an indication either of guilt or innocence. He looked as if he had never been better pleased in his life than he was now when he stood fair for the crown of martyrdom. Such an undisturbed serenity, such an undaunted courage, and such an unaccountable mixture of mildness and majesty, there was in his countenance, that everyone said he looked like an angel. There was a miraculous splendour and brightness upon his countenance, God designing thereby to put honour upon his faithful witness and confusion upon his persecutors and judges. *All that sat in the council saw it,* and an arrant shame it was that they could not but see by it that he was owned of God. Wisdom and holiness make a man's face to shine, and yet these will not secure men from the greatest indignities.

CHAPTER 7

In this chapter we have the martyrdom of Stephen, the first martyr of the Christian church. And therefore his sufferings and death are more largely related than those of any other. I. His defence of himself before the council that it was no blasphemy against God to say that the temple should be destroyed and the customs of the ceremonial law changed. And, 1. He shows this by going over the history of the Old Testament. That holy place and that law were but figures of good things to come, and it was no disparagement at all to them to say that they must give place to better things, ver. 1–50. 2. He applies this to those that prosecuted him, and sat in judgment upon him, ver. 51–53. II. The putting of him to death by stoning him, and his patient, cheerful, pious submission to it, ver. 54–60.

Verses 1–16

I. The high priest calls upon him to answer for himself, *v.* 1. You hear what is sworn against you: *Are these things so? Guilty or not guilty?*

II. He begins his defence, and it is long.

1. In this discourse he appears to be a man ready and mighty in the scriptures. He was *filled with the Holy Ghost,* not so much to reveal to him new things, but to bring to his remembrance the scriptures of the Old Testament, and to teach him how to make use of them. Those that are full of the Holy Ghost will be full of the scripture, as Stephen was.

2. He quotes the scriptures according to the Septuagint translation, by which it appears he was one of the Hellenist Jews. His preface: *Men, brethren, and fathers, hearken.* He gives them, though not flattering titles, yet civil and respectful ones. They are ready to look upon him as an apostate from the Jewish church, and an enemy to them. He addresses himself to them as *men, brethren, and fathers,* resolving to look on himself as one of them, though they would not so look on him. He craves their attention: *Hearken.* His entrance upon the discourse. It is all *to the purpose,* to show them that God, as he had a church in the world many ages before that holy place was founded and the ceremonial law given, so he would have when they should both have had their period.

[1] He begins with the call of Abraham, the father of the Old Testament church. His native country was an idolatrous country, it was Mesopotamia (*v.* 2), *the land of the Chaldeans* (*v.* 4); thence God brought him. He first brought him out of the land of the Chaldeans to Charran, or Haran, and thence five years after, when his father was dead, he *removed him into* the land of *Canaan, wherein you now dwell.* From this call of Abraham we may observe, 1. That in all our ways we must acknowledge God, and attend the directions of his providence. *God removed him into this land wherein you now dwell,* and he did but follow his Leader. 2. Those whom God takes into covenant with himself must sit loose to the world, and live above it and everything in it, even that in it which is most dear to them. God's chosen must follow him with an implicit faith and obedience But let us see what this is to Stephen's case. They had charged him as a blasphemer of God, therefore he shows that he is a son of Abraham, and values himself upon his being able to say, *Our father Abraham,* and that he is a faithful worshipper of the God of Abraham, whom therefore he here calls *the God of glory.* They were proud of their being circumcised; and therefore he shows that Abraham was taken under God's guidance, and into communion with him, before he was circumcised. They had a mighty jealousy for this holy place, which may be meant of the whole land of Canaan. "Now," says Stephen, "you need not be so proud of it; for," (1) "You came originally out of *Ur of the Chaldees,* and you were not the first planters of this country. Think of the meanness of your beginnings, and how you are entirely indebted to divine grace, and then you will see boasting to be for ever excluded." (2) "God appeared in his glory to Abraham a great way off in Mesopotamia, before he came near Canaan, so that you must not think God's visits are confined to *this land.*"

[2] The unsettled state of Abraham and his seed for many ages after he was called out of Ur of the Chaldees. God did indeed promise that he would *give it to him for a possession, and to his seed after him, v.* 5. But, *First, As yet he had no child,* nor any by Sarah for many years after. *Secondly,* He himself was but a stranger and a sojourner in that land, and God *gave him no inheritance in it, no, not so much as to set his foot on*; but there he was as in a strange country. *Thirdly,* His posterity did not come to the possession of it for a long time: *After four hundred years they shall come and serve me in this place,* and not till then, *v.* 7. *Fourthly,* They must undergo a great deal of hardship before they shall be put into the possession of that land: they shall be brought into bondage, and ill treated in a strange land. And *at the end of four hundred years that nation to whom they shall be in bondage will I judge, saith God.* When Abraham had neither inheritance nor heir, yet he was told he should have both. God's promises, though they are slow, are sure. They will be fulfilled though perhaps not so soon as we expect.

Though the people of God may be in distress and trouble for a time, yet God will at length both rescue them and reckon with those that do oppress them.

But let us see how this serves Stephen's purpose. 1. The Jewish nation was very inconsiderable in its beginnings; as their common father Abraham was fetched out of obscurity in Ur of the Chaldees, so their tribes were fetched out of servitude in Egypt. He that brought them out of Egypt can bring them into it again, and yet be no loser, while he can out of stones raise up children unto Abraham. 2. The slow steps by which the promise made to Abraham advanced towards the performance plainly show that it had a spiritual meaning, and that the land principally intended to be conveyed by it was the *better country, that is, the heavenly*. It was therefore no blasphemy to say, *Jesus shall destroy this place*, when at the same time we say, "He shall lead us to the heavenly Canaan."

[3] The building up of the family of Abraham.

First, God engaged to be a God to Abraham and his seed; and, in token of this, appointed that he and his male seed should be circumcised. He *gave him the covenant of circumcision*, and accordingly, when Abraham had a son born, he *circumcised him the eighth day* (*v.* 8). And then they began to multiply: *Isaac begat Jacob, and Jacob the twelve patriarchs*.

Secondly, Joseph, the darling and blessing of his father's house, was abused by his brethren; they *envied him* because of his dreams, and *sold him into Egypt*.

Thirdly, God owned Joseph in his troubles, and was with him by the influence of his Spirit, both on his mind, giving him comfort, and on the minds of those he was concerned with, giving him favour in their eyes. And thus at length he *delivered him out of his afflictions*.

Fourthly, Jacob was compelled to go down into Egypt by *a dearth* (which was a *great affliction*), to that degree that *our fathers found no sustenance* in Canaan, *v.* 11. But, hearing that there was *corn in Egypt* (treasured up by the wisdom of his own son), he *sent out our fathers first* to fetch corn, *v.* 12. And the *second time* that they went, Joseph made himself known to them, and it was notified to Pharaoh that they were Joseph's kindred (*v.* 13), whereupon *Joseph sent for his father Jacob to him into Egypt*, with *all his kindred and family*, to the number of *seventy-five souls, v.* 14.

Fifthly, Jacob and his sons died in Egypt (*v.* 15), but were carried over to be buried in Canaan, *v.* 16.

Let us now see what this is to Stephen's purpose. 1. He still reminds them of the mean beginning of the Jewish nation. It was by a miracle of mercy that they were raised up out of nothing to what they were. If they answer not the intention of their being so raised, they can expect no other than to be destroyed. Here it is urged upon them as an aggravation of their contempt of the gospel of Christ. 2. He reminds them likewise of the wickedness of those that were the patriarchs in envying their brother Joseph, and selling him into Egypt; and the same spirit was still working in them towards Christ. 3. Their holy land, which they doted so much upon, their fathers were long kept out of the possession of, and therefore let them not think it strange if, after it has been so long polluted with sin, it be at length destroyed.

Verses 17–29

I. The wonderful increase of the people of Israel in Egypt; it was by a wonder of providence that in a little time they advanced from a family into a nation. It was *when the time of the promise drew nigh*—the time when they were to be formed into a people. The notion of providence is sometimes quickest when it comes nearest the centre. God knows how to redeem the time that seems to have been lost, and, *when the year of the redeemed is at hand*, can do a double work in a single day. It was *in Egypt*, where they were oppressed. Suffering times have often been growing times with the church.

II. The extreme hardships which they underwent there, *v.* 18, 19. Stephen observes three things: 1. Their base ingratitude: They were oppressed by *another king that knew not Joseph*. Those that injure good people are very ungrateful, for they are the blessings of the age and place they live in. 2. Their hellish craft and policy: *They dealt subtly with our kindred. Come on*, said they, *let us deal wisely*, thinking thereby to secure themselves. Those are in a great mistake who think they deal wisely for themselves when they deal deceitfully or unmercifully with their brethren. 3. Their barbarous and inhuman cruelty. *They cast out their young children, to the end they might not live*. What they were now doing against the Christian church in its infancy was as impious and would be as fruitless as that was which the Egyptians did against the Jewish church in its infancy. In spite of your malice Christ's disciples will *increase and multiply*.

III. The raising up of *Moses to be their deliverer*. Moses was born when the persecution of Israel was at the hottest: *At that time, Moses was born* (*v.* 20), and was himself in danger of falling a sacrifice to that bloody edict. God is preparing for his people's deliverance, when their way is darkest, and their distress deepest. *He was exceedingly fair*. He was sanctified from the womb, and this made him beautiful in God's eyes. He was wonderfully preserved in his infancy, first, by the care of his tender parents, who *nourished him three months in their own house*; and then by a favourable providence that threw him *into the arms of Pharaoh's daughter, who took him up, and nourished him as her own son* (*v.* 21); for those whom God designs to make special use of he will take special care of. He became a great scholar (*v.* 22): *He was learned in all the wisdom of the Egyptians*. He became a prime minister of state in Egypt, being *mighty in words and deeds*. Though he had not a ready way of expressing himself, but stammered, yet he spoke admirably good sense, and everything he said commanded assent. Now, by all this, Stephen will make it appear that he had as high and honourable thoughts of Moses as they had.

IV. The attempts which Moses made to deliver Israel, which they spurned. This Stephen insists much upon, and it serves for a key to this story, a designed entrance upon the public service he was to be called out to (*v.* 23): *When he was full forty years old it came into his heart* (for God put it there) *to visit his brethren the children of Israel*, and to see which way he might do them any service. 1. As Israel's saviour. This he gave a specimen of in avenging an oppressed Israelite, and killing the Egyptian that abused him (*v.* 24). *Seeing one of his brethren suffer wrong, he avenged him that was oppressed, and smote the Egyptian. He supposed that his brethren would have understood that God by his hand would deliver them*. If they had but understood the signs of the times, they might have taken this for the dawning of the day of their deliverance; *but they understood not*. 2. As Israel's judge. This he gave a specimen of, *the very next day*, in offering to accommodate matters between two contending Hebrews (*v.* 26): *He showed himself to them as they strove*, and *he would have set them at one again, saying, Sirs, you are brethren, why do you wrong one to another?* For he observed that (as in most strifes) there was a fault on both sides; and therefore there must be a mutual remission and condescension. *But* the contending Israelite that was most in *the wrong thrust him away* (*v.* 27), would not bear the reproof, but was ready to fly in his face, with, *Who made thee a ruler and a judge over us?* Proud and litigious spirits are impatient of check and control. The wrong-doer was so enraged at the reproof given him that he upbraided Moses with the service he had done to their nation in killing the Egyptian: *Wilt thou kill me as thou didst the Egyptian yesterday?* (*v.* 28), charging that upon him as his crime, which was the hanging out of the flag of defiance to the Egyptians, and the banner of love and deliverance to Israel. Hereupon *Moses fled into the land of Midian.* He settled as a stranger in Midian, married, and had two sons, by Jethro's daughter, *v.* 29. How this serves Stephen's purpose. 1. They charged him with blaspheming Moses, in answer to which he retorts upon them the indignities which their fathers did to Moses, which they ought to be ashamed of, instead of picking quarrels with one that had as great a veneration for him as any of them had. 2. They persecuted him for disputing in defence of Christ and his gospel. They set up Moses and his law: "But," saith he, "you had best take heed," (1) "Lest you refuse and reject one *whom God has raised up to be to you a prince and a Saviour.* God will, by this Jesus, deliver you out of a worse slavery than that in Egypt; take heed then of thrusting him away." (2) "Lest you hereby fare as your fathers fared. You put away the gospel from you, and it will be *sent to the Gentiles*; you will not have Christ, and you shall not have him."

Verses 30-41

Stephen here proceeds in his story of Moses.

I. The vision which he saw of the glory of God at the bush (*v.* 30): *When forty years had expired*, now, at eighty years old, he enters upon that post of honour to which he was born. Where God appeared to him: *In the wilderness of Mount Sinai, v.* 30. And, when he appeared to him there, that was holy ground (*v.* 33), which Stephen takes notice of, as a check to those who prided themselves in the temple, as if there were no communion to be had with God but there. They deceive themselves if they think God is confined to places; he can bring his people into a wilderness, and there speak comfortably to them. How he appeared to him: *In a flame of fire*, and yet *the bush was not consumed.* How Moses was affected with this: (1) *He wondered at the sight, v.* 31. He had the curiosity at first to pry into it: *I will turn aside now, and see this great sight;* but the nearer he drew the more he was struck with amazement. (2) *He trembled, and durst not behold*, for he was soon aware that it was *the angel of the Lord.* This set him a trembling.

II. The declaration which he heard of the covenant of God (*v.* 32): *The voice of the Lord came to him; I am the God of thy fathers, the God of Abraham, the God of Isaac, and the God of Jacob;* and therefore, 1. "I am the same that I was." The covenant God made with Abraham was, *I will be to thee a God.* "Now," saith God, "that covenant is still in full force; I am, as I was, the God of Abraham." All the favours, all the honours God put upon Israel, were founded upon this covenant with Abraham. 2. "I will be the same that I am." He will be a God, (1) To their souls, which are now separated from their bodies. Our Saviour by this proves the future state, Matt. xxii. 31, 32. Abraham is dead, and yet God is still his God, therefore Abraham is still alive. Now this is that life and immortality which are brought to light by the gospel. Those therefore who stood up in defence of the gospel were so far from blaspheming Moses that they did the greatest honour imaginable to Moses. (2) To their seed, God, in declaring himself thus the God of their fathers, intimated his kindness to their seed, that they should be *beloved for the fathers' sakes.* Now the preachers of the gospel preached up this covenant, *the promise made of God unto the fathers*, ch. xxvi. 6, 7. And shall they, under colour of supporting the holy place and the law, oppose the covenant which was made with Abraham, before the law was given, and long before the holy place was built? God will have our salvation to be by promise, and not by the law; the Jews therefore who persecuted the Christians, under pretence that they blasphemed the law, did themselves blaspheme the promise.

III. The commission which God gave him to deliver Israel out of Egypt. When God had declared himself the God of Abraham he proceeded, 1. To order Moses into a reverent posture: *"Put off thy shoes from thy feet.* Be not hasty and rash in thy approaches to God; tread softly." 2. To order Moses into a very eminent service. He is commissioned to demand leave from Pharaoh for Israel to go out of his land, *v.* 34. Observe, (1) The notice God took both of their sufferings and of their sense of their sufferings: *I have seen, I have seen their affliction, and have heard their groaning.* Their deliverance takes rise from his pity. (2) The determination he fixed to redeem them by the hand of Moses: *I am come down to deliver them.* Moses is the man that must be employed: *Come, and I will send thee into Egypt:* and, if God send him, he will give him success.

IV. His acting in pursuance of this commission. 1. God put honour upon him whom they put contempt upon (*v.* 35): *This Moses whom they refused saying, Who made thee a ruler and a judge? did God send to be a ruler, and a deliverer, by the hand of the angel which appeared to him in the bush.* Now, by this example, Stephen would intimate to the council *that this Jesus whom they now refused saying, Who gave thee this authority?* has God advanced *to be a prince and a Saviour*, as the apostles had told them awhile ago (*ch.* v. 30, 31), *that the stone which the builders refused was become the headstone in the corner, ch.* iv. 11. 2. God showed favour to them by him. God might justly have refused them his service, but it is all forgotten, *v.* 36. *He brought them out after he had shown wonders and signs in the land of Egypt, in the Red Sea, and in the wilderness forty years.* So far is he from blaspheming Moses that he admires him as a glorious instrument in the hand of God. But it does not at all derogate from his just honour to say that he was but an instrument, and that he is outshone by this Jesus, whom he encourages these Jews yet to close with. The people of Israel were delivered by Moses, though they had once refused him.

V. His prophecy of Christ and his grace, *v.* 37. Moses spoke of him (*v.* 37): *This is that Moses who said unto the children of Israel, A prophet shall the Lord your God raise up unto you of your brethren.* This is spoken of as one of the greatest honours God put upon him, that by him he gave notice to the children of Israel of the great prophet that should come into the world. In asserting that Jesus should change the customs of the ceremonial law, he was so far from blaspheming Moses that really he did him the greatest honour imaginable. Christ told them himself, *If they had believed Moses, they would have believed him*, John v. 46. Moses told them that they should have a prophet raised up among them, one of their own nation, who should therefore have authority to change the customs that he had delivered, and to bring in a better hope, as *the Mediator of a better testament.* He charged them to hear that prophet. This will be the greatest honour you can do to Moses and to his law, who said, *Hear you him.*

VI. The eminent services which Moses continued to do to the people of Israel, after he had been instrumental to bring them out of Egypt, *v.* 38. It was the honour of Moses, 1. That *he was in the church in the wilderness*; he presided in all the affairs of it for forty years. Many a time it had been destroyed if Moses had not been in it to intercede for it. But Christ is the president and guide of a more excellent and glorious church, and is more in it, as the life and soul of it, than Moses could be in that. 2. That *he was with the angel that spoke to him in the mount Sinai, and with our fathers. Moses was in the church in the wilderness*, but it was *with the angel that spoke to him in mount Sinai*. That angel was guide to him, else he could not have been a guide to Israel Christ is himself that angel and therefore has an authority above Moses. 3. That *he received the lively oracles to give unto them*; not only the ten commandments, but the other instructions which *the Lord spoke unto Moses*. The words of God are *oracles*, certain and infallible, by them all controversies must be determined. They are *lively oracles*. The word that God speaks is spirit and life; not that the law of Moses could give life, but it showed the way to life. Moses received them from God, and delivered nothing but what *he had first received from God*. The lively oracles which he received from God he faithfully gave to the people. He that gave them those customs by his servant Moses might change the customs by his Son Jesus, who received more lively oracles to give unto us than Moses did.

VII. The contempt that was put upon him by the people. Those that charged Stephen with speaking against Moses tread in their ancestors' steps. *They would not obey him, but thrust him from them, v. 39. In their hearts they turned back again into Egypt*, and preferred their garlic and onions there before the manna they had under the guidance of Moses, or the milk and honey they hoped for in Canaan. Many that pretend to be going forward towards Canaan are, at the same time, in their hearts turning back to Egypt. Now, if the customs that Moses delivered to them could not prevail to change them, wonder not that Christ comes to change the customs. *They made a golden calf*, a great indignity to Moses: for it was upon this consideration that they made the calf, because "*as for this Moses, who brought us out of the land of Egypt, we know not what is become of him*." As if a calf were sufficient to supply the want of Moses, and as capable of going before them into the promised land. *So they made a calf in those days, and offered sacrifices unto the idol, and rejoiced in the work of their own hands*. By all this it appears that there was a great deal which the law could not do. It was therefore necessary that this law should be perfected by a better hand, and he was no blasphemer against Moses who said that Christ had done it.

Verses 42–50

I. Stephen upbraids them with the idolatry of their fathers, which God gave them up to. This was the saddest punishment of all for that sin, *that God gave them up to a reprobate mind (v.* 42): *Then God turned, and gave them up to worship the host of heaven*. For this he quotes a passage out of Amos v. 25. For it would be less invidious to tell them their own character and doom from an Old Testament prophet, who upbraids them,

1. For not sacrificing to their own God in the wilderness (*v.* 42): *Have you offered to me slain beasts, and sacrifices, by the space of forty years in the wilderness?* No: during all that time sacrifices to God were intermitted; they did not so much as keep the passover after the second year. This is also a check to their zeal for the customs that Moses delivered to them, and their fear of having them changed by *this Jesus*, that immediately after they were delivered these customs were for forty years together disused.

2. For sacrificing to other gods after they came to Canaan (*v.* 43): *You took up the tabernacle of Moloch*

Moloch was the idol of the children of Ammon, to which they barbarously offered their own children in sacrifice; yet this unnatural idolatry they arrived at, when *God gave them up to worship the host of heaven. Yea, you took up the tabernacle of Moloch*, you submitted even to that, and to the worship of *the star of your god Remphan*. Some think *Saturn*, for that planet is called *Remphan* in the Syriac. The Septuagint puts it for *Chiun*. They had images representing the star, like the silver shrines for Diana, here called *the figures which they made to worship*. A poor thing to make an idol of, and yet better than a golden calf! Now for this it is threatened, *I will carry you away beyond Babylon*. Let it not therefore seem strange to them to hear of the destruction of this place, for they had heard of it many a time from the prophets of the Old Testament.

II. He gives an answer particularly to the charge relating to the temple, *that he spoke blasphemous words against that holy place, v.* 44–50. He was accused for saying that Jesus would destroy this holy place: "And what if I did say so?" (saith Stephen) "the glory of the holy God may be preserved untouched, though this be laid in the dust"; for, 1. "It was not till our fathers came into the wilderness, that they had any fixed place of worship. He that was worshipped without a holy place in the first, and best, and purest ages of the Old Testament church, may and will be so when this holy place is destroyed." 2. The holy place was at first but a tabernacle, mean and movable, not designed to continue always. Why might not this holy place, be decently brought to its end, as well as that? 3. That tabernacle was *a tabernacle of witness*, or of testimony. This was the glory both of the tabernacle and temple, that they were erected for a testimony. 4. That tabernacle was framed *according to the fashion which Moses saw in the mount*. It had reference to good things to come. Therefore it was no diminution at all to its glory to say that this temple made with hands should be destroyed, in order to the building of *another made without hands*. 5. That tabernacle was pitched first in the wilderness; it was not a native of this land of yours, but was brought in by our fathers, into the possession of the Gentiles, *whom God drove out before the face of our fathers*. And why may not God set up his spiritual temple in those countries that were now the possession of the Gentiles? That tabernacle was brought in by those who came *with Jesus*, that is, *Joshua*. So the New-Testament Joshua should bring in the true tabernacle into the possession of the Gentiles. 6. That tabernacle continued *even to the days of David*, before there was any thought of building a temple, *v.* 45. David, having *found favour before God*, did indeed desire this further favour, to have leave to build God a constant settled tabernacle, or dwelling-place. Those who have found favour with God should show themselves forward to advance the interests of his kingdom among men. 7. God had his heart so little upon a temple that, when David desired to build one, he was forbidden to do it; God was in no haste for one. It was not he, but his son Solomon, some years after, that built him a house. 8. God often declared that temples made with hands were not his delight. Solomon acknowledged that God *dwelleth not in temples made with hands*. The whole world is his temple, in which he is everywhere present, and fills it with his glory; and what occasion has he for a temple? The one only true and living God needs no temple, for *the heaven is his throne*, in which he rests, *and the earth is his footstool*, over which he rules (*v.* 49, 50), and therefore, *What house will you build me, what is the place of my rest?* What need have I of a house, either to repose myself in or to show myself? *Hath not my hand made all these things?* And as the world is thus

God's temple, wherein he is manifested, so it is God's temple in which he will be worshipped. As the earth is full of his glory, so the earth is, or shall be, full of his praise, and upon this account it is his temple. It was therefore no reflection at all upon this holy place, to say *that Jesus should destroy this temple*, and set up another, into which all nations should be admitted, *ch.* xv. 16, 17.

Verses 51–53

Stephen was going on in his discourse (as it should seem by the thread of it) to show that, as the temple, so the temple-service must come to an end. But he perceived they could not bear it. They will not so much as give him the hearing. He breaks off abruptly and by that spirit of wisdom, courage, and power, wherewith he was filled, he sharply rebuked his persecutors. If they will not admit the testimony of the gospel to them, it shall become a testimony against them.

I. They, like their fathers, were stubborn and wilful, and would not be brought upon by the various methods God took to reclaim and reform them. 1. They were *stiff-necked* (v. 51), and would not submit their necks to the sweet and easy yoke of God's government. They would not bow their heads, no, not to God himself, would not humble themselves before him. 2. They were *uncircumcised in heart and ears.* "In name and show you are circumcised Jews, but in heart and ears you are still uncircumcised heathens, and pay no more deference to the authority of your God than they do."

II. They were not only not influenced by the methods God took to reform them, but they were enraged and incensed against them: *You do always resist the Holy Ghost.* 1. They resisted the Holy Ghost speaking to them by the prophets. *Which of the prophets have not your fathers persecuted?* Their fathers resisted the Holy Ghost in the prophets, and so did they in Christ's apostles and ministers. 2. They resisted the Holy Ghost striving with them by their own consciences. There is that in our sinful hearts that always resists the Holy Ghost, but in the hearts of God's elect, this resistance is overcome, and after a struggle the throne of Christ is set up in the soul. That grace therefore which effects this change might more fitly be called *victorious* grace than *irresistible.*

III. They, like their fathers, persecuted and slew those whom God sent unto them. 1. Their fathers had been the cruel and constant persecutors of the Old Testament prophets (v. 52): *Which of the prophets have not your fathers persecuted?* More or less, one time or other, they had a blow at them all. That which aggravated the sin of persecuting the prophets was to *show before the coming of the just One,* to give notice of God's kind intentions to send the Messiah among them. Those that were the messengers of such glad tidings should have been courted and caressed, but, instead of this, they had the treatment of the worst of malefactors. 2. They had been the *betrayers and murderers of the just One* himself, as Peter had told them, *ch.* iii. 14, 15; v. 30. They had hired Judas to betray him, and had forced Pilate to condemn him; and therefore it is charged upon them that they were his betrayers and murderers. By slaying him, they showed they would have done if they had lived then; and thus brought upon themselves the guilt of the blood of all the prophets. To which of the prophets would those have shown any respect who had no regard to the Son of God himself?

IV. They, like their fathers, put contempt upon divine revelation. God had given, as to their fathers his law, so to them his gospel, in vain. 1. Their fathers received the law, and did not observe it, v. 53. God wrote to them the great things of his law, and yet they were counted by them as a strange or foreign thing. The law is said to be *received by the disposition of angels*, because angels were employed in the solemnity of giving the law, in the thunderings, lightnings, and the sound of the trumpet. But those that thus received the law yet kept it not, but by making the golden calf broke it immediately in a capital instance. 2. They received the gospel now, by the disposition not of angels, but of the Holy Ghost, and yet they did not embrace it. They were resolved not to comply with God either in his law or in his gospel.

Verses 54–60

We have here the death of the first martyr of the Christian church. Here is hell in its fire and darkness, and heaven in its light and brightness; and these serve as foils to set off each other. It is not here said that the votes of the council were taken upon his case, and that by the majority he was found guilty, and then condemned; but, it is likely, that it was not by the violence of the people, that he was put to death; for here is the usual ceremony of regular executions—he was cast out of the city, and the hands of the witnesses were first upon him.

I. See the strength of corruption in the persecutors of Stephen.

1. *When they heard these things they were cut to the heart* (v. 54), διεπρίοντο, the same word that is used in Heb. xi. 37, and translated *they were sawn asunder.* They were put to as much torture in their minds as ever the martyrs were put to in their bodies. They were not pricked to the heart with sorrow, as those were in *ch.* ii. 37, but cut to the heart with rage and fury, as they themselves were, *ch.* v. 33. Enmity to God is a heart-cutting thing; faith and love are heart-healing. They heard how he that *looked like an angel* before he began his discourse talked like an angel before he concluded it, and despairing to run down a cause so bravely pleaded, they yet resolved not to yield to it.

2. They *gnashed upon him with their teeth.* Great malice and rage against him. They *grinned at him* as dogs at those they are enraged at. Enmity at the saints turns men into brute beasts. Great vexation within themselves; they fretted to see in him such manifest tokens of a divine power. Gnashing with the teeth is often used to express the horror and torments of the damned. Those that have the malice of hell cannot but have with it some of the pains of hell.

3. *They cried out with a loud voice* (v. 57). When he said, *I see heaven opened,* they cried with a loud voice, that he might not be heard to speak. It is very common for a righteous cause to be attempted to be run down by noise and clamour; what is wanting in reason is made up in tumult.

4. They *stopped their ears* under pretence that they could not bear to hear his blasphemies. These *stopped their ears* when Stephen said, *I now see the Son of man standing in glory.* Their stopping their ears was a manifest specimen of their wilful obstinacy; they were resolved they would not hear. It was a fatal omen of that judicial hardness to which God would give them up. They stopped their ears, and then God, in a way of righteous judgment, stopped them.

5. They *ran upon him with one accord,* they all flew upon him, as beasts upon their prey. They ran upon him, one and all, hoping thereby to put him into confusion, envying him his composure and comfort in soul. They did all they could to ruffle him.

6. They *cast him out of the city, and stoned him,* to execute the law of Moses (Lev xxiv. 16), *He that blasphemeth the name of the Lord shall surely be put to death, all the congregation shall certainly stone him.* They cast him out of the city; they treated him as the offscouring of all things. The witnesses against

him were the leaders in the execution, according to the law. Thus they were to confirm their testimony. The witnesses took off their upper garments *and they laid them down at a young man's feet, whose name was Saul.* It is the first time we find mention of his name; we shall know it and love it better when we find it changed to *Paul.* This little instance of his agency in Stephen's death he afterwards reflected upon with regret (*ch.* xxii. 20): *I kept the raiment of those that slew him.*

II. See the strength of grace in Stephen. As his persecutors were full of Satan, so was he *full of the Holy Ghost.* When he was chosen to public service, he was described to be a man *full of the Holy Ghost* (*ch.* vi. 5), and now he is called out to martyrdom he has still the same character. Those that are full of the Holy Ghost are fit for anything, either to act for Christ or to suffer for him. When the followers of Christ are for his sake *killed all the day long, and accounted as sheep for the slaughter,* does this separate them from the love of Christ? Do they love him the less? No, by no means; and so it appears by this narrative.

1. Christ's gracious manifestation of himself to Stephen. When they were cut to the heart, and gnashed upon him with their teeth, then he had a view of the glory of Christ.

(1) He, *being full of the Holy Ghost, looked up steadfastly into heaven,* v. 55. Thus he looked above the power and fury of his persecutors, and did as it were despise them. They had their eyes fixed upon him, full of malice and cruelty; but he looked up to heaven, and never minded them. He looks up to heaven; thence only comes his help, and thitherward his way is still open. They cannot interrupt his intercourse with heaven. Thus he directed his sufferings to the glory of God, and did as it were appeal to heaven concerning them. Now that he was ready to be offered he looks up steadfastly to heaven, as one willing to offer himself. Thus he lifted up his soul with his eyes to God calling upon God for wisdom and grace to carry him through this trial. God has promised that he will be with his servants whom he calls out to suffer for him; but he will for this be sought unto. Thus he breathed after the heavenly country, to which he saw the fury of his persecutors would presently send him. It is good for dying saints to look up steadfastly to heaven: "And then, O death! where is thy sting?" Thus he made it to appear that he was full of the Holy Ghost. Those that are full of the Holy Ghost will look up steadfastly to heaven, for there their heart is. If we expect to hear from heaven, we must look up steadfastly to heaven.

(2) He saw the glory of God (*v.* 55); for *he saw the heavens opened,* v. 56. The heavens were opened, to give him a view of the happiness he was going to, that he might go cheerfully through death, so great a death. Would we by faith look up steadfastly, we might see the heavens opened by the mediation of Christ. We may also see the glory of God and the sight of this will carry us through all the terrors of sufferings and death.

(3) He *saw Jesus standing on the right hand of God* (*v.* 55), *the Son of man,* so it is, *v.* 56. When the Old Testament prophets saw the glory of God it was attended with angels. But here no mention is made of the angels. The glory of God shines brightest in the face of Jesus Christ. Here is a proof of the exaltation of Christ. He saw Jesus at the right hand of God. Whatever God's right hand gives to us, or receives from us, or does concerning us, it is by him; for he is his right hand. Stephen sees him *standing* there. He stands ready to receive him and crown him, and in the meantime to give him a prospect of the joy set before him. He sees Christ is for him, and then no matter who is against him. When our Lord Jesus

was in his agony an angel appeared to him, but Stephen had Christ himself appearing to him. Nothing so comfortable nor so animating as to see Jesus at the right hand of God; by faith we may see him there.

(4) He told those about him what he saw (*v.* 56): *Behold, I see the heavens opened.* What he saw he declared, let them make what use they pleased of it. If some were exasperated by it, others perhaps might be wrought upon to consider this Jesus, and to believe in him.

2. Stephen's pious addresses to Jesus Christ. *They stoned Stephen, calling upon God,* v. 59. Though he called upon God yet they proceeded to stone him. Though they stoned him, yet he called upon God. It is the comfort of those who are unjustly hated and persecuted by men that they have a God to go to. Men stop their ears, as they did here (*v.* 57), but God does not. Stephen was now cast out of the city, but he was not cast out from his God. He was now taking his leave of the world, and therefore calls upon God. It is good to die praying. Two short prayers Stephen offered up to God in his dying moments.

(1) Here is a prayer for himself: *Lord Jesus, receive my spirit.* Thus Christ had himself resigned his spirit immediately into the hands of the Father. We are here taught to resign ours into the hands of Christ as Mediator. The soul is the man, and our great concern, living and dying, must be about our souls. "Lord," saith he, "let my spirit be safe; let it go well with my poor soul." Our Lord Jesus is God, to whom we are to seek, and in whom we comfort ourselves living and dying. Stephen here prays to Christ, and so must we. There is no venturing into another world but under his conduct, no living comforts in dying moments but what are fetched from him. Christ's receiving our spirits at death is the great thing we are to comfort ourselves with. And, if this has been our care while we live, it may be our comfort when we come to die.

(2) Here is a prayer for his persecutors, *v.* 60. The circumstances of this prayer are observable. He *knelt down,* which was an expression of his humility in prayer. He *cried with a loud voice,* which was an expression of his importunity. In his prayer for his enemies, because that is so much against the grain of corrupt nature, it was requisite he should give proofs of his being in earnest. The prayer itself: *Lord, lay not this sin to their charge.* Herein he followed the example of his dying Master, and set an example to all following sufferers in the cause of Christ. Prayer may preach. This did so to those who stoned Stephen. *First,* What they did was a sin, a great sin. *Secondly,* Notwithstanding their malice and fury against him, he was in charity with them. Let them take notice of this, and, when their thoughts were cool, surely they would not easily forgive themselves for putting him to death who could so easily forgive them. *Thirdly,* Though the sin was very heinous, yet they must not despair of the pardon of it upon their repentance. If they would lay it to their hearts, God would not lay it to their charge.

3. His expiring with this: *When he had said this, he fell asleep.* Death is but a sleep to good people. Stephen died as much in a hurry as ever any man did, and yet, when he died, he fell asleep. He fell asleep when he was praying for his persecutors; it is expressed as if he thought he could not die in peace till he had done this. If he thus sleep, he shall do well; he shall awake again in the morning of the resurrection.

CHAPTER 8

It was strange, but very true, that the disciples of Christ the more they were afflicted the more they multiplied. I. Here is the church suffering, ver. 1–3. II. Here is the church spreading. 1. The gospel brought to Samaria, preached there (ver. 4, 5), embraced there (ver. 6–8), even by Simon Magus (ver. 9–13); the gift of the Holy Ghost conferred upon some of the believing Samaritans (ver. 14–17); and the severe rebuke given by Peter to Simon Magus, ver. 18–25. 2. The gospel sent to Ethiopia, by the eunuch. He is returning home in his chariot from Jerusalem, ver. 26–28. Philip is sent to him, and in his chariot preaches Christ to him (ver. 29–35), baptizes him (ver. 36–38), and then leaves him, ver. 39, 40.

Verses 1–3

I. Something more concerning Stephen and his death; how people stood affected to it. 1. Stephen's death rejoiced in by one in particular, and that was Saul, who was afterwards called Paul; he was *consenting to his death*. We have reason to think that Paul ordered Luke to insert this, for shame to himself, and glory to free grace. 2. Stephen's death bewailed by others (*v.* 2)—*devout men*. Some of the church gathered up the poor crushed and broken remains, to which they gave a decent interment. They buried him solemnly, and made great lamentation over him. It is a bad symptom if, when such men are taken away, it is not laid to heart. Those devout men paid these their last respects to Stephen, to show that they were not ashamed of the cause for which he suffered, nor afraid of the wrath of those that were enemies to it. To show the great value and esteem they had for this faithful servant of Jesus Christ. They study to do honour to him upon whom God put honour.

II. An account of this persecution of the church, which begins upon the martyrdom of Stephen. One would have thought Stephen's dying prayers and dying comforts should have overcome them, and melted them into a better opinion, but it seems they did not. As if they hoped to be too hard for God himself, they resolve to follow their blow.

1. Against whom this persecution was raised: It was *against the church in Jerusalem*. Christ had particularly foretold that Jerusalem would soon be made too hot for his followers, for that city had been famous for killing the prophets and stoning those that were sent to it.

2. Who was an active man in it: none so zealous, so busy, as Saul, a young Pharisee, *v.* 3. As for Saul *he made havoc of the church*; he did all he could to lay it waste and ruin it. He aimed at no less than the cutting off of the gospel Israel. Saul was bred a scholar, a gentleman, and yet did not think it below him to be employed in the vilest work of that kind. He *entered into every house*. No man could be secure in his own house, though it was his castle. He haled both men and women, without any regard to the tenderness of the weaker sex. He committed them to prison, in order to their being tried and put to death.

3. What was the effect of this persecution: *They were all scattered abroad* (*v.* 1). They, remembering our Master's rule (*when they persecute you in one city, flee to another*), dispersed themselves *throughout the regions of Judæa* and of Samaria. Their work was pretty well done in Jerusalem, and now it was time to think of the necessities of other places. Though persecution may not drive us off from our work, yet it may send us to work elsewhere. The preachers were all scattered *except the apostles*. They tarried at Jerusalem, that they might be ready to go where their assistance was most needed by the other preachers that were sent to break the ice.

Verses 4–13

Christ had said, *I am come to send fire on the earth*; and they thought, by scattering those who were kindled with that fire, to have put it out, but instead of this they did but help to spread it.

I. Here is a general account of what was done by them all (*v.* 4): *They went everywhere, preaching the word*. They went everywhere, into the way of the Gentiles, and the cities of the Samaritans, which before they were forbidden to go into. They scattered into all parts, not to take their ease, but to find out work. They were now in a country where they were no strangers, for Christ and his disciples had conversed much in the regions of Judæa; so that they had a foundation laid there for them to build upon.

II. A particular account of what was done by Philip, not Philip the apostle, but Philip the deacon. Stephen was advanced to the degree of a martyr, Philip to the degree of an evangelist.

1. What wonderful success Philip had in his preaching.

(1) The place he chose was the city of Samaria, the metropolis of that country. Some think it was the same with Sychem or Sychar, that city of Samaria where Christ was, John iv. 5. The Jews would have no dealings with the Samaritans; but Christ sent his gospel to slay all enmities.

(2) The doctrine he preached was Christ: he *preached Christ to them*. The Samaritans had an expectation of the Messiah's coming, as appears by John iv. 25. Now Philip tells them that he is come, and that the Samaritans are welcome to him.

(3) The proofs he produced were miracles, *v.* 6. The miracles were undeniable; they heard and saw the miracles which he did. He was sent to break the power of Satan; and, in token of this, unclean spirits, being charged in the name of the Lord Jesus to remove, *came out of many that were possessed with them, v.* 7. Wherever the gospel gains the admission and submission it ought to have, evil spirits are dislodged. This was signified by the casting of these unclean spirits out of the bodies of people, who came out *crying with a loud voice*. They came out with great reluctancy, but were forced to acknowledge themselves overcome by a superior power. He was sent to heal, to cure a distempered world; in token of this, *many that were taken with palsies, and that were lame, were healed.* The grace of God in the gospel is designed for the healing of those that are spiritually lame and paralytic, and cannot help themselves.

(4) The acceptance which Philip's doctrine met with in Samaria (*v.* 6): *The people with one accord gave heed to those things which Philip spoke*, induced thereto by the miracles which served at first to gain attention, and so by degrees to gain assent. The common people gave heed to Philip, *a multitude of them*, not here and there one, but with one accord; they were all of a mind.

(5) The satisfaction they had in attending on Philip's preaching, and the success it had with many of them (*v.* 8): *There was great joy in that city;* for (*v.* 12) they believed Philip, and were baptized, both men and women. [1] Philip preached *the things concerning the kingdom of God*, and he preached the name of Jesus Christ, as king of that kingdom. [2] The people not only gave heed to what he said, but at length believed it, were fully convinced that it was of God and not of men. [3] When they believed *they were baptized. Men* only were capable of being admitted into the Jewish church, but, to show that *in Jesus Christ there is neither male nor female*, the initiating ordinance is such as women are capable of, for they are numbered with God's spiritual Israel. [4] This occasioned great joy. The bringing of the gospel to any place is just matter of joy, of great joy, to that place. The gospel of Christ does not make men melancholy, but fills them with joy; for it is *glad tidings of great joy to all people*, Luke ii. 10.

2. What there was at this city of Samaria that made the success of the gospel there more than ordinarily wonderful.

(1) Simon Magus had been busy there, and had gained a great interest among the people. To unlearn

that which is bad proves many times a harder task than to learn that which is good. These Samaritans had of late been drawn to follow Simon, a conjurer (for so *Magus* signifies), who had strangely *bewitched them*.

[1] How strong the delusion of Satan. He had been for a *long time, in this city, using sorceries.* Simon assumed to himself that which was considerable: *He gave out that he himself was some great one.* He had no design to reform their lives, only to make them believe that he was *some divine person.* Pride, ambition, and an affectation of grandeur, have always been the cause of abundance of mischief both to the world and to the church. The people ascribed to him what he pleased. *They all gave heed to him, from the least to the greatest. To him they had regard* (v. 10, 11). They said of him, *This man is the great power of God.* See how ignorant inconsiderate people mistake that which is done by the power of Satan, as if it were done by the power of God. They were brought to it by his sorceries: *He bewitched the people of Samaria* (v. 9), *bewitched them with sorceries* (v. 11). By his magic arts *he bewitched the minds of the people.* Satan, by God's permission, filled their hearts to follow Simon. When they knew no better, they were influenced by his sorceries; but, when they were acquainted with Philip's real miracles, they saw plainly that the one was real and the other a sham. When they saw the difference between Simon and Philip, they quitted Simon.

[2] How strong the power of Divine grace is. By that grace working with the word those that had been led captive by Satan *were brought into obedience to Christ.* Let us not despair of the worst, when even those whom Simon Magus had bewitched were brought to believe.

(2) Here is another thing yet more wonderful (v. 13): *Simon himself believed also.* He was convinced that Philip preached a true doctrine, because he saw it confirmed by real miracles, of which he was the better able to judge because he was conscious to himself of the trick of his own pretended ones. The present conviction went so far that *he was baptized.* We have no reason to think that Philip did amiss in baptizing him. Prodigals, when they return, must be joyfully welcomed home, though we cannot be sure but that they will play the prodigal again. It is God's prerogative to know the heart. The church and its ministers must go by a judgment of charity. *We must hope the best as long as we can.* The present conviction lasted so long that he continued with Philip. He that had given out himself to be some great one is content to sit at the feet of a preacher of the gospel. Even bad men, very bad, may sometimes be in a good frame, very good. The present conviction was wrought and kept up by the miracles. Many wonder at the proofs of divine truths who never experience the power of them.

Verses 14–25

The twelve kept together at Jerusalem (v. 1), and thither these good tidings were brought them *that Samaria had received the word of God* (v. 14). The word of God was not only preached to them, but received by them. *When they heard it, they sent unto them Peter and John.* Two apostles were sent, the two most eminent, to Samaria, to encourage Philip and strengthen his hands. To carry on the good work that was begun.

I. How they advanced and improved those of them that were sincere. It is said (v. 16), *The Holy Ghost was as yet fallen upon none of them,* in those extraordinary powers which were conveyed by the descent of the Spirit, *only they were baptized in the name of the Lord Jesus,* and in this they had joy and satisfaction (v. 8). Those that are indeed given up to

Christ, and have experienced the sanctifying influences of the Spirit of grace, have great reason to be thankful, and no reason to complain, though they have not those gifts that are for ornament, and would make them bright. But it is intended that they should go on to the perfection of the present dispensation. *The apostles prayed for them,* v. 15. The Spirit is given, not to ourselves only (Luke xi. 13), but to others also, in answer to prayer. We may take encouragement from this example in praying to God to give the renewing graces of the Holy Ghost to those whose spiritual welfare we are concerned for—for our children, for our friends, for our ministers. They laid their hands on them. Upon the use of this sign *they received the Holy Ghost.* The laying on of hands was anciently used in blessing. Thus the apostles blessed these new converts.

II. How they discovered and discarded Simon Magus.

1. The wicked proposal that Simon made, by which his hypocrisy was discovered (v. 18, 19): *When he saw that through laying on of the apostles' hands the Holy Ghost was given,* it gave him a notion of Christianity as no other than an exalted piece of sorcery. He was ambitious to have the honour of an apostle, but not at all solicitous to have the spirit of a Christian. He was more desirous to gain honour to himself than to do good to others. He put a great affront upon the apostles, as if they were mercenary men, would do anything for money. He put a great affront upon Christianity, as if the miracles were done by magic arts. He showed that he aimed at the rewards of divination. He showed that he had a very high conceit of himself. No less a place will serve him than to be entrusted with a power which Philip himself had not, but the apostles only.

2. The just rejection of his proposal, v. 20–23.

(1) Peter shows him his crime (v. 20): *Thou hast thought that the gift of God may be purchased with money.* He had overvalued the wealth of this world, as if it would purchase the pardon of sin, the gift of the Holy Ghost, and eternal life. He had undervalued the gift of the Holy Ghost. He thought the power of an apostle might as well be had for a good fee as the advice of a physician or a lawyer.

(2) He shows him his character, which is inferred from his crime. Peter tells him plainly, [1] That his heart was *not right in the sight of God,* v. 21. We are as our hearts are; if they be not right, we are wrong; and they are open in the sight of God, who knows them, judges them, and judges of us by them. Our great concern is to approve ourselves to him in our integrity, for otherwise we cheat ourselves into our own ruin. He does not aim at the glory of God nor the honour of Christ in it, but to make a hand of it for himself. [2] That he is *in the gall of bitterness, and in the bond of iniquity: I perceive that thou art* so, v. 23. This is plain dealing, and plain dealing is best when we are dealing about souls and eternity. *I perceive it,* saith Peter. The disguises of hypocrites many times are soon seen through; the nature of the wolf shows itself notwithstanding the cover of the sheep's clothing. Now the character here given of Simon is really the character of all wicked people. They are *in the gall of bitterness.* They are *in the bond of iniquity*—bound over to the judgment of God by the guilt of sin, and bound under the dominion of Satan by the power of sin.

(3) He reads him his doom in two things:

[1] He shall sink with his worldly wealth: *Thy money perish with thee.* Peter rejects his offer with the utmost disdain and indignation. "Away with thee and thy money too; we will have nothing to do with either." When we are tempted with money to do an evil thing, we should see what a perishing thing money is. He warns him of his danger of utter destruction if he

continued in this mind: "Thy money will perish and thou wilt lose it. But this is not the worst of it: *thou wilt perish with it, and it with thee.*"

[2] He shall come short of the spiritual blessings which he undervalued (*v.* 21): "*Thou hast neither part nor lot in this matter;* thou hast nothing to do with the gifts of the Holy Ghost, for *thy heart is not right in the sight of God,* if thou thinkest that Christianity is a trade to live by in this world."

(4) He gives him good counsel, notwithstanding, *v.* 22. Though he was angry with him, yet he did not abandon him.

[1] What it is that he advises him to. He must *repent*—must see his error and retract it. His repentance must be particular: "Repent of this, own thyself guilty in this." He must not extenuate it, by calling it a mistake, or misguided zeal, but must aggravate it by calling it *wickedness.* Those that have said and done amiss must, as far as they can, unsay it and undo it again by repentance. He must *pray* that God would give him repentance, and pardon upon repentance. Penitents must pray, which implies a desire towards God, and a confidence in Christ. Simon Magus shall not be courted into the apostles' communion upon any other terms than those upon which other sinners are admitted—repentance and prayer.

[2] What encouragement he gives him to do this: *If perhaps the thought of thy heart may be forgiven thee.* There may be a great deal of wickedness in the thought of the heart, which must be repented of, or we are undone. The thought of the heart, though ever so wicked, shall be forgiven, upon our repentance. When Peter here puts a *perhaps* upon it, the doubt is of the sincerity of his repentance, not of his pardon if his repentance be sincere.

[3] Simon's request to them to pray for him, *v.* 24. *Pray you to the Lord for me, that none of the things which you have spoken come upon me. First,* Something well that he was affected with the reproof given him. This being so, he begged the prayers of the apostles for him. *Secondly,* Something wanting. He begged of them to pray for him, but did not pray for himself. His concern is more that the judgments he had made himself liable to might be prevented than that his heart, by divine grace, be made right in the sight of God.

Lastly, Here is the return of the apostles to Jerusalem, when they had finished the business they came about. There, in the city of Samaria, they were *preachers*: They *testified the word of the Lord,* confirmed what the other ministers preached. In their road home they were itinerant preachers; as they passed through many villages of the Samaritans they preached the gospel. God has a regard to the inhabitants of his villages in Israel, and so should we.

Verses 26–40

We have here the story of the conversion of an Ethiopian eunuch to the faith of Christ.

I. Philip the evangelist is directed into the road where he would meet with this Ethiopian, *v.* 26.
1. Direction given him by an angel what course to steer: *Arise, and go towards the south.* Doubtless there is a special providence of God conversant about the removes and settlements of ministers. He will direct those who sincerely desire to follow him into that way in which he will own them. Philip must *go southward, to the way that leads from Jerusalem to Gaza,* through the desert of Judah. He would never have thought of going thither, into a desert; small probability of finding work there! Yet thither he is sent. Sometimes God opens a door of opportunity to his ministers in places very unlikely. 2. His obedience to this direction (*v.* 27): *He arose and went,* without objecting.

II. An account is given of this eunuch (*v.* 27). He was a foreigner, *a man of Ethiopia.* The Ethiopians were looked upon as the meanest of the nations, blackamoors, as if nature had stigmatized them; yet the gospel is sent to them, and divine grace looks upon them. He was a person of quality, a great man in his own country, *a eunuch*—lord chamberlain or steward of the household. He was *of great authority,* and bore a mighty sway *under Candace queen of the Ethiopians.* He *had charge of all her treasure*; so great a trust did she repose in him. *Not many mighty, not many noble, are called;* but some are. He was a proselyte for *he came to Jerusalem to worship.* Some think that there were remains of the knowledge of the true God in this country, ever since the queen of Sheba's time.

III. Philip and the eunuch are brought together, and now Philip shall know the meaning of his being sent into a desert.

1. Philip is ordered to fall into company with this traveller. He had been at Jerusalem, where the apostles were preaching the Christian faith. The grace of God pursues him, overtakes him in the desert, and there overcomes him. Philip has this order by the Spirit whispering it in his ear (*v.* 29): "*Go near, and join thyself to this chariot.*" We should study to do good to those we light in company with upon the road. We should not be so shy of all strangers as some effect to be. Of those of whom we know nothing else we know this, that they have souls.

2. He finds him reading in his Bible, as he sat in his chariot (*v.* 28): He *ran to him, and heard him read, v.* 30. He not only relieved the tediousness of the journey, but redeemed time by reading the scriptures, *the book of Esaias.* It is the duty of every one of us to converse much with the holy scriptures. Persons of quality should abound more than others in the exercises of piety, because their example will influence many. It is wisdom for men of business to redeem time for holy duties; to fill up every minute with something that will turn to a good account. Those that are diligent in searching the scriptures are in a fair way to improve in knowledge.

3. He puts a fair question to him: *Understandest thou what thou readest?* What we read and hear of the word of God we should often ask ourselves whether we understand it or no. We cannot profit by the scriptures unless we do in some measure understand them.

4. The eunuch in a sense of his need of assistance, desires Philip's company (*v.* 31): "*How can I understand,* says he, *except someone guide me?*" He speaks as one that had very low thoughts of his own capacity. He takes the question kindly, *How can I?* Those that would learn must see their need to be taught. He speaks as one very desirous to be taught, to have someone to guide him. Though there are many things in the scriptures which are *dark and hard to be understood,* yet we must not therefore throw them by, but study them for the sake of those things that are easy. Knowledge and grace grow gradually. He invited Philip to *come up and sit with him.* In order to our right understanding of the scripture, it is requisite we should have someone to guide us; some good books, and some good men, but, above all, the Spirit of grace, to lead us into all truth.

IV. The portion of scripture which the eunuch recited, with some hints of Philip's discourse upon it.

1. The chapter he was reading was the fifty-third of Isaiah, two verses of which are here quoted (*v.* 32, 33). They are set down according to the Septuagint version, which in some things differs from the original Hebrew. The greatest variation from the Hebrew is that what in the original is, *He was taken from prison and from judgment,* is here read, *In his humiliation his judgment was taken away.* He appeared

so mean and despicable in their eyes that they denied him common justice. They declared him innocent, and yet condemned him to die. He is down, and down with him. Thus *in his humiliation his judgment was taken away.* So that these verses foretold concerning the Messiah, (1) That he should die, should be *led to the slaughter*, as sheep that were offered in sacrifice. (2) That he should die wrongfully, should be hurried out of his life, and *his judgment shall be taken away.* (3) That he should die patiently. Like a *lamb dumb before the shearer*, nay, and before the butcher too, *so he opened not his mouth.* Never was there such an example of patience as our Lord Jesus. When he was accused, when he was abused, he was silent. (4) That yet he should live for ever, to ages which cannot be numbered; for so I understand those words, *Who shall declare his generation? His life is taken* only *from the earth;* in heaven he shall live to endless and innumerable ages.

2. The eunuch's question upon this is, *Of whom speaketh the prophet this? v.* 34. It is a material question he asks, and a very sensible one: "Does the prophet speak this of himself, in expectation of being used, being misused, as the other prophets were, or does he speak it *of some other man?*" He proposed this question, to draw on discourse with Philip. The way to receive good instructions is to ask good questions.

3. Philip takes this fair occasion given him to open to him the great mystery of the gospel concerning *Jesus Christ, and him crucified.* He *began at this scripture*, and *preached unto him Jesus, v.* 35. This is all the account given us of Philip's sermon. And here we have an instance of speaking of the things of God, and speaking of them to good purpose, not only as we *sit in the house*, but *as we walk by the way.*

V. The eunuch is baptized in the name of Christ, *v.* 36–38.

1. The modest proposal which the eunuch made of himself for baptism (*v.* 36): *As they went on their way* they *came unto a certain water*, the sight of which made the eunuch think of being baptized. Thus God, by hints of providence which seem casual, sometimes puts his people in mind of their duty, of which otherwise perhaps they would not have thought. The eunuch knew not how little a while Philip might be with him, and therefore, if Philip think fit, he will take the present convenience which offers itself of being baptized: "*See, here is water; what doth hinder me to be baptized?*" He does not demand baptism, does not say, "Here is water and here I am resolved I will be baptized." But he does desire it, and, unless Philip can show cause why not, he desires it now. In the solemn dedicating and devoting of ourselves to God, it is good to make haste, and not to delay; for the present time is the best time. The eunuch feared lest the good affections now working in him should cool and abate, and therefore was willing immediately to bind his soul unto the Lord.

2. The fair declaration which Philip made him (*v.* 37): "*If thou believest with all thy heart, thou mayest.*" He must believe with all his heart, for with the heart man believeth, not with the head only, by an assent to gospel truth in the understanding; but with the heart, by a consent of the will to gospel terms. "If thou do indeed believe with all thy heart, thou art by that united to Christ, and thou mayest by baptism be joined to the church."

3. The confession of faith which the eunuch made. It is very short, but it is comprehensive and much to the purpose: *I believe that Jesus Christ is the Son of God.* He was before a worshipper of the true God, so that all he had to do now was to *receive Christ Jesus the Lord.* He believes that Jesus is *the Christ*, the true Messiah promised. That Christ is *Jesus—a Saviour*, the only Saviour of his people

from their sins. That this Jesus Christ is the *Son of God*, that he has a divine nature, as the Son is of the same nature with the Father.

4. The baptizing of him hereupon. The eunuch *commanded the chariot to stand still.* It was the best waiting place he ever met with in any of his journeys. *They went down both into the water.* Going barefoot according to the custom, they went perhaps up to the ankles or mid-leg into the water, and Philip sprinkled water upon him. Though Philip had very lately been deceived in Simon Magus, yet he did not therefore scruple to baptize the eunuch upon his profession of faith immediately. If some hypocrites crowd into the church, who afterwards prove a grief and scandal to us, yet we must not therefore make the door of admission any straiter than Christ has made it; they shall answer for their apostasy, and not we.

VI. Philip and the eunuch are separated presently; and this is as surprising as the other parts of the story. As soon as they had *come up out of the water the Spirit of the Lord caught away Philip* (*v.* 39). The working of this miracle upon Philip was a confirmation of his doctrine, as much as the working of a miracle by him would have been. He was *caught away, and the eunuch saw him no more*, but, having lost his minister, returned to the use of his Bible again.

1. How the eunuch was disposed: He *went on his way rejoicing.* Business called him home, and he must hasten to it; for it was no way inconsistent with his Christianity, which is a religion which men may and ought to carry about with them into the affairs of this life. But he went on rejoicing. He was never better pleased in all his life. He rejoiced, (1) That he himself was joined to Christ. (2) That he had these good things to bring to his countrymen, and a prospect of bringing them also into fellowship with Christ.

2. How Philip was disposed of (*v.* 40): *He was found at Azotus* or *Ashdod.* But Philip, wherever he was, would not be idle. *Passing through, he preached in all the cities*, till he came to Cæsarea, and there he settled. At Cæsarea we find him in a house of his own, *ch.* xxi. 8. He that had been faithful in working for Christ as an itinerant at length gains a settlement.

CHAPTER 9

I. The famous story of St. Paul's conversion. 1. How he was first awakened and wrought upon by an appearance of Christ himself to him, and what a condition he was in while he lay under the power of those convictions and terrors, ver. 1–9. 2. How he was baptized by Ananias, ver. 10–19. 3. How he immediately preached the faith of Christ, and proved what he preached, ver. 20–22. 4. How he was persecuted, ver. 23–25. 5. How he was admitted among the brethren at Jerusalem and was persecuted there, ver. 26–30. 6. The rest and quietness which the churches enjoyed for some time after this, ver. 31. II. The cure wrought by Peter on Æneas, ver. 32–35. III. The raising of Tabitha at the prayer of Peter, ver. 36–43.

Verses 1–9

We found mention made of Saul twice or thrice in the story of Stephen. His name in Hebrew was *Saul—desired*; his Roman name was *Paul—little.* He was born in Tarsus, a city of Cilicia, a free city of the Romans, and himself a freeman of that city. His father and mother were both native Jews, therefore he calls himself a *Hebrew of the Hebrews*; he was of the tribe of Benjamin. His education was in the schools of Tarsus first, which was a little Athens for learning. Thence he was sent to Jerusalem, to study divinity and the Jewish law. His tutor was Gamaliel. He had extraordinary natural parts. He had likewise a handicraft trade (being bred to tent-making), which was common with those among the Jews who were bred scholars.

I. How bad he was, how very bad, before his conversion; just before he was an inveterate enemy to

Christianity. In other respects he was well enough, as *touching the righteousness which is of the law, blameless,* a man of no ill morals, but a persecutor of Christians. And so ill informed was his conscience that he thought that he did God service in it.

1. His general enmity and rage against the Christian religion (*v.* 1): He *yet breathed out threatenings and slaughter against the disciples of the Lord.* The persons persecuted were the disciples of the Lord; under that character he hated and persecuted them. The matter of the persecution was threatenings and slaughter. There is persecution in threatenings, they terrify and break the spirit. His breathing out threatenings and slaughter intimates that it was natural to him. His very breath, like that of some venomous creatures, was pestilential. He breathed death to the Christians, wherever he came.

2. His particular design upon the Christians at Damascus. Saul cannot be easy if he knows a Christian is quiet; and therefore, hearing that the Christians in Damascus were so, he resolves to give them disturbance. He applies to the high priest for a commission (*v.* 1) to go to Damascus, *v.* 2. The high priest needed not to be stirred up to persecute the Christians, but it seems the young persecutor drove more furiously than the old one. The proselytes which the scribes and Pharisees make often prove seven times more the children of hell than themselves. Now the commission was to empower him to enquire among the synagogues at Damascus, whether there were any that inclined to favour this heresy, that believed in Christ; and if he found any such, whether men or women, to bring them up prisoners to Jerusalem. The Christians are here said to be *those of this way.* Perhaps the Christians sometimes called themselves so, from Christ *the Way.* The high priest and sanhedrim had a deference paid to their authority in matters of religion, by all their synagogues. Even the weaker sex, who might deserve excuse, or at least compassion, shall find neither with Saul. He was ordered to bring them all bound to Jerusalem as criminals. Thus was Saul employed when the grace of God wrought that great change in him. Let not us then despair of renewing grace for the conversion of the greatest sinners, nor let such despair of the pardoning mercy of God for the greatest sin; for Paul himself obtained mercy.

II. How suddenly and strangely a blessed change was wrought in him.

1. The place and time of it: *As he journeyed, he came near to Damascus;* and there Christ met with him.

(1) He was in the way, travelling upon his journey. The work of conversion is not tied to the church. Some are reclaimed in travelling upon the road alone. There the Spirit may set in with us, for that wind blows where it listeth.

(2) He was near Damascus, almost at his journey's end. He who was to be the apostle of the Gentiles was converted to the faith of Christ in a Gentile country.

(3) He was in a wicked way, pursuing his design against the Christians at Damascus. Sometimes the grace of God works upon sinners when they are at the worst, which is much for the glory both of God's pity and of his power.

(4) The cruel edict and decree drew near to be put in execution; and now it was happily prevented. [1] A great kindness to the poor saints at Damascus, who had notice of his coming, as appears by what Ananias said (*v.* 13, 14). Christ has many ways of delivering the godly out of temptation, and sometimes does it by a change wrought in their persecutors. [2] It was also a very great mercy to Saul himself. It is to be valued as a signal token of the divine favour if God prevent us from prosecuting and executing a sinful purpose.

2. The appearance of Christ to him in his glory. Here it is only said that there *shone round about him a light from heaven;* but it appears from what follows (*v.* 17) that the Lord Jesus was in this light. This light shone upon him *suddenly.* Christ's manifestations of himself to poor souls are many times sudden and very surprising, and he anticipates them with the blessings of his goodness. It was a light from heaven. It was a light above the brightness of the sun (*ch.* xxvi. 13), for it was visible at midday. It shone *round about him,* not in his face only, but on every side of him. The devil comes to the soul in darkness; by this he gets and keeps possession of it. But Christ comes to the soul in light, for he is himself the light of the world. The first thing in this new creation, as in that of the world, is light.

3. The arresting of Saul: *He fell to the earth, v. 4.* It appears (*ch.* xxvi. 14) that all that were with him fell to the earth as well as he, but the design was upon him. The effect of Christ's appearing to him, and of the light which shone round about him. Christ's manifestations of himself to poor souls are humbling; they lay them very low. A step towards this intended advancement. Those whom Christ designs for the greatest honours are commonly first laid low. Those whom God will employ are first struck with a sense of their unworthiness to be employed.

4. The arraigning of Saul. He heard a voice saying to him (and it was distinguishing, to him only, for though those that were with him heard a sound (*v.* 7) yet they knew not the words, *ch.* xxii. 9), *Saul, Saul, why persecutest thou me?*

(1) Saul not only saw a light from heaven, but heard a voice from heaven. God's manifestations of himself were never dumb shows, for he magnifies his word above all his name, and what was seen was always designed to make way for what was said. Saul heard a voice. Faith comes by hearing. The voice he heard was the voice of Christ. The word we hear is likely to profit us when we hear it as the voice of Christ; no voice but his can reach the heart.

(2) What he heard was very awakening.

[1] He was called by his name, and that doubled: *Saul, Saul.* His calling him by name brought the conviction home to his conscience, and put it past dispute to whom the voice spoke this. What God speaks in general is then likely to do us good when we insert our own names into the precepts and promises, as if God spoke to us by name. The doubling of it, *Saul, Saul,* intimates the tender concern that the blessed Jesus had for him, and for his recovery. He speaks as one in earnest. He speaks to him as to one in imminent danger, at the pit's brink, and just ready to drop in.

[2] The charge exhibited against him is, *Why persecutest thou me?* Before Saul was made a saint, he was made to see himself a sinner. Now he was made to see that evil in himself which he never saw before. A humbling conviction of sin is the first step towards a saving conversion from sin. He is convinced of one particular sin, which he had justified himself in. The sin he is convinced of is persecution: *Why persecutest thou me?* It is a very affectionate expostulation. 1. The person sinning: "It is thou; thou that hast good parts and accomplishments, hast the knowledge of the scriptures, which, if duly considered, would show thee the folly of it. It is worse in thee than in another." 2. The person sinned against: "It is I, who was not long since crucified for thee; must I afresh be crucified by thee?" 3. The kind and continuance of the sin. It was persecution, and he was at this time engaged in it. Those that are designing mischief are, in God's account, doing mischief. 4. The question put to him upon it: "Why dost thou do it?" (1) It is complaining language. Christ never

complained so much of those who persecuted him in his own person as he did here of those who persecuted him in his followers. The sins of sinners are a very grievous burden to the Lord Jesus. (2) It is convincing language: "Why dost thou thus?" It is good for us often to ask ourselves why we do so and so, that we may discern what an unreasonable thing sin is. *Why persecutest thou me?* He thought he was persecuting only a company of poor, weak, silly people, little imagining that it was one in heaven that he was all this while insulting. Those who persecute the saints persecute Christ himself, and he takes what is done against them as done against himself.

5. Saul's question upon his indictment, and the reply to it, *v. 5.*

(1) He makes enquiry concerning Christ: *Who art thou, Lord?* He gives no direct answer to the charge preferred against him, being convicted by his own conscience. If God contend with us for our sins, we are not able to answer for one of a thousand. Convictions of sin, when they are set home with power upon the conscience, will silence all excuses and self-justifications. But he desires to know who is his judge. He who had been a blasphemer of Christ's name now speaks to him as his Lord. The question is proper: *Who art thou?* This implies his present unacquaintedness with Christ. He desired to be acquainted with him and therefore, *Lord, who art thou?* There is some hope of people when they begin to enquire after Jesus Christ.

(2) He has an answer immediately. Christ's gracious revelation of himself to him. *I am Jesus whom thou persecutest.* The name of Jesus was not unknown to him, and gladly would he bury it in oblivion. Little did he think to hear it from heaven. He said, *I am Jesus, a Saviour; I am Jesus of Nazareth,* so it is, *ch.* xxii. 8. Saul used to call him so when he blasphemed him. "*I am that Jesus whom thou persecutest.*" There is nothing more effectual to awaken and humble the soul than to see sin to be against Christ. His gentle reproof of him: *It is hard for thee to kick against the pricks,* or *goads.* Those kick at the goad that stifle and smother the convictions of conscience. Those that revolt more and more when they are stricken by the word or rod of God, kick against the pricks.

6. His surrender of himself to the Lord Jesus at length, *v. 6.*

(1) The frame and temper he was in when Christ had been dealing with him. He trembled. Strong convictions, set home by the blessed Spirit, will make an awakened soul to tremble. He was astonished, as one brought into a new world, that knew not where he was.

(2) His address to Jesus Christ: *Lord, what wilt thou have me to do?* This may be taken, [1] As a serious request for Christ's teachings. "Thou hast discovered sin to me, discover to me the way to pardon and peace." A serious desire to be instructed by Christ in the way of salvation is an evidence of a good work begun in the soul. Or, [2] As a sincere resignation of himself to the direction and government of the Lord Jesus. This was the first word that grace spoke in Paul, and with this began a spiritual life. *What wilt thou have me to do?* The great change in conversion is wrought upon the will, and consists in the resignation of that to the will of Christ.

(3) The general direction Christ gave him: *Arise, go into the city of Damascus, and it shall be told thee what thou must do.* It is encouragement enough to have further instruction promised him, but, [1] He must not have it yet. Let him consider awhile what he had done in persecuting Christ, and be deeply humbled for that, and then he shall be told what he has further to do. [2] He must not have it in this

way, by a voice from heaven, for it is plain that he cannot bear it. He shall be told therefore what he must do by a man like himself. Christ manifests himself to his people by degrees.

7. How far his fellow travellers were affected with this. *They stood speechless,* as men in confusion, and that was all, *v.* 7. We do not find that any of them were converted, though they saw the light, and were struck dumb by it. No external means will of themselves work a change in the soul, without the Spirit and grace of God. None of them said, *Who art thou, Lord?* or, *What wilt thou have me to do?* as Paul did. *They heard a voice, but saw no man;* they heard Paul speak, but saw not him to whom he spoke, nor heard distinctly what was said to him. Thus those who came hither to be the instruments of Paul's rage against the church serve for witnesses of the power of God over him.

8. What condition Saul was in after this, *v.* 8, 9. *He arose from the earth,* when Christ commanded him. *When his eyes were opened he saw no man.* It was not so much this glaring light, but it was a sight of Christ, that had this effect upon him. Thus a believing sight of the glory of God in the face of Christ dazzles the eyes to all things here below. *They led him by the hand into Damascus.* Thus he who thought to have led the disciples of Christ prisoners and captives to Jerusalem was himself led a prisoner and a captive to Christ into Damascus. He lay *without sight, neither did eat nor drink for three days, v.* 9. He was in the dark concerning his own spiritual state, and was so wounded in spirit for sin that he could relish neither meat nor drink.

Verses 10–22

A good work was begun in Saul, when he was brought to Christ's feet, in that word, *Lord, what wilt thou have me to do?* And never did Christ leave any that were brought to that. He that hath convinced will comfort.

I. Ananias is here ordered to go and look after him.

1. The person employed is *Ananias, a certain disciple at Damascus,* not lately driven thither from Jerusalem, but a native of Damascus; for it is said (*ch.* xxii. 12) *that he had a good report of all the Jews who dwelt there, as a devout man according to the law.*

2. The direction given him is to go and enquire at such a house for one *Saul of Tarsus.* Christ, in a vision, called to Ananias by name, *v.* 10. Without terror or confusion, he readily answers, "*Behold I am here, Lord.*" *Go then,* saith Christ, *into the street which is called Straight, and enquire in the house of Judas for one called Saul of Tarsus.* Christ very well knows where to find out those that are his, in their distresses. They have a friend in heaven, that knows in what street, in what house, nay, and which is more, in what frame they are.

3. Two reasons are given him why he must go.

(1) Because he prays, and his coming to him must answer his prayer. This is a reason, [1] Why Ananias needed not to be afraid of him, as we find he was, *v.* 13, 14. There is no question, saith Christ, but he is a true convert, *for behold he prayeth. Behold* denotes the certainty of it. It denotes also the strangeness of it: "Behold, and wonder." But was it such a strange thing for Saul to pray? Was he not a Pharisee? Yes; but now he began to pray after another manner than he had done; then he said his prayers, now he prayed them. You may as soon find a living man without breath as a living Christian without prayer; if breathless, lifeless; and so, if prayerless, graceless. [2] Why Ananias must go to him with all speed. It is no time to linger, *for behold he prayeth.* He was under conviction of sin. Conviction should drive us to prayer. He was under a bodily affliction, blind and sick. Christ

had promised him that it should be further told him what he should do (*v*. 6), and he prays that one may be sent to him to instruct him. What God has promised we must pray for.

(2) Because he hath seen in a vision such a man coming to him; and Ananias's coming to him must answer his dream, for it was of God (*v*. 12): *He hath seen in a vision a man named Ananias coming in and putting his hand on him that he might receive his sight.* Now this vision which Paul had may be considered: As an immediate answer to his prayer, and the keeping up of that communion with God which he had entered into by prayer. As designed to raise his expectations, and to make Ananias's coming more welcome to him. See what a great thing it is to bring a spiritual physician and his patient together: here were two visions in order to it.

II. Ananias objects against going to him.

1. Ananias pleads that this Saul was a notorious persecutor of the disciples of Christ, *v*. 13, 14: "*Lord, I have heard by many of this man, how much evil he hath done to thy saints in Jerusalem.* There was no man they were more afraid of. His errand to Damascus at this time is to persecute us Christians: *Here he has authority from the chief priests to bind all that call on thy name.*" Now, why does Ananias object to this? Not, "Therefore I do not owe him so much service." No, Christ has taught us another lesson, to render good for evil, and pray for our persecutors. Will it be safe for Ananias to go to him? If he thus bring himself into trouble, he will be blamed for his indiscretion. Will it be to any purpose to go to him? Can such a hard heart ever be softened?

2. Christ overrules the objection (*v*. 15, 16). "Go thy way with all speed *for he is a chosen vessel* unto me; thou needest not fear him." He was a vessel in which the gospel-treasure should be lodged, an earthen vessel (2. Cor. iv. 7), but a chosen vessel. He is designed, (1) for eminent services: *He is to bear my name before the Gentiles.* Saul must be a standard-bearer. He must bear Christ's name before kings, king Agrippa and Cæsar himself; nay, he must bear it before the children of Israel. (2) For eminent sufferings (*v*. 16): *I will show him how great things he must suffer for my name's sake.* He that has been a persecutor shall be himself persecuted. Those that bear Christ's name must expect to bear the cross for his name; and those that do most for Christ are often called out to suffer most for him. It is only like telling a soldier of a bold and brave spirit, that he shall take the field, and enter upon action, shortly. It is no discouragement to him to be told how great things he must suffer for Christ's name's sake.

III. Ananias goes on Christ's errand to Saul. He had started an objection against going to him, but he dropped it, and did not insist upon it. When difficulties are removed, what have we to do but to go on with our work, and not hang upon an objection?

1. Ananias delivered his message to Saul, *v*. 17. (1) *He put his hands on him.* Saul came to lay violent hands upon the disciples at Damascus, but here a disciple lays a helping healing hand upon him. (2) He called him *brother*. His readiness to own him as a brother intimated to him God's readiness to own him as a son, though he had been a blasphemer of God and a persecutor of his children. (3) He produces his commission. "That *same Jesus that appeared unto thee in the way as thou camest*, has now sent me to thee." *The hand that wounded heals.* His light struck thee blind, but *he hath sent me to thee that thou mightest receive thy sight.* Corrosives shall be no more applied, but lenitives. (4) He assures him that he shall not only have his sight restored, but be filled with the Holy Ghost.

2. Ananias saw the good issue of his mission. (1) In Christ's favour to Saul. At the word of Ananias, Saul was discharged from his confinement by the restoring of his sight. Saul is delivered from the spirit of bondage by his receiving sight (*v*. 18), which was signified by the falling of scales from his eyes; the cure was sudden, to show that it was miraculous. This signified the recovering of him, [1] From the darkness of his unconverted state. Christ often told the Pharisees that they were blind, and could not make them sensible of it. Saul is saved from his Pharisaical blindness, by being made sensible of it. Converting grace opens the eyes of the soul. This was what Saul was sent among the Gentiles to do, and therefore must first experience it in himself. [2] From the darkness of his present terrors. Now the scales fell from his eyes, the cloud was scattered, and the Sun of righteousness rose upon his soul, with healing under his wings. (2) In Saul's subjection to Christ: He was baptized, and thereby submitted to the government of Christ, and cast himself upon the grace of Christ. Saul is now a disciple of Christ, not only ceases to oppose him, but devotes himself entirely to his service.

IV. The good work that was begun in Saul is carried on wonderfully.

1. He received his bodily strength, *v*. 19. He had continued three days fasting, which had made him very weak; but, *when he had received meat, he was strengthened, v*. 19. The Lord is for the body, and therefore care must be taken of it that it may be fit to serve the soul in God's service.

2. He associated with the disciples that were at Damascus. He had lately *breathed out threatenings and slaughter against them*, but now breathes love and affection to them. Those that take God for their God take his people for their people. Thus he made profession of his Christian faith, and openly declared himself a disciple of Christ.

3. *He preached Christ in the synagogues, v*. 20. He was so full of Christ himself, that *the Spirit within him constrained him* to preach him to others. Where he preached—in the synagogues of the Jews. There they used to preach against Christ and to punish his disciples. There he would face the enemies of Christ where they were most daring, and openly profess Christianity. What he preached: *He preached Christ.* When he began to be a preacher, he fixed this for his principle, which he stuck to ever after: nothing but Christ, and him crucified. He preached concerning Christ, *that he is the Son of God*, in whom he is well pleased, and with us in him. How people were affected with it (*v*. 21): *All that heard him were amazed, and said, "Is not this he that destroyed those who called on this name in Jerusalem?"* Did he not come hither to seize all the Christians he could find, and *bring them bound to the chief priests*? Who would have thought then that he would ever preach Christ as he does? This miracle upon the mind of such a man outshone the miracles upon men's bodies; and giving a man such another heart was more than giving men to speak with other tongues.

4. He confuted and confounded those that opposed the doctrine of Christ, *v*. 22. He increased in strength. He became more intimately acquainted with the gospel of Christ, and his pious affections grew more strong. He grew more daring and resolute in defence of the gospel: *He increased the more* for the reflections that were cast upon him (*v*. 21), in which his new friends upbraided him as having been a persecutor, and his old friends upbraided him as being now a turncoat. He ran down his antagonists, and *confounded the Jews who dwelt in Damascus*; he silenced them, and shamed them. He was instrumental in converting many to the faith of Christ, and building up the church at Damascus, which he went thither to make havoc of.

Verses 23–31

Luke here makes no mention of Paul's journey into Arabia, which he tells us himself was immediately after his conversion, Gal. i. 16, 17. As soon as God *had revealed his Son in him, that he might preach him,* he went not up to Jerusalem, but he went to Arabia. Thence he returned to Damascus, and there, three years after his conversion, this happened, which is here recorded.

I. He met with difficulties at Damascus, and had a narrow escape of being killed there. What his danger was (*v.* 23): *The Jews took counsel to kill him.* He had been such a remarkable deserter, and his being a Christian was a testimony against them. It is said (*v.* 24), *The Jews watched the gates day and night to kill him.* Now Christ showed Paul *what great things he must suffer for his name* (*v.* 16). Saul was no sooner a Christian than a preacher, no sooner a preacher than a sufferer. Where God gives great grace he commonly exercises it with great trials. How he was delivered. The design against him was discovered: *Their lying in wait was known of Saul.* The disciples contrived to help him away in the night; *they let him down by the wall, in a basket,* as he himself relates it (2 Cor. xi. 33).

II. He met with difficulties at Jerusalem the first time he went thither, *v.* 26. This is thought to be that journey to Jerusalem of which he himself speaks (Gal. i. 18): *After three years I went up to Jerusalem to see Peter, and abode with him fifteen days.* But I rather incline to think that this was a journey before that, because *his coming in* and *going out, his preaching and disputing* (*v.* 28, 29), seem to be more than would consist with his fifteen days' stay. However, it might possibly be the same.

1. How shy his friends were of him (*v.* 26): *When he came to Jerusalem he assayed to join himself to the disciples.* Wherever he came, he owned himself one of that despised persecuted people. But they looked strange upon him, shut the door against him. *They were afraid of him.* The Jews had abandoned and persecuted him, and the Christians would not receive and entertain him. (1) See what was the cause of their jealousy of him: *They believed not that he was a disciple,* but that he only pretended to be so, and came among them as a spy or an informer. The disciples of Christ had need to be cautious whom they admit into communion with them. There is need of the wisdom of the serpent, to keep the mean between the extremes of suspicion on the one hand and credulity on the other; yet methinks it is safer to err on the charitable side. (2) See how it was removed (*v.* 27): *Barnabas took him to the apostles* themselves, *and he declared to them,* what Christ had done for him: *He had shown himself to him in the way* and spoken to him. What he had since done for Christ: *He had preached boldly at Damascus in the name of Jesus.* How Barnabas came to know this we are not told. Being satisfied himself, he gave satisfaction to the apostles concerning him.

2. How sharp his enemies were upon him. (1) He was admitted into the communion of the disciples. It vexed the unbelieving Jews to see Saul a trophy of Christ's victory, to see him *coming in, and going out, with the apostles* (*v.* 28). (2) He appeared vigorous in the cause of Christ, and this was yet more provoking to them (*v.* 29): *He spoke boldly in the name of the Lord Jesus.* The Grecians, or Hellenist Jews, were most offended at him, because he had been one of them; and they drew him into a dispute, in which, no doubt, he was too hard for them. That same natural quickness and fervour of spirit which made him a furious bigoted persecutor of the faith, made him a most zealous courageous defender of the faith. (3) This brought him into peril of his life: *The Grecians went about to slay him.* But notice

was given of this conspiracy too, and effectual care taken to secure this young champion (*v.* 30): *When the brethren knew they brought him down to Cæsarea.* He that flies may fight again. He that fled from Jerusalem might do service at Tarsus, the place of his nativity; and thither they desired him by all means to go. Yet it was also by direction from heaven that he left Jerusalem at this time, as he tells us himself (*ch.* xxii. 17, 18), that Christ now appeared to him, and ordered him to *go quickly out of Jerusalem,* for he must be sent *to the Gentiles, v.* 15.

III. The churches had now a comfortable gleam of liberty and peace (*v.* 31): *Then had the churches rest.* Then, when Saul was converted, those were quiet whom he used to molest. *The churches had rest.* After a storm comes a calm. This was a breathing-time allowed them, to prepare them for the next encounter. They made a good use of this lucid interval. They *were edified,* were built up in their most holy faith. They *walked in the fear of the Lord.* They so lived that all might say, Surely the fear of God reigns in those people. They *walked in the comfort of the Holy Ghost*—were not only faithful, but cheerful, in religion; they stuck to the ways of the Lord, and sang in those ways. They had recourse to the comfort of the Holy Ghost, and lived upon that, not only in days of trouble and affliction, but in days of rest and prosperity. When they walked *in the fear of the Lord,* then they walked in *the comfort of the Holy Ghost.* Those are most likely to walk cheerfully that walk circumspectly. God blessed it to them for their increase in number: They *were multiplied.* Sometimes the church multiplies the more for its being afflicted, yet if it were always so, the saints of the Most High would be worn out. At other times its rest contributes to its growth.

Verses 32–35

I. The visit Peter made to the churches that were newly planted, *v.* 32. 1. He *passed through all quarters.* As an apostle, he was not to be the resident pastor of any one church. He was, like his Master, always upon the remove, and *went about doing good;* but still his headquarters were at Jerusalem, for there we shall find him imprisoned, *ch.* xii. 4. *He came to the saints at Lydda.* The Christians are called *saints,* every sincere professor of the faith of Christ. These are the saints on the earth.

II. The cure Peter wrought on *Æneas, v.* 33. His case was very deplorable: *He was sick of the palsy.* The disease was extreme, for *he kept his bed;* it was inveterate, for he kept his bed *eight years;* and we may suppose that both he himself and all about him despaired of relief for him. Christ chose such patients as this, whose disease was incurable in a course of nature. When we were without strength, as this poor man, *he sent his word to heal us.* His cure was very admirable, *v.* 34. Peter interested Christ in his case: *Æneas, Jesus Christ maketh thee whole.* Peter declares it to be Christ's act and deed, and assures him of an *immediate* cure—not, "He *will* make thee," but, "He *does* make thee whole"; and a *perfect* cure —not, "He makes thee *easy,*" but "He makes thee *whole.*" He ordered him to bestir himself: *"Arise and make thy bed."* Let none say that because it is Christ that works all our works in us therefore we have no work, no duty, to do; for, though Jesus Christ makes thee whole, yet thou must arise and make use of the power he gives thee: *"Arise, and make thy bed,* to be to thee no longer a bed of sickness, but a bed of rest." Power went along with this word: he arose immediately.

III. The good influence this had upon many (*v.* 35): *All that dwelt at Lydda and Saron saw him, and turned to the Lord.* They all made enquiry into the truth of the miracle, and saw that it was a miraculous cure that was wrought upon him by the power of Christ. They all *turned to the Lord*, to the Lord Jesus. They turned themselves over to him to be ruled and taught and saved by him.

Verses 36–43

Here we have another miracle wrought by Peter—the raising of Tabitha to life.

I. The life, and death, and character of Tabitha, *v.* 36, 37. She lived at Joppa. Her name was *Tabitha*, a Hebrew name, the Greek for which is *Dorcas*, both signifying a *doe*. She was a disciple, eminent above many for works of charity. She showed her faith by her works, her good works. She was *full of good works*, as a tree that is full of fruit. Many are full of good words, who are empty and barren in good works; but Tabitha was a great doer, no great talker. She was remarkable for her *alms-deeds which she did*, not only her works of piety, but works of charity and beneficence, flowing from love to her neighbour. She is commended not only for the alms which she gave, but for the alms-deeds which she did. Those that have not estates wherewith to give in charity may yet be able to do in charity, working with their hands, or walking with their feet, for the benefit of the poor. And those who will not do a charitable deed, whatever they may pretend, if they were rich would not bestow a charitable gift. There is an emphasis upon her *doing* them, because what her hand found to do of this kind she did with all her might, and persevered in. This is the life and character of a certain disciple, and should be of all the disciples of Christ. She was removed in the midst of her usefulness (*v.* 37): *In those days she fell sick, and died.* Her friends and those about her *washed the dead body*, according to the custom. They *laid her out* in her grave-clothes *in an upper chamber*.

II. The request which her Christian friends sent to Peter to come to them with all speed, *v.* 38. The disciples at Joppa had heard that Peter was there, and that he had raised Æneas from a bed of languishing; and therefore they *sent him two men, desiring him that he would not delay to come to them.* Their friend was dead, and it was too late to send for a physician, but not too late to send for Peter.

III. The posture in which he found the survivors (*v.* 39): *Peter arose and went with them.* Let not faithful ministers grudge to be at everybody's beck, when the great apostle *made himself the servant of all.* He found the corpse laid in the upper chamber, and attended by widows.

1. Commending the deceased—a good work when it is done modestly and soberly, and without flattery. The commendation of Tabitha was like her own virtues, not in word, but in deed. *The widows showed the coats and garments which she made while she was with them.* It is much more honourable to clothe a company of decrepit widows with needful clothing, than to clothe a company of lazy footmen with rich liveries, who perhaps behind their backs will curse those that clothe them, for goodness is true greatness, and will pass better in the account shortly. Into what channel Tabitha turned much of her charity. She did, as it should seem with her own hands, *make coats and garments* for poor widows. And this is an excellent piece of charity, *If thou seest the naked, that thou cover him* (Isa. lviii. 7), and not think it enough to say, *Be ye warmed*, James ii. 15, 16. What a grateful sense the poor had of her kindness: *They showed the coats.* Those are horribly ungrateful indeed who have kindness shown them and will not make at least an acknowledgement of it, by showing the kindness that is done them. Those who receive alms are not obliged so industriously to conceal it, as those are who give alms. Their showing the coats

and garments which Dorcas made tended to the praise not only of her charity, but of her industry.

2. They were here lamenting the loss of her: The widows stood by Peter, weeping. They need not weep for her; *she rests from her labours and her works follow her*, but they weep for themselves and for their children, who will soon find the want of such a good woman. They take notice of what good Dorcas did *while she was with them*; but now she is gone from them, and this is their grief. The widows wept before Peter, as an inducement to him to have compassion on them, and restore one to them that used to have compassion on them. When charitable people are sick, this piece of gratitude is owing them, to pray for their recovery, that those may be spared to live who can ill be spared to die.

IV. The manner in which she was raised to life. 1. Privately: *but Peter put them all forth.* Thus Peter declined everything that looked like vainglory and ostentation; they came to see, but he did not come to be seen. 2. By prayer. In his healing Æneas there was an implied prayer, but in this greater work he addressed himself to God by solemn prayer, with the submission of a servant, and therefore he *knelt down and prayed.* 3. By the word, a quickening word. When he had prayed, he *turned to the body*, and spoke in his Master's name: *"Tabitha, arise."* Power went along with this word, and she came to life, *opened her eyes* which death had closed. When she saw Peter, she sat up (*v.* 14), *he gave her his hand and lifted her up.* Thus he would as it were welcome her to life again, and give her the right hand of fellowship among the living, from whom she had been cut off. And, *lastly*, he *called the saints and widows*, and *presented her alive* to them (*v.* 41).

V. The good effect of this miracle. 1. Many were by it convinced of the truth of the gospel, and believed in the Lord, *v.* 42. The thing was *known throughout all Joppa*, and though some never minded it many were wrought upon by it. This was the design of miracles, to confirm a divine revelation. 2. Peter was hereby induced to continue some time in this city, *v.* 43. Finding that a door of opportunity was opened for him there, he tarried there many days, till he was sent for thence upon business to another place. He took up his lodgings with one Simon a tanner. Though Peter might seem to be buried in obscurity here in the house of a poor tanner by the seaside, yet hence God fetched him to a noble piece of service.

CHAPTER 10

It is a turn very new and remarkable which the story of this chapter gives to the Acts of the apostles. Now, "Lo, we turn to the Gentiles"; and to them the door of faith is here opened. The apostle Peter is the man that is first employed to admit uncircumcised Gentiles into the Christian church; and Cornelius, a Roman centurion is the first that with his family and friends is so admitted. I. How Cornelius was directed by a vision to send for Peter, ver. 1–8. II. How Peter was directed by a vision to go to Cornelius, though he was a Gentile, ver. 9–23. III. The happy interview between Peter and Cornelius at Cæsarea, ver. 24–33. IV. The sermon Peter preached in the house of Cornelius, ver. 34–43. V. The baptizing of Cornelius and his friends with the Holy Ghost first, and then with water, ver. 44–48.

Verses 1–8

It concerns us carefully to observe all the circumstances of the beginning of this great work, this part of the *mystery of godliness—Christ preached to the Gentiles, and believed on in the world.* The gospel was never yet designedly preached to the Gentiles, nor any of them baptized—Cornelius was the first.

I. An account given us of this Cornelius, who was the first-born of the Gentiles to Christ. We are here told that he was a great man and a good man—two characters that seldom meet. Where they do meet they put a lustre upon each other: goodness makes greatness truly valuable, and greatness makes goodness much more serviceable. 1. Cornelius was an officer of the army, *v.* 1. Here there was a band, or cohort, of the Roman army, which is here called *the Italian band*, because they were all native Romans, or Italians. Cornelius had a command in this part of the army. He was an officer of considerable rank and figure, a centurion. We read of one of that rank in our Saviour's time, of whom he gave a great commendation, Matt. viii. 10. When a Gentile must be pitched upon to receive the gospel first, it is a Gentile soldier, who is a man of more free thought; and he that truly is so, when the Christian doctrine is fairly set before him, cannot but receive it and bid it welcome. Let not soldiers and officers of the army plead that their employment may excuse them if they be not religious. It was a mortification to the Jews that not only the Gentiles were taken into the church, but that the first who was taken in was an officer of the Roman army. 2. He was a religious man. It is a very good character that is given of him, *v.* 2. He was possessed with a principle of regard to the true and living God. He was *a devout man and one that feared God*. Though he was a soldier, it was no diminution of the credit of his valour to tremble before God. He kept up religion in his family. He *feared God with all his house*. He took care that not himself only, but all his, should serve the Lord. Every good man will do what he can that those about him may be good too. He was a very charitable man: He *gave much alms to the people*. He was much in prayer: He *prayed to God always*. Wherever the fear of God rules in the heart, it will appear both in works of charity and of piety.

II. The orders given him from heaven to send for Peter.

1. How, and in what way, these orders were given him. He had a vision, in which an angel delivered them to him. It was about the *ninth hour of the day*. Because it was in the temple the time of offering the evening sacrifice, it was made by devout people an *hour of prayer*. Cornelius was now at prayer: so he tells us himself, *v.* 30. An angel of God *came in to him*. He *saw him evidently* with his bodily eyes, not in a dream presented to his imagination, but in a vision presented to his sight. He called him by his name, *Cornelius*, to intimate the particular notice God took of him. This put Cornelius for the present into some confusion (*v.* 4): *When he looked on him he was afraid*. Cornelius cries, "*What is it, Lord?* What is the matter?" This he speaks as one desirous to know the mind of God, and ready to comply with it.

2. What the message was.

(1) He is assured that God accepts him (*v.* 4): *Thy prayers and thine alms are come up for a memorial before God*. Prayers and alms must go together. We must follow our prayers with alms. We must *give alms of such things as we have*; and then, behold, all things are clean to us, Luke xi. 41. And we must follow our alms with our prayers that God would graciously accept them. Cornelius prayed, and gave alms, in sincerity, as unto God; and he is here told that they were *come up for a memorial before God*. Prayers and alms are our spiritual offerings, which God is pleased to have regard to.

(2) He is appointed to enquire after a further discovery of divine grace, *v.* 5, 6. He must *send forthwith to Joppa, and enquire for one Simon Peter; he lodgeth at the house of one Simon a tanner; his house is by the sea side, when he comes he shall tell thee what thou oughtest to do.* Now here are two things very surprising: [1] Cornelius prays and gives alms in the fear of God, is religious himself and keeps up religion in his family, yet there is something further that he ought to do—he ought to embrace the Christian religion. Not, He may do it if he pleases.

But, He must do it. He that believed the promise of the Messiah must now believe the performance of that promise. Neither our prayers nor our alms can come up for a memorial before God unless we believe in Jesus Christ. [2] Cornelius has now an angel from heaven talking to him, and yet he must not receive the gospel of Christ from this angel, but all that the angel has to say is, "Send for Peter, and he shall tell thee." And as it was an honour to the apostle that he must preach that which an angel might not, so it was a further honour that an angel was despatched to order him to be sent for. To bring a faithful minister and a willing people together is a work worthy of an angel.

III. His immediate obedience to these orders, *v.* 7, 8. He sent with all speed to Joppa, to fetch Peter to him. When he sent: As soon as ever the *angel which spoke unto him had departed*. He made haste; and delayed not, to do this commandment. In any affair wherein our souls are concerned it is good for us not to lose time. Whom he sent: *Two of his household servants, and a devout soldier, that waited on him continually*. A devout centurion had devout soldiers. A little devotion commonly goes a great way with soldiers, but there would be more of it in the soldiers if there were but more of it in the commanders. When this centurion had to choose some of his soldiers to attend his person, and to be always about him, he pitched upon such of them as were devout. What instructions he gave them (*v.* 8): *He declared all these things unto them*. He does not only tell them where to find Peter, but he tells them on what errand he was to come, that they might importune him.

Verses 9–18

Cornelius had received positive orders from heaven to send for Peter, but here is another difficulty that lies in the way of bringing them together—the question is whether Peter will come to Cornelius. It sticks at a point of conscience. He is a Gentile, he is not circumcised. Peter had not got over this stingy bigoted notion of his countrymen, and therefore will be shy of coming to Cornelius. Now, to remove this difficulty, he has a vision here, to prepare him to receive the message sent him by Cornelius. Christ ordered them to *teach all nations*; and yet even Peter himself could not understand it, till it was here revealed by vision.

I. The circumstances of this vision.

1. It was when the messengers were now *nigh the city*, *v.* 9. Peter knew nothing of their approach, and they knew nothing of his praying; but he that knew both him and them was preparing things for the interview. He is pleased often to bring things to the minds of his ministers, which they had not thought of, just then when they have occasion to use them.

2. It was when *Peter went up upon the house-top to pray*. Peter was much in prayer. He prayed *about the sixth hour*, not only *morning and evening*, but *at noon*. From morning to night we should think to be too long to be without meat; yet who thinks it is too long to be without prayer? He prayed *upon the house-top*. He had this vision immediately after he had prayed. The ascent of the heart to God in prayer is an excellent preparative to receive the discoveries of the divine grace.

3. It was when he became *very hungry* (*v.* 10); and now *he would have eaten*. Now this hunger was a proper inlet to the vision about meats, as Christ's hunger in the wilderness was to Satan's temptation to turn stones into bread.

II. The vision itself. He *fell into a trance*. He quite lost himself to this world, and so had his mind entirely free for converse with divine things. The more clear we get of the world, the more near we get to heaven. He *saw heaven opened*, that he might be sure that his authority to go to Cornelius was indeed from heaven. He saw *a great sheet full of all manner of living creatures, which descended from heaven, and was let down to him to the earth.* Here were not only beasts of the earth, but fowls of the air, laid at his feet. Here were no fishes of the sea, because there were none of them in particular unclean. Some make this sheet, thus filled, to represent the church of Christ. In this we find some of all countries, without any distinction of Greek or Jew. The net of the gospel encloses all, both bad and good, those that before were clean and unclean. Or it may be applied to the bounty of the divine Providence. How should it double our comfort in the creatures, and our obligations to serve God in the use of them, to see them thus let down to us out of heaven! He was ordered by a voice from heaven to make use of this plenty and variety which God had sent him (*v.* 13): *"Rise, Peter, kill and eat."* It might be difficult for Jews to dine and sup with a Gentile, because they would have that set before them which they were not allowed to eat. Now they might fare as they feared, and therefore might eat with them. He stuck to his principles, and would by no means hearken to the motion (*v.* 14): *Not so, Lord.* Though hunger will break through stone walls, God's laws should be to us a stronger fence than stone walls. Temptations to eat forbidden fruit must not be parleyed with, but peremptorily rejected. The reason he gives is, *"For I have never eaten anything that is common or unclean;* hitherto I have kept my integrity in this matter, and will still keep it." His conscience could witness for him that he had never gratified his appetite with any forbidden food. God, by a second voice from heaven, proclaimed the repeal of the law in this case (*v.* 15): *What God hath cleansed, that call thou not common.* He that made the law might alter it when he pleased. He has now taken off that restraint, has cleansed that which was before polluted to us. We ought to welcome it as a great mercy; not so much because hereby we gain the use of swine's flesh, hares, rabbits, and other pleasant and wholesome food for our bodies, but chiefly because conscience is hereby freed from a yoke in things of this nature. *This was done thrice, v.* 16, with the same call to him, and the same reason. The instructions given us in the things of God need to be often repeated. But at last *the vessel was received up into heaven.* Those who make this vessel to represent the church, including both Jews and Gentiles, make this very aptly to signify the admission of the believing Gentiles into the church, and into heaven too. They are such as God has cleansed.

III. The providence which explained this vision, *v.* 17, 18. *He doubted within himself what this vision which he had seen should mean.* He had no reason to doubt the truth of it, all his doubt was concerning the meaning of it. Christ reveals himself to his people by degrees, and leaves them to doubt awhile, to ruminate upon a thing, and debate it to and fro in their own minds, before he clears it up to them. Yet he was made to know presently, for *the men who were sent from Cornelius* were at *the gate enquiring whether Peter lodged there*; and by their errand it will appear what was the meaning of this vision. God knows what services are before us, and therefore how to prepare us; and we then better know the meaning of what he has taught us when we find what occasion we have to make use of it.

Verses 19–33

We have here the meeting between Peter and Cornelius. Though Paul was designed to be the apostle of the Gentiles, and Peter to be the apostle of the circumcision, yet it is ordered that Peter shall break the ice, and reap the first fruits of the Gentiles, that the believing Jews might be the better reconciled to their admission into the church, when they were first brought in by their own apostle.

I. Peter is directed by the Spirit to go along with Cornelius's messengers (*v.* 19, 20). Now the riddle is unriddled: *While Peter thought on the vision;* he was musing upon it, and then it was opened to him. Those that would be taught the things of God must think on those things. 1. Whence he had the direction. The Spirit said to him what he should do. It was not spoken to him by an angel, but spoken in him by the Spirit. 2. What the direction was. He is told that three men below want to speak with him (*v.* 19), and he must arise from his musings and go down to them, *v.* 20. Those that are searching into the meaning of the words of God, and the visions of the Almighty, should not be always poring, no, nor always praying, but should sometimes look about them. He is ordered to *go along with the messengers to Cornelius, doubting nothing*, not doubting whether he might go, no, nor whether he ought to go; for it was his duty. *"Go with them, for I have sent them."* When we see our call clear to any service, we should not suffer ourselves to be perplexed with doubts and scruples, or a fear of men's censure.

II. He receives both them and their message: *He went down to them, v.* 21. 1. He favourably receives their message. He asks what their business is: *What is the cause wherefore you are come?* and they tell him their errand (*v.* 22): *"Cornelius,* an officer of the Roman army, *who fears God above many of good report among all the people of the Jews, was warned from God* by an angel to send for thee to his house, *and to hear words of thee."* These words, Peter tells us more fully, are *words whereby thou and all thy house shall be saved,* ch. xi. 14. 2. He kindly entertained the messengers (*v.* 23): *He called them in, and lodged them.* What was getting ready for him (*v.* 10) they should be welcome to share in; he little thought what company he should have when he bespoke his dinner, but God foresaw it. Peter lodged them, though they were Gentiles, to show how readily he complied with the design of the vision in eating with Gentiles. Though they were two of them servants, and the other a common soldier, yet Peter thought it not below him to take them into his house.

III. He *went with them* to Cornelius. Peter was *accompanied by certain brethren from Joppa, v.* 23. Six of them went along with him, as we find, *ch.* xi. 12. This was one way in which the primitive Christians very much showed their respect to their ministers: they accompanied them in their journeys. It is a pity that those who have skill and will to do good to others by their discourse should want an opportunity for it by travelling alone. Cornelius *had got some friends together of Cæsarea.* Now when they came into the house of Cornelius Peter found, (1) That he was expected, and this was an encouragement to him. *Cornelius waited for them,* and such a guest was worth waiting for; nor can I blame him if he waited with some impatience. (2) That he was expected by many and this was a further encouragement to him. As Peter brought some with him to partake of the spiritual gift he had now to dispense, so *Cornelius had called together,* not only his own family, but *kinsmen and near friends.* We should not covet to eat our spiritual morsels alone. It ought to be both given and taken as a piece of kindness and respect to our kindred and friends to invite them to join with us in religious exercises, to go with us to hear a sermon.

IV. Here is the first interview between Peter and Cornelius. The profound respect and honour which Cornelius paid to Peter (*v.* 25): *He met him as he was coming in,* and *he fell down at his feet and worshipped him.* His worshipping a man was indeed culpable; but, considering his present ignorance, it was excusable. No wonder if, till he was better informed, he worshipped him, whom he was ordered to send for by an angel from heaven. Peter's modest refusal of this honour that was done him (*v.* 25): *He took him up saying,* "*Stand up, I myself also am a man.*" The good angels of the churches cannot bear to have the least of that honour shown to them which is due to God only. Christ's faithful servants could better bear to be vilified than to be deified. Let him know that Peter is a man, that *the treasure is in earthen vessels,* that he may value the treasure for its own sake.

V. The account which Peter and Cornelius give to each other, and to the company, of the hand of Heaven in bringing them together: *As he talked with him he went in, v.* 27. When he came in, *he found many that were come together,* which added solemnity, as well as opportunity of doing good, to this service.

1. Peter declares the direction God gave to him to come to those Gentiles, *v.* 28, 29. They knew it had never been allowed by the Jews, but always looked upon as an *unlawful thing for a man that is a Jew to keep company or come unto one of another nation,* an uncircumcised Gentile. It was not made so by the law of God, but by the decree of their wise men. They did not forbid them to converse or traffic with Gentiles in the street or shop, or upon the exchange, but to eat with them. They might not come into the house of a Gentile. Thus scornfully did the Jews look upon the Gentiles, who were not behindhand with them in contempt. "*But now,*" saith Peter, "*God hath shown me that I should not call any man common or unclean.*" Peter, who had taught his new converts to *save themselves from the untoward generation of wicked men* (*ch.* ii. 40), is now himself taught to join himself with the towardly generation of devout Gentiles. He assures them of his readiness to do them all the good offices he could. Having now received permission, he was at their service: "*Therefore came I unto you without gainsaying, as soon as I was sent for.*" He enquires wherein he might be serviceable to them: "*I ask, therefore, for what intent you have sent for me?*"

2. Cornelius declares the directions God gave to him to send for Peter.

(1) Cornelius gives an account of the angel's appearing to him, and ordering him to send for Peter. He tells how this vision found him employed (*v.* 30): *Four days ago I was fasting until this hour. He was at the ninth hour praying in his house,* not in the synagogue, but at home. *At the ninth hour of the day,* three of the clock in the afternoon, most people were travelling or trading, working in the fields, visiting their friends, taking their pleasure, or taking a nap after dinner; yet then Cornelius was at his devotions, which shows how much he made religion his business. He describes the messenger: *There stood a man before me in bright clothing.* He repeats the message that was sent to him (*v.* 31, 32), just as we had it, *v.* 4–6. Only here it is said, *Thy prayer is heard.* We are not told what his prayer was; but if this message was an answer to it, he prayed that God would make some further discoveries of himself, and of the way of salvation to him.

(2) He declares his own and his friends' readiness to receive the message Peter had to deliver (*v.* 33): *Immediately therefore I sent to thee, and thou hast well done that thou hast come.* Faithful ministers do well to come to people that are desirous to receive instruction from them; to come when they are sent for. "*We are all here present before God. Therefore,* because thou art come to us by such a warrant, on such an errand, *we are present,* and are ready to come at a call. *We are all present.*" The whole of the man must be present; not the body here, and the

heart, with the fool's eyes, in the ends of the earth. "*We are present to hear all things that are commanded thee of God.*" Peter was there to preach all things that were commanded him of God. They were ready to hear, not whatever he pleased to say, but what he was commanded of God to say. "We are ready to hear *all* that thou art commissioned to preach, though it be ever so displeasing and ever so contrary to our former notions or present secular interests. We are ready to hear all, and therefore let nothing be kept back that is profitable for us."

Verses 34–43

We have here Peter's sermon. It is intimated that he expressed himself with a great deal of solemnity and gravity, but with freedom and copiousness, in that phrase, *he opened his mouth, and spoke, v.* 34. It was a new sermon.

I. Because they were Gentiles to whom he preached. He shows that they were interested in the gospel of Christ, and entitled to the benefit of it, upon an equal footing with the Jews. He therefore lays down this as an undoubted principle, *that God is no respecter of persons.* He doth not give judgment in favour of a man for the sake of any external advantage foreign to the merits of the cause. *But in every nation he that fears God and works righteousness is accepted of him, v.* 35. God never did, nor ever will, justify and save a wicked Jew that lived and died impenitent, whose privileges and professions, instead of screening him from the judgment of God, will but aggravate his guilt and condemnation. He never did, nor ever will, reject or refuse an honest Gentile, who like Cornelius, fears God, and worships him, and works righteousness, who lives up to the light he has. Whatever nation he is of, that shall be no prejudice to him. God judges of men by their hearts, not by their country or parentage; and, wherever he finds an upright man, he will be found an upright God. *Fearing God, and working righteousness,* must go together. But, where these are predominant, no doubt is to be made of acceptance with God. Those that have not the knowledge of him, and therefore cannot have an explicit regard to him, may yet receive grace from God for his sake, *to fear God and to work righteousness*; and wherever God gives grace to do so, as he did to Cornelius, he will, through Christ, accept the work of his own hands. This was always a truth, before Peter perceived it, *that God respecteth no man's person.* God will not ask in the great day what country men were of, but what they were. Yet now it was made more clear than it had been. Peter is here made to perceive it, by comparing the vision which he had with that which Cornelius had.

II. Because they were Gentiles inhabiting a place within the confines of the land of Israel, he refers them to what they themselves could not but know of our Lord Jesus: for these were things the report of which spread into every corner of the nation, *v.* 37.

1. They knew, in general, *the word which God sent to the children of Israel*: *That word, I say, you know, v.* 37. Though the Gentiles were not admitted to hear it, yet they could not but hear of it. We are often told in the gospels how the fame of Christ went into all parts of Canaan. That word of power and grace, *you know.* What the purport of this word was. God by it *published the glad tidings of peace by Jesus Christ,* so it should be read. It is God himself that proclaims *peace,* who justly might have proclaimed war. To whom it was sent—to the children of Israel, in the first place.

2. They knew the several matters of fact relating to this word of the gospel sent to Israel. They knew the baptism of repentance which John preached by way of introduction to it. They knew what an

extraordinary man John was, and what a direct tendency his preaching had to *prepare the way of the Lord.* They knew that immediately after John's baptism the gospel of Christ, that word of *peace, was published throughout all Judæa,* and that it took its rise from Galilee. They knew that Jesus of Nazareth *went about doing good.* They knew what a benefactor he was to that nation; how he made it his business to do good to all. He was not idle, but still doing; went about from place to place, and wherever he came he was doing good. Hereby he showed *that he was sent of God.* They knew more particularly that he *healed all that were oppressed of the devil.* He was sent to *destroy the works of the devil*; for thus he obtained many a victory over him. They knew that the Jews put him to death; they *slew* him by *hanging him on a tree.* Whom *they* slew; they, to whom he had done and designed so much good. All this they knew; but lest they should think it was only a report, Peter, for himself and the rest of the apostles, attested it (*v.* 39): *We are witnesses of all things which he did, both in the land of the Jews and in Jerusalem.*

3. They might know, by all this, that he had a commission from heaven to preach and act as he did. This Jesus *is Lord of all*; not only as *God over all blessed for evermore,* but as Mediator, *all power both in heaven and on earth* is put into his hand, and all judgment committed to him. *God anointed him with the Holy Ghost and with power,* whence he was called *Christ—the Messiah, the anointed One.* He was full of power both in preaching and working miracles, which was the seal of a divine mission. *God was with him, v.* 38. God not only sent him, but was present with him all along. Those whom God anoints he will accompany; he will himself be with those to whom he has given his Spirit.

III. Because they had had no more certain information concerning this Jesus, Peter declares to them his resurrection from the dead, and the proofs of it. Probably they had heard at Cæsarea some talk of his having risen from the dead, soon silenced by that vile suggestion of the Jews, that *his disciples came by night and stole him away.* 1. The power by which he arose is incontestably divine (*v.* 40): *Him God raised up the third day.* He did not break prison, but had a legal discharge. *God raised him up.* 2. The proofs of his resurrection were incontestably clear; for God *showed him openly.* It was such a showing of him as amounted to a demonstration of the truth of his resurrection. He showed him not publicly indeed, but evidently; *not to all the people.* By resisting all the evidences he had given them of his divine mission, they had forfeited the favour of being eye-witnesses of this great proof of it. Those who immediately forged and promoted that lie of his being stolen away were justly given up to strong delusions to believe it. A sufficient number saw him to attest the truth of his resurrection. The resurrection of Christ was proved before sufficient witnesses. They were not so by chance, but they were *chosen before of God* to be witnesses of it. They had not a sudden and transient view of him, but a great deal of free conversation with him: *They did eat and drink with him after he rose from the dead.* This was not all; they saw him without any terror or consternation, he conversed with them so familiarly, that *they did eat and drink with him.*

IV. He concludes with an inference from all this, that therefore that which they all ought to do was to believe in this Jesus: he was sent to tell Cornelius what he must do, and it is this. One thing he lacked, he must believe in Christ.

1. Why he must believe in him. The Christian faith is *built upon the foundation of the apostles and prophets,* it is built upon the testimony given by them. By the apostles. Peter as foreman speaks for the rest, that *God commanded them* to *preach to the people, and to testify* concerning Christ. Their testimony is God's testimony; and they are his witnesses to the world. By the prophets of the Old Testament (*v.* 43): *To him give all the prophets witness.* Out of the mouth of these two clouds of witnesses, *this word is established.*

2. What they must believe concerning him. That we are all accountable to Christ as our Judge. This Jesus is *ordained of God to be the Judge of the quick and dead, v.* 42. He is empowered to prescribe the terms of salvation, that rule by which we must be judged. He hath assured us of this, *in that he hath raised him from the dead* (*ch.* xvii. 31), so that it is the great concern of everyone of us to make him our friend. That if we believe in him we shall all be justified by him as our righteousness, *v.* 43. The prophets did witness this, *that through his name, whosoever believeth in him shall receive remission of sins.* This is the great thing we need, without which we are undone. And the remission of sins lays a foundation for all other favours and blessings. If sin be pardoned, all is well, and shall end everlastingly well.

Verses 44–48

We have here the issue and effect of Peter's sermon. They were all brought home to Christ.

I. God's owning Peter's word, by conferring the Holy Ghost upon the hearers of it (*v.* 44): *While Peter was yet speaking these words the Holy Ghost fell on all those who heard the word,* even as he did on the apostles at first; so Peter saith, *ch.* xi. 15. When the Holy Ghost fell upon them—while Peter was preaching. Thus God bore witness to what he said, and accompanied it with a divine power. The Holy Ghost fell upon others after they were baptized, for their confirmation; but upon these Gentiles before they were baptized: to show that God is not tied to a method, nor confines himself to external signs. How it appeared that the Holy Ghost had fallen upon them (*v.* 46): *They spoke with tongues.* When they spoke with tongues, they *magnified God,* they spoke of Christ and the benefits of redemption, which Peter had been preaching. Whatever gift we are endued with, we ought to honour God with it, and particularly the gift of speaking, and all the improvements of it. What impression it made upon the believing Jews that were present (*v.* 45): *Those of the circumcision who believed were astonished,* because *upon the Gentiles also was poured out the gift of the Holy Ghost.* Had they understood the scriptures of the Old Testament it would not have been such an astonishment to them.

II. Peter's owning God's work in baptizing those on whom the Holy Ghost fell. Though they had received the Holy Ghost, yet it was requisite they should be baptized; though God is not tied to instituted ordinances, we are. Though they were Gentiles, yet, having received the Holy Ghost, they might be admitted to baptism (*v.* 47): *Can any man forbid water, that these should not be baptized, who have received the Holy Ghost as well as we?* The argument is conclusive; can we deny the sign to those who have received the thing signified? It becomes us to follow God's indications, and to take those into communion with us whom he hath taken into communion with himself. Now it appears why the Spirit was given them before they were baptized—because otherwise Peter could not have persuaded himself to baptize them. Thus is there one unusual step of divine grace taken after another to bring the Gentiles into the church. How well is it for us that the grace of a good God is so much more extensive than the charity of some good men! Peter did not baptize them himself, but *commanded them to be baptized, v.* 48. The apostles received the commission to *go and disciple all nations by baptism.* But it was to prayer and the ministry of the word that they were to *give* themselves. The business of baptizing was therefore ordinarily devolved upon the inferior ministers; these acted by the orders of the apostles.

III. Their desire for further advantage by Peter's ministry: *They prayed him to tarry certain days.* They were not willing he should go away immediately, but earnestly begged he would stay for some time among them, that they might be further instructed by him. Those who have some acquaintance with Christ cannot but covet more. Even those that have received the Holy Ghost must see their need of the ministry of the word.

Chapter 11

I. Peter's necessary vindication of what he did in receiving Cornelius and his friends into the church, ver. 1–18. II. The good success of the gospel at Antioch, ver. 19–21. III. The carrying on of the good work that was begun at Antioch, and the lasting name of Christian first given to the disciples there, ver. 22–26. IV. A prediction of an approaching famine, and the contribution for the relief of the poor saints in Judæa, ver. 27–30.

Verses 1–18

It being so great a surprise to the believing as well as the unbelieving Jews, it is worth while to enquire how it was received.

I. Intelligence was presently brought of it to the church in Jerusalem, and thereabouts. Before he himself had returned to Jerusalem *the apostles and the brethren* there and *in Judæa heard that the Gentiles also had received the word of God,* that the Gentiles also themselves, with whom it had hitherto been thought unlawful to hold common conversation, had *received the word of God.* The word of God was preached to them, which was a greater honour put upon them than they expected. Thus often are the prejudices of pride and bigotry held fast against the clearest discoveries of divine truth. It was entertained and submitted to by them, which was a better work wrought upon them than they expected. They looked upon them as not inclined to religion, and therefore were surprised to hear that they had received the word of the Lord. We are too apt to despair of doing good to those who yet, when they are tried, prove very tractable.

II. Offence was taken at it by the believing Jews (*v.* 2, 3): *When Peter had himself come up to Jerusalem, those that were of the circumcision contended with him.* He *went in to men uncircumcised, and did eat with them*; and thereby they think he has stained, if not forfeited, the honour of his apostleship. It is the bane and damage of the church, to monopolize it, and to exclude those from it that are not in everything as we are. Christ's ministers must not think it strange if they be censured, not only by their professed enemies, but by their professing friends. But, if we have proved our own work, we may have rejoicing in ourselves, as Peter had, whatever reflections we may have from our brethren. Those that are zealous and courageous in the service of Christ must expect to be censured by those who, under pretence of being cautious, are cold and indifferent. Those who are of catholic, generous, charitable principles, must expect to be censured by such as are conceited and strait-laced.

III. Peter gave such a full and fair account of the matter of fact as was sufficient both to justify him, and to satisfy them (*v.* 4): *He rehearsed the matter from the beginning.*

1. He takes it for granted that if they had rightly understood how the matter was they would not have contended with him. We should be moderate in our censures, because if we rightly understood that which we are so forward to run down perhaps we should see cause to run in with it.

2. He is very willing to stand right in their opinion. He is ready to *give a reason of the hope that is in him* concerning the Gentiles, and why he had receded from his former sentiments, which were the same with theirs.

(1) He was instructed by a vision no longer to keep up the distinctions which were made by the ceremonial law; he relates the vision (*v.* 5, 6), as we had it before, *ch.* x. 9, &c. The sheet which was there said to be *let down to the earth* he here says came *even to him.* We should thus see all God's discoveries of himself, coming even to us, applying them by faith to ourselves. When the sheet *came to him he fastened his eyes upon it, and considered it, v.* 6. If we would be led into the knowledge of divine things, we must fix our minds upon them, and consider them. He tells them what orders he had to eat of all sorts of meat without distinction, asking no questions for conscience' sake, *v.* 7. He pleads that he was as averse to the thoughts of conversing with Gentiles, as they could be, and therefore refused the liberty given him: *Not so, Lord; for nothing common or unclean has at any time entered into my mouth, v.* 8. But he was told that God had cleansed those persons and things which were before polluted; and therefore that he must no longer call them common (*v.* 9); so that he was not to be blamed for changing his thoughts, when God had changed the thing. And, that they might be sure he was not deceived in it, he tells them it was done three times (*v.* 10). And, further to confirm him that it was a divine vision, the things he saw did not vanish away into the air, but *were drawn up again into heaven.*

(2) He was particularly directed by the Spirit to go along with the messengers that Cornelius sent. He observes to them the time when the messengers came—immediately after he had that vision; yet, lest this should not be sufficient to clear his way, the Spirit bade him *go with the men, nothing doubting* (*v.* 11, 12). He must make no scruple of going along with them.

(3) He took some of his brethren along with him, who were of the circumcision, that they might be satisfied as well as he. He did not act separately, but with advice; not rashly, but upon due deliberation.

(4) Cornelius had a vision too (*v.* 13): *He showed us how he had seen an angel in his house,* that bade him *send to Joppa for one Simon, whose surname is Peter.* Peter is the more confirmed in the truth of his vision by Cornelius's, and Cornelius by Peter's. Here is something added in what the angel said to Cornelius; before it was, *Send for Peter, and he shall speak to thee, he shall tell thee what thou oughtest to do* (*ch.* x. 6, 32); but here it is, *"He shall tell thee words whereby thou and thy house shall be saved"* (*v.* 14). The words of the gospel are words whereby we may be eternally saved; not merely by hearing them, but by believing and obeying them. They open the way of salvation to us. Those that embrace the gospel of Christ will have salvation brought by it to their families: *"Thou and all thy house shall be saved."* Thy house shall be as welcome to the benefit of the salvation as thou thyself, even the meanest servant thou hast." Now salvation is brought to the Gentiles.

(5) That which put the matter past all dispute was the descent of the Holy Ghost upon the Gentile hearers. The fact was plain and undeniable (*v.* 15): *"As I began to speak the Holy Ghost fell on them as on us at the beginning."* Thus God attested what was done, and declared his approbation of it. Peter was hereby put in mind of a saying of his Master's: *John baptized with water; but you shall be baptized*

with the Holy Ghost, v. 16. The Holy Ghost was the gift of Christ, and the product and performance of that great promise which he left with them when he went to heaven. It was therefore without doubt from him that this gift came. As it was promised by his mouth, so it was performed by his hand. The gift of the Holy Ghost was a kind of baptism. Comparing that promise, so worded, with this gift just now conferred, he concluded that the question was determined by Christ himself (*v.* 17): "*Forasmuch then as God gave them the like gift as he did to us*—gave it to us as *believing in the Lord Jesus Christ*, and to them upon their believing in him—*What was I, that I could withstand God?* Could I refuse to baptize them with water, whom God had baptized with the Holy Ghost?" Those take too much upon them who contrive how to exclude from their communion those whom God has taken into communion with himself.

IV. This account which Peter gave of the matter satisfied them. Some people, when they have fastened a censure upon a person, will stick to it, though afterwards it appear ever so plainly to be unjust and groundless. It was not so here. When they heard this they held their peace and said no more against what Peter had done. They not only held their peace from quarrelling with Peter, but opened their mouths to glorify God. They were thankful that God had shown more mercy to the poor Gentiles than they were inclined to show them, saying, *Then hath God also to the Gentiles granted repentance unto life!* He hath granted them the grace of repentance, in having given them his Holy Spirit, who gives a sight of sin and sorrow for it, and then a sight of Christ and joy in him. Repentance, if it be true, is unto life. Those that by repentance die unto sin thenceforward live unto God; and then, and not till then, we begin to live indeed, and it shall be to eternal life. Repentance is God's gift; it is not only his free grace that accepts it, but his mighty grace that works it in us. Wherever God designs to give life he gives repentance. God has exalted his Son Jesus not only to *give repentance to Israel, and the remission of sins* (*ch.* v. 31), but to the Gentiles also.

Verses 19–26

We have here an account of the planting and watering of a church at Antioch, the chief city of Syria, reckoned afterwards the third most considerable city of the empire. It is suggested that Luke, the penman of this history, as well as Theophilus, to whom he dedicates it, was of Antioch, which may be the reason why he takes more particular notice of the success of the gospel at Antioch.

I. The first preachers of the gospel there were such as were dispersed from Jerusalem by persecution, that persecution which arose at the time of Stephen's death (*v.* 19): *They travelled as far as Phenice preaching the word.* Thus what was intended for the hurt of the church was made to work for its good. The enemies designed to scatter and lose them, Christ designed to scatter and use them.

1. Those that *fled from persecution* did not flee from their work. Those that persecuted the preachers of the gospel hoped thereby to prevent their carrying it to the Gentile world; but it proved that they did but hasten it the sooner. Those that were persecuted in one city fled to another; but they carried their religion along with them.

2. They pressed forward in their work. When they had preached successfully in Judæa, Samaria, and Galilee, they travelled into Phoenicia, into the island of Cyprus, and into Syria. Though the further they travelled the more they exposed themselves, yet they travelled on; *further still*, was their motto.

3. They *preached the word to none but to the Jews only* who were dispersed in all those parts. They did

not yet understand that the Gentiles were to be fellow-heirs, but left the Gentiles either to turn Jews, or else remain as they were.

4. They particularly applied themselves to the Hellenist Jews, here called the Grecians. Many of the preachers were natives of Judæa and Jerusalem; but some of them were by birth of Cyprus and Cyrene, as Barnabas himself (*ch.* iv. 36), and Simon (Mark xv. 21). These, being themselves Grecian Jews, had a particular concern for those of their own denomination, and applied themselves closely to them at Antioch. To them they preached the Lord Jesus. This was the constant subject of their preaching; what else should the ministers of Christ preach, but Christ?

5. They had wonderful success in their preaching, *v.* 21. Their preaching was accompanied with a divine power. *The hand of the Lord was with them,* to bring that home to the hearts and consciences of men which they could but speak to the outward ear. These were not apostles, but ordinary ministers, yet they had the hand of the Lord with them, and did wonders. Abundance of good was done: *A great number believed, and turned unto the Lord.* They believed; they were convinced of the truth of the gospel. The effect of this was that they *turned unto the Lord.* They turned from a confidence in the righteousness of the law, to rely only upon the righteousness of Christ, the righteousness which is by faith. They turned to the Lord Jesus, and he became all in all with them. Whatever we profess or pretend, we do not really believe the gospel if we do not cordially embrace Christ offered to us in the gospel.

II. The good work thus begun at Antioch was carried on to great perfection; by the ministry of Barnabas and Saul.

1. The church at Jerusalem sent Barnabas thither.

(1) They heard the good news, that the gospel was received at Antioch, *v.* 22. *Tidings of these things came to the ears of the church that was in Jerusalem.*

(2) They despatched Barnabas to them. They *sent him forth* as an envoy from them. He must go *as far as Antioch.* It is probable that Barnabas had a particular genius for work of this kind, and, his talent lying this way, he was fittest to be employed in this work. God gives various gifts for various services.

(3) Barnabas was wonderfully pleased to find that the gospel got ground, and that some of his countrymen, men of Cyprus, were instrumental in it (*v.* 23): *When he came, and had seen the grace of God, he was glad.* He saw the grace of God among them. What we see which is good in any we must call God's grace in them. We must be glad to see the grace of God in others, and the more when we see it where we did not expect it.

(4) He did what he could to confirm those in the faith who were converted to the faith. He *exhorted them.* It is the same word with that by which the name of Barnabas is interpreted (*ch.* iv. 36)—a *son of exhortation;* his talent lay that way. Or, being *a son of consolation* (for so we render the word), he comforted or encouraged them with purpose of heart to cleave to the Lord. Barnabas was glad for what he saw of the grace of God among them, and therefore was the more earnest with them to persevere. To *cleave to the Lord.* Not to fall off from following him, not to flag and tire in following him. Not only to hold him fast, but to hold fast by him. To cleave to him with purpose of heart, with an intelligent, firm, and deliberate resolution.

(5) Herein he gave a proof of his good character (*v.* 24): *He was a good man, and full of the Holy Ghost, and of faith.* He was not only a righteous man, but *a good man,* a good-tempered man. Ministers that are so recommend themselves and their doctrine very much to the good opinion of those that are

without. He was a good man, that is, a charitable man; so he had approved himself, when he sold an estate, and gave the money to the poor, *ch.* iv. 37. He was richly endued with the gifts and graces of the Spirit. The goodness of his natural disposition would not have qualified him for this service if he had not been *full of the Holy Ghost.* He was full of faith, full of the grace of faith, and full of the fruits of that faith that works by love.

(6) He was instrumental to do good, by bringing in those that were without, as well as by building up those that were within: *Much people were added to the Lord.*

2. Barnabas went to fetch Saul. Barnabas takes a journey to Tarsus to tell him what a door of opportunity was opened at Antioch, and to desire him to come and spend some time with him there, *v.* 25, 26. And here also it appears that Barnabas was a good sort of a man in two things: (1) That he would take so much pains to bring an active useful man out of obscurity. It was he that brought him out of the corner into which he was driven, into a more public station. It is a very good work to fetch a candle from under a bushel, and to set it in a candlestick. (2) That he would bring in Saul at Antioch, who, being a *chief speaker* (*ch.* xiv. 12), would be likely to eclipse him there, by outshining him. Barnabas brought Saul to Antioch, though it might be the lessening of himself.

3. We are here further told,

(1) What service was now done to the church at Antioch. Paul and Barnabas continued there a whole year, presiding in their religious assemblies, and preaching the gospel, *v.* 26. *Teaching the people* is one part of the work of ministers. They are not only to be the people's mouth to God in prayer and praise, but God's mouth to the people in opening the scriptures, and teaching the good knowledge of the Lord. It is a great encouragement to ministers when they have opportunity of teaching much people, of casting the net of the gospel where there is a large shoal of fish. Preaching is not only for the conversion of those that are without, but for the instruction and edification of those that are within.

(2) What honour was now put upon the church *at Antioch: There the disciples were first called Christians.* Two such great men as Paul and Barnabas continuing there so long, being exceedingly followed, Christian assemblies made a greater figure there than anywhere, which was the reason of their being called *Christians* first there. Hitherto those who gave up their names to Christ were called *disciples, learners, scholars*; but henceforward they were called *Christians.* [1] Thus the reproachful names which their enemies had hitherto branded them with would, perhaps, be superseded. They called them *Nazarenes* (*ch.* xxiv. 5), *the men of that way, that by-way,* which had no name; and thus they prejudiced people against them. To remove the prejudice, they gave themselves a name which their enemies could not but say was proper. [2] Thus those who before their conversion had been distinguished by the names of Jews and Gentiles might after their conversion be called by one and the same name. Let not one say, "I was a *Jew*"; nor the other, "I was a *Gentile*"; when both the one and the other must now say, "I am a *Christian.*" [3] Thus they studied to do honour to their Master, and showed that they were not ashamed to own their relation to him. They took their denomination not from the name of his person, *Jesus,* but of his office, *Christ— anointed,* so putting their creed into their names, *that Jesus is the Christ.* Their enemies will turn this name to their reproach, and impute it to them as their crime, but they will glory in it. [4] Thus they now owned their dependence upon Christ. [5] Thus they laid upon themselves, and all that should ever profess that name, a strong and lasting obligation to follow the example of Christ, and to devote themselves entirely to the honour of Christ. Are we Christians? Then we ought to do nothing to the reproach of that worthy name by which we are called. And as we must look upon ourselves as Christians, and carry ourselves accordingly, so we must look upon others as Christians, and carry ourselves towards them accordingly. A Christian should be loved and respected for his sake whose name he bears, because he belongs to Christ.

Verses 27–30

When our Lord Jesus *ascended on high he gave gifts unto men,* not only *apostles and evangelists,* but *prophets.*

I. A visit which some of these prophets made to Antioch (*v.* 27): *In these days came prophets from Jerusalem to Antioch.* They came from Jerusalem. Jerusalem had been infamous for *killing the prophets* and abusing them, and therefore is now justly deprived of these prophets. They came to Antioch. Barnabas came to exhort them, and they, having received the exhortation well, now have prophets sent them *to show them things to come.*

II. A particular prediction of a famine approaching, delivered by one of these prophets, his name *Agabus*; we read of him again prophesying Paul's imprisonment, *ch.* xxi. 10, 11. Here he stood up and prophesied, *v.* 28. Whence he had his prophecy. *He signified it by the Spirit, that there should be* a famine. What the prophecy was: *There should be great dearth throughout all the world,* so that many of the poor should perish for want of bread. This should be not in one particular country, but *through all the world,* that is, all the Roman empire. Christ had foretold in general *that there should be famines*; but Agabus foretells one very remarkable famine now at hand. The accomplishment of it: *It came to pass in the days of Claudius Cæsar;* it began in the second year of his reign, and continued to the fourth, if not longer. Several of the Roman historians make mention of it, as does also Josephus.

III. The good use they made of this prediction. When they were told of a famine at hand, they did not hoard up corn for themselves; but, as became Christians, laid by for charity to relieve others.

1. What they determined—that *every man, according to his ability,* should *send relief to the brethren that dwelt in Judæa, v.* 29. The persons that were recommended to them as objects of charity were *the brethren that dwelt in Judæa.* Though we must, as we have opportunity, *do good to all men,* yet we must have a special regard *to the household of faith.* No poor must be neglected, but God's poor most particularly regarded. But the communion of saints is here extended further, and provision is made by the church at Antioch for the relief of the poor in Judæa, whom they call their brethren. Now we may suppose that the greatest part of those who turned Christians in that country were the poor. If there came a famine it would go very hard with them; and, if any of them should perish for want, it would be a great reproach to the Christian profession; and therefore this early care was taken, to send them a stock beforehand, lest, if it should be deferred till the famine came, it should be too late. The agreement there was among the disciples about it, that *every man* should contribute, *according to his ability,* to this good work. Merchants find their account in sending effects to countries that lie very remote; and so should we in giving alms to those afar off that need them, which therefore we should be forward to do when we are called to it. What may be said to be *according to our ability* we must judge for ourselves, but must be careful *that we judge righteous judgment.*

2. They did as they determined (*v.* 30). *Which also they did.* They not only talked of it, but they did it. Many a good motion of that kind is made and commended, but it is not prosecuted, and so comes to nothing. The collection was made, and was so considerable that they thought it worth while *to send Barnabas and Saul to Jerusalem.* They sent it *to the elders of the churches in Judæa,* to be by them distributed according to the necessity of the receivers, as it had been contributed according to the ability of the givers. It was sent *by Barnabas and Saul.* It is no disparagement, in an extraordinary case, for ministers of the gospel to be messengers of the church's charity.

CHAPTER 12

I. The martyrdom of James the apostle, and the imprisonment of Peter by Herod Agrippa, ver. 1–4. II. The miraculous deliverance of Peter out of prison in answer to the prayers of the church for him, ver. 6–19. III. The cutting off of Herod in the height of his pride (ver. 20–23); and this was done while Barnabas and Saul were at Jerusalem; an account of their return to Antioch, ver. 24, 25.

Verses 1–4

Ever since the conversion of Paul, we have heard no more of the agency of the priests in persecuting the saints at Jerusalem. Here the storm arises from another point. The civil power acts by itself in the persecution. But Herod, though originally of an Edomite family, yet seems to have been a proselyte to the Jewish religion; for Josephus says he was zealous for the Mosaic rites, a bigot for the ceremonies. He was not only (as Herod Antipas was) tetrarch of Galilee, but had also the government of Judæa committed to him by Claudius the emperor, and resided most at Jerusalem, where he was at this time. Three things we are here told he did:

I. He *stretched forth his hands to vex certain of the church, v.* 1. *Herod laid hands upon some of the church to afflict them,* so some read it. See how he advances gradually. He began with some of the members of the church; played first at small game, but afterwards flew at the apostles themselves. He began with vexing them only, or afflicting them. Afterwards he proceeded to greater instances of cruelty.

II. *He killed James the brother of John with the sword, v.* 2. We are here to consider, 1. Who the martyr was: it was *James the brother of John*; so called to distinguish him from the other James the brother of Joses. This who was here crowned with martyrdom was one of the first three of Christ's disciples. He was one of those whom Christ called *Boanerges—Sons of thunder*; and perhaps by his powerful awakening preaching he had provoked Herod, as John Baptist did the other Herod. He was one of those sons of Zebedee whom Christ told *that they should drink of the cup that he was to drink of, and be baptized with the baptism that he was to be baptized with,* Matt. xx. 23. And now those words of Christ were made good in him. The apostle died a martyr, to show the rest of them what they must expect. 2. What kind of death he suffered: his head was *cut off with a sword,* a more disgraceful way of being beheaded than with an axe. It is strange that we have not a more full account of the martyrdom of this great apostle, as we had of Stephen. But even this short mention is sufficient to let us know that the first preachers of the gospel were so well assured of the truth of it that they sealed it with their blood.

III. He imprisoned Peter. When he had beheaded James, *he proceeded further to take Peter also.* Blood to the bloodthirsty does but make them more so, and the way of persecution, as of other sins, is downhill; when they are in they find they must on. Those

that take one bold step in a sinful way give Satan advantage against them to tempt them to take another. It is therefore our wisdom to take heed of the beginnings of sin. He did this *because he saw it pleased the Jews.* The Jews made themselves guilty of the blood of James by showing themselves well pleased with it afterwards. Those will be reckoned with as persecutors who take pleasure in others' persecuting. Though he had no reason to fear displeasing them if he did not, yet he hoped to please them by doing it, and so make amends for displeasing them in something else. Those make themselves an easy prey to Satan who make it their business to please men. *Then were the days of unleavened bread.* It was at the feast of the passover. At the passover, when *the Jews came from all parts to Jerusalem to keep the feast,* they irritated one another against the Christians, and were then more violent than at other times. Here is an account of Peter's imprisonment (*v.* 4): *When he had laid hands on him, he put him in prison.* He was *delivered to four quaternions of soldiers,* that is, to sixteen, who were to be a guard upon him, four at a time. Thus they thought they had him fast. Herod's design was, *after Easter, to bring him forth unto the people.* He would make a spectacle of him. Herod will gratify them with the sight of Peter in bonds, of Peter upon the block, that they may feed their eyes with such a pleasing spectacle. And very ambitious surely he was to please the people who was willing thus to please them! He would do this *after Easter—after the passover,* certainly so it ought to be read, for it is the same word that is always so rendered. After the hurry of the feast was over, and the town was empty, he would entertain them with Peter's public trial and execution. And both Herod and the people long to have the feast over, that they may gratify themselves with this barbarous entertainment.

Verses 5 19

We have here an account of Peter's deliverance out of prison.

I. It was a signal answer to prayer (*v.* 5): *Peter was kept in prison. But prayer was made without ceasing of the church unto God for him,* for prayers and tears are the church's arms; therewith she fights, not only against her enemies, but for her friends. The delay of Peter's trial gave them time for prayer. James must be offered upon the sacrifice and service of their faith; but Peter must be continued to them, and therefore prayer for him is stirred up, and time is given them for it, by Herod's putting off the prosecution. They were very particular in their prayers for him, that it would please God to defeat Herod's purpose. The death of James alarmed them to a greater fervency in their prayer for Peter. Though the death and sufferings of Christ's ministers may be made greatly to serve the interests of Christ's kingdom, yet it is the duty and concern of the church earnestly to pray for their life, liberty, and tranquillity. *Prayer was made without ceasing.* It was an extended prayer. Times of public distress and danger should be praying times with the church; we must pray always, but then especially.

II. Let us observe when his deliverance came. 1. It was the very night before Herod designed to bring him forth. Herod resolves he shall die, and now God opened a door of escape for him. God's time to help is when things are brought to the last extremity. 2. It was when he was *fast bound with two chains, between two soldiers*; and, besides this, to make sure work, the *keepers before the door kept the prison,* that no one might so much as attempt to rescue him. Never could the art of man do more to secure a prisoner. When men will think to be too hard for God, God will make it appear that he is too hard for them. 3. It was when he was *sleeping between the soldiers*. Not terrified with his danger. There was but a step between him and death, and yet he could lay himself down in peace, and sleep—sleep in the midst of his enemies. Even in prison, between two soldiers, God gives him sleep. Not expecting his deliverance. He did not keep awake, and was perfectly surprised with his deliverance.

III. An *angel was sent from heaven* on purpose to rescue him.

1. *The angel of the Lord came upon him; stood over him.* He seemed as one abandoned by men, yet not forgotten of his God. Gates and guards kept all his friends from him, but could not keep the angels of God from him. Wherever the people of God are they have a way open heavenward, nor can anything intercept their intercourse with God.

2. *A light shone in the prison.* Though it is a dark place, and in the night, Peter shall see his way clear.

3. The angel awoke Peter, by giving him *a blow on his side*, a gentle touch, enough to rouse him out of his sleep. When good people slumber in a time of danger, let them expect to be smitten on the side by some sharp affliction; better be raised up so than left asleep. The language of this stroke was, *Arise up quickly*.

4. *His chains fell off from his hands.* They had handcuffed him, to make him sure, but *God loosed his hands*.

5. He was ordered to dress himself immediately, and follow the angel; and he did so, *v.* 8, 9. When Peter was awake he knew not what to do but as the angel directed him. He must *gird himself*. He must *bind on his sandals*, that he might be fit to walk. He must *cast his garments about him*, and follow the angel; and he might go with a great deal of courage and cheerfulness who had a messenger from heaven for his guide and guard. He *went out, and followed him*. Those who are delivered out of a spiritual imprisonment must follow their deliverer, as Israel did; they *went out, not knowing whither they went*, but whom they followed. When Peter went out after the angel, *he knew not that it was true which was done by the angel, but thought he saw a vision*. He thought the news was too good to be true.

6. He was led safely by the angel out of danger, *v.* 10. Guards were kept at one pass and at another, which they were to make their way through, and they did so without any opposition; nay, for aught that appears, without any discovery. The angel and Peter safely *passed the first and second ward*. But still there is an iron gate, after all, that will stop them. Up to that gate they march, and it *opened to them*. They did not so much as put a hand to it, but it opened *of its own accord*, by an invisible power. When God will work salvation for his people, no difficulties in their way are insuperable; but even gates of iron are made to open of their own accord. This iron gate led him into the city out of the castle or tower, so that, when they were through this, they were got into the street. This deliverance of Peter represents to us our redemption by Christ, which is often spoken of as the setting of prisoners free, not only the proclaiming of liberty to the captives, but the *bringing of them out of the prison-house*.

7. When this was done, *the angel departed from him*, and left him to himself. He was out of danger from his enemies, and needed no guard. He knew where he was, and how to find out his friends, and needed no guide. Miracles are not to be expected when ordinary means are to be used.

IV. Having seen how his deliverance was magnified, we are next to see how it was manifested.

1. How Peter came to himself, and so came himself to the knowledge of it, *v.* 11. So many strange and surprising things coming together upon a man just awoke out of sleep put him for the present into some confusion. At length Peter *came to himself*, and found that it was not a dream, but a real thing: "*Now I know of a surety*, now I know that it is truth, *that the Lord Jesus hath sent his angel*, and by him *hath delivered me out of the hands of Herod*, and so hath disappointed *all the expectation of the people of the Jews*." Peter, when he recollected himself, *perceived of a truth* what great things God had done for him, which at first he could not believe for joy. Thus souls who are delivered out of a spiritual bondage are not at first aware what God has wrought in them. Many have the truth of grace that want the evidence of it. But *when the Comforter comes* he will let them know of a surety what a blessed change is wrought in them.

2. How Peter came to his friends, and brought the knowledge of it to them.

(1) He *considered the thing* (*v.* 12), considered how imminent his danger was, how great his deliverance; and now what has he to do? God's providence leaves room for the use of our prudence; and, though he has undertaken to perform and perfect what he has begun, yet he expects we should consider the thing.

(2) He went directly to a friend's house; it was the house of Mary, a sister of Barnabas, and mother of John Mark. A church in the house makes it a little sanctuary.

(3) There he found *many* that were *gathered together praying*, at the dead time of the night, praying for Peter. [1] They continued in prayer, in token of their importunity. As long as we are kept waiting for a mercy we must continue praying for it. [2] It should seem that now when the affair came near to a crisis they were more fervent in prayer than before; and it was a good sign that God intended to deliver Peter when he thus stirred up a spirit of prayer for his deliverance. [3] They gathered together for prayer. They know what an encouragement Christ gave to joint-prayer. It was always the practice of God's praying people to unite their forces in prayer. [4] They were many that were got together for this work. No doubt but there were many private Christians that knew how to pray, and to pray pertinently, and to continue long in prayer. [5] Peter came to them when they were thus employed. It was as if God should say, "You are praying that Peter may be restored to you; now here he is."

(4) He knocked at the gate, and had much ado to get them to let him in (*v.* 13–16): *Peter knocked at the door of the gate*. [1] A *damsel came to hearken*; not to open the door till she knew who was there, and what their business was. It should seem, by her being named, that she was of note among the Christians, and more zealously affected to the better part than most of her age. [2] She knew Peter's voice. But, instead of letting him in immediately out of the cold, *she opened not the gate for gladness*. Thus sometimes, in a transport of affection to our friends, we do that which is unkind. [3] She ran in and told them that Peter was certainly at the gate. But, when she spoke of Peter's being there, they said, "*Thou art mad*; it is impossible, for he is in prison." Sometimes that which we most earnestly wish for we are most backward to believe, because we are afraid of imposing upon ourselves. However, she stood to it that it was he. Then said they, *It is his angel*, *v.* 15. "It is a *messenger* from him, that makes use of his name"; so some take it. When the damsel was confident it was Peter, because she knew his voice, they thought it was because he that stood at the door had called himself Peter. "It is one that comes with an errand from him, and thou didst mistake as if it had been he himself. It is his *guardian angel*." Some think that they supposed his angel to appear as a presage of his death approaching.

If so, they concluded this an ill omen, and that the language of the apparition was, "Let it suffice you, Peter must die." Others think they took this to be an angel from heaven, sent to bring them a grant to their prayers.

(5) At length they let him in (v. 16): *He continued knocking*, and at last they admitted him. The iron gate opened of itself. The door of his friend's house that was to welcome him does not open of its own accord, but must be knocked at, long knocked at. But, *when they saw him, they were astonished*, were filled with wonder and joy in him, as much as they were but just now with sorrow and fear concerning him.

(6) Peter gave them an account of his deliverance. When he came to the company they gathered about him to congratulate him on his deliverance; and herein they were so noisy that he could not make them hear him, but was forced to *beckon to them with the hand to hold their peace*, while *he declared unto them how the Lord Jesus had brought him out of prison*; and it is very likely he did not part with them till he and they had together solemnly given thanks to God for his enlargement. What is won by prayer must be worn with praise.

(7) Peter sent the account to others of his friends: *Go, show these things to James, and to the brethren with him*. He would have James and his company to know of his deliverance, not only that they might be delivered from their fears concerning Peter, but that they might return thanks to God with him and for him. Though Herod had slain one James with the sword, yet here was another James, and that in Jerusalem too, that stood up in his room to preside among the brethren there.

(8) Peter had nothing more to do for the present than to shift for his own safety. He *departed, and went into another place*. Even the Christian law of suffering for Christ has not repealed the natural law of self-preservation, as far as God gives an opportunity of providing for it.

V. Having seen the triumph of Peter's friends in his deliverance, let us next observe the confusion of his enemies thereupon. The guards were in the utmost consternation upon it (v. 18): *As soon as it was day* there was *no small stir among the soldiers, what had become of Peter*. They thought themselves as sure as could be of him but last night; yet now the bird is flown. Thus have the persecutors of the gospel of Christ been often filled with vexation to see its cause conquering. Houses were searched in vain for the rescued prisoner (v. 19): *Herod sought for him, and found him not*. Who can find whom God hath hidden? All believers have God for *their hiding-place*. The impotent world cannot reach them. The keepers were reckoned with; *Herod examined the keepers*, and *he commanded that they should be put to death*. Herod himself retired upon it: *He went down from Judæa to Caesarea, and there abode*. He was vexed to the heart, as a lion disappointed of his prey; and the more because he had so much raised the *expectation of the people of the Jews* concerning Peter. It made him ashamed to be robbed of this boasting, and to see himself disabled to make his words good. This is such a mortification to his proud spirit that he cannot bear to stay in Judæa, but away he goes to Cæsarea.

Verses 20–25

I. The death of Herod. God reckoned with him, not only for his putting James to death, but for his design to put Peter to death; for sinners will be called to an account for the mischief they have done and the mischief they would have done.

1. How the measure of his iniquity was filled up: it was *pride* that did it. The instance of it here is very remarkable, and shows how God *resists the proud*.

(1) The men of Tyre and Sidon had offended Herod. Some very small matter would serve such a man as Herod was for a provocation. He was highly displeased with this people.

(2) The offenders truckled. They submitted and were willing upon any terms to *make peace with him*. The reason why they were desirous to have the matter accommodated: *Because their country was nourished by the king's country*. Tyre and Sidon were trading cities, and were always supplied with corn from the land of Canaan. Now if Herod should make a law to prohibit the exportation of corn to Tyre and Sidon their country would be undone. And is it not then our wisdom to make our peace with God, and humble ourselves before him, who have a much more constant and necessary dependence upon him than one country can have upon another? The method they took to prevent a rupture: *They made Blastus the king's chamberlain their friend*. Blastus had Herod's ear, and has the art of mollifying his resentments; and a time is fixed for the ambassadors of Tyre and Sidon to come and make a public submission, to beg his majesty's pardon, and promise never again to offend. That which will thus feed his pride shall serve to cool his passion.

(3) Herod appeared in all the pomp and grandeur he had: He was *arrayed in his royal apparel* (v. 21), *and sat upon his throne*. Foolish people value men by their outward appearance; and no better are those who value themselves by the esteem of such as Herod did, who thought to make up the want of a royal heart with his *royal apparel; and sat upon his throne*.

(4) He made a speech to the men of Tyre and Sidon, a fine oration, and probably he kept them in suspense as to what their doom should be, till he made this oration to them, that the act of grace might come to them with the more pleasing surprise.

(5) The people applauded him. They *gave a shout*: *It is the voice of a god, and not of a man, v.* 22. It was not from any real impression made upon their minds, or any high or good thoughts they had indeed conceived of him; but they were resolved thus to curry favour with him, and strengthen the new-made peace between him and them. Thus great men are made an easy prey to flatterers if they lend an ear to them. This is a great injury to those who are thus flattered, as it makes them forget themselves, and so puffs them up with pride that they are in the utmost danger possible of falling into the condemnation of the devil.

(6) These undue praises he took to himself. This was his sin. His fault was that he said nothing, did not rebuke their flattery, nor *give God the glory* (v. 23); but was very willing that he should be thought a god and have divine honours paid him.

2. How his iniquity was punished: *Immediately* (v. 23) *the angel of the Lord smote him because he gave not God the glory; and he was eaten of worms and gave up the ghost*. Now he was reckoned with for vexing the church of Christ, killing James, imprisoning Peter, and all the other mischiefs he had done. It was no less than an angel that was the agent—*the angel of the Lord*—for those ministering spirits are the ministers either of divine justice or of divine mercy, as God is pleased to employ them. The angel smote him just at that instant when he was strutting at the applause of the people, and adoring his own shadow. The angel *smote him, because he gave not the glory to God*. It was no more than a worm that was the instrument of Herod's destruction: He was *eaten of worms—he became worm-eaten*, so it must be read; rotten he was, and he became like a piece of rotten wood. See here, What vile bodies those are which we carry about with us. We should not be proud of our bodies, we should not pamper our bodies, for this is but feeding the worms, and feeding them for the worms. See what weak and

contemptible creatures God can make the instruments of his justice. See how God delights not only to bring down proud men, but to bring them down in such a way as is most mortifying. Herod is not only destroyed, but destroyed by worms, that the pride of his glory may be effectually stained.

II. The progress of the gospel after this. 1. *The word of God grew and multiplied, v.* 24. The courage and comfort of the martyrs, and God's owning them, did more to invite people to Christianity, than their sufferings did to deter them from it. After the death of Herod the word of God gained ground. 2. Barnabas and Saul returned to Antioch: *When they had fulfilled their ministry they returned from Jerusalem.* Though they had a great many friends there, yet at present their work lay at Antioch; and where our business is there we should be. Barnabas and Saul, when they went to *Antioch, took with them John, whose surname was Mark,* at whose mother's house they had that meeting for prayer which we read of, *v.* 12. She was sister to Barnabas. It is probable that Barnabas lodged there, and perhaps Paul with him, while they were at Jerusalem, and their intimacy in that family occasioned their taking a son of that family with them when they returned, to be trained up under them. Educating young men for the ministry, and entering them into it, is a very good work for elder ministers to take care of.

CHAPTER 13

We have not yet met with anything concerning the spreading of the gospel to the Gentiles which bears any proportion to the largeness of that commission, "Go, and disciple all nations". The door was opened in the baptizing of Cornelius and his friends. But here in this chapter that work is revived. I. The solemn ordination of Barnabas and Saul to the great work of spreading the gospel among the nations about, ver. 1–3. II. Their preaching the gospel in Cyprus, and the opposition they met with there from Elymas the sorcerer, ver. 4–13. III. The heads of a sermon which Paul preached to the Jews at Antioch in Pisidia, ver. 14–41. IV. The preaching of the gospel to the Gentiles at their request, ver. 42–49. V. The trouble which the infidel Jews gave to the apostles (ver. 50–52).

Verses 1–3

We have here a divine commission to Barnabas and Saul to go and preach the gospel among the Gentiles.

I. Here is an account of the present state of the church at Antioch.

1. How well furnished it was with good ministers; there were there *certain prophets and teachers* (*v.* 1), men that were eminent for gifts, graces, and usefulness. Agabus seems to have been a prophet and not a teacher, and many were teachers who were not prophets. Antioch was a great city, and the Christians there were many; it was therefore requisite they should have many teachers. Barnabas is first named and Saul last, but afterwards the last became first. Three others are mentioned. *Simeon,* or Simon, who for distinction-sake was called *Niger, Simon the Black*; *Lucius* of Cyrene; *Manaen,* a person of some quality, as it should seem, for he was *brought up with Herod the tetrarch,* was his comrade and intimate, which gave him a fair prospect of preferment at court, and yet for Christ's sake he quitted all the hopes of it. It is better to be fellow-sufferer with a saint than fellow-persecutor with a tetrarch.

2. How well employed they were (*v.* 2): *They ministered to the Lord, and fasted.* Diligent faithful teachers do truly minister unto the Lord. Those that instruct Christians serve Christ. Ministering to the Lord, in one way or other, ought to be the stated business of churches and their teachers. Religious *fasting* is of use in our ministering to the Lord. Though it was not so much practised by the disciples of Christ, *while the bridegroom was with them,* yet,

after the bridegroom was taken away, they abounded in it.

II. The orders given by the Holy Ghost. The *Holy Ghost said: Separate me Barnabas and Saul for the work whereunto I have called them.* He does not specify the work, but refers to a former call of which they themselves knew the meaning. The matter was settled between them at Jerusalem before this, that as Peter, James, and John laid out themselves among those of the circumcision, so Paul and Barnabas should *go to the heathen.* The orders were, *Separate me Barnabas and Saul.* Christ by his Spirit has the nomination of his ministers. There are some whom the Holy Ghost has separated for the service of Christ, and concerning them directions are given to those who are competent judges: *Separate* them. Christ's ministers are separated to him and to the Holy Ghost: *Separate them to me;* they are to be employed in Christ's work and under the Spirit's guidance. All that are separated to Christ as his ministers are separated to work; Christ keeps no servants to be idle. They are separated to take pains, not to take state. The work of Christ's ministers is work which all Christ's ministers hitherto have been called to.

III. Their ordination, not to the ministry in general, but to a particular service in the ministry. Simeon, and Lucius, and Manaen, *when they had fasted and prayed, laid their hands on Barnabas and Saul, and sent them away* (*v.* 3). They prayed for them. When good men are going forth about good work, they ought to be solemnly and particularly prayed for. They joined fasting with their prayers, as they did in their other ministrations, *v.* 3. They laid their hands on them. They gave them their discharge from the present service, in the church of Antioch, acknowledging that they went off not only fairly and with consent, but honourably and with a good report. They implored a blessing upon them in their present undertaking, begged that God would be with them, and give them success. They did not envy Barnabas and Saul the honour to which they were preferred, but cheerfully committed it to them, and *they sent them away* with all expedition, out of a concern for those countries where they were to break up fallow ground.

Verses 4–13

I. A general account of the coming of Barnabas and Saul to the famous island of Cyprus. Barnabas was a native of that country (*ch.* iv. 36), and he was willing they should have the first fruits of his labours. Their being sent forth by the Holy Ghost was the great thing that encouraged them in this undertaking, *v.* 4. They came to Seleucia, thence crossed the sea to Cyprus, and the first city they came to was Salamis (*v.* 5); and, when they had sown good seed there, *thence they* went onward *through the isle* (*v.* 6) till they came to Paphos. *They preached the word of God in the synagogues of the Jews;* so far were they from excluding them that they gave them the preference. They did not act clandestinely, but laid their doctrine open to the censure of the rulers of their synagogues. *They had John for their minister;* not their servant in common things, but their assistant in the things of God. Such a one might be many ways of use to them, especially in a strange country.

II. A particular account of their encounter with *Elymas the sorcerer.*

1. There the *deputy,* a Gentile, *Sergius Paulus* by name, encouraged the apostles. He was governor *of the country,* under the Roman emperor. He had the character of *a prudent man,* that was ruled by reason, not passion, nor prejudice, which appeared by this, that he sent for them, *and desired to hear the word of God.* Those are wise people, however they may be ranked among the foolish of this world,

who are inquisitive after the mind and will of God. If they have a message from God, let him know what it is, he is ready to receive it.

2. There Elymas, a Jew, a *sorcerer*, opposed them. This Elymas was a pretender *to the gift of prophecy, a sorcerer, a false prophet*—one that would be taken for a divine. *His name was Bar-jesus—the son of Joshua;* it signifies the *son of salvation;* but the Syriac calls him, *Bar-shoma—the son of pride; the son of inflation.* He was hanging on at court, *was with the deputy* of the country. He made it his business to withstand Barnabas and Saul. *He sought to turn away the deputy from the faith* (v. 8), to keep him from receiving the gospel. Satan is in a special manner busy with great men and men of power, to keep them from being religious; because he knows that their example, whether good or bad, will have an influence upon many.

Saul (who is here for the first time called Paul) fell upon him for this with a holy indignation. *Saul, who is also called Paul*, v. 9. Saul was his name as he was a Hebrew; Paul was his name as he was a citizen of Rome. Hitherto we have had him mostly conversant among the Jews, and therefore called by his Jewish name; but now, when he is sent forth among the Gentiles, he is called by his Roman name. He was *filled with the Holy Ghost* upon this occasion; filled with power to denounce the wrath of God against him. What Paul said did not come from any personal resentment, but from the strong impressions which the Holy Ghost made upon his spirit. He *set his eyes upon him* in opposition to his wicked impudence. He gave him his true character, v. 10. He describes him to be, *First*, An agent for hell. This Elymas, though called *Bar-jesus—a son of Jesus*—was really a *child of the devil.* In two things he resembled the devil. In craftiness. Elymas, though void of all wisdom, was *full of all subtlety.* In malice. He was *full of all mischief*—a spiteful ill-conditioned man. A fulness of subtlety and mischief together make a man indeed a child of the devil. *Secondly*, An adversary to heaven. If he be a child of the devil, it follows of course that he is *an enemy to all righteousness.* He charged upon him his present crime: "*Wilt thou not cease to pervert the right ways of the Lord.*" The ways of the Lord are right; the only right ways to heaven and happiness. There are those who pervert these right ways, who not only wander out of these ways themselves, but mislead others, and suggest to them unjust prejudices against these ways, making them seem crooked ways. Those who pervert the right ways of the Lord are commonly so hardened in it that they will not cease to do it. He denounced the judgment of God upon him, in a present blindness (v. 11): "*And now, behold, the hand of the Lord is upon thee; thou shalt be blind, not seeing the sun for a season.*" He shut his eyes, the eyes of his mind, against the light of the gospel, and therefore justly were the eyes of his body shut against the light of the sun; he sought to blind the deputy, and therefore is himself struck blind. Yet it was a moderate punishment. It was only *for a season*; if he will repent, and give glory to God, his sight shall be restored; nay, it should seem, though he do not, yet his sight shall be restored. This judgment was immediately executed: *There fell on him a mist and a darkness.* Let not him any more pretend to be a guide to the deputy's conscience who is himself struck blind. *He went about seeking some to lead him by the hand;* and where now is all his skill in sorcery.

3. Notwithstanding all the endeavours of Elymas *to turn away the deputy from the faith,* he was brought to believe, and this miracle contributed to it. The deputy was a very sensible man, and observes something which intimated its divine original. In Paul's preaching: he was *astonished at the doctrine of the Lord.* The doctrine of Christ has a great deal in it that is astonishing; and the more we know of it the more reason we shall see to wonder and stand amazed at it. In this miracle: *When he saw what was done,* he believed. It is not said that he was baptized, but it is probable that he was.

III. Their departure from the island of Cyprus. They quitted the country, and *went to Perga.* Those that went were *Paul and his company.* Then John Mark *quitted them, and returned to Jerusalem,* without the consent of Paul and Barnabas. It was his fault, and we shall hear of it again.

Verses 14–41

Perga in Pamphylia was a noted place, yet nothing at all is related of what Paul and Barnabas did there, only that *thither they came* (v. 13), and *thence they departed,* v. 14. The next place we find them in is another Antioch, in Pisidia, to distinguish it from that Antioch in Syria from which they were sent out. Abundance of Jews lived there, and to them *the gospel was to be first preached*; and Paul's sermon to them is what we have in these verses.

I. The appearance which Paul and Barnabas made in a religious assembly of the Jews at Antioch, v. 14. *When they came to Antioch* they applied to the Jews, which is a further proof of their good affection to them. They observed their time of worship, *on the sabbath day,* the Jewish sabbath. *The first day of the week* they observed among themselves as a Christian sabbath; but, if they will meet the Jews, it must be on the seventh-day sabbath. They met them in their place of worship, *in the synagogue.* Paul and Barnabas were strangers; but, wherever we come, we must enquire out God's faithful worshippers, and join with them. Though they were strangers, yet they were admitted into the synagogue, and to sit down there. Care should be taken in places of public worship that strangers be accommodated, even the poorest.

II. The invitation given them to preach. 1. The usual service of the synagogue was performed (v. 15): *The law and the prophets were read,* a portion of each, the lessons for the day. 2. When that was done, they were asked by *the rulers of the synagogue* to give them a sermon (v. 15): They sent a messenger to them: *Men and brethren, if you have any word of exhortation for the people, say on.* If they had not an affection to the gospel, yet they had at least the curiosity to hear Paul preach; and therefore begged the favour of him that he would speak a *word of exhortation to the people.* The bare reading of the scriptures in the public assemblies is not sufficient, but they should be expounded, and the people exhorted out of them. Those that preside, and have power, in public assemblies, should provide for a word of exhortation to the people. Sometimes a word of exhortation from a strange minister may be of great use to the people. These were more noble, more generous, than the rulers of the synagogues generally were.

III. The sermon Paul preached. He gladly embraced the opportunity given him to preach Christ to his countrymen the Jews. He *stood up and beckoned with his hand.* He waved his hand as an orator endeavouring to move affection, and to show himself in earnest. "*Men of Israel, and you that fear God, give audience.*" Everything is touched in this sermon that might convince the judgment of the Jews, to prevail with them to receive and embrace Christ as the promised Messiah.

1. He owns them to be God's favourite people, whom he had taken into special relation to himself, and for whom he had done great things.

(1) *The God of the whole earth* was, in a particular manner, *the God of this people Israel,* a God *in covenant with them.*

(2) He had *chosen their fathers* to be his friends: Abraham was called *the friend of God*. He puts them in mind of this, to let them know that the reason why God favoured them, was because he would adhere to the choice he had made of *their fathers*.

(3) He had *exalted that people*, had advanced them into a people, and raised them from nothing, *when they dwelt as strangers in the land of Egypt*. They ought to remember this, and to infer hence that God was no debtor to them. But they were debtors to him, and obliged to receive such further discoveries as he should make of his will.

(4) He had *with a high hand brought them out of Egypt*, had delivered them at the expense of a great many miracles, both of mercy to them and judgment on their oppressors.

(5) *He had suffered their manners forty years in the wilderness*, v. 18. God made a great deal of provision for them for forty years in the wilderness: miracles were their daily bread. He exercised a great deal of patience with them. He bore with them, suffered his anger many a time to be turned away by the prayer and intercession of Moses. So many years as we have each of us lived in this world, we must own that God has thus been as a tender father to us, has been indulgent to us, a God of pardons. We have tried his patience, and yet not tired it.

(6) He had put them in possession of the land of Canaan (v. 19): *When he had destroyed seven nations in the land of Canaan, he divided their land to them by lot.*

(7) He had raised up men to deliver them out of the hands of those that oppressed them after their settlement in Canaan, v. 20, 21. He *gave them judges*. Though they were a provoking people, yet upon their petition a deliverer was raised up. He governed them by a *prophet, Samuel*. He *afterwards* at their request *set a king over them* (v. 21), *Saul, the son of Cis*. At last, he made David their king, v. 22. *When God had removed Saul, he raised up unto them David to be their king*, and made a *covenant of royalty with him, and with his seed*. He quotes the testimony God gave concerning him. That his choice was divine: *I have found David*. Finding implies seeking; as if God had ransacked all the families of Israel to find a man fit for his purpose, and this was he. That his character was divine: *A man after my own heart*, such a one as I would have, one on whom the image of God is stamped. That his conduct was under divine direction: *He shall fulfil all my will*. He shall desire and endeavour to do the will of God, and shall be enabled to do it. The changes of their government showed that it *made nothing perfect*, and therefore must give way to the spiritual kingdom of the Messiah, which was now in the setting up; and therefore they needed not conceive any jealousy at all of the preaching of the gospel.

2. He gives them a full account of our Lord Jesus, and shows that this Jesus is his promised Seed (v. 23): *Of this man's seed*, from that *man after God's own heart, hath God, according to his promise, raised unto Israel a Saviour—Jesus*, who carries salvation in his name.

(1) How welcome should the preaching of the gospel of Christ be to the Jews, and how should they embrace it, as *well worthy of all acceptation*, when it brought them the tidings of a Saviour, *a Saviour to save them from their sins*, their worst enemies. A Saviour of God's raising up. Raised up *to be a Saviour unto Israel*, to them in the first place; so far was the gospel from designing the rejection of Israel, that it designed the gathering of them. Raised up *of the seed of David*, that ancient royal family, which the people of Israel gloried so much in. Raised up *according to his promise*, the promise to David.

Why then should they entertain it so coldly, now that it was brought to them?

(2) Concerning this Jesus, he tells them,

[1] That John the Baptist was his forerunner, that great man whom all acknowledged to be a prophet. Let them not say that the Messiah's coming was a surprise upon them, for they had sufficient warning by John, who *preached before his coming*, v. 24. He made way for his entrance, by preaching *the baptism of repentance to all the people of Israel*. He showed them their sins, *called them to repentance*, and *to bring forth fruits meet for repentance*. He gave notice of his approach (v. 25): *As he fulfilled his course*. "Now," saith he, "*Whom think you that I am? You may be thinking that I am the Messiah*, whom you expect; but you are mistaken, *I am not he*, but he is at the door; *behold, there cometh one* immediately *after me, whose shoes of his feet I am not worthy to loose*, and you may guess who that must be."

[2] That the rulers and people of the Jews, who should have welcomed him, were his persecutors and murderers. When the apostles preach Christ as *the Saviour*, they are so far from concealing his ignominious death, that they always *preach Christ crucified*, yea, and crucified by his own people, by *those that dwelt in Jerusalem*, and *their rulers*, v. 27. Their sin was *that though they found no cause of death in him, yet they desired Pilate that he might be slain* (v. 28). They compelled Pilate to crucify him, not only contrary to his inclination, but contrary to his conscience; they condemned him *to so great a death*, though they could not convict him of the least sin. Justly they might have been cut off from all benefit by the Messiah, who had thus abused him, and yet they were not; notwithstanding all this, the preaching of this gospel shall begin at Jerusalem. The reason of this was because *they knew him not*, v. 27. Christ owned this in extenuation of their crime: *They know not what they do;* and so did Peter: *I wot that through ignorance you did this*, ch. iii. 17. It was also because they knew not the voice of the prophets though they heard them read every sabbath day. They did not understand nor consider that it was foretold that the Messiah should suffer. Many that read the prophets do not know the voice of the prophets. They have the sound of the gospel in their ears, but not the sense of it in their heads. God overruled them, for the accomplishment of the prophecies of the Old Testament: *Because they knew not the voice of the prophets, they fulfilled them in condemning him*. It is possible that men may be fulfilling scripture prophecies, even when they are breaking scripture precepts. All that was foretold concerning the sufferings of the Messiah was fulfilled in Christ (v. 29): *When they had fulfilled all* the rest *that was written of him*, they fulfilled what was foretold concerning his being buried. They *took him down from the tree, and laid him in a sepulchre*. This is taken notice of here as that which made his resurrection the more illustrious. They laid him in a sepulchre, and thought they had him fast.

[3] That he *rose again from the dead*. This was the great truth that was to be preached; for it is the main pillar, by which the whole fabric of the gospel is supported.

First, He rose by consent (v. 30): *God raised him from the dead*. His enemies laid him in a sepulchre, with design he should always lay there; but God said, *No*.

Secondly, There was sufficient proof of his having risen (v. 31): *He was seen many days*. They *came up with him from Galilee to Jerusalem*, and *they are his witnesses unto the people*. They have attested the thing many a time, and are ready to attest it, though they were to die for the same. Paul says nothing of his own seeing him, because it was in a vision, which was more convincing to himself than it could be to others.

Thirdly, The resurrection of Christ was the performance of the promise. It was not only true news, but good news: "In declaring this, we *declare unto you glad tidings* (v. 32, 33), which should be in a particular manner acceptable to you Jews. The doctrine we preach, if you receive it aright, brings you the greatest satisfaction imaginable; for it is in the resurrection of Christ that *the promise which was made to your fathers is fulfilled to you*." The great promise of the Old Testament was that of the Messiah, *in whom all the families of the earth should be blessed*, and not the family of Abraham only. It was to be the common benefit of all families that he should be raised up to them. God hath *raised up Jesus*; *raised* him *again* (so we read it), meaning *from the dead*. This is the fulfilling of the promises made to the fathers, the promise of sending the Messiah. "This is he that should come, and in him you have all that God promised in the Messiah, though not all that you promised yourselves." Paul puts himself into the number of the Jews, to whom the promise was fulfilled: *To us their children*. And the preaching of the gospel to the Gentiles, which was the great thing that the Jews found themselves aggrieved at, was so far from infringing the promise made to them that the promise itself that *all the families of the earth should be blessed in the Messiah*, could not otherwise be accomplished.

Fourthly, The resurrection of Christ was the great proof of his being the Son of God, and confirms what was written in the second Psalm. *Thou art my Son, this day have I begotten thee. He was declared to be the Son of God with power, by the resurrection from the dead.* When he was first raised up out of obscurity, God declared concerning him by a voice from heaven, *This is my beloved Son* (Matt. iii. 17), which has a plain reference to that in the second Psalm, *Thou art my Son*. Now all which was declared at Christ's baptism and again at his transfiguration, was undeniably proved by his resurrection. The decree which was so long before declared was then confirmed. "This day have I made it to appear that I have begotten thee."

Fifthly, His being raised the third day, so as not to see corruption, and to a heavenly life, so as no more to return to corruption, further confirms his being the Messiah promised. He rose to die no more. Lazarus came out of the grave with his grave-clothes on, because he was to use them again; but Christ, having no more occasion for them, left them behind. Now this makes them sure mercies indeed that he has risen to die no more. As, if Christ had died and had not risen again, so if he had risen to die again, we had come short of the sure mercies, or at least could not have been sure of them. He rose so soon after he was dead that his body did not see corruption. Now this was one of *the sure mercies of David*, for it was said to him, *Neither wilt thou suffer thy Holy One to see corruption*, v. 35. This promise could not have its accomplishment in David, but looked forward to Christ. It could not be accomplished in David himself (v. 36), for *David, after he had served his own generation, by the will of God, fell asleep, and was laid to his fathers, and saw corruption*. Here we have a short account of the life, death, and burial, of the patriarch David, and his continuance under the power of death. His life: *He served his own generation, by the will of God*. David was a useful good man; he did good in the world *by the will of God*. He *served his own generation* so as therein to serve God. He served the good of men, but did not serve the will of men. David was a great blessing to the age wherein he lived; he was the *servant* of his generation: many are the curse, and plague, and burden of their generation. Those that will do good in the world must make themselves *servants of all*. We were not born for ourselves, but are members of communities, to which we must study to be serviceable. Yet here is the difference between David and Christ, that David was to serve only his own generation, but Christ was to serve *all* generations, must ever live to reign for all ages, as long as the sun and moon endure. His death: *He fell asleep*. Death is a sleep, a quiet rest, to those who, while they lived, laboured in the service of God and their generation. He did not fall asleep till he had done the work for which God raised him up. God's witnesses never die till they have finished their testimony; and then *the sleep of the labouring man will be sweet*. His burial: *He was laid to his fathers*. His continuance in the grave: *He saw corruption*. We are sure he did not rise again. He saw corruption, and therefore that promise could not have its accomplishment in him. It was accomplished in the Lord Jesus (v. 37): *He whom God raised again saw no corruption*. Of him therefore the promise must be understood, and no other. Having given them this account of the Lord Jesus, he comes to make application of it. 1. In the midst of his discourse he had told his hearers that they were concerned in all this (v. 26): "*To you is the word of this salvation sent*. It is sent to you for a word of salvation; if it be not so, it is your own fault." He therefore speaks to them with tenderness and respect: You are *men and brethren*. Those to whom he does here bring the *word of salvation* are, (*a*) The native Jews, Hebrews of the Hebrews, as Paul himself was: *Children of the stock of Abraham*, to you is this word of salvation sent; nay, it is therefore sent to you, to save you from your sins. It is an advantage to be of a good stock; for, though salvation does not always follow the children of godly parents, yet the word of salvation does. (*b*) The proselytes: "*Whosoever among you that feareth God, to you is the word of this salvation sent;* you need the further discoveries and directions of revealed religion, and will bid them welcome, and therefore shall certainly be welcome to take the benefit of them." 2. In the close of his discourse he applies what he had said concerning Christ to his hearers. Now they would be ready to ask, What is all this to us? And he tells them plainly what it is to them. It will be their unspeakable advantage if they embrace Jesus Christ, and believe this word of salvation. "*Be it known unto you therefore, men and brethren*—we are warranted to proclaim it to you, and you are called to take notice of it." He did not stand up to preach before them, but to preach to them, and not without hopes of prevailing with them. They are *brethren*, spoken to, and dealt with, by men like themselves; of the same nation. It is proper for the preachers of the gospel to call their hearers brethren, with an affectionate concern for their welfare, and as being equally interested with them in the gospel they preach. Let all that hear the gospel of Christ know these two things: *First*, That it is an act of indemnity granted to the children of men. It is for and in consideration of the mediation of Christ that this act of grace is passed and proclaimed (v. 38): "*Through this man is preached unto you the forgiveness of sins*. Your sins may be forgiven. The remission of sins is *through this man*. By his merit it was purchased, in his name it is offered. We preach to you *the forgiveness of sins*. That is the salvation we bring you." *Secondly*, That it does that for us which the law of Moses could not do. "*Be it known to you that it is by Christ only that those who believe in him* are *justified from all things from which you could not be justified by the law of Moses*" (v. 39); therefore they ought to entertain and embrace the gospel, and not to adhere to the law in opposition to it. The great concern of sinners is to be justified, and accepted as righteous in God's sight. Those who are truly justified are acquitted from all their guilt. It was impossible for a sinner to be justified by the law of Moses. By Jesus Christ we obtain a complete justification; for by him a complete atonement was made for sin. All that believe in Christ, and give up themselves to be ruled by him, are justified by him. It is at their utmost peril if they reject the gospel of Christ (v. 40, 41): "*Beware therefore.* Beware lest you not only come short of the blessings and benefits spoken of in the prophets, but fall under the doom spoken of in the prophets; *lest that come upon you which is spoken of.*" The threatenings are warnings, designed to awaken us to beware lest it should come upon us. The apostle follows the Septuagint translation, which reads, *Behold, you despisers* (for, *behold, you among the heathen*). Beware lest it be said to you, *Behold, you despisers.* It is the ruin of many that they despise religion, they look upon it as a thing below them, and are not willing to stoop to it. "Take heed lest the judgment come upon you which was spoken of in the prophets: that *you shall wonder and perish.*" Those that will not wonder and be saved shall wonder and perish. Those that enjoyed the privileges of the church will wonder when they find that their privileges do but make their condemnation the more intolerable. Let the unbelieving Jews expect that God will *work a work in their days which you shall in no wise believe, though a man declare it unto you.* This may be understood as a prediction, either, (1) Of their sin, that they should be incredulous, that that great work of God, the redemption of the world by Christ, though it should be in the most solemn manner declared unto them, yet they would *in no wise believe it.* Those that had the honour and advantage to have this work wrought in their days had not the grace to believe it. Or, (2) Of their destruction, a work which one would not have believed should have ever been done, considering how much they had been the favourites of Heaven. Thus is there a *strange punishment to the workers of iniquity*, especially to the despisers of Christ.

Verses 42–52

The design of this story being to vindicate the apostles, especially Paul, it is here observed that he proceeded therein with all the caution imaginable.

I. There were some of the Jews that were so incensed against the preaching of the gospel that they would not bear to hear it, but *went out of the synagogue* (v. 42). Now this bespoke: An open infidelity. They thus publicly avowed their contempt of Christ and of his doctrine, and they thus endeavoured to beget prejudices in the minds of others. An obstinate infidelity. They went out of the synagogue to show that they did not believe the gospel, they were resolved they would not. Justly therefore was the gospel taken from them, when they first took themselves from it. For it is certainly true that God never leaves any till they first leave him.

II. The Gentiles were as willing to hear the gospel as those Jews were to get out of the hearing of it: *They besought that these words might be preached to them the next sabbath.* They begged that forgiveness of sins through Christ might be preached to them. The Jews' leavings, nay, loathings, were their longings. This justifies Paul in his preaching to them, that he was invited to it. Who could refuse to break the bread of life to those who begged so hard for it, and to give that to the poor at the door which the children at the table threw under their feet? They had heard the doctrine of Christ, but did not understand it at the first hearing, and therefore they begged it might be preached to them again. What we have heard we should desire to hear again, that it may take deep root in us, and the nail that is driven may be clenched. It aggravates the bad disposition of the Jews that the Gentiles desired to hear that often which they were not willing to hear once.

III. There were many, both of Jews and proselytes, that were wrought upon by the preaching of the gospel. *Many of the Jews and religious proselytes followed Paul and Barnabas.* They submitted to the grace of God, and were admitted to the benefit and comfort of it. They *followed Paul and Barnabas*; they became their disciples, or rather the disciples of Christ. Those that join themselves to Christ will join themselves to his ministers, and follow them. And Paul and Barnabas bade those of the Jews welcome that were willing to come under their instructions. They were exhorted and encouraged to persevere herein: *Paul and Barnabas, speaking to them, persuaded them to continue in the grace of God.* And the grace of God shall not be wanting to those who thus continue in it.

IV. The *next sabbath day* (v. 44): *Almost the whole city came together to hear the word of God.* This brought a vast concourse of people to the synagogue on the sabbath day. Some came out of curiosity, others longing to see what the Jews would do, and many who had heard something of the word of God came to hear more, and to hear it, *not as the word of men but as the word of God.* Now this justified Paul in preaching to the Gentiles, that he met with the most encouraging auditors among them.

V. The Jews were enraged at this; and not only would not receive the gospel themselves, but were filled with indignation at those that crowded after it (v. 45): *When the Jews saw the multitudes*, this *filled them with envy.* They grudged the interest the apostles had in the people. This was the same spirit that worked in the Pharisees towards Christ; they were cut to the heart when they saw *the whole world go after him.* They opposed the doctrine the apostles preached: *They spoke against those things that were spoken by Paul*, finding some fault or other with everything he said, *contradicting and blaspheming.* They contradicted for contradiction-sake, and when they could find no colour of objection, they broke out into ill language against Christ and his gospel, blaspheming him and it. Commonly those who begin with contradicting end with blaspheming.

VI. The apostles hereupon solemnly declare themselves discharged from their obligation to the Jews, and at liberty to bring the word of salvation to the Gentiles. The Jews had the tender of the gospel, and did refuse it, and therefore ought not to say anything against the Gentiles having it. In declaring this, it is said (v. 46), *Paul and Barnabas waxed bold.* There is a time for the preachers of the gospel to show as much of the boldness of the lion as of the harmlessness of the dove. When the adversaries of Christ's cause begin to be daring, it is not for its advocates to be timid. The impudence of the enemies of the gospel, instead of frightening, should rather embolden its friends. They know in whom they had trusted to bear them out. Now Paul and Barnabas, having made the Jews a fair offer of gospel grace, here give them fair notice of their bringing it to the Gentiles. 1. They own that the Jews were entitled to the first offer: "*It was necessary that the word of God should first have been spoken to you*, to whom the promise was made, to whom Christ reckoned himself first sent." 2. They charge them with the refusal of it: *You put it from you.* If men put the gospel from them, God justly takes it from them. Herein they *judge themselves unworthy of everlasting life.* In one sense we must all judge ourselves unworthy of everlasting life, for there is nothing in us by which we can pretend to merit it, but here the meaning is, "You make it to appear, that you are not meet for eternal life. *You do*, in effect, *pass this judgment* upon yourselves, and *out of your own mouth you shall be judged*; you will not have it by Christ, by whom alone it is to be had, and so shall your doom be, you shall not have it at all." 3. Upon this they ground their preaching the gospel to the uncircumcised: "*Lo, we turn to the Gentiles. If one will not, another will.*" 4. They justify themselves in this by a divine warrant (*v.* 47): "*For so hath the Lord commanded us.*" This is according to what was foretold in the Old Testament. When the Messiah, in the prospect of the Jews' infidelity, was ready to say, *I have laboured in vain*, he was told, that though *Israel were not gathered*, yet *he should be glorious.* "For *I have set thee* to be *a light of the Gentiles, that thou shouldst be for salvation unto the ends of the earth.*" He is set up to be a light; he enlightens the understanding, and so saves the soul. He is, and is to be, light and salvation to the Gentiles, to the end of the earth. All nations shall at length become his kingdom. This prophecy has had its accomplishment in part in the setting up of the kingdom of Christ in this island of ours.

VII. The Gentiles cheerfully embraced that which the Jews scornfully rejected, *v.* 48, 49. How the Gentiles welcomed this happy turn in their favour!

1. They took the comfort of it: *When they heard this they were glad.* It was good news to them. They were as welcome to the benefits of the Messiah's kingdom as the Jews themselves, and might share in their promise. When the Gentiles did but hear that the offers of grace should be made them *they were glad.* Many grieve under doubts whether they have an interest in Christ or no, when they should be rejoicing that they have an interest in him.

2. They gave God the praise of it: *They glorified the word of the Lord, the gospel;* the more they knew of it, the more they admired it. Oh! what a light, what a power, what a treasure, does this gospel bring along with it! Because now the knowledge of it was diffused, and not confined to the Jews only. It is the glory of the word of the Lord that the further it spreads the brighter it shines, which shows it to be not like the light of the candle, but like that of the sun when he goes forth in his strength. Because now the knowledge of it was brought to them. Those speak best of the honour of the word of the Lord that have themselves been subdued by its power, and comforted by its sweetness.

3. Many of them became sincerely obedient to the faith: *As many as were ordained to eternal life believed.* Those believed to whom God gave grace to believe. Those came to Christ whom the Father drew, and to whom the Spirit made the gospel call effectual. God gave this grace to believe to all those among them who were ordained to eternal life; or, *as many as were disposed to eternal life,* as many as had a concern about their eternal state, and aimed to make sure of eternal life, and it was the grace of God that wrought it in them.

4. When they believed they did what they could to spread the knowledge of Christ (*v.* 49): *And the word of the Lord was published throughout all the region.* Those new converts were themselves ready to communicate to others that which they were so full of themselves. Those that have become acquainted with Christ themselves will do what they can to bring others acquainted with him. Those in great and rich cities that have received the gospel should not think to engross it, but should do what they can to get it published in the country among the ordinary sort of people, who have souls to be saved as well as they.

VIII. Paul and Barnabas, having sown the seeds of a Christian church there, quitted the place, and went to do the like elsewhere. We read not anything of their working miracles here, to confirm their doctrine. Though God then did ordinarily make use of that

method of conviction. Begetting faith by the immediate influence of his Spirit was itself the greatest miracle to those in whom it was wrought.

1. How *the unbelieving Jews* expelled the apostles out of that country. *They raised persecution against Paul and Barnabas.* Satan and his agents are most exasperated against the preachers of the gospel when they see them go on successfully. Thus it has been the common lot of the best men in the world to suffer ill for doing well. (1) What method the Jews took to give them trouble: *They stirred up the devout and honourable women* against them. It is sad when, under colour of devotion to God, they conceive an enmity to Christ, as those here mentioned. What! women persecutors! Can they forget the tenderness and compassion of their sex? What! honourable women! Can they thus stain their honour. But, which is strangest of all, devout women! Will they kill Christ's servants, and think therein they do God service? By these devout and honourable women they stirred up likewise *the chief men of the city,* the magistrates and the rulers, and set them against the apostles. (2) How far they carried it, so far that *they expelled them out of their coasts*; they banished them. It was not by fear, but downright violence, that they were driven out. This was a method God took to make those that were well disposed the more warmly affected towards the apostles; for it is natural to us to pity those that are persecuted, and to be the more ready to help them. The expelling of the apostles out of their coasts perhaps raised them more friends than conniving at them in their coasts would have done.

2. How the apostles abandoned and rejected the unbelieving Jews (*v.* 51): *They shook off the dust of their feet against them.* They declared that they would have no more to do with them. They expressed their detestation of their infidelity. As Jews and Gentiles, if they believe, are equally acceptable to God and good men; so, if they do not, they are equally abominable. Thus they set them at defiance, and expressed their contempt of them and their malice. Thus they left a testimony behind them that they had had a fair offer made them of the grace of the gospel. Thus Christ had ordered them to do, and for this reason, Matt. x. 14; Luke ix. 5. When *they left them, they came to Iconium,* not so much for safety, as for work.

3. What frame they left the new converts in *at Antioch* (*v.* 52): *The disciples* went on with their work. They were very cheerful. One would have expected that when Paul and Barnabas were expelled out of their coasts, the disciples would have been full of grief and full of fear. But no; *they were filled with joy* in Christ. All their fears were swallowed up in their believing joys. They were courageous, wonderfully animated with a holy resolution to cleave to Christ. The more we relish the comforts and encouragements we meet with in the power of godliness the better prepared we are to face the difficulties we meet with in the profession of godliness.

CHAPTER 14

A further account of the progress of the gospel by the ministry of Paul and Barnabas among the Gentiles. Here is, I. Their successful preaching of the gospel for some time at Iconium, and their being driven thence by the violence of their persecutors, ver. 1–7. II. Their healing a lame man at Lystra, ver. 8–18. III. The outrage of the people against Paul, the effect of which was that they stoned him, as they thought to death, ver. 19, 20. IV. The visit which Paul and Barnabas made to the churches which they had planted, ver. 21–23. V. They return to Antioch, and the report they made to the church of Antioch, of their expedition, ver. 24–28.

Verses 1–7

I. The preaching of the gospel in Iconium. As the blood of the martyrs has been the seed of the church, so the banishment of the confessors has helped to scatter that seed. They made the first offer of the gospel *to the Jews in their synagogues*. Though the Jews at Antioch had used them barbarously, yet they did not therefore decline preaching the gospel to the Jews at Iconium. Let not those of any denomination be condemned in the gross, nor some suffer for others' faults. The apostles concurred herein. *They went both together into the synagogue* to testify their unanimity and mutual affection.

II. The success of their preaching there: *They so spoke that a great multitude, both of the Jews and also of the Greeks, that is the Gentiles, believed.* The gospel was now preached to Jews and Gentiles together. In the close of the foregoing chapter it was preached first to the Jews, and then to the Gentiles, but here they are put together. The Jews have not so lost their preference as to be thrown behind, only the Gentiles are brought to stand upon even terms with them, and both together admitted into the church without distinction. There seems to have been something remarkable in the manner of the apostles' preaching there: *They so spoke that a great multitude believed*—so plainly, so convincingly, so warmly, so affectionately. What they spoke came from the heart and therefore was likely to reach to the heart. So boldly and courageously, that those who heard them could not but say that *God was with them of a truth*.

III. The opposition that their preaching met with there. Unbelieving Jews were the first spring of their trouble here, as elsewhere (*v.* 2): they *stirred up the Gentiles*. The influence which the gospel had upon many of the Gentiles, and their embracing it, as it provoked some of the Jews to a holy jealousy, so it provoked others of them to a wicked jealousy. Disaffected Gentiles, irritated by the unbelieving Jews, were the instruments of their trouble. The Jews, by false suggestions, made *their minds evil affected against the brethren*. They soured and embittered their spirits against both the converters and the converted. It is no wonder if those who are ill affected towards good people wish ill to them and contrive ill against them; it is all owing to ill will. *They molested* the minds of the Gentiles (so some of the critics take it); they were continually teasing them. The tools of persecutors have a dog's life, set on continually.

IV. Their continuance in their work there, and God's owning them in it, *v.* 3. We have here, 1. The apostles working for Christ. Because the minds of *the Gentiles were evil affected against them*, one would think that therefore they should have withdrawn. On the contrary, therefore *they abode there a long time, speaking boldly in the Lord*. The more they perceived the spite against the new converts, the more they were animated to go on in their work. *They spoke boldly*, and were not afraid of giving offence to the unbelieving Jews. But observe what animated them: *They spoke boldly in the Lord*, in his strength, not depending upon anything in themselves. 2. Christ working with the apostles, according to his promise, *Lo, I am with you always*. He failed not to give testimony to the word of his grace. The gospel is a word of grace, the assurance of God's goodwill to us. It is the word of Christ's grace, for it is in him alone that we find favour with God. Christ himself has attested this word of grace; he has assured us that it is the word of God. It is said particularly concerning the apostles here *that the Lord confirmed their testimony, in granting signs and wonders to be done by their hands*—in the miracles they wrought in the kingdom of nature—as well as in the greater miracles wrought on men's minds by the power of divine grace. The Lord was with them, while they were with him.

V. The division which this occasioned in the city (*v.* 4): *The multitude of the city was divided*. It seems, this business of the preaching of the gospel was so universally taken notice of that every person, even of *the multitude of the city*, was either for it or against it; none stood neuter. We may here see the meaning of Christ's prediction that he *came not to send peace upon earth, but rather division*, Luke xii. 51–53. If all would have given in unanimously into his measures, there would have been universal concord; but, disagreeing here, the breach was wide as the sea. It is better that part of the city go to heaven than all to hell. Let us not think it strange if the preaching of the gospel occasion division, it is better to be persecuted as dividers for swimming against the stream than yield ourselves to be carried down the stream that leads to destruction.

VI. The attempt made upon the apostles by their enemies. Their evil affection against them broke out at length into violent outrages, *v.* 5. Who the plotters were: *Both the Gentiles and the Jews, with their rulers*. The Gentiles and Jews were at enmity with one another, and yet united against Christians. If the church's enemies can thus unite for its destruction, shall not its friends unite for its preservation? What the plot was. Their design was *to use the apostles despitefully*, to expose them to disgrace, and then *to stone them*.

VII. The deliverance of the apostles, *v.* 6, 7. They got away, upon notice given them of the design against them, and they made an honourable retreat (for it was not an inglorious flight) to *Lystra and Derbe*. They found safety. God has shelters for his people in a storm. They found work, and this was what they went for. To these cities they went, and there, and *in the region that lieth round about, they preached the gospel*. In times of persecution ministers may see cause to quit the spot, when yet they do not quit the work.

Verses 8–18

I. A miraculous cure wrought by Paul at Lystra upon a cripple that had been lame from his birth. The deplorable case of the poor cripple (*v.* 8): He was *impotent in his feet, disabled* (so the word is). It was well known that he had been so *from his mother's womb*, and that he *never had walked*, nor could *stand up*. The expectation that was raised in him of a cure (*v.* 9): He heard Paul preach, and, it is likely, was much affected with what he heard. This Paul was aware of, by the spirit of discerning, perhaps the aspect of his countenance did in part witness for him: *Paul perceived that he had faith to be healed*. The cure wrought: *Paul, perceiving that he had faith to be healed*, brought *the word and healed him*. Paul spoke to him with a loud voice, that the people about might take notice, and have their expectations raised of the effect. It is said (*v.* 8) *that he sat*, not that he sat begging. And we may imagine how welcome Paul's word was to him, "*Stand upright on thy feet;* help thyself, and God shall help thee." *He leaped and walked*, and not only *stood upright*, but he walked to and fro before them all. Those that by the grace of God are cured of their spiritual lameness must show it by leaping with a holy exultation and walking in a holy conversation.

II. The impression which this cure made upon the people: they were amazed at it. The working of this one miracle was enough to make them in the eyes of this people truly great and honourable, though the multitude of Christ's miracles could not screen him from the utmost contempt among the Jews. The people take them for gods (*v.* 11): *They lifted up their voices in the speech of Lycaonia, The gods are come down to us in the likeness of men*. This notion of the thing agreed well enough with the fabulous account they had of the visits which their gods made to this lower world; and proud enough they were to think that they should have a visit made to them. They carried this notion so far here that they pretended to tell which of their gods they were (*v.* 12): *They called Barnabas Jupiter;* for, if they will have him to be a god, it is as easy to make him the prince of their gods as not. And *Paul they called Mercury,* who was the messenger of the gods, for Paul was *the chief speaker.* The priest thereupon prepares *to do sacrifice to them, v.* 13. The temple of Jupiter was before the gate of their city, as its protector and guardian; and the priest, hearing the people cry out thus, thought it was time for him to do his duty. If Jupiter be among them *himself,* it concerns him to do him the utmost honours imaginable. When Christ appeared in the likeness of men, and did many, very many miracles, yet they were so far from doing sacrifice to him that they made him a sacrifice. But Paul and Barnabas, upon the working of one miracle, are immediately deified. They *brought oxen,* to be sacrificed *to them, and garlands,* with which to crown the sacrifices.

III. Paul and Barnabas protest against this, and with much ado prevent it. Many of the heathen emperors called themselves *gods,* and took a pride in having divine honours paid them: but Christ's ministers refused those honours when they were tendered. The holy indignation which Paul and Barnabas conceived at this: *When they heard this, they rent their clothes.* We do not find that they rent their clothes when the people vilified them, they could bear this without disturbance: but when they deified them, and spoke of worshipping them, they could not bear it. The pains they took to prevent it. They did not connive at it. Christ had put honour enough upon them in making them apostles, they needed not assume either the honour of princes or the honour of gods. Let us see how they prevented it. *They ran in among the people* as soon as they heard of it. They did not stand still, expecting honours to be done them, but plainly declined them by thrusting themselves into the crowd. They reasoned with them, *crying out,* "*Sirs, why do you these things?* Why do you go about to make gods of us?"

[1] "Our nature will not admit it: *We also are men of like passions with you.* You wrong God if you give that honour to us, or to any other man, which is to be given to God only. We are not only men, but sinful men and suffering men, and therefore will not be deified.

[2] "Our doctrine is directly against it. Must we be added to the number of your gods whose business it is to abolish the gods you have? *We preach unto you that you should turn from these vanities unto the living God.*" When they preached to the Jews they had nothing to do but to preach the grace of God in Christ, and needed not to preach against idolatry; but, when they had to do with the Gentiles, they must rectify their mistakes in natural religion. See here what they preached to the Gentiles.

First, The gods which they and their fathers worshipped, and all the ceremonies of their worship of them, were *vanities,* idle things, unreasonable, unprofitable. Therefore *turn from these vanities.*

Secondly, The God to whom they would have them *turn* is *the living God.* They had hitherto worshipped dead images, that were utterly unable to help them, now they are persuaded to worship a living God, who has life in himself, and life for us, and lives for evermore.

Thirdly, This God is the creator of the world, the fountain of all being and power: "He *made heaven and earth, and the sea, and all things therein.* We call you to worship *the God that made you and all the world;* worship the true God."

Fourthly, The world owed it to his patience that he had not destroyed them long ere this for their idolatry (*v.* 16): *In times past he suffered all nations to walk in their own ways.* Your serving them was a trial of God's patience. Now that he has sent his gospel into the world, if you still continue in your idolatry, he will not bear with you as he has done. Now that God has sent a revelation into the world which is to be published to *all nations* the case is altered. Now you will no longer be excused in these vanities, but must turn from them. God's patience with us hitherto should *lead us to repentance,* and not encourage us to presume. Our having done ill while we were in ignorance will not bear us out in doing ill when we are better taught.

Fifthly, Even when they were not under the direction and correction of the word of God, yet they should have known, to do better by the works of God, *v.* 17. *He left not himself without witness;* besides *the witness* for God within them (the dictates of natural conscience), they had *witnesses* for God round about them—the bounty of common providence. Their having no scriptures did in part excuse them. This however did not wholly excuse them. There were other *witnesses* for God. God, having *not left himself without witness,* has not left us without a guide, and so has left us without excuse. The bounties of common providence witness to us that there is a God. The *rain and fruitful seasons* could not come by chance. All the powers of nature witness to us a sovereign power in the God of nature. It is not the heaven that gives us rain, but God that gives us rain from heaven. The benefits we have by these bounties witness to us that we ought to make our acknowledgments to the Creator. *He left not himself without witness in that he did good.* God seems to reckon the instances of his *goodness* to be more pregnant, cogent proofs of his title to our homage than the evidences of his *greatness;* for his goodness is his glory. Because the most sensible instance of the goodness of Providence is that of the daily provision made by it of meat and drink for us, the apostle chooses to insist upon that, and shows how God does us good, (1) In preparing it for us. He does us good in giving us rain from heaven,—rain for us to drink,—rain for our land to drink, for our meat, as well as drink we have from the rain; in giving us this, he *gives us fruitful seasons.* Of all the common operations of providence, the heathen chose to form their notion of the supreme God by that which bespeaks terror, and this was *the thunder.* But the apostle sets before us his beneficence, that we may have good thoughts of him—may love him and delight in him, as one that does good, in giving *rain from heaven and fruitful seasons.* (2) In giving us the comforts of it. It is he *that fills our hearts with food and gladness.* God is not only a benefactor, but a bountiful one. *He fills our hearts with food,* not merely for necessity, but plenty, dainty, and variety. The Gentiles that *lived without God in the world,* yet lived upon God. Those heathen had *their hearts filled with food;* but *these things will not fill the soul,* nor will those that know how to value their own souls be satisfied with them. We must all own that God fills our hearts with food and gladness; not only *food,* that we may live, but *gladness,* that we may live cheerfully. We must thank God, not only for our food, but for our gladness. And, if *our hearts be filled with food and gladness,* they ought to be filled with love and thankfulness.

Lastly, The success of this prohibition which the apostles gave to *the people* (*v.* 18): *By these sayings, they restrained the people from doing sacrifice to them.* They could *scarcely* restrain them from it. Paul and Barnabas had cured a cripple, and therefore the people deified them, which should make us very cautious that we do not give that honour to another, or take it to ourselves, which is due to God only.

Verses 19–28

I. How Paul was stoned and left for dead, *v.* 19, 20. They fell upon Paul rather than Barnabas, because Paul, being the chief speaker, galled and vexed them more than Barnabas did. How the people were incensed against Paul; *there came certain Jews from Antioch,* and they incensed the people against them. See how restless the rage of the Jews was against the gospel of Christ; they could not bear that it should have footing anywhere. To what degree they were incensed by these barbarous Jews: the mob rose and *stoned Paul,* and then *drew him out of the city supposing he had been dead.* As it is with great difficulty that men are restrained from evil on one side, so it is with great ease that they are persuaded to evil on the other side. See how fickle worldly people are. Those that but the other day would have treated the apostles as more than men now treat them as worse than brutes. Today *Hosanna,* tomorrow *Crucify;* today sacrificed to, tomorrow sacrificed. Popular breath turns like the wind. How he was delivered by the power of God: When he was *drawn out of the city, the disciples stood round about him, v.* 20. It seems there were some here at Lystra that became disciples, and even these new converts had courage to own Paul when he was thus run down. They stood round about him, as a guard to him, stood about him to see whether he were alive or dead; and all of a sudden *he rose up.* God's faithful servants, though they may be brought within a step of death, shall not die as long as he has work for them to do.

II. How they went on with their work. All the stones they threw at Paul could not beat him off from his work: They *drew him out of the city* (*v.* 19), but he *came into the city* again. However, their being persecuted here is a known indication to them to seek for opportunities of usefulness elsewhere, and therefore for the present they quit Lystra.

1. They went to break up and sow fresh ground at *Derbe.* Thither the next day *Paul and Barnabas departed,* there they preached the gospel, there they *taught many, v.* 21. Nothing is recorded that happened at Derbe.

2. They returned, and went over their work again; and, having stayed as long as they thought fit at Derbe, they came back to Lystra, to Iconium, and Antioch, *v.* 21.

(1) They *confirmed the souls of the disciples, v.* 22. Young converts are apt to waver, and a little thing shocks them. The apostles come and tell them that *this is the true grace of God wherein they stand,* that there is no danger like that of losing their part in Christ, no advantage like that of keeping their hold of him; that, whatever their trials may be, they shall have strength from Christ to pass through them; and, whatever their losses may be, they shall be abundantly recompensed. And this *confirms the souls of the disciples.* Those that are converted need to be confirmed; those that are planted need to be rooted. Ministers' work is to establish saints as well as to awaken sinners. True confirmation is confirmation of the soul. It is the grace of God and nothing less, that can effectually *confirm the souls of the disciples.*

(2) They *exhorted them to continue in the faith;* or, *they encouraged them.* They told them it was both their duty and interest to persevere. Those that are in the faith are concerned to *continue in the faith.* And it is requisite that they should often be exhorted to do so.

(3) That which they insisted most upon was *that we must through much tribulation enter into the kingdom of God.* But is this the way to *confirm the souls of the disciples,* and to engage them to *continue in the faith?* One would think it would rather shock them, and make them weary. No, as the matter is fairly stated it will help to confirm them. It is true they will meet with tribulation. It is so appointed. They must undergo it, there is no remedy, all that *will live godly in Christ Jesus should suffer persecution.* All that will be Christ's disciples must *take up their cross.* When we gave up our names to Jesus Christ it was what we agreed to; when we sat down and counted the cost, if we reckoned aright, it was what we counted upon. It is the lot of the leaders in Christ's army, as well as of the soldiers. It is not only *you,* but *we,* that are subject to it. As Christ did not put the apostles upon any harder service than what he underwent before them, so neither did the apostles put the ordinary christians. It is true we must count upon *much tribulation,* but this is encouraging, that we shall get through it. We shall not only get through it, but get through it *into the kingdom of God.* It is true *we must go by the cross,* but it is as true that we shall *go to the crown.*

(4) *They ordained them elders in every church.* Now at this second visit they settled them in some order, under the guidance of a settled ministry. Every church had its governors or presidents. It is requisite that every particular church should have one or more such to preside in it. Those governors were then elders, to see to the observance and execution of the laws Christ has made. These elders were *ordained.* They, having *devoted* themselves, were solemnly set *apart* to the work of the ministry. These elders were ordained to them, to their service, for their good. Those that are in the faith have need to be build up in it, and have need of the elders' help therein.

(5) *By prayer* joined with *fasting* they *commended them to the Lord on whom they believed.* Even when persons are brought to believe, ministers' care concerning them is not over. There is still that lacking in their faith which needs to be perfected. The ministers that take most care of those that believe must after all commend them to the Lord. To his custody they must commit themselves, and their ministers must commit them. It is by prayer that they must be commended to the Lord. It is a great encouragement to us that we can say, "It is he in whom they believed; we commit to him those who have committed themselves to him." It is good to join fasting with prayer, in token of our humiliation for sin, and in order to add vigour to our prayers. When we are parting with our friends, the bare farewell is to commend them to the Lord, and to leave them with him.

3. They went on preaching the gospel in other places where they had been. From Antioch they *passed through Pisidia,* thence they came into the province of *Pamphylia,* the head-city of which was *Perga,* where they had been before (*ch.* xiii. 13), and came thither again to *preach the word* (*v.* 25). Thence they *went down to Attalia,* a city of Pamphylia. They stayed not long at a place, but wherever they came endeavoured to lay a foundation which might afterwards be built upon, and to sow the seeds which would in time produce a great increase.

III. How they at length came back to Antioch in Syria, whence they had been sent forth. From Attalia they came by sea to Antioch, *v.* 26.

1. Why they came thither: because *thence they had been recommended to the grace of God.* The brethren having recommended them to the grace of God, for the work *which they fulfilled,* they thought they owed them an account of it, that they might help them by their praises, as they had been helped by their prayers.

2. What account they gave them of their negotiation (*v.* 27): They *gathered the church together.* They

gave them an account of two things: (1) Of the tokens they had had of the divine presence with them in their labours: *They rehearsed all that God had done with them.* They did not tell what *they* had done, but what God had done. For it is he that not only worketh in us both to will and to do, but then worketh with us to make what we do successful. God's grace can do anything without ministers' preaching; but ministers' preaching can do nothing without God's grace. (2) Of the fruit of their labours among the heathen. They told how *God had opened the door of faith unto the Gentiles.* There is no entering into the kingdom of Christ but by the door of faith. It is God that opens the door of faith. We have reason to be thankful that God has *opened the door of faith to the Gentiles.* Thus the gospel was spread, and it shone more and more, and none was able to shut this door which God had opened.

3. How they disposed of themselves for the present: *There they abode a long time with the disciples* (v. 28), not because they *feared their enemies,* but because they *loved their friends.*

CHAPTER 15

In this chapter we find other work (not so pleasant) cut out for them. The Christians and ministers are engaged in controversy. When they should have been making war upon the devil's kingdom they have much ado to keep the peace in Christ's kingdom. I. A controversy raised at Antioch by the judaizing teachers, ver. 1, 2. II. A consultation held with the church at Jerusalem about this matter, ver. 3–5. III. An account of what passed in the synod that was convened upon this occasion, ver. 6. What Peter said, ver. 7–11. What Paul and Barnabas discoursed of, ver. 12. And, lastly, what James proposed for the settling of this matter, ver. 13–21. IV. The result of this debate, and the circular letter that was written to the Gentile converts, ver. 22–29. V. The delivering of this determination to the church at Antioch, ver. 30–35. VI. A second expedition designed by Paul and Barnabas to preach to the Gentiles, in which they quarrelled about their assistant, and separated upon it, ver. 36–41.

Verses 1–5

Even when things go on very smoothly and pleasantly it is folly to be secure; some uneasiness or other will arise, which is not foreseen. If ever there was a heaven upon earth, surely it was in the church at Antioch at this time. But here we have their peace disturbed, and differences arising.

I. A new doctrine started among them, obliging the Gentile converts to submit to circumcision and the ceremonial law, *v.* 1.

1. The persons that urged this were *certain men who came down from Judæa.* They came to Antioch, because that was the headquarters of those that preached to the Gentiles, and the rendezvous of the Gentile converts; and, if they could but make an interest there, this leaven would soon be diffused to all the churches of the Gentiles. *Yet one thing they lack,* they must be circumcised. Those that are ever so well taught have need to stand upon their guard that they be not untaught again, or ill taught.

2. The position they laid down was this, that except the Gentiles who turned Christians were *circumcised after the manner of Moses, they could not be saved.* Many of the Jews who embraced the faith of Christ, yet continued very *zealous for the law,* ch. xxi. 20. They knew it was from God and its authority was sacred, and had been bred up in the observance of it. Herein they were connived at, because the prejudices of education are not to be overcome all at once. But it did not suffice them that they were herein indulged themselves, they must have the Gentile converts brought under the same obligations. There is a strange proneness in us to make our own opinion and practice a rule and a law to everybody else, and to conclude that because we do well all do wrong that do not just as we do. Those Jews who believed that Christ was the Messiah could not get clear of the

notions they had of the Messiah, that he should set up a temporal kingdom in favour of the Jewish nation; it was a disappointment to them that there was as yet nothing done towards this. But now that they hear the doctrine of Christ is received among the Gentiles, and his kingdom begins to be set up in the midst of them, they hope their point will be gained, the Jewish nation will be made as considerable as they can wish, though in another way. It is no wonder if those who have wrong notions of the kingdom of Christ take wrong measures for the advancement of it. It is observable what a mighty stress they laid upon it; they do not only say, "*You ought to be circumcised after the manner of Moses. Except you be circumcised you cannot be saved.* If you be not herein of our mind and way, you will never go to heaven, and therefore of course you must go to hell." Though otherwise good men and believers in Christ, yet they cannot be saved; salvation itself cannot save them. None are in Christ, but those that are within their pale.

II. The opposition which Paul and Barnabas gave to this schismatical notion (v. 2): *They had no small dissension and disputation with them.* They would by no means yield to this doctrine. As faithful servants of Christ, they would not see his truths betrayed. They knew that Christ came to free us from the yoke of the ceremonial law, and therefore could not bear to hear of circumcising the Gentile converts, when their instructions were only to baptize them. As spiritual fathers to the Gentile converts, they would not see their liberties encroached upon. They had told the Gentiles that if they believed in Jesus Christ they should be saved. And therefore the apostles set themselves against it.

III. The expedient pitched upon for preventing the mischief of this dangerous notion. They determined that Paul and Barnabas, and some others of their number, should *go to Jerusalem to the apostles and elders.* They sent the case to Jerusalem: Because those who taught this doctrine came from Jerusalem, and pretended to have directions from the apostles there. It was therefore very proper to send to Jerusalem about it, to know if they had any such direction from the church there. And it was soon found to be all wrong. It was true that these *went out from them* (v. 24), but they never had any such orders from them. Because those who were taught this doctrine would be the better confirmed in their opposition to it, if they were sure that *the apostles and elders at Jerusalem* were against it. Because the apostles at Jerusalem were fittest to be consulted in a point not yet fully settled; their decision would be likely to end the controversy.

IV. Their journey to Jerusalem upon this errand, *v.* 3: *They were brought on their way by the church.* Thus the church showed their favour to those who stood up for them. They did good as they went along. They visited the churches by the way; they passed through Phenice and Samaria, and as they went *declared the conversion of the Gentiles,* which *caused great joy to all the brethren.* The progress of the gospel is and ought to be a matter of great joy. *All the brethren* in Christ's family rejoice when more are born into the family; for the family will be never the poorer for the multitude of its children. In Christ and heaven there is portion enough, and inheritance enough for them all.

V. Their hearty welcome at Jerusalem, *v.* 4. The good entertainment their friends gave them: They were *received of the church, and of the apostles and elders.* They received them with all possible expressions of love and friendship. The good entertainment they gave their friends: They *declared all things that God had done with them,* gave them an account of the success of their ministry among the Gentiles. As they went they had planted, as they came back they had watered; but in both they were ready to own it was God that gave the increase.

VI. The opposition they met with from the same party at Jerusalem, *v. 5. There rose up certain of the sect of the Pharisees.* They believed in Christ but thought it was needful to circumcise them. Those who have been most prejudiced against the gospel yet have been captivated by it. When Christ was here upon earth, few or none of the rulers and of the Pharisees believed on him; but now there are those of the sect of the Pharisees who believed, and many of them, we hope, in sincerity. It is very hard for men suddenly to get clear of their prejudices: those that had been Pharisees, even after they became Christians, retained some of the old leaven. All did not so, witness Paul, but some did.

Verses 6–21

We have here a council called on this occasion (*v. 6*): *The apostles and presbyters came together, to consider of this matter.* They did not give their judgment rashly, but considered of this matter. Though they were clear concerning it in their own minds, yet they would take time to consider of it, and to hear what might be said by the adverse party. Here is a direction to the pastors of the churches, when difficulties arise, to come together in solemn meetings. They may know one another's mind, and strengthen one another's hands.

I. Peter's speech. He was a faithful member of this assembly, and offered that which was very much to the purpose, and which would come better from him than from another, because he had himself been the first that preached the gospel to the Gentiles. *There had been much disputing, pro and con,* upon this question, and liberty of speech allowed, as ought to be in such cases. When both sides had been heard, *Peter rose up.*

1. He put them in mind of the commission he had some time ago *to preach the gospel to the Gentiles. You know that from the beginning of the days* of the gospel *God made choice* of one to preach the gospel to the Gentiles, and I was the person chosen, *that the Gentiles by my mouth should hear the word, and believe, v. 7.* Everybody rejoiced that *God had granted to the Gentiles repentance unto life,* and nobody said a word of circumcising them. See *ch.* xi. 18. Why should the Gentiles who hear the word of the gospel by Paul's mouth be compelled to submit to circumcision, any more than those that heard it by my mouth?

2. He puts them in mind how remarkably God owned him in preaching to the Gentiles (*v. 8*): *God, who knows the hearts, bore them witness* by *giving them the Holy Ghost, even as he did unto us apostles.*" See *ch.* xi. 15–17. Those to whom God *gives the Holy Ghost,* he thereby *bears witness* to that they are his; *sealed* with that Holy Spirit of promise—*marked* for God. "God has *put no difference between us and them* (*v. 9*); they, though Gentiles, are as welcome to the grace of Christ and the throne of grace as we Jews are." We ought not to make any conditions of our brethren's acceptance with us but such as God has made the conditions of their acceptance with him. Now the Gentiles were fitted for communion with God, in *having their hearts purified by faith,* and therefore why should we think them unfit for communion with us, unless they will submit to the ceremonial purifying enjoined by the law to us? *By faith the heart is purified.* The faith of all the saints is alike precious, and has like precious effects and those that by it are united to Christ are so to look upon themselves as joined to one another as that all distinctions even that between Jew and Gentile, are swallowed up in it.

3. He sharply reproves those teachers who went about to bring the Gentiles under the obligation of the law of Moses, *v. 10: "Now therefore, why tempt you God to put a yoke upon the neck of the disciples, a yoke which neither our fathers nor we were able to bear?"* Here he shows that, (1) They offered a very great affront to God. "By calling that in question which he has already settled by no less an indication than that of the gift of the Holy Ghost; you do, in effect, ask, 'Did he know what he did? Or was he in earnest in it?' " Those tempt God who prescribe to him, and say that people cannot be saved but upon such and such terms, which God never appointed. (2) They offered a very great wrong to the disciples: Christ came to proclaim *liberty to the captives,* and they go about to enslave those whom he has made free. This yoke Christ came to ease us of. Now for these teachers to go about to lay that yoke upon the neck of the Gentiles from which he came to free even the Jews was the greatest injury imaginable to them.

4. Whereas the Jewish teachers had urged that circumcision was necessary to salvation, Peter shows that both Jews and Gentiles were to be saved purely *through the grace of our Lord Jesus Christ,* and in no other way (*v. 11*): *We believe to be saved through that grace* only. "We that are circumcised believe to salvation, and so do those that are uncircumcised. We must depend upon the grace of Christ for salvation as well as they. There is not one way of salvation for the Jews and another for the Gentiles. Why should we burden them with the law of Moses, as necessary to their salvation, when it is not that, but the gospel of Christ, that is necessary both to our salvation and theirs?"

II. An account of what Barnabas and Paul said. *What miracles and wonders God had wrought among the Gentiles by them, v. 12.* This they had given in to the church *at Antioch* (*ch.* xiv. 27), and now again to the synod; and it was very proper to be given in here. Paul and Barnabas undertake to show, by a plain relation of matters of fact, that God owned the preaching of the pure gospel to them without the law. 1. What account they gave; they declared what signs and wonders, *God had wrought among the Gentiles by them,* what confirmation he had given by miracles wrought in the kingdom of nature, and what success by miracles wrought in the kingdom of grace. What need had they of any other advocate when God himself pleaded their cause? 2. What attention was given to them: *All the multitude kept silence, and gave audience to Paul and Barnabas;* it should seem they took more notice of their narrative than they did of all the arguments that were offered. As in natural philosophy and medicine nothing is so satisfactory as experiments, so in the things of God the best explication of the word of grace is the accounts given of the operations of the Spirit of grace. Those that fear God will most readily hear those that can tell them *what God has done for their souls,* or by their means.

III. The speech which James made to the synod. *After they had held their peace,* then James stood up. The hearing of variety of ministers may be of use when one truth does not drive out, but clench, another.

1. He addresses himself respectfully to those present: "*Men and brethren, hearken unto me.* We are all brethren, and equally concerned that nothing be done to the dishonour of Christ and the uneasiness of Christians."

2. He refers to what Peter had said concerning the conversion of the Gentiles (*v. 14*): "*Simeon hath declared how God at the first did visit the Gentiles,* in Cornelius and his friends, who were the first fruits of the Gentiles." James observes here: That the *grace of God* was the origin of it; it was God *that*

visited the Gentiles. The acquaintance began on his part; he not only *visited and redeemed his people*, but visited and redeemed those that were *not a people*. That the glory of God was the end of it: it was *to take out of them a people for his name*, who should glorify him, and in whom he would be glorified. As of old he took the Jews, so now the Gentiles.

3. He confirms this with a quotation out of the Old Testament. It was foretold in the Old Testament, and therefore it must be fulfilled, *v.* 15. *To this agree the words of the prophets;* most of the Old Testament prophets spoke more or less of the calling in of the Gentiles. It was the general expectation of the pious Jews that the Messiah should be *a light to enlighten the Gentiles* (Luke ii. 32): but James waives the more illustrious prophecies of this, and pitches upon one that seemed more obscure: *It is written*, Amos ix. 11, 12, where is foretold, (1) The setting up of the kingdom of the Messiah (*v.* 16): *I will raise up the tabernacle of David, that is fallen.* This tabernacle was ruined and *fallen down*; there had not been for many ages a king of the house of David. But God *will return, and will build it again*, raise it out of its ruins, a phœnix out of its ashes; and this was now lately fulfilled, when our Lord Jesus was raised out of that family. The church of Christ may be called the tabernacle of David. This may sometimes be brought very low, and may seem to be in ruins, but it shall be built again, its withering interests shall revive. (2) The bringing in of the Gentiles as the effect and consequence of this (*v.* 17): *That the residue of men might seek after the Lord;* not the Jews only, but *the residue of men*, such as had hitherto been left out of the pale of the visible church; they must now be brought *to seek after the Lord. That the residue of men might seek* (James here adds, *after the Lord*), *and all the Gentiles upon whom my name is called*. His name shall be declared among them, and they shall be brought both to know his name and to call upon it: they shall call themselves the people of God, and he shall call them so; and thus, by consent of both parties, *his name is called upon them*. This promise now begins to be fulfilled, for it is added, *saith the Lord, who doeth all these things. He saith it who doeth it*. Though with us saying and doing are two things they are not so with God. The uniting of *Jews and Gentiles in one body*, and all those things that were done in order to it, were, [1] What God did: whatever instruments were employed in it. [2] What God was well pleased with; for he is the God of the Gentiles, as well as the Jews.

4. He resolves it into the purpose and counsel of God (*v.* 18): *Known unto God are all his works from the beginning of the world*. He not only foretold the calling of the Gentiles by the prophets, but he foreordained it in his eternal counsels. Whatever God does, he did before design and determine to do. He not only *does whatever he determined*, which is more than we can do (our purposes are frequently broken off, and our measures broken), but he *determined whatever he does*. What we shall do in such or such a case we cannot tell till it comes to the setting to; but *known unto God are all his works*. We are poor short-sighted creatures; the wisest men can see but a little way before them, and not at all with any certainty; but this is our comfort, that there is an infallible certainty in the divine prescience: *known unto God are all his works.*

5. He gives his advice with reference *to the Gentiles* (*v.* 19): *My sentence is: I give it as my opinion*; not as having authority over the rest, but as being an adviser with them.

(1) That circumcision and the observance of the ceremonial law be by no means imposed upon the Gentile converts. I am clearly for using them with all possible tenderness, and putting no manner of discouragement upon them—*not to give them any*

molestation nor disturbance. Great care must be taken not to discourage nor disquiet young converts with matters of *doubtful disputation*. Let the essentials of religion be first impressed deeply upon them, and these will satisfy them and make them easy.

(2) That yet it would be well that in some things, which gave most offence to the Jews, the Gentiles should comply with them. It will please the Jews (and, if a little thing will oblige them, better do so than cross them) if the Gentile converts abstain, [1] *From pollutions of idols, and from fornication*, which are two bad things, and always to be abstained from. Not but that the apostles were careful to warn against *pollutions of idols*, that they should have no manner of fellowship with idolaters in their idolatrous worships, and particularly not in the feasts they held upon their sacrifices. *Fornication, and all manner of uncleanness*. How large, how pressing, is Paul in his cautions against this sin! But the Jews suggested that these were things in which the Gentiles, even after conversion, allowed themselves, and the apostle of Gentiles connived at it. Now, to obviate this suggestion, James advises that they should be publicly warned *to abstain from pollutions of idols and from fornication*. [2] *From things strangled, and from blood*, which had been forbidden before the giving of the law of Moses.

6. He gives a reason for his advice—that great respect ought to be shown to the Jews, for they have been so long accustomed to the solemn injunctions of the ceremonial law that they must be borne with, if they cannot presently come off from them (*v.* 21): *For Moses hath of old those that preach him in every city, being read in the synagogues every sabbath day*. "Moses is continually preached to them, and they are called upon *to remember the law of Moses*." Even that word of God which is written to us should also be preached. "His writings are read *in their synagogues*, and on *the sabbath day*; so that from their childhood they have been trained up in a regard to the law of Moses. This has been done *of old time*; they have received from their fathers an honour for Moses. This has been done *in every city*, so that none of them can be ignorant what stress that law laid upon these things. They cannot be blamed if they are loth to part with them, and cannot of a sudden be persuaded to look upon those things as needless and indifferent. We must therefore give them time, they must be borne with awhile, and brought on gradually." Thus does this apostle show a spirit of moderation, contriving, as much as may be, to please both sides and provoke neither.

Verses 22-35

We have here the result of the consultation. The advice which James gave was universally approved. Letters were accordingly sent by messengers of their own to the Gentile converts, which would be a great confirmation to them against the false teachers.

I. The choice of the delegates that were to be sent with Paul and Barnabas on this errand.

1. They thought fit *to send men of their own company to Antioch, with Paul and Barnabas*, *v.* 22. This was agreed to by *the apostles and elders, with the whole church*. To show their respect to the church at Antioch, as a sister-church, as also that they were desirous further to know their state. To encourage Paul and Barnabas, and to make their journey home the more pleasant. To put a reputation upon the letters they carried, that more regard might be paid to the message, which was likely to meet with opposition from some. To keep up *the communion of saints*, and to show *that, though they were many, yet they were one*.

2. Those they sent were not inferior persons, who might serve to carry the letters, but *they were chosen*

men, and chief men among the brethren. They are here named: *Judas*, who was called *Barsabas, and Silas.*

II. The drawing up of the letters to notify the sense of the synod in this matter.

1. A very obliging preamble to this decree, *v.* 23. That which intimates the humility of the apostles, that they join *the elders and brethren* in commission with them, whom they had advised with in this case. Herein they remembered the instructions their Master gave them (Matt. xxiii. 8). That which bespeaks their respect: they *send greeting,* and call them *brethren of the Gentiles,* thereby giving them the right hand of fellowship: "You are our brethren, though Gentiles." Now that *the Gentiles are fellow-heirs and of the same body,* they are to be encouraged, and called brethren.

2. A just and severe rebuke to the judaizing teachers (*v.* 24): "*We have heard that certain who went out from us have troubled you with words.* They *went out from us* indeed, but, as for their urging the law of Moses upon you, we *gave* them *no such commandment.*" They did a great deal of wrong to the Gentile converts, in saying, *You must be circumcised, and you must keep the law.* It perplexed them: "*They have troubled you with words.* You depended upon those who told you, *If you believe in the Lord Jesus Christ you shall be saved;* and now you are startled by those that tell you *you must keep the law of Moses or you cannot be saved.* They trouble you with words —mere words—sound, but no substance." How has the church been troubled with words, by the pride of men that loved to hear themselves talk! It endangered them; they *subverted* their souls, put them into disorder, and pulled down that which had been built up.

3. An honourable testimony given of the messengers.

(1) Of Paul and Barnabas, whom these judaizing teachers had censured as having done their work by the halves, because they had brought the Gentile converts to Christianity only, and not to Judaism. "They are men that are dear to us; they are *our beloved Barnabas and Paul.*" Sometimes it is good for those that are of eminence to express their esteem. They are men *that have hazarded their lives for the name of our Lord Jesus Christ* (*v.* 26). They have ventured their all for Christ, have engaged in the most dangerous services, as good soldiers of Christ. It is not likely that such faithful confessors should be unfaithful preachers.

(2) Of Judas and Silas: *They are chosen men* (*v.* 25), and they are men that have heard our debates, and will *tell you the same things by mouth, v.* 27. What is of use to us it is good to have both in writing and by word of mouth, that we may have the advantage both of reading and of hearing it.

4. Here is the direction given what to require from the Gentile converts.

(1) The matter of the injunction, which is according to the advice given by James. They should never eat anything that they knew had been offered in sacrifice to an idol, but look upon it as thereby polluted to them. This to us is an antiquated case. *That they should not eat blood. That they should not eat anything that was strangled,* or had not the blood let out. That they should be very strict in censuring those that *were guilty of fornication.* "These things are in a particular manner offensive to the Jews, and therefore do not disoblige them herein."

(2) The manner in which it is worded. They express themselves with something of authority: *It seemed good to the Holy Ghost, and to us,* that is, to us under the guidance of the Holy Ghost. They would not order anything because *it seemed good to them,* but that they knew it first *seemed good to the Holy Ghost.*

They express themselves with abundance of tenderness and fatherly concern. *First,* They are afraid of burdening them: We will *lay upon you no greater burden.* They dreaded nothing so much as imposing too far upon them, so as to discourage them at their setting out. *Secondly,* They impose upon them *no other than necessary things.* Church-rulers should impose only necessary things, things which Christ has made our duty. They have not authority to make new laws, but only to see that the laws of Christ be duly executed. *Thirdly,* They enforce their order with a commendation of those that shall comply with it, rather than with the condemnation of those that shall transgress it. "*From which if you keep yourselves you will do well.*" It is all sweetness and love and good humour. The difference of the style of the true apostles from that of the false is very observable. Those that were for imposing the ceremonial laws were positive and imperious: *Except you keep it, you cannot be saved* (*v.* 1). The apostles of Christ, who only recommend necessary things, are mild and gentle: "*From which if you keep yourselves, you will do well. Fare ye well;* we are hearty well-wishers to your honour and peace."

III. The delivering of the letters. *When they were dismissed they then came to Antioch;* they stayed no longer at Jerusalem than till their business was done, and then came back. As soon as they came to Antioch, *they gathered the multitude together, and delivered the epistle to them* (*v.* 30, 31), that they might all know what it was that was forbidden them. But this was not all; it was that they might know that *no more* than this was forbidden them. The people were wonderfully pleased (*v.* 31): *They rejoiced for the consolation.* That they were confirmed in their freedom from the yoke of the ceremonial law. That those who troubled their minds with an attempt to force circumcision upon them were hereby silenced. That the Gentiles were hereby encouraged to receive the gospel, and those that had received it to adhere to it. That the peace of the church was hereby restored. They got the strange ministers that came from Jerusalem to give them each a sermon, *v.* 32. Judas and Silas, *being prophets also themselves, exhorted the brethren with many words,* and *confirmed them.* Even those that had the constant preaching of Paul and Barnabas, yet were glad of the help of Judas and Silas; the diversity of the gifts of ministers is of use to the church. Observe what is the work of ministers with those that are in Christ. (1) To confirm them; to confirm their choice of Christ and their resolutions for Christ. (2) To exhort them to perseverance: to quicken them to that which is good, and direct them in it. They comforted the brethren (so it may be rendered), and this would contribute to the confirming of them; for the joy of the Lord will be our strength. One word would affect one, and another another; what they had to say might have been summed up in a few words, yet it was for the edification of the church that they used *many words.* The dismission of the Jerusalem ministers, *v.* 33. When they had *spent some time among them* they were let go in peace from the brethren at Antioch, to the apostles at Jerusalem. The continuance of Silas, together with Paul and Barnabas, at Antioch. Silas chose rather to *abide still at Antioch, v.* 34. We know not the reason that moved him to it. Paul and Barnabas, though their work lay chiefly among the Gentiles, yet continued for some time in Antioch. They continued there, not to take their pleasure, but *teaching and preaching the word of God.* It is probable there was a great resort of Gentiles thither from all parts, so that in preaching there they did in effect preach to many nations. And thus they were not only not idle at Antioch, but were serving their main intention. There were *many others also* there. The multitude of workmen in Christ's vineyard does not give us a writ of ease. There may be opportunity for us; the zeal and usefulness of others should excite us, not lay us asleep.

Verses 36–41

Here we have a private quarrel between two ministers, no less men than Paul and Barnabas, yet ending well.

I. Here is a good proposal Paul made to Barnabas to go and review their work among the Gentiles and renew it. Antioch was now a safe and quiet harbour for them; but Paul remembered that they only put in there to refit and refresh themselves, and therefore begins now to think of putting to sea again. Paul remembered that the work appointed him was afar off among the Gentiles, and therefore he is here meditating a second expedition among them; and this *some days after,* for his active spirit could not bear to be long out of work; no, nor his bold and daring spirit to be long out of danger. 1. To whom he makes this proposal—to Barnabas, his old friend and fellow-labourer. We have need one of another, and may be in many ways serviceable one to another; and therefore should be forward both to borrow and lend assistance. Every soldier has his comrade. 2. For whom the visit is designed: "Let us not begin new work, but let us take a view of the fields we have sown. *Let us go again and visit our brethren in every city where we have preached the word of the Lord.*" He calls all the Christians brethren. He has a concern for them in *every city.* Wherever we have *preached the word of the Lord,* let us go and water the seed sown. Those that have preached the gospel should visit those to whom they have preached it. As we must look after our praying, and hear what answer God gives to that; so we must look after our preaching, and see what success that has. 3. What was intended in this visit: "Let us *see how they do.*" He would visit them that he might acquaint himself with their case, as the physician visits his recovering patient, that he may prescribe what is proper for the perfecting of his cure, and the preventing of a relapse. Let us see how they do. (1) What spirit they are of, how they stand affected, and how they behave themselves. (2) What state they are in, that we may rejoice with them if they rejoice, and may weep with them if they weep, and may know the better how to pray for them.

II. The disagreement between Paul and Barnabas about an assistant. Barnabas would have his nephew John, whose surname was Mark, to go along with them, *v.* 37. He determined to take him, because he was his relation. We should suspect ourselves of partiality, and guard against it in preferring our relations. Paul opposed it (*v.* 38): *He thought not good to take him with them* who had *departed from them,* from Pamphylia (*ch.* xiii. 13), and *went not with them to the work.* He run his colours just as they were going to engage. It is probable that he promised very fair now that he would not do so again. But Paul thought it was not fit he should be thus honoured; at least, not till he had been longer tried. If a man deceive me once, it is his fault; but, if twice, it is my own, for trusting him.

III. The issue of this disagreement: they separated upon it. The contention was so sharp that they *departed asunder one from the other.* Neither would yield, and therefore there is no remedy but they must part. Now here is that which is just matter of lamentation, and yet very instructive. For we see, 1. That the best of men are but men, *subject to like passions* as we are, as these two good men had expressly owned concerning themselves (*ch.* xiv. 15), and now it appeared too true. I doubt there was (as usually there is in such contentions) a *fault on both*

sides. They were certainly both in fault to be hot as to let the contention be sharp, as also each to stick resolutely to his opinion, and neither to yield. It is a pity that some friend did not interpose to prevent its coming to an open rupture. We must own it was their infirmity, not that we must make use of it to excuse our own intemperate heats and passions. No; but it must check our censures of others, and moderate them. Repentance teaches us to be severe in reflections upon ourselves; but charity teaches us to be candid in our reflections upon others. It is only Christ's example that is a copy without a blot. 2. That we are not to think it strange if there be differences among wise and good men. Even those that are united to one and the same Jesus, and sanctified by one and the same Spirit, have different opinions, different views. We shall never be all of a mind till we come to heaven. 3. That these differences often prevail so far as to occasion separations. Paul and Barnabas, who were not separated by the persecutions of the unbelieving Jews, nor the impositions of the believing Jews, were yet separated by an unhappy disagreement between themselves.

IV. The good that was brought out of this evil. It was strange that even the sufferings of the apostles (as Phil. i. 12), but much more strange that even the quarrels of the apostles, should tend to the *furtherance of the gospel of Christ.* God would not permit such things to be, if he knew not how to make them to serve his own purposes. 1. More places are hereby visited. Barnabas went one way; he sailed to Cyprus (*v.* 39), where they began their work (*ch.* xiii. 4), and which was *his own country, ch.* iv. 36. Paul went another way into Cilicia, which was *his own country, ch.* xxi. 39. Each seems to be influenced by his affection to his native soil, as usual. Yet God served his own purposes by it. 2. More hands are hereby employed in the ministry of the gospel among the Gentiles. John Mark, who had been an unfaithful hand, is not rejected, and, for aught we know, proves a very useful and successful hand. Silas who was a new hand is brought in.

V. We may further observe, 1. That the church at Antioch seem to countenance Paul in what he did. Barnabas sailed with his nephew to Cyprus, and no notice was taken of him. But, when Paul departed, he was *recommended by the brethren to the grace of God.* They prayed publicly for Paul, and for the success of his ministry. They transferred the matter to the grace of God, leaving it to that grace both to work upon him and to work with him. Those are happy at all times who are enabled so to carry themselves as not to forfeit their interest in the love and prayers of good people. 2. That yet Paul afterwards seems to have had, upon further trial, a better opinion of John Mark than now he had; for he writes to Timothy (2 Tim. iv. 11), *Take Mark and bring him with thee, for he is profitable to me for the ministry.* Even those whom we justly condemn we should condemn moderately, because we know not but afterwards we may see cause to think better of them, and we should so regulate our resentments that if it should prove so we may not afterwards be ashamed of them. Even those whom we have justly condemned, if afterwards they prove more faithful, we should cheerfully receive, forgive and forget, and, as there is occasion, give a good word to. 3. That Paul went on cheerfully in his work (*v.* 41): *He went through Syria and Cilicia, confirming the churches.* Ministers are well employed when they are made use of in confirming those that believe, as well as in converting those that believe not.

CHAPTER 16

It is some rebuke to Barnabas that after he left Paul we hear no more of him. But Paul's services for Christ after this are largely recorded. I. The beginning of his acquaintance with Timothy, ver. 1–3. II. The visit he made to the churches for their establishment, ver. 4, 5. III. His call to Macedonia, his coming to Philippi, ver. 6–13. IV. The conversion of Lydia there, ver. 14, 15. V. The casting an evil spirit out of a damsel, ver. 16–18. VI. The accusing and abusing of Paul and Silas for it, their imprisonment, ver. 19–24. VII. The miraculous conversion of the jailer, ver. 25–34. VIII. The honourable discharge of Paul and Silas, ver. 35–40.

Verses 1–5

Paul was a spiritual father, and as such a one we have him here adopting Timothy: and in all he appears to have been a wise and tender father.

I. His taking Timothy into his acquaintance and under his tuition. And we are here accordingly told, 1. That he was a disciple, one that belonged to Christ. He took him to be brought up for Christ. 2. That his mother was a Jewess originally, *but believed in Christ*; her name was *Eunice*, his grandmother's name was *Lois*. Paul speaks of them both with great respect and commends them especially for their unfeigned faith (2 Tim. i. 5). 3. That his father was a Greek, a Gentile. Now because his father was a Greek he was not circumcised: his father being no Jew he was not obliged to circumcision, nor entitled to it, unless when he grew up he did himself desire it. Though his mother could not prevail to have him circumcised in his infancy, yet she educated him in the fear of God, that though he wanted the sign of the covenant he might not want the thing signified. 4. That he had gained a very good character among the Christians: he was *well reported of by the brethren* that were at Lystra and Iconium. He had a name for good things with good people. 5. That Paul would have him *to go forth with him*. Paul had a great love for him. 6. That Paul took him and circumcised him. This was strange. Had not Paul opposed those with all his might that were for imposing circumcision upon the Gentile converts? He had, and yet circumcised Timothy, not to oblige him to keep the ceremonial law, but only to render his ministry acceptable among the Jews that abounded in those quarters. Therefore, that they might not shun him as one unclean, because uncircumcised, he took him and *circumcised him*. He was against those who made circumcision necessary to salvation. Though he went not in this instance according to the letter of the decree, he went according to the spirit of it, which was a spirit of tenderness towards the Jews. Paul made no difficulty of taking Timothy to be his companion, though he was uncircumcised; but the Jews would not hear him if he were, and therefore Paul will humour them herein.

II. His confirming the churches which he had planted (v. 4, 5): *He went through the cities* where he had *preached the word of the Lord*. They delivered to them copies of the decrees of the Jerusalem synod. All the churches were concerned in that decree, and therefore it was requisite they should all have it well attested. This was of very good service to them. 1. The churches were hereby *established in the faith*, *v.* 5. They were confirmed particularly in their opinion against the imposing of the ceremonial law upon the Gentiles. When they saw the testimony, not only of the apostles and elders, but of the Holy Ghost, in them, against it, they were established. Testimonies to truth, though they may not prevail to convince those that oppose it, may be of very good use to establish those that are in doubt concerning it. And, besides, that spirit of tenderness which appeared in these letters plainly showed that the apostles and elders were herein under the guidance of him who is love itself. 2. They *increased in number daily*. The imposing of the yoke of the ceremonial law upon their converts was enough to frighten people from them. But, if they find there is no danger of being so enslaved, they are ready to embrace Christianity. And thus the church *increased in numbers daily*. And

it is a joy to those who heartily wish well to the souls of men, to see such an increase.

Verses 6–15

I. Paul's travels up and down to do good. 1. He and Silas his colleague went throughout Phrygia and the region of Galatia. 2. They were forbidden at this time to preach the gospel in Asia (the country properly so called). At this time Christ would employ Paul in a piece of new work, which was to preach the gospel to a Roman colony at Philippi, for hitherto the Gentiles to whom he had preached were Greeks. The Romans were more particularly hated by the Jews than other Gentiles. It was the Holy Ghost that forbade them. The removals of ministers are in a particular manner under a divine guidance and direction. But these New Testament ministers are only forbidden to preach in one place, while they are directed to another where there is more need. 3. They would have gone into Bithynia, but were not permitted: *the Spirit suffered them not, v.* 7. They came to Mysia. Though their judgment and inclination were to go into Bithynia, yet they were overruled. We must now follow providence, and, if this *suffer us not* to do what we assay to do, we ought to acquiesce, and believe it for the best. The *Spirit of Jesus* suffered them not; so many ancient copies read it. The servants of the Lord Jesus ought to be always under the check and conduct of the *Spirit of the Lord Jesus*. 4. They *passed by Mysia*, or passed *through it* (so some), sowing good seed, we may suppose, as they went along; and they came down to Troas, the city of Troy. Here a church was planted; for here we find one in being, *ch.* xx. 6, 7. At Troas Luke fell in with Paul, and joined himself to his company; for henceforward, when he speaks of Paul's journeys, he puts himself into the number of Paul's retinue, *we* went, *v.* 10.

II. Paul's particular call to Macedonia, that is, to Philippi, inhabited mostly by Romans, as appears, *v.* 21.

1. The vision Paul had, *v.* 9. An angel appeared to him, to intimate to him that it was the will of Christ he should go to Macedonia. Though he shall not go where he has a mind to go, he shall go where God has work for him to do. (1) The person Paul saw. There stood by him *a man of Macedonia*. Christ would have Paul directed to Macedonia, not as the apostles were at other times, by a messenger from heaven, to send him thither, but by a messenger thence to call him thither. Paul shall be called to Macedonia by a man of Macedonia, and by him speaking in the name of the rest. A man of Macedonia, not a magistrate of the country, much less a priest, but an ordinary inhabitant of that country, a plain man, that did not come to trifle with him, but in good earnest to importune his assistance. (2) The invitation given him. This honest Macedonian *prayed him, saying, Come over into Macedonia, and help us;* that is, "Come and preach the gospel to us. *Thou hast helped many*. O come and help us. It is thy business, and it is thy delight, to help poor souls; O come and help us. We have need of thy help, as much as any people, and therefore, O come, come with all speed among us. Do not only help us with thy prayers here; thou must come over and help us." People have great need of help for their souls, and it is their duty to look out for it and invite those among them that can help them.

2. The interpretation made of the vision (*v.* 10): They *gathered assuredly from this that the Lord had called them to preach the gospel* there. We may sometimes infer a call of God from a call of man. If a man of Macedonia says, *Come and help us*, Paul thence gathers assuredly that God says, Go and help them.

III. Paul's voyage to Macedonia hereupon: He *was not disobedient to the heavenly vision*, but followed this divine direction with more satisfaction than he would have followed any contrivance or inclination of his own. Thitherward he turned his thoughts. *Immediately we endeavoured to go into Macedonia.* Paul communicated it to his companions, and they all resolved for Macedonia. As Paul will follow Christ, so all his will follow him, or rather follow Christ with him. God's calls must be complied with immediately. Do it today, lest thy heart be hardened. They could not immediately go into Macedonia; but they immediately endeavoured to go. If we cannot be so quick as we would be in our performances, yet we may be in our endeavours. Thitherward he steered his course. They *set sail from Troas.* They *came with a straight course,* a prosperous voyage, *to Samothracia;* the *next day they came to Neapolis;* and at last they landed at *Philippi.* It is said (*v.* 12) to be *The chief city of that part of Macedonia;* or, as some read it, *the first city.* They began with the first city, because, if the gospel were received there, it would the more easily spread thence all the country over. It was a colony. The Romans not only had a garrison, but the inhabitants of the city were Romans.

IV. The cold entertainment which Paul and his companions met with at Philippi. One would have expected that having such a particular call from God thither they would have had a joyful welcome there. Where was the man of Macedonia that begged Paul to come thither with all speed? Why did not he stir up his countrymen, to go and meet him? It is a good while before any notice at all is taken of him: *We were in that city abiding certain days.* They had made all the haste they could thither, but, now that they are there, they are almost tempted to think they might as well have stayed where they were. Those eminent and useful men are not fit to live in this world that know not how to be slighted and overlooked. Let not ministers think it strange if they be first strongly invited to a place, and then looked shyly upon when they come. When they have an opportunity of preaching it is in an obscure place, *v.* 13. There was no synagogue of the Jews there. They found out a little meeting of good women. The place of this meeting is out of the city. It was a place *where prayer was wont to be made.* Those that worshipped the true God, and would not worship idols, met there to pray together. Each of them prayed apart every day, but, besides this, *they came together on the sabbath day.* Though they were but a few and discountenanced by the town, yet a solemn assembly the worshippers of God must have on the sabbath day. When we cannot do as we would we must do as we can; if we have not synagogues, we must be thankful for more private places, and resort to them. This place is said to be *by a river side,* which perhaps was chosen, as befriending contemplation. Thither Paul and Silas and Luke went, and *sat down.* They *spoke unto the women who resorted thither,* and led them on further to the knowledge of Christ.

V. The conversion of *Lydia.* In this story of *the Acts,* we have not only the conversion of places recorded, but of many particular persons; for such is the worth of souls that the reducing of one to God is a great matter. Nor have we only the conversions that were effected by miracle, as Paul's, but some that were brought about by the ordinary methods of grace, as Lydia's here.

1. Who this convert was. Four things are recorded of her:

(1) Her name, *Lydia.* It is an honour to her to have her name recorded here in the book of God. We cannot have our names recorded in the Bible, but, if God open our hearts, we shall find them *written in the book of life.*

(2) Her calling. She was *a seller of purple.* She had a calling, an honest calling, which the historian takes notice of to her praise. It was a mean calling. She was *a seller of purple,* not a wearer of purple, few such are called. Though she had a calling to mind, yet she was a worshipper of God. The business of our particular callings may be made to consist very well with the business of religion, and therefore it will not excuse us to say, We have shops to look after, and a trade to mind; for have we not also a God to serve and a soul to look after?

(3) The place she was of—*of the city of Thyatira,* which was a great way from Philippi. Providence brings Lydia to Philippi, to be under Paul's ministry, and there, where she met with it, she made a good use of it.

(4) Her religion before the Lord opened her heart. She worshipped God according to the knowledge she had; she was one of the devout women. Sometimes the grace of God wrought upon those who, before their conversion, were very wicked and vile, sometimes it fastened upon those who were of a good character. It is not enough to be worshippers of God, but we must be believers in Jesus Christ. To them Christ would be welcome; for those that know what it is to worship God see their need of Christ. She heard the apostles. Here, where prayer was made *the word was preached.* Can we expect God should hear our prayers if we will not hearken to his word? Those that worshipped God according to the light they had looked out for further light.

2. What the work was that was wrought upon her: *Whose heart the Lord opened.* The author of this work: it was *the Lord.* Conversion-work is God's work; it is he *that works in us both to will and to do;* not as if we had nothing to do, but of ourselves, without God's grace, we can do nothing. The salvation of those that are saved must be wholly ascribed to him. The seat of this work; it is in the heart that the change is made. Conversion-work is heart-work; it is a *renewing of the heart.* The nature of the work; she had not only her heart touched, but her heart opened. An unconverted soul is shut up, and fortified against Christ. Christ, in dealing with the soul, knocked at the door that is shut against him (Rev. iii. 20); and, when a sinner is effectually persuaded to embrace Christ, *then the heart is opened for the King of glory to come in.*

3. What were the effects of this work on the heart. She took great notice of the word of God. Her heart was so *opened that she attended to the things that were spoken by Paul. She applied to herself* (so some read it) *the things that were spoken by Paul;* and then only the word does us good, when we apply it to ourselves. She gave up her name to Jesus Christ. *She was baptized,* and with her her *household* also was baptized. She was very kind to the ministers, and very desirous to be further instructed by them: *She besought us saying, "If you have judged me to be faithful to the Lord, come into my house, and abide there."* Thus she desired an opportunity to testify her gratitude to those who had been the instruments of divine grace in this blessed change that was wrought upon her. When her heart was open to Christ, her house was open to his ministers for his sake. Nay, they are not only welcome to her house, but she is extremely pressing and importunate with them: *She constrained us;* which intimates that Paul was unwilling to go. But Lydia will have no nay. She desired an opportunity of receiving further instruction. In her own house she might not only hear them, but ask them questions; and she might have them to pray with her daily, and to bless her household.

Verses 16–24

Paul and his companions now begin to be taken notice of.

I. *A damsel that had a spirit of divination* caused them to be taken notice of.

1. The account that is given of this damsel: She was *possessed with a spirit of divination* as that damsel was by whom the oracles of Apollo at Delphos were delivered. In those times of ignorance and idolatry, the devil, thus led men captive at his will; and he could not have gained such adoration from them as he had, if he had not pretended to give oracles to them. This damsel *brought her masters much gain by soothsaying*; many came to consult this witch and none came but with the rewards of divination in their hands.

2. The testimony which this damsel gave to Paul and his companions: She *met them* in the street, as they were going to prayer, *v.* 16. They went thither publicly, everybody knew whither they were going. How subtle Satan is in taking the opportunity to give us diversion when we are going about any religious exercises, and to put us out of temper when we need to be most composed. When she met with them she followed them, crying, "*These men are the servants of the most high God; they show unto us the way of salvation.*"

(1) This witness is true. [1] "They are *the servants of the most high God*; they attend on him, are employed by him as servants; they come to us on his errands, the message they bring is from him. The gods we Gentiles worship are inferior beings, therefore not gods, but these men belong *to the most high God*, who is over all men, over all gods. They are his servants, and therefore it is our duty to hearken to them and it is at our peril if we affront them." [2] "They *show unto us the way of salvation*." Even the heathen had some notion of the miserable deplorable state of mankind, and their need of salvation. "Now," saith she, "these are the men that show us what we have in vain sought for."

(2) How came this testimony from the mouth of one that had a spirit of divination? Is Satan divided against himself? We may take it either, [1] As extorted from this spirit of divination for the honour of the gospel by the power of God; as the devil was forced to say of Christ (Mark i. 24): *I know thee who thou art, the Holy One of God*. The truth is sometimes magnified by the confession of its adversaries, in which they are witnesses against themselves. Or, [2] As designed by the evil spirit to the dishonour of the gospel. Those that were most likely to receive the apostles' doctrine were such as were prejudiced against these spirits of divination, and therefore would, by this testimony, be prejudiced against the gospel; and, as for those who regarded these diviners, the devil thought himself sure of them.

II. She continued *many days* clamouring thus (*v.* 18); and, it should seem, Paul took no notice of her; but finding perhaps that it did them a prejudice, rather than any service, he soon silenced her, by casting the devil out of her. 1. He was *grieved*. It was a disturbance to him to hear a sacred truth so profaned. Perhaps they were spoken in an ironical bantering way, and then justly might Paul be grieved, as any good man's heart would be, to hear any good truth of God bawled out in the streets in a canting, jeering way. 2. He *commanded the evil spirit to come out of her. He turned and said, I command thee in the name of Jesus Christ to come out of her;* and by this he will show *that these men are the servants of the living God*. Her silence shall demonstrate it more than her speaking could do. Power went along with the word of Christ, before which Satan could not stand, but was forced to quit his hold. *He came out the same hour*.

III. The masters of the damsel that was dispossessed caused them to be taken notice of, by bringing them before the magistrates for doing it.

1. That which provoked them was, that *her masters saw that the hope of their gain was gone, v.* 19. See here what evil *the love of money is the root of!* The power of Christ and the great kindness done to her in delivering her out of Satan's hand, made no impression upon them when they apprehended that they should hereby lose money.

2. The course they took with him was to incense the higher powers against them: *They caught them and dragged them into the market-place*, where public justice was administered. They brought them *to the rulers*, their justices of peace. From them they hurried them *to the magistrates*, the governors of the city.

3. The charge they exhibited against them was that they were the troublers of the land, *v.* 20. They take it for granted that these men are Jews. The general charge against them is *that they troubled the city*, sowed discord, and disturbed the public peace. If they troubled the city, it was but like the angel's troubling the water of Bethesda's pool, in order to healing. The proof of this charge is their teaching customs not proper to be admitted by a Roman colony, *v.* 21. The Romans were always very jealous of innovations in religion. Right or wrong, they would adhere to that which they had received by tradition from their fathers. No foreign nor upstart deity must be allowed.

IV. The magistrates caused them to be taken notice of.

1. By countenancing the persecution they raised the mob upon them (*v.* 22): *The multitude rose up together against them*. It has been the artifice of Satan to make God's ministers and people odious, by representing them as dangerous men, who aimed at the destruction of the constitution and the changing of the customs.

2. They further represented them as the vilest malefactors: *They rent off their clothes* in order to their being scourged. This was one of those three times that Paul was beaten with rods, according to the Roman usage, which was not under the compassionate limitation of the number of stripes not to exceed forty, which was provided by the Jewish law. It is here said that *they laid many stripes upon them* (*v.* 23), without counting how many. One would think, this might have satiated their cruelty; if they must be whipped, surely they must be discharged. No, they are imprisoned. The judges made their commitment very strict: They *charged the jailer to keep them safely*, as if they were dangerous men, that either would venture to break prison themselves or were in confederacy with those that would attempt to rescue them. The jailer made their confinement very severe (*v.* 24): *Having received such a charge he thrust them into the inner prison*. When magistrates are cruel, it is no wonder that the officers under them are so too. *He put them into the inner prison*, the dungeon, into which none were usually put but condemned malefactors. As if this were not enough, *he made their feet fast in the stocks*. And they were not the first of God's messengers that had their feet in the stocks. Oh what hard usage have God's servants met with, as in the former days, so in the latter times!

Verses 25–34

We have here the designs of the persecutors of Paul and Silas baffled and broken.

I. The persecutors designed to dishearten and discourage the preachers of the gospel; but here we find them both hearty and heartened.

1. They were themselves hearty, wonderfully hearty. Let us consider what their case was. The many stripes

they had laid upon them were very sore, and one might have expected to hear them complaining of them. Yet this was not all; they had reason to fear the axes next. In the meantime they were in the inner prison, their feet in the stocks, which hurt them; and yet, *at midnight* they *prayed and sang praises to God.* They prayed together, prayed to God to support them and comfort them in their afflictions—prayed that even their bonds and stripes might turn to the furtherance of the gospel,—prayed for their persecutors, that God would forgive them and turn their hearts. This was not at an hour of prayer, but at midnight; it was not in a house of prayer, but in a dungeon; yet it was seasonable to pray, and the prayer was acceptable. As in the dark, so out of the depths, we may cry unto God. No trouble, how grievous soever, should indispose us for prayer. *They sang praises to God.* We never want matter for praise, if we do not want a heart. And what should put the heart of a child of God out of tune for this duty if a dungeon and a pair of stocks will not do it? Nay, *they not only praised God, but they sang praises to him.* As our rule is that the afflicted should pray, and therefore, being in affliction, they prayed; so our rule is that the merry should sing psalms, and therefore, being merry in their affliction, *they sang psalms.* Notice is here taken of the circumstance that *the prisoners heard them.* If the prisoners did not hear them pray, yet *they heard them sing praises.* They sang so loud, that though they were in the dungeon, they were heard all the prison over. We should sing psalms with all our heart. Though they knew the prisoners would hear them, yet they sang aloud, as those that were not ashamed of their Master. Shall those that would sing psalms in their families plead, in excuse for their omission of the duty, that they are afraid their neighbours should hear them, when those that sing profane songs roar them out, and care not who hears them? The prisoners were made to hear the prison-songs of Paul and Silas, that they might be prepared for the miraculous favour shown to them all for the sake of Paul and Silas, when *the prison-doors were thrown open.*

2. God heartened them wonderfully by his signal appearances for them, *v.* 26. There was immediately a great earthquake; *the very foundations of the prison were shaken.* The Lord was in these earthquakes, to show his resentment of the indignities done to his servants. The prison doors were thrown open, and the prisoners' fetters were knocked off: *Every man's bands were loosed.* As afterwards God gave to Paul all *those that were in the ship with him* (ch. xxvii. 24), so now he gave him all those that were in the prison with him.

II. The persecutors designed to stop the progress of the gospel, but here we find converts made in the prison, the trophies of the gospel's victories erected there, and the jailer, their own servant, become a servant of Christ.

1. He is afraid he shall lose his life, and Paul makes him easy as to this care, *v.* 27, 28. (1) He *awoke out of his sleep.* It is probable that the shock of the earthquake woke him, and the prisoners' expressions of joy and amazement, when in the dark they found their bands loosed. This was enough to awaken the jailer, whose place required that he should not be hard to wake. (2) He saw the prison doors open, and supposed that the prisoners had fled; and then what would become of him? He knew the Roman law in that case. (3) In his fright *he drew his sword,* and was going *to kill himself,* to prevent a more terrible death, which he knew he was liable to for letting his prisoners escape. The philosophers generally allowed self-murder. This jailer thought there was no harm in anticipating his own death; but Christianity proves itself to be of God by this, that it keeps us to the

law of our creation, obliges us to be just to our own lives, and teaches us cheerfully to resign them to our graces, but courageously to hold them out against our corruptions. (4) Paul stopped him (*v.* 28): He *cried with a loud voice, saying, Do thyself no harm.* All the cautions of the word of God against sin have this tendency, "*Do thyself no harm.* Hurt not thyself, and then none else can hurt thee; do not sin, for nothing else can hurt thee." The jailer needs not fear being called to an account for the escape of his prisoners, for *they are all here.* It was strange that some of them did not slip away, when the prison doors were opened, and they were loosed from their bands. God showed his power in binding their spirits, as much as in loosing their feet.

2. He is afraid he shall lose his soul, and Paul makes him easy as to this care too. One concern leads him to another, and a much greater. He begins to think whither death would have brought him, and what would have become of him on the other side death.

(1) Whatever was the cause, he was put into a great consternation. The Spirit of God, that was sent to convince, in order to his being a Comforter, struck a terror upon him. *He called for a light,* and *sprang in and came trembling to Paul and Silas.* This jailer, when he was thus made to tremble, could not apply to a more proper person than to Paul, for it had once been his own case; he had been once a persecutor of good men, had cast them into prison; and therefore he was able to speak the more feelingly to the jailer.

(2) In this consternation, he applied to Paul and Silas for relief. How reverent and respectful his address to them is: *He called for a light; he fell down before them.* It is probable that he had heard what the damsel said of them, that they were *the servants of the living God, who showed to them the way of salvation.* He fell down before them, to beg their pardon, for the indignities he had done them, and to beg their advice, what he should do. He gave them a title of respect, *Sirs, lords, masters;* just now it was, *Rogues* and *villains,* and he was their master; but now, *Sirs, lords,* and they are his masters. Converting grace changes people's language. How serious his enquiry is: *What must I do to be saved? First,* His salvation is now his great concern, and lies nearest his heart, which before was the furthest thing from his thoughts. *Secondly,* He does not enquire concerning others, what they must do; but concerning himself, "What must I do?" It is his own precious soul that he is in care about. *Thirdly,* He is convinced that something must be done, and done by him too, in order to his salvation; that it is not a thing that will do itself. He asks not, "What may be done for me?" but, "What shall I do?" *Fourthly,* He is willing to do anything: "Tell me what I must do, and I am here ready to do it. Sirs, put me into the right way, though narrow, and thorny, and uphill, yet I will walk in it." Those who are thoroughly convinced of sin, and truly concerned about their salvation will be glad to have Christ upon his own terms, Christ upon any terms. *Fifthly,* He is desirous to know what he should do, and asks those that were likely to tell him. Those that set their faces Zionward must ask the way thither. We cannot know it of ourselves, but God has made it known to us by his word, has appointed his ministers to assist us, and has promised *to give his Holy Spirit to those that ask him,* to be their guide in the way of salvation. *Sixthly,* He *brought them out.* He brings them out of the dungeon, in hopes they will bring him out of a much worse.

(3) They directed him what he must do, *v.* 31. Though they are cold, and sore, and sleepy, they do not adjourn this cause to a more convenient time

and place. They strike while the iron is hot, take him now when he is in a good mind, lest the conviction should wear off. Now that God begins to work, it is time for them to set in as *workers together with God*. They are as glad to show him the way to heaven as the best friend they have. They gave him the same directions they did to others, *Believe in the Lord Jesus Christ*. Here is the sum of the whole gospel, the covenant of grace in a few words: *Believe in the Lord Jesus Christ, and thou shalt be saved, and thy house*. The happiness promised: *"Thou shalt be saved;* not only rescued from eternal ruin, but brought to eternal life and blessedness. Though a persecutor, yet thy heinous transgressions shall be all forgiven; and thy hard embittered heart shall be softened and sweetened by the grace of Christ." The condition required: *Believe in the Lord Jesus Christ*. We must approve the method God has taken of reconciling the world to himself by a Mediator; and accept of Christ as he is offered to us. This is the only way and a sure way to salvation. No other way of salvation than by Christ, and no danger of coming short if we take this way. It is the gospel that is to be preached to every creature, *He that believes shall be saved*. The extension of this to his family: *Thou shalt be saved, and thy house*. Be they ever so many, let them believe in Jesus Christ and they shall be saved.

(4) They proceeded to instruct him and his family in the doctrine of Christ (*v.* 32): They *spoke unto him the word of the Lord*. He was, for aught that appears, an utter stranger to Christ, and therefore it is requisite he should be told who this Jesus is, that he may believe in him. Christ's ministers should have the word of the Lord so ready to them, and so richly dwelling in them, as to be able to give instructions offhand to any that desire to hear and receive them. They spoke the word to *all that were in his house*. Masters of families should take care that all under their charge partake of the means of knowledge and grace, and that the word of the Lord be spoken to them; for the souls of the poorest servants are as precious as those of their masters, and are bought with the same price.

(5) The jailer and his family were immediately baptized. He was *baptized, he and all his, straightway*. The Spirit of grace worked such a strong faith in them, all on a sudden, as superseded further debate; and Paul and Silas knew by the Spirit that it was a work of God that was wrought in them.

(6) The jailer was hereupon very respectful to Paul and Silas. He *took them the same hour of the night*, would not let them lie a minute longer in the inner prison. He *washed their stripes*, to cool them, and abate the smart of them. He *brought them into his house*, bade them welcome. Now nothing was thought good enough for them, as before nothing bad enough. He *set meat before them*, and they were welcome to it. They had broken the bread of life to him and his family; and he, having reaped so plentifully of their spiritual things, thought it was but reasonable that they should reap of his carnal things. What have we houses and tables for but as we have opportunity to serve God and his people with them?

(7) The voice of rejoicing with that of salvation was heard in the jailer's house; never was such a truly merry night kept there before: *He rejoiced, believing in God, with all his house*. His believing in Christ is called believing *in God*, which intimates that Christ is God, and that the gospel has a direct tendency to bring us to God. His faith produced joy. Those that by faith have given up themselves to God in Christ as theirs have a great deal of reason to rejoice. Believing in Christ is rejoicing in Christ. He signified his joy to all about him. One cheerful Christian should make many.

Verses 35–40

I. Orders sent for the discharge of Paul and Silas, *v.* 35, 36. The magistrates that had so basely abused them the day before gave the orders *as soon as it was day*, more in haste to give them a discharge than they were to petition for one. The magistrates sent sergeants—*those that had the rods*, those that had been employed in beating them. The order was, *Let those men go*. The jailer brought them the news (*v.* 36): *The magistrates have sent to let you go: Now therefore depart*. Not that he was desirous to part with them as his guests, but as his prisoners; they shall still be welcome to his house, but he is glad they are at liberty from his stocks.

II. Paul's insisting upon the breach of privilege which the magistrates had been guilty of, *v.* 37. Paul said to the sergeants, *"They have beaten us openly, uncondemned, being Romans, and have cast us into prison* against all law and justice, and *now do they thrust us out privily? Nay verily; but let them come themselves and fetch us out*, and own that they have done us wrong."

1. Paul did not plead this before he was beaten lest he should seem to be afraid of suffering for the truth which he had preached. He had nobler things than this to comfort himself with in his affliction.

2. He did plead it afterwards, to put an honour upon the cause he suffered for, to let the world know that the preachers of the gospel merited better treatment. He did it likewise to mollify the magistrates towards the Christians at Philippi, and beget in the people a better opinion of the Christian religion.

(1) Paul lets them know how many ways they had run themselves into a premunire. They had *beaten* those that were Romans. Roman historians give instances of cities that had their charters taken from them for indignities done to Roman citizens. To tell them they had beaten those who were the messengers of Christ would have had no influence upon them; but to tell them they have abused Roman citizens will put them into a fright: so common is it for people to be more afraid of Cæsar's wrath than of Christ's. They had beaten them *uncondemned*; had not calmly examined what was said against them, much less enquired what they had to say for themselves. Christ's servants would not have been abused as they have been if they and their cause might but have had an impartial trial. It was an aggravation of this that they had done it openly. They had *cast them into prison*, without showing any cause of their commitment. They now *thrust them out privily*; they had not indeed the impudence to stand by what they had done, but yet had not the honesty to own themselves in a fault.

(2) He insists upon it that they should make them an acknowledgment of their error, and give them a public discharge, as they had done them a public disgrace: *"Let them come themselves, and fetch us out*, and give a testimony that we have done nothing worthy of stripes or of bonds." It was not a point of honour that Paul stood thus stiffly upon, but a point of justice, and not to himself so much as to his cause.

III. The reversing of the judgment given against Paul and Silas, *v.* 38, 39. The magistrates were frightened when they were told that Paul was a Roman. The proceedings of persecutors have often been illegal, even by the law of nations, and often inhuman, against the law of nature, but always sinful, and against God's law. They *came and besought them* not to take advantage of the law against them; they *brought them out* of the prison, owning that they were wrongfully put into it, and desired them that they would peaceably and quietly *depart out of the city*. Yet, if the repentance of these magistrates had been sincere, they would not have desired them to depart out of their city, but would have begged of them to continue in their city, to show them the way of salvation. But many are convinced that Christianity is not to be persecuted who yet are not convinced that it ought to be embraced. They are compelled to do honour to Christ and his servants, and yet do not go so far as to have benefit by Christ.

IV. The departure of Paul and Silas from Philippi, v. 40. They went out of the prison when they were legally discharged. They took leave of their friends: they *went to the house of Lydia, saw the brethren,* and they *comforted them.* Young converts should have a great deal said to them to comfort them, for *the joy of the Lord will be* very much *their strength. They departed.* Paul and Silas had an extraordinary call to Philippi; and yet, when they have come thither, they see little of the fruit of their labours, and are soon driven thence. Yet they did not come in vain. They laid the foundation of a church at Philippi, which became very eminent, and had people that were more generous to Paul than any other church, as appears by his epistle to the Philippians, *ch.* i. 1; iv. 15. Let not ministers be discouraged, though they see not the fruit of their labours presently; the seed sown seems to be lost under the clods, but it shall come up again in a plentiful harvest.

CHAPTER 17

We have here a further account of the travels of Paul. He was not like a candle upon a table, that gives light only to one room, but like the sun that goes its circuit to give light to many. We have him here, I. Preaching and persecuted at Thessalonica, ver. 1–9. II. Preaching at Berea, but was driven thence also by persecution, ver. 10–15. III. Disputing at Athens (ver. 16–21), and the account he gave of natural religion, to lead them to the Christian religion (ver. 22–31), together with the success of this sermon, ver. 32–34.

Verses 1–9

Paul's two epistles to the Thessalonians give such a shining character of that church, that we cannot but be glad to meet with an account of the first founding of the church there.

I. Here is Paul's coming to Thessalonica. Paul went on with his work, notwithstanding the ill usage he had met with at Philippi. He takes notice of this in his first epistle to the church here (1 Thess. ii. 2). The opposition and persecution that he met with made him the more resolute. He could never have held out, and held on, as he did, if he had not been animated by a spirit of power from on high. 2. He did but *pass through Amphipolis and Appollonia.* We may suppose though he is said only to *pass through* these cities, yet that he stayed so long in them as to publish the gospel there, and to prepare the way for the entrance of other ministers among them.

II. His preaching to the Jews first, in their synagogue at Thessalonica. He found a synagogue of the Jews there (v. 1). By it he made his entry. It was always his manner to begin with the Jews, for if they received the gospel they would cheerfully embrace the new converts; if they refused it, they might thank themselves if the apostles carried it to those that would bid it welcome. He met them in their synagogue on the sabbath day, in their place and at their time of meeting. It is good being in the house of the Lord on his day. This was Christ's manner, and Paul's manner, and has been the manner of all the saints. He *reasoned with them out of the scriptures.* They agreed with him to receive the scriptures, so far they were of a mind. But they received the scripture, and therefore thought they had reason to reject Christ; Paul received the scripture, and therefore saw great reason to embrace Christ. It was therefore requisite that he should, by reasoning with them, convince them that his inferences from the scripture

were right and theirs were wrong. The preaching of the gospel should be both scriptural preaching and rational; such Paul's was, for he *reasoned out of the scriptures*: we must reason out of them and upon them. Reason must not be set up in competition with the scripture, but it must be made use of in explaining and applying the scripture. He continued to do this *three sabbath days* successively. God waits for sinners' conversion; all the labourers come not into the vineyard at the first hour, nor are wrought upon so suddenly as the jailer. The drift and scope of his arguing was to prove that *Jesus is the Christ*; this was that which he opened and alleged, v. 3. He first explained his thesis, and opened the terms, and then alleged it, and laid it down. He opened it like one that knew it, and alleged it like one that believed it. It was necessary the Messiah should *suffer, and die, and rise again,* for the Old Testament prophecies concerning the Messiah made it necessary he should. Paul here alleges and makes it out undeniably, not only that it was possible he might be the Messiah, though he suffered, but that, being the Messiah, it was necessary he should suffer. He could not be made perfect but by sufferings; for, if he had not died, he could not have risen again from the dead. He must needs have suffered for us, because he could not otherwise purchase redemption for us; and he must needs have risen again because he could not otherwise apply the redemption to us. Jesus is the Messiah: *"This Jesus whom I preach unto you is Christ,* is the Christ, is he that should come. God has both by the scriptures and by miracles, borne witness to him." Gospel ministers should preach Jesus; he must be their principal subject. That which we are to preach concerning Jesus is that he is Christ.

III. The success of his preaching there, v. 4. Some of the Jews believed and they *consorted with Paul and Silas.* Those that believe in Jesus Christ come into communion with his faithful ministers, and associate with them. Many more of the devout Greeks, and of the chief women, embraced the gospel. These were *the worshipping Gentiles*; as in America they call those of the natives that are converted to the faith of Christ the *praying Indians.* Of these *a great multitude believed.* And not a few of the chief women of the city embraced Christianity. Particular notice is taken of this, for an example to the ladies, the chief women, to submit themselves to the commanding power of Christ's holy religion; for this intimates how acceptable it will be to God, and what great influence it may have upon many. No mention is here made of their preaching the gospel to the Gentile idolaters at Thessalonica, and yet it is certain that they did, for Paul writes to the Christians there as having *turned to God from idols* (1 Thess. i. 9), and that at the first entering in of the apostles among them.

IV. The trouble that was given to Paul and Silas at Thessalonica.

1. Who were the authors of their trouble: the *Jews who believed not, who were moved with envy,* v. 5. Some of the Jews believed the gospel and pitied and prayed for those that did not; while those that did not envied and hated those that did.

2. Who were the instruments of the trouble: the Jews made use of *certain lewd persons of the baser sort.* All wise and sober people looked upon them with respect, and none would appear against them but such as were the scum of the city. It is the honour of religion that those who hate it are generally the *lewd fellows of the baser sort.*

3. In what method they proceeded against them. (1) They *set the city in an uproar.* They began a riot, and then the mob was up presently. See how the devil carries on his designs; he sets cities in an uproar, sets souls in an uproar, and then fishes in

troubled waters. (2) They *assaulted the house of Jason*, where the apostles lodged, *to bring them out to the people*, whom they had incensed against them. The proceedings here were altogether illegal. If men have offended, magistrates are appointed to enquire into the offence, and to judge of it; but to make the rabble judges and executioners too was to make truth fall in the street, to depose equity, and enthrone fury. (3) When they could not get the apostles into their hands they fall upon an honest citizen of their own, his name *Jason*, a converted Jew, and drew him out with some others of the brethren to the rulers of the city. (4) They accused them to the rulers, and represented them as dangerous persons. The crime charged upon Jason is receiving and harbouring the apostles (*v.* 7). Two very black characters are here given them: [1] That they were enemies to the public peace, and threw everything into disorder wherever they came: *Those that have turned the world upside down are come hither also.* In one sense it is true that whereever the gospel comes in its power to any place, to any soul, it works such a change there that it may be said to turn the world upside down. The love of the world is rooted out of the heart, and the way of the world contradicted in the life; so that the world is turned upside down there. They would have it thought that the preachers of the gospel were mischief makers wherever they came. Because they persuaded people to turn from idols to the living and true God, from malice and envy to love and peace, they are charged with turning the world upside down, when it was only thus the kingdom of the devil in the world that they thus overturned. Their enemies *set the city in an uproar*, and then laid the blame upon them. If Christ's faithful ministers be thus invidiously misrepresented, let them not think it strange; we are not better than Paul and Silas, who were thus abused. The accusers cry out, "They are *come hither also*; it is therefore time for us to bestir ourselves." [2] That they were enemies to the established government (*v.* 7): They all *do contrary to the decrees of Cæsar*, for they say: *There is another king, one Jesus.* It is true the Roman government was very jealous of any governor under their dominion taking upon him the title of king. His followers said indeed, Jesus is a king, but not an earthly king. There was nothing in the doctrine of Christ that tended to the dethroning of princes. The Jews knew this very well, and of all people it ill became the Jews to do it, who hated Cæsar and his government, and who expected a Messiah that should be a temporal prince, and overturn the thrones of kingdoms, and were therefore opposing our Lord Jesus because he did not appear under that character.

4. The great uneasiness which this gave to the city (*v.* 8): *They troubled the people and the rulers of the city, when they heard these things.* They had no ill opinion of the apostles or their doctrine, but if they be represented to them by the prosecutors as enemies to Cæsar, they will be obliged to suppress them. It troubled them to be brought under a necessity of disturbing good men.

5. The issue of this troublesome affair. The magistrates had no mind to prosecute the Christians. Care was taken to secure the apostles; they fled, and kept out of their hands; so that nothing was to be done but to discharge Jason and his friends upon bail, *v.* 9. So they *took security of Jason and the other.* Among the persecutors of Christianity, as there have been instances of the madness and rage of brutes, so there have been likewise of the prudence and temper of men; moderation has been a virtue.

Verses 10–15

I. Paul and Silas removing to Berea, and employed in preaching the gospel there, *v.* 10. They had proceeded so far at Thessalonica that the foundations of a church were laid, and therefore when the storm rose they withdrew. That command of Christ to his disciples, *When they persecute you in one city flee to another*, intends their flight to be not so much for their own safety ("flee to another, to hide there") as for the carrying on of their work ("flee to another, to preach there"). The devil was outshot in his own bow; he thought by persecuting the apostles to stop the progress of the gospel, but it was so overruled as to be made to further it. 1. The care that the brethren took of Paul and Silas. They *immediately sent them away by night to Berea.* They *sent them away by night*, under the covert of that, as if they had been evil doers. 2. The constancy of Paul and Silas in their work. Though they fled from Thessalonica, they did not flee from the service of Christ. When *they came to Berea, they went into the synagogue of the Jews.* They did not decline paying their respect to the Jews, either in revenge for the injuries they had received or for fear of what they might receive. If others will not do their duty to us, yet we ought to do ours to them.

II. The good character of the Jews in Berea (*v.* 11): *These were more noble than those in Thessalonica.* They *were more noble, better bred.*

1. They had a freer thought, were willing to hear reason, and admit the force of it, though it was contrary to their former sentiments. This was more noble.

2. They had a better temper. As they were ready to come into a unity with those that they were brought to concur with, so they continued in charity with those that they saw cause to differ from. This was more noble. *They received the word with all readiness of mind;* they were very willing to hear it, and did not shut their eyes against the light. They did not pick quarrels with the word, nor seek occasion against the preachers of it; but bade it welcome. This was true nobility. The Jews thought themselves well-born and that they could not be better born. But they are here told who among them were the most noble and the best-bred men—those that were most disposed to receive the gospel. These were the most noble, and, if I may so say, the most gentleman-like men. *They searched the scriptures daily whether those things were so.* Their readiness of mind to receive the word was not such as that they took things upon trust. Since Paul reasoned out of the scriptures, and referred them to the Old Testament for the proof of what he said, they had recourse to their Bibles, examined whether Paul's arguments were cogent, and determined accordingly. The doctrine of Christ does not fear a scrutiny. The New Testament is to be examined by the Old. The Jews received the Old Testament, and those that did so could not but see cause sufficient to receive the New, because in it they see all the prophecies and promises of the Old fully and exactly accomplished. Those that read and receive the scriptures must *search them* (John v. 39), must study them, that they may find out the whole truth contained in them, and may have an intimate acquaintance with the mind of God revealed in them. Searching the scriptures must be our daily work. Those are truly noble, and are in a fair way to be more and more so, that make the scriptures their oracle and touchstone. Those that rightly study the scriptures, and *meditate therein day and night*, have their minds filled with noble thoughts. *These are more noble.*

III. The good effect of the preaching of the gospel at Berea, *v.* 12. Of the Jews there were many that believed. At Thessalonica there were only *some of them that believed* (*v.* 4), but at Berea, where they heard with unprejudiced minds, many believed. God gives grace to those whom he first inclines to make a diligent use of the means of grace, and particularly to search the scriptures. Of the Greeks likewise, many believed, both of *the honourable women and of men not a few*, men of the first rank, as should seem by their being mentioned with the honourable women. The wives first embraced the gospel, and then they persuaded their husbands to embrace it.

IV. The persecution that was raised against Paul and Silas at Berea. *The Jews at Thessalonica* were the mischief-makers at *Berea*. They *had notice that the word of God was preached at Berea*. They came thither *and they stirred up the people*, and incensed them against the preachers of the gospel. See how restless Satan's agents are in their opposition to the gospel of Christ and the salvation of the souls of men. This occasioned Paul's removal to Athens. So long Paul stayed at Berea, and such success he had there, that there were brethren there, and sensible active men too, which appeared by the care they took of Paul, *v.* 14. They were aware of the coming of the persecuting Jews from Thessalonica, and, fearing what it would come to, they lost no time, but *immediately sent Paul away*, while they retained Silas and Timothy there still, who might be sufficient to carry on the work without exposing him. They *sent Paul to go as it were to the sea*. He went out from Berea in that road which went to the sea, but he went by land to Athens. *Those that conducted Paul brought him to Athens*. The Spirit of God directed him to that famous city—famous of old for its power and dominion—famous afterwards for learning. Those who wanted learning went thither to get it, because those that had learning went thither to show it. It was a great university. Paul is sent thither, and is not ashamed nor afraid to show his face among the philosophers there, and there to preach Christ crucified. He ordered *Silas and Timothy to come to him to Athens*, when he found there was a prospect of doing good there; or because, there being none there that he knew, he was solitary and melancholy without them.

Verses 16–21

A scholar that is in love with the learning of the ancients would think he should be very happy if he were where Paul now was, at Athens, but Paul, though bred a scholar, does not make this any of his business at Athens. He has other work to mind: his business is, in God's name, *to turn them from the service of idols* to the *service of the true and living God* in Christ.

I. Here is the impression which the superstition of the Athenians made upon Paul's spirit, *v.* 16. 1. The account here given of that city: it was *wholly given to idolatry*. This agrees with the account which the heathen writers give of it, that there were more idols in Athens than there were in all Greece besides. Whatever strange gods were recommended to them, they admitted them, and allowed them a temple and an altar. It is observable that there, where human learning most flourished, idolatry most abounded. *The world by wisdom knew not God*, 1 Cor. i. 21. The greatest pretenders to reason were the greatest slaves to idols: so necessary was it that there should be a divine revelation, and that centring in Christ. 2. The disturbance which the sight of this gave to Paul. *His spirit was stirred within him*. He was filled with concern for the glory of God, which he saw given to idols, and with compassion to the souls of men, which he saw thus enslaved to Satan.

II. The testimony that he bore against their idolatry, and his endeavours to bring them to the knowledge of the truth. He *went to the synagogue of the Jews*, who, though enemies to Christianity, were free from idolatry, and took the opportunity given him there of disputing for Christ, *v.* 17. He discoursed *with the Jews*, and put it to them what reason they could give why, since they expected the Messiah, they would not receive Jesus. There he met with the devout persons that had forsaken the idol temples, and he talked with these to lead them on to the Christian church, to which the Jews' synagogue was but as a porch. He entered into conversation with all that came in his way about matters of religion: *In the market he disputed daily with those that met with him*, that were heathen, and never came to the Jews' synagogue. The zealous advocates for the cause of Christ will be ready to plead it in all companies, as occasion offers.

III. The enquiries which some of the philosophers made.

1. Who they were that entered into discourse with him: *He disputed with all that met him, in the places of concourse*. Most took no notice of him, but there were some of the philosophers that thought him worth making remarks upon. (1) *The Epicureans*, who *thought God altogether such a one as themselves*. They would not own, either that God made the world or that he governs it. The Epicureans indulged themselves in all the pleasures of sense, and placed their happiness in them, in what Christ has taught us in the first place to deny ourselves. (2) *The Stoics*, who thought themselves altogether as good as God; they made their virtuous man to be no way inferior to God himself. To which Christianity is directly opposite, as it teaches us to come off from all confidence in ourselves, that Christ may be all in all.

2. What their different sentiments were of him (*v.* 18). (1) *Some called him a babbler—this scatterer of words*, that goes about, throwing here one idle word or story and there another; or, *this picker up of seeds*. The term is used for *a little sort of bird*, that lie worth nothing at all, *that picks up the seeds that lie uncovered, either in the field or by the wayside, and hops here and there for that purpose*. Such a pitiful contemptible animal they took Paul to be, or supposed he went from place to place venting his notions to get money, a penny here and another there, as that bird picks up here and there a grain. They looked upon him as an idle fellow, and regarded him, as we say, no more than a ballad-singer. (2) *Others* called him a *setter forth of strange gods*. And, if he had strange gods to set forth, he could not bring them to a better market than to Athens. They thought he seemed to do so, *because he preached unto them Jesus, and the resurrection*. Though he did not call these gods, yet they thought he meant to make them so. "Jesus they took for a new god, and the resurrection, for a new goddess." As if believing in Jesus and looking for the resurrection, were the worshipping of new demons.

3. The proposal they made to give him a public hearing, *v.* 19, 20. They had heard some broken pieces of his doctrine, and are willing to have a more perfect knowledge of it. (1) They look upon it as strange and surprising. "It is a new doctrine. *Thou bringest certain strange things to our ears* which we never heard of before, and know not what to make of now." By this it should seem that, among all the learned books they had, they either had not, or heeded not, the books of Moses and the prophets. There was but one book in the world that was of divine inspiration, and that was the only book they were strangers to. (2) They desired to know more of it, only because it was new and strange: "*May we know what this new doctrine is? We would gladly know what these things mean*." It was fit they should know what this doctrine was before they embraced it; and they were so fair as not to condemn it till they had had some account of it. (3) The place they brought him to. It was to *Areopagus*, the same word that is translated (*v.* 22) *Mars' Hill*; it was the town-house, or guildhall of their city, where the magistrates

met upon public business, and where learned men met to communicate their notions. The court of justice which sat here was famous for its equity. Hither they brought Paul to be tried, not as a criminal but as a candidate.

4. The general character of the people of that city (*v. 21*): *All the Athenians spent their time in nothing else but either to tell or to hear some new thing.* They were inquisitive concerning Paul's doctrine, not because it was *good*, but because it was *new*. (1) They were all for conversation. It is true that good company is of great use to a man, and will polish one that has laid a good foundation in study; but that knowledge will be very flashy and superficial which is got by conversation only. (2) They affected novelty; they were for *telling and hearing some new thing*. They were for new schemes and new notions. They were given to change. (3) They meddled in other people's business and never minded their own. Tattlers are always *busy bodies*. (4) *They spent their time in nothing else*. Time is precious and it is hastening apace into eternity, but abundance of it is wasted in unprofitable converse. To set up for newsmongers, and to spend our time in nothing else, is to lose that which is very precious for the gain of that which is worth little.

Verses 22–31

We have here St. Paul's sermon at Athens. Divers sermons we have had, which the apostles preached to the Jews, or such Gentiles as were worshippers of the true God; and all they had to do with them was to open and allege *that Jesus is the Christ*; but here we have a sermon to heathens, that worshipped false gods, and to them the scope of their discourse was quite different from what it was to the other. In the former case their business was to lead their hearers by prophecies and miracles to the knowledge of the Redeemer, and faith in him; in the latter it was to lead them by the common works of providence to the knowledge of the Creator, and the worship of him.

I. He lays down this that he aimed to bring them to *the knowledge of the only living and true God*. He is here obliged to instruct them in the first principle of all religion, that there is a God, and that God, is but one. When he preached against the gods they worshipped he had no design to draw them to atheism, but to the service of the true Deity, by declaring that he does not seek to introduce any new gods, but to reduce them *to the knowledge of one God*.

1. He shows them that they had lost the knowledge of the true God that made them, in the worship of false gods that they had made. *I perceive that in all things you are too superstitious*. The crime he charges upon them is that they feared and worshipped demons, spirits that they supposed inhabited the images. "It is time for you to be told that *there is but one God*. You easily admit everything that comes under a show of religion, but it is that which corrupts it more and more; I bring you that which will reform it." They charged Paul with setting forth new demons: "Nay," says he, "you have demons enough already; I will not add to the number of them."

2. He shows them that they themselves had given a fair occasion for the declaring of this one true God to them, by *setting up an altar, To the unknown God*. It is sad to think that at Athens, a place which was supposed to have the monopoly of wisdom, the true God was an unknown God, the only God that was unknown. There, where we are sensible we are defective and come short, and just there, the gospel takes us up, and carries us on.

(1) Various conjectures the learned have concerning this *altar dedicated to the unknown God*. Some think the meaning is, *To the God whose honour it is to be unknown*, and that they intended the God of the Jews,

whose name is ineffable, and whose nature is unsearchable. The heathen called the Jews' God the God without name. *This God*, says Paul, *I now declare unto you*. Others think the meaning is, *To the God whom it is our unhappiness not to know*, that they would think it their happiness to know him.

(2) Observe, how modestly Paul mentions this. He tells them that he observed it *as he passed by, and saw their devotions*. It was public, and he could not forbear seeing it. Observe how he takes occasion from this to bring in his discourse of the true God. He tells them that the God he preached to them was one that they did already worship. He was one whom they ignorantly worshipped. "Now," says he, "I come to take away *that reproach*, that you may worship him understandingly. And it cannot but be acceptable to have your blind devotion turned into a reasonable service, that you may not worship *you know not what*."

II. He confirms his doctrine of one living and true God, by his works of creation and providence: "The God whom I call you to the worship of, is *the God that made the world*." The Gentiles in general, and the Athenians particularly, in their devotions were governed, not by their philosophers, but by their poets, and their idle fictions. Now Paul here sets himself to give them right notions of *the one only living and true God*, and then to carry the matter further for the bringing them off from their idolatry. Observe what glorious things Paul here says of that God whom he served, and would have them to serve.

1. *He is the God that made the world, and all things therein; the Father almighty, the Creator of heaven and earth*. Paul here maintains that God by the operations of an infinite power, according to the contrivance of an infinite wisdom, made the world and all things therein, the origin of which was owing to an eternal mind.

2. He is therefore *Lord of heaven and earth*. If he created all, without doubt he has the disposing of all: and, where he gives being, he has an indisputable right to give law.

3. He is, in a particular manner, the Creator of men, of all men (*v. 26*): *He made of one blood all nations of men*. He made the first man, he makes every man. He has made the nations of men, not only all men in the nations, but as nations. He is their founder and disposed them into communities. He made them all of one blood, of one and the same nature, that hereby they might be engaged in mutual affection and assistance, as fellow-creatures and brethren. *He hath made them to dwell on all the face of the earth*. He made them not to live in one place, but to be dispersed over all the earth; one nation therefore ought not to look with contempt upon another, as the Greeks did, which proud conceit of themselves, the apostle here takes down.

4. He is the great benefactor of the whole creation (*v. 25*): *He giveth to all life, and breath, and all things*. He not only *breathed into the first man the breath of life*, but still breathes it into every man. He gave us these souls; he formed the spirit of man within him He *gives to all the children of men their life and breath*; for as the meanest of the children of men live upon him, so the greatest, the wisest philosophers and mightiest potentates, cannot live without him. *He gives to all*, not only to all the children of men, but to the inferior creatures, to all animals; they have their life and breath from him, and where he gives life and breath he gives all things needful for the support of life.

5. He is the sovereign disposer of all the affairs of the children of men (*v. 26*): *He hath determined the times before appointed, and the bounds of their habitation*. (1) The sovereignty of God's disposal concerning us: he *hath determined* every event; the disposals of Providence are incontestable and must not

be disputed. (2) The wisdom of his disposals; he hath *determined* what was *before appointed*. The determinations of the Eternal Mind are not sudden resolves, but an eternal counsel. (3) The things about which his providence is conversant; these are time and place. [1] *He has determined the times* that are concerning us. *Our times are in his hand*. Whether they be prosperous times or calamitous times, it is he that has determined them. [2] He has also *determined and appointed the bounds of our habitation*. He that *appointed the earth to be a habitation for the children of men* has appointed to the children of men a distinction of habitations upon the earth. The particular habitations in which our lot is cast are of God's appointing, which is a reason why we should accommodate ourselves to the habitations we are in, and make the best of that which is.

6. *He is not far from everyone of us*, v. 27. He is *everywhere present*. He is an infinite Spirit, *that is not far from any of us*. He is nigh unto us, both to receive the homage we render him and to give the mercies we ask of him, wherever we are, though near no altar, image, or temple. Be we in a palace or in a cottage, in a crowd or in a corner, in a city or in a desert, in the depths of the sea or afar off upon the sea, this is certain, *God is not far from everyone of us*.

7. *In him we live, and move, and have our being*, v. 28. We have a necessary and constant dependence upon his providence, as the streams have upon the spring, and the beams upon the sun. (1) *In him we live*. It is not only owing to his patience that our forfeited lives are not cut off, but it is owing to his fatherly care, that our frail lives are prolonged. If he suspend the positive acts of his goodness, we die of ourselves. (2) *In him we move*. It is likewise by him that our souls move our bodies, as he is the first cause, so he is the first mover. (3) *In him we have our being;* not only from him we had it at first, but in him we have it still; we were and still are of such a noble rank of beings, capable of knowing and enjoying God; and are not thrust into the meanness of brutes, nor the misery of devils.

8. Upon the whole matter we are *God's offspring*. The apostle here quotes a saying of one of the Greek poets, Aratus, a native of Cilicia, Paul's countryman, who, speaking of the heathen *Jupiter*, that is, in the poetical dialect, the supreme *God*, says this of him, *for we are also his offspring*. By this it appears not only that Paul was himself a scholar, but that human learning is both ornamental and serviceable to a gospel minister, especially for the convincing of those that are without; for it enables him to beat them at their own weapons, and to cut off Goliath's head with his own sword. How can the adversaries of truth be beaten out of their strongholds by those that do not know them? Since in him we live, we ought to live to him; since in him we move, we ought to move towards him; and since in him we have our being, we ought to consecrate our being to him.

III. From all these great truths concerning God, he infers the absurdity of their idolatry. 1. God cannot be represented by an image. If we are *the offspring of God*, then certainly he who is *the Father of our spirits* is himself a Spirit, and we ought not to think the Godhead is *like unto gold, or silver, or stone, graven by art and man's device*, v. 29. God honoured man in making his soul after his own likeness; but man dishonours God if he makes him after the likeness of his body. 2. *He dwells not in temples made with hands*, v. 24. A temple brings him never the nearer to us, nor keeps him ever the longer among us. A temple is convenient for us to come together in to worship God; but God needs not any place of rest or residence. 3. He is *not worshipped with men's hands, as though he needed anything*, v. 25. He that

maintains all, cannot be benefited by any of our services, nor needs them. What need can God have of our services, or what benefit can he have by them, when he has all perfection in himself, and we have nothing that is good but what we have from him? 4. It concerns us all to enquire after God (v. 27): *That they should seek the Lord*. We have plain indications of God's presence among us, and his bounty to us, that we might be put upon enquiring, *Where is God our Maker*. Nothing, one would think, should be more powerful with us to convince us that there is a God, than the consideration of our own nature, especially the noble powers and faculties of our own souls. Yet so dark is this discovery, in comparison with that by divine revelation, that those who have no other could but *haply feel after God* and *find him*. It was very uncertain whether they could by this searching *find out God*; it is but a peradventure: *if haply they might*. If they did find out something of God, yet it was but some confused notions of him; they did but feel after him, as men in the dark, or blind men. It is true that by the knowledge of ourselves we may be led to the knowledge of God, but it is a very confused knowledge. We have therefore reason to be thankful that by the gospel of Christ we do not now feel after him, but *with open face behold, as in a glass, the glory of God*.

IV. He proceeds to call them all to repent of their idolatries, v. 30, 31. This is the practical part of Paul's sermon before the university; having declared God to them (v. 23), he properly presses upon them *repentance towards God*. Having shown them the absurdity of their worshipping other gods, he persuades them to return from it to the living and true God.

1. The conduct of God towards the Gentile world before the gospel came among them: *The times of this ignorance God winked at*. They were times of great ignorance. In the things of God they were grossly ignorant. Those are ignorant indeed who either know not God or worship him ignorantly; idolatry was owing to ignorance. These times of ignorance God winked at. Understand it as an act of divine patience and forbearance. He winked at these times, but gave them the gifts of his providence, *ch.* xiv. 16, 17. He was not quick and severe with them, but was long-suffering towards them, because they did it ignorantly.

2. The charge God gave to the Gentile world by the gospel: *He now commandeth all men everywhere to repent*—to change their mind and their way. It is to turn with sorrow and shame from every sin, and with cheerfulness and resolution to every duty. This is God's command. He interposes his own authority for our good, and has made that our duty which is our privilege. It is his command to *all men, everywhere*. All men have made work for repentance, and have cause enough to repent, and all men are invited to repent, and shall have the benefit of it. Now the way of remission is more opened than it had been, and the promise more fully confirmed; and therefore now he expects we should all repent.

3. The great reason to enforce this command. God commands us to repent, *because he hath appointed a day in which he will judge the world in righteousness* (v. 31). (1) The God that made the world will judge it. The God that now governs the world will reward the faithful friends of his government and punish the rebels. (2) There is a day appointed for this general review of all that men have done in time, a day of decision, a day of recompence, a day that will put a final period to all the days of time. (3) The world will be judged in righteousness; for God is not unrighteous. (4) God will judge the world *by that man whom he hath ordained*, who can be no other than the Lord Jesus, to whom all judgment is committed.

(5) God's raising Christ from the dead is the great proof of his being appointed and ordained the Judge of quick and dead. God hath *given assurance unto all men*, sufficient ground for their faith to build upon, both that there is a judgment to come and that Christ will be their Judge. Let all his enemies be assured of it, and tremble before him; let all his friends be assured of it, and triumph in him. (6) The consideration of the judgment to come, and of the great hand Christ will have in that judgment, should engage us all to repent of our sins and turn from them to God.

Verses 32–34

We have here a short account of the issue of Paul's preaching at Athens.

I. Few were the better: the gospel had as little success at Athens as anywhere. Some ridiculed Paul and his preaching. They heard him patiently till he came to speak of the resurrection of the dead (v. 32), and then they *mocked*. If he speak of a *resurrection of the dead*, though it be of the resurrection of Christ himself, it is altogether incredible to them. They had deified their heroes after their death, but never thought of their being raised from the dead. How can this be? This great doctrine, which is the saints' joy, is their jest. We are not to think it strange if sacred truths are made the scorn of profane wits. Others were willing to take time to consider of it; they said, *We will hear thee again of this matter*. They would not at present comply with what Paul said, nor oppose it. Thus many lose the benefit of the practical doctrine of Christianity, by wading beyond their depth into controversy. Those that would not yield to the present convictions of the word thought to get clear of them by putting them off to another opportunity. Thus the devil cozens them of all their time, by cozening them of the present time. Paul thereupon left them for the present to consider of it (v. 33): *He departed from amongst them*.

II. Yet there were some that were wrought upon, *v.* 34. There were certain men that adhered to him, and believed. When he departed from amongst them, they would not part with him so. Two are particularly named; one was an eminent man, *Dionysius the Areopagite*, one of that high court that sat in Aeropagus, one of those before whom Paul was summoned to appear; his judge becomes his convert. The *woman named Damaris*. Though there was not so great a harvest gathered in at Athens, yet these few being wrought upon there, Paul had no reason to say he had *laboured in vain*.

CHAPTER 18

I. Paul's coming to Corinth, his private converse with Aquila and Priscilla, and his public reasonings with the Jews, from whom, when they rejected him, he turned to the Gentiles, ver. 1–6. II. The great success of his ministry there, and the encouragement Christ gave him to continue his labours there, ver. 7–11. III. The molestations there from the Jews, which he got pretty well through by the coldness of Gallio, the Roman governor, ver. 12–17. IV. The progress Paul made through many countries, after he had continued long at Corinth, in which circuit he made a short visit to Jerusalem, ver. 18–23. V. An account of Apollos' usefulness in the church, ver. 24–28.

Verses 1–6

We do not find that Paul was much persecuted at Athens, nor that he was driven thence by any ill usage, but his reception being cold, and little prospect of doing good there, he departed from Athens, and thence he came to Corinth.

I. Paul working for his living, *v.* 2, 3. 1. Though he was bred a scholar, yet he was master of a handicraft trade. He was a tentmaker. It was the custom of the Jews to bring up their children to some trade, yea, though they gave them learning or estates. An honest trade, by which a man may get his bread, is not to be looked upon by any with contempt. Paul,

having in his youth learned to make tents, did not by disuse lose the art. 2. Though he was entitled to a maintenance from the churches he had planted, yet he worked at his calling to get bread, which is more to his praise who did not ask for supplies than to theirs who did not supply him unasked. See how humble Paul was. See how industrious he was. He that had so much to do with his mind did not think it below him to work with his hands. See how careful Paul was to recommend his ministry. He therefore maintained himself with his own labour that he might not make the gospel of Christ *burdensome*, 2 Cor. xi. 7, &c. 3. Though we may suppose he was master of his trade, yet he did not disdain to work at journey-work: He *wrought with Aquila and Priscilla*, who *were of that calling*, so that he got no more than day-wages, a bare subsistence. 4. Though he was himself a great apostle, yet he chose to work with Aquila and Priscilla, because he found them to be very intelligent in the things of God (v. 26), and he owns that they had been his *helpers in Christ Jesus*, Rom. xvi. 3. Choose to work with those that are likely to be helpers in Christ Jesus. Concerning this Aquila he was a Jew, but born in Pontus, *v.* 2. He was lately come from Italy to Corinth. The reason of his leaving Italy was because by a late edict of the emperor Claudius Cæsar all Jews were banished from Rome. Aquila, though a Christian, was banished because he had been a Jew. If Jews persecute Christians, it is not strange if heathens persecute them both.

II. We have here Paul preaching to the Jews, both the native *Jews and the Greeks*.

1. He *reasoned with them in the synagogue every sabbath*. See in what way the apostles propagated the gospel, not by force and violence, but by fair arguing. Paul was a rational as well as a scriptural preacher.

2. *He persuaded them*. It denotes the urgency of his preaching. He followed his arguments with affectionate persuasions, not to refuse the offer of salvation made to them. The good effect of his preaching. He persuaded them, that is, he prevailed with them. Some of them were convinced by his reasonings, and yielded to Christ.

3. He was yet more earnest in this matter when his fellow-labourers came up with him (v. 5): *When Silas and Timothy had come from Macedonia* and were ready to assist him here, then Paul was more than before *pressed in spirit*, which made him more than ever pressing in his preaching. And being thus pressed, he *testified to the Jews that Jesus is the Christ*.

III. We have him here abandoning the unbelieving Jews, and turning from them to the Gentiles, *v.* 6.

1. Many of the Jews persisted in their contradiction to the gospel of Christ; they *opposed themselves* and *blasphemed*; they *set themselves in battle array* (so the word signifies) against the gospel. They could not argue against it, but what was wanting in reason they made up in ill language: they *blasphemed*.

2. Paul hereupon declared himself discharged from them, and left them to perish in their unbelief. He that was *pressed in spirit to testify to them* (v. 5), was pressed in spirit to testify against them (v. 6); he *shook his raiment*, shaking off the dust from it for a testimony against them. Thus he cleared himself from them, but threatened the judgments of God against them. He had done his part, and was clean from the blood of their souls; he had, like a faithful watchman, given them warning, so that if they perish in their unbelief their blood is not to be required at his hands. It is very comfortable to a minister to have the testimony of his conscience for him, that he has faithfully discharged his trust by warning sinners. They would certainly perish if they persisted in their unbelief, and the blame would lie

wholly upon themselves: "Your *blood be upon your own heads.*" If anything would frighten them at last into a compliance with the gospel, surely this would.

3. Having given them over, yet he does not give over his work. *Henceforth I will go unto the Gentiles.* The guests that were first invited will not come; guests must be had therefore *from the highways and the hedges.* Thus the fall of the Jews became the riches of the Gentiles.

Verses 7–11

I. Paul changed his quarters. He departed out of the synagogue, and he *entered into a certain man's house, named Justus, v.* 7. It should seem, he went to this man's house, not to lodge, for he continued with Aquila and Priscilla, but to preach. This honest man opened his doors to him. When Paul could not have liberty to preach in the synagogue, he preached in a house. The man was next door to a Jew; he was one that *worshipped God*; he was not an idolater, though he was a Gentile. 2. The house was next door to the synagogue, it *joined close to it.* I rather think it was done in charity, to show that he would come as near to them as he could, and was ready to return to them if they were but willing to receive his message.

II. Paul presently saw the good fruit of his labours, both among Jews and Gentiles. *Crispus,* a Jew, an eminent one, *the chief ruler of the synagogue, believed on the Lord Jesus, with all his house, v.* 8. This would leave the Jews inexcusable, that the ruler of their synagogue believed the gospel, and yet they opposed and blasphemed it. Not only he but his house, believed. Many of the Corinthians, who were Gentiles, *hearing, believed, and were baptized.* Some perhaps came to hear Paul under some convictions of conscience, but it is probable that the most came only for curiosity. But, hearing, *they believed,* and, *believing,* they were *baptized,* and so fixed for Christ.

III. Paul was encouraged by a vision to go on with his work at Corinth (*v.* 9): *The Lord Jesus spoke to Paul in the night by a vision.* 1. He renewed his commission and charge to preach the gospel: *"Be not afraid of the Jews.* Be not afraid of the magistrates of the city. It is the cause of heaven thou art pleading, do it boldly. Do not speak shyly and with caution, but plainly and fully and with courage. Speak out." 2. He assured him of his presence with him, which was sufficient to put life and spirit into him: *"Be not afraid, for I am with thee,* to bear thee out, and to deliver thee from all thy fears, to work with thee, and to confirm the word by signs following." Those that have Christ with them need not to fear, and ought not to shrink. 3. He gave him a warrant of protection: *"No man shall set on thee to hurt thee."* He does not promise that no man should set on him (for the next news we hear is that he is set upon, and *brought to the judgment-seat, v.* 12), but *"No man shall set on thee to hurt thee.* Whatever trouble they may give thee, there is no real evil in it." 4. He gave him a prospect of success: *"For I have much people in this city.* Therefore do thou go on vigorously and cheerfully in it; for there are many in this city that are to be effectually called by thy ministry." The Lord knows those that are his. "I have them, though they yet know me not, for the Father has given them to me, and of all that were given me I will lose none." *In this city,* though it be a very profane wicked city, full of impurity, and the more so for a temple of Venus there, yet in this heap, that seems to be all chaff, there is wheat; in this ore, that seems to be all dross, there is gold. Let us not despair concerning any place, when even in Corinth Christ had *much people.*

IV. Upon this encouragement he made a long stay there (*v.* 11): He *continued at Corinth a year and six months, teaching the word of God among them.* He

stayed so long, 1. For the bringing in of those that were without. God works variously. The people Christ has at Corinth must be called in by degrees. Let Christ's ministers go on in their duty, though their work be not done all at once. 2. For the building up of those that were within. Those that are converted have still need to be *taught the word of God.* No sooner was the good seed sown in that field than the enemy came and sowed tares, the false apostles, of whom Paul in his epistles to the Corinthians complains so much. Soon after Paul came to Corinth, it is supposed, he wrote the first epistle to the Thessalonians, and the second epistle to the same church was written not long after. Ministers may be serving Christ by writing good letters, as well as by preaching good sermons.

Verses 12–17

We have here an account of some disturbance at Corinth, but no great harm done.

I. Paul is accused by the Jews before the Roman governor, *v.* 12, 13. The governor was *Gallio, deputy of Achaia.* This Gallio was elder brother to the famous Seneca, a man of great ingenuousness and great probity, and a man of wonderful good temper; he was called *Sweet Gallio,* and is said to have been universally beloved. How rudely Paul is apprehended, and brought before Gallio; *The Jews made insurrection with one accord against Paul.* They were the ringleaders. They were unanimous in it: they came upon him *with one accord.* They did it with violence and fury: *They made an insurrection* and hurried Paul away *to the judgment-seat.* How falsely Paul is accused before Gallio (*v.* 13): *This fellow persuades men to worship God contrary to the law.* They could not charge him with persuading men not to worship God at all, but only to worship God in a way contrary to the law. But the charge was unjust. The law relating to the temple-service those Jews at Corinth could not observe, and there was no part of their synagogue-worship which Paul contradicted. Thus when people are taught to worship God in Christ, and to worship him in the Spirit, they are ready to quarrel, as if they were taught to worship him contrary to the law.

II. Gallio dismisses the cause, and will not take any cognizance of it, *v.* 14, 15. Paul was going about to make his defence, but the judge, being resolved not to pass any sentence upon this cause, would not give himself the trouble of examining it.

1. He shows himself very ready to do the part of a judge in any matter that it was proper for him to take cognizance of. He *said to the Jews,* "If it were *a matter of wrong, or wicked lewdness,* I should think myself bound *to bear with you.*" It is the duty of magistrates to right the injured, and to animadvert upon the injurious; and if the complaint be not made with all the decorum that might be, yet they should hear it out.

2. He will by no means allow them to make a complaint to him of a thing that was not within his jurisdiction (*v.* 15): *"If it be a question of words and names, and of your law, look you to it; I will be no judge of such matters."* And therefore *he drove them from the judgment-seat* (*v.* 16). Here was something right in Gallio's conduct, and praiseworthy—that he would not pretend to judge of things he did not understand; that he left the Jews to themselves in matters relating to their own religion, would not himself be the tool of their malice. It was certainly wrong to speak so slightly of a law and religion which he might have known to be of God, and with which he ought to have acquainted himself. He speaks as if he boasted of his ignorance of the scriptures, as if it were below him to take notice of the law of God.

III. The abuse done to Sosthenes, and Gallio's unconcernedness in it, *v.* 17. The parties put a great contempt upon the court, when *they took Sosthenes and beat him before the judgment-seat.* Many conjectures there are concerning this matter, because it is uncertain who this Sosthenes was, and who the Greeks were that abused him. It seems most probable that Sosthenes was a Christian. It is certain that there was one Sosthenes that was a friend of Paul, and well known at Corinth; Paul calls him his brother, and joins him with himself in his first epistle to the church at Corinth (1 Cor. i. 1). He is said to be a *ruler of the synagogue.* As for the Greeks that abused him, it is very probable that they were those that joined with the Jews in opposing the gospel (*v.* 4, 6). They were so enraged against Paul that they beat Sosthenes; and so enraged against Gallio, that they beat him before the judgment-seat, whereby they tell him that they cared not for him, if he would not be their executioner, they would be their own judges. The court put no less a contempt upon the cause, and the persons too. But *Gallio cared for none of these things.* If by this he meant that he cared not for the affronts of bad men, it was commendable. But, if it be meant that he concerned not himself for the abuses done to good men, it carries his indifference too far. Gallio, as a judge, ought to have protected Sosthenes, and restrained and punished the Greeks that assaulted him. Those that see and hear of the sufferings of God's people, and have no sympathy with them, nor concern for them, it being all one to them whether the interests of religion sink or swim, are of the spirit of Gallio here, who, when a good man was abused before his face, *cared for none of these things.*

Verses 18–23

We have here Paul in motion, as we have had him at Corinth for sometime at rest, but in both busy, very busy.

I. Paul's departure from Corinth, *v.* 18. 1. He did not go away till sometime after the trouble he met with there; from other places he had departed when the storm arose, but not from Corinth, because there it had no sooner risen than it fell again. *After this he tarried there yet a good while, v.* 11. While he found he laboured not in vain, he continued labouring. 2. When he went, he took leave of the brethren, solemnly, and with much affection. 3. He took *with him Priscilla and Aquila.* They seemed disposed to remove, and not inclined to stay long at a place, a disposition which may arise from a good principle, and have good effects, and therefore ought not to be condemned in others, though it ought to be suspected in ourselves. 4. At Cenchrea, the port where those that went to sea from Corinth took ship, either Paul or Aquila (for the original does not determine which) had his head shaved, to discharge himself from the vow of a Nazarite: *Having shorn his head at Cenchrea; for he had a vow.* Those that lived in Judæa were, in such a case, bound to do it at the temple: but those who lived in other countries might do it in other places. I see no harm in admitting it concerning Paul, in compliance for a time with the Jews, to whom he *became as a Jew* (1 Cor. ix. 20), *that he might win upon them.*

II. Paul's calling *at Ephesus,* which was the metropolis of the Lesser Asia. 1. *There he left Aquila and Priscilla.* They might be serviceable to the interests of the gospel at Ephesus. Paul intended shortly to settle there for some time. Aquila and Priscilla might dispose the minds of many to give Paul, when he should come among them, a favourable reception. 2. There he preached *to the Jews in their synagogue. He entered into the synagogue,* not as a hearer, but as a preacher, for *there he reasoned with the Jews.*

Though he had abandoned the Jews at Corinth, he did not, for their sakes, decline the synagogues of the Jews in other places, but still made the first offer of the gospel to them. We must not condemn a whole body or denomination of men, for the sake of some that conduct themselves ill. 3. The Jews at Ephesus courted his stay with them (*v.* 20): *They desired him to tarry longer with them.* These were more noble, and better bred, than those Jews at Corinth, and it was a sign that God had not quite cast away his people, but had a remnant among them. 4. Paul would not stay with them now: *He consented not; but bade them farewell.* He *must by all means keep this feast at Jerusalem.* Which of the feasts it was we are not told. 5. He intimated his purpose, after this journey, to come and spend some time at Ephesus. It is good to have opportunities in reserve, when one good work is over to have another to apply ourselves to: *I will return again to you,* but he inserts that necessary proviso, *if God will.* Our times are in God's hand; we purpose, but he disposes; and therefore we must make all our promises with submission to the will of God.

III. Paul's visit to Jerusalem; a short visit it was. He came by sea to the port that lay next to Jerusalem. *He sailed from Ephesus* (*v.* 21), *and landed at Cæsarea, v.* 22. He went *up, and saluted the church,* by which, I think, is plainly meant the church at Jerusalem. It was a very friendly visit that he made them, in pure kindness to testify his hearty goodwill to them. The increase of our new friends should not make us forget our old ones, but it should be a pleasure to good men, to revive former acquaintance. He took care to keep up a good correspondence with them, that they might both congratulate and wish well to one another's comfort and success. It was but a short visit. He went *up, and saluted them,* and made no stay among them. It was designed but for a transient interview. God's people are dispersed and scattered; yet it is good to see one another sometimes.

IV. His return through those countries where he had formerly preached the gospel. *He went and spent some time in Antioch,* whence he was first sent out to preach among the Gentiles, *ch.* xiii. 1. He went down to Antioch, to refresh himself with the sight of the ministers there; and a very good refreshment it is to a faithful minister to have for awhile the society of his brethren. *Thence he went over the country of Galatia and Phrygia in order,* where he had preached the gospel, and planted churches. These country churches (for such they were, Gal. i. 2, and we read not of any city in Galatia where a church was) Paul visited *in order* as they lay, watering what he had been instrumental to plant, and *strengthening all the disciples.* Paul's countenancing them was encouraging them; but that was not all: he preached that to them which strengthened them. Disciples need to be strengthened. Ministers must do what they can to strengthen them by directing them to Christ, whose strength is perfected in their weakness.

Verses 24–28

The sacred history leaves Paul upon his travels, and goes here to meet Apollos at Ephesus.

I. Here is an account of his character.

1. He was *a Jew, born at Alexandria* in Egypt, but of Jewish parents.

2. He was a man well fitted for public service. He was *an eloquent man, and mighty in the scriptures.* He had a great command of language: He *came to Ephesus,* being *mighty in the scriptures,* having an excellent faculty of expounding scripture. He was not only ready in the scriptures, able to quote texts offhand, and tell you where to find them, but he was *mighty in the scriptures.* He understood the sense and meaning of them, he knew how to make use of them

and to apply them, how to reason out of the scriptures, and to reason strongly.

3. He *was instructed in the way of the Lord;* that is, he had some acquaintance with the doctrine of Christ, had obtained some general notions of the gospel and the principles of Christianity. He was taught something of Christ and the way of salvation by him. Those that are to teach others must first be themselves taught the word of the Lord, not only to talk of it, but to walk in it. It is not enough to have our tongues tuned to the word of the Lord, but we must have our feet directed into the way of the Lord.

4. Yet he *knew only the baptism of John.* He knew the preparing of the way of the Lord, rather than the way of the Lord itself. He had himself been baptized *only with the baptism of John,* but was not baptized with the Holy Ghost.

II. We have here the employment and improvement of his gifts at Ephesus.

1. He there made a very good use of his gifts in public. He was willing to be employed (*v.* 25): *Being fervent in the Spirit, he spoke and taught diligently the things of the Lord.* Though he had not the miraculous gifts of the Spirit, he made use of the gifts he had. We have seen how Apollos was qualified with a good head and a good tongue: he was *an eloquent man, and mighty in the scriptures.* Let us now see what he had further to recommend him as a preacher; and his example is recommended to the imitation of all preachers. He was a lively affectionate preacher; he had a good heart; he was *fervent in Spirit.* He had in him a great deal of divine fire as well as divine light. This appeared both in his forwardness to preach when he was called to it, and in his fervency in his preaching. He preached as one in earnest, and that had his heart in his work. Many are fervent in spirit, but are weak in knowledge, and, on the other hand, many are eloquent enough, and mighty in the scriptures, but they have no life or fervency. Here was a complete *man of God,* full both of divine knowledge and of divine affections. He was an industrious laborious preacher. *He spoke and taught diligently.* He took pains in his preaching, and he did not offer that to God, or to the synagogue, that either cost nothing or cost *him* nothing. *He taught diligently, accurately, exactly;* everything he said was well-weighed. He was an evangelical preacher. Though he knew only the baptism of John, yet that was the beginning of the gospel of Christ, and to that he kept close; for he taught the things of the Lord Christ, the things that tended to make way for him. He was a courageous preacher: *He began to speak boldly in the synagogue,* as one who, having put confidence in God, did not fear the face of man. *In the synagogue,* where the Jews not only were present, but had power, there he preached the things of God.

2. He there made a good increase of his gifts. *Aquila and Priscilla expounded to him the way of God more perfectly.* Aquila and Priscilla heard him preach in the synagogue. They encouraged his ministry, by a diligent and constant attendance upon it. Thus young ministers, that are hopeful, should be countenanced by grown Christians. Finding him defective in his knowledge of Christianity, *they took him to them* and *expounded to him the way of God more perfectly.* They did not despise him themselves, or disparage him to others; did not call him a young raw preacher, not fit to come into a pulpit. They communicated what they knew to him, and gave him a clear, methodical account of those things which before he had but confused notions of. See an instance of truly Christian charity in Aquila and Priscilla. Aquila did not undertake to speak in the synagogue, because he had not such gifts for public work as Apollos had; but he furnished Apollos with matter,

and then left him to clothe it with acceptable words. Instructing young Christians and young ministers privately in conversation is a piece of very good service. See an instance of great humility in Apollos. He was a very bright young man, of great parts and learning, and one mightily cried up and followed; and yet, finding that Aquila and Priscilla could speak intelligently and experimentally of the things of God, though they were but mechanics, he was glad to receive instructions from them, to be shown by them his defects and mistakes. Young scholars may gain a great deal by converse with old Christians, as young students in the law may by old practitioners. Apollos, though he *was instructed in the way of the Lord,* did not rest in the knowledge he had attained. Those that know much should covet to know more. Here is an instance of a good woman doing good with the knowledge God had given her in private converse.

III. Here is his preferment to the service of the church of Corinth. Paul had set the wheels a-going at Corinth. Many were stirred up by his preaching to receive the gospel, and they needed to be confirmed. Paul was gone and now there was a fair occasion in this vacancy for Apollos to set in, who was fitted rather to water than to plant. His call to this service. He himself inclined to do: *He was disposed to pass into Achaia.* Apollos thought there might be some work for him, and God disposed his mind that way. His friends encouraged him to go; they gave him letters of recommendation. Though those at Ephesus had a great loss of his labours, they did not grudge those in Achaia the benefit of them; but, on the contrary, used their interest in them to introduce him. His success in this service. Believers were greatly edified: *He helped those much who had believed through grace.* Those who believe in Christ, it is through grace that they believe; it is *not of themselves, it is God's gift to them.* Those who through grace do believe, yet still have need of help. Faithful ministers are capable of being in many ways helpful to those who through grace do believe, and it is their business to help them. Unbelievers were greatly mortified. Their objections were fully answered, their mouths were stopped, and their faces filled with shame (*v.* 28): *He mightily convinced the Jews, and that publicly.* He did it *earnestly,* he took pains to do it. He did it effectually and to universal satisfaction. If the Jews were but convinced of this—that Jesus is Christ, even their own law would teach them to hear him. The business of ministers is to preach Christ. The way he took to convince them was *by the scriptures;* thence he fetched his arguments. Ministers must be able not only to preach the truth, but to prove it and defend it, and to convince gainsayers with meekness and yet with power.

Chapter 19

We left Paul in his circuit visiting the churches (ch. xviii. 23), but we have not forgotten, nor has he, the promise he made to his friends at Ephesus, to return to them. Now this chapter shows us his performance of that promise. I. How he laboured there, how he taught some weak believers that had gone no further than John's baptism (ver. 1–7), how he taught three months in the synagogue (ver. 8), and how he taught the Gentiles a long time in a public school (ver. 9, 10), and how he confirmed his doctrine by miracles, ver. 11, 12. II. What was the fruit of his labour, particularly among the conjurors: some were confounded (ver. 13–17), but others were converted, ver. 18–20. III. What projects he had of further usefulness (ver. 21, 22), and what trouble at length he met with at Ephesus from the silversmiths, how a mob was raised by Demetrius to cry up Diana (ver. 23–34), and how it was suppressed and dispersed by the town-clerk, ver. 35–41.

Verses 1-7

Ephesus was a city of great note in Asia, famous for a temple built there to Diana, which was one of the wonders of the world: thither *Paul came to preach the gospel while Apollos was at Corinth* (*v.* 1); while he was watering there, Paul was planting here, and went on in the new work that was cut out for him at Ephesus with the more cheerfulness and satisfaction, because he knew that such an able minister as Apollos was now at Corinth, carrying on the good work there. Paul having gone through the country of Galatia and Phrygia, having *passed through the upper coasts, came to Ephesus*, where he had left Aquila and Priscilla, and there found them. He met with some disciples there, who professed faith in Christ as the true Messiah, but were as yet in the first and lowest form in the school of Christ, under his usher John the Baptist. They were in number *about twelve* (v. 7).

I. How Paul catechised them.

1. They did believe in the Son of God; but Paul enquires whether they had *received the Holy Ghost,*— whether they had been acquainted with, and had admitted, this revelation? This was not all; extraordinary gifts of the Holy Ghost were conferred upon the apostles and other disciples after Christ's ascension. Had they participated in these gifts? "*Have you received the Holy Ghost since you believed?* Have you had that seal of the truth of Christ's doctrine in yourselves?" There are graces of the Spirit given to all believers, which are as earnests to them. But many are deceived in this matter, thinking they have received the Holy Ghost when really they have not. As there are pretenders to the gifts of the Holy Ghost, so there are to his graces and comforts; we should therefore strictly examine ourselves, Have we received the Holy Ghost since we believed? The tree will be known by its fruits. Do we bring forth the fruits of the Spirit? Do we walk in the Spirit?

2. They owned their ignorance in this matter: *Whether there be a Holy Ghost* is more than we know. That there is a promise of the Holy Ghost we know from the scriptures and that this promise will be fulfilled in its season we doubt not. We have not so much as heard whether the Holy Ghost be indeed yet given. The gospel light, like that of the morning, shone more and more, gradually; not only clearer and clearer, but further and further.

3. Paul enquired how they came to be baptized, if they knew nothing of the Holy Ghost. *Unto what then were you baptized?* This is strange and unaccountable. What! baptized, and yet know nothing of the Holy Ghost? Ignorance of the Holy Ghost is as inconsistent with a sincere profession of Christianity as ignorance of Christ is. Let us often consider unto what we were baptized, that we may live up to our baptism.

4. They own that they were baptized *unto John's baptism*, that is, they were baptized in the name of John, by some disciple of his, that ignorantly kept up his name as the head of a party. As it is here expressed, *unto John's baptism*.

5. Paul explains to them the true intent and meaning of John's baptism, as principally referring to Jesus Christ. Those that have been left in ignorance, or led into error, by any infelicities of their education, should be compassionately instructed and better taught, as these disciples were by Paul. He owns that John's baptism was a very good thing, as far as it went: *John verily baptized with the baptism of repentance*. He shows them that John's baptism had a further reference. They should believe on him who should come after him, that is, on Christ Jesus,—that his baptism of repentance was designed only to prepare the way of the Lord, whom he directed them to: *Behold the Lamb of God*. He was only the harbinger,—Christ is the Prince. His baptism was the porch which you were to pass through, not the house you were to rest in.

6. When they were thus shown the error they thankfully accepted the discovery, and *were baptized in the name of the Lord Jesus, v. 5.* When they came

to understand things better, they desired to be *baptized in the name of the Lord Jesus*, and were so. It does not therefore follow hence that there was not an agreement between John's baptism and Christ's, for those that were here baptized *in the name of the Lord Jesus* had never been so baptized before.

II. How Paul conferred the extraordinary gifts of the Holy Ghost upon them, v. 6. Paul solemnly *prayed to God laying his hands on them*. God granted the thing he prayed for: *The Holy Ghost came upon them, and they spoke with tongues and prophesied*. They had the Spirit of prophesy, that they might understand the mysteries of the kingdom of God themselves, and the gift of tongues, that they might preach them to every nation and language. Oh, what a wonderful change was here made on a sudden in these men! those that but just now had *not so much as heard that there was any Holy Ghost* are now themselves filled with the Holy Ghost.

Verses 8–12

Paul is here very busy at Ephesus.

I. He begins, as usual, in the Jews' synagogue.

1. Where he preached to them: in their synagogue (v. 8). Where there were no Christian assemblies yet formed, he frequented the Jewish assemblies. Paul went into the synagogue, because there he had them together, and had them, it might be hoped, in a good frame.

2. What he preached to them: *The things concerning the kingdom of God* among men, the great things which concerned God's dominion over all men and favour to them, and men's subjection to God and happiness in God. Or, more particularly, *the things concerning the kingdom of the Messiah*. He gave them a right notion of this kingdom, and showed them their mistakes about it.

3. How he preached to them. He preached argumentatively: he disputed; gave reasons, and answered objections, that they might not only believe, but might see cause to believe. He preached affectionately: he persuaded. Paul was a moving preacher, and was master of the art of persuasion. He preached undauntedly, and with a holy resolution: he spoke boldly.

4. How long he preached to them: *For the space of three months*, which was a competent time allowed them to consider of it.

5. What success his preaching had among them. There were some that were persuaded to believe in Christ. Many continued in their infidelity, and were confirmed in their prejudices against Christianity. Now that he settled among them, and his word came more closely to their consciences, they were soon weary of him. They had an invincible aversion to the gospel of Christ themselves: they were *hardened, and believed not*. They did their utmost to raise and keep up in others an aversion to the gospel. *They spoke evil of that way before the multitude*, to prejudice them against it. Though they could not show any manner of evil in it, yet they said all manner of evil concerning it.

II. When he had carried the matter as far as it would go in the synagogue of the Jews, he left the synagogue. They drove him from them by their railing at those things which he spoke *concerning the kingdom of God*: they hated to be reformed, hated to be instructed, and therefore *he departed from them*.

1. When Paul departed from the Jews he took the disciples with him, and *separated them*. Lest they should be infected with the poisonous tongues of those blasphemers, he separated those who believed, to be the foundation of a Christian church. When Paul departed there needed no more to separate the disciples; let him go where he will, they will follow him.

2. When Paul separated from the synagogue he *disputed daily in the school of one Tyrannus*. He had by this separation a double advantage. (1) That now his opportunities were more frequent. In the synagogue he could only preach every sabbath day (*ch.* xiii. 43), but now he disputed daily. (2) That now they were more open. To the synagogue of the Jews none might come but Jews or proselytes; Gentiles were excluded. In the school of Tyrannus, both Jews and Greeks attended his ministry, *v.* 10. Some think this school of Tyrannus was a divinity-school of the Jews, and such a one they commonly had in their great cities besides their synagogue; they called it *Bethmidrash, the house of enquiry*. But others think it was a philosophy-school of the Gentiles, belonging to one Tyrannus. Some convenient place it was, which Paul and the disciples had the use of, either for love or money.

3. Here he continued his labours for *two years*. These two years commence from the end of the *three months* which he spent in the synagogue (*v.* 8); therefore he might justly reckon it in all three years, as he does, *ch.* xx. 31.

4. The gospel hereby spread far and near (*v.* 10): *All those that dwelt in Asia heard the word of the Lord Jesus;* not only all that dwelt in Ephesus, but all that dwelt in that large province called *Asia,* of which Ephesus was the head city. There was great resort to Ephesus from all parts of the country, which gave Paul an opportunity of sending the report of the gospel to all the towns and villages of that country. They all heard the *word of the Lord Jesus.* Some of all sects, some out of all parts both in city and country, embraced this gospel, and entertained it, and by them it was communicated to others.

III. God confirmed Paul's doctrine by miracles, *v.* 11, 12. Why did he not work miracles at Thessalonica, Berea, and Athens? Or, if he did, why are they not recorded? But here at Ephesus we have the proofs of this kind which he gave of his divine mission. They were *special miracles.* God exerted powers that were not according to the common course of nature. Or, they were not only (as all miracles are) *out of the common road,* but they were even uncommon miracles. God wrought *something above the common road of miracles.* It was not Paul that wrought them but it was God that *wrought them by the hand of Paul.* He was but the instrument.

3. He not only cured the sick that were brought to him, or to whom he was brought, but *from his body were brought to the sick handkerchiefs or aprons.* We read of one that was cured by the touch of Christ's garment when it was upon him, and he perceived that *virtue went out of him;* but here were people cured by Paul's garments when they were taken from him. Christ gave his apostles power *against unclean spirits and against all manner of sickness* (Matt. x. 1), those to whom Paul sent relief had it in both cases: *for the diseases departed from them* and the *evil spirits went out of them.*

Verses 13-20

We have here in these verses two remarkable instances of the conquest of Satan, not only in those that were violently possessed by him, but in those that were voluntarily devoted to him.

I. Here is the confusion of some of Satan's servants, some *vagabond Jews,* that were *exorcists,* who made use of Christ's name in their diabolical enchantments.

1. The general character of those who were guilty of this presumption. They were Jews, but *vagabond* Jews. They strolled about to tell people their fortunes, and pretended by spells and charms to cure diseases, and bring people to themselves that were melancholy or distracted. The superstitious Jews, to put a reputation upon these magic arts, wickedly attributed the invention of them to Solomon. And Christ seems to refer to this (Matt. xii. 27), *By whom do your children cast them out?*

2. A particular account of some at Ephesus that led this course of life. They were *seven sons of one Sceva, a Jew, and chief of the priests, v.* 14. Their father was a chief of the priests, head of one of the twenty-four courses of priests. One would think the temple would find both employment and encouragement enough for the sons of a chief priest.

3. The profaneness they were guilty of: *They took upon them to call over evil spirits the name of the Lord Jesus;* not as those who had a veneration for Christ and a confidence in his name, as we read of some who cast out devils in Christ's name and yet did not follow with his disciples (Luke ix. 49), but as those who were willing to try all methods to carry on their wicked trade. They said, *We adjure you by Jesus whom Paul preaches;* not, "whom we believe in, or depend upon," but *whom Paul preaches;* as if they had said, "We will try what that name will do."

4. The confusion they were put to in their impious operations. The evil spirit gave them a sharp reply (*v.* 15): *"Jesus I know, and Paul I know; but who are you?* What power have you to command us in his name, or who gave you any such power? What have you to do to declare the power of Jesus, seeing you hate his instructions?" *The man in whom the evil spirit was* gave them a warm reception, *leaped upon them, overcame them* and *prevailed against them,* so that *they fled out of the house,* not only *naked,* but *wounded.* A warning to all those who name the name of Christ, but do not depart from iniquity. The same enemy that overcomes them with his temptations will overcome them with his terrors. If we resist the devil by a true and lively faith in Christ, he will flee from us; but if we think to resist him by the bare using of Christ's name, as a spell or charm, he will prevail against us.

5. The general notice that was taken of this (*v.* 17): *This was known to all the Jews and Greeks also dwelling at Ephesus.* It was the common talk of the town. Men were terrified: *fear fell on them all.* In this instance they saw the malice of the devil whom they served, and the power of Christ whom they opposed. God was glorified; *the name of the Lord Jesus was the more magnified;* for now it appeared to be a name above every name.

II. Here is the conversion of others of Satan's servants.

1. Those that had been guilty of wicked practices confessed them, *v.* 18. Many that had believed and were baptized, but had not then been so particular as they might have been in the confession of their sins, came to Paul, and confessed what evil lives they had led, and what a great deal of secret wickedness their own consciences charged them with. *They showed their deeds,* took shame to themselves and gave glory to God and warning to others. Where there is true contrition for sin there will be an ingenuous confession of sin to God and to man whom we have offended when the case requires it.

2. Those that had conversed with wicked books burnt them (*v.* 19): *Many also of those who used curious arts,* that traded in the study of magic and divination. These, having their consciences more awakened than ever, *brought their books together, and burnt them before all men.* Ephesus was notorious for the use of these curious arts. It was therefore much for the honour of Christ and his gospel to have such a noble testimony borne against those *curious* arts, in a place where they were so much in vogue. Thus they showed a holy indignation at the sins they had been guilty of. Those very things were now detestable to them, as much as ever they had been

delectable. Thus they showed their resolution never to return to the use of those arts. Being steadfastly resolved never to make use of them, they burnt them. Thus they put away a temptation to return to them again. Those that truly repent of sin will keep themselves as far as possible from the occasions of it. Thus they prevented their doing mischief to others. It was the safest course to commit them all to the flames. Those that are recovered from sin themselves will do all they can to keep others from falling into it. Thus they showed a contempt of the wealth of this world; for the price of the books was cast up, and it was found to be *fifty thousand pieces of silver.* Probably they had cost them so much; yet, being the devil's books, they did not think this would justify them in being so wicked as to sell them again. Thus they publicly testified their joy for their conversion from these wicked practices. These converts joined together in making this bonfire, and made it before all men. They chose to do it together, by consent, and to do it at the high cross (as we say), that Christ and his grace in them might be the more magnified.

III. Here is a general account of the progress and success of the gospel (*v.* 20): *So mightily grew the word of God, and prevailed.* It is a blessed sight to see the word of God growing and prevailing mightily. To see it grow extensively, by the addition of many to the church. When still more and more are wrought upon by the gospel, then it grows; when those that had been most stiff in their opposition to it, are brought into obedience to it, then it may be said to *grow mightily.* To see it prevail extensively. When strong corruptions are mortified, evil customs of long standing broken off, and pleasant, gainful, fashionable sins are abandoned, then it prevails mightily; and Christ in it goes on conquering and to conquer.

Verses 21–41

I. Paul is here brought into some trouble at Ephesus, just when he is forecasting to go thence.

1. How he laid his purpose of going to other places, *v.* 21, 22. He was a man of vast designs for God, and was for making his influences as widely diffusive as might be. He designed a visit to the churches of Macedonia and Achaia, *v.* 21. There he had planted churches, and now is concerned to visit them. He *purposed in the spirit,* either in his own spirit, or by the direction of the Holy Spirit, who was his guide in all his motions. He purposed to go and see how the work of God went on in those places. Thence he designed to go to Jerusalem, to visit the brethren there, and thence he intended to go to Rome, to go and *see Rome.* It was an expression people commonly used, that they would go and see Rome, would look about them there, when that which he designed was to see the Christians there. The good people at Rome were the glory of the city which he longed for a sight of. He sent Timothy and Erastus into Macedonia, to give them notice of the visit he intended them. For the present he stayed in Asia.

2. How he was seconded in his purpose, and obliged to pursue it by the troubles which at length he met with at Ephesus. It was strange that he had been quiet there so long; yet it should seem he had met with trouble there not recorded in this story, for in his epistle he speaks of his having *fought with beasts at Ephesus* (1 Cor. xv. 32). And he speaks of the trouble which came to them in Asia, near Ephesus, when he *despaired of life,* 2 Cor. i, 8, 9.

II. But, in the trouble here related, he was worse frightened than hurt. In general, *there arose no small stir about that way, v.* 23. Let us view the particulars of it.

1. A great complaint against Paul for drawing people off from the worship of Diana, and so spoiling the trade of the silversmiths that worked for Diana's temple.

(1) The complainant is Demetrius, a silversmith. The most advantageous branch of his trade was *making silver shrines for Diana, v.* 24. Some think these were medals stamped with the effigies of Diana, others think they were representations of the temple, with the image of Diana in it in miniature, all of silver. Those that came from far to pay their devotions at the temple of Ephesus bought these little temples or shrines, to carry home with them. See how craftsmen, and crafty men too above the rank of silversmiths, make an advantage to themselves of people's superstition.

(2) The persons he appeals to are not the magistrates, but the mob; he called the *craftsmen* together, *with the workmen of like occupation,* and these he endeavoured to incense against Paul.

(3) His complaint and representation are very full. He lays it down for a principle that the making silver shrines for the worshippers of Diana was very necessary to be kept up (*v.* 25): "*You know that by this craft we have our wealth.*" It is natural for men to be jealous for that by which they get their wealth; and many have set themselves against the gospel of Christ, because it calls men off from those crafts which are unlawful, how much wealth soever is to be obtained by them. He charges it upon Paul that he had dissuaded men from worshipping idols. He had asserted, *Those are no gods which are made with hands, v.* 26. Could any truth be more plain and self-evident than this, *The workman made it, therefore it is not God?* Yet this must be looked upon as an heretical and atheistical notion, and Paul as a criminal for maintaining it. The consequence of it was that not only at Ephesus, but almost throughout all Asia, he had *persuaded and turned away much people* from the worship of Diana. There are those who will stickle for that which is most grossly absurd and unreasonable, if it have but human laws, and worldly interest on its side. He reminds them of the danger which their trade was in of going to decay. "If this doctrine gains credit, we are all undone, and may even shut up shop; *this our craft will be set at nought.*" He pretends a mighty zeal for Diana: *Not only this our craft is in danger.* All his care is lest *the temple of the great goddess Diana should be despised, and her magnificence should be destroyed;* and he would not see the diminution of the honour of that goddess, *whom all Asia and the world worship.* See what the worship of Diana had to plead for itself. It had pomp on its side; the magnificence of the temple was the thing that charmed them. It had numbers on its side; *All Asia and the world worship;* and therefore it must needs be the right way of worship, let Paul say what he will to the contrary.

2. The popular resentment of this complaint. They showed, (1) A great displeasure against the gospel and the preachers of it. *They were full of wrath* (*v.* 28). The craftsmen went stark mad when they were told that their trade and their idol were both in danger. (2) A great jealousy for the honour of their goddess: *They cried out,* "*Great is Diana of the Ephesians.* Let Paul say ever so much to prove that those are no gods which are made with hands, we will abide by it that, *Great is Diana of the Ephesians.* We must and will stand up for the religion of our country." Much more should the servants of the true God do so. (3) A great disorder among themselves (*v.* 29): *The whole city was full of confusion*— the common and natural effect of an intemperate zeal for a false religion.

3. The proceedings of the mob under the power of these resentments.

(1) They laid hands on some of Paul's companions, and hurried them into the theatre (*v.* 29). Those

whom they seized were *Gaius and Aristarchus. Gaius was of Derbe, ch. xx.* 4. *Aristarchus* is also there spoken of, and Col. iv. 10. They came with Paul *from Macedonia*, and this was their only crime, that they were Paul's companions.

(2) *Paul*, who had escaped being seized by them, when he perceived his friends in distress, for his sake *would have entered in unto the people.* It was an evidence of a generous spirit, and that he loved his neighbour as himself.

(3) He was persuaded from it by the kindness of his friends. *The disciples suffered him not*, for it better became him to offer it than it would have become them to suffer it. Others of his friends interposed, to prevent his throwing himself thus into the mouth of danger, *v.* 31. They were *certain of the chief of Asia.* Whether they were converts to the Christian faith, or whether they were only wellwishers to Paul, as an ingenuous good man, we are not told, only that they were *Paul's friends.* It is a friendly part to take more care of the lives and comforts of good men than they do themselves. Paul was overruled by his friends to obey the law of selfpreservation, and has taught us to keep out of the way of danger as long as we can without going out of the way of duty. We may be called to lay down our lives, but not to throw away our lives.

(4) The mob was in a perfect confusion (*v.* 32): *Some cried one thing and some another, the assembly was confused.* The truth was *the greater part knew not wherefore they had come together.* Upon such occasions, the greatest part come only to enquire what the matter is: they follow the cry, follow the crowd, increase like a snowball, and where there are many there will be more.

(5) The Jews would have interested themselves in this tumult, but now at Ephesus they had not interest enough to raise the mob, and yet, when it was raised, they had ill will enough to set in with it (*v.* 33): *They drew Alexander out of the multitude*, called him out to speak on the behalf of the Jews against Paul and his companions: "You have heard what Demetrius and the silversmiths have to say against them, as enemies to their religion; give us leave now to tell you what we have to say against him as an enemy to our religion." *The Jews put him forward* to do this, and therefore what he designed to say is called his apologizing to the people, not for himself in particular, but for the Jews in general. Now they would have them know that they were as much Paul's enemies as they were. *Alexander beckoned with the hand*, desiring to be heard against Paul; for it had been strange if a persecution had been carried on against the Christians and there were not Jews at one end or the other of it: if they could not begin the mischief, they would help it forward. Some think this Alexander had been a Christian, but had apostatized to Judaism, and therefore was drawn out as a proper person to accuse Paul; and that he was that *Alexander the coppersmith* that did Paul so much evil (2 Tim. iv. 14), and whom he had *delivered unto Satan*, 1 Tim. i. 20.

(6) This occasioned the prosecutors to drop the prosecution of Paul's friends, and to turn it into acclamations in honour of their goddess (*v.* 34): *When they knew that he was a Jew*, and, as such, an enemy to the worship of Diana, they were resolved not to hear him, and therefore set the mob a shouting, "*Great is Diana of the Ephesians;* whoever runs her down, be he Jew or Christian, we are resolved to cry her up." This was all the cry for *two hours* together; and it was thought a sufficient confutation of Paul's doctrine, *that those are not gods which are made with hands.* Thus the most sacred truths are often run down with nothing else but noise and clamour and popular fury.

4. The suppressing and dispersing of these rioters, by the prudence and vigilence of *the town clerk.* With much ado he, at length, stilled the noise, so as to be heard, and then made a pacific speech to them.

(1) He humours them with an acknowledgment that Diana was the celebrated goddess of the Ephesians *v.* 35. They needed not to be so loud and strenuous in asserting a truth which nobody denied. Everyone *knows that the city of the Ephesians is a worshipper of the great goddess Diana.* The temple of Diana at Ephesus was a very rich and sumptuous structure, but the *image* of Diana in the temple was had in greater veneration than the temple, for they persuaded the people that it *fell down from Jupiter*, and therefore was none of the gods that were made with men's hands. Because this image of Diana had been set up time out of mind, and nobody could tell who made it, they made the people believe it fell down from Jupiter. "Now *these things*," says the town clerk very gravely, "*cannot be spoken against*; they have obtained such universal credit that you need not fear contradiction."

(2) He cautions them against all violent and tumultuous proceedings, which their religion did not need (*v.* 36): *You ought to be quiet, and to do nothing rashly.* A very good rule this is to be observed at all times, both in private and public affairs; not to be hasty and precipitate in our motions, but to be calm and composed, and always keep reason in the throne and passion under check. *We ought to be quiet and to do nothing rashly;* to do nothing in haste, which we may repent of at leisure.

(3) He wipes off the odium that had been cast upon Paul and his associates (*v.* 37): "*You have brought hither these men.* What can you prove upon them? They are not robbers of churches. They have offered no violence to Diana's temple or the treasures of it; nor are they *blasphemers of your goddess.* Why should you prosecute those *with all this violence* who do not inveigh with any bitterness against you? Since they are calm, why should you be hot?" It was the idol in the heart that they levelled all their force against, by reason and argument; if they can but get that down, the idol in the temple will fall of course. Those that preach against idolatrous churches have truth on their side, with meekness instructing, not with passion and foul language reproaching, those that oppose themselves; for God's truth needs not man's intemperate heat.

(4) He turns them over to the regular methods of the law. A great mercy it is to live in a country where provision is made for the keeping of the peace, and the administration of public justice, and herein we of this nation are as happy as any people. If the complaint be of a private injury, let them have recourse to the judges and courts of justice. If Demetrius and the company of the silversmiths find themselves aggrieved, let them bring their action, and the matter shall be fairly tried, and justice done: *The law is open, and there are deputies*, whose business it is to hear both sides, and in their determination all parties must acquiesce, and not be their own judges, nor appeal to the people. If the complaint be of a public grievance it must be redressed, not by a confused rabble, but by a convention of the states (*v.* 39): *If you enquire anything concerning other matters it shall be determined in a lawful assembly* called together in a regular way by those in authority. Private persons should not intermeddle in public matters, we have enough to do to mind our own business.

(5) He makes them sensible of the danger they have run themselves into by this riot (*v.* 40): "It is well if we be not *called in question for this day's uproar*, for *there is no cause whereby we may give an account of this concourse.* Let the matter go no further, for it has gone too far already." Most people stand in

awe of men's judgment more than of the judgment of God. How well were it if we would thus still the tumult of our disorderly appetites and passions with the consideration of the account we must shortly give to the Judge of heaven and earth for all these disorders! We are concerned to manage ourselves *as those that must give account.*

(6) When he has thus shown them the absurdity of their riotous meeting, he advises them to separate with all speed (*v.* 41): he *dismissed the assembly.* See here how the overruling providence of God preserves the public peace, by an unaccountable power over the spirits of men. Thus the world is kept in some order, and men are restrained from being as the fishes of the sea, where the greater devour the less. Considering what an ungovernable, untameable wild beast the mob is, when it is up, we shall see reason to acknowledge God's goodness that we are not always under the tyranny of it. See how many ways God has of protecting his people. Perhaps this town clerk was no friend at all to Paul, yet his human prudence is made to serve the divine purpose.

CHAPTER 20

I. Paul's travels up and down about Macedonia, Greece, and Asia, and his coming at length to Troas, ver. 1–6. II. A particular account of his spending one Lord's day at Troas, and his raising Eutychus to life there, ver. 7–12. III. His progress in his way towards Jerusalem, ver. 13–16. IV. The farewell sermon at Ephesus, ver. 17–35. V. The very sorrowful parting between him and them, ver. 36–38.

Verses 1–6

I. Paul's departure from Ephesus. He had tarried there longer than he had done at any one place. Now it was time to think of removing, for he must *preach in other cities also*; but after this we never find him breaking up fresh ground again, for in the close of the next chapter we find him made a prisoner, and so continued, and so left, at the end of this book. Paul left Ephesus soon after the uproar had ceased, *v.* 1. His removal might somewhat appease the rage of his adversaries, and gain better quarter for the Christians there. Some think that before he now left Ephesus he wrote *the first epistle to the Corinthians,* and that his *fighting with beasts at Ephesus,* which he mentions in that epistle, was a figurative description of this uproar. He did not leave them abruptly, but took leave of them solemnly: *He called unto him the disciples, and embraced them, took leave of them* (saith the Syriac) *with the kiss of love.* Loving friends know not how well they love one another till they come to part, and then it appears how near they lay to one another's hearts.

II. His visitation of the Greek churches, which he had planted, and which appear to have laid very near his heart. He went first *to Macedonia* (*v.* 1), according to his purpose before the uproar (*ch.* xix. 21); there he visited the churches of Philippi and Thessalonica, and *gave them much exhortation, v.* 2. He had a great deal to say to them, and did not stint himself in time. He stayed *three months in Greece* (*v.* 2, 3), that is, *in Achaia,* for thither also he purposed to go, to Corinth, and thereabouts (*ch.* xix. 21).

III. The altering of his measures. *Paul was about to sail into Syria, to Antioch,* but he changed his mind, and resolved *to return to Macedonia,* the same way he came. The reason was because the Jews, expecting he would steer that course as usual, had waylaid him, designing to be the death of him.

IV. His companions in his travels when he went into Asia; they are here named, *v.* 4. *Sopater of Berea,* it is likely, is the same with *Sosipater,* who is mentioned Rom. xvi. 21. *Timothy* is reckoned among them, for though Paul, when he departed from Ephesus (*v.* 1), left Timothy there, yet he soon followed him, and accompanied him, with others here named. Now, one would think, this was no good husbandry, to have all these worthy men accompanying Paul, but so it was ordered, 1. That they might assist him in instructing such as by his preaching were awakened and startled; wherever Paul came, the waters were stirred, and then there was need of many hands to help the cripples in. 2. That they might be trained up by him, and fitted for future service.

V. His coming to Troas. They went before, and stayed for him at Troas (*v.* 5). We should not think it hard to stay awhile for good company in a journey. Paul made the best of his way thither. Luke was now in company with him; for he says, *We sailed from Philippi* (*v.* 6), and the first time we find him in his company was here at Troas, *ch.* xvi. 11. *The days of unleavened bread* are mentioned only to describe the time. He *came to them to Troas,* by sea, *in five days,* and when he was there stayed but *seven days.* There is no remedy, but a great deal of time will unavoidably be lost in travelling to and fro, by those who go about doing good, yet it shall not be put upon the score of lost time. Paul thought it worth while to bestow *five days* in going to Troas, though it was but for an opportunity of *seven days'* stay there.

Verses 7–12

We have here an account of what passed at Troas the last of the seven days that Paul stayed there.

I. There was a solemn religious assembly of the Christians that were there. 1. *The disciples came together, v.* 7. Though they read, and meditated, and prayed, and sung psalms, apart, and thereby kept up their communion with God, yet that was not enough; they must come together to worship God in concert, and so keep up their communion with one another. There ought to be stated times for the disciples of Christ to come together; though they cannot all come together in one place, yet as many as can. 2. They *came together upon the first day of the week,* which they called *the Lord's day* (Rev. i. 10). This is here said to be the day when it was their practice to come together in all the churches. The first day of the week is to be religiously observed by all the disciples of Christ; and it is a sign between Christ and them. 3. *They were gathered together in an upper chamber* (*v.* 8); they had no capacious stately chapel, but met in a private house, in a garret. As they were few, and did not need, so they were poor, and could not build, a large meeting-place; yet they came together, in that despicable inconvenient place. It will be no excuse for our absenting ourselves from religious assemblies that the place of them is not so decent nor so commodious as we would have it to be. 4. They *came together to break bread,* that is, to celebrate the ordinance of the Lord's supper. In the breaking of the bread, not only the breaking of Christ's body for us, to be a sacrifice for our sins, is commemorated, but the breaking of Christ's body to us, to be food and a feast for our souls, is signified. It was the custom of many churches to receive the Lord's supper every Lord's day, in concert, in a solemn assembly, to testify their joint concurrence in the same faith and worship.

II. In this assembly Paul gave them a sermon, a long sermon, a farewell sermon, *v.* 7. 1. He *preached to them.* The preaching of the gospel ought to accompany the sacraments. 2. It was a farewell sermon, he being *ready to depart on the morrow.* When he was gone, they might have the same gospel preached, but not as he preached it; and therefore they must make the best use of him that they could while they had him. 3. It was a very long sermon: He *continued his speech until midnight*; for he had a great deal to say, and knew not that ever he should have another opportunity of preaching to them.

There may be occasion for ministers to preach, not only in *season, but out of season.* We know some that would have reproached Paul for this as a long-winded preacher, that tired his hearers; but they were willing to hear: he saw them so, and therefore continued his speech. We wish we had the heads of this long sermon, but we may suppose it was for substance the same with his epistles. The meeting being continued till midnight, there were candles set up, *many lights* (v. 8). This might prevent the reproach of their enemies, who said they met in the night for works of darkness.

III. *A young man* in the congregation, that slept at sermon, was killed by a fall *out of the window, but raised to life again;* his name signifies *one that had good fortune,* and he answered his name.

1. The infirmity with which he was overtaken. He presumptuously *sat in the window,* unglazed perhaps, and so exposed himself; whereas, if he could have been content to sit on the floor, he had been safe. He slept, nay, he *fell into a deep sleep when Paul was preaching,* which was a sign he did not duly attend to the things that Paul spoke of. The particular notice taken of his sleeping makes us willing to hope none of the rest slept, though it was sleeping time and after supper.

2. The calamity with which he was seized herein: *He fell down from the third loft, and was taken up dead.* Some think that the hand of Satan was in it, and that he designed it for a disturbance to this assembly and a reproach to Paul. Others think that God designed it for a warning to all people to take heed of sleeping when they are hearing the word preached. We must look upon it as a bad sign of our low esteem of the word of God. We must do what we can to prevent our being sleepy, get our hearts affected with the word we hear to such a degree as may drive sleep far enough.

3. The miraculous mercy shown him in his recovery *to life again,* v. 10. It proved an occasion of that which was a great confirmation to his preaching. *Paul fell on the dead body, and embraced it,* thereby expressing a great compassion to, and an affectionate concern for, this young man. Such tender spirits as Paul had are much affected with sad accidents of this kind, and are far from judging and censuring those that fall under them. As a sign it represented the descent of that divine power upon the dead body, for the putting of life into it again, which at the same time he inwardly, earnestly, and in faith prayed for. He assured them that he had returned to life. Various speculations this ill accident had occasioned in the congregation, but Paul puts an end to them all: *"Trouble not yourselves, for his life is in him."* He returned to his work immediately after this interruption (v. 11): *He came up again* to the meeting, they broke bread together in a love-feast, and *they talked a long while, even till break of day.* Paul did not now go on in a continued discourse, as before, but he and his friends fell into a free conversation. They knew not when they should have Paul's company again, and therefore made the best use they could of it when they had it, and reckoned a night's sleep well lost for that purpose. Before they parted *they brought the young man alive* into the congregation, and *they were not a little comforted,* v. 12. It was matter of great rejoicing among them, not only to the relations of the young man, but to the whole society.

Verses 13–16

Paul is hastening towards Jerusalem. He had called at Troas, and now he makes a sort of coasting voyage, no doubt endeavouring to make every place he came to the better for him.

I. He sent his companions by sea to Assos, but he himself was *minded to go afoot,* v. 13. He would

foot it to Assos: and, if the land-way which Paul took was the shorter way, yet it is taken notice of by the ancients as a rough way. That way Paul would take, 1. That he might call on his friends by the way. Or, 2. That he might be alone, and might have the greater freedom of converse with God and his own heart in solitude. Or, 3. That he might inure himself to hardship, and not seem to indulge his ease. We should use ourselves to deny ourselves.

II. At Assos he went on board with his friends. There they *took him in.*

III. He made the best of his way to Jerusalem. His ship passed by *Chios* (v. 15), touched at *Samos,* they tarried awhile at *Trogyllium,* the seaport next to Samos, *and the next day* they came *to Miletus,* the seaport that lay next to Ephesus; for (v. 16) he had determined not to go to Ephesus at this time, *for he hasted, if it were possible for him, to be at Jerusalem on the day of pentecost.* He had been at Jerusalem about four or five years ago (*ch.* xviii. 21, 22), and now he was going thither again to pay his continued respects to that church. He aimed to be there by the feast of pentecost because it was a time of concourse, and the feast of pentecost had been particularly made famous among the Christians by the pouring out of the Spirit. Men of business must fit themselves to set time (with submission to Providence) and strive to keep it, not suffering ourselves to be diverted from it. It is a pleasure to us to be with our friends; it diverts us, nothing more; but we must not by it be diverted from our work. When Paul has a call to Jerusalem, he will not loiter away the time in Asia, though he had more and kinder friends there.

Verses 17–35

When he came to Miletus, he went ashore, and tarried there so long as to send for the elders of Ephesus to come to him thither; for if he had gone up to Ephesus, he could never have got away from them. These Paul sent for, that he might instruct and encourage them to go on in the work to which they had laid their hands.

It is a very pathetic and practical discourse with which Paul here takes leave of these elders, and has in it much of the excellent spirit of this good man.

I. He appeals to them concerning both his life and doctrine, all the time he had been in and about Ephesus (v. 18): *"You know after what manner I have been with you."* They all knew him to be a man of a serious, gracious, heavenly spirit, that he was no designing self-seeking man. He could not have been carried on with so much evenness and constancy in his services and sufferings, but by the power of divine grace. The temper of his mind, and the tenor both of his preaching and conversation, were such as plainly proved that God was with him of a truth.—He likewise makes this reference to his own conduct as an instruction to them to follow his example: *"You know after what manner I have been with you;* in like manner be you with those that are committed to your charge when I am gone."

1. His spirit and conversation were excellent and exemplary. (1) He had conducted himself well all along, *from the very first day that he came into Asia.* He appeared from the first day they knew him to be a man that aimed not only to do well, but to do good. He was a man that was consistent with himself. Take him where you would he was the same at all seasons, he did not turn with the wind nor change with the weather, but as uniform like a die, which, throw it which way you will, lights on a square side. (2) He had made it his business to serve the Lord. He never served himself, nor made himself a servant of men, nor was he a time-server. (3) He had done his work *with all humility of mind.* He never took state upon him, nor kept people at a distance, but conversed as

freely and familiarly with the meanest, for their good, as if he had stood upon a level with them. He was willing to stoop to any service. (4) He had always been very tender, affectionate, and compassionate, among them; he had *served the Lord with many tears*. Paul was herein like his Master; often in tears. In his preaching, what he had told him before he told them again, *even weeping*, Phil. iii. 18. So near did they lie to his heart that he *wept with those that wept*, which was very endearing. (5) He had struggled with many difficulties among them. He went on in his work in the face of much opposition, *many temptations*, trials of his patience and courage. These befell him *by the lying in wait of the Jews*, who still were plotting some mischief or other against him. Those are the faithful servants of the Lord that continue to serve him in the midst of troubles and perils, that care not what enemies they make, so that they can but approve themselves to their Master, and make him their friend.

2. His preaching was likewise such as it should be, *v.* 20, 21. (1) He was a plain preacher: delivered his message so as to be understood. This is intimated in two words, *I have shown you, and have taught you.* He did not amuse them with nice speculations, nor lose them in the clouds of lofty notions and expressions; but he showed them the plain truths of the gospel, and taught them as children are taught. (2) He was a powerful preacher, which is intimated in his *testifying* to them; he preached as one upon oath. He preached the gospel, not as a hawker proclaims news in the street (it is all one to him whether it be true or false), but as a conscientious witness gives in his evidence at the bar. (3) He was a profitable preacher. He studied that which was *profitable unto them*, which had a tendency to make them wise and good, wiser and better, to reform their hearts and lives. He preached such things as *brought with them* divine light, and heat, and power to their souls. It is not enough not to preach that which is hurtful, but we must preach that which is profitable. Paul aimed to please only in order to profit. (4) He was a painstaking preacher; he preached *publicly, and from house to house.* He was neither afraid nor ashamed to preach the gospel publicly, nor did he grudge to bestow his pains privately, among a few, when there was occasion for it. Ministers should in their private visits, and as they go from house to house, discourse of those things which they have taught publicly. And, especially, they should help persons to apply the truth to themselves and their own case. (5) He was a faithful preacher. He preached everything that he thought might be profitable, and kept back nothing. He declined not preaching whatever he thought might be profitable, though it was not fashionable, nor to some acceptable. He did not keep back reproofs, when they were necessary, for fear of offending; nor did he keep back the preaching of the cross, though he knew it was to the Jews a stumbling-block and to the Greeks foolishness. (6) He was a catholic preacher. He *testified both to the Jews and also to the Greeks*. Though he was born and bred a Jew, and was trained up in their prejudices against the Gentiles, yet he did not therefore confine himself to the Jews and avoid the Gentiles; but preached as readily to them as to the Jews. And, on the other hand, though he was called to be the apostle of the Gentiles, and the Jews had an implacable enmity against him upon that score, yet he did not therefore abandon them as reprobates. Ministers must preach the gospel with impartiality; for they are ministers of Christ for the universal church. (7) He was a truly Christian evangelical preacher. He did not preach philosophical notions, nor did he preach politics, but he preached faith and repentance. These he urged upon all occasions.

[1] *Repentance towards God.* He preached repentance as God's great command (*ch.* xvii. 30), *that men should repent, and turn to God, and do works meet for repentance* (so he explains it, *ch.* xxvi. 20); and he preached it as Christ's gift, in order to the *remission of sins* (*ch.* v. 31). [2] *Faith towards our Lord Jesus Christ.* We must by repentance look towards God as our end; and by faith towards Christ as our way to God. Our repentance towards God is not sufficient, we must have a true faith in Christ as our Redeemer and Saviour. For there is no coming to God, as penitent prodigals to a Father, but in the strength of Jesus Christ as Mediator.

II. He declares his expectation of sufferings and afflictions in his present journey to Jerusalem, *v.* 22–24. *Now, behold, I go bound in the spirit to Jerusalem,* which may be understood either, (1) Of the certain foresight he had of trouble before him. He was in full expectation of trouble, and made it his daily business to prepare for it. Or, (2) Of the strong impulse he was under to go this journey: "*I go bound in the spirit*, that is, firmly resolved to proceed, and not from any humour or design of my own. I go led by the Spirit, and bound to follow him wherever he leads me." He does not know particularly the things that shall befall him at Jerusalem. God had not thought fit to reveal them to him. It is good to be kept in the dark concerning future events, that we may be always waiting on God and waiting for him. We know not the things that shall befall us nor what a day, or a night, or an hour, may bring forth; and therefore must refer ourselves to God, let him do with us as seemeth good in his eyes. Yet he does know in general that there is a storm before him; for the prophets in every city he passed through told him, by the Holy Ghost, that bonds and afflictions awaited him. He fixes a brave and heroic resolution to go on with his work. It was a melancholy peal that was rung in his ears in every city, that *bonds and afflictions did abide him*; yet by the grace of God he was enabled to go on with his work. Let us take it from his own mouth here (*v.* 24): "*None of these things move me.*" Paul is here an example,

(1) Of holy courage and resolution. He made nothing of them: *None of these things move me; I make no account of them.* He did not lay these things to heart, Christ and heaven lay there. They did not drive him off from his work; he did not tack about, and go back again, when he saw the storm rise, but went on resolutely. They did not deprive him of his comfort. In the midst of troubles he was as one unconcerned. Those that have their conversation in heaven can look down, not only upon the common troubles of this earth but upon the threatening rage and malice of hell itself, and say that none of these things moved them, as knowing that none of these things can hurt them.

(2) Of a holy contempt of life: *Neither count I my life dear to myself.* Life is sweet, and is naturally dear to us. *All that a man has will he give for his life.* Yet to an eye of faith it is comparatively despicable; it is not so dear but it can be cheerfully parted with for Christ.

(3) Of a holy concern to go through with the work of life, which should be much more our care than to secure either the outward comforts of it or the countenance of it. Two things this great and good man is in care about, and if he gain them it is no matter to him what becomes of life: [1] That he may be found faithful to the trust reposed in him, that he may *finish the ministry which he has received of the Lord Jesus*, may do the work, which he was sent into the world about, or, rather, which he was sent into the church about. And may not do his work by halves. The apostleship was a ministry both to Christ and to the souls of men; and those that were called to it

considered more the ministry of it than the dignity or dominion of it. This ministry was *received from the Lord Jesus*. He entrusted them with it, and from him they received their charge; for him they do their work, in his name, in his strength. The work of this ministry was to *testify the gospel of the grace of God*. It is a proof of God's goodwill to us, and a means of his good work in us; it shows him gracious towards us, and tends to make us gracious, and so is the gospel of the grace of God. Paul desired not to live a day longer than he might be instrumental to spread the knowledge of this gospel. [2] That he may finish well. He cares not when the period of his life comes, nor how, so that he may but *finish his course with joy*. He looks upon his life as *a course, a race*, so the word is. This intimates that we have our labours appointed us, and our limits appointed us, for we were not sent into the world to be here always, but to pass through the world, nay, to run through it, and it is soon run through. He counts upon the finishing of his course, and speaks of it as sure and near. Dying is the end of our race, when we come off either with honour or shame. He is full of care to finish it well. He thinks nothing too much to do, nor too hard to suffer, so that he may but finish well, finish with joy. We must look upon it as the business of our life to provide for a joyful death, that we may not only die safely, but die comfortably.

III. Counting upon it that this was the last time they should see him, he appeals to their consciences concerning his integrity.

1. He tells them that he was now taking his last leave of them (*v.* 25): *I know that you all, among whom I have* been conversant *preaching the kingdom of God*, shall never see my face again. Paul here speaks it with assurance, that these Ephesians should *see his face no more*; and we cannot think that he who spoke so doubtfully of that which he was not sure of (*not knowing the things that shall befall me there, v.* 22) would speak this with so much confidence unless he had had a special warrant from the Spirit to say it. He would never have said thus solemnly, *Now, behold, I know it*, if he had not known it *for certain*. We ought often to think of it, that those who now are preaching to us the kingdom of God will shortly be removed and we shall see their faces no more. Yet a little while is their light with us; it concerns us therefore to improve it while we have it, that when we shall see their faces no more on earth, yet we may hope to look them in the face with comfort in the great day.

2. He appeals to them concerning the faithful discharge of his ministry among then (*v.* 26). (1) He challenges them to prove him unfaithful: *I am pure from the blood of all men*, the blood of souls. "You cannot say but I have given warning, and therefore no man's blood can be laid at my door." If a minister has approved himself faithful, he may have this rejoicing in himself, *I am pure from the blood of all men*. (2) He therefore leaves the blood of those that perish upon their own heads, because they had fair warning given them, but they would not take it. (3) He charges these ministers to look to it that they took care and pains, as he had done. *I take you to record this day*. As sometimes the heaven and earth are appealed to, so here this day shall be a witness, this parting day.

3. He proves his own fidelity with this (*v.* 27): *For I have not shunned to declare unto you all the counsel of God*. He had preached to them nothing but the counsel of God, and had not added any inventions of his own; "it was pure gospel, and nothing else." The gospel is the counsel of God. This counsel of God it is the business of ministers to declare as it is revealed, and not otherwise. He had preached to them the whole counsel of God.

As he had preached to them the gospel pure, so he had preached it to them entire. He had not wilfully nor designedly avoided the declaring of any part of the counsel of God. He had not declined preaching upon the most difficult parts of the gospel, nor declined preaching upon the most plain and easy parts of it; he had not shunned preaching those doctrines which he knew would be provoking to the watchful enemies of Christianity, or displeasing to the careless professors of it. And thus it was that he kept himself pure from the blood of all men.

IV. He charges them as ministers to be diligent and faithful in their work.

1. He commits the care of the church at Ephesus to them, who, though doubtless they were so numerous that they could not all meet in one place, are yet called here *one flock*, because they not only agreed in one faith, but in many instances they kept up communion one with another. To these elders or presbyters the apostle here commits the government of this church, and tells them that not he, but *the Holy Ghost, had made them overseers—bishops of the flock*. "You that are presbyters are bishops of the Holy Ghost's making." Now that they begin to be fledged they must learn to fly themselves, and to act without him, for the Holy Ghost had made them overseers. The Holy Ghost in them qualified them for, and enriched them to, this great undertaking, the *Holy Ghost fell upon them, ch.* xix. 6. The Holy Ghost also directed those that called, and ordained, them to this work in answer to prayer.

2. He commanded them to mind the work to which they were called. Dignity calls for duty; if the Holy Ghost has made them *overseers of the flock*, they must be true to their trust. (1) They must take heed to themselves in the first place, must walk circumspectly. "You have many eyes upon you, some to take example by you, others to pick quarrels with you, and therefore you ought to *take heed to yourselves*." Those are not likely to be skilful or faithful keepers of the vineyards of others that do not keep their own. (2) "*Take heed to the flock*." Ministers must not only take heed to their own souls, but must have a constant regard to the souls of those who are under their charge. "*Take heed to all the flock*, that none of them wander from the fold or be seized by the beasts of prey; that none of them be missing." (3) They must feed the church of God, must lead the sheep of Christ into the green pastures, must lay meat before them, must feed them with wholesome doctrine, and must see that nothing is wanting that is necessary in order to their being nourished up to eternal life. There is need of pastors, not only to gather the church of God, but to *feed* it by building up those that are within. (4) They must watch (*v.* 31), as shepherds keep watch over their flocks by night; watch against everything that will be hurtful to the flock, and watch for everything that will be advantageous to it.

3. He gives them several good reasons why they should mind the business of their ministry.

(1) Let them consider the interest of their Master, and his concern for the flock, *v.* 28. It is *the church which he has purchased with his own blood*. "It is his own; you are but his servants to take care of it for him. Your carelessness and treachery are so much the worse if you neglect your work, for you wrong God. And, if it be the church of God, he expects you should show your love to him by feeding his sheep and lambs." He has purchased it. Therefore it ought to be dear to us, for it was dear to him, because it cost him dear, and we cannot better show it than by feeding his sheep and his lambs. This church of God is what he has purchased *with his own blood*. In consideration of this, therefore, *feed the church of God*, because it is purchased at so dear a rate. Did

Christ lay down his life to purchase it, and shall his ministers be wanting in any care and pains to feed it?

(2) Let them consider the danger that the flock was in of being made a prey to its adversaries, v. 29, 30. "You are concerned to take heed both to yourselves and to it." Here are reasons for both. [1] *Take heed to the flock*, for wolves are abroad, that seek to devour (v. 29): *I know this, that after my departure grievous wolves shall enter in among you.* Some understand it of persecutors. They thought, because, while Paul was with them, the rage of the Jews was most against him, that, when he had gone out of the country, they would be quiet: "No," says he, "*after my departure* you will find the persecuting spirit still working." Ministers must take a more than ordinary care of the flock in times of persecution. It is rather to be understood of seducers and false teachers. Probably Paul has an eye to those of the circumcision, who preached up the ceremonial law; these he calls *grievous wolves.* While Paul was at Ephesus, they kept away, for they durst not face him; but, when he was gone, then they entered in among them. [2] *Take heed to yourselves*, for some shepherds will apostatise (v. 30): "*Also of your ownselves, shall men arise speaking perverse things.* They will pervert some sayings of the gospel to make them patronize their errors. But it is to *draw away disciples after them*, to make a party for themselves." Some read it, *to draw away disciples after them*—those that are already disciples of Christ draw them from him to follow them. But, though there were some such seducers in the church of Ephesus, yet it should seem by Paul's Epistle to that church that that church was not so much infested with false teachers as some other churches were; but its peace and purity were preserved by the blessing of God on the pains and vigilance of these presbyters.

(3) Let them consider the great pains that Paul had taken in planting this church (v. 31): "*Remember that for the space of three years I ceased not to warn everyone night and day with tears.*" Paul, like a faithful watchman, had warned them, and by the warnings he gave men, he prevailed with them to embrace Christianity. He warned everyone; besides the public warnings he gave in his preaching, he applied himself to particular persons according as he saw their case called for it. He was constant in giving warning; he *warned night and day*; his time was filled up with his work. He was indefatigable in it; he *ceased not* to warn. He warned those that were righteous not to turn from their righteousness, as he had warned them when they were wicked to turn from their wickedness. He spoke to them about their souls with a great deal of affection and concern: he *warned them with tears.* As he had served the Lord, so he had served them, *with many tears*, v. 19. Thus free had he been of his pains; and why then should they be sparing of their pains in carrying it on?

V. He recommends them to divine direction and influence (v. 32): "*And now, brethren, I commend you to God.*" Paul directs them to look up to God with an eye of faith, and beseeches God to look down on them with an eye of favour.

1. See here to whom he commends them. He commends them to God, begs of God to provide for them, and encourages them to cast all their care upon him: "Whatever you want, go to God. Let this be your comfort, that you have a God to go to, a God all sufficient." From whomsoever we are separated, still we have God nigh unto us. He commends them *to the word of his grace*, by which some understand Christ: he is *the word* (John i. 1). He is here called *the word of God's grace*, because *from his fulness we receive grace for grace.* Paul commends them not only to God and to his providence, but to Christ and his grace. It comes to much the same

thing, if by the word of his grace we understand the gospel of Christ. "You will find much relief by acting faith on the providence of God, but much more by acting faith on the promises of the gospel." He commends them to the word of God's grace, not only as the foundation of their hope and the fountain of their joy, but as the rule of their walking: "*I commend you to God*, as your Master, *and to the word of his grace.* Observe the precepts of this word, and then live upon the promises of it."

2. See here what he commends them to the word of God's grace for. They had received the gospel of the grace of God, and were entrusted to preach it. Now he recommends them to that, for their edification: "*It is able to build you up.* Though you are already furnished with good gifts, there is that in it with which you need to be better acquainted and more affected." Ministers must aim at their own edification as well as at the edification of others. The most advanced Christians, while they are in this world, are capable of growing. For their glorification: *It is able to give you an inheritance among all those who are sanctified.* The word of God's grace gives it, not only as it gives the knowledge of it, but as it gives the promise of it, the promise of a God *that cannot lie*; and by the word, the Spirit of grace is given (ch. x. 44), to be the seal of the promise. Heaven is an inheritance which gives an indefeasible right to all the heirs. This inheritance is secured to all those, and those only, that are sanctified; for as those cannot be welcome guests to the holy God that are unsanctified, so really heaven would be no heaven to them; but *to all that are sanctified*, that are born again, it is as sure as almighty power and eternal truth can make it. We cannot expect to be among the glorified hereafter unless we be among the sanctified here.

VI. He recommends himself to them as an example of indifference to this world. He had recommended them to God for spiritual blessings, which are the best blessings; but what shall they do for food for their families. "As to these," Paul says, "do as I did."

1. He never aimed at worldly wealth (v. 33): "*I have coveted no man's silver, or gold, or apparel.*" There were many in Ephesus who were rich, and made a very good appearance. Paul was not ambitious to live like them. We may take it in this sense: *I never coveted to have so much silver and gold at command* as I see others have. I neither condemn them nor envy them. I can live comfortably and usefully without living great. *He knew how to want and how to be abased.* He was not greedy to receive from them, silver, or gold, or apparel; so far from being always craving that he was not so much as coveting. "Whose kindness have I coveted, or asked? Or to whom have I been burdensome?"

2. He had worked for his living, and taken a great deal of pains to get bread (v. 34): "*Yea, you yourselves know that these hands of mine have ministered to my necessities, and to those that were with me.*" Paul was sometimes reduced to necessities, and the want of the common supports of life. What an unthinking, unkind, and ungrateful world is this, that could let such a man as Paul be poor in it! He desired no more than to have his necessities supplied. When he was to earn his bread, he did it by a manual occupation. Paul had a head and a tongue that he might have got money by, but they were these hands, saith he, *that ministered to my necessities.* Paul puts these presbyters (and others in them) in mind of this, that they may not think it strange if they be thus neglected. The less encouragement they have from men, the more they shall have from God. He worked not only for himself, but for the support of those also that were with him. This was hard indeed. It had better become them to have worked for him. But so it is;

those that are willing to take the labouring oar will find those about them willing they should have it.

3. Even then, when he worked for the supply of his own necessities, yet he spared something out of what he got for the relief of others; for this he here obliges them to do (*v.* 35): "*I have shown you all things, that so labouring you ought to support the weak.*" Understand it of their helping to support the sick, and the poor, and those that could not labour, because it agrees with Paul's exhortation (Eph. iv. 28): *Let him labour, working with his hands, that he may have to give to him that needeth.* We must labour in an honest employment, not only that we may be able to live, but that we may be able to give. This might seem a hard saying, and therefore Paul backs it with a saying of our Master's. An excellent saying it is, and has something of a paradox in it: *It is more blessed to give than to receive.* It is more blessed to give to others than to receive from others; not only more blessed to be rich, and so on the giving hand, than to be poor, and so on the receiving hand (everyone will own this); but more blessed to do good with what we have, be it much or little, than to increase it and make it more. The sentiment of the children of this world is contrary to this; they are afraid of giving. They are in hope of getting. Clear gain is with them the most blessed thing that can be; but Christ tells us, *It is more blessed to give than to receive.* It makes us more like to God, who gives to all, and receives from none; and to the Lord Jesus, *who went about doing good.* It is more blessed to give our pains than to receive pay for it. It is more pleasant to do good to the grateful, but it is more honourable to do good to the ungrateful, for then we have God to be our paymaster.

Verses 36–38

After the parting sermon that Paul preached to the elders of Ephesus we have here the parting prayer and tears.

I. They parted with prayer (*v.* 36): *And, when he had thus spoken, he kneeled down, and prayed with them all.* It was a joint prayer. He not only prayed for them, but prayed with them, *prayed with them all.* Public prayers are so far from being intended to supersede our own secret prayers, that they are designed to quicken and encourage them. It was a humble reverent prayer. This was expressed by the posture they used: *He kneeled down, and prayed with them,* which is significant both of adoration and of petition, especially petition for the forgiveness of sin. It was a prayer after sermon. He had committed the care of the church at Ephesus to those elders, and now he prays that God would enable them faithfully to discharge this great trust reposed in them. He prayed for the flock *that the great Shepherd of the sheep* would take care of them all, and keep them from being a prey to the grievous wolves. Thus he taught these ministers to pray for those they preached to. It was a parting prayer. It is good for friends, when they part, to part with prayer, that by praying together just at parting they may be enabled to pray the more feelingly one for another when they are separated. Paul here followed the example of Christ, who, when he took leave of his disciples, after he had preached to them, prayed with them all, John xvii. 1.

II. They parted with tears, and most affectionate embraces, *v.* 37, 38. *They all wept sorely.* He that was so often in tears while he was with them (*v.* 19, 31), no doubt shed many at parting. But the notice is taken of their tears: *They all wept sorely;* there was not a dry eye among them. These were tears of love and mutual endearment. *They fell upon Paul's neck, and kissed him.* Those that are most living are commonly best beloved. Paul, who was a most

affectionate friend himself, had friends that were very affectionate to him. That which cut them to the heart thus was *that word which Paul spoke, that* he was certain *they should see his face no more.* When they are told that they shall see his face no more in this world, that it is a final farewell they are now giving and taking, this makes it a great mourning. When our friends are separated from us by death, this is the consideration with which we raise up our mourning, that we shall see their faces no more; but we complain not of this as those that have no hope. Though we shall see their faces no more in this world, we hope to see them again in a better world, and to be there together for ever and with the Lord.

III. They *accompanied him unto the ship* that they might have a little more of his company and conversation, and see the last of him. Loth to part bids oft farewell. But this was a comfort to both sides, that the presence of Christ both went with him and stayed with them.

CHAPTER 21

Now we are to attend him to Jerusalem, and there into lasting bonds. It is a thousand pities that such a workman should be laid aside; yet so it is, and we must not only acquiesce, but we must believe that Paul in the prison is as truly glorifying God as Paul in the pulpit was. I. A journal of Paul's voyage from Ephesus to Cæsarea, ver. 1–7. II. The struggles he had with his friends at Cæsarea, who mightily opposed his going up to Jerusalem, ver. 8–14. III. Paul's journey from Cæsarea to Jerusalem, ver. 15–17. IV. His compliance with the persuasions of the brethren there to go and purify himself with an offering in the temple, that it might appear he was no such enemy to the Mosaic rites and ceremonies as he was reported to be, ver 18–26. V. The turning of this very thing against him by the Jews, ver. 27–30. VI. The narrow escape he had of being pulled to pieces by the rabble, and the taking of him into custody by the chief captain, who permitted him to speak for himself to the people, ver. 31–40.

Verses 1–7

I. How much ado Paul had to get clear from Ephesus, intimated in the first words of the chapter, *after we had gotten from them.* Paul was loth to leave them, and they were loth to part with him, but so it must be.

II. What a prosperous voyage they had thence. *They came with a straight course to Coos—the next day to Rhodes,—thence to Patara,* a famous port, the metropolis of Lycia (*v.* 1); here they very happily *found a ship sailing over into Phenicia,* the very course they were steering, *v.* 2. Providence must be acknowledged when things happen thus opportunely. This ship that was bound for Phenicia (that is, Tyre) they took the convenience of, *went on board, and set sail.* In this voyage *they discovered Cyprus,* the island that Barnabas was of, and which he took care of, and therefore Paul did not visit it, but *we left it on the left hand* (*v.* 3), *sailed* upon the coast of *Syria, and* at length *landed at Tyre, for there the ship was to unlade her burden.*

III. The halt that Paul made at Tyre.

1. *At Tyre he found disciples.* Wherever Paul came, he enquired what disciples were there, and associated with them; for we know what is the usage with birds of a feather. When Christ was upon earth, though he went sometimes into the coast of Tyre, yet he never went thither to preach the gospel there. But, after the enlarging of the gospel commission, Christ was preached at Tyre, and had disciples there.

2. Paul, *finding those disciples at Tyre, tarried there seven days.* He stayed seven days at Troas (*ch.* xx. 6), and here so many days at Tyre, that he might be sure to spend one Lord's day with them.

3. The disciples at Tyre were endowed with such gifts that they could by the Spirit foretell the troubles Paul would meet with at Jerusalem; for *the Holy Ghost witnessed it in every city, ch.* xx. 23. God saw fit to have it much prophesied of before, that people's

faith, instead of being offended, might be confirmed. Foreseeing his troubles, out of love to him, they begged of him *that he would not go up to Jerusalem.* Therefore they said to him, *by the Spirit, that he should not go up.* It was not at all their fault to think so, but it was their mistake, for his trial would be for the glory of God and the furtherance of the gospel, and he knew it.

4. The disciples of Tyre, though they were none of Paul's converts, yet showed a very great respect to Paul. Though they had had but seven days' acquaintance with him, they all came together, *with their wives and children,* solemnly to take leave of him. We should pay respect, not only to our own ministers, but we must, as there is occasion, testify our love and respect to all the faithful ministers of Christ. It is good to train up children in a respect to good people and good ministers. No doubt, gracious notice was taken of the children of the disciples at Tyre, that honoured an apostle, as Christ accepted the hosannas of the little children. We should be good husbands of our opportunities, and make the utmost we can of them for the good of our souls. *They brought Paul on his way,* that they might have so much the more of his company and his prayers.

5. They parted with prayer, as Paul and the Ephesian elders had done, *ch.* xx. 36. *We kneeled down on the shore and prayed.* As he was much in prayer so he was mighty in prayer. Those that are going to sea should commit themselves to God by prayer, and put themselves under his protection, as those that hope, even when they leave the *terra firma,* to find firm footing for their faith in the providence of God. They kneeled down on the shore, though we may suppose it either stony or dirty, and there prayed. Where he lifted up his prayer, he bowed his knees. Mr. George Herbert says, *Kneeling never spoiled silk stockings.*

6. They parted at last (*v.* 6): *When we had taken our leave one of another, we took ship,* and *they returned home again.* Paul left his blessing behind him with those that returned home, and those that stayed sent their prayers after those that went to sea.

IV. Their arrival at Ptolemais (*v.* 7): *We came to Ptolemais.* Paul begged leave to go ashore there, *to salute the brethren.* He would not pass by them without paying his respects to them, and he *abode with them one day;* better a short stay than no visit.

Verses 8–14

We have here Paul and his company arrived at length at Caesarea, it being the place where the gospel was first preached to the Gentiles, and *the Holy Ghost fell upon them, ch.* x. 1, 44.

I. Who it was that entertained Paul and his company *at Caesarea.* He seldom had occasion to go to a public house, but, wherever he came, some friend or other took him in, and bade him welcome. "We that were of Paul's company went where he went, and came to Caesarea." Those that travel together through this world will separate at death, and then it will appear who are of Paul's company and who are not.

1. They were entertained by Philip the evangelist, whom we left at Caesarea many years ago, after he had baptized the eunuch (*ch.* viii. 40), and there we now find him again. He was originally a deacon, (*ch.* vi. 5). He was now and had long been an evangelist. He had a house at Caesarea and he bade him and them very welcome to it: *We entered into the house of Philip the evangelist, and we abode with him.*

2. This Philip *had four maiden daughters, who did prophesy, v.* 9. It intimates that they prophesied of Paul's troubles at Jerusalem, or perhaps they prophesied for his comfort and encouragement.

II. A plain and full prediction of the sufferings of Paul, by a noted prophet, *v.* 10, 11. 1. Paul and his company tarried many days at Caesarea. What cause Paul saw to tarry so long there we cannot tell; but we are sure he did not stay either there or anywhere else to be idle. 2. *Agabus the prophet came to Caesarea from Judaea;* this was he of whom we read before, who came *from Jerusalem to Antioch,* to foretell a general famine, *ch.* xi. 27, 28. See how God dispenseth his gifts variously. To Paul was given the word of wisdom and knowledge, by the Spirit, and the gifts of healing; Agabus, and to Philip's daughters, was given prophecy, by the same Spirit—the foretelling of things to come. So that that which was the most eminent gift of the Spirit under the Old Testament, the foretelling of things to come, was under the New Testament quite outshone by other gifts. It should seem as if Agabus came on purpose to Caesarea, to meet Paul with this prophetic intelligence. 3. He foretold Paul's bonds at Jerusalem: By a sign, as the prophets of old did. *Agabus took Paul's girdle,* and with it *bound* first *his own hands, and then his own feet.* That which we see usually makes a greater impression upon us than that which we only hear of. By an explication of the sign: *Thus saith the Holy Ghost, So shall the Jews at Jerusalem bind the man that owneth this girdle,* and, *shall deliver him into the hands of the Gentiles.* Paul had this express warning given him of his troubles, that he might prepare for them.

III. The great importunity which his friends used with him to dissuade him from going to Jerusalem, *v.* 12. "Not only those of that place, but we that were of Paul's company, besought him with tears that he would not go up to Jerusalem." Here appeared a commendable affection to Paul. Good men that are very active sometimes need to be dissuaded from overworking themselves, and good men that are very bold need to be dissuaded from exposing themselves too far. Yet there was a mixture of infirmity, especially in those of Paul's company, who knew he undertook this journey by divine direction. But we see in them the infirmity incident to us all; when we see trouble at a distance, we can make light of it; but when it comes near we begin to shrink, and draw back.

IV. The holy bravery with which Paul persisted in his resolution, *v.* 13.

1. He reproves them for dissuading him. Here is a quarrel of love on both sides. They love him dearly, and therefore oppose his resolution; he loves them dearly, and therefore chides them for opposing it: *What mean you to weep and to break my heart?* Their weeping about him broke his heart. It was a temptation to him, it began to weaken his resolution. "I know I am appointed to suffering, and you ought to encourage me. You, with your tears, break my heart, and discourage me. Has not our Master told us to take up our cross? And would you have me to avoid mine?" It was a trouble to him that they should so earnestly press him to that in which he could not gratify them without wronging his conscience. As he was much in tears himself, so he had a compassionate regard to the tears of his friends. But now it breaks his heart, when he is under a necessity of denying the request of his weeping friends. It was an unkind kindness thus to torment him with their dissuasions. When our friends are called out to sufferings, we shall show our love rather by comforting them than by sorrowing for them. But observe, These Christians at Caesarea, if they could have foreseen the particulars of that event, would have been better reconciled to it for their own sakes; for, when Paul was made a prisoner at Jerusalem, he was presently sent to Caesarea (*ch.* xxiii. 33), and there he continued at least *two years* (*ch.* xxiv. 27), and he was a prisoner at large, as appears (*ch.* xxiv. 23). The church at

Cæsarea had much more of Paul's company and help when he was imprisoned than they could have had if he had been at liberty. That which we oppose, as thinking it to operate much against us, may be over-ruled by the providence of God to work for us.

2. He repeats his resolution to go forward, not-withstanding: "*What mean you to weep thus? I am ready* to suffer whatever is appointed for me. I am willing to suffer, and therefore why are you unwilling that I should suffer? For my part, *I am ready.*" "I was told at first *what great things I must suffer,*" *ch.* ix. 16. "I am *prepared* for it. I can *bid it welcome.* I can, through grace, not only bear it, but rejoice in it." (1) See how far his resolution extends: I tell you, *I am ready not only to be bound, but to die at Jerusalem.* It is our wisdom to think of the worst that may befall us, and to prepare accordingly. (2) See what it is that makes him willing to suffer and die: it is *for the name of the Lord Jesus.* All that a man has will he give for his life; but life itself will Paul give for the service and honour of the name of Christ.

V. The patient acquiescence of his friends in his resolution, *v.* 14. 1. They submitted to the wisdom of a good man. "*When he would not be persuaded, we ceased* our importunity. Paul knows best his own mind, and what he has to do, and it becomes us to leave it to himself. No doubt, Paul has a good reason for his resolution, and God has gracious ends to serve in confirming him in it." It is good manners not to over-press those in their own affairs that will not be persuaded. 2. They submitted to the will of a good God: *We ceased,* saying, The will of the Lord be done. They did not resolve his resolution into his stubbornness, but into his willingness to suffer, and God's will that he should. This may refer, (1) To Paul's present firmness; he is inflexible, and in this they see the will of the Lord done. (2) To his approach-ing sufferings: "If there be no remedy the will of the Lord Jesus be done. We leave it to God, we leave it to Christ, and therefore we do, not as we will, but as he will." God is wise, and knows how to make all work for good, and therefore "welcome his holy will." Not only, "The will of the Lord must be done, and there is no remedy"; but, "Let the will of the Lord be done, for his will is his wisdom." When a trouble is come, this must allay our griefs, that the will of the Lord is done; when we see it coming, this must silence our fears, that the will of the Lord shall be done.

Verses 15–26

I. Paul's journey to Jerusalem from Cæsarea, and the company that went along with him. They *took up their carriages,* their bag and baggage, like travellers or soldiers, and were their own porters. If they could have persuaded Paul to go some other way, they would gladly have gone along with him; but if he will go to Jerusalem, they do not say, "Let him go by himself then"; but, "*Let us go and die with him.*" Thus Paul's boldness emboldened them. Certain of the disciples of Cæsarea went along with them. The less while that Paul is likely to enjoy his liberty the more industrious they are to improve every opportunity of conversation with him. They brought with them an honest old gentleman that had a house of his own at Jerusalem, in which he would gladly entertain Paul and his company, *one Mnason of Cyprus* (*v.* 16), *with whom we should lodge.* Such a great concourse of people there was to the feast that it was a hard matter to get lodgings; the public houses would be taken up by those of the better sort, and it was looked upon as a scandalous thing for those that had private houses to let their rooms out at those times. Every one then would choose his friends to be his guests, and Mnason took

Paul and his company to be his lodgers. He shall be welcome to him, whatever comes of it. This Mnason is called an *old disciple*—a disciple *from the beginning.* He had been long a Christian, and was now in years. It is an honourable thing to be an old disciple of Jesus Christ, to have been enabled by the grace of God to continue long in a course of duty, steadfast in the faith. And with these old disciples one would choose to lodge; for the multitude of their years will teach wisdom.

II. Paul's welcome at Jerusalem. 1. Many of the brethren there *received him gladly, v.* 17. The word here used concerning the welcome they gave to the apostles is used concerning the welcome of the apostles' doctrine, *ch.* ii. 41. They *gladly received his word.* We think if we had Paul among us we should gladly receive him; but it is a question whether we should or no if, having his doctrine, we do not gladly receive that. 2. They paid a visit to James and the elders of the church (*v.* 18): "*The day following, Paul went in unto James,* and took us with him." It should seem that James was now the only apostle that was resident at Jerusalem. They forecasted to have an apostle at Jerusalem because there was a great resort thither from all parts. James was now upon the spot, and all the elders were present. He *saluted them.* The proper signification of salutation is, wishing salvation to you. And such mutual salutations very well become Christians, in token of their love to each other and joint regard to God.

III. The account they had from him of his ministry among the Gentiles, and their satisfaction in it. He gave them a narrative of the success of the gospel in those countries where he had been employed: *He declared particularly what things God had wrought among the Gentiles by his ministry, v.* 19. Not what things he had wrought, but what God had wrought by his ministry. It was *not I, but the grace of God which was with me.* He declared it particularly, that the grace of God might appear the more illustrious in the circumstances of his success. Hence they took occasion to give praise to God (*v.* 20): *When they heard it, they glorified the Lord.* Paul ascribed it all to God, and to God they gave the praise of it. They gave glory to the grace of God, which was extended to the Gentiles. They did not envy him, nor were they jealous of his growing reputation, but, on the contrary, *glorified the Lord.* If God be praised, Paul is pleased.

IV. The request of James and the elders to Paul, or their advice rather, that he would gratify the believing Jews by showing some compliance with the ceremonial law, and appearing publicly in the temple to offer sacrifice. The ceremonial law, though it was by no means to be imposed upon the Gentile converts, yet it was not become unlawful as yet to those that had been bred up in the observance of it. It was dead, but not buried; dead, but not yet deadly.

1. They desired him to take notice of the great numbers there were of the Jewish converts: *Thou seest, brother, how many thousands of the Jews there are who believe.* They called him brother. Though they were conformists and he a nonconformist, yet they were brethren, and owned the relation. The number of the names at first was but one hundred and twenty, yet now many thousands. Let none therefore despise the day of small things; for, though the beginning be small, God can make the latter end greatly to increase. And this account of the success of the gospel among the Jews was, no doubt, as grateful to Paul as the account which he gave them of the conversion of the Gentiles was to them; for his heart's desire and prayer to God for the Jews was *that they might be saved.*

2. They informed him of a prevailing infirmity these believing Jews laboured under: *They are all*

zealous of the law. They believe in Christ as the true Messiah, but they know the law of Moses was of God, they have found spiritual benefit in the institutions of it, and therefore they can by no means think of parting with it. This was a great weakness to be so fond of the shadows when the substance was come. But see, The power of education and long usage, and especially of a ceremonial law. The charitable allowance that must be made in consideration of these. Their being zealous of the law was capable of a good construction, which charity would put upon it; and it was capable of a good excuse.

3. They gave him to understand that these Jews were ill-affected to him, *v.* 21. Paul himself could not get the good word of all that belonged to Christ's family: "*They are informed of thee* that thou not only dost not teach the Gentiles to observe the law, but *dost teach all the Jews who are among the Gentiles to forsake Moses, not to circumcise their children nor to walk after the customs* of our nation." It was true that Paul preached the abrogation of the law of Moses, taught them that it was impossible to be justified by it. But it was false that he taught them to forsake Moses; for the religion he preached tended not to destroy the law, but to fulfil it. But even the believing Jews, having got this notion of Paul, that he was an enemy to Moses, were much exasperated against him. The elders here present, loved and honoured him, and called him brother, but the people could hardly be induced to entertain a favourable thought of him; for it is certain the least judicious are the most censorious, the weak-headed are the hot-headed.

4. They therefore desired Paul that he would by some public act make it to appear that the charge against him was false, and that he did not teach people to break the customs of the Jewish church, for he himself retained the use of them.

(1) They conclude that something of this kind must be done: "*What is it therefore?* What must be done? The *multitude will hear that thou art come* to town. When they hear thou art come, *they must needs come together*, expecting to hear thee." Now something must be done to satisfy them that Paul does not teach the people to forsake Moses, and they think it necessary, For Paul's sake, that his reputation should be cleared. For the people's sake, that they may not continue prejudiced against so good a man. For their own sake, that since they knew it was their duty to own Paul their doing it might not be turned to their reproach.

(2) They produce a fair opportunity which Paul might take to clear himself: "*Do this that we say unto thee. We have four men*, Jews who believe, and *they have a vow on them*, a vow of Nazariteship for a certain time; their time has now expired (*v.* 23), and they are to offer their offerings according to the law, when they shave the head of their separation, a he-lamb for a burnt-offering, a ewe-lamb for a sin-offering, and a ram for a peace-offering. Now Paul having so far of late complied with the law as to take upon him the vow of a Nazarite, and to signify the expiration of it by shaving his head at Cenchrea (*ch.* xviii. 18), they desire him but to go a little further, and to join with these four in offering the sacrifices of a Nazarite: "*Purify thyself with them* according to the law; and be at charges with them, in buying sacrifices for this solemn occasion, and to join with them in the sacrifice." This, they think, will effectually stop the mouth of calumny, and everyone will be convinced that Paul did not teach the Jews to forsake Moses, but that he himself kept the law.

5. They enter a protestation that this shall be no infringement at all of the decree lately made in favour of the Gentile converts (*v.* 25): "*As touching the Gentiles* who *believe, we have written and concluded that they observe no such things;* but only that they keep themselves from *things offered to idols, and from blood, and from things strangled, and from fornication.*" They knew how jealous Paul was for the preservation of the liberty of the converted Gentiles, and therefore expressly covenant to abide by that. Thus far is their proposal.

V. Here is Paul's compliance with it. Though he would not be persuaded not to go to Jerusalem, yet, when he was there, he was presuaded to do as they there did, *v.* 26. *Then Paul took the men*, and the very *next day, purifying himself with them*, and not *with multitude nor tumult*, as he himself pleads (*ch.* xxiv. 18), he *entered into the temple*, to signify the accomplishment of the days of purification to the priests. Now it has been questioned whether James and the elders did well to give Paul this advice, and whether he did well to take it. Some have blamed this occasional conformity of Paul's, as indulging the Jews too much in their adherence to the ceremonial law, and a discouragement of those who stood fast in the liberty wherewith Christ had made them free. Had it not been better to take pains with their people to convince them of their error, and to show them that they were made free from the law? To urge him to encourage them in it by his example seems to have more in it of fleshly wisdom than of the grace of God. Others think the advice was prudent and good. It was Paul's avowed principle, *To the Jews became I as a Jew, that I might gain the Jews,* 1 Cor. ix. 20. He had circumcised Timothy to please the Jews. Those that are weak in the faith are to be borne with, when those that undermine the faith must be opposed. It is true, this compliance of Paul's sped ill to him, yet this is not a sufficient ground to go upon in condemning it: Paul might do well, and yet suffer for it. Integrity and uprightness will be more likely to preserve us than sneaking compliances. And when we consider what a great trouble it must needs be to James and the presbyters, that they had by their advice brought Paul into trouble, it should be a warning to us not to press men to oblige us by doing anything contrary to their own mind.

Verses 27–40

We have here Paul brought into a captivity which we are not likely to see the end of. When we see the beginning of a trouble, we know not either how long it will last or how it will issue.

I. We have here Paul seized.

1. He was seized in the temple, when he was there attending the days of his purifying, and the solemn services of those days, *v.* 27. It was not till *the seven days were almost ended* that he was taken notice of. In the temple, where he should have been protected, as in a sanctuary, he was most violently set upon by those who did what they could to have his blood mingled with his sacrifices. The temple did they themselves thus profane.

2. The informers against him were the Jews of Asia, not those of Jerusalem—the Jews of the dispersion, who were most exasperated against him. Those who seldom came up to worship at the temple in Jerusalem themselves, yet appeared most zealous for the temple, as if thereby they would atone for their habitual neglect of it.

3. The method they took was to raise the mob. *They stirred up all the people.* Those are fittest to be employed against Christ and Christianity that are governed least by reason and most by passion.

4. The arguments wherewith they exasperated the people against him were popular, but very false and unjust. They cried out, "*Men of Israel, help.*" The enemies of Christianity, since they could never prove

it to be an ill thing, have been always very industrious to put it into an ill name, and so run it down by outrage and outcry. What is wanting in right is made up in noise.

5. They charge upon him both bad doctrine and bad practice.

(1) They charge upon him bad doctrine. Though not here at Jerusalem, yet in other places, nay in all places, he teaches all men, everywhere; as if, because he was an itinerant, he was a ubiquitary: "He spread to the utmost of his power certain damnable and heretical positions." [1] Against the people of the Jews. He had taught that Jews and Gentiles stand on the same level before God, *and neither circumcision avails anything nor uncircumcision*; nay, he had taught against the unbelieving Jews that they were rejected (and therefore had separated from them and their synagogues). Those commonly seem most jealous for the church's name that belong to it in name only. [2] Against the law. His teaching men to believe the gospel as the end of the law, and the perfection of it, was interpreted as preaching against the law. [3] Against *this place*, the temple. Because he taught men to pray everywhere, he was reproached as an enemy to the temple. Paul had himself been active in persecuting Stephen, and putting him to death for words spoken *against this holy place*, and now the same thing is laid to his charge. He that was then made use of as the tool is now set up as the butt of Jewish rage and malice.

(2) They charge upon him bad practices. They charge it upon him that he had himself polluted it. He *has brought Gentiles also into the temple*, into the inner court of the temple, which none that were uncircumcised were admitted to come into. Paul was himself a Jew, and had right to enter into the court of the Jews. And they, seeing some with him there that joined with him in his devotions, concluded that Trophimus an Ephesian, who was a Gentile, was one of them. Did they see him there? Truly no. They had seen him with him in the city, and therefore they supposed that Paul had brought him with him into the temple, which was utterly false. Innocency is no fence against calumny and false accusation. *Evil men dig up mischief*, and go far to seek proofs of their false accusations, as they did here. By such unjust and groundless suggestions have wicked men thought to justify themselves in the most barbarous outrages. Paul thought to recommend himself to their good opinion by going into the temple, and thence they take an occasion to accuse him. If he had kept further off them, he had not been so maligned by them.

II. We have Paul in danger of being pulled in pieces by the rabble. The execution shall be of a piece with the prosecution, all unjust and irregular. Therefore, as those who neither feared God nor regarded man, they resolved to knock him on the head immediately.

1. All the city was in an uproar, *v.* 30. The people heard a hue-and-cry from the temple, and were up in arms. *All the city was moved*, when they were called to from the temple, *Men of Israel, help.* Just such a zeal the Jews here show for God's temple as the Ephesians did for Diana's temple, when Paul was informed against as an enemy to that (*ch.* xix. 29): *The whole city was full of confusion.*

2. They drew Paul out of the temple, and shut the doors. In dragging him furiously out of the temple they showed a real detestation of him as one not fit to be looked upon as a member of the Jewish nation. They pretended a veneration for the temple. They condemned Paul for drawing people from the temple, and yet, when he himself was very devoutly worshipping in the temple, they drew him out of it. The officers of the temple shut the doors. Lest the crowd should by the running in of more to them

be thrust back into the temple, and some outrage should be committed, to the profanation of that holy place.

3. They went about to kill him (*v.* 31), for they fell a beating him (*v.* 32), resolving to beat him to death. Now was Paul, like a lamb, thrown into a den of lions. No doubt, he was still of the same mind as when he said, *I am ready not only to be bound, but to die at Jerusalem.*

III. We have here Paul rescued out of the hands of his Jewish enemies by a Roman enemy. Tidings were brought of the tumult *to the chief captain of the band.* Somebody that was concerned not for Paul, but for the public peace and safety, gave this information to the colonel, who had always a jealous and watchful eye upon these tumultuous Jews, and he is the man that must be instrumental to save Paul's life, when never a friend he had was capable of doing him any service. The tribune, or chief captain, got his forces together with all possible expedition, and went to suppress the mob: *He took soldiers and centurions*, and *ran down to them.* He had them near at hand, and *he ran down unto the multitude*; for at such times delays are dangerous. The very sight of the Roman general frightened them from beating Paul. They were deterred from that by the the power of the Romans from which they ought to have been restrained by the justice of God. God often makes those to be a protection to his people who yet have no affection for his people. The shepherd makes use even of his dogs for the defence of his sheep. The governor takes him into custody. He rescued him, not out of a concern for him, but out of a concern for justice, because he ought not to be put to death without trial. He therefore takes Paul out of the hands of the mob into the hands of the law (*v.* 33): *He took him, and commanded him to be bound with two chains, for he demanded who he was, and what he had done.* This violent taking of him out of the hands of the multitude, they laid to the charge of the chief captain as his crime (*ch.* xxiv. 7): *The chief captain Lysias came with great violence, and took him out of our hands.*

IV. The provision which the chief captain made to bring Paul to speak for himself. One had almost as good enter into a struggle with the winds and the waves, as with such a mob; and yet Paul made a shift to get liberty of speech among them.

1. There was no knowing the sense of the people; for when the chief captain enquired concerning Paul *some cried one thing, and some another*, so that it was impossible for the chief captain to know their mind, when really they knew not either one another's mind or their own. Those that will hearken to the clamours of the multitude will know nothing for a certainty.

2. There was no quelling the rage and fury of the people; for when *the chief captain commanded that Paul should be carried into the castle*, the tower of Antonia, where the Roman soldiers kept garrison, near the temple, the soldiers themselves had much ado to get him safely thither, the people were so violent (*v.* 35): *When he came upon the stairs*, leading up to the castle, the soldiers were forced to take him up in their arms, and carry him, to keep him from the people, who would have pulled him limb from limb if they could. When they could not reach him with their cruel hands, *They followed, crying, Away with him, v.* 36. *Take him out of the land of the living* (so the ancients expound it), chase him out of the world.

3. Paul at length begged leave of the chief captain to speak to him (*v.* 37): *As he was to be led into the castle, he said unto the chief captain, "May I speak unto thee?"* What a humble modest question was this! Paul knew how to speak to the greatest of men,

yet he humbly begs leave to speak to this commander.

4. The chief captain tells him what notion he had of him: *Canst thou speak Greek? Art not thou that Egyptian who made an uproar?* It seems, there had lately been an insurrection somewhere in that country, headed by an Egyptian. The captain here says *that he led out into the wilderness four thousand men that were murderers*. It happened in the thirteenth year of Claudius, about three years ago. The ringleader of this rebellion had made his escape, and the chief captain concluded that Paul could not be a criminal of less figure than this Egyptian. See how good men are exposed to ill will by mistake.

5. Paul rectifies his mistake concerning him, by informing him particularly what he was. *I am a man who is a Jew; I am of Tarsus, a city of Cilicia, a citizen of no mean city.* Whether he means Tarsus or Rome is not certain; they were neither of them mean cities, and he was a freeman of both. Though the chief captain had put him under such an invidious suspicion, he did not render railing for railing, but mildly denied the charge, and owned what he was.

6. He humbly desired a permission to speak to the people. He sues for it as a favour, which he will be thankful for: *I beseech thee, suffer me to speak to the people.* The chief captain rescued him with no other design than to give him a fair hearing. He desires he may have leave immediately to defend himself; for it needed no more than to be set in a true light.

7. He obtained leave to plead his own cause, for he needed not to have counsel assigned him, when the Spirit of the Father was ready to dictate to him, Matt. x. 20. *The chief captain gave him license* (v. 40). He had that justice done him by the chief captain which he could not obtain from his countrymen the Jews. This licence being obtained the people were attentive to hear: *Paul stood on the stairs.* A sorry pulpit it was, and yet better than none. There he *beckoned with the hand unto the people*, made signs to them to be quiet, and so far he gained his point that there was made a profound silence. When the cause of Christ and his gospel is to be pleaded, there ought to be a great silence, that we may *give the more earnest heed*, and all little enough. Paul addressed himself to speak: he *spoke unto them in the Hebrew tongue*, that is, in their own vulgar tongue, to which he hereby owned not only an abiding relation, but an abiding respect.

Chapter 22

In the close of the foregoing chapter we had Paul bound, yet he had his tongue set at liberty; and so intent he is upon using that liberty of speech to the honour of Christ, that he forgets the bonds he is in, but speaks of the great things Christ had done for him with as much ease as if nothing had been done to ruffle him. I. His address to the people, and their attention to it, ver. 1, 2. II. The account he gives of himself. 1. What a bigoted Jew he had been, ver. 3–5. 2. How he was miraculously converted, ver. 6–11. 3. How he was confirmed and baptized by the ministry of Ananias, ver. 12–16. 4. How he was afterwards called to be the apostle of the Gentiles, ver. 17–21. III. The interruption given him upon this by the rabble, and the violent passion they flew into upon it, ver. 22, 23. IV. Paul's second rescue out of the hands of the rabble, and the further course which the chief captain took to find out the true reason of this mighty clamour against Paul, ver. 24, 25. V. Paul's pleading his privilege as a Roman citizen, ver. 26–29. VI. The chief captain's removing the cause into the high priest's court, ver. 30.

Verses 1, 2

I. With what an admirable composure he addresses himself to speak. There appears no fright, but his mind is sedate and composed. There appears no passion. He breaks out into no angry expressions.

II. What respectful titles he gives even to those who thus abused him: "*Men, brethren, and fathers* (v. 1). *To you, O men, I call;* men, that should hear reason, and be ruled by it; men, from whom one may expect humanity. You, *brethren* of the common people; you, *fathers* of the priests." Thus he lets them know that he was one of them. Though we must not give flattering titles to any, yet we ought to give titles of due respect to all; and those we would do good to we should endeavour not to provoke. Though he was rescued out of their hands, and was taken under the protection of the chief captain, yet he does not fall foul upon them. *Hear you my defence;* a just and reasonable request, for every man that is accused has a right to answer for himself.

III. The language he spoke in, which recommended what he said to the auditory: *He spoke in the Hebrew tongue*, that is, the vulgar language of the Jews, which, at this time, was not the pure Old Testament Hebrew, but the Syriac, a dialect of the Hebrew. It showed his continued respect to his countrymen, the Jews. By this it appears he is a Jew. What he said was the more generally understood. To speak in that language was indeed to appeal to the people. *When they heard that he spoke in the Hebrew tongue, they kept the more silence.* The chief captain was surprised to hear him speak Greek (*ch.* xxi. 37), the Jews were surprised to hear him speak Hebrew, and both therefore think the better of him. Many wise and good men are therefore slighted only because they are not known.

Verses 3–21

Paul here gives an account of himself not only to satisfy the chief captain that he was not that Egyptian he took him to be, but the Jews also that he was not that enemy to their law and temple they took him to be.

I. What his extraction and education were. 1. He was one of their own nation. "*I am verily a man who is a Jew.* I am a sincere friend to your nation, for I am one of it." 2. He was born in a creditable reputable place, *in Tarsus, a city of Cilicia*, and was by his birth a freeman of that city. This was, indeed, but a small matter to make any boast of, and yet it was needful to be mentioned at this time to those who insolently trampled upon him. 3. He had a learned and liberal education. He *was brought up* in Jerusalem, the principal seat of the Jewish learning, and *at the feet of Gamaliel*, and therefore he could not be ignorant of their law, nor be thought to slight it because he did not know it. 4. He was in his early days a very forward and eminent professor of the Jews' religion. (1) He was an intelligent professor of their religion. He minded his business at Gamaliel's feet, and was there *taught according to the perfect manner of the law of the fathers.* What departures he had made from the law were not owing to any confused or mistaken notions of it, for he understood it to a nicety. Paul had as great a value for antiquity, and tradition, as any of them had; and there was never a Jew of them all that understood his religion better than Paul did, or could better give an account of it. (2) He was an active professor of their religion: *I was zealous towards God, as you all are this day.* Many that are very well skilled in the theory of religion are willing to leave the practice of it to others, but Paul was as much a zealot as a rabbi. Here he compliments his hearers *that they all were this day zealous towards God; he bears them record* (Rom. x. 2) *that they have a zeal for God, but not according to knowledge.* Though this did by no means justify their rage, yet it enabled those that prayed, *Father, forgive them*, to plead, as Christ did, *For they know not what they do.*

II. What a fiery furious persecutor he had been in the beginning of his time, *v*. 4, 5. He mentions this to make it the more plainly to appear that the change which was wrought upon him, when he was converted to the Christian faith, was purely the effect of a divine power. Immediately before that sudden change was wrought in him he had the utmost antipathy imaginable to Christianity. He may have a further view in it to invite and encourage those people to repent, for he himself had been *a blasphemer, and a persecutor,* and yet obtained mercy. Let us view Paul's picture of himself when he was a persecutor. 1. He hated Christianity with a mortal enmity: *I persecuted this way unto the death. He breathed out slaughter against them,* ch. ix. 1. When *they were put to death, he gave his voice against them,* ch. xxvi. 10. He *persecuted it to the death,* that is, he could have been willing himself to die in his opposition to Christianity, so some understand it. He would contentedly have lost his life in defence of the laws and traditions of the fathers. 2. He did all he could to frighten people from this way, and out of it, by *binding and delivering into prison both men and women.* Now that he himself was bound, he lays a particular stress upon this part of his charge against himself, that he had bound the Christians, and carried them to prison; he likewise reflects with a special regret that he had imprisoned not only the men, but the women. 3. He was employed by the great sanhedrim, the high priest, and all the estate of the elders, in suppressing this new sect, *v.* 5. When they heard that many of the Jews at Damascus had embraced the Christian faith, they resolved to proceed against them, and could not think of a fitter person to be employed in that business than Paul. They therefore sent him, and letters by him, to the Jews at Damascus, here called *the brethren,* ordering them to be assisting to Paul in seizing those among them that had turned Christians, and bringing them up prisoners to Jerusalem, to be punished, and that they might either be compelled to retract, or be put to death for a terror to others. "Such a son," says Paul, "I was at first, just such as you now are. I know the heart of a persecutor, and therefore pity you, and pray that you may know the heart of a convert, as God soon made me to do."

III. In what manner he was converted. It was not from any natural or external causes. It was the Lord's doing, and the circumstances of the doing of it were enough to justify him in the change; and none can condemn him for it, without reflecting upon that divine energy. He relates the story of his conversion here very particularly, as we had it before (*ch.* ix), aiming to show that it was purely the act of God. 1. He was as fully bent upon persecuting the Christians just before Christ arrested him as ever. He *made his journey, and was come nigh to Damascus* (*v.* 6), and had no other thought than to execute the cruel design he was sent upon. 2. It was *a light from heaven* that first startled him, *a great light,* which *shone suddenly round about him,* and the Jews knew that God is light, and that such a light as this shining at noon, must be from God. It shone upon him in the open road, at high noon, and so strongly *that it struck him to the ground* (*v.* 7), and all *that were with him,* ch. xxvi. 14. 3. It was a *voice from heaven* that first begat in him awful thoughts of Jesus Christ. The voice called to him by name, *Saul, Saul, why persecutest thou me?* And when he asked, *Who art thou, Lord?* it was answered, *I am Jesus of Nazareth, whom thou persecutest, v.* 8. 4. Lest it should be objected, "How came this light and voice to work such a change upon him, and not upon those that journeyed with him?" he observes *that his fellow travellers saw indeed the light, and were afraid;* but, though the light made them afraid, they heard not the voice of him that spoke to Paul. Now faith comes by hearing, and therefore that change was wrought upon him that heard the words, and heard them directed to himself, which was not wrought

upon those who only saw the light. 5. He assures them that when he was thus startled he referred himself entirely to a divine guidance: "*What shall I do, Lord?* Let the same voice from heaven that has stopped me in the wrong way guide me into the right way," *v.* 10. And immediately he had directions to go to Damascus, and *there it shall be told thee all things which are appointed for thee to do.* The extraordinary ways of divine revelation, by visions, and voices, and the appearance of angels, were designed only to introduce and establish the ordinary method by the scriptures and a standing ministry. The voice here tells not Paul what he shall do, but bids him go to Damascus, and there it shall be told him. 6. As a demonstration of the greatness of that light which fastened upon him, he tells them of the immediate effect it had upon his eyesight (*v.* 11): *I could not see for the glory of that light.* It struck him blind for the present. Condemned sinners are struck blind by the power of darkness, and it is a lasting blindness, but convinced sinners are struck blind, as Paul here was, not by darkness, but by light: but it is in order to their being enlightened. Those that were with Paul were not blinded, as he was. They, having their sight, led *Paul by the hand into the city.* Paul, being a Pharisee, was proud of his spiritual eyesight. The Pharisees said, *Are we blind also?* John ix. 40. Paul was thus struck with bodily blindness to make him sensible of his spiritual blindness.

IV. How he was confirmed in the change he had made, and further directed what he should do, by Ananias.

1. The character here given of Ananias. He was not a man that was any way prejudiced against the Jewish nation or religion, but was himself *a devout man according to the law*; and thence advanced further to the faith of Christ. He had a *good report of all the Jews that dwelt at Damascus.* This was the first Christian that Paul had any friendly communication with.

2. The cure immediately wrought by him upon Paul's eyes. He *came to him* (*v.* 13); and, to assure him that he came to him from Christ, he *stood by him, and said, Brother Saul, receive thy sight.* Power went along with this word, and *the same hour* he recovered his sight, and *looked up upon him,* ready to receive from him the instructions sent by him.

3. The declaration which Ananias makes to him of the favour which the Lord Jesus designed him above any other.

(1) In the present manifestation of himself to him (*v.* 14): *The God of our fathers has chosen thee.* This powerful call is the result of a particular choice; his calling God the God of our fathers intimates that Ananias was himself a Jew by birth. *This God of our fathers has chosen thee that thou shouldst* know his will. Those whom God hath chosen he hath chosen to know his will, and to do it. *That thou shouldst see that Just One, and shouldst hear the voice of his mouth,* and so shouldst know his will immediately from himself. It was a distinguishing favour, that he should see Christ here upon earth after his ascension into heaven. Stephen saw him *standing at the right hand of God,* but Paul saw him standing at his right hand. Stephen saw him, but we do not find that he heard the voice of his mouth, as Paul did. Christ is here called *that Just One*; for he is Jesus Christ the righteous, and suffered wrongfully. Those whom God has chosen to know his will must have an eye to Christ, and must see him, and hear the voice of his mouth.

(2) In the after-manifestation of himself by him to others (*v.* 15): "*Thou shalt be his witness unto all men,* Gentiles as well as Jews, *of that thou hast seen and heard.*" Paul so particularly relating the manner

of his conversion here and *ch.* xxvi, we think that he frequently related the same narrative in his preaching for the conversion of others; he told them what God had done for his soul, to encourage them to hope that he would do something for their souls.

4. The counsel he gave him to join himself to the Lord Jesus by baptism (*v.* 16): *Arise, and be baptized.* He had in his circumcision been given up to God, but he must now by baptism be given up to God in Christ. (1) The great gospel privilege which by baptism we have sealed to us is the remission of sins: *Be baptized and wash away thy sins;* that is, "Receive the comfort of the pardon of thy sins in and through Jesus Christ, and receive power against sin," for our being washed includes our being both justified and sanctified. (2) The great gospel duty which by our baptism we are bound to is *to call on the name of the Lord, the Lord Jesus*; to acknowledge him to be our Lord and our God, and to apply to him accordingly. We must *wash away our sins, calling on the name of the Lord*; that is, we must seek for the pardon of our sins in Christ's name. (3) We must do this quickly. *Why tarriest thou?* Our covenanting with God in Christ is needful work, that must not be deferred. Why should not that be done at the present time that must be done some time, or we are undone?

V. How he was commissioned to go and preach the gospel to the Gentiles. This was the great thing for which they were so angry at him, and therefore it was requisite he should for this produce a divine warrant. This commission he did not receive presently upon his conversion, for this was *at Jerusalem*. 1. He received his orders to do it when he was at prayer, begging of God to appoint him his work and to show him the course he should steer. He was *at prayer in the temple*, which was to be called *a house of prayer for all people*; not only in which all people should pray, but in which all people should be prayed for. Paul's praying in the temple was an evidence that he had a veneration for the temple. It would be a great satisfaction to Paul afterwards, in the execution of this commission, to reflect upon it that he received it when he was at prayer. 2. He received it in a vision. He fell *into a trance* (*v.* 17). In this trance he saw Jesus Christ (*v.* 18): *I saw him saying unto me.* 3. Before Christ gave him a commission to go to the Gentiles, he told him it was to no purpose for him to think of doing any good at Jerusalem; so that they must not blame him, but themselves, if he be sent to the Gentiles. "*Make haste*," says he, "*and get thee quickly out of Jerusalem*"; thou wilt find they *will not receive thy testimony concerning me.* As God knows before who will receive the gospel, so he knows who will reject it. 4. Paul renewed his petition because they knew what he had been before his conversion, and therefore must ascribe so great a change in him to the power of almighty grace. Thus he reasoned, both with himself and with the Lord, and thought he reasoned justly (*v.* 19, 20): "*Lord*," says he, "*they know* that I was as bitter an enemy as any of them to such as believed on thee, that I *imprisoned them* and *beat them in every synagogue*. Particularly in Stephen's case; they know that when he was stoned I was standing by, *consenting to his death*, and *kept the clothes of those that stoned him*. If I appear among them, preaching the doctrine that Stephen preached and suffered for, they will no doubt receive my testimony." "No," says Christ to him, "they will not; but will be more exasperated against thee as a deserter." 5. Paul's petition for a warrant to preach the gospel at Jerusalem is overruled (*v.* 21): *Depart, for I will send thee far hence, unto the Gentiles.* God often gives gracious answers to the prayers of his people, not in the thing itself that they pray for but, in something better. It is God that appoints his

labourers both their day and their place, and it is fit they should acquiesce in his appointment, though it may cross their own inclinations. Paul hankers after Jerusalem: to be a preacher there was the summit of his ambition; but Christ designs him greater preferment. So often does Providence contrive better for us than we for ourselves. Paul shall not go to preach among the Gentiles without a commission: *I will send thee.* And, if Christ send him, his Spirit will go along with him, and give him to see the fruit of his labours. He was sent to places at a distance. Surely they would see that they had no reason to be angry with Paul for preaching among the Gentiles, for he was compelled to it, by an overruling command from heaven.

Verses 22–30

Paul was going on with his account of himself. But, whatever he designs to say, they resolve he shall say no more to them: *They gave him audience to this word.* Hitherto they had heard him with patience and some attention. But when he speaks of being sent to the Gentiles they cannot bear it. Upon the mention of this, they have no manner of patience, but forget all rules of decency and equity.

Now here we are told how furious the people were against Paul, for mentioning the Gentiles as taken into the cognizance of divine grace.

I. They interrupted him that nobody might hear a word he said. Galled consciences kick at the least touch; and those who are resolved not to be ruled by reason commonly resolve not to hear it if they can help it.

II. They clamoured against him as one that was unworthy of life. They cried out with a confused noise, "*Away with such a fellow as this from the earth, it is not fit that he should live*." Thus the men that have been the greatest blessings of their age have been represented not only as the burdens of the earth, but the plague of their generation. The ungodly Jews here say of Paul that it was not fit he should live; and therefore he must be removed, that the world may be eased of the burden of him.

III. They went stark mad against Paul, and against the chief captain (*v.* 23); as men whose reason was quite lost in passion, they cried out and howled; they *cast off their clothes*. They thus showed how ready they were to stone him; those that stoned Stephen threw off their clothes, *v.* 20. Or, they *rent their clothes*, as if he had spoken blasphemy; and *threw dust into the air*, in detestation of it. All they intended was to make the chief captain sensible how much they were enraged and exasperated at Paul.

IV. The chief captain took care for his safety, by ordering him to be brought into the castle, *v.* 24. A prison sometimes has been a protection to good men from popular rage. Paul's hour was not yet come, and therefore God raised up one that took care of him.

V. He ordered him the torture. *He ordered that he should be examined by scourging, that he might know wherefore they cried so against him.* Herein he did not proceed fairly; he should have singled out some of the complainants, and should have examined them, what they had to lay to the charge of a man that could give so good an account of himself. It was proper to ask them, but not at all proper to ask Paul, *wherefore they cried so against him.* No man is bound to accuse himself, though he be guilty, much less ought he to be compelled to accuse himself when he is innocent. Is this a fair or just occasion to scourge Paul, that a rude tumultuous mob cry out against him, but cannot tell why or wherefore?

VI. Paul pleaded his privilege as a Roman citizen, by which he was exempted from all trials and punishments of this nature (*v.* 25): *As they bound him with thongs* he made no outcry against the injustice of their proceedings against an innocent man, but let them understand the illegality of their proceedings against him as a citizen of Rome. He *said to the centurion that stood by, "Is it lawful for you to scourge a man that is a Roman, and uncondemned?"* The manner of his speaking plainly intimates what a holy security and serenity of mind this good man enjoyed, not disturbed either with anger or fear in the midst of all those indignities that were done him, and the danger he was in.

VII. The chief captain was surprised at this, and put into a fright. He had taken Paul to be a vagabond Egyptian. How many men of great worth and merit are despised because they are not known! The chief captain had centurions, under-officers, attending him, *ch.* xxi. 32. One of these reports this matter to the chief captain (*v.* 26): *Take heed what thou doest, for this man is a Roman.* They all knew what a value was put upon this privilege of the Roman citizens. The chief captain would be satisfied of the truth of this from his own mouth (*v.* 27): *"Tell me, art thou a Roman? Art thou entitled to the privileges of a Roman citizen?"* "Yes," says Paul, "*I am.*" The chief captain compares notes with him upon this matter, and it appears that the privilege Paul had as a Roman citizen was more honourable than the colonel's; for the colonel owns that his was purchased: "I am a freeman of Rome; but *with a great sum obtained I this freedom.*" Says Paul, "*I was free-born.*" He pleads it for his own preservation, for which end not only we may but we ought to use all lawful means. This put an immediate stop to Paul's trouble. Those that were appointed to examine him by scourging *departed from him* (*v.* 29). The colonel himself was afraid when he heard he was a Roman, because he had bound him in order to his being beaten. Thus many are restrained from evil practices by the fear of man who would not be restrained from them by the fear of God. See here the benefit of human laws and magistracy, and what reason we have to be thankful to God for them. By the general support of equity and fair dealing between man and man, they have served to check the rage of wicked men. Therefore this service we owe to all in authority, to pray for them, because this benefit we have reason to expect from them. The governor, the next day, brought Paul before the sanhedrim, *v.* 30. He first *loosed him from his bands,* and then summoned the chief priests and all their council to come together to take cognizance of Paul's case, for he found it to be a matter of religion. This Roman, who was a military man, kept Paul in custody, and appealed from the rabble to the general assembly. We may hope that hereby he intended Paul's safety, as thinking the chief priests and elders would do him justice, and clear him; for their court governed by rules of equity. That which he is here said to aim at is the gratifying of his own curiosity: He *would have known the certainty wherefore he was accused of the Jews.*

Chapter 23

The close of the foregoing chapter left Paul in the high priest's court, and, if his enemies act there against him with less noise, yet it is with more subtlety. I. Paul's protestation of his own integrity, and of a civil respect to the high priest, however, he had upon a sudden spoken warmly to him, and justly, ver. 1–5. II. Paul's prudent contrivance to get himself clear of them, by setting the Pharisees and Sadducees at variance one with another, ver. 6–9. III. The governor's seasonable interposal, ver. 10. IV. Christ's more comfortable appearing to him, ver. 11. V. A bloody conspiracy of some desperate Jews to kill Paul, ver. 12–15. VI. The discovery of this conspiracy to Paul, and by him to the chief captain, ver. 16–22. VII. The chief captain's care of Paul's safety; he sent him away from Jerusalem to Cæsarea, and there he safely arrived, ver. 23–35.

Verses 1–5

Perhaps he thought if he were brought before the sanhedrim at Jerusalem he should be able to deal with them to some good purpose, and yet we do not find that he works at all upon them.

I. Paul's protestation of his own integrity. Paul appeared here,

1. With a good courage. He was not at all put out of countenance upon his being brought before such an august assembly, but *he earnestly beheld the council.* When Stephen was brought before them, they thought to have faced him down, but could not, such was his holy confidence. Now that Paul was brought before them he thought to have faced them down, but could not, such was their wicked impudence.

2. With a good conscience. He said, "*Men and brethren, I have lived in all good conscience before God unto this day.*" He had always been a man inclined to religion; always put a difference between moral good and evil. He was no designing man, who cared not what he did, so he could but compass his own ends. Even when he persecuted the church of God, he thought he ought to do it. Though his conscience was misinformed, yet he acted according to the dictates of it. He seems rather to speak of the time since his conversion, since he fell under their displeasure. "*Even to this day,* I have *lived in all good conscience before God.*" He had aimed at nothing but to please God and do his duty. See here the character of an honest man. He sets God before him, and lives as in his sight. He makes conscience of what he says and does, though he may be under some mistakes. He is universally conscientious; and those that are not so are not at all truly conscientious. He continues so, and perseveres in it: "I have lived so *until this day.*" Whatever changes pass over him, he is still the same, strictly conscientious.

II. The outrage of which Ananias the high priest was guilty: he *commanded those that stood by to smite him on the mouth* (*v.* 2). The high priest was highly offended at Paul. His protestation of his integrity was provocation enough to one who was resolved to run him down. When he could charge him with no crime, he thought it was crime enough that he asserted his own innocency. In his rage he ordered him to be smitten, and to be smitten, on the mouth as having offended with his lips, and in token of his enjoining him silence. If therefore we see such indignities done to good men, nay, if they be done to us for well doing and well saying, we must not think it strange: Christ will give those the *kisses of his mouth* (Song. i, 2) who for his sake receive blows on the mouth.

III. The denunciation of the wrath of God against the high priest; *God shall smite thee, thou whited wall, v.* 3. Paul did not speak this in any sinful heat or passion, but in a holy zeal against the high priest's abuse of his power, not at all with a spirit of revenge. He gives him his due character: *Thou whited wall;* that is, thou hypocrite—a mud-wall, trash and dirt and rubbish underneath, but plastered over, or whitewashed. Those that daubed with untempered mortar failed not to daub themselves over with something that made them look not only clean, but gay. He reads him his just doom: "*God shall smite thee,* shall bring upon thee his sore judgments, especially spiritual judgments." He assigns a good reason for that doom: "For *sittest thou* pretending *to judge me after the law,* and yet *commandest me to be smitten* before any crime is proved upon me, which is *contrary to the law?*" It is against all law, human and divine, natural and positive, to hinder a man from making his defence, and to condemn him unheard. It is inexcusable in a high priest that is appointed to judge according to the law.

IV. The offence which was taken at this bold word of Paul's (*v.* 4): *Those that stood by said, Revilest thou God's high priest?* See here then, What a hard game Paul had to play, when his enemies were abusive to him, and his friends were ready to find fault with his management. These were disgusted at Paul for giving him his due.

V. The excuse that Paul made for what he had said, because he found it was a stumbling-block. Though he had taken the liberty to tell the high priest his fault, yet, when he found it gave offence, he cried, *I have done wrong.* He wished he had not done it. He excuses it with this, that he did not consider when he said it to whom he spoke (*v.* 5): *I wist not, brethren, that he was the high priest.* "I did not just then think of the dignity of his place, or else I would have spoken more respectfully to him." But, says he, I did not consider it. But the Jews acknowledged that prophets might use a liberty in speaking of rulers which others might not. He takes care that what he had said should not be drawn into a precedent, to the weakening of the obligation of that law in the least: *For it is written, Thou shalt not speak evil of the ruler of thy people.* It is for the public good that the honour of magistracy should be supported, and not suffer for the miscarriages of those who are entrusted with it. Not as if great men may not hear of their faults, and public grievances be complained of by proper persons, but there must be a particular tenderness for the honour of those in authority because the law of God requires a particular reverence to be paid to them, as God's vicegerents.

Verses 6–11

And now he finds that he who has delivered does and will deliver. He that delivered him from the tumult of the people here delivers him from that of the elders.

I. His own prudence and ingenuity contribute much to his escape. Paul's greatest honour, and that upon which he most valued himself, was that he was a Christian, and an apostle of Christ; and yet he had sometimes occasion to make use of his other honours. His being a citizen of Rome saved him from his being scourged by the chief captain, and here his being a Pharisee saved him from being condemned by the sanhedrim. It will consist very well with our willingness to suffer for Christ to use all lawful methods, both to prevent suffering and to extricate ourselves out of it. The honest policy Paul used here for his own preservation was to divide his judges, and, by incensing one part of them more against him, to engage the contrary part for him.

1. The great council was made up of Sadducees and Pharisees, and Paul perceived it (*v.* 6): *One part were Sadducees and the other Pharisees.* Now these differed very much from one another, and yet they ordinarily agreed well enough to do the business of the council together. The Pharisees were bigots, zealous for the ceremonies, but at the same time they were very orthodox in the faith of the Jewish church concerning the world of spirits, the resurrection of the dead, and the life of the world to come. The Sadducees were deists—no friends to the scripture, or divine revelation. The books of Moses they admitted as containing a good history and a good law, but had little regard to the other books of the Old Testament. They *deny the resurrection*; not only the return of the body to life, but a future state of rewards and punishments. They denied the existence of angels and spirits, and allowed of no being but matter. They thought that God himself was corporeal. When they read of angels in the Old Testament, they supposed that they were impressions on the fancies of those they were sent to, and no real

existences—that they were this, or that, or anything rather than what they were. And, as for the souls of men, they denied their existence in a state of separation from the body, and any difference between the soul of a man and of a beast. These, no doubt, pretended to be free-thinkers, but really thought as meanly as possible. It is strange how men of such wicked principles could have a place in the great sanhedrim; but many of them were of quality and estate, and they complied with the public establishment, and so got in and kept in. But how degenerate was the character of the Jewish church, when such profane men as these were among their rulers!

2. In this matter of difference between the Pharisees and Sadducees Paul openly declared himself to be on the Pharisees' side against the Sadducees (*v.* 6): He *cried out, "I am a Pharisee, the son of a Pharisee. I hope for the resurrection of the dead,* and this is it for which I am now *called in question."* Paul owns himself a Pharisee, so far as the Pharisees were in the right. Though as Pharisaism was opposed to Christianity he set himself against it, yet, as it was opposed to Saduticism, he adhered to it. We must never think the worse of any truth of God, for its being held by men otherwise corrupt. He might truly say that being persecuted, as a Christian, this was the thing he was called in question for. He might truly say he was called in question for the hope of the resurrection of the dead, as he afterwards pleaded, *ch.* xxiv. 15, and *ch.* xxvi. 6, 7.

3. This occasioned a division in the council. There arose a *dissension between the Pharisees and the Sadducees* (*v.* 7), for this word of Paul's made the Sadducees more warm and the Pharisees more cool in the prosecution of him; so that *the multitude was divided.* All the cry had been against Paul, but now there arose a great cry against one another, *v.* 9. Everything was done with clamour and noise; and in such a tumultuous manner were the great principles of their religion stickled for. Gainsayers may be convinced by fair reasoning, but never by a great cry.

4. The Pharisees hereupon (would one think it?) took Paul's part (*v.* 9): *They strove, saying, We find no evil in this man.* He had given a good account of himself, and had now declared himself orthodox in the great principles of religion, and therefore they cannot see that he has *done anything worthy of death or of bonds.* Nay, they go further, "*If a spirit or an angel hath spoken to him* we ought not to oppose him, *lest we be found fighting against God*"; as Gamaliel, who was himself a Pharisee, had argued, *ch.* v. 39. We may observe, to the honour of the gospel, that it was witnessed to even by its adversaries, and confessions, not only of its innocency, but of its excellency, were extorted sometimes by the power of truth even from those that persecuted it. Pilate found no fault in Christ though he put him to death; and the Pharisees here supposed it possible that Paul might have a commission sent him from heaven by an angel to do what he did; and yet it should seem, they after this joined with the high priest in prosecuting him, *ch.* xxiv. 1. They sinned against the knowledge which they not only had, but sometimes owned. We will hope that some of them at least did henceforward conceive a better opinion of Paul than they had had, and were favourable to him. And then it must be observed to their honour that their zeal for the traditions of the elders was so far swallowed up in a zeal for the fundamental doctrines of religion, that if he will heartily join with them against the Sadducees, and adhere to the hope of the resurrection of the dead, they will charitably hope that he walks according to the light God has given him, and are so far from persecuting him that they are ready to patronize and protect him.

II. The chief captain's care and conduct stand him in more stead; for when he has thrown this bone of contention between the Pharisees and Sadducees he is never the nearer, but is in danger of being pulled in pieces by them. The chief captain is forced to come with his soldiers and rescue him, as he had done, *ch.* xxi. 32, and *ch.* xxii. 24. Paul's danger. Between his friends and his enemies he had like to have been pulled to pieces, the one hugging him to death, the other crushing him to death. His deliverance: *The chief captain ordered his soldiers to go down* and *to take him by force from among them*, and *to bring him into the castle*.

III. Divine consolations stood him in most stead of all. The chief captain had rescued him out of the hands of cruel men, but still he had him in custody. The castle was indeed a protection to him, but withal it was a confinement; and, as it was now his preservation from so great a death, it might be his reservation for a greater. Perhaps, in the night following, Paul was full of thoughts and cares what should become of him, and how his present troubles might be turned to answer some good purpose. Then did the Lord Jesus make him a kind visit (*v.* 11): *The Lord stood by him*, came to his bedside. Whoever is against us, we need not fear if the Lord stand by us. Christ bids him have a good heart upon it: *"Be of good cheer, Paul; be not discouraged."* It is the will of Christ that his servants who are faithful should be always cheerful. Christ, by his word, satisfies him that God approved of his conduct. It is a strange argument which he makes use of to encourage him: *As thou hast testified of me in Jerusalem, so must thou bear witness also at Rome*. One would think this was but cold comfort, and yet this was designed to encourage him. He had been serving Christ as a witness for him in what he had hitherto endured. He was still going on with his work. He had not yet finished his testimony, but was only reserved for further service. Nothing disheartened Paul so much as the thought of being taken off from doing service to Christ and good to souls: *Fear not*, says Christ, *I have not done with thee*. Paul seems to have had a particular fancy to go to Rome, to preach the gospel there. Being a citizen of Rome, he longed for a journey thither, and had designed it (*ch.* xix. 21): *After I have been at Jerusalem, I must also see Rome*. Now he was ready to conclude that this had broken his measures, and he should never see Rome; but even in that Christ tells him he should be gratified.

Verses 12–35

We have here the story of a plot against the life of Paul.

I. How this plot was laid. They found they could gain nothing by popular tumult, or legal process, and therefore have recourse to the barbarous method of assassination.

1. Who they were that formed this conspiracy. They were *certain Jews, v.* 12. *And they were more than forty* that were in the design, *v.* 13.

2. When the conspiracy was formed: *When it was day*. In the night Christ appeared to Paul to protect him, and, when it was day, here were forty men appearing against him to destroy him; they were not up so soon but Christ was up before them.

3. What the conspiracy was. These men *banded together*; they engaged to stand by one another, and everyone, to his power, to be aiding and assisting to murder Paul. What a monstrous idea must these men have formed of Paul, before they could be capable of forming such a monstrous design against him! What laws of truth and justice so sacred, so strong, which malice and bigotry will not break through!

4. How firm they made it: *They bound themelves under an anathema*, imprecating the heaviest curses

upon themselves if they did not kill Paul, and so quickly *that they would not eat nor drink till they had done it*. What a complication of wickedness is here! To design to kill an innocent man that had done them no harm, was *going in the way of Cain*; yet, as if this had been a small matter, they bound themselves to it. To incline to do evil, and intend to do it, is bad; but to engage to do it is much worse. This is entering into covenant with the devil; it is leaving no room for repentance. They bound one another to it, and did all they could, not only to secure the damnation of their own souls, but of theirs whom they drew into the association. They showed a great contempt of the providence of God to do such a thing within so short a time. When we say, *Tomorrow we will do this or that*, we must add, *If the Lord will*. But with what face could they insert a proviso for the permission of God's providence when what they were about was directly against the prohibitions of God's word? What a woeful dilemma did they throw themselves upon! God certainly meets them with his curse if they do go on in it, and they desire he would if they do not! Such language of hell those speak that wish God to damn them, and the devil to take them, if they do not do so and so. They showed a most eager desire to compass this matter.

5. What method they took to bring it about. There is no getting near Paul in the castle. Therefore the chief priests and elders must desire the governor of the castle to let Paul come to them, to be further examined, and then, in his passage from the castle to the council, they would put an end to all disputes about Paul by killing him, *v.* 14, 15. They come to the principal members of the great sanhedrim. They are so confident of their approbation of this villainy, that they are not ashamed to own to them *that they have bound themselves under a great curse, that they will eat nothing till they have killed Paul*. They design to breakfast the next morning upon his blood. They doubt not but the chief priests will lend them a helping hand, and be their tools, pretending to *the chief captain that they would enquire something more perfectly concerning him*. What an ill opinion had they of their priests, when they could apply to them on such an errand as this! The priests and elders consented to it without boggling at it in the least. Instead of reproving them, they bolstered them up in it, because it was against Paul whom they hated.

II. How the plot was discovered. Providence so ordered it that it was brought to light, and brought to nought.

1. How it was discovered to Paul, *v.* 16. There was a youth that was related to Paul, *his sister's son;* and somehow or other *he heard of their lying in wait*, and *he went into the castle*, and *he told Paul* what he heard. God has many ways of bringing *to light the hidden works of darkness*.

2. How it was discovered to the chief captain. Paul had got a good interest in the officers that attended, by his peaceable deportment. He could call one of the centurions to him and he was ready to come at his call (*v.* 17); and he desired that he would introduce this young man to the chief captain, to give in an information. The centurion very readily gratified him, *v.* 18. He went himself to recommend his errand to the chief captain: *"Paul the prisoner* (this was his title now) *called me to him, and prayed me to bring this young man to thee; he has something to say to thee."* It is true charity to poor prisoners to act for them as well as to give to them. *"I was sick and in prison, and you went on an errand for me,"* will pass as well in the account as, *"I was sick and in prison, and you came unto me."* Those that have acquaintance and interest should be ready to use

them for the assistance of those that are in distress. This centurion helped to save Paul's life by this piece of civility. Those that cannot give a good gift to God's prisoners may yet speak a good word for them. The chief captain received the information with a great deal of tenderness, *v.* 19. He *took the young man by the hand* to encourage him, that he might not be put out of countenance, but might be assured of a favourable audience. The notice that is taken of this circumstance should encourage great men to make themselves easy of access. This familiarity to which this Roman tribune admitted Paul's nephew is here upon record to his honour. Let no man think he disparages himself by his humility or charity. He *went with him aside privately and asked him*, "*What is it that thou hast to tell me?*" The young man delivered his errand to the chief captain very readily (*v.* 20, 21): "*The Jews have agreed to desire thee that thou wouldst bring down Paul to-morrow into the council; but do not thou yield unto them, for there lie in wait for him of them more than forty men*, who have sworn to be the death of him, *and now are they ready looking for a promise from thee.*" The captain dismissed the young man with a charge of secrecy: *See that thou tell no man that thou hast shown these things unto me, v.* 22. Those that cannot keep counsel are not fit to be employed in business.

III. How the plot was defeated: The chief captain, finding how restless they were in their designs to do him a mischief, and how near he was to become himself accessory to it, resolved to send him away with all speed out of their reach. He seemed afraid lest, if he should detain Paul in his castle here, they would find some way or other to compass their end. Whatever came of it, he would protect Paul, because he did not deserve such treatment. What a melancholy observation is it, that the Jewish *chief priests*, when they knew of this assassination-plot, should countenance it, while a Roman *chief captain*, purely from a natural sense of justice and humanity, sets himself to baffle it.

1. He orders a considerable detachment of the Roman forces under his command *to go to Cæsarea* with all expedition, and to bring Paul thither *to Felix the governor*. I see not but the chief captain might have set Paul at liberty, and given him leave to shift for his own safety. He himself owns *that nothing was laid to his charge worthy of bonds* (*v.* 29), and he ought to have had the same tenderness for his liberty that he had for his life; but he feared that this would have incensed the Jews too much against him. *Two centurions* are employed in this business, *v.* 23, 24. They must *get ready two hundred soldiers to go to Cæsarea*; and with these *seventy horse, and two hundred spearmen* besides. (1) The chief captain designed hereby to expose the Jews, as a headstrong tumultuous people, that needed to be awed by such a train as this. He thought less would not serve to defeat their attempt. (2) God designed hereby to encourage Paul. Yet Paul did not desire such a guard because he trusted in God's all-sufficiency; it was owing, however, to the governor's own care. But he was also made considerable; thus his *bonds in Christ* were made manifest all the country over (Phil. i. 13); and so great a preacher made so great a prisoner. When his enemies hate him, and I doubt his friends neglect him, then does a Roman tribune carefully provide, [1] For his ease: *Let them provide beasts, that they set Paul on.* Had his Jewish persecutors ordered his removal to Cæsarea, they would have made him run on foot, or dragged him thither in a cart. But the chief captain treats him like a gentleman, and orders him a good horse to ride upon. [2] For his security. They have a strict charge given them *to bring him safely to Felix the governor*, who was supreme in all civil affairs among the Jews, as

this chief captain was in military affairs. The Roman historians speak much of this Felix, as a man of mean extraction, but that raised himself by his shifts to be governor of Judæa. To the judgment of such a man as this is poor Paul turned over; and yet better so than in the hands of *Ananias the high priest*!

2. The chief captain orders that he be taken away at *the third hour of the night*, three hours after sunset, that they might have the cool of the night to march in.

3. *He writes a letter to Felix the governor* of this province, by which he leaves the whole matter with Felix. This letter is here inserted *verbatim, v.* 25.

(1) The compliments he passes upon *the governor, v.* 26. He is *the most excellent governor Felix*, this title being given him of course. He sends him *greeting*.

(2) The just and fair account which he gives him of Paul's case: [1] He was one that the Jews had a pique against: *They had taken him*, and would *have killed him;* and perhaps Felix did not think much the worse of him for that, *v.* 27. [2] He had protected him because he was a Roman: "When they were about to kill him, *I came with an army and rescued him*"; which action for a citizen of Rome would recommend him to the Roman governor. [3] He could not understand the merits of his cause. He took the proper method to know: he *brought him forth into their council* (*v.* 28), to be examined there, but he found *that he was accused of questions of their law* (*v.* 29), about *the hope of the resurrection of the dead, v.* 6. The Romans allowed the nations they conquered the exercise of their own religion, and never offered to impose theirs upon them; yet, as conservators of the public peace, they would not suffer them, under colour of their religion, to abuse their neighbours. [4] Thus far he understood, that there was *nothing laid to his charge worthy of death or of bonds*.

(3) His referring Paul's case to Felix (*v.* 30): "*When it was told me that the Jews laid wait for the man*, to kill him, *I sent straightway to thee*, and let *his accusers* go after him, and *say before thee what they have against him*, for, being bred a soldier, I will never pretend to be a judge, and so *farewell.*"

4. Paul was accordingly conducted to Cæsarea; the soldiers got him safely out of Jerusalem by night, and left the conspirators to consider whether they should eat and drink or no. If they would not repent of the wickedness of their oath they were now at leisure to repent to the rashness of it. If any of them did starve themselves to death, they fell unpitied. Paul was conducted to *Antipatris*, which was about the midway to Cæsarea, *v.* 31. Thence *the two hundred foot-soldiers*, and *the two hundred spearmen returned* to their quarters in *the castle*. There needed not so strong a guard, but *the horsemen* might serve to bring him to Cæsarea, and would do it with more expedition.

5. He was delivered into the hands of Felix, *v.* 33. The officers *presented the letter*, and *Paul with it, to Felix*. Paul had never affected acquaintance or society with great men, yet Providence overrules his sufferings so as by them to give him an opportunity of witnessing to Christ before great men. *The governor* enquired *of what province* the prisoner originally was, and was told *that he was a native of Cilicia, v.* 34. He promises him a speedy trial (*v.* 35): "*I will hear thee when thine accusers have come.*" He ordered him into custody, that he should *be kept* a prisoner *in Herod's judgment-hall*.

CHAPTER 24

We left Paul a prisoner at Cæsarea. His arraignment and trial before Felix the governor. I. The appearing of the prosecutors against him, ver. 1, 2. II. The opening of the indictment against him by Tertullus, ver. 2–8. III. The corroborating of the charge by the testimony of the witnesses, ver. 9. IV. The prisoner's defence, in which, with all due deference to the governor (ver. 10), he denies the charge (ver. 11–13), owns the truth, and makes an unexceptionable profession of his faith (ver. 14–16), and gives a more particular account of what had passed from their first seizing him, ver. 17–21. V. The adjourning of the cause, ver. 22, 23. VI. The private conversation that was between the prisoner and the judge, ver. 24–26. VII. The lengthening out of Paul's imprisonment for two years, till another governor came (ver. 27).

Verses 1–9

We must suppose *that Lysias, the chief captain*, gave notice to the chief priests that they must follow him to Cæsarea, and there they would find a judge ready to hear them.

I. We have here the cause followed against Paul. Here is no time lost, for they are ready for a hearing *after five days*. He says here (*v.* 11) *that it was but twelve days since he came up to Jerusalem*, and he had *spent seven in his purifying in the temple*. Those who had been his judges do themselves appear here as his prosecutors. *Ananias* himself *the high priest*, now stands to inform against him. One would wonder, That he should thus disparage himself, and forget the dignity of his place. That he should thus discover himself and his enmity against Paul! Ananias is not ashamed to own himself a sworn enemy to Paul. *The elders* attended him, to signify their concurrence with him. The pains that evil men take in an evil matter, and their unwearied industry, should shame us out of our coldness, and our indifference in that which is good.

II. We have here the cause pleaded against Paul. The prosecutors brought *with them a certain orator named Tertullus*, a Roman, and therefore fittest to be employed in a cause before *the Roman governor*, and most likely to gain favour. The high priest, and elders, though they had their own hearts spiteful enough, did not think their own tongues sharp enough. Paul is set to the bar before Felix the governor: *He was called forth, v.* 2. Tertullus's business is, on the behalf of the prosecutors, to open the information against him. His speech is made up of flattery and falsehood; it calls evil good, and good evil.

1. One of the worst of men is here applauded as one of the best of benefactors, only because he was the judge. Felix is represented by the historians of his own nation, as well as by Josephus the Jew, as a very bad man, who allowed himself in all manner of wickedness, was a great oppressor, very cruel, and very covetous. And yet Tertullus here, in the name of the high priest and elders, compliments him, and extols him to the sky, as if he were so good a magistrate as never was the like. To engage him to gratify their malice against Paul they magnify him as the greatest blessing to their church and nation that ever came among them.

(1) They are very ready to own it (*v.* 2): "*By thee we enjoy great quietness and very worthy deeds are done to the whole nation of the Jews, by thy providence.*" To give him his due, he had been instrumental to suppress the insurrection of that Egyptian of whom the chief captain spoke (*ch.* xxi. 38). The unhappiness of great men is to have their services magnified beyond measure, and never to be faithfully told of their faults. Hereby they are hardened and encouraged in evil. The policy of bad men, by flattering princes in what they do amiss is to draw them in to do worse.

(2) They promise to retain a grateful sense of it (*v.* 3): "*We accept it always, and in all places, most noble Felix, with all thankfulness.*" And, if it had been true that he was such a governor, it had been just that they should thus accept his good offices with all thankfulness. The benefits which we enjoy by government, especially by the administration of wise and good governors, are what we ought to be thankful for both to God and man.

(3) They therefore expect his favour in this cause, *v.* 4. They pretend a great care not to intrench upon his time: We will *not be further tedious to thee; I pray thee that thou wouldest hear us of thy clemency a few words*. They were so conscious to themselves that it would soon appear to have more malice than matter in it that they found it necessary thus to insinuate themselves into his favour. Everybody knew that the high priest and the elders hated Felix; and yet, to gain their ends against Paul, they show him all this respect. Princes cannot always judge of the affections of their people by their applauses; flattery is one thing, and true loyalty is another.

2. One of the best of men is here accused as one of the worst of malefactors. After a flourish of flattery he comes to his business. This part of his discourse is as nauseous for its raillery as the former part is for its flattery. As I cannot but be sorry that a man of wit and sense should have such a saleable tongue (as one calls it), so I cannot but be angry at those dignified men that put such words into his mouth. Two things Tertullus here complains of to Felix.

(1) The peace of the nation was disturbed by Paul. They could not have baited Christ's disciples if they had not first dressed them up in the skins of wild beasts. Innocence, nay excellence and usefulness, are no fence against calumny, no, nor against the impressions of calumny upon the minds both of magistrates and multitudes. Be the representation ever so unjust, when it is enforced, as here it was, with gravity, with assurance, something will stick. They do not say, "We suspect him to be a dangerous man," but, as if the thing were past dispute, "*We have found him to be so*", as if he were a traitor and rebel already convicted. Paul was a useful man, and a great blessing to his country, and yet he is here called *a pestilent fellow* (*v.* 5): "*We have found him the plague of the nation, a walking pestilence.*" They would have it thought that he had done more mischief in his time than a plague could do,—that the mischief he did was spreading and infectious,—that it was of as fatal consequence as the plague is,—that it was as much to be dreaded and guarded against as a plague is. Paul was a peace-maker; he lived peaceably and quietly himself, and taught others to do so too, and yet is here represented as *a mover of sedition among all the Jews throughout all the world*. The Jews were disaffected to the Roman government. This Felix knew. Now they would fain make him believe that this Paul was the man that made them so. They moved sedition in all places where he came, and then cast the blame unjustly upon him. Paul was a man of catholic charity, who made himself the servant of all for their good; and yet he is here charged as being a *ringleader of the sect of the Nazarenes*. Now it was true that Paul was an active leading man in propagating Christianity. But, *First*, It was utterly false that this was a sect. True Christianity establishes that which is of common concern to all mankind, publishes goodwill to men, and therefore cannot be thought to take its rise from such narrow opinions as sects owe their origin to. True Christianity has a direct tendency to the uniting of the children of men, and, as far as it obtains its just influence upon the minds of men, will make them peaceable and loving, and therefore is far from being a sect. True Christianity aims at no worldly benefit or advantage, and therefore must by no means be called a sect. Those that espouse a sect aim at wealth and honour; but the professors of Christianity expose themselves thereby to the loss of all that is dear to them in this world. *Secondly*, It is invidiously called *the sect of the Nazarenes*, by which Christ was represented as of Nazareth, whence no good thing was expected to arise; whereas he was of

Bethlehem, where the Messiah was to be born. *Thirdly,* It was false that Paul was the author or standard-bearer of this sect; for he did not draw people to himself, but to Christ. Paul had a veneration for the temple, and had lately himself with reverence attended the temple-service; and yet it is here charged upon him that he went about to *profane the temple, v.* 6.

(2) The course of justice against Paul was obstructed by the chief captain. They pleaded that they *took him, and would have judged him according to their law.* This was false; they did not go about to judge him according to their law, but went about to *beat him to death* or to *pull him to pieces,* to throw him into the hands of ruffians that lay in wait to destroy him. It is easy for men, when they know what they should have done, to say, this they would have done, when they meant something else. They reflected upon the chief captain. *The chief captain Lysias came upon us and with great violence took him out of our hands, v.* 7. See how persecutors are enraged at their disappointments, which they ought to be thankful for. These cruel men justify themselves, and reckon him their enemy who kept them from shedding blood with their own hands. They referred the matter to Felix and his judgment, the chief captain having obliged them to it (*v.* 8): "He *commanded his accusers to come to thee,* that thou mightest hear the charge. He has left it to thee to examine him, and try what thou canst get out of him."

III. The assent of the Jews to this charge (*v.* 9): *They confirmed it, saying that those things were so.* Some think this expresses the proof of their charge by witnesses upon oath. It rather seems to intimate the approbation which the high priest and the elders gave to what Tertullus said. Those that have not the wit and parts to do mischief with that some others have, yet make themselves guilty of the mischiefs others do, by assenting to that which others do. Many that have not learning enough to plead for Baal yet have wickedness enough to vote for Baal.

Verses 10–21

We have here Paul's defence of himself, and there appears in it an accomplishment of Christ's promise to his followers that when they were before governors and kings, for his sake, it should be *given them in that same hour what they should speak.* Though Tertullus had said a great many provoking things, yet Paul did not interrupt him, but let him go on to the end of his speech. And when he had done he waited for a permission from the judge to speak in his turn, and had it. The *governor beckoned to him to speak, v.* 10. He made no reflections at all upon Tertullus, and levelled his defence against those that employed him.

I. He addressed himself very respectfully to the governor. Here are no such flattering compliments as Tertullus soothed him up with, but a profession that he *answered for himself cheerfully before him,* looking upon him as one that would be fair and impartial. It was likewise the language of one that was conscious to himself of his own integrity. He did not stand trembling at the bar; he was very cheerful when he had one to be his judge that was not a party, but an indifferent person. Nay, when he considers who his judge is, *I the more cheerfully answer for myself,* because *I know thou hast been many years a judge to this nation;* and this was very true. He could say of his own knowledge that there had not formerly been any complaints against Paul. He never had Paul brought before him till now; and therefore he was not so dangerous a criminal as he was represented to be. He was well acquainted with the Jewish nation. He knew what furious zealots they were against all that did not comply

with them, and therefore would make allowances for that. Though he did not know him, he knew his prosecutors, and by this might guess what manner of man he was.

II. He denies the facts that he was charged with, upon which their character of him was grounded. *Moving sedition,* and *profaning the temple,* were the crimes for which he stood indicted, crimes which they knew the Roman governors were not accustomed to enquire into. But Paul desires that though he would not enquire into the crimes he would protect one that was unjustly charged with them. Now he would have him to understand.

1. That he came up to Jerusalem on purpose to worship God in peace and holiness. He came to keep up his communion with the Jews, not to put any affront upon them.

2. That it was but twelve days since he came up to Jerusalem, and he had been six days a prisoner; and it could not be supposed that in so short a time he could do the mischief they charged upon him.

3. That he had demeaned himself at Jerusalem very quietly and peaceably. If it had been true that he was a *mover of sedition among all the Jews,* surely he would have been industrious to make a party at Jerusalem: but he did not do so. He was in the temple, attending the public service there. He was in the synagogues where the law was read and opened. He went about in the city among his relations and friends. They could not charge him with offering anything either against the faith or against the peace of the Jewish church. (1) He had nothing in him of a contradicting spirit, as the movers of sedition have. They never found him *disputing with any man.* He was ready, if asked, to give a reason of his own hope, and to give instruction to others; but he never picked a quarrel with any man about his religion. (2) He had nothing in him of a turbulent spirit: "They never found me *raising up the people.*" He behaved as became a Christian with love and quietness, and due subjection to lawful authority. Nor did he ever mention or think of such a thing as taking up arms for the propagating of the gospel.

4. That as to what they had charged him with, of moving sedition in other countries, he was wholly innocent, and they could not make good the charge (*v.* 13): *Neither can they prove the things whereof they now accuse me.* He maintains his own innocency. He was no enemy to the public peace. He bemoans his own calamity, that he was accused of those things which could not be proved against him. And it has often been the lot of very worthy good men to be thus injured, to have things laid to their charge which they abhor the thought of. He shows the iniquity of his prosecutors, who said that which they knew they could not prove, and thereby did him wrong, and did the judge wrong too, in imposing upon him. He appeals to the equity of his judge. The judge must give sentence *according to that which is not only alleged but proved.*

III. He gives a fair and just account of himself, which does intimate what was the true reason of their prosecuting him.

1. He acknowledged himself to be one whom they looked upon as a heretic. The chief captain had observed, and the governor now cannot but observe, an uncommon violence and fury in his prosecutors. Guessing at the crime by the cry, he must needs have been a very bad man. Now Paul here unriddles the matter: *In the way which they call heresy*—or a *sect, so worship I the God of my fathers.* It is no new thing for the right way of worshipping God to be called heresy. Let us therefore never be driven off from any good way by its being put into an ill name.

2. He vindicates himself from this imputation. They call Paul a heretic, but he is not so.

(1) He *worships the God of his fathers*, and therefore is right in the object of his worship. He worships the God of Abraham, Isaac, and Jacob, the God who took them into covenant with himself. Paul adheres to that covenant, and sets up no other in opposition to it. *I worship* the same God that all my fathers worshipped. His religion gloried in its antiquity, and in an uninterrupted succession of its professors. It is very comfortable in our worshipping God to have an eye to him as the God of our fathers. He approved himself theirs, and therefore, if we serve him as they did, he will be ours.

(2) He *believed all things which are written in the law and the prophets*, and therefore is right in the rule of his worship. He received the scriptures entire, and he receives them pure. He sets not up any other rule of faith or practice but the scriptures. Divine revelation, as it is in the scripture, is that which he resolves to live and die by, and therefore he is not a heretic.

(3) He has his eye upon a future state, and therefore is right in the end of his worship. Those that turn aside to heresy have a regard to this world, but Paul aims to make heaven of his religion, and neither more nor less (*v.* 15): "*I have hope towards God; my* hope is towards God and not towards the world. I depend upon God and upon his power, that *there shall be a resurrection of the dead*, of all, both *the just and unjust*." There shall be a resurrection of the dead, of all men from the beginning to the end of time. We have not only another life to live when our present life is at an end, but there is to be another world. It shall be a resurrection *both of the just and of the unjust*, of those that did well, and to them our Saviour has told us that it will be a *resurrection of life*; and of those that did evil, he has said to them it will be a resurrection of condemnation. This implies that it will be a resurrection to a final judgment. The just shall rise by virtue of their union with Christ as their head; the unjust shall rise by virtue of Christ's dominion over them as their Judge. God is to be depended upon for the resurrection of the dead: I have *hope towards God* that there shall be a resurrection; it shall be effected by the almighty power of God. The resurrection of the dead is a fundamental article of our creed, as it was also of that of the Jewish church. It is what *they themselves also allow*, but it is more clearly revealed by the gospel. In all our religion we ought to serve God with a confidence in him *that there will be a resurrection of the dead*, expecting our recompence in that.

(4) His conversation is of a piece with his devotion (*v.* 16): *And herein do I exercise myself, to have always a conscience void of offence towards God and towards men*. This protestation of Paul's is to the same purport with that which he made before the high priest (*ch.* xxiii. 1): *I have lived in all good conscience*. [1] What was Paul's aim and desire: To *have a conscience void of offence*. Either, *First*, "A conscience not offending; not informing me wrong, nor in anything misleading me." Or, *Secondly*, A conscience, not offended. "This is what I am ambitious of, to keep upon good terms with my own conscience. I am as careful not to offend my conscience as I am not to offend a friend with whom I daily converse." [2] What was his care and endeavour, in pursuance of this: "*I exercise myself*. I make it my constant business" (those that did so were called *ascetics*, from the word here used), "that I may keep peace with my own conscience." [3] The extent of this care: *First*, To all times: *To have always a conscience void of offence*. Paul was conscious to himself that he *had not yet attained perfection*, and the evil that he would not do, yet he did. Sins of infirmity are uneasy to conscience, but they do not wound it as

presumptuous sins do; and, though offence may be given to conscience, yet care must be taken that it be not an abiding offence. This however we must always exercise ourselves in. *Secondly*, To all things: *Both towards God, and towards man*. His conscientious care extended itself to the whole of his duty, and he was afraid of breaking the law of love either to God or his neighbour. We must be very cautious that we do not think, or speak, or do anything amiss, either against God or man. [4] The inducement to it: *Herein, for this cause;* so it may be read. "Because I look for the resurrection of the dead and the life of the world to come, therefore I thus exercise myself."

IV. Having made confession of his faith, he gives a plain account of his case, and of the wrong done him by his persecutors. He challenges them to prove him guilty.

1. In the temple. Here they fell furiously upon him as an enemy to their nation and the temple, *ch.* xxi. 28. (1) It was very hard to accuse him as an *enemy to their nation*, when he came to *bring alms to his nation*, for the relief of the poor at Jerusalem. He had no malice to that people and was ready to do them all good offices. (2) It was very hard to accuse him of having profaned the temple when he brought offerings and was himself at charges therein (*ch.* xxi. 24), and was found *purifying himself in the temple*, according to the law (*v.* 18), *neither with multitude nor with tumult*. They were Jews from Asia, his enemies; they had no pretence to make a tumult and raise a multitude against him, for he had neither for him. He challenges them to prove it (*v.* 19): "Those Jews of Asia ought to have been *here before thee*, that they might have been examined, whether they had aught against me."

2. In the council. "Let *these same that are here* say whether they have *found any evil doing in me when I stood before the council* (*v.* 20). When I was there all I said was, *Touching the resurrection of the dead I am called in question by you this day* (*v.* 21), which gave no offence to anyone but the Sadducees. I stuck to that which is the faith of the whole Jewish church, excepting those whom they themselves call heretics."

Verses 22–27

I. Felix adjourned the cause (*v.* 22): He *had a more perfect knowledge of that way* than the high priest and the elders thought he had. He had got a notion of Christianity, that it was not such an evil thing as it was represented. Therefore he put off the prosecutors with an excuse: "*When the chief captain shall come down I will know the uttermost of your matter*, I shall know the truth. Either Paul deserves to be punished for raising the tumult, or you do for doing it yourselves. I will hear what he says, and determine accordingly between you." It was a disappointment to the high priest and the elders that Paul was not condemned, or remitted to their judgment. But thus sometimes God restrains the wrath of his people's enemies by the agency, not of their friends, but of such as are strangers to them. It was an injury to Paul that he was not released. But he was a judge that neither feared God nor regarded man, and what good could be expected from him?

II. He detained the prisoner in custody. Felix thought a man of such a public character as Paul was had many friends, and he might have an opportunity of obliging them, or making a hand of them. He continued him a prisoner, commanded a centurion to keep him, *v.* 23. Yet he took care he should be *a prisoner at large*, his keeper must let him have liberty, make his confinement as easy to him as possible. The high priest and the elders grudged him his life, but Felix generously allowed him a sort of liberty. He also gave orders that none of his friends should be hindered from coming to him; and a man's prison is as it were his own house if he has but his friends about him.

III. He had frequent conversation with him afterwards in private, v. 24, 25.

1. With what design *Felix sent for Paul.* He had a mind to have some talk with him *concerning the faith in Christ.* Felix had a mind to talk with Paul more freely than he could in open court *concerning the faith of Christ;* and this only to satisfy his curiosity, or rather the curiosity of *his wife Drusilla, who was a Jewess,* daughter of Herod Agrippa. Being educated in the Jewish religion, she was more inquisitive concerning the Christian religion. But it was no great matter what religion she was of; for, whatever it was, she was a reproach and scandal to it—a Jewess, but an adulteress; and was noted for an impudent woman. Many are fond of new notions and speculations in religion who yet hate to come under the power and influence of religion.

2. What the account was which Paul gave him of the Christian religion. He expected to be amused with a mystical divinity, but he is alarmed with a practical divinity. Paul, being asked *concerning the Christ, reasoned* concerning *righteousness, temperance, and judgment to come.* He discoursed with clearness and warmth *of righteousness, temperance, and judgment to come.* Faith in Christ is designed to enforce upon the children of men the great laws of justice and temperance. Justice and temperance were celebrated virtues among the heathen moralists; if the doctrine Paul preaches will but free him from an obligation to these, he will readily embrace it. "It is so far from doing so that it strengthens the obligations of those sacred laws." *Paul reasoned of righteousness and temperance,* to convince Felix of his unrighteousness and intemperance, that, seeing the odiousness of them, he might enquire concerning the faith of Christ, with a resolution to embrace it. By the doctrine of Christ is discovered to us the judgment to come. Men have their day now, Felix hath his; but God's day is coming. From this account of the heads of Paul's discourse we may gather, [1] Paul in his preaching had no respect to persons, for the word of God has not. [2] Paul in his preaching aimed at the consciences of men and led them to a sight of their sins. [3] Paul preferred the serving of Christ, and the saving of souls, before his own safety. [4] Paul was willing to run hazards, in his work, even where there was little probability of doing good. Felix and Drusilla were such hardened sinners that it was not at all likely they should be brought to repentance by Paul's preaching, and yet Paul deals with them as one that did not despair of them. Let the watchman give fair warning, and then they have delivered their own souls, though they should not prevail to deliver the souls they watch for.

3. What impressions Paul's discourse made upon this great but wicked man: *Felix trembled, being put into a fright.* Paul never trembled before him, but he was made to tremble before Paul. We do not find that Drusilla trembled, though she was equally guilty. See here, The power of the word of God. It is searching, it is startling, it can strike a terror into the heart of the most proud and daring sinner. The workings of natural conscience; when it is startled and awakened, it fills the soul with horror and amazement. A prospect of the judgment to come is enough to make the stoutest heart to tremble.

4. How Felix struggled to get clear of these impressions. He did by them as he did by Paul's prosecutors (v. 25), he *deferred them;* he said, *Go thy way for this time, when I have a convenient season I will call for thee.* He trembled and that was all. Many are startled by the word of God who are not effectually changed by it. Many are in fear of the consequences of sin, and yet continue in love and league with sin. He did not fight against his convictions. He artfully shifted off his convictions by putting off the prosecution of them to another time. Like a sorry debtor, he begs a day; Paul has spent himself, and has tired him and his lady, and therefore, "*Go thy way for this time, when I have a convenient season I will call for thee.*" Many lose all the benefit of their convictions for want of striking while the iron is hot. By dropping his convictions now, he lost them for ever, and himself with them. In the affairs of our souls, delays are dangerous. The matter is adjourned to some more convenient season, and then convictions cool and wear off. Felix put off this matter to a more convenient season, but we do not find that this more convenient season ever came. The present season is, without doubt, the most convenient season.

IV. He detained him a prisoner, and left him so, when two years after he was removed from the government, v. 26, 27. He was convinced in his conscience that Paul had done *nothing worthy of death or of bonds,* and yet had not the honesty to release him. Here we are told what principles he was governed by herein. 1. The love of money. He would not release Paul because he hoped that at length his friends would make a purse to purchase his liberty. He cannot find in his heart to do his duty as a judge, unless he can get money by it: *He hoped that money would have been given him of Paul.* In hopes of this, he detains him a prisoner, and *sends for him the oftener, and communes with him.* He sends for him to feel his pulse, and gives him an opportunity to ask what he would take to release him. And now we see what became of his promise both to Paul and to himself, that he would hear more of Christ at some other convenient season. All his business now is to get money by Paul. Paul was but a poor man, but Felix knew there were those who wished well to him who were able to assist him. Though Paul is to be commended that he would not offer money to Felix, yet I know not whether his friends are to be commended in not doing it for him. I ought not to bribe a man to do an unjust thing, but, if he will not do me justice without a fee, it is but doing myself justice to give it to him; and, if they might do it, it was a shame they did not do it. The Christians here at Cæsarea had parted with their tears to prevent his going to the prison (*ch.* xxi. 13), and could they not find in their hearts to part with their money to help him out? However, this will not excuse Felix. The judge that will not do right without a bribe will no doubt do wrong for a bribe. 2. Men-pleasing. Felix was recalled from his government about *two years after this,* and Porcius Festus was put in his place. He *left Paul bound,* and the reason here given is because he was *willing to do the Jews a pleasure.* He would continue him a prisoner rather than offend them; and he did it in hope thereby to atone for the many offences he had done against them. Thus those who do some base things are tempted to do more to screen themselves. But, when he had done it, it seems he did not gain his point. The Jews, notwithstanding this, accused him to the emperor. Those that aim to please God by doing good will have what they aim at; but so will not those that seek to please men by doing evil.

CHAPTER 25

We have here much the same management of Paul's case: cognizance is here taken of it, I. By Festus the governor, ver. 1–3. The hearing of it is appointed to be, not at Jerusalem, as the Jews desired, but at Cæsarea, ver. 4–6. The Jews appear against Paul (*ver. 7*), but he stands upon his own innocency (ver. 8); and to avoid the removing of the cause at Jerusalem, he at length appeals to Cæsar, ver. 9–12. II. By king Agrippa (ver. 13–21), and

Agrippa desires he might have the hearing of it himself, ver. 22. Paul brought to the bar (ver. 23), and Festus opens the cause (ver. 24–27).

Verses 1–12

We commonly say, "New lords, new laws, new customs"; but here was a new governor, and yet Paul had the same treatment from him. Festus, like Felix, does not release him.

I. The pressing application which the high priest and other Jews used with the governor to abandon Paul. See how speedy they were in their applications to Festus. As soon as ever he *had come into the province*, within *three days he went up to Jerusalem*. The priests were upon him to proceed against Paul. He stayed *three days at Cæsarea*, where Paul was a prisoner. As soon as ever he comes up to Jerusalem the priests are in all haste with him against Paul. See how spiteful they were in their application. They *informed the governor against Paul* (v. 2) before he was brought upon a fair trial, that so they might make him a party who was to be the judge. But this artifice, though base enough, they could not confide in. They form another project much more base, and that is to assassinate Paul before he came upon his trial. See how specious the pretence was. Now that *the governor was himself at Jerusalem they desired he would send for Paul thither*, and try him there. He was charged with having profaned the temple at Jerusalem, and it is usual for criminals to be tried in the court where the fact was committed; but that which they designed was to way-lay him and to murder him upon the road. *They desired favour against Paul*. The business of prosecutors is to demand justice against one that they suppose to be a criminal. To desire favour against a prisoner, and from the judge, too, who ought to be of counsel for them, is a very impudent thing. The favour ought to be for the prisoner, but here they desire it against him.

II. The governor's resolution that Paul shall take his trial at Cæsarea, v. 4, 5. He gave orders *that Paul should be kept at Cæsarea*. Whatever was his reason for refusing it, God made use of it as a means of preserving Paul out of the hands of his enemies. God does not bring it to light, yet he finds another way to bring it to nought, by inclining the heart of the governor, not to remove Paul to Jerusalem. God is not tied to one method, in working out salvation for his people. Yet he will do them the justice to hear what they have to say against Paul, if they will go down to Cæsarea: *"Let those among you who are able go down with me, and accuse this man.* Let them go and give in their evidence." Festus will not take it for granted that there is wickedness in him, till it is proved upon him. If he be guilty, it lies upon them to prove him so.

III. Paul's trial before Festus. Festus stayed *at Jerusalem about ten days*, and then *went down to Cæsarea*. Since they are so eager in the prosecution, he is willing this cause should be first called; he will despatch it *the next day*. 1. The court set, and the prisoner called to the bar. Festus *sat in the judgment-seat*, and he *commanded Paul to be brought*, v. 6. 2. The prosecutors exhibiting their charges against the prisoner (v. 7): *The Jews stood round about*, which intimates that they were many. They *stood round about*, if possible, to frighten the judge into a compliance with their malicious design, or, at least, to frighten the prisoner; but in vain: he had too just and strong an assurance to be frightened by them. *When they stood round about him, they brought many and grievous accusations against Paul*, so it should be read. They represented him to the court as black and odious as their wit and malice could contrive; but when they came to the evidence, there they failed: *they could not prove* what they alleged against

him, for it was all false. It is no new thing for the most excellent ones of the earth to have all manner of evil said against them falsely, even *before the judgment-seat*. 3. The prisoner's insisting upon his own vindication, v. 8. He insisted upon his general plea, Not guilty: *Neither against the law of the Jews, nor against the temple, nor yet against Cæsar, have I offended anything at all*. He had not violated the law of the Jews. *He established the law*. Preaching Christ, *the end of the law*, was no offence against the law. He had not profaned the temple. He had not offended against Cæsar, nor his government. By this it appears that they had charged him with some instances of disaffection to the present higher powers, which obliged him to purge himself as to that matter.

IV. Paul's appeal to the emperor. This gave the cause a new turn. God puts it into his heart to do it, for the bringing about of that which he had said to him, *that he must bear witness to Christ at Rome*. 1. The proposal which Festus made to Paul to go and take his trial at Jerusalem, v. 9. *Festus was willing to do the Jews a pleasure*, inclined to gratify the prosecutors rather than the prisoner, and asked him whether he would be willing to go up to Jerusalem and clear himself there. He would not offer to turn him over to the high priest and the sanhedrim, but, *Wilt thou go thither, and be judged of these things before me?* The president might have ordered him thither, but he would not do it without his own consent.

2. Paul's refusal to consent to it, and his reasons for it. (1) As a citizen of Rome, it was most proper for him to be tried in that which was properly his court, which sat at Cæsarea: *I stand at Cæsar's judgment-seat, where I ought to be judged*. The court being held in Cæsar's name, and by his authority and commission, before one that was delegated by him, it might well he said to be his judgment seat. Paul's owning that he ought to be judged at Cæsar's judgment seat plainly proves that Christ's ministers are not exempted from the jurisdiction of the civil powers, and, if they be guilty, of a real crime, to submit to their censure; if innocent, yet to submit to their enquiry. (2) As a member of the Jewish nation, he had done nothing to make himself obnoxious to them: *To the Jews have I done no wrong, as thou very well knowest*. It very well becomes those that are innocent to plead their innocency, and to insist upon it. (3) He was willing to abide by the rules of the law, and to let that take its course, v. 11. If he be guilty of any capital crime that deserves death, he will neither flee from justice nor fight with it: "I refuse not to die." If he be innocent, as he protests he is, "*If there be none of these things whereof these accuse me, no man may deliver me unto them*, no, not the governor himself; for it is his business as much to protect the innocent as to punish the guilty"; and he claims his protection.

3. His appealing to court. Since he is continually in danger of the Jews, and one attempt made after another to get him into their hands, since he cannot have justice done him in any other way: "*I appeal unto Cæsar*. Rather than be delivered to the Jews let me be delivered to Nero." It is a hard case that a son of Abraham must be forced to appeal to a Nero, from those who call themselves the seed of Abraham, and shall be safer in Rome than in Jerusalem.

V. The judgment given upon the whole matter. His enemies hoped the cause would be ended in his death; his friends hoped it would be ended in his deliverance; they are both disappointed, the thing is left as it was. It is an instance of the slow steps which Providence sometimes takes, by which we are often made ashamed both of our hopes and of our fears, and are kept still waiting on God. The president takes advice upon the matter: *He conferred with the council*—not with the council of the Jews, but with his own counsellors. He determines to send him to Rome. A Roman citizen might appeal at any time to a superior court, even to the supreme. *Hast thou appealed unto Cæsar? Unto Cæsar thou shalt go.* In our judgment before God those that by justifying themselves appeal to the law, to the law they shall go, and it will condemn them; but those that by repentance and faith appeal to the gospel, to the gospel they shall go, and it will save them.

Verses 13–27

We have here the preparation that was made for another hearing of Paul before king Agrippa, only to gratify his curiosity.

I. The friendly visit which king Agrippa made to Festus, now upon his coming into the government in that province (*v.* 13): *After certain days, king Agrippa came to Cæsarea.*

1. Who the visitants were. (1) King Agrippa, the son of that Herod (surnamed *Agrippa*) who killed James the apostle, and was himself eaten of worms; and great grandson of Herod the Great, under whom Christ was born. (2) Bernice came with him. She was his own sister, the widow of his uncle Herod, after whose death she lived with this brother of hers; after she was a second time married to Polemon, king of Cilicia, she got to be divorced from him, and returned to her brother king Agrippa. Tacitus and Suetonius speak of a criminal intimacy afterwards between her and Titus Vespasian. Drusilla, the wife of Felix, was another sister. Such lewd people were the great people generally in those times!

2. What the design of this visit was: they *came to salute Festus,* to compliment him upon his accession to the government. But it is probable they came as much to divert themselves as to show respect to him, and to share in the entertainments of his court.

II. The account which Festus gave to king Agrippa of Paul and his case.

1. To entertain him. It would be particularly acceptable to Agrippa, not only because he was a judge, and there were some points of law and practice in it well worth his notice, but much more as he was a Jew, and there were some points of religion in it much more deserving his cognizance.

2. To have his advice. *Festus* was but newly come to be a judge, and therefore was willing to have the counsel of those that were older and more experienced. The particular account he gives to king Agrippa concerning Paul, *v.* 14–21.

(1) He found him a prisoner when he came into the government of this province: *There is a certain man left in bonds by Felix;* and therefore, if there were anything amiss in the first taking of him into custody, Festus is not to answer for that.

(2) The Jewish sanhedrim were extremely set against him: "The *chief priests and the elders informed me* against him as a dangerous man, and desired he might therefore be condemned to die."

(3) He had insisted upon the Roman law in favour of the prisoner, and would not condemn him unheard (*v.* 16): "*It is not the manner of the Romans* to *deliver any man to die before the accused has the accusers face to face.*" *Hear the other side* had become a proverb among them. We must not give men bad characters, nor condemn their words and actions, till we have heard what is to be said in their vindication.

(4) He had brought him upon his trial, according to the duty of his place, *v.* 17. He had been expeditious in it *as soon as ever they had come, without any delay, on the morrow,* he had brought on the cause. He had likewise tried him in the most solemn manner: He *sat on the judgment-seat.* He called a great court

on purpose for the trial of Paul, that the sentence might be definitive, and the cause ended.

(5) He was extremely *disappointed* in the charge they brought against him (*v.* 18, 19): *When the accusers stood up against him they brought no accusations of such things as I supposed.* He supposed by the eagerness of their prosecution, and their urging it thus upon the Roman governors one after another, That they had something to accuse him of that was dangerous either to private property or the public peace. Such were the outcries against the primitive Christians, so loud, so fierce, that the standers-by could not but conclude them the worst of men; and to represent them so was the design of that clamour, as it was against our Saviour. That they had something to accuse him of that was cognizable in the Roman courts, and which the governor was properly the judge of, as Gallio expected (*ch.* xviii. 14). But he finds the matter is not so; they had *certain questions against him,* instead of proofs and evidences against him. And they were questions *of their own superstition,* so he calls their religion. The Romans protected their religion according to their law, but not their superstition. But the great question, it seems, was *concerning one Jesus that was dead, whom Paul affirmed to be alive.* See how slightly this Roman speaks of Christ, and of his death and resurrection, and of the great controversy between the Jews and the Christians whether he were the Messiah promised or no, and the great proof of his being the Messiah, his resurrection from the dead. What Paul affirmed concerning Jesus, that he is alive, is a matter of such vast importance that if it be not true we are all undone.

(6) He had proposed to Paul that the cause might be adjourned to the Jewish courts, as best able to take cognizance of an affair of this nature (*v.* 20): "*Because I doubted of such manner of questions I asked him whether he would go to Jerusalem and there be judged of these matters.*"

(7) Paul had chosen rather to remove his cause to Rome than to Jerusalem: "He *appealed to be reserved to the hearing of Augustus* (*v.* 21), and therefore I *commanded him to be kept till I might send him to Cæsar.*"

III. The bringing of him before Agrippa.

1. The king desired it (*v.* 22): "*I would also hear the man myself.*" Agrippa knows more of this matter than Festus does; he has heard of Paul. Nothing would oblige him more than to hear Paul. Agrippa would not for all the world have gone to a meeting to hear Paul preach, any more than Herod to hear Jesus; and yet they are both glad to have them brought before them, only to satisfy their curiosity.

2. Festus granted it: *Tomorrow thou shalt hear him.* There was a good providence in this, for the encouragement of Paul, who seemed buried alive in his imprisonment, and deprived of all opportunities of doing good. This gives him an opportunity of preaching Christ to a great congregation, and (which is more) to a congregatoin of great ones. Felix heard him in private concerning the faith of Christ. But Agrippa and Festus agree he shall be heard in public.

3. Great preparation was made for it (*v.* 23): *The next day* there was a great appearance *in the place of hearing.*

(1) Agrippa and Bernice took this opportunity to show themselves in state; *they came with great pomp.* They came *with great fancy,* so the word is. Great pomp is but great fancy. It neither adds any real excellency, nor gains any real respect, but feeds a vain humour. It is but a show, a dream, a fantastical thing (so the word signifies). The pomp which Agrippa and Bernice appeared in was, [1] Stained by their lewd characters, and all the beauty of it sullied, and all virtuous people that knew them could not but

contemn them in the midst of all this pomp as vile persons. [2] Outshone by the real glory of the poor prisoner at the bar. His bonds in so good a cause were more glorious than their chains of gold. Who would be fond of worldly pomp that here sees so bad a woman loaded with it and so good a man loaded with the reverse of it?

(2) The chief captains and principal men of the city took this opportunity to pay their respects to Festus and to his guests. I am apt to think that those who were to appear in pomp perplexed themselves more with care about their clothes than Paul, who was to appear as a prisoner, did with care about his cause.

IV. The speech with which Festus introduced the cause. He addressed himself respectfully to the company: "*King Agrippa, and all men who are here present with us.*" He speaks *to all the men* as if he intended a tacit reflection upon Bernice. The word used is that which signifies men in distinction from women; what had Bernice to do here? He represents the prisoner as one that the Jews had a very great spite against. *The multitude of them, both at Jerusalem and here at Cæsarea,* cry out *that he ought not to live any longer.* He confesses the prisoner's innocency (*v.* 25): *I found that he had committed nothing worthy of death.* Upon a full hearing of the case his own conscience brought in Paul *not guilty.* And why did he not discharge him then, for he stood upon his deliverance? Why, truly, because he was so much clamoured against, and he feared the clamour would turn upon himself if he should release him. It is a pity but every man that has a conscience should have courage to act according to it. He acquaints them with the present state of the case, that the prisoner had appealed to the emperor himself, and that he had admitted his appeal: *I have determined to send him.* And thus the cause now stood. He desires their assistance in examining the matter calmly and impartially, that he might have at least such an insight into the cause as was necessary to his stating it to the emperor, *v.* 36, 27. He thought it *unreasonable to send a prisoner and not withal to signify the crimes laid against him,* that the matter might be put in a readiness for the emperor's determination. He could not as yet write *anything certain* concerning Paul; so confused were the informations that were given in against him, that Festus could make nothing at all of them. He therefore desired Paul might thus be publicly examined, that he might be advised by them what to write.

CHAPTER 26

I. The account he gives of himself, 1. His humble address to king Agrippa, ver. 1–3. 2. His account of his origin, and education, his profession as a Pharisee, and his adherence still to that which was then the main article of his creed, the "resurrection of the dead", ver. 3–8. 3. Of his zeal against the Christian religion, in the beginning of his time, ver. 9–11. 4. Of his miraculous conversion, ver. 12–16. 5. Of the commission to preach the gospel to the Gentiles, ver. 17, 18. 6. Of his proceedings pursuant to that commission, ver. 19–21. 7. Of the doctrine which he had made it his business to preach to the Gentiles, ver. 22, 23. II. The remarks that were made upon his apology. 1. Festus slighted him as crazed, ver. 24. In answer to him, he appeals to king Agrippa, ver. 25–27. 2. King Agrippa owns himself almost his convert (ver. 28), and Paul heartily wishes him so, ver. 29. 3. They all agreed that he was an innocent man, that he ought to be set at liberty, and that it was a pity he was appealing to Cæsar, ver. 30–32.

Verses 1–11

Agrippa was the most honourable person in the assembly, having the title of king bestowed upon him, and, though not here superior, yet senior, to Festus. Festus having opened the cause, Agrippa intimates to Paul a licence given him to *speak for himself, v.* 1. This was a favour which the Jews would not allow him, but Agrippa freely gives it to

him. Notice is taken of his gesture: He *stretched forth his hand,* as one that had perfect freedom and command of himself.

I. Paul addressed himself with a very particular respect to Agrippa, *v.* 2, 3. He answered cheerfully before Felix, because he knew he had been *many years a judge to that nation, ch.* xxiv. 10. But his opinion of Agrippa goes further. Being accused of the Jews, and having many base things laid to his charge, he is glad he has an opportunity of clearing himself. Since he is forced to answer for himself, he is glad it is before king Agrippa, who, being himself a proselyte to the Jewish religion, understood all matters relating to it better than the other Roman governors did: *I knew thee to be expert in all customs and questions which are among the Jews.* It seems, Agrippa was expert in the customs of the Jewish religion. He was expert also in the questions that arose upon those customs. Agrippa was well versed in the scriptures of the Old Testament, and therefore could make a better judgment upon the controversy concerning Jesus being the Messiah than another could. It is an encouragement to a preacher to have those to speak to that are intelligent, and can discern things that differ. He therefore begs that he would *hear him patiently.* Paul designs a long discourse, and begs that Agrippa will hear him out, and not be weary; he designs a plain discourse, and begs that he will hear him with mildness, and not be angry. Surely the least we can expect, when we preach the faith of Christ, is to be heard patiently.

II. He professes that though he was branded as an apostate, yet he still adhered to all that good which he was first trained up in.

1. See here what his religion was in his youth: His *manner of life was well known, v.* 4, 5. He was not indeed born among his own nation, but he was bred among them at Jerusalem. His education was neither foreign nor obscure; it was among his own nation at Jerusalem. Those that *knew him from the beginning* could testify for him that he was a Pharisee, that he was of the *most strict sect of that religion.* He was not only called a Pharisee, but he *lived a Pharisee.* And he was of the better sort of Pharisees; for he was brought up at the feet of Gamaliel, who was an eminent rabbi of the school or house of Hillel. Now if Paul was a Pharisee, and lived a Pharisee, then he was a scholar, a man of learning; the Pharisees knew the law, and were well versed in it. It was a reproach to the other apostles that they had not had an academical education, but were bred fishermen, *ch.* iv. 13. Here is an apostle raised up that had sat at the feet of their most eminent doctors. Then he was a moralist, a man of virtue, and not a rake or loose debauched young man. He was, *as touching the righteousness which is in the law,* blameless. As he could not be thought to have deserted his religion because he did not know it (for he was a learned man), so he could not be thought to have deserted it because he did not love it. Then he was orthodox, sound in the faith. He was a Pharisee, in opposition to a Sadducee. They could not say, He quitted his religion for want of a due regard to divine revelation; no, he always had a veneration for the ancient *promise made of God unto the fathers.*

Now though Paul knew very well that all this would not justify him before God, yet he knew it was for his reputation among the Jews, and an argument, *such as Agrippa would feel,* that he was not such a man as they represented him to be. Though he counted it but loss that he might win Christ, yet he mentioned it when it might serve to honour Christ. He reflects upon it with some satisfaction that he had before his conversion *lived in all good conscience before God.*

2. See here what his religion is. He has not indeed such a zeal for the ceremonial law as he had in his youth. But for the main principles of his religion he is as zealous as ever.

(1) His religion is built upon the *promise made of God unto the fathers*. It is built upon divine revelation; it is built upon divine grace, and that grace manifested and conveyed by promise. The promise of God is the guide and ground of his religion, the promise *made to the fathers*, which was more ancient than the ceremonial law. Christ and heaven are the two great doctrines of the gospel—that *God has given to us eternal life, and this life is in his Son.* Now these two are the matter of the *promise made unto the fathers.*

(2) His religion consists in the hopes of this promise. He places it not, as they did, in meats and drinks, but in a believing dependence upon God's grace in the covenant, and upon the promise. He had hope in Christ as the promised seed; he hoped to be blessed in him. He had hopes of heaven. Paul had no confidence in the flesh, but in Christ.

(3) Herein he concurred with all the pious Jews. *"Our twelve tribes, instantly serving God day and night,* hope to *come to this promise.* Now all the Israelites profess to believe in this promise, both of Christ and heaven. They all hope for a Messiah to come, and we that are Christians hope in a Messiah already come; so that we all agree to build upon the same promise. They look for the *resurrection of the dead,* and this is what I look for. Why should I be looked upon as an apostate from the faith and worship of the Jewish church, when I agree with them in this fundamental article? I hope to come to the same heaven at last that they hope to come to; and, if we expect to meet so happily in our end, why should we fall out so unhappily by the way?" *Paul instantly serves God day and night* in the gospel of his Son; the twelve tribes by their representatives do so in the law of Moses, but he and they do it in hope of the same promise. Much more should Christians, who hope in the same Jesus, for the same heaven, though differing in the modes and ceremonies of worship, live together in holy love. Those only can upon good grounds hope for eternal life that are diligent and constant in the service of God; and the prospect of that eternal life should engage us to diligence and constancy in all religious exercises. And of those that *instantly serve God day and night,* though not in our way, we ought to judge charitably.

(4) This was what he was now suffering for: *I am judged for the hope of the promise made unto the fathers.* He stuck to the promise, against the ceremonial law, while his persecutors stuck to the ceremonial law, against the promise. It is common for men to hate and persecute the power of that religion in others which yet they pride themselves in the form of. Paul's hope was what *they themselves also allowed* (*ch.* xxiv. 15), and yet they were thus enraged against him for practising according to that hope.

(5) This was what he would persuade all that heard him cordially to embrace (*v.* 8): *Why should it be thought a thing incredible with you that God should raise the dead?* He explained the *promise made to the fathers* to be the promise of the resurrection and eternal life, and proved that he was in the right way because he believed in Christ who had *risen from the dead,* which was a pledge and earnest of that resurrection which the fathers hoped for. Now many of his hearers were Gentiles, Festus particularly, and we may suppose, when they heard him speak so much of Christ's resurrection, and of the resurrection from the dead, that they mocked. If it be above the power of nature, yet it is not above the power

of the God of nature. Do we not see a kind of resurrection in nature, at the return of every spring? Has the sun such a force to raise dead plants, and should it seem incredible to us that God should raise dead bodies?

III. He acknowledges that while he continued a Pharisee he was a bitter enemy to Christians and Christianity, and thought he ought to be so. His becoming a Christian and a preacher was not the result of any previous inclination that way. He did not reason himself into Christianity, but was brought into the highest degree of an assurance of it, immediately from the highest degree of prejudice against it. His conversion in such a miraculous way was not only to himself, but to others also, a convincing proof of the truth of Christianity. Perhaps he designs it for an excuse of his prosecutors. Paul himself once thought he did what he ought to do when he persecuted the disciples of Christ, and he charitably thinks they laboured under the like mistake. Observe,

(1) What a fool he was in his opinion (*v.* 9): He *thought with himself that he ought to do many things contrary to the name of Jesus of Nazareth.* Because it agreed not with the notion he had of the kingdom of the Messiah, he was for doing all he could against it. He thought he did God good service in persecuting those who called on the name of Jesus Christ. It is possible for those to be confident they are in the right who yet are evidently in the wrong.

2. What a fury he was in his practice, *v.* 10, 11. There is not a more violent principle in the world than conscience misinformed. He gives an account of what he did and aggravates it as one that was truly penitent for it. He filled the jails with Christians. *Many of the saints did I shut up in prison* (*ch.* xxvi. 10), *both men and women, ch.* viii. 3. He made himself the tool of the chief priests. Herein from them he *received authority* and proud enough he was to be a man in authority for such a purpose. He was very officious to vote the putting of Christians to death, particularly Stephen, to whose death Saul was consenting (*ch.* viii. 1). He brought them under punishments of an inferior nature, *in the synagogues,* where they were *scourged* as transgressors of the rules of the synagogue. He not only punished them for their religion, but he forced them to abjure their religion, by putting them to the torture: "*I compelled them to blaspheme* Christ." Nothing will lie heavier upon persecutors than forcing men's consciences. His rage swelled so against Christians and Christianity that Jerusalem itself was too narrow a stage for it to act upon, but, being *exceedingly mad against them, he persecuted them even to strange cities.* He was mad at them, mad to see them multiply the more for their being afflicted. He was *exceedingly mad*; the stream of his fury would admit no banks, no bounds. Persecutors are mad men, and some of them *exceedingly mad.* There is not a more restless principle than malice, especially that which pretends conscience.

This was Paul's character, and this his manner of life in the beginning of his time. All imaginable external objections lay against his being a Christian.

Verses 12–23

All who believe a God must acknowledge that those who speak and act by his direction are not to be opposed; for that *is fighting against God.* Now Paul here makes it out that he had an immediate call from heaven to preach the gospel of Christ to the Gentile world.

I. He was made a Christian by a divine power. He was brought into it on a sudden by the hand of heaven, by a divine and spiritual energy, by a revelation of Christ from above: and this when he was in the full career of his sin, going to Damascus. Nor was he tempted to give it up by the failing of his friends, for he had at this time as ample an *authority and commission from the chief priests* to persecute Christianity as ever he had. Two things bring about this surprising change, a vision from heaven and a voice from heaven.

1. He saw a heavenly vision; it was without doubt a divine appearance. He *saw a great light, a light from heaven,* such as could not be produced by any art *at midday;* it was not in a house where tricks might have been played with him, but it was *in the way,* in the open air; it was such a light as was *above the brightness of the sun,* and this could not be the product of Paul's own fancy, for it *shone round about those that journeyed with him:* made the sun itself to be in their eyes a less light. They all fell to the earth upon the sight of it, such a mighty consternation did it put them into. In the creation of grace, as of the world, the first thing created is light, 2 Cor. iv. 6. Christ himself appeared to him (*v.* 16): *I have appeared to thee for this purpose.* Christ was in this light, though those that travelled with Paul saw the light only, and not Christ in the light.

2. He heard a heavenly voice *speaking to him;* it is here said to be *in the Hebrew tongue,* his native language. He called him by his name, and repeated it (*Saul, Saul*). He convinced him of sin, the sin of persecuting the Christians. He interested himself in the sufferings of his followers: *Thou persecutest me* (*v.* 14), and again, It is *Jesus whom thou persecutest, v.* 15. Little did Paul think, when he was trampling upon those that he looked upon as the blemishes of this earth, that he was insulting one that was so much the glory of heaven. He checked him for his wilful resistance of those convictions: *It is hard for thee to kick against the pricks.* Christ made himself known to him. Paul asked (*v.* 15), "*Who art thou, Lord?*" And he said, "*I am Jesus;* he whom thou hast despised, and hated." Paul thought Jesus was buried in the earth, and, though stolen out of his own sepulchre, yet laid in some other. All the Jews were taught to say so, and therefore he is amazed to hear him speak from heaven, to see him surrounded with all this glory. This convinced him that the doctrines of Jesus were divine and heavenly, and not to be opposed, but to be cordially embraced: and this is enough to make him a Christian immediately.

II. He was made a minister by a divine authority: *That the same Jesus that appeared to him in that glorious light* ordered him *to go and preach the gospel to the Gentiles.* What is said of his being an apostle is here joined immediately to that which was said to him by the way. He puts the two together for brevity-sake: *Rise, and stand upon thy feet.* He must stand up, for Christ has work for him to do: *I have appeared to thee to make thee a minister.* Christ has the making of his own ministers. Christ will manifest himself to all those whom he makes his ministers; for how can those preach him who do not know him? And how can those know him to whom he does not by his spirit make himself known?

1. The office to which Paul is appointed: he is made a minister, to attend on Christ, and act for him, as a witness. Christ appeared to him that he might appear for Christ before men.

2. The matter of Paul's testimony: he must give an account to the world, *Of the things which he had seen.* He saw these things that he might publish them, and he did take all occasions to publish them, as here, and before, *ch.* xxii. *Of those things in which he would appear to him.* Paul at first had but confused notions of the gospel, till Christ appeared to him and gave him fuller instructions. *The gospel he preached he received from Christ* immediately (Gal. i. 12); but he received it gradually. Christ often appeared to Paul and still taught him.

3. The spiritual protection he was taken under (*v.* 17), *delivering thee from the people of the Jews and from the Gentiles.* Christ had shown Paul at this time *what great things he must suffer* (*ch.* ix. 16), and yet tells him here he will *deliver him from the people.* Great sufferings are reconcilable to the promise of the deliverance of God's people. Sometimes God delivers them into the hands of their persecutors that he may have the honour of delivering them out of their hands.

4. The special commission given him to go among the Gentiles; it was some years after Paul's conversion before he was *sent to the Gentiles.*

(1) There is great work to be done among the Gentiles, and Paul must be instrumental in doing it. A world that sits in darkness must be enlightened. He is *sent to open their eyes, and to turn them from darkness to light.* He shall open their eyes, which before were shut against the light, and they shall be willing to understand. Christ opens the heart by opening the eyes, does not lead men blindfold, but gives them to see their own way. He is sent not only to open their eyes for the present, but to keep them open, *to turn them from darkness to light,* that is, from following false and blind guides, to follow a divine revelation of unquestionable certainty and truth. This was turning them from darkness to light, from the ways of darkness to those on which the light shines. The great design of the gospel is to rectify the mistakes of those who are in error, that things may be set and seen in a true light. A world that lies in wickedness, must be reformed; it is not enough for them to have their eyes opened, they must have their hearts renewed. Satan rules by the power of darkness, and God by the convincing evidence of light. Sinners are under the power of Satan; converting grace turns them from under the dominion of Satan, and brings them into subjection to God. When gracious dispositions are strong in the soul (as corrupt and sinful dispositions had been), it is then turned from the power of Satan unto God.

(2) There is a great happiness designed for the Gentiles by this work—*that they may receive forgiveness of sins, and inheritance among those who are sanctified;* they are turned from the slavery of Satan to the service of God. That they may be restored to his favour, which by sin they have forfeited: *That they may receive forgiveness of sins.* They are persuaded to lay down their arms, and return to their allegiance, that they may have the benefit of the act of indemnity. That they may be happy in the fruition of him, *that they may have an inheritance among those who are sanctified by faith that is in me.* Heaven is an inheritance, it descends to all the children of God; for, *if children, then heirs. That they may have a right,* so some read it; not by merit, but purely by grace. All that are effectually turned from sin to God are not only pardoned, but preferred. All that shall be saved hereafter are sanctified now. None can be happy that are not holy; nor shall any be saints in heaven that are not first saints on earth. We need no more to make us happy than to have our lot among those that are sanctified, to fare as they fare. Those who are sanctified shall be glorified. Let us therefore now cast in our lot among them. We are sanctified and saved by faith in Christ. Some refer it to the word next before, *sanctified by faith,* for faith purifies the heart. Others refer it to the receiving of both pardon and the inheritance. It comes all to one; for it is by faith that we are justified, sanctified, and glorified. *By faith, that faith which is in me;* it is emphatically expressed. That faith which in a particular manner fastens upon Jesus Christ and his mediation, by which we rely upon Christ, and resign ourselves to him.

III. He had discharged his ministry by divine aid and under divine direction and protection.

1. God gave him a heart to comply with the call (*v.* 19): *I was not disobedient to the heavenly vision.* If Paul had conferred with flesh and blood, and been swayed by his secular interest, he would have done as Jonah did, gone anywhere rather than upon this errand. He accepted his commission and he applied himself to act accordingly.

2. God enabled him to go through a great deal of work, though in it he grappled with a great deal of difficulty, *v.* 20. He applied himself to the preaching of the gospel with all vigour. He began at Damascus, where he was converted. When he came to Jerusalem, where he had his education, he there witnessed for Christ, where he had most furiously set himself against him. He preached *throughout all the coasts of Judæa*; he made the first offer of the gospel to the Jews, as Christ had appointed, and did not leave them till they had wilfully thrust the gospel from them. He turned to the Gentiles.

3. His preaching was all practical. He showed them that they ought, (1) *To repent of their sins,* to be sorry for them, and enter into covenant against them. They ought to change their mind and change their way. (2) *To turn to God.* They must not only conceive an antipathy to sin, but they must come into a conformity to God; they must turn to God, in love and affection, and return to God in duty and obedience, and turn and return from the world and the flesh. (3) *To do works meet for repentance.* This was what John preached, who was the first gospel preacher, Matt. iii. 8. Those that profess repentance must practise it, must live a life of repentance. It is not enough to speak penitent words, but we must do works agreeable to those words. Now what fault could be found with such preaching as this?

4. The Jews had no quarrel with him but upon this account, that he did all he could to persuade people to be religious, and to bring them to God by bringing them to Christ (*v.* 21): It was for these causes, and no other, *that the Jews caught me in the temple, and went about to kill me*; and let anyone judge whether these were crimes worthy of death or of bonds. They caught him in the temple worshipping God, and there they set upon him, as if the better place the better deed.

5. He had no help but from heaven (*v.* 22): "*Having therefore obtained help of God, I continue unto this day.* I have stood to what I said, and have not been afraid nor ashamed to persist in it." What was it that bore him up? Not any strength of his own resolutions, but *having obtained help of God*. He could not have gone on in it, but by help obtained of God. Those who are employed in work for God shall obtain help from God. Our continuance to this day must be attributed to help obtained of God. The preachers of the gospel could never have done as they did, if they had not had immediate help from heaven.

6. He preached no doctrine but what agreed with the scriptures of the Old Testament: He *witnessed both to small and great*. It was an evidence of the grace of the gospel that it was witnessed to the meanest, and the poor were welcome to the knowledge of it; and of the incontestable truth of it that it was neither afraid nor ashamed to show itself to the greatest. The enemies of Paul objected against him that he preached something more than *that men should repent, and turn to God, and do works meet for repentance*. Besides these, he had preached Christ, and his death, and his resurrection, and this was what they quarrelled with him for. "And so I did," says Paul, "and so I do, but therein also I say *no other than that which Moses and the prophets said should come*; and what greater honour can be done to them than to show that what they foretold is accomplished?" Three things they prophesied, and Paul preached: (1) *That Christ should suffer*, that the Messiah should be a *sufferer*. His ignominious death should be not only consistent with, but pursuant of, his undertaking. The cross of Christ was a stumbling-block to the Jews; but Paul stands to it that, in preaching that, he preached the fulfilling of the Old Testament predictions. (2) *That he should be the first that should rise from the dead; that he should be the chief of the resurrection, the head, or principal one.* He was the first that rose from the dead to die no more. (3) *That he should show light unto the people, and to the Gentiles*, to the people of the Jews in the first place. To them he showed light by himself, and then to the Gentiles by the ministry of his apostles. In this Paul refers to his commission (*v.* 18), *To turn them from darkness to light.* He rose from the dead on purpose that he might show light to the people. This also was foretold by the Old Testament prophets, *that the Gentiles should be brought to the knowledge of God by the Messiah;* and what was there in all this that the Jews could justly be displeased at?

Verses 24–32

We have reason to think that Paul had a great deal more to say. He had just fallen upon that which was the life of the cause—the death and resurrection of Jesus Christ. Lead him but to this subject and he will never know when to conclude; for the power of Christ's death, and the fellowship of his sufferings, are with him inexhaustible subjects. It was a thousand pities then that he should be interrupted, and that, being permitted to speak for himself (*v.* 1), he should not be permitted to say all he designed.

I. Festus, the Roman governor, is of opinion that the poor man is crazed. He takes him to be a lunatic, a distracted man, that should be pitied, but at the same time should not be heeded. He thinks he has found out an expedient to excuse himself both from condemning Paul as a prisoner and from believing him as a preacher; for, if he be not *compos mentis—in his senses*, he is not to be either condemned or credited.

1. What it was that Festus said of him (*v.* 24): *He said with a loud voice* that he might oblige Paul to break off his discourse, and might divert the auditors from attending to it: "*Paul, thou art beside thyself. Much learning hath made thee mad,* thou hast cracked thy brains with studying." This he speaks, not so much in anger, as in scorn and contempt. He did not understand what Paul said; it was all a riddle to him, and therefore he imputes it all to a heated imagination. He owns Paul to be a scholar, and a man of learning. The apostles, who were fishermen, were despised because they had no learning; Paul who was a university-man, is despised as having too much learning. Thus the enemies of Christ's ministers will always have something or other to upbraid them with. He reproaches him as a madman. John Baptist and Christ were represented as having a devil, as being crazed. Festus put this invidious character upon him, which perhaps never a one in the company but himself thought of.

2. How Paul cleared himself from this invidious imputation. He denies the charge, protesting that there was neither ground nor colour for it (*v.* 25): "*I am not mad, most noble Festus.* I do not ramble, but speak the words of truth and soberness." He gives him all possible respect, compliments him with his title of honour, *most noble Festus*, to teach us not to render railing for railing, but to speak civilly to those who speak slightly of us. He appeals to Agrippa concerning what he spoke (*v.* 26): *For the king knows*

of these things. He therefore *spoke freely before him,* who knew something of them, and therefore would be willing to know more: *For I am persuaded that none of these things are hidden from him. This thing was not done in a corner;* all the country rang of it, and therefore it was unreasonable to censure him as a distracted man for relating it, much more for speaking of the death and resurrection of Christ, which was so universally spoken of. Agrippa could not be ignorant of it, and it was a shame for Festus that he was so.

II. Agrippa is so far from thinking him a madman that he thinks, he never heard a man talk more to the purpose.

1. Paul applies himself closely to Agrippa's conscience. He will speak to those who understand him, and whom he is likely to fasten something upon, and therefore still addresses *Agrippa:* "*King Agrippa, believest thou the prophets?*" He does not stay for an answer, but, in compliment to Agrippa, takes it for granted: *I know that thou believest;* for everyone knew that Agrippa professed the Jews' religion, and therefore both knew the writings of the prophets and gave credit to them. It is good dealing with those who have acquaintance with the scriptures and believe them; for such one has some hold of.

2. Agrippa owns there was a great deal of reason in what Paul said (*v.* 28): *Almost thou persuadest me to be a Christian.* Some understand this as spoken ironically, *Wouldest thou in so little a time persuade me to be a Christian?* But, taking it so, it is an acknowledgment that Paul spoke very much to the purpose. Others take it as spoken seriously. He is as near being persuaded to believe in Christ as Felix, when he trembled, was to leave his sins. Many are almost persuaded to be religious who are not quite persuaded; they are under strong convictions, but yet are overruled by some external inducements, and do not pursue their convictions.

3. Paul concludes with a pious wish that all his hearers were Christians, and this wish turned into a prayer: *I pray to God for it* (*v.* 29). *That not only thou but all that hear me this day were both almost, and altogether, such as I am, except these bonds.* He professes his resolution to cleave to his religion. In wishing that they were all as he was, he does in effect declare against ever being as they were, how much soever it might be to his worldly advantage. He intimates his satisfaction not only in the truth, but in the benefit and advantage of Christianity. He could not wish better to the best friend he had in the world than to wish him a faithful zealous disciple of Jesus Christ. He intimates his trouble and concern that Agrippa went no further than being almost a Christian (what good would that do?). He intimates that it would be the unspeakable happiness of every one of them to become *true Christians*—that there is grace enough in Christ for all, be they ever so many. He intimates the hearty goodwill he bore to them all; he wishes them, (1) As well as he wished his own soul. (2) Better than he now was as to his outward condition. He wishes they might all be comforted Christians as he was, but not persecuted Christians as he was. When he wished them in bonds to Christ, he desired they might never be in bonds for Christ. Nothing could be said more tenderly nor with a better grace.

III. They all agree that Paul is an innocent man. The court broke up with some precipitation (*v.* 30): *When he had spoken* the king was afraid he would say something yet more moving. The king himself found his own heart begin to yield, and durst not trust himself to hear more, but, like Felix, dismissed Paul for this time. *The king rose up, and the governor, and Bernice and those that sat with them.* They all concurred in an opinion of Paul's innocency, *v.* 31.

The court withdrew to consult, and *they talked among themselves,* all to the same purport, *that this man does nothing worthy of death;* nay, he *does nothing worthy of bonds.* Thus was he made manifest in the consciences of those who yet would not receive his doctrine; and the clamours of the hot-headed Jews, who cried out, *Away with him, it is not fit he should live,* were shamed by the moderate counsels of this court. *Agrippa* gave his judgment *that he might have been set at liberty, if he had not himself appealed to Cæsar* (*v.* 32), but by that appeal he had put a bar in his own door. Agrippa, who was but almost persuaded to be a Christian, proves no better than if he had not been at all persuaded. And now I cannot tell whether Paul repented of his having appealed to Cæsar, now he saw that was the only thing that hindered his discharge. What we think is for our welfare often proves to be a trap; such short-sighted creatures are we. Or whether, notwithstanding this, he was satisfied in what he had done, and believed there was a providence in it, and it would issue well at last. And besides, he was told in a vision that he must *bear witness at Rome,* ch. xxiii. 11. And it is all one to him whether he goes thither a prisoner or at his liberty.

CHAPTER 27

An account of Paul's voyage towards Rome. I. The beginning of the voyage was calm and prosperous, ver. 1–8. II. Paul gave them notice of a storm coming, ver. 9–11. III. They met with a great deal of tempestuous weather, and they counted upon nothing but being cast away, ver. 12–20. IV. Paul assured them that by the good providence of God, they should be brought safely through it, ver. 21–26. V. At length they were at midnight thrown upon an island, which proved to be Malta, ver. 27–36. VI. Their narrow escape with their lives, when the ship was wrecked, but all the persons wonderfully preserved, ver. 37–44.

Verses 1–11

I. How Paul was shipped off for Italy: a long voyage, but there is no remedy. He has appealed to Cæsar, and to Cæsar he must go: *It was determined that we should sail into Italy.* It was determined by the counsel of God, before it was determined by the council of Festus, that Paul should go to Rome; for God had work for him to do there. Whose custody he was committed to—to *one named Julius, a centurion of Augustus's band.* He had soldiers under him, who were a guard upon Paul. What bottom he embarked in: they went on board a ship of Adramyttium (*v.* 2), a sea-port of Africa. What company he had in this voyage; there were some prisoners who were committed to the custody of the same centurion. Paul was linked with these, as Christ with the thieves that were crucified with him, and was obliged to take his lot with them in this voyage; and we find (*v.* 42) that for their sakes he had like to have been killed, but for his sake they were preserved. But he had also some of his friends with him, Luke particularly, for he puts himself in all along, *We sailed into Italy,* and, *We launched, v.* 2. Aristarchus, a Thessalonian, is particularly named, as being now in his company. It was a comfort to Paul to have the society of some of his friends in this tedious voyage. Those that go long voyages at sea have need of wisdom, that they may do good to the bad company they are in, may make them better, or at least be made never the worse by them.

II. What course they steered, and what places they touched at. They touched at Sidon, thither they came *the next day. Julius the centurion* was extraordinarily civil to Paul. It is probable that he was one of the *chief captains, or principal men,* that heard him plead his own cause before Agrippa (*ch.* xxv. 23), and was convinced of his innocency. Though Paul was committed to him as a prisoner, he treated him as a friend, as a gentleman. He *gave him liberty to go among his friends to refresh himself.* Julius herein gives an example to those in power to be respectful to those whom they find worthy of their respect. God herein encourages those that suffer for him to trust in him; for he can put it into the hearts of those to befriend them from whom they least expect it. And it is likewise an instance of Paul's fidelity. He did not go about to make his escape. If the centurion is so civil as to take his word, he is so just and honest as to keep his word. They thence *sailed under Cyprus,* v. 4. If the wind had been fair, they had left Cyprus on the right hand; but, the wind not favouring them, they were driven to sailing with a side wind, and left it on the left hand. Sailors must do as they can, when they cannot do as they would, and make the best of their wind, whatever point it is in; so must we all in our passage over the ocean of this world. At a port called Myra they changed their ship. They went on board a vessel of Alexandria bound for Italy, v. 5, 6. Great trading there was between that city and Italy; from Alexandria they carried corn to Rome, and the East-India goods and Persian which they imported at the Red Sea they exported again, especially to Italy. And it was a particular favour shown to the Alexandrian ships in the ports of Italy that they were not obliged to strike sail, when they came into port. With much ado they made *The Fair Havens,* a port of the island of Crete, v. 7, 8. They *sailed slowly many days.* It was a great while before they made the point of Cnidus, and were forced to sail under Crete, as before under Cyprus; much difficulty they met with in passing by Salmone, a promontory on the eastern shore of the island of Crete. Though the voyage hitherto was not tempestuous, yet it was very tedious. Thus many that are not driven backward in their affairs by cross providences, yet sail slowly, and do not get forward by favourable providences. The place they came to was called *The Fair Havens.* It is known to this day by the same name, and answers the name from the pleasantness of its situation and prospect. It was not the harbour they were bound for; it was a fair haven, but it was not their haven. It was not a *commodious haven to winter in,* v. 12. Every fair haven is not a safe haven; nay, there may be most danger where there is most pleasure.

III. What advice Paul gave them—it was to be content to winter where they were. They had lost a deal of time while they were struggling with contrary winds. Sailing was now dangerous, because *the fast was already past,* that is, the famous yearly fast of the Jews, the day of atonement, which was on the tenth day of the seventh month; it was about the 20th of our September. But (which is strange) we never have any mention made in all the scripture history of the observance of it, unless it be meant here, where it serves only to describe the season of the year. Michaelmas is reckoned by mariners as bad a time of the year to be at sea in as any other. Paul put them in mind of it, and gave them notice of their danger (v. 10): "*I perceive* that *this voyage will be with hurt and damage.*" There were some good men in the ship, and many more bad men: but in things of this nature *all things come alike to all.* If both be in the same ship, they both are in the same danger. They would not be advised by Paul in this matter, v. 11. They thought him impertinent in interposing in an affair of this nature, and the centurion to whom it was referred to determine it, takes upon him to overrule. The centurion gave more regard to the opinion of the master and owner of the ship than to Paul's; for every man is to be credited in his own profession. The centurion was very civil to Paul (v. 3), and yet would not be governed by his advice.

Verses 12–20

I. The ship putting to sea again, at first with a promising gale. What induced them to leave the fair havens: it was because they thought the harbour not *commodious to winter in.* They ran upon a mischief to avoid an inconvenience, as we often do. Some of the ship's crew were for staying there. It is better to be safe in an incommodious harbour than to be lost in a tempestuous sea. But they were outvoted, and the *greater part advised to depart thence also*; yet they aimed not to go far, but only to another port of the same island, here called *Phenice.* It is here described to lie towards the south-west and north-west. Probably the haven was between two promontories, one of which pointed to the north-west and the other to the south-west, by which it was guarded against the east winds. In vain had nature provided for us the waters to sail on, if it had not likewise provided for us natural harbours to take shelter in. What encouragement they had at first to pursue their voyage. They set out with a fair wind (v. 13), the *south wind blew softly,* upon which they flattered themselves with hope that they should gain their point, and so they sailed close by the coast of Crete. Those who put to sea with ever so fair a gale know not what storms they may yet meet with, and therefore must not be secure.

II. The ship in a storm presently, a dreadful storm. They imagined that because the south wind now blew softly it would always blow so; in confidence of this, they ventured to sea, but were soon made sensible of their folly in giving more credit to a smiling wind than to the word of God in Paul's mouth.

1. What their danger and distress was. There *arose against them a tempestuous wind.* This wind the sailors called *Euroclydon,* a north-east wind, which upon those seas was in a particular manner troublesome and dangerous. The ship was *exceedingly tossed* (v. 18); it was kicked like a football from wave to wave. The ship could not possibly *bear up into the wind,* and therefore they folded up their sails, which in such a storm would endanger them rather than do them any service, and so *let the ship drive.* It is probable that they were very near the haven of Phenice, and thought they should presently be in a quiet haven, and lo, of a sudden, they are in this distress. The use of the loadstone for the direction of sailors not being then found out (so that they had no guide at all, when they could see neither sun nor stars) made the case the more hazardous. Thus melancholy sometimes is the condition of the people of God upon a spiritual account. Thus it may be with them, and yet light is sown for them. They had abundance of winter-weather: *No small tempest,* so that they were ready to perish for cold; and all this continued many days. See what hardships those often undergo who are much at sea, besides the hazards of life they run; and yet to get gain there are still those who make nothing of all this; and it is an instance of divine Providence that it disposes some to this employment, notwithstanding the difficulties that attend it. Perhaps Christ therefore chose ministers from among seafaring men, because they had been used to endure hardness.

2. What means they used for their own relief. When they could not make head against the wind, they let the ship run adrift. When it is fruitless to struggle, it is wisdom to yield. They nevertheless did what they could to avoid the present danger; there was a little island called Clauda. They took care to prevent their shipwreck, and therefore so ordered their matters that they did not run against the island, but quietly ran under it, v. 16. When they were afraid they should scarcely save the ship, they were busy to save the boat. They had *much work to come by the*

boat (v. 16), but at last they took it up, v. 17. They used means which were proper enough in those times; they *undergirded the ship*, v. 17. They bound the ship under the bottom of it with strong cables, to keep it from bulging in the extremity of the tempest. For fear of falling *into the quicksands* they *struck sail*, and then let the ship go as it would. It is strange how a ship will live at sea (so they express it), even in very stormy weather, if it have but sea-room. The next day they lightened the ship of its cargo, threw the goods and merchandise overboard. See what the wealth of this world is; the time may come when it will be a burden, not only too heavy to be carried safe of itself, but heavy enough to sink him that has it. But see the folly of the children of this world, they can be thus prodigal of their goods when it is for the saving of their lives, and yet how sparing of them in works of piety and charity, and in suffering for Christ. Any man will rather make shipwreck of his goods than of his life; but many will rather make *shipwreck of faith and a good conscience* than of their goods. The third day they *cast out the tacklings of the ship*.

3. The despair which at last they were brought to (v. 20): *All hope that we should be saved was then taken away*. The storm continued, and they saw no symptoms of its abatement. The means they had used were ineffectual, so that they were at their wits' end; and they had no heart either to eat or drink. They had provision enough on board (v. 38), but such bondage were they under, through fear of death, that they could not admit the supports of life.

Verses 21–44

We have here the issue of the distress of Paul and his fellow-travellers; they escaped with their lives and that was all. We are here told (v. 37) what number there were on board—in all two hundred and seventy-six souls, and one Paul among them worth more than all the rest. We left them in despair, giving up themselves for gone. Paul among these seamen was not, like Jonah, the cause of the storm, but the comforter in the storm.

I. The encouragement Paul gave them, by assuring them that their lives should all be saved. Paul rescued them from their despair first, that they might not die of that, and then they were in a fair way to be rescued from their distress. *After long abstinence, Paul stood forth in the midst of them*. During the distress hitherto Paul was one of the crowd, helping with the rest to *throw out the tackling* (v. 19), but now though a prisoner, he undertook to be their counsellor and comforter.

1. He reproves them for not taking his advice (v. 8): "*You should have hearkened to me and not have loosed from Crete*, and then we should not have *gained this harm and loss*." They did not hearken to Paul when he warned them of their danger, and yet he will speak comfort and relief to them now that they are in danger, so compassionate is God to those that are in misery, though they bring themselves into it by their own wilfulness. Paul, before administering comfort, will first make them sensible of their sin in not hearkening to him. That which they are blamed for is their loosing from Crete, where they were safe. Most people bring themselves into inconvenience, because they do not know when they are well off, by aiming against advice to better themselves.

2. He assures them that though they should lose the ship yet they should none of them lose their lives. "Your case is sad, but it is not desperate, now, *I exhort you to be of good cheer*." Thus we say to sinners that are convinced of their sin and folly, "*You should have hearkened unto us*, and should have had nothing to do with sin; yet now we *exhort you*

to be of good cheer: though you would not take our advice when we said, *Do not presume*, yet take it now when we say, *Do not despair*." They would use no further means, because *all hope that they should be saved was taken away*. Now Paul quickens them to bestir themselves. If they would resume their vigour they should secure their lives. They must count upon the loss of the ship. Their ship shall be wrecked. *Not a life shall be lost*. This would be good news to those that were ready to die for fear of dying.

3. He tells them what ground he had for this assurance, he has a divine revelation for it. An angel of God appeared to him in the night, and told him that for his sake they should all be preserved (v. 23–25). They should have it not only by providence, but by promise, and as a particular favour to Paul.

(1) The solemn profession Paul makes of relation to God. It is he *whose I am, and whom I serve*. He looks upon God, as his rightful owner, who has a sovereign incontestable title to him, and dominion over him: *Whose I am*. We are more his than our own. As his sovereign ruler and master, who has right to give him law: *Whom I serve*. Because his we are, therefore we are bound to serve him. He does not say, "Whose *we* are, and whom *we* serve," for most that were present were strangers to him. This he tells the company, that they might thereby be drawn in to take him for their God, and to serve him likewise.

(2) The account he gives of the vision he had: *There stood by me this night an angel of God*. Though he was *afar off upon the sea* (Ps. lxv. 5), yet this could not intercept his communion with God. Thence he can direct a prayer to God, and thither God can direct an angel to him. The *ship is tossed* with winds and waves, and yet the angel finds a way into it. No storms nor tempests can hinder the communications of God's favour to his people, for he is a very present help. We may suppose that Paul, being a prisoner, had not a cabin of his own in the ship, but was put down into the hold (any dark or dirty place was thought good enough for him in common with the rest of the prisoners), and yet there the angel of God stood by him. Meanness and poverty set none at a distance from God and his favour. Paul had this vision but *this last night*. He has this fresh vision to assure him of the safety of those with him.

(3) The encouragements that were given him in the vision, v. 14. [1] He is forbidden to fear. Though all about him are at their wits' end, and lost in despair, yet, *Fear not, Paul*. Let not the saints be afraid, no, not at sea, in a storm; for *the Lord of hosts is with them*. [2] He is assured that he shall come safely to Rome: *Thou must be brought before Cæsar*. The rage of the most stormy sea, cannot prevail against God's witnesses till they have finished their testimony. This is comfortable for the faithful servants of God in straits and difficulties, that as long as God has any work for them to do their lives shall be prolonged. [3] For his sake all that were in the ship with him should be delivered too: *God hath given thee all those that sail with thee*. God chooses by preserving them all for his sake, to show what great blessings good men are to the world. Paul here delivers a whole ship's crew, almost three hundred souls. God often spares wicked people for the sake of the godly. The good people are hated and persecuted in the world as if they were not worthy to live in it, yet really it is for their sakes that the world stands. It was a great favour to Paul, and he looked upon it to be so, that others were saved for his sake: *They are given thee*. There is no greater satisfaction to a good man than to know that he is a public blessing.

4. He comforts them (v. 25): "*Wherefore, sirs, be of good cheer, for I believe God, that it shall be even as it was told me*." He would not require them to

give credit to that to which he did not himself give credit; and therefore solemnly professes that he believes it himself. And shall it be as God hath said? Then be of good cheer, be of good courage. If with God saying and doing are not two things, then with us believing and enjoying should not be.

5. He gives them a sign, telling them particularly what this tempestuous voyage would issue in (*v.* 26): *"We must be cast upon a certain island, and that will both break the ship and save the passengers."* Providence undertakes to bring them to an island that shall be a refuge for them.

II. Their coming at length to an anchor upon an unknown shore, *v.* 27–29. They had been a full fortnight in the storm, continually expecting death: *The fourteenth night they came near land;* they were *that night driven up and down in Adria,* in the Adriatic Sea, a part of the Mediterranean, extending to the African shore; and knew not whereabouts they were. *About midnight the mariners apprehended that they drew near to some shore.* To try whether it was so or no, *they sounded;* the water would be shallower as they drew near to shore; by the first experiment *they found they drew twenty fathoms deep of water,* and by *the next fifteen fathoms,* which was a demonstration that they were near some shore. They took the hint, and, fearing rocks near the shore, *they cast anchor, and wished for the day.* When they had light, there was no land to be seen. Now they had no light to see by; no marvel then they wished for day. When those that fear God *walk in darkness, and have no light,* let them do as these mariners did, cast anchor, and wish for the day, and be assured that the day will dawn.

III. The defeating of the sailors' attempt to quit the ship. 1. The treacherous design of the seamen, and that was to leave the sinking ship (*v.* 30): *They were about to flee out of the ship,* and to save themselves, and leave all the rest to perish. They pretended they would *cast anchors out of the fore-ship,* and in order to this *they let down the boat,* and were *going into it.* Paul had, in God's name, assured them that they should come safely to land, but they will rather trust their own refuge of lies than God's word and truth. 2. Paul's discovery of it, *v.* 31. Paul saw through it, and gave notice to the centurion and the soldiers concerning it, and told them plainly, *Except these abide in the ship, you cannot be saved.* Now the greatest difficulty of all was before them, and therefore the seamen were now more necessary than ever yet. Now that they are near land, they must use their art to bring the ship to it. When God has done that for us which we could not, we must then in his strength help ourselves. God, who appointed the end, *that they should be saved,* appointed the means, that they should be saved by the help of these seamen. Duty is ours, events are God's; and we do not trust God, but tempt him, when we do not use proper means, such as are within our power, for our own preservation. 3. The effectual defeat of it by the soldiers, *v.* 32. It was no time to stand arguing the case with the seamen, and therefore they made no more ado, *but cut the ropes of the boat to let it fall off.* And now the seamen, being forced to stay in the ship, are forced likewise to work for the safety of the ship, because if the rest perish they must perish with them.

IV. The new life which Paul put into the company. Happy they who had such a one as Paul in their company. The day was coming on. The dawning of the day revived them a little, and then Paul got them together. He chid them for their neglect of themselves: *This is the fourteenth day that you have tarried, and continued fasting, having taken nothing, v.* 33. They ate very little, next to nothing. *"You have continued fasting,* that is, you have lost your stomach;

you have had no appetite at all to your food, nor any relish of it, through prevailing fear and despair." What folly it is to die for fear of dying! He courts them to their food (*v.* 34): *"Wherefore I pray you to take some meat.* We have a hard struggle before us; if our bodies be weak through fasting, we shall not be able to help ourselves."* Paul will have these people eat, or otherwise the waves will be too hard for them: *I pray you* take some nourishment; *for this is for your health,* or rather *your preservation, or safety, at this time.* You cannot without nourishment have strength to shift for your lives. As *he that will not labour, let him not eat;* so he that means to labour must eat. Weak and trembling Christians, that give way to doubts and fears, continue fasting from the Lord's supper, and fasting from divine consolations, and then complain they cannot go on in their spiritual work: and it is owing to themselves. If they would feed and feast as they ought, they would be strengthened, and it would be for their souls' health and salvation. He assured them of their preservation: *There shall not a hair fall from the head of any of you.* "You cannot eat for fear of dying; I tell you, you are sure of living, and therefore eat." He himself spread their table for them: *When he had thus spoken, he took bread.* They were not reduced to short allowance, they had plenty, but what good did that do them, when they had no stomach? We have reason to be thankful to God that we have not only food to our appetite, but appetite to our food. He was chaplain to the ship, and they had reason to be proud of their chaplain. *He gave thanks to God in presence of them all.* Whether he had before this prayed with the whole company promiscuously is not certain. Now *he gave thanks to God, in presence of them all,* that they were alive, and that they had a promise that their lives should be preserved; he gave thanks for the provision they had, and begged a blessing upon it. We must *in everything give thanks;* and must particularly have an eye to God in receiving our food. *He gave thanks in presence of them all,* not only to show that he served a Master he was not ashamed of, but to invite them into his service too. If we crave a blessing upon our meat, and give thanks for it in a right manner, we shall credit our profession, and recommend it to the good opinion of others. He set them a good example: *When he had given thanks, he broke the bread* (it was sea-biscuit) and *he began to eat.* Whether they would be encouraged or no, he would. He would eat his meat, and be thankful. The most effectual way of preaching is by example. It had a happy influence upon them all (*v.* 36): *Then were they all of good cheer.* They then ventured to believe the message God sent them by Paul when they plainly perceived that Paul believed it himself. It is an encouragement to people to commit themselves to Christ as their Saviour when those who invite them to do so make it to appear that they do so themselves. It is here that the number of the persons is set down: *they were in all two hundred threescore and sixteen souls.* See how many may be influenced by the good example of one. *They did all eat,* nay, *they did all eat enough* (*v.* 38). They once more lightened the ship. They had before thrown *the wares and the tackle overboard,* and now *the wheat;* better they should sink the food than that it should sink them. We may ourselves be under a necessity of throwing that away to save our lives which we had gathered and laid up for the support of our lives.

V. Their putting to shore, and the staving of the ship in the adventure. When it was quite day they began to look about them. *They knew not where they were;* they could not tell what country it was they were now upon the coast of. It is probable that these seamen had often sailed this way, and yet here they were at a loss. *They observed a creek with a level* shore, into which they hoped to thrust the ship, v. 39. Though they knew not what country it was, nor whether the inhabitants were civil or barbarous, they determined to cast themselves upon their mercy; it was dry land, which would be very welcome to those that had been so long at sea. It was a pity but they had had some help from the shore. Those who live on the sea-coast have often opportunity of succouring those who are in distress at sea, and of saving precious lives, and they ought to do their utmost in order to it. They made straight to the shore (v. 40): *They took up the anchors. They then committed themselves to the sea*, and *they loosed the rudder-bands*, which were fastened during the storm for the greater steadiness of the ship, but, now that they were *putting into the port, were loosed*, that the pilot might steer with the greater freedom; *they then hoisted up the main-sail to the wind, and made towards shore*. Wnen they saw the shore they hastened to it as fast as they could, and perhaps made more haste than good speed. And should not a poor soul that has long been struggling with winds and tempests in this world long to put into the safe and quiet haven of everlasting rest? And should it not hoist up the main-sail of faith to the wind of the Spirit, and so with longing desires make to shore? They made a shift among them *to run the ship aground*, in a shelf or bed of sand, or an isthmus, or neck of land, washed with the sea on both sides, and therefore two seas are said to meet upon it, and *there the forepart stuck fast. The hinder part* would soon be broken *by the violence of the waves*. The ship, that had strangely weathered the storm in the vast ocean, where it had room to roll, is dashed to pieces when it sticks fast. Thus if the heart fixes in the world it is lost. Satan's temptations beat against it, and it is gone; but, as long as it keeps above the world, though it be tossed with its cares and tumults, there is hope of it. They had the shore in view, and yet suffered shipwreck in the harbour, to teach us never to be secure.

VI. A particular danger that Paul and the rest of the prisoners were in. In this critical moment *the soldiers advised the killing of the prisoners* whom they were to give an account of, *lest any of them should swim out and escape*, v. 42. There was no great danger of that, for they could not escape far, weak and weary as they were; and, under the eye of so many soldiers that had the charge of them, it was not likely they should attempt it. But it was so much the worse that they were thus prodigal of other people's lives when without a miracle of mercy they must lose their own. The centurion, for Paul's sake, quashed this motion. Paul, who was his prisoner, had found favour with him. Julius, though he despised Paul's advice (v. 11), yet, being *willing to save Paul*, he prevented the execution of that bloody project. As God had saved all in the ship for Paul's sake, so here the centurion saves all the prisoners for his sake; such a diffusive good is a good man.

VII. The saving of the lives of all the persons in the ship. Some were saved by swimming: *The centurion commanded his soldiers, as many of them as could swim, to get to land* first, and to be ready to receive the prisoners, and prevent their escape. The rest with much ado scrambled to the shore, some on boards, and others on the *broken pieces of the ship*, and the more busy because they were assured their labour should not be in vain; but *so it came to pass* that through the good providence of God they *escaped all safely to land*. They were rescued from the dreaded sea, and brought to the desired haven. Though there be great difficulty in the way of the promised salvation, yet it shall without fail be accomplished; and even the wreck of the ship may furnish out means for the saving of the lives, and, when all seems to be gone,

all proves to be safe, though it be *on boards, and broken pieces of the ship*.

CHAPTER 28

After the story of this chapter, we hear no more of him in the sacred history, though we have a great deal of him yet before us in his epistles, and could at last have taken leave of him with the more pleasure if we had left him at liberty; but in this chapter we are to condole with him, and yet congratulate him. I. We condole with him as a poor shipwrecked passenger; and yet congratulate him, 1. As singularly owned by his God in his distress, preserved from receiving hurt by a viper that fastened on his hand (ver. 1–6), and being made an instrument of much good in the island on which they were cast, ver. 7–9. 2. As much respected by the people there, ver. 10. II. We condole with him as a poor confined prisoner (ver. 11–16), and yet we congratulate him, 1. Upon the respect shown him by the Christians at Rome, ver. 15. 2. Upon the favour he found with the captain of the guard, ver. 16. 3. Upon the free conference he had with the Jews at Rome, both about his own affair (ver. 17–22), and upon the subject of the Christian religion in general (ver. 23), the issue of which was that God was glorified, and the apostles justified in preaching the gospel to the Gentiles, ver. 24–29. 4. Upon the undisturbed liberty he had to preach the gospel in his own house for two years together, ver. 30, 31.

Verses 1–10

What a great variety of places and circumstances do we find Paul in! He was a planet, and not a fixed star. An ill wind indeed it is that blows nobody any good; this ill wind blew good to the island of Melita; for it gave them Paul's company, who was a blessing to every place he came to.

I. The kind reception which the inhabitants of this island gave (v. 2): *The barbarous people showed us no little kindness*. Providence continues its care of them, and what benefits we receive by the hand of man must be acknowledged to come from the hand of God. As he can make enemies to be at peace, so he can make strangers to be friends, friends in need, and those are friends indeed. 1. The general notice taken of the kindness which the natives of Malta showed. They are called *barbarous people*, because they did not, in language and customs, conform either to the Greeks or Romans, who looked upon all but themselves as barbarians, though otherwise civilized enough, and perhaps in some cases more civil than they. These barbarous people were full of humanity: They *showed us no little kindness*. So far were they from making a prey of this shipwreck that they laid hold of it as an opportunity of showing mercy. It is written for our imitation, that we may hence learn to be compassionate to those that are in distress and misery, and to relieve and succour them to the utmost of our ability. If Providence hath so *appointed the bounds of our habitation* as to give us an opportunity of being frequently serviceable to persons at a loss, we should not place it among the inconveniences of our lot, but the advantages of it. 2. A particular instance of their kindness: *They kindled a fire*, and *they received us every one*—made room for us about the fire, and bade us all welcome. Waters from above met those from below, and it rained so hard that this would wet them to the skin presently; and *it was a cold rain too*, so that they wanted nothing so much as a good fire *to warm them, and dry their clothes. Be you warmed*, is as necessary as, *Be you filled*.

II. The further danger that Paul was in by a viper's fastening on his hand.

1. When the fire was to be made, and to be made bigger, Paul was as busy as any of them in gathering sticks, v. 3. Paul was an industrious active man, and loved to be doing when anything was to be done, and would stoop to anything by which he might be serviceable, even to the gathering of sticks to make a fire of. We should be willing to condescend to the meanest offices for the good of our brethren. Those that receive benefit by the fire should help to carry fuel to it.

2. It happened there was a viper among them, that lay as dead till it came to the heat, and then revived, and flew at him that unawares threw it into the fire, and *fastened upon his hand*, v. 3. As there is a snake under the green grass, so there is often under the dry leaves. See how many perils human life is exposed to, and what danger we are in from the inferior creatures. We often meet with that which is mischievous where we expect that which is beneficial; and many come by hurt when they are honestly employed, and in the way of their duty.

3. The barbarous people concluded that this viper was sent by divine justice to be the avenger of blood. *When they saw the venomous animal hang on his hand*, they concluded, "*No doubt this man is a murderer* and therefore, *though he has escaped the sea, yet divine vengeance* pursues him, and will *not suffer him to live.*"

(1) Some of the discoveries of natural light. They were barbarous people and yet they knew naturally, That there is a God that governs the world and that things do not come to pass by chance but by divine direction. That evil pursues sinners, that there are good works which God will reward and wicked works which he will punish. That murder is a heinous crime, and which shall not long go unpunished. Those that think they shall go unpunished in any evil way will be judged out of the mouth of these barbarians. Learn from these illiterate people that, though malefactors have escaped the vengeance of the sea, yet there is no outrunning divine justice.

(2) Some of the mistakes of natural light. In two things their knowledge was defective: [1] They thought all wicked people were punished in this life. The day of vengeance is to come in the other world, though some are made examples of in this world, to prove that there is a God, yet many are left unpunished, to prove that there is a judgment to come. [2] They thought all who were remarkably afflicted in this life were wicked people. Divine revelation sets this matter in a true light—that all things come ordinarily alike to all, that good men are oftentimes greatly afflicted in this life, for the exercise of their faith and patience.

4. When he shook off the viper from his hand they expected *that he would have swollen*, or *that he would have fallen down dead suddenly*. See how apt men are, when once they have got an ill opinion of a man, to abide by it, and to think that God must necessarily confirm their peevish sentence.

III. Paul's deliverance from the danger, and the undue construction the people put upon this. It does not appear that it put him into any fright or confusion at all. He did not shriek or start. Such a wonderful presence of mind he had as no man could have upon such a sudden accident, but by the special aids of divine grace. He *shook off the viper into the fire*. Thus, in the strength of the grace of Christ, believers shake off the temptations of Satan. When we despise the censures and reproaches of men, having the testimony of conscience for us, then we do, as Paul here, *shake off the viper into the fire*. It does us no harm. He was none the worse. Those that thought it would have been his death *looked a great while, but saw no harm at all come to him*. God hereby intended to make way for the entertainment of the gospel among them. They then magnified him as much as before they had vilified him: *They changed their minds, and said that he was a god*; for they thought it impossible that a mortal man should have a viper hang on his hand so long and be never the worse. See the uncertainty of popular opinion, how it turns with the wind, and how apt it is to run into extremes both ways.

IV. The miraculous cure of an old gentleman that was ill of a fever, and of others, by Paul. The kind entertainment which *Publius, the chief man of the island*, gave to these distressed strangers; he *received them and lodged them three days very courteously*. It is happy when God gives a large heart to those to whom he has given a large estate. It became him, who was the chief man of the island, the richest man, to be rich in good works. The illness of *the father of Publius*: He *lay sick of a fever and a bloody flux*. Providence ordered it that he should be ill just at this time, that the cure of him might be a present recompence to Publius for his generosity, and a recompence particularly for his kindness to Paul. His cure: Paul took cognizance of his case. He entered in, not as a physician to heal him by medicines, but as an apostle to heal him by miracle; and he prayed for his cure, and then laid his hands on him, and he was perfectly well in an instant. Though he must needs be in years, yet he recovered his health. The cure of many others. If he can heal diseases so effectually, he shall soon have patients enough; and he *bade them all welcome*. He did not plead that he was a stranger there, thrown accidentally among them, and waiting to be gone by the first opportunity, and therefore might be excused. No, a good man will endeavour to do good wherever the providence of God casts him. Paul thanked God for an opportunity of being useful among them. Hereby he did in effect discharge his quarters, which should encourage us to entertain strangers, for some thereby have entertained angels and some apostles unawares. God will not be behind-hand with any for kindness shown to his people in distress. Never were any people so enriched by a shipwreck on their coasts as these Maltese were.

V. The grateful acknowledgment made of the kindness Paul had done them, v. 10. They *honoured us with many honours*. They showed them all possible respect. They justly thought nothing too much by which they might testify the esteem they had for them. *When we departed, they loaded us with such things as were necessary;* they put on board such things as we had occasion for. Paul accepted the kindness of the good people of Melita, not as a fee for his cures (freely he had received, and freely he gave), but as the relief of his wants, and theirs that were with him.

Verses 11–16

We have here the progress of Paul's voyage towards Rome, and his arrival there at length. After a storm comes a calm: the latter part of his voyage was easy and quiet.

I. Their leaving Malta. When they are refreshed they must put to sea again. The difficulties and discouragements we have met with in our Christian course must not hinder us from pressing forward. The time of their departure: *After three months*, the three winter months. Better lie by than go forward while the season was dangerous. Paul had warned them against venturing to sea in winter weather, and they would not take the warning; but, now he needed not to warn them. Experience is therefore called the mistress of fools, because those are fools that will not learn till experience has taught them. The ship in which they departed. It was in a ship of Alexandria. This ship had *wintered in that isle*, and was safe. Here were two ships, both of Alexandria, but one is wrecked there and the other is saved. Events are thus varied, that we may learn both how to want and how to abound. The sign of the ship, which probably gave it its name: it was *Castor and Pollux*. They hoped they should have better sailing under this badge than they had had before.

II. Their landing in or about Italy, and the pursuing of their journey towards Rome. They landed first at Syracuse in Sicily, the chief city of that island. There they *tarried three days*. From Syracuse they came to Rhegium, a city in Italy. There, it seems, they stayed one day. It does not appear that they did so much as go ashore, but only came to an anchor in the road. From Rhegium they came to Puteoli, a sea-port town not far from Naples. The ship of Alexandria was bound for that port, and therefore there Paul, and the rest that were bound for Rome, were put ashore, and went the remainder of their way by land. At Puteoli they *found brethren.* Who brought the knowledge of Christ hither we are not told, but here it was, so wonderfully did the leaven of the gospel diffuse itself. God has many that serve and worship him in places where we little think he has. Though it is probable there were but few brethren in Puteoli, yet Paul found them out. As it were by instinct they got together. Brethren in Christ should find out one another, as those of the same country do in a foreign land. They desired Paul and his companions to *tarry with them seven days,* that is, to forecast to stay at least one Lord's day with them. Paul was willing to allow them so much of his time; and the centurion agreed to stay one week there, to oblige Paul. From Puteoli they went forward towards Rome. This was their last stage.

III. The meeting which the Christians at Rome gave to Paul.

1. The great honour they did to Paul. They had heard much of his fame and what eminent service he had done to the kingdom of Christ. They had heard of his sufferings, and how God had owned him in them, and therefore thought themselves obliged to show him all possible respect. He had some time ago written a long epistle to them in return for which they showed him this respect. They *went to meet him,* that they might bring him in state, though he was a prisoner. Some of them went as far as *Appiforum,* which was fifty-one miles from Rome; others to a place called the *Three Taverns.* They were so far from being ashamed of him, because he was a prisoner, that for that very reason they counted him worthy of double honour.

2. The great comfort Paul had in this. Now that he was drawing near to Rome he began to have some melancholy thoughts about his appeal to Caesar, and the consequences of it. What things might befall him here he could not tell; but he began to grow dull upon it, till he met with these good people that came from Rome, and *when he saw them,* (1) He *thanked God.* If our friends be kind to us, it is God that makes them so, and we must give him the glory of it. When he saw so many Christians that were of Rome, he thanked God that the gospel of Christ had had such wonderful success there in the metropolis of the empire. When we go abroad into the world, and meet with those, even in strange places, that bear up Christ's name, and fear God, we should lift up our hearts to heaven in thanksgiving; blessed be God that there are so many excellent ones on this earth, bad as it is. (2) He *took courage.* It put new life into him, and now he can enter Rome a prisoner as cheerfully as ever he had entered Jerusalem at liberty. He finds there are those there who love and value him. It is an encouragement to those who are travelling towards heaven to meet with their fellow travellers. When we see the numerous and serious assemblies of good Christians, we should not only give thanks to God, but take courage to ourselves.

IV. The delivering of Paul into custody at Rome, *v.* 16. He is now come to his journey's end. He is still a prisoner. He had longed to see Rome, but, when he comes there, he is delivered to the *captain of the guard,* and can see no more of Rome than he will permit him. How many great men had made their entry into Rome, crowned and in triumph, who really were the plagues of their generation!

But here a good man makes his entry into Rome, chained and triumphed over as a poor captive. This thought is enough to put one for ever out of conceit with this world. Yet he has some favour shown him. He is a prisoner, but not a close prisoner: *Paul was suffered to dwell by himself,* and a soldier was appointed to be his guard, who, we hope, let him take all the liberty that could be allowed to a prisoner. This may encourage God's prisoners, that he can give them favour in the eyes of those that carry them captive. If he either makes it easy to them or them easy under it, they have reason to be thankful.

Verses 17–22

Paul must call his own cause; and here he represents it to the chief of the Jews at Rome, these *chief of the Jews* were the most distinguished men of that religion. *Paul called them together* that there might be a good understanding between him and them.

I. What account he gave them of his cause. 1. He professes his own innocency: "I have *committed nothing against the people* of the Jews; nor have I committed anything *against the customs of our fathers.*" Paul did not impose the customs of the fathers upon the Gentiles: they were never intended for them. But it is as true that he never opposed them in the Jews, but did himself conform to them. 2. He complains of the hard usage he had met with—*he was delivered prisoner from Jerusalem into the hands of the Romans.* If he had spoken the whole truth in this matter, it would have looked worse upon the Jews, for they would have murdered him if the Romans had not protected him; but, however, they accused him as a criminal, before Felix the governor, in effect, delivering him prisoner into the hands of the Romans. 3. He declares the judgment of the Roman governors concerning him, *v.* 18. They examined him, enquired into his case. The chief captain examined him, so did Felix, and Festus, and Agrippa, and they could find no cause of death in him; but, on the contrary, would have let him go. Those who most carefully examined his case acquitted him, and none condemned him but unheard, and such as were prejudiced against him. 4. He pleads the necessity he was under to remove his cause to Rome; and that it was only in his own defence, and not with any design to recriminate (*v.* 19): *When the Jews spoke against it* he was *constrained to appeal unto Caesar.* This was all he aimed at in this appeal; not to accuse his nation, but only to vindicate himself. It is an invidious thing to accuse, especially to accuse a nation. Paul made intercession for them, but never against them. The Roman government had at this time an ill opinion of the Jewish nation, and it had been an easy thing to have exasperated the emperor. But Paul would not for ever so much do such a thing; he was for making the best of everybody, and not making bad worse. 5. He puts his sufferings upon the true footing (*v.* 20): "*For this cause I have called for you,* not to quarrel with you but to *see you and speak with you* as my countrymen, because *for the hope of Israel I am bound with this chain.*" He carried the mark of his imprisonment about with him, and probably was chained to the soldier that kept him. He preached that the Messiah was come, he whom Israel hoped for. "Do not all the Jews agree in this, that the Messiah will be the glory of his people Israel? This Messiah I preach, and prove he is come. I preach such a hope in a Messiah already come as must produce a joy in him." He preached that the resurrection of the dead would come. This also was the hope of Israel. "They would have you still expect a Messiah that would free you from the Roman yoke, and make you great and prosperous upon earth. This is what they hate me for,—because I would take you off from the nation of a temporal Messiah, and lead you to that which is the true and real hope of Israel, a spiritual kingdom of holiness and love set up in the hearts of men, to be the pledge of, and preparative for, the joyful resurrection of the dead and the life of the world to come."

II. What was their reply. They own, 1. That they had nothing to say in particular against him; nor had any instructions either by letter or word of mouth (v. 21): "*We have neither received letters out of Judæa concerning thee nor have any of the brethren shown or spoken any harm of thee.*" This was very strange, that that restless rage of the Jews which had followed Paul wherever he went should not follow him to Rome. Some think they told a lie here, and had orders to prosecute him, but durst not own it. But I am apt to think that what they said was true, and Paul now found he had gained the point he aimed at in appealing to Caesar, which was to remove his cause into a court to which they durst not follow it. 2. That they desired to know particularly concerning the religion he took so much pains to propagate in the face of so much opposition (v. 22): *We desire to hear of thee what thou thinkest.* Though we know little else of Christianity, we know *it is a sect everywhere spoken against.* This was all they knew concerning the Christian religion, that it was a *sect everywhere spoken against.* They put it into an ill name, and then ran it down. They looked upon it to be a sect, and this was false. True Christianity establishes that which is of common concern to all mankind, and is not built upon such narrow opinions as sects commonly owe their original to. All its gains are spiritual and eternal. It has a direct tendency to the uniting of the children of men, and not the dividing of them. They said it was everywhere spoken against, and this was too true. It is, and always has been, the lot of Christ's holy religion to be everywhere spoken against.

Verses 23–29

We have here a short account of a long conference which Paul had with the Jews at Rome about the Christian religion. They were willing to give it a hearing, which was more than the Jews at Jerusalem would do.

I. We are here told how Paul managed this conference. The Jews appointed the time, a day was set for this dispute, v. 23. Those Jews seemed well disposed to receive conviction, and yet it did not prove that they all were so.

1. There were *many got together to Paul.* Though he was a prisoner yet they were willing to come to him to his lodging. And the confinement he was now under, instead of prejudicing them against his doctrine, ought to confirm it to them; for it was a sign that he thought it worth suffering for. One would visit such a man as Paul in his prison rather than not have instruction from him.

2. He was very full in his discourse with them, seeking their conviction more than his own vindication. He expounded the kingdom of God to them,—showed them the nature of that kingdom, that it is heavenly and spiritual, and shines not in external pomp, but in purity of heart and life. Let but that be expounded to them, and set in a true light, and they will be brought into obedience to it. He not only expounded the kingdom of God, but he testified it,—plainly declared it to them, and confirmed it by incontestable proofs. He attested the extraordinary powers in the kingdom of grace by which it was set up, and the miracles in the kingdom of nature by which it was confirmed. He bore his testimony to it from his own experience of its power. He not only expounded and testified the kingdom of God, but he pressed them with all earnestness to

embrace the kingdom of God. He followed his doctrine with a warm and lively applicaton to his hearers. He persuaded them concerning Jesus. The design and tendency of his whole discourse were to bring them to Christ, to convince them of his being the Messiah. He urged upon them *the things concerning Jesus, out of the law of Moses and out of the prophets,* and showed how they had all had their accomplishment in this Jesus. He dealt with them out of the scriptures of the Old Testament.

3. He was very long; for he continued his discourse from *morning till evening.* The subject was curious—he was full of it—it was of vast importance —he was in good earnest—he knew not when he should have such another opportunity, and therefore, he kept them all day.

II. What was the effect of this discourse. One would have thought that so good a cause and managed by such a skilful hand as Paul's, could not but carry the day. But it did not prove so: the child Jesus is set for the fall of some and the rising again of others, a foundation stone to some and a stone of stumbling to others. *They did not agree among themselves,* v. 25. His hearers could not agree about the sense and evidence of what he preached. *Some believed the things that were spoken, and some believed not,* v. 24. Some are wrought upon by the word, and others hardened; some receive the light, and others shut their eyes against it. So it was among Christ's hearers, some believed and some blasphemed.

III. The awakening word which Paul said to them at parting. He perceived by what they muttered that there were many among them, that were obstinate, and would not yield. "Hold," says Paul, "take one word with you before you go. What do you think will be the effect of your obstinate infidelity? What will it come to?"

1. "You will by the righteous judgment of God be sealed up under unbelief. Turn to that scripture (Isa. vi. 9, 10), and tremble lest the case there described should prove to be your case." As there are in the Old Testament gospel promises, which will be accomplished in all that believe, so there are gospel threatenings of spiritual judgments, which will be fulfilled in those that believe not. Isaiah the prophet is sent to make those worse that would not be made better. *Well spoke the Holy Ghost by Esaias the prophet unto our fathers.* Though what is there said had in it much of terror to the people and of grief to the prophet, yet it is here said to be well spoken. *He that believes not shall be damned* is gospel, as well as, *He that believes shall be saved,* Mark xvi. 16. "*Well did Esaias prophesy of you.* The Holy Ghost said to your fathers, that which would be fulfilled in you, *Hearing you shall hear, and shall not understand.*" (1) "That which was their great sin against God is yours. *Your eyes you have closed,*" v. 27. "As your fathers would not see God's hand lifted up against them in his judgments, so you will not see God's hand stretched out to you in gospel grace." They did not see, because they were resolved they would not, and none so blind as those that will not see. They have purposely *closed their eyes, lest they should see with their eyes* the great things which belong to their everlasting peace; will not receive the evidence of them, *lest they should hear with their ears.* And that which they are afraid of in shutting up their eyes and ears, is, *lest they should understand with their heart, and should be converted, and I should heal them.* They kept their mind in the dark, or at least in a constant confusion and tumult. God's method is to bring people first to see and hear, and so to understand with their hearts, and then to bow their wills, and so heal them, which is the regular way of dealing with a rational soul; and therefore Satan prevents the

conversion of souls to God by blinding the mind and darkening the understanding. And the case is very sad when the sinner joins with him herein, and puts out his own eyes. They are in love with their disease, and are afraid lest God should heal them. This was the sin. (2) "That which was the great judgment of God upon them for this sin is his judgment upon you, and that is, you shall be blind. *Hearing you shall hear—but you shall not understand* it; because you will not give your minds to understand it, God will not give you strength and grace to understand it. *Seeing you shall see but you shall not perceive.*" What with their resisting the grace of God and rebelling against the light, and God's withdrawing and withholding his grace and light from them,—what with their not receiving the love of the truth, and God's giving them up for that to strong delusions, to believe a lie, *the heart of this people is waxed gross, and their ears are dull of hearing.* No physic that can be given them operates upon them, and therefore their disease must be adjudged incurable. And how should those be healed that will not be converted to the use of the methods of cure? And how should those be converted that will not be convinced either of their disease or of their remedy? And how should those be convinced that *shut their eyes and stop their ears*? When once they are thus given up to hardness of heart, they are already in the suburbs of hell.

2. "Your unbelief will justify God in sending the gospel to the Gentile world (*v.* 28): therefore seeing you put the grace of God away from you, and will not submit to the power of divine truth and love, *be it known unto you that the salvation of God is sent unto the Gentiles.* They will hear it, and receive it, and be happy in it." Now Paul designs hereby, (1) To abate their displeasure at the preaching of the gospel to the Gentiles, by showing them the absurdity of it. They were angry that the salvation of God was sent to the Gentiles, but, if they thought that salvation of so small a value as not to be worthy of their acceptance, surely they could not grudge it to the Gentiles. The salvation of God was sent into the world, the Jews had the first offer of it, they would not accept the invitation which was given to them first to the wedding-feast and therefore must thank themselves if other guests be invited. (2) To improve their displeasure at the favour done to the Gentiles to their advantage, and to bring good out of that evil. The Jews have rejected the gospel of Christ, but it is not yet too late to repent of their refusal; they may say No, and take it, as the elder brother in the parable, Matt. xxi. 29. Is the gospel sent to the Gentiles? Let us go after it rather than come short of it. And will they hear it, who are thought to be out of hearing? And shall not we hear it, whose privilege it is to have God so nigh to us in all that we call upon him for? Thus he would have them shamed into the belief of the gospel by the welcome it met with among the Gentiles. And, if it had not that effect upon them, it would aggravate their condemnation.

IV. The breaking up of the assembly, as it should seem, in some disorder. They turned their backs upon Paul. *When Paul had said these words,* he had said enough for them, and *they departed,* no more affected, either with those terrible words in the close of his discourse or all the comfortable words he had spoken before, than the seats they sat on. They set their faces one against another; for they had great disputes among themselves. Those that agreed to depart from Paul, yet agreed not in the reasons why they departed, but had *great reasoning among themselves.* Many have great reasoning who yet do not reason right. Nor will men's reasoning among themselves convince them, without the grace of God to open their understandings.

Verses 30, 31

We are here taking our leave of the history of blessed Paul. We should carefully take notice of every particular of the circumstances in which we must here leave him.

I. It cannot but be trouble to us that we must leave him in bonds for Christ. *Two whole years* of that good man's life are here spent in confinement. He appealed to Cæsar, in hope of a speedy discharge from his imprisonment, and yet he is detained a prisoner. Then his bonds in Christ were manifest in Cæsar's court, as he says, Phil. i. 13. During these two years' imprisonment he wrote his epistles to the Ephesians, Philippians, Colossians, and to Philemon. How or by what means he obtained his liberty we are not told, only that two years he was a prisoner. Tradition says that after his discharge he went from Italy to Spain, thence to Crete, and so with Timothy into Judæa, and thence went to visit the churches in Asia, and at length came a second time to Rome, and there was beheaded in the last year of Nero. It would grieve one to think that such a useful man as Paul was should be so long in restraint. Two years he was a prisoner under Felix (*ch.* xxiv. 27), and he is here two years more a prisoner under Nero. How many churches might Paul have planted if he had been at liberty! But God will show that he is no debtor to the most useful instruments he employs, but will carry on his own interest, both without their services and by their sufferings. Even Paul's bonds fell out *to the furtherance of the Gospel,* Phil. i. 12–14. Yet even Paul's imprisonment was in some respects a kindness to him, for these *two years he dwelt in his own hired house,* and that was more, for aught I know, than ever he had done before. Such a retirement as this would be a refreshment to one who had been all his days an itinerant. Now he lived for two years in the same house; so that the bringing of him into this prison was like Christ's call to his disciples *to come into a desert place, and rest awhile,* Mark vi. 31. When he was at liberty, he was in continual fear by reason of *the lying in wait of the Jews* (*ch.* xx. 19), but now his prison was his castle.

II. Yet it is a pleasure to us that, though we leave him in bonds for Christ, yet we leave him at work for Christ. His prison becomes a temple, a church, and then it is to him a palace. Thanks be to God, his mouth is not stopped; a faithful zealous minister can better bear any hardship than being silenced. He is bound, but the word of the Lord is not bound. He was glad *to see some of them* (*v.* 15), but it would not be half his joy unless he could impart to them some spiritual gift, which here he has an opportunity to do.

1. To whom he preached. Whoever would had liberty to come to his house to hear, and they were welcome. Ministers' doors should be open to such as desire to receive instruction from them. When we cannot do what we would in the service of God we must do what we can. *He received all that came to him,* and was not afraid of the greatest, nor ashamed of the meanest. He might hope the better to speed because *they came in unto him,* which supposed a desire to be instructed and a willingness to learn, and where these are it is probable that some good may be done.

2. What he preached. He is God's ambassador, and therefore *preaches the kingdom of God.* He meddles not with the affairs of the kingdoms of men; let those treat of them whose work it is. He preaches the kingdom of God among men; the same that he defended in his public disputes, *testifying the kingdom of God* (*v.* 23), he enforced in his public preaching, as that which will make us all wise and good, wiser and better, which is the end of preaching. He is an agent for Christ, and therefore *teaches those*

things which concern the Lord Jesus Christ—the whole history of Christ, all that relates to the mystery of godliness. Paul stuck still to his principle—to know and preach *nothing but Christ, and him crucified.*

3. With what liberty he preached. Divine grace gave him a liberty of spirit. He preached *with all confidence.* He was *not ashamed of the gospel of Christ.* Divine Providence gave him a liberty of speech: *No man forbidding him.* The Jews that used to forbid him to speak to the Gentiles had no authority here; and the Roman government as yet took no cognizance of the profession of Christianity as a crime. It set bounds to the rage of persecutors; there were many, both Jews and Gentiles, in Rome, that hated Christianity; and yet so it was that Paul though a prisoner was connived at in preaching the gospel. Though there were so many that had it in their power to forbid Paul's preaching, yet God so ordered it, *that no man did forbid him.* See God here providing comfort for the relief of the persecuted. Though it was not a wide door that was opened to him, yet it was kept open, and it was to many an effectual door, so that there were saints even in Cæsar's household, Phil. iv. 22. When the city of our solemnities is thus made a quiet habitation at any time, we must give thanks to God for it, still longing for that holy mountain in which there shall never be any pricking brier nor grieving thorn.

AN EXPOSITION, WITH PRACTICAL OBSERVATIONS, OF

THE EPISTLE OF ST. PAUL TO THE

ROMANS

In the Old Testament David's Psalms, and in the New Testament Paul's Epistles, are stars of the first magnitude. We have upon record several particular epistles, more of Paul's than of any other. His apprehension was quick and piercing; his expressions were fluent and copious; his affections very warm and zealous, and his resolutions no less bold and daring: this made him, before his conversion, a very keen and bitter persecutor. He became the most skilful zealous preacher; never any better fitted to win souls, nor more successful.

This epistle to the Romans is placed first, not because of the priority of its date, but because of the superlative excellency of the epistle, it being one of the longest and fullest of all. It is gathered from some passages in the epistle that it was written *Anno Christi* 56, from Corinth. Paul was now going up to Jerusalem, with the money that was given to the poor saints there; and of that he speaks, *ch.* xv. 26. The great mysteries treated of in this epistle must needs produce many things dark and hard to be understood, 2 Pet. iii. 16. The former part of it doctrinal, in the first eleven chapters; the latter part practical, in the last five.

I. The doctrinal part of the epistle instructs us,

1. Concerning the way of salvation.

2. Concerning the persons saved, such as belong to the election of grace, Gentiles and Jews. Two things the Jews then stumbled at—justification by faith without the works of the law, and the admission of the Gentiles into the church; and therefore both these he studied to clear and vindicate.

II. The practical part follows.

III. As he draws towards a conclusion, he makes an apology for writing to them, sends particular salutations to many friends there, adds the salutations of his friends with him, and ends with a benediction to them and a doxology to God.

CHAPTER 1

I. The preface and introduction to the whole epistle, to ver. 16.
II. A description of the deplorable condition of the Gentile world, which begins the proof of the doctrine of justification by faith, ver. 17.

Verses 1–7

I. The person who writes the epistle described (*v.* 1): *Paul, a servant of Jesus Christ;* this is his title of honour, which he glories in, a servant. *Called to be an apostle.* Christ sought him to make an apostle of him, Acts ix. 15. He here builds his authority upon his call; he did not run without sending. *Called an apostle,* as if this were the name he would be called by, though he acknowledged himself not meet to be called so, 1 Cor. xv. 9. *Separated to the gospel of God.* The Pharisees had their name from separation, because they *separated themselves to the study of the law,* such a one Paul had formerly been; but now he had changed his studies, was a gospel Pharisee, separated by the counsel of God (Gal. i. 15), *separated from his mother's womb.* He was an entire devotee to the gospel of God.

II. Having mentioned the gospel of God, he digresses, to give us an encomium of it.

1. The antiquity of it. It was *promised before* (*v.* 2); it was of ancient standing in the promises and prophecies of the Old Testament.

2. The subject-matter of it: it is concerning Christ, *v.* 3, 4. The prophets and apostles all bear witness to him. When Paul mentions Christ, how he heaps up his names and titles, *his Son Jesus Christ our Lord.* He cannot go on in his discourse without some expression of love and honour, as here, where in one person he shows us his two distinct natures. (1) His human nature: *Made of the seed of David* (*v.* 3), that is, born of the virgin Mary, who was of the house of David (Luke i. 27). (2) His divine nature: *Declared to be the Son of God* (*v.* 4), *according to the Spirit of holiness. According to the flesh,* that is, his human nature, *he was of the seed of David;* but, *according*

to the Spirit of holiness, that is, the divine nature, he is the Son of God. The great proof or demonstration of this is *his resurrection from the dead.* Those that would not be convinced by that would be convinced by nothing. So that we have here a summary of the gospel doctrine concerning Christ's two natures in one person.

3. The fruit of it (*v.* 5): *By whom we have received grace and apostleship.* Paul reckons the apostleship a favour. We may justly reckon it a great favour to be employed in any work or service for God. This apostleship was received *for obedience to the faith,* that is, to bring people to that obedience. Paul's was for this obedience *among all nations,* for he was the *apostle of the Gentiles.* Observe the description here given of the Christian profession: it is *obedience to the faith.* It does not consist in a notional knowledge, much less does it consist in perverse disputings, but in obedience. The act of faith is the obedience of the understanding to God revealing, and the product of that is the obedience of the will to God commanding. He here speaks of Christianity as an obedience. Christ has a yoke. *"Among whom are you,* v. 6. You Romans in this stand upon the same level with other Gentile nations of less fame and wealth; you are all one in Christ."* No respect of persons with God. *The called of Jesus Christ;* all those, and those only, are brought to an obedience of the faith that are effectually called of Jesus Christ.

III. The persons to whom it is written (*v.* 7): *To all that are in Rome, beloved of God, called to be saints;* that is, to all the professing Christians that were in Rome, bond or free, learned or unlearned. Rich and poor meet together in Christ Jesus. The privilege of Christians: They are *beloved of God.* He hath a common love to all mankind and a peculiar love for true believers; and that is to be holy, for hereunto are they called, *called to be saints.* Saints, and only saints, are beloved of God with a special and peculiar love. *Called saints,* saints in profession; it were well if all that are called saints were saints indeed. It will be of little avail at the great day to have been called saints, if we be not really so.

IV. The apostolical benediction (*v.* 7): *Grace to you and peace.* It hath not only the affection of a good wish, but the authority of a blessing. The favours desired: *Grace and peace.* The Old Testament salutation was, *Peace be to you;* but now grace is prefixed—*grace,* that is, the favour of God towards us. All gospel blessings are included in these two: *grace and peace. Peace,* that is, all good. The fountain of those favours, *from God our Father, and the Lord Jesus Christ.* All good comes, From God as a Father. We are taught, when we come for grace and peace, to call him our Father. *From the Lord Jesus Christ,* as Mediator. We have them from his fulness, peace from the fulness of his merit, grace from the fulness of his Spirit.

Verses 8–15

I. His thanksgiving for them (*v.* 8): *First, I thank my God.* It is good to begin everything with blessing God. He speaks this with delight and triumph. *Through Jesus Christ.* All our duties and performances are pleasing to God only through Jesus Christ, praises as well as prayers.—*For you all.* We must express our love to our friends, not only by praying for them, but by praising God for them. When some of the Roman Christians met him (Acts xxviii. 15), he thanked God for them, and took courage; but here his true catholic love extends itself further, and he *thanks God for them all.*—*That your faith is spoken of.* Wherever he came he heard great commendations of the Christians at Rome, which he mentions, not to make them proud, but to quicken them to answer the general character people gave of them. The greater reputation a man hath for religion, the more careful he should be to preserve it.—*Throughout the whole world,* that is, the Roman empire. This was indeed a good name, a name for good things with God and good people. It is a desirable thing to be famous for faith. Rome was a city upon a hill, everyone took notice of what was done there. Thus those who have many eyes upon them have need to walk circumspectly, for what they do, good or bad, will be spoken of.

II. His prayer for them, *v.* 9. Though a famous flourishing church, yet they had need to be prayed for. One of the greatest kindnesses we can do our friends, and sometimes the only kindness that is in the power of our hands, is, by prayer to recommend them to the loving-kindness of God. From Paul's example here we may learn, Constancy in prayer: *Always without ceasing.* Charity in prayer: *I make mention of you.* He made express mention of them. It is not unfit sometimes to be express in our prayers for particular churches and places; not to inform God, but to affect ourselves. We are likely to have the most comfort in those friends that we pray most for. He makes a solemn appeal to the searcher of hearts: *For God is my witness.* It is very comfortable to be able to call God to witness to our constancy in the discharge of a duty. God is particularly a witness to our secret prayers. *God, whom I serve with my spirit.* Those that serve God with their spirits may, with a humble confidence, appeal to him; hypocrites who rest in bodily exercise cannot. His particular prayer was that he might have an opportunity of paying them a visit (*v.* 10): *Making request, if by any means,* &c. The expressions here used intimate that he was very desirous of such an opportunity: *if by any means;* that he had long and often been disappointed: *now at length;* and yet that he submitted it to the divine Providence: *a prosperous journey by the will of God.* Our journeys are prosperous or otherwise according to the will of God, comfortable or not as he pleases.

III. His great desire to see them, with the reasons of it, *v.* 11–15. Fruitful Christians are as much the joy as barren professors are the grief of faithful ministers. Accordingly, he *often purposed to come, but was let hitherto* (*v.* 13), for man purposeth, but God disposeth. Paul was for doing that first, not which was most pleasant (then he would have gone to Rome), but which was most needful.

1. That they might be edified (*v.* 11): *That I may impart unto you.* He received, that he might communicate. *To the end you may be established.* That as they grew upward in the branches they might grow downward in the root. The best saints have need to be more and more established.

2. That he might be comforted, *v.* 12. What he heard of their flourishing in grace was so much a joy to him that it must needs be much more so to behold it.—*By the mutual faith both of you and me.* It is very comfortable when there is a mutual confidence between minister and people, they confiding in him as a faithful minister, and he in them as a faithful people. It is very refreshing to Christians to compare notes about their spiritual concerns.—*That I might have some fruit, v.* 13. The more good he did the greater would be his reward be.

3. That he might discharge his trust as the apostle of the Gentiles (*v.* 14): *I am a debtor.* His receivings made him a debtor. We should think of this when we covet great things, that all our receivings put us in debt; we are but stewards of our Lord's goods. His office made him a debtor. Paul had improved his talent, and laboured in his work, and done as much good as ever any man did, and yet, he still writes himself debtor.—*Debtor to the Greeks, and to the barbarians, to the wise and to the unwise.* The Greeks fancied themselves to have the monopoly of wisdom, and looked upon all the rest of the world as barbarians. Paul was a debtor to both, and looked upon himself as obliged to do all the good he could both to the one and to the other. Accordingly, we find him paying his debt, doing good *both to Greeks and barbarians.* For these reasons he was ready, if he had an opportunity, *to preach the gospel at Rome, v.* 15. Paul was ready to run the risk at Rome, if called to it: *I am ready.* It denotes a great readiness of mind. What he did was not for filthy lucre, but of a ready mind.

Verses 16–18

Paul here enters upon a large discourse of justification, describing the deplorable condition of the Gentile world. He was ready to preach the gospel at Rome, *for, I am not ashamed of it, v.* 16. There is a great deal in the gospel which such a man as Paul might be tempted to be ashamed of, especially that he whose gospel it is was a man hanged upon a tree. Yet Paul was not ashamed to own it. I reckon him a Christian indeed that is neither ashamed of the gospel nor a shame to it.

I. The proposition, *v.* 16, 17. It reveals to us,

1. The salvation of believers as the end: *It is the power of God unto salvation.* Paul is not ashamed of the gospel; it shows us *the way of salvation. It is through the power of God;* without that power the gospel is but a dead letter. It is to those, and those only, that believe. The medicine prepared will not cure the patient if it be not taken.—*To the Jew first. The lost sheep of the house of Israel* had the first offer made them, both by Christ and his apostles. Upon their refusal the apostles turned to the Gentiles, Acts xiii. 46. Jews and Gentiles now stand upon the same level, both equally welcome to the Saviour. The long-expected Messiah proves *a light to enlighten the Gentiles,* as well as *the glory of his people Israel.*

2. The justification of believers as the way (*v.* 17): *For therein is the righteousness of God revealed.*

That which will show us the way of salvation must needs show us the way of justification. The gospel makes known a righteousness. There is such a righteousness *revealed in the gospel*. This evangelical righteousness, (1) Is called the *righteousness of God*; it is of God's appointing. It is so called to cut off all pretensions to a righteousness resulting from the merit of our own works. It is the righteousness of Christ. (2) It is said to be *from faith to faith*. From the first faith, by which we are put into a justified state, to after faith, by which we live; from faith engrafting us into Christ, to faith deriving virtue from him as our root: both implied in the next words, *The just shall live by faith. Just by faith*, there is faith justifying us; *live by faith*, there is faith maintaining us. Faith is all in all, both in the beginning and progress of a Christian life. It is increasing, continuing, persevering faith. To show that this is no novel upstart doctrine, he quotes for it that famous scripture in the Old Testament: *The just shall live by faith.* Being justified by faith he shall live by it both the life of grace and of glory. Thus is the evangelical righteousness from faith to faith—from Old Testament faith in a Christ to come to New Testament faith in a Christ already come.

II. The proof of this proposition. Justification must be either by faith or works. It cannot be by works, and therefore he concludes it must be by faith. The apostle, like a skilful surgeon, before he applies the plaster, searches the wound—endeavours first to convince of guilt and wrath, and then to show the way of salvation. This makes the gospel the more welcome. In general (*v.* 18), *the wrath of God is revealed.* The light of nature and the light of the law reveal the wrath of God from sin to sin. It is well for us that the gospel reveals the justifying righteousness of God from faith to faith.

1. The sinfulness of man described; he reduceth it to two heads, *ungodliness and unrighteousness.*

2. The cause of that sinfulness, and that is, *holding the truth in unrighteousness.* Some ideas they had of the difference of good and evil; but they held them in unrighteousness. They held the truth as a captive or prisoner, that it should not influence them. An unrighteous wicked heart is the dungeon in which many a good truth is detained and buried.

3. The displeasure of God against it: *The wrath of God is revealed from heaven;* not only in the written word, but in the providences of God, his judgments executed upon sinners. They are a revelation from heaven. Or *wrath from heaven is revealed*; it is not the wrath of a man like ourselves, *but wrath from heaven*, therefore the more terrible.

Verses 19–32

I. The means and helps they had to come to the knowledge of God. Among them *he left not himself without witness* (Acts xiv. 17).

1. What discoveries they had: *That which may be known of God is manifest among them;* that is, there were some even among them that had the knowledge of God. *That which may be known*, which implies that there is a great deal which may not be known. The being of God may be apprehended, but cannot be comprehended. Finite understandings cannot perfectly know an infinite being; but, there is that which may be known.

2. Whence they had these discoveries: *God hath shown it to them.* Those common natural notions which they had of God were imprinted upon their hearts by the God of nature himself.

3. By what means these discoveries were confirmed, namely, by the work of creation (*v.* 20): *For the invisible things of God*, &c.

(1) Observe what they knew: *The invisible things of him, even his eternal power and Godhead.* The power

and Godhead of God are invisible things, and yet are clearly seen in their products. He works in secret but manifests what he has wrought, and therein makes known his power and Godhead. They did come to the knowledge of the Godhead, at least so much knowledge as was sufficient to have kept them from idolatry. This was that truth which they held in unrighteousness.

(2) How they knew it: *By the things that are made*, which could not make themselves; and therefore must have been produced by some first cause or intelligent agent, which first cause could be no other than an eternal powerful God. The workman is known by his work. The concurrence of all the parts to the good and beauty of the whole, do abundantly prove a Creator and his eternal power and Godhead. Thus did the light shine in the darkness. And *this from the creation of the world.* To evince this truth, we have recourse to the great work of creation. The date of the discovery. It is as old as the creation of the world. These notices concerning God are ancient truths. The way of the acknowledgment of God is a good old way; it was from the beginning. Truth got the start of error.

II. Their gross idolatry, *v.* 21–23, 25. We shall the less wonder at the inefficacy of these natural discoveries to prevent the idolatry of the Gentiles if we remember how prone even the Jews were to idolatry; so miserably are the degenerate sons of men plunged in the mire of sense.

1. The inward cause of their idolatry, *v.* 21, 22. They are therefore without excuse, in that they did know God. Though some have greater light and means of knowledge than others, yet all have enough to leave them inexcusable. They *glorified him not as God.* To glorify him as God is to glorify him only; but they did not so glorify him, for they set up a multitude of other deities. To glorify him as God is to worship him with spiritual worship; but they made images of him. Not to glorify God as God is in effect not to glorify him at all. *Neither were they thankful.* Insensibleness of God's mercies is at the bottom of our sinful departures from him. *But they became vain in their imaginations, in their reasonings*, in their practical inferences. They had a great deal of knowledge of general truths (*v.* 19), but no prudence to apply them to particular cases. They soon disputed themselves into a thousand vain and foolish fancies. When truth is forsaken, errors multiply. *And their foolish heart was darkened.* The foolishness and practical wickedness of the heart cloud and darken the intellectual powers and faculties. *Professing themselves to be wise, they became fools, v.* 22. Those that had the most luxuriant fancy, in framing to themselves the idea of a God, fell into the most gross and absurd conceits. Thus the *world by wisdom knew not God.* A proud conceit of wisdom is the cause of a great deal of folly. Paul's preaching was no where so laughed at and ridiculed as among the learned Athenians—*conceiting themselves* to be wise. The plain truth of the being of God would not content them; they thought themselves above that, and so fell into the greatest errors.

2. The outward acts of their idolatry, *v.* 23–25. (1) Making images of God (*v.* 23), by which they *changed the glory of the incorruptible God.* It was the greatest honour God did to man that he made man in the image of God; but it is the greatest dishonour man has done to God that he has made God in the image of man. This is called (*v.* 25) *changing the truth of God into a lie.* Idols are called lies, for they belie God, as if he had a body, whereas he is a Spirit. (2) Giving divine honour to the creature: *Worshipped and served the creature, besides the Creator.* They did in effect disown him by the worship they paid to the creature; for God will be all or none.

Or, *above* the Creator, thinking the supreme God inaccessible. The sin itself was their worshipping the creature at all; but this is mentioned as an aggravation of the sin, that they worshipped the creature more than the Creator. This was the general wickedness of the Gentile world. Even the wise men among them, who knew and owned a supreme God and were convinced of the nonsense and absurdity of their polytheism and idolatry, yet did as the rest of their neighbours did. I mention this because methinks it doth fully explain that of the apostle here (*v.* 18): *Who hold the truth in unrighteousness.* Upon the mention of the dishonour done to God by the idolatry of the Gentiles the apostle expresses himself in an awful adoration of God: *Who is blessed for ever. Amen.* When we see or hear of any contempt cast upon God or his name, we should think and speak highly and honourably of him. In this as in other things, the worse others are, the better we should be.

III. The judgments of God upon them for this idolatry; not many temporal judgments but spiritual judgments, giving them up to the most brutish and unnatural lusts. *He gave them up;* it is thrice repeated here, *v.* 24, 26, 28. Spiritual judgments are of all judgments the sorest. By whom they were given up. God gave them up, in a way of righteous judgment, leaving them to themselves—letting them alone; for his grace is his own, he may give or withhold his grace at pleasure. This we are sure of that it is no new thing for God to give men up to their own hearts' lusts. And yet God is not the author of sin, for, though the greatest wickedness follow upon this giving up, the fault of that is to be laid upon the sinner's wicked heart. If the patient will not submit to the methods prescribed, but wilfully does that which is prejudicial to him, the physician is not to be blamed. The fatal symptoms that follow are not to be imputed to the physician, but to the disease itself and to the folly of the patient. To what they were given up.

1. *To uncleanness and vile affections, v.* 24, 26, 27. It is (as it is said here) *through the lusts of their own hearts*—there all the fault is to be laid. Those who dishonoured God were given up to dishonour themselves. A man cannot be delivered up to a greater slavery than to be given up to his own lusts. The particular instances of their uncleanness and vile affections are their unnatural lusts, for which many of the heathen, even of those among them who passed for wise men, were infamous. Perhaps the apostle especially refers to the abominations that were committed in the worship of their idol-gods. Dunghill service for dunghill gods. See what wickedness there is in the nature of man. How much are we beholden to the restraining grace of God! For, were it not for this, man, who was made but little lower than the angels, would make himself a great deal lower than the devils. This is said to be that *recompence of their error which was meet.*

2. To a reprobate mind in these abominations, *v.* 28.

(1) They *did not like to retain God in their knowledge.* The blindness of their understandings was caused by the wilful aversion of their wills and affections. They would neither know nor do anything but just what pleased themselves. There are many that have God in their knowledge, but they do not retain him there. Because it thwarts their lusts; they do not like it. There is a difference between the *knowledge* and the *acknowledgment* of God; the pagans knew God, but would not acknowledge him.

(2) Answerable to this wilfulness of theirs God gave them over to a wilfulness in the grossest sins, here called a *reprobate mind.* See whither a course of sin leads, and into what a gulf it plunges the sinner

at last. This reprobate mind was a blind seared conscience, past feeling, Eph. iv. 19. Thus wilful hardness is justly punished with judicial hardness.—*To do those things which are not convenient.* And here he subjoins a black list of those unbecoming things which the Gentiles were guilty of. No wickedness, so contrary to the light of nature, but a reprobate mind will comply with it. By the histories of those times it appears that these sins here mentioned were reigning national sins. No fewer than twenty-three several sorts of sins and sinners are here specified, *v.* 29–31. It was time to have the gospel preached among them, for the world had need of reformation.

First, Sins against the first table: *Haters of God.* Here is the devil in his own colours, sin appearing sin. Every sin has in it a hatred of God. *Proud men and boasters* put those crowns upon their own heads which must be cast before his throne.

Secondly, Sins against the second table. In general here is a charge of unrighteousness. This is put first, for every sin is unrighteousness. It is especially put for second-table sins, doing as we would not be done by. Against the fifth commandment: *Disobedient to parents*, and *without natural affection.* Disobedient children are justly punished with unnatural parents; and unnatural parents with disobedient children. Against the sixth commandment: *Wickedness* (doing mischief for mischief's sake), *maliciousness, envy, murder, debate, malignity, despiteful, implacable, unmerciful;* all expressions of that hatred of our brother which is heart-murder. Against the seventh commandment: *Fornication.* Against the eighth commandment: *Unrighteousness, covetousness.* Against the ninth commandment: *Deceit, whisperers, back-biters, covenant-breakers, inventors of evil things, and without understanding;* wise to do evil, and yet having no knowledge to do good. So quick of invention in sin, and yet without understanding (stark fools) in the thoughts of God. Every heart by nature has in it the seed and spawn of all these sins. In the close he mentions the aggravations of the sins, *v.* 32. 1. They *knew the judgment of God.* They knew the law. They knew the penalty. They knew *that those who commit such things were worthy of death;* their own consciences could not but suggest this to them. It is a great aggravation of sin when it is committed against knowledge. It is daring presumption to run upon the sword's point. 2. They *not only do the same, but have pleasure in those that do them.* To be pleased with other people's sins is to love sin for sin's sake: it is joining in a confederacy for the devil's kingdom. Our own sins are much aggravated by our concurrence with the sins of others.

Now lay all this together, and then say whether the Gentile world could be justified before God by any works of their own.

CHAPTER 2

The scope of the first two chapters of this epistle may be gathered from ch. iii. 9, "We have before proved both Jews and Gentiles that they are all under sin." In this chapter he proves it upon the Jews. I. Jews and Gentiles stand upon the same level before the justice of God, to ver. 11. II. He shows more particularly what sins the Jews were guilty of, ver. 17, to the end.

Verses 1–16

The apostle had represented the state of the Gentile world to be as bad and black as the Jews were ready enough to pronounce it. Designing to show that the state of the Jews was very bad too, he sets himself to show that God would proceed upon equal terms of justice with Jews and Gentiles.

I. He arraigns them for their censoriousness and self-conceit (*v.* 1): *Thou art inexcusable, O man, whosoever thou art that judgest.* He intends especially the Jews, and to them particularly he applies this general charge, *Thou who teachest another teachest thou not thyself?* The Jews looked with a great deal of contempt upon the poor Gentiles; while in the meantime they were themselves as bad and immoral— though not idolaters. *Therefore thou art inexcusable.* If the Gentiles, who had but the light of nature, were inexcusable, much more the Jews, who had the light of the law.

II. He asserts the invariable justice of the divine government, *v.* 2, 3. He here shows what a righteous God that is with whom we have to do. The *judgment of God is according to truth*, according to the heart, and not according to the outward appearance, according to the works, and not with respect to persons, for he would not be God if he were not just; but it behoves those especially to consider it who condemn others for those things which they themselves are guilty of, and so think to bribe the divine justice by protesting against sin. As if preaching against sin would atone for the guilt of it. But observe how he puts it to the sinner's conscience (*v.* 3): *Thinkest thou this, O man?* The case is so plain that we may venture to appeal to the sinner's own thoughts: "Canst thou think that *thou shalt escape the judgment of God?* Can the heart-searching God be imposed upon by formal pretences, the righteous Judge of all so bribed?"

III. He draws up a charge against them (*v.* 4, 5), consisting of two branches:

1. Slighting the goodness of God (*v.* 4), *the riches of his goodness.* The more light we sin against the more love we sin against. There is in every wilful sin an interpretative contempt of the goodness of God, particularly the goodness of his patience, taking occasion thence to be so much the more bold in sin. *Not knowing* that *the goodness of God leadeth thee to repentance.* What method God takes to bring sinners to repentance. He leads them, not drives them like beasts, allures them; and it is goodness that leads, bands of love. The consideration of the goodness of God, his common goodness to all, should be effectual to bring us all to repentance.

2. Provoking the wrath of God, *v.* 5. The rise of this provocation is a *hard and impenitent heart.* To sin is to walk in the way of the heart; and when that is a hard and impenitent heart, how desperate must the course needs be! The provocation is expressed by *treasuring up wrath.* A treasure denotes abundance. It is a treasure that will be spending to eternity, and yet sinners are still adding to it as to a treasure. A treasure denotes secrecy. It denotes reservation to some further occasion. These treasures will be broken open. They are treasured up *against the day of wrath.* Though the present day be a day of patience towards sinners, yet there is a day of wrath coming. And that day of wrath will be *the day of the revelation of the righteous judgment of God.* The wrath of God is not like our wrath, a heat and passion: but it is a righteous judgment, his will to punish sin. This righteous judgment of God is now many times concealed in the prosperity of sinners, but shortly it will be manifested before all the world.

IV. Having mentioned the righteous judgment of God in *v.* 5, he here illustrates that judgment, and the righteousness of it.

1. He will *render to every man according to his deeds* (*v.* 6).

(1) In dispensing his favours; and this is mentioned twice here, both in *v.* 7 and *v.* 10. For he delights to show mercy. The objects of his favour: *Those who by patient continuance*, &c. Those whom the righteous God will reward are, *First*, Such as fix to themselves the right end, that *seek for glory, and honour, and immortality.* There is a holy ambition which is at the bottom of all practical religion, This is looking in our desires and aims as high as heaven, and resolved to take up with nothing short of it. This

seeking implies a loss, desire to retrieve it, and pursuits and endeavours consonant to those desires. *Secondly*, Such as having fixed the right end, adhere to the right way: *A patient continuance in well-doing.* There must be well-doing, *v.* 10. It is not enough to know well, and promise well, but we must do well. A continuance in well doing. Not for a fit and a start, like the morning cloud and the early dew; it is perseverance that wins the crown. A patient continuance. This patience respects not only the length of the work, but the difficulties of it. Those that will do well and continue in it must put on a great deal of patience. The product of his favour. He will render to such eternal life. Heaven is life, eternal life, and it is called (*v.* 10) *glory, honour, and peace.* Those that seek for the vain glory and honour of this world often miss of them; but those that seek for immortal glory and honour shall have them, and not only *glory and honour*, but *peace.* Heavenly glory and honour have peace with them, undisturbed everlasting peace.

(2) In dispensing his frowns (*v.* 8, 9). The objects of his frowns. *Such as are contentious and do not obey the truth.* Contentious against God. Every wilful sin is a quarrel with God. *Contentious, and do not obey the truth.* The truths of religion are not only to be known, but to be obeyed. Disobedience to the truth is interpreted a striving against it. *But obey unrighteousness.* Those that refuse to be the servants of truth will soon be the slaves of unrighteousness. The products of these frowns: *Indignation and wrath, tribulation and anguish.* These are the wages of sin. And this *upon the soul*; souls are the vessels of that wrath. Sin qualifies the soul for this wrath. Hell is eternal tribulation and anguish, the product of wrath and indignation. This comes of contending with God. Those that will not bow to his golden sceptre will certainly be broken by his iron rod.

2. *There is no respect of persons with God, v.* 11. As to the spiritual state, there is a respect of persons; but not as to outward relation or condition. God does not save men with respect to their external privileges, but according as their state and disposition really are. In dispensing both his frowns and favours it is both to Jew and Gentile. If to *the Jews first*, who had greater privileges, yet *also to the Gentiles*, whose want of such privileges will neither excuse them from the punishment of their ill-doing nor bar them out from the reward of their well-doing.

V. He proves the equity of his proceedings with all (*v.* 12–16). Three degrees of light are revealed to the children of men:

1. The light of nature. This the Gentiles have, and by this they shall be judged: *As many as have sinned without law shall perish without law;* that is, the unbelieving Gentiles, who had no other guide but natural conscience, shall not be reckoned with for the transgression of the law they never had. They shall be judged by the law of nature. The light of nature was to the Gentiles instead of a written law. He had said (*v.* 12) they had *sinned without law*, which looks like a contradiction; for where there is no law there is no transgression. But, says he, though they had not the written law, they had that which was equivalent. They *had the work of the law.* The work of the law is to direct us what to do, and to examine us what we have done. (1) They had that which directed them what to do by the light of nature. They apprehended a clear and vast difference between good and evil. They *did by nature the things contained in the law.* They had a sense of justice and equity, honour and purity, love and charity. Thus they were a *law unto themselves.* (2) They had that which examined them as to what they had done: *Their conscience also bearing witness.* They had that

within them which approved what was well done and which reproached them for what was done amiss. Conscience is a witness, and first or last will bear witness, testifying of that which is most secret; and their *thought accusing or excusing*, passing a judgment upon the testimony of conscience. Conscience is that candle of the Lord which was not quite put out, no, not in the Gentile world. Their *thoughts the meanwhile*. According as they observed or broke these natural laws and dictates, their consciences did either acquit or condemn them. All this did evince that they had that which was to them instead of a law. So that the guilty Gentiles are left without excuse. God is justified in condemning them. They cannot plead ignorance.

2. The light of the law. This the Jews had, and by this they shall be judged (*v.* 12): *As many as have sinned in the law shall be judged by the law.* They sinned in the face and light of so pure and clear a law. These shall be judged *by the law*; their punishment shall be, as their sin is, so much the greater for their having the law. *The Jew first, v.* 9. The apostle shows (*v.* 13) that their having, and hearing, and knowing the law, would not justify them, but their doing it. It was a great privilege that they had the law, but not a saving privilege, unless they lived up to the law they had. We may apply it to the gospel: it is not hearing, but doing that will save us.

3. The light of the gospel: and according to this those that enjoyed the gospel shall be judged (*v.* 16): *According to my gospel;* the gospel in general, called Paul's because he was a preacher of it. Some refer those words, *according to my gospel*, to what he says of the day of judgment. It is good for us to get acquainted with what is revealed concerning that day. There is a day set for a general judgment. The judgment of that day will be put into the hands of Jesus Christ. Nothing speaks more terror to sinners, or more comfort to saints, than this, that Christ shall be the Judge. The secrets of men shall then be judged. That will be the great discovering day.

Verses 17–29

He had said (*v.* 13) that not the hearers but the doers of the law are justified; and he here applies that great truth to the Jews.

I. He allows their profession (*v.* 17–20), that they might see he did not condemn them out of ignorance. He knew the best of their cause.

1. They were a peculiar people, having the written law and the special presence of God among them. *Thou art called a Jew.* It was a very honourable title. Salvation was of the Jews; and this they were very proud of, and yet many that were so called were the vilest of men. It is no new thing for the worst practices to be shrouded under the best names. *And restest in the law.* They were mightily puffed up with this privilege, and thought this enough to bring them to heaven, though they did not live up to the law. It is a dangerous thing to rest in external privileges, and not to improve them. *And makest thy boast of God.* A believing, humble, thankful glorying in God, is the summary of all religion. Boasting in God, and in the outward profession of his name, is the summary of all hypocrisy. Spiritual pride is of all kinds of pride the most dangerous.

2. They were a knowing people (*v.* 18) *and knowest his will.* The world will then be set to rights, when God's will is the only will, and all other wills are melted into it. The will of God, that which he would have them do. *And approvest the things that are more excellent.* A good apprehension in *the things of God*, reading it thus, *Thou discernest things that differ*, knowest how to distinguish between good and evil. Good and bad lie sometimes so near together that it is

not easy to distinguish them; but the Jews were, or at least thought they were, able to distinguish, to cleave the hair in doubtful cases. Or, we may, understand *controversies.* A man may be well skilled in the controversies of religion, and yet a stranger to the power of godliness. A warm affection to the things of God, as we read it, *Approvest the things that are excellent.* There may be a consent of the practical judgment *to the law, that it is good*, and yet that consent overpowered by the lusts of the flesh, and of the mind:

I see the better, but pursue the worse.

They got this acqaintance with that which is good, by being *instructed out of the law.* It was the custom of the Jews to take a great deal of pains in teaching their children, and all their lessons were *out of the law;* it were well if Christians were but as industrious to teach their children *out of the gospel.* Now this is called (*v.* 20), *The form of knowledge, and of the truth in the law.* A form of knowledge produces but a form of godliness, 2 Tim. iii. 5. A form of knowledge may deceive men, but cannot impose upon the heart-searching God.

3. They were a teaching people, or at least thought themselves so (*v.* 19, 20): *And art confident that thou thyself art a guide of the blind.* Apply it, (1) To the Jews in general. They thought themselves guides to the poor blind Gentiles that sat in darkness. All other nations must come to school to them, to learn what is good. (2) To their rabbis, and doctors. The apostle expresses this in several terms, *a guide of the blind, a light of those who are in darkness, an instructor of the foolish, a teacher of babes*, the better to set forth their proud conceit. This was a string they loved to be harping upon. The best work, when it is prided in, is unacceptable to God. It is good to instruct the foolish, but considering our own inability to make these teachings successful without God, there is nothing in it to be proud of.

II. He aggravates their provocations (*v.* 21–24) from two things:

1. They sinned against their knowledge, did that themselves which they taught others to avoid: *Thou that teachest another, teachest thou not thyself?* Teaching is a piece of that charity which begins at home, though it must not end there. The Pharisees pulled down with their lives what they built up with their preaching. The greatest obstructors of the success of the word are those whose bad lives contradict their good doctrine, who in the pulpit preach so well that it is a pity they should ever come out, and out of the pulpit live so ill that it is a pity they should ever come in. He specifies three particular sins that abound among the Jews: (1) Stealing. (2) Adultery, *v.* 22. Many of the Jewish rabbin are said to have been notorious for this sin. (3) Sacrilege, and this is charged upon those that professed to abhor idols. It was in the latter days of the Old Testament church that they were charged *with robbing God in tithes and offerings* (Mal. iii. 8, 9), converting that to their own use which was set apart for God. And this is almost equivalent to idolatry.

2. They dishonoured God by their sin, *v.* 23, 24. While God and his law were an honour to them, which they boasted of, they were a dishonour to God and his law, by giving occasion to those that were without to reflect upon their religion. *As it is written, v.* 24. He does not mention the place, because he wrote this to those that were instructed in the law. The great evil of the sins of professors is the dishonour done to God and religion by their profession. "*Blasphemed through you.* The reproaches you bring upon yourselves reflect upon your God, and religion is wounded through your sides." A good caution to professors to walk circumspectly.

III. He asserts the utter insufficiency of their profession to clear them from the guilt of these provocations (*v.* 25–29): *Circumcision verily profiteth, if thou keep the law;* that is, obedient Jews shall not lose the reward of their obedience. He is here speaking to the Jews, whose Judaism would benefit them, if they would but live up to the laws of it; but if not "*thy circumcision is made uncircumcision. Thou wilt be no more justified than the uncircumcised Gentiles, but more condemned for sinning against greater light.*"

1. He shows that the uncircumcised Gentiles, if they live up to the light they have, stand upon the same level with the Jews; if *they keep the righteousness of the law* (*v.* 26), *fulfil the law* (*v.* 27); that is, by submitting sincerely to the conduct of natural light, perform the matter of the law. It seems to be meant of such an obedience as some of the Gentiles did attain to. Doubtless, there were many such instances: and *they were the uncircumcision, that kept the righteousness of the law.* They were accepted with God. *Their uncircumcision was counted for circumcision.* Their obedience was a great aggravation of the disobedience of the Jews, *v.* 27. *Judge thee,* who *by the letter and circumcision dost transgress.* To carnal professors the law is but the letter; they read it as a bare writing, but are not ruled by it as a law. External privileges, if they do not do us good, do us hurt. The obedience of those that enjoy less means, and make a less profession, will help to condemn those that enjoy greater means, and make a greater profession, but do not live up to it.

2. He describes the true circumcision, *v.* 28, 29. It is *not that which is outward in the flesh and in the letter.* This is not to drive us off from the observances of external institutions (they are good in their place), but from trusting to them and taking up with a name to live, without being alive indeed. *He is not a Jew.* To be Abraham's children is to do the works of Abraham. It is *that which is inward, of the heart, and in the spirit.* It is the heart that God looks at. The praise thereof, though it be *not of men,* who judge according to outward appearance, yet it is *of God,* for *he seeth not as man seeth.* Fair pretences and a plausible profession may deceive men: but God sees through shows to realities. This is alike true of Christianity. He is not a Christian that is one outwardly, nor is that baptism which is outward in the flesh.

CHAPTER 3

I. He answers some objections that might be made against what he had said about the Jews, ver. 1–8. II. He asserts the guilt and corruption of mankind in common, ver. 9–18. III. He argues thence that justification must needs be by faith, and not by the law, ver. 19, to the end.

Verses 1–18

I. Here the apostle answers several objections. Divine truths must be cleared from cavil.

Object. 1. If Jew and Gentile stand so much upon the same level before God, *what advantage then hath the Jew?* Now does not this levelling doctrine deny them all prerogatives, and reflect dishonour upon the ordinance of circumcision.

Answer. The Jews are, notwithstanding this, a people greatly privileged and honoured (*v.* 2): *Much every way.* The door is open to the Gentiles as well as the Jews, but the Jews have a fairer way up to this door. He reckons up many of the Jews' privileges Rom. ix. 4, 5; here he mentions but one *that unto them were committed the oracles of God,* that is, the scriptures of the Old Testament. The scriptures are the oracles of God: they are a divine revelation. We must have recourse to the law and to the testimony, as to an oracle. Now these oracles were committed to the Jews. The Old Testament was deposited in their hands, to be carefully preserved pure and uncorrupt. The Jews were entrusted with that sacred treasure for their own use and benefit in the first place, and then for the advantage of the world. The Jews had the means of salvation, but they had not the monopoly of salvation. Now this he mentions with a *chiefly,* this was their prime and principal privilege. The enjoyment of God's word and ordinances is the chief happiness of a people.

Object. 2. To what purpose were the oracles of God committed to them, when so many of them continued strangers to Christ, and enemies to his gospel? *Some did not believe, v.* 3.

Answer. But shall their unbelief make the faith of God without effect? The apostle startled at such a thought: *God forbid!* The obstinacy of the Jews could not invalidate those prophecies of the Messiah which were contained in the oracles committed to them. Christ will be glorious. God's words shall be accomplished, though there be a generation that by their unbelief go about to make God a liar. *Let God be true but every man a liar;* let us abide by this principle, that God is true to every word which he has spoken. Better question the credit of all the men in the world than doubt of the faithfulness of God. All men are liars, compared with God. It is very comfortable, when we find every man a liar (no faith in man), that God is faithful. He quotes Ps. li. 4, *That thou mightest be justified,* to show, 1. That God will preserve his own honour in the world, notwithstanding the sins of men. 2. That it is our duty to justify God and to assert and maintain his justice, truth, and goodness, however it goes. Thus is God justified in his sayings, and cleared when *he is judged,* as it is here rendered.

Object. 3. Carnal hearts might hence take occasion to encourage themselves in sin. If all our sin be so far from overthrowing God's honour that it commends it, and his ends are secured, is it not unjust for God to punish our sin and unbelief so severely? *If our unrighteousness commend the righteousness of God, what shall we say? v.* 5. What inference may be drawn from this? *Is God unrighteous, who taketh vengeance? I speak as a man,* that is, it is suggested like a man.

Answer. God forbid. Suggestions that reflect dishonour upon God and his justice and holiness are rather to be startled at than parleyed with. *For then how shall God judge the world? v.* 6. The sin has never the less of malignity in it though God bring glory to himself out of it. It is only accidentally that sin commends God's righteousness. No thanks to the sinner for that. It is not for us to arraign the proceedings of such an absolute Sovereign. The sentence of the supreme court, whence lies no appeal, is not to be called in question.

Object. 4. The former objection is repeated (*v.* 7, 8). But his setting off the objection in its own colours is sufficient to answer it: *If the truth of God has more abounded through my lie, why should I be judged as a sinner, and not rather* thence take encouragement to go on in my sin, that grace may abound? *Let us do evil that good may come* is oftener in the heart than in the mouth of sinners, so justifying themselves in their wicked ways. There were those who charged such doctrines as this upon Paul and his fellow-ministers: Some affirm that we say so. It is no new thing for the best of God's people and ministers to be charged with holding and teaching such things as they do most detest, and it is not to be thought strange, when our Master himself was said to be in league with Beelzebub. It is an old artifice of Satan thus to cast dirt upon Christ's ministers—*Lay slander thickly on, for some will be sure to stick.*

Answer. He says no more by way of confutation but that the damnation of those is just. Those who deliberately do evil that good may come of it will be so far from escaping, under the shelter of that excuse, that it will rather justify their damnation. Sinning upon such a surmise, and in such a confidence, argues a great deal both of the wit and of the will in the sin. Their damnation is just; and, whatever excuses of this kind they may now please themselves with, they will none of them stand good in the great day, but God will be justified in his proceedings.

II. Paul next revives his assertion of the general guilt of mankind, both of Jews and Gentiles, *v. 9–18.* "*Are we better than they,* we Jews, or will this justify us? No, by no means." or, Are we Christians (Jews and Gentiles) so much better than the unbelieving part as to have merited God's grace? Alas! no. They *are all under sin.* Under the guilt of sin. We are guilty before God, *v.* 19. And this he had proved. It is a law term: *We have charged them with it,* and have made good our charge. This charge and conviction he here further illustrates by several scriptures out of the Old Testament. The 10th, 11th, and 12th verses are taken from Ps. xiv. 1–3. The rest that follows here is found in the Septuagint translation of the 14th Psalm. What is said in Ps. xiv is expressly spoken of *all the children of men.* The *Lord looked down,* as upon the old world. He who, when he himself had made all, looked upon everything that he had made, and behold all was very good, now that man had marred all, looked, and behold all was very bad. Observe,

1. That which is habitual, which is twofold:

(1) An habitual defect of everything that is good. *There is none righteous,* none that has an honest good principle of virtue, *no, not one;* implying that, if there had been but one, God would have found him out. When all the world was corrupt, God had his eye upon one righteous Noah. No righteousness is born with us. *There is none that understandeth, v.* 11. The fault lies in the corruption of the understanding. Religion and righteousness have so much reason on their side that if people had but any understanding they would be better and do better. Sinners are fools. *None that seeketh after God,* that is, none that has any desire after him. *They are together become unprofitable, v.* 12. Those that have forsaken God soon grow good for nothing. *There is none that doeth good;* no, not a just man upon the earth, that doeth good, and sinneth not.

(2) An habitual defection to everything that is evil: *They are all gone out of the way.* God made man in the way, set him in right, but he hath forsaken it.

2. That which is actual.

(1) In their words (*v.* 13, 14), in three things particularly: [1] Cruelty: *Their throat is an open sepulchre,* waiting an opportunity to do mischief. And when they do not vent it publicly, yet they are underhand intending mischief: the *poison of asps is under their lips,* the most venomous and incurable poison, with which they blast the good name of their neighbours. [2] Cheating: *With their tongues they have used deceit.* Herein they show themselves the devil's children. They *have used* it: it intimates that they make a trade of lying. [3] Cursing: reflecting upon God, and blaspheming his holy name; wishing evil to their brethren: *Their mouth is full of cursing and bitterness.* How many, who are called Christians, do by these sins evince that they are still under the reign and dominion of sin.

(2) In their ways (*v.* 15–17): *Their feet are swift to shed blood.* Wherever they go, *destruction and misery* go along with them; these are their companions —destruction and misery to themselves at last. Destruction and misery are in their ways; their sin is its own punishment: a man needs no more to make him miserable than to be a slave to his sins. —*And the way of peace have they not known.* They

are strangers to all true peace; they know not the things that belong to their peace.

(3) The root of all this we have: *There is no fear of God before their eyes, v.* 18. The fear of God is here put for all practical religion. Wicked people have not this before their eyes; they are governed by other rules, aim at other ends. Where no fear of God is, no good is to be expected. When once fear is cast off, prayer is restrained, and then all goes to wreck and ruin quickly. So that we have here a short account of the general depravity and corruption of mankind.

Verses 19–31

From all this Paul infers that it is in vain to look for justification by the works of the law, and that it is to be had only by faith, which he lays down (*v.* 28) as the summary of his discourse. *We conclude that a man is justified by faith, without the deeds of the law.* Man, under the power of such corruption, could never, by any works of his own, gain acceptance with God; but it must be resolved purely into the free grace of God, given through Jesus Christ. There are two things from which the apostle here argues: the guiltiness of man, to prove that we cannot be justified by the works of the law, and the glory of God, to prove that we must be justified by faith.

I. He argues from man's guiltiness. The argument is very plain: we can never be justified and saved by the law that we have broken. Now concerning the guiltiness of man,

1. He fastens it particularly upon the Jews (*v.* 19). *This that the law says, it says to those who are under the law;* this conviction belongs to the Jews as well as others, for it is written in their law. "The law convicts and condemns you—you see it does." That *every mouth may be stopped.* Those that are justified have their mouths stopped by a humble conviction; those that are condemned have their mouths stopped too, for they shall at last be convinced.

2. He extends it in general to all the world: *That all the world may become guilty before God. May become guilty;* that is, may be proved guilty. They must all plead guilty. Guilty before God is a dreadful word. All are guilty, and therefore all have need of a righteousness wherein to appear before God. *For all have sinned* (*v.* 23), and *have come short of the glory of God*—have failed of that which is the chief end of man. *Come short,* as the archer comes short of the mark, as the runner comes short of the prize; so come short, as not only not to win, but to be great losers.

(1) Come short of glorifying God. *They glorified him not as God.* Man by sin comes short of this, and, instead of glorifying God, dishonours him. (2) Come short of glorying *before God.* There is no boasting of innocency: if we go about to glory before God we have all sinned, and this will silence us. We may glory before men, who cannot search our hearts, but there is no glorying before God. (3) Come short of being glorified by God. Come short of justification, which is glory begun—come short of sanctification, which is the glorious image of God upon man. It is impossible now to get to heaven in the way of spotless innocency. That passage is blocked up.

3. Further to drive us off from expecting justification by the law, he ascribes this conviction to the law (*v.* 20): *For by the law is the knowledge of sin.* That law which convicts and condemns us can never justify us. It is the proper use and intendment of the law to open our wound, and therefore not likely to be the remedy. That which is searching is not sanative. Paul makes this use of the law, *ch.* vii. 9, *Therefore by the deeds of the law shall no flesh be justified in his sight.* (1) *No flesh shall be justified.* The corruption that remained in our nature will for ever obstruct any justification by our own works. (2) Not justified

in his sight. As the conscience stands in relation to God, *in his sight*, we cannot be justified by the deeds of the law.

II. He argues from God's glory to prove that justification must be expected only by faith in Christ's righteousness. Is there no hope? Is the wound become incurable because of transgression? No, blessed be God, it is not (*v.* 21, 22); there is another way laid open for us, *the righteousness of God without the law is manifested* now under the gospel. This is called *the righteousness of God*, righteousness of his ordaining, and providing, and accepting,—righteousness which he confers upon us.

1. Now concerning this righteousness of God. It is manifested. The gospel-way of justification is a highway, it is laid open for us. It is *without the law*. The righteousness that Christ hath brought in is a complete righteousness. Yet *it is witnessed by the law and the prophets*. The law is so far from justifying us that it directs us to another way of justification, points at Christ as our righteousness, to whom bear all the prophets witness. It is by the *faith of Jesus Christ*, that faith which hath Jesus Christ for its object. It is by this that we become interested in that righteousness which God has ordained, and which Christ has brought in. It is *to all, and upon all, those that believe*. Jews and Gentiles are alike welcome to God through Christ; *for there is no difference*. It is *to all*, the gospel excludes none that do not exclude themselves; but it is *upon all that believe*, not only tendered to them, but put upon them as a crown, as a robe.

2. But now how is this for God's glory?

(1) It is for the glory of his grace (*v.* 24): *Justified freely by his grace*. It is *by his grace*. And, to make it the more emphatic, he says it is *freely by his grace*. The grace of God comes *freely, freely*; nothing in us to deserve such favours: no, it is all *through the redemption that is in Jesus Christ*. It comes freely to us, but Christ bought it, and paid dearly for it. Christ's purchase is no bar to the freeness of God's grace; for grace provided and accepted this vicarious satisfaction.

(2) It is for the glory of his justice and righteousness (*v.* 25, 26): *Whom God hath set forth to be a propitiation*, &c. [1] Jesus Christ is the great propitiation. He is our throne of grace, in and through whom atonement is made for sin. He is all in all in our reconciliation, not only the maker, but the matter of it. God was in Christ, reconciling the world unto himself. [2] *God hath set him forth*. God, the party offended, makes the first overtures towards a reconciliation. *Fore-ordained* him to this, in the counsels of his love form eternity, and has exhibited him to a guilty world as their propitiation. [3] *By faith in his blood* we become interested in this propitiation. There is the healing plaster provided. Faith is the applying of this plaster to the wounded soul. And this faith hath a special regard to *the blood of Christ*. Without blood there should be no remission, and no blood but this would do it effectually. [4] All who by faith are interested in this propitiation have *the remission of their sins that are past*. It was for this that Christ was set forth to be a propitiation. *Through the forbearance of God*. Divine patience has kept us out of hell, that we might have space to repent, and get to heaven. *Past through the forbearance of God*. It is owing to the divine forbearance that we were not taken in the very act of sin. It is owing to the master's goodness and the dresser's mediation that barren trees are let alone in the vineyard. It is owing to Christ that there is ever a sinner on this side hell. [5] God does in all this *declare his righteousness*. This he insists upon with a great deal of emphasis: *To declare, I say, at this time his righteousness*. He declares his righteousness, *First*, In the propitiation itself. It appears that he hates sin, when

nothing less than the blood of Christ would satisfy for it. Finding sin, though but imputed, upon his own Son, he did not spare him, because he had made himself sin for us. *Secondly*, In the pardon upon that propitiation. *That he might be just, and the justifier of him that believeth*. It is now become not only an act of grace and mercy, but an act of righteousness, in God, to pardon the sins of penitent believers, having accepted the satisfaction that Christ by dying made to his justice for them. He is just, that is, faithful to his word.

(3) It is for God's glory; for boasting is thus excluded, *v.* 27. Now, if justification were by the works of the law, boasting would not be excluded. If we were saved by our own works, we might put the crown upon our own heads. But the *law of faith* doth for ever exclude boasting; for faith is a depending, self-emptying, self-denying grace, and casts every crown before the throne. He speaks of *the law of faith*. Believers are not left lawless: faith is a law, it is a working grace.

From all this he draws this conclusion (*v.* 28): *That a man is justified by faith without the deeds of the law*.

III. He shows the extent of this privilege of justification by faith, and that it is not the peculiar privilege of the Jews, but pertains to the Gentiles also; for he had said (*v.* 22) that there is no difference. He asserts and proves it (*v.* 29, 30): *Is he the God of the Jews only?* It is one God of grace that *justifies the circumcision by faith, and the uncircumcision through faith*. However the Jews, in favour of themselves, will needs fancy a difference, really there is no more difference than between *by* and *through*. He obviates an objection (*v.* 31), as if this doctrine did nullify the law. "No," says he, "though we do say that the law will not justify us, yet we do not therefore say that it was given in vain. *We establish the right use of the law*, and secure its standing, by fixing it on the right basis. Though we cannot be saved by it as a covenant, yet we own it, and submit to it, as a rule in the hand of the Mediator, subordinate to the law of grace; and so are so far from overthrowing that we establish the law."

CHAPTER 4

The great gospel doctrine of justification by faith without the works of the law was so very contrary to the notions the Jews had learnt that it would hardly go down with them. Now in this chapter he proves it by example. The example he pitches upon is that of Abraham. The whole chapter is taken up with his discourse upon this instance. I. He proves that Abraham was justified not by works, but by faith, ver. 1–8. II. He observes when and why he was so justified, ver. 9–17. III. He describes and commends that faith of his, ver. 17–22. IV. He applies all this to us, ver. 22–25.

Verses 1–8

Here the apostle proves that Abraham was justified not by works, but by faith. He appeals to the case of Abraham their father, and puts his own name to the relation, being a Hebrew of the Hebrews: *Abraham our Father*. Now *what has he found?* All the world is seeking; but none can be truly reckoned to have found, but those who are justified before God; and thus Abraham found this one pearl of great price. What has he found *as pertaining to the flesh*, that is, by circumcision and his external privileges? Was he justified by them? Was it the merit of his works that recommended him to God's acceptance? No, by no means.

I. If he had been justified by works, room would have been left for boasting. If so, *he hath whereof to glory* (*v.* 2). "But was not his name made great, and then might not he glory?" Yes, but not before God; he might deserve well of men, but he could never merit of God. Paul himself had *whereof to glory before men*, and we have him sometimes glorying in it, but nothing to glory in before God. Man must not pretend to glory in anything before God; no, not Abraham.

II. It is expressly said that Abraham's faith was counted to him for righteousness. *What saith the scripture? v.* 3. In all controversies in religion this must be our question. It is not what this great man, and the other good man, say, but *What saith the scripture?* Now the scripture saith that *Abraham believed, and this was counted to him for righteousness* (Gen. xv. 6); therefore he had not whereof to glory before God, it being purely of free grace that it was so imputed. It is mentioned in Genesis, upon occasion of a very signal act of faith concerning the promised seed, and it followed upon a grievous conflict he had had with unbelief. It is not the perfect faith that is required to justification, but the prevailing faith, the faith that has the upper hand of unbelief.

III. If he had been justified by works, the reward would have been *of debt, and not of grace.* This is his argument (*v.* 4, 5): Abraham's reward was God himself; so he had told him but just before (Gen. xv. 1), *I am thy exceeding great reward.* Now, if Abraham had merited this by the perfection of his obedience, it had not been an act of grace in God. God will have free grace to have all the glory. And therefore *to him that worketh not*—that can pretend to no such merit, but casts himself wholly upon the free grace of God in Christ, by a lively, active, obedient faith—to such a one *faith is counted for righteousness. Him that justifieth the ungodly*, that is, him that was before ungodly. His former ungodliness was no bar to his justification upon his believing. No room therefore is left for despair; though God clears not the impenitent guilty; yet through Christ he justifies the ungodly.

IV. He further illustrates this by a passage out of the Psalms, where David speaks of the remission of sins, as constituting the blessedness of a man, pronouncing blessed, not the man who has no sin, but *the man to whom the Lord imputeth not sin.* 1. The nature of forgiveness. It is the remission of a debt, it is the covering of sin. God is said *to cast sin behind his back, to hide his face from it,* which implies that the ground of our blessedness is not our innocency, but God's not laying it to our charge. It is God's *not imputing sin* (*v.* 8), which makes it wholly a gracious act of God. The acceptance and the reward cannot be expected as debts; and therefore Paul infers (*v.* 6) that it is the imputing of righteousness without works. 2. The blessedness of it: *Blessed are they.* It is said, *Blessed are those whose iniquities are forgiven*, to show what that blessedness is, and what is the ground of it. Pardoned people are the only blessed people. Oh, how much therefore is it our interest to make it sure to ourselves that our sins are pardoned! For this is the foundation of all other benefits.

Verses 9–17

St. Paul observes in this paragraph when and why Abraham was thus justified.

I. It was before he was circumcised, *v.* 10. His faith was counted to him for righteousness while he was in uncircumcision. It was imputed. Now this the apostle takes notice of in answer to the question (*v.* 9), *Cometh this blessedness then on the circumcision only, or on the uncircumcision also?* Abraham was pardoned and accepted in uncircumcision. Here are two reasons why Abraham was justified by faith in circumcision:

1. That circumcision might be *a seal of the righteousness of faith, v.* 11. For the confirmation of Abraham's faith God was pleased to appoint a sealing ordinance, and Abraham received it as a special favour, *the sign*

of circumcision, &c. (1) The nature of sacraments in general; they are signs and seals. They are signs of absolute grace and favour; they are seals of the conditional promises. God does in the sacraments seal to us to be to us a God, and we do therein seal to him to be to him a people. (2) The nature of circumcision in particular: it was the initiating sacrament of the Old Testament. *A sign*—a sign of that original corruption which we are all born with, and which is cut off by spiritual circumcision. It was *an outward and sensible sign of an inward and spiritual grace signified thereby. A seal of the righteousness of the faith.* In general, it was a seal of the covenant of grace, particularly of justification by faith. Now if infants were then capable of receiving a seal of the covenant of grace, which proves that they then were within the verge of that covenant, how they come to be now cast out of the covenant, those are concerned to make out that reject the baptism of the seed of believers.

2. *That he might be the father of all those that believe.* In him commenced a much clearer and fuller dispensation of the covenant of grace than any that had been before extant; and therefore he is called *the father of all that believe. The father of all those that believe;* that is, a standing *pattern of faith*, as parents are examples to their children; and a standing precedent of justification by faith, as the liberties of the fathers descend to their children. (1) The father of believing Gentiles, *though they be not circumcised.* Abraham being himself uncircumcised when he was justified by faith, uncircumcision can never be a bar. Thus were the doubts and fears of the poor Gentiles anticipated. (2) The father of believing Jews because they *are not of the circumcision only, but walk in the steps of that faith*—not only are of Abraham's family, but follow the example of Abraham's faith. See here who are the genuine children of those that were the church's fathers. Those that tread in their steps; this is the line of succession. Those have most reason to call Christ Father, not that bear his name in being Christians in profession, but that tread in his steps.

II. It was before the giving of the law, *v.* 13–16.

1. What that promise was—*that he should be the heir of the world.* The meek are said to *inherit the earth*, and the world is theirs. Though Abraham had so little of the world in possession, yet he was heir of it all. Or, rather, it points at Christ, the seed here mentioned *To thy seed, which is Christ.* Now Christ is the heir of the world, and it is in him that Abraham was so.

2. How it was made to him: *Not through the law, but through the righteousness of faith. Not through the law;* it was upon his trusting God, in his leaving his own country when God commanded him. Now, being by faith, it could not be by the law (*v.* 14, 15): *If those who are of the law be heirs, then faith is made void;* for, if it were requisite that there should be a perfect performance of the whole law, then the promise can never take its effect, since the way to life by perfect obedience to the law, and spotless sinless innocency, is wholly blocked up, and the law in itself opens no other way. This he proves, *v.* 15. *The law worketh wrath*—wrath in us to God; as the damming up of a stream makes it swell—wrath in God against us. Now it is certain that we can never expect the inheritance by a law that worketh wrath. How the law works wrath he shows in the latter part of the verse: *Where no law is there is no transgression* (an acknowledged maxim).

3. Why the promise was made to him by faith; for three reasons, *v.* 16. (1) *That it might be by grace and not by the law; by grace, and not of debt, not of merit.* Faith hath particular reference to grace granting, as grace hath reference to faith receiving.

God will have every crown thrown at the feet of grace, free grace. (2) *That the promise might be sure.* The first covenant was not sure: but, through man's failure, the benefits designed by it were cut off. The more effectually to ensure the conveyance of the new covenant, there is another way found out, *not by works but by faith,* which received all from Christ, in whose keeping it is safe. (3) *That it might be sure to all the seed.* If it had been by the law, it had been limited to the Jews. It was by faith that Gentiles as well as Jews might become interested in it, the spiritual as well as the natural seed of faithful Abraham. God would contrive the promise in such a way as might comprehend all true believers, and for this (v. 17) he refers us to Gen. xvii. 5, where the reason of the change of his name from *Abram—a high father, to Abraham—the high father of a multitude,* is thus rendered: *For a father of many nations have I made thee;* that is, all believers should take Abraham for their pattern, and call him *father.*

Verses 17–22

I. Whom he believed: *God who quickeneth.* It is God himself that faith fastens upon. Now observe what in God Abraham's faith had an eye to. 1. *God who quickeneth the dead.* It was promised that he should be *the father of many nations,* when he and his wife were now as good as dead (Heb. xi. 11, 12), and therefore he looks upon God as a God that could breathe life into dry bones. He that quickeneth the dead can do anything, can give a child to Abraham when he is old, can bring the Gentiles, who are *dead in trespasses and sins,* to a divine and spiritual life, Eph. ii. 1. 2. *Who calleth things which are not as though they were.* The justification and salvation of sinners, the espousing of the Gentiles that had not been a people, were a gracious calling of things which are not as though they were. This expresses the sovereignty of God and his absolute power and dominion, a mighty stay to faith when all other props sink and totter. It is faith indeed to build upon the all-sufficiency of God for the accomplishment of that which is impossible to anything but that all-sufficiency. Thus Abraham became *the father of many nations before him whom he believed.* It is by faith in God that we become accepted of him.

II. How he believed. *Against hope, he believed in hope,* v. 18. There was a hope against him, a natural hope. All the arguments of sense, and reason, and experience, which in such cases usually beget and support hope, were against him. But, against all those inducements to the contrary, he believed; for he had a hope for him: *He believed in hope,* which arose, as his faith did, from the consideration of God's all-sufficiency. *That he might become the father of many nations.* Therefore God, by his almighty grace, enabled him thus to believe against hope. It was fit that he who was to be the father of the faithful should have something more than ordinary in his faith. This was that which he believed, when it was counted to him for righteousness. *Being not weak in faith, he considered not his own body,* v. 19. His own body was now dead—become utterly unlikely to beget a child. When God intends some special blessing for his people, he commonly puts a sentence of death upon the blessing itself. But Abraham did not consider this, *he did not dwell in his thoughts upon it.* His faith thought of nothing but the faithfulness of the promise, and this kept up his faith. Though it may seem to be the wisdom of carnal reason, yet it is the weakness of faith, to look into the bottom of all the difficulties that arise against the promise. *He staggered not at the promise of God through unbelief* (v. 20). *He disputed not;* he did not hold any self-consultation about it, did not take time to consider whether he should close with it or no, but by a resolute act of his soul, with a holy boldness, ventured all upon the promise. He took it not for a point that would admit of argument or debate. He *staggered not through unbelief.* Unbelief is at the bottom of all our staggerings at God's promises. It is not the promise that fails, but our faith that fails when we stagger. He *was strong in faith, giving glory to God, he was strengthened* in faith, his faith *got ground by exercise.* Though weak faith shall not be rejected, yet strong faith shall be commended and honoured. The strength of his faith appeared in the victory it won over his fears. Abraham's faith gave God the glory, especially of his faithfulness. Abraham gave glory to God by trusting him. We never hear our Lord Jesus commending anything so much as great faith (Matt. viii. 10 and xv. 28): therefore God gives honour to faith, great faith, because faith, great faith, gives honour to God. He was *fully persuaded that what God had promised he was able to perform—was carried on with the greatest confidence* and assurance; it is a metaphor taken from ships that come into the harbour with full sail. Abraham saw the storms of doubts, and fears, and temptations likely to rise against the promise. But Abraham, having taken God for his pilot, and the promise for his card and compass, like a bold adventurer sets up all his sails, regards neither winds nor clouds, but trusts to the wisdom and faithfulness of his pilot, and bravely makes to the harbour, and comes home an unspeakable gainer. Such was his full persuasion, built on the omnipotence of God: *He was able.* Our waverings rise mainly from our distrust of the divine power. It is requisite we believe not only that he is faithful, but that he is able. *And therefore it was imputed to him for righteousness,* v. 22. Because he ventured his all in the divine promise, God graciously accepted him, and not only answered, but out-did, his expectation, and justified him. This shows why faith is chosen to be the prime condition of our justification, because it is a grace that of all others gives glory to God.

Verses 23–25

In the close of the chapter, he applies all to us. He here concludes that his justification was to be the pattern of ours: *It was not written for his sake alone.* It was not intended only for an historical commendation of Abraham, or a relation of something peculiar to him. The accounts we have of the Old Testament saints were not intended for histories only, but for precedents to direct us, for ensamples (1 Cor. x. 11) for *our learning, ch.* xv. 4. And this particularly concerning Abraham was written *for us also,* to assure us what that righteousness is which God requireth. For us on whom the ends of the world are come, as well as for the patriarchs; for the grace of God is the same yesterday, today, and for ever.

I. Our common privilege; it shall be imputed to us, that is, righteousness shall. *It shall be imputed;* he uses a future verb, to signify the continuation of this mercy in the church, that as it is the same now so it will be while God has a church in the world. There is a fountain opened that is inexhaustible.

II. Our common duty, the condition of this privilege, and that is believing. The proper object of this believing is a divine revelation. The revelation to Abraham was concerning a Christ to come; the revelation to us is concerning a Christ already come, which difference in the revelation does not alter the case. Now we are to believe on him that raised up Christ; not only believe his power, but depend upon his grace. So he explains it, v. 25. He was *delivered for our offences.* He died indeed as a malefactor, because he died for sin; but it was not his own sin. He died to make atonement for our sins. He was *raised again for our justification.* By the merit of his death he paid our debt, in his resurrection he took out our acquittance. The apostle puts a special emphasis on Christ's resurrection; it is Christ that died, *yea, rather, that has risen again, ch.* viii. 34. So that upon the whole matter it is very evident that we are not justified by the merit of our own works, but by dependence upon Jesus Christ and his righteousness, which was the truth that Paul in this and the foregoing chapter had been fixing as the great spring and foundation of all our comfort.

CHAPTER 5

I. He shows the fruits of justification, ver. 1–5. II. He shows the fountain and foundation of justification in the death of Jesus Christ, in the rest of the chapter.

Verses 1–5

The precious benefits and privileges which flow from justification are such as should quicken us all to give diligence to make it sure to ourselves. The fruits of this tree of life are exceedingly precious.

I. *We have peace with God, v.* 1. It is sin that breeds the quarrel between us and God. Justification takes away the guilt, immediately upon the removing of that obstacle, the peace is made. By faith we lay hold of God's arm and of his strength, and so are at peace. There is more in this peace than barely a cessation of enmity, there is friendship and loving-kindness, for God is either the worst enemy or the best friend. Christ has called his disciples *friends,* John xv. 13–15. And surely a man needs no more to make him happy than to have God his friend! But this is *through our Lord Jesus Christ*—through him as the great peacemaker, *the Mediator between God and man,* not only the maker, but the matter and maintainer, of our peace.

II. *We have access by faith into this grace wherein we stand, v.* 2. This is a further privilege, not only peace, but grace. The saints' happy state. It is a state of grace, God's loving-kindness to us and our conformity to God. Into this grace we have access: we were not born in this state, but we are brought into it. We could not have got into it of ourselves, but we are led into it as blind, or lame, or weak people are led. *We have had access.* Paul, in his conversion, had this access; then he was made nigh. It was Christ that introduced and led him by the hand into this grace. *By whom we have access by faith.* By Christ as the author, by faith as the means of this access. Their happy standing in this state: *Wherein we stand.* Not only wherein we are, but wherein we stand. The phrase denotes also our progress; while we stand, we are going. We must not lie down, as if we had already attained, but stand as those that are pressing forward, stand as servants attending on Christ our master. The phrase denotes, further, our perseverance: we stand firmly and safely; stand as soldiers stand, that keep their ground. It is not in the court of heaven as in earthly courts, where high places are slippery places.

III. *We rejoice in hope of the glory of God.* Besides the happiness in hand, there is a happiness in hope, *the glory of God.* Those that have access by faith into the grace of God now may hope for the glory of God hereafter. Grace is glory begun, the earnest and assurance of glory. Those who hope for the glory of God hereafter, have enough to rejoice in now.

IV. *We glory in tribulations also;* not only notwithstanding our tribulations, but even in our tribulations. What a growing increasing happiness the happiness of the saints is: *Not only so. We glory in tribulations also,* especially tribulations for righteousness' sake. This being the hardest point, he sets himself to show the grounds and reasons of it. Tribulations, by a chain of causes, greatly befriend

hope, which he shows in the method of its influence. *Tribulation worketh patience,* the powerful grace of God working in and with the tribulation. It proves, and by proving improves, patience, as steel is hardened by the fire. That which worketh patience is matter of joy; for patience does us more good than tribulations can do us hurt. Tribulation in itself worketh impatience; but, as it is sanctified to the saints, it worketh patience. *Patience experience, v.* 4. It works an experience of God, the patient sufferers have the greatest experience of the divine consolations. It works an experience of ourselves. It is by tribulation that we make an experiment of our own sincerity. It works *an approbation,* as he is approved that has passed the test. *Experience hope.* He who, being thus tried, comes forth as gold, will thereby be encouraged to hope. Experience of God is a prop to our hope. Experience of ourselves helps to evidence our sincerity. This *hope maketh not ashamed,* will not deceive us. Nothing confounds more than disappointment. It maketh not ashamed of our sufferings. It is in a good cause, for a good Master, and in good hope; and therefore we are not ashamed. *Because the love of God is shed abroad.* This hope will not disappoint us, because it is sealed with the Holy Spirit as a Spirit of love. *The love of God,* that is, the sense of God's love to us, drawing out love in us to him again. The ground of all our comfort and holiness, and perseverance in both, is laid in the *shedding abroad of the love of God in our hearts.* Sense of God's love to us will make us not ashamed, either of our hope in him or our sufferings for him.

Verses 6–21

The apostle here describes the fountain and foundation of justification, laid in the death of the Lord Jesus. He enlarges upon this instance of the love of God which is shed abroad. 1. The persons he died for, *v.* 6–8. 2. The precious fruits of his death, *v.* 9–11. 3. The parallel he runs between the communication of sin and death by the first Adam and of righteousness and life by the second Adam, *v.* 12, to the end.

I. The character we were under when Christ died for us.

1. *We were without strength (v.* 6), in a sad condition; altogether unable to help ourselves out of that condition. Therefore, our salvation is here said to come *in due time.* God's time to help and save is when those that are to be saved are without strength. It is the manner of God to help at a dead lift.

2. *He died for the ungodly;* not only helpless creatures, and therefore likely to perish, but guilty sinful creatures, and therefore deserving to perish. Being ungodly, they had need of one to die for them. This he illustrates (*v.* 7, 8) as an unparalleled instance of love; herein God's thoughts and ways were above ours. (1) One would hardly *die for a righteous man,* that is, one that is unjustly condemned; everybody will pity such a one, but few will hazard their own in his stead. (2) One might perhaps be persuaded *to die for a good man,* who is more than barely a righteous man. Many that are good themselves yet do but little good to others; but those that are useful commonly get themselves well beloved. And yet observe how he qualifies this: it is but some that would do so, after all, it is but a *peradventure.* (3) *But Christ died for sinners (v.* 8), neither righteous nor good; not only such as were useless, but such as were guilty. Now herein *God commended his love,* not only proved but magnified it and made it illustrious, not only put it past dispute, but rendered it the object of the greatest wonder and admiration. *Commendeth his love* in order to the shedding abroad of his love in our hearts by the Holy Ghost. *While we were yet sinners.* He died to save us, not in our sins, but from

our sins; but we were yet sinners when he died for us. (4) Nay, which is more, *we were enemies* (v. 10), not only malefactors, but traitors and rebels. And that for such as these Christ should die is such a mystery, such an unprecedented instance of love, that it may well be our business to eternity to admire and wonder at it. Justly might he who had thus loved us make it one of the laws of his kingdom that we should love our enemies.

II. The precious fruits of his death.

1. Justification and reconciliation are the fruit of the death of Christ: *We are justified by his blood* (v. 9), *reconciled by his death*, v. 10. Sin is pardoned, the enmity slain, an end made of iniquity, and an everlasting righteousness brought in. Immediately upon our believing, we are actually put into a state of justification and reconciliation. *Justified by his blood.* Our justification is ascribed to the blood of Christ because *without blood there is no remission*, Heb. ix. 22. In all the propitiatory sacrifices, the sprinkling of the blood was of the essence of the sacrifice.

2. Hence results salvation from wrath: *Saved from wrath* (v. 9), *saved by his life*, v. 10. If God justified and reconciled us when we were enemies, much more will be save us when we are justified and reconciled. He that has done the greater, which is of enemies to make us friends, will certainly do the less, which is when we are friends to use us friendly and to be kind to us. The apostle, once and again, speaks of it with a *much more. We shall be saved from wrath.* It is the wrath of God that is the fire of hell. *Reconciled by his death, saved by his life.* His life here spoken of is not to be understood of his life in the flesh, but his life in heaven. We are reconciled by Christ humbled, we are saved by Christ exalted. The dying Jesus laid the foundation in satisfying for sin, and slaying the enmity, but it is the living Jesus that perfects the work. Christ dying was the testator, who bequeathed us the legacy; but Christ living is the executor, who pays it.

3. All this produces, as a further privilege, our *joy in God*, v. 11. God is now so far from being a terror to us that he is our *joy. We are reconciled and saved from wrath. And not only so*, there is more in it yet, a constant stream of favours; not only get into the harbour, but come in with full sail: *We joy in God*, solacing ourselves in his love. And all this (which he repeats as a string he loved to be harping upon) by virtue of the atonement, for by him we *received the atonement.* To *receive the atonement* is, (1) To give our consent to the atonement, being willing and glad to be saved in a gospel way and upon gospel terms. (2) To take the comfort of the atonement. Now *we joy in God*, now we do indeed *receive the atonement, glorying* in it.

III. The parallel that the apostle runs between the communication of sin and death by the first Adam and of righteousness and life by the second Adam (v. 12, to the end), showing a correspondence between our fall and our recovery.

1. A general truth laid down as the foundation of his discourse—that Adam was a type of Christ (v. 14): *Who is the figure of him that was to come.* God dealt with Adam and Adam acted as a common father, of and for all his posterity. Jesus Christ, the Mediator, acted as the head of all the elect, dealt with God for them, as their father, died for them, rose for them, entered within the veil for them, did all for them.

2. A more particular explication of the parallel.

(1) How Adam communicated sin and death to all his posterity (v. 12): *By one man sin entered.* We see the world under a deluge of sin and death, full of iniquities and full of calamities. It was *by one man*, and he the first man. [1] By him *sin entered.* When

God pronounced all very good (Gen. i. 31) there was no sin in the world. It never entered into the world of mankind till Adam sinned. Then entered the guilt of Adam's sin imputed to posterity, and a general depravedness of nature. *For that* (so we read it), rather *in whom, all have sinned.* Sin entered into the world by Adam, for in him we all sinned. God, as the author of nature, had made this the law of nature, that man should beget in his own likeness. In Adam therefore, as in a common receptacle, the whole nature of man was reposited. Adam therefore sinning and falling, the nature became guilty and corrupt. Thus in him all have sinned. [2] *Death by sin*, for death is the wages of sin. When sin came, of course death came with it. [3] *So death passed, passed through* all men, as an infectious disease passes through a town, so that none escape it. It is the universal fate, without exception. *Death reigned*, v. 14. None are exempted from its sceptre. It is the last enemy, 1 Cor. xv. 26. He shows that sin did not commence with the law of Moses, but was *in the world until*, or *before*, that law. Sin was in the world before the law; witness Cain's murder, the apostasy of the old world, the wickedness of Sodom. His inference hence is, Therefore there was a law; for *sin is not imputed where there is no law.* Original sin is a want of conformity to, and actual sin is a transgression of, the law of God: therefore all were under some law. His proof of it is, *Death reigned from Adam to Moses*, v. 14. This proves that sin was in the world before the law, and original sin, for death reigned over those that had not sinned any actual sin, that *had not sinned after the similitude of Adam's transgression.*

(2) How, in correspondence to this, Christ communicates righteousness and life to all true believers. He shows not only wherein the resemblance holds, but wherein the communication of grace and love by Christ *goes beyond* the communication of guilt and wrath by Adam.

[1] Wherein the resemblance holds, v. 18, 19.

First, By the offence and disobedience of one many were made sinners, and judgment came upon all men to condemnation. Adam's sin was disobedience. The thing he did was therefore evil because it was forbidden, this opened the door to other sins. The malignity and poison of sin are very strong and spreading, else the guilt of Adam's sin would not have reached so far. Who would think there should be so much evil in sin? By Adam's sin many are made sinners: *many*, that is, all his posterity. *Made sinners*, It denotes the making of us such by a judicial act. Judgment is come upon all those that by Adam's disobedience were made sinners. All the race of mankind lie under a sentence, like an attainder upon a family.

Secondly, In like manner, *by the righteousness and obedience of one are many made righteous*, and so the *free gift comes upon all.* 1. The nature of Christ's righteousness, how it is brought in; it is by his obedience. The disobedience of the first Adam ruined us, the obedience of the second Adam saves us. By his obedience he wrought out a righteousness for us, satisfied God's justice. 2. The fruit of it. There is a *free gift come upon all men.* The salvation wrought is a *common salvation*; whoever will may come, and take of these waters of life. This free gift is *unto justification of life.* It is not only a justification that frees from death, but that entitles to life. *Many shall be made righteous, shall be constituted* righteous, as by letters patent.

[2] Wherein the communication of grace and love by Christ goes beyond the communication of guilt and wrath by Adam, v. 15–17. It is designed for the magnifying of Christ's love, and for the comfort of believers. *First*, If guilt and wrath be communicated

much more shall grace and love. *Much more the grace of God, and the gift by grace.* God's goodness is, of all his attributes, in a special manner his glory. We know that God is rather inclined to show mercy; punishing is his strange work. *Secondly,* If there was so much power and efficacy in the sin of a man, to condemn us, much more are there power and efficacy in the righteousness and grace of Christ, to justify and save us. Surely Adam could not propagate so strong a poison but Jesus Christ could propagate as strong an antidote, and much stronger.

Thirdly, It is but the guilt of one single offence of Adam's that is laid to our charge: *The judgment was by one,* that is, by one offence, *v.* 16, 17. But from Jesus Christ we receive and derive an *abundance of grace, and of the gift of righteousness.* The stream of grace and righteousness is deeper and broader than the stream of guilt. God in Christ forgives all trespasses.

Fourthly, By Adam's sin *death reigned*; but by Christ's righteousness believers are preferred to *reign in life, v.* 17. We are by Christ and his righteousness entitled to, and instated in, more and greater privileges than we lost by the offence of Adam. The plaster is wider than the wound, and more healing than the wound is killing.

IV. *The law entered that the offence might abound.* Not to make sin to abound the more in itself, but to discover the abounding sinfulness of it. The glass discovers the spots, but does not cause them. The letting of a clearer light into a room discovers the dust and filth which were there before, but were not seen. *That grace might much more abound*—that the terrors of the law might make gospel-comforts so much the sweeter. The greater the strength of the enemy, the greater the honour of the conqueror. This abounding of grace he illustrates, *v.* 21. *Sin reigned unto death;* it was a cruel bloody reign. But *grace reigns* to life, *eternal life,* and this *through righteousness* by *Jesus Christ our Lord,* through the power and efficacy of Christ.

CHAPTER 6

The apostle having at large proved the great doctrine of justification by faith, he, with a like cogency of argument, presses the absolute necessity of sanctification and a holy life, as the inseparable fruit of justification; for, wherever Jesus Christ is made of God unto any soul righteousness, he is made of God unto that soul sanctification.

Verses 1–23

The apostle's transition, which joins this discourse with the former: *"What shall we say then? (v.* 1). *Shall we continue in sin that grace may abound?"* Shall we hence take encouragement to sin because the more sin we commit the more will the grace of God be magnified in our pardon? The apostle startled at the thought of it (*v.* 2): "*God forbid.*" Those opinions that give any countenance to sin are to be rejected with the greatest abhorrence. The apostle is very full in pressing the necessity of holiness in this chapter, which may be reduced to two heads: His exhortations to holiness, and his arguments to enforce those exhortations.

I. For the first, we may hence observe the nature of sanctification. It has two things in it, mortification and vivification—dying to sin and living to righteousness.

1. Mortification, putting off the old man. (1) We must *live no longer in sin (v.* 2). Though there are none that live without sin, yet there are those that do not live in sin. (2) *The body of sin must be destroyed, v.* 6. The corruption that dwelleth in us is the body of sin. This is the root to which the axe must be laid. We must not only cease from the acts of sin, but we must get the vicious habits and inclinations weakened and destroyed. *That henceforth we should not serve sin.* It is the body of sin that sways the

sceptre; destroy this, and the yoke is broken. (3) *We must be dead indeed unto sin, v.* 11. As the death of the oppressor is a release, so much more is the death of the oppressed. Thus must we be dead to sin, fulfil its will no more. He that is dead is separated from his former company. Death makes a mighty change; such a change doth sanctification make in the soul, it cuts off all correspondence with sin. (4) *Sin must not reign in our mortal bodies that we should obey it, v.* 12. Though sin may remain as an outlaw, yet let it not reign as a king. Let it not make laws, so that we should obey. Though we may be sometimes overtaken and overcome by it, yet let us never be obedient to it. *In the lusts thereof.* Sin lies very much in the gratifying of the body. And there is a reason implied in the phrase *your mortal body.* It was sin that made our bodies mortal, and therefore do not yield obedience to such an enemy. (5) We must not *yield our members as instruments of unrighteousness, v.* 13. The members of the body are made use of by the corrupt nature as tools, but we must not consent to that abuse. One sin begets another; it is like the letting forth of water, therefore leave it before it be meddled with. The members of the body may perhaps be forced to be instruments of sin; but do not yield them to be so, do not consent to it. This is one branch of sanctification, the mortification of sin.

2. Vivification, or living to righteousness. It is to *walk in newness of life, v.* 4. Newness of life supposes newness of heart; there is no way to make the stream sweet but by making the spring so. Walk by new rules. Make a new choice of the way. Choose new paths to walk in, new leaders to walk after, new companions to walk with. It is to be *alive unto God through Jesus Christ our Lord, v.* 11. To converse with God, to have a regard to him, a delight in him, this is to be alive to God. It is to have the affections and desires alive towards God. Or, *living* (our life in the flesh) *unto God,* to his honour and glory as our end, by his word and will as our rule; this is to live unto God.—*Through Jesus Christ our Lord.* Christ is our spiritual life; there is no living to God but through him. He is the Mediator; no intercourse between sinful souls and a holy God, but by the mediation of the Lord Jesus. In living to God, Christ is all in all. It is to *yield ourselves to God, as those that are alive from the dead, v.* 13. The very life and being of holiness lie in the dedication of ourselves to the Lord, giving our own selves to the Lord. "Not yield your estates to him, but yield yourselves; nothing less than your whole selves. Not only submit to him, but comply with him; be always ready to serve him. Yield yourselves to him as wax to the seal, to take any impression, to be, and have, and do, what he pleases." *As those that are alive from the dead.* To yield a dead carcase to a living God is not to please him, but to mock him: "Yield yourselves as those that are alive and good for something, a *living sacrifice, ch.* xii. 1. The surest evidence of our spiritual life is the dedication of ourselves to God. It is to yield *our members as instruments of righteousness to God.* The members of our bodies, when withdrawn from the service of sin, are not to lie idle, but to be made use of in the service of God. The body must be always ready to serve the soul in the service of God. Thus (*v.* 19), "*Yield your members servants to righteousness unto holiness.* Let them be under the conduct and at the command of the righteous law of God." *Righteousness unto holiness,* which intimates growth, and progress, and ground obtained. As every sinful act confirms the sinful habit, and makes the nature more and more prone to sin, so every gracious act confirms the gracious habit. One duty fits us for another; and the more we do the more we may do for God.

II. To show the necessity of sanctification. There is such an antipathy in our hearts by nature to holiness that it is no easy matter to bring them to submit to it: it is the Spirit's work.

1. Our baptism carries in it a great reason why we should die to sin, and live to righteousness. Observe this reasoning.

(1) In general, we are *dead to sin*. Our baptism signifies our cutting off from the kingdom of sin. We are dead to sin by our union with Christ, in and by whom it is killed. All this is in vain if we persist in sin; we return to that to which we were dead, like walking ghosts. For (*v.* 7) *he that is dead is freed from sin*; he that is dead to it is freed from the rule and dominion of it. Now shall we be such fools as to return to that slavery from which we are discharged?

(2) In particular, being *baptized into Jesus Christ, we were baptized into his death, v.* 3. Baptism binds us to Christ. Particularly, we were baptized into his death. As Christ died for sin, so we should die to sin. This was the profession and promise of our baptism, and we do not do well if we do not answer this profession, and make good this promise.

[1] Our conformity to the death of Christ obliges us to die unto sin. Thus we are here said to be *planted together in the likeness of his death* (*v.* 5), as the engrafted stock is planted together into the likeness of the shoot, of the nature of which it doth participate. We are planted in the vineyard in a likeness to Christ, which likeness we should evidence in sanctification. Our creed concerning Jesus Christ is, among other things, that he was *crucified, dead, and buried*; now baptism is a sacramental conformity to him in each of these. *First, Our old man is crucified with him, v.* 6. The death of the cross was a slow death; but it was a sure death. Such is the mortification of sin in believers. It was a cursed death. Sin dies as a malefactor, devoted to destruction. *Crucified with him.* The crucifying of Christ for us has an influence upon the crucifying of sin in us. *Secondly,* We are dead with Christ, *v.* 8. Christ was obedient to death: when he died, we might be said to die with him. Baptism signifies and seals our union with Christ, so that we are dead with him, and engaged to have no more to do with sin than he had. *Thirdly, We are buried with him by baptism, v.* 4. Our conformity is complete. We are in profession quite cut off from all commerce and communion with sin. Thus must we be, as Christ was, separate from sin and sinners. We are sealed to be the Lord's, therefore to be cut off from sin. As Christ was buried, that he might rise again to a new and more heavenly life, so we are in baptism buried, that we may rise again to a new life of faith and love.

[2] Our conformity to the resurrection of Christ obliges us to rise again to newness of life. Christ was raised up *from the dead by the glory of the Father.* Now in baptism we are obliged to conform to that pattern, to be planted in the *likeness of his resurrection* (*v.* 5), to *live with him, v.* 8. Conversion is the first resurrection from the death of sin to the life of righteousness; and this resurrection is conformable to Christ's resurrection. We have all risen with Christ. In two things we must conform to the resurrection of Christ: *First,* He rose to die no more, *v.* 9. Over Christ *death has no more dominion*; he was dead indeed, but he is alive, and so alive that he lives for evermore. Thus we must rise from the grave of sin never again to return to it. *Secondly,* He rose to live unto God (*v.* 10), to live a heavenly life. He rose again to leave the world. *Now I am no more in the world,* John xvii. 11. He rose to *live to God.* Thus must we rise to live to God: this is what he calls *newness of life* (*v.* 4), to live by other rules, with other aims, than we have done. A life devoted to God is a

new life; before, self was the chief and highest end, but now God.

2. He argues from the precious promises of the new covenant, *v.* 14. It might be objected that we cannot subdue sin, it is unavoidably too hard for us: "No," says he, "you wrestle with an enemy that may be dealt with and subdued; it is an enemy that is already foiled and baffled. *Sin shall not have dominion.*" Sin may struggle in a believer, and may create him a great deal of trouble, it may vex him, but shall not rule over him. *For we are not under the law, but under grace,* not under the law of sin and death, but under the law of the spirit of life, which is in Christ Jesus. New lords, new laws. Or, not under the covenant of works, which requires brick, and gives no straw, but under the covenant of grace, which accepts sincerity as our gospel perfection, which requires nothing but what it promises strength to perform. It does not leave our salvation in our own keeping, but lays it up in the hands of the Mediator, who undertakes for us that sin shall not have dominion over us, who hath himself condemned it, and will destroy it. Christ rules by the golden sceptre of grace. We are under grace, grace which accepts the willing mind, which leaves room for repentance, which promises pardon upon repentance. Shall we sin against so much goodness, abuse such love? See how the apostle starts at such a thought (*v.* 15): *Shall we sin because we are not under the law, but under grace? God forbid.*

3. This will be evidence of our state, for us, or against us (*v.* 16): *To whom you yield yourselves servants to obey, his servants you are.* All the children of men are either the servants of God, or the servants of sin. We must enquire to which of these masters we yield obedience. Our obeying the laws of sin will be an evidence against us that we belong to that family on which death is entailed. Our obeying the laws of Christ will evidence our relation to Christ's family.

4. He argues from their former sinfulness, *v.* 17–21.

(1) What they had been and done formerly. *You were the servants of sin.* Those that are now the servants of God would do well to remember the time when they were the servants of sin, to keep them humble, and to quicken them in the service of God. It is a reproach to the service of sin that so many thousands have quitted the service; and never any that sincerely deserted it, and gave up themselves to the service of God, have returned to the former drudgery. "*God be thanked that you were so.* God be thanked that we can speak of it as a thing past." *You have yielded your members servants to uncleanness, and to iniquity unto iniquity, v.* 19. It is the misery of a sinful state that the body is made a drudge to sin. *You have yielded.* Sinners are voluntary in the service of sin. The devil could not force them into the service, if they did not yield themselves to it. *To iniquity unto iniquity.* To iniquity as the work unto iniquity as the wages. Sow the wind, and reap the whirlwind; growing worse and worse, more and more hardened. This he speaks *after the manner of men. You were free from righteousness* (*v.* 20); not free by any liberty given, but by a liberty taken, which is licentiousness. But a freedom from righteousness is the worst kind of slavery.

(2) How the blessed change was made, and wherein it did consist.

[1] *You have obeyed from the heart that form of doctrine which was delivered to you, v.* 17. This describes conversion, it is our conformity to, and compliance with, the gospel—*Margin. Whereto you were delivered. First,* The rule of grace, *that form of doctrine.* The gospel is the great rule both of truth and holiness; it is the stamp, grace is the impression of that stamp. *Secondly,* Our conformity to that rule. It is to *obey from the heart.* The gospel is a doctrine

to be obeyed, and that from the heart; not in profession only, but in power—from the heart, the commanding part of us. It is to be *delivered into it*, as into a mould, as the wax is cast into the impression of the seal, answering it line for line.

[2] *Being made free from sin, you became servants of righteousness* (*v.* 18), *servants to God, v.* 22. Conversion is, *First*, A freedom from the service of sin. *Secondly*, A resignation of ourselves to the service of God. When we are made free from sin, it is not that we may live as we list, and be our own masters. We cannot be made the servants of God till we are freed from the power and dominion of sin; we cannot serve two masters.

(3) What apprehensions they now had of their former way. He appeals to themselves (*v.* 21), whether they had not found the service of sin, [1] An unfruitful service: "*What fruit had you then?* Did you ever get anything by it?" Besides the future losses, which are infinitely great, the very present gains of sin are not worth mentioning. *What fruit?* Nothing that deserves the name of fruit. [2] An unbecoming service; it is that of which we *are now ashamed*. Shame came into the world with sin, and is still the certain product of it. Who would wilfully do that which sooner or later he is sure to be ashamed of?

5. He argues from the end of all these things. To persuade us from sin to holiness here are good and evil, life and death, set before us; and we are put to our choice. The end of sin is death (*v.* 21): *The end of those things is death*. Though the way may seem pleasant and inviting, yet it will be bitterness in the latter end. *The wages of sin is death, v.* 23. Death is as due to a sinner as wages are to a servant. All that are sin's servants and do sin's work must expect to be thus paid. If the fruit be unto holiness the end will be everlasting life—a very happy end!—Though the way be up-hill, yet everlasting life at the end of it is sure. So, *v.* 23, *The gift of God is eternal life*. Heaven is life, and it is eternal life, no infirmities attending it, no death to put a period to it. This is the gift of God. The death is the wages of sin; but the life is a gift. Sinners merit hell, but saints do not merit heaven. We must thank God, and not ourselves, if ever we get to heaven. And this gift is *through Jesus Christ our Lord*. It is Christ that purchased it, prepares us for it, preserves us to it.

CHAPTER 7

I. Our freedom from the law an argument to press upon us sanctification, ver. 1–6. II. The excellency and usefulness of the law asserted, notwithstanding, ver. 7–14. III. The conflict between grace and corruption in the heart, ver. 14, 15, to the end.

Verses 1–6

Among other arguments to persuade us against sin, and to holiness, this was one (*v.* 14), that *we are not under the law*; and this argument is here further insisted upon (*v.* 6): *We are delivered from the law*. 1. We are delivered from that power of the law which condemns us for the sin committed by us. The law saith, *The soul that sins shall die;* but we are delivered from the law. 2. We are delivered from that power of the law which provokes the sin that dwelleth in us. This the apostle seems especially to refer to (*v.* 5): *The motions of sins which were by the law*. The law, by threatening, corrupt and fallen man, but offering no grace to cure, did but stir up the corruption. We being lamed by the fall, the law comes and directs us, but provides nothing to heal and help our lameness. We are under grace, which promises strength to do what it commands, and pardon upon repentance when we do amiss. The difference between a law-state and a gospel-state he had before illustrated by the similitude of serving a new master; now here under the similitude of being married to a new husband.

I. Our first marriage was to the law. The law of marriage is binding till the death of one of the parties, no matter which, and no longer. For this he appeals to themselves, as persons knowing the law (*v.* 1): *I speak to those that know the law*. Many of the Christians at Rome had been Jews, and so were well acquainted with the law. One has some hold of knowing people. *The law hath power over a man as long as he liveth;* in particular, the law of marriage hath power. The obligation of laws extends no further. The condemnation of laws extends no further; death is the finishing of the law. The severest laws could but kill the body, and after that there is no more that they can do. Thus while we were alive to the law we were under the power of it. Such is the law of marriage (*v.* 2), the woman is bound to her husband during life, she cannot marry another; if she do, she shall be reckoned an adulteress, *v.* 3. Thus were we married to the law (*v.* 5): *When we were in the flesh*, then *the motions of sins which were by the law did work in our members*, we were carried down the stream of sin, and the law was but as an imperfect dam, which made the stream to swell the higher. Our desire was towards sin, and sin ruled over us. We were under a law of sin and death, as the wife under the law of marriage; and the product of this marriage was fruit brought forth unto death. Lust, having conceived by the law, *bringeth forth sin, and sin, when it is finished, bringeth forth death*, Jam. i. 15. This is the posterity that springs from this marriage to sin and the law. This comes of the motions of sin working in our members.

II. Our second marriage is to Christ.

1. We are freed, by death, from our obligation to the law as a covenant, *v.* 3. *You are become dead to the law, v.* 4. He does not say, "The law is dead," but, which comes all to one, *You are dead to the law*. We are *delivered from the law* (*v.* 6); our obligation to it is as a husband is made void. And then he speaks of the law being dead as far as it was a law of bondage to us: *That being dead wherein we were held*. It is dead, it has lost its power; and this (*v.* 4) *by the body of Christ*, that is, by the sufferings of Christ in his body, by his crucified body. We are dead to the law by our union with the mystical body of Christ, but have no more to do with it than the dead servant hath to do with his master's yoke.

2. We are married to Christ. We enter upon a life of dependence on him and duty to him: *Married to another, even to him who is raised from the dead*. As our dying to sin and the law is in conformity to the death of Christ, and the crucifying of his body, so our devotedness to Christ in newness of life is in conformity to the resurrection of Christ. We are married to the raised exalted Jesus. Now we are thus married to Christ, (1) *That we should bring forth fruit unto God, v.* 4. One end of marriage is fruitfulness. Now the great end of our marriage to Christ is our fruitfulness in love, and grace, and every good work. As our old marriage to sin produced fruit unto death, so our second marriage to Christ produces fruit unto God. Good works are the children of the new nature. Whatever our professions and pretensions may be, there is no fruit brought forth to God till we are married to Christ. This distinguishes the good works of believers from the good works of hypocrites and self-justifiers that they are done in union with Christ. (2) *That we should serve in newness of spirit, and not in the oldness of the letter, v.* 6. Still we must serve, but it is a service that is perfect freedom, whereas the service of sin was a perfect drudgery. There must be a renovation of our spirits wrought by the spirit of God, and in that we must serve. *Not in the oldness of the letter;* that is, we must not rest in mere external services. The letter is said to kill with its bondage and terror, but we are delivered from that yoke that

we may serve God without fear, in holiness and righteousness, Luke i. 74, 75. It becomes us to worship within the veil, and no longer in the outward court.

Verses 7–14

What shall we say then? Is the law sin? He had said so much of the influence of the law that it might easily be misinterpreted as a reflection upon the law, to prevent which he shows the great excellency of it as a guide.

I. The great excellency of the law in itself. Far be it from Paul to reflect upon the law. It is *holy, just, and good, v.* 12. Laws are as the law-makers are. God, the great lawgiver, is holy, just, and good, therefore his law must needs be so. The ways of the Lord are right. It is good in the design of it; it was given for the good of mankind. It makes the observers of it good. Wherever there is true grace there is an assent to this—that the law is holy, just, and good. *The law is spiritual* (*v.* 14), not only in regard to the effect of it, but in regard to the extent of it; it reaches our spirits. It is given to man, whose principal part is spiritual; the soul is the best part, and therefore the law to the man must needs be a law to the soul. Herein the law of God is above all other laws, that it is a spiritual law. The law of God takes notice of the iniquity regarded in the heart. *We know this.* Wherever there is true grace there is an experimental knowledge of the spirituality of the law of God.

II. The great advantage that he had found by the law. 1. It was discovering: *I had not known sin but by the law, v.* 7. As that which is straight discovers that which is crooked, so there is no way of coming to that knowledge of sin which is necessary to repentance, but by comparing our hearts and lives with the law. Particularly he came to the knowledge of the sinfulness of lust. By lust he means sin dwelling in us. This he came to know when the law said, *Thou shalt not covet.* The law spoke in the spiritual sense and meaning of it. By this he knew that lust was sin and a very sinful sin. Paul had a very quick and piercing judgment, and yet never attained the right knowledge of indwelling sin till the Spirit by the law made it known to him. There is nothing about which the natural man is more blind than about original corruption. Thus *the law is a schoolmaster, to bring us to Christ.* Thus sin by the commandment does appear sin (*v.* 13); it appears in its own colours. Thus by the commandment it becomes *exceedingly sinful;* that is, it appears to be so. 2. It was humbling (*v.* 9): *I was alive.* He thought himself in a very good condition, very secure and confident of the goodness of his state. Thus he was *once, in times past,* when he was a Pharisee; and the reason was he was then *without the law.* Though brought up at the feet of Gamaliel, a doctor of the law, though himself a strict observer of it, yet *without the law.* He had the letter of the law, but he had not the spiritual meaning of it —the shell, but not the kernel. He had the law in his hand and in his head, but he had it not in his heart. *But when the commandment came* (not to his eyes only, but to his heart), *sin revived,* as the dust in a room rises when the sunshine is let into it. Paul then saw that in sin which he had never seen before— sin in its consequences, sin with death at the heels of it, sin and the curse entailed upon it. "The Spirit, by the commandment, convinced me that I was in a state of sin, and in a state of death because of sin." Of this excellent use is the law; it is a lamp and a light; it opens the eyes, prepares the way of the Lord.

III. The ill use that his corrupt nature made of the law. *Sin, taking occasion by the commandment, wrought in me all manner of concupiscence, v.* 8. Paul had in him all manner of concupiscence, as touching the righteousness of the law, blameless, and yet sensible of all manner of concupiscence. And it was sin that wrought it, indwelling sin, and it took occasion by the commandment. The corrupt nature would not have swelled and raged so much if it had not been for the restraints of the law. Ever since Adam ate forbidden fruit, we have all been fond of forbidden paths. *Without the law sin was dead,* as a snake in winter, which the sunbeams of the law quicken and irritate. It *deceived me.* Sin puts a cheat upon the sinner, and it is a fatal cheat, *v.* 11. *By it slew me,* It deceived and slew him. It *wrought death in me by that which is good, v.* 13. Nothing so good but a corrupt and vicious nature will pervert it, and make it an occasion of sin. Now in this sin appears sin. The worst thing that sin does is the perverting of the law. Thus the commandment, which was ordained to life, proved unto death, *v.* 10. The same word which to some is an occasion of life unto life is to others an occasion of death unto death. The same sun that makes the garden of flowers more fragrant makes the dunghill more noisome. The way to prevent this mischief is to bow our souls to the commanding authority of the law of God.

Verses 14–25

Here is a description of the conflict between grace and corruption in the heart, and it is applicable two ways: 1. To the struggles that are in a convinced soul, but yet unregenerate, in the person of whom it is supposed, by some, that Paul speaks. 2. To the struggles that are in a renewed sanctified soul, but yet in a state of imperfection, as other apprehend. And a great controversy there is of which of these we are to understand the apostle here.

I. Apply it to the struggles that are felt in a convinced soul, that is yet in a state of sin, knows his Lord's will, but does it not, continues a slave to his reigning lusts. The apostle had said (*ch.* vi. 14), *Sin shall not have dominion, because you are not under the law, but under grace,* for the proof of which he here shows that a man under the law, and not under grace, may be under the dominion of sin. The law may discover sin, and convince of sin, but it cannot conquer and subdue sin. It discovers the defilement but will not wash it off. It makes a man weary and heavy laden (Matt. xi. 28), burdens him with his sin; and yet it yields no help towards the shaking off of that burden; this is to be had only in Christ. The law may make a man cry out, *O wretched man that I am! who shall deliver me?* and yet leave him thus fettered. Now a soul advanced thus far by the law is in a fair way towards a state of liberty by Christ, though many rest here and go no further. It is possible for a man to go to hell with his eyes open, and to carry about with him a self-accusing conscience, even in the service of the devil. He may *consent to the law that it is good,* may have that within him that witnesses against sin and for holiness; and yet all this overpowered by the reigning love of sin. Drunkards and unclean persons have some faint desires to leave off their sins, and yet persist in them. Of such as these there are many that will needs have all this understood. It is very hard to imagine why, if the apostle intended this, he should speak all along in his own person; and not only so, but in the present tense.

II. It seems rather to be understood of the struggles that are maintained between grace and corruption in sanctified souls. That there are remainders of indwelling corruption, even where there is a living principle of grace, is past dispute. If we say that we have no sin, we deceive ourselves, 1 John i. 8, 10. That true grace strives against these sins and corruptions is likewise certain (Gal. v. 17): *The flesh lusteth against the spirit, and the spirit against the flesh; and these are contrary the one to the other, so that you cannot do the things that you would.* And his design is further to open the nature of sanctification, that it does not attain to a sinless perfection in this life. That which we do sincerely strive against, shall not be laid to our charge, and through grace the victory is sure at last.

1. What he complains of—the remainder of indwelling corruptions. The law is insufficient to justify even a regenerate man, which is not the fault of the law, but of our own corrupt nature, which cannot fulfil the law. Observe the particulars of this complaint. (1) *I am carnal, sold under sin, v.* 14. Even where there is spiritual life there are remainders of carnal affections, and so far a man may be *sold under sin.* (2) *What I would, that I do not; but what I hate, that do I, v.* 15. And to the same purport, *v.* 19, 21, *When I would do good, evil is present with me.* He was pressing forward towards perfection, yet he acknowledges that he had not already attained, neither was already perfect, Phil. iii. 12. Fain he would perfectly do the will of God, but his corrupt nature drew him another way: it was like the bias in a bowl, which, when it is thrown straight, yet draws it aside. (3) *In me, that is in my flesh, dwelleth no good, v.* 18. There is no good to be expected, any more than one would expect good corn growing upon a rock. As the new nature cannot commit sin (1 John iii. 9), so the flesh, the old nature, cannot perform a good duty. How should it? For the flesh serveth the law of sin (*v.* 25). (4) *I see another law in my members warring against the law of my mind, v.* 23. Christ having set up his throne in his heart, it was only the rebellious members of the body that were the instruments of sin—all that corrupt nature which is the seat not only of sensual but of more refined lusts. This wars against the law of the mind, the new nature, to which corrupt disposition and inclination are as great a burden and grief as the worst drudgery and captivity could be. *It brings me into captivity.* To the same purport (*v.* 25). *With the flesh I serve the law of sin,* the unregenerate part, is continually working towards sin. (5) His general complaint we have *v.* 24, *O wretched man that I am! who shall deliver me from the body of this death?* The thing he complains of is a body of death; either the body of flesh, which is a mortal dying body, or the body of sin, the corrupt nature, which tends to death. It was as troublesome to Paul as if he had had a dead body tied to him. This made him cry out, *O wretched man that I am!* Had I been required to speak of Paul, I should have said, "O blessed man that thou art." But in his own account he was a wretched man, because of the corruption of nature. *Who shall deliver me?* He speaks like one that was sick of it. The remainders of indwelling sin are a very grievous burden to a gracious soul.

2. What he comforts himself with. Three things comforted him:

(1) His conscience witnessed for him that he had a good principle ruling and prevailing in him, notwithstanding. The rule of this good principle which he had was the law of God, to which he here speaks of having a threefold regard. [1] *I consent unto the law that it is good, v.* 16. Here is the approbation of the judgment. Wherever there is grace there is not only a dread of the severity of the law, but a consent to the goodness of the law. This is a sign that the law is written in the heart. The sanctified judgment not only concurs to the equity of the law, but to the excellency of it. [2] *I delight in the law of God after the inward man, v.* 22. He delighted not only in the promises of the word, but in the precepts and prohibitions of the word. All that are born again do truly delight in the law of God, never better pleased than when heart and life are in the strictest conformity to the law and will of God. *After the inward man; First,* The mind or rational faculties. The soul is the inward man, and that is the seat of gracious delights, which are therefore sincere and serious, but secret. *Secondly,* The new nature. The new man is called the *inner man* (Eph. iii. 16). [3] *With the mind I myself serve the law of God, v.* 25. It is not enough to consent to the law, and to delight in the law, but we must serve the law. Thus it was with Paul's mind; this it is with every sanctified renewed mind.

(2) The fault lay in that corruption of his nature which he did really bewail and strive against: *It is no more I that do it, but sin that dwelleth in me.* This he mentions twice (*v.* 17, 20), not as an excuse for the guilt of sin, but that he might not sink in despair, but take comfort from the covenant of grace, which accepts the willingness of the spirit, and has provided pardon for the weakness of the flesh. He here professes his dissent from the law of sin. "It is not I; it is against my mind that it is done."

(3) His great comfort lay in Jesus Christ (*v.* 25) *I thank God, through Jesus Christ our Lord.* In the midst of his complaints he breaks out into praises. It is a special remedy against fears and sorrows to be much in praise: many a poor, drooping soul hath found it so. *Who shall deliver me?* says he (*v.* 24), as one at a loss for help. At length he finds an all-sufficient friend, even Jesus Christ. If it were not for Christ, this iniquity that dwells in us would certainly be our ruin. It is Christ that has purchased deliverance for us in due time. *Blessed be God that giveth us this victory through our Lord Jesus Christ!*

CHAPTER 8

The apostle, in this chapter, applies himself to the consolation of the Lord's people. It is the will of God that his people should be a comforted people. Many of the people of God have, accordingly, found this chapter a well-spring of comfort to their souls, living and dying. I. The particular instances of Christians' privileges, ver. 1–28. II. The ground thereof laid in predestination, ver. 29, 30. III. The apostle's triumph herein, in the name of all the saints ver. 31, to the end.

Verses 1–9

I. The apostle here begins with one signal privilege of true Christians, and describes the character of those to whom it belongs: *There is therefore now no condemnation to those that are in Christ Jesus, v.* 1. This is his triumph after that melancholy complaint and conflict. The complaint he takes to himself, but humbly transfers the comfort to all true believers. It is the unspeakable privilege of all those that are in Christ Jesus that there is therefore now no condemnation to them. He does not say, "There is no accusation against them", for this there is; but the accusation is thrown out. He does not say, "There is nothing in them that deserves condemnation", for this there is, and they see it, and own it; but it shall not be their ruin. He does not say, "There is no cross, no affliction to them", for this there may be; but *no condemnation.* Now this arises from their being in Christ Jesus; by virtue of their union with him through faith they are thus secured. It is the undoubted character of all those who are so in Christ Jesus that *they walk not after the flesh but after the Spirit.* The character is given from their walk, not from any one particular act.

II. How we come by this great privilege, and how we may answer this character.

1. How we come by these privileges—the privilege of justification, the privilege of sanctification. The law could not do it, *v.* 3. It could neither justify nor sanctify. The law made nothing perfect: *It was weak.* Yet that weakness was not through any defect in the law, but *through the flesh,* through the corruption

of human nature. In case of failure, the law, as a covenant of works, made no provision, and so left us as it found us. *The law of the Spirit of life in Christ Jesus* does it, *v.* 2. The covenant of grace in Christ is a treasury of merit and grace, and thence we receive pardon and a new nature, *are freed from the law of sin and death*, both from the guilt and power of sin. We are under another covenant, under the *law of the Spirit*, the law that gives the Spirit, spiritual life to qualify us for eternal. The foundation of this freedom is laid in Christ's undertaking for us, of which he speaks, *v.* 3, *God sending his own Son*. When the law failed, God provided another method. Christ comes to do that which the law could not do. The best exposition of this verse we have Heb. x. 1–10. (1) How Christ appeared: *In the likeness of sinful flesh*. Not sinful, but in the likeness of that flesh. He took upon him that nature which was corrupt, though perfectly abstracted from the corruptions of it. It was great condescension that he who was God should be made in the likeness of flesh; but much greater that he who was holy should be made in the likeness of sinful flesh. *And for sin*. God sent him *in the likeness of sinful flesh, and as a sacrifice for sin*. (2) What was done by this appearance of his: Sin *was condemned*. For all that are Christ's both the damning and the domineering power of sin is broken. Though it live and remain, its life in the saints is still but like that of a condemned malefactor. The condemning of sin saved the sinner from condemnation. Christ was made sin for us (2 Cor. v. 21). When he was condemned, sin was condemned in the flesh of Christ. So was satisfaction made to divine justice, and way made for the salvation of the sinner. (3) The happy effect of this upon us (*v.* 4): *That the righteousness of the law might be fulfilled in us*. A righteousness of satisfaction for the breach of the law is fulfilled by the imputation of Christ's perfect righteousness. A righteousness of obedience to the law is fulfilled in us, when by the Spirit the law of love is written upon the heart, and that love is the fulfilling of the law, ch. xiii. 10. *Us who walk not after the flesh, but after the Spirit*. This is the description of all those that are interested in this privilege.

2. How we may answer to this character, *v.* 5, &c. (1) By looking to our minds. By examining what we mind, the things of the flesh or the things of the spirit. The favour of God, the welfare of the soul, the concerns of eternity, are the things of the Spirit. The man is as the mind is. The mind is the forge of thoughts. Which way do the thoughts move with most pleasure? The mind is the seat of wisdom. Whether are we more wise for the world or for our souls? *They savour the things of the flesh;* so the word is rendered, Matt. xvi. 23. It is a great matter what truths, what tidings, what comforts, we do most relish. Now, to caution us against this carnal-mindedness, he shows the great misery of it, and compares it with the unspeakable comfort of spiritual-mindedness. [1] It is death, *v.* 6. It is the death of the soul; for it is its alienation from God, in union and communion with whom the life of the soul consists. A carnal soul is a dead soul, dead as a soul can die. Death includes all misery; carnal souls are miserable souls. But to be *spiritually minded* is *life and peace*. A sanctified soul is a living soul, and that life is peace; it is a very comfortable life. It is life and peace in the other world, as well as in this. Spiritual-mindedness is eternal life and peace begun. [2] It is enmity to God (*v.* 7) and this is worse than the former. The former speaks the carnal sinner a dead man, but this speaks him a devil of a man. It is not only the alienation of the soul from God, but the opposition of the soul against God. To prove this, he urges that *it is not subject to the law of God*,

neither indeed can be. The holiness of the law of God, and the unholiness of the carnal mind, are as irreconcilable as light and darkness. The carnal man may, by the power of divine grace, be made subject to the law of God, but the *carnal mind* never can; this must be broken and expelled. Hence he infers (*v.* 8), *Those that are in the flesh cannot please God*. Pleasing God is our highest end, of which those that are in the flesh cannot but fall short; they cannot please him, nay, they cannot but displease him.

(2) By enquiring whether we have the Spirit of God and Christ, or not (*v.* 9): *You are not in the flesh, but in the Spirit*. It denotes our being overcome and subdued by one of these principles. Now the great question is whether we are in the flesh or in the Spirit; and how may we come to know it? Why, by enquiring whether the Spirit of God dwell in us. The Spirit visits many that are unregenerate; but in all that are sanctified he dwells. Shall we put this question to our own hearts, Who dwells, who rules, who keeps house, here? To this he subjoins a general rule of trial: *If any man has not the Spirit of Christ, he is none of his*. To be Christ's is a privilege and honour which many pretend to that have no part nor lot in the matter. None are his but those that have his Spirit; that are spirited as he was spirited. The frame and disposition of our souls must be conformable to Christ's pattern. That are actuated and guided by the Holy Spirit of God. Having the Spirit of Christ is the same with having the Spirit of God to dwell in us. All that are actuated by the Spirit of God as their rule are conformable to the spirit of Christ as their pattern.

Verses 10–16

Two more excellent benefits, which belong to true believers.

I. Life. The happiness is not barely a negative happiness, not to be condemned; but it is positive (*v.* 10, 11): *If Christ be in you*. Now we are here told what becomes of the bodies and souls of those in whom Christ is.

1. We cannot say but that *the body is dead*; it is a frail, mortal, dying body. In the midst of life we are in death: be our bodies ever so strong, they are as good as dead, and this *because of sin*. It is sin that kills the body. Methinks, were there no other argument, love to our bodies should make us hate sin, because it is such an enemy to our bodies.

2. But the spirit, that is life. The life of the saint lies in the soul, while the life of the sinner goes no further than the body. When the body dies *the spirit is life*. Death to the saints is but the freeing of the heaven-born spirit from the clog and load of this body, that it may be fit to partake of eternal life. And this *because of righteousness*. The righteousness of Christ imputed to them secures the soul from death; the righteousness of Christ inherent in them, preserves it, and at death elevates it, and makes it meet to partake of the inheritance of the saints in light.

3. There is a reserved too for the poor body at last: *He shall also quicken your mortal bodies, v.* 11. The body shall be reunited to the soul, and clothed with a glory agreeable to it. Two great assurances of the resurrection of the body are mentioned: (1) The resurrection of Christ: He *that raised up Christ from the dead shall also quicken*. Christ rose as the forerunner of all the saints, 1 Cor. xv. 20. It is in the virtue of Christ's resurrection that we shall rise. (2) The indwelling of the Spirit. The same Spirit that raiseth the soul now will raise the body shortly: *By his Spirit that dwelleth in you*. The Spirit, breathing upon dead and dry bones, will make them live, and the saints even in their flesh shall see God. Hence the apostle infers how much it is our duty to

walk not after the flesh, but after the Spirit, *v.* 12, 13. Two motives he mentions here: [1] We are not debtors to the flesh. We are indeed bound to clothe, and feed, and take care of the body, as a servant to the soul in the service of God, but no further. We are not debtors to it. We are debtors to Christ and to the Spirit: there we owe our all. See 1 Cor. vi. 19, 20. [2] Consider what will be at the end of the way. *If you live after the flesh, you shall die;* that is, die eternally. Dying indeed is the soul's dying: the death of the saints is but a sleep. But, on the other hand, *You shall live,* that is the true life: *If you through the Spirit mortify the deeds of the body.* We cannot do it without the Spirit working it in us, and the Spirit will not do it without our doing our endeavour. We are put upon this dilemma, either to displease the body or destroy the soul.

II. The *Spirit of adoption v.* 14–16.

1. All that are Christ's are taken into the relation of children to God, *v.* 14. (1) Their property: They are *led by the Spirit of God,* not driven as beasts, but led as rational creatures. It is the undoubted character of all true believers that they are led by the Spirit of God. They do in their obedience follow that guidance, and are sweetly led into all truth and all duty. (2) Their privilege: *They are the sons of God,* owned and loved by him as his children.

2. And those that are the sons of God have the Spirit,

(1) To work in them the disposition of children. *You have not received the spirit of bondage again to fear, v.* 15. Understand it, *First,* Of that spirit of bondage which the Old Testament church was under, by reason of the darkness of that dispensation. You are not under that dispensation, you have not received that spirit. *Secondly,* Of that spirit of bondage which many of the saints themselves were under at their conversion. Then the Spirit himself was to the saints a spirit of bondage: "But," says the apostle, "with you this is over." But you *have received the Spirit of adoption.* It is God's prerogative, when he adopts, to give a spirit of adoption—the nature of children. A sanctified soul bears the image of God, as the child bears the image of the father. *Whereby we cry, Abba, Father.* Praying is here called *crying.* Children that cannot speak vent their desires by crying. Now, the Spirit teaches us in prayer to come to God as a Father. And why both, *Abba, Father?* Because Christ said so in prayer (Mark xiv. 36), *Abba, Father.* It denotes an affectionate endearing importunity. Little children, begging of their parents, can say little but *Father, Father,* and that is rhetoric enough. It also denotes that the adoption is common both to Jews and Gentiles.

(2) To witness to the relation of children, *v.* 16. *Beareth witness with our spirit.* Many speak peace to themselves to whom the God of heaven does not speak peace. But those that are sanctified have God's Spirit witnessing with their spirits. This testimony is always agreeable to the written word, and is therefore always grounded upon sanctification. The Spirit witnesses to none the privileges of chidren who have not the nature and disposition of children.

Verses 17–25

A fourth happiness of believers, namely, a title to the future glory. *If children, then heirs, v.* 17. In earthly inheritances this rule does not hold, only the first-born are heirs. Heaven is an inheritance that all the saints are heirs to. They do not come to it by any merit of their own; but as heirs, purely by the act of God. Their present state is a state of education and preparation for the inheritance. 1. *Heirs of God.* The Lord himself is the portion of the saints' inheritance. The vision of God and the fruition of God make up the inheritance the saints are heirs to.

2. *Joint-heirs with Christ.* True believers *shall inherit all things.* Those that now partake of the Spirit of Christ, as his brethren, shall partake of his glory. Lord, what is man, that thou shouldst thus magnify him! Now this future glory is the reward of present sufferings, the accomplishment of present hopes.

I. The reward of the saints' present sufferings. *If so be that we suffer with him* (*v.* 17), or *forasmuch as we suffer with him.* The state of the church in this world always is an afflicted state. He tells them that they suffered with Christ, and should be glorified with him. Though we may be losers for him, we shall not be losers by him in the end. This the gospel is filled with the assurances of. He holds the balance (*v.* 18), in a comparison between the two. 1. In one scale he puts the *sufferings of this present time.* The sufferings of the saints last no longer than the present time (2 Cor. iv. 17), light affliction, and but for a moment. So that on the sufferings he writes *tekel,* weighed in the balance and found light. 2. In the other scale he puts the glory, and finds that an exceeding and eternal weight: *Glory that shall be revealed.* In our present state we come short, not only in the enjoyment, but in the knowledge of that glory: it shall be revealed. It surpasses all that we have yet seen and known. There is something to come, something behind the curtain, that will outshine all. *Shall be revealed in us;* not only revealed to us, to be seen, but revealed in us, to be enjoyed. He concludes the sufferings *not worthy to be compared with the glory.* They cannot merit that glory; and, if suffering for Christ will not merit, much less will doing. The sufferings are small and short, and concern the body only; but the glory is rich and great, and concerns the soul, and is eternal. This he reckons as an arithmetician that is balancing an account. He first sums up what is disbursed for Christ in the sufferings of this present time, and finds they come to very little; he then sums up what is secured to us by Christ in the glory that shall be revealed, and this he finds to be an infinite sum. And who would be afraid then to suffer for Christ, who as he is beforehand with us in suffering, so he will not be behind-hand with us in recompence? He could reckon not by art only, but by experience, for he knew both. And, upon the view of both, he gives this judgment here. The reproach of Christ appears riches to those who have respect to the recompence of reward.

II. The accomplishment of the saints' present hopes and expectations, *v.* 19, &c. As the saints are suffering for it, so they are waiting for it. He will establish that word unto his servants on which he has caused them to hope. If hope deferred makes the heart sick, surely when the desire comes it will be a tree of life. Now he observes an expectation of this glory.

1. In the creatures, *v.* 19–22. That must needs be a great, a transcendent glory, which all the creatures are so earnestly expecting and longing for. By the *creature* here we understand the whole frame of nature, the whole creation. The sense of the apostle in these four verses we may take in the following observations: (1) There is a present vanity to which the creature, by reason of the sin of man, is made subject, *v.* 20. When man sinned, the ground was cursed for man's sake, and with it all the creatures. *Under the bondage of corruption, v.* 21. The creation is sullied and stained, much of the beauty of the world gone. And it is not the least part of their bondage that they are used, or abused rather, by men as instruments of sin. And this *not willingly,* not of their own choice. All the creatures desire their own perfection. When they are made instruments of sin it is not willingly. They are thus captivated, not for any sin of their own, but for man's sin: *By reason of him who hath subjected the same.* And this yoke (poor

creatures) they bear in hope that it will not be so always. We have reason to pity the poor creatures that for our sin have become subject to vanity. (2) The creatures groan and travail in pain together under this vanity and corruption, *v.* 22. Sin is a burden to the whole creation. There is a general outcry of the whole creation aganst the sin of man. (3) The creature shall be *delivered from this bondage into the glorious liberty of the children of God (v.* 21)— they shall no more be subject to vanity and corruption. This lower world shall be renewed: when there will be new heavens there will be a new earth. (4) The creature doth therefore earnestly expect the *manifestation of the children of God, v.* 19. Now the saints are God's hidden ones, the wheat seems lost in a heap of chaff; but then they shall be manifested. The children of God shall appear in their own colours. And this redemption of the creature is reserved till then. This the whole creation longs for; and it may serve as a reason why now a good man should be merciful to his beast.

2. In the saints, who are new creatures, *v.* 23–25. (1) The grounds of this expectation in the saints. It is our having received *the first-fruits of the spirit.* Grace is the first-fruits of glory, it is glory begun. We, having received such clusters in this wilderness, cannot but long for the full vintage in the heavenly Canaan. *Not only they*—not only the creatures, but even we cannot but long for something more and greater. In having the first-fruits of the Spirit we have that which is very precious, but we have not all we would have. *We groan within ourselves* with silent groans, which pierce heaven soonest of all. Or, *We groan among ourselves.* It is the unanimous vote of the whole church. Present receivings and comforts are consistent with a great many groans; as the throes of a woman in travail—groans that are symptoms of life, not of death. (2) The object of this expectation. *The adoption, to wit, the redemption of our body.* The resurrection is here called *the redemption of the body.* It shall then be rescued from the power of death and the grave. It shall be made like that glorious body of Christ, Phil. iii. 21; 1 Cor. xv. 42. This is called *the adoption.* It is the adoption manifested before all the world, angels and men. As Christ was, so the saints will be, declared to be the sons of God with power, by the resurrection from the dead, *ch.* i. 4. It is the adoption perfected and completed. The children of God have bodies as well as souls; and, till those bodies are brought into the glorious liberty of the children of God, the adoption is not perfect. (3) The agreeableness of this to our present state, *v.* 24, 25. Our happiness is not in present possession: *We are saved by hope.* Our reward is out of sight. Those that will deal with God must deal upon trust. Faith respects the promise, hope the thing promised. Faith is the evidence, hope the expectation, of things not seen. Faith is the mother of hope. *We do with patience wait.* In hoping for this glory we have need of patience. Our way is rough and long, though he seem to tarry, it becomes us to wait for him.

Verses 26–28

Two privileges more to which true Christians are entitled:

I. The help of the Spirit in prayer.

1. Our weakness in prayer: *We know not what we should pray for as we ought.* As to the matter of our requests, we know not what to ask. We are shortsighted. We are like foolish children, that are ready to cry for fruit before it is ripe and fit for them. As to the manner, we know not how to pray as we ought. The apostle speaks of this in the first person: *We know not.* He puts himself among the rest. If so great a saint as Paul knew not what to pray for, what little

reason have we to go forth about that duty in our own strength!

2. The assistances which the Spirit gives us. He *helps our infirmities,* meant especially of our praying infirmities. The Spirit in the word helps. The Spirit in the heart helps; for this end the Holy Ghost was poured out. *Helpeth, heaves with us, over against us,* helps as we help one that would lift up a burden, by lifting over against him at the other end. We must not sit still, and expect that the Spirit should do all; when the Spirit goes before us we must bestir ourselves. We cannot without God, and he will not without us. The *Spirit itself makes intercession for us.* Christ intercedes for us in heaven, the Spirit intercedes for us in our hearts; so graciously has God provided for the encouragement of the praying remnant. Now this intercession which the Spirit makes is, (1) *With groanings that cannot be uttered.* There may be praying in the Spirit where there is not a word spoken. It is not the rhetoric and eloquence, but the faith and fervency, of our prayers, that the Spirit works, in us. *Cannot be uttered;* we know not what to say, nor how to express ourselves. When we can but cry, *Abba, Father,* with a holy humble boldness, this is the work of the Spirit. (2) *According to the will of God, v.* 27. The Spirit interceding in us evermore melts our wills into the will of God.

3. The sure success of these intercessions: *He that searches the heart knoweth what is the mind of the Spirit, v.* 27. To a hypocrite, all whose religion lies in his tongue, nothing is more dreadful than that God searches the heart. To a sincere Christian, who makes heart-work of his duty, nothing is more comfortable. He will hear and answer those desires which we want words to express. He knows what we have need of before we ask. Christ had said, "Whatever you ask the Father according to his will he will give you." But how shall we learn to ask according to his will. Why, the Spirit will teach us that.

II. The concurrence of all providences for the good of those that are Christ's, *v.* 28. Notwithstanding all these privileges, we see believers compassed about with manifold afflictions, but in this the Spirit's intercession is always effectual, that all this is working together for their good.

1. The character of the saints, who are interested in this privilege. *They love God.* Those that love God make the best of all he does, and take all in good part. *They are the called according to his purpose,* not according to any merit or desert of ours, but according to God's own gracious purpose.

2. The privilege of the saints, that *all things work together for good to them.* All the providences of God are theirs—merciful providences, afflicting providences. They are all for good; perhaps for temporal good, at least, for spiritual and eternal good. Either directly or indirectly, every providence has a tendency to the spiritual good of those that love God. *They work together,* as several ingredients in a medicine concur to answer the intention. *He worketh all things together for good;* so some read it. All this *we know*— know it for a certainty, from the word of God, from our own experience, and from the experience of all the saints.

Verses 29, 30

The apostle, having reckoned up so many ingredients of the happiness of true believers, comes here to represent the ground of them all, which he lays in predestination. He here sets before us the order of the causes of our salvation, a golden chain, which cannot be broken. There are four links of it:

I. *Whom he did foreknow he also did predestinate to be conformed to the image of his Son.* All that God designed for glory and happiness as the end he decreed to grace and holiness as the way. God's fore-knowledge of the saints is the same with that ever-lasting love wherewith he is said to have loved them. *Whom he did foreknow*, that is, whom he designed for his friends and favourites. Now those whom God thus foreknew he did predestinate to be conformed to Christ. 1. Holiness consists in our conformity to the image of Christ. This takes in the whole of sanctification. Christ is the express image of his Father, and the saints are conformed to the image of Christ. Thus it is that we have God's love restored to us and God's likeness renewed upon us. 2. All that God hath from eternity foreknown with favour he hath predestinated to this conformity. It is not we that can conform ourselves to Christ. None can know their election but by their conformity to the image of Christ; for all that are chosen are chosen to sanctification. 3. That which is herein chiefly de-signed is the honour of Jesus Christ, that he might be the *first-born among many brethren*; that is, that Christ might have the honour of being the great pattern, might have pre-eminence. And blessed be God that there are many brethren; though they seem but a few in one place at one time, yet, when they come all together, they will be a great many. In spite of all the opposition of the powers of darkness, Christ will be the first-born among many, very many brethren.

II. *Whom he did predestinate those he also called*, not only with the external call, but with the internal and effectual call. The former comes to the ear only, but this to the heart. The call is then effectual when we come at the call; and we then come at the call when the Spirit draws us, persuades and enables us to embrace Christ in the promises. It is an effectual call from self and earth to God, and Christ—from sin and vanity to grace, and holiness. This is the gospel call. *Them he called*, that the purpose of God, according to election, might stand.

III. *Whom he called those he also justified*. All that are effectually called are accepted as righteous through Jesus Christ. They are no longer dealt with as criminals, but owned and loved as friends and favourites.

IV. *Whom he justified those he also glorified*. The power of corruption being broken in effectual calling, and the guilt of sin removed in justification, nothing can come between that soul and glory. It is spoken of as a thing done: *He glorified*, because of the cer-tainty of it; he *hath* saved us. God's design of love has its full accomplishment. This was what he aimed at all along—to bring them to heaven. Are they chosen? It is to salvation. Called? It is to his kingdom and glory. Begotten again? It is to an inheritance incorruptible. Afflicted? It is to work for them this exceeding and eternal weight of glory. The author of all these is the same. God himself hath undertaken the doing of it from first to last. This is a mighty encouragement to our faith and hope.

Verses 31–39

The apostle closes with a holy triumph, in the name of all the saints. *What shall we then say to these things?* What use shall we make of all that has been said? He speaks as one wondering at the height and depth, and length and breadth, of the love of Christ, which passeth knowledge. The more we know of other things the less we wonder at them; but the further we are led into an acquaintance with gospel mysteries the more we are affected with the admira-tion of them. If ever Paul rode in a triumphant chariot on this side of heaven, here it was. He here makes a challenge, dares all the enemies of the saints to do their worst: *If God be for us, who can be against us?* This includes all, that *God is for us*. All that he is, and has, and does, is for his people. And, if so, *who can be against us*, so as to prevail against us? Be

they ever so strong, ever so many, what can they do? While God is for us, and we keep in his love, we may defy all the powers of darkness. Let Satan do his worst, he is chained. Who then dares fight against us, while God himself is fighting for us? And this we say to these things.

I. We have supplies ready in all our wants (*v.* 32): *He that spared*, &c. Who can cut off our streams, while we have a fountain to go to? 1. What God has done for us, on which our hopes are built: *He spared not his own Son*. Now we may know that he loves us, in that he hath not withheld his Son. If nothing less will save man, rather than man shall perish let him go. Thus did he *deliver him up for us all*, not only for our good, but in our stead, to be a propitiation for sin. He did not *spare his own Son that served him*, that he might spare us. 2. What we may therefore expect he will do: He will *with him freely give us all things*. It is implied that he will give us Christ, for other things are bestowed with him. He will with him freely give us all things, all good things, and more we should not desire. Freely, without reluctancy; and freely, without recompence. *How shall he not?* Can it be imagined that he should give so great a gift for us when we were enemies, and should deny us any good thing, now that we are friends and children? He that hath prepared a crown and kingdom for us will be sure to give us enough to bear our charges in the way to it.

II. We have an answer ready to all accusations and a security against all condemnations (*v.* 33, 34): *Who shall lay anything?* This is enough, *It is God that justifieth*. If God justifies, this answers all. We may challenge all our accusers to come and put in their charge. This overthrows them all; it is God, the righteous faithful God, that justifieth. *Who is he that condemneth?* Though they cannot make good the charge, yet they will be ready to condemn; but we have a plea ready which cannot be overruled. *It is Christ that died*, &c. It is by Christ, and our union with him, that we are thus secured. 1. His death: *It is Christ that died*. By the merit of his death he paid our debt. 2. His resurrection: *Yea, rather, that has risen again*. This is a much greater encouragement. Therefore the apostle mentions it with a *yea, rather*. If he had died, and not risen again, we had been where we were. 3. His sitting at the right hand of God: He is *even at the right hand of God* a mighty encour-agement to us in reference to all accusations, that we have a friend, such a friend, in court. Our friend is himself the judge. 4. The intercession which he makes there. He is there, not unconcerned about us, not forgetful of us, but *making intercession*. And is not this abundant matter for comfort? What room is left for doubting and disquietment? Some under-stand the accusation and condemnation here spoken of as that which the suffering saints met with from men. The primitive Christians had many black crimes laid to their charge. For these the ruling powers condemned them: "But no matter for that" (says the apostle); "while we stand right at God's bar it is of no great moment how we stand at men's."

III. We have good assurance of our preservation and continuance in this blessed state, *v.* 35, to the end. The fears of the saints lest they should lose their hold of Christ are often very discouraging and dis-quieting, but here is that which may silence their fears, that nothing can separate them.

1. A daring challenge to all the enemies of the saints to separate them, if they could, from the love of Christ. *Who shall?* None shall, *v.* 35–37. God having manifested his love in giving his own Son for us, can we imagine that anything else should divert or dissolve that love?

(1) The present calamities of Christ's beloved ones supposed—that they meet with *tribulation*, are in

distress, are followed with *persecution* from an angry malicious world that always hated those whom Christ loved, pinched with *famine*, and starved with *nakedness*, exposed to the greatest *perils*, the *sword* of the magistrate drawn against them. Can a case be supposed more black and dismal? It is illustrated (*v.* 36) by a passage quoted from Ps. xliv. 22, *For thy sake we are killed all the day long*, that is, continually exposed to and expecting the fatal stroke. *Accounted as sheep for the slaughter;* they make no more of killing a Christian than of butchering a sheep.

(2) The inability of all these things to separate us from the love of Christ. All this will not cut the bond of love and friendship that is between Christ and true believers. [1] Christ doth not, will not, love us the less for all this. They are neither a cause nor an evidence of the abatement of his love. These things separate us from the love of other friends. When Paul was brought before Nero all men forsook him, but then the Lord stood by him, 2 Tim. iv. 16, 17. Whatever persecuting enemies may rob us of, they cannot rob us of the love of Christ, and therefore, let them do their worst, they cannot make a true believer miserable. [2] We do not, will not, love him the less for this, because we do not think that he loves us the less. A true Christian loves Christ never the less though he suffer for him, thinks never the worse of Christ though he lose all for him.

(3) The triumph of believers in this (*v.* 37): *Nay, in all these things we are more than conquerors.*

[1] We are conquerors. A strange way of conquering, but it was Christ's way. It is a surer and a nobler way of conquest by faith and patience than by fire and sword. The enemies have sometimes confessed themselves baffled and overcome by the invincible courage and constancy of the martyrs.

[2] We are more than conquerors. Those are more than conquerors that conquer, *First*, With little loss. Many conquests are dearly bought; but what do the suffering saints lose? Why, they lose that which the gold loses in the furnace, nothing but the dross. *Secondly*, With great gain. The spoils are exceedingly rich; glory, honour, and peace, a crown of righteousness that fades not away. In this the suffering saints have triumphed. As afflictions abound, consolations much more abound, 2 Cor. i. 5. Those that have gone smiling to the stake, and stood singing in the flames —these were more than conquerors.

[3] It is only *through Christ that loved us*. We are conquerors, not in our own strength, but in the grace that is in Christ Jesus. We are conquerors by virtue of Christ's victory. We have nothing to do but to pursue the victory, and to divide the spoil, and so are more than conquerors.

2. A direct and positive conclusion of the whole matter: *For I am persuaded, v.* 38, 39. And here he enumerates all those things which might separate between Christ and believers, and concludes that it could not be done. (1) *Neither death nor life*, neither the fear of death nor the hope of life. We shall not be separated from that love either in death or in life. (2) *Nor angels, nor principalities, nor powers.* The good angels will not, the bad shall not; and neither can. The good angels are engaged friends, the bad are restrained enemies. (3) *Nor things present, nor things to come*—neither the sense of troubles present nor the fear of troubles to come. Time shall not separate us, eternity shall not, from the love of Christ, whose favour is twisted in with both present things and things to come. (4) *Nor height, nor depth*— neither the height of prosperity, nor the depth of adversity, nothing from heaven above, nothing on earth below. (5) *Nor any other creature*—anything than can be named or thought of. It will not, it cannot, separate us from the love of God, which is in Christ Jesus our Lord. Nothing does it, can do

it, but sin. This is the ground of the steadfastness of the love, because Jesus Christ, in whom he loves us, is the same yesterday, today and for ever.

CHAPTER 9

What becomes of the Jews, especially those of them that do not embrace Christ, nor believe the gospel? What becomes of the promise made to the fathers, which entailed salvation upon the Jews? That the consequence of the rejection of the unbelieving Jews follows from Paul's doctrine he grants, but endeavours to soften and mollify, ver. 1–5. But that from this it follows that the word of God takes no effect, he denies (ver. 6), and proves the denial in the rest of the chapter, which serves likewise to illustrate the great doctrine of predestination.

Verses 1–5

The apostles' solemn profession of a great concern for the nation and people of the Jews—that he was heartily troubled that so many of them were enemies to the gospel. For this he had *great heaviness and continual sorrow*. It is wisdom as much as may be to mollify those truths which sound harshly: dip the nail in oil, it will drive the better. He introduces his discourse with this affectionate profession, that they might not think he triumphed over the rejected Jews. Paul was so far from desiring it that he most pathetically deprecates it.

I. He asserts it with a solemn protestation (*v.* 1): *I say the truth in Christ*, "I speak it as one of God's people, children that will not lie. I appeal to Christ concerning it." He appeals likewise to his own conscience. That which he was going to assert was a secret; it was concerning a sorrow in his heart to which none was a capable competent witness but God and his own conscience.—*That I have great heaviness, v.* 2. The very mention of it was unpleasant.

II. He backs it with a very serious imprecation out of love to the Jews. *I could wish;* he does not say, I do wish, for it was no proper means appointed for such an end; but, if it were, *I could wish that myself were accursed from Christ for my brethren*—a very high pang of zeal and affection for his countrymen. Love is apt to be thus bold, and venturous, and self-denying. Because the glory of God's grace in the salvation of many is to be preferred before the welfare and happiness of a single person, Paul would be content to forego all his own happiness to purchase theirs. 1. He would be content to be cut off from the land of the living, as an anathema. They thirsted for his blood, persecuted him as the most obnoxious person in the world. "I am willing to bear all this, and a great deal more, for your good. Your unbelief and rejection create in my heart a heaviness so much greater than all these troubles can that I could look upon them not only as tolerable, but as desirable, rather than this rejection." 2. He would be content to be excommunicated from the society of the faithful if that would do them any good. He could wish himself no more remembered among the saints. He would be content to have his name buried in oblivion or reproach, for the good of the Jews. 3. He could be content to be cut off from all his share of happiness in Christ, if that might be a means of their salvation.

III. He gives us the reason of this affection and concern.

1. Because of their relation to them: *My brethren, my kinsmen, according to the flesh*. Though they were very bitter against him upon all occasions, thus respectfully does he speak of them. It shows him to be a man of forgiving spirit. *My kinsmen.* Paul was a Hebrew of the Hebrews. We ought to be in a special manner concerned for the spiritual good of our relations. Concerning them, and our usefulness to them, we must in a special manner give account.

2. Especially because of their relation to God (*v.* 4, 5): *Who are Israelites*, distinguished by visible church privileges, many of which are here mentioned: (1) *The adoption;* not that which is saving, and which

entitles to eternal happiness, but that which was external. (2) *And the glory*. The many tokens of the divine presence and guidance, the cloud, the Shechinah, the distinguishing favours conferred upon them—these were the glory. (3) *And the covenants*—the covenant made with Abraham, and often renewed with his seed upon divers occasions. Still these pertained to Israel. (4) *And the giving of the law*. It is a great privilege to have the law of God among us, and it is to be accounted so. (5) *And the services of God*. They had the ordinances of God's worship among them—the temple, the altars, the priests, the sacrifices, the feasts. While other nations were worshipping and serving stocks, and stones, and devils, and they knew not what of other idols their own invention, the Israelites were serving the true God in the way of his own appointment. (6) *And the promises*—promises relating to the Messiah and the gospel state. The comfort of the promises is to be had in obedience to that law and attendance upon that service. (7) *Whose are the fathers* (v. 5), Abraham, Isaac, and Jacob, that stood so high in the favour of God. It was for the fathers' sake that they were taken into covenant. (8) But the greatest honour of all was that *of them as concerning the flesh, Christ came*. This was the great privilege of the Jews, that Christ was of kin to them. Mentioning Christ, he interposes a very great word concerning him, that he is *over all, God blessed for ever*. It is a very full proof of the Godhead of Christ; he is not only over all, as Mediator, but he is God blessed for ever. It was likewise the honour of the Jews that, seeing God blessed for ever would be a man, he would be a Jew.

Verses 6–13

The rejection of the Jews, by the establishment of the gospel dispensation, did not at all invalidate the word of God's promise to the patriarchs: *Not as though the word of God hath taken no effect* (v. 6). We are not to ascribe inefficacy to any word of God: nothing that he has spoken does or can fall to the ground; see Isa. lv. 10, 11. This is to be understood especially of the promise of God, which may be to a wavering faith very doubtful; but it is not, it cannot be, made of no effect.

Now the difficulty is to reconcile the rejection of the unbelieving Jews with the word of God's promise. This he does in four ways: 1. By explaining the true meaning and intention of the promise, v. 6–13. 2. By asserting the absolute sovereignty of God, v. 14–24. 3. By showing how this rejection of the Jews, and the taking in of the Gentiles, were foretold in the Old Testament, v. 25–29. 4. By fixing the true reason of the Jews' rejection, v. 30, to the end.

In this paragraph the apostle explains the true meaning and intention of the promise. When we misunderstand the promise, no marvel if we are ready to quarrel with God about the accomplishment. When God said he would be *a God to Abraham, and to his seed*, he did not mean it of all his seed according to the flesh. He intended it with a limitation. And as from the beginning it was appropriated to Isaac and not to Ishmael, to Jacob and not to Esau, and yet for all this the word of God was not made of no effect; so now the same promise is appropriated to believing Jews that embrace Christ, and, though it throws off multitudes that refuse Christ, yet the promise is not therefore invalidated.

I. He lays down this proposition—that *they are not all Israel who are of Israel* (v. 6), *neither because they are*, &c., v. 7. They are not all really Israel that are so in name and profession. Grace does not run in the blood.

II. He proves this by instances. Some of Abraham's seed were chosen, and others not; God therein wrought according to the counsel of his own will.

1. He specifies the case of Isaac and Ishmael, both of them the seed of Abraham; and yet Isaac only taken into covenant with God, and Ishmael rejected. For this he quotes Gen. xxi. 12, *In Isaac shall thy seed be called*, because the covenant was to be established with Isaac, Gen. xvii. 19. The blessings wrapt up in that great word, being communicated by God as a benefactor, he was free to determine on what head they should rest, and accordingly entailed them upon Isaac. This he explains further (v. 8, 9). The children of the flesh, as such, are not therefore the children of God, for then Ishmael had put in a good claim. This remark comes home to the unbelieving Jews. They had confidence in the flesh. Ishmael was a child of the flesh, representing those that expect justification and salvation by their own strength and righteousness. The *children of the promise are counted for the seed*. Those that have the happiness of being counted for the seed have it not for the sake of any merit of their own, but purely by virtue of the promise. Isaac was a child of promise; this he proves, v. 9. He was also conceived and born by virtue of the promise, and so a proper type of those who are now counted for the seed, even true believers, who are born, not of the will of the flesh, nor of the will of man, but of God.

2. The case of Jacob and Esau (v. 10–13), which is much stronger. There was a previous difference between Ishmael and Isaac, before Ishmael was cast out: Ishmael was of a fierce disposition, and had mocked or persecuted Isaac. But, in the case of Jacob and Esau, they were both the sons of Isaac by one mother. The difference was made between them by the divine counsel before they were born, or had done any good or evil. Both lay struggling alike in their mother's womb, when it was said, *The elder shall serve the younger, that the purpose of God according to election might stand*—that this great truth may be established, that God chooses some and refuses others by his own absolute and sovereign will. This difference that was put between Jacob and Esau he further illustrates by a quotation from Mal. i. 2, 3, where it is said, not of Jacob and Esau, but the Edomites and Israelites their posterity, *Jacob have I loved, and Esau have I hated*. The people of Israel were taken into the covenant, while the Edomites were rejected. Such a difference did God put between those two nations, that both descended from the loins of Abraham and Isaac, as at first there was a difference put between Jacob and Esau. (1) Some understand it of the election and rejection of conditions or qualifications. As God chose Isaac and Jacob, and rejected Ishmael and Esau, so he might and did choose faith to be the condition of salvation and reject the works of the law. (2) Others understand it of the election and rejection of particular persons—some loved, and others hated, from eternity. But the apostle speaks of Jacob and Esau, not in their own persons, but as ancestors. Nor does God condemn any merely because he will do it, without any reason taken from their own deserts. (3) Others therefore understand it of the election and rejection of people considered complexly. His design is to justify God, and his mercy and truth, in calling the Gentiles, while he suffered the obstinate part of the Jews to persist in unbelief. The choosing of Jacob the younger, and preferring him before Esau the elder (so crossing hands), were to intimate that the Jews, though the natural seed of Abraham, should be laid aside; and the Gentiles, who were as the younger brother, should be taken in in their stead. The Jews had for many ages been the favourites of heaven. Now that the gospel was preached, Christian churches (and in process of time Christian nations), become their successors in the divine favour.

Verses 14–24

The apostle comes here to maintain the absolute sovereignty of God, in disposing of the children of men. God is to be considered as an owner and benefactor, giving to the children of men such grace and favour as he has determined in and by his secret and eternal will.

Now this part of his discourse is in answer to two objections.

I. It might be objected, *Is there unrighteousness with God?* This the apostle startles at the thought of: *God forbid!* Far be it from us to think such a thing. He denies the consequences, and proves the denial.

1. In respect of those to whom he shows mercy, *v.* 15, 16. He quotes that scripture to show God's sovereignty in dispensing his favours (Exod. xxxiii. 19): *I will be gracious to whom I will be gracious.* All God's reasons of mercy are taken from within himself. He dispenses his gifts to whom he will, without giving us any reason. The expression is very emphatic, and the repetition makes it more so: *I will have mercy on whom I will have mercy,* he will do what he will. Therefore God's mercy endures for ever, because the reason of it is fetched from within himself; therefore his gifts and callings are without repentance. Hence he infers (*v.* 16), *It is not of him that willeth.* It is not to be ascribed to the most generous desire, nor to the most industrious endeavour, of man, but only and purely to the free grace and mercy of God. In Jacob's case it was *not of him that willeth, nor of him that runneth*; but only the mercy and grace of God. The reason why the unworthy, undeserving Gentiles are called, while the greatest part of the Jews are left to perish in unbelief, is not because those Gentiles were better deserving or better disposed for such a favour, but because of God's free grace that made that difference. Such is the method of God's grace towards all that partake of it, for he is found of those that sought him not (Isa. lxv. 1).

2. In respect of those who perish, *v.* 17. God's sovereignty is here discovered in the instance of Pharaoh. What God did with Pharaoh. He raised him up. Thus doth God raise up sinners in outward prosperity, external privileges. What he designed in it: *That I might show my power in thee.* God would, by all this, serve the honour of his name, and manifest his power. His conclusion concerning both these we have, *v.* 18. *He hath mercy on whom he will have mercy, and whom he will he hardeneth.* The various dealings of God must be resolved into his absolute sovereignty. He is debtor to no man, his grace is his own; we have none of us deserved it, nay, we have all justly forfeited it a thousand times. Those who are saved must thank God only, and those who perish must thank themselves only. We are bound to do our utmost for the salvation of all we have to do with; but God is bound no further than he has been pleased to bind himself; and that is that he will receive, and not cast out, those that come to Christ. Had he mercy on the Gentiles? It was because he would have mercy on them.

II. It might be objected, *Why doth he yet find fault? For who hath resisted his will?* (*v.* 19). He might well find fault if people refused to come up to the terms on which such a salvation is offered; the salvation being so great, the terms could not be hard. If God, while he gives effectual grace to some, denies it to others, why doth he find fault with those to whom he denies it? This objection he answers at large,

1. By reproving the objector (*v.* 20): *Nay but, O man.* This is not an objection fit to be made by the creature against his Creator, by man against God. Observe how contemptibly he speaks of man, when he comes to argue with God his Maker: "*Who art thou,* thou that art so foolish, so incompetent a judge of the divine counsels? art thou able to fathom such a depth."

That repliest against God. It becomes us to submit to him, not to reply against him; not to fly in his face, nor to charge him with folly.

2. By resolving all into the divine sovereignty. We are the thing formed, and he is the former; and it does not become us to arraign his wisdom in ordering and disposing of us into this or that shape of figure. God's sovereignty over us is fitly illustrated by the power that the potter hath over the clay; compare Jer. xviii. 6.

(1) He gives us the comparison, *v.* 21. The potter, out of the same lump, may make either a fashionable vessel, or a contemptible vessel, and herein he acts arbitrarily.

(2) The application of the comparison, *v.* 22–24. Two sorts of vessels God forms out of the great lump of fallen mankind: *Vessels of wrath.* In these God is willing to show his wrath. God will make it appear that he hates sin. He will likewise make his power known. In order to this, God *endured them with much long-suffering*—exercised a great deal of patience towards them, and so they became *fitted for destruction,* fitted by their own sin and self-hardening. The reigning corruptions and wickedness of the soul are its preparedness for hell. *Vessels of mercy.* The happiness bestowed upon the saved remnant is the fruit, not of their merit, but of God's mercy. Vessels of honour must to eternity own themselves vessels of mercy. What he designs in them: *To make known the riches of his glory,* that is, of his goodness; for God's goodness is his greatest glory. God makes known his glory, this goodness of his, in the preservation and supply of all the creatures: the earth is full of his goodness, but when he would demonstrate the riches of his goodness, he does it in the salvation of the saints. What he does for them: he does before *prepare them to glory.* This is God's work. We can destroy ourselves fast enough, but we cannot save ourselves. Sinners fit themselves for hell, but it is God that prepares saints for heaven. And would you know who these *vessels of mercy are?* Those whom he hath called (*v.* 24); for whom he did predestinate those he also called with an effectual call: and these not of the Jews only, but of the Gentiles. The question is not now whether of the seed of Abraham or no, but whether or no called according to his purpose.

Verses 25–29

The apostle here shows how the rejection of the Jews, and the taking in of the Gentiles, were foretold in the Old Testament. The Jews would, no doubt, willingly refer it to the Old Testament. Now he shows how this was there spoken of.

I. By the prophet Hosea. The Gentiles had not been the people of God: "But," says he, "*I will call them my people,* make them such and own them as such, notwithstanding all their unworthiness." Former badness is no bar to God's present grace and mercy.—*And her beloved which was not beloved.* Those whom God calls his people he calls beloved: he loves those that are his own. *In the place where it was said, &c., there shall they be called.* Wherever they are scattered over the face of the earth, there will God own them. Behold, what manner of love! This honour have all his saints.

II. By the prophet Isaiah, who speaks of the casting off of many of the Jews, in two places:

1. One is Isa. x. 22, 23, which speaks of the saving of a remnant, that is, but a remnant. It is no strange thing for God to abandon to ruin a great many of the seed of Abraham, and yet maintain his word of promise to Abraham in full force. This is intimated in the supposition that the number of children of Israel was as the sand of the sea. And yet only a remnant shall be saved; for many are called, but few

are chosen. In this salvation of the remnant we are told (v. 28) from the prophet, (1) That he will complete the work: *He will finish the work.* When God begins he will make an end, whether in ways of judgment or of mercy. As for God, his work is perfect. Margin, *He will finish the account.* God has taken an account of the children of men: and he will finish the account, call in as many as belong to the election of grace, and then the account will be finished. (2) That he will finish it quickly. Now he will *cut it short*, and make a short work upon the earth. But he will cut it short *in righteousness.* Men, when they cut short, do amiss; but, when God cuts short, it is always in righteousness. *The work (the word, the law)* was under the Old Testament very long. Our duty is now, under the gospel, summed up in much less room than it was under the law; religion is brought into a less compass. With us contractions are apt to darken things, but it is not so in this case. Though it be cut short, it is clear and plain; and, because short, the more easy.

2. Another is quoted from Isa. i. 9, where the prophet is showing how God would preserve a seed. It was no strange thing for God to leave the greatest part of the people of the Jews to ruin, and to reserve to himself only a small remnant: and they must not wonder if he did so now. What God is. He is *the Lord of sabaoth*, that is, the Lord of hosts. When God secures a seed to himself he acts as Lord of sabaoth. It is an act of almighty power and infinite sovereignty. What his people are; they are a *seed*, a small number. But they are a useful number. It is a wonder of divine power and mercy that there are any saved; for even those that are left to be a seed, if God had dealt with them according to their sins, had perished with the rest.

Verses 30–33

The true reason of the reception of the Gentiles, and the rejection of the Jews. There was a difference in the way of their seeking, and therefore there was that different success. He concludes like an orator, *What shall we say then?*

I. Concerning the Gentiles. 1. How they had been alienated from righteousness: they followed not after it. God was *found of those that sought him not*, Isa. lxv. 1. Thus doth God delight to dispense grace in a way of sovereignty and absolute dominion. 2. How they attained to righteousness, notwithstanding: *By faith;* by embracing Christ, and believing in Christ. They attained to that by the short cut of believing sincerely in Christ for which the Jews had been long in vain beating about the bush.

II. Concerning the Jews. 1. How they missed their end: they *followed after the law of righteousness* (v. 31). As many as stuck to their old Jewish principles and ceremonies, embracing the shadows now that the substance was come, these fell short of acceptance with God. 2. How they mistook their way, which was the cause of their missing the end, v. 32, 33. They sought, but not in the right way. *Not by faith*, not by depending upon the merit of Christ, and submitting to the terms of the gospel, which were the very life and end of the law. But they sought by the *works of the law.* This was the *stumbling-stone at which they stumbled.* They could by no means be reconciled to the doctrine of Christ, which brought them to expect justification through the merit of another. Christ himself is to some a stone of stumbling, for which he quotes Isa. viii. 14; xxviii. 16. It is sad that Christ should be set for the fall of any, and yet it is so (Luke ii. 34). So he is to multitudes; so he was to the unbelieving Jews. But still there is a remnant that do believe on him; and they *shall not be ashamed*, their hopes and expectations of justification by him shall not be disappointed, as theirs are

who expect it by the law. The unbelieving Jews have no reason to quarrel with God for rejecting them; they had a fair offer made to them upon gospel terms, which they did not like. If they perish, they may thank themselves.

CHAPTER 10

To two great truths I would reduce this chapter: I. That there is a great difference between the righteousness of the law, which the unbelieving Jews were wedded to, and the righteousness of faith offered in the gospel, ver. 1–11. II. That there is no difference between Jews and Gentiles; but the gospel sets them both upon the same level, ver. 12, to the end.

Verses 1–11

The scope of the apostle in this part of the chapter is to show the great pre-eminence of the righteousness of faith above that of the law; that he might persuade the Jews to believe in Christ.

I. Paul here professes his good affection to the Jews (v. 1, 2), where he gives them a good wish, and a good witness.

1. A good wish (v. 1), a wish that they might be saved. Though Paul preached against them, yet he prayed for them. This, he says, was *his heart's desire and prayer.* The strength and sincerity of his desire. It was *his heart's desire*; it was not a formal compliment, as good wishes are with many from the teeth outward, but a real desire. The soul of prayer is the heart's desire. Cold desires do but beg denials. The offering up of this desire to God. It was his prayer. There may be desires in the heart, and yet no prayer. Wishing and woulding, if that be all, are not praying.

2. A good witness, as a reason of his good wish (v. 2): *I bear them record that they have a zeal of God.* The unbelieving Jews were the most bitter enemies Paul had in the world, and yet Paul gives them as good a character as the truth would bear. Charity teaches us to put the best construction upon words and actions that they will bear. We should take notice of that which is commendable even in bad people. *They have a zeal of God.* Their opposition to the gospel is from a principle of respect to the law. There is such a thing as a blind misguided zeal: such was that of the Jews.

II. He here shows the fatal mistake that the unbelieving Jews were guilty of. Their zeal was *not according to knowledge.* It is true God gave them that law for which they were so zealous; but they might have known that, by the appearance of the promised Messiah, an end was put to it. He gave the most convincing evidence that could be of his being the Messiah; and yet they would not own him, but shut their eyes against the clear light, so that their zeal for the law was blind. This he shows further, v. 3.

1. The nature of their unbelief. They *have not submitted themselves to the righteousness of God.* Unbelief is a non-submission to the righteousness of God. *Have not submitted.* In true faith, there is need of a great deal of submission.

2. The causes of their unbelief, and these are two: (1) Ignorance of God's righteousness. They did not consider what need we have of a righteousness wherein to appear before him; if they had, they would never have expected justification by their own works, as if they could satisfy God's justice. (2) A proud conceit of their own righteousness: *Going about to establish their own*—a righteousness of their own working out, by the merit of their works. They thought they needed not to be beholden to the merit of Christ.

III. He here shows the folly of that mistake.

1. The subserviency of the law to the gospel (v. 4): *Christ is the end of the law for righteousness.* The design of the law was to lead people to Christ. The use of the law was to direct people for righteousness

to Christ. (1) Christ is the end of the ceremonial law, because he is the perfection of it. (2) Christ is the end of the moral law in that he did what the law could not do (*ch.* viii. 3). The end of the law was to bring men to perfect obedience, and so to obtain justification. The law is not destroyed, but, full satisfaction being made by the death of Christ for our breach of the law, the end is attained, and we are put in another way of justification. Christ is thus the end of the law; but it is only to *everyone that believeth.*

2. The excellency of the gospel above the law.

(1) What is the righteousness which is of the law? This he shows, *v.* 5. The tenor of it is, *Do, and live.* It owneth nothing as a righteousness sufficient to justify a man but that of perfect obedience. For this he quotes that scripture (Lev. xviii. 5), *You shall therefore keep my statutes and my judgments, which if a man do, he shall live in them.* The doing supposed must be perfect and sinless, without the least breach or violation. Now, was it not extreme folly in the Jews to adhere so closely to this way of justification and salvation, when there was a new and a living way opened?

(2) What is that righteousness which is of faith, *v.* 6, &c. This he describes in the words of Moses, in Deuteronomy. He quotes it from Deut. xxx. 11–14, and shows,

[1] That it is not at all hard or difficult. The way of justification and salvation has in it no such depths or knots as may discourage us, no insuperable difficulties attending it. *First,* We need not go to heaven to enquire into the secrets of the divine counsel. It is true Christ is in heaven; but we may be justified and saved without going thither. *Secondly,* We need not go to the deep, to fetch Christ out of the grave: *Into the deep, to bring up Christ from the dead.* It is true that Christ was in the grave, and it is as true that he is now in heaven; but we need not perplex ourselves with fancied difficulties. No, salvation is not put at so vast a distance from us.

[2] But it is very plain and easy: *The word is nigh thee.* Christ is nigh thee, for the word is nigh thee. It is *in thy mouth, and in thy heart.* The work thou hast to do lies within thee. All that which is to be done for us is already done to our hands. Those that were under the law were to do all themselves, *Do this, and live;* but the gospel discovers the greatest part of the work done already, and what remains cut short in righteousness, salvation, brought to our door, as it were. It is in our mouth—we are reading it daily; it is in our heart—we are, or should be, thinking of it daily. Even *the word of faith.* Now what is this word of faith? We have the tenor of it, *v.* 9, 10. What is promised to us: *Thou shalt be saved.* It is salvation that the gospel exhibits and tenders which Christ is the author of, a Saviour to the uttermost. Upon what terms. Two things are required as conditions of salvation: (*a*) Confessing the Lord Jesus—openly professing relation to him and dependence on him, standing by him in all weathers. Our Lord Jesus lays a great stress upon this confessing of him before men; see Matt. x. 32, 33. It was a very great thing, especially, when the profession of Christ and Christianity hazarded life, and all that is dear in this world, which was the case in the primitive times. (*b*) *Believing in the heart that God raised him from the dead.* The profession of faith with the mouth, if there be not the power of it in the heart, is but a mockery; especially concerning his resurrection, which is the fundamental article of the Christian faith. This is further illustrated (*v.* 10), and the order inverted, because there must first be faith in the heart before there can be an acceptable confession with the mouth. Concerning faith: It is *with the heart that man believeth,* which implies more than an assent of the understanding, and takes in the consent of the will.

This is *unto righteousness.* There is the righteousness of justification and the righteousness of sanctification. Faith is to both. Concerning profession: It is with *the mouth that confession is made*—confession to God in prayer and praise, confession to men by owning the ways of God before others. And this is said to be *unto salvation,* because it is the performance of the condition of that promise, Matt. x. 32. Justification by faith lays the foundation of our title to salvation; but by confession we build upon that foundation. So that we have here a brief summary of the terms of salvation, that we must give up, to God, our souls and our bodies—our souls in believing with the heart, and our bodies in confessing with the mouth. For this (*v.* 11) he quotes Isa. xlv. 17, *Whosoever believeth on him shall not be ashamed.* He will not be ashamed to own that Christ in whom he trusts; he that believes in the heart will not be ashamed to confess with the mouth. He shall not be ashamed of his hope in Christ. He shall never have cause to repent his confidence in reposing such a trust in the Lord Jesus.

Verses 12–21

There is no difference between Jews and Gentiles, but they stand upon the same level in point of acceptance with God. In Jesus Christ there is neither Greek nor Jew, Col. iii. 11. *There is no difference.*

I. God is the same to all: *The same Lord over all is rich unto all.* There is not one God to the Jews who is more kind, and another to the Gentiles who is less kind; but he is the same to all. When he proclaimed his name, The Lord, the Lord God, gracious and merciful, he thereby signified not only what he was to the Jews, but what he is and will be to all his creatures that seek unto him: liberal and bountiful in dispensing his favours *to all that call upon him.* Something must be done by us, and it is as little as can be, we must call upon him. We have nothing to do but to draw out by prayer.

II. The promise is the same to all (*v.* 13): *Whoever shall call.* Calling upon the name of the Lord is here put for all practical religion. What is the life of a Christian but a life of prayer? He that thus calls upon him shall be saved. It is but ask and have; what would we have more? For the further illustration of this he observes,

1. How necessary it was that the gospel should be preached to the Gentiles, *v.* 14, 15. This was what the Jews were so angry with Paul for. He shows how needful it was to bring them within the reach of the promise. *They cannot call on him in whom they have not believed.* Except they believe that he is God, they will not call upon him by prayer. The grace of faith is absolutely necessary to the duty of prayer; we cannot pray aright without it. He that comes to God by prayer must believe, Heb. xi. 6. *They cannot believe in him of whom they have not heard.* Some way or other the divine revelation must be made known to us, before we can receive it and assent to it; it is not born with us. *They cannot hear without a preacher.* Somebody must tell them what they are to believe. *They cannot preach except they be sent.* How shall a man act as an ambassador, unless he have both his credentials and his instructions from the prince that sends him? It is God's prerogative to send ministers. He only can qualify men for, and incline them to, the work of the ministry. But the competency of that qualification, and the sincerity of that inclination, must not be left to the judgment of every man for himself. This must needs be submitted to the judgment of those who are presumed the most able judges, and who are empowered to set apart such as they find so qualified and inclined. And those that are thus set apart, not only may, but must preach, as those that are sent.

2. How welcome the gospel ought to be to those to whom it was preached, because it showed the way to salvation, *v.* 15. For this he quotes, Isa. lii. 7. What the gospel is: It is *the gospel of peace.* Peace is put in general for all good; so it is explained here; it is *glad tidings of good things.* The things of the gospel are good things indeed, the best things; the best news that ever came from heaven to earth. What the work of ministers is: To *bring these glad tidings*; to *evangelize peace* (so the original is). Every preacher is in this sense an evangelist. How acceptable they should therefore be for their work's sake: *How beautiful are the feet,* that is, how welcome are they! Those that preach the gospel of peace should see to it that their feet (their life and conversation) be beautiful: the holiness of ministers' lives is the beauty of their feet. *How beautiful!* namely, in the eyes of those that hear them. Those that welcome the message cannot but love the messengers.

3. He answers an objection against all this (*v.* 16): *But they have not all obeyed the gospel.* All the Jews have not, all the Gentiles have not; far the greater part of both remain in unbelief and disobedience. The gospel is given us not only to be known and believed, but to be obeyed. It is no strange thing, but it is a very sad and uncomfortable thing, for the ministers of Christ to bring the report of the gospel, and not to be believed in it. He shows that the word preached is the ordinary means of working faith (*v.* 17): *So then,* though many that hear do not believe, yet those that believe have first heard. *Faith cometh by hearing.* The beginning, progress, and strength of faith, are by hearing. The word of God is therefore called *the word of faith.* God gives faith, but it is by the word as the instrument. *Hearing* is *by the word of God.* It is not hearing the enticing words of man's wisdom, but hearing the word of God, that will befriend faith. Those who would not believe the report of the gospel, yet, having heard it, were thereby left inexcusable, *v.* 18, *to the end.*

(1) The Gentiles have heard it (*v.* 18): *Have they not heard?* They have either heard the gospel, or at least heard of it. *Their sound went into all the earth;* not only a confused sound, but their *words are gone unto the ends of the world.* The commission which the apostles received runs thus: *Go you into all the world —preach to every creature—disciple all nations;* and they did with indefatigable industry and wonderful success pursue that commission. It was in order to this that the gift of tongues was poured so plentifully upon the apostles.

(2) The Jews have heard it too, *v.* 19–21. For this he appeals to two passages of the Old Testament. *Did not Israel know* that the Gentiles were to be called in? They might have known it from Moses and Isaiah.

First, One is taken from Deut. xxxii. 21, *I will provoke you to jealousy.* The Jews not only had the offer; they had the refusal. In all places where the apostles came still the Jews had the first offer, and the Gentiles had but their leavings. If one would not, another would. Now this provoked them to jealousy. The Gentiles are here called *no people,* and a *foolish nation.* How much soever there be of the wit and wisdom of the world, those that are not the people of God are a foolish people. Such was the state of the Gentile world, who yet were made the people of God, and Christ to them the wisdom of God. What a provocation it was to the Jews to see the Gentiles taken into favour we may see, especially Acts xxii. 22. It was an instance of the great wickedness of the Jews that they were thus enraged. God often makes people's sin their punishment. A man needs no greater plague than to be left to the impetuous rage of his own lusts.

Secondly, Another is taken from Isa. lxv. 1, 2, and in it Esaias is very bold. Those that will be found

faithful have need to be very bold. Those that are resolved to please God must not be afraid to displease any man. Now Esaias speaks boldly and plainly, Of the preventing grace and favour of God in the reception of the Gentiles (*v.* 20): *I was found of those that sought me not.* The prescribed method is, Seek and find; this is a rule for us, not a rule for God, who is often found of those that do not seek. Thus he manifested himself to the Gentiles, by sending the light of the gospel among them. Was not this our own particular case? Did not God begin in love, and manifest himself to us when we did not ask after him? And was not that a time of love indeed, to be often remembered with a great deal of thankfulness? Of the obstinacy and perverseness of Israel, *v.* 21. God's great goodness to them: *All day long I have stretched forth my hands.* (*a*) His offers: *I have stretched forth my hands,* offering them life and salvation. Stretching forth the hands is the gesture of those that require audience, or desire acceptance. Christ was crucified with his hands stretched out. *Stretched forth my hands* as offering reconciliation—come let us shake hands and be friends; and our duty is to give the hand to him. (*b*) His patience in making these offers: *All day long.* He waits to be gracious. He bears long, but he will not bear always. Their great badness to him. They were a *disobedient gainsaying people,* not only disobedient to the call, but gainsaying, and quarrelling with it. The Jews contradicted and blasphemed. It is a wonder of mercy in God that his goodness is not overcome by man's badness; and it is a wonder of wickedness in man that his badness is not overcome by God's goodness.

CHAPTER 11

It might be said, "Hath God then cast away his people?" The apostle therefore sets himself to make a reply to this objection, and that two ways: I. He shows at large what the mercy is that is mixed with this wrath, ver. 1–32. II. He infers thence the infinite wisdom and sovereignty of God, with the adoration of which he concludes this chapter and subject, ver. 32–36.

Verses 1–32

The apostle proposes here a plausible objection, which might be urged against the divine conduct (*v.* 1): *"Hath God cast away his people?"* Is the rejection total and final? Will he have no more a peculiar people to himself? He shows that there was a great deal of goodness and mercy expressed along with this seeming severity: 1. That, though some of the Jews were cast off, yet they were not all so. 2. That, though the body of the Jews were cast off, yet the Gentiles were taken in. And, 3. That, though the Jews were cast off at present, yet in God's due time they should be taken into his church again.

I. The Jews, it is true, were many of them cast off, but not all. The supposition of this he introduces with a *God forbid.*

1. There was a chosen remnant of believing Jews, that obtained righteousness and life by faith in Jesus Christ, *v.* 1–7. These are said to be such as he *foreknew* (*v.* 2), whom he thus foreknew he did predestinate. Here lies the ground of the difference. They are called the *election* (*v.* 7). Believers are the *election,* all those and those only whom God hath chosen. He shows that he himself was one of them: *For I also am an Israelite.* Paul was a chosen vessel (Acts ix. 15), and yet he was of the *seed of Abraham.* He suggests that as in Elias's time, so now, this chosen remnant was really more and greater than one would think it was. (1) His mistake concerning Israel; as if he himself was the only faithful servant God had in the world. He refers to 1 Kings xix. 14, where (it is here said) *he maketh intercession to God against Israel.* A strange kind of intercession! *He deals with God against Israel;* so it may be read. In

prayer we deal with God. It is said of Elijah (Jas. v. 17) that he *prayed in praying*. We are then likely to pray in praying, when we pray as those that are dealing with God. Elijah in this prayer spoke as if there were none left faithful in Israel but himself. See to what a low ebb the profession of religion may sometimes be brought. The powers of Israel were then persecuting powers: They have *killed thy prophets, and digged down thine altars*, and they *seek my life*. The multitude of Israel were then idolatrous: *I am left alone*. Thus those few that were faithful to God were not only lost in the crowd of idolaters, but crushed and driven into corners. *Digged down thine altars*. When altars were set up for Baal, it is no wonder if God's altars were pulled down; they could not endure that standing testimony against their idolatry. This was his intercession *against Israel*. It is a very sad thing for any person or people to have the prayers of God's people against them, for God espouses, and sooner or later will visibly own, the cause of his praying people. (2) The rectifying of this mistake (*v.* 4): *I have reserved*. Things are often much better with the church of God than wise and good men think they are. In times of general apostasy, there is usually a remnant that keep their integrity—all do not go one way. When there is a remnant who keep their integrity it is God that reserves to himself that remnant. It is his free and almighty grace that makes the difference between them and others.—*Seven thousand*: a competent number, and yet, compared with the many thousands of Israel, a very small number. Now the description of this remnant is that *they had not bowed the knee to the image of Baal*. In court, city, and country, Baal had the ascendant; and the generality of people, more or less, paid their respect to Baal. The best evidence of integrity is to swim against the stream when it is strong. This is thankworthy, not to bow to Baal when everybody bows. Sober singularity is commonly the badge of true sincerity. (3) The application of this instance to the case in hand: *Even so at this present time*, v. 5–7. As it has been, so it is. In Elijah's time there was a remnant, and so there is now. *A remnant*, a few of many, a remnant of believing Jews. This is called *a remnant according to the election of grace*. If the difference between them and others be made purely by the grace of God, as certainly it is (*I have reserved them*, saith he, *to myself*), then it must needs be according to the election. Now concerning this remnant we may observe, *First*, Whence it takes its rise, from the free grace of God (*v.* 6), that grace which excludes works. Election is purely according to the good pleasure of his will, Eph. i. 5. Paul's heart was so full of the freeness of God's grace that he turns aside to make this remark. *If of grace, then not of works. Secondly*, What it obtains: that which Israel in vain sought for (*v.* 7): *Israel hath not obtained that which he seeketh for*, that is, justification, and acceptance with God, but the *election have obtained it*. In them the promise of God has its accomplishment, and God's ancient kindness for that people is remembered. They were the persons whom God had in his eye in the counsels of his love.

2. *The rest were blinded*, v. 7. Some are chosen and called. But others are left to perish in their unbelief. The gospel, which to those that believed was the savour of life unto life, to the unbelieving was the savour of death unto death. The same sun softens wax and hardens clay. *They were blinded; they were hardened;* so some. They could neither see the light nor feel the touch, of gospel grace. Blindness and hardness are expressive of the same senselessness and stupidity of spirit. This seemed harsh doctrine: to qualify it, therefore, he vouches two witnesses out of the Old Testament.

(1) Isaiah, who spoke of such a judgment in his day, *ch.* xxix. 10; vi. 9. The *spirit of slumber*. They are under the power of a prevailing unconcernedness, like people that are slumbering and sleeping. *Eyes, that they should not see, and ears, that they should not hear*. They had the faculties, but in the things that belonged to their peace they had not the use of those faculties. They saw Christ, but they did not believe in him; they heard his word, but they did not receive it. It was all one as if they had neither seen nor heard—*Unto this day*. Ever since Esaias prophesied, this hardening work has been in the doing; some among them have been blind and senseless. It is still true concerning multitudes of them, even to this day in which we live.

(2) David (*v.* 9, 10), quoted from Ps. lxix. 22, 23, where David having foretold the sufferings of Christ from his own people the Jews, particularly that of their giving him *vinegar to drink*, foretells the dreadful judgments of God upon them for it: *Let their table become a snare*, which the apostle here applies to the present blindness of the Jews, and the offence they took at the gospel. He speaks here, [1] Of the ruin of their comforts: *Let their table be made a snare*, that is, as the psalmist explains it, Let that which should be for their welfare be a trap to them. The curse of God will turn meat into poison. Their very food, that should nourish them, shall choke them. [2] Of the ruin of their powers and faculties (*v.* 10), their eyes darkened, their backs bowed down, that they can neither find the right way, nor, if they could, are they able to walk in it. *They mind earthly things*. We have our eyes darkened if we are bowed down in worldly-mindedness.

II. Another thing which qualified this doctrine of the rejection of the Jews was that though they were cast off, yet the Gentiles were taken in (*v.* 11–14), which he applies by way of caution to the Gentiles, *v.* 17–22.

1. The Jews' leavings were a feast for the poor Gentiles (*v.* 11): "*Have they stumbled that they should fall?* Had God no other end in rejecting them than their destruction?" He startled at this as usually he does when anything is suggested which seems to reflect upon the wisdom, or righteousness, or goodness of God: *God forbid!* no, *through their fall salvation is come to the Gentiles*. By the divine appointment it was so ordered that the gospel should be preached to the Gentiles upon the Jews' refusal of it. And so it was in the history (Acts xiii. 46): *It was necessary that the word of God should first have been spoken to you; but, seeing you put it from you, lo, we turn to the Gentiles*. The Jews had the refusal, and so the tender came to the Gentiles. See how Infinite Wisdom brings light out of darkness, good out of evil. To the same purport he says (*v.* 12), *The fall of them was the riches of the world*. The riches of the Gentiles was the multitude of converts among them. True believers are God's jewels. To the same purport (*v.* 15): *The casting away of them is the reconciling of the world*. God's displeasure towards them made way for his favour towards the Gentiles. God was in Christ *reconciling the world*, 2 Cor. v. 19. In every nation he that feared God and wrought righteousness should be accepted of him.

2. The use that the apostle makes of this doctrine.

(1) As a kinsman to the Jews, here is a word of exhortation to them, to stir them up to receive the gospel offer. This God intended in his favour to the Gentiles, to provoke the Jews to jealousy (*v.* 11), and Paul endeavours to enforce it accordingly (*v.* 14); *If by any means I might provoke to emulation those who are my flesh*. "Shall the despised Gentiles run away with all the comforts and privileges of the gospel, and shall not we repent of our refusal, and now at last put in for a share?" There is a commendable emulation

in the affairs of our souls; why should not we be as holy and happy as any of our neighbours? The blessings are not lessened by the multitudes of the sharers.— *And might save some of them.* See what was Paul's business, to save souls; and yet the utmost he promises himself is but to save some. Of the many he dealt with he could but save some. Ministers must think their pains well bestowed if they can but be instrumental to save some.

(2) As an apostle to the Gentiles, here is a word of caution for them: "*I speak to you Gentiles.* You believing Romans, you hear what riches of salvation are come to you by the fall of the Jews, but take heed lest you do anything to forfeit it." Paul takes this, as other occasions, to apply his discourse to the Gentiles, because he was the apostle of the Gentiles. This was the purport of his extraordinary mission, Acts xxii. 21, *I will send thee far hence unto the Gentiles.* It ought to be our great and special care to do good to those that are under our charge: we must particularly mind that which is our own work. The Gentile world was a wider province; and the work to be done in it required a very able, courageous workman. God calls those to special work whom he either sees or makes fit for it.—*I magnify my office.* There were those that vilified it, and him because of it. It is a sign of true love to Jesus Christ to reckon that service for him truly honourable which the world looks upon with scorn. The office of the ministry is an office to be *magnified.* Ministers are stewards of the mysteries of God, and for their work's sake are to be esteemed highly in love.—*My office, my ministry,* my service. It was not the dignity but the work, of an apostle, that Paul was so much in love with. Now two things he exhorts the Gentiles to,

[1] To have a respect for the Jews, and to desire their conversion. The advantage that would accrue to the church by their conversion, *v.* 12, 15. It would be as life from the dead; and therefore they must long for the receiving of them in again.

[2] To take heed to themselves, lest they should stumble and fall, as the Jews had done, *v.* 17–22.

First, The privilege which the Gentiles had by being taken into the church. They were grafted in (*v.* 17), as a branch of a wild olive into a good olive, which is contrary to the custom of the husbandman, who grafts the good olive into the bad; but those that God grafts into the church he finds wild and barren, and good for nothing. Men graft to mend the tree; but God grafts to mend the branch. The church of God is an olive-tree, flourishing and fruitful, the fruit useful. Those that are out of the church are as wild olive-trees not only useless, but what they do produce is sour and unsavoury: *Wild by nature, v.* 24. It is the natural state of everyone of us to be wild by nature. Conversion is the grafting in of wild branches into the good olive. Those that are grafted into the good olive-tree partake of the root and fatness of the olive. All that are by a lively faith grafted into Christ partake of him as the branches of the root. The Gentiles, being grafted into the church, partake of the same privileges that the Jews did, *the root and fatness.* Christ only is the root. Now the believing Gentiles partake of this root.

Secondly, A caution not to abuse these privileges. 1. "Be not proud (*v.* 18): *Boast not against the branches.*" Grace is given, not to make us proud, but to make us thankful. The law of faith excludes all boasting either of ourselves or against others. "Do not say (*v.* 19): *They were broken off that I might be grafted in;* that is, do not think that thou didst merit more at the hand of God than they. But remember, *thou bearest not the root, but the root thee.* Though thou art grafted in, thou art still but a branch borne by the root; nay, and an engrafted branch, brought into the good olive *contrary to*

nature (*v.* 24), not free-born, but by an act of grace. Therefore, *if thou boast,* know (this word must be supplied to clear the sense) *thou bearest not the root but the root thee.*" 2. "Be not secure (*v.* 20): *Be not high-minded, but fear.* Be not too confident of your own strength and standing." A holy fear is an excellent preservative against high-mindedness: happy is the man that thus feareth always. *Fear* what? "Why fear lest thou lose the privileges thou now enjoyest, as they have lost theirs." The evils that befall others should be warnings to us. The patent which churches have of their privileges is not for a certain term, but it runs as long as they carry themselves well, and no longer. Consider, (1) "How they were broken off. It was not undeservedly, but *because of unbelief.*" They did by this cut themselves off. They were *natural branches* (*v.* 21), yet, when they sunk into unbelief, God did not spare them. Prescription, long usage, the faithfulness of their ancestors, would not secure them. It was in vain to plead, though they insisted much upon it, that they were Abraham's seed. This is called here *severity, v.* 22. Severity is a word that sounds harshly; and I do not remember that it is anywhere else in scripture ascribed to God. God is most severe towards those that have been in profession nearest to him, if they rebel against him. Of all judgments, spiritual judgments are the sorest; for of these he is here speaking, *v.* 8. (2) "How thou standest, thou that are engrafted in." "By what means thou standest: *By faith,* which is a depending grace. Thou dost not stand in any strength of thy own: thou art no more than the free grace of God makes thee. That which ruined them was unbelief, and by faith thou standest." On what terms (*v.* 22): "*Towards thee goodness, if thou continue in his goodness,* that is, continue in a dependence upon the free grace of God." The condition of our happiness, is to keep ourselves in the love of God.

III. Another thing that qualifies this doctrine of the Jews' rejection is that the rejection is not final.

1. How this conversion of the Jews is here described. It is said to be their fulness (*v.* 12), that is, the addition of them to the church. This would be the enriching of the world with a great deal of light and strength and beauty. It is called the receiving of them. They shall be received into the love of Christ. And this will be as *life from the dead*—so strange and surprising, and yet withal so welcome and acceptable. It is called the *grafting of them in again* (*v.* 23). That which is grafted in receives sap and virtue from the root; so does a soul that is truly grafted into the church receive life, and strength, and grace from Christ the quickening root. They shall be *grafted into their own olive-tree* (*v.* 24) to retrieve those privileges which they had so long enjoyed, but have now sinned away and forfeited by their unbelief. It is called the *saving of all Israel, v.* 26. The adding of them to the church is the saving of them.

2. What it is grounded upon, and what reason we have to look for it.

(1) Because of the holiness of the first-fruits and the root, *v.* 16. A good beginning promises a good ending. By the first-fruits understand the same with the root, namely, the patriarchs, Abraham, Isaac, and Jacob. Now, if they were holy—if they were in the covenant—then we have reason to conclude that God hath a kindness for the *lump*—the body of that people; and for the *branches*—the particular members of it. *If the root be holy, so are the branches.* Though a wise man does not beget a wise man, yet a free man begets a free man. Though grace does not run in the blood, yet external privileges do (till they are forfeited). The Jewish branches are reckoned holy, because the root was so. This is expressed more plainly (*v.* 28): *They are beloved for the fathers' sakes.* And the same love would revive their privileges for

still the ancient loving-kindness is remembered. Though, as concerning the gospel, they are enemies to it *for your sakes*, that is, for the sake of the Gentiles, against whom they have such an antipathy; yet, when God's time shall come, this will wear off, and God's love to their fathers will be remembered. Many fare the better for the sake of their godly ancestors. It is upon this account that the church is called their own *olive-tree*, which is some encouragement to us to hope that there may be room for them in it again, for old acquaintance-sake. That which hath been may be again.

(2) Because of the power of God (*v*. 23): *God is able to graft them in again.* Our comfort is that God is able to work a change, able to graft those in that have been long cast out and withered. *If they abide not still in unbelief.* So that nothing is to be done but to remove that unbelief, and God is able to take that away, though nothing less than an almighty power will do it.

(3) Because of the grace of God manifested to the Gentiles. This is his argument (*v*. 24): "If thou wast grafted into a good olive, that was wild by nature, much more shall these that were the natural branches." This is a suggestion very proper to check the insolence of those Gentile Christians that looked with disdain upon the rejected Jews. This is his argument (*v*. 30, 31): *As you in times past have not*, &c. It is good for those that have found mercy with God to be often thinking what they were in time past, and how they obtained that mercy. He argues further from the occasion of the Gentiles' call: "*You have obtained mercy through their unbelief;* much more shall they obtain mercy through your mercy. *That through your mercy they might obtain mercy*, that is, that they may be beholden to you, as you have been to them." True grace hates monopolies. Those that have found mercy themselves should endeavour that through their mercy others also may obtain mercy.

(4) Because of the promises and prophecies of the Old Testament. He quotes a very remarkable one, *v*. 26, from Isa. lix. 20, 21. [1] The coming of Christ promised: *There shall come out of Zion the deliverer.* Jesus Christ is the great deliverer. In Isaiah it is, *the Redeemer shall come to Zion.* There he is called the Redeemer; here the deliverer; he delivers in a way of redemption, by a price. There he is said to come to Zion, because when the prophet prophesied he was yet to come into the world. When the apostle wrote this, he had come, and he is speaking of the fruits of his appearing, which shall come *out of Zion*. [2] The purpose of this coming: *He shall turn away ungodliness from Jacob.* Christ's errand into the world was to turn away ungodliness, that iniquity might not be our ruin, and that it might not be our ruler. Especially to turn it away from Jacob. What greater kindness could he do them than to turn away ungodliness from them, and then make way for all good? In Isaiah it is, *The Redeemer shall come to Zion, and unto those that turn from transgression in Jacob*, those only that leave their sins and turn to God; to them Christ comes as a Redeemer.—*For this is my covenant with them*—this, that the deliverer shall come to them—this, that my Spirit shall not depart from them. The apostle adds, *When I shall take away their sins.* Pardon of sin is laid as the foundation. *For I will be merciful.* Now from all this he infers that certainly God had great mercy in store for that people, and he proves his inference (*v*. 29) by this truth: *For the gifts and callings of God are without repentance.* Those gifts and callings are immutable; whom he so loves, he loves to the end. We never find God repenting that he had given a man grace, or effectually called him.

3. The time and extent of this conversion, when and where it is to be expected. It is called a mystery (*v*. 25), that which was not obvious, and which one would not expect upon the view of the present state of that people. The case of the rejected Jews seemed as bad now as that of the Gentiles had been. Now he would have them know so much of this mystery as to keep them humble: lest *you be wise in your own conceit*. Ignorance is the cause of our self-conceitedness. (1) Their present state: *Blindness, in part, is happened to Israel*, *v*. 25. It is but in part; there is a remnant that see the things which belong to their peace, *v*. 7, 8. To the same purport (*v*. 32): *God has concluded them all in unbelief*, shut them up as in a prison. They all stand before God convicted of unbelief. They would not believe. "Why then," saith God, "you shall not." (2) When this blessed change should be: when the *fulness of the Gentiles shall come in*, when the gospel has had its intended success, and made its progress in the Gentile world. The Jews shall continue in blindness, till God hath performed his whole work among the Gentiles. God's taking them again was not because he had need of them, but of his own free grace. (3) The extent of it: *All Israel shall be saved*, *v*. 26. He will *have mercy upon all*, *v*. 32. They should be brought to believe in Christ the true Messiah whom they crucified, and become one sheep-fold with the Gentiles under Christ the great Shepherd. Some think it is done already, when before, and in, and after, the destruction of Jerusalem by the Romans, multitudes of the Jews were convinced, and turned Christians. Others think that it is yet to have its accomplishment towards the end of the world.

Verses 33–36

The apostle having insisted so largely upon reconciling the rejection of the Jews with the divine goodness, he concludes here with the acknowledgment of the divine wisdom in all this.

I. The secrecy of the divine counsels: *O the depth!* in general, the whole mystery of the gospel, which we cannot fully comprehend.—*The riches of the wisdom and knowledge of God*, a depth which the angels pry into, 1 Pet. i. 12. Much more may it puzzle any human understanding. He confesses himself at a loss in the contemplation, and, despairing to find the bottom, he humbly sits down at the brink, and adores the depth. Those that know most in this state of imperfection cannot but be most sensible of their own weakness and short-sightedness.—*The depth of the riches.* Men's riches are shallow, you may soon see the bottom; but God's riches are deep. There is not only depth in the divine counsels, but riches too, and that passing knowledge.—*Riches of the wisdom and knowledge of God.* His seeing all things—that all is naked and open before him: there is his knowledge. His ruling and ordering all things and bringing about his own purposes in all; this is his wisdom.—*How unsearchable are his judgments!* that is, his counsels and purposes: and his *ways*, that is, the execution of these counsels and purposes. We know not what he has in view; it is *past finding out*. Secret things belong not to us. What he does we know not now, John xiii. 7. We cannot give a reason of God's proceedings. The judgments of his hands, and the ways of his providence, are dark and mysterious, which therefore we must not pry into, but silently adore. The apostle speaks this especially with reference to that strange turn, the casting off of the Jews, and the entertainment of the Gentiles, with a purpose to take in the Jews again in due time. These are methods unaccountable, concerning which we must say, *O the depth!*—*Past finding out, cannot be traced.* God leaves no prints nor footsteps behind him, but his paths of providence are new every morning. He does not go the same way so often as to make a track of it. It follows (*v*. 34), *For who hath known the mind of the Lord?* Is there any creature made of his cabinet-council? Is there any to whom he has imparted his counsels, to know the way that he takes? The apostle makes the same challenge (1 Cor. ii. 16): *For who hath known the mind of the Lord?* And yet there he adds, *But we have the mind of Christ.* He that knew the mind of the Lord has declared him, John i. 18. And so, though we know not the mind of the Lord, yet if we have the mind of Christ, we have enough.—*Or who has been his counsellor?* It is nonsense for any man to prescribe to God, or to teach him how to govern the world.

II. The sovereignty of the divine counsels. In all these things God does what he will, because he will, and yet there is no unrighteousness with him.

1. He challenges any to prove God a debtor to him (*v.* 35): *Who hath first given to him?* Who is there of all the creatures that can prove God is beholden to him? *Of thine own we have given thee.* All the duties we can perform are not requitals, but rather restitutions. The apostle here proclaims, in God's name, that payment is ready: *It shall be recompenced to him again.* It is certain God will let nobody lose by him; but never anyone yet durst make a demand of this kind. This is here suggested, (1) To silence the clamours of the Jews. When God took away their visible church-privileges from them, he did but take his own. (2) To silence the insultings of the Gentiles. When God sent the gospel among them, it was not because he owed them so much favour, but of his own good pleasure.

2. He resolves all into the sovereignty of God (*v.* 36): *For of him, and through him, and to him, are all things,* that is, God is all in all. Of God as the spring and fountain of all, through Christ, as the conveyance, to God as the ultimate end. If all be of him and through him, there is all the reason in the world that all should be to him and for him. To do all to the glory of God is to make a virtue of necessity; for all shall in the end be to him, whether we will or no. And so he concludes with a short doxology: *To whom be glory for ever, Amen.* Paul had been discoursing at large of the counsels of God concerning man, but, after all, he concludes with the acknowledgment of the divine sovereignty, as that into which all these things must be ultimately resolved. Especially when we come to talk of the divine counsels and actings, it is best for us to turn our arguments into awful and serious adorations.

CHAPTER 12

The apostle comes in the next place to press the principal duties. We mistake our religion if we look upon it only as a system of notions and a guide to speculation. No, it is a practical religion. The duties are drawn from the privileges by way of inference. The foundation of Christian practice must be laid in Christian knowledge and faith. It is joined to the foregoing discourse by the word "therefore". It is the practical application of doctrinal truths that is the life of preaching. The faith that justifies is a faith that "works by love". And there is no other way to heaven but the way of holiness and obedience. The particular exhortations of this chapter are reducible to the three principal heads of Christian duty: our duty to God, to ourselves, and to our brother. The grace of God teaches us, in general, to live "godly, soberly, and righteously". Now this chapter will give us to understand what godliness, sobriety, and righteousness, are.

Verses 1–21

I. Concerning our duty to God. We see what is godliness.

1. It is to surrender ourselves to God, and so to lay a good foundation. This is here pressed as the spring of all duty and obedience, *v.* 1, 2.

(1) The body must be presented to him, *v.* 1. The exhortation is here introduced very pathetically: *I beseech you, brethren.* Though he was a great apostle, yet he calls the meanest Christians *brethren*, a term of affection and concern. He uses entreaty; this is the gospel way. This is to insinuate the exhortation,

that it might come with the more pleasing power. Many are sooner wrought upon if they be accosted kindly, are more easily led than driven.

[1] The duty pressed—to present our *bodies a living sacrifice. Your bodies*—your whole selves. Our bodies and spirits are intended. Sacrifice is here taken for whatsoever is by God's own appointment dedicated to himself. Christ, who was once offered to bear the sins of many, is the only sacrifice of atonement; but our persons and performances, tendered to God through Christ, are as sacrifices of acknowledgment to the honour of God. Presenting them denotes a voluntary act. It must be a free-will offering. The presenting of the body to God implies not only the avoiding of the sins that are committed with or against the body, but the using of the body as a servant of the soul in the service of God. It is to yield the members of our bodies as instruments of righteousness, *ch.* vi. 13. Though bodily exercise alone profits little, yet in its place it is a proof of the dedication of our souls to God. *First,* Present them a living sacrifice. A Christian makes his body a sacrifice to God. A body sincerely devoted to God is a living sacrifice. It is Christ living in the soul by faith that makes the body a living sacrifice. Holy love kindles the sacrifices, puts life into the duties. *Alive,* that is, to God, *v.* 11. *Secondly,* They must be holy. There must be that real holiness which consists in an entire rectitude of heart and life, our bodies must not be made the instruments of sin and uncleanness, but set apart for God, and put to holy uses. It is the soul that is the proper subject of holiness; but a sanctified soul communicates a holiness to the body. That is holy which is according to the will of God; when the bodily actions are so, the body is holy.

[2] The arguments to enforce this, which are three: *First,* Consider the mercies of God: *I beseech you by the mercies of God.* This is an argument most sweetly cogent. There is the mercy that is in God and the mercy that is from God—mercy in the spring and mercy in the streams: both are included here. God is a merciful God, therefore let us present our bodies to him; he will be sure to use them kindly. We receive from him every day the fruits of his mercy, particularly mercy to our bodies: he made them, he maintains them, be bought them. The greatest mercy of all is that Christ hath made not his body only, but his soul, an offering for sin. Let us render ourselves as an acknowledgment of all these favours—all we are, all we have, all we can do; and, after all, it is but very poor returns, and yet, because it is what we have, *Secondly,* It is *acceptable to God.* These living sacrifices are acceptable to God. If the presenting of ourselves will but please him, we may easily conclude that we cannot bestow ourselves better. *Thirdly,* It is our *reasonable service.* There is an act of reason in it; for it is the soul that presents the body. Our God must be served in the spirit and with the understanding. God does not impose upon us anything hard or unreasonable, but that which is altogether agreeable to the principles of right reason. That is a reasonable service which we are able and ready to give a reason for.

(2) The mind must be renewed for him. This is pressed (*v.* 2): "*Be you transformed by the renewing of your mind.*" Conversion and sanctification are the renewing of the mind, a change not of the substance, but of the qualities of the soul. The man is not what he was—old things are passed away, all things are become new. The renewing of the mind is the renewing of the whole man, for out of it are the *issues of life.* The progress of sanctification, dying to sin more and more and living to righteousness more and more, is the carrying on of this renewing work. This is called the *transforming* of us. The same word is used 2 Cor. iii. 18, where we are said to be *changed*

into the same image from glory to glory. Not that we can work such a change ourselves: we could as soon make a new world as make a new heart by any power of our own; it is God's work. "Use the means which God hath appointed and ordained for it." It is God that turns us, and then we are turned. "Lay your souls under the changing transforming influences of the blessed Spirit." Though the new man be created of God, yet we must put it on (Eph. iv. 24), and be pressing forward towards perfection.

[1] What is the great enemy to this renewing; and that is, conformity to this world: *Be not conformed to this world.* All the disciples and followers of the Lord Jesus must be nonconformists to this world. *Do not fashion yourselves* according to the world. We must not conform to the things of the world. We must not conform to the men of the world, we must not follow a multitude to do evil. If sinners entice us, we must not consent to them, but in our places witness against them. True Christianity consists much in a sober singularity. Yet we must take heed of the extreme of affected rudeness and moroseness, which some run into. The rule of the gospel is a rule of direction, not a rule of contrariety.

[2] What is the great effect of this renewing: *That you may prove what is that good, and acceptable, and perfect will of God.* By the will of God, here we are to understand his revealed will concerning our duty, that will which we pray may be done by us as it is done by the angels. *First,* The will of God is *good, and acceptable, and perfect*; three excellent properties of a law. It is good in itself. It is good for us. It is acceptable, it is pleasing to God. The only way to attain his favour as the end is to conform to his will as the rule. It is perfect, to which nothing can be added. *Secondly,* It concerns Christians to prove what is that will of God which is good, and acceptable, and perfect; to know it experimentally, to know the excellency of the will of God by the experience of a conformity to it. It is to approve *things that are excellent* (Phil. i. 10). It is to be *of quick understanding in the fear of the Lord,* Isa. xi. 3. *Thirdly,* Those are best able to prove what is the good, and acceptable, and perfect will of God, who are transformed by the renewing of their mind. It disposes the soul to receive the revelations of the divine will. The promise is (John vii. 17), *If any man will do his will, he shall know of the doctrine.* A good wit can dispute about the will of God; while an honest, humble heart loves it.

2. When this is done, to serve him (*v.* 11, 12), *Serving the Lord.* To be religious is to serve God. (1) We must make a business of it, and not be slothful in that business. *Not slothful in business.* We must not drive on slowly in religion. Slothful servants will be reckoned with as wicked servants. (2) We must be *fervent in spirit, serving the Lord.* God must be served with the spirit under the influences of the Holy Spirit. And there must be fervency in the spirit —a holy zeal, and warmth, as those that love God not only with the heart and soul, but with all our hearts, and with all our souls. This is the holy fire that kindles the sacrifice and carries it up to heaven, an offering of a sweet-smelling savour. (3) *Rejoicing in hope.* God is honoured by our hope and trust in him, especially when we rejoice in that hope. (4) *Patient in tribulation.* Thus also God is served, not only by working for him when he calls us to work, but by sitting still quietly when he calls us to suffer. Those that rejoice in hope are likely to be patient in tribulation. (5) *Continuing instant in prayer.* Prayer is a friend to hope and patience, and we do in it serve the Lord.

II. Concerning our duty which respects ourselves; this is sobriety.

1. A sober opinion of ourselves, *v.* 3. *I say, through the grace given unto me.* It is said to everyone of us,

one as well as another. Pride is a sin that is bred in the bone of all of us. *Not to think of himself more highly than he ought to think.* We must take heed of having too great an opinion of ourselves. We must not be self-conceited, nor esteem too much our own wisdom. There is a high thought of ourselves which we may and must have to think ourselves too good to be the slaves of sin and drudges to this world. We should think soberly, that is, we must have a modest opinion of ourselves and our own abilities, according to what we have received from God, and not otherwise. The words will bear yet another sense agreeable enough. *Of himself* is not in the original; therefore it may be read, *That no man be wise above what he ought to be wise, but be wise unto sobriety.* There is a knowledge that puffs up. We must take heed of this, and labour after that knowledge which tends to sobriety. To this head refers also that exhortation (*v.* 16), *Be not wise in your own conceits.* It is good to be wise, but it is bad to think ourselves so; for there is more hope of a fool than of him that is wise in his own eyes. It was an excellent thing for Moses to have his face shine and not know it. Now the reasons are these:

(1) Because whatever we have that is good, *God hath dealt* it to us. The best and most useful man in the world is no more, no better, than what the free grace of God makes him every day. When we are thinking of ourselves, we must remember to think not how we have attained; but think how kind God hath been to us.

(2) Because God deals out his gifts in a certain measure: According to *the measure of faith.* The measure of spiritual gifts he calls the measure of faith, for this is the radical grace. What we have and do that is good is so far right and acceptable as it is founded in faith. Christ had the Spirit given him without measure. But the saints have it by measure. Christ, who had gifts without measure, was meek and lowly; and shall we, that are stinted, be proud and self-conceited?

(3) Because God has dealt out gifts to others as well as to us: *Dealt to every man.* Had we the monopoly of the Spirit there might be some pretence for this conceitedness of ourselves; but others have their share as well as we. Therefore it ill becomes us to lift up ourselves, and to despise others, as if we only were the people in favour with Heaven. This reasoning he illustrates by a comparison taken from the members of the natural body. *As we have many members in one body,* &c., *v.* 4, 5. [1] All the saints make up one body in Christ, who is the head of the body. Believers lie not in the world as a confused disorderly heap, but are organized and knit together. [2] Particular believers are members of this body, deriving life and spirits from the head. Some members in the body are bigger and more useful than others, and each received according to its proportion. If the little finger should receive as much nourishment as the leg, how unseemly and prejudicial would it be! We must remember that we are not the whole; we are but parts. [3] All *the members have not the same office* (*v.* 4), but each hath its respective place and work assigned it. So in the mystical body, some are called to one sort of work; others are called to another sort of work. [4] Each member hath its place and office, for the good of the whole, and of every other member. We are not only members of Christ, but we are *members one of another, v.* 5. We are engaged to do all the good we can one to another. Whatever we have we received it not for ourselves, but for the good of others.

2. A sober use of the gifts that God hath given us. As we must not on the one hand be proud of our talents, so on the other hand we must not bury them. We must not say, "I am nothing, therefore I will sit

still, and do nothing"; but, "I am nothing in myself, and therefore I will lay out myself to the utmost in the strength of the grace of Christ." *Having gifts,* let us use them. *Gifts differing.* The immediate design is different, though the ultimate tendency of all is the same. *According to the grace.* It is grace that appoints the office, qualifies and inclines the person. Seven particular gifts he specifies (*v.* 6–8), which seem to be meant of so many distinct offices. There are two general ones here expressed by prophesying and ministering, the former the work of the bishops, the latter the work of the deacons. The five latter will therefore be reduced to the two former.

(1) *Prophecy. Whether prophecy, let us prophesy according to the proportion of faith.* It is not meant of the extraordinary gifts of foretelling things to come, but the ordinary office of preaching the word. The work of the Old Testament prophets was not only to foretell future things, but to warn the people concerning sin and duty. And thus gospel preachers are prophets. Those that preach the word must do it *according to the proportion of faith,* [1] As to the manner of our prophesying, it must be according to the proportion of the grace of faith. Let him that preaches set all the faith he hath on work, to impress the truths he preaches upon his own heart in the first place. As people cannot hear well, so ministers cannot preach well, without faith. And we must remember the proportion of faith—that, though all men have not faith, yet a great many have besides ourselves. "*Hast thou faith? Have it to thyself;* and do not make it a ruling rule to others, remembering that thou hast but thy proportion." [2] As to the matter of our prophesying, it must be according to the proportion of the doctrine of faith. There are some staple-truths, as I may call them, plainly and uniformly taught in the scripture, which are the touchstone of preaching, by which we must *prove all things,* and then *hold fast that which is good,* 1 Thess. v. 20, 21. Truths that are more dark must be examined by those that are more clear, for it is certain one truth can never contradict another. See here what ought to be the great care of preachers—to preach sound doctrine. It is necessary that it be according to the proportion of faith: for it is the word of faith that we preach. Now there are two particular works which he that prophesieth hath to mind—teaching and exhorting. *First,* Let him that teacheth wait on teaching. Teaching is the bare explaining and proving of gospel truths, without practical application. Now he that has a faculty of teaching, and has undertaken that province, let him stick to it. It is a good gift, let him use it, and give his mind to it. *Secondly,* Let him that *exhorteth* wait *on exhortation.* Let him give himself to that. This is the work of the pastor, to apply gospel truths and rules more closely to the people, and to press upon them that which is more practical. Many that are very accurate in teaching may yet be very cold and unskilful in exhorting; and on the contrary. The one requires a clearer head, the other a warmer heart. To wait on our work is to bestow the best of our time and thoughts upon it, and to study not only to do it, but to do it well.

(2) *Ministry.* If a man hath *the office of a deacon* let him use that office well. It includes all those offices which concern *the outward business of the house of God. Serving tables,* Acts vi. 2. Now let him on whom this care of ministering is devolved attend to it with faithfulness and diligence. [1] *He that giveth, let him do it with simplicity.* Those church-officers that were the stewards of the church's alms. Let them do it *liberally* and faithfully, with all sincerity and integrity, having no other intention in it than to glorify God and do good. He that hath wherewithal, let him give, and give plentifully and liberally. God loves a cheerful bountiful giver. [2] *He that ruleth*

with diligence. It should seem, he means those that were assistants to the pastors in exercising church-discipline. Now such must do it with diligence. The word denotes both care and industry to discover what is amiss to keep the church pure. [3] *He that showeth mercy with cheerfulness.* Some think it is meant in general of all that in anything show mercy; Let them be willing to do it, and take a pleasure in it. But it seems to be meant of some particular church-officers, whose work it was to take care of the sick and strangers. Now this must be done with cheerfulness. A pleasing countenance in acts of mercy is a great relief and comfort to the miserable; when they see it is not done grudgingly and unwillingly, but with pleasant looks and gentle words. Those that have to do with such as are sick and sore, and commonly cross and peevish, have need to put on not only patience, but cheerfulness.

III. Concerning that part of our duty which respects our brethren. Now all our duty towards one another is summed up in one word, and that a sweet word, *love.* Therefore the apostle mentions this first: *Let love be without dissimulation;* not in compliment and pretence, but in reality. There is a love owing to our friends, and to our enemies. He specifies both.

1. To our friends. There is a mutual love that Christians owe, and must pay.

(1) An affectionate love (*v.* 10): *Be kindly affectioned one to another, with brotherly love*—it signifies not only love, but a readiness and inclination to love, kindness flowing out as from a spring. It properly denotes the love of parents to their children. Such must our love be to one another, and such it will be where there is a new nature and the law of love is written in the heart. *One to another.* This may recommend the grace of love to us, that, as it is made our duty to love others, so it is as much their duty to love us. And what can be sweeter on this side heaven than to love and be beloved?

(2) A respectful love: *In honour preferring one another.* Let us be forward to give to others the pre-eminence. We should be forward to take notice of the gifts, and graces, and performances of our brethren, and value them accordingly, be more pleased to hear another praised than ourselves; *going before,* or *leading one another in honour;* so some read it: not in taking honour, but in giving honour. Though we must prefer others (as our translation reads it) as more capable and deserving than ourselves, yet we must not make that an excuse for doing nothing, nor under a pretence of honouring others, indulge ourselves in ease and slothfulness. Therefore he immediately adds (*v.* 11), *Not slothful in business.*

(3) A liberal love (*v.* 13): *Distributing to the necessities of saints.* It is but a mock love which rests in the verbal expressions of kindness and respect, while the wants of our brethren call for real supplies, and it is in the power of our hands to furnish them. It is no strange thing for saints in this world to want necessaries for the support of their natural life. Surely the things of this world are not the best things; if they were, the saints would not be put off with so little of them. It is the duty of those who have wherewithal to *distribute,* or (as it might better be read) to *communicate* to those necessities. It is not enough to draw out the soul, but we must draw out the purse, to the hungry. *Communicating.* Our poor brethren have a kind of interest in that which God hath given us; and our relieving them should come from a fellow-feeling of their wants. The charitable benevolence of the Philippians to Paul is called their communicating with his affliction, Phil. iv. 14. We are in a special manner bound to communicate to the saints. There is a common love owing to our fellow-creatures, but a special love owing to our fellow-christians. He mentions another branch of this

bountiful love: *Given to hospitality*. As there is occasion, we must welcome strangers. *I was a stranger, and you took me in*, is mentioned as one instance of the mercifulness of those that shall obtain mercy. It intimates, not only that we must take opportunity, but that we must seek opportunity, thus to show mercy.

(4) A sympathizing love (*v.* 15): *Rejoice with those that do rejoice, and weep with those that weep*. True love will interest us in the sorrows and joys of one another, and teach us to make them our own. Some rejoicing, and others weeping for the trial, as of other graces, so of brotherly love and Christian sympathy. Not that we must participate in the sinful mirths or mournings of any. Not envying those that prosper, but rejoicing with them; not despising those that are in trouble, but concerned for them, and ready to help them.

(5) A united love: "*Be of the same mind one towards another* (*v.* 16). Agree in affection; endeavour to be all one; *wishing the same good* to others that you do to yourselves"; so some understand it. This is to love our brethren as ourselves.

(6) A condescending love: *Mind not high things, but condescend to men of low estate*, *v.* 16. True love cannot be without lowliness. To love one another aright is to be willing to stoop to the meanest offices of kindness for the good of one another. Love is a condescending grace. *Mind not high things*. We must not be ambitious of honour and preferment. The Romans, living in the imperial city, were perhaps ready to take occasion thence to think the better of themselves. Therefore the apostle so often cautions them against high-mindedness; compare *ch.* xi. 20. *Condescend to men of low estate*. It may be meant of *mean things*, to which we must condescend. If our condition in the world be poor and low, yet we must bring our minds to it, and acquiesce in it. So the margin: *Be contented with mean things*. Be reconciled to the place which God in his providence hath put us in. We must account nothing below us but sin. It may be meant of *mean persons*; so we read it (I think both are to be included): *Condescend to men of low estate*. We need not be ashamed to converse with the lowly, while the great God overlooks heaven and earth to look at such. True love values grace in rags as well as in scarlet. A jewel is a jewel, though it lie in the dirt. *Condescend;* that is, suit yourselves to them, stoop to them for their good. He adds, *Be not wise in your own conceits;* to the same purport with *v.* 3. We shall never find in our hearts to condescend to others while we find there so great a conceit of ourselves: and therefore this must needs be mortified. "*Be not wise by yourselves*, be not confident of the sufficiency of your own wisdom, nor be shy of communicating what you have to others. It is the merchandise of wisdom that we profess; now merchandise consists in commerce, receiving and returning."

(7) A love that engages us, as much as lies in us, *to live peaceably with all men*, *v.* 18. Even those with whom we cannot live intimately and familiarly, yet we must with such live peaceably. Thus must we labour to preserve the peace, that it be not broken, and to piece it again when it is broken. It is not expressed so as to oblige us to impossibilities: *If it be possible, as much as lies in you*. Study the things that make for peace.—*If it be possible*. It is not possible to preserve the peace when we cannot do it without offending God and wounding conscience. The wisdom that is from above is first pure and then peaceable, Jas. iii. 17. Peace without purity is the peace of the devil's palace.—*As much as lieth in you*. There must be two words to the bargain of peace. We may be unavoidably striven with. Our care must be that nothing be wanting on our parts to preserve the peace.

2. To our enemies. Those that embrace religion have reason to expect to meet with enemies in a world whose smiles seldom concur with Christ's. Now Christianity teaches us how to behave towards our enemies; and it quite differs from all other rules and methods, which generally aim at victory and dominion; but this at inward peace. Whoever are our enemies, our rule is to do them all the good we can.

(1) To do them no hurt (*v.* 17): *Recompence to no man evil for evil*. We have so learned God, who does so much for his enemies (Matt. v. 45), much more have we so learned Christ, who died for us when we were enemies (*ch.* v. 8, 10).—"*To no man;* not to one that has been thy friend, for by recompencing evil for evil thou wilt certainly lose him; not to one that has been thine enemy, for by not recompencing evil for evil thou mayest perhaps gain him." To the same purport, *v.* 19, *Dearly beloved, avenge not yourselves*. He addresses himself to such in this endearing language, to mollify them. Anything that breathes love sweetens the blood. Would you pacify a brother offended? Call him dearly beloved. Such a soft word may be effectual to turn away wrath. *Avenge not yourselves*. It forbids private revenge, which flows from anger and ill-will. See how strict the law of Christ is in this matter, Matt. v. 38–40. It is forbidden not only to take it into our own hands to avenge ourselves, but to thirst after even that judgment in our case which the law affords, for the satisfying of a revengeful humour. This is a hard lesson to corrupt nature; and therefore he subjoins, [1] A remedy against it: *Rather give place unto wrath*. Not to our own wrath; to give place to this is to give place to the devil. We must resist and suppress this. *First*, To the wrath of our enemy. "Give place to it; do not answer wrath with wrath, but with love rather." When men's passions are up, and the stream is strong, let it have its course, lest it be made to rage and swell the more. When others are angry, let us be calm. *Secondly*, Many apply it to the wrath of God: "Give place to this, and let him alone to deal with thine adversary." [2] A reason against it: *For it is written, Vengeance is mine*. God is the sovereign King, the righteous Judge, and to him it belongs to administer justice. Some of this power he hath trusted in the hands of the civil magistrates; their legal punishments therefore are to be looked upon as a branch of God's revengings. If vengeance be God's we may not do it. We step into the throne of God if we do. We need not do it. For God will, if we meekly leave the matter with him.

(2) We must not only not do hurt to our enemies, but do them all the good we can. It is a command peculiar to Christianity: *Love your enemies*, Matt. v. 44. We are here taught to show that love to them both in word and deed.

[1] In word: *Bless those who persecute you, v.* 14. It has been the common lot of God's people to be persecuted. Now we are here taught to bless those that so persecute us. *Bless* them; "Speak well of them. Speak respectfully to them, not rendering railing for railing." We must wish well to them. We must offer up that desire to God, by prayer for them. We can testify our goodwill by praying for them.—*Bless and curse not*. It denotes a thorough goodwill; not, "Bless them when you are at prayer, and curse them at other times;" but, "Bless them always, and curse not at all." Cursing ill becomes the mouths of those whose work it is to bless God.

[2] In deed (*v.* 20): "*If thine enemy hunger* be ready to show him any kindness, and be never the less forward for his having been thine enemy, that thou mayest thereby testify the sincerity of thy forgiveness of him." *First*, What we must do. We must do good to our enemies. "*If he hunger*, do not say, Now God

is avenging me of him. But *feed him. Then,* when he has need of thy help, and thou hast an opportunity of starving him, *feed him* (a significant word)—feed him abundantly; feed him, as we do children and sick people, with much tenderness. Contrive to do it so as to express thy love. *If he thirst, give him drink:* in token of reconciliation and friendship. So confirm your love to him." *Secondly,* Why we must do this. *Thou shalt heap coals of fire on his head;* that is, "Thou shalt either," 1. "Melt him into repentance and friendship" (alluding to those who melt metals; they not only put fire under them, but heap fire upon them) "thou wilt win a friend by it, and if thy kindness have not that effect then," 2. "It will make his malice against thee the more inexcusable." Not that this must be our intention in showing him kindness, but such will be the effect. Those that revenge are the conquered, and those that forgive are the conquerors. (1) "*Be not overcome of evil.* Let not the evil of any provocation that is given you have such a power over you as to disturb your peace, to destroy your love, or to bring you to study or attempt any revenge." He that cannot quietly bear an injury is perfectly conquered by it. (2) "*But overcome evil with good,* with the good of patience and forbearance, nay, and of kindness and beneficence to those that wrong you." He that hath this rule over his spirit is better than the mighty.

3. There remain two exhortations which recommend all the rest as good in themselves, and of good report.

(1) As good in themselves (*v.* 9): *Abhor that which is evil, cleave to that which is good.* We must not only not do evil, but we must *abhor that which is evil.* We must hate sin with an utter and irreconcilable hatred. We must not only do that which is good, but we must cleave to it. It denotes a deliberate choice of, a sincere affection for, and a constant perseverance in, that which is good.

(2) As of good report (*v.* 17): "*Provide things honest in the sight of all men;* study and take care to do, that which recommends religion to all with whom you converse."

CHAPTER 13

There are three good lessons taught us in this chapter. I. A lesson of subjection to lawful authority, ver. 1–6. II. A lesson of justice and love to our brethren, ver. 7–10. III. A lesson of sobriety and godliness in ourselves, ver. 11, to the end.

Verses 1–6

We are here taught how to conduct ourselves towards magistrates, and those that are in authority over us, called here the *higher powers,* intimating their authority (they are powers), and their dignity (they are higher powers). The just power which they have must be submitted to and obeyed.

I. The duty enjoined: *Let every soul be subject.* Every soul—every person, one as well as another, not excluding the clergy.—*Every soul.* Not that our consciences are to be subjected to the will of any man. It is God's prerogative to make laws immediately to bind conscience. Our subjection must be free and voluntary, sincere and hearty. The subjection of soul here required includes inward honour and outward reverence and respect, both in speaking to them and in speaking of them. "They are *higher powers;* be content they should be so, and submit to them accordingly." Now there was good reason for the pressing of this duty, 1. Because of the reproach which the Christian religion lay under in the world, as an enemy to public peace, order, and government. Our Lord Jesus was so reproached, though he told them his kingdom was not of this world: no marvel, then, if his followers have been loaded in all ages with the like calumnies, called *facetious, seditious,* and *turbulent.* The apostle therefore shows

that obedience to civil magistrates is one of the laws of Christ, whose religion helps to make people good subjects. 2. Because of the temptation which the Christians lay under to be otherwise affected to civil magistrates. The apostle enjoins obedience to civil government, which was the more necessary to be pressed now because the magistrates were heathens and unbelievers, which yet did not destroy their civil power and authority.

II. The reasons to enforce this duty.

1. For *wrath's sake.* Magistrates bear the sword; it is to no purpose to contend with him that bears the sword. The least show of resistance in a Christian would be very prejudicial to the whole society; and therefore they had more need than others to be exact in their subjection. To this head must that argument be referred (*v.* 2), *Those that resist shall receive to themselves damnation:* they shall be called to an account for it. God will reckon with them for it, because the resistance reflects upon him. The magistrates will reckon with them for it. So it follows (*v.* 3), *Rulers are a terror.* This is a good argument, but it is low for a Christian.

2. We must be subject, *not only for wrath, but for conscience' sake;* not so much *from the fear of punishment,* as *from the love of virtue.* Now to oblige conscience to this subjection he argues, *v.* 1–4, 6,

(1) From the institution of magistracy: *There is no power but of God.* God as the ruler of the world hath appointed the ordinance of magistracy, so that all civil power is derived from him. The usurpation of power and the abuse of power are not of God, but the power itself is. The most unjust and oppressive princes in the world have no power but what is given them from above (John xix. 11). It is an instance of God's wisdom, power, and goodness, in the management of mankind, that he has disposed them into such a state as distinguishes between governors and governed, and has not left them like the fishes of the sea, where the greater devour the less.—*The powers that be:* whatever the particular form and method of government are. It is an ordinance of God, and it is to be received and submitted to accordingly.—*Ordained of God.* Hence it follows (*v.* 2) that whosoever *resisteth the power resisteth the ordinance of God.* Magistracy is from God as an ordinance, that is, it is a great law, and it is a great blessing. And those who spurn at their power reflect upon God himself. Magistrates are here again and again called God's ministers. He is the *minister of God, v.* 4, 6. Magistrates are in a more peculiar manner God's servants; the dignity they have calls for duty. Though they are lords to us, they are servants to God.

(2) From the intention of magistracy: *Rulers are not a terror to good works, but to the evil,* &c. Magistracy was designed to be,

[1] A terror to evil works and evil workers. They bear the sword; not only the sword of war, but the sword of justice. Such is the power of sin and corruption that many will not be restrained from the greatest enormities by any regard to the law of God and nature; but only by the fear of temporal punishments. Laws with penalties for the lawless and disobedient (1 Tim. i. 9) must be constituted in Christian nations, and are agreeable with, and not contradictory to, the gospel. In this work the magistrate is the *minister of God, v.* 4. He acts as God's agent, and therefore must take heed of infusing into his judgments any private personal resentments of his own.—*To execute wrath upon him that doeth evil.* The judicial processes of the most vigilant faithful magistrates yet come far short of the judgment of God: they reach only to the evil act, on him that *doeth* evil.—*He beareth not the sword in vain.* It is not for nothing that God hath put such a power into the magistrate's hand. And therefore, "*If thou do*

that which is evil, be afraid; for civil powers have quick eyes and long arms." It is a good thing when the punishment of malefactors is managed as an ordinance of God. As a holy God, that hates sin. As King of nations, and the God of peace and order. As the protector of the good. As one that by the punishment of some would terrify others, and so prevent the like wickedness.

[2] A praise to those that do well. "Do that which is good (v. 3), and thou needest not be afraid of the power, nay, thou shalt have praise of it." This is the intention of magistracy, and therefore we must, for conscience' sake, be subject to it, as a constitution designed for the public good. But pity it is that ever this gracious intention should be perverted. Yet even then the blessing and benefit of a common protection, and a face of government and order, are such that it is our duty rather to submit to persecution for well-doing, than by any irregular and disorderly practices to attempt a redress. Better a bad government than none at all.

(3) From our interest in it: "He is the minister of God to thee for good." Protection draws allegiance. By upholding the government, we keep up our own hedge. This subjection is likewise consented to by the tribute we pay (v. 6): "For this cause pay you tribute, as a testimony of your submission, and an acknow-ledgment that in conscience you think it to be due. By your paying tribute you not only own the magis-trate's authority, but the blessing of that authority to yourselves. Honour is a burden: and, if he do as he ought, he is attending continually upon this very thing, in consideration of which fatigue, we pay tribute." He does not say, "You give it as an alms," but, "You pay it as a just debt." This is the lesson the apostle teaches, and it becomes all Christians to learn and practise it, that the godly in the land may be found (whatever others are) the quiet and the peace-able in the land.

Verses 7–10

We are here taught a lesson of justice and charity.

I. Of justice (v. 7): Render therefore to all their dues. What we have we have as stewards; others have an interest in it, and must have their dues. Render to all their dues; and that readily and cheer-fully, not tarrying till you are by law compelled to it. Due taxes: Tribute to whom tribute is due, custom to whom custom. He wrote this to the Romans, who, as they were rich, so they were drained by taxes and impositions, to the just and honest payment of which they are here pressed by the apostle. Our Lord was born when his mother went to be taxed; and he en-joined the payment of tribute to Cæsar. Many, who in other things seem to be just, yet make no conscience of this, but pass it off with a false ill-favoured maxim, that it is no sin to cheat the king. Due respect: Fear to whom fear, honour to whom honour. This sums up the duty which we owe not only to magistrates, but to all that are over us in the Lord, according to the fifth commandment: Honour thy father and mother. Where there is not this respect in the heart to our superiors, no other duty will be paid aright. Due payment of debts (v. 8): "Owe no man any thing; do not continue in anyone's debt, while you are able to pay it." Many that are very sensible of the trouble think little of the sin of being in debt.

II. Of charity: Owe no man any thing. "Whatever you owe, it is eminently summed up in this debt of love. But to love one another, this is a debt that must be always in the paying, and yet always owing." Love is a debt. Love is the fulfilling of the law; not perfectly, but it is a good step towards it. It is in-clusive of all the duties of the second table, which he specifies, v. 9, and these suppose the love of God. If the love be sincere, it is accepted as the fulfilling of

the law. Surely we serve a good master, that has summed up all our duty in one word, and that a short word and a sweet word—love, the beauty and harmony of the universe. Loving and being loved is all the pleasure, joy, and happiness, of an intelligent being. God is love (1 John iv. 16), and love is his image upon the soul. Now, to prove that love is the fulfilling of the law, he gives us, 1. An induction of particular precepts, v. 9. He specifies the last five of the ten commandments, which he observes to be all summed up in this royal law, Thou shalt love thy neighbour as thyself. On this is built that golden rule of doing as we would be done by. Were there no restraints of human laws in these things the law of love would of itself be effectual to keep peace and good order among us. The apostle puts the seventh before the sixth, and mentions this first, Thou shalt not commit adultery; for though this commonly goes under the name of love (pity it is that so good a word should be so abused) yet it is really as great a violation of it as killing and stealing. He that tempts others to sin, though he may pretend the most passionate love does really hate them. 2. A general rule concerning the nature of brotherly love: Love worketh no ill (v. 10)—he that walks in love worketh no ill to his neighbour, to anyone that he has any-thing to do with. Love intends and designs no ill to anybody. More is implied than is expressed; it not only worketh no ill, but it worketh all the good that may be. Love is a living active principle of obedience to the whole law. The whole law is written in the heart, if the law of love be there.

Verses 11–14

We are here taught a lesson of sobriety and god-liness in ourselves. Four things we are here taught, as a Christian's directory for his day's work: when to awake, how to dress ourselves, how to walk, and what provision to make.

I. When to awake: Now it is high time to awake (v. 11). We have need to be often excited and stirred up to awake. The word of command to all Christ's disciples is, Watch. "Awake—be concerned about your souls and your eternal interest. Considering," 1. "The time we are cast into: Knowing the time. Con-sider what time of day it is with us, and you will see it is high time to awake. It is gospel time, it is a time when more is expected than was in the times of that ignorance which God winked at, when people sat in darkness. It is high time to awake; for the sun has been up a great while, and shines in our faces. It is high time to awake; for others are awake and up about us. Know the time to be a busy time; we have a great deal of work to do. Know the time to be a perilous time. We are in the midst of enemies and snares. It is time to awake, for we have slept enough." 2. "The salvation we are upon the brink of: Now is our salvation nearer than when we believed. The eternal happiness we chose for our portion is now nearer to us than it was when we became Christians. Let us mind our way and mend our pace. The nearer we are to our centre the quicker should our motion be. Is there but a step between us and heaven, and shall we be so very slow and dull in our Christian course?"

II. How to dress ourselves. This is the next care, when we are awake and up: "The night is far spent, the day is at hand; therefore it is time to dress our-selves." Clearer discoveries will be quickly made of gospel grace than have been yet made, as light gets ground.

1. "What we must put off; our night-clothes, which it is a shame to appear abroad in: Cast off the works of darkness." Sinful works are works of darkness. Let us therefore, who are of the day, cast them off, and have no more to do with them.

2. "What we must put on." Our care must be *wherewithal we shall be clothed*, how shall we dress our souls? (1) *Put on the armour of light.* Christians are soldiers in the midst of enemies, therefore their array must be armour. A Christian may reckon himself undressed if he be unarmed. The graces of the Spirit are this armour, to secure the soul from Satan's temptations. This is called the armour of light. The graces of the Spirit are suitable splendid ornaments. (2) *Put on the Lord Jesus Christ, v.* 14. This stands in opposition to a great many base lusts, mentioned, *v.* 13. *Rioting and drunkenness* must be cast off. "*Put on Christ*, this includes all. Put on the righteousness of Christ for justification; be found in him (Phil. iii. 9) as a man is found in his clothes. Put on the spirit and grace of Christ for sanctification; put on the *new man* (Eph. iv. 24)." Jesus Christ is the best clothing for Christians to adorn themselves with, to arm themselves with. All other things are filthy rags. By baptism we have in profession put on Christ. Let us do it in truth and sincerity. *The Lord Jesus Christ.* "Put him on as Lord to rule you, as Jesus to save you, and in both as Christ, appointed by the Father to this ruling saving work."

III. How to walk. When we are up and dressed, we are not to sit still. What have we good clothes for, but to appear abroad in them?—*Let us walk.* Christianity teaches us how to walk so as to please God. Our conversation must be as becomes the gospel. *Walk honestly; decently* and becomingly. Christians should be careful to conduct themselves well in those things wherein men have an eye upon them, and to study that which is lovely and of good report. We must not walk in *rioting and drunkenness;* we must abstain from all excess in eating and drinking. We must not give the least countenance to revelling. *Not in chambering and wantonness;* not in any of those lusts of the flesh, those works of darkness—whatsoever transgresseth the pure and sacred law of chastity and modesty. Not in *strife and envying.* These are also works of darkness; for, though the acts and instances of strife and envy are very common, yet none are willing to acknowledge themselves envious and contentious. To strive and to envy ill becomes the disciples and followers of the peaceable and humble Jesus. Where there are riot and drunkenness, there usually are chambering and wantonness, and strife and envy.

IV. What provision to make (*v.* 14): "*Make not provision for the flesh.* Be not careful about the body." Our great care must be to provide for our souls; but must we take no care about our bodies? Two things are here forbidden: 1. Perplexing ourselves with an inordinate care; do not stretch your wits, nor set your thoughts upon the tenter-hooks, in making this provision. It forbids an anxious encumbering care. 2. Indulging ourselves in an irregular desire. The necessities of the body must be considered, but the lusts of it must not be gratified. Natural desires must be answered but wanton appetites must be checked and denied.

CHAPTER 14

The apostle having directed our conduct one towards another in civil things, comes in this to direct our demeanour one towards another in sacred things. It seems there was something amiss among the Roman Christians which he here labours to redress. But the rules are general, and of standing use in the church. Nothing is more threatening, nor more often fatal, to Christian societies than the contentions and divisions of their members.

Verses 1–23

I. An account of the unhappy contention which had broken out in the Christian church.

1. There was a difference among them about the distinction of meats and days. The members of the Christian church at Rome were some of them originally Gentiles, and others of them Jews. Now those that had been Jews were trained up in the observance of the ceremonial appointments touching meats and days, and therefore retained the ceremonial institutions, while other Christians made no such difference. Concerning meats (*v.* 2): *One believeth that he may eat all things*—he is well satisfied that every creature of God is good, and nothing to be refused; nothing *unclean of itself, v.* 14. This the strong Christian is clear in, and practises accordingly, eating what is set before him. On the other hand, *another, who is weak*, is dissatisfied in this point; he will eat no flesh at all, but *eateth herbs*, contenting himself with only the fruits of the earth. Concerning days, *v.* 5. Those who thought themselves still under some kind of obligation by the ceremonial law esteemed *one day above another*—kept up a respect to the times of the passover, pentecost, new moons, and feast of tabernacles. Those who knew that all these things were abolished by Christ's coming esteemed every day alike. We must understand it with an exception of the Lord's day, which all Christians unanimously observed. The apostle seems willing to let the ceremonial law wither by degrees, and to let it have an honourable burial.

2. It was not so much the difference itself that did the mischief as the mismanagement of the difference, making it a bone of contention. Those who were strong, and knew their Christian liberty, despised the weak, who did not. They should have pitied them, and helped them. So apt are those who have knowledge to be puffed up with it, and to look disdainfully and scornfully upon their brethren. Those who were weak, and durst not use their Christian liberty, judged and censured the strong, who did, as if they were loose Christians. They judged them as breakers of the law. Well, this was the disease, and we see it remaining in the church to this day.

II. We have proper suggestions laid down for allaying this contention. Not by excommunicating, suspending, and silencing either side, but by persuading them both to a mutual forbearance: reasoning the case with the strong that they should not be so scornful, and with the weak that they should not be so censorious. Let us observe the rules he gives, some to the strong and some to the weak, and some to both.

1. Those who are weak must be *received, but not to doubtful disputations, v.* 1. Spend your zeal in those things wherein you and all the people of God are agreed. *Receive him, take him to you, lend him your hand*, to help him. Receive him into your company. Receive him: not to quarrel with him, and to argue about uncertain points that are in controversy. Let not your Christian friendship be disturbed with such vain janglings and strifes of words.—*Not to judge his doubtful thoughts* (so the margin). Receive him, not to expose him, but to instruct and strengthen him.

2. Those who are strong must by no means despise the weak; nor those who are weak judge the strong, *v.* 3. This is levelled directly against the fault of each party. It is seldom that any such contention exists but there is a fault on both sides. We must not despise nor judge our brethren. Why so?

(1) Because God hath received them. Strong believers and weak believers, if they be true believers, are accepted of God. "Nay, God doth not only receive him, but *hold him up* (*v.* 4). If they have true faith, they shall be held up—the one in his integrity, and the other in his comfort. This hope is built upon the power of God, for *God is able to make him stand.*"

(2) Because they are servants to their own master (*v.* 4): *Who art thou that judgest another man's servant?*

We reckon it a piece of ill manners to meddle with other people's servants. Weak and strong Christians are indeed our brethren, but they are not our servants. We make ourselves our brethren's masters, and do in effect usurp the throne of God, when we take upon us thus to judge them. God sees not as man sees; and he is their master, and not we. If we must needs be judging, let us exercise our faculty upon our own hearts and ways.—*To his own master he stands or falls.* How well for us is it that we are not to stand nor fall by the judgment one of another, but by the judgment of God.

(3) Because both the one and the other, if they be true believers, have an eye to God, and do approve themselves to God in what they do, *v.* 6. He *that regards the day*—it is well. We have reason to think, because in other things he conducts himself like a good Christian, that *he regardeth it unto the Lord*; and God will accept of his honest intention. The sincerity and uprightness of the heart were never rejected for the weakness and infirmity of the head: so good a master do we serve. On the other hand, he *that regards not the day*, but esteems every day alike—he does not do it out of a spirit of contradiction, or contempt of his brother. If he be a good Christian we charitably conclude that to the *Lord he does not regard it.* He makes no such difference of days only because he knows God hath made none; and therefore intends his honour in endeavouring to dedicate every day to him. So for the other instance: *He that eateth* whatever is set before him he *eateth to the Lord.* He understands the liberty that God has granted him, and uses it to the glory of God. He *giveth God thanks* for the variety of food he has, and the liberty he has to eat it. On the other hand, *he that eateth not, to the Lord he eateth not.* It is for God's sake, because he is afraid of offending God by eating that which he is sure was once prohibited; and he *giveth God thanks too* that there is enough besides. Thus, while both approve themselves to him in their integrity, why should either of them be judged or despised? Whether we eat flesh, or eat herbs, it is a thankful regard to God, the author and giver of all our mercies, that sanctifies and sweetens it. It appears by this that *saying grace* (as we commonly call it), before and after meat was the common known practice of the church. Blessing the creatures in the name of God before we use them, and blessing the name of God for them after, are both included. Observe his description of true Christians, taken from their end and aim (*v.* 7, 8), and the ground of it, *v.* 9.

[1] Our end and aim: not self, but the Lord. If we would know what way we walk in, we must enquire what end we walk towards. *First*, Not to self. We have learned to deny ourselves: *None of us liveth to himself.* This is a thing in which all the people of God are one, however they differ in other things. Not one that hath given up his name to Christ is allowedly a self-seeker; it is contrary to the foundation of true Christianity. We neither *live to ourselves nor die to ourselves.* The business of our lives is not to please ourselves, but to please God. When we come to die it is to the Lord, that we may depart and be with Christ. *Secondly*, But *to the Lord* (*v.* 8), to the Lord Christ. Christ is the gain we aim at, living and dying. We live to glorify him; we die to glorify him, and to go to be glorified with him. Christ is the centre, in which all the lines of life and death do meet. So that, *whether we live or die, we are the Lord's.* Though some Christians are weak and others strong, yet they are all the Lord's, and are accordingly owned and accepted of him. Is it for us then to judge or despise them, as if we were their masters?

[2] The ground of this, *v.* 9. It is grounded upon Christ's absolute sovereignty, the fruit and end of his

death and resurrection. *To this end he both died, and rose, and revived, that he might be Lord both of dead and living.* He is head over all things to the church. He is Lord of those that are living to rule them, of those that are dead to receive them and raise them up. We must consider that Christ is Lord of the dead, as well as of the living. If they are dead, they have already given up their account, and let that suffice. And this leads to another reason against judging and despising.

(4) Because both the one and the other must shortly give an account, *v.* 10–12. *Why dost thou* that are weak *judge thy brother* that is strong? And *why dost thou* that art strong *set at nought thy brother* that is weak? Why is all this clashing, and contradicting, and censuring, among Christians? *We shall all stand before the judgment-seat of Christ.* Christ will be the Judge, and before him we shall stand as persons to be tried. To illustrate this (*v.* 11), he quotes a passage out of the Old Testament, which speaks of Christ's universal sovereignty and dominion, and that established with an oath: *As I live* (saith the Lord), *every knee shall bow to me.* It is a prophecy, in general, of Christ's dominion. Here is a proof of Christ's Godhead. Divine honour is due to him, and must be paid. The bowing of the knee to him, and the confession made with the tongue, are but outward expressions of inward adoration and praise. *Every knee* and *every tongue*, either freely or by force.

[1] All his friends shall do it freely. Bowing to him—the understanding bowed to his truths, the will to his laws, the whole man to his authority; and this expressed by the bowing of the knee, the posture of adoration and prayer. Confessing to him—acknowledging his glory, grace, and greatness—acknowledging our own meanness and vileness, confessing our sins to him.

[2] All his foes shall be constrained to do it. Hence he concludes (*v.* 12), *Everyone of us shall give account of himself to God.* We must not give account for others, nor they for us; but everyone for himself. We have little to do to judge others, for they are not accountable to us, nor are we accountable for them. They must give account to their own master, and not to us; if we can in anything be helpers of their joy, it is well; but we have not dominion over their faith. We have the more to do to judge ourselves. We have an account of our own to make up. Let this take up his thoughts, and he that is strict in judging himself will not be apt to judge and despise his brother.

(5) Because the stress of Christianity is not to be laid upon these things, nor are they at all essential to religion. Why should you spend your zeal either for or against those things which are so minute and inconsiderable in religion? *The kingdom of God is not meat,* &c. Observe here,

[1] The nature of true Christianity. It is here called, *The kingdom of God;* it is a religion intended to rule us. *First,* It is *not meat and drink*: it does not consist either in using or in abstaining from such and such meats and drinks. Christianity gives no rule in that case. The matter is left at large. Every *creature of God is good,* 1 Tim. iv. 4. It is not being of this party and persuasion, of this or the other opinion in minor things, that will recommend us to God. But it will be asked, "Who feared God and worked righteousness, and who did not?" *Secondly, It is righteousness, and peace, and joy in the Holy Ghost.* These are some of the essentials of Christianity in the pursuit of which we must spend our zeal. Righteousness, peace, and joy, are very comprehensive words. As to God, our great concern is *righteousness,* for the righteous Lord loveth righteousness. As to our brethren, it is *peace*— to live in peace and love, and charity with them. Christ came into the world to be the great peacemaker. As to ourselves, it is *joy in the Holy Ghost.*

Next to our compliance with God, to delight ourselves always in the Lord. Surely we serve a good Master, who makes peace and joy so essential to our religion. *Thirdly,* It is in these things to *serve Christ* (*v.* 18), to do all this out of respect to Christ himself as our Master, to his will as our rule and to his glory as our end. What is Christianity but the serving of Christ?

[2] The advantages of it. He that duly observeth these things is acceptable to God. He has the love and favour of God, and we need no more to make us happy. Those are most pleasing to God that are best pleased with him. He is approved of men—of all wise and good men, and the opinion of others is not to be regarded. The approbation of men is not to be slighted; for we must provide things honest in the sight of all men: but the acceptance of God is to be aimed at in the first place.

3. In these doubtful things everyone not only may, but must, walk according to the light that God hath given him. This is laid down, *v.* 5, *Let every man be fully persuaded in his own mind;* that is, "Practise according to your own judgment in these things, and leave others to do so too. If your sober sentiments be otherwise, do not make their practice a rule to you, any more than you must prescribe yours as a rule to them. First be persuaded that what you do is lawful, before you venture to do it." In doubtful things, it is good keeping on the sure side of the hedge. To this purport he argues, *v.* 14 and 23, which two verses give us a rule not to act against the dictates,

(1) Of a mistaken conscience, *v.* 14. If we really think it a sin to do it it is to us a sin, because we act against our consciences, though mistaken and misinformed.

[1] His own clearness in this matter. "*I know and am persuaded*—I am fully persuaded that there *is nothing unclean of itself,* that is, no kind of meat that lies under any ceremonial uncleanness, nor is forbidden to be eaten." Sin had brought a curse upon the whole creation. Now that Christ has removed the curse the matter is set at large again. Therefore Paul says that he was persuaded by the Lord Jesus, not only as the author of that persuasion, but as the ground of it. So that now there is nothing unclean of itself, every creature of God is good; nothing *common;* nothing profane; in this sense the Jews used the word *common.* This was Paul's own clearness, and he practised accordingly.

[2] But here is a caution: *To him that esteemeth anything to be unclean, to him it is unclean.* He who does a thing which he verily believes to be unlawful, however the thing be in itself, to him it is a sin. Our wills, in all their choices should follow the dictates of our understandings. This order is broken if the understanding (though misguided) tells us that such a thing is a sin, and yet we will do it. This is a *will* to do evil; there is the same corruption of the will in the doing of it as if really it were a sin. It must be understood likewise with this proviso, though men's judgments and opinions may make that which is good in itself to become evil to them, yet they cannot make that which is evil in itself to become good.

(2) Nor must we act against the dictates of a doubting conscience. He *that doubteth is damned if he eat* (*v.* 23), that is, it turns into sin to him; *he is condemned* of his own conscience, because he *eateth not of faith,* because he does that which he is not fully persuaded he may lawfully do. Here his own heart cannot but condemn him as a transgressor.— *For whatsoever is not of faith is sin.* Whatever is done while we are not clearly persuaded of the lawfulness of it, is a sin against conscience. He that will venture to do that which his own conscience suggests to him to be unlawful, when it is not so in itself, will by a like temptation be brought to do that which his

conscience tells him is unlawful when it is really so. It is a dangerous thing to put a force upon conscience, though it be under a mistake (*v.* 22). *Happy is he that condemns not himself in that thing which he allows.* Many a one allows himself in practice to do that which yet in his judgment and conscience he condemns himself for. Whilst he does it his own heart gives him the lie, and his conscience condemns him for it. Now, happy is the man who so orders his conversation as not to expose himself to the reproaches of his own conscience. He is happy that has peace and quietness within.

4. Another rule here prescribed is to those who know their Christian liberty, yet to take heed of using it so as to give offence to a weak brother. This is laid down *v.* 13, *Let us not judge one another any more.* "*Judge this rather,* instead of censuring the practice of others, let us look to our own, that no *man put a stumbling-block, or an occasion to fall, in his brother's way.*" We must take heed of saying or doing anything which may occasion our brother to stumble or fall; which may be an occasion,

(1) Of grief to our brother, "One that is weak, and thinks it unlawful to eat such and such meats, will be greatly troubled to see thee eat them." Christians should take heed of grieving one another, and of saddening the hearts of Christ's little ones.

(2) Of guilt to our brother. The former is a *stumbling-block,* that gives our brother a great shake; but this is an *occasion to fall.* "If thy weak brother, purely by thy example and influence, be drawn to act against his conscience and to walk contrary to the light he has, and so to contract guilt upon his soul, thou art to be blamed for giving the occasion." To the same purport (*v.* 21) he recommends it to our care not to give offence by the use of lawful things: *It is good neither to eat flesh nor to drink wine;* these are things not necessary to the support of human life, and therefore we must deny ourselves in them, rather than give offence. *It is good*—pleasing to God, profitable to our brother, and no harm to ourselves. This is to be extended to all things whereby thy brother stumbleth, or is offended, is involved either in sin or in trouble: or *is made weak*—his graces weakened, his comforts weakened, his resolutions weakened. Observe the motives to enforce this caution.

[1] Consider the royal law of Christian love and charity, which is hereby broken (*v.* 15): *If thy brother be grieved with thy meat.* Possibly thou art ready to say, "Now he talks foolishly and weakly." We are apt, in such a case, to lay all the blame on that side. But the reproof is here given to the stronger: *Now walkest thou not charitably.* Thus the apostle takes part with the weakest, and condemns the defect in love on the one side more than the defect in knowledge on the other side. Charity to the souls of our brethren is the best charity. True love would make us tender of their peace and purity, and beget a regard to their consciences as well as to our own. Christ deals gently with those that have true grace, though they are weak in it.

[2] Consider the design of Christ's death: *Destroy not him with thy meat for whom Christ died, v.* 15. *First,* Drawing a soul to sin threatens the destruction of that soul. It denotes an utter destruction. *Secondly,* The consideration of the love of Christ in dying for souls should make us very tender of the happiness and salvation of souls. Did Christ quit a life for souls, such a life, and shall not we quit a morsel of meat for them? Did he think it worth while to deny himself so much for them as to die for them, and shall not we think it worth while to deny ourselves so little for them?—*With thy meat.* Thou pleadest that it is thy own meat, but remember that, though the meat is thine, the brother offended by it is Christ's.

While thou destroyest thy brother thou art helping forward the devil's design, and, as much as in thee lies, thou art crossing the design of Christ, and dost not only offend thy brother, but offend Christ. But are any destroyed for whom Christ died? No thanks to thee if they be not destroyed; by doing that which has a tendency to it, thou dost manifest a great opposition to Christ.

[3] Consider the work of God (*v.* 20): "*For meat destroy not the work of God.*" Do not undo that which God hath done. You should work together with God, do not countermine his work. The work of grace and peace is the work of God. The same for whom Christ died (*v.* 15) are here called the work of God; besides the work that is wrought for us there is a work to be wrought in us. Every saint is God's workmanship. We must be very careful to do nothing which tends to the destruction of this work, either in ourselves or others. We must deny ourselves rather than obstruct and prejudice our own or others' grace and peace. Many do for meat and drink destroy the work of God in themselves, so likewise in others. Think what thou destroyest—*the work of God*; think for what thou destroyest it—*for meat*, which was but for the belly, and the belly for it.

[4] Consider the evil of giving offence. He grants that *all things indeed are pure.* But, if we abuse this liberty, it turns into sin to us: *It is evil to him that eats with offence.* Lawful things may be done unlawfully. It is observable that the apostle directs his reproof most against those who gave the offence. He directs his speech to the strong, because they were better able to bear the reproof, and to begin the reformation. For the further pressing of this rule, we may here observe two directions.—*First, Let not then your good be evil spoken of* (*v.* 16)—take heed of doing any thing which may give occasion to others to speak evil, either of the Christian religion in general, or of your Christian liberty in particular. It is true we cannot hinder loose and ungoverned tongues from speaking evil of us, and of the best things we have; but we must not (if we can help it) give them any occasion to do it. We must deny ourselves in many cases for the preservation of our credit and reputation, forbearing to do that which we rightly know we may lawfully do, when our doing it may be a prejudice to our good name. In such a case we must rather cross ourselves than shame ourselves. We should manage all our good duties in such a manner that they may not be evil spoken of. As we tender the reputation of the good we profess and practise, let us so order it that it may not be evil spoken of. *Secondly, Hast thou faith? Have it to thyself before God, v.* 22. "Art thou satisfied that thou mayest eat all meats, and observe all days (except the Lord's day) alike? *Have it to thyself,* and do not trouble others by the imprudent use of it." In these indifferent things, though we must never contradict our persuasion, yet we may sometimes conceal it, when the avowing of it will do more hurt than good. A rule to thyself (not to be imposed upon others, or made a rule to them), or a rejoicing to thyself. Paul had faith in these things: *I am persuaded that there is nothing unclean of itself;* but he had it to himself, so as not to use his liberty to the offence of others. In things necessary let there be unity, in things unnecessary let there be liberty, and in both let there be charity.—*Have it to thyself before God.* The end of such knowledge is that we may have a conscience void of offence towards God. Those are right indeed that are so in God's sight.

5. There is one rule more laid down here: *Let us therefore follow after the things which make for peace, and things wherewith one may edify another,* (*v.* 19).We must study mutual peace. Many wish for peace, and talk loudly for it, that do not follow the

things that make for peace. Meekness, humility, self-denial, and love, are the springs of peace, the things that make for our peace. We are not always so happy as to obtain peace; there are so many that delight in war: but the God of peace will accept us if we follow after the things that make for peace. We must study mutual edification. We cannot edify one another, while we are quarrelling and contending. We are God's building, God's temple, and have need to be edified. None so strong but they may be edified; none so weak but may edify.

CHAPTER 15

The apostle, in this chapter, continues the discourse of the former, concerning mutual forbearance in indifferent things; and so draws towards a conclusion of the epistle. I. His precepts to them. II. His prayers for them. III. His apology for writing to them. IV. His account of himself and his own affairs. V. His declaration of his purpose to come and see them. VI. His desire of a share in their prayers.

Verses 1–4

The apostle here lays down two precepts, showing the duty of the strong Christian to consider the weakest.

I. We must *bear the infirmities of the weak, v.* 1. We all have our infirmities; but the weak are more subject to them than others. We must bear with their infirmities, and not have our affections alienated from them. Thus Christ bore with his weak disciples. We must also bear their infirmities by sympathizing with them, ministering strength to them. This is bearing one another's burdens.

II. We must not please ourselves, but our neighbour, *v.* 1, 2.

1. Christians must not please themselves. It is good for us to cross ourselves sometimes, and then we shall the better bear others crossing of us. We shall be spoiled if we be always humoured. The first lesson we have to learn is to deny ourselves, Matt. xvi. 24.

2. Christians must please their brethren. Christians should study to be pleasing. How amiable and comfortable a society would the church of Christ be if Christians would study to please one another!—*Please his neighbour,* not in everything, but *for his good,* especially for the good of his soul. *To edification,* that is, not only for his profit, but for the profit of others, to edify the body of Christ. The closer the stones lie, and the better they are squared to fit one another, the stronger is the building. *For even Christ pleased not himself.* The self-denial of our Lord Jesus is the best argument against the selfishness of Christians.

(1) Christ pleased not himself. He did not consult his own worldly credit, ease, safety, nor pleasure; he emptied himself, and made himself of no reputation: and all this for our sakes, and to set us an example. His whole life was a self-denying, self-displeasing life.

(2) Herein the scripture was fulfilled: *As it is written, The reproaches of those that reproached thee fell on me.* It is quoted to show that Christ was so far from pleasing himself that he did in the highest degree displease himself. In his humiliation the content and satisfaction of natural inclination were altogether crossed and denied. He preferred our benefit before his own ease and pleasure. This the apostle chooses to express in scripture language. The shame of those reproaches, which Christ underwent. Whatever dishonour was done to God was a trouble to the Lord Jesus. Christ also did himself endure the greatest indignities; there was much of reproach in his suffering. The sin of those reproaches. Every sin is a kind of reproach to God. Now the guilt of these fell upon Christ, when he was made a sin-offering for us.

Nothing could be more contrary to him, nor more against him, than to be made sin and a curse for us, and to have the reproaches of God fall upon him. We must not please ourselves, for Christ pleased not himself; we must bear the infirmities of the weak, for Christ bore the reproaches of those that reproached God. He bore the guilt of sin and the curse for it; we are only called to bear a little of the trouble of it. He bore the presumptuous sins of the wicked; we are called only to bear the infirmities of the weak.—*Even Christ*. Even he pleased not himself, even he bore our sins. And should not we be humble, and self-denying, and ready to consider one another.

(3) Therefore we must go and do likewise: *For whatsoever things were written aforetime were written for our learning*. [1] That which is written of Christ, is *written for our learning*; he hath left us an example. The example of Christ is recorded for our imitation. [2] That which is written in the scriptures of the Old Testament is written for our learning. What happened to the Old Testament saints happened to them for ensample. They are *written*, that they might remain for our use and benefit. *First*, For our learning. We must therefore labour, not only to understand the literal meaning of the scripture, but to learn out of it that which will do us good. Practical observations are more necessary than critical expositions. *Secondly, That we through patience and comfort of the scriptures might have hope*. The scripture was written that we might know what to hope for from God. Now the way of attaining this hope is *through patience and comfort of the scripture*. Patience and comfort suppose trouble and sorrow; such is the lot of the saints in this world. But both these befriend that hope which is the life of our souls. Patience works experience, and experience hope, which maketh not ashamed, *ch.* v. 3–5. The more patience we exercise under troubles the more hopefully we may look through our troubles; nothing more destructive to hope than impatience. And the *comfort of the scriptures*, that comfort which springs from the word of God is likewise a great stay to hope, as it is an earnest in hand of the good hoped for.

Verses 5, 6

The apostle, having delivered two exhortations, intermixes here a prayer for the success of what he had said.

I. The title he gives to God: *The God of patience and consolation*. He gives the grace of patience; he confirms and keeps it up as the God of consolation. When he comes to beg the pouring out of the spirit of love and unity he addresses himself to God as the God of patience and consolation. 1. As a God that bears with us and comforts us, is not extreme to mark what we do amiss—to teach us so to testify our love to our brethren. Or, 2. As a God that gives us patience and comfort. He had spoken (*v.* 4) of patience and comfort of the scriptures; it comes through the scripture as the conduit-pipe, but from God as the fountain-head. Nothing breaks the peace more than an impatient, and peevish, melancholy temper.

II. The mercy he begs of God: *Grant you to be like-minded one towards another, according to Christ Jesus*. The foundation of Christian love and peace is laid in likemindedness. This like-mindedness must be *according to Christ Jesus*, according to the precept of Christ, the royal law of love, according to the pattern and example of Christ, which he had propounded to them for their imitation, *v.* 3. The method of our prayer must be first for truth, and then for peace; for such is the method of the wisdom that is from above: *it is first pure, then peaceable*. This is to be like-minded according to Christ Jesus. Like-mindedness among Christians, according to Christ Jesus, is

the gift of God. We are taught to pray that the will of God may be done on earth as it is done in heaven: now there it is done unanimously, among the angels; and our desire must be that the saints on earth may do so too.

III. The end of his desire: that God may be glorified, *v.* 6. We should have the glory of God in our eye in every prayer. Like-mindedness among Christians is in order to our glorifying God, 1. *With one mind and one mouth*. It will not suffice that there be one mouth, but there must be one mind; nay, there will hardly be one mouth where there is not one mind. 2. As *the Father of our Lord Jesus Christ*. God must be glorified as he has now revealed himself in the face of Jesus Christ, in whom he is our Father. The unity of Christians glorifies *God as the Father of our Lord Jesus Christ*.

Verses 7–12

He had exhorted the strong to receive the weak (*ch.* xiv. 1), here, *Receive one another;* for sometimes the prejudices of the weak Christian make him shy of the strong, as much as the pride of the strong Christian makes him shy of the weak, neither of which ought to be. Let there be a mutual embracing among Christians. Now the reason why Christians must receive one another is taken, as before, from the condescending love of Christ to us: *As Christ also received us, to the glory of God*. Has Christ been so kind to us, and shall we be so unkind to those that are his? Christ has received us into the nearest and dearest relations to himself. He has received us (though we were strangers and enemies, and had played the prodigal) into fellowship and communion with himself. Those words, *to the glory of God*, may refer both to Christ's receiving us, which is our pattern, and to our receiving one another, which is our practice according to that pattern.

I. Christ hath received us to the glory of God. The end of our reception by Christ is that we might glorify God in this world, and be glorified with him in that to come. We are called to an eternal glory by Christ Jesus, John xvii. 24.

II. We must receive one another to the glory of God. This must be our great end in all our actions, that God may be glorified; and nothing more conduces to this than the mutual love and kindness of those that profess religion; compare *v.* 6, *That you may with one mind and one mouth glorify God*. He shows how Jesus Christ has received both Jews and Gentiles; in him they are both one, *one new man*, Eph. ii. 14–16. Those that agree in Christ may well afford to agree among themselves.

1. He received the Jews, *v.* 8. Let not any think hardly or scornfully therefore of those that were originally Jews. (1) Jesus Christ was a *minister of the circumcision*. He was a *minister—a servant*. Christ blessed them, looked upon himself as primarily sent to the *lost sheep of the house of Israel, laid hold of the seed of Abraham* (Heb. ii. 16, margin), and by them, as it were, caught at the whole body of mankind. Christ's personal ministry was appropriated to them. (2) He was so for the truth of God. That is, to make good the promises given to the patriarchs concerning the special mercy God had in store for their seed.— *To confirm the promises made unto the fathers*. The best confirmation of promises is the performance of them. When Messiah the Prince appeared in the fulness of time, as a minister of the circumcision, all these promises were confirmed. In Christ all the promises of God are Yea, and in him Amen.

2. He received the Gentiles likewise. This he shows, *v.* 9–12.

(1) Christ's favour to the Gentiles. One design of Christ was that the Gentiles likewise might be converted. A good reason why they should not think the

worse of any Christian for his having been formerly a Gentile; for Christ has received him. *That the Gentiles might glorify God for his mercy.* They shall have matter for praise, even the mercy of God. Considering the miserable and deplorable condition that the Gentile world was in, the receiving of them appears more as an act of mercy than the receiving of the Jews. The greatest mercy of God to any people is the receiving of them into covenant with himself. They shall have a heart for praise. They shall glorify God for his mercy. God intended to reap a harvest of glory from the Gentiles, who had been so long turning his glory into shame.

(2) The fulfilling of the scriptures in this. The favour of God to the Gentiles was not only mercy, but truth. Though there were not promises directly given to them, yet there were many prophesies concerning them, which related to the calling of them, some of which he mentioned. Thus, by referring them to the Old Testament, he labours to qualify their dislike of the Gentiles. [1] It was foretold that the Gentiles should have the gospel preached to them: "*I will confess to thee among the Gentiles* (v. 9), *thy name shall be known and owned in the Gentile world.*" Christ, and in by his apostles and ministers, whom he sent to disciple all nations, did confess to God among the Gentiles. Christ's declaring God's name to his brethren is called *his praising God in the midst of the congregation,* Ps. xxii. 22. When David's psalms are read and sung among the Gentiles, to the praise and glory of God, it may be said that David is *confessing to God among the Gentiles, and singing to his name.* He that was the sweet psalmist of Israel is now the sweet psalmist of the Gentiles. Converting grace makes people greatly in love with David's psalms. If any confess to God among the Gentiles, and sing to his name, it is not they, but Christ and his grace in them. [2] The Gentiles should *rejoice with his people,* v. 10. Those Jews that retain a prejudice against the Gentiles will by no means admit them to any of their joyful festivities. But, the partition-wall being taken down, the Gentiles are welcome to rejoice with his people. [3] They should praise God (v. 11): *Praise the Lord, all ye Gentiles.* Converting grace sets people praising God. The Gentiles had been, for many ages, praising their idols of wood and stone, but now they are brought to praise the Lord. [4] They should believe in Christ (v. 12), quoted from Isa. xi. 10. *First,* The revelation of Christ, as the Gentiles' king. He is here called *the root of Jesse.* Christ, as God, was David's root; Christ, as man, was David's offspring.—*And he that shall rise to reign over the Gentiles.* When Christ rose from the dead, when he scended on high, it was to reign over the Gentiles. *Secondly,* The recourse of the Gentiles to him: *In him shall the Gentiles trust.* The prophet has it, *to him shall the Gentiles seek.* The method of faith is first to seek unto Christ, as to one proposed to us for a Saviour; and, finding him able and willing to save, then to trust in him. Those that know him will trust in him. This seeking to him is the effect of a trust in him. We shall never seek to Christ till we trust in him. Trust is the mother; diligence in the use of means the daughter. Jews and Gentiles being thus united in Christ's love, why should they not be united in one another's love?

Verse 13

Here is another prayer directed to God, as the God of hope.

I. He addresses himself to God, as the *God of hope.* He is the foundation on which our hope is built, and he is the builder that doth himself raise it: he is both the object of our hope, and the author of it. That hope is but fancy, which is not fastened upon God and which is not of his working in us.

II. What he asks of God, not for himself, but for them.

1. *That they might be filled with all joy and peace in believing.* Joy and peace are two of those things in which the kingdom of God consists, *ch.* xiv. 17. (1) How desirable this joy and peace are; they are filling. Carnal joy puffs up the soul, but cannot fill it. True, heavenly, spiritual joy is filling to the soul; it has a satisfaction in it, answerable to the soul's vast and just desires. Nothing more than this joy, only more of it, even the perfection of it in glory, is the desire of the soul that hath it. (2) How it is attainable. By prayer. Prayer fetches in spiritual joy and peace. By believing. True substantial joy is the fruit of faith. It is owing to the weakness of our faith that we are so much wanting in joy and peace. Only believe; believe the goodness of Christ, the love of Christ, and the result must needs be joy and peace. It is *all* joy and peace—all sorts of true joy and peace. When we come to God by prayer we must enlarge our desires. Ask for all joy.

2. That they might *abound in hope through the power of the Holy Ghost.* What is laid out upon them is but little, compared with what is laid up for them; therefore the more hope they have the more joy and peace they have. Christians should desire and labour after an abundance of hope, such hope as will not make ashamed. This is through the power of the Holy Ghost. Our own power will never reach it; and therefore where this hope is, and is abounding, the blessed spirit must have all the glory.

Verses 14–16

I. He commends these Christians. He began his epistle with their praises (*ch.* i. 8), *Your faith is spoken of throughout the world.* Because sometimes he had reproved them sharply, he now concludes with the like commendation, to part friends. It was not a piece of idle flattery, but a due acknowledgment of their worth, and of the grace of God in them. We must be forward to observe and commend in others that which is excellent and praiseworthy. Paul had no personal acquaintance with these Christians, and yet he says he was persuaded of their excellencies, though he knew them only by hearsay. As we must not, on the one hand, be so simple as to believe every word; so, on the other hand, we must not be so sceptical as to believe nothing; but especially we must be forward to believe good concerning others. It is safer to err on this side. They *were full of goodness;* therefore the more likely to take in good part what he had written, and to account it a kindness; and not only so, but to put it in practice, especially that which relates to the healing of their differences. A good understanding of one another, and a goodwill to one another, would soon put an end to strife. *Filled with all knowledge.* Goodness and knowledge together! A very rare and an excellent conjunction! the head and the heart of the new man. *Able to admonish one another.* Those that have goodness and knowledge should communicate what they have. "You that excel so much in good gifts may think you have no need of any instructions of mine." How gladly would ministers leave off their admonishing work, if people were able and willing to admonish one another! Would to God that all the Lord's people were prophets.

II. He clears himself from the suspicion of intermeddling needlessly with that which did not belong to him, v. 15. Observe how affectionately he speaks to them: *My brethren* (v. 14), and again, *brethren,* v. 15. He had himself, and taught others, the art of obliging. He acknowledges he had written *boldly in some sort.*

1. He did it only as their remembrancer: *As putting you in mind.* People commonly excuse themselves

from hearing the word with this, that the minister can tell them nothing but what they knew before. Yet have they not need to know it better, and to be put in mind of it?

2. He did it as the apostle of the Gentiles. It was in pursuance of his office: *Because of the grace given to me of God*, to be the minister *of Jesus Christ to the Gentiles, v.* 16. He thus laid out himself among the Gentiles, that he might not receive that grace of God in vain. Christ received that he might give; so did Paul; so have we talents which must not be buried. Paul was a minister. Whose minister he was: the *minister of Jesus Christ*; his we are, and him we serve. To whom: to the Gentiles. These Romans were Gentiles: "Now," says he, "I do not thrust myself upon you, I am appointed to it: my commission is my warrant. What he ministered: the *gospel of God—ministering as about holy things* (so the word signifies). For what end: *that the offering up of the Gentiles might be acceptable.* Paul laid out himself thus to bring about something that might be acceptable to God. It is the *offering up of the Gentiles; the oblation of the Gentiles*, in which the Gentiles are looked upon either, (1) As the priests, offering the oblation of prayer and praise. Long had the Jews been the holy nation, the kingdom of priests, but now the Gentiles are made priests unto God. Or, (2) The Gentiles are themselves the sacrifice offered up to God by Paul. Paul gathered in souls by his preaching, not to keep them to himself, but to offer them up to God. And it is an acceptable offering, *being sanctified by the Holy Ghost.* That which made them sacrifices to God was their sanctification; and this was not his work, but the work of the Holy Ghost. None are acceptably offered to God but those that are sanctified.

Verses 17–21

He goes on further to magnify his office in the efficacy of it, and to mention to the glory of God the wonderful things that God had done by him. Though, compared with the multitude of their idolatrous neighbours, they were but a little flock, yet, there were many that were their companions in the kingdom and patience of Jesus Christ. It was likewise a great confirmation of the truth of the Christian doctrine that it had such strange success. Therefore Paul gives them this account, which he makes the matter of his glorying; not vain glory, but holy gracious glorying; it is *through Jesus Christ.* Thus does he centre all his glorying in Christ. And it is *in those things which pertain to God. Whereof I may glory.* I would rather read it thus: *Therefore I have a rejoicing in Christ Jesus concerning the things of God.* Paul would have them to rejoice with him in the efficacy of his ministry, of which he speaks not only with the greatest deference possible to the power of Christ, but with a protestation of the truth of what he said (*v.* 18): *I will not dare to speak of any of those things which Christ hath not wrought by me.* He would not take the praise of another man's work, for (says he) I dare not do it.

I. His unwearied diligence and industry in his work. 1. He preached in many places: *From Jerusalem* and *round about unto Illyricum.* We have in the book of the Acts an account of Paul's travels. There we find him, after he was sent forth to preach to the Gentiles (Acts xiii), labouring in Seleucia, Cyprus, Pamphylia, Pisidia, and Lycaonia (Acts xiii, xiv), afterwards travelling through Syria and Cilicia, Phrygia, Galatia, Mysia, Troas, and thence called over to Macedonia, and so into Europe, Acts xv, xvi. Then we find him very busy at Thessalonica, Berea, Athens, Corinth, Ephesus, and the parts adjacent. Now it might be suspected that if Paul undertook so much work, surely he did it by the halves. "No," says he, "*I have fully preached the Gospel of Christ*—have given them a full account of the truth and terms of the gospel, have not shunned to declare the whole counsel of God."

2. He preached in places that had not heard the gospel before, *v.* 20, 21. He broke up the fallow ground, and introduced Christianity where nothing had reigned for many ages but idolatry and witchcraft. Paul broke the ice, and therefore must needs meet with the more difficulties and discouragements in his work. Paul was called out to the hardest work. He was a bold man that made the first attack upon the palace of the strong man armed in the Gentile world, and Paul was that man who ventured the first onset in many places, and suffered greatly for it. He mentions this as a proof of his apostleship; for the office of the apostles was especially to bring in those that were without. He principally laid himself out for the good of those that sat in darkness. He was in care not to *build upon another man's foundation.* He quotes a scripture for this out of Isa. lii. 15, *To whom he was not spoken of, they shall see.* The transition from darkness to light is more sensible than the after-growth and increase of that light. And commonly the greatest success of the gospel is at its first coming to a place; afterwards most people become sermonproof.

II. The great success that he had in his work: It was effectual to *make the Gentiles obedient.* The design of the gospel is to bring people to be *obedient.* This Paul aimed at in all his travels. Now how was this great work wrought? Christ was the principal agent. He does not say, "which I worked," but "which Christ wrought by me," *v.* 18. Whatever good we do, it is not we, but Christ by us, that does it. Paul takes all occasions to own this. Paul was a very active instrument: *By word and deed*, that is, by his preaching, and by the miracles he wrought, or his preaching and his living. Those ministers are likely to win souls that preach both by word and deed. This is according to Christ's example, who began both to do and teach.—*Through mighty signs and wonders.* These made the preaching of the word so effectual. The *power of the Spirit of God* made this effectual, *v.* 19. (1) The power of the Spirit in Paul, as in the other apostles, for the working of those miracles. Miracles were wrought by the power of the Holy Ghost. Or, (2) The power of the Spirit in the hearts of those who saw the miracles. Paul himself could not make one soul obedient further than the power of the Spirit of God accompanied his labours. This is an encouragement to faithful ministers, who labour under the sense of great weakness and infirmity. The same almighty Spirit that wrought with Paul often perfects strength in weakness. The converted nations were his joy and crown of rejoicing: and he tells them of it, that they might rejoice with him.

Verses 22–29

St. Paul here declares his purpose to come and see the Christians at Rome. The manner of his expression is gracious, and for our imitation. Even our common discourse should have an air of grace; by this it will appear what country we belong to. It should seem that Paul's company was very much desired at Rome. Should the apostle of the Gentiles be a stranger at Rome, the metropolis of the Gentile world? He promises to come shortly, and gives a good reason why he could not come now.

I. He excuses it that he never came yet. 1. He assures them that he had a great desire to see them; not to see Rome, but *to come unto you* (*v.* 3), a company of poor despised saints in Rome. These were the men that Paul was ambitious of an acquaintance with at Rome. And he had a special desire to see them, because of the great character they had in all the churches for faith and holiness. This desire Paul had had for many years, and yet could never compass it. God's dearest servants are not always gratified in everything that they have a mind to. 2. He tells them that the reason why he could not come to them was because he had so much work cut out for him elsewhere. *For which cause* he was so much *hindered*. God had opened a wide door for him in other places, and so turned him aside. (1) The gracious providence of God about his ministers, casting their lot, not according to their contrivance, but according to his own purpose. Man purposes but God disposes. The gospel does not come by chance to any place, but by the will and counsel of God. (2) The gracious prudence of Paul, in bestowing his time and pains where there was most need. Had Paul consulted his own honour, the greatness of the work would never have hindered him from seeing Rome. Paul sought the things of Christ more than his own things. There was now a gale of opportunity, the fields were white unto the harvest; such a season slipped might never be retrieved. It concerns us all to do that first which is most needful. This Paul mentions as a sufficient satisfying reason. We must not take it ill of our friends if they prefer necessary work, which is pleasing to God, before unnecessary visits and compliments.

II. He promised to come and see them shortly, *v.* 23, 24, 29. *Having no more place in these parts,* namely, in Greece, where he then was. He had driven the chariot of the gospel to the sea-coast, and having thus conquered Greece he is ready to wish there were another Greece to conquer.

1. How he forecasted his intended visit. His project was to see them in his way to Spain. It appears by this that Paul intended a journey into Spain. But it is not certain whether ever he fulfilled his purpose, and went to Spain. He did indeed come to Rome, but he was brought thither a prisoner, and there was detained two years; and whither he went after is uncertain. The grace of God often with favour accepts the sincere intention, when the providence of God in wisdom prohibits the execution. Now, in his way to Spain he proposed to come to them. *I trust to see you:* not, "I am resolved I will," but, "I hope I shall." We must purpose all our purposes in like manner with a submission to the divine providence.

2. What he expected in his intended visit. (1) What he expected from them. He expected they would bring him on his way towards Spain. It was not a stately attendance but a loving attendance, such as friends give, that Paul expected. They might be helpful to Paul in his voyage thither; and it was not barely their accompanying him part of the way, but their furthering him in his expedition, that he counted upon. (2) What he expected in them: to *be somewhat filled with their company.* That which Paul desired was their company and conversation. Paul was himself a man of great attainments in knowledge and grace, and yet see how he pleased himself with the thoughts of good company. He intended to make some stay with them, for he would be filled with their company; not just look at them, and away. It is but somewhat filled, he thought he should leave them with a desire of more of their company. The satisfaction we have in communion with the saints in this world is but partial. It is partial compared with our communion with Christ. That will fill the soul. It is partial compared with the communion we hope to have with the saints in the other world. (3) What he expected from God with them, *v.* 29. He expected to come *in the fulness of the blessing of the gospel of Christ.* Concerning what he *expected* from *them* he speaks doubtfully: *I trust to be brought on my way,*

and to be filled with your company. Paul had learnt not to be too confident of the best. These very men slipped from him afterwards, *At my first answer, no man stood by me;* none of the Christians at Rome. But concerning what he expected from God he speaks confidently. *I am sure when I do come I shall come in the fulness,* &c. We cannot expect too little from man, nor too much from God. Now Paul expected that God would bring him to them, loaded with blessings. Compare *ch.* i. 11, *That I may impart unto you some spiritual gift.* The blessing of the gospel of Christ is the best and most desirable blessing. There is then a happy meeting between people and ministers, when they are both under the fulness of the blessing. When ministers are fully prepared to give out, and people fully prepared to receive, this blessing, both are happy.

III. He gives them a good reason why he could not come and see them now. He must first make a journey to Jerusalem, *v.* 25–28. He was going to Jerusalem, as the messenger of the church's charity.

1. Concerning this charity itself. And he speaks of that probably to excite the Roman Christians to do the like. Examples are moving, and Paul was very ingenious at begging, not for himself, but for others. (1) For whom it was intended: *For the poor saints which are at Jerusalem, v.* 26. It is no strange thing for saints to be poor. Riches are not the best things, nor is poverty a curse. It seems, the saints at Jerusalem were poorer than other saints because the famine that was over all the world in the days of Claudius Cæsar did in a special manner prevail in Judæa. This was the occasion of that contribution mentioned, Acts xi. 28–30. Though the saints at Jerusalem were at a great distance from them, yet they thus extended their bounty to them, to teach us to stretch out the hand of our charity to all that are of the household of faith, though in places distant from us. We must extend our bounty, as the sun his beams. (2) By whom it was collected: *By those of Macedonia* (the chief of whom were the Philippians) *and Achaia* (the chief of whom were the Corinthians). It seems those of Macedonia and Achaia were rich and wealthy, while those at Jerusalem were poor and needy, so that some should have what others want, and so this mutual dependence of Christians one upon another might be maintained.—*It pleased them.* This intimates how ready they were to it, and how cheerful they were in it.— *To make a certain contribution; a communication,* in token of the communion of saints, as in the natural body one member communicates to the relief of another, as there is occasion. Time was when the saints at Jerusalem were on the giving hand, when they laid their estates at the apostles' feet for charitable uses, and took special care that the Grecian widows should not be neglected in the daily ministration. And now that the providence of God had turned the scale, and made them necessitous, they found the Grecians kind to them; for the merciful shall obtain mercy. (3) What reason there was for it (*v.* 27): *And their debtors they are.* The Gentiles were greatly beholden to the Jews, and were bound in gratitude to be very kind to them. From the stock of Israel came Christ himself; out of the same stock came the prophets, and apostles, and first preachers of the gospel. The Jews, having had the lively oracles committed to them, were the Christians' library-keepers. They were cut off, that the Gentiles might be admitted in. Thus did the Gentiles partake of their spiritual things, and receive the gospel of salvation as it were at secondhand from the Jews; and therefore *their duty is to minister unto them in carnal things*: it is the least they can do.

2. Concerning Paul's agency in this business. He *ministered unto the saints (v.* 25) by stirring up others, receiving what was gathered, and transmitting it to

Jerusalem. Many good works of that kind stand at a stay for want of some one active person to lead in them, and to set the wheels going. Besides this, Paul had other business in this journey, to visit and confirm the churches. Paul was one that laid out himself to do good every way, like his Master, to the bodies as well as to the souls of people. This Paul had undertaken, and therefore he resolves to go through with it, before he fell upon other work (v. 28): *When I have sealed to them this fruit.* He calls the alms *fruit*, for it is one of the fruits of righteousness; it sprang from a root of grace in the givers. And his sealing it intimates his great care about it. Paul was very solicitous to approve himself faithful in the management of this matter.

Verses 30–33

I. St. Paul's desire of a share in the prayers of the Romans for him, expressed very earnestly, v. 30–32. He had prayed much for them, and this he desires as the return of his kindness. Interchanging prayers is an excellent token of the interchanging of loves. How careful should we be lest we do anything to forfeit our interest in the love and prayers of God's praying people!

1. Why they must pray for him. *I beseech you, "For the Lord Jesus Christ's sake.* You love Christ, and own Christ; for his sake then do me this kindness. *For the love of the Spirit.* As a proof of that love which the Spirit works in the hearts of believers one to another, pray for me. If ever you experienced the Spirit's love to you, and would be found returning your love to the Spirit, be not wanting in this office of kindness."

2. How they must pray for him: *That you strive together.* That *you strive in prayer.* We must put forth all that is within us in that duty; pray with fixedness, faith, and fervency. This not only when we are praying for ourselves, but when we are praying for our friends. True love to our brethren should make us as earnest for them as sense of our own need makes us for ourselves. "*Strive together with me*, who am wrestling with God daily, upon my own and my friends' account." He would have them to ply the same oar. Those who are put far asunder by the disposal of God's providence may yet meet together at the throne of his grace.

3. What they must beg of God for him. In praying both for ourselves and for our friends, it is good to be particular. He recommends himself to their prayers, with reference to three things: (1) The dangers which he was exposed to: *That I may be delivered from those that do not believe in Judæa.* Some prospect he had of trouble from them in this journey; and therefore they must pray that God would deliver him. We may, and must, pray against persecution. (2) His services: *Pray that my service which I have for Jerusalem may be accepted of the saints.* Why, was there any danger that it would not be accepted? Paul was the apostle of the Gentiles, and as the unbelieving Jews looked spitefully at him, which was their wickedness, so those that believed were shy of him, which was their weakness. "Pray that it may be accepted." As God must be sought unto for the restraining of the ill will of our enemies, so also for the preserving and increasing of the goodwill of our friends. (3) His journey to them. To engage their prayers for him, he interests them in his concerns (v. 32): *That I may come unto you with joy.* If he should not do good, and prosper, in one visit, he thought he should have small joy of the next: may *come with joy, by the will of God.* All our joy depends upon the will of God.

II. Here is another prayer of the apostle for them (v. 33): *Now the God of peace be with you all, Amen.* He describes God under this title here, because of the divisions among them; if God be the God of peace, let us be men of peace. Those who have the fountain cannot want any of the streams. *With you all;* both weak and strong. Those who are united in the blessing of God should be united in affection one to another.

CHAPTER 16

Paul is now concluding this long and excellent epistle, and he does it with a great deal of affection. He appears to have been a very loving man. It is observable how often Paul speaks as if he were concluding, and yet takes fresh hold again. These repeated benedictions, which stand for valedictions, speak Paul loth to part. I. His recommendation of one friend to the Roman Christians, and his particular salutation of several among them, ver. 1–16. II. A caution to take heed of those who caused divisions, ver. 17–20. III. Salutations added from some who were with Paul, ver. 21–24. IV. He concludes with a solemn celebration of the glory of God, ver. 25–27.

Verses 1–16

I. Here is the recommendation of a friend, by whom (as some think) this epistle was sent—one *Phebe, v. 1, 2.* It should seem that she was a person of quality and estate, who had business which called her to Rome, where she was a stranger; and therefore Paul recommends her to the acquaintance of the Christians there. Courtesy and Christianity agree well together.

1. He gives a very good character of her. (1) As a sister to Paul: *Phebe our sister;* not in nature, but in grace. Both Christ and his apostles had some of their best friends among the devout (and upon that account honourable) women. (2) As a *servant to the church at Cenchrea*: a servant by office, not to preach the word (that was forbidden to women), but in acts of charity and hospitality. Phebe seems to have been a person of some account; and yet it was no disparagement to her to be a servant to the church. Everyone in his place should strive to serve the church, for therein he serves Christ. Cenchrea was a small sea-port town adjoining to Corinth. (3) As a *succourer of many*, and particularly of Paul, *v. 2.* She relieved many that were in want and distress. Her bounty was extensive, she was a succourer of many. Observe the gratitude of Paul in mentioning her particular kindness to him: *And to myself also.* Acknowledgment of favours is the least return we can make.

2. He recommends her to their care. "*Receive her in the Lord.* Entertain her; bid her welcome, as a servant and friend of Christ." *As it becometh saints* to receive, who love Christ, and therefore love all that are his for his sake; or, as *becometh saints* to be received, with love and honour. *Assist her in whatsoever business she has need of you.* Being a woman, a stranger, a Christian, she had need of help: and Paul engaged them to be assistant to her. It becomes Christians to be helpful one to another in their affairs, especially to be helpful to strangers; for we are members one of another. Paul bespeaks help for one that had been so helpful to many.

II. Here are commendations to some particular friends among those to whom he wrote. Though the care of all the churches came upon Paul daily, enough to distract an ordinary head, yet he could retain the remembrance of so many; and his heart was so full of love and affection as to send salutations to each of them. *Greet* them, *salute* them; it is the same word, "Let them know that I remember them."

1. Concerning Aquila and Priscilla, a famous couple, that Paul had a special kindness for. They were originally of Rome, but were banished thence by the edict of Claudius, Acts xviii. 2. At Corinth, Paul became acquainted with them, wrought with them at the trade of tent-making; after some time, they returned to Rome. He calls them his *helpers in Christ Jesus.* Nay, they did not only do much, but they

ventured much, for Paul: They have *for my life laid down their own necks*. They exposed themselves to secure Paul, hazarded their own lives for the preservation of his. Paul was in a great deal of danger at Corinth; but they sheltered him. It was a good while ago that they had done Paul this kindness; and yet he speaks as feelingly of it as if it had been but yesterday. *To whom not only I give thanks, but also all the churches of the Gentiles;* who were all beholden to these good people for helping to save the life of him that was the apostle of the Gentiles. He sends likewise greeting to the *church in their house, v.* 5. Religion reigning in a family, will turn a house into a church. It had a good influence upon this that Priscilla the good wife of the family was so very eminent and forward in religion, so eminent that she is often named first. When Priscilla and Aquila were at Ephesus, though but sojourners there, yet there also they had a church in their house, 1 Cor. xvi. 19. A truly godly man will be careful to take religion along with him wherever he goes.

2. Concerning Epenetus, *v.* 5. He calls him his *well-beloved*. Endearing language should pass among Christians to express love, and to engage love. So he calls Amplias, *beloved in the Lord*; and Stachys, his *beloved*. Of Epenetus it is further said that he was the *first-fruit of Achaia unto Christ*: one that was offered up to God by Paul, as the first-fruits of his ministry there; an earnest of a great harvest; for in Corinth, the chief city of Achaia, God had much people, Acts xviii. 10. Special respect is to be paid to those that set out early, and come to work in the vineyard at the first hour.

3. Concerning Mary, and some others. *Mary,* who *bestowed much labour on us*. True love never sticks at labour, but rather takes a pleasure in it; where there is much love there will be much labour. He says of Tryphena and Tryphosa that they laboured in the Lord (*v.* 12), and of the beloved Persis, that she laboured much in the Lord, abounding more in the work of the Lord.

4. Concerning Andronicus and Junia, *v.* 7. Some take them for a man and his wife. They were Paul's *cousins*, akin to him; so was Herodion, *v.* 11. Religion does not take away, but sanctifies, and improves, our respect to our kindred, engaging us to rejoice in them the more, when we find them related to Christ by faith. They were his fellow-prisoners. Partnership in suffering sometimes does much towards the union of souls and the knitting of affections. They were *of note among the apostles*. They were eminent for knowledge, and gifts, and graces, which made them famous among the apostles. *Who also were in Christ before me*. In time they had the start of Paul. How ready was Paul to acknowledge in others any kind of precedency!

5. Concerning Apelles, who is here said to be *approved in Christ* (*v.* 10), a high character! One that had been tried; his friends and enemies had tried him, and he was as gold, a man that one might trust and repose a confidence in.

6. Concerning Aristobulus and Narcissus; notice is taken of their household, *v.* 10, 11. Those of their household who *are in the Lord* (as it is limited, *v.* 11), that were Christians. How studious was Paul to leave none out of his salutations that he had any knowledge of or acquaintance with!

7. Concerning Rufus (*v.* 13), *chosen in the Lord*. He was a choice Christian, whose gifts and graces evinced that he was eternally chosen in Christ Jesus. *—And his mother and mine*, his mother by nature and mine by Christian love. This good woman, upon some occasion, or other, had been as a mother to Paul, and Paul here gratefully owns it.

8. Concerning the rest, he salutes the *brethren who are with them* (*v.* 14), and the *saints who are with them*

(*v.* 15). It is the good property of saints to delight in being together; and Paul thus joins them together in his salutations to endear them one to another. In Christian congregations there should be smaller societies linked together in love and converse.

Lastly, He concludes with the recommendation of them to the love and embraces one of another: *Salute one another with a holy kiss.* Mutual salutations, as they express love, so they increase and strengthen love. Paul here encourages the use of them, and only directs that they may be holy. He adds, in the close, a general salutation to them all, in the name of the churches of Christ (*v.* 16): *"The churches of Christ salute you;* that is, the churches which I am with desire me to testify their affection to you and good wishes for you." This is one way of maintaining the communion of saints.

Verses 17–20

A caution to take heed of those whose principles and practices were destructive to Christian love.

I. The caution itself: *I beseech you, brethren.* He does not will and command, but for love's sake beseeches. He teaches them, 1. To see their danger: *Mark those who cause divisions and offences.* Our Master had himself foretold that divisions and offences would come, and against such we are here cautioned. Those who burden the church with dividing and offending impositions cause divisions and offences, contrary to, or different from, the *doctrine which we have learned.* If truth be once deserted, unity and peace will not last long. Now, *mark* those that thus cause divisions. There is need of a piercing watchful eye to discern the danger we are in from such people; for commonly the pretences are plausible, when the projects are very pernicious. A danger discovered is half prevented. 2. To shun it: *"Avoid them.* Shun all unnecessary communion and communication with them, lest you be leavened and infected by them. —*Their word will eat as doth a canker."* Some think he especially warns them to take heed of the judaizing teachers.

II. The reasons to enforce this caution.

1. Because of the pernicious policy of these seducers, *v.* 18. His description of them, in two things: (1) The master they serve: not *our Lord Jesus Christ.* Though they call themselves Christians, they do not serve Christ, whatever they pretend. But they *serve their own belly.* It is some base lust or other that they are pleasing. Their *God is their belly,* Phil. iii. 19. What a base master do they serve, and how unworthy to come in competition with Christ. (2) The method they take to compass their design: *By good words and fair speeches they deceive the hearts of the simple.* Their words and speeches have a show of holiness and zeal for God (it is an easy thing to be godly from the teeth outward), and a show of kindness and love to those into whom they instil their corrupt doctrines. We have great need therefore to keep our hearts with all diligence.

2. Because of the peril we are in: "For *your obedience has come abroad unto all men*—you are noted in all the churches for a willing, tractable, complying people." (1) Therefore, because it was so, these seducing teachers would be the more apt to assault them. "The false teachers hear that you are an obedient people, and therefore they will be likely to come among you, to see if you will be obedient to them." (2) Though it were so, yet they were in danger from these seducers. This Paul suggests, not as one suspicious of them, but as one solicitous for them: "Your *obedience has come abroad unto all men; I am glad therefore on your behalf.*" Thus does he insinuate their commendation, the better to make way for the caution. "You must not be secure: *I would have you wise unto that which is good, and*

simple concerning evil." A pliable temper is good when it is under good government; but otherwise it may be very ensnaring. Two general rules: [1] To be *wise unto that which is good.* There is need of a great deal of wisdom in our adherence to good truths, and good duties, and good people, lest in any of these we be imposed upon and deluded. [2] To be *simple concerning evil*—so wise as not to be *deceived, and* yet so simple as not to be deceivers. The wisdom of the serpent becomes Christians, but not the subtlety of the old serpent. That is a wisely simple man that knows not how to do anything against the truth. Now Paul was the more solicitous for the Roman church, because it was so famous; it was a city upon a hill, and many eyes were upon the Christians there.

3. Because of the promise of God, that we shall have victory at last (*v.* 20): *The God of peace shall bruise Satan under your feet.*

(1) The titles he gives to God: *The God of peace.* When we come to God for spiritual victories, we must not only eye him as the Lord of hosts, whose all power is, but as the God of peace, a God at peace with us, creating peace for us. Victory comes from God more as the God of peace than as the God of war.

(2) The blessing he expects from God—a victory over Satan. Satan tempting and troubling, acting as a deceiver and as a destroyer, the *God of peace* will *bruise under our feet.* "Though you cannot overcome in your own strength and wisdom, yet the God of peace will do it for you." [1] The victory shall be complete: *He shall bruise Satan under your feet,* plainly alluding to the first promise the Messiah made in paradise (Gen. iii. 15). Christ hath overcome for us, and we have nothing to do but to pursue the victory. Let this quicken us to our spiritual conflict, to fight the good fight of faith. [2] The victory shall be speedy: He shall do it *shortly.* It will encourage soldiers when they know the war will be at an end quickly, in such a victory. It is the victory which all the saints shall have over Satan when they come to heaven, together with the present victories which through grace they obtain in earnest of that. Hold out therefore, faith and patience, yet a little while! *The grace of our Lord Jesus Christ be with you.* If the grace of Christ be with us, who can be against us so as to prevail? Paul, not only as a friend, but as an apostle, thus with authority blesses them, and repeats it, *v.* 24.

Verses 21–24

He here adds an affectionate remembrance of them from some particular persons who were now with him. 1. Some that were his particular friends. *Timotheus my work-fellow.* Paul sometimes calls Timothy his son; but here he styles him his work-fellow, as one equal with him. *Lucius,* probably Lucius of Cyrene, a noted man in the church of Antioch (Acts xiii. 1). *Sosipater,* supposed to be the same with Sopater of Berea, mentioned Acts xx. 4. These Paul calls his kinsmen. It is a very great comfort to see the holiness and usefulness of our kindred. 2. One that was Paul's amanuensis (*v.* 22): *I Tertius, who wrote this epistle.* Paul made use of a scribe because he wrote a bad hand, which was not very legible, which he excuses, when he writes to the Galatians with his own hand (Gal. vi. 11). The least piece of service done to the church shall not pass without a remembrance and a recompence. 3. Some others that were of note among the Christians (*v.* 23): *Gaius my host.* Paul commends him for his great hospitality; not only my host, but of the *whole church.* *Erastus, the chamberlain of the city,* is another; he means the city of Corinth. It seems he was a person of honour and account, one in public place. Not

many mighty, not many noble, are called, but some are. *Quartus* is likewise mentioned, and called a brother.

Verses 25–27

Here the apostle solemnly closes his epistle with a magnificent ascription of glory to the blessed God. He does, as it were, breathe out his soul to these Romans in the praise of God.

I. A description of the gospel of God, which comes in in a parenthesis. *To establish you according to my gospel.* Paul calls it his gospel, because he was the preacher of it. Paul had his head and heart so full of the gospel that he could scarcely mention it without a digression to set forth the nature and excellency of it.

1. It is the *preaching of Jesus Christ.* The sum and substance of the whole gospel is Jesus Christ and him crucified. We preach not ourselves, says Paul, but Christ Jesus the Lord. That which establishes souls is the plain preaching of Jesus Christ.

2. *It is the revelation of the mystery which was kept secret since the world began, and by the scriptures of the prophets made known.* The subject-matter of the gospel is a mystery. Blessed be God, there is as much of this mystery made plain as will suffice to bring us to heaven, if we do not wilfully neglect so great salvation.

(1) This mystery was kept secret since the world began: It was *wrapped up in silence from eternity*; so some. Before the foundation of the world was laid, the mystery was hid in God, Eph. iii. 9. Or, *since the world began,* so we translate it. During all the times of the Old Testament this mystery was comparatively kept secret. Thus it was hid from ages and generations, even among the Jews, much more among the Gentiles. Even the disciples of Christ themselves, before his resurrection and ascension, were very much in the dark about the mystery of redemption.

(2) It is now made manifest. The shadows of the evening are done away, and the Sun of righteousness has risen upon the world. But how is it made manifest by the scriptures of the prophets? Surely, because now the event has given the best exposition to the prophecies of the Old Testament. Being accomplished, they are explained. The Old Testament does not only borrow light from, but return light to, the revelation of the New Testament. Now Christ appears to have been the treasure hid in the field of the Old Testament. To him bear *all the prophets witness.* See Luke xxiv. 27.

(3) It is manifested *according to the commandment of the everlasting God.* Lest any should object, "Why was this mystery kept secret so long, and why made manifest now?"—he resolves it into the will of God. *The everlasting God.* He is from everlasting. He is to everlasting. We must never look for any new revelation, but abide by this, for this is according to the commandment of the everlasting God. Christ, in the gospel, is the same yesterday, today, and for ever.

(4) It is *made known to all nations for the obedience of faith.* The extent of this revelation he often takes notice of. Christ is salvation to the ends of the earth, to all nations. And the design of it is very observable; it is for the obedience of faith. The gospel is revealed, not to be talked of, and disputed about, but to be submitted to. See here what is the right faith—even that which works in obedience; and what is the right obedience—even that which springs from faith; and what is the design of the gospel—to bring us to both.

II. A doxology to that God whose gospel it is, ascribing glory to him for ever (*v.* 27).

1. The matter of this praise. In thanking God, we fasten upon his favours, to us; in praising and adoring God, we fasten upon his perfections in himself. Two

of his principal attributes are here taken notice of: (1) His power (*v.* 25): *To him that is of power to establish you.* It is no less than a divine power that establishes the saints. In giving God the glory of this power we may, and must, take to ourselves the comfort of it—that whatever our doubts, and difficulties, and fears, may be, our God, whom we serve, is of power to establish us. (2) His wisdom (*v.* 27): *To God only wise,* Power to effect without wisdom to contrive, and wisdom to contrive without power to effect, are alike vain and fruitless; but both together, and both infinite, make a perfect being. He is only perfectly and infallibly wise. He is the spring and fountain of all the wisdom of the creatures. With him are strength and wisdom.

2. The Mediator of this praise: *Through Jesus Christ. To God only wise through Jesus Christ;* so some. It is in and through Christ that God is manifested to the world as the only wise God. Or rather, as we read it, *glory through Jesus Christ.* All the glory that passes from fallen man to God must go through the hands of the Lord Jesus. As he is the Mediator of all our prayers, so he is, and I believe will be to eternity, the Mediator of all our praises.

AN EXPOSITION, WITH PRACTICAL OBSERVATIONS, OF

THE FIRST EPISTLE TO THE

CORINTHIANS

Corinth was a principal city of Greece. It was situated on the isthmus that joined Peloponnesus to the rest of Greece, and had two ports adjoining, one called *Lechæum*, not far from the city, whence they traded to Italy and the west, the other, called *Cenchrea*, at a more remote distance, whence they traded to Asia. From this situation, it is no wonder that Corinth should be a place of great trade and wealth; and neither is it to be wondered at if a place so famous for wealth and arts should be infamous for vice. Yet in this lewd city did Paul plant and raise a Christian church, chiefly among the Gentiles. *You know that you were Gentiles, carried away to those dumb idols even as you were led,* though it is not improbable that many Jewish converts might be also among them, for we are told that *Crispus, the chief ruler of the synagogue, believed on the Lord, with all his house,* Acts xviii. 8. He continued in this city nearly two years, being encouraged by a divine vision assuring him God *had much people in that city,* Acts xviii. 9, 10.

Some time after he left them he wrote this epistle to them, to water what he had planted and rectify some gross disorders which during his absence had been introduced. Pride, avarice, luxury, lust, with all these either the body of this people or some particular persons among them are here charged by the apostle. Their pride discovered itself in their parties and factions. And this vice was not wholly fed by their wealth, but by the insight they had into the Greek learning and philosophy. Their avarice was manifest in their law-suits before heathen judges. Their luxury appeared in more instances than one, in their dress, in their debauching themselves even at the Lord's table. Their lust broke out in a most flagrant and infamous instance—that a man should have his father's wife. And it is plain from other passages of the epistle that they were not so entirely free from their former lewd inclinations as not to need very strict cautions against fornication. The pride of their learning had also carried many of them so far as to disbelieve or dispute against the doctrine of the resurrection.

It is manifest that there was much that deserved reprehension, and needed correction, in this church. And the apostle sets himself to do both with all wisdom and faithfulness, and with a due mixture of tenderness and authority. After a short introduction he first blames them for their discord and factions, and prescribes humility as a remedy for the evils that abounded amongst them. This he does through the first four chapters. In the fifth he treats of the case of the incestuous person. In the sixth chapter he blames them for their law-suits, carried on before heathen judges, and in the close of the chapter warns them against the sin of fornication. In the seventh chapter he gives advice upon a case of conscience about marriage. He gives also some directions here about virgins. In the eighth he directs them about meats offered to idols. From this he also takes occasion, in the ninth chapter, to expatiate a little on his own conduct. In the tenth chapter he dissuades them against having communion with idolaters, by eating of their sacrifices, inasmuch as they could not be at once partakers of the Lord's table and the table of devils. In the eleventh chapter he gives direction about their habit in public worship, blames them for their gross irregularities and scandalous disorders in receiving the Lord's supper. In the twelfth chapter he enters on the consideration of spiritual gifts, which were poured forth in great abundance on this church. Towards the close he informs them that he could recommend to them something far more excellent, upon which he breaks out, in the thirteenth chapter, into the commendation and characteristics of charity. And then, in the fourteenth, he directs them how to keep up decency and order in the churches in the use of their spiritual gifts. The fifteenth chapter is taken up in confirming and explaining the great doctrine of the resurrection. The last chapter consists of some particular advices and salutations.

CHAPTER 1

I. The preface or introduction to the whole epistle, ver. 1–9. II. One principal occasion of writing it, their divisions and the origin of them, ver. 10–13. III. An account of Paul's ministry among them, ver. 14–17. IV. The manner wherein he preached the gospel, ver. 17, to the end.

Verses 1–9

We have here the apostle's preface to his whole epistle.

I. The inscription. It is an epistle from Paul to the church of Corinth, which he himself had planted, though there were some among them that now questioned his apostleship (*ch.* ix. 1, 2). The most faithful and useful ministers are not secure from this contempt. *Paul, called to be an apostle of Jesus Christ, through the will of God.* He had not taken this honour to himself, but had a divine commission for it. It was necessary at this time, to assert his character, and magnify his office, when false teachers made a merit of running him down. It was not pride in Paul, but faithfulness to his trust to maintain his apostolical character and authority. He joins Sosthenes with him

in writing. Paul, and Sosthenes his brother, once a ruler of the Jewish synagogue, afterwards a convert to Christianity. He speaks, through the rest of the epistle, in his own name, and in the singular number. The persons to whom this epistle was directed were *the church of God that was at Corinth, sanctified in Christ Jesus, and called to be saints.* All Christians are thus far sanctified in Christ Jesus, that they are by baptism dedicated and devoted to him. If they be not truly holy, it is their own fault and reproach. It is the design of Christianity to sanctify us in Christ. He directs the epistle *to all that in every place call on the name of Christ Jesus our Lord, both theirs and ours.* God hath a remnant in all places; and we should have a common concern for and hold communion with all that call on Christ's name.

II. The apostolical benediction. *Grace be to you, and peace, from God our Father, and from the Lord Jesus Christ.* Grace and peace—the favour of God, and reconciliation to him. It is indeed the summary of all blessings. This advantage we have by the gospel, 1. That we are directed how to obtain that peace from God: it is in and by Christ. 2. We are told what must qualify us for this peace; namely, grace: first grace, and then peace.

III. The apostle's thanksgiving to God on their behalf. Paul begins most of his epistles with thanksgiving to God for his friends and prayer for them. He gives thanks, 1. For their conversion to the faith of Christ: *For the grace which was given you through Jesus Christ, v.* 4. Those who are united to him by faith, are the objects of divine favour. God loves them. 2. For the abundance of their spiritual gifts. They did not come behind any of the churches in any gift, *v.* 7. He specifies *utterance and knowledge, v.* 5. Many have the flower of utterance that have not the root of knowledge, and their converse is barren. Many have the treasure of knowledge, and want utterance to employ it for the good of others, and then it is in a manner wrapped up in a napkin. But, where God gives both, a man is qualified for eminent usefulness. These gifts were a confirmation of the testimony of Christ among them, *v.* 6. So that the more plentifully they were poured forth on any church the more confirming evidence they had of their divine mission. And it is no wonder that when they had such a foundation for their faith they should live in expectation of the coming of their Lord Jesus Christ, *v.* 7. It is the character of Christians that they wait for Christ's second coming. And the more confirmed we are in the Christian faith the more earnest our expectation of it.

IV. The encouraging hopes the apostle had of them for the time to come, founded on the power and love of Christ, and the faithfulness of God, *v.* 8, 9. He who had begun a good work in them, would not leave it unfinished. Those that wait for the coming of our Lord Jesus Christ will be kept by him, and those that are so *will be blameless in the day of Christ.* How glorious are the hopes of such a privilege, whether for ourselves or others! O glorious expectation, especially when the faithfulness of God comes in to support our hopes! Those that come at his call shall never be disappointed in their hopes in him. If we approve ourselves faithful to God, we shall never find him unfaithful to us.

Verses 10–13

Here the apostle enters on his subject.

I. He exhorts them to unity and brotherly love, and reproves them for their divisions. He had received an account from some that wished them well of some unhappy differences among them. He writes to them in a very engaging way: *"I beseech you, brethren, by the name of our Lord Jesus Christ;* be unanimous. *Speak all the same thing;* avoid *divisions* or *schisms. Be perfectly joined together in the same mind.* In the great things of religion be of a mind: but, when there is not a unity of sentiment, let there be a union of affections."

II. He hints at the origin of these contentions. Pride lay at the bottom, and this made them factious. They quarrelled about their ministers. Those who were disposed to be contentious broke into parties, and set their ministers at the head of their several factions: some cried up Paul, others cried up Apollos, some Cephas, or Peter, and some were for none of them, but Christ only. So liable are the best things in the world to be corrupted, and the gospel and its institutions, which are at perfect harmony with themselves and one another, to be made the engines of variance, discord, and contention. How far will pride carry Christians in opposition to one another! Even so far as to set Christ and his own apostles at variance, and make them rivals and competitors.

III. He expostulates with them upon their discord and quarrels: *"Is Christ divided?* No, there is but one Christ, and therefore Christians should be of one heart. *Was Paul crucified for you?* Was he your

sacrifice and atonement? Or, *were you baptized in the name of Paul?* Were you devoted to my service, or engaged to be my disciples, by that sacred rite?" Ministers, however instrumental they are of good to us, are not to be put in Christ's stead. And happy were it for the churches if there were no name of distinction among them, as Christ is not divided.

Verses 14–16

Here the apostle gives an account of his ministry among them. He thanks God he had baptized but a few among them, *Crispus,* who had been a ruler of a synagogue at Corinth (Acts xviii. 8), *Gaius, and the household of Stephanas,* besides whom, he says, he did not remember that he had baptized any. He is not to be understood in such a sense as if he were thankful for not having baptized at all, but for not having done it in present circumstances. He left it to other ministers to baptize, while he filled up his time with preaching the gospel. This, he thought, was more his business. In this sense he says, *Christ sent him not to baptize, but to preach the gospel*—not so much to baptize as to preach. Ministers should consider themselves set apart more especially to that service in which Christ will be most honoured and the salvation of souls promoted, and for which they are best fitted. The principal business Paul did among them was to preach *the gospel* (*v.* 17), *the cross* (*v.* 18), *Christ crucified, v.* 23. He did not preach his own fancy, but the gospel. Christ crucified is the foundation of all our hopes and the fountain of all our joys. By his death we live. This is what Paul preached, what all ministers should preach, and what all the saints live upon.

Verses 17–31

I. The manner in which Paul preached the gospel, and the cross of Christ: *Not with the wisdom of words* (*v.* 17), *the enticing words of man's wisdom* (*ch.* ii. 4), lest *the cross of Christ should be of no effect,* lest the success should be ascribed to the force of art, and not of truth; not to the plain doctrine of a crucified Jesus, but to the powerful oratory of those who spread it. He preached a crucified Jesus in plain language, and told the people that that Jesus who was crucified at Jerusalem was the Son of God and Saviour of men, and that all who would be saved must repent of their sins, and believe in him. This truth needed no artificial dress; it shone out with the greatest majesty in its own light, and prevailed in the world by its divine authority, without any human helps. The plain preaching of a crucified Jesus was more powerful than all the oratory and philosophy of the heathen world.

II. We have the different effects of this preaching: To those who perish it is foolishness, *but to those who are saved it is the power of God, v.* 18. *It is to the Jews a stumbling-block, and to the Greeks foolishness; but unto those who are called, both Jews and Greeks, Christ the power of God and the wisdom of God, v.* 23, 24. 1. Christ crucified is a stumbling-block to the Jews. They despised him, and looked upon him as execrable, because he did not gratify them with a sign to their mind, though his divine power shone out in innumerable miracles. The Jews require a sign, *v.* 22. 2. He was to the Greeks foolishness. They laughed at the story of a crucified Saviour. They sought for wisdom. There was nothing in the plain doctrine of the cross to suit their taste: they entertained it therefore with scorn and contempt. What, hope to be saved by one that could not save himself! And trust in one who was condemned and crucified as a malefactor, a man of mean birth and poor condition in life! This was what the pride of human reason and learning could not relish. It is just with God to leave those to themselves who pour such proud contempt on divine wisdom and grace. 3. To those who are saved *he is the wisdom of God, and the power of God.* Those who are enlightened by the Spirit of God, discern more glorious discoveries of God's wisdom and power in the doctrine of Christ crucified than in all his other works.

III. We have here the triumphs of the cross over human wisdom, according to the ancient prophecy (Isa. xxix. 14): *I will destroy the wisdom of the wise, and bring to nothing the understanding of the prudent. Where is the wise? Where is the scribe? Where is the disputer of this world? Hath not God made foolish the wisdom of this world?* (v. 19, 20). All the valued learning of this world was confounded by the Christian revelation and the glorious triumphs of the cross. When God would save the world, he took a way by himself; and good reason, for *the world by wisdom knew not God*, v. 21. All the boasted science of the heathen world did not, could not, effectually bring home the world to God. Men were puffed up by their imaginary knowledge, and therefore *it pleased him, by the foolishness of preaching, to save those that believe.*

1. The thing preached was foolishness in the eyes of worldly-wise men. Our living through one who died, our being blessed by one who was made a curse, our being justified by one who was himself condemned, was all folly.

2. The manner of preaching the gospel was foolishness to them too. None of the famous men for wisdom or eloquence were employed. A few fishermen were called out, and sent upon this errand. These were commissioned to disciple the nations. The proud pretenders to learning and wisdom despised the doctrine for the sake of those who dispensed it. And yet *the foolishness of God is wiser than men*, v. 25. "*You see your calling, brethren, how that not many wise men after the flesh, not many mighty, not many noble, are called,*" v. 26, &c. There is a great deal of meanness and weakness in the outward appearance of our religion. Few of distinguished character in any of these respects were chosen for the work of the ministry. Not the wise men after the flesh. Not the mighty and noble. But God seeth not as man seeth. He hath chosen the foolish things of the world, the weak things of the world, the base and despicable things of the world, men of mean birth, of low rank, of no liberal education, to be the preachers of the gospel. He is a better judge than we what instruments and measures will best serve the purposes of his glory. Few of distinguished rank and character were called to be Christians. As the preachers were poor and mean, so generally were the converts. Few of the wise, and mighty, and noble, embraced the doctrine of the cross. Yet what glorious discoveries are there of divine wisdom in the whole scheme of the gospel.

IV. We have an account how admirably all is fitted, 1. To beat down the pride and vanity of men. God hath chosen *the foolish things of the world to confound the wise, the weak things of the world to confound the mighty, and base things, and things which are despised, and things which are not, to bring to nought (to abolish) things that are*; the conversion of the Gentiles was to open a way to the abolishing of that constitution upon which they valued themselves so much. It is common for the Jews to speak of the Gentiles under this character, as *things that are not.* The gospel is fitted to bring down the pride of both Jews and Greeks, *that no flesh should glory in his presence* (v. 29), that there might be no pretence for boasting. Divine wisdom alone had the contrivance of the method of redemption; divine grace alone revealed it, and made it known. It lay, in both respects, out of human reach. The gospel dispensation is a contrivance to humble man. 2. It is as admirably fitted to glorify God. The hand of the Lord went along with the preachers, and was mighty in the hearts of the hearers; and Jesus Christ was made both to ministers and Christians what was truly great and honourable. All we have we have from God as the fountain, and in and through Christ as the channel of conveyance. He is made of God to us *wisdom, righteousness, sanctification, and redemption* (v. 30). We are foolishness and he is made wisdom to us. We are guilty and he is made righteousness. We are depraved and corrupt; and he is made sanctification. We are in bonds, and he is made redemption to us. And what is designed in all is *that all flesh may glory in the Lord*, v. 31. Man is humbled, and God glorified by the whole scheme.

CHAPTER 2

The apostle, I. Reminds the Corinthians of the plain manner wherein he delivered the gospel to them, ver. 1–5. II. Shows them that he had communicated to them a treasure of the highest wisdom, such as could never have entered into the heart of man if it had not been revealed, nor can be received but by the light and influence of that Spirit who revealed it, ver. 6, to the end.

Verses 1–5

The apostle reminds the Corinthians how he acted when he first preached the gospel among them.

I. As to the matter or subject he tells us (v. 2), *He determined to know nothing among them but Jesus Christ and him crucified.* Christ, in his person and offices, is the sum and substance of the gospel, and ought to be the great subject of a gospel minister's preaching. Anyone that heard Paul preach found him to harp so continuously on this string that he would say he knew nothing but Christ and him crucified.

II. The manner wherein he preached Christ. Negatively. *He came not among them with excellency of speech or wisdom*, v. 1. *His speech and preaching were not with enticing words of man's wisdom*, v. 4. He did not set himself to captivate the ear by eloquent expressions, nor to entertain the fancy with lofty flights. Divine wisdom needed not to be set off with such human ornaments. Positively. He came among them *declaring the testimony of God*, v. 1. He published a divine revelation. Ornaments of speech and philosophical skill and argument could add no weight to what came recommended by such authority. *He was also among them in weakness and fear, and in much trembling;* and yet *his speech and preaching were in demonstration of the Spirit and of power*, v. 3, 4. His enemies in the church of Corinth spoke very contemptuously of him: *His bodily presence, say they, is weak, and his speech contemptible*, 2 Cor. x. 10. Possibly he had a little body, and a low voice; but, it is plain that he was no mean speaker. Nor did he want courage nor resolution, he was in *nothing terrified by his adversaries.* Yet he was no boaster. He did not proudly vaunt himself, like his opposers. None know the fear and trembling of faithful ministers; and a deep sense of their own weakness is the occasion of this fear and trembling. They know how insufficient they are. Yet he spoke with authority: *In the demonstration of the Spirit and of power.* He preached the truths of Christ in their native dress, with plainness of speech. He laid down the doctrine as the Spirit delivered it; and left the Spirit to demonstrate the truth of it.

III. Here is the end mentioned for which he preached Christ crucified: *That your faith should not stand in the wisdom of man, but the power of God* (v. 5)— that they might not be drawn by human motives, nor overcome by mere human arguments. When nothing but Christ crucified was plainly preached, the success must be entirely attributed to a divine power.

Verses 6–16

The apostle shows them that he had communicated to them a treasure of the truest and the highest wisdom: *We speak wisdom among those who are perfect* (v. 6). Those that receive the doctrine as divine, and have looked well into it, discover true wisdom in it. Though what we preach is foolishness to the world, it is wisdom to them. Those who are wise themselves are the only proper judges of what is wisdom: *not, indeed the wisdom of this world, nor of the princes of this world,* but *the wisdom of God in a mystery* (v. 6, 7); not worldly wisdom, but divine; not such as the men of this world could have discovered, nor such as worldly men, destitute of the Spirit of God, can receive. How different is the judgment of God from that of the world! The wisdom he teaches is of a quite different kind from what passes under that notion in the world. *But the wisdom of God in a mystery, the hidden wisdom of God.* The depth of which, now it is revealed, none but himself can fathom. Now, concerning this wisdom, observe,

I. The rise and origin of it: *It was ordained of God, before the world, to our glory,* v. 7. It was ordained of God; he had determined long ago to make it known; and that to our glory, *the glory of us,* either us apostles or us Christians. It was a great honour put upon the apostles, to be entrusted with the revelation of this wisdom. It was a great privilege for Christians to have this glorious wisdom discovered to them. And the wisdom of God taught by the gospel prepares for our everlasting glory and happiness in the world to come. What honour does he put on his saints!

II. The ignorance of the great men of the world about it: *Which none of the princes of this world knew* (v. 8). The Roman governor, and the rulers of the Jewish nation, seem to be the persons here chiefly meant. Jesus Christ is the Lord of glory, and the reason why he was hated was because he was not known. Had his crucifiers known him, known who and what he was, they would have withheld their impious hands. Thus he pleaded with his Father for their pardon: *Father, forgive them, for they know not what they do,* Luke xxiii. 34.

III. It is such wisdom as could not have been discovered without a revelation, according to what the prophet Isaiah says (Isa. lxiv. 4), *Eye hath not seen, nor ear heard, nor have entered into the heart of man the things which God hath prepared for those that love him*—for *him that waiteth for him,* that waiteth for his mercy, so the LXX. Waiting upon God is an evidence of love to him. There are things which God hath prepared for those that love him, and wait for him. But the apostle speaks here of the divine revelation under the gospel. The great truths of the gospel are things lying out of the sphere of human discovery: *Eye hath not seen, nor ear heard them, nor have they entered into the heart of man.* Were they objects of sense there had been no need of a revelation. But, lying out of the sphere of nature, we cannot discover them but by the light of revelation.

IV. By whom this wisdom is discovered to us: *God hath revealed them to us by his Spirit,* v. 10. The scripture is given by inspiration of God. And the apostles spoke by inspiration of the same Spirit. What he taught was revealed of God by his Spirit, *that Spirit that searches all things, yea, the deep things of God, and knows the things of God, as the spirit of a man that is in him knows the things of a man,* v. 11. A double argument in proof of the divinity of the Holy Ghost: 1. Omniscience is attributed to him: *He searches all things, even the deep things of God.* He enters into the very depths of God, penetrates into his most secret counsels. Now who can have such a thorough knowledge of God but God? 2. This allusion seems to imply that the Holy Spirit is as much in God as a man's mind is in himself. He is as much and as intimately one with God as the man's mind is with the man. The Spirit of God knows the things of God because he is one with God. Neither can we know the secret counsels and purposes of God till they are made known to us by his Holy Spirit. And it was by this Spirit that the apostles had received the *wisdom of God in a mystery.* "*Now we have received not the spirit of the world, but the Spirit which is of God, that we might know the things freely given to us of God* (v. 12). We have what we deliver in the name of God by inspiration from him; and it is by his gracious illumination that *we know the things freely given to us of God* unto salvation" —that is, "the great privileges of the gospel." Though these things are given to us, we cannot know them to any saving purpose till we have the Spirit.

V. In what manner this wisdom was taught: *Which things we speak, not in the words which man's wisdom teaches, but which the Holy Ghost teaches,* v. 13. They had received the wisdom they taught from the Spirit of God. Nor did they put a human dress on it, but plainly declared the doctrine of Christ, in terms also taught them by the Holy Spirit. The truths of God need no garnishing by human skill or eloquence, but look best in the words which the Holy Ghost teaches. *Comparing spiritual things with spiritual*—one part of revelation with another. Spiritual things, when brought together, will help to illustrate one another; but, if the principles of human art and science are to be made a test of revelation, we shall certainly judge amiss concerning it. The language of the Spirit of God is the most proper to convey his meaning.

VI. How this wisdom is received.

1. *The natural man receiveth not the things of God, for they are foolishness to him, neither can he know them, because they are spiritually discerned,* v. 14. Either, (1) The man under the power of corruption, and never yet illuminated by the Spirit of God. Men unsanctified receive not the things of God. The truths of God are foolishness to such a mind. Evil inclinations and wicked principles render the man unwilling to enter into the mind of God. It is the quickening beams of the Spirit of truth and holiness that must help the mind to discern their excellency. Thus the natural man cannot know them, because they are spiritually discerned. Or, (2) The natural man, that is, the wise man of the world (ch. i. 19, 20), one who hath the wisdom of the world, man's wisdom (ch. ii. 4–6), a man that would receive nothing by faith, nor own any need of supernatural assistance. This was very much the character of the philosophy and the Grecian learning and wisdom in that day. Such a man receives not the things of the Spirit of God. Revelation is not with him a principle of science; he looks upon it as the extravagant thought of some deluded dreamer. For that reason he can have no knowledge of things revealed, because they are only spiritually discerned.

2. *But he that is spiritual judgeth all things, yet he himself is judged of no man,* v. 15. He who is sanctified is capable of judging about matters of human wisdom, and has also a relish and savour of divine truths. It is the sanctified mind that must discern the real beauties of holiness; but they do not lose their power of discerning about common and natural things. The spiritual man may judge of all things, natural and supernatural, human and divine. But he himself is judged or discerned of no man. The carnal man knows no more of a spiritual man than he does of other spiritual things. The spiritual man does not lie open to his observation. *He that is spiritual* can judge both of common things and things divine. He does not lose the power of reasoning by founding his religion on revelation.

But *he himself is judged of no man*—can be judged, so as to be confuted, by no man. He who founds all his knowledge upon principles of science, and the mere light of reason, can never be a judge of the truth or falsehood of what is received by revelation. *For who hath known the mind of the Lord, that he may instruct him* (v. 16), that is, the *spiritual man*? Who can enter so far into the mind of God as to instruct him who has the Spirit of God, and is under his inspiration? Very few have known anything of the mind of God by a natural power. *But*, adds the apostle, *we have the mind of Christ*: and the mind of Christ is the mind of God. It is the great privilege of Christians that they have the mind of Christ.

CHAPTER 3

The apostle, I. Blames the Corinthians for their carnality and divisions, ver. 1–4. II. He instructs them how what was amiss among them might be rectified, by remembering, 1. That their ministers were no more than ministers, ver. 5. 2. That they carried on the same design, ver. 6–10. 3. That they built on one and the same foundation, ver. 11–15. III. He exhorts them to give due honour to their bodies (ver. 16, 17), and to humility, ver. 18–21. IV. And dehorts them from glorying in particular ministers, ver. 22, to the end.

Verses 1–4

Here, I. Paul blames the Corinthians for their weakness. Those who are renewed to a spiritual life may yet in many things be defective. The apostle tells *them he could not speak to them as unto spiritual* men, *but as unto carnal* men, *as to babes in Christ*, v. 1. It was but too evident they were much under the command of carnal and corrupt affections. They were still mere babes in Christ. They had received some of the first principles of Christianity, but had not grown up to maturity. He had communicated no more of the deep things of it to them. They could not bear such food; they needed to be fed with milk, not with meat, v. 2. It is the duty of a faithful minister of Christ to consult the capacities of his hearers and teach them as they can bear. And yet it is natural for babes to grow up to men; and babes in Christ should endeavour to grow in stature, and become men in Christ. Christians are utterly to blame who do not endeavour to grow in grace and knowledge.

II. He blames them for their carnality, and mentions their contention and discord about their ministers as evidence of it: *For you are yet carnal; for whereas there are among you envyings, and strifes, and divisions, are you not carnal, and walk as men?* (v. 3). *While one said, I am of Paul;* and *another, I am of Apollos*, v. 4. Contentions and quarrels about religion are sad evidences of remaining carnality. True religion makes men peaceable and not contentious. *Do not you walk as men?* It is to be lamented that many who should walk as Christians, above the common rate of men, do indeed walk as men, live and act too much like other men.

Verses 5–10

Here the apostle instructs them how to cure this humour.

I. By reminding them that the ministers about whom they contended were but ministers: *Who then is Paul, and who is Apollos, but ministers by whom you believed? Even as the Lord gave to every man*, v. 5, mere instruments used by the God of all grace. We should take care not to deify ministers, nor put them into the place of God. All the gifts and powers that even apostles discovered and exerted in the work of the ministry were from God. They were intended to manifest their mission and doctrine to be divine. *Paul had planted and Apollos had watered*, v. 6. Both were useful, one for one purpose, the other for another. Paul was fitted for planting work, and Apollos for watering work, but God gave the increase.

The success of the ministry must be derived from the divine blessing: *Neither he that planteth is anything, nor he that watereth, but God who giveth the increase*, v. 7. Even apostolical ministers can do nothing with efficacy and success unless God give the increase. Paul and Apollos are nothing at all in their own account, but God is all in all.

II. By representing to them the unanimity of Christ's ministers: *He that planteth and he that watereth are one* (v. 8), employed by one Master, busied in one work, in harmony with one another, however they may be set in opposition to each other by factious party-makers. All the faithful ministers of Christ are one in the great business and intention of their ministry. All such may expect a glorious recompence of their fidelity, and in proportion to it: *Every man shall receive his own reward, according to his own labour.* Those that work hardest shall fare best. Those that are most faithful shall have the greatest reward. *They are labourers with God, fellow-labourers* (v. 9). They are engaged in his business. They are working together with God, and he who knows their work will take care they do not labour in vain. The judgment of God is according to truth. He ever rewards in proportion to the diligence and faithfulness of his servants. They are always under his eye, employed in his husbandry and building; and therefore, to be sure, he will carefully look over them: "*You are God's husbandry, you are God's building;* and therefore are neither of Paul nor of Apollos. It is all for God that we have been doing among you." *According to the grace of God which is given unto me, as a wise master-builder, I have laid the foundation, and another buildeth thereon.* It was honourable to be a master-builder in the edifice of God; but it added to his character to be a wise one. But, though he gives himself such a character, it is not to gratify his own pride, but to magnify divine grace. He was a wise master-builder, but the grace of God made him such. Spiritual pride is abominable. But to take notice of the favours of God to promote our gratitude to him, and to speak of them to his honour, is but a proper expression of the duty and regard we owe him. Ministers should not be proud of their gifts or graces; but the better qualified they are for their work, and the more success they have in it, the more thankful should they be to God. *I have laid the foundation, and another buildeth thereon.* It was Paul that laid the foundation of a church among them. He would derogate from none that had done service among them, nor would he be robbed of his own honour and respect. Faithful ministers may and ought to have a concern for their own reputation. Their usefulness depends much upon it. *But let every man take heed how he buildeth thereon.* There may be very indifferent building on a good foundation. Nothing must be laid upon it but what the foundation will bear, and what is of a piece with it. Gold and dirt must not be mingled together. Ministers of Christ should take great care that they do not build their own fancies or false reasonings on the foundation of divine revelation.

Verses 11–15

Here the apostle informs us what foundation he had laid. *Other foundation can no man lay besides what is laid—even Jesus Christ.* The doctrine of our Saviour and his mediation is the principal doctrine of Christianity. It lies at the bottom, and is the foundation, of all the rest. But of those that hold the foundation there are two sorts:

I. Some build upon this foundation *gold, silver, and precious stones* (v. 12), namely, those who hold nothing but the *truth as it is in Jesus*, and preach nothing else. This is building well upon a good foundation.

II. Others *build wood, hay, and stubble*, on this foundation; that is, though they adhere to the foundation, they depart from the mind of Christ in many particulars, and build upon the good foundation what will not abide the test when the day of trial shall come. There is a time coming when a discovery will be made of what men have built on this foundation: *Every man's work shall be made manifest.* Every man's work shall be made manifest to himself, and made manifest to others, both those that have been misled by him and those that have escaped his errors. There is a day coming that will show us ourselves, and show us our actions in the true light, without covering or disguise: *For the day shall declare it* (that is, every man's work), *because it shall be revealed by fire; and the fire shall try every man's work, of what sort it is*, v. 13. The day shall declare and make it manifest, the last day, the great day of trial; see *ch.* iv. 5. There is a day coming that will distinguish one man from another, and one man's work from another's, as the fire distinguishes gold from dross, or metal that will bear the fire from other materials that will be consumed in it. Some men's works will *abide the trial.* It will appear that they not only held the foundation, but that they built regularly and well upon it. The foundation and the superstructure were all of a piece. And such a builder shall not, cannot fail of a reward. He will have praise and honour in that day, and eternal recompence after it. Fidelity in the ministers of Christ will meet with a full and ample reward in a future life. And, Lord, how great! how much exceeding their deserts! There are others *whose works shall be burnt* (v. 15). The great day will pluck off all disguises, and make things appear as they are: *He whose work shall be burnt will suffer loss.* If he have built upon the right foundation wood and hay and stubble, he will suffer loss, though he may in the general have been an honest and an upright Christian. This part of his work will be lost, though he himself may be saved. Those who hold the foundation of Christianity, though they build hay, wood, and stubble, upon it, may be saved. This may help to enlarge our charity. Nothing will damn men but wickedness. He shall be saved, *yet so as by fire*, saved out of the fire. God will have no mercy on their works, though he may pluck them as brands out of the burning.

Verses 16, 17

Here the apostle resumes his argument, founding it on his former allusion, *You are God's building*, v. 9. *Know you not that you are the temple of God, and the Spirit of God dwelleth in you? If any man defile* (corrupt and destroy) *the temple of God, him shall God destroy* (the same word is in the original in both clauses), *for the temple of God is holy, which temple you are.* It looks from other parts of the epistle (see *ch.* vi. 13-20), as if the false teachers among the Corinthians were not only loose livers, but taught licentious doctrines. Such doctrine was not to be reckoned among hay and stubble, which would be consumed while the person who laid them on the foundation escaped the burning. Those who spread principles of this sort would provoke God to destroy them. *Know you not that you are the temple of God, and that the Spirit of God dwelleth in you?* Christian churches are temples of God. He dwells among them by his Holy Spirit. Every Christian is a living temple of the living God. Christ by his Spirit dwells in all true believers. The temple was set apart from every common to a holy use, to the immediate service of God. So all Christians are separated from common uses, and set apart for God and his service. They are sacred to him. Christians are holy by profession, and should be pure and clean both in heart and conversation.

Verses 18–20

Here he prescribes humility for the remedy of the irregularities in the Church of Corinth: "*Let no man deceive himself* (v. 18). Do not be led away from the truth and simplicity of the gospel." We are in great danger of deceiving ourselves when we have too high an opinion of human wisdom and arts. But *he who seems to be wise must become a fool that he may be wise.* He must be sensible of his own ignorance, and lament it; he must distrust his own understanding, and not lean on it. The person who resigns his own understanding, that he may follow the instruction of God, is in the way to true and everlasting wisdom. He that has a low opinion of his own knowledge and powers will submit to better information; but the proud man, conceited of his own wisdom and understanding, will undertake to correct even divine wisdom itself. We must abase ourselves before God if we would be either truly wise or good: *For the wisdom of this world is foolishness with God*, v. 19. There can be no more comparison between his wisdom and ours than between his power and being and ours. There is no common measure by which to compare finite and infinite. And much more is the wisdom of man foolishness with God when set in competition with his. How justly does he despise, how easily can he baffle and confound it! *He knows the thoughts of the wise, that they are vain* (v. 20). God has a perfect knowledge of the thoughts of men, their most secret counsels and purposes. And he knows them to be vanity. And should not all this teach us modesty, and a deference to the wisdom of God? He who would be wise indeed must learn of God, and not set his own wisdom up in competition with God's.

Verses 21–23

An exhortation against over-valuing their teachers. They had an equal interest in all their ministers: *Therefore let no man glory in men* (v. 21)—forget that their ministers are men, or pay that deference to them that is due only to God, set them at the head of parties. The only way to avoid this mischief is to have a due sense of the common weakness of human understanding, and an entire deference to the wisdom of God. Ministers are not to be set up in competition with one another. They were appointed of Christ, for the common benefit of the church: "*Paul, and Apollos, and Cephas, are all yours.* All are to be valued and used for your own spiritual benefit." Upon this occasion also he gives in an inventory of the church's possessions, the spiritual riches of a true believer: "*All is yours.* Nay, the world itself is yours. *Life is yours*, that you may prepare for the life of heaven; and *death is yours*, that you may go to the possession of it. It is the kind messenger that will fetch you to your Father's house. *Things present* are yours, for your support on the road; *things to come* are yours, to enrich you for ever at your journey's end." All is ours, time and eternity, earth and heaven, life and death. But it must be remembered, at the same time, *that we are Christ's.* All things are ours, upon no other ground than our being Christ's. Those that would be safe for time, and happy to eternity, must be Christ's. *And Christ is God's.* He is the Christ of God, anointed of God, and commissioned by him. God in Christ reconciling a sinful world to himself, and shedding abroad the riches of his grace on a reconciled world, is the sum and substance of the gospel.

CHAPTER 4

The apostle, I. Directs them how to account of him and his fellow-ministers, ver. 1-6. II. He cautions them against pride and self-elation, ver. 7-13. III. He challenges their regard to him as their father in Christ, ver. 14-16. IV. He tells them of his having sent Timothy to them, and of his own purpose to come to them shortly, ver. 17 to the end.

Verses 1-6

I. The apostle challenges the respect due to him on account of his character and office. *Let a man so account of us as of the ministers of Christ, and stewards of the mysteries of God* (v. 1). In our opinion of ministers we should be careful to avoid extremes. Apostles themselves were, 1. Not to be overvalued, for they were ministers, not masters. They were servants of Christ, and no more. They had no authority to propagate their own fancies, but to spread Christian faith. 2. Apostles were not to be undervalued; for, they were ministers of Christ. They are not stewards of the common things of the world, but of divine mysteries. They did not set up for masters, but they deserved respect and esteem in this honourable service. Especially,

II. When they did their duty in it. *It is required in stewards that a man be found faithful* (v. 2), trustworthy. The stewards in Christ's family must appoint what he hath appointed. They must teach what he hath commanded. When they have the testimony of a good conscience, and the approbation of their Master, they must slight the opinions and censures of their fellow-servants: *But with me,* saith the apostle, *it is a small thing that I should be judged of you, or of man's judgment, v. 3.* Indeed, reputation and esteem among men are a good step towards usefulness in the ministry. But he that would make it his chief endeavour to please men would hardly approve himself a faithful servant of Christ, Gal. i. 10. He that would be faithful to Christ must despise the censures of men for his sake. The best of men are too apt to judge rashly, and harshly. It is a comfort that men are not to be our final judges. Nay, we are not thus to judge ourselves: "*Yea, I judge not myself. For though I know nothing by myself,* cannot charge myself with unfaithfulness, *yet am I not thereby justified; but he that judgeth me is the Lord.* It is his judgment that must determine me. Such I am as he shall find and judge me to be."

III. The apostle takes occasion hence to caution the Corinthians against censoriousness: *Therefore judge nothing before the time, until the Lord come, v. 5.* It is judging out of season, judging persons' future state, or the secret springs and principles of their actions. To judge in these cases is to assume the seat of God. How bold a sinner is the forward and severe censurer! How ill-timed and arrogant are his censures! But there is one who will judge the censurer, and those he censures. This should make them now cautious of judging others, and careful in judging themselves. There is a time coming when *the Lord will bring to light the hidden things of darkness, and make manifest the counsels of the hearts.* There is a day coming that will fetch men's secret sins into open day and discover the secrets of their hearts. The Lord Jesus Christ will manifest the counsels of the heart, of all hearts. The Lord Jesus Christ must have the knowledge of the counsels of the heart, else he could not make them manifest. We should be very careful how we censure others, when we have to do with a Judge from whom we cannot conceal ourselves. When he shall come to judge, *every man shall have praise of God. Every man,* that is, everyone qualified for it. Christians may well be patient under unjust censures, when they know such a day as this is coming. But how fearful should they be of loading any with reproaches now whom their common Judge shall hereafter commend.

IV. The apostle here lets us into the reason why he had used his own name and that of Apollos in this discourse of his. He had done *it in a figure,* and *he had done it for their sakes.* He chose rather to mention his own name, and the name of a faithful fellow-labourer, than the names of any heads of factions among them, that hereby he might avoid what would provoke. *That they might learn not to think of men above what is written, nor be puffed up for one against another* (v. 6). Apostles were not to be esteemed other than servants of Christ. We must be very careful not to transfer the honour and authority of the Master to his servant. We must not think of them above what is written. Pride commonly lies at the bottom of these quarrels. We shall not be puffed up for one against another if we remember that they are all instruments employed by God in his husbandry and building, and endowed by him with their various talents and qualifications.

Verses 7-13

Here the apostle improves the foregoing hint to a caution against pride and self-conceit.

I. He cautions them against pride; all the distinction made among them was owing to God: *Who maketh thee to differ? And what hast thou that thou didst not receive? (v. 7).* Here the apostle turns his discourse to the ministers who set themselves at the head of these factions. What had they to glory in, when all their peculiar gifts were from God? But it may be taken as a general maxim: We have no reason to be proud of our attainments, or performances; all that we have, or are, or do, that is good, is owing to the free and rich grace of God. Boasting is for ever excluded. Those who receive all should be proud of nothing. Due attention to our obligations to divine grace would cure us of arrogance and self-conceit.

II. He presses the duty of humility upon them by a very smart irony: "*You are full, you are rich, you have reigned as kings without us.* You have not only a sufficiency, but an affluence, of spiritual gifts; nay, you can make them the matter of your glory *without us.*" There is a very elegant gradation from sufficiency to wealth, and thence to royalty, to intimate how much the Corinthians were elated by the abundance of their wisdom and spiritual gifts. "*You have reigned as kings,*" says the apostle, "that is, in your own conceit; and *I would to God you did reign, that we also might reign with you.* I wish you had as much of the true glory of a Christian church upon you as you arrogate to yourselves." Those do not commonly know themselves best who think best of themselves. The Corinthians might have reigned, and the apostle with them, if they had not been blown up with an imaginary royalty. Pride is a great prejudice to our improvement. He is stopped from growing wiser or better who thinks himself at the height; not only full, but rich, nay, a king.

III. He comes to set forth his own circumstances and those of the other apostles, and compares them with theirs. 1. To set forth the case of the apostles: *For I think it hath pleased God to set forth us the apostles last, as it were appointed to death. For we are made a spectacle to the world, and to angels, and to men.* Never were any men in this world so hunted and worried. An allusion is made to some of the bloody spectacles in the Roman amphitheatres, where the victor did not escape with his life, but was only reserved for another combat, so that such wretched criminals might very properly be called *persons devoted or appointed to death.* They are said to be set forth last, because those who combated one another in the after-part of the day, were most exposed, being obliged to fight naked. The general meaning is that the apostles were exposed to continual danger of death. God had set them forth. The apostles were shown to manifest the power of divine grace, to confirm the truth of their mission and doctrine. These were ends worthy of God—noble views, fit to animate them to the combat. The office of an apostle was, as an honourable, so a hard and hazardous one: "*For we are made a spectacle to the world, and to angels, and to men, v. 9.* A show. Angels and men are witnesses to our persecutions, patience, and magnanimity. They all see that we suffer for our fidelity to Christ. How sharp our sufferings, and how patiently we endure them, by the power of divine grace. Ours is hard work, but honourable; it is hazardous, but glorious. The world cannot but see and wonder at our undaunted resolution, our invincible patience." 2. He compares his own case with that of the Corinthians: "*We are fools for Christ's sake, but you are wise in Christ; we are weak, but you are strong; you are honourable, but we are despised, v. 10.* We can pass for fools in the world, and be despised as such, so that the honour of the gospel may by this means be secured and displayed. *But you are wise in Christ.* You have the fame of being wise and learned Christians, and you do not a little value yourselves upon it. *We are weak, but you are strong.* We are suffering for Christ's sake when you are in easy and flourishing circumstances." All Christians are not alike exposed. The standard-bearers in an army are most struck at. So ministers in a time of persecution are commonly the first and greatest sufferers. Those are not always the greatest proficients in Christianity who think thus of themselves, or pass for such upon others. The Corinthians may think themselves, and be esteemed by others, as wiser and stronger men in Christ than the apostles themselves. But O! how gross is the mistake!

IV. He enters into some particularities of their sufferings: *Even to this present hour; we hunger and thirst, and are naked, and are buffeted, and have no certain dwelling-place, and labour, working with our own hands, v.* 11, 12. Nay, they were *made as the filth of the world, and the off-scouring of all things, v.* 13. Poor circumstances indeed, for the prime ministers of our Saviour's kingdom to have no house nor home, and to be destitute of food and raiment! But yet no poorer than his who had not *where to lay his head,* Luke ix. 58. But O glorious charity and devotion, that would carry them through all these hardships! How ardently did they love God. They thought they had a rich amends for all the outward good things they wanted, if they might but serve Christ and save souls. Nay, though they *were made the filth of the world, and the off-scouring of all things.* They were treated as men not fit to live. And apostles could not meet with better usage. They suffered in their persons and characters as the very worst and vilest men. Nay, as the *off-scouring of all things.* To be the off-scouring of anything is bad, but what is it to be the off-scouring of all things! How much did the apostles resemble their Master! They suffered for him, and they suffered after his example. Those may be very dear to God, and honourable in his esteem, whom men may think unworthy to live, and use and scorn as the very dirt and refuse of the world.

V. We have here the apostles' behaviour under all: *Being reviled, we bless; being persecuted, we suffer it; being defamed, we entreat, v.* 12, 13. They returned blessings for reproaches, and were patient under the sharpest persecutions. The disciples of Christ, and especially his ministers, should hold fast their integrity, and keep a good conscience. They must be content, with him and for him, to be despised and abused.

Verses 14–16

Here Paul challenges their regard to him as their father. 1. What he had written was not for their reproach, but admonition (v. 14): *I write not to shame you, but as my beloved children I warn you.* Reproofs that expose commonly do but exasperate, when those that kindly and affectionately warn are likely to reform; to lash like an enemy or executioner will provoke and render obstinate. To expose to open

shame is but the way to render shameless. 2. He shows them upon what foundation he called them his sons. He was their father: *for in Christ Jesus he had begotten them by the gospel, v.* 15. They were made Christians by his ministry. He was the instrument of their new birth, and therefore claimed the relation of a father to them. There commonly is, and always ought to be, an endeared affection between faithful ministers and those they beget in Christ Jesus through the gospel. They should love like parents and children. 3. We have here the special advice he urges on them: *Wherefore I beseech you be you followers of me, v.* 16. This he elsewhere explains and limits (ch. xi. 1): "*Be you followers of me, as I also am of Christ.* Follow me as far as I follow Christ. I would not have you be my disciples, but his." Ministers should so live that their people may live after their copy. They should guide them by their lives as well as their lips, go before them in the way to heaven, and not content themselves with pointing it out.

Verses 17–21

I. He tells them of his having sent Timothy to them, *to bring them into remembrance of his ways in Christ, as he taught everywhere in every church (v.* 17). Those who have had ever so good teaching are apt to forget and need to have their memories refreshed. He had not one doctrine for one place and people, and another for another. He therefore taught the same things in every church, and lived after the same manner in all times and places. The truth of Christ is one and invariable. What one apostle taught at one time and in one place, he taught at all times and in all places. To render their regard to Timothy the greater, he gives them his character. He was *his beloved son,* a spiritual child of his, as well as themselves. The children of one father should have one heart. But he adds, "*He is faithful in the Lord* trustworthy, as one that feared the Lord." It is a great commendation of any minister that he is faithful in the Lord; this must go a great way in procuring regard to his message.

II. He rebukes those who imagined he would not come to them, by letting them know this was his purpose: "*I will come to you shortly.*" But he adds, *if the Lord will.* All our purposes must be formed with a dependence on Providence.

III. He lets them know what would follow upon his coming to them: *I will know, not the speech of those that are puffed up, but the power, v.* 19. He would bring the great pretenders among them to a trial, would know what they were by the authority and efficacy of what they taught, and whether it was accompanied with divine influences and saving effects on the minds of men. For, adds he, *the kingdom of God is not in word, but in power,* the powerful influence of divine truth on the minds and manners of men. It is a good way in the general to judge of a preacher's doctrine, to see whether the effects of it upon men's hearts be truly divine. That is most likely to come from God which in its own nature is most fit, and in event is found to produce most likeness to God.

IV. He puts it to their choice how he should come among them, *whether with a rod or in love and the spirit of meekness (v.* 21); that is, according as they were they would find him. Stubborn offenders must be used with severity. In families, in Christian communities, paternal pity and tenderness, Christian love and compassion, will sometimes force the use of the rod. But this is far from being desirable, if it may be prevented. *Or in love and the spirit of meekness.* As much as if he had said, "Take warning, cease your unchristian feuds, and you shall find me as gentle and benign as you can wish. I had rather come and display the tenderness of a father among you than assert his authority." It is a happy temper in a minister to have the spirit of love and meekness predominant, and yet to maintain his just authority.

CHAPTER 5

The apostle, I. Blames them for their indulgence in the case of the incestuous person, ver. 1–6. II. He exhorts them to Christian purity, ver. 7, 8. And, III. Directs them to shun Christians who were guilty of any notorious and flagitious wickedness, ver. 9, to the end.

Verses 1–6

I. One of their community was guilty of fornication, *v*. 1. It was told in all places, to their dishonour. The heinous sins of professed Christians are quickly noted and noised abroad. We should walk circumspectly, for many eyes are upon us. This was not a common instance of fornication, but *such as was not so much as named among the Gentiles, that a man should have his father's wife*. Not that there were no such instances of incestuous marriages among the heathens; but, whenever they happened, they gave a shock to every man of virtue and probity among them. They could not mention them without detestation. Yet such a horrible wickedness was committed by one in the church of Corinth. The best churches are, in this state of imperfection, liable to very great corruptions.

II. He greatly blames them for their own conduct hereupon: *They were puffed up* (*v*. 2), *they gloried*. Perhaps on account of this very scandalous person. He might be a man very greatly esteemed. Instead of mourning for his fall, and their own reproach upon his account, they continued to applaud him and pride themselves in him. Pride or self-esteem often lies at the bottom of our immoderate esteem of others, and this makes us as blind to their faults as to our own. Or else some of the opposite party were puffed up. It is a very wicked thing to glory over the miscarriages and sins of others. Probably this was one effect of the divisions among them. The opposite party made their advantage of this scandalous lapse, and were glad of the opportunity. The sins of others should be our sorrow.

III. We have the apostle's direction to them how they should now proceed with this scandalous sinner. He would have him excommunicated and delivered to Satan (*v*. 3–5); *as absent in body, yet present in spirit, he had judged already as if he had been present*. He says this to let them know that, though he was at a distance, he did not pass an unrighteous sentence, nor judge without having as full cognizance of the case as if he had been on the spot. The apostle adds, *him who hath so done this deed*. He had so committed the evil as to heighten the guilt by the manner of doing it. In dealing with scandalous sinners, not only are they to be charged with the fact, but the aggravating circumstances of it. Paul had judged that *he should be delivered to Satan* (*v*. 5), and this was to be done *in the name of Christ*, and in a full assembly, where the apostle would be also present in spirit. Some think that this is to be understood of mere ordinary excommunication, and that delivering him to Satan is only meant of disowning him, that by this means he might be brought to repentance, and his flesh might be mortified. Those that live in sin, when they profess relation to Christ, belong to another master, and by excommunication should be delivered up to him; and this in the name of Christ. It was to be done also *when they were gathered together*. The more public the more solemn, and the more solemn the more likely to have a good effect on the offender. Others think the apostle is not to be understood of mere excommunication, but of a miraculous power or authority they had of delivering a scandalous sinner into the power of Satan, which is the meaning

of the *destruction of the flesh*. In this sense the destruction of the flesh has been a happy occasion of the salvation of the spirit. The great end of church-censures is the good of those who fall under them. It is that their spirit may be saved in the day of the Lord Jesus, *v*. 5.

IV. He hints the danger of contagion from this example: *Your glorying is not good. Know you not that a little leaven leaveneth the whole lump?* The bad example of a man in rank and reputation is very mischievous, spreads the contagion far and wide. A little leaven will quickly spread the ferment through a great lump.

Verses 7, 8

Here the apostle exhorts them to purity.

I. The advice itself, addressed either, 1. To the church in general; and so purging out the old leaven, that they might be a new lump, refers to the *putting away from themselves that wicked person*, *v*. 13. Or, 2. To each particular member of the church. And so it implies that they should purge themselves from all impurity of heart and life. Christians should be careful to keep themselves clean, as well as purge polluted members out of their society. They were also to purge themselves from malice and wickedness. This is leaven that sours the mind to a great degree. Christians should be careful to keep free from malice and mischief. Love is the very essence and life of the Christian religion. It is the fairest image of God, *for God is love* (1 John iv. 16), and therefore it is no wonder if it be the greatest beauty and ornament of a Christian.

II. The reason with which this advice is enforced: *For Christ our passover is sacrificed for us, v*. 7. The Jews, after they had killed the passover, kept the feast of unleavened bread. So must we; not for seven days only, but all our days. The whole life of a Christian must be a feast of unleavened bread. *He must purge out the old leaven, and keep the feast of unleavened bread of sincerity and truth*. He must be without guilt in his conduct towards God and man. The sacrifice of our Redeemer is the strongest argument with a gracious heart for purity and sincerity. Heinous evil could not be expiated but with the blood of the Son of God! And shall a Christian love the murderer of his Lord? God forbid.

Verses 9–13

Here the apostle advises them to shun the company of scandalous professors.

I. The advice itself: *I wrote to you in a letter not to company with fornicators, v*. 9. Some think this was an epistle written to them before, which is lost. Some think it is to be understood of this very epistle, but thought it needful now to be more particular. And therefore he tells them that if any man called a brother, and being a member of a Christian church, were *a fornicator, or covetous, or an idolater, or a railer*, that they should not *keep company with him, not so much as eat with such a one*. They were to avoid all familiarity with him; but, that they might shame him, and bring him to repentance, must disclaim and shun him. They may call themselves *brethren in Christ*, but they are not Christian brethren. They are only fit companions for their brethren in iniquity.

II. How he limits this advice. He does not forbid their eating nor conversing with the *fornicators of this world*, &c. They know no better. They profess no better. "*You must needs go out of the world* if you will have no conversation with such men. It is impossible, as long as you are in the world, but you must fall into their company. This cannot be wholly avoided."

III. The reason of this limitation is here assigned. Christians must have gone out of the world to avoid the company of loose heathens. But the dread of sin wears off by familiar converse with the wicked. Besides, heathens were such as Christians had nothing to do to judge and censure, and avoid upon a censure passed; for *they are without* (*v.* 12), and must be left to *God's judgment, v.* 13. But, as to members of the church, they are within, are professedly bound by the laws and rules of Christianity, and not only liable to the judgment of God, but to the censures of the fellow-members of the same body, when they transgress those rules. They are to be punished, by having this mark of disgrace put upon them, that they may be shamed, and, if possible, reclaimed thereby. Though the church has nothing to do with those without, it must endeavour to keep clear of the guilt and reproach of those within.

IV. How he applies the argument to the case before him: *"Therefore put away from among yourselves that wicked person, v.* 13. Cast him out of your fellowship."

CHAPTER 6

The apostle, I. Reproves them for going to law with one another, and bringing the cause before heathen judges, ver. 1–8. II. He takes occasion hence to warn them against many gross sins, ver. 9–11. III. And he vehemently dehorts them from fornication, ver. 12, to the end.

Verses 1–8

Here the apostle reproves them for going to law with one another before heathen judges for little matters; and therein blames all *vexatious law-suits.*

I. The fault he blames them for. *Brother went to law with brother* (*v.* 6). The bonds of fraternal love were broken through. Christians should not contend with one another, for they are brethren. They brought the matter before the heathen magistrates: *they went to law before the unjust, not before the saints* (*v.* 1), brought the controversy before unbelievers (*v.* 6). This tended much to the reproach of Christianity. And therefore, says the apostle, *"Dare any of you,* having a controversy with another, go to law before the unjust?" Here is at least an intimation that they went to law for trivial matters, for the apostle blames them that they did not suffer wrong rather than go to law (*v.* 7). Christians should be of a forgiving temper. And it is more for their honour to suffer small injuries than seem to be contentious.

II. He lays before them the aggravations of their fault: *Do you not know that the saints shall judge the world* (*v.* 2), *shall judge angels?* (*v.* 3). And are they unworthy *to judge the smallest matters, the things of this life?* It was a dishonour to their Christian character, as saints, for them to carry little matters, about the things of life, before heathen magistrates. When they were to judge the world, nay, to judge angels, it is unaccountable that they could not determine little controversies among one another. They are not partners in their Lord's commission, but see his proceeding against the wicked world, and approve it. Others understand it as condemning the world by their faith and practice. The first sense seems to be most natural. "Shall Christians have the honour to sit with the sovereign Judge, and are they not worthy to judge of the trifles about which you contend before heathen magistrates? Cannot they make up your mutual differences? Must you, about *the affairs of this life, set those to judge who are of no esteem in the church?"* i.e., *heathen* magistrates (so some read, and perhaps most properly, *v.* 4). "Must those be called in to judge in your controversies of whom you ought to entertain so low an opinion? Is not this shameful?" *v.* 5. Some who read it as our translators make it an ironical speech: "If you have such controversies depending, set those to judge who are of least esteem among yourselves. They are trifles not worth

contending about. *Bear and forbear,* and the men of meanest skill among you may end your quarrels. *I speak it to your shame," v.* 5.

III. He puts them on a method to remedy this fault. 1. By referring it to some to make it up: *"Is it so that there is no wise man among you, no one able to judge between his brethren?* (*v.* 5). You who value yourselves so much upon your wisdom and knowledge, is there none among you that has wisdom enough to judge in these differences? Must brethren quarrel, and the heathen magistrate judge, in a church so famous as yours for knowledge and wisdom?" 2. By suffering wrong rather than taking this method to right themselves: *It is utterly a fault among you to go to law in this matter:* it is always a fault of one side to go to law, except in a case where the title is indeed dubious, and there is a friendly agreement of both parties to refer it to the judgment of those learned in the law to decide it. *Should you not rather take wrong, rather suffer yourselves to be defrauded?* A Christian should rather put up with a little injury than tease himself, and provoke others, by a litigious contest. The peace of his own mind, and the calm of his neighbourhood, are of more worth than any victory in such a contest. But the apostle tells them they were so far from bearing injuries *that they actually did wrong, and defrauded, and that their brethren.* It is utterly a fault to wrong and defraud any; but it is an aggravation of this fault to defraud our Christian brethren.

Verses 9–11

Here he takes occasion to warn them against many heinous evils, to which they had been formerly addicted.

I. He puts it to them as a plain truth, that such sinners should not inherit the kingdom of God. The meanest among them must know this much, that *the unrighteous shall not inherit the kingdom of God* (*v.* 9). He specifies several sorts of sins: against the first and second commandments, as *idolaters*; against the seventh, as *adulterers, fornicators, effeminate,* and *Sodomites*; against the eighth, as *thieves* and *extortioners*; against the ninth, as *revilers*; and against the tenth, as *covetous* and *drunkards.* Heaven could never be intended for these. The scum of the earth are no ways fit to fill the heavenly mansions.

II. Yet he warns them against deceiving themselves: *Be not deceived.* Those who cannot but know the fore-mentioned truth are but too apt not to attend to it. Men are very much inclined to flatter themselves that they may live in sin and yet die in Christ, may lead the life of the devil's children and yet go to heaven with the children of God. But this is all a gross cheat. We cannot hope to sow to the flesh and yet reap everlasting life.

III. He puts them in mind what a change the gospel and grace of God had made in them: *Such were some of you* (*v.* 11). Some that are eminently good after their conversion have been as remarkably wicked before. *How glorious a change does grace make!* It changes the vilest of men into saints and the children of God. You are not what you were. *You are washed, you are sanctified, you are justified in the name of Christ, and by the Spirit of our God. The washing of regeneration* can purge away all guilt and defilement. *You are sanctified, you are justified.* None are cleansed from the guilt of sin, and reconciled to God through Christ, but those who are also sanctified by his Spirit. All who are made righteous in the sight of God are made holy by the grace of God.

Verses 12–20

The twelfth verse and former part of the thirteenth seem to relate to that early dispute among Christians about the distinction of meats, and yet to be prefatory to the caution that follows against fornication. The connection seems plain enough if we attend to the famous determination of the apostles, Acts xv, where the prohibition of certain foods was joined with that of fornication. Now some among the Corinthians seem ready to say, even in the case of fornication, *All things are lawful for me.* This pernicious conceit Paul here sets himself to oppose: he tells them that many things lawful in themselves were not expedient. Christians should not barely consider what is in itself lawful to be done, but what is fit for them to do. They should be very careful that by carrying this maxim too far they be not brought into bondage, either to a crafty deceiver or a carnal inclination. *All things are lawful for me,* says he, *but I will not be brought under the power of any, v.* 12. There is a liberty wherewith Christ has made us free, in which we must stand fast. But surely he would never carry this liberty so far as to put himself into the power of any bodily appetite. He would not become a glutton nor a drunkard. And much less would he abuse the maxim of lawful liberty to countenance the sin of fornication. He would not abuse this maxim about eating and drinking to encourage any intemperance, nor indulge a carnal appetite: *"Though meats are for the belly and the belly for meats (v.* 13). If I am in danger of being subjected to my belly and appetite, I will abstain. *But God shall destroy both it and them."* There is a time coming when the need and use of food shall be abolished. The transition to his arguments against fornication seems very natural: *But the body is not for fornication, but for the Lord, and the Lord for the body, v.* 13. Meats and the belly are for one another; not so fornication and the body.

I. The body is not for fornication, but for the Lord. This is the first argument he uses against this sin, for which the heathen inhabitants of Corinth were infamous. The *body is not for fornication;* it was never formed for any such purpose, *but for the Lord.* It is to be a member of Christ, and therefore must not be made the member of a harlot, *v.* 15. And *the Lord is for the body,* that is, as some think, Christ is to be Lord of the body, to have property in it and dominion over it. We must take care that we do not use what belongs to Christ as if it were our own, and much less to his dishonour.

II. Some understand this last passage, *The Lord is for the body,* thus: He is for its resurrection and glorification, according to what follows, *v.* 14, which is a second argument against this sin, the honour intended to be put on our bodies: *God hath both raised up our Lord, and will raise us up by his power (v.* 14). It will be an honour to our bodies that they will be raised. Let us not abuse those bodies by sin which, if they be kept pure, shall be made like to *Christ's glorious body.*

III. A third argument is the honour already put on them: *Know you not that your bodies are the members of Christ? v.* 15. If the soul be united to Christ by faith, the whole man is become a member of his mystical body. The body is in union with Christ as well as the soul. *But now,* says the apostle, *shall I take the members of Christ, and make them the members of a harlot? God forbid.* Would it not be dishonouring Christ, and dishonouring ourselves to the very last degree? What, make Christ's members the members of a harlot? God forbid. *Know you not that he who is joined to a harlot is one body* with hers? *For two,* says he, *shall be one flesh. But he who is joined to the Lord is one spirit, v.* 16, 17. He is joined to the Lord in union with Christ, and made partaker by faith of his Spirit. How shall one in so close a union with Christ as to be one spirit with him yet be so united to a harlot as to become one flesh with her? Can anything be more inconsistent with our profession or relation? It is no wonder

therefore that the apostle should say, *"Flee fornication" (v.* 18). *Other vices may be conquered in fight, this only by flight;* so speak many of the fathers.

IV. A fourth argument is that it is a sin against our own bodies. *Every sin that a man does is without the body; he that committeth fornication sinneth against his own body (v.* 18); every sin, that is, every external act of sin besides, is without the body. This sin is in a peculiar manner styled uncleanness, pollution, because no sin has so much external turpitude in it, especially in a Christian. He sins against his own body; he defiles it, he degrades it. He casts vile reproach on what his Redeemer has dignified to the last degree by taking it into union with himself. We should not make our present vile bodies more vile by sinning against them.

V. The fifth argument against this sin is that the bodies of Christians are *the temples of the Holy Ghost which is in them, and which they have of God, v.* 19. He that is joined to Christ is one spirit. He is yielded up to him and is hereupon possessed, and inhabited, by his Holy Spirit. This is the proper notion of a temple—a place where God dwells, and sacred to his use. Such temples real Christians are of the Holy Ghost. Hence we are not our own. We are possessed by and for God; nay, and this in virtue of a purchase made of us: *You are bought with a price.* In short, our bodies were made for God, they were purchased for him. And shall we desecrate his temple, and offer it up to the use and service of a harlot? The temple of the Holy Ghost must be kept holy. Our bodies must be kept as his whose they are, and fit for his use and residence.

VI. The apostle argues from the obligation we are under *to glorify God both with our body and spirit, which are his, v.* 20. He made both, he bought both. They must be kept as vessels fitted for our Master's use. We must look upon our whole selves as holy to the Lord. We are to honour *him with our bodies and spirits, which are his.* Body and spirit are to be kept clean, that God may be honoured by both. But God is dishonoured when either is defiled by so beastly a sin. Therefore flee fornication, nay, and every sin. Use your bodies for the glory and service of their Lord and Maker.

CHAPTER 7

The apostle answers some cases proposed to him by the Corinthians about marriage. I. He shows them that marriage was appointed as a remedy against fornication, ver. 1–9. II. He gives direction to those who are married to continue together, though they might have an unbelieving relative, unless the unbeliever would part, ver. 10–16. III. He shows them that becoming Christians does not change their external state, ver. 17–24. IV. He advises them, by reason of the present distress, to keep themselves unmarried; and shows them how worldly cares distract them in the service of God, ver. 25–35. V. He directs them in the disposal of their virgins, ver. 36–38. VI. And closes the chapter with advice to widows how to dispose of themselves in that state, ver. 39, 40.

Verses 1–9

The apostle comes now to answer some cases of conscience which the Corinthians had proposed to him. They were *things whereof they wrote to him, v.* 1. The apostle was as ready to resolve as they were to propose their doubts. In the former chapter, he warns them to avoid fornication; here he gives some directions about marriage.

I. It was good to abstain from marriage altogether: *It is good for a man not to touch a woman* (not to take her to wife), by good here not understanding what is so conformable to the mind of God as if to do otherwise were sin, an extreme into which many of the ancients have run in favour of celibacy and virginity. *At this juncture* it would be a convenience for Christians to keep themselves single, provided they can keep themselves chaste.

II. He informs them that marriage, and the comforts and satisfactions of that state, are by divine wisdom prescribed for preventing fornication (v. 2). And, when they are married, let each render the other *due benevolence* (v. 3). And therefore they should not defraud one another of the use of their bodies, except it be *with mutual consent* (v. 5) and *for a time* only, while they employ themselves in some extraordinary duties of religion, *or give themselves to fasting and prayer*. Seasons of deep humiliation require abstinence from lawful pleasures.

III. The apostle limits what he had said (v. 2). Paul did not bind every man to marry. No, he *could wish all men were as himself* (v. 7). Natural constitutions vary.

IV. He sums up (v. 9, 10): Marriage, with all its inconveniences, is much better than to burn with impure and lustful desires.

Verses 10–16

The apostle gives them direction in a case which must have been frequent in that age of the world, whether they were to live with heathen relatives in a married state. Moses's law permitted divorce. This might move a scruple in many minds.

I. Marriage, by Christ's command, is for life. The wife *must not depart from the husband* (v. 10), nor the *husband put away his wife*, v. 11. The Lord himself had forbidden such separations, Matt. v. 32. They must not separate for any other cause than what Christ allows. Husbands and wives should not quarrel at all, or should be quickly reconciled. They are bound to each other for life. They cannot throw off the burden, and therefore should set their shoulders to it, and endeavour to make it as light to each other as they can.

II. The case of such as had an unbelieving mate (v. 12). It does not mean that the apostle decided this case by his own wisdom. He closes this subject with a declaration to the contrary (v. 40).

1. The advice itself, that if an unbelieving husband or wife were pleased to dwell with a Christian relative, the other should not separate, v. 12, 13. The Christian calling did not dissolve the marriage covenant, but bind it the faster. Yet, if the unbelieving relative desert the believer, in such *a case a brother or sister is not in bondage* (v. 15). In such a case the deserted person must be free to marry again. The apostle says (v. 11), *If the woman depart from her husband let her remain unmarried*.

2. The reasons of this advice. (1) The relation is sanctified by the holiness of either party (v. 14). The apostle tells them that, though they were yoked with unbelievers, yet, if they themselves were holy, marriage was to them a holy state. He is sanctified for the wife's sake. She is sanctified for the husband's sake. *Else were your children unclean, but now are they holy* (v. 14). The children born to Christians, though married to unbelievers, are not to be reckoned as part of the world, but of the church. (2) Another reason is that *God hath called Christians to peace*, v. 15. (3) It is possible for the believing relative to be an instrument of the other's salvation (v. 16). Should a Christian desert a mate, when an opportunity offers to give the most glorious proof of love? Endeavour to save a soul. It is not impossible. *What know I but I may save his soul?* should move me to attempt it.

Verses 17–24

I. He lays down this rule in general—*as God hath distributed to everyone*. And again, *As the Lord hath called everyone, so let him walk*. In every state a man may live so as to be a credit to it. The apostle adds that this was a general rule, to be observed in all places: *So ordain I in all churches*.

II. He specifies particular cases: 1. That of circumcision. It matters not whether a man be a Jew or Gentile (v. 19). External observances without internal piety are as nothing. Therefore let every man abide *in the calling* (the state) *wherein he was called*, v. 20. 2. That of servitude and freedom. "Now," says the apostle, "*art thou called being a servant? Care not for it*. It is not inconsistent with thy duty, profession, or hopes, as a Christian. *Yet, if thou mayest be made free, use it rather*," v. 21. There are many conveniences in a state of freedom above that of servitude. But men's outward condition does neither hinder nor promote their acceptance with God. He who is a slave may yet be a Christian freeman; he who is a freeman may yet be Christ's servant. He must not be so the servant of men, that Christ's will is not obeyed, and regarded, more than his master's. The servants of Christ should be at the absolute command of no other master besides himself.

III. He sums up his advice (v. 24). He should quietly abide in the condition in which he is; and this he may well do, when he may abide therein with God. The presence and favour of God are not limited to any outward condition. He who is bound may have it as well as he who is free. The favour of God is not bound.

Verses 25–35

The apostle here gives directions to virgins how to act.

I. The manner wherein he introduces them, v. 25. Though Christ had before delivered no universal law about that matter, he now gives direction by an inspired apostle.

II. A state of celibacy was preferable. It is worded with modesty, but delivered with apostolical authority. Ministers do not lose their authority by prudent condescensions. The married state would bring more care and cumber along with it (v. 33, 34), and would therefore make persecution more terrible.

III. He is very careful to satisfy them that he does not condemn marriage, nor declare it unlawful. Though he says, "If thou *art loosed from a wife do not seek a wife*," yet he adds, "*If thou art bound to a wife, do not seek to be loosed*. It is thy duty to continue in the married relation." Duty must be done, and God trusted with events. Marrying is not in itself a sin, but marrying at that time was likely to add to the calamities of the times.

IV. General rules to all Christians to carry themselves with a holy indifference towards the world. Those *that had wives must be as though they had none*. They know not how soon they shall have none. Those that have children should be as though they had none. Those that are their comfort now may prove their greatest cross. *Those that weep must be as though they wept not*. Even in sorrow the heart may be joyful, and the end of our grief may be gladness. *Those that rejoice should be as though they rejoiced not*. Here is not their rest, nor are these things their portion. *Those that buy must be as though they possessed not*. Buying and possessing should not too much engage our minds. They hinder many people altogether from minding the better part. *Those that use this world as not abusing it*, v. 31. The world may be used, but must not be abused. It is abused when, instead of being oil to the wheels of our obedience, it is made fuel to lust. We must keep the world out of our hearts, that we may not abuse it when we have it in our hands.

V. Two reasons, v. 29. We have but little time to continue in this world. Therefore do not set your hearts on worldly enjoyments. Do not be overwhelmed with worldly cares and troubles (v. 31). It is not so much a world as the appearance of one. All is show with nothing solid in it; and it is transient show too, and will quickly be gone.

VI. The embarrassment of worldly cares, v. 32. A wise concern about worldly interests is a duty; but to be careful, full of care, is a sin. God must *be attended upon without distraction, v.* 35. But how is this possible when the mind is swallowed up of the cares of this life? This is the general maxim by which the apostle would have Christians govern themselves. In the application of it Christian prudence must direct. The unmarried man and woman mind the things of the Lord, that they may please the Lord, and be holy both in body and spirit, v. 32, 34. Not but the married person may be holy both in body and spirit too. It is the constant care of those in that relation to please each other. At that season, therefore, the apostle advises that those who were single should abstain from marriage. And the very same rule must determine persons for marriage, if in the unmarried state persons are likely to be more distracted in the service of God than if they were married. That condition of life should be chosen by the Christian in which it is most likely he will have the best helps, and the fewest hindrances, in the service of God.

Verses 36-38

Advice about the disposal of children in marriage. It was in that age reckoned a disgrace for a woman to remain unmarried past a certain number of years. "Now," says the apostle, "if any man thinks he behaves unhandsomely towards his daughter, he may use his pleasure. It is no sin in him to dispose of her to a suitable mate. But if a man has determined in himself to keep her a virgin with her consent, he does well."

Verses 39, 40

Advice to widows. Death only can annul the bond. Second marriages are not unlawful. She has such a liberty only with a limitation that *she marry in the Lord, v.* 40. It will be much more for the peace and quiet of such, and give them less hindrance in the service of God, to continue unmarried.

CHAPTER 8

Eating those things that had been sacrificed to idols. I. A caution against too high an esteem of their knowledge, ver. 1-3. II. The vanity of idols, ver. 4-6. III. Regard must be had to the weakness of Christian brethren, ver. 7, to the end.

Verses 1-3

Things that had been offered to idols. It was a custom among the heathens to make feasts of their sacrifices. These were usually kept in the temple, where the sacrifice was offered (v. 10). What remained, after all, belonged to the priests, who sometimes sold it in the markets. See *ch.* x. 25. It was accounted a very profane thing among them to eat at their private tables any meat whereof they had not first sacrificed. What should Christians do if anything that had been sacrificed should be set before them? What, if they should be invited to feast with them in their temples? The Corinthians had an opinion that even this might be done, because they knew an idol was nothing in the world, v. 4. Paul says, "We who abstain know as much of the vanity of idols, and that they are nothing. *Knowledge puffeth up, but charity edifieth,*" v. 1. The preference of charity to conceited knowledge. There is no evidence of ignorance more common than a conceit of knowledge. He that knows most best understands his own ignorance. He that imagines himself a knowing man has reason to suspect that he knows nothing aright. Much may be known when nothing is known to any good purpose. *But,* adds the apostle, *if any*

man love God, the same is known of God. He shall be approved of God; he will accept him and have pleasure in him. The charitable person is most likely to have God's favour. How much better is it to be approved of God than to have a vain opinion of ourselves!

Verses 4-6

The vanity of idols. Heathen idols have no divinity in them. They are merely imaginary gods. The gods of the heathen have nothing of real godhead belonging to them; for there is no other God but one. We Christians well know there is but one God. All things are of him, and we, and all things else, are for him. It is the great privilege of us Christians that we know the true God, and true Mediator between God and man.

Verses 7-13

Their inference was not just, namely, that therefore they might go into the idol-temple and feast there with their heathen neighbours. He does not so much insist upon the unlawfulness as the mischief such freedom might do to weaker Christians.

I. Every Christian man, at that time, was not so fully convinced that an idol was nothing. Weak Christians may be ignorant, or have but a confused knowledge of the greatest and plainest truths. *So their conscience, being weak, was defiled.* They were weak in their understanding, and, while they ate what was sacrificed contracted the guilt of idolatry and so greatly polluted themselves. We should be careful to do nothing that may occasion weak Christians to defile their consciences.

II. He tells them that mere eating and drinking had nothing in them virtuous nor criminal, v. 8. Some of the Corinthians made a merit of their eating what had been offered to idols, and that in their very temples too (v. 10), because it plainly showed that they thought the idols nothing. Eating this food, and forbearing that, have nothing in them to recommend a person to God.

III. He cautions them against abusing their liberty. Even upon the supposition that they had such power, they must be cautious how they use it; it might be a *stumbling-block to the weak* (v. 9). We must deny ourselves rather than occasion their stumbling, and endanger their souls (v. 11): *Through thy knowledge shall thy weak brother perish, for whom Christ died?* If he had such compassion as to die for them, we should have so much compassion for them as to deny ourselves, for their sakes. That man has very little of the spirit of the Redeemer who had rather his brother should perish than himself be abridged of his liberty. The hurt done to them Christ takes as done to himself, v. 12. Injuries done to Christians are injuries to Christ. Shall we be void of compassion for those to whom Christ has shown so much? Shall we sin against Christ who suffered for us?

IV. His own example (v. 13). We must not rigorously claim our own rights, to the hurt and ruin of a brother's soul, and so to the injury of our Redeemer, who died for him. And, if we must be so careful not to occasion other men's sins, how careful should we be to avoid sin ourselves!

CHAPTER 9

I. He asserts his apostolical mission and authority, ver. 1, 2. II. He claims a right to subsist by his ministry, ver. 3-14. III. He shows that he had willingly waived this privilege, ver. 15-18. IV. He specifies several other things, in which he had denied himself, ver. 19-23. And, V. Concludes his argument by showing what animated him to this course, ver. 24, to the end.

Verses 1, 2

Paul not only met with opposition from those without, but discouragement from those within.

Some among the Corinthians questioned, if they did not disown, his apostolical character. He asserts his apostolical mission and character: *Am I not an apostle? Have I not seen Jesus Christ our Lord?* To be a witness of his resurrection was one great branch of the apostolical charge. *"Am I not free?"* It was not because he had no right to live of the gospel that he maintained himself with his own hands. He offers the success of his ministry among them as a proof of his apostleship. He justly upbraids the Corinthians with their disrespect, v. 2. "You, above all others, should own my character, and not call it in question." It was aggravated ingratitude for this people to call in question his authority.

Verses 3–14

He proceeds to claim the rights belonging to his office.

I. These he states, v. 3–6.

II. He proceeds to prove his claim, from the common practice of mankind. Those who give themselves up to any way of business in the world expect to live out of it (v. 7–9). It is very reasonable for ministers to expect a livelihood out of their labours, v. 8. It is also consonant to the old law. But this law was not chiefly given out of God's regard to oxen, but to teach mankind that all due encouragement should be given to those who are labouring for our good—that the labourers should taste of the fruit of their labours, v. 10. Those that lay themselves out to do our souls good should not have their mouths muzzled. He argues from common equity. What they had sown was much better than they expected to reap. They had been instruments of conveying to them the greater spiritual blessings; and had they no claim to a share in their carnal things? What, get so much good by them, and yet grudge to do so little good to them! He argues from the maintenance they afforded others. Who has so just a claim as I from the church of Corinth? Who has laboured so much for your good? He renounced his right, rather than by claiming it he would hinder his success, but asserted his right lest his self-denial should prove prejudicial to the ministry. He argues from the old Jewish establishment: *"Do you not know that those who minister about holy things live of the things of the temple, and those who wait at the altar are partakers with the altar?* (v. 13). He asserts it to be the institution of Christ: *"Even so hath the Lord ordained that those who preach the gospel should live of the gospel"* (v. 14). But those transgress an appointment of Christ who deny or withhold it.

Verses 15–18

I. He had neglected to claim his right in times past, v. 15. Nor did he write this to make his claim now.

II. He would not have his glorying made void, v. 15, to have it justly said that he preferred his wages to his work. It is the glory of a minister to deny himself, that he may serve Christ, and save souls.

III. This self-denial yielded him much more content than his preaching did, v. 16. This is a duty expressly bound upon him. Those who are set apart to the office of the ministry have it in charge to preach the gospel. Woe be to them if they do not. But it is not given in charge to all, nor any preacher of the gospel, to do his work gratis. It may be his duty to preach under some circumstances, without receiving a maintenance for it; but he has a right to it. It may sometimes be his duty to insist on his maintenance for so doing, and whenever he forbears he parts with his right.

IV. *If I do this thing willingly, I have a reward.* Indeed, it is willing service only that is capable of reward from God. Leave the heart out of our duties,

and God abhors them: they are but the carcasses, without the life and spirit, of religion. Ministers have a dispensation of the gospel committed to them. Christ's willing servants shall not fail of a recompence, and his slothful and unwilling servants shall all be called to an account.

V. *What is my reward then?* (v. 18). *That when I preach the gospel I may make it without charge, that I abuse not my power in the gospel.* It is an abuse of power to employ it against the very ends for which it is given. And the apostle would never use his so as to frustrate the ends of it, but would willingly and cheerfully deny himself.

Verses 19–23

I. He asserts his liberty (v. 19). He was free-born, a citizen of Rome. He was in bondage to none, *yet he made himself a servant to all, that he might gain the more.* He made himself a servant, that they might be made free.

II. He accommodated himself to all sorts of people. *To the Jews, and those under the law, he became a Jew.* He submitted to it, that he might prevail with them and win them over to Christ. *To those that are without the law, as without law,* that is, to the Gentiles. In innocent things he could comply with people's usages for their advantage. He behaved among them as one that was not under the bondage of the Jewish laws. He did not stand on privileges and punctilios. *To the weak he became as weak, that he might gain the weak,* v. 22. He did not despise nor judge them, but became as one of them. He denied himself for their sakes, that he might gain their souls. The rights of God he could not give up, but he might resign his own, and he very often did so for the good of others.

III. His reason for acting in this manner (v. 23): *This I do for the gospel's sake, and that I may be partaker thereof with you.* A heart warmed with zeal for God, and breathing after the salvation of men, will not plead and insist upon rights and privileges.

Verses 24–27

He had a glorious prize, an incorruptible crown, in view. *"Know you not that those who run in a race run all, but one obtaineth the prize?"* (v. 24).

I. It is quite otherwise in the Christian race than in your races; where only one wins the prize. You may all run so as to obtain. You cannot fail if you run well. And it is a glorious contest who shall get first to heaven.

II. He directs them in their course, by setting more fully to view his own example. 1. Those that ran in their games were kept to a set diet, v. 23. "The fighters and wrestlers in your exercises are kept to strict diet and discipline. They use a very spare diet and deny themselves much; so do I; so should you." 2. They were not only temperate, but inured themselves to hardships. Those who fought with one another prepared themselves by beating the air, as the apostle calls it. There is no room for any such exercise in the Christian warfare. Christians are ever in close combat. One enemy the apostle here mentions, namely, the body; this must be kept under, beaten black and blue.

III. The apostle presses this advice by proper arguments drawn from the same contenders. Those who conquered in these games were crowned only with the withering leaves or boughs of trees, of olive, bays, or laurel. But Christians have an incorruptible crown in view. Can they expose their bodies to so much hardship who have no more in view than the trifling huzzas of a giddy multitude, or a crown of leaves? And shall not Christians, who hope for a crown of glory, exert themselves in beating down their fleshly inclinations? All run, but one receives the prize, *v.* 24. But the Christian racer is at no such uncertainty. Everyone may run here so as to obtain; but then he must keep to the path of duty prescribed, which is the meaning of *running not as uncertainly, v.* 26. And would the Grecian racers exert themselves to the very last, when one only could win? And shall not Christians be much more vigorous when all are sure of a crown? The danger of yielding to fleshly inclinations: *I keep my body under, lest by any means, when I have preached to others, I myself should be a castaway* (*v.* 27), *rejected,* one to whom the *judge* or *umpire,* will not decree the crown. A preacher of salvation may yet miss it. He may show others the way to heaven, and never get thither himself. A holy fear of himself was necessary to preserve the fidelity of an apostle; and how much more necessary is it to our preservation?

CHAPTER 10

The apostle, I. Warns the Corinthians against security, by the example of the Jews, ver. 1-14. II. He resumes his former argument (*ch.* 8), about eating things offered to idols, ver. 15-22. III. They might buy such flesh in the markets, or eat it at the table of heathen acquaintances, without asking any questions. Yet liberty of this kind must be used with a due regard to weak consciences, ver. 23, to the end.

Verses 1–5

He sets before them the example of the Jews. They enjoyed great privileges, but they fell under very grievous punishments.

I. The providence of God towards them, and what happened to them ought to be warnings to us.

II. He specifies some of their privileges. 1. Their deliverance from Egypt. They were miraculously conducted through the Red Sea, where the pursuing Egyptians were drowned: it was a lane to them, but a grave to these. They were very dear to God when he would work such miracles for their deliverance. 2. They had sacraments like ours. *They were all baptized unto Moses in the cloud, and in the sea* (*v.* 2). *They did all eat of the same spiritual meat, and drink of the same spiritual drink.* These were great privileges. One would think that this should have saved them. Yet was it otherwise, *v.* 5. Men may enjoy many and great spiritual privileges in this world, and yet come short of eternal life. Let none presume upon their great privileges.

Verses 6–14

I. Several of their sins are specified as cautions to us. We should shun inordinate desires after carnal objects, *v.* 6. God fed them with manna, but they must have flesh, Num. xi. 4. Carnal desires get head by indulgence. If once they prevail, and bear sway in us, we know not whither they will carry us. He warns against idolatry (*v.* 7). The apostle is speaking to the case of the Corinthians, who were tempted to feast on the heathen sacrifices. He cautions against fornication, a sin to which the inhabitants of Corinth were in a peculiar manner addicted. How needful was a caution against fornication to those who lived in so corrupt a city! Let us fear the sins of Israel, if we would shun their plagues. He warns us against *tempting Christ* (*as some of them tempted, and were destroyed of serpents, v.* 9), or provoking him to jealousy, *v.* 22. For which reason God sent fiery serpents among them (Num. xxi. 5, 6). And it is but just to fear that such as tempt Christ under the present dispensation will be left by him in the power of the old serpent. He warns against murmuring (*v.* 10). When they met with discouragements in the way to Canaan, they were very apt to fly in the face of their leaders. Something like this seems to have been the case of the Corinthians; they murmured against Paul, and in him against Christ.

II. The apostle subjoins to these particular cautions a more general one (*v.* 11). Their sins against God were typical of the infidelity of many under the gospel. God's judgments on them were types of spiritual judgments now. Their history was written, to be a standing monitor to the church. Nothing in scripture is written in vain, and it is our wisdom and duty to receive instruction from it. A caution (*v.* 12). Others have fallen, and so may we. God has not promised to keep us from falling, if we do not look to ourselves: his protection supposes our own care.

III. He adds a word of comfort, *v.* 13. Though it is displeasing to God for us to presume, it is not pleasing to him for us to despair. Either our trials will be proportioned to our strength, or strength will be supplied in proportion to our temptations. Others have the like temptations; what they bear up under, and break through, we may also. Men may be false, and the world may be false; but God is faithful, and our strength and security are in him. He is wise as well as faithful. He knows what we can bear. He will take care that we be not overcome, if we rely upon him. *He will make a way to escape.* There is no valley so dark but he can find a way through it.

IV. *"Flee idolatry;* shun it." Idolatry is the most heinous affront to the true God. "Seeing you have such encouragement to trust God, be not shaken by any discouragements. God will help you in your trials, and help you out of them." We cannot fall by a temptation if we cleave fast to him.

Verses 15–22

The apostle urges the general caution against idolatry.

I. An appeal to their own reason and judgment: "*I speak to wise men, judge you what I say,*" *v.* 15.

II. He lays down his argument from the Lord's supper. Is not this sacred rite a token whereby we professedly hold communion with Christ? Thus to partake of the Lord's table is to profess ourselves his guests and covenant people; and this in conjunction with all true Christians, with whom we have communion also in this ordinance (*v.* 17).

III. He confirms this from the Jewish worship and customs. Those who were admitted to eat of the offerings were reckoned to partake of the sacrifice itself, and therefore surely to worship God.

IV. He applies this to the argument against feasting with idolaters on their sacrifices. An idol was nothing. What was sacrificed to idols was nothing. But the eating of it as a part of a heathen sacrifice was, (1) A partaking with them in their idolatry, just as he who eats the Lord's supper is supposed to partake in the Christian sacrifice. "Therefore do not feast on their sacrifices. I would not have you be in communion with devils." (2) It was a virtual renouncing of Christianity, *v.* 21. Communion with Christ, and communion with devils, could never be had at once. One must be renounced, if the other was maintained. How much reason have we to look to it that every sin and idol be renounced by us, when we eat and drink at the Lord's table.

V. He warns them that God is a jealous God (*v.* 22). Those who have fellowship with other gods provoke him to jealousy. And, before this be done, persons should consider whether they are stronger than he. It is a dangerous thing to provoke God's anger, unless we could withstand his power. Shall we rouse almighty wrath? Are we a match for God?

Verses 23–33

In what instances Christians might lawfully eat what had been sacrificed to idols.

I. That may be lawful which is not expedient, which will not edify. He must be concerned not to hurt his neighbour, nay, he must be concerned to promote his welfare. Those who allow themselves in everything not plainly sinful in itself will often run into what is evil by accident. The welfare of others, as well as our own convenience, must be consulted in many things we do.

II. He tells them that what was *sold in the shambles they might eat without asking questions.* They need not be so scrupulous as to ask the butcher whether the meat he sold had been offered to an idol? It was there sold as common food, and as such might be bought and used; *for the earth is the Lord's, and the fulness thereof* (v. 26).

III. If they were invited by any heathen acquaintances to a feast, *they might go, and eat what was set before them, without asking questions* (v. 27). There is a civility owing even to infidels and heathens. Anything fit to be eaten, that was set before them, they might lawfully eat. It is to be understood of civil feasting, not religious. At a common feast they might expect common food.

IV. Yet, if any should say it was a thing that had been offered to idols, they should refrain. They should refrain for his sake who suggested this to them, and for conscience' sake, out of regard to conscience. Christians should be very cautious of doing what may thus prejudice the consciences of others.

V. He urges them to refrain where they will give offence. Christians should take care not to use their liberty to the hurt of others, nor their own reproach.

VI. The apostle takes occasion from this discourse to lay down a general rule for Christians' conduct (v. 31, 32). In all we do, we should aim at the glory of God. And therefore nothing should be done by us to offend any, *whether Jew, or Gentile, or the church,* v. 32. Our own humour and appetite must not determine our practice, but the honour of God and the good and edification of the church.

VII. He presses all upon them by his own example, v. 33. A preacher may press his advice home with boldness and authority when he can enforce it with his own example. And it is highly commendable in a minister to neglect his own advantage that he may promote the salvation of his hearers.

Chapter 11

The apostle blames, and endeavours to rectify, some manifest disorders in the church of Corinth; as, I. The misconduct of their women in the public assembly, who laid by their veils. This behaviour he reprehends, asserts the superiority of the husband, yet so as to remind the husband that both were made for mutual help and comfort, ver. 1–16. II. He blames them for their discord, and contempt of the poor, at the Lord's supper, ver. 17–22. III. He sets before them the intentions of this holy institution, ver. 23, to the end.

Verses 1–16

Be ye followers of me, as I also am of Christ (v. 1). It is plain that Paul not only preached such doctrine as they ought to believe, but led such a life as they ought to imitate. Ministers are likely to preach most to the purpose when they can press their hearers to follow their example. Yet would not Paul be followed blindly. He would be followed himself no further than he followed Christ. Christ's pattern is a copy without a blot; so is no man's else. He passes next to reprehend an indecency among them, of which the women were more especially guilty.

I. A commendation of what was praiseworthy in them (v. 2). When we reprove what is amiss in any, it is very prudent and fit to commend what is good in them.

II. The superiority of the man over the woman. Christ is at the head of mankind. In this high office he has a superior, God being his head. And as God is the head of Christ, and Christ the head of the whole human kind, so the man is the head of the two sexes: and the woman should be in subjection and not usurp the man's place. The women of the church of Corinth prayed and prophesied even in their assemblies, v. 5. It is indeed an apostolical canon, that the women *should keep silence in the churches* (ch. xiv. 34; 1 Tim. ii. 12). The apostle does not in this place prohibit the thing, but reprehend the manner of doing it. The manner of doing a thing enters into the morality of it. We must not only be concerned to do good, but that the good we do be well done.

III. The thing he reprehends is the woman's praying or prophesying uncovered, or the man's doing either covered, v. 4, 5.

IV. The reasons on which he grounds his reprehension. *The man that prays or prophesies with his head covered dishonoureth his head,* namely, Christ, the head of every man (v. 3). *The woman who prays or prophesies with her head uncovered dishonoureth her head,* namely, the man, v. 3. She appears in the dress of her superior, and throws off the token of her subjection. The sexes should not affect to change places. The woman should keep to the rank God has chosen for her. *The man is the image and glory of God.* It is the man who is set at the head of this lower creation, and therein he bears the resemblance of God. The woman, on the other hand, *is the glory of the man* (v. 7). She is the image of God, inasmuch as she is the image of the man, v. 8. *The woman was made for the man, and not the man for the woman.* And she should do nothing that looks like an affectation of equality. *She ought to have power on her head, because of the angels.* Power, that is, a veil, the token that she is under the power of her husband. Jews and Christians have had an opinion that these ministering spirits are present in their assemblies.

V. A caution lest the inference be carried too far (v. 11, 12). They were made to be a mutual comfort and blessing, not one a slave and the other a tyrant. As it is the will of God that the woman know her place, so it is his will also that the man abuse not his power.

VI. The woman's hair is a natural covering; to wear it long is a glory to her; but for a man to have long hair is a token of softness and effeminacy.

VII. He sums up all by referring to the usages and customs of the churches, v. 16. The common practice of the churches is what he would have them govern themselves by.

Verses 17–22

The apostle sharply rebukes them for much greater disorders in their partaking of the Lord's supper.

I. Such scandalous disorders as they were guilty of, called for a sharp reprehension. The ordinances of Christ, if they do not make us better, will be very apt to make us worse; if they do not melt and mend, they will harden.

II. His charge against them. Upon coming together, they fell into *divisions.* They fell a quarrelling with one another. The apostle had heard a report of the Corinthians' divisions, and he tells them he had too much reason to believe it. There must be heresies also. No marvel there should be breaches of Christian love in the churches, when such offences will come. Such offences must come. God permits them, that those who are approved (such honest hearts as will bear the trial) may be set to view, and appear faithful. The wisdom of God can make the wickedness of others a foil to the integrity of the saints. He charges them with scandalous disorder, v. 21. They would not stay for one another. Thus some wanted, while others had more than enough. The poor were deprived of the food prepared for them, and the rich turned a feast of charity into a debauch.

III. The apostle lays the blame of this conduct closely on them. 1. Their conduct perfectly destroyed the purpose and use of such an institution, *v.* 20. They might as well have stayed away. 2. Their conduct carried in it a contempt of the church, *v.* 22. If they had a mind to feast, they might do it at home in their own houses. Religious feasts should be attended religiously.

Verses 23–34

The apostle sets the sacred institution here to view.

I. He tells us how he came by the knowledge of it. *He had received from the Lord what he delivered to them, v.* 23.

II. He gives us a more particular account of the institution than we meet with elsewhere.

1. The author—our Lord Jesus Christ.

2. The time of the institution: *It was the very night wherein he was betrayed;* just as he was entering on his sufferings which are therein to be commemorated.

3. The institution itself. Our Saviour took bread, and when he had given thanks, *he broke, and said, Take, eat; this is my body, broken for you; this do in remembrance of me. And in like manner he took the cup, when he had supped, saying, This cup is the New Testament in my blood; this do, as oft as you drink it, in remembrance of me, v.* 24, 25.

(1) The materials of this sacrament, [1] The visible signs; these are bread and the cup. What is eaten is called bread, though it is at the same time said to be *the body of the Lord.* Bread and the cup are both made use of, because it is a holy feast. The cup is put for what was in it, without once specifying what the liquor was. [2] The things signified by these outward signs: they are Christ's body and blood, his body broken, his blood shed.

(2) The sacramental actions. Our Saviour did, at the institution, deliver his body and blood, with all the benefits procured by his death, to his disciples, and continues to do the same every time the ordinance is administered to true believers. They are to take him as their Lord and life, yield themselves up to him, and live upon him.

(3) An account of the ends of this institution. It was appointed to be done *in remembrance of Christ,* to keep fresh in our minds his dying for us, as well as to remember an absent friend, even Christ interceding for us. The motto on this ordinance, and the very meaning of it, is, *When this you see, remember me.* It was *to show forth Christ's death.* It is not barely in remembrance of Christ, but to commemorate his glorious condescension and grace in our redemption. We own before the world, by this very service, that we are the disciples of Christ, who trust in him alone for salvation and acceptance with God.

(4) It should be frequent. Our bodily meals return often. And it is fit that this spiritual diet should be taken often too. It must be perpetual. It is to be celebrated *till the Lord shall come.* The Lord's supper is not a temporary, but a standing and perpetual ordinance.

III. The danger of receiving unworthily and using it to the purposes of feasting and faction. 1. They shall *be guilty of the body and blood of the Lord (v.* 27). Instead of being cleansed by his blood, they are guilty of his blood. 2. *They eat and drink judgment to themselves, v.* 29. They provoke God, and are likely to bring down punishment on themselves. But fearful believers should not be discouraged from attending at this holy ordinance by the sound of these words. The Holy Spirit never indited this to deter serious Christians from their duty, though the devil has often made this advantage of it, and robbed good Christians of their choicest comforts. The Corinthians came to the Lord's table *not discerning the Lord's body*—not making a distinction between that and common food. *For this cause many are weak and sickly among you, and many sleep.* Even those who were thus punished were in a state of favour with God: *They were chastened of the Lord, that they should not be condemned with the world, v.* 32. He frequently punishes those whom he tenderly loves. It is kindness to use the rod to prevent the child's ruin. They were punished by him out of fatherly goodwill, punished now that they might not perish for ever.

IV. The duty of those who would come to the Lord's table (*v.* 28). Such self-examination is necessary to a right attendance at this holy ordinance. Those should have the wedding-garment on who would be welcome at this marriage-feast—grace in habit, and grace in exercise, *v.* 31. To be exact and severe on ourselves is the most proper way not to fall under the just severity of our heavenly Father. We must not judge others, lest we be judged (Matt. vii. 1); but we must judge ourselves, to prevent our being judged and condemned by God.

V. A caution against the irregularities of which they were guilty (*v.* 33, 34). They were to eat for hunger and pleasure only at home. Our holy duties, through our own abuse, may prove matter of condemnation. Holy things are to be used in a holy manner, or else they are profaned.

CHAPTER 12

The apostle, I. Considers the case of spiritual gifts. He considers their original, that they are from God; their variety and use, ver. 1–11. II. He illustrates this by an allusion to a human body, ver. 12–26. III. He tells us that the church is the body of Christ, ver. 27–30. IV. Closes with an exhortation to seek somewhat more beneficial than these gifts, ver. 31.

Verses 1–11

Of spiritual gifts. Where grace is given it is for the salvation of those who have it. Gifts are bestowed for the advantage and salvation of others. And there may be great gifts where there is not a dram of grace. This church was rich in gifts, but there were many things scandalously out of order in it.

I. Gifts come from God, and are to be used for him.

II. He puts them in mind of the sad state out of which they had been recovered, *v.* 2. Their former character: they *were Gentiles.* Not God's peculiar people, but of the nations whom he had in a manner abandoned. What a change was here! Christian Corinthians were once Gentiles. It is of great use to the Christian, and a proper consideration to stir him up both to duty and thankfulness, to think what once he was. The conduct they were under: *Carried away to these dumb idols, even as you were led.* Miserable abjectness of mind! And those who despised these gross conceptions of the vulgar yet countenanced them by their practice. Could the Spirit of God be among such stupid idolaters?

III. How they might discern those gifts that were from the Spirit of God: *No man, speaking by the Spirit, calls Jesus accursed.* Thus did both Jews and Gentiles: they blasphemed him as an imposter, and execrated his name. None could act under the influence, nor by the power of the Spirit of God, who disowned and blasphemed Christ: for the Spirit of God could never so far contradict itself as to declare him accursed. No man can call Christ *Lord,* with a believing dependence upon him, unless that faith be wrought by the Holy Ghost.

IV. The same giver may bestow various gifts, *v.* 4. There are different offices, and officers to discharge them (see *v.* 28–30), but the same Lord, who appointed all, *v.* 6. *There are diversities of operations (v.* 10), *but it is the same God that worketh all in all.* However different they may be in themselves, in this they agree; all are from God. And several of the kinds are here specified, *v.* 8–10. To one was given the *word of wisdom*; a knowledge of the mysteries of the gospel, and ability to explain them. *To another the word of knowledge, by the same Spirit;* that is, say some, the knowledge of mysteries (*ch.* ii. 13): say others, a skill and readiness to give advice and counsel in perplexed cases. *To another faith, by the same Spirit*, whereby they were enabled to trust God in any emergency. *To another the gift of healing, by the same Spirit;* that is, healing the sick. *To another the working of miracles. To another prophecy;* to explain scripture by a peculiar gift of the Spirit. *To another the discerning of spirits*, power to distinguish between true and false prophets. *To another divers kinds of tongues*, or ability to speak languages by inspiration. *To another the interpretation of tongues*, or ability to render foreign languages.

V. The end for which these gifts were bestowed, *v.* 7. They were not distributed for the advantage of those who had them, but for the benefit of the church. Whatever gifts God confers on any man, he confers them that he may do good with them. They are a trust put into his hands. They are not given for show, but for service.

VI. *All these worketh one and the same Spirit, dividing to every man as he will.* Shall not the Spirit of God do what he will with his own? It is not as men will, nor as they may think fit, but as the Spirit pleases.

Verses 12–26

The apostle puts the gifted men among the Corinthians in mind of their duty, by comparing the church of Christ to a human body.

I. One body may have many members, the many members of the same body make but one body (*v.* 12). All the members are *baptized into the same body, and made to drink of the same Spirit*, *v.* 13. Christians become members of this body by baptism: they are baptized into one body. And by communion at the other ordinance we are sustained by drinking into one Spirit. It is baptism by the Spirit, it is internal renovation and drinking into one Spirit that makes us true members of Christ's body. All who have the spirit of Christ are the members of Christ, whether Jew or Gentile, bond or free.

II. Each member has its particular form, place, and use. The meanest member makes a part of the body. The foot and ear are less useful, perhaps, than the hand and eye; shall they say, therefore, that they do not belong to the body? *v.* 15, 16. So every member of the body mystical cannot have the same place and office. The meanest member of his body is as much a member as the noblest. All his members are dear to him. There must be a distinction of members in the body: *They are many members, and yet are but one body*, *v.* 20. So it is in the body of Christ. Variety in the members of the body contributes to the beauty of it. So it is for the beauty and good appearance of the church that there should be diversity of gifts. The disposal of members and their situation, are as God pleases, *v.* 18. So is it also in the members of Christ's body. We should be doing the duties of our own place, and not quarrelling with others, that we are not in theirs. All the members of the body are useful and necessary to each other. Those members of the body *which seem to be more feeble are necessary* (*v.* 21, 22). Every member serves some good purpose or other. Nor is there a member of the body of Christ but ought to be useful to his fellow-members, and in some cases, is needful to them. Those who excel in any gift cannot say that they have no need of those who in that gift are their

inferiors, while perhaps, in other gifts, they exceed them. The eye has need of the hand, and the head of the feet. Such is the man's concern for his whole body that *on the less honourable members more abundant honour is bestowed, and our uncomely parts have more abundant comeliness, v.* 24. So should the members of Christ's body behave towards their fellow-members. Divine wisdom has ordered things in this manner that the members of the body should not be schismatics. That *there might be no schism in the body* (*v.* 25). The members of the natural body are made to have a care and concern for each other. So should it be in Christ's body. Christian sympathy is a great branch of Christian duty.

Verses 27–31

I. Here the apostle applies this similitude to the church of Christ.

1. The relation wherein Christians stand to Christ and one another. *Now you are the body of Christ, and members in particular.* All have a common relation to one another.

2. The variety of offices instituted by Christ, and gifts or favours dispensed by him (*v.* 28). Observe, (1) The plenteous variety of these gifts and offices. He was no niggard of his benefits and favours. They had no want, but a store—all that was necessary, and even more. (2) Observe the order of these offices and gifts. Those of most value have the first place. God does, and we should, value things according to their real worth. What holds the last and lowest rank in this enumeration is diversity of tongues. It is by itself the most useless and insignificant of all these gifts. The Corinthians valued themselves exceedingly on this gift. How proper a method it is to beat down pride to let persons know the true value of what they pride themselves in! It is but too common a thing for men to value themselves most on what is least worth. (3) The various distribution of these gifts. All members and officers had not the same endowments (*v.* 29, 30). The Spirit distributes to everyone as he will. We must be content with our own rank and share. All are to minister to one another, and promote the good of the body in general.

II. He closes this chapter with an advice and a hint. An advice to covet the best gifts. We should desire that most which is best, and most worth. Grace is therefore to be preferred before gifts. But some read this passage, not as an advice, but a charge: *You are envious* at each other's gifts. You quarrel and contend about them. It was a quarrel about precedency; and it is no wonder that a quarrel about precedency should extinguish charity. When all would stand in the first rank, no wonder if they jostle. To have the heart glow with mutual love is vastly better than to glare with the most pompous titles, offices, or powers.

CHAPTER 13

The apostle goes on to show that more excellent way. I. By showing the necessity of it, ver. 1–3. II. By giving a description of its properties, ver. 4–7. III. By showing how much it excels the best of gifts and other graces, by its continuance, when they shall be no longer in being, ver. 8, to the end.

Verses 1–3

Here the apostle shows what more excellent way he meant, *charity*, or *love*: love in its fullest meaning, true love to God and man. Without this the most glorious gifts are nothing. 1. The gift of tongues (*v.* 1). It is the charitable heart, not the voluble tongue, that is acceptable with God. 2. Prophecy, and the understanding of mysteries, and all knowledge. This without charity is as nothing, *v.* 2. A clear and deep head is of no signification, without a benevolent and charitable heart. It is not great knowledge that God sets a value upon, but true and hearty devotion and love. 3. Miraculous faith. Moving mountains is a great achievement in the account of men; but one dram of charity is, in God's account, of much greater worth than all the faith of this sort in the world. Saving faith is ever in conjunction with charity, but the faith of miracles may be without it. 4. The outward acts of charity, *v.* 3. There may be an open and lavish hand, where there is no liberal and charitable heart. If we give away all we have, while we withhold the heart from God, it will not profit. 5. Even sufferings, *v.* 3. Should we sacrifice our lives for the faith of the gospel; this will stand us in no stead without charity. True charity is the very heart and spirit of religion. If we feel none of its sacred heat in our hearts, it will profit nothing, though we be burnt to ashes for the truth.

Verses 4–7

Some of the properties and effects of charity.

I. *It is long suffering.* It can endure evil and provocation, without being filled with resentment or revenge. It will put up with many slights from the person it loves, and wait long to see the kindly effects of such patience on him.

II. *It is kind. The law of kindness is in her lips.* It seeks to be useful; and not only seizes on opportunities of doing good, but searches for them.

III. *It envieth not;* it is not grieved at the good of others. Envy is the effect of ill-will. The mind which is bent on doing good to all can never wish ill to any.

IV. *It vaunteth not itself, is not puffed up,* is not bloated with self-conceit. True love will give us an esteem of our brethren, and this will limit our esteem of ourselves. The word rendered in our translation *vaunteth itself* bears other significations, but in every sense and meaning true charity stands in opposition to it. The Syriac renders it—*does not raise tumults* and disturbances. Charity calms the angry passions, instead of raising them. Others render it—*It does not act insidiously,* does not seek to ensnare them. It is not froward nor apt to be cross and contradictory. Some understand it of dissembling and flattery. Charity abhors such falsehood and flattery.

V. *It behaveth not unseemly.* It does nothing out of place or time; but behaves with courtesy and good-will towards all men.

VI. Charity is an utter enemy to selfishness: *Seeketh not its own.* Indeed self-love, in some degree, is natural to all men. And a reasonable love of self is by our Saviour made the measure of our love to others. *Thou shalt love thy neighbour as thyself.* But charity never seeks its own to the hurt of others. It often neglects its own for the sake of others.

VII. *It is not exasperated.* Where the fire of love is kept in, the flames of wrath will not easily kindle, nor long keep burning. Anger cannot rest in the bosom where love reigns. It is hard to be angry with those we love.

VIII. Charity *thinks no evil.* It cherishes no malice, nor gives way to revenge: so some understand it. It is not soon, nor long, angry. It does not suspect evil of others. It will hide faults that appear, instead of hunting and raking out those that lie covered and concealed.

IX. The matter of its joy and pleasure is here suggested. *It rejoiceth not in iniquity.* It wishes ill to none, much less will it make this the matter of its delight, or rejoice in doing harm and mischief. The sins of others stir all its compassion, but can give it no entertainment. *It rejoiceth in the truth.* It gives it much satisfaction to see truth and justice prevail among men, and mutual faith and trust established.

X. *It beareth all things, it endureth all things.* Some read the first, *covers all things.* It is not for blazing nor publishing the faults of a brother. Though such a man be free to tell his brother his faults in private, he is very unwilling to expose him by making them public. Thus we do by our own faults, and thus charity would teach us to do by the faults of others. Or, it *beareth all things*—will be patient upon provocation, and long patient. What a fortitude and firmness fervent love will give the mind! What cannot a lover endure for the beloved and for his sake!

XI. *Believeth all things; hopeth all things.* Indeed charity does by no means destroy prudence. Wisdom may dwell with love, and charity be cautious. But it is apt to believe well of all. All charity is apt to make the best of everything; it will judge well, and believe well. And, when in spite of inclination, it cannot believe well of others, it will yet hope well. How lovely a mind is that which is tinctured throughout with such benevolence! Happy the man who has this heavenly fire glowing in his heart!

Verses 8–13

How much it is preferable to the gifts on which the Corinthians were so apt to pride themselves.

I. *Charity never faileth.* It is a permanent and perpetual grace, lasting as eternity. *Prophecy must fail. Tongues will cease.* There will be but one language in heaven. There is no confusion of tongues in the region of perfect tranquillity. And *knowledge will vanish away.* Not that holy and happy souls shall be unknowing: it is a very poor happiness that can consist with utter ignorance. The apostle is here setting the grace of charity in opposition to supernatural gifts. And it is more valuable, because more durable; *it* shall enter into heaven, where *they* will have no place.

II. *We know in part, and we prophesy in part, v.* 9. How little a portion of God was heard even by apostles and inspired men! These gifts were fitted to the present imperfect state of the church, whereas charity was to last for ever.

III. How much better it will be with the church hereafter (*v.* 10). When the end is once attained, the means will of course be abolished. Then the church will be in a state of perfection, complete both in knowledge and holiness. God will be known then clearly. What confused and indistinct notions of things, have children, in comparison of grown men! And how naturally do men despise and relinquish their infant thoughts! The things to be known will be open to our eyes; and our knowledge will be free from all obscurity and error. God is to be seen *face to face*; and we *are to know him* as *we are known by him.* O glorious change! To pass from darkness to light, from clouds to the clear sunshine of our Saviour's face, and in God's own light to see light! It is at best but twilight while we are in this world; there it will be perfect and eternal day.

IV. Faith, hope, and love, are the three principal graces, of which charity is the chief. Faith fixes on the divine revelation, and assents to that: hope fastens on future felicity, and waits for that. But love fastens on the divine perfections themselves. These will all shine forth in the most glorious splendours in another world, and there will love be made perfect; there we shall perfectly love God. And there shall we perfectly love one another. When faith and hope are at an end, true charity will burn for ever with the brightest flame. Where God is to be seen as he is, and face to face, there charity is in its greatest height—there, and there only, will it be perfected.

CHAPTER 14

The apostle directs them about spiritual gifts. I. Advising them of all spiritual gifts to prefer prophesying, ver. 1-5. II. How

unprofitable the speaking of foreign languages is, ver. 6–14.
III. Worship should be celebrated so that the most ignorant
might understand, ver. 15–20. IV. Tongues were a sign for unbelievers, ver. 21–25. V. He blames them for the disorder they
had brought into the assembly, ver. 26–33. VI. He forbids
women speaking in the church, ver. 34, to the end.

Verses 1–5

He teaches them, among spiritual gifts, which
they should prefer.

I. An exhortation to charity (v. 1). See you do not
miss this, the principal of all graces.

II. He directs them which spiritual gift to prefer:
"*Desire spiritual gifts, but rather that you may prophesy.*" Gifts are fit objects of our desire and pursuit,
in subordination to grace and charity.

III. The reasons of this preference. He only compares prophesying with speaking with tongues.
This was more ostentatious than the plain interpretation of scripture, but less fit to pursue the purposes
of Christian charity. He that spoke with tongues
must wholly speak between God and himself, v. 2.
What cannot be understood can never edify. But he
that prophesies speaks to the advantage of his hearers.
They may be exhorted and comforted by it, v. 3.
He that speaks with tongues may edify himself, v. 4,
others can reap no benefit from his speech. Whereas
the end of speaking in the church is to edify the
church (v. 4), to which prophesying is immediately
adapted. That is the best gift which does most good.
Every gift of God is a favour from God, but then
those are to be most valued that are most useful.
Greater is he who interprets scripture to edify the
church than he who speaks tongues to recommend
himself. That makes most for the honour of a minister
which is most for the church's edification, not that
which shows his gifts to most advantage.

Verses 6–14

*If I come to you speaking with tongues, what will
it profit you, unless I speak to you by revelation, or by
knowledge, or by prophesying, or by doctrine?* (v. 6).
It would signify nothing to utter any of these in an
unknown tongue.

I. Unintelligible language is like piping or harping
without distinction of sounds: it gives no more
direction than a pipe with but one stop or a harp
with but one string can direct a dancer how he should
order his steps, v. 7. A trumpet giving an *uncertain
sound.* If, instead of sounding an onset, it sounded
a retreat, or sounded one knew not what, who would
prepare for the battle? Words without a meaning
can convey no notion nor instruction to the mind;
and words not understood have no meaning. He
compares the speaking in an unknown tongue to
the gibberish of barbarians. There are (v. 10) many
kinds of voices in the world, none of which is without
its proper signification. But whatever proper signification the words of any language may have to
those who understand them, they are perfect gibberish
to men of another language. In this case, speaker
and hearers are barbarians to each other (v. 11),
they talk and hear only sounds without sense. To
speak in the church in an unknown tongue is to talk
gibberish.

II. Be chiefly desirous of those gifts that are most
for the church's edification, v. 12. "Covet those gifts
most that will do the best service to men's souls."
If they did speak a foreign language, they should beg
of God the gift of interpreting it, v. 13. The church
must understand, that it might be edified. The sum
is that they should perform all religious exercises in
their assemblies so that all might join in them and
profit by them. He enforces this advice. His own
mind might be devoutly engaged, *but his understanding
would be unfruitful* (v. 14), he would not be understood, nor therefore would others join with him in

his devotions. Language that is most obvious and
easy to be understood is the most proper for public
devotion.

Verses 15–20

The apostle,

I. Directs them how they should sing and pray in
public (v. 15). He would have them perform both so
as to be understood by others, that others might join
with them. Public worship should be performed so
as to be understood.

II. He enforces the argument with several reasons.

1. Otherwise the unlearned could not say Amen
to their prayers or thanksgivings, could not join in
the worship, for they did not understand it, v. 16.
All should say *Amen* inwardly; and it is not improper
to testify this inward concurrence in public prayers
and devotions, by an audible *Amen.* Now, how should
the people say *Amen* to what they did not understand?
The intention of public devotions is therefore entirely
destroyed if they are performed in an unknown
tongue. Others are not, cannot be, edified (v. 17)
by what they understand not.

2. He alleges his own example, to make the greater
impression. (1) He did not come behind any of them
in this spiritual gift. It was not envy that made Paul
depreciate what they so highly valued and so much
vaunted of; he surpassed them all in this very gift
of tongues. There was more ground for them to
envy him upon this head than for him to envy them.
When we beat down men's unreasonable value for
themselves, we should let them see that this does not
proceed from an envious and grudging spirit. (2) He
had rather *speak five words with understanding than
ten thousand words in an unknown tongue,* v. 19.
A truly Christian minister will value himself much
more upon doing good to men's souls than upon
procuring the greatest applause.

3. The fondness then discovered for this gift was
but too plain an indication of the immaturity of their
judgment, v. 20. Children are apt to be struck with
novelty and strange appearances. Do not you act
like them, and prefer noise and show to worth and
substance; be like children in nothing but an innocent
and inoffensive disposition. Christians should have
wisdom and knowledge that are ripe and mature.

Verses 21–25

The apostle pursues the argument.

I. Tongues, as the Corinthians used them, were
rather a token of judgment from God than mercy
to any people (v. 21). It is an evidence that a people
are abandoned of God when he gives them up to the
discipline of those who speak in another language.
They can never be benefited by such teaching as this;
and, when they are left to it, it is a sad sign that God
gives them over as past cure. Yet thus did the Corinthian preachers who would always deliver their
inspirations in an unknown tongue.

II. Tongues were rather a sign to unbelievers
than to believers, v. 22. The gift of tongues was
necessary to spread Christianity. It was proper
and intended to convince unbelievers; interpreting
scripture in their own language, as most for the
edification of such as did already believe. That gifts
may be rightly used, it is proper to know the ends
which they are intended to serve. To go about the
conversion of infidels had been a vain undertaking
without the gift of tongues, but, in an assembly of
Christians it would be perfectly impertinent.

III. The credit and reputation of their assemblies
required them to prefer prophesying before speaking
with tongues. If their ministers, or all employed
in public worship, should talk unintelligible language,
and infidels should drop in, they would conclude
them to be mad. What sort of religion is that which

leaves out sense and understanding? Would not this make Christianity ridiculous to a heathen? If, instead of speaking with tongues, those who minister plainly interpret scripture, a heathen or unlearned person, coming in, will probably be convinced, and become a convert to Christianity (*v.* 24, 25); and so will be brought to confess his guilt, to pay his homage to God, and own that he is indeed among you. Prophesying would certainly edify the church, and might probably convert infidels. The ministry was not instituted to make ostentation of gifts and parts, but to save souls.

Verses 26–33

I. He blames them for the confusion they introduced into the assembly (*v.* 26). "You are apt to confound the several parts of worship"; or else, "You are apt to be confused if you do not stay for one another. Can this be edifying? *Let all things be done to edifying.*"

II. He corrects their faults. 1. As to speaking in an unknown tongue, he orders that no more than two or three should do it at one meeting, and this one after another. And even this was not to be done unless there were someone to interpret (*v.* 27, 28). But, if there were none to interpret, he was to be silent in the church, and only exercise his gift between God and himself (*v.* 28). 2. As to prophesying he orders, (1) That two or three only should speak at one meeting (*v.* 29). There might be false prophets, and the true prophets were to judge of these and discover who was divinely inspired and who was not. (2) He orders that, if any assistant prophet had a revelation, while another was prophesying, the other should hold his peace, be silent (*v.* 30). He who had the new revelation might claim liberty of speech in his turn. The reason annexed (*v.* 31): *That all might prophesy*, one after another. Divine inspirations are not, like the diabolical possessions of heathen priests, violent and ungovernable; but are sober and calm, and capable of regular conduct. The man inspired by the Spirit of God may still observe the rules of natural order and decency in delivering his revelations.

III. The apostle gives the reasons of these regulations. They would be for the church's benefit, their instruction and consolation. Divine inspiration should by no means throw Christian assemblies into confusion. If they are managed in a tumultuous and confused manner, what a notion must this give of the God who is worshipped! Does it look as if he were the God of peace and order, and an enemy to confusion? Things were thus orderly managed in all the other churches. And it would be perfectly scandalous for them, who exceeded most churches in spiritual gifts, to be more disorderly than any in the exercise of them.

Verses 34, 35

Here the apostle, 1. Enjoins silence on their women in public assemblies, who must not ask questions for their own information in the church, but ask their husbands at home. There is indeed an intimation (*ch.* xi. 5) as if the women sometimes did pray and prophesy in their assemblies. But here he seems to forbid all public performances of theirs. They are not permitted to speak (*v.* 34) in the church. Nor must she therefore be allowed to teach in a congregation; nor so much as to ask questions in the church, but learn in silence there; and, if difficulties occurred, *ask their own husbands at home*. As it is the woman's duty to learn in subjection, it is the man's duty to keep up his superiority, by being able to instruct her. If it be a shame for her to speak in the church, where she should be silent, it is a shame for him to be silent when he should speak, and not be able to give an answer, when she asks him at home. 2. The apostle concludes it was a shame for women to speak in the church. Shame is the mind's uneasy reflection on having done an indecent thing. And what more indecent than for a woman to quit her rank. The woman was made subject to the man, and she should keep her station and be content with it.

Verses 36–40

A just rebuke of the Corinthians for their extravagant pride and self-conceit. Are you the only church favoured with divine revelations. How intolerably assuming is this behaviour! What he said to them was the command of God; nor durst any true prophet deny it (*v.* 37). "If their revelations contradict mine, they do not come from the same Spirit; either I or they must be false prophets. But if any continue after all, uncertain or ignorant whether they or I speak by the Spirit of God, they must be left under the power of this ignorance." It is just with God to leave those to the blindness of their own minds who wilfully shut out the light. Though they should not despise the gift of tongues, yet they should prefer prophesying. It was the more useful gift. He charges them to let all things be done decently and in order (*v.* 40). They must do nothing that was manifestly childish (*v.* 20), or that would give occasion to say they were mad (*v.* 23), nor must they act so as to breed confusion, *v.* 33. All parts of divine worship should be carried on in a composed and orderly manner.

CHAPTER 15

I. He establishes the certainty of our Saviour's resurrection, ver. 1–11. II. He sets himself to refute those who said, There is no resurrection of the dead, ver. 12–19. III. From our Saviour's resurrection he establishes the resurrection of the dead, ver. 20–34. IV. He answers an objection and takes occasion thence to show what a vast change will be made in the bodies of believers at the resurrection, ver. 35–50. V. He informs us what a change will be made in those who shall be living at the sound of the last trumpet, ver. 51–57. And, VI. He sums up the argument with a very serious exhortation to Christians, ver. 58.

Verses 1–11

It is the apostle's business in this chapter to establish the doctrine of the resurrection of the dead, which some of the Corinthians flatly denied, *v.* 12. And they disowned a future state of recompences, by denying the resurrection of the dead. He begins with an epitome of the gospel. Now concerning the gospel observe,

I. What a stress he lays upon it (*v.* 1, 2). It was what he constantly preached. The doctrine which Paul had heretofore taught, he still taught. It was what they had received. It was no strange doctrine. It was that very gospel in which they had hitherto stood, and must continue to stand. The doctrine of Christ's death and resurrection is at the foundation of Christianity. Remove this foundation, and the whole fabric falls. It was that alone by which they could hope for salvation (*v.* 2). There is no salvation in his name, but upon supposition of his death and resurrection. These are the saving truths of our holy religion. They must be retained in mind, they must be held fast. We believe in vain, unless we continue and persevere in the faith of the gospel. We shall be never the better for a temporary faith. And in vain is it to profess faith in Christ, if we deny the resurrection. Take away this, you make nothing of Christianity.

II. What this gospel is. It was that doctrine which he had received, and delivered to them, *among the first, the principal*. It was a doctrine of the first rank, a most necessary truth. Christ's death and resurrection are the very sum and substance of evangelical truth.

III. This truth is confirmed,

1. By Old Testament predictions. He died for our sins; he was buried, and rose from the dead, according

to the scripture-prophecies. It is a great confirmation of our faith of the gospel to see how it corresponds with ancient prophecies.

2. By the testimony of many eye-witnesses, who saw Christ after he had risen from the dead. How uncontrollably evident was Christ's resurrection from the dead, when so many eyes saw him at so many different times. Even Paul himself was last of all favoured with the sight of him. The Lord Jesus appeared to him by the way to Damascus, Acts ix. 17. He was highly favoured of God, but he always endeavoured to keep up a mean opinion of himself. So he does here, by observing, (1) That he was *one born out of due time* (v. 8). He was not matured for the apostolic function, as the others were, who had personal converse with our Lord. He was out of time for it. (2) By owning himself inferior to the other apostles. The least and not worthy to be called an apostle, because he had been *a persecutor of the church of God*, v. 9. A humble spirit, in the midst of high attainments, is a great ornament to any man. What kept Paul low was the remembrance of his former wickedness, his raging zeal against Christ and his members. How easily God can bring a good out of the greatest evil! When sinners are by divine grace turned into saints, he makes the remembrance of their former sins very serviceable, to make them humble, and diligent, and faithful. (3) By ascribing all that was valuable in him to divine grace. We are nothing but what God makes us. Though he was conscious of his own zeal, and service, he thought himself so much more the debtor to divine grace. *Yet not I, but the grace of God which was with me.* The more he laboured, and the more good he did, the more humble he was and the more disposed to own the favour of God towards him. The apostle tells them (v. 11) that he not only preached the same gospel himself at all times, and in all places, but that all the apostles preached the same. All agreed in this that Jesus Christ, and him crucified and slain, and then rising from the dead, was the very sum and substance of Christianity. By this faith they live. In this faith they die.

Verses 12–19

If Christ be preached that he rose from the dead, how say some among you that there is no resurrection of the dead? (v. 12). The apostle produces an incontestable fact, namely, the resurrection of Christ.

I. It was foretold in ancient prophecies that he should rise; and it has been proved by multitudes of eye-witnesses that he has risen.

II. This supposition decried, would destroy the principal evidence of Christianity; and so, 1. Make preaching vain. "*We* apostles should *be found false witnesses of God*. Would not our labour be wholly in vain? If Christ be not raised, the gospel is a jest; it is chaff and emptiness." 2. It would make the faith of Christians vain because it is through his death and sacrifice for sin alone that forgiveness is to be had. Had he remained under the power of death, how could he have delivered us from its power? And how vain a thing would faith in him be. There had been no justification nor salvation if Christ had not risen.

III. They took death to be the destruction and extinction of the man, and not merely of the bodily life. "Upon supposition there is no resurrection, no after-state and life, then dead Christians are quite lost. How vain a thing were our faith and religion upon this supposition!" And this,

IV. Would infer that Christ's ministers and servants were *of all men most miserable*, as having *hope in him in this life only* (v. 19). If there be no resurrection, or state of future recompence, and, if all their hopes in Christ lie within the compass of this life, they are in a much worse condition than the rest of mankind. Better be anything than a Christian upon these terms. They fare much harder than other men in this life, and yet have no further nor better hopes. The Christian is by his religion crucified to this world, and taught to live upon the hope of another.

Verses 20–34

The apostle establishes the truth of the resurrection of the dead, the dead in Christ.

I. On the resurrection of Christ. He has truly risen himself, as the first-fruits of those who sleep in him. As he has risen, they shall rise. Christ's resurrection is a pledge and earnest of ours. This is the first argument used by the apostle in confirmation of the truth: and it is illustrated by a parallel between the first and second Adam, v. 21. All who die die through the sin of Adam; all who are raised, rise through the merit and power of Christ. But the meaning is not that, as all men died in Adam, so all men, without exception, shall be made alive in Christ. Christ rose as the first-fruits; therefore *those that are Christ's* (v. 23) shall rise too. All who thus rise, rise in virtue of Christ's resurrection, and so, as by man came death, by man came deliverance. He states that there will be an order observed in their resurrection. What that precisely will be we are nowhere told. It is only here said that the first-fruits are supposed to rise first, and afterwards all who are Christ's, when he shall come again.

II. He argues from the continuance of the mediatorial kingdom till all Christ's enemies are destroyed, the last of which is death, v. 24–26.

1. This argument implies: (1) That our Saviour rose from the dead to have all power put into his hands. (2) That this mediatorial kingdom is to have an end, v. 24. (3) That it is not to have an end till all opposing power be put down, v. 24, 25. (4) That, among other enemies, death must be destroyed (v. 26). Therefore the saints must rise, else death and the grave would have power over them. When saints shall live again, and die no more, then, and not till then, will death be abolished.

2. Our Saviour, as man and mediator between God and man, has a delegated royalty. As man, all his authority must be delegated. As Mediator, a middle person between God and man, partaking of both natures, he was to reconcile both parties, God and man. Upon his ascension, he was made head over all things to the church, had power given him to govern and protect it against all its enemies, and in the end destroy them and complete the salvation of all that believe in him. This delegated royalty must at length *be delivered up to the Father*, from whom it was received (v. 24); for it is a power received for particular ends (v. 25, 26). The Redeemer must reign till his enemies be destroyed, and, when this end is attained, then will he deliver up the power. The Redeemer shall certainly reign till the last enemy of his people be destroyed, till death itself be abolished. He shall have all power in heaven and earth till then. What support should this be to his saints in every hour of distress and temptation! When this is done, *and all things are put under his feet*, v. 28, then the man Christ Jesus shall appear upon giving it up to be a subject of the Father. And it will appear to the divine glory, that God may be all in all, that the accomplishment of our salvation may appear altogether divine. Though the human nature must be employed in the work of our redemption, yet God was all in all in it.

III. He argues for the resurrection, from the case of those who were baptized for the dead (v. 29). But what is this baptism for the dead? Some understand the passage of the martyrs: Why do they suffer martyrdom for their religion? This is sometimes called the baptism of blood by the ancients. Some understand it of a custom that was observed among many who professed the Christian name in the first ages, of baptizing some in the name and stead of catechumens dying without baptism. But whether this be the meaning, or whatever else be, doubtless the apostle's argument was good and intelligible to the Corinthians. And his next is as plain to us.

IV. He argues from the absurdity of his own conduct and that of other Christians.

1. It would be a foolish thing for them to run so many hazards (*v.* 30). Christianity were a foolish profession if it proposed no hopes beyond this life, required men to risk all the blessings and comforts of this life, and to face and endure all the evils of it, without any future prospects. And must he not fix this character on it if he give up his future hopes, and deny the resurrection of the dead? "*I die daily,*" *v.* 31. He was in continual danger of death, and carried his life, as we say, in his hand. He had encountered very great difficulties and fierce enemies; he had *fought with beasts at Ephesus* (*v.* 32), and was in danger of being pulled to pieces by an enraged multitude (Acts xix. 24, &c.). I take it that this fighting with beasts is a figurative expression, that the beasts intended were men of a fierce and ferine disposition. "Now," says he, "what advantage have I from such contests, if the dead rise not? *If I am to perish by death,* and expect nothing after it, could anything be more weak?" Was Paul so senseless? Could anything but the sure hopes of a better life after death have extinguished the love of life in him to this degree? "*What advantageth it me, if the dead rise not?*" It is very lawful and fit for a Christian to propose advantage to himself by his fidelity to God. Thus did Paul.

2. It would be a much wiser thing to take the comforts of this life (*v.* 32). Let us even live like beasts, if we must die like them. This would be a wiser course, if there were no resurrection. If there were no hopes after death, would not every wise man prefer an easy comfortable life, and endeavour to enjoy the comforts of life as fast as possible, because the continuance of it is short? Nothing but the hopes of better things hereafter can enable a man to forgo all the comforts and pleasures here.

V. The apostle closes his argument with a caution, exhortation, and reproof. 1. A caution against men of loose lives and principles, *v.* 33. Possibly, some of those who said that there was no resurrection of the dead were men of loose lives, and had that speech often in their mouths *Let us eat and drink, for tomorrow we die.* He now warns the Corinthians how dangerous such men's conversation must prove. They would probably be corrupted by them, and fall in with their course of life Those who would keep their innocence must keep good company Error and vice are infectious. 2. Here is an exhortation to break off their sins, and lead a more holy and righteous life (*v.* 34): "Rouse yourselves, break off your sins. Do not, by sloth and stupidity, be led away into such conversation as will sap your Christian hopes." The disbelief of a future state destroys all virtue and piety. If there will be a resurrection and a future life, we should live and act as those who believe it. 3. Here is a reproof to some at least among them. It is a shame in Christians not to have the knowledge of God. Those who profess this religion reproach themselves, by remaining without the knowledge of God; for it must be owing to their own sloth. It must be ignorance of God that leads men into the disbelief of a resurrection and future life. Those who know God know that he is not unfaithful nor unkind, to forget their labour and patience, their faithful services and cheerful sufferings, or let their *labour be in vain.* Those who own a God and observe how unequal the distributions of the present life are, and how frequently the best men fare worst, can hardly doubt an after state, where everything will be set to rights.

Verses 35–50

A plausible objection against doctrine of the resurrection of the dead, *v.* 35. The objection is plainly twofold. *How are they raised up?* that is, "By what means? What power is equal to this effect?" The other part of the objection is about the quality of their bodies: "*With what body will they come?*" The former objection is that of those who opposed the doctrine, the latter the enquiry of curious doubters.

I. To the former the apostle replies by telling them this was to be brought about by divine power, that very power which they had all observed to do something very like it, year after year, in the death and revival of the corn, *v.* 36. It not only sprouts after it is dead, but it must die that it may live. It is a foolish thing to question the divine power to raise the dead, when we see it every day quickening and reviving things that are dead.

II. But he is longer in replying to the second enquiry.

1. There is a change made in the grain that is sown. God gives it such a body as he will. Every seed sown has its *proper body.* It is certain the grain undergoes a great change, so will the dead, when they rise again.

2. There is a great deal of variety among other bodies. (1) In bodies of flesh (*v.* 39). (2) In bodies celestial and terrestrial there is also a difference. (3) There is a variety of glory among heavenly bodies themselves, *v.* 41. The bodies of the dead, when they rise, will be so far changed that there will be a variety of glories. It must be as easy to divine power to raise the dead, as out of the same materials to form so many different kinds of flesh and plants, and celestial bodies as well as terrestrial ones. And can he, out of the same materials, form such various beings, and yet not be able to raise the dead?

3. *So also,* says he, *is the resurrection of the dead.* Burying the dead is like sowing them; it is like committing the seed to the earth, that it may spring out of it again. When we rise, they will be out of the power of the grave, and never more be liable to corruption. Ours is at present a vile body, Phil. iii. 21. But at the resurrection it will be made like the glorious body of our Saviour, and shine out with a splendour resembling his. It is laid in the earth, a poor helpless thing, wholly in the power of death. But when we arise our bodies will have heavenly life and vigour infused into them. When we rise our body will rise spiritual. We shall at the resurrection have bodies made fit to be perpetual associates of spirits made perfect. And why should it not be in the power of God to raise incorruptible spiritual bodies as first to make matter out of nothing, and then produce such variety of beings, both in earth and heaven? *To God all things are possible.*

4. He illustrates this by a comparison of the first and second Adam. (1) As we have our natural body, from the first Adam, we expect our spiritual body from the second. (2) *The first Adam was made a living soul,* such a being as ourselves. The *second Adam is a quickening Spirit*; he is the resurrection and the life. If the first Adam could communicate to us natural and animal bodies, cannot the second Adam make our bodies spiritual ones? (3) We must first have natural bodies from the first Adam before we can have spiritual bodies from the second (*v.* 49). It is as certain that we shall have spiritual bodies as it is now that we have natural or animal ones. We

are as certainly intended to bear the one as we have borne the other.

5. The reason of this change (*v.* 50). Corruption cannot inherit incorruption. The bodies of the saints, when they shall rise again, will be greatly changed from what they are now, and much for the better. They are now corruptible; they will be then incorruptible, glorious, and spiritual bodies, fitted to the celestial world, where they are ever afterwards to have their eternal inheritance.

Verses 51–57

I. He here tells them that all the saints would not die, but all would be changed. It will not be without changing from corruption to incorruption, *v.* 52. Changed they must be as well as the dead, because flesh and blood cannot inherit the kingdom of God. The apostle here makes known a truth unknown before, which is that the saints living at our Lord's second coming will not die, but be changed, that this change will be made in a moment, in the twinkling of an eye, and *at the sound of the last trump*. At this summons the graves shall open, the dead saints shall rise incorruptible, and the living saints be changed to the same incorruptible state, *v.* 52.

II. The reason of this change (*v.* 53). This corruptible body must be made incorruptible, this mortal body must be changed into immortal. What is sown must be quickened.

III. What will follow upon this change of the living and dead in Christ: *Then shall be brought to pass that saying, Death is swallowed up in victory.* Christ hinders it from swallowing his saints when they die; but, when they rise again, death shall be swallowed for ever.

1. They will glory over death as a vanquished enemy: "*O death! where is thy sting?* We fear no further mischiefs from thee, but defy thy power. *O grave! where is thy victory?* Once we were thy prisoners, but the prison-doors are burst open, and we are for ever released. Captivity is taken captive. Thy triumphs, grave, are at an end."

2. The foundation for this triumph, (1) Whence death had its power to hurt: *The sting of death is sin.* This gives venom to his dart. Sin is the parent of death, and gives it all its hurtful power. It is its cursed progeny and offspring. (2) The victory saints obtain over it through Jesus Christ, *v.* 56. *The sting of death is sin;* but Christ, by dying, has taken out this sting. It may hiss therefore, but it cannot hurt. *The strength of sin is the law;* but the curse of the law is removed by our Redeemer's *becoming a curse for us,* so that sin is deprived of its strength and sting, through Christ. There is a day coming when the grave shall open, the dead saints revive, and become immortal, and put out of the reach of death for ever. They often rejoice beforehand, in the hope of this victory; and, when they arise glorious from the grave, they will boldly triumph over death. It is altogether owing to the grace of God in Christ that sin is pardoned and death disarmed. This triumph of the saints over death should issue in thanksgiving to God: *Thanks be to God, who giveth us the victory through Christ Jesus, our Lord* (*v.* 57). Then only do we enjoy our blessings and honours when God has his revenue of glory out of it. And this really improves and exalts our satisfaction. We are conscious at once of having done our duty and enjoyed our pleasure. Those who remain under the power of death can have no heart to praise; but such conquests and triumphs will certainly tune the tongues of the saints to thankfulness and praise. With what acclamations will saints rising from the dead applaud him! *Thanks be to God* will be the burden of their song; and angels will join the chorus, and declare their consent with a loud Amen, Hallelujah.

Verse 58

I. An exhortation, and this threefold: 1. That they should be steadfast, fixed in faith of the gospel. "Do not let your belief of these truths be shaken. They are most certain, and of the last importance." Christians should be steadfast believers of this great article of the resurrection of the dead. A disbelief of a future life will open a way to all manner of licentiousness. It will be easy and natural to infer hence that we may live like beasts, and eat and drink, for tomorrow we die. 2. He exhorts them to be *immovable* in their expectation of being raised incorruptible and immortal. Christians should not be moved away from this hope of the gospel (Col. i. 23). This hope should be an anchor to their souls, firm and sure, Heb. vi. 19, 3. He exhorts them *to abound in the work of the Lord,* and that *always.* What vigour and resolution, what constancy and patience, should those hopes inspire!

II. They have the best grounds in the world to build upon. As surely as Christ is risen, they shall rise. The labour of Christians will not be lost labour; they may lose for God, but they will lose nothing by him. He will never be found unjust to forget their labour of love. Nay, he will do exceedingly abundantly above what they can now ask or think. Those who serve God have good wages; they cannot do too much nor suffer too much for so good a Master. If they serve him now, they shall see him hereafter; they shall rise again from the dead, be crowned with glory, honour, and immortality, and inherit eternal life.

CHAPTER 16

I. The apostle gives directions about some charitable collection to be made for the churches in Judæa, ver. 1–4. II. He talks of paying them a visit, ver. 5–9. III. He recommends Timothy to them, and tells them Apollos intended to come to them, ver. 10–12. IV. He presses them to watchfulness, constancy, charity, and to pay a due regard to all his fellow labourers, ver. 13–19. V. After salutations from others, and his own, he closes the epistle, ver. 20, to the end.

Verses 1–4

In this chapter Paul closes this long epistle. He begins with directing them about a charitable collection on a particular occasion, the distresses and poverty of Christians in Judæa.

I. How he introduces his direction. He had given similar *orders to the churches of Galatia, v.* 1. He desired them only to conform to the same rules which he had given to other churches on a similar occasion. He also prudently mentions these orders of his to the churches of Galatia, to excite emulation, and stir them up to be liberal. Those who exceeded most churches in spiritual gifts, surely would not suffer themselves to come behind any in their bounty to their afflicted brethren. It is becoming a Christian not to bear to be outdone by a fellow-christian in anything virtuous and praise-worthy, provided this consideration only makes him exert himself, not envy others. The church of Corinth should not be outdone in this service of love by the churches of Galatia.

II. The direction itself.

1. The manner in which the collection was to be made: *Everyone was to lay by in store* (*v.* 2). He should lay by as he could spare from time to time. It is a good thing to lay up in store for good uses. The best way in the world for them to get a treasury for this purpose is to lay by from time to time, as they can afford. "Every little," as the proverb says, "would make a mickle." We may cheerfully give when we know that we can spare, and that we have been laying by in store that we may.

2. The measure in which they are to lay by: *As God hath prospered them.* All our business and labour are that to us which God is pleased to make them. It is not the diligent hand that will make rich by itself, without the divine blessing. It is his bounty and blessing to which we owe all we have. And what argument more proper to excite us to charity to the people of God than to consider all we have as his gift? When his bounty flows forth upon us we should not confine it to ourselves, but let it stream out to others. The more good we receive from God the more we should do good to others. They were to lay by as God had blessed them. God expects that our beneficence to others should hold some proportion to his bounty to us. The greater ability he gives, the more enlarged should our hearts be, and the more open our hands; but, where the ability is less, the hands cannot be as open, however willing the mind and however large the heart; nor does God expect it.

3. The time when this is to be done: *The first day of the week*, the Lord's day. It is a day of holy rest; and the more vacation the mind has from worldly cares and toils the more disposition has it to show mercy: and the other duties of the day should stir us up to the performance of this; works of charity should always accompany works of piety. Works of mercy are the genuine fruits of true love to God, and therefore are a proper service on his own day.

4. The apostle would have everything ready against his coming. As to the disposal of it, he would leave it much to themselves. Paul no more pretended to lord it over the purses of his hearers than over their faith; he would not meddle with their contributions without their consent. They should give letters of credence, and send messengers of their own with their liberality, v. 3. This would be a proper testimony of their respect and brotherly love to their distressed brethren. It would argue that they were very hearty in this service, when they should send some of their own body on so long and hazardous a journey to convey their liberality. We should not only charitably relieve our poor fellow-christians but do it in such a way as will best signify our compassion to them. He offers to go with their messengers, if they think proper, v. 4. Ministers are doing their proper business when they are promoting or helping in works of charity.

Verses 5–9

The apostle notifies his purpose of visiting them. 1. His purpose: he intended to pass out of Asia, and to go through Macedonia, and to stay some time with them, and perhaps the winter, v. 5, 6. He had long laboured in this church, and done much good among them. The heart of a truly Christian minister must be much towards that people among whom he has long laboured, and with remarkable success. Though some among this people made a faction against him, doubtless there were many who loved him tenderly. And is it any wonder that he should be willing to visit them, and stay with them? It is plain that he hoped for some good effect, because he says he intended to stay, *that they might bring him on his journey whithersoever he went* (v. 6); not that they might accompany him a little way on the road, but help and encourage him to it, and provide him for it. His stay among them, he hoped, would cure their factious humour. 2. His excuse for not seeing them now (v. 7). He would not see them because he could not stay with them. Such a visit would give neither him nor them any satisfaction. He loved them so much that he longed for an opportunity to take up his abode among them for some length of time. This would be more pleasing to himself, and more serviceable to them, than a cursory visit in his

way. 3. We have the limitation of this purpose: *I trust to tarry awhile with you, if the Lord permit,* v. 7. Concerning all our purposes it is fit we should say, "We will execute them if the Lord permit." It is not in us to effect our own designs, without the divine leave. It is by God's power and permission. 4. We have his purpose expressed of staying at Ephesus for the present. He says he would stay there till pentecost, v. 8. It is very probably that at the time of writing this epistle he was in Ephesus, from this passage, compared with v. 19, where he says, *The churches of Asia salute you.* 5. We have the reason given for his staying at Ephesus for the present, v. 9. God gave him great success among them. For this reason he determined to stay awhile at Ephesus. Success, and a fair prospect of more, was a just reason to determine an apostle to stay and labour in a particular place. And there were many adversaries. Great success in the work of the gospel commonly creates many enemies. The devil opposes those most who most heartily set themselves to destroy his kingdom. There were many adversaries; and therefore the apostle determined to stay. True courage is whetted by opposition. The opposition of adversaries only animated his zeal. Adversaries and opposition do not break the spirits of faithful ministers, but only enkindle their zeal. To labour in vain is heartless and discouraging. This damps the spirits, and breaks the heart. But success will give life and vigour to a minister. It is not the opposition of enemies, but the hardness of his hearers, and the backslidings of professors, that damp a faithful minister, and break his heart.

Verses 10–12

I. He recommends Timothy to them, v. 10. Timothy was sent by the apostle to correct the abuses which had crept in among them; and not only to direct, but to reprove, those who were culpable. No doubt the mutual strife and hatred ran very high among them. Proud spirits cannot easily bear reproof. It was reasonable therefore to think young Timothy might be roughly used. It was their duty to behave themselves well towards him, and not dishearten him in his Lord's work. They should not fly out into resentment at his reproof. He warns them against despising him, v. 11. He was but a young man, and his own youthful face and years commanded but little reverence. Pride was a reigning sin among the Corinthians, and such a caution was but too necessary. Christians should be very careful not to pour contempt on any, but especially on ministers. He tells them they should use him well while he was with them; and they should send him away in friendship, and well prepared for his journey back again to Paul. This is the meaning of bringing him on his journey in peace, v. 11.

II. The reasons why they should behave thus towards Timothy. He was employed in the same work as Paul, and acted in it by the same authority, v. 10. He did not come on Paul's errand among them, nor to do his work, but the work of the Lord. Those who work the work of the Lord should be treated with all tenderness and respect. Pastors and teachers, as well as apostles and evangelists, are to be treated with honour and respect. As they were to esteem him for his work's sake, so also for Paul's sake, who had sent him to Corinth (v. 11). "I am expecting his return and shall judge by your conduct towards him what your regard and respect for me will be." They would hardly dare to send back Timothy with a report that would grieve or provoke the apostle.

III. He informs them of Apollos's purpose to see them. He himself had greatly desired him to come to them, *v.* 12. Though one party among them had declared for Apollos against Paul, yet Paul did not hinder Apollos from going to Corinth in his own absence. Faithful ministers are not apt to entertain jealousies of each other. True charity and brotherly love think no evil. Apollos could not be prevailed on for the present to come. He would not go to be set at the head of a party. When this had subsided he might conclude a visit would be more proper. Apostles did not vie with each other, but consulted each other's comfort and usefulness. Apollos shows his respect to Paul by declining the journey till the Corinthians were in better temper.

Verses 13–18

I. Some general advices. They should watch (*v.* 13). The Corinthians were in manifest danger upon many accounts: their feuds ran high, the irregularities among them were very great, there were deceivers among them. In such dangerous circumstances it was their concern to watch. If a Christian would be secure, he must be on his guard. He advises them to *stand fast in the faith.* A Christian should be fixed in the faith of the gospel. It is by this faith alone that he will be able to keep his ground in an hour of temptation; it is by this that we must overcome the world (1 John v. 4), both when it fawns and when it frowns. He advises them to act like men and be strong. "Show yourselves men in Christ, by your steadiness, by your sound judgment and firm resolution." Christians should be manly and firm in defending their faith. He advises them to do everything in charity, *v.* 14. When the apostle would have us play the man for our faith or religion, he puts in a caution against playing the devil for it. Christians should be careful that charity not only reign in their hearts, but shine out in their lives. Christianity never appears to so much advantage as when the charity of Christians is most conspicuous, when they can bear with their mistaken brethren, and oppose the open enemies of their holy faith in love.

II. Particular directions how they should behave towards some that had been eminently serviceable among them.

1. He gives us their character. (1) The household of Stephanas is mentioned by him. They were the first-fruits of Achaia. It is an honourable character to any man to be early a Christian, betimes in Christ. But they had moreover addicted themselves to the ministry of the saints, to serve the saints. It is not meant of the ministry of the word properly, but of serving them in other respects, and assisting them upon all occasions. (2) He mentions Stephanas, and Fortunatus, and Achaicus, as coming to him from the church of Corinth. They supplied the deficiencies of the church towards him, and by so doing *refreshed his spirit and theirs, v.* 17, 18. They gave him a more perfect account of the state of the church by word of mouth than he could acquire by their letter. Report had made their cause much worse than it was in fact; but he had been made more easy by converse with them. They came to him as peace-makers. It is a great refreshment to the spirit of a faithful minister to hear better of a people by wise and good men of their own body than by common report. It is a grief to him to hear ill of those he loves; it gladdens his heart to hear the report thereof is false.

2. He directs how they should behave towards them. He would have them acknowledged (*v.* 11), that is, owned and respected. They deserve it for their good offices. Those who discover so good a spirit cannot easily be over-valued, *v.* 16. They were persons to whom they owed peculiar respect, and whom they should have in veneration.

Verses 19–24

The apostle closes his epistle,

I. With salutations to the church of Corinth, first from those of Asia, from *Priscilla* and *Aquila* (who seem to have been at this time inhabitants of Ephesus), *with the church in their house* (v. 19), and from *all the brethren* (v. 20) at Ephesus. Paul could find room in an epistle treating of very important matters to send the salutations of friends. Religion should promote a courteous and obliging temper towards all. Those misrepresent and reproach it who would have any encouragement from it to be sour and morose. Some of these *salute them much in the Lord.* Christian salutations are attended with hearty recommendations to the divine grace and blessing. We read also of a church in a private family, *v.* 19. Every Christian family should in some respects be a Christian church. Wherever two or three are gathered together, and Christ is among them, there is a church. He subjoins, 1. An advice, that *they should greet one another with a holy kiss* (v. 20), or with sincere goodwill, a tacit reproof of their feuds and factions. The love of the brethren should be a powerful incentive to mutual love. 2. His own salutation: *The salutation of me Paul with my own hand, v.* 21. At the close it was fit that himself should sign it, that they might know it to be genuine. So he wrote in every epistle which he did not wholly pen, as he did that to the Galatians, Gal. vi. 11.

II. With a very solemn warning to them, *v.* 22. We sometimes need words of threatening, that we may fear. Holy fear is a very good friend both to holy faith and holy living. 1. The person described, who is liable to this doom: *He that loveth not the Lord Jesus Christ.* It stands here as a warning to the Corinthians and a rebuke of their criminal behaviour. Professed Christians will, by contempt of Christ, and revolt from him, bring upon themselves the most dreadful destruction. Many who have his name much in their mouths have no true love to him in their hearts. And none love him in truth who do not love his laws and keep his commandments. What, not love the most glorious lover in the world! What had we a power of loving for, if we are unmoved with such love as this, and without affection to such a Saviour? 2. The doom of the person described: "*Let him be Anathema, Maran-atha,* lie under the heaviest and most dreadful curse." *Maran-atha* is a Syriac phrase, and signifies *The Lord cometh.* That very Lord whom they do not love is coming to execute judgment. Those who fall under his condemning sentence must perish. True faith in Christ will evermore be productive of sincere love to him. Those who love him not cannot be believers in him.

III. With his good wishes for them and expressions of goodwill to them. 1. With his good wishes, *v.* 23. The grace of our Lord Jesus Christ comprehends in it all that is good, for time or eternity. We can wish them nothing more, and we should wish them nothing less. The most solemn warnings are the result of the tenderest affection and the greatest goodwill. And therefore it is no wonder that the apostle should close all, 2. With the declaration of his love to them in Christ Jesus, *v.* 24. He parts with them in love. His heart would be with them, and he would bear them dear affection as long as their hearts were with Christ. We should be cordial lovers of all who are in Christ. Not but we should love all men, but *those* must have our dearest affection who are dear to Christ, and lovers of him. May our love be with all those who are in Christ Jesus! Amen.

AN EXPOSITION, WITH PRACTICAL OBSERVATIONS, OF

THE SECOND EPISTLE OF ST. PAUL TO

THE CORINTHIANS

The apostle had signified his intentions of *coming to Corinth, as he passed through Macedonia* (*ch.* xvi. 5), but, being providentially hindered, he writes this second epistle to them. There seem to be these two urgent occasions: 1. The case of the incestuous person. This therefore he gives directions about (*ch.* ii), and afterwards (*ch.* vii) he declares the satisfaction he had upon their good behaviour in that affair. 2. There was a contribution now making for the poor saints at Jerusalem, in which he exhorts the Corinthians to join, *ch.* viii, ix.

Other things very observable in this epistle, I. The account the apostle gives of his labours and success in preaching the gospel in several places, *ch.* ii. II. The comparison he makes between the Old and New Testament dispensation, *ch.* iii. III. The manifold sufferings that he and his fellow-labourers met with, *ch.* iv, v. IV. The caution he gives the Corinthians against mingling with unbelievers, *ch.* vi. V. The way in which he justifies himself and his apostleship, *ch.* x–xii, and throughout the whole epistle.

CHAPTER 1

After the introduction (ver. 1, 2) the apostle begins with the narrative of his troubles and God's goodness by way of thanksgiving to God (ver. 3–6), and for the edification of the Corinthians, ver. 7–11. Then he attests his and his fellow-labourers' integrity (ver. 12–14), and afterwards vindicates himself, ver. 15–24.

Verses 1, 2

I. The inscription. The apostleship itself was ordained by Jesus Christ, according to the will of God; and Paul was called to it by Jesus Christ, according to the will of God. He joins Timotheus with himself in writing this epistle. His dignifying Timothy with the title of *brother* shows the humility of this great apostle, and his desire to recommend Timothy to the esteem of the Corinthians. The persons to whom this epistle was sent, *the church of God at Corinth*: and also *to all the saints in all Achaia*, that is, to all the Christians who lived in the region round about.

II. The salutation. Therein the apostle desires the two great and comprehensive blessings, grace and peace, for those Corinthians. These two benefits are fitly joined together, because there is no good and lasting peace without true grace; and both of them come *from God our Father, and from the Lord Jesus Christ.*

Verses 3–6

The apostle begins with the narrative of God's goodness to him and his fellow-labourers in their manifold tribulations, which he speaks of by way of thanksgiving to God (*v.* 3–6).

I. The object of the apostle's thanksgiving, the blessed God. 1. *The God and Father of our Lord Jesus Christ.* In the New Testament God is styled *the God and Father of our Lord Jesus Christ*, to denote his covenant-relation to the Mediator and his spiritual seed. 2. *The Father of mercies.* All mercies are from God originally: mercy is his genuine offspring and his delight. 3. *The God of all comfort;* from him proceedeth the COMFORTER. All our comforts come from God.

II. The reasons of the apostle's thanksgivings.

1. The benefits that he himself and his companions had received from God, *v.* 4. In the world they had trouble, but in Christ they had peace. Their sufferings called *the sufferings of Christ* (*v.* 5), did abound, but their consolation by Christ did abound also. Then we speak best of God and his goodness when we speak from our own experience, and, in telling others, tell God also what he has done for our souls.

2. The advantage which others might receive (*v.* 4). What favours God bestows on us are intended not only to make us cheerful ourselves, but also that we may be useful to others.

Verses 7–11

The apostle speaks for the encouragement of the Corinthians; and tells them (*v.* 7) of his steadfast hope that they should receive benefit by the troubles he and his companions had met with. What their sufferings had been (*v.* 8). It is not certain what particular troubles in Asia are here referred to, for the apostle was in deaths often. This however is evident, that they were great tribulations. They *despaired even of life* (*v.* 8). And they were brought to this extremity in order *that they should not trust in themselves but in God*, *v.* 9. God often brings his people into great straits, that they may be induced to place their trust and hope in his all-sufficiency. Our extremity is God's opportunity. We may safely trust in *God, who raiseth the dead*, *v.* 9. He that can do this can do anything, and is worthy to be trusted in at all times. What the deliverance was that they had obtained. Their hope and trust were not in vain. God had delivered them, and did still deliver them, *v.* 10. What use they made of this deliverance. Past experiences are great encouragements to faith and hope. We reproach our experiences if we distrust God in future straits, who hath delivered as in former troubles. What was desired of the Corinthians upon this account (*v.* 11). He desires the help of others' prayers. If we thus help one another by our prayers, we may hope for an occasion of *giving thanks by many* for answer of prayer.

Verses 12–14

The apostle attests their integrity by the sincerity of their conversation.

I. He appeals to the testimony of conscience with rejoicing (*v.* 12). The witness appealed to, namely, conscience. This is God's deputy in the soul, and the voice of conscience is the voice of God. They rejoiced in the testimony of conscience. The testimony of conscience for us will be matter of rejoicing at all times and in all conditions. The testimony this witness gave. Conscience witnessed, (1) Concerning their conversation, their constant course of life: by that we may judge of ourselves, and not by this or that single act. (2) Concerning the manner of their conversation; that it was in simplicity and godly sincerity. This blessed apostle was a man of plain dealing; you might know where to have him. He was not a man who seemed to be one thing and was another, but a man of sincerity. (3) Concerning the principle they acted from in all their conversation, and that was not fleshly wisdom, but it was the grace of God.

II. He appeals to the knowledge of the Corinthians with hope and confidence, v. 13, 14. They never found anything in him unbecoming an honest man. This they had acknowledged in part already, and he doubted not but they would still do so to the end. And so there would be mutual rejoicing in one another.

Verses 15–24

The apostle here vindicates himself from the imputation of levity and inconstancy, in that he did not hold his purpose of coming to them at Corinth.

I. He avers the sincerity of his intention (v. 15–17), and he does this in confidence of their good opinion of him. He assured them he *was minded to come* to them that they might receive a *second benefit*. He tells them that he had not herein *used lightness* (v. 17), for his purpose was not *according to the flesh*. It was for some weighty reasons that he had altered his purpose; with him there was not yea yea, and nay nay, v. 17.

II. He would not have the Corinthians to infer that his gospel was false or uncertain, v. 18, 19. For *God is true*, and *the Son of God, Jesus Christ*, is true. Jesus Christ is not *yea* and *nay*, but in him was *yea* (v. 19), nothing but infallible truth. And the promises of God in Christ are not yea and nay, but yea and amen, v. 20. There is an inviolable constancy and certainty in all the parts of the gospel of Christ. The promises of the gospel covenant stand firm and inviolable. Bad men are false; good men are fickle; but *God is true*, neither fickle nor false. 1. They are the promises of the God of truth (v. 20). 2. They are made in Christ Jesus (v. 20), the Amen, the true and faithful witness. 3. They are confirmed by the Holy Spirit. He is given *as an earnest in their hearts*, v. 21, 22. An earnest secures the promise, and is part of the payment. And the accomplishment of them shall be to the *glory of God* (v. 20).

III. The apostle gives a good reason why he did not come to Corinth, v. 23. It was that he might spare them. He knew there were things amiss among them, and such as deserved censure, but was desirous to show tenderness. He assures them that this is the true reason. He adds that he did not pretend to have any dominion over their faith, v. 24. Christ only is the Lord of our faith. He reveals to us what we must believe. Paul, and Apollos, were *but ministers by whom they believed* (1 Cor. iii. 5), and so the *helpers of their joy*, even the joy of faith. Our strength and ability are owing to faith, and our comfort and joy must flow from faith.

CHAPTER 2

The apostle proceeds in the account of the reasons why he did not come to Corinth, ver. 1–4. Then he writes concerning the incestuous person (ver. 5–11), and afterwards informs them of his labours and success in preaching the gospel, ver. 12–17.

Verses 1–4

An account of the reason why he did not come to Corinth. He was unwilling to grieve them, or be grieved by them, v. 1, 2. If he had made them sorry, that would have been a sorrow to himself, for there would have been none to have made him glad. He tells them it was to the same intent that he wrote his former epistle, v. 3, 4. The particular thing referred to was the case of the incestuous person. He assures them that he did not design to grieve them. He wrote to them with much *anguish and affliction* in his own heart, and with great affection to them.

Verses 5–11

The apostle treats concerning the incestuous person. He tells them that the punishment which had been inflicted upon this offender was sufficient, v. 6. The desired effect was obtained. He therefore directs them, with all speed, to receive him again to their communion, v. 7, 8. He beseeches them to forgive him. They must also confirm their love to him; show that their reproofs proceeded from love to his person, as well as hatred to his sin. He was in danger of being *swallowed up with over-much sorrow, v. 7*. He was in danger of falling into despair. When sorrow is excessive it does hurt; and even sorrow for sin is too great when it drives men to despair. He would have them comply with his desire to restore him, v. 9. He mentions his readiness to concur with them in this matter, v. 10. And this he would do for their sakes, and for Christ's sake, in conformity to his doctrine and example, which are so full of kindness and tender mercy towards all those who truly repent. Not only was there danger lest Satan should get an advantage against the penitent, by driving him to despair; but against the apostles or ministers of Christ, by representing them as too rigid and severe. Satan is a subtle enemy, and we should not be *ignorant of his devices*: he is also a watchful adversary, ready to take all advantages against us.

Verses 12–17

The apostle makes a long digression, to give the Corinthians an account of his travels and labours, declaring at the same time how he *had no rest in his spirit*, when he found not Titus at Troas (v. 13). And we find afterwards (*ch.* vii. 5–7) that when the apostle had come into Macedonia he was comforted by the coming of Titus.

I. Paul's unwearied labour and diligence in his work, v. 12, 13. He went to Troas from Philippi by sea (Acts xx. 6), and thence he went to Macedonia. He was prevented in his design as to the place of working, yet he was unwearied in his work.

II. His success in his work, v. 12. God *made manifest the savour of his knowledge* by him in every place where he came. The apostle speaks of this as a matter of thankfulness to God. In ourselves we are weak, and have neither joy nor victory; but in Christ we may rejoice and triumph.

III. The comfort that the apostle found, even when the gospel was not successful to the salvation of some who heard it, v. 15–17.

1. The success is different; for some are saved by it, while others perish under it. (1) Unto some it is a *savour of death unto death*, as men dislike an ill savour, and therefore they are blinded and hardened by it. They reject the gospel, to their ruin, even to spiritual death. (2) Unto others the gospel is a *savour of life unto life*. To humble and gracious souls the preaching of the word is most delightful and profitable. As it quickened them at first, *when they were dead in trespasses and sins*, so it will end in eternal life.

2. The awful impressions this matter made upon the apostle, v. 16. Who is *worthy* to be employed in such weighty work? Who is able to perform such a difficult work? The work is great and our strength is small; *all our sufficiency is of God*.

3. The comfort which the apostle had. (1) Because faithful ministers shall be accepted of God, whatever their success be (v. 15), in those who are saved and in those also who perish. Ministers shall be accepted, and recompensed, not according to their success, but according to their fidelity. (2) Because his conscience witnessed to his faithfulness, v. 17. Though many *did corrupt the word of God*, yet the apostle's conscience witnessed to his fidelity. His aim was to approve himself to God; he therefore spoke and

acted always as in the sight of God, and therefore in sincerity.

CHAPTER 3

The apostle makes an apology for his seeming to commend himself, ver. 1-5. He then draws a comparison between the Old Testament and the New (ver. 6-11), whence he infers what is the duty of gospel ministers, and the advantage of those who live under the gospel, ver. 12, to the end.

Verses 1-5

I. The apostle makes an apology for seeming to commend himself. He neither needed nor desired any verbal commendation to them, nor letters testimonial from them, as some others did, meaning the false apostles or teachers, *v.* 1. The Corinthians themselves were his real commendation, *v.* 2. They were written *in his heart; known and read of all men.*

II. The apostle is careful to ascribe all the praise to God. He says they were the *epistle of Christ, v.* 3. The apostle and others were but instruments. This epistle was not written with *ink, but with the Spirit of the living God;* nor was it written in *tables of stone,* but on the *heart,* upon the *fleshy* (not *fleshly,* as fleshliness denotes sensuality) *tables of the heart,* that is, upon hearts that are softened by divine grace. He utterly disclaims the taking of any praise to themselves, and ascribes all the glory to God, *v.* 5. *All our sufficiency is of God;* to him therefore are owing all the praise and glory of that good which is done. The best are no more than what the grace of God makes them.

Verses 6-11

The apostle makes a comparison between the Old Testament and the New and values himself and his fellow-labourers by this, that *they were able ministers of the New Testament,* that God had made them so, *v.* 6.

I. He distinguishes between the letter and the spirit even of the New Testament, *v.* 6. They were ministers not merely of the letter, but they were ministers of the Spirit also. The *letter killeth,* but the Spirit of the gospel giveth life eternal.

II. He shows the excellency of the gospel above the law. The Old Testament dispensation was the *ministration of death (v.* 7), whereas that of the New Testament is the *ministration of life.* The law was the *ministration of condemnation,* but the gospel is the *ministration of righteousness.* This reveals the grace and mercy of God through Jesus Christ, for obtaining the remission of sins and eternal life. The gospel therefore so much exceeds in glory that in a manner it eclipses the glory of the legal dispensation, *v.* 10. The law is done away, but the gospel does and shall *remain, v.* 11. That dispensation was only to continue for a time; whereas the gospel shall remain to the end of the world.

Verses 12-18

I. The duty of the ministers of the gospel to use great clearness of speech. The gospel is a more clear dispensation than the law. Though the Israelites could not look *steadfastly to the end* of what was commanded, yet we may.

II. The privilege of those who enjoy the gospel, above those who lived under the law. Those who lived under the legal dispensation had their minds blinded (*v.* 14), and there was a *veil upon their hearts, v.* 15. There is a time coming when this *veil also shall be taken away,* and *when it* (the body of that people) *shall turn to the Lord, v.* 16. The condition of those who believe the gospel is much more happy. They have liberty (*v.* 17). They have *light;* for with *open face* we behold the glory of the Lord, *v.* 18. It was the peculiar privilege of Moses for God to converse with him face to face; but now all true Christians see him with open face. This light and liberty *are transforming (v.* 18), till grace here be consummated in glory for ever.

CHAPTER 4

I. Of the constancy of the apostle and his fellow-labourers in their work. II. Of their courage and patience under their sufferings.

Verses 1-7

In this chapter his design is to vindicate their ministry from the accusation of false teachers. He tells them how they believed, and how they showed their value for their office as ministers of the gospel.

I. Their constancy and perseverance in their work are declared (*v.* 1). And this their steadfastness was owing to the *mercy of God.* The best men in the world would faint in their work, and under their burdens, if they did not receive mercy from God. Their sincerity in their work is avouched (*v.* 2). They had no base and wicked designs covered with fair and specious pretences of something that was good. Nor did they in their preaching *handle the word of God deceitfully;* but they used *great plainness of speech.* They *manifested the truth to every man's conscience,* declaring nothing but what in their own conscience they believed to be true. And all this they did *as in the sight of God,* desirous thus to commend themselves to God, and to the consciences of men.

II. An objection is obviated. "How then does it come to pass, that the gospel is hid, as to some who hear it?" The true reasons of this are, 1. *Those are lost souls* to whom the gospel is hid, *v.* 3. 2. *The god of this world hath blinded their minds, v.* 4. They are under the influence of the devil, who is here called *the god of this world,* because of the great interest he has in this world. And as he is the prince of darkness, and ruler of the darkness of this world, so he darkens the understandings of men. Christ's design by his gospel is to make a glorious discovery of God to the minds of men. The design of the devil is to keep men in ignorance.

III. A proof of their integrity is given, *v.* 5. They made it their business to preach Christ and not themselves. But they *preached Christ Jesus the Lord,* as being Christ's servants. All the lines of Christian doctrine centre in Christ; and in preaching Christ we preach all we should preach. Ministers should not be of proud spirits who are servants to the souls of men: yet, at the same time, they must avoid becoming the servants of the humours or the lusts of men. Why they should preach Christ. For by gospel light we have the *knowledge of the glory of God,* which shines in the *face of Jesus Christ, v.* 6. It is a pleasant thing for the eye to behold the sun in the firmament; but it is more pleasant and profitable when the gospel shines in the heart. Why they should not preach themselves: because they were but earthen vessels. The ministers of the gospel are weak and frail creatures; they are mortal, and soon broken in pieces. And God has so ordered it that the weaker the vessels are the stronger his power may appear to be, that the treasure itself should be valued the more.

Verses 8-18

I. How their sufferings, and patience under them, are declared, *v.* 8-12. "*We are troubled on every side, yet not distressed,*" *v.* 8. We can see help in God, and help from God. "*We are perplexed, yet not in despair (v.* 8), knowing that God is able to support us, and to deliver us. We are *persecuted; yet not forsaken* of God," *v.* 9. "We are *cast down;* yet we are *not destroyed,*" *v.* 9. Still they were preserved, and kept their heads above water. Whatever condition the children of God may be in, in this world they have a *"but not"* to comfort themselves with. The apostle speaks of their sufferings as a counterpart of the sufferings of Christ, *v.* 10. Thus did they *bear about the dying of the Lord Jesus* in their body, *that the life of Jesus might also be made manifest*, though they were always *delivered to death* (*v.* 11), and though *death worked in them* (*v.* 12). *Death worketh in us; but life in you*, *v.* 12.

II. What it was that kept them from sinking and fainting under their sufferings, *v.* 13–18.

1. Faith kept them from fainting (*v.* 13). The grace of faith is a sovereign cordial against fainting-fits in troublous times. As the apostle had David's example to imitate, who said (Ps. cxvi. 10), *I have believed, and therefore have I spoken*, so he leaves us his example to imitate: *We also believe*, says he, *and therefore speak*.

2. Hope of the resurrection kept them from sinking, *v.* 14. Their hope was firm, being well grounded, that he who raised up Christ the head will also raise up all his members. What reason has a good Christian to fear death, that dies in hope of a joyful resurrection?

3. The consideration of the benefit of the church kept them from fainting, *v.* 15. We may well afford to bear sufferings patiently when we see others are the better for them.

4. The thoughts of the advantage their souls would reap kept them from fainting, *v.* 16. It is our happiness if when the body is sick the soul is vigorous. The best of men have need of further renewing of the inward man, even day by day. As in wicked men things grow every day worse and worse, so in godly men they grow better and better.

5. The prospect of eternal life and happiness kept them from fainting. The apostle and his fellow-sufferers saw their afflictions working towards heaven, and that they would end at last (*v.* 17), whereupon they weighed things aright in the balance of the sanctuary. They found afflictions to be light, and the glory of heaven to be *a far more exceeding weight*. That which sense was ready to pronounce heavy and long, faith perceived to be light and short, and but for a moment. Their faith enabled them to make this right judgment of things, *v.* 18. Unseen things are eternal, seen things but temporal. By faith we not only discern these things, and the great difference between them, but by this also we take our aim at unseen things.

CHAPTER 5

The reasons why they did not faint under their afflictions, namely, their assurance of happiness after death (ver. 1–5). An inference for the comfort of believers (ver. 6–8), and another to quicken them in their duty, ver. 9–11. An apology for seeming to commend himself (ver. 12–15). Two things that are necessary in order to our living to Christ, ver. 16, to the end.

Verses 1–11

I. He mentions their expectation, and desire, and assurance, of eternal happiness, *v.* 1–5.

1. The believer's expectation of eternal happiness after death, *v.* 1. "We know that we have a building of God, we have a firm expectation of the future felicity." (1) What heaven is in the eye and hope of a believer. He looks upon it as a house, or habitation, our Father's house, and our everlasting home. It is a house in the heavens. It is a building of God. It is eternal in the heavens, not like the earthly tabernacles, the poor cottages of clay in which our souls now dwell. (2) When it is expected this happiness shall be enjoyed—so soon as *our house of this earthly tabernacle is dissolved*. Then comes the house not made with hands. Such as have walked with God here shall dwell with God for ever.

2. The believer's earnest desire after this future blessedness—*we groan*. (1) A groaning of sorrow under

a heavy load, *v.* 2. *We that are in this tabernacle groan, being burdened*, *v.* 4. Believers groan because burdened with a body of sin. (2) There is a groaning of desire after the happiness of another life; and thus believers groan. The believer is *willing rather to be absent from the body, that he may be present with the Lord* (*v.* 8), to put off these rags of mortality that he may put on the robes of glory. Gracious souls are not found naked in the other world; no, they are clothed with garments of praise.

3. The believer's assurance of this future blessedness, from the experience of the grace of God, making him meet for this blessedness, *v.* 5. All who are designed for heaven hereafter are wrought or prepared for heaven while they are here; the stones of that spiritual building above are squared and fashioned here below. No hand less than the hand of God can work us for this thing. The *earnest of the Spirit* gave them this assurance.

II. An inference for the comfort of believers in their present state in this world, *v.* 6–8. What their present state is: they *are absent from the Lord* (*v.* 6). God is with us here, yet we are not with him as we hope to be: for *We walk by faith, not by sight*, *v.* 7. Faith is for this world, and sight is reserved for the other world. How comfortable and courageous we ought to be in the hour of death (*v.* 6) and again (*v.* 8). They should be willing rather to die than live, when it is the will of God that they should *put off this tabernacle*, to close their eyes to all things in this world, and open them in a world of glory. Faith will be turned into sight.

III. An inference to quicken himself and others to duty, *v.* 9–11. Well-grounded hopes of heaven will be far from giving the least encouragement to sloth, *v.* 9. *We are ambitious.* The apostle was thus ambitious to *be accepted of him*, the Lord (*v.* 9). It was the summit of ambition. Further quickening motives from the consideration of the judgment to come, *v.* 10, 11. The certainty of this judgment, for we must appear; the universality of it, for we must all appear; the great Judge before whose judgment-seat we must appear, the Lord Jesus Christ; the recompence to be then received, for things done in the body. The apostle calls this awful judgment *the terror of the Lord* (*v.* 11), and was excited to persuade men to repent, and live a holy life, that, when Christ shall appear terribly, they may appear before him comfortably.

Verses 12–15

I. The apostle makes an apology for seeming to commend himself and his fellow-labourers (*v.* 13). The true reason was this, to put an argument in their mouths wherewith to answer his accusers.

II. He gives good reasons for their great zeal and diligence. The apostle tells them, 1. It was for the glory of God, and the good of the church, that he was thus zealous and industrious, *v.* 13. 2. *The love of Christ constrained them*, *v.* 14. Love has a constraining virtue to excite ministers and private Christians in their duty. Our love to Christ will have this virtue; and Christ's love to us will have this effect upon us. (1) What we must have continued to be, had not Christ died for us, *v.* 14. *If one died for all, then were all dead;* dead in sins and trespasses, spiritually dead. (2) What such should do, for whom Christ died; they should live to him. They should not live *to themselves*, *v.* 15. Then do we live as we ought to live when we live to Christ, who died for us.

Verses 16–21

Two things that are necessary in order to our living to Christ: regeneration and reconciliation.

I. Regeneration. 1. Weanedness from the world, *v.* 16. The love of Christ is in our hearts, and the world is under our feet. *Yea, though we have known Christ after the flesh, yet, says the apostle, we know him no more.* We must live upon his spiritual presence and the comfort it affords. 2. A thorough change of the heart: *He is a new creature, v. 17.* Some read it, *Let him be a new creature,* not only that they wear a new livery, but that they have a new heart and new nature. *Old things are passed away,* and *all these things must become new.*

II. Reconciliation.

1. An unquestionable privilege, *v. 18, 19.* Reconciliation supposes a quarrel, or breach of friendship. Yet, behold, there may be a reconciliation. He has reconciled us to himself by Jesus Christ, *v. 18.* All things relating to our reconciliation by Jesus Christ are of God, who by the mediation of Jesus Christ has reconciled the world to himself. He has appointed the *ministry of reconciliation, v. 18.* He has appointed the office of the ministry, which is a *ministry of reconciliation.*

2. Our indispensable duty, *v. 20.* As God is willing to be reconciled to us, we ought to be reconciled to God. Though God can be no loser by the quarrel, nor gainer by the peace, yet by his ministers he beseeches sinners that they would be reconciled to him. And for our encouragement so to do the apostle subjoins what should be well known by us (*v. 21*). The purity of the Mediator: *He knew no sin.* The sacrifice he offered: *He was made sin; that* is, a sin-offering, a sacrifice for sin. That *we might be made the righteousness of God in him.* As Christ, who knew no sin of his own, was made sin for us, so we, who have no righteousness of our own, are made the righteousness of God in him.

CHAPTER 6

An account of his general errand to all to whom he preached, ver. 1–10. Then he addresses himself particularly to the Corinthians, with great affection, ver. 11–18.

Verses 1–10

An account of the apostle's general errand and exhortation to all to whom he preached.

I. The errand or exhortation itself, *v. 1.* As it is the duty of the ministers of the gospel to exhort their hearers to accept of grace and mercy, so they are honoured with this high title of *co-workers with* God. They are workers with God, yet under him. If they be faithful, they may hope to find God working with them, and their labour will be effectual. Observe the way of the gospel: it is not with roughness and severity, but with all mildness and gentleness, to beseech and entreat.

II. The arguments and method which the apostle used.

1. The present time is the only proper season to accept of the grace that is offered: Now *is the accepted time,* NOW *is the day of salvation, v. 2.* The morrow is none of ours: we know not what will be on the morrow.

2. What caution they used not to give offence that might hinder the success of their preaching, *v. 3.* When others are too apt to take offence, we should be cautious lest we give offence; and ministers especially should be careful.

3. Their constant aim in all things to approve themselves faithful, as became the ministers of God, *v. 4.* His great desire was to be the servant of God, and to approve himself so. (1) By much patience in afflictions. He was a great sufferer, and met with many afflictions, but he exercised much patience in all, *v. 4, 5.* Those who would approve themselves to God must approve themselves faithful in trouble as well as in peace, not only in doing the work of God diligently, but also in bearing the will of God

patiently. (2) By acting from good principles. What his principles were (*v. 6, 7*); namely, pureness; and there is no piety without purity. Knowledge was another principle; and zeal without this is but madness. He also acted with *long-suffering and kindness,* bearing with the hardness of men's hearts, and hard treatment from their hands. He acted under the influence of the Holy Ghost, from the noble principle of unfeigned love, according to the rule of the word of truth, under the power of God, having on the armour of righteousness, which is the best defence against the temptations of prosperity on the right hand, and of adversity on the left. (3) By a due temper and behaviour under all the variety of conditions, *v. 8–10.* The apostles met with honour and dishonour, good report and evil report. We stand in need of the grace of God to arm us against the temptations of honour on the one hand, so as to bear good report without pride, and of dishonour on the other hand, so as to bear reproaches without recrimination. Some represented them as the best, and others as the worst, of men: by some they were counted deceivers, by others as true. They were slighted by the men of the world as unknown, not worth taking notice of; yet in all the churches of Christ they were well known, and of great account: they were looked upon as dying, "and yet behold, we live." They were chastened, and often fell under the lash of the law, yet not killed: and though it was thought that they were sorrowful, a company of mopish and melancholy men, yet they were always rejoicing in God. They were despised as poor, and yet they made many rich, by preaching the unsearchable riches of Christ. They were thought to have nothing, yet they possessed all things. They had nothing in themselves, but possessed all things in Christ. Such a paradox is a Christian's life.

Verses 11–18

The apostle cautions them against mingling with unbelievers.

I. The caution is introduced with a profession of the most tender affection to them, *v. 11–13.* He seemed to want words to express the warm affections he had for these Corinthians. *Our mouth is open unto you, and our heart is enlarged unto you. "You are not,"* says he, *"straitened in us;* we would gladly do you all the service we can, and if it be otherwise, the fault is in yourselves; it is because you are straitened in yourselves. All we desire as a recompence is only that you would be proportionally affected towards us, as children should love their father."

II. The caution itself, not to mingle with unbelievers, not to be *unequally yoked* with them, *v. 14.* It is wrong for good people to join in affinity with the wicked and profane. There is more danger that the bad will damage the good than hope that the good will benefit the bad. We should not yoke ourselves in friendship with wicked men and unbelievers. We should never choose them for our bosom-friends. Much less should we join in religious communion with them. It is a very great absurdity, *v. 14, 15.* Believers are righteous; but unbelievers are unrighteous. Believers are made light in the Lord, but unbelievers are in darkness; and what comfortable communion can these have together? Christ and Belial are contrary one to the other. It is a dishonour to the Christian's profession (*v. 16*); for Christians are the *temples of the living God.* Now there can be no agreement between *the temple of God and idols.* There is a great deal of danger in communicating with unbelievers, danger of being defiled and of being rejected; therefore the exhortation is (*v. 17*) *to come out from among them, to be separate,* as one would avoid the society of those who have the leprosy or the plague, and not *to touch the unclean thing.* Who can touch pitch, and not be defiled by it? We must take care not to defile ourselves by converse with those who defile themselves with sin. It is base ingratitude to God for all the favours he has bestowed upon believers and promised to them, *v.* 18. God has promised to be a Father to them, and that they shall be his sons and his daughters; and is there a greater honour or happiness than this?

CHAPTER 7

An exhortation to progressive holiness, ver. 1–4. Then the apostle returns to speak further of the incestuous person, and tells them what comfort he received upon his meeting with Titus (ver. 5–7), and how he rejoiced in their repentance, ver. 8–11. He concludes with endeavouring to comfort the Corinthians, ver. 12–16.

Verses 1–4

These verses contain a double exhortation:

I. To make a progress in holiness, *v.* 1. 1. The dying unto sin. We must *cleanse ourselves from all filthiness of flesh and spirit*. There are sins of the flesh, that are committed with the body, and sins of the spirit; and we must cleanse ourselves from the filthiness of both. 2. The living unto righteousness and holiness. We must be still perfecting holiness, and not be contented with sincerity (which is our gospel perfection), without aiming at sinless perfection. This we must do in the *fear of God*; there is no holiness without it.

II. To show a due regard to the ministers of the gospel: *Receive us, v.* 2. If the ministers of the gospel are thought contemptible because of their office, there is danger lest the gospel itself be contemned also. He had done nothing to forfeit their esteem (*v.* 2). He did not herein reflect upon them for want of affection to him, *v.* 3. He assures them again of his great affection to them, insomuch that he could spend his last breath at Corinth, and *live and die with them*. It was his great affection to them that made him use such *boldness of speech towards them*, and caused him to *glory*, or make his boast of them.

Verses 5–11

I. How he was distressed, *v.* 5. He was troubled when he did not meet with Titus at Troas, and afterwards when for some time he did not meet with him in Macedonia. There were *fightings without* and there were *fears within*.

II. How he was comforted, *v.* 6, 7. The very coming of Titus was some comfort to him. The good news which Titus brought concerning the Corinthians was matter of greater consolation. He found Titus to be comforted in them; and this filled the apostle with comfort. He ascribes all his comfort to God as the author. It was God who comforted him by the coming of Titus, *v.* 6.

III. How greatly he rejoiced at their repentance. The apostle was sorry that it was needful he should make those sorry whom he would rather have made glad, *v.* 8. But now he rejoiced, when he found they had *sorrowed to repentance, v.* 9. The effect of it (*repentance unto salvation, v.* 10), made him rejoice.

1. The antecedent of true repentance is godly sorrow. It was a godly sorrow, because a sorrow for sin. Godly sorrow will end in salvation; but worldly sorrow worketh death. The sorrows of worldly men for worldly things will bring down grey hairs the sooner to the grave. Humiliation and godly sorrow are previously necessary in order to repentance, and both of them are from God, the giver of all grace.

2. The happy fruits and consequences of true repentance are mentioned (*v.* 11). Where the heart is changed, the life and actions will be changed too. It wrought indignation at sin; it wrought fear, a fear of reverence, an awful fear of God, a cautious fear of sin, and a jealous fear of themselves. It wrought

vehement desires after a thorough reformation of what had been amiss. It wrought zeal, a mixture of love and anger, a zeal for duty, and against sin. And thus *in all things had they approved themselves to be clear in that matter*. They were penitent, and therefore clear of guilt before God, who would pardon and not punish them.

Verses 12–16

The apostle endeavours to comfort the Corinthians. He had a good design in his former epistle, which might be thought severe, *v.* 12. It was not chiefly *for his cause that did the wrong*, nor was it merely *for his cause that suffered wrong*, but it was also to manifest his sincere concern and *care for them.* Titus was rejoiced, and his spirit refreshed, with their comfort, and this comforted and rejoiced the apostle also (*v.* 13); and, as Titus was comforted while he was with them, so when he remembered his reception among them, the thought of these things increased his affections to them, *v.* 15. Great comfort and joy follow upon godly sorrow. Paul was glad, and Titus was glad, and the Corinthians were comforted. Well may all this joy be on earth, when there is joy in heaven over one sinner that repenteth. He was not ashamed of his boasting concerning them to Titus (*v.* 14); for he was not disappointed in his expectation concerning them, and he could now with great joy declare what confidence he still had in them as to all things.

CHAPTER 8

Paul is exhorting and directing the Corinthians about a particular work of charity—to relieve the necessities of the poor saints at Jerusalem and in Judæa. The apostle stirred them up to contribute liberally for their relief. He acquaints the Corinthians with the good example of the Macedonians. Titus was sent to Corinth to collect their bounty, ver. 1–6. He then proceeds to urge this duty (ver. 7–15), and commends the persons who were employed in this affair, ver. 16–24.

Verses 1–6

I. The apostle takes occasion from the good example of the churches of Macedonia to exhort the Corinthians to the good work of charity.

1. He acquaints them with their great liberality, *v.* 1. It is great grace and favour from God, if we are made useful to others.

2. He commends the charity of the Macedonians. They were themselves in distress, yet they contributed to the relief of others, *v.* 2. As they had abundance of joy in the midst of tribulation, they abounded in their liberality; they gave out of a little, trusting in God to provide for them. They gave very largely, with *the riches of liberality* (*v.* 2); it was *according to*, yea *beyond, their power* (*v.* 3), as much as could well be expected from them, if not more. *They were willing of themselves* (*v.* 3), and were so far from needing that Paul should urge and press them that they *prayed him with much entreaty to receive the gift, v.* 4. Their charity was founded in true piety (*v.* 5). They solemnly made a fresh surrender of themselves, and all they had, unto the Lord Jesus Christ, sanctifying their contributions to God's honour, by first giving themselves to the Lord. We should give ourselves to God; we cannot bestow ourselves better. What we give or bestow for charitable uses will not be accepted of God, unless we first give ourselves to the Lord.

II. The apostle tells them that Titus was desired to go and make a collection among them (*v.* 6). Titus had already begun this work among them, therefore he was desired to finish it. When so good a work had already prospered in so good a hand, it would be a pity if it should not proceed and be finished. The work of charity will often succeed the best when the most proper persons are employed to solicit contributions and dispose of them.

Verses 7–15

I. He urges upon them the consideration of their eminence in other gifts and graces, and would have them excel in this of charity also, *v.* 7. When he would persuade the Corinthians to this good thing, he commends them for other good things. Most people love to be complimented, especially when we ask a gift of them; and it is a justice we owe to those in whom God's grace shines to give them their due commendation. What it was that the Corinthians abounded in. Faith is mentioned first, for that is the root. Those who abound in faith will abound in other graces and good works also. To their faith was added utterance. Many have faith who want utterance. With their utterance there appeared knowledge. They abounded also in all diligence. Those who have great knowledge and ready utterance are not always the most diligent Christians. Great talkers are not always the best doers. And further, they had abundant love to their ministers. Now to all these good things the apostle desires them to add this grace also, to abound in charity to the poor. He takes care to prevent any misapprehensions, and tells them (*v.* 8) he does not speak by commandment. I give *my advice, v.* 10. Many a thing which is good for us to do, yet cannot be said to be, by express and indispensable commandment, our duty at this or that time.

II. Another argument is taken from the consideration of the grace of our Lord Jesus Christ. And *you know,* saith the apostle, *the grace of our Lord Jesus Christ* (*v.* 9), *that though he was rich, yet for your sakes he became poor;* that ye thereby might be made rich, rich in the love of God, rich in the blessings of the new covenant, rich in the hopes of eternal life. We should be charitable to the poor out of what we have, because we ourselves live upon the charity of the Lord Jesus Christ.

III. Another argument is taken from their forwardness to begin this good work. It was expedient for them to finish what they had begun, *v.* 10, 11. Good purposes, indeed, are good things; they are like buds and blossoms, pleasant to behold, and give hopes of good fruit; but they are lost, and signify nothing, without performances which would be acceptable to God (*v.* 12). When men purpose that which is good, and endeavour to perform also, God will accept of what they can do, and not reject them for what is not in their power to do. This scripture will by no means justify those who think good meanings are enough.

IV. Another argument is taken from the distribution of the things of this world, and the mutability of human affairs, *v.* 13–15. Those who have a greater *abundance may supply those who are in want,* that there may be room for charity. It is the will of God that, by our mutually supplying one another, there should *be some sort of equality.* All should think themselves concerned to supply those who are in want. This is illustrated by the instance of gathering and distributing manna in the wilderness: *he that had gathered much* had nothing over.

Verses 16–24

I. He commends Titus for his earnest care for them. This is mentioned with thankfulness to God (*v.* 16), and it is cause of thankfulness if God hath put it into the hearts of any to do us or others any good. He commends him for his readiness to this present service, *v.* 17. Asking charity for the relief of others is looked upon as a thankless office; yet it is a good office.

II. He commends another brother, who was sent with Titus. It is generally thought that this was Luke. He is commended as a man whose *praise was in the gospel through all the churches, v.* 18. As one chosen of the churches (*v.* 19). This was done, it is most

likely, at the request of Paul himself; *that no man might blame him in that abundance which was administered by him* (*v.* 20). He would not give occasion to any to accuse him of partiality, and thought it to be his duty, *to provide for things honest, not only in the sight of the Lord, but also in the sight of men.* We live in a censorious world, and should cut off occasion from those who seek occasion to speak reproachfully.

III. He commends also another brother. This brother is thought to be Apollos. Whoever he was, he had *approved himself diligent in many things;* and therefore was fit to be employed in this affair.

IV. He concludes with a general good character of them all (*v.* 23). Wherefore, he exhorts them to show their liberality that these messengers of the churches, and the churches themselves, might see a full *proof of their love,* and that it was with good reason the apostle had even *boasted on their behalf, v.* 24.

CHAPTER 9

The apostle seems to excuse his earnestness in pressing the Corinthians to the duty of charity (ver. 1–5), and proceeds to give directions about the acceptable manner of performing it, ver. 6, to the end.

Verses 1–5

I. It was needless to press them with further arguments to afford relief to their poor brethren (*v.* 1). *He knew their forwardness* to every good work, and how they had begun this good work a year ago. He had boasted of their zeal to the Macedonians, and this had provoked many of them to do as they had done. As they had begun well, they would go on well.

II. He sends Titus and the other brethren to them, that, having this timely notice, they might be fully ready (*v.* 3), when he should come to them. When we would have others to do that which is good we must give them time. Another reason was that he might not be ashamed of his boasting concerning them, if they should be found unready, *v.* 3, 4. Some from Macedonia might *haply come with him:* and, if the collection should not then be made, this would make him, not to say them, ashamed.

Verses 6–16

I. Proper directions to be observed about the right manner of bestowing charity. It should be bountifully. Men who expect a good return at harvest are not wont to pinch and spare in sowing their seed. It should be deliberately: *Every man, according as he purposes in his heart, v.* 7. Works of charity, like other good works, should be done with thought and design. It should be freely given: *Not grudgingly, nor of necessity,* but cheerfully, *v.* 7. Persons sometimes will give merely to satisfy the importunity of those who ask their charity, and what they give is in a manner squeezed or forced from them, and this unwillingness spoils all they do.

II. Good encouragement to perform this work of charity.

1. They themselves would be no losers by what they gave in charity. What is given to the poor is far from being lost; as the precious seed which is cast into the ground is not lost, for it will spring up, and bear fruit; the sower shall receive it again with increase, *v.* 6. God loveth a cheerful giver (*v.* 7). Can a man be a loser by doing that with which God is pleased? God is able to make our charity redound to our advantage, *v.* 8. We have no reason to distrust the goodness of God; he is *able to make all grace abound.* The honour of it is lasting, the reward of it eternal. A prayer to God that they might be gainers, and not losers, *v.* 10, 11. To whom the prayer is made —to God, *who ministereth seed to the sower,* who giveth such an increase of the fruits of the earth

that we have not only bread sufficient to eat for one year, but enough to sow again for a future supply. For what he prayeth. That they may have *bread for their food*, always a competency for themselves—that God will *multiply their seed sown*, that they may still be able to do more good—and that there may be *an increase of the fruits of righteousness*, so as to be *enriched in everything to all bountifulness* (v. 11). Works of charity are so far from impoverishing us that they are the proper means truly to enrich us, or make us truly rich.

2. While they would be no losers, the poor would be gainers, v. 12.

3. This would redound to the praise and glory of God. All who wished well to the gospel would *glorify God for this* proof *of subjection to the gospel of Christ*, and true love to all men, v. 13.

4. Those whose wants were supplied would make the best return they were able, by sending up many prayers to God for those who had relieved them, v. 14. As this is the only recompence the poor can make, so it is often greatly for the advantage of the rich.

Lastly, The apostle concludes this whole matter with this doxology, *Thanks be to God for his unspeakable gift*, v. 15. He means Jesus Christ, who is indeed the unspeakable gift of God unto this world.

Chapter 10

The apostle asserts the power of his preaching, and his power to punish offenders, ver. 1–6, asserting his relation to Christ, and his authority as an apostle of Christ (ver. 7–11), and refuses to justify himself, or to act by such rules as the false teachers did, ver. 12, to the end.

Verses 1–6

I. He addresses them in a very mild and humble manner, v. 1. In the midst of the greatest provocations he shows mildness. How humbly also does this great apostle speak of himself, as *one in presence base among them*! So his enemies spoke of him with contempt. He is desirous that no occasion may be given to use severity, v. 2. *He beseeches them* to give no occasion for him to be bold, or to exercise his authority against them in general.

II. He asserts the power of his preaching and his power to punish offenders.

1. The power of his preaching, v. 3, 5. The work of the ministry is a warfare, not *after the flesh* indeed, for it is a spiritual warfare, with spiritual enemies and for spiritual purposes. The doctrines of the gospel are the weapons. Outward force, therefore, is not the method of the gospel, but strong persuasions. People must be persuaded to God and their duty, not driven by force of arms. What opposition is made against the gospel by the powers of sin and Satan in the hearts of men, but these strongholds are pulled down by the gospel, through the grace and power of God.

2. The apostle's power to punish offenders is asserted in v. 6. Though the apostle showed meekness and gentleness, yet he would not betray his authority.

Verses 7–11

"*Do you,*" says he, "*look on things after the outward appearance?* (v. 7). Is this a fit rule to make an estimate of things or persons by?" In outward appearance, Paul was mean and despicable with some. But there are often false appearances.

I. His relation to Christ, v. 7. Now the apostle reasons thus with the Corinthians: "Suppose it to be so, allowing what they say to be true, yet they ought also to allow this to us, that *we also are Christ's*." There is room in Christ for many; and those who differ much from one another may yet be one in

him. It would help to heal the differences that are among us if we would remember that those who differ from us may belong to Christ too. We must not think that we are the people, and that none belong to Christ but ourselves. This we may plead for ourselves, against those who judge us and despise us that, how weak soever we are, yet, as they are Christ's, so are we.

II. His authority from Christ as an apostle. The *Lord had given it to him*, and it was more than his adversaries could justly pretend to. It was certainly what he should not be ashamed of, v. 8. The nature of his authority: it was for *edification, and not for destruction*. The caution with which he speaks of his authority, professing that his design was not to terrify them with big words, nor by angry letters, v. 9. The apostle declares he did not intend to frighten those who were obedient. He would have his adversaries *know this* (v. 11), that he would, by the exercise of his apostolical power make it appear to have a real efficacy.

Verses 12–18

I. The apostle refuses to justify himself as the false apostles did, v. 12. He plainly intimates that they took a wrong method to commend themselves. They were pleased, and did pride themselves, in their own attainments. We should be pleased and thankful for what we have of gifts or graces, but never pride ourselves therein, as if there were none to be compared with us. The apostle would not be of the number of such vain men.

II. He fixes a better rule for his conduct, v. 13. He would not go beyond the line prescribed to him, which the false apostles did, while they *boasted of other men's labours*.

III. He acted according to this rule, v. 14. He acted according to this rule in preaching at Corinth, for he came thither by divine direction. In boasting of them as his charge, he boasted not of *other men's labours*, v. 15.

IV. He declares his success in observing this rule. His hope was that their faith was increased, and that others would embrace the gospel also.

V. He seems to check himself as if he had spoken too much in his own praise. He is afraid of boasting, or taking any praise to himself, v. 17. Ministers in particular must be careful not to glory in their performances, but must give God the glory of their work, and the success thereof, v. 18. Of all flattery, self-flattery is the worst. Instead of praising or commending ourselves, we should strive to approve ourselves to God, and his approbation will be our best commendation.

Chapter 11

The apostle goes on with his discourse, in opposition to the false apostles. I. He apologizes for going about to commend himself, ver. 1–4. II. His equality with the other apostles, and with the false apostles in this particular of preaching the gospel to the Corinthians freely, without wages, ver. 5–15. III. He makes another preface to what he was about further to say in his own justification, ver. 16–21. And, IV. He gives a large account of his labours, and sufferings, in which he exceeded the false apostles, ver. 22, to the end.

Verses 1–4

1. The apology the apostle makes for going about to commend himself, v. 1. As much against the grain as it is with a proud man to acknowledge his infirmities, so much is it against the grain with a humble man to speak in his own praise. 2. The reasons for what the apostle did. To preserve the Corinthians from being corrupted by the insinuations of the false apostles, v. 2, 3. *He was jealous over them with godly jealousy*. He had *espoused them to one husband*, and he was desirous to *present them as a chaste virgin*—pure, and spotless, and faithful, not having *their minds corrupted*

by false teachers. To vindicate himself against the false apostles. They could not pretend they had another Jesus, or another Spirit, or another gospel, to preach to them, *v.* 4. But seeing there is but one Jesus, one Spirit, and one gospel preached to them and received by them, what reason could there be why the Corinthians should be prejudiced against him, who first converted them to the faith?

Verses 5–15

I. His equality with the other apostles, *v.* 5. This he expresses very modestly: *I suppose so.* He might have spoken very positively. He speaks modestly of himself, and humbly owns his personal infirmity, that he was *rude in speech.* However, he was not rude *in knowledge*; much less was he ignorant of the mysteries of the kingdom of heaven.

II. His equality with the false apostles in this particular. They ought to acknowledge he had been a good friend to them. He had preached the gospel to them freely, *v.* 7–10. He says he himself had *taken wages of other churches* (*v.* 8), so that he had a right to have asked and received from them: yet he waived his right, and chose rather to abase himself. He chose rather to be supplied from Macedonia than to be chargeable unto them. He informs them of the reason. It was not because *he did not love them* (*v.* 11), but it was to avoid offence. He would not give occasion for any to accuse him of worldly designs in preaching the gospel, or that he intended to enrich himself, *v.* 12.

III. The false apostles are charged *as deceitful workers* (*v.* 13), and though they were the ministers of Satan, would seem to be the *ministers of righteousness.* Hypocrisy is a thing not to be much wondered at in this world, especially when we consider the great influence Satan has. As he can turn himself into any shape, and look sometimes *like an angel of light*, in order to promote his kingdom of darkness, so he will teach his instruments to do the same. But it follows, *Their end is according to their works* (*v.* 15).

Verses 16–21

Let no man think me a fool, v. 16. Boasting of ourselves is usually not only a sign of a proud mind, but a mark of folly also, *v.* 17. He would not have them think that boasting of ourselves is a thing commanded by the Lord in general unto Christians. It is the duty and practice of Christians rather to humble and abase themselves; yet prudence must direct in what circumstances it is needful to speak of what God has wrought for us, and in us, and by us too, *v.* 18. But he gloried in his infirmities, as he tells them afterwards. These words, *You suffer fools gladly seeing you yourselves are wise* (*v.* 19), may be ironical. "Notwithstanding all your wisdom, you willingly suffer yourselves to be *brought into bondage*, or suffer others to lord it over you; nay, even to *smite you on the face*, or impose upon you to your very faces" (*v.* 20). The circumstances of the case were such as made it needful that *whereinsoever any were bold* he should be *bold also, v.* 21.

Verses 22–33

I. The privilege of his birth (*v.* 22). He was a Hebrew of the Hebrews; of a family among the Jews that never intermarried with the Gentiles. He was also an Israelite, and was also of the seed of Abraham.

II. He makes mention also of his apostleship, *v.* 23. They had found full proofs of his ministry: *Are they ministers of Christ? I am more so.*

III. He chiefly insists upon this, that he had been an extraordinary sufferer for Christ, *v.* 23. When the apostle would prove himself an extraordinary minister, he proves that he had been an extraordinary sufferer.

Bonds and imprisonments were familiar to him. He says that *thrice he suffered shipwreck. A night and a day he had been in the deep* (*v.* 25). Wherever he went, he went in perils. If he journeyed by land, or voyaged by sea, he was in perils of robbers; his own countrymen sought to kill him; the heathen were not more kind to him, for among them he was in peril. If he was in the city, or in the wilderness, still he was in peril. He was in peril not only among avowed enemies, but among those also who called themselves brethren, but were false brethren, *v.* 26. He was in *watchings often*, and exposed to *hunger and thirst*; in *fastings often*; and endured *cold and nakedness, v.* 27. Thus he was used as if he·had been the burden of the earth, and the plague of his generation. As an apostle, the *care of all the churches* lay on him, *v.* 28. He mentions this last, as if this lay the heaviest upon him, *v.* 29. There was not a weak Christian with whom he did not sympathize, nor any one scandalized, but he was affected therewith. Nor was he ashamed of all this; it was what he accounted his honour, *v.* 30.

He mentions one particular part of his sufferings out of its place, as if he had forgotten it before, namely, the danger he was in at Damascus, soon after he was converted. This was his first great danger and difficulty, and the rest of his life was of a piece with this. The apostle confirms this narrative with a solemn oath, *v.* 31. It is a great comfort to a good man that *the God and Father of our Lord Jesus Christ* knows the truth of all he says, and knows all he does and all he suffers for his sake.

CHAPTER 12

The apostle proceeds in maintaining the honour of his apostleship. He makes mention of the favour God had shown him, and the use he made of this dispensation, ver. 1–10. Then he addresses himself to the Corinthians, giving a large account of his behaviour and kind intentions towards them, ver. 11, to the end.

Verses 1–10

I. The narrative the apostle gives of the favours God had shown him, for doubtless he himself is the man in Christ of whom he speaks. He was *caught up into the third heaven, v.* 2. When this was we cannot say, much less can we pretend to say *how* this was. In some sense he was caught up into the *third heaven.* This third heaven is called paradise (*v.* 4). The apostle does not mention what he saw in the third heaven or paradise, but tells us that *he heard unspeakable words*: nor was it lawful to utter those words. The modest manner in which the apostle mentions this matter, *v.* 1. He therefore did not mention this till *above fourteen years* after, *v.* 2. Again, his humility appears by the check he seems to put upon himself (*v.* 6). It is an excellent thing to have a lowly spirit in the midst of high advancements; and those who abase themselves shall be exalted.

II. The methods God took to prevent his *being lifted up above measure.* When God's people communicate their experiences, let them always remember to take notice of what God has done to keep them humble.

1. The apostle was pained with a thorn in the flesh, and buffeted with a messenger of Satan, *v.* 7. We are much in the dark about what this was. Some think it was an acute bodily pain or sickness. This is certain, that what the apostle calls a thorn in his flesh was for a time very grievous to him: but the thorns Christ wore for us, sanctify and make easy all the thorns in the flesh we may at any time be afflicted with.

2. The design of this was to keep the apostle humble, *v.* 7. If God loves us, he will hide pride from us, and keep us from being exalted above measure. This thorn in the flesh is said to be a messenger of

Satan, which he did not send with a good design, but with ill intentions. But God overruled it for good.

3. The apostle prayed earnestly to God for the removal of this sore grievance. If an answer be not given to the first prayer, nor to the second, we must hold on, and hold out, till we receive an answer. As troubles are sent to teach us to pray, so they are continued to teach us to continue instant in prayer.

4. *My grace is sufficient for thee.* Though God accepts the prayer of faith, yet he does not always answer it in the letter; as he sometimes grants in wrath, so he sometimes denies in love. It is a great comfort to us, whatever thorns in the flesh we are pained with, that God's grace is sufficient for us. Grace signifies two things: (1) The goodwill of God towards us, and this is sufficient to strengthen and comfort us. (2) The good work of God in us. Christ Jesus will proportion the remedy to our malady.

III. The use which the apostle makes of this dispensation: *He gloried in his infirmities* (v. 9), and took pleasure in them for Christ's sake, v. 10. They were fair opportunities for Christ to manifest the power and sufficiency of his grace resting upon him. When we are weak in ourselves, then we are strong in the grace of our Lord Jesus Christ.

Verses 11–21

I. He blames them that they had not stood up in his defence. They compelled him to commend himself, v. 11. They in particular had good reason to speak well of him. It is a debt we owe to good men to stand up in the defence of their reputation. How much soever we are esteemed by others, we ought always to think humbly of ourselves. See an example of this in this great apostle, who thought himself to be nothing, though in truth he was not behind the greatest apostles.

II. His behaviour and kind intentions towards them. He says (v. 13) he had not been burdensome to them, for the time past, and tells them (v. 14) he would not be burdensome to them when he should come to them. He spared their purses to save their souls. Those who aim at clothing themselves with the fleece of the flock, and take no care of the sheep, are hirelings, and not good shepherds. He would gladly spend and be spent for them (v. 15); so spend as to be spent, and be like a candle, which consumes itself to give light to others. He did not abate in his love to them, v. 15. He was careful not only that he himself should not be burdensome, but that none he employed should. He was a man who did all things for edifying, v. 19. He would not shrink from his duty. Therefore he was resolved to be faithful in reproving sin, v. 20. Faithful ministers must not fear offending the guilty by sharp reproofs as they are needful, in public and in private. He was grieved at the apprehension that he should find scandalous sins among them not duly repented of. This would be the cause of great humiliation and lamentation. We have reason to *bewail many that have sinned, and have not repented,* v. 21. Those who love God, and love them, should mourn for them.

CHAPTER 13

The apostle threatens to be severe against obstinate sinners (ver. 1–6); then he makes a suitable prayer to God on the behalf of the Corinthians (ver. 7–10), and concludes his epistle, ver. 11–14.

Verses 1–6

I. The apostle threatens to be severe against obstinate sinners when he should come. He was not hasty in using severity, but gave a first and second admonition (v. 1), referring to his first and second epistles, by which he admonished them, as if he were present with them, though in person he was absent, v. 2. We should go, or send, to our brother, once and again, to tell him of his fault. Now he tells them to exercise severity. The threatening itself: *That he would not spare* such as were impenitent. Though it is God's gracious method to bear long with sinners, yet he will not bear always.

II. Why he would be thus severe, v. 3. It was the design of the false teachers to make the Corinthians call this matter into question, of which yet they had not weak, but strong and mighty proofs (v. 3). Even as Christ himself *was crucified through weakness but liveth by the power of God* (v. 4), so the apostles did yet manifest the power of God, and particularly the power of his grace, in converting the world to Christianity. He puts them upon proving their Christianity (v. 5). If Jesus Christ was in them, this was a proof that Christ spoke in him. If therefore they could prove themselves *not to be reprobates,* he trusted they would know that he was not a reprobate (v. 6). We should examine whether we be in faith; *prove our own selves* whether Christ be in us, or not.

Verses 7–10

I. The apostle's prayer to God on the behalf of the Corinthians, v. 7. We are more concerned to pray that we may not do evil than that we may not suffer evil.

II. The reasons why the apostle put up this prayer to God, v. 7. The best way to adorn our holy religion is *to do that which is honest,* and of good report. Further that they might be free from all blame when he should come to them. This is intimated in v. 8. If therefore they did not do evil the apostle had no power to punish them (v. 9), "Though we are weak through persecutions and contempt, we bear it joyfully, while we see that you are strong and persevering in well-doing." He desired their perfection (v. 9). He not only desired that they might be kept from sin, but also that they might grow in grace. This was the great end of his writing this epistle.

Verses 11–14

I. A valediction.

1. He gives them several good exhortations. To be perfect, or to be knit together in love. To be of good comfort. To be of one mind, for the more easy we are with our brethren the more ease we shall have in our own souls. He exhorts them to live in peace, that difference in opinion should not cause an alienation of affections.

2. He encourages them with the promise of God's presence among them, v. 11. God is the God of love and peace. God will be with those who live in love and peace. He will love those who love peace.

3. He gives directions to them to salute each other, and sends kind salutations to them from those who were with him, v. 12, 13.

II. The apostolical benediction (v. 14). Thus the apostle concludes his epistle. This is a very solemn benediction, and we should give all diligence to inherit this blessing.

AN EXPOSITION, WITH PRACTICAL OBSERVATIONS, OF

THE EPISTLE OF ST. PAUL TO

THE GALATIANS

While he was with them, they had expressed the greatest esteem and affection both for his person and ministry. Some judaizing teachers got in among them. That which these false teachers chiefly aimed at was to draw them off from the truth as it is in Jesus, particularly in the great doctrine of justification, asserting the necessity of joining the observance of the law of Moses with faith in Christ in order to it. They did all they could to lessen the character and reputation of the apostle, representing him as one who, if he was to be owned as an apostle, yet was much inferior to others, and particularly who deserved not such a regard as Peter, James, and John. In both these attempts they had but too great success. This was the occasion of his writing this epistle, wherein he expresses his great concern that they had suffered themselves to be so soon turned aside, vindicates his own character and authority as an apostle, and shows he was not *behind the very chief of the apostles.* He then sets himself to assert and maintain the great gospel doctrine of justification by faith without the works of the law, and he exhorts them to stand fast in the liberty wherewith Christ had made them free, gives them several very needful counsels and directions and then concludes the epistle.

CHAPTER 1

After the preface or introduction (v. 1-5), the apostle severely reproves these churches (ver. 6-9), and then proves his own apostleship, I. From his preaching the gospel, ver. 10. II. From his having received it by immediate revelation, ver. 11, 12. For the proof of which he acquaints them, 1. What his former conversation was, ver. 13, 14. 2. How he was converted, ver. 15, 16. 3. How he behaved himself afterwards, ver. 16, to the end.

Verses 1–5

I. The person or persons from whom this epistle is sent—from Paul *an apostle,* &c., *and all the brethren that were with him.* 1. He gives a general account both of his office and of the manner in which he was called to it. As to his office, he was an apostle. He acquaints them how he was called to this office, and assures them that his commission to it was wholly divine. He was an apostle *by Jesus Christ*, he had his commission immediately from him, and consequently from *God the Father.* Furthermore his call to the apostleship was after Christ's resurrection from the dead. He had his call from him when in heaven. 2. He joins all the brethren that were with him in the inscription of the epistle. Hereby it would appear that he had their concurrence with him in the doctrine which he had preached, and was now about to confirm.

II. To whom this epistle is sent. It should seem that all of them were more or less corrupted through the arts of those seducers who had crept in among them.

III. The apostolical benediction, *v.* 3. Grace includes God's goodwill towards us and his good work upon us; and peace implies in it all that inward comfort or outward prosperity which is really needful for us. Both these the apostle wishes for these Christians. First grace, and then peace, for there can be no true peace without grace. Having mentioned the Lord Jesus Christ, he cannot pass without enlarging upon his love (*v.* 4). This present world is an evil world: it has become so by the sin of man. Jesus Christ has died to deliver us from this present evil world, not to remove his people out of it, but to rescue them from the power of it. This, the apostle informs us, he has done *according to the will of God and our Father.* Hence we have encouragement to look upon God as our Father. As he is the Father of our Lord Jesus, so in and through him he is also the Father of all true believers.

The apostle concludes this preface with a solemn ascription of praise and glory to him (*v.* 5).

Verses 6–9

I. How much he was concerned at their defection. There were several things by which their defection was greatly aggravated: 1. That they were *removed from him that had called them;* not only from the apostle, but from God himself. They had been guilty of a great abuse of his kindness and mercy towards them. 2. They had been called to partake of the greatest blessings and benefits. In proportion to the greatness of the privilege they enjoyed, such were their sin and folly in deserting it. 3. That they were *so soon removed.* In a very little time they lost that esteem of this grace of Christ which they seemed to have. This, as it was an instance of their weakness, so it was a further aggravation of their guilt. 4. That they were removed to *another gospel, which yet was not another.* You will find it to be no gospel at all, but the perverting of the gospel of Christ. Those who go about to establish any other way to heaven than what the gospel of Christ has revealed will find themselves wretchedly mistaken.

II. The gospel he had preached to them was the only true gospel. He pronounced an anathema upon those who pretended to preach any other gospel (*v.* 8). "If you have any other gospel preached to you under our name, or under colour of having it from an angel himself, you must conclude that you are imposed upon: and whoever preaches another gospel lays himself under a curse."

Verses 10–24

What Paul had said in the preface of this epistle he now proceeds to enlarge upon. There he had declared himself to be an apostle of Christ; and here he comes more directly to support his claim to that character and office.

I. From the scope and design of his ministry. As he professed to act by a commission from God, so that which he chiefly aimed at was to promote his glory, by recovering sinners into a state of subjection to him. He did not accommodate himself to the humours of persons, but his great care was to approve himself to God. No man could serve two such masters, and therefore he dare not allow himself to gratify men at the expense of his faithfulness to Christ. Thus, he proves that he was truly an apostle of Christ. The great end which ministers of the gospel should aim at is to bring men to God. They must not be solicitous to please men, if they would approve themselves faithful servants to Christ.

II. From the manner wherein he received the gospel which he preached to them (v. 11, 12). One thing peculiar in the character of an apostle was that he had been called to, and instructed for, this office immediately by Christ himself. He had his knowledge of the gospel, as well as his authority to preach it, directly from the Lord Jesus.

1. He tells them what his conversation in time past had been, v. 13, 14. It must be something very extraordinary which had made so great a change in him, and brought him not only to profess, but to preach, that doctrine, which he had before so vehemently opposed.

2. In how wonderful a manner he was brought to the knowledge and faith of Christ, and appointed to the office of an apostle, v. 15, 16. There was something peculiar in the case of Paul, both in the suddenness and in the greatness of the change wrought in him, and also in the manner wherein it was effected. He had Christ *revealed in him*. It will but little avail us to have Christ revealed to us if he is not also revealed in us. It pleased God *to reveal his Son in him* that he should preach him among the heathen. So that he was both a Christian and an apostle by revelation.

3. How he behaved himself hereupon, from v. 16. *He conferred not with flesh and blood*. So that it could not well be pretended that he was indebted to any other either for his knowledge of the gospel or his authority to preach it. This account being of importance, to establish his claim to this office, he confirms it by a solemn oath (v. 20), which, though it will not justify us in solemn appeals to God upon every occasion, yet shows that, in matters of weight and moment, this may sometimes not only be lawful, but duty. He had no communication at that time with the *churches of Christ in Judæa*, they had not so much as *seen his face*. The very report of this mighty change in him, as it filled them with joy, so it excited them to give glory to God on the account of it.

CHAPTER 2

The apostle makes it appear that he was not beholden to them either for his knowledge of the gospel or his authority as an apostle; he was owned and approved even by them, as having an equal commission with them to this office. I. He particularly informs them of another journey which he took to Jerusalem, ver. 1–10. And, II. Gives them an account of another interview he had with the apostle Peter at Antioch, and how he was obliged to behave himself towards him there. He proceeds to discourse on the great doctrine of justification by faith in Christ, without the works of the law, which it was the main design of this epistle to establish.

Verses 1–10

From the very first preaching of Christianity there was a difference of apprehension between those Christians who had first been Jews and those who had first been Gentiles. Peter was the apostle of the circumcision. But Paul was the apostle of the Gentiles. He informs us of another journey which he took to Jerusalem, v. 1–10.

I. It was not till *fourteen years* after the former (mentioned *ch.* i. 18). It was some evidence that he had no dependence upon the other apostles, that he had been so long absent from them, and was all the while employed in preaching pure Christianity, without being called into question by them for it. *He went up with Barnabas, and took with him Titus also*. If the journey here spoken of was the same with that recorded Acts xv, then we have a plain reason why Barnabas went along with him; for he was chosen by the Christians at Antioch to be his companion and associate. Though Titus had now become not only a convert to the Christian faith, but a preacher of it too, yet he was by birth a Gentile and uncircumcised, and therefore, by making him his companion, it appeared that their doctrine and practice were of a piece. *He went up by revelation.* It was a privilege with which this apostle was often favoured to be under a special divine direction. It should teach us to endeavour to see our way made plain before us, and to commit ourselves to the guidance of Providence.

II. An account of his behaviour while he was at Jerusalem.

1. *He there communicated the gospel to them, which he preached among the Gentiles, but privately, &c.* Observe both the faithfulness and prudence of our great apostle. (1) His faithfulness in giving them a fair account of the doctrine which he had all along preached among the Gentiles, and was still resolved to preach. (2) He uses prudence and caution herein. He chooses rather to do it in a more private than in a public way. The reason of this his caution was lest he should stir up opposition against himself and thereby either the success of his past labours should be lessened, or his future usefulness be obstructed. It was enough to his purpose to have his doctrine owned by those who were of greatest authority, whether it was approved by others or not.

2. In his practice he firmly adhered to the doctrine which he had preached. Though he had Titus with him, who was a Greek, yet he would not suffer him to be circumcised. It does not appear that the apostles at all insisted upon this; they were not for imposing it upon the Gentiles. But there were others who did, *false brethren, unawares brought in*, to *spy out their liberty which they had in Christ Jesus*. Their design herein was *to bring them into bondage*. Had they prevailed with Paul to have circumcised Titus, they would easily have imposed circumcision upon other Gentiles, and so have brought them under the bondage of the Law of Moses. But Paul would not *give place by subjection, no, not for an hour, that the truth of the gospel might continue with them*. He would not yield to those who were for the Mosaic rites and ceremonies, but would stand fast in the liberty wherewith Christ hath made us free.

3. Though he conversed with the other apostles, yet he did not receive any addition to his knowledge or authority from them, v. 6. That they were apostles first was no prejudice to his being equally an apostle with them. They told him nothing but what he before knew by revelation, nor could they except against the doctrine which he communicated to them.

4. The other apostles were fully convinced of his divine mission and authority, and accordingly acknowledged him as their fellow-apostle, v. 7–10. They justly concluded *that the gospel of the uncircumcision was committed to Paul, as the gospel of the circumcision was to Peter. They gave unto him and Barnabas the right hand of fellowship*, and agreed that *these should go to the heathen, while they continued to preach to the circumcision*. And thus this meeting ended in an entire harmony and agreement; they approved both Paul's doctrine and conduct, and had nothing further to add, *only that they would remember the poor*, which of his own accord *he was very forward to do*. Herein he has given us an excellent pattern of Christian charity and we should by no means confine it to those who are just of the same sentiments with us, but be ready to extend it to all whom we have reason to look upon as the disciples of Christ.

Verses 11–21

I. He acquaints them with another interview which he had with the apostle Peter at Antioch, and what passed between them there, v̄. 11–14. In their other meeting, there had been good harmony and agreement. But in this Paul finds himself obliged to oppose Peter.

1. Peter's fault. When he came among the Gentile

churches, he complied with them, and did eat with them. But, when there came some Jewish Christians from Jerusalem, *he withdrew, and separated himself.* His fault herein had a bad influence upon others. Barnabas himself, one of the apostles of the Gentiles, *was carried away with their dissimulation.* Here note, (1) The weakness and inconstancy of the best of men, and how apt they are to falter in their duty to God, out of an undue regard to the pleasing of men. (2) The great force of bad examples, especially the examples of great men and good men.

2. The rebuke which Paul gave him. When he observes him thus behaving he is not afraid to reprove him for it. Paul adhered resolutely to his principles, when others faltered in theirs. He was as good a Jew as any and the Gentiles must comply with the Jews, or else not be admitted into Christian communion.

II. He takes occasion to speak of that great fundamental doctrine of the gospel—That justification is only by faith in Christ, and not by the works of the law. This was the doctrine which Paul had preached among the Galatians, to which he still adhered, and which it is his great business in this epistle to confirm.

1. The practice of the Jewish Christians themselves: "What did we believe in Christ for? Was it not that we might be justified by the faith of Christ? And, if so, is it not folly to go back to the law?" To give the greater weight to this he adds (v. 17), "*But if, while we seek to be justified by Christ, we ourselves also are found sinners, is Christ the minister of sin?* Will it not follow that he is so, if he engage us to receive a doctrine by which we are so far from being justified that we remain impure sinners?" But he rejects it with abhorrence: "*God forbid,*" says he, "that thereby we should direct us into a way of justification that is defective and ineffectual. *For,*" says he (v. 18), "*if I build again the things which I destroyed I make myself a transgressor;* I own myself to remain under the guilt of sin, notwithstanding my faith in Christ."

2. What his own judgment and practice were. (1) He was dead to the law, *through the law itself.* He saw that justification was not to be expected by the works of it and that there was now no further need of the sacrifices since they were done away in Christ, by his offering up himself a sacrifice for us. But, though he was thus *dead to the law,* yet he did not look upon himself as *without law.* He was dead to the law, *that he might live unto God.* The doctrine of the gospel, instead of weakening the bond of duty, did but the more strengthen and confirm it; and therefore, though he was dead to the law, yet it was only in order to his living a new and better life to God. (2) As he was dead to the law, so he was alive unto God through Jesus Christ (v. 20). He is crucified, and yet he lives; the old man is crucified, but the new man is living. Sin is mortified, and grace quickened. *I live, and yet not I.* He has the comforts and the triumphs of grace; and yet that grace is not from himself, but from another. *He is crucified with Christ,* and yet *Christ lives in him.* He is interested in the death of Christ, so as to die unto sin; and yet interested in the life of Christ, so as to live unto God. *He lives in the flesh,* and yet *lives by faith*; to outward appearance he lives as other people do, yet he has a higher and nobler principle that supports him, that of faith in Christ. Those who have true faith live by that faith.

Lastly, By the doctrine of justification by faith in Christ, without the works of the law, he avoided two great difficulties. 1. *He did not frustrate the grace of God. If it be of works, it is no more of grace.* 2. He did not frustrate the death of Christ; for, if we look for salvation by the law of Moses, then we render the death of Christ needless.

CHAPTER 3

The apostle, I. Reproves the Galatians for their folly, in suffering themselves to be drawn away from the faith of the gospel. II. He proves the doctrine of justification by faith without the works of the law, 1. From the example of Abraham's justification. 2. From the nature of the law. 3. From the express testimony of the Old Testament; and, 4. From the covenant of God with Abraham. Lest any should hereupon say, "Wherefore than serveth the law?" he answers, (1) It was added because of transgressions. (2) It was given to convince the world of the necessity of a Saviour. (3) It was designed as a schoolmaster, to bring us to Christ. He concludes the chapter by acquainting us with the privilege of Christians.

Verses 1–5

The apostle is here dealing with those who, having embraced the faith of Christ, still continued to seek for justification by the works of the law.

He reproves them, v. 1. He asks, *Who hath bewitched you?* They did not adhere to the gospel way of justification, wherein they had been taught. It is not enough to know the truth, and to say we believe it, but we must obey it too. Several things proved the folly of these Christians.

1. *Jesus Christ had been evidently set forth as crucified among them;* they had had the doctrine of the cross preached to them, and the sacrament of the Lord's supper administered among them, in both which Christ crucified had been set before them.

2. He appeals to the experiences they had had of the working of the Spirit upon their souls (v. 2). He desires to know how they came by these gifts and graces: Was it *by the works of the law*? Or was it by the *hearing of faith.* The latter, if they would say the truth, they were obliged to own.

3. He calls upon them to consider their past and present conduct (v. 3, 4). They had begun well; but now they were turning to the law, and expected to be advanced to higher degrees of perfection by adding the observance of it to faith in Christ, in order to their justification. This, instead of being an improvement upon the gospel, was really a perversion of it; they were so far from being more perfect Christians that they were more in danger of becoming no Christians at all. They had not only embraced the Christian doctrine, but suffered for it too; and therefore their folly would be the more aggravated, if now they should desert it.

4. They had *ministered the Spirit to them, and wrought miracles among them*: and he appeals to them whether they did it *by the works of the law or by the hearing of faith.* They very well knew that it was not the former, but the latter; and therefore must needs be inexcusable in forsaking a doctrine which had been so signally owned and attested.

Verses 6–18

He largely proves the doctrine which he had reproved them for rejecting.

I. From the example of Abraham's justification (v. 6). His faith fastened upon the promise of God, and upon his believing he was owned and accepted of God as a righteous man. *Those who are of faith are the children of Abraham* (v. 7). Abraham was justified by faith, and so are they (v. 8). God would justify the heathen world in the way of faith; and therefore in Abraham, that is, in the seed of Abraham, which is Christ, not the Jews only, but the Gentiles also, should be blessed as Abraham was, being justified as he was. It was through faith in the promise of God that he was blessed, and it is only in the same way that others obtain this privilege.

II. We cannot be justified but by faith fastening on the gospel, because the law condemns us. If we put ourselves upon trial in that court, we are certainly lost and undone, v. 10. The condition of life, by the law, is perfect, personal, and perpetual obedience; the language of it is as v. 12. Unless our obedience be universal, and unless it be perpetual too, we fall under the curse of the law. If, as transgressors of the law, we are under the curse of it, it must be a vain thing to look for justification by it. Yet the apostle afterwards acquaints us that there is a way open to our escaping this curse, through faith in Christ (as he says, *v.* 13). A strange method it was which Christ took to redeem us from the curse of the law; it was *by his being himself made a curse for us.* The design of this was *that the blessing of Abraham might come on the Gentiles through Jesus Christ*—that all who believed on Christ might become heirs of Abraham's blessing, and particularly of that great promise of the Spirit. Hence it appeared that it was not by putting themselves under the law, but by faith in Christ, that they became the people of God and heirs of the promise.

III. The apostle alleges the express testimony of the Old Testament, *v.* 11. *The just shall live by faith.* It is only through faith that persons become righteous, and as such obtain this life and happiness. *The law is not of faith*, but the language of it is, *The man that doeth them shall live in them.* It requires perfect obedience as the condition of life, and therefore now can by no means be the rule of our justification.

IV. The apostle urges the stability of the covenant which God made with Abraham, which was not disannulled by the giving of the law to Moses, *v.* 15, &c. Faith had the precedence of the law, for Abraham was justified by faith. God entered into covenant with Abraham (*v.* 8). The original word signifies both a covenant and a testament. If it should be said that a testament may be defeated for want of persons to claim the benefit of it (*v.* 16), he shows that there is no danger of that. Abraham is dead, and the prophets are dead, but the covenant is made with Abraham and his seed. Says the apostle, "It points at a single person—*that seed is Christ.*" So that the covenant is still in force; for Christ abideth for ever. The subsequent law could not disannul the previous covenant or promise (*v.* 18). If the inheritance was given to Abraham by promise, we may be sure that God would not retract that promise; for he is not a man that he should repent.

Verses 19–29

Why did God give the law by Moses?

I. The law *was added because of transgressions*, *v.* 19. The Israelites were sinners as well as others, and therefore the law was given to convince them of their sin. And it was also intended to restrain them from the commission of sin. The law was given for this purpose *till the seed should come to whom the promise was made.* The law was added because of transgressions, till this fulness of time should come. But when a fuller discovery of divine grace in the promise was made, then the law, as given by Moses, was to cease. And though the law, considered as the law of nature, is always in force, yet we are now no longer under the bondage and terror of that legal covenant. The law then was only to lead men to see their need of the promise, by showing them the sinfulness of sin, and to point them to Christ. Whereas the promise was given immediately by God himself, the law was given *by the ministry of angels, and the hand of a mediator.* Hence it appeared that the law could not be designed to set aside the promise; for (*v.* 20), *God is one*, and therefore it is not to be supposed that he should make void a promise which he had long before made to Abraham. This would not have been consistent with his truth and faithfulness. Moses was only a mediator, and therefore the law that was given by him could not affect the promise.

II. The law was given to convince men of the necessity of a Saviour (*v.* 21). The law is by no means inconsistent with the promise. The design of it is to discover men's transgressions, and to show them the need they have of a better righteousness than that of the law. *The scripture hath concluded all under sin* (*v.* 22). The law discovered their wounds, but could not afford them a remedy. The great design of it was *that the promise by faith of Jesus Christ might be given to those that believe*, that being convinced of the insufficiency of the law to effect a righteousness for them, they might be persuaded to believe on Christ, and so obtain the benefit of the promise.

III. The law was designed for *a schoolmaster, to bring men to Christ*, *v.* 24. They were shut up, held under the terror and discipline of it, as prisoners in a state of confinement. Hereby they might be disposed more readily to accept Christ when he came into the world. It was proper to convince them of their lost and undone condition in themselves, and to let them see the weakness and insufficiency of their own righteousness. And thus it was their schoolmaster, to instruct and govern them in their state of minority, their *servant*, to lead and conduct them to Christ (as children were wont to be led to school by those servants who had the care of them); that they might be more fully instructed by him as their schoolmaster, in the true way of justification and salvation, which is only by faith in him. The apostle adds (*v.* 25) *after faith has come, we are no longer under a schoolmaster* —we have no such need of the law to direct us to him as there was then.

1. The goodness of God to his people of old, in giving the law to them. It furnished them with sufficient helps both to direct them in their duty to God and to encourage their hopes in him.

2. The great fault and folly of the Jews, in mistaking the design of the law. They expected to be justified by the works of it, whereas it was never designed to be the rule of their justification, but only a means of convincing them of their guilt and of their need of a Saviour.

3. The great advantage of the gospel state above the legal. We are not now treated as children in a state of minority, but as sons grown up to a full age.

(1) *We are the children of God by faith in Christ Jesus*, *v.* 26. The great privilege which real Christians enjoy under the gospel: They are no longer accounted servants, but *sons.* They are admitted into the number, and have a right to all the privileges of his children. How they come to obtain this privilege *by faith in Christ Jesus.* This faith in Christ, whereby they became the children of God (*v.* 27), was what they professed in baptism. Having thus become the members of Christ, they were owned as the children of God. Baptism is now the solemn rite of our admission into the Christian church. *Those who are baptized into Christ have put on Christ;* under the gospel baptism comes in the room of circumcision. Being baptized into Christ, we are baptized into his death, that as he died and rose again, so we should die unto sin, and walk in newness of life; it would be of great advantage to us did we oftener remember this.

(2) This privilege of being the children of God is now enjoyed in common by all real Christians. The law indeed made a difference between Jew and Greek, between *bond and free*, and between *male and female.* But it is not so now; they all stand on the same level, *and are all one in Christ Jesus.* All who sincerely believe on Christ, of what nation, or sex, or condition, soever they be, are accepted of him, and become the children of God through faith in him.

(3) *Being Christ's, we are Abraham's seed, and heirs according to the promise.* "You therefore become the true *seed of Abraham*, and as such *are heirs according to the promise*, and consequently are entitled to the great blessings and privileges of it." They were very unreasonable and unwise, in hearkening to those

who at once endeavoured to deprive them of the truth and liberty of the gospel.

CHAPTER 4

The apostle is still carrying on the same general design. For this purpose he makes use of various considerations, I. The great excellence of the gospel state above the legal, ver. 1–7. II. The happy change that was made in them at their conversion, ver. 8–11. III. The affection they had had for him, ver. 12–16. IV. The character of the false teachers, ver. 17, 18. V. The very tender affection he had for them, ver. 19, 20. VI. The history of Isaac and Ishmael.

Verses 1–7

The apostle deals plainly with those who hearkened to the judaizing teachers.

I. He acquaints us with the state of the Old Testament church: it was like a child under age. That was indeed a dispensation of grace, and yet it was comparatively a dispensation of darkness; for as the heir, in his minority, is *under tutors and governors till the time appointed of his father*, so it was with the Old Testament church. And as that was a dispensation of darkness, so of bondage too. The church then lay more under the character of *a servant*. The time appointed of the Father having come, we are under a dispensation of greater light and liberty.

II. He acquaints us with the much happier state under the gospel-dispensation, v. 4–7. *When the fulness of time had come he sent forth his Son*, &c. He, in pursuance of the great design he had undertaken, submitted to be *made of a woman*—there is his incarnation; and to be *made under the law*—there is his subjection. One great end of all this was *to redeem those that were under the law*. He was sent to redeem us, *that we might receive the adoption of sons*—that we might no longer be accounted as servants, but as sons grown up to maturity. Under the gospel, particular believers receive the adoption. They have together therewith the Spirit of adoption, enabling them in prayer to eye God as a Father (*v.* 6): *Because you are sons, God hath sent forth the Spirit of his Son into your hearts, crying Abba, Father.* And hereupon (*v.* 7) the apostle concludes this argument: *Wherefore thou art no more a servant, but a son; and, if a son, then an heir of God through Christ;* we are no longer under the servitude of the law, but, upon our believing in Christ, become the sons of God, and, being the sons, we are also heirs of God.

1. The wonders of divine love and mercy towards us, particularly of God the Father, in sending his Son into the world to redeem and save us—of the Son of God, in suffering so much, for us—and of the Holy Spirit, in condescending to dwell in the hearts of believers for such gracious purposes.

2. The great and invaluable advantages which Christians enjoy under the gospel. We receive *the adoption of sons*. We who by nature are children of wrath and disobedience have become by grace children of love. We receive *the Spirit of adoption*. All who are received into the number partake of the nature of the children of God; for he will have all his children to resemble him. Those who have the nature of sons shall have the inheritance of sons.

Verses 8–11

I. He reminds them what they were before the gospel was preached to them. Then *they knew not God*. They were under the worst of slaveries, for *they did service to those which by nature were no gods*, and therefore were utterly unable to hear and help them. Those who are ignorant of the true God cannot but be inclined to false gods.

II. He calls upon them to consider the happy change made in them by the preaching of the gospel. *They had known God or rather were known of God;* this happy change in their state was not owing to themselves, but to him. All our acquaintance with God begins with him; we know him, because we are known of him.

III. The unreasonableness of their suffering themselves to be brought again into a state of bondage. *How turn you again*, &c., says he, *v.* 9. "How is it that you, who have been taught to worship God in the gospel way, should now be persuaded to comply with the ceremonial way of worship? They were more inexcusable than the Jews themselves, who might be supposed to have some fondness for that which had been of such long standing among them. Besides, what they suffered themselves to be brought into bondage to were but *weak and beggarly elements*, such things as had no power in them to cleanse the soul. Their weakness and folly were the more aggravated, in submitting to them, and in observing their various festivals, *days, and months, and times, and years.* It is possible for those who have made great professions of religion to be afterwards drawn into very great defections from the purity and simplicity of it. This the apostle lays a special stress upon, that after they had known God, or rather were known of him, they desired to be in bondage under the weak and beggarly elements of the law.

IV. He expresses his fears concerning them, *lest he had bestowed on them labour in vain.* He had been at a great deal of pains about them, but now they were rendering his labour among them fruitless, and with the thoughts of this he could not but be deeply affected.

Verses 12–16

I. How affectionately he addresses himself to them. He styles them brethren, though he knew their hearts were in a great measure alienated from him. He would have them *to be as he was, for he was as they were, they had not injured him at all.* He had no quarrel with them upon his own account. Thus he endeavours to mollify their spirits towards him, that so they might receive the admonitions he was giving them. In reproving others we should take care to convince them that our reproofs do not proceed from any private pique but from a sincere regard to the honour of God and their truest welfare.

II. He magnifies their former affection. He puts them in mind of the difficulty under which he laboured when he came first among them: *I knew how, through infirmity of the flesh, I preached the gospel unto you at the first.* When this *infirmity of the flesh* was, which in the following words he expresses by *his temptation that was in his flesh*, we can now have no certain knowledge of. It seems it made no impression on them to his disadvantage. They did not despise him on the account of it, but on the contrary, *received him as an angel of God, even as Christ Jesus.* He was a welcome messenger to them; yea, so great was their esteem of him, that *they could have plucked out their own eyes, and have given them to him.* How uncertain the respects of people are, how apt they are to change their minds, so that they are ready to pluck out the eyes of those for whom they would before have plucked out their own!

III. He expostulates with them hereupon: *Where is then, the blessedness you spoke of?* "You once thought yourselves happy in receiving the gospel; have you now any reason to think otherwise?" Those who have left their first love would do well to consider, Where is now the blessedness they once spoke of? He again asks (*v.* 16), "*Am I become your enemy, because I tell you the truth?* How is it that I, who was heretofore your favourite, am now accounted your enemy? It is no uncommon thing for men to account those their enemies who are really their best friends; for so, undoubtedly, those are who tell them the truth.

Ministers sometimes create enemies to themselves by the faithful discharge of their duty. Yet ministers must not forbear speaking the truth, for fear of offending others. If others have become their enemies, it is only for telling them the truth.

Verses 17, 18
He here gives them the character of those false teachers. He tells them they were designing men, who were aiming to set up themselves. "*They zealously affect you,*" says he; "*and pretend a great deal of affection to you, but not well*; for *they would exclude you, that you might affect them.* That which they are chiefly aiming at is to engage your affections to them.*" There may appear to be a great deal of zeal where yet there is but little truth and sincerity. The apostle gives us that excellent rule which we have, v. 18, *It is good to be zealously affected always in a good thing.* What our translation renders *in a good thing* some choose to render *to a good man,* and so consider the apostle as pointing to himself; *and not only when I am present with you.* It is a very good rule that zeal be exercised only upon that which is good; for zeal is then only good when it is in a good thing. It is good to be zealous always in a good thing; not for a time only, or now and then, like the heat of an ague-fit, but, like the natural heat of the body, constant. Happy would it be for the church of Christ if this rule were better observed among Christians!

Verses 19, 20
He here expresses his great affection to them. He was not like them—one thing when among them and another when absent from them. Nor was he like their false teachers, who pretended a great deal of affection to them, when at the same time they were only consulting their own interest. He calls them *his children,* as he justly might, yea, he styles them his *little children,* which may possibly have a respect to their present behaviour, whereby they showed themselves too much like little children. He expresses his concern for them. *He travailed in birth for them that Christ might be formed in them,* that they might become Christians indeed. From this we may note, 1. The very tender affection which faithful ministers bear towards those among whom they are employed; it is like that of the most affectionate parents to their little children. 2. That the chief thing they are longing for, on their account, is that Christ may be formed in them. How unreasonably must those people act who suffer themselves to be prevailed upon to desert or dislike such ministers! He adds (v. 20) that *he desired to be then present with them,* that thereupon he might find occasion to *change his voice* towards them; for at present *he stood in doubt of them.* He knew not well what to think of them. But he would be glad to find that matters were better with them than he feared, and that he might have occasion to commend them, instead of thus reproving and chiding them.

Verses 21–31
The apostle illustrates the difference between believers who rested in Christ only and those judaizers who trusted in the law, by a comparison taken from the story of Isaac and Ishmael. *Tell me,* says he, *you that desire to be under the law, do you not hear the law?* He sets before them the history itself (v. 22, 23): *For it is written, Abraham had two sons,* &c. The one, Ishmael, *was by a bond-maid,* and the other, Isaac, *by a free-woman*; the former *was born after the flesh,* or by the ordinary course of nature, the other *was by promise,* when in the course of nature there was no reason to expect that Sarah should have a son. He acquaints them with the meaning of this history

(v. 24–27): *These things,* says he, *are an allegory.* These two, Agar and Sarah, *are the two covenants.* The former, Agar, represented that which was given from mount Sinai, and *which gendereth to bondage. For this Agar is mount Sinai in Arabia and it answereth to Jerusalem which now is, and is in bondage with her children;* it justly represents the present state of the Jews, who adhering to that covenant, are still in bondage with their children. But the other, Sarah, was intended to prefigure Jerusalem which is above, which is free both from the curse of the moral and the bondage of the ceremonial law, and *is the mother of us all*—a state into which all, both Jews and Gentiles, are admitted, upon their believing in Christ. And to this greater freedom the apostle refers that of the prophet, Isa. liv. 1, where it is written, *Rejoice, thou barren that bearest not; break forth and cry, thou that travailest not: for the desolate hath many more children than she who hath a husband.* He applies the history to the present case (v. 28): *Now we, brethren, as Isaac was, are the children of the promise.* We Christians, who have accepted Christ and look for justification and salvation by him alone, are entitled to the promised inheritance. He tells them that *as then he that was born after the flesh persecuted him that was born after the Spirit,* they must expect it would be *so now.* But, he desires them to consider what the scripture saith (Gen. xxi. 10), *Cast out the bond-woman and her son, for the son of the bond-woman shall not be heir with the son of the free-woman.* He concludes (v. 31), *So then, brethren, we are not children of the bond-woman, but of the free.*

CHAPTER 5

He begins it with a general exhortation (ver. 1), which he afterwards enforces by several considerations, ver. 2–12. He then presses them to serious practical godliness. I. That they should not strive with one another, ver. 13–15. II. That they would strive against sin, 1. There is in everyone a struggle between flesh and spirit, ver. 17. 2. It is our duty to side with the better part, ver. 16, 18. 3. He specifies the works of the flesh and the fruits of the Spirit, ver. 19–24. And then concludes the chapter with a caution against pride and envy.

Verses 1–12
Since it appeared by what had been said that we can be justified only by faith in Jesus Christ, and that the law of Moses was no longer in force, he would have them to *stand fast in the liberty wherewith Christ hath made us free, and not to be again entangled with the yoke of bondage.* Under the gospel we are enfranchised, we are brought into a state of liberty. We owe this liberty to Jesus Christ. It is he who *has made us free.* It is therefore our duty to *stand fast in this liberty, and not to suffer ourselves to be again entangled in the yoke of bondage.*

I. Their submitting to circumcision, and depending on the works of the law for righteousness, were a forfeiture of all their advantages by Jesus Christ, v. 2–4. 1. With what solemnity the apostle declares this: *Behold, I Paul say unto you* (v. 2), and he repeats it (v. 3), *I testify unto you that if you be circumcised Christ shall profit you nothing,* &c. He looked upon it as a matter of the greatest consequence that they did not submit to it. That this is his meaning appears from v. 4, where he expresses the same thing by their being *justified by the law. Christ would profit them nothing, that were debtors to do the whole law; Christ* had become of no effect to them, they were fallen from grace. Thereby they renounced that way of justification which God had established. They became debtors to do the whole law, which required such an obedience as they were not capable of performing. Having thus revolted from Christ, and built their hopes upon the law, Christ would profit them nothing. He will not be the Saviour of any who will not own and rely upon him as their only Saviour.

II. To persuade them to steadfastness he sets before them his own example, and acquaints them what their hopes were; *through the Spirit they were waiting for the hope of righteousness by faith.* 1. What it is that Christians are waiting for: it is *the hope of righteousness,* by which we are chiefly to understand the happiness of the other world. It is the great object of their hope, which they are above everything else desiring and pursuing. It is the righteousness of Christ alone which has procured it for us, and on account of which we can expect to be brought to the possession of it. 2. How they hope to obtain this happiness, namely, by faith in our Lord Jesus Christ, not by the works of the law. 3. Whence it is that they are thus waiting for the hope of righteousness: it is *through the Spirit.* It is under his conduct, and by his assistance, that they are enabled to believe on Christ, and to look for the hope of righteousness through him.

III. He tells them (*v.* 6) that *in Christ Jesus neither circumcision availeth anything nor uncircumcision.* Christ, who is *the end of the law,* having come, now it was neither here nor there whether a man were circumcised or uncircumcised; he was neither the better for the one nor the worse for the other, nor would either the one or the other recommend him to God. Yet he informs them what would do so; *faith, which worketh by love.* Without it nothing else would stand them in any stead. Faith, where it is true, is a working grace: it works by love, love to God and love to our brethren; and faith, thus working by love, is all in all in our Christianity.

IV. To recover them from their backslidings he puts them in mind of their good beginnings.

1. *They did run well.* The life of a Christian is a race, wherein he must run, and hold on, if he would obtain the prize. It is not enough that we run in this race, but we must run well. Thus these Christians had done for awhile, but they were either turned out of the way or at least made to flag and falter in it.

2. He asks them, and calls upon them to ask themselves, *Who did hinder you?* He very well knew who they were, and what it was that hindered them; but he would have them to put the question to themselves. Many who set out fair in religion, and run well for awhile—are yet by some means or other hindered in their progress, or turned out of the way. It concerns those who have run well, but now begin either to turn out of the way or to tire in it, to enquire what it is that hinders them. Young converts must expect that Satan will be doing all he can to divert them from the course they are in. The apostle tells them that by hearkening to them they were kept from *obeying the truth.* The gospel which he had preached to them was the truth. It was necessary that they should obey it, that they should continue to govern their lives and hopes according to the directions of it. The truth is not only to be believed, but to be obeyed, to be received not only in the light of it, but in the love and power of it. Those do not rightly obey the truth, who do not steadfastly adhere to it.

V. He argues from the ill rise of that persuasion whereby they were drawn away (*v.* 8): *This persuasion,* says he, *cometh not of him that calleth you.* That is, either of God, or of the apostle himself. It could not come from God, for it was contrary to that way of justification and salvation which he had established; nor from Paul himself, for he had all along been an opposer and not a preacher of circumcision, he had never pressed the use of it upon Christians, much less imposed it upon them as necessary to salvation. He leaves them to judge whence it must arise; it could be owing to none but Satan and his instruments. The Galatians had every reason to reject it, and to continue steadfast in the truth which they had before embraced.

VI. The danger there was of the spreading of this infection, is a further argument which the apostle urges against their complying with false teachers. To convince them that there was more danger in it than they were aware of, he tells them (*v.* 9) that *a little leaven leaveneth the whole lump.* The whole lump of the Christian society may be infected by one member of it, and therefore they were greatly concerned, to purge out the infection from among them. The doctrine which the false teachers were industrious to spread, and which some in these churches had been drawn into, was subversive of Christianity itself, and therefore considering the fatal tendency of it, he would not have them to be easy and unconcerned.

VII. He expresses the hopes he had concerning them (*v.* 10): *I have confidence in you, through the Lord, that you will be none otherwise minded.* He hoped that they might be brought to be of the same mind with him, and to own and abide by that truth and that liberty of the gospel which he had preached to them. We ought to hope the best even of those concerning whom we have cause to fear the worst. He lays the blame of it more upon others than themselves; for he adds, *But he that troubleth you shall bear his judgment, whosoever he be.* In reproving sin and error, we should always distinguish between the leaders and the led. Thus the apostle softens and alleviates the fault of these Christians, even while he is reproving them. But as for him or those that troubled them, he declares they *should bear their judgment.* He did not doubt but God would deal with them according to their deserts. He wishes that *they were even cut off*—not cut off from Christ and all hopes of salvation by him, but cut off by the censures of the church, which ought to witness against those teachers who thus corrupted the purity of the gospel.

VIII. To dissuade these Christians from hearkening to their judaizing teachers, he represents them as men who had used very base methods to compass their designs: for they had misrepresented him. They had given out among them that Paul himself was a preacher of circumcision: for when he says (*v.* 11), *And I brethren, if I yet preach circumcision,* it plainly appears that they had reported him to have done so. Yet that he was a preacher of it he utterly denies. If he would have preached circumcision, he might have avoided persecution. If I yet preach circumcision, says he, *why do I yet suffer persecution?* If he had fallen in with them herein, instead of being exposed to their rage he might have been received into their favour. He was so far from preaching the doctrine he was charged with, that, rather than do so, he was willing to expose himself to the greatest hazards. If he had yielded to the Jews herein, *then would the offence of the cross have ceased.* He rather chose to hazard his ease and credit, yea his very life itself, than thus to corrupt the truth and give up the liberty of the gospel.

Verses 13–26

The apostle comes to exhort these Christians to serious practical godliness.

I. They should not strive with one another, but love one another. He tells them (*v.* 13) that *they had been called unto liberty,* but yet he would have them be very careful that they did not *use this liberty as an occasion to the flesh.* On the contrary, he would have them *by love to serve one another.* The liberty we enjoy as Christians is not a licentious liberty: though Christ has redeemed us from the curse of the law, yet he has not freed us from the obligation of it. Though we ought to stand fast in our Christian liberty, yet we should not insist upon it to the breach of Christian charity, but should always maintain such a temper towards each other as may dispose us by love to serve one another. Two considerations for this purpose: (1) *That all the law is fulfilled in one word, even in this, Thou shalt love thy neighbour as thyself, v.* 14. Love is the sum of the whole law. It will appear that we are the disciples of Christ indeed when we have love one to another (John xiii. 35); and, if it do not wholly extinguish those unhappy discords that are among Christians, yet at least the fatal consequences of them will be prevented. (2) The dangerous tendency of a contrary behaviour (*v.* 15): *But,* says he, if *you bite and devour one another, take heed that you be not consumed one of another.* Mutual strifes among brethren, if persisted in, are likely to prove a common ruin. Christian churches can only be ruined by their own hands; if Christians be as brute beasts, biting and devouring each other, what can be expected but that the God of love should deny his grace to them, and the Spirit of love should depart from them, and that the evil spirit should prevail?

II. They should all strive against sin; and happy would it be for the church if Christians would let all their quarrels be swallowed up of this, even a quarrel against sin. This is what we are chiefly concerned to fight against.

1. That there is in everyone a struggle between the flesh and the spirit (*v.* 17): *The flesh lusts against the spirit.* On the other hand, *the spirit* (the renewed part of us) strives *against the flesh,* hence it comes to pass *that we cannot do the things that we would.* Even as in a natural man there is something of this struggle (the convictions of his conscience and the corruption of his own heart strive with one another) so in a renewed man, there is a struggle between the old nature and the new nature, the remainders of sin and the beginnings of grace; and this Christians must expect as long as they continue in this world.

2. That it is our duty and interest in this struggle to side with the better part and with our graces against our lusts. He gives us this one general rule, to walk in the Spirit (*v.* 16): *This I say, then, Walk in the Spirit, and you shall not fulfil the lust of the flesh.* The duty here recommended to us is that we set ourselves to act under the guidance and influence of the blessed Spirit. We may depend upon it that, though we may not be freed from the stirrings of our corrupt nature, though it remain in us, yet it shall not obtain a dominion over us. The best antidote against the poison of sin is to walk in the Spirit. So it would be a good evidence that they were Christians indeed; for, says the apostle (*v.* 18), *If you be led by the Spirit, you are not under the law.* If, in the prevailing bent and tenor of your lives, you be *led by the Spirit,* it will hence appear that you are not under the law, not under the condemning, though you are still under the commanding, power of it.

3. The apostle specifies the works of the flesh and the fruits of the Spirit, which must be cherished and brought forth (*v.* 19), &c. He begins with *the works of the flesh,* which, as they are many, so they are manifest. Some are sins against the seventh commandment, such as *adultery, fornication, uncleanness, lasciviousness.* Some are sins against the first and second commandments, as *idolatry* and *witchcraft.* Others are sins against our neighbour, such as *hatred, variance, emulations, wrath, strife, seditions, heresies, envyings,* and sometimes break out into *murders,* not only of the names and reputation, but even of the very lives of our fellow-creatures. Others are sins against ourselves, such as *drunkenness and revellings.* Of these and *such like,* says he, *I tell you before, as I have also told you in times past, that those who do such things, shall not inherit the kingdom of God.* These are sins which will undoubtedly shut men out of heaven. He specifies the fruits of the Spirit, which as Christians we are

concerned to bring forth, *v.* 22, 23. As sin is called *the work of the flesh,* because the flesh is the principle that moves men to it, so grace is said to be *the fruit of the Spirit,* because it wholly proceeds from the Spirit, as the fruit does from the root. He particularly commends to us, *love* and *joy,* by which may be understood constant delight in God,—*peace,* with God, or a peaceableness towards others,—*long-suffering,*—*gentleness,*—a sweetness of temper, easy to be entreated when any have wronged us,—*goodness,* readiness to do good to all as we have opportunity,—*faith,* in what we profess and promise to others,—*meekness,* not to be easily provoked, and, when we are so, to be soon pacified,—and *temperance.* Concerning those in whom these fruits of the Spirit are found, the apostle says, *There is no law against them.* They are not under the law, but under grace; for these fruits of the Spirit, in whomsoever they are found, plainly show that such are *led by the Spirit.* So (*v.* 24) he informs us that this is the sincere care and endeavour of all real Christians: *And those that are Christ's have crucified the flesh with the affections and lusts.* They are now sincerely endeavouring to die unto sin, as he had died for it. They have not yet obtained a complete victory over it; they have still flesh as well as Spirit in them, and that has its affections and lusts, which continue to give them no little disturbance, but they are seeking the utter ruin and destruction of it. If we would approve ourselves to be Christ's, we must make it our constant care to crucify the flesh. Christ will never own those as his who yield themselves the servants of sin. It is not enough that we cease to do evil, but we must learn to do well. Our Christianity obliges us not only to oppose the works of the flesh, but to bring forth the fruits of the Spirit too. This must be our sincere care and endeavour as well as the other; and that it was the design of the apostle to represent both of these as our duty may be gathered from what follows (*v.* 25): *If we live in the Spirit, let us also walk in the Spirit.* He had before told us that the Spirit of Christ is a privilege bestowed on all the children of God, *ch.* iv. 6. Let us show it by behaviour agreeable hereunto; let us evidence our good principles by good practices. It must be by our *walking not after the flesh, but after the spirit.* We must set ourselves in good earnest both to mortify the deeds of the body, and to walk in newness of life.

4. The apostle concludes this chapter with a caution against pride and envy, *v.* 26. He here cautions them against being desirous of vainglory, because this would certainly lead them to provoke one another and to envy one another. Thus a foundation is laid for those quarrels and contentions which are inconsistent with that love which Christians ought to maintain towards each other. This therefore the apostle would have us by all means to watch against. (1) The glory which comes from men is vain-glory, which, instead of being desirous of, we should be dead to. (2) An undue regard to the applause of men is one great ground of the unhappy strifes and contentions that exist among Christians.

CHAPTER 6

This chapter chiefly consists of two parts. In the former the apostle gives us several practical directions, which more especially tend to instruct Christians in their duty to one another, ver. 1–10. In the latter he revives the main design of the epistle, which was to fortify the Galatians against the arts of their judaizing teachers. I. The true character of these teachers, ver. 11–14. II. He acquaints them with his own temper and behaviour. And then he concludes the epistle with a solemn benediction.

Verses 1–10

I. We are here taught to deal tenderly with those who are overtaken in a fault, *v.* 1; *if a man be overtaken in a fault,* brought to sin by the surprise of temptation. It is one thing to overtake a fault by contrivance and deliberation, and another thing to be overtaken in a fault. Great tenderness should be used. *Those who are spiritual* must *restore such a one with the spirit of meekness.* 1. The duty we are directed to—to restore such. The original word signifies *to set in joint,* as a dislocated bone. We should endeavour to set them in joint again, comforting them in a sense of pardoning mercy, confirming our love to them. 2. The manner wherein this is to be done: *With the spirit of meekness;* not in wrath and passion, as those who triumph in a brother's falls. Many needful reproofs lose their efficacy by being given in wrath; but when they are managed with tenderness, and from sincere concern for the welfare of those to whom they are given, they are likely to make a due impression. 3. A very good reason why this should be done with meekness: *Considering thyself, lest thou also be tempted.* We ought to deal very tenderly with those who are overtaken in sin, it may some time or other be our own case. This will dispose us to do by others as we desire to be done by in such a case.

II. We are here directed *to bear one another's burdens, v.* 2. This may be considered either as referring to what goes before, and so may teach us to exercise forbearance and compassion towards one another, or a more general precept it directs us to sympathize with one another under the various trials and troubles that we may meet with. So we shall *fulfil the law of Christ.* This is to act agreeably to the law of his precept, which is the law of love, and it would also be agreeable to his pattern and example, which have the force of a law to us. Though as Christians we are freed from the law of Moses, yet we are under the law of Christ; and therefore, instead of laying unnecessary burdens upon others, it much more becomes us to fulfil the law of Christ by bearing one another's burdens. The apostle being aware how great a hindrance pride would be to the mutual condescension which he had been recommending (*v.* 3) takes care to caution us against this; he supposes it as a very possible thing for a man to think himself to be something—when in truth he is nothing. Such a one does but deceive himself; while he imposes upon others, by pretending to what he has not, he puts the greatest cheat upon himself. He is neither the freer from mistakes nor will he be the more secure against temptations for the good opinion he has of his own sufficiency, but rather the more liable to fall into them; for *he that thinks he stands has need to take heed lest he fall.* Self-conceit is but self-deceit. There is not a more dangerous cheat in the world than self-deceit.

III. We are advised everyone to prove his own work, *v.* 4. By our own work is chiefly meant our own actions or behaviour. These the apostle directs us to prove, that is, seriously to examine them by the rule of God's word. Instead of being forward to judge and censure others, it would much more become us to search and try our own ways; our business lies more at home than abroad, with ourselves than with other men. The best way to keep us from being proud of ourselves is to prove our ownselves: the better we are acquainted with our own hearts and ways, the less liable shall we be to despise and the more disposed to compassionate and help others.

1. This is the way to *have rejoicing in ourselves alone.* If we set ourselves in good earnest to *prove our own work,* this, he intimates, would be a much better ground of joy and satisfaction than to be able to rejoice *in another,* either in the good opinion which others may have of us, or by comparing ourselves with others. The joy that results thence is nothing to that which arises from trial of ourselves by the rule of God's word, and our being able thereupon to approve ourselves to him. Though we have nothing in ourselves to boast of, yet we may have the matter of rejoicing in ourselves. If our consciences can witness for us we may upon good ground rejoice therein. The true way to have *rejoicing in ourselves* is to be much in *proving our own works.* If we have the testimony of our consciences that we are accepted of God, we need not much concern ourselves about what others think or say of us.

2. The other argument which the apostle uses is that every man shall bear his own burden (*v.* 5). There is a day come when we must all give an account of ourselves to God; and he declares that then the judgment will proceed, and the sentence pass, according as our state and behaviour have really been in the sight of God. If we must certainly be called to an account hereafter, surely we ought to be often calling ourselves to an account here, to see whether or no we are such as God will own and approve then. If it were more our practice instead of bearing hard upon one another, we should be more ready to fulfil that law of Christ by which we must be judged in bearing one another's burdens.

IV. Christians are here exhorted to be free and liberal in maintaining their ministers (*v.* 6): *Let him that is taught in the word communicate to him that teacheth, in all good things.* As there are some to be taught, so there are others who are appointed to teach them. Reason itself directs us to put a difference between the teachers and the taught, and the scriptures sufficiently declare that it is the will of God we should do so. It is the word of God wherein ministers are to teach and instruct others. It is the word of God which is the only rule of faith and life. They are no further to be regarded than as they speak according to this rule. It is the duty of those who are taught in the word to support those who are appointed to teach them; for they are *to communicate to them in all good things.* It is but fit and equitable that, while they are *sowing to others spiritual things, they should reap their carnal things.*

V. A caution to take heed of mocking God, or of deceiving ourselves, by imagining that he can be imposed upon by mere professions (*v.* 7): *Be not deceived, God is not mocked.* Many are apt to excuse themselves from the work of religion, though at the same time they may make a show of it. Hereby they may possibly impose upon others, yet they do but deceive themselves if they think to impose upon God. As he cannot be deceived, so he will not be mocked. *Whatsoever a man soweth that shall he also reap.* Our present time is seed-time: in the other world there will be a great harvest. We shall reap then as we sow now. And he further informs us (*v.* 8) that, as there are two sorts of seedness, so accordingly will the reckoning be hereafter: *If we sow to the flesh, we shall of the flesh reap corruption*; a mean and short-lived satisfaction at present, and ruin and misery at the end of it. But, on the other hand, *those who sow to the Spirit,* may depend upon it that *of the Spirit they shall reap life everlasting*—they shall have the truest comfort in their present course, and an eternal life and happiness at the end of it. The God we have to do with will certainly deal with us hereafter, not according to our professions, but our practices.

VI. A further caution, *not to be weary in well doing, v.* 9. There is in all of us too great a proneness to this; we are very apt to flag and tire in duty. *In due season we shall reap, if we faint not.* There is a recompence of reward in reserve for all who sincerely employ themselves in well doing. Though our reward may be delayed, yet it will surely come.

VII. An exhortation to all Christians to do good in their places (*v.* 10): *As we have therefore an opportunity,* &c. It is not enough that we be good ourselves, but we must do good to others. 1. The objects of this duty are more generally all men. We are not to confine our charity and beneficence within too narrow bounds, but should be ready to extend it to all as far as we are capable. We are to have a special regard to the household of faith. Though others are not to be excluded, yet these are to be preferred. 2. The rule which we are to observe in doing good *as we have opportunity*. (1) We should be sure to do it while we have opportunity, or while our life lasts. We must not, as too many do, neglect it in our lifetime, and defer it till we come to die, under a pretence of doing something of this nature then: by leaving something behind us for the good of others, when we can no longer keep it ourselves. But we should take care to do good in our lifetime, yea, to make this the business of our lives. (2) We should be ready to improve every opportunity for it. Whenever God gives us an opportunity of being useful to others, he expects we should improve it, according to our capacity and ability. None who stand in need of us are to be wholly overlooked, yet there is a difference to be made between some and others.

Verses 11–18

The apostle seems as if he intended here to have put an end to the epistle. As a particular mark of his respect for them, he had written this large letter with his own hand, and had not made use of another as his amanuensis. But such is his affection to them that he cannot break off till he has once again given them the true character of those teachers.

I. False teachers were men who *desired to make a fair show in the flesh*, v. 12. They were very zealous for the externals of religion, though they had little or no regard to real piety, for, *neither do they themselves keep the law*. Frequently those have least of the substance of religion who are most solicitous to make a show of it. They constrained the Gentile Christians to be circumcised, *only lest they should suffer persecution for the cross of Christ*. They were willing to sleep in a whole skin, and to save their worldly cargo, and cared not though they made shipwreck of faith and a good conscience. They were men who had no further zeal for the law than as it subserved their carnal designs; for they desired to have these Christians circumcised, *that they might glory in their flesh* (v. 13), that they might say they had gained them over to their side.

II. He acquaints us, on the other hand, with his own temper and behaviour.

1. His principal glory was in the cross of Christ: *God forbid that I should glory, save in the cross of our Lord Jesus Christ, v. 14.* This was what the Jews stumbled at and the Greeks accounted foolishness; and the judaizing teachers themselves were for mixing the observance of the law of Moses with faith in Christ, as necessary to salvation. But Paul was so far from being offended at the cross of Christ that he gloried in it, and rejected the thought of setting up anything in competition with it, with the utmost abhorrence. *God forbid*, &c. This was the ground of all his hope as a Christian, and whatever trials his firm adherence to it might bring upon him, he was ready not only to submit to them, but to rejoice in them. There is the greatest reason why we should glory in it, for to it we owe all our joys and hopes.

2. He was dead to the world. By Christ *the world was crucified to him, and he to the world.* He had got above both the smiles and the frowns of it, and had become as indifferent to it as one who is dying out of it. The more we contemplate the sufferings our dear Redeemer met with from the world the less likely shall we be to be in love with it.

3. He did not lay the stress of his religion on one side or the other of the contesting interests, but on sound Christianity, v. 15. What they laid so great a

stress upon Paul made very little account of. He very well knew that *in Jesus Christ neither circumcision availed anything nor uncircumcision*, as to men's acceptance with God, *but a new creature.* Here he instructs us both wherein real religion does not and wherein it does consist. It does not consist in our being in this or the other denomination of Christians; but it consists in our being new creatures; in our being renewed in the spirit of our minds and having Christ formed in us. It is a change of mind and heart, whereby we are enabled to believe in the Lord Jesus and to live a life of devotedness to God. No outward professions, nor particular names, will ever be sufficient to recommend us to him. Were Christians duly concerned to experience this in themselves, and to promote it in others, if it did not make them lay aside their distinguishing names, yet it would at least take them off from laying so great a stress upon them as they too often do. *And as many as walk according to this rule peace be upon them, and mercy upon the Israel of God.* The blessings which he desires or which he gives them the hope and prospect of (for the words may be taken either as a prayer or a promise), are *peace and mercy.* A foundation is laid for these in that gracious change which is wrought in them. These, he declares, shall be the portion of *all the Israel of God*, all sincere Christians, whether Jews or Gentiles, all who are Israelites indeed. The Jews and judaizing teachers were for confining these blessings to such as were circumcised. Real Christians are such as walk by rule; not a rule of their own devising, but that which God himself has prescribed to them. Even those who walk according to this rule do yet stand in need of the mercy of God. All who sincerely endeavour to walk according to this rule may be assured that peace and mercy will be upon them: this is the best way to have peace with God. As we may be sure of the favour of God now, so we may be sure that we shall find mercy with him hereafter.

4. He had cheerfully suffered persecution for the sake of Christ and Christianity, v. 17. He had already suffered much in the cause of Christ, for *he bore in his body the marks of the Lord Jesus*, the scars of those wounds which he had sustained from persecuting enemies, for his steady adherence to him. With a becoming warmth and vehemence, suitable to his authority as an apostle and to the deep concern of mind he was under, he insists upon it that no man should henceforth trouble him, by opposing his doctrine or authority, or by any such reproaches as had been cast upon him. It may justly be presumed that men are fully persuaded of those truths in the defence of which they are willing to suffer. It is very unjust to charge those things upon others which are contrary not only to their profession, but their sufferings too.

III. The apostle concludes the epistle with his apostolical benediction, v. 18. He calls them his brethren, and takes his leave of them with this very affectionate prayer, that *the grace of our Lord Jesus Christ may be with their spirit.* This was a usual farewell wish of the apostle's. And herein he prays that they might enjoy the favour of Christ, all that grace which was needful to establish them in their Christian course, and to encourage and comfort them under all the trials of life and the prospect of death itself. Though these churches had done enough to forfeit it, yet, out of his great concern for them, he earnestly desires it on their behalf; yea, that it might *be with their spirit*, that they might continually experience the influence of it upon their souls. We need desire no more to make us happy than the grace of our Lord Jesus Christ. And, both for their and our encouragement to hope for it, he adds his *Amen.*

AN EXPOSITION, WITH PRACTICAL OBSERVATIONS, OF

THE EPISTLE OF ST. PAUL TO

THE EPHESIANS

Some think that this epistle to the Ephesians was a circular letter sent to several churches. It is the only one of all Paul's epistles that has nothing in it peculiarly adapted to the case of that particular church; but it has much of common concernment to all Christians. It is an epistle that bears date out of a prison: and some have observed that what this apostle wrote when he was a prisoner had the greatest relish and savour in it of the things of God. When his tribulations did abound, his consolations did much more abound. The apostle's design is to settle and establish the Ephesians in the truth, and further to acquaint them with the mystery of the gospel. In the former part he represents the great privilege of the Ephesians, who were now converted to Christianity and received into covenant with God, *ch.* i–iii. In the latter part he instructs them in the principal duties of religion.

CHAPTER 1

I. The introduction to the whole epistle, ver. 1, 2. II. The apostle's thanksgiving and praises to God for his inestimable blessings bestowed on the believing Ephesians, ver. 3–14. III. His earnest prayers to God in their behalf, ver. 15–23.

Verses 1, 2

1. The title St. Paul takes to himself—*Paul, an apostle of Jesus Christ*, &c. Such a one Paul was *by the will of God*. Every faithful minister of Christ may, with our apostle, reflect on it as an honour that he is what he is *by the will of God*. 2. The persons to whom this epistle is sent: *To the saints who are at Ephesus*. He calls them saints, for such they were in profession, and many of them were such. All Christians must be saints. He calls them *the faithful in Christ Jesus*. Those are not saints who are not faithful; *in Christ Jesus*, from whom they derive all their grace and spiritual strength. 3. The apostolical benediction: *Grace be to you*, &c. By *grace* we are to understand the free and undeserved love and favour of God, and those graces of the Spirit which proceed from it; by *peace* all other blessings, the fruits and product of the former. No peace without grace. No peace, nor grace, but *from God the Father, and from the Lord Jesus Christ*. These peculiar blessings proceed from God not as a Creator, but as a Father, and they come from our Lord Jesus Christ, who has a right to bestow them. The saints, and the faithful in Christ Jesus, had already received grace and peace. The best saints stand in need of fresh supplies of the graces of the Spirit: and therefore they should pray, each one for himself and all for one another, that such blessings may still abound unto them. The Spirit of God saw fit that his discourse of divine things in this chapter should be cast into prayers and praises. Prayer may preach; and praise may do so too.

Verses 3–14

He begins with thanksgivings and praise, and enlarges upon the exceedingly great and precious benefits which we enjoy by Jesus Christ.

I. He blesses God for *spiritual blessings*, *v.* 3, where he styles him *the God and Father of our Lord Jesus Christ*. All blessings come from God as the Father of our Lord Jesus Christ. *He hath blessed us with all spiritual blessings*. Spiritual blessings are the best blessings. He blesses us by bestowing such things upon us as make us really blessed. We cannot thus bless God in return; but by praising. Those whom God blesses with some he blesses with all spiritual blessings. It is not so with temporal blessings. They are *spiritual blessings in heavenly places*. Or it may be read, *in heavenly things*, such as come from

heaven, and are designed to prepare men for it. We should hence learn to mind spiritual and heavenly blessings as the best blessings with which we cannot be miserable, and without which we cannot but be so.

II. Particular spiritual blessings enlarged upon. 1. Election and predestination, *v.* 4, 5, 11. *Election*, or choice, respects that lump or mass of mankind from which they are separated. Predestination has respect to the blessings they are designed for; particularly *the adoption of children*, that in due time we should become his adopted children, and so have a right to all the privileges of children. *Before the foundation of the world* they were chosen in the counsel of God from all eternity. The alms which you give to beggars at your doors proceed from a sudden resolve; but the provision which a parent makes for his children is the result of many thoughts. He acts in pursuance of his eternal purpose in bestowing spiritual blessings upon his people. *He hath blessed us—according as he hath chosen us in him*, in Christ the great head of the election. One great end and design of this choice: *chosen—that we should be holy*. All who are chosen to happiness as the end are chosen to holiness as the means. *And without blame before him*—that their holiness might not be merely external and in outward appearance, but internal and real, such holiness as proceeds from love to God and to our fellow-creatures, this charity being the principle of all true holiness. Here is also the rule and the fontal cause of God's election: it is *according to the good pleasure of his will* (*v.* 5), because it was his sovereign will. It is *according to the purpose of him who worketh all things after the counsel of his own will* (*v.* 11). The last and great end is his own glory: *To the praise of the glory of his grace* (*v.* 6), *that we should be to the praise of his glory* (*v.* 12). The glory of God is his own end, and it should be ours in all that we do. 2. The next is acceptance with God through Jesus Christ: *Wherein he hath made us accepted in the beloved*, *v.* 6. We cannot be thus accepted of God, but in and through Jesus Christ. He loves his people for the sake of the beloved. 3. Remission of sins, and redemption through the blood of Jesus, *v.* 7. No remission without redemption. The guilt and the stain of sin could be no otherwise removed than by the blood of Jesus. All our spiritual blessings flow down to us in that stream. It is according to the riches of God's grace. It was rich grace to provide such a surety as his own Son, when nothing of that nature could have entered into our thoughts, nor have been otherwise found out for us. He has not only manifested riches of grace, but *has abounded towards us in all wisdom and prudence* (*v.* 8). 4. Another privilege is divine revelation—

that God hath *made known to us the mystery of his will* (v. 9). This we owe to Christ, who came to declare his will to the children of men: *According to his good pleasure which he had purposed.* It is described (v. 13) *as the word of truth, and the gospel of our salvation.* O, how ought we to prize this glorious gospel and to bless God for it! 5. Union in and with Christ is a great privilege. *He gathers together in one all things in Christ,* v. 10. All the lines of divine revelation meet in Christ; all religion centres in him. Jews and Gentiles were united to each other by being both united to Christ. *Things in heaven and things on earth* are gathered together in him; peace made between heaven and earth through him. The innumerable company of angels become one with the church through Christ: this God *purposed in himself.* 6. The eternal inheritance is the great blessing with which we are blessed in Christ: *In whom also we have obtained an inheritance,* v. 11. Heaven is the inheritance. *If children, then heirs.* All the blessings that we have in hand are but small if compared with the inheritance. What is laid out upon an heir in his minority is nothing to what is reserved for him when he comes to age. 7. The seal and earnest of the Spirit. We are said to be *sealed with that Holy Spirit of promise,* v. 13. He makes us holy. He is the promised Spirit. By him believers are sealed and set apart for God. The Spirit *is the earnest of our inheritance,* v. 14. The earnest is part of payment, and it secures the full sum. All his influences are heaven begun, glory in the seed and bud. His comforts are earnests of everlasting joys. He is said to be the earnest, *until the redemption of the purchased possession.* This earnest makes it as sure to the heirs as though they were already possessed of it; and it is purchased for them by the blood of Christ. The great end and design of God in bestowing all these spiritual privileges is *that we should be to the praise of his glory who first trusted in Christ.* Seniority in grace is a preferment: those who have for a longer time experienced the grace of Christ are under more special obligations to glorify God. This is the great design of God in all that he has done for us: it is *unto the praise of his glory,* v. 14.

Verses 15–23

Paul's earnest prayer to God in behalf of these Ephesians. He has laid up these spiritual blessings for us in the hands of his Son. He has appointed us to draw them out, and fetch them in, by prayer. We have no part nor lot in the matter, any further than we claim it by faith and prayer. Note, the good account he had of them, *of their faith in the Lord Jesus and love to all the saints,* v. 15. Those who love saints, as such, love all saints, how weak in grace, how mean in the world, how fretful and peevish soever, some of them may be. Another inducement to pray for them was because they had received the earnest of the inheritance. *Wherefore—I cease not to give thanks for you, making mention of you in my prayers,* v. 16. While he blessed God for giving them the Spirit, he ceases not to pray (v. 17), that he would give greater measures of the Spirit. The great thing he prays for is the illumination of their understandings, and that their knowledge might increase and abound; he means it of a practical and experimental knowledge. The graces and comforts of the Spirit are communicated to the soul by the enlightening of the understanding. Satan takes a contrary way: he gets possession by the senses and passions, Christ by the understanding. I. Whence this knowledge must come; from *the God of our Lord Jesus Christ,* v. 17. The Lord *is a God of knowledge,* and there is no sound saving knowledge but what comes from him. He gives knowledge by giving the Spirit of knowledge; for the

Spirit of God is the teacher of the saints, *the Spirit of wisdom and revelation.* We have the revelation of the Spirit in the word: but will that avail us, if we have not the wisdom of the Spirit in the heart? *In the knowledge of him.* This knowledge is first in the understanding. He prays that *the eyes of their understanding may be enlightened,* v. 18. Christians should not think it enough to have warm affections, but they should labour to have clear understandings; they should be ambitious of being knowing Christians, and judicious Christians.

II. What it is that he more particularly desires they should grow in the knowledge of. 1. *The hope of his calling,* v. 18. There is a hope in this calling; for those who deal with God deal upon trust. We ought to labour after, and pray earnestly for, a clearer insight into, and a fuller acquaintance with, the great objects of a Christian's hopes. 2. *The riches of the glory of his inheritance in the saints.* There is a present inheritance in the saints; for grace is glory begun, and holiness is happiness in the bud. There is a glory in this inheritance, and it is desirable to know this experimentally. It may be understood of the glorious inheritance in heaven, where God does, as it were, lay forth all his riches. Let us endeavour then, by reading, contemplation, and prayer, to know as much of heaven as we can, that we may be desiring and longing to be there. 3. *The exceeding greatness of God's power towards those who believe,* v. 19. It is a difficult thing to bring a soul to believe in Christ. It is nothing less than an almighty power that will work this in us. The apostle speaks as if he wanted words to express the *exceeding greatness of God's almighty power,* that power which God exerts towards his people, and by which *he raised Christ from the dead,* v. 20. That indeed was the great proof of the truth of the gospel to the world: but the transcript of that in ourselves is the great proof to us. Many understand the apostle here as speaking of that *exceeding greatness of power* which God will exert for raising believers to eternal life, even the same *mighty power which he wrought in Christ when he raised him,* &c. And how desirable a thing must it be to become at length acquainted with that power, by being raised thereby unto eternal life!

The apostle digresses a little to make mention of the Lord Jesus and his exaltation. He sits at the Father's *right hand in the heavenly places,* &c., v. 20, 21. The Father *hath put all things under his feet* (v. 22). God GAVE *him to be head over all things.* It was a gift to Christ, and it was a gift to the church, to be provided with a head endued with so much power and authority. He gave him all power both in heaven and in earth. *The Father loves the Son, and hath given* ALL *things into his hands.* But that which completes the comfort of this is that he is the head over all things to the church. The same power that supports the world supports the church; and we are sure he loves his church, for it *is his body* (v. 23), and he will care for it. It is *the fulness of him that filleth all in all.* Jesus Christ filleth all in all. Christ as Mediator would not be complete if he had not a church. How could he be a king if he had not a kingdom?

CHAPTER 2

An account, I. Of the miserable condition of these Ephesians by nature (ver. 1–3) and again, ver. 11, 12. II. Of the glorious change that was wrought in them (ver. 4–10) and again, ver. 13. III. Of the great privileges that both converted Jews and Gentiles receive from Christ, ver. 14–22. We have here a lively picture both of the misery of unregenerate men and of the happy condition of converted souls.

Verses 1–3

Unregenerate souls are dead in trespasses and sins. All those who are in their sins, are dead in sins,

Sin is the death of the soul. Wherever that prevails there is a privation of all spiritual life. A state of sin is a state of conformity to this world, *v.* 2. *Wherein in time past you walked*; you lived and behaved yourselves in such a manner as the men of the world are used to do. We are by nature bond-slaves to sin and Satan. Those who walk according to the course of this world, walk *according to the prince of the power of the air.* Wicked men are slaves to Satan. The course and tenor of their lives are according to his suggestions; they are subject to him, and are led captive by him at his will, whereupon he is called the god of this world, and *the spirit that now worketh in the children of disobedience.* As the good Spirit works that which is good in obedient souls, so this evil spirit works that which is evil in wicked men; and he now works, not only heretofore. *Among whom also we all had our conversation in times past.* We are by nature drudges to the flesh, and to our corrupt affections, *v.* 3, *fulfilling the desires of the flesh and of the mind.* We lived in the actual commission of all those sins to which corrupt nature inclined us. The carnal mind makes a man a perfect slave to his vicious appetite.—*The fulfilling of the wills of the flesh,* so the words may be rendered. We are *by nature the children of wrath, even as others.* One man is as much so as another by nature, not only by custom and imitation, but by reason of our natural inclinations and appetites. Our state and course are such as deserve wrath, and would end in eternal wrath, if divine grace did not interpose. What reason have sinners then to be looking out for that grace that will make them children of God and heirs of glory!

Verses 4–10

The glorious change that was wrought in them by converting grace.

I. By whom, and in what manner, it was brought about. *Not of yourselves, v.* 8. *Not of works, lest any man should boast, v.* 9. These things are not brought to pass by anything done by us. There is no room for any man's boasting of his own abilities and power; or as though he had done anything that might deserve such immense favours from God. *But God, who is rich in mercy,* &c., *v.* 4. God himself is the author of this great and happy change. Love is his inclination to do us good considered simply as creatures: mercy respects us as apostate and as miserable creatures. That love of God is great love, and that mercy of his is rich mercy. *By grace you are saved* (*v.* 5), and *by grace are you saved through faith—it is the gift of God, v.* 8. Every converted sinner is a saved sinner. The grace that saves them is the free undeserved goodness and favour of God; and he saves them, not *by the works of the law,* but through faith in Christ Jesus. Both that faith and that salvation are the gift of God. God has ordered all so that the whole shall appear to be of grace.

II. Wherein this change consists. 1. We who were dead are quickened (*v.* 5). Grace in the soul is a new life in the soul. As death seals up all the powers and faculties, so does a state of sin, as to anything that is good. Grace unlocks and opens all, and enlarges the soul. A regenerate sinner becomes a living soul, being born of God: *He hath quickened us together with Christ.* It is in him that we live: *Because I live, you shall live also.* 2. We who were buried are raised up, *v.* 6. When he raised Christ from the dead, he did in effect raise up all believers together with him, and when he placed him at his right hand in heavenly places, he advanced and glorified them in and with him.—*And made us sit together in heavenly places in Christ Jesus.* Sinners roll themselves in the dust; sanctified souls sit in heavenly places; the world is as nothing to them, compared with what it has been,

and compared with what the other world is. They are exalted to reign with him; they sit upon the throne with Christ.

III. The great design of God in producing and effecting this change. 1. With respect to others: *That in the ages to come he might show,* &c. (*v.* 7), that he might give a proof of his great goodness and mercy, for the encouragement of sinners in future time. The goodness of God in saving sinners heretofore is a proper encouragement to others in after-time to hope in his grace and mercy. God having this in his design, poor sinners should take great encouragement from it. 2. With respect to the regenerated sinners themselves: *For we are his workmanship, created in Christ Jesus unto good works,* &c., *v.* 10. *We are his workmanship;* not only as men, but as saints. The new man is a new creature; and God is its Creator. *In Christ Jesus,* that is, on the account of what he has done and suffered. *Unto good works,* &c. Lest he should seem to discourage good works, he here observes that God, in his new creation, has designed us for good works: *Created unto good works; which God hath before ordained, that we should walk in them,* or glorify God by an exemplary conversation and by our perseverance in holiness.

Verses 11–13

The miserable condition of these Ephesians by nature. *Wherefore remember,* &c., *v.* 11. Converted sinners ought frequently to reflect upon the sinfulness and misery of the state they were in by nature. *Gentiles in the flesh,* that is, living in the corruption of their natures. *Who are called uncircumcision by that,* &c., "You were reproached and upbraided for it by the formal Jews." The misery of their case, *v.* 12. "*At that time* you were," 1. "In a Christless condition without any saving relation to him." It must be a sad and deplorable thing for a soul to be without a Christ. Being without Christ, they were, 2. *Aliens from the commonwealth of Israel;* they did not belong to Christ's church. It is no small privilege to be placed in the church of Christ, and to share in the advantages peculiar to it. 3. *They are strangers from the covenants of promise;* the covenants of promise, because it is made up of promises. The Ephesians, in their gentilism, were strangers to this covenant, and all unregenerate sinners are strangers to it. 4. They had no hope. Those who are without Christ, and strangers from the covenant, can have no good hope. They were in a state of estrangement from God: *Without God in the world.* The words are, *atheists in the world*; for, though they worshipped many gods, yet they were without the true God.

The happy change that was made in their state: *But now, in Christ Jesus, you who sometimes were far off,* &c. They were far off from Christ, and from God himself; and therefore from all good. "*But now in Christ Jesus,* &c., you are made nigh." They were brought home to God. God is a help at hand to his people; and this is *by the blood of Christ.* Every believing sinner owes his nearness to God, to the death and sacrifice of Christ.

Verses 14–22

The great privileges that converted Jews and Gentiles both receive from Christ. Those who were in a state of enmity are reconciled. Jesus Christ is our peace, *v.* 14. He made peace and came to reconcile, 1. Jews and Gentiles to each other. He *made both one.* He *broke down the middle wall of partition,* the ceremonial law, called *the partition-wall* by way of allusion to the partition in the temple, which separated the court of the Gentiles from that into which the Jews only had liberty to enter. Thus

he abolished in his flesh the enmity, v. 15. By his
sufferings in the flesh, he took away the binding power
of the ceremonial law, *the law of commandments
contained in ordinances.* By taking these out of the
way, he formed one church of believers, whether
they had been Jews or Gentiles. Thus he made *in
himself of twain one new man.* He framed both these
parties into one new society, *so making peace.*
2. God and sinners, whether Jews or Gentiles.
Christ came to slay that enmity, and to reconcile
them both to God, v. 16. Sin breeds a quarrel
between God and men. Christ came to take up
the quarrel, and to bring it to an end, and
this *by the cross, having slain the enmity thereby.*
The great advantages which both parties gain, v. 17.
Christ came, partly in his own person, as to the Jews,
who are here said to have been nigh, and partly in
his apostles to the Gentiles, who are said to have
been afar off. *And preached peace,* reconciliation
with God. Now the effect of this peace is the free
access which both Jews and Gentiles have unto God
(v. 18): *For through him we both have access.* The
throne of grace is erected for us to come to, and
liberty of approach to that throne is allowed us.
Christ purchased for us leave to come to God, and
the Spirit gives us a heart to come. *Now therefore
you are no more strangers and foreigners,* v. 19.
They were now no longer *aliens from the commonwealth of Israel, but fellow-citizens with the saints,
and of the household of God.* The church is compared
to a city, and every converted sinner is free of it.
It is also compared to a house, and every converted
sinner is one of the family, a servant and a child in
God's house. In *v.* 20 the church is compared to a
building. The apostles and prophets are *the foundation* of that building. *Jesus Christ himself being the
chief corner-stone.* Christ supports the building by
his strength: *In whom all the building, fitly framed
together,* &c., v. 21. All believers being united to
Christ by faith, and among themselves by Christian
charity, *grow unto a holy temple,* in which there is
much communion between God and his people.
The church is the place which God hath chosen to
put his name there, and it becomes such a temple
by grace and strength derived from himself—*in the
Lord. In whom you also are built together,* &c., v. 22.
Every true believer is a living temple, is *a habitation
of God through the Spirit.* God dwells in all believers
now, an earnest of their dwelling together with him
to eternity.

CHAPTER 3

This chapter consists of two parts. I. Of the account which Paul
gives the Ephesians concerning himself, ver. 1–13. II. Of his
devout and affectionate prayer to God for the Ephesians, ver.
14–21. We may observe it to have been very much the practice
of this apostle to intermix, with his instructions and counsels,
intercessions and prayers to God. All his instructions and teachings would be useless and vain, except God did co-operate with
them, and render them effectual.

Verses 1–13

I. The tribulations and sufferings which he endured, *v.* 1. *"For this cause,*—for asserting that the
great privileges of the gospel belong not only to the
Jews, but to believing Gentiles also,—for this I
am now a prisoner, but a *prisoner of Jesus Christ."*
Christ's servants, if they come to be prisoners, are his
prisoners. Paul adhered to Christ, and Christ owned
him, when he was in prison. *For you, Gentiles* the
faithful ministers of Christ are to dispense his sacred
truths whatever they themselves may suffer for doing
so. He speaks again of his sufferings: *Wherefore
I desire that you faint not at my tribulation for you,
which is your glory,* v. 13. While he was in prison,
he suffered much there; yet he would not have them
discouraged nor dismayed at this. The apostle seems
to have been more solicitous lest they should be

discouraged and faint upon his tribulations than about
what he himself endured. His sufferings, he says,
were their glory. God not only sent his apostles to
preach the gospel to them, but even to suffer for them.
II. The apostle informs them of God's appointing
him to the office by a special revelation that he made
unto him. 1. God appointed him to the office: *If
you have heard of the dispensation of the grace of
God, which is given me to you-ward,* v. 2. He styles
the gospel *the grace of God* because it is the gift of
divine grace to sinful men; and it is also the great
instrument in the hands of the Spirit by which God
works grace in the souls of men. *Whereof I was made
a minister,* &c., *v.* 7. He was MADE a minister—he did
not make himself such—*according to the gift of the
grace of God unto* him. God supplied and furnished
him for his work *by the effectual working of his
power,* in himself more especially, and also in great
numbers of those to whom he preached. What God
calls men to he fits them for, and does it with an
almighty power. 2. God eminently qualified him for
it, by a special revelation. (1) The mystery revealed
is *that the Gentiles should be fellow-heirs, and of the
same body, and partakers of his promise in Christ, by
the gospel* (v. 6). And this *in Christ,* being united to
Christ, *in whom all the promises are yea and amen;
and by the gospel.* This was the great truth revealed
to the apostles. (2) Of the revelation of this truth he
speaks, *v.* 3–5. The coalition of Jews and Gentiles
in the gospel church was a mystery. It is called a
mystery because the several circumstances of it were
concealed and kept secret in God's own breast. And
it is called the mystery of Christ because it was revealed by him, and because it relates so very much
to him. Of this the apostle has given some hints
afore in the preceding chapters. *Whereby, when you
read;* or, as those words may be read, *unto which
attending* (and it is not enough for us barely to read
the scriptures, unless we attend to them) *you may
understand my knowledge in the mystery of Christ.
This mystery in other ages was not made known unto
the sons of men, as it is now revealed unto his holy
apostles and prophets by the Spirit* (v. 5). Who would
have imagined that those who had been so long in
the dark, and at so great a distance, would be enlightened with the marvellous light, and be made
nigh? Let us learn hence not to despair of the worst,
of the worst of persons, and the worst of nations.
None so unworthy but God may please to confer
great grace upon them.
III. How he was employed in this office with respect
to the Gentiles, and to all men.
1. With respect to the Gentiles, he *preached* to
them *the unsearchable riches of Christ,* v. 8. (1) How
humbly he speaks of himself: *I am less than the least
of all saints.* St. Paul, who was the chief of the
apostles, calls himself *less than the least of all saints.*
What can be less than the least? To speak himself
as little as could be, he speaks himself less than
could be. Where God gives grace to be humble,
there he gives all other grace. While he magnifies
his office, he debases himself. (2) How highly he
speaks of Jesus Christ: *The unsearchable riches of
Christ.* There is a mighty treasury of mercy, grace,
and love, laid up in Christ Jesus, and that both for
Jews and Gentiles. And they are unsearchable
riches, which we cannot find the bottom of. It was
the apostle's business and employment to *preach* these
unsearchable riches of Christ among the Gentiles.
"Unto me is this grace given; this special favour God
has granted to such an unworthy creature as I am."
And it is an unspeakable favour to the Gentile world
that to them *the unsearchable riches of Christ* are
preached. Though many remain poor, and are not
enriched with these riches, yet if we are not enriched
with them, it is our own fault.

2. With respect to all men, *v. 9. To make all men see what is the fellowship of the mystery which from the beginning of the world hath been hid in God who created all things by Jesus Christ.* No wonder that he saves the Gentiles as well as the Jews; for he is the common Creator of them both. *To the intent that now unto the principalities and powers in heavenly places might be known, by the church, the manifold wisdom of God, v. 10. Of the manifold wisdom of God;* that is, of the great variety with which God wisely dispenses things, or of the many ways he takes in ordering his church, and especially in receiving the Gentiles into it. And this is *according to the eternal purpose which he purposed in Christ Jesus our Lord, v.* 11. The apostle, having mentioned our Lord Jesus Christ, subjoins concerning him, *In whom we have boldness and access with confidence by the faith of him* (*v.* 12). We have liberty to open our minds freely to God, as to a Father. We may come with humble boldness to hear from God, and we may expect to hear from him good words and comfortable.

Verses 14–21

Paul's affectionate prayer to God for his beloved Ephesians.—*For this cause.* This may be referred either to the immediately foregoing verse, *That you faint not*, &c., or, rather, the apostle is here resuming what he began at the first verse.

I. To whom he prays—to God, as *the Father of our Lord Jesus Christ.*

II. *I bow my knees.* When we draw nigh to God, we should reverence him in our hearts, and express our reverence in the most becoming behaviour. The universal church has a dependence upon the Lord Jesus Christ: *Of whom the whole family in heaven and earth is named.* Understand it of the saints in heaven, who wear the crown of glory, and of saints on earth who are going on in the work of grace here. Both the one and the other make but one family; and from him they are *named* CHRISTIANS.

III. What the apostle asks of God for these his friends—spiritual blessings. 1. Spiritual strength for the work to which they were called. *That he would grant you, according to the riches of his grace, to be strengthened*, &c. And the apostle prays that this may be *according to the riches of his glory*, or according to his glorious riches, and this by his Spirit. Strength from the Spirit of God in the inner man is the best and most desirable strength. 2. The indwelling of Christ in their hearts, *v.* 17. Christ is an inhabitant in the soul of every good Christian. Where his Spirit dwells, there he dwells; and he dwells in the heart by faith. Faith opens the door of the soul, to receive Christ, faith admits him, and submits to him. By faith we are united to Christ. 3. The fixing of devout affections in the soul: *That you being rooted and grounded in love.* Many have some love to God and to his servants, but it is a flash, like the crackling of thorns under a pot, it makes a great noise, but is gone presently. We should earnestly desire that good affections may be fixed in us. Some understand it of their being settled and established in the sense of God's love to them. And how very desirable it is to have a settled fixed sense of the love of God and Christ to our souls, so as to be able to say with the apostle at all times, *He has loved me!* Now the best way to attain this is to be careful that we maintain a constant love to God in our souls. 4. For their experimental acquaintance with the love of Jesus Christ. *That you may be able to comprehend with all saints*, &c. (*v.* 18, 19). Christians should not aim to comprehend above all saints; we should desire to comprehend *with all saints*, to have so much knowledge as the saints are allowed to have in this world. How magnificently the apostle speaks of the love of Christ. The dimensions of redeeming love are admirable: *The breadth, and length, and depth, and height.* By enumerating these dimensions, the apostle designs to signify the exceeding greatness of the love of Christ, the unsearchable riches of his love. We should desire to comprehend this love: it is the character of all the saints that they do so. *And to know the love of Christ which passeth knowledge, v.* 19. If it passeth knowledge, how can we know it? We must pray and endeavour to know something, and should still covet to know more and more of it, though none can fully comprehend it: in its full extent it surpasses knowledge. 5. He prays that they may be *filled with all the fulness of God.* It is a high expression: we should not dare to use it if we did not find it in the scriptures. Such a fulness as God is ready to bestow, who is willing to fill them all to the utmost of their capacity, and that with all those gifts and graces which he sees they need. Those who receive grace for grace from Christ's fulness may be said to be *filled with the fulness of God*, according to their capacity.

The apostle closes the chapter with a doxology, *v.* 20, 21. How he describes God, and how he ascribes glory to him. He describes him as a God that *is able to do exceedingly abundantly above all that we ask or think.* There is an inexhaustible fulness of grace and mercy in God, which the prayers of all the saints can never draw dry. We should encourage our faith by a consideration of his all-sufficiency and almighty power. *According to the power which worketh in us.* We have already had a proof of this power of God, in what he hath wrought in us and done for us. The power that still worketh for the saints is according to that power that hath wrought in them. He ascribes glory to him. Unto him be glory in the church by Christ Jesus. The seat of God's praises is in the church. That little rent of praise which God receives from this world is from the church, every particular member of which, both Jew and Gentile, concurs in this work of praising God. The Mediator of these praises is Jesus Christ. All God's gifts come from him to us through the hand of Christ; and all our praises pass from us to him through the same hand. And God should and will be praised thus *throughout all ages, world without end. Amen.* So be it; and so it will certainly be.

CHAPTER 4

In what has gone before we have heard of Christian privileges. In what follows we shall hear of Christian duties. Christian faith and Christian practice mutually befriend each other. In this chapter we have divers exhortations to important duties. I. One that is more general, ver. 1. II. An exhortation to mutual love, ver. 2–16. III. An exhortation to Christian purity and holiness of life; and that both more general (ver. 17–24) and in several particular instances, ver. 25, to the end.

Verse 1

This is a general exhortation to walk as becomes our Christian profession. Paul was now a prisoner at Rome; and he was the *prisoner of the Lord.* He mentions this once and again, to show that he was not ashamed of his bonds. We have here the petition of a poor prisoner: "*I therefore, the prisoner of the Lord, beseech you*, &c. Considering what God has done for you I now come with an earnest request to you not to send me relief, nor to use your interest for the obtaining of my liberty, but, that you would approve yourselves good Christians: *That you walk worthily.*" We are called Christians; we must answer that name, and live like Christians. We are called to God's kingdom and glory; we must walk as becomes the heirs of them.

Verses 2–16

Exhortation to mutual love. Love is the law of Christ's kingdom, the lesson of his school, the livery of his family.

I. The means of unity: *Lowliness and meekness, long-suffering, and forbearing one another in love, v. 2.* By lowliness we are to understand humility opposed to pride, by *meekness,* that excellent disposition of soul which makes men unwilling to provoke others, and not easily to be provoked. *Long-suffering* implies a patient bearing of injuries, without seeking revenge. *Forbearing one another in love.* The best Christians have need to make the best one of another, to provoke one another's graces and not their passions. We find much in ourselves which it is hard to forgive ourselves; and therefore we must not think it much if we find that in others which we think hard to forgive them, and yet we must forgive them. Now without these things unity cannot be preserved. The first step towards unity is humility. Pride and passion break the peace, and make all the mischief. Humility and meekness restore the peace. The more lowly-mindedness the more like-mindedness.

II The nature of that unity: it is *the unity of the Spirit, v.* 3. The seat of Christian unity is in the heart or spirit: it does not lie in one set of thoughts, nor in one form and mode of worship, but in one heart and one soul. This we should endeavour to keep. *Endeavouring* is a gospel word. We must do our utmost. If others will quarrel with us, we must take all possible care not to quarrel with them. *In the bond of peace.* Peace is a bond. Many slender twigs, bound together, become strong. The bond of peace is the strength of society. Not that it can be imagined that all good people, should be in everything just of the same length, and the same sentiments. As in a bundle of rods, they may be of different lengths and different strength; but, when they are tied together by one bond, they are stronger than any, even than the thickest and strongest was of itself.

III. The motives proper to promote this Christian unity and concord.

1. Consider how many unities there are. There should be one heart; for *there is one body, and one Spirit, v.* 4. Two hearts in one body would be monstrous. If there be but one body, all that belong to that body should have one heart. If we belong to Christ, we are all actuated by one and the same Spirit, and therefore should be one. *Even as you are called in one hope of your calling.* There is one Christ that they all hope in, and one heaven that they are all hoping for; and therefore they should be of one heart. *One Lord (v.* 5), that is, Christ. *One faith,* that is, the gospel, or, it is the same grace of faith whereby all Christians are saved. *One baptism,* by by which we profess our faith. *One God and Father of all, v.* 6. One God, who owns all the true members of the church for his children; and he *is above all, and through all,* by his providence upholding them: *and in you all,* in all believers, by his Spirit. If then there be so many *ones,* it is a pity but there should be one more—one heart, or one soul.

2. Consider the variety of gifts that Christ has bestowed among Christians: *But unto everyone of us is given grace according to the measure of the gift of Christ.* Though the members of Christ's church agree in so many things, yet there are some things wherein they differ: but this should breed no difference of affection among them, since they are all derived from the same bountiful author. They had no reason to quarrel about them because all was given *according to the measure of the gift of Christ.* All the ministers, and all the members of Christ, owe all the gifts and graces that they are possessed of to him; and this is a good reason why we should love one another, *because to everyone of us is given grace.* All to whom Christ has given grace, and on whom he has bestowed his gifts *ought to love one another.* The apostle takes this occasion to specify some of the gifts. And that they were bestowed by Christ he makes appear by those words of David (Ps. lxviii. 18), *Wherefore he saith* (v. 8), *When he ascended up on high, he led captivity captive, and gave gifts unto men.* Let us set ourselves to think of the ascension of Jesus Christ: that our blessed Redeemer, having risen from the dead, is gone to heaven, where he sits at the right hand of the majesty on high. Christ, when he ascended into heaven, as a triumphant conqueror, *led captivity captive.* It is a phrase used in the Old Testament to signify a conquest over enemies, especially over such as formerly had led others captive. He conquered those who had conquered us; such as sin, the devil, and death. Indeed, he triumphed over these *on the cross;* but the triumph was completed at his ascension, when he became Lord over all. *And he gave gifts unto men:* in the psalm it is, *He received gifts for men.* He received for them, that he might give to them. The apostle takes notice that he *descended first, v.* 9, *into the lower parts of the earth.* He descended to the earth in his incarnation. He descended into the earth in his burial. *He that descended is the same also that ascended up far above all heavens (v.* 10) into the heaven of heavens *that he might fill all things,* all the members of his church, with gifts and graces. The apostle next tells us what were Christ's gifts at his ascension: *He gave some apostles,* &c., *v.* 11. The great gift that Christ gave to the church at his ascension was that of the ministry of peace and reconciliation. The gift of the ministry is the fruit of Christ's ascension. The officers which Christ gave to his church were of two sorts—*extraordinary* ones: such were *apostles, prophets,* and *evangelists.* The apostles were chief. They having been the witnesses of his miracles and doctrine, he sent them forth to spread the gospel. The prophets seem to have been such as expounded the writings of the Old Testament. The evangelists were ordained persons whom the apostles took for their companions in travel. And then there are *ordinary* ministers, as *pastors* and *teachers.* Some take these two names to signify one office. Others think they design two distinct offices, and then pastors are such as are fixed at the head of particular churches; and they are frequently called bishops and elders: and the teachers were those whose work it was to instruct the people by way of exhortation. How rich is the church that has still such a variety of gifts! How kind is Christ to his church!

3. Christ's great end and design in giving gifts unto men. The gifts of Christ were intended for the good of his church. All are *for the perfecting of the saints (v.* 12); to bring into an orderly spiritual state those who had been dislocated and disjointed by sin, and then to advance them therein, that so each might contribute to the good of the whole.—*For the work of the ministry. For the edifying of the body of Christ;* that is, to build up the church, which is Christ's mystical body, by an increase of their graces, and an addition of new members. All are designed to prepare us for heaven: *Till we all come,* &c., *v.* 13. *Till they all come in the unity of the faith and of the knowledge of the Son of God,* not a bare speculative knowledge, but such as is attended with appropriation and affection.—*Unto a perfect man,* to our full growth of gifts and graces, free from those childish infirmities that we are subject to in the present world.—*Unto the measure of the stature of the fulness of Christ,* so as to be Christians of a full maturity in all the graces derived from Christ's fulness. We shall never come to the perfect man, till we come to the perfect world. God's children, as long as they are in this world, are growing. Now see God's design in his sacred institutions, and what effect they ought to have upon us. (1) *We henceforth be no more children,* &c. (*v.* 14); no longer children in knowledge, weak in the faith, and inconstant in our judgments, easily

yielding to every temptation, and being at everyone's beck. Children are easily imposed upon. We must take care of this, and of being *tossed to and fro*, like ships without ballast, *and carried about*, like clouds in the air, with such doctrines as have no truth nor solidity in them, and are therefore compared to wind. *By the sleight of men, and cunning craftiness, whereby they lie in wait to deceive*, as in an ambush, in order to circumvent the weak. The best method we can take to fortify ourselves against such is to study the sacred oracles, and to pray for the illumination and grace of the Spirit of Christ. (2) We should *speak the truth in love* (v. 15). Love is an excellent thing; but we must be careful to preserve truth together with it. Truth is an excellent thing; yet it is requisite that we speak it in love, and not in contention. These two should go together—truth and peace. (3) We should *grow up into Christ in all things*. Into Christ, so as to be more deeply rooted in him. In all things; in knowledge, love, faith. We should grow up towards maturity, which is opposed to being children. The more we grow into an acquaintance with Christ, faith in him, love to him, dependence upon him, the more we shall flourish in every grace. (4) We should be helpful one to another, as members of the same body, v. 16. Here the apostle makes a comparison between the natural body and Christ's mystical body. As there must be communion of the members of the body among themselves, so there must be mutual love and unity among Christians, in order to their spiritual improvement and growth in grace. Particular Christians receive their gifts and graces from Christ for the sake and benefit of the whole body. *Unto the edifying of itself in love*. Mutual love among Christians is a great friend to spiritual growth: it is in love that the body edifies itself.

Verses 17–32

There follows an exhortation to Christian purity and holiness of heart and life, and that both more general (v. 17–24) and in several particular instances, v. 25–32. This is solemnly introduced: *"This I say therefore, and testify in the Lord."*

I. The more general exhortation to purity and holiness of heart and life.

1. *"That you henceforth walk not as other Gentiles walk."* Converted Gentiles must not live as unconverted Gentiles do. Though they live among them, they must not live like them.

(1) The wickedness of the Gentile world. [1] Their *understandings were darkened*, v. 18. They were void of all saving knowledge. They sat in darkness, and they loved it rather than light: and by their ignorance they were *alienated from the life of God*. They were estranged from a life of holiness. Their wilful ignorance was the cause of their estrangement from this life of God. And what was the cause of their being thus ignorant? It was *because of the blindness* or the hardness *of their heart*. It was not because God did not make himself known to them by his works. They were ignorant because they would be so. Their ignorance proceeded from their obstinacy. [2] Their consciences were debauched and seared: *Who being past feeling*, v. 19. They had no sense of their sin, nor of the danger of their case. They *gave themselves over unto lasciviousness*. They indulged themselves in their filthy lusts. They became the slaves and drudges of sin and the devil, *working all uncleanness with greediness*. When men's consciences are once seared, there are no bounds to their sins.

(2) These Christians must distinguish themselves from such Gentiles: *You have not so learned Christ*, v. 20. It may be read, *But you not so; you have learned Christ*. Those who have learned Christ are saved from the darkness which others lie under; and, as they know more, they are obliged to live in a better manner than others. Learn Christ! Is Christ a book, a lesson, a way, a trade? *"If so be that you have heard him* (v. 21), *and have been taught by him."* Christ is the lesson; we must learn Christ: and Christ is the teacher; we are taught by him. *As the truth is in Jesus.* "You have been taught the real truth, as held forth by Christ himself, both in his doctrine and in his life." The truth of Christ then appears in its beauty and power, when it appears as in Jesus.

2. Another branch of the general exhortation follows. *That you put off, concerning the former conversation, the old man*, &c., v. 22–24. Here the apostle expresses himself in metaphors taken from garments. There must be sanctification, which consists of these two things: (1) The old man must be put off. The corrupt nature is called a man. It is the old man, as old Adam, from whom we derive it. It is bred in the bone, and we brought it into the world with us. It is said to be corrupt; for sin in the soul is the corruption of its faculties: and where it is not mortified, it grows daily worse and worse. *According to the deceitful lusts.* They promise men happiness, but render them more miserable. These therefore must be put off as an old garment that we should be ashamed to be seen in. These lusts prevailed in their *former conversation*. (2) The new man must be put on. It is not enough to shake off corrupt principles, but we must be actuated by gracious ones. *"Be renewed in the spirit of your mind* (v. 23), *And that you put on the new man,"* v. 24. By the new man is meant the new nature, the new creature. This new man *is created*, or produced out of confusion and emptiness, by God's almighty power. *After God:* The loss of God's image upon the soul was both the sinfulness and misery of man's fallen state; and that resemblance which it bears to God is the glory, and the happiness, of the new creature. *In righteousness* towards men *and in holiness* towards God. *True holiness* in opposition to the ceremonial holiness of the Jews. We are said to put on this new man when we are endeavouring after this divine nature.

II. Those particular limbs of the old man that must be mortified, those filthy rags of the old nature that must be put off, and what are the peculiar ornaments of the new man. 1. Take heed of lying, and be ever careful to speak the truth (v. 25): *"Wherefore, putting away lying."* Of this sin the heathen were very guilty, affirming that a profitable lie was better than a hurtful truth. That branch of the new man that must be put on in opposition to it is *speaking the truth* in all our converse with others. All who have grace make conscience of speaking the truth. *We are members one of another.* Truth is a debt we owe to one another; and, if we love one another, we shall not deceive one another. We belong to the same society or body, which falsehood or lying tends to dissolve; and therefore we should avoid it, and speak truth. Lying is a very great sin. 2. "Take heed of anger and ungoverned passions. *Be you angry, and sin not,"* v. 26. Here is an easy concession; for as such we should consider it. *Be you angry.* This we are apt enough to be, God knows: but we find it difficult enough to observe the restriction, *and sin not*. If we would be angry and not sin (says one), we must be angry at nothing but sin. One great and common sin in anger is to suffer it to burn into wrath, and then to let it rest. Before night calm and quiet your spirits, be reconciled to the offender: *Let not the sun go down upon your wrath.* Though anger in itself is not sinful, yet there is the utmost danger of its becoming so if it be not carefully watched. *Neither give place to the devil*, v. 27. Those who persevere in sinful anger and in wrath let the devil into their hearts. "*Neither give place to the* calumniator, or the false accuser" (so some read the words); "let your ears be deaf to whisperers, tale-bearers, and slanderers." 3. We are here warned against the sin of stealing, and advised to honest industry and to beneficence: *Let him that stole steal no more, v. 28.* But we must not only take heed of the sin, but conscientiously abound in the opposite duty: not only not steal, *but rather let him labour, working with his hands the thing that is good.* Idleness makes thieves. Men should therefore be diligent and industrious, not in any unlawful way, but in some honest calling: *Working the thing which is good.* Industry will keep people out of temptation of doing wrong. But there is another reason that they may be capable of doing some good. *That he may have to give to him that needeth.* They must labour not only that they may live themselves. Those who have but little for themselves, must cast their mite into the treasury. God must have his dues and the poor are his receivers. 4. We are here warned against corrupt communication; and directed to that which is useful and edifying, *v. 29.* Filthy and unclean words and discourse are poisonous and infectious, as putrid rotten meat. Christians should beware of all such discourse. We must not only put off corrupt communication, but *put on that which is good to the use of edifying.* Christians should endeavour to promote a useful conversation: *that it may minister grace unto the hearers.* It is the great duty of Christians to take care that they offend not with their lips, and that they improve discourse for the good of others. 5. Another caution against wrath and anger, with further advice to mutual love, *v. 31, 32.* By *bitterness, wrath,* and *anger,* are meant violent inward resentment against others: and, by *clamour,* intemperate speeches, by which bitterness, wrath, and anger, vent themselves. Christians should not be clamorous with their tongues. *Evil speaking* signifies all railing against such as we are angry with. *Malice,* that rooted anger which prompts men to design mischief to others. The contrary to all this follows: *Be you kind one to another.* This implies the principle of love in the heart, and the outward expression of it. *Tender-hearted;* that is, merciful, so as to be quickly moved to compassion and pity. *Forgiving one another.* Occasions of difference will happen among Christ's disciples; and therefore they must be ready to forgive, therein resembling God himself, who *for Christ's sake hath forgiven them.* Those who are forgiven of God should be of a forgiving spirit, and should forgive even as God forgives. All these particulars that the apostle has insisted on belong to the second table. He who does not conscientiously discharge them can never fear nor love God in truth and in sincerity, whatever he may pretend to.

And grieve not the Holy Spirit of God, v. 30. We must not do that which is contrary to his holy nature and his will; we must not refuse to hearken to his counsels, nor rebel against his government. Provoke not the blessed Spirit of God to withdraw his presence and his gracious influences from you! *By him we are sealed unto the day of redemption.* The body is to be redeemed from the power of the grave at the resurrection-day; then our full and complete happiness commences. All true believers are sealed to that day. God has distinguished them from others, and the Spirit of God is the seal. We should be undone should God take away his Holy Spirit from us.

CHAPTER 5

Verses 1, 2

Exhortation to mutual love. "Because God, for Christ's sake, has forgiven you, therefore be you followers of God, or *imitators* of him"; for so the word signifies. This puts a great honour upon practical religion, that it is the imitating of God. We must be holy as God is holy, merciful as he is merciful, perfect as he is perfect. But there is no one attribute of God more recommended to our imitation than that of his goodness. Be you imitators of God, especially in his love. *As dear children,* as children (who are wont to be greatly beloved by their parents) usually resemble them in the features of their faces, and in the dispositions of their minds. Children are obliged to imitate their parents in what is good, especially when dearly beloved by them. The character that we bear of God's children obliges us to resemble him. And those only are God's dear children who imitate him. *And walk in love, v. 2.* It should be the principle from which we act; it should direct the ends at which we aim. *As Christ also hath loved us.* We are all joint sharers in that love and therefore should love one another, Christ having loved us all, *he hath given himself for us. An offering and a sacrifice to God;* or an offering, even a sacrifice, *for a sweet-smelling savour.* As he offered himself with a design to be accepted of God, so God did accept, was pleased with, that sacrifice. His example should be prevailing with us, and we should carefully copy it.

Verses 3–20

Filthy lusts must be suppressed, in order to the supporting of holy love. *Walk in love,* and *shun fornication and all uncleanness.* Now these sins must be dreaded and detested in the highest degree: *Let it not be once named among you as becometh saints.* The apostle not only cautions against the gross acts of sin, but against what some may be apt to make light of, and think to be excusable. *Neither filthiness (v. 4), nor foolish talking,* such vain discourse as betrays much folly and indiscretion, *nor jesting.* There is no doubt an innocent and inoffensive jesting, which we cannot suppose the apostle here forbids. But the context seems to restrain it to such pleasantry of discourse as is filthy and obscene. *They are not convenient.* Indeed there is more than inconvenience, even a great deal of mischief, in them. Those things do not become Christians. Christians are allowed to be cheerful and pleasant; but they must be merry and wise. *But rather giving of thanks:* that he may delight his mind, and make himself cheerful, by a grateful remembrance of God's goodness and mercy to him, and by blessing and praising him on account of these. A reflection on the grace and goodness of God to us, to excite our thankfulness to him, is proper to delight the Christian's mind, and to make him cheerful. If men abounded more in good and pious expressions, they would not be so apt to utter ill and unbecoming words.

I. To fortify us against the sins of uncleanness, &c., the apostle urges several arguments, and prescribes several remedies.

1. He urges several arguments, (1) Consider that these are sins which shut persons out of heaven: *For this you know, &c., v. 5.* There is spiritual idolatry in the love of this world. As the epicure makes a god of his belly, so the covetous man makes a god of his money. He serves mammon instead of God. Of these persons it is said that they *have no inheritance in the kingdom of Christ and of God.* In this kingdom the saints and servants of God have an inheritance. But those who allow themselves either in the lusts of the flesh or the love of the world, belong not to the kingdom of grace, nor shall they ever come to the kingdom of glory. Let us then be on our guard

against those sins which would shut us out of heaven. (2) These sins bring the wrath of God upon those who are guilty of them: "*Let no man deceive you with vain words*," &c., *v.* 6. Those who flatter themselves with hopes of impunity in sin do but put a cheat upon themselves. They are *vain words* indeed, *for because of these things cometh the wrath of God upon the children of disobedience*. Disobedience is the very malignity of sin. *The wrath of God comes upon* such, sometimes in this world, but more especially in the next. And dare we make light of that which will lay us under the wrath of God? *Be not you therefore partakers with them, v.* 7. "Do not partake with them in their sins, that you may not share in their punishment." (3) Consider what obligations Christians are under to live at another rate, *For you were sometimes darkness, but now*, &c., *v.* 8. The apostles call their former condition *darkness*. A state of sin is a state of darkness. Sinners, like men in the dark, are going they know not whither, and doing they know not what. *Now are you light in the Lord. Walk as children of light*. "Now, being such, live up to the obligation you are under by that knowledge and those advantages you enjoy".—*Proving what is acceptable unto the Lord* (*v.* 10), searching diligently what God has revealed to be his will. We must not only dread and avoid that which is displeasing to God, but enquire and consider what will be acceptable to him. 2. Some remedies against them. (1) We must bring forth *the fruits of the Spirit, v.* 9. This is expected from the children of light, that they be also sanctified by the Spirit, and thereupon bring forth his fruit, which *is in all goodness and righteousness*. All religion is goodness and righteousness. With these must be *truth*. (2) We must have no fellowship with sin nor sinners, *v.* 11. Sinful works are works of darkness. These works of darkness are *unfruitful works*; there is nothing got by them in the long run, whatever profit is pretended by sin, it will by no means balance the loss. We must therefore *have no fellowship* with these unfruitful works. If we share with others in their sin, we must expect to share with them in their plagues. Rather than have fellowship with them, we must *reprove them*. We must witness against the sins of others, and endeavour to convince them of their sinfulness in our words; but especially by the holiness of our lives. Reprove their sins by abounding in the contrary duties. *For it is a shame even to speak of those things*, &c., *v.* 12; much more must it be a shame to have any fellowship with them. *The things which are done of them in secret*. A good man is ashamed to speak that which many wicked people are not ashamed to act. *But all things that are reproved are made manifest by the light, v.* 13. By that instructive light which is diffused by the holiness of your lives and by your exemplary walk. *For whatsoever doth make manifest is light*, and accordingly it becomes those who are *children of light*, who are *light in the Lord*, to discover to others their sins, thus shining as lights in the world. The apostle further urges this duty from the example of God or Christ: *Wherefore he saith*, &c. (*v.* 14). *Awake, thou that sleepest, and arise from the dead*. They would break off their sins by repentance, and he encourages them to do their utmost that way, by that gracious promise, *And Christ shall give thee light*. When we are endeavouring to convince sinners, and to reform them from their sins, we are imitating God and Christ in that which is their great design throughout the gospel. (3) Another remedy against sin is circumspection, (*v.* 15): *See then*, &c. "If you are to reprove others for their sins you must look well to yourselves, and to your own behaviour and conduct." We have here another preservative from the before-mentioned sins; it being impossible to maintain purity and holiness of heart and life without

great circumspection and care. *Walk circumspectly*, exactly in the right way, in order to which we must be frequently consulting our rule. *Not as fools*, who walk at all adventures, and who through neglect, and want of care, fall into sin, and destroy themselves; *but as wise*, as persons taught of God. Circumspect walking is the effect of true wisdom, but the contrary is the effect of folly. *Redeeming the time* (*v.* 16), literally, *buying the opportunity*. It is a metaphor taken from merchants and traders who diligently observe and improve the seasons for merchandise and trade. Good Christians must be good husbands of their time. They should make the best use they can of the present seasons of grace. Our time is a talent given us by God for some good end, and it is misspent and lost when it is not employed according to his design. If we have lost our time heretofore, we must endeavour to redeem it by doubling our diligence for the future. *Because the days are evil*. Those were times of persecution wherein the apostle wrote this: the Christians were in jeopardy every hour. When the days are evil we know not how soon they may be worse. People are very apt to complain of bad times; it were well if that would stir them up to redeem time. "*Wherefore* (*v.* 17), *be you not unwise, but understanding what the will of the Lord is*." Acquaintance with the will of God, and a care to comply with it, bespeak the best and truest wisdom.

II. The apostle warns against some other particular sins, and urges some other duties. 1. He warns against the sin of drunkenness: *And be not drunk with wine, v.* 18. The apostle adds, *wherein is excess*. Drunkenness is a sin that seldom goes alone, but often involves men in other instances of guilt: it is a great hindrance to the spiritual life. 2. Instead of being filled with wine, he exhorts them to be *filled with the Spirit*. Those who are full of drink are not likely to be full of the Spirit. Men should labour for a plentiful measure of the graces of the Spirit, that would fill their souls with great joy, and courage, which things sensual men expect their wine should inspire them with. We ought not to be satisfied with a little of the Spirit, but to be filled with the Spirit. Now by this means we shall come to *understand what the will of the Lord is*. The apostle exhorts, 3. To sing unto the Lord, *v.* 19. Drunkards are wont to sing obscene and profane songs. The joy of Christians should express itself in songs of praise to their God. In these they should *speak to themselves* in their assemblies. Though Christianity is an enemy to profane mirth, yet it encourages joy and gladness. God's people have reason to rejoice, and to sing for joy. They are to *sing and to make melody in their hearts;* not only with their voices, but with inward affection, and then it will be done to the Lord. 4. Thanksgiving is another duty, *v.* 20. We should be *always giving thanks;* and we should give thanks *for all things*. It is our duty in *everything to give thanks unto God and the Father*.

Verses 21–33

The discharge of relative duties. As a general foundation for these duties, he lays down that rule, *v.* 21. There is a mutual submission that Christians owe one to another. *In the fear of God*, for his sake, that hereby we may give proof that we truly fear him. Where there is this mutual submission, the duties of all relations will be the better performed.

I. The duty prescribed to wives is submission to their husbands in the Lord (*v.* 22). The reason of this submission from wives: *For the husband is the head of the wife, v.* 23. God has given the man the pre-eminence and a right to direct and govern by creation. Generally, too, the man has (what he ought to have) a superiority in wisdom and knowledge. He is therefore the head, *even as Christ is the head* of the church, and he is the Saviour of the body. Christ's authority is exercised over the church for the saving of her from evil, and the supplying of her with everything good for her. In like manner should the husband be employed for the protection and comfort of his spouse. *Therefore as the church is subject unto Christ* (v. 24), with cheerfulness, with fidelity, with humility, *so let the wives be to their own husbands in everything.*

II. The duty of husbands is to love their wives (v. 25); for without this they would abuse their superiority, it being a special and peculiar affection that is required in her behalf. The love of Christ to the church is proposed as an example of this, which love of his is a constant affection, and that notwithstanding the imperfections and failures that she is guilty of. The greatness of his love to the church appeared in his giving himself unto the death for it. The love which God requires from the husband in behalf of his wife will make amends for the subjection which he demands from her to her husband; and the prescribed subjection of the wife will be an abundant return for that love of the husband which God has made her due. The reason why he gave himself for it: *That he might sanctify and cleanse it, with the washing of water by the word* (v. 26). *That he might present it to himself, a glorious church, not having spot, nor wrinkle, nor any such thing, holy and without blemish*, free from the least remains of sin. The church in general, and particular believers, will not be without spot or wrinkle till they come to glory. Those, and those only, who are sanctified now, will be glorified hereafter.—*So ought men to love their wives as their own bodies, &c.,* v. 28. The wife being made one with her husband this is an argument why he should love her with as ardent an affection as that with which he loves himself. *For no man ever yet hated his own flesh*, v. 29—*he nourishes and cherishes it: even as the Lord the church. For we are members of his body, of his flesh and of his bones*, v. 30. *For this cause* (because they are one, as Christ and his church are one) *shall a man leave his father and mother.* This relation is to be preferred to all others, there being a nearer union between these two than between any others.—*And they two shall be one flesh. This is a great mystery*, v. 32. Those words have also a hidden mystical sense in them, relating to the union between Christ and his church. *I speak concerning Christ and the church.*

A brief summary of the duty of husbands and wives, v. 33. "*Nevertheless let everyone of you in particular so love his wife even as himself. And the wife see that she reverence her husband.*" Reverence consists of love and esteem. That the wife thus reverence her husband is the will of God and the law of the relation.

CHAPTER 6

I. The apostle proceeds in the exhortation to relative duties, particularly he insists on the duties of children and parents, and of servants and masters, ver. 1–9. II. He directs Christians how to behave themselves in the spiritual warfare with the enemies of their souls; and to the exercise of several Christian graces, which he proposes to them as so many pieces of spiritual armour, ver. 10–18. III. The conclusion of the epistle, ver. 19–24.

Verses 1–9

I. The duty of children to their parents: to obey their parents (v. 1). That obedience which God demands from their children includes an inward reverence, as well as the outward expressions and acts. Obey in the Lord. "Obey your parents, especially in those things which relate to the Lord. Your parents teach you good manners, and therein you must obey them. They teach you what is for your health, and in this you must obey them: but the chief things in which you are to do it are the things pertaining to the Lord." In these things especially they

must see that they be obedient. *For this is right*, there is a natural equity in it, God has enjoined it. It is the order of nature that parents command and children obey. The apostle quotes the law of the fifth commandment. *Honour thy father and mother* (v. 2), *which is the first commandment with promise.* The promise is, *That it may be well with thee*, &c., v. 3. Outward prosperity and long life are blessings promised to those who keep this commandment. Obedient children are often rewarded with outward prosperity. Not indeed that it is always so; but *ordinarily* obedience is thus rewarded. The gospel has its temporal promises, as well as spiritual ones. We are allowed to have respect to the promised reward. This may be considered as a motive and encouragement to our obedience.

II. The duty of parents: *And you fathers*, v. 4. 1. "*Do not provoke your children to wrath.* Your children are pieces of yourselves, and therefore ought to be governed with great tenderness and love. When you caution them, when you counsel them, when you reprove them, do it in such a manner as not to *provoke them to wrath*, endeavouring to convince their judgments and to work upon their reason." 2. "*Bring them up* well, *in the nurture and admonition of the Lord.* Give them a good education." It is the great duty of parents to be careful in the education of their children. Not only bring them up as men, but as Christians, in the admonition of the Lord. Let them have a religious education.

III. The duty of servants. This also is summed up in one word, *obedience.* These servants were generally slaves. Civil servitude is not inconsistent with Christian liberty. Those may be the Lord's freemen who are slaves to men. "*Your masters according to the flesh* (v. 5), who have the command of your bodies, but not of your souls and consciences." 1. That they obey *with fear and trembling.* They are to reverence those who are over them. 2. That they be sincere in their obedience: *In singleness of heart:* serving them with faithfulness. 3. They should have an eye to Jesus Christ in all the service that they perform to their masters (v. 5–7), *doing service as to the Lord, and not to men.* Service done to their earthly masters, with an eye to him, becomes acceptable service to him also. 4. They must not serve their masters *with eye-service* (v. 6)—that is, only when their master's eye is upon them. Their Master in heaven beholds them: and therefore they must not act as *men-pleasers.* A steady regard to the Lord Jesus Christ will make men faithful and sincere in every station of life. 5. What they do they must do cheerfully: *Doing the will of God from the heart*, serving their masters as God wills they should. This is *doing it with goodwill* (v. 7). Service, performed with conscience, and from a regard to God, though it be to unrighteous masters, will be accounted by Christ as service done to himself. 6. Let faithful servants trust God for their wages, while they do their duty in his fear: *Knowing that whatsoever good thing* (v. 8)—*the same shall he receive of the Lord.* Though his master on earth should neglect or abuse him, instead of rewarding him, he shall certainly be rewarded by the Lord Christ, *whether he be bond or free.* Christ regards not these differences of men at present; nor will he in the great and final judgment.

IV. The duty of masters: *And you masters, do the same things unto them* (v. 9). Masters are under as strict obligations to discharge their duty to their servants as servants are to be obedient and dutiful to them. "*Forbearing threatening.* Be not tyrannical and imperious over them, *knowing that your Master also is in heaven*; you and they are but fellow-servants in respect of Christ. You are therefore to show favour to others, as ever you expect to find favour with him; and you will never be a match for him, though you may be too hard for your servants." *Neither is there respect of persons with him.* He will call masters and servants to an impartial account for their conduct one to another. If both masters and servants would consider their relation to God and the account they must shortly give to him, they would be more careful of their duty to each other.

Verses 10–18

Is not our life a warfare? It is so; for we struggle with the common calamities of human life. Is not our religion much more a warfare? It is so; for we struggle with the opposition of the powers of darkness. "*Finally, my brethren (v.* 10), it yet remains that you apply yourselves to your work and duty as Christian soldiers."

I. They must see that they be stout-hearted. *Be strong in the Lord,* &c. Those who have so many battles to fight, and who, in their way to heaven, must dispute every pass, with dint of sword, have need of a great deal of courage. *Be strong therefore.* Let a soldier be ever so well armed without, if he have not within a good heart, his armour will stand him in little stead. Spiritual strength and courage are very necessary for our spiritual warfare. We have no sufficient strength of our own. All our sufficiency is of God. In his strength we must go forth and go on. We must fetch in grace and help from heaven to enable us to do that which of ourselves we cannot do in our Christian work and warfare.

II. They must be well armed: "*Put on the whole armour of God (v.* 11). Get and exercise all the Christian graces, the whole armour, that no part be naked and exposed to the enemy." Those who would have true grace must aim at all grace, the whole armour. We have no armour of our own that will be armour of proof in a trying time. Nothing will stand us in stead but the armour of God. This armour is prepared for us, but we must put it on. The Christian should be completely armed *that he may be able to stand against the wiles of the devil*—that he may be able to hold out, and to overcome.

1. What our danger is, and what need we have to put on this whole armour. *For we wrestle not against flesh and blood,* &c., *v.* 12. The combat is not against ordinary human enemies, not barely against men compounded of *flesh and blood.* (1) We have to do with an enemy who uses wiles and stratagems, as *v.* 11. He has a thousand ways of beguiling unstable souls. (2) He is a powerful enemy: *Principalities,* and *powers,* and *rulers.* They are numerous, they are vigorous, and rule in those heathen nations which are yet in darkness. Satan's is a kingdom of darkness; whereas Christ's is a kingdom of light. (3) They are spiritual enemies: *Spiritual wickedness in high places,* or wicked spirits, as some translate it. Our danger is the greater from our enemies because they are unseen, and assault us ere we are aware of them. These enemies are said to be *in high places,* or in heavenly places, so the word is. Our enemies strive to prevent our ascent to heaven. They assault us in the things that belong to our souls. We have need of faith in our Christian warfare, because we have spiritual enemies to grapple with, as well as of faith in our Christian work, because we have spiritual strength to fetch in.

2. What our duty is: to put on the whole armour of God, and then to stand our ground, and withstand our enemies.

(1) We must *withstand, v.* 13. We must not yield to the devil's allurements and assaults, but oppose them. If he stand up against us, we must stand against him. To stand against Satan is to strive against sin. *That you may be able to withstand in the evil day,* in the day of temptation, or of any sore affliction.

(2) We must stand our ground: *And, having done all, to stand.* Resist him, and he will flee. If we give back, he will get ground. Our present business is to withstand the assaults of the devil, and to stand it out; and then our warfare will be accomplished, and we shall be finally victorious.

(3) We must stand armed. Here is a Christian in complete armour: and the armour is divine: *Armour of God.* The apostle specifies the particulars of this armour, both offensive and defensive. The military girdle or belt, the breast-plate, the greaves (or soldier's shoes), the shield, the helmet, and the sword. It is observable that, among them all, there is none for the back; if we turn our back upon the enemy, we lie exposed. [1] Truth is our girdle, *v.* 14. This is the strength of our loins; and it girds on all other pieces of our armour, and therefore is first mentioned. I know no religion without sincerity. [2] Righteousness must be our breast-plate. The breast-plate secures the vitals, shelters the heart. The righteousness of Christ implanted in us is our breast-plate to fortify the heart against the attacks which Satan makes against us. [3] Resolution must be as the greaves to our legs: *And their feet shod with the preparation of the gospel of peace, v.* 15. Shoes, or greaves of brass, were formerly part of the military armour to defend the feet against the gall-traps, and sharp sticks, which were wont to be laid to obstruct the marching of the enemy, those who fell upon them being unfit to march. *The preparation of the gospel of peace* signifies a resolved frame of heart which will enable us to walk with a steady pace in the way of religion. It is styled *the gospel of peace* because it brings all sorts of peace. This will certainly preserve you from many great temptations and persecutions, as did those shoes of brass the soldiers from those gall-traps. [4] Faith must be our shield: *Above all, taking the shield of faith, v.* 16. This is more necessary than any of them. Faith is all in all to us in an hour of temptation. The breast-plate secures the vitals; but with the shield we turn every way. Faith is like a shield, a sort of universal defence. Our enemy the devil is here called *the wicked one.* He is wicked himself, and he endeavours to make us wicked. His temptations are called *fiery darts,* by way of allusion to the poisonous darts which were wont to inflame the parts which were wounded. Violent temptations, by which the soul is set on fire of hell, are the darts which Satan shoots at us. Faith is the shield with which we must quench these fiery darts, that they may not hit us, or at least that they may not hurt us. [5] Salvation must be our helmet (*v.* 17); that is, hope, which has salvation for its object. He would tempt us to despair; but good hope keeps us trusting in God, and rejoicing in him. [6] The word of God is the sword of the Spirit. It is called *the sword of the Spirit,* because he renders it efficacious and powerful. This, being hid in the heart, will preserve from sin. [7] Prayer must buckle on all the other parts of our Christian armour, *v.* 18. We must join prayer with all these graces, and we must pray always. Not as though we were to do nothing else but pray, for there are other duties that are to be done in their place and season; but we should keep up constant times of prayer. We must pray upon all occasions. We must intermix ejaculatory prayers with other duties, and with common business. Though set and solemn prayer may sometimes be unseasonable, yet pious ejaculations *can* never be so. We must pray *with all prayer and supplications,* with all kinds of prayer. We must pray *in the Spirit.* We must do it by the grace of God's good Spirit. We must *watch thereunto,* endeavouring to keep our hearts in a praying frame, and taking all occasions for the duty. This we must do *with all perseverance.* We must continue in it as long as we live in the world. And we must pray *with supplication,* not for ourselves only,

but *for all saints.* None are so much saints, and in so good a condition in this world, but they need our prayers, and they ought to have them.

Verses 19–24

I. He desires their prayers for him, *v.* 19. Having mentioned *supplication for all saints,* he puts himself into the number. We must pray for all saints, and particularly for God's faithful ministers. *"That utterance may be given unto me; and that I may open my mouth boldly. To make known the mystery of the gospel."* The whole gospel was a mystery, till made known by divine revelation. Paul had a great command of language; they called him Mercury, because he was the chief speaker (Acts xiv. 12), and yet he would have his friends ask of God the gift of utterance for him. He was a man of great courage, yet he would have them pray that God would give him boldness. He knew as well what to say as any man; yet he desires them to pray for him, that he may *speak as he ought to speak.* For the sake of the gospel he was *an ambassador in bonds, v.* 20. He was persecuted and imprisoned for preaching the gospel; though, notwithstanding, he continued in the embassy committed to him by Christ. The best ministers may receive advantage by the prayers of good Christians; and therefore should earnestly desire them.

II. He recommends Tychicus unto them, *v.* 21, 22. He sent him with this epistle, that he might acquaint them how he did, and what he did. It is desirable to good ministers both that their Christian friends should know their state and that they should be acquainted with the condition of their friends; for by this means they may the better help each other in their prayers.—*And that he might comfort their hearts,* by giving such an account of his sufferings, as might prevent their fainting at his tribulations and even minister matter of joy and thanksgiving unto them. Tychicus was *a beloved brother and faithful minister in the Lord.* He was very dear to Paul, which makes Paul's love to these Christian Ephesians the more observable, in that he should now part with so good and dear a friend for their sakes. But the faithful servants of Jesus Christ are wont to prefer the public good to their own personal interests.

III. He concludes with his good wishes and prayers for them, and not for them only, but for all the brethren, *v.* 23, 24. *Peace be to the brethren, and love with faith;* faith and love including all the rest. It is the continuance and increase of these that he desires for them, in whom they were already begun. *From God the Father,* &c. The closing benediction is more extensive than the former; for in this he prays for all true believers at Ephesus, and everywhere else. Our love to Christ is not acceptable, unless it be in sincerity: indeed there is no such thing as love to Christ, whatever men may pretend, where there is not sincerity. Grace, that is, the favour of God, and all good, the product of it, are and shall be with all those who thus love our Lord Jesus Christ. And it is, or ought to be, the prayer of every lover of Christ that it may be so with all his fellow-christians. *Amen,* so be it.

AN EXPOSITION, WITH PRACTICAL OBSERVATIONS, OF

THE EPISTLE OF ST. PAUL TO

THE PHILIPPIANS

Philippi was a chief city of the western part of Macedonia. It is most remarkable among Christians for this epistle, which was written when Paul was a prisoner at Rome. Paul seems to have had a very particular kindness for the church at Philippi, which he himself had been instrumental in planting; he had, upon that account, a particular fatherly tender care of this. He looked upon them as his children, and, having *begotten them by the gospel*, he was desirous by the same gospel to nourish and nurse them up. I. He was called in an extraordinary manner to preach the gospel at Philippi. A vision appeared to Paul in the night: *There stood a man of Macedonia, and prayed him, saying, Come over into Macedonia, and help us.* He saw God going before him. II. At Philippi he suffered hard things; yet he had not the less kindness for the place. We must never love our friends the less for the ill treatment which our enemies give us. III. The beginnings of that church were very small; yet that did not discourage him. If good be not done at first, it may be done afterwards and the last works may be more abundant. IV. It seems that this church at Philippi grew into a flourishing church, and particularly that the brethren were very kind to Paul. He acknowledges the receipt of a present they had sent him (*ch.* iv. 18), and this when no other church communicated with him as concerning giving and receiving (*v.* 15).

CHAPTER 1

The inscription and benediction, ver. 1, 2. He gives thanks for the saints at Philippi, ver. 3–6. He speaks of his great affection (ver. 7, 8), his prayers for them (ver. 9–11), his care to prevent their offence at his sufferings (ver. 12–20), his readiness to glorify Christ by life or death (ver. 21–26), and then concludes with a double exhortation to strictness and constancy, ver. 27–30.

Verses 1, 2

I. The persons writing the epistle—*Paul and Timotheus, the servants of Jesus Christ.* The highest honour of the greatest apostle, and most eminent ministers, is to be the servants of Jesus Christ; not the masters of the churches, but the servants of Christ. II. The persons to whom it is directed. 1. To *all the saints in Christ who are at Philippi.* He mentions the church before the ministers, because the ministers are for the church, not the churches for the ministers. They are not only the servants of Christ, but the servants of the church for his sake. It is directed to *all the saints*, one as well as another, even the meanest, the poorest, and those of the least gifts. Christ makes no difference; the rich and the poor meet together in him: *Saints in Christ Jesus.* Out of Christ the best saints will appear sinners, and unable to stand before God. 2. *With the bishops and deacons*, the bishops or elders, whose office it was to teach and rule, and the deacons, or overseers of the poor, who took care of the outward business of the house of God. These were all the offices which were then known in the church, and which were of divine appointment. III. The apostolical benediction: *Grace be unto you, and peace, from God our Father, and from the Lord Jesus Christ, v.* 2. This is the same, almost word for word, in all the epistles, we must not be shy of forms, though we are not to be tied down to them. *Grace and peace*—the free favour and goodwill of God, and all the blessed fruits and effects of it, and that *from God our Father, and from the Lord Jesus Christ.* No peace without grace. Inward peace springs from a sense of divine favour. No grace and peace but from God our Father, the fountain and original of all blessings. No grace and peace from God our Father, but in and through our Lord Jesus Christ.

Verses 3–6

The apostle proceeds to thanksgiving for the saints at Philippi.

I. Paul remembered them: he bore them much in his thoughts. *Upon every mention of you.* As he often thought of them, so he often spoke of them, and delighted to hear them spoken of. It is a pleasure to hear of the welfare of an absent friend.

II. He remembered them with joy. At Philippi he was maltreated; and yet he remembers Philippi with joy. So far was he from being ashamed of them, or loth to hear of the scene of his sufferings, that he remembered it with joy.

III. He remembered them in prayer: *Always in every prayer of mine for you all, v.* 4. The best remembrance of our friends is to remember them at the throne of grace. He had seasons of prayer for the church at Philippi. God gives us leave to be thus free with him, though, for our comfort, he knows whom we mean when we do not name them.

IV. He thanked God upon every joyful remembrance of them. Thanksgiving must have a part in every prayer. What we have the comfort of, God must have the glory of. He thanked God, as well as made requests with joy.

V. *I thank my God.* It encourages us in prayer, and enlarges the heart in praise, to see every mercy coming from the hand of God as our God.—*I thank my God upon every remembrance of you.* He gives thanks to God. 1. For the comfort he had in them: for *your fellowship in the gospel, from the first day until now, v.* 5. Gospel fellowship is a good fellowship. Those who sincerely receive the gospel have fellowship in it *from the very first day*: a new-born Christian, if he is true-born, is interested in all the promises of the gospel from the first day of his becoming such. —*Until now.* It is a great comfort to ministers when those who begin well hold on and persevere. 2. For the confidence he had concerning them (*v.* 6): *Being confident of this very thing*, &c. The confidence of Christians is the great comfort of Christians, and we may fetch matter of praise from our hopes as well as from our joys. Paul speaks with much confidence. *That he who has begun a good work in you will perform it unto the day of Jesus Christ.* A good work *among you*—he who hath planted Christianity in the world will preserve it as long as the world stands. But it is rather to be applied to particular persons, and then it speaks of the certain accomplishment of the work of grace wherever it is begun. (1) The work of grace is a good work. It makes us like God, and fits us for the enjoyment of God.

(2) Wherever this good work is begun it is of God's beginning: *He has begun a good work in you.* We could not begin it ourselves, for we are by nature *dead in trespasses and sins:* and what can dead men do towards raising themselves to life? It is God who quickens those who are thus dead. (3) The work of grace is but begun in this life; it is not finished here. (4) If the same God who begins the good work did not undertake the carrying on and finishing of it, it would lie for ever unfinished. (5) We may be confident that God will finish the work of his own hands. (6) The work of grace will never be perfected *till the day of Jesus Christ.* When he shall come to judge the world, then this work will be complete.

Verses 7, 8

The ardent affection he had for them: *I have you in my heart, v.* 7. 1. Why he had them in his heart: *Inasmuch as both in my bonds, and in the defence and confirmation of the gospel, you are all partakers of my grace;* they were partakers of that grace of God which by him was communicated to them. This makes people dear to their ministers—their receiving benefit by their ministry. Or, *"You are partakers of my grace,* you have joined with me in doing and suffering." They were partakers of his affliction by sympathy and concern, and readiness to assist him. Those shall share in the reward, who bear their part of the burden. He loved them because they adhered to him in his bonds, and in the *defence and confirmation of the gospel:* they were as ready to appear in their places for the defence of the gospel, as the apostle was in his. Fellow sufferers should be dear one to another. 2. The evidence of it: *It is meet for me to think this of you all, because I have you in my heart.* By this it appeared that he had them in his heart, because he had a good opinion of them. It is very proper to think the best of other people, and as well as we can of them. 3. An appeal to God concerning the truth of this (*v.* 8): *For God is my record how greatly I long after you all in the bowels of Jesus Christ.* Having them in his heart, he longed after them. He had *joy in them* (*v.* 4), because of the good he saw and heard of among them. He *longed after them all,* not only those among them who were witty and wealthy, but even the meanest and poorest; and he *longed greatly* after them. And this *in the bowels of Jesus Christ,* with that tender concern which Christ himself has and has shown to precious souls. Paul was herein a follower of Christ, and all good ministers should aim to be so. Shall not we pity and love those souls whom Christ had such a love and pity for? For this he appeals to God: *God is my record.* "Whether you know it or not, God, who knows the heart, knows it."

Verses 9–11

The prayers he put up for them. Paul often let his friends know what it was he begged of God for them, that they might know what to beg for themselves, and that they might be encouraged to hope they should receive from God the comforting grace which Paul asked of God for them. He prayed, 1. That they might be a loving people: *That your love might abound yet more and more.* Those who abound much in any grace have still need to abound more and more, because we are imperfect in our best attainments. 2. That they might be a knowing and judicious people: that love might abound *in knowledge and in all judgment.* It is not a blind love that will recommend us to God. Strong passions, without knowledge and a settled judgment, will not make us complete in the will of God, and sometimes do more hurt than good. 3. That they might be a discerning people. *That you may approve the things which are excellent* (*v.* 10); or, as it is in the margin, *Try the things which differ;*

that we may approve the things which are excellent upon the trial of them, and discern their difference from other things. The truths and laws of Christ are excellent things. We only need to try them, to approve of them. 4. That they might be an honest upright-hearted people: *That you may be sincere.* Sincerity is our gospel perfection. When we are really what we appear to be, and mean honestly, then we are sincere. 5. That they might be an inoffensive people: that you may be *without offence until the day of Christ;* not apt to take offence; and very careful not to give offence to God or their brethren. And we must continue to the end *blameless,* that we may be presented so at the *day of Christ.* 6. That they might be a fruitful useful people (*v.* 11): *Being filled with the fruits of righteousness,* &c. From God is our fruit found, and therefore from him it must be asked. *Being filled* with them. Fear not being emptied by bringing forth the fruits of righteousness, for you will be filled with them. These fruits are *by Jesus Christ,* and they are *unto the glory and praise of God.* We must not aim at our own glory in our fruitfulness. It is much for the honour of God, when Christians not only are good, but do good, and *abound in good works.*

Verses 12–20

He was now a prisoner at Rome; this might be a stumbling-block to those who had received the gospel by his ministry. They might be shy of owning this doctrine, lest they should be involved in the same trouble themselves. Now to take off the offence of the cross, he expounds this dark and hard chapter of his sufferings.

I. He suffered by the sworn enemies of the gospel; but they should not be stumbled at this, for good was brought out of it, and it tended to the furtherance of the gospel (*v.* 12): *The things which happened unto me have fallen out rather unto the furtherance of the gospel.*

A strange chemistry of Providence this, to extract so great a good as the enlargement of the gospel out of so great an evil as the confinement of the apostle. 1. It alarmed those who were without (*v.* 13): *My bonds in Christ are manifest in all the palace and in all other places.* Paul's sufferings made him known at court, and this might lead some of them to enquire after the gospel for which he suffered, which they might otherwise have never heard of. When his bonds were manifest in the palace, they were manifest in all other places. 2. It emboldened those who were within. As his enemies were startled at his sufferings, so his friends were encouraged by them. *Many of the brethren in the Lord waxing confident by my bonds, v.* 14. When they saw Paul imprisoned for Christ, they were so far from being deterred from preaching Christ and praising his name, that it made them the more bold. If they should be hurried from the pulpit to the prison, they could be reconciled to it, because they would be there in such good company. Besides, the comfort which Paul had in his sufferings greatly encouraged them. They saw that those who served Christ served a good Master, who could both bear them up and bear them out. *Waxing confident by my bonds.* That which was intended by the enemy to discourage the preachers of the gospel was overruled for their encouragement. And *are much more bold to speak the word without fear:* they see the worst of it, and therefore are not afraid to venture.

II. He suffered from false friends as well as from enemies (*v.* 15, 16): *Some preach Christ even of envy and strife. The one preach Christ of contention, not sincerely.* There were those who envied Paul's reputation in the churches, and endeavoured to supplant and undermine him. *Supposing to add affliction to my bonds.* However, there were others who were animated by Paul's sufferings to preach Christ the more vigorously: *Some also of goodwill, and love.—Knowing that I am set for the defence of the gospel.* This made them the more bold to preach the word.

III. How easy he was in the midst of all: *Notwithstanding every way, whether in pretence or in truth, Christ is preached; and I therein do rejoice, yea, and I will rejoice, v.* 18. It is God's prerogative to judge of the principles men act upon; this is out of our line. Paul was so far from envying those who had liberty to preach the gospel that he rejoiced in the preaching of it even by those who do it in pretence, and not in truth.

1. It tended to the salvation of the souls of men: *I know that this shall turn to my salvation, v.* 19. God can bring good out of evil. What reward can those expect who preach Christ out *of strife, and envy, and contention,* and to add affliction to a faithful minister's bonds? who preach in pretence, and not in truth? And yet even this may turn to the salvation of others; and Paul's rejoicing in it turned to his salvation too. *Through your prayers, and the supply of the Spirit of Christ.* The prayers of the people may bring a supply of the Spirit to their ministers, to support them in suffering, as well as in preaching the gospel.

2. It would turn to the glory of Christ, *v.* 20. *According to my earnest expectation and hope, that in nothing I shall be ashamed,* &c. The great desire of every true Christian is that Christ may be magnified and glorified. Those who truly desire that Christ may be magnified desire that he may be *magnified in their body.* They are willing to serve his designs with every member of their body, as well as faculty of their soul. *That in nothing I shall be ashamed, but that with all boldness Christ may be magnified.* The boldness of Christians is the honour of Christ. Those who make Christ's glory their desire may make it their expectation and hope. If it be truly aimed at, it shall certainly be attained. Those who desire that Christ may be magnified in their bodies have a holy indifference *whether it be by life or by death.* They refer it to him which way he will make them serviceable to his glory, whether by their living to his honour in working for him or dying to his honour in suffering for him.

Verses 21–26

We have here an account of the life and death of blessed Paul: his life was Christ, and his death was gain. It is the undoubted character of every good Christian that to him to live is Christ. The glory of Christ ought to be the end of our life. All those to whom to live is Christ to them to die *will be gain.* Death is a great loss to a carnal worldly man; but to a good Christian it is gain. It delivers him from all the evils of life, and brings him to the possession of the chief good. Some read the whole expression thus: *To me, living and dying, Christ is gain.* "I desire no more, neither while I live nor when I die, but to win Christ and be found in him."

I. *If I live in the flesh, this is the fruit of my labour* (*v.* 22), that is, Christ is. He reckoned his labour well bestowed, if he could be instrumental to advance the kingdom of Christ in the world. It is worth while for a good Christian and a good minister to live in the world as long as he can glorify God and do good to his church. *Yet what I shall choose I wot not; for I am in a strait betwixt two.* It was a blessed strait which Paul was in, not between two evil things, but between two good things. Paul was in a strait between two blessings—living to Christ, and being with him.

1. His inclination was for death. We have naturally an aversion to death, but he had an inclination to it

(*v.* 23); *Having a desire to depart, and to be with Christ.* It is being with Christ which makes a departure desirable to a good man. If I cannot be with Christ without departing, I shall reckon it desirable on that account to depart. *Which is far better.* Those who know the value of Christ and heaven will readily acknowledge it far better to be in heaven than to be in this world, to be with Christ. If we come to be with Christ, farewell sin and temptation, farewell sorrow and death, for ever.

2. His judgment was rather to live awhile longer in this world, for the service of the church (*v.* 24): *Nevertheless to abide in the flesh is more needful for you.* Paul's strait was not between living in this world and living in heaven; between these two there is no comparison: but his strait was between serving Christ in this world and enjoying him in another. To advance the interest of Christ and his church, he chose rather to tarry here, where he met with oppositions and difficulties, and to deny himself for awhile the satisfaction of his reward.

II. *And, having this confidence, I know that I shall abide and continue with you all for your furtherance and joy of faith, v.* 25. What a great confidence Paul had in the divine Providence, that it would order all for the best to him. Whatsoever is best for the church, we may be sure God will do. What ministers are continued for: *For our furtherance and joy of faith,* our further advancement in holiness and comfort. What promotes our *faith and joy of faith* is very much for our furtherance in the way to heaven. The more faith the more joy, and the more faith and joy the more we are furthered in our Christian course.

III. *That your rejoicing may be more abundant in Jesus Christ for me, by my coming to you again, v.* 26. They rejoiced in the hope of seeing him, and enjoying his further labours among them. All our joys should terminate in Christ. Our joy in good ministers should be our joy *in Christ Jesus for them.*

Verses 27–30

I. He exhorts them to strictness of conversation (*v.* 27): *Only let your conversation be as becometh the gospel of Christ.* Let it be in all respects as those who belong to the kingdom of God among men. It is an ornament to our profession when our conversation is of a piece with it.—*That whether I come and see you, or else be absent, I may hear of your affairs.* Our religion must not be bound up in the hands of our ministers. Whether ministers come or no, Christ is always at hand. Let me hear of you *that you stand fast in one spirit, with one mind striving together for the faith of the gospel.* It becomes those who profess the gospel to strive for it. There is much opposition, and there is need of striving. A man may sleep and go to hell; but he who will go to heaven must look about him and be diligent. The unity and unanimity of Christians become the gospel: *Strive together,* not strive one with another. One spirit and one mind become the gospel. Steadfastness becomes the gospel: *Stand fast in one spirit, with one mind.* It is a shame to religion when the professors of it are off and on, unfixed in their minds, and unstable as water. Those who would strive for the faith of the gospel must stand firm to it.

II. He exhorts them to courage and constancy in suffering: *And in nothing terrified by your adversaries, v.* 28. Whatever oppositions we meet with, we must not be frightened at them. Persecuting is an *evident token of perdition.* Those who oppose the gospel of Christ are marked out for ruin. But being persecuted is a token of salvation. Not that it is a certain mark; many hypocrites have suffered for their religion; but it is a good sign that we are in good earnest in religion, when we are enabled in a right manner to suffer for the cause of Christ.—*For to you it is given* on the behalf of Christ not only to believe, but also to suffer for his name, v. 29. To believe in him. Faith is God's gift on the behalf of Christ. To suffer for the sake of Christ is a valuable gift too. If we suffer reproach and loss for Christ, we are to reckon it a great gift, always provided we behave under our sufferings with the genuine temper of martyrs (v. 30): "*Having the same conflict which you saw in me, and now hear to be in me,* suffering in the same manner as you saw and now hear of me that I suffer." It is not simply the suffering, but the cause, and not only the cause, but the spirit, which makes the martyr.

CHAPTER 2

Further exhortations to be like-minded, and lowly-minded, which he presses from the example of Christ (ver. 1-11), to be diligent and serious (ver. 12, 13), and to adorn their Christian profession, ver. 14-18. Particular notice and commendation of Timothy and Epaphroditus, whom he designed to send to them, ver. 19-30.

Verses 1–11

Further exhortations to Christian duties.

I. The great gospel precept pressed upon us; to love one another. This he represents (v. 2) by being *like-minded, having the same love, being of one accord, of one mind.* Christians should be one in affection, whether they can be one in apprehension or no. *Having the same love.* Christian love ought to be mutual love. Love, and you shall be loved. *Being of one accord, and of one mind;* unanimously agreeing in the great things of God and keeping the *unity of the Spirit* in other differences.

1. The pathetic pressing of the duty. The inducements to brotherly love are these: (1) "If there is any *consolation in Christ.* Have you experienced consolation in Christ? Evidence that experience by loving one another." Do we expect consolation in Christ? If we would not be disappointed, we must love one another. (2) "*Comfort of love.* If there is any comfort in God's love to you, in your love to God, or in your brethren's love to us, be you like-minded." (3) "*Fellowship of the Spirit.* If there is such a thing as communion with God and Christ by the Spirit, such a thing as the communion of saints, be you like-minded." (4) "*Any bowels and mercies,* in God and Christ, towards you. If you expect the benefit of God's compassions to yourselves, be you compassionate one to another." (5) Another argument is the comfort it would be to him: *Fulfil you my joy.* It is the joy of ministers to see people like-minded and living in love. He had been instrumental in bringing them to the grace of Christ and the love of God. "Now," says he, "*fulfil the joy* of your poor minister, who preached the gospel to you."

2. Some means to promote it. (1) *Do nothing through strife and vain glory, v.* 3. Christ came to slay all enmities; therefore let there not be among Christians a spirit of opposition. Christ came to humble us, and therefore let there not be among us a spirit of pride. (2) We must *esteem others in lowliness of mind better than ourselves,* be severe upon our own faults and charitable in our judgment of others. We must esteem the good which is in others above that which is in ourselves; for we best know our own unworthiness and imperfections. (3) We must interest ourselves in the concerns of others, in Christian love and sympathy: *Look not every man on his own things, but every man also on the things of others, v.* 4. A selfish spirit is destructive of Christian love. We must love our neighbour as ourselves, and make his case our own.

II. A gospel pattern proposed is the example of our Lord Jesus Christ: *Let this mind be in you which was also in Christ Jesus, v.* 5. Christians must be of Christ's mind. We must bear a resemblance to his

life, if we would have the benefit of his death. He was eminently humble, and this is what we are peculiarly to learn of him. If we were lowly-minded, we should be like-minded; and, if we were like Christ, we should be lowly-minded. Walk in the same spirit with the Lord Jesus, who humbled himself to sufferings and death for us.

1. Here are the two natures of Christ. His divine nature: *Who being in the form of God (v. 6),* partaking of the divine nature, as the eternal Son of God. *He thought it no robbery to be equal with God;* did not think himself guilty of any invasion of what did not belong to him. It is the highest degree of robbery for any mere man or mere creature to pretend to be equal with God. His human nature: He was *made in the likeness of men,* and *found in fashion as a man.* He was really and truly man. And he voluntarily assumed human nature; it was his own act. We cannot say that our participation of the human nature is so. Herein he *emptied himself,* to clothe himself with the rags of human nature. Here are,

2. His two estates, of humiliation and exaltation. (1) His humiliation. The *form of a servant.* He was not only God's servant, but he came to minister to men, and was among them as one who serveth. One would think that the Lord Jesus, if he would be a man, should have been a prince. But quite the contrary: *He took upon him the form of a servant.* He was brought up meanly, probably working with his supposed father at his trade. His whole life was a life of humiliation. But the lowest step of his humiliation was his dying the death of the cross. *He became obedient to death, even the death of the cross.* He not only suffered, but was voluntarily obedient. There is an emphasis laid upon the manner of his dying, which had in it all the circumstances possible which are humbling: *Even the death of the cross,* a cursed, shameful death,—full of pain,—and the death of a malefactor and a slave, not of a freeman, exposed as a public spectacle. (2) His exaltation: *Wherefore God also hath highly exalted him.* Because he humbled himself, God exalted him; and he *highly exalted him.* He exalted his whole person, the human nature as well as the divine. His exaltation here is made to consist in honour and power. *He had a name above every name. Every knee must bow to him.* The whole creation must be in subjection to him: *things in heaven, and things in earth, and things under the earth,* the inhabitants of heaven and earth, the living and the dead. *At the name of Jesus* all should pay a solemn homage. *Every tongue should confess that Jesus Christ is Lord.* The kingdom of Christ reaches to heaven and earth, and to all the creatures in each, and to the dead as well as the living.—*To the glory of God the Father.* Whatever respect is paid to Christ redounds to the honour of the Father.

Verses 12, 13

I. He exhorts them to diligence and seriousness in the Christian course: *Work out your own salvation.* It concerns us above all things to secure the welfare of our souls: whatever becomes of other things, let us take care of our best interests. It is our own salvation. It is not for us to judge other people; we have enough to do to look to ourselves. We are required to *work out our salvation.* The word signifies *working thoroughly* and taking *true pains.* We must not only work at our salvation, by doing something now and then about it; but we must work out our salvation, by doing all that is to be done, and persevering therein to the end. We cannot attain salvation without the utmost care and diligence. *With fear and trembling,* that is, with great care and circumspection. Fear is a great guard and preservative from evil.

II. He urges this from the consideration of their readiness always to obey the gospel: "*As you have always obeyed, not as in my presence only, but now much more in my absence*," *v.* 12. They were not merely awed by the apostle's presence, but did it even *much more in his absence.* "*And because it is God who worketh in you*, do you work out your salvation. Work, for he worketh." God is ready to concur with his grace, and assist our faithful endeavours. The operations of God's grace in us are so far from excusing, that they are intended to quicken our endeavours. "And work out our salvation *with fear and trembling*, for *he worketh in you*. Work with *fear*, for he works of his *good pleasure*."—*To will and to do.* It is the grace of God which inclines the will to that which is good: and then enables us to perform it. *Of his good pleasure.* As we cannot act without God's grace, so we cannot pretend to deserve it.

Verses 14–18

The apostle exhorts them to adorn their Christian profession by a suitable temper and behaviour. 1. By a cheerful obedience to the commands of God (*v.* 14): "*Do all things without murmurings.* Mind your work, and do not quarrel with it." God's commands were given to be obeyed, not to be disputed. 2. By peaceableness and love one to another. "Do all things *without disputing.* The light of truth and the life of religion are often lost in the heats and mists of disputation." 3. By a blameless conversation towards all men (*v.* 15): "*That you may be blameless and harmless, the sons of God, without rebuke.*" We should endeavour not only not to do hurt, but not to come under the just suspicion of it. The *sons of God.* The children of God should differ from the sons of men. *Without rebuke.* We should endeavour, not only to get to heaven, but to get thither without a blot. *In the midst of a crooked and perverse generation.* Where there is no true religion, little is to be expected but crookedness and perverseness; and the more crooked and perverse others are among whom we live, the more careful we should be to keep ourselves blameless and harmless. *Among whom you shine as lights in the world.* Good Christians are lights in the world. When God raises up a good man in any place, he sets up a light in that place. They must shine as well as be sincere.— *Holding forth the word of life, v.* 16. It is our duty not only to hold fast, but to hold forth the word of life; to hold it forth for the benefit of others, to hold it forth as the candlestick holds forth the candle. "*That I may rejoice in the day of Christ;* not only rejoice in your steadfastness, but in your usefulness." He would have them think that *he had not run in vain, nor laboured in vain.* Running denotes vehemence and vigour; labour denotes constancy and close application. It is a great joy to ministers when they perceive that they have not *run in vain, nor laboured in vain*; and it will be their rejoicing in the day of Christ, when their converts will be their crown. The apostle not only ran and laboured for them with satisfaction, he was ready to suffer for their good (*v.* 17): *Yea, and if I be offered upon the sacrifice and service of your faith, I joy and rejoice with you all.* He could willingly be a sacrifice at their altars, to serve the faith of God's elect. Could Paul think it worth while to shed his blood for the service of the church, and shall we think it much to take a little pains? He could rejoice to seal his doctrine with his blood (*v.* 18): *For the same cause also do you joy and rejoice with me.* It is the will of God that good Christians should be much in rejoicing; and those who are happy in good ministers have a great deal of reason to joy and rejoice with them.

I. He speaks of Timothy, whom he intended to send to the Philippians. *For I have no man likeminded, who will naturally care for your state.* Timothy was a non-such. None comparable to Timothy, a man of an excellent spirit and tender heart. *Who will naturally care for your state.* It is best with us when our duty becomes in a manner natural to us. *Naturally*, that is, sincerely, and not in pretence only. It is the duty of ministers to care for the state of their people and be concerned for their welfare. It is a rare thing to find one who does it naturally. *All seek their own, not the things which are Jesus Christ's, v.* 21. Did Paul say this in haste, as David said, *All men are liars?* He means the generality; *all*, either the most, or all in comparison of Timothy. Many prefer their own credit, ease, and safety, before truth, holiness, and duty, but Timothy was none of these.— *You know the proof of him, v.* 22. Timothy was a man who had been tried, and was faithful in all that befell him. All the churches with whom he had acquaintance knew the proof of him. He was a man as good as he seemed to be. *As a son with a father, he hath served with me in the gospel.* He was Paul's assistant in many places. Their ministrations together were with great respect on the one side and great tenderness and kindness on the other—an admirable example to elder and younger ministers united in the same service. *Him therefore I hope to send presently, as soon as I shall see how it will go with me, v.* 23. He was now a prisoner, and did not know what would be the issue. He hoped to come himself (*v.* 24): *But I trust in the Lord that I also myself shall come shortly.* Paul desired his liberty, not that he might take his pleasure, but that he might do good.— *I trust in the Lord.* He expresses his hope of seeing them, with a humble submission to the divine will.

II. Concerning Epaphroditus, whom he calls *his brother, and companion in labour, and fellow-soldier, who ministered to my wants.* He had an earnest desire to come to them, and Paul was willing he should. 1. Epaphroditus had been sick: *They had heard that he had been sick, v.* 26. And *indeed he was sick, nigh unto death, v.* 27. 2. The Philippians were exceedingly sorry to hear of his sickness. He was one for whom they had a particular respect and affection, and thought fit to choose out to send to the apostle. 3. It pleased God to recover and spare him: *But God had mercy on him, v.* 27. The apostle owns it is a great mercy to himself, as well as to Epaphroditus and others. He was sensibly touched with the thoughts of so great a loss: *Lest I should have sorrow upon sorrow.* "Lest, besides the sorrow of my own imprisonment, I should have the sorrow of his death." 4. Epaphroditus was willing to pay a visit to the Philippians, that he might be comforted with those who had sorrowed for him when he was sick: "*That when you see him again you may rejoice*" (*v.* 28). He gave himself the pleasure of comforting them by the sight of so dear a friend. "*Receive him therefore in the Lord with all gladness, and hold such in reputation:* account such men valuable, who are zealous and faithful, and let them be highly loved and regarded." It seems he had caught his illness in the work of God: *It was for the work of Christ that he was nigh to death, and to supply their lack of service to him.* The apostle reckons they ought to love him the more upon that account. What is given us in answer to prayer should be received with great thankfulness and joy.

Chapter 3

Verses 1–3

It seems the church of the Philippians, though a faithful and flourishing church, was disturbed by the judaizing teachers.

I. He exhorts them to *rejoice in the Lord* (v. 1). The more we take of the comfort of our religion the more closely we shall cleave to it: the more we rejoice in Christ the more willing we shall be to suffer for him, and the less danger of being drawn away from him.

II. He cautions them to take heed of those false teachers: *To write the same thing to you to me indeed is not grievous, but for you it is safe.* Ministers must not think anything grievous to themselves which they have reason to believe is safe and edifying to the people. It is good for us often to hear the same truths. It is a wanton curiosity to desire always to hear some new thing. *Beware of dogs, v.* 2. *Dogs,* for their malice against the faithful professors of the gospel of Christ, barking at them and biting them. They cried up good works in opposition to the faith of Christ; but Paul calls them evil workers: they boasted themselves to be of the circumcision; but he calls them the concision.

III. He describes true Christians. *We are the circumcision, who worship God in the spirit, and rejoice in Christ Jesus, and have no confidence in the flesh.* Here are three characters: 1. They worshipped in the spirit, in opposition to the carnal ordinances of the Old Testament. Christianity teaches us to be inward with God in all the duties of religious worship. The work of religion is to no purpose any further than the heart is employed in it. 2. They *rejoice in Christ Jesus.* Now that the substance has come the shadows are done away, and we are to rejoice in Christ Jesus only. 3. They have no *confidence in the flesh,* in those carnal ordinances and outward performances. Our confidence, as well as our joy, is proper to him.

Verses 4–8

The apostle here proposes himself for an example of trusting in Christ only.

I. He shows what he had to boast of as a Jew and a Pharisee. *If any other man thinketh that he hath whereof to trust in the flesh, I more, v.* 4. He had as much to boast of as any Jew of them all. 1. His birth-right privileges. He was not a proselyte, but a native Israelite: *of the stock of Israel.* And he was *of the tribe of Benjamin. A Hebrew of the Hebrews,* an Israelite on both sides, and from one generation to another; none of his ancestors had matched with Gentiles. 2. He could boast of his relations to the covenant, for he was *circumcised the eighth day.* 3. For learning, he was a Pharisee, brought up at the feet of Gamaliel. He was a *Pharisee, the son of a Pharisee* (Acts xxiii. 6). 4. He had a blameless conversation: *Touching the righteousness which is of the law, blameless.* As to the mere letter of the law and outward observance of it, he could acquit himself from the breach of it and could not be accused by any. 5. He had been an active man for his religion. *Concerning zeal, persecuting the church.* He showed that he was in good earnest, though he had a zeal without knowledge. All this was stock sufficient to set up with for his justification.

II. How little account he made of these: *But what things were gain to me those have I counted loss for Christ* (v. 7). "I should have reckoned myself an unspeakable loser if, to adhere to them, I had lost Jesus Christ." The apostle did not persuade them to quit anything but what he had himself quitted.— *Yea doubtless, and I count all things but loss for the excellency of the knowledge of Christ Jesus my Lord, v.* 8. 1. He tells us what it was that he reached after: it was the knowledge of Christ Jesus his Lord, a

believing experimental acquaintance with Christ as Lord; not a speculative, but a practical knowledge of him. And it is the excellency of knowledge. There is an abundant and transcendent excellency in the doctrine of Christ, above all the knowledge of nature, and improvements of human wisdom. 2. He shows how he had quitted his privileges as a Jew and a Pharisee: *Yea doubtless;* his expression rises with a holy triumph and elevation. *But indeed even also do I count all things but loss.* He had spoken before of *those things,* his Jewish privileges: here he speaks of *all things.* There he had said that he did count them but loss; but it might be asked, "Did he continue still in the same mind?" Now he speaks in the present tense: *Yea doubtless, I do count them but loss.* He tells us that he had himself practised according to this estimate of the case: *For whom I have suffered the loss of all things.* When he embarked in the bottom of the Christian religion, he ventured all in it, and suffered the loss of all for the privileges of a Christian. He not only counted them loss, but dung—*offals* thrown to dogs; they are not only less valuable than Christ, but in the highest degree contemptible, when they come in competition with him.

Verses 9–14

What he laid hold on: Christ and heaven.

I. The apostle had his heart upon Christ. 1. He desired to win Christ. *That I may win him;* as the runner wins the prize, as the sailor makes the port he is bound for. 2. That he *might be found in him* (v. 9). We are undone without a righteousness wherein to appear before God. There is a righteousness provided for us in Jesus Christ. *"Not having my own righteousness, which is of the law;* not thinking that my outward observances and good deeds are able to atone for my bad ones. The righteousness is that *which is through the faith of Christ,* not a legal, but evangelical righteousness: *The righteousness which is of God by faith,* ordained and appointed of God." Faith is the ordained means of saving benefit in all the purchase of his blood. 3. That he might know Christ (v. 10): *That I may know him, and the power of his resurrection, and the fellowship of his sufferings.* Knowing him here is believing in him: it is an experimental knowledge. The apostle was as ambitious of being sanctified as he was of being justified. 4. That he might be conformable unto him. We are then made conformable to his death when we die to sin, as Christ died for sin, when we are crucified with Christ, and the *world is crucified to us.*

II. The apostle had his heart upon heaven as his happiness: *If by any means I might attain to the resurrection of the dead, v.* 11.

1. The happiness of heaven is here called the resurrection of the dead. This the apostle had his eye upon; this he would attain. There will be a resurrection of the unjust, and our care must be to escape that: but the joyful and glorious resurrection of saints is called *the resurrection by eminence.* To the saints it will be indeed a resurrection, while the resurrection of the wicked is a rising from the grave, but a return to a second death.

2. This joyful resurrection the apostle pressed towards. He speaks as if they were in danger of missing it, and coming short of it. A holy fear of coming short is an excellent means of perseverance. Paul himself did not hope to attain it through his own merit, but through the merit of Jesus Christ.

(1) He looks upon himself to be in a state of imperfection and trial: *Not as though I had already attained, or were already perfect, v.* 12. The best men in the world will readily own their imperfection in the present state. If Paul had not attained to perfection, much less have we. *Brethren, I count*

not myself to have apprehended (v. 13). Those who think they have grace enough give proof that they have little enough, or rather that they have none at all; because, wherever there is true grace, there is a desire of more grace.

(2) What the apostle's actings were under this conviction. "*I follow after* (v. 12), *I pursue* with vigour. *If that I may apprehend that for which also I am apprehended of Christ Jesus.*" It is not our laying hold of Christ first, but his laying hold of us, which is our happiness and salvation. Not our keeping hold of Christ, but his keeping hold of us, is our safety. *To apprehend that for which we are apprehended of Christ.* To apprehend that for which he apprehended us is to attain the perfection of our bliss. He adds further (v. 13): *This one thing I do, forgetting those things which are behind, and reaching forth to those things which are before.* Paul forgot the things which were behind, he was still for having more and more. So he *reached forth.*

(3) The apostle's aim. *I press towards the mark, for the prize of the high calling of God in Christ Jesus,* v. 14. The fitter we grow for heaven the faster we must press towards it. Heaven is the *prize of the high calling;* what we aim at in all we do, and what will reward all our pains. It is of God, from whom we are to expect it. But it is in Christ Jesus; through his hand it must come to us. There is no getting to heaven as our home but by Christ as our way.

Verses 15, 16

This was the thing wherein all good Christians were agreed, to make Christ all in all, and set their hearts upon another world. This is that whereto we have all attained. Therefore let us walk by the same rule, and mind the same thing. Having made Christ our all, *to us to live must be Christ.* Christians who differ in smaller matters should yet bear with one another, because they are agreed in the main matter: "*If in anything you be otherwise minded,* you must not judge one another, while you all meet now in Christ as your centre, and hope to meet shortly in heaven as your home. *God shall reveal even this unto you.* Whatever it is wherein you differ, you must wait till God give you a better understanding. *As far as you have attained, you* must go together in the ways of God, and wait for further light in the minor things wherein you differ."

Verses 17–21

I. He warns them against following the examples of evil teachers (v. 18, 19): *Many walk, of whom I have told you often, and now tell you weeping, that they are the enemies of the cross of Christ.*

1. There are many called by Christ's name who are enemies to Christ's cross. Their walk is a surer evidence what they are than their profession. *I have told you often.* We so little heed the warnings given us that we have need to have them repeated. *I now tell you weeping.* What we say often we may say again, if we say it affectionately.

2. The characters of those who were the enemies of the cross of Christ. (1) *Whose God is their belly.* They minded nothing but their sensual appetites. The same observance which good people give to God epicures give to their appetites. (2) They glory in their shame. "They value themselves for what is their blemish and reproach." (3) They mind earthly things. Those who mind earthly things act directly contrary to the cross of Christ. They set their hearts and affections on earthly things. How absurd it would be for Christians to follow the example of such! To deter us all from so doing, he reads their doom. (4) *Whose end is destruction.* Their way seems pleasant, but death and hell are at the end of it. If we choose their way, we have reason to fear their end.

II. He proposes himself and his brethren for an example: *Brethren, be followers together of me, and mark those who walk as you have us for an example,* v. 17. He explains himself (v. 20) by their regard to Christ and heaven: *For our conversation is in heaven.* Good Christians, even while they are here on earth, have their conversation in heaven. This world is not our home, but that is. The life of a Christian is in heaven, where his home is, and where he hopes to be shortly. It is good having fellowship with those who have fellowship with Christ, and conversation with those whose conversation is in heaven.

1. We look for the Saviour from heaven (v. 20): *Whence also we look for the Saviour, the Lord Jesus Christ.* We expect his second coming thence.

2. At the second coming of Christ we expect to be happy and glorified there. *Who shall change our vile bodies, that they may be fashioned like unto his glorious body,* v. 21. There is a glory reserved for the saints, which they will be instated in at the resurrection. The body is now at the best a *vile body, the body of our humiliation.* But it will be made a glorious body. *According to the working whereby he is able even to subdue all things unto himself.* It is matter of comfort to us that he can subdue all things to himself. And the resurrection will be wrought by this power. Let this confirm our faith of the resurrection, that we not only have the scriptures, which assure us it shall be, but we *know the power of God,* which can effect it. As Christ's resurrection was a glorious instance of the divine power, so will our resurrection be. And then all the enemies of the Redeemer's kingdom will be completely conquered.

CHAPTER 4

Exhortations to several Christian duties, ver. 1–9. The apostle's grateful acknowledgments of the Philippians' kindness to him, ver. 10–19. He concludes the epistle with praise, salutations, and blessing, ver. 20–23.

Verses 1–9

I. Steadfastness in our Christian profession, v. 1. Seeing our *conversation is in heaven,* and we look for the Saviour to come thence and fetch us thither, *therefore let us stand fast.* The believing prospect of eternal life should engage us to be constant, in our Christian course. *My brethren, dearly beloved and longed for, my joy and crown;* and again, *My dearly beloved.* Thus he expresses the pleasure he took in them to convey his exhortations to them with so much the greater advantage. Being brethren he loved them, and loved them dearly: *Dearly beloved;* and again, *My dearly beloved.* Brotherly love must always go along with the brotherly relation. He loved them and longed for them. He loved them and rejoiced in them. They were his joy. He loved them and gloried in them. They were his crown as well as his joy. *So stand fast in the Lord.* Being in Christ, they must stand fast in him, close and constant unto the end. Or, To *stand fast in the Lord* is to stand fast in his strength and by his grace; not trusting in ourselves.

II. He exhorts them to unanimity and mutual assistance (v. 2, 3): *I beseech Euodias and Syntyche that they be of the same mind in the Lord.* This is directed to some particular persons. Sometimes there is need of applying the general precepts of the gospel to particular persons and cases. Euodias and Syntyche, it seems, were at variance, either one with the other or with the church. "Desire them from me to be of the same mind in the Lord, to keep the peace and live in love, to be of the same mind with the rest of the church." Then he exhorts to mutual assistance (v. 3), and this exhortation he directs to particular persons: *I entreat thee also, true yoke-fellow.* Who this person was whom he calls true yoke-fellow is uncertain. He exhorts his yoke-fellow to *help the women who laboured with him.* Whoever was the yoke-fellow with the apostle must be a yoke-fellow too with his friends. It seems, there were women who laboured with Paul in the gospel. Women may be helpful to ministers in the work of the gospel. *Do thou help them.* Those who help others should be helped themselves when there is occasion.—*With Clement also, and other my fellow-labourers.* Paul had a kindness for all his fellow-labourers, *Whose names are in the book of life.* There is a book of life; there are names in that book and not characters and conditions only. We cannot search into that book, or know whose names are written there; but we may conclude that those who labour in the gospel have their names in the book of life.

III. *Rejoice in the Lord always, and again I say, Rejoice, v.* 4. All our joy must terminate in God; and our thoughts of God must be delightful thoughts. It is our duty and privilege to rejoice in God, and to rejoice in him always; at all times, in all conditions. There is enough in God to furnish us with matter of joy in the worst circumstance on earth. *Rejoice in the Lord always; and again I say, Rejoice.* If good men have not a continual feast, it is their own fault.

IV. We are here exhorted to gentleness, and good temper towards our brethren: "*Let your moderation be known to all men, v.* 5. In things indifferent do not run into extremes; judge charitably concerning one another." Some understand it of the patient bearing of afflictions, or the sober enjoyment of worldly good. *The Lord is at hand.* "He will take vengeance on your enemies, and reward your patience."

V. A caution against disquieting perplexing care (*v.* 6): *Be careful for nothing.* Avoid anxious care and distracting thought in the wants and difficulties of life. It is the duty and interest of Christians to live without care. There is a care of diligence which is our duty, but there is a care of distrust which is our sin and folly.

VI. He recommends to us constant prayer: *In everything by prayer and supplication, with thanksgiving, let your requests be made known to God.* We must pray upon every particular emergency: *In everything by prayer.* When anything burdens our spirits, we must ease our minds by prayer; when our affairs are perplexed or distressed, we must seek direction and support. We must join thanksgiving with our prayers and supplications. We must not only seek supplies of good, but own receipts of mercy. Prayer is the offering up of our desires to God: *Let your requests be made known to God.* Not that God needs to be told either our wants or desires; but he will know them from us. The effect of this will be the *peace of God keeping our hearts, v.* 7. The *peace of God which passeth all understanding* is a greater good than can be sufficiently valued or duly expressed. This peace will *keep our hearts and minds through Christ Jesus*; it will keep us from sinning under our troubles, and from sinking under them.

VII. We are exhorted to get and keep a good name: *Whatsoever things are true and honest (v.* 8), a regard to truth and to becomingness in our behaviour. Whatsoever things are *just and pure,* without the impurity or mixture of sin. Whatsoever things are *lovely and of good report,* that will render us beloved, and make us well spoken of. *If there is any virtue, if there is any praise.* The apostle would have the Christians learn anything which was good of their heathen neighbours: "*If there be any virtue, think of these things*—imitate them in what is truly excellent among them." We should not be ashamed to learn any good thing of bad men. Virtue has its praise, and will have. *Those things which you have learned, and received, and heard and seen in me, do.* Paul's

doctrine and life were of a piece. He could propose himself as well as his doctrine to their imitation. It gives a great force to what we say to others when we can appeal to what they have seen in us.

Verses 10–19

Grateful acknowledgment of the kindness of the Philippians.

I. He takes occasion to acknowledge their former kindnesses to him, *v.* 15, 16. Paul had a grateful spirit. Wherever this epistle shall be read there shall this which they did to Paul be told for a memorial of them. Surely never was present so well repaid. *In the beginning of the gospel no church communicated with me as to giving and receiving but ye only, v.* 15, not only while he was with them, but when *he departed from Macedonia*; and this when no other church did so. They were the only church who were thus just and generous. *Even in Thessalonica you sent once and again to my necessity, v.* 16. Just such things as he had need of; he did not desire superfluities nor dainties. *You sent once and again.* Many people make it an excuse for their charity that they have given once; why should the charge come upon them again? But the Philippians sent once and again.

II. He excuses their neglect of late. *Now at the last their care of him flourished again (v.* 10), like a tree in the spring, which seemed all the winter to be quite dead. He makes an excuse for them: *Wherein you were also careful, but you lacked opportunity.* They would have done it if a fair opportunity had offered.

III. He commends their present liberality: *Notwithstanding, you have well done that you did communicate with my affliction, v.* 14. Here see Christian sympathy; not only to be concerned for our friends in their troubles, but to do what we can to help them. He rejoiced greatly in it (*v.* 10), because it was an evidence of their affection to him and the success of his ministry among them.

IV. *Not that I speak in respect of want (v.* 11); not in respect of any want he felt, nor of any want he feared. As to the former, he was content with the little he had, and that satisfied him; as to the latter, he depended upon the providence of God to provide for him from day to day, and that satisfied him. *For I have learned, in whatsoever state I am, therewith to be content.* That was the lesson he had as much need to learn as most men, considering the hardships and sufferings with which he was exercised.—*I know both how to be abased and I know how to abound, v.* 12. This is a special act of grace, to accommodate ourselves to every condition of life. To accommodate ourselves to an afflicted condition—to know how to be abased. To a prosperous condition—to know how to abound, how to be full, so as not to be proud, or secure. And this is as hard a lesson as the other; for the temptations of fulness and prosperity are not less than those of affliction and want. *I can do all things through Christ who strengthens me, v.* 13. We need his strength to teach us to be content in every condition. The apostle had seemed to boast of himself, and of his own strength: *I know how to be abased (v.* 12); but here he transfers all the praise to Christ. It is by his constant and renewed strength I am enabled to act in everything. "*Not because I desired a gift (v.* 17). I welcome your kindness because it adds to your account. *I desire fruit that may abound to your account. I have all, and abound, v.* 18. What can a man desire more than enough?" *I am full, having received from Epaphroditus the things which were sent by you.* A covetous worldling, if he has ever so much, would still have more; but a heavenly Christian, though he has little, has enough.

V. The apostle assures them that God did accept, and would recompense, their kindness to him. He did accept it: *It is an odour of a sweet smell, a sacrifice acceptable, well-pleasing to God.* A sacrifice of acknowledgment, and *well-pleasing to God.* It was more acceptable to God as it was the fruit of their grace than it was to Paul as it was the supply of his want. He would recompense it: *But my God shall supply all your wants according to his riches in glory by Christ Jesus, v.* 19. He does as it were draw a bill upon the exchequer in heaven, and leaves it to God. "You have supplied my needs, according to your poverty; and he shall supply yours, according to his riches." But still it is by Christ Jesus. Not of debt, but of grace.

Verses 20–23

1. Praises to God: *Now unto God and our Father be glory for ever and ever, Amen, v.* 20. God is to be considered by us as our Father. It is a title peculiar to the gospel dispensation. We should look upon God, under all our weaknesses and fears, not as a tyrant, but as a Father, who is disposed to pity us and help us. We must thankfully own the receipt of all from him, and give the praise of all to him. And our praise must be constant and perpetual; it must be *glory for ever and ever.*

2. Salutations to his friends at Philippi: *Salute every saint in Christ Jesus (v.* 21). Paul had a kind affection to all good Christians.

3. Salutations from those who were at Rome: "*The brethren who are with me salute you;* all the saints here. *Chiefly those who are of Cæsar's household;* the Christian converts who belonged to the emperor's court." There were saints in Cæsar's household. The gospel early obtained among some of the rich and great.

4. The apostolical benediction, as usual: "*The grace of our Lord Jesus Christ be with you all, Amen.*"

AN EXPOSITION, WITH PRACTICAL OBSERVATIONS, OF

THE EPISTLE OF ST. PAUL TO

THE COLOSSIANS

Colosse was a considerable city of Phrygia, and probably not far from Laodicea and Hierapolis; we find these mentioned together, *ch.* iv. 13. It is now buried in ruins, and the memory of it chiefly preserved in this epistle. The design of the epistle is to warn them of the danger of the Jewish zealots. He professes a great satisfaction in their steadfastness and constancy. It was written while he was now a prisoner at Rome. He was not idle in his confinement, and the word of God was not bound.

The epistle, like that to the Romans, was written to those he had never seen. The church planted at Colosse was not by Paul's ministry, but by the ministry of Epaphras, whom he delegated to preach the gospel among the Gentiles; and yet, I. There was a flourishing church at Colosse, and one which was eminent and famous among the churches. God is sometimes pleased to make use of the ministry of those who are of less note, and lower gifts, for doing great service to his church. God uses what hands he pleases, and is not tied to those of note. II. Though Paul had not the planting of this church, yet he did not therefore neglect it. The Colossians were as dear to him as the Philippians, or any others who were converted by his ministry.

CHAPTER 1

I. The inscription, ver. 1, 2. II. His thanksgiving to God for their faith, love, and hope, ver. 3–8. III. His prayer for their knowledge, fruitfulness, and strength, ver. 9–11. IV. The operation of the Spirit, the person of the Redeemer, the work of redemption, and the preaching of it in the gospel, ver. 12–29.

Verses 1, 2

I. He calls himself an *apostle of Jesus Christ by the will of God.* He thought himself engaged to do his utmost, as an apostle, because he was made so by the will of God. He joins Timothy in commission with himself, and, though he elsewhere calls him his son, yet here he calls him his brother. He calls the Christians at Colosse *saints, and faithful brethren in Christ.* All good Christians are brethren one to another. Towards God they must be saints. And in both these, as saints to God and as brethren to one another, they must be faithful. Faithfulness runs through every character and relation of the Christian life, and is the crown and glory of them all.

II. *Grace be unto you, and peace, from God our Father, and the Lord Jesus Christ.* He wishes them *grace and peace,* the free favour of God and all the blessed fruits of it.

Verses 3–8

I. He gave thanks to God for them. In his prayers for them he gave thanks for them. Thanksgiving ought to be a part of every prayer. 1. Whom he gives thanks to: *To God, even the Father of our Lord Jesus Christ.* In our thanksgiving we must have an eye to God as God, and as the Father of our Lord Jesus Christ, in and through whom all good comes to us. 2. What he gives thanks to God for—for the graces of God in them. *Since we heard of your faith in Christ Jesus, and of the love you have to all the saints; for the hope which is laid up for you in heaven,* v. 4, 5. Faith, hope, and love, are the three principal graces in the Christian life. (1) He gives thanks for their faith in Christ Jesus, that they were brought to believe in him. (2) For their love. Besides the general love which is due to all men, there is a particular love owing to the saints. We must love all the saints, notwithstanding smaller points of difference, and many real weaknesses. (3) For their hope: *The hope which is laid up for you in heaven,* v. 5. What is laid out upon believers in this world is much; but what is laid up for them in heaven is much more. The more we fix our hopes on the recompence of reward in the other world, the more free shall we be of our earthly treasure upon all occasions of doing good.

II. He blesses God for the means of grace which they enjoyed: *Wherein you heard before in the word of the truth of the gospel.* The gospel is the word of truth, and what we may safely venture our immortal souls upon. He calls it *the grace of God in truth,* v. 6. It is a great mercy to hear this word of truth. *"Which has come unto you, as it hath to all the world, and bringeth forth fruit, as it doth also in you,"* v. 6. All who hear the word of the gospel ought to bring forth the fruit of the gospel. Wherever the gospel comes, it will bring forth fruit to the honour and glory of God. We mistake, if we think to monopolise the comforts and benefits of the gospel to ourselves.

III. The minister by whom they believed (*v.* 7, 8): *As you also learned of Epaphras, our dear fellow-servant, who is for you a faithful minister of Christ.* He calls him his fellow-servant. They were fellow-labourers in the work of the Lord. He calls him his dear fellow-servant: it is an endearing consideration that they are engaged in the same service. He represents him as one who was a faithful minister of Christ to them. He does not say who is your minister; but *who is the minister of Christ for you.* It is by his authority and appointment. He represents him as one who gave them a good word: *Who also declared unto us your love in the Spirit,* v. 8. He recommends him to their affection, from the good report he made of their sincere love, which was wrought in them by the Spirit. Faithful ministers are glad to be able to speak well of their people.

Verses 9–11

He heard that they were good, and he prayed that they might be better. *We do not cease to pray for you.* It may be he could hear of them but seldom, but he constantly prayed for them.

I. *Filled with the knowledge of his will, in all wisdom and spiritual understanding.* A mere empty notion of the greatest truths is insignificant. Our knowledge of the will of God must be always practical: we must know it, in order to do it. Our knowledge is then a blessing indeed when it is in wisdom, when we know how to apply our general knowledge to our particular occasions. Christians should endeavour to be filled with knowledge; not only to know the will of God, but to know more of it, and to *increase in the knowledge of God* (as it is *v.* 10).

II. Good knowledge without a good life will not

profit. *That you may walk worthy of the Lord unto all pleasing* (v. 10). The agreeableness of our conversation to our religion is pleasing to God as well as to good men. *Being fruitful in every good work.* Good words will not do without good works. We must abound in good works, and in every good work. There must be a regular uniform regard to all the will of God. And the more fruitful we are in good works the more we shall *increase in the knowledge of God.*

III. *Strengthened with all might, according to his glorious power* (v. 11). Where there is spiritual life there is still need of spiritual strength. To be strengthened is to be furnished by the grace of God for every good work, and fortified by that grace against every evil one. In the praying for spiritual strength we are not straitened in the promises, and therefore should not be straitened in our own hopes and desires. He prayed that they might be strengthened with might: that they might be mightily strengthened. It is with all might. With all that might which we have occasion for, to enable us to discharge our duty or preserve our innocence, that grace which is sufficient for us in all the trials of life. It is *according to his glorious power.* The grace of God in the hearts of believers is the power of God; and there is a glory in this power. The communications of strength are not according to our weakness, but according to his power. *That you may be strengthened unto all patience and long-suffering with joyfulness.* He prays not only that they may be *supported* under their troubles, but *strengthened* for them. Strengthened *according to his glorious power.* 1. To all patience. Then we are strengthened to all patience—when we not only bear our troubles patiently, but receive them as gifts from God, and are thankful for them. 2. This is even unto long-suffering, not only to bear trouble awhile, but to bear it as long as God pleases to continue it. 3. It is with joyfulness, to rejoice in tribulation, to rejoice that we are counted worthy to suffer for his name, to have joy as well as patience in the troubles of life. This we could never do by any strength of our own, but as we are strengthened by the grace of God.

Verses 12–29

Here is a summary of the doctrine of the gospel concerning the great work of our redemption by Christ. It comes in here as the matter of a thanksgiving: *Giving thanks unto the Father, v.* 12.

I. The operations of the Spirit of grace. We must give thanks for them: *Giving thanks to the Father, &c., v.* 12, 13. Those in whom the work of grace is wrought must give thanks unto the Father. 1. "He hath *delivered us from the power of darkness, v.* 13. He hath saved us from the dominion of sin, which is darkness." 2. "He hath *translated us into the kingdom of his dear Son,* made us members of the church of Christ, which is a state of light and purity." The conversion of a sinner is the translation of a soul into the kingdom of Christ out of the kingdom of the devil. It is the kingdom of his dear Son. 3. "He hath *made us meet to partake of the inheritance of the saints in light, v.* 12." God gives *grace and glory.* (1) What that glory is. It is the *inheritance of the saints in light.* It is an inheritance, and belongs to them as children. And it is an inheritance of the saints. Those who are not saints on earth will never be saints in heaven. And it is an inheritance in light; by communion with God, who is light. (2) What this grace is. It is a meetness for the inheritance: "*He hath made us meet to be partakers.*" All who are designed for heaven hereafter are prepared for heaven now. Those who are sanctified and renewed go out of the world with their heaven about them. Those who have the inheritance of sons have the education of sons. This

meetness for heaven is the earnest of the Spirit in our heart, which is part of payment, and assures the full payment.

II. The Redeemer. Glorious things are here said of him; for blessed Paul was full of Christ. He speaks of him distinctly as God, and as Mediator. 1. As God he speaks of him, *v.* 15–17. (1) He is the *image of the invisible God.* He is so the image of God as the son is the image of his father, who has a natural likeness to him. (2) He is the *first-born of every creature.* Born or *begotten before all the creation,* which is the scripture-way of representing eternity. It signifies his dominion over all things, as the first-born in a family is heir and lord of all. (3) He is so far from being himself a creature that he is the Creator: *For by him were all things created, which are in heaven and earth, visible and invisible, v.* 16. He speaks here as if there were several orders of angels: *Whether thrones, or dominions, or principalities, or powers. All things are created by him and for him.* He is the end, as well as the cause of all things. (4) He *was before all things.* He had a being before the world was made, and therefore from all eternity. He not only had a being before he was born of the virgin, but he had a being before all time. (5) *By him all things consist.* The whole creation is kept together by the power of the Son of God, and made to consist in its proper frame.

2. What he is as Mediator, *v.* 18, 19. (1) He is the *head of the body the church:* not only a head of government and direction, but a head of vital influence, as the head in the natural body: for all grace and strength are derived from him. (2) He is the *beginning, the first-born from the dead,* the principle of our resurrection. The first and only one who rose by his own power, and has given us evidence of our resurrection from the dead. (3) He hath in *all things the pre-eminence,* preferred above angels and all the powers in heaven. Among men he should have the pre-eminence. (4) All fulness dwells in him, and it pleased the Father it should do so (v. 19), not only a fulness of abundance for himself, but abundance for us.

III. The work of redemption.

1. Wherein it consists. (1) In the remission of sin: *In whom we have redemption, even the forgiveness of sins, v.* 14. If we are redeemed, we must be redeemed from sin; and this is by forgiveness. (2) In reconciliation to God. God by him *reconciled all things to himself, v.* 20. He is the Mediator of reconciliation, who procures peace as well as pardon for sinners, and will bring all holy creatures into one blessed society at last: *things in earth, or things in heaven.* The Gentiles, who were alienated, and *enemies in their minds by wicked works, yet now hath he reconciled, v.* 21. This *enmity is slain,* and we are now reconciled. The greatest enemies to God may be reconciled, if it be not their own fault.

2. How the redemption is procured: *it is through his blood* (v. 14); he has *made peace through the blood of his cross* (v. 20), and it is *in the body of his flesh through death, v.* 22. There was such a value in the blood of Christ that, on account of Christ's shedding it, God was willing to deal with men upon new terms, to pardon and accept to favour all who comply with them.

IV. The preaching of this redemption.

1. To whom it was preached: *To every creature under heaven* (v. 23). The gospel excludes none who do not exclude themselves.

2. By whom it was preached: *Whereof I Paul am made a minister.* He looks upon it as the highest of his titles of honour to be a minister of the gospel of Jesus Christ.

(1) Whence Paul had his ministry: it was *according to the dispensation of God which was given to him*

(v. 25). He received it from God as a gift, and took it as a favour.

(2) For whose sake he had his ministry: *It is for you.* We are Christ's ministers for the good of his people, to *fulfil the word of God* (that is, fully to preach it).

(3) What kind of preacher Paul was.

[1] He was a suffering preacher: *Who now rejoice in my sufferings for you,* v. 24. He suffered for preaching the gospel to them. And, while he suffered in so good a cause, he could rejoice in his sufferings. *And fill up that which is behind of the afflictions of Christ in my flesh.* The suffering of Paul and other good ministers made them conformable to Christ. They are said to fill up what was behind of the sufferings of Christ, as the wax fills up the vacuities of the seal, when it receives the impression of it. Or it may be meant of his suffering for Christ. He *filled that which was behind.* He was still filling up more and more what was behind, or remained of them to his share.

[2] He was a close preacher. *Whom we preach, warning every man, and teaching every man in all wisdom,* v. 28. When we warn people of what they do amiss, we must teach them to do better: warning and teaching must go together. Men must be warned and taught in all wisdom. We must choose the fittest seasons, and accommodate ourselves to the different capacities of those we have to do with. That which he aimed at was to *present every men perfect in Christ Jesus.* Ministers ought to aim at the improvement and salvation of every particular person who hears them. He was a laborious preacher (v. 29): *Whereunto I also labour, striving according to his working, which worketh in me mightily.* As Paul laid out himself to do much good, so he had this favour, that the power of God wrought in him the more effectually.

3. The gospel which was preached. *Even the mystery which hath been hid from ages, and from generations, but is now made manifest to his saints,* v. 26, 27. The mystery of the gospel was long hidden. This mystery now is made manifest to the saints. And what is this mystery? It is the riches of God's glory among the Gentiles. This mystery, thus made known, *is Christ in you, the hope of glory.* Christ is the hope of glory. The ground of our hope is Christ in the world. The evidence of our hope is Christ in the heart.

4. The duty of those who are interested in this redemption: *If you continue in the faith, grounded and settled, and be not moved away from the hope of the gospel which you have heard,* v. 23. We can expect the happy end of our faith only when we continue in the faith, and are so far grounded and settled in it as not to be moved from it.

CHAPTER 2

I. The apostle expresses concern for the Colossians, ver. 1–3. II. He repeats it again, ver. 5. III. He cautions them against false teachers among the Jews (ver. 4, 6, 7), and against the Gentile philosophy, ver. 8–12. IV. He represents the privileges of Christians, ver. 13–15. And, V. Concludes with a caution against those who would introduce the worship of angels, ver. 16–23.

Verses 1–3

The apostle had never been at Colosse, and yet he had as tender a care of it as if it had been the only people of his charge (v. 1): *For I would that you knew what great conflict I have for you, and for those at Laodicea, and for as many as have not seen my face in the flesh.* Paul's care of the church was such as amounted to a conflict. He was in a sort of agony. We may keep up a communion by faith, hope, and holy love, even with those of whom we have no personal knowledge. Those we never saw in the flesh we may hope to meet in heaven.

I. What was it that the apostle desired for them? *That their hearts may be comforted, being knit together in love,* &c., v. 2. It was their spiritual welfare about which he was solicitous, that their *hearts may be comforted.* The prosperity of the soul is the best prosperity. A description of soul-prosperity.

1. When our knowledge grows to an understanding of the mystery of God, and of the Father, and of Christ. *To understand the mystery.* Not barely to speak of it by rote, but to enter into the meaning and design of it.

2. When our faith grows to a full assurance and bold acknowledgment of this mystery. To a full assurance, or a well-settled judgment. To a free acknowledgment, and we not only believe with the heart, but are ready to make confession with our mouth. This is called the *riches of the full assurance of understanding.* Great knowledge and strong faith make a soul rich.

3. *That their hearts might be comforted.* The soul prospers when it is filled with joy and peace.

4. *Being knit together in love.* The stronger our faith is, and the warmer our love, the greater will our comfort be. Having occasion to mention Christ (v. 2), he makes this remark to his honour (v. 3): *In whom are hidden all the treasures of wisdom and knowledge.* The treasures of wisdom are hidden not from us, but for us, in Christ. We must spend upon the stock which is laid up for us in him, and draw from the treasures which are hidden in him.

II. His concern for them is repeated (v. 5): *Though I am absent in the flesh, yet am I with you in the spirit, joying, and beholding your order, and the steadfastness of your faith in Christ.* We may be present in spirit with those from whom we are absent in body. Though he had never seen them he tells them he could easily think himself among them, and look with pleasure upon their good behaviour. The more steadfast our faith in Christ is, the better order there will be in our whole conversation.

Verses 4–12

The apostle cautions the Colossians against deceivers (v. 4): *And this I say lest any man beguile you with enticing words;* and v. 8, *Lest any man spoil you.* Satan spoils souls by beguiling them. He deceives them, and by this means slays them. He could not ruin us if he did not cheat us; and he could not cheat us but by our own folly. Satan's agents beguile them with enticing words. How many are ruined by the flattery of those who lie in wait to deceive! "That which they aim at is to spoil you."

I. A sovereign antidote against seducers (v. 6, 7): *As you have therefore received Christ Jesus the Lord, so walk you in him, rooted and built up,* &c. All Christians have, in profession at least, *received Jesus Christ the Lord,* consented to him, taken him for theirs in every relation and every capacity. The great concern of those who have received Christ is *to walk in him.* We must walk with him in our daily course and keep up our communion with him. The more closely we walk with Christ the more we are *rooted and established in the faith.* If we walk in him, we shall be rooted in him; and the more firmly we are rooted in him the more closely we shall walk in him: *Rooted and built up.—As you have been taught.* A good education has a good influence upon our establishment. We must be *established in the faith, as we have been taught, abounding therein.* And this with thanksgiving.

II. The fair warning given us of our danger: *Beware lest any man spoil you through philosophy and vain deceit, after the tradition of men, after the rudiments of the world, and not after Christ,* v. 8. There is a philosophy which is a noble exercise of our reasonable faculties. But there is a philosophy which is vain and deceitful. *After the tradition of men, after the rudiments of the world*. The Jews governed themselves by the traditions of their elders. The Gentiles mixed their maxims of philosophy with their Christian principles; and both alienated their minds from Christ. Those who pin their faith on other men's sleeves have turned away from following after Christ.

1. We have in Christ the substance of all the shadows of the ceremonial law. Had they then the Shechinah, or special presence of God? So have we now in Jesus Christ (v. 9): *For in him dwelleth all the fulness of the Godhead bodily*. It dwells in him bodily; not as the body is opposed to the spirit, but as the body is opposed to the shadow. The fulness of the Godhead dwells in Christ really, and not figuratively. Had they circumcision, which was the seal of the covenant? In Christ we are *circumcised with the circumcision made without hands* (v. 11). *It is made without hands;* not by the power of any creature, but by the power of the blessed Spirit of God. Again, The Jews thought themselves complete in the ceremonial law; but we are *complete in Christ*, v. 10. That was imperfect and defective. But all the defects of it are made up in the gospel of Christ. *Which is the head of all principality and power*. As the Old Testament priesthood had its perfection in Christ, so likewise had the kingdom of David. He is the Lord and head of all the powers in heaven and earth.

2. We have communion with Christ in his whole undertaking (v. 12): *Buried with him in baptism, wherein also you have risen with him*. We are both buried and rise with him, and both are signified by our baptism. He is speaking of the *circumcision made without hands*; and says it is *through the faith of the operation of God*. God in baptism engages to be to us a God, and we become engaged to be his people, and by his grace to die to sin and to live to righteousness.

Verses 13–15

The privileges we Christians have above the Jews.

I. Christ's death is our life: *And you, being dead in your sins and the uncircumcision of your flesh, hath he quickened together with him*, v. 13. A state of sin is a state of spiritual death. Those who are in sin are dead in sin. As the death of the body is the corruption of it, so sin is the corruption of the soul. As a man who is dead is unable to help himself by any power of his own, so an habitual sinner is morally impotent. This is our state. Now through Christ we, who were dead in sins, are quickened. *Quickened together with him*. Christ's death was the death of our sins; Christ's resurrection is the quickening of our souls.

II. Through him we have the remission of sin: *Having forgiven you all trespasses*. The pardon of the crime is the life of the criminal.

III. Whatever was in force against us is taken out of the way. He has obtained for us a legal discharge from the *hand-writing of ordinances, which was against us* (v. 14). *Cursed is everyone who continues not in everything*. This was a hand-writing which was *against us, and contrary to us*. When he was nailed to the cross, the curse was as it were nailed to the cross. It must be understood of the ceremonial law, the *hand-writing of ordinances*. The Lord Jesus *took it out of the way, nailed it to his cross;* disannulled the obligation of it. When the substance came, the shadows fled away.

IV. He has obtained a glorious victory for us over the powers of darkness: *And, having spoiled principalities and powers, he made a show of them openly, triumphing over them in it*, v. 15. As the curse of the law was against us, so the power of Satan was against us. Out of the hands of Satan the executioner he redeemed us by power and with a high hand. The devil and all the powers of hell were conquered and disarmed by the dying Redeemer. The Redeemer conquered by dying. See his crown of thorns turned into a crown of laurels. He *spoiled them* and *made a show of them openly*. Never had the devil's kingdom such a mortal blow given to it as was given by the Lord Jesus. *Triumphing over them in it*; in His Cross and by His death.

Verses 16–23

I. A caution to take heed of judaizing teachers. *Let no man therefore judge you in meat nor in drink*, &c., v. 16. "Let no man impose those things upon you, for God has not imposed them." These things *were shadows of things to come* (v. 17): they are now done away. *But the body is of Christ:* the body, of which they were shadows, has come. They had the shadows, we have the substance.

II. He cautions them to take heed of those who would introduce the worship of angels as the Gentile philosophers did: *Let no man beguile you of your reward, in a voluntary humility and worshipping of angels*, v. 18. Though it has a show of humility, it is a voluntary, not a commanded humility; and therefore it is not acceptable, yea, it is not warrantable. Besides, the notions upon which this practice was grounded were merely the inventions of men—the proud conceits of human reason: *Intruding into those things which he hath not seen, vainly puffed up by his fleshly mind*. Though there was a show of humility in the practice, there was a real pride in the principle. Pride is at the bottom of a great many errors and corruptions, and even of many evil practices, which have a great show and appearance of humility. Those who do so do *not hold the head*, v. 19. When men let go their hold of Christ, they catch at that which is next them and will stand them in no stead.—*From which all the body, by joints and bands, having nourishment ministered, and knit together, increaseth with the increase of God*. Jesus Christ is not only a head of government over the church, but a head of vital influence to it. The body of Christ is a growing body: *it increaseth with the increase of God*, with a large and abundant increase.

III. He takes occasion hence to warn them again: "*Wherefore, if you be dead with Christ from the rudiments of the world, why, as though living in the world, are you subject to ordinances?* (v. 20). Such observances as, *Touch not, taste not, handle not*," v. 21, 22, *which all are to perish with the using*, having no other authority than the traditions and injunctions of men. *Which things have indeed a show of wisdom in will-worship and humility*. They thought themselves wiser than their neighbours. There is nothing of true devotion in these things, for the gospel teaches us to worship God in spirit and truth and not by ritual observances, and through the mediation of Christ alone and not of any angels. Such things have only a show of wisdom, but are really folly. It is true wisdom to keep close to the appointments of the gospel, and an entire subjection to Christ, the only head of the church.

CHAPTER 3

I. The apostle exhorts us to set our hearts upon heaven, ver. 1–4. II. The mortification of sin, ver. 5–11. III. Mutual love and compassion, ver. 12–17. Exhortations to relative duties, ver. 18–25.

Verses 1–4

Though we are made free from the ceremonial law, it does not therefore follow that we may live as we list. We must walk the more closely with God. *If you then have risen with Christ, seek those things which are above*. We must mind the concerns of another world more than the concerns of this. *Christ sits at the right hand of God*. He who is our best friend has gone before to secure to us the heavenly happiness; and therefore we should seek what he has purchased at so vast an expense.

I. He explains this duty (*v.* 2): *Set your affections on things above, not on things on the earth.* Upon the wings of affection the heart soars upwards. *Things on earth* are here set in opposition to *things above.* Heaven and earth are contrary one to the other, and the prevalence of our affection to one will proportionably weaken our affection to the other.

II. He assigns three reasons for this, *v.* 3, 4.

1. We are dead to present things. And if we are dead to the earth, and have renounced it as our happiness, it is absurd for us to *set our affections* upon it, and *seek* it.

2. Our true life lies in the other world: *You are dead, and your life is hid with Christ in God, v.* 3. The new man has its livelihood thence. It is *hid with Christ*: not hid from us only, in point of secrecy, but hid for us, denoting security. This is our comfort, that our *life is hid with him,* and laid up safely with him.

3. At the second coming of Christ we hope for the perfection of our happiness. *When Christ, who is our life, shall appear, we shall also appear with him in glory, v.* 4. Christ is a believer's life. He is the principle and end of the Christian's life. Christ will appear again. He is now *hid,* but he will appear in *his own glory and his Father's glory.* We shall then appear with him in glory. It will be his glory to have his redeemed with him, and it will be their glory to come with him. Do we look for such a happiness, and should we not set our affections upon that world, and live above this? Our head is there, our home is there, our treasure is there, and we hope to be there for ever.

Verses 5–7

It is our duty to mortify our *members which are upon the earth,* and which naturally incline us to the things of the world.

I. The lusts of the flesh: *Fornication, uncleanness, inordinate affection, evil concupiscence*—which were so contrary to the Christian state and the heavenly hope.

II. The love of the world: *And covetousness, which is idolatry;* that is, an inordinate love of present good and outward enjoyments. Covetousness is spiritual idolatry: it is the giving of that love and regard to worldly wealth which are due to God only. Among all the instances of sin which good men are recorded in the scripture to have fallen into there is no instance of any good man charged with covetousness. How necessary it is to mortify sins, *v.* 6, 7. If we do not kill them, they will kill us: *For which things' sake the wrath of God cometh on the children of disobedience, v.* 6. See what we are all by nature more or less: we are *children of disobedience.* The wrath of God comes upon all the children of disobedience. Those who do not obey the precepts of the law incur the penalties of it. We should mortify these sins because they have lived in us: *In which you also walked some time, when you lived in them, v.* 7. The consideration that we have formerly lived in sin is a good argument why we should now forsake it. We have walked in by-paths, therefore let us walk in them no more. *When you lived among those who did such things* (so some understand it), then you walked in those evil practices. Let us keep out of the way of evil-doers.

Verses 8–11

We are to mortify inordinate passions (*v.* 8): *But now you also put off all these, anger, wrath, malice.* Anger and wrath are bad, but malice is worse; it is anger heightened and settled. So the product of them in the tongue; as *blasphemy,* which seems there to mean, not so much speaking ill of God as speaking

ill of men,—*filthy communication,* all lewd and wanton discourse, which propagates the same defilements in the hearers. *Lie not one to another* (*v.* 9). Lying makes us like the devil (who is the *father of lies*). Seeing *you have put off the old man with his deeds, and have put on the new man, v.* 10. Those who have put off the old man have put it off with its deeds; and those who have put on the new man must put on all its deeds, *renewed in knowledge,* because an ignorant soul cannot be a good soul. Light is the first thing in the new creation, as it was in the first: *after the image of him who created him.* It was the honour of man in innocence that he was made after the image of God. In the privilege of sanctification *there is neither Greek nor Jew, circumcision nor uncircumcision, Barbarian, Scythian, bond nor free, v.* 11. It is as much the duty of the one as of the other to be holy, and as much the privilege of the one as of the other to receive from God the grace to be so. *Christ is all in all.* Christ is a Christian's all, all his hope and happiness.

Verses 12–17

Put on therefore bowels of mercy, v. 12. We must not only put off anger and wrath (as *v.* 8), but we must put on compassion and kindness.

I. *Put on, as the elect of God, holy and beloved.* Those who are the elect of God, are beloved, and ought to conduct themselves in everything as becomes them. What we must put on. 1. Compassion towards the miserable: *Bowels of mercy.* Those who owe so much to mercy ought to be merciful. 2. *Kindness.* The design of the gospel is not only to soften the minds of men, but to sweeten them, and to promote friendship among men as well as reconciliation with God. 3. *Humbleness of mind.* There must not only be a humble demeanour, but a humble mind. 4. *Meekness.* Prudently bridle our own anger, and patiently bear the anger of others. 5. *Long-suffering.* Many can bear a short provocation who are weary of bearing when it grows long. If God is long-suffering to us we should exercise long-suffering to others. 6. Mutual forbearance: *Forbearing one another.* We have all of us something which needs to be borne with. We need the same good turn from others which we are bound to show them. 7. *Forgiving one another, if any man have a quarrel against any.* Quarrels will sometimes happen, even among the elect of God, who are holy and beloved. But it is our duty to forgive one another in such cases. *Even as Christ forgave you, so also do you.* It is a branch of his example which we are obliged to follow, if we ourselves would be forgiven.

II. In order to all this, we are exhorted: 1. To clothe ourselves with love (*v.* 14): *Above all things put on charity.* He lays the foundation in faith, and the top-stone in charity, *which is the bond of perfectness.* Christian unity consists of unanimity and mutual love. 2. To submit ourselves to the government of the *peace of God* (*v.* 15): *Let the peace of God rule in your hearts,* prevail and govern there, or as an umpire decide all matters of difference among you.—*To which you are called in one body.* Being united in one body, we are called to be at peace one with another. We must be thankful. The work of thanksgiving to God is such a sweet and pleasant work that it will help to make us sweet and pleasant towards all men. 3. To let the *word of Christ dwell in us richly, v.* 16. It must dwell in us, or *keep house,* not as a servant but as a master. It must dwell in us; that is, be always ready and at hand to us in everything. It must dwell in us richly: not only keep house in our hearts, but keep a good house. Many have the word of Christ dwelling in them, but it dwells in them but poorly. The soul prospers when the word of God *dwells in us richly.* And this in all wisdom. The word of Christ must dwell in us, not in all notion and speculation, to make us doctors, but in all wisdom, to make us good Christians. 4. To teach and admonish one another. We sharpen ourselves by quickening others. We must *admonish one another in psalms and hymns.* Religious poesy seems countenanced by these expressions and is capable of great edification. But, when we sing psalms, we make no melody unless we sing with grace in our hearts. And we are not only to quicken and encourage ourselves, but to *teach and admonish one another.* 5. That all must be done in the name of Christ (*v.* 17): *And whatsoever you do in word or deed, do all in the name of the Lord Jesus. Giving thanks to God and the Father by him.* Those who do all things in Christ's name will never want matter of thanksgiving to God, even the Father.

Verses 18–25

Exhortations to relative duties. We must never separate the privileges and duties of the gospel religion.

I. The duties of wives and husbands (*v.* 18): *Wives, submit yourselves unto your own husbands, as it is fit in the Lord.* Submission is the duty of wives. It is agreeable to the order of nature and the reason of things, as well as the appointment and will of God. It is submission to a husband, and to her own husband, who stands in the nearest relation, and is under strict engagements to proper duty too. And *this is fit in the Lord. Husbands must love their wives, and not be bitter against them, v.* 19. They must love them with tender and faithful affection, as Christ loved the church. And they must not be bitter against them, but be kind and obliging to them in all things.

II. The duties of children and parents: *Children, obey your parents in all things, for this is well-pleasing unto the Lord, v.* 20. They must be willing to do all their lawful commands, as those who have a natural right and are fitter to direct them than themselves. And this is *well-pleasing to God.* And parents must be tender, as well as children obedient (*v.* 21): *"Fathers, provoke not your children to anger, lest they be discouraged.* Let not your authority over them be exercised with rigour and severity, but with kindness and gentleness, lest you, by holding the reins too tight make them fly out with the greater fierceness."

III. Servants and masters: *Servants, obey your masters in all things according to the flesh, v.* 22. Servants must do the duty of the relation in which they stand in *all things*—not only when their master's eye is upon them. *In singleness of heart, fearing God.* The fear of God ruling in the heart will make people good in every relation. *"And whatsoever you do, do it heartily* (*v.* 23), with diligence, not idly and slothfully."—*As to the Lord, and not as to men.* It sanctifies a servant's work when it is done as unto God, and not merely as unto men. We are really doing our duty to God when we are faithful in our duty to men. A good and faithful servant is never the further from heaven for his being a servant: *"Knowing that of the Lord you shall receive the reward of the inheritance, for you serve the Lord Christ, v.* 24. Serving your masters according to the command of Christ, you serve Christ, and he will be your paymaster. Though you are now servants, you will receive the inheritance of sons." *He who does wrong will receive for the wrong which he has done, v.* 25. He will be sure to punish the unjust as well as reward the faithful servant: as well if masters wrong their servants.—*And there is no respect of persons with him.* The righteous Judge of the earth will be impartial, and carry it with an equal hand towards master and servant. How happy would the gospel religion make the world, if it everywhere prevailed; and how much would it influence every state of things and every relation of life!

CHAPTER 4

I. He continues his account of the duty of masters, ver. 1. II. He exhorts to the duty of prayer (ver. 2–4), and to a prudent conduct towards those with whom we converse, ver. 5, 6. III. He closes the epistle with the mention of several of his friends, ver. 7-18.

Verse 1

The apostle proceeds with the duty of masters to their servants. Justice is required of them: *Give unto your servants that which is just and equal* (*v.* 1), not only strict justice, but equity and kindness. *"Knowing that you also have a Master in heaven.* You who are masters of others have a Master yourself, and are accountable to one above you. Deal with your servants as you expect God should deal with you. You are both servants of the same Lord and are equally accountable to him at last."

Verses 2–4

This is the duty of everyone—to *continue in prayer. Watching in the same.* Christians should lay hold of all opportunities for prayer, and choose the fittest seasons, and keep their minds lively in the duty.— *With thanksgiving.* Thanksgiving must have a part in every prayer.—*Withal praying also for us, v.* 3. The people must pray particularly for their ministers, and bear them upon their hearts at all times at the throne of grace. As if he had said, "Do not forget us, whenever you pray for yourselves." *That God would open to us a door of utterance,* that is, either afford opportunity to preach the gospel, or else give me ability and courage. *And for me, that utterance may be given to me, that I may open my mouth boldly, to speak the mystery of Christ, for which I am also in bonds.* He would have them pray for him, that he might not be discouraged in his work, nor driven from it by his sufferings: *That I may make it manifest, as I ought to speak, v.* 4. He had been particular in telling them what he prayed for on their behalf, *ch.* i. Here he tells them particularly what he would have them pray for on his behalf. Paul knew as well as any man how to speak; and yet he begged their prayers for him, that he might be taught to speak.

Verses 5, 6

The apostle exhorts them further to a prudent conduct towards the heathen world, or those out of the Christian church among whom they lived (*v.* 5): *Walk in wisdom towards those who are without.* Be careful to get no hurt by them, and to do no hurt to them, or increase their prejudices against religion. Do them all the good you can, and by all the fittest means recommend religion to them.—*Redeeming the time;* either "improving every opportunity of doing them good," or else "walking with circumspection, to give them no advantage against you. Let *your speech be always with grace v.* 6. Let all your discourse be as becomes Christians—savoury, discreet, seasonable." Though it be not always of grace, it must be always with grace. It must be in a Christian manner: *seasoned with salt.* Grace is the salt which seasons our discourse, makes it savoury, and keeps it from corrupting. *That you may know how to answer every man.* We have need of a great deal of wisdom and grace to give proper answers to every man, particularly in answering the questions and objections of adversaries against our religion, giving the reasons of our faith.

Verses 7–18

I. Concerning Tychicus, *v.* 7. By him this epistle was sent. He knew they would be glad to hear how it fared with him. The churches cannot but be concerned for good ministers and desirous to know their state. *A beloved brother and faithful minister.* Faithfulness in any one is truly lovely, and renders him worthy our affection and esteem. *And a fellow-servant in the Lord.* It adds much to the beauty and strength of the gospel ministry when ministers are thus loving one to another. *Whom I have sent unto you for the same purpose, that he might know your estate, and comfort your hearts, v. 8.* He was as willing to hear from them as they could be to hear from him. It is a great comfort to have the mutual concern of fellow-christians.

II. Concerning Onesimus (*v.* 9): *With Onesimus, a faithful and beloved brother, who is one of you.* This was he whom Paul had begotten in his bonds, Philem. 10. He was converted at Rome, whither he had fled from his master's service. Though he was a poor servant, and had been a bad man, yet, being now a convert, Paul calls him a *faithful and beloved brother.* The meanest circumstance of life, and greatest wickedness of former life, make no difference in the spiritual relation among sincere Christians.

III. *Aristarchus, a fellow-prisoner.* Those who join in services and sufferings should be thereby engaged to one another in holy love.

IV. *Marcus, sister's son to Barnabas,* who wrote the gospel which bears his name. *If he come unto you receive him.* Paul had a quarrel with Barnabas upon the account of this Mark, yet Paul is not only reconciled to him himself, but recommends him to the respect of the churches. If men have been guilty of a fault, it must not be always remembered against them. We must forget as well as forgive.

V. Here is one who is called *Jesus,* which is the Greek name for the Hebrew *Joshua. Who is called Justus. These are my fellow-labourers unto the kingdom of God, who have been a comfort unto me.* One is his fellow-servant, another his fellow-prisoner, and all his fellow-workers.

VI. *Epaphras* (*v.* 12). He is *one of you; he salutes you. Always labouring fervently for you in prayers.*

Epaphras has learned of Paul to be much in prayer for his friends. We must be earnest in prayer, not only for ourselves, but for others also. *That you may stand perfect and complete in all the will of God.* To stand perfect and complete in the will of God is what we should earnestly desire both for ourselves and others. He had a great zeal for them: "*I bear him record.*" And his zeal extended to all about them: to *those who are in Laodicea and Hierapolis.*

VII. *Luke* is another here mentioned, whom he calls the *beloved physician.* This is he who wrote the Gospel and Acts, and was Paul's companion.

VIII. *Demas.* We read (2 Tim. iv. 10), *Demas hath forsaken me, having loved this present world.* Many who have made a great figure in profession, and gained a great name among Christians, have yet shamefully apostatized.

IX. The *brethren in Laodicea* living in the neighbourhood of Colosse: and Paul sends salutations to them, and orders that this epistle should be read in the church of the Laodiceans (*v.* 16). And some think Paul sent another epistle at this time to Laodicea: *And that you likewise read the epistle from Laodicea.* If so, that epistle is now lost.

X. *Nymphas* is mentioned (*v.* 15) as one who lived at Colosse, and had a church in his house.

XI. Concerning *Archippus.* They are bidden to admonish him to mind his work as a minister, to *take heed to it, and to fulfil it.* The ministry we have received is a great honour; for it is *received in the Lord,* and is by his appointment. The people may put their ministers in mind of their duty, and excite them to it: *Say to Archippus, Take heed to the ministry.*

XII. Concerning himself (*v.* 18): *The salutation of me Paul. Remember my bonds.* These words he wrote with his own hand. "*Grace be with you.* The favour of God, and all good, be with you, and be your portion."

AN EXPOSITION, WITH PRACTICAL OBSERVATIONS, OF

THE FIRST EPISTLE OF ST. PAUL TO

THE THESSALONIANS

Thessalonica was formerly the metropolis of Macedonia. The apostle Paul, being directed after an extraordinary manner to preach the gospel in Macedonia (Acts xvi. 9, 10), went from Troas to Samothracia, thence to Neapolis, and then to Philippi, where he had good success in his ministry, but met with hard usage, being cast into prison with Silas, from which being wonderfully delivered, they comforted the brethren there, and departed. Passing through Amphipolis and Apollonia, they came to Thessalonica, where the apostle planted a church. But a tumult being raised in the city, Paul and Silas, for their safety, were sent away by night unto Berea, and afterwards Paul was conducted to Athens, leaving Silas and Timotheus behind him. When they came, Timotheus was sent to Thessalonica, to enquire after their welfare and to establish them in the faith (1 Thess. iii. 2), and, as was sent again, together with Silas, to visit the churches in Macedonia. So that Paul, being left at Athens alone (1 Thess. iii. 1), departed thence to Corinth, where he continued a year and a half, and then he wrote this epistle to the church of Christ at Thessalonica, which, though it is placed after the other epistles of this apostle, is supposed to be first in time of all Paul's epistles.

CHAPTER 1

After the introduction (ver. 1) the apostle begins with a thanksgiving to God, ver. 2-5. And then mentions the good success of the gospel among them, ver. 6-10.

Verse 1

I. The inscription. The persons from whom this epistle came. Paul was the writer of this epistle. He joins Silvanus (or Silas) and Timotheus with himself. The persons to whom this epistle is written, the church of the Thessalonians, the converted Jews and Gentiles. This church is said to *be in God the Father and in the Lord Jesus Christ*. The Gentiles among them were turned to God from idols, and the Jews among them believed Jesus to be the promised Messias. All of them were devoted and dedicated to God the Father and the Lord Jesus Christ.

II. The salutation. *Grace be with you, and peace from God our Father and the Lord Jesus Christ.* The free grace or favour of God is the spring of all the peace and prosperity we can enjoy. As all good comes from God, so no good can be hoped for by sinners but from God in Christ. And the best good may be expected from God as our Father for the sake of Christ.

Verses 2–5

I. The apostle begins with thanksgiving to God. Being about to mention the things that were matter of joy to him, and highly praiseworthy in them, he chooses to do this by way of thanksgiving to God. Even when we do not actually give thanks to God by our words, we should have a grateful sense of God's goodness upon our minds.

II. He joined prayer with his praise or thanksgiving. When we give thanks for any benefit we receive we should join prayer. As there is much that we ought to be thankful for, so there is much occasion of constant prayer for further supplies of good.

III. The particulars for which he was so thankful to God.

1. The saving benefits bestowed on them. (1) Their faith and their work of faith. Their faith was a true and living faith, because a working faith. Wherever there is a true faith, it will work. (2) Their love and the labour of love. Love will show itself by labour. (3) Their hope and the patience of hope. Wherever there is a well-grounded hope of eternal life, it will appear by the exercise of patience.

2. The apostle not only mentions these three cardinal graces, faith, hope, and love, but also takes notice of the sincerity of them: being in the *sight of God even our Father*. Then is the work of faith, or labour of love, or patience of hope, sincere, when it is done as under the eye of God. He mentions the fountain whence these graces flow, God's electing love: *Knowing, brethren beloved, your election of God, v. 4.* Thus he runs up these streams to the fountain, and that was God's eternal election. He calls them, *brethren beloved.* It is a good reason why we should *love one another*, because we are all beloved of God. The election of God is of his own good pleasure and mere grace, not for the sake of any merit in those who are chosen. The election of God may be known by the fruits thereof.

3. Another ground of the apostle's thanksgiving is the success of his ministry among them. He was thankful on his own account as well as theirs, that he had not laboured in vain. Their ready entertainment of the gospel he preached to them was an evidence of their being elected and beloved of God. The gospel came to them also not in word only, but in power. It did not merely tickle the ear and please the fancy, but it affected their hearts: a divine power went along with it. By this we may know our election, if we not only speak of the things of God by rote as parrots, but feel the influence of these things in our hearts. It came in the Holy Ghost. Unless the Spirit of God accompany the word of God it will be to us but as a dead letter; and the letter killeth, it is the Spirit that giveth life. The gospel came to them in much assurance. They were fully convinced of the truth of it. They were willing to leave all for Christ, and to venture their souls upon the verity of the gospel revelation. The Thessalonians thus knew what manner of men the apostle and his fellow-labourers were among them, and what they did for their sake.

Verses 6–10

The evidence of the apostle's success among the Thessalonians.

I. They were careful to imitate the good examples of the apostles and ministers of Christ, *v. 6*. The Thessalonians showed a conscientious care to be followers of them. Herein they became also followers of the Lord, who is the perfect example we must strive to imitate. The Thessalonians acted thus, notwithstanding their affliction. They were willing to share in the sufferings that attended the embracing of Christianity. Perhaps this made the word more precious, being dear-bought. *With joy in the Holy*

Ghost, who, when our afflictions abound, makes our consolations much more to abound.

II. They were themselves examples to all about them, v. 7, 8.

1. Their example was very effectual to make good impressions upon many others. They were *stamps*, or instruments to make impression with. They had themselves received good impressions, and they made good impressions. Christians should be so good as by their example to influence others.

2. It was very extensive, and reached beyond the confines of Thessalonica, even to the believers of all Macedonia, and further in Achaia.

3. It was very famous. The word of the Lord was famous and well known, in the regions round about that city, and *in every place*; so that, from the good success of the gospel among them, many others were encouraged to entertain it, and to be willing, when called, to suffer for it. The readiness of their faith was famed abroad. These Thessalonians embraced the gospel as soon as it was preached to them. The effects of their faith were famous. They quitted their idolatry. They gave themselves up to God, to the living and true God. They set themselves to wait for the Son of God from heaven, v. 10. And this is one of the peculiarities of our holy religion, to wait for Christ's second coming, as those who believe he will come and hope he will come to our joy.

CHAPTER 2

The apostle puts the Thessalonians in mind of the manner of his preaching among them, ver. 1–6. Then of the manner of his conversation among them, ver. 7–12. Afterwards of the success of his ministry (ver. 13–16), and then apologizes for his absence, ver. 17–20.

Verses 1–6

He could appeal to the Thessalonians how faithfully he, and Silas, and Timotheus, had discharged their office: *You yourselves, brethren, know our entrance in unto you. His preaching was not in vain*, or, as some read it, *was not vain*. It was not fruitless or in vain (according to our translation), or, as others think, it was not vain and empty. The subject-matter of the apostle's preaching was sound and solid truth. He had no worldly design in his preaching, which he puts them in mind to have been,

I. With courage and resolution: *We were bold in our God to speak unto you the gospel of God, v.* 2. The apostle was inspired with a holy boldness, nor was he discouraged at the afflictions he met with. He had met with ill usage at Philippi, as these Thessalonians well know. There it was that he and Silas were put in the stocks; yet no sooner were they set at liberty than they went to Thessalonica, and preached the gospel with as much boldness as ever. Suffering in a good cause should rather sharpen than blunt the edge of holy resolution. Those who preached it preached it *with contention*, which denoted either the apostles' striving in their preaching or their striving against the opposition they met with. Paul was neither daunted in his work, nor driven from it.

II. With great simplicity and godly sincerity: *Our exhortation was not of deceit, nor of uncleanness, nor in guile, v.* 3. This, no doubt, was matter of the greatest comfort to the apostle—the consciousness of his own incerity; and was one reason of his success. The gospel he preached was without deceit, it was true and faithful. Nor was it of uncleanness. His gospel was pure and holy, and, as the matter of the apostle's exhortation was thus true and pure, the manner of his speaking was without guile. The apostle not only asserts his sincerity, but subjoins the reasons and evidences thereof.

1. They were stewards, *put in trust* with the gospel. The gospel which Paul preached was not his own, but the gospel of God. Ministers have a great favour

shown them, and honour put upon them, and trust committed to them.

2. Their design was to please God and not men. If sincerity be wanting, all that we do cannot please God. The gospel of Christ is not accommodated to the vain fancies and lusts of men, but, on the contrary, it was designed for the mortifying of their corrupt affections, that they might be brought under the power of faith.

3. They acted as in the sight of him who *tries our hearts*. He is well acquainted with all our aims and designs, as well as our actions. And it is from this God who trieth our hearts that we must receive our reward. The evidences of the apostles' sincerity: (1) He avoided flattery: *Neither at any time used we flattering words, as you know, v.* 5. He and his fellow-labourers preached Christ and him crucified, and did not aim to gain an interest in men's affections for themselves, nor did he flatter men in their sins. He did not flatter them with vain hopes. (2) He avoided covetousness. He did not make the ministry *a cloak*, or a covering, for *covetousness, as God was witness, v.* 5. His design was not to enrich himself by preaching the gospel: so far from this, he did not stipulate with them for bread. (3) He avoided ambition and vain-glory: *Nor of men sought we glory, neither of you nor yet of others, v.* 6. They expected neither people's purses nor their caps.

Verses 7–12

I. He mentions the gentleness of their behaviour: *We were gentle among you, v.* 7. He showed the kindness and care of a nurse that cherishes her children. This is the way to win people, rather than to rule with rigour. As a nursing mother bears with frowardness in a child, and condescends to mean offices for its good, cherishing it in her bosom, so in like manner should the ministers of Christ behave towards their people. This gentleness the apostle expressed several ways. 1. By the most affectionate desire of their welfare: *Being affectionately desirous of you, v.* 8. It was their spiritual and eternal welfare that he was earnestly desirous of. 2. By great readiness to do them good, willingly imparting to them, *not the gospel of God only, but also our own souls, v.* 8. He was willing to spend and be spent in the service of men's souls. 3. By bodily labour that his ministry might not be burdensome to them: *You remember our labour and travail; for, labouring night and day, &c., v.* 9. To the labour of the ministry he added that of his calling, as a tent-maker, that he might get his own bread. He spent part of the night, as well as the day, in this work; that he might have an opportunity to do good to the souls of men in the day time. 4. By the holiness of their conversation, concerning which he appeals not only to them, but to God also (v. 10): *You are witnesses, and God also*. They were observers of their outward conversation in public before men, and God was witness not only of their behaviour in secret, but of the inward principles from which they acted.

II. He mentions their faithful discharge of the work of the ministry, v. 11, 12. Paul and his fellow-labourers were not only good Christians, but faithful ministers. Paul exhorted the Thessalonians, and he comforted them also, *and charged every one* of them by personal addresses: this is intended by the similitude of a father's charging his children. He was their spiritual father; and, as he cherished them like a nursing mother, so he charged them as a father, with a father's affection rather than a father's authority. That *they would walk worthy of God, who hath called them to his kingdom and glory, v.* 12. 1. What is our great gospel privilege—that God has called us to his kingdom and glory. 2. What is our great gospel duty —that we walk worthy of God.

Verses 13–16

I. The success of his ministry among these Thessalonians (*v.* 13).

1. The manner of their receiving the word of God: *When you received the word of God, which you heard of us, you received it, not as the word of men, but (as it is in truth) the word of God.* The word of the gospel is preached by men like ourselves, men of like passions and infirmities with others. However, it is in truth the word of God. Such was the word the apostles preached by divine inspiration, and such is that which is left upon record, and such is that word which in our days is preached. Those are greatly to blame who give out their own fancies or injunctions for the word of God. Those are also to blame who, in hearing the word, look no further than to the ministry of men, or the words of men. We should receive the word of God as the word of God. The words of men are frail and perishing, like themselves, and sometimes false, foolish, and fickle: but God's word is holy, wise, just, and faithful, and abides for ever.

2. The wonderful operation of this word they received: *It effectually worketh in those that believe, v.* 13. Such as have this inward testimony of the truth of the scriptures have the best evidence of their divine original, though this is not sufficient to convince others who are strangers thereto.

II. The good effects which his successful preaching had,

1. Upon himself and fellow-labourers. It was a constant cause of thankfulness: *For this cause thank we God without ceasing, v.* 13. He never could be sufficiently thankful that God had counted him faithful, and made his ministrations successful.

2. Upon them. The word wrought effectually in them. In constancy and patience under sufferings: *You became followers of the churches of God, and have suffered like things as they have done* (*v.* 14). The cross is the Christian's mark. It is a good effect of the gospel when we are enabled to suffer for its sake. The sufferings of the churches of God, which *in Judæa were in Christ Jesus.* Those in Judæa first heard the gospel, and they first suffered for it: for the Jews were the most bitter enemies Christianity had. Bitter zeal and fiery persecution will set countrymen at variance. They were the ringleaders of persecution in all places; so in particular it was at Thessalonica. Upon this occasion, the apostle gives a character of the unbelieving Jews (*v.* 15). They *killed the Lord Jesus.* They killed *their own prophets.* They hated the apostles, and did them all the mischief they could. No marvel, if they killed the Lord Jesus, that they persecuted his followers. They *pleased not God.* They had quite lost all sense of religion. They were *contrary to all men.* Their persecuting spirit was a perverse spirit. *Forbidding the apostles to speak to the Gentiles, that they might be saved.* They were envious against the Gentiles, and angry that they should be admitted to share in the means of salvation. Thus did the Jews fill up their sins. For the sake of these things *wrath has come upon them to the uttermost;* wrath was determined against them, and would soon overtake them. It was not many years after this that Jerusalem was destroyed, and the Jewish nation cut off by the Romans.

Verses 17–20

The apostle apologizes for his absence: *We, brethren, were taken from you, v.* 17. He was unwillingly sent away by night to Berea. Though he was absent in body, yet he was present in heart. Even his bodily absence was but for a short time. This world is not a place where we are always, or long, to be together. It is in heaven that holy souls shall meet, and never part more. He earnestly desired and endeavoured to see them again: *We endeavoured more abundantly to see your face with great desire, v.* 17. But men of business are not masters of their own time. Paul did his endeavour, and he could do no more, *v.* 18. Satan hindered his return (*v.* 18). Satan is a constant enemy to the work of God, and does all he can to obstruct it. He assures them of his affection and high esteem for them. They were his *hope, and joy, and crown of rejoicing; his glory and joy.* Those that sow and those that reap shall rejoice together, *in the presence of our Lord Jesus Christ at his coming.* Though he should never be able to come to them, yet our Lord Jesus Christ will come.

CHAPTER 3

The apostle gives further evidence of his love to the Thessalonians, ver. 1–5. The return of Timothy, with good tidings concerning them, ver. 6–10. He concludes with fervent prayer for them, ver. 11, to the end.

Verses 1–5

An account of his sending Timothy to the Thessalonians. Paul was content, for their good, *to be left alone at Athens.*

I. The character he gives of Timothy (*v.* 2): *We sent Timotheus, our brother.* Elsewhere he calls him his son; here he calls him brother. He calls him also a minister of God. He calls him also his fellow-labourer in the gospel of Christ. Ministers should strengthen one another's hands, not strive and contend one with another (which will hinder their work), but strive together to carry on the great work they are engaged in.

II. The end why Paul sent Timothy: *To establish you and to comfort you concerning your faith, v.* 2. He was desirous that they might be confirmed and comforted. The more we are comforted, the more we shall be confirmed. The apostle's design was to establish and comfort the Thessalonians concerning their faith,—concerning the object of their faith,—concerning the recompence of faith.

III. The motive, a godly fear lest they should be moved from the faith of Christ, *v.* 3.

1. He apprehended there was danger, and feared the consequence.

(1) There was danger by reason of *affliction* and persecution for the sake of the gospel, *v.* 3. Those who made profession of the gospel were persecuted, and without doubt these Thessalonians themselves were afflicted. The apostle was afraid lest by any means the tempter had tempted him, *v.* 5. The devil is a subtle and unwearied tempter. He has often been successful in his attacks upon persons under afflictions.

(2) The consequence the apostle feared was lest his labour should be in vain. It is the devil's design to hinder the good fruit and effect of the preaching of the gospel. If he cannot hinder ministers from labouring he will, if he be able, hinder them of the success of their labours.

2. The apostle tells them what care he took in sending Timothy, (1) To put them in mind of what he had told them before concerning suffering tribulation (*v.* 4), he says (*v.* 3), *We are appointed thereunto.* Their troubles and persecutions did not come merely from the malice of the enemies of religion, but by the *appointment of God.* Being fore-warned, they should be fore-armed. Besides, it might prove a confirmation of their faith, when they perceived that it only happened to them as was predicted before. (2) To know their faith, whether they remained steadfast. If their faith did not fail, they would be able to stand their ground against the tempter and all his temptations.

Verses 6–10

Paul's great satisfaction upon the return of Timothy with good tidings.

I. The good report Timothy made concerning them, *v.* 6. *Concerning their faith*, that they were not shaken in mind, nor turned aside. *Their love* also continued; their love to the gospel, and the ministers of the gospel. They *desired greatly to see them again*, and there was no love lost for the apostle was as desirous to see them.

II. The great comfort the apostle had in this good report (*v.* 7, 8): *Therefore, brethren, we were comforted in all our affliction and distress.* The apostle thought this good news of them was sufficient to balance all the troubles he met with. This put new life and spirit into the apostle. Thus he was not only comforted, but greatly rejoiced also: *Now we live, if you stand fast in the Lord, v.* 8. It would have been a killing thing if the professors of religion had been unsteady, whereas nothing was more encouraging than their constancy.

III. The effects of this were thankfulness and prayer to God on their behalf. 1. How thankful the apostle was, *v.* 9. When we are most cheerful we should be most thankful. Paul speaks as if he could not tell how to express his thankfulness to God, or his joy and rejoicing for their sakes. His heart was enlarged with love to them and with thanksgiving to God. 2. He prayed for them night and day (*v.* 10), in the midst of the business of the day or slumber of the night lifting up his heart to God in prayer. He prayed exceedingly. When we are most thankful we should always give ourselves to prayer. There was something still lacking in their faith; Paul desired that this might be perfected, and to see their face in order thereunto. The best of men have something wanting in their faith, if not as to the matter of it, yet as to the clearness and certainty of their faith.

Verses 11–13

He desired to be instrumental in the further benefit of the Thessalonians; and the only way to be so while at a distance was by prayer for them, together with his writing or sending to them.

I. Whom he prays to, namely, God and Christ. Prayer is not only to be offered in the name of Christ, but offered up to Christ himself, as our Lord and our Saviour.

II. What he prays for.

1. He prays that their way might be directed to them, *v.* 11. The taking of a journey to this or that place, one would think, is a thing depending on a man's own will, and lies in his own power. But the apostle knew that God our Father directs and orders his children whither they shall go and what they shall do. Let us acknowledge God in all our ways, and he will direct our paths.

2. He prays for the prosperity of the Thessalonians. (1) That they might increase and abound in love (*v.* 12), in love to one another and in love to all men. Love is of God, and is the fulfilling of the gospel as well as of the law. Timothy brought good tidings of their faith, yet something was lacking therein; and of their charity, yet the apostle prays that this might increase and abound. We are beholden to God not only for the stock put into our hands at first, but for the improvement of it also. And to our prayer we must add endeavour. The apostle again mentions his abounding love, towards them. The more we are beloved, the more affectionate we should be. (2) That they might be established unblameable in holiness, *v.* 13. *To the end that he* (the Lord) *may establish your hearts.* Holiness is required of all those who would go to heaven, and therein we must be unblameable. Our desire should be to have our hearts established in holiness before God, and that we may be unblameable before God, even the Father, now, and be presented blameless when the Lord Jesus shall come with all his saints.

CHAPTER 4

The apostle gives earnest exhortations to abound in holiness, ver. 1–8. The great duties of brotherly love, and quietness with industry in our callings, ver. 9–12. He concludes with comforting those who mourned for their relations and friends that died in the Lord, ver. 13–18.

Verses 1–8

I. An exhortation to *abound more and more* in that which is good, *v.* 1, 2.

1. The manner in which the exhortation is given— very affectionately. The apostle entreats them as brethren; he exhorts them very earnestly: *We beseech and exhort you.*

2. The matter of his exhortation—that they would abound more and more in holy walking. The apostle would have them further to excel others. Those who most excel others fall short of perfection. We must not only persevere to the end, but we should grow better.

3. The arguments with which the apostle enforces his exhortation. They had been informed of their duty. They had received or been taught, *how they ought to walk.* The design of the gospel is to teach men not only what they should believe, but also how they ought to live. The apostle taught them how to walk, not how to talk. To talk well without living well will never bring us to heaven. The apostle taught and exhorted them in the name of the Lord Jesus Christ. Herein they would please God. We should not be men-pleasers, but should walk so as to please God. The rule according to which they ought to walk and act—*the commandments they had given them by the Lord Jesus Christ.* Though they had great authority from Christ, yet that was to teach men what Christ had commanded, not to give forth commandments of their own. The Thessalonians knew what commandments he gave them, that they were no other than what he had received from the Lord Jesus.

II. A caution against uncleanness.

1. *That you should abstain from fornication* (*v.* 3), by which we are to understand all uncleanness whatsoever. All that is contrary to chastity in heart, speech, and behaviour, is contrary to the command of God and contrary to that holiness which the gospel requires.

2. This branch of sanctification in particular is the will of God, *v.* 3. Not only does God require holiness in the heart, but also purity in our bodies. This will be greatly for our honour: so much is plainly implied, *v.* 4. The body is here called the vessel of the soul, which dwells therein, and it must be kept pure from defiling lusts. What can be more dishonourable than for a rational soul to be enslaved by bodily affections and brutal appetites? To indulge the lust of concupiscence is to live and act like heathens. *Even as the Gentiles who know not God, v.* 5. Christians should not walk as unconverted Gentiles. The sin of uncleanness, especially adultery, is a great piece of injustice that God will be the avenger of; so we may understand those words, *That no man go beyond or defraud his brother* (*v.* 6) *in any matter.* Some understand these words as a further warning and caution against injustice and oppression, which are certainly contrary to the gospel. But the meaning may rather be to show the injustice and wrong that are done by the sin of uncleanness. And, as this sin is of such a heinous nature, so it follows that God will be the avenger of it. The sin of uncleanness is contrary to the design of our Christian calling: *For God hath called us not unto uncleanness, but unto holiness, v.* 7.

The contempt therefore of God's law and gospel is the contempt of God himself: *He that despises, despises God, not man* only. *God hath given Christians his Spirit.* The Holy Ghost is given unto us to arm us against these sins.

Verses 9–12

I. Of brotherly love. This he exhorts them to increase in yet more and more. They were remarkable in the exercise of it, which made it less needful that he should write to them about it, *v.* 9. Thus by his good opinion of them he insinuated himself into their affections, and so made way for his exhortation to them.

1. What it is that the apostle commends in them. It was not so much their own virtue as God's grace. God had taught them this good lesson: *You yourselves are taught of God to love one another, v.* 9. Whoever does that which is good is taught of God to do it. All who are savingly taught of God are taught this lesson, to love one another. This is the livery of Christ's family. The Thessalonians gave good evidence of their being taught of God by *their love to the brethren in all Macedonia, v.* 10. Their love was extensive. And a true Christian's is so to all the saints.

2. The exhortation itself is to increase more and more in brotherly love, *v.* 10. They must be exhorted to pray for more, and labour for more. There are none on this side heaven who love in perfection.

II. Of quietness and industry in their callings. *Study to be quiet, v.* 11. It is the most desirable thing to have a calm and quiet temper, and to be of a peaceable and quiet behaviour. Satan is very busy to disquiet us; and we have that in our own hearts that disposes us to be disquiet; therefore let us study to be quiet. *Do your own business.* Those who are busy-bodies, meddling in other men's matters, generally have but little quiet in their own minds and cause great disturbances among their neighbours; at least they seldom mind the other exhortation, to be diligent in their own calling, *to work with their own hands.* Christianity does not discharge us from the work of our particular callings, but teaches us to be diligent therein. Thus we shall walk honestly, or decently and creditably, towards those that are without, *v.* 12. This will be to act as becomes the gospel, and will gain a good report from those that are strangers, yea, enemies to it. We shall live comfortably, and have lack of nothing, *v.* 12. Such as are diligent in their own business live comfortably and have lack of nothing. They earn their own bread, and have the greatest pleasure in so doing.

Verses 13–18

The apostle comforts the Thessalonians who mourned for the death of their relations and friends that died in the Lord. His design is to dissuade them from excessive grief. *All* grief for the death of friends is far from being unlawful; we may weep for our own loss, though it may be their gain. Yet we must not be immoderate in our sorrows.

I. This looks as if we had no hope, *v.* 13. It is to act too much like the Gentiles, who had no hope of a better life after this. This hope is more than enough to balance all our griefs.

II. This is an effect of ignorance concerning those who are dead, *v.* 13. There are some things which we cannot but be ignorant of concerning those that are asleep. Yet there are some things concerning those especially who die in the Lord that we need not be ignorant of. They will be sufficient to allay our sorrow concerning them.

1. They sleep in Jesus. They are asleep, *v.* 13. They have retired out of this troublesome world, to rest from all their labours and sorrows, and they sleep in Jesus, *v.* 14. They are not lost, nor are they losers,

but great gainers by death, and their removal out of this world is into a better.

2. They shall be raised up from the dead, and awakened out of their sleep, for *God will bring them with him, v.* 14. They then are with God, and are better where they are than when they were here; and when God comes he will bring them with him. The doctrine of the resurrection and the second coming of Christ is a great antidote against the fear of death and inordinate sorrow for the death of our Christian friends; and this doctrine we have a full assurance of, because we *believe that Jesus died and rose again, v.* 14.

3. Their state and condition shall be glorious and happy at the second coming of Christ. This the apostle informs the Thessalonians of *by the word of the Lord (v.* 15). The Lord Jesus will come down from heaven in all the pomp and power of the upper world (*v.* 16): *The Lord himself shall descend from heaven with a shout.* He will descend from heaven into this our air, *v.* 17. The appearance will be with pomp and power, *with a shout*—with *the voice of the archangel.* The glorious appearance of this great Redeemer and Judge will be proclaimed and ushered in by the *trump of God.* The dead shall be raised: *The dead in Christ shall rise first (v.* 16). Those who shall then *be found alive shall not prevent those that are asleep, v.* 15. Those that shall be found alive will then be changed. They shall *be caught up together with them in the clouds, to meet the Lord in the air, v.* 17. Those who are raised, and thus changed, shall meet together in the clouds, and there meet with their Lord. Here is the bliss of the saints at that day: they shall *be ever with the Lord, v.* 17. The principal happiness of heaven is this, *to be with the Lord,* to see him, live with him, and enjoy him, for ever. This should comfort the saints upon the death of their friends. We and they with all the saints shall meet our Lord, and be with him for ever, no more to be separated either from him or from one another for ever. And the apostle would have us *comfort one another with these words, v.* 18.

CHAPTER 5

The apostle, having spoken in the end of the foregoing chapter concerning the resurrection, and the second coming of Christ, proceeds to speak concerning the uselessness of enquiring after the particular time of Christ's coming, which would be sudden and terrible to the wicked, but comfortable to the saints, ver. 1–5. He then exhorts them to the duties of watchfulness, sobriety, and the exercise of faith, love, and hope, as being suitable to their state, ver. 6–10. In the next words he exhorts them to several duties they owed to others, or to one another (ver. 11–15), afterwards to several other Christian duties of great importance (ver. 16–22), and then concludes this epistle, ver. 23–28.

Verses 1–5

I. The apostle tells the Thessalonians it was needless or useless to enquire about the particular time of Christ's coming: *Of the times and seasons you need not that I write unto you, v.* 1. There is a certain time appointed for his coming; but he had no revelation given him; nor should they or we enquire into this secret. There are times and seasons for us to do our work in: these it is our duty and interest to know and observe; but the time and season when we must give up our account we know not. There are many things which our vain curiosity desires to know which there is no necessity at all of our knowing, nor would our knowledge of them do us good.

II. He tells them that the coming of Christ would be a great surprise to most men, *v.* 2. *As a thief in the night.* As the thief usually cometh in the dead time of the night, when he is least expected, such a *surprise* will the day of the Lord be.

III. He tells them how terrible Christ's coming would be to the ungodly, *v.* 3. It will be to their destruction in that day of the Lord. It will be sudden. It will overtake them in the midst of their carnal security and jollity, when they say in their hearts, *Peace and safety*, and think not of it,—*as travail cometh upon a woman with child*, at the set time indeed, but not perhaps just then expected. It will be unavoidable destruction too: *They shall not escape*.

IV. He tells them how comfortable this day will be to the righteous, *v.* 4, 5. Their character and privilege. They are the children of the light, &c. This was the happy condition of the Thessalonians as it is of all true Christians. They were not in a state of sin and ignorance as the heathen world. They were the *children of the day*, for the day-star had risen upon them. They were no longer under the darkness of heathenism, but under the gospel, which brings life and immortality to light. Their great advantage on this account: that *that day should not overtake them as a thief, v.* 4. They had fair warning, and might hope to stand with comfort and confidence before the Son of man, as a friend in the day, not as a thief in the night.

Verses 6–10

Exhortations to several needful duties.

I. To watchfulness and sobriety, *v.* 6. These duties are distinct, yet they mutually befriend one another. We shall not keep sober, unless we be upon our guard, and, unless we keep sober, we shall not long watch. 1. Then *let us not sleep as do others, but let us watch;* we must not be secure and careless, nor indulge spiritual sloth and idleness. The generality of men are too careless of their duty and regardless of their spiritual enemies. Either they do not consider the things of another world at all, because they are asleep; or they do not consider them aright, because they dream. But let us watch, and act like men that are awake, and that stand upon their guard. 2. Let us also *be sober*. Let us keep our natural desires and appetites after the things of this world within due bounds. Watchfulness and sobriety are most suitable to the Christian's character and privilege, as being *children of the day*; because *those that sleep, sleep in the night, and those that are drunken are drunken in the night, v.* 7. They were not sensible of their danger, therefore they *slept*; they were not sensible of their duty, therefore they were drunk: but it ill becomes Christians to do thus.

II. To be well armed as well as watchful. Our spiritual enemies are many, and mighty, and malicious. We have need to arm ourselves against their attempts, and this spiritual armour consists of the three great graces of Christians, faith, love, and hope, *v.* 8. 1. We must live by faith, and this will keep us watchful and sober. Faith will be our best defence against the assaults of our enemies. 2. We must get a heart inflamed with love. True and fervent love to God, and the things of God, will keep us watchful and sober. 3. We must make salvation our hope. This good hope of eternal life, will be as a helmet to defend the head, and hinder our being intoxicated with the pleasures of sin, which are but for a season. The apostle shows what grounds Christians have to hope for this salvation. He says nothing of their meriting it. No, the doctrine of our merits is altogether unscriptural and antiscriptural. But our hopes are to be grounded, (1) Upon God's appointment: because *God hath not appointed us to wrath, but to obtain salvation, v.* 9. If we would trace our salvation to the first cause, that is God's appointment. On this we build unshaken hope, especially when we consider, (2) Christ's merit and grace, and that salvation is by our Lord Jesus Christ, who died for us. Our salvation therefore is owing to, and our hopes of it are grounded on, Christ's atonement as well as God's appointment.

That whether we wake or sleep we should live together with Christ, live in union and in glory with him for ever. Christ died for us, that, living and dying, we might be his; that we might live to him while we are here, and live with him when we go hence.

Verses 11–15

Several duties.

I. Towards those who were nearly related one to another. Such should comfort themselves, or exhort one another, and edify one another, *v.* 11. They must comfort or exhort themselves and one another. We should not only be careful about our own comfort and welfare, but of others also. They must edify one another. We should communicate our knowledge and experiences one to another. We should join in prayer and praise one with another. We should set a good example one before another. This the Thessalonians did (*which also you do*). Those who do that which is good have need of further exhortations to excite them to do more good, as well as continue in doing what they do.

II. Towards their ministers, *v.* 12, 13. 1. How the ministers of the gospel are described by the work of their office. Ministers must labour among their people, labour with diligence, and unto weariness (so the word in the original imports). They are called labourers, and should not be loiterers. Ministers are to rule their people also. They must rule, not with rigour, but with love. They must rule as spiritual guides, by setting a good example to the flock. They are over the people in the Lord, and must rule the people by Christ's laws. They must also admonish the people. They must instruct them to do well, and should reprove when they do ill. 2. What the duty of the people is towards their ministers. The people must know them. As the shepherd should know his flock, so the sheep must know their shepherd. They must esteem their ministers highly in love; and this for their work's sake, because their business is to promote the honour of Christ and the welfare of men's souls. Faithful ministers ought to be so far from being lightly esteemed because of their work that they should be highly esteemed on account of it.

III. Touching the duty Christians owe to one another. *To be at peace among themselves, v.* 13. The people should be at peace among themselves, doing all they can to hinder any differences from rising or continuing among them, and using all proper means to preserve peace and harmony. *To warn the unruly, v.* 14. There will be in all societies some who walk disorderly. Such should be reproved and told plainly of the injury they do their own souls, and the hurt they may do to others. *To comfort the feeble-minded, v.* 14, the timorous and faint-hearted, or such as are dejected and of a sorrowful spirit. Such should be encouraged; we should not despise them, but comfort them; and who knows what good a kind and comfortable word may do them? *To support the weak, v.* 15. Some are not well able to perform their work, nor bear up under their burdens; we should therefore help their infirmities, and lift at one end of the burden, and so help to bear it. *To be patient towards all men, v.* 14. We must bear and forbear. And this duty must be exercised towards all men, good and bad, high and low. We must endeavour to make the best we can of everything, and think the best we can of everybody. *Not to render evil for evil to any man, v.* 15. We must by all means forbear to avenge ourselves. It becomes us to forgive, as those that are, and that hope to be, forgiven of God. *Ever to follow that which is good, v.* 15. We must study to do what is pleasing to God. Whatever men do to us, we must do good to others, both among ourselves and then, *as we have opportunity, unto all men.*

Verses 16–22

Here we have divers short exhortations. The duties are of great importance, and we may observe how they are connected together. 1. *Rejoice evermore, v.* 16. If we do rejoice in God we may do that evermore. A religious life is a pleasant life, it is a life of constant joy. 2. *Pray without ceasing, v.* 17. The way to rejoice evermore is to pray without ceasing. We should rejoice more if we prayed more. The meaning is not that men should do nothing but pray, but that nothing else we do should hinder prayer in its proper season. Prayer will help forward and not hinder all other lawful business, and every good work. 3. *In everything give thanks, v.* 18. If we pray without ceasing, we shall not want matter for thanksgiving *in everything.* We should be thankful in every condition, even in adversity as well as prosperity. It is never so bad with us but it might be worse. We never can have any reason to complain of God, and have always much reason to praise and give thanks. This is the *will of God in Christ Jesus concerning us, that we give thanks.* He allows us to rejoice evermore, and appoints us in everything to give thanks. 4. *Quench not the Spirit* (*v.* 19). Christians are said to *be baptized with the Holy Ghost and with fire.* We must be careful not to quench this holy fire. As fire is put out by withdrawing fuel, so we quench the Spirit if we do not stir up our spirits. And as fire is quenched by pouring water, or putting a great quantity of dirt upon it, so we must be careful not to quench the Holy Spirit by indulging carnal lusts and affections, or minding only earthly things. 5. *Despise not prophesyings* (*v.* 20). By *prophesyings* here we are to understand the preaching of the word. We must not despise preaching, though it be plain, and though we be told no more than what we knew before. It is useful, and many times needful, to have our affections and resolutions excited, to those things that we knew before to be our interest and our duty. 6. *Prove all things, but hold fast that which is good, v.* 21. We must not take things upon trust from the preacher. We must search the scriptures, whether what they say be true or not. But we must not be always trying, always unsettled; no, at length we must be settled, and hold fast that which is good. Proving all things must be in order to holding fast that which is good. 7. *Abstain from all appearance of evil, v.* 22. Corrupt affections indulged in the heart, and evil practices allowed of in the life, will greatly tend to promote fatal errors in the mind; whereas purity of heart, and integrity of life, will dispose men to receive the truth in the love of it. He who is not shy of the appearances of sin will not long abstain from the actual commission of sin.

Verses 23–29

I. Paul's prayer for them, *v.* 23. 1. To whom the apostle prays, *The very God of peace.* By their peaceableness and unity those things would best be obtained which he prays for. 2. The things he prays for are their sanctification, that *God would sanctify them wholly*; and their preservation, that they might be *preserved blameless.* All those who are sanctified in Christ Jesus shall be preserved to the coming of our Lord Jesus Christ. We should pray to God to perfect his work, and *preserve us blameless,* till at length we are *presented faultless before the throne of his glory with exceeding joy.*

II. His comfortable assurance that God would hear his prayer: *Faithful is he who calleth you, who will also do it, v.* 24. The faithfulness of God was their security that they should persevere to the end. God would do what he desired; he would accomplish all the good pleasure of his goodness towards them. Our fidelity to God depends upon his faithfulness to us.

III. His request of their prayers: *Brethren, pray for us, v.* 25. Brethren should thus express brotherly love. The more people pray for their ministers the more good ministers may have from God, and the more benefit people may receive by their ministry.

IV. His salutation: *Greet all the brethren with a holy kiss, v.* 26. Thus the apostle sends a friendly salutation from himself, and Silvanus, and Timotheus, and would have them salute each other in their names; and thus he would have them signify their mutual love and affection to one another.

V. His solemn charge for the reading of this epistle, *v.* 27. This is not only an exhortation, but an adjuration by the Lord. And this epistle was to be read to all the holy brethren. In order to this, these holy oracles should not be kept concealed in an unknown tongue, but translated into the vulgar languages. The scriptures should be read in the public assemblies of Christians also.

VI. The apostolical benediction that is usual in other epistles: *The grace of our Lord Jesus Christ be with you. Amen, v.* 28. We need no more to make us happy than to know that grace which our Lord Jesus Christ has manifested. This is an ever-flowing and overflowing fountain of grace to supply all our wants.

AN EXPOSITION, WITH PRACTICAL OBSERVATIONS, OF

THE SECOND EPISTLE OF ST. PAUL TO

THE THESSALONIANS

This Second Epistle was written soon after the former, and seems to have been designed to prevent a mistake concerning the second coming of Christ, as if it were near at hand. The apostle informs them that there were many intermediate counsels yet to be fulfilled before that day of the Lord should come, though, because it is sure, he had spoken of it as near.

CHAPTER 1

After the introduction (ver. 1, 2) the apostle begins this epistle with an account of his high esteem for these Thessalonians, ver. 3, 4. He then comforts them under their afflictions and persecutions, ver. 5–10, and tells them what his prayers were to God for them, ver. 11, 12.

Verses 1–4

I. The introduction (*v.* 1, 2), in the same words as in the former epistle. This church of the Thessalonians was built, as all true churches are; *in God our Father and the Lord Jesus Christ.*

II. The apostle's expression of the high esteem he had for them.

1. How his esteem of them is expressed. (1) He glorified God on their behalf, *v.* 3. It is our duty to be thankful to God for all the good that is found in us or others: and it not only is an act of kindness to our fellow-christians, but our duty, to thank God on their behalf. (2) He also *glories in them before the churches of God, v.* 4. The apostle never flattered his friends, but he took pleasure in speaking well of them, to the glory of God.

2. For what he esteemed them and thanked God. In his former epistle (*ch.* i. 3) he gave thanks for their faith, love, and patience; here he gives thanks for the increase of all those graces. Where there is the truth of grace there will be increase of it. And where there is the increase of grace God must have all the glory of it. We are as much indebted to him for the improvement of grace, as we are for the very beginning of it. We may be tempted to think that though when we were bad we could not make ourselves good, yet when we are good we can easily make ourselves better. Their faith grew exceedingly, *v.* 3. The growth of their faith appeared by the works of faith; and, where faith grows, all other graces grow proportionably. Their charity abounded (*v.* 3). Where faith grows love will abound. Their patience as well as faith increased in all their persecutions and tribulations. And patience has then its perfect work when it extends itself to all trials. They endured all these by faith, and endured them with patience, not with an insensibility under them, but with patience arising from Christian principles.

Verses 5–10

I. The present happiness and advantage of their sufferings, *v.* 5. They were improved by their sufferings, were *counted worthy of the kingdom of God.* Religion, if it is worth anything, is worth everything, and those either have no religion at all, or know not how to value it, that cannot find in their hearts to suffer for it.

II. The future recompence that shall be given to persecutors and persecuted.

1. In this future recompence there will be, (1) A punishment inflicted on persecutors, *v.* 6. And there is nothing that more infallibly marks a man for eternal ruin than a spirit of persecution. God will render a recompence, and will trouble those that trouble his people. (2) A reward for those that are persecuted, *v.* 7. There is a rest that remains for the people of God, a rest from sin and sorrow. The future rest will abundantly recompence all their present troubles. There is enough in heaven to countervail all that we may lose or suffer for the name of Christ in this world.

2. Concerning this future recompence.

(1) The certainty of it: *It is a righteous thing with God* (*v.* 6). God's suffering people will lose nothing by their sufferings, and their enemies will gain nothing.

(2) When this righteous recompence shall be made, *v.* 7. The Lord Jesus will in that day appear from heaven. He will be revealed with his mighty angels (*v.* 7). He will come in flaming fire, *v.* 8. A refining fire, to purify the saints. A consuming fire to the wicked. The effects of this appearance will be terrible to some and joyful to others.

First, They will be terrible to some. Those that sinned against the principles of natural religion, and rebelled against the light of nature (*v.* 8). Those that rebel against the light of revelation. To such persons the revelation of our Lord Jesus Christ will be terrible, because of their doom, *v.* 9. They will then be punished. They did sin's work, and must receive sin's wages. Their punishment will be no less than destruction. This destruction shall come from the *presence of the Lord.* It shall come from the *glory of his power.*

Secondly, It will be a joyful day to some, even to the saints. Christ Jesus will be glorified and admired by his saints. Christ will be glorified and admired in them. His grace and power will be magnified in the salvation of his saints. How will they be wondered at in this great and glorious day; or, rather, how will Christ be admired!

Verses 11, 12

His earnest and constant prayer for them: *Wherefore also we pray,* &c.

I. What the apostle prayed for, *v.* 11. 1. That God would begin his good work of grace in them; so we may understand this expression: *That our God would count you* (or, as it might be read, *make you*) *worthy of this calling.* We are called to God's kingdom and glory. Now, if this be our calling, our great concern should be to be worthy of it. We should pray that he would make us worthy. 2. That God would carry on the good work that is begun. The good pleasure of God denotes his gracious purposes towards his people. Now, there are various and manifold purposes of grace and goodwill in God towards his people; and the apostle prays that all of them may be fulfilled towards these Thessalonians. In particular, the apostle prays that God would fulfil in them the *work of faith with power.*

II. Why the apostle prayed for these things (*v.* 12). Our good works should so shine before men that others may glorify God, that Christ may be glorified in and by us, and then we shall be glorified in and with him.

CHAPTER 2

An error into which some among them had fallen concerning the coming of Christ, as being very near, ver. 1–3. Then he proceeds to confute the error he cautioned them against, ver. 4–12. He then comforts them and exhorts them to steadfastness, ver. 13–15. And concludes with a prayer for them, ver. 16–17.

Verses 1–3

Some among the Thessalonians had mistaken the apostle's meaning about the coming of Christ, by thinking that it was near at hand. The apostle is careful to rectify this mistake. If errors and mistakes arise among Christians, we should take the first opportunity to rectify them, and good men will be especially careful to suppress errors that may arise from a mistake of their words and actions. We have a subtle adversary, who will sometimes promote errors even by means of the words of scripture.

I. How very earnest this apostle was, v. 1. He entreats them as brethren who might have charged them as a father charges his children. And this is the best way to deal with men when we would preserve or recover them from errors, to deal gently and affectionately with them.

1. It is most certain that the Lord Jesus Christ will come to judge the world. Whatever mistakes may arise about the time of his coming, his coming itself is certain.

2. At the second coming of Christ all the saints will be gathered together to him. It will be the completing of the happiness of his saints. There will then be a general meeting of all the saints, and none but saints; all the Old Testament saints, and all the New Testament saints. They shall be gathered *together to Christ*. He will be the great centre of their unity. To be with him for ever, and altogether happy in his presence to all eternity.

II. The Thessalonians should not be deceived about the time of Christ's coming, and so *be shaken in mind, or be troubled*. Errors in the mind tend greatly to weaken our faith, and such as are weak in faith and of troubled minds are oftentimes apt to be deceived. The apostle would not have them be deceived, v. 3. There are many who lie in wait to deceive, and they have many ways of deceiving; we have reason therefore to stand upon our guard. The apostle cautions them not to be deceived about the near approach of Christ's coming, as if it was to have been in the apostle's days. He gives them warning. He would not have their faith weakened. They ought not to waver in their minds as to this great thing, which is the faith and hope of all the saints. False doctrines are like the winds, that toss the water to and fro, and they are apt to unsettle the minds of men, who are sometimes as unstable as water. He would not have their comforts lessened with false alarms. In itself it should be matter of the believer's hope and joy. We should always watch and pray, but must not be discouraged nor uncomfortable at the thought of Christ's coming.

Verses 3–12

The apostle confutes the error against which he had cautioned them. There are several events previous to the second coming of Christ.

I. A general apostasy, v. 3. The apostle speaks of some very great apostasy such as should give occasion to the revelation or rise of that *man of sin*. This, he says (v. 5), he had told them of when he was with them. No sooner was Christianity planted and rooted in the world than there began to be a defection in the Christian church. It was so in the Old Testament church, and therefore it was no strange thing that

after the planting of Christianity there should come a falling away.

II. A revelation of that man of sin (v. 3). The apostle afterwards speaks of the revelation of that wicked one (v. 8): here he seems to speak of his rise. He is called the man of sin, and he is the son of perdition, because he himself is devoted to certain destruction, and is the instrument of destroying many others. The characters here given, v. 4. The antichrist is some usurper of God's authority who claims divine honours. His rise is mentioned, v. 6, 7. There was something that hindered, or *let, until it was taken away*. This mystery of iniquity was gradually to arrive at its height. The apostle calls it a *mystery of iniquity*. This mystery of iniquity did *already work*. While the apostles were yet living *the enemy came and sowed tares*. The fall or ruin of the antichristian state is declared, v. 8. The head of this antichristian kingdom is called *that wicked one*. The revelation or discovery of this to the world would be the sure presage of his ruin. The apostle assures the Thessalonians that the Lord would destroy him. The power of antichrist in due time will be totally and finally destroyed, and this will be by the brightness of Christ's coming. The apostle further describes the rule of this man of sin. A divine power is pretended for the support of this kingdom, but it is only after the working of Satan. The apostle calls it *all deceiveableness of unrighteousness*, v. 10. Many are the subtle artifices the man of sin has used. His willing subjects, v. 10. Had they loved the truth, they would have persevered in it, and been preserved by it; but no wonder if they easily parted with what they never had any love to. The *sin and ruin of the subjects* of antichrist's kingdom declared, v. 11, 12. An erroneous mind and vicious life often go together and help forward one another. He will punish men for their unbelief, and for their dislike of the truth and love to sin and wickedness. He sometimes withdraws his grace from such sinners as are here mentioned; he gives them up to their own hearts' lusts, and leaves them to themselves, and then sin will follow of course.

Verses 13–15

I. The consolation the Thessalonians might take, v. 13, 14. The apostle reckoned himself bound in duty to be thankful to God on this account. And there was good reason, because they were beloved by the Lord.

1. The stability of the election of grace, v. 13. God had chosen them from the beginning. He had loved them with an everlasting love. (1) The eternal date of it—it is from the beginning. (2) The end to which they were chosen—salvation, complete and eternal salvation. (3) The means in order to obtaining this end—*sanctification of the spirit and belief of the truth*. We are not elected of God because we were holy, but that we might be holy. Being chosen of God, we must not live as we list. Faith and holiness must be joined together, as well as holiness and happiness.

2. The efficacy of the gospel call, v. 14. They were called thereunto by the gospel. It is a call to honour and happiness, even the *glory of our Lord Jesus Christ*. Such shall be with Christ, to behold his glory, and they shall be glorified with Christ and partake of his glory.

II. He does not say, "You are chosen to salvation, and therefore you may be careless and secure"; but *therefore stand fast*. The Thessalonians are exhorted to steadfastness in their Christian profession.

Verses 16, 17

The apostle's earnest prayer for them.

I. To whom he prays: *Our Lord Jesus Christ himself, and God, even our Father*. We may and should direct our prayers, not only to God the Father, but also *to our Lord Jesus Christ himself*.

II. From what he takes encouragement—from the consideration of what God had already done for him and them (*v*. 16). The love of God is the spring and fountain of all the good we have or hope for. From this fountain all our consolation flows. And the consolation of the saints is an everlasting consolation. The comforts of the saints are not dying things. Their consolation is founded on the hope of eternal life. The free grace and mercy of God are what they hope for, and what their hopes are founded on.

III. What it is that he asks of God for them, *v*. 17. He prayed that they might have more abundant consolation, and he prayed that they might be established. Comfort is a means of establishment; for the more pleasure we take in the ways of God, the more likely we shall be to persevere therein. Our establishment in the ways of God is a likely means in order to comfort. If we are halting and faltering in our duty, no wonder if we are strangers to the pleasures and joys of religion. We must be established in every good word and work. Christ must be honoured by our good works and good words.

CHAPTER 3

The apostle had prayed earnestly for the Thessalonians, and now he desires their prayers, ver. 1–5. Commands and directions for correcting some things amiss among them, ver. 6–15, and a conclusion with benedictions and prayers, ver. 16–18.

Verses 1–5

I. The apostle desires the prayers of his friends, *v*. 1. He always remembered them in his prayers, and would not have them forget him and his fellow-labourers. This is one way by which the communion of saints is kept up, not only by their praying together but by their praying for one another when they are absent one from another. What they are desired to pray for: 1. For the success of the gospel ministry, *v*. 1. He desired that the word of the Lord might run (so it is in the original), that it might get ground, and not only go forward, but go apace. We should pray that the gospel may have free course to the hearts and the consciences of men, that it may be glorified in the conversion of sinners. God will glorify the gospel, and so will glorify his own name. 2. For the safety of gospel ministers. He asks their prayers, not for preferment, but for preservation, *v*. 2. Those who are enemies to the preaching of the gospel are unreasonable and wicked men. There is the greatest absurdity in the world, as well as impiety. Godly and faithful ministers are as the standard-bearers, who are most struck at. Many do not believe the gospel; no wonder if such are restless in their endeavours to oppose the gospel, and disgrace the ministers of the word; and too many have not common faith or honesty; there is no confidence that we can safely put in them, and we should pray to be delivered from those who have no conscience nor honour.

II. He encourages them to trust in God.

1. What the good is which we may expect from the grace of God—establishment, and preservation from evil. We stand no longer than God holds us up. We have as much need of the grace of God for our perseverance to the end as for the beginning of the good work.

2. What encouragement we have to depend upon the grace of God. He is faithful to his promises. When once the promise is made, performance is sure and certain. He is a faithful God and a faithful friend. Let it be our care to be true and faithful in our promises, and to the relations we stand in to this faithful God.

3. A further ground of hope that God would do this for them, *v*. 4. The apostle had this confidence in them, and this was founded upon his confidence in God; for there is otherwise no confidence in man.

III. He makes a short prayer for them, *v*. 5, that their hearts may be brought into the love of God. This is not only most reasonable in order to our happiness, but is our happiness itself. We can never attain to this unless God by his grace direct our hearts aright, for our love is apt to go astray after other things. We must wait for Christ, which supposes our faith in him, that we believe he came once in flesh and will come again in glory. We *have need of patience*, patience for Christ's sake and after Christ's example.

Verses 6–15

Commands and directions to some who were faulty, correcting some things that were amiss among them. The best society of Christians may have some faulty persons among them. Perfection is not to be found on this side heaven: but evil manners beget good laws.

I. That which was amiss among the Thessalonians.

1. There were some who *walked disorderly*, *not after the tradition they received* from the apostle, *v*. 6.

2. There were among them some *idle persons and busy-bodies*, *v*. 11. It does not appear that they were gluttons or drunkards, but idle, and therefore disorderly people. It is not enough for any to say they do no hurt; for it is required of all persons that they do good. It is probable that these persons had a notion concerning the near approach of the coming of Christ, which served them for a pretence to leave off the work of their calling, and live in idleness. Industry in our particular callings as men is a duty required of us by our general calling as Christians. There were busy-bodies among them. The same persons who were idle were busy-bodies also. Most commonly those persons who have no business of their own to do, or who neglect it, busy themselves in other men's matters. If we are idle, the devil will soon find us something to do. The mind of man is a busy thing; if it be not employed in doing good, it will be doing evil.

II. The good laws which were occasioned by these evil manners.

1. Whose laws they are: they are commands of the apostles of our Lord, that is, the commands of our Lord himself, *v*. 6, 12. The authority of Christ should awe our minds to obedience, and his grace and goodness should allure us.

2. What the good laws and rules are.

(1) His commands and directions to the whole church. [1] Their behaviour towards the disorderly persons (*v*. 6). Note that man is charged with not obeying the word of God. We must have sufficient proof of his fault before we proceed further. Admonish him in a friendly manner; we must put him in mind of his sin, and of his duty. If he will not hear do not keep company with him, that ye may not learn his evil ways; for he who follows vain persons is in danger of becoming like them. Another reason is for the shaming, and so the reforming, of those that offend. Love therefore to the persons of our offending brethren should be the motive of our withdrawing from them; and even those who are under the censures of the church must not be accounted as enemies (*v*. 15). [2] Their general conduct ought to be according to the good example the apostle had given them, *v*. 7. The particular good example the apostle mentions was their diligence: "*We behaved not ourselves disorderly among you* (*v*. 7), we did not spend our time idly." They took pains in their ministry and in getting their own living, *v*. 8.

Those who preach the gospel may of right expect to live by the gospel. This is a just debt that people owe to their ministers, and the apostle had power or authority to have demanded this (*v.* 9); but he waived his right from affection to them, and that he might be an example for them to follow (*v.* 9).

(2) He commands those that lived idle lives to reform, *v.* 10. The labourer is worthy of his meat; but what is the loiterer worthy of? None should live like useless drones in the world. It was not the mere humour of the apostle, it was the command of our Lord Jesus Christ, that *with quietness we work, and eat our own bread, v.* 12. Men ought some way or other to earn their own living, otherwise they do not eat their own bread. We must study to be quiet, and do our own business. This is an excellent but rare composition, to be of an active yet quiet spirit, active in our own business and yet quiet as to other people's.

(3) He exhorts *those that did well, not* to be *weary in well-doing* (*v.* 13). You must never give over, nor tire in your work. It will be time enough to rest when you come to heaven.

Verses 16–18

The apostle's benediction and prayers for these Thessalonians.

I. That God would give them peace. Peace is the blessing pronounced or desired. This peace is desired for them always. Peace by all means: for peace is often difficult, as it is always desirable. If we have any peace that is desirable, God must give it.

II. That the presence of God might be with them. We need nothing more to make us safe and happy, nor can we desire anything better for ourselves and our friends. It is the presence of God that makes heaven to be heaven, and this will make this earth to be like heaven.

III. That the *grace of our Lord Jesus Christ might be with them.* It is through the grace of our Lord Jesus Christ that we may comfortably hope to have peace with God and enjoy the presence of God. It is this grace that is all in all to make us happy.

AN EXPOSITION, WITH PRACTICAL OBSERVATIONS, OF

THE FIRST EPISTLE OF ST. PAUL TO

TIMOTHY

Hitherto Paul's epistles were directed to churches; now follow some to particular persons: two to Timothy, one to Titus, and another to Philemon. Timothy and Titus were evangelists. Their commission and work was much the same with that of the apostles, and accordingly they were itinerants, as we find Timothy was. Timothy was first converted by Paul, and therefore he calls him his *own son in the faith.*

The scope of these two epistles is to direct Timothy how to discharge his duty as an evangelist at Ephesus, where he now was.

CHAPTER 1

After the inscription (ver. 1, 2) we have, I. The charge given to Timothy, ver. 3, 4. II. The true end of the law (ver. 5–11). III. He mentions his own call to be an apostle, ver. 12–16. IV. His doxology, ver. 17. V. A renewal of the charge to Timothy, ver. 18. And of Hymenæus and Alexander, ver. 19, 20.

Verses 1–4

I. The inscription of the epistle. His credentials were unquestionable. He had a commandment, not only from God our Saviour, but from Jesus Christ. Jesus Christ is a Christian's hope; all our hope of eternal life is built upon him. He calls Timothy his own son, because he had been an instrument of his conversion, and because he had been a son that served him. Timothy had not been wanting in the duty of a son to Paul, and Paul was not wanting in the care and tenderness of a father to him.

II. The benediction. In all the epistles to the churches the apostolic benediction is *grace and peace*; in these two epistles to Timothy and that to Titus it is *grace, mercy, and peace.* Ministers need more mercy than others. If Timothy needed the increase and continuance of it, how much more do we ministers.

III. Paul tells Timothy what was the end of his appointing him to this office. His business was to take care to fix both the ministers and the people of that church, that they do not add to the Christian doctrine, that they do not alter it, but cleave to it as it was delivered to them. In the times of the apostles there were attempts made to corrupt Christianity, otherwise this charge to Timothy might have been spared. He must not only see to it that he did not preach any other doctrine, but he must charge others that they preach it pure and uncorrupt. They will be the corrupting and ruining of religion among you, for *they minister questions rather than edifying.* That which gives occasion for doubtful disputes pulls down the church rather than builds it up. Godly edifying is the end ministers should aim at in all their discourses. Godly edifying must be in faith. It is by faith that we come to God at first, and it must be in the same way, and by the same principle of faith, that we must be edified. Ministers should avoid what will occasion disputes. Even disputes about great and necessary truths eat out the vitals of religion, which consist in practice and obedience as well as in faith.

Verses 5–11

Here the apostle shows the use of the law, and the glory of the gospel.

I. The end and uses of the law: it is intended to promote love.

1. The main scope and drift of the divine law are to engage us to the love of God and one another. Surely the gospel, which obliges us to love our enemies, to do good to those who hate us (Matt. *v.* 44), does not design to supersede a commandment the end whereof is love? Those therefore who boasted of their knowledge of the law, but used it only as a colour for the disturbance that they gave to the preaching of the gospel, defeated that which was the very end of the commandment, and that is love, love *out of a pure heart.* Our hearts must be cleansed from all sinful love; our love must arise *out of a good conscience*; a real belief of the truth of the word of God, here called a *faith unfeigned.* It is love without dissimulation: the faith that works by it must be of the like nature, genuine and sincere. When persons swerve from the great law of charity they will turn aside to vain jangling; when a man misses his end it is no wonder that every step he takes is out of the way. Jangling, especially in religion, is vain, and yet many people's religion consists of little else but vain jangling.

2. The use of the law (*v.* 8). The Jews used it unlawfully. They set it up for justification, and so used it unlawfully. Call it back to its right use and take away the abuses, for the law is still very useful as a rule of life. It is good to teach us what is sin and what is duty. It is the grace of God that changes men's hearts; but the terrors of the law may be of use to tie their hands and restrain their tongues. The law is not made primarily for the righteous, but for sinners of all sorts, whether in a greater or less measure, *v.* 9, 10.

II. He shows the glory and grace of the gospel. The glorious gospel, for so it is: much of the glory of God appears in the works of creation and providence, but much more in the gospel, where it shines in the face of Jesus Christ. Paul reckoned it a great honour put upon him, and a great favour done him, that this glorious gospel was committed to his trust.

Verses 12–17

I. Thanks to Jesus Christ for putting him into the ministry. It is Christ's work to put men into the ministry. Ministers cannot make ministers, much less can persons make themselves ministers; for it is Christ's work. Those whom he puts into the ministry he fits for it; whom he calls he qualifies. Christ gives not only ability, but fidelity, to those whom he puts into the ministry. Christ's ministers are trusty servants. A call to the ministry is a great favour.

II. He gives an account of his conversion.

1. What he was before his conversion. Frequently those who are designed for great and eminent services are left to themselves before their conversion. The greatness of sin is no bar to our acceptance with God, nor to our being employed for him, if it be truly repented of. True penitents will not be backward to

own their former condition. This good apostle often confessed what his former life had been.

2. The great favour of God to him.

(1) Because he did it ignorantly and in unbelief, he obtained mercy. What we do ignorantly is a less crime than what we do knowingly; yet a sin of ignorance is a sin. Ignorance in some cases will extenuate a crime, though it does not take it away. Unbelief is at the bottom of what sinners do ignorantly. For these reasons Paul obtained mercy.

(2) The abundant grace of Jesus Christ, v. 14, that grace of Christ which appears in his glorious gospel (v. 15). Here we have the sum of the whole gospel, *that Jesus Christ came into the world.* It is good news, worthy of all acceptation; and yet not too good to be true, for it is a faithful saying. Paul was a sinner of the first rank; so he acknowledges himself to have been. Persecutors are some of the worst of sinners: such a one Paul had been. He that elsewhere calls himself the *least of all saints* (Eph. iii. 8) here calls himself the chief of sinners. The chief of sinners may become the chief of saints. This is a faithful saying which may be depended on.

(3) The mercy which Paul found with God.

[1] For the encouragement of others to repent and believe (v. 16). It was an instance of the long-suffering of Christ that he would bear so much with one who had been so very provoking; and it was designed for a pattern to all others, that the greatest sinners might not despair of mercy with God.

[2] He mentions it to the glory of God. He could not go on with his letter without inserting a thankful acknowledgement of God's goodness to him. Those who are sensible of their obligations to the mercy and grace of God will have their hearts enlarged in his praise. When we have found God good we must not forget to pronounce him great; and his kind thoughts of us must not at all abate our high thoughts of him, but rather increase them. God's gracious dealings with us should fill us with admiration of his glorious attributes. *"To him be glory for ever and ever."*

Verses 18–20

The charge he gives to Timothy to proceed in his work with resolution, v. 18. It seems, there had been prophecies before concerning Timothy. This encouraged Paul to commit this charge to him. The ministry is a good warfare against sin and Satan. Ministers must war this good warfare diligently and courageously. The prophecies which went before concerning Timothy are a motive to stir him up to a vigorous discharge of his duty; so the good hopes that others have entertained concerning us should excite us to our duty. *Holding faith and a good conscience,* v. 19. Those that put away a good conscience will soon make shipwreck of faith; we must look to the one as well as the other. As for those who had made shipwreck of the faith, he specifies two, *Hymenæus and Alexander,* who had made a profession of the Christian religion. Paul had delivered them to Satan, had declared them to belong to the kingdom of Satan *that they might learn not to blaspheme.* God can, if he please, work by contraries: *Hymenæus and Alexander* are delivered to Satan, that they may learn not to blaspheme, when one would rather think they would learn of Satan to blaspheme the more. Let us hold faith and a good conscience, for if we once let go our hold of these we do not know where we shall stop.

CHAPTER 2

I. Of prayer, ver. 1–8. II. Of women's apparel, ver. 9, 10. III. Of their subjection, ver. 11–14. IV. A promise given for their encouragement in child-bearing, ver. 15.

Verses 1–8

I. A charge given to Christians to pray for all men in general, and particularly for all in authority. Paul does not send him any prescribed form of prayer. Paul thought it enough to give them general heads; they, having the scripture to direct them in prayer and the Spirit of prayer poured out upon them, needed not any further directions. The disciples of Christ must be praying people. There must be prayers for ourselves in the first place; this is implied here. We must also pray *for all men.* See how far the Christian religion was from being a sect, when it taught men this diffusive charity, to pray for all men. Pray for kings (v. 2); though the kings at this time were heathens, yet they must pray for them. *For kings, and all that are in authority.* We must give thanks for them, pray for their welfare and for the welfare of their kingdoms, that in the peace thereof we may have peace. He does not say, "that we may get preferments under them, grow rich, and be in honour and power under them"; no, the summit of the ambition of a good Christian is to lead a quiet and peaceable life. We cannot expect to be kept quiet and peaceable unless we keep in all godliness and honesty. Here we have our duty as Christians summed up in two words: godliness, that is, the right worshipping of God; and honesty, that is, a good conduct towards all men. These two must go together. Christians are to be men much given to prayer. In our prayers we are to have a generous concern for others as well as for ourselves; we are to pray for all men, and to give thanks for all men. Kings themselves, and those who are in authority, are to be prayed for. They want our prayers, for they have many difficulties to encounter, many snares to which their exalted stations expose them.

II. He shows God's love to mankind in general, v. 4.

1. God bears a goodwill to all mankind. There is one God (v. 5), and one only. This one *God will have all men to be saved, and to come to the knowledge of the truth.* It concerns us to get the knowledge of the truth, because that is the way to be saved.

2. There is one Mediator, and that Mediator gave himself a ransom for all. As the mercy of God extends itself to all his works, so the mediation of Christ extends to all the children of men, so that they are not now under the law as a covenant of works, but as a rule of life. They are under grace. We deserved to have died. Christ died for us. He put himself into the office of Mediator between God and man. A mediator supposes a controversy. Sin had made a quarrel between us and God. Jesus Christ is a Mediator who undertakes to make peace, to bring God and man together. He is a ransom that *was to be testified in due time.* This doctrine of Christ's mediation Paul was entrusted to preach to every creature. He was commissioned particularly to preach to the Gentiles, faithfully and truly. God has a goodwill to the salvation of all; so that it is not so much the want of a will in God to save them as it is a want of will in themselves to be saved in God's way. Those who are saved must come to the knowledge of the truth. Without knowledge the heart cannot be good; if we do not know the truth, we cannot be ruled by it. Paul was ordained a minister, to declare this to the Gentiles, that Christ is the one Mediator between God and men, who gave himself a ransom for all. Ministers must preach the truth; they are, like our apostle, to preach in faith and verity, and they must also be faithful and trusty.

III. A direction how to pray, v. 8. Men must pray everywhere: no place is amiss for prayer, no place more acceptable to God than another. *Lifting up holy hands,* or pure hands, pure from the pollution of sin.

We must pray in charity: *Without wrath*, or malice, or anger at any person. We must pray in faith *without doubting*, or as some read it, *without disputing*.

Verses 9–15

I. Women who profess the Christian religion should be modest, sober, silent, and submissive. They must be very modest in their apparel (you may read the vanity of a person's mind in the gaiety and gaudiness of his habit), because they have better ornaments with which they should *adorn themselves*. Good works are the best ornament. Those that profess godliness should, in their dress, as well as other things, act as becomes their profession. Women must learn the principles of their religion, learn Christ, learn the scriptures. They must be silent, submissive, and not usurp authority. *Adam was first formed, then Eve* out of him. And as she was last in the creation, so she was first in the transgression. A word of comfort (*v.* 15) that those who continue in sobriety shall be *saved in child-bearing*, or *with* child-bearing. The sentence which they are under for sin shall be no bar to their acceptance with Christ.

II. The extensiveness of the rules of Christianity; they reach not only to men, but to women. Women are to profess godliness as well as men, and, to their honour be it spoken, many of them were eminent professors of Christianity in the days of the apostles, as the book of Acts will inform us. The best ornaments for professors of godliness are good works. Women must be learners, and are not allowed to be public teachers in the church; the woman must not usurp authority over the man, but is to be in silence. But, notwithstanding this prohibition, good women ought to teach their children at home the principles of religion. Timothy from a child had known the holy scriptures; and who should teach him but his mother and grandmother? Two very good reasons given for the man's authority over the woman, and her subjection to the man, *v.* 13, 14. Here is much for her support and encouragement, *v.* 15. Though in sorrow, yet she shall bring forth, and be a living mother of living children.

CHAPTER 3

I. The qualification of a person to be admitted to the office of a bishop, ver. 1–7. II. The qualifications of deacons (ver. 8–10), and of their wives (ver. 11), again of the deacons, ver. 12, 13. III. The reasons of his writing to Timothy, ver. 14, to the end.

Verses 1–7

Timothy, we suppose, was an evangelist who was left at Ephesus. They were very loth to part with Paul, especially because he told them they should *see his face no more* (Acts xx. 38), and therefore Paul left Timothy with them.

I. The ministry is a work. The office of a scripture-bishop is an office of divine appointment, and not of human invention. This office of a Christian bishop is a work which requires diligence and application. Ministers should always look more to their work than to the honour and advantage of their office. It is a good work, a work of the greatest importance. The ministry is conversant about no lower concerns than the life and happiness of immortal souls. There ought to be an earnest desire of the office in those who would be put into it.

II. The workman must be duly qualified. 1. A minister must be blameless, he must not lie under any scandal. 2. He must be the husband of one wife. 3. He must be vigilant and watchful against Satan. 4. He must be sober, temperate, moderate in all his actions, and in the use of all creature-comforts. 5. He must be of good behaviour, and not light, vain, and frothy. 6. He must be given to hospitality. 7. Apt to teach, both able and willing to communicate to others the knowledge which God has given him. 8. No drunkard. 9. No striker; one who is not quarrelsome, but does everything with mildness, love, and gentleness. 10. One who is not greedy of filthy lucre, who is dead to the wealth of this world, lives above it. 11. He must be patient, and not a brawler, of a mild disposition. As not a striker with his hands, so not a brawler with his tongue. 12. Not covetous. Covetousness is bad in any, but it is worst in a minister. 13. He must be one who keeps his family in good order. The families of ministers ought to be examples of good to all other families.—*With all gravity*. The best way to keep inferiors in subjection, is to be grave with them. Not having his children in subjection with all austerity, but with all gravity. 14. He must not be a novice, who knows no more of religion than the surface of it, for such a one is apt to be lifted up with pride: the more ignorant men are the more proud they are. We should take heed of pride, because it is a sin that turned angels into devils. 15. He must be of good reputation among his neighbours.

III. What great reason we have to cry out, as Paul does, *Who is sufficient for these things?* (2 Cor. ii. 16). What holy watchfulness is necessary in this work! Have not the most faithful and concientious ministers just reason to complain against themselves? How far short do the best come of what they should be and what they should do! Yet let those bless God, and be thankful, whom the Lord has enabled, and counted faithful. He will fit us for our work and reward our faithfulness with a crown of glory.

Verses 8–13

The character of deacons. They must be *grave*. Gravity becomes all Christians, but especially those who are in office in the church. *Not doubled-tongued;* a double tongue comes from a double heart; flatterers and slanderers are double-tongued. *Not given to much wine;* for this opens the door to many temptations. *Not greedy of filthy lucre;* this would especially be bad in the deacons, who were entrusted with the church's money, *v.* 9. If we keep a pure conscience, this will preserve in our souls the mystery of faith, *v.* 10. The soundness of their judgments, their zeal for Christ, and the blamelessness of their conversation, must be proved. Their wives likewise must have a good character (*v.* 11). All who are related to ministers must double their care to walk as becomes the gospel of Christ, lest the ministry be blamed. As he said before of the bishops or ministers, so here of the deacons, they must be *the husband of one wife;* they must *rule their children and their own houses well:* the families of deacons should be examples to other families. The reason why the deacons must be thus qualified (*v.* 13). In the primitive church there were but two orders of ministers or officers, *bishops* and *deacons*. The design of the deacon's office was to mind the temporal concerns of the church, such as the salaries of the ministers and providing for the poor. Integrity and uprightness in an inferior office are the way to be preferred to a higher station in the church: *They purchase to themselves a good degree.* This will also give a man great boldness in the faith, whereas a want of integrity and uprightness will make a man timorous.

Verses 14–16

He hoped shortly to come to him, to give him further directions and assistance in his work, and he therefore wrote the more briefly to him. But he wrote *lest he should tarry long, that* Timothy *might know how to behave himself in the house of God.*

I. Ministers ought to behave themselves well: their office binds them to their good behaviour, for any behaviour will not do in this case. The church is the house of God, he dwells there.

II. It is the great support of the church that it is the church of the living *God*.

1. It is *the pillar and ground of truth*. (1) The church itself is the pillar and ground of truth. The church holds forth the scripture and the doctrine of Christ, as the pillar to which a proclamation is affixed holds forth the proclamation. (2) Others understand it of Timothy. He as an evangelist, he and other faithful ministers, are the pillars and ground of truth; it is their business to maintain the truths of Christ in the church. Let us be diligent and impartial in our own enquiries after truth; let us buy the truth at any rate, and not think much of any pains to discover it. Let us be careful to keep and preserve it. Let us take care to publish it.

2. But what is the truth which the churches and ministers are the pillars and grounds of? He tells us (*v*. 16).

(1) Christianity is a mystery that could not have been found out by reason or the light of nature, because it is above reason, though not contrary thereto. It is a mystery of godliness, and herein it exceeds all the mysteries of the Gentiles.

(2) It is Christ. [1] He is God manifest in the flesh. [2] He is *justified in the Spirit*. Whereas he was reproached as a sinner, and put to death as a malefactor, being raised again, he was justified in the Spirit. [3] He was *seen of angels*. Angels ministered to him, for he is the Lord of angels. [4] He is *preached unto the Gentiles*. This is a great part of the mystery of godliness, that Christ was offered to the Gentiles a Redeemer and Saviour. [5] He was *believed on in the world*. Who would have thought that the world, which lay in wickedness, would believe in the Son of God, would take him to be their Saviour who was himself crucified at Jerusalem? [6] He was *received up into glory*. It is not only his ascension that is meant, but his sitting at the right hand of God, where he ever lives. He who was manifest in flesh was God, really and truly God. This makes it to be a mystery. Godliness is a mystery in all its parts and branches. It being a great mystery, we should rather humbly adore it, than curiously pry into it.

CHAPTER 4

I. A dreadful apostasy, ver. 1–3. II. He treats of Christian liberty, ver. 4, 5. III. He gives Timothy divers directions, ver. 6, to the end.

Verses 1–5

A prophecy of the apostasy of the latter times.

I. The prophecies concerning antichrist, as well as the prophecies concerning Christ, came from the Spirit. *Some shall depart from the faith*, an apostasy from the faith. Some, not all; for in the worst of times God will have a remnant.

1. One of the great instances of the apostasy, giving heed to doctrines of demons, or concerning demons.

2. The instruments of promoting and propagating this apostasy and delusion. It will be done by hypocrisy of those that speak lies, *v*. 2, who have *their consciences seared with a red-hot iron*, who are perfectly lost to the very first principles of virtue and moral honesty. Another part of their character is that they forbid to marry, and that they command *to abstain from meats*, and place religion in such abstinence at certain times and seasons.

3. The apostasy of the latter times should not surprise us, because it was expressly foretold by the Spirit. The Spirit speaks expressly, but the oracles of the heathen were always doubtful and uncertain. In such general apostasies all are not carried away, but only some. Men must be hardened, and their consciences seared, before they can depart from the faith, and draw in others to side with them.

II. The apostle takes occasion to lay down the doctrine of the Christian liberty,—that, whereas under the law there was a distinction of meats between clean and unclean, all this is now taken away. We are to look upon our food as that which God has created; we have it from him, and therefore must use it for him. We must not refuse the gifts of God's bounty, nor be scrupulous in making differences where God has made none; but receive them, and be thankful, *v*. 4. God's good creatures are then good, and doubly sweet to us, when they are received with thanksgiving, *v*. 5. It is a desirable thing to have a sanctified use of our creature-comforts. Now they are sanctified to us: By the word of God. By prayer, which blesses our meat to us. Every creature is God's, for he made all. Every creature of God is good. The blessing of God makes every creature nourishing to us, and therefore nothing ought to be refused. We ought therefore to sanctify the creatures we receive by prayer.

Verses 6–16

The apostles reckoned it a main part of their work to put their hearers in remembrance; for we are apt to forget, and slow to learn and remember, the things of God. The best way for ministers to grow in knowledge and faith is to put the brethren in remembrance; while we teach others, we teach ourselves.

I. Godliness is here pressed upon him and others, *v*, 7, 8. Those who would be godly must exercise themselves unto godliness; it requires a constant exercise. What will it avail us to mortify the body if we do not mortify sin? There is a great deal to be got by godliness. The promises made to godly people relate to the life that now is, but especially they relate to the life that is to come. If godly people have but little of the good things of the life that now is, yet it shall be made up to them in the good things of the life that is to come. It is not enough that we refuse profane and old wives' fables, but we must exercise ourselves to godliness.

II. The encouragement which we have to proceed in the ways of godliness (*v*. 8). Will the profit balance the loss? Here is another of Paul's faithful sayings, worthy of all acceptation—that all our labours and losses in the service of God will be abundantly recompenced, so that though we lose for Christ we shall not lose by him, *v*. 10.

1. Toil and trouble are to be expected by us in this world, not only as men, but as saints.

2. Those who labour and suffer reproach in the service of God may depend upon the living God that they shall not lose by it. Let this encourage them. He is *the Saviour of all men*. Now, if he be thus the Saviour of all men, we may hence infer that much more he will be the rewarder of those who seek and serve him. The salvation he has in store for those that believe is sufficient to recompence them for all their services and sufferings. The life of a Christian is a life of labour and suffering: *We labour and suffer*. The best we can expect to suffer in the present life is reproach for our well-doing, for our work of faith and labour of love.

III. An exhortation to Timothy,

1. To *command and teach these things* that he had now been teaching him.

2. To conduct himself with that gravity and prudence which might gain him respect, notwithstanding his youth. Men's youth will not be despised if they do not by youthful vanities and follies make themselves despicable; and this men may do who are old, who may therefore thank themselves if they be despised.

3. To confirm his doctrine by a good example. Those who teach by their doctrine must teach by their

life, else they pull down with one hand what they build up with the other.

4. He charges him to study hard, *v.* 13. Though Timothy had extraordinary gifts, yet he must use ordinary means. Or it may be meant of the public reading of the scriptures; he must *read and exhort.* He must teach them both what to do and what to believe. The best way for ministers to avoid being despised is to teach and practise the things that are given them in charge. Those ministers that are the best accomplished for their work must yet mind their studies, and they must mind also their work.

5. He charges him to beware of negligence, *v.* 14. The gifts of God will wither if they be neglected. Here see the scripture-way of ordination: it was by the laying on of hands, and the laying on of the hands of the presbytery. The office of the ministry is a gift, it is the gift of Christ, and this was a very kind gift to his church. Ministers ought not to neglect the gift bestowed upon them, whether the office of the ministry or the qualifications for that office.

6. Having this work committed to him, he must *give himself wholly* to it, and make it appear that he improved in knowledge. Ministers are to be much in meditation. They are to meditate on the great trust committed to them. Ministers must be wholly in these things. By this means their profiting will appear in all things.

7. He presses it upon him to be very cautious. This will be the way to *save thyself, and those that hear thee.* "Save thyself in the first place, so shalt thou be instrumental to save those that hear thee." The best way to answer both these ends is to take heed to ourselves.

CHAPTER 5

Here the apostle, I. Directs Timothy how to reprove, ver. 1, 2. II. Adverts to widows, ver. 3–16. III. To elders, ver. 17–19. IV. Treats of public reproof, ver. 20. V. Gives a solemn charge concerning ordinations, ver. 21, 22. VI. Refers to his health (ver. 23), and states men's sins to be very different in their effects, ver. 24, 25.

Verses 1, 2

Ministers are reprovers by office; it is a part, though the least pleasing part, of their office. Be very tender in rebuking elders. Respect must be had to the dignity of their years and place. The younger must be rebuked as brethren, with love and tenderness. There is need of a great deal of meekness in reproving those who deserve reproof. The elder women must be reproved, as mothers. The younger women must be reproved, but reproved as *sisters, with all purity.*

Verses 3–16

The general rule is to *honour widows that are widows indeed,* to maintain them, to relieve them with respect and tenderness.

I. She is to be reckoned a widow indeed, who, being *desolate, trusteth in God, v.* 5, 6. Those who trust in God must *continue in prayer.* But she is not a widow indeed *that lives in pleasure* (*v.* 6). A jovial widow is not a widow indeed. *She that lives in pleasure is dead while she lives,* is no living member of the church, but as a carcase in it, or a mortified member. They are in the world to no purpose, buried alive as to the great ends of living.

II. The church should not be charged with the maintenance of those widows who had relations of their own that were able to maintain them (*v.* 4). So *v.* 16. The respect of children to their parents, with their care of them, is fitly called piety. Children can never sufficiently requite their parents for the care they have taken of them, but they must endeavour

to do it. He speaks of this again (*v.* 8). If they spend that upon their lusts which should maintain their families, they have denied the faith (*v.* 16). There should be prudence in the choice of the objects of charity, that it may not be thrown away upon those who are not properly so, that there may be the more for those who are real objects of charity.

III. Directions concerning the characters of the widows that were to receive the church's charity. Particular care ought to be taken to relieve those who, when they had wherewithal, were ready to every good work. Those who would find mercy when they are in distress must show mercy when they are in prosperity.

IV. Take heed of admitting into the number those who are likely to be no credit to them (*v.* 11): *The younger widows refuse;* they will be weary of living by rule, as they must do; so they *will marry, and cast off their first faith.* The apostle here advises the younger widows to marry (*v.* 14). It is seldom that those who are idle are idle only; they learn to make mischief among neighbours, and sow discord among brethren. If housekeepers do not mind their business, but are tattlers, they give occasion to the adversaries of Christianity to reproach the Christian name. In the primitive church there was care taken of poor widows, and the churches of Christ in these days should follow so good an example. Great care is to be taken that those share in the public bounty who most want it and best deserve it. The credit of religion, and the reputation of Christian churches, are very much concerned in the character and behaviour of those that receive alms of the church. Christianity obliges its professors to relieve their indigent friends. Rich people should be ashamed to burden the church with their poor relations.

Verses 17–25

I. Concerning the supporting of ministers. Care must be taken that they be honourably maintained (*v.* 17). They had not, in the primitive church, one to preach to them and another to rule them, but ruling and teaching were performed by the same persons. The work of ministers consists principally in two things: ruling well and labouring in the word and doctrine. Those who were not idle, but laborious in this work, were worthy of double honour. *Thou shalt not muzzle the ox that treads out the corn.* Does God take care for oxen, and will he not take care of his own servants? The ox only treads out the corn of which they make the bread that perishes; but ministers break the bread of life which endures for ever. Those who would have ministers starved, or not comfortably provided for, God will require it of them another day.

II. Concerning the accusation of ministers (*v.* 19). There must be an accusation; it must not be a flying uncertain report. This accusation is not to be received unless supported by two or three credible witnesses; and the accusation must be received before them, that is, the accused must have the accusers face to face. Great care should be taken that the thing alleged against him be well proved, "but (*v.* 20) *those that sin rebuke before all;* that the plaster may be as wide as the wound, and that those who are in danger of sinning by the example of their fall may take warning by the rebuke given them for it, *that others also may fear.*" Public rebuke is designed for the good of others as well as for the good of the party rebuked.

III. Concerning the ordination of ministers (*v.* 22), it seems to be meant of the ordaining of men to the office of the ministry. Some understand it of absolution: "Be not too hasty in laying hands on any." Those who are rash will make themselves partakers in other men's sins.

IV. Concerning absolution, to which *v.* 24, 25, seem to refer. Some men's sins are so plain and obvious that there is no dispute concerning the bringing of them under the censures of the church.— *Others they follow after;* their wickedness does not presently appear, nor till after a due search has been made concerning it. So also, as to the evidences of repentance. There are secret, and there are open sins. Some are humbled and brought to repentance while it is quite otherwise with others. The incorrigible cannot be hid.

V. Concerning Timothy himself. A charge to him to be careful of his office, *v.* 21. He charges him to guard against partiality. Ministers must give an account to God and the Lord Jesus Christ, and woe to them if they have been partial in their ministrations. To take care of his health Paul advises him to use wine for the helping of his stomach and the recruiting of his nature. It is the will of God that people should take all due care of their bodies, to use them so that they may be most fit and helpful to us in the service of God. Wine should be used as a help, and not a hindrance, to our work and usefulness.

CHAPTER 6

I. He treats of the duty of servants, ver. 1, 2. II. Of false teachers, ver. 3–5. III. Of godliness and covetousness, ver. 6–10. IV. What Timothy was to flee, and what to follow, ver. 11, 12. V. A solemn charge, ver. 13–16. VI. A charge for the rich, ver. 17–19. And lastly, A charge to Timothy, ver. 20, 21.

Verses 1–5

I. Here is the duty of servants. They are yoked to work, not to be idle. They must respect their masters, they must count them worthy of all that honour which was fit for them to receive. If servants that embraced the Christian religion should grow disobedient to their masters, the doctrine of Christ would be reflected on for their sakes. If the professors of religion misbehave themselves, *the name of God and his doctrine* are in danger of being blasphemed. And this is a good reason why we should all conduct ourselves well. Or suppose the master were a Christian, and a believer, and the servant a believer too? They must think themselves the more obliged to serve them because the faith and love that bespeak men Christians oblige them to do good. Believing masters and servants are brethren, and partakers of the benefit.

II. Paul here warns Timothy to withdraw from those who corrupted the doctrine of Christ. *If any man teach otherwise* (*v.* 3–5). We are not required to consent to any words as wholesome words except the words of our Lord Jesus Christ. But he that does not consent to the words of Christ *is proud* (*v.* 4), knowing nothing. Commonly those are most proud who know least. Those who fall off from the plain practical doctrines of Christianity fall in with controversies. When men are not content with the words of the Lord Jesus Christ, but will frame notions of their own and impose them, they sow the seeds of all mischief in the church (*v.* 5); disputes that are all subtlety, and no solidity. Men of corrupt minds are *destitute of the truth.* The words of our Lord Jesus Christ are wholesome words, they are the fittest to prevent or heal the church's wounds, as well as to heal a wounded conscience. When men leave the wholesome words of our Lord Jesus Christ, they will never agree in other words, either of their own or other men's invention, but will perpetually wrangle and quarrel about them. Such persons as are given to perverse disputings appear to be men of corrupt minds, and destitute of the truth; especially such as act in this manner for the sake of gain, which is all their godliness. Christians will withdraw themselves from such.

Verses 6–12

I. The excellency of contentment and the evil of covetousness.

1. The excellency of contentment, *v.* 6–8. Though Christianity is the worst trade, it is the best calling in the world. Those that make a trade of it, merely to serve their turn for this world, will find it a sorry trade; but those that mind it as their calling, and make a business of it, will find it a gainful calling.

(1) The truth he lays down is that *godliness with contentment is great gain.* Godliness is itself great gain, and, wherever there is true godliness, there will be contentment. Christian contentment is great gain. He that is godly is sure to be happy in another world; and if withal he do by contentment accommodate himself to his condition in this world he has enough. It is not like the little gain of worldlings, who are so fond of a little worldly advantage. Godliness is ever accompanied with contentment. All truly godly people have learned with Paul, in whatever state they are, to be therewith content.

(2) The reason he gives for it, *v.* 7. We can challenge nothing as a debt that is due to us, for we came naked into the world. Whatever we have had since, we are obliged to the providence of God for it. We cannot be poorer than when we came into this world, and yet then we were provided for; therefore let us trust in God for the remaining part of our pilgrimage. We shall carry nothing with us out of this world. Why should we not be content with a little, because, how much soever we have, we must leave it behind us?

(3) Hence he infers, *v.* 8. If God give us the necessary supports of life, we ought to be content therewith. What will worldlings do when death shall strip them of their happiness and portion, and they must take an everlasting farewell of all these things, on which they have so much doted? The necessaries of life are the bounds of a true Christian's desire. A few comforts of this life, will serve him, and these he may hope to enjoy.

2. The evil of covetousness *v.* 9. It is not said, those that are rich, but those that will be rich, that place their happiness in worldly wealth. When the devil sees which way their lusts carry them, he will soon bait his hook accordingly.

(1) Some will be rich; they are resolved upon it. Such will not be safe nor innocent. Worldly lusts are foolish and hurtful, for they drown men in destruction and perdition.

(2) The apostle affirms that *the love of money is the root of all evil, v.* 10. People may have money, and yet not love it; but, if they love it inordinately, it will push them on to all evil. Covetous persons will quit the faith, if that be the way to get money. Those that depart from God do but treasure up sorrows for themselves.

II. Hence he takes occasion to caution Timothy. He addresses himself to him as *a man of God.* Ministers are men of God, and ought to conduct themselves accordingly. He charges Timothy to take heed of the love of money. It ill becomes men of God to set their hearts upon the things of this world; men of God should be taken up with the things of God. To arm him against the love of the world, he directs him to follow that which is good. It is not enough that men of God flee these things, but they must follow after what is directly contrary thereto. What excellent persons are men of God who follow after righteousness! They are the excellent of the earth, they should be approved of men. He exhorts him to do the part of a soldier. Those who will get to heaven must fight their way thither. It is a good fight, it is a good cause, and it will have a good issue. It is the fight of faith. Eternal life is the crown proposed to us. This we must lay hold on, as those that are afraid of coming short of it and losing it. Lay hold, and take heed of losing your hold.

Verses 13–21

I. He gives him a solemn charge. He charges him as he will answer it at the great day to that God whose eyes are upon us all, who sees what we are and what we do. This should quicken us to the service of God that we serve a God who quickens all things. He charges him before Christ Jesus. Christ died not only as a sacrifice, but as a martyr; and he witnessed a good confession when he was arraigned before Pilate. That good confession of his before Pilate, *My kingdom is not of this world*, should be effectual to draw off all his followers from the love of this world.

II. He reminds him of the confession that he himself had made, *v.* 12. The obligation of that was still upon him, and he must live up to that.

III. He reminds him of Christ's second coming. The Lord Jesus Christ will appear, and it will be a glorious appearing. Ministers should have an eye to this appearing of the Lord Jesus Christ, and, till his appearing, they are to keep this commandment without spot, unrebukable. The appearing of Christ is certain, but it is not for us to know the time and season of it. Let this suffice us, that in time he will show it.

1. Concerning Christ and God the Father the apostle here speaks great things. God is the only Potentate; the powers of earthly princes are all derived from him. He is the blessed and the only Potentate, infinitely happy. He only has immortality. He dwells in inaccessible light. No man can get to heaven but those whom he is pleased to bring thither, and admit into his kingdom. He is invisible. It is impossible that mortal eyes should bear the brightness of the divine glory. No man can see God and live.

2. He concludes with a doxology. What an evil is sin when committed against such a God! What are we then, that the blessed God, the King of kings and Lord of lords, should seek after us? Blessed are those who are admitted to dwell with this great and blessed Potentate.

IV. The apostle adds a lesson for rich people, *v.* 17–19.

1. Timothy must charge those that are rich to beware of the temptations, and improve the opportunities of their prosperous estate. He must caution them to take heed of pride. He must caution them against vain confidence in their wealth. Nothing is more uncertain than the wealth of this world; many have had much of it one day and been stripped of all the next. Those who are rich must see God giving them their riches, and giving them to enjoy them richly; for many have riches, but enjoy them poorly, not having a heart to use them. He must charge them to do good with what they have. Those are truly rich who are rich in good works. He must charge them to think of another world, and prepare for that which is to come by works of charity.

2. Ministers must not be afraid of the rich. They must caution them against pride, and vain confidence in their riches. A lesson for ministers in the charge given to Timothy: *Keep that which is committed to thy trust.* Every minister is a trustee. The truths of God, the ordinances of God, keep these. Keep close to the written word, for that is committed to our trust. Some who have been very proud of their learning, their *science, which is falsely so called,* have by that been drawn away from the faith of Christ, which is a good reason why we should keep to the plain word of the gospel. *O Timothy, keep that which is committed to thy trust!* as if he had said, "I cannot conclude without charging thee again; whatever thou doest, be sure to keep this trust, for it is too great a trust to be betrayed." That science which opposes the truth of the gospel is falsely so called. Those who are for advancing reason above faith are in danger of leaving faith.

V. Our apostle concludes with a solemn prayer and benediction. Grace is an earnest, yea, a beginning, of glory; for, wherever God gives grace, he will give glory. Grace be with you all. Amen.

AN EXPOSITION, WITH PRACTICAL OBSERVATIONS, OF

THE SECOND EPISTLE OF ST. PAUL TO

TIMOTHY

This second epistle Paul wrote to Timothy from Rome, when he was a prisoner there and in danger of his life; *I am now ready to be offered, and the time of my departure is at hand,* ch. iv. 6. He had been brought before the emperor Nero, which he calls *his first answer, when no man stood with him, but all men forsook him,* ch. iv. 16. And interpreters agree that this was the last epistle he wrote. Where Timothy now was is not certain.

CHAPTER 1

After the introduction (ver. 1, 2) we have, I. Paul's sincere love to Timothy, ver. 3–5. II. Divers exhortations given to him, ver. 6–14. III. He speaks of Phygellus and Hermogenes, with others, and closes with Onesiphorus, ver. 15, to the end.

Verses 1–5

I. The inscription of the epistle. The gospel is the promise of life in Christ Jesus; life is the end, and Christ the way. Paul was an apostle of Jesus Christ by the will of God; his commission to be an apostle was not by the will of man. God called him to be an apostle. We have the promise of life. This, as well as all other promises, is in and through Jesus Christ. The grace, mercy, and peace, which Timothy wanted, comes from God the Father and Christ Jesus our Lord. The best want these blessings, and they are the best we can ask for our dearly-beloved friends.

II. Paul's thanksgiving to God for Timothy's faith and holiness. Paul was much in prayer, he prayed night and day. Prayer was his constant business, and he never forgot his friends in his prayers, as we often do. It was a comfort to him that he was of the seed of those that served God; as likewise that he had served him with a pure conscience. Timothy was sorry to part with Paul, he wept at parting, and therefore Paul desired to see him again, because he had perceived by that what a true affection he had for him. He thanks God that Timothy kept up the religion of his ancestors, v. 5. It is a comfortable thing when children imitate the faith and holiness of their godly parents, and tread in their steps. The faith that dwells in real believers is unfeigned; it is a faith that will stand the trial, and it dwells in them as a living principle. It was the matter of Paul's thanksgiving that Timothy inherited the faith of his mother Eunice and his grandmother Lois.

Verses 6–14

Exhortation and excitation of Timothy to his duty (v. 6). The best men need remembrancers.

I. Stir up the gift that is in them as fire under the embers. Use gifts, and have gifts. He must take all opportunities to use these gifts, for that is the best way of increasing them. The great hindrance of usefulness in the increase of our gifts is slavish fear. Paul therefore warns Timothy against this, v. 7. God hath delivered us from the spirit of fear, and hath given us the spirit *of power, and of love, and of a sound mind.* The spirit of power, or of courage and resolution; the spirit of love to God which will set us above the fear of man, and the spirit of a sound mind, or quietness of mind, for we are oftentimes discouraged in our work by the creatures of our own imagination, which a sober, thinking mind would obviate.

II. He exhorts him to count upon afflictions, and get ready for them. Be not thou ashamed of the gospel.

1. We must not be ashamed of those who are suffering for the gospel of Christ. Timothy must not be ashamed of good old Paul, though he was now in bonds. The gospel is the testimony of our Lord; in and by this he bears testimony of himself to us, and by professing our adherence to it we bear testimony of him and for him. Paul was the Lord's prisoner. For his sake he was bound with a chain. If we are ashamed of either now, Christ will be ashamed of us hereafter. "Expect afflictions for the gospel's sake, be willing to take thy lot with the suffering saints in this world. *Be partaker of the afflictions of the gospel.*"

2. He takes notice what great things God has done for us by the gospel, v. 9, 10.

(1) The nature of that gospel and the glorious designs of it. The gospel aims at our salvation: and we must not think much to suffer for that which we hope to be saved by. It is designed for our sanctification. All who shall be saved hereafter are sanctified now. Wherever the call of the gospel is an effectual call, it is found to be a holy call. The origin of it is the free grace and eternal purpose of God in Christ Jesus. If we had merited it, it had been hard to suffer for it; but our salvation by it is of free grace, and therefore we must not think much to suffer for it. *In Christ Jesus,* for all the gifts that come from God to sinful man come in and through Christ Jesus. The gospel is the manifestation of this purpose and grace. Did Jesus Christ suffer for it, and shall we think much to suffer for it? By the gospel of Christ death is abolished. Death once an enemy has become a friend; it is the gate by which we pass out of a troublesome, sinful world, into a world of perfect peace and purity. Death does not triumph over those who believe the gospel, but they triumph over it. He has *brought life and immortality to light by the gospel.* He has brought it to light, not only set it before us, but offered it to us, by the gospel.

(2) Consider the example of blessed Paul, v. 11, 12. He was appointed to preach the gospel, and particularly appointed to teach the Gentiles. He thought it a cause worth suffering for, and why should not Timothy think so too? No man needs to be afraid nor ashamed to suffer for the cause of the gospel. Good men often suffer many things for the best cause in the world. They need not be ashamed, the cause will bear them out. Those who trust in Christ know whom they have trusted. What must we commit to Christ? The salvation of our souls, and their preservation to the heavenly kingdom; and what we so commit to him he will keep. There is a day coming when we must give an account of our souls: now, if by an active obedient faith we commit it to Jesus Christ, we may be sure he is able to keep it.

III. He exhorts him to *hold fast the form of sound words,* v. 13. Adhere to it in opposition to all heresies and false doctrine. But how must it be held fast? Faith and love must go together; it is not enough to believe the sound words, but we must love them, believe their truth and love their goodness. It must be faith and love fastening upon Jesus Christ. *Of hearing words*, so it may read; there is a healing virtue in the word of God. To the same purport is *v.* 14. That good thing was the form of sound words, the Christian doctrine, which was committed to Timothy in his baptism, and in his ordination. The Christian doctrine is a trust committed to us. It is a good thing, of unspeakable value in itself, and which will be of unspeakable advantage to us. It is committed to us to be preserved pure and entire, and to be transmitted to those who shall come after us. Even those who are ever so well taught cannot keep what they have learned, any more than they could at first learn it, without the assistance of the Holy Spirit. We must not think to keep it by our own strength, but keep it by the Holy Ghost. The assistance and indwelling of the Holy Ghost do not exclude men's endeavours, but they very well consist together.

Verses 15–18

I. He mentions the apostasy of many from the doctrine of Christ, *v.* 15. He does not say that they had turned away from the doctrine of Christ, but they had turned away from him.

II. He mentions the constancy of Onesiphorus, *v.* 16. He often refreshed him and he was not ashamed of his chains. When Onesiphorus was at Rome he took care to seek Paul out, *v.* 17. A good man will seek opportunities of doing good. At Ephesus he had ministered to him, and been very kind to him. How Paul returns his kindness, *v.* 16–18. He repays him with his prayers.

III. He prays for Onesiphorus himself, as well as for his house: *That he may find mercy in that day*, in the day of death and of judgment. We need desire no more to make us happy than to find mercy of the Lord in that day. If you would have mercy then, you must seek for it now of the Lord. The best thing we can ask, either for ourselves or our friends, is that the Lord will grant to them that they may find mercy of the Lord in that day.

CHAPTER 2

I. He encourages him in his work, showing him whence he must fetch help, ver. 1. II. He must take care of a succession in the ministry, ver. 2. III. He exhorts him to constancy and perseverance in this work, considering what would be the end of all his suffering, &c., ver. 3–15. IV. He must shun profane and vain babblings (ver. 16–18). V. He speaks of the foundation of God, which standeth sure, ver. 19–21. VI. What he is to avoid and what to do, ver. 22, to the end.

Verses 1–7

Paul encourages Timothy to constancy and perseverance in his work, *v.* 1. Those who have work to do for God must strengthen themselves for it. Where there is the truth of grace there must be a labouring after the strength of grace. We have need to grow stronger and stronger in that which is good. Or it may be understood in opposition to our being strong in our own strength: "Be strong, not confiding in thy own sufficiency, but in the grace that is in Jesus Christ." There is grace enough in him for all of us. We must be strong in this grace; not in ourselves, or in the grace we have already received, but in the grace that is in him.

I. Timothy must count upon sufferings, even unto blood, and therefore he must train up others to succeed him in the ministry of the gospel, *v.* 2. He must lodge the gospel as a trust in their hands, and so commit to them the things which he had heard. Two things he must have an eye to in ordaining ministers: Their fidelity or integrity, and also their ministerial ability. They must not only be knowing themselves, but be apt to teach.

II. He must *endure hardness* (*v.* 3). All Christians, but especially ministers, *are soldiers of Jesus Christ*. The soldiers of Jesus Christ must approve themselves good soldiers, faithful to their captain, resolute in his cause. Those who would approve themselves good soldiers of Jesus Christ must endure hardness; we must count upon it in this world, and bear it patiently when it comes.

III He must not entangle himself in the affairs of this world, *v* 4. If we have given up ourselves to be Christ's soldiers, we must sit loose to this world; and though we must employ ourselves in the affairs of this life while we are here (we have something to do here), we must not entangle ourselves with those affairs. The great care of a soldier should be to please his general; so the great care of a Christian should be to please Christ.

IV. He must see to it that in carrying on the spiritual warfare he went by rule, that he observed the laws of war (*v.* 5). In doing that which is good we must take care that we do it in a right manner, that our good may not be evil spoken of. Those who do so shall be crowned at last.

V. He must be willing to wait for a recompence (*v.* 6). If we would be partakers of the fruits, we must labour. We must do the will of God, before we receive the promises.

The apostle further commends what he had said to the attention of Timothy. Timothy must be reminded to use his considering faculties about the things of God. Consideration is as necessary to a good conversation as to a sound conversion. He prays for him: *The Lord give thee understanding in all things.* The most intelligent man needs more and more of this gift. If he who gave the revelation in the word does not give the understanding in the heart, we are nothing.

Verses 8–13

I. To encourage Timothy in suffering, the apostle puts him in mind of the resurrection of Christ (*v.* 8). The consideration of it should make us faithful to our Christian profession. The incarnation and resurrection of Jesus Christ, heartily believed and rightly considered, will support a Christian under all sufferings in the present life.

II. Another thing to encourage him in suffering was that he had Paul for an example.

1. How the apostle suffered (*v.* 9). We must not think it strange if those who do well fare ill in this world, and if the best of men meet with the worst of treatment; but this was his comfort *that the word of God was not bound.* Persecuting powers cannot hinder the operation of the word of God upon men's hearts and consciences; that cannot be bound by any human force. This might encourage Timothy not to be afraid of bonds for the testimony of Jesus.

2. Why he suffered cheerfully, *v.* 10. Next to the salvation of our own souls we should be willing to do and suffer any thing to promote the salvation of the souls of others.

III. Another thing with which he encourages Timothy is the prospect of a future state.

1. Those who faithfully adhere to Christ, whatever it cost them, will certainly have the advantage of it in another world, *v.* 11. If we be dead to this world we shall go to live with him in a better world, to be for ever with him. *Those who suffer for Christ* on earth shall reign with Christ in heaven, *v.* 12.

2. It is at our peril if we prove unfaithful to him. That man must needs be for ever miserable whom Christ disowns at last. This will certainly be the issue, whether we believe it or no (*v.* 13). If we be faithful to Christ, he will certainly be faithful to us. If we be false to him, he will be faithful to his threatenings

This is a faithful saying, and may be depended on and ought to be believed.

Verses 14-18

He comes in the next place to direct him in his work.

I. He must make it his business to edify those who were under his charge. This is the work of ministers; not to tell people that which they never knew before, but to put them in mind of that which they do know, *charging them that they strive not about words.* If people did but consider of what little use most of the controversies in religion are, they would not be so zealous in their strifes of words. People are very prone to strive about words, and such strifes never answer any other ends than to shake some and subvert others. *Study to show thyself approved unto God, v. 15, a workman that need not be ashamed.* Workmen that are unskilful, or unfaithful, or lazy, have need to be ashamed; but those who mind their business, and keep to their work, are workmen that need not be ashamed. And what is their work? Not to invent a new gospel, but rightly to divide the gospel that is committed to their trust.

II. He must take heed of that which would be a hindrance to him in his work, *v.* 16. He must take heed of error: *Shun profane and vain babblings.* When once men became fond of those *they will increase unto more ungodliness.* The way of error is down-hill. The infecting of one often proves the infecting of many, or the infecting of the same person with one error often proves the infecting of him with many errors. The apostle mentions some who had lately advanced erroneous doctrines: *Hymeneus and Philetus.* They did not deny the resurrection, but they put a corrupt interpretation upon that true doctrine, saying that the resurrection was past already. By this they *overthrew the faith of some.* Whatever takes away the doctrine of a future state overthrows the faith of Christians. Error is very productive and on that account the more dangerous. When men err concerning the truth, they always endeavour to have some plausible pretence for it.

Verses 19-21

I. The unbelief of men cannot make the promise of God of no effect. The prophets and apostles, that is, the doctrines of the Old and New Testament, are still firm; and they have a seal with two mottoes upon it, one on the one side, and the other on the other, as is usual in a broad seal. One expresses our comfort—that *the Lord knows those that are his.* He will never lose them. Another declares our duty—that everyone who names the name of Christ must depart from iniquity. We must depart from iniquity, else he will not own us.

II. Though there are some whose faith is overthrown, yet there are others who keep their integrity, and hold it fast (*v.* 20). There are some professors of religion that are like the vessels of wood and earth, they are vessels of dishonour. But at the same time all are not vessels of dishonour. When we are discouraged by the badness of some, we must encourage ourselves by the goodness of others. Now we should see to it that we be vessels of honour: sanctified for our Master's use. Every vessel must be fit for its Master's use; everyone in the church whom God approves must be devoted to his Master's service and meet for his use.

Verses 22-26

I. Paul here exhorts Timothy to beware of *youthful lusts, v.* 22. The lusts of the flesh are youthful lusts, which young people must carefully watch against. He prescribes an excellent remedy against youthful lusts. Youthful lusts are very dangerous, for they

war against the soul. The exciting of our graces will be the extinguishing of our corruptions; the more we follow that which is good the faster and the further we shall flee from that which is evil. Our prayers to God and Christ are not acceptable except they come out of a pure heart.

II. He cautions him against contention, and (*v.* 23) cautions him against *foolish and unlearned questions,* strifes of words. Those who advanced them thought themselves wise and learned; but Paul calls them foolish and unlearned. They breed debates and quarrels among Christians. Religion consists more in believing and practising what God requires than in subtle disputes.—*The servant of the Lord must not strive, v.* 24. The servant of the Lord must be *gentle to all men.—Apt to teach.* Those are unapt to teach who are apt to strive. In *meekness instructing* (*v.* 25) not only those who subject themselves, but those who oppose themselves. This is the way to convey truth in its light and power, and to overcome evil with good. That which ministers must have in their eyes, in instructing those who oppose themselves, is their recovery. Repentance is God's gift. It is a gift with a *peradventure* in the case of those who oppose themselves. The same God who gives us the discovery of the truth does by his grace bring us to the acknowledging of it, otherwise our hearts would continue in rebellion against it. And thus sinners recover themselves out of the snare of the devil. The misery of sinners, *v.* 26. They are slaves to the worst of task-masters. They are taken in a snare, and in the worst snare, because it is the devil's. The happiness of those who repent: they recover themselves out of this snare. Those who before were led captive by the devil at his will come to be led into the glorious liberty of the children of God.

CHAPTER 3

I. The apostle forewarns Timothy what the last days would be, ver. 1-9. II. Prescribes various remedies against them (ver. 10, to the end), particularly his own example, and the knowledge of the holy scriptures. Paul tells Timothy how bad others would be, and therefore how good he should be.

Verses 1-9

Timothy must not think it strange if there were in the church bad men; for the net of the gospel was to enclose both good fish and bad, Matt. xiii. 47, 48. Even in gold ore there will be dross, and a great deal of chaff among the wheat when it lies on the floor.

I. In the *last days* (*v.* 1), in gospel times, there would *come perilous times,* not so much on account of persecution from without as on account of corruptions within. Two traitors within the garrison may do more hurt to it than two thousand besiegers without. Perilous times shall come, for men shall be wicked. Sin makes the time perilous.

II. Paul tells Timothy what shall be the marks and signs whereby these times may be known, *v.* 2, &c. Self-love will make the times perilous. Instead of Christian charity, which takes care for the good of others, they will mind themselves only. Covetousness. When men are lovers of themselves, no good can be expected from them, as good may be expected from those who love God. When every man is for what he can get and for keeping what he has, this makes men dangerous to one another. Pride and vain-glory. When men are *boasters and blasphemers.* When men do not fear God they will not regard man. When children are disobedient to their parents. What wickedness will those stick at who will be abusive to their own parents and rebel against them? Unthankfulness and unholiness make the times perilous. What is the reason that men are unholy and without the fear of God, but that they are unthankful for the mercies of God? When they are *without natural affection,* and *truce-breakers, v.* 3. When children are disobedient to their parents (*v.* 2) and when parents are without natural affection to their children, *v.* 3. And those who will not be bound by natural affection, no marvel that they will not be bound by the most solemn leagues and covenants. *They are truce-breakers.* When men are *false accusers* one of another—*devils* one to another. When men have no government of themselves and their own appetites: they are *incontinent,* they are *fierce.* When that which is good and ought to be honoured is generally despised. When men are generally treacherous, wilful, and haughty (*v.* 4). When men are puffed up, behaving scornfully to all about them, then the times are perilous. When men are generally *lovers of pleasure more than lovers of God.* That is a carnal mind, and is full of enmity against him, which prefers anything before him, especially such a sordid thing as carnal pleasure is. When they *have the form of godliness* (*v.* 5). A form of godliness is a very different thing from the power of it; men may have the one and be wholly destitute of the other.

III. Paul warns Timothy to take heed of certain seducers. He shows how industrious they were to make proselytes (*v.* 6). They crept into houses, to insinuate themselves into the good opinion of people, and so to draw them over to their party. And see what sort of people those were that they gained; they were such as were weak, and such as were wicked. A foolish head and a filthy heart make persons an easy prey to seducers. He shows how far they were from coming to the knowledge of the truth, though they pretended to be *ever learning, v.* 7. He foretells the certain stop that should be put to their progress (*v.* 8, 9). Those heretics *resisted the truth* and were men *of corrupt minds, reprobate concerning the faith, but they shall proceed no further.* Though the spirit of error may be let loose for a time, God has it in a chain. *Their folly shall be manifest,* it shall appear that they are impostors, and every man shall abandon them.

Verses 10–17

I. The apostle sets before him his own example (*v.* 10). Christ's apostles had no enemies but those who did not know them, or did not know them fully; those who knew them best loved and honoured them the most. Paul kept back nothing from his hearers, but declared to them the whole counsel of God, so that if it were not their own fault they might fully know it. He had fully known his conversation. His manner of life was of a piece with his doctrine, and did not contradict it. Those cannot expect to profit the people at all that preach well and live ill. Timothy fully knew what was the great thing that Paul had in view: "Thou hast known *my purpose,* what I drive at." Timothy fully knew Paul's good character. He knew that he had suffered ill for doing well (*v.* 11), (he mentions those only which happened to him while Timothy was with him, *at Antioch, at Iconium, at Lystra*). He knew what care God had taken of him. As he never failed his cause, so his God never failed him. Thou hast fully known my *afflictions.* When we *fully* know the afflictions, not only how they suffer, but how they are supported and comforted under their sufferings, then, instead of being discouraged, we shall be animated by them, especially considering that we are told before that we must count upon such things (*v.* 12). Those who will live godly must expect it; especially those who will live godly *in Christ Jesus,* especially when they are resolute in it. The apostle's life was very exemplary for three things: for his *doctrine,* for his *life,* and for his *persecutions and sufferings.* His life was a life of great usefulness, yet it was a life of great sufferings. The apostle mentions the Lord's delivering him out of them all,

for Timothy's and our encouragement under sufferings.

II. He warns Timothy of the fatal end of seducers, *v.* 13. As good men, by the grace of God, grow better and better, so bad men, through the subtlety of Satan and the power of their own corruptions, grow worse and worse.

III. He directs him particularly to what he had learned out of the holy scriptures (*v.* 14, 15). It is not enough to learn that which is good, but we must continue in it, and persevere in it unto the end. If Timothy would adhere to the truth as he had been taught it, this would arm him against the snares and insinuations of seducers.

1. It is a great happiness to know the certainty of the things wherein we have been instructed. Consider of *whom thou hast learned them*; not of evil men and seducers, but good men, who had themselves experienced the power of the truths they taught thee. "Knowing especially the firm foundation upon which thou hast built (*v.* 15): *That from a child thou hast known the holy scriptures.*"

2. Those who would acquaint themselves with the things of God, must know the holy scriptures.

3. It is a great happiness to know the holy scriptures from our childhood. The age of children is the learning age; and those who would get true learning must get it out of the scriptures.

4. They must not lie by us neglected, and seldom or never looked into.

(1) What is the excellency of the scripture (*v.* 16). The prophets and apostles did not speak from themselves, but what they received of the Lord that they delivered unto us.

(2) What use it will be of to us. *It is able to make us wise to salvation.* Those are wise indeed who are wise to salvation. "*Through faith.*" The scriptures will make us wise to salvation, if they be mixed with faith. For, if we do not believe their truth and goodness, they will do us no good. It is *profitable* to us for all the purposes of the Christian life. It instructs us in that which is true, reproves us for that which is amiss, directs us in that which is good. *That the man of God may be perfect, v.* 17. That which furnishes a man of God in this world is the scripture. By it we are *thoroughly furnished for every good work.* Scripture has various uses, and answers divers ends and purposes. Scripture is a perfect rule of faith and practice. If we consult the scripture which was given by inspiration of God, and follow its directions, we shall be made men of God, *perfect and thoroughly furnished to every good work.* O that we may love our Bibles more, and keep closer to them than ever!

CHAPTER 4

I. Paul presses Timothy to the diligent and conscientious discharge of his work as an evangelist, ver. 1-5. II. The reason of his concern in this case. His departure was at hand, ver. 6-8. III. Divers particular matters, ver. 9-15. IV. He informs him of what befell him at his first answer; though men forsook him, the Lord stood by him, ver. 16-18. And then he concludes with salutations and a benediction, ver. 19, to the end.

Verses 1–8

I. How awfully this charge is introduced (*v.* 1). The best of men have need to be awed into the discharge of their duty. The eye of God and Jesus Christ was upon him: *I charge thee before God and the Lord Jesus Christ.* He charges him as he will answer it at the great day, reminding him of the judgment to come. He will appear; he will come the second time, and it will be a glorious appearance. Then his kingdom shall appear in its glory: *At his appearing and kingdom;* for he will then appear in his kingdom.

II. What is the matter of the charge, v. 2–5.

1. To *preach the word*. This is ministers' business. It is not their own notions and fancies that they are to preach, but the pure plain word of God.

2. To urge what he preached: "*Be instant in season and out of season, reprove, rebuke, exhort;* do this work with all fervency of spirit. *In season,* when some special opportunity offers itself of speaking to them with advantage. *Out of season,* because thou dost not know but the Spirit of God may fasten upon them."

3. He must tell people of their faults. Endeavour, by dealing plainly with them, to bring them to repentance.

4. He must direct, encourage, and quicken those who began well. "*Exhort them with all longsuffering and doctrine.*" He must do it very patiently. While God shows to them all longsuffering, let ministers exhort with all longsuffering. He must do it rationally, not with passion, but *with doctrine.* Teach them the truth as it is in Jesus, and this will be a means both to reclaim them from evil and to bring them to good.

5. He must *watch in all things.* "Watch to thy work; watch against the temptations of Satan; watch over the souls of those who are committed to thy charge."

6. He must count upon afflictions and endure them. "Inure thyself to hardships."

7. He must remember his office, and discharge its duties. The office of the evangelist was, as the apostles' deputy, to water the churches that they planted. This was Timothy's work.

8. He must fulfil his ministry: *Make full proof of it.* Perform all the parts of his office with diligence and care. The best way to make full proof of our ministry is to fulfil it, to fill it up in all its parts with proper work.

III. The reasons to enforce the charge.

1. Because errors and heresies were likely to creep into the church (v. 3, 4). "Improve the present time when they will endure it." They will grow weary of the old plain gospel of Christ, and then they will be greedy of fables. False teachers were not of God's sending; but they chose them to please their itching ears. People do so when they will not endure sound doctrine; that preaching which is searching, plain, and to the purpose. There is a wide difference between the word of God and the word of such teachers; the one is sound doctrine, the word of truth, the other is only fables.

2. Because Paul for his part had almost done his work, v. 6.

(1) "Therefore there will be the more occasion for thee." The fewer hands there are to work the more industrious those hands must be that are at work.

(2) "I have done the work of my day and generation; do thou in like manner do the work of thy day and generation."

(3) The comfort and cheerfulness of Paul, in the prospect of his approaching departure, might encourage Timothy. "I can look back upon my warfare with a great deal of satisfaction; and therefore be not afraid of the difficulties thou must meet with. The crown of life is as sure to thee as if it were already upon thy head." Here the apostle looks forward, upon his death approaching, and he looks upon it now as near at hand: I am *already poured out.* Observe,

[1] With what pleasure he speaks of dying. He calls it his departure, or his release. Death to a good man is his release from the imprisonment of this world and his departure to the enjoyments of another world; he does not cease to be, but is only removed from one world to another.

[2] With what pleasure he looks back upon the life he had lived (v. 7). He did not fear death, because

he had the testimony of his conscience that by the grace of God he had in some measure answered the ends of living. He had fought a good fight. His life was a course, and he had now finished it; as his warfare was accomplished, so his race was run. "*I have kept the faith.*" We must fight this good fight; we must fight it out, and finish our course. Towards the end of our days to be able to speak in this manner, what comfort, unspeakable comfort, will it afford!

[3] With what pleasure he looks forward to the life he was to live hereafter (v. 8). Let this encourage Timothy to endure hardness as a good soldier of Jesus Christ that there is a crown of life before us. It is called *a crown of righteousness,* because our holiness and righteousness will there be perfected, and will be our crown. And yet this crown of righteousness was not peculiar to Paul, as if it belonged only to apostles and martyrs, but *to all those also that love his appearing.* It is the character of all the saints that they love the appearing of Jesus Christ: they love his second appearing at the great day; love it, and long for it. This crown, which believers shall wear, is laid up for them; they have it not at present, for here they are but heirs; they have it not in possession, and yet it is sure.

Verses 9–15

1. He bids him hasten to him (v. 9). Paul wanted Timothy's company and help; and the reason he gives is because several had left him (v. 10): *Demas hath forsaken me, having loved this present world.* Love to this present world is often the cause of apostasy from the truths and ways of Jesus Christ. *Crescens* had gone one way and *Titus* another way. *Luke* ever remained with Paul (v. 11, 12). 2. He speaks respectfully concerning *Mark.* This Mark was he about whom Paul and Barnabas had contended, Acts xv. 39. Paul would not take him with him to the work, because he had once flinched and drawn back: but now, says he, *Take Mark, and bring him with thee.* By this it appears that Paul was now reconciled to Mark. We must not disclaim for ever making use of those that are profitable and useful, though they may have done amiss. 3. Paul orders Timothy as he came through Troas to bring with him thence those things which he had left behind him there (v. 13), the cloak he had left there, which Paul had the more occasion for in a cold prison. He would have his books with him. Whereas he had exhorted Timothy to give attendance to reading, so he did himself. 4. He mentions *Alexander,* and the mischief that he had done him, v. 14, 15. Paul foretells that God would reckon with him. The Lord *will reward him according to his works.* Some who were once Paul's hearers and admirers did not give him reason to remember them with much pleasure; for one forsook him, and another did him much evil. At the same time he mentions some with pleasure; the badness of some did not make him forget the goodness of others.

Verses 16–22

I. He gives Timothy an account of his own present circumstances.

1. He had lately been called to appear before the emperor (v. 16). The Christians at Rome were forward to go and meet him (Acts xxviii); but when it came to the pinch, and they would be in danger of suffering with him, then they all forsook him. Paul had his trials in his friends' forsaking him in a time of danger as well as in the opposition made by enemies: all forsook him. God might lay it to their charge, but Paul endeavours to prevent it by his earnest prayers.

2. When he had nobody to keep him in countenance, God made his face to shine. Paul knew

how to preach at the bar as well as in the pulpit. *And that all the Gentiles might hear;* the emperor himself and the great men who would never have heard Paul preach if he had not been brought before them. *And I was delivered out of the mouth of the lion. And the Lord shall deliver me from every evil work.* See how Paul improved his experiences. "*And shall preserve me to his heavenly kingdom.*" If the Lord stand by us, he will strengthen us, and his presence will more than supply everyone's absence. Former deliverances should encourage future hopes. We ought to give God the glory of all past, present, and future deliverances: *To whom be glory for ever and ever. Amen.*

II. He sends salutations, *v.* 19. He mentions his leaving *Trophimus sick at Miletum* (*v.* 20).

III. He hastens Timothy to *come to him before winter* (*v.* 21).

IV. He sends commendations to him from *Eubulus, Pudens, Linus, Claudia,* and all the *brethren.*

V. He concludes with a prayer, that the *Lord Jesus would be with his spirit.* We need no more to make us happy than to have the Lord Jesus Christ with our spirits. And it is the best prayer we can put up for our friends. *Grace be with you. Amen.* And if grace be with us here to convert and change us, to make us holy, to keep us humble, and to enable us to persevere to the end, glory will crown us hereafter.

AN EXPOSITION, WITH PRACTICAL OBSERVATIONS, OF

THE EPISTLE OF ST. PAUL TO

TITUS

This Epistle of Paul to Titus is much of the same nature with those to Timothy. We read much of this Titus. He was a Greek, Gal. ii. 3. Paul called him *his son* (Titus i. 4), *his brother* (2 Cor. ii. 13), *his partner and fellow-helper* (2 Cor. viii. 23). He went up with the apostles to the church at Jerusalem (Gal. ii. 1), was much conversant at Corinth, for which church he had *an earnest care*, 2 Cor. viii. 16. Paul's second epistle to them was sent by his hand, 2 Cor. viii. 16–18, 23; ix. 2–4; xii. 18. He was with the apostle at Rome, and thence went into Dalmatia (2 Tim. iv. 10), after which no more occurs of him in the scriptures. In Crete the gospel had got some footing; and here were Paul and Titus in one of their travels; but the apostle could not himself tarry long at this place. He therefore left Titus some time there, to carry on the work which had been begun, wherein, probably, meeting with more difficulty than ordinary, Paul wrote this epistle to him; and yet perhaps not so much for his own sake as for the people's, that the endeavours of Titus might be more significant and effectual among them.

CHAPTER 1

I. The preface to the epistle with the apostle's salutations and prayer for Titus, ver. 1–4. II. The end of Titus's being left at Crete, ver. 5. III. How that end should be pursued in reference both to good and bad ministers, ver. 6, to the end.

Verses 1–4

I. The writer. *Paul*, a Gentile name taken by the apostle of the Gentiles, Acts xiii. 9, 46, 47. Ministers will accommodate even smaller matters, so that there may be any furthering of acceptance in their work. *A servant of God, and an apostle of Jesus Christ.* The highest officers in the church are but servants. (Much divinity and devotion are comprehended in the inscriptions of the epistles.) *According to the faith of God's elect.* Their doctrine agreed with the faith of all the elect. Faith is the first principle of sanctification. The gospel is truth; the great, sure, and saving truth. Divine faith rests not on fallible reasonings and profitable opinions, but on the truth itself, *which is after godliness.* All gospel truth is after godliness; it is truth not only to be known, but acknowledged; it must be held forth in word and practice. To bring to this knowledge and faith, and to the acknowledging of the truth which is after godliness, is the great end of the gospel ministry, *v.* 2. This is the further intent of the gospel, to beget hope as well as faith. The faith and godliness of Christians lead to eternal life, and give hope of it; for *God, that cannot lie, hath promised it.* Here is the stability and antiquity of the promise of eternal life to the saints. God, who cannot lie, hath promised before the world began. No wonder if the contempt of it be punished severely, since he has not only promised it of old, *but* (*v.* 3) *has in due times manifested his word through preaching.* That which some called *foolishness of preaching* has been thus honoured. *Which is committed unto me.* The ministry is a trust; none taketh this honour, but he who is thereunto appointed; and whoso is appointed and called must preach the word. *According to the commandment of God our Saviour.* Let none rest therefore in men's calling, without God's.

II. The person written to, *Titus*, a Gentile Greek, yet called both to the faith and ministry. The grace of God is free and powerful. What worthiness or preparation was there in one of heathen stock and education? *My own* (or *my genuine*) *son*, not by natural generation, but by supernatural regeneration. "*After the common faith*, that faith which is common to all the regenerate, and which thou hast in truth, and expressest in the life."

III. The salutation and prayer, wishing all blessings to him. The blessings wished: *Grace, mercy, and peace.* Grace is the fountain of all blessings. Mercy, and peace, and all good, spring out of this. Get into God's favour, and all must be well; for, the persons from whom blessings are wished: *From God the Father*, the fountain of all good. Every blessing, every comfort, comes to us from God, as a Father. *And the Lord Jesus Christ our Saviour.* All is from the Father by the Son.

Verse 5

I. More generally. Titus was to go on in settling what the apostle himself had not time for, in his short stay there. 1. The apostle's great diligence in the gospel; when he had set things on foot in one place, he hastened away to another. 2. His faithfulness and prudence. He neglected not the places that he went from; but left some to cultivate the young plantation. 3. His humility; he disdained not to be helped in his work, and that by such as were not of so great gifts as himself. 4. Titus, though inferior to an apostle, was yet above the ordinary fixed pastors or bishops, who were to tend particular churches as their peculiar stated charge; but Titus was in a higher sphere, to ordain such ordinary pastors where wanting, and settle things in their first state and form, and then to pass to other places. Here at Crete Titus was but occasionally, and for a short time; Paul willed him to despatch the business he was left for, and come to him at Nicopolis, where he purposed to winter; after this he was sent to Corinth, was with the apostle at Rome, and was sent thence into Dalmatia, which is the last we read of him in scripture. Their work was spiritual. The *things wanting* were divine and spiritual ordinances, and appointments for spiritual ends, derived from Christ. For settling these was Titus left. No easy thing is it to raise churches, and bring them to perfection. Paul had himself been here labouring, and yet were there things wanting. The best are apt to decay and to go out of order. This in general was Titus's work in Crete.

II. In special: *To ordain elders in every city.* These presbyters or elders were to have the ordinary and stated care and charge of the churches. Presbyters here therefore are gospel ministers, to dispense Christ's ordinances, and to *feed the church of God.* A church without a fixed and standing ministry in it is imperfect and wanting. Where a fit number of believers is, presbyters or elders must be set; their continuance in churches is as necessary as their first appointment, for *perfecting the saints, and edifying the body of Christ. Faith comes by hearing*, and is preserved through it also. Ignorance and corruption, decays of good and increase of all evil, come by want of a teaching and quickening ministry. On such accounts therefore was *Titus left in Crete, to set in order the things that were wanting.*

III. The rule of his proceeding. As under the law all things were to be made according to the pattern shown to Moses in the mount; so under the gospel all must be ordered and managed according to the direction of Christ, and of his chief ministers. Human traditions and inventions may not be brought into the church of God. If an evangelist might not do any thing but by appointment, much less may others.

Verses 6–16

The apostle here gives Titus directions about ordination.

I. Of those whom he should ordain.

1. Their qualifications respecting their life.

(1) More general: *If any be blameless;* not absolutely without fault, so none are; nor altogether unblamed, this is rare and difficult; for Christ himself and his apostles were blamed. But he must be one who lies not under an ill character.

(2) More particularly.

[1] There is his relative character. In his own person, he must be of conjugal chastity. And, as to his children, *having faithful children*, obedient and good, brought up in the true Christian faith, and living according to it, at least as far as the endeavours of the parents can avail. *Not accused of riot, nor unruly.* The most innocent may be falsely so charged; they must look to it therefore that there be no colour for such censure. Children so faithful and obedient, will be a good sign of faithfulness and diligence in the parent. From his faithfulness in the less, there may be encouragement to commit to him the greater, the rule of the church of God. The ground of this qualification is shown from the nature of his office (*v.* 7). Being such bishops and overseers of the flock, who were to be examples to them, and God's stewards to take care of the affairs of his house, there is great reason that they should be blameless.

[2] The more absolute ones are expressed, *First*, Negatively. *Not self-willed.* The prohibition is of large extent, excluding self-opinion,—self-love, making self the centre of all,—also self-confidence and self-pleasing, set on one's own will and way. A great honour it is to a minister to be ready to ask and to take advice, to be ready to defer to the mind and will of others, becoming all things to all men, that they may gain some. *Not soon angry.* How unfit are those to govern a church who cannot govern themselves. *Not given to wine.* Moderate use of this, as of the other good creatures of God, is not unlawful. But excess therein is shameful in all, especially in a minister. *Not given to filthy lucre;* not entering into the ministry with base worldly views. Nothing is more unbecoming a minister, who is to direct his own and others' eyes to another world, than to be too intent upon this. *Secondly*, Positively: he must be (*v.* 8) *a lover of hospitality.* Such a spirit and practice, according to ability and occasion, are very becoming such as should be examples of good works. *A lover of good men*, or of *good things;* ministers should be exemplary in both. *Sober*, or *prudent; a* needful grace in a minister both for his ministerial and personal carriage and management. *Just in* things belonging to civil life. *Holy* in what concerns religion. *Temperate;* it comes from a word that signifies *strength*, and denotes one who has power over his appetite and affections.

2. As to doctrine,

(1) Here is his duty: *Holding fast the faithful word, as he has been taught*—holding it fast in his own belief and profession, and in teaching others. Ministers must hold fast, and hold forth, the faithful word in their teaching and life.

(2) Here is the end: *That he may be able, by sound doctrine, both to exhort, and to convince the gain-sayers.* How should he do this if he himself were uncertain or unsteady, not holding fast that *faithful word and sound doctrine.*

II. Whom he should reject or avoid. The reasons he takes both from bad teachers and hearers among them, *v.* 10, to the end.

1. From bad teachers. (1) Those false teachers are described. They were *unruly*, headstrong and ambitious of power, refractory and untractable. *And vain talkers and deceivers*, falling into errors and mistakes, and fond of them, and studious and industrious to draw others into the same. Many such there were, *especially those of the circumcision*, who yet were for mingling Judaism and Christianity together, and so making a corrupt medley. (2) Here is the apostle's direction how to deal with them (*v.* 11): *Their mouths must be stopped* by confutation and conviction. (3) The reasons are given for this. From the pernicious effects of their errors. Their base end in what they do: serving a worldly interest under pretence of religion.

2. In reference to their people or hearers, who are described from ancient testimony given of them.

(1) Here is the witness (*v.* 12): One of the Cretans, likely to know and unlikely to slander them. *A prophet of their own;* so their poets were accounted.

(2) Here is the matter of his testimony: *The Cretans are always liars, evil beasts, slow bellies.* Even to a proverb, they were infamous for falsehood and lying; to play the *Cretan*, or to lie, is the same; and they were compared to evil beasts for their sly hurtfulness and savage nature, and called slow bellies for their laziness and sensuality, more inclined to eat than to work.

(3) Here is the verification of this by the apostle himself: *v.* 13. The apostle saw too much ground for that character.

(4) He instructs Titus how to deal with them. When Paul wrote to Timothy he bade him instruct with meekness; but now, when he writes to Titus, he bids him rebuke them sharply. Timothy had a more polite people to deal with, and therefore he must rebuke them with meekness; and Titus had to do with those who were more rough and uncultivated. Their corruptions were many and gross, and therefore should be dealt with accordingly. There must in reproving be a distinguishing between sins and sins; some are more gross and heinous in their nature: and between sinners and sinners; some are of a more tender and tractable temper, apter to be wrought on by gentleness; others are more hardy and stubborn, and need more cutting language.

(5) Here is the end of it noted (*v.* 14), that they may show themselves truly and effectually changed. The sharpest reproofs must aim at the good of the reproved, to reclaim and reform the erroneous and the guilty. Soundness in the faith is most desirable and necessary. This is the soul's health and vigour. A special means to soundness in the faith is to turn away the ear from fables and the fancies of men. Fancies and devices of men in the worship of God are contrary to truth and piety.

(6) He gives the reasons of this. To good Christians that are sound in the faith and thereby purified *all things are pure, but to those that are defiled and unbelieving nothing is pure.* They suck poison out of that from which others draw sweetness; their mind and conscience, being defiled, a taint is communicated to all they do.

There are many who profess to know God, and yet in their lives deny and reject him; their practice is a contradiction to their profession. The apostle, instructing Titus to rebuke sharply, does himself rebuke sharply; he gives them very hard words, yet doubtless no harder than their case warranted, and their need required. *Being abominable*, deserving that God and good men should turn away their eyes from them as nauseous and offensive. *And disobedient*. They might do divers things; but it was not the obedience of faith. *To every good work reprobate*, without skill or judgment to do anything aright. See the miserable condition of hypocrites. Let us not be so ready to fix this charge on others as careful that it agree not to ourselves.

CHAPTER 2

The apostle here directs Titus about the faithful discharge of his own office generally (ver. 1), and particularly as to several sorts of persons (ver. 2–10) and gives the grounds of these and of other following directions (ver. 11–14), with a summary direction in the close, ver. 15.

Verses 1–10

Here he exhorts him,

I. Generally, to a faithful discharge of his own office. His ordaining others to preach would not excuse himself from preaching, nor might he take care of ministers and elders only, but he must instruct private Christians also in their duty. The true doctrines of the gospel are *sound doctrines*, they are in themselves good and holy, and make the believers so.

II. Specially and particularly, he instructs him to apply this sound doctrine to several sorts of persons, from *v.* 2–10. Ministers must be particular as well as practical in their preaching; they must teach men their duty, and must teach all and each his duty.

1. To the aged men. Old disciples of Christ must conduct themselves in everything agreeably to the Christian doctrine. *That the aged men be sober;* they must keep measure in things, both for health and for fitness, for counsel and example to the younger. *Grave:* levity is unbecoming in any, but especially in the aged. *Temperate. Sound in the faith*, sincere and steadfast. Those who are full of years should be full of grace and goodness, the inner man renewing more and more as the outer decays. *In charity*, or love; this is fitly joined with *faith*, which works by, and must be seen in, love. It must be sincere love, without dissimulation: love of God for himself, and of men for God's sake. And *in patience*. Aged persons are apt to be peevish and therefore need to be on their guard against such infirmities. Faith, love, and patience, are three main Christian graces, and soundness in these is much of gospel perfection.

2. To the aged women. These also must be instructed and warned. Those virtues before mentioned (*sobriety, gravity, temperance, soundness in the faith, charity, and patience*) recommended to aged men, are not proper to them only, but applicable to both sexes. There is not one way of salvation for one sex or sort, and another for another; but both must learn and practise the same things; the virtues and duties are common. *That the aged women likewise be in behaviour as becometh holiness;* or as beseems and is proper for holy persons, such as they profess to be. Whatsoever things are beseeming or unbeseeming holiness form a measure and rule of conduct to be looked to. *Not false accusers*—slandering and backbiting their neighbours, a great and too common fault; not only loving to speak, but to speak ill, of people, and to separate very friends. *Not given to much wine*. This is unseemly and evil in any, but especially in this sex and age, and was too much to be found among the Greeks of that time and place. *Teachers of good things*. Not public preachers, that is forbidden, but otherwise teach they may and should, by example and good life. Those whose actions and behaviour become holiness are thereby teachers of good things; and, besides this, they may and should also teach by doctrinal instruction at home, and in a private way. Their business is, and they may be called on to it, to be teachers of good things.

3. There are lessons for young women also, whom the aged women must teach. For teaching such things aged women have often better access than the men, even than ministers have. *To be sober and discreet*, contrary to the vanity and rashness which younger years are subject to. *Discreet* and *chaste* stand well together; many expose themselves to fatal temptations by that which at first might be but indiscretion. *Chaste*, and *keepers at home*, are well joined too. Not but there are occasions of going abroad; but a gadding temper for merriment and company sake is the opposite evil intended. *Good*, generally, in opposition to all vice; and specially kind, helpful, and charitable. It may also have a more particular sense; one of a meek and yet cheerful spirit and temper, not sullen nor bitter. *To love their husbands, and to be obedient to them:* and where there is true love this will be no difficult command. God would have a resemblance of Christ's authority over the church held forth in the husband's over the wife. Christ is the head of the church, to protect and save it, to supply it with all good, and secure it from evil; and so is the husband over the wife, to keep her from injuries, and to provide comfortably for her. It is not then a slavish subjection that is required; but a loving subordination. *And to love their children*, not with a natural affection only, but a spiritual; not a fond foolish love, neglecting due reproof and correction where necessary, but a regular Christian love, forming their life and manners aright, taking care of their souls as well as of their bodies. *That the word of God may not be blasphemed*. "What are these the better for this their new religion?" would the infidels be ready to say. "Judge what a God he is by these his servants; and what his word, and doctrine, and religion, are by these his followers."

4. Here is the duty of young men. They are apt to be eager and hot, therefore they must be earnestly exhorted to be considerate, not rash; humble and mild, not haughty and proud; for there are more young people ruined by pride than by any other sin.

5. With these instructions to Titus the apostle inserts some directions to himself. For his conversation, *v.* 7. Without this, he would pull down with one hand what he built with the other. Good doctrine and good life must go together. *In all things;* some read, *above all things*. Above all things, example, especially that of the teacher himself, is needful; hereby both light and influence are more likely to go together. Ministers must be examples to the flock, and the people followers of them, as they are of Christ. For his teaching and doctrine, as well as for his life, *v.* 7, 8. In their preaching, therefore, the display of human learning or oratory, is not to be affected; but sound speech must be used, which cannot be *condemned*; scripture-language in expressing scripture-truths. This is sound speech, that cannot be condemned. Thus be an example *in word*; and *in conversation*, the life corresponding with the doctrine. The reason both for the strictness of the minister's life and the gravity and soundness of his preaching. Adversaries would be seeking occasion to reflect, and would do so could they find anything amiss in doctrine or life. Faithful ministers will have enemies watching, such as will endeavour to find or pick holes in their teaching or behaviour; the more need therefore for them to look to themselves.

6. The directions respecting servants. Servants must know and do their duty to their earthly masters, but with an eye to their heavenly one.

(1) The duties themselves are these:

[1] *v.* 9: Obedience the prime duty, that by which they are characterized. Their will must be subject to their master's will, and their time and labour at their master's disposal and command. If he be a master, the duties of a servant are to be paid to him as such.

[2] *To please them well in all things.* We are not to understand it either of obeying or pleasing them, without any limitation; but always with a reserve of God's right. If his command and the earthly master's come in competition, we are instructed to obey God rather than man. And not only must the will of God be the measure of the servant's obedience, but the reason of it also. All must be done with a respect to him, in virtue of his authority, and for pleasing him primarily and chiefly. Christian liberty comports well with civil servitude and subjection. Persons may serve men, and yet be the servants of Christ. Servants therefore should not be troubled at their condition, but be faithful and cheerful in the station wherein God hath set them, striving to please their masters in all things. Hard it may be, but it must be aimed at as much as possible.

[3] *Not answering again.* When conscious of a fault, to palliate or stand in justification of it doubles it. Yet this not answering again excludes not turning away wrath with a soft answer, when season and circumstances admit. Good and wise masters will be ready to hear and do right.

[4] *Not purloining, but showing all good fidelity.* This is another great essential of good servants, to be *honest.* They must be just and true, and do for their masters as they would or should for themselves. Be it so that the master is hard and strait, scarcely making sufficient provision for servants; yet they must not be their own carvers, nor go about by theft to right themselves. He must not only not steal nor waste, but must improve his master's goods, and promote his prosperity to his utmost. He that increased not his master's talent is accused of unfaithfulness, though he had not embezzled nor lost it.

(2) The consideration with which Titus was to enforce them: *That they may adorn the doctrine of God our Saviour in all things.* If they be careful to do their duty, it will redound to the glory of God and the credit of religion. The unbelieving masters would think the better of that despised way when they found that those of their servants who were Christians were better than their other servants. True religion is an honour to the professors of it; and they should see that they do not any dishonour to it.

Verses 11–14

The grounds upon which all the foregoing directions are urged.

I. From the nature and design of the gospel. Let all sorts do their respective duties, for this is the very aim and business of Christianity, to instruct persons, to a right frame and conduct.

1. They are put under the dispensation of *the grace of God.* Now grace is obliging and constraining to goodness. Without this effect, grace is received in vain.

2. This gospel grace *brings salvation.* Hence it is called *the word of life*; it brings to faith, and so to life.

3. *It hath appeared.* The old dispensation was comparatively dark and shadowy; this is a clear and shining light.

4. It hath appeared *to all men.* Gospel grace is open to all, and all are invited to come and partake of the benefit of it. The doctrine of grace and salvation by the gospel is for all ranks and conditions of men (slaves and servants, as well as masters).

5. This gospel revelation is to *teach.* It directs what to shun and what to follow, what to avoid and what to do. The gospel is not for speculation only or chiefly, but for practice and right ordering of life.

(1) *Denying ungodliness and worldly lusts.* "Put away ungodliness and irreligion, all unbelief of the divine Being, not loving, nor fearing, nor trusting in him, nor obeying him as we should. *And worldly lusts*, all corrupt and vicious desires and affections that prevail in worldly men." An earthly sensual conversation suits not a heavenly calling.

(2) *To live soberly, righteously, and godly,* &c. Religion is not made up of negatives only; there must be doing good as well as eschewing evil. We should live soberly with respect to ourselves, keeping the limits of moderation and temperance; and righteously towards all men, rendering to all their due, and injuring none, but rather doing good to others. Selfishness is a sort of unrighteousness; it robs others of that share in us which is their due. Live righteously therefore as well as soberly. And godly towards God. Regard to him indeed should run through all. But there is an express and direct duty also that we owe to God, belief and acknowledgment of his being and perfections,—loving, fearing, and trusting in him,—depending on him, and devoting ourselves to him,—praying to him, praising him, and meditating on his word and works. This is godliness, looking and coming to God, as he has manifested himself in Christ. Thus must we exercise ourselves to godliness, without which there can be no adorning of that gospel which is according to it. The gospel teaches us not only how to believe and hope well, but also to live well, as becomes that faith and hope in this present world, and as expectants of another and better.

(3) *Looking for that blessed hope, and the glorious appearing of the great God and our Saviour Jesus Christ.* Hope is put for the thing hoped for, heaven and the felicities thereof, called emphatically *that hope*, because it is the great thing we look for; and a *blessed hope*, because, when attained, we shall be completely happy for ever. This denotes both the time of the accomplishing of our hope and the sureness and greatness of it. *The great God and our Saviour* (or *even our Saviour*) *Jesus Christ.* Christ then is the *great God*, not figuratively, but properly and absolutely, *the true God.* In his second coming he will reward his servants, and bring them to glory with him. [1] There is a common and blessed hope for all true Christians in the other world. By hope is meant the thing hoped for, Christ himself, who is called *our hope*, and blessedness in and through him, hence fitly termed here *that blessed hope.* [2] The design of the gospel is to stir up all to a good life by this blessed hope. *Denying ungodliness and worldly lusts, live soberly, righteously, and godly, in this present world, looking for the blessed hope;* not as mercenaries, but as dutiful and thankful Christians. [3] At the glorious appearing of Christ will the blessed hope of Christians be attained. The glory of the great God and our Saviour will then break out as the sun. The work and design of the gospel are to raise the heart to wait for this second appearing of Christ. Let us then look to this hope. [4] The comfort and joy of Christians are that their Saviour is the great God, and will gloriously manifest himself.

II. From the end of Christ's death, *v.* 14. To bring us to holiness and happiness was the end of Christ's death, as well as the scope of his doctrine.

1. The purchaser of salvation—Jesus Christ, *that great God and our Saviour*, who saves not simply as God, much less as man alone; but as God-man. Man, that he might obey, and suffer, and die, for man; and God, that he might support the manhood.

2. The price of our redemption: *He gave himself.* The Father gave him, but he gave himself too; and, in the freeness and voluntariness, as well as the

greatness of the offering, lay the acceptableness and merit of it. The human nature was the offering, and the divine the altar, sanctifying the gift.

3. The persons for whom He died. He gave himself *for us*, not only for our good, but in our stead. *He loved us, and gave himself for us;* what can we do less than love and give up ourselves to him?

4. The ends of his giving himself for us, (1) *That he might redeem us from all iniquity.* This is fitted to the first lesson, *denying ungodliness and worldly lusts.* Christ gave himself to redeem us from these, therefore put them away. To love and live in sin is to trample under foot redeeming blood. But how could the short sufferings of Christ redeem us from all iniquity? Through the infinite dignity of his person. He who was God suffered, though not as God. *The great God and our Saviour gave himself for us;* this accounts for it. Happy end and fruit of Christ's death, redemption from all iniquity! Christ died for this: and, (2) *To purify to himself a peculiar people.* This enforces the second lesson: *To live soberly, righteously, and godly, in this present world.* Christ died to purify as well as to pardon—to heal the nature, as well as to free from guilt and condemnation. Thus does he make *to himself a peculiar people,* by purifying them. Thus are they distinguished from the world that lies in wickedness. Redemption from sin and sanctification of the nature go together, and both made a peculiar people unto God. And (3) *Zealous of good works.* This peculiar people must be seen to be so by doing good, and having a zeal therein.

Verse 15

A summary direction to Titus in which we have the matter and manner of ministers' teaching.

I. The matter of ministers' teaching: *These things,* namely, those before mentioned: the truths and duties of the gospel, of avoiding sin, and living soberly, righteously, and godly, in this present world.

II. The manner; by doctrine, and exhortation, and reproof with all authority. The great and necessary truths and duties of the gospel, especially, these *speak and exhort, press with much earnestness.* Ministers must not be cold and lifeless in delivering heavenly doctrine and precepts, as if they were indifferent things; but they must urge them with earnestness. *And rebuke;* convince and reprove such as contradict or gainsay, or neglect and do not receive the truth as they should. *Rebuke with all authority,* as coming in the name of God. Ministers are reprovers in the gate.

III. "*Let no man despise thee. Speak and exhort these things,* press them upon all, with boldness and faithfulness reprove sin, and carefully look to thyself and thy own conduct, and then none will despise thee." The most effectual way for ministers to secure themselves from contempt is to keep close to the doctrine of Christ, and do their duty with prudence and courage.

Perhaps too an admonition might be here intended to the people—that Titus, though young, yet should not be contemned by them.

CHAPTER 3

Of duties which concern Christians more in common, ver. 1-8. What Titus in teaching should avoid, with some other directions (ver. 9-14), and salutations in the close, ver. 15.

Verses 1–8

The apostle had directed Titus in reference to the particular duties of several sorts of persons; now he bids him exhort to what concerned them more in common. Ministers are people's remembrancers of their duty. Forgetfulness of duty is a common frailty; there is need therefore of reminding and quickening them thereto.

I. The duties themselves. 1. *Put them in mind to be subject to principalities and powers, to obey magistrates,* that is, all civil rulers. That they be subject to them and obey them in things lawful and honest. The Christian religion was misrepresented by its adversaries as prejudicial to the rights of princes and civil powers, and tending to faction and sedition, and to rebellion against lawful authority. Christians must be reminded to show themselves examples rather of all due subjection and obedience to the government that is over them. 2. *To be ready to every good work.* The precept regards doing good of every kind and on every occasion that may offer, whether respecting God, ourselves, or our neighbour. Mere harmlessness, or good words and good meanings only, are not enough without good works. "Not only take, but seek, occasion for doing good. Put all in mind of this." And, 3. *To speak evil of no man.* If no good can be spoken, rather than speak evil unnecessarily, say nothing. We must never take pleasure in speaking ill of others, nor make the worst of anything, but the best that we can. We must not go up and down as tale-bearers, carrying ill-natured stories. As this evil is too common, so it is of great malignity. This is among the sins to be put off, for, if indulged, it unfits for Christian communion here and the society of the blessed in heaven. Remind them therefore to avoid this. 4. *To be no brawlers; no fighters,* either with hand or tongue. Contention and strife arise from men's lusts, which must be curbed, not indulged; and Christian's need to be reminded of these things. 5. *But gentle, equitable and just,* not taking words or actions in the worst sense; and for peace sometimes yielding somewhat of strict right. 6. *Showing all meekness to all men.* Not only have meekness in our hearts, but show it in our speech and conduct. *All meekness*—meekness in all instances and occasions, not towards friends only, but *to all men.* Meekness of spirit and demeanour renders religion amiable; it is a commanded imitation of Christ, and brings its own reward with it.

II. He adds the reasons.

1. From their own past condition. *We ourselves also were sometimes,* (1) *Foolish;* without true spiritual understanding, ignorant of heavenly things. Those should be most disposed to bear with others' follies who may remember many of their own. And, (2) *Disobedient;* heady and unpersuadable, resisting the word. Well are these set together, *foolish* and *disobedient.* For what folly like this, to disobey God and his laws, natural or revealed? (3) *Deceived,* or wandering, out of the ways of truth and holiness. Man in this his degenerate state is of straying nature. He is weak, and ready to be imposed upon by the wiles of Satan, and of men lying in wait to seduce and mislead. (4) *Serving divers lusts and pleasures.* Carnal people think they enjoy their pleasures; the word calls it servitude and vassalage. It is the misery of the servants of sin that they have many masters, one lust hurrying them one way, and another another. The lusts that tempt them promise them liberty, but in yielding they become the servants of corruption. (5) *Living in malice.* Malice desires hurt to another and rejoices in it. (6) *And envy,* which grudges and repines at another's good. Both are roots of bitterness, whence many evils spring. These were some of the sins in which we lived in our natural state. (7) *Hateful.* (8) *And hating one another.* It is the misery of sinners that they hate one another, as it is the duty and happiness of saints to love one another. The consideration of its having been thus with us should dispose us to be more meek and tender-hearted, towards those who are such.

2. From their present state. "We are delivered out of that our miserable condition by no merit

nor strength of our own." The apostle again opens the causes of our salvation, *v.* 4-7.

(1) The prime author of our salvation—God the Father, therefore termed here *God our Saviour.* All things belonging to the new creation, and recovery of fallen man to life and happiness, are of God the Father. The Father begins, the Son manages, and the Holy Spirit works and perfects all.

(2) The spring and rise of it—the divine *philanthropy,* or *kindness and love of God to man.* By grace we are saved from first to last. This is the ground and motive. The occasion is in man, his misery and wretchedness. Sin bringing that misery, wrath might have issued out rather than compassion; but God would pity and save rather than destroy. He delights in mercy.

(3) Here is the means—the shining out of this love and grace of God in the gospel, *after it appeared.* The appearing of love and grace has, through the Spirit, great virtue to change and turn to God.

(4) False grounds are here removed: *Not by works of righteousness which we have done, but according to his mercy, he saved us.* Works must be in the saved but not among the causes of his salvation; they are the way to the kingdom, not the meriting price of it. Faith and all saving graces are God's free gift and his work; the beginning, increase, and perfection of them in glory, all are from him.

(5) The formal cause of salvation, regeneration or spiritual renewing, as it is here called. A new prevailing principle of grace and holiness is wrought, which makes the man a new man, having new thoughts, desires, and affections. *He saved us.* What is so begun, as sure to be perfected in time, is expressed as if it already were so. We must be initially saved now, by regeneration, if on good ground we would expect complete salvation in heaven. The change then will be but in degree, not in kind. Grace is glory begun, as glory is but grace in its perfection.

(6) The outward sign and seal thereof in baptism, called therefore *the washing of regeneration.* The work itself is inward and spiritual; but it is outwardly signified and sealed in this ordinance. Baptism saves figuratively and sacramentally, where it is rightly used. Slight not this outward sign and seal, yet rest not in the outward washing. The covenant sealed in baptism binds to duties, as well as conveys benefits and privileges; if the former be not minded, in vain are the latter expected.

(7) The principal efficient, the *renewing of the Holy Ghost.* In the economy of our salvation, the applying and effecting part is especially attributed to the Holy Spirit. We are said to be born of the Spirit, to be quickened and sanctified by the Spirit, to be led and guided, strengthened and helped, by the Spirit. Earnestly therefore is he to be sought, and greatly to be heeded by us, that we quench not his holy motions. As we act towards him, so may we expect he will to us; if we slight, and resist, and oppose his workings, he will slacken them; if we continue to vex him, he will retire.

(8) The manner of God's communicating this Spirit in the gifts and graces of it; not with a scanty and niggardly hand, but most freely and plentifully: *Which he shed on us abundantly.* More of the Spirit in its gifts and graces is poured out under the gospel than was under the law. A measure of the Spirit the church has had in all ages, but more since the coming of Christ, than before. There was then great abundance of common gifts of illumination, outward calling and profession, and general faith, and of more special gifts of sanctification too, such as faith, and hope, and love. Let us get a share in these. What will it signify if much be shed forth and we remain dry? This is the manner of God's communicating grace and all spiritual blessings under the gospel —*plentifully;* he is not straitened towards us.

(9) The procuring cause of all, namely, Christ: *Through Jesus Christ our Saviour.* All come through him, and through him as a Saviour. Let us praise God for him above all; let us go to the Father by him. Have we grace? Let us thank him with the Father and Spirit for it, and grow and increase therein more and more.

(10) The ends why we are brought into this new spiritual condition, justification, and heirship, and hope of eternal life: *That being justified by his grace, we should be made heirs according to the hope of eternal life.* Justification is the free remission of a sinner, and accepting him as righteous through the righteousness of Christ received by faith. This God does freely as to us, yet through the intervention of Christ's sacrifice and righteousness, laid hold on by faith. It is by grace, as the spring and rise, though *through the redemption that is in Christ,* and by faith applying that redemption. Inherent righteousness we must have, and the fruits of it in works of obedience; as fruits of our justification, and evidences of our interest in Christ and qualification for life and happiness, and the very beginning and part of it; but the procuring of all this is by Christ, that, *being justified by his grace, we should be made heirs.* Our justification is *by the grace of God,* and our justification by that grace is necessary in order to our being made *heirs of eternal life.* Eternal life is set before us in the promise. The Spirit works faith in us and hope of that life, and so are we made heirs of it; faith and hope bring it near, and fill with joy in the well-grounded expectation of it. The meanest believer is a great heir. All this gives good reason why we should *show all meekness to all men,* because we have experienced so much benefit by the kindness and love of God to us, and may hope that they, in God's time, may be partakers of the like grace as we are.

III. When he has opened the grace of God towards us, he immediately presses the necessity of good works; for we must not expect the benefit of God's mercy unless we make conscience of our duty (*v.* 8). It must be an operative working faith. They must make it their care *to maintain good works,* not to do them occasionally only. *These things are good and profitable unto men;* these *good works,* say some, or *the teaching of these things,* rather than idle questions, as follows.

Verses 9-15

What Titus should avoid in teaching; how he should deal with a heretic; with some other directions.

I. He tells Titus what, in teaching, he should shun, *v.* 9. Idle and foolish enquiries must be shunned.— *And genealogies.* Some lawful and useful enquiries might be made into these things, to see the fulfilling of the scriptures in some cases, and especially in the descent of Christ the Messiah; but all that served to pomp only, and to feed vanity, in boasting of a long pedigree, these Titus must withstand as foolish and vain.—*And contentions, and strivings about the law.* There were those who were for the Mosaic rites and ceremonies, and would have them continued in the church. Titus must give no countenance to these, but avoid and oppose them; *for they are unprofitable and vain:* this is to be referred to all those *foolish questions and genealogies,* as well as those *strivings about the law.* They are so far from instructing and building up in godliness, that they are hindrances of it rather. Ministers must not only teach things good and useful, but shun and oppose the contrary; nor should people have itching ears, but love and embrace sound doctrine.

II. But because there will be *heresies* and *heretics* in the church, the apostle next directs Titus how to deal with such, *v.* 10. "Admonish him once and again, that, if possible he may be brought back, and thou mayest gain thy brother; but, if this will not reduce him, cast him out of the communion. Those who will not be reclaimed by admonitions, but are obstinate in their sins and errors, *are subverted and self-condemned*. How great an evil real heresy is. Such a one is *subverted* or perverted—a metaphor from a building so ruined as to render it difficult if not impossible to repair and raise it up again. Real heretics have seldom been recovered to the true faith: not so much defect of judgment, as perverseness of the will, being in the case. Pains and patience must be used about those that err most grievously. They must be admonished, instructed, and warned. Upon continued obstinacy the church is obliged, to preserve its own purity, by severing such a corrupt member; which discipline may by God's blessing become effectual to reform the offender.

III. The apostle subjoins some further directions, *v*. 12, 13.

1. Titus should hold himself ready to come to Paul at *Nicopolis*, as soon as *Artemas* or *Tychicus* should be sent to Crete, to supply his place. Of Artemas we read little, but Tychicus is mentioned on many occasions with respect. Paul calls him *a beloved brother, and faithful minister, and fellow-servant in the Lord*: one fit therefore for the service intimated.

2. The other personal charge to Titus is that he would bring two of his friends on their journey diligently, and see them furnished, so that nothing should be wanting to them. *Zenas* is styled *the lawyer*. *Apollos* was an eminent and faithful minister. Accompanying such persons part of their way, and accommodating them for their work and journeys, was a pious and needful service. Let Christians learn to *maintain good works, that they be not unfruitful*. Christianity is not a fruitless profession. It is not enough that they be harmless, but they must be profitable, doing good, as well as eschewing evil.—"*Let ours* set up and maintain some honest labour and employment, to provide for themselves and their families, that they be not unprofitable burdens on the earth"; so some understand it. Let them not think that Christianity gives them a writ of ease. *To maintain good works for necessary uses;* not living like drones on the labours of others, but themselves fruitful to the common benefit.

IV. The apostle concludes with salutations and benedictions, *v*. 15. Great comfort and encouragement it is to have the heart and prayers of other Christians with and for us. *Grace be with you all. Amen.* This is the apostle's wish and prayer. Grace is the chief thing to be wished and begged for, with respect to ourselves or others; it is, summarily, all good. *Amen* shuts up the prayer, expressing desire and hope, that so it may, and so it shall be.

AN EXPOSITION, WITH PRACTICAL OBSERVATIONS, OF

THE EPISTLE OF ST. PAUL TO

PHILEMON

Philemon, one of note and probably a minister in the church of Colosse, a city of Phrygia, had a servant named *Onesimus*, who, having purloined his goods, ran away from him, and came to Rome, where Paul was then a prisoner for the gospel, and was, by the blessing of God, converted by him, after which he ministered awhile to the apostle in bonds. Understanding him to be another man's servant, Paul would not, without his consent, detain him, but sends him back with this letter-commendatory, wherein he earnestly sues for his pardon and kind reception. There is no reason to doubt but Paul prevailed with Philemon to forgive and receive Onesimus.

In this epistle we have, I. The preface, ver. 1–7. II. The substance and body of it, ver. 8–21. And then the conclusion, ver. 22, to the end.

Verses 1–7

I. In the first two verses of the preface we have the persons from and to whom it is written,

1. The persons writing: Paul, the principal, who calls himself *a prisoner of Jesus Christ.* This was proper to move Philemon upon the request made to him by such a one, especially when strengthened too with the concurrence of Timothy. What could be denied to two such petitioners?

2. The persons written to are *Philemon and Apphia,* and with them Archippus, and the church in Philemon's house. Philemon, the master of Onesimus, was the principal; a good man he was, and probably a minister, and on both accounts dearly beloved by Paul. With Philemon Apphia is joined, probably his yoke-fellow. She was a party offended and injured by Onesimus, and therefore proper to be taken notice of in a letter for reconciliation and forgiveness. These are the principal parties written to. The less principal are, *Archippus, and the church in Philemon's house.* Archippus was a minister in the church of Colosse, Philemon's friend. Paul might think him one whom Philemon would advise with, and who might be capable of furthering the good work of peace-making and forgiveness. *And to the church in thy house,* his whole family, in which the worship of God was kept up. Families which generally may be most pious and orderly may yet have one or other in them impious and wicked. This was the aggravation of Onesimus's sin, that it was where he might have learned better. This one evil servant did not hinder Philemon's house from being called a church. Such should all families be—nurseries of religion. Wicked families are nurseries for hell, as good ones are for heaven. Paul, for some concern that all might have in this matter of Onesimus, directs to them all, that their affection as well as Philemon's might return to him, and that they might further, and not hinder, the reconciliation wished and sought.

II. The apostle's salutation of those named by him (*v.* 3). He wishes for them the best things; not gold, nor silver, nor any earthly good, but *grace and peace from God in Christ. Grace,* the spring and fountain of all blessings; *and peace,* all good, as the fruit and effect of that grace. *From God our Father and the Lord Jesus Christ.* From the Father, who is our Father in Christ; and from Christ, his favour and goodwill as God, and the fruits of it through him as Mediator. The favour of God and peace with him, as in itself it is the best and most desirable good, so is it the cause of all other, and what puts sweetness into every mercy and can make happy even in the want of all earthly things.

III. He expresses the singular affection he had for him, by thanksgiving and prayer to God in his behalf, and the great joy for the many good things he knew and heard to be in him, *v.* 4–7.

1. The object of Paul's praises and prayers for Philemon, *v.* 4. It is the privilege of good men that in their praises and prayers they come to God as their God: *I thank my God,* said Paul. Our prayers and praises should be offered up to God, not for ourselves only, but for others also. In this lies no little part of the communion of saints. Paul, in his private thanksgivings and prayers, was often particular in remembering his friends. This is a means of exercising love, and obtaining good for others.

2. The circumstance: *Always making mention of thee.* So must we remember Christian friends much and often, as their case may need.

3. The matter both of his praises and prayers, in reference to Philemon.

(1) Of his praises. He thanks God for the love which he heard Philemon had towards the Lord Jesus. For his faith in Christ also. Love to Christ, and faith in him, are prime Christian graces, for which there is great ground of praise to God. He praises God likewise for Philemon's love to all the saints. These two must go together. Different sentiments and ways in what is not essential will not make a difference of affection as to the truth. Mere external differences are nothing here. Paul calls a poor converted slave *his bowels.* We must love, as God does, all saints. *Hearing of thy love and faith, which thou hast towards the Lord Jesus, and towards all saints.* Love to saints, if it be sincere, will be catholic and universal love towards all saints; faith and love, though in the heart they are hidden things, are known by the effects of them.

(2) The apostle joins prayer with his praises, that the fruits of Philemon's faith and love might be more and more conspicuous, that the communication of them might constrain others to the acknowledgment of all the good things that were in him and in his house towards Christ Jesus.

4. He adds a reason, both of his prayer and his praises (*v.* 7). The good thou hast done and still doest is abundant matter of joy and comfort to me and others, who therefore desire you may continue and abound in such good fruits more and more.

Verses 8–25

I. The main business of the epistle, which was to plead with Philemon on behalf of Onesimus. Many arguments Paul urges for this purpose, *v.* 8–21. The *1st Argument* is taken from what was before noted: "Seeing so much good is reported of thee and found in thee, especially thy love to all saints, now let me see it on a fresh and further occasion." A disposition to do good, together with past instances and expressions of it, is a good handle to take hold of for pressing to more.

2nd Argument is from the authority of him that was now making this request to him, *v.* 8. This was a matter within the compass of the apostle's power to require, though he would not in this instance act up to it.

3rd Argument. He chooses to entreat it of him (*v.* 9). He argues from love rather than authority, which doubtless must carry engaging influence with it.

4th Argument. Being such a one as Paul the aged, and now also a prisoner of Jesus Christ. Years bespeak respect. The request of an aged apostle, and now suffering for Christ and his gospel, should be tenderly considered.

5th Argument. From the spiritual relation now between Onesimus and himself, *v.* 10. *My son, whom I have begotten in my bonds;* he was dear to him, and he hoped would be so to Philemon, under this consideration. Prison mercies are sweet.

6th Argument is from Philemon's own interest, *v.* 11. Unsanctified persons are unprofitable persons. Grace makes good for somewhat: "*In time past unprofitable but now profitable,* as he has since his conversion been here to me, ministering to me in my confinement." There seems an allusion to the name Onesimus, which signifies *profitable.* Now he will answer to his name. How tenderly does Paul here speak, when he is pleading with Philemon not to make severe reflections on his servant's misconduct, but to forgive. What happy changes conversion makes—of evil good! of unprofitable useful!

7th Argument. He urges Philemon from the strong affection that he had to Onesimus, *v.* 12. Even good men may sometimes need great earnestness and entreaty to forgive those who have injured and offended them.

8th Argument is from the apostle's denying himself in sending back Onesimus, *v.* 13, 14. Paul was now in prison, and wanted a friend or servant to assist him, for which he found Onesimus fit and ready, and therefore would have detained him to minister to him. Yet he would not take this liberty, though his circumstances needed it: *I have sent him back* to thee, that any good office of thine to me might not be *of necessity, but willingly.* He might indeed have presumed on Philemon's willingness; but, notwithstanding his need, he would deny himself rather than take that way.

9th Argument. Such a change was now wrought in Onesimus that Philemon needed not fear his ever running from him, or injuring him any more, *v.* 15. Charity would so hope and judge, yea, so it would be. How tenderly still the sins of penitents are spoken of; he calls it a *departure for a season* instead of giving it the term that it deserved. True penitents will not return to folly. Observe the goodness, and power of God, that he should be led into the way of salvation who had fled from it, and find means made effectual at Rome who had been hardened under them at Colosse.

10th Argument is taken from the capacity under which Onesimus now would return, and must be received by Philemon (*v.* 16). There is a spiritual brotherhood between all true believers, however distinguished in civil and outward respects; they are all children of the same heavenly Father. Christianity does not annul nor confound the respective civil duties, but strengthens the obligation to them. Religious servants are more than mere ordinary servants; they have grace in their hearts, and have found grace in God's sight, and so will in the sight of religious masters. "*A brother beloved, specially to me, but how much more to thee, both in the flesh and in the Lord.*

He is God's servant and thine too; here are more ties than he is under to me."

11th Argument. From the communion of saints, *v.* 17. Own and treat him as thou wouldst me, with a like ready and true, though perhaps not equal, affection.

12th Argument. A promise of satisfaction to Philemon, *v.* 18, 19.

(1) A confession of Onesimus's debt to Philemon. True penitents will be ingenuous in owning their faults, and especially is this to be done in cases of injury to others.

(2) Paul here engages for satisfaction. The communion of saints does not destroy distinction of property: Onesimus is yet Philemon's servant still, and indebted to him for wrongs that he had done. Suretiship is not in all cases unlawful, but in some is a good and merciful undertaking. Hereby he expresses his real and great affection for Onesimus, and his full belief of the sincerity of his conversion.

(3) The reason of things between him and Philemon: "*Albeit, I do not say to thee how thou owest unto me even thy own self besides.*" The apostle glances at the benefits he had conferred on Philemon. I have been the instrument of all that spiritual good to thee; and what thy obligation to me on this account is I leave to thee to consider.

13th Argument is from the joy and comfort the apostle hereby would have on Philemon's own account, as well as on Onesimus's, *v.* 20. Philemon was Paul's son in the faith, yet he entreats him as a brother: Onesimus a poor slave, yet he solicits for him as if he were seeking some great thing for himself. Christians should do the things that may rejoice the hearts of one another. From the world they expect trouble; and where may they look for comfort and joy but in one another? It is not any selfish respect I am actuated by, but what is pleasing to Christ.

14th Argument. This lies in the good hope and opinion which he expresses of Philemon, *v.* 21. Good thoughts and expectations of us more strongly move and engage us to do the things expected from us. Good persons will be ready for good works, and not narrow and pinching, but abundant in them.

II. The conclusion.

1. He signifies his good hope of deliverance, through their prayers, and that shortly he might see them, desiring Philemon to make provision for him, *v.* 22.

(1) *Prepare me also a lodging.* He wills Philemon to do it, intending to be his guest. Who would not show the utmost of affectionate regards to such a one?

(2) *For I trust that through your prayers I shall be given unto you.* He did not know how God might deal with him, but the benefit of prayer he had often found, and hoped he should again, for deliverance, and liberty to come to them. Trust must be with the use of means, prayer especially; this hath unlocked heaven and opened prison-doors. The least may in this way be helpful to the greatest. Though prayer obtains, yet it does not merit the things obtained: they are God's gift, and Christ's purchase. *I trust that through your prayers I shall be freely bestowed on you.* In praying for faithful ministers, people in effect pray for themselves: "*I trust I shall be given unto you,* for your service, and comfort."

2. He sends salutations from one who was his fellow-prisoner, and four more who were his fellow-labourers, *v.* 23, 24. *Epaphras, my fellow-prisoner in Christ Jesus.* He was of Colosse, and so countryman and fellow-citizen with Philemon, who, being at Rome, perhaps accompanying Paul, was confined in the same prison, and for the same cause. *My fellow-prisoner in Christ Jesus* is mentioned as his glory and the apostle's comfort. So God sometimes lightens

the sufferings of his servants by the communion of saints, the sweet fellowship they have one with another in their bonds. Never more enjoyment of God have they found than when suffering together for God.—*Marcus, Aristarchus, Demas, Lucas, my fellow-labourers.* The mention of these seems in a manner to interest them in the business of the letter. How ill would it look by denial of the request of it to slight so many worthy names as most of these, at least, were! *Marcus,* cousin of Barnabas, and son of Mary, who was so hospitable to the saints at Jerusalem. Though some failing seems to have been in him when Paul and he parted, yet in conjunction with Barnabas he went on with his work, and here Paul and he, we perceive, were reconciled. *Aristarchus* is mentioned with Marcus (Col. iv. 10), and called there by Paul his fellow-prisoner. Next is *Demas*: no mark of disgrace lay on him here, but he is joined with others who were faithful. *Lucas* is the last, that

beloved physician and evangelist, who came to Rome, companion with Paul.

3. Here is the apostle's closing prayer and benediction, *v.* 25. What is wished and prayed for: *Grace,* the free favour and love of God; with this the apostle begins and ends. From whom: *Our Lord Jesus Christ.* All grace to us is from Christ; he purchased, and he bestows it. To whom: *Your spirit,* not of Philemon only, but of all who were named in the inscription. All the house saluted are here joined in the closing benediction, the more to quicken all to further the end of the epistle.

Amen is added, not only for strong and affectionate summing up the prayer and wish, *so let it be*; but as an expression of faith that it will be heard, *so shall it be.* The grace of Christ with their spirits, Philemon's especially, would sweeten and mollify them, and dispose to forgive others as God for Christ's sake hath forgiven us.

AN EXPOSITION, WITH PRACTICAL OBSERVATIONS, OF

THE EPISTLE TO

THE HEBREWS

Concerning this epistle we must enquire, I. Into the divine authority of it; for this has been questioned by some. The divine original of it shines forth with such strong and unclouded rays that he who runs may read it as an eminent part of the canon of scripture. Its general reception in the church of God in all ages—these are the evidences of its divine authority. II. As to the penman of this epistle, we are not so certain; it does not bear the name of any in the front of it, as the rest of the epistles do, and there has been some dispute among the learned to whom they should ascribe it. But it is generally assigned to the apostle Paul. In the primitive times it was generally ascribed to him. III. As to the scope and design of this epistle, it is very evident that it was clearly to inform the minds, and strongly to confirm the judgment, of the Hebrews in the transcendent excellency of the gospel above the law. The design of this epistle was to press the believing Hebrews to a constant adherence to the Christian faith, and perseverance in it, notwithstanding all the sufferings they might meet with in so doing. It must be acknowledged that there are many things in this epistle hard to be understood, but the sweetness we shall find therein will make us abundant amends for all the pains we take to understand it.

CHAPTER 1

In this chapter we have a twofold comparison stated: I. Between the evangelical and legal dispensation, ver. 1–3. II. Between the glory of Christ and that of the highest creatures, the angels, ver. 4, to the end.

Verses 1–3

The apostle begins with a general declaration of the excellency of the gospel dispensation above that of the law.

I. The way wherein God communicated himself and his will to men under the Old Testament. The persons by whom God delivered his mind under the Old Testament; they were *the prophets*, that is, persons chosen of God, and qualified by him, for that office of revealing the will of God to men. The persons to whom God spoke by the prophets: *To the fathers*, to all the Old Testament saints. The order in which God spoke to men in those past times: he spoke to his ancient people *at sundry times and in divers manners. By several parts*, as the word signifies, which may refer either to the several ages of the Old Testament dispensation; or to the several gradual openings of his mind concerning the Redeemer. *In divers manners*, according to the different ways in which God thought fit to communicate his mind to his prophets.

II. God's method of communicating his mind and will under the New Testament dispensation, these last days as they are called. Now we must expect no new revelation, but only more of the Spirit of Christ to help us better to understand what is already revealed. It is the final, the finishing revelation. It is a revelation which God has made by his Son, the most excellent messenger that was ever sent into the world.

1. The glory of his office. God hath appointed him to be heir of all things. By him God made the worlds, both visible and invisible, the heavens and the earth. By him he made the old creation, by him he makes the new creature, and by him he rules and governs both. He upholds all things by the word of his power. The weight of the whole creation is laid upon Christ: he supports the whole and all the parts.

2. Hence the apostle passes to the glory of the person of Christ, *v.* 3. He is the only-begotten Son of God, and as such he must have the same nature. The person of the Son is the glory of the Father, shining forth with a truly divine splendour. Jesus Christ in his person is God manifest in the flesh. The person of the Son is the true image and character of the person of the Father. In beholding the power, wisdom, and goodness, of the Lord Jesus Christ, we behold the power, wisdom, and goodness, of the Father. This is the glory of the person of Christ; the fulness of the Godhead dwells in him.

3. From the glory of the person of Christ he proceeds to mention the glory of his grace. The sufferings of Christ had this great honour in them, to be a full satisfaction for the sins of his people: *By himself he purged away our sins*; he has made atonement for sin. Himself, the glory of his person and nature, gave to his sufferings such merit as was a sufficient reparation of honour to God, who had suffered injury and affront by the sins of men.

4. From the glory of his sufferings we are at length led to consider the glory of his exaltation. Having assumed our nature, and suffered in it on earth, he has taken it up with him to heaven.

Now it was by no less a person than this that God in these last days spoke to men. The dispensations of the gospel must therefore exceed, very far exceed, the dispensation of the law.

Verses 4–14

The apostle now proceeds to show that he is much superior not only to the prophets, but to the angels themselves. Both in nature and office Christ is vastly superior to the angels themselves.

I. The superior nature of Christ is proved from his superior name.

II. The superiority of the name and nature of Christ above the angels is declared in the holy scriptures, and is to be deduced thence. Now here are several passages of scripture cited, in which those things are said of Christ that were never said of the angels.

1. It was said of Christ, *Thou art my Son, this day have I begotten thee* (Ps. ii. 7). Now this was never said concerning the angels, and therefore by inheritance he has a more excellent nature and name than they.

2. It is said concerning Christ, but never concerning the angels, *I will be to him a Father, and he shall be to me a Son.*

3. It is said of Christ, *When God bringeth his First-begotten into the world, let all the angels of God worship him.* The proof of this is taken out of Ps. xcvii 7, *Worship him, all you gods*, "All you that are superior to men, own yourselves to be inferior to Christ in nature and power."

4. God has said concerning Christ, *Thy throne, O God, is for ever and ever,* &c., *v.* 8–12. But of the angels he has only said that *he hath made them spirits, and his ministers a flame of fire, v.* 7.

(1) What does God say here of the angels? *He maketh his angels spirits, and his ministers a flame of fire.* The office of the angels: they are God's ministers, or *servants, to do his pleasure.* He endows them with light and zeal, readiness and resolution to do his pleasure: they are no more than what God has made them to be.

(2) How much greater things are said of Christ by the Father. Here two passages of scripture are quoted.

[1] One of these is out of Ps. xlv. 5, 7, where God declares of Christ, *First,* His true and real divinity, *Thy throne, O God.* And, if God the Father declares him to be so, he must be really and truly so. *Secondly,* God declares his dignity and dominion, as having a throne, a kingdom, and a sceptre of that kingdom. *Thirdly,* God declares the eternal duration of the dominion and dignity of Christ: *Thy throne, O God, is for ever and ever.* This distinguishes Christ's throne from all earthly thrones, which are tottering, and will at length tumble down; but the throne of Christ shall be as the days of heaven. *Fourthly,* God declares of Christ the perfect equity of his administration, *v.* 8. He came righteously to the sceptre, and he uses it in perfect righteousness, *v.* 9. Christ came to fulfil all righteousness. He came to finish transgression, and to make an end of sin as a hateful as well as hurtful thing. *Fifthly,* God declares of Christ how he was qualified for the office of Mediator, and how he was installed and confirmed in it (*v.* 9). Christ has the name Messiah from his being anointed. This anointing of Christ was *with the oil of gladness,* that joy which was set before him as the reward of his service and sufferings, that crown of glory and gladness which he should wear for ever after the suffering of death. This anointing of Christ was above the anointing of his fellows. All God's other anointed ones had only the Spirit in a certain measure; Christ had the Spirit above measure, without any limitation.

[2] The other passage of scripture is taken out of Ps. cii. 25–27, and is recited in *v.* 10–12, where the omnipotence of the Lord Jesus Christ is declared as it appears both in creating the world and in changing it. In creating the world (*v.* 10). His right, as God with the Father, was absolute, resulting from his creating power. This power he had before the beginning of the world, and he exerted it in giving a beginning and being to the world. He not only founded the earth, but the heavens too are the work of his hands, the hosts of heaven, the angels themselves; and therefore he must needs be infinitely superior to them. In changing the world that he has made. *a* This world is mutable, all created nature is so; this world has passed through many changes, and shall pass through more (*v.* 11, 12). Not only men and beasts and trees grow old, but this world itself grows old, and is hastening to its dissolution; it changes like a garment, has lost much of its beauty and strength. It bears the symptoms of a dying world. But then its dissolution will not be its utter destruction, but its change. Christ will fold up this world as a garment not to be abused any longer. Sin has made a great change in the world for the worse, and Christ will make a great change in it for the better. *b* Christ is immutable. Thus the Father testifies of him, *Thou remainest, thy years shall not fail.* Christ is the same in himself, and the same to his people in all the changes of time. Christ is immutable and immortal: his years shall not fail. Christ lives to take care of us while we live, and of ours when we are gone.

III. The superiority of Christ to the angels appears in this that God never said to the angels what he has said to Christ, *v.* 13, 14.

1. What has God said to Christ? He has said, "*Sit thou at my right hand, till I make thy enemies thy footstool,* Ps. cx. 1. Christ Jesus has his enemies, enemies even among men. Let us not think it strange then if we have our enemies. Christ never did anything to make men his enemies; he has done a great deal to make them all his friends and his Father's friends, and yet he has his enemies. All the enemies of Christ shall be made his footstool. God the Father has undertaken for this, and, though it be not done presently, it shall certainly be done. Christ shall go on to rule and reign till this be done; he shall not leave any of his great designs unfinished. And it becomes his people to go on in their duty, till he make them conquerors over all their spiritual enemies.

2. What has God said to the angels? *They are ministering spirits, sent forth to minister for those who shall be the heirs of salvation.* (1) What the angels are as to their nature: they are spirits. (2) What the angels are as to their office: they are ministering spirits. They are the ministers of divine Providence. The angels are sent forth for this end—to minister to those who shall be the heirs of salvation. The description given of the saints—they are *heirs of salvation*; at present they are under age, heirs, not inheritors. They are heirs because they are children of God. The dignity and privilege of the saints—the angels are sent forth to minister for them. Bless God for the ministration of angels.

Chapter 2

The apostle, I. Makes some application of the doctrine laid down concerning the excellency of the person of Christ, ver. 1–4. II. Enlarges further upon the pre-eminence of Christ above the angels, ver. 5–9. III. Proceeds to remove the scandal of the cross, ver. 10–15. IV. Asserts the incarnation of Christ, and assigns the reason of his so doing, ver. 16, to the end.

Verses 1–4

He now comes to apply this doctrine both by way of exhortation and argument.

I. By way of exhortation, *v.* 1. It is the great concern of everyone under the gospel to give the most earnest heed to all gospel discoveries and directions. We must embrace them in our hearts and affections, retain them in our memories, and finally regulate our words and actions according to them.

II. He adds strong motives to enforce the exhortation.

1. From the great loss we shall sustain if we do not take this earnest heed to the things which we have heard: *We shall let them slip.* Our minds and memories are like a leaky vessel, they do not without much care retain what is poured into them. Those meet with an inconceivable loss who let gospel truths slip out of their minds. All is lost, if the gospel be lost. If we do not well attend, we shall not long retain the word of God; inattentive hearers will soon be forgetful hearers.

2. Another argument is taken from the dreadful punishment we shall incur if we do not do this duty, *v.* 2, 3. (1) How the law is described: it was the *word spoken by angels, and declared to be steadfast.* It is like the promise, *yea and amen*; it is truth and faithfulness, and it will abide and have its force whether men obey it or no; *for every transgression and disobedience will receive a just recompence of reward.* If men trifle with the law of God, the law will not trifle with them. Punishments are as just, and as much due to sin as rewards are to obedience. (2) How the gospel is described. It is salvation, a great salvation, so great that none can fully express, no, nor yet conceive, how great it is. It shows how we may be saved from so great sin and so great misery, and be restored to so great holiness and so great happiness. (3) How sinning against the gospel is described: it is declared to be a *neglect of this great salvation*; it is a

contempt put upon the saving grace of God in Christ, making light of it, not caring for it. Let us all take heed that we be not found among those wicked wretched sinners who neglect the grace of the gospel. (4) How the misery of such sinners is described: it is declared to be unavoidable (*v.* 3): *How shall we escape?* The despoilers of this salvation are condemned already, under arrest and in the hands of justice already. There is no escaping out of this condemned state, but by accepting the great salvation discovered in the gospel; as for those who neglect it, the wrath of God is upon them, and it abides upon them. There is no door of mercy left open for them; there will be no more sacrifice for sin.

3. Another argument to enforce the exhortation is taken from the person by whom the gospel began to be spoken (*v.* 3): that is, the Lord Jesus Christ. Now surely it may be expected that all will reverence this Lord, and take heed to a gospel that began to be spoken by one who spoke so as never *man spoke*.

4. Another argument is taken from the character of those who were witnesses to Christ and the gospel (*v.* 3, 4). (1) The promulgation of the gospel was continued and confirmed by the evangelists and apostles, who were eye and ear-witnesses of what Jesus Christ began both to do and to teach, Acts i. 1. These witnesses could have no worldly end to serve hereby. They exposed themselves by their testimony to the loss of all that was dear to them in this life, and many of them sealed it with their blood. (2) *God himself bore witness* to those who were witnesses for Christ. He bore them witness *by signs, and wonders, and divers miracles, and gifts of the Holy Ghost, according to his will.* It was the will of God that we should have sure footing for our faith, and a strong foundation for our hope in receiving the gospel. As at the giving forth of the law there were signs and wonders, so he witnesses to the gospel by more and greater miracles, as to a more excellent and abiding dispensation.

Verses 5–9

For to the angels hath he not put in subjection the world to come, whereof we speak.

I. Here the apostle lays down a negative proposition, including a positive one—That the state of the gospel-church, which is here called *the world to come*, is *not subjected to the angels.* This new world is committed to Christ, and put in absolute subjection to him only. His angels were too weak for such a charge.

II. A scripture-account of that blessed Jesus. It is taken from Ps. viii. 4–6. These words are to be considered both as applicable to mankind in general, and as applied here to the Lord Jesus Christ.

1. As applicable to mankind in general, an affectionate thankful expostulation with the great God concerning his kindness to the sons of men. (1) In remembering them, or being mindful of them. God is always mindful of us, let us never be forgetful of him. (2) In visiting them. He comes to see us, how it is with us; and by his visitation our spirit is preserved. (3) In making man the head of all the creatures in this lower world. (4) In crowning him with glory and honour, the honour of having noble powers and faculties. (5) In giving him dominion over the inferior creatures.

2. As applied to the Lord Jesus Christ, *v.* 8, 9. The moving cause of all the kindness God shows to men is the grace of God. The fruits of this free grace of God is that God crowned the human nature of Christ with glory and honour, in his being perfectly holy; that by his sufferings he might make satisfaction, tasting death for every man. As a reward of his humiliation in suffering death, he was crowned with glory and honour.

Verses 10–13

The apostle here proceeds to remove the scandal of the cross.

I. It became God that Christ should suffer, *v.* 10.

1. God is described as the final end and first cause of all things, and as such it became him to secure his own glory in all that he did.

2. He is declared to have acted up to this glorious character in the work of redemption.

(1) In the choice of the end; and that was to bring many sons to glory. We must be the sons of God both by adoption and regeneration, before we can be brought to the glory of heaven. Though the sons of God are but a few in one place and at one time, yet when they shall be all brought together it will appear that they are many.

(2) In the choice of the means. In finding out such a person as should be the captain of our salvation. In making this captain of our salvation perfect through sufferings. He perfected the work of our redemption by shedding his blood. He found his way to the crown by the cross, and so must his people too.

II. How much they should be benefited by the cross and sufferings of Christ. Hereby they are brought into a near union with Christ, and into a very endearing relation.

1. Into a near union (*v.* 11). Christ, who is the agent in this work of sanctification, and Christians, are all of one. They are all of one heavenly Father. They are of one earthly father, Adam. Christ and believers have the same human nature. They are of one spirit, the same mind is in them that was in Christ.

2. Into an endearing relation.

(1) He declares what this relation is: he is not ashamed to call them *brethren.* Christ and believers are brethren in what is heavenly as well as in what is earthly. He will never be ashamed of any who are not ashamed of him, and who take care not to be a shame and reproach to him and to themselves.

(2) He illustrates this from three texts of scripture.

[1] The first is out of Ps. xxii. 22. Christ should have a church or *congregation* in the world, a company of volunteers, freely willing to follow him. These should not only be brethren to one another, but to Christ himself. He would declare his Father's name to them.

[2] The second scripture is quoted from Ps. xviii. 2. His brethren must suffer and trust too.

[3] The third scripture is taken from Isa. viii. 18. Christ's children were given him of the Father. And they are given to Christ at their conversion. Christ receives them, rejoices in them, takes them up to heaven, and there presents them to his Father.

Verses 14–18

I. The incarnation of Christ is asserted (*v.* 16). He took our nature into union with his divine nature, and became really and truly man. He did not lay hold of angels, but he laid hold of the seed of Abraham. The nature of angels could not be an atoning sacrifice for the sin of man. He took upon him the human nature from one descended from the loins of Abraham, that the same nature that had sinned might suffer. Now there is hope and help for the chief of sinners in and through Christ.

II. The reasons and designs of the incarnation of Christ are declared.

1. For no higher nor lower nature than man's that had sinned could so suffer for the sin of man as to satisfy the justice of God, and raise man up to a state of hope.

2. He became man that he might die. The legal sacrifices and offerings God could not accept as a propitiation. A body was prepared for Christ.

3. The devil was the first sinner, and the first

tempter to sin, and sin was the procuring cause of death. He draws men into sin, the ways whereof are death. In these respects he may be said to have had the power of death. But now Christ has so far destroyed him who had the power of death that he can keep none under the power of spiritual death; nor can he draw any into sin.

4. That he might deliver his own people from the slavish fear of death to which they are often subject, Christ became man, and died, to deliver them from perplexities of soul, by letting them know that death is not only a conquered enemy, but a reconciled friend. Death is not now in the hand of Satan, but in the hand of Christ.

5. He must be faithful to God and merciful to men. In things pertaining to God, to his justice, and to his honour—to make reconciliation for the sins of the people. In things pertaining to his people, to their support and comfort, *v.* 18. Christ's passion: *He suffered being tempted;* and his temptations were not the least part of his sufferings. Christ's compassion: *He is able to succour those that are tempted.* He knows how to deal with tempted sorrowful souls, because he has been himself sick of the same disease, not of sin, but of temptation and trouble of soul. The best of Christians are subject to many temptations. Temptations bring our souls into such distress and danger that they need support and succour.

CHAPTER 3

The apostle applies what he had said concerning the priesthood of Christ, ver. 1–6. He then adds many weighty counsels and cautions, from ver. 7, to the end.

Verses 1–6

The application of the doctrine concerning the priesthood of our Lord Jesus Christ.

I. The apostle exhorts Christians to have this high priest much in their thoughts.

1. The honourable compellation used towards those to whom he wrote: *Holy brethren, partakers of the heavenly calling.* Brethren, not only my brethren, but the brethren of Christ, and in him brethren to all the saints. Holy brethren; holy not only in profession and title, but in principle and practice, in heart and life. *Partakers of the heavenly calling—* partakers of the means of grace, and of the Spirit of grace, that came from heaven; that calling which brings down heaven into the souls of men.

2. The titles he gives to Christ, whom he would have them consider, (1) As the apostle of our profession, the great revealer of that faith which we profess to hold and of that hope which we profess to have. (2) Not only the apostle, but the high priest, too, of our profession, upon whose satisfaction and intercession we profess to depend for pardon of sin, and acceptance with God. (3) As Christ, the Messiah. (4) As Jesus, our Saviour, our healer.

II. The duty we owe to him who bears all these high and honourable titles. Look unto Jesus, the author and finisher of your faith. Even those that are holy brethren, and partakers of the heavenly calling, have need to stir up one another to think more of Christ than they do; the best of his people think too seldom and too slightly of him.

III. Several arguments to enforce this duty of considering Christ the apostle and high priest of our profession.

1. The first is taken from his fidelity, *v.* 2. He was faithful to him that appointed him, as Moses was in all his house. Moses was faithful in the discharge of his office to the Jewish church in the Old Testament, and so is Christ under the New; this was a proper argument to urge upon the Jews.

2. The superior glory and excellence of Christ above Moses (*v.* 3–6). (1) Christ was a maker of the house,

Moses but a member in it. Christ, who is God, drew the ground-plan of the church, provided the materials, and disposed them to receive the form; he has compacted and united this his house, and crowned all with his own presence, which is the true glory of this house of God. (2) Christ was the master of this house, as well as the maker, *v.* 5, 6. Moses was only a faithful servant. Christ, as the eternal Son of God, is the rightful owner and sovereign ruler of the church. Christ is worthy of more glory than Moses, and of greater regard and consideration. Now follows a comfortable accommodation of it to himself and all true believers. *Whose house we are.* A characteristic description of those persons who constitute this house: "*If we hold fast the confidence, and the rejoicing of the hope, firmly to the end.*" There must not only be a setting out well in the ways of Christ, but a steadfastness and perseverance therein unto the end.

Verses 7–19

Here the apostle proceeds in pressing upon them serious counsels and cautions; and he recites a passage out of Ps. xcv. 7, &c.

I. What he counsels them to do—to give a speedy and present attention to the call of Christ. "Hear his voice; apply it to yourselves and set about it this very day, for to-morrow it may be too late."

II. What he cautions them against—hardening their hearts, turning the deaf ear to the calls and counsels of Christ. The hardening of our hearts is the spring of all our other sins.

III. Whose example he warns them by—that of the Israelites their fathers in the wilderness: *As in the provocation and day of temptation;* this refers to Exod. xvii. 2–7. Days of temptation are often days of provocation. The sins of others should be a warning to us. Our fathers' sins and punishments should be remembered by us, to deter us from following their evil examples. The sin they were guilty of: they distrusted God, murmured against Moses, and would not attend to the voice of God. The aggravations of their sin: they sinned when they saw his works— works of wonder wrought for their deliverance out of Egypt, and their support and supply in the wilderness. They continued thus to sin against God for forty years. The source and spring of such aggravated sins. They erred in their hearts; and these heart-errors produced many other errors in their lips and lives. They did not know God's ways, though he had walked before them. They did not observe either his providences or his ordinances. The just resentment God had at their sins, and yet the great patience he exercised towards them (*v.* 10). All sin does not only anger and affront God, but it grieves him. If they by their sins continue to grieve the Spirit of God, their sins shall be made grievous to their own spirits, either in a way of judgment or mercy. God swore in his wrath that they should not enter into his rest. Sin, long continued in, will kindle the divine wrath. His wrath will make their condition a restless condition; there is no resting under the wrath of God.

IV. What use the apostle makes of their awful example, *v.* 12, 13, &c.

1. He gives the Hebrews a proper caution; the word is, *Take heed—look to it.* "Look about you; be upon your guard against enemies both within and without." The ruin of others should be a warning to us to take heed of the rock they split upon.

2. He enlarges upon the matter of the admonition: *Take heed, brethren, lest there be in any of you an evil heart of unbelief in departing from the living God.* A heart of unbelief is an evil heart. An evil heart of unbelief is at the bottom of all our sinful departures from God; if once we allow ourselves to distrust God, we may soon desert him.

3. That which would be a remedy against this evil heart of unbelief, *v.* 13. Since tomorrow is none of ours, we must make the best improvement of today. There is a great deal of deceitfulness in sin; it promises much, but performs nothing. The deceitfulness of sin is of a hardening nature. Every act of sin confirms the habit.

4. He conforts those who not only set out well, but hold on well, and hold out to the end (*v.* 14). The saints' privilege: they are made partakers of Christ, in all that he is, in all that he has done, or can do. The condition on which they hold that privilege, their perseverance. Not but they shall persevere, being kept by the mighty power of God through faith to salvation, but to be pressed thus to it is one means by which Christ helps his people to persevere. The same spirit with which Christians set out in the ways of God they should maintain to the end. There are a great many who in the beginning show a great deal of courage and confidence, but do not hold them fast to the end.

5. The apostle resumes what he had quoted before, *v.* 15, 16, &c. The apostle tells them that though some who had heard the voice of God did provoke him, yet all did not so. God will have a remnant that shall be obedient to his voice.

6. The apostle puts some queries upon what had been before mentioned (*v.* 17–19). God is grieved only with those of his people who sin against him, and continue in sin. Unbelief (with rebellion which is the consequent of it) is the great damning sin of the world. This sin shuts up the heart of God, and shuts up the gate of heaven, against them.

CHAPTER 4

The apostle proceeds, I. To declare that our privileges by Christ under the gospel exceed the privileges of the Jewish church under Moses, ver. 1–4. II. He assigns the cause why the ancient Hebrews did not profit by their religious privileges, ver. 2. Then, III. Confirms the privileges of those who believe, and the misery of those who continue in unbelief, 3–10. IV. Concludes with arguments and motives to faith and obedience.

Verses 1–10

I. Our privileges by Christ under the gospel are not only as great, but greater than those enjoyed under the Mosaic law. We have a promise left us of entering into his rest. This promise of spiritual rest is a promise left us by the Lord Jesus Christ in his last will and testament, as a precious legacy. Our business is to see to it that we be the legatees, and so have the prospect and earnest of perfect and everlasting rest in heaven.

II. We have as great advantages as they (*v.* 2); the same gospel for substance was preached under both Testaments. We have the gospel as well as they, and in greater purity and perspicuity than they had.

III. The reason why so few of the ancient Jews profited by that dispensation of the gospel was their want of faith, *v.* 2. The word is preached to us that we may profit by it; it is a price put into our hands to get wisdom. There have been in all ages a great many unprofitable hearers. Those who are not gainers by hearing are great losers. That which is at the bottom of all our unprofitableness is our unbelief. If the hearers have not faith in their souls to mix with the word, they will be never the better for it. This faith must mingle with every word, and be in act and exercise while we are hearing.

IV. Those who enjoy the gospel should maintain a holy fear and jealousy over themselves, *v.* 1. Those who might have attained salvation by faith may fall short by unbelief. It is a dreadful thing so much as to seem to fall short of the gospel salvation. It is much more dreadful really to fall short. Maintain a holy and religious fear lest we should fall short. Presumption is the high road to ruin.

V. The apostle confirms the happiness of all those who truly believe the gospel.

1. By asserting so positively the truth of it, from the experience of himself and others: "*We who have believed, do enter into rest,*" *v.* 3.

2. He illustrates and confirms it. (1) From God's finishing his work of creation, and so entering into his rest (*v.* 3, 4). He will cause those who believe to finish their work, and then to enjoy their rest. (2) From God's continuing the observance of the sabbath. There is a more spiritual sabbath remaining for the people of God than that into which Joshua led the Jews (*v.* 6–9). Believers shall enter into their rest, *v.* 10.

VI. The apostle confirms the misery of those who do not believe; they shall never enter into this spiritual rest, either of grace here or glory hereafter. It remains only for the people of God; others by their sin abandon themselves to eternal restlessness.

Verses 11–16

I. A serious exhortation, *v.* 11. The end proposed —rest in Christ on earth, with Christ in heaven. The way to this end prescribed—labour, diligent labour; this is the only way to rest; those who will not work now shall not rest hereafter. Let us therefore labour, let us all call upon one another to this diligence. Now is our working time, our rest remains.

II. Powerful motives to make the advice effectual.

1. *Lest any man fall after the same example of unbelief.* To have seen so many fall before us will be a great aggravation of our sin, if we will not take warning by them.

2. The great help we may have from the word of God that we may obtain this rest, *v.* 12. It is *quick*; it is very lively and active, in seizing the conscience of the sinner, in cutting him to the heart, and in comforting him and binding up the wounds of the soul. It is *powerful*. It convinces powerfully, converts powerfully, and comforts powerfully. It is powerful to batter down Satan's kingdom, and to set up the kingdom of Christ upon the ruins thereof. It is *sharper than any two-edged sword*. It will enter where no other sword can, and make a more critical dissection: it *pierces to the dividing asunder of the soul and the spirit*, the soul and its habitual prevailing temper; it makes a soul that has been a long time of a proud spirit to be humble, of a perverse spirit to be meek and obedient. This sword divides between *the joints and the marrow*. This sword can make men willing to undergo the sharpest operation for the mortifying of sin. It is *a discerner of the thoughts and intents of the heart*. The word will turn the inside of a sinner out, and let him see all that is in his heart.

3. The perfections of the Lord Jesus Christ.

(1) His person, particularly his omniscience, *v.* 13. None of the creatures can be concealed from Christ; and there are none of the motions and workings of our heads and hearts but what are open and manifest to him. This omniscience of Christ should engage us to persevere in faith and obedience.

(2) His office, and this particular office of our high priest.

[1] What kind of high priest Christ is (*v.* 14). *First*, A great high priest. The greatness of our high priest is set forth by his having passed into the heavens. Christ executed one part of his priesthood on earth, in dying for us; the other he executes in heaven, by pleading the cause of his people. The greatness of Christ is set forth by his name, *Jesus*—a physician and a Saviour, able to save to the uttermost all who come to God by him. *Secondly*, He is not only a great, but a gracious high priest, merciful, compassionate, and sympathizing with his people, *v.* 15. He is touched with the feeling of our infirmities, not

only that he might be able to satisfy for us, but to sympathize with us. *Thirdly*, He is a sinless high priest: *He was in all things tempted as we are, yet without sin.* We seldom meet with temptations but they give us some shock. We are apt to give back, though we do not yield; but our great high priest came off clear in his encounter with the devil.

[2] How we should demean ourselves towards him. Let us hold fast our profession of faith in him, *v.* 14. Let us never deny him, never be ashamed of him before men. Christians must not only set out well, but they must hold out. We should encourage ourselves to come boldly to the throne of grace, *v.* 16. There is a throne of grace set up. God might have set up a tribunal of strict justice, but he has chosen to set up a throne of grace. There grace reigns, and acts with sovereign freedom, power, and bounty. It is our duty to be often found before this throne of grace. It is good for us to be there. Our business at the throne of grace should be that we *may obtain mercy and find grace to help in time of need.* Mercy and grace are the things we want, mercy to pardon all our sins and grace to purify our souls. In all our approaches to this throne of grace for mercy, we should come with a humble freedom and boldness; we should ask in faith, nothing doubting. We are indeed to come with reverence and godly fear; not as if we were dragged before the tribunal of justice, but kindly invited to the mercy-seat, where grace reigns, and loves to exert and exalt itself towards us. The office of Christ, as being our high priest, and such a high priest, should be the ground of our confidence in all our approaches to the throne of grace.

CHAPTER 5

The apostle continues his discourse upon the priesthood of Christ. I. He explains the nature of the priestly office in general, ver. 1–3. II. The proper call there must be to this office, ver. 4–6. III. The requisite qualifications for the work, ver. 7–9. IV. The peculiar order of the priesthood of Christ, ver. 6, 7, 10. V. He reproves the Hebrews, that they had not made those improvements in knowledge which might have made them capable of looking into the more abstruse parts of scripture, ver. 11–14.

Verses 1–9

An account of the nature of the priestly office in general.

I. Of what kind of beings the high priest must be. He must be taken from among men; he must be a man, one of ourselves. This implies that God would not admit sinful man to come to him immediately and alone; that God was pleased to take one from among men, by whom they might approach God in hope.

II. For whom every high priest is ordained: *For men in things pertaining to God*, for the glory of God and the good of men.

III. For what purpose every high priest was ordained: *That he might offer both gifts and sacrifices for sin.*

1. That he might offer gifts or free-will offerings, as an acknowledgment that our all is of him and from him. All we bring to God must be free and not forced; it must be a gift.

2. That he might offer sacrifices for sin. Christ is constituted a high priest for both these ends. Our good deeds must be presented by Christ, and our evil deeds must be expiated by the sacrifice of himself.

IV. How this high priest must be qualified, *v.* 2.

1. He must be one that can have compassion *on the ignorant.* He must be one who can find in his heart to pity them, one that is willing to instruct those that are dull of understanding. *On those that are out of the way.* He must be one who has tenderness enough to lead them back from the by-paths of error, sin, and misery, into the right away: this will require great patience and compassion, even the compassion of a God.

2. He must also be compassed with infirmity; and so be able from himself to sympathize with us. Thus Christ was qualified.

V. How the high priest was to be called of God. (*v.* 4). The office of the priesthood was a very great honour. Those only can expect his presence and blessing on them and their administrations, that are called of God; others may expect a blast instead of a blessing.

VI. How this is brought home and applied to Christ, *v.* 5. Though Christ reckoned it his glory to be made a high priest, yet he would not assume that glory to himself. He did not run without being sent; and, if he did not, surely others should be afraid to do it.

VII. The apostle prefers Christ before Aaron. In the manner of his call, in which God said unto him, *Thou art my Son, this day have I begotten thee.* Now God never said thus to Aaron. Another expression that God used in the call of Christ, *v.* 6. God the Father appointed him a priest of a higher order than that of Aaron. The priesthood of Aaron was to be but temporary; the priesthood of Christ was to be perpetual. In the holiness of his person. Other priests were to offer up sacrifices, as for the *sins of others, so for themselves, v.* 3. But Christ needed not to offer for sins for himself.

VIII. Christ's discharge of this his office, and the consequences of that discharge, *v.* 7–9.

1. The discharge of his office of the priesthood (*v.* 7). He took to him flesh; he became a mortal man. Christ, in the days of his flesh, subjected himself to death; he was a tempted, bleeding, dying Jesus! God the Father was able to save him from death. What would have become of us if God had saved Christ from dying? It was in kindness to us that the Father would not suffer that bitter cup to pass away from him; for then we must have drunk the dregs of it. Christ, in the days of his flesh, offered up prayers and supplications to his Father. A great many instances we have of Christ's praying. This refers to his prayer in his agony, and to that before his agony. The prayers and supplications that Christ offered up were joined with strong cries and tears, herein setting us an example. How many dry prayers, how few wet ones, do we offer up to God! Christ was heard in that he feared. He was answered by present supports in his agonies, and in being carried well through death, and delivered from it by a glorious resurrection. He was carried through death; and there is no real deliverance from death but to be carried well through it. We may have many recoveries from sickness, but we are never saved from death till we are carried well through it.

2. The consequences of this discharge of his office, *v.* 8, 9, &c.

(1) By these his sufferings *he learned obedience, though he was a Son, v.* 8. Let none then who are the children of God by adoption expect an absolute freedom from suffering. Though he never was disobedient, yet he never performed such an act of obedience as when he became obedient to death, even to the death of the cross. We should learn by all our afflictions a humble obedience to the will of God.

(2) Hereby he has become the author of eternal salvation to men. This salvation is actually bestowed on none but those who obey Christ. We must hearken to his word, and obey him. He is exalted to be a prince to rule us, as well as a Saviour to deliver us; and he will be a Saviour to none but to those to whom he is a prince. But to those who obey him, he will be the author—the grand cause of their salvation.

Verses 10–14

I. He had many things which he could say to them concerning this mysterious person called Melchisedec, whose priesthood was eternal. There are great mysteries in the person and offices of the Redeemer; Christianity is the great mystery of godliness.

II. The reason why he did not say all those things concerning Christ, our Melchisedec, that he had to say: *You are dull of hearing.* Dull hearers make the preaching of the gospel a difficult thing, and even many who have some faith are but dull hearers.

III. It was not a mere natural infirmity, but it was a sinful infirmity, *v.* 12.

1. They might have been so well instructed in the doctrine of the gospel as to have been teachers of others.

2. *You have need that one should teach you again,* &c. In the oracles of God there are some first principles, plain to be understood and necessary to be learned. There are also deep and sublime mysteries.

IV. There are in the church babes and persons of full age (*v.* 12–14), and there are in the gospel milk and strong meat. Those that are babes, unskilful in the word of righteousness, must be fed with milk. Christ despises not his babes; he has provided suitable food for them. There is strong meat for those that are of full age, *v.* 14. The deeper mysteries of religion belong to those that are of a higher class in the school of Christ. Every true Christian stands in need of nourishment. The word of God is food and nourishment to the life of grace. There are spiritual senses as well as those that are natural. The soul has its sensations as well as the body; these are much depraved and lost by sin, but they are recovered by grace. It is by use and exercise that these senses are improved, made more quick and strong to taste the sweetness of what is good and true, and the bitterness of what is false and evil.

CHAPTER 6

The best way to prevent apostasy, the dreadful nature of which sin he sets forth (ver. 1–8), and then expresses his good hopes concerning them, and sets before them the great encouragement they had from God, ver. 9, to the end.

Verses 1–8

In order to their growth, Christians must leave the principles of the doctrine of Christ. They must not lose them, they must not despise them, they must not forget them. But they must not rest in them, they must not be always laying the foundation, they must go on, and build upon it. Though some of them were but weak, yet others of them had gained more strength; and they must be provided for suitably. He hoped they would be growing and so be able to digest stronger meat.

I. Several foundation-principles, which must be well laid at first, and then built upon.

1. Repentance from dead works. Take care that you return not to sin again, for then you must have the foundation to lay again. Repentance for and from dead works is a foundation-principle, which must not be laid again, though we must renew our repentance daily.

2. Faith towards God. Repentance from dead works, and faith towards God, are connected, and always go together; they are inseparable twins, the one cannot live without the other.

3. The doctrine of baptisms. This ordinance of baptism is a foundation to be rightly laid, and daily remembered, but not repeated.

4. Laying on of hands, on persons passing solemnly from their initiated state by baptism to the confirmed state. Or by this may be meant ordination of persons to the ministerial office. This is to be done but once.

5. The resurrection of the dead.

6. Eternal judgment.

These are the great foundation-principles, and from these they must never depart.

II. The apostle declares his readiness to assist the Hebrews in building themselves up on these foundations, *v.* 3. That resolution is right which is not only made in the sincerity of our hearts, but in a humble dependence upon God. Ministers should not only teach people what to do, but go before them, and along with them, in the way of duty.

III. Spiritual growth is the surest way to prevent apostasy from the faith.

1. He shows how far persons may go in religion, and, after all, fall away, and perish for ever, *v.* 4, 5. (1) They may be *enlightened.* It is rather to be understood of notional knowledge and common illumination, of which persons may have a great deal, and yet come short of heaven. (2) They may *taste of the heavenly gift* like persons in the market, who taste of what they will not come up to the price of, and so but take a taste, and leave it. (3) They may be *made partakers of the Holy Ghost,* of his extraordinary and miraculous gifts. Such gifts in the apostolic age were sometimes bestowed upon those who had no true saving grace. (4) They may *taste of the good word of God*; they may hear the word with pleasure, and talk well of it, and yet never have it dwelling richly in them. (5) They may have *tasted of the powers of the world to come.* These lengths hypocrites may go, and, after all, turn apostates.

2. The dreadful case of such as fall away. The greatness of the sin of apostasy. It is *crucifying the Son of God afresh, and putting him to open shame.* They declare that they approve of what the Jews did in crucifying Christ, and that they would be glad to do the same thing again, and would have him to be a public shame and reproach. The great misery of apostates. It is impossible to renew them again unto repentance. God can renew them to repentance, but he seldom does it; and with men themselves it is impossible. Their misery is exemplified by a proper similitude, *v.* 8. To give this the greater force, here is observed the difference that there is between the good ground and the bad. A description of the good ground: It *drinketh in the rain that cometh often upon it.* Believers do not only taste of the word of God, but they drink it in; and this good ground bringeth forth fruit. And this fruit-field or garden receives the blessing. Here is the different case of the bad ground: It *bears briers and thorns*; it is not only barren of good fruit, but fruitful in that which is bad, briers and thorns. Such ground is rejected. And that is not all, but such ground *is nigh unto cursing*; so far is it from receiving the blessing. Its end is to be burned. This is the sad end to which apostasy leads, and therefore Christians should go on and grow in grace, lest, if they do not go forward, they should go backward.

Verses 9–20

The apostle proceeds to apply himself to their hopes.

I. He declares the good hope he had concerning them, *v.* 9. There are things that accompany salvation, things that are never separated from salvation. Ministers must sometimes speak by way of caution to those of whose salvation they have good hopes. And those who have in themselves good hopes should yet consider seriously how fatal a disappointment it would be if they should fall short. Thus they are to work out their salvation with fear and trembling.

II. Encouragements to them to go on. God had wrought a principle of holy love and charity in them, *v.* 10. Good works and labour proceeding from love to God are commendable; and what is done to any in the name of God shall not go unrewarded. Those who expect a gracious reward for the labour of love must continue in it as long as they have ability and opportunity. Those who persevere in a diligent discharge of their duty shall attain to the full assurance of hope in the end. Full assurance is a higher degree of hope; they differ not in nature, but only in degree. Full assurance is attainable by great diligence and perseverance to the end.

III. Caution and counsel how to attain this full assurance of hope to the end. They should not be slothful. They must not love their ease, nor lose their opportunities. They should follow the good examples of those who had gone before, *v.* 12. There are some who from assurance have gone to inherit the promises. The way by which they came to the inheritance was that of faith and patience. We must follow them in the way of faith and patience.

IV. The assured truth of the promises of God, *v.* 13, *to the end.*

1. They are all confirmed by the oath of God. Those whom he has blessed indeed he will go on to bless. *He swore by himself.* No greater security can be given or desired. It was made good to him after he had patiently endured. There is always an interval, and sometimes a long one, between the promise and the performance. That interval is a trying time to believers. Those who patiently endure shall assuredly obtain the blessedness promised, as sure as Abraham did, *v.* 16. This is the nature and design of an oath, in which men swear by the greater, by the Lord himself. Now, if God would condescend to take an oath to his people, he will surely remember the nature and design of it.

2. The promises of God are all founded in his eternal counsel; and this counsel of his is an immutable counsel. God never needs to change his counsels.

3. The promises of God may safely be depended upon.

(1) Who they are to whom God has given such full security of happiness. They are the heirs of the promise. They are such as have fled for refuge to the hope set before them. Here is a refuge for all sinners who shall have the heart to flee to it.

(2) What God's design towards them is—that they might have strong consolation. God is concerned for the consolation of believers. The consolations of God are strong enough to support his people under their strongest trials. The comforts of this world are too weak, but the consolations of the Lord are neither few nor small.

(3) What use the people of God should make of their hope and comfort, *v.* 19. We are in this world as a ship at sea, in danger of being cast away. Heaven is the harbour to which we sail. We have need of an anchor to keep us sure and steady. Gospel hope is our anchor. It is sure and steadfast. It is sure in its own nature; it is not a flattering hope made out of the spider's web, but it is a true work of God. It is steadfast as to its object; it is an anchor that has taken good hold. It does not seek to fasten in the sands, but enters within the veil, and fixes there upon Christ; he is the anchor-hold of the believer's hope.

Chapter 7

Now the apostle assures them that by receiving the Lord Jesus they would have a much better high priest, a priesthood of a higher order. I. We have a more particular account of Melchisedec, ver. 1–3. II. The superiority of his priesthood to that of Aaron, ver. 4–10. III. An accommodation of all to Christ, to show the superior excellency of his person, office, and covenant, ver. 11, to the end.

Verses 1–10

Here the apostle sets before them some of the strong meat he had spoken of before.

1. The great question that first offers itself is, Who was this Melchisedec? All the account we have of him in the Old Testament is in Gen. xiv. 18, &c., and in Ps. cx. 4. We are much in the dark about him.

1. The opinions concerning him that are best worthy our consideration are these three: (1) The rabbin, and most of the Jewish writers, think he was Shem the son of Noah. (2) Many Christian writers have thought him to be Jesus Christ himself. (3) The most general opinion is that he was a Canaanite king, who reigned in Salem.

2. How Christ is represented thereby, *v.* 1–3. (1) Melchisedec was a king, and so is the Lord Jesus. (2) He was *king of righteousness*: his name signifies *the righteous king.* Jesus Christ is a rightful and a righteous king. (3) He was king of Salem, that is, king of peace; first king of righteousness, and after that king of peace. So is our Lord Jesus. (4) He was *priest of the most high God.* So is the Lord Jesus. (5) The scripture has chosen to set him forth as an extraordinary person, without giving us his genealogy, that he might be a fitter type of Christ, whose priesthood is without descent, but is personal and perpetual. (6) He *met Abraham returning from the slaughter of the kings, and blessed him.* He gave as a king, and blessed as a priest. Thus our Lord Jesus meets his people, refreshes them, renews their strength, and blesses them. (7) *Abraham gave him a tenth part of all* (*v.* 2). And thus are we obliged to make all possible returns of love and gratitude to the Lord Jesus for all the favours we receive from him. (8) This Melchisedec was *made like unto the Son of God, and abideth a priest continually.* He bore the image of God in his piety and authority, and stands upon record as an immortal high priest.

II. Let us now consider how great this Melchisedec was, and how far his priesthood was above that of the order of Aaron (*v.* 4, 5, &c.). The greatness of this man and his priesthood appears from Abraham's paying the tenth of the spoils unto him; and it is well observed that Levi paid tithes to Melchisedec in Abraham, *v.* 9. Levi paid tithes to Melchisedec, as to a greater and higher priest than himself. It appears also it was Melchisedec's blessing of Abraham, *v.* 6, 7. Abraham's great dignity and felicity—was that he had the promises. That man is rich and happy indeed who has an estate in bills and bonds under God's own hand and seal. Melchisedec's greater honour—was his privilege to bless Abraham; and it is an incontested maxim *that the less is blessed of the greater, v.* 7.

Verses 11–28

The necessity there was of raising up another priest, after the order of Melchisedec and not after the order of Aaron, *v.* 11, 12, &c.

I. It is asserted that perfection could not come by the Levitical priesthood and the law.

II. Therefore another priest must be raised up, after the order of Melchisedec, by whom perfection might come.

III. It is asserted that the priesthood being changed there must of necessity be a change of the law.

IV. It is not only asserted, but proved, that the priesthood and law are changed, *v.* 13, 14. A dispensation is now set up, by which true believers may be made perfect.

1. There is a change in the tribe of which the priesthood comes, *v.* 14. This change of the family shows a real change of the law of priesthood.

2. There is a change in the form and order of making the priests. The law by which Christ was constituted a priest, after the order of Melchisedec, was the power of an endless life. This gives the preference infinitely to Christ and the gospel. The high priest of our profession holds his office by that innate power of endless life which he has in himself, to communicate eternal life to all those who duly rely upon his sacrifice and intercession.

3. There is a change in the efficacy of the priesthood, *v.* 18, 19. The Levitical priesthood brought nothing to perfection. But the priesthood of Christ brings along with it a better hope; it shows us the

true foundation of all the hope we have towards God for pardon and salvation. By this hope we are encouraged to draw nigh unto God, to live a life of communion with him.

4. There is a change in God's way of acting in this priesthood. Christ was made a priest with the oath of God, *v.* 21.

5. There is a change in the dispensation of that covenant. The gospel dispensation is more full, free, and efficacious, than that of the law. He, as surety, has united the divine and human nature together in his own person, and therein given assurance of reconciliation; and he has, as surety, united God and man together in the bond of the everlasting covenant.

6. There is a remarkable change in the number of the priests. In that of Aaron there was a multitude of priests; but in this of Christ there is but one and the same. *They were not suffered to continue by reason of death.* Our high priest continues for ever, and his priesthood is *an unchangeable one.* There can be no vacancy in this priesthood, no hour nor moment in which the people are without a priest to negotiate their spiritual concerns in heaven. This ever-living high priest is able to save to the utmost all who come to God by him, *v.* 25.

7. There is a remarkable difference in the moral qualifications of the priests. He is *such a high priest as became us, holy, harmless, and undefiled,* &c., *v.* 26–28. Our case, as sinners, needed a high priest to make satisfaction and intercession for us. No priest could be suitable or sufficient for our reconciliation to God but one who was perfectly righteous. The Lord Jesus was exactly such a high priest as we wanted, for he has a personal holiness, absolutely perfect. He is holy. No sin dwells in him, though it does in the best of Christians. He is harmless, never did the least wrong to God or man. He is undefiled, though he took upon him the guilt of our sins, yet he never involved himself in the fact and fault of them. He is separate from sinners. Though he took a true human nature, yet the miraculous way in which it was conceived set him upon a separate footing from all the rest of mankind. He is made higher than the heavens, for he is exalted at the right hand of God, to perfect the design of his priesthood. The validity and prevalency of Christ's priesthood in *v.* 27 are placed in the impartiality and disinterestedness of it. He needed not to offer up for himself: it was a disinterested mediation; he mediated for that mercy for others which he did not need for himself.

CHAPTER 8

The priesthood of Christ. I. He sums up what he had already said, ver. 1, 2. II. He sets before them the necessary parts of the priestly office, ver. 3–5. And, III. Largely illustrates the excellency of the priesthood of Christ, ver. 6, to the end.

Verses 1–5

I. A summary recital of what had been said before concerning the excellency of Christ's priesthood, *v.* 1, 2. What we have in Christ; we have a high priest, and such a high priest as no other people ever had; all others were but types and shadows of this high priest. Where he now resides: *He sits on the right hand of the throne of the Majesty on high.* This is the reward of his humiliation. What is that sanctuary of which he is a minister, *v.* 2. There was an outer part, in which was the altar where they were to offer their sacrifices, which typified Christ dying; and there was an interior part within the veil, which typified Christ interceding for the people in heaven. Having finished the work of satisfaction in the true tabernacle of his own body, he is now a minister of the sanctuary, the holy of holies, the true tabernacle in heaven. He is not only in heaven enjoying great dominion and dignity, but as the high priest of his church.

II. The apostle sets before the Hebrews what it was that belonged to that office, *v.* 3, 4. It necessarily belongs to the priesthood of Christ that he should have somewhat to offer; and he had himself to offer, as the great atoning sacrifice. Christ must now execute his priesthood in heaven; having finished the work of sacrificing here, he must go into heaven, to present his righteousness and to make intercession there. *If Christ were on earth, he would not be a priest* (*v.* 4), that is, not according to the Levitical law. If he had still continued on earth, he could not have been a perfect priest; and an imperfect one he could not be.

Verses 6–13

The apostle illustrates and confirms the superior excellency of the priesthood of Christ. His ministry is more excellent, by how much he is the Mediator of a better covenant.

I. What is here said of the old covenant. 1. That it was made with the fathers of the Jewish nation at Mount Sinai (*v.* 9). 2. That this covenant was not found faultless (*v.* 7, 8). It was perfect in its kind, and fitted to answer its end, but very imperfect in comparison of the gospel. 3. That it was not sure or steadfast, *v.* 9. God will regard those who remain in his covenant, but will reject those who cast away his yoke from them. 4. That it is decayed, grown old, and vanisheth away, *v.* 13. It is antiquated, of no more use in gospel times than candles are when the sun has risen.

II. What is here said of the New Testament dispensation.

1. That it is a better covenant (*v.* 6). It is without fault, well ordered in all things. It requires nothing but what it promises grace to perform. All is put into a good and safe hand.

2. That it is established upon better promises. This covenant contains in it promises of assistance and acceptance in duty, promises of progress and perseverance in grace and holiness, of bliss and glory in heaven.

3. It is a new covenant. This will always be a new covenant, in which all who truly take hold of it shall be always found preserved by the power of God.

4. The articles of this covenant are sealed between God and his people by baptism and the Lord's supper.

(1) God articles with his people, *v.* 10. He once wrote his laws to them, now he will write his laws in them. Their souls shall be a table and transcript of the law of God.

(2) He articles with them to take them into a near and very honourable relation to himself. He will be to them a God. Nothing more can be said in a thousand volumes than is comprehended in these few words: *I will be a God to them.* They shall be to him a people, to love, honour, observe, and obey him in all things. This those must do and will do who have God for their God; this they shall do, for God will enable them to do it. It is God himself who first founds the relation, and then fills it up with grace suitable and sufficient, and helps them in their measure to fill it up with love and duty.

(3) He articles with them that they shall grow more and more acquainted with their God (*v.* 11). There shall not be so much need of one neighbour teaching another the knowledge of God. This private instruction shall not be so necessary under the New Testament as it was under the Old. There shall be a mighty increase and spreading of Christian knowledge in persons of all sorts, of each sex, and of all ages. O that this promise might be fulfilled in our days!

(4) God articles with them about the pardon of their sins (*v.* 12). The freeness of this pardon. It does not result from merit in man, but from mercy in God. The fulness of this pardon; it extends to

all kinds of sin. The fixedness of this pardon. It is so final and so fixed that God will remember their sins no more; he will not recall his pardon. It is the effect of that mercy that is from everlasting, and the earnest of that mercy that shall be to everlasting. Therefore we have great reason to rejoice that the former dispensation is antiquated and has vanished away.

CHAPTER 9

The Old Testament was never intended to be rested in, but to prepare for the institutions of the gospel. And here he treats, I. Of the tabernacle, the place of worship, ver. 1–5. II. Of the worship and services performed in the tabernacle, ver. 6–7. III. Of the spiritual sense and the main design of all, ver. 8, to the end.

Verses 1–7

I. The apostle gives an account of the tabernacle. It was divided into two parts, called a first and a second tabernacle, an inner and an outer part. We are also told what was placed in each part of the tabernacle.

1. In the outer part. (1) The candlestick; doubtless not an empty and unlighted one, but where the lamps were always burning. And there was need of it, for there were no windows in the sanctuary. Their light was only candle-light, in comparison of the fulness of light which Christ, the Sun of righteousness, would bring along with him. (2) The table and the show-bread set upon it. This table was set directly opposite to the candlestick. We must not come in the dark to his table, but by light from Christ must discern the Lord's body. He is the bread of life; in our Father's house there is bread enough and to spare; we may have fresh supplies from Christ, especially every Lord's day.

2. We have an account of what was in the inner part of the sanctuary, which was within the second veil, and is called *the holiest of all*. Now in this part were, (1) The golden censer, which was to hold the incense, or the golden altar set up to burn the incense upon. (2) The ark of the covenant overlaid round about with pure gold, *v.* 4. Now here we are told both what was in this ark and what was over it. [1] What was in it. *First, The golden pot that had manna.* This was a memorial of God's miraculously feeding his people in the wilderness, that they might never forget such signal favour, nor distrust God for the time to come. *Secondly, Aaron's rod that budded.* This was that rod of God with which Moses and Aaron wrought such wonders; and this was a type of Christ, by whom God has wrought wonders for his people. *Thirdly, The tables of the covenant,* in which the moral law was written, signifying the regard God has to the preservation of his holy law, and the care we all ought to have that we keep the law of God. [2] What was over the ark (*v.* 5). The mercy-seat, which was the covering of the ark. It was of pure gold, as long and as broad as the ark in which the tables of the law were laid. It was an eminent type of Christ, and of his perfect righteousness, ever adequate to the dimensions of the law of God, and covering all our transgressions. *The cherubim of glory* shadowing the mercy-seat, represented the holy angels of God.

II. The apostle proceeds to speak of the duties and services performed in those places, *v.* 6.

1. The ordinary priests went always into the first tabernacle, to accomplish the service of God. None but priests were to enter into the first part of the tabernacle. The ordinary priests were only to enter into the first part of the tabernacle, it would have been fatal presumption in them to have gone into the holiest of all.

2. Into the second, the interior part, went the high priest alone, *v.* 7. None but the high priest must go into the holiest; so none but Christ could

enter into heaven by his own right, and by his own merits. The high priest must not enter without blood. None of us can enter either into God's gracious presence here or his glorious presence hereafter, but by the blood of Jesus. The high priest offered up that blood for himself and his own errors first, and then for the errors of the people, *v.* 7. Christ is a more excellent person and high priest than any under the law, for he has no errors of his own to offer for. Ministers, when in the name of Christ they intercede for others, must first apply the blood of Christ to themselves for their pardon. When the legal high priest had offered for himself, he must not stop there, but must also offer for the errors of the people. Our high priest forgets not to offer for his people; he pleads the merit of his sufferings for the benefit of his people on earth.

Verses 8–14

The apostle undertakes to deliver to us the mind and meaning of the Holy Ghost in all the ordinances of the tabernacle.

I. The way into the holiest of all was not yet made manifest, *v.* 8. There was not that free access to God then that there is now; God has now opened a wider door.

II. The first tabernacle was only a figure for the time then present, *v.* 9.

III. None of the gifts and sacrifices there offered could make the offerers perfect as pertaining to conscience (*v.* 9); they could not deliver conscience from a dread of the wrath of God. He might thereby be saved from temporal punishments, but he could not be saved by them from sin.

IV. The Old Testament institutions were but imposed upon them until the time of reformation, *v.* 10. These were never designed for a perpetuity, but only till the better things provided for them were actually bestowed upon them. We have far greater advantages under the gospel than they had under the law; and either we must be better or we shall be worse.

V. As he writes to those who believed that Jesus was the Christ, so he very justly infers that he is infinitely above all legal high priests (*v.* 11, 12).

1. *Christ is a high priest of good things to come.* The Old Testament set forth in shadows what was to come; the New Testament is the accomplishment of the Old. All the good things yet to come, when the promises shall be accomplished; all these depend upon Christ and his priesthood, and shall be fulfilled; all the good things to come in the heavenly state, which will perfect both the Testaments; as the state of glory will perfect the state of grace.

2. Christ is a high priest *by a greater and more perfect tabernacle* (*v.* 11), his own body, or rather human nature, conceived by the Holy Ghost overshadowing the blessed virgin. This was a new fabric, a new order of building.

3. Christ, our high priest, has entered into heaven, not as their high priest entered into the holiest, with the blood of bulls and of goats, but by his own blood.

4. Our high priest entered into heaven *once for all*, and has obtained eternal redemption.

5. The Holy Ghost showed what was the efficacy of the blood of the Old Testament sacrifices. The efficacy of the blood of the legal sacrifices extended to the purifying of the flesh (*v.* 13): from ceremonial uncleanness. The far greater efficacy of the blood of Christ (*v.* 14). What it was that gave such efficacy to the blood of Christ. It was his offering himself to God. It was Christ's offering up himself to God through the eternal Spirit. It was Christ's offering himself to God without spot, without any sinful stain. What the efficacy of Christ's blood is. It is sufficient to purge the conscience from dead works, it reaches to the very soul and conscience. It is sufficient

to enable us to serve the living God by sanctifying and renewing the soul through the gracious influences of the Holy Spirit.

Verses 15–22

I. The gospel is here considered as a testament. A covenant is an agreement between two or more parties about things that are in their own power; this agreement takes effect at such time and in such manner as therein declared. A testament is a voluntary act and deed of a single person, bestowing legacies on such legatees as are described by the testator, and which can only take effect upon his death. Christ is the Mediator of a New Testament (v. 15), to redeem persons from their transgressions committed against the law or first testament; to qualify all those that are effectually called to receive the promise of an eternal inheritance.

II. To make this New Testament effectual, it was necessary that Christ should die. This he proves by two arguments: 1. From the general nature of every will or testamentary disposition, v. 16. No estate, no right, is conveyed by will, till the testator's death has made it effectual. 2. From the particular method that was taken by Moses in the ratification of the first testament, which was not done without blood, v. 18, 19, &c. God accepted the blood of bulls and goats; and by these means the covenant of grace was ratified under the former dispensation. Moses spoke every precept to all the people, according to the law, v. 19. Then he took the blood of calves and of goats, with water, and scarlet wool, and hyssop, and applied this blood by sprinkling it. With these Moses sprinkled, (1) The book of the law and covenant. (2) The people. The blood of Christ will be no advantage to us if it be not applied to us. Moses at the same time used these words, *This is the blood of the testament which God hath enjoined unto you.* (3) The tabernacle and all the utensils of it. All the sacrifices offered up and services performed there were accepted only through the blood of Christ.

Verses 23–29

I. The necessity of purifying the patterns of the things in heaven, v. 23. The sanctuary of God on earth is a pattern of heaven, and communion with God in his sanctuary is to his people a heaven upon earth.

II. The things themselves are better than the patterns, and must therefore be consecrated with better sacrifices. These heavenly things are the privileges of the gospel state, begun in grace, perfected in glory. Now it is very evident that the sacrifice of Christ is infinitely better than those of the law, 1. From the places in which the sacrifices were offered. Those under the law were the holy places made with hands, v. 24. Christ's sacrifice was by himself carried up into heaven, for he appears in the presence of God for us. 2. From the sacrifices themselves, v. 26. Those under the law were the lives and blood of other creatures. The sacrifice of Christ was the oblation of himself; he offered his own blood, and it was of infinite value. 3. From the frequent repetition of the legal sacrifices. This showed the imperfection of that law; but it is the perfection of Christ's sacrifice, that being once offered, it was sufficient to all the ends of it. *But now once in the end of the world hath he appeared, to put away sin by the sacrifice of himself.* 4. From the inefficacy of the legal sacrifices, and the efficacy of Christ's sacrifice. The legal sacrifices could not of themselves put away sin. Jesus Christ by one sacrifice has made an end of sin.

III. The apostle illustrates the argument from the appointment of God concerning men (v. 27, 28).

1. The appointment of God concerning men contains in it two things. They must once die. This is matter of comfort to the godly, that they shall die well and die but once; but it is matter of terror to the wicked, who die in their sin. After death they shall come to judgment. This is the unalterable decree of God concerning men—they must die, and they must be judged.

2. The appointment of God concerning Christ. He must be once offered to bear the sins of many. He was not offered for any sin of his own; he was wounded for our transgressions. Christ shall appear the second time without sin, to the salvation of those who look for him. He appeared in the form of sinful flesh; but his second appearance will be without any such charge upon him. This will be to the salvation of all who look for him; he will then perfect their holiness, their happiness.

CHAPTER 10

The apostle proceeds in this chapter, I. To lay low the whole of that priesthood and sacrifice, ver. 1–6. II. He raises and exalts the priesthood of Christ very high, ver. 7–18. III. He shows to believers the honours of their state, and calls them to suitable duties, ver. 19, to the end.

Verses 1–6

Here the apostle sets himself to lay low the Levitical dispensation.

I. The law had but a shadow, of good things to come. These good things were to come, not clearly discovered. The Jews then had but the shadow of the good things of Christ; we under the gospel have the substance.

II. The law was not the very image of the good things to come, but was only a shadow. The law was a very rough draught of the great design of divine grace, and therefore not to be so much doted on.

III. The legal sacrifices, being offered year by year, could never make the comers thereunto perfect, v. 1, 2. Under the gospel, the atonement is perfect, and the sinner, once pardoned, is ever pardoned as to his state, and only needs to renew his repentance and faith.

IV. As the legal sacrifices did not of themselves take away sin, so it was impossible they should, v. 4. The atoning sacrifice must be one capable of consenting, and must voluntarily substitute himself in the sinner's stead: Christ did so.

V. There was a time fixed and foretold by the great God, and that time had now come, when these legal sacrifices would be no longer accepted by him nor useful to men. This time of the repeal of the Levitical laws was foretold by David (Ps. xl. 6, 7).

Verses 7–18

He recommends Christ to them as the true high priest, the true atoning sacrifice. This he illustrates,

I. From the purpose and promise of God concerning Christ, which are frequently recorded in the volume of the book of God, v. 7.

II. From what God had done in preparing a body for Christ (that is, a human nature), that he might be qualified to be our Redeemer and Advocate.

III. From the readiness and willingness that Christ discovered to engage in this work, when no other sacrifice would be accepted, v. 7–9. Christ voluntarily came into it: "*Lo, I come! I delight to do thy will, O God!*" This should endear Christ and our Bibles to us, that in Christ we have the fulfilling of the scriptures.

IV. From the errand and design upon which Christ came. Christ came to do the will of God in two instances. 1. In taking away the first priesthood, which God had no pleasure in. 2. In establishing the second, his own priesthood and the everlasting gospel. This is the great design upon which the heart of God was set from all eternity. And it is not more agreeable to the will of God than it is advantageous to the souls of men.

V. From the perfect efficacy of the priesthood of Christ (v. 14). This is what the Levitical priesthood could never do; and, if we indeed are aiming at a perfect state, we must receive the Lord Jesus as the only high priest that can bring us to that state.

VI. From the place to which our Lord Jesus is now exalted, v. 12, 13. 1. To what honour Christ is exalted—to the right hand of God, the seat of power, the giving hand; the receiving hand; the working hand; this is the highest post of honour. 2. How Christ came to this honour—as a reward due to his sufferings. He will never quit it, nor cease to employ it for his people's good. This is his rest for ever. He has further expectations, which shall not be disappointed. One would think such a person as Christ could have no enemies except in hell; but it is certain that he has enemies on earth. Let not Christians then wonder that they have enemies. But Christ's enemies shall be made his footstool; this he is expecting. When his enemies shall be subdued, their enemies shall be subdued also.

VII. The apostle recommends Christ from the witness the Holy Ghost has given in the scriptures concerning him (v. 15): *Whereof the Holy Ghost is a witness.* The passage is cited from Jer. xxxi. 31. God promises that he will pour out his Spirit upon his people; he will put his laws in their hearts, and write them in their minds, v. 16. Their sins and iniquities he will remember no more (v. 17), which will alone show the sufficiency of Christ's satisfaction, that it needs not be repeated, v. 18. This was much more than the Levitical priesthood and sacrifices could effect.

Verses 19–39

I. Here the apostle sets forth the dignities of the gospel state. The privileges are, 1. Boldness to enter into the holiest. They have access to God till they are prepared to enter into his glorious presence in heaven. 2. A high priest over the house of God, even this blessed Jesus. God is willing to dwell with men on earth, and to have them dwell with him in heaven; but fallen man cannot dwell with God without a high priest.

II. The way and means by which Christians enjoy such privileges—*by the blood of Jesus.* The apostle enters further into the particulars of it, v. 20. 1. It is the only way. 2. It is a new way. It is a way that will always be effectual. 3. It is a living way. This way we may come to God, and live. It is by a living Saviour who, though he was dead is alive; and it is a way that gives life and lively hope to those who enter into it. 4. It is a way that Christ has consecrated for us through the veil, that is, his flesh. Our way to heaven is by a crucified Saviour; his death is to us the way of life.

III. The duties binding upon them on account of these privileges, v. 22, 23, &c.

1. They must draw near to God, and that in a right manner. They must draw near in conformity to God, and communion with him, still endeavouring to get nearer and nearer, till they come to dwell in his presence. (1) With a true heart. God is the searcher of hearts, and he requires truth in the inward parts. (2) In full assurance of faith. We should lay aside all sinful distrust. Without faith it is impossible to please God. (3) Having our hearts sprinkled from an evil conscience. They may be cleansed from guilt, and whatever evils the consciences of men are subject to by reason of sin. (4) Our bodies washed with pure water, that is, with the water of baptism, or with the sanctifying virtue of the Holy Spirit, cleansing from the filthiness of the flesh as well as of the spirit.

2. The apostle exhorts believers to hold fast the profession of their faith, v. 23. (1) The duty itself—

to hold fast the profession of our faith. Our spiritual enemies will do what they can to wrest our faith, and hope, out of our hands, but we must hold fast. (2) The manner in which we must do this—without wavering. Those who begin to waver are in danger of falling away. (3) The motive or reason enforcing this duty: *He is faithful that hath promised.* There is no fickleness with him, and there should be none with us. We must depend more upon his promises to us than upon our promises to him.

IV. We have the means prescribed for promoting our fidelity and perseverance, v. 24, 25, &c. 1. We should *consider one another, to provoke to love and to good works.* Christians ought to have a tender consideration and concern for one another. A good example given to others is the best and most effectual provocation to love and good works. 2. *Not to forsake the assembling of ourselves together, v* 25. Even in those times there were some who forsook these assemblies. The communion of saints is a great help and privilege, and a good means of steadiness and perseverance. 3. To exhort one another, to watch over one another, and be jealous of ourselves and one another with a godly jealousy. This, would be the best friendship. 4. We should observe the approaching of times of trial. Christians ought to observe the signs of the times, such as God has foretold. There is a trying day coming on us all, the day of our death, and we should observe all the signs of its approaching, and improve them to greater watchfulness and diligence in duty.

V. The apostle proceeds to enforce his exhortations (v. 26, 27, &c.).

1. From the description he gives of the sin of apostasy. It is *sinning wilfully after we have received the knowledge of the truth.* The sin here mentioned is a total and final apostasy, when men reject Christ, the only Saviour, and renounce the gospel, the only way of salvation, and the words of eternal life, after they have professed the Christian religion.

2. From the dreadful doom of such apostates. (1) There remains no more sacrifice for such sins, no other Christ to come to save such sinners. Those under the gospel who will not accept of Christ, that they may be saved by him, have no other refuge left them. (2) There remains for them only a certain fearful looking for of judgment, v. 27. God gives some notorious sinners, while on earth, a fearful foreboding in their own consciences, with a despair of ever being able either to endure or escape it.

3. From the methods of divine justice with those who despised Moses's law. These, when convicted by two or three witnesses, were put to death; they died without mercy. Hence the apostle infers the heavy doom that will fall upon those that apostatize from Christ. They have *trodden under foot the Son of God.* What punishment can be too great for such men? They have *counted the blood of the covenant, wherewith he was sanctified, an unholy thing.* Men who have seemed before to have the blood of Christ in high esteem may come to account it an unholy thing. *Those have done despite unto the Spirit of grace.* They have grieved, resisted, yea, done despite to him, which is the highest act of wickedness, and makes the case of the sinner desperate, refusing to have the gospel salvation applied to him.

4. From the description we have of the nature of God's vindictive justice, v. 30. The terrors of the Lord are known both by revelation and reason. The other quotation is from Deut. xxxii. 36, *The Lord will judge his people;* he will search and try his visible church, and will punish the sinners in Zion with the greatest severity. Now those who know him who hath said, *Vengeance belongeth to me, I will recompense,* must needs conclude, as the apostle does (v. 31). Those who know the joy that results from the favour

of God can thereby judge of the power and dread of his vindictive wrath.

5. He presses them to perseverance by putting them in mind of their former sufferings for Christ. When they had suffered: *In former days, after* they were *illuminated.* A natural state is a dark state, and those who continue in that state meet with no disturbance from Satan and the world; but a state of grace is a state of light, and therefore the powers of darkness will violently oppose it. What they suffered: they *endured a great fight of afflictions.* They were afflicted in themselves. In their own persons. In their names and reputations (v. 33), by many reproaches. Christians ought to value their reputation, because the reputation of religion is concerned: this makes reproach a great affliction. They were afflicted in the afflictions of their brethren. The Christian spirit is a sympathizing spirit, not a selfish spirit, but a compassionate spirit. Christians are one body, the children of that God who is afflicted in all the afflictions of his people. If one member of the body suffers, all the rest suffer with it. The apostle takes particular notice how they had sympathized with him (v. 34). How they had suffered. They took their sufferings patiently, and not only so, but joyfully received it from God, that they should be thought worthy to suffer reproach for the name of Christ. What it was that enabled them thus to bear up under their sufferings. They knew in themselves that they had in heaven a better and a more enduring substance. The happiness of the saints in heaven is substance. All things here are but shadows. It is a better substance than any thing they can have or lose here. It will out-live time and run parallel with eternity. In heaven they shall have everything better. Christians should know this in themselves. The assured knowledge of this will help them to endure any fight of afflictions they may be encountered with in this world.

6. He presses them to persevere (v. 35). He exhorts them not to cast away their confidence, but to hold fast that profession for which they had suffered so much. The reward of their holy confidence would be very great. It carries a present reward in it, in holy peace and joy, and it shall have a great recompence of reward hereafter. He shows them how necessary a grace the grace of patience is in our present state (v. 36). They must first do the will of God before they receive the promise; and, after they have done the will of God, they have need of patience to wait for the time when the promise shall be fulfilled. We must be God's waiting servants when we can be no longer his working servants. To help their patience, he assures them of the near approach of Christ's coming (v. 37). There is an appointed time and beyond that time he will not tarry.

7. He presses them to perseverance, by telling them that this will be their happiness, whereas apostasy is the reproach, and will be the ruin, of all who are guilty of it (v. 38, 39). It is the honourable character of just men that in times of the greatest affliction they can live by faith. Faith puts life and vigour into them. They can trust God, and live upon him. As their faith maintains their spiritual life now, it shall be crowned with eternal life hereafter. Apostasy is the mark of those in whom God takes no pleasure; and it is a cause of God's severe displeasure and anger. The apostle concludes with declaring his good hope concerning himself and these Hebrews (v. 39). Professors may go a great way, and after all draw back; and this drawing back from God is drawing on to perdition: the further we depart from God the nearer we approach to ruin. Those who have been kept faithful in great trials for the time past have reason to hope that the same grace will be sufficient to help them still to live by faith. If we live by faith, and die in faith, our souls will be safe for ever.

CHAPTER 11

The nature and fruits of this excellent grace. I. The nature of it, ver. 1–3. II. The great examples we have in the Old Testament of those who lived by faith, ver. 4–38. III. The advantages that we have in the gospel for the exercise of this grace, above what those had who lived in the times of the Old Testament, ver. 39, 40.

Verses 1–3

I. A definition of the grace of faith in two parts. It *is the substance of things hoped for.* Faith and hope go together; and the same things that are the object of our hope are the object of our faith. It is a firm persuasion and expectation that God will perform all that he has promised to us in Christ. Believers in the exercise of faith *are filled with joy unspeakable and full of glory.* It is *the evidence of things not seen.* Faith demonstrates to the eye of the mind the reality of those things that cannot be discerned by the eye of the body. It is designed to serve the believer instead of sight, and to be to the soul all that the senses are to the body.

II. An account of the honour it reflects upon all those who have lived in the exercise of it (v. 2). True faith is an old grace, and has the best plea to antiquity: it is not a new invention, a modern fancy. The eldest and best men that ever were in the world were believers. They were an honour to their faith, and their faith was an honour to them. It put them upon doing *the things that were of good report.*

III. We have here one of the first articles of faith, the creation of the *worlds by the word of God,* not out of pre-existent matter, but out of nothing, v. 3. The grace of faith has a retrospect as well as prospect; it looks not only forward to the end of the world, but back to the beginning of the world. Now what does faith give us to understand concerning *the worlds.* 1. *That these worlds were* not eternal, nor did they produce themselves, but they were made by another. 2. That the maker of the worlds is God. 3. That God made the world by his word and by his active will. 4. That the world was thus framed out of nothing. These things we understand by faith.

Verses 4–31

The apostle now proceeds to set before us some illustrious examples of it in the Old Testament times, and these may be divided into two classes: 1. Those whose names are mentioned, and the particular actings of whose faith are specified. 2. Those whose names are barely mentioned, and an account given in general of the exploits of their faith.

I. The leading instance and example of faith here recorded is that of Abel. It begins with Abel, one who lived by faith, and died for it, and therefore a fit pattern for the Hebrews to imitate.

1. *He offered up a more acceptable sacrifice than Cain.* After the fall, God opened a new way for the children of men to return to him in religious worship. After the fall, God must be worshipped by sacrifices. Cain was the elder brother, but Abel has the preference. It is not seniority of birth, but grace, that makes men truly honourable. Abel brought a sacrifice of atonement, *brought of the firstlings of the flock.* Cain brought only a sacrifice of acknowledgment, a mere thank-offering, *the fruit of the ground.*

2. What Abel gained by his faith. In this place we are told that he obtained by his faith some special advantages: *Witness that he was righteous.* God gave witness to the righteousness of his person, by testifying his acceptance of his gifts. *By it he, being dead, yet speaketh.* He had the honour to leave behind him an instructive speaking case; and what does it speak to us? That fallen man has leave to go in to worship God, with hope of acceptance. That God will not suffer the injuries done to his people to remain unpunished, nor their sufferings unrewarded.

II. The faith of Enoch, *v.* 5.

1. What is here reported of him. (1) *He walked with God.* (2) *He was translated, that he should not see death,* nor any part of him be found upon earth. (3) *Before his translation he had this testimony, that he pleased God.* He had the evidence of it in his own conscience, and the Spirit of God witnessed with his spirit.

2. What is here said of his faith, *v.* 6. We cannot please God without such a faith as helps us to walk with God, an active faith. God is again to be found of us through Christ. God has prescribed means and ways wherein he may be found. Those who would find God must *seek him diligently*; and when once they have found him, they will never repent the pains they have spent in seeking after him.

III. The faith of Noah, *v.* 7.

1. The ground of Noah's faith—a warning he had received from God of things as yet not seen. God usually warns sinners before he strikes, and, where his warnings are slighted, the blow will fall the heavier.

2. The actings of Noah's faith, and the influence it had both upon his mind and practice. He was *moved with fear.* Faith first influences our affections, then our actions; and faith works upon those affections that are suitable to the matter revealed. If it be some good thing, faith stirs up love and desire; if some evil thing, faith stirs up fear. His faith influenced his practice. His fear moved him to prepare an ark. His faith set him to work in earnest.

3. The rewards of Noah's faith. (1) Hereby himself and his house were saved, when a whole world of sinners were perishing about them. (2) Hereby he judged and condemned the world; his holy fear condemned their vain confidence; his faith condemned their unbelief; his obedience condemned their contempt. Good examples will either convert sinners or condemn them. This is the best way the people of God can take to condemn the wicked; not by harsh and censorious language, but by a holy exemplary conversation. (3) Hereby *he became an heir of the righteousness which is by faith.* He was possessed of a true justifying righteousness; he was *heir to it.*

IV. The faith of Abraham, the friend of God, and father of the faithful, in whom the Hebrews boasted. The apostle enlarges more upon the heroic achievements of Abraham's faith than of that of any other of the patriarchs; and in the midst of his account of the faith of Abraham he inserts the story of Sarah's faith.

1. The ground of Abraham's faith, the call and promise of God, *v.* 8. (1) This call was the call of God. This was an effectual call, by which he was converted from the idolatry of his father's house, Gen. xii. 1. The grace of God is absolutely free, in taking some of the worst of men. God must come to us before we come to him. This calls us not only to leave sin, but sinful company. (2) The promise of God. God promised Abraham that the place he was called to he should afterwards receive for an inheritance. God calls his people to an inheritance. This inheritance is not immediately possessed by them, but the promise is sure.

2. The exercise of Abraham's faith. *He went out, not knowing whither he went.* He put himself into the hand of God, to send him whithersoever he pleased. All that are effectually called resign up their own will and wisdom to the will and wisdom of God. Though they know not always their way, yet they know their guide. *He sojourned in the land of promise as in a strange country.* This was an exercise of his faith. Abraham lived in Canaan as a sojourner only. He dwelt in tabernacles with Isaac and Jacob, heirs with him of the same promise. The promise is made to believers and their children, and it is pleasant to see parents and children sojourning together in this world as heirs of the heavenly inheritance.

3. The supports of Abraham's faith (*v.* 10). It is a city that hath foundations, even the immutable purposes and almighty power of God. The due regard that Abraham had to this heavenly city: he looked for it. He waited for it, and in the mean time he conversed in it by faith. It was a support to him under all the trials of his sojourning state.

V. The faith of Sarah.

1. The difficulties of Sarah's faith. The prevalency of unbelief for a time: she laughed at the promise, as impossible to be made good. The great improbability of the thing promised, that she should be the mother of a child.

2. The actings of her faith. Her unbelief is pardoned and forgotten, but her faith prevailed and is recorded, *v.* 11.

3. The rewards of her faith. *She received strength to conceive seed.* He can make the barren soul fruitful, as well as the barren womb. *She was delivered of a child,* a child of the promise. From them, by this son, sprang a numerous progeny of illustrious persons, *as the stars of the sky* (*v.* 12).

VI. The faith of the other patriarchs, *v.* 13.

1. The trial of their faith. They had not received the promises. One imperfection of the present state of the saints on earth is that their happiness lies more in promise than in actual enjoyment and possession.

2. The actings of their faith. Though they had not received the promises, yet,

(1) They saw them afar off. Faith has a clear and a strong eye, and can see promised mercies at a great distance.

(2) They were persuaded of them, that they were true and should be fulfilled.

(3) They embraced them. Faith has a long arm, and can lay hold of blessings at a great distance.

(4) They *confessed that they were strangers and pilgrims on earth.* They are strangers as saints, whose home is heaven; they are pilgrims as they are travelling towards their home.

(5) Hereby they declared plainly that they sought another country (*v.* 14), heaven.

(6) They gave full proof of their sincerity. They were not mindful of that country whence they came, *v.* 15. Those that are once savingly called out of a sinful state have no mind to return into it again; they now know better things. They did not take the opportunity that offered itself for their return. But they steadfastly adhered to God. We must show the truth of our faith and profession by a steady adherence to him. Their sincerity appeared not only in not returning to their former country, but in desiring a better country, that is, a heavenly. All true believers desire this better country. The stronger faith is the more fervent those desires will be.

(7) They died in the faith of those promises, *v.* 13. That faith held out to the last.

3. The gracious reward of their faith, *v.* 16. He is called their God. He calls himself so; he gives them leave to call him so. God is not ashamed to be called *their God*: such is his love to them. Let them take care that they be not a shame and reproach to their God, and so provoke him to be ashamed of them. As the proof of this, God has prepared for them a city, a happiness suitable to the relation into which he has taken them. If God neither could nor would give his people anything better than this world affords, he would be ashamed to be called their God.

VII. Now after the apostle has given this account of the faith of others, with Abraham, he returns to him again, and gives us an instance of the greatest trial and act of faith that stands upon record. This was his offering up Isaac, *v.* 17.

1. The trial of Abraham's faith. God had before this tempted or tried the faith of Abraham. But this trial was greater than all; he was commanded to offer

up his son Isaac. "Take thy son, thy only son by Sarah, Isaac thy laughter, the child of thy joy and delight; take him away to the land of Moriah; do not only leave him there, but offer him for a burnt-offering." Some things that very much added to the greatness of this trial. He was put upon it after he had received the promises (*v.* 18). In being called to offer up his Isaac, he seemed to be called to cut off his own family, to cancel the promises of God. This Isaac was his only-begotten son by his wife Sarah, the only one he was to have by her, and the only one that was to be the child and heir of the promise. Besides his most tender affection to this his son, all his expectations were bound up in him, and, if he perished, must perish with him. To have this son offered up as a sacrifice, and that by his own hand; it was a trial that would have overset the firmest and the strongest mind.

2. The actings of Abraham's faith in so great a trial: he obeyed. He went as far in it as to the very critical moment, and would have gone through with it if God had not prevented him.

3. The supports of his faith, *v.* 19. He knew that God was able to raise him from the dead, and he believed that God would do so. God is able to raise the dead, to raise dead bodies, and to raise dead souls.

4. The reward of his faith in this great trial (*v.* 19). He received his son. He had parted with him to God, and God gave him back again. He received him from the dead, for he gave him up for dead.

VIII. The faith of Isaac, *v.* 20.

1. The actings of his faith: He *blessed Jacob and Esau concerning things to come.* Both Jacob and Esau were blessed as Isaac's children. Jacob had the pre-cedency and the principal blessing. If one has his portion in this world, and the other in the better world, it is God who makes the difference; for even the comforts of this life are more and better than any of the children of men deserve.

2. The difficulties Isaac's faith struggled with. He seemed to have forgotten how God had determined the matter at the birth of these his sons, Gen. xxv. 23. When he came to pronounce the blessing, *he trembled very exceedingly* (Gen. xxvii. 33); and he charged Jacob that he had subtly taken away Esau's blessing. But, notwithstanding all this, Isaac's faith recovered itself, and he ratified the blessing: *I have blessed him, yea, and he shall be blessed.* Now, the faith of Isaac thus prevailing over his unbelief, it has pleased the God of Isaac to pass by the weakness of his faith, to commend the sincerity of it.

IX. The faith of Jacob (*v.* 21). There were a great many instances of the faith of Jacob; his life was a life of faith.

1. The actings of his faith.

(1) *He blessed both the sons of Joseph,* Ephraim and Manasseh. He made them both heads of different tribes, as if they had been his own immediate sons. As Isaac did before, so now Jacob prefers the younger, Ephraim; though Joseph had placed them so that the right hand of his father should be laid on Man-asseh, the elder.

(2) *He worshipped, leaning on his staff;* he praised God for what he had done for him, and for the pros-pect he had of approaching blessedness. He was not able to support himself, so far as to sit up in his bed without a staff, and yet he would not make this an excuse for neglecting the worshipping of God; he would do it as well as he could with his body, as well as with his spirit.

2. When Jacob thus acted his faith: when he was dying. He lived by faith, and he died by faith and in faith.

X. The faith of Joseph, *v.* 22.

1. What he did by his faith. He made mention by faith of the departing of the children of Israel, that the time should come when they should be delivered out of Egypt. Though he should not live to see their deliverance, yet he could die in the faith of it. He gave commandment concerning his bones, that they should preserve them unburied in Egypt. Though he had lived and died in Egypt, yet he did not live and die an Egyptian, but an Israelite. He preferred a significant burial in Canaan before a magnificent one in Egypt.

2. When the faith of Joseph acted after this manner: when he was dying. God often gives his people living comforts in dying moments.

XI. The faith of the parents of Moses. 1. The acting of their faith: they hid this their son three months. Moses was persecuted betimes, and forced to be concealed; in this he was a type of Christ, who was persecuted almost as soon as he was born, and his parents were obliged to flee with him into Egypt for his preservation. 2. The reasons of their thus acting. No doubt, natural affection could not but move them; but there was something further. They *saw he was a proper child.* There appeared in him something uncommon; the beauty of the Lord sat upon him. Sometimes, not always, the countenance is the index of the mind. 3. The prevalency of their faith over their fear. They were not afraid of the king's commandment. They believed that God would preserve his people, and that the time was coming when it would be worth while for an Israelite to live. Some must hazard their own lives to preserve their children, and they were resolved to do it. Faith is a great preservative against the sinful slavish fear of men.

XII. The faith of Moses himself (*v.* 24, 25, &c.).

1. An instance of his faith in conquering the world.

(1) He *refused to be called the son of Pharaoh's daughter,* whose foundling he was, and her fondling too. How glorious was the triumph of his faith. He *refused to be called the son of Pharaoh's daughter* lest he should undervalue the truer honour of being a son of Abraham, the father of the faithful; lest it should look like renouncing his religion as well as his relation to Israel; and no doubt both these he must have done if he had accepted this honour.

(2) He was willing to take his lot with the people of God here, though it was a suffering lot, that he might have his portion with them hereafter (*v.* 25). Herein he acted rationally as well as religiously. The pleasures of sin must end in speedy repentance or in speedy ruin. The pleasures of this world, and especially those of a court, are too often the pleasures of sin. A true believer will despise them. Suffering is to be chosen rather than sin, there being more evil in the least sin than there can be in the greatest suffering.

(3) See how Moses weighed matters: in one scale he put the worst of religion—*the reproaches of Christ,* in the other scale the best of the world—*the treasures of Egypt* (*v.* 26). The worst of religion weighed down the best of the world. The reproaches of the church of God are *the reproaches of Christ.* God's people are, and always have been, a reproached people. Christ accounts himself reproached in their reproaches and, while he thus interests himself in their reproaches, they become riches. Faith discerns this, and acts accordingly.

2. The circumstance of time is taken notice of, when Moses by his faith gained this victory (*v.* 24); not only in years of discretion, but of experience, to the age of forty years. He made this choice when he had grown ripe for judgment and enjoyment, able to know what he did and why he did it. It was not the act of a child, but it proceeded from mature deliberation. It is an excellent thing for persons to despise the world when they are most capable of relishing and enjoying it.

3. What it was that supported and strengthened the faith of Moses: *He had respect unto the recompence of reward.* Believers may and ought to have respect to this recompence of reward. It will prove a land-mark to direct their course, a load-stone to draw their hearts, and a cordial to refresh them.

4. We have another instance of the faith of Moses, *v.* 27. (1) The product of his faith: *He forsook Egypt.* Twice Moses forsook Egypt: As a supposed criminal, when the king's wrath was incensed against him for killing the Egyptian. As a commander after God had employed him to humble Pharaoh and make him willing to let Israel go. (2) The prevalency of his faith. It raised him above the fear of the king's wrath. Those who forsook Egypt must expect the wrath of men; but they need not fear it. (3) The principle upon which his faith acted in these his motions: *He endured, as seeing him that was invisible.* By faith we may see this invisible God. We may be fully assured of his existence, and of his gracious and powerful presence with us. Such a sight of God will enable believers to endure to the end.

5. We have yet another instance of the faith of Moses, *v.* 28. The passover was one of the most solemn institutions of the Old Testament, and a very significant type of Christ. To entitle them to this distinguishing favour, a lamb must be slain; the blood of it must be sprinkled with a bunch of hyssop upon the lintel of the door, and on the two side-posts. Christ is that Lamb, he is our Passover, he was sacrificed for us. His blood must be sprinkled; it must be applied to those who have the saving benefit of it. It is not owing to our inherent righteousness that we are saved from the wrath of God, but to the blood of Christ and his imputed righteousness. Wherever this blood is applied, the soul receives Christ by faith, and lives upon him. All our spiritual privileges on earth should quicken us to set out early, and get forward, in our way to heaven.

XIII. The Israelites passing through the Red Sea under the conduct of Moses their leader, *v.* 29.

1. The safe passage of the Israelites through the Red Sea, when there was no other way to escape from Pharaoh and his host. Israel's danger was very great. Their deliverance was very glorious. The grace of faith will help us through all the dangers we meet with in our way to heaven.

2. The destruction of the Egyptians. Their rashness was great, and their ruin was grievous. When God judges, he will overcome; and it is plain that the destruction of sinners is of themselves.

XIV. The Israelites, under Joshua their leader, before the walls of Jericho. The story we have Joshua vi. 5, &c. The means prescribed of God to bring down the walls of Jericho. Here was a great trial of their faith. The method prescribed seemed very improbable to answer such an end. But this was the way God commanded them to take, and he loves to do great things by small and contemptible means, that his own arm may be made bare. The powerful success of the prescribed means. The walls of Jericho fell before them. God can in his own time cause all the powerful opposition that is made to his interest to fall down, and the grace of faith is mighty through God for the pulling down of strongholds. When he has some great thing to do for them, he raises up great and strong faith in them.

XV. The faith of Rahab, *v.* 31.

1. Who this Rahab was. She was a Canaanite, a *stranger to the commonwealth of Israel,* and had but little help for faith, and yet she was a believer. She was a harlot, and lived in a way of sin. Christ has saved the chief of sinners. *Where sin has abounded, grace has superabounded.*

2. What she did by her faith: *She received the spies in peace.* She not only bade them welcome, but she concealed them from their enemies, and she made a noble confession of her faith. True faith will show itself in good works, especially towards the people of God. Faith will venture all hazards in the cause of God and his people. A true believer is desirous, not only to be in covenant with God, but in communion with the people of God.

3. What she gained by her faith. She escaped perishing with those that believed not. It was an utter destruction that befell that city: man and beast were cut off. The signal preservation of Rahab. Joshua gave a strict charge that she should be spared, and none but she and hers. Singular faith, when the generality are not only unbelievers, but against believers, will be rewarded with singular favours.

Verses 32–40

The apostle now concludes his narrative with a more summary account of another set of believers. He prefaces this part of the narrative with an elegant expostulation: *What shall I say more? Time would fail me.* We should be pleased to think how great the number of believers was under the Old Testament, and how strong their faith. We should lament it, that now, when the rule of faith is more clear and perfect, the number of believers should be so small and their faith so weak.

I. The apostle mentions,

1. Gideon. He was an eminent instrument raised up of God to deliver his people from the oppression of the Midianites. God put the whole army of the Midianites to confusion and ruin.

2. Barak. He obtained a great victory by his faith over all the host of Sisera.

3. Samson. If Samson had not had a strong faith as well as a strong arm, he had never performed such exploits. True faith is acknowledged and accepted, even when mingled with many failings. The believer's faith endures to the end, and, in dying, gives him victory over death and all his deadly enemies; his greatest conquest he gains by dying.

4. Jephthah. As various and new enemies rise up against the people of God, various and new deliverers are raised up for them. The grace of God often finds out, and fastens upon, the most undeserving and ill-deserving persons, to do great things for them and by them. Jephthah was the son of a harlot. Faith will not only put men upon making their vows to God, but paying their vows after the mercy received; yea, though they have vowed to their own great grief, as in the case of Jephthah and his daughter.

5. David that great man after God's own heart. Few ever met with greater trials, and few ever discovered a more lively faith. The same faith made him a very successful and victorious prince, and, after a long life of virtue and honour (though not without some foul stains of sin), he died in faith, and he has left behind him such excellent memoirs of the trials and acts of faith in the book of Psalms as will ever be of great esteem and use.

6. Samuel, raised up to be a most eminent prophet of the Lord to Israel, as well as a ruler over them. God revealed himself to Samuel when he was but a child, and continued to do so till his death.

7. To Samuel he adds, *and of the prophets,* who were employed of God sometimes to denounce judgment, sometimes to promise mercy, always to reprove sin; sometimes to foretell remarkable events; and chiefly to give notice of the Messiah. A true faith was very requisite for the right discharge of such an office as this.

II. What things were done by their faith.

1. *By faith they subdued kingdoms, v.* 33. The interests and powers of kings and kingdoms are often set up in opposition to God and his people. God can

easily subdue all those kings and kingdoms that set themselves to oppose him.

2. They *wrought righteousness*. They believed God, and it was imputed to them for righteousness. It is a greater happiness to work righteousness than to work miracles.

3. They *obtained promises*. It is by faith that we are prepared to wait for the promises, and in due time to receive them.

4. They *stopped the mouths of lions*. Faith engages the power of God for his people, whenever it shall be for his glory, to overcome brute beasts and brutish men.

5. They *quenched the violence of the fire*, v. 34. So did the three children, or rather mighty champions, Dan. iii. 17–27. Never was the grace of faith more severely tried, never more nobly exerted, nor ever more gloriously rewarded, than theirs was.

6. They *escaped the edge of the sword*. The swords of men are held in the hand of God. Faith takes hold of that hand of God which has hold of the swords of men; and God had often suffered himself to be prevailed upon by the faith of his people.

7. *Out of weakness they were made strong*. It is the same grace of faith that from spiritual weakness helps men to recover and renew their strength.

8. They *grew valiant in fight*. True faith gives truest courage and patience, as it discerns the strength of God, and thereby the weakness of all his enemies. And they were not only valiant, but successful. God, as a reward and encouragement of their faith, *put to flight the armies of the aliens*; God made them flee and fall before his faithful servants.

9. *Women received their dead raised to life again*, v. 35. Many of the weaker sex have been strong in faith. God has sometimes yielded so far to the tender affections of sorrowful women as to restore their dead children to life again.

III. The apostle tells us what these believers endured by faith. They *were tortured, not accepting deliverance*, v. 35. They bore the torture, and would not accept of deliverance. That which animated them thus to suffer was the hope they had of *obtaining a better resurrection*. They endured *trials of cruel mockings and scourgings, and bonds and imprisonment*, v. 36. They were persecuted in their reputation by *mockings*, which are cruel to an ingenuous mind; in their persons by *scourging*, the punishment of slaves; in their liberty by *bonds and imprisonment*. They were put to death in the most cruel manner. Their enemies clothed death in all the array of cruelty and terror, and yet they boldly met it and endured it. Those who escaped death were used so ill that death might seem more eligible than such a life. Their enemies spared them, only to prolong their misery, v. 37, 38. Such sufferings as these they endured then for their faith; and such they endured through the power of the grace of faith: and which shall we most admire, the wickedness of human nature, or the excellency of divine grace, that is able to bear up the faithful under such cruelties, and to carry them safely through all?

IV. What they obtained by their faith. 1. A most honourable commendation from God—that *the world was not worthy* of such men; the world did not deserve such blessings. The righteous are not worthy to live in the world, and God declares the world is not worthy of them. 2. They *obtained a good report* (v. 39) of all good men, add the truth itself. 3. They had a title to the promises, though they received not the great things promised. They had shadows, but had not seen the substance; and yet, under this imperfect dispensation, they discovered this precious faith. This the apostle insists upon to render their faith more illustrious. He tells the Hebrews that God had *provided some better things for* them (v. 40), and therefore they might be assured

that he expected at least as good things from them. Their faith should be much more perfect than the faith of the Old Testament saints; for their state and dispensation were more perfect than the former.

CHAPTER 12

The apostle presses home the argument, I. From a greater example than he had yet mentioned, Christ himself, ver. 1–3. II. From the gentle nature of the afflictions they endured in their Christian course, ver. 4–17. III. From the conformity between the state of the gospel-church on earth and the triumphant church in heaven, ver. 18, to the end.

Verses 1–3

The great duty which the apostle urges upon the Hebrews. The duty consists of two parts.

I. Preparatory: *Lay aside every weight, and the sin, &c. Every weight*, that is, all inordinate affection and concern for the body, and the present life and world. *The sin that doth so easily beset us;* the sin that has the greatest advantage against us, by the circumstances we are in, our constitution, our company.

II. Perfective: *Run with patience the race that is set before us*.

1. Christians have a race to run.

2. This race is set before them; it is marked out unto them, both by the word of God and the examples of the faithful servants of God, that cloud of witnesses with which they are compassed about.

3. This race must be run with patience and perseverance. Faith and patience are the conquering graces, and therefore must be always cultivated.

4. Christians have a greater example to encourage them than any who have been mentioned before, v. 2.

(1) What our Lord Jesus is to his people: he is *the author and finisher of* their *faith*, not only the object, but the author. He is the great leader and precedent of our faith. He is *the finisher of our faith*. He is the finisher of grace, and of the work of faith with power in the souls of his people; and he is the judge and the rewarder of their faith.

(2) What trials Christ met with in his race and course. He *endured the contradiction of sinners against himself* (v. 3), yet he endured their evil manners with great patience. He endured all. He *endured the cross*—all those sufferings that he met with in the world; for he took up his cross betimes, and was at length nailed to it. Yet all this he endured with invincible patience and resolution. He *despised the shame*. All the reproaches that were cast upon him, both in his life and at his death, he despised.

(3) What it was that supported the human soul of Christ, *the joy that was set before him*. He rejoiced to see that by his sufferings he should make satisfaction to the injured justice of God, that he should make peace between God and man, that he should open a way of salvation.

(4) The reward of his suffering: he *has sat down at the right hand of the throne of God*. He ever lives *to make intercession for* his people.

(5) What is our duty. We must look unto him; we must set him continually before us as our example. We must consider him, meditate much upon him. We shall find that as his sufferings far exceeded ours, so his patience far excels ours.

(6) The advantage we shall reap by thus doing: it will be a means to prevent our weariness and fainting (v. 3). There is a proneness in the best to grow weary and to faint under their trials and afflictions. The best way to prevent this is to look unto Jesus. Faith and meditation will fetch in fresh supplies of strength, comfort, and courage.

Verses 4–17

I. The gentle and moderate measure of their sufferings, v. 4. He owns that they had suffered much;

they had been striving to an agony against sin. He puts them in mind that they might have suffered more; for they had *not yet resisted unto blood.* Our Lord Jesus does not call his people out to the hardest trials at first, but wisely trains them up by less sufferings to be prepared for greater. The gentleness of Christ in accommodating their trials to their strength. They should not magnify their afflictions, but should take notice of the mercy that is mixed with them.

II. He argues from the nature of those sufferings. They are divine chastisements; their heavenly Father has his hand in all; of this he has given them due notice, and they should not forget it, *v.* 5.

1. Those afflictions which may be truly persecution as far as men are concerned in them are fatherly rebukes and chastisements as far as God is concerned in them. Men persecute them because they are religious; God chastises them because they are not more so.

2. God has directed his people how they ought to behave themselves under all their afflictions. They must not despise the chastening of the Lord. Those who make light of affliction make light of God and make light of sin. They must not faint when they are rebuked.

3. Afflictions, though they may be the fruits of God's displeasure, are yet proofs of his paternal love to his people and care for them (*v.* 6, 7). The best of God's children have their faults and follies, which need to be corrected. He will correct sin in his own children; they are of his family. In this he acts as becomes a father; no wise and good father will wink at faults in his own children as he would in others. To be suffered to go on in sin without a rebuke is a sad sign of alienation from God; such are bastards, not sons. They are the spurious offspring of another father, not of God, *v.* 7, 8.

4. Those that are impatient under the discipline of their heavenly father behave worse towards him than they would do towards earthly parents, *v.* 9, 10. It is the duty of children to give the reverence of submission to their correction when they have been disobedient. He recommends humble and submissive behaviour towards our heavenly Father, when under his correction. (1) Our earthly fathers are but *the fathers of our flesh,* but God is *the Father of our spirits.* Our fathers on earth were instrumental in the production of our bodies, which are but flesh. We must owe much more to him who is the Father of our spirits. (2) Our earthly parents *chastened us for their own pleasure.* Sometimes they did it to gratify their passion rather than to reform our manners. This is a weakness the fathers of our flesh are subject to. It should be *for our profit.* God loves his children so that he would have them to be as like himself as can be, and for this end he chastises them when they need it. (3) The fathers of our flesh corrected us for *a few days,* in our state of childhood, and when we came to maturity we loved and honoured them the more for it. Our whole life here is a state of childhood; when we come to a state of perfection we shall be fully reconciled to all the measures of God's discipline over us now. (4) God's correction is no condemnation. He does it to prevent the death and destruction of their souls, that they may live to God, and be like God, and be for ever with him.

5. The children of God ought not to judge of his dealings with them by present sense, but by reason, and faith, and experience, *v.* 11.

(1) The judgment of sense. Afflictions are not grateful to the sense, but grievous.

(2) The judgment of faith. Affliction produces peace, by producing more righteousness; for the fruit of righteousness is peace. Their great concern is that the chastening they are under may be endured by them with patience, and improved to a greater degree of holiness. [1] That their affliction may be endured with patience, *v.* 12. A burden of affliction is apt to make the Christian's hands hang down, and his knees grow feeble, to dispirit him and discourage him; but this he must strive against; that he may the better run his spiritual race. Faith, and patience, and holy courage and resolution, will make him walk more steadily. He must encourage and not dispirit others. There are many that are in the way to heaven who yet walk but weakly and lamely in it. Such are apt to discourage one another; but it is their duty to help one another forward in the way to heaven. [2] That their affliction may be improved to a greater degree of holiness, *v.* 14. Faith and patience will enable them to follow peace and holiness too. Sufferings are apt to sour the spirit and sharpen the passions; but the children of God must follow peace with all men. Peace and holiness are connected together. This true Christian peaceableness is never found separate from holiness. *Without holiness no man shall see the Lord.*

6. Where afflictions and sufferings for the sake of Christ are not considered by men as the chastisement of their heavenly Father, they will be a dangerous temptation to apostasy (*v.* 15, 16).

(1) A serious caveat against apostasy.

[1] The nature of apostasy. It is *failing of the grace of God,* coming short of a principle of true grace in the soul, and so coming short of the love and favour of God here and hereafter. The consequences of apostasy: where persons fail of having the true grace of God, a root of bitterness will spring up, corruption will prevail and break forth. It produces to themselves corrupt principles. It also produces bitter fruits to others. *Many are defiled,* tainted with those bad principles, and drawn into defiling practices.

[2] The apostle backs the caution with an awful example, that of Esau. Esau's sin. He profanely despised and sold the birthright, and all the advantages attending it. So do apostates. Esau's punishment. His conscience was convinced of his sin and folly, when it was too late. He now saw that the blessing he had made so light of was worth the having. He was rejected of God: *He found no place of repentance.* Esau, in his great wickedness, had made the bargain, and God, in his righteous judgment, ratified and confirmed it.

(2) Apostasy from Christ is the fruit of preferring the gratification of the flesh to the blessing of God. Sinners will not always have such mean thoughts of the divine blessing and inheritance as now they have. When the day of grace is over they will find no place for repentance. Christians should never give up their hope of their Father's blessings by deserting their holy religion, to avoid suffering.

Verses 18–29

I. He shows how much the gospel church differs from the Jewish church, and how much it excels, *v.* 18–21. 1. It was a gross sensible state. Mount Sinai was a *mount that might be touched* (*v.* 18), a gross palpable place; so was the dispensation. The state of the gospel church on Mount Zion is more spiritual. 2. It was a dark dispensation. Upon that mount there were blackness and darkness. The gospel state is clear and bright. 3. It was a dreadful and terrible dispensation; the Jews could not bear the terror of it, *v.* 19. Yea, Moses himself said, *I exceedingly fear and quake.* The gospel state is mild, and kind, suited to our weak frame. 4. It was a limited dispensation; all might not approach to that mount. Under the gospel we have all access with boldness to God. This was the state of the Jewish church, fitted to set forth the strict and tremendous justice of God.

II. He shows how much the gospel church represents the church triumphant in heaven. The gospel church is called *Mount Zion, the heavenly Jerusalem.* In coming to Mount Zion, believers come into heavenly places, and into a heavenly society.

1. Into heavenly places. (1) *Unto the city of the living God.* God has taken up his gracious residence in the gospel church, which on that account is an emblem of heaven. (2) To *the heavenly Jerusalem,* as free denizens there.

2. To a heavenly society. (1) *To an innumerable company of angels.* Those who by faith are joined to the gospel church are joined to the angels, and shall at length be like them. (2) *To the general assembly and church of the first-born, that are written in heaven,* to the universal church, however dispersed. By faith we come to them, have communion with them in the same blessed hope, and walk in the same way of holiness. Here will be the general assembly of the first-born, the saints of former and earlier times. The names of these are written in heaven: they have a name in God's house, and are enrolled in the Lamb's book of life, as citizens are enrolled in the livery-books. (3) *To God the Judge of all,* that great God who will judge both Jew and Gentile according to the law they are under. (4) *To the spirits of just men made perfect;* to the best sort of men, the righteous, to the best part of just men, their spirits, and to these in their best state, made perfect. (5) *To Jesus the Mediator of the new covenant, and to the blood of sprinkling, that speaketh better things than that of Abel.* This is none of the least of the many encouragements there are to perseverance. [1] The gospel covenant is a new covenant, distinct from the covenant of works. [2] Christ is the Mediator of this new covenant. [3] This covenant is ratified by the blood of Christ sprinkled upon our consciences. This blood of Christ pacifies God and purifies the consciences of men. [4] This is speaking blood, and it speaks better things than that of Abel. It speaks to God in behalf of sinners; it pleads not for vengeance, but for mercy. It speaks to sinners, in the name of God. It speaks pardon to their sins, peace to their souls.

III. The apostle closes the chapter by improving the argument in a manner suitable to the weight of it (*v.* 25, &c.). Then he spoke on earth, now he speaks from heaven.

1. When God speaks to men in the most excellent manner he justly expects from them the most strict attention. He now speaks from a higher and more glorious throne—heaven. He speaks now more powerfully and effectually. Then indeed his voice shook the earth, but now he hath shaken not only the earth, but the heavens. It is by the gospel from heaven that God shook to pieces the Jewish nation, and introduced a new state of the church.

2. When God speaks to men in the most excellent manner, the guilt of those who refuse him is the greater, *v.* 25. It was by the sound of the gospel trumpet that a new kingdom was erected for God in the world, which can never be so shaken as to be removed. This was a change made once for all. The apostle justly concludes, (1) How necessary it is for us to obtain *grace from God, to serve him acceptably.* We lose all our labour in religion if we be not accepted of God. (2) We cannot worship God acceptably, unless we worship him with *godly reverence and fear.* As faith, so holy fear, is necessary to acceptable worship. (3) It is only the grace of God that enables us to worship God in a right manner. (4) God is the same just and righteous God under the gospel that he appeared to be under the law. He is in himself a consuming fire; that is, a God of strict justice.

CHAPTER 13

The apostle recommends several excellent duties to them as the proper fruits of faith (ver. 1–17); he then bespeaks their prayers for him, and offers up his prayers to God for them, gives them some hope of seeing himself and Timothy, and ends with the general salutation and benediction, ver. 18, to the end.

Verses 1–17

The apostle calls the believing Hebrews to the performance of many excellent duties.

I. To brotherly love (*v.* 1). The spirit of Christianity is a spirit of love. Faith works by love. The true religion is the strongest bond of friendship. This brotherly love was in danger of being lost, and that in a time of persecution, when it would be most necessary. Christians should always love and live as brethren, and the more they grow in devout affection to God their heavenly Father, the more they will grow in love to one another for his sake.

II. To hospitality, *v.* 2. We must add to brotherly kindness, charity. The duty required—*to entertain strangers.* Seeing they are without any certain dwelling place, we should allow them room in our hearts and in our houses, as we have opportunity and ability. The motive: *Thereby some have entertained angels unawares.* God has often bestowed honours and favours upon his hospitable servants, beyond all their thoughts, *unawares.*

III. To Christian sympathy, *v.* 3.

1. The duty. Those that are themselves at liberty must sympathise with those that are in bonds and adversity, as if they were bound with them in the same chain.

2. The reason of the duty: *As being yourselves in the body;* not only in the body natural, but in the same mystical body. It would be unnatural in Christians not to bear each other's burdens.

IV. To purity and chastity, *v.* 4. A recommendation of God's ordinance of marriage, that it *is honourable in all.* It is *honourable* and happy, when persons come together pure and chaste, and preserve the marriage bed undefiled. A dreadful but just censure of impurity and lewdness: *Whoremongers and adulterers God will judge.* He will call such sins by their proper names, not by the names of love and gallantry, but of whoredom and adultery. He will bring them into judgment. He will convict them, condemn them.

V. To Christian contentment, *v.* 5, 6. The sin that is contrary to his grace and duty—*covetousness.* We must take care not only to keep this sin down, but to root it out of our souls. The duty that is contrary to covetousness—being satisfied and pleased *with such things as we have.* What God gives us from day to day we must be content with. We must bring our minds to our present condition. Those who cannot do it would not be contented though God should raise their condition to their minds, for the mind would rise with the condition. Paul, though abased and empty, had *learned in* every *state, in* any *state, therewith to be content.* What reason Christians have to be contented with their lot, *v.* 5, 6. This promise contains the sum and substance of all the promises. From this comprehensive promise they may assure themselves of help from God, *v.* 6. Men can do nothing against God, and God can make all that men do against his people to turn to their good.

VI. To the duty Christians owe to their ministers, and that both to those that are dead and to those that are yet alive.

1. To those that are dead, *v.* 7.

(1) The description given of them. They were such as had the rule over them, and had spoken to them the word of God.

(2) The duties owing to them. "*Remember them. Follow* their *faith;* labour after the grace of faith by which they lived and died so well. *Consider the end*

of their conversation!" Now this duty of following the same true faith in which they had been instructed the apostle enlarges much upon by referring to the immutability and eternity of the Lord Jesus Christ. The great head of the church ever lives, and is ever the same; and they should be steadfast and immovable, in imitation of Christ. Furthermore he describes erroneous doctrines which they must avoid.

[1] They were divers and various (v. 9), different from what they had received and inconsistent with themselves.

[2] They were strange doctrines.

[3] They were of an unsettling, distracting nature. They were quite contrary to that grace of God which fixes and establishes the heart.

[4] They were about external, little, perishing things, such as *meats and drinks*, &c.

[5] They were unprofitable. They did not make them more holy, nor more humble, nor more thankful, nor more heavenly.

[6] They would exclude those who embraced them from the privileges of the Christian altar (v. 10): *We have an altar*. The Christian church has its altar. Not a material altar, but a personal one, and that is Christ; he is both our altar, and our sacrifice. This altar furnishes out a feast for true believers. The Lord's supper is the feast of the gospel passover. Those who adhere to the tabernacle or the Levitical dispensation, or return to it again, exclude themselves from the privileges of this altar. This part of the argument he first proves and then improves.

a. This servile adherence to the Jewish state is a bar to the privileges of the gospel altar. The gospel feast is the fruit of the sacrifice, which those have no right to who do not acknowledge the sacrifice itself. He proceeds,

b. To improve this argument (v. 13–15): *Let us go forth therefore unto him without the camp.* Let us be willing to *bear his reproach.* We must submit to it; and we have the more reason because we must necessarily go forth in a little time by death; for *here we have no continuing city.* We should go forth now by faith, and seek in Christ the rest and settlement which this world cannot afford us, v. 14. Let us make a right use of this altar. Let us bring our sacrifices to this altar, v. 15, 16. 1. The sacrifice of praise to God, which we should offer up to God continually. In this are included all adoration and prayer, as well as thanksgiving; this is *the fruit of our lips.* 2. The sacrifice of alms-deeds, and Christian charity, v. 16, not contending ourselves to offer the sacrifice of our lips, mere words, but the sacrifice of good deeds.

2. To their living ministers (v. 17). The duty—to obey them, and submit themselves to them. Christians must submit to be instructed by their ministers, and not think themselves too wise, too good, or too great, to learn from them; and they must obey them. The motives to this duty. (1) They have the rule over the people; their office is truly authoritative. (2) They watch for the souls of the people. They are to watch against everything that may be hurtful. They are to watch for all opportunities of helping the souls of men forward in the way to heaven. (3) They must give an account how they have discharged their duty. They would be glad to give a good account. If they can then give in an account of their own fidelity and success, it will be a joyful day to them. If they give up their account with grief, it will be the people's loss as well as theirs.

Verses 18–25

I. The apostle recommends himself, and his fellow-sufferers, to the prayers of the Hebrew believers (v. 18).

1. This is one part of the duty which people owe to their ministers. Ministers need the prayers of the people; and the more earnestly the people pray for their ministers the more benefit they may expect to reap from their ministry.

2. There are good reasons why people should pray for their ministers.

(1) *We trust we have a good conscience, &c.*, v. 18. Many of the Jews had a bad opinion of Paul. He here modestly asserts his own integrity. *We trust!* he might have said, *We know;* but he chose to speak in a humble style. "We trust we have a good conscience *in all things.* We would act honestly and sincerely in all things." A good conscience has a respect to all God's commands and all our duty. Those who have this good conscience, yet need the prayers of others.

(2) Another reason why he desires their prayers, v. 19, intimating that, now he was absent from them, he had a great desire and real intention to come again to them,—and that the best way to facilitate his return to them, was to make it a matter of their prayer.

II. He offers up his prayers to God for them: *Now the God of peace, &c.*, v. 20. The title given to God—*the God of peace*, who has found out a way for peace and reconciliation between himself and sinners. The great work ascribed to him: *He hath brought again from the dead our Lord Jesus, &c.* That divine power by which he was raised is able to do everything for us that we stand in need of. The titles given to Christ—our Lord Jesus, our sovereign, our Saviour, and the great shepherd of the sheep. They are the flock of his pasture, and his care and concern are for them. The way and method in which God is reconciled, and Christ raised from the dead: *Through the blood of the everlasting covenant.* This blood is the sanction and seal of an everlasting covenant between God and his people. The mercy prayed for, v. 21. The perfection of the saints in every good work is the great thing desired by them and for them. The way in which God makes his people perfect; it is by working in them always what is pleasing in his sight. To this every one should say, *Amen.*

III. He was pleased with the hopes of not only seeing Timothy, but seeing the Hebrews with him, v. 23.

IV. He closes with salutations, and a solemn, though short benediction (v. 22).

1. The salutation. From himself to them all, ministers and people. From the Christians in Italy to them.

2. The solemn, though short benediction (v. 25).

AN EXPOSITION, WITH PRACTICAL OBSERVATIONS, OF

THE GENERAL EPISTLE OF

JAMES

The writer of this epistle was not James the son of Zebedee; for he was put to death by Herod (Acts xii). It is called a general epistle, because (as some think) not directed to any particular person or church, but such a one as we call a circular letter. The time when this epistle was written is uncertain. The design of it is to reprove Christians for their great degeneracy both in faith and manners. It was also a special intention of the author of this epistle to awaken the Jewish nation to a sense of the greatness and nearness of those judgments which were coming upon them; and to support all true Christians in the way of their duty, under the calamities and persecutions they might meet with.

CHAPTER 1

After the inscription and salutation (ver. 1), Christians are taught how to conduct themselves when under the cross. Those who endure their trials and afflictions are pronounced blessed, ver. 2–12. But those sins which bring sufferings, are by no means to be imputed to God, who cannot be the author of sin, but is the author of all good, ver. 13–18. The word of God should be made our chief study; and what we hear and know of it we must take care to practise. To this is added an account wherein pure religion consists, ver. 19–27.

Verse 1

The inscription of this epistle.

I. The character by which our author desires to be known: *James, a servant of God, and of the Lord Jesus Christ.* Though James is called by the evangelist *the brother of our Lord,* yet it was his glory to serve Christ in the spirit, rather than to boast of his being akin according to the flesh. Hence let us learn to prize this title above all others in the world—*the servants of God and of Christ.* We cannot acceptably serve the Father, unless we are also servants of the Son.

II. *The twelve tribes which are scattered abroad.* They were dispersed in mercy. They were scattered in several countries for the diffusing of the light of divine revelation. They began now to be scattered in wrath. Even good people among them shared in the common calamity. These Jews of the dispersion were those who had embraced the Christian faith. It is often the lot even of God's own tribes to be scattered abroad. While God's tribes are scattered abroad, he will send to look after them. Here is an apostle writing to the scattered; an epistle from God to them. We should not despond and think ourselves rejected, under outward calamities, God remembers and sends comfort to his scattered people.

III. James here shows the respect he had even for the dispersed: *greeting.* It was the desire of this apostle's heart that those who were scattered might be comforted.

Verses 2–12

I. The suffering state of Christians in this world is represented. It is implied that troubles and afflictions may be the lot of the best Christians. Such as have a title to the greatest joy may yet endure very grievous afflictions. The trials of a good man are such as he does not create to himself, nor sinfully pull upon himself; but they are such as he is said to fall into.

II. The graces and duties of a state of trial and affliction.

1. One Christian grace to be exercised is joy, *v.* 2. We must not sink into a sad and disconsolate frame of mind, which would make us faint under our trials. Philosophy may instruct men to be calm under their troubles; but Christianity teaches them to be joyful. Our trials will brighten our graces now and our crown at last. There is the more reason for joy in afflictions if we consider the other graces that are promoted by them.

2. Faith, *v.* 3; and then in *v.* 6. There must be a sound believing of the great truths of Christianity, and a resolute cleaving to them, in times of trial.

3. There must be patience: *The trial of faith worketh patience.* The trying of one grace produces another. To exercise Christian patience aright, we must let it work. Stoical apathy and Christian patience are very different: by the one men become, in some measure, insensible of their afflictions; but by the other they become triumphant in and over them. Let us give it leave to work, and it will work wonders in a time of trouble. We must let it have its perfect work. When we bear all that God appoints, and as long as he appoints, and when we not only bear troubles, but rejoice in them, then patience hath its perfect work. When the work of patience is complete, then the Christian is entire, and nothing will be wanting.

4. Prayer. What we ought more especially to pray for—wisdom. We should not pray so much for the removal of an affliction as for wisdom to make a right use of it. To be wise in trying times is a special gift of God. In what way this is to be obtained—upon our asking for it. Let the foolish become beggars at the throne of grace, and they are in a fair way to be wise. We have the greatest encouragement to do this: *he giveth to all men liberally, and upbraideth not. It shall be given, v.* 5. He to whom we are sent, has it to give: and he is of a giving disposition. Nor is there any fear of his favours being limited to some for *he gives to all men.* If you should say you want a great deal of wisdom, a small portion will not serve your turn, he *gives liberally*; and lest you should be afraid of being put to shame for your folly, he *upbraideth not.* Ask when you will, and as often as you will, you will meet with no upbraidings. The promise is: *It shall be given him.* There is one thing necessary to be observed in our asking, *v.* 6. There must be *no wavering*, no staggering at the promise of God through unbelief.

5. Sincerity of intention, and a steadiness of mind, constitute another duty required under affliction: *He that wavereth is like a wave of the sea, driven with the wind, and tossed.* To be sometimes lifted up by faith, and then thrown down again by distrust—this is very fitly compared to a wave of the sea, that rises and falls, swells and sinks, just as the wind tosses it higher or lower, that way or this. The success of prayer is spoiled hereby, *v.* 7. Such a distrustful shifting, unsettled person is not likely to value a favour from God as he should do, and therefore cannot expect to

receive it. A wavering faith and spirit has a bad influence upon our conversations, *v.* 8. There will be great unsteadiness in all our conversation and actions. He that is unstable as water shall not excel.

III. Both poor and rich are directed on what grounds to build their joy and comfort, *v.* 9–11. Those of low degree are to be looked upon as brethren. Good Christians may be rich in the world, *v.* 10. Grace and wealth are not wholly inconsistent. Both these are allowed to rejoice. No condition of life puts us out of a capacity of rejoicing in God. All who are brought low, and made lowly by grace, may rejoice in the prospect of their exaltation at the last in heaven. What reason rich people have to be humble: *As the flower of the grass he shall pass away.* He, and his wealth with him, *v.* 11. *For the sun has no sooner risen with a burning heat than it withereth the grass.* As a flower fades before the heat of the scorching sun, *so shall the rich man fade away in his ways.* For this reason let him that is rich rejoice, not so much in the providence of God, that makes him rich, as in the grace of God, that makes and keeps him humble.

IV. A blessing is pronounced on those who endure their exercises and trials, *v.* 12. It is not the man who suffers only that is blessed, but he who endures. Afflictions cannot make us miserable. A blessing may arise from them. Sufferings and temptations are the way to eternal blessedness: *When he is tried, he shall receive the crown of life, when he is approved,* when his graces are found to be true and of the highest worth (so metals are tried as to their excellency by the fire). The tried Christian shall be a crowned one: and the crown he shall wear will be a crown of life. We only bear the cross for a while, but we shall wear the crown to eternity. This blessedness is a promised thing to the righteous sufferer. It is therefore what we may most surely depend upon. Our enduring temptations must be from a principle of love to God and to our Lord Jesus Christ: *The Lord hath promised to those that love him.* The crown of life is promised to all those who have the love of God reigning in their hearts.

Verses 13–18

I. God is not the author of any man's sin. Some professors might fall in the hour of temptation. The blame of their misconduct must lie entirely upon themselves. There is nothing in the nature of God that they can lay the blame upon. There is nothing in the providential dispensations of God that the blame of any man's sin can be laid upon (*v.* 13). As God cannot be tempted with evil himself, so neither can he be a tempter of others. It is very bad to sin; but it is much worse, when we have done amiss, to charge it upon God, and say it was owing to him. Afflictions are designed to draw out our graces, but not our corruptions.

II. Where the true cause of evil lies, and where the blame ought to be laid (*v.* 14). The true original of evil and temptation is in our own hearts. The combustible matter is in us, though the flame may be blown up by some outward causes. The method of sin in its proceeding. First it draws away, then entices. The heart is carried from that which is good, and enticed to cleave to that which is evil, estranged from the life of God, and then by degrees fixed in a course of sin. The word here rendered *drawn away* signifies a being forcibly haled or compelled. The word translated *enticed* signifies being wheedled and beguiled. The force and power of sin could never prevail, were it not for its cunning and guile. The success of corruption in the heart (*v.* 15). Sin being allowed to excite desires in us, it will soon ripen those desires into consent, and then it is said to have *conceived.* The final issue of sin: *Sin, when it is finished,*

bringeth forth death. There is death upon the soul, and death comes upon the body.

III. We are taught yet further that *God is the Father and fountain of all good, v.* 16, 17. We should take particular care not to err in our conceptions of God: "*Do not err, my beloved brethren, do not wander.*" God is not, cannot be, the author of anything that is evil; but must be acknowledged as the cause and spring of everything that is good, *v.* 17. God is unchangeable, and our changes and shadows are not from any mutability or shadowy alterations in him, but from ourselves. The Father of lights, *with whom there is no variableness, neither shadow of turning.* Every good gift is from him. He gives the light of reason. He gives also the light of learning. The light of divine revelation is more immediately from above. So that we have nothing good but what we receive from God. Our regeneration, and all the holy happy consequences of it, must be ascribed to him (*v.* 18). A true Christian is a creature begotten anew. It is of God's own will; not by our skill or power; but purely from the goodwill and grace of God. The means whereby this is effected, *the word of truth,* that is, the gospel. This gospel is indeed a word of truth, or else it could never produce such real, such lasting, such great and noble effects. The end and design of God's giving renewing grace, *That we should be a kind of first-fruits of his creatures.* Christ is the first-fruits of Christians, Christians are the first-fruits of creatures.

Verses 19–27

We are required,

I. To restrain the workings of passion. This we shall learn if we are indeed begotten again by the word of truth, *v.* 19. Be ready to hear and consider what God's word teaches. This may be applied to the afflictions and temptations spoken of in the beginning of the chapter. Instead of censuring God under our trials, let us open our ears and hearts to hear what he will say to us. This may be understood as referring to the disputes and differences that Christians were running into among themselves. We should be swift to hear reason and truth on all sides, and be slow to speak: and, when we do speak, there should be nothing of wrath. If men would govern their tongues, they must govern their passions. If we would be slow to speak, we must be slow to wrath.

II. A very good reason is given for suppressing anger, *v.* 20. The worst thing we can bring to a religious controversy is anger. *Wrath* is a human thing, and the wrath of man stands opposed to the righteousness of God. Those who pretend to serve the cause of God hereby show that they are acquainted neither with God nor his cause.

III. We are called upon to suppress other corrupt affections, as well as rash anger, *v.* 21. Hereby we are taught, as Christians, to watch against, and lay aside, all the disorders of a corrupt heart, which would prejudice it against the word and ways of God. There is abundance of that which is evil in us, to be watched against; there is *superfluity of naughtiness.* It is not enough to restrain evil affections, but *they must be cast from us, or laid apart.* This must extend not only to outward sins, but to all sin of thought and affection as well as speech and practice; *all filthiness.*

IV. Concerning hearing the word of God.

1. We are required to prepare ourselves for it (*v.* 21).

2. How to hear it: *Receive with meekness the engrafted word, which is able to save your souls.* In hearing the word of God, we are to receive it; receive it as the stock does the graft; so that the fruit which is produced may be, not according to the nature of the sour stock, but according to the nature of the gospel which is engrafted into our souls. We must

therefore yield ourselves to the word of God, with most submissive tempers: this is to *receive it with meekness*. Being willing to hear of our faults, and taking it not only patiently, but thankfully. In all our hearing we should aim at the salvation of our souls. It is the design of the word of God to make us wise to salvation.

3. What is to be done after hearing (v. 22). Hearing is in order to doing; the most attentive and the most frequent hearing of the word of God will not avail us, unless we be also doers of it. It is not enough to remember what we hear. Bare hearers are self-deceivers. Self-deceit will be found the worst deceit at last.

4. What is the proper use of the word of God, v. 23–24. The use we are to make of God's word may be learnt from its being compared to a glass, in which a man may *behold his natural face*. As a looking-glass shows us the spots and defilements upon our faces, so the word of God shows us our sins. It shows us what is amiss, that it may be amended. When we attend to *the word of God*, so as to see ourselves, our true state and condition, and dress ourselves anew by the glass of God's word, this is to make a proper use of it. We have here an account of those who do not use this glass of the word as they ought, v. 24. In vain do we hear God's word, and look into the gospel glass, if we go away, and forget our spots, and forget our remedy. This is the case of those who do not hear the word as they ought. Those also are described who hear aright, and who use the glass of God's word as they should do (v. 25). The gospel is a law of liberty, or *of liberation*. The ceremonial law was a yoke of bondage; the gospel of Christ is a law of liberty. It is a perfect law. In hearing the word, we look into this perfect law. Then only do we look into the law of liberty as we should when we *continue therein*. Those who thus do, and *continue in the law and word of God*, are, and *shall be, blessed in their deed*. This blessedness does not lie in knowing, but in doing the will of God. It is not talking, but walking, that will bring us to heaven.

V. How we may distinguish between a vain religion and that which is pure and approved of God.

1. What is a vain religion: *If any man among you seemeth to be religious, and bridleth not his tongue, but deceives his own heart, this man's religion is vain*. In a vain religion there is much of show. When men are more concerned to seem religious than really to be so, it is a sign that their religion is but vain. In a vain religion there is much censuring of others. When we hear people ready to speak of the faults of others, that they themselves may seem the wiser and better, this is a sign that they have but a vain religion. The man who has a detracting tongue cannot have a truly humble gracious heart. There is no strength nor power in that religion which will not enable a man to bridle his tongue. In a vain religion a man deceives his own heart. When once religion comes to be a vain thing, how great is the vanity!

2. Wherein true religion consists, v. 27. It is the glory of religion to be pure and undefiled. A holy life and a charitable heart show a true religion. That religion is pure and undefiled which is so before God and the Father. True religion teaches us to do everything as in the presence of God. Compassion and charity to the poor and distressed form a very great and necessary part of true religion: *Visiting the fatherless and widow in their affliction*. By them we are to understand all who are proper objects of charity, all who are in affliction. If the sum of religion be drawn up in two articles this is one—to be charitable and relieve the afflicted. An unspotted life must accompany an unfeigned love and charity: *To keep himself unspotted from the world*. The world is apt to spot and blemish the soul, and it is hard to live in it, and

have to do with it, and not be defiled; but this must be our constant endeavour. Herein consists pure and undefiled religion.

CHAPTER 2

The apostle condemns a sinful regarding of the rich, and despising the poor, ver. 1–7. Mercy should be followed, as well as justice, ver. 8–13. He exposes the error and folly of those who boast of faith without works, ver. 14, to the end.

Verses 1–7

He shows how much mischief there is in the sin of *respect of persons*.

I. A caution against this sin laid down in general, v. 1. The character of Christians fully implied: they are such as have the faith of our Lord Jesus Christ. They have it as a trust; they have it as a treasure. How honourably James speaks of Jesus Christ; he calls him *the Lord of glory*. Christ's being the Lord of glory should teach us not to respect Christians for anything so much as their conformity to Christ. We should not show respect to men, so as to cloud or lessen the glory of our glorious Lord. This is certainly a very heinous sin.

II. We have this sin described and cautioned against, by an example of it (v. 2, 3). You act partially, and determine wrong, merely because the one makes a better appearance than the other. God has his remnant among all sorts of people, among those that wear soft and gay clothing, and among those that wear poor and vile raiment. In matters of religion, rich and poor stand upon a level; no man's riches set him in the least nearer to God, nor does any man's poverty set him at a distance from God. All undue honouring of worldly greatness and riches should especially be watched against in Christian societies. If a poor man be a good man, we must not value him a whit the less for his poverty; and, if a rich man be a bad man, we must not value him any whit the more for his riches. There is many a humble, heavenly, good Christian, who is clothed meanly; but neither should he nor his Christianity be thought the worse of on this account.

III. We have the greatness of this sin set forth, v. 4, 5. *Are you not then partial in yourselves?* According to the strict rendering of the original, the question is, "*Have you not made a difference?* And, in that difference, do you not judge by a false rule, and go upon false measures?" This respect of persons is owing to the evil and injustice of the thoughts. "*You have become judges of evil thoughts;* you are judges according to those unjust estimations and corrupt opinions which you have formed to yourselves. You secretly prefer outward pomp before inward grace, and the things that are seen before those which are not seen." The deformity of sin is never truly and fully discerned till the evil of our thoughts be disclosed. This respect of persons is a heinous sin, because it is to show ourselves most directly contrary to God (v. 5–6). God has made those heirs of a kingdom whom you make of no reputation. Many of the poor of this world are the chosen of God. Their being God's chosen does not prevent their being poor; their being poor does not at all prejudice the evidences of their being chosen. God designed to recommend his holy religion, not by the external advantages of gaiety and pomp, but by its intrinsic worth; and therefore chose the poor of this world. Many poor of the world are rich in faith; thus the poorest may become rich. It is expected from those who have wealth that they be rich in good works; but it is expected from the poor in the world that they be rich in faith. Believing Christians are heirs of a kingdom, though they may be very poor as to present possessions. Where any are rich in faith, there will be also divine love. We read of the crown promised to those that love God, in the former chapter (*v.* 12); we here find there is a kingdom too. And, as the crown is a crown of life, so the kingdom will be an everlasting kingdom. After such considerations as these, the charge is cutting indeed, *v.* 6. Respecting persons on account of their riches or outward figure, is shown to be a very great sin, because of the mischiefs which are owing to worldly wealth and greatness, *v.* 7. This will make your sin appear exceedingly sinful and foolish, in setting up that which tends to pull you down, and to dishonour that worthy name by which you are called.

Verses 8–13

How the matter may be mended.

I. The law that is to guide us, *v.* 8. As the scripture teaches us to love all our neighbours, be they rich or poor, as ourselves, so, in our having a steady regard to this rule, *we shall do well.* The rule for Christians to walk by is settled in the scriptures. The scripture gives us this as a law, to love our neighbour as ourselves. This law is a royal law, it comes from the King of kings. Its own worth and dignity deserve it should be thus honoured. A pretence of observing this royal law, when it is interpreted with partiality, will not excuse men in any unjust proceedings.

II. This general law is to be considered together with a particular law, *v.* 9. The very royal law itself, rightly explained, would serve to convict them, because it teaches them to put themselves as much in the places of the poor as in those of the rich.

III. The extent of the law, and how far obedience must be paid to it. They must fulfil the royal law, have a regard to one part as well as another, *v.* 10. Do you plead for your respect to the rich, because you are to love your neighbour as yourselves? Well then show also an equitable and due regard to the poor, because you are to love your neighbour as yourself: or else your offending in one point will spoil your pretence of observing that law at all. This is further illustrated by putting a case different from that before mentioned (*v.* 11). One, perhaps, is very severe in the case of adultery; but less ready to condemn murder: another has a prodigious dread of murder, but has more easy thoughts of adultery; whereas one who looks at the authority of the Lawgiver, will see the same reason for condemning the one as the other. If we offend in one point, we contemn the authority of him who gave the whole law, and so far are guilty of all.

IV. James directs Christians to govern and conduct themselves by the law of Christ, *v.* 12. The gospel is called a law. It prescribes duty, as well as administers comfort; and Christ is a king to rule us as well as a prophet to teach us, and a priest to sacrifice and intercede for us. It is a *law of liberty*, the service of God, according to the gospel, is perfect freedom. We must all be judged by this law of liberty. It concerns us therefore so to speak and act now as becomes those who must shortly be judged by this law of liberty; that we be of a gospel temper, and that our conversation be a gospel conversation. The consideration of our being judged by the gospel should engage us more especially to be merciful in our regards to the poor (*v.* 13). Such as show no mercy now shall find no mercy in the great day. There will be such as shall become instances of the triumph of mercy, in whom mercy rejoices against judgment.

Verses 14–26

The apostle shows the error of those who rested in a bare profession of the Christian faith, as if that would save them. A man is justified, not by faith only, but by works.

I. Upon this arises a very great question, namely, how to reconcile Paul and James. Paul, in his epistles to the Romans and Galatians, seems to assert the directly contrary thing, *that we are justified by faith only, and not by the works of the law.* It may be sufficient only to observe these few things following: When Paul says that *a man is justified by faith, without the deeds of the law* (Rom. iii. 28), he plainly speaks of another sort of work than James does, but not of another sort of faith. Paul speaks of works wrought in obedience to the law of Moses, and before men's embracing the faith of the gospel. James speaks of works done in obedience to the gospel. Both are concerned to magnify the faith of the gospel, as that which alone could save us and justify us. Paul had to do with those who depended on the merit of their works in the sight of God. James had to do with those who cried up faith, but would not allow works to be used even as evidences. Those who cry up the gospel so as to set aside the law, and those who cry up the law so as to set aside the gospel, are both in the wrong. The justification of which Paul speaks is different from that spoken of by James; the one speaks of our persons being justified before God, the other speaks of our faith being justified before men: "*Show me thy faith by thy works,*" says James. Paul speaks of justification in the sight of God.

II. Let us see what is more particularly to be learnt from this excellent passage of James.

1. Faith without works will not profit, and cannot save us. *What doth it profit, my brethren, if a man say he hath faith, and have not works? Can faith save him?* Faith which does not save will not really profit us. All things should be accounted profitable or unprofitable to us as they tend to forward or hinder the salvation of our souls. For a man to have faith, and to say he has faith, are two different things. Men may boast of that to others, and be conceited of that in themselves, of which they are really destitute.

2. As love or charity is an operative principle, so is faith. By trying how it looks for a person to pretend he is very charitable who yet never does any works of charity, you may judge what sense there is in pretending to have faith without the fruits of it, *v.* 15–17. What will such a charity as this, that consists in bare words, avail either you or the poor? You might as well pretend that your love and charity will stand the test without acts of mercy as think that a profession of faith will bear you out before God without works of piety and obedience, *v.* 17. We are too apt to rest in a bare profession of faith, and to think that this will save us. Mock-faith is as hateful as mock-charity, and both show a heart dead to all real godliness.

3. Compare a faith boasting of itself without works and a faith evidenced by works, by looking on both together, to try how this comparison will work upon our minds, *v.* 18. "Thou makest a profession, and sayest thou hast faith; I make no such boasts, but leave my works to speak for me." This is the evidence by which the scriptures all along teach men to judge both of themselves and others. And this is the evidence according to which Christ will proceed at the day of judgment.

4. Look upon a faith of bare speculation and knowledge as the faith of devils, *v.* 19. That instance of faith which the apostle here chooses to mention is the first principle of all religion. But to rest here, and take up a good opinion of thy state towards God, merely on account of thy believing in him, this will render thee miserable: *The devils also believe, and tremble.* If thou contentest thyself with a bare assent to articles of faith, and some speculations upon them, thus far the devils go. They tremble, not out of reverence, but hatred and opposition to that one God on whom they believe.

5. He who boasts of faith without works is to be looked upon at present as a foolish condemned person, *v.* 20. Faith without works is said to be *dead*, not only as void of all those operations which are the proofs of spiritual life, but as unavailable to eternal life.

6. A justifying faith cannot be without works, from two examples.

(1) The first instance is that of Abraham (*v.* 21). By what Abraham did, it appeared that he truly believed. The faith of Abraham was a working faith (*v.* 22). Abraham believed God, *and it was imputed unto him for righteousness,* v. 23. And thus he became the *friend of God.* You see then (*v.* 24) how that *by works a man is justified, and not by faith only;* not by believing without obeying, but by having such a faith as is productive of good works. Those who would have Abraham's blessings must be careful to copy after his faith: to boast of being Abraham's seed will not avail any. Those works which evidence true faith must be such as God himself commands, and not the mere fruits of our own imagination and devising. The actings of faith make it grow perfect, as the truth of faith makes it act. Such an acting faith will make others, as well as Abraham, friends of God.

(2) The second example is Rahab, *v.* 25. The former instance was of one renowned for his faith all his life long. This is of one noted for sin. The strongest faith will not do, nor the meanest be allowed to go without works. That which proved her faith sincere was, that, to the hazard of her life, she *received the messengers, and sent them out another way.* Where great sins are pardoned, there must be great acts of self-denial. Her former acquaintance must be discarded, her former course of life entirely abandoned, and she must give signal proof and evidence of this.

7. The apostle draws this conclusion, *As the body without the spirit is dead, so faith without works is dead also,* v. 26. The best works, without faith, are dead; they want their root and principle. It is by faith that anything we do is really good. The most plausible profession of faith, without works, is dead: as the root is dead when it produces nothing green, nothing of fruit. Faith is the root, good works are the fruits, and we must see to it that we have both. We must not think that either, without the other, will justify and save us.

CHAPTER 3

Those who profess religion ought especially to govern their tongues, ver. 1–12. True wisdom makes men meek, and hereby it may easily be distinguished from a wisdom that is earthly, ver. 13, to the end.

Verses 1–12

The foregoing chapter shows how unprofitable and dead faith is without works. Such a faith is, however, apt to make men conceited in their tempers and their talk. The best need to be cautioned against a dictating, censorious use of their tongues. We are therefore taught,

I. Not to use our tongues so as to lord it over others, *v.* 1. We must not affect to speak and act as those who are continually assuming the chair, we must not prescribe to one another, so as to make our own sentiments a standard by which to try all others. "Therefore be not many *masters* (or *teachers,* as some read it); but rather speak with the humility and spirit of learners." Those who thus set up for judges and censurers *shall receive the greater condemnation.* Our judging others will but make our own judgment the more strict and severe, Matt. vii. 1, 2. Another reason is because we are all sinners, *v.* 2. Were we to think more of our own mistakes

and offences, we should be less apt to judge other people. Self-justifiers are commonly self-deceivers. Their magisterial deportment, and censorious tongues, may prove worse than any faults they condemn in others.

II. To govern our tongue so as to prove ourselves perfect and upright men, and such as have an entire government over ourselves. But, on the other hand, *if a man seemeth to be religious and bridleth not his tongue, that man's religion is vain.* Further, he that offends not in word will not only prove himself a sincere Christian, but a very much advanced Christian. For the wisdom and grace which enable him to rule his tongue will enable him also to rule all his actions. This we have illustrated by two comparisons: 1. The governing and guiding of all the motions of a horse, by the bit which is put into his mouth, *v.* 3. There is a great deal of brutish fierceness and wantonness in us. This shows itself very much by the tongue, so that this must be bridled. As an unruly and ungovernable horse runs away with his rider, or throws him, so an unruly tongue will serve those who have no command over it. 2. The governing of a ship by the right management of the helm, *v.* 4, 5. As the helm is a very small part of the ship, so is the tongue a very small part of the body: but the right governing of the helm will steer and turn the ship, and a right management of the tongue is, in a great measure, the government of the whole man. Things of small bulk may yet be of vast use. We should learn to make the due management of our tongues more our study, because, though they are little members, they are capable of doing a great deal of good or a great deal of hurt.

III. To dread an unruly tongue as one of the greatest and most pernicious evils, *v.* 5, 6. There is such an abundance of sin in the tongue that it may be called *a world of iniquity. So is the tongue among the members that it defileth the whole body.* The whole body is often drawn into sin and guilt by the tongue. *It setteth on fire the course of nature.* The affairs of mankind and of societies are often thrown into confusion, and all is on a flame, by the tongues of men. *And it is set on fire of hell.* Hell has more to do in promoting the fire of the tongue than men are generally aware of. When it is set on fire of hell, as in all undue heats it is, there it is mischievous, producing rage and hatred, and those things which serve the purposes of the devil.

IV. We are next taught how very difficult a thing it is to govern the tongue, *v.* 7, 8. Fierce creatures have not been subdued nor tamed by miracle only. What is here spoken of is something commonly done; not only hath been tamed, but is tamed of mankind. Yet the tongue is worse than these, and cannot be tamed by the power and art which serves to tame these things. The apostle does not intend to represent it as a thing impossible, but as a thing extremely difficult, which therefore will require great watchfulness, and pains, and prayer. And sometimes all is too little; *for it is an unruly evil, full of deadly poison.* The tongue is apt to break through all bounds and rules, and to spit out its poison on one occasion or other, notwithstanding the utmost care.

V. We are taught to think of the use we make of our tongues in religion and in the service of God, *v.* 9, 10. How absurd it is that those who use their tongues in prayer and praise should ever use them in cursing, slandering, and the like! That tongue which addresses with reverence the divine Being cannot, without the greatest inconsistency, turn upon fellow-creatures with reviling brawling language. *These things ought not so to be;* and, if such considerations were always at hand, surely they would not be. Further, to fix this thought, the apostle shows that contrary effects from the same causes are monstrous, and not to be found in nature, and therefore cannot be consistent with grace, v. 11, 12. True religion will not admit of contradictions; and a truly religious man can never allow of them either in his words or his actions.

Verses 13–18

The difference between men's pretending to be wise and their being really so, and between the wisdom which is from beneath and that which is from above.

I. We have some account of true wisdom, v. 13. A wise man will not value himself merely upon knowing things, if he has not wisdom to make a right application of that knowledge. These two things must be put together to make up the account of true wisdom. A good conversation. If we are wiser than others, this should be evidenced by the goodness of our conversation, not by the roughness or vanity of it. True wisdom may be known by its works. The conversation here does not refer only to words, but to the whole of men's practice; therefore it is said, Let him show out of a good conversation his works. Not he who thinks well, or he who talks well, is allowed to be wise, if he do not live and act well. True wisdom may be known by the meekness of the spirit and temper. It is a great instance of wisdom prudently to bridle our own anger, and patiently to bear the anger of others. When we are mild and calm, we are best able to hear reason, and best able to speak it. Wisdom produces meekness, and meekness increases wisdom.

II. We have the glorying taken away of those who are of a contrary character, v. 14–16. Envying and strife are opposed to the meekness of wisdom. The heart is the seat of both; but envy and wisdom cannot dwell together in the same heart. The order of things here laid down. Envying is first and excites strife; strife, vain-glorying and lying; and then (v. 16) hereupon ensue confusion and every evil work. One sin begets another, and it cannot be imagined how much mischief is produced: *there* is every evil work. Whence such wisdom cometh, v. 15. It springs from earthly principles. It is sensual, indulging the flesh. It is devilish. And therefore those who are lifted up with such wisdom as this must fall into the condemnation of the devil.

III. We have the lovely picture of that wisdom which is from above more fully drawn, v. 17, 18. True wisdom is God's gift. It comes from above. It is pure, without mixture of maxims or aims that would debase it: studious of holiness both in heart and life. The wisdom that is from above is peaceable. Those who are truly wise do what they can to preserve peace, that it may not be broken; and to make peace, that where it is lost it may be restored. Heavenly wisdom makes men peaceable. It is gentle, not being rude and overbearing in conversation, nor harsh and cruel in temper. Heavenly wisdom is *easy to be entreated*, it is very *persuadable*, either to what is good or from what is evil. There is an easiness that is weak and faulty; but it is not a blameable easiness to yield ourselves to the persuasions of God's word, and to all just requests of our fellow-creatures. Heavenly wisdom is full of mercy and good fruits, both to relieve those who want and to forgive those who offend. Heavenly wisdom is without partiality. The margin reads it, *without wrangling*. The wisest men are least apt to be censurers. That wisdom which is from above is without hypocrisy. It has no disguises nor deceits. It is sincere and open, steady and uniform, and consistent with itself. True wisdom will go on to sow the fruits of righteousness in peace, and thus, to make peace in the world, v. 18. And that which is sown in peace will produce a harvest of joys.

CHAPTER 4

I. Some causes of contention, ver. 1–5. II. We are taught to abandon the friendship of this world, ver. 4–10. III. All detraction and rash judgment of others are to be carefully avoided, ver. 11, 12. IV. We must preserve a constant regard to the disposals of divine Providence, ver. 13, to the end.

Verses 1–10

This chapter speaks of a lust after worldly things as that which carried their divisions to a shameful height.

I. The apostle here reproves the Jewish Christians for their wars, and for their lusts as the cause of them, v. 1. The origin of their wars and fightings was not (as they pretended) a true zeal for their country, and for the honour of God, their prevailing lusts were the cause of all. What is shrouded under a specious pretence of zeal for God and religion often comes from men's pride. They make a war within as well as fightings without. From lust of power and dominion, lust of pleasure, or lust of riches, arise all the broils and contentions that are in the world. It is therefore the right method for the cure of contention to lay the axe to the root, and mortify those lusts that war in the members. It should kill these lusts to think of their disappointment, v. 2. Inordinate desires are either totally disappointed, or they are not to be appeased and satisfied by obtaining the things desired. Worldly and fleshly lusts are the distemper which will not allow of contentment or satisfaction in the mind. Sinful desires and affections generally exclude prayer: "*You fight and war, yet you have not, because you ask not.* You do not consult God in your undertakings, and you do not commit your way to him, but follow your own corrupt views and inclinations: therefore you meet with continual disappointments. Your lusts spoil your prayers," v. 3. Pride, vanity, luxury, and sensuality, are what you would serve by your successes, and by your very prayers. You disgrace devotion and dishonour God by such gross and base ends; and therefore your prayers are rejected. They ask God to give them success in their callings or undertakings; not that they may glorify their heavenly Father and do good with what they have, but that they may *consume it upon their lusts.* When we speed not in our prayers it is *because we ask amiss*; either we do not ask for right ends or not in a right manner. When our prayers are rather the language of our lusts than of our graces, they will return empty.

II. We have fair warning to avoid all criminal friendships with this world, v. 4. There is this brand put upon worldly-mindedness—that it is enmity to God. A man may have a competent portion of the good things of this life, and yet may keep himself in the love of God, but it is constructive treason and rebellion against God to set the world upon his throne in our hearts. *Whosoever therefore is the friend of the world is the enemy of God.* Hence arise wars and fightings, even from this adulterous idolatrous love of the world. What peace can there be among men, so long as there is enmity towards God? (v. 5). Natural corruption principally shows itself by envying, and there is a continual propensity to this. Now this way of the world, affecting pomp and pleasure, and falling into strifes and quarrels for the sake of these things, is the certain consequence of being friends to the world. Christians, to avoid contentions, must avoid the friendship of the world. If we belong to God, he gives more grace than to live and act as the generality of the world do. The grace of God will correct and cure the spirit that naturally dwells in us; where he giveth grace, he giveth another spirit than that of the world.

III. The difference God makes between pride and humility, v. 6. This is represented as the language of scripture in the Old Testament. 1. The disgrace cast upon the proud: God resists them. The proud resists God. Let proud spirits hear this and tremble—*God resists them.* He will certainly fill with shame the faces of such as have filled their hearts with pride. 2. The honour and help God gives to the humble. Grace, as opposed to disgrace, is honour; this God gives to the humble. Wherever God gives true grace, he will give more. He will especially give more grace to the humble, because they see their need of it, will pray for it and be thankful for it; and such shall have it.

IV. We are taught to submit ourselves entirely to God, *v.* 7. Christians should forsake the friendship of the world, and should by grace learn to glory in their submissions to God We are subjects, and as such must be submissive; not only through fear, but through love. Now, as this subjection and submission to God are what the devil most industriously strives to hinder, so we ought with great care and steadiness to resist his suggestions. "*Resist him and he will flee from you.*" If we basely yield to temptations, the devil will continually follow us; but if we stand it out against him, he will be gone from us. Resolution shuts and bolts the door against temptation.

V. We are directed how to act towards God, *v.* 8–10. 1. *Draw nigh to God.* The heart that has rebelled must be brought to the foot of God; the spirit that was estranged from a life of communion with God must become acquainted with him. 2. *Cleanse your hands.* He who comes unto God must have clean hands. The hands must be cleansed or it will be in vain for us to draw nigh to God. 3. The hearts of the double-minded must be purified. To *purify the heart* is to be sincere. 4. *Be afflicted, and mourn, and weep.* "What afflictions God sends take them as he would have you, and be duly sensible of them. Times of contention and division are times to mourn in, and the sins that occasion wars and fightings should be mourned for. *Let your laughter be turned to mourning and your joy to heaviness.*" This may be taken either as a prediction of sorrow or a prescription of seriousness. They are directed, before things come to the worst, to lay aside their vain mirth and their sensual pleasures, that they might indulge godly sorrow and penitential tears. 5. "*Humble yourselves in the sight of the Lord.* Let there be a thorough humiliation in bewailing everything that is evil; let there be great humility in doing that which is good."

VI. We have great encouragement to act thus towards God (*v.* 8–10). Those that draw nigh to God in a way of duty shall find God drawing nigh to them in a way of mercy. If there be not a close communion between God and us, it is our fault, and not his. *He shall lift up the humble.* If we be truly penitent and humble under the marks of God's displeasure, we shall in a little time know the advantages of his favour; he will lift us up out of trouble, or he will lift us up in our spirits and comfort us under trouble. The highest honour in heaven will be the reward of the greatest humility on earth.

Verses 11–17

I. We are cautioned against the sin of evil-speaking, *v.* 11. We must not speak evil things of others, though they be true, unless there be some necessary occasion for it; much less must we report evil things when they are false. Our lips must be guided by the law of kindness, as well as truth and justice. 1. Because you are brethren. It is required of us that we be tender of the good name of our brethren; where we cannot speak well, we had better say nothing than speak evil. 2. Because this is to judge the law. He who quarrels with his brother, and condemns him for the sake of anything not determined in the

word of God, does thereby reflect on that word of God, as if it were not a perfect rule. Let us take heed of judging the law, for the law of the Lord is perfect; if men break the law, leave that to judge them; if they do not break it, let us not judge them. Those who are most ready to set up for judges of the law generally fail most in their obedience to it. 3. Because God, the Lawgiver, has reserved the power of passing the final sentence on men wholly to himself, *v.* 12. God is the supreme Lawgiver, who only can give law to the conscience, and who alone is to be absolutely obeyed. His right to enact laws is incontestable, because he has such a power to enforce them. He *is able to save, and to destroy.* He has power fully to reward the observance of his laws, and to punish all disobedience. Here he cautions against being many judges. Let us not prescribe to our brethren. It is sufficient that we have the law of God, which is a rule to us all; and therefore we should not set up other rules.

II. We are cautioned against a presumptuous confidence of the continuance of our lives, *v.* 13, 14. Reflect a little on this way of thinking and talking; call yourselves to account for it. There were some who said of old, as too many say still, *We will go to such a city, and do this or that,* while all serious regards to the disposals of Providence were neglected. 1. How apt worldly men are to leave God out of their schemes. 2. How much of worldly happiness lies in the promises men make to themselves beforehand. Their heads are full of fine visions, as to what they shall do in some future time. 3. How vain a thing it is to look for anything good in futurity, without the concurrence of Providence. *We will go to such a city* (say they). Something might possibly stop their way, or call them elsewhere. Many who have set out on a journey have gone to their long home, and never reached their journey's end. But, suppose they should reach the city they designed, how did they know they should continue there? Something might happen to shorten their stay They could not be certain that they should buy and sell there. Suppose they should go to that city, and continue there a year, yet they might not get gain; getting of gain in this world is at best but an uncertain thing. The frailty, shortness, and uncertainty of life, ought to check the presumptuous confidence of such projectors for futurity, *v.* 14. God hath wisely left us in the dark concerning future events. We *know not what shall be on the morrow;* we may know what we intend to do and to be, but a thousand things may happen to prevent us. We are not sure of life itself, since it is but as a *vapour. It appears but for a little time, and then vanisheth away.*

III. We are taught to keep up a constant sense of our dependence on the will of God, *v.* 15. The apostle now directs them how to be and do better: "You ought to say it in your hearts at all times, that if the Lord will give leave, you have such and such designs to accomplish." *With the leave and blessing of God* was used by the Greeks in the beginning of every undertaking. *If the Lord will, we shall live.* We must remember that our times are not in our own hands, but at the disposal of God, and therefore must be submissive to him. *If the Lord will, we shall do this or that.* All our actions and designs are under the control of Heaven. Therefore both our counsels for action and our conduct in action should be entirely referred to God.

IV. We are directed to avoid vain boasting, *v.* 16. They promised themselves life and prosperity, and great things in the world, without any just regard to God; and then they boasted of these things. *Such rejoicing is evil;* it is foolish and it is hurtful. If we rejoice in God that our times are in his hand, that all events are at his disposal, and that he is our God, this rejoicing is good. But, if we rejoice in our own vain confidences and presumptuous boasts, this is evil.

V. We are taught to act up to our own convictions, that we never go contrary to our own knowledge (*v.* 17). It is aggravated sin; it is sinning with a witness; and it is to have the worst witness against a man that can be, when he sins against his own conscience. Omissions are sins which will come into judgment, as well as commissions. He that does not the good he knows should be done, as well as he who does the evil he knows should not be done, will be condemned.

CHAPTER 5

The apostle denounces the judgments of God upon those rich men who oppress the poor, ver. 1–6. Hereupon, all the faithful are exhorted to patience under their trials and sufferings, ver. 7–11. The sin of swearing is cautioned against, ver. 12. We are directed how to act, both under affliction and in prosperity, ver. 13. Prayer for the sick, and anointing with oil, are prescribed, ver. 14, 15. Christians are directed to acknowledge their faults one to another, and to pray one for another, ver. 16–18. And, lastly, it is recommended to us to do what we can for bringing back those that stray from the ways of truth.

Verses 1–11

The apostle is here addressing first sinners and then saints.

I. The address to sinners; and here we find James seconding what his great Master had said: *Woe unto you that are rich; for you have received your consolation*, Luke vi. 24. The poor among the Jews received the gospel, and many of them believed; but the generality of the rich rejected Christianity, and persecuted those who believed on Christ.

1. He foretells the judgments of God that should come upon them, *v.* 1–3. They should have miseries come upon them, misery that should arise from the very things in which they placed their happiness. *Go to now, you rich men.* Rich men are apt to say to themselves (and others are ready to say to them), *Eat, drink, and be merry;* but God says, *Weep and howl.* Those who live like beasts are called to howl like such. "Corruption, decay, rust, and ruin, will come upon all your goodly things (*v.* 2). Those things which you now inordinately affect will be of no worth, of no use to you," *v.* 3. They think to heap up treasure for their latter days, but, alas! they are only heaping up treasures that will prove at last to be only treasures of wrath.

2. What those sins are which should bring such miseries. Covetousness is laid to the charge of this people. God gives us our worldly possessions that we may honour him and do good with them; but if, instead of this, we sinfully hoard them up, this is a very heinous crime, and will be witnessed against by the very rust and corruption of the treasure thus heaped together. Another sin is oppression, *v.* 4. Those who have wealth in their hands get power into their hands, and then they are tempted to abuse that power to oppress such as are under them. They made as hard bargains with the poor as they could, and even after that would not make good their bargains as they should have done. Another sin is sensuality and voluptuousness, *v.* 5. God does not forbid us to use pleasure; but to live in them as if we lived for nothing else is a very provoking sin. Luxury makes people wanton. Wantonness and luxury are commonly the effects of great plenty and abundance. "*You have nourished your hearts as in a day of slaughter:* you live as if it were every day a day of sacrifices, a festival." Some may say, "What harm is there in good cheer, provided people do not spend above what they have?" What! Is it no harm for people to make gods of their bellies, and to give all to these, instead of abounding in acts of charity

and piety? Pride, and idleness, and fulness of bread, mean the same thing with living in pleasure, and being wanton, and nourishing the heart as in a day of slaughter. Another sin is persecution, *v.* 6. This fills up the measure of their iniquity. When such do suffer, and yield without resistance to the unjust sentence of oppressors, this is marked by God, to the honour of the sufferers and the infamy of their persecutors.

II. An address to saints. From what has been said concerning wicked and oppressing rich men, occasion is given to administer comfort to God's afflicted people.

1. Attend to your duty. (1) "*Be patient* though God should not appear for you immediately. Wait for him." When we have done our work, we have need of patience to stay for our reward. This Christian patience is not a mere yielding to necessity, as the moral patience taught by some philosophers was, but it is a humble acquiescence in the wisdom and will of God. *Be patient to the coming of the Lord.* And because this is a lesson Christians must learn, though ever so hard or difficult to them, it is repeated in *v.* 8. (2) "*Establish your hearts*—let your faith be firm, your practice of what is good constant and continued, and your resolutions for God and heaven fixed, in spite of all sufferings or temptations." (3) *Grudge not one against another; Groan* not one against another. Do not make yourselves uneasy and make one another uneasy by groaning to and grieving one another. Those who are in the midst of common enemies, and in any suffering circumstances, should be more especially careful not to groan against one another, otherwise judgments will come upon them as well as others.

2. Consider what encouragement here is for Christians to be patient. "Look to the example of the husbandman. When you sow your corn in the ground, you wait many months for the former and latter rain, and are willing to stay till harvest for the fruit of your labour. Consider him that waits for a crop of corn; and will not you wait for a crown of glory? If you should be called to wait a little longer than the husbandman does, is it not something proportionably greater and infinitely more worth your waiting for? Think how short your waiting time may possibly be (*v.* 8–9). Do not be impatient, do not quarrel with one another; the great Judge is at hand: as near as one who is just knocking at the door." *Grudge not, lest you be condemned.* Fretfulness and discontent expose us to the just judgment of God, and we bring more calamities upon ourselves by our groans and grudgings against one another, than we are aware of. We are encouraged to be patient by the example of the prophets (*v.* 10). When we think that the best men have had the hardest usage in this world, we should hereby be reconciled to affliction. Those who were the greatest examples of suffering affliction were also the best and greatest examples of patience. *We count those happy who endure* (*v.* 11). Job also is proposed as an example, *v.* 11. Under all he could bless God and what came to him in the end? God accomplished those things for him which plainly prove that *the Lord is very pitiful, and of tender mercy.* The tender mercy of God is such that he will make his people an abundant amends for all their sufferings and afflictions. Let us serve our God, and endure our trials, as those who believe the end will crown all.

Verses 12–20

I. The sin of swearing is cautioned against, *v.* 12. Some have translated the words, *before all things;* they should not, in common conversation, *before everything they say*, put an oath. All customary needless swearing is all along in scripture condemned, as a very grievous sin. Profane swearing was very customary among the Jews. Some of the looser sort of those who were called Christians might be guilty also of this.

1. *Above all things, swear not;* but how many are there who mind this the least of all things, and who make light of nothing so much as common profane swearing! It strikes most directly at the honour of God and most expressly throws contempt upon his name and authority. This sin has, of all sins, the least temptation to it. It is with most difficulty left off when once men are accustomed to it, therefore it should above all things he watched against. "*Above all things swear not.*" But "all this is so far from forbidding necessary oaths that it is but to conform them, by preserving the due reverence of them." The Jews thought if they did but omit the great oath they were safe. But they grew so profane as to swear by the creature, as if it were God. On the other hand, those who swear commonly and profanely by the name of God do hereby put him upon the level with every common thing.

2. *But let your yea be yea, and your nay nay; lest you fall into condemnation.* Be sure to stand to your word, and be true to it, so as to give no occasion for your being suspected of falsehood. It is being suspected of falsehood that leads men to swearing.

II. As Christians we are taught to suit ourselves to the dispensations of Providence (*v.* 13). Our condition in this world is various; and our wisdom is to submit to its being so, and to behave as becomes us both in prosperity and under affliction. Afflictions should put us upon prayer, and prosperity should make us abound in praise. 1. In a day of affliction nothing is more seasonable than prayer. Times of affliction should be praying times. God sends afflictions, that we may be engaged to seek him early; and that those who at other times have neglected him may be brought to enquire after him. Afflictions naturally draw out complaints; and to whom should we complain but to God in prayer? It is necessary to exercise faith and hope under afflictions; and prayer is the appointed means both for obtaining and increasing these graces in us. 2. In a day of mirth and prosperity singing psalms is very proper and seasonable. This we are sure of, that the singing of psalms is a gospel ordinance, and that our joy should be holy joy, consecrated to God. Holy mirth becomes families and retirements, as well as public assemblies.

III. We have particular directions given as to sick persons, *v.* 14, 15. It lies upon sick people as a duty to send for ministers, and to desire their assistance and their prayers. It is the duty of ministers to pray over the sick, when thus desired and called for. The *sick were to be anointed with oil in the name of the Lord.* When miracles ceased, this institution ceased also. Some have thought that it should not be wholly laid aside in any age, but that where there are extraordinary measures of faith in the person anointing, and in those who are anointed, an extraordinary blessing may attend the observance of this direction for the sick. There is one thing carefully to be observed here, that the saving of the sick is not ascribed to the *anointing with oil*, but to prayer, *v.* 15. Prayer over the sick must proceed from, and be accompanied with, a lively faith. There must be faith both in the person praying and in the person prayed for. *And, if he have committed sins, they shall be forgiven him.* The great thing therefore we should beg of God for ourselves and others in the time of sickness is the pardon of sin. Sin is both the root of sickness and the sting of it. If sin be pardoned, either

affliction shall be removed in mercy or we shall see there is mercy in the continuance of it.

IV. Christians are directed to *confess their faults one to another*, *v.* 16. The confession here required is that of Christians to one another. Where persons have injured one another. Where persons have tempted one another to sin, or have consented in the same evil actions. So far as confession is necessary to our reconciliation with such as are at variance with us, or for reparation of wrongs done to any, making our own spirits quiet and easy, so far we should be ready to confess our faults. And sometimes also it may be of good use to Christians to disclose their peculiar weaknesses and infirmities to one another. Those who make confession of their faults one to another should thereupon pray with and for one another.

V. The great advantage and efficacy of prayer are declared and proved, *v.* 17, 18. He who prays must be a righteous man. The prayer itself must be a fervent, in-wrought, well-wrought prayer. Such prayer avails much. It is of great advantage to ourselves, it may be very beneficial to our friends, and we are assured of its being acceptable to God. Elijah was *a man of like passions with us.* He was a zealous good man and a very great man, but he had his infirmities. In prayer we must not look to the merit of man, but to the grace of God. He prayed earnestly, or, as it is in the original, *in prayer he prayed.* It is not enough to say a prayer, but we must pray in prayer. Elijah *prayed that it might not rain*; and God heard him, so that *it rained not on the earth for the space of three years and six months. Again he prayed, and the heaven gave rain*, &c. This is recorded for encouragement even to ordinary Christians to be instant and earnest in prayer. Where there may not be so much of miracle in God's answering our prayers, yet there may be as much of grace.

VI. The epistle concludes with an exhortation to do all we can to promote the conversion and salvation of others, *v.* 19, 20. "If any err, and one convert him, let him be who he will that does so good an office for another, he is therein an instrument of saving a soul from death." Be they ever so great, you must not be afraid to show them their error; and, be they ever so weak and little, you must not disdain to make them wiser and better. If they err from the truth, whether it be in opinion or practice, you must endeavour to bring them again to the rule. Errors in judgment and in life generally go together. If we are instrumental in the conversion of any, *we* are said to convert them, though this be the work of God. And, if we can do no more towards the conversion of sinners, yet we may do this—pray for the grace and Spirit of God to convert and change them. He that is said to *err from the truth* in *v.* 19 is described as *erring in his way* in *v.* 20 and we cannot be said to convert any merely by altering their opinions, unless we can bring them to correct and amend their ways. This is conversion. He who thus converteth a sinner from the error of his ways *shall save a soul from death.* By such conversion of heart and life, a *multitude of sins shall be hid.* Though our sins are many, even a multitude, yet they may be hid or pardoned. Let people contrive to cover their sin as they will, there is no way effectually to hide it but by forsaking it. Some make the sense of this text to be, that conversion shall *prevent* a multitude of sins; and it is a truth beyond dispute that many sins are prevented in the party converted, many also may be prevented in others that he may have an influence upon.

AN EXPOSITION, WITH PRACTICAL OBSERVATIONS, OF

THE FIRST EPISTLE GENERAL OF

PETER

Two epistles we have enrolled in the sacred canon of the scripture written by Peter. When our Saviour called his apostles, and gave them their commission, he nominated him first in the list; and by his behaviour towards him he seems to have distinguished him as a special favourite among the twelve. Many instances of our Lord's affection to him, both during his life and after his resurrection, are upon record. Peter himself modestly styles himself an *apostle of Jesus Christ*; and, when he writes to the presbyters of the church, he humbly places himself in the same rank with them: *The elders who are among you I exhort, who am also an elder, ch.* v. 1.

The design of this first epistle is, I. To explain more fully the doctrines of Christianity to these newly-converted Jews. II. To direct and persuade them to a holy conversation. III. To prepare them for sufferings. This seems to be his principal intention; for he has something to this purport in every chapter.

CHAPTER 1

The apostle describes the persons to whom he writes, and salutes them (ver. 1, 2), blesses God for their regeneration to a lively hope of eternal salvation (ver. 3–5), in the hope of this salvation he shows they had great cause of rejoicing, ver. 6–9. This is that salvation which the ancient prophets foretold and the angels desire to look into, ver. 10–12. He exhorts them to sobriety and holiness (ver. 13–21), and to brotherly love, ver. 22–25.

Verses 1, 2

I. The author of it, described, 1. By his name— *Peter.* Jesus Christ gave him the surname of *Peter,* which signifies *a rock,* as a commendation of his faith. 2. By his office—*an apostle of Jesus Christ.* It signifies the highest office in the Christian church. Peter, (1) Asserts his own character as an apostle. To pretend to what we have not is hypocrisy; and to deny what we have is ingratitude. (2) He mentions his apostolical function as his warrant and call to write this epistle to these people.

II. The persons to whom this epistle was addressed are described,

1. By their external condition—*Strangers dispersed throughout Pontus, Galatia, &c.* At present their circumstances were poor and afflicted. The best of God's servants may, through the hardships of times, be dispersed about, and forced to leave their native countries. The value of good people ought not to be estimated by their present external condition.

2. They are described by their spiritual condition.

(1) *Elect according to the foreknowledge of God the Father.* Election is either to an office, or it is to the enjoyment of special privileges, or it is to eternal salvation. This is the election here spoken of. [1] This election is said to be *according to the fore-knowledge of God.* Foreknowledge may be taken in two ways: *First,* For mere prescience, foresight, or understanding, that such a thing will be, before it comes to pass. Thus a mathematician certainly fore-knows that at such a time there will be an eclipse. But such a prescience is not the cause why anything is so or so. *Secondly,* Foreknowledge sometimes signifies counsel, appointment, and approbation. The death of Christ was not only foreseen, but fore-ordained, as *v.* 20. Take it thus here; so the sense is, *elect according to the counsel, ordination, and free grace of God.* [2] It is added, according to the fore-knowledge of *God the Father.* In the affair of man's redemption, election is ascribed to the Father, as reconciliation is ascribed to the Son and sanctification to the Holy Ghost.

(2) They were elect *through sanctification of the Spirit, unto obedience, and sprinkling of the blood of Jesus Christ.* Every elect person must be sanctified by the Spirit, and justified by the blood of Jesus.

By sanctification here understand living to God in all the duties of a Christian life, which is here summed up in one word, *obedience.* By *the Spirit* is meant the Holy Ghost, the author of sanctification. *Unto obedience.* This word denotes the end of sanctifica-tion, which is, to bring rebellious sinners to obedience again, *You have purified your souls in obeying the truth through the Spirit,* v. 22.

(3) They were elected also to the *sprinkling of the blood of Jesus.* Here is a manifest allusion to the typical sprinklings of blood under the law. The blood of Christ, the grand and all-sufficient sacrifice, was not only shed, but must be sprinkled and com-municated to every one of these elect Christians. All that are chosen to eternal life as the end are chosen to obedience as the way. Unless a person be sanctified by the Spirit, and sprinkled with the blood of Jesus, there will be no true obedience in the life.

III. The salutation follows. The blessings desired for them are *grace and peace. Grace*—the free favour of God, with all its proper effects. *Peace.* All sorts of peace may be here intended: peace with God, with the feeling of it in our own consciences. The request or prayer, in relation to these blessings—that they may be multiplied. He wishes them the con-tinuation, the increase, and the perfection of them. The best blessings we can desire for ourselves, or one for another, are grace and peace, with the multi-plication of them. Peace cannot be enjoyed where there is no true grace; first grace, then peace. Peace without grace is mere stupidity; but grace may be true where there is for a time no actual peace. Christ was once in an agony. The increase of grace and peace, as well as the first gift of them, is from God.

Verses 3–5

I. A thanksgiving to God.

1. The duty performed, which is blessing God.

2. The object of this blessing described by his relation to Jesus Christ: *The God and Father of our Lord Jesus Christ.* Here are three names of one person, denoting his threefold office. He is *Lord,* a universal king. *Jesus,* a priest or Saviour. *Christ,* a prophet.

3. The reasons that oblige us to this duty of blessing God, which are comprised in *his abundant mercy.* He *hath begotten us again,* and this deserves our thanksgiving to God, especially if we consider the fruit it produces in us, which is that excellent grace of hope, a lively hope, a living, durable hope, as that hope must needs be that has such a solid foundation as *the resurrection of Jesus Christ from the dead.* A good Christian's condition is never so bad but he has great reason still to bless God. In our prayers

and praises we should address God as *the Father of our Lord Jesus Christ*; it is only through him that we and our services are accepted. The best of men owe their best blessings to the abundant mercy of God. All the evil in the world is from man's sin, but all the good in it is from *God's mercy*. We subsist entirely upon divine mercy. Regeneration produces a lively hope of eternal life. Those who are begotten to a new and spiritual life are begotten to a new and spiritual hope. The hope of a Christian has this excellency, it is a living hope. The hope of eternal life in a true Christian is a hope that keeps him alive, quickens him, supports him, and conducts him to heaven. The delusive hopes of the unregenerate are vain and perishing; the hypocrite and his hope expire and die both together. *The resurrection of Jesus Christ from the dead* is the ground or foundation of a Christian's hope. There being an inseparable union between Christ and his flock, they rise by virtue of his resurrection as a head.

II. The apostle goes on to describe that life under the notion of *an inheritance*. He tells them they were new-born to a new inheritance, infinitely better than what they had lost. They are put in mind of a noble inheritance reserved in heaven for them.

1. Heaven is the undoubted inheritance of all the children of God. God giveth his gifts unto all, but the inheritance to none but his children. This inheritance is not our purchase, but our Father's gift; not wages that we merit, but the effect of grace.

2. The incomparable excellencies of this inheritance. It is incorruptible, in which respect it is like its Maker. All corruption is a change from better to worse, but heaven is without change and without end; the house is eternal in the heavens. This inheritance is undefiled. Sin and misery have no place there. It fadeth not away, but always retains its vigour and beauty. *"Reserved in heaven for you."* It is certain, a reversion in another world, safely kept and preserved till we come to the possession of it. The persons for whom it is reserved are described by their character: everyone that is *begotten again to a lively hope*.

III. The apostle supposes some doubt or uneasiness whether they might not possibly fall short by the way. He answers that they should be kept and preserved from all such destructive temptations as would prevent their safe arrival at eternal life. The heirs of heaven shall certainly be conducted safely to the possession of it. The blessing here promised is preservation: You *are kept*; the author of it is *God*; the means in us made use of for that end are our own *faith* and care; the end to which we are preserved is *salvation*; and the time when we shall see the safe end and issue of all is *the last time*. Their being kept implies both danger and deliverance; they may be attacked, but shall not be overcome. The preservation of the regenerate to eternal life is the effect of God's power. Preservation by God's power does not supersede man's endeavour and care for his own salvation. Faith is a sovereign preservative of the soul through a state of grace unto a state of glory. This salvation is *ready to be revealed in the last time*. It is now prepared and reserved in heaven for them. Though it be made ready now, yet it is in a great measure hidden and unrevealed at present, even to the heirs of salvation themselves. It shall be fully and completely *revealed in the last time*. *Life and immortality are now brought to light by the gospel*, but this life will be revealed more gloriously at death, when the soul shall be admitted into the presence of Christ, and behold his glory.

Verses 6–9

The first word, *wherein*, refers to the apostle's foregoing discourse about the excellency of their present state, and their grand expectations for the future, v. 6.

I. Several things in mitigation of their sorrows. Every sound Christian has always something wherein he may greatly rejoice. The chief joy of a good Christian arises from things spiritual and heavenly. His joy arises from his treasure, which consists of matters of great value, and the title to them is sure. The best Christians may yet be in great heaviness through manifold temptations. All sorts of adversities are temptations, or trials. These seldom go singly, but are manifold, and come from different quarters, the effect of all which is great heaviness. The afflictions and sorrows of good people are but for a season. The shortness of any affliction does much abate the heaviness of it. Great heaviness is often necessary to a Christian's good: *If need be, you are in heaviness*. God does not afflict his people willingly, but acts with judgment, in proportion to our needs. These troubles, that lie heavy, never come upon us but when we have need, and never stay any longer than needs must.

II. He expresses the end of their afflictions and the ground of their joy under them, v. 7. The afflictions of serious Christians are designed for the trial of their faith. God's design in afflicting his people is their probation, not their destruction. This trial is made upon faith principally, because the trial of this is, in effect, the trial of all that is good in us. Christ prays for this apostle, *that his faith might not fail;* if that be supported, all the rest will stand firm. A tried faith is much more precious than tried gold. Here is a double comparison of faith and gold. Gold is the most valuable and durable of all the metals; so is faith among the Christian virtues; it lasts till it brings the soul to heaven. The trial of faith is much more precious than the trial of gold. Gold does not increase and multiply by trial in the fire, it rather grows less; but *faith* is established and multiplied by the afflictions that it meets with. *Gold* must perish at last—*gold that perisheth*; but *faith* never will. The trial of faith will be found to praise, and honour and glory. If a tried faith be found to praise, honour, and glory, let this recommend faith to you, as much more precious than gold, though it be assaulted and tried by afflictions. Jesus Christ will appear again in glory. The trial will soon be over, but the glory, honour, and praise will last to eternity.

III. He particularly commends the faith of these primitive Christians.

1. The excellency of its object, the unseen Jesus, *v.* 8. It is one thing to believe God, or Christ (so the devils believe), and another thing to believe in him.

2. Two notable productions or effects of their faith, *love* and *joy*, and this joy so great as to be above description.

(1) Sense converses with things sensible and present; reason is a higher guide, but faith ascends further still. It is *the evidence of things not seen*.

(2) True faith is never alone, but produces a strong love to Jesus Christ. True Christians have a sincere love to Jesus, because they believe in him.

(3) Where there are true faith and love to Christ there is *joy unspeakable and full of glory*. It cannot be described by words; the best discovery is by an experimental taste of it; it is *full of glory*, full of heaven. There is much of heaven and the future glory in the present joys of improved Christians; their faith removes the causes of sorrow, and affords the best reasons for joy. Well might these primitive Christians rejoice with joy unspeakable, since they were every day *receiving the end of their faith, the salvation of their souls*, *v.* 4. The blessing they were receiving: *The salvation of their souls*, which salvation is here called *the end of their faith*, the end wherein faith terminates. The salvation of the soul was the prize

these Christians sought for, the end they aimed at, which came nearer and more within their reach every day. Every faithful Christian is daily receiving the salvation of his soul. These believers had the beginnings of heaven in the possession of holiness and a heavenly mind. They were on the losing side in the world, but the apostle puts them in mind of what they were receiving; if they lost an inferior good, they were all the while receiving the salvation of their souls. The glory of God and our own felicity are so connected that if we regularly seek the one we must attain the other.

Verses 10–12

The apostle goes on to show them what warrant he had for what he had delivered. He produces the authority of the prophets to convince them that the doctrine of salvation by faith in Jesus Christ was no new doctrine.

I. Who made this diligent search—*the prophets*, who were persons inspired by God.

II. The object of their search, which was *salvation*, and *the grace of God which should come unto you*. They foresaw glorious times of light, grace, and comfort, which made the prophets and righteous men desire to see and hear the things which came to pass in the days of the gospel.

III. The manner of their enquiry: they *enquired and searched diligently*. The words are strong and emphatic, alluding to miners, who dig to the bottom, and break through not only the earth, but the rock, to come to the ore; so these holy prophets had an earnest desire to know, and were proportionably diligent in their enquiries. Their being inspired did not make their industrious search needless. The doctrine of man's salvation by Jesus Christ has been the study and admiration of the greatest and wisest of men. Those who would be acquainted with this great salvation, and the grace that shines therein, must enquire and search diligently into it.

IV. The particular matters which the ancient prophets chiefly searched into, *v.* 11. Jesus Christ was the main subject of their studies.

1. His humiliation and death, and the glorious consequences of it. This enquiry would lead them into a view of the whole gospel.

2. Undoubtedly these holy prophets earnestly desired to see the days of the Son of man; and therefore their minds were set upon the time of its accomplishment, so far as the Spirit of Christ, which was in them, had signified anything towards that purpose. The nature of the times was also under their strict consideration. From the example of Christ Jesus learn to expect a time of services and sufferings before you are received to glory. It was so with him, and *the disciple is not above his Lord*.

V. The success with which their enquiries were crowned. God gave them a satisfactory revelation to quiet and comfort their minds. They were informed that these things should not come to pass in their time: *Not unto themselves, but to us;* and we must report them, under the infallible direction of the Holy Ghost, to all the world. *Which things the angels*, &c.

You have here three sorts of enquirers: 1. *The prophets*, who *searched diligently* into it. 2. The apostles, who consulted all the prophecies of them, and were witnesses of the accomplishment of them, and so reported what they knew to others in the preaching of the gospel. 3. The angels, who most attentively pry into these matters. A diligent endeavour after the knowledge of Christ will certainly be answered with good success. The holiest and best of men sometimes have their lawful and pious requests denied. God is pleased to answer our necessities rather than our requests. It is the practice of a Christian to be

useful to others rather than to himself. The prophets ministered to others, not unto themselves. The revelations of God to his church are all perfectly consistent; the doctrine of the prophets and that of the apostles exactly agree, as coming from the same Spirit of God. The gospel is the ministration of the Spirit; the success of it depends upon his operation and blessing. The mysteries of the gospel are so glorious that the blessed angels earnestly desire to look into them.

Verses 13–23

I. He exhorts them to sobriety and holiness.

1. *Wherefore gird up the loins of your mind*, &c., *v.* 13. Let the loins or strength and vigour of your minds be exerted in your duty; disengage yourselves from all that would hinder you, and go on resolutely in your obedience. *Be sober*, be vigilant against all your spiritual dangers and enemies, and be temperate and modest in the whole of your behaviour. Be sober-minded also in opinion, as well as in practice. The main work of a Christian lies in the right management of his heart and mind. The best Christians have need to be exhorted to sobriety. A Christian's work is not over as soon as he has got into a state of grace; he must still hope and strive for more grace. We must hope perfectly, and yet gird up our loins, and address ourselves vigorously to the work we have to do, encouraging ourselves from the grace of Jesus Christ.

2. *As obedient children*, &c., *v.* 14. An argument to press them to holiness from the consideration of what they now are, children of obedience, and what they were when they lived in lust and ignorance. The children of God ought to prove themselves to be such by their obedience to God. The best of God's children have had their times of lust and ignorance. Persons, when converted, differ exceedingly from what they were formerly.

3. *But as he who hath called you*, &c., *v.* 15, 16. It is required in strong terms, and enforced by three reasons, taken from the grace of God in calling us,—from his command, *it is written*,—and from his example. *Be you holy, for I am holy*. It is a great favour to be called effectually by divine grace into the possession of all the blessings of the new covenant; and great favours are strong obligations; they enable as well as oblige to be holy. Complete holiness is the desire and duty of every Christian. It must, for the extent of it, be universal. We must *be holy*, and be so *in all manner of conversation*, towards all people, friends and enemies; in all our intercourse and business still we must be holy. For the pattern of it, we must *be holy, as God is holy*: we must imitate him, though we can never equal him. The consideration of the holiness of God should oblige us to the highest degree of holiness we can attain unto.

4. *If you call on the Father*, &c., *v.* 17. The whole time of our sojourning here is to be passed in the fear of God. Holy confidence in God as a Father, and an awful fear of him as a Judge, are very consistent. The judgment of God will be without respect of persons: *According to every man's work*. God will not respect persons from personal considerations, but judge them according to their work.

5. He adds (*v.* 18) a second argument. Herein he puts them in mind, (1) That they were redeemed by a ransom paid to the Father. (2) What the price paid for their redemption was. (3) From what they were redeemed. (They knew this, and cannot pretend ignorance.) The consideration of our redemption ought to be a constant and powerful inducement to holiness, and the fear of God. God expects that a Christian should live answerably to what he knows. Neither silver nor gold, nor any of the corruptible things of this world, can redeem so much as one soul.

They are corruptible, and therefore cannot redeem an incorruptible and immortal soul. The blood of Jesus Christ is the only price of man's redemption. The design of Christ in shedding his most precious blood was to redeem us, not only from eternal misery hereafter, but from a vain conversation in this world. Not only the open wickedness, but the vanity and unprofitableness of our conversation are highly dangerous. A man's conversation may plead antiquity, custom, and tradition, in its defence, and yet after all be a most vain conversation. Antiquity is no certain rule of verity.

6. Some things relating both to the Redeemer and the redeemed, *v.* 20, 21.

(1) The Redeemer is further described as one, [1] That was *fore-ordained before the foundation of the world.* It imports an act of the will, a resolution that the thing shall be. [2] That was *manifested in these last days for them.* He was manifested to be that Redeemer whom God had fore-ordained. "This was done in these last times of the New Testament and of the gospel. You have the comfort of the manifestation and appearance of Christ, if you believe on him." [3] That was raised from the dead by the Father, who gave him glory, proclaimed him to all the world to be his Son by his resurrection from the dead, and glorified him with that glory which he had with God before the world was.

(2) The redeemed are also described here by their faith and hope, the cause of which is Jesus Christ: "*You do by him believe in God.*"

(3) The decree of God to send Christ to be a Mediator was from everlasting. God had purposes of special favour towards his people long before he made any manifestations of such grace to them. Great is the happiness of the last times in comparison with what the former ages of the world enjoyed. Our gratitude and services should be suitable to such favours.

II. He exhorts them to brotherly love.

1. He supposes that the gospel had already produced at least an *unfeigned love of the brethren, v.* 22. It is not to be doubted but that every sincere Christian purifies his soul. The apostle takes this for granted: *Seeing you have,* &c. The word of God is the great instrument of a sinner's purification. Many hear the truth, but are never purified by it, because they will not submit to it nor obey it. The Spirit of God is the great agent in the purification of man's soul. The Spirit excites our endeavours, and makes them successful. The aid of the Spirit does not supersede our own industry; these people purified their own souls, but it was through the Spirit. The souls of Christians must be purified before they can so much as love one another unfeignedly. There is no charity but out of a pure heart.

2. He further presses upon Christians the duty of loving one another with a pure heart fervently from the consideration of their spiritual relation. All Christians are born again. They are brought into a new and a near relation to one another, they become brethren by their new birth. This new and second birth is much more desirable and excellent than the first. By the one we become the children of men, by the other the sons and daughters of the Most High. Brethren by nature are bound to love one another; but the obligation is double where there is a spiritual relation.

Verses 24, 25

He now sets before us the vanity of the natural man. Nothing can make him a solid substantial being, but the being born again of the incorruptible seed, the word of God; and this word is daily set before you in the preaching of the gospel. Man, in his utmost flourish and glory, is still a withering, fading, dying creature. His wit, beauty, strength, vigour, wealth, honour—these are but as the flower of grass, which soon withers and dies away. The only way to render this perishing creature solid and incorruptible is for him to entertain and receive the word of God; for this will preserve him to everlasting life, and abide with him for ever.

CHAPTER 2

The general exhortation to holiness is continued. The means of obtaining it, the word of God, is recommended, ver. 1–12. Particular directions are given, ver. 13, to the end.

Verses 1–3

I. Lay aside or put off what is evil.

1. The sins to be put off, or thrown aside. *Malice.* Malice is settled overgrown anger, retained till it inflames a man to design mischief. *Guile,* or deceit in words. *Hypocrisies.* The word being plural comprehends all sorts of hypocrisies. *Envies;* which is a grieving at the good and welfare of another. *Evil speaking,* speaking against another, or defaming him.

2. The best Christians have need to be cautioned and warned against the worst sins. They are but sanctified in part, and are still liable to temptations. Our best services towards God will neither please him nor profit us if we be not conscientious in our duties to men. One sin, not laid aside, will hinder our spiritual profit and everlasting welfare.

II. The apostle, like a wise physician, goes on to direct to wholesome food, that they may grow thereby. The duty exhorted to is a strong and constant desire for the *word of God.* This milk of the word must be *sincere,* not adulterated by the mixtures of men: *As new-born babes.* A new life requires suitable food. Infants desire common milk, and their desires towards it are fervent and frequent. Such must Christians' desires be for the word of God: that they may grow thereby. Strong desires and affections to the word of God are a sure evidence of a person's being born again. Growth and improvement in wisdom and grace are the desire of every Christian. The word of God, does not leave a man as it finds him.

III. He adds an argument from their own experience, *v.* 3. The apostle does not express a doubt, but affirms that these good Christians had tasted the goodness of God. Our Lord Jesus Christ is very gracious to his people; he has in him a fulness of grace. The graciousness of our Redeemer is best discovered by an experimental taste of it. We cannot taste at a distance, as we may see, and hear, and smell. To taste the graciousness of Christ experimentally supposes our being united to him by faith. The best of God's servants have in this life but a taste of the grace of Christ.

Verses 4–12

I. A description of Jesus Christ as a living stone.

1. He is called a stone, to denote his invincible strength and everlasting duration, and to teach his servants that he is the foundation on which they are built. He is the living stone, having eternal life in himself. The reputation and respect he has with God and man are very different. He is disallowed of men, but chosen of God, and gracious. *To whom coming;* by faith, whereby we are united to him at first, and draw nigh to him afterwards. Jesus Christ is the very foundation-stone of all our hopes and happiness. However Christ may be disallowed by an ungrateful world, yet he is chosen of God, and precious in his account. Those who expect mercy from this gracious Redeemer must come to him, which is our act, though done by God's grace—a real endeavour, not a fruitless wish.

2. The apostle goes on to speak of the super-structure, the materials built upon him, *v.* 6. The apostle is recommending the Christian church and constitution to these dispersed Jews. The Christian church is a much nobler fabric than the Jewish temple; it is a living temple. Christ, the foundation, is a living stone. Christians are lively stones, and they are a holy priesthood. They offer spiritual sacrifices, acceptable to God by Jesus Christ. All sincere Christians have in them a principle of spiritual life communicated to them from Christ; not dead in trespasses and sins, but alive to God. The church of God is a spiritual house. This house is daily built up, every part of it improving, and the whole supplied in every age by the addition of new particular members. All good Christians are a holy priesthood. This holy priesthood must and will offer up spiritual sacrifices to God. The most spiritual sacrifices of the best men are not acceptable to God, but through Jesus Christ; therefore bring all your oblations to him, and by him present them to God.

II. He confirms what he had asserted of Christ being a *living stone,* &c., from Isa. xxviii. 16. In their quotations they kept rather to the sense than the words of scripture. The true sense of scripture may be justly and fully expressed in other than scripture-words, but in the weighty matters of religion we must depend entirely upon scripture-proof. The word of God is the only rule God hath given us. The accounts that God hath given us in scripture concerning his Son Jesus Christ are what require our strictest attention. *Behold, I lay,* &c. The constituting of Christ Jesus head of the church is an eminent work of God: *I lay in Zion.* Jesus Christ is the chief corner-stone that God hath laid in his spiritual building. The corner-stone stays inseparably with the building, supports it, unites it, and adorns it. So does Christ by his holy church, his spiritual house.

III. He deduces an important inference, *v.* 7. "You who believe will be so far from being ashamed of him that you will boast of him and glory in him for ever." The disobedient will go on to disallow Jesus Christ; but God is resolved that he shall be, in despite of all opposition, the head of the corner. The apostle draws an inference from the prophet's testimony. The prophet did not expressly say so, but yet he said that from which the consequence was unavoidable. The business of a faithful minister is to apply general truths to the particular condition and state of his hearers. The apostle quotes a passage (*v.* 6) out of the prophet, and applies it severally to good and bad. This requires wisdom, courage, and fidelity; but it is very profitable to the hearers. Disobedient people have no true faith. These may have some right notions, but no solid faith. Those that ought to be builders of the church of Christ are often the worst enemies that Christ has in the world. God will carry on his own work notwithstanding the falseness of pretended friends and the opposition of his worst enemies.

IV. The apostle adds a further description, still preserving the metaphor of a stone, *v.* 8. The words are taken from Isa. viii. 13, 14.

1. The builders, the chief-priests, refused him, and the people followed their leaders; and so Christ became to them *a stone of stumbling, and a rock of offence.* All those that are disobedient take offence at the word of God. They are offended with Christ himself, with his doctrine and the purity of his precepts. The same blessed Jesus who is the author of salvation to some is to others the occasion of their sin and destruction. Those who reject him as a Saviour will split upon him as a Rock.

2. Those who received him were highly privileged, *v.* 9. The Jews were exceedingly tender of their ancient privileges.

(1) The apostle answers, that if they did not submit they were ruined (*v.* 7, 8), but that if they did submit they should lose no real advantage, but continue still *a chosen generation, a royal priesthood,* &c. All true Christians *are a chosen generation*; they all make one family, a sort and species of people distinct from the common world. All the true servants of Christ are a royal priesthood, separated from sin and sinners, consecrated to God, and offering to God spiritual services and oblations, acceptable to God through Jesus Christ. All Christians, wheresoever they be, compose one holy nation. It is the honour of the servants of Christ that they are God's peculiar people. These dignities and virtues of Christians are not natural to them; for their first state is a state of horrid darkness, but they are effectually called out of darkness that they should show forth the virtues and praises of him who hath called them.

(2) The apostle advises them to compare their former and their present state. Time was when they were not a people, nor had they obtained mercy, but now they are taken in again to be the people of God, and have obtained mercy.

V. He warns them to beware of fleshly lusts, *v.* 11. Knowing the difficulty, and yet the importance of the duty, he uses his utmost interest in them: *Dearly beloved, I beseech you.* The duty is to abstain from fleshly lusts. These Christians ought to avoid, considering, 1. The respect they have with God: They are *dearly beloved.* 2. Their condition in the world: *They are strangers and pilgrims,* and should not impede their passage by giving in to the lusts of the country through which they pass. 3. The grand mischief that sin does to man is this, it *wars against the soul.* Of all sorts of sin, none are more injurious to the soul than *fleshly lusts.*

VI. He exhorts them further to an honest conversation. They lived among the Gentiles who were inveterate enemies to them, and constantly spoke evil of them *as of evil-doers.* "A good conversation may not only stop their mouths, but may possibly be a means to bring them to glorify God, and turn to you, when they shall see you excel all others in good works. Vindicate yourselves by good works, this is the way to convince them. When the gospel shall come among them, and take effect, a good conversation will encourage them in their conversion, but an evil one will obstruct it."

Verses 13–25

A Christian conversation must be honest.

I. The case of subjects. Christians were not only reputed innovators in religion, but disturbers of the state; it was highly necessary, therefore, that the apostle should settle the rules of obedience to the civil magistrate.

1. The duty required is submission.

2. The persons or objects to whom this submission is due are described. More generally: *Every ordinance of man.* Magistracy is certainly of divine right; and this is a general rule, binding in all nations, let the established form of government be what it will. Particularly: *To the king, as supreme, or unto governors,* who *are sent by him,* commissioned by him to govern.

3. The reasons to enforce this duty are,

(1) *For the Lord's sake,* who has ordained magistracy for the good of mankind.

(2) From the end and use of the magistrate's office, which are, to punish evil-doers and to praise and encourage all those that do well. True religion is the best support of civil government. The best way the magistrate can take to discharge his own duty, and to amend the world, is to punish well and reward well.

(3) Christians should submit to the civil magistrate, *v.* 15. *The will of God is,* to a good man, the strongest

reason for any duty. A Christian must endeavour, in all relations, to behave himself so as to put to silence the unreasonable reproaches of the most ignorant and foolish men.

(4) The spiritual nature of Christian liberty. The apostle tells the Christians that they were free, but from what? Not from duty or obedience to God's law, which requires subjection to the civil magistrate. They were free spiritually, but must still remember they were *the servants of God.* All the servants of Christ are free men. The servants of Jesus Christ ought to be very careful not to abuse their Christian liberty.

4. The apostle concludes with four admirable precepts: (1) *Honour all men.* A due respect is to be given to all men; the poor are not to be despised; the wicked must be honoured, not for their wickedness, but for any other qualities. (2) *Love the brotherhood.* All Christians are a fraternity. They should therefore love one another with an especial affection. (3) *Fear God* with the highest reverence. If this be wanting, none of the other three duties can be performed as they ought. (4) *Honour the king.*

II. The case of servants. They imagined that their Christian liberty set them free from their unbelieving and cruel masters; *Servants, be subject, v.* 18.

1. He orders them to *be subject,* and that *not only to the good and gentle,* but even to the crooked and perverse. The sinful misconduct of one relation does not justify the sinful behaviour of the other; the servant is bound to do his duty, though the master be sinfully froward and perverse. Good people are meek and gentle to their servants and inferiors.

2. He condescends to reason with them about it.

(1) If they were patient under their hardships, while they suffered unjustly, this would be acceptable to God, *v.* 19, 20. There is no condition so mean but a man may glorify God in it; the meanest servant may do so. The most conscientious persons are very often the greatest sufferers. *For conscience towards God, they suffer wrongfully; they do well, and suffer for it;* but sufferers of this sort are praiseworthy, they do honour to God and they are accepted of him. Deserved sufferings must be endured with patience.

(2) More reasons to encourage Christian servants to patience under unjust sufferings, *v.* 21. From their Christian calling. From the example of Christ. Good Christians are a sort of people called to be sufferers, and therefore they must expect it; they are bound to deny themselves, and take up the cross. Jesus Christ *suffered for* you, or *for us,* in our stead and for our good, *v.* 24. The sufferings of Christ should quiet us under the most unjust and cruel sufferings we meet with in the world. Shall not we sinners submit to the light afflictions of this life, which work for us unspeakable advantages afterwards?

3. The example of Christ's subjection and patience is here explained: *Christ suffered,* (1) Wrongfully, *v.* 22. His words, as well as his actions, were all sincere, just, and right. (2) Patiently, *v.* 23. Provocations to sin can never justify the commission of it. The reasons for sin can never be so great, but we have always stronger reasons to avoid it.

4. Lest any should think that Christ's death was designed merely for an example of patience under sufferings, the apostle here adds a more glorious design and effect of it: *Who his own self.* The person suffering—Jesus Christ: *His own self—in his own body.* The expression *his own self* is emphatic to distinguish him from the Levitical priests (who offered the blood of others). The sufferings he underwent were *stripes and the death of the cross*—servile and ignominious punishments! The reason of his sufferings: He *bore our sins.* Christ, in his sufferings, stood charged with our sins. He bore the punishment of

them. As the scape-goat did typically bear the sins of the people on his head, and then carried them quite away, so the Lamb of God does first bear our sins in his own body, and thereby take away the sins of the world. The fruits of Christ's sufferings. Our sanctification. Our justification. *By his stripes we are healed.*

5. The difference between their former and present condition, *v.* 25. (1) Man's sin: he goes astray; it is his own act. (2) His misery: he goes astray from the shepherd, and from the flock. (3) The recovery of these by conversion. This return is to Christ, who is the true careful shepherd, that loves his sheep, who is the most vigilant pastor, and bishop, or overseer of souls.

CHAPTER 3

The duties of husbands and wives one to another, ver. 1–7. He exhorts Christians to unity and patience under sufferings; to oppose the slanders of their enemies, ver. 8–17. To encourage them to this he proposes the example of Christ, ver. 18, to the end.

Verses 1–7

I. Lest the Christian matrons should imagine that their conversion to Christ exempted them from subjection to their pagan or Jewish husbands, the apostle here tells them,

1. In what the duty of wives consists.

(1) In *subjection,* which obliging conduct would be the most likely way to win those unbelieving husbands who had rejected the word, or who attended to no other evidence of the truth of it than what they saw in the exemplary *conversation of their wives.* A cheerful *subjection,* and a loving, reverential respect, are duties which Christian women owe their husbands, whether they be good or bad. There is nothing more powerful, next to the word of God, to win people, than a good conversation.

(2) In *fear,* or reverence to their husbands.

(3) In a *chaste conversation.* Evil men are strict observers of the conversation of the professors of religion. *A chaste conversation* is an excellent means to win them to the faith of the gospel.

(4) In preferring the ornaments of the mind to those of the body, *v.* 3. Here are three sorts of ornaments forbidden: *plaiting of hair,* which was commonly used in those times by lewd women; *wearing of gold; putting on of apparel* with too much nicety and costliness in it. Religious people should take care that all their external behaviour be answerable to their profession. The outward adorning of the body is very often sensual and excessive. The attire of a harlot can never become a chaste Christian matron. He directs Christian wives to put on much more excellent and beautiful ornaments, *v.* 4. *First,* The part to be adorned: *The hidden man of the heart.* Take care to adorn and beautify your souls rather than your bodies. *Secondly,* The ornament prescribed. It must be something *not corruptible.* The ornaments of the body perish in the using; but the grace of God, the longer we wear it, the brighter and better it is. The finest ornament of Christian women is *a meek and quiet spirit.* If the husband be harsh, and averse to religion, there is no way so likely to win him as a prudent meek behaviour. A true Christian's chief care lies in the right ordering and commanding of his own spirit. Where the hypocrite's work ends, there the true Christian's work begins. The endowments of the inner man are the chief ornaments of a Christian; but especially a composed, calm, and quiet spirit, renders either man or woman beautiful and lovely.

2. The apostle enforces them by the example, (1) Of the holy women of old, who trusted in God, *v.* 5. "The duties imposed upon you are not new, but what have ever been practised by the greatest

and best women in the world." (2) Of Sara, who obeyed her husband, and followed him. "*Whose daughters you are* if you imitate her in faith and good works." The subjection of wives to their husbands is a duty which has been practised universally by holy women in all ages. Christians ought to do their duty to one another, not out of fear, nor from force, but from a willing mind, and in obedience to the command of God.

II. The husband's duty to the wife.

1. The particulars are: *Cohabitation. Dwelling with the wife according to knowledge*, as wise and sober men, who know the word of God and their own duty. *Giving honour to the wife*—giving due respect to her, and placing a due trust and confidence in her.

2. The reasons are, Because she is *the weaker vessel*. The wife is, in other and higher respects, equal to her husband; they are *heirs together of the grace of life*, and therefore should live peaceable one with another, and, if they do not, their prayers one with another and one for another will be hindered.

Verses 8–15

I. How Christians and friends should treat one another. Christians should endeavour to be all of one mind in the great points of faith, in real affection, and in Christian practice. Though Christians cannot be exactly of the same mind, yet they should have compassion one for another, and love as brethren. Christianity requires pity to the distressed, and civility to all.

II. He instructs us how to behave towards enemies.

1. "When they rail at you, do you bless them; when they give you evil words, do you give them good ones; for Christ has called you to bless those that curse you, and has settled a blessing on you as your everlasting inheritance." The laws of Christ oblige us to return blessing for railing (Matt. v. 44). We must bless, pray for, and love those who rail at us. A Christian's calling, as it invests him with glorious privileges, so it obliges him to difficult duties.

2. An excellent prescription for a comfortable happy life in this quarrelsome ill-natured world (*v.* 10): it is quoted from Ps. xxxiv. 12-14. It is lawful to consider temporal advantages as motives and encouragements to religion. The practice of religion, particularly the right government of the tongue, is the best way to make this life comfortable and prosperous; a sincere, inoffensive, discreet tongue, is a singular means to pass us peaceably and comfortably through the world. It is the duty of Christians not only to embrace peace when it is offered, but to seek and pursue it when it is denied.

3. Christians need not fear that such patient inoffensive behaviour will invite the cruelty of their enemies (*v.* 12). *His ears are open to their prayers. But the face of the Lord is against those that do evil.* He is more an enemy to wicked persecutors than men are. God hath a special care and paternal affection towards all his righteous people. God doth always hear the prayers of the faithful.

4. This patient humble behaviour of Christians is further urged. This will be the best and surest way to prevent suffering, *v.* 13. "Ordinarily, there will be but few so diabolical and impious as to harm those who live so innocently and usefully as you do." But if you suffer for righteousness' sake (*v.* 14), it will be your glory and your happiness. "You need not be afraid of anything they can do to strike you with terror, neither be much troubled nor concerned about the rage or force of your enemies." To follow always that which is good is the best course we can take to keep out of harm's way. To suffer for righteousness' sake is the honour and happiness of a Christian. Christians have no reason to be afraid of the threats or rage of any of their enemies. Instead of terrifying yourselves with the fear of men, be sure to *sanctify the Lord God in your hearts* (*v.* 15). "When this principle is laid deeply into your hearts, the next thing, as to men, is to be always ready *to give an answer to every man that asketh a reason of your hope*. The hope and faith of a Christian are defensible against all the world. Every Christian is bound to answer for the hope that is in him. Christians should have a reason ready for their Christianity, that it may appear they are not actuated either by folly or fancy. These confessions of our faith ought to be made *with meekness and fear*.

Verses 16, 17

The confession of a Christian's faith cannot credibly be supported but by *a good conscience* and a *good conversation*. Conscience is good when it is kept clear from guilt. *A good conversation in Christ* is a holy life. "Look well to your conscience, and to your conversation; and then, though men falsely accuse you as evil-doers, you will bring them to shame. Be not discouraged, for it is better for you, though worse for your enemies, that you suffer for well-doing than for evil-doing." The most conscientious persons cannot escape the censures and slanders of evil men. Christ and his apostles were so used. False accusation generally turns to the accuser's shame. As well-doing sometimes exposes a good man to suffering, so evil-doing will not exempt an evil man from it. If the sufferings of good people for well-doing be so severe, what will the sufferings of wicked people be for evil-doing?

Verses 18–20

I. The example of Christ is proposed as an argument for patience. Jesus Christ himself was not exempted from sufferings in this life. The reason of Christ's suffering was the sins of men: *Christ suffered for sins*. In the case of our Lord's suffering, it was the just that suffered for the unjust. He that knew no sin suffered instead of those that knew no righteousness. The merit and perfection of Christ's sacrifice. The legal sacrifices were repeated but the sacrifice of Christ, once suffered, purgeth away sin. The blessed design of our Lord's sufferings was to bring us to God. The issue of Christ's suffering. He was put to death in his human nature, but he was quickened and raised again by the Spirit. If Christ was not exempted from sufferings, why should Christians expect it? If he, though perfectly just, why should not we, who are all criminals? If he once suffered, and then entered into glory, shall not we be patient under trouble?

II. The apostle passes from the example of Christ to that of the old world. They had now an offer of mercy; those that accepted of it should be saved, but those who rejected Christ should be as certainly destroyed as ever the disobedient in the times of Noah were. 1. The preacher—Christ Jesus. *He went and preached*, by his Spirit striving with them. 2. The hearers. He properly calls them spirits now *in prison*; not that they were *in prison when Christ preached to them*. 3. The sin of these people: They were *disobedient*. This their sin is aggravated from the patience and *long-suffering of God*. 4. The event of all: Their bodies were drowned. Noah and his family, who believed and were obedient, *were saved in the ark*. Though the patience of God wait long upon sinners, yet it will expire at last; it is beneath the majesty of the great God always to wait upon man in vain. The way of the most is neither the best, the wisest, nor the safest way to follow: better to follow the eight in the ark.

Verses 21, 22

Noah's salvation in the ark upon the water prefigured the salvation of all good Christians by baptism.

I. What he means by saving baptism; not the outward ceremony of washing with water, but it is that baptism wherein there is a faithful answer of a resolved good conscience.

II. The efficacy of baptism to salvation depends not upon the work done, but upon the resurrection of Christ. The sacrament of baptism, rightly received, is a means and a pledge of salvation. *Baptism now saveth us.* The external participation of baptism will save no man without an answerable good conscience and conversation. There must be the answer of a good conscience towards God.

III. The apostle proceeds to speak of his ascension, and sitting at the right hand of the Father, *v.* 22. If the advancement of Christ was so glorious after his deep humiliation, let not his followers despair, but expect that after these short distresses they shall be advanced to transcendent joy and glory. Upon his ascension into heaven, Christ is enthroned at the right hand of the Father. Angels, authorities, and powers, are all made subject to Christ Jesus.

CHAPTER 4

The work of a Christian is twofold—doing the will of God and suffering his pleasure. This chapter directs us in both. The duties we are here exhorted to employ ourselves in, ver. 1–11. The directions for sufferings are that we should not be surprised at them, but rejoice in them. The best way to preserve their souls is to commit them to God in well-doing.

Verses 1–3

I. How the exhortation is expressed. *Christ had suffered* for us in the flesh, or in his human nature. "*Arm* and fortify *yourselves likewise with the same mind.* As Christ suffered in his human nature, do you make your corrupt nature suffer, by putting to death the body of sin by self-denial and mortification. *Cease from sin.*" Some of the strongest and best arguments against all sorts of sin are taken from the sufferings of Christ. All sympathy and tenderness for Christ as a sufferer are lost if you do not put away sin. The beginning of all true mortification lies in the mind, not in penances and hardships upon the body.

II. How it is further explained, *v.* 2. Negatively, a Christian ought *no longer to live the rest of his time in the flesh*, but, positively, he ought to conform himself to the revealed will of the holy God. The lusts of men are the springs of all their wickedness. Let occasional temptations be what they will, they could not prevail, were it not for men's own corruptions. True conversion makes a marvellous change in the heart and life of everyone who partakes of it. It alters the mind and conversation of everyone who has experienced it.

III. How it is enforced (*v.* 3). "It is but just that as you have hitherto all the former part of your life served sin and Satan, so you should now serve the living God." When a man is truly converted, it is very grievous to him to think how the time past of his life has been spent. While the will of man is unsanctified and corrupt, he walks continually in wicked ways, and he makes a bad condition daily worse and worse. One sin, allowed, draws on another. Here are six named. (1) *Lasciviousness*, expressed in looks, gesture, or behaviour. (2) *Lusts*, acts of lewdness. (3) *Excess of wine*. (4) *Revellings*, too frequent, too full, or too expensive. (5) *Banquetings*, by which is meant gluttony. (6) *Abominable* idolatry; the idol-worship of the Gentiles. It is a Christian's duty not only to abstain from what is grossly wicked, but also from those things that are generally the occasions of sin.

Verses 4–6

I. Here you have the visible change wrought in those who were represented as having been in the former part of their life very wicked. The conduct of their wicked acquaintance towards them. 1. *They think it strange* that their old friends should not run with as much violence as they used to do *to the same excess of riot.* 2. *They speak evil of them.* Those that are once really converted will not return to their former course of life. Neither persuasion nor reproach will prevail with them to be or to do as they were wont to do. The temper and behaviour of true Christians seem very strange to ungodly men. The ungodly cannot comprehend. The best actions of religious people cannot escape the censures and slanders of those who are irreligious. They will speak evil of good people, though they themselves reap the fruits of their charity, piety, and goodness.

II. For the comfort of the servants of God, it is here added,

1. That all wicked people shall *give an account* to him who is ready to judge. The malignant world shall in a little time give an account to the great God of all their evil speeches against his people.

2. That *for this cause was the gospel preached also to those that are dead, v.* 6. The mortifying of our sins and living to God are the expected effects of the gospel preached to us. God will certainly reckon with all those who have had the gospel preached to them, but without these good effects produced by it. It is no matter how we are judged according to men in the flesh, if we do but live according to God in the Spirit.

Verses 7–11

We have here an awful position and an inference drawn from it. The position is that the *end of all things is at hand.* Consequently, the time of their persecution is but very short. Your own life and that of your enemies will soon come to their utmost period. Nay, the world itself will not continue very long. The inference from this comprises a series of exhortations.

1. To sobriety and watchfulness, *v.* 7. Do not suffer yourselves to be caught with your former sins and temptations, *v.* 3. *And watch unto prayer.* Take care that you be frequent in prayers, lest this end come upon you unawares. Those who would pray to purpose must *watch unto prayer*.

2. To charity, *v.* 8. Christians ought to love one another. This mutual affection must not be cold, but fervent, that is, sincere, strong, and lasting. This sort of earnest affection is recommended *above all things*, which shows the importance of it. One excellent effect of it is that it will *cover a multitude of sins. Have charity among yourselves.* There is a special relation between all sincere Christians, and a particular amiableness and good in them, which require special affection. It is not enough for Christians not to bear malice, nor to have common respect for one another, they must intensely and fervently love each other. It is the property of true charity *to cover a multitude of sins.* It inclines people to forgive and forget offences against themselves, to cover the sins of others, rather than aggravate them and spread them abroad. It prepares for mercy at the hand of God, who hath promised to forgive those that forgive others.

3. To hospitality, *v.* 9. The proper objects of Christian hospitality are one another. The manner of performing this duty is this: it must be done in an easy, kind, handsome manner, *without grudging* or grumbling at the expense or trouble. Christians ought not only to be charitable, but hospitable, one to another.

4. To the improvement of talents, *v.* 11.

(1) Whatever gift, whatever power, of doing good is given to us, we should minister with the same *one to another.* In receiving and using the manifold

gifts of God we must look upon ourselves as stewards only.

(2) The apostle exemplifies his direction about gifts in two particulars—speaking and ministering. *If any man speak* or teach, he must do it *as the oracles of God.* What Christians in private, or ministers in public, teach and speak must be the pure word and oracles of God. *If any man minister let him do it as of the ability which God giveth. That God in all things* may be glorified, *through Jesus Christ,* to whom *be praise and dominion for ever and ever. Amen. First,* It is the duty of Christians in private, as well as ministers in public, to speak to one another of the things of God. *Secondly,* It highly concerns all preachers of the gospel to keep close to the word of God, and to treat that word as becomes the oracles of God. *Thirdly,* Whatever we are called to do for the honour of God and the good of others we should do it with all our might. *Fourthly,* In all the duties and services of life we should aim at the glory of God; all other views must be subservient to this. *Fifthly, God in all things must be glorified through Jesus Christ,* who is the only way to the Father.

Verses 12–19

The frequent repetition of comfort to Christians, considered as sufferers, in every chapter of this epistle, shows that the greatest danger these new converts were in arose from the persecutions to which their embracing Christianity exposed them. The apostle comes here to direct them in the necessary duty of patience under sufferings.

I. The apostle's kind manner of address: they were his *beloved, v.* 9.

II. His advice to them, relating to their sufferings.

1. They should not think them strange, nor be surprised at them.

(1) Though they be sharp and fiery, yet they are designed only to try, not to ruin them. They ought rather to rejoice under their sufferings, because theirs may properly be called Christ's sufferings. He suffers in them, and feels in our infirmities; and, if we be partakers of his sufferings, we shall also be made *partakers of his glory.* The apostle owns these poor afflicted Christians, and calls them his beloved. True Christians never look more amiable one to another than in their adversities. There is no reason for Christians to wonder at the unkindnesses and persecutions of the world, because they are forewarned of them. Christ himself endured them. Christians ought not only to be patient, but to rejoice, in their sharpest sorest sufferings for Christ. Those who rejoice in their sufferings for Christ shall eternally triumph and rejoice with him in glory.

(2) The apostle descends to a lower degree of persecution, *v.* 14. They would be reviled, evil-spoken of, and slandered for the name or sake of Christ. In such case he asserts, *Happy are you.* "You have the Spirit of God with you and the Spirit of God is also the Spirit of glory. This glorious Spirit *resteth upon you.* By your patience and fortitude in suffering *he is on your part glorified;* but by the contempt and reproaches cast upon you *the Spirit itself* is evil-spoken of and blasphemed." The happiness of good people not only consists with, but even flows from, their afflictions: *Happy are you.* That man who hath the Spirit of God resting upon him cannot be miserable, let his afflictions be ever so great. When good people are vilified *for the name of Christ* his Holy Spirit is glorified in them.

2. They should take care they did not suffer justly, as evil-doers, *v.* 15. Their enemies charged them with these and other foul crimes: therefore the apostle thought these cautions necessary. *If any man suffer* for the cause of Christianity, and with a patient Christian spirit, he ought not to account it a shame, and ought to glorify God who hath thus dignified him, *v.* 16. But there is very little comfort in sufferings when we bring them upon ourselves by our own sin and folly. It is not the suffering, but the cause, that makes the martyr.

3. Their trials were now at hand, *v.* 17, 18.

(1) The time had come when *judgment must begin at the house of God.* This renders all the foregoing exhortations to patience necessary for you. These judgments will but *begin* with you that are God's house. "Your troubles will be but light and short, in comparison of what shall befall the wicked world. *What shall the end be of those who obey not the gospel of God?*" The best of God's servants have so much amiss in them as renders it fit and necessary that God should sometimes correct and punish them. *Judgment* begins at the house of God. Those who are the family of God have their worst things in this life. Their worst condition is tolerable, and will soon be over. The apostle distinguishes the disobedient from the house of God. *What shall the end be of those that obey not the gospel?*

(2) He intimates the irremediable doom of the wicked, *v.* 18. The grievous sufferings of good people in this world are sad presages of much heavier judgments coming upon impenitent sinners. It is as much as the righteous can do to be saved. Let the absolute necessity of salvation balance the difficulty of it. Your difficulties are greatest at first; God offers his grace and help.

4. When called to suffer, *according to the will of God,* they should look chiefly to the safety of their souls, *committing them to God,* who will undertake the charge, for he is their Creator, *v.* 19. All the sufferings that befall good people come upon them *according to the will of God.* It is the duty of Christians to look more to the keeping of their souls than to the preserving of their bodies. Good people have great encouragement to commit their souls to God, because he is their Creator, and faithful in all his promises.

CHAPTER 5

In which the apostle gives particular directions, first to the elders, ver. 1–4; then to the younger, ver. 5–7. He then exhorts all, praying earnestly for them; and so concludes his epistle.

Verses 1–4

I. The persons to whom this exhortation is given— elders by office, rather than by age, ministers of those churches to whom he wrote this epistle.

II. He tells them he was their fellow-elder, and so puts nothing upon them but what he was ready to perform himself. He was also *a witness of the sufferings of Christ.* He was also *a partaker of the glory* that shall be completely enjoyed at the second coming of Jesus Christ. It was the peculiar honour of Peter, and a few more, to be the witnesses of Christ's sufferings; but it is the privilege of all true Christians to be partakers of the glory that shall be revealed.

III. The pastor's duty described. 1. *To feed the flock,* by preaching to them the sincere word of God. 2. The pastors of the church must *take the oversight thereof.* 3. They must be *examples to the flock,* and practice the holiness which they preach and recommend to their people. These duties must be performed, *not by constraint,* but from a willing mind that takes pleasure in the work: *not for filthy lucre, but of a ready mind,* regarding the flock more than the fleece; *neither as being lords over God's heritage,* tyrannizing over them. These poor, dispersed, suffering Christians were the flock of God. The rest of the world is a brutal herd. These are an orderly flock, redeemed to God by the great Shepherd. They are also dignified with the title of God's *heritage,* chosen out of the common multitude for his own people. They are God's people, and should be treated with love, meekness, and tenderness, for the sake of him to whom they belong.

IV. In opposition to that filthy lucre the apostle sets before them the crown of glory designed by the great shepherd for all his faithful ministers. Jesus Christ is *the chief shepherd* of the whole flock and heritage of God. He is also the chief shepherd over all inferior shepherds. This chief shepherd will appear, to judge all ministers and undershepherds. Those that are found to have done their duty shall receive from the grand shepherd *a crown of glory that fadeth not away.*

Verses 5–7

The apostle comes now to instruct the flock.

I. He exhorts those that are younger and inferior to *submit themselves to the elder.* As to one another, the rule is that they should all *be subject one to another,* so far as to receive the reproofs and counsels one of another. He advises them to *be clothed with humility.* "If you be disobedient and proud, God will set himself to oppose you; for *he resisteth the proud,* when he *giveth grace to the humble.*" Humility is the great preserver of peace and order in all Christian societies, consequently pride is the great disturber of them. There is a mutual opposition between God and the proud. Where God giveth grace to be humble, he will give more grace and humility. Hence the apostle adds: "Since God resisteth the proud, but giveth grace to the humble, therefore humble yourselves, not only one to another, but to the great God. His hand is almighty, and can easily pull you down if you be proud, or exalt you if you be humble." Humbling ourselves to God under his hand is the next way to deliverance and exaltation.

II. The apostle rightly supposes that what he had foretold of greater hardships yet coming might excite in them abundance of care. Foreseeing this anxious care would be a heavy burden, and a sore temptation, he gives them the best advice. His advice is to *cast all their care,* or *all care of themselves, upon God.* Trust in him with a firm, composed mind, *for he careth for you.* He is willing to release you of your care, and take the care of you upon himself. The best of Christians are apt to labour under the burden of anxious and excessive care. The cares even of good people are very burdensome, and too often very sinful. The best remedy against immoderate care is to *cast our care upon God.* A firm belief of the rectitude of the divine will calms the spirit of man.

Verses 8, 9

I. He shows them their danger from an enemy whom he describes,

1. By his characters and names. He is an adversary: *"That adversary of yours." The devil, the grand accuser of all the brethren.* He is *a roaring lion,* the fierce and greedy pursuer of souls.

2. By his business: *He walks about, seeking whom he may devour;* his whole design is to devour and destroy souls.

II. Hence he infers that it is their duty to *be sober,* to *be vigilant,* to be watchful and diligent to prevent his designs and save their souls. To resist him *steadfast in the faith.* It was the faith of these people that Satan aimed at. This strong trial and temptation they must resist, by being steadfast in the faith.

III. The like afflictions befell their brethren in all parts of the world, all the people of God were their fellow-soldiers in this warfare. The devil is the grand persecutor, as well as *the deceiver and accuser, of the brethren.* Sobriety and watchfulness are necessary virtues at all times, but especially in times of suffering and persecution. If your faith give way, you are gone. The consideration of what others suffer is proper to encourage us to bear our own share in any affliction: *The same afflictions are accomplished in your brethren.*

Verses 10–14

We come now to the conclusion of this epistle.

I. The apostle begins with a most weighty prayer, which he addresses to God as *the God of all grace.*

1. What he prays for on their account. *After they had suffered awhile* that God would perfect his work in them. Those who are called to be heirs of eternal life through Jesus Christ must, nevertheless, suffer in this world, but their sufferings will be but for a little while. Therefore he is earnestly to be sought unto by continual prayer, and dependence upon his promises.

2. His doxology, v. 11.

II. He recapitulates the design of his writing this epistle to them (v. 12). The doctrine of salvation, which he had explained and they had embraced, was the true account of the grace of God, foretold by the prophets and published by Jesus Christ. As they had embraced the gospel, they would continue steadfast in it. A firm persuasion that we are in the true way to heaven will be the best motive to stand fast, and persevere therein.

III. He recommends *Silvanus,* the person by whom he sent them this brief epistle. The prejudices that some of these Jews might have against Silvanus, as a minister of the Gentiles, would soon wear off when they were once convinced that he was a faithful brother.

IV. He closes with salutations and a solemn benediction. In this salutation he particularly joins Mark the evangelist, who was then with him, and who was his son in a spiritual sense. All the churches of Jesus Christ ought to have a most affectionate concern one for another; they should love and pray for one another. He exhorts them to fervent love and charity one towards another, and to express this by giving *the kiss of peace* (v. 14), and so concludes with a benediction, which he confines to those *that are in Christ Jesus.* The blessing he pronounces upon them is *peace,* by which he means all necessary good.

AN EXPOSITION, WITH PRACTICAL OBSERVATIONS, OF

THE SECOND EPISTLE GENERAL OF

PETER

The design of this second epistle is the same with that of the former, as is evident from the first verse of the third chapter, whence observe that, in the things of God, we have need of *precept upon precept, and line upon line*, and all little enough to keep them in remembrance; and yet these are the things which should be most faithfully recorded and frequently remembered by us.

CHAPTER 1

I. An introduction leading to what is principally designed by the apostle, ver. 1–4. II. An exhortation to advance and improve in all Christian graces, ver. 5–7. III. To enforce this exhortation he adds, 1. A representation of the very great advantage which will thereby accrue to them, ver. 8–11. 2. A promise of the best assistance the apostle was able to give, ver. 12–15. 3 A declaration of the certain truth of the gospel of Christ.

Verses 1–4

I. We have here a description of the person who wrote the epistle, by the name of *Simon*, as well as *Peter*, and by the title of *servant*, as well as that of *apostle*. He here styles himself *a servant* (as well as an apostle) *of Jesus Christ*. How great an honour is it to be the servants of this Master! This is what we cannot, without sin, be ashamed of.

II. We have an account of the people to whom the epistle is written. They are described as *having obtained precious faith in our Lord Jesus Christ*. True saving faith is a precious grace. True faith is very excellent and of very great use and advantage to those who have it. *The just lives by faith*. Faith is alike precious in the private Christian and in the apostle; it produces the same precious effects in the one and in the other. Faith, in whomsoever it exists, takes hold of the same *precious* Saviour, and applies the same precious promises. This precious faith is obtained of God. Faith is the gift of God. The preciousness of faith, as well as our obtaining it, is through the righteousness of Christ.

III. We have the apostolical benediction.

1. An account of the way and means whereby *grace and peace are multiplied*—it is *through the knowledge of God and Jesus Christ*.

2. What we have already received should encourage us to ask for more. All things that have any relation to, and influence upon, the true spiritual life, the life and power of godliness, are from Jesus Christ. Knowledge of God, and faith in him, are the channel whereby all spiritual supports and comforts are conveyed to us; but then we must own and acknowledge God as the author of our effectual calling, for so he is here described: *Him that hath called us to glory and virtue*. The design of God in calling or converting men is to bring them to *glory and virtue*. It is the glory of God's power to convert sinners. The apostle goes on to encourage their faith and hope in looking for an increase of grace and peace. (1) The good things which the promises make over are exceedingly great. Pardon of sin is one of the blessings here intended. To pardon sins that are numerous and heinous is a wonderful thing. (2) The promised blessings of the gospel are very precious. The great promise of the New Testament is the *Holy Ghost*. (3) Those who receive the promises of the gospel *partake of the divine nature*. Their hearts are set for God and his service. (4) Those in whom the Spirit works the divine nature are freed from the bondage

of corruption. The dominion that sin has in the men of the world is through lust; their desires are to it, and therefore it rules over them. The dominion that sin has over us is according to the delight we have in it.

Verses 5–11

Having already obtained precious faith, and been made partakers of the divine nature is a very good beginning, but it is not to be rested in, as if we were already perfect. He exhorts them to press forward for the obtaining of more grace. Those who will make any progress in religion must be very industrious in their endeavours. Without *giving all diligence*, there is no gaining any ground in the work of holiness.

I. The believer's way is marked out step by step. 1. He must get *virtue*, by which some understand *justice*; and then the *knowledge, temperance, and patience* that follow. By *virtue* here we may understand *strength* and *courage*, without which the believer cannot stand up for good works. A cowardly Christian must expect that Christ will be ashamed of him another day. We have need of virtue while we live, and it will be of excellent use when we come to die. 2. The believer must add *knowledge* to his virtue, prudence to his courage. Christian prudence regards the persons we have to do with and the place and company we are in. 3. We must add *temperance to our knowledge*. We must be moderate in desiring and using the good things of natural life; an inordinate desire after these is inconsistent with an earnest desire after God and Christ. 4. Add to temperance *patience*, which must *have its perfect work*. We are born to trouble, and must through many tribulations enter into the kingdom of heaven. Our sufferings are less than our sins deserve. 5. To patience we must add *godliness*. When Christians bear afflictions patiently, they get an experimental *knowledge of the loving-kindness of their heavenly Father*, and hereby they are brought to the child-like fear and reverential love wherein true godliness consists. 6. We must add *brotherly-kindness*, a tender affection to all our fellow-christians, who are children of the same Father, and therefore are to be loved, as those who are peculiarly near and dear to us. 7. *Charity*, or a love of goodwill to all mankind. God has made of one blood all nations, and all the children of men are partakers of the same human nature, are all capable of the same mercies, and liable to the same afflictions. Thus must all believers in Christ evidence that they are the children of God, who is good to all.

II. All the forementioned graces must be had. The advantages that redound to all who successfully labour so as to get these things to *be and abound in them*, v. 8–11.

1. More generally, *v.* 8. The being and abounding of all Christian graces in us will make us neither inactive nor unfruitful, it will make us very zealous

and lively, and eminently fruitful in the works of righteousness. These will bring much glory to God, by bringing forth much fruit among men, being *fruitful in knowledge, or the acknowledging of our Lord Jesus Christ.* This is the necessary consequence of adding one grace to another; for, where all Christian graces are in the heart, they improve and strengthen one another. Wherever grace abounds there will be an abounding in good works. How desirable it is to be in such a case the apostle evidences, *v.* 9. He who has not the forementioned graces *is blind,* that is, as to spiritual and heavenly things. *He cannot see far off.* This present evil world he can see, and dotes upon, but has no discerning at all of the world to come. How wretched is their condition who are thus blind as to the awfully great things of the other world. But this is not all the misery of those who do not *add to their faith virtue, knowledge,* &c. They are as unable to look backward as forward, their memories are slippery and unable to retain what is past. Often call to mind, and seriously meditate on, your solemn engagement to be the Lord's, to lay aside *all filthiness of flesh and spirit.*

2. Two particular advantages: stability in grace, and a triumphant entrance into glory. *Giving diligence to make our calling and election sure.* It requires a great deal of diligence and labour to make sure our calling and election; there must be a very close examination of ourselves. "But, how great soever the labour is, do not think much of it, for great is the advantage you gain by it. By this you will be kept from falling." When many fall into errors, they shall be preserved sound in the faith, and stand perfect and complete in all the will of God. Those who are *growing in grace,* and *abounding in the work of the Lord,* shall have an *abundant entrance into the joy of their Lord,* and they shall *reign with him for ever and ever.*

Verses 12–15

I. Peter *will not be negligent,* but will be exemplarily diligent, and that in the work of a remembrancer. We need to be put in mind of what we already know to prevent our forgetting it, and to improve our knowledge, and reduce all to practice. We must be established in the belief of the truth, that we may not be shaken by every wind of doctrine, and especially in that which is the present truth, the truth more peculiarly necessary for us to know in our day. If the people need teaching and exhortation while they are in the body, it is very meet and just that ministers should, as long as they are in this tabernacle, instruct and exhort them, and bring those truths to their remembrance that they have formerly heard.

II. The apostle tells us (*v.* 14) what makes him earnest in this matter. The body is but the tabernacle of the soul. This tabernacle must be put off. We are not to continue long in this earthly house. The nearness of death makes the apostle diligent in the business of life. He must soon be removed from those to whom he wrote; and his ambition being that they should remember the doctrine he had delivered to them, after he himself was taken away from them, he commits his exhortation to writing.

Verses 16–18

These things are not idle tales, or a vain thing, but of undoubted truth and vast concern. The gospel is not a *cunningly devised fable.* The apostle's preaching was a making of these things known. 1. The preaching of the gospel is a making known the power of Christ. 2. The coming of Christ also is made known by the preaching of the gospel. This coming of Christ the gospel is very plain and circumstantial in setting forth; but there is a second coming, which it likewise mentions. He will come to judge the world in righteousness by the everlasting gospel. During our blessed Saviour's abode here on earth he sometimes manifested himself to be God, and particularly to our apostle and the two sons of Zebedee, who *were eye-witnesses of his divine majesty, when he was transfigured before them.* Besides the visible glory there was an audible voice from heaven. What a gracious declaration was made: *This is my beloved Son, in whom I am well pleased*—the best voice that ever came from heaven to earth; God is well pleased with Christ. *He received honour and glory from God the Father.* This is the person whom God delights to honour. This voice is from heaven, called here *the excellent glory.* This voice was heard, and that so as to be understood, by Peter, James, and John. They not only heard a sound, but they understood the sense. God opens the ears and understandings of his people to receive what they are concerned to know. Blessed are those who not only hear, but understand, who believe the truth, and feel the power of the voice from heaven.

Verses 19–21

In these words the apostle lays down another argument to prove the truth and reality of the gospel. For this is foretold by the prophets of the Old Testament, who spoke and wrote according to the direction of the Spirit of God.

I. The description that is given of the scriptures of the Old Testament: they are called *a more sure word of prophecy.* It is a prophetical declaration of the power and coming of our Saviour. But the New Testament is a history of that whereof the Old Testament is a prophecy. Read the Old Testament as a prophecy of Christ, and with diligence and thankfulness use the New as the best exposition of the Old. How firm and sure should our faith be, who have such a firm and sure word to rest upon! All the prophecies of the Old Testament are more sure and certain to us who have the history of the accomplishment of them.

II. The encouragement the apostle gives us to search the scriptures. *We do well if we take heed to them;* apply our minds to understand the sense, and our hearts to believe the truth, of this sure word. If we thus apply ourselves to the word of God, we certainly do well in all respects, what is pleasing to God and profitable to ourselves. They must use the scripture as a light which God hath sent into the world, to dispel that darkness which is upon the face of the whole earth. They must acknowledge their own darkness. Every man in the world is naturally without that knowledge which is necessary in order to attain eternal life. If ever men are made wise to salvation, it is by the shining of the word of God into their hearts. Natural notions of God are not sufficient for fallen man. When the light of the scripture is darted into the dark understanding by the Holy Spirit of God, then the *spiritual day dawns and the day-star arises in that soul.* This enlightening of a dark benighted mind is like the day-break that spreads and diffuses itself through the whole soul, till it makes perfect day. It is a growing knowledge. All who do truth come to this light, while evil-doers keep at a distance from it.

III. The apostle lays down one thing as previously necessary, and that is the knowing that all prophecy is of divine origin. No scripture prophecy is of private interpretation, but the revelation of the mind of God. This was the difference between the prophets of the Lord and the false prophets. The prophets of the Lord did not speak nor do anything of their own mind. The prophets and penmen of the scripture spoke and wrote what was the mind of God. Every private man ought to search it, and come to understand the sense and meaning thereof. This important truth of the divine origin of the scriptures is to be known and owned by all who will give heed to the sure word of prophecy. As a man not barely believes, but knows assuredly that that very person is his particular friend in whom he sees all the distinguishing marks and characters of his friend, so the Christian knows that book to be the word of God in which he sees all the proper marks and characters of a divinely inspired book. The divinity of the scriptures must be known and acknowledged in the first place, before men can give good heed to them.

IV. The apostle (*v.* 21) tells us how the Old Testament came to be compiled. 1. They were holy men of God who were employed about that book which we receive as the word of God. All the penmen of the scriptures were holy men of God. 2. *These holy men were moved by the Holy Ghost.* The Holy Ghost is the supreme agent, the holy men are but instruments. The Holy Ghost inspired and dictated to them what they were to deliver of the mind of God. He effectually engaged them to speak (and write) what he had put into their mouths. Mix faith therefore with what you find in the scriptures; esteem and reverence your Bible as a book written by holy men, inspired, influenced, and assisted by the Holy Ghost.

CHAPTER 2

The apostle now comes to remove what he could not but apprehend would hinder their complying with his exhortation. He therefore gives them fair warning of false teachers. I. He describes these seducers as impious in themselves, and very pernicious to others, ver. 1–3. II. He assures them of the punishment that shall be inflicted on them, ver. 3–6. III. He tells us how contrary the method is which God takes with those who fear him, ver. 7–9. IV. A further description of those seducers.

Verses 1–3

I. In all ages of the church the devil sends some to deceive, false prophets in the Old Testament, and seducing teachers in the New. Their business is to bring in destructive errors, *even damnable heresies.* Those who introduce destructive heresies *deny the Lord that bought them.* Those who bring in errors destructive to others bring swift (and therefore sure) *destruction upon themselves.* Self destroyers are soon destroyed.

II. The consequence with respect to others. Corrupt leaders seldom fail of many to follow them. Men drink in iniquity like water, and are pleased to live in error. The spreading of error will bring up an evil report on the way of truth; the way of salvation by Jesus Christ.

III. The method seducers take to draw disciples after them: they use *feigned words*; they flatter, and by good words and fair speeches deceive the hearts of the simple. All this is through covetousness, with design to get more wealth, or credit, or commendation, by increasing the number of their followers.

Verses 3–6

How successful and prosperous soever false teachers may be, yet their *judgment lingereth not.* Such unbelievers are condemned already. Examples of the righteous judgment of God.

I. The angels who sinned. No excellency will exempt a sinner from punishment. God did not spare them. By how much the more excellent the offender, by so much the more severe the punishment. Sin debases and degrades the persons who commit it. The angels of heaven are divested of all their glory upon their disobedience. Sin is the work of darkness, and darkness is the wages of sin. Those who will not walk according to the light and direction of God's law shall be deprived of the light of God's countenance.

II. He spared not the old world. If the sin be universal, the punishment shall likewise extend to all.

But if there be but a few righteous, they shall be preserved. God does not destroy the good with the bad. In wrath he remembers mercy. The procuring cause of destruction: *it was a world of ungodly men.* Ungodliness puts men out of the divine protection, and exposes them to utter destruction.

III. Sodom and Gomorrah. He destroys the *old world by water*, and Sodom by fire. He who keeps fire and water from hurting his people can make either to destroy his enemies; therefore they are never safe. Those who are sinners exceedingly before the Lord must expect the most dreadful vengeance. The punishment of sinners in former ages is designed for the example of those who come after. Men who live ungodly must see what they are to expect if they go on still in a course of impiety.

Verses 7–9

When God sends destruction on the ungodly, he commands deliverance for the righteous. This we have an instance of in his preserving Lot. 1. The character given of Lot; he is called *a just man.* He does not follow the multitude to do evil, but in a city of injustice he walks uprightly. 2. The impression the sins of others made upon this righteous man. In bad company we cannot escape either guilt or grief. 3. The duration and continuance of this good man's grief and vexation: it was *from day to day.* Being accustomed to hear and see their wickedness did not reconcile him to it. (1) *The Lord knows those that are his.* He has set apart him who is godly for himself; and, if there is but one in five cities, he knows him. (2) The wisdom of God is never at a loss about ways and means to deliver his people. They are often utterly at a loss; but he can find a way of escape. (3) The deliverance of the godly is the work of God, both his wisdom to contrive the way and his power to work out the deliverance *out of temptation.* (4) The unjust has no share in the salvation God works out for the righteous. The wicked are *reserved to the day of judgment.*

Verses 10–22

The apostle's design being to warn us of seducers, he now returns to discourse more particularly of them.

I. *These walk after the flesh.* They, in their lives, act directly contrary to God's righteous precepts, and comply with the demands of corrupt nature. Evil opinions are often accompanied with evil practices; and those who are for propagating error are for improving in wickedness. They go on in their sinful course, and increase unto more ungodliness. They also pour contempt on those whom God has set in authority over them and requires them to honour.

II. This he aggravates, by setting forth the very different conduct of more excellent creatures, even the *angels.* They *are greater in power and might,* and that even than those who are clothed with authority and power among the sons of men. *Angels bring* their *accusations of sinful creatures before the Lord.* It is before the Lord, who is the Judge, and will be the avenger, of all impiety and injustice. Good angels mingle no bitter revilings nor base reproaches with any of the accusations they bring. Let us imitate the angels. If we complain of wicked men, let it be to God, and that not with rage and reviling, but with compassion, that may evidence that we belong to him who is meek and merciful.

III. The apostle proceeds (*v.* 12) to show how like they are to the most inferior. Men, under the power of sin, are so far from observing divine revelation that they do not exercise reason. Brute-creatures follow the instinct of their sensitive appetite, and sinful man follows the inclination of his carnal mind. These persons shall be utterly destroyed in their own corruption. Whatever they meet with is the just *reward of their unrighteousness.* Such sinners as sport themselves in mischief deceive themselves and disgrace all they belong to, for by one sort of sins they prepare themselves for another; so that their *eyes are full of adultery*, their wanton looks show their own impure lusts and are directed to kindle the like in others; and this is what they *cannot cease* from. Those who are themselves incessant in sin are very often successful in drawing others into the same excess of riot. Those who are in the greatest danger of being led away into error and impiety, are the *unstable*. Those whose hearts are not established with grace are easily turned into the way of sin. These are not only riotous and lascivious, but *covetous* also; they pant after riches, and the desire of their souls is to the wealth of this world. If men abandon themselves to all sorts of lusts, we cannot wonder that the apostle should call them *cursed children*.

IV. The apostle (*v.* 15, 16) proves that they are *cursed children*. They *have forsaken the right way*. They have gone into a wrong way: they have erred and strayed from the way of life. This he makes out by showing it to be *the way of Balaam, the son of Bosor*. The love of riches and honour turned Balaam out of the way of his duty, although he knew that the way he took displeased the Lord. Hardened sinners sometimes meet with rebukes for their iniquity. God stops them in their way. If rebuking a sinner for his iniquity would have made a man return to his duty, surely the rebuke of Balaam must have produced this effect. *The dumb ass* is enabled to speak, and she exposes *the madness* of his conduct and opposes his going on in this evil way, and yet all in vain.

V. The apostle proceeds (*v.* 17) to a further description of seducing teachers.

1. As *wells*, or fountains, *without water*. The word of truth is the water of life, but these deceivers are set upon spreading and promoting error, and therefore are set forth as empty, because there is no truth in them.

2. As *clouds carried with a tempest*. These are clouds which yield no rain, for they are driven with the wind, but not of the Spirit, but the stormy tempest of their own ambition. Clouds obstruct the light of the sun, and darken the air, and, seeing these men are for promoting darkness in this world, it is very just that the mist of darkness should be their portion in the next. They allure those they deal with. It is *with great swelling words of vanity* which have a great sound but little sense. They work upon *the corrupt affections* and *carnal fleshly lusts of men*. By application and industry men attain a skilfulness and dexterity in promoting error. They are as artful and as successful as the fisher, who makes angling his daily employment. Persons who have for a while adhered to the truth, and kept clear of errors, may be so far deceived as to fall into those errors they had for a while *clean escaped*. To prevent these men's gaining proselytes, he tells us that they are the servants of corruption; their own lusts have gotten a complete victory over them, and they are actually in bondage to them. This consideration should prevent our being led away by these seducers; and to this he adds another (*v.* 20). It is a real detriment to those who have clean escaped from those who live in error, for hereby their latter end is made worse than their beginning. Some men are, for a time, *kept from the pollutions of the world, by the knowledge of Christ*. A religious education has restrained many whom the grace of God has not renewed, but we must receive the love of the truth, and hide God's word in our heart, or it will not sanctify and save us. When men are once entangled, they are easily overcome. If men who have once *escaped are again entangled, the latter end is worse with them than the beginning.*

VI. A state of apostasy is worse than a state of ignorance; for it is a *condemning of the way of right-* *eousness*, after they have had some knowledge of it. The misery of such deserters of Christ and his gospel is more intolerable than that of other offenders. God is more highly provoked by those who by their conduct despise the gospel, and pour contempt upon his grace. No wonder it should be so when they have licked up their own vomit again, returning to the same impieties that they had once cast off, and wallowing in that filthiness from which they appeared once to be really cleansed.

CHAPTER 3

The apostle begins this last chapter with repeating the account of his design in writing a second time to them, ver. 1-2. II. One thing that induced him to write this second epistle, namely, the coming of scoffers, ver. 3-7. III. He instructs them in the coming of our Lord Jesus Christ to judgment, ver. 8-10. IV. The use Christians ought to make of Christ's second coming, ver. 11-18.

Verses 1, 2

The better to recommend the matter, he tells them that what he would have them to remember are, *The words spoken by the holy prophets*, who were divinely inspired. *The commandments of the apostles of the Lord and Saviour*. What God has spoken by the prophets of the Old Testament, and Christ has commanded by the apostles of the New, cannot but demand and deserve to be frequently remembered. It is by these things the pure minds of Christians are to be stirred up.

Verses 3–7

There will be *scoffers*, men who will *make a mock of sin*, and of salvation from it. God's way of saving sinners by Jesus Christ is what men will scoff at, and that *in the last days*, under the gospel. The spirituality and simplicity of New Testament worship are directly contrary to the carnal mind of man. This is mentioned as a thing well known to all Christians.

I. What sort of persons they are: they *walk after their own lusts*, they follow the devices and desires of their own hearts. They live as they list, and they speak as they list. As they will walk in their own way, and talk their own language, so will they also think their own thoughts, and form principles which are altogether their own.

II. They will scoffingly say, *Where is the promise of his coming?* (*v.* 4). Without this, all the other articles of the Christian faith will signify very little; this is that which fills up and gives the finishing stroke to all the rest. Till our Lord shall have come, they will not themselves believe that he will come; nay, they will laugh at the very mention of his second coming. The believer not only desires that he may come, but, having a promise that he will come, he is also firmly and fully persuaded that he will come: on the other hand, these seducers, because they wish he never may, therefore do all that in them lies to cheat themselves and others into a persuasion that he never will come. They will laugh at that very promise: *Where is the promise*, say they, *of his coming?*

III. While they laugh they will pretend to argue too, *v.* 4. This is a subtle, though not a solid way of reasoning; it is apt to make impressions upon weak minds, and especially upon wicked hearts. Those are all dead to whom *the promise was made*, and it was never made good in their time, and there is no likelihood that it ever will be in any time; why should we trouble ourselves about it? To this very day *all things continue as they were*, without any change, even *from the beginning of the creation*. What he never has done they would conclude he never can do or never will.

IV. The apostle puts us in remembrance of a change already past, which was the drowning of the world in the days of Noah. *This they willingly are ignorant* of (*v.* 5), they choose to pass it over in silence. It is hard to persuade men to believe what they are not willing to find true. They do not know because they do not care to know. But let not sinners think that such ignorance as this will be admitted as an excuse for whatever sin it may betray them into.

1. The apostle's account of the destruction which has once already come upon the world (*v.* 5, 6). At the time of the universal deluge, the case is strangely altered; the waters which God had divided before, now does he, in anger, throw together again in a heap. All this was done by the word of God; it was by his powerful word that the world was made at first. *By the word of the Lord the heavens were of old and the earth standing out of the water and in the water.* The after-confusion and ruin of the world, as well as the utter destruction of its inhabitants, were also by the same word. This was the change which God had before brought upon the world, and which these scoffers had overlooked.

2. What the apostle says of the destructive change which is yet to come upon it, *v.* 7. Here we have an awful account of the final dissolution of the world. The judgment here spoken of is yet to come, and will surely come, though we know not when. That the world has once been destroyed by a universal deluge renders it the more credible that it may be again ruined by a universal conflagration. Let therefore the scoffers, who laugh at the coming of our Lord to judgment, at least consider that it *may be. The heavens and the earth which now are, are kept in store.* They are *reserved unto fire.* The day of judgment is the day of *the perdition of ungodly men.* Those who now scoff at a future judgment shall find it a day of vengeance. "Give diligence therefore to be found in Christ, that that may be a time of refreshment and day of redemption to you."

Verse 8

We may clearly discern the tenderness and affection wherewith he speaks to them, calling them *beloved*; he had a compassionate concern and a love of good-will for the ungodly wretches who refused to believe divine revelation, but he has a peculiar respect for the true believers.

I. The truth which the apostle asserts—*that with the Lord one day is as a thousand years, and a thousand years are as one day.* All things past, present, and future, are ever before him.

II. The importance of this truth: This is the *one thing* the apostle would not have us ignorant of. This is a truth that belongs to our peace, and therefore he endeavours that it may not be hidden from our eyes; as it is in the original, *Let not this one thing be hidden from you.* Yet how hard is it to conceive of eternity!

Verses 9, 10

We are here told that *the Lord is not slack*—he does not delay beyond the appointed time; he will keep to the time appointed in coming to judge the world. Good men are apt to think God stays beyond the appointed time, that is, the time which they have set, but they set one time and God sets another.

I. What men count slackness is truly *longsuffering*, and that *to us-ward*; it is giving more time to his own people that they may bring glory to God, and improve in a meetness for heaven; for God is not willing that any of these should perish, but that all of them should come to repentance. God has no delight in the death of sinners. His goodness and forbearance do in their own nature call to repentance all those to whom they are exercised; and, if men continue impenitent when God gives them space to repent, he will deal more severely with them.

II. *The day of the Lord will come as a thief in the night, v.* 10. 1. The certainty of the day of the Lord.

The day has not yet come, it assuredly will come. God has *appointed a day* and he will keep his appointment. 2. The suddenness of this day: It *will come as a thief in the night*, at a time when men are sleeping and secure. The time which men think to be the most improper and unlikely, and when therefore they are most secure, will be the time of the Lord's coming. 3. The solemnity of this coming. *The heavens shall pass away with a great noise. The elements shall melt with fervent heat. The earth also, and all the works that are therein, shall be burnt up.* All must pass through the fire, which shall be a consuming fire to all that sin has brought into the world, though it may be but a refining fire to the works of God's hand.

What a difference there will be between the first coming of Christ and the second! May we be so wise as to prepare for it, that it may not be a day of vengeance and destruction unto us.

Verses 11–18

The apostle, having instructed them in the doctrine of Christ's second coming,

I. Takes occasion thence to exhort them to purity and godliness in their whole conversation. *Seeing all these things must be dissolved, how holy should we be.* Inasmuch as this dissolution is in order to their being restored to their primitive beauty and excellency, how pure and holy should we be, in order to our being fit for the *new heaven and new earth, wherein dwelleth righteousness!* Those things which we now see must in a little while pass away, and be no more as they now are: let us look therefore at what shall abide and continue. This *looking for the day of God* is one of the directions the apostle gives us, in order to our being eminently *holy and godly in all manner of conversation. The coming of the day of God* is what every Christian must hope for and earnestly expect. Though it cannot but affright the ungodly to see the visible heavens and the elements melting, yet the believer can rejoice in hope of more glorious heavens after these have been refined by that dreadful fire which shall burn up all the dross of this visible creation. 1. What true Christians look for: *new heavens and a new earth.* In these new heavens and earth only righteousness shall dwell. 2. What is the ground and foundation of this expectation and hope—*the promise of God.* To look for anything which God has not promised is presumption; but if our expectations are according to the promise, we cannot meet with a disappointment.

II. In *v.* 14 he resumes his exhortation from the consideration that they shall be again renewed. It nearly concerns you to see in what state you will be when the Judge of all the world shall come to pass sentence upon men, therefore get ready to *appear before the judgment-seat of Christ.*

1. "That you be *found of him in peace*, in a state of peace and reconciliation with God through Christ. Those whose sins are pardoned and their peace made with God are the only safe and happy people; therefore follow after peace." Peace with God through our Lord Jesus Christ. Peace in our own consciences. Peace with men.

2. That you be *found of Christ without spot, and blameless. Follow after holiness* as well as peace. We must be pressing towards spotless purity, absolute perfection. Christians must be *perfecting holiness.* It is only the diligent Christian who will be the happy Christian in the day of the Lord. He will certainly reward us if we be diligent in the work he has allotted us; now, that you may be diligent, *account the longsuffering of our Lord to be salvation.* "Does your Lord delay his coming? It is so much space to repent that men may have time to prepare for eternity." Our apostle quotes St. Paul as directing men to make the same good use of the divine forbearance. What an

honourable mention does this apostle of the circumcision make of that very man who had openly, *before all, reproved him*. He calls him *brother*, not only that he is a fellow-christian, but a fellow-apostle. Though many seducing teachers denied Paul's apostleship, yet Peter owns him to be an apostle. He calls him *beloved*. He mentions Paul as one who had an uncommon measure of wisdom given unto him. How desirable is it that those who preach the same gospel should treat one another according to the pattern Peter here sets them! (1) The excellent wisdom that was in Paul is said to be *given* him. The understanding and knowledge that qualify men to preach the gospel are the gift of God. (2) The apostle imparts to men according as he had received from God. He endeavours to lead others as far as he himself was led into the knowledge of the mysteries of the gospel. But the apostle Peter proceeds to tell us that in those things which are to be met with in Paul's epistles there are some things hard to be understood. Some are not easy to be understood because of their own obscurity, others cannot be so easily understood because of their excellency and sublimity, and others are with difficulty taken in because of the weakness of men's minds. And here the unlearned and unstable make wretched work; for they wrest and torture the scriptures. Those who are not well instructed and well established in the truth are in great danger of perverting the word of God. Where there is a divine power to establish as well as to instruct men in divine truth, persons are effectually secured from falling into errors. How great a blessing this is we learn by observing what is the pernicious consequence of the errors that ignorant and unstable men fall into—even their own destruction.

III. The apostle gives them a word of caution, *v.* 17, 18.

1. The knowledge we have of these things should make us very watchful, inasmuch as there is a twofold danger, *v.* 17. (1) We are in great danger *of* being seduced, and turned away from the truth. Many who have the scriptures and read them do not understand what they read; and too many of those who have a right understanding are not established in the belief of the truth, and all these are liable to fall into error. (2) We are in great danger *by* being seduced. If men corrupt the word of God, it tends to their own utter ruin. When men wrest the word of God, *they fall into the error of the wicked*. If we imbibe their opinions, we shall too soon imitate their practices. Those who are led away by error *fall from their own steadfastness*. They are wholly unhinged and unsettled, and know not where to rest.

2. The apostle directs us what to do, *v.* 18. We must *grow in grace*. By how much the stronger grace is in us, by so much the more steadfast shall we be in the truth. We must grow *in the knowledge of our Lord Jesus Christ*. Such a knowledge of Christ as conforms us more to him, and endears him more to us, must needs preserve us from falling off in times of general apostasy. *To him be glory both now and for ever. Amen.*

AN EXPOSITION, WITH PRACTICAL OBSERVATIONS, OF

THE FIRST EPISTLE GENERAL OF

JOHN

The continued tradition of the church attests that this epistle came from John the apostle. There is scarcely a critic or competent judge of diction, or style of argument and spirit, but will adjudge this epistle to the writer of that gospel that bears the name of the apostle John.

The epistle is styled *general*, as being not inscribed to any particular church; it is, as a circular letter sent to divers churches in order to confirm them in their steadfast adherence to the Lord Christ, against seducers; and to instigate them to adorn that doctrine by love to God and man, and particularly to each other.

CHAPTER 1

Concerning Christ's person and excellency, ver. 1, 2. The knowledge thereof gives us communion with God and Christ (ver. 3), and joy, ver. 4. A description of God, ver. 5. How we are thereupon to walk, ver. 6. The benefit of such walking, ver. 7. The way to forgiveness, ver. 9. The evil of denying our sin, ver. 8–10.

Verses 1–4

I. An account of the Mediator's person. 1. *As the Word of life, v.* 1. He is not a mere vocal word, but a vital one: *the Word of life.* 2. *As eternal life*, He was from eternity. He is the eternal Word of the eternal living Father. 3. *As life manifested (v.* 2), manifested in the flesh. Kindness indeed, that eternal life should come to visit mortals, and to procure eternal life for them, and then confer it on them!

II. The evidences that the apostle and his brethren had of the Mediator's presence in this world. *The life, the word of life, the eternal life*, as such, could not be seen and felt; but the life manifested might be, and was so. 1. To their ears, *v.* 1, 3. The life assumed a mouth and tongue, that he might utter words of life. The divine word would employ the ear, and the ear should be devoted to the word of life. 2. To their eyes, *v.* 1–3. The Word would become visible, would not only be heard, but seen *with our eyes*—with all the use and exercise that we could make of our eyes. His apostles must be eye-witnesses as well as ear-witnesses of him. 3. To their internal sense, to the eyes of their mind: for so (possibly) may the next clause be interpreted: *Which we have looked upon.* The word is not applied to the immediate object of the eye, but to that which was rationally collected from what they saw. The senses are to be the informers of the mind. 4. To their hands and sense of feeling: *And our hands have handled of the Word of life.* The invisible life and Word was no despiser of the testimony of sense. Sense is a means that God has appointed for our information. Our Lord took care to satisfy all the senses of his apostles, that they might be the more authentic witnesses of him to the world. The apostles could not be deceived in such long and various exercise of their sense. Sense must minister to reason and judgment; and reason and judgment must minister to the reception of the Lord Jesus Christ and his gospel.

III. The apostles publish these assurances for our satisfaction, *v.* 2, 3. It became the apostles to open to the disciples the evidence by which they were led. It concerned the disciples to be well assured of the truth of the institution they had embraced. They should see the evidences of their holy religion.

IV. The reason of the apostle's asserting this summary of sacred faith.

1. That the believers of it may be advanced to the same happiness with them (with the apostles themselves), *v.* 3. It is communion with heaven, and in

blessings that come thence and tend thither. There is a communion (or common participation of privilege and dignity) belonging to all saints, from the highest apostle to the lowest believer. What it is and where it is: *And truly our fellowship* (or communion) *is with the Father and his Son Jesus Christ.* See to what the gospel revelation tends—to advance us far above sin and earth and to carry us to blessed communion with the Father and the Son. See for what end the eternal life was made flesh—that he might advance us to eternal life in communion with the Father and himself.

2. That believers may be enlarged and advanced in holy joy, *v.* 4. The mystery of the Christian religion is for the joy of mortals. Those live beneath the use and end of the Christian revelation who are not filled with spiritual joy. Were they confirmed in their holy faith, how would they rejoice!

Verses 5–7

I. Here is the message from the Lord Jesus (*v.* 5). The apostles are the messengers of the Lord Jesus; it is their honour to bring his messages to the world. He that put on human nature will honour earthen vessels. It was the ambition of the apostles faithfully to deliver the messages they had received. The present one is this—*That God is light, and in him is no darkness at all.* He is all that beauty and perfection that can be represented to us by light. There is no defect or imperfection, *v.* 5. It is meet that to this dark world the great God should be represented as pure and perfect light. What more could be included in one word than in this, *God is light, and in him is no darkness at all?*

II. There is a just conclusion to be drawn from this message. 1. For the conviction of such professors as have no true fellowship with God: *If we say we have fellowship with him, and walk in darkness, we lie, and do not the truth.* To walk in darkness is to live and act according to such ignorance, and erroneous practice, as are contrary to our holy religion. They may profess to have communion with God; and yet their lives may be irreligious, immoral, and impure. To such the apostle would not fear to give the lie: *They lie, and do not the truth.* Their practice gives their profession and pretences the lie, and demonstrates the folly and falsehood of them. 2. For the conviction and consequent satisfaction of those that are near to God: *But, if we walk in the light, we have fellowship one with another, and the blood of Jesus Christ his Son cleanseth us from all sin.* Those that so walk show that they know God. *Then we have fellowship one with another*, they with us and we with them, and both with God. *The blood of Jesus Christ his Son cleanseth us from all sin.* His blood procures for us those sacred influences by which sin is to be subdued more and more, till it is quite abolished.

Verses 8–10

I. The apostle, having supposed that even those of this heavenly communion have yet their sin, proceeds here to justify that supposition, *v.* 8. We must beware of deceiving ourselves in denying or excusing our sins. The Christian religion is the religion of sinners. The Christian life is a life of continued repentance, of continual faith in, thankfulness for, and love to the Redeemer, *v.* 10. The denial of our sin not only deceives ourselves, it challenges his veracity. God has given his testimony to the continued sinfulness of the world, by providing a sacrifice for sin, that will be needed in all ages, and to the continued sinfulness of believers themselves by requiring them continually to confess their sins.

II. The way to the continued pardon of the believer's sin. 1. His duty in order thereto, *v.* 9. Penitent confession and acknowledgment of sin are the means of his deliverance from his guilt. 2. His encouragement thereto. This is the righteousness, and clemency of God, to whom he makes such confession, *v.* 9. God is faithful to his word, wherein he has promised forgiveness to penitent believing confessors. He is clement and gracious also, and so will forgive, to the contrite confessor, all his sins and cleanse him from the guilt of all unrighteousness.

CHAPTER 2

Here the apostle encourages against sins of infirmity (ver. 1, 2), shows the true knowledge and love of God (ver. 3–6), renews the precept for fraternal love (ver. 7–11), addresses the several ages of Christians (ver. 12–14), warns against worldly love (ver. 15–17), against seducers (ver. 18, 19), shows the security of true Christians (ver. 20–27), and advises to abide in Christ, ver. 28, 29.

Verses 1, 2

He gives them both dissuasion and support.

1. Dissuasion. He would leave no room for sin, *v.* 1. The design of this letter is to dissuade and drive them from sin. See the familiar affectionate compellation with which he introduces his admonition. Certainly the gospel most prevailed where such ministerial love most abounded.

II. The believer's support and relief in case of sin, *v.* 1. Believers themselves have yet their sins. There are some who, though they really sin, yet, in comparison with others, are said *not to sin.* And this must be the support and refuge of believers: *We have an Advocate.* Here is an advocate in heaven and with the Father. The Judge with whom our advocate pleads is the Father. He who was our Judge in the legal court (the court of the violated law) is our Father in the gospel court, the court of heaven and of grace. His throne or tribunal is the mercy-seat. Our advocate is recommended to us upon these considerations: 1. By his person and personal names. *It is Jesus Christ the Son of the Father,* one anointed by the Father for the whole work of salvation, and consequently for that of the intercessor. 2. By his qualification for the office. *It is Jesus Christ the righteous.* The clients are guilty; their innocence and legal righteousness cannot be pleaded. It is the advocate's own righteousness that he must plead for the criminals. He has been righteous to the death, righteous for them. Upon this score he pleads, that the clients' sins may not be imputed to them. 3. By the plea he has to make, the ground and basis of his advocacy, *v.* 2. He is the propitiatory sacrifice. The Mediator of intercession, the Advocate for us, is the Mediator of redemption, the propitiation for our sins. It is his propitiation that he pleads. *He ever lives to make intercession for those that come*

to God through him. 4. By the extent of his plea. It is not confined to one nation, *v.* 2; not only for the past, or us present believers, but for the sins of all who shall hereafter come to God through him. The extent and intent of the Mediator's death reach to all tribes, nations, and countries.

Verses 3–6

Here now succeeds the trial or test of our light and of our love.

I. The trial of our light, *v.* 3. Divine light and knowledge are the beauty and improvement of the mind. Young Christians are apt to magnify their new light and applaud their own knowledge; and old ones are apt to suspect the sufficiency and fulness of their knowledge. Here is the evidence of the soundness of our knowledge, if it constrain us to *keep God's commandments.* A careful conscientious obedience to his commands shows that the apprehension and knowledge of these things are graciously impressed upon the soul; and therefore it must follow in the reverse that *he that saith, I know him, and keepeth not his commandments, is a liar, and the truth is not in him, v.* 4. A disobedient life is the confutation and shame of pretended religious knowledge.

II. The trial of our love, *v.* 5. To keep the word of God, or of Christ, is sacredly to attend thereto in all the conduct and motion of life; in him that does so is the love of God perfected. The phrase denotes here our love to God; so *v.* 15, so *ch.* iii. 17. We know that we belong to him, and that we are united to him by that Spirit which assists us to this obedience; and if we acknowledge our relation to him, and our union with him, it must have this continued enforcement upon us: *He that saith he abideth in him ought himself to walk even as he walked, v.* 6. Those who profess to be on his side, and to abide with him, must walk with him, walk after his pattern and example.

Verses 7–11

The precept of fraternal love is recommended,

I. As an old one, *v.* 7. The precept of love must be as old as human nature. And so it is the *old commandment.*

II. As a new one: "*Again, a new commandment I write unto you, which thing is true in him,* and it is true *in you;* this law is in some measure written upon your hearts; you are taught of God to love one another, and that *because the darkness is past,* your deplorable ignorance of God and of Christ is now past, *and the true light now shineth*" (*v.* 8). We should see that that grace which was true in Christ be true also in us. The more our darkness is past, and gospel light shines unto us, the deeper should our subjection be to the commandments of our Lord, whether considered as old or new. Another trial of our Christian light; before, it was to be approved by obedience to God; here by Christian love. 1. He who wants such love in vain pretends his light, *v.* 9. These cannot be swayed by the sense of the love of Christ to their brethren, and therefore remain in their dark state. 2. He who is governed by such love approves his light to be good and genuine, *v.* 10. He sees how meet it is that we should love those whom Christ hath loved; *there is no occasion of stumbling in him* (*v.* 10). Christian love teaches us highly to value our brother's soul, and to dread everything that will be injurious to his innocence and peace. 3. Hatred is a sign of spiritual darkness, *v.* 11. He then who is possessed with malignity towards a Christian brother must needs be destitute of spiritual light; consequently *he walks in darkness, and he knows not whither he goes, because darkness hath blinded his eyes, v.* 11. It is the Lord Jesus that is the great Master of love: it is his school that is the school of love. His disciples are the disciples of love, and his family must be the family of love.

Verses 12–17

I. All Christians are not of the same standing and stature; there are babes in Christ, there are grown men, and old disciples. There are precepts and a correspondent obedience common to them all, as particularly mutual love and contempt of the world. 1. The lowest in the Christian school, v. 12. There are novices in religion, babes in Christ. He addresses *the children* in Christianity, (1) *Because their sins were forgiven them for his name's sake*, v. 12. The youngest sincere disciple is pardoned. Sins are forgiven either for God's 'name's sake, or *for Christ's name's sake*, and those that are forgiven of God are strongly obliged to relinquish this world. (2) Because of their knowledge of God, v. 13. We say, It is a wise child that knows his father. These children cannot but know theirs. Those that know the Father may well be withdrawn from the love of this world. 2. To those of the highest station, to the seniors in Christianity (v. 13, 14). The apostle immediately passes from the bottom to the top of the school. Those that are of longest standing in Christ's school have need of further advice and instruction. None are too old to learn. He writes to them upon the account of their knowledge, v. 13, 14. Those who know him that was from the beginning may well be induced thereby to relinquish this world. 3. To the middle age of Christians, v. 13, 14. There are the adults in Christ Jesus. The apostle applies to them, (1) Upon the account of their martial exploits. Dexterous soldiers they are in the camp of Christ, v. 13. Those that are well taught in Christ's school can handle their arms and vanquish the evil one; and those that can vanquish him may be called to vanquish the world too. (2) Upon the account of their strength, discovered in this their achievement, v. 14. Young men are wont to glory in their strength. It will be their glory, and it will try their strength, to overcome the devil. The same strength must be exerted in overcoming the world as is employed in overcoming the devil. (3) Because of their acquaintance with the word of God, v. 14. Those in whom the word of God dwells are well furnished for the conquest of the world. II. A caution fundamental to vital practical religion, v. 15. Be crucified to the world. Their love should be reserved for God; throw it not away upon the world. The reasons of this dissuasion and caution. 1. The inconsistency of this love with the love of God, v. 15. The heart of man is narrow, and cannot contain both loves. 2. The prohibition of worldly love or lust; it is not ordained of God, v. 16. This love or lust is not appointed of God but it intrudes itself from the world. The things of the world are distinguished into three classes, according to the three predominant inclinations of depraved nature, (1) There is *the lust of the flesh.* This lust is usually called *luxury.* (2) There is *the lust of the eyes.* This is the lust of covetousness. (3) There is *the pride of life.* This is ambition. The objects of these appetites must be abandoned and renounced, v. 16. The Father disallows them. The lust or appetite to these things must be mortified and subdued. 3. The vain and vanishing state of earthly things, v. 17. The things of the world are fading and dying apace. 4. The immortality of the lover of God, v. 17. The object of his love in opposition to *the world* that *passeth away*, abideth for ever. Love shall never fail; and he himself is an heir of immortality and endless life.

Verses 18, 19

I. The end is coming, v. 18. It is meet that the disciples should be warned of the haste and end of time.

II. The sign of this last time (v. 18), that many oppose the kingdom of Christ. It should be no great offence nor prejudice to the disciples that there are such antichrists: 1. One great one has been foretold, v. 18. *Even now there are many antichrists*, the mystery of iniquity already worketh. 2. They were foretold also as the sign of this last time, v. 18.

III. Some account of these seducers or antichrists: "*They went out from us* (v. 19), from our company and communion." The purest churches may have their apostates. "*For, if they had been of us, they would have continued with us* (v. 19); had the sacred truth been rooted in their hearts it would have held them with us." Those that apostatize from religion sufficiently indicate that, before, they were hypocrites in religion. *But* this was done (or *they went out) that they might be made manifest that they were not all of us*, v. 19. Some of the hypocritical must be manifested here, and that for their own shame and benefit too, in their reduction to the truth.

Verses 20–27

Here, I. The apostle encourages the disciples in this hour of seducers. *But you have an unction from the Holy One, and you know all* things. 1. The blessing wherewith they were enriched: *You have an unction.* True Christians are anointed ones, their name intimates as much. They are anointed by the Spirit of grace. 2. From whom this blessing comes—*from the Holy One.* The Lord Christ disposes of the graces of the divine Spirit, and he anoints the disciples to make them like himself. 3. The effect of this unction: "*And thereby you know all things* (v. 20), all these things concerning Christ and his religion."

II. The mind and meaning with which he wrote to them. 1. By way of negation; not as suspecting their knowledge, v. 21. It is good to surmise well concerning our Christian brethren. A just confidence in religious persons may both encourage and contribute to their fidelity. 2. By way of assertion, *But because you know it* (you know *the truth in Jesus), and that no lie is of the truth.* Those who know the truth in any respect are thereby prepared to discern what is inconsistent therewith. No lie belongs to religion, either natural or revealed. *No lie is of the truth;* frauds and impostures then are very unfit means to support and propagate the truth.

III. The apostle further arraigns these seducers. 1. They are *liars: Who is a liar, but ye that denieth that Jesus is the Christ?* There is no truth so sacred and fully attested but some or other will contradict or deny it. 2. They are direct enemies to God as well as to the Lord Christ, v. 22. He that opposes Christ denies the witness and testimony of the father. The apostle may well infer, *Whosoever denies the Son the same has not the Father. But he that acknowledgeth the Son has the Father also*, v. 23.

IV. The apostle advises the disciples to continue in the old doctrines at first communicated to them, v. 24. Truth is older than error. The truth concerning Christ, that was at first delivered to the saints, is not to be exchanged for novelties. The Christian truth may plead antiquity, and be recommended thereby. 1. The sacred advantage they will receive by adhering to the primitive truth and faith. (1) They will continue thereby in holy union with God and Christ, v. 24. It is the truth of Christ abiding in us that is the means of severing us from sin and uniting us to the Son of God. (2) They will thereby secure the promise of eternal life, v. 25. Great is the promise that God makes to his faithful adherents. It is *eternal life*, which none but God can give. 2. The design of the apostle's writing to them. This letter is to fortify them against the deceivers of the age (v. 26), and therefore, if you continue not in what *you have heard from the beginning*, my writing and service will be in vain.

3. The instructive blessing they had received from heaven, *v.* 27. True Christians have an inward confirmation of the divine truth they have imbibed. This sacred chrism is commended on these accounts: (1) It is durable and lasting, *v.* 27. Divine illumination must be something continued. Temptations, snares, and seductions, arise. The anointing must abide. (2) It is better than human instruction, *v.* 27. You were instructed by us before you were anointed; but now our teaching is nothing in comparison to that. (3) It is a sure evidence of truth, *v.* 27. The Holy Spirit must needs be *the Spirit of truth*. The Spirit of truth will not lie; and he teacheth all things. (4) It will preserve those in whom it abides against seducers and their seduction, *v.* 27. It teaches you to abide in Christ; and, as it teaches you, it secures you.

Verses 28, 29

And now, little children, abide in him, *v.* 28. He would persuade by love, and prevail by endearment as well as by reason. Those that are anointed by the Lord Jesus are highly obliged to abide with him. This duty of perseverance and constancy is strongly urged: 1. From the consideration of his return at the great day of account, *v.* 28. It is here taken for granted that the Lord Jesus will come again. This was part of that truth they had heard from the beginning. Those who have continued with him throughout all their temptations shall have confidence, and joy, in the sight of him. On the contrary, those that have deserted him *shall be ashamed before him*. The apostle includes himself in the number. "Let not us be ashamed of you," as well as, "you will not be ashamed of yourselves." 2. From the consideration of the dignity of those who still adhere to Christ, *v.* 29. He that doeth righteousness may here be justly enough assumed as another name for him that abideth in Christ. Such a one must needs *be born of him*. He is renewed by the Spirit of Christ, after the image of Christ. He that is constant to the practice of religion in trying times gives good evidence that he is born from above, from the Lord Christ.

CHAPTER 3

The love of God in our adoption, ver. 1, 2. He thereupon argues for holiness (ver. 3), and against sin, ver. 4–10. He presses brotherly love, ver. 11–18. How to assure our hearts before God, ver. 19–22. The precept of faith, ver. 23. And the good of obedience, ver. 24.

Verses 1–3

The apostle,

I. Breaks forth into the admiration of that grace that is the spring of such a wonderful vouchsafement: *Behold what manner of love the Father hath bestowed upon us, that we should be called the sons of God!* It is wonderful condescending love of the eternal Father, that such as we should be made and called his sons. Strange, that the holy God is not ashamed to be called our Father, and to call us his sons!

II. Infers the honour of believers above the cognizance of the world, *v.* 1. Little does the world perceive the happiness of the genuine followers of Christ. Little does the world think that these poor, humble, contemned ones are the favourites of heaven, and will be inhabitants there ere long. Their Lord was here unknown as well as they, *v.* 1. Let the followers of Christ be content with hard fare here, since they are in a land of strangers, among those who little know them, and their Lord was so treated before them.

III. Exalts these persevering disciples in the prospect of the certain revelation of their state and dignity.

1. Their present honourable relation is asserted, *v.* 2. We have the nature of sons by regeneration. 2. The glory pertaining to the sonship and adoption is reserved for another world. The sons of God must walk by faith, and live by hope. 3. The time of the revelation of the sons of God is determined: *But we know that when he shall appear we shall be like him*. The sons of God will be known and be made manifest by their likeness to their head. 4. Their likeness to him is argued from the sight they shall have of him: *We shall be like him, for we shall see him as he is*. All shall see him, but not as *he is*, to those in heaven. The wicked shall see him in his frowns; but these shall see him in the smiles and beauty of his face. Their likeness shall enable them to see him as the blessed do in heaven.

IV. Urges to the prosecution of holiness, *v.* 3. The sons of God know that their Lord is holy and pure. Those then who hope to live with him must study the utmost purity, their hope of heaven will dictate and constrain them so to do. It is a contradiction to such hope to indulge sin and impurity. As we are sanctified by faith, we must be sanctified by hope. That we may be saved by hope we must be purified by hope.

Verses 4–10

Multiplied arguments against sin, and all communion with the works of darkness.

I. From the nature of sin. It is a contrariety to the divine law, *v.* 4. Commission of sin now is the rejection of the divine law, and this is the rejection of the divine authority, and consequently of God himself.

II. From the errand of the Lord Jesus in this world, which was to remove sin, *v.* 5. He takes sin away, that he may conform us to himself, *and in him is no sin*. Those that expect communion with Christ above should study communion with him here in the utmost purity.

III. From the opposition between sin and a real union with the Lord Christ, *v.* 6. He that abideth in Christ continues not in the practice of sin. Those that abide in Christ abide in their covenant with him. They abide in the potent light and knowledge of him; and therefore it may be concluded *that he that sinneth hath not seen him, neither known him*. Practical renunciation of sin is the great evidence of saving knowledge of the Lord Christ.

IV. From the connection between the practice of righteousness and a state of righteousness. The practice of sin and a justified state are inconsistent: "*Little children, let no man deceive you. He that doeth righteousness is righteous.*" It may appear that righteousness may in several places of scripture be justly rendered *religion*, as Matt. v. 10, *Blessed are those that are persecuted for righteousness' sake*, that is, for religion's sake. To do righteousness then is to practise religion. The practice of religion cannot subsist without a principle of integrity and conscience.

V. From the relation between the sinner and the devil, and thereupon from the design of the Lord Christ. 1. From the relation between the sinner and the devil. *To commit sin* is here to live under the power and dominion of it; and he who does so *is of the devil*. 2. From the design and office of the Lord Christ against the devil, *v.* 8. He came into our world that he might conquer him. Sin will he loosen and dissolve more and more, till he has quite destroyed it. Let not us serve or indulge what the Son of God came to destroy.

VI. From the connection between regeneration and the relinquishment of sin: *Whosoever is born of God doth not commit sin*. To be born of God is to be inwardly renewed, and restored to a holy rectitude of nature by the power of the Spirit of God. *Such a* one committeth not sin, his seed remaineth in him. Renewing grace is an abiding principle. Religion is not an art, an acquired dexterity and skill, but a new nature. And thereupon the consequence is the regenerate person *cannot sin*. He cannot continue in the course and practice of sin. And the reason is *because he is born of God*. There is that light in his mind which shows him the evil and malignity of sin. There is that bias upon his heart which disposes him to loathe and hate sin. There is the spiritual disposition, that breaks the force and fulness of the sinful acts. It is not reckoned the person's sin, in the gospel account, where the bent and frame of the mind and spirit are against it. The unregenerate person is morally unable for what is religiously good. The regenerate person is happily disabled for sin.

VII. From the discrimination between the children of God and the children of the devil. They have their distinct characters, v. 10. Now the seed of the serpent is known: 1. By neglect of religion: *Whosoever doeth not righteously is not of God*, but, on the contrary, of the devil. 2. By hatred of fellow-christians, v. 10.

Verses 11–13

I. He recommends fraternal Christian love, v. 11. We should love the Lord Jesus, and value his love, and consequently love all the objects of it.

II. He dissuades from what is contrary thereto and that by the example of Cain. He was as the first-born of the serpent's seed; was of *the wicked one*. He imitated and resembled the first wicked one, the devil. His ill-will had no restraint; it proceeded so far as to accomplish murder, v. 12. Sin, indulged, knows no bound. He was vexed with the superiority of Abel's service, and envied him the favour and acceptance he had with God. And for these he martyred his brother, v. 12. Ill-will will teach us to hate and revenge what we should admire and imitate.

III. He infers that it is no wonder that good men are so served now, v. 13. The serpentine nature still continues in the world. Wonder not then that the serpentine world hates and hisses at you.

Verses 14–19

The beloved apostle can scarcely touch upon the mention of sacred love, but he must enlarge upon the enforcement of it.

I. It is a mark of our transition into a state of life, v. 14. We may know it by the evidences of our faith in Christ, of which this love to our brethren is one. This love,

1. Supposes a general love to mankind. Mankind are to be loved: (1) As the excellent work of God, made by him, and made in wonderful resemblance of him. (2) As being beloved in Christ. A world so beloved of God should accordingly be loved by us. This love will include all due love to enemies themselves.

2. It includes a peculiar love to the Christian society. They are not so much loved for their own sakes as for the sake of God and Christ, who have loved them. This is the issue of faith in Christ, of our passage from death to life.

II. The hatred of our brethren is a sign of our deadly state, v. 14. This the apostle argues, v. 15. Hatred of the person is a hatred of life and welfare, and naturally tends to desire the extinction of it. Now he who by the disposition of his heart is a mur-derer *cannot have eternal life abiding in him*.

III. The example of God and Christ should inflame our hearts with this holy love, v. 16. The great God has given his Son to the death for us. Surely we should love those whom God hath loved, and so loved.

IV. The apostle proceeds to show us what should be the effect of this our Christian love. 1. It must be

so fervent as to make us willing to suffer even to death for the safety and salvation of the dear brethren, v. 16. How mortified should the Christian be to this life, and how well assured of a better! 2. It must be compassionate, liberal, and communicative to the necessities of the brethren, v. 17. Those who have this world's good must love a good God more, and their good brethren more, and be ready to distribute it for their sakes. This love to the brethren is love to God in them; and where there is none of this love to them there is no true love to God at all. There may be other fruits of this love, v. 18. Compliments and flatteries become not Christians; but the sincere expressions of sacred affection, and the services or labours of love, do.

V. This love will evince our sincerity in religion, and give us hope towards God, v. 19. It is a great happiness to be assured of our integrity in religion. The way to secure our inward peace, is to abound in love and in the works of love.

Verses 20–22

The apostle proceeds here,

I. To establish the court of conscience, v. 20. Our heart here is our self-reflecting judicial power, whereby we can take cognizance of ourselves, and accordingly pass a judgment upon our state towards God; and so it is the same with conscience. Conscience is God's vicegerent, calls the court in his name, and acts for him. If conscience condemn us, God does so too. God is a greater witness than our conscience, and knoweth more against us than it does: *he knoweth all things*. If conscience acquit us, God does so too (v. 21). Then have we assurance that he accepts us now, and will acquit us in the great day of account. Let conscience therefore be heard, be well-informed, and diligently attended to.

II. To indicate the privilege of those who have a good conscience towards God. They have interest in heaven; their suits are heard there, v. 22. Obedient souls are prepared for blessings, and they have promise of audience.

Verses 23–24

I. What his commandments are, v. 23. To discern what he is, according to his name, the Son of God, and the anointed Saviour of the world. To approve him in judgment and conscience. To consent to him as our Redeemer. To trust to him for the full discharge of his saving office. This faith is a needful requisite to those who would be prevalent petitioners with God, because it is by the Son that we must come to the Father. That we *love one another, as he gave us commandment*, v. 23. As goodwill to men was proclaimed from heaven, so goodwill to men must be carried in the hearts of those who go to God and heaven.

II. The blessedness of obedience to these commands. The obedient enjoy communion with God, v. 24. We dwell in God and God dwells in us. The trial of his divine inhabitation (v. 24), is by the frame of soul that he hath conferred upon us.

CHAPTER 4

The apostle exhorts to try spirits (ver. 1), gives a note to try by (ver. 2, 3), shows who are of the world and who of God (ver. 4–6), urges Christian love (ver. 7–16), describes our love to God, and the effect of it, ver. 17–21.

Verses 1–3

I. He calls the disciples to caution and scrutiny about the spirits that had now risen. 1. To caution: *"Beloved, believe not every spirit;* follow not every pretender to the Spirit of God."* There had been real communications from the divine Spirit and therefore others pretended thereto. 2. To scrutiny, to examination of the claims that are laid to the Spirit, *v.* 1. To the disciples is allowed a judgment of discretion. A reason is given for this trial, *v.* 1. It should not seem strange to us that false teachers set themselves up in the church: it was so in the apostles' times.

II. He gives a test whereby the disciples may try these pretending spirits. They were to be tried by their doctrine, *v.* 2. He who confesses and preaches Christ, does it by the Spirit of God. The sum of revealed religion is comprehended in the doctrine concerning Christ, his person and office. We see then the aggravation of a systematic opposition to him and it, *v.* 3. The anti-christian spirit began betimes, even in the apostles' days. But we have been forewarned that such opposition would arise, and the more we see the word of Christ fulfilled the more confirmed we should be in the truth of it.

Verses 4–6

The apostle encourages the disciples against this seducing antichristian spirit. He assures them of a more divine principle in them, *v.* 4, 6. *We are born of God.* He gives them hope of victory, *v.* 4. "There is a strong preserver within you, *v.* 4. The Spirit of God dwells in you, and that Spirit is more mighty than men or devils." The Spirit of God hath framed your mind for God and heaven; *but they are of the world, and therefore speak they of the world.* This worldly design procures them proselytes, *v.* 5. They are followed by such as themselves: the world will love its own, and its own will love it. "*He that knoweth God heareth us.* He who knows the purity and holiness of God, the love and grace of God, must know that he is with us; and he who knows this will attend to us, and abide with us. *He that is not of God heareth not us.* Thus you have a distinction between us and others," *v.* 6.

Verses 7–13

The Spirit of truth is known by love, *v.* 7. The apostle would unite them in his love, that he might unite them in love to each other.

I. The high and heavenly descent of love: *For love is of God, v.* 7. The Spirit of God is the Spirit of love. Love comes down from heaven.

II. Love argues a true apprehension of the divine nature, *v.* 7, 8. What attribute of the divine Majesty so clearly shines in all the world as his communicative goodness, which is love. *He that loveth not knoweth not God.* Knowledge of God dwells not in such a soul; *for God is love* (*v.* 8). Love is natural and essential to the divine Majesty: *God is love.* He hath loved us, such as we are (*v.* 9). Strange that God should love impure dust and ashes! He has loved us at such an incomparable value as he has given for us, *v.* 9. Mystery and miracle of divine love that such a Son should be sent into our world for us! God loved us first, *v.* 10. He loved us, when we had no love for him, when we lay in our guilt. He gave us his Son for such service and such an end. For such service, *to be the propitiation for our sins.* For such an end (*v.* 9), that we might live with God, and live in eternal glory and blessedness with him. O what love is here! III. Divine love to the brethren should constrain ours, *v.* 11. This should be an invincible argument. Shall we refuse to love those whom the eternal God hath loved? We should be admirers of his love, and lovers of his love, and consequently lovers of those whom he loves.

IV. The Christian love is an assurance of the divine inhabitation, *v.* 12. The sacred lovers of the brethren are the temples of God; the divine Majesty has a peculiar residence there.

V. Herein the divine love attains accomplishment in us, *v.* 12. God's love is not perfected in him, but in and with us. Faith is perfected by its works, and love perfected by its operations. When the divine love has wrought us to the love of God, and thereupon to the love of the brethren, for his sake, it is therein perfected. How ambitious should we be of this love, when God reckons his own love to us perfected thereby, *v.* 13. One would think that to speak of God dwelling in us, and we in him, were to use words too high for mortals, had not God gone before us therein. What it fully is must be left to the revelation of the blessed world. But this mutual inhabitation we know, says the apostle, *because he hath given us of his Spirit.*

Verses 14–16

I. The fundamental article of the Christian religion, *v.* 14. 1. The Lord Jesus's relation to God; he is Son to the Father. 2. His relation and office towards us—*the Saviour of the world.* 3. The ground on which he became so: *The Father sent the Son.* 4. The apostle's assurance of this—he and his brethren had seen it; they had seen the Son of God in his human nature. 5. The apostle's attestation of this: "*We have seen and do testify.*"

II. The excellent privilege attending the due acknowledgment of this truth, *v.* 15. He who thus confesses Christ, and God in him, is possessed by the Spirit of God.

III. God's love is thus seen and exerted in Christ Jesus, *v.* 16. The Christian revelation is the revelation of the divine love; the articles of our revealed faith are but so many articles relating to the divine love. The history of the Lord Christ is the history of God's love to us.

1. *God is love;* he is essential boundless love; he has incomprehensible love for us of this world, which he has demonstrated in the mission of his beloved Son. What will he not do then when he designs to demonstrate his love, that he himself is love? In such a dispensation as that of giving an eternal Son for us and to us, he will commend his love to us indeed. Then may it well be inscribed upon the whole creation of God, *God is love.*

2. *He that dwelleth in love dwelleth in God, and God in him.* He that dwells in sacred love has *the love of God shed abroad upon his heart*, and will ere long go to dwell with God for ever.

Verses 17–21

He recommends it in both the branches of it, both as love to God, and love to our brother.

I. As love to God. 1. It will give us peace and satisfaction of spirit in the day when it will be most needed, *v.* 17. There must be a day of universal judgment. Happy they who shall have boldness before the Judge at that day, who shall be able to lift up their heads, and to look him in the face, as knowing he is their friend. So may do the lovers of God. And we have this boldness towards Christ because of our conformity to him, *v.* 17. Love hath conformed us to him. 2. It prevents servile fear (*v.* 18); so far as love prevails, fear ceases. We must here distinguish between the fear of God and being afraid of him. The fear of God is often mentioned and commanded as the substance of religion. Such fear is consistent with love, yea, with perfect love. But then there is a being afraid of God, which arises from a sense of guilt; and so fear here may be rendered *dread*: *There is no dread in love.* Love puts off dread, and puts on joy in him; and, as love grows, joy grows too; so that *perfect love casteth out fear* or dread. They well know that God loves them, and they thereupon triumph in his love. *Because fear hath torment* (*v.* 18) —fear is known to be a disquieting passion, but perfect love casteth out torment, for it teaches the mind a perfect acquiescence in the beloved, and therefore perfect love casteth out fear. He that feareth is not made perfect in love, it is a sign that our love is far from being perfect. 3. We cannot but love so good a God, who loved us when we were both unloving and unlovely. The divine love stamped love upon our souls.

II. As love to our brother in Christ; such love is urged on these accounts: 1. As consonant to our Christian profession. In the profession of Christianity we profess to love God as the root of religion (*v.* 20). That such a one loves not God the apostle proves, *v.* 20. The eye is wont to affect the heart; things unseen less catch the mind, and thereby the heart. The member of Christ has much of God visible in him. How then shall the hater of a visible image of God pretend to love the invisible God himself? 2. As suitable to the express law of God, *v.* 21. We must love God originally and supremely, and others in him. It cannot but be a natural suitable obligation *that he who loves God should love his brother also.*

CHAPTER 5

I. The dignity of believers, ver. 1. II. Their obligation to love, ver. 1–3. III. Their victory, ver. 4, 5. IV. The confirmation of their faith, ver. 6–10. V. The advantage of their faith in eternal life, ver. 11–13. VI. The audience of their prayers, ver. 14–17. VII. Their preservation from sin and Satan, ver. 18. VIII. Their happy distinction from the world, ver. 19. IX. Their true knowledge of God (ver. 20), upon which they must depart from idols, ver. 21.

Verses 1–5

I. Our Christian brethren are nearly related to God; they are his children, *v.* 1. Here the Christian brother is, 1. Described by his faith; he that *believeth that Jesus is the Christ* accordingly yields himself up to his care and direction. 2. Dignified by his descent, *v.* 1. All believers, though by nature sinners, are spiritually descended from God, and accordingly are to be beloved, *v.* 1. It seems but natural that he who loves the Father should love the children also.

II. The apostle shows, 1. How we may discern the truth of our love to the regenerate. The ground of it must be our love to God, *v.* 2. Our love to them appears to be sound and genuine when we love them because they are God's children, and so in them God himself is loved. 2. How we may learn the truth of our love to God, *v.* 2. Then we truly love God: *For this is the love of God, that we keep his commandments;* and the keeping of his commandments requires a spirit delighting therein, *v.* 3. His commandments are thereby made easy and pleasant to us. 3. What is the result of regeneration, *v.* 4. He that is born of God is born *for God,* and consequently for another world. He can repel and conquer this, *v.* 4. Faith is the cause of victory. In and by faith we cleave to Christ in opposition to the world. It receives and derives strength from the object of it, the Son of God, for conquering the world.

III. It is the real Christian that is the true conqueror of the world, *v.* 5. He who believes that Jesus is the Son of God believes therein that Jesus came from God to be the Saviour of the world. And he who so believes must needs by this faith overcome the world. He sees it must be a great part of the Saviour's work, and of his own salvation, to be redeemed and rescued from this malignant world. He perceives that the Lord Jesus conquered the world, not for himself only, but for his followers. He is possessed with a spirit and disposition that cannot be satisfied with this world, that looks beyond it. It is the Christian revelation that is the great means of conquering the world, and gaining another that is blessed and eternal. The Saviour designs not this world for the inheritance and portion of his saved company. It is the real Christian that is the proper hero, who vanquishes

the world. Who in all the world but the believer on Jesus Christ can thus overcome the world?

Verses 6–9

The faith of the Christian believer had need to be well founded, and it is so; Christ brings his credentials along with him.

I. In the way and manner by which he came: *This is he that came by water and blood* (*v.* 6).

1. We are inwardly and outwardly defiled. Inwardly, by the pollution of sin in our nature. For our cleansing from this we need spiritual water. We are defiled outwardly by the guilt of sin upon our persons. From this we must be purged by atoning blood.

2. Both these ways of cleansing were represented in the old ceremonial institutions of God. Persons and things must be purified by water and blood.

3. Upon the death of Jesus Christ, his side being pierced with a soldier's spear, out of the wound there immediately issued water and blood. This the beloved apostle saw. Now this water and blood are comprehensive of all that is necessary to our salvation. By the water our souls are washed and purified. By the blood God is glorified, his law is honoured. By the blood we are justified, reconciled, and presented righteous to God. The water and the blood then comprehend all things that can be requisite to our salvation.

II. In the witness that attends him, *v.* 6. The apostle adds the commendation of this witness. He is the Spirit of God, and cannot lie. He is indeed the Spirit of truth. And that the Spirit is truth, and a witness worthy of all acceptation, appears in that he is a heavenly witness. But here,

1. We are stopped in our course by the contest there is about the genuineness of *v.* 7. It is alleged that many old Greek manuscripts have it not. We shall not here enter into the controversy. It can scarcely be supposed that, when the apostle is representing the Christian's faith in overcoming the world, and the foundation it relies upon in adhering to Jesus Christ, he should omit the supreme testimony that attended him (*v.* 9). Upon our present reading here is a noble enumeration of the several witnesses and testimonies supporting the truth of the Lord Jesus.

2. The apostle, having told us that the Spirit that bears witness to Christ is truth, shows us that he is so, by assuring us that he is in heaven, *v.* 7.

(1) Here is a trinity of heavenly witnesses, such as have testified and vouched to the world the authority of the Lord Jesus in his claims. The first that occurs in order is *the Father*; he set his seal to the commission of the Lord Christ all the while he was here. The second witness is the Word, a mysterious name. He must bear witness to the human nature, or to the man Christ Jesus. The third witness is the Holy Ghost. True and faithful must he be to whom the Spirit of holiness sets his seal. These are witnesses in heaven; and they bear record from heaven; and they are one.

(2) To these there is opposed, though with them joined, a trinity of witnesses on earth, *v.* 8. Of these witnesses the first is the *spirit*. The regeneration or renovation of souls is a testimony to the Saviour. It is a testimony on earth, because it continues with the church here. To this Spirit belong not only the regeneration and conversion of the church, but its progressive sanctification, victory over the world. The second is the *water*. This was before considered as a means of salvation, now as a testimony to the Saviour himself, and intimates his purity and purifying power. And so it seems to comprehend the testimony of John's baptism, who bore witness of him and to the purity of his own doctrine, by which souls are purified and washed. The baptism that he has appointed for the initiation of his disciples. The third witness is

the blood; this he shed, and this was our ransom. This testifies for Jesus Christ; in that it demonstrated unspeakable love to us; and none will deceive those whom they entirely love. In that it lays obligation on his disciples to suffer and die for him. This shows that neither he nor his kingdom is of this world. These are signified and sealed in the institution of his own supper. Such are the witnesses on earth. These three witnesses *agree in one*, in one and the same thing among themselves.

III. The apostle concludes, *v*. 9. *Here is the* witness whereby God hath testified of his Son. He has by himself proclaimed him to the world. The authority and acceptableness of his testimony. It is truth itself, of highest authority and most unquestionable infallibility. The application of the rule to the present case. *God, that cannot lie*, hath given sufficient assurance to the world that Jesus Christ is his Son, the Son of his love, to reconcile the world unto himself; he testified therefore the truth and divine origin of the Christian religion, and that it is the sure appointed way of bringing us to God.

Verses 10–13

I. The privilege and stability of the real Christian, *v*. 10. He hath not only the outward evidence that others have, but he hath in his own heart a testimony for Jesus Christ. He can allege what Christ and the truth of Christ have done for his soul and what he has seen and found in him. Christ is formed in him, and he is growing up to the fulness and perfection, or perfect image of Christ, in heaven.

II. The aggravation of the unbeliever's sin, the sin of unbelief, *v*. 10. He must believe that God did not send his Son into the world, or that Jesus Christ was not the Son of God.

III. The matter of all this divine testimony concerning Jesus Christ, *v*. 11. This is the sum of the gospel. 1. *God hath given to us eternal life*. He has designed it for us. He has made it over to us. 2. *This life is in the Son*. He is eternal life to us. It must follow, (1) He that is united to the Son is united to life (*v*. 12). (2) He who refuses the Son, who is life itself, and the way to it refuses life.

IV. The end of the apostle's preaching this to believers. 1. For their satisfaction and comfort: These believers have eternal life. These believers may come to know that they have eternal life, and should be encouraged, and comforted, in the prospect of it. 2. For their confirmation and progress in their holy faith (*v*. 13). Believers must persevere, or they do nothing.

Verses 14–17

I. A privilege belonging to faith in Christ, audience in prayer: *v*. 14. The Lord Christ emboldens us to come to God in all circumstances. Through him our petitions are accepted of God. The matter of our prayer must be agreeable to the declared will of God. We may have confidence that the prayer of faith shall be heard in heaven.

II. The advantage accruing to us by such privilege, *v*. 15. To know that his petitions are heard or accepted is as good as to know that they are answered.

III. Direction in prayer in reference to the sins of others, *v*. 16. 1. We ought to pray for others as well as for ourselves. 2. There is a great distinction in the heinousness and guilt of sin (*v*. 16), and (*v*. 17). (1) *There is a sin unto death*. There is a sin unto death in opposition to such sin as is here said *not to be unto death*. There is, therefore, (2) *A sin not unto death*. The gospel does not positively and peremptorily threaten death to the more visible sins of the members of Christ but only some gospel-chastise-

ment. There is room left for divine wisdom or goodness, or even gospel severity, to determine how far the chastisement or the scourge shall proceed. There are sins which are unto death spiritual and evangelical, that is, are inconsistent with spiritual life in the soul and with an evangelical right to life above, such as total impenitence and unbelief.

IV. The direction for prayer according to the different sorts of sin. The prayer is supposed to be for life: *He shall ask, and he shall give them life.* Life is to be asked of God. He is the God of life; he gives it when and to whom he pleases. In the case of a brother's sin, which is not unto death, we may in faith and hope pray for him. But, in case of the sin unto death we have no allowance to pray. Perhaps the apostle's expression, *I do not say, He shall pray for it*, may intend no more than, "I have no promise for you in that case." The removal of evangelical penalties, or the prevention of death, can be prayed for only conditionally or provisionally. We cannot pray that the sins of the impenitent and unbelieving should, while they are such, be forgiven them. But we may pray for their repentance, for their being enriched with faith in Christ, and thereupon for all other saving mercies. The apostle seems to argue that there is sin that is not unto death (*v*. 17); for, were all unrighteousness unto death, then we were all peremptorily bound over to death, and, since it is not so, there must be sin that is not to death. Though there is no venial sin there is pardoned sin.

Verses 18–21

I. A recapitulation of the privileges of sound Christian believers. 1. They are secured against sin (*v*. 18); secured against that sin which is unto death. The new nature, and the inhabitation of the divine Spirit thereby, prevent the admission of such unpardonable sin. 2. They are fortified against the devil's destructive attempts (*v*. 18). It seems not to be barely a narration of the duty of the regenerate; but an indication of their power. 3. They are on God's side in opposition to the world, *v*. 19. Mankind are divided into two great parties, that which belongs to God and that which belongs to wickedness. The Christian believers belong to God. They are of God, and from him, and to him, and for him. On the contrary, *the whole world*, the rest, being by far the major part, *lieth in wickedness.* May the God of the Christian world continually demolish the devil's dominion, and translate souls into *the kingdom of his dear Son!* 4. They are enlightened in the knowledge of the true eternal God, *v*. 20. The Son of God has come into our world, and we have seen him, and know him. He has revealed unto us the true God, and he has opened our minds too to understand that revelation; and we are assured that it is the true God that he hath discovered to us. It is a great happiness to know the true God, to know him in Christ; it is eternal life. 5. They have a happy union with God and his Son, *v*. 20. The Son leads us to the Father, and we are in both, in the love and favour of both. In union with either, much more with both, we are united to *the true God and eternal life.*

II. The apostle's concluding monition, *v*. 21. Since you know the true God, and are in him, let your light and love guard you. Flee from the false gods of the heathen world. The God whom you have known is he who redeemed you by his Son, who has pardoned your sins, and given you eternal life. Cleave to him in faith, and love, and constant obedience. To this living and true God be glory and dominion for ever and ever. *Amen.*

AN EXPOSITION, WITH PRACTICAL OBSERVATIONS, OF

THE SECOND EPISTLE OF

JOHN

Here we find a canonical epistle inscribed, principally, not only to a single person, but to one also of the softer sex. And why not to one of that sex? In gospel redemption, privilege, and dignity, *there is neither male nor female;* they are both one *in Christ Jesus.* No wonder then that a heroine in the Christian religion should be dignified also by an apostolical epistle.

The apostle here salutes an honourable matron and her children, ver. 1–3. Recommends to them faith and love, ver. 5, 6. Warns them of deceivers (ver. 7), and to take heed to themselves, ver. 8. Teaches how to treat those who bring not the doctrine of Christ, ver. 10, 11. Concludes the epistle, ver. 12, 13.

Verses 1–4

I. The saluter, not expressed by name, but by a chosen character: *The elder.* The expression, and style, and love, intimate that the penman was the same with that of the foregoing epistle. Possibly the oldest apostle now living. He was now old in holy service and experience, had seen and tasted much of heaven, and was much nearer than when at first he believed.

II. The saluted: *To the elect lady and her children.* A lady, a person of eminent quality. It is well that the gospel has got among such. It is a pity but lords and ladies should be acquainted with the Lord Christ and his religion. *The elect lady;* not only a choice one, but one chosen of God. *And her children;* probably the lady was a widow. We see that children may well be taken notice of in Christian letters, and they should know it too; it may avail to their encouragement. The respect paid them, 1. By the apostle himself: *Whom I love in the truth,* whom I sincerely and heartily love. He who was the beloved disciple had learnt the art or exercise of love. 2. By all her Christian acquaintance; *And not I only, but also all those that have known the truth.* Truth demands acknowledgment, and those who see the evidences of pure religion should confess and attest them. The ground of this love and respect was their regard to the truth: *For the truth's sake which dwelleth in us, and shall be with us for ever.* Those who love truth and piety in themselves should love it in others too. Religion should still dwell within us, in our minds and hearts, in our faith and love.

III. The salutation, which is indeed an apostolical benediction, *v.* 3. Sacred love pours out blessings upon this honourable Christian family; to those who have shall more be given.

1. From whom these blessings are craved, (1) *From God the Father.* He is the fountain of blessedness. (2) *From the Lord Jesus Christ.* He is also author and communicator of these heavenly blessings, *the Son of the Father.*

2. What the apostle craves, (1) *Grace*—divine favour and goodwill. (2) *Mercy*—free pardon and forgiveness; those who are already rich in grace have need of continual forgiveness. (3) *Peace*—tranquillity of spirit and serenity of conscience. And these are desired *in truth and love.* These blessings will continually preserve true faith and love *in the elect lady and her children.*

IV. The congratulation upon the prospect of the exemplary behaviour of other children of this excellent lady, *v.* 4. Possibly the lady's sons travelled abroad, and in their travels might come to Ephesus, where the apostle is supposed to have now resided, and might there happily converse with him. Let young travellers learn to carry their religion along with them, and not either leave it at home or learn the ill customs of the countries where they come. It is pleasant to see children treading in good parent's steps. How great a joy must it be to her ladyship to hear so good an account of them from so good a judge! We see here also the rule of true walking: *the commandment of the Father.* Then is our walk true, our converse right, when it is managed by the word of God.

Verses 5, 6

I. The apostle's request. Whether out of deference to her ladyship, or apostolical meekness, or both, he condescends to beseech: *And now I beseech thee, lady.* Love will avail where authority will not; and we may often see that the more authority is urged the more it is slighted.

II. The thing requested—growth in love. Those that are eminent in any Christian virtue have yet room to grow therein.

1. This love is recommended: From the obligation thereto—*the commandment.* From the antiquity of the obligation, *v.* 5. This commandment must everywhere attend Christianity, that the disciples of it must love one another.

2. Then this love is illustrated, *v.* 5. This is the evidence of our sincere, mutual, Christian love—that we walk after God's commands. Universal obedience is the proof of the sincerity of Christian virtues. This is a fundamental duty in the gospel-charter (*v.* 6), that is, walk in this love.

Verses 7–9

I. The ill news communicated to the lady, *For many deceivers have entered into the world.* Your stability is likely to be tried. 1. The description of the deceiver and his deceit (*v.* 7); he brings some error or other concerning the person of the Lord Jesus. Strange that after such evidence any should deny that the Lord Jesus is the Son of God and Saviour of the world! 2. The aggravation of the case (*v.* 7); he deludes souls and undermines the kingdom of the Lord Christ.

II. The counsel given hereupon, *v.* 8. Two things they must beware of, for some begin well, but at last lose all their pains. 1. Professors should take care not to lose what they have gained. Sad it is that fair and splendid attainments in the school of Christ should all be lost at last. 2. That they lose not their reward, none of it. *That we receive a full reward.* The way to attain the full reward is to abide true to Christ, and constant in religion to the end.

III. The reason of the apostle's counsel. 1. The danger and evil of departure from gospel light. It is in reality a departure from God himself: *Whosoever transgresseth and abideth not in the doctrine of Christ, hath not God.* Those who revolt thence, in so doing revolt from God. 2. The advantage and happiness of firm adherence to Christian truth. *He that abideth in the doctrine of Christ, he hath both the Father and the Son.* We must retain that holy doctrine in faith and love, as we hope or desire to arrive at blessed communion with the Father and the Son.

Verses 10, 11

I. The apostle gives direction concerning the treatment of such: *If there come any unto you, and bring not this doctrine, receive him not into your house. Neither bid him God speed.* Bad work should not be consecrated or recommended to the divine benediction. God will be no patron of falsehood and sin. The propagation of fatal error we must not dare to countenance.

II. The reason of such direction: *For he that biddeth him God speed is partaker of his evil deeds.* Favour and affection partake of the sin. We may be sharers in the iniquities of others.

Verses 12, 13

The apostle concludes this letter, for some things are better spoken than written. The use of pen and ink may be a mercy and a pleasure; but a personal interview may be more so. *The children of thy elect sister greet thee.* Grace was abundant towards this family; here are two elect sisters, and probably their elect children. May there be many such gracious ladies rejoicing in their gracious descendants and other relations! *Amen.*

AN EXPOSITION, WITH PRACTICAL OBSERVATIONS, OF

THE THIRD EPISTLE OF

JOHN

The apostle sends this encouraging epistle to his friend Gaius, in which also he complains of the quite opposite spirit of a certain minister, and confirms the good report concerning another.

In this epistle the apostle congratulates Gaius upon the prosperity of his soul (ver. 1, 2), upon the fame he had among good Christians (ver. 3, 4), and upon his hospitality to the servants of Christ, ver. 5, 6. He complains of Diotrephes (ver. 9, 10), recommends Demetrius (ver. 12), and expresses his hope of visiting Gaius shortly, ver. 13, 14.

Verses 1, 2

I. The sacred penman who writes and sends the letter; not here indeed notified by his name: *The elder.* Some have questioned whether this were John the apostle or no; but his style and spirit seem to shine in the epistle. Gaius could not question from whom the letter came.

II. The person saluted and honoured by the letter. He is notified, 1. By his name,—*Gaius.* We read of several of that name, particularly of one whom the apostle Paul baptized at Corinth. 2. By the kind expressions of the apostle to him: *The well-beloved,* and *whom I love in the truth.* Love expressed is wont to kindle love. To love our friends for the truth's sake is true love, gospel love.

III. The salutation or greeting. 1. The apostle's good opinion of his friend, that his *soul prospered,* the greatest blessing on this side heaven. 2. His good wish for his friend that his body may *prosper and be in health* as well as his soul. Grace will improve health, health will employ grace.

Verses 3–8

I. The good report that the apostle had received concerning this friend of his (*v.* 3–6). 1. The testimony concerning Gaius—the truth that was in him, and this evinced by his charity. Faith should work by love. 2. The witnesses—brethren that came from Gaius testified. A good report is due from those who have received good. 3. The auditory before which the report and testimony were given—*before the church.* This seems to be the church at which the apostle now resided. They could not but testify what they found and felt.

II. The report the apostle himself gives of him, *v.* 5. He was hospitable, good to the brethren, even to strangers. All who were of the household of faith were welcome to him. He was conscientious in what he did: "*Thou doest faithfully whatsoever thou doest;* thou doest it as a faithful servant, and from the Lord Christ mayest thou expect the reward."

III. The apostle's joy therein, *v.* 3. The best evidence of our having the truth is our *walking in the truth.*

IV. Concerning further treatment of the brethren that were with him. It seems to have been customary in those days of love to attend travelling ministers and Christians, at least some part of their road. It is a kindness to a stranger to be guided in his way, and a pleasure to travellers to meet with suitable company: this is a work that may be done *after a godly sort.*

V. The reasons of this directed conduct: *Because that for his name's sake these brethren went forth, taking nothing of the Gentiles.* They went forth to preach the gospel; possibly they might be sent out by this apostle himself: they went forth to convert the Gentiles; they went forth for God and his name's sake; they went forth also to carry a free gospel about with them: *Taking nothing of the Gentiles.* There are those who are not called to preach the gospel themselves who may yet contribute to the progress of it. The gospel should be made without charge to those to whom it is first preached. *We ought therefore to receive such, that we may be fellow-helpers to the truth.* Those who cannot themselves proclaim it may yet help and countenance those who do.

Verses 9–11

I. Here is a very different example and character. 1. His name—a Gentile name: *Diotrephes,* attended with an unchristian spirit. 2. His temper and spirit—full of pride and ambition: *He loves to have the pre-eminence.* 3. His contempt of the apostle's authority, and letter, and friends. Of his authority: *The deeds which he doeth prating against us with malicious words.* Malice and ill-will in the heart will be apt to vent themselves by the lips. Of his letter (*v.* 9). To an ambitious aspiring spirit apostolical authority or epistle signifies but little. Of his friends, the brethren he recommended, *v.* 10. There might be some differences or different customs between the Jewish and Gentile Christians. Many are cast out of the church who should be received there with satisfaction and welcome. 4. The apostle's menace of this proud domineerer (*v.* 10). This seems to intimate apostolical authority.

II. Here is counsel upon that different character, *v.* 11. Caution and counsel are not needless to those who are good already. To this caution and counsel a reason is respectively subjoined. To the counsel: *Follow that which is good;* for he that doeth good is of God. To the caution: *Follow not that which is evil,* for *he that doeth evil hath not seen God.* Evil-workers vainly pretend or boast an acquaintance with God.

Verses 12–14

I. The character of another person, one *Demetrius,* not much known otherwise. But here his name will live. His commendation was, 1. General: *Demetrius has a good report of all men.* Few are well spoken of by all. But universal integrity and goodness are the way to (and sometimes obtain) universal applause. 2. Deserved and well founded, *v.* 12. 3. Confirmed by the apostle's and his friends' testimony: *Yea, and we also bear record; And you know that our record is true.* It is good to be well known, or known for good.

II. The conclusion of the epistle. The referring of some things to personal interview, *v.* 13, 14. Many things may be more proper for immediate communication than for letter. Good Christians may well be glad to see one another. The benediction: *Peace be to you.* The public salutation sent to Gaius: *Our friends salute thee.* The apostle's particular salutation of the Christians in Gaius's church or vicinity: *Greet the friends by name.* Those may well salute and greet one another on earth who hope to live together in heaven.

AN EXPOSITION, WITH PRACTICAL OBSERVATIONS, OF

THE GENERAL EPISTLE OF

JUDE

This epistle is styled (as are some few others) *general* or *Catholic*, because it is not immediately directed to any particular person, family, or church, but to the whole society of Christians. The general scope of it is much the same with that of the second chapter of the second epistle of Peter. It is designed to warn us against seducers, to inspire us with a warm love to, and a hearty concern for, truth and that in the closest conjunction with holiness, of which charity is a most essential character.

I. An account of the penman of this epistle, ver. 1, 2. II. The occasion of writing this epistle, ver. 3. III. A character of evil and perverse men, ver. 4. IV. A caution against hearkening to and following after such, ver. 5–7. V. The seducers against whom he was warning them, from ver. 8 to 13. VI. He cites an ancient prophecy of Enoch, ver. 14, 15. VII. He enlarges on the seducers' character, ver. 16–19. VIII. Exhorts them, ver. 20, 21. IX. Directs them how to act towards the erroneous and scandalous, ver. 22, 23. X. Closes with an admirable doxology.

Verses 1, 2

I. We have an account of the penman of this epistle, *Jude*, or *Judas*. He was name-sake to one of his ancestors, the patriarch-son of Jacob. This was a name of worth, eminency, and honour; yet, 1. He had a wicked name-sake. There was one Judas who was the betrayer of his and our Lord. The same names may be common to the best and worst persons. It may be instructive to be called after the names of eminently good men, but there can be no inference drawn thence as to what we shall prove, though we may conclude what sort of persons our good parents hoped we should be. But, 2. Our Judas was quite another man. He was a faithful servant of Jesus Christ, the other was his betrayer and murderer. Our apostle here calls himself a servant of Jesus Christ, esteeming that a most honourable title. He might have claimed kindred to Christ according to the flesh, but he waives this, and rather glories in being his servant. It is a great honour to the meanest sincere minister (and it holds proportionably as to every upright Christian) that he is *the servant of Christ Jesus*. The apostles were servants before they were apostles, and they were but servants still. *And brother of James*, to wit, of him whom the ancients style *the first bishop of Jerusalem*. Of this James our Jude was brother, whether in the strictest or a larger acceptation I determine not.

II. To whom this epistle is directed; to all those *who are sanctified by God the Father, and preserved in Jesus Christ, and called*. The apostle may speak of their being *called to be Christians*. Christians are the called, called out of the world,—called from sin to Christ. Sanctified: *Sanctified by God the Father*. All who are effectually called are sanctified. Our sanctification is not our own work. Our corruption and pollution are of ourselves; but our sanctification and renovation are of God and his grace. The called and sanctified are *preserved in Christ Jesus*. Where he begins he will perfect; though we are fickle, he is constant.

III. We have the apostolical benediction: *Mercy to you*, &c. The *mercy* of God is the spring and fountain of all the good we have or hope for. Next to mercy is *peace*, which we have from the sense of having obtained mercy. As from mercy springs peace, so from peace springs *love*, his love to us, our love to him, and our brotherly love to one another. These the apostle prays may be multiplied, that Christians

may not be content with scraps and narrow scantlings of them.

Verses 3–7

I. The design of the apostle in writing this epistle: to establish them in the Christian faith, and a practice and conversation truly conformable thereunto, and in an open and bold profession thereof. 1. The gospel salvation is a common salvation, in a most sincere offer and tender of it to all mankind. None are excluded from the benefit of these gracious offers and invitations, but those who exclude themselves. It is made to all believers; it is made to the weak as well as to the strong. Here let us abide; here we are safe; if we stir a step further, we are in danger of being either entangled or seduced. The apostles and evangelists all wrote to us of this common salvation. They have fully declared to us all that is necessary *for every one to believe and do*, in order to obtain a personal interest in the common salvation. The apostle (though inspired) gave all diligence to write of the common salvation. Those who speak of sacred things ought always to speak of them with the greatest reverence, care, and diligence. Those who have received the doctrine of this common salvation must contend earnestly for it. *Earnestly*, not *furiously*. But how? As the apostles did; by suffering patiently and courageously for it.

II. The occasion the apostle had to write to this purport. As evil manners give rise to good laws, so dangerous errors often give just occasion to the proper defence of important truths. 1. Ungodly men are the great enemies of the faith of Christ and the peace of the church. Those who deny or corrupt the one, and disturb the other, are here expressly styled *ungodly men*. Ungodly men raise scruples, start questions, cause divisions, widen breaches. Nothing cuts us off from the church but that which cuts us off from Christ; namely, reigning infidelity and ungodliness. Those are ungodly men who live *without God in the world*, who have no regard to God and conscience. 2. Those are *the worst of ungodly men who turn the grace of God into lasciviousness*, who take encouragement to sin more boldly because the grace of God has abounded, and still abounds, so wonderfully. 3. Those who turn the grace of God into lasciviousness do in effect *deny the Lord God, and our Lord Jesus Christ*; they deny both natural and revealed religion. They strike at the foundation of natural religion, for they *deny the only Lord God*; and they overturn all the frame of revealed religion, for they deny *the Lord Jesus Christ*. These stand or fall together, and they mutually yield light and force to each other. Never two tallies answered more exactly to each other than these do. 4. Those who turn the grace of God into lasciviousness are ordained unto condemnation. Those who thus sin must needs die of their wounds, of their disease. 5. We ought to contend earnestly for the faith, in opposition to those who would corrupt or deprave it, such as have *crept in unawares*. The more busy and crafty the instruments and agents of Satan are, to rob us of the truth, the more solicitous should we be to hold it fast.

III. The fair warning which the apostle, in Christ's name, gives to those who, having professed his holy religion, do afterwards prove false to it, *v. 5–7. I will put you in remembrance*. What we already know we still need to be put in remembrance of. Preaching is not designed to teach us something new in every sermon; but *to put us in remembrance*, to call to mind things forgotten. *Though you know these things*, yet you still need to *know them better*.

1. The destruction of the unbelieving Israelites in the wilderness, *v. 5*. They had miracles in abundance: they were their daily bread; yet even they perished in unbelief. We have greater advantages than they had; let their error be our awful warning.

2. We are here put in remembrance of the fall of the angels, *v. 6*. There were a great number of the angels who *left their own habitation*. They quitted their post, and rebelled against God. But God did not spare them. Those who would not be servants to their Maker were made captives to his justice, and are *reserved in everlasting chains under darkness*. Hear and fear, O sinful mortals of mankind!

3. The apostle here calls to our remembrance the destruction of Sodom and Gomorrah, *v. 7*. Their ruin is a particular warning to all people to take heed of, and fly *from, fleshly lusts that war against the soul*. God is the same holy, just, pure Being now as then; and can the beastly pleasures of a moment make amends for your suffering the vengeance of eternal fire?

Verses 8–15

A charge against deceivers who were now seducing the disciples of Christ. He calls them *filthy dreamers*, forasmuch as delusion is a dream, and the beginning of, and inlet to, all manner of filthiness. *These filthy dreamers* dream themselves into a fool's paradise on earth, and into a real hell at last.

I. The character of these deceivers is described.

1. They *defile the flesh*. The flesh or body is the immediate seat, and often the irritating occasion, of many horrid pollutions; yet these, though done in and against the body, do greatly defile and grievously maim and wound the soul.

2. They *despise dominion, and speak evil of dignities*. Such evil-speakers despise the dominion of conscience, make a jest of it, and would banish it out of the world; and as for the word of God, the rule of conscience, they despise it. Religion and its serious professors have been always and everywhere evil spoken of.

The apostle brings in *Michael the archangel*, &c., *v. 9*. Interpreters are at a loss what is here meant by *the body of Moses. He durst not bring*, &c. Not that he was afraid of the devil, but he believed God would be offended if, in such a dispute, he went that way to work. A memorandum to all disputants, never to bring railing accusations into their disputes. Truth needs no supports from falsehood or scurrility. *The Lord rebuke thee*. He would not stand disputing with the devil. Divine rebukes are harder to be borne than careless sinners now think for.

3. *They speak evil of the things which they know not*, &c., *v. 10*. If they had known them, they would have spoken well of them, for nothing but good and excellent can be truly said of religion. Men are most apt to speak evil of those persons and things that they know least of. On the other hand, retirement screens some even from just censure. *But what they know naturally*, &c. The apostle likens such to *brute beasts*, though they often think and boast themselves if not as the wisest, yet at least as the wittiest part of mankind. *In those things they corrupt themselves*. The fault, whatever it is, lies in their depraved wills.

4. In *v. 11* the apostle represents them as followers *of Cain*, and in *v. 12, 13*, as atheistical and profane people,—as greedy and covetous, who, so they could but gain present worldly advantages, cared not what came next—who, like Core, ran into attempts in which they must assuredly perish, as he did. *These are spots in your feasts of charity*, or *love-feasts*. Yet how common in all Christian societies here on earth, the very best not excepted, are such blemishes! *When they feast with you, they feed themselves without fear*. Arrant gluttons, no doubt, they were; such as minded only the gratifying of their appetites. In common eating and drinking a holy fear is necessary, much more in feasting. *Clouds they are without water*, which promise rain in time of drought, but perform nothing of what they promise. Such is the case of formal professors. *Carried about of winds*, easily driven about as the wind happens to set; such are empty, ungrounded professors, an easy prey to every seducer. How happy would our world be if men either knew more or practically knew how little they know! *Trees whose fruit withereth*, &c. Trees they are, for they are planted in the Lord's vineyard, yet fruitless ones. *Twice dead*. One would think to be once dead were enough. They had been once dead in their natural state; but they seemed to recover, and to be brought to life again, when they took upon them the profession of the Christian religion. But now they are dead again by the evident proofs they have given of their hypocrisy: whatever they seemed, they had nothing truly vital in them.— *Plucked up by the roots*, as we commonly serve dead trees, from which we expect no more fruit. *Raging waves of the sea*, full of talk and turbulency, *foaming out their own shame*, creating much uneasiness to men of calmer tempers, which yet will in the end turn to their own greater shame and just reproach. Raging waves are a terror to sailing passengers; but, when they have got to port, the waves are forgotten, their noise and terror are for ever ended. *Wandering stars*. A very lively emblem of false teachers, who are sometimes here and sometimes there, so that one knows not where nor how to fix them.

II. The doom of this wicked people is declared. False teachers are to expect the worst of punishments in this and a future world. If this will not make both ministers and people cautious, I know not what will.

Of the prophecy of Enoch (*v. 14, 15*) we have no mention made in any other part or place of scripture. *The Lord cometh with* his holy myriads, including both angels and the spirits of just men made perfect. What a glorious time will that be, when Christ shall *come with ten thousand of these*! He cometh, *To execute judgment upon* the wicked; *to convince* them. They shall have no excuse or apology to make that they either can or dare then stand by.

I cannot pass *v. 15* without taking notice how often, and how emphatically, the word *ungodly* is repeated in it, no fewer than four times: ungodly men, ungodly sinners, ungodly deeds, ungodly committed. Godly or ungodly signifies little with men nowadays, unless it be to scoff at and deride even the very expressions; but it is not so in the language of the Holy Ghost. Hard speeches of one another, especially if ill-grounded, will most certainly come into account at *the judgment of the great day*.

Verses 15–25

Here, I. The apostle enlarges further on the character of these evil men and seducers, *v. 16*. A murmuring complaining temper lays men under a very bad character; such are very weak at least, and for the most part very wicked. They are angry at everything that happens, and never pleased with their own state and condition in the world, as not thinking it good enough for them. Their will, their appetite, their fancy, are their only rule.

II. He proceeds to caution and exhort those to whom he is writing, *v.* 17–23.

1. He calls them to remember how they had been forewarned, *v.* 17. The accomplishment of it is a confirmation of their faith, instead of being in the least an occasion of shaking and unsettling them therein. Those who would persuade must make it evident that they sincerely love those whom they would persuade. Bitter words and hard usage never did nor ever will convince, much less persuade anybody. We must not think it strange, but comfort ourselves with this, that in the midst of all this confusion Christ will maintain his church, and make good his promise. The more religion is ridiculed and persecuted the faster hold we should take and keep of it; being forewarned, we should show that we are fore-armed; under such trials we should stand firm.

2. He guards them against seducers by a further description of their odious character, &c., *v.* 19. Sensual men have not the Spirit, that is, of God and Christ, the Spirit of holiness. The worse others are the better should we endeavour to be; the more busy Satan, the more tenacious should we be of sound doctrine and a good conversation.

3. He exhorts them to persevering constancy in truth and holiness.

(1) *Building up yourselves in your most holy faith, v.* 20. Having laid our foundation well in a sound faith, we must build upon it; and we should take care with what materials we carry on our building. Right principles will stand the test even of the fiery trial.

(2) *Praying in the Holy Ghost.* Prayer is the nurse of faith. Our prayers are then most likely to prevail when we *pray in the Holy Ghost,* under his guidance and influence.

(3) *Keep yourselves in the love of God, v.* 21. Keep yourselves in the way of God, if you would continue in his love.

(4) *Looking for the mercy,* &c. Eternal life is to be looked for only through *mercy;* mercy is our only plea, not merit. Through the mercy of *our Lord Jesus Christ* as Redeemer; all who come to heaven must come thither through our Lord Jesus Christ. A lively faith of the blessed hope will help us to mortify our cursed lusts.

4. He directs them how to behave towards erring brethren, *v.* 22, 23. We ought to do all we can to rescue others out of the snare of the devil. We are not only our own keepers, but every man ought to be, as much as in him lies, his *brother's keeper.* This must be done with *compassion, making a difference.* We must distinguish between the weak and the wilful. *Of some* we *must have compassion,* treat them with all tenderness, not be needlessly harsh and severe in our censures of them. If God has forgiven them, why should not we? We infinitely more need his forgiveness than they do ours. *Others save with fear,* urging upon them *the terrors of the Lord:* "Endeavour to frighten them out of their sins. Fear lest you frustrate your own good intentions, do not harden, instead of reclaiming." We are often apt to over-do, when we are sure we mean honestly, and think we are right in the main. "*Hating even the garment spotted with the flesh,* keeping yourselves at the utmost distance from what is or appears evil."

III. The apostle concludes this epistle with a solemn ascription of glory to the great God, *v.* 24, 25. God is able, and he is as willing as able, *to keep us from falling and to present us faultless before the presence of his glory;* not as those who never have been faulty, but as those whose faults shall not be imputed.— *Before the presence of his glory.* The glory of the Lord will shortly be present. This is now the object of our faith, but hereafter it will be the object of our sense; whom we now believe in, him we shall shortly see. When believers shall be presented faultless it will be with exceeding joy. Where there is no sin there will be no sorrow; where there is the perfection of holiness, there will be the perfection of joy. Surely, the God who can and will do all this is worthy to have *glory, majesty, dominion, and power,* ascribed to him, *both now and for ever! Amen.*

AN EXPOSITION, WITH PRACTICAL OBSERVATIONS, OF

THE

REVELATION OF ST. JOHN

It ought to be no prejudice to the credit and authority of this book that it has been rejected by men of corrupt minds. The church of God has generally received it, and found good counsel and great comfort in it. Christ himself prophesied of the destruction of Jerusalem; and, about the time in which that was accomplished, he entrusted the apostle John with this book of revelation for the support of the faith of his people and the direction of their hope.

CHAPTER 1

This chapter is a general preface to the whole book. I. An inscription, ver. 1, 2. II. The apostolic benediction, ver. 3–8. III. A glorious appearance of the Lord Jesus Christ to the apostle John, when he delivered to him this revelation, ver. 9, to the end.

Verses 1, 2

I. It is *the revelation of Jesus Christ*. As the prophet of the church, he has made known to us the things that shall be hereafter. It is a revelation *which God gave unto Christ*. Our Lord Jesus is the great trustee of divine revelation; it is to him that we owe the knowledge we have of what we are to expect from God and what he expects from us. This revelation Christ *sent and signified by his angel*. Christ employed an angel to communicate it to the churches. The angels are God's messengers. The angels *signified it to the apostle John*. John was the apostle chosen for this service. Some think he was the only one surviving, the rest having sealed their testimony with their blood. John was to deliver this revelation to the church, to all his servants. They have all a right to the oracles of God.

II. The subject-matter of this revelation, the things that must shortly come to pass. We have in this revelation a general idea of the methods of divine providence. These events were such as should come to pass not only *surely*, but *shortly*.

III. Here is an attestation of the prophecy, *v*. 2. He was one who bore record of the word of God in general, and of the testimony of Jesus in particular, and of all things that he saw; he was an eye-witness, and he concealed nothing that he saw. As he added nothing to it, so he kept back no part of the counsels of God.

Verses 3–8

We have here an apostolic benediction on those who should give a due regard to this divine revelation.

I. More generally, to all who either read or hear the words of the prophecy. It is a blessed privilege to enjoy the oracles of God. It is a blessed thing to study the scriptures. It is a privilege not only to read the scriptures ourselves, but to hear them read by others. It is not sufficient to our blessedness that we read and hear the scriptures, but we must keep the things that are written.

II. The apostolic benediction is pronounced more especially and particularly to the seven Asian churches, *v*. 4. These seven churches are named in *v*. 11, and distinct messages sent to each of them.

1. What the blessing is. *Grace*, that is, the goodwill of God towards us and his good work in us; and *peace*, that is, the sweet evidence and assurance of this grace.

2. Whence this blessing is to come. In the name of God, of the whole Trinity. (1) The Father is first named: God the Father, *who is, and who was, and who is to come*, eternal, unchangeable. (2) The Holy Spirit, called *the seven spirits*, the infinite perfect Spirit of God, in whom there is a diversity of gifts and operations. He is before the throne; for, as God made, so he governs, all things by his Spirit. (3) The Lord Jesus Christ. Observe the particular account we have here of Christ, *v*. 5. *The faithful witness;* upon his testimony we may safely depend, for he is a faithful witness, cannot be deceived and cannot deceive us. The first-begotten or first-born from the dead. The prince of the kings of the earth; by him their power is limited; by him their counsels are over-ruled, and to him they are accountable. The great friend of his church and people. He has loved them. *First, He has washed them from their sins in his own blood*. Sins leave a stain upon the soul. Nothing can fetch out this stain but the blood of Christ; and, rather than it should not be washed out, Christ was willing to shed his own blood. *Secondly,* He has *made them kings and priests to God and his Father*. Having justified and sanctified them, he makes them kings to his Father. As kings, they overcome the world. He hath made them priests, given them access to God. For these high honours and favours they are bound to ascribe to him dominion and glory for ever. He will be the Judge of the world, *v*. 7. This book, the Revelation, begins and ends with a prediction of the second coming of the Lord Jesus Christ. John speaks as if he saw that day: "*Behold, he cometh*, as sure as if you beheld him with your eyes. *He cometh with clouds*, which are his chariot and pavilion. *Every eye shall see him*, the eye of his people, the eye of his enemies, every eye, yours and mine." He shall come, to the terror of those who have pierced him and have not repented and of all who have wounded and crucified him afresh by their apostasy from him, and to the astonishment of the pagan world. This account of Christ is ratified and confirmed by himself, *v*. 8. He is the beginning and the end; all things are from him and for him; he is the Almighty; he is the same eternal and unchangeable one.

Verses 9–20

I. The person who was favoured with this vision. His present state and condition. A persecuted man, banished, and perhaps imprisoned, for his adherence to Christ. He was their *brother*, though an apostle. He was their companion in tribulation: the persecuted servants of God did not suffer alone. He was their companion in patience, not only a sharer with them in suffering circumstances, but in suffering graces. By this account he acknowledges his engagements to sympathize with them, and to endeavour to give them counsel and comfort. The place where he was when he was favoured with this vision: he was in *the isle Patmos.* Under this confinement it was the apostle's comfort that he did not suffer as an evil-doer, but that it was for the testimony of Jesus. This was a cause worth suffering for; and the Spirit of glory and of God rested upon this persecuted apostle. The day and time in which he had this vision: it was *the Lord's day. He was in the Spirit.* He was not only in a rapture when he received the vision, but before he received it. God usually prepares the souls of his people for uncommon manifestations of himself, by the quickening influences of his good Spirit.

II. What he heard. An alarm was given as with the sound of a trumpet, and then *he heard a voice,* the voice of Christ, *the first and the last,* commanding the apostle to commit to writing the things that were now to be revealed to him, and to send it immediately *to the seven Asian churches.*

III. An account of what he saw. *He turned to see the voice,* and then a wonderful scene of vision opened itself to him.

1. He saw a representation of the church under the emblem of *seven golden candlesticks.* The churches are compared to candlesticks, because they hold forth the light of the gospel to advantage.

2. He saw a representation of the Lord Jesus Christ in the midst of the golden candlesticks.

(1) The glorious form in which Christ appeared.

(2) The impression this appearance of Christ made upon the apostle John (*v.* 17). He was overpowered with the greatness of the lustre and glory in which Christ appeared, though he had been so familiar with him before.

(3) The condescending goodness of the Lord Jesus to his disciple, *v.* 17. He raised him up; he put strength into him, he spoke kind words to him. Words of comfort and encouragement: *Fear not.* Words of instruction, telling him particularly who he was that thus appeared to him. He acquaints him, *First,* With his divine nature: *The first and the last. Secondly,* With his former sufferings: *I was dead. Thirdly,* With his resurrection and life: "*I live, and am alive for evermore,* have conquered death, and am partaker of an endless life." *Fourthly,* With his office and authority: *I have the keys of hell and of death,* a sovereign dominion in and over the invisible world. *Fifthly,* With his will and pleasure: *Write the things which thou hast seen, and the things which are, and which shall be hereafter. Sixthly,* With the meaning of the seven stars, and of the seven candlesticks.

Chapter 2

I. The message sent to Ephesus, ver. 1–7. II. To Smyrna, ver. 8–11. III. To Pergamos, ver. 12–17. IV. To Thyatira, ver. 18, &c.

Verses 1–7

I. The inscription. 1. *To the church of Ephesus.* 2. From whom this epistle to Ephesus was sent. *He that holds the stars in his right hand.* The ministers of Christ are under his special care and protection. The ministers of the gospel are in his hand. He supports them, or else they would soon be falling stars; and all the good they do is done by his hand with them. *He walks in the midst of the golden candlesticks.* This intimates his relation to his churches. Though Christ is in heaven, he walks in the midst of his churches on earth.

II. The contents of the epistle.

1. The commendation Christ gave this church, which he brings in by declaring that he knows their works, and therefore both his commendation and reprehension are to be strictly regarded; for he does not in either speak at a venture: he knows what he says. Now the church of Ephesus is commended, (1) For their diligence in duty, *v.* 2–3. (2) For their

patience in suffering, *v.* 2. It is not enough that we be diligent, but we must be patient—no Christian can be without it. There must be bearing patience, and there must be waiting patience, that they may receive the promise, *v.* 3. (3) For their zeal against what was evil, *v.* 2. We must show all meekness to men, yet we must show a just zeal against their sins. True zeal proceeds with discretion; none should be cast off till they be tried.

2. The rebuke given to this church, *v.* 4. Those that have much good in them may have something much amiss in them. *Thou hast left thy first love;* not left and forsaken the object of it, but lost the fervent degree of it that at first appeared. The first affections of men towards Christ are usually lively and warm. These lively affections will abate and cool if great care be not taken.

3. The advice and counsel given them from Christ. Those that have lost their first love *must remember whence they have fallen;* they must compare their present with their former state, and consider how much better it was with them then than now. They must repent. They must return and do their first works. They must as it were begin again. They must endeavour to revive and recover their first zeal.

4. This good advice is enforced and urged, (1) By a severe threatening, if it should be neglected. If the presence of Christ's grace and Spirit be slighted, we may expect the presence of his displeasure. (2) By an encouraging mention of what was yet good among them, *v.* 6. "Though thou hast declined in thy love to what is good, yet thou retainest thy hatred to what is evil." An indifference of spirit between truth and error, good and evil, may be called *charity* and *meekness,* but it is not pleasing to Christ.

III. We have the conclusion of this epistle.

1. A call to attention. What is said to one church concerns all the churches, in every place and age.

2. A promise of great mercy to those who overcome. We must never yield to our spiritual enemies, but fight the good fight, till we gain the victory, and the warfare and victory shall have a glorious triumph and reward. They shall *eat of the tree of life which is in the midst of the paradise of God,* not in the earthly paradise, but the heavenly.

Verses 8–11

I. The preface or inscription in both parts. 1. The superscription: *To the angel of the church in Smyrna.* 2. The subscription. Jesus Christ is the *first and the last.* It is but a little scantling of time that is allowed to us in this world, but our Redeemer is the first and the last. *He was dead and is alive.* He was dead, and died for our sins; he is alive, and he ever lives to make intercession for us.

II. The subject-matter of this epistle.

1. The improvement they had made in their spiritual state. But thou art rich. Some who are poor outwardly are inwardly rich, rich in faith and in good works. Where there is spiritual plenty, outward poverty may be better borne.

2. Their sufferings: *I know thy tribulation and thy poverty.* Jesus Christ takes particular notice of all their troubles.

3. He knows the wickedness and the falsehood of their enemies: *I know the blasphemy of those that say they are Jews, but are not;* that is, of those who pretend to be the only peculiar covenant-people of God, when indeed *they are the synagogue of Satan.* For the synagogues of Satan to give themselves out to be the church or Israel of God is no less than blasphemy.

4. He foreknows the future trials of his people. (1) He forewarns them of future trials, *v.* 10. They had been impoverished by their tribulations before; now they must be imprisoned. (2) Christ forearms

them against these approaching troubles, [1] By his counsel: *Fear none of these things.* This is not only a word of command, but of efficacy. [2] By showing them how their sufferings would be alleviated and limited. They should not be universal. It would be some of them, not all. They were not to be perpetual, but for a short time: *Ten days.* It should be to try them, not to destroy them. [3] By proposing a glorious reward to their fidelity: *Be thou faithful to death, and I will give thee a crown of life.* He has said it that is able to do it; and he has undertaken that he will do it. The suitableness of it. *A crown,* to reward their poverty, their fidelity, and their conflict. *A crown of life,* to reward those who are faithful even unto death.

III. The conclusion of this message. A call to universal attention. It concerns all the inhabitants of the world to observe God's dealings with his own people. A gracious promise to the conquering Christian, *v.* 11. There is not only a first, but a second death. This second death is unspeakably worse than the first death. It is *eternal death.* From this death Christ will save all his faithful servants. The first death shall not hurt them, and the second death shall have no power over them.

Verses 12–17

I. The inscription of this message. *To the angel of the church of Pergamos.* The church of Pergamos was infested with men of corrupt minds, and Christ, being resolved to fight against them by the sword of his word, takes the title of him that *hath the sharp sword with two edges.* The word of God is a sword; it is a weapon both offensive and defensive. It is a *sharp sword.* No heart is so hard but it is able to wound it. It is a *sword with two edges.* There is the *edge* of the law against the transgressors of that dispensation, and the *edge* of the gospel against the despisers of that dispensation.

II. The contents of the epistle.

1. Christ takes notice of the trials and difficulties this church encountered, *v.* 13. Now that which added very much lustre to the good works of this church was the circumstance of the place where this church was planted, a place where *Satan's seat* was. His *circuit* is throughout the world, his *seat* is in some places that are infamous for wickedness, error, and cruelty.

2. He commends their steadfastness. *"Thou holdest fast my name;* thou art not ashamed of thy relation to me, but accountest it thine honour that my name is named on thee. That which has made thee thus faithful is the grace of faith: *thou hast not denied,* nor departed from the Christian faith." They had been steadfast *even in those days wherein Antipas his faithful martyr was slain among them.* He sealed his faith and fidelity with his blood in the place where Satan dwelt. They were not discouraged nor drawn away from their steadfastness.

3. He reproves them for their sinful failures (*v.* 14). The filthiness of the spirit and the filthiness of the flesh often go together. To continue in communion with persons of corrupt principles and practices draws a guilt and blemish upon the whole society.

4. He calls them to repentance, *v.* 16. It is the duty of churches and communities as well as particular persons; those who sin together should repent together. When God comes to punish the corrupt members of a church, he rebukes that church itself for allowing such to continue in its communion, and some drops of the storm fall upon the whole society. The word of God will take hold of sinners, sooner or later, either for their conviction or their confusion.

III. There is the promise of great favour to those that overcome, *v.* 17. 1. The hidden manna, the influences and comforts of the Spirit of Christ,

coming down from heaven into the soul, from time to time. This is hidden from the rest of the world, and it is laid up in Christ. 2. The white stone, with a new name engraven upon it. This white stone is absolution from the guilt of sin, alluding to the ancient custom of giving a white stone to those acquitted on trial and a black stone to those condemned. The new name is the name of adoption. None can read the evidence of a man's adoption but himself.

Verses 18–29

I. The inscription. *To the angel of the church of Thyatira.* By whom it was sent: by *the Son of God,* who is here described as having *eyes like a flame of fire, and feet like as fine brass.* His eyes are like a flame of fire, signifying his piercing insight into all persons and all things. His feet are like fine brass. As he judges with perfect wisdom, so he acts with perfect strength and steadiness.

II. The contents of this epistle.

1. The honourable character and commendation Christ gives of this church. Christ makes honourable mention of their *charity*: there is no religion where there is no charity. Their *service.* Their *faith,* which was the grace that actuated all the rest. Their *patience.* Their growing fruitfulness: their last works were better than the first. It should be the ambition and earnest desire of all Christians that their last works may be their best works.

2. A faithful reproof for what was amiss. These wicked seducers are compared to Jezebel, and called by her name. The sin of these seducers was that they attempted to draw the servants of God into fornication, and to offer sacrifices to idols. They abused the patience of God to harden themselves in their wickedness. God gave them space for repentance, but they repented not.

3. The punishment of this seducer, *v.* 22, 23. *I will cast her into a bed,* into a bed of pain, not of pleasure. *I will kill her children with death;* that is, the second death.

4. The design of Christ in the destruction of these wicked seducers, was the instruction of others. God is known by *the judgments that he executes.*

5. The encouragement given to those who keep themselves pure and undefiled, *v.* 24. (1) What these seducers called their doctrines—*depths,* profound mysteries. (2) What Christ called them—*depths of Satan,* Satanical delusions and devices. (3) How tender Christ is of his faithful servants, *v.* 24, 25. "I only require your attention to what you have received." If they hold fast faith and a good conscience till he come, all the difficulty and danger will be over.

III. The conclusion of this message, *v.* 26–29. 1. The promise of an ample reward to the persevering victorious believer: Very great power and dominion over the rest of the world: *Power over the nations.* Knowledge and wisdom, suitable to such power and dominion: *I will give him the morning-star.* Christ is the morning-star. He brings day with him into the soul, the light of grace and of glory. 2. This epistle ends with the usual demand of attention.

CHAPTER 3

Here we have three more of the epistles of Christ to the churches: I. To Sardis, ver. 1–6. II. To Philadelphia, ver. 7–13. III. To Laodicea, ver. 14, to the end.

Verses 1–6

I. The preface. *To the angel of the church of Sardis,* said to have been the first city in that part of the world that was converted by the preaching of John; and, some say, the first that revolted from Christianity. By whom this message was sent—the Lord Jesus, *that hath the seven spirits of God, and the seven stars.* (1) He hath the seven spirits, that is, the Holy Spirit with his various powers. This epistle being sent to a languishing ministry and church, they are very fitly put in mind that Christ has the seven spirits, the Spirit without measure and in perfection, to whom they may apply themselves for the reviving of his work among them. (2) He hath the seven stars, the angels of the churches. The Holy Spirit usually works by the ministry, and the ministry will be of no efficacy without the Spirit; the same divine hand holds them both.

II. The body of this epistle. In this (and in the epistle to Laodicea) he begins,

1. With a reproof, and a very severe one. Hypocrisy, and a lamentable decay in religion, are the sins charged upon this church. This church had gained a great reputation; it had a name for a flourishing church. We read not of any unhappy divisions among themselves. Everything appeared well, as to what falls under the observation of men. This church was not really what it was reputed to be. There was a form of godliness, but not the power, *a name to live,* but not a principle of life. What little life was yet left among them was expiring, ready to die.

2. Our Lord proceeds to give this degenerate church the best advice, *v.* 2. (1) He advises them to be upon their watch. Whenever we are off our watch, we lose ground, and therefore must return to our watchfulness against sin, and Satan. (2) To strengthen the things that remain, and that are ready to die. Some understand this of persons. It is a difficult thing to keep up to the life and *power of godliness* ourselves, when we see a universal deadness and declension prevailing round about us. Or it may be understood of practices: *I have not found thy works perfect before God*; there is something wanting in them; there is the shell, but not the kernel. The inward thing is wanting, thy works are hollow and empty. When the spirit is wanting the form cannot long subsist. (3) To recollect themselves (*v.* 3); to remember what they had received and heard, how welcome the gospel and the grace of God were to them when they first received them. (4) To hold fast what they had received, that they might not lose all *and repent.*

3. Christ enforces his counsel with a dreadful threatening, *v.* 3. (1) When Christ leaves a people as to his gracious presence, he comes to them in judgment. (2) His judicial approach to a dead declining people will be surprising; their deadness will keep them in security.

4. Our blessed Lord does not leave this sinful people without some comfort and encouragement (*v.* 4). He makes honourable mention of the faithful remnant in Sardis, though but small. God takes notice of the smallest number of those who abide with him; and the fewer they are the more precious in his sight. He makes a very gracious promise to them. They shall walk with Christ, and what delightful converse will there be between Christ and them when they thus walk together! Those who walk with Christ shall walk with Christ in the white robes of honour and glory in the other world.

III. The conclusion of this epistle.

1. A great reward promised to the conquering Christian (*v.* 5). The purity of grace shall be rewarded with the perfect purity of glory. Holiness, when perfected, shall be its own reward; glory is the perfection of grace. To this is added another promise. Christ has his book of life. Christ will not blot the names of his chosen and faithful ones out of this book of life. The names of those that overcome shall never be blotted out. Christ will produce this book of life, and confess the names of the faithful who

stand there, before God, and all the angels. How great will this honour and reward be!

2. The demand of universal attention finishes the message. Every word from God deserves attention from men.

Verses 7–13

I. The inscription.

1. For whom it was designed: *The angel of the church of Philadelphia.* It was its ancient name, on account of the love and kindness which the citizens had and showed to each other. This was an excellent spirit, and would render them an excellent church, as indeed they were, for here is no one fault found with this church.

2. By whom this letter was signed; even by the same Jesus. You have his personal character: *He that is holy* and *he that is true*; holy in his nature, and therefore he cannot but be true to his word. The acts of his government. [1] He opens. He opens a door of opportunity to his churches; he opens a door of entrance, opens the heart; and he opens the door of admission into the church triumphant. [2] He shuts the door. When he pleases, he shuts the door of opportunity, and he shuts the door of heaven against the workers of iniquity. The way and manner in which he performs these acts is absolute sovereignty. When he works, none can hinder.

II. The subject-matter of this epistle.

1. Christ puts them in mind of what he had done for them, *v.* 8. I have set it open, and kept it open, though there be many adversaries. Wicked men envy the people of God their door of liberty, and would be glad to shut it against them. If we do not provoke Christ to shut this door against us, men cannot do it.

2. This church is commended, *v.* 8. In this there seems to be couched a gentle reproof: "*Thou hast a little strength,* a little grace." True grace, though weak, has the divine approbation; yet believers should not rest satisfied in a little, but should strive to grow in grace. True grace, though weak, will enable the Christian to keep the word of Christ, and not to deny his name.

3. The great favour God would bestow on this church, *v.* 9, 10.

(1) Christ would make this church's enemies subject to her. [1] Those enemies are described to be such as *said they were Jews,* but were really *the synagogue of Satan.* [2] Their subjection to the church is described: *They shall worship at thy feet;* shall be convinced that they have been in the wrong. How shall this great change be wrought? By the power of God upon the hearts of his enemies, and by signal discoveries of his peculiar favour to his church: *They shall know that I have loved thee.* Christ can discover this his favour to his people in such a manner that their very enemies shall see it, and be forced to acknowledge it. This will, by the grace of Christ, soften the hearts of their enemies.

(2) Another instance of favour that Christ promises (*v.* 10). The gospel of Christ is the word of his patience. It is the fruit of the patience of God to a sinful world. After a day of patience we must expect an hour of temptation. Those who keep the gospel in a time of peace shall be kept by Christ in an hour of temptation.

4. Christ calls the church to persevere. "*Hold fast that which thou hast*; thou hast been possessed of this excellent treasure, hold it fast. *Behold, I come quickly.* I am just coming to relieve them under the trial, to reward their fidelity, and to punish those who fall away. The persevering Christian shall win the prize from backsliding professors."

III. The conclusion of this epistle, *v.* 12, 13.

1. Our Saviour promises a glorious reward to the victorious believer in two things: (1) He shall be a monumental *pillar in the temple of God*; not a pillar to support the temple, but a monument of the grace of God, a monument that shall never be defaced nor removed, as many stately pillars erected in honour to the Roman emperors and generals have been. (2) On this there shall be an honourable inscription, as in those cases is usual. [1] *The name of God, and the name of the city of God, the new Jerusalem, which came down from heaven.* [2] The *new name* of Christ. By this it will appear under whose banner this conquering believer had enlisted, and under whose influence he fought the good fight, and came off victorious.

2. The epistle is closed up with the demand of attention.

Verses 14–22

We now come to the last and worst of all the seven Asian churches. Here is nothing commended.

I. The inscription. *To the angel of the church of Laodicea.* The apostle Paul was very instrumental in planting the gospel in this city, from which he wrote a letter, as he mentions in *the epistle to the Colossians.* Here our Lord Jesus styles himself *the Amen, the faithful and true witness, the beginning of the creation of God.* The Amen, one that is steady and unchangeable in all his purposes and promises. *The faithful and true witness,* whose testimony of God to men ought to be received. *The beginning of the creation of God,* either of the first creation, or of the second creation, the church; as it is in *ch. i.* 5.

II. The subject-matter.

1. The heavy charge drawn up against this church, *v.* 15. Lukewarmness or indifference in religion is the worst temper in the world. If religion is worth anything, it is worth everything. Here is no room for neutrality. Christ expects that men should declare themselves in earnest either for him or against him.

2. A severe punishment threatened: *I will spew thee out of my mouth.* As lukewarm water turns the stomach, and provokes to a vomit, lukewarm professors turn the heart of Christ against them. He is sick of them, and cannot long bear them. They shall be rejected.

3. We have one cause of this indifference assigned, and that is self-conceitedness or self-delusion, *v.* 17. What a difference there was between the thoughts they had of themselves and the thoughts that Christ had of them. The high thoughts they had of themselves. Perhaps they were well provided for as to their bodies, and this made them overlook the necessities of their souls. Or they thought themselves well furnished in their souls. How careful should we be not to put the cheat upon our own souls! Doubtless there are many in hell that once thought themselves to be in the way to heaven. The mean thoughts that Christ had of them. They were poor, really poor, when they said and thought they were rich. Their souls were starving in the midst of their abundance. They were *blind*; they could not see their state, nor their way; they could not see into themselves; yet they thought they saw. They could not see Christ. They could not see God. They were naked. They were without clothing, had neither the garment of justification nor that of sanctification.

4. We have good counsel given by Christ to this sinful people, *v.* 18. Our Lord Jesus Christ continues to give good counsel to those who have cast his counsels behind their backs. These people were poor; Christ counsels them to buy of him gold tried in the fire, that they might be rich. He lets them know where they might have true riches and how they might have them. Where they might have them—

from himself. How must they have this true gold from him? They must buy it. "Part with self-sufficiency, and come to Christ with your poverty and emptiness, that you may be filled with his hidden treasure." These people were naked; Christ tells them where they might have clothing. This they must receive from Christ; and they must only put off their filthy rags that they might put on the white raiment which he had provided for them. They were blind; and he *counsels them to buy of him eye-salve, that they might see,* to give up their own wisdom and reason, and resign themselves to his word and Spirit, and their eyes shall be opened.

5. Great and gracious encouragement to this sinful people to take the admonition well that Christ had given them, *v.* 19, 20. "You may think I have given you hard words and severe reproofs; it is all out of love to your souls." Sinners ought to take the rebukes of God's word as tokens of his goodwill to their souls. Better are the frowns and wounds of a friend than the flattering smiles of an enemy. If they would comply with his admonitions, he was ready to make them good to their souls, *v.* 20. Christ is graciously pleased by his word and Spirit to come to the door of the heart of sinners. He finds this door shut against him; the heart of man is by nature shut up against Christ. When he finds the heart shut, he does not immediately withdraw, but he waits to be gracious. Those who open to him shall enjoy his presence. He will sup with them; he will accept of what is good in them; and he will bring the best part of the entertainment with him.

III. The conclusion of this epistle.

1. The promise made to the overcoming believer. It was possible that by the reproofs and counsels of Christ they might be inspired with fresh zeal and vigour, and might come off conquerors in their spiritual warfare. If they did so they should have a great reward, *v.* 21. Christ himself had met with his temptations and conflicts. He overcame them all, and was more than a conqueror. Those who are conformed to Christ in his trials and victories shall be conformed to him in his glory.

2. All is closed up with the general demand of attention (*v.* 22). Thus end the messages of Christ to the Asian churches.

CHAPTER 4

In this chapter the prophetical scene opens. He, I. Records the heavenly sight he saw, ver. 1–7. And then, II. The heavenly songs he heard, ver. 8, to the end.

Verses 1–8

We have here an account of a second vision with which the apostle John was favoured.

I. The preparation made for the apostle's having this vision.

1. *A door was opened in heaven.* We can know nothing of future events but what God is pleased to discover to us; they are within the veil, till God opens the door.

2. To prepare John for the vision, a trumpet was sounded, and he was called up into heaven, to have a sight there of the things which were to be hereafter.

3. To prepare for this vision, *the apostle was in the Spirit.* He was in a rapture. His spirit was possessed with the spirit of prophecy, and wholly under a divine influence.

II. The vision itself. 1. He saw *a throne set in heaven,* the seat of honour, and authority, and judgment. All earthly thrones are under the jurisdiction of this throne that is set in heaven. 2. He saw a glorious one upon the throne. There was one in it who filled it, and that was God. *His countenance was like a jasper and a sardine-stone;* he is not described by any human features, so as to be represented by an image, but only by his transcendent brightness. 3. He saw *a rainbow about the throne, like unto an emerald, v.* 3. The rainbow was the seal and token of the covenant of providence that God made with Noah. This rainbow looked like *the emerald*; the most prevailing colour was a pleasant green, to show the reviving and refreshing nature of the new covenant. 4. He saw *four-and-twenty seats* round about the throne, with *four-and-twenty elders. They are clothed in white raiment*, the righteousness of the saints; they *had on their heads crowns of gold*, signifying the honour and authority given them of God, and the glory they have with him. 5. He perceived lightnings and voices proceeding out of the throne. Thus he gave forth the law on mount Sinai; and the gospel has not less glory and authority than the law. 6. He saw *seven lamps of fire burning before the throne* (*v.* 5), the various gifts, graces, and operations of the Spirit of God. 7. He saw *before the throne a sea of glass like unto crystal.* In this all those must be washed that are admitted into the gracious presence of God. 8. He saw *four animals*, living creatures, between the throne and the circle of the elders (as seems most probable), standing between God and the people; these seem to signify the ministers of the gospel. The elders sit and are ministered unto; these stand and minister: they rest not night nor day.

Verses 8–11

We have considered the sights that the apostle saw in heaven: now let us observe the songs that he heard.

I. He heard the song of the four living creatures, which refers to the prophet Isaiah's vision, *ch.* vi. They adore one God, and one only, *the Lord God Almighty.* They adore three holies in this one God.

II. He heard the adorations of the *four-and-twenty elders, v.* 10, 11.

1. The object of their worship: *Him that sat on the throne*, the eternal everliving God. There is but one God, and he alone, as God, is worshipped by the church on earth and in heaven.

2. The acts of adoration. They *fell down before him that sat on the throne.* They *cast their crowns before the throne*; they gave God the glory of the holiness wherewith he had crowned their souls on earth and the honour and happiness with which he crowns them in heaven. It is their glory to be glorifying God.

3. The words of adoration, *v.* 11. In this they tacitly acknowledge that God is exalted far above all blessing and praise. He was worthy to receive glory, but they were not worthy to praise.

4. We have the ground of their adoration. (1) He is the Creator of all things; and none but the Creator of all things should be adored; no made thing can be the object of religious worship. (2) He is the preserver of all things. All beings but God are dependent upon the will and power of God, and no dependent being must be set up as an object of religious worship. (3) He is the final cause of all things: *For thy pleasure they are and were created.* It was his will and pleasure to create all things.

CHAPTER 5

Now the counsels and decrees of God are set before the apostle, as in a book, and this book is represented, I. As sealed in the hand of God, ver. 1–9. II. As taken into the hand of Christ the Redeemer, to be unsealed and opened, ver. 6, to the end.

Verses 1–5

Hitherto the apostle had seen only the great God, the governor of all things. Now,

I. He is favoured with a sight of the methods of his government, as they are all written down in a book which he holds in his hand; and this we are now to consider as shut up and sealed. But there is

a transcript of so much as was necessary to be known in the book of the scripture in general, in the prophetical part of scripture especially. God holds this book in his right hand, to declare the authority of the book. It is known to none but himself, till he allows it to be opened. It is *sealed with seven seals.* Each part seems to have its particular seal. These seven parts are not unsealed and opened at once, but successively, one scene of Providence introducing another, and explaining it.

II. He heard a proclamation made concerning this sealed book. The crier was *a strong angel.* This angel seems to come out as a champion, with a challenge to any or all the creatures to try the strength of their wisdom in opening the counsels of God. The cry or challenge, *v.* 2. None in heaven or earth could accept the challenge and undertake the task. *None under the earth*, none of the fallen angels. Satan himself, with all his subtlety, cannot do it; the creatures cannot open it, nor look on it; they cannot read it. God only can do it.

III. The apostle *wept much*; it was a great disappointment to him. By what he had seen in him who sat upon the throne, he was very desirous to see and know more of his mind and will. Those who have seen his glory desire to know his will.

IV. The apostle was comforted and encouraged to hope this sealed book would yet be opened. Who it was that gave John the hint: *One of the elders.* God had revealed it to his church. Who it was that would do the thing—the Lord Jesus Christ, called *the lion of the tribe of Judah*, according to his human nature, and *the root of David* according to his divine nature. He who bears the office of Mediator between God and man, is fit and worthy to open and execute all the counsels of God towards men.

Verses 6–14

I. The apostle beholds this book taken into the hands of the Lord Jesus Christ. His place and station. He was on the same throne with the Father. Christ, as man and Mediator, is subordinate to God the Father, but is nearer to him than all the creatures. The form in which he appeared. Before he is called *a lion*; here he appears *as a lamb slain.* He is a lion to conquer Satan, a lamb to satisfy the justice of God. He appears as a *lamb, having seven horns and seven eyes*, perfect power to execute all the will of God and perfect wisdom to understand it all. *For he hath the seven Spirits of God*, he has received the Holy Spirit without measure. His act and deed (*v.* 7), not by violence, nor by fraud, but he prevailed to do it (as *v.* 5), he prevailed by his merit and worthiness.

II. No sooner had Christ received this book out of the Father's hand than he received the applauses and adorations of angels and men, yea, of *every creature.*

1. The church begins the doxology, as being more immediately concerned in it (*v.* 8). (1) The object of their worship—*the Lamb*, the Lord Jesus Christ. (2) Their posture: They *fell down before him*, gave him the most profound adoration. (3) The instruments used in their adoration—*harps and vials*; the harps were the instruments of praise, the vials were full of odours or incense, which signify *the prayers of the saints.* (4) The matter of their song. *Thou art worthy to take the book, and to open the seals thereof.* They mention the grounds of this worthiness, yet they chiefly insist upon the merit of his sufferings; these more sensibly struck their souls with thankfulness and joy. They mention his suffering: "*Thou wast slain.*" The fruits of his sufferings. [1] Redemption to God. [2] High exaltation, *v.* 10.

2. The doxology is carried on by the angels, *v.* 11. They are said to be *innumerable*, and to be the attendants on the throne of God. Though they did not

need a Saviour themselves, yet they rejoice in the redemption and salvation of sinners, and they agree with the church that he is *worthy to receive power, and riches, and wisdom, and strength, and honour, and glory, and blessing.*

3. This doxology is resounded by the whole creation, *v.* 13. Heaven and earth ring with the high praises of the Redeemer. The whole creation fares the better for Christ. That part which is made for the whole creation is a song of *blessing, and honour, and glory, and power. To him that sits on the throne,* to God the Father. *To the Lamb,* the Mediator of the new covenant. We worship and glorify one and the same God for our creation and for our redemption. Thus we have seen this sealed book passing with great solemnity from the hand of the Creator into the hand of the Redeemer.

CHAPTER 6

Now we are to launch into the deep, and our business is not so much to fathom it as to let down our net to take a draught. We shall only hint at what seems most obvious. In this chapter six of the seven seals are opened, and the visions attending them are related; the first seal in ver. 1, 2, the second seal in ver. 3, 4, the third seal in ver. 5, 6, the fourth seal in ver. 7, 8, the fifth seal in ver. 9–11, the sixth seal in ver. 12, 13, &c.

Verses 1, 2

Christ, the Lamb, opens the first seal. We have the vision itself, *v.* 2. 1. The Lord Jesus appears riding on *a white horse.* 2. *He had a bow* in his hand. The convictions impressed by the word of God are sharp arrows, they reach at a distance. 3. *A crown was given him.* When Christ was going to war, one would think a helmet had been more proper than a crown; but a crown is given him as the earnest of victory. 4. *He went forth conquering, and to conquer.* As long as the church continues militant Christ will be conquering. He conquers his enemies in his people; their sins are their enemies and his enemies; when Christ comes with power into their soul he begins to conquer these enemies, and he goes on conquering, in the progressive work of sanctification, till he has gained us a complete victory. And he conquers his enemies in the world, wicked men. The successful progress of the gospel of Christ in the world is a glorious sight, worth beholding. Christ's work is not all done at once. We are ready to think, when the gospel goes forth, it should carry all the world before it, but it often meets with opposition, and moves slowly. Christ will do his own work effectually, in his own time and way.

Verses 3–8

The next three seals give us a sad prospect of judgments with which God punishes those who abuse the everlasting gospel.

I. Upon opening the second seal *another horse* appears, *a red horse, v.* 4. This signifies the desolating judgment of war. The sword of war is a dreadful judgment; it takes away peace from the earth. Men, who should love one another and help one another, are, in a state of war, set upon killing one another.

II. Upon opening the third seal another horse appears, *a black horse,* signifying famine (*v.* 5). One judgment seldom comes alone; the judgment of war naturally draws after it that of famine. The famine of bread is a terrible judgment; but the famine of the word is more so.

III. Upon opening the fourth seal there appears another horse, of a pale colour. 1. The name of the rider—*Death,* the king of terrors. 2. The attendants of this king of terrors—*hell.* There is a natural connection between one judgment and another: war is a wasting calamity, and draws scarcity and famine after it; and famine draws the pestilence after it. God has

published threatenings against the wicked as well as promises to the righteous; and it is our duty to believe the threatenings as well as the promises.

IV. After the opening of these seals we have this general observation, *v.* 8. To the three great judgments of war, famine, and pestilence, is here added *the beasts of the earth,* another of God's sore judgments. When a nation is depopulated by the sword, famine, and pestilence, the small remnant that continue become an easy prey. Others, by *the beasts of the field,* understand brutish, cruel, savage men.

Verses 9–17

I. The fifth seal. It does not contain a new prophecy, but rather opens a spring of consolation to those who still were under great tribulation.

1. The sight this apostle saw at the opening of the fifth seal (*v.* 9). He saw the souls of the martyrs. Where he saw them—in the most holy place; he saw them in heaven, at the foot of Christ. God has provided a good place in the better world for those who are faithful to death and are not allowed a place any longer on earth. The cause in which they suffered —*the word of God and the testimony which they held.* A noble cause, the best that any man can lay down his life for.

2. The cry he heard, *v.* 10. Even *the spirits of just men made perfect* retain a proper resentment of the wrong they have sustained by their cruel enemies. They commit their cause to him to whom vengeance belongeth; they are not for avenging themselves, but leave all to God.

3. The kind return that was made to this cry (*v.* 11). What was given to them—*white robes,* the robes of victory and of honour. What was said to them—that they should be easy in themselves, for it would not be long ere the number of their fellow-sufferers *should be fulfilled.* He will recompence tribulation to those who trouble them, and to those that are troubled full and uninterrupted rest.

II. We have here the sixth seal opened, *v.* 12.

1. The tremendous events that were hastening; and here are several occurrences that contribute to make that day and dispensation very dreadful (*v.* 13). It would be a judgment that should astonish all the world.

2. The dread and terror that would seize upon all sorts of men in that great and awful day, *v.* 15. The degree of their terror and astonishment; it should prevail so far as to make them call *to the mountains to fall upon them, and to the hills to cover them.* The cause of their terror—*the wrath of the Lamb.* Though God be invisible, he can make the inhabitants of this world sensible of his awful frowns. Though Christ be a lamb, yet he can be angry, and *the wrath of the Lamb* is exceedingly dreadful. As men have their day of opportunity, and their seasons of grace, so God has his day of righteous wrath.

CHAPTER 7

This comfortable chapter secures the graces and comforts of the people of God in times of common calamity. I. An account of the restraint laid upon the winds, ver. 1–3. II. The sealing of the servants of God, ver. 4–8. III. The songs of angels and saints on this occasion, ver. 9–12. IV. A description of the honour and happiness of those who had faithfully served Christ, and suffered for him, ver. 13, &c.

Verses 1–12

I. An account of the restraint laid upon the winds. By these winds we suppose are meant those errors which would occasion a great deal of trouble and mischief to the church of God. The spirits of error are compared to *the four winds,* contrary one to another, but doing much hurt to the garden and vineyard of God. Errors are as wind, by which those who are unstable are shaken. They are restrained by the ministry of angels, *standing on the four corners of the earth*; the spirit of error cannot go forth till God permits it. Angels minister to the good of the church by restraining its enemies. Their restraint was only for a season, and that was *till the servants of God were sealed in their foreheads.*

II. An account of the sealing of the servants of God. 1. To whom this work was committed—to an angel. Another angel was employed to mark out and distinguish the faithful servants of God. 2. How they were distinguished—the seal of God was set upon their foreheads. By this mark they were set apart for mercy and safety in the worst of times. 3. The number of those that were sealed. A particular account of those that were sealed of the twelve tribes of Israel—twelve thousand out of every tribe. A general account of those who were saved out of other nations (*v.* 9). Though the church of God is but a little flock, in comparison of the wicked world, yet it is no contemptible society, but really large, and to be still more enlarged.

III. We have the songs of saints and angels, *v.* 9–12.

1. The praises offered up by the saints. (1) The posture of these praising saints: they *stood before the throne, and before the Lamb*, before the Creator and the Mediator. The throne of God would be inaccessible to sinners were it not for a Mediator. (2) Their habit: they were *clothed with white robes, and had palms in their hands*, as conquerors used to appear in their triumphs. (3) Their employment: they *cried with a loud voice, saying, Salvation to our God who sitteth upon the throne, and to the Lamb*. This may be understood either as a *hosannah*, or as a *hallelujah*. Both the Father and the Son are joined together in these praises; the Father contrived this salvation, the Son purchased it, and those who enjoy it must and will bless the Lord and the Lamb.

2. Here is the song of the angels as they fell on their faces and worshipped (*v.* 11, 12). What humility then, and what profound reverence, become us vile frail creatures, when we come into the presence of God! They consented to the praises of the saints, their *Amen* thereto; and then they added more of their own. We see what is the work of heaven, and we ought to get our hearts tuned for it, and to long for that world where our praises, as well as happiness, will be perfected.

Verses 13–17

A description of the happiness of those who have faithfully served the Lord Jesus Christ.

I. A question asked by one of the elders, not for his own information, but for John's instruction. The lowest saint in heaven knows more than the greatest apostle in the world.

II. The answer returned by the apostle, in which he tacitly acknowledges his own ignorance: *Thou knowest.*

III. The account given to the apostle concerning that noble army of martyrs. 1. The low and desolate state they had formerly been in; they had been in great tribulation. The way to heaven lies through many tribulations; but tribulation shall not *separate us from the love of God*. 2. The means by which they had been prepared for the great happiness they now enjoyed, *v.* 14. This is the only blood that makes the robes of the saints white and clean. 3. The blessedness to which they are now advanced. (1) They are happy in their station, for *they are before the throne of God night and day*; and he *dwells among them.* (2) They are happy in their employment, for they serve God continually. (3) They are happy in their freedom from all the inconveniences of this present life. From all want and sense of want: *They hunger and thirst no more;* all their wants are supplied. From all sickness and pain: they shall never be scorched

by *the heat of the sun any more.* (4) They are happy in the love and guidance of the Lord Jesus: *He shall feed them, he shall lead them to living fountains of waters.* (5) They are happy in being delivered from all sorrow. *God shall wipe away all tears from their eyes.* God himself, with his own gentle and gracious hand, will wipe those tears away, and they would not have been without those tears, when God comes to wipe them away. In this he deals with them as a tender father who finds his beloved child in tears, he comforts him, he wipes his eyes, and turns his sorrow into rejoicing.

CHAPTER 8

In this chapter we have, I. The preface to the sounding of the trumpets, ver. 1–6. II. The sounding of four of the trumpets, ver. 7, &c.

Verses 1–6

I. The opening of the last seal. This was to introduce a new set of events.

II. A profound *silence in heaven for the space of half an hour*. A silence of expectation; great things were upon the wheel of providence, and the church of God, both in heaven and earth, stood silent, to see what God was doing.

III. The trumpets were delivered to the angels who were to sound them.

IV. To prepare for this, another angel must first offer incense, *v.* 3. This incense he was to offer up, *with the prayers of all the saints, upon the golden altar.* 1. All the saints are a praying people; none of the children of God are born dumb. 2. Times of danger should be praying times, and so should times of great expectation; both our fears and our hopes should put us upon prayer. 3. The prayers of the saints themselves stand in need of the incense and intercession of Christ to make them acceptable and effectual. No prayer, thus recommended, was ever denied audience or acceptance. These prayers that were thus accepted in heaven produced great changes upon earth. The same angel in the same censer *took of the fire of the altar, and cast it into the earth*, and this presently caused strange commotions, *voices, and thunderings, and lightnings, and an earthquake.* And now, all things being thus prepared, the angels discharge their duty.

Verses 7–13

I. *The first angel sounded* the first trumpet, *v.* 7. It was a very terrible storm—fire, and hail, and blood: a strange mixture! The limitation of it: it fell on *the third part of the trees*, and on the third part of *the grass*, and blasted and burnt it up. The most severe calamities have their bounds and limits set them by the great God.

II. *The second angel sounded*, *v.* 8. Here was still a limitation to the third part, for *in the midst of judgment God remembers mercy.*

III. *The third angel sounded*, *v.* 10. A star from heaven fell: *Upon a third part of the rivers, and upon the fountains of waters.* It turned those springs and streams into wormwood, made them very bitter, that men were poisoned by them. The souls of men found their ruin where they sought for their refreshment.

IV. *The fourth angel sounded.* The nature of this calamity; it was darkness; it fell therefore upon the great luminaries of the heaven, that give light to the world—*the sun, and the moon, and the stars.* The limitation: it was confined to a third part of these luminaries; there was some light both of the sun by day, and of the moon and stars by night. Where the gospel comes to a people, and is but coldly received, it is usually followed with dreadful judgments. God gives warning to men of his judgments before he sends them, so that, if a people be surprised, it is their own fault. Yet God does not in this world stir up all his wrath, but sets bounds to the most terrible judgments.

V. Before the other three trumpets are sounded here is solemn warning how terrible the calamities would be that should follow them, v. 13. The messenger was *an angel flying in the midst of heaven*, as in haste. Here are three woes, to show how much the calamities coming should exceed those that had been already. If less judgments do not take effect, but the church and the world grow worse under them, they must expect greater.

CHAPTER 9

The sounding of the fifth and sixth trumpets, the appearance that attended them, and the events that were to follow; the fifth trumpet, ver. 1–12, the sixth, ver. 13, &c.

Verses 1–12

1. *A star falling from heaven to the earth.* 2. To this fallen star *was given the key of the bottomless pit.* It becomes the devil's turnkey, to let loose the powers of hell against the churches of Christ. 3. Upon the opening of the bottomless pit *there arose a great smoke*, which darkened the sun and the air. The devil carries on his designs by extinguishing light and knowledge. Wretched souls follow him in the dark, or they durst not follow him. 4. Out of this dark smoke there came a swarm of locusts, and these had, by the just permission of God, power to hurt those who had not the mark of God in their foreheads. 5. The hurt they were to do them was not a bodily, but a spiritual hurt. They should not in a military way destroy all by fire and sword; the trees and the grass should be untouched, and those they hurt should not be slain. 6. They had no power so much as to hurt those who had the seal of God in their foreheads. 7. The power given to these factors for hell is limited in point of time: *five months*, a certain season, and but a short season. 8. Though it would be short, it would be very sharp, v. 6. 9. These locusts were of a monstrous size and shape, v. 7, 8, &c. They were equipped for their work like horses prepared to battle. *They had crowns like gold on their heads;* it was not a true, but a counterfeit authority. They had the show of wisdom and sagacity, *the faces of men*, though the spirit of devils. They had all the allurements of seeming beauty—*hair like women.* Though they appeared with the tenderness of women, they were really cruel creatures. They had the defence and protection of earthly powers—*breastplates of iron.* They made a mighty noise in the world, and the noise of their motion was like that of an army with chariots and horses. Though at first they soothed and flattered men with a fair appearance, there was a sting in their tails. The king and commander of this hellish squadron is here described as an angel. *The angel of the bottomless pit;* an angel still, but a fallen angel, fallen into the bottomless pit. His true name is *Abaddon, Apollyon—a destroyer*, for that is his business, to which he diligently attends.

Verses 13–21

I. The preface to this vision, v. 13, 14. When nations are ripe for punishment, those instruments of God's anger that were before restrained are let loose upon them, v. 14.

II. The vision itself, v. 15, 16. 1. The time of their military operations is limited to *an hour, and a day, and a month, and a year.* Prophetic characters of time are hardly to be understood by us. How far the execution shall prevail, even to a third part of the inhabitants of the earth. 2. The army that was to execute this great commission is mustered, and the number found to be of horsemen *two hundred thousand thousand*; but we are left to guess what the infantry must be. In general, it tells us, the armies should be vastly great. 3. Their formidable equipage and appearance, v. 17. As the horses were fierce, like lions, so those who sat upon them were clad in bright and costly armour. 4. The vast havoc and desolation that they made. 5. Their artillery, by which they made such slaughter, described *by fire, smoke, and brimstone*, issuing out of the mouths of their horses, and the stings that were in their tails. 6. The impenitancy of the antichristian generation under these dreadful judgments (v. 20). They still persisted in those sins for which God was so severely punishing them. Though God has revealed his wrath from heaven against them, they are obstinate, and impenitent. Impenitency under divine judgments is an iniquity that will be the ruin of sinners; for where God judges he will overcome.

CHAPTER 10

This chapter is an introduction to the latter part of the prophecies of this book. I. A remarkable description of a very glorious angel with an open book in his hand, ver. 1–3. II. An account of seven thunders which the apostle heard, as echoing to the voice of this angel, ver. 4. III. The solemn oath taken by him who had the book in his hand, ver. 5–7. IV. The charge given to the apostle, and observed by him, ver. 8–11.

Verses 1–7

Another vision the apostle was favoured with.

I. The person communicating this discovery to John—an angel from heaven, *another mighty angel.*

II. His station and posture: *He set his right foot upon the sea and his left foot upon the earth. And he held in his hand a little book opened*, probably the same that was before sealed, but was now opened, and gradually fulfilled by him.

III. His awful voice (v. 3) was echoed by *seven thunders*, seven solemn and terrible ways of discovering the mind of God.

IV. The prohibition given to the apostle, v. 4. The apostle was for preserving and publishing everything he saw and heard in these visions, but the time had not yet come.

V. The solemn oath taken by this mighty angel. *He lifted up his hand to heaven, and swore by him that liveth for ever*, that *there shall be time no longer;* either, 1. That there shall be now no longer delay in fulfilling the predictions of this book than till the last angel should sound, v. 7. Or, 2. That when this mystery of God is finished time itself shall be no more.

Verses 8–11

I. A strict charge given to the apostle, 1. That he should *go and take the little book* out of the hands of that mighty angel. 2. To eat the book. Before he should publish what he had discovered he must more thoroughly digest the predictions.

II. An account of the taste which this little book would have; at first, while *in his mouth, sweet.* But, when this book of prophecy was more thoroughly digested by the apostle, the contents would be bitter; these were things so awful and terrible, that the foresight of them would not be pleasant.

III. The apostle's discharge of the duty he was called to (v. 10): he found the relish to be as was told him.

IV. This book of prophecy was not given him merely to gratify his own curiosity, but to be communicated by him to the world. He is ordered to prepare for another embassy, to convey those declarations of the mind and will of God to all the world, and such should be read and recorded in many languages.

CHAPTER 11

In this chapter we have an account, I. Of the measuring-reed given to the apostle, to take the dimensions of the temple, ver. 1, 2. II. Of the two witnesses of God, ver. 3–13. III. Of the sounding of the seventh trumpet, and what followed upon it, ver. 14, &c.

Verses 1, 2

This prophetical passage about measuring the temple is a plain reference to what we find in Ezekiel's vision, Ezek. xl. 3, &c. The design of this measurement seems to be the preservation of it in those times of public danger and calamity that are here foretold.

I. How much was to be measured. 1. *The temple;* the gospel church in general. 2. *The altar.* Whether the church has the true altars. 3. The worshippers too must be measured, whether they make God's glory their end and his word their rule.

II. What was not to be measured (*v.* 2): *The court which is without the temple measure it not.* Herod, in the additions made to the temple, built an outer court, and called it *the court of the Gentiles.* This was no part of the temple, and therefore God would have no regard to it. Both that and the city were trodden under foot for a certain time—*forty and two months.* Those who worship in the outer court are either such as worship in a false manner or with hypocritical hearts. Those who worship in the outer court will be rejected, and only those who worship within the veil accepted.

Verses 3–13

God has reserved to himself his faithful witnesses.
I. The number of these witnesses. 1. It is but small. One witness, when the cause is upon trial, is worth many at other times. 2. It is a sufficient number; for in the mouth of two witnesses every cause shall be established. Christ sent out his disciples two by two, to preach the gospel.

II. The time of their prophesying. *A thousand two hundred and threescore days,* that is (as many think), to the period of the reign of antichrist.

III. Their habit: they prophesy in sackcloth, as those that are deeply affected with the low and distressed state of the churches.

IV. How they were supported: they stood before the God of the whole earth. He made them to be like Zerubbabel and Joshua, the two olive-trees and candlestick in the vision of Zechariah, *ch.* iv. 2, &c.

V. Their security and defence during the time of their prophesying, *v.* 5. Some think this alludes to Elias's calling for fire from heaven, to consume the captains and their companies that came to seize him, 2 Kings i. 12, and restraining the dews of heaven, shutting heaven up, that no rain should fall for many days, as God did at the prayers of Elias, 1 Kings xvii. 1.

VI. The slaying of the witnesses. To make their testimony more strong, they must seal it with their blood. The time when they should be killed: *When they have finished their testimony.* They are immortal, till their work be done. The enemy that should overcome and slay them—*the beast that ascendeth out of the bottomless pit.* Antichrist should make war against them with open force and violence; and God would permit his enemies to prevail against his witnesses for a time. The barbarous usage of these slain witnesses; the malice of their enemies, pursued even their dead bodies. They would not allow them a quiet grave; their bodies were cast out in the open street. Their death was a matter of mirth and joy to the antichristian world, *v.* 10.

VII. The resurrection of these witnesses. The time of their rising again (*v.* 11). God's witnesses may be slain, but they shall rise again. God will revive his work, when it seems to be dead in the world. *The Spirit of life from God entered into them,*

and they stood upon their feet. God put not only life, but courage into them. The effect of their resurrection upon their enemies: *Great fear fell upon them.* A persecuting spirit, though cruel, is not a courageous, but a cowardly spirit.

VIII. The ascension of the witnesses into heaven, *v.* 12, 13. 1. Their ascension. To this honour they did not attempt to ascend, till God called them, and said, *Come up hither.* The Lord's witnesses must wait for their advancement, till God calls them. 2. The consequences of their ascension—a mighty shock and convulsion and the fall of *a tenth part of the city. The fear of God fell upon many. They gave glory to the God of heaven.* Thus, when God's work and witnesses revive, the devil's work and witnesses fall before him.

Verses 14–19

What he before expected he now heard—the seventh angel sounding.

I. Loud and joyful acclamations of the saints and angels in heaven. They rose from their seats, *and fell upon their faces, and worshipped God.* They thankfully recognise the right of our God and Saviour to rule and reign over all the world, *v.* 15. They give him thanks because he had taken to him his great power. They rejoice that this his reign shall never end. None shall ever wrest the sceptre out of his hand.

II. Angry resentments in the world at these actings of the power of God (*v.* 18): *The nations were angry;* their hearts rose up against God. They fretted against God, and so increased their guilt and hastened their destruction.

III. The opening of the temple of God in heaven. What was seen there: the *ark of God's testament.* This was in the holy of holies; in this ark the tables of the law were kept. As before Josiah's time the law of God had been lost, but was then found, so in the reign of antichrist God's law was laid aside. Now the scriptures are opened, now they are brought to the view of all. What was heard and felt there: *Lightnings, voices, thunderings, an earthquake, and great hail.* By terrible things in righteousness God would answer those prayers that were presented in his holy temple, now opened.

CHAPTER 12

In this chapter we have an account of the contest between the church and antichrist, the seed of the woman and the seed of the serpent. I. As it was begun in heaven, ver. 1–11. II. As it was carried on in the wilderness, ver. 12, &c.

Verses 1–11

I. The attempts of Satan to prevent the increase of the church.

1. The church is represented, (1) As a *woman,* the spouse of Christ, and the mother of the saints. (2) As *clothed with the sun.* Having put on Christ, who is the Sun of righteousness, she shines in his rays. (3) As having *the moon under her feet.* Her heart and hope are not set upon sublunary things, but on the things that are in heaven, where her head is. (4) As having on her head *a crown of twelve stars,* that is, the doctrine of the gospel preached by the twelve apostles. (5) As in travail and now in pain, to bring forth a holy progeny to Christ.

2. How the grand enemy of the church is represented. (1) A dragon for strength and terror—a red dragon for fierceness and cruelty. (2) As *having seven heads.* It is probable that pagan Rome is here meant. (3) As having *ten horns,* divided into ten provinces, as the Roman empire was by Augustus Cæsar. (4) As having *seven crowns upon his head,* which is afterwards expounded to be seven kings, *ch.* xvii. 10. (5) As drawing with his tail a *third part of the stars in heaven,*

and *casting them down to the earth.* (6) As standing *before the woman, to devour her child as soon as it should be born,* very vigilant to crush the Christian religion in its birth.

II. The unsuccessfulness of these attempts. She was safely delivered of a *man-child* (*v.* 5). Care was taken of this child. The Christian religion has been from its infancy the special care of *the great God and our Saviour Jesus Christ.* Care was taken of the mother as well as of the child, *v.* 6. Furthermore her obscure and private state was for a limited time.

III. The attempts of the dragon not only proved unsuccessful against the church, but fatal to his own interests (*v.* 7). *Heaven* will espouse the quarrel of the church.

1. The seat of this war—*in heaven,* in the church, which is *the kingdom of heaven* on earth, under the care of heaven.

2. The parties: Christ, the great Angel of the covenant, and his faithful followers; and Satan and all his instruments. The strength of the church lies in having the Lord Jesus for the captain of their salvation.

3. The success of the battle: *The dragon and his angels fought and prevailed not.* The victory fell to Christ and his church, and the dragon and his angels were not only conquered, but cast out.

4. The triumphant song that was composed and used on this occasion, *v.* 10, 11. The conqueror is adored. The salvation and strength of the church are all to be ascribed to the king and head of the church. The conquered enemy is described. By his malice he appeared before God as an adversary to the church. Though he hates the presence of God, yet he is willing to appear there to accuse the people of God. How the victory was gained. How the servants of God overcame Satan, (1) *By the blood of the Lamb.* (2) *By the word of their testimony*—by a resolute powerful preaching of the everlasting gospel. By their courage and patience in sufferings; *they loved not their lives unto the death;* their love to their own lives was overcome by stronger affections of another nature.

Verses 12–17

I. The warning given of the distress that should fall upon the inhabitants of the world in general. Being defeated in his designs against the church, he is resolved to give all the disturbance he can to the world in general, *v.* 12.

II. His second attempt upon the church now in the wilderness, *v.* 13. 1. The care that God had taken of his church. He had conveyed her as on eagles' wings, into a place of safety provided for her. 2. The continual malice of the dragon against the church. Her obscurity could not altogether protect her. 3. The seasonable help provided in this dangerous juncture, *v.* 16. 4. His malice against the woman pushes him on to *make war with the remnant of her seed.* Fidelity will expose men still, to the end of the world, when *the last enemy shall be destroyed.*

CHAPTER 13

A further description of the church's enemies after another manner. They are represented as two beasts; the first you have an account of, ver. 1–10, the second, ver. 11, &c.

Verses 1–10

An account of the first beast. He seemed to the apostle to stand upon *the sea-shore.* Whence this beast came—*out of the sea.* The form and shape of this beast. In some part of this description there seems to be an allusion to Daniel's vision of the four beasts, which represented the four monarchies, Dan. vii. 1–3, &c. The seven heads and the ten horns seem to design its several powers; the ten crowns, its tributary princes; the word blasphemy on its forehead proclaims

its direct enmity to the glory of God. The source and spring of his authority—*the dragon.* He was set up by the devil, and the devil lent him all the assistance he could. A dangerous wound given him, and yet unexpectedly healed, *v.* 3. The honour and worship paid to this infernal monster: *All the world wondered after the beast.* They paid honour and subjection to the devil and his instruments, and thought there was no power able to withstand them. How he exercised his infernal power and policy: He had *a mouth, speaking great things, and blasphemies; and he made war with the saints, and overcame them.* And *against those that dwell in heaven.* The malice of the devil shows itself against heaven and the blessed inhabitants of heaven. These are above the reach of his power. All he can do is to blaspheme them; but the saints on earth are more exposed to his cruelty, and he sometimes is permitted to triumph over them. The limitation of the devil's power and success. He is limited in point of time (*v.* 5). He is also limited as to the persons that he shall entirely subject to his will. It will be only those *whose names are not written in the Lamb's book of life.* Those who have killed with the sword shall themselves fall by the sword (*v.* 10), and those who led the people of God into captivity shall themselves be made captives.

Verses 11–18

I. The form and shape of this second beast: *He had two horns like a lamb,* but a mouth that *spoke like the dragon.* All agree that this must be some great impostor, who, under a pretence of religion, shall deceive the souls of men.

II. The power which he exercises (*v.* 12) to draw men off from worshipping the true God to worship those who by nature are no gods.

III. The methods by which this second beast carried on his designs. Lying wonders, pretended miracles, by which they should be deceived. They would pretend to bring down fire from heaven. God sometimes permits his enemies to do things that seem very wonderful, and by which unwary persons may be deluded. They have *the mark of the beast in their forehead* and *in their right hand,* and they have *the name of the beast* and *the number of his name.* They make an open profession of their subjection.

IV. We have here *the number of the beast,* given in such a manner as will sufficiently exercise all the wisdom and accuracy of men: *The number is the number of a man,* and it is 666. Only this we know, God has written *Mene Tekel* upon all his enemies; he has numbered their days, and they shall be finished; but his own kingdom shall endure for ever.

CHAPTER 14

The day begins now to dawn, and here we have represented, I. The Lord Jesus at the head of his faithful followers, ver. 1–5. II. Three angels sent successively to proclaim the fall of Babylon, ver. 6–13. III. The vision of the harvest, ver. 14, &c.

Verses 1–5

The Lord Jesus Christ at the head of his faithful.
1. How Christ appears: as a Lamb standing upon *Mount Zion.* A counterfeit lamb is mentioned as rising out of the earth in the last chapter, which was really a dragon; here Christ appears as the true paschal Lamb. 2. How his people appear. All who were sealed; not one of them lost in all the tribulations through which they had gone. They had *the name of God written in their foreheads.* Their songs of praise (*v.* 3). They are described by their chastity and purity: *They are virgins.* They had not defiled themselves either with corporal or spiritual adultery. By their loyalty and steadfast adherence to Christ: *They follow the Lamb whithersoever he goes.* By their former

designation to this honour, *v. 4. They were the first-fruits to God and to the Lamb,* and the earnest of many more who should *be followers of them, as they were of Christ. There was no guile found in them,* and *they were without fault before the throne of God.* Their hearts were right with God, and they were freely pardoned in Christ.

Verses 6–12

Three angels or messengers sent from heaven to give notice of the fall of Babylon.

I. The first angel was sent on an errand antecedent to it, *v.* 6, 7. The gospel is an everlasting gospel. It is a work fit for an angel to preach this everlasting gospel. The everlasting gospel is of great concern to all the world. The gospel is the great means whereby men are brought to fear God, and to give glory to him. It is by the preaching of the gospel that men are *turned from idols to serve the living God, v.* 7.

II. The second angel follows the other, and proclaims the actual fall of Babylon. By Babylon is generally understood Rome. The wickedness of Babylon will make her fall just, *v.* 8.

III. A third angel follows the other two, *v.* 9, 10. If after this any should persist in their idolatry, they must expect *to drink deep of the wine of the wrath of God.* Those who refuse to come out of Babylon must receive of her plagues. When the treachery and rebellion of others shall be punished, then it will be said, to the honour of the faithful (*v.* 12): *Here is the patience of the saints;* you have before seen their patience exercised, now you see it rewarded.

Verses 13–20

The vision of the harvest and vintage.

I. The preface, *v.* 13. This prophecy came down from heaven, and not from men, and therefore it is of certain truth. It was to be preserved and published—by writing; it was to be matter of record, that the people of God might have recourse to it for their comfort upon all occasions. It principally intended to show the blessedness of all the faithful servants of God, both in death and after death: *Blessed are the dead that die in the Lord from henceforth,* &c. The description of those that are and shall be blessed—such as die in the Lord. They are blessed in their rest. They are blessed in their recompence: *Their works follow them;* as their evidence of having lived and died in the Lord.

II. The vision itself.

1. A harvest (*v.* 14, 15), an emblem that sometimes signifies the cutting down of the wicked, and sometimes the gathering in of the righteous. This seems rather to represent God's judgments against the wicked.

(1) The Lord of the harvest—one so *like unto the Son of man* that he was the same, even the Lord Jesus. The chariot in which he sat—*a white cloud,* a cloud that had a bright side turned to the church, how dark soever it might be to the wicked. The ensign of his power: *On his head was a golden crown,* authority to do whatsoever he would do. The instrument of his providences: *In his hand a sharp sickle.*

(2) The harvest-work, to thrust the sickle into the corn, and reap the field.

(3) The harvest-time; when the corn is ripe, when the measure of the sin of men is filled up. Then he will spare them no longer; he will thrust in his sickle, and the earth shall be reaped.

2. A vintage, *v.* 17. To whom this vintage-work was committed—*another angel that came out from the altar.* The work of the vintage, which consists of two parts: (1) *Gathering the clusters of the vine, fully ripe, v.* 18. (2) Casting these grapes *into the wine-press* (*v.* 19). It was *the wrath of God, without*

the city, where the army lay that came against Babylon. The quantity of the wine, that is, of the blood that was drawn forth by this judgment (*v.* 20). But here we are left to doubtful conjectures.

CHAPTER 15

The vision of the seven vials. I. A sight of those angels in heaven who were to have the execution of this great work, ver. 1–4. II. A sight of these angels coming out of heaven to receive those vials which they were to pour out, ver. 5, &c.

Verses 1–4

The pouring out of the seven vials, which was committed to seven angels. The work they had to do, which was to finish the destruction of antichrist. The spectators and witnesses of this their commission: all *that had gotten the victory over the beast,* &c. These stood on a *sea of glass singing the song of Moses.* They extol the greatness of God's works. They call upon all nations to render unto God the fear due to such a discovery of his truth and justice: *Who shall not fear thee?* (*v.* 4).

Verses 5–8

I. How these angels appeared, *v.* 5. Here is an allusion to the holiest of all in the tabernacle and temple, where was *the mercy-seat, covering the ark of the testimony.* In the judgments God was now about to execute he was fulfilling the prophecies and promises of his word and covenant, which were there always before him.

II. How they were equipped. Their array, *v.* 6. This was the habit of the high priests when they went in to enquire of God, and came out with an answer from him. They do everything in a pure and holy manner. Their artillery was *seven vials filled with the wrath of God;* they were armed with the wrath of God against his enemies.

III. They were all wrapt up in clouds of smoke, which filled the temple, from the glorious and powerful presence of God; so that *no man was able to enter into the temple,* till the work was finished. God himself was now preaching to the church and to all the world, by terrible things in righteousness; but when this work was done, the temple would be opened.

CHAPTER 16

The pouring forth of these vials that were filled with the wrath of God. I. Upon the earth, ver. 2. II. Upon the sea, ver. 3. III. Upon the rivers and fountains of water, ver. 4. Here the heavenly hosts applaud the righteousness of the judgments of God. IV. The fourth vial was poured out on the sun, ver. 8. V. The fifth on the seat of the beast. VI. The sixth on the river Euphrates. VII. The seventh in the air, upon which the cities of the nations fell.

Verses 1–7

I. Though everything was made ready before, yet nothing was to be put in execution without an order from God; and this he gave out of the temple.

II. No sooner was the word of command given than it was immediately obeyed. God says, *Go your ways, and pour out the vials;* and immediately the work is begun. We have here a reference and allusion to several of the plagues of Egypt. Their sins were alike, and so were their punishments. These vials have a plain reference to the seven trumpets, which represented the rise of antichrist. The fall of antichrist shall be gradual; as Rome was not built in one day, so neither shall it fall in one day. The fall of the antichristian interest shall be universal. Everything that any ways belonged to them, all consigned over to ruin, all accursed for the sake of the wickedness of that people.

1. The first angel, *v.* 2. Where the vial fell—*upon the earth,* upon the common people. What it produced—

noisome and grievous sores on all who had the mark of the beast. They had marked themselves by their sin, now God marks them out by his judgments.

2. *The second angel poured out his vial.* Where it fell—*upon the sea.* It turned the sea into blood, *as the blood of a dead man, and every living soul died in the sea.* God discovered not only the vanity and falsehood of their religion, but the pernicious and deadly nature of it.

The next angel poured out his vial. Where it fell—*upon the rivers, and upon the fountains of waters. It turned them into blood.* The following doxology (*v.* 5, 6). The instrument that God makes use of in this work is here called *the angel of the waters,* who extols the righteousness of God in this retaliation, to which another angel answered by full consent, *v.* 7.

Verses 8–11

The fourth angel poured out his vial, and that fell upon the sun. That sun which before cherished them with warm and benign influences shall now grow hot against these idolaters, and shall scorch them, which yet will be so far from bringing them to repentance, that it will cause them to curse God. They will be hardened to their ruin. The fifth angel, *v.* 10. Where this vial fell—*upon the seat of the beast,* upon Rome itself. The whole kingdom of the beast *was full of darkness.* Darkness is opposed to wisdom and penetration, and forebodes the confusion and folly which the idolaters should discover at that time. It is opposed to pleasure and joy.

Verses 12–16

The sixth angel poured out his vial.

I. Where it fell—*upon the great river Euphrates.* Some take it literally. Others take it for the river Tiber.

II. What did this vial produce? The drying up of the river. A way is hereby prepared *for the kings of the east.* The last effort of the great dragon; he is resolved to have another push for it. The instruments he makes use of: *Three unclean spirits like frogs.* These would muster up the devil's forces for a decisive battle. The means these instruments would use. They would work pretended miracles. The field of battle—a place called *Armageddon;* that is, say some, the mount of Megiddo. The further account of it is suspended till we come to the nineteenth chapter, *v.* 19, 20. The warning which God gives of this great and decisive trial, *v.* 15. When God's cause comes to be tried, and his battles to be fought, all his people shall be ready and be faithful and valiant in his service.

Verses 17–21

An account of the seventh and last angel pouring forth his vial, which was the finishing stroke.

I. Where this plague fell—*on the air,* upon the prince of the power of the air, that is, the devil. Here is a vial poured out upon his kingdom, and he is not able to support his tottering cause and interest any longer.

II. What it produced. 1. A thankful voice from heaven, pronouncing that now the work was done. It is finished. 2. An earthquake, so great as never was before, and this ushered in by thunder and lightnings. 3. The fall of Babylon (*v.* 19). God now remembered this great and wicked city. Now he gives unto her *the cup of the wine of the fierceness of his wrath,* and every island and every mountain, that seemed by nature and situation the most secured, were carried away in the deluge of this ruin.

III. How the antichristian party were affected with it. Though it fell upon them as a dreadful storm, as if the stones of the city, tossed up into the air, came down upon their heads, like hailstones of a talent weight each, yet they were so far from repenting that they blasphemed that God who thus punished them.

CHAPTER 17

This antichrist is now described as a great whore. I. The apostle is invited to see this vile woman, ver. 1, 2. II. He tells us what an appearance she made, ver. 3-6. III. The mystery of it is explained to him, ver. 7-12. And, IV. Her ruin foretold, ver. 13, &c.

Verses 1–6

Here we have a new vision. 1. The invitation given to the apostle, *v.* 1. This is a name of great infamy. She had been a prostitute to the kings of the earth, whom she had intoxicated *with the wine of her fornication.* 2. The appearance she made, *v.* 4. 3. Her principal seat and residence—*upon the beast that had seven heads and ten horns;* that is to say, Rome, the city on seven hills. 4. Her name, which *was written on her forehead.* She is named from her place of residence—*Babylon the great.* She is named from her infamous way and practice; not only a harlot, but a mother of harlots. 5. Her diet: she satiated herself with *the blood of the saints and martyrs of Jesus.* She drank their blood with such greediness that she intoxicated herself with it.

Verses 7–13

Here we have the mystery of this vision explained. But it is so explained as still to need further explanation. 1. This beast *was, and is not, and yet is;* it *was* a seat of idolatry and persecution; *and is not,* not in the ancient form, *and yet it is* truly the seat of idolatry and tyranny. *It ascends out of the bottomless pit,* and it shall return thither and go into perdition. 2. *This beast has seven heads,* which have a double signification. *Seven mountains*—the seven hills on which Rome stands. *Seven kings*—seven sorts of government. Five of these were extinct; one was then in being; and the other was yet to come, *v.* 10. This beast makes an eighth. 3. This beast had ten horns; which are said to be *ten kings which have as yet received no kingdoms.*

Verses 14–18

I. War begun between the beast and his followers, and the Lamb and his followers. One would think an army with a lamb at the head of them could not stand before *the great red dragon.*

II. Victory gained by the Lamb: *The Lamb shall overcome.* He will be sure to meet with many enemies, but he will also be sure to gain the victory.

III. The ground or reason of the victory. 1. From the character of the Lamb: *He is King of kings and Lord of lords.* All the powers of earth and hell are subject to his check and control. 2. From the character of his followers: *They are called, and chosen, and faithful.* Such an army, under such a commander, will at length carry all the world before them.

IV. The victory is justly aggrandized. 1. By the vast multitude who paid obedience and subjection to the beast and to the whore, *v.* 15, 18. 2. By the powerful influence which God hereby showed he had over the minds of great men. It was of God, and to fulfil his will, that these kings *agreed to give their kingdom unto the beast.* It was of God that afterwards their hearts were turned against the whore.

CHAPTER 18

I. An angel proclaiming the fall of Babylon, ver. 1, 2. II. Assigning the reasons of her fall, ver. 3. III. Giving warning to all who belonged to God to come out of her (ver. 4, 5), and to assist in her destruction, ver. 6-8. IV. The great lamentation made for her by those who had been large sharers in her sinful pleasures and profits, ver. 9-19. V. The great joy that there would be among others at the sight of her irrecoverable ruin, ver. 20, &c.

Verses 1–8

Here is another angel sent from heaven, *v*. 1. He had not only light in himself, to discern the truth of his own prediction, but to inform and enlighten the world about that great event. This angel publishes the fall of Babylon, as a thing already come to pass. Here seems to be an allusion to the prediction of the fall of pagan Babylon (Isa. xxi. 9), where the word is repeated as it is here: *has fallen, has fallen, v.* 2. This is also borrowed from Isa. xxi. 9, and seems to describe not so much her sin as her punishment, it being a common notion that unclean spirits, as well as ominous and hateful birds, used to haunt a city or house that lay in its ruins. The reason of this ruin is declared (*v*. 3). She had not only forsaken the true God herself, and set up idols, but had drawn all sorts of men into the spiritual adultery, and by her wealth and luxury had retained them in her interest. All that expect mercy from God should not only *come out of her*, but be assisting in her destruction, *v*. 4, 5. God may have a people even in Babylon. Those that are resolved to partake with wicked men in their sins must receive of their plagues. Though private revenge is forbidden, yet God will have his people act under him, when called to it, in pulling down his and their implacable enemies, *v*. 6. God will proportion the punishment of sinners to the measure of their pride, and security, *v*. 7. When destruction comes on a people suddenly, the surprise is a great aggravation of their misery, *v*. 8.

Verses 9–24

I. A doleful lamentation made by Babylon's friends for her fall.

1. The mourners, those who had been bewitched by her fornication, and those who had been gainers by her wealth and trade—the kings and the merchants of the earth.

2. The manner of their mourning. They stood afar off. Even Babylon's friends will stand at a distance from her fall. Though they had been partakers with her in her sinful pleasures and profits, they were not willing to bear a share in her plagues. They made a grievous outcry, *v*. 19. Those who have most indulged themselves in pride and pleasure are the least able to bear calamities.

3. The cause of their mourning; not their sin, but their punishment. The spirit of antichrist is a worldly spirit, and their sorrow is a mere worldly sorrow. The wealth and merchandise of this city, all which was suddenly lost (*v*. 12, 13), and lost irrecoverably (*v*. 14). The church of God may fall for a time, but she shall rise again; but the fall of Babylon will be an utter overthrow. Godly sorrow is some support under affliction, but mere worldly sorrow adds to the calamity.

II. The joy and triumph there was both in heaven and earth at the irrecoverable fall of Babylon, *v*. 20. 1. How universal this joy would be: heaven and earth, angels and saints, would join in it. 2. How just and reasonable. (1) Because the fall of Babylon was an act of God's justice. Though they did not take pleasure in the miseries of any, yet they had reason to rejoice in the discoveries of the glorious justice of God. (2) Because it was an irrecoverable ruin (*v*. 21). The place shall be no longer habitable by man, no work shall be done there, no comfort enjoyed, no light seen there, but utter darkness and desolation, as the reward of her great wickedness, *v*. 24. Such abominable sins deserved so great a ruin.

Chapter 19

I. A further account of the triumphant song of angels and saints for the fall of Babylon, ver. 1–4. II. The marriage between Christ and the church proclaimed, ver. 5–10. III. Another warlike expedition of the glorious head of the church, ver. 10, &c.

Verses 1–4

The fall of Babylon being finished, and declared to be irrecoverable, this begins with a holy triumph over her. The form of their thanksgiving, *Alleluia, praise you the Lord*: with this they begin, with this they go on, and with this they end (*v*. 4); their prayers are now turned into praises, their hosannas end in halleluias. They praise him for the truth of his word, and the righteousness of his providential conduct, especially in this great event—the ruin of Babylon (*v*. 2). When the angels and saints cried *Alleluia*, her fire burned more fiercely, *v*. 3. Praising God for what we have is praying in the most effectual manner for what is yet further to be done for us; the praises of the saints blow up the fire of God's wrath against the common enemy. The blessed harmony between the angels and the saints in this triumphant song, *v*. 4.

Verses 5–10

An epithalamium, or marriage-song, begins, *v*. 6.

I. The concert of heavenly music. The chorus was large and loud, *as the voice of many waters and of mighty thunderings*.

II. The occasion of this song, *v*. 7. 1. A description of the bride, how she appeared; not in the gay and gaudy dress of the mother of harlots, but *in fine linen, clean and white*, which *is the righteousness of saints*; in the robes of Christ's righteousness. These her nuptial ornaments she did not purchase by any price of her own, but received them as the grant of her blessed Lord. 2. The marriage-feast which is declared to be such as would make all those happy who were called to it, a feast made up of the promises of the gospel, *the true sayings of God, v*. 9. 3. The transport of joy which the apostle felt. *He fell down at the feet of the angel to worship him*. The angel refused it, and this was with some resentment: "*See thou do it not. I am thy fellow-servant, and of thy brethren which have the testimony of Jesus*. Thou, as an apostle, having *the Spirit of prophecy*, hast the same testimony to give in; and therefore we are in this brethren and fellow-servants. *Worship God*, and him alone."

Verses 11–21

The glorious head of the church is called out to a new expedition, which seems to be the great battle that was to be fought at Armageddon.

I. The description of the great Commander. The seat of his empire; and that is *heaven*. His equipage: he is again described as sitting *on a white horse*. He is *faithful and true*, he is righteous in all his proceedings, he has a penetrating insight into all the strength of his enemies, he has a large and extensive dominion, many crowns. His armour; and that is *a vesture dipped in blood*. His name: *The Word of God*, a name that none fully knows but himself. His perfections are incomprehensible by any creature.

II. The army which he commands (*v*. 14).

III. The weapons of his warfare—*a sharp sword* proceeding from *his mouth* (*v*. 15).

IV. The ensigns of his authority, his coat of arms, *v*. 16.

V. An invitation given *to the fowls of heaven*, that they should come and share in the spoil and pillage of the field (*v*. 17, 18).

VI. The battle joined. The enemy falls on with great fury; the powers of earth and hell gathered, to make their utmost effort, *v*. 19.

VII. The victory gained by the great head of the church: *The beast and the false prophet* are taken prisoners, and *cast into the burning lake*, and their followers are given up to military execution, and made a feast for *the fowls of heaven*.

CHAPTER 20

Here we have an account, I. Of the binding of Satan for a thousand years, ver. 1–3. II. The reign of the saints with Christ for the same time, ver. 4–6. III. Of the loosing of Satan, and the conflict of the church, with Gog and Magog, ver. 7–10. IV. Of the day of judgment, ver. 11, &c.

Verses 1–10

I. A prophecy of *the binding of Satan*. To whom this work of binding Satan is committed—to *an angel from heaven*. Christ never wants proper powers and instruments to break the power of Satan. The execution of this work, *v.* 2, 3. Neither the strength of the dragon, nor the subtlety of the serpent, was sufficient to rescue him. He *cast him into the bottomless pit*. He is brought back to that prison, and there laid in chains. He is *shut up, and a seal set upon him*. We have the term of this confinement of Satan—*a thousand years*, after which he was to *be loosed* again for *a little season*.

II. An account of the reign of the saints for the same space of time in which Satan continued bound (*v.* 4–6). Who those were that received such honour—those who had suffered for Christ, and all who had faithfully adhered to him. The honour bestowed upon them. They were raised from the dead, and restored to life. *They reigned with Christ a thousand years.* Those who suffer with Christ shall reign with Christ. This is called *the first resurrection*, which none but those who have served Christ and suffered for him shall be favoured with. The happiness of these servants of God. They are *blessed and holy*, *v.* 6. None can be blessed but those that are holy; and all that are holy shall be blessed. They are secured from the power of the second death. Those who have had experience of a spiritual resurrection are saved from the power of the second death.

III. An account of another mighty conflict, very sharp, but short and decisive. The restraints laid on Satan are at length taken off. While this world lasts, Satan's power in it will not be wholly destroyed. No sooner is Satan let loose than he falls to his old work, *deceiving the nations*, and so stirring them up to make a war with the saints and servants of God. His last efforts seem to be the greatest, *v.* 8. The principal commanders in this army under the dragon—*Gog and Magog*. Of *Gog and Magog* together we only read in Ezek. xxxviii. 2, a prophecy whence this in the Revelation borrows many of its images. The march and military disposition of this formidable army (*v.* 9). The doom and punishment of the grand enemy, *the devil*: he is now cast into hell, with his two great officers, *the beast and the false prophet*, to be there *tormented night and day, for ever and ever*.

Verses 11–15

The utter destruction of the devil's kingdom leads to an account of the day of judgment. This will be a great day, *the great day, when all shall appear before the judgment-seat of Christ*. 1. We behold *the throne, great and white*, very glorious and perfectly just and righteous. 2. The Judge, the Lord Jesus Christ. *The earth and the heaven flee from his face, and there is no place found for them.* 3. The persons to be judged (*v.* 12). None are so mean but they have some talents to account for, and none so great as to avoid the jurisdiction of this court; not only those that are found alive at the coming of Christ, but all who have died before. 4. The rule of judgment settled: *The books were opened*. The book of God's omniscience, and the book of the sinner's conscience. *And another book* shall be *opened*—the book of the scriptures, the statute-book of heaven, the rule of life. 5. The cause to be tried; *the works of men*, what they have done and whether it

be good or evil. 6. The issue of the trial and judgment. All those who have *made a covenant with death*, and an *agreement with hell*, shall then be condemned with their infernal confederates, cast with them into the lake of fire. But those whose names are written in that book shall then be justified and acquitted by the Judge.

CHAPTER 21

The day breaks, and the shadows flee away; a new world now appears, the former having passed away. I. An introduction to the vision of the new Jerusalem, ver. 1–9. II. The vision itself, ver. 10, &c.

Verses 1–8

I. A new world now opens to our view (*v.* 1). To make way for the commencement of this new world, the old world *passed away*.

II. In this new world the apostle *saw the holy city, the new Jerusalem, coming down from heaven*. This new Jerusalem is the church of God in its new and perfect state, *prepared as a bride adorned for her husband*.

III. The blessed presence of God with his people is here proclaimed, *v.* 3. The presence of God with his church is the glory of the church. The presence of God with his people in heaven will not be interrupted as it is on earth, but he will dwell with them continually. *They shall be his people. God himself will be their God.*

IV. This new and blessed state will be free from all trouble and sorrow. *All tears shall be wiped away.* God himself, as their tender Father, with his own kind hand, *shall wipe away the tears* of his children; and they would not have been without those tears when God shall come and wipe them away. All the causes of future sorrow shall be for ever removed: *There shall be neither death nor pain;* and therefore *no sorrow nor crying; former things have passed away.*

V. The truth and certainty of this blessed state are ratified by the word and promise of God, *v.* 5, 6. God would have it committed to writing, for perpetual memory, and continual use to his people. *These words are faithful and true;* and it follows, *It is done*, is as sure as if it were done already. We may and ought to take God's promise as present payment; if he has said that he *makes all things new, it is done*. His titles of honour as a pledge of the full performance, *Alpha and Omega, the beginning and the end*. As his power and will were the first cause of all things, his pleasure and glory are the last end, and he will not lose his design. Men may begin designs which they can never bring to perfection; but *the counsel of God shall stand*. It would be inconsistent with the goodness of God, and his love to his people, to create in them holy desires, and then deny them their proper satisfaction; and therefore they may be assured that *he will give them of the fountain of the water of life freely*.

VI. The greatness of this future felicity is declared. The freeness of it: *He gives of the water of life freely.* The fulness of it. They *inherit all things* (*v.* 7). He is all in all. The tenure and title by which they enjoy this blessedness as *the sons of God*, a title most sure and indefeasible. The vastly different state of the wicked, *v.* 8. The sins of those who perish. *The fearful* lead the van in this black list. Those who were so dastardly as not to dare to take up the cross of Christ, were yet so desperate as to run into all manner of abominable wickedness. Their punishment. They could not burn at a stake for Christ, but they must burn in hell for sin. They must die another death after their natural death; the agonies and terrors of the first death will consign them over to the far greater terrors and agonies of eternal death.

Verses 9–27

We now come to the vision itself.

I. The person that opened the vision to the apostle, v. 9. God has a variety of work and employment for his holy angels. They readily execute every commission they receive from God.

II. The place from which the apostle had this glorious view. He was taken into *a high mountain*. Those who would have clear views of heaven must get as near heaven as they can, into the mount of vision.

III. The subject-matter of the vision (v. 10); the church of God in her glorious, perfect, triumphant state.

1. The exterior part of the city—*the wall* and *the gates*.

(1) The wall for security. Heaven is a safe state. The height of it (v. 17), sufficient both for ornament and security. The matter of it: *It was as jasper*, v. 11. This city has a wall that is impregnable as well as precious. The form of it: In the new Jerusalem all shall be equal in purity and perfection. The measure of the wall (v. 15, 16). Here is room sufficient for all the people of God—*many mansions in their Father's house*. The foundation of the wall (v. 19). The foundations are described by their number—*twelve*, alluding to the twelve apostles (v. 14). The matter of these foundations, it was various and precious, set forth by twelve sorts of precious stones.

(2) The gates for entrance. Heaven is not inaccessible; there is a free admission to all those that are sanctified. Their number—*twelve gates*, answering to the twelve tribes of Israel. All the true Israel of God shall have entrance into the new Jerusalem. Their guards—*twelve angels*, to admit and receive the several tribes of the spiritual Israel. The inscription on the gates—*the names of the twelve tribes*, to show that they have a right to the tree of life, and to enter through the gates into the city. The situation of the gates. As the city had four equal sides, answering to the four quarters of the world, so on each side there were three gates, signifying that there is as free entrance from one part of the world as from the other. The materials of these gates—they were all of pearls: *Every gate one pearl*. Christ is the pearl of great price, and he is our way to God. There is nothing magnificent enough in this world fully to set forth the glory of heaven.

2. The interior part of the new Jerusalem, v. 22–27. The first thing which we observe there is the street of the city, v. 21. The saints in heaven tread upon gold. The saints are then at rest, but it is not a mere passive rest; but a state of delightful motion: *The nations that are saved walk in the light of it*. They walk with Christ in white. They have communion not only with God, but with one another.

(1) The temple of the new Jerusalem, which was no material temple, *for the Lord God Almighty, and the Lamb, are the temple thereof*.

(2) The light of this city, v. 23. There is no want of the light of the sun, *for the glory of God lightens that city, and the Lamb is the light thereof*. There is no need of the sun or moon, any more than we here need to set up candles at noon day.

(3) The inhabitants of this city. Their numbers—whole nations of saved souls. All those multitudes who were sealed on earth are saved in heaven. Their dignity—some of the kings and princes of the earth. God will have some of all ranks and degrees of men to fill the heavenly mansions, high and low. Their continual accession and entrance into this city: *The gates shall never be shut*. Those that are sanctified always find the gates open.

(4) The accommodations of this city: All the *glory and honour of the nations shall be brought into it*.

Whatever is excellent and valuable in this world shall be there enjoyed in a more refined kind, and to a far greater degree.

(5) The unmixed purity of all who belong to the new Jerusalem, v. 27. There the saints shall have no impure thing remaining in them. Now they feel a sad mixture of corruption with their graces; but, at their entance into the holy of holies, they are washed in the laver of Christ's blood, and presented to the Father without spot. There the saints shall have no impure persons admitted among them. In the new Jerusalem there is a society perfectly pure. Free from such as are openly profane. There are none admitted into heaven who work abominations. Free from hypocrites, such as make lies. They cannot intrude into the new Jerusalem.

CHAPTER 22

I. A further description of the heavenly state of the church, ver. 1–5. II. A confirmation of this and all the other visions of this book, ver. 6–19. III. The conclusion, ver. 20, 21.

Verses 1–5

The heavenly state is here described as a paradise. A paradise in a city, or a whole city in a paradise! In the first paradise there were only two persons to behold the beauty of it; but in this second paradise whole cities and nations shall find abundant delight and satisfaction.

I. The river of paradise. Its fountain-head—*the throne of God and the Lamb*. All our springs of grace, comfort, and glory, are in God; and all our streams from him are through the Lamb. Its quality —*pure and clear as crystal*. All the streams of earthly comfort are muddy; but these are clear, giving life, to those who drink of them.

II. The tree of life, in this paradise. Such a tree there was in the earthly paradise, Gen. ii. 9. This far excels it. The situation of it—*in the midst of the street, and on either side the river*. This tree of life is fed by the pure waters of the river that comes from the throne of God. The fruitfulness of this tree. It brings forth many sorts of fruit—*twelve sorts*. It brings forth fruit at all times—*yields its fruit every month*. There is always fruit upon it. The fruit is not only pleasant, but wholesome. The presence of God in heaven is the health and happiness of the saints.

III. The perfect freedom of this paradise from everything that is evil (v. 3). No serpent there, as there was in the earthly paradise. The devil has nothing to do there.

IV. The supreme felicity of this paradisaical state. There the saints shall see the face of God. God will own them, as having his seal and name on their foreheads. *They shall reign with him for ever*. All this shall be with perfect knowledge and joy, walking in the light of the Lord; and this not for a time, *but for ever and ever*.

Verses 6–19

We have here a solemn ratification of the contents of this book. 1. This is confirmed by the name and nature of that God who gave out these discoveries: he is *the Lord God, faithful and true*. 2. By the messengers he chose. The holy angels showed them to holy men of God. 3. They will soon be confirmed by their accomplishment. Christ will make haste, *he will come quickly*. 4. By the integrity of that angel who had been the apostle's guide and interpreter in these visions. 5. By the order given to leave the book of the prophecy open, to be perused by all. He does not speak in secret. 6. By the effect this book will have upon men; those that are filthy and unjust will take occasion thence to be more so, but it will further sanctify those that are upright with God. 7. It will be Christ's rule of judgment at the great day; he will dispense rewards and punishments to men according as their works agree or disagree with the word of God. 8. It is the word of him who is the author, finisher, and rewarder of the faith and holiness of his people, *v.* 13, 14. He is *the first and the last.* He will by this word give to his people *a right to the tree of life,* and an entrance into heaven. 9. It condemns and excludes from heaven all wicked persons, and particularly *those that love and make lies* (*v.* 15). 10. It is confirmed by *the testimony of Jesus, which is the Spirit of prophecy.* He is the fountain of all light, the *bright and the morning star,* and has given to his churches this morning light of prophecy, to assure them of the light of that perfect day which is approaching. 11. It is confirmed by an open invitation to all to come and partake of the streams of the water of life; these are tendered to all who feel in their souls a thirst which nothing in this world can quench. 12. It is confirmed by the joint testimony of the Spirit of God, and that gracious Spirit that is in all the true members of the church of God; *the Spirit and the bride.* 13. It is confirmed by a most solemn sanction, *v.* 18, 19. This sanction is like a flaming sword, to guard the canon of the scripture from profane hands.

Verses 20, 21

We have now come to the conclusion of the whole.

I. Christ's farewell to his church. *Behold, I come quickly.* As when he ascended into heaven, after his resurrection, he parted with a promise of his gracious presence, so here he parts with a promise of a speedy return. The vision is for an appointed time, and will not tarry. *He will come quickly.*

II. The church's hearty echo to Christ's promise. Her firm belief of it: *Amen, so it is,* so it shall be. Her earnest desire of it: *Even so, come, Lord Jesus.* We should never be satisfied till we find such a spirit breathing in us. This is the language of the church of the first-born, and we should join with them. What comes from heaven in a promise should be sent back to heaven in a prayer, "*Come, Lord Jesus.* Finish thy great design, and fulfil all that word in which thou hast caused thy people to hope."

III. The apostolical benediction, which closes the whole: *The grace of our Lord Jesus Christ be with you all, Amen.* Nothing should be more desired by us than that the grace of Christ may be with us in this world, to prepare us for the glory of Christ in the other world. To this most comprehensive prayer we should all add our hearty *Amen,* most earnestly thirsting after greater measures of the gracious influences of the blessed Jesus in our souls, and his gracious presence with us, till glory has perfected all his grace towards us.